THE NEW AMERICAN EPHEMERIS for the 20TH CENTURY 1900 TO 2000 at NOON

Michelsen Memorial Edition

compiled and programmed by

Rique Pottenger

based on the earlier work of

Neil F. Michelsen

Starcrafts Publishing

New Hampshire

The New American Ephemeris for the 20th Century
1900-2000 at Noon

Michelsen Memorial Edition
First printing 2009

Compiled and programmed by Rique Pottenger
Based on the earlier work of Neil F. Michelsen

Cover and compilation of introductory text by Maria Kay Simms

Library of Congress Control Number 2009928823

ISBN 978-1-9349760-9-8

Published by Starcrafts Publishing, Starcrafts LLC
PO Box 446, Exeter, NH 03833-0446
http://www.starcraftspublishing.com

Printed in the United States of America

Dedication

Neil F. Michelsen

May 11, 1931 — May 15, 1990

The American Ephemeris 1931-1980, first published in 1976, began the series of computer-generated ephemerides that are Neil Michelsen's most enduring legacy. As a primary pioneer of computer technology for astrology, he set the standards for accuracy, and always insisted on updating his published work as new data or refinements in calculation became available. In the photograph above, Neil holds his most popular reference, ***The American Ephemeris for the 20th Century, 1900-2000 at Midnight.*** Published through the 5th Edition in both midnight and noon versions, this book has been quite likely the most widely used of its type internationally. As Neil would be the first to agree though, new data and improved calculation methods now call for Rique Pottenger, his chosen successor, to program substantially updated new editions.

Therefore, it is with deep respect and great pleasure that we dedicate ***The New American Ephemeris for the 20th Century, 1900-2000 at Noon*** to the memory of its inspired originator, **Neil F. Michelsen.**

Introduction to The New American Ephemeris

In 1976, Neil F. Michelsen compiled, programmed, printed and published the first edition of ***The American Ephemeris, 1931-1980***, thus providing more comprehensive data at a lower cost than had been previously available, and setting a standard for accuracy previously unmatched in astrology. His subsequent publication of ***The American Ephemeris for the 20th Century 1900-2000***, made available in both Midnight and Noon versions, became highly popular internationally. It was subsequently updated through 5th Edition, each time with revisions according to the latest and most accurate orbital data available. Since 1988, files and algorithms from the Jet Propulsion Laboratory export ephemeris files have been used.

Michelsen also programmed and published specialty versions of his ephemeris, including T***he American Heliocentric Ephemeris*** and ***The American Sidereal Ephemeris.*** In 1982, a first printing of ***The American Ephemeris for the 21st Century*** was published in one relatively small first printing for the entire century. Because many users appeared not quite ready to buy a book that looked so very far into the future, subsequent 21st century editions were published as half-century books, for 2000-2050.

In 2006, Rique Pottenger, who has revised ***The American Ephemeris*** series since Michelsen's passing in 1990, reintroduced the concept of a full 21st century ephemeris in his ***The New American Ephemeris for the 21st Century, 2000-2100 at Midnight.*** This new version was fully updated with the latest Jet Propulsion Laboratory data, and it included several new refinements in calculation. Also, Rique and Starcrafts Publishing (along with numerous school textbook publishers) held up publication of our new book so that we could properly address the vote to be taken by the International Astronomer's Union, following their debate about redefining the parameters of our solar system.

In 2008, with the highly popular "red book" (the 20th Midnight version Neil holds in the photograph) nearly out-of-print, Rique compiled and programmed ***The New American Ephemeris for the 20th Century, 1900-2000 at Midnight*** including all of the new features and programming refinements of the new 21st century ephemeris. Since we'd already used red for the new 21st midnight ephemeris, the cover of our newly updated replacement for the "red book" was given a sunny gold cover. Now, we are also updating the noon version with ***The New American Ephemeris for the 20th Century, 1900-2000 at Noon.*** As with other "New American" versions, features in this ephemeris include the 2006 decisions of the International Astronomers Union to change our solar system. They first decided to demote Pluto to a new classification of "dwarf planet," and then subsequently promoted Ceres, the largest asteroid among those orbiting between Mars and Jupiter, to the dwarf planet category. A new planet, orbiting far beyond the orbit of Pluto, became the third body added to this new classification and was named Eris, for the mythical goddess of chaos. Knowing that few, if any, astrologers would be willing to accept leaving Pluto out of daily planetary order, we decided to leave Pluto in his customary position and revise the table of daily planetary positions to include Ceres, between Mars and Jupiter. Eris, orbiting so far beyond Pluto that her positions change only a few minutes from one month to the next, is listed with her monthly positions in the Astro Data box at lower right of each page along with the Galactic Center and Chiron. Also, monthly positions are given for astrology's now 'major three" of the former major four asteroids: Pallas, Juno and Vesta.

Rique's new computation program is now Windows™ based, offering some improvements in calculation that enable advantages such as checking for double ingresses on the same day. Some station times may also show as slightly different from prior versions of the ephemeris. A significantly more accurate formula was obtained for the Galactic Center, so it may also show as slightly different from the prior versions. Also, phenomena in the far left Astro Data column are sorted by time as well as date. In the prior ACS Publication of the 20th century ephemeris, they were not sorted by time, so if two events occurred on the same day, the later one might be higher in the column. Planetary ingress data include R after the sign if a planet is retrograde when it ingresses.

General Information

The New American Ephemeris for the 20th Century, 1900-2000 at Noon, like its ACS Publications predecessor, is a noon ephemeris based on Universal Time (UT), which is for all practical purposes the same as Greenwich Mean Time (GMT) except that the UT is expressed in military style, 00:00 to 24:00 hours. All positions are given for 00:00 hours UT, and the times for phenomena are given in UT. As with all of our other "century" ephemerides, this is actually a 101 year ephemeris. Although technically, the 20th century begins on 1/1/1901, we follow expressed user preference for including 1900.

Other tropical ephemerides are based on Ephemeris Time (ET), which must be used to determine planetary positions because their calculation requires a uniform meansurement of time. Because of earthquakes, tidal coupling with the Moon and other disturbances, the Earth's rotation, upon which our clocks depend, either speeds up or slows down by small amounts at irregular time intervals. (How much can only be determined after the fact by observation.)

For example, at the beginning of 1987, the difference between UT and ET, called Delta T, was about 55 seconds. In order to accurately calculate a horoscope using an ephemeris based on ET, Delta T must be added to the birth time before interpolating to find the planetary positions. Many astrologers bypass this correction because they don't know about it, or don't need the additional accuracy it provides. This ephemeris completely eliminates the consideration because the positions are calculated for Universal Time.

Accuracy of Planetary Positions

Successive editions of this ephemeris differ slightly from earlier versions because of increased accuracy of data from the Jet Propulsion Laboratory (JPL). Since 1984, JPL data has been used in ***The Astronomical Almanac***, a joint publication of the US Naval Observatory and the Royal Greenwich Observatory. Differences are so small that they show up mainly in the times of aspects, sign ingresses, 0 declinations and stations that appear in the phenomena section at the bottom of each page. The most dramatic changes are seen in a few void-of-course Moon times where an aspect time that previously started the void period shifts to just after the Moon enters a new sign, so that an earlier aspect becomes the determining time for the beginning of the void Moon.

Positions of Chiron are determined by numerical integration using elements from the *Soviet Asteroid Ephemeris*. The integration program is an adaptation of the A.P.A.E. Volume XXII procedure as implemented by Mark Pottenger.

All positions are apparent, meaning that they are corrected for light time. For example, the light from the Sun takes 8 ½ minutes to reach the Earth, and in that time the Sun moves about 20.5"(seconds of arc). So the Sun's apparent position is 20.4" less than the geometric one. Finally, the planet positions are transformed to the ecliptic of date, which means that precession and nutation (the wobble of the Earth on its axis) are applied

Eclipses

The solar and lunar eclipses were recalculated using JPL data. Because of the accuracy of this data, it was justifiable to list the duration of the geocentric maximum of total and annular solar eclipses to the second of time. This edition identifies six different types of solar eclipses. Since the method of calculation is improved over other editions published prior to 1997, solar eclipse times may be up to several minutes more accurate. See **Key to the Phenomena Section** for further explanation.

Additional Features

Sun and Moon positions are given to the nearest second of arc; all other positions are given to the nearest tenth of a minute. Because of its irregular movement, the **True Node of Moon** is listed daily. The **Mean Node of Moon** is listed once each month. **Direct/Retrograde indicators** are given on the day that the planet goes direct or retrograde. Look in the far left Astro Data section at the bottom of the page for the exact UT time of the station. If the planet's station is marked D, those persons born prior to that time have the planet retrograde; after that time, direct. **Phenomena sections for each month** give all lunar phases, solar and lunar eclipses, stations, ingresses, outer planet aspects, planetary crossings of the celestial equator and void-of-course Moon data. See **Key to Phenomena Section** for details.

Summary of Differences from Prior Editions of 20th Century Ephemeris

- The position of the Galactic Center is given in place of Delta T.
- Improvements in the ephemeris generating program enable finding double ingresses in a single day and more accurate station times.
- Daily positions for Ceres have been inserted between Mars and Jupiter.
- A new formula more accurately determines the position of Galactic Center.
- Monthly positions of Eris plus asteroids Pallas, Juno and Vesta are added to the far right Astro Data box, along with the monthly position of Chiron.
- Planetary Ingress Astro Data includes R after the sign if the planet is retrograde at ingress.
- Phenomena in the far left Astro Data column are sorted by time as well as date.

LONGITUDE — January 1900

Day	Sid.Time	☉	0 hr ☽	Noon ☽	True ☊	☿	♀	♂	⚳	♃	♄	♅	♆	♇
1 M	18 42 43	10♑39 47	2♑24 58	9♑36 58	20♐15.8	19♐38.4	6♒59.8	14♑15.2	1♑13.6	1♐14.0	27♐46.5	10♐10.0	25♊12.3	15♊14.6
2 Tu	18 46 40	11 40 59	16 53 08	24 12 39	20R 13.8	20 56.5	8 14.4	15 01.4	1 38.0	1 25.7	27 53.5	10 13.3	25R 10.7	15R 13.5
3 W	18 50 37	12 42 10	1♒34 38	8♒58 07	20 10.9	22 15.9	9 28.9	15 47.7	2 02.3	1 37.3	28 00.4	10 16.6	25 09.1	15 12.5
4 Th	18 54 33	13 43 21	16 22 08	23 45 42	20 07.5	23 36.6	10 43.5	16 34.1	2 26.6	1 48.8	28 07.3	10 19.8	25 07.5	15 11.5
5 F	18 58 30	14 44 32	1♓07 56	8♓28 00	20 04.2	24 58.4	11 58.0	17 20.4	2 50.9	2 00.2	28 14.2	10 23.0	25 05.9	15 10.5
6 Sa	19 02 26	15 45 42	15 45 09	22 58 49	20 01.6	26 21.3	13 12.5	18 06.8	3 15.2	2 11.6	28 21.1	10 26.2	25 04.3	15 09.5
7 Su	19 06 23	16 46 52	0♈08 30	7♈13 55	20D 00.1	27 45.0	14 26.9	18 53.3	3 39.4	2 22.9	28 28.0	10 29.4	25 02.7	15 08.6
8 M	19 10 19	17 48 01	14 14 49	21 11 07	19 59.8	29 09.7	15 41.4	19 39.8	4 03.6	2 34.1	28 34.8	10 32.5	25 01.2	15 07.6
9 Tu	19 14 16	18 49 10	28 02 50	4♉50 03	20 00.6	0♑35.1	16 55.8	20 26.3	4 27.7	2 45.3	28 41.6	10 35.6	24 59.7	15 06.6
10 W	19 18 12	19 50 18	11♉32 54	18 11 35	20 02.2	2 01.2	18 10.1	21 12.8	4 51.9	2 56.3	28 48.4	10 38.7	24 58.1	15 05.7
11 Th	19 22 09	20 51 26	24 46 18	1♊11 18	20 03.9	3 28.1	19 24.5	21 59.4	5 16.0	3 07.3	28 55.2	10 41.7	24 56.6	15 04.8
12 F	19 26 06	21 52 33	7♊44 48	14 09 02	20R 05.0	4 55.7	20 38.8	22 46.0	5 40.1	3 18.2	29 01.9	10 44.8	24 55.2	15 03.9
13 Sa	19 30 02	22 53 40	20 30 11	26 48 29	20 04.9	6 23.9	21 53.1	23 32.6	6 04.1	3 29.0	29 08.6	10 47.7	24 53.7	15 03.0
14 Su	19 33 59	23 54 46	3♋04 05	9♋17 09	20 03.2	7 52.7	23 07.3	24 19.2	6 28.1	3 39.7	29 15.3	10 50.7	24 52.2	15 02.1
15 M	19 37 55	24 55 51	15 27 50	21 36 15	19 59.7	9 22.2	24 21.5	25 05.9	6 52.1	3 50.3	29 21.9	10 53.6	24 50.8	15 01.3
16 Tu	19 41 52	25 56 56	27 42 33	3♌46 52	19 54.3	10 52.2	25 35.7	25 52.6	7 16.0	4 00.8	29 28.5	10 56.5	24 49.4	15 00.4
17 W	19 45 48	26 58 00	9♌49 21	15 50 08	19 47.6	12 22.8	26 49.8	26 39.4	7 39.9	4 11.3	29 35.1	10 59.4	24 48.0	14 59.6
18 Th	19 49 45	27 59 04	21 49 25	27 47 25	19 40.1	13 54.0	28 03.9	27 26.2	8 03.7	4 21.6	29 41.6	11 02.2	24 46.6	14 58.8
19 F	19 53 41	29 00 07	3♍44 21	9♍40 32	19 32.6	15 25.8	29 17.9	28 13.0	8 27.6	4 31.9	29 48.1	11 04.9	24 45.3	14 58.0
20 Sa	19 57 38	0♒01 10	15 36 15	21 31 53	19 25.7	16 58.2	0♓31.9	28 59.8	8 51.3	4 42.0	29 54.6	11 07.7	24 43.9	14 57.2
21 Su	20 01 35	1 02 12	27 27 51	3♎24 35	19 20.3	18 31.1	1 45.9	29 46.6	9 15.1	4 52.1	0♑01.0	11 10.4	24 42.6	14 56.4
22 M	20 05 31	2 03 14	9♎22 35	15 22 21	19 16.6	20 04.7	2 59.8	0♒33.5	9 38.8	5 02.0	0 07.4	11 13.1	24 41.3	14 55.7
23 Tu	20 09 28	3 04 15	21 24 29	27 29 32	19D 14.9	21 38.8	4 13.7	1 20.4	10 02.4	5 11.9	0 13.8	11 15.7	24 40.1	14 54.9
24 W	20 13 24	4 05 16	3♏38 07	9♏50 51	19 14.9	23 13.6	5 27.6	2 07.4	10 26.0	5 21.6	0 20.1	11 18.3	24 38.8	14 54.2
25 Th	20 17 21	5 06 16	16 08 19	22 31 07	19 16.0	24 49.0	6 41.4	2 54.3	10 49.6	5 31.3	0 26.3	11 20.8	24 37.6	14 53.5
26 F	20 21 17	6 07 16	28 59 47	5♐34 49	19 17.3	26 25.0	7 55.1	3 41.3	11 13.1	5 40.8	0 32.6	11 23.4	24 36.4	14 52.8
27 Sa	20 25 14	7 08 15	12♐16 35	19 05 23	19R 18.0	28 01.6	9 08.8	4 28.3	11 36.6	5 50.2	0 38.7	11 25.8	24 35.2	14 52.2
28 Su	20 29 10	8 09 13	26 01 21	3♑04 29	19 17.1	29 38.9	10 22.5	5 15.4	12 00.0	5 59.5	0 44.9	11 28.3	24 34.1	14 51.5
29 M	20 33 07	9 10 11	10♑14 35	17 31 13	19 14.1	1♒16.9	11 36.1	6 02.4	12 23.4	6 08.7	0 51.0	11 30.7	24 33.0	14 50.9
30 Tu	20 37 04	10 11 08	24 53 46	2♒21 23	19 08.7	2 55.6	12 49.7	6 49.5	12 46.7	6 17.8	0 57.0	11 33.0	24 31.9	14 50.3
31 W	20 41 00	11 12 04	9♒53 03	17 27 34	19 01.4	4 34.9	14 03.3	7 36.6	13 10.0	6 26.8	1 03.0	11 35.3	24 30.8	14 49.7

LONGITUDE — February 1900

Day	Sid.Time	☉	0 hr ☽	Noon ☽	True ☊	☿	♀	♂	⚳	♃	♄	♅	♆	♇
1 Th	20 44 57	12♒12 58	25♒03 38	2♓39 53	18♐52.9	6♒15.0	15♓16.7	8♒23.7	13♑33.2	6♐35.6	1♑08.9	11♐37.6	24♊29.8	14♊49.2
2 F	20 48 53	13 13 51	10♓14 58	17 47 36	18R 44.3	7 55.8	16 30.1	9 10.9	13 56.4	6 44.4	1 14.8	11 39.8	24R 28.8	14R 48.6
3 Sa	20 52 50	14 14 43	25 16 37	2♈41 02	18 36.9	9 37.3	17 43.5	9 58.0	14 19.5	6 52.9	1 20.6	11 42.0	24 27.8	14 48.1
4 Su	20 56 46	15 15 34	10♈00 04	17 13 07	18 31.4	11 19.6	18 56.8	10 45.2	14 42.5	7 01.4	1 26.4	11 44.1	24 26.8	14 47.6
5 M	21 00 43	16 16 23	24 19 50	1♉20 02	18 28.1	13 02.7	20 10.1	11 32.3	15 05.5	7 09.8	1 32.1	11 46.2	24 25.9	14 47.1
6 Tu	21 04 39	17 17 10	8♉13 43	15 01 02	18D 27.0	14 46.5	21 23.2	12 19.5	15 28.4	7 18.0	1 37.8	11 48.3	24 25.0	14 46.6
7 W	21 08 36	18 17 56	21 42 16	28 17 47	18 27.3	16 31.1	22 36.3	13 06.7	15 51.3	7 26.1	1 43.4	11 50.3	24 24.1	14 46.2
8 Th	21 12 33	19 18 41	4♊47 58	11♊13 19	18R 28.1	18 16.4	23 49.4	13 53.9	16 14.1	7 34.0	1 48.9	11 52.2	24 23.3	14 45.7
9 F	21 16 29	20 19 24	17 34 17	23 51 21	18 28.1	20 02.6	25 02.4	14 41.2	16 36.8	7 41.9	1 54.4	11 54.1	24 22.5	14 45.3
10 Sa	21 20 26	21 20 05	0♋04 59	6♋15 37	18 26.5	21 49.5	26 15.3	15 28.4	16 59.5	7 49.6	1 59.9	11 56.0	24 21.7	14 45.0
11 Su	21 24 22	22 20 45	12 23 38	18 29 25	18 22.3	23 37.2	27 28.1	16 15.6	17 22.1	7 57.1	2 05.2	11 57.8	24 20.9	14 44.6
12 M	21 28 19	23 21 23	24 33 16	0♌35 29	18 15.3	25 25.6	28 40.9	17 02.9	17 44.6	8 04.5	2 10.5	11 59.5	24 20.2	14 44.3
13 Tu	21 32 15	24 22 00	6♌36 19	12 35 58	18 05.5	27 14.7	29 53.5	17 50.1	18 07.1	8 11.8	2 15.8	12 01.3	24 19.5	14 43.9
14 W	21 36 12	25 22 35	18 34 38	24 32 30	17 53.5	29 04.5	1♈06.2	18 37.4	18 29.5	8 19.0	2 20.9	12 02.9	24 18.9	14 43.6
15 Th	21 40 08	26 23 08	0♍29 41	6♍26 22	17 40.2	0♓54.9	2 18.7	19 24.7	18 51.8	8 26.0	2 26.1	12 04.5	24 18.2	14 43.4
16 F	21 44 05	27 23 40	12 22 43	18 18 53	17 26.6	2 45.9	3 31.1	20 12.0	19 14.1	8 32.8	2 31.1	12 06.1	24 17.7	14 43.1
17 Sa	21 48 02	28 24 11	24 15 04	0♎11 30	17 13.9	4 37.3	4 43.5	20 59.3	19 36.3	8 39.5	2 36.1	12 07.6	24 17.1	14 42.9
18 Su	21 51 58	29 24 40	6♎08 26	12 06 09	17 03.1	6 29.0	5 55.8	21 46.6	19 58.4	8 46.1	2 41.0	12 09.1	24 16.6	14 42.6
19 M	21 55 55	0♓25 08	18 05 01	24 05 25	16 54.9	8 21.0	7 08.0	22 33.9	20 20.4	8 52.5	2 45.8	12 10.5	24 16.1	14 42.5
20 Tu	21 59 51	1 25 34	0♏07 47	6♏12 34	16 49.5	10 13.0	8 20.1	23 21.2	20 42.4	8 58.8	2 50.6	12 11.9	24 15.6	14 42.3
21 W	22 03 48	2 26 00	12 20 19	18 31 35	16 46.8	12 04.8	9 32.1	24 08.5	21 04.3	9 04.9	2 55.3	12 13.2	24 15.2	14 42.1
22 Th	22 07 44	3 26 23	24 46 55	1♐06 55	16D 46.0	13 56.3	10 44.1	24 55.8	21 26.1	9 10.9	2 59.9	12 14.4	24 14.8	14 42.0
23 F	22 11 41	4 26 46	7♐32 10	14 03 14	16R 46.1	15 47.2	11 56.0	25 43.1	21 47.8	9 16.7	3 04.5	12 15.6	24 14.4	14 41.9
24 Sa	22 15 37	5 27 07	20 40 39	27 24 51	16 45.8	17 37.1	13 07.7	26 30.5	22 09.5	9 22.3	3 09.0	12 16.8	24 14.1	14 41.8
25 Su	22 19 34	6 27 27	4♑16 11	11♑14 52	16 43.9	19 25.7	14 19.4	27 17.8	22 31.0	9 27.8	3 13.4	12 17.9	24 13.8	14 41.8
26 M	22 23 31	7 27 45	18 20 58	25 34 18	16 39.6	21 12.7	15 31.0	28 05.1	22 52.5	9 33.1	3 17.7	12 19.0	24 13.5	14 41.7
27 Tu	22 27 27	8 28 01	2♒54 32	10♒21 01	16 32.5	22 57.5	16 42.5	28 52.4	23 13.9	9 38.3	3 22.0	12 20.0	24 13.3	14D 41.7
28 W	22 31 24	9 28 16	17 52 55	25 29 09	16 22.9	24 39.7	17 53.9	29 39.8	23 35.2	9 43.3	3 26.1	12 20.9	24 13.1	14 41.7

Astro Data

	Dy Hr Mn
☽ 0N	6 3:26
☽ 0S	20 4:51
☽ 0N	2 12:34
♀ 0N	14 22:38
☽ 0S	16 12:01
♇ D	27 14:48

Planet Ingress

	Dy Hr Mn
☿ ♑	9 2:10
♀ ♓	20 1:39
☉ ♒	20 11:33
♄ ♑	21 8:10
♂ ♒	21 18:51
☿ ♒	28 17:11
♀ ♈	13 14:08
☿ ♓	15 0:04
☉ ♓	19 2:01
♂ ♓	28 22:15

Last Aspect / ☽ Ingress

Last Aspect Dy Hr Mn		☽ Ingress Dy Hr Mn
1 20:06	♂ ☌	♒ 2 21:26
4 19:09	♄ ⚹	♓ 4 22:09
6 21:04	♄ □	♈ 6 23:46
9 1:03	♄ △	♉ 9 3:26
10 17:50	♂ △	♊ 11 9:37
13 16:30	♄ ☍	♋ 13 18:06
15 19:20	♂ ☍	♌ 16 4:31
18 15:52	♄ △	♍ 18 16:27
21 5:06	♄ □	♎ 21 5:07
23 6:27	♆ △	♏ 23 16:55
25 16:53	☿ ⚹	♐ 26 1:51
27 21:31	♆ ☍	♑ 28 6:48
29 1:21	♀ ⚹	♒ 30 8:13

Last Aspect / ☽ Ingress

Last Aspect Dy Hr Mn		☽ Ingress Dy Hr Mn
31 23:07	♆ △	♓ 1 7:48
2 22:42	♆ □	♈ 3 7:38
5 0:11	♆ ⚹	♉ 5 9:42
7 0:35	♀ ⚹	♊ 7 15:08
9 14:31	♀ □	♋ 9 23:50
12 7:46	♀ △	♌ 12 10:49
14 22:48	☿ ☍	♍ 14 23:00
17 0:05	♆ □	♎ 17 11:37
19 12:21	♆ △	♏ 19 23:45
21 23:30	♂ □	♐ 22 9:54
24 10:18	♂ ⚹	♑ 24 16:33
26 3:46	☿ ⚹	♒ 26 19:16
28 18:55	♂ ☌	♓ 28 19:05

☽ Phases & Eclipses

Dy Hr Mn	
1 13:52	● 10♑45
8 5:40	☽ 17♈32
15 19:07	○ 25♋14
23 23:53	☾ 3♏34
31 1:23	● 10♒45
6 16:23	☽ 17♉28
14 13:50	○ 25♌27
22 16:44	☾ 3♐38

Astro Data

1 January 1900
Julian Day # 1
SVP 6♓39'04"
GC 25♐26.6 ⚵ 20♐49.7
Eris 21♓35.2 ✱ 22♑32.7
⚷ 18♐57.2 ⚶ 17♈26.6
☽ Mean ☊ 19♐08.1

1 February 1900
Julian Day # 32
SVP 6♓38'59"
GC 25♐26.6 ⚵ 3♑10.4
Eris 21♓50.2 ✱ 5♒17.8
⚷ 22♐05.4 ⚶ 25♈38.4
☽ Mean ☊ 17♐29.6

March 1900 — LONGITUDE

Day	Sid.Time	☉	0 hr ☽	Noon☽	True☊	☿	♀	♂	⚳	♃	♄	♅	♆	♇
1 Th	22 35 20	10♓28 29	3♓08 25	10♓49 17	16♐11.6	26♓18.9	19♈05.2	0♓27.1	23♑56.4	9♐48.1	3♑30.2	12♐21.8	24♊12.9	14♊41.8
2 F	22 39 17	11 28 41	18 30 15	26 09 47	16R 00.1	27 54.4	20 16.4	1 14.4	24 17.5	9 52.8	3 34.3	12 22.7	24R 12.8	14 41.8
3 Sa	22 43 13	12 28 50	3♈46 27	11♈18 56	15 49.7	29 25.7	21 27.5	2 01.7	24 38.5	9 57.3	3 38.2	12 23.5	24 12.7	14 41.9
4 Su	22 47 10	13 28 58	18 46 06	26 07 04	15 41.4	0♈52.3	22 38.5	2 49.0	24 59.4	10 01.6	3 42.1	12 24.2	24 12.6	14 42.0
5 M	22 51 06	14 29 03	3♉21 10	10♉28 00	15 35.9	2 13.5	23 49.4	3 36.3	25 20.3	10 05.8	3 45.8	12 24.9	24D 12.6	14 42.1
6 Tu	22 55 03	15 29 06	17 27 23	24 19 21	15 33.1	3 28.8	25 00.2	4 23.6	25 41.0	10 09.8	3 49.5	12 25.5	24 12.6	14 42.3
7 W	22 59 00	16 29 08	1♊04 06	7♊41 57	15 32.2	4 37.7	26 10.8	5 10.9	26 01.6	10 13.6	3 53.1	12 26.1	24 12.7	14 42.4
8 Th	23 02 56	17 29 07	14 13 23	20 38 53	15 32.1	5 39.6	27 21.4	5 58.2	26 22.1	10 17.2	3 56.6	12 26.6	24 12.8	14 42.6
9 F	23 06 53	18 29 03	26 59 02	3♋14 26	15 31.6	6 34.2	28 31.8	6 45.5	26 42.5	10 20.7	4 00.1	12 27.1	24 12.9	14 42.8
10 Sa	23 10 49	19 28 58	9♋25 41	15 33 21	15 29.6	7 21.1	29 42.1	7 32.7	27 02.9	10 24.0	4 03.4	12 27.5	24 13.0	14 43.1
11 Su	23 14 46	20 28 50	21 38 01	27 40 12	15 25.0	7 59.8	0♉52.2	8 20.0	27 23.1	10 27.1	4 06.7	12 27.9	24 13.2	14 43.3
12 M	23 18 42	21 28 41	3♌40 23	9♌39 02	15 17.5	8 30.1	2 02.2	9 07.2	27 43.2	10 30.0	4 09.9	12 28.2	24 13.4	14 43.6
13 Tu	23 22 39	22 28 29	15 36 33	21 33 15	15 07.2	8 52.0	3 12.1	9 54.4	28 03.1	10 32.8	4 13.0	12 28.4	24 13.7	14 43.9
14 W	23 26 35	23 28 15	27 29 29	3♍25 29	14 54.5	9 05.2	4 21.8	10 41.6	28 23.0	10 35.4	4 16.0	12 28.6	24 13.9	14 44.2
15 Th	23 30 32	24 27 58	9♍21 30	15 17 44	14 40.4	9R 10.0	5 31.4	11 28.8	28 42.8	10 37.8	4 18.9	12 28.8	24 14.3	14 44.5
16 F	23 34 29	25 27 40	21 14 20	27 11 29	14 26.0	9 06.3	6 40.9	12 15.9	29 02.4	10 40.0	4 21.7	12 28.9	24 14.6	14 44.9
17 Sa	23 38 25	26 27 20	3♎09 19	9♎08 00	14 12.5	8 54.5	7 50.2	13 03.1	29 21.9	10 42.0	4 24.4	12R 28.9	24 15.0	14 45.3
18 Su	23 42 22	27 26 58	15 07 41	21 08 34	14 00.8	8 35.0	8 59.4	13 50.2	29 41.4	10 43.9	4 27.1	12 28.9	24 15.4	14 45.7
19 M	23 46 18	28 26 34	27 10 50	3♏14 45	13 51.9	8 08.3	10 08.4	14 37.4	0♒00.6	10 45.5	4 29.6	12 28.9	24 15.9	14 46.1
20 Tu	23 50 15	29 26 08	9♏20 35	15 28 39	13 45.9	7 35.1	11 17.2	15 24.5	0 19.8	10 47.0	4 32.1	12 28.7	24 16.4	14 46.5
21 W	23 54 11	0♈25 40	21 39 17	27 52 55	13 42.7	6 56.3	12 26.0	16 11.6	0 38.9	10 48.3	4 34.4	12 28.6	24 16.9	14 47.0
22 Th	23 58 08	1 25 11	4♐09 57	10♐30 52	13D 41.6	6 12.6	13 34.5	16 58.7	0 57.8	10 49.4	4 36.7	12 28.4	24 17.4	14 47.5
23 F	0 02 04	2 24 39	16 56 07	23 26 11	13R 41.8	5 25.2	14 42.9	17 45.7	1 16.6	10 50.3	4 38.9	12 28.1	24 18.0	14 48.0
24 Sa	0 06 01	3 24 07	0♑01 32	6♑42 37	13 41.9	4 35.0	15 51.1	18 32.8	1 35.2	10 51.1	4 41.0	12 27.8	24 18.6	14 48.5
25 Su	0 09 58	4 23 32	13 29 47	20 23 19	13 40.9	3 43.3	16 59.2	19 19.8	1 53.8	10 51.6	4 43.0	12 27.4	24 19.3	14 49.1
26 M	0 13 54	5 22 55	27 23 24	4♒30 04	13 37.8	2 50.9	18 07.0	20 06.8	2 12.2	10 52.0	4 44.9	12 27.0	24 20.0	14 49.7
27 Tu	0 17 51	6 22 17	11♒43 07	19 02 14	13 32.2	1 59.2	19 14.7	20 53.8	2 30.4	10R 52.1	4 46.7	12 26.5	24 20.7	14 50.3
28 W	0 21 47	7 21 37	26 26 51	3♓56 10	13 24.4	1 08.9	20 22.3	21 40.7	2 48.5	10 52.1	4 48.4	12 26.0	24 21.4	14 50.9
29 Th	0 25 44	8 20 55	11♓29 11	19 04 46	13 14.9	0 21.1	21 29.6	22 27.7	3 06.5	10 51.9	4 50.0	12 25.4	24 22.2	14 51.5
30 F	0 29 40	9 20 11	26 41 35	4♈18 16	13 05.1	29♓36.5	22 36.8	23 14.6	3 24.3	10 51.5	4 51.5	12 24.7	24 23.0	14 52.1
31 Sa	0 33 37	10 19 25	11♈53 27	19 25 46	12 56.0	28 55.8	23 43.7	24 01.5	3 42.0	10 50.9	4 52.9	12 24.1	24 23.9	14 52.8

April 1900 — LONGITUDE

Day	Sid.Time	☉	0 hr ☽	Noon☽	True☊	☿	♀	♂	⚳	♃	♄	♅	♆	♇
1 Su	0 37 33	11♈18 37	26♈54 01	4♉17 08	12♐48.8	28♓19.6	24♉50.5	24♓48.4	3♒59.6	10♐50.1	4♑54.2	12♐23.3	24♊24.8	14♊53.5
2 M	0 41 30	12 17 47	11♉34 16	18 44 46	12R 44.1	27R 48.2	25 57.1	25 35.2	4 16.9	10R 49.2	4 55.4	12R 22.5	24 25.7	14 54.2
3 Tu	0 45 26	13 16 55	25 48 13	2♊44 25	12D 41.8	27 22.0	27 03.4	26 22.0	4 34.2	10 48.0	4 56.5	12 21.7	24 26.6	14 54.9
4 W	0 49 23	14 16 00	9♊33 21	16 15 11	12 41.4	27 01.2	28 09.6	27 08.8	4 51.2	10 46.7	4 57.5	12 20.8	24 27.6	14 55.7
5 Th	0 53 20	15 15 03	22 50 12	29 18 49	12 42.1	26 45.9	29 15.5	27 55.5	5 08.1	10 45.2	4 58.4	12 19.9	24 28.6	14 56.5
6 F	0 57 16	16 14 04	5♋41 31	11♋58 53	12R 42.8	26 36.2	0♊21.2	28 42.3	5 24.9	10 43.4	4 59.3	12 18.9	24 29.6	14 57.2
7 Sa	1 01 13	17 13 03	18 11 30	24 19 58	12 42.6	26D 31.9	1 26.6	29 28.9	5 41.5	10 41.6	5 00.0	12 17.9	24 30.7	14 58.0
8 Su	1 05 09	18 11 59	0♌24 55	6♌26 57	12 40.7	26 33.1	2 31.8	0♈15.6	5 57.9	10 39.5	5 00.6	12 16.8	24 31.8	14 58.9
9 M	1 09 06	19 10 53	12 26 39	18 24 36	12 36.6	26 39.5	3 36.8	1 02.2	6 14.1	10 37.2	5 01.1	12 15.7	24 32.9	14 59.7
10 Tu	1 13 02	20 09 44	24 21 17	0♍17 13	12 30.3	26 51.0	4 41.5	1 48.8	6 30.2	10 34.8	5 01.5	12 14.6	24 34.1	15 00.6
11 W	1 16 59	21 08 33	6♍12 49	12 08 30	12 22.2	27 07.5	5 45.9	2 35.4	6 46.1	10 32.2	5 01.9	12 13.4	24 35.2	15 01.4
12 Th	1 20 55	22 07 21	18 04 38	24 01 30	12 12.9	27 28.8	6 50.1	3 21.9	7 01.9	10 29.4	5 02.1	12 12.1	24 36.4	15 02.3
13 F	1 24 52	23 06 06	29 59 22	5♎58 30	12 03.3	27 54.6	7 54.0	4 08.4	7 17.4	10 26.4	5R 02.2	12 10.8	24 37.7	15 03.2
14 Sa	1 28 49	24 04 49	11♎59 04	18 01 15	11 54.3	28 24.8	8 57.6	4 54.8	7 32.8	10 23.3	5 02.2	12 09.5	24 38.9	15 04.1
15 Su	1 32 45	25 03 30	24 05 14	0♏11 07	11 46.6	28 59.2	10 00.9	5 41.2	7 48.0	10 19.9	5 02.2	12 08.1	24 40.2	15 05.1
16 M	1 36 42	26 02 09	6♏19 03	12 29 11	11 40.9	29 37.5	11 03.9	6 27.6	8 03.0	10 16.4	5 02.0	12 06.7	24 41.6	15 06.0
17 Tu	1 40 38	27 00 46	18 41 40	24 56 38	11 37.3	0♈19.6	12 06.6	7 14.0	8 17.8	10 12.8	5 01.7	12 05.2	24 42.9	15 07.0
18 W	1 44 35	27 59 21	1♐14 16	7♐34 47	11D 35.9	1 05.3	13 09.0	8 00.3	8 32.4	10 09.0	5 01.4	12 03.7	24 44.3	15 08.0
19 Th	1 48 31	28 57 55	13 58 23	20 25 20	11 36.1	1 54.5	14 11.0	8 46.6	8 46.9	10 05.0	5 00.9	12 02.1	24 45.7	15 09.0
20 F	1 52 28	29 56 27	26 55 52	3♑30 14	11 37.4	2 47.0	15 12.7	9 32.8	9 01.1	10 00.8	5 00.4	12 00.6	24 47.1	15 10.0
21 Sa	1 56 24	0♉54 58	10♑08 44	16 51 35	11 38.7	3 42.5	16 14.1	10 19.0	9 15.2	9 56.5	4 59.7	11 58.9	24 48.6	15 11.0
22 Su	2 00 21	1 53 27	23 39 02	0♒31 13	11R 39.5	4 41.1	17 15.1	11 05.2	9 29.0	9 52.0	4 59.0	11 57.3	24 50.0	15 12.1
23 M	2 04 18	2 51 54	7♒28 15	14 30 08	11 38.9	5 42.6	18 15.8	11 51.4	9 42.6	9 47.4	4 58.1	11 55.6	24 51.6	15 13.1
24 Tu	2 08 14	3 50 19	21 36 48	28 47 59	11 36.7	6 46.8	19 16.1	12 37.5	9 56.1	9 42.6	4 57.2	11 53.8	24 53.1	15 14.2
25 W	2 12 11	4 48 43	6♓03 21	13♓22 22	11 33.0	7 53.6	20 16.0	13 23.5	10 09.3	9 37.6	4 56.1	11 52.1	24 54.6	15 15.3
26 Th	2 16 07	5 47 06	20 44 24	28 08 38	11 28.2	9 03.1	21 15.6	14 09.5	10 22.3	9 32.5	4 55.0	11 50.3	24 56.2	15 16.4
27 F	2 20 04	6 45 26	5♈34 11	13♈00 03	11 23.0	10 14.9	22 14.7	14 55.5	10 35.0	9 27.3	4 53.8	11 48.4	24 57.8	15 17.5
28 Sa	2 24 00	7 43 46	20 25 13	27 48 38	11 18.2	11 29.2	23 13.4	15 41.5	10 47.6	9 21.9	4 52.5	11 46.5	24 59.4	15 18.6
29 Su	2 27 57	8 42 03	5♉09 18	12♉26 17	11 14.4	12 45.8	24 11.7	16 27.3	10 59.9	9 16.4	4 51.0	11 44.6	25 01.1	15 19.8
30 M	2 31 53	9 40 19	19 38 47	26 46 08	11 12.2	14 04.6	25 09.5	17 13.2	11 12.0	9 10.8	4 49.5	11 42.7	25 02.7	15 20.9

Astro Data

	Dy Hr Mn
☽ 0N	1 23:47
☿ 0N	2 21:25
♆ D	5 16:55
☿ R	15 13:22
☽ 0S	15 18:17
♅ R	17 19:27
☉ 0N	21 1:39
♃ R	27 21:19
☽ 0N	29 10:46
☿ 0S	3 2:53
☿ D	7 18:52
♂ 0N	11 0:39
☽ 0S	12 0:14
♄ R	14 6:59
☿ 0N	23 22:50

Planet Ingress

		Dy Hr Mn
☿	♈	3 21:21
♀	♉	10 18:08
⚳	♒	19 11:12
☉	♈	21 1:39
☿	♓R	29 23:07
♀	♊	6 4:15
♂	♈	8 3:58
☿	♈	17 1:05
☉	♉	20 13:27

☽ 0N25 19:35

Last Aspect / ☽ Ingress

Last Aspect Dy Hr Mn			☽ Ingress	Dy Hr Mn
2 15:03	☿	☌	♈	2 18:02
4 8:52	♆	⚹	♉	4 18:25
5 19:24	☉	⚹	♊	6 22:05
9 2:01	♀	⚹	♋	9 5:46
10 20:26	☉	△	♌	11 16:39
13 17:24	♆	⚹	♍	14 5:04
16 8:12	☉	☍	♎	16 17:39
18 18:12	♆	△	♏	19 5:35
20 11:51	♂	△	♐	21 16:03
23 13:35	♆	☍	♑	23 23:57
25 10:03	♂	⚹	♒	26 4:26
27 20:37	♆	△	♓	28 5:42
30 4:56	☿	☌	♈	30 5:13

Last Aspect / ☽ Ingress

Last Aspect Dy Hr Mn			☽ Ingress	Dy Hr Mn
31 19:59	♆	⚹	♉	1 5:01
3 2:57	☿	⚹	♊	3 7:14
5 9:15	♂	□	♋	5 13:17
7 22:51	♂	△	♌	7 23:11
10 0:25	♆	⚹	♍	10 11:25
12 19:12	☿	☍	♎	13 0:01
15 1:08	♆	△	♏	15 11:38
15 21:30	♄	⚹	♐	17 21:39
20 4:59	☉	△	♑	20 5:37
20 23:36	♂	□	♒	22 11:06
24 5:28	♆	△	♓	24 14:00
26 6:48	♆	□	♈	26 15:00
28 7:24	♆	⚹	♉	28 15:34
29 5:23	☉	☌	♊	30 17:30

☽ Phases & Eclipses

Dy Hr Mn		
1 11:25	●	10♓27
8 5:34	☽	17♊13
16 8:12	○	25♍18
24 5:37	☾	3♑08
30 20:30	●	9♈41
6 20:55	☽	16♋36
15 1:02	○	24♎37
22 14:33	☾	2♒00
29 5:23	●	8♉26

Astro Data

1 March 1900
Julian Day # 60
SVP 6♓38'56"
GC 25♐26.7 ⚴ 13♑06.2
Eris 22♓10.7 ⚵ 17♒05.5
⚷ 24♐05.0 ⚶ 5♉25.4
☽ Mean ☊ 16♐00.7

1 April 1900
Julian Day # 91
SVP 6♓38'53"
GC 25♐26.8 ⚴ 21♑50.3
Eris 22♓35.6 ⚵ 0♓06.4
⚷ 24♐59.3 ⚶ 17♉42.1
☽ Mean ☊ 14♐22.1

LONGITUDE May 1900

Day	Sid.Time	☉	0 hr ☽	Noon ☽	True ☊	☿	♀	♂	⚳	♃	♄	♅	♆	♇
1 Tu	2 35 50	10♉38 33	3♊47 47	10♊43 22	11♐11.4	15♈25.6	26♊06.9	17♈59.0	11♒23.8	9♐05.0	4♑47.9	11♐40.7	25♊04.4	15♊22.1
2 W	2 39 47	11 36 45	17 32 42	24 15 43	11D 11.9	16 48.8	27 03.7	18 44.8	11 35.5	8R 59.1	4R 46.3	11R 38.7	25 06.2	15 23.3
3 Th	2 43 43	12 34 55	0♋52 30	7♋23 15	11 13.3	18 14.1	28 00.1	19 30.5	11 46.8	8 53.0	4 44.5	11 36.7	25 07.9	15 24.4
4 F	2 47 40	13 33 03	13 48 17	20 08 00	11 15.0	19 41.5	28 56.0	20 16.2	11 58.0	8 46.9	4 42.6	11 34.6	25 09.7	15 25.6
5 Sa	2 51 36	14 31 09	26 22 50	2♌33 21	11 16.3	21 11.0	29 51.4	21 01.8	12 08.9	8 40.6	4 40.7	11 32.5	25 11.4	15 26.9
6 Su	2 55 33	15 29 13	8♌40 04	14 43 33	11R 16.9	22 42.4	0♋46.1	21 47.4	12 19.5	8 34.2	4 38.6	11 30.4	25 13.2	15 28.1
7 M	2 59 29	16 27 15	20 44 26	26 43 15	11 16.4	24 15.9	1 40.3	22 32.9	12 29.9	8 27.7	4 36.5	11 28.2	25 15.0	15 29.3
8 Tu	3 03 26	17 25 16	2♍40 37	8♍37 06	11 14.8	25 51.5	2 34.0	23 18.4	12 40.0	8 21.1	4 34.3	11 26.1	25 16.9	15 30.5
9 W	3 07 22	18 23 14	14 33 13	20 29 29	11 12.3	27 29.0	3 27.0	24 03.8	12 49.9	8 14.4	4 32.0	11 23.9	25 18.7	15 31.8
10 Th	3 11 19	19 21 11	26 26 24	2♎24 24	11 09.1	29 08.5	4 19.3	24 49.2	12 59.5	8 07.6	4 29.6	11 21.7	25 20.6	15 33.0
11 F	3 15 16	20 19 06	8♎23 53	14 25 13	11 05.8	0♉50.1	5 11.0	25 34.5	13 08.9	8 00.8	4 27.1	11 19.4	25 22.5	15 34.3
12 Sa	3 19 12	21 16 59	20 28 44	26 34 42	11 02.6	2 33.6	6 02.0	26 19.8	13 17.9	7 53.8	4 24.6	11 17.2	25 24.4	15 35.6
13 Su	3 23 09	22 14 51	2♏43 21	8♏54 53	10 59.9	4 19.1	6 52.3	27 05.0	13 26.7	7 46.8	4 22.0	11 14.9	25 26.3	15 36.9
14 M	3 27 05	23 12 41	15 09 26	21 27 08	10 58.1	6 06.7	7 41.9	27 50.2	13 35.3	7 39.7	4 19.3	11 12.6	25 28.3	15 38.2
15 Tu	3 31 02	24 10 29	27 48 03	4♐12 16	10D 57.2	7 56.3	8 30.7	28 35.3	13 43.5	7 32.5	4 16.5	11 10.3	25 30.2	15 39.5
16 W	3 34 58	25 08 17	10♐39 47	17 10 39	10 57.2	9 47.9	9 18.7	29 20.4	13 51.5	7 25.2	4 13.6	11 07.9	25 32.2	15 40.8
17 Th	3 38 55	26 06 03	23 44 50	0♑22 20	10 57.9	11 41.4	10 05.9	0♉05.5	13 59.2	7 17.9	4 10.7	11 05.6	25 34.2	15 42.1
18 F	3 42 51	27 03 47	7♑03 07	13 47 10	10 58.9	13 37.0	10 52.2	0 50.5	14 06.6	7 10.5	4 07.7	11 03.2	25 36.2	15 43.4
19 Sa	3 46 48	28 01 31	20 34 25	27 24 50	11 00.0	15 34.5	11 37.7	1 35.4	14 13.8	7 03.1	4 04.7	11 00.8	25 38.2	15 44.7
20 Su	3 50 45	28 59 13	4♒18 20	11♒14 49	11 00.9	17 33.9	12 22.2	2 20.3	14 20.6	6 55.7	4 01.5	10 58.5	25 40.2	15 46.1
21 M	3 54 41	29 56 55	18 14 11	25 16 17	11R 01.3	19 35.2	13 05.9	3 05.1	14 27.1	6 48.2	3 58.3	10 56.0	25 42.3	15 47.4
22 Tu	3 58 38	0♊54 35	2♓20 54	9♓27 48	11 01.2	21 38.3	13 48.5	3 49.9	14 33.3	6 40.6	3 55.0	10 53.6	25 44.3	15 48.8
23 W	4 02 34	1 52 14	16 36 41	23 47 12	11 00.7	23 43.1	14 30.1	4 34.7	14 39.2	6 33.0	3 51.7	10 51.2	25 46.4	15 50.1
24 Th	4 06 31	2 49 53	0♈58 54	8♈11 21	11 00.0	25 49.4	15 10.7	5 19.4	14 44.8	6 25.4	3 48.3	10 48.8	25 48.5	15 51.5
25 F	4 10 27	3 47 30	15 24 01	22 36 19	10 59.1	27 57.2	15 50.2	6 04.0	14 50.1	6 17.8	3 44.8	10 46.3	25 50.6	15 52.8
26 Sa	4 14 24	4 45 07	29 47 39	6♉57 26	10 58.4	0♊06.2	16 28.6	6 48.6	14 55.0	6 10.2	3 41.3	10 43.8	25 52.7	15 54.2
27 Su	4 18 20	5 42 42	14♉05 02	21 09 53	10 57.9	2 16.4	17 05.7	7 33.1	14 59.7	6 02.5	3 37.7	10 41.4	25 54.8	15 55.6
28 M	4 22 17	6 40 17	28 11 26	5♊09 11	10D 57.6	4 27.4	17 41.7	8 17.6	15 04.0	5 54.9	3 34.1	10 38.9	25 56.9	15 56.9
29 Tu	4 26 14	7 37 50	12♊02 43	18 51 42	10 57.7	6 39.0	18 16.4	9 02.0	15 08.0	5 47.2	3 30.4	10 36.4	25 59.1	15 58.3
30 W	4 30 10	8 35 23	25 35 52	2♋15 05	10 57.8	8 50.9	18 49.8	9 46.4	15 11.7	5 39.6	3 26.6	10 34.0	26 01.2	15 59.7
31 Th	4 34 07	9 32 54	8♋49 16	15 18 28	10 58.0	11 03.0	19 21.8	10 30.7	15 15.0	5 32.0	3 22.8	10 31.5	26 03.4	16 01.1

LONGITUDE June 1900

Day	Sid.Time	☉	0 hr ☽	Noon ☽	True ☊	☿	♀	♂	⚳	♃	♄	♅	♆	♇
1 F	4 38 03	10♊30 24	21♋42 48	28♋02 28	10♐58.1	13♊14.9	19♋52.4	11♉14.9	15♒18.0	5♐24.4	3♑18.9	10♐29.0	26♊05.5	16♊02.5
2 Sa	4 42 00	11 27 52	4♌17 44	10♌28 59	10R 58.1	15 26.3	20 21.5	11 59.1	15 20.6	5R 16.8	3R 15.0	10R 26.5	26 07.7	16 03.8
3 Su	4 45 56	12 25 20	16 36 36	22 41 03	10 58.0	17 37.0	20 49.0	12 43.2	15 22.9	5 09.2	3 11.1	10 24.1	26 09.9	16 05.2
4 M	4 49 53	13 22 46	28 42 49	4♍42 27	10D 57.9	19 46.8	21 15.0	13 27.3	15 24.9	5 01.7	3 07.1	10 21.6	26 12.1	16 06.6
5 Tu	4 53 49	14 20 11	10♍40 30	16 37 31	10 57.9	21 55.3	21 39.3	14 11.3	15 26.5	4 54.2	3 03.1	10 19.1	26 14.3	16 08.0
6 W	4 57 46	15 17 34	22 34 05	28 30 47	10 58.0	24 02.3	22 01.8	14 55.3	15 27.8	4 46.8	2 59.0	10 16.7	26 16.5	16 09.4
7 Th	5 01 43	16 14 57	4♎28 11	10♎26 49	10 58.4	26 07.8	22 22.6	15 39.2	15 28.7	4 39.4	2 54.9	10 14.2	26 18.7	16 10.8
8 F	5 05 39	17 12 19	16 27 14	22 29 56	10 58.9	28 11.5	22 41.6	16 23.0	15 29.3	4 32.1	2 50.8	10 11.7	26 20.9	16 12.2
9 Sa	5 09 36	18 09 39	28 35 23	4♏44 01	10 59.6	0♋13.2	22 58.6	17 06.8	15R 29.6	4 24.8	2 46.6	10 09.3	26 23.1	16 13.6
10 Su	5 13 32	19 06 59	10♏56 11	17 12 14	11 00.3	2 12.9	23 13.7	17 50.5	15 29.4	4 17.6	2 42.4	10 06.9	26 25.3	16 15.0
11 M	5 17 29	20 04 18	23 32 26	29 56 56	11R 00.8	4 10.4	23 26.8	18 34.2	15 29.0	4 10.5	2 38.1	10 04.4	26 27.5	16 16.3
12 Tu	5 21 25	21 01 36	6♐25 54	12♐59 21	11 01.0	6 05.8	23 37.8	19 17.8	15 28.2	4 03.4	2 33.9	10 02.0	26 29.8	16 17.7
13 W	5 25 22	21 58 53	19 37 16	26 19 33	11 00.7	7 58.8	23 46.6	20 01.3	15 27.0	3 56.4	2 29.6	9 59.6	26 32.0	16 19.1
14 Th	5 29 18	22 56 10	3♑06 00	9♑56 23	10 59.8	9 49.6	23 53.3	20 44.8	15 25.4	3 49.5	2 25.3	9 57.2	26 34.2	16 20.5
15 F	5 33 15	23 53 27	16 50 24	23 47 41	10 58.4	11 38.0	23 57.7	21 28.2	15 23.6	3 42.7	2 21.0	9 54.8	26 36.5	16 21.9
16 Sa	5 37 12	24 50 42	0♒47 49	7♒50 24	10 56.7	13 24.0	23R 59.8	22 11.6	15 21.3	3 36.0	2 16.6	9 52.5	26 38.7	16 23.3
17 Su	5 41 08	25 47 58	14 54 57	22 01 01	10 55.0	15 07.6	23 59.7	22 54.9	15 18.7	3 29.4	2 12.2	9 50.1	26 40.9	16 24.7
18 M	5 45 05	26 45 13	29 08 10	6♓15 59	10 53.7	16 48.8	23 57.2	23 38.1	15 15.7	3 22.9	2 07.9	9 47.8	26 43.2	16 26.0
19 Tu	5 49 01	27 42 28	13♓24 01	20 31 55	10D 52.9	18 27.6	23 52.3	24 21.3	15 12.4	3 16.4	2 03.5	9 45.4	26 45.4	16 27.4
20 W	5 52 58	28 39 42	27 39 19	4♈45 55	10 52.9	20 04.0	23 45.0	25 04.5	15 08.7	3 10.1	1 59.1	9 43.1	26 47.6	16 28.8
21 Th	5 56 54	29 36 57	11♈51 25	18 55 33	10 53.5	21 37.9	23 35.4	25 47.5	15 04.7	3 03.9	1 54.7	9 40.8	26 49.9	16 30.1
22 F	6 00 51	0♋34 11	25 58 04	2♉58 44	10 54.7	23 09.4	23 23.4	26 30.6	15 00.3	2 57.8	1 50.2	9 38.6	26 52.1	16 31.5
23 Sa	6 04 47	1 31 26	9♉57 21	16 53 42	10 56.1	24 38.4	23 09.0	27 13.5	14 55.6	2 51.9	1 45.8	9 36.3	26 54.3	16 32.8
24 Su	6 08 44	2 28 40	23 47 33	0♊38 43	10R 57.0	26 04.9	22 52.3	27 56.4	14 50.5	2 46.1	1 41.4	9 34.1	26 56.6	16 34.2
25 M	6 12 41	3 25 55	7♊27 00	14 12 12	10 57.3	27 28.8	22 33.3	28 39.2	14 45.0	2 40.3	1 37.0	9 31.9	26 58.8	16 35.5
26 Tu	6 16 37	4 23 09	20 54 08	27 32 38	10 56.5	28 50.2	22 12.0	29 22.0	14 39.2	2 34.8	1 32.6	9 29.7	27 01.0	16 36.9
27 W	6 20 34	5 20 23	4♋07 35	10♋38 51	10 54.4	0♌09.0	21 48.6	0♊04.7	14 33.1	2 29.3	1 28.2	9 27.6	27 03.3	16 38.2
28 Th	6 24 30	6 17 36	17 06 22	23 30 08	10 51.3	1 25.2	21 23.1	0 47.4	14 26.6	2 24.0	1 23.8	9 25.5	27 05.5	16 39.5
29 F	6 28 27	7 14 50	29 50 09	6♌06 30	10 47.3	2 38.6	20 55.6	1 29.9	14 19.7	2 18.9	1 19.4	9 23.4	27 07.7	16 40.9
30 Sa	6 32 23	8 12 03	12♌19 20	18 28 50	10 42.9	3 49.3	20 26.3	2 12.5	14 12.6	2 13.9	1 15.0	9 21.3	27 09.9	16 42.2

Astro Data

	Dy Hr Mn
☽0S	9 6:45
☽0N	23 2:00
☽0S	5 14:20
⚳R	9 16:07
♀R	16 22:20
☽0N	19 7:28

Planet Ingress

	Dy Hr Mn
♀ ♋	5 15:46
☿ ♉	11 0:14
♂ ♉	17 9:05
☉ ♊	21 13:17
☿ ♊	26 10:51
☿ ♋	9 9:23
☉ ♋	21 21:40
☿ ♌	27 9:13
♂ ♊	27 9:21

Last Aspect / ☽ Ingress

Last Aspect Dy Hr Mn		☽ Ingress Dy Hr Mn
2 17:27 ♀ ☌	♋	2 22:24
4 12:17 ♂ □	♌	5 7:01
7 9:02 ♆ ⚹	♍	7 18:36
9 21:45 ♆ □	♎	10 7:10
12 11:29 ♂ ☍	♏	12 18:42
14 15:37 ☉ ☍	♐	15 4:08
17 3:17 ♆ ☍	♑	17 11:20
19 13:09 ☉ △	♒	19 16:31
21 12:44 ♆ △	♓	21 20:02
23 15:19 ♆ □	♈	23 22:22
25 17:25 ♆ ⚹	♉	26 0:21
27 4:47 ♀ ⚹	♊	28 3:06
30 0:44 ♆ ☌	♋	30 7:55

Last Aspect / ☽ Ingress

Last Aspect Dy Hr Mn		☽ Ingress Dy Hr Mn
31 19:54 ♀ ☌	♌	1 15:45
3 18:56 ♆ ⚹	♍	4 2:34
6 7:28 ♆ □	♎	6 15:00
9 1:27 ♆ △	♏	9 2:46
10 23:37 ♆ △	♐	11 12:06
13 12:22 ♆ ☍	♑	13 18:31
15 12:17 ♀ ☍	♒	15 22:38
17 19:53 ♆ △	♓	18 1:27
20 0:57 ☉ □	♈	20 3:57
22 1:31 ♆ ⚹	♉	22 6:54
24 7:00 ♂ ☌	♊	24 10:52
26 11:03 ♆ ☌	♋	26 16:28
28 8:09 ♀ ☌	♌	29 0:19

☽ Phases & Eclipses

Dy Hr Mn	
6 13:39	☽ 15♌33
14 15:37	○ 23♏21
21 20:31	☾ 0♓17
28 14:50	● 6♊47
28 14:53:57	T 02'10"
5 6:59	☽ 14♍08
13 3:39	○ 21♐39
13 3:28	A 1.001
20 0:57	☾ 28♓13
27 1:27	● 4♋55

Astro Data

1 May 1900
Julian Day # 121
SVP 6♓38'50"
GC 25♐26.8 ⚴ 26♑41.1
Eris 22♓56.3 ⚵ 12♓16.6
⚷ 24♐26.7R ⚶ 0♊20.2
☽ Mean ☊ 12♐46.8

1 June 1900
Julian Day # 152
SVP 6♓38'45"
GC 25♐26.9 ⚴ 26♑08.7R
Eris 23♓09.0 ⚵ 23♓52.1
⚷ 22♐44.5R ⚶ 13♊43.4
☽ Mean ☊ 11♐08.3

July 1900 LONGITUDE

Day	Sid.Time	☉	0 hr ☽	Noon ☽	True ☊	☿	♀	♂	⚳	♃	♄	♅	♆	♇
1 Su	6 36 20	9♋09 16	24♌35 15	0♍38 54	10♐38.6	4♌57.1	19♋55.2	2♊54.9	14♒05.1	2♐09.0	1♑10.6	9♐19.3	27♊12.1	16♊43.5
2 M	6 40 16	10 06 28	6♍40 09	12 39 25	10R 35.0	6 02.1	19R 22.7	3 37.3	13R 57.3	2R 04.3	1R 06.3	9R 17.2	27 14.3	16 44.8
3 Tu	6 44 13	11 03 40	18 37 09	24 33 52	10 32.4	7 04.0	18 48.7	4 19.6	13 49.2	1 59.7	1 01.9	9 15.3	27 16.5	16 46.1
4 W	6 48 10	12 00 52	0♎30 05	6♎26 22	10D 31.1	8 02.9	18 13.6	5 01.8	13 40.7	1 55.3	0 57.6	9 13.3	27 18.7	16 47.3
5 Th	6 52 06	12 58 04	12 23 20	18 21 32	10 31.1	8 58.6	17 37.6	5 44.0	13 32.0	1 51.1	0 53.4	9 11.4	27 20.8	16 48.6
6 F	6 56 03	13 55 15	24 21 37	0♏24 09	10 32.1	9 51.0	17 00.8	6 26.1	13 23.0	1 47.0	0 49.1	9 09.5	27 23.0	16 49.9
7 Sa	6 59 59	14 52 27	6♏29 45	12 39 00	10 33.7	10 39.9	16 23.5	7 08.2	13 13.7	1 43.1	0 44.9	9 07.6	27 25.2	16 51.1
8 Su	7 03 56	15 49 38	18 52 23	25 10 26	10 35.2	11 25.4	15 46.0	7 50.2	13 04.1	1 39.3	0 40.7	9 05.8	27 27.3	16 52.4
9 M	7 07 52	16 46 49	1♐33 33	8♐02 06	10R 36.0	12 07.1	15 08.4	8 32.1	12 54.2	1 35.7	0 36.5	9 04.0	27 29.5	16 53.6
10 Tu	7 11 49	17 44 00	14 36 19	21 16 21	10 35.5	12 45.1	14 31.1	9 13.9	12 44.1	1 32.3	0 32.4	9 02.3	27 31.6	16 54.8
11 W	7 15 45	18 41 12	28 02 14	4♑53 53	10 33.4	13 19.1	13 54.2	9 55.7	12 33.7	1 29.1	0 28.3	9 00.5	27 33.7	16 56.1
12 Th	7 19 42	19 38 23	11♑51 02	18 53 18	10 29.7	13 49.0	13 18.1	10 37.4	12 23.0	1 26.0	0 24.3	8 58.9	27 35.8	16 57.3
13 F	7 23 39	20 35 35	26 00 12	3♒11 05	10 24.4	14 14.7	12 42.8	11 19.1	12 12.1	1 23.1	0 20.3	8 57.2	27 37.9	16 58.5
14 Sa	7 27 35	21 32 47	10♒25 13	17 41 48	10 18.4	14 36.1	12 08.8	12 00.7	12 01.0	1 20.3	0 16.3	8 55.6	27 40.0	16 59.6
15 Su	7 31 32	22 30 00	24 59 57	2♓18 48	10 12.3	14 52.9	11 36.0	12 42.2	11 49.7	1 17.8	0 12.4	8 54.0	27 42.1	17 00.8
16 M	7 35 28	23 27 13	9♓37 32	16 55 19	10 07.0	15 05.1	11 04.8	13 23.7	11 38.2	1 15.4	0 08.5	8 52.5	27 44.1	17 02.0
17 Tu	7 39 25	24 24 27	24 11 29	1♈25 24	10 03.2	15 12.5	10 35.4	14 05.1	11 26.4	1 13.2	0 04.7	8 51.0	27 46.2	17 03.1
18 W	7 43 21	25 21 41	8♈36 34	15 44 36	10D 01.2	15R 15.1	10 07.7	14 46.4	11 14.5	1 11.2	0 00.9	8 49.6	27 48.2	17 04.3
19 Th	7 47 18	26 18 57	22 49 13	29 50 16	10 00.8	15 12.9	9 42.1	15 27.7	11 02.4	1 09.3	29♐57.1	8 48.1	27 50.2	17 05.4
20 F	7 51 14	27 16 13	6♉47 40	13♉41 23	10 01.6	15 05.7	9 18.6	16 08.9	10 50.1	1 07.6	29 53.5	8 46.8	27 52.3	17 06.5
21 Sa	7 55 11	28 13 30	20 31 29	27 18 03	10R 02.8	14 53.6	8 57.2	16 50.0	10 37.7	1 06.2	29 49.8	8 45.4	27 54.2	17 07.6
22 Su	7 59 08	29 10 48	4♊01 10	10♊40 58	10 03.3	14 36.7	8 38.1	17 31.1	10 25.1	1 04.9	29 46.3	8 44.2	27 56.2	17 08.7
23 M	8 03 04	0♌08 07	17 17 34	23 51 04	10 02.4	14 15.1	8 21.3	18 12.1	10 12.4	1 03.7	29 42.8	8 42.9	27 58.2	17 09.8
24 Tu	8 07 01	1 05 26	0♋21 33	6♋49 05	9 59.4	13 49.0	8 06.9	18 53.0	9 59.5	1 02.8	29 39.3	8 41.7	28 00.1	17 10.8
25 W	8 10 57	2 02 47	13 13 44	19 35 32	9 54.0	13 18.7	7 54.9	19 33.9	9 46.6	1 02.0	29 35.9	8 40.6	28 02.1	17 11.9
26 Th	8 14 54	3 00 08	25 54 31	2♌10 44	9 46.5	12 44.6	7 45.2	20 14.6	9 33.6	1 01.5	29 32.6	8 39.5	28 04.0	17 12.9
27 F	8 18 50	3 57 29	8♌24 13	14 35 01	9 37.2	12 07.0	7 37.9	20 55.4	9 20.5	1 01.1	29 29.3	8 38.4	28 05.9	17 13.9
28 Sa	8 22 47	4 54 52	20 43 14	26 48 58	9 27.1	11 26.6	7 33.0	21 36.0	9 07.4	1D 00.9	29 26.2	8 37.4	28 07.8	17 14.9
29 Su	8 26 44	5 52 15	2♍52 22	8♍53 38	9 16.9	10 43.8	7D 30.4	22 16.6	8 54.2	1 00.9	29 23.0	8 36.4	28 09.6	17 15.9
30 M	8 30 40	6 49 38	14 53 01	20 50 47	9 07.8	9 59.6	7 30.2	22 57.1	8 40.9	1 01.0	29 20.0	8 35.5	28 11.5	17 16.9
31 Tu	8 34 37	7 47 03	26 47 18	2♎42 57	9 00.4	9 14.4	7 32.2	23 37.5	8 27.7	1 01.4	29 17.0	8 34.6	28 13.3	17 17.8

August 1900 LONGITUDE

Day	Sid.Time	☉	0 hr ☽	Noon ☽	True ☊	☿	♀	♂	⚳	♃	♄	♅	♆	♇
1 W	8 38 33	8♌44 28	8♎38 11	14♎33 30	8♐55.2	8♌29.3	7♋36.5	24♊17.9	8♒14.5	1♐01.9	29♐14.1	8♐33.8	28♊15.1	17♊18.8
2 Th	8 42 30	9 41 54	20 29 24	26 26 29	8R 52.2	7R 45.0	7 43.0	24 58.1	8R 01.2	1 02.6	29R 11.3	8R 33.0	28 16.9	17 19.7
3 F	8 46 26	10 39 20	2♏25 22	8♏26 38	8D 51.2	7 02.3	7 51.7	25 38.4	7 48.0	1 03.5	29 08.5	8 32.2	28 18.7	17 20.6
4 Sa	8 50 23	11 36 47	14 30 58	20 39 01	8 51.5	6 22.0	8 02.4	26 18.5	7 34.9	1 04.6	29 05.8	8 31.5	28 20.4	17 21.5
5 Su	8 54 19	12 34 15	26 51 24	3♐08 44	8R 52.1	5 45.0	8 15.3	26 58.6	7 21.7	1 05.9	29 03.2	8 30.9	28 22.1	17 22.4
6 M	8 58 16	13 31 44	9♐31 37	16 00 32	8 52.0	5 12.1	8 30.1	27 38.5	7 08.7	1 07.3	29 00.7	8 30.3	28 23.8	17 23.2
7 Tu	9 02 13	14 29 13	22 35 57	29 18 09	8 50.3	4 43.7	8 46.8	28 18.5	6 55.7	1 09.0	28 58.3	8 29.8	28 25.5	17 24.1
8 W	9 06 09	15 26 44	6♑07 20	13♑03 32	8 46.3	4 20.7	9 05.5	28 58.3	6 42.9	1 10.8	28 55.9	8 29.3	28 27.2	17 24.9
9 Th	9 10 06	16 24 15	20 06 36	27 16 11	8 39.9	4 03.5	9 25.9	29 38.1	6 30.1	1 12.8	28 53.7	8 28.8	28 28.8	17 25.7
10 F	9 14 02	17 21 47	4♒31 44	11♒52 32	8 31.3	3 52.6	9 48.2	0♋17.8	6 17.5	1 14.9	28 51.5	8 28.5	28 30.4	17 26.5
11 Sa	9 17 59	18 19 21	19 17 39	26 46 00	8 21.4	3D 48.3	10 12.1	0 57.4	6 05.0	1 17.3	28 49.4	8 28.1	28 32.0	17 27.3
12 Su	9 21 55	19 16 55	4♓16 25	11♓47 41	8 11.4	3 50.8	10 37.7	1 36.9	5 52.6	1 19.8	28 47.3	8 27.8	28 33.6	17 28.0
13 M	9 25 52	20 14 31	19 18 33	26 47 50	8 02.4	4 00.5	11 05.0	2 16.4	5 40.4	1 22.5	28 45.4	8 27.6	28 35.1	17 28.8
14 Tu	9 29 48	21 12 09	4♈14 30	11♈37 37	7 55.4	4 17.4	11 33.7	2 55.8	5 28.4	1 25.4	28 43.6	8 27.4	28 36.7	17 29.5
15 W	9 33 45	22 09 47	18 56 26	26 10 23	7 50.8	4 41.6	12 04.0	3 35.1	5 16.5	1 28.4	28 41.8	8 27.2	28 38.1	17 30.2
16 Th	9 37 41	23 07 28	3♉19 06	10♉22 22	7D 48.7	5 13.0	12 35.7	4 14.4	5 04.8	1 31.6	28 40.1	8 27.1	28 39.6	17 30.9
17 F	9 41 38	24 05 10	17 20 07	24 12 27	7 48.2	5 51.7	13 08.8	4 53.6	4 53.3	1 35.0	28 38.5	8D 27.1	28 41.1	17 31.5
18 Sa	9 45 35	25 02 54	0♊59 31	7♊41 35	7R 48.3	6 37.5	13 43.2	5 32.7	4 42.1	1 38.6	28 37.1	8 27.1	28 42.5	17 32.2
19 Su	9 49 31	26 00 39	14 18 58	20 51 58	7 47.8	7 30.3	14 18.9	6 11.7	4 31.0	1 42.3	28 35.7	8 27.2	28 43.9	17 32.8
20 M	9 53 28	26 58 27	27 20 57	3♋46 15	7 45.5	8 29.9	14 55.8	6 50.7	4 20.2	1 46.2	28 34.3	8 27.3	28 45.3	17 33.4
21 Tu	9 57 24	27 56 15	10♋08 11	16 27 02	7 40.5	9 35.9	15 34.0	7 29.5	4 09.7	1 50.3	28 33.1	8 27.5	28 46.6	17 34.0
22 W	10 01 21	28 54 06	22 43 05	28 56 33	7 33.0	10 48.2	16 13.2	8 08.3	3 59.4	1 54.5	28 32.0	8 27.7	28 47.9	17 34.5
23 Th	10 05 17	29 51 58	5♌07 39	11♌16 31	7 22.6	12 06.4	16 53.6	8 47.1	3 49.3	1 58.9	28 31.0	8 28.0	28 49.2	17 35.1
24 F	10 09 14	0♍49 51	17 23 20	23 28 13	7 09.9	13 30.1	17 35.0	9 25.7	3 39.6	2 03.5	28 30.1	8 28.3	28 50.5	17 35.6
25 Sa	10 13 10	1 47 46	29 31 16	5♍32 38	6 56.0	14 59.0	18 17.5	10 04.2	3 30.1	2 08.2	28 29.2	8 28.6	28 51.7	17 36.1
26 Su	10 17 07	2 45 43	11♍32 26	17 30 49	6 42.1	16 32.5	19 00.9	10 42.7	3 20.9	2 13.1	28 28.5	8 29.1	28 52.9	17 36.6
27 M	10 21 04	3 43 41	23 27 58	29 24 03	6 29.3	18 10.3	19 45.2	11 21.1	3 12.0	2 18.1	28 27.8	8 29.5	28 54.1	17 37.1
28 Tu	10 25 00	4 41 40	5♎19 21	11♎14 07	6 18.6	19 51.8	20 30.5	11 59.4	3 03.4	2 23.3	28 27.3	8 30.1	28 55.2	17 37.5
29 W	10 28 57	5 39 41	17 08 43	23 03 31	6 10.5	21 36.7	21 16.6	12 37.6	2 55.1	2 28.7	28 26.8	8 30.6	28 56.3	17 37.9
30 Th	10 32 53	6 37 43	28 58 57	4♏55 30	6 05.2	23 24.3	22 03.6	13 15.7	2 47.1	2 34.2	28 26.5	8 31.3	28 57.4	17 38.3
31 F	10 36 50	7 35 47	10♏53 41	16 54 04	6 02.5	25 14.3	22 51.4	13 53.8	2 39.5	2 39.9	28 26.2	8 32.0	28 58.5	17 38.7

Astro Data	Dy Hr Mn
☽ 0S	2 22:41
☽ 0N	16 14:00
☿ R	18 12:54
♃ D	29 2:23
♀ D	30 2:29
☽ 0S	30 6:56
☿ D	11 15:11
☽ 0N	12 22:41
♄☍♆	16 15:58
♅ D	17 18:17
☽ 0S	26 14:15

Planet Ingress	Dy Hr Mn
♄ ♐R	18 17:32
☉ ♌	23 8:36
♂ ♋	10 1:15
☉ ♍	23 15:20

Last Aspect Dy Hr Mn		☽ Ingress	Dy Hr Mn
1 5:09	♆ ⚹	♍	1 10:43
3 17:30	♆ □	♎	3 22:59
6 6:00	♆ △	♏	6 11:12
7 18:53	♀ △	♐	8 21:05
10 23:08	♆ ☍	♑	11 3:27
12 13:22	☉ ☍	♒	13 6:41
15 4:25	♆ △	♓	15 8:12
17 5:55	♆ □	♈	17 9:38
19 12:12	♄ △	♉	19 12:17
21 13:46	☉ ⚹	♊	21 16:49
23 22:45	♄ ☍	♋	23 23:20
24 14:23	♀ ☌	♌	26 7:49
28 17:10	♄ △	♍	28 18:18
31 5:05	♄ □	♎	31 6:30

Last Aspect Dy Hr Mn		☽ Ingress	Dy Hr Mn
2 17:30	♄ ⚹	♏	2 19:09
3 16:46	☉ □	♐	5 6:01
7 11:25	♄ ☌	♑	7 13:14
8 5:00	♀ ☍	♒	9 16:32
11 15:17	♄ ⚹	♓	11 17:10
13 15:09	♄ □	♈	13 17:09
15 16:13	♄ △	♉	15 18:25
17 11:46	☉ □	♊	17 22:14
20 2:36	♆ ☌	♋	20 4:56
21 10:13	♀ ☌	♌	22 14:03
24 22:40	♆ ⚹	♍	25 0:57
27 10:59	♆ □	♎	27 13:13
29 23:56	♆ △	♏	30 2:03

☽ Phases & Eclipses Dy Hr Mn	
5 0:13	☽ 12♎30
12 13:22	○ 19♑42
19 5:31	☾ 26♈03
26 13:43	● 3♌04
3 16:46	☽ 10♏51
10 21:30	○ 17♒45
17 11:46	☾ 24♉05
25 3:53	● 1♍28

Astro Data

1 July 1900
Julian Day # 182
SVP 6♓38'40"
GC 25♐27.0 ⚵ 19♑51.2R
Eris 23♓10.3R ⚶ 3♈15.7
⚷ 20♐44.4R ⚴ 26♊42.5
☽ Mean ☊ 9♐33.0

1 August 1900
Julian Day # 213
SVP 6♓38'35"
GC 25♐27.1 ⚵ 11♑52.2R
Eris 23♓00.2R ⚶ 9♈27.7
⚷ 19♐14.7R ⚴ 9♋53.8
☽ Mean ☊ 7♐54.5

LONGITUDE — September 1900

Day	Sid.Time	☉	0 hr ☽	Noon ☽	True ☊	☿	♀	♂	⚳	♃	♄	♅	♆	♇
1 Sa	10 40 46	8♍33 53	22♏57 16	29♏03 55	6♐01.7	27♌06.3	23♋40.0	14♋31.7	2♒32.2	2♐45.8	28♐26.0	8♐32.7	28♊59.5	17♊39.1
2 Su	10 44 43	9 31 59	5♐14 38	11♐30 06	6R 01.6	28 59.7	24 29.3	15 09.6	2R 25.2	2 51.7	28D 26.0	8 33.5	29 00.5	17 39.4
3 M	10 48 39	10 30 07	17 50 56	24 17 44	6 01.2	0♍54.3	25 19.4	15 47.4	2 18.6	2 57.9	28 26.0	8 34.3	29 01.5	17 39.7
4 Tu	10 52 36	11 28 17	0♑51 05	7♑31 24	5 59.3	2 49.6	26 10.2	16 25.0	2 12.3	3 04.2	28 26.1	8 35.2	29 02.4	17 40.0
5 W	10 56 33	12 26 28	14 19 04	21 14 17	5 55.2	4 45.4	27 01.7	17 02.7	2 06.3	3 10.6	28 26.4	8 36.2	29 03.4	17 40.3
6 Th	11 00 29	13 24 41	28 17 05	5♒27 18	5 48.5	6 41.4	27 53.8	17 40.2	2 00.7	3 17.2	28 26.7	8 37.1	29 04.2	17 40.5
7 F	11 04 26	14 22 55	12♒44 33	20 08 11	5 39.5	8 37.3	28 46.6	18 17.6	1 55.5	3 23.9	28 27.1	8 38.2	29 05.1	17 40.8
8 Sa	11 08 22	15 21 10	27 37 21	5♓10 59	5 29.0	10 32.9	29 40.0	18 54.9	1 50.6	3 30.8	28 27.6	8 39.3	29 05.9	17 41.0
9 Su	11 12 19	16 19 28	12♓47 49	20 26 29	5 18.2	12 28.1	0♌34.0	19 32.2	1 46.0	3 37.8	28 28.3	8 40.4	29 06.7	17 41.2
10 M	11 16 15	17 17 47	28 05 31	5♈43 31	5 08.3	14 22.8	1 28.6	20 09.3	1 41.8	3 44.9	28 29.0	8 41.6	29 07.4	17 41.3
11 Tu	11 20 12	18 16 08	13♈19 06	20 51 03	5 00.5	16 16.7	2 23.8	20 46.4	1 38.0	3 52.2	28 29.8	8 42.8	29 08.2	17 41.5
12 W	11 24 08	19 14 31	28 18 19	5♉40 05	4 55.4	18 09.9	3 19.5	21 23.4	1 34.5	3 59.6	28 30.7	8 44.1	29 08.8	17 41.6
13 Th	11 28 05	20 12 57	12♉55 43	20 04 51	4 52.8	20 02.3	4 15.8	22 00.3	1 31.4	4 07.2	28 31.7	8 45.5	29 09.5	17 41.7
14 F	11 32 02	21 11 24	27 07 18	4♊03 02	4D 52.1	21 53.7	5 12.6	22 37.1	1 28.6	4 14.8	28 32.8	8 46.8	29 10.1	17 41.8
15 Sa	11 35 58	22 09 54	10♊52 12	17 35 05	4R 52.3	23 44.2	6 09.9	23 13.8	1 26.2	4 22.7	28 34.0	8 48.3	29 10.7	17 41.9
16 Su	11 39 55	23 08 26	24 12 02	0♋43 28	4 52.1	25 33.7	7 07.6	23 50.4	1 24.2	4 30.6	28 35.3	8 49.8	29 11.3	17 41.9
17 M	11 43 51	24 07 00	7♋09 50	13 31 38	4 50.5	27 22.2	8 05.9	24 26.9	1 22.5	4 38.7	28 36.7	8 51.3	29 11.8	17R 41.9
18 Tu	11 47 48	25 05 37	19 49 19	26 03 21	4 46.6	29 09.7	9 04.6	25 03.3	1 21.2	4 46.9	28 38.2	8 52.9	29 12.3	17 41.9
19 W	11 51 44	26 04 15	2♌14 11	8♌22 13	4 40.0	0♎56.2	10 03.7	25 39.6	1 20.2	4 55.2	28 39.8	8 54.5	29 12.8	17 41.9
20 Th	11 55 41	27 02 56	14 27 50	20 31 20	4 30.8	2 41.7	11 03.3	26 15.9	1 19.6	5 03.7	28 41.5	8 56.2	29 13.2	17 41.8
21 F	11 59 37	28 01 39	26 33 04	2♍33 15	4 19.6	4 26.2	12 03.3	26 52.0	1D 19.4	5 12.3	28 43.2	8 57.9	29 13.6	17 41.8
22 Sa	12 03 34	29 00 23	8♍32 08	14 29 56	4 07.2	6 09.7	13 03.6	27 28.0	1 19.5	5 21.0	28 45.1	8 59.6	29 14.0	17 41.7
23 Su	12 07 31	29 59 10	20 26 50	26 23 00	3 54.7	7 52.2	14 04.4	28 03.9	1 20.0	5 29.8	28 47.1	9 01.5	29 14.3	17 41.6
24 M	12 11 27	0♎57 59	2♎18 39	8♎13 55	3 43.2	9 33.8	15 05.5	28 39.7	1 20.8	5 38.7	28 49.1	9 03.3	29 14.6	17 41.4
25 Tu	12 15 24	1 56 50	14 09 01	20 04 11	3 33.6	11 14.4	16 07.1	29 15.3	1 22.0	5 47.8	28 51.3	9 05.2	29 14.8	17 41.3
26 W	12 19 20	2 55 43	25 59 37	1♏55 38	3 26.4	12 54.1	17 08.9	29 50.9	1 23.6	5 56.9	28 53.5	9 07.2	29 15.1	17 41.1
27 Th	12 23 17	3 54 37	7♏52 31	13 50 38	3 21.9	14 32.9	18 11.1	0♌26.4	1 25.5	6 06.2	28 55.9	9 09.2	29 15.3	17 40.9
28 F	12 27 13	4 53 34	19 50 23	25 52 10	3D 19.8	16 10.8	19 13.6	1 01.7	1 27.7	6 15.6	28 58.3	9 11.2	29 15.4	17 40.7
29 Sa	12 31 10	5 52 32	1♐56 30	8♐03 53	3 19.6	17 47.7	20 16.5	1 37.0	1 30.3	6 25.1	29 00.8	9 13.3	29 15.5	17 40.4
30 Su	12 35 06	6 51 33	14 14 50	20 29 56	3 20.4	19 23.9	21 19.7	2 12.1	1 33.3	6 34.8	29 03.5	9 15.4	29 15.6	17 40.1

LONGITUDE — October 1900

Day	Sid.Time	☉	0 hr ☽	Noon ☽	True ☊	☿	♀	♂	⚳	♃	♄	♅	♆	♇
1 M	12 39 03	7♎50 35	26♐49 45	3♑14 50	3♐21.2	20♎59.2	22♌23.2	2♌47.1	1♒36.5	6♐44.5	29♐06.2	9♐17.6	29♊15.7	17♊39.9
2 Tu	12 42 59	8 49 39	9♑45 44	16 22 55	3R 21.0	22 33.6	23 27.0	3 22.0	1 40.2	6 54.3	29 09.0	9 19.8	29R 15.7	17R 39.6
3 W	12 46 56	9 48 44	23 06 49	29 57 44	3 19.1	24 07.2	24 31.0	3 56.8	1 44.1	7 04.3	29 11.8	9 22.1	29 15.7	17 39.2
4 Th	12 50 53	10 47 51	6♒55 50	14♒01 10	3 15.1	25 40.0	25 35.4	4 31.4	1 48.4	7 14.3	29 14.8	9 24.3	29 15.7	17 38.9
5 F	12 54 49	11 47 00	21 13 31	28 32 32	3 09.2	27 12.0	26 40.1	5 05.9	1 53.0	7 24.4	29 17.9	9 26.7	29 15.6	17 38.5
6 Sa	12 58 46	12 46 11	5♓57 35	13♓27 51	3 01.9	28 43.2	27 45.0	5 40.3	1 58.0	7 34.7	29 21.0	9 29.1	29 15.5	17 38.1
7 Su	13 02 42	13 45 24	21 02 18	28 39 44	2 54.3	0♏13.7	28 50.2	6 14.6	2 03.2	7 45.0	29 24.3	9 31.5	29 15.3	17 37.7
8 M	13 06 39	14 44 38	6♈18 47	13♈58 05	2 47.2	1 43.3	29 55.6	6 48.8	2 08.8	7 55.4	29 27.6	9 33.9	29 15.2	17 37.3
9 Tu	13 10 35	15 43 55	21 36 13	29 11 49	2 41.7	3 12.1	1♍01.3	7 22.8	2 14.7	8 06.0	29 31.0	9 36.4	29 14.9	17 36.8
10 W	13 14 32	16 43 14	6♉43 40	14♉10 43	2 38.3	4 40.2	2 07.3	7 56.7	2 20.9	8 16.6	29 34.5	9 38.9	29 14.7	17 36.4
11 Th	13 18 28	17 42 35	21 32 05	28 47 07	2D 36.9	6 07.4	3 13.5	8 30.5	2 27.4	8 27.3	29 38.0	9 41.5	29 14.4	17 35.9
12 F	13 22 25	18 41 58	5♊55 22	12♊56 36	2 37.2	7 33.8	4 20.0	9 04.2	2 34.2	8 38.1	29 41.7	9 44.1	29 14.1	17 35.4
13 Sa	13 26 22	19 41 24	19 50 46	26 37 58	2 38.4	8 59.4	5 26.7	9 37.7	2 41.3	8 49.0	29 45.4	9 46.8	29 13.8	17 34.8
14 Su	13 30 18	20 40 52	3♋18 26	9♋52 31	2R 39.8	10 24.2	6 33.6	10 11.1	2 48.7	9 00.0	29 49.2	9 49.5	29 13.4	17 34.3
15 M	13 34 15	21 40 23	16 20 39	22 43 19	2 40.3	11 48.0	7 40.8	10 44.4	2 56.4	9 11.0	29 53.1	9 52.2	29 13.0	17 33.7
16 Tu	13 38 11	22 39 55	29 01 02	5♌14 21	2 39.4	13 11.0	8 48.1	11 17.5	3 04.4	9 22.2	29 57.1	9 54.9	29 12.5	17 33.1
17 W	13 42 08	23 39 30	11♌23 46	17 29 51	2 36.7	14 33.0	9 55.7	11 50.4	3 12.6	9 33.4	0♑01.2	9 57.7	29 12.1	17 32.5
18 Th	13 46 04	24 39 07	23 33 06	29 34 00	2 32.3	15 54.0	11 03.5	12 23.3	3 21.2	9 44.7	0 05.3	10 00.5	29 11.6	17 31.9
19 F	13 50 01	25 38 47	5♍33 01	11♍30 34	2 26.5	17 13.9	12 11.5	12 55.9	3 30.0	9 56.1	0 09.5	10 03.4	29 11.0	17 31.3
20 Sa	13 53 57	26 38 28	17 27 02	23 22 47	2 19.8	18 32.7	13 19.7	13 28.5	3 39.1	10 07.6	0 13.8	10 06.3	29 10.5	17 30.6
21 Su	13 57 54	27 38 12	29 18 07	5♎13 20	2 13.0	19 50.3	14 28.0	14 00.8	3 48.5	10 19.2	0 18.2	10 09.2	29 09.9	17 29.9
22 M	14 01 51	28 37 58	11♎08 43	17 04 28	2 06.8	21 06.7	15 36.6	14 33.1	3 58.2	10 30.8	0 22.6	10 12.1	29 09.2	17 29.2
23 Tu	14 05 47	29 37 46	23 00 51	28 58 03	2 01.7	22 21.6	16 45.3	15 05.1	4 08.1	10 42.5	0 27.1	10 15.1	29 08.6	17 28.5
24 W	14 09 44	0♏37 35	4♏56 18	10♏55 47	1 58.1	23 34.9	17 54.2	15 37.0	4 18.3	10 54.3	0 31.7	10 18.1	29 07.9	17 27.8
25 Th	14 13 40	1 37 27	16 56 45	22 59 25	1D 56.2	24 46.6	19 03.3	16 08.7	4 28.8	11 06.1	0 36.4	10 21.2	29 07.1	17 27.0
26 F	14 17 37	2 37 21	29 04 02	5♐10 52	1 55.9	25 56.5	20 12.6	16 40.3	4 39.5	11 18.1	0 41.1	10 24.3	29 06.4	17 26.3
27 Sa	14 21 33	3 37 17	11♐20 13	17 32 24	1 56.8	27 04.4	21 22.0	17 11.7	4 50.4	11 30.1	0 45.9	10 27.4	29 05.6	17 25.5
28 Su	14 25 30	4 37 14	23 47 46	0♑06 39	1 58.3	28 10.0	22 31.5	17 42.9	5 01.6	11 42.1	0 50.8	10 30.5	29 04.8	17 24.7
29 M	14 29 26	5 37 13	6♑29 26	12 56 30	2 00.0	29 13.2	23 41.2	18 14.0	5 13.1	11 54.3	0 55.7	10 33.7	29 03.9	17 23.9
30 Tu	14 33 23	6 37 13	19 28 13	26 04 56	2R 01.3	0♐13.6	24 51.1	18 44.8	5 24.8	12 06.4	1 00.7	10 36.8	29 03.1	17 23.1
31 W	14 37 20	7 37 16	2♒46 57	9♒34 31	2 01.6	1 11.0	26 01.1	19 15.5	5 36.7	12 18.7	1 05.8	10 40.0	29 02.1	17 22.2

Astro Data

	Dy Hr Mn
♄ D	2 15:16
☽ 0N	9 9:11
♇ R	17 19:23
☿0S	20 8:53
⚳ D	21 15:47
☽ 0S	22 20:23
☉0S	23 12:20
♆ R	2 17:47
♄☍♆	4 18:33
☽ 0N	6 20:02
☽ 0S	20 1:58
♃☌♅	20 8:14

Planet Ingress

		Dy Hr Mn
☿	♍	3 0:39
♀	♌	8 20:55
☿	♎	18 23:18
☉	♎	23 12:20
♂	♌	26 18:08
☿	♏	7 8:22
♀	♍	8 13:36
♄	♑	17 5:03
☉	♏	23 20:55
☿	♐	30 6:29

Last Aspect / ☽ Ingress

Last Aspect Dy Hr Mn			☽ Ingress	Dy Hr Mn
1 7:28	☿	□	♐	1 13:49
3 20:41	♆	☍	♑	3 22:27
5 22:31	♀	☍	♒	6 2:53
8 2:20	♆	△	♓	8 3:47
10 1:37	♆	□	♈	10 3:00
12 1:21	♆	⚹	♉	12 2:45
13 15:25	♂	⚹	♊	14 4:58
16 9:09	♆	☌	♋	16 10:40
18 19:02	☿	⚹	♌	18 19:39
21 5:20	♆	⚹	♍	21 6:53
23 17:47	♆	□	♎	23 19:19
26 7:35	♂	□	♏	26 8:06
27 21:31	♀	□	♐	28 20:10

Last Aspect / ☽ Ingress

Last Aspect Dy Hr Mn			☽ Ingress	Dy Hr Mn
1 4:34	♆	☍	♑	1 5:57
3 0:27	☿	□	♒	3 12:04
5 13:14	♄	⚹	♓	5 14:22
7 13:10	♄	□	♈	7 14:06
9 12:31	♄	△	♉	9 13:16
10 1:33	♂	□	♊	11 14:02
13 17:37	♄	☍	♋	13 18:02
15 9:51	☉	□	♌	16 1:53
18 11:15	♆	⚹	♍	18 12:52
20 23:44	♆	□	♎	21 1:25
23 13:27	☉	☌	♏	23 14:05
25 15:55	☿	☌	♐	26 1:50
28 10:03	♆	☍	♑	28 11:47
30 9:34	♀	△	♒	30 19:02

☽ Phases & Eclipses

Dy Hr Mn		
2 7:56	☽	9♐22
9 5:06	○	16♓03
15 20:57	☾	22♊32
23 19:57	●	0♎19
1 21:10	☽	8♑13
8 13:18	○	14♈48
15 9:51	☾	21♋35
23 13:27	●	29♎41
31 8:17	☽	7♒28

Astro Data

1 September 1900
Julian Day # 244
SVP 6♓38'32"
GC 25♐27.1 ⚴ 8♑29.7R
Eris 22♓41.5R ⚵ 9♈40.2R
⚷ 18♐59.3 ⚶ 22♋31.4
☽ Mean ☊ 6♐16.0

1 October 1900
Julian Day # 274
SVP 6♓38'29"
GC 25♐27.2 ⚴ 10♑43.2
Eris 22♓20.3R ⚵ 3♈45.6R
⚷ 20♐05.2 ⚶ 3♌42.6
☽ Mean ☊ 4♐40.7

November 1900 LONGITUDE

Day	Sid.Time	☉	0 hr ☽	Noon ☽	True ☊	☿	♀	♂	⚳	♃	♄	♅	♆	♇
1 Th	14 41 16	8♏37 19	16♒27 50	23♒26 58	2♐00.9	2♐04.9	27♍11.2	19♌46.0	5♒48.9	12♐31.0	1♑10.9	10♐43.3	29♊01.2	17♊21.4
2 F	14 45 13	9 37 25	0♓31 52	7♓42 21	1R59.1	2 55.1	28 21.5	20 16.3	6 01.3	12 43.4	1 16.1	10 46.5	29R00.3	17R20.5
3 Sa	14 49 09	10 37 31	14 58 05	22 18 35	1 56.6	3 41.0	29 32.0	20 46.4	6 13.9	12 55.8	1 21.4	10 49.8	28 59.3	17 19.6
4 Su	14 53 06	11 37 40	29 43 10	7♈11 01	1 53.8	4 22.2	0♎42.5	21 16.4	6 26.8	13 08.3	1 26.7	10 53.1	28 58.2	17 18.7
5 M	14 57 02	12 37 50	14♈41 10	22 12 36	1 51.2	4 58.0	1 53.2	21 46.1	6 39.8	13 20.8	1 32.1	10 56.5	28 57.2	17 17.8
6 Tu	15 00 59	13 38 02	29 44 09	7♉14 41	1 49.3	5 28.0	3 04.0	22 15.6	6 53.1	13 33.4	1 37.6	10 59.8	28 56.1	17 16.8
7 W	15 04 55	14 38 15	14♉43 05	22 08 18	1D48.2	5 51.5	4 15.0	22 45.0	7 06.6	13 46.1	1 43.1	11 03.2	28 55.0	17 15.9
8 Th	15 08 52	15 38 30	29 29 21	6♊45 27	1 48.0	6 07.8	5 26.1	23 14.1	7 20.3	13 58.8	1 48.6	11 06.6	28 53.9	17 14.9
9 F	15 12 49	16 38 48	13♊55 54	21 00 14	1 48.7	6R16.2	6 37.3	23 43.0	7 34.2	14 11.5	1 54.3	11 10.0	28 52.8	17 14.0
10 Sa	15 16 45	17 39 07	27 58 06	4♋49 22	1 49.8	6 16.0	7 48.6	24 11.8	7 48.4	14 24.3	1 59.9	11 13.4	28 51.6	17 13.0
11 Su	15 20 42	18 39 28	11♋33 59	18 12 06	1 51.0	6 06.6	9 00.1	24 40.3	8 02.7	14 37.2	2 05.7	11 16.9	28 50.4	17 12.0
12 M	15 24 38	19 39 51	24 43 57	1♌09 53	1 52.0	5 47.5	10 11.6	25 08.6	8 17.2	14 50.1	2 11.5	11 20.4	28 49.2	17 11.0
13 Tu	15 28 35	20 40 16	7♌30 18	13 45 41	1R52.6	5 18.2	11 23.3	25 36.6	8 31.9	15 03.0	2 17.3	11 23.8	28 48.0	17 10.0
14 W	15 32 31	21 40 43	19 56 35	26 03 31	1 52.6	4 38.7	12 35.1	26 04.4	8 46.8	15 16.0	2 23.2	11 27.3	28 46.7	17 09.0
15 Th	15 36 28	22 41 11	2♍07 05	8♍07 50	1 52.2	3 49.0	13 47.0	26 32.0	9 01.9	15 29.0	2 29.1	11 30.9	28 45.4	17 07.9
16 F	15 40 24	23 41 42	14 06 21	20 03 12	1 51.4	2 49.9	14 59.0	26 59.4	9 17.1	15 42.1	2 35.1	11 34.4	28 44.1	17 06.9
17 Sa	15 44 21	24 42 14	25 58 54	1♎53 58	1 50.4	1 42.4	16 11.1	27 26.5	9 32.6	15 55.2	2 41.2	11 37.9	28 42.7	17 05.8
18 Su	15 48 18	25 42 48	7♎48 53	13 44 06	1 49.5	0 28.1	17 23.3	27 53.3	9 48.2	16 08.4	2 47.3	11 41.5	28 41.4	17 04.8
19 M	15 52 14	26 43 23	19 40 02	25 37 04	1 48.7	29♏08.9	18 35.5	28 19.9	10 04.0	16 21.5	2 53.4	11 45.1	28 40.0	17 03.7
20 Tu	15 56 11	27 44 01	1♏35 33	7♏35 45	1 48.1	27 47.5	19 47.9	28 46.2	10 20.0	16 34.8	2 59.6	11 48.7	28 38.6	17 02.6
21 W	16 00 07	28 44 40	13 37 59	19 42 27	1D47.8	26 26.4	21 00.4	29 12.2	10 36.2	16 48.0	3 05.8	11 52.3	28 37.2	17 01.5
22 Th	16 04 04	29 45 20	25 49 23	1♐58 56	1 47.8	25 08.4	22 12.9	29 38.0	10 52.5	17 01.3	3 12.1	11 55.9	28 35.8	17 00.4
23 F	16 08 00	0♐46 02	8♐11 16	14 26 31	1 47.8	23 55.9	23 25.6	0♍03.5	11 09.0	17 14.6	3 18.4	11 59.5	28 34.3	16 59.3
24 Sa	16 11 57	1 46 45	20 44 48	27 06 13	1R47.9	22 51.4	24 38.3	0 28.7	11 25.7	17 28.0	3 24.7	12 03.1	28 32.9	16 58.2
25 Su	16 15 53	2 47 30	3♑30 50	9♑58 47	1 47.8	21 56.3	25 51.0	0 53.6	11 42.5	17 41.4	3 31.1	12 06.8	28 31.4	16 57.1
26 M	16 19 50	3 48 15	16 30 07	23 04 54	1 47.6	21 12.0	27 03.9	1 18.2	11 59.5	17 54.8	3 37.6	12 10.4	28 29.9	16 56.0
27 Tu	16 23 47	4 49 02	29 43 15	6♒25 11	1 47.3	20 39.2	28 16.8	1 42.5	12 16.7	18 08.2	3 44.1	12 14.1	28 28.4	16 54.9
28 W	16 27 43	5 49 50	13♒10 47	20 00 03	1 47.1	20 17.9	29 29.8	2 06.5	12 34.0	18 21.7	3 50.6	12 17.7	28 26.8	16 53.7
29 Th	16 31 40	6 50 38	26 53 02	3♓49 40	1D46.9	20D08.0	0♏42.9	2 30.2	12 51.4	18 35.2	3 57.1	12 21.4	28 25.3	16 52.6
30 F	16 35 36	7 51 27	10♓49 54	17 53 36	1 47.0	20 09.1	1 56.0	2 53.6	13 09.0	18 48.7	4 03.7	12 25.0	28 23.7	16 51.4

December 1900 LONGITUDE

Day	Sid.Time	☉	0 hr ☽	Noon ☽	True ☊	☿	♀	♂	⚳	♃	♄	♅	♆	♇
1 Sa	16 39 33	8♐52 18	25♓00 34	2♈10 32	1♐47.4	20♏20.4	3♏09.2	3♍16.6	13♒26.7	19♐02.2	4♑10.3	12♐28.7	28♊22.1	16♊50.3
2 Su	16 43 29	9 53 09	9♈23 09	16 37 59	1 48.0	20 41.0	4 22.4	3 39.3	13 44.6	19 15.7	4 16.9	12 32.4	28R20.5	16R49.1
3 M	16 47 26	10 54 01	23 54 32	1♉12 11	1 48.8	21 10.3	5 35.7	4 01.6	14 02.6	19 29.3	4 23.6	12 36.1	28 18.9	16 48.0
4 Tu	16 51 22	11 54 53	8♉30 18	15 48 09	1 49.5	21 47.2	6 49.1	4 23.6	14 20.8	19 42.8	4 30.3	12 39.7	28 17.3	16 46.8
5 W	16 55 19	12 55 47	23 04 59	0♊20 02	1R49.8	22 31.0	8 02.5	4 45.3	14 39.0	19 56.4	4 37.1	12 43.4	28 15.7	16 45.7
6 Th	16 59 16	13 56 42	7♊32 35	14 41 53	1 49.6	23 20.8	9 16.0	5 06.6	14 57.5	20 10.0	4 43.8	12 47.1	28 14.1	16 44.5
7 F	17 03 12	14 57 38	21 47 17	28 48 14	1 48.6	24 15.9	10 29.6	5 27.5	15 16.0	20 23.7	4 50.6	12 50.8	28 12.4	16 43.4
8 Sa	17 07 09	15 58 35	5♋44 14	12♋34 55	1 47.0	25 15.7	11 43.2	5 48.1	15 34.7	20 37.3	4 57.4	12 54.4	28 10.8	16 42.2
9 Su	17 11 05	16 59 33	19 20 03	25 59 29	1 44.9	26 19.5	12 56.9	6 08.3	15 53.5	20 50.9	5 04.3	12 58.1	28 09.1	16 41.1
10 M	17 15 02	18 00 31	2♌33 14	9♌01 23	1 42.5	27 26.9	14 10.6	6 28.0	16 12.4	21 04.6	5 11.1	13 01.8	28 07.5	16 39.9
11 Tu	17 18 58	19 01 31	15 24 09	21 41 50	1 40.4	28 37.4	15 24.3	6 47.4	16 31.4	21 18.2	5 18.0	13 05.4	28 05.8	16 38.7
12 W	17 22 55	20 02 32	27 54 49	4♍03 33	1 38.7	29 50.5	16 38.2	7 06.4	16 50.6	21 31.9	5 24.9	13 09.1	28 04.1	16 37.6
13 Th	17 26 51	21 03 34	10♍08 32	16 10 20	1D37.8	1♐06.0	17 52.0	7 24.9	17 09.9	21 45.5	5 31.8	13 12.8	28 02.4	16 36.4
14 F	17 30 48	22 04 37	22 09 32	28 06 43	1 37.9	2 23.5	19 05.9	7 43.0	17 29.3	21 59.2	5 38.8	13 16.4	28 00.7	16 35.3
15 Sa	17 34 45	23 05 41	4♎02 32	9♎57 35	1 38.8	3 42.7	20 19.9	8 00.6	17 48.8	22 12.9	5 45.7	13 20.1	27 59.1	16 34.1
16 Su	17 38 41	24 06 46	15 52 28	21 47 49	1 40.3	5 03.5	21 33.9	8 17.8	18 08.4	22 26.5	5 52.7	13 23.7	27 57.4	16 32.9
17 M	17 42 38	25 07 51	27 44 12	3♏42 09	1 42.2	6 25.6	22 47.9	8 34.6	18 28.2	22 40.2	5 59.7	13 27.3	27 55.7	16 31.8
18 Tu	17 46 34	26 08 58	9♏42 12	15 44 48	1 43.8	7 48.9	24 02.0	8 50.8	18 48.0	22 53.9	6 06.7	13 30.9	27 54.0	16 30.7
19 W	17 50 31	27 10 05	21 50 23	27 59 18	1R44.6	9 13.2	25 16.1	9 06.6	19 07.9	23 07.5	6 13.7	13 34.5	27 52.3	16 29.5
20 Th	17 54 27	28 11 13	4♐11 53	10♐28 20	1 44.4	10 38.4	26 30.3	9 21.9	19 28.0	23 21.2	6 20.8	13 38.1	27 50.5	16 28.4
21 F	17 58 24	29 12 22	16 48 51	23 13 30	1 42.7	12 04.5	27 44.5	9 36.7	19 48.2	23 34.9	6 27.8	13 41.7	27 48.8	16 27.2
22 Sa	18 02 20	0♑13 31	29 42 19	6♑15 15	1 39.6	13 31.2	28 58.7	9 50.9	20 08.4	23 48.5	6 34.9	13 45.3	27 47.1	16 26.1
23 Su	18 06 17	1 14 41	12♑52 12	19 32 58	1 35.3	14 58.6	0♐13.0	10 04.7	20 28.8	24 02.1	6 42.0	13 48.9	27 45.4	16 25.0
24 M	18 10 14	2 15 50	26 17 19	3♒05 00	1 30.2	16 26.5	1 27.3	10 17.9	20 49.2	24 15.8	6 49.0	13 52.4	27 43.7	16 23.9
25 Tu	18 14 10	3 17 00	9♒55 41	16 49 04	1 25.1	17 55.0	2 41.6	10 30.5	21 09.8	24 29.4	6 56.1	13 55.9	27 42.1	16 22.8
26 W	18 18 07	4 18 10	23 44 50	0♓42 37	1 20.6	19 23.9	3 55.9	10 42.6	21 30.4	24 43.0	7 03.2	13 59.4	27 40.4	16 21.7
27 Th	18 22 03	5 19 20	7♓42 09	14 43 07	1 17.3	20 53.4	5 10.3	10 54.1	21 51.2	24 56.6	7 10.3	14 02.9	27 38.7	16 20.6
28 F	18 26 00	6 20 30	21 45 16	28 48 21	1D15.6	22 23.2	6 24.6	11 05.0	22 12.0	25 10.2	7 17.4	14 06.4	27 37.0	16 19.5
29 Sa	18 29 56	7 21 39	5♈52 08	12♈56 27	1 15.5	23 53.4	7 39.0	11 15.4	22 32.9	25 23.7	7 24.4	14 09.9	27 35.3	16 18.4
30 Su	18 33 53	8 22 49	20 01 06	27 05 53	1 16.5	25 24.1	8 53.5	11 25.1	22 53.9	25 37.2	7 31.5	14 13.3	27 33.6	16 17.3
31 M	18 37 49	9 23 58	4♉10 36	11♉15 03	1 18.1	26 55.1	10 07.9	11 34.3	23 14.9	25 50.7	7 38.6	14 16.8	27 32.0	16 16.3

Astro Data (Dy Hr Mn)

	Dy Hr Mn
☽0N	3 5:24
♀0S	7 0:03
☿R	9 23:37
☽0S	16 8:15
♃☍♇	22 10:31
☿D	29 21:36
☽0N	30 12:29
☽0S	13 16:10
☽0N	27 18:21

Planet Ingress (Dy Hr Mn)

		Dy Hr Mn
♀	♎	3 21:33
☿	♏R	18 20:38
☉	♐	22 17:48
♂	♍	23 8:41
♀	♏	28 21:55
☿	♐	12 15:03
☉	♑	22 6:42
♀	♐	23 7:48

Last Aspect / ☽ Ingress (Dy Hr Mn)

Last Aspect		☽ Ingress
1 21:27	♆ △	♓ 1 23:06
3 22:48	♆ □	♈ 4 0:27
5 22:44	♆ ⚹	♉ 6 0:25
7 13:02	♂ □	♊ 8 0:50
10 1:34	♆ ☌	♋ 10 3:32
11 12:54	☉ △	♌ 12 9:49
14 17:22	♆ ⚹	♍ 14 19:48
17 5:33	♆ □	♎ 17 8:09
19 18:07	♆ △	♏ 19 20:48
22 7:17	☉ ☌	♐ 22 8:09
24 14:42	♆ ☍	♑ 24 17:26
26 19:56	♀ □	♒ 27 0:30
29 2:41	♆ △	♓ 29 5:24

Last Aspect / ☽ Ingress (Dy Hr Mn)

Last Aspect		☽ Ingress
1 5:39	♆ □	♈ 1 8:22
3 7:16	♆ ⚹	♉ 3 10:01
4 22:21	☿ ☍	♊ 5 11:27
7 10:59	♆ ☌	♋ 7 14:04
9 12:40	♆ △	♌ 9 19:19
12 2:50	☿ □	♍ 12 4:04
14 11:48	♆ □	♎ 14 15:49
17 0:25	♆ △	♏ 17 4:34
19 6:07	♀ ☌	♐ 19 15:54
22 0:01	☉ ☌	♑ 22 0:33
22 18:39	♂ △	♒ 24 6:34
26 6:47	♆ △	♓ 26 10:47
28 9:59	♆ □	♈ 28 14:02
30 12:47	♆ ⚹	♉ 30 16:55

☽ Phases & Eclipses (Dy Hr Mn)

Dy Hr Mn	
6 23:00	○ 14♉06
14 2:37	☾ 21♌17
22 7:17	● 29♏33
22 7:19:44	● A 06'42"
29 17:35	☽ 7♓05
6 10:38	○ 13♊53
6 10:26	[eclipse] A 0.818
13 22:42	☾ 21♍31
22 0:01	● 29♐43
29 1:48	☽ 6♈56

Astro Data

1 November 1900
Julian Day # 305
SVP 6♓38'26"
GC 25♐27.3 ⚴ 17♑01.0
Eris 22♓01.7R ⚵ 28♓13.0R
⚷ 22♐24.4 ⚶ 13♌17.6
☽ Mean ☊ 3♐02.2

1 December 1900
Julian Day # 335
SVP 6♓38'21"
GC 25♐27.3 ⚴ 25♑25.2
Eris 21♓52.5R ⚵ 0♈08.5
⚷ 25♐24.3 ⚶ 19♌07.1
☽ Mean ☊ 1♐26.9

LONGITUDE — January 1901

Day	Sid.Time	☉	0 hr ☽	Noon ☽	True ☊	☿	♀	♂	⚳	♃	♄	♅	♆	♇
1 Tu	18 41 46	10♑25 07	18♉18 58	25♉22 06	1♐19.2	28♐26.5	11♐22.4	11♍42.8	23♒36.1	26♐04.2	7♑45.7	14♐20.2	27♊30.3	16♊15.2
2 W	18 45 43	11 26 16	2♊24 07	9♊24 41	1R19.0	29 58.3	12 36.8	11 50.7	23 57.3	26 17.7	7 52.8	14 23.5	27R28.7	16R14.2
3 Th	18 49 39	12 27 25	16 23 26	23 19 58	1 17.0	1♑30.4	13 51.4	11 58.0	24 18.6	26 31.1	7 59.8	14 26.9	27 27.0	16 13.2
4 F	18 53 36	13 28 34	0♋13 51	7♋04 43	1 12.8	3 02.9	15 05.9	12 04.6	24 40.0	26 44.6	8 06.9	14 30.3	27 25.4	16 12.1
5 Sa	18 57 32	14 29 42	13 52 10	20 35 51	1 06.6	4 35.8	16 20.4	12 10.5	25 01.5	26 58.0	8 14.0	14 33.6	27 23.8	16 11.1
6 Su	19 01 29	15 30 51	27 15 27	3♌50 44	0 58.8	6 09.1	17 35.0	12 15.8	25 23.0	27 11.3	8 21.0	14 36.9	27 22.2	16 10.1
7 M	19 05 25	16 31 59	10♌21 34	16 47 50	0 50.3	7 42.8	18 49.6	12 20.4	25 44.6	27 24.6	8 28.1	14 40.1	27 20.6	16 09.1
8 Tu	19 09 22	17 33 07	23 09 34	29 26 52	0 42.0	9 16.8	20 04.2	12 24.3	26 06.3	27 37.9	8 35.1	14 43.4	27 19.0	16 08.2
9 W	19 13 19	18 34 15	5♍39 55	11♍49 00	0 34.7	10 51.3	21 18.8	12 27.4	26 28.0	27 51.2	8 42.1	14 46.6	27 17.4	16 07.2
10 Th	19 17 15	19 35 23	17 54 28	23 56 45	0 29.1	12 26.3	22 33.4	12 29.9	26 49.8	28 04.5	8 49.1	14 49.8	27 15.9	16 06.2
11 F	19 21 12	20 36 31	29 56 19	5♎53 44	0 25.6	14 01.6	23 48.1	12 31.6	27 11.7	28 17.7	8 56.1	14 53.0	27 14.3	16 05.3
12 Sa	19 25 08	21 37 39	11♎49 36	17 44 30	0D 24.1	15 37.5	25 02.8	12R32.6	27 33.6	28 30.8	9 03.1	14 56.1	27 12.8	16 04.4
13 Su	19 29 05	22 38 47	23 39 07	29 34 06	0 24.2	17 13.8	26 17.5	12 32.8	27 55.7	28 43.9	9 10.1	14 59.2	27 11.3	16 03.5
14 M	19 33 01	23 39 55	5♏30 08	11♏27 53	0 25.3	18 50.6	27 32.2	12 32.3	28 17.7	28 57.0	9 17.0	15 02.3	27 09.8	16 02.6
15 Tu	19 36 58	24 41 02	17 28 01	23 31 09	0R 26.4	20 27.9	28 46.9	12 31.0	28 39.9	29 10.1	9 24.0	15 05.4	27 08.3	16 01.7
16 W	19 40 54	25 42 09	29 37 54	5♐48 47	0 26.4	22 05.7	0♑01.6	12 28.9	29 02.1	29 23.1	9 30.9	15 08.4	27 06.9	16 00.8
17 Th	19 44 51	26 43 16	12♐04 18	18 24 51	0 24.6	23 44.1	1 16.4	12 26.0	29 24.3	29 36.1	9 37.8	15 11.4	27 05.4	16 00.0
18 F	19 48 48	27 44 23	24 50 45	1♑22 12	0 20.5	25 23.0	2 31.1	12 22.3	29 46.6	29 49.0	9 44.7	15 14.3	27 04.0	15 59.1
19 Sa	19 52 44	28 45 29	7♑59 16	14 41 55	0 13.8	27 02.4	3 45.9	12 17.9	0♓09.0	0♑01.8	9 51.5	15 17.3	27 02.6	15 58.3
20 Su	19 56 41	29 46 34	21 29 59	28 23 09	0 04.9	28 42.5	5 00.6	12 12.6	0 31.4	0 14.7	9 58.3	15 20.2	27 01.2	15 57.5
21 M	20 00 37	0♒47 39	5♒20 58	12♒22 54	29♏54.6	0♒23.1	6 15.4	12 06.5	0 53.9	0 27.4	10 05.1	15 23.0	26 59.9	15 56.7
22 Tu	20 04 34	1 48 43	19 28 17	26 36 26	29 44.0	2 04.3	7 30.2	11 59.6	1 16.4	0 40.2	10 11.9	15 25.9	26 58.5	15 56.0
23 W	20 08 30	2 49 46	3♓46 36	10♓58 01	29 34.4	3 46.1	8 45.0	11 51.9	1 39.0	0 52.8	10 18.7	15 28.6	26 57.2	15 55.2
24 Th	20 12 27	3 50 48	18 09 58	25 21 46	29 26.7	5 28.4	9 59.8	11 43.5	2 01.6	1 05.4	10 25.4	15 31.4	26 55.9	15 54.5
25 F	20 16 23	4 51 49	2♈32 51	9♈42 41	29 21.6	7 11.4	11 14.5	11 34.2	2 24.3	1 18.0	10 32.1	15 34.1	26 54.6	15 53.7
26 Sa	20 20 20	5 52 48	16 50 54	23 57 09	29D 19.0	8 55.0	12 29.3	11 24.1	2 47.0	1 30.5	10 38.7	15 36.8	26 53.4	15 53.0
27 Su	20 24 17	6 53 47	1♉01 16	8♉03 05	29 18.5	10 39.1	13 44.1	11 13.2	3 09.7	1 42.9	10 45.3	15 39.4	26 52.1	15 52.3
28 M	20 28 13	7 54 44	15 02 33	21 59 40	29R 18.8	12 23.7	14 58.9	11 01.6	3 32.5	1 55.3	10 51.9	15 42.0	26 50.9	15 51.7
29 Tu	20 32 10	8 55 40	28 54 25	5♊46 51	29 18.8	14 08.9	16 13.7	10 49.2	3 55.4	2 07.6	10 58.5	15 44.6	26 49.7	15 51.0
30 W	20 36 06	9 56 35	12♊36 59	19 24 50	29 17.2	15 54.5	17 28.5	10 36.0	4 18.3	2 19.9	11 05.0	15 47.1	26 48.6	15 50.4
31 Th	20 40 03	10 57 29	26 10 22	2♋53 32	29 13.0	17 40.5	18 43.3	10 22.1	4 41.2	2 32.0	11 11.5	15 49.6	26 47.5	15 49.8

LONGITUDE — February 1901

Day	Sid.Time	☉	0 hr ☽	Noon ☽	True ☊	☿	♀	♂	⚳	♃	♄	♅	♆	♇
1 F	20 43 59	11♒58 21	9♋34 17	16♋12 28	29♏05.8	19♒26.9	19♑58.1	10♍07.4	5♓04.1	2♑44.2	11♑17.9	15♐52.1	26♊46.4	15♊49.2
2 Sa	20 47 56	12 59 12	22 47 59	29 20 40	28R55.8	21 13.6	21 12.9	9R52.1	5 27.1	2 56.2	11 24.3	15 54.5	26R45.3	15R48.6
3 Su	20 51 52	14 00 02	5♌50 22	12♌16 55	28 43.5	23 00.4	22 27.7	9 36.0	5 50.2	3 08.2	11 30.7	15 56.9	26 44.2	15 48.1
4 M	20 55 49	15 00 51	18 40 14	25 00 11	28 30.0	24 47.2	23 42.5	9 19.2	6 13.2	3 20.1	11 37.0	15 59.2	26 43.2	15 47.5
5 Tu	20 59 46	16 01 38	1♍16 45	7♍29 56	28 16.4	26 34.0	24 57.3	9 01.8	6 36.3	3 31.9	11 43.3	16 01.5	26 42.2	15 47.0
6 W	21 03 42	17 02 24	13 39 48	19 46 29	28 04.0	28 20.4	26 12.1	8 43.7	6 59.4	3 43.7	11 49.5	16 03.7	26 41.2	15 46.5
7 Th	21 07 39	18 03 10	25 50 12	1♎51 13	27 53.8	0♓06.3	27 26.9	8 25.0	7 22.6	3 55.4	11 55.7	16 05.9	26 40.3	15 46.1
8 F	21 11 35	19 03 54	7♎49 53	13 46 37	27 46.3	1 51.4	28 41.7	8 05.7	7 45.8	4 07.0	12 01.9	16 08.0	26 39.4	15 45.6
9 Sa	21 15 32	20 04 37	19 41 53	25 36 14	27 41.6	3 35.4	29 56.5	7 45.8	8 09.0	4 18.5	12 08.0	16 10.2	26 38.5	15 45.2
10 Su	21 19 28	21 05 19	1♏30 14	7♏24 29	27 39.3	5 17.9	1♒11.4	7 25.4	8 32.3	4 30.0	12 14.0	16 12.2	26 37.6	15 44.8
11 M	21 23 25	22 06 00	13 19 41	19 16 29	27 38.7	6 58.7	2 26.2	7 04.5	8 55.6	4 41.4	12 20.0	16 14.2	26 36.8	15 44.4
12 Tu	21 27 21	23 06 39	25 15 36	1♐17 44	27 38.7	8 37.1	3 41.0	6 43.1	9 18.9	4 52.6	12 26.0	16 16.2	26 36.0	15 44.0
13 W	21 31 18	24 07 18	7♐23 35	13 33 48	27 38.1	10 12.8	4 55.8	6 21.2	9 42.2	5 03.9	12 31.9	16 18.1	26 35.3	15 43.7
14 Th	21 35 15	25 07 55	19 49 03	26 09 52	27 35.7	11 45.2	6 10.6	5 59.0	10 05.6	5 15.0	12 37.8	16 20.0	26 34.5	15 43.3
15 F	21 39 11	26 08 32	2♑36 47	9♑10 10	27 30.9	13 13.6	7 25.5	5 36.4	10 29.0	5 26.0	12 43.6	16 21.9	26 33.8	15 43.0
16 Sa	21 43 08	27 09 07	15 50 17	22 37 15	27 23.3	14 37.5	8 40.3	5 13.5	10 52.4	5 37.0	12 49.3	16 23.6	26 33.1	15 42.7
17 Su	21 47 04	28 09 40	29 31 01	6♒31 21	27 13.1	15 56.2	9 55.1	4 50.3	11 15.8	5 47.8	12 55.0	16 25.4	26 32.5	15 42.5
18 M	21 51 01	29 10 12	13♒37 50	20 49 51	27 01.3	17 09.0	11 09.9	4 26.8	11 39.2	5 58.6	13 00.6	16 27.1	26 31.9	15 42.2
19 Tu	21 54 57	0♓10 43	28 06 38	5♓27 14	26 48.9	18 15.3	12 24.7	4 03.2	12 02.7	6 09.2	13 06.2	16 28.7	26 31.3	15 42.0
20 W	21 58 54	1 11 12	12♓50 38	20 15 44	26 37.5	19 14.3	13 39.5	3 39.4	12 26.2	6 19.8	13 11.7	16 30.3	26 30.8	15 41.8
21 Th	22 02 50	2 11 39	27 41 25	5♈06 37	26 28.1	20 05.4	14 54.3	3 15.6	12 49.7	6 30.2	13 17.2	16 31.8	26 30.3	15 41.7
22 F	22 06 47	3 12 04	12♈30 20	19 51 43	26 21.7	20 48.1	16 09.1	2 51.7	13 13.2	6 40.6	13 22.6	16 33.3	26 29.8	15 41.5
23 Sa	22 10 43	4 12 27	27 10 02	4♉24 42	26 18.1	21 21.8	17 23.8	2 27.8	13 36.8	6 50.9	13 27.9	16 34.8	26 29.3	15 41.4
24 Su	22 14 40	5 12 49	11♉35 19	18 41 37	26D 16.8	21 46.2	18 38.6	2 03.9	14 00.3	7 01.0	13 33.2	16 36.2	26 28.9	15 41.3
25 M	22 18 37	6 13 08	25 43 30	2♊40 55	26R 16.7	22 01.0	19 53.4	1 40.2	14 23.9	7 11.1	13 38.4	16 37.5	26 28.5	15 41.2
26 Tu	22 22 33	7 13 26	9♊33 59	16 22 50	26 16.5	22R06.0	21 08.1	1 16.6	14 47.5	7 21.0	13 43.6	16 38.8	26 28.2	15 41.1
27 W	22 26 30	8 13 41	23 07 40	29 48 41	26 14.9	22 01.3	22 22.9	0 53.2	15 11.0	7 30.9	13 48.7	16 40.0	26 27.9	15 41.1
28 Th	22 30 26	9 13 55	6♋26 06	13♋00 09	26 10.9	21 47.0	23 37.6	0 30.0	15 34.6	7 40.6	13 53.7	16 41.2	26 27.6	15D 41.1

Astro Data Dy Hr Mn	Planet Ingress Dy Hr Mn	Last Aspect Dy Hr Mn	☽ Ingress Dy Hr Mn	Last Aspect Dy Hr Mn	☽ Ingress Dy Hr Mn	☽ Phases & Eclipses Dy Hr Mn	Astro Data
♃☌♆ 7 5:29	☿ ♑ 2 12:27	31 12:33 ♂ △	♊ 1 19:54	1 19:33 ♀ ☍	♌ 2 13:12	5 0:13 ○ 14♋00	1 January 1901
☽0S 10 1:28	♀ ♑ 16 11:29	3 19:08 ♆ ☌	♋ 3 23:36	4 15:16 ♆ ✶	♍ 4 21:33	12 20:38 ☾ 22♎00	Julian Day # 366
♂R 13 7:04	⚳ ♓ 19 2:22	5 0:13 ☉ ☍	♌ 6 4:59	7 2:12 ♀ △	♎ 7 8:18	20 14:36 ● 29♑53	SVP 6♓38'16"
☽0N 24 1:13	♃ ♑ 19 8:33	8 8:28 ♃ △	♍ 8 13:04	9 14:06 ♆ △	♏ 9 20:56	27 9:52 ☽ 6♉48	GC 25♐27.4 ⚴ 5♒23.1
♅☌♇ 31 13:15	☉ ♒ 20 17:17	10 20:25 ♃ □	♎ 11 0:07	11 18:12 ☉ □	♐ 12 9:26		Eris 21♓55.3 ⚵ 9♈15.9
	☊ ♏R 20 23:36	13 10:16 ♃ ✶	♏ 13 12:52	14 12:46 ♆ ☍	♑ 14 19:10	3 15:30 ○ 14♌09	⚷ 28♐46.8 ⚶ 19♌16.3R
☽0S 6 10:42	☿ ♒ 21 6:30	15 14:30 ☉ ✶	♐ 16 0:43	15 20:12 ☿ ✶	♒ 17 0:50	11 18:12 ☾ 22♏22	☽ Mean ☊ 29♏48.4
☽0N 20 10:22		18 9:07 ♃ ☌	♑ 18 9:30	19 2:45 ☉ ☌	♓ 19 3:06	19 2:45 ● 29♒47	
☿R 26 12:18	☿ ♓ 7 10:35	20 14:36 ☉ ☌	♒ 20 14:48	20 22:06 ☿ □	♈ 21 3:44	25 18:38 ☽ 6♊30	1 February 1901
♇D 28 18:17	♀ ♒ 9 13:07	22 12:37 ♆ △	♓ 22 17:41	22 22:53 ♆ ✶	♉ 23 4:41		Julian Day # 397
	☉ ♓ 19 7:45	24 14:37 ♆ □	♈ 24 19:45	24 17:21 ♆ ✶	♊ 25 7:22		SVP 6♓38'11"
		26 16:58 ♆ ✶	♉ 26 22:16	27 5:59 ♆ ☌	♋ 27 12:20		GC 25♐27.5 ⚴ 15♒52.7
		27 22:42 ♀ △	♊ 29 1:54				Eris 22♓10.0 ⚵ 22♈54.3
		31 1:07 ♆ ☌	♋ 31 6:50				⚷ 1♑54.1 ⚶ 12♌51.6R
							☽ Mean ☊ 28♏09.9

March 1901 — LONGITUDE

Day	Sid.Time	☉	0 hr ☽	Noon ☽	True ☊	☿	♀	♂	⚳	♃	♄	♅	♆	♇
1 F	22 34 23	10♓14 06	19♋31 01	25♋58 51	26♏04.0	21♓23.7	24♒52.3	0♍07.1	15♓58.2	7♑50.2	13♑58.6	16♐42.3	26♊27.4	15♊41.1
2 Sa	22 38 19	11 14 15	2♌23 49	8♌46 00	25R 54.3	20R 51.9	26 07.0	29♌44.5	16 21.9	7 59.7	14 03.5	16 43.4	26R 27.2	15 41.1
3 Su	22 42 16	12 14 23	15 05 30	21 22 23	25 42.4	20 12.4	27 21.7	29R 22.2	16 45.5	8 09.1	14 08.3	16 44.5	26 27.0	15 41.1
4 M	22 46 12	13 14 28	27 36 41	3♍48 27	25 29.2	19 26.3	28 36.4	29 00.4	17 09.1	8 18.4	14 13.0	16 45.4	26 26.8	15 41.2
5 Tu	22 50 09	14 14 31	9♍57 44	16 04 36	25 15.9	18 34.7	29 51.1	28 38.9	17 32.7	8 27.5	14 17.7	16 46.4	26 26.7	15 41.3
6 W	22 54 06	15 14 33	22 09 07	28 11 24	25 03.7	17 38.9	1♓05.8	28 17.9	17 56.3	8 36.6	14 22.3	16 47.2	26 26.6	15 41.4
7 Th	22 58 02	16 14 32	4♎11 37	10♎09 57	24 53.5	16 40.3	2 20.5	27 57.5	18 20.0	8 45.5	14 26.8	16 48.1	26D 26.6	15 41.6
8 F	23 01 59	17 14 30	16 06 39	22 02 00	24 46.0	15 40.3	3 35.2	27 37.5	18 43.6	8 54.3	14 31.3	16 48.8	26 26.6	15 41.7
9 Sa	23 05 55	18 14 26	27 56 21	3♏50 07	24 41.2	14 40.3	4 49.8	27 18.1	19 07.3	9 02.9	14 35.7	16 49.6	26 26.6	15 41.9
10 Su	23 09 52	19 14 21	9♏43 45	15 37 44	24D 38.9	13 41.6	6 04.5	26 59.2	19 30.9	9 11.5	14 40.0	16 50.2	26 26.7	15 42.1
11 M	23 13 48	20 14 14	21 32 38	27 29 02	24 38.5	12 45.4	7 19.1	26 41.0	19 54.5	9 19.9	14 44.2	16 50.8	26 26.8	15 42.3
12 Tu	23 17 45	21 14 05	3♐27 34	9♐28 52	24 39.1	11 52.7	8 33.8	26 23.4	20 18.2	9 28.2	14 48.3	16 51.4	26 26.9	15 42.6
13 W	23 21 41	22 13 54	15 33 38	21 42 30	24R 39.6	11 04.5	9 48.4	26 06.5	20 41.8	9 36.4	14 52.4	16 51.9	26 27.1	15 42.8
14 Th	23 25 38	23 13 42	27 56 09	4♑15 13	24 38.9	10 21.4	11 03.0	25 50.2	21 05.5	9 44.4	14 56.4	16 52.3	26 27.3	15 43.1
15 F	23 29 35	24 13 28	10♑40 17	17 11 52	24 36.4	9 43.9	12 17.7	25 34.6	21 29.1	9 52.3	15 00.3	16 52.7	26 27.5	15 43.5
16 Sa	23 33 31	25 13 12	23 50 24	0♒36 11	24 31.6	9 12.4	13 32.3	25 19.8	21 52.8	10 00.0	15 04.1	16 53.1	26 27.8	15 43.8
17 Su	23 37 28	26 12 55	7♒29 21	14 29 53	24 24.7	8 47.0	14 46.9	25 05.6	22 16.4	10 07.7	15 07.9	16 53.4	26 28.1	15 44.1
18 M	23 41 24	27 12 35	21 37 34	28 51 57	24 16.2	8 28.0	16 01.5	24 52.2	22 40.0	10 15.1	15 11.5	16 53.6	26 28.4	15 44.5
19 Tu	23 45 21	28 12 14	6♓12 23	13♓38 02	24 07.1	8 15.2	17 16.1	24 39.6	23 03.7	10 22.5	15 15.1	16 53.8	26 28.8	15 44.9
20 W	23 49 17	29 11 51	21 07 51	28 40 40	23 58.6	8D 08.6	18 30.6	24 27.7	23 27.3	10 29.7	15 18.6	16 53.9	26 29.2	15 45.3
21 Th	23 53 14	0♈11 26	6♈15 14	13♈50 15	23 51.6	8 08.0	19 45.2	24 16.6	23 50.9	10 36.7	15 22.0	16R 54.0	26 29.6	15 45.8
22 F	23 57 10	1 10 58	21 24 25	28 56 33	23 46.9	8 13.1	20 59.8	24 06.3	24 14.5	10 43.6	15 25.4	16 54.0	26 30.1	15 46.2
23 Sa	0 01 07	2 10 29	6♉25 36	13♉50 37	23D 44.6	8 23.9	22 14.3	23 56.8	24 38.1	10 50.3	15 28.6	16 54.0	26 30.6	15 46.7
24 Su	0 05 04	3 09 57	21 10 54	28 25 53	23 44.3	8 39.9	23 28.8	23 48.1	25 01.7	10 56.9	15 31.7	16 53.9	26 31.1	15 47.2
25 M	0 09 00	4 09 23	5♊35 13	12♊38 42	23 45.2	9 01.0	24 43.3	23 40.1	25 25.2	11 03.4	15 34.8	16 53.8	26 31.7	15 47.8
26 Tu	0 12 57	5 08 47	19 36 17	26 28 02	23R 46.2	9 26.9	25 57.8	23 33.0	25 48.8	11 09.7	15 37.8	16 53.6	26 32.3	15 48.3
27 W	0 16 53	6 08 09	3♋14 09	9♋54 53	23 46.5	9 57.3	27 12.3	23 26.7	26 12.3	11 15.8	15 40.7	16 53.4	26 32.9	15 48.9
28 Th	0 20 50	7 07 28	16 30 31	23 01 24	23 45.1	10 32.1	28 26.8	23 21.1	26 35.8	11 21.8	15 43.5	16 53.1	26 33.6	15 49.5
29 F	0 24 46	8 06 44	29 27 53	5♌50 20	23 41.7	11 10.8	29 41.2	23 16.3	26 59.3	11 27.6	15 46.2	16 52.8	26 34.3	15 50.1
30 Sa	0 28 43	9 05 59	12♌09 05	18 24 29	23 36.4	11 53.4	0♈55.7	23 12.3	27 22.8	11 33.3	15 48.8	16 52.4	26 35.0	15 50.7
31 Su	0 32 39	10 05 11	24 36 49	0♍46 23	23 29.5	12 39.6	2 10.1	23 09.1	27 46.3	11 38.8	15 51.3	16 51.9	26 35.8	15 51.4

April 1901 — LONGITUDE

Day	Sid.Time	☉	0 hr ☽	Noon ☽	True ☊	☿	♀	♂	⚳	♃	♄	♅	♆	♇
1 M	0 36 36	11♈04 20	6♍53 26	12♍58 15	23♏21.7	13♓29.2	3♈24.5	23♌06.7	28♓09.7	11♑44.2	15♑53.7	16♐51.4	26♊36.6	15♊52.0
2 Tu	0 40 32	12 03 28	19 01 00	25 01 56	23R 13.7	14 22.0	4 38.9	23R 05.0	28 33.2	11 49.4	15 56.1	16R 50.9	26 37.4	15 52.7
3 W	0 44 29	13 02 33	1♎01 15	6♎59 08	23 06.4	15 17.9	5 53.3	23D 04.0	28 56.6	11 54.4	15 58.3	16 50.3	26 38.3	15 53.4
4 Th	0 48 26	14 01 37	12 55 46	18 51 24	23 00.4	16 16.6	7 07.6	23 03.8	29 20.0	11 59.2	16 00.5	16 49.6	26 39.2	15 54.1
5 F	0 52 22	15 00 38	24 46 15	0♏40 33	22 56.2	17 18.2	8 22.0	23 04.3	29 43.3	12 03.9	16 02.5	16 48.9	26 40.1	15 54.9
6 Sa	0 56 19	15 59 38	6♏34 34	12 28 38	22D 53.8	18 22.3	9 36.3	23 05.6	0♈06.7	12 08.5	16 04.5	16 48.2	26 41.0	15 55.6
7 Su	1 00 15	16 58 35	18 23 04	24 18 14	22 53.3	19 29.0	10 50.7	23 07.5	0 30.0	12 12.8	16 06.4	16 47.4	26 42.0	15 56.4
8 M	1 04 12	17 57 31	0♐14 33	6♐12 28	22 54.0	20 38.1	12 05.0	23 10.2	0 53.3	12 17.0	16 08.2	16 46.6	26 43.1	15 57.2
9 Tu	1 08 08	18 56 25	12 12 27	18 15 01	22 55.6	21 49.4	13 19.3	23 13.5	1 16.6	12 21.0	16 09.8	16 45.7	26 44.1	15 58.0
10 W	1 12 05	19 55 17	24 20 42	0♑30 03	22 57.3	23 03.0	14 33.6	23 17.6	1 39.9	12 24.8	16 11.4	16 44.8	26 45.2	15 58.9
11 Th	1 16 01	20 54 08	6♑43 37	13 01 57	22R 58.5	24 18.7	15 47.9	23 22.3	2 03.1	12 28.5	16 12.9	16 43.8	26 46.3	15 59.7
12 F	1 19 58	21 52 56	19 25 37	25 55 06	22 58.7	25 36.5	17 02.1	23 27.6	2 26.3	12 32.0	16 14.3	16 42.7	26 47.4	16 00.6
13 Sa	1 23 55	22 51 43	2♒30 50	9♒13 13	22 57.6	26 56.3	18 16.4	23 33.7	2 49.5	12 35.3	16 15.6	16 41.7	26 48.6	16 01.5
14 Su	1 27 51	23 50 28	16 02 30	22 58 49	22 55.3	28 18.1	19 30.7	23 40.3	3 12.6	12 38.4	16 16.8	16 40.5	26 49.8	16 02.4
15 M	1 31 48	24 49 12	0♓02 08	7♓12 18	22 51.9	29 41.7	20 44.9	23 47.6	3 35.8	12 41.4	16 17.9	16 39.4	26 51.0	16 03.3
16 Tu	1 35 44	25 47 54	14 28 54	21 51 22	22 48.1	1♈07.2	21 59.1	23 55.5	3 58.8	12 44.2	16 18.9	16 38.2	26 52.2	16 04.2
17 W	1 39 41	26 46 34	29 18 55	6♈50 38	22 44.4	2 34.6	23 13.4	24 04.1	4 21.9	12 46.8	16 19.8	16 36.9	26 53.5	16 05.2
18 Th	1 43 37	27 45 12	14♈25 24	22 02 01	22 41.5	4 03.7	24 27.6	24 13.2	4 44.9	12 49.2	16 20.6	16 35.6	26 54.8	16 06.1
19 F	1 47 34	28 43 48	29 39 12	7♉15 41	22 39.7	5 34.6	25 41.8	24 22.9	5 07.9	12 51.4	16 21.3	16 34.3	26 56.2	16 07.1
20 Sa	1 51 30	29 42 22	14♉50 14	22 21 43	22D 39.1	7 07.3	26 55.9	24 33.2	5 30.9	12 53.4	16 21.9	16 32.9	26 57.5	16 08.1
21 Su	1 55 27	0♉40 55	29 49 06	7♊11 33	22 39.5	8 41.7	28 10.1	24 44.1	5 53.8	12 55.3	16 22.4	16 31.4	26 58.9	16 09.1
22 M	1 59 24	1 39 25	14♊28 22	21 39 04	22 40.7	10 17.9	29 24.3	24 55.6	6 16.7	12 56.9	16 22.9	16 30.0	27 00.3	16 10.2
23 Tu	2 03 20	2 37 53	28 43 20	5♋41 00	22 42.1	11 55.8	0♉38.4	25 07.6	6 39.5	12 58.4	16 23.2	16 28.5	27 01.8	16 11.2
24 W	2 07 17	3 36 19	12♋32 05	19 16 43	22 43.2	13 35.4	1 52.5	25 20.1	7 02.3	12 59.7	16 23.4	16 26.9	27 03.2	16 12.3
25 Th	2 11 13	4 34 43	25 55 06	2♌27 33	22R 43.7	15 16.7	3 06.6	25 33.2	7 25.1	13 00.8	16R 23.5	16 25.3	27 04.7	16 13.4
26 F	2 15 10	5 33 05	8♌54 28	15 16 16	22 43.5	16 59.8	4 20.7	25 46.8	7 47.8	13 01.7	16 23.5	16 23.7	27 06.2	16 14.4
27 Sa	2 19 06	6 31 24	21 33 24	27 46 19	22 42.4	18 44.7	5 34.8	26 00.8	8 10.5	13 02.4	16 23.5	16 22.0	27 07.8	16 15.5
28 Su	2 23 03	7 29 42	3♍55 30	10♍01 25	22 40.7	20 31.2	6 48.9	26 15.4	8 33.1	13 03.0	16 23.3	16 20.3	27 09.3	16 16.7
29 M	2 26 59	8 27 57	16 04 30	22 05 12	22 38.7	22 19.6	8 02.9	26 30.5	8 55.7	13 03.3	16 23.0	16 18.6	27 10.9	16 17.8
30 Tu	2 30 56	9 26 10	28 03 55	4♎01 02	22 36.7	24 09.6	9 16.9	26 46.0	9 18.3	13R 03.5	16 22.6	16 16.8	27 12.5	16 18.9

Astro Data	Dy Hr Mn
☽0S	5 18:26
♆D	8 6:24
☽0N	19 21:03
☿D	21 2:30
☉0N	21 7:23
♅R	22 11:26
♄⊼♇	31 12:37
♀0N	1 10:10
☽0S	2 0:26
♂D	4 6:52
☽0N	16 7:31
☿0N	19 19:54
♄R	26 4:34
♄⊻♅	26 14:17
☽0S	29 5:51

Planet Ingress	Dy Hr Mn
♂ ♌R	1 19:28
♀ ♓	5 14:51
☉ ♈	21 7:24
♀ ♈	29 18:03
⚳ ♈	6 5:07
☿ ♈	15 17:10
☉ ♉	20 19:14
♀ ♉	22 23:34
♅☍☍	29 18:34
♃ R	30 20:41

Last Aspect Dy Hr Mn		☽ Ingress	Dy Hr Mn
1 3:45	☿ △	♌	1 19:30
4 2:57	♂ ☌	♍	4 4:37
6 8:31	♆ □	♎	6 15:37
8 23:03	♂ ⚹	♏	9 4:12
11 10:26	♂ □	♐	11 17:04
13 21:09	♆ ☍	♑	14 3:56
16 1:42	☉ ⚹	♒	16 10:56
18 8:03	♆ △	♓	18 13:52
20 12:53	☉ ☌	♈	20 14:06
22 8:06	♆ ⚹	♉	22 13:41
24 4:24	♂ □	♊	24 14:37
26 12:08	♆ ☌	♋	26 18:15
28 23:10	♀ △	♌	29 1:00
31 3:51	♆ ⚹	♍	31 10:29

Last Aspect Dy Hr Mn		☽ Ingress	Dy Hr Mn
2 15:11	♆ □	♎	2 21:57
5 3:51	♆ △	♏	5 10:38
7 9:36	♂ □	♐	7 23:31
10 4:42	♆ ☍	♑	10 11:02
12 11:22	☿ ⚹	♒	12 19:27
14 18:35	♆ △	♓	14 23:56
16 20:05	♆ □	♈	17 1:06
18 21:37	☉ ☌	♉	19 0:33
20 15:34	♂ □	♊	21 0:18
22 21:05	♆ ☌	♋	23 2:11
24 6:50	♄ ☍	♌	25 7:28
27 10:45	♆ ⚹	♍	27 16:20
29 22:15	♆ □	♎	30 3:54

☽ Phases & Eclipses Dy Hr Mn	
5 8:04	○ 14♍05
13 13:06	☾ 22♐17
20 12:53	● 29♓14
27 4:39	☽ 5♋50
4 1:20	○ 13♎35
12 3:57	☾ 21♑33
18 21:37	● 28♈09
25 16:15	☽ 4♌45

Astro Data

1 March 1901
Julian Day # 425
SVP 6♓38'08"
GC 25♐27.5 ⚴ 25♒18.5
Eris 22♓30.3 ⚵ 7♉23.3
⚷ 4♑04.0 ⚶ 6♌23.8R
☽ Mean ☊ 26♏40.9

1 April 1901
Julian Day # 456
SVP 6♓38'05"
GC 25♐27.6 ⚴ 5♓11.2
Eris 22♓55.2 ⚵ 24♉36.4
⚷ 5♑20.4 ⚶ 5♌08.5
☽ Mean ☊ 25♏02.4

LONGITUDE — May 1901

Day	Sid.Time	☉	0 hr ☽	Noon☽	True☊	☿	♀	♂	⚳	♃	♄	♅	♆	♇
1 W	2 34 53	10♉24 22	9♎56 55	15♎51 56	22♏34.8	26♈01.5	10♉30.9	27♌02.0	9♈40.8	13♑03.5	16♑22.2	16♐15.0	27♊14.2	16♊20.1
2 Th	2 38 49	11 22 32	21 46 22	27 40 32	22R33.4	27 55.1	11 44.9	27 18.4	10 03.3	13R03.2	16R21.6	16R13.1	27 15.8	16 21.2
3 F	2 42 46	12 20 40	3♏34 45	9♏29 15	22 32.6	29 50.5	12 58.9	27 35.3	10 25.7	13 02.8	16 20.9	16 11.3	27 17.5	16 22.4
4 Sa	2 46 42	13 18 46	15 24 21	21 20 17	22D32.3	1♉47.6	14 12.9	27 52.6	10 48.0	13 02.3	16 20.2	16 09.3	27 19.2	16 23.6
5 Su	2 50 39	14 16 50	27 17 20	3♐15 48	22 32.4	3 46.5	15 26.9	28 10.3	11 10.3	13 01.5	16 19.3	16 07.4	27 20.9	16 24.8
6 M	2 54 35	15 14 54	9♐15 56	15 18 03	22 32.9	5 47.0	16 40.8	28 28.4	11 32.6	13 00.5	16 18.4	16 05.4	27 22.7	16 26.0
7 Tu	2 58 32	16 12 55	21 22 27	27 29 29	22 33.6	7 49.2	17 54.8	28 47.0	11 54.8	12 59.4	16 17.4	16 03.4	27 24.4	16 27.2
8 W	3 02 28	17 10 55	3♑39 29	9♑52 47	22 34.2	9 52.9	19 08.7	29 05.9	12 17.0	12 58.0	16 16.2	16 01.4	27 26.2	16 28.4
9 Th	3 06 25	18 08 54	16 09 46	22 30 48	22 34.7	11 58.2	20 22.6	29 25.2	12 39.1	12 56.5	16 15.0	15 59.3	27 28.0	16 29.7
10 F	3 10 22	19 06 51	28 56 15	5♒26 28	22 35.0	14 04.8	21 36.5	29 44.9	13 01.2	12 54.8	16 13.7	15 57.3	27 29.8	16 30.9
11 Sa	3 14 18	20 04 47	12♒01 46	18 42 26	22R35.1	16 12.7	22 50.4	0♍05.0	13 23.2	12 52.9	16 12.3	15 55.1	27 31.7	16 32.2
12 Su	3 18 15	21 02 42	25 28 44	2♓20 47	22 35.0	18 21.6	24 04.3	0 25.4	13 45.2	12 50.8	16 10.8	15 53.0	27 33.5	16 33.5
13 M	3 22 11	22 00 36	9♓18 42	16 22 24	22D35.0	20 31.5	25 18.2	0 46.2	14 07.0	12 48.6	16 09.2	15 50.8	27 35.4	16 34.7
14 Tu	3 26 08	22 58 28	23 31 45	0♈46 25	22 35.0	22 42.1	26 32.1	1 07.4	14 28.9	12 46.1	16 07.5	15 48.6	27 37.3	16 36.0
15 W	3 30 04	23 56 19	8♈05 59	15 29 49	22 35.1	24 53.1	27 45.9	1 28.9	14 50.7	12 43.5	16 05.7	15 46.4	27 39.2	16 37.3
16 Th	3 34 01	24 54 09	22 57 12	0♉27 14	22 35.2	27 04.4	28 59.8	1 50.7	15 12.4	12 40.7	16 03.8	15 44.2	27 41.2	16 38.6
17 F	3 37 57	25 51 58	7♉58 56	15 31 15	22R35.3	29 15.6	0♊13.7	2 12.9	15 34.0	12 37.7	16 01.9	15 41.9	27 43.1	16 39.9
18 Sa	3 41 54	26 49 45	23 03 05	0♊33 18	22 35.3	1♊26.4	1 27.5	2 35.4	15 55.6	12 34.5	15 59.8	15 39.7	27 45.1	16 41.2
19 Su	3 45 51	27 47 31	8♊00 52	15 24 46	22 35.1	3 36.7	2 41.3	2 58.2	16 17.2	12 31.2	15 57.7	15 37.4	27 47.1	16 42.6
20 M	3 49 47	28 45 16	22 44 08	29 58 13	22 34.6	5 46.1	3 55.1	3 21.4	16 38.6	12 27.6	15 55.5	15 35.1	27 49.0	16 43.9
21 Tu	3 53 44	29 42 59	7♋06 27	14♋08 24	22 33.8	7 54.3	5 09.0	3 44.9	17 00.0	12 23.9	15 53.2	15 32.7	27 51.1	16 45.2
22 W	3 57 40	0♊40 40	21 03 48	27 52 32	22 32.9	10 01.0	6 22.8	4 08.6	17 21.3	12 20.1	15 50.8	15 30.4	27 53.1	16 46.6
23 Th	4 01 37	1 38 20	4♌34 39	11♌10 19	22 32.1	12 06.2	7 36.5	4 32.7	17 42.6	12 16.1	15 48.4	15 28.0	27 55.1	16 47.9
24 F	4 05 33	2 35 59	17 39 47	24 03 27	22D31.6	14 09.4	8 50.3	4 57.0	18 03.8	12 11.9	15 45.8	15 25.6	27 57.2	16 49.3
25 Sa	4 09 30	3 33 35	0♍21 44	6♍35 07	22 31.5	16 10.6	10 04.1	5 21.7	18 24.9	12 07.5	15 43.2	15 23.2	27 59.2	16 50.6
26 Su	4 13 26	4 31 11	12 44 08	18 49 21	22 31.9	18 09.6	11 17.8	5 46.6	18 45.9	12 03.0	15 40.5	15 20.8	28 01.3	16 52.0
27 M	4 17 23	5 28 45	24 51 20	0♎50 37	22 32.8	20 06.3	12 31.5	6 11.7	19 06.9	11 58.3	15 37.7	15 18.4	28 03.4	16 53.4
28 Tu	4 21 20	6 26 17	6♎47 48	12 43 24	22 34.0	22 00.5	13 45.3	6 37.2	19 27.7	11 53.5	15 34.9	15 16.0	28 05.5	16 54.7
29 W	4 25 16	7 23 48	18 37 56	24 31 55	22 35.3	23 52.1	14 59.0	7 02.9	19 48.5	11 48.5	15 32.0	15 13.6	28 07.6	16 56.1
30 Th	4 29 13	8 21 18	0♏25 49	6♏20 03	22 36.4	25 41.1	16 12.7	7 28.8	20 09.3	11 43.4	15 29.0	15 11.1	28 09.7	16 57.5
31 F	4 33 09	9 18 47	12 15 03	18 11 10	22R37.0	27 27.4	17 26.3	7 55.0	20 29.9	11 38.1	15 25.9	15 08.7	28 11.9	16 58.9

LONGITUDE — June 1901

Day	Sid.Time	☉	0 hr ☽	Noon☽	True☊	☿	♀	♂	⚳	♃	♄	♅	♆	♇
1 Sa	4 37 06	10♊16 15	24♏08 44	0♐08 04	22♏36.9	29♊11.0	18♊40.0	8♍21.5	20♈50.5	11♑32.7	15♑22.8	15♐06.2	28♊14.0	17♊00.2
2 Su	4 41 02	11 13 42	6♐09 26	12 13 05	22R35.9	0♋51.8	19 53.7	8 48.2	21 11.0	11R27.2	15R19.6	15R03.8	28 16.1	17 01.6
3 M	4 44 59	12 11 07	18 19 13	24 28 03	22 34.0	2 29.8	21 07.4	9 15.1	21 31.4	11 21.5	15 16.3	15 01.3	28 18.3	17 03.0
4 Tu	4 48 55	13 08 32	0♑39 43	6♑54 24	22 31.3	4 05.0	22 21.0	9 42.2	21 51.7	11 15.7	15 13.0	14 58.9	28 20.5	17 04.4
5 W	4 52 52	14 05 56	13 12 14	19 33 21	22 28.1	5 37.3	23 34.7	10 09.6	22 11.9	11 09.7	15 09.6	14 56.4	28 22.6	17 05.8
6 Th	4 56 49	15 03 19	25 57 52	2♒25 53	22 24.8	7 06.8	24 48.3	10 37.2	22 32.0	11 03.7	15 06.1	14 53.9	28 24.8	17 07.2
7 F	5 00 45	16 00 42	8♒57 32	15 32 55	22 22.0	8 33.3	26 01.9	11 05.0	22 52.1	10 57.5	15 02.6	14 51.5	28 27.0	17 08.6
8 Sa	5 04 42	16 58 04	22 12 08	28 55 16	22 19.9	9 56.9	27 15.5	11 33.1	23 12.0	10 51.2	14 59.0	14 49.0	28 29.2	17 10.0
9 Su	5 08 38	17 55 25	5♓42 25	12♓33 36	22D18.9	11 17.5	28 29.1	12 01.3	23 31.9	10 44.7	14 55.4	14 46.5	28 31.4	17 11.4
10 M	5 12 35	18 52 46	19 28 51	26 28 09	22 18.9	12 35.1	29 42.8	12 29.8	23 51.7	10 38.2	14 51.7	14 44.1	28 33.6	17 12.8
11 Tu	5 16 31	19 50 07	3♈31 25	10♈38 30	22 19.9	13 49.6	0♋56.4	12 58.5	24 11.3	10 31.6	14 47.9	14 41.6	28 35.8	17 14.2
12 W	5 20 28	20 47 27	17 49 10	25 03 08	22 21.3	15 01.0	2 10.0	13 27.3	24 30.9	10 24.8	14 44.1	14 39.1	28 38.0	17 15.6
13 Th	5 24 24	21 44 47	2♉19 57	9♉39 08	22R22.5	16 09.3	3 23.5	13 56.4	24 50.4	10 18.0	14 40.3	14 36.7	28 40.3	17 16.9
14 F	5 28 21	22 42 06	17 00 04	24 22 03	22 22.9	17 14.3	4 37.1	14 25.7	25 09.8	10 11.1	14 36.4	14 34.3	28 42.5	17 18.3
15 Sa	5 32 18	23 39 25	1♊44 19	9♊06 00	22 22.0	18 16.0	5 50.7	14 55.2	25 29.0	10 04.0	14 32.5	14 31.8	28 44.7	17 19.7
16 Su	5 36 14	24 36 44	16 26 15	23 44 12	22 19.6	19 14.4	7 04.3	15 24.8	25 48.2	9 56.9	14 28.5	14 29.4	28 46.9	17 21.1
17 M	5 40 11	25 34 02	0♋58 59	8♋09 51	22 15.7	20 09.2	8 17.9	15 54.7	26 07.2	9 49.8	14 24.4	14 27.0	28 49.2	17 22.5
18 Tu	5 44 07	26 31 19	15 16 05	22 17 07	22 10.8	21 00.5	9 31.4	16 24.8	26 26.2	9 42.5	14 20.4	14 24.6	28 51.4	17 23.9
19 W	5 48 04	27 28 36	29 12 28	6♌01 50	22 05.4	21 48.2	10 45.0	16 55.0	26 45.0	9 35.2	14 16.3	14 22.2	28 53.7	17 25.3
20 Th	5 52 00	28 25 51	12♌45 04	19 22 06	22 00.3	22 32.0	11 58.5	17 25.4	27 03.7	9 27.8	14 12.1	14 19.8	28 55.9	17 26.6
21 F	5 55 57	29 23 07	25 53 03	2♍18 09	21 56.1	23 12.0	13 12.0	17 56.0	27 22.3	9 20.4	14 08.0	14 17.5	28 58.1	17 28.0
22 Sa	5 59 53	0♋20 21	8♍37 42	14 52 07	21 53.3	23 47.9	14 25.5	18 26.8	27 40.8	9 12.9	14 03.7	14 15.1	29 00.4	17 29.4
23 Su	6 03 50	1 17 35	21 01 55	27 07 37	21D52.0	24 19.8	15 39.1	18 57.7	27 59.1	9 05.4	13 59.5	14 12.8	29 02.6	17 30.7
24 M	6 07 47	2 14 49	3♎09 48	9♎09 07	21 52.2	24 47.4	16 52.5	19 28.8	28 17.4	8 57.8	13 55.2	14 10.5	29 04.8	17 32.1
25 Tu	6 11 43	3 12 01	15 06 10	21 01 36	21 53.3	25 10.7	18 06.0	20 00.1	28 35.5	8 50.2	13 51.0	14 08.2	29 07.1	17 33.5
26 W	6 15 40	4 09 14	26 56 03	2♏50 08	21 54.9	25 29.6	19 19.5	20 31.5	28 53.5	8 42.6	13 46.6	14 05.9	29 09.3	17 34.8
27 Th	6 19 36	5 06 26	8♏44 27	14 39 35	21R56.1	25 44.0	20 33.0	21 03.1	29 11.3	8 34.9	13 42.3	14 03.7	29 11.5	17 36.1
28 F	6 23 33	6 03 37	20 36 03	26 34 22	21 56.2	25 53.8	21 46.4	21 34.9	29 29.0	8 27.3	13 38.0	14 01.4	29 13.7	17 37.5
29 Sa	6 27 29	7 00 48	2♐34 58	8♐38 14	21 54.7	25R59.0	22 59.9	22 06.8	29 46.6	8 19.6	13 33.6	13 59.2	29 16.0	17 38.8
30 Su	6 31 26	7 57 59	14 44 32	20 54 08	21 51.2	25 59.6	24 13.3	22 38.8	0♉04.1	8 11.9	13 29.2	13 57.0	29 18.2	17 40.1

Astro Data (Dy Hr Mn)

- ♄⚻♇ 2 16:58
- ☽0N 13 16:21
- ☽0S 26 12:19
- ⚳0N 31 11:30

- ☽0N 9 23:22
- ♄⚺♅ 15 21:45
- ☽0S 22 20:34
- ☿R 30 2:52

Planet Ingress (Dy Hr Mn)

- ☿ ♉ 3 13:58
- ♂ ♍ 11 6:05
- ♀ ♊ 17 7:34
- ☿ ♊ 17 20:08
- ☉ ♊ 21 19:05

- ☿ ♋ 1 23:35
- ♀ ♋ 10 17:37
- ☉ ♋ 22 3:28
- ⚳ ♉ 30 6:23

Last Aspect / ☽ Ingress (Dy Hr Mn)

Last Aspect		☽ Ingress	
2 12:35	☿ ☍	♏	2 16:44
5 1:31	♂ □	♐	5 5:27
7 14:35	♂ △	♑	7 16:54
9 7:33	♀ △	♒	10 1:58
12 3:38	♆ △	♓	12 7:55
14 6:47	♆ □	♈	14 10:44
16 7:34	♆ ⚹	♉	16 11:17
18 5:38	☉ ☌	♊	18 11:07
20 8:24	♆ ☌	♋	20 12:03
21 15:00	♄ ☍	♌	22 15:47
24 19:25	♆ ⚹	♍	24 23:18
27 6:23	♆ □	♎	27 10:18
29 19:20	♆ △	♏	29 23:07

Last Aspect / ☽ Ingress (Dy Hr Mn)

Last Aspect		☽ Ingress	
31 6:28	♄ ⚹	♐	1 11:44
3 19:28	♆ ☍	♑	3 22:43
5 3:45	♄ ☌	♒	6 7:30
8 11:14	♆ △	♓	8 13:55
10 15:35	♆ □	♈	10 18:01
12 17:56	♆ ⚹	♉	12 20:10
13 23:29	☿ ⚹	♊	14 21:10
16 20:22	♆ ☌	♋	16 22:22
18 9:40	☿ ☌	♌	19 1:23
21 6:05	☉ ⚹	♍	21 7:40
23 15:49	♆ □	♎	23 17:42
26 4:29	♆ △	♏	26 6:14
28 10:38	☿ △	♐	28 18:51

☽ Phases & Eclipses (Dy Hr Mn)

- 3 18:19 ○ 12♏36
- 3 18:31 • A 1.043
- 11 14:38 ☾ 20♒11
- 18 5:38 ● 26♉34
- 18 5:33:49 • T 06'29"
- 25 5:40 ☽ 3♍18

- 2 9:53 ○ 11♐09
- 9 22:00 ☾ 18♓19
- 16 13:33 ● 24♊40
- 23 20:59 ☽ 1♎39

Astro Data

1 May 1901
Julian Day # 486
SVP 6♓38'02"
GC 25♐27.7 ⚴ 13♓37.6
Eris 23♓15.9 ⚵ 11♊40.9
⚷ 5♑14.8R ⚶ 10♌16.4
☽ Mean ☊ 23♏27.1

1 June 1901
Julian Day # 517
SVP 6♓37'58"
GC 25♐27.8 ⚴ 20♓23.0
Eris 23♓28.8 ⚵ 29♊12.7
⚷ 3♑55.5R ⚶ 19♌55.6
☽ Mean ☊ 21♏48.6

July 1901 LONGITUDE

Day	Sid.Time	☉	0 hr ☽	Noon ☽	True ☊	☿	♀	♂	⚳	♃	♄	♅	♆	♇
1 M	6 35 22	8♋55 10	27♐07 15	3♑24 02	21♏45.8	25♋55.5	25♋26.7	23♍11.0	0♉21.4	8♑04.2	13♑24.8	13♐54.9	29♊20.4	17♊41.5
2 Tu	6 39 19	9 52 21	9♑44 34	16 08 54	21R 38.7	25R 46.9	26 40.1	23 43.4	0 38.6	7R 56.5	13R 20.4	13R 52.7	29 22.6	17 42.8
3 W	6 43 16	10 49 31	22 36 59	29 08 45	21 30.6	25 33.8	27 53.5	24 15.9	0 55.6	7 48.8	13 16.0	13 50.6	29 24.8	17 44.1
4 Th	6 47 12	11 46 42	5♒44 05	12♒22 49	21 22.2	25 16.4	29 06.9	24 48.5	1 12.5	7 41.2	13 11.6	13 48.5	29 27.0	17 45.4
5 F	6 51 09	12 43 53	19 04 46	25 49 46	21 14.6	24 54.8	0♌20.3	25 21.3	1 29.3	7 33.5	13 07.2	13 46.5	29 29.2	17 46.7
6 Sa	6 55 05	13 41 04	2♓37 36	9♓28 04	21 08.5	24 29.5	1 33.6	25 54.3	1 45.9	7 25.9	13 02.8	13 44.4	29 31.4	17 47.9
7 Su	6 59 02	14 38 15	16 21 02	23 16 18	21 04.4	24 00.7	2 47.0	26 27.3	2 02.3	7 18.3	12 58.4	13 42.4	29 33.6	17 49.2
8 M	7 02 58	15 35 26	0♈13 44	7♈13 12	21D 02.5	23 28.7	4 00.3	27 00.5	2 18.6	7 10.7	12 53.9	13 40.5	29 35.7	17 50.5
9 Tu	7 06 55	16 32 39	14 14 36	21 17 47	21 02.3	22 54.2	5 13.7	27 33.9	2 34.8	7 03.2	12 49.5	13 38.5	29 37.9	17 51.7
10 W	7 10 51	17 29 51	28 22 37	5♉28 58	21 03.0	22 17.6	6 27.0	28 07.4	2 50.8	6 55.7	12 45.1	13 36.6	29 40.0	17 53.0
11 Th	7 14 48	18 27 05	12♉36 38	19 45 23	21R 03.5	21 39.5	7 40.3	28 41.0	3 06.6	6 48.3	12 40.7	13 34.7	29 42.2	17 54.2
12 F	7 18 45	19 24 18	26 54 55	4♊04 51	21 02.9	21 00.6	8 53.7	29 14.8	3 22.3	6 40.9	12 36.4	13 32.9	29 44.3	17 55.4
13 Sa	7 22 41	20 21 33	11♊14 48	18 24 14	21 00.1	20 21.4	10 07.0	29 48.7	3 37.8	6 33.6	12 32.0	13 31.1	29 46.5	17 56.6
14 Su	7 26 38	21 18 48	25 32 38	2♋39 23	20 55.0	19 42.7	11 20.3	0♎22.7	3 53.1	6 26.4	12 27.6	13 29.3	29 48.6	17 57.8
15 M	7 30 34	22 16 03	9♋43 53	16 45 31	20 47.3	19 05.1	12 33.6	0 56.9	4 08.2	6 19.2	12 23.3	13 27.5	29 50.7	17 59.0
16 Tu	7 34 31	23 13 19	23 43 41	0♌37 51	20 37.9	18 29.4	13 46.8	1 31.2	4 23.2	6 12.1	12 19.0	13 25.8	29 52.8	18 00.2
17 W	7 38 27	24 10 35	7♌27 33	14 12 24	20 27.6	17 56.1	15 00.1	2 05.6	4 38.0	6 05.1	12 14.7	13 24.1	29 54.9	18 01.4
18 Th	7 42 24	25 07 51	20 52 06	27 26 31	20 17.4	17 26.0	16 13.4	2 40.2	4 52.6	5 58.2	12 10.5	13 22.5	29 56.9	18 02.5
19 F	7 46 20	26 05 07	3♍55 36	10♍19 24	20 08.4	16 59.4	17 26.6	3 14.9	5 07.0	5 51.3	12 06.2	13 20.9	29 59.0	18 03.7
20 Sa	7 50 17	27 02 24	16 38 08	22 52 03	20 01.4	16 37.0	18 39.8	3 49.7	5 21.2	5 44.6	12 02.0	13 19.3	0♋01.0	18 04.8
21 Su	7 54 14	27 59 41	29 01 33	5♎07 05	19 56.8	16 19.2	19 53.0	4 24.6	5 35.2	5 38.0	11 57.8	13 17.8	0 03.1	18 05.9
22 M	7 58 10	28 56 59	11♎09 10	17 08 24	19 54.4	16 06.3	21 06.2	4 59.6	5 49.1	5 31.4	11 53.7	13 16.3	0 05.1	18 07.0
23 Tu	8 02 07	29 54 16	23 05 23	29 00 47	19D 53.7	15D 58.8	22 19.4	5 34.8	6 02.7	5 25.0	11 49.6	13 14.9	0 07.1	18 08.1
24 W	8 06 03	0♌51 35	4♏55 16	10♏49 31	19R 53.9	15 56.8	23 32.5	6 10.1	6 16.1	5 18.7	11 45.5	13 13.5	0 09.1	18 09.2
25 Th	8 10 00	1 48 53	16 44 12	22 39 59	19 54.1	16 00.6	24 45.7	6 45.5	6 29.3	5 12.5	11 41.5	13 12.1	0 11.0	18 10.3
26 F	8 13 56	2 46 12	28 37 31	4♐37 25	19 53.1	16 10.4	25 58.8	7 21.0	6 42.4	5 06.5	11 37.6	13 10.8	0 13.0	18 11.3
27 Sa	8 17 53	3 43 32	10♐40 16	16 46 34	19 50.3	16 26.2	27 11.9	7 56.6	6 55.2	5 00.5	11 33.6	13 09.5	0 14.9	18 12.3
28 Su	8 21 49	4 40 52	22 56 46	29 11 15	19 45.0	16 48.1	28 25.0	8 32.4	7 07.8	4 54.7	11 29.7	13 08.3	0 16.9	18 13.4
29 M	8 25 46	5 38 13	5♑30 20	11♑54 12	19 37.1	17 16.2	29 38.1	9 08.2	7 20.1	4 49.0	11 25.9	13 07.1	0 18.8	18 14.4
30 Tu	8 29 43	6 35 34	18 22 58	24 56 37	19 27.0	17 50.5	0♍51.1	9 44.2	7 32.3	4 43.5	11 22.1	13 06.0	0 20.6	18 15.4
31 W	8 33 39	7 32 57	1♒35 02	8♒18 02	19 15.5	18 30.8	2 04.1	10 20.3	7 44.2	4 38.1	11 18.4	13 04.9	0 22.5	18 16.4

August 1901 LONGITUDE

Day	Sid.Time	☉	0 hr ☽	Noon ☽	True ☊	☿	♀	♂	⚳	♃	♄	♅	♆	♇
1 Th	8 37 36	8♌30 20	15♒05 18	21♒56 27	19♏03.7	19♋17.3	3♍17.1	10♎56.4	7♉55.9	4♑32.9	11♑14.7	13♐03.8	0♋24.4	18♊17.3
2 F	8 41 32	9 27 43	28 51 03	5♓48 34	18R 52.8	20 09.8	4 30.1	11 32.7	8 07.4	4R 27.7	11R 11.1	13R 02.8	0 26.2	18 18.3
3 Sa	8 45 29	10 25 08	12♓48 32	19 50 25	18 43.8	21 08.2	5 43.1	12 09.1	8 18.6	4 22.8	11 07.5	13 01.9	0 28.0	18 19.2
4 Su	8 49 25	11 22 35	26 53 43	3♈57 59	18 37.4	22 12.3	6 56.0	12 45.6	8 29.6	4 18.0	11 04.0	13 00.9	0 29.8	18 20.1
5 M	8 53 22	12 20 02	11♈02 49	18 07 52	18 33.8	23 22.2	8 09.0	13 22.2	8 40.4	4 13.3	11 00.5	13 00.1	0 31.6	18 21.0
6 Tu	8 57 18	13 17 31	25 12 52	2♉17 34	18D 32.3	24 37.5	9 21.9	13 58.9	8 50.9	4 08.8	10 57.1	12 59.2	0 33.3	18 21.9
7 W	9 01 15	14 15 01	9♉21 49	16 25 29	18R 32.1	25 58.1	10 34.8	14 35.8	9 01.1	4 04.5	10 53.8	12 58.5	0 35.1	18 22.8
8 Th	9 05 12	15 12 32	23 28 27	0♊30 37	18 31.9	27 23.7	11 47.7	15 12.7	9 11.1	4 00.3	10 50.5	12 57.7	0 36.8	18 23.6
9 F	9 09 08	16 10 05	7♊31 52	14 32 06	18 30.4	28 54.2	13 00.5	15 49.7	9 20.9	3 56.3	10 47.3	12 57.0	0 38.5	18 24.4
10 Sa	9 13 05	17 07 40	21 31 09	28 28 49	18 26.6	0♌29.1	14 13.4	16 26.9	9 30.3	3 52.4	10 44.2	12 56.4	0 40.2	18 25.3
11 Su	9 17 01	18 05 15	5♋24 53	12♋19 03	18 20.0	2 08.3	15 26.2	17 04.1	9 39.5	3 48.8	10 41.2	12 55.8	0 41.8	18 26.0
12 M	9 20 58	19 02 52	19 11 02	26 00 28	18 10.7	3 51.3	16 39.0	17 41.5	9 48.5	3 45.3	10 38.2	12 55.3	0 43.5	18 26.8
13 Tu	9 24 54	20 00 31	2♌47 02	9♌30 23	17 59.2	5 37.8	17 51.8	18 18.9	9 57.1	3 41.9	10 35.3	12 54.8	0 45.1	18 27.6
14 W	9 28 51	20 58 10	16 10 12	22 46 12	17 46.6	7 27.4	19 04.6	18 56.5	10 05.5	3 38.8	10 32.4	12 54.4	0 46.6	18 28.3
15 Th	9 32 47	21 55 51	29 18 09	5♍45 53	17 34.0	9 19.7	20 17.3	19 34.1	10 13.5	3 35.8	10 29.7	12 54.0	0 48.2	18 29.1
16 F	9 36 44	22 53 33	12♍09 20	18 28 30	17 22.7	11 14.3	21 30.0	20 11.9	10 21.3	3 33.0	10 27.0	12 53.6	0 49.7	18 29.8
17 Sa	9 40 41	23 51 16	24 43 28	0♎54 23	17 13.5	13 10.8	22 42.7	20 49.8	10 28.8	3 30.4	10 24.4	12 53.4	0 51.2	18 30.4
18 Su	9 44 37	24 49 00	7♎01 33	13 05 17	17 07.0	15 08.7	23 55.4	21 27.7	10 36.0	3 28.0	10 21.8	12 53.1	0 52.7	18 31.1
19 M	9 48 34	25 46 46	19 06 00	25 04 10	17 03.1	17 07.8	25 08.0	22 05.8	10 42.9	3 25.8	10 19.4	12 52.9	0 54.2	18 31.8
20 Tu	9 52 30	26 44 33	1♏00 21	6♏55 06	17D 01.4	19 07.7	26 20.7	22 43.9	10 49.5	3 23.7	10 17.0	12 52.8	0 55.6	18 32.4
21 W	9 56 27	27 42 21	12 49 04	18 42 54	17R 01.1	21 08.0	27 33.3	23 22.2	10 55.8	3 21.8	10 14.7	12 52.7	0 57.0	18 33.0
22 Th	10 00 23	28 40 10	24 37 17	0♐32 54	17 01.2	23 08.4	28 45.8	24 00.5	11 01.8	3 20.1	10 12.5	12D 52.7	0 58.4	18 33.6
23 F	10 04 20	29 38 00	6♐30 26	12 30 34	17 00.6	25 08.8	29 58.4	24 39.0	11 07.4	3 18.7	10 10.4	12 52.7	0 59.8	18 34.2
24 Sa	10 08 16	0♍35 52	18 33 59	24 41 16	16 58.3	27 08.9	1♎10.9	25 17.5	11 12.8	3 17.4	10 08.4	12 52.8	1 01.1	18 34.7
25 Su	10 12 13	1 33 44	0♑53 01	7♑09 44	16 53.7	29 08.4	2 23.3	25 56.2	11 17.8	3 16.2	10 06.5	12 52.9	1 02.4	18 35.2
26 M	10 16 10	2 31 38	13 31 51	19 59 42	16 46.7	1♍07.3	3 35.8	26 34.9	11 22.5	3 15.3	10 04.6	12 53.1	1 03.7	18 35.8
27 Tu	10 20 06	3 29 34	26 33 28	3♒13 17	16 37.5	3 05.3	4 48.2	27 13.7	11 26.8	3 14.6	10 02.9	12 53.3	1 04.9	18 36.2
28 W	10 24 03	4 27 31	9♒59 03	16 50 37	16 26.8	5 02.5	6 00.6	27 52.6	11 30.9	3 14.0	10 01.2	12 53.6	1 06.1	18 36.7
29 Th	10 27 59	5 25 29	23 47 36	0♓49 32	16 15.7	6 58.6	7 12.9	28 31.6	11 34.6	3 13.7	9 59.6	12 53.9	1 07.3	18 37.2
30 F	10 31 56	6 23 29	7♓55 49	15 05 44	16 05.4	8 53.7	8 25.2	29 10.7	11 37.9	3D 13.5	9 58.1	12 54.3	1 08.5	18 37.6
31 Sa	10 35 52	7 21 30	22 18 32	29 33 22	15 56.9	10 47.7	9 37.5	29 49.8	11 40.9	3 13.5	9 56.7	12 54.7	1 09.6	18 38.0

Astro Data	Dy Hr Mn
☽0N	7 5:32
♂0S	15 5:26
☽0S	20 6:01
☿ D	24 8:16
☽0N	3 12:19
☽0S	16 15:19
♅ D	22 13:55
♀0S	25 3:21
☽0N	30 20:41
♃ D	30 21:46

Planet Ingress		Dy Hr Mn
♀	♌	5 5:22
♂	♎	13 19:59
♆	♋	19 23:55
☉	♌	23 14:24
♀	♍	29 19:13
☿	♌	10 4:45
♀	♎	23 12:33
☉	♍	23 21:08
☿	♍	25 22:24
♂	♏	31 18:13

Last Aspect Dy Hr Mn			☽ Ingress	Dy Hr Mn
1 4:14	♆	☍	♑	1 5:31
3 9:28	♀	☍	♒	3 13:34
5 18:29	♆	△	♓	5 19:22
7 22:53	♆	□	♈	7 23:36
10 2:09	♆	⚹	♉	10 2:45
12 3:34	♂	△	♊	12 5:10
14 7:11	♆	☌	♋	14 7:31
15 22:10	☉	☌	♌	16 10:54
18 16:38	♆	⚹	♍	18 16:43
20 20:48	☉	⚹	♎	21 1:55
23 13:58	☉	□	♏	23 14:00
25 16:42	♀	□	♐	26 2:45
28 10:22	♀	△	♑	28 13:33
29 22:23	☿	☍	♒	30 21:09

Last Aspect Dy Hr Mn			☽ Ingress	Dy Hr Mn
1 5:37	♇	△	♓	2 1:59
3 14:23	☿	△	♈	4 5:16
5 21:43	☿	□	♉	6 8:07
8 6:04	☿	⚹	♊	8 11:08
9 18:39	♇	☌	♋	10 14:38
11 20:41	♂	□	♌	12 19:04
14 8:27	☉	☌	♍	15 1:17
16 18:25	♀	☌	♎	17 10:14
19 13:34	☉	⚹	♏	19 21:58
22 7:59	♀	⚹	♐	22 10:54
24 17:42	☿	△	♑	24 22:18
27 0:40	♂	□	♒	27 6:13
29 7:54	♂	△	♓	29 10:36
30 17:53	♇	□	♈	31 12:44

☽ Phases & Eclipses Dy Hr Mn		
1 23:18	○	9♑22
9 3:20	☾	16♈12
15 22:10	●	22♋40
23 13:58	☽	29♎59
31 10:34	○	7♒30
7 8:02	☾	14♉06
14 8:27	●	20♌50
22 7:52	☽	28♏30
29 20:21	○	5♓46

Astro Data

1 July 1901
Julian Day # 547
SVP 6♓37'53"
GC 25♐27.8 ⚴ 23♓53.2
Eris 23♓30.3R ⚵ 15♋43.6
⚷ 2♑01.5R ⚶ 1♍49.3
☽ Mean ☊ 20♏13.3

1 August 1901
Julian Day # 578
SVP 6♓37'48"
GC 25♐27.9 ⚴ 22♓51.9R
Eris 23♓20.5R ⚵ 2♌05.3
⚷ 0♑17.2R ⚶ 15♍45.6
☽ Mean ☊ 18♏34.8

LONGITUDE — September 1901

Day	Sid.Time	☉	0 hr ☽	Noon ☽	True ☊	☿	♀	♂	⚳	♃	♄	♅	♆	♇
1 Su	10 39 49	8♍19 33	6♈49 26	14♈05 57	15♏51.0	12♍40.5	10♎49.8	0♏29.1	11♉43.6	3♑13.7	9♑55.4	12♐55.2	1♋10.7	18♊38.4
2 M	10 43 45	9 17 39	21 22 10	28 37 26	15R47.7	14 32.1	12 02.0	1 08.4	11 45.9	3 14.1	9R54.2	12 55.7	1 11.8	18 38.8
3 Tu	10 47 42	10 15 46	5♉51 12	13♉02 59	15D46.6	16 22.6	13 14.2	1 47.9	11 47.9	3 14.7	9 53.1	12 56.3	1 12.9	18 39.1
4 W	10 51 39	11 13 55	20 12 27	27 19 21	15 46.8	18 11.9	14 26.3	2 27.4	11 49.5	3 15.5	9 52.1	12 57.0	1 13.9	18 39.4
5 Th	10 55 35	12 12 06	4♊23 30	11♊24 47	15R47.2	19 59.9	15 38.5	3 07.0	11 50.7	3 16.4	9 51.1	12 57.7	1 14.9	18 39.7
6 F	10 59 32	13 10 19	18 23 09	25 18 36	15 46.6	21 46.8	16 50.6	3 46.8	11 51.6	3 17.6	9 50.3	12 58.4	1 15.8	18 40.0
7 Sa	11 03 28	14 08 35	2♋11 07	9♋00 44	15 44.1	23 32.5	18 02.7	4 26.6	11R52.1	3 18.9	9 49.6	12 59.2	1 16.8	18 40.3
8 Su	11 07 25	15 06 52	15 47 26	22 31 14	15 39.1	25 17.0	19 14.7	5 06.5	11 52.2	3 20.5	9 48.9	13 00.0	1 17.6	18 40.5
9 M	11 11 21	16 05 11	29 12 06	5♌49 59	15 31.8	27 00.4	20 26.7	5 46.4	11 52.0	3 22.2	9 48.4	13 00.9	1 18.5	18 40.7
10 Tu	11 15 18	17 03 33	12♌24 51	18 56 37	15 22.5	28 42.6	21 38.7	6 26.5	11 51.4	3 24.1	9 47.9	13 01.9	1 19.3	18 40.9
11 W	11 19 14	18 01 56	25 25 14	1♍50 36	15 12.3	0♎23.7	22 50.6	7 06.7	11 50.4	3 26.2	9 47.6	13 02.9	1 20.1	18 41.1
12 Th	11 23 11	19 00 21	8♍12 42	14 31 29	15 02.0	2 03.7	24 02.5	7 46.9	11 49.0	3 28.5	9 47.3	13 03.9	1 20.9	18 41.3
13 F	11 27 08	19 58 48	20 46 57	26 59 08	14 52.8	3 42.6	25 14.4	8 27.3	11 47.3	3 30.9	9 47.2	13 05.0	1 21.7	18 41.4
14 Sa	11 31 04	20 57 17	3♎08 09	9♎14 06	14 45.4	5 20.4	26 26.2	9 07.7	11 45.1	3 33.6	9D47.1	13 06.1	1 22.4	18 41.5
15 Su	11 35 01	21 55 48	15 17 13	21 17 43	14 40.2	6 57.2	27 38.0	9 48.2	11 42.6	3 36.4	9 47.2	13 07.3	1 23.0	18 41.6
16 M	11 38 57	22 54 20	27 15 54	3♏12 10	14D37.4	8 32.9	28 49.8	10 28.8	11 39.7	3 39.4	9 47.3	13 08.6	1 23.7	18 41.6
17 Tu	11 42 54	23 52 55	9♏06 54	15 00 36	14 36.6	10 07.6	0♏01.5	11 09.5	11 36.5	3 42.6	9 47.5	13 09.9	1 24.3	18 41.7
18 W	11 46 50	24 51 31	20 53 45	26 46 55	14 37.3	11 41.2	1 13.2	11 50.3	11 32.8	3 46.0	9 47.9	13 11.2	1 24.9	18R41.7
19 Th	11 50 47	25 50 08	2♐40 42	8♐35 43	14 38.6	13 13.9	2 24.9	12 31.2	11 28.8	3 49.6	9 48.3	13 12.6	1 25.4	18 41.7
20 F	11 54 43	26 48 48	14 32 36	20 32 02	14R39.6	14 45.5	3 36.5	13 12.1	11 24.4	3 53.3	9 48.8	13 14.0	1 25.9	18 41.7
21 Sa	11 58 40	27 47 29	26 34 41	2♑41 10	14 39.7	16 16.1	4 48.0	13 53.1	11 19.6	3 57.3	9 49.5	13 15.5	1 26.4	18 41.6
22 Su	12 02 36	28 46 12	8♑52 08	15 08 11	14 38.2	17 45.6	5 59.5	14 34.2	11 14.5	4 01.4	9 50.2	13 17.1	1 26.8	18 41.6
23 M	12 06 33	29 44 56	21 29 50	27 57 35	14 34.8	19 14.2	7 11.0	15 15.4	11 08.9	4 05.6	9 51.0	13 18.7	1 27.3	18 41.5
24 Tu	12 10 30	0♎43 43	4♒31 47	11♒12 40	14 29.8	20 41.8	8 22.4	15 56.7	11 03.1	4 10.1	9 52.0	13 20.3	1 27.6	18 41.4
25 W	12 14 26	1 42 31	18 00 23	24 54 54	14 23.5	22 08.3	9 33.7	16 38.0	10 56.8	4 14.7	9 53.0	13 22.0	1 28.0	18 41.3
26 Th	12 18 23	2 41 20	1♓55 59	9♓03 17	14 16.8	23 33.7	10 45.1	17 19.4	10 50.2	4 19.5	9 54.1	13 23.7	1 28.3	18 41.1
27 F	12 22 19	3 40 12	16 16 14	23 34 09	14 10.5	24 58.1	11 56.3	18 00.9	10 43.2	4 24.4	9 55.4	13 25.5	1 28.6	18 40.9
28 Sa	12 26 16	4 39 06	0♈56 10	8♈21 19	14 05.4	26 21.4	13 07.5	18 42.5	10 35.9	4 29.5	9 56.7	13 27.3	1 28.8	18 40.7
29 Su	12 30 12	5 38 01	15 48 35	23 16 54	14 02.0	27 43.6	14 18.7	19 24.2	10 28.2	4 34.8	9 58.1	13 29.1	1 29.0	18 40.5
30 M	12 34 09	6 36 59	0♉45 12	8♉12 29	14D00.5	29 04.7	15 29.8	20 05.9	10 20.1	4 40.3	9 59.6	13 31.0	1 29.2	18 40.3

LONGITUDE — October 1901

Day	Sid.Time	☉	0 hr ☽	Noon ☽	True ☊	☿	♀	♂	⚳	♃	♄	♅	♆	♇
1 Tu	12 38 05	7♎35 59	15♉37 51	23♉00 28	14♏00.6	0♏24.5	16♏40.8	20♏47.7	10♉11.8	4♑45.9	10♑01.2	13♐33.0	1♋29.3	18♊40.0
2 W	12 42 02	8 35 02	0♊19 41	7♊34 56	14 01.8	1 43.1	17 51.8	21 29.6	10R03.1	4 51.6	10 02.9	13 35.0	1 29.4	18R39.7
3 Th	12 45 59	9 34 06	14 45 50	21 52 07	14 03.3	3 00.4	19 02.7	22 11.6	9 54.0	4 57.6	10 04.7	13 37.0	1 29.5	18 39.4
4 F	12 49 55	10 33 13	28 53 35	5♋50 13	14R04.2	4 16.3	20 13.6	22 53.7	9 44.7	5 03.7	10 06.6	13 39.1	1R29.6	18 39.1
5 Sa	12 53 52	11 32 23	12♋42 01	19 29 05	14 04.0	5 30.8	21 24.5	23 35.8	9 35.0	5 09.9	10 08.6	13 41.3	1 29.6	18 38.8
6 Su	12 57 48	12 31 34	26 11 34	2♌49 38	14 02.4	6 43.7	22 35.3	24 18.0	9 25.0	5 16.3	10 10.7	13 43.4	1 29.6	18 38.4
7 M	13 01 45	13 30 49	9♌23 29	15 53 19	13 59.4	7 55.0	23 46.0	25 00.3	9 14.7	5 22.9	10 12.9	13 45.6	1 29.5	18 38.0
8 Tu	13 05 41	14 30 05	22 19 22	28 41 49	13 55.2	9 04.5	24 56.7	25 42.7	9 04.1	5 29.6	10 15.1	13 47.9	1 29.4	18 37.6
9 W	13 09 38	15 29 23	5♍00 53	11♍16 45	13 50.4	10 12.1	26 07.3	26 25.1	8 53.2	5 36.5	10 17.5	13 50.2	1 29.3	18 37.2
10 Th	13 13 34	16 28 44	17 29 36	23 39 37	13 45.6	11 17.6	27 17.8	27 07.7	8 42.0	5 43.5	10 20.0	13 52.5	1 29.1	18 36.8
11 F	13 17 31	17 28 07	29 46 59	5♎51 52	13 41.3	12 20.8	28 28.3	27 50.3	8 30.6	5 50.7	10 22.5	13 54.9	1 28.9	18 36.3
12 Sa	13 21 28	18 27 32	11♎54 27	17 54 56	13 37.9	13 21.6	29 38.8	28 33.0	8 18.9	5 58.0	10 25.2	13 57.3	1 28.7	18 35.8
13 Su	13 25 24	19 26 59	23 53 31	29 50 26	13 35.9	14 19.8	0♐49.1	29 15.7	8 07.0	6 05.4	10 27.9	13 59.8	1 28.4	18 35.3
14 M	13 29 21	20 26 28	5♏45 57	11♏40 19	13D35.1	15 15.0	1 59.4	29 58.6	7 54.9	6 13.0	10 30.7	14 02.3	1 28.1	18 34.8
15 Tu	13 33 17	21 25 59	17 33 53	23 26 58	13 35.4	16 07.0	3 09.6	0♐41.5	7 42.5	6 20.8	10 33.6	14 04.8	1 27.8	18 34.2
16 W	13 37 14	22 25 32	29 19 57	5♐13 16	13 36.6	16 55.4	4 19.8	1 24.5	7 30.0	6 28.7	10 36.6	14 07.4	1 27.4	18 33.7
17 Th	13 41 10	23 25 07	11♐07 21	17 02 40	13 38.2	17 40.0	5 29.9	2 07.5	7 17.2	6 36.7	10 39.7	14 10.0	1 27.0	18 33.1
18 F	13 45 07	24 24 43	22 59 46	28 59 09	13 39.8	18 20.2	6 39.9	2 50.7	7 04.3	6 44.9	10 42.9	14 12.6	1 26.6	18 32.5
19 Sa	13 49 03	25 24 22	5♑01 25	11♑07 06	13 41.1	18 55.7	7 49.8	3 33.9	6 51.2	6 53.2	10 46.2	14 15.3	1 26.2	18 31.9
20 Su	13 53 00	26 24 02	17 16 48	23 31 05	13R41.6	19 26.0	8 59.6	4 17.2	6 38.0	7 01.6	10 49.5	14 18.0	1 25.7	18 31.2
21 M	13 56 56	27 23 44	29 50 29	6♒15 33	13 41.5	19 50.6	10 09.4	5 00.5	6 24.6	7 10.2	10 53.0	14 20.8	1 25.1	18 30.6
22 Tu	14 00 53	28 23 27	12♒46 44	19 24 25	13 40.5	20 08.9	11 19.0	5 43.9	6 11.2	7 18.9	10 56.5	14 23.6	1 24.6	18 29.9
23 W	14 04 50	29 23 12	26 08 53	3♓00 21	13 39.0	20 20.3	12 28.6	6 27.4	5 57.6	7 27.7	11 00.1	14 26.4	1 24.0	18 29.2
24 Th	14 08 46	0♏22 59	9♓58 49	17 04 11	13 37.3	20R24.2	13 38.1	7 11.0	5 43.9	7 36.7	11 03.8	14 29.3	1 23.4	18 28.5
25 F	14 12 43	1 22 48	24 16 09	1♈34 15	13 35.7	20 20.2	14 47.5	7 54.6	5 30.2	7 45.7	11 07.6	14 32.1	1 22.7	18 27.7
26 Sa	14 16 39	2 22 38	8♈57 50	16 26 04	13 34.4	20 07.6	15 56.7	8 38.3	5 16.4	7 54.9	11 11.4	14 35.1	1 22.0	18 27.0
27 Su	14 20 36	3 22 31	23 57 58	1♉32 27	13D33.7	19 46.1	17 05.9	9 22.1	5 02.6	8 04.3	11 15.4	14 38.0	1 21.3	18 26.2
28 M	14 24 32	4 22 25	9♉08 19	16 44 23	13 33.6	19 15.3	18 14.9	10 05.9	4 48.7	8 13.7	11 19.4	14 41.0	1 20.6	18 25.5
29 Tu	14 28 29	5 22 21	24 19 24	1♊52 15	13 33.9	18 35.2	19 23.9	10 49.8	4 34.9	8 23.3	11 23.5	14 44.0	1 19.8	18 24.7
30 W	14 32 25	6 22 20	9♊21 52	16 47 19	13 34.4	17 46.0	20 32.7	11 33.7	4 21.0	8 33.0	11 27.7	14 47.1	1 19.0	18 23.9
31 Th	14 36 22	7 22 20	24 07 51	1♋22 50	13 35.1	16 48.2	21 41.4	12 17.8	4 07.2	8 42.7	11 31.9	14 50.1	1 18.2	18 23.0

Astro Data

	Dy Hr Mn
⚳ R	8 8:49
☿0S	12 1:46
☽0S	12 23:11
♄ D	14 14:09
♇ R	19 0:36
☉0S	23 18:09
☽0N	27 6:38
♆ R	5 6:56
☽0S	10 5:20
☿ R	24 12:10
☽0N	24 17:07

Planet Ingress

		Dy Hr Mn
☿	♎	11 6:21
♀	♏	17 11:29
☉	♎	23 18:09
☿	♏	1 4:35
♀	♐	12 19:15
♂	♐	14 12:48
☉	♏	24 2:46

Last Aspect / ☽ Ingress (September)

Last Aspect Dy Hr Mn			☽ Ingress	Dy Hr Mn
1 19:30	♇	⚹	♉	2 14:17
3 18:23	☿	△	♊	4 16:32
6 4:58	☿	□	♋	6 20:11
8 17:41	☿	⚹	♌	9 1:26
10 17:30	♀	⚹	♍	11 8:33
12 21:19	☉	☌	♎	13 17:52
16 2:10	♀	☌	♏	16 5:31
18 7:44	☉	⚹	♐	18 18:33
21 1:33	☉	□	♑	21 6:44
23 15:33	☉	△	♒	23 15:45
25 6:39	☿	△	♓	25 20:43
27 3:59	♇	□	♈	27 22:29
29 19:51	☿	☍	♉	29 22:47

Last Aspect / ☽ Ingress (October)

Last Aspect Dy Hr Mn			☽ Ingress	Dy Hr Mn
1 8:13	♂	☍	♊	1 23:28
3 6:34	♇	☌	♋	4 1:54
5 19:45	♂	△	♌	6 6:52
8 6:02	♂	□	♍	8 14:28
10 19:52	♀	⚹	♎	11 0:26
12 13:22	♇	△	♏	13 12:19
14 19:53	☿	☌	♐	16 1:22
18 2:01	☉	⚹	♑	18 14:01
20 17:58	☉	□	♒	21 0:18
23 5:12	☉	△	♓	23 6:46
24 17:34	☿	△	♈	25 9:26
26 15:13	♇	⚹	♉	27 9:34
28 15:49	☿	☍	♊	29 9:01
30 18:38	♀	☍	♋	31 9:42

☽ Phases & Eclipses

Dy Hr Mn	
5 13:27	☾ 12♊16
12 21:19	● 19♍23
21 1:33	☽ 27♐22
28 5:36	○ 4♈23
4 20:52	☾ 10♋55
12 13:11	● 18♎30
20 17:58	☽ 26♑39
27 15:06	○ 3♉30
27 15:15	P 0.221

Astro Data

1 September 1901
Julian Day # 609
SVP 6♓37'45"
GC 25♐28.0 ⚴ 16♓43.5R
Eris 23♓01.9R ⚵ 17♌31.7
⚷ 29♐31.7R ⚶ 0♎48.3
☽ Mean ☊ 16♏56.3

1 October 1901
Julian Day # 639
SVP 6♓37'42"
GC 25♐28.0 ⚴ 9♓19.1R
Eris 22♓40.7R ⚵ 1♍20.2
⚷ 0♑03.4 ⚶ 16♎04.6
☽ Mean ☊ 15♏20.9

November 1901 LONGITUDE

Day	Sid.Time	☉	0 hr ☽	Noon ☽	True ☊	☿	♀	♂	⚳	♃	♄	♅	♆	♇
1 F	14 40 19	8♏22 23	8♋31 50	15♋34 36	13♏35.6	15♏42.8	22♐50.0	13♐01.9	3♉53.4	8♑52.7	11♑36.3	14♐53.2	1♋17.3	18♊22.2
2 Sa	14 44 15	9 22 28	22 31 00	29 21 02	13R 35.9	14R 31.1	23 58.5	13 46.0	3R 39.6	9 02.7	11 40.7	14 56.4	1R 16.5	18R 21.3
3 Su	14 48 12	10 22 35	6♌04 51	12♌42 41	13 35.9	13 14.9	25 06.9	14 30.3	3 25.9	9 12.8	11 45.1	14 59.5	1 15.5	18 20.5
4 M	14 52 08	11 22 44	19 14 50	25 41 39	13 35.8	11 56.4	26 15.1	15 14.6	3 12.3	9 23.0	11 49.7	15 02.7	1 14.6	18 19.6
5 Tu	14 56 05	12 22 55	2♍03 32	8♍20 54	13 35.7	10 38.0	27 23.2	15 59.0	2 58.8	9 33.4	11 54.3	15 05.9	1 13.6	18 18.7
6 W	15 00 01	13 23 08	14 34 12	20 43 50	13D 35.6	9 22.2	28 31.2	16 43.4	2 45.4	9 43.8	11 59.0	15 09.1	1 12.6	18 17.8
7 Th	15 03 58	14 23 23	26 50 16	2♎53 52	13 35.7	8 11.5	29 39.1	17 27.9	2 32.1	9 54.4	12 03.8	15 12.4	1 11.6	18 16.8
8 F	15 07 54	15 23 40	8♎55 04	14 54 12	13 35.8	7 08.1	0♑46.8	18 12.5	2 19.0	10 05.1	12 08.6	15 15.7	1 10.5	18 15.9
9 Sa	15 11 51	16 23 59	20 51 37	26 47 41	13 36.0	6 13.7	1 54.3	18 57.1	2 06.1	10 15.8	12 13.5	15 19.0	1 09.4	18 14.9
10 Su	15 15 48	17 24 20	2♏42 40	8♏36 53	13R 36.2	5 29.7	3 01.7	19 41.8	1 53.3	10 26.7	12 18.5	15 22.3	1 08.3	18 14.0
11 M	15 19 44	18 24 43	14 30 36	20 24 07	13 36.2	4 57.0	4 09.0	20 26.5	1 40.7	10 37.7	12 23.6	15 25.6	1 07.2	18 13.0
12 Tu	15 23 41	19 25 07	26 17 40	2♐11 32	13 35.9	4 36.0	5 16.1	21 11.4	1 28.3	10 48.7	12 28.7	15 29.0	1 06.0	18 12.0
13 W	15 27 37	20 25 33	8♐05 59	14 01 19	13 35.2	4D 26.7	6 23.0	21 56.3	1 16.1	10 59.9	12 33.8	15 32.4	1 04.8	18 11.0
14 Th	15 31 34	21 26 00	19 57 48	25 55 46	13 34.2	4 28.7	7 29.7	22 41.2	1 04.2	11 11.1	12 39.1	15 35.8	1 03.6	18 10.0
15 F	15 35 30	22 26 29	1♑55 32	7♑57 28	13 32.9	4 41.3	8 36.3	23 26.2	0 52.5	11 22.5	12 44.4	15 39.2	1 02.4	18 09.0
16 Sa	15 39 27	23 27 00	14 01 55	20 09 18	13 31.6	5 03.9	9 42.6	24 11.3	0 41.1	11 33.9	12 49.8	15 42.7	1 01.1	18 07.9
17 Su	15 43 23	24 27 31	26 20 01	2♒34 30	13 30.5	5 35.6	10 48.8	24 56.4	0 29.9	11 45.4	12 55.2	15 46.2	0 59.9	18 06.9
18 M	15 47 20	25 28 04	8♒53 10	15 16 28	13D 29.7	6 15.5	11 54.8	25 41.6	0 19.0	11 57.0	13 00.7	15 49.6	0 58.6	18 05.8
19 Tu	15 51 17	26 28 39	21 44 49	28 18 36	13 29.5	7 02.7	13 00.5	26 26.8	0 08.4	12 08.7	13 06.3	15 53.1	0 57.2	18 04.8
20 W	15 55 13	27 29 14	4♓58 12	11♓43 53	13 29.9	7 56.3	14 06.1	27 12.1	29♈58.1	12 20.5	13 11.9	15 56.7	0 55.9	18 03.7
21 Th	15 59 10	28 29 50	18 35 53	25 34 19	13 30.8	8 55.6	15 11.4	27 57.4	29 48.2	12 32.4	13 17.5	16 00.2	0 54.5	18 02.6
22 F	16 03 06	29 30 28	2♈39 10	9♈50 18	13 32.1	9 59.8	16 16.4	28 42.8	29 38.5	12 44.3	13 23.2	16 03.7	0 53.1	18 01.5
23 Sa	16 07 03	0♐31 07	17 07 24	24 30 00	13 33.2	11 08.3	17 21.2	29 28.3	29 29.1	12 56.3	13 29.0	16 07.3	0 51.7	18 00.4
24 Su	16 10 59	1 31 47	1♉57 27	9♉28 54	13R 33.8	12 20.4	18 25.8	0♑13.8	29 20.1	13 08.4	13 34.8	16 10.8	0 50.3	17 59.3
25 M	16 14 56	2 32 28	17 03 23	24 39 47	13 33.6	13 35.6	19 30.0	0 59.3	29 11.5	13 20.6	13 40.7	16 14.4	0 48.9	17 58.2
26 Tu	16 18 52	3 33 11	2♊16 53	9♊53 26	13 32.3	14 53.6	20 34.1	1 44.9	29 03.2	13 32.8	13 46.7	16 18.0	0 47.4	17 57.1
27 W	16 22 49	4 33 55	17 28 10	24 59 52	13 30.0	16 13.9	21 37.8	2 30.6	28 55.2	13 45.1	13 52.6	16 21.6	0 45.9	17 56.0
28 Th	16 26 46	5 34 40	2♋27 27	9♋49 55	13 27.1	17 36.1	22 41.2	3 16.3	28 47.6	13 57.5	13 58.7	16 25.2	0 44.5	17 54.9
29 F	16 30 42	6 35 27	17 06 30	24 16 33	13 23.8	18 59.9	23 44.3	4 02.1	28 40.3	14 09.9	14 04.8	16 28.8	0 42.9	17 53.7
30 Sa	16 34 39	7 36 15	1♌19 41	8♌15 40	13 20.8	20 25.2	24 47.1	4 47.9	28 33.5	14 22.5	14 10.9	16 32.5	0 41.4	17 52.6

December 1901 LONGITUDE

Day	Sid.Time	☉	0 hr ☽	Noon ☽	True ☊	☿	♀	♂	⚳	♃	♄	♅	♆	♇
1 Su	16 38 35	8♐37 05	15♌04 27	21♌46 08	13♏18.6	21♏51.6	25♑49.6	5♑33.7	28♈27.0	14♑35.1	14♑17.1	16♐36.1	0♋39.9	17♊51.4
2 M	16 42 32	9 37 56	28 20 59	4♍49 22	13D 17.5	23 19.1	26 51.8	6 19.7	28R 20.9	14 47.7	14 23.3	16 39.7	0R 38.3	17R 50.3
3 Tu	16 46 28	10 38 48	11♍11 43	17 28 34	13 17.6	24 47.4	27 53.6	7 05.6	28 15.1	15 00.4	14 29.6	16 43.4	0 36.8	17 49.1
4 W	16 50 25	11 39 42	23 40 28	29 48 01	13 18.8	26 16.4	28 55.0	7 51.6	28 09.8	15 13.2	14 35.9	16 47.0	0 35.2	17 48.0
5 Th	16 54 21	12 40 37	5♎51 49	11♎52 28	13 20.5	27 46.0	29 56.1	8 37.7	28 04.8	15 26.0	14 42.2	16 50.7	0 33.6	17 46.8
6 F	16 58 18	13 41 34	17 50 32	23 46 35	13 22.4	29 16.1	0♒56.8	9 23.8	28 00.2	15 38.9	14 48.6	16 54.3	0 32.0	17 45.7
7 Sa	17 02 15	14 42 31	29 41 10	5♏34 47	13R 23.7	0♐46.7	1 57.1	10 10.0	27 56.0	15 51.9	14 55.0	16 58.0	0 30.3	17 44.5
8 Su	17 06 11	15 43 30	11♏27 54	17 20 56	13 23.9	2 17.6	2 57.0	10 56.2	27 52.3	16 04.9	15 01.5	17 01.7	0 28.7	17 43.3
9 M	17 10 08	16 44 30	23 14 16	29 08 16	13 22.6	3 48.9	3 56.4	11 42.4	27 48.9	16 18.0	15 08.0	17 05.4	0 27.1	17 42.2
10 Tu	17 14 04	17 45 31	5♐03 14	10♐59 27	13 19.4	5 20.4	4 55.5	12 28.7	27 45.9	16 31.1	15 14.6	17 09.0	0 25.4	17 41.0
11 W	17 18 01	18 46 33	16 57 08	22 56 31	13 14.6	6 52.1	5 54.0	13 15.1	27 43.3	16 44.3	15 21.2	17 12.7	0 23.8	17 39.9
12 Th	17 21 57	19 47 35	28 57 48	5♑01 08	13 08.2	8 24.1	6 52.1	14 01.5	27 41.2	16 57.5	15 27.8	17 16.3	0 22.1	17 38.7
13 F	17 25 54	20 48 38	11♑06 42	17 14 38	13 01.0	9 56.2	7 49.6	14 47.9	27 39.4	17 10.8	15 34.4	17 20.0	0 20.5	17 37.5
14 Sa	17 29 50	21 49 42	23 25 06	29 38 16	12 53.7	11 28.5	8 46.7	15 34.4	27 38.0	17 24.1	15 41.1	17 23.6	0 18.8	17 36.4
15 Su	17 33 47	22 50 47	5♒54 19	12♒13 25	12 47.1	13 01.0	9 43.2	16 20.9	27 37.1	17 37.5	15 47.8	17 27.3	0 17.1	17 35.2
16 M	17 37 44	23 51 52	18 35 48	25 01 41	12 41.8	14 33.7	10 39.1	17 07.4	27D 36.5	17 50.9	15 54.6	17 31.0	0 15.4	17 34.1
17 Tu	17 41 40	24 52 57	1♓31 18	8♓04 54	12 38.4	16 06.5	11 34.4	17 54.0	27 36.4	18 04.4	16 01.3	17 34.6	0 13.7	17 32.9
18 W	17 45 37	25 54 02	14 42 46	21 25 07	12D 36.9	17 39.4	12 29.1	18 40.6	27 36.6	18 17.9	16 08.1	17 38.2	0 12.0	17 31.7
19 Th	17 49 33	26 55 08	28 12 12	5♈04 12	12 37.1	19 12.5	13 23.2	19 27.3	27 37.2	18 31.4	16 14.9	17 41.9	0 10.3	17 30.6
20 F	17 53 30	27 56 14	12♈01 15	19 03 27	12 38.2	20 45.8	14 16.6	20 14.0	27 38.2	18 45.0	16 21.8	17 45.5	0 08.6	17 29.5
21 Sa	17 57 26	28 57 20	26 10 43	3♉22 57	12R 39.4	22 19.3	15 09.3	21 00.7	27 39.7	18 58.6	16 28.7	17 49.1	0 06.9	17 28.3
22 Su	18 01 23	29 58 27	10♉39 50	18 00 56	12 39.6	23 53.0	16 01.3	21 47.4	27 41.5	19 12.3	16 35.6	17 52.7	0 05.2	17 27.2
23 M	18 05 19	0♑59 33	25 25 40	2♊53 15	12 37.9	25 26.8	16 52.5	22 34.2	27 43.6	19 25.9	16 42.5	17 56.3	0 03.5	17 26.0
24 Tu	18 09 16	2 00 40	10♊22 49	17 53 19	12 33.9	27 00.9	17 42.9	23 21.0	27 46.2	19 39.7	16 49.4	17 59.9	0 01.8	17 24.9
25 W	18 13 13	3 01 47	25 23 38	2♋52 37	12 27.6	28 35.2	18 32.5	24 07.9	27 49.1	19 53.4	16 56.4	18 03.5	0 00.1	17 23.8
26 Th	18 17 09	4 02 55	10♋19 05	17 41 57	12 19.6	0♑09.8	19 21.2	24 54.8	27 52.5	20 07.2	17 03.3	18 07.1	29♊58.4	17 22.7
27 F	18 21 06	5 04 03	25 00 11	2♌12 56	12 10.7	1 44.6	20 09.1	25 41.7	27 56.1	20 21.0	17 10.3	18 10.6	29 56.7	17 21.6
28 Sa	18 25 02	6 05 11	9♌19 29	16 19 20	12 02.1	3 19.7	20 56.0	26 28.6	28 00.2	20 34.8	17 17.3	18 14.1	29 55.0	17 20.5
29 Su	18 28 59	7 06 19	23 12 09	29 57 50	11 54.7	4 55.0	21 42.0	27 15.6	28 04.6	20 48.7	17 24.3	18 17.7	29 53.3	17 19.4
30 M	18 32 55	8 07 28	6♍36 26	13♍08 08	11 49.4	6 30.7	22 27.0	28 02.6	28 09.4	21 02.6	17 31.4	18 21.2	29 51.7	17 18.3
31 Tu	18 36 52	9 08 37	19 33 18	25 52 22	11 46.2	8 06.7	23 10.9	28 49.6	28 14.5	21 16.5	17 38.4	18 24.7	29 50.0	17 17.2

Astro Data	Dy Hr Mn
☽0S	6 10:46
☿D	13 19:44
☽0N	21 2:40
♃☌♄	28 16:29
☽0S	3 17:21
♃⚺♅	14 10:49
♃⚻♇	15 8:14
♅☍♇	17 3:30
⚳D	17 9:54
☽0N	18 10:24
♄⚻♇	28 21:23
☽0S	31 2:17

Planet Ingress		Dy Hr Mn
♀	♑	7 19:25
⚳	♈R	20 7:37
☉	♐	22 23:41
♂	♑	24 4:44
♀	♒	5 13:32
☿	♐	6 23:38
☉	♑	22 12:37
♆	♊R	25 13:33
☿	♑	26 9:31

Last Aspect Dy Hr Mn		☽ Ingress Dy Hr Mn
1 12:13	☿ △	♌ 2 13:09
4 13:09	♀ △	♍ 4 20:06
7 4:54	♀ □	♎ 7 6:15
8 19:06	♂ ⚹	♏ 9 18:30
11 7:34	☉ ☌	♐ 12 7:32
14 5:03	♂ ☌	♑ 14 20:09
16 18:59	☉ ⚹	♒ 17 7:04
19 8:24	♂ ⚹	♓ 19 15:04
21 17:22	☉ △	♈ 21 19:32
23 20:26	♂ △	♉ 23 20:52
25 3:15	♀ △	♊ 25 20:24
27 0:45	♇ ☌	♋ 27 20:02
29 11:01	♀ ☍	♌ 29 21:43

Last Aspect Dy Hr Mn		☽ Ingress Dy Hr Mn
1 12:11	☿ □	♍ 2 3:02
4 10:06	♀ △	♎ 4 12:24
5 23:51	♇ △	♏ 7 0:38
8 9:22	♃ ⚹	♐ 9 13:45
11 2:53	☉ ☌	♑ 12 2:04
13 11:52	♃ ☌	♒ 14 12:42
16 9:39	☉ ⚹	♓ 16 21:12
18 20:35	☉ □	♈ 19 3:09
21 4:05	☉ △	♉ 21 6:23
22 18:28	♂ △	♊ 23 7:22
25 4:18	☿ ☍	♋ 25 7:23
27 0:32	♂ ☍	♌ 27 8:18
29 11:52	♆ ⚹	♍ 29 12:04
31 19:36	♆ □	♎ 31 19:56

☽ Phases & Eclipses Dy Hr Mn	
3 7:24	☾ 10♌11
11 7:34	● 18♏14
11 7:28:22	● A 11'01"
19 8:23	☽ 26♒20
26 1:18	○ 3♊06
2 21:50	☾ 10♍03
11 2:53	● 18♐23
18 20:35	☽ 26♓16
25 12:16	○ 3♋02

Astro Data

1 November 1901
Julian Day # 670
SVP 6♓37'39"
GC 25♐28.1 ⚴ 5♓35.1R
Eris 22♓22.1R ⚵ 14♍00.1
⚷ 1♑50.1 ⚶ 2♏18.9
☽ Mean ☊ 13♏42.4

1 December 1901
Julian Day # 700
SVP 6♓37'34"
GC 25♐28.2 ⚴ 7♓22.8
Eris 22♓12.8R ⚵ 23♍57.7
⚷ 4♑25.4 ⚶ 18♏12.3
☽ Mean ☊ 12♏07.1

LONGITUDE — January 1902

Day	Sid.Time	☉	0 hr ☽	Noon ☽	True ☊	☿	♀	♂	⚳	♃	♄	♅	♆	♇
1 W	18 40 49	10♑09 47	2♎05 54	8♎14 30	11♏45.1	9♑43.0	23♒53.8	29♑36.7	28♈20.0	21♑30.4	17♑45.5	18♐28.1	29♊48.3	17♊16.2
2 Th	18 44 45	11 10 57	14 18 49	20 19 33	11D45.5	11 19.7	24 35.6	0♒23.7	28 25.8	21 44.4	17 52.5	18 31.6	29R46.6	17R15.1
3 F	18 48 42	12 12 07	26 17 22	2♏12 57	11R46.3	12 56.7	25 16.2	1 10.9	28 32.0	21 58.4	17 59.6	18 35.1	29 45.0	17 14.1
4 Sa	18 52 38	13 13 18	8♏07 00	14 00 10	11 46.6	14 34.1	25 55.5	1 58.0	28 38.5	22 12.4	18 06.7	18 38.5	29 43.3	17 13.0
5 Su	18 56 35	14 14 28	19 53 03	25 46 15	11 45.5	16 11.9	26 33.7	2 45.2	28 45.4	22 26.4	18 13.8	18 41.9	29 41.7	17 12.0
6 M	19 00 31	15 15 39	1♐40 17	7♐35 39	11 42.0	17 50.1	27 10.5	3 32.3	28 52.6	22 40.4	18 20.9	18 45.3	29 40.0	17 11.0
7 Tu	19 04 28	16 16 50	13 32 46	19 32 01	11 35.8	19 28.6	27 46.0	4 19.6	29 00.1	22 54.5	18 28.0	18 48.6	29 38.4	17 10.0
8 W	19 08 24	17 18 00	25 33 42	1♑38 03	11 26.8	21 07.6	28 20.1	5 06.8	29 08.0	23 08.5	18 35.1	18 52.0	29 36.8	17 09.0
9 Th	19 12 21	18 19 11	7♑45 17	13 55 31	11 15.5	22 46.9	28 52.6	5 54.0	29 16.1	23 22.6	18 42.2	18 55.3	29 35.2	17 08.0
10 F	19 16 18	19 20 21	20 08 49	26 25 13	11 02.8	24 26.7	29 23.7	6 41.3	29 24.6	23 36.7	18 49.3	18 58.6	29 33.6	17 07.1
11 Sa	19 20 14	20 21 31	2♒44 42	9♒07 14	10 49.8	26 06.8	29 53.1	7 28.6	29 33.5	23 50.8	18 56.4	19 01.9	29 32.0	17 06.1
12 Su	19 24 11	21 22 41	15 32 46	22 01 12	10 37.6	27 47.3	0♓20.9	8 15.9	29 42.6	24 04.9	19 03.5	19 05.1	29 30.5	17 05.2
13 M	19 28 07	22 23 49	28 32 30	5♓06 35	10 27.5	29 28.1	0 47.0	9 03.2	29 52.0	24 19.0	19 10.6	19 08.3	29 28.9	17 04.2
14 Tu	19 32 04	23 24 58	11♓43 27	18 23 05	10 20.1	1♒09.2	1 11.3	9 50.6	0♉01.8	24 33.1	19 17.7	19 11.5	29 27.4	17 03.3
15 W	19 36 00	24 26 05	25 05 29	1♈50 43	10 15.6	2 50.5	1 33.7	10 37.9	0 11.8	24 47.2	19 24.8	19 14.7	29 25.9	17 02.4
16 Th	19 39 57	25 27 12	8♈38 51	15 29 59	10D13.6	4 32.1	1 54.2	11 25.3	0 22.1	25 01.3	19 31.9	19 17.9	29 24.4	17 01.5
17 F	19 43 53	26 28 18	22 24 12	29 21 34	10R13.3	6 13.8	2 12.7	12 12.7	0 32.7	25 15.4	19 39.0	19 21.0	29 22.9	17 00.6
18 Sa	19 47 50	27 29 23	6♉22 08	13♉25 54	10 13.4	7 55.5	2 29.2	13 00.1	0 43.6	25 29.5	19 46.0	19 24.1	29 21.4	16 59.8
19 Su	19 51 47	28 30 27	20 32 48	27 42 39	10 12.5	9 37.2	2 43.5	13 47.5	0 54.8	25 43.6	19 53.1	19 27.1	29 20.0	16 58.9
20 M	19 55 43	29 31 31	4♊55 11	12♊10 01	10 09.4	11 18.7	2 55.6	14 34.9	1 06.3	25 57.7	20 00.1	19 30.1	29 18.6	16 58.1
21 Tu	19 59 40	0♒32 33	19 26 37	26 44 22	10 03.5	12 59.9	3 05.5	15 22.3	1 18.0	26 11.8	20 07.2	19 33.1	29 17.1	16 57.3
22 W	20 03 36	1 33 35	4♋02 30	11♋20 13	9 54.6	14 40.5	3 13.0	16 09.7	1 30.0	26 25.9	20 14.2	19 36.1	29 15.8	16 56.5
23 Th	20 07 33	2 34 35	18 36 35	25 50 43	9 43.4	16 20.4	3 18.2	16 57.1	1 42.3	26 40.0	20 21.2	19 39.0	29 14.4	16 55.7
24 F	20 11 29	3 35 35	3♌01 43	10♌08 44	9 30.8	17 59.3	3R21.0	17 44.6	1 54.8	26 54.1	20 28.2	19 41.9	29 13.0	16 55.0
25 Sa	20 15 26	4 36 34	17 11 03	24 08 02	9 18.4	19 36.9	3 21.3	18 32.0	2 07.5	27 08.1	20 35.1	19 44.8	29 11.7	16 54.2
26 Su	20 19 22	5 37 32	0♍59 13	7♍44 18	9 07.2	21 12.9	3 19.1	19 19.5	2 20.5	27 22.2	20 42.1	19 47.6	29 10.4	16 53.5
27 M	20 23 19	6 38 30	14 23 06	20 55 38	8 58.4	22 46.8	3 14.4	20 06.9	2 33.8	27 36.2	20 49.0	19 50.4	29 09.1	16 52.8
28 Tu	20 27 16	7 39 26	27 22 04	3♎42 39	8 52.3	24 18.3	3 07.2	20 54.4	2 47.3	27 50.3	20 55.9	19 53.2	29 07.8	16 52.1
29 W	20 31 12	8 40 22	9♎57 48	16 07 59	8 48.9	25 46.7	2 57.5	21 41.8	3 01.0	28 04.3	21 02.8	19 55.9	29 06.6	16 51.4
30 Th	20 35 09	9 41 18	22 13 48	28 15 50	8D47.6	27 11.6	2 45.3	22 29.3	3 15.0	28 18.3	21 09.7	19 58.6	29 05.4	16 50.8
31 F	20 39 05	10 42 12	4♏14 47	10♏11 19	8R47.5	28 32.2	2 30.6	23 16.7	3 29.2	28 32.2	21 16.6	20 01.3	29 04.2	16 50.2

LONGITUDE — February 1902

Day	Sid.Time	☉	0 hr ☽	Noon ☽	True ☊	☿	♀	♂	⚳	♃	♄	♅	♆	♇
1 Sa	20 43 02	11♒43 06	16♏06 10	22♏00 01	8♏47.3	29♒48.0	2♓13.4	24♒04.2	3♉43.6	28♑46.2	21♑23.4	20♐03.9	29♊03.0	16♊49.5
2 Su	20 46 58	12 43 59	27 53 35	3♐47 33	8R45.9	0♓58.1	1R53.8	24 51.7	3 58.3	29 00.1	21 30.2	20 06.5	29R01.9	16R48.9
3 M	20 50 55	13 44 51	9♐42 34	15 39 14	8 42.3	2 01.8	1 32.0	25 39.2	4 13.1	29 14.1	21 37.0	20 09.0	29 00.8	16 48.4
4 Tu	20 54 51	14 45 42	21 38 08	27 39 46	8 36.0	2 58.3	1 07.9	26 26.6	4 28.2	29 28.0	21 43.7	20 11.5	28 59.7	16 47.8
5 W	20 58 48	15 46 33	3♑44 34	9♑52 55	8 26.9	3 46.8	0 41.7	27 14.1	4 43.5	29 41.8	21 50.4	20 14.0	28 58.6	16 47.3
6 Th	21 02 45	16 47 22	16 05 06	22 21 20	8 15.3	4 26.6	0 13.4	28 01.6	4 59.1	29 55.7	21 57.1	20 16.4	28 57.6	16 46.7
7 F	21 06 41	17 48 10	28 41 43	5♒06 17	8 02.1	4 57.0	29♒43.4	28 49.0	5 14.8	0♒09.5	22 03.8	20 18.8	28 56.6	16 46.2
8 Sa	21 10 38	18 48 57	11♒35 00	18 07 43	7 48.5	5 17.4	29 11.7	29 36.5	5 30.7	0 23.3	22 10.4	20 21.1	28 55.6	16 45.8
9 Su	21 14 34	19 49 42	24 44 14	1♓24 18	7 35.7	5R27.3	28 38.5	0♓23.9	5 46.8	0 37.0	22 17.0	20 23.4	28 54.6	16 45.3
10 M	21 18 31	20 50 26	8♓07 37	14 53 51	7 24.9	5 26.6	28 04.0	1 11.4	6 03.2	0 50.8	22 23.5	20 25.7	28 53.7	16 44.9
11 Tu	21 22 27	21 51 09	21 42 41	28 33 48	7 16.9	5 15.0	27 28.5	1 58.8	6 19.7	1 04.5	22 30.1	20 27.9	28 52.8	16 44.5
12 W	21 26 24	22 51 50	5♈26 54	12♈21 44	7 12.0	4 53.0	26 52.1	2 46.2	6 36.4	1 18.1	22 36.5	20 30.1	28 51.9	16 44.1
13 Th	21 30 20	23 52 29	19 18 05	26 15 45	7D09.8	4 20.9	26 15.1	3 33.7	6 53.3	1 31.7	22 43.0	20 32.2	28 51.1	16 43.7
14 F	21 34 17	24 53 07	3♉14 38	10♉14 37	7 09.5	3 39.5	25 37.8	4 21.1	7 10.4	1 45.3	22 49.4	20 34.3	28 50.3	16 43.3
15 Sa	21 38 14	25 53 43	17 15 38	24 17 36	7R09.7	2 50.0	25 00.4	5 08.5	7 27.6	1 58.9	22 55.7	20 36.3	28 49.5	16 43.0
16 Su	21 42 10	26 54 17	1♊20 28	8♊24 07	7 09.2	1 53.6	24 23.2	5 55.8	7 45.1	2 12.4	23 02.1	20 38.3	28 48.7	16 42.7
17 M	21 46 07	27 54 49	15 28 25	22 33 13	7 06.9	0 51.9	23 46.4	6 43.2	8 02.7	2 25.8	23 08.3	20 40.2	28 48.0	16 42.4
18 Tu	21 50 03	28 55 20	29 38 13	6♋43 09	7 02.0	29♒46.6	23 10.2	7 30.5	8 20.4	2 39.2	23 14.6	20 42.1	28 47.3	16 42.1
19 W	21 54 00	29 55 49	13♋47 37	20 51 10	6 54.5	28 39.4	22 35.0	8 17.9	8 38.4	2 52.6	23 20.8	20 44.0	28 46.7	16 41.9
20 Th	21 57 56	0♓56 15	27 53 18	4♌53 30	6 44.7	27 32.2	22 01.0	9 05.2	8 56.5	3 05.9	23 26.9	20 45.8	28 46.1	16 41.7
21 F	22 01 53	1 56 41	11♌51 12	18 45 53	6 33.7	26 26.4	21 28.3	9 52.5	9 14.7	3 19.2	23 33.0	20 47.6	28 45.5	16 41.5
22 Sa	22 05 49	2 57 04	25 37 00	2♍24 08	6 22.7	25 23.7	20 57.2	10 39.8	9 33.1	3 32.4	23 39.0	20 49.3	28 44.9	16 41.3
23 Su	22 09 46	3 57 25	9♍06 53	15 44 57	6 12.7	24 25.3	20 27.8	11 27.0	9 51.7	3 45.6	23 45.0	20 50.9	28 44.4	16 41.1
24 M	22 13 43	4 57 45	22 18 08	28 46 22	6 04.7	23 32.3	20 00.4	12 14.3	10 10.4	3 58.8	23 51.0	20 52.5	28 43.9	16 41.0
25 Tu	22 17 39	5 58 04	5♎09 40	11♎28 09	5 59.2	22 45.3	19 35.0	13 01.5	10 29.3	4 11.8	23 56.9	20 54.1	28 43.4	16 40.9
26 W	22 21 36	6 58 21	17 42 03	23 51 41	5D56.3	22 05.0	19 11.8	13 48.7	10 48.3	4 24.9	24 02.7	20 55.6	28 43.0	16 40.8
27 Th	22 25 32	7 58 36	29 57 27	5♏59 49	5 55.4	21 31.7	18 50.9	14 35.9	11 07.5	4 37.8	24 08.5	20 57.1	28 42.6	16 40.7
28 F	22 29 29	8 58 50	11♏59 20	17 56 35	5 56.0	21 05.5	18 32.3	15 23.1	11 26.8	4 50.7	24 14.2	20 58.5	28 42.2	16 40.7

Astro Data	Dy Hr Mn	Planet Ingress	Dy Hr Mn	Last Aspect Dy Hr Mn	☽ Ingress Dy Hr Mn	Last Aspect Dy Hr Mn	☽ Ingress Dy Hr Mn	☽ Phases & Eclipses Dy Hr Mn	
♄⊻♅	12 22:02	♂ ♒	1 23:54	3 7:01 ♆ △	♏ 3 7:30	2 2:04 ♃ ⚹	♐ 2 4:17	1 16:08	☾ 10♎20
☽0N	14 16:56	♀ ♓	11 17:47	5 13:42 ♀ □	♐ 5 20:36	4 14:38 ♆ ☍	♑ 4 16:38	9 21:14	● 18♑43
♀R	25 3:02	☿ ♒	13 19:35	8 8:02 ♆ ☍	♑ 8 8:47	6 11:13 ♄ ☌	♒ 7 2:27	17 6:38	☽ 26♈15
☽0S	27 12:52	⚳ ♉	14 7:43	10 7:39 ♆ △	♒ 10 18:48	9 7:32 ♆ △	♓ 9 9:29	24 0:06	○ 3♌05
		☉ ♒	20 23:12	13 1:45 ♆ △	♓ 13 2:40	11 12:33 ♆ □	♈ 11 14:31	31 13:08	☾ 10♏45
♃⊼♆	2 14:46			15 7:44 ♆ □	♈ 15 8:44	13 16:27 ♆ ⚹	♉ 13 18:26		
☿R	9 22:20	☿ ♓	1 15:58	17 12:02 ♆ ⚹	♉ 17 13:06	15 14:56 ☉ □	♊ 15 21:43	8 13:21	● 18♒52
☽0N	10 23:54	♃ ♒	6 19:31	19 13:26 ☉ △	♊ 19 15:49	17 22:34 ♆ ☌	♋ 18 0:37	15 14:56	☽ 26♉01
♃Q♇	14 8:35	♀ ♒R	6 22:55	21 16:11 ♆ ☌	♋ 21 17:21	19 16:17 ♄ ☍	♌ 20 3:37	22 13:03	○ 3♍00
☽0S	23 23:02	♂ ♓	8 23:54	23 13:23 ♃ ☍	♌ 23 18:56	22 5:32 ♆ ⚹	♍ 22 7:44		
		☿ ♒R	18 7:09	25 20:50 ♆ ⚹	♍ 25 22:16	24 11:55 ♆ □	♎ 24 14:18		
		☉ ♓	19 13:40	28 3:20 ♆ □	♎ 28 4:57	26 21:33 ♆ △	♏ 27 0:05		
				30 13:39 ♆ △	♏ 30 15:28				

Astro Data

1 January 1902
Julian Day # 731
SVP 6♓37'29"
GC 25♐28.2 ⚴ 13♓35.5
Eris 22♓15.3 ⚵ 0♎34.3
⚷ 7♑32.1 ⚶ 4♐28.3
☽ Mean ☊ 10♏28.6

1 February 1902
Julian Day # 762
SVP 6♓37'25"
GC 25♐28.3 ⚴ 22♓42.1
Eris 22♓29.7 ⚵ 1♎35.6R
⚷ 10♑34.2 ⚶ 20♐08.7
☽ Mean ☊ 8♏50.1

March 1902 LONGITUDE

Day	Sid.Time	☉	0 hr ☽	Noon☽	True☊	☿	♀	♂	⚳	♃	♄	♅	♆	♇
1 Sa	22 33 25	9♓59 02	23♏52 10	29♏46 45	5♏57.0	20♒46.5	18♒16.2	16♓10.2	11♉46.2	5♒03.6	24♑19.9	20♐59.9	28♊41.9	16♊40.7
2 Su	22 37 22	10 59 13	5♐41 00	11♐35 35	5R57.5	20R34.5	18R02.5	16 57.3	12 05.8	5 16.4	24 25.6	21 01.2	28R41.6	16D40.7
3 M	22 41 18	11 59 22	17 31 11	23 28 28	5 56.6	20D29.4	17 51.4	17 44.4	12 25.5	5 29.1	24 31.1	21 02.4	28 41.4	16 40.7
4 Tu	22 45 15	12 59 30	29 28 04	5♑30 36	5 53.8	20 30.7	17 42.7	18 31.5	12 45.4	5 41.8	24 36.6	21 03.7	28 41.1	16 40.7
5 W	22 49 11	13 59 36	11♑36 37	17 46 38	5 48.9	20 38.3	17 36.5	19 18.6	13 05.3	5 54.4	24 42.1	21 04.8	28 40.9	16 40.8
6 Th	22 53 08	14 59 41	24 01 06	0♒20 21	5 42.0	20 51.8	17 32.7	20 05.6	13 25.4	6 07.0	24 47.5	21 05.9	28 40.8	16 40.9
7 F	22 57 05	15 59 44	6♒44 40	13 14 13	5 33.7	21 10.9	17D31.4	20 52.6	13 45.7	6 19.5	24 52.8	21 07.0	28 40.6	16 41.0
8 Sa	23 01 01	16 59 45	19 49 03	26 29 06	5 24.9	21 35.2	17 32.6	21 39.6	14 06.0	6 31.9	24 58.1	21 08.0	28 40.6	16 41.1
9 Su	23 04 58	17 59 44	3♓14 12	10♓04 04	5 16.5	22 04.3	17 36.0	22 26.6	14 26.5	6 44.2	25 03.3	21 09.0	28 40.5	16 41.3
10 M	23 08 54	18 59 41	16 58 21	23 56 33	5 09.6	22 38.1	17 41.8	23 13.5	14 47.1	6 56.5	25 08.4	21 09.9	28D40.5	16 41.4
11 Tu	23 12 51	19 59 36	0♈58 10	8♈02 36	5 04.6	23 16.1	17 49.9	24 00.4	15 07.8	7 08.7	25 13.5	21 10.7	28 40.5	16 41.6
12 W	23 16 47	20 59 30	15 09 16	22 17 34	5D01.8	23 58.0	18 00.2	24 47.3	15 28.7	7 20.8	25 18.5	21 11.5	28 40.5	16 41.9
13 Th	23 20 44	21 59 21	29 26 56	6♉36 49	5 01.2	24 43.7	18 12.6	25 34.1	15 49.6	7 32.9	25 23.4	21 12.3	28 40.6	16 42.1
14 F	23 24 40	22 59 10	13♉46 44	20 56 16	5 01.9	25 32.9	18 27.0	26 21.0	16 10.7	7 44.8	25 28.3	21 13.0	28 40.7	16 42.4
15 Sa	23 28 37	23 58 57	28 05 02	5♊12 44	5 03.3	26 25.4	18 43.5	27 07.7	16 31.8	7 56.7	25 33.1	21 13.6	28 40.9	16 42.7
16 Su	23 32 34	24 58 42	12♊19 06	19 23 56	5R04.3	27 20.9	19 02.0	27 54.5	16 53.1	8 08.5	25 37.8	21 14.2	28 41.0	16 43.0
17 M	23 36 30	25 58 24	26 27 03	3♋28 17	5 04.1	28 19.2	19 22.3	28 41.2	17 14.5	8 20.3	25 42.5	21 14.7	28 41.3	16 43.3
18 Tu	23 40 27	26 58 04	10♋27 31	17 24 36	5 02.4	29 20.3	19 44.5	29 27.9	17 35.9	8 31.9	25 47.1	21 15.2	28 41.5	16 43.7
19 W	23 44 23	27 57 41	24 19 24	1♌11 46	4 58.9	0♓24.0	20 08.4	0♈14.5	17 57.5	8 43.5	25 51.6	21 15.6	28 41.8	16 44.0
20 Th	23 48 20	28 57 17	8♌01 33	14 48 34	4 54.1	1 30.0	20 34.0	1 01.1	18 19.2	8 55.0	25 56.0	21 16.0	28 42.1	16 44.4
21 F	23 52 16	29 56 50	21 32 40	28 13 41	4 48.3	2 38.3	21 01.3	1 47.7	18 41.0	9 06.3	26 00.4	21 16.3	28 42.5	16 44.9
22 Sa	23 56 13	0♈56 21	4♍51 26	11♍25 47	4 42.5	3 48.9	21 30.2	2 34.2	19 02.8	9 17.6	26 04.7	21 16.6	28 42.9	16 45.3
23 Su	0 00 09	1 55 49	17 56 36	24 23 48	4 37.3	5 01.5	22 00.6	3 20.7	19 24.8	9 28.8	26 08.9	21 16.8	28 43.3	16 45.8
24 M	0 04 06	2 55 16	0♎47 20	7♎07 11	4 33.2	6 16.1	22 32.5	4 07.2	19 46.8	9 39.9	26 13.0	21 17.0	28 43.7	16 46.2
25 Tu	0 08 03	3 54 41	13 23 25	19 34 06	4 30.6	7 32.6	23 05.8	4 53.6	20 08.9	9 51.0	26 17.1	21 17.1	28 44.2	16 46.7
26 W	0 11 59	4 54 03	25 45 25	1♏51 35	4D29.6	8 50.9	23 40.5	5 40.0	20 31.1	10 01.9	26 21.1	21R17.2	28 44.7	16 47.3
27 Th	0 15 56	5 53 24	7♏54 51	13 55 34	4 30.0	10 11.1	24 16.5	6 26.3	20 53.4	10 12.7	26 25.0	21 17.2	28 45.3	16 47.8
28 F	0 19 52	6 52 43	19 54 06	25 50 52	4 31.3	11 33.0	24 53.7	7 12.7	21 15.8	10 23.4	26 28.8	21 17.1	28 45.9	16 48.4
29 Sa	0 23 49	7 52 00	1♐46 22	7♐41 05	4 33.0	12 56.6	25 32.2	7 58.9	21 38.3	10 34.1	26 32.5	21 17.0	28 46.5	16 48.9
30 Su	0 27 45	8 51 15	13 35 35	19 30 26	4 34.8	14 21.8	26 11.8	8 45.2	22 00.9	10 44.6	26 36.2	21 16.9	28 47.1	16 49.5
31 M	0 31 42	9 50 29	25 26 13	1♑23 33	4R35.9	15 48.6	26 52.5	9 31.4	22 23.5	10 55.0	26 39.7	21 16.7	28 47.8	16 50.2

April 1902 LONGITUDE

Day	Sid.Time	☉	0 hr ☽	Noon☽	True☊	☿	♀	♂	⚳	♃	♄	♅	♆	♇
1 Tu	0 35 38	10♈49 41	7♑23 03	13♑25 20	4♏36.2	17♓17.1	27♒34.3	10♈17.5	22♉46.2	11♒05.4	26♑43.2	21♐16.4	28♊48.5	16♊50.8
2 W	0 39 35	11 48 51	19 31 00	25 40 36	4R35.4	18 47.0	28 17.2	11 03.7	23 09.0	11 15.6	26 46.6	21R16.1	28 49.3	16 51.5
3 Th	0 43 32	12 47 59	1♒54 42	8♒13 47	4 33.7	20 18.6	29 01.0	11 49.7	23 31.9	11 25.7	26 50.0	21 15.8	28 50.1	16 52.2
4 F	0 47 28	13 47 05	14 38 16	21 08 30	4 31.2	21 51.6	29 45.8	12 35.8	23 54.8	11 35.7	26 53.2	21 15.4	28 50.9	16 52.9
5 Sa	0 51 25	14 46 09	27 44 43	4♓27 04	4 28.4	23 26.2	0♓31.5	13 21.8	24 17.8	11 45.6	26 56.3	21 14.9	28 51.7	16 53.6
6 Su	0 55 21	15 45 12	11♓15 32	18 10 02	4 25.6	25 02.2	1 18.0	14 07.7	24 40.9	11 55.4	26 59.4	21 14.4	28 52.6	16 54.3
7 M	0 59 18	16 44 13	25 10 18	2♈15 55	4 23.3	26 39.8	2 05.4	14 53.7	25 04.1	12 05.0	27 02.4	21 13.8	28 53.5	16 55.1
8 Tu	1 03 14	17 43 11	9♈26 22	16 41 00	4 21.8	28 18.9	2 53.6	15 39.5	25 27.3	12 14.6	27 05.2	21 13.2	28 54.4	16 55.9
9 W	1 07 11	18 42 08	23 59 04	1♉19 45	4D21.2	29 59.5	3 42.5	16 25.4	25 50.6	12 24.0	27 08.0	21 12.6	28 55.4	16 56.7
10 Th	1 11 07	19 41 03	8♉42 10	16 05 26	4 21.4	1♈41.6	4 32.2	17 11.2	26 14.0	12 33.3	27 10.7	21 11.9	28 56.4	16 57.5
11 F	1 15 04	20 39 56	23 28 41	0♊51 04	4 22.2	3 25.2	5 22.6	17 56.9	26 37.4	12 42.5	27 13.4	21 11.1	28 57.4	16 58.3
12 Sa	1 19 00	21 38 46	8♊11 49	15 30 15	4 23.2	5 10.3	6 13.6	18 42.6	27 00.9	12 51.5	27 15.9	21 10.3	28 58.5	16 59.2
13 Su	1 22 57	22 37 34	22 45 46	29 57 53	4 24.2	6 57.0	7 05.3	19 28.2	27 24.5	13 00.5	27 18.3	21 09.4	28 59.6	17 00.0
14 M	1 26 54	23 36 20	7♋06 13	14♋10 30	4R24.7	8 45.3	7 57.7	20 13.8	27 48.1	13 09.3	27 20.6	21 08.5	29 00.7	17 00.9
15 Tu	1 30 50	24 35 04	21 10 32	28 06 12	4 24.9	10 35.0	8 50.6	20 59.4	28 11.7	13 18.0	27 22.9	21 07.6	29 01.9	17 01.8
16 W	1 34 47	25 33 45	4♌57 29	11♌44 24	4 24.5	12 26.4	9 44.1	21 44.9	28 35.5	13 26.5	27 25.0	21 06.6	29 03.0	17 02.7
17 Th	1 38 43	26 32 24	18 27 02	25 05 29	4 23.8	14 19.3	10 38.2	22 30.4	28 59.3	13 34.9	27 27.1	21 05.6	29 04.3	17 03.7
18 F	1 42 40	27 31 01	1♍39 53	8♍10 24	4 23.0	16 13.7	11 32.8	23 15.8	29 23.1	13 43.2	27 29.1	21 04.5	29 05.5	17 04.6
19 Sa	1 46 36	28 29 35	14 37 11	21 00 24	4 22.2	18 09.8	12 28.0	24 01.1	29 47.0	13 51.4	27 30.9	21 03.3	29 06.8	17 05.6
20 Su	1 50 33	29 28 08	27 20 14	3♎36 52	4 21.5	20 07.4	13 23.6	24 46.4	0♊11.0	13 59.4	27 32.7	21 02.2	29 08.0	17 06.6
21 M	1 54 29	0♉26 38	9♎50 27	16 01 11	4 21.1	22 06.5	14 19.8	25 31.7	0 35.0	14 07.3	27 34.4	21 00.9	29 09.4	17 07.6
22 Tu	1 58 26	1 25 07	22 09 15	28 14 50	4D20.9	24 07.1	15 16.4	26 16.9	0 59.0	14 15.0	27 35.9	20 59.7	29 10.7	17 08.6
23 W	2 02 23	2 23 34	4♏18 09	10♏19 24	4 20.9	26 09.1	16 13.5	27 02.1	1 23.1	14 22.6	27 37.4	20 58.4	29 12.1	17 09.6
24 Th	2 06 19	3 21 58	16 18 50	22 16 41	4 21.0	28 12.5	17 11.0	27 47.2	1 47.3	14 30.1	27 38.8	20 57.0	29 13.5	17 10.6
25 F	2 10 16	4 20 21	28 13 15	4♐08 50	4R21.0	0♉17.3	18 09.0	28 32.2	2 11.5	14 37.4	27 40.1	20 55.6	29 14.9	17 11.7
26 Sa	2 14 12	5 18 43	10♐03 45	15 58 24	4 21.0	2 23.2	19 07.3	29 17.3	2 35.7	14 44.6	27 41.3	20 54.2	29 16.3	17 12.8
27 Su	2 18 09	6 17 03	21 53 08	27 48 24	4 20.8	4 30.2	20 06.1	0♉02.2	3 00.0	14 51.6	27 42.4	20 52.7	29 17.8	17 13.8
28 M	2 22 05	7 15 21	3♑44 39	9♑42 21	4 20.5	6 38.1	21 05.2	0 47.1	3 24.4	14 58.5	27 43.4	20 51.2	29 19.3	17 14.9
29 Tu	2 26 02	8 13 37	15 42 01	21 44 09	4 20.2	8 46.8	22 04.8	1 32.0	3 48.7	15 05.2	27 44.3	20 49.6	29 20.8	17 16.1
30 W	2 29 58	9 11 52	27 49 18	3♒58 00	4D20.0	10 56.0	23 04.6	2 16.8	4 13.2	15 11.8	27 45.2	20 48.0	29 22.4	17 17.2

Astro Data	Dy Hr Mn
♇ D	2 1:05
☿ D	3 18:51
♃∠♅	6 9:48
♀ D	7 12:46
☽ 0N	10 8:21
♆ D	10 18:15
♂0N	21 11:38
☉0N	21 13:17
☽ 0S	23 7:10
♅ R	27 3:49
☽ 0N	6 18:07
☿0N	12 12:57
☽ 0S	19 13:17
♃⊼♆	21 19:47

Planet Ingress		Dy Hr Mn
☿	♓	19 3:04
♂	♈	19 4:31
☉	♈	21 13:17
♀	♓	4 19:31
☿	♈	9 12:07
⚳	♊	20 1:02
☉	♉	21 1:04
☿	♉	25 8:41
♂	♉	27 10:49

Last Aspect Dy Hr Mn			☽ Ingress	Dy Hr Mn
1 0:51	♄	⚹	♐	1 12:27
3 22:27	♆	☍	♑	4 1:04
6 1:24	♄	☌	♒	6 11:22
8 15:55	♆	△	♓	8 18:16
10 20:05	♆	□	♈	10 22:21
12 22:42	♆	⚹	♉	13 0:55
14 21:37	♂	⚹	♊	15 3:13
17 3:49	♆	☌	♋	17 6:04
19 5:54	☉	△	♌	19 9:54
21 12:52	♆	⚹	♍	21 15:12
23 20:07	♆	□	♎	23 22:31
26 5:52	♆	△	♏	26 8:20
28 13:17	♄	⚹	♐	28 20:24
31 6:46	♆	☍	♑	31 9:12

Last Aspect Dy Hr Mn			☽ Ingress	Dy Hr Mn
2 14:08	♄	☌	♒	2 20:20
5 2:00	♆	△	♓	5 4:03
7 6:18	♆	□	♈	7 8:11
9 8:04	♆	⚹	♉	9 9:50
11 6:04	♄	△	♊	11 10:37
13 10:22	♆	☌	♋	13 12:04
15 10:44	♄	☍	♌	15 15:18
17 19:16	♆	⚹	♍	17 20:57
20 3:25	♆	□	♎	20 5:05
22 13:51	♆	△	♏	22 15:28
24 22:52	♄	⚹	♐	25 3:36
27 15:01	♆	☍	♑	27 16:26
29 23:51	♄	☌	♒	30 4:16

☽ Phases & Eclipses Dy Hr Mn		
2 10:39	☾	10♐56
10 2:50	●	18♓37
16 22:13	☽	25♊24
24 3:21	○	2♎34
1 6:24	☾	10♑36
8 13:50	●	17♈48
8 14:05:03	☀	P 0.064
15 5:26	☽	24♋19
22 18:50	○	1♏42
22 18:53	☍	T 1.333
30 22:58	☾	9♒38

Astro Data

1 March 1902
Julian Day # 790
SVP 6♓37'22"
GC 25♐28.4 ⚴ 2♈31.5
Eris 22♓49.9 ⚵ 27♍05.1R
⚷ 12♑49.0 ⚶ 3♑17.0
☽ Mean ☊ 7♏21.2

1 April 1902
Julian Day # 821
SVP 6♓37'19"
GC 25♐28.5 ⚴ 14♈33.5
Eris 23♓14.7 ⚵ 19♍46.4R
⚷ 14♑20.8 ⚶ 15♑52.1
☽ Mean ☊ 5♏42.7

LONGITUDE — May 1902

Day	Sid.Time	☉	0 hr ☽	Noon ☽	True ☊	☿	♀	♂	⚳	♃	♄	♅	♆	♇
1 Th	2 33 55	10♉10 06	10♒10 47	16♒28 12	4♏20.1	13♉05.5	24♓04.9	3♉01.6	4♊37.6	15♒18.2	27♑45.9	20♐46.4	29♊24.0	17♊18.3
2 F	2 37 52	11 08 18	22 50 42	29 18 47	4 20.3	15 15.1	25 05.4	3 46.3	5 02.2	15 24.5	27 46.5	20R 44.7	29 25.6	17 19.5
3 Sa	2 41 48	12 06 28	5♓52 50	12♓33 10	4 20.9	17 24.4	26 06.3	4 31.0	5 26.7	15 30.6	27 47.0	20 43.0	29 27.2	17 20.6
4 Su	2 45 45	13 04 37	19 20 01	26 13 30	4 21.7	19 33.2	27 07.5	5 15.6	5 51.3	15 36.5	27 47.4	20 41.3	29 28.8	17 21.8
5 M	2 49 41	14 02 45	3♈13 35	10♈20 07	4 22.4	21 41.2	28 08.9	6 00.2	6 16.0	15 42.3	27 47.7	20 39.5	29 30.5	17 23.0
6 Tu	2 53 38	15 00 51	17 32 45	24 51 00	4R 22.9	23 48.1	29 10.7	6 44.7	6 40.7	15 48.0	27 48.0	20 37.7	29 32.2	17 24.2
7 W	2 57 34	15 58 56	2♉14 11	9♉41 29	4 23.0	25 53.6	0♈12.7	7 29.2	7 05.4	15 53.4	27R 48.1	20 35.8	29 33.9	17 25.4
8 Th	3 01 31	16 56 59	17 11 57	24 44 30	4 22.5	27 57.4	1 15.0	8 13.6	7 30.1	15 58.7	27 48.1	20 34.0	29 35.6	17 26.6
9 F	3 05 27	17 55 00	2♊18 01	9♊51 18	4 21.3	29 59.3	2 17.6	8 58.0	7 54.9	16 03.9	27 48.0	20 32.0	29 37.4	17 27.8
10 Sa	3 09 24	18 53 00	17 23 14	24 52 43	4 19.7	1♊58.9	3 20.4	9 42.3	8 19.8	16 08.8	27 47.9	20 30.1	29 39.1	17 29.1
11 Su	3 13 21	19 50 58	2♋18 46	9♋40 31	4 17.9	3 56.2	4 23.5	10 26.6	8 44.6	16 13.6	27 47.6	20 28.1	29 40.9	17 30.3
12 M	3 17 17	20 48 54	16 57 16	24 08 29	4 16.2	5 50.9	5 26.7	11 10.8	9 09.5	16 18.3	27 47.2	20 26.1	29 42.8	17 31.6
13 Tu	3 21 14	21 46 49	1♌13 48	8♌12 59	4 15.0	7 42.9	6 30.2	11 54.9	9 34.5	16 22.7	27 46.8	20 24.1	29 44.6	17 32.9
14 W	3 25 10	22 44 41	15 06 00	21 52 55	4D 14.6	9 31.9	7 33.9	12 39.0	9 59.4	16 27.0	27 46.2	20 22.0	29 46.4	17 34.1
15 Th	3 29 07	23 42 32	28 33 52	5♍09 09	4 14.9	11 18.0	8 37.9	13 23.1	10 24.4	16 31.1	27 45.6	20 19.9	29 48.3	17 35.4
16 F	3 33 03	24 40 21	11♍39 05	18 04 02	4 16.0	13 00.9	9 42.0	14 07.1	10 49.4	16 35.0	27 44.8	20 17.8	29 50.2	17 36.7
17 Sa	3 37 00	25 38 08	24 24 24	0♎40 37	4 17.4	14 40.6	10 46.3	14 51.0	11 14.5	16 38.8	27 44.0	20 15.7	29 52.1	17 38.0
18 Su	3 40 56	26 35 53	6♎53 06	13 02 16	4 19.0	16 17.1	11 50.9	15 34.9	11 39.6	16 42.4	27 43.0	20 13.5	29 54.0	17 39.3
19 M	3 44 53	27 33 37	19 08 31	25 12 15	4R 20.0	17 50.2	12 55.6	16 18.7	12 04.7	16 45.8	27 42.0	20 11.3	29 56.0	17 40.7
20 Tu	3 48 50	28 31 20	1♏13 48	7♏13 32	4 20.3	19 20.0	14 00.5	17 02.5	12 29.8	16 49.0	27 40.8	20 09.1	29 57.9	17 42.0
21 W	3 52 46	29 29 01	13 11 45	19 08 45	4 19.4	20 46.4	15 05.6	17 46.2	12 54.9	16 52.0	27 39.6	20 06.9	29 59.9	17 43.3
22 Th	3 56 43	0♊26 41	25 04 50	1♐00 15	4 17.3	22 09.2	16 10.9	18 29.8	13 20.1	16 54.9	27 38.3	20 04.6	0♋01.9	17 44.6
23 F	4 00 39	1 24 19	6♐55 15	12 50 05	4 13.9	23 28.6	17 16.3	19 13.4	13 45.3	16 57.6	27 36.9	20 02.4	0 03.9	17 46.0
24 Sa	4 04 36	2 21 57	18 45 01	24 40 18	4 09.5	24 44.4	18 21.9	19 57.0	14 10.6	17 00.1	27 35.4	20 00.1	0 05.9	17 47.3
25 Su	4 08 32	3 19 33	0♑36 11	6♑32 58	4 04.5	25 56.6	19 27.7	20 40.5	14 35.8	17 02.4	27 33.8	19 57.8	0 07.9	17 48.7
26 M	4 12 29	4 17 08	12 30 56	18 30 25	3 59.5	27 05.1	20 33.6	21 23.9	15 01.1	17 04.5	27 32.1	19 55.4	0 09.9	17 50.1
27 Tu	4 16 25	5 14 42	24 31 46	0♒35 20	3 55.0	28 10.0	21 39.7	22 07.3	15 26.4	17 06.5	27 30.4	19 53.1	0 12.0	17 51.4
28 W	4 20 22	6 12 15	6♒41 31	12 50 45	3 51.5	29 11.0	22 46.0	22 50.7	15 51.7	17 08.2	27 28.5	19 50.7	0 14.1	17 52.8
29 Th	4 24 19	7 09 48	19 03 29	25 20 08	3 49.4	0♋08.2	23 52.4	23 34.0	16 17.1	17 09.8	27 26.6	19 48.4	0 16.1	17 54.2
30 F	4 28 15	8 07 19	1♓41 12	8♓07 07	3D 48.7	1 01.5	24 58.9	24 17.2	16 42.4	17 11.2	27 24.6	19 46.0	0 18.2	17 55.5
31 Sa	4 32 12	9 04 50	14 38 21	21 15 17	3 49.2	1 50.8	26 05.6	25 00.4	17 07.8	17 12.4	27 22.4	19 43.6	0 20.3	17 56.9

LONGITUDE — June 1902

Day	Sid.Time	☉	0 hr ☽	Noon ☽	True ☊	☿	♀	♂	⚳	♃	♄	♅	♆	♇
1 Su	4 36 08	10♊02 20	27♓58 17	4♈47 38	3♏50.5	2♋36.0	27♈12.4	25♉43.5	17♊33.2	17♒13.3	27♑20.2	19♐41.2	0♋22.4	17♊58.3
2 M	4 40 05	10 59 49	11♈43 31	18 46 02	3 51.9	3 17.0	28 19.4	26 26.6	17 58.6	17 14.2	27R 17.9	19R 38.8	0 24.6	17 59.7
3 Tu	4 44 01	11 57 17	25 55 04	3♉10 24	3R 52.6	3 53.9	29 26.5	27 09.6	18 24.1	17 14.8	27 15.6	19 36.3	0 26.7	18 01.1
4 W	4 47 58	12 54 45	10♉31 36	17 58 04	3 51.8	4 26.4	0♉33.7	27 52.6	18 49.5	17 15.2	27 13.1	19 33.9	0 28.8	18 02.5
5 Th	4 51 54	13 52 12	25 28 58	3♊03 19	3 49.4	4 54.5	1 41.0	28 35.5	19 15.0	17R 15.4	27 10.6	19 31.5	0 31.0	18 03.9
6 F	4 55 51	14 49 38	10♊39 58	18 17 40	3 45.1	5 18.2	2 48.4	29 18.4	19 40.5	17 15.5	27 08.0	19 29.0	0 33.2	18 05.3
7 Sa	4 59 48	15 47 03	25 55 06	3♋30 55	3 39.4	5 37.4	3 56.0	0♊01.2	20 06.0	17 15.3	27 05.3	19 26.6	0 35.3	18 06.7
8 Su	5 03 44	16 44 28	11♋03 51	18 32 42	3 33.1	5 52.0	5 03.6	0 44.0	20 31.6	17 14.9	27 02.5	19 24.1	0 37.5	18 08.1
9 M	5 07 41	17 41 51	25 56 29	3♌14 21	3 27.1	6 02.0	6 11.4	1 26.7	20 57.1	17 14.4	26 59.7	19 21.7	0 39.7	18 09.5
10 Tu	5 11 37	18 39 13	10♌25 40	17 30 00	3 22.1	6R 07.4	7 19.3	2 09.3	21 22.7	17 13.7	26 56.8	19 19.2	0 41.9	18 10.9
11 W	5 15 34	19 36 35	24 27 10	1♍17 07	3 18.7	6 08.3	8 27.2	2 51.9	21 48.2	17 12.7	26 53.8	19 16.7	0 44.1	18 12.3
12 Th	5 19 30	20 33 55	8♍00 00	14 36 05	3D 17.2	6 04.7	9 35.3	3 34.4	22 13.8	17 11.6	26 50.7	19 14.3	0 46.3	18 13.7
13 F	5 23 27	21 31 14	21 05 45	27 29 30	3 17.2	5 56.7	10 43.4	4 16.9	22 39.4	17 10.3	26 47.6	19 11.8	0 48.5	18 15.0
14 Sa	5 27 23	22 28 32	3♎47 50	10♎01 20	3 18.1	5 44.5	11 51.7	4 59.3	23 05.0	17 08.8	26 44.4	19 09.4	0 50.7	18 16.4
15 Su	5 31 20	23 25 50	16 10 34	22 16 09	3R 19.3	5 28.3	13 00.1	5 41.6	23 30.6	17 07.1	26 41.1	19 06.9	0 52.9	18 17.8
16 M	5 35 17	24 23 06	28 18 38	4♏18 34	3 19.8	5 08.2	14 08.5	6 23.9	23 56.2	17 05.2	26 37.8	19 04.4	0 55.2	18 19.2
17 Tu	5 39 13	25 20 22	10♏16 30	16 12 55	3 18.8	4 44.7	15 17.0	7 06.2	24 21.8	17 03.2	26 34.4	19 02.0	0 57.4	18 20.6
18 W	5 43 10	26 17 37	22 08 16	28 02 58	3 15.8	4 18.1	16 25.7	7 48.4	24 47.4	17 00.9	26 30.9	18 59.6	0 59.6	18 22.0
19 Th	5 47 06	27 14 52	3♐57 23	9♐51 51	3 10.5	3 48.8	17 34.4	8 30.5	25 13.0	16 58.5	26 27.4	18 57.1	1 01.8	18 23.4
20 F	5 51 03	28 12 06	15 46 40	21 42 07	3 03.0	3 17.3	18 43.2	9 12.6	25 38.7	16 55.9	26 23.8	18 54.7	1 04.1	18 24.8
21 Sa	5 54 59	29 09 20	27 38 24	3♑35 45	2 53.6	2 44.1	19 52.1	9 54.6	26 04.3	16 53.1	26 20.2	18 52.3	1 06.3	18 26.2
22 Su	5 58 56	0♋06 33	9♑34 20	15 34 22	2 43.2	2 09.7	21 01.1	10 36.6	26 30.0	16 50.1	26 16.5	18 49.9	1 08.5	18 27.5
23 M	6 02 52	1 03 46	21 36 00	27 39 26	2 32.6	1 34.7	22 10.2	11 18.5	26 55.7	16 47.0	26 12.7	18 47.5	1 10.8	18 28.9
24 Tu	6 06 49	2 00 58	3♒44 50	9♒52 25	2 22.8	0 59.8	23 19.3	12 00.4	27 21.3	16 43.6	26 08.9	18 45.1	1 13.0	18 30.3
25 W	6 10 46	2 58 11	16 02 26	22 15 06	2 14.6	0 25.6	24 28.6	12 42.2	27 47.0	16 40.1	26 05.1	18 42.8	1 15.2	18 31.6
26 Th	6 14 42	3 55 23	28 30 42	4♓49 34	2 08.7	29♊52.5	25 37.9	13 24.0	28 12.7	16 36.4	26 01.2	18 40.4	1 17.5	18 33.0
27 F	6 18 39	4 52 35	11♓12 02	17 38 25	2 05.1	29 21.2	26 47.3	14 05.7	28 38.3	16 32.6	25 57.3	18 38.1	1 19.7	18 34.4
28 Sa	6 22 35	5 49 48	24 09 07	0♈44 30	2D 03.7	28 52.3	27 56.8	14 47.4	29 04.0	16 28.5	25 53.3	18 35.8	1 21.9	18 35.7
29 Su	6 26 32	6 47 00	7♈24 54	14 10 39	2 03.8	28 26.2	29 06.4	15 29.0	29 29.7	16 24.3	25 49.2	18 33.5	1 24.2	18 37.0
30 M	6 30 28	7 44 13	21 02 03	27 59 16	2R 04.2	28 03.4	0♊16.1	16 10.5	29 55.4	16 19.9	25 45.2	18 31.2	1 26.4	18 38.4

Astro Data

	Dy Hr Mn
☽0N	4 4:06
♄ R	8 6:18
♀0N	10 3:20
☽0S	16 18:56
☽0N	31 13:13
♃ R	6 4:31
☿ R	11 4:41
☽0S	13 1:55
☽0N	27 20:57
♅☍♇	28 12:31
♃⚼♆	29 12:33

Planet Ingress

		Dy Hr Mn
♀	♈	7 7:05
☿	♊	9 12:09
♆	♋	21 13:33
☉	♊	22 0:54
☿	♋	29 8:28
♀	♉	3 23:59
♂	♊	7 11:20
☉	♋	22 9:15
☿	♊R	26 6:27
♀	♊	30 6:28
⚳	♋	30 16:19

Last Aspect / ☽ Ingress (May)

Last Aspect Dy Hr Mn			☽ Ingress	Dy Hr Mn
2 12:12	♆	△	♓	2 13:16
4 17:37	♆	□	♈	4 18:30
6 19:38	♆	✶	♉	6 20:23
8 17:54	☿	☌	♊	8 20:21
10 19:43	♆	☌	♋	10 20:15
12 18:09	♄	☍	♌	12 21:54
15 2:13	♆	✶	♍	15 2:36
17 10:26	♆	□	♎	17 10:42
19 21:26	♆	△	♏	19 21:33
22 5:12	♄	✶	♐	22 9:58
24 12:09	☿	☍	♑	24 22:47
27 5:55	♄	☌	♒	27 10:50
29 8:57	♀	✶	♓	29 20:50

Last Aspect / ☽ Ingress (June)

Last Aspect Dy Hr Mn			☽ Ingress	Dy Hr Mn
31 22:55	♄	✶	♈	1 3:35
3 5:20	♀	☌	♉	3 6:46
5 4:35	♂	☌	♊	5 7:10
6 13:52	♅	☍	♋	7 6:26
9 1:45	♄	☍	♌	9 6:39
10 15:07	♅	△	♍	11 9:44
13 10:41	♄	△	♎	13 16:45
15 20:43	♄	□	♏	16 3:22
18 8:54	♄	✶	♐	18 15:58
21 2:17	☉	☍	♑	21 4:46
23 9:09	♄	☌	♒	23 16:37
25 16:43	♀	□	♓	26 2:50
28 8:43	☿	□	♈	28 10:39
30 12:07	☿	✶	♉	30 15:26

☽ Phases & Eclipses

Dy Hr Mn		
7 22:45	●	16♉25
7 22:34:16	●	P 0.859
14 13:40	☽	22♌49
22 10:46	○	0♐24
30 12:00	☾	8♓07
6 6:11	●	14♊36
12 23:54	☽	21♍02
21 2:17	○	28♐46
28 21:52	☾	6♈13

Astro Data

1 May 1902
Julian Day # 851
SVP 6♓37'16"
GC 25♐28.5 ⚴ 27♈00.4
Eris 23♓35.4 ⚵ 16♍14.8R
⚷ 14♑36.9R ⚶ 24♑44.8
☽ Mean ☊ 4♏07.3

1 June 1902
Julian Day # 882
SVP 6♓37'12"
GC 25♐28.6 ⚴ 10♉28.5
Eris 23♓48.5 ⚵ 18♍05.9
⚷ 13♑39.4R ⚶ 28♑20.6R
☽ Mean ☊ 2♏28.8

July 1902 — LONGITUDE

Day	Sid.Time	☉	0 hr ☽	Noon ☽	True ☊	☿	♀	♂	⚳	♃	♄	♅	♆	♇
1 Tu	6 34 25	8♋41 26	5♉02 24	12♉11 26	2♏03.9	27♊44.3	1♊25.8	16♊52.0	0♋21.1	16♒15.4	25♑41.1	18♐28.9	1♋28.6	18♊39.7
2 W	6 38 21	9 38 39	19 26 10	26 46 14	2R 01.9	27R 29.3	2 35.6	17 33.5	0 46.8	16R 10.7	25R 36.9	18R 26.7	1 30.8	18 41.0
3 Th	6 42 18	10 35 52	4♊11 07	11♊40 02	1 57.4	27 18.6	3 45.5	18 14.9	1 12.5	16 05.8	25 32.7	18 24.5	1 33.0	18 42.3
4 F	6 46 15	11 33 06	19 12 05	26 46 09	1 50.4	27D 12.5	4 55.4	18 56.2	1 38.2	16 00.8	25 28.5	18 22.3	1 35.3	18 43.7
5 Sa	6 50 11	12 30 19	4♋21 02	11♋55 26	1 41.3	27 11.2	6 05.4	19 37.5	2 03.8	15 55.6	25 24.3	18 20.1	1 37.5	18 45.0
6 Su	6 54 08	13 27 33	19 28 01	26 57 31	1 31.1	27 14.8	7 15.5	20 18.8	2 29.5	15 50.3	25 20.0	18 17.9	1 39.7	18 46.3
7 M	6 58 04	14 24 46	4♌22 47	11♌42 46	1 21.1	27 23.5	8 25.7	21 00.0	2 55.2	15 44.8	25 15.7	18 15.8	1 41.9	18 47.5
8 Tu	7 02 01	15 22 00	18 56 39	26 03 48	1 12.3	27 37.3	9 35.9	21 41.1	3 20.9	15 39.2	25 11.4	18 13.7	1 44.1	18 48.8
9 W	7 05 57	16 19 13	3♍03 48	9♍56 27	1 05.7	27 56.3	10 46.2	22 22.2	3 46.6	15 33.5	25 07.1	18 11.6	1 46.2	18 50.1
10 Th	7 09 54	17 16 26	16 41 46	23 19 55	1 01.4	28 20.6	11 56.5	23 03.2	4 12.2	15 27.6	25 02.7	18 09.6	1 48.4	18 51.3
11 F	7 13 50	18 13 40	29 51 13	6♎16 05	0 59.4	28 50.0	13 06.9	23 44.1	4 37.9	15 21.5	24 58.3	18 07.5	1 50.6	18 52.6
12 Sa	7 17 47	19 10 53	12♎35 05	18 48 46	0 58.9	29 24.6	14 17.4	24 25.0	5 03.5	15 15.4	24 53.9	18 05.5	1 52.7	18 53.8
13 Su	7 21 44	20 08 06	24 57 47	1♏02 49	0 59.0	0♋04.3	15 27.9	25 05.9	5 29.2	15 09.1	24 49.5	18 03.6	1 54.9	18 55.1
14 M	7 25 40	21 05 19	7♏04 30	13 03 30	0 58.6	0 49.2	16 38.5	25 46.7	5 54.8	15 02.7	24 45.1	18 01.6	1 57.0	18 56.3
15 Tu	7 29 37	22 02 32	19 00 27	24 55 58	0 56.5	1 39.2	17 49.2	26 27.4	6 20.4	14 56.2	24 40.7	17 59.7	1 59.2	18 57.5
16 W	7 33 33	22 59 46	0♐50 37	6♐44 57	0 52.2	2 34.2	18 59.9	27 08.1	6 46.1	14 49.6	24 36.3	17 57.9	2 01.3	18 58.7
17 Th	7 37 30	23 57 00	12 39 25	18 34 28	0 45.2	3 34.1	20 10.7	27 48.8	7 11.7	14 42.9	24 31.8	17 56.0	2 03.4	18 59.9
18 F	7 41 26	24 54 14	24 30 30	0♑27 49	0 35.5	4 39.0	21 21.5	28 29.3	7 37.3	14 36.0	24 27.4	17 54.2	2 05.5	19 01.0
19 Sa	7 45 23	25 51 28	6♑26 43	12 27 26	0 23.7	5 48.6	22 32.4	29 09.9	8 02.9	14 29.1	24 23.0	17 52.5	2 07.6	19 02.2
20 Su	7 49 19	26 48 43	18 30 09	24 34 59	0 10.5	7 03.0	23 43.4	29 50.3	8 28.4	14 22.1	24 18.5	17 50.7	2 09.6	19 03.3
21 M	7 53 16	27 45 58	0♒42 06	6♒51 33	29♎57.1	8 22.1	24 54.4	0♋30.8	8 54.0	14 15.0	24 14.1	17 49.0	2 11.7	19 04.5
22 Tu	7 57 13	28 43 14	13 03 25	19 17 45	29 44.6	9 45.6	26 05.5	1 11.1	9 19.5	14 07.8	24 09.7	17 47.4	2 13.8	19 05.6
23 W	8 01 09	29 40 31	25 34 38	1♓54 09	29 34.0	11 13.6	27 16.7	1 51.5	9 45.1	14 00.5	24 05.3	17 45.7	2 15.8	19 06.7
24 Th	8 05 06	0♌37 48	8♓16 21	14 41 23	29 26.0	12 45.9	28 27.9	2 31.7	10 10.6	13 53.1	24 00.9	17 44.1	2 17.8	19 07.8
25 F	8 09 02	1 35 06	21 09 23	27 40 31	29 20.9	14 22.3	29 39.2	3 11.9	10 36.1	13 45.7	23 56.5	17 42.6	2 19.8	19 08.9
26 Sa	8 12 59	2 32 25	4♈14 58	10♈52 58	29 18.4	16 02.6	0♋50.6	3 52.1	11 01.6	13 38.2	23 52.2	17 41.1	2 21.8	19 10.0
27 Su	8 16 55	3 29 45	17 34 43	24 20 29	29 17.7	17 46.6	2 02.0	4 32.2	11 27.1	13 30.7	23 47.8	17 39.6	2 23.8	19 11.0
28 M	8 20 52	4 27 06	1♉10 26	8♉04 46	29 17.6	19 34.0	3 13.5	5 12.3	11 52.6	13 23.1	23 43.5	17 38.2	2 25.8	19 12.1
29 Tu	8 24 48	5 24 28	15 03 36	22 06 59	29 17.0	21 24.6	4 25.0	5 52.3	12 18.0	13 15.5	23 39.2	17 36.8	2 27.7	19 13.1
30 W	8 28 45	6 21 51	29 14 50	6♊26 58	29 14.7	23 18.1	5 36.6	6 32.3	12 43.4	13 07.8	23 34.9	17 35.4	2 29.6	19 14.1
31 Th	8 32 42	7 19 16	13♊43 04	21 02 37	29 09.9	25 14.2	6 48.3	7 12.2	13 08.9	13 00.1	23 30.7	17 34.1	2 31.6	19 15.1

August 1902 — LONGITUDE

Day	Sid.Time	☉	0 hr ☽	Noon ☽	True ☊	☿	♀	♂	⚳	♃	♄	♅	♆	♇
1 F	8 36 38	8♌16 41	28♊25 01	5♋49 26	29♎02.5	27♋12.5	8♋00.0	7♋52.1	13♋34.3	12♒52.3	23♑26.4	17♐32.9	2♋33.5	19♊16.1
2 Sa	8 40 35	9 14 08	13♋14 58	20 40 35	28R 52.9	29 12.7	9 11.8	8 31.9	13 59.6	12R 44.5	23R 22.3	17R 31.6	2 35.4	19 17.1
3 Su	8 44 31	10 11 35	28 05 12	5♌27 43	28 42.0	1♌14.4	10 23.7	9 11.6	14 25.0	12 36.7	23 18.1	17 30.5	2 37.2	19 18.0
4 M	8 48 28	11 09 04	12♌47 05	20 02 19	28 31.1	3 17.2	11 35.6	9 51.3	14 50.3	12 28.9	23 14.0	17 29.3	2 39.1	19 19.0
5 Tu	8 52 24	12 06 33	27 12 34	4♍17 09	28 21.5	5 20.9	12 47.5	10 31.0	15 15.6	12 21.1	23 09.9	17 28.2	2 40.9	19 19.9
6 W	8 56 21	13 04 03	11♍15 31	18 07 22	28 13.9	7 25.1	13 59.5	11 10.6	15 40.9	12 13.3	23 05.9	17 27.2	2 42.7	19 20.8
7 Th	9 00 17	14 01 34	24 52 31	1♎30 59	28 08.9	9 29.4	15 11.6	11 50.1	16 06.2	12 05.4	23 01.9	17 26.2	2 44.5	19 21.7
8 F	9 04 14	14 59 06	8♎02 56	14 28 41	28 06.4	11 33.7	16 23.7	12 29.6	16 31.4	11 57.6	22 57.9	17 25.2	2 46.2	19 22.6
9 Sa	9 08 11	15 56 39	20 48 38	27 03 18	28D 05.6	13 37.7	17 35.9	13 09.0	16 56.6	11 49.8	22 54.0	17 24.3	2 48.0	19 23.4
10 Su	9 12 07	16 54 13	3♏13 14	9♏19 04	28R 05.9	15 41.1	18 48.1	13 48.4	17 21.8	11 42.1	22 50.1	17 23.5	2 49.7	19 24.3
11 M	9 16 04	17 51 47	15 21 26	21 21 02	28 06.0	17 43.9	20 00.3	14 27.7	17 46.9	11 34.3	22 46.3	17 22.6	2 51.4	19 25.1
12 Tu	9 20 00	18 49 23	27 18 31	3♐14 32	28 04.9	19 45.7	21 12.7	15 07.0	18 12.0	11 26.6	22 42.6	17 21.9	2 53.1	19 25.9
13 W	9 23 57	19 46 59	9♐09 44	15 04 45	28 01.9	21 46.5	22 25.0	15 46.2	18 37.1	11 18.9	22 38.9	17 21.2	2 54.8	19 26.7
14 Th	9 27 53	20 44 37	21 00 08	26 56 27	27 56.6	23 46.3	23 37.5	16 25.4	19 02.2	11 11.3	22 35.2	17 20.5	2 56.4	19 27.4
15 F	9 31 50	21 42 15	2♑54 09	8♑53 42	27 48.8	25 44.8	24 50.0	17 04.5	19 27.2	11 03.7	22 31.6	17 19.9	2 58.0	19 28.2
16 Sa	9 35 46	22 39 55	14 55 27	20 59 45	27 39.1	27 42.1	26 02.5	17 43.5	19 52.2	10 56.2	22 28.1	17 19.3	2 59.6	19 28.9
17 Su	9 39 43	23 37 35	27 06 49	3♒16 53	27 28.0	29 38.1	27 15.1	18 22.5	20 17.1	10 48.8	22 24.6	17 18.8	3 01.2	19 29.6
18 M	9 43 40	24 35 17	9♒30 02	15 46 24	27 16.7	1♍32.7	28 27.7	19 01.5	20 42.1	10 41.4	22 21.2	17 18.3	3 02.7	19 30.3
19 Tu	9 47 36	25 33 00	22 05 58	28 28 44	27 06.2	3 26.0	29 40.4	19 40.4	21 06.9	10 34.0	22 17.9	17 17.9	3 04.3	19 31.0
20 W	9 51 33	26 30 45	4♓54 40	11♓23 40	26 57.4	5 17.9	0♌53.2	20 19.2	21 31.8	10 26.8	22 14.6	17 17.5	3 05.8	19 31.7
21 Th	9 55 29	27 28 31	17 55 40	24 30 34	26 50.8	7 08.4	2 06.0	20 58.0	21 56.6	10 19.6	22 11.4	17 17.2	3 07.2	19 32.3
22 F	9 59 26	28 26 18	1♈08 17	7♈48 44	26 46.9	8 57.5	3 18.8	21 36.7	22 21.4	10 12.5	22 08.3	17 16.9	3 08.7	19 32.9
23 Sa	10 03 22	29 24 07	14 31 54	21 17 42	26D 45.3	10 45.3	4 31.8	22 15.4	22 46.1	10 05.6	22 05.2	17 16.7	3 10.1	19 33.5
24 Su	10 07 19	0♍21 58	28 06 09	4♉57 15	26 45.4	12 31.7	5 44.7	22 54.1	23 10.8	9 58.7	22 02.2	17 16.5	3 11.5	19 34.1
25 M	10 11 15	1 19 51	11♉51 00	18 47 25	26R 46.2	14 16.8	6 57.7	23 32.6	23 35.5	9 51.9	21 59.3	17 16.4	3 12.9	19 34.6
26 Tu	10 15 12	2 17 46	25 46 28	2♊48 08	26 46.7	16 00.5	8 10.8	24 11.2	24 00.1	9 45.2	21 56.4	17D 16.3	3 14.2	19 35.2
27 W	10 19 09	3 15 42	9♊52 20	16 58 52	26 45.9	17 43.0	9 24.0	24 49.7	24 24.7	9 38.6	21 53.6	17 16.3	3 15.5	19 35.7
28 Th	10 23 05	4 13 40	24 07 34	1♋18 04	26 43.1	19 24.1	10 37.2	25 28.1	24 49.2	9 32.1	21 50.9	17 16.3	3 16.8	19 36.2
29 F	10 27 02	5 11 41	8♋29 59	15 42 49	26 38.2	21 03.9	11 50.4	26 06.5	25 13.7	9 25.8	21 48.3	17 16.4	3 18.1	19 36.7
30 Sa	10 30 58	6 09 43	22 55 58	0♌08 47	26 31.5	22 42.4	13 03.7	26 44.8	25 38.1	9 19.6	21 45.8	17 16.5	3 19.3	19 37.1
31 Su	10 34 55	7 07 46	7♌20 34	14 30 35	26 23.8	24 19.7	14 17.0	27 23.1	26 02.5	9 13.5	21 43.3	17 16.7	3 20.5	19 37.6

Astro Data

	Dy Hr Mn
☿ D	5 6:25
☽ 0S	10 10:56
☽ 0N	25 3:36
☽ 0S	6 21:13
☽ 0N	21 10:13
♅ D	27 10:18

Planet Ingress

		Dy Hr Mn
☿	♋	13 9:32
♂	♋	20 17:44
☊	♎R	21 6:43
☉	♌	23 20:10
♀	♋	25 18:59
☿	♌	2 21:22
☿	♍	17 16:34
♀	♌	19 18:28
☉	♍	24 2:53

Last Aspect / ☽ Ingress (July)

Last Aspect Dy Hr Mn			☽ Ingress	Dy Hr Mn
2 10:08	♄	△	♊	2 17:14
4 12:41	☿	☌	♋	4 17:07
6 9:24	♄	☍	♌	6 16:54
8 14:43	☿	⚹	♍	8 18:43
10 21:33	☿	□	♎	11 0:16
12 23:48	♄	□	♏	13 9:56
15 11:29	♄	⚹	♐	15 22:17
18 7:47	♂	☍	♑	18 11:04
20 16:45	☉	☍	♒	20 22:38
23 2:20	♀	△	♓	23 8:24
25 15:59	♀	□	♈	25 16:15
27 11:03	♄	□	♉	27 21:57
29 14:35	♄	△	♊	30 1:16

Last Aspect / ☽ Ingress (August)

Last Aspect Dy Hr Mn			☽ Ingress	Dy Hr Mn
31 9:04	♇	☌	♋	1 2:34
2 16:20	♄	☍	♌	3 3:06
4 10:48	♇	⚹	♍	5 4:43
6 20:47	♄	△	♎	7 9:15
9 4:02	♄	□	♏	9 17:43
11 14:51	♄	⚹	♐	12 5:26
14 4:19	☿	△	♑	14 18:10
16 22:59	♀	☍	♒	17 5:38
19 6:03	☉	☍	♓	19 14:51
21 7:48	♄	⚹	♈	21 21:57
23 13:47	♂	□	♉	24 3:20
25 20:34	♂	⚹	♊	26 7:13
27 16:24	♇	☌	♋	28 9:50
30 6:05	♂	☌	♌	30 11:45

☽ Phases & Eclipses

Dy Hr Mn		
5 12:59	●	12♋33
12 12:47	☽	19♎13
20 16:45	○	27♑00
28 5:15	☾	4♉11
3 20:17	●	10♌31
11 4:24	☽	17♏34
19 6:03	○	25♒19
26 11:04	☾	2♊16

Astro Data

1 July 1902
Julian Day # 912
SVP 6♓37'07"
GC 25♐28.7 ⚴ 23♉56.6
Eris 23♓50.2R ⚵ 23♍48.8
⚷ 11♑56.4R ⚶ 24♑49.5R
☽ Mean ☊ 0♏53.5

1 August 1902
Julian Day # 943
SVP 6♓37'02"
GC 25♐28.7 ⚴ 8♊06.3
Eris 23♓40.6R ⚵ 2♎10.1
⚷ 10♑06.4R ⚶ 17♑44.4R
☽ Mean ☊ 29♎15.0

LONGITUDE — September 1902

Day	Sid.Time	☉	0 hr ☽	Noon ☽	True ☊	☿	♀	♂	⚳	♃	♄	♅	♆	♇
1 M	10 38 51	8♍05 52	21♌38 04	28♌42 21	26♎16.0	25♍55.8	15♌30.4	28♋01.3	26♋26.9	9♒07.5	21♑41.0	17♐16.9	3♋21.7	19♊38.0
2 Tu	10 42 48	9 03 59	5♍42 46	12♍38 46	26R 09.0	27 30.5	16 43.8	28 39.4	26 51.2	9R 01.7	21R 38.7	17 17.2	3 22.9	19 38.4
3 W	10 46 44	10 02 08	19 29 54	26 15 49	26 03.7	29 04.1	17 57.3	29 17.5	27 15.4	8 56.0	21 36.5	17 17.5	3 24.0	19 38.8
4 Th	10 50 41	11 00 18	2♎56 18	9♎31 16	26 00.3	0♎36.4	19 10.8	29 55.6	27 39.6	8 50.4	21 34.3	17 17.9	3 25.1	19 39.1
5 F	10 54 38	11 58 30	16 00 45	22 24 54	25D 59.0	2 07.5	20 24.4	0♌33.6	28 03.7	8 45.1	21 32.3	17 18.4	3 26.1	19 39.4
6 Sa	10 58 34	12 56 44	28 43 59	4♏58 19	25 59.3	3 37.3	21 38.0	1 11.5	28 27.8	8 39.8	21 30.4	17 18.9	3 27.2	19 39.8
7 Su	11 02 31	13 54 59	11♏08 21	17 14 34	26 00.6	5 05.9	22 51.7	1 49.4	28 51.8	8 34.7	21 28.5	17 19.4	3 28.2	19 40.0
8 M	11 06 27	14 53 16	23 17 29	29 17 43	26 02.1	6 33.2	24 05.4	2 27.2	29 15.7	8 29.8	21 26.7	17 20.0	3 29.1	19 40.3
9 Tu	11 10 24	15 51 34	5♐15 52	11♐12 32	26R 03.1	7 59.3	25 19.1	3 04.9	29 39.6	8 25.1	21 25.1	17 20.7	3 30.1	19 40.6
10 W	11 14 20	16 49 54	17 08 23	23 04 01	26 03.0	9 24.1	26 32.9	3 42.6	0♌03.5	8 20.5	21 23.5	17 21.4	3 31.0	19 40.8
11 Th	11 18 17	17 48 15	29 00 06	4♑57 11	26 01.3	10 47.6	27 46.7	4 20.2	0 27.2	8 16.0	21 22.0	17 22.1	3 31.9	19 41.0
12 F	11 22 13	18 46 38	10♑55 52	16 56 41	25 58.1	12 09.8	29 00.6	4 57.8	0 50.9	8 11.8	21 20.6	17 22.9	3 32.7	19 41.2
13 Sa	11 26 10	19 45 02	23 00 08	29 06 39	25 53.4	13 30.6	0♍14.5	5 35.3	1 14.5	8 07.7	21 19.3	17 23.8	3 33.5	19 41.3
14 Su	11 30 06	20 43 29	5♒16 37	11♒30 21	25 47.9	14 50.0	1 28.4	6 12.8	1 38.1	8 03.8	21 18.1	17 24.7	3 34.3	19 41.5
15 M	11 34 03	21 41 56	17 48 06	24 10 02	25 42.0	16 07.9	2 42.4	6 50.2	2 01.6	8 00.0	21 17.0	17 25.6	3 35.1	19 41.6
16 Tu	11 38 00	22 40 26	0♓36 16	7♓06 48	25 36.4	17 24.3	3 56.4	7 27.5	2 25.0	7 56.5	21 16.0	17 26.6	3 35.8	19 41.7
17 W	11 41 56	23 38 57	13 41 35	20 20 29	25 31.9	18 39.2	5 10.5	8 04.8	2 48.4	7 53.1	21 15.0	17 27.7	3 36.5	19 41.7
18 Th	11 45 53	24 37 31	27 03 20	3♈49 52	25 28.7	19 52.4	6 24.6	8 42.1	3 11.7	7 49.9	21 14.2	17 28.8	3 37.1	19 41.8
19 F	11 49 49	25 36 06	10♈39 48	17 32 50	25D 27.2	21 03.9	7 38.7	9 19.2	3 34.9	7 46.9	21 13.5	17 29.9	3 37.8	19R 41.8
20 Sa	11 53 46	26 34 43	24 28 36	1♉26 47	25 27.0	22 13.6	8 52.9	9 56.3	3 58.0	7 44.1	21 12.8	17 31.1	3 38.4	19 41.8
21 Su	11 57 42	27 33 23	8♉27 02	15 28 59	25 28.0	23 21.4	10 07.2	10 33.4	4 21.1	7 41.5	21 12.3	17 32.4	3 38.9	19 41.8
22 M	12 01 39	28 32 04	22 32 21	29 36 49	25 29.5	24 27.1	11 21.4	11 10.4	4 44.1	7 39.0	21 11.9	17 33.7	3 39.5	19 41.8
23 Tu	12 05 35	29 30 48	6♊42 05	13♊47 53	25 30.8	25 30.6	12 35.7	11 47.3	5 07.0	7 36.7	21 11.5	17 35.0	3 40.0	19 41.7
24 W	12 09 32	0♎29 35	20 53 57	28 00 02	25R 31.5	26 31.8	13 50.1	12 24.2	5 29.8	7 34.7	21 11.3	17 36.4	3 40.4	19 41.6
25 Th	12 13 29	1 28 23	5♋05 53	12♋11 13	25 31.2	27 30.5	15 04.5	13 01.0	5 52.5	7 32.8	21D 11.1	17 37.9	3 40.8	19 41.5
26 F	12 17 25	2 27 14	19 15 46	26 19 14	25 29.7	28 26.4	16 18.9	13 37.8	6 15.2	7 31.1	21 11.1	17 39.4	3 41.2	19 41.4
27 Sa	12 21 22	3 26 07	3♌21 21	10♌21 46	25 27.4	29 19.5	17 33.3	14 14.5	6 37.7	7 29.7	21 11.1	17 40.9	3 41.6	19 41.3
28 Su	12 25 18	4 25 03	17 20 10	24 16 14	25 24.5	0♏09.4	18 47.8	14 51.1	7 00.2	7 28.4	21 11.3	17 42.5	3 41.9	19 41.1
29 M	12 29 15	5 24 00	1♍09 36	7♍59 59	25 21.5	0 55.8	20 02.4	15 27.7	7 22.6	7 27.3	21 11.5	17 44.1	3 42.2	19 40.9
30 Tu	12 33 11	6 23 00	14 47 04	21 30 35	25 18.9	1 38.6	21 16.9	16 04.2	7 44.8	7 26.4	21 11.9	17 45.8	3 42.5	19 40.7

LONGITUDE — October 1902

Day	Sid.Time	☉	0 hr ☽	Noon ☽	True ☊	☿	♀	♂	⚳	♃	♄	♅	♆	♇
1 W	12 37 08	7♎22 01	28♍10 18	4♎46 03	25♎17.0	2♏17.2	22♍31.5	16♌40.6	8♌07.0	7♒25.7	21♑12.4	17♐47.5	3♋42.7	19♊40.5
2 Th	12 41 04	8 21 05	11♎17 43	17 45 14	25D 16.0	2 51.5	23 46.1	17 17.0	8 29.1	7R 25.2	21 12.9	17 49.3	3 42.9	19R 40.2
3 F	12 45 01	9 20 11	24 08 35	0♏27 52	25 16.0	3 20.9	25 00.8	17 53.3	8 51.1	7D 24.9	21 13.6	17 51.1	3 43.1	19 39.9
4 Sa	12 48 58	10 19 19	6♏43 13	12 54 50	25 16.6	3 45.1	26 15.5	18 29.5	9 12.9	7 24.8	21 14.3	17 53.0	3 43.2	19 39.6
5 Su	12 52 54	11 18 29	19 02 59	25 07 59	25 17.7	4 03.7	27 30.2	19 05.7	9 34.7	7 24.9	21 15.2	17 54.9	3 43.3	19 39.3
6 M	12 56 51	12 17 40	1♐10 13	7♐10 07	25 19.0	4 16.1	28 44.9	19 41.8	9 56.3	7 25.2	21 16.1	17 56.9	3 43.3	19 39.0
7 Tu	13 00 47	13 16 54	13 08 10	19 04 51	25 20.2	4R 22.0	29 59.7	20 17.8	10 17.9	7 25.7	21 17.2	17 58.9	3R 43.4	19 38.6
8 W	13 04 44	14 16 09	25 00 43	0♑56 19	25 21.0	4 20.7	1♎14.5	20 53.8	10 39.3	7 26.4	21 18.3	18 00.9	3 43.4	19 38.2
9 Th	13 08 40	15 15 26	6♑52 16	12 49 07	25R 21.4	4 12.0	2 29.3	21 29.6	11 00.6	7 27.3	21 19.6	18 03.0	3 43.3	19 37.8
10 F	13 12 37	16 14 45	18 47 30	24 47 58	25 21.2	3 55.4	3 44.1	22 05.5	11 21.8	7 28.4	21 20.9	18 05.2	3 43.2	19 37.4
11 Sa	13 16 33	17 14 05	0♒51 07	6♒57 29	25 20.7	3 30.6	4 59.0	22 41.2	11 42.9	7 29.7	21 22.4	18 07.3	3 43.1	19 37.0
12 Su	13 20 30	18 13 27	13 07 36	19 21 57	25 20.0	2 57.6	6 13.8	23 16.8	12 03.8	7 31.2	21 23.9	18 09.6	3 43.0	19 36.5
13 M	13 24 26	19 12 52	25 40 55	2♓04 54	25 19.1	2 16.2	7 28.7	23 52.4	12 24.7	7 32.9	21 25.6	18 11.8	3 42.8	19 36.0
14 Tu	13 28 23	20 12 17	8♓34 08	15 08 49	25 18.4	1 26.8	8 43.6	24 27.9	12 45.4	7 34.8	21 27.3	18 14.1	3 42.6	19 35.5
15 W	13 32 20	21 11 45	21 49 02	28 34 46	25 17.9	0 30.0	9 58.6	25 03.4	13 05.9	7 36.9	21 29.1	18 16.5	3 42.3	19 35.0
16 Th	13 36 16	22 11 15	5♈25 53	12♈22 08	25D 17.7	29♎26.6	11 13.5	25 38.7	13 26.4	7 39.2	21 31.1	18 18.8	3 42.1	19 34.5
17 F	13 40 13	23 10 46	19 23 09	26 28 28	25 17.6	28 17.8	12 28.5	26 14.0	13 46.7	7 41.7	21 33.1	18 21.2	3 41.8	19 33.9
18 Sa	13 44 09	24 10 20	3♉37 33	10♉49 45	25 17.6	27 05.3	13 43.5	26 49.3	14 06.8	7 44.3	21 35.2	18 23.7	3 41.4	19 33.3
19 Su	13 48 06	25 09 56	18 04 21	25 20 39	25R 17.7	25 50.9	14 58.6	27 24.4	14 26.8	7 47.2	21 37.4	18 26.2	3 41.0	19 32.7
20 M	13 52 02	26 09 34	2♊37 54	9♊55 21	25 17.6	24 36.8	16 13.6	27 59.5	14 46.7	7 50.2	21 39.7	18 28.7	3 40.6	19 32.1
21 Tu	13 55 59	27 09 14	17 12 19	24 28 08	25 17.5	23 25.2	17 28.7	28 34.5	15 06.5	7 53.5	21 42.1	18 31.3	3 40.2	19 31.5
22 W	13 59 55	28 08 57	1♋42 14	8♋54 05	25 17.3	22 18.1	18 43.8	29 09.4	15 26.1	7 56.9	21 44.6	18 33.9	3 39.7	19 30.8
23 Th	14 03 52	29 08 42	16 03 16	23 09 27	25D 17.2	21 17.8	19 58.9	29 44.2	15 45.5	8 00.5	21 47.2	18 36.6	3 39.2	19 30.2
24 F	14 07 49	0♏08 29	0♌12 22	7♌11 49	25 17.2	20 25.8	21 14.0	0♍18.9	16 04.8	8 04.3	21 49.9	18 39.3	3 38.7	19 29.5
25 Sa	14 11 45	1 08 18	14 07 41	20 59 55	25 17.5	19 43.7	22 29.2	0 53.6	16 23.9	8 08.3	21 52.7	18 42.0	3 38.1	19 28.8
26 Su	14 15 42	2 08 10	27 48 29	4♍33 23	25 18.0	19 12.3	23 44.4	1 28.2	16 42.9	8 12.4	21 55.5	18 44.7	3 37.5	19 28.0
27 M	14 19 38	3 08 04	11♍14 40	17 52 23	25 18.7	18 52.2	24 59.6	2 02.7	17 01.7	8 16.8	21 58.5	18 47.5	3 36.9	19 27.3
28 Tu	14 23 35	4 07 59	24 26 37	0♎57 26	25 19.5	18D 43.6	26 14.8	2 37.1	17 20.3	8 21.3	22 01.5	18 50.4	3 36.2	19 26.5
29 W	14 27 31	5 07 57	7♎24 55	13 49 08	25R 20.1	18 46.3	27 30.0	3 11.4	17 38.7	8 26.0	22 04.7	18 53.2	3 35.5	19 25.8
30 Th	14 31 28	6 07 57	20 10 11	26 28 10	25 20.3	19 00.0	28 45.2	3 45.6	17 57.0	8 30.9	22 07.9	18 56.1	3 34.8	19 25.0
31 F	14 35 24	7 07 59	2♏43 10	8♏55 18	25 20.0	19 23.9	0♏00.5	4 19.8	18 15.1	8 36.0	22 11.2	18 59.0	3 34.0	19 24.2

Astro Data

	Dy Hr Mn
☽0S	3 7:17
☿0S	4 1:52
☽0N	17 17:54
♇ R	20 6:48
☉0S	23 23:55
♄ D	26 10:54
☽0S	30 15:46
♃ D	4 11:13
♆ R	7 17:36
☿ R	7 20:00
♀0S	10 5:25
☽0N	15 3:06
☽0S	27 22:22
☿ D	28 18:08

Planet Ingress

		Dy Hr Mn
☿	♎	4 2:30
♂	♌	4 14:48
⚳	♌	10 8:31
♀	♍	13 7:18
☉	♎	23 23:55
☿	♏	28 7:22
♀	♎	7 12:06
☿	♎R	15 23:38
♂	♍	23 22:55
☉	♏	24 8:36
♀	♏	31 11:51

Last Aspect / ☽ Ingress (September)

Last Aspect Dy Hr Mn			☽ Ingress	Dy Hr Mn
31 20:37	♇	⚹	♍	1 14:12
3 17:42	♂	⚹	♎	3 18:42
5 10:21	♄	□	♏	6 2:26
8 0:24	♀	□	♐	8 13:25
10 19:51	♀	△	♑	11 2:01
12 20:42	♄	☌	♒	13 13:44
15 3:35	♇	△	♓	15 22:53
17 18:23	☉	☍	♈	18 5:14
19 18:40	☿	☍	♉	20 9:31
22 10:02	☉	△	♊	22 12:39
24 9:20	☿	△	♋	24 15:23
26 15:52	☿	□	♌	26 18:16
28 4:03	♇	⚹	♍	28 21:58

Last Aspect / ☽ Ingress (October)

Last Aspect Dy Hr Mn			☽ Ingress	Dy Hr Mn
30 11:33	♀	☌	♎	1 3:19
2 18:29	♄	□	♏	3 11:07
5 17:14	♀	⚹	♐	5 21:40
7 14:35	♂	△	♑	8 10:06
10 5:06	♄	☌	♒	10 22:19
12 19:49	♂	☍	♓	13 8:07
14 23:23	♄	⚹	♈	15 14:30
17 14:50	☿	☍	♉	17 17:56
19 15:32	♂	□	♊	19 19:40
21 19:05	♂	⚹	♋	21 21:10
23 22:58	☉	□	♌	23 23:39
25 14:53	♀	⚹	♍	26 3:53
27 19:30	♄	△	♎	28 10:14
30 16:52	♀	☌	♏	30 18:46

☽ Phases & Eclipses

Dy Hr Mn		
2 5:19	●	8♍48
9 22:15	☽	16♐16
17 18:23	○	23♓55
24 16:32	☾	0♋41
1 17:09	●	7♎35
9 17:21	☽	15♑29
17 6:01	○	22♈56
17 6:03	☍	T 1.456
23 22:58	☾	29♋36
31 8:14	●	6♏59
31 8:00:17	☌	P 0.696

Astro Data

1 September 1902
Julian Day # 974
SVP 6♓36'59"
GC 25♐28.8 ⚵ 22♊05.3
Eris 23♓22.2R ⚴ 11♎57.0
⚷ 8♑59.8R ⚶ 15♑21.5
☽ Mean ☊ 27♎36.5

1 October 1902
Julian Day # 1004
SVP 6♓36'56"
GC 25♐28.9 ⚵ 4♋30.9
Eris 23♓01.1R ⚴ 22♎07.4
⚷ 9♑03.5 ⚶ 19♑43.4
☽ Mean ☊ 26♎01.2

November 1902 LONGITUDE

Day	Sid.Time	☉	0 hr ☽	Noon☽	True☊	☿	♀	♂	⚳	♃	♄	♅	♆	♇
1 Sa	14 39 21	8♏08 03	15♏04 42	21♏11 30	25♎18.9	19♎57.3	1♏15.7	4♍53.8	18♌33.0	8♒41.2	22♑14.6	19♐02.0	3♋33.2	19♊23.3
2 Su	14 43 18	9 08 09	27 15 55	3♐18 06	25R17.2	20 39.4	2 31.0	5 27.7	18 50.7	8 46.6	22 18.1	19 05.0	3R32.4	19R22.5
3 M	14 47 14	10 08 16	9♐18 20	15 16 52	25 15.0	21 29.3	3 46.3	6 01.6	19 08.3	8 52.2	22 21.7	19 08.0	3 31.6	19 21.6
4 Tu	14 51 11	11 08 25	21 14 00	27 10 07	25 12.4	22 26.0	5 01.6	6 35.3	19 25.6	8 58.0	22 25.3	19 11.0	3 30.7	19 20.8
5 W	14 55 07	12 08 36	3♑05 33	9♑00 47	25 10.0	23 28.9	6 16.9	7 09.0	19 42.7	9 03.9	22 29.1	19 14.1	3 29.8	19 19.9
6 Th	14 59 04	13 08 49	14 56 13	20 52 24	25 07.9	24 37.0	7 32.2	7 42.5	19 59.7	9 10.0	22 32.9	19 17.2	3 28.8	19 19.0
7 F	15 03 00	14 09 02	26 49 49	2♒49 01	25 06.6	25 49.7	8 47.5	8 15.9	20 16.4	9 16.3	22 36.8	19 20.3	3 27.9	19 18.1
8 Sa	15 06 57	15 09 18	8♒50 35	14 55 06	25D06.1	27 06.3	10 02.9	8 49.3	20 32.9	9 22.8	22 40.8	19 23.5	3 26.9	19 17.1
9 Su	15 10 53	16 09 35	21 03 08	27 15 16	25 06.5	28 26.3	11 18.2	9 22.5	20 49.2	9 29.4	22 44.9	19 26.7	3 25.9	19 16.2
10 M	15 14 50	17 09 53	3♓32 04	9♓54 03	25 07.7	29 49.0	12 33.6	9 55.6	21 05.3	9 36.1	22 49.0	19 29.9	3 24.8	19 15.3
11 Tu	15 18 47	18 10 12	16 21 41	22 55 23	25 09.3	1♏14.1	13 48.9	10 28.6	21 21.1	9 43.0	22 53.3	19 33.1	3 23.8	19 14.3
12 W	15 22 43	19 10 34	29 35 28	6♈22 10	25 10.7	2 41.2	15 04.3	11 01.5	21 36.7	9 50.1	22 57.6	19 36.3	3 22.7	19 13.3
13 Th	15 26 40	20 10 56	13♈15 33	20 15 35	25R11.6	4 09.9	16 19.6	11 34.3	21 52.1	9 57.3	23 01.9	19 39.6	3 21.5	19 12.3
14 F	15 30 36	21 11 20	27 22 01	4♉34 29	25 11.4	5 39.9	17 35.0	12 07.0	22 07.3	10 04.7	23 06.4	19 42.9	3 20.4	19 11.3
15 Sa	15 34 33	22 11 46	11♉52 24	19 15 01	25 09.9	7 11.1	18 50.4	12 39.6	22 22.2	10 12.3	23 10.9	19 46.2	3 19.2	19 10.3
16 Su	15 38 29	23 12 13	26 41 28	4♊10 43	25 07.0	8 43.1	20 05.8	13 12.1	22 36.9	10 20.0	23 15.5	19 49.6	3 18.0	19 09.3
17 M	15 42 26	24 12 42	11♊41 38	19 13 04	25 03.0	10 15.7	21 21.2	13 44.4	22 51.4	10 27.8	23 20.2	19 53.0	3 16.8	19 08.3
18 Tu	15 46 22	25 13 13	26 43 50	4♋12 50	24 58.6	11 49.0	22 36.6	14 16.6	23 05.6	10 35.8	23 25.0	19 56.3	3 15.6	19 07.2
19 W	15 50 19	26 13 45	11♋39 01	19 01 31	24 54.4	13 22.7	23 52.0	14 48.8	23 19.5	10 43.9	23 29.8	19 59.7	3 14.3	19 06.2
20 Th	15 54 16	27 14 19	26 19 33	3♌32 33	24 51.1	14 56.6	25 07.4	15 20.7	23 33.2	10 52.2	23 34.7	20 03.2	3 13.0	19 05.1
21 F	15 58 12	28 14 55	10♌40 07	17 42 00	24D49.2	16 30.9	26 22.8	15 52.6	23 46.6	11 00.6	23 39.7	20 06.6	3 11.7	19 04.0
22 Sa	16 02 09	29 15 33	24 38 08	1♍28 31	24 48.7	18 05.2	27 38.2	16 24.3	23 59.8	11 09.2	23 44.7	20 10.1	3 10.4	19 02.9
23 Su	16 06 05	0♐16 12	8♍13 21	14 52 50	24 49.5	19 39.7	28 53.7	16 56.0	24 12.6	11 17.8	23 49.8	20 13.5	3 09.0	19 01.9
24 M	16 10 02	1 16 53	21 27 18	27 57 05	24 51.1	21 14.3	0♐09.1	17 27.4	24 25.2	11 26.7	23 54.9	20 17.0	3 07.6	19 00.8
25 Tu	16 13 58	2 17 35	4♎22 32	10♎44 02	24 52.6	22 48.8	1 24.6	17 58.8	24 37.5	11 35.6	24 00.2	20 20.5	3 06.2	18 59.7
26 W	16 17 55	3 18 19	17 01 59	23 16 42	24R53.5	24 23.4	2 40.0	18 30.0	24 49.5	11 44.7	24 05.5	20 24.1	3 04.8	18 58.5
27 Th	16 21 51	4 19 05	29 28 32	5♏37 47	24 52.8	25 57.9	3 55.5	19 01.0	25 01.2	11 54.0	24 10.8	20 27.6	3 03.4	18 57.4
28 F	16 25 48	5 19 52	11♏44 45	17 49 39	24 50.2	27 32.4	5 10.9	19 31.9	25 12.6	12 03.4	24 16.3	20 31.1	3 01.9	18 56.3
29 Sa	16 29 45	6 20 41	23 52 45	29 54 13	24 45.5	29 06.9	6 26.4	20 02.7	25 23.7	12 12.8	24 21.7	20 34.7	3 00.5	18 55.2
30 Su	16 33 41	7 21 30	5♐54 16	11♐53 04	24 38.8	0♐41.3	7 41.9	20 33.3	25 34.5	12 22.5	24 27.3	20 38.3	2 59.0	18 54.0

December 1902 LONGITUDE

Day	Sid.Time	☉	0 hr ☽	Noon☽	True☊	☿	♀	♂	⚳	♃	♄	♅	♆	♇
1 M	16 37 38	8♐22 21	17♐50 48	23♐47 38	24♎30.5	2♐15.7	8♐57.4	21♍03.8	25♌45.0	12♒32.2	24♑32.9	20♐41.9	2♋57.5	18♊52.9
2 Tu	16 41 34	9 23 13	29 43 46	5♑39 26	24R21.3	3 50.0	10 12.9	21 34.1	25 55.1	12 42.1	24 38.6	20 45.4	2R56.0	18R51.7
3 W	16 45 31	10 24 06	11♑34 49	17 30 14	24 12.2	5 24.2	11 28.3	22 04.2	26 05.0	12 52.1	24 44.3	20 49.1	2 54.4	18 50.6
4 Th	16 49 27	11 25 00	23 25 57	29 22 20	24 03.9	6 58.4	12 43.8	22 34.2	26 14.4	13 02.2	24 50.1	20 52.7	2 52.9	18 49.4
5 F	16 53 24	12 25 55	5♒19 44	11♒18 36	23 57.3	8 32.6	13 59.3	23 04.0	26 23.6	13 12.4	24 55.9	20 56.3	2 51.3	18 48.3
6 Sa	16 57 20	13 26 51	17 19 22	23 22 33	23 52.8	10 06.8	15 14.8	23 33.7	26 32.4	13 22.8	25 01.8	20 59.9	2 49.7	18 47.1
7 Su	17 01 17	14 27 47	29 28 41	5♓38 19	23D50.4	11 41.0	16 30.2	24 03.1	26 40.8	13 33.2	25 07.7	21 03.5	2 48.1	18 46.0
8 M	17 05 14	15 28 44	11♓52 02	18 10 25	23 50.0	13 15.1	17 45.7	24 32.4	26 49.0	13 43.8	25 13.7	21 07.2	2 46.5	18 44.8
9 Tu	17 09 10	16 29 42	24 34 03	1♈03 29	23 50.8	14 49.3	19 01.2	25 01.6	26 56.7	13 54.5	25 19.8	21 10.8	2 44.9	18 43.6
10 W	17 13 07	17 30 40	7♈39 13	14 21 42	23R51.8	16 23.5	20 16.6	25 30.5	27 04.1	14 05.3	25 25.8	21 14.4	2 43.3	18 42.5
11 Th	17 17 03	18 31 39	21 11 16	28 08 09	23 52.1	17 57.8	21 32.1	25 59.3	27 11.1	14 16.2	25 32.0	21 18.1	2 41.7	18 41.3
12 F	17 21 00	19 32 38	5♉12 22	12♉23 49	23 50.5	19 32.2	22 47.6	26 27.9	27 17.8	14 27.2	25 38.2	21 21.7	2 40.0	18 40.1
13 Sa	17 24 56	20 33 38	19 42 10	27 06 50	23 46.7	21 06.6	24 03.0	26 56.2	27 24.1	14 38.3	25 44.4	21 25.4	2 38.4	18 39.0
14 Su	17 28 53	21 34 39	4♊37 01	12♊11 43	23 40.3	22 41.1	25 18.5	27 24.5	27 30.0	14 49.5	25 50.7	21 29.0	2 36.7	18 37.8
15 M	17 32 49	22 35 41	19 49 42	27 29 37	23 31.9	24 15.7	26 34.0	27 52.5	27 35.5	15 00.8	25 57.0	21 32.7	2 35.1	18 36.7
16 Tu	17 36 46	23 36 43	5♋10 01	12♋49 24	23 22.4	25 50.5	27 49.4	28 20.3	27 40.6	15 12.2	26 03.4	21 36.3	2 33.4	18 35.5
17 W	17 40 43	24 37 46	20 26 22	27 59 34	23 13.1	27 25.4	29 04.9	28 47.9	27 45.4	15 23.7	26 09.8	21 40.0	2 31.7	18 34.3
18 Th	17 44 39	25 38 50	5♌27 53	12♌50 22	23 05.0	29 00.5	0♑20.3	29 15.3	27 49.7	15 35.3	26 16.2	21 43.6	2 30.0	18 33.2
19 F	17 48 36	26 39 54	20 06 19	27 15 16	22 59.1	0♑35.7	1 35.8	29 42.5	27 53.7	15 46.9	26 22.7	21 47.3	2 28.3	18 32.0
20 Sa	17 52 32	27 41 00	4♍16 58	11♍11 22	22 55.6	2 11.1	2 51.2	0♎09.5	27 57.2	15 58.7	26 29.2	21 50.9	2 26.6	18 30.9
21 Su	17 56 29	28 42 06	17 58 39	24 39 04	22D54.3	3 46.7	4 06.7	0 36.2	28 00.3	16 10.6	26 35.8	21 54.5	2 24.9	18 29.7
22 M	18 00 25	29 43 12	1♎13 02	7♎41 02	22 54.4	5 22.5	5 22.1	1 02.7	28 03.0	16 22.5	26 42.4	21 58.2	2 23.2	18 28.6
23 Tu	18 04 22	0♑44 20	14 03 35	20 21 16	22R54.8	6 58.4	6 37.6	1 29.0	28 05.3	16 34.6	26 49.0	22 01.8	2 21.5	18 27.4
24 W	18 08 18	1 45 28	26 34 40	2♏44 20	22 54.4	8 34.6	7 53.1	1 55.1	28 07.2	16 46.7	26 55.6	22 05.4	2 19.8	18 26.3
25 Th	18 12 15	2 46 37	8♏50 48	14 54 36	22 52.1	10 10.9	9 08.5	2 20.9	28 08.6	16 58.9	27 02.3	22 09.0	2 18.1	18 25.2
26 F	18 16 12	3 47 47	20 56 11	26 56 01	22 47.0	11 47.4	10 24.0	2 46.5	28 09.6	17 11.2	27 09.1	22 12.6	2 16.4	18 24.1
27 Sa	18 20 08	4 48 57	2♐54 27	8♐51 50	22 38.9	13 24.1	11 39.4	3 11.8	28R10.2	17 23.6	27 15.8	22 16.2	2 14.7	18 22.9
28 Su	18 24 05	5 50 07	14 48 28	20 44 36	22 28.0	15 01.0	12 54.9	3 36.8	28 10.3	17 36.0	27 22.6	22 19.8	2 13.0	18 21.8
29 M	18 28 01	6 51 17	26 40 27	2♑36 13	22 14.7	16 37.9	14 10.3	4 01.6	28 10.0	17 48.5	27 29.4	22 23.4	2 11.3	18 20.7
30 Tu	18 31 58	7 52 28	8♑32 03	14 28 07	22 00.1	18 14.9	15 25.7	4 26.1	28 09.3	18 01.2	27 36.3	22 26.9	2 09.6	18 19.6
31 W	18 35 54	8 53 39	20 24 34	26 21 34	21 45.4	19 51.9	16 41.2	4 50.3	28 08.1	18 13.8	27 43.2	22 30.5	2 08.0	18 18.5

Astro Data	Planet Ingress	Last Aspect	☽ Ingress	Last Aspect	☽ Ingress	☽ Phases & Eclipses
Dy Hr Mn	Dy Hr Mn	Dy Hr Mn	Dy Hr Mn	Dy Hr Mn	Dy Hr Mn	Dy Hr Mn
♅☍♇ 6 22:42	☿ ♏ 10 15:08	1 14:05 ♄ ⚹	♐ 2 5:26	1 6:14 ♂ □	♑ 2 0:33	8 12:30 ☽ 15♒11
☽0N 11 13:18	☉ ♐ 23 5:36	4 1:34 ☿ ⚹	♑ 4 17:44	4 2:46 ♄ ☌	♒ 4 13:16	15 17:06 ○ 22♉25
☽0S 24 4:17	♀ ♐ 24 9:06	6 20:23 ☿ □	♒ 7 6:22	6 7:16 ♅ ⚹	♓ 7 1:01	22 7:47 ☾ 29♌05
	☿ ♐ 30 1:30	9 14:33 ☿ △	♓ 9 17:16	9 1:20 ♄ ⚹	♈ 9 10:03	30 2:04 ● 6♐56
☽0N 8 23:09		11 11:56 ♄ ⚹	♈ 12 0:44	11 7:30 ♄ □	♉ 11 15:11	
☽0S 21 11:31	♀ ♑ 18 5:32	13 16:44 ♄ □	♉ 14 4:24	13 11:42 ♂ △	♊ 13 16:38	8 6:27 ☽ 15♓15
♃⚼♆ 26 20:58	☿ ♑ 19 3:01	15 18:23 ♄ △	♊ 16 5:19	15 12:37 ♂ □	♋ 15 15:55	15 3:47 ○ 22♊15
⚳R 28 7:39	♂ ♎ 20 3:33	17 13:04 ♅ ☍	♋ 18 5:14	17 13:20 ♂ ⚹	♌ 17 15:13	21 20:00 ☾ 29♍02
♃△♇ 31 20:12	☉ ♑ 22 18:36	20 0:44 ☉ △	♌ 20 6:05	19 10:56 ☉ △	♍ 19 16:40	29 21:25 ● 7♑15
		22 7:47 ☉ □	♍ 22 9:24	21 20:00 ☉ □	♎ 21 21:46	
		24 4:29 ♄ △	♎ 24 15:49	24 0:35 ♄ □	♏ 24 6:39	
		26 13:35 ♄ □	♏ 27 1:01	26 12:26 ♄ ⚹	♐ 26 18:09	
		29 10:11 ☿ ☌	♐ 29 12:12	28 15:14 ♅ ☌	♑ 29 6:44	
				31 14:46 ♄ ☌	♒ 31 19:20	

Astro Data

1 November 1902
Julian Day # 1035
SVP 6♓36'54"
GC 25♐28.9 ⚵ 14♋01.8
Eris 22♓42.4R ⚶ 2♏52.4
⚷ 10♑21.2 ⚴ 29♑03.8
☽ Mean ☊ 24♎22.7

1 December 1902
Julian Day # 1065
SVP 6♓36'49"
GC 25♐29.0 ⚵ 16♋02.2R
Eris 22♓32.9R ⚶ 13♏03.0
⚷ 12♑33.2 ⚴ 10♒50.3
☽ Mean ☊ 22♎47.3

LONGITUDE — January 1903

Day	Sid.Time	☉	0 hr ☽	Noon ☽	True ☊	☿	♀	♂	⚳	♃	♄	♅	♆	♇
1 Th	18 39 51	9♑54 50	2♒19 16	8♒17 52	21♎31.8	21♑28.9	17♑56.6	5♎14.3	28♌06.5	18♒26.6	27♑50.1	22♐34.0	2♋06.3	18♊17.5
2 F	18 43 47	10 56 01	14 17 36	20 18 42	21R20.3	23 05.8	19 12.0	5 37.9	28R04.4	18 39.4	27 57.0	22 37.5	2R04.6	18R16.4
3 Sa	18 47 44	11 57 11	26 21 29	2♓26 18	21 11.6	24 42.5	20 27.5	6 01.3	28 01.9	18 52.3	28 03.9	22 41.0	2 02.9	18 15.3
4 Su	18 51 41	12 58 22	8♓33 30	14 43 33	21 06.0	26 18.9	21 42.9	6 24.3	27 59.0	19 05.2	28 10.9	22 44.5	2 01.2	18 14.3
5 M	18 55 37	13 59 32	20 56 53	27 14 01	21 03.1	27 54.9	22 58.3	6 47.1	27 55.6	19 18.3	28 17.8	22 48.0	1 59.6	18 13.2
6 Tu	18 59 34	15 00 41	3♈35 28	10♈01 47	21 02.3	29 30.3	24 13.6	7 09.5	27 51.8	19 31.3	28 24.8	22 51.5	1 57.9	18 12.2
7 W	19 03 30	16 01 50	16 33 29	23 11 05	21 02.2	1♒04.9	25 29.0	7 31.6	27 47.6	19 44.5	28 31.9	22 54.9	1 56.3	18 11.2
8 Th	19 07 27	17 02 59	29 55 00	6♉45 38	21 01.7	2 38.5	26 44.4	7 53.4	27 42.9	19 57.7	28 38.9	22 58.3	1 54.6	18 10.2
9 F	19 11 23	18 04 08	13♉43 14	20 47 55	20 59.4	4 10.9	27 59.8	8 14.9	27 37.8	20 10.9	28 45.9	23 01.7	1 53.0	18 09.2
10 Sa	19 15 20	19 05 15	27 59 37	5♊18 05	20 54.6	5 41.7	29 15.1	8 36.0	27 32.2	20 24.3	28 53.0	23 05.1	1 51.4	18 08.2
11 Su	19 19 16	20 06 23	12♊42 47	20 13 01	20 46.9	7 10.6	0♒30.4	8 56.8	27 26.3	20 37.6	29 00.1	23 08.5	1 49.8	18 07.2
12 M	19 23 13	21 07 30	27 47 47	5♋25 55	20 36.7	8 37.3	1 45.8	9 17.2	27 19.9	20 51.1	29 07.1	23 11.8	1 48.2	18 06.3
13 Tu	19 27 10	22 08 36	13♋06 02	20 46 42	20 25.1	10 01.2	3 01.1	9 37.2	27 13.1	21 04.6	29 14.2	23 15.1	1 46.6	18 05.3
14 W	19 31 06	23 09 42	28 26 22	6♌03 34	20 13.4	11 21.7	4 16.4	9 56.9	27 06.0	21 18.1	29 21.3	23 18.4	1 45.1	18 04.4
15 Th	19 35 03	24 10 48	13♌36 54	21 05 11	20 03.0	12 38.4	5 31.7	10 16.2	26 58.4	21 31.7	29 28.5	23 21.7	1 43.5	18 03.5
16 F	19 38 59	25 11 53	28 27 23	5♍42 44	19 54.9	13 50.6	6 47.0	10 35.2	26 50.4	21 45.3	29 35.6	23 24.9	1 42.0	18 02.6
17 Sa	19 42 56	26 12 58	12♍50 44	19 51 06	19 49.6	14 57.5	8 02.2	10 53.7	26 42.0	21 59.0	29 42.7	23 28.2	1 40.5	18 01.7
18 Su	19 46 52	27 14 02	26 43 46	3♎28 52	19 47.0	15 58.4	9 17.5	11 11.8	26 33.2	22 12.7	29 49.8	23 31.4	1 38.9	18 00.8
19 M	19 50 49	28 15 06	10♎06 42	16 37 43	19 46.2	16 52.3	10 32.8	11 29.5	26 24.1	22 26.5	29 57.0	23 34.5	1 37.4	17 59.9
20 Tu	19 54 46	29 16 10	23 02 24	29 21 22	19 46.3	17 38.6	11 48.0	11 46.8	26 14.5	22 40.3	0♒04.1	23 37.7	1 36.0	17 59.1
21 W	19 58 42	0♒17 14	5♏35 14	11♏44 40	19 45.8	18 16.2	13 03.2	12 03.7	26 04.7	22 54.1	0 11.2	23 40.8	1 34.5	17 58.3
22 Th	20 02 39	1 18 17	17 50 18	23 52 46	19 43.7	18 44.3	14 18.5	12 20.1	25 54.4	23 08.0	0 18.3	23 43.9	1 33.1	17 57.4
23 F	20 06 35	2 19 20	29 52 43	5♐50 41	19 39.2	19 02.3	15 33.7	12 36.1	25 43.9	23 22.0	0 25.5	23 46.9	1 31.7	17 56.6
24 Sa	20 10 32	3 20 22	11♐47 14	17 42 51	19 31.7	19R09.4	16 48.9	12 51.6	25 33.0	23 35.9	0 32.6	23 50.0	1 30.3	17 55.9
25 Su	20 14 28	4 21 24	23 37 58	29 32 58	19 21.4	19 05.2	18 04.1	13 06.6	25 21.8	23 49.9	0 39.8	23 53.0	1 28.9	17 55.1
26 M	20 18 25	5 22 24	5♑28 12	11♑23 58	19 08.8	18 49.6	19 19.2	13 21.1	25 10.3	24 04.0	0 46.9	23 56.0	1 27.5	17 54.3
27 Tu	20 22 21	6 23 25	17 20 30	23 18 00	18 54.8	18 22.6	20 34.4	13 35.1	24 58.5	24 18.1	0 54.0	23 58.9	1 26.2	17 53.6
28 W	20 26 18	7 24 24	29 16 39	5♒16 36	18 40.6	17 44.7	21 49.6	13 48.7	24 46.4	24 32.2	1 01.1	24 01.8	1 24.9	17 52.9
29 Th	20 30 15	8 25 22	11♒17 57	17 20 51	18 27.4	16 56.8	23 04.7	14 01.7	24 34.1	24 46.3	1 08.2	24 04.7	1 23.6	17 52.2
30 F	20 34 11	9 26 19	23 25 23	29 31 43	18 16.3	16 00.2	24 19.8	14 14.1	24 21.5	25 00.5	1 15.3	24 07.5	1 22.3	17 51.5
31 Sa	20 38 08	10 27 16	5♓39 57	11♓50 17	18 07.8	14 56.3	25 34.9	14 26.1	24 08.7	25 14.7	1 22.4	24 10.3	1 21.0	17 50.9

LONGITUDE — February 1903

Day	Sid.Time	☉	0 hr ☽	Noon ☽	True ☊	☿	♀	♂	⚳	♃	♄	♅	♆	♇
1 Su	20 42 04	11♒28 11	18♓02 55	24♓18 04	18♎02.4	13♒47.1	26♒50.0	14♎37.4	23♌55.7	25♒28.9	1♒29.5	24♐13.1	1♋19.8	17♊50.2
2 M	20 46 01	12 29 04	0♈36 00	6♈57 02	17D59.8	12R34.6	28 05.0	14 48.3	23R42.5	25 43.1	1 36.5	24 15.8	1R18.6	17R49.6
3 Tu	20 49 57	13 29 57	13 21 30	19 49 47	17 59.2	11 21.0	29 20.1	14 58.5	23 29.1	25 57.4	1 43.6	24 18.5	1 17.4	17 49.0
4 W	20 53 54	14 30 48	26 22 13	2♉59 12	17R59.7	10 08.3	0♓35.1	15 08.2	23 15.6	26 11.7	1 50.6	24 21.2	1 16.3	17 48.4
5 Th	20 57 50	15 31 37	9♉41 06	16 28 14	18 00.1	8 58.5	1 50.1	15 17.3	23 01.9	26 26.0	1 57.6	24 23.8	1 15.1	17 47.9
6 F	21 01 47	16 32 25	23 20 51	0♊19 07	17 59.2	7 53.1	3 05.0	15 25.8	22 48.2	26 40.3	2 04.6	24 26.4	1 14.0	17 47.3
7 Sa	21 05 43	17 33 12	7♊23 07	14 32 45	17 56.2	6 53.6	4 20.0	15 33.7	22 34.3	26 54.7	2 11.6	24 29.0	1 13.0	17 46.8
8 Su	21 09 40	18 33 57	21 47 45	29 07 42	17 50.9	6 00.9	5 34.9	15 40.9	22 20.3	27 09.0	2 18.6	24 31.5	1 11.9	17 46.3
9 M	21 13 37	19 34 40	6♋31 58	13♋59 45	17 43.4	5 15.8	6 49.8	15 47.6	22 06.3	27 23.4	2 25.5	24 34.0	1 10.9	17 45.8
10 Tu	21 17 33	20 35 22	21 30 03	29 01 45	17 34.5	4 38.6	8 04.7	15 53.6	21 52.2	27 37.8	2 32.4	24 36.4	1 09.9	17 45.3
11 W	21 21 30	21 36 03	6♌33 38	14♌04 28	17 25.4	4 09.5	9 19.5	15 58.9	21 38.1	27 52.2	2 39.3	24 38.8	1 08.9	17 44.9
12 Th	21 25 26	22 36 42	21 32 59	28 58 01	17 17.2	3 48.5	10 34.3	16 03.6	21 24.0	28 06.6	2 46.2	24 41.1	1 08.0	17 44.5
13 F	21 29 23	23 37 20	6♍18 32	13♍33 39	17 10.8	3 35.3	11 49.1	16 07.6	21 09.9	28 21.0	2 53.0	24 43.4	1 07.1	17 44.1
14 Sa	21 33 19	24 37 56	20 42 38	27 45 01	17 06.8	3D29.8	13 03.9	16 10.9	20 55.9	28 35.4	2 59.8	24 45.7	1 06.2	17 43.7
15 Su	21 37 16	25 38 31	4♎40 29	11♎28 55	17D05.0	3 31.4	14 18.6	16 13.6	20 41.8	28 49.8	3 06.6	24 47.9	1 05.3	17 43.3
16 M	21 41 12	26 39 05	18 10 24	24 45 07	17 05.1	3 39.9	15 33.3	16 15.5	20 27.9	29 04.3	3 13.4	24 50.1	1 04.5	17 43.0
17 Tu	21 45 09	27 39 37	1♏13 27	7♏35 48	17 06.2	3 54.7	16 48.0	16 16.7	20 14.0	29 18.7	3 20.1	24 52.3	1 03.7	17 42.7
18 W	21 49 06	28 40 08	13 52 42	20 04 45	17R07.4	4 15.4	18 02.7	16R17.2	20 00.2	29 33.2	3 26.8	24 54.4	1 03.0	17 42.4
19 Th	21 53 02	29 40 38	26 12 32	2♐16 41	17 07.7	4 41.6	19 17.3	16 16.9	19 46.6	29 47.6	3 33.5	24 56.4	1 02.2	17 42.1
20 F	21 56 59	0♓41 07	8♐17 52	14 16 42	17 06.5	5 12.9	20 31.9	16 15.9	19 33.1	0♓02.1	3 40.1	24 58.4	1 01.5	17 41.9
21 Sa	22 00 55	1 41 35	20 13 47	26 09 45	17 03.4	5 49.0	21 46.5	16 14.1	19 19.7	0 16.5	3 46.8	25 00.4	1 00.9	17 41.6
22 Su	22 04 52	2 42 01	2♑05 07	8♑00 25	16 58.2	6 29.3	23 01.0	16 11.6	19 06.5	0 31.0	3 53.3	25 02.3	1 00.2	17 41.4
23 M	22 08 48	3 42 25	13 56 09	19 52 43	16 51.4	7 13.7	24 15.6	16 08.3	18 53.5	0 45.4	3 59.9	25 04.2	0 59.6	17 41.2
24 Tu	22 12 45	4 42 48	25 50 31	1♒49 53	16 43.5	8 01.8	25 30.1	16 04.2	18 40.7	0 59.8	4 06.4	25 06.0	0 59.0	17 41.1
25 W	22 16 41	5 43 10	7♒51 06	13 54 25	16 35.3	8 53.3	26 44.5	15 59.4	18 28.2	1 14.3	4 12.8	25 07.8	0 58.5	17 40.9
26 Th	22 20 38	6 43 30	20 00 01	26 08 03	16 27.7	9 48.0	27 59.0	15 53.8	18 15.9	1 28.7	4 19.2	25 09.5	0 58.0	17 40.8
27 F	22 24 35	7 43 48	2♓18 38	8♓31 52	16 21.3	10 45.6	29 13.4	15 47.3	18 03.8	1 43.1	4 25.6	25 11.2	0 57.5	17 40.7
28 Sa	22 28 31	8 44 04	14 47 49	21 06 32	16 16.7	11 45.9	0♈27.7	15 40.1	17 52.0	1 57.5	4 31.9	25 12.8	0 57.1	17 40.7

Astro Data Dy Hr Mn	Planet Ingress Dy Hr Mn	Last Aspect Dy Hr Mn	☽ Ingress Dy Hr Mn	Last Aspect Dy Hr Mn	☽ Ingress Dy Hr Mn	☽ Phases & Eclipses Dy Hr Mn
♂0S 2 7:37	☿ ♒ 6 19:31	2 16:37 ♅ ⚹	♓ 3 7:12	1 11:51 ♅ □	♈ 1 22:52	6 21:57 ☽ 15♈26
☽0N 5 7:28	♀ ♒ 11 2:18	5 14:02 ♄ ⚹	♈ 5 17:14	3 23:27 ♃ ⚹	♉ 4 6:36	13 14:17 ○ 22♋14
☽0S 17 21:13	♄ ♒ 19 22:15	7 21:38 ♄ □	♉ 8 0:09	6 5:38 ♃ □	♊ 6 11:27	20 11:49 ☾ 29♎16
☿R 24 15:16	☉ ♒ 21 5:14	10 1:23 ♄ △	♊ 10 3:19	8 8:43 ♃ △	♋ 8 13:25	28 16:38 ● 7♒36
♃⚹♅ 25 18:36		11 16:39 ♅ ☍	♋ 12 3:28	9 14:54 ♂ □	♌ 10 13:33	
♄⊼♆ 31 8:01	♀ ♓ 4 0:47	14 1:21 ♄ ☍	♌ 14 2:27	12 10:35 ♃ ☍	♍ 12 13:41	5 10:12 ☽ 15♉27
	☉ ♓ 19 19:41	15 15:42 ♅ △	♍ 16 2:32	14 6:52 ♅ □	♎ 14 15:53	12 0:58 ○ 22♌09
☽0N 1 14:19	♃ ♓ 20 8:35	18 5:26 ♄ △	♎ 18 5:47	16 20:08 ♃ △	♏ 16 21:43	19 6:23 ☾ 29♏26
♄⚼♇ 12 6:22	♀ ♈ 28 3:03	20 11:49 ☉ □	♏ 20 13:14	19 6:58 ♃ □	♐ 19 7:29	27 10:19 ● 7♓40
☽0S 14 8:27		22 10:29 ♃ □	♐ 23 0:15	21 9:39 ♅ ☌	♑ 21 19:46	
☿D 14 18:21		25 0:28 ♅ ☌	♑ 25 12:55	23 21:51 ♀ ⚹	♒ 24 8:20	
♂R 18 15:34		26 16:02 ♂ □	♒ 28 1:27	26 10:06 ♅ ⚹	♓ 26 19:31	
♃△♆ 24 10:43		30 2:57 ♃ ☌	♓ 30 12:55			
☽0N 28 20:53						

Astro Data

1 January 1903
Julian Day # 1096
SVP 6♓36'44"
GC 25♐29.1 ⚵ 8♋11.4R
Eris 22♓35.2 ⚴ 22♏45.8
⚷ 15♑23.3 ⚶ 24♒34.2
☽ Mean ☊ 21♎08.9

1 February 1903
Julian Day # 1127
SVP 6♓36'39"
GC 25♐29.2 ⚵ 1♋03.7R
Eris 22♓49.4 ⚴ 0♐51.9
⚷ 18♑17.8 ⚶ 9♓06.1
☽ Mean ☊ 19♎30.4

March 1903 LONGITUDE

Day	Sid.Time	☉	0 hr ☽	Noon ☽	True ☊	☿	♀	♂	⚳	♃	♄	♅	♆	♇
1 Su	22 32 28	9♓44 19	27♓28 03	3♈52 27	16♎14.1	12♒48.9	1♈42.1	15♎32.1	17♌40.5	2♓11.9	4♒38.2	25♐14.4	0♋56.7	17♊40.6
2 M	22 36 24	10 44 31	10♈19 45	16 50 01	16D 13.3	13 54.2	2 56.4	15R 23.4	17R 29.3	2 26.3	4 44.5	25 15.9	0R 56.3	17D 40.6
3 Tu	22 40 21	11 44 42	23 23 21	29 59 49	16 14.0	15 01.7	4 10.6	15 13.8	17 18.4	2 40.7	4 50.7	25 17.4	0 55.9	17 40.6
4 W	22 44 17	12 44 51	6♉39 31	13♉22 34	16 15.5	16 11.4	5 24.9	15 03.5	17 07.8	2 55.0	4 56.8	25 18.9	0 55.6	17 40.6
5 Th	22 48 14	13 44 57	20 09 04	26 59 06	16 17.1	17 23.1	6 39.1	14 52.4	16 57.6	3 09.4	5 02.9	25 20.3	0 55.3	17 40.6
6 F	22 52 10	14 45 02	3♊52 44	10♊49 59	16R 18.0	18 36.6	7 53.2	14 40.6	16 47.7	3 23.7	5 09.0	25 21.6	0 55.1	17 40.7
7 Sa	22 56 07	15 45 04	17 50 49	24 55 09	16 17.7	19 52.0	9 07.3	14 28.0	16 38.2	3 38.0	5 15.0	25 22.9	0 54.9	17 40.8
8 Su	23 00 04	16 45 04	2♋02 47	9♋13 26	16 16.0	21 09.1	10 21.4	14 14.7	16 29.0	3 52.3	5 21.0	25 24.1	0 54.7	17 40.9
9 M	23 04 00	17 45 02	16 26 43	23 42 07	16 13.2	22 27.8	11 35.4	14 00.6	16 20.3	4 06.5	5 26.9	25 25.3	0 54.6	17 41.0
10 Tu	23 07 57	18 44 58	0♌59 04	8♌16 53	16 09.4	23 48.1	12 49.4	13 45.9	16 11.9	4 20.8	5 32.7	25 26.4	0 54.5	17 41.2
11 W	23 11 53	19 44 51	15 34 47	22 51 59	16 05.5	25 09.9	14 03.3	13 30.5	16 03.9	4 35.0	5 38.5	25 27.5	0 54.4	17 41.3
12 Th	23 15 50	20 44 43	0♍07 39	7♍20 58	16 01.9	26 33.2	15 17.2	13 14.4	15 56.3	4 49.2	5 44.3	25 28.6	0D 54.4	17 41.5
13 F	23 19 46	21 44 32	14 31 10	21 37 33	15 59.2	27 58.0	16 31.0	12 57.6	15 49.0	5 03.3	5 50.0	25 29.5	0 54.3	17 41.7
14 Sa	23 23 43	22 44 20	28 39 29	5♎36 30	15D 57.7	29 24.1	17 44.8	12 40.2	15 42.2	5 17.5	5 55.6	25 30.5	0 54.4	17 42.0
15 Su	23 27 39	23 44 05	12♎28 12	19 14 20	15 57.4	0♓51.7	18 58.6	12 22.2	15 35.9	5 31.6	6 01.2	25 31.3	0 54.4	17 42.2
16 M	23 31 36	24 43 49	25 54 47	2♏29 32	15 58.1	2 20.6	20 12.3	12 03.6	15 29.9	5 45.6	6 06.7	25 32.2	0 54.5	17 42.5
17 Tu	23 35 32	25 43 31	8♏58 44	15 22 35	15 59.5	3 50.8	21 25.9	11 44.4	15 24.3	5 59.7	6 12.2	25 32.9	0 54.7	17 42.8
18 W	23 39 29	26 43 11	21 41 24	27 55 34	16 01.0	5 22.4	22 39.6	11 24.7	15 19.2	6 13.7	6 17.6	25 33.7	0 54.8	17 43.2
19 Th	23 43 26	27 42 49	4♐05 32	10♐11 49	16 02.4	6 55.3	23 53.1	11 04.4	15 14.5	6 27.6	6 22.9	25 34.3	0 55.0	17 43.5
20 F	23 47 22	28 42 26	16 14 56	22 15 29	16R 03.2	8 29.5	25 06.7	10 43.7	15 10.2	6 41.6	6 28.2	25 35.0	0 55.3	17 43.9
21 Sa	23 51 19	29 42 01	28 14 03	4♑11 12	16 03.3	10 05.0	26 20.2	10 22.6	15 06.3	6 55.5	6 33.4	25 35.5	0 55.5	17 44.3
22 Su	23 55 15	0♈41 34	10♑07 33	16 03 42	16 02.6	11 41.7	27 33.6	10 01.0	15 02.9	7 09.4	6 38.6	25 36.0	0 55.8	17 44.7
23 M	23 59 12	1 41 05	22 00 11	27 57 34	16 01.3	13 19.8	28 47.0	9 39.1	14 59.9	7 23.2	6 43.7	25 36.5	0 56.2	17 45.1
24 Tu	0 03 08	2 40 35	3♒56 23	9♒57 05	15 59.5	14 59.2	0♉00.4	9 16.9	14 57.4	7 37.0	6 48.7	25 36.9	0 56.5	17 45.6
25 W	0 07 05	3 40 02	16 00 07	22 05 53	15 57.6	16 39.9	1 13.7	8 54.3	14 55.3	7 50.7	6 53.6	25 37.3	0 56.9	17 46.0
26 Th	0 11 01	4 39 28	28 14 44	4♓26 56	15 55.9	18 22.0	2 26.9	8 31.5	14 53.6	8 04.4	6 58.5	25 37.6	0 57.4	17 46.5
27 F	0 14 58	5 38 52	10♓42 44	17 02 18	15 54.5	20 05.3	3 40.1	8 08.5	14 52.4	8 18.1	7 03.3	25 37.8	0 57.8	17 47.1
28 Sa	0 18 55	6 38 14	23 25 45	29 53 08	15 53.7	21 50.0	4 53.3	7 45.4	14 51.5	8 31.7	7 08.1	25 38.0	0 58.3	17 47.6
29 Su	0 22 51	7 37 34	6♈24 26	12♈59 37	15D 53.3	23 36.1	6 06.4	7 22.1	14D 51.2	8 45.2	7 12.8	25 38.2	0 58.9	17 48.2
30 M	0 26 48	8 36 52	19 38 34	26 21 08	15 53.4	25 23.5	7 19.4	6 58.8	14 51.2	8 58.8	7 17.4	25 38.2	0 59.4	17 48.7
31 Tu	0 30 44	9 36 07	3♉07 07	9♉56 20	15 53.8	27 12.3	8 32.4	6 35.4	14 51.7	9 12.2	7 21.9	25R 38.3	1 00.0	17 49.3

April 1903 LONGITUDE

Day	Sid.Time	☉	0 hr ☽	Noon ☽	True ☊	☿	♀	♂	⚳	♃	♄	♅	♆	♇
1 W	0 34 41	10♈35 21	16♉48 31	23♉43 25	15♎54.3	29♓02.5	9♉45.4	6♎12.1	14♌52.7	9♓25.6	7♒26.3	25♐38.3	1♋00.7	17♊50.0
2 Th	0 38 37	11 34 32	0♊40 47	7♊40 19	15 54.8	0♈54.0	10 58.2	5R 48.9	14 54.0	9 39.0	7 30.7	25R 38.2	1 01.3	17 50.6
3 F	0 42 34	12 33 41	14 41 46	21 44 51	15 55.2	2 47.0	12 11.1	5 25.8	14 55.8	9 52.3	7 35.0	25 38.1	1 02.0	17 51.3
4 Sa	0 46 30	13 32 48	28 49 16	5♋54 44	15R 55.3	4 41.3	13 23.8	5 02.9	14 58.0	10 05.6	7 39.2	25 37.9	1 02.8	17 52.0
5 Su	0 50 27	14 31 52	13♋00 59	20 07 43	15 55.3	6 37.0	14 36.6	4 40.2	15 00.6	10 18.7	7 43.4	25 37.7	1 03.5	17 52.7
6 M	0 54 24	15 30 54	27 14 37	4♌21 22	15D 55.3	8 34.1	15 49.2	4 17.7	15 03.7	10 31.9	7 47.5	25 37.4	1 04.3	17 53.4
7 Tu	0 58 20	16 29 54	11♌27 38	18 33 05	15 55.3	10 32.6	17 01.8	3 55.6	15 07.1	10 45.0	7 51.5	25 37.1	1 05.2	17 54.1
8 W	1 02 17	17 28 51	25 37 21	2♍40 04	15 55.4	12 32.3	18 14.3	3 33.7	15 10.9	10 58.0	7 55.4	25 36.7	1 06.0	17 54.9
9 Th	1 06 13	18 27 46	9♍40 51	16 39 21	15 55.6	14 33.3	19 26.8	3 12.3	15 15.2	11 10.9	7 59.2	25 36.3	1 06.9	17 55.6
10 F	1 10 10	19 26 39	23 35 11	0♎28 01	15 55.9	16 35.5	20 39.2	2 51.3	15 19.8	11 23.8	8 03.0	25 35.8	1 07.8	17 56.4
11 Sa	1 14 06	20 25 30	7♎17 32	14 03 27	15R 56.0	18 38.9	21 51.5	2 30.7	15 24.8	11 36.6	8 06.6	25 35.3	1 08.8	17 57.2
12 Su	1 18 03	21 24 18	20 45 30	27 23 32	15 55.9	20 43.2	23 03.7	2 10.6	15 30.3	11 49.4	8 10.2	25 34.7	1 09.8	17 58.1
13 M	1 21 59	22 23 05	3♏57 23	10♏27 00	15 55.4	22 48.5	24 15.9	1 51.0	15 36.1	12 02.1	8 13.7	25 34.1	1 10.8	17 58.9
14 Tu	1 25 56	23 21 50	16 52 24	23 13 37	15 54.7	24 54.5	25 28.1	1 31.9	15 42.2	12 14.7	8 17.1	25 33.4	1 11.8	17 59.8
15 W	1 29 53	24 20 33	29 30 48	5♐44 08	15 53.6	27 01.0	26 40.1	1 13.4	15 48.8	12 27.2	8 20.5	25 32.7	1 12.9	18 00.7
16 Th	1 33 49	25 19 14	11♐53 55	18 00 27	15 52.4	29 07.9	27 52.1	0 55.5	15 55.7	12 39.7	8 23.7	25 31.9	1 14.0	18 01.6
17 F	1 37 46	26 17 54	24 04 08	0♑05 21	15 51.2	1♉14.8	29 04.0	0 38.3	16 02.9	12 52.1	8 26.9	25 31.1	1 15.1	18 02.5
18 Sa	1 41 42	27 16 31	6♑04 37	12 02 25	15 50.3	3 21.7	0♊15.9	0 21.6	16 10.6	13 04.5	8 30.0	25 30.3	1 16.3	18 03.4
19 Su	1 45 39	28 15 08	17 59 18	23 55 48	15D 49.8	5 28.1	1 27.7	0 05.7	16 18.6	13 16.7	8 33.0	25 29.4	1 17.5	18 04.4
20 M	1 49 35	29 13 42	29 52 31	5♒50 02	15 49.8	7 33.7	2 39.4	29♍50.4	16 26.9	13 28.9	8 35.9	25 28.4	1 18.7	18 05.3
21 Tu	1 53 32	0♉12 15	11♒48 56	17 49 47	15 50.5	9 38.3	3 51.1	29 35.8	16 35.6	13 41.0	8 38.7	25 27.4	1 20.0	18 06.3
22 W	1 57 28	1 10 46	23 53 10	29 59 37	15 51.6	11 41.5	5 02.7	29 22.0	16 44.6	13 53.0	8 41.4	25 26.3	1 21.2	18 07.3
23 Th	2 01 25	2 09 15	6♓09 39	12♓23 42	15 52.9	13 42.9	6 14.2	29 08.9	16 53.9	14 05.0	8 44.0	25 25.2	1 22.5	18 08.3
24 F	2 05 21	3 07 43	18 42 12	25 05 28	15 54.2	15 42.4	7 25.6	28 56.5	17 03.6	14 16.8	8 46.6	25 24.1	1 23.9	18 09.3
25 Sa	2 09 18	4 06 09	1♈33 48	8♈07 20	15R 55.0	17 39.5	8 37.0	28 44.9	17 13.6	14 28.6	8 49.0	25 22.9	1 25.2	18 10.4
26 Su	2 13 15	5 04 33	14 46 11	21 30 19	15 55.1	19 34.1	9 48.3	28 34.1	17 24.0	14 40.3	8 51.4	25 21.7	1 26.6	18 11.4
27 M	2 17 11	6 02 56	28 19 35	5♉13 45	15 54.2	21 25.7	10 59.5	28 24.1	17 34.6	14 51.9	8 53.6	25 20.4	1 28.0	18 12.5
28 Tu	2 21 08	7 01 16	12♉12 28	19 15 16	15 52.3	23 14.3	12 10.7	28 14.9	17 45.6	15 03.4	8 55.8	25 19.1	1 29.5	18 13.6
29 W	2 25 04	7 59 35	26 21 37	3♊30 53	15 49.6	24 59.6	13 21.7	28 06.5	17 56.9	15 14.8	8 57.9	25 17.7	1 30.9	18 14.7
30 Th	2 29 01	8 57 52	10♊42 25	17 55 30	15 46.4	26 41.4	14 32.7	27 58.8	18 08.5	15 26.2	8 59.9	25 16.3	1 32.4	18 15.8

Astro Data	Dy Hr Mn
♀0N	2 3:04
♇ D	3 7:11
♆ D	13 5:33
☽0S	13 19:09
♃⚺♄	18 22:54
☉0N	21 19:15
☽0N	28 4:26
⚳ D	29 20:28
♂0N	29 21:52
♅ R	31 17:50
☿0N	4 6:36
☽0S	10 3:50
☽0N	24 13:21

Planet Ingress		Dy Hr Mn
☿	♓	14 21:52
☉	♈	21 19:15
♀	♉	24 11:53
☿	♈	2 0:25
☿	♉	16 21:51
♀	♊	18 6:41
♂	♍R	19 20:46
☉	♉	21 6:59

Last Aspect Dy Hr Mn			☽ Ingress	Dy Hr Mn
28 19:46	♅	□	♈	1 4:45
3 3:27	♅	△	♉	3 12:00
4 17:28	☿	□	♊	5 17:16
7 12:47	♅	☍	♋	7 20:34
9 1:26	☉	△	♌	9 22:23
11 16:17	♅	△	♍	11 23:47
13 18:35	♅	□	♎	14 2:18
15 23:18	♅	⚹	♏	16 7:26
18 9:28	☉	△	♐	18 16:01
21 2:08	☉	□	♑	21 3:33
23 13:51	♀	□	♒	23 16:06
25 18:54	♅	⚹	♓	26 3:24
28 4:07	♅	□	♈	28 12:13
30 10:44	♅	△	♉	30 18:29

Last Aspect Dy Hr Mn			☽ Ingress	Dy Hr Mn
1 22:35	☿	⚹	♊	1 22:50
3 18:36	♅	☍	♋	4 2:00
5 1:51	☉	□	♌	6 4:39
7 23:59	♅	△	♍	8 7:27
10 3:30	♅	□	♎	10 11:11
12 8:43	♅	⚹	♏	12 16:45
14 16:43	♀	☍	♐	15 0:56
17 3:46	☉	△	♑	17 11:49
20 0:11	♂	△	♒	20 0:15
22 3:04	♅	⚹	♓	22 12:01
24 19:03	♂	☍	♈	24 21:07
26 18:47	♅	△	♉	27 2:55
29 3:01	♂	△	♊	29 6:07

☽ Phases & Eclipses Dy Hr Mn	
6 19:14	☽ 15♊03
13 12:13	○ 21♍45
21 2:08	☾ 29♐18
29 1:26	● 7♈11
29 1:35:21	A 01'53"
5 1:51	☽ 14♋07
12 0:18	○ 20♎56
12 0:13	P 0.968
19 21:30	☾ 28♑38
27 13:31	● 6♉07

Astro Data

1 March 1903
Julian Day # 1155
SVP 6♓36'36"
GC 25♐29.2 ⚴ 3♋21.1
Eris 23♓09.4 ⚵ 5♐51.2
⚷ 20♑34.0 ⚶ 22♓28.4
☽ Mean ☊ 18♎01.4

1 April 1903
Julian Day # 1186
SVP 6♓36'34"
GC 25♐29.3 ⚴ 12♋43.1
Eris 23♓34.1 ⚵ 7♐26.6R
⚷ 22♑16.4 ⚶ 7♈12.1
☽ Mean ☊ 16♎22.9

LONGITUDE May 1903

Day	Sid.Time	☉	0 hr ☽	Noon ☽	True ☊	☿	♀	♂	⚳	♃	♄	♅	♆	♇
1 F	2 32 57	9♉56 08	25♊09 28	2♋23 36	15♎43.3	28♉19.5	15♊43.6	27♍52.0	18♌20.4	15♓37.4	9♒01.8	25♐14.9	1♋33.9	18♊16.9
2 Sa	2 36 54	10 54 21	9♋37 16	16 49 54	15R 40.9	29 53.9	16 54.5	27R 46.0	18 32.5	15 48.5	9 03.6	25R 13.4	1 35.5	18 18.1
3 Su	2 40 50	11 52 32	24 00 57	1♌10 02	15D 39.3	1♊24.3	18 05.2	27 40.8	18 45.0	15 59.6	9 05.3	25 11.9	1 37.0	18 19.2
4 M	2 44 47	12 50 41	8♌16 45	15 20 51	15 39.0	2 50.8	19 15.8	27 36.4	18 57.7	16 10.5	9 06.9	25 10.3	1 38.6	18 20.4
5 Tu	2 48 44	13 48 48	22 22 07	29 20 25	15 39.7	4 13.2	20 26.4	27 32.8	19 10.8	16 21.4	9 08.4	25 08.7	1 40.2	18 21.6
6 W	2 52 40	14 46 53	6♍15 40	13♍07 49	15 41.1	5 31.4	21 36.8	27 30.0	19 24.1	16 32.1	9 09.8	25 07.0	1 41.8	18 22.7
7 Th	2 56 37	15 44 56	19 56 51	26 42 45	15 42.6	6 45.4	22 47.2	27 28.0	19 37.6	16 42.7	9 11.1	25 05.4	1 43.5	18 23.9
8 F	3 00 33	16 42 57	3♎25 34	10♎05 16	15R 43.6	7 55.0	23 57.5	27 26.7	19 51.4	16 53.3	9 12.3	25 03.6	1 45.2	18 25.1
9 Sa	3 04 30	17 40 56	16 41 53	23 15 26	15 43.4	9 00.3	25 07.6	27D 26.2	20 05.5	17 03.7	9 13.4	25 01.9	1 46.9	18 26.4
10 Su	3 08 26	18 38 54	29 45 54	6♏13 18	15 41.8	10 01.2	26 17.7	27 26.5	20 19.9	17 14.0	9 14.5	25 00.1	1 48.6	18 27.6
11 M	3 12 23	19 36 50	12♏37 38	18 58 54	15 38.5	10 57.5	27 27.6	27 27.5	20 34.4	17 24.2	9 15.4	24 58.3	1 50.3	18 28.8
12 Tu	3 16 19	20 34 44	25 17 09	1♐32 24	15 33.7	11 49.3	28 37.5	27 29.3	20 49.3	17 34.3	9 16.2	24 56.4	1 52.1	18 30.1
13 W	3 20 16	21 32 37	7♐44 45	13 54 17	15 27.7	12 36.5	29 47.3	27 31.8	21 04.3	17 44.3	9 16.9	24 54.6	1 53.9	18 31.3
14 Th	3 24 13	22 30 29	20 01 10	26 05 34	15 21.2	13 18.9	0♋56.9	27 35.0	21 19.7	17 54.2	9 17.6	24 52.7	1 55.7	18 32.6
15 F	3 28 09	23 28 19	2♑07 44	8♑07 56	15 14.8	13 56.7	2 06.5	27 38.9	21 35.2	18 04.0	9 18.1	24 50.7	1 57.5	18 33.9
16 Sa	3 32 06	24 26 08	14 06 31	20 03 50	15 09.1	14 29.6	3 15.9	27 43.5	21 51.0	18 13.6	9 18.6	24 48.7	1 59.3	18 35.2
17 Su	3 36 02	25 23 56	26 00 19	1♒56 26	15 04.8	14 57.7	4 25.2	27 48.9	22 06.9	18 23.2	9 18.9	24 46.7	2 01.2	18 36.5
18 M	3 39 59	26 21 42	7♒52 41	13 49 38	15 02.2	15 20.9	5 34.5	27 54.9	22 23.2	18 32.6	9 19.2	24 44.7	2 03.1	18 37.8
19 Tu	3 43 55	27 19 28	19 47 50	25 47 53	15D 01.2	15 39.3	6 43.6	28 01.6	22 39.6	18 41.9	9 19.3	24 42.6	2 04.9	18 39.1
20 W	3 47 52	28 17 12	1♓50 23	7♓55 58	15 01.6	15 52.8	7 52.6	28 08.9	22 56.2	18 51.0	9R 19.4	24 40.5	2 06.9	18 40.4
21 Th	3 51 48	29 14 55	14 05 14	20 18 47	15 02.9	16 01.4	9 01.5	28 16.9	23 13.1	19 00.1	9 19.3	24 38.4	2 08.8	18 41.7
22 F	3 55 45	0♊12 37	26 37 11	3♈00 56	15R 04.2	16R 05.3	10 10.2	28 25.6	23 30.1	19 09.0	9 19.2	24 36.3	2 10.7	18 43.1
23 Sa	3 59 42	1 10 18	9♈30 30	16 06 14	15 04.7	16 04.4	11 18.9	28 34.9	23 47.4	19 17.8	9 18.9	24 34.1	2 12.7	18 44.4
24 Su	4 03 38	2 07 58	22 48 23	29 37 05	15 03.7	15 59.0	12 27.4	28 44.8	24 04.9	19 26.4	9 18.6	24 31.9	2 14.7	18 45.7
25 M	4 07 35	3 05 37	6♉32 19	13♉33 53	15 00.8	15 49.3	13 35.8	28 55.3	24 22.5	19 35.0	9 18.1	24 29.7	2 16.7	18 47.1
26 Tu	4 11 31	4 03 15	20 41 27	27 54 28	14 55.8	15 35.3	14 44.1	29 06.5	24 40.4	19 43.3	9 17.6	24 27.5	2 18.7	18 48.5
27 W	4 15 28	5 00 51	5♊12 15	12♊33 55	14 49.0	15 17.5	15 52.2	29 18.2	24 58.4	19 51.6	9 17.0	24 25.2	2 20.7	18 49.8
28 Th	4 19 24	5 58 27	19 58 30	27 24 56	14 41.4	14 56.0	17 00.2	29 30.5	25 16.7	19 59.7	9 16.2	24 23.0	2 22.7	18 51.2
29 F	4 23 21	6 56 01	4♋52 07	12♋18 56	14 33.7	14 31.4	18 08.1	29 43.4	25 35.1	20 07.7	9 15.4	24 20.7	2 24.8	18 52.6
30 Sa	4 27 17	7 53 34	19 44 21	27 07 26	14 27.1	14 04.0	19 15.8	29 56.9	25 53.7	20 15.5	9 14.5	24 18.4	2 26.8	18 53.9
31 Su	4 31 14	8 51 06	4♌27 19	11♌43 22	14 22.2	13 34.3	20 23.4	0♎11.0	26 12.5	20 23.2	9 13.5	24 16.1	2 28.9	18 55.3

LONGITUDE June 1903

Day	Sid.Time	☉	0 hr ☽	Noon ☽	True ☊	☿	♀	♂	⚳	♃	♄	♅	♆	♇
1 M	4 35 11	9♊48 36	18♌55 02	26♌01 59	14♎19.5	13♊02.7	21♋30.9	0♎25.5	26♌31.4	20♓30.8	9♒12.4	24♐13.7	2♋31.0	18♊56.7
2 Tu	4 39 07	10 46 05	3♍04 01	10♍01 04	14D 18.6	12R 30.0	22 38.2	0 40.6	26 50.5	20 38.2	9R 11.2	24R 11.4	2 33.1	18 58.1
3 W	4 43 04	11 43 33	16 53 09	23 40 26	14 19.1	11 56.5	23 45.3	0 56.3	27 09.8	20 45.4	9 09.9	24 09.0	2 35.2	18 59.5
4 Th	4 47 00	12 40 59	0♎23 07	7♎01 25	14R 19.8	11 22.9	24 52.2	1 12.4	27 29.3	20 52.5	9 08.5	24 06.6	2 37.3	19 00.9
5 F	4 50 57	13 38 24	13 35 39	20 06 05	14 19.9	10 49.9	25 59.0	1 29.0	27 48.9	20 59.5	9 07.0	24 04.2	2 39.4	19 02.3
6 Sa	4 54 53	14 35 48	26 33 00	2♏56 40	14 18.2	10 17.8	27 05.6	1 46.1	28 08.6	21 06.3	9 05.4	24 01.8	2 41.6	19 03.7
7 Su	4 58 50	15 33 11	9♏17 19	15 35 12	14 14.3	9 47.3	28 12.1	2 03.7	28 28.5	21 13.0	9 03.8	23 59.4	2 43.7	19 05.1
8 M	5 02 46	16 30 33	21 50 29	28 03 21	14 07.7	9 18.9	29 18.4	2 21.8	28 48.6	21 19.5	9 02.0	23 57.0	2 45.9	19 06.5
9 Tu	5 06 43	17 27 54	4♐13 55	10♐22 21	13 58.7	8 53.1	0♌24.4	2 40.3	29 08.8	21 25.8	9 00.2	23 54.6	2 48.0	19 07.9
10 W	5 10 40	18 25 14	16 28 45	22 33 14	13 47.9	8 30.3	1 30.3	2 59.3	29 29.2	21 32.0	8 58.3	23 52.1	2 50.2	19 09.3
11 Th	5 14 36	19 22 34	28 35 55	4♑36 56	13 36.0	8 10.9	2 36.0	3 18.7	29 49.7	21 38.1	8 56.2	23 49.7	2 52.4	19 10.7
12 F	5 18 33	20 19 53	10♑36 28	16 34 41	13 24.2	7 55.2	3 41.5	3 38.5	0♍10.3	21 43.9	8 54.1	23 47.2	2 54.6	19 12.1
13 Sa	5 22 29	21 17 11	22 31 48	28 28 05	13 13.4	7 43.4	4 46.9	3 58.8	0 31.1	21 49.6	8 52.0	23 44.8	2 56.8	19 13.5
14 Su	5 26 26	22 14 29	4♒23 51	10♒19 27	13 04.5	7 35.8	5 52.0	4 19.5	0 52.0	21 55.2	8 49.7	23 42.3	2 59.0	19 14.9
15 M	5 30 22	23 11 46	16 15 15	22 11 45	12 57.9	7D 32.6	6 56.9	4 40.6	1 13.0	22 00.6	8 47.3	23 39.9	3 01.2	19 16.3
16 Tu	5 34 19	24 09 03	28 09 24	4♓08 44	12 53.9	7 33.8	8 01.5	5 02.0	1 34.2	22 05.8	8 44.9	23 37.4	3 03.4	19 17.7
17 W	5 38 15	25 06 19	10♓10 21	16 14 49	12D 52.1	7 39.6	9 06.0	5 23.9	1 55.5	22 10.8	8 42.4	23 35.0	3 05.6	19 19.1
18 Th	5 42 12	26 03 36	22 22 47	28 34 53	12 51.8	7 50.1	10 10.3	5 46.2	2 16.9	22 15.7	8 39.8	23 32.5	3 07.8	19 20.5
19 F	5 46 09	27 00 52	4♈51 43	11♈13 55	12R 52.0	8 05.1	11 14.3	6 08.8	2 38.4	22 20.4	8 37.1	23 30.1	3 10.0	19 21.8
20 Sa	5 50 05	27 58 07	17 42 03	24 16 37	12 51.6	8 24.8	12 18.1	6 31.8	3 00.1	22 24.9	8 34.3	23 27.6	3 12.2	19 23.2
21 Su	5 54 02	28 55 23	0♉58 04	7♉46 40	12 49.6	8 49.1	13 21.6	6 55.2	3 21.9	22 29.3	8 31.5	23 25.2	3 14.5	19 24.6
22 M	5 57 58	29 52 39	14 42 36	21 45 50	12 45.2	9 18.0	14 24.9	7 18.9	3 43.8	22 33.5	8 28.6	23 22.8	3 16.7	19 26.0
23 Tu	6 01 55	0♋49 54	28 56 10	6♊13 10	12 38.3	9 51.5	15 27.9	7 43.0	4 05.8	22 37.5	8 25.6	23 20.3	3 18.9	19 27.4
24 W	6 05 51	1 47 09	13♊36 10	21 04 18	12 29.1	10 29.4	16 30.7	8 07.4	4 28.0	22 41.3	8 22.6	23 17.9	3 21.2	19 28.8
25 Th	6 09 48	2 44 24	28 36 29	6♋11 29	12 18.7	11 11.7	17 33.3	8 32.2	4 50.3	22 44.9	8 19.4	23 15.5	3 23.4	19 30.2
26 F	6 13 45	3 41 39	13♋47 59	21 24 34	12 08.1	11 58.3	18 35.5	8 57.3	5 12.6	22 48.4	8 16.2	23 13.1	3 25.6	19 31.5
27 Sa	6 17 41	4 38 53	28 59 52	6♌32 37	11 58.6	12 49.2	19 37.5	9 22.8	5 35.1	22 51.7	8 13.0	23 10.7	3 27.9	19 32.9
28 Su	6 21 38	5 36 07	14♌01 40	21 26 04	11 51.3	13 44.4	20 39.2	9 48.6	5 57.7	22 54.8	8 09.6	23 08.3	3 30.1	19 34.2
29 M	6 25 34	6 33 20	28 45 02	5♍58 01	11 46.6	14 43.7	21 40.5	10 14.7	6 20.4	22 57.7	8 06.2	23 05.9	3 32.4	19 35.6
30 Tu	6 29 31	7 30 33	13♍04 44	20 04 59	11 44.3	15 47.1	22 41.6	10 41.1	6 43.2	23 00.4	8 02.8	23 03.6	3 34.6	19 36.9

Astro Data	Dy Hr Mn
☽0S	7 10:34
♂ D	9 15:26
♃□♇	19 3:37
♄ R	20 12:08
☽0N	21 23:04
☿ R	22 19:40
♄∠♅	2 16:00
☽0S	3 16:47
♂0S	4 15:12
☿ D	15 17:25
☽0N	18 8:28
♄∠♅	29 18:46
♃∠♄	30 21:27

Planet Ingress		Dy Hr Mn
☿	♊	2 13:36
♀	♋	13 16:23
☉	♊	22 6:45
♂	♎	30 17:20
♀	♌	9 3:07
⚳	♍	12 0:03
☉	♋	22 15:05

Last Aspect Dy Hr Mn			☽ Ingress	Dy Hr Mn
1 4:33	♂	□	♋	1 8:02
3 6:11	♂	✶	♌	3 10:02
5 4:47	♅	△	♍	5 13:08
7 13:20	♂	☌	♎	7 17:52
9 15:47	♀	△	♏	10 0:26
12 4:12	♂	✶	♐	12 9:02
14 14:58	♂	□	♑	14 19:46
17 3:36	♂	△	♒	17 8:05
19 15:18	☉	□	♓	19 20:21
22 6:20	☉	✶	♈	22 6:22
24 3:05	♅	△	♉	24 12:40
26 14:00	♂	△	♊	26 15:27
28 15:25	♂	□	♋	28 16:10
30 16:41	♂	✶	♌	30 16:42

Last Aspect Dy Hr Mn			☽ Ingress	Dy Hr Mn
1 8:57	♅	△	♍	1 18:45
3 12:51	♅	□	♎	3 23:18
5 23:59	♀	□	♏	6 6:28
8 14:40	♀	△	♐	8 15:46
10 14:36	♅	☌	♑	11 2:47
12 22:28	♃	✶	♒	13 15:06
15 14:57	♅	✶	♓	16 3:42
18 6:44	☉	□	♈	18 14:43
20 19:09	☉	✶	♉	20 22:17
22 13:21	♃	✶	♊	23 1:46
24 15:33	♅	☍	♋	25 2:12
26 14:13	♃	△	♌	27 1:35
28 14:47	♅	△	♍	29 2:04

☽ Phases & Eclipses Dy Hr Mn		
4 7:26	☽	12♌40
11 13:18	○	19♏40
19 15:18	☾	27♒27
26 22:50	●	4♊29
2 13:24	☽	10♍49
10 3:08	○	18♐04
18 6:44	☾	25♓51
25 6:11	●	2♋31

Astro Data

1 May 1903
Julian Day # 1216
SVP 6♓36'31"
GC 25♐29.4 ⚴ 24♋58.0
Eris 23♓54.9 ⚵ 4♐08.5R
⚷ 22♑49.5R ⚶ 21♈05.9
☽ Mean ☊ 14♎47.5

1 June 1903
Julian Day # 1247
SVP 6♓36'27"
GC 25♐29.4 ⚴ 8♌56.0
Eris 24♓08.1 ⚵ 27♏29.4R
⚷ 22♑11.4R ⚶ 4♉48.4
☽ Mean ☊ 13♎09.0

July 1903 — LONGITUDE

Day	Sid.Time	☉	0 hr ☽	Noon☽	True☊	☿	♀	♂	⚳	♃	♄	♅	♆	♇
1 W	6 33 27	8♋27 45	26♍58 50	3♎46 27	11♎43.6	16♊54.6	23♌42.3	11♎07.8	7♍06.0	23♓02.9	7♒59.3	23♐01.2	3♋36.8	19♊38.3
2 Th	6 37 24	9 24 57	10♎28 06	17 04 08	11R43.6	18 06.0	24 42.7	11 34.8	7 29.0	23 05.3	7R55.7	22R58.9	3 39.0	19 39.6
3 F	6 41 20	10 22 09	23 35 00	0♏01 07	11 42.9	19 21.4	25 42.7	12 02.1	7 52.1	23 07.4	7 52.0	22 56.6	3 41.3	19 40.9
4 Sa	6 45 17	11 19 20	6♏22 56	12 40 55	11 40.5	20 40.7	26 42.4	12 29.7	8 15.3	23 09.4	7 48.3	22 54.3	3 43.5	19 42.3
5 Su	6 49 13	12 16 31	18 55 30	25 07 04	11 35.6	22 03.9	27 41.7	12 57.5	8 38.5	23 11.1	7 44.6	22 52.0	3 45.7	19 43.6
6 M	6 53 10	13 13 42	1♐16 01	7♐22 39	11 27.9	23 30.8	28 40.6	13 25.7	9 01.9	23 12.7	7 40.8	22 49.8	3 47.9	19 44.9
7 Tu	6 57 07	14 10 53	13 27 18	19 30 12	11 17.5	25 01.5	29 39.1	13 54.1	9 25.3	23 14.1	7 36.9	22 47.6	3 50.1	19 46.2
8 W	7 01 03	15 08 04	25 31 35	1♑31 40	11 05.1	26 35.8	0♍37.3	14 22.8	9 48.8	23 15.3	7 33.1	22 45.4	3 52.3	19 47.5
9 Th	7 05 00	16 05 15	7♑30 36	13 28 35	10 51.5	28 13.7	1 34.9	14 51.7	10 12.5	23 16.3	7 29.1	22 43.2	3 54.5	19 48.8
10 F	7 08 56	17 02 27	19 25 46	25 22 19	10 37.9	29 55.1	2 32.2	15 20.9	10 36.1	23 17.1	7 25.1	22 41.0	3 56.7	19 50.0
11 Sa	7 12 53	17 59 38	1♒18 25	7♒14 15	10 25.3	1♋39.9	3 29.0	15 50.3	10 59.9	23 17.8	7 21.1	22 38.9	3 58.9	19 51.3
12 Su	7 16 49	18 56 50	13 10 02	19 06 02	10 14.8	3 27.9	4 25.4	16 20.0	11 23.8	23 18.2	7 17.0	22 36.7	4 01.1	19 52.6
13 M	7 20 46	19 54 02	25 02 33	0♓59 54	10 06.9	5 18.9	5 21.3	16 49.9	11 47.7	23R18.4	7 12.9	22 34.6	4 03.2	19 53.8
14 Tu	7 24 43	20 51 14	6♓58 28	12 58 41	10 01.8	7 12.9	6 16.6	17 20.1	12 11.7	23 18.5	7 08.7	22 32.6	4 05.4	19 55.0
15 W	7 28 39	21 48 27	19 01 00	25 05 55	9 59.1	9 09.4	7 11.5	17 50.5	12 35.8	23 18.3	7 04.5	22 30.5	4 07.6	19 56.3
16 Th	7 32 36	22 45 41	1♈14 00	7♈25 47	9D58.4	11 08.4	8 05.9	18 21.1	13 00.0	23 17.9	7 00.3	22 28.5	4 09.7	19 57.5
17 F	7 36 32	23 42 55	13 41 53	20 02 52	9R58.5	13 09.5	8 59.7	18 52.0	13 24.2	23 17.4	6 56.1	22 26.5	4 11.8	19 58.7
18 Sa	7 40 29	24 40 10	26 29 20	3♉01 48	9 58.3	15 12.5	9 53.0	19 23.1	13 48.5	23 16.6	6 51.8	22 24.6	4 14.0	19 59.9
19 Su	7 44 25	25 37 25	9♉40 45	16 26 37	9 56.8	17 17.0	10 45.7	19 54.4	14 12.9	23 15.7	6 47.5	22 22.7	4 16.1	20 01.0
20 M	7 48 22	26 34 42	23 19 39	0♊20 00	9 53.1	19 22.8	11 37.8	20 26.0	14 37.3	23 14.6	6 43.1	22 20.8	4 18.2	20 02.2
21 Tu	7 52 18	27 31 59	7♊27 38	14 42 19	9 47.1	21 29.4	12 29.2	20 57.7	15 01.9	23 13.2	6 38.8	22 18.9	4 20.3	20 03.4
22 W	7 56 15	28 29 17	22 03 33	29 30 39	9 38.9	23 36.7	13 20.1	21 29.7	15 26.5	23 11.7	6 34.4	22 17.1	4 22.4	20 04.5
23 Th	8 00 12	29 26 36	7♋02 42	14♋38 33	9 29.3	25 44.2	14 10.3	22 01.9	15 51.1	23 10.0	6 30.0	22 15.3	4 24.4	20 05.7
24 F	8 04 08	0♌23 56	22 16 54	29 56 22	9 19.4	27 51.7	14 59.8	22 34.3	16 15.8	23 08.0	6 25.6	22 13.5	4 26.5	20 06.8
25 Sa	8 08 05	1 21 16	7♌35 29	15♌12 50	9 10.5	29 59.0	15 48.6	23 07.0	16 40.6	23 05.9	6 21.2	22 11.8	4 28.5	20 07.9
26 Su	8 12 01	2 18 37	22 47 05	0♍17 03	9 03.6	2♌05.8	16 36.6	23 39.8	17 05.5	23 03.6	6 16.7	22 10.1	4 30.6	20 09.0
27 M	8 15 58	3 15 58	7♍41 45	15 00 23	8 59.2	4 11.8	17 23.9	24 12.8	17 30.4	23 01.1	6 12.3	22 08.5	4 32.6	20 10.1
28 Tu	8 19 54	4 13 20	22 12 26	29 17 33	8D57.1	6 17.0	18 10.3	24 46.0	17 55.4	22 58.4	6 07.8	22 06.8	4 34.6	20 11.1
29 W	8 23 51	5 10 42	6♎15 37	13♎06 41	8 56.9	8 21.1	18 56.0	25 19.5	18 20.4	22 55.5	6 03.4	22 05.3	4 36.6	20 12.2
30 Th	8 27 47	6 08 04	19 50 56	26 28 43	8R57.4	10 24.0	19 40.7	25 53.1	18 45.5	22 52.5	5 58.9	22 03.7	4 38.5	20 13.2
31 F	8 31 44	7 05 28	3♏00 25	9♏26 32	8 57.6	12 25.6	20 24.6	26 26.9	19 10.7	22 49.2	5 54.5	22 02.2	4 40.5	20 14.2

August 1903 — LONGITUDE

Day	Sid.Time	☉	0 hr ☽	Noon☽	True☊	☿	♀	♂	⚳	♃	♄	♅	♆	♇
1 Sa	8 35 41	8♌02 52	15♏47 33	22♏04 01	8♎56.6	14♌25.9	21♍07.5	27♎00.9	19♍35.9	22♓45.8	5♒50.0	22♐00.8	4♋42.4	20♊15.2
2 Su	8 39 37	9 00 16	28 16 27	4♐25 24	8R53.6	16 24.7	21 49.4	27 35.1	20 01.1	22R42.2	5R45.6	21R59.3	4 44.4	20 16.2
3 M	8 43 34	9 57 41	10♐31 21	16 34 47	8 48.2	18 22.1	22 30.4	28 09.4	20 26.4	22 38.4	5 41.1	21 58.0	4 46.3	20 17.2
4 Tu	8 47 30	10 55 07	22 36 08	28 35 49	8 40.6	20 17.9	23 10.2	28 43.9	20 51.8	22 34.4	5 36.7	21 56.6	4 48.2	20 18.2
5 W	8 51 27	11 52 34	4♑34 10	10♑31 33	8 31.2	22 12.2	23 49.0	29 18.6	21 17.2	22 30.3	5 32.3	21 55.3	4 50.0	20 19.1
6 Th	8 55 23	12 50 01	16 28 14	22 24 29	8 20.9	24 05.0	24 26.6	29 53.5	21 42.6	22 25.9	5 27.9	21 54.1	4 51.9	20 20.0
7 F	8 59 20	13 47 30	28 20 33	4♒16 38	8 10.5	25 56.2	25 03.0	0♏28.6	22 08.1	22 21.4	5 23.5	21 52.9	4 53.7	20 21.0
8 Sa	9 03 16	14 44 59	10♒12 56	16 09 40	8 01.0	27 45.8	25 38.2	1 03.8	22 33.7	22 16.8	5 19.1	21 51.7	4 55.6	20 21.9
9 Su	9 07 13	15 42 30	22 07 00	28 05 09	7 53.1	29 33.9	26 12.2	1 39.1	22 59.3	22 12.0	5 14.7	21 50.6	4 57.3	20 22.7
10 M	9 11 10	16 40 01	4♓04 21	10♓04 49	7 47.3	1♍20.4	26 44.8	2 14.7	23 24.9	22 07.0	5 10.4	21 49.5	4 59.1	20 23.6
11 Tu	9 15 06	17 37 34	16 06 48	22 10 38	7 43.8	3 05.4	27 16.0	2 50.4	23 50.6	22 01.8	5 06.1	21 48.5	5 00.9	20 24.4
12 W	9 19 03	18 35 08	28 16 36	4♈25 04	7D42.5	4 48.9	27 45.8	3 26.2	24 16.3	21 56.5	5 01.8	21 47.5	5 02.6	20 25.3
13 Th	9 22 59	19 32 44	10♈36 26	16 51 06	7 42.8	6 30.9	28 14.1	4 02.2	24 42.1	21 51.1	4 57.6	21 46.5	5 04.3	20 26.1
14 F	9 26 56	20 30 21	23 09 31	29 32 08	7 43.9	8 11.4	28 40.9	4 38.4	25 07.9	21 45.4	4 53.4	21 45.6	5 06.0	20 26.9
15 Sa	9 30 52	21 28 00	5♉59 24	12♉31 45	7R45.1	9 50.3	29 06.1	5 14.7	25 33.8	21 39.7	4 49.2	21 44.8	5 07.7	20 27.6
16 Su	9 34 49	22 25 40	19 09 35	25 53 17	7 45.3	11 27.9	29 29.7	5 51.2	25 59.7	21 33.8	4 45.0	21 44.0	5 09.4	20 28.4
17 M	9 38 45	23 23 22	2♊43 07	9♊39 16	7 44.1	13 03.9	29 51.5	6 27.8	26 25.6	21 27.7	4 40.9	21 43.2	5 11.0	20 29.1
18 Tu	9 42 42	24 21 05	16 41 47	23 50 34	7 41.2	14 38.5	0♎11.6	7 04.6	26 51.6	21 21.6	4 36.9	21 42.5	5 12.6	20 29.9
19 W	9 46 38	25 18 50	1♋05 20	8♋25 38	7 36.6	16 11.7	0 29.9	7 41.6	27 17.6	21 15.2	4 32.8	21 41.9	5 14.2	20 30.6
20 Th	9 50 35	26 16 37	15 50 48	23 20 00	7 30.9	17 43.3	0 46.4	8 18.7	27 43.7	21 08.8	4 28.8	21 41.2	5 15.7	20 31.3
21 F	9 54 32	27 14 25	0♌52 12	8♌26 18	7 24.9	19 13.5	1 00.9	8 55.9	28 09.8	21 02.2	4 24.9	21 40.7	5 17.3	20 31.9
22 Sa	9 58 28	28 12 15	16 01 01	23 35 07	7 19.5	20 42.3	1 13.4	9 33.3	28 35.9	20 55.5	4 21.0	21 40.2	5 18.8	20 32.6
23 Su	10 02 25	29 10 06	1♍07 20	8♍36 28	7 15.3	22 09.5	1 23.8	10 10.9	29 02.1	20 48.7	4 17.2	21 39.7	5 20.3	20 33.2
24 M	10 06 21	0♍07 58	16 01 29	23 21 27	7D12.9	23 35.3	1 32.2	10 48.5	29 28.3	20 41.8	4 13.4	21 39.3	5 21.7	20 33.8
25 Tu	10 10 18	1 05 52	0♎35 39	7♎43 32	7 12.2	24 59.5	1 38.4	11 26.4	29 54.6	20 34.8	4 09.6	21 38.9	5 23.2	20 34.4
26 W	10 14 14	2 03 47	14 44 46	21 39 11	7 12.8	26 22.2	1 42.3	12 04.3	0♎20.8	20 27.7	4 06.0	21 38.6	5 24.6	20 34.9
27 Th	10 18 11	3 01 44	28 26 48	5♏07 44	7 14.2	27 43.3	1R44.0	12 42.4	0 47.1	20 20.5	4 02.3	21 38.3	5 26.0	20 35.5
28 F	10 22 07	3 59 42	11♏42 15	18 10 44	7 15.7	29 02.8	1 43.4	13 20.7	1 13.4	20 13.2	3 58.8	21 38.1	5 27.3	20 36.0
29 Sa	10 26 04	4 57 41	24 33 38	0♐51 25	7R16.6	0♎20.6	1 40.4	13 59.1	1 39.8	20 05.8	3 55.3	21 38.0	5 28.7	20 36.5
30 Su	10 30 01	5 55 41	7♐04 37	13 13 49	7 16.4	1 36.7	1 35.1	14 37.6	2 06.2	19 58.3	3 51.8	21 37.9	5 30.0	20 37.0
31 M	10 33 57	6 53 43	19 19 32	25 22 22	7 14.9	2 51.0	1 27.3	15 16.2	2 32.6	19 50.8	3 48.5	21D37.8	5 31.2	20 37.5

Astro Data	Dy Hr Mn
☽0S	1 0:07
♃□♅	1 3:39
♃R	14 4:20
☽0N	15 16:39
☽0S	28 9:19
♀0S	5 23:48
♄⚼♇	7 23:25
☽0N	11 23:27
♄⚻♆	12 8:51
♃□♅	14 11:05
☽0S	24 19:51
♃□♇	25 13:19
♀R	27 17:37
☿0S	27 17:43

Planet Ingress		Dy Hr Mn
♀	♍	7 20:36
☿	♋	10 13:08
☉	♌	24 1:59
☿	♌	25 12:11
♂	♏	6 16:27
☿	♍	9 17:51
♀	♎	17 21:51
☉	♍	24 8:42
⚳	♎	25 16:59
☿	♎	29 5:36

Last Aspect Dy Hr Mn		☽ Ingress Dy Hr Mn
30 17:09	☿ □	♎ 1 5:19
3 3:17	♀ ⚹	♏ 3 11:58
5 17:27	♀ □	♐ 5 21:31
8 0:38	☿ ☍	♑ 8 8:56
10 7:47	♃ ⚹	♒ 10 21:21
12 19:04	♅ ⚹	♓ 13 9:59
15 8:28	♃ ☌	♈ 15 21:36
17 19:24	☉ □	♉ 18 6:28
20 5:07	☉ ⚹	♊ 20 11:26
22 1:51	♃ □	♋ 22 12:47
24 8:13	☿ ☌	♌ 24 12:06
26 1:00	♂ ⚹	♍ 26 11:33
28 1:19	♃ ☍	♎ 28 13:13
30 10:52	♂ ☌	♏ 30 18:27

Last Aspect Dy Hr Mn		☽ Ingress Dy Hr Mn
1 13:20	♃ △	♐ 2 3:21
4 12:17	♂ ⚹	♑ 4 14:49
6 16:20	♀ △	♒ 7 3:21
9 15:29	☿ ☍	♓ 9 15:50
11 22:27	☿ ☍	♈ 12 3:23
13 21:22	♅ △	♉ 14 12:52
16 18:32	♀ △	♊ 16 19:15
18 12:54	☉ ⚹	♋ 18 22:12
20 8:32	♃ △	♌ 20 22:37
22 19:51	☉ ☌	♍ 22 22:13
24 12:25	☿ ☌	♎ 24 23:01
26 11:59	♅ ⚹	♏ 27 2:46
28 15:47	♃ △	♐ 29 10:21
31 4:34	♅ ☌	♑ 31 21:14

☽ Phases & Eclipses Dy Hr Mn	
1 21:02	☽ 8♎49
9 17:43	○ 16♑19
17 19:24	☾ 24♈01
24 12:46	● 0♌26
31 7:15	☽ 6♏54
8 8:54	○ 14♒38
16 5:23	☾ 22♉10
22 19:51	● 28♌31
29 20:34	☽ 5♐18

Astro Data

1 July 1903
Julian Day # 1277
SVP 6♓36'22"
GC 25♐29.5 ⚴ 22♌53.7
Eris 24♓10.0R ⚵ 22♏36.0R
⚷ 20♑41.4R ⚶ 17♉05.8
☽ Mean ☊ 11♎33.7

1 August 1903
Julian Day # 1308
SVP 6♓36'18"
GC 25♐29.6 ⚴ 7♍25.9
Eris 24♓00.6R ⚵ 22♏18.3
⚷ 18♑51.6R ⚶ 28♉13.5
☽ Mean ☊ 9♎55.2

LONGITUDE September 1903

Day	Sid.Time	☉	0 hr ☽	Noon ☽	True ☊	☿	♀	♂	⚳	♃	♄	♅	♆	♇
1 Tu	10 37 54	7♍51 46	1♑22 49	7♑21 25	7♎12.1	4♎03.4	1♎17.2	15♏55.0	2♎59.0	19♓43.2	3♒45.2	21♐37.8	5♋32.5	20♊37.9
2 W	10 41 50	8 49 51	13 18 40	19 15 02	7R 08.2	5 14.0	1R 04.7	16 33.9	3 25.5	19R 35.5	3R 41.9	21 37.8	5 33.7	20 38.3
3 Th	10 45 47	9 47 57	25 10 56	1♒06 47	7 03.6	6 22.5	0 49.7	17 12.9	3 52.0	19 27.8	3 38.8	21 37.9	5 34.9	20 38.7
4 F	10 49 43	10 46 05	7♒02 55	12 59 41	6 59.0	7 28.9	0 32.5	17 52.0	4 18.5	19 20.0	3 35.7	21 38.1	5 36.1	20 39.1
5 Sa	10 53 40	11 44 14	18 57 22	24 56 15	6 54.8	8 33.1	0 12.9	18 31.3	4 45.0	19 12.2	3 32.7	21 38.3	5 37.2	20 39.5
6 Su	10 57 36	12 42 25	0♓56 33	6♓58 29	6 51.4	9 35.0	29♍51.1	19 10.7	5 11.6	19 04.3	3 29.7	21 38.5	5 38.3	20 39.8
7 M	11 01 33	13 40 37	13 02 16	19 08 06	6 49.1	10 34.3	29 27.1	19 50.2	5 38.1	18 56.4	3 26.8	21 38.8	5 39.4	20 40.1
8 Tu	11 05 30	14 38 52	25 16 08	1♈26 34	6D 48.1	11 31.1	29 01.1	20 29.8	6 04.7	18 48.5	3 24.0	21 39.1	5 40.4	20 40.4
9 W	11 09 26	15 37 08	7♈39 34	13 55 20	6 48.1	12 25.0	28 33.2	21 09.6	6 31.4	18 40.6	3 21.3	21 39.5	5 41.5	20 40.7
10 Th	11 13 23	16 35 26	20 14 04	26 35 57	6 49.0	13 15.9	28 03.5	21 49.4	6 58.0	18 32.6	3 18.7	21 40.0	5 42.4	20 41.0
11 F	11 17 19	17 33 46	3♉01 11	9♉30 01	6 50.4	14 03.6	27 32.2	22 29.4	7 24.7	18 24.6	3 16.1	21 40.5	5 43.4	20 41.2
12 Sa	11 21 16	18 32 09	16 02 39	22 39 17	6 51.8	14 47.8	26 59.4	23 09.5	7 51.3	18 16.6	3 13.6	21 41.0	5 44.3	20 41.4
13 Su	11 25 12	19 30 33	29 20 07	6♊05 20	6 52.8	15 28.4	26 25.4	23 49.7	8 18.0	18 08.7	3 11.3	21 41.6	5 45.2	20 41.6
14 M	11 29 09	20 29 00	12♊55 03	19 49 21	6R 53.2	16 05.0	25 50.4	24 30.0	8 44.7	18 00.7	3 08.9	21 42.3	5 46.1	20 41.8
15 Tu	11 33 05	21 27 28	26 48 14	3♋51 37	6 52.9	16 37.3	25 14.5	25 10.5	9 11.5	17 52.7	3 06.7	21 43.0	5 46.9	20 41.9
16 W	11 37 02	22 25 59	10♋59 20	18 11 05	6 51.9	17 05.0	24 38.0	25 51.1	9 38.2	17 44.8	3 04.6	21 43.8	5 47.7	20 42.0
17 Th	11 40 59	23 24 33	25 26 27	2♌44 56	6 50.5	17 27.8	24 01.1	26 31.7	10 05.0	17 36.9	3 02.5	21 44.6	5 48.5	20 42.1
18 F	11 44 55	24 23 08	10♌05 53	17 28 32	6 48.9	17 45.4	23 24.2	27 12.5	10 31.8	17 29.0	3 00.6	21 45.4	5 49.3	20 42.2
19 Sa	11 48 52	25 21 45	24 52 05	2♍15 37	6 47.5	17 57.3	22 47.3	27 53.4	10 58.6	17 21.2	2 58.7	21 46.3	5 50.0	20 42.3
20 Su	11 52 48	26 20 25	9♍38 13	16 58 59	6 46.6	18R 03.2	22 10.8	28 34.4	11 25.4	17 13.3	2 56.9	21 47.3	5 50.6	20 42.3
21 M	11 56 45	27 19 06	24 17 01	1♎31 30	6D 46.1	18 02.8	21 34.9	29 15.6	11 52.2	17 05.6	2 55.2	21 48.3	5 51.3	20R 42.3
22 Tu	12 00 41	28 17 49	8♎41 42	15 47 01	6 46.2	17 55.6	20 59.8	29 56.8	12 19.1	16 57.9	2 53.6	21 49.4	5 51.9	20 42.3
23 W	12 04 38	29 16 35	22 46 58	29 41 11	6 46.6	17 41.4	20 25.7	0♐38.1	12 45.9	16 50.3	2 52.1	21 50.5	5 52.5	20 42.3
24 Th	12 08 34	0♎15 22	6♏29 29	13♏11 45	6 47.2	17 20.1	19 52.8	1 19.6	13 12.8	16 42.7	2 50.7	21 51.6	5 53.0	20 42.2
25 F	12 12 31	1 14 11	19 48 03	26 18 33	6 47.8	16 51.3	19 21.4	2 01.1	13 39.6	16 35.2	2 49.4	21 52.9	5 53.5	20 42.1
26 Sa	12 16 27	2 13 01	2♐43 29	9♐03 13	6 48.3	16 15.3	18 51.6	2 42.8	14 06.5	16 27.8	2 48.2	21 54.1	5 54.0	20 42.0
27 Su	12 20 24	3 11 54	15 18 10	21 28 48	6 48.6	15 32.1	18 23.5	3 24.5	14 33.4	16 20.5	2 47.1	21 55.4	5 54.4	20 41.9
28 M	12 24 21	4 10 48	27 35 38	3♑39 12	6R 48.7	14 42.1	17 57.3	4 06.4	15 00.3	16 13.2	2 46.1	21 56.8	5 54.9	20 41.8
29 Tu	12 28 17	5 09 44	9♑40 05	15 38 52	6 48.7	13 46.0	17 33.2	4 48.4	15 27.2	16 06.1	2 45.2	21 58.2	5 55.2	20 41.6
30 W	12 32 14	6 08 42	21 36 06	27 32 22	6D 48.6	12 44.7	17 11.2	5 30.4	15 54.1	15 59.0	2 44.3	21 59.7	5 55.6	20 41.4

LONGITUDE October 1903

Day	Sid.Time	☉	0 hr ☽	Noon ☽	True ☊	☿	♀	♂	⚳	♃	♄	♅	♆	♇
1 Th	12 36 10	7♎07 41	3♒28 12	9♒24 10	6♎48.6	11♎39.2	16♍51.5	6♐12.6	16♎21.0	15♓52.1	2♒43.6	22♐01.2	5♋55.9	20♊41.2
2 F	12 40 07	8 06 42	15 20 46	21 18 27	6 48.7	10R 31.1	16R 34.0	6 54.8	16 47.9	15R 45.3	2R 43.0	22 02.7	5 56.2	20R 41.0
3 Sa	12 44 03	9 05 45	27 17 41	3♓18 51	6 48.9	9 22.0	16 18.9	7 37.1	17 14.8	15 38.6	2 42.4	22 04.3	5 56.4	20 40.8
4 Su	12 48 00	10 04 50	9♓22 19	15 28 25	6 49.2	8 13.6	16 06.3	8 19.6	17 41.7	15 32.0	2 42.0	22 06.0	5 56.6	20 40.5
5 M	12 51 56	11 03 57	21 37 25	27 49 31	6R 49.4	7 08.0	15 56.0	9 02.1	18 08.6	15 25.5	2 41.7	22 07.6	5 56.8	20 40.2
6 Tu	12 55 53	12 03 06	4♈04 55	10♈23 45	6 49.4	6 06.8	15 48.3	9 44.7	18 35.5	15 19.2	2 41.4	22 09.4	5 56.9	20 39.9
7 W	12 59 50	13 02 17	16 46 05	23 12 00	6 49.2	5 11.8	15 42.9	10 27.4	19 02.4	15 13.0	2D 41.3	22 11.2	5 57.1	20 39.6
8 Th	13 03 46	14 01 30	29 41 28	6♉14 29	6 48.6	4 24.6	15D 40.0	11 10.2	19 29.3	15 07.0	2 41.3	22 13.0	5 57.1	20 39.2
9 F	13 07 43	15 00 45	12♉51 00	19 30 54	6 47.7	3 46.4	15 39.6	11 53.1	19 56.2	15 01.0	2 41.3	22 14.9	5R 57.2	20 38.8
10 Sa	13 11 39	16 00 02	26 14 07	3♊00 30	6 46.6	3 18.2	15 41.5	12 36.0	20 23.2	14 55.3	2 41.5	22 16.8	5 57.2	20 38.4
11 Su	13 15 36	16 59 22	9♊49 56	16 42 15	6 45.4	3 00.6	15 45.8	13 19.1	20 50.1	14 49.6	2 41.8	22 18.8	5 57.2	20 38.0
12 M	13 19 32	17 58 44	23 37 19	0♋34 56	6 44.5	2D 53.9	15 52.4	14 02.2	21 17.0	14 44.2	2 42.1	22 20.8	5 57.1	20 37.6
13 Tu	13 23 29	18 58 09	7♋34 57	14 37 10	6D 44.0	2 58.1	16 01.3	14 45.5	21 43.9	14 38.9	2 42.6	22 22.8	5 57.0	20 37.1
14 W	13 27 25	19 57 35	21 41 22	28 47 18	6 44.1	3 13.0	16 12.3	15 28.8	22 10.8	14 33.7	2 43.2	22 24.9	5 56.9	20 36.6
15 Th	13 31 22	20 57 04	5♌54 42	13♌03 01	6 44.8	3 38.2	16 25.6	16 12.2	22 37.7	14 28.7	2 43.9	22 27.1	5 56.7	20 36.2
16 F	13 35 19	21 56 36	20 12 43	27 22 36	6 45.9	4 13.0	16 40.9	16 55.7	23 04.6	14 23.9	2 44.6	22 29.2	5 56.5	20 35.6
17 Sa	13 39 15	22 56 09	4♍32 33	11♍42 05	6 47.1	4 56.7	16 58.2	17 39.3	23 31.5	14 19.3	2 45.5	22 31.5	5 56.3	20 35.1
18 Su	13 43 12	23 55 45	18 50 45	25 58 00	6R 48.0	5 48.6	17 17.5	18 22.9	23 58.4	14 14.8	2 46.5	22 33.7	5 56.0	20 34.5
19 M	13 47 08	24 55 23	3♎03 22	10♎06 17	6 48.2	6 47.8	17 38.8	19 06.7	24 25.3	14 10.5	2 47.5	22 36.0	5 55.7	20 34.0
20 Tu	13 51 05	25 55 06	17 06 15	24 02 49	6 47.5	7 53.5	18 01.8	19 50.5	24 52.1	14 06.4	2 48.7	22 38.4	5 55.4	20 33.4
21 W	13 55 01	26 54 45	0♏55 31	7♏44 01	6 45.7	9 04.9	18 26.6	20 34.4	25 19.0	14 02.4	2 50.0	22 40.8	5 55.0	20 32.8
22 Th	13 58 58	27 54 29	14 27 59	21 07 12	6 42.9	10 21.3	18 53.1	21 18.4	25 45.8	13 58.7	2 51.4	22 43.2	5 54.7	20 32.1
23 F	14 02 54	28 54 15	27 41 34	4♐11 01	6 39.5	11 42.0	19 21.3	22 02.5	26 12.7	13 55.1	2 52.8	22 45.7	5 54.2	20 31.5
24 Sa	14 06 51	29 54 03	10♐35 37	16 55 30	6 35.9	13 06.3	19 51.1	22 46.6	26 39.5	13 51.8	2 54.4	22 48.2	5 53.8	20 30.8
25 Su	14 10 47	0♏53 53	23 10 56	29 22 11	6 32.5	14 33.6	20 22.4	23 30.9	27 06.3	13 48.6	2 56.1	22 50.7	5 53.3	20 30.1
26 M	14 14 44	1 53 44	5♑29 39	11♑33 47	6 29.9	16 03.5	20 55.2	24 15.2	27 33.1	13 45.6	2 57.9	22 53.3	5 52.8	20 29.4
27 Tu	14 18 41	2 53 37	17 35 04	23 34 03	6D 28.2	17 35.4	21 29.4	24 59.6	27 59.9	13 42.8	2 59.7	22 55.9	5 52.2	20 28.7
28 W	14 22 37	3 53 32	29 31 18	5♒27 24	6 27.8	19 09.1	22 05.0	25 44.0	28 26.7	13 40.2	3 01.7	22 58.6	5 51.6	20 28.0
29 Th	14 26 34	4 53 28	11♒22 59	17 18 40	6 28.5	20 44.1	22 41.9	26 28.5	28 53.4	13 37.9	3 03.8	23 01.3	5 51.0	20 27.2
30 F	14 30 30	5 53 26	23 15 04	29 12 48	6 30.0	22 20.2	23 20.1	27 13.1	29 20.2	13 35.7	3 05.9	23 04.0	5 50.3	20 26.4
31 Sa	14 34 27	6 53 26	5♓12 27	11♓14 36	6 31.9	23 57.1	23 59.5	27 57.8	29 46.9	13 33.7	3 08.2	23 06.7	5 49.7	20 25.6

Astro Data	Planet Ingress	Last Aspect	☽ Ingress	Last Aspect	☽ Ingress	☽ Phases & Eclipses	Astro Data
Dy Hr Mn	Dy Hr Mn	Dy Hr Mn	Dy Hr Mn	Dy Hr Mn	Dy Hr Mn	Dy Hr Mn	1 September 1903
♅ D 1 4:19	♀ ♍R 6 2:28	2 12:41 ♃ ⚹	♒ 3 9:45	2 13:29 ♅ ⚹	♓ 3 5:24	7 0:20 ○ 13♓12	Julian Day # 1339
☽ 0N 8 5:40	♂ ♐ 22 13:52	5 5:23 ♅ ⚹	♓ 5 22:07	5 0:57 ♅ □	♈ 5 16:11	14 13:14 ☾ 20♊32	SVP 6♓36'14"
♃∠♄ 13 0:55	☉ ♎ 24 5:44	8 7:28 ♀ ☍	♈ 8 9:12	7 10:07 ♅ △	♉ 8 0:34	21 4:31 ● 27♍01	GC 25♐29.6 ⚴ 21♍55.3
☿ R 20 22:22		10 2:42 ♅ △	♉ 10 18:22	9 5:04 ♀ △	♊ 10 6:41	21 4:39:49 T 02'12"	Eris 23♓42.4R ⚵ 26♏34.1
☽ 0S 21 6:26	☉ ♏ 24 14:23	12 19:29 ♀ △	♊ 13 1:11	11 21:45 ♅ ☍	♋ 12 11:00	28 13:08 ☽ 4♑14	⚷ 17♑30.9R ⚶ 6♊45.0
♇ R 21 12:38	⚳ ♏ 31 23:48	14 21:56 ♀ □	♋ 15 5:27	13 19:57 ☉ □	♌ 14 14:03		☽ Mean ☊ 8♎16.7
☉0S 24 5:44		17 1:18 ♂ △	♌ 17 7:30	16 3:47 ♅ △	♍ 16 16:24	6 15:23 ○ 12♈11	
⚳0S 30 11:59		19 4:34 ♂ □	♍ 19 8:20	18 6:14 ♅ □	♎ 18 18:49	6 15:18 P 0.865	1 October 1903
☽ 0N 5 12:38		21 8:03 ♂ ⚹	♎ 21 9:28	20 15:30 ☉ ☌	♏ 20 22:23	13 19:57 ☾ 19♋18	Julian Day # 1369
♀0N 6 5:55		22 22:22 ♅ ⚹	♏ 23 12:33	22 7:49 ♀ ⚹	♐ 23 4:15	20 15:30 ● 26♎04	SVP 6♓36'12"
♄ D 8 8:06		24 23:40 ♀ ⚹	♐ 25 18:53	24 23:56 ♂ ☌	♑ 25 13:14	28 8:33 ☽ 3♒45	GC 25♐29.7 ⚴ 5♎47.7
♀ D 9 4:36		27 12:52 ♅ ☌	♑ 28 4:45	27 7:37 ♀ △	♒ 28 0:58		Eris 23♓21.4R ⚵ 3♐44.5
♆ R 10 6:37		29 15:43 ♀ △	♒ 30 16:59	30 7:43 ♂ ⚹	♓ 30 13:35		⚷ 17♑12.4 ⚶ 10♊53.2
☿ D 12 14:41							☽ Mean ☊ 6♎41.4
☽ 0S 18 15:44							

November 1903 LONGITUDE

Day	Sid.Time	☉	0 hr ☽	Noon ☽	True ☊	☿	♀	♂	⚳	♃	♄	♅	♆	♇
1 Su	14 38 23	7♏53 27	17♓19 45	23♓28 25	6♎33.4	25♎34.5	24♍40.2	28♐42.5	0♏13.6	13♓31.9	3♒10.5	23♐09.5	5♋48.9	20♊24.8
2 M	14 42 20	8 53 30	29 41 00	5♈57 53	6R 34.1	27 12.4	25 21.9	29 27.3	0 40.2	13R 30.3	3 13.0	23 12.4	5R 48.2	20R 24.0
3 Tu	14 46 16	9 53 34	12♈19 20	18 45 34	6 33.4	28 50.6	26 04.8	0♑12.1	1 06.9	13 28.9	3 15.5	23 15.2	5 47.4	20 23.2
4 W	14 50 13	10 53 41	25 16 42	1♉52 44	6 31.1	0♏29.0	26 48.8	0 57.0	1 33.5	13 27.8	3 18.1	23 18.1	5 46.6	20 22.3
5 Th	14 54 10	11 53 49	8♉33 35	15 19 05	6 27.0	2 07.3	27 33.7	1 42.0	2 00.1	13 26.8	3 20.9	23 21.0	5 45.8	20 21.4
6 F	14 58 06	12 53 59	22 08 56	29 02 47	6 21.7	3 45.7	28 19.7	2 27.1	2 26.7	13 26.0	3 23.7	23 24.0	5 44.9	20 20.6
7 Sa	15 02 03	13 54 11	6♊00 10	13♊00 36	6 15.5	5 24.0	29 06.6	3 12.2	2 53.3	13 25.5	3 26.6	23 27.0	5 44.0	20 19.7
8 Su	15 05 59	14 54 25	20 03 32	27 08 24	6 09.5	7 02.1	29 54.5	3 57.3	3 19.9	13 25.1	3 29.6	23 30.0	5 43.1	20 18.8
9 M	15 09 56	15 54 41	4♋14 41	11♋21 48	6 04.3	8 40.1	0♎43.3	4 42.6	3 46.4	13D 25.0	3 32.7	23 33.0	5 42.2	20 17.8
10 Tu	15 13 52	16 54 59	18 29 17	25 36 40	6 00.5	10 17.8	1 32.9	5 27.9	4 12.9	13 25.0	3 35.9	23 36.1	5 41.2	20 16.9
11 W	15 17 49	17 55 18	2♌43 35	9♌49 42	5D 58.6	11 55.3	2 23.3	6 13.2	4 39.4	13 25.3	3 39.2	23 39.2	5 40.2	20 16.0
12 Th	15 21 45	18 55 40	16 54 45	23 58 32	5 58.4	13 32.5	3 14.5	6 58.6	5 05.8	13 25.7	3 42.5	23 42.3	5 39.2	20 15.0
13 F	15 25 42	19 56 04	1♍00 52	8♍01 39	5 59.4	15 09.5	4 06.5	7 44.1	5 32.2	13 26.4	3 46.0	23 45.5	5 38.1	20 14.0
14 Sa	15 29 39	20 56 30	15 00 46	21 58 07	6 00.7	16 46.2	4 59.2	8 29.6	5 58.6	13 27.3	3 49.5	23 48.7	5 37.0	20 13.0
15 Su	15 33 35	21 56 57	28 53 36	5♎47 06	6R 01.4	18 22.7	5 52.7	9 15.2	6 25.0	13 28.4	3 53.1	23 51.9	5 35.9	20 12.0
16 M	15 37 32	22 57 27	12♎38 30	19 27 38	6 00.5	19 58.9	6 46.8	10 00.9	6 51.3	13 29.7	3 56.8	23 55.1	5 34.8	20 11.0
17 Tu	15 41 28	23 57 58	26 14 20	2♏58 25	5 57.4	21 34.8	7 41.6	10 46.6	7 17.6	13 31.1	4 00.6	23 58.3	5 33.6	20 10.0
18 W	15 45 25	24 58 31	9♏39 39	16 17 51	5 51.9	23 10.5	8 37.0	11 32.4	7 43.9	13 32.8	4 04.5	24 01.6	5 32.4	20 09.0
19 Th	15 49 21	25 59 05	22 52 49	29 24 21	5 44.2	24 45.9	9 33.0	12 18.2	8 10.1	13 34.7	4 08.5	24 04.9	5 31.2	20 07.9
20 F	15 53 18	26 59 41	5♐52 18	12♐16 33	5 34.9	26 21.1	10 29.5	13 04.0	8 36.3	13 36.9	4 12.5	24 08.2	5 30.0	20 06.9
21 Sa	15 57 14	28 00 19	18 37 04	24 53 51	5 24.8	27 56.1	11 26.7	13 50.0	9 02.5	13 39.2	4 16.6	24 11.6	5 28.7	20 05.8
22 Su	16 01 11	29 00 57	1♑06 58	7♑16 33	5 14.9	29 30.9	12 24.4	14 35.9	9 28.6	13 41.7	4 20.9	24 14.9	5 27.4	20 04.7
23 M	16 05 08	0♐01 37	13 22 51	19 26 07	5 06.3	1♐05.6	13 22.6	15 22.0	9 54.7	13 44.4	4 25.1	24 18.3	5 26.1	20 03.6
24 Tu	16 09 04	1 02 18	25 26 44	1♒25 06	4 59.5	2 40.0	14 21.3	16 08.0	10 20.7	13 47.3	4 29.5	24 21.7	5 24.8	20 02.6
25 W	16 13 01	2 03 01	7♒21 42	13 17 05	4 55.1	4 14.3	15 20.5	16 54.2	10 46.8	13 50.4	4 34.0	24 25.2	5 23.5	20 01.5
26 Th	16 16 57	3 03 44	19 11 49	25 06 31	4D 53.0	5 48.4	16 20.2	17 40.3	11 12.7	13 53.7	4 38.5	24 28.6	5 22.1	20 00.3
27 F	16 20 54	4 04 29	1♓01 49	6♓58 25	4 52.6	7 22.5	17 20.3	18 26.5	11 38.6	13 57.2	4 43.1	24 32.0	5 20.7	19 59.2
28 Sa	16 24 50	5 05 14	12 56 57	18 58 08	4 53.3	8 56.4	18 20.9	19 12.8	12 04.5	14 00.9	4 47.7	24 35.5	5 19.3	19 58.1
29 Su	16 28 47	6 06 00	25 02 37	1♈11 02	4R 54.0	10 30.2	19 21.8	19 59.0	12 30.3	14 04.8	4 52.5	24 39.0	5 17.9	19 57.0
30 M	16 32 43	7 06 48	7♈24 01	13 42 06	4 53.7	12 03.9	20 23.3	20 45.4	12 56.1	14 08.9	4 57.3	24 42.5	5 16.4	19 55.9

December 1903 LONGITUDE

Day	Sid.Time	☉	0 hr ☽	Noon ☽	True ☊	☿	♀	♂	⚳	♃	♄	♅	♆	♇
1 Tu	16 36 40	8♐07 36	20♈05 45	26♈35 22	4♎51.4	13♐37.6	21♎25.1	21♑31.7	13♏21.9	14♓13.1	5♒02.2	24♐46.0	5♋15.0	19♊54.7
2 W	16 40 37	9 08 25	3♉11 13	9♉53 26	4R 46.7	15 11.2	22 27.3	22 18.1	13 47.6	14 17.6	5 07.1	24 49.5	5R 13.5	19R 53.6
3 Th	16 44 33	10 09 16	16 42 02	23 36 49	4 39.3	16 44.8	23 29.9	23 04.6	14 13.2	14 22.2	5 12.2	24 53.1	5 12.0	19 52.4
4 F	16 48 30	11 10 07	0♊37 28	7♊43 29	4 29.7	18 18.4	24 32.8	23 51.0	14 38.8	14 27.0	5 17.3	24 56.6	5 10.5	19 51.3
5 Sa	16 52 26	12 11 00	14 54 12	22 08 50	4 18.8	19 51.9	25 36.1	24 37.5	15 04.3	14 32.0	5 22.4	25 00.2	5 09.0	19 50.1
6 Su	16 56 23	13 11 53	29 26 30	6♋46 13	4 07.9	21 25.4	26 39.8	25 24.1	15 29.8	14 37.2	5 27.7	25 03.8	5 07.4	19 49.0
7 M	17 00 19	14 12 48	14♋06 59	21 27 51	3 58.0	22 58.8	27 43.8	26 10.7	15 55.3	14 42.6	5 32.9	25 07.3	5 05.9	19 47.8
8 Tu	17 04 16	15 13 44	28 47 54	6♌06 18	3 50.4	24 32.3	28 48.1	26 57.3	16 20.7	14 48.1	5 38.3	25 10.9	5 04.3	19 46.7
9 W	17 08 12	16 14 41	13♌22 22	20 35 31	3 45.4	26 05.7	29 52.7	27 43.9	16 46.0	14 53.9	5 43.7	25 14.5	5 02.7	19 45.5
10 Th	17 12 09	17 15 39	27 45 21	4♍51 34	3D 43.1	27 39.1	0♏57.6	28 30.6	17 11.3	14 59.8	5 49.2	25 18.1	5 01.1	19 44.3
11 F	17 16 06	18 16 39	11♍54 01	18 52 38	3 42.5	29 12.5	2 02.9	29 17.3	17 36.5	15 05.8	5 54.8	25 21.8	4 59.5	19 43.2
12 Sa	17 20 02	19 17 39	25 47 28	2♎38 37	3R 42.7	0♑45.7	3 08.4	0♒04.0	18 01.7	15 12.1	6 00.4	25 25.4	4 57.9	19 42.0
13 Su	17 23 59	20 18 41	9♎26 13	16 10 26	3 42.2	2 18.9	4 14.1	0 50.8	18 26.8	15 18.5	6 06.0	25 29.0	4 56.3	19 40.8
14 M	17 27 55	21 19 44	22 51 27	29 29 26	3 39.8	3 52.0	5 20.2	1 37.6	18 51.9	15 25.0	6 11.8	25 32.6	4 54.7	19 39.7
15 Tu	17 31 52	22 20 47	6♏04 30	12♏36 47	3 34.7	5 24.9	6 26.5	2 24.4	19 16.8	15 31.8	6 17.5	25 36.3	4 53.0	19 38.5
16 W	17 35 48	23 21 52	19 06 21	25 33 15	3 26.4	6 57.6	7 33.0	3 11.3	19 41.8	15 38.7	6 23.4	25 39.9	4 51.4	19 37.3
17 Th	17 39 45	24 22 57	1♐57 30	8♐19 06	3 15.1	8 30.0	8 39.8	3 58.1	20 06.6	15 45.8	6 29.3	25 43.5	4 49.7	19 36.2
18 F	17 43 41	25 24 04	14 38 02	20 54 17	3 01.6	10 02.0	9 46.8	4 45.1	20 31.4	15 53.0	6 35.2	25 47.2	4 48.0	19 35.0
19 Sa	17 47 38	26 25 10	27 07 50	3♑18 41	2 47.0	11 33.6	10 54.0	5 32.0	20 56.2	16 00.4	6 41.2	25 50.8	4 46.3	19 33.8
20 Su	17 51 35	27 26 18	9♑26 52	15 32 27	2 32.5	13 04.6	12 01.4	6 18.9	21 20.8	16 08.0	6 47.3	25 54.4	4 44.7	19 32.7
21 M	17 55 31	28 27 26	21 35 33	27 36 20	2 19.4	14 34.9	13 09.1	7 05.9	21 45.4	16 15.7	6 53.4	25 58.1	4 43.0	19 31.5
22 Tu	17 59 28	29 28 34	3♒35 02	9♒31 55	2 08.6	16 04.3	14 16.9	7 52.9	22 09.9	16 23.6	6 59.5	26 01.7	4 41.3	19 30.4
23 W	18 03 24	0♑29 42	15 27 20	21 21 41	2 00.6	17 32.7	15 24.9	8 39.9	22 34.3	16 31.6	7 05.7	26 05.3	4 39.6	19 29.2
24 Th	18 07 21	1 30 50	27 15 27	3♓09 08	1 55.7	18 59.8	16 33.1	9 27.0	22 58.7	16 39.8	7 12.0	26 09.0	4 37.9	19 28.1
25 F	18 11 17	2 31 59	9♓03 18	14 58 34	1 53.3	20 25.3	17 41.5	10 14.0	23 23.0	16 48.1	7 18.3	26 12.6	4 36.2	19 26.9
26 Sa	18 15 14	3 33 08	20 55 35	26 55 02	1 52.6	21 49.0	18 50.1	11 01.1	23 47.2	16 56.5	7 24.6	26 16.2	4 34.5	19 25.8
27 Su	18 19 10	4 34 16	2♈57 36	9♈03 59	1 52.6	23 10.5	19 58.8	11 48.1	24 11.3	17 05.1	7 31.0	26 19.8	4 32.8	19 24.7
28 M	18 23 07	5 35 25	15 14 53	21 30 59	1 51.9	24 29.4	21 07.7	12 35.2	24 35.4	17 13.9	7 37.4	26 23.4	4 31.1	19 23.6
29 Tu	18 27 04	6 36 34	27 52 54	4♉21 12	1 49.6	25 45.2	22 16.7	13 22.3	24 59.3	17 22.8	7 43.9	26 27.0	4 29.4	19 22.5
30 W	18 31 00	7 37 42	10♉56 21	17 38 42	1 44.7	26 57.4	23 25.9	14 09.4	25 23.2	17 31.8	7 50.4	26 30.6	4 27.7	19 21.3
31 Th	18 34 57	8 38 51	24 28 26	1♊25 36	1 37.1	28 05.4	24 35.3	14 56.5	25 47.0	17 41.0	7 57.0	26 34.2	4 26.0	19 20.2

Astro Data (Dy Hr Mn)

Astro Data	Dy Hr Mn
☽0N	1 21:15
♀0S	8 21:13
♃ D	9 17:32
☽0S	14 23:11
☽0N	29 7:14
♄♃♇	30 6:15
♄⚻♆	3 11:28
☽0S	12 5:42
☽0N	26 17:11

Planet Ingress (Dy Hr Mn)

Planet Ingress	Dy Hr Mn
♂ ♑	3 5:31
☿ ♏	4 4:56
♀ ♎	8 14:44
☿ ♐	22 19:22
☉ ♐	23 11:22
♀ ♏	9 14:42
☿ ♑	12 0:14
♂ ♒	12 9:56
☉ ♑	23 0:21

Last Aspect / ☽ Ingress (November)

Last Aspect Dy Hr Mn		☽ Ingress	Dy Hr Mn
1 22:46	♂ □	♈	2 0:36
3 20:19	♅ △	♉	4 8:36
6 10:41	♀ △	♊	6 13:39
8 5:49	♅ ☍	♋	8 16:50
9 20:15	☉ △	♌	10 19:24
12 11:32	♅ △	♍	12 22:16
14 15:12	♅ □	♎	15 1:55
16 19:55	♅ ⚹	♏	17 6:41
19 5:10	☉ ☌	♐	19 13:06
21 10:39	♅ ☌	♑	21 21:50
23 3:23	♂ ☌	♒	24 9:09
26 10:43	♅ ⚹	♓	26 21:55
28 23:10	♅ □	♈	29 9:42

Last Aspect / ☽ Ingress (December)

Last Aspect Dy Hr Mn		☽ Ingress	Dy Hr Mn
1 8:38	♅ △	♉	1 18:14
3 11:01	♂ △	♊	3 22:56
5 18:08	♀ △	♋	6 0:55
7 23:03	♀ □	♌	8 1:58
9 22:20	☿ △	♍	10 3:47
12 7:12	♂ △	♎	12 7:21
14 4:49	♅ ⚹	♏	14 12:56
15 17:26	♃ △	♐	16 20:19
18 21:27	♅ ☌	♑	19 5:34
20 13:11	♃ ⚹	♒	21 16:48
23 21:40	♅ ⚹	♓	24 5:35
26 10:42	♅ □	♈	26 18:08
28 21:15	♅ △	♉	29 3:57
31 5:46	☿ △	♊	31 9:33

☽ Phases & Eclipses (Dy Hr Mn)

Dy Hr Mn	
5 5:27	○ 11♉37
12 2:46	☾ 18♌32
19 5:10	● 25♏42
27 5:37	☽ 3♓48
4 18:13	○ 11♊26
11 10:53	☾ 18♍14
18 21:26	● 25♐48
27 2:22	☽ 4♈10

Astro Data

1 November 1903
Julian Day # 1400
SVP 6♓36'09"
GC 25♐29.8 ⚴ 19♎49.5
Eris 23♓02.6R ⚵ 13♐11.0
⚷ 18♑04.9 ⚶ 8♊53.3R
☽ Mean ☊ 5♎02.9

1 December 1903
Julian Day # 1430
SVP 6♓36'05"
GC 25♐29.8 ⚴ 2♏50.9
Eris 22♓52.9R ⚵ 23♐31.7
⚷ 19♑55.5 ⚶ 1♊45.7R
☽ Mean ☊ 3♎27.5

LONGITUDE — January 1904

Day	Sid.Time	☉	0 hr ☽	Noon ☽	True ☊	☿	♀	♂	⚳	♃	♄	♅	♆	♇
1 F	18 38 53	9♑39 59	8♊30 02	15♊41 19	1♎27.1	29♑08.5	25♏44.8	15♒43.7	26♏10.7	17♓50.3	8♒03.5	26♐37.8	4♋24.3	19♊19.2
2 Sa	18 42 50	10 41 07	22 58 53	0♋21 54	1R 15.5	0♒05.9	26 54.4	16 30.8	26 34.4	17 59.7	8 10.2	26 41.3	4R 22.6	19R 18.1
3 Su	18 46 46	11 42 16	7♋49 22	15 20 07	1 03.6	0 56.9	28 04.2	17 17.9	26 57.9	18 09.3	8 16.8	26 44.9	4 20.9	19 17.0
4 M	18 50 43	12 43 24	22 52 53	0♌26 23	0 52.9	1 40.6	29 14.1	18 05.1	27 21.3	18 19.0	8 23.5	26 48.4	4 19.2	19 15.9
5 Tu	18 54 40	13 44 33	7♌59 17	15 30 24	0 44.3	2 16.1	0♐24.2	18 52.2	27 44.7	18 28.8	8 30.2	26 51.9	4 17.6	19 14.9
6 W	18 58 36	14 45 41	22 58 38	0♍23 02	0 38.6	2 42.4	1 34.4	19 39.4	28 07.9	18 38.7	8 37.0	26 55.5	4 15.9	19 13.8
7 Th	19 02 33	15 46 50	7♍42 53	14 57 38	0 35.7	2R 58.7	2 44.7	20 26.5	28 31.1	18 48.8	8 43.8	26 59.0	4 14.2	19 12.8
8 F	19 06 29	16 47 58	22 06 56	29 10 35	0D 34.9	3 04.3	3 55.1	21 13.7	28 54.2	18 58.9	8 50.6	27 02.4	4 12.6	19 11.8
9 Sa	19 10 26	17 49 07	6♎08 35	13♎01 00	0R 35.1	2 58.5	5 05.7	22 00.8	29 17.2	19 09.2	8 57.4	27 05.9	4 10.9	19 10.8
10 Su	19 14 22	18 50 16	19 48 04	26 30 03	0 34.9	2 40.9	6 16.3	22 48.0	29 40.0	19 19.6	9 04.3	27 09.4	4 09.3	19 09.8
11 M	19 18 19	19 51 24	3♏07 16	9♏40 03	0 33.2	2 11.5	7 27.1	23 35.2	0♐02.8	19 30.2	9 11.2	27 12.8	4 07.7	19 08.8
12 Tu	19 22 15	20 52 33	16 08 46	22 33 45	0 29.0	1 30.7	8 38.0	24 22.3	0 25.5	19 40.8	9 18.1	27 16.2	4 06.0	19 07.8
13 W	19 26 12	21 53 42	28 55 20	5♐13 47	0 22.0	0 39.1	9 49.0	25 09.5	0 48.0	19 51.6	9 25.1	27 19.6	4 04.4	19 06.8
14 Th	19 30 09	22 54 51	11♐29 24	17 42 23	0 12.2	29♑38.2	11 00.0	25 56.7	1 10.5	20 02.5	9 32.0	27 23.0	4 02.8	19 05.9
15 F	19 34 05	23 55 59	23 52 57	0♑01 16	0 00.4	28 29.5	12 11.2	26 43.8	1 32.8	20 13.4	9 39.0	27 26.4	4 01.2	19 04.9
16 Sa	19 38 02	24 57 07	6♑07 28	12 11 42	29♍47.4	27 15.2	13 22.4	27 31.0	1 55.1	20 24.5	9 46.0	27 29.7	3 59.7	19 04.0
17 Su	19 41 58	25 58 14	18 14 04	24 14 43	29 34.5	25 57.7	14 33.8	28 18.2	2 17.2	20 35.7	9 53.1	27 33.0	3 58.1	19 03.1
18 M	19 45 55	26 59 21	0♒13 45	6♒11 20	29 22.7	24 39.3	15 45.2	29 05.3	2 39.2	20 47.0	10 00.1	27 36.3	3 56.6	19 02.2
19 Tu	19 49 51	28 00 28	12 07 38	18 02 52	29 13.0	23 22.5	16 56.7	29 52.5	3 01.1	20 58.4	10 07.2	27 39.6	3 55.0	19 01.3
20 W	19 53 48	29 01 33	23 57 15	29 51 06	29 05.9	22 09.5	18 08.3	0♓39.6	3 22.8	21 09.9	10 14.3	27 42.8	3 53.5	19 00.5
21 Th	19 57 44	0♒02 38	5♓44 43	11♓38 31	29 01.6	21 02.0	19 19.9	1 26.7	3 44.5	21 21.5	10 21.4	27 46.1	3 52.0	18 59.6
22 F	20 01 41	1 03 42	17 32 54	23 28 21	28D 59.8	20 01.7	20 31.6	2 13.9	4 06.0	21 33.2	10 28.5	27 49.3	3 50.5	18 58.8
23 Sa	20 05 38	2 04 45	29 25 23	5♈24 34	28 59.8	19 09.4	21 43.4	3 01.0	4 27.4	21 45.0	10 35.6	27 52.4	3 49.1	18 57.9
24 Su	20 09 34	3 05 47	11♈26 30	17 31 48	29 00.7	18 25.8	22 55.2	3 48.1	4 48.6	21 56.8	10 42.8	27 55.6	3 47.6	18 57.1
25 M	20 13 31	4 06 47	23 41 07	29 55 06	29R 01.6	17 51.3	24 07.2	4 35.2	5 09.8	22 08.8	10 49.9	27 58.7	3 46.2	18 56.4
26 Tu	20 17 27	5 07 47	6♉14 23	12♉39 33	29 01.3	17 25.9	25 19.1	5 22.2	5 30.7	22 20.8	10 57.1	28 01.8	3 44.8	18 55.6
27 W	20 21 24	6 08 46	19 11 10	25 49 43	28 59.3	17 09.3	26 31.2	6 09.3	5 51.6	22 33.0	11 04.2	28 04.8	3 43.4	18 54.8
28 Th	20 25 20	7 09 44	2♊35 33	9♊28 55	28 55.2	17D 01.3	27 43.3	6 56.3	6 12.3	22 45.2	11 11.4	28 07.9	3 42.0	18 54.1
29 F	20 29 17	8 10 40	16 29 51	23 38 16	28 49.0	17 01.4	28 55.4	7 43.4	6 32.9	22 57.5	11 18.6	28 10.9	3 40.7	18 53.4
30 Sa	20 33 13	9 11 35	0♋53 47	8♋15 51	28 41.5	17 09.0	0♑07.6	8 30.4	6 53.3	23 09.9	11 25.7	28 13.9	3 39.4	18 52.7
31 Su	20 37 10	10 12 29	15 43 40	23 16 15	28 33.6	17 23.6	1 19.9	9 17.3	7 13.6	23 22.3	11 32.9	28 16.8	3 38.1	18 52.0

LONGITUDE — February 1904

Day	Sid.Time	☉	0 hr ☽	Noon ☽	True ☊	☿	♀	♂	⚳	♃	♄	♅	♆	♇
1 M	20 41 07	11♒13 22	0♌52 23	8♌30 47	28♍26.3	17♑44.7	2♑32.2	10♓04.3	7♐33.8	23♓34.9	11♒40.1	28♐19.7	3♋36.8	18♊51.3
2 Tu	20 45 03	12 14 14	16 10 02	23 48 46	28R 20.5	18 11.7	3 44.5	10 51.2	7 53.8	23 47.5	11 47.3	28 22.6	3R 35.5	18R 50.7
3 W	20 49 00	13 15 04	1♍25 36	8♍59 19	28 16.9	18 44.2	4 57.0	11 38.2	8 13.7	24 00.2	11 54.4	28 25.4	3 34.3	18 50.1
4 Th	20 52 56	14 15 54	16 28 50	23 53 14	28D 15.4	19 21.7	6 09.4	12 25.1	8 33.4	24 12.9	12 01.6	28 28.2	3 33.1	18 49.5
5 F	20 56 53	15 16 43	1♎11 51	8♎24 10	28 15.7	20 03.7	7 22.0	13 12.0	8 52.9	24 25.8	12 08.8	28 31.0	3 31.9	18 48.9
6 Sa	21 00 49	16 17 30	15 29 55	22 28 59	28 16.9	20 49.9	8 34.5	13 58.8	9 12.3	24 38.7	12 16.0	28 33.8	3 30.7	18 48.3
7 Su	21 04 46	17 18 17	29 21 25	6♏07 23	28R 18.3	21 39.8	9 47.2	14 45.7	9 31.6	24 51.6	12 23.1	28 36.5	3 29.6	18 47.7
8 M	21 08 42	18 19 03	12♏47 11	19 21 09	28 18.8	22 33.2	10 59.8	15 32.5	9 50.6	25 04.7	12 30.3	28 39.1	3 28.5	18 47.2
9 Tu	21 12 39	19 19 48	25 49 41	2♐13 15	28 17.9	23 29.8	12 12.5	16 19.3	10 09.5	25 17.8	12 37.5	28 41.8	3 27.4	18 46.7
10 W	21 16 36	20 20 32	8♐32 18	14 47 17	28 15.2	24 29.3	13 25.3	17 06.0	10 28.3	25 30.9	12 44.6	28 44.4	3 26.3	18 46.2
11 Th	21 20 32	21 21 15	20 58 39	27 06 50	28 10.7	25 31.5	14 38.1	17 52.8	10 46.9	25 44.2	12 51.8	28 46.9	3 25.3	18 45.7
12 F	21 24 29	22 21 57	3♑12 15	9♑15 15	28 04.9	26 36.1	15 50.9	18 39.5	11 05.3	25 57.5	12 58.9	28 49.5	3 24.3	18 45.3
13 Sa	21 28 25	23 22 38	15 16 12	21 15 25	27 58.3	27 43.0	17 03.7	19 26.2	11 23.5	26 10.8	13 06.0	28 52.0	3 23.3	18 44.9
14 Su	21 32 22	24 23 17	27 13 12	3♒09 49	27 51.7	28 52.0	18 16.6	20 12.9	11 41.5	26 24.2	13 13.1	28 54.4	3 22.3	18 44.5
15 M	21 36 18	25 23 55	9♒05 32	15 00 33	27 45.7	0♒03.0	19 29.6	20 59.6	11 59.4	26 37.7	13 20.2	28 56.8	3 21.4	18 44.1
16 Tu	21 40 15	26 24 31	20 55 07	26 49 27	27 40.8	1 15.9	20 42.5	21 46.2	12 17.0	26 51.2	13 27.3	28 59.2	3 20.5	18 43.7
17 W	21 44 11	27 25 06	2♓43 47	8♓38 22	27 37.5	2 30.4	21 55.5	22 32.8	12 34.5	27 04.8	13 34.3	29 01.5	3 19.6	18 43.4
18 Th	21 48 08	28 25 39	14 33 26	20 29 16	27D 35.9	3 46.6	23 08.5	23 19.3	12 51.8	27 18.4	13 41.4	29 03.8	3 18.8	18 43.0
19 F	21 52 04	29 26 11	26 26 10	2♈24 27	27 35.7	5 04.3	24 21.5	24 05.9	13 08.9	27 32.1	13 48.4	29 06.0	3 18.0	18 42.7
20 Sa	21 56 01	0♓26 41	8♈24 29	14 26 39	27 36.7	6 23.5	25 34.6	24 52.4	13 25.8	27 45.8	13 55.4	29 08.2	3 17.2	18 42.5
21 Su	21 59 58	1 27 09	20 31 22	26 39 04	27 38.4	7 44.0	26 47.7	25 38.9	13 42.5	27 59.6	14 02.4	29 10.4	3 16.5	18 42.2
22 M	22 03 54	2 27 35	2♉50 14	9♉05 21	27 40.1	9 05.9	28 00.8	26 25.3	13 59.0	28 13.4	14 09.3	29 12.5	3 15.8	18 42.0
23 Tu	22 07 51	3 27 59	15 24 53	21 49 20	27R 41.4	10 29.1	29 13.9	27 11.7	14 15.2	28 27.2	14 16.3	29 14.5	3 15.1	18 41.8
24 W	22 11 47	4 28 22	28 19 09	4♊54 46	27 41.9	11 53.6	0♒27.0	27 58.1	14 31.3	28 41.1	14 23.2	29 16.6	3 14.4	18 41.6
25 Th	22 15 44	5 28 43	11♊36 33	18 24 46	27 41.3	13 19.2	1 40.2	28 44.4	14 47.2	28 55.1	14 30.0	29 18.5	3 13.8	18 41.4
26 F	22 19 40	6 29 01	25 19 37	2♋21 08	27 39.8	14 46.1	2 53.4	29 30.7	15 02.8	29 09.0	14 36.9	29 20.5	3 13.2	18 41.3
27 Sa	22 23 37	7 29 18	9♋29 13	16 43 36	27 37.5	16 14.0	4 06.6	0♈16.9	15 18.2	29 23.0	14 43.7	29 22.4	3 12.7	18 41.1
28 Su	22 27 33	8 29 32	24 03 50	1♌29 16	27 34.9	17 43.2	5 19.8	1 03.2	15 33.4	29 37.1	14 50.5	29 24.2	3 12.2	18 41.0
29 M	22 31 30	9 29 45	8♌59 04	16 32 15	27 32.4	19 13.4	6 33.0	1 49.3	15 48.4	29 51.2	14 57.3	29 26.0	3 11.7	18 41.0

Astro Data	Planet Ingress	Last Aspect	☽ Ingress	Last Aspect	☽ Ingress	☽ Phases & Eclipses	Astro Data
Dy Hr Mn	Dy Hr Mn	Dy Hr Mn	Dy Hr Mn	Dy Hr Mn	Dy Hr Mn	Dy Hr Mn	1 January 1904
☿R 8 11:56	☿ ♒ 2 9:24	2 6:01 ♅ ☍	♋ 2 11:25	2 19:12 ♅ △	♍ 2 21:45	3 5:47 ○ 11♋26	Julian Day # 1461
☽0S 8 13:10	♀ ♐ 5 3:43	4 9:56 ♀ △	♌ 4 11:18	4 19:32 ♅ □	♎ 4 22:01	9 21:10 ☾ 18♎12	SVP 6♓36'00"
♃□♇ 9 15:15	⚳ ♐ 11 9:02	6 6:22 ♅ △	♍ 6 11:23	6 22:38 ♅ ✶	♏ 7 1:08	17 15:47 ● 26♑08	GC 25♐29.9 ⚵ 15♏15.6
☽0N 23 1:41	☿ ♑R 14 3:47	8 8:20 ♅ □	♎ 8 13:25	8 22:47 ♃ △	♐ 9 7:49	25 20:41 ☽ 4♉29	Eris 22♓55.0 ✱ 4♑52.9
☿D 28 23:49	☊ ♍R 15 12:40	10 13:11 ♅ ✶	♏ 10 18:20	11 15:17 ♅ ☌	♑ 11 17:41		⚷ 22♑29.2 ⚶ 25♉53.5R
	♂ ♓ 19 15:50	12 15:38 ♂ □	♐ 13 2:03	14 2:23 ♅ ☌	♒ 14 5:36	1 16:33 ○ 11♌25	☽ Mean ☊ 1♎49.1
☽0S 4 22:47	☉ ♒ 21 10:58	15 6:55 ♅ ☌	♑ 15 11:58	16 16:25 ♅ ✶	♓ 16 18:27	8 9:56 ☾ 18♏14	
☽0N 19 8:28	♀ ♑ 30 9:28	17 15:47 ☉ ☌	♒ 17 23:32	19 5:20 ♅ □	♈ 19 7:10	16 11:05 ● 26♒22	1 February 1904
♄∠♅ 23 3:33		20 7:38 ♅ ✶	♓ 20 12:18	21 16:55 ♅ △	♉ 21 18:31	24 11:08 ☽ 4♊26	Julian Day # 1492
♃□♅ 27 10:38	☿ ♒ 15 10:59	22 20:49 ♅ □	♈ 23 1:10	24 3:04 ♀ △	♊ 24 3:05		SVP 6♓35'55"
♂0N 28 22:48	☉ ♓ 20 1:25	25 8:16 ♅ △	♉ 25 12:09	26 6:53 ♂ □	♋ 26 8:00		GC 25♐30.0 ⚵ 25♏46.6
	♀ ♒ 24 3:08	27 6:01 ♃ ✶	♊ 27 19:26	28 8:56 ♃ △	♌ 28 9:36		Eris 23♓08.9 ✱ 16♑23.7
	♂ ♈ 27 3:12	29 21:33 ♀ ☍	♋ 29 22:32				⚷ 25♑14.9 ⚶ 26♉34.3
		31 12:10 ♃ △	♌ 31 22:38				☽ Mean ☊ 0♎10.6

March 1904 — LONGITUDE

Day	Sid.Time	☉	0 hr ☽	Noon ☽	True ☊	☿	♀	♂	⚳	♃	♄	♅	♆	♇
1 Tu	22 35 27	10♓29 55	24♌07 43	1♍44 14	27♍30.6	20♒44.8	7♒46.3	2♈35.5	16♐03.2	0♈05.3	15♒04.0	29♐27.7	3♋11.2	18♊40.9
2 W	22 39 23	11 30 04	9♍20 33	16 55 26	27D 29.5	22 17.2	8 59.6	3 21.6	16 17.7	0 19.4	15 10.7	29 29.4	3R 10.8	18R 40.9
3 Th	22 43 20	12 30 11	24 27 41	1♎56 12	27 29.4	23 50.8	10 12.9	4 07.7	16 32.0	0 33.6	15 17.4	29 31.1	3 10.4	18D 40.9
4 F	22 47 16	13 30 16	9♎20 01	16 38 22	27 29.9	25 25.5	11 26.2	4 53.7	16 46.0	0 47.8	15 24.1	29 32.7	3 10.0	18 40.9
5 Sa	22 51 13	14 30 19	23 50 38	0♏56 22	27 30.9	27 01.2	12 39.5	5 39.7	16 59.8	1 02.1	15 30.7	29 34.2	3 09.7	18 40.9
6 Su	22 55 09	15 30 21	7♏55 20	14 47 26	27 32.0	28 38.1	13 52.9	6 25.6	17 13.4	1 16.3	15 37.2	29 35.8	3 09.4	18 41.0
7 M	22 59 06	16 30 22	21 32 43	28 11 23	27 32.8	0♓16.1	15 06.2	7 11.5	17 26.7	1 30.6	15 43.8	29 37.2	3 09.1	18 41.0
8 Tu	23 03 02	17 30 20	4♐43 44	11♐10 08	27R 33.3	1 55.2	16 19.6	7 57.4	17 39.7	1 44.9	15 50.3	29 38.6	3 08.9	18 41.1
9 W	23 06 59	18 30 18	17 31 01	23 46 54	27 33.4	3 35.4	17 33.0	8 43.2	17 52.5	1 59.3	15 56.7	29 40.0	3 08.7	18 41.3
10 Th	23 10 56	19 30 13	29 58 18	6♑05 44	27 33.0	5 16.8	18 46.4	9 29.0	18 05.1	2 13.6	16 03.1	29 41.3	3 08.6	18 41.4
11 F	23 14 52	20 30 07	12♑09 45	18 10 53	27 32.3	6 59.4	19 59.9	10 14.8	18 17.4	2 28.0	16 09.5	29 42.6	3 08.4	18 41.6
12 Sa	23 18 49	21 29 59	24 09 39	0♒06 34	27 31.5	8 43.1	21 13.3	11 00.5	18 29.4	2 42.4	16 15.8	29 43.8	3 08.3	18 41.8
13 Su	23 22 45	22 29 49	6♒02 04	11 56 39	27 30.7	10 27.9	22 26.8	11 46.2	18 41.1	2 56.8	16 22.1	29 44.9	3 08.3	18 42.0
14 M	23 26 42	23 29 37	17 50 41	23 44 36	27 30.1	12 14.0	23 40.2	12 31.8	18 52.6	3 11.3	16 28.4	29 46.0	3D 08.3	18 42.2
15 Tu	23 30 38	24 29 24	29 38 45	5♓33 27	27 29.7	14 01.3	24 53.7	13 17.4	19 03.7	3 25.7	16 34.5	29 47.1	3 08.3	18 42.5
16 W	23 34 35	25 29 09	11♓29 00	17 25 43	27D 29.5	15 49.7	26 07.2	14 02.9	19 14.6	3 40.2	16 40.7	29 48.1	3 08.3	18 42.8
17 Th	23 38 31	26 28 51	23 23 50	29 23 36	27 29.5	17 39.4	27 20.7	14 48.4	19 25.2	3 54.7	16 46.8	29 49.1	3 08.4	18 43.1
18 F	23 42 28	27 28 32	5♈25 15	11♈29 01	27R 29.5	19 30.4	28 34.2	15 33.9	19 35.5	4 09.1	16 52.8	29 50.0	3 08.5	18 43.4
19 Sa	23 46 25	28 28 11	17 35 06	23 43 45	27 29.4	21 22.5	29 47.7	16 19.3	19 45.5	4 23.6	16 58.8	29 50.8	3 08.7	18 43.7
20 Su	23 50 21	29 27 47	29 55 10	6♉09 34	27 29.3	23 15.9	1♓01.2	17 04.7	19 55.2	4 38.2	17 04.8	29 51.6	3 08.8	18 44.1
21 M	23 54 18	0♈27 21	12♉27 12	18 48 18	27 28.9	25 10.5	2 14.7	17 50.0	20 04.6	4 52.7	17 10.7	29 52.4	3 09.0	18 44.5
22 Tu	23 58 14	1 26 53	25 13 06	1♊41 50	27 28.5	27 06.3	3 28.2	18 35.3	20 13.7	5 07.2	17 16.5	29 53.0	3 09.3	18 44.9
23 W	0 02 11	2 26 23	8♊14 44	14 52 01	27 28.1	29 03.2	4 41.7	19 20.5	20 22.5	5 21.7	17 22.3	29 53.7	3 09.6	18 45.3
24 Th	0 06 07	3 25 51	21 33 54	28 20 32	27D 27.9	1♈01.4	5 55.2	20 05.7	20 31.0	5 36.2	17 28.0	29 54.3	3 09.9	18 45.8
25 F	0 10 04	4 25 16	5♋12 01	12♋08 26	27 28.0	3 00.5	7 08.8	20 50.9	20 39.1	5 50.8	17 33.7	29 54.8	3 10.3	18 46.2
26 Sa	0 14 00	5 24 39	19 09 44	26 15 49	27 28.3	5 00.7	8 22.3	21 36.0	20 47.0	6 05.3	17 39.3	29 55.3	3 10.6	18 46.7
27 Su	0 17 57	6 23 59	3♌26 28	10♌41 22	27 29.0	7 01.9	9 35.8	22 21.0	20 54.5	6 19.8	17 44.9	29 55.7	3 11.1	18 47.3
28 M	0 21 53	7 23 17	18 00 02	25 21 54	27 29.8	9 03.8	10 49.3	23 06.0	21 01.6	6 34.4	17 50.4	29 56.1	3 11.5	18 47.8
29 Tu	0 25 50	8 22 33	2♍46 18	10♍12 24	27 30.5	11 06.4	12 02.9	23 50.9	21 08.5	6 48.9	17 55.8	29 56.5	3 12.0	18 48.4
30 W	0 29 47	9 21 47	17 39 21	25 06 11	27R 30.9	13 09.6	13 16.4	24 35.8	21 15.0	7 03.4	18 01.2	29 56.7	3 12.5	18 48.9
31 Th	0 33 43	10 20 58	2♎31 55	9♎55 36	27 30.7	15 13.0	14 29.9	25 20.7	21 21.2	7 17.9	18 06.5	29 57.0	3 13.1	18 49.5

April 1904 — LONGITUDE

Day	Sid.Time	☉	0 hr ☽	Noon ☽	True ☊	☿	♀	♂	⚳	♃	♄	♅	♆	♇
1 F	0 37 40	11♈20 08	17♎16 18	24♎33 07	27♍29.7	17♈16.6	15♓43.5	26♈05.4	21♐27.0	7♈32.4	18♒11.8	29♐57.1	3♋13.7	18♊50.1
2 Sa	0 41 36	12 19 15	1♏45 19	8♏52 15	27R 28.1	19 20.1	16 57.0	26 50.2	21 32.5	7 46.9	18 16.9	29 57.3	3 14.3	18 50.8
3 Su	0 45 33	13 18 21	15 53 23	22 48 23	27 26.1	21 23.2	18 10.5	27 34.9	21 37.7	8 01.4	18 22.1	29R 57.3	3 14.9	18 51.4
4 M	0 49 29	14 17 24	29 37 02	6♐19 16	27 23.9	23 25.5	19 24.1	28 19.5	21 42.5	8 15.9	18 27.1	29 57.3	3 15.6	18 52.1
5 Tu	0 53 26	15 16 26	12♐55 08	19 24 52	27 21.8	25 26.8	20 37.7	29 04.1	21 46.9	8 30.4	18 32.1	29 57.3	3 16.3	18 52.8
6 W	0 57 22	16 15 26	25 48 43	2♑07 06	27 20.4	27 26.7	21 51.2	29 48.7	21 51.0	8 44.8	18 37.0	29 57.2	3 17.1	18 53.5
7 Th	1 01 19	17 14 25	8♑20 29	14 29 22	27D 19.7	29 24.9	23 04.8	0♉33.2	21 54.7	8 59.3	18 41.9	29 57.1	3 17.9	18 54.3
8 F	1 05 16	18 13 22	20 34 19	26 35 55	27 19.9	1♉20.9	24 18.3	1 17.7	21 58.1	9 13.7	18 46.7	29 56.9	3 18.7	18 55.0
9 Sa	1 09 12	19 12 16	2♒34 47	8♒31 30	27 21.0	3 14.5	25 31.9	2 02.1	22 01.1	9 28.1	18 51.4	29 56.7	3 19.5	18 55.8
10 Su	1 13 09	20 11 10	14 26 42	20 20 58	27 22.5	5 05.2	26 45.5	2 46.4	22 03.7	9 42.5	18 56.0	29 56.4	3 20.4	18 56.6
11 M	1 17 05	21 10 01	26 14 52	2♓08 57	27 24.3	6 52.8	27 59.1	3 30.8	22 05.9	9 56.9	19 00.6	29 56.0	3 21.3	18 57.4
12 Tu	1 21 02	22 08 50	8♓03 43	13 59 40	27 25.7	8 36.9	29 12.6	4 15.0	22 07.8	10 11.3	19 05.1	29 55.6	3 22.2	18 58.2
13 W	1 24 58	23 07 38	19 57 15	25 56 50	27R 26.4	10 17.2	0♈26.2	4 59.2	22 09.3	10 25.7	19 09.5	29 55.2	3 23.2	18 59.1
14 Th	1 28 55	24 06 24	1♈58 47	8♈03 25	27 25.9	11 53.5	1 39.8	5 43.4	22 10.4	10 40.0	19 13.9	29 54.7	3 24.2	18 59.9
15 F	1 32 51	25 05 07	14 10 57	20 21 38	27 24.0	13 25.4	2 53.4	6 27.5	22 11.1	10 54.3	19 18.1	29 54.2	3 25.2	19 00.8
16 Sa	1 36 48	26 03 49	26 35 36	2♉52 59	27 20.8	14 52.9	4 06.9	7 11.6	22R 11.4	11 08.6	19 22.3	29 53.6	3 26.3	19 01.7
17 Su	1 40 45	27 02 29	9♉13 49	15 38 10	27 16.5	16 15.7	5 20.5	7 55.6	22 11.4	11 22.8	19 26.4	29 52.9	3 27.4	19 02.6
18 M	1 44 41	28 01 07	22 06 01	28 37 21	27 11.6	17 33.7	6 34.1	8 39.6	22 10.9	11 37.0	19 30.5	29 52.2	3 28.5	19 03.5
19 Tu	1 48 38	28 59 43	5♊12 06	11♊50 13	27 06.5	18 46.7	7 47.6	9 23.5	22 10.1	11 51.2	19 34.4	29 51.5	3 29.6	19 04.5
20 W	1 52 34	29 58 17	18 31 36	25 16 12	27 02.1	19 54.6	9 01.2	10 07.4	22 08.9	12 05.4	19 38.3	29 50.7	3 30.8	19 05.5
21 Th	1 56 31	0♉56 49	2♋03 55	8♋54 39	26 58.8	20 57.3	10 14.7	10 51.2	22 07.3	12 19.5	19 42.1	29 49.9	3 32.0	19 06.4
22 F	2 00 27	1 55 18	15 48 21	22 44 54	26D 57.0	21 54.6	11 28.3	11 35.0	22 05.3	12 33.6	19 45.8	29 49.0	3 33.3	19 07.4
23 Sa	2 04 24	2 53 45	29 44 12	6♌46 09	26 56.8	22 46.5	12 41.8	12 18.7	22 03.0	12 47.7	19 49.5	29 48.1	3 34.5	19 08.4
24 Su	2 08 20	3 52 10	13♌50 36	20 57 23	26 57.6	23 33.0	13 55.4	13 02.3	22 00.2	13 01.8	19 53.0	29 47.1	3 35.8	19 09.5
25 M	2 12 17	4 50 33	28 06 15	5♍16 57	26 59.0	24 14.0	15 08.9	13 45.9	21 57.1	13 15.8	19 56.5	29 46.1	3 37.1	19 10.5
26 Tu	2 16 14	5 48 54	12♍29 09	19 42 25	27R 00.1	24 49.3	16 22.4	14 29.5	21 53.6	13 29.7	19 59.8	29 45.0	3 38.5	19 11.6
27 W	2 20 10	6 47 13	26 56 18	4♎10 15	27 00.1	25 19.1	17 36.0	15 13.0	21 49.7	13 43.6	20 03.1	29 43.9	3 39.8	19 12.6
28 Th	2 24 07	7 45 29	11♎23 39	18 35 52	26 58.3	25 43.2	18 49.5	15 56.4	21 45.4	13 57.5	20 06.3	29 42.7	3 41.2	19 13.7
29 F	2 28 03	8 43 44	25 46 14	2♏54 03	26 54.6	26 01.7	20 03.0	16 39.8	21 40.8	14 11.4	20 09.5	29 41.5	3 42.6	19 14.8
30 Sa	2 32 00	9 41 57	9♏58 40	16 59 29	26 49.1	26 14.7	21 16.5	17 23.2	21 35.7	14 25.2	20 12.5	29 40.3	3 44.1	19 15.9

Astro Data Dy Hr Mn	Planet Ingress Dy Hr Mn	Last Aspect Dy Hr Mn	☽ Ingress Dy Hr Mn	Last Aspect Dy Hr Mn	☽ Ingress Dy Hr Mn	☽ Phases & Eclipses Dy Hr Mn	Astro Data
♃∠♄ 1 7:56	♃ ♈ 1 3:00	1 8:24 ♅ △	♍ 1 9:16	1 20:59 ♅ ✱	♏ 1 21:04	2 2:48 ○ 11♍07	1 March 1904
☽0S 3 9:59	☿ ♓ 7 8:05	3 8:06 ♅ □	♎ 3 8:53	3 4:14 ♄ □	♐ 4 0:41	2 3:02 • A 0.175	Julian Day # 1521
♇D 3 13:41	♀ ♓ 19 16:01	5 9:40 ♅ ✱	♏ 5 10:24	6 7:52 ♅ ☌	♑ 6 7:57	9 1:01 ☾ 18♐03	SVP 6♓35'52"
♃0N 11 17:05	⊙ ♈ 21 0:59	6 13:29 ♄ □	♐ 7 15:18	8 6:54 ♀ ✱	♒ 8 18:49	17 5:39 ● 26♓13	GC 25♐30.1 ⚳ 2♐38.2
♃□♆ 14 7:01	☿ ♈ 23 23:34	9 23:26 ♅ ☌	♑ 10 0:03	11 7:30 ♅ ✱	♓ 11 7:38	17 5:40:41 • A 08'07"	Eris 23♓29.5 ⚵ 26♑51.1
♆D 14 17:03		11 17:04 ⊙ ✱	♒ 12 11:47	13 19:54 ♅ □	♈ 13 20:04	24 21:37 ☽ 3♋50	⚷ 27♑34.6 ⚶ 2♊22.6
☽0N 17 14:34	♂ ♉ 6 18:06	15 0:16 ♅ ✱	♓ 15 0:43	16 6:19 ♅ △	♉ 16 6:31	31 12:44 ○ 10♎23	☽ Mean ☊ 28♍38.4
⊙0N 21 0:59	☿ ♉ 7 19:13	17 12:51 ♅ □	♈ 17 13:13	17 19:07 ♄ □	♊ 18 14:31	31 12:32 • A 0.704	
☿0N 25 13:39	♀ ♈ 13 3:27	19 23:52 ♅ △	♉ 20 0:09	20 20:05 ♅ ☍	♋ 20 20:22		1 April 1904
☽0S 30 21:00	⊙ ♉ 20 12:42	22 2:01 ☿ ✱	♊ 22 8:52	22 10:27 ♅ ✱	♌ 23 0:27	7 17:53 ☾ 17♑29	Julian Day # 1552
♄⚻♆ 1 21:56		24 14:45 ♅ ☍	♋ 24 14:55	25 2:48 ♅ △	♍ 25 3:10	15 21:53 ● 25♈29	SVP 6♓35'50"
♅R 4 9:09		26 3:42 ♂ □	♌ 26 18:16	27 4:39 ♅ □	♎ 27 5:05	23 4:54 ☽ 2♌36	GC 25♐30.1 ⚳ 4♐41.0R
♄△♇ 10 15:25		28 19:25 ♅ △	♍ 28 19:31	29 6:36 ♅ ✱	♏ 29 7:06	29 22:36 ○ 9♏09	Eris 23♓54.1 ⚵ 7♒06.6
☽0N 13 21:26	⚳ R16 20:50	30 19:49 ♅ □	♎ 30 19:54				⚷ 29♑22.1 ⚶ 12♊00.5
♀0N 16 1:19	☽0S27 6:24						☽ Mean ☊ 26♍59.9

LONGITUDE — May 1904

Day	Sid.Time	☉	0 hr ☽	Noon ☽	True ☊	☿	♀	♂	⚳	♃	♄	♅	♆	♇
1 Su	2 35 56	10♉40 08	23♏55 56	0♐47 33	26♍42.2	26♉22.2	22♈30.1	18♉06.5	21♐30.3	14♈38.9	20♒15.4	29♐39.0	3♋45.6	19♊17.0
2 M	2 39 53	11 38 18	7♐34 00	14 15 01	26R34.8	26R24.3	23 43.6	18 49.7	21R24.6	14 52.7	20 18.3	29R37.7	3 47.1	19 18.2
3 Tu	2 43 49	12 36 26	20 50 29	27 20 23	26 27.6	26 21.2	24 57.1	19 32.9	21 18.5	15 06.4	20 21.1	29 36.3	3 48.6	19 19.3
4 W	2 47 46	13 34 33	3♑44 51	10♑04 06	26 21.5	26 13.0	26 10.6	20 16.0	21 12.0	15 20.0	20 23.7	29 34.9	3 50.1	19 20.5
5 Th	2 51 42	14 32 38	16 18 27	22 28 18	26 17.1	26 00.1	27 24.2	20 59.1	21 05.2	15 33.6	20 26.3	29 33.4	3 51.7	19 21.7
6 F	2 55 39	15 30 42	28 34 08	4♒36 29	26D14.6	25 42.8	28 37.7	21 42.2	20 58.0	15 47.1	20 28.8	29 31.9	3 53.3	19 22.9
7 Sa	2 59 36	16 28 44	10♒35 56	16 33 08	26 13.8	25 21.4	29 51.2	22 25.2	20 50.4	16 00.6	20 31.2	29 30.4	3 54.9	19 24.1
8 Su	3 03 32	17 26 45	22 28 41	28 23 17	26 14.4	24 56.3	1♉04.7	23 08.1	20 42.5	16 14.0	20 33.5	29 28.8	3 56.6	19 25.3
9 M	3 07 29	18 24 44	4♓17 34	10♓12 11	26 15.5	24 28.0	2 18.3	23 51.0	20 34.3	16 27.4	20 35.8	29 27.2	3 58.2	19 26.5
10 Tu	3 11 25	19 22 43	16 07 47	22 04 59	26R16.4	23 57.1	3 31.8	24 33.9	20 25.8	16 40.8	20 37.9	29 25.6	3 59.9	19 27.7
11 W	3 15 22	20 20 39	28 04 22	4♈06 26	26 16.1	23 24.1	4 45.3	25 16.7	20 16.9	16 54.0	20 39.9	29 23.9	4 01.6	19 29.0
12 Th	3 19 18	21 18 35	10♈11 43	16 20 36	26 14.1	22 49.6	5 58.8	25 59.4	20 07.7	17 07.3	20 41.9	29 22.2	4 03.3	19 30.2
13 F	3 23 15	22 16 29	22 33 28	28 50 34	26 09.7	22 14.2	7 12.4	26 42.1	19 58.2	17 20.4	20 43.7	29 20.4	4 05.1	19 31.5
14 Sa	3 27 11	23 14 22	5♉12 07	11♉38 12	26 03.0	21 38.5	8 25.9	27 24.8	19 48.4	17 33.5	20 45.5	29 18.6	4 06.8	19 32.7
15 Su	3 31 08	24 12 13	18 08 51	24 43 58	25 54.4	21 03.3	9 39.4	28 07.4	19 38.3	17 46.6	20 47.1	29 16.8	4 08.6	19 34.0
16 M	3 35 05	25 10 03	1♊23 25	8♊06 55	25 44.7	20 29.0	10 53.0	28 49.9	19 28.0	17 59.6	20 48.7	29 15.0	4 10.4	19 35.3
17 Tu	3 39 01	26 07 52	14 54 11	21 44 50	25 34.7	19 56.3	12 06.5	29 32.4	19 17.3	18 12.5	20 50.1	29 13.1	4 12.3	19 36.6
18 W	3 42 58	27 05 39	28 38 29	5♋34 42	25 25.7	19 25.6	13 20.0	0♊14.9	19 06.4	18 25.3	20 51.5	29 11.1	4 14.1	19 37.9
19 Th	3 46 54	28 03 24	12♋33 05	19 33 11	25 18.5	18 57.6	14 33.5	0 57.3	18 55.3	18 38.1	20 52.8	29 09.2	4 16.0	19 39.2
20 F	3 50 51	29 01 08	26 34 40	3♌37 10	25 13.7	18 32.6	15 47.1	1 39.6	18 43.9	18 50.9	20 53.9	29 07.2	4 17.9	19 40.5
21 Sa	3 54 47	29 58 50	10♌40 24	17 44 08	25D11.2	18 10.9	17 00.6	2 21.9	18 32.4	19 03.5	20 55.0	29 05.2	4 19.8	19 41.9
22 Su	3 58 44	0♊56 31	24 48 08	1♍52 14	25 10.6	17 52.9	18 14.1	3 04.2	18 20.6	19 16.1	20 56.0	29 03.2	4 21.7	19 43.2
23 M	4 02 40	1 54 10	8♍56 19	16 00 13	25R11.0	17 38.9	19 27.6	3 46.4	18 08.6	19 28.6	20 56.8	29 01.1	4 23.6	19 44.5
24 Tu	4 06 37	2 51 47	23 03 49	0♎06 58	25 11.1	17 29.1	20 41.1	4 28.5	17 56.4	19 41.0	20 57.6	28 59.0	4 25.6	19 45.9
25 W	4 10 34	3 49 23	7♎09 29	14 11 09	25 09.8	17D23.6	21 54.6	5 10.6	17 44.0	19 53.4	20 58.3	28 56.9	4 27.5	19 47.2
26 Th	4 14 30	4 46 57	21 11 42	28 10 51	25 06.2	17 22.5	23 08.1	5 52.7	17 31.5	20 05.7	20 58.9	28 54.8	4 29.5	19 48.6
27 F	4 18 27	5 44 30	5♏08 15	12♏03 32	24 59.9	17 25.9	24 21.6	6 34.7	17 18.9	20 17.9	20 59.4	28 52.6	4 31.5	19 50.0
28 Sa	4 22 23	6 42 02	18 56 18	25 46 08	24 51.0	17 33.7	25 35.1	7 16.6	17 06.1	20 30.0	20 59.8	28 50.4	4 33.5	19 51.3
29 Su	4 26 20	7 39 33	2♐32 39	9♐15 30	24 40.1	17 46.1	26 48.7	7 58.5	16 53.2	20 42.1	21 00.0	28 48.2	4 35.5	19 52.7
30 M	4 30 16	8 37 02	15 54 21	22 28 58	24 28.3	18 02.9	28 02.2	8 40.4	16 40.2	20 54.1	21 00.2	28 46.0	4 37.6	19 54.1
31 Tu	4 34 13	9 34 31	28 59 09	5♑24 50	24 16.7	18 24.2	29 15.7	9 22.2	16 27.1	21 06.0	21R00.3	28 43.7	4 39.6	19 55.5

LONGITUDE — June 1904

Day	Sid.Time	☉	0 hr ☽	Noon ☽	True ☊	☿	♀	♂	⚳	♃	♄	♅	♆	♇
1 W	4 38 09	10♊31 59	11♑46 00	18♑02 45	24♍06.4	18♉49.7	0♊29.2	10♊03.9	16♐13.9	21♈17.8	21♒00.3	28♐41.4	4♋41.7	19♊56.9
2 Th	4 42 06	11 29 25	24 15 15	0♒23 49	23R58.1	19 19.6	1 42.7	10 45.6	16R00.7	21 29.5	21R00.2	28R39.2	4 43.8	19 58.3
3 F	4 46 03	12 26 51	6♒28 45	12 30 31	23 52.3	19 53.6	2 56.3	11 27.3	15 47.4	21 41.2	21 00.0	28 36.9	4 45.9	19 59.6
4 Sa	4 49 59	13 24 17	18 29 37	24 26 34	23 49.0	20 31.7	4 09.8	12 08.9	15 34.1	21 52.7	20 59.7	28 34.5	4 48.0	20 01.0
5 Su	4 53 56	14 21 40	0♓21 59	6♓16 31	23D47.7	21 13.8	5 23.4	12 50.5	15 20.7	22 04.2	20 59.3	28 32.2	4 50.1	20 02.4
6 M	4 57 52	15 19 05	12 10 48	18 05 32	23R47.5	21 59.7	6 36.9	13 32.0	15 07.4	22 15.6	20 58.8	28 29.9	4 52.2	20 03.8
7 Tu	5 01 49	16 16 29	24 01 24	29 59 04	23 47.4	22 49.5	7 50.5	14 13.5	14 54.0	22 26.9	20 58.3	28 27.5	4 54.3	20 05.2
8 W	5 05 45	17 13 51	5♈59 14	12♈02 31	23 46.4	23 43.0	9 04.0	14 54.9	14 40.7	22 38.1	20 57.6	28 25.1	4 56.5	20 06.6
9 Th	5 09 42	18 11 14	18 09 32	24 20 50	23 43.6	24 40.1	10 17.6	15 36.3	14 27.4	22 49.1	20 56.8	28 22.7	4 58.6	20 08.0
10 F	5 13 38	19 08 35	0♉36 54	6♉58 08	23 38.3	25 40.7	11 31.2	16 17.7	14 14.2	23 00.2	20 55.9	28 20.3	5 00.8	20 09.4
11 Sa	5 17 35	20 05 57	13 24 50	19 57 12	23 30.3	26 44.9	12 44.8	16 59.0	14 01.1	23 11.1	20 54.9	28 17.9	5 02.9	20 10.9
12 Su	5 21 32	21 03 17	26 35 19	3♊19 05	23 20.2	27 52.5	13 58.4	17 40.2	13 48.0	23 21.9	20 53.9	28 15.5	5 05.1	20 12.3
13 M	5 25 28	22 00 37	10♊08 20	17 02 42	23 08.6	29 03.4	15 11.9	18 21.4	13 35.0	23 32.6	20 52.7	28 13.1	5 07.3	20 13.7
14 Tu	5 29 25	22 57 57	24 01 44	1♋04 52	22 56.7	0♊17.7	16 25.6	19 02.6	13 22.2	23 43.2	20 51.4	28 10.6	5 09.5	20 15.1
15 W	5 33 21	23 55 16	8♋11 26	15 20 43	22 45.8	1 35.2	17 39.2	19 43.7	13 09.5	23 53.7	20 50.1	28 08.2	5 11.7	20 16.5
16 Th	5 37 18	24 52 34	22 31 57	29 44 25	22 37.0	2 56.0	18 52.8	20 24.8	12 56.9	24 04.0	20 48.6	28 05.8	5 13.9	20 17.9
17 F	5 41 14	25 49 51	6♌57 22	14♌10 09	22 30.8	4 19.9	20 06.4	21 05.8	12 44.5	24 14.3	20 47.1	28 03.3	5 16.1	20 19.3
18 Sa	5 45 11	26 47 08	21 22 13	28 33 04	22 27.4	5 47.0	21 20.0	21 46.8	12 32.2	24 24.5	20 45.5	28 00.9	5 18.3	20 20.7
19 Su	5 49 08	27 44 24	5♍42 18	12♍49 38	22D26.1	7 17.3	22 33.6	22 27.7	12 20.2	24 34.5	20 43.7	27 58.4	5 20.5	20 22.1
20 M	5 53 04	28 41 39	19 54 51	26 57 49	22R26.0	8 50.6	23 47.3	23 08.6	12 08.3	24 44.5	20 41.9	27 56.0	5 22.7	20 23.5
21 Tu	5 57 01	29 38 53	3♎58 28	10♎56 44	22 25.7	10 27.1	25 00.9	23 49.5	11 56.6	24 54.3	20 40.0	27 53.5	5 25.0	20 24.9
22 W	6 00 57	0♋36 06	17 52 37	24 46 06	22 24.1	12 06.6	26 14.5	24 30.3	11 45.2	25 04.0	20 38.0	27 51.1	5 27.2	20 26.3
23 Th	6 04 54	1 33 19	1♏37 09	8♏25 46	22 20.2	13 49.0	27 28.2	25 11.0	11 34.0	25 13.6	20 36.0	27 48.6	5 29.4	20 27.6
24 F	6 08 50	2 30 32	15 11 52	21 55 22	22 13.6	15 34.5	28 41.8	25 51.7	11 23.0	25 23.1	20 33.8	27 46.2	5 31.7	20 29.0
25 Sa	6 12 47	3 27 43	28 36 10	5♐14 08	22 04.4	17 22.8	29 55.5	26 32.4	11 12.3	25 32.4	20 31.6	27 43.8	5 33.9	20 30.4
26 Su	6 16 43	4 24 55	11♐49 08	18 21 01	21 53.2	19 13.9	1♋09.1	27 13.0	11 01.8	25 41.7	20 29.2	27 41.3	5 36.1	20 31.8
27 M	6 20 40	5 22 06	24 49 39	1♑14 55	21 40.9	21 07.7	2 22.8	27 53.6	10 51.6	25 50.8	20 26.8	27 38.9	5 38.4	20 33.2
28 Tu	6 24 37	6 19 17	7♑36 43	13 55 02	21 28.8	23 04.1	3 36.5	28 34.1	10 41.7	25 59.8	20 24.3	27 36.5	5 40.6	20 34.5
29 W	6 28 33	7 16 28	20 09 51	26 21 14	21 17.9	25 02.9	4 50.2	29 14.6	10 32.1	26 08.6	20 21.7	27 34.1	5 42.8	20 35.9
30 Th	6 32 30	8 13 39	2♒29 19	8♒34 17	21 09.1	27 03.9	6 03.9	29 55.1	10 22.7	26 17.4	20 19.1	27 31.7	5 45.0	20 37.2

Astro Data Dy Hr Mn	Planet Ingress Dy Hr Mn	Last Aspect Dy Hr Mn	☽ Ingress Dy Hr Mn	Last Aspect Dy Hr Mn	☽ Ingress Dy Hr Mn	☽ Phases & Eclipses Dy Hr Mn	Astro Data
☿R 2 9:34	♀♉ 7 14:52	1 4:12 ☿☍	♐ 1 10:36	1 18:22 ♃☐	♒ 2 11:13	7 11:50 ☾ 16♒28	1 May 1904
☽0N 11 5:46	♂♊ 18 3:35	3 16:13 ♅☌	♑ 3 16:58	4 20:20 ♅✱	♓ 4 23:15	15 10:58 ● 24♉10	Julian Day # 1582
☽0S 24 13:55	☉♊ 21 12:29	5 22:47 ♀☐	♒ 6 2:50	7 8:57 ♅☐	♈ 7 12:02	22 10:19 ☽ 0♍52	SVP 6♓35'47"
♃✱♇ 24 22:34		8 14:13 ♅✱	♓ 8 15:17	9 19:43 ♅△	♉ 9 22:50	29 8:55 ○ 7♐32	GC 25♐30.2 ⚴ 29♏45.7R
☿D 26 5:56	♀♊ 1 2:28	11 2:40 ♅☐	♈ 11 3:51	12 1:24 ☿☌	♊ 12 6:06		Eris 24♓14.8 ✱ 15♒20.3
♃✱♄ 31 0:32	☿♊ 14 6:23	13 12:56 ♅△	♉ 13 14:12	14 7:05 ♅☍	♋ 14 10:10	6 5:53 ☾ 15♓04	⚷ 0♒06.4 ⚶ 23♊16.7
♄R 31 23:27	☉♋ 21 20:51	15 18:28 ♂☌	♊ 15 21:30	16 2:27 ♃☐	♌ 16 12:26	13 21:10 ● 22♊23	☽ Mean ☊ 25♍24.6
	♀♋ 25 13:29	18 0:58 ♅☍	♋ 18 2:21	18 11:06 ♅△	♍ 18 14:26	20 15:10 ☽ 28♍49	
☽0N 7 15:12	♂♋ 30 14:56	20 3:35 ☉✱	♌ 20 5:50	20 15:10 ☉☐	♎ 20 17:11	27 20:23 ○ 5♑42	1 June 1904
☽0S 20 20:29		22 7:14 ♅△	♍ 22 8:49	22 17:23 ♅✱	♏ 22 21:09		Julian Day # 1613
♄☐♆ 24 23:36		24 10:05 ♅☐	♎ 24 11:48	24 9:34 ♄☐	♐ 25 2:31		SVP 6♓35'42"
♄△♇ 25 19:30		26 13:15 ♅✱	♏ 26 15:08	27 5:22 ♂☍	♑ 27 9:40		GC 25♐30.3 ⚴ 20♏49.9R
		28 11:39 ♀☍	♐ 28 19:29	29 11:35 ♃☐	♒ 29 19:07		Eris 24♓27.8 ✱ 20♒47.5
		30 23:34 ♅☌	♑ 31 1:53				⚷ 29♑43.1R ⚶ 6♋04.2
							☽ Mean ☊ 23♍46.1

July 1904 LONGITUDE

Day	Sid.Time	☉	0 hr ☽	Noon ☽	True ☊	☿	♀	♂	⚳	♃	♄	♅	♆	♇
1 F	6 36 26	9♋10 50	14♒36 24	20♒35 59	21♍02.7	29♊07.0	7♋17.6	0♋35.5	10♐13.7	26♈26.0	20♒16.4	27♐29.3	5♋47.3	20♊38.6
2 Sa	6 40 23	10 08 01	26 33 25	2♓29 09	20R 59.0	1♋11.9	8 31.3	1 15.8	10R 04.9	26 34.4	20R 13.5	27R 27.0	5 49.5	20 39.9
3 Su	6 44 19	11 05 12	8♓23 40	14 17 32	20D 57.4	3 18.3	9 45.0	1 56.2	9 56.5	26 42.8	20 10.7	27 24.6	5 51.7	20 41.3
4 M	6 48 16	12 02 23	20 11 20	26 05 41	20 57.3	5 26.0	10 58.7	2 36.5	9 48.4	26 51.0	20 07.7	27 22.3	5 54.0	20 42.6
5 Tu	6 52 12	12 59 34	2♈01 14	7♈58 40	20R 57.7	7 34.7	12 12.5	3 16.7	9 40.6	26 59.0	20 04.6	27 19.9	5 56.2	20 43.9
6 W	6 56 09	13 56 46	13 58 38	20 01 50	20 57.7	9 44.2	13 26.2	3 56.9	9 33.1	27 06.9	20 01.5	27 17.6	5 58.4	20 45.2
7 Th	7 00 06	14 53 58	26 08 56	2♉20 32	20 56.2	11 54.0	14 40.0	4 37.1	9 26.0	27 14.7	19 58.3	27 15.3	6 00.6	20 46.5
8 F	7 04 02	15 51 11	8♉37 14	14 59 33	20 52.7	14 03.9	15 53.8	5 17.2	9 19.2	27 22.4	19 55.1	27 13.0	6 02.8	20 47.8
9 Sa	7 07 59	16 48 24	21 27 56	28 02 41	20 46.9	16 13.7	17 07.6	5 57.3	9 12.8	27 29.9	19 51.8	27 10.8	6 05.0	20 49.1
10 Su	7 11 55	17 45 37	4♊44 02	11♊32 01	20 39.1	18 23.1	18 21.4	6 37.4	9 06.7	27 37.2	19 48.4	27 08.5	6 07.2	20 50.4
11 M	7 15 52	18 42 51	18 26 32	25 27 21	20 30.0	20 31.8	19 35.2	7 17.4	9 00.9	27 44.4	19 44.9	27 06.3	6 09.4	20 51.7
12 Tu	7 19 48	19 40 05	2♋33 59	9♋45 51	20 20.4	22 39.6	20 49.0	7 57.4	8 55.5	27 51.5	19 41.4	27 04.1	6 11.6	20 52.9
13 W	7 23 45	20 37 20	17 02 11	24 22 07	20 11.6	24 46.4	22 02.9	8 37.3	8 50.5	27 58.4	19 37.8	27 01.9	6 13.8	20 54.2
14 Th	7 27 41	21 34 35	1♌44 41	9♌08 53	20 04.5	26 52.0	23 16.7	9 17.2	8 45.8	28 05.1	19 34.2	26 59.8	6 16.0	20 55.4
15 F	7 31 38	22 31 50	16 33 41	23 58 08	19 59.8	28 56.2	24 30.6	9 57.0	8 41.6	28 11.7	19 30.5	26 57.6	6 18.1	20 56.6
16 Sa	7 35 35	23 29 05	1♍21 18	8♍42 25	19D 57.4	0♌59.0	25 44.5	10 36.9	8 37.6	28 18.1	19 26.8	26 55.5	6 20.3	20 57.9
17 Su	7 39 31	24 26 21	16 00 47	23 15 53	19 56.9	3 00.2	26 58.3	11 16.6	8 34.1	28 24.4	19 22.9	26 53.4	6 22.5	20 59.1
18 M	7 43 28	25 23 36	0♎27 17	7♎34 42	19 57.6	4 59.9	28 12.2	11 56.4	8 30.9	28 30.5	19 19.1	26 51.4	6 24.6	21 00.3
19 Tu	7 47 24	26 20 52	14 37 59	21 37 02	19R 58.3	6 57.8	29 26.1	12 36.1	8 28.0	28 36.5	19 15.2	26 49.3	6 26.7	21 01.5
20 W	7 51 21	27 18 08	28 31 51	5♏22 31	19 58.1	8 54.1	0♌40.0	13 15.7	8 25.6	28 42.2	19 11.2	26 47.3	6 28.8	21 02.6
21 Th	7 55 17	28 15 24	12♏09 07	18 51 48	19 56.2	10 48.7	1 53.9	13 55.3	8 23.5	28 47.9	19 07.2	26 45.4	6 31.0	21 03.8
22 F	7 59 14	29 12 41	25 30 41	2♐05 56	19 52.2	12 41.5	3 07.8	14 34.9	8 21.8	28 53.3	19 03.2	26 43.4	6 33.1	21 05.0
23 Sa	8 03 10	0♌09 57	8♐37 40	15 06 01	19 46.1	14 32.6	4 21.7	15 14.4	8 20.4	28 58.6	18 59.1	26 41.5	6 35.1	21 06.1
24 Su	8 07 07	1 07 15	21 31 06	27 53 01	19 38.5	16 21.9	5 35.6	15 53.9	8 19.4	29 03.7	18 54.9	26 39.6	6 37.2	21 07.2
25 M	8 11 04	2 04 33	4♑11 53	10♑27 46	19 30.2	18 09.5	6 49.5	16 33.4	8 18.8	29 08.7	18 50.8	26 37.8	6 39.3	21 08.3
26 Tu	8 15 00	3 01 51	16 40 46	22 50 59	19 21.8	19 55.3	8 03.5	17 12.8	8D 18.5	29 13.5	18 46.6	26 36.0	6 41.3	21 09.4
27 W	8 18 57	3 59 10	28 58 32	5♒03 32	19 14.4	21 39.5	9 17.4	17 52.2	8 18.6	29 18.1	18 42.3	26 34.2	6 43.4	21 10.5
28 Th	8 22 53	4 56 30	11♒06 09	17 06 35	19 08.5	23 21.9	10 31.4	18 31.5	8 19.1	29 22.5	18 38.1	26 32.5	6 45.4	21 11.6
29 F	8 26 50	5 53 51	23 05 02	29 01 46	19 04.4	25 02.6	11 45.3	19 10.8	8 19.9	29 26.7	18 33.8	26 30.7	6 47.4	21 12.7
30 Sa	8 30 46	6 51 12	4♓57 05	10♓51 20	19D 02.4	26 41.5	12 59.3	19 50.1	8 21.0	29 30.8	18 29.4	26 29.1	6 49.4	21 13.7
31 Su	8 34 43	7 48 35	16 44 55	22 38 15	19 02.1	28 18.8	14 13.3	20 29.4	8 22.6	29 34.7	18 25.1	26 27.4	6 51.4	21 14.7

August 1904 LONGITUDE

Day	Sid.Time	☉	0 hr ☽	Noon ☽	True ☊	☿	♀	♂	⚳	♃	♄	♅	♆	♇
1 M	8 38 39	8♌45 58	28♓31 48	4♈26 06	19♍03.0	29♌54.4	15♌27.3	21♋08.6	8♐24.4	29♈38.4	18♒20.7	26♐25.8	6♋53.3	21♊15.7
2 Tu	8 42 36	9 43 23	10♈21 40	16 19 05	19 04.6	1♍28.3	16 41.2	21 47.7	8 26.6	29 42.0	18R 16.3	26R 24.3	6 55.3	21 16.7
3 W	8 46 33	10 40 49	22 18 58	28 21 55	19 06.0	3 00.5	17 55.3	22 26.9	8 29.2	29 45.3	18 11.9	26 22.7	6 57.2	21 17.7
4 Th	8 50 29	11 38 16	4♉28 32	10♉39 28	19R 06.7	4 30.9	19 09.3	23 06.0	8 32.1	29 48.5	18 07.4	26 21.2	6 59.1	21 18.7
5 F	8 54 26	12 35 44	16 55 17	23 16 34	19 06.1	5 59.7	20 23.3	23 45.1	8 35.3	29 51.4	18 03.0	26 19.8	7 01.0	21 19.6
6 Sa	8 58 22	13 33 14	29 43 48	6♊17 26	19 04.1	7 26.7	21 37.3	24 24.1	8 38.9	29 54.2	17 58.5	26 18.4	7 02.9	21 20.6
7 Su	9 02 19	14 30 45	12♊57 48	19 45 07	19 00.7	8 52.0	22 51.4	25 03.1	8 42.8	29 56.8	17 54.1	26 17.0	7 04.8	21 21.5
8 M	9 06 15	15 28 18	26 39 28	3♋40 44	18 56.3	10 15.4	24 05.4	25 42.1	8 47.0	29 59.2	17 49.6	26 15.7	7 06.6	21 22.4
9 Tu	9 10 12	16 25 51	10♋48 41	18 02 53	18 51.5	11 37.1	25 19.5	26 21.0	8 51.6	0♉01.4	17 45.1	26 14.4	7 08.5	21 23.3
10 W	9 14 08	17 23 27	25 22 40	2♌47 15	18 47.0	12 57.0	26 33.6	26 59.9	8 56.4	0 03.5	17 40.6	26 13.2	7 10.3	21 24.2
11 Th	9 18 05	18 21 03	10♌15 42	17 46 56	18 43.5	14 14.9	27 47.6	27 38.8	9 01.7	0 05.3	17 36.1	26 12.0	7 12.1	21 25.0
12 F	9 22 02	19 18 40	25 19 48	2♍53 08	18 41.3	15 30.9	29 01.7	28 17.6	9 07.2	0 06.9	17 31.6	26 10.8	7 13.8	21 25.9
13 Sa	9 25 58	20 16 19	10♍25 48	17 56 40	18D 40.5	16 44.9	0♍15.8	28 56.4	9 13.0	0 08.3	17 27.1	26 09.7	7 15.6	21 26.7
14 Su	9 29 55	21 13 58	25 24 46	2♎49 13	18 41.0	17 56.8	1 29.9	29 35.2	9 19.2	0 09.6	17 22.6	26 08.6	7 17.3	21 27.5
15 M	9 33 51	22 11 39	10♎09 19	17 24 29	18 42.3	19 06.6	2 44.0	0♌13.9	9 25.7	0 10.6	17 18.2	26 07.6	7 19.0	21 28.3
16 Tu	9 37 48	23 09 20	24 34 20	1♏38 34	18 43.7	20 14.2	3 58.1	0 52.6	9 32.4	0 11.4	17 13.7	26 06.6	7 20.7	21 29.0
17 W	9 41 44	24 07 03	8♏37 06	15 29 55	18R 44.7	21 19.4	5 12.2	1 31.3	9 39.5	0 12.1	17 09.2	26 05.7	7 22.4	21 29.8
18 Th	9 45 41	25 04 47	22 17 05	28 51 49	18 44.8	22 22.2	6 26.3	2 09.9	9 46.9	0 12.5	17 04.8	26 04.8	7 24.0	21 30.5
19 F	9 49 37	26 02 32	5♐35 19	12♐06 53	18 44.0	23 22.5	7 40.4	2 48.5	9 54.6	0R 12.8	17 00.4	26 04.0	7 25.6	21 31.2
20 Sa	9 53 34	27 00 18	18 33 48	24 56 25	18 42.1	24 20.1	8 54.5	3 27.0	10 02.5	0 12.8	16 56.0	26 03.2	7 27.2	21 31.9
21 Su	9 57 31	27 58 05	1♑15 04	7♑30 03	18 39.5	25 14.9	10 08.6	4 05.5	10 10.8	0 12.7	16 51.6	26 02.5	7 28.8	21 32.6
22 M	10 01 27	28 55 53	13 41 43	19 50 22	18 36.5	26 06.7	11 22.7	4 44.0	10 19.3	0 12.3	16 47.3	26 01.8	7 30.4	21 33.2
23 Tu	10 05 24	29 53 43	25 56 18	1♒59 48	18 33.5	26 55.3	12 36.8	5 22.5	10 28.1	0 11.8	16 43.0	26 01.1	7 31.9	21 33.9
24 W	10 09 20	0♍51 34	8♒01 10	14 00 38	18 30.9	27 40.7	13 50.9	6 00.9	10 37.2	0 11.0	16 38.7	26 00.5	7 33.4	21 34.5
25 Th	10 13 17	1 49 26	19 58 29	25 54 58	18 29.0	28 22.5	15 05.0	6 39.3	10 46.5	0 10.0	16 34.4	26 00.0	7 34.9	21 35.1
26 F	10 17 13	2 47 20	1♓50 20	7♓44 51	18D 27.8	29 00.5	16 19.1	7 17.6	10 56.1	0 08.9	16 30.2	25 59.5	7 36.3	21 35.6
27 Sa	10 21 10	3 45 16	13 38 48	19 32 28	18 27.5	29 34.5	17 33.2	7 56.0	11 06.0	0 07.6	16 26.0	25 59.0	7 37.7	21 36.2
28 Su	10 25 06	4 43 13	25 26 09	1♈20 11	18 27.9	0♎04.3	18 47.3	8 34.2	11 16.1	0 06.0	16 21.8	25 58.6	7 39.1	21 36.7
29 M	10 29 03	5 41 11	7♈14 54	13 10 40	18 28.8	0 29.6	20 01.4	9 12.5	11 26.5	0 04.3	16 17.7	25 58.3	7 40.5	21 37.2
30 Tu	10 32 59	6 39 12	19 07 55	25 07 02	18 29.9	0 50.1	21 15.5	9 50.7	11 37.1	0 02.3	16 13.7	25 58.0	7 41.8	21 37.7
31 W	10 36 56	7 37 14	1♉08 30	7♉12 45	18 31.0	1 05.6	22 29.6	10 28.9	11 48.0	0 00.2	16 09.6	25 57.7	7 43.2	21 38.2

Astro Data	Planet Ingress	Last Aspect	☽ Ingress	Last Aspect	☽ Ingress	☽ Phases & Eclipses	Astro Data
Dy Hr Mn	Dy Hr Mn	Dy Hr Mn	Dy Hr Mn	Dy Hr Mn	Dy Hr Mn	Dy Hr Mn	1 July 1904
☽0N 5 0:36	☿ ♋ 1 22:14	2 1:50 ♅ ⚹	♓ 2 6:58	31 19:46 ♅ □	♈ 1 2:59	5 22:54 ☾ 13♈26	Julian Day # 1643
♃△♅ 7 13:24	☿ ♌ 16 0:26	4 14:35 ♅ □	♈ 4 19:55	3 14:45 ♃ ☌	♉ 3 15:13	13 5:27 ● 20♋22	SVP 6♓35'37"
☽0S 18 3:36	♀ ♌ 19 23:01	7 2:11 ♅ △	♉ 7 7:29	5 12:56 ♂ ⚹	♊ 6 0:30	19 20:48 ☽ 26♎42	GC 25♐30.3 ⚴ 16♏08.0R
⚳ D 26 17:43	☉ ♌ 23 7:50	8 21:07 ♄ □	♊ 9 15:32	8 5:42 ♃ ⚹	♋ 8 5:44	27 9:42 ○ 3♒54	Eris 24♓29.6R ⚵ 21♒23.1R
		11 15:54 ♃ ⚹	♋ 11 19:41	10 2:12 ♂ ☌	♌ 10 7:30		⚷ 28♑24.8R ⚶ 19♋05.5
☽0N 1 8:50	☿ ♍ 1 13:25	13 17:55 ♃ □	♌ 13 21:10	12 5:20 ♀ ☌	♍ 12 7:25	4 14:03 ☾ 11♉43	☽ Mean ☊ 22♍10.8
☽0S 14 12:18	♃ ♉ 8 20:11	15 18:55 ♃ △	♍ 15 21:48	14 6:31 ♂ ⚹	♎ 14 7:25	11 12:58 ● 18♌23	
♃ R 20 5:28	♀ ♍ 13 6:53	17 18:45 ♀ ⚹	♎ 17 23:14	16 2:37 ♅ ⚹	♏ 16 9:12	18 4:27 ☽ 24♏47	1 August 1904
☿0S 21 3:05	♂ ♌ 15 3:22	20 0:13 ♃ ☍	♏ 20 2:34	18 4:27 ☉ □	♐ 18 13:50	26 1:02 ○ 2♓21	Julian Day # 1674
☽0N 28 15:33	☉ ♍ 23 14:37	22 6:19 ☉ △	♐ 22 8:10	20 16:14 ☉ △	♑ 20 21:37		SVP 6♓35'33"
	☿ ♎ 28 8:17	24 14:15 ♃ △	♑ 24 16:01	23 1:14 ☿ △	♒ 23 8:02		GC 25♐30.4 ⚴ 18♏04.3
	♃ ♈R 31 13:54	27 0:34 ♃ □	♒ 27 2:01	25 12:10 ♅ ⚹	♓ 25 20:16		Eris 24♓20.1R ⚵ 16♒15.0R
		29 12:51 ♃ ⚹	♓ 29 13:58	28 1:06 ♅ □	♈ 28 9:17		⚷ 26♑38.7R ⚶ 2♌54.2
				30 13:42 ♅ △	♉ 30 21:44		☽ Mean ☊ 20♍32.3

LONGITUDE — September 1904

Day	Sid.Time	☉	0 hr ☽	Noon ☽	True ☊	☿	♀	♂	⚳	♃	♄	♅	♆	♇
1 Th	10 40 53	8♍35 19	13♉20 18	19♉31 38	18♍31.8	1♎15.8	23♍43.7	11♌07.1	11♐59.1	29♈57.8	16♒05.6	25♐57.5	7♋44.4	21♊38.7
2 F	10 44 49	9 33 25	25 47 15	2♊07 38	18R 32.3	1R 20.3	24 57.8	11 45.2	12 10.5	29R 55.3	16R 01.7	25R 57.4	7 45.7	21 39.1
3 Sa	10 48 46	10 31 33	8♊33 16	15 04 35	18 32.4	1 18.9	26 12.0	12 23.3	12 22.1	29 52.6	15 57.8	25 57.3	7 47.0	21 39.5
4 Su	10 52 42	11 29 44	21 41 57	28 25 42	18 32.1	1 11.5	27 26.1	13 01.4	12 33.9	29 49.7	15 54.0	25D 57.2	7 48.2	21 39.9
5 M	10 56 39	12 27 56	5♋16 01	12♋13 01	18 31.6	0 57.7	28 40.2	13 39.5	12 46.0	29 46.6	15 50.2	25 57.2	7 49.3	21 40.3
6 Tu	11 00 35	13 26 11	19 16 40	26 26 46	18 31.0	0 37.5	29 54.3	14 17.5	12 58.3	29 43.3	15 46.5	25 57.3	7 50.5	21 40.6
7 W	11 04 32	14 24 27	3♌42 58	11♌04 44	18 30.5	0 10.9	1♎08.4	14 55.4	13 10.8	29 39.8	15 42.8	25 57.4	7 51.6	21 40.9
8 Th	11 08 28	15 22 45	18 31 22	26 02 00	18 30.2	29♍37.8	2 22.6	15 33.4	13 23.6	29 36.1	15 39.2	25 57.5	7 52.7	21 41.2
9 F	11 12 25	16 21 06	3♍35 38	11♍11 08	18D 30.0	28 58.5	3 36.7	16 11.3	13 36.6	29 32.2	15 35.7	25 57.7	7 53.8	21 41.5
10 Sa	11 16 22	17 19 28	18 47 19	26 23 00	18 30.0	28 13.3	4 50.8	16 49.2	13 49.7	29 28.2	15 32.2	25 58.0	7 54.8	21 41.8
11 Su	11 20 18	18 17 51	3♎56 57	11♎28 03	18R 30.0	27 22.8	6 04.9	17 27.1	14 03.1	29 23.9	15 28.8	25 58.3	7 55.8	21 42.0
12 M	11 24 15	19 16 17	18 55 18	26 17 47	18 30.0	26 27.7	7 19.0	18 04.9	14 16.8	29 19.5	15 25.4	25 58.6	7 56.8	21 42.2
13 Tu	11 28 11	20 14 44	3♏34 47	10♏45 45	18 29.9	25 28.9	8 33.1	18 42.7	14 30.6	29 14.9	15 22.1	25 59.1	7 57.7	21 42.4
14 W	11 32 08	21 13 13	17 50 17	24 48 11	18 29.7	24 27.5	9 47.3	19 20.4	14 44.6	29 10.2	15 18.9	25 59.5	7 58.7	21 42.6
15 Th	11 36 04	22 11 44	1♐39 24	8♐23 59	18 29.4	23 24.7	11 01.4	19 58.1	14 58.8	29 05.2	15 15.8	26 00.0	7 59.5	21 42.8
16 F	11 40 01	23 10 16	15 02 10	21 34 13	18D 29.3	22 22.2	12 15.5	20 35.8	15 13.2	29 00.1	15 12.7	26 00.6	8 00.4	21 42.9
17 Sa	11 43 57	24 08 50	28 00 30	4♑21 29	18 29.4	21 21.2	13 29.5	21 13.5	15 27.8	28 54.9	15 09.8	26 01.2	8 01.2	21 43.0
18 Su	11 47 54	25 07 25	10♑37 37	16 49 22	18 29.8	20 23.4	14 43.6	21 51.1	15 42.6	28 49.4	15 06.8	26 01.9	8 02.0	21 43.1
19 M	11 51 51	26 06 02	22 57 17	29 01 50	18 30.5	19 30.2	15 57.7	22 28.7	15 57.6	28 43.9	15 04.0	26 02.6	8 02.8	21 43.1
20 Tu	11 55 47	27 04 41	5♒03 31	11♒02 50	18 31.3	18 43.0	17 11.8	23 06.2	16 12.8	28 38.1	15 01.3	26 03.4	8 03.5	21 43.2
21 W	11 59 44	28 03 22	17 00 13	22 56 06	18 32.2	18 03.1	18 25.8	23 43.7	16 28.1	28 32.2	14 58.6	26 04.2	8 04.2	21R 43.2
22 Th	12 03 40	29 02 04	28 50 55	4♓45 02	18 33.0	17 31.5	19 39.9	24 21.2	16 43.6	28 26.2	14 56.0	26 05.1	8 04.8	21 43.2
23 F	12 07 37	0♎00 48	10♓38 49	16 32 35	18R 33.3	17 09.0	20 53.9	24 58.6	16 59.3	28 20.0	14 53.5	26 06.0	8 05.5	21 43.2
24 Sa	12 11 33	0 59 34	22 26 39	28 21 18	18 33.1	16D 56.1	22 08.0	25 36.1	17 15.2	28 13.7	14 51.1	26 07.0	8 06.0	21 43.1
25 Su	12 15 30	1 58 22	4♈16 49	10♈13 28	18 32.2	16 53.3	23 22.0	26 13.4	17 31.2	28 07.3	14 48.7	26 08.0	8 06.6	21 43.1
26 M	12 19 26	2 57 13	16 11 29	22 11 08	18 30.6	17 00.5	24 36.0	26 50.8	17 47.4	28 00.7	14 46.5	26 09.1	8 07.1	21 43.0
27 Tu	12 23 23	3 56 05	28 12 40	4♉16 20	18 28.5	17 17.8	25 50.0	27 28.1	18 03.8	27 54.0	14 44.3	26 10.2	8 07.6	21 42.9
28 W	12 27 19	4 54 59	10♉22 24	16 31 08	18 26.0	17 44.9	27 04.0	28 05.4	18 20.3	27 47.2	14 42.2	26 11.4	8 08.1	21 42.7
29 Th	12 31 16	5 53 56	22 42 49	28 57 44	18 23.6	18 21.4	28 18.0	28 42.7	18 37.0	27 40.2	14 40.3	26 12.6	8 08.5	21 42.6
30 F	12 35 13	6 52 55	5♊16 13	11♊38 33	18 21.4	19 06.7	29 32.0	29 19.9	18 53.8	27 33.2	14 38.4	26 13.9	8 08.9	21 42.4

LONGITUDE — October 1904

Day	Sid.Time	☉	0 hr ☽	Noon ☽	True ☊	☿	♀	♂	⚳	♃	♄	♅	♆	♇
1 Sa	12 39 09	7♎51 56	18♊05 04	24♊36 05	18♍20.0	20♍00.2	0♏46.0	29♌57.1	19♐10.8	27♈26.0	14♒36.6	26♐15.2	8♋09.3	21♊42.2
2 Su	12 43 06	8 51 00	1♋11 53	7♋52 44	18D 19.5	21 01.3	2 00.0	0♍34.3	19 27.9	27R 18.7	14R 34.9	26 16.5	8 09.6	21R 42.0
3 M	12 47 02	9 50 06	14 38 53	21 30 30	18 19.8	22 09.2	3 14.0	1 11.4	19 45.2	27 11.4	14 33.2	26 18.0	8 09.9	21 41.7
4 Tu	12 50 59	10 49 15	28 27 42	5♌30 30	18 20.9	23 23.1	4 28.0	1 48.5	20 02.7	27 03.9	14 31.7	26 19.4	8 10.2	21 41.5
5 W	12 54 55	11 48 25	12♌38 47	19 52 20	18 22.4	24 42.5	5 42.0	2 25.6	20 20.2	26 56.4	14 30.3	26 20.9	8 10.4	21 41.2
6 Th	12 58 52	12 47 38	27 10 47	4♍33 38	18R 23.6	26 06.5	6 55.9	3 02.6	20 38.0	26 48.8	14 29.0	26 22.5	8 10.6	21 40.9
7 F	13 02 48	13 46 53	12♍00 12	19 29 40	18 24.0	27 34.5	8 09.9	3 39.6	20 55.8	26 41.0	14 27.7	26 24.1	8 10.8	21 40.6
8 Sa	13 06 45	14 46 10	27 01 06	4♎33 27	18 23.3	29 05.9	9 23.9	4 16.6	21 13.8	26 33.3	14 26.6	26 25.8	8 10.9	21 40.2
9 Su	13 10 42	15 45 30	12♎05 36	19 36 23	18 21.1	0♎40.2	10 37.8	4 53.5	21 32.0	26 25.4	14 25.5	26 27.5	8 11.0	21 39.8
10 M	13 14 38	16 44 51	27 04 42	4♏29 26	18 17.7	2 16.8	11 51.8	5 30.4	21 50.2	26 17.5	14 24.6	26 29.2	8 11.0	21 39.4
11 Tu	13 18 35	17 44 15	11♏49 39	19 04 31	18 13.5	3 55.3	13 05.7	6 07.3	22 08.6	26 09.6	14 23.8	26 31.0	8R 11.1	21 39.0
12 W	13 22 31	18 43 40	26 13 20	3♐15 38	18 09.0	5 35.3	14 19.6	6 44.1	22 27.2	26 01.6	14 23.0	26 32.9	8 11.1	21 38.6
13 Th	13 26 28	19 43 07	10♐11 05	16 59 35	18 04.8	7 16.4	15 33.6	7 20.9	22 45.9	25 53.6	14 22.4	26 34.7	8 11.0	21 38.1
14 F	13 30 24	20 42 36	23 41 07	0♑15 54	18 01.7	8 58.3	16 47.5	7 57.6	23 04.6	25 45.5	14 21.9	26 36.7	8 10.9	21 37.7
15 Sa	13 34 21	21 42 07	6♑44 12	13 06 27	18D 00.0	10 40.8	18 01.4	8 34.3	23 23.6	25 37.4	14 21.4	26 38.7	8 10.8	21 37.2
16 Su	13 38 17	22 41 40	19 23 08	25 34 47	17 59.6	12 23.7	19 15.3	9 11.0	23 42.6	25 29.3	14 21.1	26 40.7	8 10.7	21 36.7
17 M	13 42 14	23 41 14	1♒42 00	7♒45 25	18 00.5	14 06.8	20 29.1	9 47.6	24 01.7	25 21.2	14 20.9	26 42.7	8 10.5	21 36.1
18 Tu	13 46 11	24 40 50	13 45 39	19 43 19	18 02.1	15 49.9	21 43.0	10 24.2	24 21.0	25 13.1	14D 20.7	26 44.8	8 10.3	21 35.6
19 W	13 50 07	25 40 28	25 39 03	1♓33 26	18 03.8	17 33.0	22 56.8	11 00.8	24 40.4	25 05.0	14 20.7	26 47.0	8 10.1	21 35.0
20 Th	13 54 04	26 40 07	7♓27 03	13 20 25	18R 04.9	19 15.8	24 10.7	11 37.3	24 59.8	24 56.9	14 20.8	26 49.2	8 09.8	21 34.4
21 F	13 58 00	27 39 49	19 14 02	25 08 22	18 04.8	20 58.4	25 24.5	12 13.7	25 19.4	24 48.7	14 20.9	26 51.4	8 09.5	21 33.8
22 Sa	14 01 57	28 39 32	1♈03 49	7♈00 46	18 02.8	22 40.6	26 38.3	12 50.2	25 39.1	24 40.7	14 21.2	26 53.7	8 09.1	21 33.2
23 Su	14 05 53	29 39 17	12 59 30	19 00 19	17 58.9	24 22.5	27 52.1	13 26.6	25 58.9	24 32.6	14 21.6	26 56.0	8 08.7	21 32.5
24 M	14 09 50	0♏39 04	25 03 27	1♉09 04	17 53.0	26 04.0	29 05.9	14 02.9	26 18.8	24 24.6	14 22.1	26 58.4	8 08.3	21 31.9
25 Tu	14 13 46	1 38 53	7♉17 20	13 28 22	17 45.6	27 45.0	0♐19.6	14 39.2	26 38.9	24 16.6	14 22.7	27 00.7	8 07.9	21 31.2
26 W	14 17 43	2 38 44	19 42 14	25 59 01	17 37.3	29 25.5	1 33.4	15 15.5	26 59.0	24 08.6	14 23.3	27 03.2	8 07.4	21 30.5
27 Th	14 21 39	3 38 37	2♊18 47	8♊41 33	17 28.9	1♏05.6	2 47.1	15 51.8	27 19.2	24 00.7	14 24.1	27 05.6	8 06.9	21 29.8
28 F	14 25 36	4 38 32	15 07 24	21 36 23	17 21.4	2 45.2	4 00.8	16 28.0	27 39.5	23 52.8	14 25.0	27 08.2	8 06.4	21 29.0
29 Sa	14 29 33	5 38 30	28 08 32	4♋43 57	17 15.5	4 24.3	5 14.6	17 04.1	27 59.9	23 45.0	14 26.0	27 10.7	8 05.8	21 28.3
30 Su	14 33 29	6 38 29	11♋22 44	18 04 59	17 11.6	6 02.9	6 28.3	17 40.3	28 20.4	23 37.3	14 27.1	27 13.3	8 05.2	21 27.5
31 M	14 37 26	7 38 31	24 50 48	1♌40 18	17D 09.9	7 41.1	7 41.9	18 16.4	28 41.0	23 29.7	14 28.3	27 15.9	8 04.6	21 26.7

Astro Data

Astro Data	Dy Hr Mn
☿R	2 18:37
♅D	4 23:11
♀0S	8 16:59
☽0S	10 22:38
☿0N	16 5:02
♇R	21 20:45
☉0S	23 11:41
☽0N	24 21:32
☿D	25 6:45
☽0S	8 9:38
♃△♅	9 6:54
♆R	11 17:47
☿0S	11 20:38
♄D	19 6:57
☽0N	22 4:08

Planet Ingress

Planet Ingress	Dy Hr Mn
♀ ♎	6 13:50
☿ ♍R	7 20:25
☉ ♎	23 11:40
♀ ♏	30 21:04
♂ ♍	1 13:52
☿ ♎	9 1:51
☉ ♏	23 20:19
♀ ♐	25 5:37
☿ ♏	26 20:16

Last Aspect / ☽ Ingress (September)

Last Aspect Dy Hr Mn		☽ Ingress	Dy Hr Mn
1 20:57	♀ △	♊	2 7:59
4 14:28	♃ ⚹	♋	4 14:47
6 17:24	♃ □	♌	6 17:53
8 17:39	♃ △	♍	8 18:18
10 14:46	☿ ☌	♎	10 17:44
12 16:57	♃ ☍	♏	12 18:05
14 11:27	☿ ⚹	♐	14 21:05
17 1:46	♃ △	♑	17 3:45
19 11:25	♃ □	♒	19 13:55
21 23:16	♃ ⚹	♓	22 2:20
24 7:27	♅ □	♈	24 15:20
26 23:30	♃ ☌	♉	27 3:33
29 11:30	♂ □	♊	29 13:59

Last Aspect / ☽ Ingress (October)

Last Aspect Dy Hr Mn		☽ Ingress	Dy Hr Mn
1 17:07	♃ ⚹	♋	1 21:50
3 21:44	♃ □	♌	4 2:38
5 23:30	♃ △	♍	6 4:36
8 2:20	☿ ☌	♎	8 4:45
9 23:01	♅ ⚹	♏	10 4:43
11 4:15	♄ □	♐	12 6:25
14 5:18	♅ ☌	♑	14 11:31
16 11:50	♃ □	♒	16 20:39
19 2:16	♅ ⚹	♓	19 8:50
21 15:30	♅ □	♈	21 21:51
24 3:45	♅ △	♉	24 9:44
25 14:24	♂ △	♊	26 19:38
28 22:12	♅ ☍	♋	29 3:24
30 21:45	♃ □	♌	31 9:04

☽ Phases & Eclipses

Dy Hr Mn	
3 2:58	☾ 10♊10
9 20:43	● 16♍42
9 20:44:17	● T 06'20"
16 15:13	☽ 23♐18
24 17:50	○ 1♈14
24 17:35	• A 0.544
2 13:52	☾ 8♋56
9 5:25	● 15♎29
16 5:54	☽ 22♑27
24 10:56	○ 0♉36
31 23:13	☾ 8♌07

Astro Data

1 September 1904
Julian Day # 1705
SVP 6♓35'30"
GC 25♐30.5 ⚵ 24♏58.3
Eris 24♓01.8R ✱ 9♒10.1R
⚷ 25♑10.7R ⚶ 16♌50.0
☽ Mean ☊ 18♍53.8

1 October 1904
Julian Day # 1735
SVP 6♓35'28"
GC 25♐30.5 ⚵ 4♐24.2
Eris 23♓40.9R ✱ 6♒52.5
⚷ 24♑36.9R ⚶ 0♍10.0
☽ Mean ☊ 17♍18.4

November 1904 — LONGITUDE

Day	Sid.Time	☉	0 hr ☽	Noon ☽	True ☊	☿	♀	♂	⚳	♃	♄	♅	♆	♇
1 Tu	14 41 22	8♏38 35	8♌33 35	15♌30 42	17♍09.9	9♏18.8	8♐55.6	18♍52.4	29♐01.6	23♈22.1	14♒29.6	27♐18.6	8♋03.9	21♊25.9
2 W	14 45 19	9 38 41	22 31 42	29 36 32	17 10.8	10 56.0	10 09.3	19 28.4	29 22.4	23R14.6	14 31.0	27 21.3	8R03.2	21R25.1
3 Th	14 49 15	10 38 49	6♍45 06	13♍57 11	17R11.6	12 32.8	11 22.9	20 04.4	29 43.3	23 07.2	14 32.5	27 24.0	8 02.5	21 24.3
4 F	14 53 12	11 38 59	21 12 29	28 30 31	17 11.1	14 09.2	12 36.6	20 40.3	0♑04.2	22 59.9	14 34.1	27 26.8	8 01.7	21 23.4
5 Sa	14 57 08	12 39 11	5♎50 46	13♎12 30	17 08.5	15 45.2	13 50.2	21 16.1	0 25.2	22 52.6	14 35.8	27 29.6	8 00.9	21 22.6
6 Su	15 01 05	13 39 25	20 34 56	27 57 11	17 03.3	17 20.7	15 03.8	21 52.0	0 46.3	22 45.5	14 37.6	27 32.4	8 00.1	21 21.7
7 M	15 05 02	14 39 41	5♏18 17	12♏37 16	16 55.7	18 55.9	16 17.4	22 27.7	1 07.5	22 38.5	14 39.5	27 35.2	7 59.3	21 20.8
8 Tu	15 08 58	15 39 59	19 53 10	27 05 07	16 46.3	20 30.8	17 31.0	23 03.5	1 28.8	22 31.7	14 41.5	27 38.1	7 58.4	21 19.9
9 W	15 12 55	16 40 19	4♐12 18	11♐14 03	16 36.2	22 05.3	18 44.6	23 39.2	1 50.2	22 24.9	14 43.6	27 41.1	7 57.5	21 19.0
10 Th	15 16 51	17 40 40	18 09 51	24 59 20	16 26.4	23 39.4	19 58.1	24 14.8	2 11.6	22 18.3	14 45.8	27 44.0	7 56.5	21 18.0
11 F	15 20 48	18 41 03	1♑42 19	8♑18 47	16 18.1	25 13.3	21 11.7	24 50.4	2 33.1	22 11.8	14 48.0	27 47.0	7 55.6	21 17.1
12 Sa	15 24 44	19 41 27	14 48 50	21 12 44	16 11.9	26 46.8	22 25.2	25 25.9	2 54.7	22 05.5	14 50.4	27 50.0	7 54.6	21 16.1
13 Su	15 28 41	20 41 53	27 30 53	3♒43 44	16 08.1	28 20.1	23 38.7	26 01.4	3 16.4	21 59.2	14 52.9	27 53.1	7 53.6	21 15.1
14 M	15 32 37	21 42 20	9♒51 51	15 55 51	16D06.6	29 53.1	24 52.1	26 36.8	3 38.1	21 53.2	14 55.5	27 56.2	7 52.5	21 14.1
15 Tu	15 36 34	22 42 48	21 56 23	27 54 08	16 06.5	1♐25.8	26 05.6	27 12.2	3 59.9	21 47.3	14 58.2	27 59.3	7 51.4	21 13.1
16 W	15 40 31	23 43 17	3♓49 48	9♓44 05	16R07.0	2 58.3	27 19.0	27 47.5	4 21.7	21 41.5	15 01.0	28 02.4	7 50.3	21 12.1
17 Th	15 44 27	24 43 48	15 37 38	21 31 10	16 07.0	4 30.5	28 32.4	28 22.7	4 43.7	21 35.9	15 03.8	28 05.5	7 49.2	21 11.1
18 F	15 48 24	25 44 20	27 25 17	3♈20 35	16 05.5	6 02.5	29 45.7	28 57.9	5 05.6	21 30.5	15 06.8	28 08.7	7 48.1	21 10.1
19 Sa	15 52 20	26 44 54	9♈17 37	15 16 53	16 01.6	7 34.2	0♑59.1	29 33.1	5 27.7	21 25.2	15 09.8	28 11.9	7 46.9	21 09.0
20 Su	15 56 17	27 45 28	21 18 50	27 23 49	15 55.0	9 05.7	2 12.4	0♎08.2	5 49.8	21 20.1	15 13.0	28 15.1	7 45.7	21 08.0
21 M	16 00 13	28 46 04	3♉32 09	9♉44 03	15 45.6	10 37.0	3 25.6	0 43.2	6 12.0	21 15.2	15 16.2	28 18.4	7 44.5	21 06.9
22 Tu	16 04 10	29 46 42	15 59 39	22 19 03	15 34.0	12 08.0	4 38.9	1 18.2	6 34.2	21 10.4	15 19.5	28 21.7	7 43.2	21 05.8
23 W	16 08 06	0♐47 20	28 42 15	5♊09 09	15 21.1	13 38.8	5 52.1	1 53.2	6 56.5	21 05.8	15 22.9	28 25.0	7 42.0	21 04.8
24 Th	16 12 03	1 48 01	11♊39 39	18 13 35	15 08.0	15 09.4	7 05.3	2 28.0	7 18.8	21 01.4	15 26.4	28 28.3	7 40.7	21 03.7
25 F	16 16 00	2 48 42	24 50 43	1♋30 51	14 55.9	16 39.6	8 18.4	3 02.9	7 41.2	20 57.2	15 30.0	28 31.6	7 39.4	21 02.6
26 Sa	16 19 56	3 49 26	8♋13 43	14 59 06	14 46.0	18 09.5	9 31.5	3 37.6	8 03.7	20 53.2	15 33.7	28 35.0	7 38.0	21 01.5
27 Su	16 23 53	4 50 10	21 46 48	28 36 39	14 39.0	19 39.1	10 44.6	4 12.3	8 26.2	20 49.3	15 37.5	28 38.4	7 36.7	21 00.4
28 M	16 27 49	5 50 56	5♌28 28	12♌22 11	14 34.8	21 08.4	11 57.7	4 47.0	8 48.8	20 45.7	15 41.3	28 41.8	7 35.3	20 59.2
29 Tu	16 31 46	6 51 44	19 17 42	26 14 59	14D33.2	22 37.1	13 10.7	5 21.6	9 11.4	20 42.2	15 45.2	28 45.2	7 33.9	20 58.1
30 W	16 35 42	7 52 33	3♍14 01	10♍14 46	14R32.9	24 05.4	14 23.7	5 56.1	9 34.0	20 39.0	15 49.2	28 48.6	7 32.5	20 57.0

December 1904 — LONGITUDE

Day	Sid.Time	☉	0 hr ☽	Noon ☽	True ☊	☿	♀	♂	⚳	♃	♄	♅	♆	♇
1 Th	16 39 39	8♐53 24	17♍17 12	24♍21 16	14♍32.8	25♐33.2	15♑36.6	6♎30.5	9♑56.7	20♈35.9	15♒53.3	28♐52.1	7♋31.1	20♊55.9
2 F	16 43 35	9 54 16	1♎26 50	8♎33 44	14R31.3	27 00.3	16 49.5	7 04.9	10 19.5	20R33.0	15 57.5	28 55.5	7R29.6	20R54.7
3 Sa	16 47 32	10 55 09	15 41 43	22 50 26	14 27.5	28 26.6	18 02.4	7 39.3	10 42.3	20 30.4	16 01.8	28 59.0	7 28.1	20 53.6
4 Su	16 51 29	11 56 04	29 59 28	7♏08 18	14 20.6	29 52.1	19 15.2	8 13.5	11 05.2	20 27.9	16 06.1	29 02.5	7 26.6	20 52.4
5 M	16 55 25	12 57 00	14♏16 20	21 22 56	14 10.8	1♑16.6	20 28.0	8 47.7	11 28.1	20 25.6	16 10.5	29 06.0	7 25.1	20 51.3
6 Tu	16 59 22	13 57 57	28 27 25	5♐29 06	13 58.8	2 39.9	21 40.8	9 21.8	11 51.0	20 23.6	16 15.0	29 09.5	7 23.6	20 50.1
7 W	17 03 18	14 58 55	12♐27 20	19 21 32	13 45.6	4 01.8	22 53.5	9 55.8	12 14.0	20 21.7	16 19.6	29 13.1	7 22.1	20 48.9
8 Th	17 07 15	15 59 55	26 11 09	2♑55 46	13 32.7	5 22.0	24 06.1	10 29.8	12 37.0	20 20.1	16 24.3	29 16.6	7 20.5	20 47.8
9 F	17 11 11	17 00 55	9♑35 07	16 09 01	13 21.3	6 40.5	25 18.7	11 03.7	13 00.1	20 18.7	16 29.0	29 20.2	7 19.0	20 46.6
10 Sa	17 15 08	18 01 55	22 37 24	29 00 23	13 12.3	7 56.7	26 31.3	11 37.5	13 23.2	20 17.4	16 33.8	29 23.7	7 17.4	20 45.4
11 Su	17 19 05	19 02 57	5♒18 09	11♒31 02	13 06.1	9 10.3	27 43.8	12 11.2	13 46.4	20 16.4	16 38.7	29 27.3	7 15.8	20 44.3
12 M	17 23 01	20 03 59	17 39 26	23 43 51	13 02.7	10 21.0	28 56.3	12 44.9	14 09.5	20 15.6	16 43.6	29 30.9	7 14.2	20 43.1
13 Tu	17 26 58	21 05 01	29 44 51	5♓43 01	13D01.4	11 28.3	0♒08.6	13 18.5	14 32.7	20 15.0	16 48.7	29 34.5	7 12.6	20 41.9
14 W	17 30 54	22 06 04	11♓39 03	17 33 36	13R01.3	12 31.5	1 21.0	13 51.9	14 56.0	20 14.6	16 53.8	29 38.1	7 11.0	20 40.8
15 Th	17 34 51	23 07 07	23 27 24	29 21 08	13 01.2	13 30.2	2 33.2	14 25.3	15 19.3	20D14.5	16 58.9	29 41.7	7 09.4	20 39.6
16 F	17 38 47	24 08 11	5♈15 31	11♈11 14	13 00.0	14 23.6	3 45.4	14 58.7	15 42.6	20 14.5	17 04.1	29 45.3	7 07.7	20 38.4
17 Sa	17 42 44	25 09 15	17 08 56	23 09 17	12 56.7	15 11.0	4 57.6	15 31.9	16 05.9	20 14.7	17 09.4	29 48.9	7 06.1	20 37.2
18 Su	17 46 40	26 10 19	29 12 49	5♉20 03	12 50.9	15 51.6	6 09.6	16 05.0	16 29.3	20 15.2	17 14.8	29 52.5	7 04.4	20 36.1
19 M	17 50 37	27 11 24	11♉31 28	17 47 23	12 42.3	16 24.4	7 21.6	16 38.1	16 52.7	20 15.9	17 20.2	29 56.1	7 02.7	20 34.9
20 Tu	17 54 33	28 12 29	24 08 05	0♊33 45	12 31.4	16 48.7	8 33.5	17 11.1	17 16.1	20 16.7	17 25.7	29 59.8	7 01.1	20 33.8
21 W	17 58 30	29 13 35	7♊04 25	13 40 03	12 19.1	17R03.5	9 45.3	17 43.9	17 39.5	20 17.8	17 31.3	0♑03.4	6 59.4	20 32.6
22 Th	18 02 27	0♑14 41	20 20 28	27 05 25	12 06.4	17 07.9	10 57.1	18 16.7	18 03.0	20 19.1	17 36.9	0 07.0	6 57.7	20 31.4
23 F	18 06 23	1 15 47	3♋54 32	10♋47 23	11 54.8	17 01.3	12 08.8	18 49.4	18 26.5	20 20.6	17 42.6	0 10.6	6 56.0	20 30.3
24 Sa	18 10 20	2 16 54	17 43 29	24 42 18	11 45.2	16 43.0	13 20.3	19 22.0	18 50.0	20 22.3	17 48.3	0 14.2	6 54.3	20 29.2
25 Su	18 14 16	3 18 01	1♌43 18	8♌45 58	11 38.4	16 13.0	14 31.8	19 54.5	19 13.5	20 24.2	17 54.1	0 17.9	6 52.6	20 28.0
26 M	18 18 13	4 19 09	15 49 47	22 54 20	11 34.5	15 31.3	15 43.2	20 26.9	19 37.1	20 26.3	17 59.9	0 21.5	6 50.9	20 26.9
27 Tu	18 22 09	5 20 17	29 59 14	7♍04 08	11D33.1	14 38.5	16 54.5	20 59.2	20 00.7	20 28.6	18 05.8	0 25.1	6 49.2	20 25.8
28 W	18 26 06	6 21 26	14♍08 48	21 13 02	11 33.2	13 35.8	18 05.8	21 31.4	20 24.2	20 31.1	18 11.8	0 28.7	6 47.5	20 24.6
29 Th	18 30 03	7 22 35	28 16 40	5♎19 36	11R33.7	12 24.9	19 16.9	22 03.5	20 47.9	20 33.8	18 17.8	0 32.3	6 45.8	20 23.5
30 F	18 33 59	8 23 44	12♎21 43	19 22 57	11 33.2	11 07.9	20 27.9	22 35.5	21 11.5	20 36.7	18 23.9	0 35.9	6 44.1	20 22.4
31 Sa	18 37 56	9 24 54	26 23 11	3♏22 19	11 30.7	9 47.3	21 38.8	23 07.4	21 35.1	20 39.8	18 30.0	0 39.5	6 42.4	20 21.3

Astro Data Dy Hr Mn	Planet Ingress Dy Hr Mn	Last Aspect Dy Hr Mn	☽ Ingress Dy Hr Mn	Last Aspect Dy Hr Mn	☽ Ingress Dy Hr Mn	☽ Phases & Eclipses Dy Hr Mn
☽0S 4 19:49	⚳ ♑ 4 7:12	2 8:11 ♅ △	♍ 2 12:40	1 19:40 ♅ □	♎ 1 21:33	7 15:37 ● 14♏49
☽0N 18 12:20	☿ ♐ 14 13:47	4 10:15 ♅ □	♎ 4 14:27	3 22:27 ☿ ⚹	♏ 4 0:01	15 0:35 ☽ 22♒14
♃⚹♇ 23 19:32	♀ ♑ 18 16:40	6 11:19 ♅ ⚹	♏ 6 15:20	5 10:18 ♀ ⚹	♐ 6 2:38	23 3:12 ○ 0♊25
♂0S 26 10:47	♂ ♎ 20 6:24	8 4:59 ♂ ⚹	♐ 8 16:54	8 5:27 ♅ ☌	♑ 8 6:46	30 7:38 ☾ 7♍41
	☉ ♐ 22 17:16	10 16:54 ♅ ☌	♑ 10 20:56	10 6:49 ♀ ☌	♒ 10 13:53	
☽0S 2 4:04		13 0:06 ☿ ⚹	♒ 13 4:47	12 23:36 ♅ ⚹	♓ 13 0:30	7 3:46 ● 14♐38
♃ D 15 19:58	☿ ♑ 4 14:14	15 12:10 ♅ ⚹	♓ 15 16:14	15 12:42 ♅ □	♈ 15 13:19	14 22:07 ☽ 22♓32
☽0N 15 21:56	♀ ♒ 13 9:08	18 3:55 ♀ □	♈ 18 5:14	18 1:15 ♅ △	♉ 18 1:33	22 18:01 ○ 0♋30
☿ R 22 9:49	♅ ♑ 20 13:37	20 13:41 ♅ △	♉ 20 17:06	19 11:08 ♄ □	♊ 20 10:57	29 15:46 ☾ 7♎32
♃⚹♇ 26 16:14	☉ ♑ 22 6:14	21 22:40 ♄ □	♊ 23 2:25	22 0:21 ♇ ☌	♋ 22 17:08	
☽0S 29 10:47		25 6:37 ♅ ☍	♋ 25 9:17	24 4:33 ♃ □	♌ 24 21:04	
		26 22:23 ♃ □	♌ 27 14:26	26 7:50 ♇ ⚹	♍ 27 0:01	
		29 16:19 ♅ △	♍ 29 18:27	28 10:38 ♇ □	♎ 29 2:56	
				30 17:43 ♂ ☌	♏ 31 6:12	

Astro Data

1 November 1904
Julian Day # 1766
SVP 6♓35'24"
GC 25♐30.6 ⚴ 15♐42.7
Eris 23♓22.3R ⚵ 11♒07.1
⚷ 25♑10.1 ⚶ 13♍23.4
☽ Mean ☊ 15♍39.9

1 December 1904
Julian Day # 1796
SVP 6♓35'20"
GC 25♐30.7 ⚴ 27♐23.6
Eris 23♓12.7R ⚵ 20♒06.7
⚷ 26♑42.9 ⚶ 25♍00.2
☽ Mean ☊ 14♍04.6

LONGITUDE — January 1905

Day	Sid.Time	☉	0 hr ☽	Noon ☽	True ☊	☿	♀	♂	⚳	♃	♄	♅	♆	♇
1 Su	18 41 52	10♑26 04	10♏20 10	17♏16 33	11♍25.7	8♑25.7	22♒49.7	23♎39.2	21♑58.8	20♈43.1	18♒36.1	0♑43.1	6♋40.7	20♊20.2
2 M	18 45 49	11 27 15	24 11 15	1♐03 59	11R 18.1	7R 05.9	24 00.4	24 10.9	22 22.5	20 46.6	18 42.4	0 46.7	6R 39.0	20R 19.1
3 Tu	18 49 45	12 28 26	7♐54 28	14 42 21	11 08.5	5 50.3	25 11.0	24 42.4	22 46.2	20 50.3	18 48.6	0 50.3	6 37.3	20 18.0
4 W	18 53 42	13 29 37	21 27 20	28 09 05	10 57.9	4 40.9	26 21.5	25 13.8	23 09.9	20 54.2	18 55.0	0 53.8	6 35.7	20 17.0
5 Th	18 57 38	14 30 48	4♑47 19	11♑21 46	10 47.4	3 39.5	27 31.9	25 45.1	23 33.6	20 58.3	19 01.3	0 57.4	6 34.0	20 15.9
6 F	19 01 35	15 31 59	17 52 14	24 18 35	10 38.1	2 47.1	28 42.2	26 16.3	23 57.4	21 02.5	19 07.7	1 00.9	6 32.3	20 14.9
7 Sa	19 05 32	16 33 10	0♒40 45	6♒58 45	10 30.7	2 04.5	29 52.3	26 47.3	24 21.1	21 07.0	19 14.2	1 04.5	6 30.6	20 13.8
8 Su	19 09 28	17 34 20	13 12 40	19 22 42	10 25.8	1 31.9	1♓02.3	27 18.2	24 44.8	21 11.7	19 20.7	1 08.0	6 29.0	20 12.8
9 M	19 13 25	18 35 30	25 29 05	1♓32 11	10D 23.3	1 09.2	2 12.2	27 49.0	25 08.6	21 16.5	19 27.2	1 11.5	6 27.3	20 11.8
10 Tu	19 17 21	19 36 39	7♓32 22	13 30 08	10 22.9	0D 56.2	3 21.9	28 19.6	25 32.4	21 21.5	19 33.8	1 15.0	6 25.6	20 10.8
11 W	19 21 18	20 37 48	19 25 58	25 20 29	10 23.8	0 52.4	4 31.5	28 50.1	25 56.1	21 26.7	19 40.4	1 18.4	6 24.0	20 09.8
12 Th	19 25 14	21 38 56	1♈14 14	7♈07 54	10 25.2	0 57.1	5 40.9	29 20.5	26 19.9	21 32.1	19 47.0	1 21.9	6 22.4	20 08.8
13 F	19 29 11	22 40 04	13 02 08	18 57 35	10R 26.1	1 09.9	6 50.2	29 50.7	26 43.7	21 37.7	19 53.7	1 25.4	6 20.7	20 07.8
14 Sa	19 33 07	23 41 11	24 54 56	0♉54 52	10 25.9	1 29.9	7 59.3	0♏20.7	27 07.4	21 43.4	20 00.4	1 28.8	6 19.1	20 06.9
15 Su	19 37 04	24 42 17	6♉58 01	13 05 01	10 23.9	1 56.5	9 08.3	0 50.6	27 31.2	21 49.3	20 07.2	1 32.2	6 17.5	20 05.9
16 M	19 41 01	25 43 23	19 16 25	25 32 45	10 19.9	2 29.2	10 17.1	1 20.4	27 55.0	21 55.4	20 14.0	1 35.6	6 15.9	20 05.0
17 Tu	19 44 57	26 44 28	1♊54 27	8♊21 51	10 14.2	3 07.3	11 25.7	1 50.0	28 18.7	22 01.6	20 20.8	1 39.0	6 14.4	20 04.1
18 W	19 48 54	27 45 32	14 55 12	21 34 36	10 07.3	3 50.4	12 34.1	2 19.5	28 42.5	22 08.1	20 27.7	1 42.3	6 12.8	20 03.2
19 Th	19 52 50	28 46 35	28 20 04	5♋11 26	10 00.0	4 37.9	13 42.3	2 48.8	29 06.3	22 14.7	20 34.5	1 45.7	6 11.3	20 02.3
20 F	19 56 47	29 47 37	12♋08 25	19 10 34	9 53.1	5 29.4	14 50.4	3 17.9	29 30.0	22 21.4	20 41.4	1 49.0	6 09.7	20 01.4
21 Sa	20 00 43	0♒48 39	26 17 20	3♌28 04	9 47.6	6 24.5	15 58.2	3 46.9	29 53.8	22 28.3	20 48.4	1 52.3	6 08.2	20 00.6
22 Su	20 04 40	1 49 40	10♌42 00	17 58 21	9 43.8	7 22.9	17 05.8	4 15.7	0♒17.5	22 35.4	20 55.3	1 55.5	6 06.7	19 59.7
23 M	20 08 36	2 50 40	25 16 17	2♍35 00	9D 42.1	8 24.2	18 13.2	4 44.3	0 41.3	22 42.6	21 02.3	1 58.8	6 05.2	19 58.9
24 Tu	20 12 33	3 51 40	9♍53 42	17 11 40	9 42.1	9 28.2	19 20.4	5 12.8	1 05.0	22 50.0	21 09.3	2 02.0	6 03.7	19 58.1
25 W	20 16 30	4 52 39	24 28 15	1♎42 55	9 43.2	10 34.6	20 27.4	5 41.1	1 28.7	22 57.6	21 16.4	2 05.2	6 02.3	19 57.3
26 Th	20 20 26	5 53 37	8♎55 11	16 04 43	9 44.8	11 43.2	21 34.2	6 09.2	1 52.4	23 05.3	21 23.4	2 08.4	6 00.8	19 56.5
27 F	20 24 23	6 54 35	23 11 12	0♏14 28	9R 45.9	12 53.9	22 40.7	6 37.1	2 16.2	23 13.1	21 30.5	2 11.5	5 59.4	19 55.7
28 Sa	20 28 19	7 55 32	7♏14 23	14 10 52	9 45.9	14 06.4	23 47.0	7 04.8	2 39.9	23 21.1	21 37.6	2 14.6	5 58.0	19 55.0
29 Su	20 32 16	8 56 29	21 03 53	27 53 26	9 44.4	15 20.6	24 53.0	7 32.3	3 03.5	23 29.3	21 44.7	2 17.7	5 56.7	19 54.3
30 M	20 36 12	9 57 25	4♐39 32	11♐22 12	9 41.6	16 36.5	25 58.8	7 59.6	3 27.2	23 37.6	21 51.8	2 20.8	5 55.3	19 53.6
31 Tu	20 40 09	10 58 20	18 01 29	24 37 23	9 37.5	17 53.8	27 04.4	8 26.7	3 50.9	23 46.0	21 59.0	2 23.8	5 54.0	19 52.9

LONGITUDE — February 1905

Day	Sid.Time	☉	0 hr ☽	Noon ☽	True ☊	☿	♀	♂	⚳	♃	♄	♅	♆	♇
1 W	20 44 05	11♒59 15	1♑09 58	7♑39 13	9♍32.9	19♑12.5	28♓09.6	8♏53.6	4♒14.5	23♈54.6	22♒06.1	2♑26.8	5♋52.6	19♊52.2
2 Th	20 48 02	13 00 08	14 05 12	20 27 55	9R 28.2	20 32.4	29 14.6	9 20.3	4 38.2	24 03.3	22 13.3	2 29.8	5R 51.4	19R 51.6
3 F	20 51 59	14 01 01	26 47 26	3♒03 47	9 24.1	21 53.6	0♈19.3	9 46.8	5 01.8	24 12.2	22 20.5	2 32.8	5 50.1	19 50.9
4 Sa	20 55 55	15 01 52	9♒17 03	15 27 20	9 21.0	23 16.0	1 23.7	10 13.0	5 25.4	24 21.1	22 27.7	2 35.7	5 48.8	19 50.3
5 Su	20 59 52	16 02 42	21 34 44	27 39 26	9D 19.2	24 39.4	2 27.9	10 39.0	5 49.0	24 30.3	22 34.9	2 38.6	5 47.6	19 49.7
6 M	21 03 48	17 03 31	3♓41 38	9♓41 34	9 18.6	26 04.0	3 31.7	11 04.7	6 12.5	24 39.5	22 42.1	2 41.4	5 46.4	19 49.1
7 Tu	21 07 45	18 04 18	15 39 31	21 35 47	9 19.1	27 29.5	4 35.1	11 30.2	6 36.1	24 48.9	22 49.3	2 44.2	5 45.2	19 48.6
8 W	21 11 41	19 05 04	27 30 45	3♈24 50	9 20.4	28 56.0	5 38.3	11 55.5	6 59.6	24 58.4	22 56.6	2 47.0	5 44.1	19 48.0
9 Th	21 15 38	20 05 48	9♈18 28	15 12 09	9 22.1	0♒23.5	6 41.0	12 20.5	7 23.1	25 08.1	23 03.8	2 49.8	5 43.0	19 47.5
10 F	21 19 34	21 06 31	21 06 23	27 01 43	9 23.7	1 51.9	7 43.5	12 45.2	7 46.6	25 17.9	23 11.0	2 52.5	5 41.9	19 47.0
11 Sa	21 23 31	22 07 13	2♉58 44	8♉58 02	9 24.9	3 21.3	8 45.5	13 09.7	8 10.0	25 27.8	23 18.3	2 55.2	5 40.8	19 46.6
12 Su	21 27 28	23 07 52	15 00 12	21 05 51	9R 25.4	4 51.5	9 47.2	13 33.9	8 33.4	25 37.8	23 25.5	2 57.8	5 39.7	19 46.1
13 M	21 31 24	24 08 30	27 15 35	3♊29 57	9 25.2	6 22.7	10 48.4	13 57.8	8 56.8	25 47.9	23 32.8	3 00.4	5 38.7	19 45.7
14 Tu	21 35 21	25 09 07	9♊49 31	16 14 44	9 24.2	7 54.8	11 49.3	14 21.5	9 20.2	25 58.1	23 40.0	3 03.0	5 37.7	19 45.3
15 W	21 39 17	26 09 41	22 46 03	29 23 47	9 22.8	9 27.7	12 49.7	14 44.9	9 43.5	26 08.5	23 47.2	3 05.5	5 36.8	19 44.9
16 Th	21 43 14	27 10 14	6♋08 08	12♋59 14	9 21.2	11 01.6	13 49.7	15 07.9	10 06.8	26 19.0	23 54.5	3 08.0	5 35.8	19 44.5
17 F	21 47 10	28 10 45	19 56 59	27 01 13	9 19.6	12 36.4	14 49.2	15 30.7	10 30.1	26 29.6	24 01.7	3 10.4	5 34.9	19 44.2
18 Sa	21 51 07	29 11 15	4♌11 33	11♌27 28	9 18.4	14 12.0	15 48.2	15 53.2	10 53.3	26 40.2	24 08.9	3 12.9	5 34.1	19 43.8
19 Su	21 55 03	0♓11 43	18 48 16	26 13 07	9D 17.7	15 48.6	16 46.7	16 15.4	11 16.5	26 51.0	24 16.2	3 15.2	5 33.2	19 43.5
20 M	21 59 00	1 12 09	3♍41 04	11♍11 05	9 17.6	17 26.1	17 44.8	16 37.2	11 39.7	27 01.9	24 23.4	3 17.6	5 32.4	19 43.2
21 Tu	22 02 57	2 12 33	18 42 07	26 13 02	9 17.8	19 04.6	18 42.3	16 58.8	12 02.8	27 12.9	24 30.6	3 19.9	5 31.6	19 43.0
22 W	22 06 53	3 12 56	3♎42 48	11♎10 26	9 18.3	20 44.0	19 39.2	17 20.0	12 25.9	27 24.0	24 37.8	3 22.1	5 30.8	19 42.7
23 Th	22 10 50	4 13 18	18 35 01	25 55 48	9 18.8	22 24.3	20 35.6	17 40.8	12 49.0	27 35.2	24 44.9	3 24.3	5 30.1	19 42.5
24 F	22 14 46	5 13 38	3♏12 09	10♏23 35	9 19.2	24 05.7	21 31.4	18 01.3	13 12.0	27 46.5	24 52.1	3 26.5	5 29.4	19 42.3
25 Sa	22 18 43	6 13 56	17 29 45	24 30 26	9R 19.4	25 48.0	22 26.7	18 21.5	13 35.0	27 57.9	24 59.3	3 28.6	5 28.7	19 42.2
26 Su	22 22 39	7 14 14	1♐25 34	8♐15 09	9 19.5	27 31.3	23 21.3	18 41.3	13 58.0	28 09.4	25 06.4	3 30.7	5 28.1	19 42.0
27 M	22 26 36	8 14 30	14 59 19	21 38 15	9 19.5	29 15.7	24 15.3	19 00.7	14 20.9	28 20.9	25 13.5	3 32.7	5 27.5	19 41.9
28 Tu	22 30 32	9 14 44	28 12 12	4♑41 25	9D 19.4	1♓01.1	25 08.6	19 19.7	14 43.8	28 32.6	25 20.7	3 34.7	5 26.9	19 41.8

Astro Data	Planet Ingress	Last Aspect	☽ Ingress	Last Aspect	☽ Ingress	☽ Phases & Eclipses	Astro Data
Dy Hr Mn	Dy Hr Mn	Dy Hr Mn	Dy Hr Mn	Dy Hr Mn	Dy Hr Mn	Dy Hr Mn	1 January 1905
☿ D 11 10:25	♀ ♓ 7 14:38	1 22:32 ♀ □	♐ 2 10:08	2 18:53 ♃ □	♒ 3 6:08	5 18:17 ● 14♑47	Julian Day # 1827
☽ 0N 12 7:35	♂ ♏ 13 19:26	4 8:28 ♀ ✶	♑ 4 15:20	5 5:41 ♃ ✶	♓ 5 16:39	13 20:11 ☽ 23♈01	SVP 6♓35'15"
♄△♇ 15 7:59	☉ ♒ 20 16:52	6 15:50 ♂ □	♒ 6 22:43	8 1:37 ☿ ✶	♈ 8 5:03	21 7:14 ○ 0♌37	GC 25♐30.8 ⚴ 9♑38.1
♄⚼♆ 23 20:10	⚳ ♒ 21 18:17	9 4:17 ♂ △	♓ 9 8:57	10 8:27 ♃ ☌	♉ 10 18:00	28 0:20 ☾ 7♏26	Eris 23♓14.9 ⚵ 2♓44.1
☽ 0S 25 17:47		11 1:32 ☉ ✶	♈ 11 21:29	12 16:36 ♄ □	♊ 13 5:17		⚷ 29♑02.1 ⚶ 4♎35.6
	♀ ♈ 3 4:49	13 20:11 ☉ □	♉ 14 10:11	15 6:03 ♃ ✶	♋ 15 13:05	4 11:06 ● 15♒00	☽ Mean ☊ 12♍26.1
♀0N 2 15:02	☿ ♒ 9 5:35	16 12:22 ☉ △	♊ 16 20:25	17 11:06 ♃ □	♌ 17 17:00	12 16:20 ☽ 23♉19	
☽ 0N 8 15:57	☉ ♓ 19 7:21	18 13:00 ♃ ✶	♋ 19 2:56	19 13:02 ♃ △	♍ 19 18:05	19 18:52 ○ 0♍29	1 February 1905
☽ 0S 22 2:42	☿ ♓ 27 22:07	20 17:25 ♃ □	♌ 21 6:13	21 1:37 ♇ □	♎ 21 18:03	19 19:00 ☍ P 0.405	Julian Day # 1858
		22 19:39 ♃ △	♍ 23 7:46	23 14:46 ♃ ☍	♏ 23 18:42	26 10:04 ☾ 7♐09	SVP 6♓35'10"
		24 16:34 ♇ □	♎ 25 9:09	25 14:33 ☿ □	♐ 25 21:31		GC 25♐30.8 ⚴ 21♑31.5
		26 23:57 ♃ ☍	♏ 27 11:35	28 0:27 ♃ △	♑ 28 3:19		Eris 23♓29.0 ⚵ 17♓35.3
		29 6:14 ♀ △	♐ 29 15:44				⚷ 1♒38.6 ⚶ 9♎41.0
		31 16:53 ♀ □	♑ 31 21:51				☽ Mean ☊ 10♍47.6

March 1905 LONGITUDE

Day	Sid.Time	☉	0 hr ☽	Noon ☽	True ☊	☿	♀	♂	⚳	♃	♄	♅	♆	♇
1 W	22 34 29	10♓14 57	11♑06 14	17♑26 59	9♍19.5	2♓47.5	26♈01.2	19♏38.3	15♒06.6	28♈44.4	25♒27.8	3♑36.7	5♋26.4	19♊41.7
2 Th	22 38 26	11 15 09	23 43 57	29 57 29	9 19.7	4 35.0	26 53.2	19 56.5	15 29.4	28 56.2	25 34.8	3 38.6	5R 25.9	19R 41.6
3 F	22 42 22	12 15 18	6♒07 54	12♒15 29	9 19.9	6 23.5	27 44.4	20 14.4	15 52.2	29 08.1	25 41.9	3 40.4	5 25.4	19 41.6
4 Sa	22 46 19	13 15 26	18 20 32	24 23 20	9 20.2	8 13.1	28 34.8	20 31.7	16 14.9	29 20.2	25 48.9	3 42.2	5 25.0	19D 41.6
5 Su	22 50 15	14 15 32	0♓24 08	6♓23 11	9R 20.4	10 03.8	29 24.5	20 48.7	16 37.5	29 32.3	25 55.9	3 44.0	5 24.6	19 41.6
6 M	22 54 12	15 15 37	12 20 45	18 17 05	9 20.3	11 55.5	0♉13.3	21 05.2	17 00.1	29 44.4	26 02.9	3 45.7	5 24.2	19 41.6
7 Tu	22 58 08	16 15 39	24 12 26	0♈07 02	9 19.9	13 48.2	1 01.3	21 21.2	17 22.7	29 56.7	26 09.9	3 47.4	5 23.8	19 41.7
8 W	23 02 05	17 15 40	6♈01 11	11 55 09	9 19.0	15 42.0	1 48.4	21 36.8	17 45.2	0♉09.0	26 16.8	3 49.0	5 23.5	19 41.7
9 Th	23 06 01	18 15 38	17 49 15	23 43 47	9 17.8	17 36.8	2 34.5	21 51.9	18 07.7	0 21.4	26 23.8	3 50.6	5 23.3	19 41.8
10 F	23 09 58	19 15 34	29 39 08	5♉35 40	9 16.4	19 32.5	3 19.7	22 06.5	18 30.1	0 33.9	26 30.6	3 52.1	5 23.0	19 41.9
11 Sa	23 13 54	20 15 29	11♉33 47	17 33 56	9 14.9	21 29.1	4 03.9	22 20.7	18 52.4	0 46.5	26 37.5	3 53.6	5 22.8	19 42.1
12 Su	23 17 51	21 15 21	23 36 33	29 42 07	9 13.6	23 26.5	4 47.1	22 34.3	19 14.7	0 59.1	26 44.3	3 55.0	5 22.6	19 42.2
13 M	23 21 48	22 15 11	5♊51 08	12♊04 06	9D 12.8	25 24.6	5 29.2	22 47.4	19 36.9	1 11.8	26 51.1	3 56.4	5 22.5	19 42.4
14 Tu	23 25 44	23 14 59	18 21 32	24 43 55	9 12.6	27 23.3	6 10.2	23 00.0	19 59.1	1 24.5	26 57.9	3 57.7	5 22.4	19 42.6
15 W	23 29 41	24 14 44	1♋11 44	7♋45 24	9 13.0	29 22.5	6 50.0	23 12.1	20 21.2	1 37.3	27 04.6	3 59.0	5 22.3	19 42.9
16 Th	23 33 37	25 14 27	14 25 18	21 11 43	9 14.0	1♈21.9	7 28.5	23 23.6	20 43.3	1 50.2	27 11.3	4 00.2	5D 22.3	19 43.1
17 F	23 37 34	26 14 08	28 04 52	5♌04 49	9 15.2	3 21.4	8 05.8	23 34.6	21 05.3	2 03.2	27 18.0	4 01.4	5 22.3	19 43.4
18 Sa	23 41 30	27 13 47	12♌11 29	19 24 40	9 16.4	5 20.8	8 41.8	23 45.1	21 27.2	2 16.2	27 24.6	4 02.5	5 22.3	19 43.7
19 Su	23 45 27	28 13 24	26 43 55	4♍08 41	9R 17.1	7 19.7	9 16.5	23 54.9	21 49.1	2 29.2	27 31.2	4 03.6	5 22.4	19 44.0
20 M	23 49 23	29 12 58	11♍38 10	19 11 25	9 16.9	9 17.9	9 49.7	24 04.2	22 10.9	2 42.4	27 37.7	4 04.6	5 22.5	19 44.4
21 Tu	23 53 20	0♈12 30	26 47 22	4♎24 47	9 15.7	11 15.1	10 21.4	24 12.9	22 32.6	2 55.5	27 44.3	4 05.6	5 22.6	19 44.7
22 W	23 57 17	1 12 00	12♎02 25	19 38 58	9 13.5	13 10.8	10 51.6	24 21.0	22 54.3	3 08.8	27 50.7	4 06.5	5 22.8	19 45.1
23 Th	0 01 13	2 11 28	27 13 12	4♏43 55	9 10.5	15 04.7	11 20.2	24 28.4	23 15.9	3 22.0	27 57.1	4 07.4	5 22.9	19 45.5
24 F	0 05 10	3 10 55	12♏10 07	19 30 55	9 07.3	16 56.4	11 47.2	24 35.3	23 37.5	3 35.4	28 03.5	4 08.2	5 23.2	19 45.9
25 Sa	0 09 06	4 10 19	26 45 38	3♐53 47	9 04.3	18 45.4	12 12.4	24 41.4	23 58.9	3 48.7	28 09.9	4 09.0	5 23.4	19 46.4
26 Su	0 13 03	5 09 42	10♐55 05	17 49 23	9 02.1	20 31.4	12 36.0	24 47.0	24 20.3	4 02.2	28 16.2	4 09.7	5 23.7	19 46.8
27 M	0 16 59	6 09 04	24 36 46	1♑17 24	9D 01.0	22 13.8	12 57.7	24 51.9	24 41.7	4 15.7	28 22.4	4 10.4	5 24.1	19 47.3
28 Tu	0 20 56	7 08 23	7♑51 35	14 19 44	9 01.2	23 52.4	13 17.6	24 56.1	25 02.9	4 29.2	28 28.6	4 11.0	5 24.5	19 47.9
29 W	0 24 52	8 07 41	20 42 17	26 59 44	9 02.3	25 26.7	13 35.5	24 59.6	25 24.1	4 42.8	28 34.8	4 11.6	5 24.9	19 48.4
30 Th	0 28 49	9 06 57	3♒12 37	9♒21 28	9 03.9	26 56.2	13 51.4	25 02.4	25 45.2	4 56.4	28 40.9	4 12.1	5 25.3	19 48.9
31 F	0 32 46	10 06 11	15 26 50	21 29 13	9 05.6	28 20.8	14 05.3	25 04.5	26 06.2	5 10.0	28 47.0	4 12.6	5 25.8	19 49.5

April 1905 LONGITUDE

Day	Sid.Time	☉	0 hr ☽	Noon ☽	True ☊	☿	♀	♂	⚳	♃	♄	♅	♆	♇
1 Sa	0 36 42	11♈05 23	27♒29 08	3♓27 01	9♍06.7	29♈40.1	14♉17.1	25♏05.8	26♒27.2	5♉23.7	28♒53.0	4♑13.0	5♋26.3	19♊50.1
2 Su	0 40 39	12 04 33	9♓23 21	15 18 31	9R 06.7	0♉53.7	14 26.7	25R 06.5	26 48.1	5 37.5	28 58.9	4 13.3	5 26.8	19 50.7
3 M	0 44 35	13 03 41	21 12 54	27 06 50	9 05.1	2 01.5	14 34.0	25 06.4	27 08.8	5 51.2	29 04.8	4 13.6	5 27.4	19 51.4
4 Tu	0 48 32	14 02 47	3♈00 38	8♈54 34	9 01.7	3 03.3	14 39.1	25 05.5	27 29.5	6 05.0	29 10.7	4 13.9	5 28.0	19 52.0
5 W	0 52 28	15 01 52	14 48 54	20 43 52	8 56.7	3 58.7	14R 41.9	25 03.9	27 50.2	6 18.9	29 16.5	4 14.1	5 28.6	19 52.7
6 Th	0 56 25	16 00 54	26 39 43	2♉36 40	8 50.3	4 47.8	14 42.3	25 01.6	28 10.7	6 32.8	29 22.2	4 14.2	5 29.3	19 53.4
7 F	1 00 21	16 59 54	8♉34 55	14 34 42	8 43.2	5 30.4	14 40.2	24 58.5	28 31.1	6 46.7	29 27.9	4 14.3	5 30.0	19 54.1
8 Sa	1 04 18	17 58 52	20 36 15	26 39 50	8 36.0	6 06.4	14 35.8	24 54.6	28 51.5	7 00.6	29 33.5	4R 14.4	5 30.7	19 54.8
9 Su	1 08 14	18 57 48	2♊45 42	8♊54 09	8 29.5	6 35.8	14 28.8	24 49.9	29 11.7	7 14.6	29 39.1	4 14.4	5 31.5	19 55.6
10 M	1 12 11	19 56 42	15 05 31	21 20 07	8 24.4	6 58.4	14 19.4	24 44.5	29 31.9	7 28.6	29 44.6	4 14.3	5 32.3	19 56.3
11 Tu	1 16 08	20 55 33	27 38 20	4♋00 32	8 21.0	7 14.5	14 07.5	24 38.4	29 51.9	7 42.6	29 50.0	4 14.2	5 33.1	19 57.1
12 W	1 20 04	21 54 23	10♋27 07	16 58 28	8D 19.5	7R 24.0	13 53.2	24 31.4	0♓11.9	7 56.7	29 55.4	4 14.1	5 33.9	19 57.9
13 Th	1 24 01	22 53 09	23 34 58	0♌16 58	8 19.7	7 27.0	13 36.4	24 23.7	0 31.8	8 10.8	0♓00.7	4 13.8	5 34.8	19 58.7
14 F	1 27 57	23 51 54	7♌04 47	13 58 37	8 20.7	7 23.8	13 17.2	24 15.3	0 51.5	8 24.9	0 06.0	4 13.6	5 35.8	19 59.6
15 Sa	1 31 54	24 50 36	20 58 39	28 04 53	8R 21.9	7 14.6	12 55.6	24 06.1	1 11.2	8 39.0	0 11.2	4 13.3	5 36.7	20 00.5
16 Su	1 35 50	25 49 16	5♍17 12	12♍35 19	8 22.1	6 59.7	12 31.8	23 56.1	1 30.8	8 53.1	0 16.3	4 12.9	5 37.7	20 01.3
17 M	1 39 47	26 47 54	19 58 47	27 26 56	8 20.7	6 39.6	12 05.9	23 45.5	1 50.2	9 07.3	0 21.4	4 12.5	5 38.7	20 02.2
18 Tu	1 43 43	27 46 30	4♎58 55	12♎33 44	8 17.1	6 14.6	11 37.9	23 34.0	2 09.6	9 21.4	0 26.3	4 12.0	5 39.7	20 03.2
19 W	1 47 40	28 45 04	20 10 12	27 47 03	8 11.4	5 45.3	11 08.0	23 21.9	2 28.8	9 35.6	0 31.3	4 11.5	5 40.8	20 04.1
20 Th	1 51 37	29 43 35	5♏22 57	12♏56 36	8 04.1	5 12.4	10 36.4	23 09.0	2 48.0	9 49.8	0 36.1	4 11.0	5 41.9	20 05.0
21 F	1 55 33	0♉42 05	20 26 44	27 52 13	7 56.1	4 36.4	10 03.3	22 55.5	3 07.0	10 04.0	0 40.9	4 10.3	5 43.0	20 06.0
22 Sa	1 59 30	1 40 34	5♐12 05	12♐25 32	7 48.3	3 58.1	9 28.7	22 41.3	3 25.9	10 18.3	0 45.6	4 09.7	5 44.2	20 07.0
23 Su	2 03 26	2 39 00	19 32 02	26 31 13	7 41.8	3 18.2	8 53.1	22 26.3	3 44.7	10 32.5	0 50.2	4 09.0	5 45.4	20 08.0
24 M	2 07 23	3 37 26	3♑22 56	10♑07 15	7 37.1	2 37.5	8 16.6	22 10.8	4 03.4	10 46.8	0 54.8	4 08.2	5 46.6	20 09.0
25 Tu	2 11 19	4 35 49	16 44 23	23 14 39	7D 34.6	1 56.7	7 39.3	21 54.6	4 22.0	11 01.1	0 59.3	4 07.4	5 47.9	20 10.0
26 W	2 15 16	5 34 11	29 38 32	5♒56 34	7 33.9	1 16.6	7 01.7	21 37.7	4 40.4	11 15.3	1 03.7	4 06.6	5 49.1	20 11.0
27 Th	2 19 12	6 32 31	12♒09 21	18 17 31	7 34.4	0 37.8	6 23.8	21 20.3	4 58.7	11 29.6	1 08.1	4 05.7	5 50.4	20 12.1
28 F	2 23 09	7 30 50	24 21 42	0♓22 35	7R 35.2	0 01.1	5 46.1	21 02.4	5 17.0	11 43.9	1 12.3	4 04.7	5 51.8	20 13.2
29 Sa	2 27 06	8 29 07	6♓20 47	12 16 56	7 35.2	29♈26.9	5 08.6	20 43.9	5 35.0	11 58.2	1 16.5	4 03.8	5 53.1	20 14.2
30 Su	2 31 02	9 27 23	18 11 37	24 05 23	7 33.7	28 55.8	4 31.7	20 24.9	5 53.0	12 12.5	1 20.6	4 02.7	5 54.5	20 15.3

Astro Data	Dy Hr Mn
♇ D	4 18:29
☽ 0N	7 22:42
☿ 0N	16 17:21
♆ D	17 2:34
☉ 0N	21 6:58
☽ 0S	21 13:29
♃△♅	27 2:11
♃∠♇	29 22:21
♃⚹♆	1 16:37
♂ R	2 20:46
☽ 0N	4 4:43
♀ R	6 3:53
♅ R	8 21:19
☿ R	13 11:35
☽ 0S	18 0:41

Planet Ingress		Dy Hr Mn
♀	♉	6 5:26
♃	♉	7 18:28
☿	♈	15 19:33
☉	♈	21 6:58
☿	♉	1 18:19
⚳	♓	11 21:40
♄	♓	13 8:39
☉	♉	20 18:44
☿	♈R	28 12:43

Last Aspect Dy Hr Mn		☽ Ingress	Dy Hr Mn
2 10:00	♃ □	♒	2 12:05
4 22:02	♃ ⚹	♓	4 23:12
6 17:48	♂ △	♈	7 11:46
9 17:28	♄ ⚹	♉	10 0:42
12 6:07	♄ □	♊	12 12:35
14 17:51	☿ □	♋	14 21:48
16 19:37	☉ △	♌	17 3:19
19 1:12	♄ ☍	♍	19 5:18
21 4:55	☉ ☍	♎	21 5:03
23 1:05	♄ △	♏	23 4:26
25 2:17	♄ □	♐	25 5:25
27 6:42	♄ ⚹	♑	27 9:40
29 8:37	☿ □	♒	29 17:47

Last Aspect Dy Hr Mn		☽ Ingress	Dy Hr Mn
1 3:28	☿ ⚹	♓	1 5:03
3 7:55	♂ △	♈	3 17:52
6 5:25	♄ ⚹	♉	6 6:44
8 17:45	♄ □	♊	8 18:35
11 4:06	♄ △	♋	11 4:28
13 1:34	♂ △	♌	13 11:30
15 6:09	☉ △	♍	15 15:13
17 6:09	♂ ⚹	♎	17 16:04
19 13:38	☉ ☍	♏	19 15:30
21 4:07	♂ ☌	♐	21 15:28
23 1:00	♇ ☍	♑	23 18:03
25 9:34	♂ ⚹	♒	26 0:41
27 17:52	♂ □	♓	28 11:15

☽ Phases & Eclipses Dy Hr Mn	
6 5:19	● 14♓59
6 5:12:21	● A 07'58"
14 8:59	☽ 23♊07
21 4:55	○ 29♍55
27 21:35	☾ 6♑33
4 23:23	● 14♈31
12 21:41	☽ 22♋18
19 13:38	○ 28♎49
26 11:13	☾ 5♒32

Astro Data

1 March 1905
Julian Day # 1886
SVP 6♓35'07"
GC 25♐30.9 ⚴ 1♒29.9
Eris 23♓48.8 ⚵ 2♈18.2
⚷ 3♒51.1 ⚶ 8♎19.6R
☽ Mean ☊ 9♍18.6

1 April 1905
Julian Day # 1917
SVP 6♓35'05"
GC 25♐31.0 ⚴ 11♒03.5
Eris 24♓13.3 ⚵ 19♈34.5
⚷ 5♒43.3 ⚶ 1♎11.7R
☽ Mean ☊ 7♍40.1

LONGITUDE — May 1905

Day	Sid.Time	☉	0 hr ☽	Noon ☽	True ☊	☿	♀	♂	⚳	♃	♄	♅	♆	♇
1 M	2 34 59	10♉25 37	29♓58 45	5♈52 10	7♍29.9	28♈28.2	3♉55.6	20♏05.4	6♓10.8	12♉26.8	1♓24.7	4♑01.6	5♋55.9	20♊16.4
2 Tu	2 38 55	11 23 49	11♈46 04	17 40 48	7R 23.6	28R 04.5	3R 20.5	19R 45.5	6 28.5	12 41.1	1 28.6	4R 00.5	5 57.3	20 17.6
3 W	2 42 52	12 22 00	23 36 42	29 34 02	7 14.6	27 45.1	2 46.6	19 25.2	6 46.0	12 55.4	1 32.5	3 59.3	5 58.8	20 18.7
4 Th	2 46 48	13 20 09	5♉33 02	11♉33 54	7 03.7	27 30.0	2 14.1	19 04.6	7 03.4	13 09.7	1 36.3	3 58.1	6 00.3	20 19.8
5 F	2 50 45	14 18 16	17 36 46	23 41 48	6 51.5	27 19.6	1 43.3	18 43.6	7 20.7	13 24.0	1 40.0	3 56.9	6 01.8	20 21.0
6 Sa	2 54 41	15 16 22	29 49 06	5♊58 46	6 39.2	27D 13.8	1 14.2	18 22.4	7 37.8	13 38.3	1 43.6	3 55.6	6 03.3	20 22.2
7 Su	2 58 38	16 14 26	12♊10 54	18 25 36	6 27.8	27 12.7	0 47.0	18 01.0	7 54.8	13 52.6	1 47.1	3 54.2	6 04.9	20 23.4
8 M	3 02 35	17 12 29	24 43 00	1♋03 14	6 18.3	27 16.3	0 21.8	17 39.4	8 11.6	14 06.9	1 50.6	3 52.8	6 06.5	20 24.6
9 Tu	3 06 31	18 10 29	7♋26 28	13 52 52	6 11.4	27 24.6	29♈58.7	17 17.7	8 28.3	14 21.2	1 54.0	3 51.4	6 08.1	20 25.8
10 W	3 10 28	19 08 28	20 22 41	26 56 07	6 07.1	27 37.5	29 37.9	16 55.9	8 44.9	14 35.4	1 57.2	3 50.0	6 09.7	20 27.0
11 Th	3 14 24	20 06 25	3♌33 26	10♌14 54	6D 05.3	27 54.9	29 19.3	16 34.1	9 01.2	14 49.7	2 00.4	3 48.4	6 11.3	20 28.2
12 F	3 18 21	21 04 20	17 00 45	23 51 13	6R 05.0	28 16.7	29 03.1	16 12.3	9 17.5	15 04.0	2 03.5	3 46.9	6 13.0	20 29.5
13 Sa	3 22 17	22 02 13	0♍46 30	7♍46 42	6 05.1	28 42.8	28 49.3	15 50.5	9 33.5	15 18.2	2 06.6	3 45.3	6 14.7	20 30.7
14 Su	3 26 14	23 00 04	14 51 52	22 01 53	6 04.4	29 13.2	28 37.9	15 28.8	9 49.4	15 32.4	2 09.5	3 43.7	6 16.4	20 32.0
15 M	3 30 10	23 57 54	29 16 33	6♎35 29	6 01.8	29 47.5	28 28.9	15 07.3	10 05.2	15 46.6	2 12.3	3 42.0	6 18.2	20 33.3
16 Tu	3 34 07	24 55 42	13♎58 09	21 23 50	5 56.5	0♉25.8	28 22.3	14 46.0	10 20.7	16 00.8	2 15.1	3 40.4	6 19.9	20 34.5
17 W	3 38 03	25 53 28	28 51 39	6♏20 37	5 48.7	1 07.9	28 18.1	14 25.0	10 36.1	16 15.0	2 17.7	3 38.6	6 21.7	20 35.8
18 Th	3 42 00	26 51 13	13♏49 37	21 17 30	5 38.7	1 53.6	28D 16.3	14 04.2	10 51.4	16 29.2	2 20.3	3 36.9	6 23.5	20 37.1
19 F	3 45 57	27 48 56	28 43 04	6♐05 13	5 27.6	2 43.0	28 16.9	13 43.7	11 06.4	16 43.3	2 22.8	3 35.1	6 25.3	20 38.4
20 Sa	3 49 53	28 46 39	13♐22 56	20 35 19	5 16.7	3 35.7	28 19.8	13 23.6	11 21.3	16 57.4	2 25.2	3 33.2	6 27.1	20 39.8
21 Su	3 53 50	29 44 20	27 41 39	4♑41 26	5 07.1	4 31.8	28 25.0	13 03.8	11 36.1	17 11.5	2 27.5	3 31.4	6 29.0	20 41.1
22 M	3 57 46	0♊41 59	11♑34 18	18 20 09	4 59.7	5 31.1	28 32.4	12 44.5	11 50.6	17 25.6	2 29.7	3 29.5	6 30.9	20 42.4
23 Tu	4 01 43	1 39 38	24 59 01	1♒31 05	4 54.9	6 33.6	28 42.0	12 25.7	12 04.9	17 39.7	2 31.8	3 27.6	6 32.8	20 43.7
24 W	4 05 39	2 37 16	7♒56 43	14 16 21	4 52.4	7 39.1	28 53.8	12 07.4	12 19.1	17 53.7	2 33.8	3 25.6	6 34.7	20 45.1
25 Th	4 09 36	3 34 53	20 30 31	26 39 50	4 51.6	8 47.6	29 07.5	11 49.5	12 33.1	18 07.7	2 35.7	3 23.6	6 36.6	20 46.4
26 F	4 13 33	4 32 28	2♓44 56	8♓46 31	4 51.6	9 59.0	29 23.3	11 32.3	12 46.9	18 21.7	2 37.6	3 21.6	6 38.5	20 47.8
27 Sa	4 17 29	5 30 03	14 45 14	20 41 48	4 51.1	11 13.2	29 41.0	11 15.7	13 00.5	18 35.7	2 39.3	3 19.6	6 40.5	20 49.2
28 Su	4 21 26	6 27 37	26 36 52	2♈31 04	4 49.2	12 30.2	0♉00.6	10 59.6	13 13.8	18 49.6	2 40.9	3 17.5	6 42.5	20 50.5
29 M	4 25 22	7 25 10	8♈25 03	14 19 21	4 45.1	13 50.0	0 22.0	10 44.3	13 27.0	19 03.5	2 42.5	3 15.4	6 44.4	20 51.9
30 Tu	4 29 19	8 22 42	20 14 31	26 11 02	4 38.3	15 12.5	0 45.1	10 29.6	13 40.0	19 17.4	2 43.9	3 13.3	6 46.4	20 53.3
31 W	4 33 15	9 20 14	2♉09 17	8♉09 40	4 28.8	16 37.7	1 09.9	10 15.6	13 52.8	19 31.2	2 45.3	3 11.2	6 48.5	20 54.6

LONGITUDE — June 1905

Day	Sid.Time	☉	0 hr ☽	Noon ☽	True ☊	☿	♀	♂	⚳	♃	♄	♅	♆	♇
1 Th	4 37 12	10♊17 44	14♉12 28	20♉17 56	4♍17.2	18♉05.5	1♉36.3	10♏02.4	14♓05.3	19♉45.0	2♓46.5	3♑09.0	6♋50.5	20♊56.0
2 F	4 41 08	11 15 14	26 26 14	2♊37 30	4R 04.2	19 36.0	2 04.3	9R 49.9	14 17.7	19 58.8	2 47.7	3R 06.8	6 52.5	20 57.4
3 Sa	4 45 05	12 12 42	8♊51 48	15 09 09	3 51.0	21 09.1	2 33.7	9 38.1	14 29.8	20 12.5	2 48.7	3 04.6	6 54.6	20 58.8
4 Su	4 49 02	13 10 10	21 29 34	27 53 00	3 38.8	22 44.7	3 04.6	9 27.2	14 41.7	20 26.2	2 49.7	3 02.4	6 56.7	21 00.2
5 M	4 52 58	14 07 37	4♋19 24	10♋48 43	3 28.5	24 23.0	3 36.9	9 17.0	14 53.4	20 39.9	2 50.5	3 00.1	6 58.7	21 01.6
6 Tu	4 56 55	15 05 02	17 20 53	23 55 52	3 20.9	26 03.8	4 10.5	9 07.7	15 04.8	20 53.5	2 51.3	2 57.8	7 00.8	21 03.0
7 W	5 00 51	16 02 27	0♌33 39	7♌14 14	3 16.2	27 47.2	4 45.4	8 59.2	15 16.0	21 07.1	2 51.9	2 55.6	7 02.9	21 04.4
8 Th	5 04 48	16 59 50	13 57 40	20 43 59	3D 14.0	29 33.1	5 21.5	8 51.5	15 27.0	21 20.6	2 52.5	2 53.2	7 05.1	21 05.8
9 F	5 08 44	17 57 13	27 33 15	4♍25 33	3 13.6	1♊21.5	5 58.8	8 44.6	15 37.7	21 34.1	2 52.9	2 50.9	7 07.2	21 07.2
10 Sa	5 12 41	18 54 34	11♍20 58	18 19 32	3R 13.7	3 12.4	6 37.2	8 38.6	15 48.2	21 47.6	2 53.3	2 48.6	7 09.3	21 08.6
11 Su	5 16 37	19 51 54	25 21 15	2♎26 04	3 13.3	5 05.8	7 16.7	8 33.4	15 58.5	22 01.0	2 53.5	2 46.2	7 11.5	21 10.1
12 M	5 20 34	20 49 14	9♎33 52	16 44 25	3 11.0	7 01.5	7 57.3	8 29.0	16 08.5	22 14.3	2 53.7	2 43.9	7 13.6	21 11.5
13 Tu	5 24 31	21 46 32	23 57 22	1♏12 16	3 06.5	8 59.5	8 38.8	8 25.5	16 18.2	22 27.6	2R 53.8	2 41.5	7 15.8	21 12.9
14 W	5 28 27	22 43 49	8♏28 35	15 45 36	2 59.4	10 59.7	9 21.4	8 22.7	16 27.7	22 40.9	2 53.7	2 39.1	7 17.9	21 14.3
15 Th	5 32 24	23 41 06	23 02 36	0♐18 44	2 50.3	13 01.9	10 04.9	8 20.9	16 36.9	22 54.1	2 53.6	2 36.7	7 20.1	21 15.7
16 F	5 36 20	24 38 22	7♐33 08	14 44 58	2 40.2	15 06.1	10 49.3	8D 19.8	16 45.9	23 07.2	2 53.4	2 34.3	7 22.3	21 17.1
17 Sa	5 40 17	25 35 37	21 53 24	28 57 41	2 30.1	17 12.1	11 34.6	8 19.6	16 54.6	23 20.4	2 53.0	2 31.9	7 24.5	21 18.5
18 Su	5 44 13	26 32 52	5♑57 11	12♑51 23	2 21.1	19 19.5	12 20.7	8 20.1	17 03.1	23 33.4	2 52.6	2 29.5	7 26.7	21 19.9
19 M	5 48 10	27 30 06	19 39 55	26 22 32	2 14.2	21 28.3	13 07.7	8 21.5	17 11.3	23 46.4	2 52.1	2 27.1	7 28.9	21 21.3
20 Tu	5 52 06	28 27 21	2♒59 10	9♒29 53	2 09.6	23 38.2	13 55.4	8 23.6	17 19.2	23 59.3	2 51.5	2 24.6	7 31.1	21 22.7
21 W	5 56 03	29 24 34	15 54 51	22 14 22	2D 07.4	25 48.8	14 43.9	8 26.5	17 26.8	24 12.2	2 50.8	2 22.2	7 33.3	21 24.1
22 Th	6 00 00	0♋21 48	28 28 51	4♓38 46	2 07.0	28 00.0	15 33.1	8 30.2	17 34.1	24 25.0	2 49.9	2 19.8	7 35.5	21 25.5
23 F	6 03 56	1 19 01	10♓44 39	16 47 08	2 07.6	0♋11.5	16 23.0	8 34.7	17 41.2	24 37.8	2 49.0	2 17.3	7 37.8	21 26.9
24 Sa	6 07 53	2 16 15	22 46 48	28 44 36	2R 08.2	2 22.9	17 13.6	8 39.9	17 47.9	24 50.5	2 48.0	2 14.9	7 40.0	21 28.3
25 Su	6 11 49	3 13 28	4♈40 21	10♈35 34	2 07.9	4 34.0	18 04.8	8 45.9	17 54.4	25 03.2	2 46.9	2 12.4	7 42.2	21 29.7
26 M	6 15 46	4 10 41	16 30 36	22 26 05	2 06.1	6 44.5	18 56.7	8 52.7	18 00.6	25 15.7	2 45.7	2 10.0	7 44.4	21 31.1
27 Tu	6 19 42	5 07 54	28 22 38	4♉20 47	2 02.1	8 54.3	19 49.1	9 00.1	18 06.5	25 28.2	2 44.4	2 07.6	7 46.7	21 32.5
28 W	6 23 39	6 05 08	10♉21 05	16 24 00	1 56.1	11 03.0	20 42.2	9 08.3	18 12.0	25 40.7	2 43.0	2 05.1	7 48.9	21 33.8
29 Th	6 27 35	7 02 21	22 29 56	28 39 14	1 48.2	13 10.6	21 35.8	9 17.2	18 17.3	25 53.1	2 41.5	2 02.7	7 51.1	21 35.2
30 F	6 31 32	7 59 35	4♊52 10	11♊08 56	1 39.1	15 16.7	22 29.9	9 26.9	18 22.2	26 05.4	2 40.0	2 00.3	7 53.4	21 36.6

Astro Data

	Dy Hr Mn
☽0N	1 11:18
☿ D	7 5:34
☽0S	15 10:42
♀ D	18 18:04
♃⚼♅	26 11:53
☽0N	28 19:11
♃⚺♇	7 6:44
♄⚹♅	8 18:35
☽0S	11 18:42
♃∠♆	12 10:29
♄ R	13 15:10
♂ D	17 7:24
☽0N	25 4:08

Planet Ingress

		Dy Hr Mn
♀	♈R	9 10:37
☿	♉	15 20:06
☉	♊	21 18:31
♀	♉	28 11:18
☿	♊	8 18:00
☉	♋	22 2:51
☿	♋	23 9:54

Last Aspect / ☽ Ingress (May)

Last Aspect Dy Hr Mn			☽ Ingress	Dy Hr Mn
30 4:43	♂	△	♈	1 0:03
3 8:26	☿	☌	♉	3 12:52
5 2:29	♂	☍	♊	6 0:21
8 4:48	☿	⚹	♋	8 10:01
10 16:47	♀	□	♌	10 17:34
12 20:52	♀	△	♍	12 22:40
14 13:44	☉	△	♎	15 1:12
16 23:09	♀	☍	♏	17 1:50
18 21:36	☉	☍	♐	19 2:05
21 1:09	♀	△	♑	21 3:56
23 6:44	♀	□	♒	23 9:12
25 16:56	♀	⚹	♓	25 18:34
27 12:15	♇	□	♈	28 6:53
30 1:17	♇	⚹	♉	30 19:41

Last Aspect / ☽ Ingress (June)

Last Aspect Dy Hr Mn			☽ Ingress	Dy Hr Mn
1 10:54	♃	☌	♊	2 6:55
3 23:03	♇	☌	♋	4 15:57
6 16:26	☿	⚹	♌	6 22:59
8 13:06	♃	□	♍	9 4:17
10 18:02	♃	△	♎	11 7:53
12 19:25	♇	△	♏	13 10:01
14 23:35	♃	☍	♐	15 11:29
17 5:51	☉	☍	♑	17 13:46
19 7:15	♃	△	♒	19 18:33
21 20:19	☿	△	♓	22 2:57
24 4:00	♃	⚹	♈	24 14:33
26 10:08	♇	⚹	♉	27 3:16
29 6:31	♃	☌	♊	29 14:37

☽ Phases & Eclipses

Dy Hr Mn		
4 15:50	●	13♉29
12 6:46	☽	20♌52
18 21:36	○	27♏14
26 2:50	☾	4♓10
3 5:56	●	11♊58
10 13:04	☽	18♍57
17 5:51	○	25♐21
24 19:46	☾	2♈35

Astro Data

1 May 1905
Julian Day # 1947
SVP 6♓35'02"
GC 25♐31.0 ⚴ 17♒57.7
Eris 24♓34.0 ⚵ 6♉55.4
⚷ 6♒38.2 ⚶ 26♍05.5R
☽ Mean ☊ 6♍04.8

1 June 1905
Julian Day # 1978
SVP 6♓34'58"
GC 25♐31.1 ⚴ 21♒19.5
Eris 24♓47.1 ⚵ 25♉10.6
⚷ 6♒29.4R ⚶ 28♍02.2
☽ Mean ☊ 4♍26.3

July 1905 — LONGITUDE

Day	Sid.Time	☉	0 hr ☽	Noon ☽	True ☊	☿	♀	♂	ʡ	♃	♄	♅	♆	♇
1 Sa	6 35 29	8♋56 48	17♊29 40	23♊54 25	1♍29.7	17♋21.4	23♉24.5	9♏37.2	18♓26.8	26♉17.6	2♓38.3	1♑57.9	7♋55.6	21♊37.9
2 Su	6 39 25	9 54 02	0♋23 10	6♋55 49	1R 21.0	19 24.4	24 19.7	9 48.2	18 31.1	26 29.8	2R 36.5	1R 55.4	7 57.8	21 39.3
3 M	6 43 22	10 51 15	13 32 14	20 12 14	1 13.8	21 25.7	25 15.3	9 59.9	18 35.1	26 41.9	2 34.7	1 53.0	8 00.1	21 40.6
4 Tu	6 47 18	11 48 29	26 55 34	3♌42 00	1 08.7	23 25.3	26 11.4	10 12.3	18 38.8	26 53.9	2 32.7	1 50.6	8 02.3	21 42.0
5 W	6 51 15	12 45 42	10♌31 16	17 23 07	1D 05.9	25 23.0	27 07.9	10 25.3	18 42.1	27 05.8	2 30.7	1 48.3	8 04.5	21 43.3
6 Th	6 55 11	13 42 55	24 17 16	1♍13 30	1 05.0	27 18.7	28 04.9	10 39.0	18 45.1	27 17.7	2 28.6	1 45.9	8 06.8	21 44.6
7 F	6 59 08	14 40 08	8♍11 37	15 11 24	1 05.6	29 12.6	29 02.2	10 53.3	18 47.8	27 29.4	2 26.4	1 43.5	8 09.0	21 46.0
8 Sa	7 03 04	15 37 21	22 12 40	29 15 16	1 06.8	1♌04.5	0♊00.0	11 08.2	18 50.1	27 41.1	2 24.1	1 41.2	8 11.2	21 47.3
9 Su	7 07 01	16 34 33	6♎19 02	13♎23 48	1R 07.6	2 54.5	0 58.2	11 23.7	18 52.1	27 52.7	2 21.7	1 38.8	8 13.4	21 48.6
10 M	7 10 58	17 31 46	20 29 23	27 35 33	1 07.2	4 42.5	1 56.7	11 39.9	18 53.7	28 04.3	2 19.2	1 36.5	8 15.6	21 49.9
11 Tu	7 14 54	18 28 58	4♏42 03	11♏48 36	1 05.1	6 28.6	2 55.6	11 56.6	18 55.0	28 15.7	2 16.7	1 34.2	8 17.8	21 51.1
12 W	7 18 51	19 26 10	18 54 51	26 00 24	1 01.3	8 12.7	3 54.9	12 13.9	18 56.0	28 27.1	2 14.1	1 31.9	8 20.0	21 52.4
13 Th	7 22 47	20 23 23	3♐04 51	10♐07 43	0 56.1	9 54.9	4 54.6	12 31.8	18 56.6	28 38.3	2 11.4	1 29.6	8 22.2	21 53.7
14 F	7 26 44	21 20 35	17 08 32	24 06 48	0 50.0	11 35.0	5 54.5	12 50.2	18R 56.9	28 49.5	2 08.6	1 27.4	8 24.4	21 54.9
15 Sa	7 30 40	22 17 48	1♑02 03	7♑53 52	0 43.9	13 13.3	6 54.8	13 09.1	18 56.8	29 00.6	2 05.7	1 25.2	8 26.6	21 56.2
16 Su	7 34 37	23 15 01	14 41 50	21 25 37	0 38.6	14 49.6	7 55.5	13 28.6	18 56.3	29 11.6	2 02.8	1 23.0	8 28.8	21 57.4
17 M	7 38 33	24 12 15	28 04 59	4♒39 46	0 34.6	16 23.9	8 56.4	13 48.6	18 55.6	29 22.5	1 59.8	1 20.8	8 31.0	21 58.7
18 Tu	7 42 30	25 09 29	11♒09 51	17 35 17	0 32.2	17 56.2	9 57.7	14 09.1	18 54.4	29 33.3	1 56.7	1 18.6	8 33.1	21 59.9
19 W	7 46 27	26 06 43	23 56 07	0♓12 34	0D 31.4	19 26.6	10 59.2	14 30.0	18 52.9	29 44.0	1 53.5	1 16.5	8 35.3	22 01.1
20 Th	7 50 23	27 03 58	6♓24 53	12 33 23	0 32.0	20 55.0	12 01.1	14 51.5	18 51.1	29 54.6	1 50.3	1 14.3	8 37.4	22 02.3
21 F	7 54 20	28 01 14	18 38 29	24 40 38	0 33.4	22 21.4	13 03.2	15 13.5	18 48.9	0♊05.1	1 47.0	1 12.2	8 39.6	22 03.5
22 Sa	7 58 16	28 58 30	0♈40 20	6♈38 07	0 35.2	23 45.7	14 05.6	15 35.9	18 46.3	0 15.5	1 43.6	1 10.2	8 41.7	22 04.6
23 Su	8 02 13	29 55 48	12 34 35	18 30 17	0 36.5	25 08.0	15 08.3	15 58.7	18 43.3	0 25.8	1 40.2	1 08.1	8 43.8	22 05.8
24 M	8 06 09	0♌53 06	24 25 51	0♉21 54	0R 37.1	26 28.1	16 11.2	16 22.1	18 40.1	0 36.0	1 36.7	1 06.1	8 45.9	22 06.9
25 Tu	8 10 06	1 50 25	6♉19 02	12 17 51	0 36.6	27 46.2	17 14.4	16 45.8	18 36.4	0 46.1	1 33.1	1 04.1	8 48.0	22 08.1
26 W	8 14 02	2 47 45	18 18 56	24 22 51	0 34.9	29 02.0	18 17.9	17 10.0	18 32.4	0 56.0	1 29.5	1 02.1	8 50.1	22 09.2
27 Th	8 17 59	3 45 06	0♊30 06	6♊41 08	0 32.0	0♍15.6	19 21.5	17 34.7	18 28.0	1 05.9	1 25.8	1 00.2	8 52.1	22 10.3
28 F	8 21 56	4 42 28	12 56 23	19 16 11	0 28.5	1 26.9	20 25.5	17 59.7	18 23.3	1 15.7	1 22.0	0 58.3	8 54.2	22 11.4
29 Sa	8 25 52	5 39 52	25 40 48	2♋10 24	0 24.6	2 35.8	21 29.6	18 25.2	18 18.2	1 25.3	1 18.2	0 56.4	8 56.3	22 12.5
30 Su	8 29 49	6 37 16	8♋45 04	15 24 47	0 21.0	3 42.2	22 34.0	18 51.1	18 12.8	1 34.8	1 14.4	0 54.6	8 58.3	22 13.6
31 M	8 33 45	7 34 41	22 09 28	28 58 54	0 18.1	4 46.1	23 38.5	19 17.4	18 07.0	1 44.2	1 10.4	0 52.8	9 00.3	22 14.6

August 1905 — LONGITUDE

Day	Sid.Time	☉	0 hr ☽	Noon ☽	True ☊	☿	♀	♂	ʡ	♃	♄	♅	♆	♇
1 Tu	8 37 42	8♌32 07	5♌52 46	12♌50 43	0♍16.3	5♍47.3	24♊43.3	19♏44.1	18♓00.9	1♊53.5	1♓06.5	0♑51.0	9♋02.3	22♊15.6
2 W	8 41 38	9 29 33	19 52 18	26 57 01	0D 15.5	6 45.8	25 48.3	20 11.2	17R 54.4	2 02.7	1R 02.5	0R 49.3	9 04.3	22 16.7
3 Th	8 45 35	10 27 01	4♍04 19	11♍13 38	0 15.7	7 41.3	26 53.5	20 38.6	17 47.6	2 11.7	0 58.4	0 47.6	9 06.3	22 17.7
4 F	8 49 31	11 24 29	18 24 24	25 36 04	0 16.7	8 33.8	27 58.9	21 06.5	17 40.4	2 20.6	0 54.3	0 45.9	9 08.2	22 18.7
5 Sa	8 53 28	12 21 58	2♎48 06	10♎00 00	0 17.9	9 23.1	29 04.4	21 34.6	17 32.9	2 29.4	0 50.2	0 44.3	9 10.2	22 19.6
6 Su	8 57 25	13 19 28	17 11 17	24 21 33	0 19.0	10 09.1	0♋10.2	22 03.2	17 25.1	2 38.1	0 46.0	0 42.7	9 12.1	22 20.6
7 M	9 01 21	14 16 59	1♏30 25	8♏37 33	0R 19.6	10 51.6	1 16.1	22 32.1	17 17.0	2 46.6	0 41.7	0 41.2	9 14.0	22 21.5
8 Tu	9 05 18	15 14 30	15 42 41	22 45 33	0 19.5	11 30.4	2 22.2	23 01.3	17 08.5	2 55.0	0 37.5	0 39.7	9 15.9	22 22.5
9 W	9 09 14	16 12 02	29 45 56	6♐43 39	0 18.8	12 05.4	3 28.5	23 30.9	16 59.8	3 03.3	0 33.2	0 38.2	9 17.8	22 23.4
10 Th	9 13 11	17 09 35	13♐38 31	20 30 23	0 17.6	12 36.2	4 34.9	24 00.8	16 50.7	3 11.4	0 28.9	0 36.8	9 19.6	22 24.3
11 F	9 17 07	18 07 09	27 19 08	4♑04 39	0 16.1	13 02.7	5 41.6	24 31.1	16 41.4	3 19.4	0 24.5	0 35.4	9 21.5	22 25.2
12 Sa	9 21 04	19 04 44	10♑46 49	17 25 33	0 14.5	13 24.8	6 48.4	25 01.6	16 31.7	3 27.3	0 20.1	0 34.0	9 23.3	22 26.0
13 Su	9 25 00	20 02 20	24 00 46	0♒32 27	0 13.3	13 42.1	7 55.3	25 32.4	16 21.8	3 35.0	0 15.7	0 32.7	9 25.1	22 26.9
14 M	9 28 57	20 59 57	7♒00 33	13 25 04	0 12.5	13 54.5	9 02.5	26 03.6	16 11.6	3 42.6	0 11.3	0 31.4	9 26.9	22 27.7
15 Tu	9 32 54	21 57 35	19 46 04	26 03 35	0D 12.1	14R 01.7	10 09.7	26 35.0	16 01.2	3 50.0	0 06.8	0 30.2	9 28.6	22 28.5
16 W	9 36 50	22 55 15	2♓17 45	8♓28 42	0 12.2	14 03.6	11 17.2	27 06.7	15 50.5	3 57.3	0 02.4	0 29.0	9 30.4	22 29.3
17 Th	9 40 47	23 52 56	14 36 37	20 41 44	0 12.5	14 00.0	12 24.8	27 38.8	15 39.5	4 04.4	29♒57.9	0 27.9	9 32.1	22 30.1
18 F	9 44 43	24 50 38	26 44 20	2♈44 43	0 13.1	13 50.8	13 32.6	28 11.0	15 28.3	4 11.4	29 53.4	0 26.8	9 33.8	22 30.8
19 Sa	9 48 40	25 48 22	8♈43 16	14 40 20	0 13.6	13 35.8	14 40.5	28 43.6	15 16.9	4 18.3	29 48.9	0 25.7	9 35.5	22 31.6
20 Su	9 52 36	26 46 07	20 36 24	26 31 54	0 14.0	13 15.1	15 48.5	29 16.4	15 05.3	4 25.0	29 44.3	0 24.7	9 37.1	22 32.3
21 M	9 56 33	27 43 54	2♉27 21	8♉23 15	0 14.3	12 48.7	16 56.7	29 49.5	14 53.4	4 31.5	29 39.8	0 23.8	9 38.7	22 33.0
22 Tu	10 00 29	28 41 43	14 20 11	20 18 40	0R 14.4	12 16.7	18 05.1	0♐22.9	14 41.4	4 37.9	29 35.3	0 22.8	9 40.4	22 33.7
23 W	10 04 26	29 39 34	26 19 27	2♊22 38	0D 14.4	11 39.5	19 13.6	0 56.5	14 29.2	4 44.1	29 30.7	0 22.0	9 41.9	22 34.3
24 Th	10 08 23	0♍37 26	8♊29 15	14 39 41	0 14.4	10 57.4	20 22.2	1 30.4	14 16.8	4 50.2	29 26.2	0 21.2	9 43.5	22 35.0
25 F	10 12 19	1 35 20	20 54 27	27 14 03	0 14.5	10 10.9	21 31.0	2 04.5	14 04.2	4 56.1	29 21.7	0 20.4	9 45.0	22 35.6
26 Sa	10 16 16	2 33 16	3♋38 54	10♋09 21	0 14.7	9 20.7	22 39.9	2 38.9	13 51.5	5 01.8	29 17.2	0 19.7	9 46.6	22 36.2
27 Su	10 20 12	3 31 13	16 45 41	23 28 03	0 15.0	8 27.6	23 48.9	3 13.5	13 38.7	5 07.4	29 12.6	0 19.0	9 48.0	22 36.8
28 M	10 24 09	4 29 13	0♌16 33	7♌11 05	0 15.3	7 32.5	24 58.1	3 48.4	13 25.7	5 12.8	29 08.1	0 18.3	9 49.5	22 37.3
29 Tu	10 28 05	5 27 14	14 11 29	21 17 23	0R 15.6	6 36.5	26 07.4	4 23.5	13 12.6	5 18.0	29 03.6	0 17.8	9 51.0	22 37.9
30 W	10 32 02	6 25 17	28 28 20	5♍43 43	0 15.6	5 40.8	27 16.8	4 58.8	12 59.5	5 23.1	28 59.1	0 17.2	9 52.4	22 38.4
31 Th	10 35 58	7 23 21	13♍02 49	20 24 47	0 15.3	4 46.4	28 26.3	5 34.4	12 46.2	5 28.0	28 54.7	0 16.7	9 53.8	22 38.9

Astro Data Dy Hr Mn	Planet Ingress Dy Hr Mn	Last Aspect Dy Hr Mn	☽ Ingress Dy Hr Mn	Last Aspect Dy Hr Mn	☽ Ingress Dy Hr Mn	☽ Phases & Eclipses Dy Hr Mn
☽0S 9 1:11	☿ ♌ 7 22:07	1 7:45 ♇ ☌	♋ 1 23:17	2 9:54 ♀ ⚹	♍ 2 17:09	2 17:50 ● 10♋08
ʡR 14 18:28	♀ ♊ 8 12:00	3 23:46 ♃ ⚹	♌ 4 5:27	4 16:18 ♀ □	♎ 4 19:20	9 17:46 ☽ 16♎48
☽0N 22 13:12	♃ ♊ 21 0:23	6 6:10 ☿ □	♍ 6 9:53	6 8:37 ♇ △	♏ 6 21:28	16 15:32 ○ 23♑23
♃⊼♅ 27 0:24	☉ ♌ 23 13:46	8 9:18 ♃ △	♎ 8 13:16	8 12:28 ♂ ☌	♐ 9 0:24	24 13:09 ☾ 0♉56
♃□♄ 28 23:21	☿ ♍ 27 6:51	10 2:15 ♇ △	♏ 10 16:04	10 15:20 ♇ ☍	♑ 11 4:45	
		12 16:12 ♃ ☍	♐ 12 18:46	13 2:25 ♂ ⚹	♒ 13 11:00	1 4:02 ● 8♌13
☽0S 5 7:36	♀ ♋ 6 8:18	14 8:12 ♇ ☍	♑ 14 22:12	15 13:03 ♂ □	♓ 15 19:34	7 22:16 ☽ 14♏42
♄⚹♅ 7 17:01	♄ ♒R 17 0:42	17 2:13 ♃ △	♒ 17 3:29	18 2:27 ♂ △	♈ 18 6:30	15 3:31 ○ 21♒37
☿R 16 8:22	♂ ♐ 21 19:33	19 11:04 ♃ □	♓ 19 11:36	20 18:27 ♄ ⚹	♉ 20 19:02	15 3:41 ☍ P 0.287
☽0N 18 21:22	☉ ♍ 23 20:29	21 19:16 ☉ △	♈ 21 22:39	23 6:22 ♄ □	♊ 23 7:18	23 6:10 ☾ 29♉25
		24 3:08 ☿ △	♉ 24 11:16	25 15:58 ♄ △	♋ 25 17:12	30 13:13 ● 6♍28
		26 22:09 ☿ □	♊ 26 23:01	27 12:40 ☿ ☌	♌ 27 23:31	30 13:07:20 ● T 03'46"
		28 17:30 ♇ ☌	♋ 29 8:00	30 0:55 ♄ ☍	♍ 30 2:32	
		30 18:20 ♂ △	♌ 31 13:47			

Astro Data

1 July 1905
Julian Day # 2008
SVP 6♓34'53"
GC 25♐31.2 ⚳ 19♒30.1R
Eris 24♓49.1R ⚵ 12♊49.2
⚷ 5♒23.7R ⚶ 5♎46.3
☽ Mean ☊ 2♍51.0

1 August 1905
Julian Day # 2039
SVP 6♓34'48"
GC 25♐31.2 ⚳ 12♒40.2R
Eris 24♓39.8R ⚵ 0♋37.2
⚷ 3♒43.2R ⚶ 17♎30.0
☽ Mean ☊ 1♍12.5

LONGITUDE — September 1905

Day	Sid.Time	☉	0 hr ☽	Noon ☽	True ☊	☿	♀	♂	⚳	♃	♄	♅	♆	♇
1 F	10 39 55	8♍21 27	27♍48 45	5♎13 45	0♍14.7	3♍54.7	29♋36.0	6♐10.2	12♓32.9	5♊32.7	28♒50.2	0♑16.3	9♋55.1	22♊39.4
2 Sa	10 43 51	9 19 34	12♎38 50	20 03 07	0R 13.7	3R 06.9	0♌45.8	6 46.2	12R 19.6	5 37.3	28R 45.8	0R 15.9	9 56.4	22 39.8
3 Su	10 47 48	10 17 43	27 25 41	4♏45 47	0 12.6	2 23.9	1 55.6	7 22.4	12 06.2	5 41.6	28 41.4	0 15.6	9 57.8	22 40.3
4 M	10 51 45	11 15 53	12♏02 43	19 15 56	0 11.6	1 47.0	3 05.6	7 58.8	11 52.8	5 45.8	28 37.0	0 15.3	9 59.0	22 40.7
5 Tu	10 55 41	12 14 05	26 24 58	3♐29 30	0D 11.0	1 16.9	4 15.7	8 35.5	11 39.4	5 49.8	28 32.6	0 15.1	10 00.3	22 41.1
6 W	10 59 38	13 12 19	10♐29 21	17 24 24	0 10.9	0 54.4	5 25.9	9 12.4	11 26.0	5 53.6	28 28.3	0 14.9	10 01.5	22 41.5
7 Th	11 03 34	14 10 33	24 14 39	1♑00 10	0 11.4	0 40.2	6 36.3	9 49.4	11 12.6	5 57.3	28 24.0	0 14.7	10 02.7	22 41.8
8 F	11 07 31	15 08 50	7♑41 05	14 17 34	0 12.4	0D 34.6	7 46.7	10 26.7	10 59.3	6 00.8	28 19.8	0 14.7	10 03.9	22 42.2
9 Sa	11 11 27	16 07 08	20 49 51	27 18 08	0 13.7	0 38.0	8 57.2	11 04.1	10 46.0	6 04.0	28 15.6	0D 14.6	10 05.0	22 42.5
10 Su	11 15 24	17 05 27	3♒42 40	10♒03 43	0 14.9	0 50.4	10 07.9	11 41.7	10 32.8	6 07.1	28 11.4	0 14.6	10 06.1	22 42.8
11 M	11 19 20	18 03 48	16 21 28	22 36 12	0R 15.7	1 12.0	11 18.6	12 19.6	10 19.6	6 10.0	28 07.3	0 14.7	10 07.2	22 43.0
12 Tu	11 23 17	19 02 11	28 48 06	4♓57 24	0 15.8	1 42.4	12 29.4	12 57.6	10 06.6	6 12.7	28 03.2	0 14.8	10 08.2	22 43.3
13 W	11 27 14	20 00 35	11♓04 19	17 09 01	0 15.0	2 21.6	13 40.4	13 35.7	9 53.6	6 15.3	27 59.1	0 15.0	10 09.3	22 43.5
14 Th	11 31 10	20 59 01	23 11 44	29 12 40	0 13.0	3 09.1	14 51.5	14 14.1	9 40.8	6 17.6	27 55.1	0 15.2	10 10.3	22 43.7
15 F	11 35 07	21 57 30	5♈12 01	11♈10 01	0 10.2	4 04.5	16 02.6	14 52.6	9 28.1	6 19.7	27 51.2	0 15.5	10 11.2	22 43.9
16 Sa	11 39 03	22 56 00	17 06 55	23 02 59	0 06.5	5 07.3	17 13.9	15 31.3	9 15.6	6 21.7	27 47.3	0 15.8	10 12.1	22 44.0
17 Su	11 43 00	23 54 32	28 58 30	4♉53 47	0 02.5	6 17.0	18 25.2	16 10.1	9 03.2	6 23.4	27 43.5	0 16.2	10 13.0	22 44.2
18 M	11 46 56	24 53 06	10♉49 12	16 45 07	29♌58.7	7 32.9	19 36.7	16 49.1	8 51.0	6 25.0	27 39.7	0 16.6	10 13.9	22 44.3
19 Tu	11 50 53	25 51 43	22 41 58	28 40 11	29 55.4	8 54.4	20 48.2	17 28.3	8 39.0	6 26.4	27 36.0	0 17.1	10 14.7	22 44.4
20 W	11 54 49	26 50 22	4♊40 16	10♊42 42	29 53.0	10 21.0	21 59.9	18 07.6	8 27.2	6 27.5	27 32.3	0 17.6	10 15.6	22 44.4
21 Th	11 58 46	27 49 03	16 48 01	22 56 47	29D 51.9	11 51.9	23 11.6	18 47.1	8 15.5	6 28.5	27 28.7	0 18.2	10 16.3	22 44.5
22 F	12 02 43	28 47 46	29 09 31	5♋26 47	29 51.9	13 26.6	24 23.5	19 26.8	8 04.1	6 29.3	27 25.2	0 18.8	10 17.1	22R 44.5
23 Sa	12 06 39	29 46 32	11♋49 07	18 17 00	29 53.0	15 04.6	25 35.4	20 06.6	7 53.0	6 29.8	27 21.7	0 19.5	10 17.8	22 44.5
24 Su	12 10 36	0♎45 19	24 50 53	1♌31 10	29 54.5	16 45.2	26 47.4	20 46.5	7 42.0	6 30.2	27 18.3	0 20.2	10 18.5	22 44.5
25 M	12 14 32	1 44 09	8♌18 08	15 11 57	29 56.0	18 28.1	27 59.5	21 26.6	7 31.4	6R 30.4	27 14.9	0 21.0	10 19.1	22 44.5
26 Tu	12 18 29	2 43 02	22 12 40	29 20 08	29R 56.6	20 12.6	29 11.7	22 06.9	7 20.9	6 30.3	27 11.7	0 21.9	10 19.7	22 44.4
27 W	12 22 25	3 41 56	6♍34 03	13♍53 56	29 55.9	21 58.5	0♍24.0	22 47.3	7 10.8	6 30.1	27 08.5	0 22.7	10 20.3	22 44.3
28 Th	12 26 22	4 40 52	21 19 04	28 48 36	29 53.6	23 45.4	1 36.3	23 27.9	7 00.9	6 29.6	27 05.3	0 23.7	10 20.8	22 44.2
29 F	12 30 18	5 39 51	6♎21 29	13♎56 31	29 49.6	25 33.0	2 48.8	24 08.5	6 51.3	6 29.0	27 02.3	0 24.7	10 21.4	22 44.1
30 Sa	12 34 15	6 38 51	21 32 28	29 08 00	29 44.5	27 21.0	4 01.3	24 49.4	6 42.0	6 28.1	26 59.3	0 25.7	10 21.8	22 43.9

LONGITUDE — October 1905

Day	Sid.Time	☉	0 hr ☽	Noon ☽	True ☊	☿	♀	♂	⚳	♃	♄	♅	♆	♇
1 Su	12 38 11	7♎37 54	6♏41 53	14♏12 53	29♌38.9	29♍09.1	5♍13.9	25♐30.4	6♓33.1	6♊27.1	26♒56.4	0♑26.8	10♋22.3	22♊43.8
2 M	12 42 08	8 36 58	21 39 57	29 02 10	29R 33.6	0♎57.3	6 26.5	26 11.5	6R 24.4	6R 25.8	26R 53.6	0 27.9	10 22.7	22R 43.6
3 Tu	12 46 05	9 36 04	6♐18 48	13♐29 19	29 29.5	2 45.3	7 39.3	26 52.7	6 16.1	6 24.4	26 50.9	0 29.1	10 23.1	22 43.4
4 W	12 50 01	10 35 12	20 33 25	27 30 57	29 27.0	4 33.0	8 52.1	27 34.1	6 08.1	6 22.7	26 48.3	0 30.4	10 23.4	22 43.1
5 Th	12 53 58	11 34 22	4♑21 55	11♑06 29	29D 26.2	6 20.4	10 04.9	28 15.6	6 00.4	6 20.8	26 45.7	0 31.6	10 23.7	22 42.9
6 F	12 57 54	12 33 33	17 44 56	24 17 37	29 26.8	8 07.2	11 17.9	28 57.2	5 53.1	6 18.8	26 43.3	0 33.0	10 24.0	22 42.6
7 Sa	13 01 51	13 32 47	0♒44 57	7♒07 24	29 28.1	9 53.5	12 30.9	29 38.9	5 46.1	6 16.5	26 40.9	0 34.4	10 24.3	22 42.3
8 Su	13 05 47	14 32 01	13 25 26	19 39 32	29R 29.4	11 39.2	13 44.0	0♑20.8	5 39.4	6 14.1	26 38.6	0 35.8	10 24.5	22 42.0
9 M	13 09 44	15 31 18	25 50 11	1♓57 50	29 29.8	13 24.2	14 57.1	1 02.7	5 33.2	6 11.4	26 36.4	0 37.3	10 24.7	22 41.6
10 Tu	13 13 40	16 30 37	8♓02 54	14 05 46	29 28.6	15 08.6	16 10.3	1 44.8	5 27.2	6 08.6	26 34.3	0 38.8	10 24.8	22 41.3
11 W	13 17 37	17 29 57	20 06 48	26 06 20	29 25.2	16 52.3	17 23.6	2 27.0	5 21.6	6 05.5	26 32.2	0 40.4	10 24.9	22 40.9
12 Th	13 21 34	18 29 19	2♈04 39	8♈02 01	29 19.4	18 35.4	18 37.0	3 09.3	5 16.4	6 02.3	26 30.3	0 42.0	10 25.0	22 40.5
13 F	13 25 30	19 28 44	13 58 39	19 54 47	29 11.6	20 17.7	19 50.4	3 51.6	5 11.6	5 58.9	26 28.5	0 43.7	10R 25.0	22 40.0
14 Sa	13 29 27	20 28 10	25 50 37	1♉46 19	29 02.1	21 59.3	21 03.8	4 34.1	5 07.1	5 55.3	26 26.7	0 45.4	10 25.0	22 39.6
15 Su	13 33 23	21 27 39	7♉42 07	13 38 11	28 51.7	23 40.3	22 17.4	5 16.7	5 03.0	5 51.5	26 25.1	0 47.1	10 25.0	22 39.1
16 M	13 37 20	22 27 09	19 34 45	25 32 02	28 41.4	25 20.5	23 31.0	5 59.4	4 59.2	5 47.5	26 23.5	0 48.9	10 24.9	22 38.6
17 Tu	13 41 16	23 26 42	1♊30 20	7♊29 55	28 32.1	27 00.1	24 44.6	6 42.2	4 55.8	5 43.3	26 22.0	0 50.8	10 24.9	22 38.1
18 W	13 45 13	24 26 17	13 31 07	19 34 19	28 24.5	28 39.0	25 58.4	7 25.1	4 52.8	5 39.0	26 20.7	0 52.7	10 24.7	22 37.6
19 Th	13 49 09	25 25 55	25 39 54	1♋48 19	28 19.3	0♏17.4	27 12.2	8 08.1	4 50.2	5 34.5	26 19.4	0 54.6	10 24.6	22 37.1
20 F	13 53 06	26 25 34	8♋00 04	14 15 37	28 16.4	1 55.0	28 26.0	8 51.2	4 47.9	5 29.8	26 18.3	0 56.6	10 24.4	22 36.5
21 Sa	13 57 03	27 25 16	20 35 30	27 00 14	28D 15.6	3 32.1	29 39.9	9 34.4	4 46.0	5 24.9	26 17.2	0 58.6	10 24.2	22 35.9
22 Su	14 00 59	28 25 00	3♌30 21	10♌06 20	28 16.0	5 08.6	0♎53.8	10 17.6	4 44.5	5 19.8	26 16.2	1 00.7	10 23.9	22 35.3
23 M	14 04 56	29 24 47	16 48 37	23 37 34	28R 16.7	6 44.5	2 07.9	11 01.0	4 43.3	5 14.6	26 15.4	1 02.8	10 23.6	22 34.7
24 Tu	14 08 52	0♏24 36	0♍33 27	7♍36 23	28 16.4	8 19.9	3 21.9	11 44.4	4 42.5	5 09.2	26 14.6	1 05.0	10 23.3	22 34.0
25 W	14 12 49	1 24 26	14 46 19	22 03 02	28 14.2	9 54.7	4 36.0	12 28.0	4D 42.1	5 03.7	26 13.9	1 07.2	10 22.9	22 33.4
26 Th	14 16 45	2 24 19	29 26 04	6♎54 45	28 09.5	11 29.0	5 50.2	13 11.6	4 42.1	4 57.9	26 13.4	1 09.4	10 22.5	22 32.7
27 F	14 20 42	3 24 14	14♎28 11	22 05 14	28 02.2	13 02.8	7 04.4	13 55.3	4 42.4	4 52.1	26 12.9	1 11.7	10 22.1	22 32.0
28 Sa	14 24 38	4 24 12	29 44 36	7♏24 54	27 52.9	14 36.1	8 18.7	14 39.1	4 43.1	4 46.1	26 12.6	1 14.0	10 21.6	22 31.3
29 Su	14 28 35	5 24 11	15♏04 38	22 42 21	27 42.5	16 08.9	9 33.0	15 23.0	4 44.2	4 39.9	26 12.3	1 16.4	10 21.1	22 30.6
30 M	14 32 32	6 24 12	0♐16 39	7♐46 19	27 32.5	17 41.2	10 47.3	16 07.0	4 45.6	4 33.6	26D 12.2	1 18.8	10 20.6	22 29.8
31 Tu	14 36 28	7 24 14	15 10 16	22 27 43	27 24.0	19 13.1	12 01.7	16 51.0	4 47.4	4 27.1	26 12.1	1 21.3	10 20.1	22 29.0

Astro Data

	Dy Hr Mn
☽0S	1 15:30
☿ D	8 15:02
♅ D	9 15:17
☽0N	15 4:17
♇ R	23 7:12
☉0S	23 17:30
♃ R	25 19:20
☽0S	29 1:31
☿0S	4 3:04
☽0N	12 10:31
♆ R	14 5:22
♀0S	24 17:12
⚳ D	26 2:36
☽0S	26 12:49
♄ D	31 9:03

Planet Ingress

		Dy Hr Mn
♀	♌	1 20:16
☊	♌R	18 3:28
☉	♎	23 17:30
♀	♍	27 4:02
☿	♎	1 23:17
♂	♑	8 0:06
☿	♏	19 7:45
♀	♎	21 18:32
☉	♏	24 2:08

Last Aspect / ☽ Ingress (September)

Last Aspect Dy Hr Mn			☽ Ingress	Dy Hr Mn
1 2:07	♀	✶	♎	1 3:32
3 2:06	♄	△	♏	3 4:12
5 3:38	♄	□	♐	5 6:04
7 7:23	♄	✶	♑	7 10:13
8 13:41	☉	△	♒	9 17:02
11 22:37	♄	☌	♓	12 2:20
13 23:04	♇	□	♈	14 13:35
16 21:33	♄	✶	♉	17 2:05
19 9:52	♄	□	♊	19 14:40
21 22:13	☉	□	♋	22 1:37
23 5:12	☿	✶	♌	24 9:17
26 11:45	♀	☌	♍	26 13:07
28 3:03	♂	□	♎	28 13:54
30 8:37	♄	△	♏	30 13:22

Last Aspect / ☽ Ingress (October)

Last Aspect Dy Hr Mn			☽ Ingress	Dy Hr Mn
2 8:31	♄	□	♐	2 13:35
4 12:06	♂	☌	♑	4 16:20
5 12:54	☉	□	♒	6 22:36
9 1:32	♄	☌	♓	9 8:09
11 5:08	♇	□	♈	11 19:49
14 1:15	♄	✶	♉	14 8:25
16 13:43	♄	□	♊	16 20:59
19 2:01	♀	□	♋	19 8:29
21 17:27	♀	✶	♌	21 17:33
23 22:48	☉	✶	♍	23 23:03
25 12:49	♇	□	♎	26 0:55
27 18:28	♄	△	♏	28 0:24
29 17:32	♄	□	♐	29 23:33

☽ Phases & Eclipses

Dy Hr Mn		
6 4:09	☽	12♐53
13 18:10	○	20♓16
21 22:13	☾	28♊14
28 21:59	●	5♎05
5 12:54	☽	11♑37
13 11:02	○	19♈26
21 12:50	☾	27♋27
28 6:58	●	4♏12

Astro Data

1 September 1905
Julian Day # 2070
SVP 6♓34'45"
GC 25♐31.3 ⚴ 5♒26.7R
Eris 24♓21.7R ⚵ 17♋27.7
⚷ 2♒10.1R ⚶ 1♏29.4
☽ Mean ☊ 29♌34.0

1 October 1905
Julian Day # 2100
SVP 6♓34'43"
GC 25♐31.4 ⚴ 2♒50.6
Eris 24♓00.8R ⚵ 2♌10.1
⚷ 1♒22.7R ⚶ 16♏20.9
☽ Mean ☊ 27♌58.6

November 1905 LONGITUDE

Day	Sid.Time	☉	0 hr ☽	Noon ☽	True ☊	☿	♀	♂	⚳	♃	♄	♅	♆	♇
1 W	14 40 25	8♏24 19	29♐38 03	6♑40 58	27♌17.8	20♏44.6	13♎16.1	17♑35.1	4♓49.6	4♊20.6	26♒12.2	1♑23.7	10♋19.5	22♊28.3
2 Th	14 44 21	9 24 25	13♑36 19	20 24 10	27R14.2	22 15.5	14 30.6	18 19.3	4 52.1	4R13.8	26 12.4	1 26.3	10R18.8	22R27.5
3 F	14 48 18	10 24 32	27 04 48	3♒38 34	27D12.7	23 46.1	15 45.1	19 03.6	4 55.0	4 07.0	26 12.6	1 28.8	10 18.2	22 26.6
4 Sa	14 52 14	11 24 41	10♒05 58	16 27 32	27R12.6	25 16.1	16 59.6	19 47.9	4 58.2	4 00.1	26 13.0	1 31.4	10 17.5	22 25.8
5 Su	14 56 11	12 24 51	22 43 53	28 55 37	27 12.8	26 45.7	18 14.1	20 32.3	5 01.8	3 53.0	26 13.5	1 34.0	10 16.8	22 25.0
6 M	15 00 07	13 25 03	5♓03 24	11♓07 49	27 12.0	28 14.9	19 28.7	21 16.8	5 05.7	3 45.8	26 14.1	1 36.7	10 16.1	22 24.1
7 Tu	15 04 04	14 25 17	17 09 28	23 08 55	27 09.2	29 43.6	20 43.4	22 01.3	5 10.0	3 38.5	26 14.8	1 39.4	10 15.3	22 23.2
8 W	15 08 01	15 25 32	29 06 41	5♈03 14	27 03.8	1♐11.8	21 58.0	22 45.8	5 14.6	3 31.1	26 15.6	1 42.1	10 14.5	22 22.3
9 Th	15 11 57	16 25 48	10♈59 00	16 54 21	26 55.3	2 39.5	23 12.7	23 30.5	5 19.6	3 23.7	26 16.5	1 44.9	10 13.6	22 21.4
10 F	15 15 54	17 26 07	22 49 37	28 45 05	26 44.1	4 06.7	24 27.5	24 15.2	5 24.8	3 16.1	26 17.4	1 47.7	10 12.8	22 20.5
11 Sa	15 19 50	18 26 26	4♉41 00	10♉37 33	26 30.6	5 33.3	25 42.2	24 59.9	5 30.4	3 08.5	26 18.5	1 50.5	10 11.9	22 19.6
12 Su	15 23 47	19 26 48	16 34 56	22 33 17	26 16.0	6 59.3	26 57.0	25 44.7	5 36.4	3 00.7	26 19.8	1 53.4	10 11.0	22 18.6
13 M	15 27 43	20 27 11	28 32 44	4♊33 26	26 01.3	8 24.7	28 11.9	26 29.6	5 42.6	2 52.9	26 21.1	1 56.3	10 10.0	22 17.7
14 Tu	15 31 40	21 27 36	10♊35 31	16 39 08	25 47.9	9 49.4	29 26.7	27 14.5	5 49.2	2 45.1	26 22.5	1 59.2	10 09.0	22 16.7
15 W	15 35 36	22 28 03	22 44 26	28 51 39	25 36.7	11 13.3	0♏41.6	27 59.4	5 56.0	2 37.2	26 24.0	2 02.2	10 08.0	22 15.7
16 Th	15 39 33	23 28 31	5♋00 58	11♋12 42	25 28.3	12 36.3	1 56.5	28 44.4	6 03.2	2 29.2	26 25.6	2 05.2	10 07.0	22 14.7
17 F	15 43 30	24 29 02	17 27 08	23 44 37	25 23.0	13 58.4	3 11.5	29 29.5	6 10.7	2 21.2	26 27.3	2 08.2	10 06.0	22 13.7
18 Sa	15 47 26	25 29 34	0♌05 32	6♌30 18	25 20.4	15 19.4	4 26.4	0♒14.6	6 18.5	2 13.1	26 29.1	2 11.3	10 04.9	22 12.7
19 Su	15 51 23	26 30 07	12 59 20	19 33 06	25 19.7	16 39.2	5 41.4	0 59.7	6 26.6	2 05.0	26 31.0	2 14.3	10 03.8	22 11.6
20 M	15 55 19	27 30 43	26 12 00	2♍56 26	25 19.7	17 57.6	6 56.5	1 44.9	6 35.0	1 56.9	26 33.1	2 17.4	10 02.6	22 10.6
21 Tu	15 59 16	28 31 20	9♍46 44	16 43 09	25 18.9	19 14.6	8 11.5	2 30.1	6 43.7	1 48.7	26 35.2	2 20.6	10 01.5	22 09.5
22 W	16 03 12	29 31 59	23 45 49	0♎54 44	25 16.4	20 29.7	9 26.6	3 15.4	6 52.7	1 40.5	26 37.4	2 23.7	10 00.3	22 08.5
23 Th	16 07 09	0♐32 40	8♎09 42	15 30 20	25 11.1	21 42.9	10 41.7	4 00.7	7 01.9	1 32.3	26 39.7	2 26.9	9 59.1	22 07.4
24 F	16 11 05	1 33 22	22 56 03	0♏26 01	25 03.1	22 53.9	11 56.8	4 46.1	7 11.5	1 24.1	26 42.1	2 30.1	9 57.8	22 06.3
25 Sa	16 15 02	2 34 06	7♏59 15	15 34 32	24 52.7	24 02.2	13 12.0	5 31.5	7 21.3	1 15.9	26 44.6	2 33.3	9 56.6	22 05.2
26 Su	16 18 59	3 34 51	23 10 34	0♐45 58	24 41.0	25 07.6	14 27.1	6 16.9	7 31.4	1 07.8	26 47.2	2 36.6	9 55.3	22 04.1
27 M	16 22 55	4 35 38	8♐19 21	15 49 24	24 29.5	26 09.7	15 42.3	7 02.4	7 41.8	0 59.6	26 49.9	2 39.9	9 54.0	22 03.0
28 Tu	16 26 52	5 36 26	23 14 54	0♑34 50	24 19.4	27 07.9	16 57.5	7 47.9	7 52.4	0 51.5	26 52.7	2 43.2	9 52.7	22 01.9
29 W	16 30 48	6 37 15	7♑48 24	14 55 00	24 11.7	28 01.7	18 12.7	8 33.5	8 03.3	0 43.3	26 55.6	2 46.5	9 51.3	22 00.8
30 Th	16 34 45	7 38 05	21 54 17	28 46 06	24 06.8	28 50.5	19 27.9	9 19.1	8 14.5	0 35.3	26 58.6	2 49.8	9 50.0	21 59.7

December 1905 LONGITUDE

Day	Sid.Time	☉	0 hr ☽	Noon ☽	True ☊	☿	♀	♂	⚳	♃	♄	♅	♆	♇
1 F	16 38 41	8♐38 56	5♒30 30	12♒07 42	24♌04.5	29♐33.6	20♏43.2	10♒04.7	8♓25.9	0♊27.2	27♒01.7	2♑53.2	9♋48.6	21♊58.5
2 Sa	16 42 38	9 39 48	18 38 06	25 02 09	24D04.0	0♑10.4	21 58.4	10 50.3	8 37.6	0R19.2	27 04.9	2 56.6	9R47.2	21R57.4
3 Su	16 46 34	10 40 40	1♓20 24	7♓33 31	24R04.3	0 39.9	23 13.7	11 36.0	8 49.5	0 11.3	27 08.2	3 00.0	9 45.7	21 56.3
4 M	16 50 31	11 41 34	13 42 06	19 46 51	24 04.0	1 01.4	24 29.0	12 21.7	9 01.7	0 03.4	27 11.6	3 03.4	9 44.3	21 55.1
5 Tu	16 54 28	12 42 28	25 48 26	1♈47 30	24 02.2	1R14.0	25 44.2	13 07.4	9 14.1	29♉55.6	27 15.0	3 06.8	9 42.8	21 54.0
6 W	16 58 24	13 43 23	7♈44 41	13 40 35	23 58.0	1 17.0	26 59.5	13 53.1	9 26.8	29 47.9	27 18.5	3 10.2	9 41.3	21 52.8
7 Th	17 02 21	14 44 18	19 35 46	25 30 44	23 51.1	1 09.4	28 14.8	14 38.9	9 39.6	29 40.2	27 22.2	3 13.7	9 39.9	21 51.6
8 F	17 06 17	15 45 15	1♉25 57	7♉21 49	23 41.5	0 50.9	29 30.1	15 24.7	9 52.7	29 32.7	27 25.9	3 17.2	9 38.3	21 50.5
9 Sa	17 10 14	16 46 12	13 18 43	19 16 55	23 29.9	0 20.9	0♐45.4	16 10.5	10 06.1	29 25.2	27 29.7	3 20.7	9 36.8	21 49.3
10 Su	17 14 10	17 47 10	25 16 42	1♊18 15	23 17.1	29♐39.6	2 00.8	16 56.3	10 19.6	29 17.8	27 33.6	3 24.2	9 35.3	21 48.1
11 M	17 18 07	18 48 09	7♊21 44	13 27 16	23 04.2	28 47.2	3 16.1	17 42.1	10 33.4	29 10.5	27 37.6	3 27.7	9 33.7	21 47.0
12 Tu	17 22 03	19 49 08	19 34 57	25 44 51	22 52.4	27 44.8	4 31.5	18 27.9	10 47.4	29 03.3	27 41.7	3 31.2	9 32.2	21 45.8
13 W	17 26 00	20 50 09	1♋57 02	8♋11 33	22 42.6	26 33.8	5 46.8	19 13.8	11 01.6	28 56.2	27 45.8	3 34.7	9 30.6	21 44.6
14 Th	17 29 57	21 51 10	14 28 27	20 47 51	22 35.4	25 16.2	7 02.2	19 59.6	11 16.0	28 49.3	27 50.0	3 38.3	9 29.0	21 43.5
15 F	17 33 53	22 52 12	27 09 48	3♌34 27	22 31.0	23 54.5	8 17.6	20 45.5	11 30.6	28 42.5	27 54.3	3 41.8	9 27.4	21 42.3
16 Sa	17 37 50	23 53 15	10♌01 58	16 32 30	22D29.2	22 31.5	9 32.9	21 31.3	11 45.4	28 35.7	27 58.7	3 45.4	9 25.8	21 41.1
17 Su	17 41 46	24 54 19	23 06 18	29 43 33	22 29.2	21 09.9	10 48.3	22 17.2	12 00.4	28 29.2	28 03.2	3 49.0	9 24.1	21 39.9
18 M	17 45 43	25 55 24	6♍24 31	13♍09 26	22 30.0	19 52.5	12 03.7	23 03.1	12 15.6	28 22.7	28 07.8	3 52.6	9 22.5	21 38.8
19 Tu	17 49 39	26 56 29	19 58 31	26 51 56	22R30.6	18 41.5	13 19.1	23 49.0	12 31.0	28 16.4	28 12.4	3 56.1	9 20.9	21 37.6
20 W	17 53 36	27 57 35	3♎49 48	10♎52 09	22 29.8	17 38.8	14 34.6	24 34.9	12 46.6	28 10.2	28 17.1	3 59.7	9 19.2	21 36.4
21 Th	17 57 32	28 58 42	17 58 55	25 09 53	22 26.9	16 45.9	15 50.0	25 20.9	13 02.4	28 04.2	28 21.9	4 03.3	9 17.5	21 35.3
22 F	18 01 29	29 59 50	2♏24 44	9♏42 57	22 21.8	16 03.4	17 05.4	26 06.8	13 18.3	27 58.3	28 26.7	4 06.9	9 15.9	21 34.1
23 Sa	18 05 26	1♑00 59	17 03 55	24 26 50	22 14.7	15 31.7	18 20.9	26 52.7	13 34.5	27 52.6	28 31.7	4 10.5	9 14.2	21 32.9
24 Su	18 09 22	2 02 08	1♐50 48	9♐14 50	22 06.5	15 10.8	19 36.3	27 38.6	13 50.8	27 47.1	28 36.7	4 14.1	9 12.5	21 31.8
25 M	18 13 19	3 03 18	16 37 54	23 58 55	21 58.2	15D00.3	20 51.8	28 24.6	14 07.3	27 41.7	28 41.8	4 17.8	9 10.8	21 30.6
26 Tu	18 17 15	4 04 28	1♑16 54	8♑30 56	21 51.0	14 59.6	22 07.2	29 10.5	14 23.9	27 36.5	28 46.9	4 21.4	9 09.1	21 29.5
27 W	18 21 12	5 05 38	15 40 11	22 43 59	21 45.5	15 08.1	23 22.7	29 56.5	14 40.8	27 31.4	28 52.1	4 25.0	9 07.4	21 28.4
28 Th	18 25 08	6 06 49	29 41 52	6♒33 27	21 42.2	15 25.1	24 38.1	0♓42.4	14 57.8	27 26.6	28 57.4	4 28.6	9 05.7	21 27.2
29 F	18 29 05	7 07 59	13♒18 37	19 57 21	21D41.0	15 49.7	25 53.6	1 28.4	15 15.0	27 21.9	29 02.8	4 32.2	9 04.1	21 26.1
30 Sa	18 33 01	8 09 10	26 29 47	2♓56 12	21 41.5	16 21.2	27 09.0	2 14.3	15 32.3	27 17.4	29 08.2	4 35.8	9 02.4	21 25.0
31 Su	18 36 58	9 10 20	9♓16 57	15 32 31	21 43.0	16 59.0	28 24.5	3 00.3	15 49.8	27 13.1	29 13.7	4 39.4	9 00.6	21 23.9

Astro Data Dy Hr Mn	Planet Ingress Dy Hr Mn	Last Aspect Dy Hr Mn	☽ Ingress Dy Hr Mn	Last Aspect Dy Hr Mn	☽ Ingress Dy Hr Mn	☽ Phases & Eclipses Dy Hr Mn	Astro Data
☽0N 8 17:05	☿ ♐ 7 16:27	31 18:14 ♄ ⚹	♑ 1 0:37	2 15:54 ♄ ☌	♓ 2 21:26	4 1:39 ☽ 10♒59	1 November 1905
♃⚻♅ 18 15:58	♀ ♏ 14 22:40	2 15:44 ☿ ⚹	♒ 3 5:19	5 8:18 ♃ ⚹	♈ 5 8:24	12 5:11 ○ 19♉10	Julian Day # 2131
☽0S 22 23:33	♂ ♒ 18 4:15	5 7:13 ♄ ☌	♓ 5 14:06	7 15:47 ♄ ⚹	♉ 7 21:06	20 1:34 ☾ 27♌04	SVP 6♓34'40"
	☉ ♐ 22 23:05	7 10:28 ♇ □	♈ 8 1:48	10 8:03 ♃ ☌	♊ 10 9:24	26 16:47 ● 3♐47	GC 25♐31.5 ⚴ 5♒20.7
☽0N 6 0:50		10 7:01 ♄ ⚹	♉ 10 14:32	12 15:48 ♄ △	♋ 12 20:14		Eris 23♓42.2R ⚵ 14♌38.6
☿R 6 6:57	☿ ♑ 2 4:46	12 19:35 ♄ □	♊ 13 2:54	15 2:59 ♃ ⚹	♌ 15 5:19	3 18:37 ☽ 10♓57	⚷ 1♒37.7 ⚶ 2♐31.7
♃□♄ 19 20:51	♃ ♉R 4 22:31	15 7:10 ♄ △	♋ 15 14:14	17 9:47 ♃ □	♍ 17 12:30	11 23:25 ○ 19♊17	☽ Mean ☊ 26♌20.1
☽0S 20 8:02	♀ ♐ 8 21:31	17 23:33 ♂ ☍	♌ 17 23:50	19 14:25 ♃ △	♎ 19 17:25	19 12:08 ☾ 26♍57	
☿D 26 1:34	☿ ♐R 10 0:57	20 1:34 ☉ □	♍ 20 6:47	21 18:48 ☉ ⚹	♏ 21 20:01	26 4:04 ● 3♑44	1 December 1905
	☉ ♑ 22 12:04	22 9:31 ☉ ⚹	♎ 22 10:29	23 18:39 ♄ □	♐ 23 21:00		Julian Day # 2161
	♂ ♓ 27 13:50	24 6:01 ♄ △	♏ 24 11:19	25 19:47 ♄ ⚹	♑ 25 21:53		SVP 6♓34'35"
		26 5:41 ♄ □	♐ 26 10:47	27 20:11 ♃ △	♒ 28 0:32		GC 25♐31.5 ⚴ 11♒21.5
		28 5:57 ☿ ☌	♑ 28 11:03	30 4:51 ♄ ☌	♓ 30 6:30		Eris 23♓32.5R ⚵ 22♌23.6
		29 18:11 ♀ ⚹	♒ 30 14:11				⚷ 2♒53.1 ⚶ 18♐37.2
							☽ Mean ☊ 24♌44.8

LONGITUDE — January 1906

Day	Sid.Time	☉	0 hr ☽	Noon ☽	True ☊	☿	♀	♂	⚳	♃	♄	♅	♆	♇
1 M	18 40 55	10♑11 30	21♓43 25	27♓50 15	21♌44.5	17♐42.3	29♐39.9	3♓46.2	16♓07.4	27♉08.9	29♒19.2	4♑43.0	8♋58.9	21♊22.8
2 Tu	18 44 51	11 12 39	3♈53 36	9♈54 08	21R45.2	18 30.5	0♑55.4	4 32.1	16 25.2	27R05.0	29 24.9	4 46.6	8R57.2	21R21.7
3 W	18 48 48	12 13 49	15 52 28	21 49 15	21 44.6	19 23.2	2 10.8	5 18.0	16 43.1	27 01.2	29 30.5	4 50.2	8 55.5	21 20.6
4 Th	18 52 44	13 14 58	27 45 07	3♉40 39	21 42.3	20 19.8	3 26.2	6 03.9	17 01.2	26 57.6	29 36.3	4 53.8	8 53.9	21 19.5
5 F	18 56 41	14 16 07	9♉36 26	15 33 01	21 38.3	21 19.8	4 41.7	6 49.8	17 19.5	26 54.3	29 42.1	4 57.4	8 52.2	21 18.4
6 Sa	19 00 37	15 17 15	21 30 53	27 30 28	21 32.8	22 23.0	5 57.1	7 35.7	17 37.8	26 51.1	29 47.9	5 00.9	8 50.5	21 17.3
7 Su	19 04 34	16 18 24	3♊32 12	9♊36 23	21 26.4	23 29.0	7 12.5	8 21.5	17 56.3	26 48.1	29 53.8	5 04.5	8 48.8	21 16.3
8 M	19 08 30	17 19 32	15 43 21	21 53 18	21 19.9	24 37.4	8 28.0	9 07.4	18 15.0	26 45.3	29 59.8	5 08.0	8 47.1	21 15.2
9 Tu	19 12 27	18 20 39	28 06 24	4♋22 47	21 13.8	25 48.1	9 43.4	9 53.2	18 33.8	26 42.7	0♓05.8	5 11.6	8 45.4	21 14.2
10 W	19 16 24	19 21 46	10♋42 30	17 05 36	21 08.9	27 00.8	10 58.8	10 39.0	18 52.7	26 40.4	0 11.9	5 15.1	8 43.8	21 13.2
11 Th	19 20 20	20 22 53	23 32 01	0♌01 44	21 05.5	28 15.2	12 14.2	11 24.8	19 11.7	26 38.2	0 18.0	5 18.6	8 42.1	21 12.2
12 F	19 24 17	21 24 00	6♌34 39	13 10 42	21D03.8	29 31.3	13 29.7	12 10.6	19 30.9	26 36.2	0 24.2	5 22.1	8 40.5	21 11.2
13 Sa	19 28 13	22 25 06	19 49 45	26 31 42	21 03.7	0♑48.9	14 45.1	12 56.4	19 50.1	26 34.4	0 30.5	5 25.6	8 38.8	21 10.2
14 Su	19 32 10	23 26 12	3♍16 28	10♍03 57	21 04.7	2 07.8	16 00.5	13 42.1	20 09.5	26 32.9	0 36.7	5 29.1	8 37.2	21 09.2
15 M	19 36 06	24 27 18	16 54 03	23 46 42	21 06.3	3 27.9	17 15.9	14 27.9	20 29.1	26 31.5	0 43.1	5 32.6	8 35.5	21 08.3
16 Tu	19 40 03	25 28 23	0♎41 47	7♎39 16	21 07.8	4 49.2	18 31.3	15 13.6	20 48.7	26 30.4	0 49.4	5 36.1	8 33.9	21 07.3
17 W	19 43 59	26 29 29	14 39 00	21 40 53	21R08.6	6 11.6	19 46.7	15 59.3	21 08.5	26 29.4	0 55.9	5 39.5	8 32.3	21 06.4
18 Th	19 47 56	27 30 34	28 44 45	5♏50 24	21 08.5	7 34.9	21 02.1	16 44.9	21 28.3	26 28.7	1 02.3	5 42.9	8 30.7	21 05.4
19 F	19 51 53	28 31 38	12♏57 36	20 06 01	21 07.2	8 59.2	22 17.6	17 30.6	21 48.3	26 28.1	1 08.8	5 46.3	8 29.1	21 04.5
20 Sa	19 55 49	29 32 43	27 15 18	4♐25 01	21 05.0	10 24.4	23 33.0	18 16.2	22 08.4	26 27.8	1 15.4	5 49.7	8 27.6	21 03.6
21 Su	19 59 46	0♒33 47	11♐34 40	18 43 44	21 02.2	11 50.4	24 48.4	19 01.8	22 28.6	26D27.7	1 22.0	5 53.1	8 26.0	21 02.8
22 M	20 03 42	1 34 51	25 51 38	2♑57 47	20 59.2	13 17.2	26 03.8	19 47.4	22 49.0	26 27.7	1 28.6	5 56.4	8 24.5	21 01.9
23 Tu	20 07 39	2 35 54	10♑01 37	17 02 33	20 56.7	14 44.7	27 19.2	20 33.0	23 09.4	26 28.0	1 35.3	5 59.8	8 23.0	21 01.1
24 W	20 11 35	3 36 56	24 00 03	0♒53 41	20 54.9	16 13.1	28 34.6	21 18.6	23 29.9	26 28.5	1 42.0	6 03.1	8 21.4	21 00.2
25 Th	20 15 32	4 37 58	7♒43 01	14 27 45	20D54.0	17 42.1	29 50.0	22 04.1	23 50.5	26 29.2	1 48.8	6 06.4	8 19.9	20 59.4
26 F	20 19 29	5 38 58	21 07 40	27 42 40	20 54.0	19 11.9	1♒05.3	22 49.6	24 11.2	26 30.1	1 55.6	6 09.6	8 18.5	20 58.6
27 Sa	20 23 25	6 39 58	4♓12 41	10♓37 50	20 54.7	20 42.3	2 20.7	23 35.1	24 32.1	26 31.2	2 02.4	6 12.9	8 17.0	20 57.8
28 Su	20 27 22	7 40 56	16 58 15	23 14 11	20 55.9	22 13.5	3 36.1	24 20.5	24 53.0	26 32.6	2 09.3	6 16.1	8 15.6	20 57.1
29 M	20 31 18	8 41 53	29 25 58	5♈33 58	20 57.1	23 45.3	4 51.4	25 06.0	25 14.0	26 34.1	2 16.2	6 19.3	8 14.1	20 56.3
30 Tu	20 35 15	9 42 49	11♈38 40	17 40 32	20 58.2	25 17.9	6 06.8	25 51.4	25 35.1	26 35.8	2 23.1	6 22.5	8 12.7	20 55.6
31 W	20 39 11	10 43 44	23 40 06	29 37 56	20 58.9	26 51.1	7 22.1	26 36.7	25 56.2	26 37.7	2 30.0	6 25.6	8 11.3	20 54.9

LONGITUDE — February 1906

Day	Sid.Time	☉	0 hr ☽	Noon ☽	True ☊	☿	♀	♂	⚳	♃	♄	♅	♆	♇
1 Th	20 43 08	11♒44 37	5♉34 36	11♉30 44	20♌59.2	28♑25.1	8♒37.4	27♓22.1	26♓17.5	26♉39.9	2♓37.0	6♑28.7	8♋10.0	20♊54.2
2 F	20 47 04	12 45 30	17 26 54	23 23 43	20R59.0	29 59.7	9 52.7	28 07.4	26 38.9	26 42.2	2 44.0	6 31.8	8R08.6	20R53.5
3 Sa	20 51 01	13 46 20	29 21 45	5♊21 35	20 58.4	1♒35.1	11 08.0	28 52.6	27 00.3	26 44.7	2 51.0	6 34.9	8 07.3	20 52.8
4 Su	20 54 57	14 47 10	11♊23 44	17 28 44	20 57.7	3 11.2	12 23.3	29 37.9	27 21.8	26 47.4	2 58.1	6 37.9	8 06.0	20 52.2
5 M	20 58 54	15 47 58	23 37 01	29 49 00	20 57.0	4 48.1	13 38.6	0♈23.1	27 43.4	26 50.3	3 05.2	6 40.9	8 04.7	20 51.6
6 Tu	21 02 51	16 48 44	6♋05 03	12♋25 25	20 56.3	6 25.7	14 53.8	1 08.2	28 05.1	26 53.4	3 12.3	6 43.9	8 03.5	20 51.0
7 W	21 06 47	17 49 30	18 50 21	25 19 57	20 55.9	8 04.0	16 09.1	1 53.4	28 26.8	26 56.7	3 19.4	6 46.9	8 02.2	20 50.4
8 Th	21 10 44	18 50 13	1♌54 17	8♌33 19	20D55.7	9 43.2	17 24.3	2 38.5	28 48.6	27 00.2	3 26.5	6 49.8	8 01.0	20 49.8
9 F	21 14 40	19 50 56	15 16 54	22 04 52	20 55.7	11 23.1	18 39.6	3 23.5	29 10.5	27 03.9	3 33.7	6 52.7	7 59.9	20 49.3
10 Sa	21 18 37	20 51 37	28 56 54	5♍52 41	20R55.7	13 03.9	19 54.8	4 08.6	29 32.5	27 07.8	3 40.9	6 55.5	7 58.7	20 48.8
11 Su	21 22 33	21 52 17	12♍51 48	19 53 47	20 55.7	14 45.4	21 10.0	4 53.5	29 54.5	27 11.8	3 48.1	6 58.3	7 57.6	20 48.3
12 M	21 26 30	22 52 55	26 58 10	4♎04 26	20 55.5	16 27.9	22 25.2	5 38.5	0♈16.6	27 16.0	3 55.3	7 01.1	7 56.4	20 47.8
13 Tu	21 30 26	23 53 33	11♎12 05	18 20 37	20 55.2	18 11.1	23 40.4	6 23.4	0 38.8	27 20.5	4 02.5	7 03.9	7 55.4	20 47.3
14 W	21 34 23	24 54 09	25 29 33	2♏38 26	20 54.9	19 55.3	24 55.6	7 08.3	1 01.0	27 25.0	4 09.7	7 06.6	7 54.3	20 46.9
15 Th	21 38 20	25 54 44	9♏46 52	16 54 29	20D54.6	21 40.3	26 10.8	7 53.1	1 23.3	27 29.8	4 17.0	7 09.3	7 53.3	20 46.5
16 F	21 42 16	26 55 18	24 00 56	1♐05 57	20 54.6	23 26.2	27 25.9	8 38.0	1 45.7	27 34.8	4 24.3	7 11.9	7 52.3	20 46.1
17 Sa	21 46 13	27 55 50	8♐09 15	15 10 39	20 54.9	25 13.0	28 41.1	9 22.7	2 08.1	27 39.9	4 31.5	7 14.5	7 51.3	20 45.7
18 Su	21 50 09	28 56 22	22 09 55	29 06 53	20 55.4	27 00.7	29 56.2	10 07.5	2 30.6	27 45.2	4 38.8	7 17.1	7 50.3	20 45.4
19 M	21 54 06	29 56 52	6♑01 23	12♑53 16	20 56.3	28 49.3	1♓11.3	10 52.2	2 53.1	27 50.7	4 46.1	7 19.7	7 49.4	20 45.0
20 Tu	21 58 02	0♓57 21	19 42 24	26 28 37	20 57.1	0♓38.7	2 26.5	11 36.8	3 15.8	27 56.3	4 53.4	7 22.2	7 48.5	20 44.7
21 W	22 01 59	1 57 48	3♒11 48	9♒51 50	20R57.8	2 29.0	3 41.6	12 21.5	3 38.4	28 02.1	5 00.7	7 24.6	7 47.7	20 44.4
22 Th	22 05 55	2 58 14	16 28 36	23 02 00	20 58.0	4 20.1	4 56.7	13 06.1	4 01.1	28 08.1	5 08.0	7 27.0	7 46.8	20 44.2
23 F	22 09 52	3 58 38	29 31 57	5♓58 24	20 57.5	6 12.0	6 11.7	13 50.6	4 23.9	28 14.3	5 15.3	7 29.4	7 46.0	20 43.9
24 Sa	22 13 49	4 59 01	12♓21 21	18 40 48	20 56.3	8 04.7	7 26.8	14 35.2	4 46.7	28 20.6	5 22.6	7 31.8	7 45.3	20 43.7
25 Su	22 17 45	5 59 21	24 56 49	1♈09 32	20 54.4	9 58.0	8 41.8	15 19.6	5 09.6	28 27.0	5 29.9	7 34.1	7 44.5	20 43.5
26 M	22 21 42	6 59 40	7♈19 05	13 25 41	20 51.9	11 51.8	9 56.9	16 04.1	5 32.6	28 33.7	5 37.3	7 36.3	7 43.8	20 43.3
27 Tu	22 25 38	7 59 57	19 29 36	25 31 09	20 49.2	13 46.2	11 11.9	16 48.5	5 55.5	28 40.5	5 44.6	7 38.5	7 43.1	20 43.1
28 W	22 29 35	9 00 12	1♉30 41	7♉28 37	20 46.6	15 40.9	12 26.9	17 32.8	6 18.6	28 47.4	5 51.9	7 40.7	7 42.5	20 43.0

Astro Data

	Dy Hr Mn
☽0N	2 9:47
☽0S	16 14:21
♃ D	21 14:25
☽0N	29 19:02
♂0N	6 8:15
☽0S	12 20:33
☽0N	26 3:30

Planet Ingress

		Dy Hr Mn
♀	♑	1 18:23
♄	♓	8 12:47
☿	♑	12 20:56
☉	♒	20 22:43
♀	♒	25 15:12
☿	♒	2 12:04
♂	♈	4 23:45
⚳	♈	11 17:58
♀	♓	18 13:13
☉	♓	19 13:15
☿	♓	20 3:32

Last Aspect / ☽ Ingress

Last Aspect Dy Hr Mn			☽ Ingress	Dy Hr Mn
1 16:02	♀	□	♈	1 16:16
4 3:41	♄	✶	♉	4 4:33
6 16:36	♄	□	♊	6 16:58
8 17:50	☿	☍	♋	9 3:38
11 5:46	♃	✶	♌	11 11:57
13 12:05	♃	□	♍	13 18:11
15 16:46	♃	△	♎	15 22:48
17 20:49	☉	□	♏	18 2:08
20 3:13	☉	✶	♐	20 4:36
21 15:53	♇	☍	♑	22 6:59
24 7:33	♀	☌	♒	24 10:26
26 9:47	♃	□	♓	26 16:12
28 18:24	♃	✶	♈	29 1:06
31 5:34	☿	□	♉	31 12:45

Last Aspect / ☽ Ingress

Last Aspect Dy Hr Mn			☽ Ingress	Dy Hr Mn
2 22:09	♂	✶	♊	3 1:17
4 18:38	♇	☌	♋	5 12:21
7 14:58	♃	✶	♌	7 20:32
9 20:46	♃	□	♍	10 1:50
12 0:27	♃	△	♎	12 5:07
13 22:01	☉	△	♏	14 7:34
16 6:00	♃	☍	♐	16 10:08
18 11:40	☉	✶	♑	18 13:32
20 14:37	♃	△	♒	20 18:17
22 21:29	♃	□	♓	23 0:52
25 6:43	♃	✶	♈	25 9:45
27 2:26	♇	✶	♉	27 20:58

☽ Phases & Eclipses

Dy Hr Mn		
2 14:52	☽	11♈20
10 16:36	○	19♋34
17 20:49	☾	26♎52
24 17:09	●	3♒50
1 12:31	☽	11♉46
9 7:46	○	19♌40
9 7:47	◐	T 1.625
16 4:22	☾	26♏36
23 7:57	●	3♓48
23 7:43:14	◐	P 0.539

Astro Data

1 January 1906
Julian Day # 2192
SVP 6♓34'30"
GC 25♐31.6 ⚴ 19♒49.8
Eris 23♓34.4 ⚵ 23♌30.5R
⚷ 4♒57.8 ⚶ 5♑21.9
☽ Mean ☊ 23♌06.3

1 February 1906
Julian Day # 2223
SVP 6♓34'26"
GC 25♐31.7 ⚴ 29♒33.6
Eris 23♓48.2 ⚵ 17♌18.7R
⚷ 7♒25.3 ⚶ 21♑53.9
☽ Mean ☊ 21♌27.8

March 1906 — LONGITUDE

Day	Sid.Time	☉	0 hr ☽	Noon ☽	True ☊	☿	♀	♂	⚳	♃	♄	♅	♆	♇
1 Th	22 33 31	10♓00 25	13♉25 24	19♉21 31	20♌44.5	17♓35.7	13♓41.9	18♈17.1	6♈41.6	28♉54.5	5♓59.2	7♑42.8	7♋41.9	20♊42.9
2 F	22 37 28	11 00 36	25 17 30	1♊13 54	20D 43.2	19 30.6	14 56.8	19 01.4	7 04.7	29 01.8	6 06.5	7 44.9	7R 41.3	20R 42.8
3 Sa	22 41 24	12 00 45	7♊11 17	13 10 15	20 42.8	21 25.2	16 11.8	19 45.6	7 27.9	29 09.2	6 13.8	7 47.0	7 40.7	20 42.7
4 Su	22 45 21	13 00 52	19 11 25	25 15 21	20 43.4	23 19.3	17 26.7	20 29.8	7 51.1	29 16.7	6 21.0	7 49.0	7 40.2	20 42.7
5 M	22 49 18	14 00 57	1♋22 39	7♋33 54	20 44.7	25 12.6	18 41.6	21 14.0	8 14.3	29 24.4	6 28.3	7 50.9	7 39.7	20D 42.7
6 Tu	22 53 14	15 01 00	13 49 36	20 10 15	20 46.4	27 04.8	19 56.4	21 58.1	8 37.6	29 32.2	6 35.6	7 52.9	7 39.3	20 42.7
7 W	22 57 11	16 01 00	26 36 17	3♌08 02	20 47.9	28 55.6	21 11.3	22 42.1	9 00.9	29 40.2	6 42.8	7 54.7	7 38.8	20 42.7
8 Th	23 01 07	17 00 59	9♌45 44	16 29 33	20R 48.8	0♈44.4	22 26.1	23 26.1	9 24.3	29 48.3	6 50.1	7 56.6	7 38.4	20 42.8
9 F	23 05 04	18 00 55	23 19 28	0♍15 23	20 48.5	2 30.8	23 41.0	24 10.1	9 47.7	29 56.6	6 57.3	7 58.3	7 38.1	20 42.8
10 Sa	23 09 00	19 00 49	7♍17 00	14 23 56	20 46.9	4 14.4	24 55.8	24 54.0	10 11.1	0♊05.0	7 04.5	8 00.1	7 37.8	20 42.9
11 Su	23 12 57	20 00 42	21 35 34	28 51 15	20 43.9	5 54.7	26 10.5	25 37.9	10 34.6	0 13.5	7 11.7	8 01.7	7 37.5	20 43.0
12 M	23 16 53	21 00 32	6♎10 08	13♎31 21	20 39.8	7 31.1	27 25.3	26 21.7	10 58.0	0 22.1	7 18.9	8 03.4	7 37.2	20 43.2
13 Tu	23 20 50	22 00 21	20 53 56	28 16 55	20 35.2	9 03.3	28 40.0	27 05.5	11 21.6	0 30.9	7 26.1	8 05.0	7 37.0	20 43.3
14 W	23 24 47	23 00 07	5♏39 22	13♏00 23	20 30.7	10 30.5	29 54.7	27 49.2	11 45.1	0 39.8	7 33.2	8 06.5	7 36.8	20 43.5
15 Th	23 28 43	23 59 53	20 19 21	27 35 08	20 27.1	11 52.5	1♈09.4	28 32.9	12 08.7	0 48.9	7 40.3	8 08.0	7 36.6	20 43.7
16 F	23 32 40	24 59 36	4♐43 36	11♐56 12	20D 24.8	13 08.6	2 24.1	29 16.6	12 32.3	0 58.0	7 47.4	8 09.5	7 36.5	20 43.9
17 Sa	23 36 36	25 59 18	19 00 37	26 00 42	20 24.1	14 18.5	3 38.8	0♉00.2	12 56.0	1 07.3	7 54.5	8 10.9	7 36.4	20 44.2
18 Su	23 40 33	26 58 58	2♑56 23	9♑47 40	20 24.7	15 21.7	4 53.4	0 43.7	13 19.7	1 16.7	8 01.6	8 12.2	7 36.4	20 44.4
19 M	23 44 29	27 58 37	16 34 41	23 17 33	20 26.1	16 18.0	6 08.0	1 27.3	13 43.4	1 26.2	8 08.6	8 13.5	7D 36.3	20 44.7
20 Tu	23 48 26	28 58 14	29 56 27	6♒31 37	20 27.6	17 07.0	7 22.6	2 10.7	14 07.1	1 35.9	8 15.7	8 14.8	7 36.4	20 45.1
21 W	23 52 22	29 57 49	13♒03 14	19 31 30	20R 28.3	17 48.5	8 37.2	2 54.2	14 30.9	1 45.6	8 22.7	8 16.0	7 36.4	20 45.4
22 Th	23 56 19	0♈57 22	25 56 38	2♓18 47	20 27.6	18 22.3	9 51.8	3 37.6	14 54.7	1 55.5	8 29.6	8 17.1	7 36.5	20 45.7
23 F	0 00 15	1 56 53	8♓38 07	14 54 47	20 24.9	18 48.3	11 06.3	4 20.9	15 18.5	2 05.5	8 36.6	8 18.2	7 36.6	20 46.1
24 Sa	0 04 12	2 56 22	21 08 54	27 20 35	20 20.1	19 06.4	12 20.8	5 04.2	15 42.3	2 15.6	8 43.5	8 19.3	7 36.7	20 46.5
25 Su	0 08 09	3 55 49	3♈29 55	9♈37 03	20 13.4	19R 16.7	13 35.3	5 47.5	16 06.1	2 25.7	8 50.3	8 20.3	7 36.9	20 46.9
26 M	0 12 05	4 55 14	15 42 03	21 45 06	20 05.2	19 19.3	14 49.8	6 30.7	16 30.0	2 36.0	8 57.2	8 21.2	7 37.1	20 47.4
27 Tu	0 16 02	5 54 37	27 46 19	3♉45 54	19 56.3	19 14.3	16 04.3	7 13.9	16 53.9	2 46.5	9 04.0	8 22.1	7 37.4	20 47.9
28 W	0 19 58	6 53 58	9♉44 05	15 41 06	19 47.5	19 02.2	17 18.7	7 57.0	17 17.8	2 57.0	9 10.8	8 23.0	7 37.7	20 48.3
29 Th	0 23 55	7 53 17	21 37 16	27 32 57	19 39.6	18 43.2	18 33.1	8 40.1	17 41.7	3 07.6	9 17.5	8 23.7	7 38.0	20 48.8
30 F	0 27 51	8 52 33	3♊28 30	9♊24 24	19 33.5	18 17.9	19 47.5	9 23.1	18 05.7	3 18.3	9 24.2	8 24.5	7 38.3	20 49.4
31 Sa	0 31 48	9 51 48	15 21 06	21 19 09	19 29.3	17 46.9	21 01.8	10 06.1	18 29.6	3 29.1	9 30.9	8 25.2	7 38.7	20 49.9

April 1906 — LONGITUDE

Day	Sid.Time	☉	0 hr ☽	Noon ☽	True ☊	☿	♀	♂	⚳	♃	♄	♅	♆	♇
1 Su	0 35 44	10♈50 59	27♊19 04	3♋21 29	19♌27.3	17♈10.9	22♈16.1	10♉49.1	18♈53.6	3♊40.0	9♓37.5	8♑25.8	7♋39.1	20♊50.5
2 M	0 39 41	11 50 09	9♋26 59	15 36 12	19D 27.1	16R 30.7	23 30.4	11 32.0	19 17.6	3 51.0	9 44.1	8 26.4	7 39.6	20 51.1
3 Tu	0 43 38	12 49 16	21 49 44	28 08 13	19 27.9	15 47.2	24 44.7	12 14.8	19 41.6	4 02.1	9 50.7	8 27.0	7 40.1	20 51.7
4 W	0 47 34	13 48 21	4♌32 13	11♌02 15	19R 28.9	15 01.2	25 59.0	12 57.6	20 05.6	4 13.2	9 57.2	8 27.4	7 40.6	20 52.3
5 Th	0 51 31	14 47 24	17 38 48	24 22 11	19 29.0	14 13.8	27 13.2	13 40.4	20 29.6	4 24.5	10 03.6	8 27.9	7 41.2	20 53.0
6 F	0 55 27	15 46 24	1♍12 41	8♍10 20	19 27.5	13 25.9	28 27.3	14 23.1	20 53.6	4 35.8	10 10.1	8 28.3	7 41.7	20 53.7
7 Sa	0 59 24	16 45 23	15 15 04	22 26 36	19 23.7	12 38.4	29 41.5	15 05.7	21 17.7	4 47.2	10 16.4	8 28.6	7 42.4	20 54.3
8 Su	1 03 20	17 44 18	29 44 25	7♎07 48	19 17.5	11 52.2	0♉55.6	15 48.3	21 41.7	4 58.7	10 22.8	8 28.9	7 43.0	20 55.1
9 M	1 07 17	18 43 12	14♎35 53	22 07 32	19 09.4	11 08.1	2 09.7	16 30.9	22 05.8	5 10.3	10 29.0	8 29.1	7 43.7	20 55.8
10 Tu	1 11 13	19 42 04	29 41 33	7♏16 37	19 00.3	10 26.9	3 23.8	17 13.4	22 29.8	5 22.0	10 35.3	8 29.3	7 44.4	20 56.5
11 W	1 15 10	20 40 54	14♏51 24	22 24 36	18 51.3	9 49.1	4 37.8	17 55.9	22 53.9	5 33.7	10 41.5	8 29.4	7 45.1	20 57.3
12 Th	1 19 07	21 39 42	29 55 02	7♐21 37	18 43.5	9 15.2	5 51.9	18 38.3	23 18.0	5 45.6	10 47.6	8R 29.5	7 45.9	20 58.1
13 F	1 23 03	22 38 29	14♐43 29	21 59 57	18 37.7	8 45.8	7 05.9	19 20.7	23 42.1	5 57.4	10 53.7	8 29.5	7 46.7	20 58.9
14 Sa	1 27 00	23 37 14	29 10 32	6♑14 58	18 34.3	8 21.2	8 19.8	20 03.0	24 06.1	6 09.4	10 59.8	8 29.5	7 47.6	20 59.7
15 Su	1 30 56	24 35 57	13♑13 08	20 05 08	18D 33.0	8 01.5	9 33.8	20 45.3	24 30.2	6 21.5	11 05.8	8 29.4	7 48.5	21 00.6
16 M	1 34 53	25 34 39	26 51 07	3♒31 23	18 33.1	7 46.9	10 47.7	21 27.6	24 54.3	6 33.6	11 11.7	8 29.3	7 49.4	21 01.4
17 Tu	1 38 49	26 33 18	10♒06 18	16 36 16	18R 33.5	7 37.6	12 01.6	22 09.8	25 18.4	6 45.7	11 17.6	8 29.1	7 50.3	21 02.3
18 W	1 42 46	27 31 57	23 01 43	29 23 05	18 33.0	7D 33.4	13 15.5	22 52.0	25 42.5	6 58.0	11 23.4	8 28.9	7 51.3	21 03.2
19 Th	1 46 42	28 30 33	5♓40 48	11♓55 16	18 30.7	7 34.3	14 29.3	23 34.1	26 06.6	7 10.3	11 29.2	8 28.6	7 52.3	21 04.1
20 F	1 50 39	29 29 08	18 06 53	24 15 57	18 25.7	7 40.3	15 43.2	24 16.2	26 30.7	7 22.7	11 34.9	8 28.2	7 53.3	21 05.0
21 Sa	1 54 36	0♉27 40	0♈22 48	6♈27 42	18 17.9	7 51.3	16 57.0	24 58.2	26 54.8	7 35.1	11 40.6	8 27.8	7 54.3	21 06.0
22 Su	1 58 32	1 26 11	12 30 52	18 32 32	18 07.4	8 07.0	18 10.7	25 40.2	27 18.9	7 47.6	11 46.2	8 27.4	7 55.4	21 06.9
23 M	2 02 29	2 24 41	24 32 51	0♉32 00	17 54.8	8 27.5	19 24.5	26 22.2	27 43.0	8 00.2	11 51.7	8 26.9	7 56.5	21 07.9
24 Tu	2 06 25	3 23 08	6♉30 08	12 27 24	17 41.2	8 52.4	20 38.2	27 04.1	28 07.1	8 12.8	11 57.2	8 26.4	7 57.7	21 08.9
25 W	2 10 22	4 21 34	18 23 57	24 19 59	17 27.6	9 21.6	21 51.9	27 46.0	28 31.2	8 25.5	12 02.6	8 25.8	7 58.8	21 09.9
26 Th	2 14 18	5 19 57	0♊15 42	6♊11 19	17 15.1	9 54.9	23 05.5	28 27.8	28 55.3	8 38.2	12 07.9	8 25.2	8 00.1	21 10.9
27 F	2 18 15	6 18 19	12 07 06	18 03 23	17 04.8	10 32.2	24 19.2	29 09.6	29 19.4	8 51.0	12 13.2	8 24.5	8 01.3	21 12.0
28 Sa	2 22 11	7 16 39	24 00 31	29 58 54	16 57.1	11 13.4	25 32.8	29 51.3	29 43.4	9 03.8	12 18.4	8 23.8	8 02.5	21 13.0
29 Su	2 26 08	8 14 57	5♋58 58	12♋01 13	16 52.3	11 58.1	26 46.3	0♊33.0	0♉07.5	9 16.7	12 23.6	8 23.0	8 03.8	21 14.1
30 M	2 30 04	9 13 12	18 06 11	24 14 26	16 49.9	12 46.4	27 59.9	1 14.6	0 31.5	9 29.7	12 28.7	8 22.2	8 05.1	21 15.2

Astro Data

	Dy Hr Mn
♅☍♆	1 3:16
♇D	5 21:25
☿0N	8 2:17
☽0S	12 4:40
♄△♆	14 23:46
♀0N	16 22:50
♆D	19 15:17
♄✶♅	20 8:16
☉0N	21 12:53
☽0N	25 10:42
⚳0N	25 23:07
☿R	26 8:03
☽0S	8 14:59
♅R	13 11:54
☿D	18 19:33

Planet Ingress

	Dy Hr Mn
☿ ♈	8 2:10
♃ ♊	9 21:48
♀ ♈	14 13:42
♂ ♉	17 11:54
☉ ♈	21 12:53
♀ ♉	7 17:59
☉ ♉	21 0:39
♂ ♊	28 17:00
⚳ ♉	29 4:32
☽0N	21 17:06
♃××	23 4:22
♃⊼⊼	25 12:37

Last Aspect / ☽ Ingress

Last Aspect Dy Hr Mn		☽ Ingress Dy Hr Mn
2 7:30 ♃☌	♊	2 9:31
4 7:29 ☿□	♋	4 21:19
7 5:35 ♃✶	♌	7 6:16
9 11:27 ♃□	♍	9 11:34
11 7:10 ♀☍	♎	11 13:53
13 9:58 ♂☍	♏	13 14:48
15 5:38 ☉△	♐	15 16:01
17 11:57 ☉□	♑	17 18:54
19 21:08 ☉✶	♒	20 0:06
21 14:18 ♇△	♓	22 7:38
23 23:16 ♇□	♈	24 17:10
26 10:05 ♇✶	♉	27 4:27
27 22:45 ♄✶	♊	29 16:58

Last Aspect Dy Hr Mn		☽ Ingress Dy Hr Mn
31 11:21 ♀✶	♋	1 5:20
3 4:52 ♀□	♌	3 15:31
5 17:31 ♀△	♍	5 21:53
7 9:27 ♇□	♎	8 0:25
9 10:06 ♇△	♏	10 0:29
11 4:32 ♂☍	♐	12 0:08
13 13:09 ☉△	♑	14 1:23
15 20:37 ☉□	♒	16 5:39
18 8:12 ☉✶	♓	18 13:10
20 12:00 ♂✶	♈	20 23:15
22 17:09 ♇✶	♉	23 10:56
25 19:23 ♂☌	♊	25 23:28
27 18:21 ♇☌	♋	28 12:02
30 20:05 ♀✶	♌	30 23:09

☽ Phases & Eclipses

Dy Hr Mn		
3 9:28	☽	11♊54
10 20:17	○	19♍21
17 11:57	☾	25♐59
24 23:52	●	3♈26
2 4:02	☽	11♋31
9 6:12	○	18♎29
15 20:37	☾	24♑57
23 16:06	●	2♉35

Astro Data

1 March 1906
Julian Day # 2251
SVP 6♓34'23"
GC 25♐31.7 ⚴ 8♓49.3
Eris 24♓07.9 ⚵ 11♌00.9R
⚷ 9♒34.8 ⚶ 6♒21.6
☽ Mean ☊ 19♌58.9

1 April 1906
Julian Day # 2282
SVP 6♓34'20"
GC 25♐31.8 ⚴ 19♓05.0
Eris 24♓32.3 ⚵ 9♌46.4
⚷ 11♒29.9 ⚶ 21♒28.6
☽ Mean ☊ 18♌20.3

LONGITUDE — May 1906

Day	Sid.Time	☉	0 hr ☽	Noon ☽	True ☊	☿	♀	♂	⚳	♃	♄	♅	♆	♇
1 Tu	2 34 01	10♉11 26	0♌26 34	6♌43 10	16♌49.2	13♈38.0	29♉13.4	1♊56.3	0♉55.6	9♊42.6	12♓33.7	8♑21.3	8♋06.5	21♊16.3
2 W	2 37 58	11 09 38	13 04 52	19 32 14	16R 49.2	14 32.8	0♊26.9	2 37.8	1 19.6	9 55.7	12 38.6	8R 20.4	8 07.9	21 17.4
3 Th	2 41 54	12 07 47	26 05 49	2♍46 06	16 48.6	15 30.7	1 40.3	3 19.3	1 43.6	10 08.7	12 43.5	8 19.4	8 09.2	21 18.5
4 F	2 45 51	13 05 55	9♍33 30	16 28 15	16 46.4	16 31.5	2 53.7	4 00.8	2 07.6	10 21.9	12 48.3	8 18.4	8 10.7	21 19.6
5 Sa	2 49 47	14 04 01	23 30 29	0♎40 06	16 41.8	17 35.3	4 07.1	4 42.2	2 31.6	10 35.0	12 53.1	8 17.4	8 12.1	21 20.8
6 Su	2 53 44	15 02 04	7♎56 50	15 20 09	16 34.6	18 41.8	5 20.5	5 23.6	2 55.6	10 48.2	12 57.7	8 16.3	8 13.6	21 21.9
7 M	2 57 40	16 00 06	22 49 16	0♏23 11	16 25.1	19 50.9	6 33.8	6 04.9	3 19.6	11 01.5	13 02.3	8 15.1	8 15.1	21 23.1
8 Tu	3 01 37	16 58 07	8♏00 44	15 40 31	16 14.4	21 02.7	7 47.1	6 46.2	3 43.5	11 14.7	13 06.8	8 14.0	8 16.6	21 24.3
9 W	3 05 33	17 56 05	23 21 05	1♐00 56	16 03.6	22 17.0	9 00.3	7 27.5	4 07.5	11 28.1	13 11.3	8 12.7	8 18.1	21 25.5
10 Th	3 09 30	18 54 03	8♐38 37	16 12 49	15 54.0	23 33.7	10 13.5	8 08.7	4 31.4	11 41.4	13 15.6	8 11.5	8 19.7	21 26.7
11 F	3 13 27	19 51 58	23 42 20	1♑06 13	15 46.6	24 52.9	11 26.7	8 49.9	4 55.3	11 54.8	13 19.9	8 10.2	8 21.3	21 27.9
12 Sa	3 17 23	20 49 53	8♑23 44	15 34 24	15 41.9	26 14.4	12 39.9	9 31.0	5 19.2	12 08.2	13 24.2	8 08.8	8 22.9	21 29.2
13 Su	3 21 20	21 47 46	22 37 55	29 34 15	15 39.6	27 38.2	13 53.0	10 12.1	5 43.1	12 21.7	13 28.3	8 07.4	8 24.5	21 30.4
14 M	3 25 16	22 45 38	6♒23 30	13♒05 56	15 39.0	29 04.4	15 06.1	10 53.1	6 07.0	12 35.2	13 32.4	8 06.0	8 26.2	21 31.7
15 Tu	3 29 13	23 43 29	19 41 55	26 11 54	15 39.0	0♉32.8	16 19.2	11 34.2	6 30.8	12 48.7	13 36.3	8 04.5	8 27.9	21 32.9
16 W	3 33 09	24 41 18	2♓36 24	8♓55 58	15 38.4	2 03.4	17 32.2	12 15.1	6 54.6	13 02.2	13 40.2	8 03.0	8 29.6	21 34.2
17 Th	3 37 06	25 39 07	15 11 08	21 22 27	15 36.1	3 36.2	18 45.2	12 56.1	7 18.4	13 15.8	13 44.0	8 01.4	8 31.3	21 35.5
18 F	3 41 02	26 36 54	27 30 27	3♈35 38	15 31.4	5 11.3	19 58.2	13 37.0	7 42.2	13 29.4	13 47.8	7 59.8	8 33.0	21 36.8
19 Sa	3 44 59	27 34 40	9♈38 27	15 39 20	15 23.9	6 48.5	21 11.2	14 17.8	8 06.0	13 43.0	13 51.4	7 58.2	8 34.8	21 38.1
20 Su	3 48 56	28 32 25	21 38 40	27 36 46	15 13.7	8 28.0	22 24.1	14 58.7	8 29.7	13 56.6	13 55.0	7 56.6	8 36.6	21 39.4
21 M	3 52 52	29 30 08	3♉33 57	9♉30 29	15 01.5	10 09.6	23 37.0	15 39.4	8 53.4	14 10.3	13 58.5	7 54.9	8 38.4	21 40.7
22 Tu	3 56 49	0♊27 51	15 26 35	21 22 28	14 48.2	11 53.4	24 49.8	16 20.2	9 17.1	14 24.0	14 01.8	7 53.1	8 40.2	21 42.0
23 W	4 00 45	1 25 32	27 18 19	3♊14 18	14 35.0	13 39.5	26 02.7	17 00.9	9 40.8	14 37.7	14 05.2	7 51.3	8 42.1	21 43.3
24 Th	4 04 42	2 23 12	9♊10 36	15 07 25	14 22.8	15 27.6	27 15.5	17 41.6	10 04.4	14 51.5	14 08.4	7 49.5	8 43.9	21 44.7
25 F	4 08 38	3 20 51	21 04 55	27 03 20	14 12.6	17 18.0	28 28.2	18 22.2	10 28.0	15 05.2	14 11.5	7 47.7	8 45.8	21 46.0
26 Sa	4 12 35	4 18 28	3♋02 55	9♋03 55	14 05.0	19 10.5	29 41.0	19 02.8	10 51.6	15 19.0	14 14.5	7 45.8	8 47.7	21 47.4
27 Su	4 16 31	5 16 05	15 06 41	21 11 33	14 00.2	21 05.1	0♋53.6	19 43.4	11 15.2	15 32.8	14 17.5	7 43.9	8 49.6	21 48.7
28 M	4 20 28	6 13 39	27 18 55	3♌29 12	13D 57.9	23 01.9	2 06.3	20 23.9	11 38.7	15 46.6	14 20.4	7 42.0	8 51.6	21 50.1
29 Tu	4 24 25	7 11 13	9♌42 54	16 00 29	13 57.4	25 00.7	3 18.9	21 04.4	12 02.2	16 00.4	14 23.1	7 40.0	8 53.5	21 51.5
30 W	4 28 21	8 08 45	22 22 27	28 49 19	13R 57.9	27 01.4	4 31.5	21 44.8	12 25.6	16 14.2	14 25.8	7 38.1	8 55.5	21 52.9
31 Th	4 32 18	9 06 15	5♍21 35	11♍59 42	13 58.1	29 04.1	5 44.0	22 25.2	12 49.1	16 28.0	14 28.4	7 36.0	8 57.4	21 54.2

LONGITUDE — June 1906

Day	Sid.Time	☉	0 hr ☽	Noon ☽	True ☊	☿	♀	♂	⚳	♃	♄	♅	♆	♇
1 F	4 36 14	10♊03 44	18♍44 05	25♍35 03	13♌57.0	1♊08.5	6♋56.5	23♊05.6	13♉12.5	16♊41.8	14♓30.9	7♑34.0	8♋59.4	21♊55.6
2 Sa	4 40 11	11 01 12	2♎32 47	9♎37 20	13R 54.0	3 14.7	8 09.0	23 45.9	13 35.8	16 55.7	14 33.3	7R 31.9	9 01.4	21 57.0
3 Su	4 44 07	11 58 39	16 48 37	24 06 17	13 48.7	5 22.3	9 21.4	24 26.2	13 59.1	17 09.5	14 35.6	7 29.8	9 03.5	21 58.4
4 M	4 48 04	12 56 05	1♏29 50	8♏58 29	13 41.5	7 31.2	10 33.8	25 06.5	14 22.4	17 23.4	14 37.8	7 27.7	9 05.5	21 59.8
5 Tu	4 52 00	13 53 29	16 31 19	24 07 09	13 33.1	9 41.3	11 46.1	25 46.7	14 45.7	17 37.3	14 39.9	7 25.6	9 07.6	22 01.2
6 W	4 55 57	14 50 52	1♐44 44	9♐22 41	13 24.4	11 52.3	12 58.4	26 26.9	15 08.9	17 51.1	14 42.0	7 23.4	9 09.6	22 02.6
7 Th	4 59 54	15 48 15	16 59 37	24 34 10	13 16.8	14 03.9	14 10.7	27 07.0	15 32.1	18 05.0	14 43.9	7 21.2	9 11.7	22 04.0
8 F	5 03 50	16 45 37	2♑05 06	9♑31 18	13 10.9	16 15.9	15 22.9	27 47.1	15 55.2	18 18.9	14 45.8	7 19.0	9 13.8	22 05.4
9 Sa	5 07 47	17 42 58	16 51 51	24 06 04	13 07.2	18 28.0	16 35.1	28 27.2	16 18.3	18 32.7	14 47.5	7 16.8	9 15.9	22 06.8
10 Su	5 11 43	18 40 19	1♒13 27	8♒13 44	13D 05.8	20 39.9	17 47.2	29 07.2	16 41.4	18 46.6	14 49.1	7 14.5	9 18.0	22 08.2
11 M	5 15 40	19 37 39	15 06 51	21 52 53	13 05.9	22 51.4	18 59.3	29 47.3	17 04.4	19 00.5	14 50.7	7 12.3	9 20.1	22 09.6
12 Tu	5 19 36	20 34 58	28 32 04	5♓04 46	13 06.9	25 02.1	20 11.4	0♋27.2	17 27.3	19 14.3	14 52.2	7 10.0	9 22.2	22 11.1
13 W	5 23 33	21 32 17	11♓31 24	17 52 30	13R 07.7	27 12.0	21 23.4	1 07.2	17 50.3	19 28.2	14 53.5	7 07.7	9 24.4	22 12.5
14 Th	5 27 30	22 29 36	24 08 37	0♈20 19	13 07.4	29 20.6	22 35.3	1 47.1	18 13.2	19 42.1	14 54.8	7 05.3	9 26.5	22 13.9
15 F	5 31 26	23 26 54	6♈28 10	12 32 45	13 05.4	1♋27.9	23 47.3	2 27.0	18 36.0	19 55.9	14 55.9	7 03.0	9 28.7	22 15.3
16 Sa	5 35 23	24 24 12	18 34 37	24 34 19	13 01.4	3 33.7	24 59.2	3 06.8	18 58.8	20 09.8	14 57.0	7 00.7	9 30.8	22 16.7
17 Su	5 39 19	25 21 29	0♉32 20	6♉29 09	12 55.5	5 37.7	26 11.0	3 46.7	19 21.6	20 23.6	14 57.9	6 58.3	9 33.0	22 18.1
18 M	5 43 16	26 18 47	12 25 11	18 20 49	12 48.1	7 40.0	27 22.8	4 26.4	19 44.3	20 37.4	14 58.8	6 55.9	9 35.2	22 19.5
19 Tu	5 47 12	27 16 04	24 16 25	0♊12 17	12 39.7	9 40.3	28 34.6	5 06.2	20 06.9	20 51.2	14 59.6	6 53.5	9 37.4	22 20.9
20 W	5 51 09	28 13 20	6♊08 41	12 05 54	12 31.3	11 38.6	29 46.3	5 45.9	20 29.5	21 05.0	15 00.2	6 51.1	9 39.6	22 22.4
21 Th	5 55 05	29 10 37	18 04 08	24 03 35	12 23.6	13 34.8	0♌58.0	6 25.7	20 52.1	21 18.8	15 00.8	6 48.7	9 41.8	22 23.8
22 F	5 59 02	0♋07 53	0♋04 27	6♋06 55	12 17.3	15 28.9	2 09.6	7 05.3	21 14.6	21 32.6	15 01.3	6 46.3	9 44.0	22 25.2
23 Sa	6 02 59	1 05 08	12 11 09	18 17 21	12 12.8	17 20.9	3 21.2	7 45.0	21 37.0	21 46.4	15 01.6	6 43.9	9 46.2	22 26.6
24 Su	6 06 55	2 02 23	24 25 43	0♌36 28	12D 10.3	19 10.6	4 32.7	8 24.6	21 59.4	22 00.1	15 01.9	6 41.5	9 48.4	22 28.0
25 M	6 10 52	2 59 38	6♌49 49	13 06 03	12 09.7	20 58.2	5 44.2	9 04.2	22 21.7	22 13.9	15 02.0	6 39.1	9 50.6	22 29.4
26 Tu	6 14 48	3 56 52	19 25 25	25 48 14	12 10.4	22 43.6	6 55.6	9 43.7	22 44.0	22 27.6	15R 02.1	6 36.6	9 52.8	22 30.8
27 W	6 18 45	4 54 06	2♍14 48	8♍45 26	12 11.8	24 26.7	8 07.0	10 23.2	23 06.2	22 41.3	15 02.1	6 34.2	9 55.1	22 32.2
28 Th	6 22 41	5 51 19	15 20 27	22 00 08	12 13.2	26 07.6	9 18.3	11 02.7	23 28.4	22 54.9	15 01.9	6 31.8	9 57.3	22 33.5
29 F	6 26 38	6 48 31	28 44 46	5♎34 32	12R 13.8	27 46.2	10 29.5	11 42.2	23 50.5	23 08.6	15 01.7	6 29.3	9 59.5	22 34.9
30 Sa	6 30 34	7 45 44	12♎29 36	19 29 59	12 13.3	29 22.6	11 40.7	12 21.6	24 12.5	23 22.2	15 01.3	6 26.9	10 01.7	22 36.3

Astro Data

Dy Hr Mn	
☽0S	6 2:08
♅☍♆	7 12:39
☽0N	18 23:35
♃□♄	20 8:03
☽0S	2 12:13
☽0N	15 6:55
♄ R	26 14:36
♃☌♇	26 18:12
☽0S	29 20:08

Planet Ingress

		Dy Hr Mn
♀	♊	2 3:13
☿	♉	15 3:10
☉	♊	22 0:25
♀	♋	26 18:17
☿	♊	31 22:49
♂	♋	11 19:39
☿	♋	14 19:24
♀	♌	20 16:36
☉	♋	22 8:42
☿	♌	30 21:27

Last Aspect / ☽ Ingress (May)

Dy Hr Mn	Last Aspect	☽ Ingress	Dy Hr Mn
2 15:14	♇ ⚹	♍	3 7:03
4 20:19	♇ □	♎	5 10:53
6 21:41	♇ △	♏	7 11:23
8 14:09	☉ ☍	♐	9 10:24
11 0:54	☿ △	♑	11 10:12
13 8:15	☿ □	♒	13 12:45
15 7:03	☉ □	♓	15 19:06
17 21:04	☉ ⚹	♈	18 4:54
20 0:20	♀ ⚹	♉	20 16:49
21 21:04	♄ ⚹	♊	23 5:27
25 15:09	♀ ☌	♋	25 17:54
27 11:45	☿ ⚹	♌	28 5:14
30 8:03	☿ □	♍	30 14:11

Last Aspect / ☽ Ingress (June)

Dy Hr Mn	Last Aspect	☽ Ingress	Dy Hr Mn
1 7:26	♂ □	♎	1 19:38
3 12:34	♂ △	♏	3 21:35
4 21:01	♄ △	♐	5 21:15
7 16:15	♂ ☍	♑	7 20:40
8 22:25	♀ ☍	♒	9 21:55
11 14:05	☿ △	♓	12 2:40
14 9:40	☿ □	♈	14 11:20
16 12:55	♀ □	♉	16 22:55
19 8:20	♀ ⚹	♊	19 11:35
21 23:05	☉ ☌	♋	21 23:51
23 9:49	☿ ☌	♌	24 10:49
26 5:49	♇ ⚹	♍	26 19:50
28 20:23	☿ ⚹	♎	29 2:13

☽ Phases & Eclipses

Dy Hr Mn	
1 19:07	☽ 10♌29
8 14:09	○ 17♏03
15 7:03	☾ 23♒32
23 8:01	● 1♊16
31 6:23	☽ 8♍53
6 21:12	○ 15♐13
13 19:34	☾ 21♓50
21 23:05	● 29♊37
29 14:19	☽ 6♎54

Astro Data

1 May 1906
Julian Day # 2312
SVP 6♓34'17"
GC 25♐31.9 ⚳ 28♓33.6
Eris 24♓53.0 ⚵ 14♌17.0
⚷ 12♒33.3 ⚶ 4♓43.5
☽ Mean ☊ 16♌45.0

1 June 1906
Julian Day # 2343
SVP 6♓34'12"
GC 25♐31.9 ⚳ 7♈18.7
Eris 25♓06.3 ⚵ 22♌32.7
⚷ 12♒36.8R ⚶ 16♓11.0
☽ Mean ☊ 15♌06.5

July 1906 LONGITUDE

Day	Sid.Time	☉	0 hr ☽	Noon ☽	True ☊	☿	♀	♂	⚳	♃	♄	♅	♆	♇
1 Su	6 34 31	8♋42 55	26♎35 37	3♏46 20	12♌11.3	0♌56.8	12♌51.9	13♋01.0	24♉34.4	23♊35.8	15♓00.9	6♑24.5	10♋04.0	22♊37.7
2 M	6 38 28	9 40 07	11♏01 44	18 21 22	12R 08.0	2 28.7	14 02.9	13 40.4	24 56.3	23 49.4	15R 00.4	6R 22.0	10 06.2	22 39.0
3 Tu	6 42 24	10 37 18	25 44 32	3♐10 28	12 04.0	3 58.3	15 14.0	14 19.7	25 18.2	24 02.9	14 59.7	6 19.6	10 08.4	22 40.4
4 W	6 46 21	11 34 29	10♐38 13	18 06 47	11 59.7	5 25.6	16 24.9	14 59.0	25 39.9	24 16.4	14 59.0	6 17.2	10 10.7	22 41.7
5 Th	6 50 17	12 31 40	25 35 06	3♑02 03	11 55.9	6 50.5	17 35.8	15 38.3	26 01.6	24 29.9	14 58.2	6 14.8	10 12.9	22 43.1
6 F	6 54 14	13 28 51	10♑26 36	17 47 46	11 53.1	8 13.1	18 46.6	16 17.6	26 23.3	24 43.4	14 57.3	6 12.4	10 15.1	22 44.4
7 Sa	6 58 10	14 26 02	25 04 39	2♒16 31	11D 51.6	9 33.3	19 57.4	16 56.8	26 44.8	24 56.8	14 56.2	6 10.0	10 17.4	22 45.8
8 Su	7 02 07	15 23 13	9♒22 47	16 23 00	11 51.3	10 51.1	21 08.1	17 36.0	27 06.3	25 10.2	14 55.1	6 07.6	10 19.6	22 47.1
9 M	7 06 03	16 20 24	23 16 54	0♓04 24	11 52.2	12 06.4	22 18.7	18 15.2	27 27.7	25 23.6	14 53.9	6 05.2	10 21.8	22 48.4
10 Tu	7 10 00	17 17 36	6♓45 30	13 20 23	11 53.6	13 19.1	23 29.3	18 54.3	27 49.0	25 36.9	14 52.6	6 02.8	10 24.0	22 49.7
11 W	7 13 57	18 14 48	19 49 18	26 12 37	11 55.1	14 29.3	24 39.8	19 33.5	28 10.3	25 50.2	14 51.2	6 00.4	10 26.3	22 51.0
12 Th	7 17 53	19 12 01	2♈30 46	8♈44 14	11R 56.2	15 36.7	25 50.2	20 12.6	28 31.5	26 03.4	14 49.7	5 58.1	10 28.5	22 52.3
13 F	7 21 50	20 09 14	14 53 34	20 59 17	11 56.6	16 41.5	27 00.6	20 51.6	28 52.6	26 16.6	14 48.1	5 55.7	10 30.7	22 53.6
14 Sa	7 25 46	21 06 28	27 01 59	3♉02 13	11 56.0	17 43.3	28 10.9	21 30.7	29 13.6	26 29.8	14 46.4	5 53.4	10 32.9	22 54.9
15 Su	7 29 43	22 03 42	9♉00 33	14 57 33	11 54.6	18 42.3	29 21.1	22 09.7	29 34.6	26 43.0	14 44.6	5 51.1	10 35.1	22 56.1
16 M	7 33 39	23 00 57	20 53 45	26 49 38	11 52.4	19 38.1	0♍31.2	22 48.7	29 55.4	26 56.1	14 42.8	5 48.8	10 37.3	22 57.4
17 Tu	7 37 36	23 58 13	2♊45 41	8♊42 22	11 49.9	20 30.8	1 41.3	23 27.7	0♊16.2	27 09.1	14 40.8	5 46.5	10 39.5	22 58.6
18 W	7 41 32	24 55 29	14 40 03	20 39 09	11 47.2	21 20.3	2 51.3	24 06.7	0 36.9	27 22.1	14 38.7	5 44.3	10 41.6	22 59.9
19 Th	7 45 29	25 52 46	26 39 58	2♋42 48	11 44.8	22 06.3	4 01.3	24 45.7	0 57.5	27 35.1	14 36.6	5 42.0	10 43.8	23 01.1
20 F	7 49 26	26 50 03	8♋47 56	14 55 33	11 42.9	22 48.7	5 11.2	25 24.6	1 18.0	27 48.0	14 34.4	5 39.8	10 46.0	23 02.3
21 Sa	7 53 22	27 47 21	21 05 52	27 19 02	11 41.7	23 27.4	6 20.9	26 03.5	1 38.4	28 00.9	14 32.0	5 37.6	10 48.2	23 03.5
22 Su	7 57 19	28 44 40	3♌35 11	9♌54 25	11D 41.3	24 02.2	7 30.7	26 42.4	1 58.7	28 13.7	14 29.6	5 35.4	10 50.3	23 04.7
23 M	8 01 15	29 41 59	16 16 51	22 42 33	11 41.5	24 33.0	8 40.3	27 21.2	2 18.9	28 26.4	14 27.1	5 33.3	10 52.4	23 05.9
24 Tu	8 05 12	0♌39 18	29 11 34	5♍43 59	11 42.2	24 59.5	9 49.8	28 00.1	2 39.0	28 39.2	14 24.6	5 31.1	10 54.6	23 07.1
25 W	8 09 08	1 36 38	12♍19 49	18 59 08	11 43.0	25 21.7	10 59.3	28 38.9	2 59.0	28 51.8	14 21.9	5 29.0	10 56.7	23 08.2
26 Th	8 13 05	2 33 59	25 41 56	2♎28 15	11 43.9	25 39.4	12 08.6	29 17.7	3 19.0	29 04.4	14 19.2	5 26.9	10 58.8	23 09.3
27 F	8 17 01	3 31 20	9♎18 05	16 11 23	11 44.5	25 52.3	13 17.9	29 56.4	3 38.8	29 17.0	14 16.3	5 24.9	11 00.9	23 10.5
28 Sa	8 20 58	4 28 41	23 08 06	0♏08 08	11R 44.8	26 00.4	14 27.1	0♌35.2	3 58.5	29 29.5	14 13.4	5 22.8	11 03.0	23 11.6
29 Su	8 24 55	5 26 03	7♏11 20	14 17 29	11 44.7	26R 03.5	15 36.2	1 13.9	4 18.1	29 41.9	14 10.5	5 20.8	11 05.1	23 12.7
30 M	8 28 51	6 23 25	21 26 19	28 37 28	11 44.4	26 01.5	16 45.2	1 52.6	4 37.5	29 54.2	14 07.4	5 18.9	11 07.1	23 13.8
31 Tu	8 32 48	7 20 48	5♐50 32	13♐05 01	11 44.0	25 54.3	17 54.0	2 31.3	4 56.9	0♋06.6	14 04.3	5 16.9	11 09.2	23 14.9

August 1906 LONGITUDE

Day	Sid.Time	☉	0 hr ☽	Noon ☽	True ☊	☿	♀	♂	⚳	♃	♄	♅	♆	♇
1 W	8 36 44	8♌18 12	20♐20 23	27♐36 00	11♌43.6	25♌42.0	19♍02.8	3♌09.9	5♊16.2	0♋18.8	14♓01.1	5♑15.0	11♋11.2	23♊15.9
2 Th	8 40 41	9 15 36	4♑51 14	12♑05 23	11R 43.3	25R 24.5	20 11.5	3 48.5	5 35.3	0 31.0	13R 57.8	5R 13.1	11 13.3	23 17.0
3 F	8 44 37	10 13 01	19 17 48	26 27 47	11 43.2	25 01.9	21 20.0	4 27.2	5 54.3	0 43.1	13 54.4	5 11.3	11 15.3	23 18.0
4 Sa	8 48 34	11 10 27	3♒34 42	10♒37 59	11 43.2	24 34.4	22 28.5	5 05.8	6 13.2	0 55.1	13 51.0	5 09.5	11 17.3	23 19.0
5 Su	8 52 30	12 07 53	17 37 06	24 31 39	11 43.2	24 02.4	23 36.8	5 44.3	6 32.0	1 07.1	13 47.6	5 07.7	11 19.2	23 20.0
6 M	8 56 27	13 05 21	1♓21 18	8♓05 48	11 43.1	23 26.0	24 45.0	6 22.9	6 50.7	1 19.0	13 44.0	5 05.9	11 21.2	23 21.0
7 Tu	9 00 24	14 02 50	14 45 02	21 18 58	11 42.9	22 45.8	25 53.1	7 01.4	7 09.2	1 30.9	13 40.4	5 04.2	11 23.2	23 22.0
8 W	9 04 20	15 00 20	27 47 41	4♈11 22	11 42.6	22 02.4	27 01.1	7 39.9	7 27.6	1 42.6	13 36.7	5 02.5	11 25.1	23 22.9
9 Th	9 08 17	15 57 51	10♈30 15	16 44 40	11 42.1	21 16.3	28 09.0	8 18.4	7 45.9	1 54.3	13 33.0	5 00.9	11 27.0	23 23.9
10 F	9 12 13	16 55 24	22 55 00	29 01 43	11 41.7	20 28.4	29 16.7	8 56.9	8 04.0	2 05.9	13 29.2	4 59.3	11 28.9	23 24.8
11 Sa	9 16 10	17 52 58	5♉05 18	11♉06 17	11D 41.4	19 39.4	0♎24.4	9 35.4	8 22.0	2 17.5	13 25.3	4 57.7	11 30.8	23 25.7
12 Su	9 20 06	18 50 34	17 05 12	23 02 38	11 41.4	18 50.4	1 31.9	10 13.9	8 39.9	2 28.9	13 21.4	4 56.1	11 32.7	23 26.6
13 M	9 24 03	19 48 11	28 59 10	4♊55 23	11 41.7	18 02.1	2 39.2	10 52.3	8 57.6	2 40.3	13 17.5	4 54.6	11 34.5	23 27.4
14 Tu	9 27 59	20 45 49	10♊51 50	16 49 06	11 42.4	17 15.6	3 46.5	11 30.7	9 15.2	2 51.6	13 13.5	4 53.2	11 36.3	23 28.3
15 W	9 31 56	21 43 30	22 47 42	28 48 09	11 43.3	16 31.8	4 53.6	12 09.1	9 32.7	3 02.8	13 09.4	4 51.8	11 38.2	23 29.1
16 Th	9 35 53	22 41 11	4♋50 57	10♋56 31	11 44.3	15 51.7	6 00.6	12 47.5	9 49.9	3 14.0	13 05.3	4 50.4	11 40.0	23 29.9
17 F	9 39 49	23 38 54	17 05 15	23 17 30	11 45.2	15 16.0	7 07.4	13 25.9	10 07.1	3 25.0	13 01.1	4 49.0	11 41.7	23 30.7
18 Sa	9 43 46	24 36 39	29 33 31	5♌53 33	11R 45.8	14 45.5	8 14.1	14 04.3	10 24.0	3 36.0	12 56.9	4 47.8	11 43.5	23 31.5
19 Su	9 47 42	25 34 25	12♌17 45	18 46 12	11 45.7	14 21.0	9 20.7	14 42.6	10 40.9	3 46.9	12 52.7	4 46.5	11 45.2	23 32.3
20 M	9 51 39	26 32 12	25 18 55	1♍55 50	11 45.0	14 03.1	10 27.1	15 21.0	10 57.5	3 57.7	12 48.4	4 45.3	11 46.9	23 33.0
21 Tu	9 55 35	27 30 01	8♍36 52	15 21 48	11 43.5	13D 52.1	11 33.3	15 59.3	11 14.0	4 08.3	12 44.1	4 44.1	11 48.6	23 33.8
22 W	9 59 32	28 27 50	22 10 24	29 02 25	11 41.5	13 48.6	12 39.4	16 37.6	11 30.3	4 18.9	12 39.7	4 43.0	11 50.3	23 34.5
23 Th	10 03 28	29 25 42	5♎57 29	12♎55 16	11 39.1	13 52.7	13 45.4	17 15.9	11 46.5	4 29.4	12 35.4	4 41.9	11 51.9	23 35.2
24 F	10 07 25	0♍23 34	19 55 25	26 57 32	11 36.9	14 04.6	14 51.1	17 54.2	12 02.4	4 39.8	12 30.9	4 40.9	11 53.5	23 35.8
25 Sa	10 11 22	1 21 28	4♏01 14	11♏06 11	11 35.1	14 24.5	15 56.7	18 32.4	12 18.2	4 50.1	12 26.5	4 39.9	11 55.1	23 36.5
26 Su	10 15 18	2 19 23	18 12 00	25 18 23	11D 34.2	14 52.4	17 02.1	19 10.6	12 33.8	5 00.3	12 22.0	4 38.9	11 56.7	23 37.1
27 M	10 19 15	3 17 19	2♐24 59	9♐31 32	11 34.1	15 28.0	18 07.3	19 48.9	12 49.3	5 10.4	12 17.5	4 38.0	11 58.3	23 37.7
28 Tu	10 23 11	4 15 17	16 37 44	23 43 19	11 35.0	16 11.5	19 12.4	20 27.1	13 04.5	5 20.4	12 13.0	4 37.2	11 59.8	23 38.3
29 W	10 27 08	5 13 16	0♑48 02	7♑51 36	11 36.3	17 02.4	20 17.2	21 05.3	13 19.6	5 30.3	12 08.5	4 36.4	12 01.3	23 38.9
30 Th	10 31 04	6 11 16	14 53 46	21 54 14	11 37.7	18 00.5	21 21.8	21 43.4	13 34.4	5 40.1	12 04.0	4 35.6	12 02.8	23 39.4
31 F	10 35 01	7 09 17	28 52 45	5♒49 00	11R 38.6	19 05.6	22 26.2	22 21.6	13 49.1	5 49.7	11 59.4	4 34.9	12 04.2	23 40.0

Astro Data	Planet Ingress	Last Aspect	☽ Ingress	Last Aspect	☽ Ingress	☽ Phases & Eclipses	Astro Data
Dy Hr Mn	Dy Hr Mn	Dy Hr Mn	Dy Hr Mn	Dy Hr Mn	Dy Hr Mn	Dy Hr Mn	1 July 1906
☽0N 12 15:13	♀ ♍ 16 1:18	30 18:40 ♃ △	♏ 1 5:43	1 8:55 ☿ △	♑ 1 15:58	6 4:27 ○ 13♑11	Julian Day # 2373
☽0S 27 2:05	⚳ ♊ 16 17:18	2 6:32 ♄ △	♐ 3 6:53	3 2:40 ♀ △	♒ 3 17:57	13 10:13 ☾ 20♈05	SVP 6♓34'08"
☿ R 29 14:38	☉ ♌ 23 19:33	4 22:03 ♃ ☍	♑ 5 7:06	5 11:11 ☿ ☍	♓ 5 21:36	21 12:59 ● 27♋50	GC 25♐32.0 ⚴ 13♈58.6
	♂ ♌ 27 14:13	6 9:25 ♂ ☍	♒ 7 8:11	7 21:16 ♀ ☍	♈ 8 4:07	21 13:14:15 ● P 0.336	Eris 25♓08.5R ⚵ 2♍24.9
☽0N 8 24:00	♃ ♋ 30 23:12	9 3:34 ♃ △	♓ 9 11:52	10 0:57 ♇ ⚹	♉ 10 13:55	28 19:56 ☽ 4♏48	⚷ 11♒43.0R ⚶ 23♓49.4
♀0S 11 13:20		11 11:17 ♃ □	♈ 11 19:12	12 4:04 ☿ □	♊ 13 2:03		☽ Mean ☊ 13♌31.2
☿ D 22 11:16	♀ ♎ 11 3:21	14 1:15 ♀ △	♉ 14 5:55	15 1:22 ♇ ☌	♋ 15 14:23	4 13:00 ○ 11♒13	
☽0S 23 7:44	☉ ♍ 24 2:14	16 3:37 ☉ ⚹	♊ 16 18:25	16 16:11 ♄ △	♌ 18 0:50	4 13:00 ● T 1.780	1 August 1906
♃☍♅ 24 14:14		19 1:39 ♃ ☌	♋ 19 6:37	20 1:27 ☉ ☌	♍ 20 8:31	12 2:47 ☾ 18♉28	Julian Day # 2404
♄△♆ 30 16:50		21 12:59 ☉ ☌	♌ 21 17:09	22 2:27 ♇ □	♎ 22 13:40	20 1:27 ● 26♌07	SVP 6♓34'03"
		23 22:47 ♃ ⚹	♍ 24 1:29	24 6:16 ♇ △	♏ 24 17:10	20 1:12:42 ● P 0.315	GC 25♐32.1 ⚴ 17♈39.7
		26 6:06 ♂ ⚹	♎ 26 7:38	26 1:10 ♂ □	♐ 26 19:55	27 0:42 ☽ 2♐50	Eris 24♓59.4R ⚵ 13♍35.7
		28 10:53 ♃ △	♏ 28 11:46	28 11:51 ♇ ☍	♑ 28 22:38		⚷ 10♒09.3R ⚶ 26♓05.3R
		30 7:41 ☿ □	♐ 30 14:17	30 11:00 ♀ □	♒ 31 1:56		☽ Mean ☊ 11♌52.7

LONGITUDE — September 1906

Day	Sid.Time	☉	0 hr ☽	Noon ☽	True ☊	☿	♀	♂	⚳	♃	♄	♅	♆	♇
1 Sa	10 38 57	8♍07 20	12♒42 44	19♒33 37	11♌38.5	20♌17.2	23♎30.4	22♌59.7	14♊03.6	5♋59.3	11♓54.9	4♑34.3	12♋05.6	23♊40.5
2 Su	10 42 54	9 05 25	26 21 24	3♓05 49	11R 37.0	21 34.8	24 34.4	23 37.9	14 17.8	6 08.7	11R 50.3	4R 33.7	12 07.0	23 41.0
3 M	10 46 51	10 03 31	9♓46 38	16 23 39	11 34.2	22 58.1	25 38.2	24 16.0	14 31.9	6 18.1	11 45.7	4 33.1	12 08.4	23 41.4
4 Tu	10 50 47	11 01 39	22 56 43	29 25 43	11 30.2	24 26.6	26 41.7	24 54.1	14 45.7	6 27.3	11 41.1	4 32.6	12 09.8	23 41.9
5 W	10 54 44	11 59 49	5♈50 37	12♈11 27	11 25.2	25 59.6	27 44.9	25 32.2	14 59.4	6 36.4	11 36.5	4 32.1	12 11.1	23 42.3
6 Th	10 58 40	12 58 00	18 28 19	24 41 22	11 20.0	27 36.8	28 48.0	26 10.3	15 12.8	6 45.4	11 31.9	4 31.7	12 12.4	23 42.7
7 F	11 02 37	13 56 14	0♉50 50	6♉57 01	11 15.1	29 17.5	29 50.8	26 48.4	15 26.0	6 54.2	11 27.4	4 31.3	12 13.6	23 43.1
8 Sa	11 06 33	14 54 29	13 00 17	19 01 02	11 11.1	1♍01.3	0♏53.3	27 26.4	15 38.9	7 02.9	11 22.8	4 31.0	12 14.9	23 43.4
9 Su	11 10 30	15 52 47	24 59 45	0♊56 56	11 08.4	2 47.7	1 55.5	28 04.5	15 51.7	7 11.6	11 18.2	4 30.7	12 16.1	23 43.8
10 M	11 14 26	16 51 06	6♊53 09	12 48 58	11D 07.1	4 36.1	2 57.5	28 42.5	16 04.2	7 20.1	11 13.7	4 30.5	12 17.3	23 44.1
11 Tu	11 18 23	17 49 28	18 44 59	24 41 51	11 07.3	6 26.2	3 59.2	29 20.6	16 16.5	7 28.4	11 09.1	4 30.3	12 18.4	23 44.4
12 W	11 22 19	18 47 52	0♋40 09	6♋40 32	11 08.4	8 17.6	5 00.7	29 58.6	16 28.5	7 36.6	11 04.6	4 30.2	12 19.6	23 44.7
13 Th	11 26 16	19 46 18	12 43 36	18 49 56	11 10.1	10 09.9	6 01.8	0♍36.6	16 40.3	7 44.7	11 00.1	4D 30.1	12 20.7	23 44.9
14 F	11 30 13	20 44 46	25 00 06	1♌14 36	11R 11.4	12 02.7	7 02.6	1 14.6	16 51.8	7 52.7	10 55.6	4 30.1	12 21.7	23 45.2
15 Sa	11 34 09	21 43 16	7♌33 52	13 58 17	11 11.8	13 55.9	8 03.1	1 52.6	17 03.1	8 00.5	10 51.1	4 30.2	12 22.8	23 45.4
16 Su	11 38 06	22 41 48	20 28 08	27 03 36	11 10.6	15 49.1	9 03.3	2 30.6	17 14.1	8 08.2	10 46.6	4 30.2	12 23.8	23 45.6
17 M	11 42 02	23 40 22	3♍44 43	10♍31 28	11 07.5	17 42.2	10 03.2	3 08.6	17 24.9	8 15.8	10 42.2	4 30.4	12 24.8	23 45.7
18 Tu	11 45 59	24 38 58	17 23 37	24 20 52	11 02.5	19 35.0	11 02.7	3 46.5	17 35.3	8 23.2	10 37.8	4 30.6	12 25.7	23 45.9
19 W	11 49 55	25 37 36	1♎22 45	8♎28 43	10 55.9	21 27.3	12 01.8	4 24.5	17 45.6	8 30.5	10 33.5	4 30.8	12 26.6	23 46.0
20 Th	11 53 52	26 36 16	15 38 04	22 50 06	10 48.7	23 19.0	13 00.6	5 02.4	17 55.5	8 37.6	10 29.1	4 31.1	12 27.5	23 46.1
21 F	11 57 48	27 34 58	0♏04 01	7♏19 01	10 41.6	25 10.1	13 59.0	5 40.3	18 05.1	8 44.5	10 24.8	4 31.4	12 28.3	23 46.2
22 Sa	12 01 45	28 33 41	14 34 20	21 49 14	10 35.5	27 00.5	14 57.0	6 18.3	18 14.5	8 51.4	10 20.6	4 31.8	12 29.2	23 46.2
23 Su	12 05 42	29 32 27	29 03 04	6♐15 15	10 31.3	28 50.0	15 54.5	6 56.2	18 23.5	8 58.0	10 16.4	4 32.3	12 30.0	23 46.3
24 M	12 09 38	0♎31 14	13♐25 20	20 32 57	10D 29.1	0♎38.7	16 51.6	7 34.1	18 32.3	9 04.6	10 12.2	4 32.8	12 30.7	23R 46.3
25 Tu	12 13 35	1 30 02	27 37 49	4♑39 47	10 28.7	2 26.6	17 48.3	8 11.9	18 40.8	9 10.9	10 08.1	4 33.3	12 31.4	23 46.3
26 W	12 17 31	2 28 53	11♑38 45	18 34 40	10 29.5	4 13.5	18 44.5	8 49.8	18 49.0	9 17.1	10 04.0	4 33.9	12 32.1	23 46.2
27 Th	12 21 28	3 27 45	25 27 34	2♒17 28	10R 30.4	5 59.6	19 40.2	9 27.7	18 56.8	9 23.2	10 00.0	4 34.6	12 32.8	23 46.2
28 F	12 25 24	4 26 39	9♒04 27	15 48 32	10 30.5	7 44.7	20 35.4	10 05.5	19 04.4	9 29.1	9 56.1	4 35.3	12 33.4	23 46.1
29 Sa	12 29 21	5 25 34	22 29 46	29 08 12	10 28.9	9 29.0	21 30.1	10 43.3	19 11.6	9 34.8	9 52.1	4 36.0	12 34.0	23 46.0
30 Su	12 33 17	6 24 32	5♓43 50	12♓16 39	10 24.8	11 12.3	22 24.2	11 21.2	19 18.6	9 40.4	9 48.3	4 36.8	12 34.6	23 45.9

LONGITUDE — October 1906

Day	Sid.Time	☉	0 hr ☽	Noon ☽	True ☊	☿	♀	♂	⚳	♃	♄	♅	♆	♇
1 M	12 37 14	7♎23 31	18♓46 37	25♓13 42	10♌18.3	12♎54.8	23♏17.7	11♍59.0	19♊25.2	9♋45.8	9♓44.5	4♑37.7	12♋35.1	23♊45.7
2 Tu	12 41 11	8 22 32	1♈37 51	7♈59 01	10R 09.3	14 36.4	24 10.7	12 36.8	19 31.4	9 51.0	9R 40.7	4 38.6	12 35.6	23R 45.6
3 W	12 45 07	9 21 35	14 17 11	20 32 21	9 58.8	16 17.2	25 03.0	13 14.6	19 37.4	9 56.1	9 37.1	4 39.5	12 36.1	23 45.4
4 Th	12 49 04	10 20 40	26 44 31	2♉53 47	9 47.5	17 57.1	25 54.8	13 52.4	19 43.0	10 01.0	9 33.4	4 40.5	12 36.5	23 45.2
5 F	12 53 00	11 19 48	9♉00 15	15 04 04	9 36.5	19 36.2	26 45.8	14 30.1	19 48.2	10 05.7	9 29.9	4 41.6	12 36.9	23 44.9
6 Sa	12 56 57	12 18 58	21 05 30	27 04 48	9 26.7	21 14.5	27 36.2	15 07.9	19 53.1	10 10.3	9 26.4	4 42.7	12 37.3	23 44.7
7 Su	13 00 53	13 18 10	3♊02 20	8♊58 29	9 19.0	22 52.0	28 25.8	15 45.7	19 57.7	10 14.7	9 23.0	4 43.8	12 37.6	23 44.4
8 M	13 04 50	14 17 24	14 53 42	20 48 30	9 13.8	24 28.7	29 14.8	16 23.4	20 01.9	10 18.9	9 19.7	4 45.0	12 37.9	23 44.1
9 Tu	13 08 46	15 16 41	26 43 27	2♋39 07	9 10.9	26 04.7	0♐02.9	17 01.2	20 05.8	10 22.9	9 16.4	4 46.3	12 38.2	23 43.8
10 W	13 12 43	16 15 59	8♋36 09	14 35 12	9D 10.0	27 40.0	0 50.3	17 38.9	20 09.3	10 26.8	9 13.2	4 47.6	12 38.4	23 43.5
11 Th	13 16 39	17 15 21	20 36 55	26 41 59	9 10.3	29 14.5	1 36.9	18 16.7	20 12.4	10 30.5	9 10.1	4 48.9	12 38.6	23 43.1
12 F	13 20 36	18 14 44	2♌51 05	9♌04 51	9R 10.6	0♏48.3	2 22.6	18 54.4	20 15.1	10 33.9	9 07.1	4 50.3	12 38.8	23 42.7
13 Sa	13 24 33	19 14 10	15 23 53	21 48 45	9 09.9	2 21.4	3 07.4	19 32.1	20 17.5	10 37.3	9 04.1	4 51.8	12 38.9	23 42.3
14 Su	13 28 29	20 13 38	28 19 54	4♍57 41	9 07.3	3 53.9	3 51.3	20 09.8	20 19.5	10 40.4	9 01.2	4 53.3	12 39.0	23 41.9
15 M	13 32 26	21 13 08	11♍42 22	18 33 59	9 02.1	5 25.7	4 34.2	20 47.5	20 21.1	10 43.3	8 58.4	4 54.8	12 39.0	23 41.5
16 Tu	13 36 22	22 12 40	25 32 29	2♎37 33	8 54.3	6 56.8	5 16.1	21 25.2	20 22.3	10 46.0	8 55.7	4 56.4	12R 39.1	23 41.0
17 W	13 40 19	23 12 15	9♎48 43	17 05 19	8 44.3	8 27.2	5 57.0	22 02.9	20 23.2	10 48.6	8 53.1	4 58.0	12 39.0	23 40.5
18 Th	13 44 15	24 11 52	24 26 29	1♏51 12	8 33.1	9 57.0	6 36.8	22 40.6	20R 23.6	10 51.0	8 50.5	4 59.7	12 39.0	23 40.0
19 F	13 48 12	25 11 30	9♏18 22	16 46 49	8 22.0	11 26.1	7 15.4	23 18.3	20 23.6	10 53.1	8 48.1	5 01.4	12 38.9	23 39.5
20 Sa	13 52 08	26 11 11	24 15 21	1♐42 49	8 12.2	12 54.6	7 52.9	23 55.9	20 23.3	10 55.1	8 45.7	5 03.2	12 38.8	23 39.0
21 Su	13 56 05	27 10 53	9♐08 12	16 30 35	8 04.8	14 22.4	8 29.1	24 33.6	20 22.6	10 56.9	8 43.4	5 05.0	12 38.7	23 38.4
22 M	14 00 02	28 10 37	23 49 14	1♑03 33	8 00.1	15 49.5	9 04.1	25 11.2	20 21.4	10 58.5	8 41.3	5 06.9	12 38.5	23 37.8
23 Tu	14 03 58	29 10 23	8♑13 08	15 17 47	7 57.9	17 15.8	9 37.7	25 48.8	20 19.9	10 59.9	8 39.2	5 08.8	12 38.3	23 37.2
24 W	14 07 55	0♏10 11	22 17 24	29 12 01	7 57.4	18 41.5	10 09.8	26 26.4	20 17.9	11 01.1	8 37.2	5 10.8	12 38.0	23 36.6
25 Th	14 11 51	1 10 00	6♒01 47	12♒46 54	7 57.4	20 06.4	10 40.6	27 04.0	20 15.6	11 02.1	8 35.3	5 12.8	12 37.8	23 36.0
26 F	14 15 48	2 09 51	19 27 38	26 04 17	7 56.6	21 30.5	11 09.8	27 41.6	20 12.8	11 02.9	8 33.5	5 14.8	12 37.5	23 35.3
27 Sa	14 19 44	3 09 43	2♓37 07	9♓06 27	7 53.7	22 53.8	11 37.4	28 19.2	20 09.7	11 03.5	8 31.8	5 16.9	12 37.1	23 34.6
28 Su	14 23 41	4 09 37	15 32 32	21 55 36	7 48.0	24 16.2	12 03.4	28 56.7	20 06.1	11 03.9	8 30.2	5 19.0	12 36.7	23 33.9
29 M	14 27 37	5 09 33	28 15 53	4♈33 32	7 39.3	25 37.7	12 27.7	29 34.3	20 02.2	11R 04.1	8 28.7	5 21.2	12 36.3	23 33.2
30 Tu	14 31 34	6 09 31	10♈48 43	17 01 31	7 27.8	26 58.1	12 50.2	0♎11.8	19 57.8	11 04.1	8 27.3	5 23.4	12 35.9	23 32.5
31 W	14 35 31	7 09 30	23 12 03	29 20 24	7 14.2	28 17.5	13 10.8	0 49.4	19 53.0	11 03.9	8 25.9	5 25.7	12 35.4	23 31.7

Astro Data Dy Hr Mn	Planet Ingress Dy Hr Mn	Last Aspect Dy Hr Mn	☽ Ingress Dy Hr Mn	Last Aspect Dy Hr Mn	☽ Ingress Dy Hr Mn	☽ Phases & Eclipses Dy Hr Mn	Astro Data
☽0N 5 8:31	♀ ♏ 7 15:33	1 19:33 ♀ △	♓ 2 6:28	1 9:16 ♇ □	♈ 1 20:56	2 23:36 ○ 9♓34	1 September 1906
♅D 14 8:12	☿ ♍ 7 21:54	4 1:23 ♇ □	♈ 4 13:04	3 18:13 ♇ ✶	♉ 4 6:20	10 20:54 ☾ 17♊13	Julian Day # 2435
☽0S 19 15:00	♂ ♍ 12 12:53	6 20:45 ♀ ☍	♉ 6 22:21	6 13:08 ♀ ☍	♊ 6 17:52	18 12:33 ● 24♍40	SVP 6♓33'59"
☉0S 23 23:15	☉ ♎ 23 23:15	9 5:52 ♂ □	♊ 9 10:05	8 20:37 ☿ △	♋ 9 6:38	25 6:11 ☽ 1♑16	GC 25♐32.2 ⚴ 16♈12.0R
♇R 24 14:11	☿ ♎ 24 3:26	11 21:52 ♂ ✶	♋ 11 22:40	11 17:42 ☿ □	♌ 11 18:27		Eris 24♓41.5R ✵ 25♍12.5
☿0S 25 19:55		13 14:00 ☉ ✶	♌ 14 9:37	13 15:30 ♇ ✶	♍ 14 3:02	2 12:48 ○ 8♈25	⚷ 8♒34.0R ⚶ 21♓20.7R
	♀ ♐ 9 10:31	16 6:01 ♇ ✶	♍ 16 17:18	15 20:50 ♇ □	♎ 16 7:34	10 15:39 ☾ 16♋25	☽ Mean ☊ 10♌14.2
♃△♄ 1 8:36	☿ ♏ 11 23:37	18 12:33 ☉ ☌	♎ 18 21:39	17 22:45 ♇ △	♏ 18 9:00	17 22:43 ● 23♎39	
☽0N 2 16:13	☉ ♏ 24 7:55	20 13:33 ♇ △	♏ 20 23:53	19 22:56 ♂ ✶	♐ 20 9:14	24 13:50 ☽ 0♒15	1 October 1906
♆R 16 16:57	♂ ♎ 30 4:26	23 0:00 ☉ ✶	♐ 23 1:35	22 6:51 ☉ ✶	♑ 22 10:14		Julian Day # 2465
☽0S 17 0:44		24 17:27 ♇ ☍	♑ 25 4:02	24 6:58 ♂ △	♒ 24 13:24		SVP 6♓33'57"
⚳R 19 2:42		26 12:18 ♀ ✶	♒ 27 7:58	26 7:29 ♇ △	♓ 26 19:11		GC 25♐32.2 ⚴ 9♈19.1R
☽0N 29 23:04		29 2:17 ♇ △	♓ 29 13:34	29 1:59 ♂ ☍	♈ 29 3:18		Eris 24♓20.7R ✵ 6♎29.1
♃R 30 0:16				31 0:39 ♇ ✶	♉ 31 13:18		⚷ 7♒36.3R ⚶ 14♓12.6R
							☽ Mean ☊ 8♌38.9

November 1906 LONGITUDE

Day	Sid.Time	☉	0 hr ☽	Noon ☽	True ☊	☿	♀	♂	⚳	♃	♄	♅	♆	♇
1 Th	14 39 27	8♏09 31	5♉26 38	11♉30 49	6♌59.7	29♏35.7	13♐29.6	1♎26.9	19♊47.9	11♋03.5	8♓24.7	5♑28.0	12♋34.9	23♊31.0
2 F	14 43 24	9 09 35	17 33 04	23 33 30	6R45.4	0♐52.6	13 46.4	2 04.4	19R42.4	11R02.9	8R23.6	5 30.3	12R34.3	23R30.2
3 Sa	14 47 20	10 09 40	29 32 16	5♊29 32	6 32.5	2 08.1	14 01.2	2 41.9	19 36.4	11 02.1	8 22.6	5 32.7	12 33.8	23 29.4
4 Su	14 51 17	11 09 47	11♊25 33	17 20 35	6 21.9	3 22.0	14 14.0	3 19.4	19 30.1	11 01.1	8 21.7	5 35.1	12 33.2	23 28.6
5 M	14 55 13	12 09 56	23 14 59	29 09 08	6 14.2	4 34.2	14 24.6	3 56.9	19 23.4	10 59.9	8 20.9	5 37.5	12 32.5	23 27.8
6 Tu	14 59 10	13 10 07	5♋03 27	10♋58 27	6 09.4	5 44.5	14 33.0	4 34.4	19 16.3	10 58.5	8 20.2	5 40.0	12 31.9	23 26.9
7 W	15 03 06	14 10 20	16 54 39	22 52 39	6 07.2	6 52.7	14 39.1	5 11.9	19 08.8	10 56.9	8 19.6	5 42.6	12 31.2	23 26.1
8 Th	15 07 03	15 10 35	28 53 04	4♌56 33	6 06.6	7 58.4	14 43.0	5 49.3	19 00.9	10 55.1	8 19.1	5 45.1	12 30.5	23 25.2
9 F	15 11 00	16 10 52	11♌03 45	17 15 22	6 06.7	9 01.5	14R44.5	6 26.8	18 52.7	10 53.1	8 18.7	5 47.7	12 29.7	23 24.3
10 Sa	15 14 56	17 11 11	23 32 04	29 54 29	6 06.1	10 01.5	14 43.7	7 04.2	18 44.1	10 50.9	8 18.4	5 50.4	12 28.9	23 23.4
11 Su	15 18 53	18 11 33	6♍23 12	12♍58 45	6 03.9	10 58.2	14 40.5	7 41.7	18 35.2	10 48.5	8 18.3	5 53.0	12 28.1	23 22.5
12 M	15 22 49	19 11 55	19 41 33	26 31 52	5 59.3	11 51.0	14 34.8	8 19.1	18 25.9	10 45.9	8D18.2	5 55.7	12 27.2	23 21.5
13 Tu	15 26 46	20 12 20	3♎29 49	10♎35 20	5 52.0	12 39.5	14 26.7	8 56.5	18 16.2	10 43.1	8 18.2	5 58.5	12 26.4	23 20.6
14 W	15 30 42	21 12 47	17 48 07	25 07 37	5 42.4	13 23.2	14 16.2	9 33.9	18 06.2	10 40.2	8 18.4	6 01.3	12 25.4	23 19.6
15 Th	15 34 39	22 13 16	2♏33 06	10♏03 34	5 31.5	14 01.5	14 03.3	10 11.3	17 55.9	10 37.0	8 18.6	6 04.1	12 24.5	23 18.6
16 F	15 38 35	23 13 46	17 37 50	25 14 37	5 20.4	14 33.7	13 47.9	10 48.7	17 45.3	10 33.6	8 18.9	6 06.9	12 23.5	23 17.7
17 Sa	15 42 32	24 14 18	2♐52 28	10♐30 00	5 10.6	14 59.1	13 30.2	11 26.0	17 34.3	10 30.1	8 19.4	6 09.8	12 22.6	23 16.7
18 Su	15 46 29	25 14 51	18 05 51	25 38 44	5 03.0	15 17.1	13 10.2	12 03.4	17 23.1	10 26.3	8 20.0	6 12.7	12 21.5	23 15.7
19 M	15 50 25	26 15 26	3♑07 33	10♑31 26	4 58.2	15R26.7	12 48.0	12 40.7	17 11.6	10 22.4	8 20.6	6 15.6	12 20.5	23 14.6
20 Tu	15 54 22	27 16 02	17 49 41	25 01 50	4D56.1	15 27.3	12 23.6	13 18.0	16 59.8	10 18.3	8 21.4	6 18.6	12 19.4	23 13.6
21 W	15 58 18	28 16 39	2♒07 36	9♒06 55	4 55.8	15 18.2	11 57.2	13 55.3	16 47.7	10 14.0	8 22.3	6 21.6	12 18.3	23 12.6
22 Th	16 02 15	29 17 18	15 59 51	22 46 37	4R56.2	14 58.9	11 28.8	14 32.6	16 35.4	10 09.5	8 23.3	6 24.6	12 17.2	23 11.5
23 F	16 06 11	0♐17 57	29 27 31	6♓02 54	4 56.2	14 28.8	10 58.7	15 09.9	16 22.9	10 04.8	8 24.4	6 27.7	12 16.0	23 10.4
24 Sa	16 10 08	1 18 37	12♓33 12	18 58 51	4 54.6	13 48.0	10 27.1	15 47.2	16 10.2	10 00.0	8 25.6	6 30.8	12 14.9	23 09.4
25 Su	16 14 04	2 19 19	25 20 16	1♈37 55	4 50.6	12 56.7	9 54.0	16 24.4	15 57.2	9 55.0	8 26.9	6 33.9	12 13.7	23 08.3
26 M	16 18 01	3 20 01	7♈52 12	14 03 29	4 44.0	11 55.6	9 19.8	17 01.6	15 44.1	9 49.9	8 28.3	6 37.0	12 12.4	23 07.2
27 Tu	16 21 58	4 20 45	20 12 08	26 18 27	4 35.0	10 46.1	8 44.6	17 38.8	15 30.8	9 44.5	8 29.8	6 40.2	12 11.2	23 06.1
28 W	16 25 54	5 21 30	2♉22 43	8♉25 10	4 24.1	9 29.7	8 08.8	18 16.0	15 17.3	9 39.1	8 31.4	6 43.3	12 09.9	23 05.0
29 Th	16 29 51	6 22 16	14 26 03	20 25 33	4 12.4	8 08.9	7 32.4	18 53.2	15 03.7	9 33.4	8 33.1	6 46.5	12 08.6	23 03.9
30 F	16 33 47	7 23 03	26 23 49	2♊21 03	4 00.8	6 46.3	6 55.9	19 30.4	14 50.0	9 27.6	8 35.0	6 49.8	12 07.3	23 02.8

December 1906 LONGITUDE

Day	Sid.Time	☉	0 hr ☽	Noon ☽	True ☊	☿	♀	♂	⚳	♃	♄	♅	♆	♇
1 Sa	16 37 44	8♐23 52	8♊17 24	14♊13 04	3♌50.4	5♐24.6	6♐19.4	20♎07.5	14♊36.1	9♋21.7	8♓36.9	6♑53.0	12♋06.0	23♊01.6
2 Su	16 41 40	9 24 41	20 08 12	26 03 03	3R41.9	4R06.6	5R43.2	20 44.7	14R22.2	9R15.6	8 38.9	6 56.3	12R04.6	23R00.5
3 M	16 45 37	10 25 32	1♋57 49	7♋52 48	3 35.9	2 54.8	5 07.6	21 21.8	14 08.2	9 09.4	8 41.0	6 59.6	12 03.3	22 59.4
4 Tu	16 49 33	11 26 24	13 48 19	19 44 41	3 32.4	1 51.2	4 32.9	21 58.9	13 54.1	9 03.0	8 43.3	7 02.9	12 01.9	22 58.2
5 W	16 53 30	12 27 17	25 42 18	1♌41 38	3D31.2	0 57.5	3 59.1	22 36.0	13 39.9	8 56.5	8 45.6	7 06.2	12 00.5	22 57.1
6 Th	16 57 27	13 28 12	7♌43 08	13 47 19	3 31.7	0 14.6	3 26.7	23 13.1	13 25.8	8 49.9	8 48.0	7 09.6	11 59.0	22 55.9
7 F	17 01 23	14 29 07	19 54 43	26 05 56	3 32.9	29♏43.1	2 55.7	23 50.2	13 11.6	8 43.1	8 50.5	7 13.0	11 57.6	22 54.8
8 Sa	17 05 20	15 30 04	2♍21 32	8♍42 06	3R34.0	29 23.0	2 26.4	24 27.2	12 57.4	8 36.2	8 53.1	7 16.4	11 56.1	22 53.6
9 Su	17 09 16	16 31 02	15 08 11	21 40 21	3 34.1	29D14.0	1 59.0	25 04.2	12 43.3	8 29.2	8 55.9	7 19.8	11 54.6	22 52.4
10 M	17 13 13	17 32 02	28 19 02	5♎04 38	3 32.5	29 15.4	1 33.5	25 41.3	12 29.2	8 22.1	8 58.7	7 23.2	11 53.1	22 51.3
11 Tu	17 17 09	18 33 02	11♎57 24	18 57 28	3 29.0	29 26.7	1 10.2	26 18.2	12 15.1	8 14.9	9 01.6	7 26.6	11 51.6	22 50.1
12 W	17 21 06	19 34 04	26 04 47	3♏19 05	3 23.7	29 47.0	0 49.1	26 55.2	12 01.2	8 07.6	9 04.6	7 30.1	11 50.1	22 48.9
13 Th	17 25 02	20 35 06	10♏39 54	18 06 33	3 17.2	0♐15.4	0 30.3	27 32.2	11 47.3	8 00.2	9 07.7	7 33.6	11 48.5	22 47.7
14 F	17 28 59	21 36 10	25 38 07	3♐13 30	3 10.4	0 51.1	0 13.8	28 09.1	11 33.5	7 52.7	9 10.9	7 37.1	11 46.9	22 46.6
15 Sa	17 32 56	22 37 15	10♐51 28	18 30 38	3 04.3	1 33.4	29♏59.8	28 46.0	11 19.9	7 45.1	9 14.2	7 40.6	11 45.4	22 45.4
16 Su	17 36 52	23 38 20	26 09 37	3♑47 02	2 59.7	2 21.4	29 48.3	29 22.9	11 06.4	7 37.4	9 17.6	7 44.1	11 43.8	22 44.2
17 M	17 40 49	24 39 26	11♑21 36	18 52 08	2D57.0	3 14.5	29 39.2	29 59.8	10 53.0	7 29.7	9 21.1	7 47.6	11 42.2	22 43.0
18 Tu	17 44 45	25 40 32	26 17 39	3♒37 21	2 56.3	4 12.1	29 32.6	0♏36.7	10 39.9	7 21.9	9 24.7	7 51.1	11 40.6	22 41.9
19 W	17 48 42	26 41 39	10♒50 40	17 57 14	2 57.0	5 13.6	29 28.5	1 13.5	10 26.9	7 14.0	9 28.3	7 54.7	11 39.0	22 40.7
20 Th	17 52 38	27 42 46	24 56 50	1♓49 29	2 58.5	6 18.6	29D26.8	1 50.3	10 14.2	7 06.1	9 32.1	7 58.2	11 37.3	22 39.5
21 F	17 56 35	28 43 53	8♓35 18	15 14 34	3 00.0	7 26.6	29 27.6	2 27.1	10 01.7	6 58.1	9 35.9	8 01.8	11 35.7	22 38.3
22 Sa	18 00 31	29 45 00	21 47 38	28 14 55	3R00.7	8 37.3	29 30.8	3 03.8	9 49.4	6 50.1	9 39.8	8 05.3	11 34.0	22 37.2
23 Su	18 04 28	0♑46 07	4♈36 54	10♈54 05	3 00.2	9 50.3	29 36.3	3 40.5	9 37.4	6 42.0	9 43.9	8 08.9	11 32.4	22 36.0
24 M	18 08 25	1 47 15	17 07 00	23 16 10	2 58.2	11 05.4	29 44.1	4 17.2	9 25.6	6 34.0	9 48.0	8 12.5	11 30.7	22 34.9
25 Tu	18 12 21	2 48 23	29 22 04	5♉25 12	2 54.7	12 22.3	29 54.2	4 53.9	9 14.1	6 25.9	9 52.2	8 16.1	11 29.0	22 33.7
26 W	18 16 18	3 49 30	11♉26 03	17 25 01	2 50.1	13 40.7	0♐06.5	5 30.5	9 03.0	6 17.7	9 56.4	8 19.6	11 27.3	22 32.5
27 Th	18 20 14	4 50 38	23 22 31	29 18 55	2 44.9	15 00.6	0 21.0	6 07.1	8 52.1	6 09.6	10 00.8	8 23.2	11 25.7	22 31.4
28 F	18 24 11	5 51 46	5♊14 33	11♊09 44	2 39.8	16 21.8	0 37.5	6 43.7	8 41.5	6 01.5	10 05.2	8 26.8	11 24.0	22 30.2
29 Sa	18 28 07	6 52 54	17 04 45	22 59 51	2 35.2	17 44.0	0 56.1	7 20.3	8 31.2	5 53.3	10 09.7	8 30.4	11 22.3	22 29.1
30 Su	18 32 04	7 54 03	28 55 17	4♋51 16	2 31.6	19 07.3	1 16.7	7 56.8	8 21.3	5 45.2	10 14.3	8 34.0	11 20.6	22 28.0
31 M	18 36 00	8 55 11	10♋48 02	16 45 49	2 29.3	20 31.6	1 39.2	8 33.4	8 11.8	5 37.1	10 19.0	8 37.6	11 18.9	22 26.9

Astro Data

	Dy Hr Mn
♂0S	3 16:03
♀ R	9 15:36
♄ D	12 17:09
☽0S	13 11:58
☿ R	20 1:39
☽0N	26 5:36
♃△♄	6 16:54
☿ D	9 20:30
☽0S	10 22:29
♃☍♅	15 21:45
♀ D	20 16:26
☽0N	23 12:42

Planet Ingress

		Dy Hr Mn
☿	♐	1 19:33
☉	♐	23 4:54
☿	♏R	6 22:06
☿	♐	12 23:49
♀	♏R	15 11:42
♂	♏	17 12:07
☉	♑	22 17:53
♀	♐	25 23:49

Last Aspect / ☽ Ingress

Last Aspect Dy Hr Mn			☽ Ingress	Dy Hr Mn
1 14:07	♆	⚹	♊	3 0:56
5 0:27	♇	☌	♋	5 13:43
6 16:51	☉	△	♌	8 2:13
9 23:44	♇	⚹	♍	10 12:10
12 6:28	♇	□	♎	12 18:00
14 9:04	♇	△	♏	14 19:54
16 8:36	☉	☌	♐	16 19:29
18 8:12	♇	☍	♑	18 18:58
20 16:03	☉	⚹	♒	20 20:23
23 0:39	☉	□	♓	23 0:59
24 19:51	♇	□	♈	25 8:53
27 5:42	♇	⚹	♉	27 19:17
28 19:27	♆	⚹	♊	30 7:15

Last Aspect / ☽ Ingress

Last Aspect Dy Hr Mn			☽ Ingress	Dy Hr Mn
2 5:50	♇	☌	♋	2 20:01
4 16:45	♂	□	♌	5 8:37
7 18:44	☿	□	♍	7 19:30
10 1:37	☿	⚹	♎	10 3:00
12 0:56	♂	☌	♏	12 6:31
13 1:52	♆	△	♐	14 6:55
16 4:46	♂	⚹	♑	16 6:02
18 5:21	♀	⚹	♒	18 6:03
20 7:50	♀	□	♓	20 8:48
22 15:04	☉	□	♈	22 15:17
24 10:39	♇	⚹	♉	25 1:15
26 0:04	♆	⚹	♊	27 13:23
29 10:58	♇	☌	♋	30 2:11

☽ Phases & Eclipses

Dy Hr Mn		
1 4:46	○	7♉51
9 9:45	☾	16♌05
16 8:36	●	23♏05
23 0:39	☽	29♒49
30 23:07	○	7♊51
9 1:45	☾	16♍05
15 18:54	●	22♐55
22 15:04	☽	29♓53
30 18:44	○	8♋11

Astro Data

1 November 1906
Julian Day # 2496
SVP 6♓33'54"
GC 25♐32.3 ⚵ 1♈12.4R
Eris 24♓02.0R ⚶ 17♎48.3
⚷ 7♒35.8 ⚴ 11♓47.3
☽ Mean ☊ 7♌00.4

1 December 1906
Julian Day # 2526
SVP 6♓33'50"
GC 25♐32.4 ⚵ 28♓38.0
Eris 23♓52.1R ⚶ 27♎59.6
⚷ 8♒35.6 ⚴ 15♓52.6
☽ Mean ☊ 5♌25.0

LONGITUDE — January 1907

Day	Sid.Time	☉	0 hr ☽	Noon ☽	True ☊	☿	♀	♂	⚳	♃	♄	♅	♆	♇
1 Tu	18 39 57	9♑56 19	22♋44 50	28♋45 18	2♌28.3	21♐56.6	2♐03.5	9♏09.8	8♊02.5	5♋29.0	10♓23.7	8♑41.2	11♋17.2	22♊25.7
2 W	18 43 54	10 57 28	4♌47 31	10♌51 42	2D 28.5	23 22.4	2 29.6	9 46.3	7R 53.7	5R 20.9	10 28.6	8 44.8	11R 15.5	22R 24.6
3 Th	18 47 50	11 58 37	16 58 11	23 07 15	2 29.6	24 48.9	2 57.4	10 22.7	7 45.2	5 12.9	10 33.5	8 48.4	11 13.8	22 23.5
4 F	18 51 47	12 59 45	29 19 15	5♍34 32	2 31.1	26 16.1	3 26.9	10 59.1	7 37.0	5 04.9	10 38.5	8 52.0	11 12.1	22 22.4
5 Sa	18 55 43	14 00 54	11♍53 28	18 16 26	2 32.7	27 43.9	3 58.0	11 35.5	7 29.3	4 57.0	10 43.5	8 55.6	11 10.4	22 21.3
6 Su	18 59 40	15 02 04	24 43 48	1♎15 57	2 33.8	29 12.2	4 30.6	12 11.9	7 21.9	4 49.0	10 48.6	8 59.1	11 08.7	22 20.3
7 M	19 03 36	16 03 13	7♎53 14	14 35 55	2R 34.3	0♑41.2	5 04.7	12 48.2	7 14.9	4 41.2	10 53.8	9 02.7	11 07.0	22 19.2
8 Tu	19 07 33	17 04 22	21 24 16	28 18 25	2 34.0	2 10.6	5 40.2	13 24.5	7 08.4	4 33.4	10 59.1	9 06.3	11 05.3	22 18.1
9 W	19 11 29	18 05 32	5♏18 27	12♏24 17	2 33.0	3 40.6	6 17.1	14 00.7	7 02.2	4 25.7	11 04.4	9 09.9	11 03.6	22 17.1
10 Th	19 15 26	19 06 41	19 35 42	26 52 21	2 31.6	5 11.1	6 55.2	14 36.9	6 56.4	4 18.0	11 09.8	9 13.4	11 02.0	22 16.0
11 F	19 19 23	20 07 51	4♐13 42	11♐39 05	2 29.9	6 42.0	7 34.7	15 13.1	6 51.1	4 10.4	11 15.3	9 17.0	11 00.3	22 15.0
12 Sa	19 23 19	21 09 01	19 07 39	26 38 26	2 28.5	8 13.5	8 15.3	15 49.3	6 46.1	4 02.9	11 20.8	9 20.5	10 58.6	22 14.0
13 Su	19 27 16	22 10 10	4♑10 22	11♑42 20	2 27.4	9 45.5	8 57.1	16 25.4	6 41.6	3 55.5	11 26.4	9 24.1	10 57.0	22 13.0
14 M	19 31 12	23 11 19	19 13 12	26 41 49	2D 27.0	11 18.0	9 40.0	17 01.5	6 37.5	3 48.2	11 32.1	9 27.6	10 55.3	22 12.0
15 Tu	19 35 09	24 12 28	4♒07 10	11♒28 16	2 27.0	12 50.9	10 23.9	17 37.5	6 33.8	3 41.0	11 37.8	9 31.1	10 53.6	22 11.0
16 W	19 39 05	25 13 35	18 44 20	25 54 42	2 27.4	14 24.4	11 08.8	18 13.5	6 30.5	3 33.9	11 43.6	9 34.6	10 52.0	22 10.1
17 Th	19 43 02	26 14 43	2♓58 53	9♓56 33	2 28.1	15 58.3	11 54.8	18 49.4	6 27.7	3 27.0	11 49.5	9 38.1	10 50.4	22 09.1
18 F	19 46 59	27 15 49	16 47 33	23 31 53	2 28.7	17 32.8	12 41.6	19 25.3	6 25.3	3 20.1	11 55.4	9 41.6	10 48.8	22 08.2
19 Sa	19 50 55	28 16 54	0♈09 40	6♈41 10	2 29.1	19 07.8	13 29.3	20 01.2	6 23.3	3 13.3	12 01.4	9 45.0	10 47.1	22 07.2
20 Su	19 54 52	29 17 59	13 06 42	19 26 43	2R 29.3	20 43.4	14 17.9	20 37.0	6 21.7	3 06.7	12 07.4	9 48.5	10 45.5	22 06.3
21 M	19 58 48	0♒19 03	25 41 41	1♉52 08	2 29.4	22 19.5	15 07.4	21 12.8	6 20.6	3 00.2	12 13.5	9 51.9	10 44.0	22 05.4
22 Tu	20 02 45	1 20 05	7♉58 38	14 01 45	2 29.3	23 56.2	15 57.6	21 48.5	6 19.9	2 53.9	12 19.6	9 55.3	10 42.4	22 04.5
23 W	20 06 41	2 21 07	20 02 03	26 00 07	2D 29.3	25 33.5	16 48.6	22 24.2	6D 19.6	2 47.7	12 25.8	9 58.7	10 40.8	22 03.7
24 Th	20 10 38	3 22 08	1♊56 30	7♊51 45	2 29.4	27 11.3	17 40.3	22 59.8	6 19.7	2 41.6	12 32.1	10 02.1	10 39.3	22 02.8
25 F	20 14 34	4 23 08	13 46 21	19 40 48	2 29.5	28 49.8	18 32.8	23 35.4	6 20.2	2 35.7	12 38.4	10 05.5	10 37.7	22 02.0
26 Sa	20 18 31	5 24 06	25 35 34	1♋31 02	2 29.8	0♒28.9	19 25.9	24 10.9	6 21.2	2 29.9	12 44.7	10 08.8	10 36.2	22 01.1
27 Su	20 22 28	6 25 04	7♋27 37	13 25 38	2 30.2	2 08.7	20 19.7	24 46.4	6 22.5	2 24.3	12 51.1	10 12.2	10 34.7	22 00.3
28 M	20 26 24	7 26 01	19 25 23	25 27 11	2R 30.4	3 49.1	21 14.1	25 21.9	6 24.3	2 18.9	12 57.5	10 15.5	10 33.2	21 59.6
29 Tu	20 30 21	8 26 56	1♌31 13	7♌37 44	2 30.4	5 30.2	22 09.1	25 57.3	6 26.5	2 13.6	13 04.0	10 18.7	10 31.8	21 58.8
30 W	20 34 17	9 27 51	13 46 54	19 58 52	2 30.1	7 12.0	23 04.8	26 32.6	6 29.0	2 08.4	13 10.6	10 22.0	10 30.3	21 58.0
31 Th	20 38 14	10 28 45	26 13 47	2♍31 45	2 29.4	8 54.5	24 01.0	27 07.9	6 32.0	2 03.5	13 17.1	10 25.2	10 28.9	21 57.3

LONGITUDE — February 1907

Day	Sid.Time	☉	0 hr ☽	Noon ☽	True ☊	☿	♀	♂	⚳	♃	♄	♅	♆	♇
1 F	20 42 10	11♒29 38	8♍52 53	15♍17 16	2♌28.3	10♒37.6	24♐57.7	27♏43.2	6♊35.4	1♋58.7	13♓23.7	10♑28.5	10♋27.5	21♊56.6
2 Sa	20 46 07	12 30 29	21 44 59	28 16 08	2R 26.9	12 21.5	25 55.0	28 18.4	6 39.1	1R 54.1	13 30.4	10 31.7	10R 26.1	21R 55.9
3 Su	20 50 03	13 31 20	4♎50 47	11♎29 01	2 25.6	14 06.1	26 52.7	28 53.5	6 43.3	1 49.6	13 37.1	10 34.8	10 24.7	21 55.2
4 M	20 54 00	14 32 10	18 10 53	24 56 26	2 24.4	15 51.3	27 51.0	29 28.6	6 47.8	1 45.3	13 43.8	10 38.0	10 23.4	21 54.5
5 Tu	20 57 57	15 32 59	1♏45 43	8♏38 44	2D 23.8	17 37.3	28 49.8	0♐03.7	6 52.7	1 41.3	13 50.6	10 41.1	10 22.0	21 53.9
6 W	21 01 53	16 33 48	15 35 28	22 35 52	2 23.7	19 23.9	29 48.9	0 38.6	6 58.0	1 37.3	13 57.4	10 44.2	10 20.7	21 53.2
7 Th	21 05 50	17 34 35	29 39 47	6♐47 04	2 24.4	21 11.2	0♑48.6	1 13.6	7 03.6	1 33.6	14 04.3	10 47.2	10 19.4	21 52.6
8 F	21 09 46	18 35 22	13♐57 26	21 10 34	2 25.5	22 59.1	1 48.6	1 48.4	7 09.6	1 30.1	14 11.2	10 50.3	10 18.2	21 52.1
9 Sa	21 13 43	19 36 07	28 26 01	5♑43 18	2 26.7	24 47.5	2 49.1	2 23.2	7 16.0	1 26.8	14 18.1	10 53.3	10 16.9	21 51.5
10 Su	21 17 39	20 36 52	13♑01 47	20 20 50	2R 27.7	26 36.4	3 49.9	2 58.0	7 22.8	1 23.6	14 25.1	10 56.3	10 15.7	21 50.9
11 M	21 21 36	21 37 35	27 39 41	4♒57 35	2 28.0	28 25.8	4 51.1	3 32.6	7 29.9	1 20.6	14 32.0	10 59.2	10 14.5	21 50.4
12 Tu	21 25 32	22 38 17	12♒13 44	19 27 21	2 27.3	0♓15.4	5 52.7	4 07.2	7 37.3	1 17.9	14 39.1	11 02.1	10 13.3	21 49.9
13 W	21 29 29	23 38 57	26 37 40	3♓44 02	2 25.5	2 05.2	6 54.5	4 41.7	7 45.2	1 15.3	14 46.1	11 05.0	10 12.2	21 49.4
14 Th	21 33 26	24 39 36	10♓45 49	17 42 31	2 22.6	3 55.1	7 56.8	5 16.2	7 53.3	1 12.9	14 53.2	11 07.9	10 11.1	21 49.0
15 F	21 37 22	25 40 13	24 33 45	1♈19 16	2 19.1	5 44.8	8 59.3	5 50.6	8 01.8	1 10.7	15 00.3	11 10.7	10 10.0	21 48.5
16 Sa	21 41 19	26 40 49	7♈58 55	14 32 43	2 15.3	7 34.1	10 02.1	6 24.9	8 10.6	1 08.8	15 07.4	11 13.5	10 08.9	21 48.1
17 Su	21 45 15	27 41 23	21 00 47	27 23 19	2 11.9	9 22.8	11 05.3	6 59.1	8 19.8	1 07.0	15 14.6	11 16.3	10 07.8	21 47.7
18 M	21 49 12	28 41 55	3♉40 39	9♉53 12	2 09.2	11 10.6	12 08.7	7 33.2	8 29.3	1 05.4	15 21.7	11 19.0	10 06.8	21 47.3
19 Tu	21 53 08	29 42 26	16 01 26	22 05 53	2D 07.8	12 57.2	13 12.4	8 07.3	8 39.1	1 04.0	15 28.9	11 21.7	10 05.8	21 46.9
20 W	21 57 05	0♓42 54	28 07 07	4♊05 44	2 07.5	14 42.2	14 16.3	8 41.3	8 49.2	1 02.8	15 36.1	11 24.3	10 04.9	21 46.6
21 Th	22 01 01	1 43 21	10♊02 23	15 57 41	2 08.4	16 25.1	15 20.5	9 15.2	8 59.6	1 01.9	15 43.4	11 26.9	10 03.9	21 46.3
22 F	22 04 58	2 43 46	21 52 15	27 46 44	2 10.1	18 05.6	16 25.0	9 49.0	9 10.4	1 01.1	15 50.6	11 29.5	10 03.0	21 46.0
23 Sa	22 08 55	3 44 09	3♋41 42	9♋37 46	2 12.0	19 42.9	17 29.7	10 22.7	9 21.4	1 00.5	15 57.9	11 32.1	10 02.2	21 45.7
24 Su	22 12 51	4 44 30	15 35 28	21 35 18	2R 13.4	21 16.7	18 34.7	10 56.4	9 32.8	1 00.1	16 05.2	11 34.6	10 01.3	21 45.5
25 M	22 16 48	5 44 49	27 37 44	3♌43 10	2 13.9	22 46.4	19 39.8	11 30.0	9 44.4	0D 59.9	16 12.5	11 37.0	10 00.5	21 45.2
26 Tu	22 20 44	6 45 06	9♌51 58	16 04 25	2 12.9	24 11.3	20 45.2	12 03.5	9 56.3	1 00.0	16 19.8	11 39.5	9 59.7	21 45.0
27 W	22 24 41	7 45 22	22 20 44	28 41 04	2 10.2	25 30.7	21 50.8	12 36.9	10 08.5	1 00.2	16 27.1	11 41.9	9 59.0	21 44.8
28 Th	22 28 37	8 45 35	5♍05 29	11♍34 01	2 05.8	26 44.2	22 56.6	13 10.2	10 21.0	1 00.6	16 34.4	11 44.2	9 58.2	21 44.7

Astro Data Dy Hr Mn	Planet Ingress Dy Hr Mn	Last Aspect Dy Hr Mn	☽ Ingress Dy Hr Mn	Last Aspect Dy Hr Mn	☽ Ingress Dy Hr Mn	☽ Phases & Eclipses Dy Hr Mn	Astro Data
☽0S 7 6:24	☿ ♑ 7 0:55	31 1:04 ♆ ☌	♌ 1 14:29	2 12:04 ♂ ⚹	♎ 2 15:10	7 14:47 ☾ 16♎10	1 January 1907
♄△♆ 9 9:22	☉ ♒ 21 4:31	3 15:44 ☿ △	♍ 4 1:19	4 17:32 ♀ ⚹	♏ 4 20:55	14 5:57 ● 22♑56	Julian Day # 2557
☽0N 19 21:00	☿ ♒ 26 5:00	6 7:45 ☿ □	♎ 6 9:41	6 5:44 ☿ □	♐ 7 0:34	14 6:05:38 ● T 02'25"	SVP 6♓33'44"
⚳D 23 17:02		8 1:35 ♇ △	♏ 8 14:55	8 15:25 ☿ ⚹	♑ 9 2:35	21 8:42 ☽ 0♉11	GC 25♐32.4 ⚴ 2♈39.2
	♂ ♐ 5 9:29	9 22:14 ☉ ⚹	♐ 10 17:07	10 2:12 ♄ ⚹	♒ 11 3:50	29 13:45 ○ 8♌31	Eris 23♓53.8 ⚵ 7♏03.2
♅☍♆ 1 6:53	♀ ♑ 6 16:28	12 4:58 ♇ ☍	♑ 12 17:21	12 17:43 ☉ ☌	♓ 13 5:41	29 13:38 ● P 0.711	⚷ 10♒26.9 ⚶ 24♓40.2
☽0S 3 11:59	☿ ♓ 12 8:38	14 5:57 ☉ ☌	♒ 14 17:20	14 19:10 ♇ □	♈ 15 9:38		☽ Mean ☊ 3♌46.6
☽0N 16 6:13	☉ ♓ 19 18:58	16 5:43 ♇ △	♓ 16 18:55	17 12:37 ☉ ⚹	♉ 17 16:58	6 0:52 ☾ 16♏06	
♃D 25 21:40		18 19:18 ☉ ⚹	♈ 18 23:42	18 22:48 ♄ ⚹	♊ 20 3:46	12 17:43 ● 22♒53	1 February 1907
☿0N 28 17:06		20 17:05 ♇ ⚹	♉ 21 8:21	21 23:48 ♇ ☌	♋ 22 16:30	20 4:35 ☽ 0♊24	Julian Day # 2588
		23 10:58 ☿ △	♊ 23 20:04	24 11:18 ☿ △	♌ 25 4:41	28 6:23 ○ 8♍31	SVP 6♓33'39"
		25 16:46 ♇ ☌	♋ 26 8:56	26 22:52 ♇ ⚹	♍ 27 14:28		GC 25♐32.5 ⚴ 11♈38.7
		28 11:49 ♂ △	♌ 28 21:00				Eris 24♓07.3 ⚵ 13♏35.5
		31 1:13 ♂ □	♍ 31 7:12				⚷ 12♒45.4 ⚶ 6♈07.2
							☽ Mean ☊ 2♌08.1

March 1907 LONGITUDE

Day	Sid.Time	☉	0 hr ☽	Noon ☽	True ☊	☿	♀	♂	⚳	♃	♄	♅	♆	♇
1 F	22 32 34	9♓45 47	18♍06 35	24♍43 04	2♌00.0	27♓51.1	24♑02.7	13♐43.4	10♊33.7	1♋01.2	16♓41.8	11♑46.5	9♋57.6	21♊44.5
2 Sa	22 36 30	10 45 57	1♎23 16	8♎06 59	1R 53.4	28 50.8	25 08.9	14 16.5	10 46.7	1 02.0	16 49.1	11 48.8	9R 56.9	21R 44.4
3 Su	22 40 27	11 46 06	14 53 55	21 43 48	1 46.7	29 42.8	26 15.3	14 49.5	11 00.0	1 03.0	16 56.5	11 51.0	9 56.3	21 44.3
4 M	22 44 23	12 46 12	28 36 20	5♏31 12	1 41.0	0♈26.7	27 21.9	15 22.5	11 13.5	1 04.2	17 03.9	11 53.2	9 55.6	21 44.3
5 Tu	22 48 20	13 46 18	12♏28 08	19 26 51	1 36.7	1 02.0	28 28.6	15 55.3	11 27.3	1 05.6	17 11.2	11 55.3	9 55.1	21 44.2
6 W	22 52 17	14 46 21	26 27 05	3♐28 39	1D 34.3	1 28.6	29 35.6	16 28.0	11 41.3	1 07.2	17 18.6	11 57.4	9 54.5	21D 44.2
7 Th	22 56 13	15 46 24	10♐31 19	17 34 55	1 33.7	1 46.1	0♒42.7	17 00.6	11 55.6	1 09.0	17 26.0	11 59.5	9 54.0	21 44.2
8 F	23 00 10	16 46 24	24 39 17	1♑44 14	1 34.4	1R 54.5	1 50.0	17 33.1	12 10.2	1 10.9	17 33.4	12 01.5	9 53.6	21 44.2
9 Sa	23 04 06	17 46 23	8♑49 36	15 55 11	1 35.7	1 53.9	2 57.4	18 05.5	12 24.9	1 13.1	17 40.8	12 03.5	9 53.1	21 44.2
10 Su	23 08 03	18 46 21	23 00 44	0♒06 01	1R 36.4	1 44.4	4 05.0	18 37.8	12 39.9	1 15.5	17 48.2	12 05.4	9 52.7	21 44.3
11 M	23 11 59	19 46 17	7♒10 41	14 14 24	1 35.7	1 26.5	5 12.7	19 10.0	12 55.2	1 18.0	17 55.5	12 07.3	9 52.3	21 44.4
12 Tu	23 15 56	20 46 10	21 16 46	28 17 19	1 32.9	1 00.6	6 20.6	19 42.0	13 10.7	1 20.7	18 02.9	12 09.1	9 52.0	21 44.5
13 W	23 19 52	21 46 03	5♓15 37	12♓11 11	1 27.6	0 27.4	7 28.6	20 13.9	13 26.4	1 23.7	18 10.3	12 10.9	9 51.7	21 44.6
14 Th	23 23 49	22 45 53	19 03 33	25 52 18	1 20.2	29♓47.8	8 36.7	20 45.7	13 42.3	1 26.8	18 17.7	12 12.7	9 51.4	21 44.8
15 F	23 27 46	23 45 41	2♈37 02	9♈17 26	1 11.1	29 02.7	9 44.9	21 17.3	13 58.4	1 30.0	18 25.1	12 14.4	9 51.2	21 44.9
16 Sa	23 31 42	24 45 27	15 53 15	22 24 20	1 01.4	28 13.2	10 53.3	21 48.8	14 14.8	1 33.5	18 32.4	12 16.0	9 51.0	21 45.1
17 Su	23 35 39	25 45 11	28 50 37	5♉12 09	0 52.0	27 20.4	12 01.8	22 20.2	14 31.4	1 37.2	18 39.8	12 17.6	9 50.8	21 45.4
18 M	23 39 35	26 44 52	11♉29 04	17 41 35	0 44.0	26 25.6	13 10.4	22 51.4	14 48.1	1 41.0	18 47.1	12 19.2	9 50.7	21 45.6
19 Tu	23 43 32	27 44 32	23 50 03	29 54 50	0 37.8	25 29.9	14 19.1	23 22.5	15 05.1	1 45.0	18 54.5	12 20.7	9 50.5	21 45.9
20 W	23 47 28	28 44 09	5♊56 26	11♊55 22	0 34.0	24 34.7	15 27.9	23 53.4	15 22.3	1 49.2	19 01.8	12 22.2	9 50.5	21 46.2
21 Th	23 51 25	29 43 44	17 52 13	23 47 35	0D 32.3	23 40.9	16 36.8	24 24.2	15 39.7	1 53.6	19 09.1	12 23.6	9D 50.4	21 46.5
22 F	23 55 21	0♈43 17	29 42 09	5♋36 34	0 32.2	22 49.6	17 45.8	24 54.8	15 57.3	1 58.1	19 16.4	12 24.9	9 50.4	21 46.8
23 Sa	23 59 18	1 42 48	11♋31 31	17 27 40	0 32.9	22 01.7	18 54.9	25 25.3	16 15.0	2 02.8	19 23.7	12 26.3	9 50.5	21 47.2
24 Su	0 03 15	2 42 16	23 25 42	29 26 15	0R 33.5	21 18.0	20 04.1	25 55.6	16 32.9	2 07.7	19 31.0	12 27.5	9 50.5	21 47.5
25 M	0 07 11	3 41 42	5♌29 56	11♌37 19	0 32.8	20 38.9	21 13.4	26 25.8	16 51.1	2 12.7	19 38.2	12 28.7	9 50.6	21 47.9
26 Tu	0 11 08	4 41 06	17 48 54	24 05 08	0 30.2	20 05.1	22 22.7	26 55.8	17 09.4	2 17.9	19 45.5	12 29.9	9 50.8	21 48.3
27 W	0 15 04	5 40 27	0♍26 22	6♍52 52	0 25.1	19 36.8	23 32.2	27 25.6	17 27.8	2 23.3	19 52.7	12 31.0	9 50.9	21 48.8
28 Th	0 19 01	6 39 46	13 24 46	20 02 07	0 17.5	19 14.2	24 41.7	27 55.3	17 46.5	2 28.8	19 59.9	12 32.1	9 51.1	21 49.2
29 F	0 22 57	7 39 03	26 44 48	3♎32 36	0 07.8	18 57.4	25 51.4	28 24.8	18 05.3	2 34.5	20 07.0	12 33.1	9 51.4	21 49.7
30 Sa	0 26 54	8 38 18	10♎25 12	17 22 07	29♋56.8	18 46.4	27 01.1	28 54.1	18 24.3	2 40.4	20 14.2	12 34.1	9 51.6	21 50.2
31 Su	0 30 50	9 37 31	24 22 50	1♏26 43	29 45.7	18D 41.3	28 10.9	29 23.2	18 43.4	2 46.4	20 21.3	12 35.0	9 51.9	21 50.8

April 1907 LONGITUDE

Day	Sid.Time	☉	0 hr ☽	Noon ☽	True ☊	☿	♀	♂	⚳	♃	♄	♅	♆	♇
1 M	0 34 47	10♈36 42	8♏33 06	15♏41 18	29♋35.7	18♓41.8	29♒20.8	29♐52.1	19♊02.7	2♋52.5	20♓28.4	12♑35.9	9♋52.3	21♊51.3
2 Tu	0 38 43	11 35 51	22 50 39	0♐00 31	29R 27.8	18 47.8	0♓30.7	0♑20.9	19 22.2	2 58.8	20 35.5	12 36.7	9 52.6	21 51.9
3 W	0 42 40	12 34 59	7♐10 19	14 19 32	29 22.6	18 59.1	1 40.8	0 49.5	19 41.8	3 05.3	20 42.6	12 37.5	9 53.0	21 52.5
4 Th	0 46 37	13 34 05	21 27 47	28 34 43	29 19.9	19 15.5	2 50.9	1 17.8	20 01.5	3 11.9	20 49.6	12 38.2	9 53.5	21 53.1
5 F	0 50 33	14 33 09	5♑40 05	12♑43 44	29D 19.1	19 36.8	4 01.1	1 46.0	20 21.5	3 18.7	20 56.6	12 38.8	9 53.9	21 53.7
6 Sa	0 54 30	15 32 11	19 45 32	26 45 27	29R 19.2	20 02.7	5 11.3	2 13.9	20 41.5	3 25.6	21 03.6	12 39.5	9 54.4	21 54.3
7 Su	0 58 26	16 31 12	3♒43 25	10♒39 26	29 18.9	20 33.1	6 21.6	2 41.6	21 01.7	3 32.6	21 10.5	12 40.0	9 55.0	21 55.0
8 M	1 02 23	17 30 10	17 33 27	24 25 27	29 16.9	21 07.7	7 32.0	3 09.1	21 22.1	3 39.8	21 17.4	12 40.5	9 55.5	21 55.7
9 Tu	1 06 19	18 29 07	1♓15 20	8♓03 01	29 12.3	21 46.3	8 42.4	3 36.3	21 42.6	3 47.2	21 24.3	12 41.0	9 56.1	21 56.4
10 W	1 10 16	19 28 02	14 48 22	21 31 12	29 04.8	22 28.7	9 52.9	4 03.3	22 03.2	3 54.6	21 31.1	12 41.4	9 56.8	21 57.1
11 Th	1 14 12	20 26 56	28 11 21	4♈48 37	28 54.5	23 14.7	11 03.5	4 30.1	22 24.0	4 02.2	21 37.9	12 41.8	9 57.4	21 57.9
12 F	1 18 09	21 25 47	11♈22 46	17 53 38	28 42.1	24 04.1	12 14.1	4 56.6	22 44.9	4 10.0	21 44.7	12 42.1	9 58.1	21 58.6
13 Sa	1 22 06	22 24 36	24 21 03	0♉44 52	28 28.7	24 56.8	13 24.8	5 22.9	23 05.9	4 17.9	21 51.4	12 42.3	9 58.9	21 59.4
14 Su	1 26 02	23 23 24	7♉05 01	13 21 29	28 15.6	25 52.5	14 35.5	5 48.8	23 27.1	4 25.9	21 58.1	12 42.5	9 59.6	22 00.2
15 M	1 29 59	24 22 09	19 34 18	25 43 36	28 03.9	26 51.2	15 46.2	6 14.6	23 48.4	4 34.0	22 04.8	12 42.7	10 00.4	22 01.0
16 Tu	1 33 55	25 20 52	1♊49 35	7♊52 31	27 54.4	27 52.7	16 57.0	6 40.0	24 09.8	4 42.3	22 11.4	12 42.8	10 01.2	22 01.9
17 W	1 37 52	26 19 33	13 52 44	19 50 38	27 47.7	28 56.9	18 07.9	7 05.2	24 31.3	4 50.7	22 18.0	12R 42.8	10 02.1	22 02.7
18 Th	1 41 48	27 18 12	25 46 42	1♋41 28	27 43.7	0♈03.7	19 18.8	7 30.0	24 53.0	4 59.2	22 24.5	12 42.8	10 03.0	22 03.6
19 F	1 45 45	28 16 49	7♋35 29	13 29 24	27 42.0	1 12.9	20 29.7	7 54.6	25 14.7	5 07.8	22 31.0	12 42.7	10 03.9	22 04.5
20 Sa	1 49 41	29 15 23	19 23 51	25 19 31	27 41.6	2 24.6	21 40.7	8 18.9	25 36.6	5 16.6	22 37.4	12 42.6	10 04.9	22 05.4
21 Su	1 53 38	0♉13 56	1♌17 06	7♌17 16	27 41.5	3 38.5	22 51.7	8 42.8	25 58.6	5 25.5	22 43.8	12 42.5	10 05.8	22 06.3
22 M	1 57 35	1 12 26	13 20 44	19 28 10	27 40.6	4 54.6	24 02.7	9 06.5	26 20.7	5 34.5	22 50.2	12 42.3	10 06.8	22 07.3
23 Tu	2 01 31	2 10 54	25 40 10	1♍57 20	27 38.0	6 13.0	25 13.8	9 29.8	26 43.0	5 43.6	22 56.5	12 42.0	10 07.9	22 08.2
24 W	2 05 28	3 09 20	8♍20 10	14 49 05	27 32.9	7 33.4	26 25.0	9 52.8	27 05.3	5 52.8	23 02.7	12 41.7	10 09.0	22 09.2
25 Th	2 09 24	4 07 43	21 24 22	28 06 12	27 25.3	8 55.9	27 36.1	10 15.5	27 27.7	6 02.1	23 08.9	12 41.4	10 10.1	22 10.2
26 F	2 13 21	5 06 05	4♎54 36	11♎49 24	27 15.4	10 20.4	28 47.3	10 37.9	27 50.2	6 11.6	23 15.1	12 41.0	10 11.2	22 11.2
27 Sa	2 17 17	6 04 25	18 50 18	25 56 48	27 04.1	11 46.9	29 58.6	10 59.8	28 12.9	6 21.1	23 21.2	12 40.5	10 12.3	22 12.2
28 Su	2 21 14	7 02 43	3♏08 14	10♏23 51	26 52.6	13 15.4	1♈09.9	11 21.5	28 35.6	6 30.8	23 27.2	12 40.0	10 13.5	22 13.3
29 M	2 25 10	8 00 59	17 42 42	25 03 50	26 42.2	14 45.8	2 21.2	11 42.7	28 58.4	6 40.5	23 33.2	12 39.4	10 14.7	22 14.3
30 Tu	2 29 07	8 59 13	2♐26 14	9♐48 56	26 33.8	16 18.1	3 32.5	12 03.6	29 21.3	6 50.4	23 39.2	12 38.8	10 16.0	22 15.4

Astro Data Dy Hr Mn	Planet Ingress Dy Hr Mn	Last Aspect Dy Hr Mn	☽ Ingress Dy Hr Mn	Last Aspect Dy Hr Mn	☽ Ingress Dy Hr Mn	☽ Phases & Eclipses Dy Hr Mn
☽0S 2 17:33	☿ ♈ 3 20:52	1 18:08 ☿ ☍	♎ 1 21:31	1 20:06 ♄ △	♐ 2 11:59	7 8:42 ☾ 15♐38
♇D 7 4:16	♀ ♒ 6 20:44	3 20:36 ♀ □	♏ 4 2:26	4 0:42 ♇ ☍	♑ 4 14:24	14 6:05 ● 22♓31
☿R 8 22:21	☿ ♓R 14 4:59	6 4:48 ♀ ⚹	♐ 6 6:04	6 2:09 ♄ ⚹	♒ 6 17:35	22 1:10 ☽ 0♋16
☽0N 15 15:22	☉ ♈ 21 18:33	7 19:03 ♇ ☍	♑ 8 9:03	8 7:38 ♇ △	♓ 8 21:47	29 19:44 ○ 7♎58
☉0N 21 18:33	☊ ♋R 30 5:08	9 15:22 ☉ ⚹	♒ 10 11:50	10 13:49 ☿ ☌	♈ 11 3:16	
☿0S 21 19:11		12 0:47 ♇ △	♓ 12 14:56	12 19:35 ♇ ⚹	♉ 13 10:35	5 15:21 ☾ 14♑41
♆D 22 1:59	♂ ♑ 1 18:33	14 18:37 ☿ ☌	♈ 14 19:20	15 14:24 ☿ ⚹	♊ 15 20:24	12 19:06 ● 21♈43
☽0S 30 1:09	♀ ♓ 2 1:28	16 10:52 ♂ △	♉ 17 2:10	18 8:20 ☿ □	♋ 18 8:34	20 20:38 ☽ 29♋36
☿D 31 21:52	☿ ♈ 18 10:42	19 7:19 ☉ ⚹	♊ 19 12:10	20 20:38 ☉ □	♌ 20 21:25	28 6:05 ○ 6♏48
☽0N 11 23:29	☉ ♉ 21 6:17	21 13:18 ♂ ☍	♋ 22 0:36	22 17:09 ♇ ⚹	♍ 23 8:17	
♄□♇ 14 20:36	♀ ♈ 27 12:29	23 20:39 ☿ △	♌ 24 13:07	25 11:01 ♀ ☍	♎ 25 15:22	
♅R 17 22:42		26 17:37 ♂ △	♍ 26 23:11	27 5:41 ♇ △	♏ 27 18:47	
☿0N 23 14:44		29 2:37 ♂ □	♎ 29 5:46	29 9:31 ♄ △	♐ 29 20:02	
☽0S 26 10:57		31 8:23 ♂ ⚹	♏ 31 9:33			
♀0N 30 15:07						

Astro Data

1 March 1907
Julian Day # 2616
SVP 6♓33'36"
GC 25♐32.6 ⚴ 22♈38.3
Eris 24♓26.8 ⚵ 16♏07.6
⚷ 14♒51.6 ⚶ 17♈41.6
☽ Mean ☊ 0♌39.1

1 April 1907
Julian Day # 2647
SVP 6♓33'33"
GC 25♐32.6 ⚴ 7♉01.9
Eris 24♓51.2 ⚵ 14♏00.0R
⚷ 16♒48.4 ⚶ 1♉10.0
☽ Mean ☊ 29♋00.6

LONGITUDE — May 1907

Day	Sid.Time	☉	0 hr ☽	Noon ☽	True ☊	☿	♀	♂	⚳	♃	♄	♅	♆	♇
1 W	2 33 04	9♉57 26	17♐10 58	24♐31 31	26♋28.2	17♈52.3	4♈43.9	12♑24.1	29♊44.3	7♋00.3	23♓45.1	12♑38.2	10♋17.3	22♊16.5
2 Th	2 37 00	10 55 38	1♑49 51	9♑05 21	26R 25.2	19 28.4	5 55.4	12 44.3	0♋07.4	7 10.4	23 50.9	12R 37.5	10 18.6	22 17.6
3 F	2 40 57	11 53 48	16 17 35	23 26 13	26D 24.3	21 06.4	7 06.8	13 04.0	0 30.6	7 20.5	23 56.7	12 36.8	10 19.9	22 18.7
4 Sa	2 44 53	12 51 56	0♒31 02	7♒31 57	26R 24.4	22 46.3	8 18.3	13 23.2	0 53.9	7 30.8	24 02.4	12 36.0	10 21.2	22 19.8
5 Su	2 48 50	13 50 04	14 28 58	21 22 07	26 24.3	24 28.1	9 29.9	13 42.1	1 17.3	7 41.1	24 08.1	12 35.1	10 22.6	22 20.9
6 M	2 52 46	14 48 09	28 11 30	4♓57 17	26 22.8	26 11.7	10 41.5	14 00.5	1 40.8	7 51.6	24 13.7	12 34.2	10 24.0	22 22.1
7 Tu	2 56 43	15 46 14	11♓39 34	18 18 30	26 19.0	27 57.3	11 53.1	14 18.5	2 04.3	8 02.1	24 19.2	12 33.3	10 25.4	22 23.2
8 W	3 00 39	16 44 16	24 54 12	1♈26 46	26 12.5	29 44.7	13 04.7	14 35.9	2 28.0	8 12.7	24 24.7	12 32.3	10 26.9	22 24.4
9 Th	3 04 36	17 42 18	7♈56 19	14 22 52	26 03.5	1♉34.1	14 16.3	14 52.9	2 51.7	8 23.4	24 30.1	12 31.3	10 28.4	22 25.6
10 F	3 08 33	18 40 18	20 46 29	27 07 12	25 52.5	3 25.3	15 28.0	15 09.5	3 15.5	8 34.2	24 35.4	12 30.2	10 29.9	22 26.8
11 Sa	3 12 29	19 38 16	3♉25 01	9♉39 58	25 40.7	5 18.5	16 39.7	15 25.5	3 39.4	8 45.1	24 40.7	12 29.1	10 31.4	22 28.0
12 Su	3 16 26	20 36 13	15 52 06	22 01 27	25 29.0	7 13.5	17 51.5	15 41.0	4 03.3	8 56.0	24 45.9	12 28.0	10 33.0	22 29.2
13 M	3 20 22	21 34 09	28 08 07	4♊12 13	25 18.5	9 10.4	19 03.2	15 56.0	4 27.4	9 07.1	24 51.1	12 26.8	10 34.5	22 30.5
14 Tu	3 24 19	22 32 03	10♊13 53	16 13 22	25 10.1	11 09.1	20 15.0	16 10.4	4 51.5	9 18.2	24 56.1	12 25.5	10 36.1	22 31.7
15 W	3 28 15	23 29 56	22 10 53	28 06 45	25 04.1	13 09.6	21 26.8	16 24.4	5 15.7	9 29.4	25 01.2	12 24.2	10 37.8	22 33.0
16 Th	3 32 12	24 27 46	4♋01 21	9♋55 04	25 00.6	15 11.9	22 38.7	16 37.7	5 39.9	9 40.7	25 06.1	12 22.9	10 39.4	22 34.2
17 F	3 36 08	25 25 36	15 48 23	21 41 48	24D 59.3	17 15.9	23 50.5	16 50.5	6 04.3	9 52.0	25 11.0	12 21.6	10 41.1	22 35.5
18 Sa	3 40 05	26 23 23	27 35 53	3♌31 12	24 59.6	19 21.4	25 02.4	17 02.8	6 28.7	10 03.4	25 15.8	12 20.1	10 42.8	22 36.8
19 Su	3 44 02	27 21 09	9♌28 23	15 28 05	25 00.4	21 28.3	26 14.3	17 14.4	6 53.1	10 14.9	25 20.5	12 18.7	10 44.5	22 38.1
20 M	3 47 58	28 18 53	21 30 58	27 37 40	25R 00.9	23 36.6	27 26.2	17 25.5	7 17.7	10 26.5	25 25.1	12 17.2	10 46.2	22 39.4
21 Tu	3 51 55	29 16 36	3♍48 52	10♍05 10	25 00.3	25 46.0	28 38.1	17 36.0	7 42.3	10 38.1	25 29.7	12 15.7	10 48.0	22 40.7
22 W	3 55 51	0♊14 17	16 27 10	22 55 23	24 57.8	27 56.3	29 50.1	17 45.8	8 06.9	10 49.8	25 34.2	12 14.1	10 49.7	22 42.0
23 Th	3 59 48	1 11 56	29 30 14	6♎12 02	24 53.4	0♊07.4	1♉02.1	17 55.0	8 31.7	11 01.6	25 38.6	12 12.5	10 51.5	22 43.3
24 F	4 03 44	2 09 34	13♎00 58	19 57 04	24 47.1	2 19.0	2 14.0	18 03.6	8 56.4	11 13.4	25 43.0	12 10.9	10 53.3	22 44.7
25 Sa	4 07 41	3 07 11	27 00 09	4♏09 53	24 39.6	4 30.8	3 26.1	18 11.6	9 21.3	11 25.3	25 47.2	12 09.2	10 55.2	22 46.0
26 Su	4 11 37	4 04 46	11♏25 44	18 46 56	24 31.7	6 42.5	4 38.1	18 18.9	9 46.2	11 37.3	25 51.4	12 07.5	10 57.0	22 47.3
27 M	4 15 34	5 02 20	26 12 36	3♐41 41	24 24.6	8 54.0	5 50.2	18 25.6	10 11.2	11 49.3	25 55.6	12 05.7	10 58.9	22 48.7
28 Tu	4 19 31	5 59 53	11♐13 03	18 45 29	24 18.9	11 04.8	7 02.2	18 31.6	10 36.2	12 01.3	25 59.6	12 04.0	11 00.8	22 50.1
29 W	4 23 27	6 57 25	26 17 50	3♑48 55	24 15.3	13 14.8	8 14.4	18 36.9	11 01.3	12 13.5	26 03.5	12 02.2	11 02.7	22 51.4
30 Th	4 27 24	7 54 55	11♑17 43	18 43 19	24D 13.8	15 23.7	9 26.5	18 41.5	11 26.4	12 25.7	26 07.4	12 00.3	11 04.6	22 52.8
31 F	4 31 20	8 52 25	26 04 56	3♒21 58	24 13.9	17 31.2	10 38.7	18 45.4	11 51.6	12 37.9	26 11.2	11 58.5	11 06.5	22 54.2

LONGITUDE — June 1907

Day	Sid.Time	☉	0 hr ☽	Noon ☽	True ☊	☿	♀	♂	⚳	♃	♄	♅	♆	♇
1 Sa	4 35 17	9♊49 54	10♒34 00	17♒40 45	24♋15.0	19♊37.2	11♉50.8	18♑48.6	12♋16.9	12♋50.2	26♓14.9	11♑56.5	11♋08.5	22♊55.6
2 Su	4 39 13	10 47 23	24 42 03	1♓37 53	24R 16.1	21 41.4	13 03.0	18 51.0	12 42.2	13 02.5	26 18.5	11R 54.6	11 10.5	22 57.0
3 M	4 43 10	11 44 50	8♓28 20	15 13 34	24 16.4	23 43.6	14 15.3	18 52.7	13 07.5	13 14.9	26 22.1	11 52.6	11 12.5	22 58.3
4 Tu	4 47 06	12 42 17	21 53 46	28 29 14	24 15.2	25 43.8	15 27.5	18R 53.7	13 32.9	13 27.4	26 25.5	11 50.7	11 14.4	22 59.7
5 W	4 51 03	13 39 43	5♈00 13	11♈27 00	24 12.2	27 41.8	16 39.8	18 53.9	13 58.4	13 39.9	26 28.9	11 48.6	11 16.5	23 01.1
6 Th	4 55 00	14 37 09	17 49 54	24 09 10	24 07.5	29 37.6	17 52.1	18 53.3	14 23.9	13 52.4	26 32.1	11 46.6	11 18.5	23 02.5
7 F	4 58 56	15 34 34	0♉25 06	6♉37 57	24 01.6	1♋30.9	19 04.4	18 52.0	14 49.5	14 05.0	26 35.3	11 44.5	11 20.5	23 03.9
8 Sa	5 02 53	16 31 58	12 47 56	18 55 18	23 55.0	3 21.9	20 16.8	18 50.0	15 15.1	14 17.6	26 38.4	11 42.4	11 22.6	23 05.3
9 Su	5 06 49	17 29 22	25 00 15	1♊03 00	23 48.4	5 10.3	21 29.1	18 47.1	15 40.7	14 30.3	26 41.4	11 40.3	11 24.6	23 06.8
10 M	5 10 46	18 26 45	7♊03 46	13 02 43	23 42.6	6 56.3	22 41.5	18 43.5	16 06.4	14 43.0	26 44.4	11 38.1	11 26.7	23 08.2
11 Tu	5 14 42	19 24 07	19 00 06	24 56 07	23 38.0	8 39.8	23 53.9	18 39.2	16 32.2	14 55.8	26 47.2	11 36.0	11 28.8	23 09.6
12 W	5 18 39	20 21 28	0♋51 01	6♋45 05	23 35.1	10 20.7	25 06.4	18 34.1	16 58.0	15 08.6	26 49.9	11 33.8	11 30.9	23 11.0
13 Th	5 22 35	21 18 49	12 38 36	18 31 53	23D 33.7	11 59.0	26 18.8	18 28.2	17 23.8	15 21.5	26 52.6	11 31.5	11 33.0	23 12.4
14 F	5 26 32	22 16 09	24 25 18	0♌19 14	23 33.8	13 34.7	27 31.3	18 21.6	17 49.7	15 34.3	26 55.1	11 29.3	11 35.2	23 13.8
15 Sa	5 30 29	23 13 28	6♌14 07	12 10 25	23 34.9	15 07.8	28 43.8	18 14.3	18 15.7	15 47.2	26 57.6	11 27.1	11 37.3	23 15.3
16 Su	5 34 25	24 10 46	18 08 35	24 09 11	23 36.6	16 38.3	29 56.3	18 06.2	18 41.6	16 00.2	26 59.9	11 24.8	11 39.4	23 16.7
17 M	5 38 22	25 08 04	0♍12 44	6♍19 47	23 38.2	18 06.1	1♊08.8	17 57.5	19 07.6	16 13.2	27 02.2	11 22.5	11 41.6	23 18.1
18 Tu	5 42 18	26 05 20	12 30 55	18 46 42	23R 39.2	19 31.2	2 21.3	17 48.0	19 33.7	16 26.2	27 04.4	11 20.2	11 43.7	23 19.5
19 W	5 46 15	27 02 36	25 07 39	1♎34 18	23 39.3	20 53.6	3 33.9	17 37.9	19 59.8	16 39.2	27 06.4	11 17.9	11 45.9	23 20.9
20 Th	5 50 11	27 59 51	8♎07 06	14 46 26	23 38.4	22 13.3	4 46.5	17 27.1	20 25.9	16 52.3	27 08.4	11 15.5	11 48.1	23 22.4
21 F	5 54 08	28 57 05	21 32 35	28 25 43	23 36.3	23 30.1	5 59.0	17 15.7	20 52.0	17 05.4	27 10.3	11 13.2	11 50.3	23 23.8
22 Sa	5 58 04	29 54 19	5♏25 53	12♏32 55	23 33.6	24 44.2	7 11.7	17 03.7	21 18.2	17 18.5	27 12.1	11 10.8	11 52.4	23 25.2
23 Su	6 02 01	0♋51 32	19 46 31	27 06 10	23 30.6	25 55.3	8 24.3	16 51.1	21 44.4	17 31.6	27 13.8	11 08.5	11 54.6	23 26.6
24 M	6 05 58	1 48 44	4♐31 11	12♐00 42	23 27.8	27 03.4	9 37.0	16 37.9	22 10.7	17 44.8	27 15.4	11 06.1	11 56.8	23 28.0
25 Tu	6 09 54	2 45 57	19 33 42	27 09 03	23 25.7	28 08.6	10 49.7	16 24.2	22 37.0	17 58.0	27 16.9	11 03.7	11 59.1	23 29.4
26 W	6 13 51	3 43 09	4♑45 33	12♑21 57	23D 24.5	29 10.6	12 02.4	16 09.9	23 03.3	18 11.2	27 18.3	11 01.3	12 01.3	23 30.8
27 Th	6 17 47	4 40 20	19 57 03	27 29 41	23 24.2	0♌09.4	13 15.1	15 55.2	23 29.7	18 24.5	27 19.6	10 58.9	12 03.5	23 32.2
28 F	6 21 44	5 37 32	4♒58 49	12♒23 33	23 24.8	1 04.9	14 27.9	15 40.0	23 56.1	18 37.7	27 20.8	10 56.5	12 05.7	23 33.6
29 Sa	6 25 40	6 34 43	19 43 08	26 57 01	23 25.9	1 57.0	15 40.7	15 24.4	24 22.5	18 51.0	27 21.9	10 54.1	12 07.9	23 35.0
30 Su	6 29 37	7 31 55	4♓04 47	11♓06 11	23 27.1	2 45.6	16 53.5	15 08.3	24 48.9	19 04.3	27 22.9	10 51.7	12 10.1	23 36.4

Astro Data Dy Hr Mn	Planet Ingress Dy Hr Mn	Last Aspect Dy Hr Mn	☽ Ingress Dy Hr Mn	Last Aspect Dy Hr Mn	☽ Ingress Dy Hr Mn	☽ Phases & Eclipses Dy Hr Mn	Astro Data
☽0N 9 6:20	⚳ ♋ 2 4:17	1 10:43 ♄ □	♑ 1 20:59	1 20:58 ♇ △	♓ 2 9:10	4 21:53 ☾ 13♒16	1 May 1907
♃☌♆ 22 11:47	☿ ♉ 8 15:23	3 12:52 ♄ ✶	♒ 3 23:07	4 8:13 ♄ ☌	♈ 4 14:46	12 8:59 ● 20♉29	Julian Day # 2677
☽0S 23 21:30	☉ ♊ 22 6:03	5 18:13 ☿ ✶	♓ 6 3:12	6 9:53 ♇ ✶	♉ 6 23:12	20 13:27 ☽ 28♌22	SVP 6♓33'30"
♃☍♅ 28 16:32	♀ ♉ 22 15:18	7 23:01 ♄ ☌	♈ 8 9:20	9 3:18 ♄ ✶	♊ 9 9:55	27 14:18 ○ 5♐08	GC 25♐32.7 ⚴ 22♉37.4
	☿ ♊ 23 10:39	10 3:08 ♇ ✶	♉ 10 17:29	11 15:46 ♄ □	♋ 11 22:16		Eris 25♓11.9 ⚵ 7♏53.8R
♂R 5 6:42		12 17:25 ♄ ✶	♊ 13 3:41	14 5:40 ♀ ✶	♌ 14 11:21	3 5:20 ☾ 11♓29	⚷ 17♒58.4 ⚶ 14♉25.8
☽0N 5 12:34	☿ ♋ 6 16:43	15 5:42 ♄ □	♋ 15 15:50	16 12:03 ☉ ✶	♍ 16 23:35	10 23:50 ● 18♊55	☽ Mean ☊ 27♋25.3
♅☍♆ 13 3:47	♀ ♊ 16 13:14	17 20:16 ☉ ✶	♌ 18 4:52	19 3:41 ♄ ☍	♎ 19 9:05	19 2:55 ☽ 26♍41	
☽0S 20 6:57	☉ ♋ 22 14:23	20 13:27 ☉ □	♍ 20 16:37	21 12:58 ☉ △	♏ 21 14:43	25 21:27 ○ 3♑08	1 June 1907
	☿ ♌ 27 8:05	22 22:58 ☿ △	♎ 23 0:54	23 12:12 ♄ △	♐ 23 16:42		Julian Day # 2708
		24 16:47 ♇ △	♏ 25 5:03	25 12:12 ♄ □	♑ 25 16:30		SVP 6♓33'25"
		26 23:29 ♄ △	♐ 27 6:05	27 11:44 ♄ ✶	♒ 27 16:00		GC 25♐32.8 ⚴ 10♊01.7
		28 23:34 ♄ □	♑ 29 5:54	29 6:23 ♇ △	♓ 29 17:07		Eris 25♓25.4 ⚵ 1♏58.8R
		31 0:07 ♄ ✶	♒ 31 6:26				⚷ 18♒12.7R ⚶ 28♉02.8
							☽ Mean ☊ 25♋46.8

July 1907 — LONGITUDE

Day	Sid.Time	☉	0 hr ☽	Noon ☽	True ☊	☿	♀	♂	⚳	♃	♄	♅	♆	♇
1 M	6 33 33	8♋29 06	18♓01 10	24♓49 44	23♋28.0	3♌30.7	18♊06.3	14♑51.9	25♋15.4	19♋17.6	27♓23.8	10♑49.2	12♋12.4	23♊37.8
2 Tu	6 37 30	9 26 18	1♈32 05	8♈08 26	23R28.3	4 11.9	19 19.2	14R35.2	25 41.9	19 30.9	27 24.6	10R46.8	12 14.6	23 39.1
3 W	6 41 27	10 23 30	14 39 06	21 04 28	23 28.1	4 49.3	20 32.1	14 18.2	26 08.5	19 44.3	27 25.3	10 44.4	12 16.8	23 40.5
4 Th	6 45 23	11 20 42	27 24 57	3♉40 58	23 27.3	5 22.8	21 45.0	14 01.0	26 35.0	19 57.6	27 25.9	10 42.0	12 19.1	23 41.9
5 F	6 49 20	12 17 55	9♉52 57	16 01 21	23 26.1	5 52.1	22 57.9	13 43.5	27 01.6	20 11.0	27 26.4	10 39.5	12 21.3	23 43.2
6 Sa	6 53 16	13 15 08	22 06 36	28 09 07	23 24.7	6 17.2	24 10.9	13 26.0	27 28.3	20 24.4	27 26.8	10 37.1	12 23.5	23 44.6
7 Su	6 57 13	14 12 21	4♊09 18	10♊07 32	23 23.3	6 37.9	25 23.9	13 08.3	27 54.9	20 37.8	27 27.0	10 34.7	12 25.7	23 45.9
8 M	7 01 09	15 09 34	16 04 11	21 59 36	23 22.2	6 54.1	26 36.9	12 50.5	28 21.6	20 51.2	27 27.2	10 32.3	12 28.0	23 47.3
9 Tu	7 05 06	16 06 48	27 54 05	3♋47 58	23 21.4	7 05.8	27 50.0	12 32.8	28 48.3	21 04.6	27R27.3	10 29.8	12 30.2	23 48.6
10 W	7 09 03	17 04 01	9♋41 33	15 35 07	23D21.1	7R12.7	29 03.1	12 15.1	29 15.0	21 18.0	27 27.3	10 27.4	12 32.4	23 49.9
11 Th	7 12 59	18 01 15	21 28 57	27 23 20	23 21.0	7 15.0	0♋16.2	11 57.4	29 41.8	21 31.4	27 27.2	10 25.0	12 34.7	23 51.2
12 F	7 16 56	18 58 30	3♌18 34	9♌14 57	23 21.2	7 12.4	1 29.3	11 40.0	0♌08.6	21 44.9	27 27.0	10 22.6	12 36.9	23 52.6
13 Sa	7 20 52	19 55 44	15 12 45	21 12 20	23 21.5	7 05.1	2 42.4	11 22.7	0 35.4	21 58.3	27 26.7	10 20.2	12 39.1	23 53.9
14 Su	7 24 49	20 52 58	27 14 01	3♍18 08	23 21.8	6 53.1	3 55.6	11 05.6	1 02.2	22 11.7	27 26.3	10 17.9	12 41.3	23 55.1
15 M	7 28 45	21 50 13	9♍25 05	15 35 13	23 22.1	6 36.5	5 08.8	10 48.9	1 29.0	22 25.2	27 25.8	10 15.5	12 43.5	23 56.4
16 Tu	7 32 42	22 47 27	21 48 56	28 06 39	23R22.2	6 15.4	6 22.0	10 32.4	1 55.9	22 38.6	27 25.2	10 13.1	12 45.8	23 57.7
17 W	7 36 38	23 44 42	4♎28 44	10♎55 36	23 22.2	5 50.0	7 35.2	10 16.4	2 22.8	22 52.0	27 24.4	10 10.8	12 48.0	23 59.0
18 Th	7 40 35	24 41 57	17 27 37	24 05 05	23D22.2	5 20.8	8 48.5	10 00.7	2 49.7	23 05.4	27 23.6	10 08.5	12 50.2	24 00.2
19 F	7 44 31	25 39 12	0♏48 18	7♏37 29	23 22.2	4 47.9	10 01.8	9 45.6	3 16.6	23 18.9	27 22.7	10 06.2	12 52.3	24 01.5
20 Sa	7 48 28	26 36 28	14 32 44	21 34 06	23 22.4	4 11.9	11 15.1	9 30.9	3 43.5	23 32.3	27 21.7	10 03.9	12 54.5	24 02.7
21 Su	7 52 25	27 33 43	28 41 27	5♐54 34	23 22.7	3 33.4	12 28.5	9 16.7	4 10.5	23 45.7	27 20.6	10 01.6	12 56.7	24 03.9
22 M	7 56 21	28 30 59	13♐13 01	20 36 17	23 23.1	2 52.8	13 41.8	9 03.1	4 37.4	23 59.1	27 19.4	9 59.3	12 58.9	24 05.1
23 Tu	8 00 18	29 28 15	28 03 38	5♑34 13	23 23.5	2 10.9	14 55.2	8 50.1	5 04.4	24 12.5	27 18.1	9 57.1	13 01.0	24 06.3
24 W	8 04 14	0♌25 32	13♑07 05	20 41 08	23R23.7	1 28.4	16 08.6	8 37.7	5 31.4	24 25.9	27 16.7	9 54.8	13 03.2	24 07.5
25 Th	8 08 11	1 22 50	28 15 14	5♒48 15	23 23.6	0 45.9	17 22.1	8 25.9	5 58.4	24 39.2	27 15.2	9 52.6	13 05.3	24 08.7
26 F	8 12 07	2 20 08	13♒19 03	20 46 34	23 23.1	0 04.4	18 35.5	8 14.8	6 25.4	24 52.6	27 13.6	9 50.4	13 07.5	24 09.8
27 Sa	8 16 04	3 17 26	28 09 50	5♓28 02	23 22.1	29♋24.5	19 49.0	8 04.4	6 52.5	25 05.9	27 11.9	9 48.3	13 09.6	24 11.0
28 Su	8 20 01	4 14 46	12♓40 28	19 46 38	23 20.9	28 47.0	21 02.6	7 54.7	7 19.5	25 19.3	27 10.2	9 46.1	13 11.7	24 12.1
29 M	8 23 57	5 12 06	26 46 12	3♈38 59	23 19.6	28 12.6	22 16.1	7 45.7	7 46.6	25 32.6	27 08.3	9 44.0	13 13.8	24 13.2
30 Tu	8 27 54	6 09 28	10♈24 58	17 04 16	23 18.5	27 42.0	23 29.7	7 37.5	8 13.6	25 45.9	27 06.3	9 41.9	13 15.9	24 14.4
31 W	8 31 50	7 06 51	23 37 08	0♉03 54	23D17.8	27 15.7	24 43.3	7 30.0	8 40.7	25 59.2	27 04.3	9 39.8	13 18.0	24 15.5

August 1907 — LONGITUDE

Day	Sid.Time	☉	0 hr ☽	Noon ☽	True ☊	☿	♀	♂	⚳	♃	♄	♅	♆	♇
1 Th	8 35 47	8♌04 14	6♉24 59	12♉40 51	23♋17.8	26♋54.4	25♋57.0	7♑23.3	9♌07.8	26♋12.4	27♓02.1	9♑37.8	13♋20.1	24♊16.5
2 F	8 39 43	9 01 39	18 52 02	24 59 04	23 18.3	26R38.5	27 10.6	7R17.3	9 34.9	26 25.7	26R59.9	9R35.8	13 22.1	24 17.6
3 Sa	8 43 40	9 59 06	1♊02 32	7♊03 00	23 19.5	26 28.3	28 24.3	7 12.2	10 02.0	26 38.9	26 57.6	9 33.8	13 24.2	24 18.7
4 Su	8 47 36	10 56 33	13 01 01	18 57 07	23 20.9	26D24.3	29 38.1	7 07.9	10 29.2	26 52.1	26 55.1	9 31.8	13 26.2	24 19.7
5 M	8 51 33	11 54 02	24 51 49	0♋45 39	23 22.3	26 26.6	0♌51.8	7 04.4	10 56.3	27 05.3	26 52.6	9 29.9	13 28.2	24 20.7
6 Tu	8 55 30	12 51 31	6♋39 03	12 32 29	23R23.4	26 35.5	2 05.6	7 01.8	11 23.5	27 18.5	26 50.0	9 28.0	13 30.2	24 21.7
7 W	8 59 26	13 49 02	18 26 19	24 20 57	23 23.8	26 51.1	3 19.4	7 00.0	11 50.6	27 31.6	26 47.4	9 26.1	13 32.2	24 22.7
8 Th	9 03 23	14 46 34	0♌16 42	6♌13 54	23 23.2	27 13.5	4 33.3	6D59.0	12 17.8	27 44.7	26 44.6	9 24.3	13 34.2	24 23.7
9 F	9 07 19	15 44 07	12 12 48	18 13 40	23 21.5	27 42.6	5 47.2	6 58.9	12 45.0	27 57.8	26 41.8	9 22.5	13 36.2	24 24.7
10 Sa	9 11 16	16 41 41	24 16 44	0♍22 11	23 18.8	28 18.5	7 01.1	6 59.6	13 12.1	28 10.8	26 38.9	9 20.7	13 38.1	24 25.6
11 Su	9 15 12	17 39 17	6♍30 12	12 41 00	23 15.2	29 01.2	8 15.0	7 01.2	13 39.3	28 23.9	26 35.9	9 19.0	13 40.0	24 26.5
12 M	9 19 09	18 36 53	18 54 44	25 11 33	23 11.2	29 50.4	9 28.9	7 03.6	14 06.5	28 36.9	26 32.8	9 17.3	13 41.9	24 27.5
13 Tu	9 23 05	19 34 30	1♎31 39	7♎55 10	23 07.2	0♌46.2	10 42.9	7 06.9	14 33.7	28 49.8	26 29.6	9 15.6	13 43.8	24 28.4
14 W	9 27 02	20 32 08	14 22 17	20 53 11	23 03.8	1 48.3	11 56.9	7 10.9	15 00.9	29 02.7	26 26.4	9 14.0	13 45.7	24 29.2
15 Th	9 30 58	21 29 48	27 28 01	4♏06 56	23 01.5	2 56.5	13 10.9	7 15.9	15 28.1	29 15.6	26 23.1	9 12.4	13 47.6	24 30.1
16 F	9 34 55	22 27 28	10♏50 07	17 37 41	23D00.4	4 10.6	14 24.9	7 21.6	15 55.2	29 28.5	26 19.7	9 10.8	13 49.4	24 30.9
17 Sa	9 38 52	23 25 09	24 29 44	1♐26 19	23 00.5	5 30.3	15 39.0	7 28.2	16 22.4	29 41.3	26 16.2	9 09.3	13 51.2	24 31.8
18 Su	9 42 48	24 22 51	8♐27 26	15 33 00	23 01.6	6 55.3	16 53.1	7 35.6	16 49.6	29 54.0	26 12.7	9 07.8	13 53.0	24 32.6
19 M	9 46 45	25 20 35	22 42 52	29 56 45	23 03.0	8 25.4	18 07.2	7 43.7	17 16.8	0♌06.8	26 09.1	9 06.4	13 54.8	24 33.4
20 Tu	9 50 41	26 18 19	7♑14 16	14♑34 56	23R04.1	10 00.0	19 21.3	7 52.7	17 44.0	0 19.4	26 05.5	9 05.0	13 56.6	24 34.1
21 W	9 54 38	27 16 05	21 58 07	29 23 06	23 04.2	11 38.8	20 35.4	8 02.4	18 11.2	0 32.1	26 01.8	9 03.6	13 58.3	24 34.9
22 Th	9 58 34	28 13 52	6♒49 01	14♒14 57	23 02.7	13 21.4	21 49.6	8 12.8	18 38.3	0 44.7	25 58.0	9 02.3	14 00.0	24 35.6
23 F	10 02 31	29 11 40	21 39 58	29 03 02	22 59.6	15 07.4	23 03.8	8 24.0	19 05.5	0 57.2	25 54.2	9 01.0	14 01.7	24 36.3
24 Sa	10 06 28	0♍09 30	6♓23 15	13♓39 39	22 54.9	16 56.3	24 18.0	8 36.0	19 32.7	1 09.7	25 50.3	8 59.8	14 03.4	24 37.0
25 Su	10 10 24	1 07 21	20 51 26	27 57 55	22 49.2	18 47.7	25 32.2	8 48.6	19 59.9	1 22.2	25 46.3	8 58.6	14 05.1	24 37.7
26 M	10 14 21	2 05 14	4♈58 33	11♈52 55	22 43.2	20 41.0	26 46.5	9 01.9	20 27.0	1 34.6	25 42.3	8 57.4	14 06.7	24 38.4
27 Tu	10 18 17	3 03 08	18 40 47	25 22 06	22 37.6	22 36.1	28 00.8	9 16.0	20 54.2	1 47.0	25 38.3	8 56.3	14 08.3	24 39.0
28 W	10 22 14	4 01 05	1♉56 54	8♉25 25	22 33.3	24 32.3	29 15.1	9 30.7	21 21.3	1 59.3	25 34.2	8 55.3	14 09.9	24 39.6
29 Th	10 26 10	4 59 03	14 47 57	21 04 56	22 30.5	26 29.4	0♍29.4	9 46.1	21 48.5	2 11.5	25 30.0	8 54.3	14 11.5	24 40.2
30 F	10 30 07	5 57 03	27 16 51	3♊24 16	22D29.4	28 27.1	1 43.8	10 02.1	22 15.6	2 23.7	25 25.8	8 53.3	14 13.0	24 40.8
31 Sa	10 34 03	6 55 05	9♊27 47	15 28 02	22 29.7	0♍25.0	2 58.2	10 18.8	22 42.7	2 35.9	25 21.6	8 52.4	14 14.5	24 41.4

Astro Data

	Dy Hr Mn
☽0N	2 19:12
♄R	9 22:15
☿R	11 11:17
☽0S	17 14:10
♃⊻♇	22 23:53
☽0N	30 2:58
☿D	4 15:19
♃△♄	4 16:37
♂D	9 3:28
☽0S	13 19:30
☽0N	26 11:55

Planet Ingress

		Dy Hr Mn
♀	♋	11 6:42
⚳	♌	12 4:19
☉	♌	24 1:18
☿	♋R	26 14:36
♀	♌	4 19:08
☿	♌	12 16:20
♃	♌	18 23:15
☉	♍	24 8:03
♀	♍	29 2:30
☿	♍	31 6:54

Last Aspect / ☽ Ingress

Dy Hr Mn	Aspect		☽ Ingress Dy Hr Mn
1 16:35	♄ ☌	♈	1 21:14
3 16:55	♇ ⚹	♉	4 4:56
6 10:36	♄ ⚹	♊	6 15:41
8 23:06	♄ □	♋	9 4:16
11 12:08	♄ △	♌	11 17:18
13 17:23	♇ ⚹	♍	14 5:29
16 10:41	♄ ☍	♎	16 15:34
18 13:11	☉ □	♏	18 22:34
20 21:46	♄ △	♐	21 2:11
22 22:48	♄ □	♑	23 3:06
24 22:26	♄ ⚹	♒	25 2:46
26 17:30	♇ △	♓	27 3:00
29 2:52	♇ △	♈	29 5:37
31 6:55	☿ □	♉	31 11:53

Last Aspect / ☽ Ingress

Dy Hr Mn	Aspect		☽ Ingress Dy Hr Mn
2 16:49	♀ ⚹	♊	2 21:56
5 4:07	♄ □	♋	5 10:27
7 18:33	♃ ☌	♌	7 23:26
10 0:17	♇ ⚹	♍	10 11:16
12 18:36	♃ ⚹	♎	12 21:07
15 3:06	♃ □	♏	15 4:35
17 8:56	♃ △	♐	17 9:31
19 5:45	♄ □	♑	19 12:05
21 6:36	♄ ⚹	♒	21 13:00
23 12:15	☉ ☍	♓	23 13:33
25 8:18	♄ ☌	♈	25 15:28
27 17:18	♀ △	♉	27 20:26
30 0:26	☿ □	♊	30 5:19

☽ Phases & Eclipses

Dy Hr Mn		
2 14:34	☾	9♈32
10 15:17	●	17♋12
10 15:24:27	●	A 07'22"
18 13:11	☽	24♎45
25 4:29	○	1♒05
25 4:22	•	P 0.615
1 2:26	☾	7♉41
9 6:36	●	15♌31
16 21:05	☽	22♏49
23 12:15	○	29♒12
30 17:28	☾	6♊10

Astro Data

1 July 1907
Julian Day # 2738
SVP 6♓33'20"
GC 25♐32.8 ⚵ 27♊43.4
Eris 25♓27.7R ⚴ 0♏28.3
⚷ 17♒29.7R ⚶ 10♊52.7
☽ Mean ☊ 24♋11.5

1 August 1907
Julian Day # 2769
SVP 6♓33'16"
GC 25♐32.9 ⚵ 16♋22.3
Eris 25♓18.9R ⚴ 3♏34.2
⚷ 16♒03.4R ⚶ 23♊27.9
☽ Mean ☊ 22♋33.0

LONGITUDE — September 1907

Day	Sid.Time	☉	0 hr ☽	Noon ☽	True ☊	☿	♀	♂	⚳	♃	♄	♅	♆	♇
1 Su	10 38 00	7♍53 09	21♊25 40	27♊21 20	22♋30.9	2♍23.0	4♍12.6	10♑36.1	23♌09.9	2♌48.0	25♓17.3	8♑51.5	14♋16.0	24♊41.9
2 M	10 41 56	8 51 15	3♋15 40	9♋09 18	22 32.3	4 20.7	5 27.0	10 54.1	23 37.0	3 00.0	25R 13.0	8R 50.6	14 17.5	24 42.4
3 Tu	10 45 53	9 49 23	15 02 51	20 56 53	22R 33.1	6 18.0	6 41.4	11 12.7	24 04.1	3 12.0	25 08.6	8 49.9	14 18.9	24 42.9
4 W	10 49 50	10 47 32	26 51 55	2♌48 28	22 32.5	8 14.7	7 55.9	11 31.8	24 31.2	3 23.9	25 04.2	8 49.1	14 20.3	24 43.4
5 Th	10 53 46	11 45 44	8♌46 57	14 47 47	22 29.9	10 10.7	9 10.4	11 51.6	24 58.3	3 35.7	24 59.8	8 48.4	14 21.7	24 43.8
6 F	10 57 43	12 43 57	20 51 18	26 57 45	22 25.2	12 05.9	10 24.9	12 12.0	25 25.4	3 47.5	24 55.3	8 47.8	14 23.1	24 44.3
7 Sa	11 01 39	13 42 12	3♍07 22	9♍20 19	22 18.3	14 00.2	11 39.4	12 32.9	25 52.4	3 59.2	24 50.8	8 47.2	14 24.4	24 44.7
8 Su	11 05 36	14 40 29	15 36 41	21 56 32	22 09.7	15 53.5	12 54.0	12 54.4	26 19.5	4 10.8	24 46.3	8 46.6	14 25.7	24 45.1
9 M	11 09 32	15 38 47	28 19 50	4♎46 35	22 00.2	17 45.8	14 08.5	13 16.4	26 46.5	4 22.4	24 41.7	8 46.1	14 27.0	24 45.4
10 Tu	11 13 29	16 37 08	11♎16 41	17 50 02	21 50.7	19 37.1	15 23.1	13 39.0	27 13.5	4 33.9	24 37.2	8 45.7	14 28.3	24 45.8
11 W	11 17 25	17 35 30	24 26 33	1♏06 06	21 42.3	21 27.3	16 37.7	14 02.1	27 40.5	4 45.3	24 32.6	8 45.3	14 29.5	24 46.1
12 Th	11 21 22	18 33 53	7♏48 34	14 33 53	21 35.7	23 16.4	17 52.3	14 25.7	28 07.5	4 56.7	24 28.0	8 44.9	14 30.7	24 46.4
13 F	11 25 19	19 32 18	21 21 56	28 12 41	21 31.4	25 04.5	19 07.0	14 49.9	28 34.4	5 08.0	24 23.4	8 44.6	14 31.9	24 46.7
14 Sa	11 29 15	20 30 45	5♐06 03	12♐02 02	21D 29.4	26 51.4	20 21.6	15 14.5	29 01.4	5 19.2	24 18.7	8 44.4	14 33.0	24 47.0
15 Su	11 33 12	21 29 14	19 00 34	26 01 38	21 29.2	28 37.2	21 36.2	15 39.6	29 28.3	5 30.3	24 14.1	8 44.2	14 34.1	24 47.2
16 M	11 37 08	22 27 44	3♑05 08	10♑10 59	21R 29.8	0♎22.0	22 50.9	16 05.2	29 55.2	5 41.3	24 09.5	8 44.0	14 35.2	24 47.4
17 Tu	11 41 05	23 26 16	17 19 01	24 29 01	21 30.1	2 05.7	24 05.6	16 31.2	0♍22.1	5 52.3	24 04.8	8 44.0	14 36.3	24 47.6
18 W	11 45 01	24 24 49	1♒40 40	8♒53 36	21 28.9	3 48.4	25 20.3	16 57.7	0 48.9	6 03.2	24 00.2	8D 43.9	14 37.3	24 47.8
19 Th	11 48 58	25 23 24	16 07 19	23 21 15	21 25.4	5 30.0	26 35.0	17 24.6	1 15.7	6 14.0	23 55.5	8 43.9	14 38.3	24 48.0
20 F	11 52 54	26 22 01	0♓34 45	7♓47 08	21 19.3	7 10.5	27 49.7	17 51.9	1 42.5	6 24.7	23 50.9	8 44.0	14 39.2	24 48.1
21 Sa	11 56 51	27 20 39	14 57 38	22 05 30	21 10.7	8 50.1	29 04.4	18 19.7	2 09.3	6 35.3	23 46.3	8 44.1	14 40.2	24 48.2
22 Su	12 00 48	28 19 19	29 10 02	6♈10 32	21 00.3	10 28.7	0♎19.1	18 47.8	2 36.0	6 45.8	23 41.6	8 44.2	14 41.1	24 48.3
23 M	12 04 44	29 18 02	13♈06 25	19 57 12	20 49.2	12 06.3	1 33.9	19 16.3	3 02.8	6 56.3	23 37.0	8 44.4	14 41.9	24 48.3
24 Tu	12 08 41	0♎16 46	26 42 30	3♉22 07	20 38.6	13 43.0	2 48.6	19 45.2	3 29.5	7 06.6	23 32.4	8 44.7	14 42.8	24 48.4
25 W	12 12 37	1 15 33	9♉55 55	16 23 58	20 29.5	15 18.7	4 03.4	20 14.5	3 56.1	7 16.9	23 27.8	8 45.0	14 43.6	24R 48.4
26 Th	12 16 34	2 14 22	22 46 26	29 03 34	20 22.7	16 53.5	5 18.2	20 44.1	4 22.8	7 27.0	23 23.3	8 45.3	14 44.3	24 48.4
27 F	12 20 30	3 13 13	5♊15 46	11♊23 31	20 18.3	18 27.4	6 33.0	21 14.1	4 49.4	7 37.1	23 18.7	8 45.8	14 45.1	24 48.4
28 Sa	12 24 27	4 12 06	17 27 20	23 27 50	20D 16.1	20 00.4	7 47.8	21 44.4	5 16.0	7 47.0	23 14.2	8 46.2	14 45.8	24 48.3
29 Su	12 28 23	5 11 02	29 25 38	5♋21 26	20 15.6	21 32.5	9 02.6	22 15.1	5 42.5	7 56.9	23 09.7	8 46.7	14 46.5	24 48.3
30 M	12 32 20	6 10 00	11♋15 54	17 09 45	20R 15.8	23 03.8	10 17.4	22 46.1	6 09.0	8 06.7	23 05.2	8 47.3	14 47.1	24 48.2

LONGITUDE — October 1907

Day	Sid.Time	☉	0 hr ☽	Noon ☽	True ☊	☿	♀	♂	⚳	♃	♄	♅	♆	♇
1 Tu	12 36 17	7♎09 00	23♋03 39	28♋58 18	20♋15.6	24♎34.1	11♎32.3	23♑17.4	6♍35.5	8♌16.3	23♓00.8	8♑47.9	14♋47.7	24♊48.1
2 W	12 40 13	8 08 03	4♌54 20	10♌52 22	20R 13.9	26 03.6	12 47.1	23 49.0	7 02.0	8 25.9	22R 56.4	8 48.6	14 48.3	24R 47.9
3 Th	12 44 10	9 07 08	16 52 59	22 56 41	20 09.9	27 32.2	14 02.0	24 21.0	7 28.4	8 35.3	22 52.0	8 49.3	14 48.9	24 47.8
4 F	12 48 06	10 06 15	29 03 57	5♍15 08	20 03.2	28 59.9	15 16.9	24 53.3	7 54.7	8 44.6	22 47.7	8 50.1	14 49.4	24 47.6
5 Sa	12 52 03	11 05 24	11♍30 32	17 50 23	19 53.8	0♏26.7	16 31.7	25 25.8	8 21.1	8 53.9	22 43.4	8 50.9	14 49.9	24 47.4
6 Su	12 55 59	12 04 35	24 14 47	0♎43 44	19 42.2	1 52.6	17 46.6	25 58.7	8 47.4	9 03.0	22 39.1	8 51.8	14 50.3	24 47.1
7 M	12 59 56	13 03 48	7♎17 11	13 54 57	19 29.4	3 17.5	19 01.5	26 31.8	9 13.6	9 11.9	22 34.9	8 52.7	14 50.7	24 46.9
8 Tu	13 03 52	14 03 04	20 36 46	27 22 20	19 16.5	4 41.5	20 16.4	27 05.3	9 39.8	9 20.8	22 30.7	8 53.6	14 51.1	24 46.6
9 W	13 07 49	15 02 21	4♏11 16	11♏03 10	19 04.9	6 04.6	21 31.4	27 39.0	10 06.0	9 29.6	22 26.6	8 54.7	14 51.5	24 46.3
10 Th	13 11 45	16 01 41	17 57 35	24 54 07	18 55.5	7 26.6	22 46.3	28 12.9	10 32.1	9 38.2	22 22.6	8 55.7	14 51.8	24 46.0
11 F	13 15 42	17 01 02	1♐52 21	8♐51 56	18 49.1	8 47.5	24 01.2	28 47.2	10 58.2	9 46.7	22 18.5	8 56.9	14 52.0	24 45.7
12 Sa	13 19 39	18 00 25	15 52 34	22 53 59	18 45.5	10 07.4	25 16.1	29 21.7	11 24.2	9 55.1	22 14.6	8 58.0	14 52.3	24 45.3
13 Su	13 23 35	18 59 50	29 55 57	6♑58 20	18 44.1	11 26.0	26 31.1	29 56.4	11 50.2	10 03.3	22 10.7	8 59.3	14 52.5	24 45.0
14 M	13 27 32	19 59 17	14♑00 59	21 03 51	18 44.0	12 43.4	27 46.0	0♒31.4	12 16.1	10 11.5	22 06.9	9 00.5	14 52.7	24 44.6
15 Tu	13 31 28	20 58 45	28 06 48	5♒09 45	18 43.7	13 59.5	29 00.9	1 06.6	12 42.0	10 19.4	22 03.1	9 01.9	14 52.8	24 44.2
16 W	13 35 25	21 58 15	12♒12 37	19 15 13	18 41.8	15 14.2	0♏15.9	1 42.0	13 07.8	10 27.3	21 59.4	9 03.2	14 52.9	24 43.7
17 Th	13 39 21	22 57 47	26 17 22	3♓18 50	18 37.6	16 27.3	1 30.8	2 17.6	13 33.6	10 35.0	21 55.7	9 04.6	14 53.0	24 43.3
18 F	13 43 18	23 57 21	10♓19 17	17 18 23	18 30.4	17 38.8	2 45.8	2 53.5	13 59.3	10 42.6	21 52.2	9 06.1	14R 53.1	24 42.8
19 Sa	13 47 14	24 56 56	24 15 42	1♈10 50	18 20.4	18 48.5	4 00.7	3 29.6	14 24.9	10 50.1	21 48.7	9 07.6	14 53.1	24 42.3
20 Su	13 51 11	25 56 33	8♈03 17	14 52 38	18 08.5	19 56.2	5 15.6	4 05.8	14 50.5	10 57.4	21 45.2	9 09.2	14 53.0	24 41.8
21 M	13 55 08	26 56 12	21 38 26	28 20 19	17 55.7	21 01.8	6 30.6	4 42.2	15 16.1	11 04.6	21 41.9	9 10.8	14 53.0	24 41.2
22 Tu	13 59 04	27 55 53	4♉57 57	11♉31 07	17 43.2	22 05.1	7 45.5	5 18.9	15 41.6	11 11.6	21 38.6	9 12.4	14 52.9	24 40.7
23 W	14 03 01	28 55 37	17 59 39	24 23 30	17 32.3	23 05.8	9 00.5	5 55.7	16 07.0	11 18.5	21 35.4	9 14.1	14 52.8	24 40.1
24 Th	14 06 57	29 55 22	0♊42 42	6♊57 25	17 23.7	24 03.6	10 15.4	6 32.7	16 32.3	11 25.3	21 32.2	9 15.9	14 52.6	24 39.5
25 F	14 10 54	0♏55 10	13 07 52	19 14 24	17 17.9	24 58.2	11 30.4	7 09.9	16 57.6	11 31.9	21 29.2	9 17.7	14 52.4	24 38.9
26 Sa	14 14 50	1 54 59	25 17 25	1♋17 24	17 14.7	25 49.4	12 45.4	7 47.2	17 22.9	11 38.3	21 26.2	9 19.5	14 52.2	24 38.3
27 Su	14 18 47	2 54 51	7♋14 53	13 10 29	17D 13.6	26 36.7	14 00.3	8 24.7	17 48.0	11 44.6	21 23.3	9 21.4	14 51.9	24 37.6
28 M	14 22 43	3 54 45	19 04 48	24 58 31	17R 13.7	27 19.7	15 15.3	9 02.4	18 13.1	11 50.8	21 20.5	9 23.3	14 51.6	24 36.9
29 Tu	14 26 40	4 54 42	0♌52 20	6♌46 55	17 13.9	27 57.9	16 30.3	9 40.2	18 38.2	11 56.8	21 17.8	9 25.3	14 51.3	24 36.2
30 W	14 30 37	5 54 40	12 42 59	18 41 13	17 13.1	28 30.8	17 45.3	10 18.2	19 03.1	12 02.6	21 15.2	9 27.3	14 50.9	24 35.5
31 Th	14 34 33	6 54 41	24 42 18	0♍46 50	17 10.4	28 57.9	19 00.2	10 56.3	19 28.0	12 08.3	21 12.6	9 29.3	14 50.5	24 34.8

Astro Data

	Dy Hr Mn
♄□♇	8 17:54
☽0S	10 0:43
☿0S	17 11:05
♅D	18 22:04
☽0N	22 21:21
⊙0S	24 5:08
♀0S	24 16:53
♇R	25 20:52
♃⚼♄	30 9:35
♃⚻♅	5 3:29
☽0S	7 7:42
♃∠♇	11 9:18
♆R	19 4:32
☽0N	20 6:11

Planet Ingress

		Dy Hr Mn
☿	♎	16 6:56
⚳	♍	16 16:18
♀	♎	22 5:52
⊙	♎	24 5:09
☿	♏	5 4:36
♂	♒	13 14:29
♀	♏	16 6:55
⊙	♏	24 13:52

Last Aspect / ☽ Ingress (September)

Last Aspect Dy Hr Mn		☽ Ingress	Dy Hr Mn
1 7:50	♄ □	♋	1 17:22
3 20:28	♄ △	♌	4 6:20
6 7:38	♇ ✱	♍	6 17:56
8 17:18	♄ ☍	♎	9 3:07
11 0:35	♇ △	♏	11 10:01
13 5:41	☿ ✱	♐	13 15:07
15 17:03	☿ □	♑	15 18:46
17 11:20	♄ ✱	♒	17 21:12
19 14:24	♇ △	♓	19 23:02
22 0:59	♀ ☍	♈	22 1:25
23 20:36	♇ ✱	♉	24 5:55
26 1:14	♄ ✱	♊	26 13:49
28 14:42	♇ ☌	♋	29 1:09

Last Aspect / ☽ Ingress (October)

Last Aspect Dy Hr Mn		☽ Ingress	Dy Hr Mn
1 1:46	☿ □	♌	1 14:05
3 22:14	☿ ✱	♍	4 1:49
6 2:50	♂ △	♎	6 10:39
8 11:28	♂ □	♏	8 16:38
10 17:57	♂ ✱	♐	10 20:47
12 16:26	♀ ✱	♑	13 0:07
15 0:31	♀ □	♒	15 3:13
16 21:20	♇ △	♓	17 6:20
19 0:46	♇ □	♈	19 9:57
21 9:17	⊙ ☍	♉	21 15:00
23 9:21	☿ ☍	♊	23 22:38
25 22:43	♇ ☌	♋	26 9:25
28 17:05	☿ △	♌	28 22:14
31 8:18	☿ □	♍	31 10:28

☽ Phases & Eclipses

Dy Hr Mn		
7 21:04	●	14♍04
15 3:40	☽	21♐09
21 21:34	○	27♓44
29 11:37	☾	5♋10
7 10:20	●	13♎00
14 10:02	☽	19♑54
21 9:17	○	26♈49
29 7:51	☾	4♌44

Astro Data

1 September 1907
Julian Day # 2800
SVP 6♓33'12"
GC 25♐33.0 ⚴ 4♌45.3
Eris 25♓01.1R ⚵ 10♏04.4
⚷ 14♒27.9R ⚶ 4♋52.4
☽ Mean ☊ 20♋54.5

1 October 1907
Julian Day # 2830
SVP 6♓33'09"
GC 25♐33.1 ⚴ 21♌36.8
Eris 24♓40.4R ⚵ 18♏26.0
⚷ 13♒22.4R ⚶ 13♋58.3
☽ Mean ☊ 19♋19.1

November 1907 LONGITUDE

Day	Sid.Time	☉	0 hr ☽	Noon ☽	True ☊	☿	♀	♂	⚳	♃	♄	♅	♆	♇
1 F	14 38 30	7♏54 43	6♍55 24	13♍08 33	17♋05.3	29♏18.4	20♏15.2	11♒34.6	19♍52.8	12♌13.8	21♓10.2	9♑31.4	14♋50.1	24♊34.1
2 Sa	14 42 26	8 54 48	19 26 43	25 50 14	16R 57.6	29 31.9	21 30.2	12 13.0	20 17.6	12 19.1	21R 07.8	9 33.6	14R 49.6	24R 33.3
3 Su	14 46 23	9 54 55	2♎19 21	8♎54 13	16 47.8	29R 37.7	22 45.2	12 51.6	20 42.2	12 24.3	21 05.6	9 35.8	14 49.2	24 32.5
4 M	14 50 19	10 55 04	15 34 48	22 20 58	16 36.8	29 35.0	24 00.2	13 30.3	21 06.8	12 29.3	21 03.4	9 38.0	14 48.6	24 31.7
5 Tu	14 54 16	11 55 15	29 12 28	6♏08 52	16 25.5	29 23.4	25 15.2	14 09.1	21 31.3	12 34.2	21 01.3	9 40.3	14 48.1	24 30.9
6 W	14 58 12	12 55 27	13♏09 41	20 14 16	16 15.3	29 02.3	26 30.2	14 48.1	21 55.7	12 38.9	20 59.3	9 42.6	14 47.5	24 30.1
7 Th	15 02 09	13 55 42	27 21 58	4♐32 03	16 07.1	28 31.4	27 45.2	15 27.2	22 20.0	12 43.4	20 57.4	9 44.9	14 46.9	24 29.2
8 F	15 06 06	14 55 58	11♐43 46	18 56 26	16 01.6	27 50.7	29 00.2	16 06.5	22 44.2	12 47.7	20 55.7	9 47.3	14 46.2	24 28.4
9 Sa	15 10 02	15 56 16	26 09 21	3♑21 54	15D 58.8	27 00.3	0♐15.2	16 45.8	23 08.4	12 51.9	20 54.0	9 49.7	14 45.5	24 27.5
10 Su	15 13 59	16 56 35	10♑33 36	17 43 59	15 58.2	26 00.8	1 30.2	17 25.3	23 32.4	12 55.8	20 52.4	9 52.2	14 44.8	24 26.6
11 M	15 17 55	17 56 56	24 52 43	1♒59 33	15 58.7	24 53.4	2 45.2	18 04.9	23 56.4	12 59.6	20 50.9	9 54.7	14 44.1	24 25.7
12 Tu	15 21 52	18 57 18	9♒04 15	16 06 43	15R 59.4	23 39.5	4 00.2	18 44.6	24 20.2	13 03.3	20 49.5	9 57.2	14 43.3	24 24.8
13 W	15 25 48	19 57 41	23 06 53	0♓04 39	15 58.9	22 21.1	5 15.2	19 24.4	24 44.0	13 06.7	20 48.2	9 59.8	14 42.5	24 23.9
14 Th	15 29 45	20 58 06	7♓00 01	13 52 55	15 56.5	21 00.6	6 30.2	20 04.3	25 07.6	13 10.0	20 47.1	10 02.4	14 41.7	24 22.9
15 F	15 33 41	21 58 32	20 43 19	27 31 09	15 51.8	19 40.6	7 45.1	20 44.3	25 31.2	13 13.1	20 46.0	10 05.1	14 40.8	24 22.0
16 Sa	15 37 38	22 58 59	4♈16 20	10♈58 47	15 44.8	18 23.7	9 00.1	21 24.4	25 54.6	13 16.0	20 45.0	10 07.8	14 39.9	24 21.0
17 Su	15 41 35	23 59 28	17 38 22	24 14 57	15 36.1	17 12.5	10 15.1	22 04.6	26 18.0	13 18.7	20 44.1	10 10.5	14 39.0	24 20.0
18 M	15 45 31	24 59 58	0♉48 24	7♉18 37	15 26.7	16 09.1	11 30.0	22 44.9	26 41.2	13 21.2	20 43.4	10 13.2	14 38.0	24 19.0
19 Tu	15 49 28	26 00 29	13 45 27	20 08 50	15 17.5	15 15.2	12 45.0	23 25.2	27 04.3	13 23.5	20 42.7	10 16.0	14 37.0	24 18.0
20 W	15 53 24	27 01 03	26 28 44	2♊45 06	15 09.4	14 32.2	14 00.0	24 05.7	27 27.4	13 25.7	20 42.2	10 18.8	14 36.0	24 17.0
21 Th	15 57 21	28 01 37	8♊58 01	15 07 34	15 03.2	14 00.6	15 14.9	24 46.2	27 50.3	13 27.6	20 41.7	10 21.7	14 35.0	24 16.0
22 F	16 01 17	29 02 14	21 13 55	27 17 17	14 59.2	13 40.7	16 29.9	25 26.8	28 13.1	13 29.4	20 41.4	10 24.6	14 33.9	24 14.9
23 Sa	16 05 14	0♐02 51	3♋17 57	9♋16 15	14D 57.4	13D 32.3	17 44.8	26 07.4	28 35.7	13 31.0	20 41.2	10 27.5	14 32.9	24 13.9
24 Su	16 09 10	1 03 31	15 12 35	21 07 25	14 57.4	13 35.0	18 59.8	26 48.2	28 58.3	13 32.4	20D 41.0	10 30.4	14 31.8	24 12.8
25 M	16 13 07	2 04 12	27 01 14	2♌54 35	14 58.6	13 48.1	20 14.7	27 29.0	29 20.7	13 33.6	20 41.0	10 33.4	14 30.6	24 11.7
26 Tu	16 17 04	3 04 54	8♌48 04	14 42 16	15 00.3	14 10.8	21 29.7	28 09.8	29 43.0	13 34.6	20 41.1	10 36.4	14 29.5	24 10.6
27 W	16 21 00	4 05 38	20 37 49	26 35 24	15R 01.6	14 42.1	22 44.6	28 50.8	0♎05.2	13 35.4	20 41.3	10 39.4	14 28.3	24 09.6
28 Th	16 24 57	5 06 24	2♍35 40	8♍39 16	15 01.8	15 21.3	23 59.6	29 31.8	0 27.2	13 36.0	20 41.6	10 42.5	14 27.1	24 08.5
29 F	16 28 53	6 07 11	14 46 50	20 58 59	15 00.5	16 07.4	25 14.5	0♓12.8	0 49.2	13 36.4	20 42.0	10 45.6	14 25.8	24 07.3
30 Sa	16 32 50	7 08 00	27 16 17	3♎39 13	14 57.6	16 59.6	26 29.4	0 54.0	1 10.9	13R 36.6	20 42.5	10 48.7	14 24.6	24 06.2

December 1907 LONGITUDE

Day	Sid.Time	☉	0 hr ☽	Noon ☽	True ☊	☿	♀	♂	⚳	♃	♄	♅	♆	♇
1 Su	16 36 46	8♐08 50	10♎08 13	16♎43 35	14♋53.0	17♏57.1	27♐44.4	1♓35.2	1♎32.6	13♌36.6	20♓43.2	10♑51.8	14♋23.3	24♊05.1
2 M	16 40 43	9 09 41	23 25 32	0♏14 06	14R 47.5	18 59.4	28 59.3	2 16.4	1 54.1	13R 36.4	20 43.9	10 55.0	14R 22.0	24R 04.0
3 Tu	16 44 39	10 10 34	7♏09 13	14 10 36	14 41.7	20 05.7	0♑14.2	2 57.7	2 15.4	13 36.0	20 44.7	10 58.1	14 20.6	24 02.8
4 W	16 48 36	11 11 28	21 17 51	28 30 23	14 36.3	21 15.5	1 29.2	3 39.1	2 36.6	13 35.4	20 45.7	11 01.4	14 19.3	24 01.7
5 Th	16 52 33	12 12 24	5♐47 29	13♐08 18	14 32.1	22 28.4	2 44.1	4 20.5	2 57.7	13 34.7	20 46.7	11 04.6	14 17.9	24 00.6
6 F	16 56 29	13 13 20	20 31 54	27 57 17	14 29.5	23 43.9	3 59.0	5 01.9	3 18.5	13 33.7	20 47.9	11 07.8	14 16.5	23 59.4
7 Sa	17 00 26	14 14 18	5♑23 28	12♑49 27	14D 28.5	25 01.6	5 13.9	5 43.5	3 39.3	13 32.5	20 49.2	11 11.1	14 15.1	23 58.2
8 Su	17 04 22	15 15 16	20 14 20	27 37 14	14 29.0	26 21.3	6 28.8	6 25.0	3 59.9	13 31.1	20 50.6	11 14.4	14 13.7	23 57.1
9 M	17 08 19	16 16 15	4♒57 27	12♒14 22	14 30.4	27 42.7	7 43.7	7 06.7	4 20.3	13 29.6	20 52.0	11 17.7	14 12.3	23 55.9
10 Tu	17 12 15	17 17 14	19 27 30	26 36 29	14 31.9	29 05.5	8 58.6	7 48.3	4 40.5	13 27.8	20 53.6	11 21.1	14 10.8	23 54.8
11 W	17 16 12	18 18 14	3♓41 04	10♓41 08	14R 32.9	0♐29.5	10 13.5	8 30.0	5 00.6	13 25.8	20 55.3	11 24.4	14 09.3	23 53.6
12 Th	17 20 08	19 19 15	17 36 36	24 27 31	14 33.0	1 54.6	11 28.4	9 11.7	5 20.4	13 23.6	20 57.1	11 27.8	14 07.8	23 52.4
13 F	17 24 05	20 20 16	1♈13 57	7♈56 01	14 31.9	3 20.6	12 43.2	9 53.5	5 40.2	13 21.3	20 59.0	11 31.2	14 06.3	23 51.2
14 Sa	17 28 02	21 21 17	14 33 54	21 07 44	14 29.7	4 47.5	13 58.1	10 35.3	5 59.7	13 18.7	21 01.0	11 34.6	14 04.8	23 50.1
15 Su	17 31 58	22 22 19	27 37 44	4♉04 04	14 26.6	6 15.0	15 12.9	11 17.1	6 19.1	13 16.0	21 03.1	11 38.0	14 03.3	23 48.9
16 M	17 35 55	23 23 22	10♉26 54	16 46 26	14 23.2	7 43.2	16 27.7	11 59.0	6 38.2	13 13.1	21 05.4	11 41.5	14 01.7	23 47.7
17 Tu	17 39 51	24 24 25	23 02 49	29 16 13	14 19.8	9 11.8	17 42.5	12 40.8	6 57.2	13 10.0	21 07.7	11 44.9	14 00.1	23 46.5
18 W	17 43 48	25 25 28	5♊26 49	11♊34 46	14 16.9	10 41.0	18 57.3	13 22.7	7 16.0	13 06.7	21 10.1	11 48.4	13 58.5	23 45.3
19 Th	17 47 44	26 26 32	17 40 13	23 43 22	14 14.8	12 10.6	20 12.1	14 04.6	7 34.6	13 03.2	21 12.6	11 51.9	13 57.0	23 44.2
20 F	17 51 41	27 27 37	29 44 24	5♋43 32	14D 13.6	13 40.6	21 26.8	14 46.6	7 53.0	12 59.5	21 15.2	11 55.4	13 55.4	23 43.0
21 Sa	17 55 37	28 28 42	11♋40 59	17 37 00	14 13.5	15 11.0	22 41.6	15 28.6	8 11.2	12 55.6	21 17.9	11 58.9	13 53.7	23 41.8
22 Su	17 59 34	29 29 48	23 31 53	29 25 58	14 14.0	16 41.7	23 56.3	16 10.5	8 29.2	12 51.6	21 20.8	12 02.4	13 52.1	23 40.6
23 M	18 03 31	0♑30 55	5♌19 34	11♌13 05	14 15.2	18 12.7	25 11.0	16 52.5	8 47.0	12 47.4	21 23.7	12 05.9	13 50.5	23 39.5
24 Tu	18 07 27	1 32 01	17 06 56	23 01 35	14 16.5	19 44.0	26 25.7	17 34.6	9 04.6	12 43.0	21 26.7	12 09.4	13 48.8	23 38.3
25 W	18 11 24	2 33 09	28 57 30	4♍55 12	14 17.7	21 15.6	27 40.4	18 16.6	9 21.9	12 38.5	21 29.8	12 13.0	13 47.2	23 37.1
26 Th	18 15 20	3 34 17	10♍55 15	16 58 10	14 18.7	22 47.5	28 55.1	18 58.6	9 39.0	12 33.7	21 33.0	12 16.5	13 45.5	23 36.0
27 F	18 19 17	4 35 25	23 04 32	29 14 56	14R 19.1	24 19.7	0♒09.7	19 40.7	9 55.9	12 28.8	21 36.3	12 20.1	13 43.8	23 34.8
28 Sa	18 23 13	5 36 35	5♎29 55	11♎50 03	14 19.1	25 52.2	1 24.3	20 22.8	10 12.6	12 23.8	21 39.7	12 23.6	13 42.2	23 33.7
29 Su	18 27 10	6 37 44	18 15 48	24 47 38	14 18.7	27 24.9	2 39.0	21 04.9	10 29.1	12 18.5	21 43.2	12 27.2	13 40.5	23 32.5
30 M	18 31 06	7 38 54	1♏25 56	8♏10 58	14 18.1	28 58.0	3 53.6	21 47.0	10 45.3	12 13.2	21 46.7	12 30.8	13 38.8	23 31.4
31 Tu	18 35 03	8 40 05	15 02 54	22 01 46	14 17.3	0♑31.3	5 08.2	22 29.1	11 01.2	12 07.6	21 50.4	12 34.3	13 37.1	23 30.2

Astro Data	Planet Ingress	Last Aspect	☽ Ingress	Last Aspect	☽ Ingress	☽ Phases & Eclipses	Astro Data
Dy Hr Mn	Dy Hr Mn	Dy Hr Mn	Dy Hr Mn	Dy Hr Mn	Dy Hr Mn	Dy Hr Mn	1 November 1907
☿ R 3 16:40	♀ ♐ 9 7:08	2 18:56 ☿ ⚹	♎ 2 19:43	2 9:36 ♀ ⚹	♏ 2 11:35	5 22:39 ● 12♏22	Julian Day # 2861
☽ 0S 3 17:04	☉ ♐ 23 10:52	4 15:49 ♇ △	♏ 5 1:23	3 23:05 ♄ △	♐ 4 14:28	12 17:14 ☽ 19♒10	SVP 6♓33'06"
☽ 0N 16 13:35	⚳ ♎ 27 6:21	7 2:19 ☿ ☌	♐ 7 4:25	6 5:36 ♇ ☍	♑ 6 15:18	20 0:04 ○ 26♉31	GC 25♐33.1 ⚴ 7♍17.3
☿ D 23 17:57	♂ ♓ 29 4:30	8 21:12 ♇ ☍	♑ 9 6:24	8 9:44 ☿ ⚹	♒ 8 15:53	28 4:21 ☾ 4♍47	Eris 24♓21.6R ⚵ 28♏21.6
♄ D 25 4:06		11 0:55 ☿ ⚹	♒ 11 8:38	10 16:39 ☿ □	♓ 10 17:44		⚷ 13♒08.8 ⚶ 19♋52.0
	♀ ♑ 3 7:26	13 2:13 ♇ △	♓ 13 11:52	12 10:58 ♇ □	♈ 12 21:48	5 10:22 ● 12♐08	☽ Mean ☊ 17♋40.6
♃ R 1 1:20	☿ ♐ 11 3:37	15 6:26 ♇ □	♈ 15 16:24	14 16:58 ♇ ⚹	♉ 15 4:24	12 2:16 ☽ 18♓54	
☽ 0S 1 3:33	☉ ♑ 22 23:52	17 12:09 ♇ ⚹	♉ 17 22:31	16 20:16 ♄ ⚹	♊ 17 13:25	19 17:55 ○ 26♊42	1 December 1907
☽ 0N 13 19:44	♀ ♒ 27 8:53	20 0:04 ☉ ☍	♊ 20 6:43	19 17:55 ☉ ☍	♋ 20 0:31	27 23:10 ☾ 5♎04	Julian Day # 2891
♃⚻♅ 28 12:24	☿ ♑ 31 3:57	22 8:07 ♂ △	♋ 22 17:24	21 23:31 ♀ ☍	♌ 22 13:09		SVP 6♓33'02"
☽ 0S 28 12:56		24 11:06 ♄ △	♌ 25 6:04	24 13:14 ♇ ⚹	♍ 25 2:06		GC 25♐33.2 ⚴ 19♍46.7
		27 16:48 ♂ ☍	♍ 27 18:50	27 1:05 ☿ □	♎ 27 13:27		Eris 24♓11.5R ⚵ 8♐37.3
		29 21:02 ♀ □	♎ 30 5:09	29 17:24 ☿ ⚹	♏ 29 21:26		⚷ 13♒54.8 ⚶ 20♋05.2R
							☽ Mean ☊ 16♋05.3

LONGITUDE — January 1908

Day	Sid.Time	☉	0 hr ☽	Noon ☽	True ☊	☿	♀	♂	⚳	♃	♄	♅	♆	♇
1 W	18 39 00	9♑41 16	29♏07 25	6♐19 34	14♋16.7	2♑05.0	6♒22.7	23♓11.2	11♎16.9	12♌01.9	21♓54.2	12♑37.9	13♋35.4	23♊29.1
2 Th	18 42 56	10 42 27	13♐37 43	21 01 12	14R 16.3	3 39.0	7 37.3	23 53.3	11 32.4	11R 56.1	21 58.0	12 41.5	13R 33.7	23R 28.0
3 F	18 46 53	11 43 38	28 29 14	6♑00 47	14D 16.2	5 13.3	8 51.8	24 35.5	11 47.6	11 50.1	22 02.0	12 45.1	13 32.0	23 26.9
4 Sa	18 50 49	12 44 50	13♑34 48	21 10 04	14 16.2	6 48.0	10 06.3	25 17.7	12 02.5	11 44.0	22 06.0	12 48.7	13 30.3	23 25.8
5 Su	18 54 46	13 46 01	28 45 25	6♒19 37	14R 16.2	8 23.1	11 20.8	25 59.8	12 17.2	11 37.7	22 10.1	12 52.3	13 28.6	23 24.7
6 M	18 58 42	14 47 12	13♒51 33	21 20 10	14 16.2	9 58.5	12 35.3	26 42.0	12 31.6	11 31.3	22 14.3	12 55.8	13 26.9	23 23.6
7 Tu	19 02 39	15 48 23	28 44 33	6♓03 57	14 16.1	11 34.2	13 49.7	27 24.2	12 45.7	11 24.8	22 18.6	12 59.4	13 25.2	23 22.5
8 W	19 06 36	16 49 33	13♓17 46	20 25 36	14 15.9	13 10.4	15 04.1	28 06.4	12 59.6	11 18.1	22 23.0	13 03.0	13 23.5	23 21.4
9 Th	19 10 32	17 50 43	27 27 11	4♈22 25	14 15.7	14 47.0	16 18.5	28 48.6	13 13.1	11 11.4	22 27.4	13 06.6	13 21.8	23 20.3
10 F	19 14 29	18 51 52	11♈11 21	17 54 07	14D 15.5	16 24.1	17 32.9	29 30.7	13 26.4	11 04.5	22 32.0	13 10.1	13 20.2	23 19.3
11 Sa	19 18 25	19 53 00	24 30 58	1♉02 13	14 15.7	18 01.6	18 47.2	0♈12.9	13 39.4	10 57.5	22 36.6	13 13.7	13 18.5	23 18.2
12 Su	19 22 22	20 54 08	7♉28 15	13 49 28	14 16.1	19 39.5	20 01.5	0 55.1	13 52.0	10 50.4	22 41.3	13 17.3	13 16.8	23 17.2
13 M	19 26 18	21 55 16	20 06 17	26 19 09	14 16.8	21 17.9	21 15.7	1 37.3	14 04.4	10 43.2	22 46.1	13 20.8	13 15.1	23 16.2
14 Tu	19 30 15	22 56 23	2♊28 30	8♊34 45	14 17.7	22 56.8	22 29.9	2 19.4	14 16.5	10 36.0	22 50.9	13 24.4	13 13.4	23 15.2
15 W	19 34 11	23 57 29	14 38 18	20 39 32	14 18.6	24 36.2	23 44.1	3 01.6	14 28.3	10 28.6	22 55.9	13 27.9	13 11.8	23 14.2
16 Th	19 38 08	24 58 34	26 38 50	2♋36 31	14R 19.3	26 16.1	24 58.2	3 43.7	14 39.7	10 21.2	23 00.9	13 31.5	13 10.1	23 13.2
17 F	19 42 05	25 59 39	8♋32 55	14 28 19	14 19.6	27 56.5	26 12.3	4 25.9	14 50.9	10 13.6	23 05.9	13 35.0	13 08.5	23 12.2
18 Sa	19 46 01	27 00 44	20 23 00	26 17 15	14 19.3	29 37.4	27 26.4	5 08.0	15 01.7	10 06.0	23 11.1	13 38.5	13 06.8	23 11.3
19 Su	19 49 58	28 01 48	2♌11 19	8♌05 27	14 18.2	1♒18.8	28 40.4	5 50.1	15 12.1	9 58.4	23 16.3	13 42.0	13 05.2	23 10.3
20 M	19 53 54	29 02 51	13 59 54	19 54 56	14 16.4	3 00.7	29 54.4	6 32.2	15 22.3	9 50.7	23 21.6	13 45.5	13 03.6	23 09.4
21 Tu	19 57 51	0♒03 54	25 50 50	1♍47 52	14 14.0	4 43.1	1♓08.3	7 14.3	15 32.1	9 42.9	23 27.0	13 49.0	13 01.9	23 08.5
22 W	20 01 47	1 04 56	7♍46 20	13 46 34	14 11.3	6 25.9	2 22.2	7 56.4	15 41.6	9 35.1	23 32.4	13 52.4	13 00.3	23 07.5
23 Th	20 05 44	2 05 57	19 48 55	25 53 45	14 08.5	8 09.2	3 36.0	8 38.5	15 50.7	9 27.2	23 37.9	13 55.9	12 58.7	23 06.7
24 F	20 09 40	3 06 58	2♎01 28	8♎12 28	14 06.2	9 52.9	4 49.8	9 20.6	15 59.5	9 19.3	23 43.5	13 59.3	12 57.2	23 05.8
25 Sa	20 13 37	4 07 58	14 27 11	20 46 03	14 04.6	11 37.0	6 03.6	10 02.6	16 07.9	9 11.3	23 49.1	14 02.8	12 55.6	23 04.9
26 Su	20 17 34	5 08 58	27 09 32	3♏38 03	14D 04.0	13 21.3	7 17.3	10 44.6	16 15.9	9 03.4	23 54.8	14 06.2	12 54.0	23 04.1
27 M	20 21 30	6 09 58	10♏12 00	16 51 47	14 04.3	15 05.9	8 31.0	11 26.7	16 23.6	8 55.4	24 00.6	14 09.6	12 52.5	23 03.2
28 Tu	20 25 27	7 10 56	23 37 40	0♐29 56	14 05.5	16 50.5	9 44.6	12 08.7	16 30.9	8 47.4	24 06.4	14 12.9	12 51.0	23 02.4
29 W	20 29 23	8 11 55	7♐28 41	14 33 55	14 07.0	18 35.2	10 58.2	12 50.7	16 37.8	8 39.3	24 12.3	14 16.3	12 49.5	23 01.6
30 Th	20 33 20	9 12 52	21 45 32	29 03 11	14 08.3	20 19.6	12 11.7	13 32.7	16 44.4	8 31.3	24 18.3	14 19.6	12 48.0	23 00.9
31 F	20 37 16	10 13 49	6♑26 24	13♑54 31	14R 08.9	22 03.8	13 25.2	14 14.7	16 50.5	8 23.3	24 24.3	14 23.0	12 46.5	23 00.1

LONGITUDE — February 1908

Day	Sid.Time	☉	0 hr ☽	Noon ☽	True ☊	☿	♀	♂	⚳	♃	♄	♅	♆	♇
1 Sa	20 41 13	11♒14 45	21♑26 40	29♑01 50	14♋08.3	23♒47.4	14♓38.6	14♈56.6	16♎56.3	8♌15.3	24♓30.4	14♑26.3	12♋45.1	22♊59.4
2 Su	20 45 09	12 15 40	6♒38 51	14♒16 29	14R 06.1	25 30.3	15 52.0	15 38.6	17 01.7	8R 07.3	24 36.5	14 29.6	12R 43.6	22R 58.6
3 M	20 49 06	13 16 33	21 53 25	29 28 21	14 02.6	27 12.1	17 05.3	16 20.5	17 06.6	7 59.4	24 42.7	14 32.8	12 42.2	22 57.9
4 Tu	20 53 03	14 17 26	7♓00 04	14♓27 24	13 58.2	28 52.4	18 18.6	17 02.4	17 11.2	7 51.4	24 48.9	14 36.1	12 40.8	22 57.2
5 W	20 56 59	15 18 17	21 49 25	29 05 18	13 53.5	0♓31.0	19 31.8	17 44.3	17 15.3	7 43.5	24 55.2	14 39.3	12 39.4	22 56.6
6 Th	21 00 56	16 19 06	6♈14 28	13♈16 34	13 49.2	2 07.4	20 44.9	18 26.2	17 19.1	7 35.6	25 01.6	14 42.5	12 38.0	22 55.9
7 F	21 04 52	17 19 55	20 11 22	26 58 54	13 46.0	3 41.0	21 58.0	19 08.1	17 22.4	7 27.8	25 08.0	14 45.6	12 36.7	22 55.3
8 Sa	21 08 49	18 20 41	3♉39 19	10♉12 54	13D 44.2	5 11.4	23 11.0	19 50.0	17 25.3	7 20.1	25 14.4	14 48.8	12 35.4	22 54.7
9 Su	21 12 45	19 21 26	16 40 05	23 01 19	13 44.0	6 38.0	24 23.9	20 31.8	17 27.8	7 12.4	25 20.9	14 51.9	12 34.1	22 54.1
10 M	21 16 42	20 22 10	29 17 10	5♊28 13	13 45.0	8 00.0	25 36.8	21 13.6	17 29.9	7 04.7	25 27.4	14 55.0	12 32.8	22 53.5
11 Tu	21 20 38	21 22 52	11♊35 03	17 38 19	13 46.6	9 16.9	26 49.6	21 55.4	17 31.6	6 57.1	25 34.0	14 58.0	12 31.5	22 52.9
12 W	21 24 35	22 23 32	23 38 34	29 36 25	13 48.3	10 27.9	28 02.3	22 37.1	17 32.8	6 49.7	25 40.6	15 01.1	12 30.3	22 52.4
13 Th	21 28 32	23 24 11	5♋32 25	11♋27 05	13R 49.2	11 32.2	29 14.9	23 18.9	17 33.6	6 42.2	25 47.3	15 04.1	12 29.1	22 51.9
14 F	21 32 28	24 24 48	17 20 54	23 14 19	13 48.7	12 29.2	0♈27.5	24 00.6	17R 34.0	6 34.9	25 54.0	15 07.1	12 27.9	22 51.4
15 Sa	21 36 25	25 25 24	29 07 44	5♌01 31	13 46.3	13 18.2	1 39.9	24 42.3	17 33.9	6 27.7	26 00.8	15 10.0	12 26.8	22 50.9
16 Su	21 40 21	26 25 57	10♌55 59	16 51 26	13 41.8	13 58.4	2 52.3	25 23.9	17 33.4	6 20.5	26 07.6	15 12.9	12 25.6	22 50.5
17 M	21 44 18	27 26 30	22 48 06	28 46 13	13 35.3	14 29.4	4 04.6	26 05.6	17 32.5	6 13.5	26 14.4	15 15.8	12 24.5	22 50.1
18 Tu	21 48 14	28 27 01	4♍45 58	10♍47 31	13 27.2	14 50.7	5 16.9	26 47.2	17 31.2	6 06.5	26 21.3	15 18.7	12 23.4	22 49.6
19 W	21 52 11	29 27 30	16 51 03	22 56 42	13 18.2	15R 01.9	6 29.0	27 28.7	17 29.4	5 59.7	26 28.2	15 21.5	12 22.4	22 49.3
20 Th	21 56 07	0♓27 58	29 04 38	5♎15 00	13 09.2	15 02.9	7 41.1	28 10.3	17 27.2	5 53.0	26 35.1	15 24.3	12 21.4	22 48.9
21 F	22 00 04	1 28 24	11♎28 00	17 43 47	13 01.1	14 53.7	8 53.0	28 51.8	17 24.5	5 46.4	26 42.1	15 27.0	12 20.4	22 48.5
22 Sa	22 04 01	2 28 49	24 02 36	0♏24 39	12 54.6	14 34.6	10 04.9	29 33.3	17 21.4	5 39.9	26 49.1	15 29.8	12 19.4	22 48.2
23 Su	22 07 57	3 29 13	6♏50 14	13 19 35	12 50.3	14 06.1	11 16.7	0♉14.8	17 17.9	5 33.5	26 56.2	15 32.5	12 18.4	22 47.9
24 M	22 11 54	4 29 35	19 53 01	26 30 49	12D 48.2	13 28.9	12 28.4	0 56.3	17 14.0	5 27.3	27 03.2	15 35.1	12 17.5	22 47.6
25 Tu	22 15 50	5 29 56	3♐13 16	10♐00 38	12 48.0	12 44.0	13 40.0	1 37.7	17 09.6	5 21.2	27 10.3	15 37.7	12 16.6	22 47.4
26 W	22 19 47	6 30 15	16 53 08	23 50 56	12 48.8	11 52.5	14 51.5	2 19.1	17 04.8	5 15.2	27 17.5	15 40.3	12 15.8	22 47.1
27 Th	22 23 43	7 30 33	0♑54 05	8♑02 35	12R 49.6	10 55.7	16 02.9	3 00.5	16 59.6	5 09.4	27 24.6	15 42.9	12 14.9	22 46.9
28 F	22 27 40	8 30 50	15 16 14	22 34 44	12 49.3	9 55.3	17 14.2	3 41.9	16 53.9	5 03.8	27 31.8	15 45.4	12 14.1	22 46.7
29 Sa	22 31 36	9 31 05	29 57 34	7♒24 06	12 47.0	8 52.7	18 25.4	4 23.2	16 47.8	4 58.2	27 39.0	15 47.9	12 13.4	22 46.6

Astro Data

	Dy Hr Mn
☽0N	10 2:03
♂0N	12 2:42
♅☍♆	12 9:43
♄□♇	18 12:35
☽0S	24 19:47
♃⚼♄	27 2:51
♃∠♇	3 16:43
☽0N	6 10:04
⚳R	14 21:01
♀0N	15 10:46
☿R	20 2:19
☽0S	21 0:53

Planet Ingress

		Dy Hr Mn
♂	♈	11 4:39
☿	♒	18 17:22
♀	♓	20 13:50
☉	♒	21 10:28
☿	♓	5 4:24
♀	♈	14 2:55
☉	♓	20 0:54
♂	♉	23 3:25

Last Aspect / ☽ Ingress (January)

Last Aspect Dy Hr Mn		☽ Ingress	Dy Hr Mn
31 12:49	♂ △	♐	1 1:28
2 16:51	♂ □	♑	3 2:25
4 18:50	♂ ⚹	♒	5 1:58
6 15:19	♇ △	♓	7 2:03
9 1:49	♂ ☌	♈	9 4:24
10 21:48	♇ ⚹	♉	11 10:05
13 5:05	♄ ⚹	♊	13 19:10
15 18:52	♀ △	♋	16 6:45
18 13:37	☉ ☍	♌	18 19:33
20 18:33	♇ ⚹	♍	21 8:23
23 7:31	♄ ☍	♎	23 20:03
25 16:21	♇ △	♏	26 5:17
28 0:46	♄ △	♐	28 11:08
30 4:09	♄ □	♑	30 13:33

Last Aspect / ☽ Ingress (February)

Last Aspect Dy Hr Mn		☽ Ingress	Dy Hr Mn
1 4:48	♄ ⚹	♒	1 13:32
3 7:57	☿ ☌	♓	3 12:50
5 5:03	♄ ☌	♈	5 13:31
7 4:48	♇ ⚹	♉	7 17:24
9 16:29	♄ ⚹	♊	10 1:23
12 8:29	♀ □	♋	12 12:48
14 17:29	♄ △	♌	15 1:46
17 9:05	☉ ☍	♍	17 14:28
19 18:58	♄ ☍	♎	20 1:48
22 10:18	♂ ☍	♏	22 11:14
24 12:59	♄ △	♐	24 18:15
26 17:56	♄ □	♑	26 22:28
28 20:08	♄ ⚹	♒	29 0:04

☽ Phases & Eclipses

Dy Hr Mn	
3 21:43	● 12♑08
3 21:45:14	● T 04'14"
10 13:53	☽ 18♈57
18 13:37	○ 27♋05
18 13:21	☍ A 0.537
26 15:01	☾ 5♏17
2 8:36	● 12♒07
9 4:27	☽ 19♉02
17 9:05	○ 27♌19
25 3:24	☾ 5♐08

Astro Data

1 January 1908
Julian Day # 2922
SVP 6♓32'56"
GC 25♐33.3 ⚵ 28♍15.3
Eris 24♓13.0 ⚴ 19♐22.3
⚷ 15♒33.6 ⚶ 13♋55.7R
☽ Mean ☊ 14♋26.8

1 February 1908
Julian Day # 2953
SVP 6♓32'51"
GC 25♐33.3 ⚵ 29♍36.4R
Eris 24♓26.3 ⚴ 29♐42.5
⚷ 17♒43.5 ⚶ 6♋44.8R
☽ Mean ☊ 12♋48.4

March 1908 LONGITUDE

Day	Sid.Time	☉	0 hr ☽	Noon ☽	True ☊	☿	♀	♂	⚳	♃	♄	♅	♆	♇
1 Su	22 35 33	10♓31 18	14♒53 28	22♒24 42	12♋42.1	7♓49.4	19♈36.5	5♉04.5	16♎41.4	4♌52.9	27♓46.3	15♑50.3	12♋12.6	22♊46.4
2 M	22 39 30	11 31 30	29 56 41	7♓28 13	12R34.8	6R46.9	20 47.5	5 45.8	16R34.5	4R47.7	27 53.5	15 52.7	12R11.9	22R46.3
3 Tu	22 43 26	12 31 40	14♓58 04	22 25 02	12 25.6	5 46.7	21 58.4	6 27.1	16 27.2	4 42.6	28 00.8	15 55.1	12 11.2	22 46.2
4 W	22 47 23	13 31 48	29 48 00	7♈05 57	12 15.7	4 49.9	23 09.2	7 08.3	16 19.5	4 37.7	28 08.1	15 57.4	12 10.6	22 46.1
5 Th	22 51 19	14 31 54	14♈18 01	21 23 36	12 06.2	3 57.5	24 19.9	7 49.5	16 11.4	4 33.0	28 15.4	15 59.7	12 10.0	22 46.1
6 F	22 55 16	15 31 58	28 22 12	5♉13 36	11 58.1	3 10.4	25 30.4	8 30.7	16 03.0	4 28.5	28 22.8	16 01.9	12 09.4	22D46.0
7 Sa	22 59 12	16 31 59	11♉57 44	18 34 45	11 52.3	2 29.1	26 40.8	9 11.9	15 54.2	4 24.1	28 30.1	16 04.1	12 08.8	22 46.0
8 Su	23 03 09	17 31 59	25 04 53	1♊28 35	11 48.9	1 54.1	27 51.1	9 53.0	15 45.0	4 19.9	28 37.5	16 06.2	12 08.3	22 46.0
9 M	23 07 05	18 31 57	7♊46 19	13 58 42	11D47.5	1 25.5	29 01.3	10 34.1	15 35.5	4 15.8	28 44.9	16 08.4	12 07.8	22 46.1
10 Tu	23 11 02	19 31 52	20 06 20	26 09 55	11 47.6	1 03.7	0♉11.4	11 15.2	15 25.7	4 12.0	28 52.3	16 10.4	12 07.4	22 46.1
11 W	23 14 58	20 31 45	2♋10 08	8♋07 39	11R48.0	0 48.4	1 21.3	11 56.2	15 15.5	4 08.3	28 59.7	16 12.4	12 07.0	22 46.2
12 Th	23 18 55	21 31 36	14 03 09	19 57 18	11 47.8	0D39.6	2 31.0	12 37.3	15 05.0	4 04.8	29 07.1	16 14.4	12 06.6	22 46.3
13 F	23 22 52	22 31 25	25 50 44	1♌44 02	11 45.8	0 37.1	3 40.7	13 18.2	14 54.2	4 01.5	29 14.6	16 16.4	12 06.2	22 46.4
14 Sa	23 26 48	23 31 11	7♌37 43	13 32 19	11 41.5	0 40.8	4 50.2	13 59.2	14 43.1	3 58.4	29 22.0	16 18.3	12 05.9	22 46.6
15 Su	23 30 45	24 30 56	19 28 16	25 25 56	11 34.3	0 50.2	5 59.5	14 40.1	14 31.8	3 55.4	29 29.4	16 20.1	12 05.6	22 46.7
16 M	23 34 41	25 30 38	1♍25 39	7♍27 43	11 24.4	1 05.2	7 08.7	15 21.0	14 20.1	3 52.7	29 36.9	16 21.9	12 05.4	22 46.9
17 Tu	23 38 38	26 30 18	13 32 18	19 39 36	11 12.4	1 25.5	8 17.7	16 01.9	14 08.3	3 50.1	29 44.3	16 23.7	12 05.1	22 47.2
18 W	23 42 34	27 29 56	25 49 41	2♎02 39	10 59.1	1 50.7	9 26.6	16 42.7	13 56.1	3 47.7	29 51.8	16 25.4	12 04.9	22 47.4
19 Th	23 46 31	28 29 32	8♎18 30	14 37 16	10 45.8	2 20.6	10 35.3	17 23.5	13 43.8	3 45.5	29 59.3	16 27.0	12 04.8	22 47.6
20 F	23 50 27	29 29 06	20 58 53	27 23 22	10 33.5	2 54.9	11 43.8	18 04.2	13 31.2	3 43.5	0♈06.7	16 28.7	12 04.7	22 47.9
21 Sa	23 54 24	0♈28 38	3♏50 41	10♏20 49	10 23.3	3 33.4	12 52.2	18 45.0	13 18.5	3 41.6	0 14.2	16 30.2	12 04.6	22 48.2
22 Su	23 58 21	1 28 09	16 53 46	23 29 35	10 16.0	4 15.7	14 00.4	19 25.7	13 05.6	3 40.0	0 21.7	16 31.8	12 04.5	22 48.6
23 M	0 02 17	2 27 37	0♐08 20	6♐50 05	10 11.5	5 01.7	15 08.5	20 06.4	12 52.5	3 38.6	0 29.1	16 33.2	12D04.5	22 48.9
24 Tu	0 06 14	3 27 04	13 34 57	20 23 04	10 09.5	5 51.1	16 16.3	20 47.0	12 39.2	3 37.3	0 36.6	16 34.7	12 04.5	22 49.3
25 W	0 10 10	4 26 29	27 14 33	4♑09 32	10 09.2	6 43.8	17 24.0	21 27.6	12 25.9	3 36.2	0 44.1	16 36.1	12 04.5	22 49.7
26 Th	0 14 07	5 25 53	11♑08 05	18 10 15	10 09.1	7 39.5	18 31.5	22 08.2	12 12.4	3 35.4	0 51.5	16 37.4	12 04.6	22 50.1
27 F	0 18 03	6 25 15	25 16 00	2♒25 11	10 08.0	8 38.1	19 38.9	22 48.8	11 58.8	3 34.7	0 59.0	16 38.7	12 04.7	22 50.5
28 Sa	0 22 00	7 24 34	9♒37 36	16 52 51	10 04.7	9 39.5	20 46.0	23 29.3	11 45.2	3 34.2	1 06.4	16 39.9	12 04.9	22 51.0
29 Su	0 25 56	8 23 53	24 10 27	1♓29 46	9 58.7	10 43.4	21 52.9	24 09.9	11 31.4	3 33.9	1 13.9	16 41.1	12 05.1	22 51.5
30 M	0 29 53	9 23 09	8♓50 03	16 10 27	9 49.8	11 49.8	22 59.7	24 50.3	11 17.7	3D33.8	1 21.3	16 42.3	12 05.3	22 52.0
31 Tu	0 33 50	10 22 23	23 30 02	0♈47 50	9 38.8	12 58.6	24 06.2	25 30.8	11 03.9	3 33.9	1 28.7	16 43.3	12 05.5	22 52.5

April 1908 LONGITUDE

Day	Sid.Time	☉	0 hr ☽	Noon ☽	True ☊	☿	♀	♂	⚳	♃	♄	♅	♆	♇
1 W	0 37 46	11♈21 35	8♈02 54	15♈14 18	9♋26.7	14♓09.6	25♉12.6	26♉11.2	10♎50.1	3♌34.2	1♈36.1	16♑44.4	12♋05.8	22♊53.0
2 Th	0 41 43	12 20 45	22 21 14	29 22 59	9R14.8	15 22.7	26 18.7	26 51.6	10R36.3	3 34.6	1 43.5	16 45.4	12 06.1	22 53.6
3 F	0 45 39	13 19 53	6♉18 59	13♉08 53	9 04.5	16 37.9	27 24.6	27 32.0	10 22.5	3 35.3	1 50.9	16 46.3	12 06.5	22 54.2
4 Sa	0 49 36	14 18 59	19 52 25	26 29 23	8 56.5	17 55.1	28 30.2	28 12.4	10 08.9	3 36.2	1 58.2	16 47.2	12 06.9	22 54.8
5 Su	0 53 32	15 18 03	3♊00 22	9♊25 06	8 51.2	19 14.3	29 35.7	28 52.7	9 55.2	3 37.2	2 05.6	16 48.0	12 07.3	22 55.4
6 M	0 57 29	16 17 04	15 44 06	21 57 49	8 48.5	20 35.3	0♊40.9	29 33.0	9 41.7	3 38.4	2 12.9	16 48.8	12 07.7	22 56.0
7 Tu	1 01 25	17 16 03	28 06 49	4♋11 40	8D47.6	21 58.1	1 45.8	0♊13.2	9 28.3	3 39.8	2 20.3	16 49.6	12 08.2	22 56.7
8 W	1 05 22	18 15 00	10♋13 02	16 11 35	8R47.6	23 22.7	2 50.5	0 53.5	9 15.0	3 41.4	2 27.6	16 50.2	12 08.7	22 57.4
9 Th	1 09 19	19 13 55	22 08 01	28 03 00	8 47.4	24 49.1	3 54.9	1 33.7	9 01.8	3 43.2	2 34.8	16 50.9	12 09.3	22 58.1
10 F	1 13 15	20 12 47	3♌57 15	9♌51 25	8 45.8	26 17.2	4 59.1	2 13.8	8 48.8	3 45.2	2 42.1	16 51.5	12 09.9	22 58.8
11 Sa	1 17 12	21 11 37	15 46 09	21 42 03	8 42.1	27 46.9	6 02.9	2 54.0	8 35.9	3 47.4	2 49.3	16 52.0	12 10.5	22 59.6
12 Su	1 21 08	22 10 25	27 39 39	3♍39 30	8 35.9	29 18.3	7 06.5	3 34.1	8 23.3	3 49.7	2 56.5	16 52.5	12 11.1	23 00.3
13 M	1 25 05	23 09 10	9♍42 01	15 47 35	8 27.0	0♈51.4	8 09.8	4 14.2	8 10.8	3 52.2	3 03.7	16 52.9	12 11.8	23 01.1
14 Tu	1 29 01	24 07 54	21 56 31	28 09 03	8 16.1	2 26.1	9 12.8	4 54.2	7 58.6	3 54.9	3 10.9	16 53.3	12 12.5	23 01.9
15 W	1 32 58	25 06 35	4♎25 21	10♎45 29	8 03.9	4 02.5	10 15.4	5 34.2	7 46.6	3 57.8	3 18.0	16 53.6	12 13.3	23 02.7
16 Th	1 36 54	26 05 14	17 09 29	23 37 16	7 51.5	5 40.5	11 17.8	6 14.2	7 34.8	4 00.8	3 25.1	16 53.9	12 14.0	23 03.5
17 F	1 40 51	27 03 51	0♏08 43	6♏43 41	7 40.1	7 20.1	12 19.8	6 54.2	7 23.3	4 04.0	3 32.2	16 54.1	12 14.9	23 04.4
18 Sa	1 44 47	28 02 27	13 21 57	20 03 18	7 30.6	9 01.3	13 21.4	7 34.1	7 12.0	4 07.4	3 39.2	16 54.3	12 15.7	23 05.3
19 Su	1 48 44	29 01 00	26 47 28	3♐34 15	7 23.9	10 44.2	14 22.7	8 14.0	7 01.0	4 11.0	3 46.2	16 54.4	12 16.6	23 06.2
20 M	1 52 41	29 59 32	10♐23 25	17 14 46	7 19.8	12 28.8	15 23.7	8 53.9	6 50.4	4 14.7	3 53.2	16 54.5	12 17.5	23 07.1
21 Tu	1 56 37	0♉58 03	24 08 09	1♑03 26	7D18.3	14 15.0	16 24.3	9 33.7	6 40.0	4 18.6	4 00.2	16R54.5	12 18.4	23 08.0
22 W	2 00 34	1 56 31	8♑00 29	14 59 14	7 18.3	16 02.9	17 24.5	10 13.5	6 29.9	4 22.7	4 07.1	16 54.5	12 19.4	23 08.9
23 Th	2 04 30	2 54 58	21 59 37	29 01 33	7R18.7	17 52.4	18 24.3	10 53.3	6 20.1	4 27.0	4 14.0	16 54.4	12 20.4	23 09.9
24 F	2 08 27	3 53 24	6♒04 58	13♒09 43	7 18.5	19 43.7	19 23.8	11 33.1	6 10.7	4 31.4	4 20.9	16 54.3	12 21.4	23 10.9
25 Sa	2 12 23	4 51 48	20 15 39	27 22 33	7 16.4	21 36.6	20 22.8	12 12.8	6 01.6	4 35.9	4 27.7	16 54.1	12 22.4	23 11.8
26 Su	2 16 20	5 50 10	4♓30 08	11♓38 03	7 12.1	23 31.2	21 21.4	12 52.6	5 52.9	4 40.7	4 34.5	16 53.9	12 23.5	23 12.9
27 M	2 20 16	6 48 31	18 45 50	25 53 01	7 05.4	25 27.4	22 19.5	13 32.3	5 44.5	4 45.5	4 41.2	16 53.6	12 24.6	23 13.9
28 Tu	2 24 13	7 46 50	2♈59 02	10♈03 18	6 56.8	27 25.3	23 17.2	14 11.9	5 36.4	4 50.6	4 47.9	16 53.3	12 25.8	23 14.9
29 W	2 28 10	8 45 07	17 05 13	24 04 12	6 47.2	29 24.9	24 14.5	14 51.6	5 28.8	4 55.8	4 54.5	16 52.9	12 26.9	23 16.0
30 Th	2 32 06	9 43 23	0♉59 39	7♉51 06	6 37.8	1♉26.0	25 11.2	15 31.2	5 21.5	5 01.2	5 01.2	16 52.5	12 28.1	23 17.0

Astro Data Dy Hr Mn	Planet Ingress Dy Hr Mn	Last Aspect Dy Hr Mn	☽ Ingress Dy Hr Mn	Last Aspect Dy Hr Mn	☽ Ingress Dy Hr Mn	☽ Phases & Eclipses Dy Hr Mn	Astro Data
☽0N 4 19:50	♀ ♉ 10 8:06	1 12:35 ♇ △	♓ 2 0:05	2 0:54 ♇ ⚹	♉ 2 13:04	2 18:57 ● 11♓49	1 March 1908
♇ D 7 11:13	♄ ♈ 19 14:23	3 21:10 ♄ ☌	♈ 4 0:20	4 16:01 ♀ ☌	♊ 4 18:26	9 21:42 ☽ 18♊56	Julian Day # 2982
☿ D 13 9:32	☉ ♈ 21 0:27	5 17:30 ♀ ☌	♉ 6 2:50	6 13:53 ♇ ☌	♋ 7 3:43	18 2:28 ○ 27♍06	SVP 6♓32'47"
☽0S 19 6:23		8 6:34 ♄ ⚹	♊ 8 9:13	9 4:31 ☿ △	♌ 9 15:58	25 12:32 ☾ 4♑28	GC 25♐33.4 ⚴ 23♍07.0R
☉0N 21 0:27	♀ ♊ 5 20:57	10 17:27 ♄ □	♋ 10 19:39	11 14:37 ♇ ⚹	♍ 12 4:41		Eris 24♓46.4 ⚵ 8♑23.6
♆ D 23 15:01	♂ ♊ 7 4:06	13 6:52 ♄ △	♌ 13 8:28	14 2:06 ♇ □	♎ 14 15:33	1 5:02 ● 11♈04	⚷ 19♒50.2 ⚶ 5♋20.4
♃ D 30 13:16	☿ ♈ 12 22:48	15 6:40 ♇ ⚹	♍ 15 21:09	16 16:55 ☉ ☍	♏ 16 23:44	8 16:31 ☽ 18♋26	☽ Mean ☊ 11♋16.2
	☉ ♉ 20 12:11	18 7:45 ♄ ☍	♎ 18 8:04	18 6:22 ♅ ⚹	♐ 19 5:41	16 16:55 ○ 26♎17	
☽0N 1 5:59	☿ ♉ 29 19:00	20 3:25 ♇ △	♏ 20 16:52	20 22:14 ♇ ☍	♑ 21 10:10	23 19:07 ☾ 3♒12	1 April 1908
☽0S 15 13:42		22 4:13 ♂ ☍	♐ 22 23:45	22 15:18 ♅ ☌	♒ 23 13:40	30 15:33 ● 9♉52	Julian Day # 3013
☿0N 16 13:12		24 16:17 ♇ ☍	♑ 25 4:48	25 4:57 ♇ △	♓ 25 16:25		SVP 6♓32'45"
♅ R 21 12:18		26 19:03 ♂ △	♒ 27 7:57	27 7:31 ♇ □	♈ 27 18:57		GC 25♐33.5 ⚴ 13♍52.8R
☽0N 28 14:55		28 23:24 ♂ □	♓ 29 9:33	29 12:19 ♀ ⚹	♉ 29 22:16		Eris 25♓10.7 ⚵ 15♑44.0
♄0N 29 17:08		31 2:53 ♂ ⚹	♈ 31 10:41				⚷ 21♒46.8 ⚶ 10♋06.9
♃△♄ 30 12:12							☽ Mean ☊ 9♋37.7

LONGITUDE May 1908

Day	Sid.Time	☉	0 hr ☽	Noon ☽	True ☊	☿	♀	♂	⚳	♃	♄	♅	♆	♇
1 F	2 36 03	10♉41 37	14♉38 06	21♉20 20	6♋29.5	3♉28.7	26♊07.5	16♊10.8	5♎14.6	5♌06.7	5♈07.7	16♑52.0	12♋29.4	23♊18.1
2 Sa	2 39 59	11 39 49	27 57 33	4♊29 39	6R 23.2	5 32.8	27 03.2	16 50.3	5R 08.1	5 12.4	5 14.3	16R 51.4	12 30.6	23 19.2
3 Su	2 43 56	12 37 59	10♊56 38	17 18 35	6 19.1	7 38.3	27 58.4	17 29.9	5 02.0	5 18.2	5 20.7	16 50.9	12 31.9	23 20.3
4 M	2 47 52	13 36 08	23 35 43	29 48 21	6D 17.2	9 45.1	28 53.1	18 09.4	4 56.3	5 24.2	5 27.2	16 50.3	12 33.2	23 21.4
5 Tu	2 51 49	14 34 15	5♋56 50	12♋01 39	6 17.2	11 53.0	29 47.2	18 48.9	4 50.9	5 30.3	5 33.6	16 49.6	12 34.6	23 22.6
6 W	2 55 45	15 32 20	18 03 19	24 02 23	6 18.2	14 01.9	0♋40.7	19 28.4	4 46.0	5 36.6	5 39.9	16 48.9	12 35.9	23 23.7
7 Th	2 59 42	16 30 22	29 59 27	5♌55 10	6R 19.3	16 11.6	1 33.5	20 07.8	4 41.5	5 43.0	5 46.2	16 48.1	12 37.3	23 24.9
8 F	3 03 39	17 28 23	11♌50 09	17 45 05	6 19.9	18 21.8	2 25.7	20 47.2	4 37.4	5 49.5	5 52.4	16 47.3	12 38.7	23 26.1
9 Sa	3 07 35	18 26 23	23 40 36	29 37 21	6 19.1	20 32.4	3 17.3	21 26.6	4 33.7	5 56.2	5 58.6	16 46.4	12 40.2	23 27.2
10 Su	3 11 32	19 24 20	5♍35 57	11♍36 59	6 16.5	22 43.0	4 08.1	22 06.0	4 30.4	6 03.0	6 04.8	16 45.5	12 41.6	23 28.4
11 M	3 15 28	20 22 15	17 41 00	23 48 29	6 12.1	24 53.4	4 58.3	22 45.3	4 27.6	6 10.0	6 10.9	16 44.6	12 43.1	23 29.6
12 Tu	3 19 25	21 20 09	29 59 54	6♎15 36	6 06.0	27 03.4	5 47.7	23 24.6	4 25.1	6 17.1	6 16.9	16 43.6	12 44.6	23 30.9
13 W	3 23 21	22 18 01	12♎35 51	19 00 53	5 58.9	29 12.5	6 36.3	24 03.9	4 23.0	6 24.3	6 22.9	16 42.5	12 46.2	23 32.1
14 Th	3 27 18	23 15 51	25 30 47	2♏05 35	5 51.6	1♊20.7	7 24.1	24 43.1	4 21.4	6 31.7	6 28.8	16 41.4	12 47.7	23 33.3
15 F	3 31 14	24 13 40	8♏45 10	15 29 23	5 44.8	3 27.5	8 11.1	25 22.4	4 20.1	6 39.2	6 34.6	16 40.3	12 49.3	23 34.6
16 Sa	3 35 11	25 11 27	22 17 56	29 10 31	5 39.3	5 32.7	8 57.2	26 01.6	4 19.3	6 46.8	6 40.4	16 39.1	12 50.9	23 35.9
17 Su	3 39 08	26 09 13	6♐06 42	13♐06 03	5 35.6	7 36.0	9 42.4	26 40.8	4D 18.8	6 54.6	6 46.2	16 37.9	12 52.6	23 37.1
18 M	3 43 04	27 06 57	20 08 04	27 12 17	5D 33.7	9 37.4	10 26.7	27 19.9	4 18.8	7 02.4	6 51.9	16 36.7	12 54.2	23 38.4
19 Tu	3 47 01	28 04 41	4♑18 11	11♑25 19	5 33.6	11 36.5	11 10.0	27 59.1	4 19.2	7 10.4	6 57.5	16 35.4	12 55.9	23 39.7
20 W	3 50 57	29 02 23	18 33 14	25 41 32	5 34.6	13 33.2	11 52.4	28 38.2	4 19.9	7 18.6	7 03.0	16 34.0	12 57.6	23 41.0
21 Th	3 54 54	0♊00 04	2♒49 50	9♒57 50	5 36.0	15 27.4	12 33.7	29 17.3	4 21.0	7 26.8	7 08.5	16 32.7	12 59.3	23 42.3
22 F	3 58 50	0 57 44	17 05 13	24 11 43	5R 37.0	17 18.9	13 13.9	29 56.4	4 22.6	7 35.1	7 14.0	16 31.2	13 01.1	23 43.7
23 Sa	4 02 47	1 55 24	1♓17 08	8♓21 12	5 37.0	19 07.7	13 53.1	0♋35.4	4 24.5	7 43.6	7 19.4	16 29.8	13 02.8	23 45.0
24 Su	4 06 43	2 53 02	15 23 43	22 24 28	5 35.6	20 53.6	14 31.1	1 14.4	4 26.8	7 52.2	7 24.7	16 28.3	13 04.6	23 46.3
25 M	4 10 40	3 50 39	29 23 14	6♈19 48	5 32.8	22 36.6	15 07.9	1 53.5	4 29.5	8 00.9	7 29.9	16 26.7	13 06.4	23 47.7
26 Tu	4 14 37	4 48 15	13♈13 57	20 05 25	5 28.9	24 16.7	15 43.4	2 32.4	4 32.6	8 09.7	7 35.1	16 25.2	13 08.2	23 49.0
27 W	4 18 33	5 45 50	26 54 00	3♉39 28	5 24.4	25 53.9	16 17.7	3 11.4	4 36.0	8 18.6	7 40.2	16 23.6	13 10.1	23 50.4
28 Th	4 22 30	6 43 25	10♉21 36	17 00 14	5 19.9	27 28.0	16 50.7	3 50.4	4 39.8	8 27.6	7 45.2	16 21.9	13 11.9	23 51.7
29 F	4 26 26	7 40 58	23 35 10	0♊06 19	5 16.0	28 59.0	17 22.2	4 29.3	4 44.0	8 36.8	7 50.2	16 20.2	13 13.8	23 53.1
30 Sa	4 30 23	8 38 30	6♊33 35	12 56 58	5 13.1	0♋26.9	17 52.3	5 08.2	4 48.6	8 46.0	7 55.1	16 18.5	13 15.7	23 54.5
31 Su	4 34 19	9 36 02	19 16 29	25 32 13	5D 11.6	1 51.7	18 21.0	5 47.1	4 53.5	8 55.4	7 59.9	16 16.8	13 17.6	23 55.8

LONGITUDE June 1908

Day	Sid.Time	☉	0 hr ☽	Noon ☽	True ☊	☿	♀	♂	⚳	♃	♄	♅	♆	♇
1 M	4 38 16	10♊33 32	1♋44 20	7♋53 02	5♋11.2	3♋13.3	18♋48.0	6♋26.0	4♎58.8	9♌04.8	8♈04.6	16♑15.0	13♋19.5	23♊57.2
2 Tu	4 42 13	11 31 01	13 58 34	20 01 17	5 11.9	4 31.8	19 13.5	7 04.9	5 04.5	9 14.4	8 09.3	16R 13.1	13 21.5	23 58.6
3 W	4 46 09	12 28 29	26 01 33	1♌59 46	5 13.3	5 46.9	19 37.3	7 43.7	5 10.5	9 24.0	8 13.9	16 11.3	13 23.4	24 00.0
4 Th	4 50 06	13 25 56	7♌56 25	13 51 59	5 15.0	6 58.8	19 59.4	8 22.6	5 16.8	9 33.8	8 18.4	16 09.4	13 25.4	24 01.4
5 F	4 54 02	14 23 21	19 47 01	25 42 05	5 16.4	8 07.3	20 19.6	9 01.4	5 23.5	9 43.6	8 22.8	16 07.5	13 27.4	24 02.8
6 Sa	4 57 59	15 20 46	1♍37 45	7♍34 36	5R 17.4	9 12.4	20 38.0	9 40.1	5 30.5	9 53.5	8 27.2	16 05.6	13 29.4	24 04.2
7 Su	5 01 55	16 18 09	13 33 15	19 34 17	5 17.5	10 14.0	20 54.5	10 18.9	5 37.9	10 03.5	8 31.5	16 03.6	13 31.4	24 05.6
8 M	5 05 52	17 15 31	25 38 17	1♎45 50	5 16.9	11 12.0	21 09.0	10 57.7	5 45.5	10 13.7	8 35.7	16 01.6	13 33.5	24 07.0
9 Tu	5 09 48	18 12 52	7♎57 26	14 13 35	5 15.5	12 06.3	21 21.5	11 36.4	5 53.6	10 23.8	8 39.8	15 59.5	13 35.5	24 08.5
10 W	5 13 45	19 10 12	20 34 42	27 01 10	5 13.6	12 57.0	21 31.9	12 15.1	6 01.9	10 34.1	8 43.8	15 57.5	13 37.6	24 09.9
11 Th	5 17 42	20 07 31	3♏33 13	10♏11 04	5 11.6	13 43.8	21 40.1	12 53.8	6 10.5	10 44.5	8 47.8	15 55.4	13 39.6	24 11.3
12 F	5 21 38	21 04 50	16 54 45	23 44 14	5 09.7	14 26.7	21 46.1	13 32.4	6 19.5	10 55.0	8 51.7	15 53.3	13 41.7	24 12.7
13 Sa	5 25 35	22 02 07	0♐39 21	7♐39 48	5 08.2	15 05.5	21 49.8	14 11.1	6 28.7	11 05.5	8 55.5	15 51.2	13 43.8	24 14.1
14 Su	5 29 31	22 59 24	14 45 10	21 54 56	5D 07.3	15 40.3	21R 51.3	14 49.7	6 38.3	11 16.1	8 59.2	15 49.0	13 45.9	24 15.6
15 M	5 33 28	23 56 40	29 08 27	6♑25 01	5 07.1	16 10.9	21 50.4	15 28.3	6 48.1	11 26.8	9 02.8	15 46.9	13 48.0	24 17.0
16 Tu	5 37 24	24 53 56	13♑43 52	21 04 12	5 07.4	16 37.1	21 47.1	16 06.9	6 58.3	11 37.6	9 06.3	15 44.7	13 50.1	24 18.4
17 W	5 41 21	25 51 11	28 28 12	5♒46 05	5 08.0	16 59.0	21 41.5	16 45.5	7 08.7	11 48.4	9 09.8	15 42.5	13 52.3	24 19.8
18 Th	5 45 17	26 48 26	13♒06 04	20 24 29	5 08.7	17 16.4	21 33.4	17 24.1	7 19.4	11 59.4	9 13.1	15 40.2	13 54.4	24 21.3
19 F	5 49 14	27 45 41	27 40 42	4♓54 11	5 09.3	17 29.2	21 23.0	18 02.7	7 30.4	12 10.4	9 16.4	15 38.0	13 56.6	24 22.7
20 Sa	5 53 11	28 42 55	12♓04 29	19 11 16	5R 09.7	17 37.6	21 10.1	18 41.2	7 41.6	12 21.4	9 19.6	15 35.7	13 58.7	24 24.1
21 Su	5 57 07	29 40 10	26 14 15	3♈13 16	5 09.8	17R 41.3	20 54.9	19 19.7	7 53.1	12 32.6	9 22.7	15 33.4	14 00.9	24 25.5
22 M	6 01 04	0♋37 24	10♈08 11	16 58 58	5 09.6	17 40.5	20 37.4	19 58.2	8 04.9	12 43.8	9 25.7	15 31.1	14 03.1	24 26.9
23 Tu	6 05 00	1 34 38	23 45 37	0♉28 11	5 09.3	17 35.2	20 17.6	20 36.7	8 17.0	12 55.1	9 28.6	15 28.8	14 05.3	24 28.3
24 W	6 08 57	2 31 52	7♉06 43	13 41 21	5 09.0	17 25.5	19 55.6	21 15.2	8 29.3	13 06.4	9 31.4	15 26.5	14 07.5	24 29.8
25 Th	6 12 53	3 29 06	20 12 11	26 39 21	5 08.7	17 11.5	19 31.4	21 53.7	8 41.8	13 17.9	9 34.2	15 24.1	14 09.7	24 31.2
26 F	6 16 50	4 26 20	3♊02 59	9♊23 13	5D 08.6	16 53.4	19 05.2	22 32.2	8 54.7	13 29.3	9 36.8	15 21.8	14 11.9	24 32.6
27 Sa	6 20 46	5 23 34	15 40 14	21 54 10	5 08.6	16 31.5	18 37.1	23 10.7	9 07.7	13 40.9	9 39.4	15 19.4	14 14.1	24 34.0
28 Su	6 24 43	6 20 48	28 05 11	4♋13 28	5R 08.6	16 06.1	18 07.2	23 49.1	9 21.0	13 52.5	9 41.8	15 17.0	14 16.3	24 35.4
29 M	6 28 40	7 18 01	10♋19 12	16 22 35	5 08.6	15 37.4	17 35.7	24 27.5	9 34.6	14 04.2	9 44.2	15 14.6	14 18.5	24 36.8
30 Tu	6 32 36	8 15 15	22 23 52	28 23 16	5 08.4	15 06.1	17 02.7	25 06.0	9 48.3	14 15.9	9 46.4	15 12.2	14 20.7	24 38.2

Astro Data	Dy Hr Mn
♃△♄	12 7:05
☽0S	12 22:42
⚳D	18 2:33
☽0N	25 21:55
♃∠♇	31 13:26
☽0S	9 8:04
♀R	14 14:51
☿R	21 19:47
☽0N	22 3:38

Planet Ingress		Dy Hr Mn
♀	♋	5 17:44
☿	♊	13 20:52
☉	♊	21 11:58
♂	♋	22 14:14
☿	♋	30 4:34
☉	♋	21 20:19

Last Aspect Dy Hr Mn			☽ Ingress	Dy Hr Mn
1 3:59	♅	△	♊	2 3:44
4 10:04	♀	☌	♋	4 12:23
5 21:32	♅	☍	♌	7 0:01
8 23:32	♇	⚹	♍	9 12:46
11 14:33	☿	△	♎	12 0:00
13 21:50	♂	△	♏	14 8:12
16 4:32	☉	☍	♐	16 13:26
18 12:14	♂	☍	♑	18 16:44
20 18:02	☉	△	♒	20 19:14
22 11:12	♇	△	♓	22 21:49
24 14:21	♇	□	♈	25 1:03
26 20:23	☿	⚹	♉	27 5:30
28 11:42	♀	⚹	♊	29 11:48
31 8:54	♇	☌	♋	31 20:37

Last Aspect Dy Hr Mn			☽ Ingress	Dy Hr Mn
2 10:22	♀	☌	♌	3 7:59
5 8:38	♇	⚹	♍	5 20:42
7 20:58	♇	□	♎	8 8:33
10 6:42	♇	△	♏	10 17:30
12 8:32	♀	△	♐	12 22:52
14 15:55	♇	☍	♑	15 1:25
16 13:10	♀	☍	♒	17 2:35
18 23:18	☉	△	♓	19 3:51
21 5:26	☉	□	♈	21 6:27
23 1:15	♇	⚹	♉	23 11:09
25 2:40	♂	⚹	♊	25 18:16
27 17:10	♇	☌	♋	28 3:44
30 5:02	♂	☌	♌	30 15:14

☽ Phases & Eclipses Dy Hr Mn	
8 11:23	☽ 17♌27
16 4:32	○ 24♏53
23 0:17	☾ 1♓27
30 3:14	● 8♊18
7 4:56	☽ 16♍01
14 13:55	○ 23♐04
14 14:06	◑ A 0.813
21 5:26	☾ 29♓25
28 16:31	● 6♋32
28 16:29:42	● A 03'60"

Astro Data

1 May 1908
Julian Day # 3043
SVP 6♓32'41"
GC 25♐33.5 ⚴ 10♍59.4
Eris 25♓31.3 ⚵ 19♑40.7
⚷ 23♒00.7 ⚶ 18♋52.3
☽ Mean ☊ 8♋02.4

1 June 1908
Julian Day # 3074
SVP 6♓32'37"
GC 25♐33.6 ⚴ 14♍57.9
Eris 25♓44.5 ⚵ 18♑56.4R
⚷ 23♒22.4R ⚶ 0♌27.9
☽ Mean ☊ 6♋23.9

July 1908 — LONGITUDE

Day	Sid.Time	☉	0 hr ☽	Noon ☽	True ☊	☿	♀	♂	⚳	♃	♄	♅	♆	♇
1 W	6 36 33	9♋12 28	4♌21 05	10♌17 37	5♋08.0	14♋32.4	16♋28.4	25♋44.4	10♎02.4	14♌27.7	9♈48.6	15♑09.8	14♋22.9	24♊39.6
2 Th	6 40 29	10 09 41	16 13 10	22 08 08	5R07.4	13R57.1	15R53.0	26 22.8	10 16.6	14 39.5	9 50.6	15R07.4	14 25.2	24 40.9
3 F	6 44 26	11 06 54	28 02 54	3♍57 52	5 06.7	13 20.6	15 16.7	27 01.2	10 31.0	14 51.4	9 52.6	15 05.0	14 27.4	24 42.3
4 Sa	6 48 22	12 04 06	9♍53 31	15 50 18	5 05.9	12 43.5	14 39.8	27 39.5	10 45.7	15 03.4	9 54.5	15 02.6	14 29.6	24 43.7
5 Su	6 52 19	13 01 18	21 48 45	27 49 23	5 05.3	12 06.5	14 02.5	28 17.9	11 00.6	15 15.4	9 56.2	15 00.2	14 31.9	24 45.1
6 M	6 56 15	13 58 30	3♎52 44	9♎59 20	5D05.0	11 30.3	13 25.0	28 56.3	11 15.7	15 27.4	9 57.9	14 57.8	14 34.1	24 46.4
7 Tu	7 00 12	14 55 42	16 09 45	22 24 30	5 05.1	10 55.4	12 47.5	29 34.6	11 31.0	15 39.5	9 59.5	14 55.3	14 36.3	24 47.8
8 W	7 04 09	15 52 54	28 44 07	5♏09 04	5 05.6	10 22.4	12 10.3	0♌12.9	11 46.5	15 51.7	10 00.9	14 52.9	14 38.5	24 49.1
9 Th	7 08 05	16 50 06	11♏39 45	18 16 33	5 06.4	9 52.1	11 33.7	0 51.2	12 02.2	16 03.9	10 02.3	14 50.5	14 40.8	24 50.5
10 F	7 12 02	17 47 17	24 59 44	1♐49 27	5 07.4	9 24.8	10 57.8	1 29.6	12 18.2	16 16.1	10 03.6	14 48.1	14 43.0	24 51.8
11 Sa	7 15 58	18 44 29	8♐45 45	15 48 31	5 08.3	9 01.2	10 22.9	2 07.8	12 34.3	16 28.4	10 04.8	14 45.7	14 45.2	24 53.1
12 Su	7 19 55	19 41 41	22 57 31	0♑12 17	5R08.9	8 41.6	9 49.3	2 46.1	12 50.5	16 40.8	10 05.8	14 43.2	14 47.5	24 54.4
13 M	7 23 51	20 38 53	7♑32 17	14 56 44	5 08.7	8 26.4	9 17.0	3 24.4	13 07.0	16 53.1	10 06.8	14 40.8	14 49.7	24 55.7
14 Tu	7 27 48	21 36 05	22 24 46	29 55 22	5 07.8	8 16.0	8 46.3	4 02.7	13 23.7	17 05.5	10 07.7	14 38.4	14 51.9	24 57.0
15 W	7 31 44	22 33 18	7♒27 27	14♒59 52	5 06.2	8D10.7	8 17.3	4 40.9	13 40.5	17 18.0	10 08.5	14 36.1	14 54.1	24 58.3
16 Th	7 35 41	23 30 31	22 31 29	0♓01 13	5 04.0	8 10.6	7 50.2	5 19.2	13 57.5	17 30.5	10 09.1	14 33.7	14 56.3	24 59.6
17 F	7 39 38	24 27 45	7♓28 03	14 51 05	5 01.7	8 16.0	7 25.2	5 57.4	14 14.7	17 43.0	10 09.7	14 31.3	14 58.5	25 00.9
18 Sa	7 43 34	25 24 59	22 09 35	29 22 56	4 59.7	8 26.9	7 02.3	6 35.7	14 32.0	17 55.6	10 10.1	14 28.9	15 00.7	25 02.1
19 Su	7 47 31	26 22 14	6♈30 42	13♈32 38	4 58.3	8 43.5	6 41.6	7 13.9	14 49.5	18 08.2	10 10.5	14 26.6	15 02.9	25 03.4
20 M	7 51 27	27 19 30	20 28 36	27 18 37	4D57.8	9 05.8	6 23.2	7 52.1	15 07.2	18 20.8	10 10.8	14 24.2	15 05.1	25 04.6
21 Tu	7 55 24	28 16 46	4♉02 48	10♉41 22	4 58.3	9 33.8	6 07.1	8 30.4	15 25.1	18 33.5	10 10.9	14 21.9	15 07.3	25 05.8
22 W	7 59 20	29 14 04	17 14 36	23 42 50	4 59.5	10 07.6	5 53.4	9 08.6	15 43.1	18 46.2	10R11.0	14 19.6	15 09.5	25 07.1
23 Th	8 03 17	0♌11 23	0♊06 27	6♊25 50	5 01.0	10 47.0	5 42.1	9 46.8	16 01.2	18 58.9	10 10.9	14 17.3	15 11.7	25 08.3
24 F	8 07 13	1 08 42	12 41 23	18 53 28	5 02.5	11 32.2	5 33.2	10 25.0	16 19.5	19 11.7	10 10.8	14 15.0	15 13.8	25 09.5
25 Sa	8 11 10	2 06 02	25 02 29	1♋08 47	5R03.3	12 22.9	5 26.6	11 03.2	16 38.0	19 24.5	10 10.5	14 12.7	15 16.0	25 10.6
26 Su	8 15 07	3 03 23	7♋12 42	13 14 33	5 03.1	13 19.2	5 22.5	11 41.5	16 56.6	19 37.3	10 10.2	14 10.4	15 18.2	25 11.8
27 M	8 19 03	4 00 45	19 14 38	25 13 14	5 01.5	14 20.9	5D20.7	12 19.7	17 15.4	19 50.1	10 09.7	14 08.2	15 20.3	25 13.0
28 Tu	8 23 00	4 58 08	1♌10 36	7♌07 00	4 58.5	15 28.0	5 21.3	12 57.9	17 34.3	20 03.0	10 09.2	14 06.0	15 22.4	25 14.1
29 W	8 26 56	5 55 31	13 02 38	18 57 47	4 54.1	16 40.3	5 24.1	13 36.1	17 53.4	20 15.9	10 08.5	14 03.8	15 24.6	25 15.3
30 Th	8 30 53	6 52 55	24 52 40	0♍47 33	4 48.7	17 57.7	5 29.1	14 14.3	18 12.6	20 28.8	10 07.7	14 01.6	15 26.7	25 16.4
31 F	8 34 49	7 50 20	6♍42 42	12 38 23	4 42.8	19 20.1	5 36.4	14 52.4	18 31.9	20 41.7	10 06.9	13 59.5	15 28.8	25 17.5

August 1908 — LONGITUDE

Day	Sid.Time	☉	0 hr ☽	Noon ☽	True ☊	☿	♀	♂	⚳	♃	♄	♅	♆	♇
1 Sa	8 38 46	8♌47 46	18♍34 55	24♍32 39	4♋37.1	20♋47.2	5♋45.7	15♌30.6	18♎51.4	20♌54.7	10♈05.9	13♑57.3	15♋30.9	25♊18.6
2 Su	8 42 42	9 45 12	0♎31 56	6♎33 10	4R32.2	22 18.9	5 57.2	16 08.8	19 10.9	21 07.7	10R04.8	13R55.2	15 32.9	25 19.6
3 M	8 46 39	10 42 39	12 36 46	18 43 11	4 28.5	23 54.9	6 10.7	16 47.0	19 30.7	21 20.6	10 03.6	13 53.1	15 35.0	25 20.7
4 Tu	8 50 36	11 40 07	24 52 54	1♏06 24	4D26.4	25 35.0	6 26.2	17 25.1	19 50.5	21 33.6	10 02.4	13 51.1	15 37.1	25 21.7
5 W	8 54 32	12 37 35	7♏24 12	13 46 46	4 25.8	27 18.9	6 43.5	18 03.3	20 10.5	21 46.7	10 01.0	13 49.1	15 39.1	25 22.8
6 Th	8 58 29	13 35 04	20 14 38	26 48 13	4 26.5	29 06.2	7 02.8	18 41.5	20 30.6	21 59.7	9 59.6	13 47.1	15 41.1	25 23.8
7 F	9 02 25	14 32 34	3♐27 58	10♐14 11	4 27.9	0♌56.6	7 23.8	19 19.6	20 50.8	22 12.7	9 58.0	13 45.1	15 43.1	25 24.8
8 Sa	9 06 22	15 30 05	17 07 09	24 06 59	4R29.1	2 49.8	7 46.6	19 57.8	21 11.1	22 25.8	9 56.3	13 43.1	15 45.1	25 25.8
9 Su	9 10 18	16 27 37	1♑13 39	8♑26 59	4 29.4	4 45.4	8 11.0	20 36.0	21 31.6	22 38.9	9 54.6	13 41.2	15 47.1	25 26.8
10 M	9 14 15	17 25 10	15 46 36	23 11 55	4 28.1	6 43.0	8 37.1	21 14.1	21 52.2	22 51.9	9 52.7	13 39.3	15 49.1	25 27.7
11 Tu	9 18 12	18 22 43	0♒42 10	8♒16 21	4 24.8	8 42.1	9 04.8	21 52.3	22 12.8	23 05.0	9 50.8	13 37.5	15 51.0	25 28.7
12 W	9 22 08	19 20 18	15 53 21	23 31 53	4 19.8	10 42.6	9 34.0	22 30.4	22 33.6	23 18.1	9 48.8	13 35.7	15 53.0	25 29.6
13 Th	9 26 05	20 17 54	1♓10 34	8♓48 04	4 13.4	12 43.9	10 04.6	23 08.6	22 54.5	23 31.2	9 46.6	13 33.9	15 54.9	25 30.5
14 F	9 30 01	21 15 31	16 23 02	23 54 13	4 06.5	14 45.8	10 36.7	23 46.7	23 15.5	23 44.3	9 44.4	13 32.1	15 56.8	25 31.4
15 Sa	9 33 58	22 13 10	1♈20 33	8♈41 09	4 00.1	16 48.0	11 10.2	24 24.9	23 36.6	23 57.4	9 42.1	13 30.4	15 58.7	25 32.2
16 Su	9 37 54	23 10 50	15 55 18	23 02 34	3 54.9	18 50.1	11 44.9	25 03.0	23 57.8	24 10.5	9 39.7	13 28.7	16 00.5	25 33.1
17 M	9 41 51	24 08 32	0♉02 40	6♉55 33	3 51.6	20 52.0	12 21.0	25 41.2	24 19.1	24 23.6	9 37.2	13 27.1	16 02.4	25 33.9
18 Tu	9 45 47	25 06 15	13 41 19	20 20 15	3D50.2	22 53.5	12 58.2	26 19.3	24 40.4	24 36.7	9 34.6	13 25.4	16 04.2	25 34.7
19 W	9 49 44	26 04 00	26 52 41	3♊19 06	3 50.3	24 54.3	13 36.7	26 57.5	25 01.9	24 49.8	9 32.0	13 23.9	16 06.0	25 35.5
20 Th	9 53 40	27 01 47	9♊40 00	15 55 56	3 51.2	26 54.3	14 16.3	27 35.7	25 23.5	25 02.9	9 29.2	13 22.3	16 07.8	25 36.3
21 F	9 57 37	27 59 36	22 07 29	28 15 14	3R52.1	28 53.4	14 57.0	28 13.8	25 45.2	25 16.0	9 26.4	13 20.8	16 09.6	25 37.1
22 Sa	10 01 34	28 57 26	4♋19 43	10♋21 28	3 52.0	0♍51.5	15 38.7	28 52.0	26 07.0	25 29.1	9 23.5	13 19.4	16 11.4	25 37.8
23 Su	10 05 30	29 55 18	16 21 02	22 18 50	3 50.2	2 48.4	16 21.4	29 30.2	26 28.8	25 42.2	9 20.5	13 17.9	16 13.1	25 38.6
24 M	10 09 27	0♍53 11	28 15 20	4♌10 54	3 46.0	4 44.2	17 05.1	0♍08.4	26 50.8	25 55.3	9 17.4	13 16.6	16 14.8	25 39.3
25 Tu	10 13 23	1 51 06	10♌05 54	16 00 39	3 39.3	6 38.8	17 49.8	0 46.6	27 12.8	26 08.4	9 14.2	13 15.2	16 16.5	25 39.9
26 W	10 17 20	2 49 03	21 55 24	27 50 25	3 30.2	8 32.2	18 35.3	1 24.7	27 35.0	26 21.5	9 11.0	13 13.9	16 18.2	25 40.6
27 Th	10 21 16	3 47 01	3♍45 54	9♍42 03	3 19.5	10 24.3	19 21.7	2 02.9	27 57.2	26 34.5	9 07.7	13 12.7	16 19.8	25 41.3
28 F	10 25 13	4 45 01	15 39 04	21 37 08	3 07.8	12 15.1	20 08.9	2 41.1	28 19.5	26 47.6	9 04.3	13 11.4	16 21.4	25 41.9
29 Sa	10 29 09	5 43 02	27 36 25	3♎37 07	2 56.2	14 04.7	20 56.9	3 19.3	28 41.9	27 00.6	9 00.8	13 10.3	16 23.0	25 42.5
30 Su	10 33 06	6 41 05	9♎39 28	15 43 41	2 45.8	15 53.0	21 45.7	3 57.5	29 04.3	27 13.6	8 57.3	13 09.1	16 24.6	25 43.1
31 M	10 37 03	7 39 09	21 50 02	27 58 49	2 37.4	17 40.0	22 35.3	4 35.7	29 26.9	27 26.6	8 53.7	13 08.0	16 26.2	25 43.6

Astro Data

	Dy Hr Mn
♃⊻♆	1 0:06
♃⊼♅	4 10:42
☽0S	6 16:20
♅☍♆	11 14:13
☿D	16 0:21
☽0N	19 9:36
♄R	22 12:46
⚳0S	25 0:44
♀D	27 18:25
☽0S	2 22:44
☽0N	15 17:12
♃⚼♄	18 8:52
♃✱♇	23 4:52
☽0S	30 3:52

Planet Ingress

	Dy Hr Mn
♂ ♌	8 3:54
☉ ♌	23 7:14
☿ ♌	6 23:47
☿ ♍	22 1:31
☉ ♍	23 13:57
♂ ♍	24 6:44

Last Aspect / ☽ Ingress

Last Aspect Dy Hr Mn	☽ Ingress Dy Hr Mn	Last Aspect Dy Hr Mn	☽ Ingress Dy Hr Mn
2 17:11 ♇ ✱	♍ 3 3:58	1 13:32 ♇ □	♎ 1 22:56
5 13:00 ♂ ✱	♎ 5 16:20	4 0:55 ♇ △	♏ 4 9:53
8 2:18 ♂ □	♏ 8 2:23	6 16:49 ☿ △	♐ 6 17:47
9 9:12 ☉ △	♐ 10 8:49	8 14:14 ♇ ☍	♑ 8 21:57
12 3:14 ♇ ☍	♑ 12 11:40	10 0:02 ♆ ☍	♒ 10 22:53
13 21:48 ☉ ☍	♒ 14 12:07	12 15:05 ♇ △	♓ 12 22:09
16 3:56 ♇ △	♓ 16 11:58	14 14:36 ♇ □	♈ 14 21:49
18 4:56 ☉ △	♈ 18 13:02	16 16:17 ♇ ✱	♉ 16 23:55
20 12:02 ☉ □	♉ 20 16:46	18 23:32 ♂ □	♊ 19 5:48
22 23:12 ☉ ✱	♊ 22 23:48	21 13:30 ☿ ✱	♋ 21 15:26
25 0:15 ♇ ☌	♋ 25 9:44	22 23:42 ♆ ☌	♌ 24 3:32
26 16:08 ♆ ☌	♌ 27 21:38	26 8:56 ♃ ☌	♍ 26 16:23
30 0:47 ♇ ✱	♍ 30 10:24	28 20:11 ♇ □	♎ 29 4:47
		31 10:56 ♃ ✱	♏ 31 15:55

☽ Phases & Eclipses

Dy Hr Mn	
6 20:25	☽ 14♎19
13 21:48	○ 21♑02
13 21:34	☊ A 0.229
20 12:02	☾ 27♈20
28 7:17	● 4♌47
5 9:40	☽ 12♏32
12 4:59	○ 19♒03
18 21:25	☾ 25♉29
26 22:59	● 3♍16

Astro Data

1 July 1908
Julian Day # 3104
SVP 6♓32'31"
GC 25♐33.7 ⚴ 23♍02.9
Eris 25♓46.7R ⚵ 13♑25.3R
⚷ 22♒47.7R ⚶ 13♌11.5
☽ Mean ☊ 4♋48.6

1 August 1908
Julian Day # 3135
SVP 6♓32'26"
GC 25♐33.8 ⚴ 3♎53.0
Eris 25♓37.7R ⚵ 6♑45.3R
⚷ 21♒27.9R ⚶ 27♌20.7
☽ Mean ☊ 3♋10.1

LONGITUDE — September 1908

Day	Sid.Time	☉	0 hr ☽	Noon☽	True☊	☿	♀	♂	⚳	♃	♄	♅	♆	♇
1 Tu	10 40 59	8♍37 14	4♏10 22	10♏25 03	2♋31.5	19♍25.7	23♋25.6	5♍13.9	29♎49.5	27♌39.6	8♈50.0	13♑07.0	16♋27.7	25♊44.2
2 W	10 44 56	9 35 22	16 43 15	23 05 24	2R 28.1	21 10.2	24 16.5	5 52.2	0♏12.2	27 52.6	8R 46.3	13R 06.0	16 29.2	25 44.7
3 Th	10 48 52	10 33 30	29 31 55	6♐03 15	2D 26.9	22 53.5	25 08.2	6 30.4	0 34.9	28 05.6	8 42.5	13 05.1	16 30.7	25 45.2
4 F	10 52 49	11 31 40	12♐39 50	19 22 03	2R 26.9	24 35.6	26 00.5	7 08.6	0 57.8	28 18.5	8 38.6	13 04.2	16 32.1	25 45.7
5 Sa	10 56 45	12 29 52	26 10 17	3♑04 47	2 27.2	26 16.4	26 53.4	7 46.8	1 20.7	28 31.4	8 34.7	13 03.3	16 33.5	25 46.2
6 Su	11 00 42	13 28 05	10♑05 42	17 13 06	2 26.5	27 56.1	27 47.0	8 25.0	1 43.7	28 44.3	8 30.7	13 02.5	16 35.0	25 46.6
7 M	11 04 38	14 26 19	24 26 50	1♒46 34	2 23.8	29 34.6	28 41.1	9 03.3	2 06.7	28 57.1	8 26.7	13 01.7	16 36.3	25 47.0
8 Tu	11 08 35	15 24 35	9♒11 47	16 41 44	2 18.4	1♎11.9	29 35.8	9 41.5	2 29.8	29 10.0	8 22.6	13 01.0	16 37.7	25 47.4
9 W	11 12 32	16 22 53	24 15 29	1♓51 53	2 10.6	2 48.1	0♌31.1	10 19.7	2 53.0	29 22.8	8 18.5	13 00.3	16 39.0	25 47.8
10 Th	11 16 28	17 21 12	9♓29 39	17 07 24	2 00.7	4 23.2	1 26.9	10 58.0	3 16.2	29 35.6	8 14.3	12 59.7	16 40.3	25 48.2
11 F	11 20 25	18 19 33	24 43 45	2♈17 17	1 50.0	5 57.1	2 23.2	11 36.2	3 39.5	29 48.3	8 10.0	12 59.1	16 41.6	25 48.5
12 Sa	11 24 21	19 17 56	9♈46 46	17 11 03	1 39.8	7 30.0	3 20.1	12 14.5	4 02.8	0♍01.0	8 05.7	12 58.6	16 42.8	25 48.8
13 Su	11 28 18	20 16 21	24 29 13	1♉40 34	1 31.0	9 01.7	4 17.5	12 52.8	4 26.3	0 13.7	8 01.4	12 58.1	16 44.0	25 49.1
14 M	11 32 14	21 14 48	8♉44 39	15 41 12	1 24.6	10 32.3	5 15.3	13 31.0	4 49.7	0 26.4	7 57.0	12 57.7	16 45.2	25 49.4
15 Tu	11 36 11	22 13 18	22 30 11	29 11 46	1 20.8	12 01.8	6 13.6	14 09.3	5 13.3	0 39.0	7 52.6	12 57.3	16 46.4	25 49.6
16 W	11 40 07	23 11 49	5♊46 15	12♊14 04	1D 19.1	13 30.3	7 12.4	14 47.6	5 36.9	0 51.6	7 48.2	12 57.0	16 47.5	25 49.8
17 Th	11 44 04	24 10 23	18 35 44	24 51 50	1R 18.8	14 57.6	8 11.6	15 25.9	6 00.5	1 04.2	7 43.7	12 56.7	16 48.6	25 50.0
18 F	11 48 01	25 08 59	1♋03 02	7♋09 58	1 18.7	16 23.7	9 11.2	16 04.2	6 24.2	1 16.7	7 39.2	12 56.5	16 49.7	25 50.2
19 Sa	11 51 57	26 07 37	13 13 18	19 13 42	1 17.8	17 48.8	10 11.2	16 42.6	6 48.0	1 29.2	7 34.6	12 56.3	16 50.7	25 50.4
20 Su	11 55 54	27 06 17	25 11 47	1♌08 09	1 15.0	19 12.6	11 11.7	17 20.9	7 11.8	1 41.6	7 30.1	12 56.2	16 51.7	25 50.5
21 M	11 59 50	28 05 00	7♌03 22	12 57 56	1 09.5	20 35.3	12 12.5	17 59.2	7 35.7	1 54.0	7 25.5	12 56.1	16 52.7	25 50.6
22 Tu	12 03 47	29 03 44	18 52 20	24 47 00	1 01.2	21 56.8	13 13.7	18 37.6	7 59.6	2 06.4	7 20.9	12D 56.1	16 53.6	25 50.7
23 W	12 07 43	0♎02 31	0♍42 15	6♍38 27	0 50.1	23 17.0	14 15.2	19 16.0	8 23.5	2 18.7	7 16.2	12 56.1	16 54.5	25 50.8
24 Th	12 11 40	1 01 20	12 35 49	18 34 37	0 36.9	24 35.9	15 17.2	19 54.3	8 47.6	2 31.0	7 11.6	12 56.2	16 55.4	25 50.9
25 F	12 15 36	2 00 11	24 35 00	0♎37 07	0 22.7	25 53.4	16 19.4	20 32.7	9 11.6	2 43.2	7 06.9	12 56.3	16 56.3	25R 50.9
26 Sa	12 19 33	2 59 03	6♎41 06	12 47 02	0 08.5	27 09.5	17 22.0	21 11.1	9 35.7	2 55.4	7 02.2	12 56.5	16 57.1	25 50.9
27 Su	12 23 29	3 57 58	18 55 02	25 05 10	29♊55.6	28 24.2	18 24.9	21 49.5	9 59.9	3 07.5	6 57.5	12 56.7	16 57.9	25 50.9
28 M	12 27 26	4 56 55	1♏17 33	7♏32 18	29 45.0	29 37.2	19 28.1	22 27.9	10 24.1	3 19.5	6 52.8	12 57.0	16 58.6	25 50.8
29 Tu	12 31 23	5 55 53	13 49 34	20 09 31	29 37.3	0♏48.6	20 31.6	23 06.3	10 48.4	3 31.6	6 48.1	12 57.3	16 59.4	25 50.8
30 W	12 35 19	6 54 54	26 32 23	2♐58 22	29 32.5	1 58.2	21 35.5	23 44.7	11 12.6	3 43.5	6 43.4	12 57.7	17 00.1	25 50.7

LONGITUDE — October 1908

Day	Sid.Time	☉	0 hr ☽	Noon☽	True☊	☿	♀	♂	⚳	♃	♄	♅	♆	♇
1 Th	12 39 16	7♎53 56	9♐27 46	16♐00 51	29♊30.4	3♏05.9	22♌39.6	24♍23.2	11♏37.0	3♍55.4	6♈38.7	12♑58.1	17♋00.7	25♊50.6
2 F	12 43 12	8 53 00	22 37 58	29 19 23	29R 29.9	4 11.5	23 44.0	25 01.6	12 01.3	4 07.3	6R 34.0	12 58.6	17 01.4	25R 50.4
3 Sa	12 47 09	9 52 06	6♑05 26	12♑56 20	29 29.9	5 14.9	24 48.6	25 40.1	12 25.8	4 19.0	6 29.3	12 59.2	17 02.0	25 50.3
4 Su	12 51 05	10 51 14	19 52 19	26 53 28	29 29.2	6 16.0	25 53.6	26 18.5	12 50.2	4 30.8	6 24.6	12 59.7	17 02.5	25 50.1
5 M	12 55 02	11 50 23	3♒59 49	11♒11 13	29 26.5	7 14.5	26 58.8	26 57.0	13 14.7	4 42.4	6 19.9	13 00.4	17 03.1	25 49.9
6 Tu	12 58 58	12 49 34	18 27 22	25 47 49	29 21.3	8 10.1	28 04.2	27 35.5	13 39.2	4 54.0	6 15.2	13 01.1	17 03.6	25 49.7
7 W	13 02 55	13 48 47	3♓11 56	10♓38 52	29 13.5	9 02.7	29 10.0	28 14.0	14 03.8	5 05.6	6 10.6	13 01.8	17 04.0	25 49.5
8 Th	13 06 52	14 48 02	18 07 39	25 37 12	29 03.6	9 51.9	0♍15.9	28 52.5	14 28.3	5 17.0	6 06.0	13 02.6	17 04.4	25 49.2
9 F	13 10 48	15 47 18	3♈06 20	10♈33 51	28 52.7	10 37.5	1 22.1	29 31.0	14 53.0	5 28.4	6 01.4	13 03.4	17 04.8	25 48.9
10 Sa	13 14 45	16 46 37	17 58 34	25 19 22	28 42.1	11 19.1	2 28.6	0♎09.5	15 17.6	5 39.8	5 56.8	13 04.3	17 05.2	25 48.6
11 Su	13 18 41	17 45 57	2♉35 18	9♉45 34	28 33.0	11 56.3	3 35.2	0 48.0	15 42.3	5 51.0	5 52.2	13 05.3	17 05.5	25 48.3
12 M	13 22 38	18 45 20	16 49 31	23 46 45	28 26.1	12 28.6	4 42.1	1 26.6	16 07.0	6 02.2	5 47.7	13 06.3	17 05.8	25 47.9
13 Tu	13 26 34	19 44 45	0♊37 01	7♊20 19	28 21.9	12 55.7	5 49.3	2 05.1	16 31.7	6 13.3	5 43.2	13 07.3	17 06.1	25 47.6
14 W	13 30 31	20 44 13	13 56 44	20 26 35	28D 20.0	13 17.1	6 56.6	2 43.7	16 56.5	6 24.4	5 38.7	13 08.4	17 06.3	25 47.2
15 Th	13 34 27	21 43 43	26 50 13	3♋08 10	28 19.8	13 32.2	8 04.2	3 22.3	17 21.3	6 35.3	5 34.3	13 09.5	17 06.5	25 46.8
16 F	13 38 24	22 43 15	9♋20 58	15 29 16	28R 20.3	13R 40.5	9 11.9	4 00.9	17 46.1	6 46.2	5 29.9	13 10.7	17 06.7	25 46.3
17 Sa	13 42 21	23 42 49	21 33 41	27 34 54	28 20.5	13 41.5	10 19.9	4 39.5	18 11.0	6 57.0	5 25.5	13 12.0	17 06.8	25 45.9
18 Su	13 46 17	24 42 25	3♌33 36	9♌30 25	28 19.2	13 34.6	11 28.1	5 18.2	18 35.9	7 07.8	5 21.2	13 13.3	17 06.9	25 45.4
19 M	13 50 14	25 42 04	15 26 01	21 21 00	28 15.8	13 19.5	12 36.4	5 56.8	19 00.8	7 18.4	5 16.9	13 14.6	17 07.0	25 44.9
20 Tu	13 54 10	26 41 45	27 15 57	3♍11 24	28 09.9	12 55.8	13 45.0	6 35.5	19 25.7	7 28.9	5 12.7	13 16.0	17R 07.0	25 44.4
21 W	13 58 07	27 41 28	9♍07 50	15 05 40	28 01.7	12 23.1	14 53.7	7 14.1	19 50.7	7 39.4	5 08.5	13 17.4	17 07.0	25 43.9
22 Th	14 02 03	28 41 14	21 05 18	27 07 03	27 51.6	11 41.7	16 02.6	7 52.8	20 15.7	7 49.8	5 04.4	13 18.9	17 06.9	25 43.3
23 F	14 06 00	29 41 01	3♎11 10	9♎17 52	27 40.5	10 51.6	17 11.7	8 31.5	20 40.7	8 00.1	5 00.4	13 20.4	17 06.9	25 42.7
24 Sa	14 09 56	0♏40 51	15 27 17	21 39 33	27 29.3	9 53.4	18 20.9	9 10.2	21 05.7	8 10.3	4 56.4	13 22.0	17 06.8	25 42.1
25 Su	14 13 53	1 40 42	27 54 41	4♏12 44	27 19.1	8 48.2	19 30.3	9 49.0	21 30.7	8 20.4	4 52.4	13 23.6	17 06.6	25 41.5
26 M	14 17 50	2 40 36	10♏33 40	16 57 29	27 10.9	7 37.2	20 39.9	10 27.7	21 55.8	8 30.4	4 48.5	13 25.3	17 06.4	25 40.9
27 Tu	14 21 46	3 40 31	23 24 09	29 53 37	27 05.0	6 22.2	21 49.6	11 06.5	22 20.9	8 40.3	4 44.7	13 27.0	17 06.2	25 40.3
28 W	14 25 43	4 40 29	6♐25 52	13♐00 55	27 01.8	5 05.3	22 59.4	11 45.2	22 46.0	8 50.1	4 40.9	13 28.8	17 06.0	25 39.6
29 Th	14 29 39	5 40 28	19 38 45	26 19 26	27D 00.8	3 48.7	24 09.4	12 24.0	23 11.1	8 59.8	4 37.2	13 30.6	17 05.7	25 38.9
30 F	14 33 36	6 40 29	3♑03 00	9♑49 32	27 01.3	2 34.9	25 19.6	13 02.8	23 36.2	9 09.4	4 33.6	13 32.4	17 05.4	25 38.2
31 Sa	14 37 32	7 40 31	16 39 06	23 31 47	27 02.5	1 26.2	26 29.9	13 41.6	24 01.4	9 18.9	4 30.1	13 34.3	17 05.0	25 37.5

Astro Data

	Dy Hr Mn
♃□♅	3 11:09
☿0S	8 6:19
☽0N	12 2:48
♃∠♆	21 9:10
♅D	22 13:25
☉0S	23 10:59
♇R	26 2:04
☽0S	26 9:16
♄0S	7 9:22
☽0N	9 13:22
♃⊼♄	11 13:48
♂0S	13 20:08
☿R	17 3:09
♆R	20 17:12
☽0S	23 16:12

Planet Ingress

		Dy Hr Mn
⚳	♏	1 23:08
☿	♎	7 18:14
♀	♌	8 22:32
♃	♍	12 10:02
☉	♎	23 10:58
☊	♊R	27 3:29
☿	♏	28 19:36
♀	♍	8 6:13
♂	♎	10 6:05
☉	♏	23 19:37

Last Aspect / ☽ Ingress (September)

Last Aspect Dy Hr Mn			☽ Ingress	Dy Hr Mn
2 21:05	♃	□	♐	3 0:52
5 3:59	♃	△	♑	5 6:40
7 7:58	☿	△	♒	7 9:06
9 8:02	♃	☍	♓	9 9:04
11 1:42	♇	□	♈	11 8:21
13 2:12	♇	⚹	♉	13 9:11
14 22:32	☉	△	♊	15 13:27
17 13:52	♇	☌	♋	17 21:57
20 3:07	☉	⚹	♌	20 9:42
22 14:09	♇	⚹	♍	22 22:34
25 2:31	♇	□	♎	25 10:46
27 19:08	☿	☌	♏	27 21:30
29 17:51	♂	⚹	♐	30 6:28

Last Aspect / ☽ Ingress (October)

Last Aspect Dy Hr Mn			☽ Ingress	Dy Hr Mn
2 5:46	♇	☍	♑	2 13:12
4 10:58	♂	△	♒	4 17:16
6 15:59	♀	☍	♓	6 18:49
8 17:27	♂	☍	♈	8 19:01
10 12:48	♇	⚹	♉	10 19:42
12 0:28	♆	⚹	♊	12 22:55
14 22:01	♇	☌	♋	15 6:00
17 3:35	☉	□	♌	17 16:51
19 21:38	☉	⚹	♍	20 5:32
22 9:14	♇	□	♎	22 17:43
24 19:46	♇	△	♏	25 3:59
26 19:36	♀	⚹	♐	27 12:12
29 10:47	♇	☍	♑	29 18:34
31 17:38	♀	△	♒	31 23:12

☽ Phases & Eclipses

Dy Hr Mn		
3 20:51	☽	10♐55
10 12:23	○	17♓22
17 10:33	☾	24♊07
25 14:59	●	2♎07
3 6:13	☽	9♑38
9 21:03	○	16♈10
17 3:35	☾	23♋22
25 6:46	●	1♏28

Astro Data

1 September 1908
Julian Day # 3166
SVP 6♓32'23"
GC 25♐33.8 ⚴ 16♎10.4
Eris 25♓19.9R ⚵ 4♑30.0
⚷ 19♒53.7R ⚶ 12♍10.8
☽ Mean ☊ 1♋31.6

1 October 1908
Julian Day # 3196
SVP 6♓32'20"
GC 25♐33.9 ⚴ 28♎52.2
Eris 24♓59.2R ⚵ 7♑45.8
⚷ 18♒43.7R ⚶ 26♍56.9
☽ Mean ☊ 29♊56.3

November 1908 LONGITUDE

Day	Sid.Time	☉	0 hr ☽	Noon ☽	True ☊	☿	♀	♂	⚳	♃	♄	♅	♆	♇
1 Su	14 41 29	8♏40 35	0♒27 39	7♒26 41	27♊03.2	0♏24.7	27♍40.3	14♎20.4	24♏26.5	9♍28.3	4♈26.6	13♑36.3	17♋04.7	25♊36.7
2 M	14 45 25	9 40 40	14 28 53	21 34 09	27R 02.5	29♎32.1	28 50.8	14 59.2	24 51.7	9 37.6	4R 23.2	13 38.3	17R 04.2	25R 36.0
3 Tu	14 49 22	10 40 47	28 42 16	5♓52 58	26 59.9	28R 49.9	0♎01.5	15 38.1	25 16.9	9 46.8	4 19.9	13 40.3	17 03.8	25 35.2
4 W	14 53 19	11 40 56	13♓05 52	20 20 27	26 55.4	28 18.8	1 12.3	16 16.9	25 42.1	9 55.8	4 16.6	13 42.4	17 03.3	25 34.4
5 Th	14 57 15	12 41 06	27 36 08	4♈52 12	26 49.2	27 59.3	2 23.3	16 55.8	26 07.2	10 04.8	4 13.5	13 44.5	17 02.8	25 33.6
6 F	15 01 12	13 41 17	12♈07 55	19 22 28	26 42.3	27D 51.4	3 34.3	17 34.7	26 32.4	10 13.6	4 10.4	13 46.7	17 02.3	25 32.8
7 Sa	15 05 08	14 41 30	26 35 01	3♉44 47	26 35.3	27 54.9	4 45.5	18 13.5	26 57.7	10 22.3	4 07.4	13 48.9	17 01.7	25 31.9
8 Su	15 09 05	15 41 45	10♉51 01	17 53 02	26 29.4	28 09.1	5 56.8	18 52.4	27 22.9	10 30.9	4 04.5	13 51.1	17 01.1	25 31.1
9 M	15 13 01	16 42 02	24 50 16	1♊42 18	26 25.1	28 33.4	7 08.2	19 31.4	27 48.1	10 39.4	4 01.6	13 53.4	17 00.4	25 30.2
10 Tu	15 16 58	17 42 21	8♊28 48	15 09 36	26D 22.7	29 06.8	8 19.7	20 10.3	28 13.3	10 47.8	3 58.9	13 55.7	16 59.8	25 29.3
11 W	15 20 54	18 42 41	21 44 39	28 14 02	26 22.1	29 48.6	9 31.4	20 49.3	28 38.6	10 56.0	3 56.3	13 58.1	16 59.1	25 28.4
12 Th	15 24 51	19 43 03	4♋37 58	10♋56 43	26 22.9	0♏37.8	10 43.1	21 28.2	29 03.8	11 04.1	3 53.7	14 00.5	16 58.4	25 27.5
13 F	15 28 48	20 43 27	17 10 41	23 20 20	26 24.6	1 33.6	11 55.0	22 07.2	29 29.1	11 12.1	3 51.2	14 02.9	16 57.6	25 26.6
14 Sa	15 32 44	21 43 53	29 26 11	5♌28 47	26 26.3	2 35.1	13 07.0	22 46.2	29 54.3	11 20.0	3 48.9	14 05.4	16 56.8	25 25.6
15 Su	15 36 41	22 44 21	11♌28 46	17 26 42	26R 27.4	3 41.5	14 19.1	23 25.2	0♐19.6	11 27.7	3 46.6	14 07.9	16 56.0	25 24.7
16 M	15 40 37	23 44 51	23 23 16	29 19 03	26 27.4	4 52.3	15 31.2	24 04.3	0 44.8	11 35.3	3 44.4	14 10.4	16 55.1	25 23.7
17 Tu	15 44 34	24 45 22	5♍14 43	11♍10 50	26 25.9	6 06.8	16 43.5	24 43.3	1 10.1	11 42.8	3 42.3	14 13.0	16 54.3	25 22.7
18 W	15 48 30	25 45 56	17 08 01	23 06 47	26 23.0	7 24.5	17 55.8	25 22.4	1 35.4	11 50.1	3 40.3	14 15.6	16 53.3	25 21.7
19 Th	15 52 27	26 46 31	29 07 40	5♎11 07	26 19.0	8 44.8	19 08.3	26 01.5	2 00.6	11 57.3	3 38.4	14 18.3	16 52.4	25 20.7
20 F	15 56 23	27 47 07	11♎17 34	17 27 21	26 14.2	10 07.4	20 20.8	26 40.5	2 25.9	12 04.3	3 36.6	14 21.0	16 51.4	25 19.7
21 Sa	16 00 20	28 47 45	23 40 45	29 57 59	26 09.2	11 31.9	21 33.4	27 19.7	2 51.1	12 11.2	3 34.9	14 23.7	16 50.4	25 18.6
22 Su	16 04 17	29 48 25	6♏19 13	12♏44 31	26 04.7	12 58.0	22 46.1	27 58.8	3 16.4	12 18.0	3 33.3	14 26.5	16 49.4	25 17.6
23 M	16 08 13	0♐49 07	19 13 54	25 47 18	26 01.2	14 25.4	23 58.9	28 37.9	3 41.7	12 24.6	3 31.8	14 29.3	16 48.4	25 16.6
24 Tu	16 12 10	1 49 50	2♐24 36	9♐05 38	25 58.9	15 53.9	25 11.8	29 17.1	4 06.9	12 31.0	3 30.5	14 32.1	16 47.3	25 15.5
25 W	16 16 06	2 50 34	15 50 10	22 37 59	25D 58.0	17 23.4	26 24.7	29 56.3	4 32.1	12 37.3	3 29.2	14 35.0	16 46.2	25 14.4
26 Th	16 20 03	3 51 20	29 28 47	6♑22 18	25 58.2	18 53.6	27 37.7	0♏35.4	4 57.4	12 43.5	3 28.0	14 37.9	16 45.1	25 13.3
27 F	16 23 59	4 52 06	13♑18 13	20 16 16	25 59.3	20 24.4	28 50.8	1 14.6	5 22.6	12 49.5	3 26.9	14 40.8	16 43.9	25 12.2
28 Sa	16 27 56	5 52 54	27 16 09	4♒17 36	26 00.8	21 55.8	0♏03.9	1 53.8	5 47.8	12 55.3	3 26.0	14 43.7	16 42.8	25 11.1
29 Su	16 31 52	6 53 43	11♒20 21	18 24 11	26 02.1	23 27.5	1 17.1	2 33.1	6 13.0	13 01.0	3 25.1	14 46.7	16 41.6	25 10.0
30 M	16 35 49	7 54 32	25 28 48	2♓34 01	26R 02.8	24 59.6	2 30.4	3 12.3	6 38.2	13 06.6	3 24.4	14 49.7	16 40.3	25 08.9

December 1908 LONGITUDE

Day	Sid.Time	☉	0 hr ☽	Noon ☽	True ☊	☿	♀	♂	⚳	♃	♄	♅	♆	♇
1 Tu	16 39 46	8♐55 22	9♓39 32	16♓45 08	26♊02.7	26♏31.9	3♏43.7	3♏51.5	7♐03.4	13♍11.9	3♈23.7	14♑52.8	16♋39.1	25♊07.8
2 W	16 43 42	9 56 13	23 50 31	0♈55 26	26R 01.8	28 04.5	4 57.1	4 30.8	7 28.6	13 17.1	3R 23.2	14 55.8	16R 37.8	25R 06.7
3 Th	16 47 39	10 57 05	7♈59 32	15 02 30	26 00.2	29 37.2	6 10.5	5 10.1	7 53.7	13 22.2	3 22.8	14 58.9	16 36.5	25 05.5
4 F	16 51 35	11 57 58	22 03 59	29 03 38	25 58.4	1♐10.1	7 24.0	5 49.4	8 18.8	13 27.0	3 22.5	15 02.0	16 35.2	25 04.4
5 Sa	16 55 32	12 58 51	6♉01 04	12♉55 55	25 56.5	2 43.1	8 37.5	6 28.7	8 43.9	13 31.8	3 22.3	15 05.2	16 33.9	25 03.2
6 Su	16 59 28	13 59 46	19 47 51	26 36 30	25 55.0	4 16.1	9 51.1	7 08.0	9 09.1	13 36.3	3D 22.2	15 08.3	16 32.5	25 02.1
7 M	17 03 25	15 00 41	3♊21 36	10♊02 53	25 54.0	5 49.3	11 04.8	7 47.3	9 34.1	13 40.7	3 22.2	15 11.5	16 31.1	25 00.9
8 Tu	17 07 21	16 01 38	16 40 10	23 13 16	25D 53.6	7 22.5	12 18.5	8 26.7	9 59.2	13 44.9	3 22.3	15 14.7	16 29.7	24 59.8
9 W	17 11 18	17 02 35	29 42 09	6♋06 48	25 53.7	8 55.9	13 32.2	9 06.0	10 24.3	13 48.9	3 22.5	15 18.0	16 28.3	24 58.6
10 Th	17 15 15	18 03 33	12♋27 17	18 43 43	25 54.2	10 29.2	14 46.0	9 45.4	10 49.3	13 52.8	3 22.9	15 21.2	16 26.9	24 57.4
11 F	17 19 11	19 04 33	24 56 18	1♌05 20	25 55.0	12 02.7	15 59.9	10 24.8	11 14.3	13 56.5	3 23.3	15 24.5	16 25.4	24 56.3
12 Sa	17 23 08	20 05 33	7♌11 07	13 14 02	25 55.7	13 36.2	17 13.8	11 04.2	11 39.3	14 00.0	3 23.9	15 27.8	16 24.0	24 55.1
13 Su	17 27 04	21 06 34	19 14 31	25 13 04	25 56.3	15 09.9	18 27.8	11 43.6	12 04.3	14 03.3	3 24.5	15 31.1	16 22.5	24 53.9
14 M	17 31 01	22 07 36	1♍10 10	7♍06 22	25 56.7	16 43.6	19 41.8	12 23.1	12 29.2	14 06.4	3 25.3	15 34.5	16 21.0	24 52.7
15 Tu	17 34 57	23 08 39	13 02 14	18 58 23	25R 56.8	18 17.4	20 55.8	13 02.5	12 54.1	14 09.4	3 26.2	15 37.8	16 19.4	24 51.5
16 W	17 38 54	24 09 43	24 55 22	0♎53 48	25 56.8	19 51.4	22 09.9	13 42.0	13 19.0	14 12.2	3 27.2	15 41.2	16 17.9	24 50.4
17 Th	17 42 50	25 10 48	6♎54 17	12 57 23	25D 56.8	21 25.4	23 24.0	14 21.5	13 43.9	14 14.8	3 28.3	15 44.6	16 16.4	24 49.2
18 F	17 46 47	26 11 54	19 03 38	25 13 35	25 56.7	22 59.7	24 38.2	15 01.0	14 08.8	14 17.2	3 29.5	15 48.0	16 14.8	24 48.0
19 Sa	17 50 44	27 13 01	1♏27 41	7♏46 22	25 56.8	24 34.1	25 52.4	15 40.6	14 33.6	14 19.4	3 30.8	15 51.4	16 13.2	24 46.8
20 Su	17 54 40	28 14 08	14 09 58	20 38 45	25 57.0	26 08.6	27 06.6	16 20.1	14 58.4	14 21.5	3 32.2	15 54.8	16 11.6	24 45.6
21 M	17 58 37	29 15 16	27 12 54	3♐52 31	25 57.3	27 43.4	28 20.9	16 59.7	15 23.2	14 23.3	3 33.8	15 58.3	16 10.0	24 44.4
22 Tu	18 02 33	0♑16 25	10♐37 33	17 27 51	25R 57.5	29 18.3	29 35.2	17 39.2	15 47.9	14 25.0	3 35.4	16 01.7	16 08.4	24 43.3
23 W	18 06 30	1 17 34	24 23 12	1♑23 13	25 57.6	0♑53.5	0♐49.5	18 18.8	16 12.6	14 26.5	3 37.2	16 05.2	16 06.8	24 42.1
24 Th	18 10 26	2 18 44	8♑27 26	15 35 17	25 57.3	2 28.9	2 03.9	18 58.4	16 37.3	14 27.7	3 39.0	16 08.7	16 05.2	24 40.9
25 F	18 14 23	3 19 54	22 46 09	29 59 19	25 56.6	4 04.6	3 18.2	19 38.0	17 01.9	14 28.8	3 41.0	16 12.2	16 03.5	24 39.8
26 Sa	18 18 20	4 21 04	7♒14 06	14♒29 45	25 55.7	5 40.5	4 32.6	20 17.6	17 26.5	14 29.7	3 43.0	16 15.7	16 01.9	24 38.6
27 Su	18 22 16	5 22 13	21 45 32	29 00 49	25 54.6	7 16.6	5 47.1	20 57.3	17 51.1	14 30.4	3 45.2	16 19.2	16 00.2	24 37.4
28 M	18 26 13	6 23 23	6♓14 56	13♓27 22	25 53.6	8 53.1	7 01.5	21 36.9	18 15.6	14 30.9	3 47.5	16 22.8	15 58.5	24 36.3
29 Tu	18 30 09	7 24 33	20 37 38	27 45 20	25D 52.9	10 29.8	8 16.0	22 16.6	18 40.1	14 31.2	3 49.9	16 26.3	15 56.9	24 35.1
30 W	18 34 06	8 25 43	4♈50 10	11♈51 55	25 52.8	12 06.9	9 30.5	22 56.2	19 04.6	14R 31.3	3 52.3	16 29.8	15 55.2	24 34.0
31 Th	18 38 02	9 26 52	18 50 24	25 45 33	25 53.2	13 44.2	10 45.0	23 35.9	19 29.0	14 31.3	3 54.9	16 33.4	15 53.5	24 32.8

Astro Data

	Dy Hr Mn
☽0N	5 23:04
♀0S	6 13:53
☿ D	6 16:33
☽0S	20 0:46
☽0N	3 6:27
♄ D	6 21:04
☽0S	17 9:47
♅☍♆	23 19:23
☽0N	30 11:54
♃ R	30 14:22

Planet Ingress

		Dy Hr Mn
☿	♎R	1 22:44
♀	♎	3 11:29
☿	♏	11 17:53
⚳	♐	14 17:23
☉	♐	22 16:35
♂	♏	25 14:18
♀	♏	28 10:43
☿	♐	3 17:54
☉	♑	22 5:34
♀	♐	22 20:01
☿	♑	22 22:31

Last Aspect / ☽ Ingress (November)

Last Aspect Dy Hr Mn			☽ Ingress	Dy Hr Mn
3 0:44	☿	△	♓	3 2:10
4 20:38	♇	□	♈	5 3:58
7 2:09	☿	☍	♉	7 5:43
8 10:31	♆	⚹	♊	9 9:00
11 15:08	☿	△	♋	11 15:18
13 9:29	♂	□	♌	14 1:07
16 4:04	♇	⚹	♍	16 13:23
18 17:47	☉	⚹	♎	19 1:44
21 6:42	♂	☌	♏	21 12:04
22 19:33	♆	△	♐	23 19:39
25 19:17	♀	⚹	♑	26 0:55
28 4:06	♀	□	♒	28 4:40
29 23:27	♇	△	♓	30 7:39

Last Aspect / ☽ Ingress (December)

Last Aspect Dy Hr Mn			☽ Ingress	Dy Hr Mn
2 6:35	☿	△	♈	2 10:26
4 5:10	♇	⚹	♉	4 13:37
5 18:20	♆	⚹	♊	6 18:01
8 15:16	♇	☌	♋	9 0:33
10 7:38	♆	☌	♌	11 9:52
13 11:22	♇	⚹	♍	13 21:38
15 23:51	♇	□	♎	16 10:12
18 14:03	☉	⚹	♏	18 21:12
21 1:02	♀	☌	♐	21 5:02
23 0:34	♇	☍	♑	23 9:38
24 17:56	♂	⚹	♒	25 12:01
27 4:45	♇	△	♓	27 13:38
29 6:40	♇	□	♈	29 15:48
31 9:54	♇	⚹	♉	31 19:24

☽ Phases & Eclipses

Dy Hr Mn		
1 14:16	☽	8♒46
8 7:58	○	15♉32
15 23:41	☾	23♌14
23 21:53	●	1♐14
30 21:44	☽	8♓19
7 21:44	○	15♊25
7 21:55	☍	A 1.034
15 21:12	☾	23♍32
23 11:50	●	1♑17
23 11:44:17	●	AT00'12"
30 5:40	☽	8♈10

Astro Data

1 November 1908
Julian Day # 3227
SVP 6♓32'16"
GC 25♐34.0 ⚵ 12♏24.1
Eris 24♓40.6R ⚴ 15♑26.7
⚷ 18♒20.9 ⚶ 12♎23.5
☽ Mean ☊ 28♊17.8

1 December 1908
Julian Day # 3257
SVP 6♓32'12"
GC 25♐34.0 ⚵ 25♏31.5
Eris 24♓30.7R ⚴ 25♑41.0
⚷ 18♒56.4 ⚶ 27♎12.3
☽ Mean ☊ 26♊42.4

LONGITUDE — January 1909

Day	Sid.Time	☉	0 hr ☽	Noon ☽	True ☊	☿	♀	♂	⚳	♃	♄	♅	♆	♇
1 F	18 41 59	10♑28 01	2♉37 18	9♉25 38	25♊54.3	15♑21.9	11♐59.5	24♏15.6	19♐53.3	14♍31.0	3♈57.6	16♑36.9	15♋51.8	24♊31.7
2 Sa	18 45 55	11 29 10	16 10 36	22 52 12	25 55.6	16 59.8	13 14.1	24 55.3	20 17.6	14R 30.5	4 00.4	16 40.5	15R 50.1	24R 30.6
3 Su	18 49 52	12 30 19	29 30 30	6♊05 32	25 56.8	18 38.1	14 28.6	25 35.0	20 41.9	14 29.9	4 03.3	16 44.0	15 48.4	24 29.4
4 M	18 53 49	13 31 28	12♊37 23	19 06 05	25R 57.6	20 16.6	15 43.2	26 14.7	21 06.2	14 29.0	4 06.3	16 47.6	15 46.7	24 28.3
5 Tu	18 57 45	14 32 36	25 31 40	1♋54 13	25 57.6	21 55.4	16 57.8	26 54.5	21 30.4	14 28.0	4 09.3	16 51.2	15 45.1	24 27.2
6 W	19 01 42	15 33 44	8♋13 46	14 30 23	25 56.6	23 34.5	18 12.4	27 34.2	21 54.5	14 26.8	4 12.5	16 54.8	15 43.4	24 26.1
7 Th	19 05 38	16 34 52	20 44 09	26 55 09	25 54.5	25 13.8	19 27.1	28 14.0	22 18.6	14 25.3	4 15.8	16 58.3	15 41.7	24 25.0
8 F	19 09 35	17 36 00	3♌03 30	9♌09 21	25 51.4	26 53.2	20 41.7	28 53.8	22 42.7	14 23.7	4 19.2	17 01.9	15 40.0	24 24.0
9 Sa	19 13 31	18 37 08	15 12 54	21 14 21	25 47.5	28 32.8	21 56.4	29 33.6	23 06.7	14 21.9	4 22.6	17 05.5	15 38.3	24 22.9
10 Su	19 17 28	19 38 16	27 13 58	3♍12 02	25 43.3	0♒12.5	23 11.1	0♐13.4	23 30.6	14 19.9	4 26.2	17 09.0	15 36.6	24 21.8
11 M	19 21 24	20 39 23	9♍08 55	15 05 00	25 39.3	1 52.1	24 25.8	0 53.2	23 54.5	14 17.7	4 29.8	17 12.6	15 34.9	24 20.8
12 Tu	19 25 21	21 40 30	21 00 42	26 56 29	25 36.0	3 31.6	25 40.5	1 33.1	24 18.4	14 15.3	4 33.6	17 16.2	15 33.2	24 19.7
13 W	19 29 18	22 41 37	2♎52 52	8♎50 24	25 33.8	5 10.8	26 55.2	2 12.9	24 42.2	14 12.8	4 37.4	17 19.7	15 31.5	24 18.7
14 Th	19 33 14	23 42 44	14 49 37	20 51 08	25D 32.8	6 49.7	28 09.9	2 52.8	25 05.9	14 10.0	4 41.3	17 23.3	15 29.8	24 17.7
15 F	19 37 11	24 43 51	26 55 32	3♏03 26	25 33.0	8 28.0	29 24.7	3 32.7	25 29.6	14 07.1	4 45.3	17 26.8	15 28.1	24 16.7
16 Sa	19 41 07	25 44 58	9♏15 24	15 32 02	25 34.3	10 05.6	0♑39.5	4 12.6	25 53.2	14 03.9	4 49.4	17 30.4	15 26.5	24 15.7
17 Su	19 45 04	26 46 04	21 53 52	28 21 23	25 36.0	11 42.1	1 54.3	4 52.5	26 16.8	14 00.6	4 53.6	17 33.9	15 24.8	24 14.7
18 M	19 49 00	27 47 10	4♐55 01	11♐35 05	25 37.6	13 17.4	3 09.0	5 32.4	26 40.3	13 57.1	4 57.9	17 37.4	15 23.2	24 13.7
19 Tu	19 52 57	28 48 16	18 21 47	25 15 12	25R 38.3	14 51.0	4 23.8	6 12.4	27 03.8	13 53.4	5 02.3	17 41.0	15 21.5	24 12.8
20 W	19 56 53	29 49 21	2♑15 16	9♑21 43	25 37.5	16 22.7	5 38.7	6 52.3	27 27.2	13 49.6	5 06.7	17 44.5	15 19.9	24 11.8
21 Th	20 00 50	0♒50 26	16 34 09	23 51 56	25 35.0	17 51.9	6 53.5	7 32.3	27 50.5	13 45.6	5 11.3	17 48.0	15 18.2	24 10.9
22 F	20 04 47	1 51 30	1♒14 17	8♒40 18	25 30.8	19 18.1	8 08.3	8 12.3	28 13.8	13 41.4	5 15.9	17 51.5	15 16.6	24 10.0
23 Sa	20 08 43	2 52 33	16 08 53	23 38 54	25 25.3	20 40.8	9 23.1	8 52.3	28 37.0	13 37.0	5 20.6	17 55.0	15 15.0	24 09.1
24 Su	20 12 40	3 53 35	1♓09 12	8♓38 35	25 19.2	21 59.4	10 38.0	9 32.2	29 00.1	13 32.4	5 25.4	17 58.5	15 13.4	24 08.2
25 M	20 16 36	4 54 36	16 06 00	23 30 25	25 13.5	23 13.2	11 52.8	10 12.2	29 23.2	13 27.7	5 30.2	18 01.9	15 11.8	24 07.4
26 Tu	20 20 33	5 55 36	0♈51 01	8♈07 05	25 08.9	24 21.3	13 07.6	10 52.2	29 46.2	13 22.9	5 35.2	18 05.4	15 10.3	24 06.5
27 W	20 24 29	6 56 35	15 18 09	22 23 50	25 06.1	25 23.2	14 22.4	11 32.2	0♑09.1	13 17.8	5 40.2	18 08.8	15 08.7	24 05.7
28 Th	20 28 26	7 57 33	29 24 00	6♉18 35	25D 05.1	26 17.8	15 37.3	12 12.3	0 31.9	13 12.7	5 45.3	18 12.2	15 07.2	24 04.9
29 F	20 32 22	8 58 29	13♉07 41	19 51 29	25 05.5	27 04.4	16 52.1	12 52.3	0 54.7	13 07.3	5 50.4	18 15.6	15 05.6	24 04.1
30 Sa	20 36 19	9 59 25	26 30 16	3♊04 19	25 06.9	27 42.2	18 06.9	13 32.3	1 17.4	13 01.8	5 55.7	18 19.0	15 04.1	24 03.3
31 Su	20 40 16	11 00 18	9♊34 00	15 59 41	25R 08.2	28 10.4	19 21.8	14 12.4	1 40.0	12 56.2	6 01.0	18 22.4	15 02.6	24 02.5

LONGITUDE — February 1909

Day	Sid.Time	☉	0 hr ☽	Noon ☽	True ☊	☿	♀	♂	⚳	♃	♄	♅	♆	♇
1 M	20 44 12	12♒01 11	22♊21 42	28♊40 24	25♊08.4	28♒28.4	20♑36.6	14♐52.4	2♑02.6	12♍50.4	6♈06.4	18♑25.7	15♋01.1	24♊01.8
2 Tu	20 48 09	13 02 02	4♋56 07	11♋09 08	25R 07.0	28R 35.6	21 51.4	15 32.5	2 25.0	12R 44.5	6 11.8	18 29.1	14R 59.7	24R 01.0
3 W	20 52 05	14 02 53	17 19 42	23 28 05	25 03.2	28 31.8	23 06.3	16 12.6	2 47.4	12 38.5	6 17.3	18 32.4	14 58.2	24 00.3
4 Th	20 56 02	15 03 41	29 34 28	5♌39 03	24 57.0	28 17.0	24 21.1	16 52.7	3 09.7	12 32.3	6 22.9	18 35.7	14 56.8	23 59.6
5 F	20 59 58	16 04 29	11♌41 59	17 43 25	24 48.6	27 51.2	25 36.0	17 32.8	3 31.9	12 26.0	6 28.6	18 38.9	14 55.4	23 58.9
6 Sa	21 03 55	17 05 15	23 43 30	29 42 24	24 38.5	27 15.1	26 50.8	18 12.9	3 54.0	12 19.6	6 34.3	18 42.2	14 54.0	23 58.3
7 Su	21 07 51	18 06 00	5♍40 16	11♍37 16	24 27.6	26 29.5	28 05.6	18 53.0	4 16.1	12 13.1	6 40.1	18 45.4	14 52.6	23 57.6
8 M	21 11 48	19 06 44	17 33 37	23 29 34	24 16.9	25 35.6	29 20.5	19 33.1	4 38.0	12 06.4	6 45.9	18 48.6	14 51.3	23 57.0
9 Tu	21 15 45	20 07 27	29 25 22	5♎21 21	24 07.3	24 34.9	0♒35.3	20 13.3	4 59.9	11 59.6	6 51.8	18 51.8	14 49.9	23 56.4
10 W	21 19 41	21 08 08	11♎17 52	17 15 20	23 59.6	23 29.2	1 50.1	20 53.4	5 21.7	11 52.8	6 57.8	18 55.0	14 48.6	23 55.8
11 Th	21 23 38	22 08 49	23 14 10	29 14 54	23 54.3	22 20.3	3 05.0	21 33.6	5 43.4	11 45.8	7 03.8	18 58.1	14 47.3	23 55.3
12 F	21 27 34	23 09 28	5♏18 02	11♏24 09	23 51.4	21 10.1	4 19.8	22 13.8	6 04.9	11 38.7	7 09.9	19 01.2	14 46.1	23 54.7
13 Sa	21 31 31	24 10 06	17 33 49	23 47 40	23D 50.6	20 00.5	5 34.7	22 54.0	6 26.4	11 31.6	7 16.1	19 04.3	14 44.8	23 54.2
14 Su	21 35 27	25 10 43	0♐06 18	6♐30 19	23 51.0	18 53.3	6 49.5	23 34.1	6 47.8	11 24.3	7 22.3	19 07.4	14 43.6	23 53.7
15 M	21 39 24	26 11 19	13 00 16	19 36 41	23R 51.6	17 49.9	8 04.4	24 14.4	7 09.1	11 17.0	7 28.5	19 10.4	14 42.4	23 53.2
16 Tu	21 43 20	27 11 54	26 19 59	3♑10 30	23 51.3	16 51.7	9 19.2	24 54.6	7 30.4	11 09.6	7 34.9	19 13.4	14 41.3	23 52.8
17 W	21 47 17	28 12 28	10♑08 24	17 13 42	23 49.1	15 59.5	10 34.0	25 34.8	7 51.5	11 02.2	7 41.2	19 16.4	14 40.1	23 52.3
18 Th	21 51 14	29 13 00	24 26 12	1♒45 31	23 44.3	15 14.2	11 48.9	26 15.0	8 12.5	10 54.6	7 47.7	19 19.4	14 39.0	23 51.9
19 F	21 55 10	0♓13 31	9♒10 59	16 41 44	23 36.9	14 36.2	13 03.7	26 55.2	8 33.3	10 47.0	7 54.1	19 22.3	14 37.9	23 51.5
20 Sa	21 59 07	1 14 00	24 16 40	1♓54 30	23 27.4	14 05.6	14 18.5	27 35.5	8 54.1	10 39.4	8 00.7	19 25.2	14 36.8	23 51.2
21 Su	22 03 03	2 14 27	9♓33 51	17 13 15	23 16.9	13 42.6	15 33.4	28 15.7	9 14.8	10 31.7	8 07.2	19 28.0	14 35.8	23 50.8
22 M	22 07 00	3 14 53	24 51 14	2♈26 24	23 06.6	13 27.1	16 48.2	28 55.9	9 35.4	10 24.0	8 13.8	19 30.9	14 34.8	23 50.5
23 Tu	22 10 56	4 15 17	9♈57 32	17 23 34	22 57.8	13D 18.7	18 03.0	29 36.2	9 55.8	10 16.2	8 20.5	19 33.7	14 33.8	23 50.2
24 W	22 14 53	5 15 39	24 43 39	1♉57 12	22 51.4	13 17.3	19 17.8	0♑16.4	10 16.1	10 08.4	8 27.2	19 36.4	14 32.8	23 49.9
25 Th	22 18 49	6 15 59	9♉03 49	16 03 23	22 47.6	13 22.5	20 32.6	0 56.6	10 36.3	10 00.6	8 34.0	19 39.1	14 31.9	23 49.6
26 F	22 22 46	7 16 17	22 55 54	29 41 35	22D 46.1	13 34.0	21 47.3	1 36.9	10 56.4	9 52.7	8 40.8	19 41.8	14 31.0	23 49.4
27 Sa	22 26 43	8 16 33	6♊20 45	12♊53 49	22R 45.9	13 51.3	23 02.1	2 17.1	11 16.4	9 44.9	8 47.6	19 44.5	14 30.1	23 49.2
28 Su	22 30 39	9 16 47	19 21 17	25 43 39	22 46.0	14 14.1	24 16.9	2 57.4	11 36.2	9 37.0	8 54.5	19 47.1	14 29.3	23 49.0

Astro Data

	Dy Hr Mn
☽0S	13 17:43
♄0N	24 0:14
☽0N	26 17:41
☿R	2 15:52
☽0S	9 23:59
☽0N	23 1:53
☿D	24 4:54

Planet Ingress

	Dy Hr Mn
♂ ♐	10 3:55
☿ ♒	10 9:00
♀ ♑	15 23:20
☉ ♒	20 16:11
⚳ ♑	27 2:28
♀ ♒	9 0:41
☉ ♓	19 6:38
♂ ♑	24 2:13

Last Aspect / ☽ Ingress (January)

Last Aspect Dy Hr Mn		☽ Ingress Dy Hr Mn
2 15:53	♂ ☍	♊ 3 0:54
4 22:00	♇ ☌	♋ 5 8:24
7 14:42	♂ △	♌ 7 18:01
9 18:17	♇ ⚹	♍ 10 5:34
12 9:08	♀ □	♎ 12 18:11
15 4:04	♀ ⚹	♏ 15 6:02
17 8:49	☉ ⚹	♐ 17 15:01
19 10:12	♇ ☍	♑ 19 20:09
21 2:00	♅ ☌	♒ 21 22:00
23 12:48	♇ △	♓ 23 22:09
25 13:00	♇ □	♈ 25 22:36
27 17:29	☿ ⚹	♉ 28 1:02
30 1:43	☿ □	♊ 30 6:22

Last Aspect / ☽ Ingress (February)

Last Aspect Dy Hr Mn		☽ Ingress Dy Hr Mn
1 11:37	☿ △	♋ 1 14:32
3 11:12	♀ ☍	♌ 4 0:50
6 7:20	☿ ☍	♍ 6 12:35
8 12:56	♇ □	♎ 9 1:10
11 1:23	♇ △	♏ 11 13:30
13 12:47	☉ □	♐ 13 23:48
16 0:41	☉ ⚹	♑ 16 6:27
17 15:26	♅ ☌	♒ 18 9:08
20 4:54	♂ ⚹	♓ 20 9:00
22 6:11	♂ □	♈ 22 8:08
23 22:32	♇ ⚹	♉ 24 8:44
25 20:35	♀ □	♊ 26 12:33
28 8:58	♀ △	♋ 28 20:08

☽ Phases & Eclipses

Dy Hr Mn	
6 14:12	○ 15♋39
14 18:11	☾ 23♎58
22 0:12	● 1♒21
28 15:07	☽ 8♉05
5 8:25	○ 15♌55
13 12:47	☾ 24♏12
20 10:52	● 1♓11
27 2:49	☽ 7♊53

Astro Data

1 January 1909
Julian Day # 3288
SVP 6♓32'06"
GC 25♐34.1 ⚳ 8♐40.7
Eris 24♓32.3 ⚵ 8♒10.0
⚷ 20♒25.1 ⚶ 11♏54.7
☽ Mean ☊ 25♊04.0

1 February 1909
Julian Day # 3319
SVP 6♓32'01"
GC 25♐34.2 ⚳ 20♐49.4
Eris 24♓45.8 ⚵ 21♒55.9
⚷ 22♒27.4 ⚶ 25♏16.0
☽ Mean ☊ 23♊25.5

March 1909 LONGITUDE

Day	Sid.Time	☉	0 hr ☽	Noon ☽	True ☊	☿	♀	♂	⚳	♃	♄	♅	♆	♇
1 M	22 34 36	10♓16 59	2♋01 29	8♋15 18	22♊45.1	14♒42.0	25♒31.6	3♑37.6	11♑55.9	9♍29.1	9♈01.4	19♑49.7	14♋28.5	23♊48.8
2 Tu	22 38 32	11 17 09	14 25 39	20 33 02	22R 42.2	15 14.7	26 46.4	4 17.9	12 15.5	9R 21.3	9 08.4	19 52.3	14R 27.7	23R 48.6
3 W	22 42 29	12 17 17	26 37 53	2♌40 39	22 36.5	15 51.8	28 01.1	4 58.1	12 35.0	9 13.4	9 15.4	19 54.8	14 26.9	23 48.5
4 Th	22 46 25	13 17 22	8♌41 42	14 41 22	22 27.7	16 33.0	29 15.8	5 38.4	12 54.3	9 05.6	9 22.4	19 57.3	14 26.2	23 48.4
5 F	22 50 22	14 17 26	20 39 56	26 37 41	22 16.2	17 18.1	0♓30.5	6 18.7	13 13.5	8 57.8	9 29.4	19 59.7	14 25.5	23 48.3
6 Sa	22 54 18	15 17 28	2♍34 48	8♍31 29	22 02.6	18 06.7	1 45.3	6 58.9	13 32.6	8 50.0	9 36.5	20 02.1	14 24.9	23 48.2
7 Su	22 58 15	16 17 28	14 27 55	20 24 14	21 47.9	18 58.7	2 59.9	7 39.2	13 51.5	8 42.3	9 43.6	20 04.5	14 24.2	23 48.2
8 M	23 02 12	17 17 26	26 20 37	2♎17 12	21 33.3	19 53.7	4 14.6	8 19.5	14 10.3	8 34.5	9 50.8	20 06.8	14 23.6	23D 48.2
9 Tu	23 06 08	18 17 22	8♎14 10	14 11 43	21 19.9	20 51.7	5 29.3	8 59.7	14 29.0	8 26.9	9 58.0	20 09.1	14 23.1	23 48.2
10 W	23 10 05	19 17 16	20 10 04	26 09 29	21 08.9	21 52.4	6 44.0	9 40.0	14 47.5	8 19.2	10 05.2	20 11.3	14 22.5	23 48.2
11 Th	23 14 01	20 17 09	2♏10 16	8♏12 45	21 00.7	22 55.6	7 58.7	10 20.3	15 05.8	8 11.7	10 12.4	20 13.5	14 22.0	23 48.3
12 F	23 17 58	21 17 00	14 17 19	20 24 26	20 55.5	24 01.3	9 13.3	11 00.6	15 24.1	8 04.2	10 19.7	20 15.7	14 21.5	23 48.3
13 Sa	23 21 54	22 16 49	26 34 32	2♐48 09	20 52.9	25 09.2	10 28.0	11 40.9	15 42.1	7 56.7	10 27.0	20 17.8	14 21.1	23 48.4
14 Su	23 25 51	23 16 37	9♐05 48	15 28 03	20 52.2	26 19.3	11 42.6	12 21.1	16 00.1	7 49.3	10 34.3	20 19.9	14 20.7	23 48.6
15 M	23 29 47	24 16 23	21 55 27	28 28 31	20 52.2	27 31.5	12 57.3	13 01.4	16 17.8	7 42.0	10 41.6	20 21.9	14 20.3	23 48.7
16 Tu	23 33 44	25 16 07	5♑07 46	11♑53 36	20 51.5	28 45.6	14 11.9	13 41.7	16 35.4	7 34.8	10 49.0	20 23.9	14 20.0	23 48.9
17 W	23 37 41	26 15 49	18 46 22	25 46 15	20 49.2	0♓01.5	15 26.5	14 22.0	16 52.9	7 27.7	10 56.4	20 25.9	14 19.7	23 49.1
18 Th	23 41 37	27 15 30	2♒53 16	10♒07 17	20 44.3	1 19.3	16 41.1	15 02.3	17 10.2	7 20.6	11 03.8	20 27.8	14 19.4	23 49.3
19 F	23 45 34	28 15 09	17 27 55	24 54 33	20 36.7	2 38.8	17 55.7	15 42.6	17 27.3	7 13.6	11 11.2	20 29.6	14 19.2	23 49.5
20 Sa	23 49 30	29 14 46	2♓26 19	10♓02 09	20 26.9	3 59.9	19 10.3	16 22.8	17 44.3	7 06.8	11 18.6	20 31.5	14 19.0	23 49.8
21 Su	23 53 27	0♈14 21	17 40 48	25 20 50	20 15.7	5 22.7	20 24.9	17 03.1	18 01.0	7 00.0	11 26.1	20 33.2	14 18.8	23 50.0
22 M	23 57 23	1 13 54	3♈00 47	10♈39 09	20 04.7	6 47.0	21 39.5	17 43.3	18 17.7	6 53.4	11 33.5	20 35.0	14 18.6	23 50.3
23 Tu	0 01 20	2 13 25	18 14 32	25 45 38	19 55.0	8 12.9	22 54.0	18 23.5	18 34.1	6 46.8	11 41.0	20 36.6	14 18.5	23 50.6
24 W	0 05 16	3 12 54	3♉11 22	10♉30 50	19 47.7	9 40.3	24 08.6	19 03.8	18 50.3	6 40.4	11 48.5	20 38.3	14 18.5	23 51.0
25 Th	0 09 13	4 12 21	17 43 25	24 48 43	19 43.1	11 09.1	25 23.1	19 44.0	19 06.4	6 34.1	11 56.0	20 39.8	14D 18.4	23 51.4
26 F	0 13 09	5 11 45	1♊46 33	8♊36 56	19D 41.1	12 39.5	26 37.6	20 24.2	19 22.3	6 28.0	12 03.5	20 41.4	14 18.4	23 51.7
27 Sa	0 17 06	6 11 07	15 20 06	21 56 21	19 40.7	14 11.2	27 52.1	21 04.4	19 38.0	6 21.9	12 11.0	20 42.9	14 18.5	23 52.2
28 Su	0 21 03	7 10 27	28 26 09	4♋50 01	19R 40.9	15 44.4	29 06.6	21 44.5	19 53.5	6 16.0	12 18.6	20 44.3	14 18.5	23 52.6
29 M	0 24 59	8 09 45	11♋08 32	17 22 17	19 40.6	17 19.0	0♈21.1	22 24.7	20 08.8	6 10.2	12 26.1	20 45.7	14 18.6	23 53.0
30 Tu	0 28 56	9 09 00	23 31 55	29 38 00	19 38.6	18 55.0	1 35.5	23 04.9	20 23.9	6 04.6	12 33.6	20 47.1	14 18.8	23 53.5
31 W	0 32 52	10 08 12	5♌41 08	11♌41 52	19 34.3	20 32.4	2 50.0	23 45.0	20 38.9	5 59.1	12 41.2	20 48.4	14 18.9	23 54.0

April 1909 LONGITUDE

Day	Sid.Time	☉	0 hr ☽	Noon ☽	True ☊	☿	♀	♂	⚳	♃	♄	♅	♆	♇
1 Th	0 36 49	11♈07 23	17♌40 45	23♌38 13	19♊27.3	22♓11.2	4♈04.4	24♑25.1	20♑53.6	5♍53.8	12♈48.7	20♑49.6	14♋19.1	23♊54.5
2 F	0 40 45	12 06 31	29 34 45	5♍30 42	19R 17.8	23 51.5	5 18.8	25 05.3	21 08.1	5R 48.6	12 56.3	20 50.8	14 19.3	23 55.1
3 Sa	0 44 42	13 05 37	11♍26 26	17 22 14	19 06.4	25 33.1	6 33.2	25 45.4	21 22.4	5 43.5	13 03.8	20 52.0	14 19.6	23 55.6
4 Su	0 48 38	14 04 41	23 18 23	29 15 05	18 54.0	27 16.2	7 47.6	26 25.5	21 36.5	5 38.7	13 11.4	20 53.1	14 19.9	23 56.2
5 M	0 52 35	15 03 42	5♎12 33	11♎10 57	18 41.6	29 00.8	9 02.0	27 05.5	21 50.4	5 33.9	13 18.9	20 54.1	14 20.2	23 56.8
6 Tu	0 56 32	16 02 42	17 10 27	23 11 11	18 30.4	0♈46.8	10 16.3	27 45.6	22 04.1	5 29.4	13 26.5	20 55.2	14 20.6	23 57.4
7 W	1 00 28	17 01 40	29 13 20	5♏17 02	18 21.1	2 34.3	11 30.7	28 25.7	22 17.6	5 24.9	13 34.0	20 56.1	14 21.0	23 58.1
8 Th	1 04 25	18 00 35	11♏22 28	17 29 51	18 14.3	4 23.2	12 45.0	29 05.7	22 30.8	5 20.7	13 41.5	20 57.0	14 21.4	23 58.7
9 F	1 08 21	18 59 29	23 39 25	29 51 25	18 10.1	6 13.7	13 59.3	29 45.7	22 43.9	5 16.6	13 49.1	20 57.9	14 21.9	23 59.4
10 Sa	1 12 18	19 58 21	6♐06 09	12♐23 57	18D 08.4	8 05.6	15 13.6	0♒25.7	22 56.7	5 12.7	13 56.6	20 58.7	14 22.4	24 00.1
11 Su	1 16 14	20 57 12	18 45 10	25 10 12	18 08.5	9 59.0	16 27.9	1 05.7	23 09.2	5 09.0	14 04.1	20 59.4	14 22.9	24 00.8
12 M	1 20 11	21 56 00	1♑39 24	8♑13 12	18 09.3	11 53.9	17 42.2	1 45.7	23 21.6	5 05.4	14 11.6	21 00.2	14 23.5	24 01.6
13 Tu	1 24 07	22 54 47	14 51 58	21 36 02	18R 09.3	13 50.3	18 56.5	2 25.6	23 33.7	5 02.0	14 19.2	21 00.8	14 24.1	24 02.3
14 W	1 28 04	23 53 32	28 25 42	5♒21 09	18 09.3	15 48.2	20 10.7	3 05.6	23 45.5	4 58.8	14 26.6	21 01.4	14 24.7	24 03.1
15 Th	1 32 01	24 52 16	12♒22 30	19 29 41	18 06.8	17 47.5	21 25.0	3 45.5	23 57.1	4 55.7	14 34.1	21 02.0	14 25.4	24 03.9
16 F	1 35 57	25 50 58	26 42 31	4♓00 37	18 02.2	19 48.3	22 39.2	4 25.3	24 08.5	4 52.8	14 41.6	21 02.5	14 26.1	24 04.7
17 Sa	1 39 54	26 49 38	11♓23 25	18 50 11	17 55.8	21 50.4	23 53.4	5 05.2	24 19.6	4 50.1	14 49.0	21 02.9	14 26.8	24 05.5
18 Su	1 43 50	27 48 16	26 19 58	3♈51 42	17 48.3	23 53.7	25 07.7	5 45.0	24 30.5	4 47.6	14 56.5	21 03.3	14 27.6	24 06.4
19 M	1 47 47	28 46 52	11♈24 13	18 56 17	17 40.7	25 58.3	26 21.9	6 24.8	24 41.1	4 45.3	15 03.9	21 03.7	14 28.4	24 07.3
20 Tu	1 51 43	29 45 27	26 26 38	3♉54 05	17 34.0	28 04.0	27 36.0	7 04.5	24 51.4	4 43.2	15 11.3	21 04.0	14 29.2	24 08.1
21 W	1 55 40	0♉44 00	11♉17 34	18 36 07	17 29.0	0♉10.6	28 50.2	7 44.2	25 01.5	4 41.2	15 18.7	21 04.2	14 30.0	24 09.0
22 Th	1 59 36	1 42 30	25 48 58	2♊55 32	17 26.1	2 18.0	0♉04.4	8 23.9	25 11.2	4 39.4	15 26.1	21 04.4	14 30.9	24 10.0
23 F	2 03 33	2 40 59	9♊55 26	16 48 29	17D 25.2	4 26.1	1 18.5	9 03.5	25 20.8	4 37.8	15 33.4	21 04.6	14 31.8	24 10.9
24 Sa	2 07 30	3 39 26	23 34 39	0♋14 04	17 25.8	6 34.5	2 32.7	9 43.1	25 30.0	4 36.4	15 40.7	21 04.7	14 32.8	24 11.9
25 Su	2 11 26	4 37 50	6♋47 00	13 13 49	17 27.1	8 43.1	3 46.8	10 22.6	25 39.0	4 35.2	15 48.1	21R 04.7	14 33.8	24 12.8
26 M	2 15 23	5 36 13	19 35 00	25 51 03	17R 28.4	10 51.5	5 00.9	11 02.1	25 47.6	4 34.1	15 55.3	21 04.7	14 34.8	24 13.8
27 Tu	2 19 19	6 34 33	2♌02 32	8♌10 02	17 28.8	12 59.6	6 15.0	11 41.6	25 56.0	4 33.3	16 02.6	21 04.7	14 35.8	24 14.8
28 W	2 23 16	7 32 51	14 14 11	20 15 32	17 27.8	15 07.0	7 29.0	12 21.0	26 04.1	4 32.6	16 09.8	21 04.6	14 36.9	24 15.8
29 Th	2 27 12	8 31 07	26 14 43	2♍12 17	17 25.2	17 13.3	8 43.1	13 00.4	26 11.9	4 32.1	16 17.0	21 04.4	14 38.0	24 16.9
30 F	2 31 09	9 29 21	8♍08 46	14 04 41	17 20.9	19 18.4	9 57.1	13 39.7	26 19.5	4 31.8	16 24.2	21 04.2	14 39.1	24 17.9

Astro Data

	Dy Hr Mn
♃⚻♄	3 8:54
♇ D	8 19:55
☽0S	9 5:27
☉0N	21 6:14
☽0N	22 12:22
♆ D	26 2:12
♀0N	31 21:07
♃♇♅	2 3:29
☽0S	5 11:20
☿0N	8 17:59
♄□♆	14 5:19
☽0N	18 23:14
♅ R	25 22:27

Planet Ingress

	Dy Hr Mn
♀ ♓	5 2:11
☿ ♓	17 11:31
☉ ♈	21 6:13
♀ ♈	29 5:12
☿ ♈	6 1:27
♂ ♒	9 20:34
☉ ♉	20 17:58
☿ ♉	21 10:00
♀ ♉	22 10:35

Last Aspect / ☽ Ingress

Last Aspect Dy Hr Mn		☽ Ingress Dy Hr Mn
2 10:40	♅ ☍	♌ 3 6:41
5 6:19	♇ ⚹	♍ 5 18:48
7 18:52	♇ □	♎ 8 7:23
10 7:17	♇ △	♏ 10 19:40
12 19:45	☿ □	♐ 13 6:37
15 10:06	☿ ⚹	♑ 15 14:46
17 12:54	☉ ⚹	♒ 17 19:09
19 10:16	♇ △	♓ 19 20:08
21 9:38	♇ □	♈ 21 19:17
23 8:56	♇ ⚹	♉ 23 18:50
25 13:05	♀ ⚹	♊ 25 20:55
28 0:07	♀ □	♋ 28 2:55
29 22:22	♂ ☍	♌ 30 12:43

Last Aspect / ☽ Ingress

Last Aspect Dy Hr Mn		☽ Ingress Dy Hr Mn
1 12:33	♇ ⚹	♍ 2 0:51
4 7:19	☿ ☍	♎ 4 13:31
6 21:38	♂ □	♏ 7 1:33
9 11:48	♂ ⚹	♐ 9 12:17
11 9:51	♇ ☍	♑ 11 20:57
13 14:30	☉ □	♒ 14 2:44
15 21:36	☉ ⚹	♓ 16 5:26
17 20:26	♇ □	♈ 18 5:51
20 4:51	☉ ☌	♉ 20 5:43
21 16:05	♅ △	♊ 22 7:02
24 1:06	♇ ☌	♋ 24 11:34
26 2:51	♅ ☍	♌ 26 20:02
28 20:02	♇ ⚹	♍ 29 7:33

☽ Phases & Eclipses

Dy Hr Mn	
7 2:56	○ 15♍55
15 3:41	☾ 23♐56
21 20:11	● 0♈35
28 16:49	☽ 7♋22
5 20:28	○ 15♎25
13 14:30	☾ 23♑01
20 4:51	● 29♈28
27 8:36	☽ 6♌26

Astro Data

1 March 1909
Julian Day # 3347
SVP 6♓31'57"
GC 25♐34.2 ⚳ 0♑13.1
Eris 25♓05.1 ⚵ 5♓05.4
⚷ 24♒26.0 ⚶ 5♐09.5
☽ Mean ☊ 21♊56.5

1 April 1909
Julian Day # 3378
SVP 6♓31'54"
GC 25♐34.3 ⚳ 7♑40.0
Eris 25♓29.3 ⚵ 20♓10.4
⚷ 26♒22.9 ⚶ 11♐52.7
☽ Mean ☊ 20♊18.0

LONGITUDE May 1909

Day	Sid.Time	☉	0 hr ☽	Noon ☽	True ☊	☿	♀	♂	⚳	♃	♄	♅	♆	♇
1 Sa	2 35 05	10♉27 33	20♍00 30	25♍56 40	17♊15.3	21♉21.9	11♉11.1	14♒19.0	26♑26.7	4♍31.7	16♈31.3	21♑03.9	14♋40.3	24♊19.0
2 Su	2 39 02	11 25 44	1♎53 33	7♎51 30	17R 09.0	23 23.5	12 25.1	14 58.2	26 33.6	4D 31.8	16 38.4	21R 03.6	14 41.4	24 20.1
3 M	2 42 59	12 23 52	13 50 51	19 51 50	17 02.6	25 22.9	13 39.1	15 37.4	26 40.2	4 32.1	16 45.5	21 03.3	14 42.7	24 21.2
4 Tu	2 46 55	13 21 58	25 54 43	1♏59 40	16 56.8	27 19.9	14 53.1	16 16.6	26 46.5	4 32.5	16 52.6	21 02.9	14 43.9	24 22.3
5 W	2 50 52	14 20 03	8♏06 52	14 16 28	16 52.1	29 14.3	16 07.1	16 55.6	26 52.5	4 33.1	16 59.6	21 02.4	14 45.2	24 23.4
6 Th	2 54 48	15 18 06	20 28 35	26 43 20	16 48.9	1♊05.8	17 21.0	17 34.7	26 58.2	4 33.9	17 06.6	21 01.9	14 46.5	24 24.5
7 F	2 58 45	16 16 08	3♐00 51	9♐21 12	16D 47.4	2 54.3	18 35.0	18 13.7	27 03.5	4 34.9	17 13.5	21 01.4	14 47.8	24 25.7
8 Sa	3 02 41	17 14 08	15 44 32	22 10 56	16 47.2	4 39.7	19 48.9	18 52.6	27 08.6	4 36.1	17 20.4	21 00.8	14 49.1	24 26.8
9 Su	3 06 38	18 12 06	28 40 33	5♑13 31	16 48.2	6 21.8	21 02.8	19 31.5	27 13.3	4 37.4	17 27.3	21 00.1	14 50.5	24 28.0
10 M	3 10 34	19 10 04	11♑49 58	18 30 02	16 49.7	8 00.4	22 16.7	20 10.3	27 17.7	4 38.9	17 34.1	20 59.5	14 51.9	24 29.2
11 Tu	3 14 31	20 08 00	25 13 50	2♒01 31	16 51.2	9 35.6	23 30.6	20 49.0	27 21.7	4 40.6	17 40.9	20 58.7	14 53.3	24 30.4
12 W	3 18 28	21 05 54	8♒53 08	15 48 43	16R 52.0	11 07.3	24 44.5	21 27.7	27 25.4	4 42.5	17 47.7	20 57.9	14 54.8	24 31.6
13 Th	3 22 24	22 03 48	22 48 16	29 51 42	16 51.9	12 35.3	25 58.4	22 06.3	27 28.8	4 44.6	17 54.4	20 57.1	14 56.3	24 32.8
14 F	3 26 21	23 01 40	6♓58 49	14♓09 20	16 50.7	13 59.6	27 12.2	22 44.9	27 31.8	4 46.8	18 01.1	20 56.2	14 57.8	24 34.1
15 Sa	3 30 17	23 59 31	21 22 54	28 39 01	16 48.6	15 20.2	28 26.1	23 23.3	27 34.5	4 49.2	18 07.7	20 55.3	14 59.3	24 35.3
16 Su	3 34 14	24 57 20	5♈57 05	13♈16 26	16 45.9	16 36.9	29 39.9	24 01.7	27 36.9	4 51.8	18 14.3	20 54.3	15 00.8	24 36.6
17 M	3 38 10	25 55 09	20 36 17	27 55 50	16 43.0	17 49.9	0♊53.8	24 40.0	27 38.8	4 54.5	18 20.8	20 53.3	15 02.4	24 37.8
18 Tu	3 42 07	26 52 56	5♉14 13	12♉30 37	16 40.6	18 58.9	2 07.6	25 18.2	27 40.5	4 57.4	18 27.3	20 52.3	15 04.0	24 39.1
19 W	3 46 03	27 50 42	19 44 13	26 54 16	16 38.8	20 03.9	3 21.4	25 56.3	27 41.8	5 00.5	18 33.8	20 51.2	15 05.6	24 40.4
20 Th	3 50 00	28 48 27	4♊00 06	11♊01 11	16D 38.0	21 04.9	4 35.3	26 34.4	27 42.7	5 03.8	18 40.2	20 50.0	15 07.3	24 41.7
21 F	3 53 57	29 46 10	17 57 04	24 47 26	16 38.1	22 01.8	5 49.1	27 12.3	27 43.3	5 07.2	18 46.5	20 48.8	15 08.9	24 43.0
22 Sa	3 57 53	0♊43 52	1♋32 07	8♋11 04	16 38.8	22 54.6	7 02.9	27 50.1	27R 43.5	5 10.8	18 52.8	20 47.6	15 10.6	24 44.3
23 Su	4 01 50	1 41 33	14 44 20	21 12 05	16 40.0	23 43.1	8 16.6	28 27.9	27 43.3	5 14.6	18 59.1	20 46.3	15 12.3	24 45.6
24 M	4 05 46	2 39 12	27 34 36	3♌52 13	16 41.2	24 27.3	9 30.4	29 05.5	27 42.8	5 18.6	19 05.3	20 45.0	15 14.1	24 47.0
25 Tu	4 09 43	3 36 49	10♌05 22	16 14 29	16 42.2	25 07.1	10 44.2	29 43.0	27 41.9	5 22.6	19 11.4	20 43.7	15 15.8	24 48.3
26 W	4 13 39	4 34 25	22 20 07	28 22 47	16R 42.8	25 42.5	11 57.9	0♓20.4	27 40.7	5 26.9	19 17.5	20 42.3	15 17.6	24 49.6
27 Th	4 17 36	5 32 00	4♍23 04	10♍21 31	16 42.8	26 13.4	13 11.6	0 57.7	27 39.1	5 31.3	19 23.5	20 40.8	15 19.4	24 51.0
28 F	4 21 32	6 29 33	16 18 44	22 15 16	16 42.4	26 39.6	14 25.3	1 34.9	27 37.2	5 35.9	19 29.5	20 39.4	15 21.2	24 52.3
29 Sa	4 25 29	7 27 05	28 11 41	4♎08 31	16 41.5	27 01.3	15 39.0	2 12.0	27 34.8	5 40.6	19 35.4	20 37.8	15 23.0	24 53.7
30 Su	4 29 26	8 24 35	10♎06 17	16 05 28	16 40.5	27 18.3	16 52.7	2 49.0	27 32.2	5 45.5	19 41.3	20 36.3	15 24.8	24 55.1
31 M	4 33 22	9 22 04	22 06 30	28 09 48	16 39.4	27 30.7	18 06.4	3 25.8	27 29.1	5 50.5	19 47.1	20 34.7	15 26.7	24 56.5

LONGITUDE June 1909

Day	Sid.Time	☉	0 hr ☽	Noon ☽	True ☊	☿	♀	♂	⚳	♃	♄	♅	♆	♇
1 Tu	4 37 19	10♊19 32	4♏15 44	10♏24 38	16♊38.6	27♊38.4	19♊20.1	4♓02.5	27♑25.7	5♍55.7	19♈52.8	20♑33.1	15♋28.6	24♊57.8
2 W	4 41 15	11 16 59	16 36 44	22 52 16	16R 38.0	27R 41.4	20 33.7	4 39.1	27R 21.9	6 01.1	19 58.5	20R 31.4	15 30.5	24 59.2
3 Th	4 45 12	12 14 25	29 11 24	5♐34 15	16D 37.6	27 39.9	21 47.4	5 15.6	27 17.8	6 06.6	20 04.1	20 29.7	15 32.4	25 00.6
4 F	4 49 08	13 11 50	12♐00 53	18 31 18	16 37.6	27 34.0	23 01.0	5 51.9	27 13.4	6 12.2	20 09.6	20 28.0	15 34.3	25 02.0
5 Sa	4 53 05	14 09 14	25 05 29	1♑43 21	16 37.6	27 23.7	24 14.6	6 28.1	27 08.5	6 18.0	20 15.1	20 26.2	15 36.3	25 03.4
6 Su	4 57 01	15 06 37	8♑24 49	15 09 43	16 37.8	27 09.4	25 28.3	7 04.2	27 03.4	6 23.9	20 20.5	20 24.4	15 38.3	25 04.8
7 M	5 00 58	16 03 59	21 57 54	28 49 10	16R 37.9	26 51.3	26 41.9	7 40.1	26 57.8	6 30.0	20 25.9	20 22.6	15 40.2	25 06.2
8 Tu	5 04 55	17 01 21	5♒43 17	12♒40 04	16 37.9	26 29.6	27 55.5	8 15.9	26 52.0	6 36.2	20 31.2	20 20.8	15 42.2	25 07.6
9 W	5 08 51	17 58 42	19 39 15	26 40 34	16 37.8	26 04.7	29 09.1	8 51.5	26 45.7	6 42.5	20 36.4	20 18.9	15 44.2	25 09.1
10 Th	5 12 48	18 56 03	3♓43 48	10♓48 38	16D 37.8	25 37.0	0♋22.6	9 26.9	26 39.2	6 49.0	20 41.5	20 16.9	15 46.3	25 10.5
11 F	5 16 44	19 53 23	17 54 48	25 02 00	16 37.7	25 07.1	1 36.2	10 02.2	26 32.3	6 55.6	20 46.6	20 15.0	15 48.3	25 11.9
12 Sa	5 20 41	20 50 43	2♈09 55	9♈18 11	16 37.9	24 35.3	2 49.8	10 37.3	26 25.0	7 02.4	20 51.6	20 13.0	15 50.3	25 13.3
13 Su	5 24 37	21 48 02	16 26 29	23 34 25	16 38.3	24 02.2	4 03.4	11 12.2	26 17.5	7 09.3	20 56.6	20 11.0	15 52.4	25 14.7
14 M	5 28 34	22 45 21	0♉41 35	7♉47 36	16 38.8	23 28.4	5 16.9	11 47.0	26 09.6	7 16.3	21 01.4	20 09.0	15 54.5	25 16.2
15 Tu	5 32 30	23 42 40	14 52 01	21 54 26	16 39.3	22 54.5	6 30.5	12 21.5	26 01.3	7 23.4	21 06.2	20 06.9	15 56.6	25 17.6
16 W	5 36 27	24 39 58	28 54 26	5♊51 36	16R 39.8	22 21.1	7 44.0	12 55.9	25 52.8	7 30.7	21 10.9	20 04.8	15 58.7	25 19.0
17 Th	5 40 24	25 37 16	12♊45 34	19 35 59	16 39.9	21 48.6	8 57.6	13 30.0	25 44.0	7 38.1	21 15.6	20 02.7	16 00.8	25 20.5
18 F	5 44 20	26 34 34	26 22 32	3♋05 00	16 39.5	21 17.7	10 11.1	14 03.9	25 34.9	7 45.6	21 20.1	20 00.6	16 02.9	25 21.9
19 Sa	5 48 17	27 31 51	9♋43 12	16 16 59	16 38.7	20 48.9	11 24.6	14 37.7	25 25.4	7 53.3	21 24.6	19 58.4	16 05.0	25 23.3
20 Su	5 52 13	28 29 07	22 46 20	29 11 16	16 37.3	20 22.6	12 38.2	15 11.2	25 15.7	8 01.1	21 29.0	19 56.3	16 07.2	25 24.7
21 M	5 56 10	29 26 23	5♌31 52	11♌48 21	16 35.6	19 59.4	13 51.7	15 44.4	25 05.7	8 09.0	21 33.3	19 54.1	16 09.3	25 26.2
22 Tu	6 00 06	0♋23 38	18 00 55	24 09 53	16 33.8	19 39.6	15 05.2	16 17.5	24 55.5	8 17.0	21 37.6	19 51.8	16 11.5	25 27.6
23 W	6 04 03	1 20 52	0♍15 38	6♍18 34	16 32.1	19 23.6	16 18.6	16 50.2	24 45.0	8 25.1	21 41.7	19 49.6	16 13.6	25 29.0
24 Th	6 08 00	2 18 06	12 19 10	18 17 54	16 30.9	19 11.6	17 32.1	17 22.8	24 34.2	8 33.4	21 45.8	19 47.3	16 15.8	25 30.4
25 F	6 11 56	3 15 19	24 15 19	0♎12 00	16D 30.4	19 03.9	18 45.6	17 55.1	24 23.3	8 41.8	21 49.8	19 45.1	16 18.0	25 31.9
26 Sa	6 15 53	4 12 32	6♎08 29	12 05 22	16 30.5	19D 00.7	19 59.0	18 27.2	24 12.1	8 50.2	21 53.7	19 42.8	16 20.2	25 33.3
27 Su	6 19 49	5 09 44	18 03 15	24 02 42	16 31.4	19 02.2	21 12.4	18 58.9	24 00.6	8 58.8	21 57.6	19 40.5	16 22.4	25 34.7
28 M	6 23 46	6 06 56	0♏04 17	6♏08 33	16 32.7	19 08.5	22 25.9	19 30.5	23 49.0	9 07.5	22 01.3	19 38.2	16 24.6	25 36.1
29 Tu	6 27 42	7 04 08	12 16 00	18 27 07	16 34.2	19 19.6	23 39.3	20 01.7	23 37.2	9 16.3	22 05.0	19 35.8	16 26.8	25 37.5
30 W	6 31 39	8 01 19	24 42 20	1♐02 00	16 35.5	19 35.6	24 52.7	20 32.7	23 25.2	9 25.2	22 08.5	19 33.5	16 29.0	25 38.9

Astro Data (Dy Hr Mn)

	Dy Hr Mn
♃ D	1 14:51
☽ 0S	2 18:18
☽ 0N	16 8:26
⚳ R	22 14:04
♃⚼♅	29 1:23
☽ 0S	30 2:07
☿ R	2 16:03
♄□♅	7 1:04
☽ 0N	12 15:09
☽ 0S	26 10:03
☿ D	26 16:25

Planet Ingress

	Dy Hr Mn
☿ ♊	5 21:46
♀ ♊	16 18:31
☉ ♊	21 17:45
♂ ♓	25 22:54
♀ ♋	10 4:37
☉ ♋	22 2:06

Last Aspect / ☽ Ingress (May)

Last Aspect Dy Hr Mn		☽ Ingress Dy Hr Mn
1 8:42	♇ □	♎ 1 20:11
3 20:56	♇ △	♏ 4 8:04
6 1:05	♅ ✶	♐ 6 18:16
8 16:12	♇ ☍	♑ 9 2:26
10 19:26	♀ △	♒ 11 8:26
13 4:46	♀ □	♓ 13 12:14
15 11:37	♀ ✶	♈ 15 14:13
17 6:35	♇ ✶	♉ 17 15:24
19 13:42	☉ ☌	♊ 19 17:13
21 16:29	♂ △	♋ 21 21:15
23 11:12	♅ ☍	♌ 24 4:36
26 6:26	♅ ✶	♍ 26 15:14
28 21:12	☿ □	♎ 29 3:39
31 10:42	☿ △	♏ 31 15:37

Last Aspect / ☽ Ingress (June)

Last Aspect Dy Hr Mn		☽ Ingress Dy Hr Mn
2 7:31	♅ ✶	♐ 3 1:32
5 4:18	☿ ☍	♑ 5 8:54
6 21:14	♅ ☌	♒ 7 14:04
9 16:37	♀ △	♓ 9 17:40
11 12:17	♇ □	♈ 11 20:22
13 14:49	♇ ✶	♉ 13 22:50
15 8:57	♅ △	♊ 16 1:53
17 23:28	☉ ☌	♋ 18 6:28
19 21:31	♄ □	♌ 20 13:32
22 14:33	♇ ✶	♍ 22 23:29
25 2:33	♇ □	♎ 25 11:36
27 15:04	♇ △	♏ 27 23:52
29 23:04	♀ △	♐ 30 10:03

☽ Phases & Eclipses

Dy Hr Mn	
5 12:08	○ 14♏20
12 21:45	☾ 21♒29
19 13:42	● 27♉55
27 1:28	☽ 5♍07
4 1:24	○ 12♐46
4 1:29	☍ T 1.158
11 2:43	☾ 19♓31
17 23:28	● 26♊05
17 23:18:27	● AT00'24"
25 18:43	☽ 3♎31

Astro Data

1 May 1909
Julian Day # 3408
SVP 6♓31'51"
GC 25♐34.4 ⚴ 10♑09.2R
Eris 25♓49.9 ⚵ 5♈03.7
⚷ 27♒41.4 ⚶ 11♐51.6R
☽ Mean ☊ 18♊42.7

1 June 1909
Julian Day # 3439
SVP 6♓31'46"
GC 25♐34.5 ⚴ 6♑07.6R
Eris 26♓03.3 ⚵ 20♈31.2
⚷ 28♒11.2 ⚶ 5♐30.2R
☽ Mean ☊ 17♊04.2

July 1909 LONGITUDE

Day	Sid.Time	☉	0 hr ☽	Noon ☽	True ☊	☿	♀	♂	⚳	♃	♄	♅	♆	♇
1 Th	6 35 35	8♋58 30	7♐26 24	13♐55 45	16♊36.1	19♊56.5	26♋06.1	21♓03.4	23♑13.0	9♍34.2	22♈12.0	19♑31.1	16♋31.2	25♊40.3
2 F	6 39 32	9 55 40	20 30 12	27 09 44	16R 35.8	20 22.3	27 19.4	21 33.8	23R 00.7	9 43.4	22 15.4	19R 28.8	16 33.4	25 41.7
3 Sa	6 43 29	10 52 51	3♑54 18	10♑43 44	16 34.4	20 53.0	28 32.8	22 03.9	22 48.2	9 52.6	22 18.7	19 26.4	16 35.6	25 43.1
4 Su	6 47 25	11 50 02	17 37 44	24 35 56	16 31.8	21 28.6	29 46.2	22 33.7	22 35.6	10 01.9	22 21.9	19 24.0	16 37.8	25 44.5
5 M	6 51 22	12 47 12	1♒37 52	8♒43 00	16 28.4	22 09.0	0♌59.5	23 03.2	22 22.9	10 11.3	22 25.1	19 21.6	16 40.1	25 45.8
6 Tu	6 55 18	13 44 23	15 50 45	23 00 29	16 24.7	22 54.2	2 12.8	23 32.4	22 10.1	10 20.8	22 28.1	19 19.2	16 42.3	25 47.2
7 W	6 59 15	14 41 34	0♓11 34	7♓23 22	16 21.1	23 44.1	3 26.1	24 01.2	21 57.2	10 30.4	22 31.0	19 16.8	16 44.5	25 48.6
8 Th	7 03 11	15 38 46	14 35 17	21 46 45	16 18.3	24 38.6	4 39.4	24 29.7	21 44.1	10 40.1	22 33.9	19 14.4	16 46.8	25 49.9
9 F	7 07 08	16 35 57	28 57 17	6♈06 27	16D 16.6	25 37.8	5 52.7	24 57.8	21 31.1	10 49.9	22 36.6	19 12.0	16 49.0	25 51.3
10 Sa	7 11 04	17 33 10	13♈13 52	20 19 16	16 16.2	26 41.5	7 06.0	25 25.6	21 17.9	10 59.8	22 39.3	19 09.6	16 51.2	25 52.6
11 Su	7 15 01	18 30 22	27 22 23	4♉23 05	16 17.0	27 49.8	8 19.3	25 52.9	21 04.7	11 09.8	22 41.9	19 07.2	16 53.4	25 54.0
12 M	7 18 58	19 27 36	11♉21 12	18 16 39	16 18.4	29 02.4	9 32.6	26 19.9	20 51.5	11 19.8	22 44.3	19 04.8	16 55.7	25 55.3
13 Tu	7 22 54	20 24 50	25 09 22	1♊59 17	16 19.7	0♋19.4	10 45.8	26 46.5	20 38.3	11 30.0	22 46.7	19 02.3	16 57.9	25 56.6
14 W	7 26 51	21 22 04	8♊46 21	15 30 31	16R 20.4	1 40.7	11 59.1	27 12.6	20 25.1	11 40.2	22 49.0	18 59.9	17 00.1	25 57.9
15 Th	7 30 47	22 19 20	22 11 43	28 49 53	16 19.7	3 06.2	13 12.3	27 38.4	20 11.9	11 50.5	22 51.2	18 57.5	17 02.4	25 59.3
16 F	7 34 44	23 16 35	5♋24 59	11♋56 55	16 17.4	4 35.8	14 25.6	28 03.7	19 58.7	12 00.9	22 53.3	18 55.1	17 04.6	26 00.5
17 Sa	7 38 40	24 13 51	18 25 38	24 51 06	16 13.2	6 09.5	15 38.8	28 28.5	19 45.6	12 11.4	22 55.3	18 52.7	17 06.8	26 01.8
18 Su	7 42 37	25 11 08	1♌13 17	7♌32 11	16 07.5	7 46.9	16 52.0	28 52.9	19 32.5	12 22.0	22 57.1	18 50.3	17 09.0	26 03.1
19 M	7 46 33	26 08 25	13 47 51	20 00 20	16 00.6	9 28.1	18 05.2	29 16.8	19 19.5	12 32.6	22 58.9	18 47.9	17 11.2	26 04.4
20 Tu	7 50 30	27 05 42	26 09 46	2♍16 19	15 53.4	11 12.9	19 18.3	29 40.3	19 06.6	12 43.4	23 00.6	18 45.5	17 13.4	26 05.6
21 W	7 54 27	28 02 59	8♍20 14	14 21 47	15 46.5	13 01.0	20 31.5	0♈03.2	18 53.8	12 54.1	23 02.2	18 43.1	17 15.6	26 06.9
22 Th	7 58 23	29 00 17	20 21 18	26 19 10	15 40.7	14 52.2	21 44.6	0 25.7	18 41.1	13 05.0	23 03.7	18 40.8	17 17.8	26 08.1
23 F	8 02 20	29 57 35	2♎15 49	8♎11 45	15 36.4	16 46.3	22 57.8	0 47.6	18 28.5	13 16.0	23 05.0	18 38.4	17 20.0	26 09.3
24 Sa	8 06 16	0♌54 54	14 07 28	20 03 32	15D 34.0	18 42.9	24 10.9	1 09.0	18 16.1	13 27.0	23 06.3	18 36.1	17 22.2	26 10.6
25 Su	8 10 13	1 52 13	26 00 33	1♏59 08	15 33.2	20 41.9	25 24.0	1 29.9	18 03.8	13 38.0	23 07.5	18 33.7	17 24.4	26 11.8
26 M	8 14 09	2 49 33	7♏59 53	14 03 26	15 33.8	22 42.8	26 37.0	1 50.2	17 51.7	13 49.2	23 08.6	18 31.4	17 26.6	26 12.9
27 Tu	8 18 06	3 46 53	20 10 26	26 21 28	15 35.0	24 45.3	27 50.1	2 10.0	17 39.8	14 00.4	23 09.5	18 29.1	17 28.7	26 14.1
28 W	8 22 02	4 44 13	2♐37 07	8♐57 54	15R 36.1	26 49.2	29 03.1	2 29.3	17 28.0	14 11.7	23 10.4	18 26.8	17 30.9	26 15.3
29 Th	8 25 59	5 41 34	15 24 17	21 56 39	15 36.1	28 53.9	0♍16.1	2 47.9	17 16.5	14 23.0	23 11.2	18 24.5	17 33.0	26 16.4
30 F	8 29 56	6 38 56	28 35 17	5♑20 19	15 34.3	0♌59.4	1 29.1	3 06.0	17 05.2	14 34.5	23 11.8	18 22.3	17 35.2	26 17.6
31 Sa	8 33 52	7 36 18	12♑11 47	19 09 30	15 30.5	3 05.1	2 42.1	3 23.5	16 54.1	14 45.9	23 12.4	18 20.0	17 37.3	26 18.7

August 1909 LONGITUDE

Day	Sid.Time	☉	0 hr ☽	Noon ☽	True ☊	☿	♀	♂	⚳	♃	♄	♅	♆	♇
1 Su	8 37 49	8♌33 42	26♑13 12	3♒22 23	15♊24.6	5♌10.9	3♍55.0	3♈40.3	16♑43.2	14♍57.4	23♈12.9	18♑17.8	17♋39.4	26♊19.8
2 M	8 41 45	9 31 06	10♒36 24	17 54 29	15R 17.0	7 16.4	5 07.9	3 56.5	16R 32.6	15 09.0	23 13.2	18R 15.6	17 41.5	26 20.9
3 Tu	8 45 42	10 28 31	25 15 42	2♓39 03	15 08.7	9 21.5	6 20.8	4 12.1	16 22.2	15 20.7	23 13.5	18 13.4	17 43.6	26 22.0
4 W	8 49 38	11 25 56	10♓03 31	17 28 03	15 00.6	11 26.0	7 33.7	4 27.0	16 12.0	15 32.4	23R 13.6	18 11.3	17 45.7	26 23.1
5 Th	8 53 35	12 23 24	24 51 40	2♈13 25	14 53.8	13 29.6	8 46.6	4 41.3	16 02.2	15 44.1	23 13.6	18 09.1	17 47.7	26 24.1
6 F	8 57 31	13 20 52	9♈32 32	16 48 21	14 49.0	15 32.2	9 59.4	4 54.9	15 52.6	15 55.9	23 13.6	18 07.0	17 49.8	26 25.2
7 Sa	9 01 28	14 18 22	24 00 21	1♉08 10	14 46.3	17 33.7	11 12.2	5 07.7	15 43.3	16 07.8	23 13.4	18 04.9	17 51.9	26 26.2
8 Su	9 05 25	15 15 53	8♉11 35	15 10 30	14D 45.6	19 34.0	12 25.1	5 19.9	15 34.2	16 19.7	23 13.1	18 02.9	17 53.9	26 27.2
9 M	9 09 21	16 13 25	22 04 55	28 54 56	14 46.0	21 33.0	13 37.8	5 31.3	15 25.5	16 31.7	23 12.8	18 00.8	17 55.9	26 28.2
10 Tu	9 13 18	17 10 59	5♊40 43	12♊22 26	14R 46.5	23 30.7	14 50.6	5 41.9	15 17.1	16 43.7	23 12.3	17 58.8	17 57.9	26 29.2
11 W	9 17 14	18 08 35	19 00 19	25 34 36	14 46.0	25 27.0	16 03.3	5 51.8	15 09.0	16 55.8	23 11.7	17 56.8	17 59.9	26 30.2
12 Th	9 21 11	19 06 12	2♋05 31	8♋33 14	14 43.6	27 21.9	17 16.1	6 00.9	15 01.2	17 07.9	23 11.0	17 54.9	18 01.9	26 31.1
13 F	9 25 07	20 03 50	14 57 58	21 19 51	14 38.6	29 15.3	18 28.8	6 09.3	14 53.7	17 20.0	23 10.3	17 52.9	18 03.9	26 32.0
14 Sa	9 29 04	21 01 29	27 39 02	3♌55 37	14 31.0	1♍07.3	19 41.5	6 16.8	14 46.5	17 32.2	23 09.4	17 51.0	18 05.8	26 32.9
15 Su	9 33 00	21 59 10	10♌09 41	16 21 20	14 20.8	2 57.8	20 54.1	6 23.5	14 39.7	17 44.5	23 08.4	17 49.2	18 07.7	26 33.8
16 M	9 36 57	22 56 53	22 30 37	28 37 37	14 09.0	4 46.9	22 06.8	6 29.5	14 33.2	17 56.8	23 07.3	17 47.3	18 09.6	26 34.7
17 Tu	9 40 54	23 54 36	4♍42 26	10♍45 11	13 56.4	6 34.6	23 19.4	6 34.6	14 27.1	18 09.1	23 06.1	17 45.5	18 11.5	26 35.6
18 W	9 44 50	24 52 21	16 46 01	22 45 07	13 44.1	8 20.8	24 32.0	6 38.8	14 21.3	18 21.5	23 04.8	17 43.7	18 13.4	26 36.4
19 Th	9 48 47	25 50 06	28 42 41	4♎39 02	13 33.2	10 05.6	25 44.5	6 42.3	14 15.9	18 33.9	23 03.4	17 42.0	18 15.3	26 37.2
20 F	9 52 43	26 47 54	10♎34 27	16 29 19	13 24.5	11 48.9	26 57.1	6 44.9	14 10.8	18 46.3	23 01.9	17 40.3	18 17.1	26 38.1
21 Sa	9 56 40	27 45 42	22 24 05	28 19 11	13 18.4	13 30.9	28 09.6	6 46.6	14 06.0	18 58.8	23 00.3	17 38.6	18 18.9	26 38.8
22 Su	10 00 36	28 43 31	4♏15 10	10♏12 35	13 14.9	15 11.5	29 22.0	6R 47.5	14 01.7	19 11.3	22 58.6	17 37.0	18 20.7	26 39.6
23 M	10 04 33	29 41 22	16 12 02	22 14 10	13D 13.5	16 50.7	0♎34.5	6 47.6	13 57.7	19 23.8	22 56.8	17 35.4	18 22.5	26 40.4
24 Tu	10 08 29	0♍39 14	28 19 37	4♐29 02	13R 13.3	18 28.6	1 46.9	6 46.9	13 54.0	19 36.4	22 54.9	17 33.8	18 24.3	26 41.1
25 W	10 12 26	1 37 08	10♐43 06	17 02 25	13 13.4	20 05.1	2 59.3	6 45.3	13 50.7	19 49.0	22 52.9	17 32.3	18 26.0	26 41.8
26 Th	10 16 23	2 35 02	23 27 37	29 59 13	13 12.5	21 40.2	4 11.7	6 42.9	13 47.8	20 01.7	22 50.8	17 30.8	18 27.7	26 42.5
27 F	10 20 19	3 32 58	6♑37 39	13♑23 16	13 09.7	23 14.0	5 24.0	6 39.6	13 45.2	20 14.3	22 48.6	17 29.4	18 29.4	26 43.2
28 Sa	10 24 16	4 30 55	20 16 14	27 16 35	13 04.5	24 46.5	6 36.3	6 35.5	13 43.0	20 27.0	22 46.4	17 28.0	18 31.1	26 43.8
29 Su	10 28 12	5 28 54	4♒24 06	11♒38 26	12 56.7	26 17.7	7 48.5	6 30.6	13 41.1	20 39.7	22 44.0	17 26.6	18 32.8	26 44.5
30 M	10 32 09	6 26 54	18 58 56	26 24 46	12 46.8	27 47.5	9 00.7	6 24.9	13 39.6	20 52.5	22 41.6	17 25.3	18 34.4	26 45.1
31 Tu	10 36 05	7 24 56	3♓54 54	11♓28 09	12 35.8	29 16.0	10 12.9	6 18.4	13 38.5	21 05.2	22 39.0	17 24.0	18 36.0	26 45.7

Astro Data	Planet Ingress	Last Aspect	☽ Ingress	Last Aspect	☽ Ingress	☽ Phases & Eclipses	Astro Data
Dy Hr Mn	Dy Hr Mn	Dy Hr Mn	Dy Hr Mn	Dy Hr Mn	Dy Hr Mn	Dy Hr Mn	
☽0N 9 20:15	♀ ♌ 4 16:32	2 9:22 ♇ ☍	♑ 2 17:04	31 18:54 ♄ □	♒ 1 6:22	3 12:17 ○ 10♑54	1 July 1909
☽0S 23 17:20	☿ ♋ 13 6:04	4 8:23 ♂ ⚹	♒ 4 21:14	3 1:47 ♇ △	♓ 3 7:42	10 6:58 ☾ 17♈21	Julian Day # 3469
	♂ ♈ 21 8:36	6 16:39 ♇ △	♓ 6 23:41	5 2:30 ♇ □	♈ 5 8:22	17 10:45 ● 24♋11	SVP 6♓31'41"
♄ R 5 9:32	☉ ♌ 23 13:01	8 18:47 ♇ □	♈ 9 1:45	7 4:04 ♇ ⚹	♉ 7 10:05	25 11:45 ☽ 1♏52	GC 25♐34.5 ⚴ 27♐54.1R
☽0N 6 1:49	♀ ♍ 29 6:42	10 23:46 ☿ ⚹	♉ 11 4:29	8 20:54 ☿ □	♊ 9 13:55		Eris 26♓05.7R ⚵ 5♉15.4
♅☍♆ 10 17:21	☿ ♌ 30 0:39	13 2:32 ♂ ⚹	♊ 13 8:30	11 13:42 ♇ ☌	♋ 11 20:08	1 21:14 ○ 8♒56	⚷ 27♒45.7R ⚶ 0♐20.5R
♃△♅ 15 19:57		15 9:46 ♂ □	♋ 15 14:07	13 15:29 ♄ □	♌ 14 4:29	8 12:10 ☾ 15♉16	☽ Mean ☊ 15♊28.9
♃⚹♆ 17 17:34	☿ ♍ 13 21:32	17 19:02 ♂ △	♌ 17 21:41	16 7:58 ♇ ⚹	♍ 16 14:42	15 23:55 ● 22♌28	
☽0S 19 23:41	♀ ♎ 23 0:34	19 23:51 ♇ ⚹	♍ 20 7:32	18 19:46 ♇ □	♎ 19 2:36	24 3:55 ☽ 0♐20	1 August 1909
♂ R 23 2:20	☉ ♍ 23 19:44	22 17:53 ☉ ⚹	♎ 22 19:26	21 10:46 ☉ ⚹	♏ 21 15:24	31 5:08 ○ 7♓08	Julian Day # 3500
♀0S 24 14:55		25 0:21 ♇ △	♏ 25 8:01	23 6:16 ♃ ⚹	♐ 24 3:16		SVP 6♓31'35"
☿0S 31 11:37		27 15:09 ♀ □	♐ 27 19:00	26 5:59 ♇ ☍	♑ 26 12:01		GC 25♐34.6 ⚴ 21♐57.9R
		29 19:51 ♇ ☍	♑ 30 2:32	28 7:13 ☿ △	♒ 28 16:37		Eris 25♓56.9R ⚵ 19♉43.5
				30 12:33 ♇ △	♓ 30 17:45		⚷ 26♒33.4R ⚶ 1♐57.2
							☽ Mean ☊ 13♊50.4

LONGITUDE — September 1909

Day	Sid.Time	☉	0 hr ☽	Noon ☽	True ☊	☿	♀	♂	⚳	♃	♄	♅	♆	♇
1 W	10 40 02	8♍22 59	19♓03 12	26♓38 42	12♊25.0	0♎43.1	11♎25.0	6♈11.1	13♑37.7	21♍18.0	22♈36.4	17♑22.8	18♋37.6	26♊46.3
2 Th	10 43 58	9 21 04	4♈13 19	11♈45 47	12R 15.6	2 08.8	12 37.2	6R 03.0	13D 37.2	21 30.8	22R 33.7	17R 21.6	18 39.2	26 46.8
3 F	10 47 55	10 19 10	19 14 57	26 39 52	12 08.6	3 33.2	13 49.2	5 54.1	13 37.2	21 43.6	22 30.8	17 20.5	18 40.7	26 47.3
4 Sa	10 51 52	11 17 19	3♉59 46	11♉14 04	12 04.3	4 56.2	15 01.3	5 44.5	13 37.4	21 56.5	22 28.0	17 19.3	18 42.2	26 47.9
5 Su	10 55 48	12 15 30	18 22 27	25 24 42	12 02.3	6 17.7	16 13.3	5 34.2	13 38.1	22 09.3	22 25.0	17 18.3	18 43.7	26 48.4
6 M	10 59 45	13 13 43	2♊20 51	9♊11 00	12 01.9	7 37.8	17 25.3	5 23.1	13 39.0	22 22.2	22 21.9	17 17.3	18 45.2	26 48.8
7 Tu	11 03 41	14 11 58	15 55 25	22 34 24	12 01.8	8 56.3	18 37.2	5 11.3	13 40.4	22 35.1	22 18.8	17 16.3	18 46.6	26 49.3
8 W	11 07 38	15 10 15	29 08 20	5♋37 38	12 00.8	10 13.3	19 49.1	4 58.9	13 42.0	22 48.0	22 15.6	17 15.4	18 48.1	26 49.7
9 Th	11 11 34	16 08 35	12♋02 40	18 23 53	11 57.8	11 28.7	21 01.0	4 45.8	13 44.1	23 00.9	22 12.2	17 14.5	18 49.4	26 50.1
10 F	11 15 31	17 06 56	24 41 39	0♌56 19	11 52.1	12 42.3	22 12.9	4 32.2	13 46.4	23 13.9	22 08.9	17 13.6	18 50.8	26 50.5
11 Sa	11 19 27	18 05 19	7♌08 14	13 17 40	11 43.4	13 54.2	23 24.7	4 17.9	13 49.1	23 26.8	22 05.4	17 12.8	18 52.2	26 50.9
12 Su	11 23 24	19 03 44	19 24 53	25 30 06	11 32.1	15 04.3	24 36.4	4 03.2	13 52.2	23 39.8	22 01.9	17 12.1	18 53.5	26 51.2
13 M	11 27 21	20 02 11	1♍33 31	7♍35 18	11 18.9	16 12.4	25 48.2	3 47.9	13 55.5	23 52.7	21 58.3	17 11.4	18 54.7	26 51.5
14 Tu	11 31 17	21 00 40	13 35 36	19 34 34	11 04.9	17 18.5	26 59.9	3 32.2	13 59.2	24 05.7	21 54.6	17 10.8	18 56.0	26 51.8
15 W	11 35 14	21 59 11	25 32 20	1♎29 05	10 51.1	18 22.4	28 11.6	3 16.1	14 03.3	24 18.7	21 50.9	17 10.2	18 57.2	26 52.1
16 Th	11 39 10	22 57 44	7♎24 57	13 20 11	10 38.8	19 23.9	29 23.2	2 59.7	14 07.7	24 31.6	21 47.0	17 09.6	18 58.4	26 52.4
17 F	11 43 07	23 56 18	19 14 58	25 09 36	10 28.8	20 23.0	0♏34.8	2 42.9	14 12.4	24 44.6	21 43.2	17 09.1	18 59.6	26 52.6
18 Sa	11 47 03	24 54 55	1♏04 24	6♏59 42	10 21.6	21 19.4	1 46.3	2 25.9	14 17.4	24 57.6	21 39.2	17 08.6	19 00.7	26 52.8
19 Su	11 51 00	25 53 33	12 55 55	18 53 30	10 17.2	22 13.0	2 57.8	2 08.7	14 22.7	25 10.6	21 35.2	17 08.2	19 01.8	26 53.0
20 M	11 54 56	26 52 13	24 52 58	0♐54 50	10D 15.3	23 03.5	4 09.2	1 51.3	14 28.4	25 23.6	21 31.2	17 07.9	19 02.9	26 53.2
21 Tu	11 58 53	27 50 55	6♐59 41	13 08 07	10 15.0	23 50.7	5 20.6	1 33.8	14 34.3	25 36.6	21 27.1	17 07.6	19 04.0	26 53.3
22 W	12 02 50	28 49 38	19 20 46	25 38 15	10R 15.2	24 34.3	6 32.0	1 16.3	14 40.6	25 49.5	21 22.9	17 07.3	19 05.0	26 53.4
23 Th	12 06 46	29 48 23	2♑01 11	8♑30 10	10 15.0	25 14.0	7 43.3	0 58.8	14 47.2	26 02.5	21 18.7	17 07.1	19 06.0	26 53.5
24 F	12 10 43	0♎47 10	15 05 43	21 48 17	10 13.1	25 49.6	8 54.6	0 41.3	14 54.1	26 15.5	21 14.4	17 07.0	19 07.0	26 53.6
25 Sa	12 14 39	1 45 58	28 38 11	5♒35 38	10 09.1	26 20.6	10 05.8	0 23.9	15 01.3	26 28.4	21 10.1	17 06.9	19 07.9	26 53.7
26 Su	12 18 36	2 44 49	12♒40 38	19 53 00	10 02.7	26 46.7	11 16.9	0 06.7	15 08.7	26 41.4	21 05.7	17D 06.8	19 08.8	26R 53.7
27 M	12 22 32	3 43 41	27 12 18	4♓37 53	9 54.2	27 07.5	12 28.0	29♓49.6	15 16.5	26 54.3	21 01.3	17 06.8	19 09.7	26 53.7
28 Tu	12 26 29	4 42 34	12♓08 53	19 44 11	9 44.6	27 22.6	13 39.0	29 32.8	15 24.5	27 07.3	20 56.9	17 06.9	19 10.5	26 53.7
29 W	12 30 25	5 41 30	27 22 31	5♈02 29	9 35.0	27R 31.6	14 50.0	29 16.2	15 32.9	27 20.2	20 52.4	17 06.9	19 11.3	26 53.7
30 Th	12 34 22	6 40 28	12♈42 36	20 21 27	9 26.6	27 34.0	16 00.9	29 00.0	15 41.5	27 33.1	20 47.9	17 07.1	19 12.1	26 53.6

LONGITUDE — October 1909

Day	Sid.Time	☉	0 hr ☽	Noon ☽	True ☊	☿	♀	♂	⚳	♃	♄	♅	♆	♇
1 F	12 38 18	7♎39 27	27♈57 39	5♉29 58	9♊20.3	27♎29.5	17♏11.8	28♓44.1	15♑50.4	27♍46.0	20♈43.3	17♑07.3	19♋12.8	26♊53.5
2 Sa	12 42 15	8 38 30	12♉57 22	20 19 00	9R 16.6	27R 17.7	18 22.6	28R 28.6	15 59.5	27 58.9	20R 38.7	17 07.5	19 13.5	26R 53.4
3 Su	12 46 12	9 37 34	27 34 15	4♊42 44	9D 15.2	26 58.2	19 33.4	28 13.5	16 08.9	28 11.7	20 34.1	17 07.8	19 14.2	26 53.3
4 M	12 50 08	10 36 41	11♊44 15	18 38 49	9 15.3	26 30.9	20 44.1	27 59.0	16 18.6	28 24.6	20 29.5	17 08.2	19 14.9	26 53.2
5 Tu	12 54 05	11 35 50	25 26 34	2♋07 48	9R 16.1	25 55.7	21 54.7	27 44.9	16 28.5	28 37.4	20 24.8	17 08.6	19 15.5	26 53.0
6 W	12 58 01	12 35 01	8♋42 52	15 12 12	9 16.4	25 12.7	23 05.3	27 31.3	16 38.7	28 50.2	20 20.1	17 09.1	19 16.1	26 52.8
7 Th	13 01 58	13 34 15	21 36 18	27 55 40	9 15.3	24 22.3	24 15.8	27 18.3	16 49.2	29 03.0	20 15.4	17 09.6	19 16.6	26 52.6
8 F	13 05 54	14 33 31	4♌10 48	10♌22 13	9 12.0	23 25.1	25 26.2	27 05.9	16 59.9	29 15.8	20 10.7	17 10.1	19 17.1	26 52.4
9 Sa	13 09 51	15 32 49	16 30 23	22 35 45	9 06.4	22 21.9	26 36.6	26 54.2	17 10.9	29 28.5	20 06.0	17 10.7	19 17.6	26 52.1
10 Su	13 13 47	16 32 10	28 38 46	4♍39 49	8 58.7	21 14.1	27 47.0	26 43.1	17 22.1	29 41.2	20 01.2	17 11.4	19 18.1	26 51.8
11 M	13 17 44	17 31 32	10♍39 13	16 37 19	8 49.3	20 03.2	28 57.2	26 32.6	17 33.5	29 53.9	19 56.5	17 12.1	19 18.5	26 51.5
12 Tu	13 21 41	18 30 57	22 34 23	28 30 40	8 39.3	18 51.0	0♐07.4	26 22.9	17 45.2	0♎06.6	19 51.7	17 12.9	19 18.8	26 51.2
13 W	13 25 37	19 30 24	4♎26 25	10♎21 50	8 29.4	17 39.4	1 17.5	26 13.9	17 57.1	0 19.2	19 46.9	17 13.7	19 19.2	26 50.9
14 Th	13 29 34	20 29 53	16 17 07	22 12 28	8 20.6	16 30.5	2 27.6	26 05.7	18 09.3	0 31.8	19 42.1	17 14.5	19 19.5	26 50.5
15 F	13 33 30	21 29 24	28 08 06	4♏04 11	8 13.6	15 26.4	3 37.6	25 58.2	18 21.6	0 44.4	19 37.4	17 15.5	19 19.8	26 50.1
16 Sa	13 37 27	22 28 57	10♏01 00	15 58 46	8 08.8	14 28.9	4 47.5	25 51.5	18 34.2	0 56.9	19 32.6	17 16.4	19 20.0	26 49.7
17 Su	13 41 23	23 28 32	21 57 46	27 58 20	8D 06.2	13 39.8	5 57.3	25 45.6	18 47.1	1 09.4	19 27.8	17 17.4	19 20.2	26 49.3
18 M	13 45 20	24 28 09	4♐00 48	10♐05 32	8 05.6	13 00.1	7 07.0	25 40.5	19 00.1	1 21.9	19 23.1	17 18.5	19 20.4	26 48.8
19 Tu	13 49 16	25 27 48	16 12 59	22 23 34	8 06.5	12 31.1	8 16.7	25 36.2	19 13.4	1 34.3	19 18.4	17 19.6	19 20.6	26 48.4
20 W	13 53 13	26 27 29	28 37 46	4♑56 04	8 08.0	12 13.0	9 26.3	25 32.7	19 26.8	1 46.7	19 13.6	17 20.8	19 20.7	26 47.9
21 Th	13 57 10	27 27 11	11♑18 58	17 46 57	8R 09.3	12D 06.3	10 35.8	25 30.0	19 40.5	1 59.0	19 08.9	17 22.0	19 20.7	26 47.4
22 F	14 01 06	28 26 55	24 20 29	1♒00 00	8 09.6	12 10.8	11 45.1	25 28.2	19 54.4	2 11.3	19 04.3	17 23.3	19R 20.8	26 46.8
23 Sa	14 05 03	29 26 41	7♒45 49	14 38 12	8 08.5	12 26.0	12 54.4	25D 27.1	20 08.5	2 23.6	18 59.6	17 24.6	19 20.8	26 46.3
24 Su	14 08 59	0♏26 28	21 37 17	28 43 03	8 05.8	12 51.5	14 03.6	25 26.9	20 22.8	2 35.8	18 55.0	17 25.9	19 20.8	26 45.7
25 M	14 12 56	1 26 17	5♓55 18	13♓13 41	8 01.6	13 26.5	15 12.7	25 27.4	20 37.3	2 47.9	18 50.4	17 27.3	19 20.7	26 45.1
26 Tu	14 16 52	2 26 08	20 37 35	28 06 15	7 56.5	14 10.2	16 21.6	25 28.8	20 51.9	3 00.0	18 45.8	17 28.8	19 20.6	26 44.5
27 W	14 20 49	3 26 00	5♈38 42	13♈13 49	7 51.2	15 01.8	17 30.5	25 30.9	21 06.8	3 12.1	18 41.3	17 30.3	19 20.5	26 43.9
28 Th	14 24 45	4 25 54	20 50 23	28 27 05	7 46.6	16 00.4	18 39.2	25 33.9	21 21.8	3 24.1	18 36.8	17 31.8	19 20.3	26 43.3
29 F	14 28 42	5 25 50	6♉02 36	13♉35 41	7 43.3	17 05.2	19 47.8	25 37.6	21 37.1	3 36.1	18 32.3	17 33.4	19 20.1	26 42.6
30 Sa	14 32 39	6 25 48	21 05 09	28 30 00	7D 41.5	18 15.4	20 56.3	25 42.0	21 52.5	3 48.0	18 27.9	17 35.1	19 19.9	26 41.9
31 Su	14 36 35	7 25 49	5♊49 22	13♊02 37	7 41.3	19 30.2	22 04.7	25 47.2	22 08.0	3 59.8	18 23.5	17 36.8	19 19.6	26 41.2

Astro Data (Dy Hr Mn)	Planet Ingress (Dy Hr Mn)	Last Aspect (Dy Hr Mn)	☽ Ingress (Dy Hr Mn)	Last Aspect (Dy Hr Mn)	☽ Ingress (Dy Hr Mn)	☽ Phases & Eclipses (Dy Hr Mn)	Astro Data
☽0N 2 9:38	☿ ♎ 1 0:05	1 12:12 ♇ □	♈ 1 17:19	30 23:21 ☿ ☍	♉ 1 3:14	6 19:44 ☾ 13♊33	1 September 1909
⚳ D 3 5:25	♀ ♏ 17 0:21	3 12:12 ♇ ⚹	♉ 3 17:26	3 1:17 ♂ ⚹	♊ 3 4:04	14 15:08 ● 21♍08	Julian Day # 3531
♃⚻♄ 6 11:35	☉ ♎ 23 16:45	5 6:20 ♃ △	♊ 5 19:55	5 5:35 ♃ □	♋ 5 8:09	22 18:31 ☽ 29♐06	SVP 6♓31'31"
☽0S 16 5:30	♂ ♓R 26 21:19	7 19:45 ♇ ☌	♋ 8 1:35	7 14:11 ♃ ⚹	♌ 7 15:58	29 13:05 ○ 5♈44	GC 25♐34.7 ⚳ 22♐18.8
☉0S 23 16:44		9 20:57 ♃ ⚹	♌ 10 10:11	9 20:49 ♀ □	♍ 10 2:42		Eris 25♓39.3R ⚵ 2♊22.9
♅ D 27 1:29	♃ ♎ 11 23:33	12 14:40 ♇ ⚹	♍ 12 20:54	12 8:39 ♇ □	♎ 12 15:01	6 6:44 ☾ 12♋22	⚷ 25♒01.3R ⚶ 9♐44.9
♇ R 27 10:43	♀ ♐ 12 9:28	15 2:41 ♇ □	♎ 15 9:00	14 21:23 ♇ △	♏ 15 3:46	14 8:13 ● 20♎21	☽ Mean ☊ 12♊11.9
♃□♇ 27 10:51	☉ ♏ 24 1:23	17 15:29 ♇ △	♏ 17 21:49	17 7:37 ♂ △	♐ 17 16:02	22 7:03 ☽ 28♑15	
☽0N 29 19:56		20 3:15 ☉ ⚹	♐ 20 10:11	19 20:30 ♇ ☍	♑ 20 2:37	28 22:07 ○ 4♉51	1 October 1909
☿ R 30 8:34		22 18:31 ☉ □	♑ 22 20:13	22 7:03 ☉ □	♒ 22 10:13		Julian Day # 3561
☽0S 13 11:29		24 19:58 ♃ △	♒ 25 2:22	24 8:43 ♇ △	♓ 24 14:09		SVP 6♓31'29"
♄□♆ 19 1:09		26 23:36 ☿ △	♓ 27 4:32	26 9:49 ♇ □	♈ 26 15:02		GC 25♐34.7 ⚳ 27♐27.7
☿ D 21 14:22		29 3:08 ♂ ☌	♈ 29 4:07	28 9:16 ♇ ⚹	♉ 28 14:27		Eris 25♓18.7R ⚵ 11♊00.6
♆ R 23 5:03	♂ D24 7:15			30 7:26 ♂ ⚹	♊ 30 14:27		⚷ 23♒46.8R ⚶ 20♐55.0
♃0S 24 6:42	☽0N27 7:12						☽ Mean ☊ 10♊36.6

November 1909 LONGITUDE

Day	Sid.Time	☉	0 hr ☽	Noon ☽	True ☊	☿	♀	♂	⚳	♃	♄	♅	♆	♇
1 M	14 40 32	8♏25 51	20♊09 15	27♊09 02	7♊42.3	20♎49.0	23♐12.9	25♓53.2	22♑23.8	4♎11.6	18♈19.2	17♑38.5	19♋19.3	26♊40.5
2 Tu	14 44 28	9 25 55	4♋01 51	10♋47 46	7 43.9	22 11.2	24 21.0	25 59.8	22 39.7	4 23.4	18R 14.9	17 40.3	19R 19.0	26R 39.8
3 W	14 48 25	10 26 02	17 27 00	23 59 50	7 45.4	23 36.3	25 29.0	26 07.2	22 55.8	4 35.1	18 10.7	17 42.1	19 18.6	26 39.0
4 Th	14 52 21	11 26 10	0♌26 42	6♌48 02	7R 46.3	25 03.7	26 36.8	26 15.3	23 12.1	4 46.7	18 06.5	17 44.0	19 18.3	26 38.2
5 F	14 56 18	12 26 21	13 04 21	19 16 12	7 46.2	26 33.1	27 44.5	26 24.1	23 28.5	4 58.3	18 02.3	17 45.9	19 17.8	26 37.4
6 Sa	15 00 14	13 26 34	25 24 09	1♍28 43	7 44.9	28 04.1	28 52.1	26 33.6	23 45.1	5 09.8	17 58.3	17 47.9	19 17.4	26 36.6
7 Su	15 04 11	14 26 48	7♍30 29	13 29 57	7 42.5	29 36.4	29 59.5	26 43.8	24 01.8	5 21.2	17 54.3	17 49.9	19 16.9	26 35.8
8 M	15 08 08	15 27 05	19 27 38	25 24 00	7 39.3	1♏09.7	1♑06.7	26 54.7	24 18.8	5 32.6	17 50.3	17 51.9	19 16.3	26 35.0
9 Tu	15 12 04	16 27 23	1♎19 31	7♎14 35	7 35.7	2 43.9	2 13.8	27 06.2	24 35.8	5 43.9	17 46.4	17 54.0	19 15.8	26 34.1
10 W	15 16 01	17 27 44	13 09 34	19 04 50	7 32.0	4 18.7	3 20.7	27 18.3	24 53.0	5 55.1	17 42.6	17 56.1	19 15.2	26 33.2
11 Th	15 19 57	18 28 06	25 00 40	0♏57 23	7 28.9	5 53.9	4 27.5	27 31.1	25 10.4	6 06.2	17 38.8	17 58.3	19 14.6	26 32.4
12 F	15 23 54	19 28 30	6♏55 12	12 54 24	7 26.5	7 29.5	5 34.1	27 44.6	25 27.9	6 17.3	17 35.1	18 00.5	19 13.9	26 31.5
13 Sa	15 27 50	20 28 56	18 55 09	24 57 41	7 25.1	9 05.4	6 40.5	27 58.6	25 45.6	6 28.3	17 31.5	18 02.8	19 13.2	26 30.5
14 Su	15 31 47	21 29 23	1♐02 12	7♐08 54	7D 24.6	10 41.3	7 46.7	28 13.3	26 03.4	6 39.2	17 28.0	18 05.1	19 12.5	26 29.6
15 M	15 35 43	22 29 52	13 17 57	19 29 35	7 25.0	12 17.4	8 52.7	28 28.5	26 21.3	6 50.1	17 24.5	18 07.4	19 11.8	26 28.7
16 Tu	15 39 40	23 30 23	25 44 00	2♑01 25	7 25.9	13 53.4	9 58.5	28 44.4	26 39.4	7 00.9	17 21.1	18 09.8	19 11.0	26 27.7
17 W	15 43 37	24 30 55	8♑22 04	14 46 13	7 27.1	15 29.4	11 04.1	29 00.8	26 57.6	7 11.5	17 17.8	18 12.2	19 10.2	26 26.7
18 Th	15 47 33	25 31 28	21 14 05	27 45 56	7 28.3	17 05.4	12 09.5	29 17.7	27 15.9	7 22.1	17 14.6	18 14.7	19 09.3	26 25.8
19 F	15 51 30	26 32 02	4♒22 00	11♒02 31	7 29.1	18 41.2	13 14.7	29 35.2	27 34.4	7 32.6	17 11.5	18 17.2	19 08.5	26 24.8
20 Sa	15 55 26	27 32 38	17 47 40	24 37 36	7R 29.5	20 16.9	14 19.6	29 53.3	27 53.0	7 43.1	17 08.4	18 19.7	19 07.6	26 23.8
21 Su	15 59 23	28 33 15	1♓32 24	8♓32 05	7 29.3	21 52.5	15 24.2	0♈11.8	28 11.7	7 53.4	17 05.5	18 22.3	19 06.6	26 22.7
22 M	16 03 19	29 33 53	15 36 33	22 45 37	7 28.8	23 27.9	16 28.6	0 30.9	28 30.6	8 03.6	17 02.6	18 24.9	19 05.7	26 21.7
23 Tu	16 07 16	0♐34 31	29 58 59	7♈16 12	7 28.1	25 03.2	17 32.8	0 50.4	28 49.6	8 13.8	16 59.8	18 27.5	19 04.7	26 20.7
24 W	16 11 12	1 35 11	14♈36 42	21 59 49	7 27.3	26 38.3	18 36.6	1 10.4	29 08.7	8 23.9	16 57.1	18 30.2	19 03.7	26 19.6
25 Th	16 15 09	2 35 53	29 24 44	6♉50 35	7 26.8	28 13.3	19 40.2	1 30.9	29 27.9	8 33.8	16 54.5	18 32.9	19 02.7	26 18.5
26 F	16 19 06	3 36 35	14♉16 25	21 41 16	7 26.4	29 48.2	20 43.4	1 51.8	29 47.2	8 43.7	16 52.0	18 35.6	19 01.6	26 17.5
27 Sa	16 23 02	4 37 19	29 04 08	6♊24 08	7D 26.3	1♐22.9	21 46.4	2 13.1	0♒06.6	8 53.4	16 49.6	18 38.4	19 00.5	26 16.4
28 Su	16 26 59	5 38 04	13♊40 23	20 52 08	7 26.4	2 57.5	22 49.0	2 34.9	0 26.1	9 03.1	16 47.3	18 41.2	18 59.4	26 15.3
29 M	16 30 55	6 38 50	27 58 44	4♋59 43	7R 26.5	4 32.1	23 51.3	2 57.1	0 45.8	9 12.7	16 45.1	18 44.0	18 58.3	26 14.2
30 Tu	16 34 52	7 39 38	11♋54 42	18 43 29	7 26.5	6 06.5	24 53.3	3 19.7	1 05.5	9 22.1	16 42.9	18 46.9	18 57.1	26 13.1

December 1909 LONGITUDE

Day	Sid.Time	☉	0 hr ☽	Noon ☽	True ☊	☿	♀	♂	⚳	♃	♄	♅	♆	♇
1 W	16 38 48	8♐40 27	25♋26 00	2♌02 19	7♊26.4	7♐40.8	25♑54.9	3♈42.7	1♒25.4	9♎31.5	16♈40.9	18♑49.8	18♋55.9	26♊12.0
2 Th	16 42 45	9 41 18	8♌32 36	14 57 09	7R 26.2	9 15.1	26 56.1	4 06.1	1 45.4	9 40.8	16R 39.0	18 52.7	18R 54.7	26R 10.8
3 F	16 46 41	10 42 09	21 16 19	27 30 33	7 26.0	10 49.4	27 57.0	4 29.8	2 05.4	9 49.9	16 37.2	18 55.7	18 53.5	26 09.7
4 Sa	16 50 38	11 43 02	3♍40 21	9♍46 16	7D 25.9	12 23.6	28 57.4	4 53.9	2 25.6	9 58.9	16 35.4	18 58.7	18 52.2	26 08.6
5 Su	16 54 35	12 43 57	15 48 52	21 48 44	7 26.0	13 57.8	29 57.5	5 18.4	2 45.9	10 07.8	16 33.8	19 01.7	18 50.9	26 07.4
6 M	16 58 31	13 44 52	27 46 27	3♎42 38	7 26.3	15 32.0	0♒57.1	5 43.2	3 06.2	10 16.6	16 32.3	19 04.7	18 49.6	26 06.3
7 Tu	17 02 28	14 45 49	9♎37 52	15 32 41	7 27.0	17 06.2	1 56.3	6 08.4	3 26.7	10 25.3	16 30.9	19 07.8	18 48.3	26 05.1
8 W	17 06 24	15 46 47	21 27 39	27 23 16	7 27.9	18 40.4	2 55.1	6 33.9	3 47.2	10 33.9	16 29.6	19 10.9	18 46.9	26 04.0
9 Th	17 10 21	16 47 47	3♏20 01	9♏18 20	7 28.9	20 14.7	3 53.3	6 59.7	4 07.8	10 42.3	16 28.4	19 14.0	18 45.6	26 02.8
10 F	17 14 17	17 48 47	15 18 38	21 21 15	7 29.7	21 49.1	4 51.1	7 25.9	4 28.6	10 50.7	16 27.3	19 17.2	18 44.2	26 01.6
11 Sa	17 18 14	18 49 48	27 26 29	3♐34 37	7R 30.1	23 23.5	5 48.4	7 52.3	4 49.4	10 58.9	16 26.3	19 20.3	18 42.8	26 00.4
12 Su	17 22 10	19 50 50	9♐45 52	16 00 22	7 30.0	24 58.0	6 45.2	8 19.1	5 10.3	11 06.9	16 25.4	19 23.5	18 41.3	25 59.3
13 M	17 26 07	20 51 54	22 18 16	28 39 37	7 29.2	26 32.6	7 41.4	8 46.2	5 31.3	11 14.9	16 24.7	19 26.7	18 39.9	25 58.1
14 Tu	17 30 04	21 52 57	5♑04 29	11♑32 49	7 27.7	28 07.3	8 37.0	9 13.5	5 52.4	11 22.7	16 24.0	19 30.0	18 38.4	25 56.9
15 W	17 34 00	22 54 02	18 04 38	24 39 52	7 25.5	29 42.0	9 32.1	9 41.2	6 13.5	11 30.4	16 23.5	19 33.2	18 37.0	25 55.7
16 Th	17 37 57	23 55 07	1♒18 25	8♒00 12	7 23.1	1♑16.9	10 26.5	10 09.1	6 34.8	11 37.9	16 23.1	19 36.5	18 35.5	25 54.5
17 F	17 41 53	24 56 12	14 45 08	21 33 05	7 20.8	2 51.9	11 20.3	10 37.3	6 56.1	11 45.3	16 22.7	19 39.8	18 33.9	25 53.4
18 Sa	17 45 50	25 57 18	28 23 57	5♓17 37	7 19.0	4 27.0	12 13.4	11 05.7	7 17.5	11 52.6	16 22.5	19 43.1	18 32.4	25 52.2
19 Su	17 49 46	26 58 24	12♓13 57	19 12 49	7D 17.9	6 02.1	13 05.7	11 34.5	7 38.9	11 59.7	16D 22.4	19 46.5	18 30.9	25 51.0
20 M	17 53 43	27 59 30	26 14 05	3♈17 33	7 17.8	7 37.3	13 57.4	12 03.4	8 00.5	12 06.7	16 22.4	19 49.8	18 29.3	25 49.8
21 Tu	17 57 40	29 00 36	10♈23 04	17 30 22	7 18.6	9 12.6	14 48.3	12 32.6	8 22.1	12 13.6	16 22.6	19 53.2	18 27.7	25 48.6
22 W	18 01 36	0♑01 42	24 39 11	1♉49 13	7 20.0	10 47.8	15 38.4	13 02.0	8 43.7	12 20.3	16 22.8	19 56.6	18 26.2	25 47.4
23 Th	18 05 33	1 02 49	9♉00 06	16 11 23	7 21.5	12 23.1	16 27.6	13 31.7	9 05.5	12 26.8	16 23.1	20 00.0	18 24.6	25 46.2
24 F	18 09 29	2 03 55	23 22 36	0♊33 13	7R 22.4	13 58.3	17 16.0	14 01.5	9 27.3	12 33.2	16 23.6	20 03.4	18 23.0	25 45.1
25 Sa	18 13 26	3 05 03	7♊42 42	14 50 28	7 22.4	15 33.4	18 03.5	14 31.6	9 49.2	12 39.5	16 24.2	20 06.9	18 21.3	25 43.9
26 Su	18 17 22	4 06 10	21 55 53	28 58 25	7 21.0	17 08.2	18 50.0	15 01.9	10 11.1	12 45.6	16 24.8	20 10.3	18 19.7	25 42.7
27 M	18 21 19	5 07 17	5♋57 29	12♋52 36	7 18.1	18 42.9	19 35.6	15 32.3	10 33.1	12 51.6	16 25.6	20 13.8	18 18.1	25 41.6
28 Tu	18 25 15	6 08 25	19 43 20	26 29 18	7 14.0	20 17.1	20 20.1	16 03.0	10 55.1	12 57.4	16 26.5	20 17.2	18 16.4	25 40.4
29 W	18 29 12	7 09 33	3♌10 17	9♌46 06	7 09.0	21 50.8	21 03.6	16 33.8	11 17.3	13 03.1	16 27.5	20 20.7	18 14.8	25 39.2
30 Th	18 33 09	8 10 41	16 16 43	22 42 10	7 03.7	23 23.9	21 46.0	17 04.8	11 39.4	13 08.6	16 28.6	20 24.2	18 13.1	25 38.1
31 F	18 37 05	9 11 50	29 02 37	5♍18 19	6 58.9	24 56.1	22 27.3	17 36.0	12 01.7	13 13.9	16 29.9	20 27.7	18 11.5	25 36.9

Astro Data	Planet Ingress	Last Aspect	☽ Ingress	Last Aspect	☽ Ingress	☽ Phases & Eclipses	Astro Data
Dy Hr Mn	Dy Hr Mn	Dy Hr Mn	Dy Hr Mn	Dy Hr Mn	Dy Hr Mn	Dy Hr Mn	1 November 1909
♄□♅ 8 5:29	♀ ♑ 7 12:11	1 11:11 ♇ ☌	♋ 1 16:57	30 23:56 ♀ ☍	♌ 1 8:17	4 21:38 ☾ 11♌50	Julian Day # 3592
☽0S 9 18:06	☿ ♏ 7 18:06	3 15:58 ♂ △	♌ 3 23:10	3 9:24 ♇ ⚹	♍ 3 16:50	13 2:18 ● 20♏05	SVP 6♓31'25"
☽0N 23 17:00	♂ ♈ 20 20:48	6 6:18 ♀ △	♍ 6 9:04	5 20:39 ♇ □	♎ 6 4:30	20 17:29 ☽ 27♒46	GC 25♐34.8 ⚵ 5♑48.5
♂0N 25 20:58	☉ ♐ 22 22:20	8 15:06 ♂ ☍	♎ 8 21:19	8 9:20 ♇ △	♏ 8 17:17	27 8:52 ○ 4♊29	Eris 25♓00.0R ⚴ 13♊08.0R
	☿ ♐ 26 14:59	11 3:06 ♇ △	♏ 11 10:04	10 7:53 ♅ ⚹	♐ 11 5:01	27 8:54 ☍ T 1.366	⚷ 23♒14.5R ⚶ 4♑37.0
♅☍♆ 2 23:19	⚳ ♒ 27 3:52	13 18:05 ♂ △	♐ 13 21:57	13 7:27 ☿ ☌	♑ 13 14:31		☽ Mean ☊ 8♊58.1
☽0S 7 1:25		16 5:37 ♂ □	♑ 16 8:09	15 2:40 ♅ ☌	♒ 15 21:39	4 16:12 ☾ 11♍54	
♄ D 19 21:51	♀ ♒ 5 13:01	18 14:51 ♂ ⚹	♒ 18 16:05	17 19:36 ♇ △	♓ 18 2:48	12 19:58 ● 20♐11	1 December 1909
☽0N 20 23:47	☿ ♑ 15 16:33	20 17:29 ☉ □	♓ 20 21:20	20 2:17 ☉ □	♈ 20 6:25	12 19:44:36 ☌ P 0.542	Julian Day # 3622
	☉ ♑ 22 11:20	22 17:59 ♇ □	♈ 23 0:02	22 8:46 ☉ △	♉ 22 8:57	20 2:17 ☽ 27♓35	SVP 6♓31'20"
		24 19:00 ♇ ⚹	♉ 25 0:57	23 18:23 ♅ △	♊ 24 11:04	26 21:30 ○ 4♋30	GC 25♐34.9 ⚵ 15♑31.3
		26 10:19 ♀ △	♊ 27 1:31	26 6:26 ♇ ☌	♋ 26 13:45		Eris 24♓50.0R ⚴ 7♊53.1R
		28 21:04 ♇ ☌	♋ 29 3:26	28 0:57 ♅ ☍	♌ 28 18:17		⚷ 23♒38.9 ⚶ 19♑03.7
				30 17:31 ♇ ⚹	♍ 31 1:49		☽ Mean ☊ 7♊22.8

LONGITUDE — January 1910

Day	Sid.Time	☉	0 hr ☽	Noon ☽	True ☊	☿	♀	♂	⚳	♃	♄	♅	♆	♇
1 Sa	18 41 02	10♑12 59	11♍29 36	17♍36 52	6♊55.1	26♑27.4	23♒07.3	18♈07.4	12♒23.9	13♎19.1	16♈31.2	20♑31.2	18♋09.8	25♊35.8
2 Su	18 44 58	11 14 08	23 40 37	29 41 22	6R52.8	27 57.3	23 46.1	18 39.0	12 46.3	13 24.1	16 32.6	20 34.7	18R08.1	25R34.6
3 M	18 48 55	12 15 17	5♎39 41	11♎36 12	6D51.9	29 25.7	24 23.7	19 10.7	13 08.7	13 28.9	16 34.2	20 38.2	18 06.4	25 33.5
4 Tu	18 52 51	13 16 27	17 31 31	23 26 19	6 52.5	0♒52.2	24 59.9	19 42.5	13 31.1	13 33.6	16 35.8	20 41.8	18 04.7	25 32.4
5 W	18 56 48	14 17 36	29 21 12	5♏16 51	6 54.0	2 16.3	25 34.7	20 14.6	13 53.6	13 38.1	16 37.6	20 45.3	18 03.0	25 31.2
6 Th	19 00 44	15 18 46	11♏13 53	17 12 53	6 55.8	3 37.8	26 08.1	20 46.8	14 16.2	13 42.5	16 39.5	20 48.9	18 01.3	25 30.1
7 F	19 04 41	16 19 56	23 14 27	29 19 06	6R57.1	4 56.0	26 40.0	21 19.1	14 38.8	13 46.7	16 41.5	20 52.4	17 59.6	25 29.0
8 Sa	19 08 38	17 21 07	5♐27 19	11♐39 31	6 57.3	6 10.5	27 10.4	21 51.6	15 01.4	13 50.7	16 43.6	20 56.0	17 57.9	25 27.9
9 Su	19 12 34	18 22 17	17 56 02	24 17 07	6 55.7	7 20.4	27 39.1	22 24.2	15 24.1	13 54.5	16 45.7	20 59.5	17 56.2	25 26.8
10 M	19 16 31	19 23 27	0♑42 58	7♑13 40	6 52.0	8 25.2	28 06.2	22 57.0	15 46.9	13 58.2	16 48.1	21 03.1	17 54.5	25 25.8
11 Tu	19 20 27	20 24 36	13 49 09	20 29 20	6 46.3	9 24.0	28 31.5	23 29.9	16 09.6	14 01.7	16 50.5	21 06.6	17 52.9	25 24.7
12 W	19 24 24	21 25 46	27 13 59	4♒02 48	6 39.1	10 16.0	28 55.0	24 03.0	16 32.5	14 05.0	16 53.0	21 10.2	17 51.2	25 23.7
13 Th	19 28 20	22 26 55	10♒55 23	17 51 17	6 31.0	11 00.3	29 16.6	24 36.2	16 55.3	14 08.1	16 55.6	21 13.8	17 49.5	25 22.6
14 F	19 32 17	23 28 03	24 50 01	1♓51 04	6 23.1	11 36.1	29 36.3	25 09.5	17 18.3	14 11.0	16 58.3	21 17.3	17 47.8	25 21.6
15 Sa	19 36 14	24 29 11	8♓53 54	15 58 01	6 16.3	12 02.4	29 54.0	25 42.9	17 41.2	14 13.8	17 01.1	21 20.9	17 46.1	25 20.5
16 Su	19 40 10	25 30 17	23 02 56	0♈08 15	6 11.4	12R18.5	0♓09.5	26 16.5	18 04.2	14 16.4	17 04.0	21 24.4	17 44.4	25 19.5
17 M	19 44 07	26 31 23	7♈13 35	14 18 37	6D08.7	12 23.6	0 23.0	26 50.2	18 27.2	14 18.8	17 07.0	21 28.0	17 42.7	25 18.5
18 Tu	19 48 03	27 32 29	21 23 08	28 26 54	6 08.0	12 17.3	0 34.2	27 24.0	18 50.2	14 21.0	17 10.2	21 31.5	17 41.0	25 17.5
19 W	19 52 00	28 33 33	5♉29 47	12♉31 40	6 08.6	11 59.3	0 43.2	27 57.9	19 13.3	14 23.0	17 13.4	21 35.1	17 39.4	25 16.6
20 Th	19 55 56	29 34 36	19 32 25	26 31 59	6R09.6	11 29.7	0 49.8	28 31.9	19 36.4	14 24.8	17 16.7	21 38.6	17 37.7	25 15.6
21 F	19 59 53	0♒35 39	3♊30 13	10♊27 01	6 09.8	10 49.0	0 54.0	29 06.0	19 59.6	14 26.5	17 20.1	21 42.1	17 36.1	25 14.7
22 Sa	20 03 49	1 36 40	17 22 12	24 15 37	6 08.3	9 58.1	0R55.8	29 40.2	20 22.8	14 28.0	17 23.6	21 45.6	17 34.4	25 13.7
23 Su	20 07 46	2 37 41	1♋07 00	7♋56 09	6 04.3	8 58.2	0 55.1	0♉14.5	20 46.0	14 29.2	17 27.2	21 49.2	17 32.8	25 12.8
24 M	20 11 43	3 38 41	14 42 45	21 26 32	5 57.6	7 51.2	0 51.9	0 48.8	21 09.2	14 30.3	17 30.9	21 52.7	17 31.2	25 11.9
25 Tu	20 15 39	4 39 40	28 07 13	4♌44 32	5 48.4	6 39.0	0 46.2	1 23.3	21 32.4	14 31.2	17 34.7	21 56.2	17 29.6	25 11.0
26 W	20 19 36	5 40 38	11♌18 14	17 48 07	5 37.6	5 23.8	0 37.9	1 57.8	21 55.7	14 32.0	17 38.6	21 59.6	17 28.0	25 10.2
27 Th	20 23 32	6 41 35	24 14 02	0♍35 56	5 26.1	4 08.0	0 27.1	2 32.5	22 19.0	14 32.5	17 42.5	22 03.1	17 26.4	25 09.3
28 F	20 27 29	7 42 31	6♍53 49	13 07 45	5 15.0	2 53.6	0 13.8	3 07.2	22 42.4	14 32.8	17 46.6	22 06.6	17 24.8	25 08.5
29 Sa	20 31 25	8 43 26	19 17 54	25 24 31	5 05.3	1 42.8	29♒58.0	3 42.0	23 05.7	14R33.0	17 50.7	22 10.0	17 23.2	25 07.6
30 Su	20 35 22	9 44 21	1♎27 54	7♎28 28	4 57.9	0 37.1	29 39.8	4 16.9	23 29.1	14 32.9	17 55.0	22 13.5	17 21.7	25 06.8
31 M	20 39 18	10 45 15	13 26 40	19 23 02	4 52.9	29♑38.0	29 19.2	4 51.8	23 52.5	14 32.7	17 59.3	22 16.9	17 20.1	25 06.0

LONGITUDE — February 1910

Day	Sid.Time	☉	0 hr ☽	Noon ☽	True ☊	☿	♀	♂	⚳	♃	♄	♅	♆	♇
1 Tu	20 43 15	11♒46 08	25♎18 06	1♏12 31	4♊50.4	28♑46.5	28♒56.3	5♉26.8	24♒15.9	14♎32.2	18♈03.7	22♑20.3	17♋18.6	25♊05.3
2 W	20 47 12	12 47 00	7♏06 55	13 01 59	4D49.8	28R03.0	28R31.2	6 01.9	24 39.3	14R31.6	18 08.2	22 23.7	17R17.1	25R04.5
3 Th	20 51 08	13 47 51	18 58 23	24 56 50	4R50.1	27 28.1	28 04.1	6 37.1	25 02.8	14 30.8	18 12.8	22 27.1	17 15.6	25 03.8
4 F	20 55 05	14 48 42	0♐58 00	7♐02 35	4 50.3	27 01.6	27 35.1	7 12.3	25 26.3	14 29.8	18 17.4	22 30.4	17 14.2	25 03.0
5 Sa	20 59 01	15 49 32	13 11 11	19 24 25	4 49.4	26 43.6	27 04.2	7 47.6	25 49.7	14 28.6	18 22.2	22 33.8	17 12.7	25 02.3
6 Su	21 02 58	16 50 21	25 42 48	2♑06 46	4 46.2	26D33.7	26 31.9	8 23.0	26 13.3	14 27.2	18 27.0	22 37.1	17 11.3	25 01.7
7 M	21 06 54	17 51 08	8♑36 40	15 12 43	4 40.5	26 31.6	25 58.1	8 58.4	26 36.8	14 25.7	18 31.9	22 40.4	17 09.8	25 01.0
8 Tu	21 10 51	18 51 55	21 55 01	28 43 29	4 31.9	26 36.7	25 23.2	9 33.9	27 00.3	14 23.9	18 36.9	22 43.7	17 08.4	25 00.3
9 W	21 14 47	19 52 40	5♒37 54	12♒37 52	4 21.2	26 48.7	24 47.3	10 09.5	27 23.9	14 22.0	18 42.0	22 47.0	17 07.1	24 59.7
10 Th	21 18 44	20 53 25	19 42 53	26 52 14	4 09.2	27 07.0	24 10.7	10 45.1	27 47.4	14 19.8	18 47.1	22 50.3	17 05.7	24 59.1
11 F	21 22 41	21 54 07	4♓05 08	11♓20 43	3 57.2	27 31.2	23 33.6	11 20.8	28 11.0	14 17.5	18 52.3	22 53.5	17 04.4	24 58.5
12 Sa	21 26 37	22 54 48	18 38 04	25 56 14	3 46.6	28 00.7	22 56.3	11 56.6	28 34.6	14 15.0	18 57.6	22 56.7	17 03.0	24 57.9
13 Su	21 30 34	23 55 28	3♈14 21	10♈31 37	3 38.4	28 35.3	22 19.1	12 32.4	28 58.1	14 12.3	19 03.0	22 59.9	17 01.7	24 57.4
14 M	21 34 30	24 56 06	17 47 17	25 00 47	3 33.1	29 14.5	21 42.1	13 08.2	29 21.7	14 09.4	19 08.4	23 03.0	17 00.5	24 56.9
15 Tu	21 38 27	25 56 42	2♉11 39	9♉19 32	3 30.5	29 57.8	21 05.7	13 44.1	29 45.3	14 06.4	19 13.9	23 06.2	16 59.2	24 56.4
16 W	21 42 23	26 57 16	16 24 13	23 25 36	3 29.8	0♒45.0	20 30.0	14 20.1	0♓08.9	14 03.1	19 19.5	23 09.3	16 58.0	24 55.9
17 Th	21 46 20	27 57 49	0♊23 38	7♊18 23	3 29.8	1 35.8	19 55.4	14 56.1	0 32.5	13 59.7	19 25.1	23 12.4	16 56.8	24 55.4
18 F	21 50 16	28 58 20	14 09 56	20 58 23	3 29.1	2 29.8	19 22.0	15 32.1	0 56.1	13 56.1	19 30.8	23 15.4	16 55.6	24 55.0
19 Sa	21 54 13	29 58 49	27 43 51	4♋26 28	3 26.4	3 26.9	18 50.1	16 08.2	1 19.7	13 52.4	19 36.6	23 18.5	16 54.5	24 54.5
20 Su	21 58 10	0♓59 16	11♋06 18	17 43 26	3 21.0	4 26.8	18 19.8	16 44.3	1 43.3	13 48.4	19 42.5	23 21.5	16 53.3	24 54.1
21 M	22 02 06	1 59 41	24 17 53	0♌49 40	3 12.5	5 29.2	17 51.3	17 20.5	2 06.9	13 44.3	19 48.4	23 24.4	16 52.2	24 53.8
22 Tu	22 06 03	3 00 05	7♌18 46	13 45 07	3 01.2	6 34.1	17 24.8	17 56.7	2 30.5	13 40.1	19 54.3	23 27.4	16 51.1	24 53.4
23 W	22 09 59	4 00 27	20 08 40	26 29 21	2 47.9	7 41.3	17 00.3	18 32.9	2 54.1	13 35.7	20 00.4	23 30.3	16 50.1	24 53.1
24 Th	22 13 56	5 00 47	2♍47 08	9♍01 58	2 33.7	8 50.5	16 38.1	19 09.2	3 17.7	13 31.1	20 06.4	23 33.2	16 49.1	24 52.8
25 F	22 17 52	6 01 05	15 13 51	21 22 50	2 19.8	10 01.7	16 18.2	19 45.5	3 41.3	13 26.3	20 12.6	23 36.1	16 48.1	24 52.5
26 Sa	22 21 49	7 01 22	27 29 00	3♎32 29	2 07.4	11 14.9	16 00.7	20 21.8	4 04.9	13 21.4	20 18.8	23 38.9	16 47.1	24 52.2
27 Su	22 25 45	8 01 37	9♎33 29	15 32 17	1 57.4	12 29.7	15 45.7	20 58.2	4 28.5	13 16.4	20 25.1	23 41.7	16 46.2	24 51.9
28 M	22 29 42	9 01 50	21 29 12	27 24 36	1 50.3	13 46.3	15 33.1	21 34.6	4 52.1	13 11.2	20 31.4	23 44.4	16 45.2	24 51.7

Astro Data

	Dy Hr Mn
☽ 0S	3 9:00
☽ 0N	17 4:32
☿ R	17 10:52
♀ R	22 17:24
♄□♆	24 13:15
♃ R	29 18:10
☽ 0S	30 16:25
☿ D	7 6:52
☽ 0N	13 10:14
☽ 0S	26 23:25

Planet Ingress

	Dy Hr Mn
☿ ♒	3 21:27
♀ ♓	15 20:56
☉ ♒	20 21:59
♂ ♉	23 1:54
♀ ♒R	29 9:12
☿ ♑R	31 2:44
☿ ♒	15 13:10
⚳ ♓	16 2:56
☉ ♓	19 12:28

Last Aspect / ☽ Ingress (January)

Last Aspect Dy Hr Mn		☽ Ingress Dy Hr Mn
2 8:02 ☿ △	♎	2 12:37
4 16:15 ♇ △	♏	5 1:19
7 6:33 ♀ □	♐	7 13:20
9 18:32 ♀ ✶	♑	9 22:40
11 17:36 ♂ □	♒	12 4:53
14 8:05 ♀ ☌	♓	14 8:50
16 3:52 ♇ □	♈	16 11:46
18 10:20 ☉ □	♉	18 14:38
20 17:39 ☉ △	♊	20 17:58
22 21:52 ♂ ✶	♋	22 22:02
24 12:47 ♅ ☍	♌	25 3:24
27 1:44 ♇ ✶	♍	27 10:52
29 11:27 ♇ □	♎	29 21:05

Last Aspect / ☽ Ingress (February)

Last Aspect Dy Hr Mn		☽ Ingress Dy Hr Mn
1 7:32 ♀ △	♏	1 9:33
3 18:00 ♀ □	♐	3 22:05
6 1:58 ♀ ✶	♑	6 8:03
8 8:15 ☿ ☌	♒	8 14:14
10 8:51 ♇ △	♓	10 17:13
12 15:32 ☿ ✶	♈	12 18:41
14 19:25 ☿ □	♉	14 20:19
16 18:32 ☉ □	♊	16 23:19
19 3:22 ☉ △	♋	19 4:03
20 22:19 ♅ ☍	♌	21 10:28
23 8:57 ♇ ✶	♍	23 18:41
25 18:51 ♇ □	♎	26 4:58
28 6:50 ♇ △	♏	28 17:16

☽ Phases & Eclipses

Dy Hr Mn		
3 13:27	☾	12♎19
11 11:51	●	20♑24
18 10:20	☽	27♈28
25 11:50	○	4♌39
2 11:27	☾	12♏46
10 1:13	●	20♒26
16 18:32	☽	27♉14
24 3:36	○	4♍40

Astro Data

1 January 1910
Julian Day # 3653
SVP 6♓31'14"
GC 25♐34.9 ⚴ 26♑21.9
Eris 24♓51.3 ⚵ 3♊00.6R
⚷ 24♒57.0 ⚶ 4♒37.1
☽ Mean ☊ 5♊44.3

1 February 1910
Julian Day # 3684
SVP 6♓31'09"
GC 25♐35.0 ⚴ 7♒22.7
Eris 25♓04.5 ⚵ 5♊56.3
⚷ 26♒51.4 ⚶ 20♒22.8
☽ Mean ☊ 4♊05.8

March 1910 LONGITUDE

Day	Sid.Time	☉	0 hr ☽	Noon ☽	True ☊	☿	♀	♂	⚳	♃	♄	♅	♆	♇
1 Tu	22 33 38	10♓02 02	3♏18 58	9♏12 46	1♊46.0	15♒04.5	15♒23.0	22♉11.0	5♓15.6	13♎05.8	20♈37.7	23♑47.2	16♋44.3	24♊51.5
2 W	22 37 35	11 02 12	15 06 35	21 01 00	1D44.1	16 24.2	15R15.4	22 47.5	5 39.2	13R00.3	20 44.2	23 49.9	16R43.5	24R51.3
3 Th	22 41 32	12 02 21	26 56 38	2♐54 11	1R43.8	17 45.3	15 10.2	23 24.0	6 02.7	12 54.7	20 50.6	23 52.5	16 42.7	24 51.2
4 F	22 45 28	13 02 29	8♐54 19	14 57 44	1 43.8	19 08.0	15D07.6	24 00.5	6 26.3	12 48.9	20 57.2	23 55.2	16 41.9	24 51.0
5 Sa	22 49 25	14 02 34	21 05 08	27 17 11	1 43.2	20 31.9	15 07.4	24 37.0	6 49.8	12 43.0	21 03.8	23 57.8	16 41.1	24 50.9
6 Su	22 53 21	15 02 39	3♑34 32	9♑57 46	1 40.8	21 57.3	15 09.6	25 13.6	7 13.4	12 37.0	21 10.4	24 00.3	16 40.4	24 50.8
7 M	22 57 18	16 02 41	16 27 22	23 03 46	1 36.0	23 23.9	15 14.2	25 50.2	7 36.9	12 30.8	21 17.1	24 02.8	16 39.7	24 50.8
8 Tu	23 01 14	17 02 42	29 47 13	6♒37 51	1 28.6	24 51.8	15 21.1	26 26.9	8 00.4	12 24.5	21 23.8	24 05.3	16 39.0	24 50.7
9 W	23 05 11	18 02 41	13♒35 37	20 40 15	1 18.9	26 21.0	15 30.2	27 03.5	8 23.9	12 18.1	21 30.6	24 07.8	16 38.3	24D50.7
10 Th	23 09 07	19 02 39	27 51 18	5♓08 07	1 07.9	27 51.5	15 41.5	27 40.2	8 47.4	12 11.6	21 37.4	24 10.2	16 37.7	24 50.7
11 F	23 13 04	20 02 34	12♓29 52	19 55 33	0 56.8	29 23.1	15 54.9	28 16.9	9 10.8	12 05.0	21 44.2	24 12.5	16 37.1	24 50.7
12 Sa	23 17 01	21 02 28	27 24 01	4♈54 06	0 46.9	0♓56.0	16 10.4	28 53.7	9 34.3	11 58.3	21 51.1	24 14.9	16 36.6	24 50.8
13 Su	23 20 57	22 02 19	12♈24 34	19 54 15	0 39.1	2 30.1	16 27.9	29 30.4	9 57.7	11 51.4	21 58.1	24 17.2	16 36.1	24 50.8
14 M	23 24 54	23 02 09	27 22 05	4♉47 06	0 34.1	4 05.4	16 47.3	0♊07.2	10 21.1	11 44.5	22 05.0	24 19.4	16 35.6	24 50.9
15 Tu	23 28 50	24 01 56	12♉08 29	19 25 37	0D31.8	5 41.9	17 08.5	0 44.0	10 44.5	11 37.5	22 12.1	24 21.6	16 35.1	24 51.0
16 W	23 32 47	25 01 41	26 38 02	3♊45 28	0 31.3	7 19.6	17 31.6	1 20.9	11 07.8	11 30.4	22 19.1	24 23.8	16 34.7	24 51.2
17 Th	23 36 43	26 01 24	10♊47 45	17 44 53	0R31.8	8 58.5	17 56.4	1 57.7	11 31.2	11 23.2	22 26.2	24 25.9	16 34.3	24 51.3
18 F	23 40 40	27 01 05	24 36 57	1♋24 08	0 31.9	10 38.7	18 22.8	2 34.6	11 54.5	11 16.0	22 33.3	24 28.0	16 34.0	24 51.5
19 Sa	23 44 36	28 00 43	8♋06 39	14 44 46	0 30.6	12 20.1	18 50.9	3 11.5	12 17.8	11 08.7	22 40.5	24 30.1	16 33.6	24 51.7
20 Su	23 48 33	29 00 19	21 18 45	27 48 54	0 26.9	14 02.8	19 20.5	3 48.3	12 41.0	11 01.3	22 47.7	24 32.1	16 33.3	24 51.9
21 M	23 52 30	29 59 53	4♌15 27	10♌38 42	0 20.8	15 46.7	19 51.6	4 25.3	13 04.3	10 53.9	22 54.9	24 34.0	16 33.1	24 52.2
22 Tu	23 56 26	0♈59 24	16 58 50	23 16 04	0 12.3	17 31.8	20 24.2	5 02.2	13 27.5	10 46.4	23 02.1	24 35.9	16 32.9	24 52.5
23 W	0 00 23	1 58 53	29 30 35	5♍42 31	0 02.1	19 18.3	20 58.1	5 39.1	13 50.7	10 38.8	23 09.4	24 37.8	16 32.7	24 52.8
24 Th	0 04 19	2 58 20	11♍52 02	17 59 14	29♉51.1	21 06.0	21 33.4	6 16.0	14 13.8	10 31.3	23 16.7	24 39.6	16 32.5	24 53.1
25 F	0 08 16	3 57 45	24 04 15	0♎07 13	29 40.4	22 55.1	22 10.0	6 53.0	14 36.9	10 23.6	23 24.0	24 41.4	16 32.4	24 53.4
26 Sa	0 12 12	4 57 08	6♎08 15	12 07 31	29 30.8	24 45.5	22 47.8	7 30.0	15 00.0	10 16.0	23 31.4	24 43.2	16 32.3	24 53.8
27 Su	0 16 09	5 56 28	18 05 12	24 01 31	29 23.1	26 37.2	23 26.8	8 06.9	15 23.1	10 08.3	23 38.8	24 44.8	16 32.2	24 54.1
28 M	0 20 05	6 55 47	29 56 41	5♏51 02	29 17.8	28 30.2	24 07.0	8 43.9	15 46.1	10 00.6	23 46.2	24 46.5	16D32.2	24 54.5
29 Tu	0 24 02	7 55 04	11♏44 52	17 38 34	29D14.9	0♈24.6	24 48.2	9 20.9	16 09.1	9 52.9	23 53.6	24 48.1	16 32.2	24 55.0
30 W	0 27 59	8 54 19	23 32 33	29 27 18	29 14.1	2 20.2	25 30.5	9 57.9	16 32.1	9 45.2	24 01.0	24 49.6	16 32.3	24 55.4
31 Th	0 31 55	9 53 33	5♐23 20	11♐21 09	29 14.7	4 17.2	26 13.8	10 34.9	16 55.1	9 37.4	24 08.5	24 51.2	16 32.4	24 55.9

April 1910 LONGITUDE

Day	Sid.Time	☉	0 hr ☽	Noon ☽	True ☊	☿	♀	♂	⚳	♃	♄	♅	♆	♇
1 F	0 35 52	10♈52 44	17♐21 23	23♐24 36	29♉16.0	6♈15.4	26♒58.1	11♊12.0	17♓18.0	9♎29.7	24♈16.0	24♑52.6	16♋32.5	24♊56.4
2 Sa	0 39 48	11 51 54	29 31 27	5♑42 33	29R17.1	8 14.9	27 43.3	11 49.0	17 40.8	9R22.0	24 23.5	24 54.0	16 32.6	24 56.9
3 Su	0 43 45	12 51 02	11♑58 31	18 19 57	29 17.1	10 15.5	28 29.5	12 26.1	18 03.7	9 14.2	24 31.0	24 55.4	16 32.8	24 57.4
4 M	0 47 41	13 50 08	24 47 25	1♒21 23	29 15.5	12 17.3	29 16.4	13 03.1	18 26.5	9 06.5	24 38.6	24 56.7	16 33.0	24 58.0
5 Tu	0 51 38	14 49 13	8♒02 16	14 50 20	29 12.1	14 20.1	0♓04.2	13 40.2	18 49.2	8 58.9	24 46.1	24 58.0	16 33.3	24 58.6
6 W	0 55 34	15 48 15	21 45 43	28 48 23	29 07.0	16 23.7	0 52.8	14 17.3	19 11.9	8 51.2	24 53.7	24 59.2	16 33.6	24 59.2
7 Th	0 59 31	16 47 16	5♓58 06	13♓14 27	29 00.8	18 28.2	1 42.2	14 54.4	19 34.6	8 43.6	25 01.2	25 00.4	16 33.9	24 59.8
8 F	1 03 28	17 46 15	20 36 47	28 04 17	28 54.4	20 33.2	2 32.3	15 31.5	19 57.2	8 36.0	25 08.8	25 01.5	16 34.2	25 00.4
9 Sa	1 07 24	18 45 12	5♈35 53	13♈10 28	28 48.5	22 38.7	3 23.0	16 08.6	20 19.8	8 28.4	25 16.4	25 02.6	16 34.6	25 01.1
10 Su	1 11 21	19 44 07	20 46 46	28 23 28	28 44.0	24 44.3	4 14.5	16 45.7	20 42.4	8 21.0	25 24.0	25 03.6	16 35.0	25 01.7
11 M	1 15 17	20 43 00	5♉59 17	13♉32 59	28 41.4	26 49.9	5 06.6	17 22.8	21 04.9	8 13.5	25 31.6	25 04.6	16 35.5	25 02.4
12 Tu	1 19 14	21 41 51	21 03 29	28 29 50	28D40.5	28 55.2	5 59.3	18 00.0	21 27.3	8 06.1	25 39.2	25 05.5	16 35.9	25 03.2
13 W	1 23 10	22 40 40	5♊51 14	13♊07 05	28 41.2	0♉59.8	6 52.6	18 37.1	21 49.7	7 58.8	25 46.9	25 06.4	16 36.5	25 03.9
14 Th	1 27 07	23 39 27	20 16 59	27 20 42	28 42.5	3 03.5	7 46.4	19 14.3	22 12.1	7 51.6	25 54.5	25 07.2	16 37.0	25 04.6
15 F	1 31 03	24 38 11	4♋18 08	11♋09 21	28 43.9	5 05.9	8 40.8	19 51.4	22 34.4	7 44.4	26 02.1	25 08.0	16 37.6	25 05.4
16 Sa	1 35 00	25 36 53	17 54 30	24 33 50	28R44.6	7 06.7	9 35.8	20 28.6	22 56.6	7 37.3	26 09.8	25 08.7	16 38.2	25 06.2
17 Su	1 38 57	26 35 33	1♌07 40	7♌36 22	28 44.0	9 05.5	10 31.2	21 05.8	23 18.8	7 30.3	26 17.4	25 09.4	16 38.9	25 07.0
18 M	1 42 53	27 34 10	14 00 19	20 19 55	28 42.0	11 02.0	11 27.2	21 42.9	23 41.0	7 23.4	26 25.0	25 10.0	16 39.5	25 07.9
19 Tu	1 46 50	28 32 46	26 35 34	2♍47 40	28 38.6	12 55.9	12 23.6	22 20.1	24 03.1	7 16.6	26 32.6	25 10.6	16 40.2	25 08.7
20 W	1 50 46	29 31 19	8♍56 37	15 02 45	28 34.3	14 46.9	13 20.5	22 57.3	24 25.1	7 09.9	26 40.3	25 11.1	16 41.0	25 09.6
21 Th	1 54 43	0♉29 50	21 06 25	27 07 58	28 29.4	16 34.7	14 17.8	23 34.4	24 47.1	7 03.2	26 47.9	25 11.6	16 41.8	25 10.5
22 F	1 58 39	1 28 19	3♎07 39	9♎05 48	28 24.7	18 19.1	15 15.5	24 11.6	25 09.0	6 56.7	26 55.5	25 12.0	16 42.6	25 11.4
23 Sa	2 02 36	2 26 46	15 02 39	20 58 27	28 20.5	19 59.8	16 13.7	24 48.8	25 30.9	6 50.3	27 03.1	25 12.4	16 43.4	25 12.3
24 Su	2 06 32	3 25 11	26 53 29	2♏47 59	28 17.3	21 36.7	17 12.3	25 26.0	25 52.7	6 44.0	27 10.7	25 12.7	16 44.3	25 13.2
25 M	2 10 29	4 23 34	8♏42 12	14 36 23	28 15.3	23 09.5	18 11.3	26 03.2	26 14.4	6 37.8	27 18.3	25 13.0	16 45.2	25 14.2
26 Tu	2 14 25	5 21 55	20 30 50	26 25 49	28D14.5	24 38.2	19 10.6	26 40.4	26 36.1	6 31.8	27 25.9	25 13.2	16 46.1	25 15.1
27 W	2 18 22	6 20 15	2♐21 40	8♐18 43	28 14.9	26 02.6	20 10.3	27 17.5	26 57.7	6 25.9	27 33.5	25 13.4	16 47.1	25 16.1
28 Th	2 22 19	7 18 33	14 17 19	20 17 52	28 16.0	27 22.6	21 10.4	27 54.7	27 19.3	6 20.1	27 41.0	25 13.5	16 48.0	25 17.1
29 F	2 26 15	8 16 50	26 20 48	2♑26 31	28 17.5	28 38.1	22 10.8	28 31.9	27 40.8	6 14.4	27 48.6	25R13.6	16 49.1	25 18.1
30 Sa	2 30 12	9 15 05	8♑35 30	14 48 14	28 19.0	29 48.9	23 11.5	29 09.1	28 02.2	6 08.9	27 56.1	25 13.6	16 50.1	25 19.2

Astro Data Dy Hr Mn	Planet Ingress Dy Hr Mn	Last Aspect Dy Hr Mn	☽ Ingress Dy Hr Mn	Last Aspect Dy Hr Mn	☽ Ingress Dy Hr Mn	☽ Phases & Eclipses Dy Hr Mn
♀ D 5 1:55	☿ ♓ 11 21:34	2 17:44 ♅ ✶	♐ 3 6:10	1 19:27 ♀ ✶	♑ 2 0:56	4 7:52 ☾ 12♐52
♇ D 10 1:17	♂ ♊ 14 7:17	5 7:18 ♇ ☍	♑ 5 17:12	4 0:16 ♅ ☌	♒ 4 9:32	11 12:12 ● 20♓03
☽ 0N 12 18:49	☉ ♈ 21 12:03	7 17:13 ♂ △	♒ 8 0:23	6 5:31 ♇ △	♓ 6 14:01	18 3:37 ☽ 26♊40
☉0N 21 12:03	☊ ♉R 23 16:42	9 23:09 ♂ □	♓ 10 3:33	8 7:06 ♅ ✶	♈ 8 15:05	25 20:21 ○ 4♎18
☽ 0S 26 5:56	☿ ♈ 29 6:52	12 1:59 ♂ ✶	♈ 12 4:10	10 7:15 ♄ ☌	♉ 10 14:32	
♆ D 28 16:14		13 19:56 ♇ ✶	♉ 14 4:15	12 6:29 ♅ △	♊ 12 14:26	3 0:47 ☾ 12♑23
☿0N 31 6:11	♀ ♓ 5 9:53	15 20:13 ☉ ✶	♊ 16 5:39	14 9:31 ♄ ✶	♋ 14 16:33	9 21:25 ● 19♈08
	☿ ♉ 13 0:28	18 3:37 ☉ □	♋ 18 9:31	16 14:56 ♄ □	♌ 16 21:56	16 14:04 ☽ 25♋42
♅⚻♇ 6 9:48	☉ ♉ 20 23:46	20 14:24 ☉ △	♌ 20 16:03	19 3:04 ☉ △	♍ 19 6:35	24 13:22 ○ 3♏29
♄✶♇ 7 6:57	☿ ♊ 30 15:54	22 15:05 ♇ ✶	♍ 23 0:57	21 8:08 ♅ △	♎ 21 17:44	
♄□♅ 7 8:49		25 1:37 ♇ □	♎ 25 11:46	24 0:28 ♄ ☍	♏ 24 6:19	
☽ 0N 9 5:37		27 13:47 ♇ △	♏ 28 0:07	26 9:33 ♅ ✶	♐ 26 19:14	
☽ 0S 22 12:10		30 3:29 ♀ □	♐ 30 13:06	29 3:54 ♂ ☍	♑ 29 7:12	
♅⚻♇ 23 15:59						
♅ R 30 10:51						

Astro Data

1 March 1910
Julian Day # 3712
SVP 6♓31'05"
GC 25♐35.1 ⚵ 17♒00.4
Eris 25♓23.7 ✱ 14♊06.0
⚷ 28♒46.2 ⚶ 4♓29.8
☽ Mean ☊ 2♊36.9

1 April 1910
Julian Day # 3743
SVP 6♓31'02"
GC 25♐35.2 ⚵ 26♒47.1
Eris 25♓47.8 ✱ 26♊22.7
⚷ 0♓43.0 ⚶ 19♓42.5
☽ Mean ☊ 0♊58.3

LONGITUDE — May 1910

Day	Sid.Time	☉	0 hr ☽	Noon ☽	True ☊	☿	♀	♂	⚳	♃	♄	♅	♆	♇
1 Su	2 34 08	10♉13 18	21♑05 11	27♑26 50	28♉20.1	0♊55.1	24♓12.6	29♊46.3	28♓23.5	6♎03.5	28♈03.7	25♑13.5	16♋51.2	25♊20.2
2 M	2 38 05	11 11 30	3♒53 37	10♒26 00	28R 20.5	1 56.6	25 13.9	0♋23.5	28 44.8	5R 58.2	28 11.2	25R 13.5	16 52.3	25 21.3
3 Tu	2 42 01	12 09 41	17 04 20	23 48 55	28 20.2	2 53.2	26 15.6	1 00.7	29 06.1	5 53.1	28 18.7	25 13.3	16 53.5	25 22.4
4 W	2 45 58	13 07 50	0♓39 59	7♓37 37	28 19.2	3 44.9	27 17.6	1 38.0	29 27.2	5 48.1	28 26.2	25 13.2	16 54.6	25 23.5
5 Th	2 49 55	14 05 57	14 41 48	21 52 19	28 17.7	4 31.7	28 19.8	2 15.2	29 48.3	5 43.3	28 33.6	25 12.9	16 55.8	25 24.6
6 F	2 53 51	15 04 03	29 08 49	6♈30 46	28 16.0	5 13.4	29 22.3	2 52.4	0♈09.3	5 38.6	28 41.1	25 12.7	16 57.0	25 25.7
7 Sa	2 57 48	16 02 08	13♈57 28	21 28 01	28 14.5	5 50.1	0♈25.0	3 29.6	0 30.2	5 34.1	28 48.5	25 12.3	16 58.3	25 26.8
8 Su	3 01 44	17 00 11	29 01 26	6♉36 34	28 13.5	6 21.8	1 28.0	4 06.9	0 51.1	5 29.8	28 55.9	25 11.9	16 59.6	25 28.0
9 M	3 05 41	17 58 13	14♉12 15	21 47 16	28D 13.0	6 48.2	2 31.2	4 44.1	1 11.9	5 25.6	29 03.3	25 11.5	17 00.9	25 29.1
10 Tu	3 09 37	18 56 13	29 20 25	6♊50 36	28 13.0	7 09.6	3 34.7	5 21.4	1 32.6	5 21.5	29 10.6	25 11.0	17 02.2	25 30.3
11 W	3 13 34	19 54 12	14♊16 48	21 38 09	28 13.5	7 25.8	4 38.3	5 58.6	1 53.2	5 17.7	29 17.9	25 10.5	17 03.6	25 31.5
12 Th	3 17 30	20 52 09	28 53 57	6♋03 40	28 14.1	7 36.9	5 42.2	6 35.9	2 13.7	5 14.0	29 25.3	25 10.0	17 04.9	25 32.7
13 F	3 21 27	21 50 04	13♋06 55	20 03 32	28 14.7	7R 43.0	6 46.3	7 13.1	2 34.2	5 10.5	29 32.5	25 09.3	17 06.4	25 33.9
14 Sa	3 25 24	22 47 57	26 53 27	3♌36 46	28 15.2	7 44.1	7 50.6	7 50.4	2 54.5	5 07.1	29 39.8	25 08.7	17 07.8	25 35.1
15 Su	3 29 20	23 45 48	10♌13 41	16 44 31	28R 15.4	7 40.4	8 55.1	8 27.6	3 14.8	5 03.9	29 47.0	25 08.0	17 09.3	25 36.4
16 M	3 33 17	24 43 38	23 09 38	29 29 29	28 15.5	7 32.1	9 59.8	9 04.9	3 35.0	5 00.9	29 54.2	25 07.2	17 10.8	25 37.6
17 Tu	3 37 13	25 41 26	5♍44 32	11♍55 18	28 15.3	7 19.4	11 04.6	9 42.1	3 55.0	4 58.1	0♉01.3	25 06.4	17 12.3	25 38.9
18 W	3 41 10	26 39 12	18 02 16	24 05 58	28 15.2	7 02.5	12 09.6	10 19.4	4 15.0	4 55.4	0 08.5	25 05.5	17 13.8	25 40.1
19 Th	3 45 06	27 36 57	0♎06 54	6♎05 35	28D 15.0	6 41.8	13 14.9	10 56.7	4 34.9	4 52.9	0 15.5	25 04.6	17 15.4	25 41.4
20 F	3 49 03	28 34 40	12 02 27	17 57 59	28 15.0	6 17.6	14 20.2	11 33.9	4 54.7	4 50.6	0 22.6	25 03.7	17 16.9	25 42.7
21 Sa	3 52 59	29 32 21	23 52 36	29 46 42	28 15.1	5 50.5	15 25.8	12 11.2	5 14.4	4 48.5	0 29.6	25 02.7	17 18.5	25 44.0
22 Su	3 56 56	0♊30 01	5♏40 40	11♏34 50	28 15.3	5 20.9	16 31.5	12 48.4	5 34.1	4 46.5	0 36.6	25 01.7	17 20.2	25 45.3
23 M	4 00 53	1 27 40	17 29 32	23 25 05	28R 15.4	4 49.3	17 37.4	13 25.7	5 53.6	4 44.7	0 43.6	25 00.6	17 21.8	25 46.6
24 Tu	4 04 49	2 25 18	29 21 45	5♐19 48	28 15.4	4 16.3	18 43.4	14 03.0	6 13.0	4 43.2	0 50.5	24 59.5	17 23.5	25 47.9
25 W	4 08 46	3 22 54	11♐19 31	17 21 08	28 15.1	3 42.5	19 49.6	14 40.2	6 32.3	4 41.7	0 57.3	24 58.3	17 25.2	25 49.3
26 Th	4 12 42	4 20 29	23 24 54	29 31 03	28 14.6	3 08.4	20 56.0	15 17.5	6 51.5	4 40.5	1 04.2	24 57.1	17 26.9	25 50.6
27 F	4 16 39	5 18 03	5♑39 51	11♑51 31	28 13.8	2 34.6	22 02.5	15 54.8	7 10.6	4 39.4	1 11.0	24 55.9	17 28.6	25 51.9
28 Sa	4 20 35	6 15 36	18 06 19	24 24 31	28 12.8	2 01.8	23 09.1	16 32.0	7 29.6	4 38.6	1 17.7	24 54.6	17 30.4	25 53.3
29 Su	4 24 32	7 13 09	0♒46 21	7♒12 06	28 11.8	1 30.5	24 15.9	17 09.3	7 48.5	4 37.9	1 24.4	24 53.2	17 32.2	25 54.7
30 M	4 28 28	8 10 40	13 42 00	20 16 19	28 11.0	1 01.2	25 22.8	17 46.6	8 07.3	4 37.3	1 31.1	24 51.9	17 34.0	25 56.0
31 Tu	4 32 25	9 08 10	26 55 15	3♓39 00	28D 10.5	0 34.3	26 29.8	18 23.9	8 25.9	4 37.0	1 37.7	24 50.5	17 35.8	25 57.4

LONGITUDE — June 1910

Day	Sid.Time	☉	0 hr ☽	Noon ☽	True ☊	☿	♀	♂	⚳	♃	♄	♅	♆	♇
1 W	4 36 22	10♊05 40	10♓27 43	17♓21 31	28♉10.5	0♊10.4	27♈37.0	19♋01.2	8♈44.5	4♎36.8	1♉44.2	24♑49.0	17♋37.6	25♊58.8
2 Th	4 40 18	11 03 09	24 20 24	1♈24 18	28 11.1	29♉49.8	28 44.3	19 38.4	9 02.9	4D 36.9	1 50.8	24R 47.5	17 39.5	26 00.2
3 F	4 44 15	12 00 37	8♈33 05	15 46 26	28 12.0	29R 32.8	29 51.7	20 15.7	9 21.2	4 37.1	1 57.2	24 46.0	17 41.4	26 01.5
4 Sa	4 48 11	12 58 05	23 04 00	0♉25 14	28 13.0	29 19.7	0♉59.2	20 53.1	9 39.4	4 37.5	2 03.7	24 44.4	17 43.2	26 02.9
5 Su	4 52 08	13 55 32	7♉49 29	15 15 59	28R 13.9	29 10.8	2 06.8	21 30.4	9 57.5	4 38.0	2 10.0	24 42.8	17 45.1	26 04.3
6 M	4 56 04	14 52 58	22 43 54	0♊12 14	28 14.1	29D 06.0	3 14.6	22 07.7	10 15.4	4 38.8	2 16.4	24 41.2	17 47.1	26 05.8
7 Tu	5 00 01	15 50 23	7♊40 02	15 06 17	28 13.6	29 05.7	4 22.5	22 45.0	10 33.2	4 39.7	2 22.6	24 39.5	17 49.0	26 07.2
8 W	5 03 57	16 47 48	22 29 58	29 50 11	28 12.2	29 09.8	5 30.4	23 22.3	10 50.9	4 40.8	2 28.8	24 37.8	17 51.0	26 08.6
9 Th	5 07 54	17 45 12	7♋06 04	14♋16 53	28 09.9	29 18.5	6 38.5	23 59.7	11 08.5	4 42.1	2 35.0	24 36.1	17 52.9	26 10.0
10 F	5 11 51	18 42 35	21 22 04	28 21 10	28 07.2	29 31.6	7 46.6	24 37.0	11 25.9	4 43.5	2 41.1	24 34.3	17 54.9	26 11.4
11 Sa	5 15 47	19 39 56	5♌13 53	12♌00 05	28 04.4	29 49.3	8 54.9	25 14.4	11 43.2	4 45.2	2 47.2	24 32.5	17 56.9	26 12.8
12 Su	5 19 44	20 37 17	18 39 48	25 13 10	28 02.0	0♊11.4	10 03.2	25 51.7	12 00.3	4 47.0	2 53.1	24 30.7	17 59.0	26 14.3
13 M	5 23 40	21 34 37	1♍40 26	8♍01 58	28 00.3	0 38.0	11 11.7	26 29.1	12 17.3	4 49.0	2 59.1	24 28.8	18 01.0	26 15.7
14 Tu	5 27 37	22 31 56	14 18 12	20 29 38	27D 59.6	1 08.9	12 20.2	27 06.4	12 34.1	4 51.1	3 04.9	24 26.9	18 03.0	26 17.1
15 W	5 31 33	23 29 14	26 36 50	2♎40 20	27 59.9	1 44.1	13 28.8	27 43.8	12 50.8	4 53.5	3 10.7	24 25.0	18 05.1	26 18.6
16 Th	5 35 30	24 26 31	8♎40 46	14 38 43	28 01.1	2 23.6	14 37.5	28 21.1	13 07.3	4 56.0	3 16.5	24 23.0	18 07.1	26 20.0
17 F	5 39 26	25 23 47	20 34 48	26 29 36	28 02.7	3 07.2	15 46.3	28 58.5	13 23.7	4 58.7	3 22.2	24 21.0	18 09.2	26 21.4
18 Sa	5 43 23	26 21 03	2♏23 41	8♏17 36	28 04.4	3 55.0	16 55.1	29 35.9	13 40.0	5 01.5	3 27.8	24 19.0	18 11.3	26 22.8
19 Su	5 47 20	27 18 18	14 11 52	20 06 57	28R 05.6	4 46.7	18 04.1	0♌13.2	13 56.1	5 04.5	3 33.3	24 17.0	18 13.4	26 24.3
20 M	5 51 16	28 15 32	26 03 18	2♐01 19	28 05.8	5 42.4	19 13.1	0 50.6	14 12.0	5 07.7	3 38.8	24 14.9	18 15.5	26 25.7
21 Tu	5 55 13	29 12 46	8♐01 23	14 03 46	28 04.7	6 41.9	20 22.2	1 28.0	14 27.8	5 11.1	3 44.3	24 12.8	18 17.6	26 27.1
22 W	5 59 09	0♋09 59	20 08 47	26 16 38	28 02.0	7 45.3	21 31.4	2 05.4	14 43.4	5 14.6	3 49.6	24 10.7	18 19.8	26 28.6
23 Th	6 03 06	1 07 12	2♑27 30	8♑41 32	27 58.0	8 52.5	22 40.7	2 42.8	14 58.8	5 18.3	3 54.9	24 08.6	18 21.9	26 30.0
24 F	6 07 02	2 04 24	14 58 49	21 19 26	27 52.8	10 03.4	23 50.1	3 20.2	15 14.1	5 22.1	4 00.1	24 06.4	18 24.1	26 31.4
25 Sa	6 10 59	3 01 37	27 43 26	4♒10 50	27 47.1	11 17.9	24 59.5	3 57.6	15 29.2	5 26.1	4 05.3	24 04.2	18 26.2	26 32.9
26 Su	6 14 56	3 58 49	10♒41 37	17 15 47	27 41.5	12 36.1	26 09.1	4 35.0	15 44.1	5 30.2	4 10.3	24 02.0	18 28.4	26 34.3
27 M	6 18 52	4 56 01	23 53 18	0♓34 10	27 36.7	13 57.9	27 18.7	5 12.4	15 58.9	5 34.6	4 15.3	23 59.8	18 30.6	26 35.7
28 Tu	6 22 49	5 53 13	7♓18 21	14 05 49	27 33.2	15 23.2	28 28.3	5 49.8	16 13.4	5 39.0	4 20.3	23 57.6	18 32.7	26 37.1
29 W	6 26 45	6 50 25	20 56 33	27 50 32	27D 31.3	16 52.0	29 38.1	6 27.2	16 27.8	5 43.7	4 25.1	23 55.3	18 34.9	26 38.5
30 Th	6 30 42	7 47 37	4♈47 41	11♈47 58	27 31.0	18 24.2	0♊47.9	7 04.7	16 42.0	5 48.4	4 29.9	23 53.0	18 37.1	26 39.9

Astro Data

	Dy Hr Mn
☽ 0N	6 16:25
♀ 0N	9 23:38
☿ R	14 5:29
☽ 0S	19 18:24
♃ D	1 21:14
☽ 0N	3 1:10
☿ D	7 1:49
☽ 0S	16 1:00
☽ 0N	30 7:14

Planet Ingress

	Dy Hr Mn
♂ ♋	1 20:49
⚳ ♈	6 1:21
♀ ♈	7 2:27
♄ ♉	17 7:30
☉ ♊	21 23:30
☿ ♉R	1 23:39
♀ ♉	3 14:58
☿ ♊	12 0:14
♂ ♌	19 3:30
☉ ♋	22 7:49
♀ ♊	29 19:32

Last Aspect / ☽ Ingress (May)

Last Aspect Dy Hr Mn		☽ Ingress	Dy Hr Mn
1 13:10	♄ □	♒	1 16:46
3 19:58	♄ ⚹	♓	3 22:50
5 23:29	♀ ☌	♈	6 1:24
7 23:45	♄ ☌	♉	8 1:33
9 17:24	♅ △	♊	10 1:03
12 0:46	♄ ⚹	♋	12 1:50
14 4:52	♄ □	♌	14 5:32
16 12:48	♄ △	♍	16 12:58
18 17:32	☉ △	♎	18 23:46
21 3:45	♇ △	♏	21 12:27
23 15:13	♅ ⚹	♐	24 1:17
26 4:46	♇ ☍	♑	26 12:57
28 12:57	♅ ☌	♒	28 22:33
30 22:15	♇ △	♓	31 5:31

Last Aspect / ☽ Ingress (June)

Last Aspect Dy Hr Mn		☽ Ingress	Dy Hr Mn
2 9:24	☿ ⚹	♈	2 9:37
4 4:52	♇ ⚹	♉	4 11:19
6 10:14	☿ ☌	♊	6 11:40
8 5:56	♇ ☌	♋	8 12:16
10 14:05	☿ ⚹	♌	10 14:51
12 13:53	♇ ⚹	♍	12 20:52
15 1:40	♂ ⚹	♎	15 6:42
17 17:19	♂ □	♏	17 19:08
19 20:24	♅ ⚹	♐	20 7:56
22 12:23	♇ ☍	♑	22 19:14
24 17:13	♅ ☌	♒	25 4:15
27 5:36	♀ □	♓	27 10:59
29 15:23	♀ ⚹	♈	29 15:44

☽ Phases & Eclipses

Dy Hr Mn		
2 13:29	☾	11♒15
9 5:33	●	17♉43
9 5:42:03	●	T 04'15"
16 2:13	☽	24♌20
24 5:39	○	2♐10
24 5:34	○	T 1.095
31 22:24	☾	9♓33
7 13:16	●	15♊53
14 16:19	☽	22♍42
22 20:12	○	0♑30
30 4:39	☾	7♈30

Astro Data

1 May 1910
Julian Day # 3773
SVP 6♓30'58"
GC 25♐35.2 ⚴ 4♓44.0
Eris 26♓08.5 ⚵ 9♋44.4
⚷ 2♓05.4 ⚶ 3♈43.6
☽ Mean ☊ 29♉23.0

1 June 1910
Julian Day # 3804
SVP 6♓30'53"
GC 25♐35.3 ⚴ 10♓24.9
Eris 26♓22.0 ⚵ 24♋05.1
⚷ 2♓42.5 ⚶ 17♈06.8
☽ Mean ☊ 27♉44.5

July 1910 LONGITUDE

Day	Sid.Time	☉	0 hr ☽	Noon ☽	True ☊	☿	♀	♂	⚳	♃	♄	♅	♆	♇
1 F	6 34 38	8♋44 50	18♈51 17	25♈57 29	27♉31.9	19♊59.9	1♊57.8	7♌42.1	16♈56.0	5♎53.4	4♉34.6	23♑50.7	18♋39.3	26♊41.4
2 Sa	6 38 35	9 42 03	3♉06 22	10♉17 42	27 33.1	21 38.9	3 07.8	8 19.6	17 09.8	5 58.5	4 39.3	23R 48.4	18 41.5	26 42.8
3 Su	6 42 31	10 39 16	17 31 08	24 46 16	27R 33.9	23 21.2	4 17.9	8 57.1	17 23.5	6 03.7	4 43.8	23 46.1	18 43.7	26 44.2
4 M	6 46 28	11 36 29	2♊02 34	9♊19 28	27 33.4	25 06.6	5 28.0	9 34.5	17 36.9	6 09.1	4 48.3	23 43.8	18 46.0	26 45.6
5 Tu	6 50 25	12 33 42	16 36 18	23 52 22	27 31.0	26 55.2	6 38.2	10 12.0	17 50.1	6 14.6	4 52.7	23 41.4	18 48.2	26 46.9
6 W	6 54 21	13 30 56	1♋06 54	8♋19 08	27 26.6	28 46.7	7 48.4	10 49.5	18 03.1	6 20.3	4 57.0	23 39.1	18 50.4	26 48.3
7 Th	6 58 18	14 28 10	15 28 18	22 33 43	27 20.3	0♋40.9	8 58.8	11 27.1	18 15.9	6 26.1	5 01.2	23 36.7	18 52.6	26 49.7
8 F	7 02 14	15 25 23	29 34 43	6♌30 47	27 12.7	2 37.8	10 09.1	12 04.6	18 28.5	6 32.1	5 05.4	23 34.4	18 54.9	26 51.1
9 Sa	7 06 11	16 22 37	13♌21 29	20 06 31	27 04.8	4 37.1	11 19.6	12 42.1	18 40.9	6 38.2	5 09.4	23 32.0	18 57.1	26 52.5
10 Su	7 10 07	17 19 51	26 45 43	3♍19 03	26 57.4	6 38.6	12 30.1	13 19.7	18 53.0	6 44.5	5 13.4	23 29.6	18 59.3	26 53.8
11 M	7 14 04	18 17 04	9♍46 37	16 08 37	26 51.4	8 41.9	13 40.6	13 57.2	19 05.0	6 50.9	5 17.3	23 27.2	19 01.5	26 55.2
12 Tu	7 18 00	19 14 18	22 25 23	28 37 19	26 47.2	10 46.9	14 51.3	14 34.8	19 16.7	6 57.4	5 21.1	23 24.8	19 03.8	26 56.5
13 W	7 21 57	20 11 31	4♎44 54	10♎48 41	26D 45.0	12 53.3	16 01.9	15 12.3	19 28.1	7 04.1	5 24.8	23 22.4	19 06.0	26 57.9
14 Th	7 25 54	21 08 45	16 49 17	22 47 18	26 44.5	15 00.6	17 12.7	15 49.9	19 39.4	7 10.9	5 28.5	23 20.0	19 08.2	26 59.2
15 F	7 29 50	22 05 59	28 43 24	4♏38 14	26 45.1	17 08.7	18 23.5	16 27.5	19 50.4	7 17.8	5 32.0	23 17.6	19 10.4	27 00.5
16 Sa	7 33 47	23 03 13	10♏32 28	16 26 46	26R 46.1	19 17.3	19 34.3	17 05.1	20 01.1	7 24.9	5 35.4	23 15.1	19 12.7	27 01.8
17 Su	7 37 43	24 00 27	22 21 44	28 18 00	26 46.5	21 25.9	20 45.3	17 42.7	20 11.6	7 32.1	5 38.8	23 12.7	19 14.9	27 03.1
18 M	7 41 40	24 57 41	4♐16 08	10♐16 38	26 45.5	23 34.4	21 56.2	18 20.3	20 21.9	7 39.4	5 42.1	23 10.3	19 17.1	27 04.4
19 Tu	7 45 36	25 54 56	16 20 01	22 26 39	26 42.4	25 42.6	23 07.3	18 57.9	20 31.9	7 46.8	5 45.3	23 07.9	19 19.3	27 05.7
20 W	7 49 33	26 52 10	28 36 55	4♑51 05	26 37.0	27 50.0	24 18.4	19 35.6	20 41.7	7 54.4	5 48.4	23 05.5	19 21.6	27 07.0
21 Th	7 53 29	27 49 26	11♑09 20	17 31 48	26 29.4	29 56.7	25 29.6	20 13.2	20 51.2	8 02.1	5 51.3	23 03.1	19 23.8	27 08.2
22 F	7 57 26	28 46 42	23 58 31	0♒29 26	26 19.9	2♌02.3	26 40.8	20 50.9	21 00.4	8 09.9	5 54.3	23 00.7	19 26.0	27 09.5
23 Sa	8 01 23	29 43 58	7♒04 25	13 43 18	26 09.5	4 06.8	27 52.1	21 28.5	21 09.4	8 17.8	5 57.1	22 58.3	19 28.2	27 10.7
24 Su	8 05 19	0♌41 15	20 25 49	27 11 42	25 59.2	6 10.1	29 03.4	22 06.2	21 18.1	8 25.9	5 59.8	22 56.0	19 30.4	27 12.0
25 M	8 09 16	1 38 33	4♓00 37	10♓52 14	25 50.0	8 11.9	0♋14.8	22 43.9	21 26.6	8 34.1	6 02.4	22 53.6	19 32.6	27 13.2
26 Tu	8 13 12	2 35 51	17 46 14	24 42 17	25 42.9	10 12.3	1 26.3	23 21.6	21 34.7	8 42.3	6 04.9	22 51.2	19 34.8	27 14.4
27 W	8 17 09	3 33 11	1♈40 06	8♈39 25	25 38.2	12 11.1	2 37.8	23 59.3	21 42.6	8 50.7	6 07.3	22 48.8	19 36.9	27 15.6
28 Th	8 21 05	4 30 31	15 40 01	22 41 43	25D 36.0	14 08.4	3 49.4	24 37.1	21 50.2	8 59.2	6 09.7	22 46.5	19 39.1	27 16.8
29 F	8 25 02	5 27 53	29 44 21	6♉47 47	25 35.5	16 04.1	5 01.0	25 14.8	21 57.5	9 07.9	6 11.9	22 44.2	19 41.3	27 18.0
30 Sa	8 28 58	6 25 16	13♉51 54	20 56 35	25R 35.7	17 58.2	6 12.7	25 52.6	22 04.5	9 16.6	6 14.0	22 41.8	19 43.4	27 19.1
31 Su	8 32 55	7 22 40	28 01 39	5♊06 58	25 35.5	19 50.7	7 24.5	26 30.4	22 11.3	9 25.4	6 16.0	22 39.5	19 45.6	27 20.3

August 1910 LONGITUDE

Day	Sid.Time	☉	0 hr ☽	Noon ☽	True ☊	☿	♀	♂	⚳	♃	♄	♅	♆	♇
1 M	8 36 52	8♌20 05	12♊12 17	19♊17 20	25♉33.7	21♌41.5	8♋36.3	27♌08.2	22♈17.7	9♎34.4	6♉18.0	22♑37.2	19♋47.7	27♊21.4
2 Tu	8 40 48	9 17 31	26 21 48	3♋25 18	25R 29.4	23 30.7	9 48.2	27 46.0	22 23.8	9 43.4	6 19.8	22R 35.0	19 49.9	27 22.5
3 W	8 44 45	10 14 59	10♋27 23	17 27 34	25 22.3	25 18.3	11 00.2	28 23.8	22 29.6	9 52.6	6 21.5	22 32.7	19 52.0	27 23.6
4 Th	8 48 41	11 12 27	24 25 23	1♌20 19	25 12.6	27 04.3	12 12.2	29 01.7	22 35.1	10 01.8	6 23.2	22 30.4	19 54.1	27 24.7
5 F	8 52 38	12 09 57	8♌11 52	14 59 35	25 01.3	28 48.7	13 24.2	29 39.5	22 40.3	10 11.2	6 24.7	22 28.2	19 56.2	27 25.8
6 Sa	8 56 34	13 07 27	21 43 05	28 22 03	24 49.2	0♍31.4	14 36.3	0♍17.4	22 45.1	10 20.7	6 26.1	22 26.0	19 58.3	27 26.9
7 Su	9 00 31	14 04 58	4♍56 16	11♍25 35	24 37.6	2 12.6	15 48.5	0 55.3	22 49.6	10 30.2	6 27.4	22 23.8	20 00.4	27 27.9
8 M	9 04 27	15 02 30	17 49 59	24 09 35	24 27.6	3 52.2	17 00.7	1 33.2	22 53.8	10 39.9	6 28.6	22 21.6	20 02.4	27 29.0
9 Tu	9 08 24	16 00 03	0♎24 32	6♎35 08	24 20.0	5 30.2	18 13.0	2 11.1	22 57.7	10 49.6	6 29.7	22 19.5	20 04.5	27 30.0
10 W	9 12 21	16 57 37	12 41 45	18 44 50	24 14.9	7 06.6	19 25.3	2 49.1	23 01.2	10 59.5	6 30.7	22 17.4	20 06.5	27 31.0
11 Th	9 16 17	17 55 12	24 44 54	0♏42 32	24 12.2	8 41.5	20 37.6	3 27.0	23 04.4	11 09.4	6 31.6	22 15.3	20 08.6	27 32.0
12 F	9 20 14	18 52 48	6♏38 20	12 32 57	24 11.3	10 14.8	21 50.1	4 05.0	23 07.3	11 19.4	6 32.4	22 13.2	20 10.6	27 32.9
13 Sa	9 24 10	19 50 25	18 27 03	24 21 21	24 11.3	11 46.6	23 02.5	4 43.0	23 09.8	11 29.5	6 33.1	22 11.1	20 12.6	27 33.9
14 Su	9 28 07	20 48 03	0♐16 31	6♐13 14	24 11.0	13 16.7	24 15.0	5 21.0	23 11.9	11 39.7	6 33.7	22 09.1	20 14.6	27 34.8
15 M	9 32 03	21 45 42	12 12 11	18 13 59	24 09.4	14 45.3	25 27.6	5 59.0	23 13.8	11 50.0	6 34.2	22 07.1	20 16.5	27 35.7
16 Tu	9 36 00	22 43 21	24 19 14	0♑28 28	24 05.7	16 12.3	26 40.2	6 37.1	23 15.2	12 00.4	6 34.5	22 05.1	20 18.5	27 36.7
17 W	9 39 56	23 41 02	6♑42 09	13 00 41	23 59.4	17 37.7	27 52.9	7 15.1	23 16.4	12 10.8	6 34.8	22 03.2	20 20.4	27 37.5
18 Th	9 43 53	24 38 44	19 24 22	25 53 23	23 50.6	19 01.4	29 05.6	7 53.2	23 17.1	12 21.4	6 35.0	22 01.3	20 22.3	27 38.4
19 F	9 47 50	25 36 28	2♒27 48	9♒07 35	23 39.8	20 23.5	0♌18.4	8 31.3	23R 17.5	12 32.0	6R 35.0	21 59.4	20 24.2	27 39.3
20 Sa	9 51 46	26 34 12	15 52 34	22 42 27	23 27.8	21 43.9	1 31.2	9 09.4	23 17.6	12 42.7	6 35.0	21 57.6	20 26.1	27 40.1
21 Su	9 55 43	27 31 58	29 36 49	6♓35 11	23 15.8	23 02.5	2 44.1	9 47.5	23 17.3	12 53.4	6 34.8	21 55.7	20 28.0	27 40.9
22 M	9 59 39	28 29 45	13♓36 59	20 41 34	23 05.1	24 19.4	3 57.0	10 25.6	23 16.6	13 04.3	6 34.5	21 54.0	20 29.8	27 41.7
23 Tu	10 03 36	29 27 34	27 48 18	4♈56 32	22 56.7	25 34.4	5 10.0	11 03.8	23 15.5	13 15.2	6 34.2	21 52.2	20 31.7	27 42.5
24 W	10 07 32	0♍25 25	12♈05 38	19 15 02	22 51.0	26 47.5	6 23.0	11 42.0	23 14.1	13 26.2	6 33.7	21 50.5	20 33.5	27 43.3
25 Th	10 11 29	1 23 17	26 24 16	3♉32 52	22 48.0	27 58.6	7 36.1	12 20.2	23 12.3	13 37.3	6 33.1	21 48.8	20 35.3	27 44.0
26 F	10 15 25	2 21 11	10♉40 31	17 46 57	22D 47.1	29 07.7	8 49.3	12 58.4	23 10.2	13 48.4	6 32.5	21 47.1	20 37.0	27 44.7
27 Sa	10 19 22	3 19 07	24 51 58	1♊55 26	22R 47.1	0♎14.6	10 02.5	13 36.7	23 07.7	13 59.6	6 31.7	21 45.5	20 38.8	27 45.4
28 Su	10 23 19	4 17 05	8♊57 14	15 57 19	22 46.8	1 19.3	11 15.7	14 14.9	23 04.8	14 10.9	6 30.8	21 44.0	20 40.5	27 46.1
29 M	10 27 15	5 15 05	22 55 36	29 52 03	22 44.9	2 21.6	12 29.0	14 53.2	23 01.5	14 22.2	6 29.8	21 42.4	20 42.3	27 46.8
30 Tu	10 31 12	6 13 07	6♋46 33	13♋39 01	22 40.5	3 21.5	13 42.4	15 31.5	22 57.9	14 33.6	6 28.7	21 40.9	20 43.9	27 47.4
31 W	10 35 08	7 11 10	20 29 19	27 17 16	22 33.5	4 18.7	14 55.8	16 09.9	22 53.9	14 45.1	6 27.5	21 39.5	20 45.6	27 48.0

Astro Data	Dy Hr Mn
☽0S	13 8:05
☽0N	27 11:54
☽0S	9 15:32
♄ R	19 12:50
⚳ R	20 3:11
☽0N	23 17:28
☿0S	24 15:15

Planet Ingress		Dy Hr Mn
☿	♋	7 3:28
☿	♌	21 12:38
☉	♌	23 18:43
♀	♋	25 7:01
♂	♍	6 0:58
☿	♍	6 4:37
♀	♌	19 5:56
☉	♍	24 1:27
☿	♎	27 6:42

Last Aspect Dy Hr Mn			☽ Ingress	Dy Hr Mn
1 13:14	♇	⚹	♉	1 18:48
3 10:21	♅	△	♊	3 20:38
5 17:47	☿	☌	♋	5 22:09
7 13:47	♅	☍	♌	8 0:43
10 0:14	♇	⚹	♍	10 5:54
12 8:44	♇	□	♎	12 14:41
14 20:30	♇	△	♏	15 2:35
17 2:34	☉	△	♐	17 15:25
19 21:04	♇	☍	♑	20 2:41
22 8:37	☉	☍	♒	22 11:06
24 15:36	♀	△	♓	24 16:57
26 16:23	♇	□	♈	26 21:08
28 19:49	♇	⚹	♉	29 0:27
30 20:45	♂	□	♊	31 3:20

Last Aspect Dy Hr Mn			☽ Ingress	Dy Hr Mn
2 1:56	♂	⚹	♋	2 6:11
3 20:44	♅	☍	♌	4 9:40
6 10:20	♇	⚹	♍	6 14:58
8 18:22	♇	□	♎	8 23:13
11 5:35	♇	△	♏	11 10:34
13 9:02	♀	△	♐	13 23:27
16 6:26	♇	☍	♑	16 11:05
18 18:28	♀	☍	♒	18 19:31
20 20:38	♇	△	♓	21 0:40
22 23:50	♇	□	♈	23 3:42
25 2:13	♇	⚹	♉	25 6:02
26 18:46	♅	△	♊	27 8:43
29 8:23	♇	☌	♋	29 12:14
31 2:05	♅	☍	♌	31 16:48

☽ Phases & Eclipses Dy Hr Mn	
6 21:20	● 13♋53
14 8:24	☽ 21♎00
22 8:37	○ 28♑39
29 9:34	☾ 5♉22
5 6:37	● 11♌57
13 2:01	☽ 19♏26
20 19:14	○ 26♒52
27 14:33	☾ 3♊25

Astro Data

1 July 1910
Julian Day # 3834
SVP 6♓30'48"
GC 25♐35.4 ⚴ 12♓10.1R
Eris 26♓24.6R ⚵ 8♌00.2
⚷ 2♓25.4R ⚶ 28♈28.0
☽ Mean ☊ 26♉09.2

1 August 1910
Julian Day # 3865
SVP 6♓30'43"
GC 25♐35.4 ⚴ 8♓51.0R
Eris 26♓16.0R ⚵ 22♌08.6
⚷ 1♓20.4R ⚶ 7♉34.6
☽ Mean ☊ 24♉30.8

LONGITUDE — September 1910

Day	Sid.Time	☉	0 hr ☽	Noon ☽	True ☊	☿	♀	♂	⚳	♃	♄	♅	♆	♇
1 Th	10 39 05	8♍09 15	4♌02 40	10♌45 19	22♉23.8	5♎13.1	16♌09.2	16♍48.3	22♈49.5	14♎56.6	6♉26.2	21♑38.0	20♋47.3	27♊48.7
2 F	10 43 01	9 07 23	17 24 59	24 01 27	22R 12.4	6 04.5	17 22.7	17 26.6	22R 44.8	15 08.2	6R 24.8	21R 36.7	20 48.9	27 49.2
3 Sa	10 46 58	10 05 31	0♍34 31	7♍03 58	22 00.2	6 52.8	18 36.2	18 05.0	22 39.6	15 19.9	6 23.3	21 35.3	20 50.5	27 49.8
4 Su	10 50 54	11 03 42	13 29 42	19 51 36	21 48.5	7 37.7	19 49.8	18 43.5	22 34.1	15 31.6	6 21.6	21 34.0	20 52.1	27 50.3
5 M	10 54 51	12 01 54	26 09 40	2♎23 55	21 38.2	8 19.1	21 03.5	19 21.9	22 28.3	15 43.4	6 19.9	21 32.8	20 53.6	27 50.9
6 Tu	10 58 48	13 00 08	8♎34 29	14 41 32	21 30.2	8 56.6	22 17.1	20 00.4	22 22.1	15 55.2	6 18.1	21 31.5	20 55.1	27 51.4
7 W	11 02 44	13 58 23	20 45 21	26 46 15	21 24.9	9 29.9	23 30.8	20 38.9	22 15.5	16 07.1	6 16.2	21 30.4	20 56.6	27 51.8
8 Th	11 06 41	14 56 40	2♏44 39	8♏40 59	21 22.0	9 58.9	24 44.6	21 17.4	22 08.6	16 19.0	6 14.2	21 29.2	20 58.1	27 52.3
9 F	11 10 37	15 54 59	14 35 47	20 29 37	21D 21.2	10 23.2	25 58.4	21 55.9	22 01.3	16 31.0	6 12.1	21 28.1	20 59.6	27 52.7
10 Sa	11 14 34	16 53 19	26 23 04	2♐16 47	21 21.6	10 42.4	27 12.2	22 34.5	21 53.7	16 43.1	6 09.9	21 27.1	21 01.0	27 53.1
11 Su	11 18 30	17 51 41	8♐11 26	14 07 42	21R 22.1	10 56.3	28 26.1	23 13.1	21 45.7	16 55.2	6 07.6	21 26.1	21 02.4	27 53.5
12 M	11 22 27	18 50 04	20 06 15	26 07 46	21 21.9	11R 04.6	29 40.0	23 51.7	21 37.5	17 07.3	6 05.2	21 25.2	21 03.8	27 53.9
13 Tu	11 26 23	19 48 29	2♑12 55	8♑22 20	21 20.1	11 06.8	0♍54.0	24 30.3	21 28.8	17 19.5	6 02.7	21 24.2	21 05.1	27 54.3
14 W	11 30 20	20 46 56	14 36 35	20 56 12	21 16.1	11 02.7	2 08.0	25 09.0	21 19.9	17 31.7	6 00.1	21 23.4	21 06.5	27 54.6
15 Th	11 34 17	21 45 24	27 21 37	3♒53 09	21 09.9	10 52.0	3 22.0	25 47.6	21 10.7	17 44.0	5 57.5	21 22.6	21 07.8	27 54.9
16 F	11 38 13	22 43 54	10♒31 03	17 15 23	21 01.9	10 34.5	4 36.1	26 26.3	21 01.1	17 56.3	5 54.7	21 21.8	21 09.0	27 55.2
17 Sa	11 42 10	23 42 26	24 06 04	1♓02 54	20 52.8	10 10.1	5 50.2	27 05.1	20 51.3	18 08.7	5 51.8	21 21.1	21 10.3	27 55.5
18 Su	11 46 06	24 40 59	8♓05 29	15 13 17	20 43.5	9 38.7	7 04.3	27 43.8	20 41.1	18 21.1	5 48.9	21 20.4	21 11.5	27 55.7
19 M	11 50 03	25 39 34	22 25 37	29 41 41	20 35.3	9 00.4	8 18.5	28 22.6	20 30.7	18 33.5	5 45.9	21 19.8	21 12.7	27 55.9
20 Tu	11 53 59	26 38 11	7♈00 37	14♈21 30	20 28.8	8 15.6	9 32.7	29 01.4	20 20.0	18 46.0	5 42.8	21 19.2	21 13.8	27 56.1
21 W	11 57 56	27 36 51	21 43 23	29 05 21	20 24.8	7 24.6	10 47.0	29 40.2	20 09.0	18 58.5	5 39.6	21 18.7	21 14.9	27 56.3
22 Th	12 01 52	28 35 32	6♉26 34	13♉46 17	20D 23.0	6 28.2	12 01.3	0♎19.0	19 57.8	19 11.1	5 36.3	21 18.2	21 16.0	27 56.4
23 F	12 05 49	29 34 16	21 03 49	28 18 39	20 23.0	5 27.3	13 15.6	0 57.9	19 46.4	19 23.7	5 33.0	21 17.8	21 17.1	27 56.6
24 Sa	12 09 45	0♎33 02	5♊30 22	12♊38 38	20 24.0	4 23.2	14 30.0	1 36.8	19 34.7	19 36.3	5 29.6	21 17.4	21 18.2	27 56.7
25 Su	12 13 42	1 31 50	19 43 17	26 44 09	20R 24.8	3 17.1	15 44.4	2 15.7	19 22.7	19 49.0	5 26.1	21 17.1	21 19.2	27 56.8
26 M	12 17 39	2 30 41	3♋41 14	10♋34 31	20 24.6	2 10.6	16 58.9	2 54.7	19 10.6	20 01.6	5 22.5	21 16.8	21 20.1	27 56.8
27 Tu	12 21 35	3 29 33	17 24 04	24 09 56	20 22.7	1 05.4	18 13.4	3 33.7	18 58.2	20 14.4	5 18.8	21 16.6	21 21.1	27 56.9
28 W	12 25 32	4 28 29	0♌52 13	7♌31 00	20 18.7	0 03.3	19 27.9	4 12.7	18 45.7	20 27.1	5 15.1	21 16.4	21 22.0	27R 56.9
29 Th	12 29 28	5 27 26	14 06 21	20 38 22	20 12.8	29♍06.0	20 42.4	4 51.8	18 33.0	20 39.9	5 11.3	21 16.2	21 22.9	27 56.9
30 F	12 33 25	6 26 26	27 07 07	3♍32 38	20 05.5	28 14.9	21 57.0	5 30.8	18 20.1	20 52.7	5 07.4	21 16.2	21 23.8	27 56.9

LONGITUDE — October 1910

Day	Sid.Time	☉	0 hr ☽	Noon ☽	True ☊	☿	♀	♂	⚳	♃	♄	♅	♆	♇
1 Sa	12 37 21	7♎25 27	9♍54 58	16♍14 11	19♉57.6	27♍31.4	23♍11.6	6♎09.9	18♈07.1	21♎05.5	5♉03.5	21♑16.1	21♋24.6	27♊56.8
2 Su	12 41 18	8 24 31	22 30 19	28 43 27	19R 50.0	26R 56.8	24 26.3	6 49.1	17R 53.9	21 18.4	4R 59.5	21D 16.2	21 25.4	27R 56.7
3 M	12 45 14	9 23 37	4♎53 39	11♎01 02	19 43.5	26 31.9	25 41.0	7 28.2	17 40.6	21 31.2	4 55.5	21 16.2	21 26.1	27 56.7
4 Tu	12 49 11	10 22 45	17 05 44	23 07 54	19 38.5	26D 17.2	26 55.7	8 07.4	17 27.2	21 44.1	4 51.3	21 16.3	21 26.9	27 56.5
5 W	12 53 08	11 21 55	29 07 47	5♏05 36	19 35.5	26 13.1	28 10.4	8 46.6	17 13.8	21 57.0	4 47.2	21 16.5	21 27.5	27 56.4
6 Th	12 57 04	12 21 07	11♏01 41	16 56 20	19D 34.3	26 19.6	29 25.2	9 25.9	17 00.2	22 10.0	4 42.9	21 16.7	21 28.2	27 56.2
7 F	13 01 01	13 20 20	22 49 59	28 43 02	19 34.6	26 36.6	0♎40.0	10 05.1	16 46.6	22 22.9	4 38.6	21 17.0	21 28.8	27 56.0
8 Sa	13 04 57	14 19 36	4♐35 58	10♐29 18	19 36.0	27 03.5	1 54.8	10 44.4	16 32.9	22 35.9	4 34.3	21 17.3	21 29.4	27 55.8
9 Su	13 08 54	15 18 54	16 23 36	22 19 25	19 37.8	27 40.0	3 09.6	11 23.8	16 19.2	22 48.9	4 29.9	21 17.7	21 30.0	27 55.6
10 M	13 12 50	16 18 13	28 17 23	4♑18 06	19 39.3	28 25.3	4 24.5	12 03.1	16 05.5	23 01.9	4 25.5	21 18.2	21 30.5	27 55.4
11 Tu	13 16 47	17 17 34	10♑22 13	16 30 20	19R 40.0	29 18.7	5 39.3	12 42.5	15 51.8	23 14.9	4 21.0	21 18.6	21 31.0	27 55.1
12 W	13 20 43	18 16 57	22 43 06	29 01 03	19 39.4	0♎19.5	6 54.3	13 21.9	15 38.2	23 27.9	4 16.5	21 19.2	21 31.5	27 54.8
13 Th	13 24 40	19 16 22	5♒24 45	11♒54 39	19 37.5	1 26.9	8 09.2	14 01.4	15 24.5	23 40.9	4 12.0	21 19.8	21 31.9	27 54.5
14 F	13 28 37	20 15 48	18 31 08	25 14 28	19 34.3	2 40.0	9 24.1	14 40.8	15 10.9	23 54.0	4 07.4	21 20.4	21 32.3	27 54.2
15 Sa	13 32 33	21 15 16	2♓04 46	9♓02 02	19 30.4	3 58.3	10 39.1	15 20.3	14 57.4	24 07.0	4 02.8	21 21.1	21 32.7	27 53.8
16 Su	13 36 30	22 14 46	16 06 06	23 16 35	19 26.2	5 20.9	11 54.1	15 59.8	14 43.9	24 20.1	3 58.1	21 21.8	21 33.0	27 53.4
17 M	13 40 26	23 14 18	0♈32 57	7♈54 29	19 22.5	6 47.2	13 09.1	16 39.4	14 30.6	24 33.1	3 53.4	21 22.6	21 33.3	27 53.0
18 Tu	13 44 23	24 13 52	15 20 20	22 49 30	19 19.7	8 16.6	14 24.1	17 19.0	14 17.3	24 46.2	3 48.7	21 23.4	21 33.6	27 52.6
19 W	13 48 19	25 13 28	0♉20 54	7♉53 23	19D 18.1	9 48.7	15 39.1	17 58.6	14 04.2	24 59.2	3 44.0	21 24.3	21 33.8	27 52.1
20 Th	13 52 16	26 13 05	15 25 49	22 57 05	19 17.8	11 22.9	16 54.2	18 38.2	13 51.2	25 12.3	3 39.3	21 25.3	21 34.0	27 51.7
21 F	13 56 12	27 12 46	0♊26 11	7♊52 11	19 18.5	12 58.8	18 09.3	19 17.9	13 38.4	25 25.3	3 34.5	21 26.3	21 34.1	27 51.2
22 Sa	14 00 09	28 12 28	15 14 18	22 31 53	19 19.8	14 36.0	19 24.4	19 57.6	13 25.7	25 38.4	3 29.7	21 27.3	21 34.3	27 50.7
23 Su	14 04 06	29 12 13	29 44 29	6♋51 44	19 21.2	16 14.4	20 39.5	20 37.4	13 13.2	25 51.4	3 24.9	21 28.4	21 34.4	27 50.2
24 M	14 08 02	0♏12 00	13♋53 26	20 49 32	19R 22.1	17 53.5	21 54.6	21 17.1	13 00.8	26 04.5	3 20.1	21 29.5	21 34.4	27 49.6
25 Tu	14 11 59	1 11 49	27 40 02	4♌25 05	19 22.3	19 33.1	23 09.8	21 57.0	12 48.7	26 17.5	3 15.3	21 30.7	21R 34.4	27 49.1
26 W	14 15 55	2 11 40	11♌04 52	17 39 37	19 21.7	21 13.2	24 25.0	22 36.8	12 36.8	26 30.6	3 10.5	21 32.0	21 34.4	27 48.5
27 Th	14 19 52	3 11 34	24 09 37	0♍35 10	19 20.2	22 53.5	25 40.2	23 16.7	12 25.1	26 43.6	3 05.6	21 33.2	21 34.4	27 47.9
28 F	14 23 48	4 11 29	6♍56 36	13 14 12	19 18.3	24 33.8	26 55.4	23 56.6	12 13.7	26 56.6	3 00.8	21 34.6	21 34.3	27 47.3
29 Sa	14 27 45	5 11 27	19 28 19	25 39 14	19 16.1	26 14.2	28 10.6	24 36.5	12 02.5	27 09.7	2 56.0	21 35.9	21 34.2	27 46.6
30 Su	14 31 41	6 11 27	1♎47 14	7♎52 37	19 14.0	27 54.4	29 25.9	25 16.5	11 51.6	27 22.7	2 51.2	21 37.4	21 34.1	27 46.0
31 M	14 35 38	7 11 29	13 55 39	19 56 34	19 12.3	29 34.4	0♏41.1	25 56.5	11 40.9	27 35.7	2 46.3	21 38.9	21 33.9	27 45.3

Astro Data

	Dy Hr Mn
☽0S	5 23:00
☿R	13 8:36
☽0N	20 1:37
☉0S	23 22:31
♅☍♆	23 23:05
♂0S	24 23:21
♇R	28 20:28
☿0N	1 8:21
♅D	1 15:05
♃□♅	2 7:52
♃□♆	3 1:53
☽0S	3 6:02
☿D	5 9:15
♀0S	9 16:17
☿0S	15 21:55

Planet Ingress

		Dy Hr Mn
♀	♍	12 18:29
♂	♎	22 0:15
☉	♎	23 22:31
☿	♍R	28 13:20
♀	♎	6 23:11
☿	♎	12 4:36
☉	♏	24 7:11
♀	♏	30 22:53
☿	♏	31 18:09

☽0N17 12:11
♆ R25 17:30
♅☍♂28 7:50
☽0S30 12:21

Last Aspect / ☽ Ingress (September)

Last Aspect Dy Hr Mn			☽ Ingress	Dy Hr Mn
2 18:57	♇	⚹	♍	2 22:57
5 3:14	♇	□	♎	5 7:22
7 14:12	♇	△	♏	7 18:29
10 0:28	♀	□	♐	10 7:22
12 15:30	♇	☍	♑	12 19:39
14 20:18	♂	△	♒	15 4:53
17 6:37	♇	△	♓	17 10:12
19 9:44	♂	☍	♈	19 12:30
21 10:07	♇	⚹	♉	21 13:29
23 14:15	☉	△	♊	23 14:49
25 14:05	♇	☌	♋	25 17:37
27 6:59	♆	☌	♌	27 22:26
30 1:33	♇	⚹	♍	30 5:22

Last Aspect / ☽ Ingress (October)

Last Aspect Dy Hr Mn			☽ Ingress	Dy Hr Mn
2 10:30	♇	□	♎	2 14:28
4 21:37	♇	△	♏	5 1:45
7 7:34	☿	⚹	♐	7 14:37
9 23:26	☿	□	♑	10 3:25
12 1:15	♃	□	♒	12 13:51
14 16:41	♇	△	♓	14 20:22
16 19:38	♇	□	♈	16 23:06
18 20:03	♇	⚹	♉	18 23:27
20 9:47	♆	⚹	♊	20 23:18
22 22:08	☉	△	♋	23 0:26
24 21:21	♃	□	♌	25 4:08
27 6:47	♇	⚹	♍	27 10:54
29 16:08	♇	□	♎	29 20:30

☽ Phases & Eclipses

Dy Hr Mn		
3 18:06	●	10♍20
11 20:10	☽	18♐12
19 4:52	○	25♓22
25 20:54	☾	1♋54
3 8:32	●	9♎15
11 13:40	☽	17♑22
18 14:24	○	24♈20
25 5:48	☾	0♌56

Astro Data

1 September 1910
Julian Day # 3896
SVP 6♓30'38"
GC 25♐35.5 ⚵ 1♓28.7R
Eris 25♓58.6R ⚶ 5♍50.2
⚷ 29♒51.0R ⚴ 12♉21.0
☽ Mean ☊ 22♉52.3

1 October 1910
Julian Day # 3926
SVP 6♓30'35"
GC 25♐35.6 ⚵ 25♒18.2R
Eris 25♓38.0R ⚶ 18♍27.1
⚷ 28♒33.5R ⚴ 10♉51.7R
☽ Mean ☊ 21♉16.9

November 1910 — LONGITUDE

Day	Sid.Time	☉	0 hr ☽	Noon ☽	True ☊	☿	♀	♂	⚳	♃	♄	♅	♆	♇
1 Tu	14 39 35	8♏11 32	25♎55 39	1♏53 07	19♉11.1	1♏14.2	1♏56.4	26♎36.5	11♈30.6	27♎48.6	2♉41.5	21♑40.4	21♋33.7	27♊44.6
2 W	14 43 31	9 11 38	7♏49 14	13 44 14	19D 10.6	2 53.8	3 11.7	27 16.6	11R 20.5	28 01.6	2R 36.7	21 41.9	21R 33.4	27R 43.9
3 Th	14 47 28	10 11 46	19 38 24	25 31 58	19 10.6	4 33.0	4 27.0	27 56.7	11 10.7	28 14.5	2 32.0	21 43.6	21 33.1	27 43.1
4 F	14 51 24	11 11 55	1♐25 16	7♐18 35	19 11.0	6 11.9	5 42.3	28 36.9	11 01.3	28 27.5	2 27.2	21 45.2	21 32.8	27 42.4
5 Sa	14 55 21	12 12 06	13 12 16	19 06 40	19 11.7	7 50.5	6 57.6	29 17.0	10 52.1	28 40.4	2 22.5	21 46.9	21 32.5	27 41.6
6 Su	14 59 17	13 12 19	25 02 10	0♑59 12	19 12.4	9 28.7	8 12.9	29 57.2	10 43.3	28 53.3	2 17.8	21 48.7	21 32.1	27 40.8
7 M	15 03 14	14 12 34	6♑58 13	12 59 39	19 13.1	11 06.5	9 28.2	0♏37.5	10 34.9	29 06.1	2 13.1	21 50.5	21 31.7	27 40.0
8 Tu	15 07 10	15 12 50	19 04 02	25 11 51	19 13.5	12 44.0	10 43.6	1 17.7	10 26.8	29 19.0	2 08.5	21 52.4	21 31.2	27 39.2
9 W	15 11 07	16 13 07	1♒23 37	7♒39 51	19R 13.7	14 21.1	11 58.9	1 58.0	10 19.0	29 31.8	2 03.9	21 54.3	21 30.7	27 38.4
10 Th	15 15 04	17 13 26	14 01 04	20 27 44	19 13.8	15 57.9	13 14.3	2 38.3	10 11.6	29 44.6	1 59.3	21 56.2	21 30.2	27 37.5
11 F	15 19 00	18 13 46	27 00 19	3♓39 10	19 13.7	17 34.3	14 29.6	3 18.7	10 04.5	29 57.3	1 54.7	21 58.2	21 29.7	27 36.6
12 Sa	15 22 57	19 14 08	10♓24 36	17 16 49	19D 13.7	19 10.3	15 45.0	3 59.1	9 57.8	0♏10.0	1 50.2	22 00.2	21 29.1	27 35.7
13 Su	15 26 53	20 14 31	24 15 53	1♈21 45	19 13.7	20 46.1	17 00.4	4 39.5	9 51.5	0 22.7	1 45.8	22 02.3	21 28.5	27 34.8
14 M	15 30 50	21 14 55	8♈34 09	15 52 43	19 13.9	22 21.6	18 15.7	5 20.0	9 45.6	0 35.4	1 41.4	22 04.4	21 27.9	27 33.9
15 Tu	15 34 46	22 15 21	23 16 50	0♉45 45	19 14.1	23 56.8	19 31.1	6 00.4	9 40.0	0 48.0	1 37.0	22 06.5	21 27.2	27 33.0
16 W	15 38 43	23 15 48	8♉18 32	15 54 06	19R 14.2	25 31.7	20 46.5	6 41.0	9 34.8	1 00.6	1 32.7	22 08.7	21 26.5	27 32.1
17 Th	15 42 39	24 16 17	23 31 17	1♊08 50	19 14.1	27 06.3	22 01.9	7 21.5	9 30.0	1 13.2	1 28.4	22 11.0	21 25.7	27 31.1
18 F	15 46 36	25 16 48	8♊45 30	16 20 04	19 13.8	28 40.7	23 17.3	8 02.1	9 25.6	1 25.7	1 24.2	22 13.2	21 25.0	27 30.1
19 Sa	15 50 33	26 17 20	23 51 21	1♋18 22	19 13.1	0♐14.9	24 32.7	8 42.7	9 21.6	1 38.2	1 20.1	22 15.5	21 24.2	27 29.2
20 Su	15 54 29	27 17 54	8♋40 14	15 56 14	19 12.2	1 48.9	25 48.1	9 23.4	9 17.9	1 50.6	1 16.0	22 17.9	21 23.4	27 28.2
21 M	15 58 26	28 18 29	23 05 52	0♌08 48	19 11.2	3 22.7	27 03.5	10 04.1	9 14.6	2 03.0	1 12.0	22 20.3	21 22.5	27 27.2
22 Tu	16 02 22	29 19 07	7♌04 52	13 54 05	19 10.4	4 56.3	28 18.9	10 44.8	9 11.8	2 15.4	1 08.0	22 22.7	21 21.6	27 26.1
23 W	16 06 19	0♐19 46	20 36 34	27 12 35	19D 10.0	6 29.7	29 34.4	11 25.6	9 09.3	2 27.7	1 04.1	22 25.2	21 20.7	27 25.1
24 Th	16 10 15	1 20 26	3♍42 29	10♍06 41	19 10.2	8 03.0	0♐49.8	12 06.4	9 07.2	2 39.9	1 00.3	22 27.7	21 19.8	27 24.1
25 F	16 14 12	2 21 08	16 25 39	22 39 53	19 10.9	9 36.2	2 05.3	12 47.2	9 05.4	2 52.2	0 56.5	22 30.2	21 18.8	27 23.0
26 Sa	16 18 08	3 21 52	28 49 54	4♎56 13	19 12.0	11 09.2	3 20.7	13 28.1	9 04.1	3 04.3	0 52.8	22 32.8	21 17.8	27 21.9
27 Su	16 22 05	4 22 37	10♎59 21	16 59 49	19 13.5	12 42.1	4 36.2	14 09.0	9 03.2	3 16.4	0 49.2	22 35.4	21 16.8	27 20.9
28 M	16 26 02	5 23 24	22 58 04	28 54 34	19 14.8	14 14.9	5 51.6	14 50.0	9D 02.6	3 28.5	0 45.7	22 38.1	21 15.8	27 19.8
29 Tu	16 29 58	6 24 12	4♏49 43	10♏43 57	19R 15.7	15 47.6	7 07.1	15 31.0	9 02.5	3 40.5	0 42.2	22 40.8	21 14.7	27 18.7
30 W	16 33 55	7 25 02	16 37 35	22 30 59	19 15.9	17 20.2	8 22.6	16 12.0	9 02.7	3 52.5	0 38.8	22 43.5	21 13.6	27 17.6

December 1910 — LONGITUDE

Day	Sid.Time	☉	0 hr ☽	Noon ☽	True ☊	☿	♀	♂	⚳	♃	♄	♅	♆	♇
1 Th	16 37 51	8♐25 53	28♏24 27	4♐18 15	19♉15.1	18♐52.7	9♐38.0	16♏53.0	9♈03.3	4♏04.4	0♉35.5	22♑46.2	21♋12.4	27♊16.5
2 F	16 41 48	9 26 45	10♐12 40	16 07 56	19R 13.3	20 25.0	10 53.5	17 34.1	9 04.3	4 16.2	0R 32.3	22 49.0	21R 11.3	27R 15.4
3 Sa	16 45 44	10 27 38	22 04 18	28 02 00	19 10.4	21 57.3	12 09.0	18 15.3	9 05.7	4 28.0	0 29.2	22 51.8	21 10.1	27 14.2
4 Su	16 49 41	11 28 33	4♑01 17	10♑02 22	19 06.7	23 29.4	13 24.4	18 56.4	9 07.5	4 39.7	0 26.2	22 54.7	21 08.9	27 13.1
5 M	16 53 38	12 29 28	16 05 30	22 10 58	19 02.7	25 01.3	14 39.9	19 37.6	9 09.6	4 51.4	0 23.2	22 57.6	21 07.7	27 12.0
6 Tu	16 57 34	13 30 24	28 19 02	4♒30 00	18 58.7	26 33.0	15 55.4	20 18.8	9 12.2	5 03.0	0 20.4	23 00.5	21 06.4	27 10.8
7 W	17 01 31	14 31 21	10♒44 11	17 01 55	18 55.4	28 04.6	17 10.9	21 00.1	9 15.0	5 14.5	0 17.6	23 03.4	21 05.2	27 09.7
8 Th	17 05 27	15 32 18	23 23 33	29 49 26	18 53.1	29 35.8	18 26.3	21 41.4	9 18.3	5 25.9	0 14.9	23 06.4	21 03.9	27 08.5
9 F	17 09 24	16 33 16	6♓19 55	12♓55 22	18D 52.0	1♑06.8	19 41.8	22 22.7	9 21.9	5 37.3	0 12.3	23 09.4	21 02.5	27 07.3
10 Sa	17 13 20	17 34 15	19 36 04	26 22 20	18 52.3	2 37.3	20 57.3	23 04.1	9 25.9	5 48.6	0 09.9	23 12.4	21 01.2	27 06.2
11 Su	17 17 17	18 35 14	3♈14 21	10♈12 17	18 53.5	4 07.4	22 12.7	23 45.4	9 30.3	5 59.9	0 07.5	23 15.5	20 59.8	27 05.0
12 M	17 21 13	19 36 14	17 16 09	24 25 52	18 55.0	5 36.9	23 28.2	24 26.9	9 35.0	6 11.0	0 05.2	23 18.5	20 58.5	27 03.8
13 Tu	17 25 10	20 37 14	1♉41 13	9♉01 48	18R 56.3	7 05.8	24 43.7	25 08.3	9 40.0	6 22.1	0 03.0	23 21.6	20 57.1	27 02.6
14 W	17 29 07	21 38 15	16 27 04	23 56 17	18 56.5	8 33.9	25 59.1	25 49.8	9 45.4	6 33.1	0 00.9	23 24.8	20 55.6	27 01.5
15 Th	17 33 03	22 39 16	1♊28 33	9♊02 50	18 55.2	10 01.0	27 14.6	26 31.3	9 51.2	6 44.0	29♈59.0	23 27.9	20 54.2	27 00.3
16 F	17 37 00	23 40 19	16 37 58	24 12 43	18 52.0	11 27.0	28 30.0	27 12.9	9 57.3	6 54.9	29 57.1	23 31.1	20 52.7	26 59.1
17 Sa	17 40 56	24 41 21	1♋45 52	9♋16 10	18 47.3	12 51.7	29 45.5	27 54.5	10 03.7	7 05.7	29 55.3	23 34.3	20 51.3	26 57.9
18 Su	17 44 53	25 42 25	16 42 29	24 03 49	18 41.6	14 14.8	1♑00.9	28 36.1	10 10.4	7 16.4	29 53.6	23 37.5	20 49.8	26 56.7
19 M	17 48 49	26 43 29	1♌19 18	8♌28 16	18 35.6	15 35.9	2 16.3	29 17.8	10 17.5	7 26.9	29 52.1	23 40.8	20 48.3	26 55.5
20 Tu	17 52 46	27 44 34	15 30 15	22 25 01	18 30.2	16 54.9	3 31.8	29 59.5	10 24.9	7 37.5	29 50.6	23 44.0	20 46.8	26 54.3
21 W	17 56 42	28 45 40	29 12 27	5♍52 40	18 26.0	18 11.2	4 47.2	0♐41.3	10 32.6	7 47.9	29 49.3	23 47.3	20 45.2	26 53.2
22 Th	18 00 39	29 46 46	12♍25 54	18 52 33	18D 23.6	19 24.5	6 02.7	1 23.1	10 40.6	7 58.2	29 48.0	23 50.6	20 43.7	26 52.0
23 F	18 04 36	0♑47 53	25 13 04	1♎28 00	18 22.8	20 34.2	7 18.1	2 04.9	10 49.0	8 08.4	29 46.9	23 53.9	20 42.1	26 50.8
24 Sa	18 08 32	1 49 01	7♎37 58	13 43 35	18 23.5	21 39.7	8 33.6	2 46.7	10 57.6	8 18.6	29 45.8	23 57.2	20 40.5	26 49.6
25 Su	18 12 29	2 50 09	19 45 30	25 44 24	18 25.0	22 40.4	9 49.0	3 28.6	11 06.5	8 28.6	29 44.9	24 00.6	20 38.9	26 48.4
26 M	18 16 25	3 51 18	1♏40 53	7♏35 37	18R 26.5	23 35.5	11 04.4	4 10.6	11 15.8	8 38.6	29 44.1	24 04.0	20 37.3	26 47.2
27 Tu	18 20 22	4 52 27	13 29 10	19 22 06	18 27.1	24 24.3	12 19.9	4 52.5	11 25.3	8 48.4	29 43.4	24 07.4	20 35.7	26 46.0
28 W	18 24 18	5 53 37	25 14 57	1♐08 10	18 26.0	25 05.9	13 35.3	5 34.5	11 35.2	8 58.2	29 42.8	24 10.8	20 34.1	26 44.9
29 Th	18 28 15	6 54 48	7♐02 13	12 57 26	18 22.8	25 39.5	14 50.7	6 16.6	11 45.3	9 07.8	29 42.4	24 14.2	20 32.5	26 43.7
30 F	18 32 11	7 55 58	18 54 11	24 52 44	18 17.1	26 04.0	16 06.2	6 58.6	11 55.7	9 17.4	29 42.0	24 17.6	20 30.8	26 42.5
31 Sa	18 36 08	8 57 09	0♑53 20	6♑56 09	18 09.2	26R 18.6	17 21.6	7 40.7	12 06.4	9 26.8	29 41.7	24 21.1	20 29.2	26 41.4

Astro Data

	Dy Hr Mn
♃△♇	1 4:53
☽0N	13 23:12
♃☍♇	18 9:55
☽0S	26 18:12
⚳D	29 9:42
☽0N	11 8:08
☽0S	24 0:22

Planet Ingress

	Dy Hr Mn
♂ ♏	6 13:39
♃ ♏	11 17:04
☿ ♐	19 8:12
☉ ♐	23 4:11
♀ ♐	23 20:09
☿ ♑	8 18:22
♄ ♈R	14 23:09
♀ ♑	17 16:38
♂ ♐	20 12:16
☉ ♑	22 17:12

Last Aspect / ☽ Ingress (November)

Last Aspect Dy Hr Mn		☽ Ingress Dy Hr Mn
1 3:40	♇ △	♏ 1 8:12
3 4:14	♅ ⚹	♐ 3 21:06
6 9:48	♂ ⚹	♑ 6 10:01
8 20:08	♃ □	♒ 8 21:19
11 5:14	♃ △	♓ 11 5:26
13 5:38	♇ □	♈ 13 9:43
15 6:52	♇ ⚹	♉ 15 10:47
17 4:54	☿ ☍	♊ 17 10:12
19 5:50	♇ ☌	♋ 19 9:53
21 8:37	☉ △	♌ 21 11:45
23 16:48	♀ □	♍ 23 17:08
25 21:09	♇ □	♎ 26 2:17
28 8:49	♇ △	♏ 28 14:12

Last Aspect / ☽ Ingress (December)

Last Aspect Dy Hr Mn		☽ Ingress Dy Hr Mn
30 12:26	♅ ⚹	♐ 1 3:15
3 10:24	♇ ☍	♑ 3 15:57
5 13:32	♅ ☌	♒ 6 3:17
8 11:31	☿ ⚹	♓ 8 12:20
10 13:17	♇ □	♈ 10 18:22
12 16:22	♇ ⚹	♉ 12 21:13
14 15:10	♂ ☍	♊ 14 21:39
16 21:06	♄ ⚹	♋ 16 21:11
18 21:37	♄ □	♌ 18 21:48
21 1:07	♄ △	♍ 21 1:25
23 3:08	♇ □	♎ 23 9:10
25 20:05	♄ ☍	♏ 25 20:36
27 22:57	☿ ⚹	♐ 28 9:41
30 21:38	♄ △	♑ 30 22:14

☽ Phases & Eclipses

Dy Hr Mn	
2 1:56	● 8♏46
2 2:08:21	● P 0.852
10 5:29	☽ 16♒57
17 0:25	○ 23♉47
17 0:21	● T 1.125
23 18:13	☾ 0♍35
1 21:10	● 8♐49
9 19:05	☽ 16♓51
16 11:05	○ 23♊38
23 10:36	☾ 0♎44
31 16:21	● 9♑08

Astro Data

1 November 1910
Julian Day # 3957
SVP 6♓30'32"
GC 25♐35.6 ⚴ 23♒54.3
Eris 25♓19.3R ⚵ 0♎30.4
⚷ 27♒53.0R ⚶ 3♉43.3R
☽ Mean ☊ 19♉38.4

1 December 1910
Julian Day # 3987
SVP 6♓30'27"
GC 25♐35.7 ⚴ 27♒22.2
Eris 25♓09.1R ⚵ 10♎42.0
⚷ 28♒07.3 ⚶ 27♈52.7R
☽ Mean ☊ 18♉03.1

LONGITUDE — January 1911

Day	Sid.Time	☉	0 hr ☽	Noon ☽	True ☊	☿	♀	♂	⚳	♃	♄	♅	♆	♇
1 Su	18 40 05	9♑58 20	13♑01 21	19♑09 03	17♉59.6	26♑22.5	18♑37.0	8♐22.9	12♈17.4	9♏36.1	29♈41.6	24♑24.5	20♋27.5	26♊40.2
2 M	18 44 01	10 59 31	25 19 21	1♒32 19	17R 49.1	26R 15.0	19 52.4	9 05.1	12 28.7	9 45.3	29D 41.6	24 28.0	20R 25.9	26R 39.1
3 Tu	18 47 58	12 00 42	7♒48 00	14 06 29	17 38.7	25 55.8	21 07.8	9 47.3	12 40.2	9 54.4	29 41.7	24 31.5	20 24.2	26 37.9
4 W	18 51 54	13 01 52	20 27 50	26 52 07	17 29.4	25 24.7	22 23.2	10 29.5	12 51.9	10 03.4	29 41.9	24 34.9	20 22.5	26 36.8
5 Th	18 55 51	14 03 02	3♓19 25	9♓49 52	17 22.1	24 42.0	23 38.6	11 11.8	13 04.0	10 12.3	29 42.2	24 38.4	20 20.8	26 35.6
6 F	18 59 47	15 04 12	16 23 36	23 00 47	17 17.2	23 48.6	24 54.0	11 54.1	13 16.3	10 21.0	29 42.6	24 41.9	20 19.1	26 34.5
7 Sa	19 03 44	16 05 22	29 41 35	6♈26 10	17D 14.9	22 45.6	26 09.4	12 36.4	13 28.8	10 29.7	29 43.1	24 45.5	20 17.4	26 33.4
8 Su	19 07 40	17 06 31	13♈14 45	20 07 27	17 14.4	21 34.9	27 24.7	13 18.8	13 41.6	10 38.2	29 43.8	24 49.0	20 15.7	26 32.3
9 M	19 11 37	18 07 39	27 04 25	4♉05 44	17R 15.0	20 18.6	28 40.1	14 01.2	13 54.7	10 46.6	29 44.5	24 52.5	20 14.1	26 31.2
10 Tu	19 15 34	19 08 47	11♉11 21	18 21 12	17 15.5	18 59.3	29 55.4	14 43.6	14 08.0	10 54.8	29 45.4	24 56.0	20 12.4	26 30.1
11 W	19 19 30	20 09 55	25 35 03	2♊52 32	17 14.5	17 39.4	1♒10.7	15 26.1	14 21.5	11 03.0	29 46.4	24 59.6	20 10.7	26 29.0
12 Th	19 23 27	21 11 02	10♊13 08	17 36 13	17 11.1	16 21.4	2 26.0	16 08.6	14 35.2	11 11.0	29 47.5	25 03.1	20 09.0	26 27.9
13 F	19 27 23	22 12 08	25 00 59	2♋26 31	17 05.0	15 07.7	3 41.3	16 51.2	14 49.2	11 18.8	29 48.7	25 06.6	20 07.3	26 26.9
14 Sa	19 31 20	23 13 14	9♋51 48	17 15 47	16 56.3	14 00.1	4 56.6	17 33.7	15 03.4	11 26.6	29 50.0	25 10.2	20 05.6	26 25.8
15 Su	19 35 16	24 14 19	24 37 23	1♌55 33	16 45.8	13 00.2	6 11.9	18 16.4	15 17.8	11 34.2	29 51.5	25 13.7	20 03.9	26 24.8
16 M	19 39 13	25 15 24	9♌09 21	16 17 56	16 34.5	12 08.9	7 27.2	18 59.0	15 32.4	11 41.7	29 53.0	25 17.3	20 02.2	26 23.8
17 Tu	19 43 10	26 16 29	23 20 38	0♍16 57	16 23.8	11 26.8	8 42.4	19 41.7	15 47.3	11 49.0	29 54.6	25 20.8	20 00.5	26 22.7
18 W	19 47 06	27 17 33	7♍06 34	13 49 19	16 14.8	10 54.3	9 57.7	20 24.4	16 02.3	11 56.2	29 56.4	25 24.4	19 58.8	26 21.7
19 Th	19 51 03	28 18 36	20 25 16	26 54 36	16 08.1	10 31.2	11 12.9	21 07.2	16 17.6	12 03.3	29 58.3	25 27.9	19 57.1	26 20.7
20 F	19 54 59	29 19 40	3♎17 38	9♎34 49	16 04.0	10 17.3	12 28.1	21 49.9	16 33.1	12 10.2	0♉00.2	25 31.4	19 55.5	26 19.8
21 Sa	19 58 56	0♒20 43	15 46 40	21 53 48	16D 02.2	10D 12.2	13 43.3	22 32.8	16 48.7	12 17.0	0 02.3	25 35.0	19 53.8	26 18.8
22 Su	20 02 52	1 21 45	27 56 53	3♏56 35	16 02.0	10 15.3	14 58.5	23 15.6	17 04.6	12 23.7	0 04.5	25 38.5	19 52.1	26 17.8
23 M	20 06 49	2 22 47	9♏53 36	15 48 40	16R 02.1	10 26.0	16 13.7	23 58.5	17 20.6	12 30.1	0 06.8	25 42.0	19 50.5	26 16.9
24 Tu	20 10 45	3 23 49	21 42 28	27 35 41	16 01.6	10 43.8	17 28.9	24 41.5	17 36.9	12 36.5	0 09.2	25 45.6	19 48.8	26 16.0
25 W	20 14 42	4 24 50	3♐28 58	9♐22 57	15 59.3	11 08.1	18 44.1	25 24.4	17 53.3	12 42.7	0 11.7	25 49.1	19 47.2	26 15.1
26 Th	20 18 39	5 25 50	15 18 11	21 15 11	15 54.5	11 38.3	19 59.2	26 07.4	18 09.9	12 48.7	0 14.3	25 52.6	19 45.6	26 14.2
27 F	20 22 35	6 26 50	27 14 26	3♑16 18	15 46.7	12 13.9	21 14.4	26 50.5	18 26.7	12 54.6	0 17.0	25 56.1	19 44.0	26 13.3
28 Sa	20 26 32	7 27 49	9♑21 09	15 29 12	15 36.1	12 54.4	22 29.5	27 33.5	18 43.7	13 00.3	0 19.8	25 59.6	19 42.3	26 12.4
29 Su	20 30 28	8 28 47	21 40 40	27 55 38	15 23.3	13 39.3	23 44.6	28 16.6	19 00.8	13 05.9	0 22.7	26 03.1	19 40.8	26 11.6
30 M	20 34 25	9 29 44	4♒14 10	10♒36 14	15 09.3	14 28.3	24 59.7	28 59.7	19 18.2	13 11.3	0 25.7	26 06.6	19 39.2	26 10.7
31 Tu	20 38 21	10 30 40	17 01 45	23 30 37	14 55.3	15 20.9	26 14.8	29 42.9	19 35.7	13 16.6	0 28.8	26 10.0	19 37.6	26 09.9

LONGITUDE — February 1911

Day	Sid.Time	☉	0 hr ☽	Noon ☽	True ☊	☿	♀	♂	⚳	♃	♄	♅	♆	♇
1 W	20 42 18	11♒31 35	0♓02 39	6♓37 42	14♉42.6	16♑16.8	27♒29.8	0♑26.1	19♈53.3	13♏21.6	0♉32.0	26♑13.5	19♋36.0	26♊09.1
2 Th	20 46 14	12 32 29	13 15 34	19 56 05	14R 32.3	17 15.7	28 44.8	1 09.3	20 11.1	13 26.6	0 35.4	26 16.9	19R 34.5	26R 08.3
3 F	20 50 11	13 33 22	26 39 06	3♈24 29	14 25.0	18 17.5	29 59.8	1 52.6	20 29.1	13 31.3	0 38.8	26 20.4	19 33.0	26 07.6
4 Sa	20 54 08	14 34 13	10♈12 09	17 02 02	14 20.7	19 21.7	1♓14.8	2 35.8	20 47.3	13 35.9	0 42.3	26 23.8	19 31.5	26 06.8
5 Su	20 58 04	15 35 03	23 54 07	0♉48 23	14D 19.0	20 28.3	2 29.8	3 19.1	21 05.6	13 40.3	0 45.9	26 27.2	19 30.0	26 06.1
6 M	21 02 01	16 35 51	7♉44 52	14 43 35	14R 18.8	21 37.0	3 44.7	4 02.5	21 24.0	13 44.6	0 49.6	26 30.6	19 28.5	26 05.4
7 Tu	21 05 57	17 36 38	21 44 32	28 47 41	14 18.6	22 47.7	4 59.7	4 45.9	21 42.6	13 48.7	0 53.4	26 34.0	19 27.0	26 04.7
8 W	21 09 54	18 37 23	5♊52 58	13♊00 14	14 17.1	24 00.3	6 14.6	5 29.2	22 01.4	13 52.6	0 57.3	26 37.3	19 25.6	26 04.0
9 Th	21 13 50	19 38 06	20 09 14	27 19 39	14 13.2	25 14.5	7 29.4	6 12.7	22 20.2	13 56.3	1 01.2	26 40.7	19 24.1	26 03.4
10 F	21 17 47	20 38 49	4♋31 04	11♋42 55	14 06.5	26 30.4	8 44.3	6 56.1	22 39.3	13 59.9	1 05.3	26 44.0	19 22.7	26 02.8
11 Sa	21 21 43	21 39 29	18 54 37	26 05 27	13 57.0	27 47.7	9 59.1	7 39.6	22 58.4	14 03.3	1 09.5	26 47.3	19 21.4	26 02.1
12 Su	21 25 40	22 40 08	3♌14 41	10♌21 34	13 45.4	29 06.5	11 13.9	8 23.1	23 17.7	14 06.5	1 13.7	26 50.6	19 20.0	26 01.5
13 M	21 29 37	23 40 46	17 25 21	24 25 30	13 32.8	0♒26.7	12 28.6	9 06.7	23 37.1	14 09.5	1 18.0	26 53.8	19 18.6	26 01.0
14 Tu	21 33 33	24 41 22	1♍20 55	8♍11 35	13 20.7	1 48.1	13 43.4	9 50.3	23 56.7	14 12.4	1 22.5	26 57.1	19 17.3	26 00.4
15 W	21 37 30	25 41 56	14 56 54	21 36 39	13 10.2	3 10.8	14 58.1	10 33.9	24 16.4	14 15.0	1 27.0	27 00.3	19 16.0	25 59.9
16 Th	21 41 26	26 42 30	28 10 42	4♎39 03	13 02.1	4 34.7	16 12.7	11 17.5	24 36.2	14 17.5	1 31.5	27 03.5	19 14.7	25 59.4
17 F	21 45 23	27 43 02	11♎01 51	17 19 21	12 56.8	5 59.7	17 27.4	12 01.2	24 56.1	14 19.9	1 36.2	27 06.7	19 13.4	25 58.9
18 Sa	21 49 19	28 43 32	23 31 56	29 40 03	12 54.1	7 25.8	18 42.0	12 44.9	25 16.1	14 22.0	1 41.0	27 09.8	19 12.2	25 58.4
19 Su	21 53 16	29 44 01	5♏44 14	11♏45 04	12D 53.4	8 53.0	19 56.6	13 28.7	25 36.3	14 23.9	1 45.8	27 13.0	19 11.0	25 57.9
20 M	21 57 12	0♓44 30	17 43 11	23 39 15	12R 53.6	10 21.3	21 11.2	14 12.4	25 56.6	14 25.7	1 50.7	27 16.1	19 09.8	25 57.5
21 Tu	22 01 09	1 44 56	29 33 58	5♐28 02	12 53.7	11 50.6	22 25.7	14 56.2	26 17.0	14 27.3	1 55.7	27 19.2	19 08.6	25 57.1
22 W	22 05 06	2 45 22	11♐22 08	17 16 57	12 52.6	13 21.0	23 40.2	15 40.1	26 37.5	14 28.7	2 00.8	27 22.2	19 07.5	25 56.7
23 Th	22 09 02	3 45 46	23 13 09	29 11 21	12 49.4	14 52.4	24 54.7	16 23.9	26 58.2	14 29.9	2 06.0	27 25.3	19 06.4	25 56.3
24 F	22 12 59	4 46 08	5♑12 09	11♑16 04	12 43.8	16 24.8	26 09.2	17 07.8	27 18.9	14 30.9	2 11.2	27 28.3	19 05.3	25 56.0
25 Sa	22 16 55	5 46 30	17 23 34	23 35 04	12 35.6	17 58.3	27 23.6	17 51.7	27 39.7	14 31.7	2 16.5	27 31.2	19 04.2	25 55.7
26 Su	22 20 52	6 46 49	29 50 51	6♒11 09	12 25.3	19 32.7	28 38.0	18 35.7	28 00.7	14 32.4	2 21.9	27 34.2	19 03.2	25 55.4
27 M	22 24 48	7 47 07	12♒36 06	19 05 44	12 13.8	21 08.2	29 52.3	19 19.6	28 21.7	14 32.8	2 27.3	27 37.1	19 02.2	25 55.1
28 Tu	22 28 45	8 47 24	25 39 57	2♓18 37	12 02.2	22 44.7	1♈06.6	20 03.6	28 42.9	14R 33.1	2 32.8	27 40.0	19 01.2	25 54.9

Astro Data

	Dy Hr Mn
☿ R	1 8:25
♄ D	2 5:19
☽ 0N	7 13:58
♃□♇	14 9:54
☽ 0S	20 7:42
☿ D	21 14:44
⚳ 0N	22 3:37
♅⚻♇	31 11:21
☽ 0N	3 18:27
☽ 0S	16 16:11

Planet Ingress

		Dy Hr Mn
♀	♒	10 13:28
♄	♉	20 9:21
☉	♒	21 3:52
♂	♑	31 21:30
♀	♓	3 12:03
☿	♒	13 4:03
☉	♓	19 18:20
♀	♈	27 14:29

Last Aspect / ☽ Ingress (January)

Last Aspect Dy Hr Mn			☽ Ingress	Dy Hr Mn
2 8:27	♄	□	♒	2 9:02
4 17:16	♄	⚹	♓	4 17:50
6 18:24	♇	□	♈	7 0:33
9 4:34	♄	☌	♉	9 5:01
10 22:58	♅	△	♊	11 7:17
13 7:45	♄	⚹	♋	13 8:03
15 8:35	♄	□	♌	15 8:49
17 11:21	♄	△	♍	17 11:30
19 14:51	☉	△	♎	19 17:47
21 20:44	♇	△	♏	22 4:06
24 8:14	♅	⚹	♐	24 16:54
26 22:23	♂	☌	♑	27 5:30
29 8:24	♅	☌	♒	29 15:57
31 17:34	♀	☌	♓	31 23:55

Last Aspect / ☽ Ingress (February)

Last Aspect Dy Hr Mn			☽ Ingress	Dy Hr Mn
2 23:23	♅	⚹	♈	3 5:57
5 4:25	♅	□	♉	5 10:36
7 8:12	♅	△	♊	7 14:03
9 9:53	♇	☌	♋	9 16:28
11 15:08	☿	☍	♌	11 18:33
13 14:45	♇	⚹	♍	13 21:39
15 21:53	♅	△	♎	16 3:22
18 9:59	☉	△	♏	18 12:39
20 19:22	♅	⚹	♐	21 0:53
23 5:29	♇	☍	♑	23 13:37
25 20:07	♀	⚹	♒	26 0:17
28 0:27	♇	△	♓	28 7:51

☽ Phases & Eclipses

Dy Hr Mn		
8 6:20	☽	16♈52
14 22:26	○	23♋40
22 6:21	☾	1♏07
30 9:44	●	9♒24
6 15:27	☽	16♉45
13 10:37	○	23♌37
21 3:44	☾	1♐24

Astro Data

1 January 1911
Julian Day # 4018
SVP 6♓30'21"
GC 25♐35.8 ⚴ 4♓25.0
Eris 25♓10.2 ⚵ 18♎48.4
⚷ 29♒15.6 ⚶ 28♈15.4
☽ Mean ☊ 16♉24.7

1 February 1911
Julian Day # 4049
SVP 6♓30'15"
GC 25♐35.9 ⚴ 13♓39.2
Eris 25♓23.2 ⚵ 23♎01.5
⚷ 1♓02.6 ⚶ 4♉26.7
☽ Mean ☊ 14♉46.2

March 1911 — LONGITUDE

Day	Sid.Time	☉	0 hr ☽	Noon ☽	True ☊	☿	♀	♂	⚳	♃	♄	♅	♆	♇
1 W	22 32 41	9♓47 38	9♓01 28	15♓48 11	11♉51.7	24♒22.2	2♈20.9	20♑47.7	29♈04.2	14♏33.2	2♉38.4	27♑42.9	19♋00.2	25♊54.6
2 Th	22 36 38	10 47 51	22 38 24	29 31 41	11R 43.2	26 00.8	3 35.2	21 31.7	29 25.5	14R 33.0	2 44.1	27 45.7	18R 59.3	25R 54.4
3 F	22 40 35	11 48 02	6♈27 36	13♈25 42	11 37.3	27 40.4	4 49.4	22 15.8	29 47.0	14 32.7	2 49.8	27 48.5	18 58.4	25 54.2
4 Sa	22 44 31	12 48 10	20 25 35	27 26 50	11 34.1	29 21.0	6 03.6	22 59.8	0♉08.5	14 32.2	2 55.6	27 51.3	18 57.5	25 54.0
5 Su	22 48 28	13 48 17	4♉29 08	11♉32 09	11D 33.3	1♓02.7	7 17.7	23 44.0	0 30.2	14 31.5	3 01.5	27 54.0	18 56.7	25 53.9
6 M	22 52 24	14 48 22	18 35 38	25 39 23	11 33.8	2 45.5	8 31.8	24 28.1	0 51.9	14 30.7	3 07.4	27 56.7	18 55.9	25 53.8
7 Tu	22 56 21	15 48 25	2♊43 13	9♊47 00	11R 34.5	4 29.4	9 45.9	25 12.2	1 13.7	14 29.6	3 13.4	27 59.3	18 55.1	25 53.7
8 W	23 00 17	16 48 25	16 50 35	23 53 50	11 34.4	6 14.5	10 59.9	25 56.4	1 35.6	14 28.4	3 19.5	28 02.0	18 54.3	25 53.6
9 Th	23 04 14	17 48 23	0♋56 37	7♋58 45	11 32.6	8 00.6	12 13.9	26 40.6	1 57.6	14 26.9	3 25.6	28 04.6	18 53.6	25 53.6
10 F	23 08 10	18 48 19	15 00 02	22 00 13	11 28.5	9 47.8	13 27.8	27 24.8	2 19.7	14 25.3	3 31.8	28 07.1	18 52.9	25D 53.5
11 Sa	23 12 07	19 48 13	28 59 02	5♌56 09	11 22.2	11 36.2	14 41.7	28 09.1	2 41.8	14 23.5	3 38.0	28 09.7	18 52.3	25 53.5
12 Su	23 16 04	20 48 05	12♌51 14	19 43 54	11 14.3	13 25.8	15 55.5	28 53.3	3 04.0	14 21.5	3 44.3	28 12.2	18 51.7	25 53.5
13 M	23 20 00	21 47 54	26 33 46	3♍20 29	11 05.7	15 16.5	17 09.3	29 37.6	3 26.3	14 19.3	3 50.7	28 14.6	18 51.1	25 53.6
14 Tu	23 23 57	22 47 42	10♍03 43	16 43 09	10 57.2	17 08.4	18 23.0	0♒21.9	3 48.7	14 17.0	3 57.1	28 17.0	18 50.5	25 53.6
15 W	23 27 53	23 47 27	23 18 33	29 49 44	10 49.9	19 01.4	19 36.7	1 06.3	4 11.1	14 14.4	4 03.5	28 19.4	18 50.0	25 53.7
16 Th	23 31 50	24 47 11	6♎16 36	12♎39 07	10 44.3	20 55.6	20 50.4	1 50.6	4 33.7	14 11.7	4 10.0	28 21.7	18 49.4	25 53.8
17 F	23 35 46	25 46 52	18 57 22	25 11 28	10 40.9	22 50.8	22 04.0	2 35.0	4 56.3	14 08.8	4 16.6	28 24.0	18 49.0	25 54.0
18 Sa	23 39 43	26 46 32	1♏21 39	7♏28 13	10D 39.6	24 47.2	23 17.5	3 19.4	5 18.9	14 05.8	4 23.2	28 26.3	18 48.5	25 54.1
19 Su	23 43 39	27 46 10	13 31 33	19 32 04	10 39.9	26 44.6	24 31.0	4 03.8	5 41.7	14 02.5	4 29.8	28 28.5	18 48.1	25 54.3
20 M	23 47 36	28 45 46	25 30 15	1♐26 39	10 41.2	28 43.0	25 44.5	4 48.3	6 04.5	13 59.1	4 36.5	28 30.7	18 47.8	25 54.5
21 Tu	23 51 32	29 45 20	7♐21 50	13 16 24	10 42.9	0♈42.4	26 57.9	5 32.7	6 27.3	13 55.5	4 43.3	28 32.8	18 47.4	25 54.7
22 W	23 55 29	0♈44 53	19 10 59	25 06 14	10R 44.0	2 42.5	28 11.3	6 17.2	6 50.3	13 51.7	4 50.1	28 34.9	18 47.1	25 55.0
23 Th	23 59 26	1 44 24	1♑02 47	7♑01 18	10 44.0	4 43.3	29 24.6	7 01.7	7 13.3	13 47.8	4 56.9	28 37.0	18 46.8	25 55.2
24 F	0 03 22	2 43 53	13 02 23	19 06 40	10 42.5	6 44.7	0♉37.9	7 46.3	7 36.3	13 43.7	5 03.8	28 39.0	18 46.6	25 55.5
25 Sa	0 07 19	3 43 21	25 14 42	1♒27 00	10 39.4	8 46.5	1 51.1	8 30.8	7 59.5	13 39.5	5 10.8	28 40.9	18 46.4	25 55.8
26 Su	0 11 15	4 42 46	7♒44 02	14 06 11	10 34.9	10 48.5	3 04.3	9 15.3	8 22.6	13 35.0	5 17.7	28 42.9	18 46.2	25 56.2
27 M	0 15 12	5 42 10	20 33 44	27 06 53	10 29.4	12 50.4	4 17.4	9 59.9	8 45.9	13 30.5	5 24.8	28 44.8	18 46.1	25 56.5
28 Tu	0 19 08	6 41 32	3♓45 43	10♓30 12	10 23.7	14 51.9	5 30.5	10 44.5	9 09.2	13 25.7	5 31.8	28 46.6	18 46.0	25 56.9
29 W	0 23 05	7 40 52	17 20 08	24 15 17	10 18.4	16 52.9	6 43.5	11 29.1	9 32.6	13 20.8	5 38.9	28 48.4	18 45.9	25 57.3
30 Th	0 27 01	8 40 09	1♈15 13	8♈19 27	10 14.3	18 53.0	7 56.4	12 13.7	9 56.0	13 15.8	5 46.0	28 50.1	18D 45.9	25 57.7
31 F	0 30 58	9 39 25	15 27 23	22 38 21	10 11.7	20 51.7	9 09.4	12 58.3	10 19.5	13 10.6	5 53.2	28 51.8	18 45.9	25 58.1

April 1911 — LONGITUDE

Day	Sid.Time	☉	0 hr ☽	Noon ☽	True ☊	☿	♀	♂	⚳	♃	♄	♅	♆	♇
1 Sa	0 34 55	10♈38 39	29♈51 39	7♉06 35	10♉10.6	22♈48.8	10♉22.2	13♒43.0	10♉43.0	13♏05.2	6♉00.4	28♑53.5	18♋45.9	25♊58.6
2 Su	0 38 51	11 37 51	14♉22 24	21 38 27	10D 11.0	24 43.8	11 35.0	14 27.6	11 06.6	12R 59.8	6 07.6	28 55.1	18 45.9	25 59.1
3 M	0 42 48	12 37 00	28 54 05	6♊08 43	10 12.2	26 36.5	12 47.8	15 12.3	11 30.2	12 54.2	6 14.9	28 56.7	18 46.0	25 59.6
4 Tu	0 46 44	13 36 07	13♊21 51	20 33 02	10 13.6	28 26.3	14 00.4	15 56.9	11 53.9	12 48.4	6 22.2	28 58.2	18 46.2	26 00.1
5 W	0 50 41	14 35 12	27 41 56	4♋48 15	10R 14.8	0♉12.9	15 13.1	16 41.6	12 17.6	12 42.5	6 29.5	28 59.7	18 46.3	26 00.7
6 Th	0 54 37	15 34 15	11♋51 44	18 52 15	10 15.0	1 55.9	16 25.6	17 26.3	12 41.4	12 36.5	6 36.9	29 01.1	18 46.5	26 01.3
7 F	0 58 34	16 33 15	25 49 39	2♌43 50	10 14.2	3 35.0	17 38.1	18 10.9	13 05.2	12 30.4	6 44.2	29 02.5	18 46.8	26 01.9
8 Sa	1 02 30	17 32 13	9♌34 44	16 22 19	10 12.2	5 10.0	18 50.5	18 55.6	13 29.0	12 24.2	6 51.6	29 03.8	18 47.0	26 02.5
9 Su	1 06 27	18 31 08	23 06 32	29 47 22	10 09.5	6 40.4	20 02.9	19 40.3	13 52.9	12 17.8	6 59.1	29 05.1	18 47.3	26 03.1
10 M	1 10 24	19 30 01	6♍24 48	12♍58 49	10 06.4	8 06.0	21 15.2	20 25.0	14 16.9	12 11.4	7 06.5	29 06.3	18 47.7	26 03.8
11 Tu	1 14 20	20 28 52	19 29 25	25 56 37	10 03.4	9 26.7	22 27.4	21 09.7	14 40.9	12 04.8	7 14.0	29 07.5	18 48.0	26 04.4
12 W	1 18 17	21 27 41	2♎20 26	8♎40 55	10 00.8	10 42.1	23 39.6	21 54.4	15 04.9	11 58.1	7 21.5	29 08.7	18 48.4	26 05.1
13 Th	1 22 13	22 26 28	14 58 07	21 12 07	9 59.0	11 52.2	24 51.6	22 39.1	15 28.9	11 51.4	7 29.0	29 09.7	18 48.9	26 05.8
14 F	1 26 10	23 25 13	27 23 02	3♏31 02	9D 58.1	12 56.7	26 03.7	23 23.9	15 53.0	11 44.5	7 36.5	29 10.8	18 49.3	26 06.6
15 Sa	1 30 06	24 23 56	9♏36 18	15 39 02	9 58.1	13 55.6	27 15.6	24 08.6	16 17.2	11 37.6	7 44.1	29 11.8	18 49.8	26 07.3
16 Su	1 34 03	25 22 37	21 39 32	27 38 06	9 58.8	14 48.7	28 27.5	24 53.3	16 41.3	11 30.6	7 51.7	29 12.7	18 50.4	26 08.1
17 M	1 37 59	26 21 16	3♐35 04	9♐30 49	9 59.9	15 36.0	29 39.3	25 38.1	17 05.5	11 23.5	7 59.3	29 13.6	18 50.9	26 08.9
18 Tu	1 41 56	27 19 54	15 25 46	21 20 24	10 01.1	16 17.3	0♊51.0	26 22.8	17 29.8	11 16.3	8 06.9	29 14.5	18 51.5	26 09.7
19 W	1 45 53	28 18 30	27 15 11	3♑10 40	10 02.3	16 52.6	2 02.7	27 07.6	17 54.1	11 09.1	8 14.5	29 15.3	18 52.1	26 10.5
20 Th	1 49 49	29 17 04	9♑07 21	15 05 50	10 03.1	17 21.8	3 14.3	27 52.3	18 18.4	11 01.8	8 22.1	29 16.0	18 52.8	26 11.4
21 F	1 53 46	0♉15 36	21 06 40	27 10 27	10R 03.5	17 45.1	4 25.8	28 37.1	18 42.7	10 54.4	8 29.8	29 16.7	18 53.5	26 12.2
22 Sa	1 57 42	1 14 07	3♒17 45	9♒29 07	10 03.4	18 02.4	5 37.2	29 21.8	19 07.1	10 47.0	8 37.4	29 17.4	18 54.2	26 13.1
23 Su	2 01 39	2 12 37	15 45 06	22 06 11	10 02.9	18 13.7	6 48.6	0♓06.6	19 31.5	10 39.5	8 45.1	29 17.9	18 55.0	26 14.0
24 M	2 05 35	3 11 04	28 32 48	5♓05 19	10 02.2	18R 19.2	7 59.9	0 51.3	19 56.0	10 32.0	8 52.7	29 18.5	18 55.8	26 14.9
25 Tu	2 09 32	4 09 30	11♓44 01	18 29 04	10 01.5	18 19.0	9 11.1	1 36.1	20 20.4	10 24.4	9 00.4	29 19.0	18 56.6	26 15.9
26 W	2 13 28	5 07 54	25 20 32	2♈18 18	10 00.8	18 13.3	10 22.3	2 20.8	20 44.9	10 16.9	9 08.1	29 19.4	18 57.4	26 16.8
27 Th	2 17 25	6 06 17	9♈22 10	16 31 44	10 00.4	18 02.4	11 33.4	3 05.5	21 09.5	10 09.2	9 15.8	29 19.8	18 58.3	26 17.8
28 F	2 21 22	7 04 38	23 46 29	1♉05 44	10D 00.2	17 46.5	12 44.3	3 50.3	21 34.0	10 01.6	9 23.5	29 20.2	18 59.2	26 18.7
29 Sa	2 25 18	8 02 57	8♉28 42	15 54 28	10 00.2	17 26.1	13 55.3	4 35.0	21 58.6	9 54.0	9 31.2	29 20.5	19 00.2	26 19.7
30 Su	2 29 15	9 01 14	23 22 05	0♊50 31	10 00.3	17 01.5	15 06.1	5 19.7	22 23.2	9 46.3	9 38.9	29 20.7	19 01.2	26 20.8

Astro Data

	Dy Hr Mn
♃ R	1 8:49
♀0N	1 14:12
☽0N	3 0:28
♇ D	11 5:19
☽0S	16 0:44
☉0N	21 17:55
☿0N	22 11:00
☽0N	30 9:12
♆ D	31 4:41
☽0S	12 8:13
♃♇♇	19 7:43
☿ R	24 23:10
☽0N	26 19:31
♃☍♄	30 23:34

Planet Ingress

		Dy Hr Mn
⚳	♉	4 2:31
☿	♓	4 21:14
♂	♒	14 0:07
☿	♈	21 3:30
☉	♈	21 17:54
♀	♉	23 23:35
☿	♉	5 9:04
♀	♊	17 18:56
☉	♉	21 5:36
♂	♓	23 8:28

Last Aspect / ☽ Ingress

Last Aspect Dy Hr Mn			☽ Ingress	Dy Hr Mn
2 8:55	♅	⚹	♈	2 12:49
4 15:41	☿	⚹	♉	4 16:21
6 15:54	♅	△	♊	6 19:23
8 15:24	♇	☌	♋	8 22:24
10 22:33	♅	☍	♌	11 1:45
12 22:49	♇	⚹	♍	13 6:04
15 9:13	♅	△	♎	15 12:19
17 18:15	♅	□	♏	17 21:21
20 6:05	☉	△	♐	20 9:05
22 18:57	♀	△	♑	22 21:53
25 6:39	♅	☌	♒	25 9:13
27 9:52	♇	△	♓	27 17:14
29 19:50	♅	⚹	♈	29 21:52

Last Aspect / ☽ Ingress

Last Aspect Dy Hr Mn			☽ Ingress	Dy Hr Mn
31 22:22	♅	□	♉	1 0:14
3 0:03	♅	△	♊	3 1:49
5 3:09	☿	⚹	♋	5 3:53
7 5:34	♅	☍	♌	7 7:15
9 5:16	♇	⚹	♍	9 12:23
11 17:58	♅	△	♎	11 19:36
14 3:30	♅	□	♏	14 5:06
16 15:11	♅	⚹	♐	16 16:46
19 1:15	☉	△	♑	19 5:34
21 16:09	♅	☌	♒	21 17:33
23 19:43	♇	△	♓	24 2:41
26 6:53	♅	⚹	♈	26 8:03
28 9:07	♅	□	♉	28 10:13
30 9:36	♅	△	♊	30 10:39

☽ Phases & Eclipses

Dy Hr Mn		
1 0:31	●	9♓19
7 23:01	☽	16♊16
14 23:58	○	23♍17
23 0:26	☾	1♑16
30 12:38	●	8♈42
6 5:55	☽	15♋19
13 14:36	○	22♎33
21 18:35	☾	0♒32
28 22:25	●	7♉30
28 22:27:10	●	T 04'57"

Astro Data

1 March 1911
Julian Day # 4077
SVP 6♓30'11"
GC 25♐35.9 ⚴ 23♓06.6
Eris 25♓42.2 ⚵ 22♎09.6R
⚷ 2♓53.6 ⚶ 13♉08.6
☽ Mean ☊ 13♉17.2

1 April 1911
Julian Day # 4108
SVP 6♓30'08"
GC 25♐36.0 ⚴ 4♈15.7
Eris 26♓06.3 ⚵ 16♎17.0R
⚷ 4♓50.0 ⚶ 24♉43.0
☽ Mean ☊ 11♉38.7

LONGITUDE — May 1911

Day	Sid.Time	☉	0 hr ☽	Noon ☽	True ☊	☿	♀	♂	⚳	♃	♄	♅	♆	♇
1 M	2 33 11	9♉59 30	8♊18 46	15♊45 50	10♉00.3	16♉33.3	16♊16.8	6♓04.3	22♉47.9	9♏38.6	9♉46.6	29♑20.9	19♋02.2	26♊21.8
2 Tu	2 37 08	10 57 44	23 10 49	0♋32 53	10R 00.3	16R 02.0	17 27.5	6 49.0	23 12.5	9R 31.0	9 54.3	29 21.0	19 03.2	26 22.9
3 W	2 41 04	11 55 55	7♋51 19	15 05 32	10 00.1	15 28.1	18 38.0	7 33.7	23 37.2	9 23.3	10 02.0	29 21.1	19 04.3	26 23.9
4 Th	2 45 01	12 54 05	22 15 06	29 19 40	10 00.0	14 52.4	19 48.5	8 18.3	24 01.9	9 15.7	10 09.7	29R 21.2	19 05.4	26 25.0
5 F	2 48 57	13 52 13	6♌19 04	13♌13 12	9D 59.9	14 15.4	20 58.9	9 02.9	24 26.6	9 08.1	10 17.4	29 21.2	19 06.5	26 26.1
6 Sa	2 52 54	14 50 18	20 02 05	26 45 50	10 00.0	13 37.9	22 09.2	9 47.5	24 51.3	9 00.5	10 25.1	29 21.1	19 07.6	26 27.2
7 Su	2 56 51	15 48 22	3♍24 36	9♍58 36	10 00.3	13 00.5	23 19.3	10 32.1	25 16.1	8 52.9	10 32.8	29 21.0	19 08.8	26 28.3
8 M	3 00 47	16 46 24	16 28 06	22 53 22	10 00.9	12 23.8	24 29.4	11 16.6	25 40.9	8 45.3	10 40.4	29 20.8	19 10.0	26 29.5
9 Tu	3 04 44	17 44 23	29 14 42	5♎32 23	10 01.6	11 48.6	25 39.4	12 01.2	26 05.6	8 37.8	10 48.1	29 20.6	19 11.3	26 30.6
10 W	3 08 40	18 42 21	11♎46 44	17 58 00	10 02.4	11 15.3	26 49.3	12 45.7	26 30.4	8 30.4	10 55.8	29 20.4	19 12.5	26 31.8
11 Th	3 12 37	19 40 18	24 06 30	0♏12 29	10R 02.9	10 44.6	27 59.0	13 30.2	26 55.3	8 23.0	11 03.4	29 20.1	19 13.8	26 32.9
12 F	3 16 33	20 38 12	6♏16 12	12 17 56	10 03.1	10 16.8	29 08.7	14 14.7	27 20.1	8 15.6	11 11.1	29 19.7	19 15.1	26 34.1
13 Sa	3 20 30	21 36 05	18 17 54	24 16 21	10 02.7	9 52.4	0♋18.2	14 59.2	27 44.9	8 08.3	11 18.7	29 19.3	19 16.5	26 35.3
14 Su	3 24 26	22 33 57	0♐13 33	6♐09 44	10 01.7	9 31.8	1 27.7	15 43.6	28 09.8	8 01.1	11 26.3	29 18.9	19 17.8	26 36.5
15 M	3 28 23	23 31 48	12 05 10	18 00 09	10 00.1	9 15.1	2 37.0	16 28.1	28 34.7	7 53.9	11 33.9	29 18.4	19 19.2	26 37.7
16 Tu	3 32 20	24 29 36	23 54 58	29 49 55	9 58.0	9 02.7	3 46.2	17 12.5	28 59.6	7 46.8	11 41.5	29 17.8	19 20.7	26 39.0
17 W	3 36 16	25 27 24	5♑45 22	11♑41 41	9 55.7	8 54.7	4 55.3	17 56.8	29 24.5	7 39.8	11 49.0	29 17.2	19 22.1	26 40.2
18 Th	3 40 13	26 25 11	17 39 15	23 38 30	9 53.5	8D 51.2	6 04.3	18 41.2	29 49.4	7 32.8	11 56.6	29 16.6	19 23.6	26 41.5
19 F	3 44 09	27 22 56	29 39 51	5♒43 49	9 51.7	8 52.2	7 13.1	19 25.5	0♊14.3	7 26.0	12 04.1	29 15.9	19 25.1	26 42.8
20 Sa	3 48 06	28 20 40	11♒50 50	18 01 27	9D 50.5	8 57.8	8 21.9	20 09.8	0 39.3	7 19.2	12 11.7	29 15.2	19 26.6	26 44.0
21 Su	3 52 02	29 18 23	24 16 08	0♓35 25	9 50.2	9 07.9	9 30.5	20 54.1	1 04.2	7 12.5	12 19.1	29 14.4	19 28.1	26 45.3
22 M	3 55 59	0♊16 05	6♓59 45	13 29 37	9 50.6	9 22.6	10 39.0	21 38.3	1 29.2	7 05.9	12 26.6	29 13.6	19 29.7	26 46.6
23 Tu	3 59 55	1 13 46	20 05 25	26 47 29	9 51.8	9 41.7	11 47.3	22 22.5	1 54.1	6 59.5	12 34.1	29 12.7	19 31.3	26 47.9
24 W	4 03 52	2 11 25	3♈36 05	10♈31 21	9 53.2	10 05.1	12 55.6	23 06.7	2 19.1	6 53.1	12 41.5	29 11.8	19 32.9	26 49.2
25 Th	4 07 49	3 09 04	17 33 18	24 41 49	9 54.4	10 32.8	14 03.7	23 50.8	2 44.1	6 46.8	12 48.9	29 10.8	19 34.6	26 50.6
26 F	4 11 45	4 06 42	1♉56 35	9♉17 07	9R 54.9	11 04.7	15 11.6	24 34.9	3 09.1	6 40.7	12 56.3	29 09.8	19 36.2	26 51.9
27 Sa	4 15 42	5 04 19	16 42 46	24 12 41	9 54.4	11 40.6	16 19.5	25 18.9	3 34.1	6 34.7	13 03.6	29 08.7	19 37.9	26 53.2
28 Su	4 19 38	6 01 55	1♊45 52	9♊21 12	9 52.6	12 20.4	17 27.2	26 02.9	3 59.1	6 28.8	13 11.0	29 07.6	19 39.6	26 54.6
29 M	4 23 35	6 59 30	16 57 27	24 33 22	9 49.7	13 04.1	18 34.7	26 46.9	4 24.1	6 23.0	13 18.3	29 06.5	19 41.3	26 55.9
30 Tu	4 27 31	7 57 03	2♋07 42	9♋39 15	9 46.0	13 51.5	19 42.2	27 30.8	4 49.1	6 17.4	13 25.5	29 05.3	19 43.1	26 57.3
31 W	4 31 28	8 54 35	17 06 56	24 29 49	9 42.1	14 42.5	20 49.4	28 14.6	5 14.2	6 11.9	13 32.8	29 04.1	19 44.8	26 58.7

LONGITUDE — June 1911

Day	Sid.Time	☉	0 hr ☽	Noon ☽	True ☊	☿	♀	♂	⚳	♃	♄	♅	♆	♇
1 Th	4 35 25	9♊52 06	1♌47 08	8♌58 19	9♉38.6	15♉37.0	21♋56.5	28♓58.4	5♊39.2	6♏06.5	13♉40.0	29♑02.8	19♋46.6	27♊00.1
2 F	4 39 21	10 49 36	16 02 59	23 00 57	9R 36.2	16 35.0	23 03.4	29 42.2	6 04.2	6R 01.3	13 47.1	29R 01.5	19 48.4	27 01.4
3 Sa	4 43 18	11 47 04	29 52 09	6♍36 43	9D 35.0	17 36.3	24 10.2	0♈25.9	6 29.2	5 56.2	13 54.3	29 00.2	19 50.3	27 02.8
4 Su	4 47 14	12 44 31	13♍14 54	19 47 01	9 35.1	18 40.9	25 16.8	1 09.5	6 54.2	5 51.2	14 01.4	28 58.8	19 52.1	27 04.2
5 M	4 51 11	13 41 57	26 13 30	2♎34 47	9 36.2	19 48.7	26 23.2	1 53.1	7 19.2	5 46.5	14 08.4	28 57.4	19 54.0	27 05.6
6 Tu	4 55 07	14 39 21	8♎51 22	15 03 45	9 37.8	20 59.6	27 29.5	2 36.6	7 44.2	5 41.8	14 15.5	28 55.9	19 55.8	27 07.0
7 W	4 59 04	15 36 45	21 12 27	27 17 58	9 39.2	22 13.7	28 35.5	3 20.1	8 09.3	5 37.3	14 22.5	28 54.4	19 57.7	27 08.4
8 Th	5 03 00	16 34 07	3♏20 46	9♏21 19	9R 39.8	23 30.8	29 41.4	4 03.5	8 34.3	5 33.0	14 29.4	28 52.9	19 59.7	27 09.8
9 F	5 06 57	17 31 28	15 20 01	21 17 17	9 39.1	24 50.9	0♌47.0	4 46.9	8 59.3	5 28.8	14 36.3	28 51.3	20 01.6	27 11.3
10 Sa	5 10 53	18 28 49	27 13 28	3♐08 53	9 36.6	26 13.9	1 52.5	5 30.2	9 24.3	5 24.8	14 43.2	28 49.7	20 03.5	27 12.7
11 Su	5 14 50	19 26 09	9♐03 51	14 58 39	9 32.3	27 40.0	2 57.8	6 13.4	9 49.3	5 21.0	14 50.0	28 48.0	20 05.5	27 14.1
12 M	5 18 47	20 23 28	20 53 31	26 48 41	9 26.3	29 08.9	4 02.8	6 56.6	10 14.2	5 17.3	14 56.8	28 46.3	20 07.5	27 15.5
13 Tu	5 22 43	21 20 46	2♑44 24	8♑40 53	9 19.1	0♊40.8	5 07.6	7 39.7	10 39.2	5 13.8	15 03.5	28 44.6	20 09.5	27 17.0
14 W	5 26 40	22 18 04	14 38 22	20 37 03	9 11.2	2 15.5	6 12.3	8 22.8	11 04.2	5 10.4	15 10.2	28 42.9	20 11.5	27 18.4
15 Th	5 30 36	23 15 21	26 37 13	2♒39 07	9 03.5	3 53.1	7 16.7	9 05.8	11 29.2	5 07.3	15 16.9	28 41.1	20 13.5	27 19.8
16 F	5 34 33	24 12 38	8♒43 02	14 49 16	8 56.8	5 33.5	8 20.8	9 48.7	11 54.2	5 04.2	15 23.5	28 39.3	20 15.5	27 21.3
17 Sa	5 38 29	25 09 54	20 58 11	27 10 08	8 51.5	7 16.7	9 24.8	10 31.5	12 19.1	5 01.4	15 30.0	28 37.4	20 17.6	27 22.7
18 Su	5 42 26	26 07 10	3♓25 30	9♓44 42	8 48.2	9 02.7	10 28.5	11 14.3	12 44.1	4 58.7	15 36.5	28 35.5	20 19.6	27 24.1
19 M	5 46 23	27 04 26	16 08 09	22 36 18	8D 46.8	10 51.5	11 31.9	11 57.0	13 09.0	4 56.2	15 43.0	28 33.6	20 21.7	27 25.6
20 Tu	5 50 19	28 01 41	29 09 33	5♈48 17	8 46.9	12 42.8	12 35.1	12 39.6	13 34.0	4 53.9	15 49.4	28 31.7	20 23.8	27 27.0
21 W	5 54 16	28 58 57	12♈32 52	19 23 36	8 47.9	14 36.8	13 38.0	13 22.2	13 58.9	4 51.7	15 55.8	28 29.7	20 25.9	27 28.4
22 Th	5 58 12	29 56 12	26 20 39	3♉24 08	8R 48.8	16 33.3	14 40.7	14 04.6	14 23.8	4 49.8	16 02.1	28 27.7	20 28.0	27 29.9
23 F	6 02 09	0♋53 27	10♉33 58	17 49 55	8 48.5	18 32.1	15 43.1	14 47.0	14 48.7	4 48.0	16 08.3	28 25.7	20 30.1	27 31.3
24 Sa	6 06 05	1 50 42	25 11 36	2♊38 23	8 46.5	20 33.1	16 45.3	15 29.3	15 13.6	4 46.4	16 14.5	28 23.7	20 32.2	27 32.7
25 Su	6 10 02	2 47 57	10♊09 29	17 43 53	8 42.2	22 36.2	17 47.1	16 11.5	15 38.5	4 44.9	16 20.6	28 21.6	20 34.4	27 34.2
26 M	6 13 58	3 45 12	25 20 26	2♋57 52	8 35.8	24 41.2	18 48.7	16 53.6	16 03.4	4 43.7	16 26.7	28 19.5	20 36.5	27 35.6
27 Tu	6 17 55	4 42 27	10♋34 49	18 09 57	8 27.9	26 47.7	19 49.9	17 35.6	16 28.2	4 42.6	16 32.7	28 17.4	20 38.7	27 37.1
28 W	6 21 52	5 39 41	25 41 58	3♌09 40	8 19.4	28 55.7	20 50.9	18 17.5	16 53.1	4 41.7	16 38.7	28 15.2	20 40.8	27 38.5
29 Th	6 25 48	6 36 55	10♌32 01	17 48 12	8 11.5	1♋04.7	21 51.5	18 59.4	17 17.9	4 41.0	16 44.6	28 13.1	20 43.0	27 39.9
30 F	6 29 45	7 34 08	24 57 35	1♍59 46	8 05.0	3 14.6	22 51.7	19 41.1	17 42.7	4 40.5	16 50.4	28 10.9	20 45.2	27 41.3

Astro Data (Dy Hr Mn)

♅ R 4 20:18
☽ 0S 9 14:17
♄∠♇ 16 2:34
☿ D 18 18:37
☽ 0N 24 5:20

☽ 0S 5 19:39
♂0N 9 5:18
☽ 0N 20 13:02

Planet Ingress (Dy Hr Mn)

♀ ♋ 13 5:42
⚳ ♊ 18 22:12
☉ ♊ 22 5:19

♂ ♈ 2 21:48
♀ ♌ 8 18:48
☿ ♊ 13 1:26
☉ ♋ 22 13:36
☿ ♋ 28 23:59

Last Aspect / ☽ Ingress (May)

Dy Hr Mn		☽ Ingress Dy Hr Mn
2 5:12	♇ ☌	♋ 2 11:06
4 12:03	♅ ☍	♌ 4 13:09
6 11:27	♇ ⚹	♍ 6 17:49
9 0:11	♅ △	♎ 9 1:26
11 10:17	♅ □	♏ 11 11:35
13 22:10	♅ ⚹	♐ 13 23:33
16 5:32	♇ ☍	♑ 16 12:20
18 23:13	♅ ☌	♒ 19 0:40
21 9:23	☉ □	♓ 21 10:53
23 16:17	♅ ⚹	♈ 23 17:41
25 19:26	♅ □	♉ 25 20:48
27 19:50	♅ △	♊ 27 21:12
29 15:46	♇ ☌	♋ 29 20:37
31 19:30	♅ ☍	♌ 31 21:03

Last Aspect / ☽ Ingress (June)

Dy Hr Mn		☽ Ingress Dy Hr Mn
2 19:00	♇ ⚹	♍ 3 0:14
5 5:09	♅ △	♎ 5 7:07
7 15:10	♅ □	♏ 7 17:21
10 3:16	♅ ⚹	♐ 10 5:37
12 12:54	♇ ☍	♑ 12 18:27
15 4:08	♅ ☌	♒ 15 6:44
17 12:24	♇ △	♓ 17 17:27
19 22:53	♅ ⚹	♈ 20 1:32
22 5:42	☉ ⚹	♉ 22 6:14
24 5:11	♅ △	♊ 24 7:46
26 3:32	♇ ☌	♋ 26 7:20
28 4:07	♅ ☍	♌ 28 6:54
30 4:37	♇ ⚹	♍ 30 8:34

☽ Phases & Eclipses (Dy Hr Mn)

5 13:14 ☽ 13♌55
13 6:09 ○ 21♏22
13 5:56 ☍ A 0.799
21 9:23 ☾ 29♒12
28 6:24 ● 5♊48

3 22:04 ☽ 12♍11
11 21:50 ○ 19♐50
19 20:50 ☾ 27♓26
26 13:19 ● 3♋48

Astro Data

1 May 1911
Julian Day # 4138
SVP 6♓30'05"
GC 25♐36.1 ⚴ 15♈20.9
Eris 26♓26.9 ⚵ 9♎52.6R
⚷ 6♓15.6 ⚶ 6♊59.3
☽ Mean ☊ 10♉03.4

1 June 1911
Julian Day # 4169
SVP 6♓29'59"
GC 25♐36.1 ⚴ 26♈46.6
Eris 26♓40.6 ⚵ 7♎26.3
⚷ 6♓59.1 ⚶ 20♊13.5
☽ Mean ☊ 8♉24.9

July 1911 LONGITUDE

Day	Sid.Time	☉	0 hr ☽	Noon ☽	True ☊	☿	♀	♂	⚳	♃	♄	♅	♆	♇
1 Sa	6 33 41	8♋31 21	8♍54 34	15♍42 00	8♉00.6	5♋25.0	23♌51.7	20♈22.7	18♊07.5	4♏40.2	16♉56.2	28♑08.7	20♋47.4	27♊42.8
2 Su	6 37 38	9 28 33	22 22 14	28 55 36	7D 58.4	7 35.7	24 51.2	21 04.2	18 32.3	4D 40.0	17 01.9	28R 06.4	20 49.5	27 44.2
3 M	6 41 34	10 25 45	5♎22 31	11♎43 29	7 57.9	9 46.4	25 50.4	21 45.6	18 57.0	4 40.0	17 07.5	28 04.2	20 51.7	27 45.6
4 Tu	6 45 31	11 22 57	17 59 07	24 09 59	7 58.3	11 56.7	26 49.2	22 26.8	19 21.7	4 40.2	17 13.1	28 01.9	20 53.9	27 47.0
5 W	6 49 27	12 20 09	0♏16 45	6♏20 02	7R 58.8	14 06.5	27 47.6	23 08.0	19 46.4	4 40.6	17 18.6	27 59.7	20 56.1	27 48.4
6 Th	6 53 24	13 17 20	12 20 27	18 18 36	7 58.3	16 15.5	28 45.6	23 49.1	20 11.1	4 41.2	17 24.1	27 57.4	20 58.4	27 49.8
7 F	6 57 21	14 14 32	24 15 02	0♐10 18	7 56.0	18 23.6	29 43.1	24 30.0	20 35.8	4 41.9	17 29.4	27 55.1	21 00.6	27 51.2
8 Sa	7 01 17	15 11 43	6♐04 53	11 59 12	7 51.2	20 30.5	0♍40.3	25 10.9	21 00.4	4 42.8	17 34.7	27 52.7	21 02.8	27 52.6
9 Su	7 05 14	16 08 54	17 53 40	23 48 37	7 43.8	22 36.0	1 36.9	25 51.6	21 25.1	4 43.9	17 40.0	27 50.4	21 05.0	27 53.9
10 M	7 09 10	17 06 05	29 44 22	5♑41 10	7 34.0	24 40.1	2 33.1	26 32.2	21 49.6	4 45.2	17 45.1	27 48.1	21 07.2	27 55.3
11 Tu	7 13 07	18 03 17	11♑39 16	17 38 49	7 22.4	26 42.7	3 28.8	27 12.7	22 14.2	4 46.7	17 50.2	27 45.7	21 09.5	27 56.7
12 W	7 17 03	19 00 29	23 40 01	29 43 00	7 09.9	28 43.6	4 24.0	27 53.0	22 38.8	4 48.3	17 55.2	27 43.4	21 11.7	27 58.0
13 Th	7 21 00	19 57 41	5♒47 54	11♒54 50	6 57.5	0♌42.9	5 18.7	28 33.2	23 03.3	4 50.1	18 00.2	27 41.0	21 13.9	27 59.4
14 F	7 24 57	20 54 53	18 03 58	24 15 25	6 46.3	2 40.3	6 12.9	29 13.4	23 27.8	4 52.1	18 05.0	27 38.6	21 16.1	28 00.7
15 Sa	7 28 53	21 52 06	0♓29 22	6♓45 59	6 37.3	4 36.0	7 06.5	29 53.3	23 52.2	4 54.2	18 09.8	27 36.2	21 18.4	28 02.1
16 Su	7 32 50	22 49 19	13 05 31	19 28 11	6 30.8	6 29.9	7 59.5	0♉33.2	24 16.7	4 56.6	18 14.6	27 33.8	21 20.6	28 03.4
17 M	7 36 46	23 46 32	25 54 16	2♈24 04	6 27.1	8 22.0	8 51.9	1 12.9	24 41.1	4 59.1	18 19.2	27 31.4	21 22.8	28 04.7
18 Tu	7 40 43	24 43 47	8♈57 53	15 36 03	6D 25.5	10 12.3	9 43.7	1 52.4	25 05.5	5 01.7	18 23.7	27 29.0	21 25.0	28 06.0
19 W	7 44 39	25 41 02	22 18 52	29 06 38	6R 25.3	12 00.7	10 34.9	2 31.8	25 29.8	5 04.6	18 28.2	27 26.6	21 27.3	28 07.3
20 Th	7 48 36	26 38 18	5♉59 36	12♉57 54	6 25.3	13 47.3	11 25.5	3 11.1	25 54.1	5 07.6	18 32.6	27 24.2	21 29.5	28 08.6
21 F	7 52 32	27 35 35	20 01 37	27 10 44	6 24.2	15 32.1	12 15.4	3 50.2	26 18.4	5 10.8	18 36.9	27 21.8	21 31.7	28 09.9
22 Sa	7 56 29	28 32 53	4♊25 01	11♊44 07	6 21.0	17 15.1	13 04.5	4 29.2	26 42.7	5 14.1	18 41.2	27 19.4	21 33.9	28 11.2
23 Su	8 00 26	29 30 12	19 07 29	26 34 25	6 15.2	18 56.3	13 53.0	5 08.0	27 06.9	5 17.6	18 45.3	27 17.0	21 36.2	28 12.4
24 M	8 04 22	0♌27 31	4♋03 59	11♋35 08	6 06.8	20 35.7	14 40.7	5 46.6	27 31.1	5 21.3	18 49.4	27 14.6	21 38.4	28 13.7
25 Tu	8 08 19	1 24 51	19 06 44	26 37 31	5 56.4	22 13.2	15 27.7	6 25.1	27 55.2	5 25.2	18 53.4	27 12.2	21 40.6	28 14.9
26 W	8 12 15	2 22 12	4♌06 16	11♌31 45	5 45.3	23 49.0	16 13.8	7 03.4	28 19.4	5 29.2	18 57.3	27 09.8	21 42.8	28 16.2
27 Th	8 16 12	3 19 34	18 52 55	26 08 46	5 34.6	25 22.9	16 59.1	7 41.5	28 43.4	5 33.4	19 01.1	27 07.4	21 45.0	28 17.4
28 F	8 20 08	4 16 56	3♍18 34	10♍21 44	5 25.6	26 55.1	17 43.5	8 19.5	29 07.5	5 37.7	19 04.8	27 05.0	21 47.2	28 18.6
29 Sa	8 24 05	5 14 18	17 17 55	24 06 56	5 18.9	28 25.4	18 26.9	8 57.2	29 31.4	5 42.2	19 08.4	27 02.7	21 49.3	28 19.8
30 Su	8 28 01	6 11 41	0♎48 50	7♎23 47	5 14.8	29 53.9	19 09.5	9 34.8	29 55.4	5 46.9	19 11.9	27 00.3	21 51.5	28 21.0
31 M	8 31 58	7 09 05	13 52 08	20 14 20	5 12.9	1♍20.5	19 51.0	10 12.2	0♋19.3	5 51.7	19 15.4	26 57.9	21 53.7	28 22.1

August 1911 LONGITUDE

Day	Sid.Time	☉	0 hr ☽	Noon ☽	True ☊	☿	♀	♂	⚳	♃	♄	♅	♆	♇
1 Tu	8 35 55	8♌06 29	26♎30 54	2♏42 27	5♉12.5	2♍45.2	20♍31.6	10♉49.3	0♋43.1	5♏56.6	19♉18.7	26♑55.6	21♋55.9	28♊23.3
2 W	8 39 51	9 03 54	8♏49 37	14 53 03	5R 12.4	4 08.1	21 11.0	11 26.3	1 07.0	6 01.8	19 22.0	26R 53.2	21 58.0	28 24.4
3 Th	8 43 48	10 01 19	20 53 27	26 51 28	5 11.7	5 29.0	21 49.3	12 03.1	1 30.7	6 07.1	19 25.1	26 50.9	22 00.1	28 25.6
4 F	8 47 44	10 58 45	2♐47 45	8♐42 56	5 09.2	6 47.9	22 26.5	12 39.7	1 54.4	6 12.5	19 28.2	26 48.6	22 02.3	28 26.7
5 Sa	8 51 41	11 56 12	14 37 37	20 32 20	5 04.2	8 04.8	23 02.5	13 16.1	2 18.1	6 18.1	19 31.2	26 46.3	22 04.4	28 27.8
6 Su	8 55 37	12 53 40	26 27 35	2♑23 49	4 56.7	9 19.6	23 37.2	13 52.3	2 41.7	6 23.8	19 34.1	26 44.0	22 06.5	28 28.9
7 M	8 59 34	13 51 09	8♑21 26	14 20 47	4 46.6	10 32.3	24 10.6	14 28.3	3 05.3	6 29.7	19 36.9	26 41.8	22 08.6	28 30.0
8 Tu	9 03 30	14 48 38	20 22 08	26 25 44	4 34.5	11 42.8	24 42.7	15 04.1	3 28.8	6 35.7	19 39.6	26 39.5	22 10.7	28 31.0
9 W	9 07 27	15 46 09	2♒31 45	8♒40 19	4 21.5	12 50.9	25 13.4	15 39.6	3 52.3	6 41.9	19 42.1	26 37.3	22 12.8	28 32.1
10 Th	9 11 24	16 43 40	14 51 31	21 05 25	4 08.7	13 56.7	25 42.6	16 14.9	4 15.7	6 48.2	19 44.6	26 35.1	22 14.9	28 33.1
11 F	9 15 20	17 41 13	27 22 01	3♓41 21	3 57.0	15 00.1	26 10.3	16 50.0	4 39.1	6 54.6	19 47.0	26 32.9	22 16.9	28 34.1
12 Sa	9 19 17	18 38 47	10♓03 26	16 28 14	3 47.5	16 00.8	26 36.4	17 24.9	5 02.4	7 01.2	19 49.3	26 30.7	22 19.0	28 35.1
13 Su	9 23 13	19 36 22	22 55 48	29 26 10	3 40.8	16 58.8	27 00.9	17 59.5	5 25.6	7 07.9	19 51.5	26 28.5	22 21.0	28 36.1
14 M	9 27 10	20 33 58	5♈59 23	12♈35 33	3 36.8	17 54.0	27 23.8	18 33.9	5 48.8	7 14.8	19 53.6	26 26.4	22 23.0	28 37.0
15 Tu	9 31 06	21 31 36	19 14 45	25 57 08	3D 35.2	18 46.2	27 44.9	19 08.1	6 11.9	7 21.8	19 55.6	26 24.3	22 25.0	28 38.0
16 W	9 35 03	22 29 16	2♉42 50	9♉32 00	3 35.1	19 35.3	28 04.2	19 42.0	6 35.0	7 28.9	19 57.5	26 22.2	22 27.0	28 38.9
17 Th	9 38 59	23 26 57	16 24 46	23 21 15	3R 35.3	20 21.1	28 21.7	20 15.6	6 58.0	7 36.2	19 59.3	26 20.1	22 29.0	28 39.8
18 F	9 42 56	24 24 40	0♊21 28	7♊25 25	3 34.7	21 03.3	28 37.3	20 49.0	7 21.0	7 43.5	20 01.0	26 18.1	22 31.0	28 40.7
19 Sa	9 46 53	25 22 25	14 33 00	21 43 59	3 32.3	21 41.9	28 51.0	21 22.1	7 43.9	7 51.1	20 02.6	26 16.1	22 32.9	28 41.6
20 Su	9 50 49	26 20 11	28 58 02	6♋14 42	3 27.4	22 16.6	29 02.6	21 54.9	8 06.7	7 58.7	20 04.0	26 14.1	22 34.9	28 42.5
21 M	9 54 46	27 17 59	13♋33 20	20 53 16	3 20.2	22 47.2	29 12.2	22 27.4	8 29.5	8 06.5	20 05.4	26 12.2	22 36.8	28 43.3
22 Tu	9 58 42	28 15 49	28 13 37	5♌33 31	3 11.2	23 13.3	29 19.6	22 59.6	8 52.2	8 14.4	20 06.7	26 10.2	22 38.7	28 44.1
23 W	10 02 39	29 13 40	12♌52 01	20 08 09	3 01.2	23 34.9	29 24.8	23 31.5	9 14.8	8 22.4	20 07.9	26 08.3	22 40.6	28 44.9
24 Th	10 06 35	0♍11 32	27 21 00	4♍29 46	2 51.7	23 51.6	29R 27.9	24 03.2	9 37.3	8 30.6	20 08.9	26 06.5	22 42.4	28 45.7
25 F	10 10 32	1 09 26	11♍33 43	18 32 15	2 43.5	24 03.1	29 28.6	24 34.5	9 59.8	8 38.9	20 09.9	26 04.6	22 44.3	28 46.5
26 Sa	10 14 28	2 07 21	25 24 57	2♎11 33	2 37.5	24R 09.3	29 27.1	25 05.4	10 22.2	8 47.2	20 10.7	26 02.8	22 46.1	28 47.3
27 Su	10 18 25	3 05 18	8♎51 56	15 26 08	2 33.9	24 09.9	29 23.2	25 36.1	10 44.5	8 55.8	20 11.4	26 01.1	22 47.9	28 48.0
28 M	10 22 22	4 03 16	21 54 19	28 16 47	2D 32.4	24 04.6	29 16.9	26 06.4	11 06.7	9 04.4	20 12.1	25 59.3	22 49.7	28 48.7
29 Tu	10 26 18	5 01 15	4♏33 55	10♏46 13	2 32.6	23 53.4	29 08.2	26 36.4	11 28.9	9 13.1	20 12.6	25 57.6	22 51.4	28 49.4
30 W	10 30 15	5 59 16	16 54 13	22 58 30	2 33.5	23 36.0	28 57.2	27 06.0	11 50.9	9 22.0	20 13.0	25 56.0	22 53.2	28 50.1
31 Th	10 34 11	6 57 18	28 59 43	4♐58 30	2R 34.1	23 12.5	28 43.7	27 35.3	12 12.9	9 30.9	20 13.3	25 54.3	22 54.9	28 50.7

Astro Data	Planet Ingress	Last Aspect	☽ Ingress	Last Aspect	☽ Ingress	☽ Phases & Eclipses	Astro Data
Dy Hr Mn	Dy Hr Mn	Dy Hr Mn	Dy Hr Mn	Dy Hr Mn	Dy Hr Mn	Dy Hr Mn	
♃ D 2 21:30	♀ ♍ 7 19:04	2 10:30 ♅ △	♎ 2 13:59	1 3:36 ♇ △	♏ 1 6:44	3 9:20 ☽ 10♎19	1 July 1911
☽0S 3 1:34	☿ ♌ 13 3:20	4 19:33 ♅ □	♏ 4 23:27	3 11:59 ♅ ⚹	♐ 3 18:21	11 12:53 ○ 18♑05	Julian Day # 4199
♅⊼♇ 8 13:17	♂ ♉ 15 16:01	7 11:00 ♀ □	♐ 7 11:39	6 4:05 ♇ ☍	♑ 6 7:10	19 5:31 ☾ 25♈26	SVP 6♓29'53"
☽0N 17 18:28	☉ ♌ 24 0:29	9 20:18 ♇ ☍	♑ 10 0:32	8 12:27 ♅ ☌	♒ 8 19:02	25 20:12 ● 1♌44	GC 25♐36.2 ⚵ 7♉26.6
☽0S 30 8:58	☿ ♍ 30 13:41	12 9:39 ☿ ☍	♒ 12 12:34	11 2:16 ♇ △	♓ 11 5:00		Eris 26♓43.4R ⚶ 9♎53.2
	⚳ ♋ 30 16:38	14 22:06 ♂ ⚹	♓ 14 23:04	13 10:28 ♇ □	♈ 13 13:02	1 23:29 ☽ 8♏34	⚷ 6♓49.9R ⚴ 3♋14.8
♀0S 6 7:46		17 4:01 ♇ □	♈ 17 7:35	15 16:47 ♇ ⚹	♉ 15 19:12	10 2:54 ○ 16♒22	☽ Mean ☊ 6♉49.6
☽0N 13 23:07	☉ ♍ 24 7:13	19 10:16 ♇ ⚹	♉ 19 13:34	17 20:46 ♀ △	♊ 17 23:23	17 12:11 ☾ 23♉27	
☿0S 21 4:38		21 12:44 ☉ ⚹	♊ 21 16:42	19 23:58 ♀ □	♋ 20 1:42	24 4:14 ● 29♌53	1 August 1911
♀ R 25 7:54		23 14:37 ♇ ☌	♋ 23 17:30	22 1:43 ♀ ⚹	♌ 22 2:54	31 16:20 ☽ 7♐08	Julian Day # 4230
☽0S 26 17:43		25 12:55 ♅ ☍	♌ 25 17:24	24 4:14 ☉ ☌	♍ 24 4:26		SVP 6♓29'48"
☿ R 27 2:24		27 15:35 ♇ ⚹	♍ 27 18:26	26 7:08 ♀ ☌	♎ 26 8:06		GC 25♐36.3 ⚵ 17♉27.8
		29 19:32 ♇ □	♎ 29 22:32	28 13:01 ♇ △	♏ 28 15:16		Eris 26♓35.1R ⚶ 15♎59.9
				30 23:42 ♀ ⚹	♐ 31 2:01		⚷ 5♓52.0R ⚴ 16♋39.6
							☽ Mean ☊ 5♉11.1

LONGITUDE — September 1911

Day	Sid.Time	☉	0 hr ☽	Noon ☽	True ☊	☿	♀	♂	⚳	♃	♄	♅	♆	♇
1 F	10 38 08	7♍55 22	10♐55 31	16♐51 25	2♉33.6	22♍42.9	28♍27.9	28♉04.2	12♋34.8	9♏40.0	20♉13.5	25♑52.8	22♋56.6	28♊51.3
2 Sa	10 42 04	8 53 27	22 46 49	28 42 22	2R 31.4	22R 07.3	28R 09.7	28 32.8	12 56.6	9 49.2	20R 13.6	25R 51.2	22 58.3	28 52.0
3 Su	10 46 01	9 51 33	4♑38 37	10♑36 09	2 27.1	21 26.0	27 49.3	29 01.0	13 18.3	9 58.5	20 13.6	25 49.7	22 59.9	28 52.6
4 M	10 49 57	10 49 41	16 35 28	22 37 00	2 20.7	20 39.6	27 26.7	29 28.8	13 39.9	10 07.9	20 13.5	25 48.2	23 01.6	28 53.1
5 Tu	10 53 54	11 47 51	28 41 10	4♒48 18	2 12.8	19 48.5	27 01.9	29 56.2	14 01.5	10 17.4	20 13.2	25 46.8	23 03.2	28 53.7
6 W	10 57 51	12 46 01	10♒58 39	17 12 27	2 04.0	18 53.5	26 35.2	0♊23.2	14 22.9	10 27.0	20 12.9	25 45.4	23 04.8	28 54.2
7 Th	11 01 47	13 44 14	23 29 49	29 50 50	1 55.2	17 55.8	26 06.5	0 49.9	14 44.3	10 36.7	20 12.5	25 44.0	23 06.3	28 54.7
8 F	11 05 44	14 42 28	6♓15 30	12♓43 48	1 47.2	16 56.2	25 36.1	1 16.1	15 05.5	10 46.4	20 11.9	25 42.7	23 07.9	28 55.2
9 Sa	11 09 40	15 40 44	19 15 37	25 50 50	1 40.9	15 56.2	25 04.2	1 41.9	15 26.6	10 56.3	20 11.2	25 41.4	23 09.4	28 55.7
10 Su	11 13 37	16 39 02	2♈29 17	9♈10 48	1 36.6	14 56.9	24 30.8	2 07.2	15 47.7	11 06.3	20 10.5	25 40.2	23 10.9	28 56.1
11 M	11 17 33	17 37 22	15 55 12	22 42 18	1D 34.5	13 59.9	23 56.3	2 32.2	16 08.6	11 16.4	20 09.6	25 39.0	23 12.3	28 56.5
12 Tu	11 21 30	18 35 43	29 31 55	6♉23 55	1 34.3	13 06.5	23 20.8	2 56.7	16 29.5	11 26.6	20 08.6	25 37.8	23 13.8	28 56.9
13 W	11 25 26	19 34 07	13♉18 09	20 14 29	1 35.2	12 18.0	22 44.5	3 20.7	16 50.2	11 36.8	20 07.6	25 36.7	23 15.2	28 57.3
14 Th	11 29 23	20 32 33	27 12 48	4♊12 59	1 36.6	11 35.7	22 07.8	3 44.2	17 10.8	11 47.2	20 06.4	25 35.7	23 16.6	28 57.7
15 F	11 33 19	21 31 02	11♊14 54	18 18 26	1R 37.4	11 00.5	21 30.8	4 07.3	17 31.3	11 57.6	20 05.1	25 34.6	23 18.0	28 58.0
16 Sa	11 37 16	22 29 32	25 23 24	2♋29 37	1 37.0	10 33.5	20 53.7	4 29.8	17 51.7	12 08.2	20 03.7	25 33.7	23 19.3	28 58.4
17 Su	11 41 13	23 28 05	9♋36 48	16 44 40	1 35.0	10 15.3	20 16.9	4 51.9	18 12.0	12 18.8	20 02.2	25 32.7	23 20.6	28 58.6
18 M	11 45 09	24 26 40	23 52 50	1♌00 53	1 31.4	10D 06.3	19 40.5	5 13.4	18 32.1	12 29.5	20 00.6	25 31.9	23 21.9	28 58.9
19 Tu	11 49 06	25 25 17	8♌08 20	15 14 41	1 26.5	10 07.0	19 04.8	5 34.4	18 52.2	12 40.3	19 58.9	25 31.0	23 23.2	28 59.2
20 W	11 53 02	26 23 56	22 19 22	29 21 50	1 21.0	10 17.3	18 30.1	5 54.9	19 12.1	12 51.2	19 57.1	25 30.2	23 24.4	28 59.4
21 Th	11 56 59	27 22 37	6♍21 32	13♍17 58	1 15.6	10 37.3	17 56.4	6 14.8	19 31.8	13 02.1	19 55.2	25 29.5	23 25.6	28 59.6
22 F	12 00 55	28 21 21	20 10 38	26 59 09	1 11.1	11 06.8	17 24.1	6 34.1	19 51.5	13 13.2	19 53.2	25 28.8	23 26.7	28 59.8
23 Sa	12 04 52	29 20 06	3♎43 11	10♎22 29	1 07.9	11 45.3	16 53.3	6 52.8	20 11.0	13 24.3	19 51.1	25 28.1	23 27.9	28 59.9
24 Su	12 08 48	0♎18 53	16 56 56	23 26 29	1D 06.3	12 32.4	16 24.1	7 11.0	20 30.4	13 35.5	19 48.8	25 27.5	23 29.0	29 00.1
25 M	12 12 45	1 17 42	29 51 11	6♏11 11	1 06.1	13 27.5	15 56.8	7 28.5	20 49.6	13 46.7	19 46.5	25 27.0	23 30.1	29 00.2
26 Tu	12 16 42	2 16 33	12♏26 43	18 38 06	1 07.1	14 30.1	15 31.4	7 45.4	21 08.7	13 58.1	19 44.1	25 26.5	23 31.1	29 00.3
27 W	12 20 38	3 15 25	24 45 43	0♐50 01	1 08.8	15 39.5	15 08.1	8 01.7	21 27.6	14 09.5	19 41.6	25 26.0	23 32.2	29 00.4
28 Th	12 24 35	4 14 20	6♐51 28	12 50 38	1 10.5	16 55.0	14 47.0	8 17.4	21 46.4	14 21.0	19 39.0	25 25.6	23 33.2	29 00.4
29 F	12 28 31	5 13 16	18 48 05	24 44 23	1R 11.8	18 15.9	14 28.2	8 32.4	22 05.0	14 32.5	19 36.4	25 25.3	23 34.1	29R 00.4
30 Sa	12 32 28	6 12 15	0♑40 10	6♑36 02	1 12.3	19 41.6	14 11.6	8 46.7	22 23.5	14 44.2	19 33.6	25 25.0	23 35.0	29 00.4

LONGITUDE — October 1911

Day	Sid.Time	☉	0 hr ☽	Noon ☽	True ☊	☿	♀	♂	⚳	♃	♄	♅	♆	♇
1 Su	12 36 24	7♎11 15	12♑32 35	18♑30 26	1♉11.7	21♍11.4	13♍57.5	9♊00.4	22♋41.8	14♏55.8	19♉30.7	25♑24.7	23♋35.9	29♊00.4
2 M	12 40 21	8 10 16	24 30 10	0♒32 20	1R 10.0	22 44.7	13R 45.7	9 13.4	23 00.0	15 07.6	19R 27.8	25R 24.5	23 36.8	29R 00.4
3 Tu	12 44 17	9 09 20	6♒37 27	12 45 59	1 07.5	24 20.9	13 36.4	9 25.7	23 18.0	15 19.4	19 24.7	25 24.4	23 37.7	29 00.3
4 W	12 48 14	10 08 25	18 58 22	25 14 56	1 04.4	25 59.5	13 29.5	9 37.2	23 35.9	15 31.3	19 21.6	25 24.3	23 38.5	29 00.2
5 Th	12 52 11	11 07 32	1♓36 00	8♓01 45	1 01.3	27 40.1	13 25.0	9 48.1	23 53.5	15 43.2	19 18.4	25D 24.2	23 39.2	29 00.1
6 F	12 56 07	12 06 41	14 32 19	21 07 45	0 58.4	29 22.2	13D 23.0	9 58.2	24 11.0	15 55.2	19 15.1	25 24.2	23 40.0	29 00.0
7 Sa	13 00 04	13 05 52	27 47 58	4♈32 50	0 56.3	1♎05.5	13 23.3	10 07.6	24 28.4	16 07.3	19 11.7	25 24.3	23 40.7	28 59.8
8 Su	13 04 00	14 05 04	11♈22 08	18 15 33	0D 55.0	2 49.6	13 26.1	10 16.2	24 45.5	16 19.4	19 08.3	25 24.4	23 41.4	28 59.7
9 M	13 07 57	15 04 19	25 12 43	2♉13 12	0 54.7	4 34.3	13 31.1	10 24.0	25 02.5	16 31.5	19 04.7	25 24.5	23 42.0	28 59.5
10 Tu	13 11 53	16 03 36	9♉16 31	16 22 11	0 55.1	6 19.4	13 38.5	10 31.1	25 19.3	16 43.7	19 01.1	25 24.7	23 42.6	28 59.2
11 W	13 15 50	17 02 56	23 29 40	0♊38 29	0 56.0	8 04.6	13 48.1	10 37.4	25 35.9	16 56.0	18 57.4	25 25.0	23 43.2	28 59.0
12 Th	13 19 46	18 02 18	7♊48 06	14 58 03	0 57.1	9 49.8	13 59.9	10 42.8	25 52.3	17 08.3	18 53.7	25 25.3	23 43.7	28 58.7
13 F	13 23 43	19 01 42	22 07 54	29 17 14	0 58.0	11 34.9	14 13.8	10 47.4	26 08.5	17 20.7	18 49.8	25 25.6	23 44.3	28 58.4
14 Sa	13 27 40	20 01 08	6♋25 40	13♋32 53	0R 58.5	13 19.8	14 29.8	10 51.2	26 24.5	17 33.1	18 45.9	25 26.0	23 44.7	28 58.1
15 Su	13 31 36	21 00 37	20 38 34	27 42 28	0 58.5	15 04.3	14 47.8	10 54.2	26 40.3	17 45.6	18 42.0	25 26.5	23 45.2	28 57.8
16 M	13 35 33	22 00 08	4♌44 21	11♌43 59	0 58.0	16 48.4	15 07.8	10 56.2	26 55.9	17 58.1	18 37.9	25 27.0	23 45.6	28 57.5
17 Tu	13 39 29	22 59 41	18 41 12	25 35 47	0 57.3	18 32.1	15 29.6	10R 57.4	27 11.3	18 10.7	18 33.8	25 27.5	23 46.0	28 57.1
18 W	13 43 26	23 59 17	2♍27 36	9♍16 29	0 56.4	20 15.3	15 53.3	10 57.8	27 26.5	18 23.3	18 29.7	25 28.1	23 46.3	28 56.7
19 Th	13 47 22	24 58 55	16 02 17	22 44 51	0 55.5	21 57.9	16 18.7	10 57.2	27 41.4	18 36.0	18 25.5	25 28.8	23 46.6	28 56.3
20 F	13 51 19	25 58 34	29 24 06	5♎59 54	0 54.9	23 40.0	16 45.8	10 55.7	27 56.1	18 48.7	18 21.2	25 29.5	23 46.9	28 55.8
21 Sa	13 55 15	26 58 16	12♎32 12	19 00 55	0D 54.6	25 21.5	17 14.6	10 53.4	28 10.6	19 01.4	18 16.9	25 30.3	23 47.2	28 55.4
22 Su	13 59 12	27 58 01	25 26 02	1♏47 35	0 54.5	27 02.4	17 44.9	10 50.1	28 24.9	19 14.2	18 12.5	25 31.1	23 47.4	28 54.9
23 M	14 03 09	28 57 47	8♏05 36	14 20 10	0 54.6	28 42.8	18 16.7	10 45.9	28 38.9	19 27.0	18 08.0	25 32.0	23 47.5	28 54.4
24 Tu	14 07 05	29 57 35	20 31 27	26 39 38	0R 54.7	0♏22.6	18 50.0	10 40.9	28 52.6	19 39.8	18 03.6	25 32.9	23 47.7	28 53.9
25 W	14 11 02	0♏57 25	2♐44 56	8♐47 38	0 54.8	2 01.8	19 24.7	10 34.9	29 06.2	19 52.7	17 59.0	25 33.8	23 47.8	28 53.3
26 Th	14 14 58	1 57 17	14 48 05	20 46 38	0 54.7	3 40.5	20 00.8	10 28.1	29 19.4	20 05.6	17 54.5	25 34.8	23 47.9	28 52.8
27 F	14 18 55	2 57 10	26 43 43	2♑39 46	0 54.5	5 18.6	20 38.2	10 20.3	29 32.5	20 18.6	17 49.9	25 35.9	23R 47.9	28 52.2
28 Sa	14 22 51	3 57 05	8♑35 18	14 30 48	0 54.3	6 56.2	21 16.8	10 11.7	29 45.2	20 31.6	17 45.2	25 37.0	23 47.9	28 51.6
29 Su	14 26 48	4 57 02	20 26 51	26 24 00	0D 54.0	8 33.3	21 56.6	10 02.2	29 57.7	20 44.6	17 40.6	25 38.2	23 47.9	28 51.0
30 M	14 30 44	5 57 01	2♒22 50	8♒23 56	0 54.0	10 09.9	22 37.6	9 51.8	0♌09.9	20 57.6	17 35.9	25 39.4	23 47.8	28 50.3
31 Tu	14 34 41	6 57 01	14 27 53	20 35 15	0 54.2	11 46.0	23 19.8	9 40.6	0 21.9	21 10.7	17 31.1	25 40.7	23 47.7	28 49.7

Astro Data	Dy Hr Mn	Planet Ingress	Dy Hr Mn
♄ R	2 20:57	♂ ♊	5 15:21
☿0N	5 5:53	☉ ♎	24 4:18
☽0N	10 5:01		
☿ D	18 22:25	☿ ♎	6 20:49
☽0S	23 2:45	☿ ♏	24 6:33
☉0S	24 4:18	☉ ♏	24 12:58
♃□♇	26 16:42	⚳ ♌	29 16:29
♇ R	30 4:37		
♀0N	1 1:35		
♅ D	6 1:53		
♀ D	6 20:24		
☽0N	7 13:16		
☿0S	9 8:11		
♂ R	18 8:37	☽0S	20 10:42
♃☍♄	18 21:06	♆ R	28 4:02

Last Aspect Dy Hr Mn		☽ Ingress Dy Hr Mn
2 12:19	♇ ☍	♑ 2 14:37
5 2:05	♂ △	♒ 5 2:35
7 10:14	♇ △	♓ 7 12:17
9 17:35	♇ □	♈ 9 19:31
11 22:58	♇ ⚹	♉ 12 0:49
13 21:14	♅ △	♊ 14 4:47
16 6:03	♇ ☌	♋ 16 7:47
18 2:47	♅ ☍	♌ 18 10:18
20 11:22	♇ ⚹	♍ 20 13:05
22 15:34	♇ □	♎ 22 17:21
24 22:24	♇ △	♏ 25 0:17
27 1:20	♅ ⚹	♐ 27 10:21
29 20:38	♇ ☍	♑ 29 22:39

Last Aspect Dy Hr Mn		☽ Ingress Dy Hr Mn
2 1:49	♅ ☌	♒ 2 10:56
4 19:07	♇ △	♓ 4 20:59
7 2:09	♇ □	♈ 7 3:56
9 6:29	♇ ⚹	♉ 9 8:12
11 3:14	♅ △	♊ 11 10:55
13 11:29	♇ ☌	♋ 13 13:12
15 8:09	♅ ☍	♌ 15 15:54
17 17:51	♇ ⚹	♍ 17 19:41
19 23:09	♇ □	♎ 20 1:05
22 6:34	♇ △	♏ 22 8:36
24 9:49	♅ ⚹	♐ 24 18:34
27 4:20	♇ ☍	♑ 27 6:37
29 10:28	♅ ☌	♒ 29 19:14

☽ Phases & Eclipses Dy Hr Mn	
8 15:56	○ 14♓52
15 17:51	☾ 21♊45
22 14:37	● 28♍28
30 11:08	☽ 6♑10
8 4:11	○ 13♈46
14 23:46	☾ 20♋30
22 4:09	● 27♎38
22 4:12:49	● A 03'47"
30 6:41	☽ 5♒44

Astro Data

1 September 1911
Julian Day # 4261
SVP 6♓29'44"
GC 25♐36.3 ⚴ 25♉17.1
Eris 26♓17.8R ⚵ 24♎22.5
⚷ 4♓25.9R ⚶ 29♋45.0
☽ Mean ☊ 3♉32.7

1 October 1911
Julian Day # 4291
SVP 6♓29'41"
GC 25♐36.4 ⚴ 28♉33.9
Eris 25♓57.3R ⚵ 3♏45.1
⚷ 3♓06.2R ⚶ 11♌42.8
☽ Mean ☊ 1♉57.3

November 1911 — LONGITUDE

Day	Sid.Time	☉	0 hr ☽	Noon ☽	True ☊	☿	♀	♂	⚳	♃	♄	♅	♆	♇
1 W	14 38 38	7♏57 03	26♒46 36	3♓02 26	0♉54.7	13♏21.6	24♍03.0	9♊28.6	0♌33.5	21♏23.8	17♉26.4	25♑42.0	23♋47.6	28♊49.0
2 Th	14 42 34	8 57 06	9♓23 13	15 49 23	0 55.4	14 56.7	24 47.3	9R 15.8	0 44.9	21 36.9	17R 21.6	25 43.3	23R 47.4	28R 48.3
3 F	14 46 31	9 57 11	22 21 15	28 59 03	0 56.2	16 31.5	25 32.5	9 02.1	0 56.0	21 50.0	17 16.8	25 44.7	23 47.2	28 47.6
4 Sa	14 50 27	10 57 18	5♈42 57	12♈32 56	0 57.0	18 05.8	26 18.8	8 47.7	1 06.8	22 03.2	17 12.0	25 46.2	23 47.0	28 46.9
5 Su	14 54 24	11 57 26	19 28 55	26 30 37	0R 57.4	19 39.7	27 06.0	8 32.5	1 17.3	22 16.3	17 07.1	25 47.7	23 46.7	28 46.1
6 M	14 58 20	12 57 36	3♉37 40	10♉49 32	0 57.3	21 13.2	27 54.1	8 16.6	1 27.6	22 29.5	17 02.3	25 49.2	23 46.4	28 45.3
7 Tu	15 02 17	13 57 48	18 05 32	25 24 54	0 56.5	22 46.3	28 43.0	8 00.0	1 37.5	22 42.7	16 57.4	25 50.8	23 46.1	28 44.6
8 W	15 06 13	14 58 02	2♊46 47	10♊10 15	0 55.1	24 19.1	29 32.8	7 42.7	1 47.1	22 56.0	16 52.5	25 52.5	23 45.7	28 43.8
9 Th	15 10 10	15 58 18	17 34 22	24 58 10	0 53.2	25 51.6	0♎23.5	7 24.8	1 56.4	23 09.2	16 47.7	25 54.2	23 45.3	28 42.9
10 F	15 14 07	16 58 35	2♋20 47	9♋41 22	0 51.3	27 23.7	1 14.9	7 06.2	2 05.3	23 22.5	16 42.8	25 55.9	23 44.9	28 42.1
11 Sa	15 18 03	17 58 55	16 59 12	24 13 40	0 49.5	28 55.4	2 07.1	6 47.1	2 14.0	23 35.7	16 37.9	25 57.7	23 44.4	28 41.3
12 Su	15 22 00	18 59 17	1♌24 18	8♌30 42	0D 48.4	0♐26.9	3 00.0	6 27.4	2 22.3	23 49.0	16 33.0	25 59.5	23 43.9	28 40.4
13 M	15 25 56	19 59 40	15 32 38	22 29 59	0 48.1	1 58.0	3 53.6	6 07.2	2 30.2	24 02.3	16 28.2	26 01.4	23 43.4	28 39.5
14 Tu	15 29 53	21 00 06	29 22 42	6♍10 51	0 48.7	3 28.8	4 47.9	5 46.5	2 37.9	24 15.6	16 23.3	26 03.3	23 42.9	28 38.6
15 W	15 33 49	22 00 33	12♍54 32	19 33 54	0 50.0	4 59.3	5 42.9	5 25.4	2 45.1	24 28.9	16 18.4	26 05.3	23 42.3	28 37.7
16 Th	15 37 46	23 01 02	26 09 10	2♎40 32	0 51.6	6 29.4	6 38.4	5 03.9	2 52.1	24 42.2	16 13.6	26 07.3	23 41.6	28 36.8
17 F	15 41 42	24 01 33	9♎08 14	15 32 30	0 53.0	7 59.3	7 34.6	4 42.1	2 58.6	24 55.6	16 08.8	26 09.3	23 41.0	28 35.8
18 Sa	15 45 39	25 02 06	21 53 30	28 11 30	0R 53.7	9 28.7	8 31.4	4 20.1	3 04.8	25 08.9	16 04.0	26 11.4	23 40.3	28 34.9
19 Su	15 49 36	26 02 40	4♏26 38	10♏39 07	0 53.4	10 57.8	9 28.7	3 57.8	3 10.7	25 22.2	15 59.2	26 13.5	23 39.6	28 33.9
20 M	15 53 32	27 03 16	16 49 06	22 56 45	0 51.6	12 26.5	10 26.5	3 35.3	3 16.1	25 35.5	15 54.5	26 15.7	23 38.8	28 32.9
21 Tu	15 57 29	28 03 54	29 02 14	5♐05 41	0 48.5	13 54.7	11 24.9	3 12.7	3 21.2	25 48.9	15 49.7	26 17.9	23 38.0	28 31.9
22 W	16 01 25	29 04 33	11♐07 17	17 07 14	0 44.0	15 22.5	12 23.8	2 50.1	3 25.9	26 02.2	15 45.0	26 20.2	23 37.2	28 30.9
23 Th	16 05 22	0♐05 14	23 05 42	29 02 57	0 38.7	16 49.8	13 23.2	2 27.4	3 30.2	26 15.5	15 40.4	26 22.5	23 36.4	28 29.9
24 F	16 09 18	1 05 55	4♑59 13	10♑54 49	0 33.0	18 16.4	14 23.0	2 04.8	3 34.1	26 28.9	15 35.8	26 24.8	23 35.5	28 28.9
25 Sa	16 13 15	2 06 38	16 50 03	22 45 18	0 27.6	19 42.4	15 23.3	1 42.3	3 37.7	26 42.2	15 31.2	26 27.2	23 34.6	28 27.8
26 Su	16 17 11	3 07 22	28 40 58	4♒37 31	0 23.0	21 07.7	16 24.0	1 20.0	3 40.8	26 55.5	15 26.7	26 29.6	23 33.7	28 26.8
27 M	16 21 08	4 08 07	10♒35 25	16 35 10	0 19.8	22 32.1	17 25.1	0 57.8	3 43.5	27 08.8	15 22.2	26 32.0	23 32.7	28 25.7
28 Tu	16 25 05	5 08 54	22 37 21	28 42 30	0D 18.2	23 55.5	18 26.6	0 35.9	3 45.9	27 22.1	15 17.7	26 34.5	23 31.7	28 24.6
29 W	16 29 01	6 09 41	4♓51 14	11♓04 07	0 18.1	25 17.8	19 28.6	0 14.3	3 47.8	27 35.3	15 13.3	26 37.0	23 30.7	28 23.6
30 Th	16 32 58	7 10 29	17 21 44	23 44 40	0 19.1	26 38.9	20 30.9	29♉53.1	3 49.3	27 48.6	15 09.0	26 39.6	23 29.7	28 22.5

December 1911 — LONGITUDE

Day	Sid.Time	☉	0 hr ☽	Noon ☽	True ☊	☿	♀	♂	⚳	♃	♄	♅	♆	♇
1 F	16 36 54	8♐11 17	0♈13 25	6♈48 27	0♉20.7	27♐58.4	21♎33.5	29♉32.2	3♌50.4	28♏01.9	15♉04.7	26♑42.2	23♋28.6	28♊21.4
2 Sa	16 40 51	9 12 07	13 30 10	20 18 50	0R 22.1	29 16.3	22 36.6	29R 11.8	3 51.1	28 15.1	15R 00.4	26 44.8	23R 27.5	28R 20.2
3 Su	16 44 47	10 12 58	27 14 36	4♉17 26	0 22.4	0♑32.2	23 40.0	28 51.8	3R 51.3	28 28.3	14 56.3	26 47.5	23 26.4	28 19.1
4 M	16 48 44	11 13 50	11♉27 11	18 43 26	0 21.0	1 45.9	24 43.7	28 32.4	3 51.2	28 41.5	14 52.1	26 50.2	23 25.3	28 18.0
5 Tu	16 52 40	12 14 42	26 05 36	3♊32 53	0 17.6	2 56.9	25 47.8	28 13.5	3 50.6	28 54.7	14 48.1	26 52.9	23 24.1	28 16.9
6 W	16 56 37	13 15 36	11♊04 17	18 38 41	0 12.3	4 05.0	26 52.1	27 55.2	3 49.6	29 07.8	14 44.1	26 55.7	23 22.9	28 15.7
7 Th	17 00 34	14 16 31	26 14 47	3♋51 17	0 05.7	5 09.6	27 56.8	27 37.5	3 48.2	29 21.0	14 40.2	26 58.5	23 21.7	28 14.6
8 F	17 04 30	15 17 27	11♋26 48	19 00 05	29♈58.6	6 10.2	29 01.8	27 20.4	3 46.4	29 34.1	14 36.4	27 01.3	23 20.5	28 13.4
9 Sa	17 08 27	16 18 24	26 29 57	3♌55 23	29 52.0	7 06.3	0♏07.1	27 04.0	3 44.1	29 47.2	14 32.6	27 04.2	23 19.2	28 12.3
10 Su	17 12 23	17 19 22	11♌15 33	18 29 48	29 46.8	7 57.2	1 12.7	26 48.3	3 41.4	0♐00.2	14 28.9	27 07.1	23 17.9	28 11.1
11 M	17 16 20	18 20 21	25 37 44	2♍39 08	29 43.5	8 42.1	2 18.5	26 33.2	3 38.2	0 13.3	14 25.3	27 10.0	23 16.6	28 09.9
12 Tu	17 20 16	19 21 22	9♍33 57	16 22 18	29D 42.2	9 20.3	3 24.7	26 18.9	3 34.7	0 26.3	14 21.7	27 12.9	23 15.3	28 08.8
13 W	17 24 13	20 22 23	23 04 24	29 40 37	29 42.5	9 50.9	4 31.0	26 05.4	3 30.7	0 39.2	14 18.2	27 15.9	23 13.9	28 07.6
14 Th	17 28 10	21 23 25	6♎11 20	12♎37 01	29 43.6	10 13.1	5 37.6	25 52.6	3 26.3	0 52.2	14 14.9	27 18.9	23 12.6	28 06.4
15 F	17 32 06	22 24 29	18 58 09	25 15 11	29R 44.6	10R 26.0	6 44.5	25 40.5	3 21.4	1 05.1	14 11.6	27 21.9	23 11.2	28 05.2
16 Sa	17 36 03	23 25 33	1♏28 37	7♏38 53	29 44.3	10 28.7	7 51.6	25 29.3	3 16.1	1 18.0	14 08.3	27 25.0	23 09.8	28 04.0
17 Su	17 39 59	24 26 39	13 46 26	19 51 37	29 42.0	10 20.5	8 58.9	25 18.9	3 10.4	1 30.8	14 05.2	27 28.1	23 08.3	28 02.8
18 M	17 43 56	25 27 45	25 54 48	1♐56 17	29 37.2	10 00.9	10 06.4	25 09.3	3 04.3	1 43.6	14 02.2	27 31.2	23 06.9	28 01.6
19 Tu	17 47 52	26 28 52	7♐56 22	13 55 15	29 29.6	9 29.6	11 14.1	25 00.5	2 57.8	1 56.4	13 59.2	27 34.3	23 05.4	28 00.4
20 W	17 51 49	27 29 59	19 53 11	25 50 19	29 19.6	8 46.7	12 22.0	24 52.5	2 50.8	2 09.1	13 56.4	27 37.5	23 03.9	27 59.3
21 Th	17 55 45	28 31 07	1♑46 51	7♑42 57	29 07.9	7 52.9	13 30.1	24 45.4	2 43.5	2 21.8	13 53.6	27 40.7	23 02.4	27 58.1
22 F	17 59 42	29 32 16	13 38 46	19 34 29	28 55.4	6 49.1	14 38.4	24 39.1	2 35.7	2 34.4	13 50.9	27 43.9	23 00.9	27 56.9
23 Sa	18 03 39	0♑33 24	25 30 18	1♒26 26	28 43.1	5 37.2	15 46.9	24 33.7	2 27.6	2 47.0	13 48.4	27 47.1	22 59.4	27 55.7
24 Su	18 07 35	1 34 33	7♒23 07	13 20 39	28 32.2	4 19.2	16 55.5	24 29.0	2 19.0	2 59.6	13 45.9	27 50.3	22 57.8	27 54.5
25 M	18 11 32	2 35 43	19 19 22	25 19 38	28 23.5	2 57.6	18 04.3	24 25.2	2 10.1	3 12.1	13 43.5	27 53.6	22 56.3	27 53.3
26 Tu	18 15 28	3 36 52	1♓21 51	7♓26 29	28 17.4	1 35.3	19 13.3	24 22.3	2 00.8	3 24.5	13 41.3	27 56.9	22 54.7	27 52.1
27 W	18 19 25	4 38 01	13 34 02	19 45 01	28 14.0	0 14.9	20 22.4	24 20.1	1 51.2	3 36.9	13 39.1	28 00.2	22 53.1	27 50.9
28 Th	18 23 21	5 39 10	26 00 01	2♈19 35	28D 12.9	28♐59.0	21 31.7	24 18.8	1 41.2	3 49.2	13 37.0	28 03.5	22 51.5	27 49.7
29 F	18 27 18	6 40 20	8♈44 18	15 14 44	28R 13.0	27 49.7	22 41.1	24D 18.2	1 30.9	4 01.5	13 35.1	28 06.9	22 49.9	27 48.5
30 Sa	18 31 14	7 41 29	21 51 24	28 34 46	28 13.3	26 48.7	23 50.7	24 18.5	1 20.2	4 13.7	13 33.2	28 10.2	22 48.3	27 47.4
31 Su	18 35 11	8 42 38	5♉25 11	12♉22 54	28 12.6	25 57.1	25 00.4	24 19.5	1 09.3	4 25.9	13 31.4	28 13.6	22 46.7	27 46.2

Astro Data Dy Hr Mn	Planet Ingress Dy Hr Mn	Last Aspect Dy Hr Mn	☽ Ingress Dy Hr Mn	Last Aspect Dy Hr Mn	☽ Ingress Dy Hr Mn	☽ Phases & Eclipses Dy Hr Mn	Astro Data
☽0N 3 23:15	♀ ♎ 9 0:55	1 3:56 ♇ △	♓ 1 6:12	3 1:51 ♇ ⚹	♉ 3 4:43	6 15:48 ○ 13♉07	1 November 1911
♀0S 9 22:34	☿ ♐ 12 4:56	3 11:39 ♇ □	♈ 3 13:49	5 4:26 ♃ ☍	♊ 5 6:18	6 15:36 • A 0.815	Julian Day # 4322
♃△♆ 12 3:10	☉ ♐ 23 9:56	5 15:49 ♇ ⚹	♉ 5 17:54	7 3:10 ♇ ☌	♋ 7 5:55	13 7:19 ☾ 19♌48	SVP 6♓29'37"
☽0S 16 16:47	♂ ♉R 30 4:07	7 17:42 ♀ △	♊ 7 19:29	9 5:21 ♀ □	♌ 9 5:39	20 20:49 ● 27♏26	GC 25♐36.5 ⚴ 24♉20.4R
♃⚹♅ 24 3:05		9 18:05 ♇ ☌	♋ 9 20:11	11 4:19 ♇ ⚹	♍ 11 7:27	29 1:42 ☽ 5♓44	Eris 25♓38.5R ✱ 14♏07.2
	☿ ♑ 3 1:44	11 20:46 ☿ △	♌ 11 21:39	13 9:10 ♇ □	♎ 13 12:35		⚷ 2♓18.8R ⚶ 22♌39.2
☽0N 1 8:56	☊ ♈R 8 7:07	13 22:44 ♇ ⚹	♍ 14 1:05	15 17:26 ♇ △	♏ 15 21:09	6 2:52 ○ 12♊52	☽Mean ☊ 0♉18.8
♃⊼♇ 2 20:39	♀ ♏ 9 9:23	16 4:31 ♇ □	♎ 16 7:04	18 3:09 ♅ ⚹	♐ 18 8:08	12 17:46 ☾ 19♍36	
⚳R 3 15:20	♃ ♐ 10 11:36	18 12:45 ♇ △	♏ 18 15:28	20 16:20 ♇ ☍	♑ 20 20:24	20 15:40 ● 27♐39	1 December 1911
☽0S 13 21:45	☉ ♑ 22 22:53	20 20:49 ☉ ☌	♐ 21 1:54	23 4:35 ♅ ☌	♒ 23 9:05	28 18:47 ☽ 5♈56	Julian Day # 4352
♅R 16 6:09	☿ ♐R 27 16:35	23 10:53 ♇ ☍	♑ 23 13:55	25 17:05 ♇ △	♓ 25 21:18		SVP 6♓29'32"
♅⊼♇ 25 10:20		25 20:09 ♃ ⚹	♒ 26 2:40	28 6:14 ☿ □	♈ 28 7:36		GC 25♐36.6 ⚴ 14♉42.8R
☽0N 28 16:25		28 11:25 ♇ △	♓ 28 14:32	30 11:16 ♅ □	♉ 30 14:31		Eris 25♓28.2R ✱ 24♏19.0
♂ D 29 16:25		30 23:05 ♂ ⚹	♈ 30 23:35				⚷ 2♓24.0 ⚶ 0♍40.1
							☽Mean ☊ 28♈43.5

LONGITUDE — January 1912

Day	Sid.Time	☉	0 hr ☽	Noon ☽	True ☊	☿	♀	♂	⚳	♃	♄	♅	♆	♇
1 M	18 39 08	9♑43 46	19♉28 01	26♉40 25	28♈09.7	25♐15.8	26♏10.2	24♉21.3	0♌58.0	4♐38.0	13♉29.8	28♑17.0	22♋45.0	27♊45.0
2 Tu	18 43 04	10 44 55	3♊59 47	11♊25 35	28R 04.1	24R 44.8	27 20.2	24 23.9	0R 46.4	4 50.1	13R 28.3	28 20.4	22R 43.4	27R 43.9
3 W	18 47 01	11 46 04	18 57 01	26 33 01	27 55.8	24 24.1	28 30.3	24 27.2	0 34.6	5 02.1	13 26.8	28 23.8	22 41.7	27 42.7
4 Th	18 50 57	12 47 12	4♋12 23	11♋53 41	27 45.5	24D 13.3	29 40.6	24 31.2	0 22.4	5 14.0	13 25.5	28 27.2	22 40.1	27 41.6
5 F	18 54 54	13 48 21	19 35 25	27 16 03	27 34.2	24 11.9	0♐50.9	24 36.0	0 10.1	5 25.9	13 24.3	28 30.7	22 38.4	27 40.4
6 Sa	18 58 50	14 49 29	4♌54 05	12♌28 09	27 23.4	24 19.3	2 01.4	24 41.4	29♋57.5	5 37.7	13 23.2	28 34.1	22 36.7	27 39.3
7 Su	19 02 47	15 50 38	19 57 04	27 19 51	27 14.2	24 34.8	3 12.0	24 47.6	29 44.6	5 49.4	13 22.2	28 37.6	22 35.1	27 38.2
8 M	19 06 44	16 51 46	4♍35 46	11♍44 21	27 07.6	24 57.7	4 22.7	24 54.4	29 31.6	6 01.0	13 21.3	28 41.0	22 33.4	27 37.0
9 Tu	19 10 40	17 52 54	18 45 21	25 38 44	27 03.7	25 27.2	5 33.5	25 01.9	29 18.3	6 12.6	13 20.6	28 44.5	22 31.7	27 35.9
10 W	19 14 37	18 54 03	2♎24 40	9♎03 29	27D 02.1	26 02.8	6 44.4	25 10.0	29 04.9	6 24.2	13 19.9	28 48.0	22 30.0	27 34.8
11 Th	19 18 33	19 55 11	15 35 37	22 01 34	27R 01.9	26 43.8	7 55.5	25 18.8	28 51.3	6 35.6	13 19.3	28 51.5	22 28.3	27 33.7
12 F	19 22 30	20 56 20	28 21 55	4♏37 18	27 01.8	27 29.6	9 06.6	25 28.3	28 37.5	6 47.0	13 18.9	28 55.0	22 26.6	27 32.6
13 Sa	19 26 26	21 57 28	10♏48 20	16 55 37	27 00.6	28 19.9	10 17.8	25 38.3	28 23.7	6 58.3	13 18.6	28 58.5	22 24.9	27 31.5
14 Su	19 30 23	22 58 36	22 59 45	29 01 18	26 57.2	29 14.0	11 29.1	25 49.0	28 09.7	7 09.5	13 18.4	29 02.0	22 23.2	27 30.5
15 M	19 34 19	23 59 44	5♐00 48	10♐58 43	26 50.9	0♑11.7	12 40.5	26 00.2	27 55.6	7 20.6	13D 18.3	29 05.6	22 21.5	27 29.4
16 Tu	19 38 16	25 00 52	16 55 29	22 51 30	26 41.4	1 12.5	13 52.0	26 12.1	27 41.5	7 31.7	13 18.3	29 09.1	22 19.8	27 28.4
17 W	19 42 13	26 02 00	28 47 04	4♑42 29	26 29.2	2 16.1	15 03.6	26 24.5	27 27.3	7 42.6	13 18.4	29 12.6	22 18.1	27 27.3
18 Th	19 46 09	27 03 07	10♑38 01	16 33 50	26 14.8	3 22.3	16 15.2	26 37.5	27 13.0	7 53.5	13 18.7	29 16.2	22 16.4	27 26.3
19 F	19 50 06	28 04 13	22 30 09	28 27 06	25 59.4	4 30.8	17 26.9	26 51.0	26 58.8	8 04.3	13 19.0	29 19.7	22 14.7	27 25.3
20 Sa	19 54 02	29 05 19	4♒24 49	10♒23 28	25 44.3	5 41.4	18 38.7	27 05.1	26 44.5	8 15.0	13 19.5	29 23.2	22 13.0	27 24.3
21 Su	19 57 59	0♒06 24	16 23 10	22 24 04	25 30.6	6 53.9	19 50.6	27 19.7	26 30.3	8 25.6	13 20.1	29 26.7	22 11.4	27 23.3
22 M	20 01 55	1 07 28	28 26 23	4♓30 17	25 19.4	8 08.1	21 02.5	27 34.8	26 16.1	8 36.1	13 20.8	29 30.3	22 09.7	27 22.3
23 Tu	20 05 52	2 08 31	10♓36 02	16 43 54	25 11.3	9 23.9	22 14.5	27 50.4	26 02.0	8 46.5	13 21.6	29 33.8	22 08.0	27 21.4
24 W	20 09 48	3 09 34	22 54 14	29 07 22	25 06.2	10 41.2	23 26.5	28 06.5	25 48.0	8 56.9	13 22.5	29 37.3	22 06.3	27 20.4
25 Th	20 13 45	4 10 35	5♈23 45	11♈43 47	25 03.9	11 59.8	24 38.6	28 23.1	25 34.0	9 07.1	13 23.5	29 40.9	22 04.7	27 19.5
26 F	20 17 42	5 11 35	18 07 57	24 36 44	25 03.4	13 19.7	25 50.8	28 40.1	25 20.2	9 17.2	13 24.7	29 44.4	22 03.0	27 18.6
27 Sa	20 21 38	6 12 34	1♉10 37	7♉50 01	25 03.4	14 40.8	27 03.0	28 57.7	25 06.5	9 27.2	13 26.0	29 47.9	22 01.4	27 17.7
28 Su	20 25 35	7 13 32	14 35 23	21 27 01	25 02.8	16 03.0	28 15.3	29 15.6	24 53.0	9 37.2	13 27.3	29 51.4	21 59.8	27 16.8
29 M	20 29 31	8 14 29	28 25 09	5♊29 54	25 00.2	17 26.2	29 27.6	29 34.0	24 39.6	9 47.0	13 28.8	29 54.9	21 58.1	27 15.9
30 Tu	20 33 28	9 15 24	12♊41 09	19 58 41	24 55.2	18 50.4	0♑40.0	29 52.8	24 26.5	9 56.7	13 30.4	29 58.4	21 56.5	27 15.1
31 W	20 37 24	10 16 19	27 21 58	4♋50 20	24 47.5	20 15.6	1 52.4	0♊12.0	24 13.5	10 06.3	13 32.1	0♒01.9	21 54.9	27 14.2

LONGITUDE — February 1912

Day	Sid.Time	☉	0 hr ☽	Noon ☽	True ☊	☿	♀	♂	⚳	♃	♄	♅	♆	♇
1 Th	20 41 21	11♒17 12	12♋22 50	19♋58 22	24♈37.6	21♑41.8	3♑04.9	0♊31.6	24♋00.8	10♐15.8	13♉33.9	0♒05.4	21♋53.4	27♊13.4
2 F	20 45 17	12 18 04	27 35 38	5♌13 15	24R 26.6	23 08.8	4 17.4	0 51.6	23R 48.3	10 25.2	13 35.8	0 08.9	21R 51.8	27R 12.6
3 Sa	20 49 14	13 18 54	12♌49 48	20 23 52	24 15.9	24 36.6	5 30.0	1 12.0	23 36.1	10 34.5	13 37.9	0 12.4	21 50.2	27 11.8
4 Su	20 53 11	14 19 44	27 54 10	5♍19 32	24 06.7	26 05.4	6 42.6	1 32.7	23 24.1	10 43.6	13 40.0	0 15.8	21 48.7	27 11.0
5 M	20 57 07	15 20 32	12♍39 01	19 51 51	23 59.9	27 34.9	7 55.2	1 53.8	23 12.4	10 52.7	13 42.2	0 19.3	21 47.1	27 10.3
6 Tu	21 01 04	16 21 20	26 57 34	3♎55 51	23 55.8	29 05.3	9 08.0	2 15.3	23 00.9	11 01.6	13 44.6	0 22.7	21 45.6	27 09.6
7 W	21 05 00	17 22 06	10♎46 40	17 30 06	23D 54.1	0♒36.6	10 20.7	2 37.1	22 49.8	11 10.4	13 47.0	0 26.1	21 44.1	27 08.8
8 Th	21 08 57	18 22 51	24 06 26	0♏36 04	23 54.0	2 08.6	11 33.5	2 59.2	22 39.0	11 19.1	13 49.6	0 29.5	21 42.6	27 08.1
9 F	21 12 53	19 23 36	6♏59 30	13 17 19	23R 54.6	3 41.5	12 46.3	3 21.6	22 28.5	11 27.7	13 52.3	0 32.9	21 41.1	27 07.5
10 Sa	21 16 50	20 24 19	19 30 07	25 38 34	23 54.6	5 15.1	13 59.2	3 44.4	22 18.4	11 36.1	13 55.0	0 36.3	21 39.7	27 06.8
11 Su	21 20 46	21 25 02	1♐43 17	7♐44 56	23 53.0	6 49.6	15 12.1	4 07.4	22 08.6	11 44.4	13 57.9	0 39.7	21 38.3	27 06.2
12 M	21 24 43	22 25 43	13 44 08	19 41 30	23 49.2	8 24.9	16 25.1	4 30.8	21 59.1	11 52.6	14 00.9	0 43.0	21 36.8	27 05.5
13 Tu	21 28 40	23 26 23	25 37 35	1♑32 53	23 42.9	10 01.1	17 38.1	4 54.5	21 50.0	12 00.7	14 03.9	0 46.4	21 35.4	27 04.9
14 W	21 32 36	24 27 02	7♑27 55	13 23 05	23 34.1	11 38.1	18 51.1	5 18.4	21 41.3	12 08.6	14 07.1	0 49.7	21 34.1	27 04.3
15 Th	21 36 33	25 27 40	19 18 46	25 15 18	23 23.5	13 16.0	20 04.1	5 42.7	21 33.0	12 16.4	14 10.4	0 53.0	21 32.7	27 03.8
16 F	21 40 29	26 28 16	1♒12 58	7♒11 59	23 12.0	14 54.7	21 17.2	6 07.2	21 25.1	12 24.0	14 13.8	0 56.3	21 31.4	27 03.2
17 Sa	21 44 26	27 28 51	13 12 34	19 14 52	23 00.6	16 34.3	22 30.3	6 32.0	21 17.6	12 31.6	14 17.2	0 59.5	21 30.1	27 02.7
18 Su	21 48 22	28 29 24	25 19 01	1♓25 08	22 50.3	18 14.8	23 43.4	6 57.1	21 10.5	12 38.9	14 20.8	1 02.8	21 28.8	27 02.2
19 M	21 52 19	29 29 56	7♓33 20	13 43 41	22 42.0	19 56.2	24 56.6	7 22.4	21 03.8	12 46.2	14 24.4	1 06.0	21 27.5	27 01.7
20 Tu	21 56 15	0♓30 26	19 56 19	26 11 21	22 36.1	21 38.6	26 09.7	7 48.0	20 57.5	12 53.3	14 28.2	1 09.2	21 26.2	27 01.3
21 W	22 00 12	1 30 54	2♈28 54	8♈49 09	22 32.8	23 21.8	27 22.9	8 13.8	20 51.6	13 00.2	14 32.0	1 12.4	21 25.0	27 00.8
22 Th	22 04 09	2 31 20	15 12 16	21 38 29	22D 31.7	25 06.0	28 36.1	8 39.9	20 46.2	13 07.0	14 36.0	1 15.5	21 23.8	27 00.4
23 F	22 08 05	3 31 45	28 08 01	4♉41 07	22 32.3	26 51.2	29 49.4	9 06.2	20 41.2	13 13.7	14 40.0	1 18.7	21 22.6	27 00.0
24 Sa	22 12 02	4 32 08	11♉18 05	17 59 10	22 33.5	28 37.4	1♒02.6	9 32.7	20 36.6	13 20.2	14 44.2	1 21.8	21 21.5	26 59.7
25 Su	22 15 58	5 32 29	24 44 36	1♊34 36	22R 34.4	0♓24.5	2 15.9	9 59.4	20 32.5	13 26.5	14 48.4	1 24.8	21 20.3	26 59.3
26 M	22 19 55	6 32 48	8♊29 21	15 28 53	22 34.1	2 12.6	3 29.1	10 26.4	20 28.8	13 32.8	14 52.7	1 27.9	21 19.2	26 59.0
27 Tu	22 23 51	7 33 05	22 33 13	29 42 12	22 32.0	4 01.7	4 42.4	10 53.6	20 25.6	13 38.8	14 57.1	1 30.9	21 18.2	26 58.7
28 W	22 27 48	8 33 19	6♋55 33	14♋12 51	22 28.0	5 51.8	5 55.8	11 20.9	20 22.7	13 44.7	15 01.6	1 33.9	21 17.1	26 58.4
29 Th	22 31 44	9 33 32	21 33 30	28 56 48	22 22.4	7 42.8	7 09.1	11 48.5	20 20.4	13 50.5	15 06.1	1 36.9	21 16.1	26 58.1

Astro Data Dy Hr Mn	Planet Ingress Dy Hr Mn	Last Aspect Dy Hr Mn	☽ Ingress Dy Hr Mn	Last Aspect Dy Hr Mn	☽ Ingress Dy Hr Mn	☽ Phases & Eclipses Dy Hr Mn
☿ D 5 3:32	♀ ♐ 4 18:38	1 14:40 ♅ △	♊ 1 17:28	1 15:01 ♆ ☌	♌ 2 3:47	4 13:29 ○ 12♋51
☽ 0S 10 3:42	⚳ ♋R 6 7:12	3 13:49 ♇ ☌	♋ 3 17:25	3 22:51 ♇ ⚹	♍ 4 3:23	11 7:43 ☾ 19♎44
♃⚼♆ 15 13:41	☿ ♑ 15 7:15	5 13:57 ♅ ☍	♌ 5 16:17	6 2:38 ♅ △	♎ 6 5:12	19 11:10 ● 28♑02
♄ D 15 20:23	☉ ♒ 21 9:29	7 12:30 ♇ ⚹	♍ 7 16:23	8 5:35 ♇ △	♏ 8 10:53	27 8:51 ☽ 6♉05
☽ 0N 24 21:38	♀ ♑ 29 22:45	9 17:29 ♅ △	♎ 9 19:42	10 4:13 ♆ △	♐ 10 20:35	
	♂ ♊ 30 21:02	12 1:00 ♅ □	♏ 12 3:07	13 2:57 ♇ ☍	♑ 13 8:52	2 23:58 ○ 12♌48
☽ 0S 6 12:06	♅ ♒ 30 22:42	14 12:01 ♅ ⚹	♐ 14 13:57	15 4:32 ♅ ☌	♒ 15 21:33	10 0:50 ☾ 19♏56
☽ 0N 21 2:30		16 21:20 ♇ ☍	♑ 17 2:28	18 5:44 ☉ ☌	♓ 18 9:13	18 5:44 ● 28♒14
	☿ ♒ 7 2:24	19 13:46 ♅ ☌	♒ 19 15:07	20 13:35 ♇ □	♈ 20 19:17	25 19:26 ☽ 5♊51
	☉ ♓ 19 23:56	21 22:00 ♂ □	♓ 22 3:06	23 2:11 ♀ □	♉ 23 3:26	
	♀ ♒ 23 15:29	24 12:58 ♅ ⚹	♈ 24 13:41	24 18:00 ♆ ⚹	♊ 25 9:15	
	☿ ♓ 25 6:32	26 21:26 ♅ □	♉ 26 21:52	27 7:26 ♇ ☌	♋ 27 12:30	
		29 2:31 ♅ △	♊ 29 2:42	28 23:33 ♆ ☌	♌ 29 13:42	
		30 23:48 ♇ ☌	♋ 31 4:15			

Astro Data

1 January 1912
Julian Day # 4383
SVP 6♓29'26"
GC 25♐36.6 ⚴ 10♉19.4
Eris 25♓29.1 ⚵ 4♐29.1
⚷ 3♓23.0 ⚶ 4♍13.4
☽ Mean ☊ 27♈05.0

1 February 1912
Julian Day # 4414
SVP 6♓29'20"
GC 25♐36.7 ⚴ 16♉02.2
Eris 25♓41.8 ⚵ 13♐36.8
⚷ 5♓02.9 ⚶ 0♍51.0R
☽ Mean ☊ 25♈26.6

March 1912 — LONGITUDE

Day	Sid.Time	☉	0 hr ☽	Noon ☽	True ☊	☿	♀	♂	⚳	♃	♄	♅	♆	♇
1 F	22 35 41	10♓33 43	6♌21 51	13♌47 43	22♈15.9	9♓34.8	8♒22.4	12♊16.3	20♋18.4	13♐56.0	15♉10.8	1♒39.9	21♋15.1	26♊57.9
2 Sa	22 39 38	11 33 52	21 13 20	28 37 40	22R 09.4	11 27.8	9 35.8	12 44.2	20R 16.9	14 01.5	15 15.5	1 42.8	21R 14.1	26R 57.7
3 Su	22 43 34	12 33 59	5♍59 37	13♍18 14	22 03.8	13 21.6	10 49.2	13 12.3	20 15.8	14 06.7	15 20.3	1 45.7	21 13.2	26 57.5
4 M	22 47 31	13 34 03	20 32 37	27 42 00	21 59.8	15 16.3	12 02.6	13 40.6	20D 15.2	14 11.8	15 25.2	1 48.5	21 12.3	26 57.3
5 Tu	22 51 27	14 34 06	4♎45 45	11♎43 28	21D 57.6	17 11.7	13 16.0	14 09.1	20 15.0	14 16.8	15 30.2	1 51.3	21 11.4	26 57.2
6 W	22 55 24	15 34 08	18 34 51	25 19 47	21 57.2	19 07.9	14 29.4	14 37.8	20 15.2	14 21.6	15 35.2	1 54.1	21 10.5	26 57.0
7 Th	22 59 20	16 34 08	1♏58 18	8♏30 35	21 58.1	21 04.6	15 42.8	15 06.6	20 15.8	14 26.2	15 40.4	1 56.9	21 09.7	26 56.9
8 F	23 03 17	17 34 06	14 56 56	21 17 43	21 59.8	23 01.8	16 56.3	15 35.5	20 16.9	14 30.6	15 45.6	1 59.6	21 08.9	26 56.8
9 Sa	23 07 13	18 34 02	27 33 24	3♐44 30	22 01.4	24 59.3	18 09.8	16 04.7	20 18.4	14 34.9	15 50.9	2 02.3	21 08.2	26 56.8
10 Su	23 11 10	19 33 57	9♐51 36	15 55 17	22R 02.3	26 56.9	19 23.3	16 34.0	20 20.3	14 39.0	15 56.2	2 05.0	21 07.4	26 56.7
11 M	23 15 07	20 33 50	21 56 10	27 54 52	22 02.1	28 54.4	20 36.8	17 03.4	20 22.6	14 42.9	16 01.6	2 07.6	21 06.7	26D 56.7
12 Tu	23 19 03	21 33 42	3♑51 59	9♑48 07	22 00.5	0♈51.5	21 50.3	17 33.0	20 25.4	14 46.7	16 07.2	2 10.2	21 06.0	26 56.7
13 W	23 23 00	22 33 32	15 43 50	21 39 42	21 57.5	2 48.0	23 03.8	18 02.7	20 28.5	14 50.3	16 12.7	2 12.8	21 05.4	26 56.8
14 Th	23 26 56	23 33 20	27 36 12	3♒33 48	21 53.4	4 43.6	24 17.3	18 32.6	20 32.1	14 53.7	16 18.4	2 15.3	21 04.8	26 56.8
15 F	23 30 53	24 33 06	9♒32 56	15 33 59	21 48.8	6 37.8	25 30.9	19 02.6	20 36.1	14 56.9	16 24.1	2 17.8	21 04.2	26 56.9
16 Sa	23 34 49	25 32 50	21 37 17	27 43 07	21 44.0	8 30.3	26 44.4	19 32.8	20 40.4	15 00.0	16 29.9	2 20.3	21 03.7	26 57.0
17 Su	23 38 46	26 32 33	3♓51 42	10♓03 15	21 39.7	10 20.6	27 58.0	20 03.1	20 45.2	15 02.8	16 35.7	2 22.7	21 03.1	26 57.1
18 M	23 42 42	27 32 13	16 17 52	22 35 40	21 36.4	12 08.4	29 11.5	20 33.5	20 50.4	15 05.5	16 41.6	2 25.1	21 02.7	26 57.3
19 Tu	23 46 39	28 31 52	28 56 42	5♈21 00	21 34.2	13 53.1	0♓25.1	21 04.1	20 55.9	15 08.0	16 47.6	2 27.4	21 02.2	26 57.4
20 W	23 50 35	29 31 28	11♈48 34	18 19 23	21D 33.4	15 34.3	1 38.7	21 34.8	21 01.8	15 10.4	16 53.7	2 29.7	21 01.8	26 57.6
21 Th	23 54 32	0♈31 03	24 53 26	1♉30 38	21 33.6	17 11.6	2 52.3	22 05.6	21 08.2	15 12.5	16 59.8	2 32.0	21 01.4	26 57.8
22 F	23 58 29	1 30 35	8♉10 58	14 54 23	21 34.6	18 44.5	4 05.8	22 36.5	21 14.9	15 14.5	17 05.9	2 34.2	21 01.0	26 58.1
23 Sa	0 02 25	2 30 05	21 40 49	28 30 13	21 36.0	20 12.6	5 19.4	23 07.6	21 21.9	15 16.2	17 12.2	2 36.4	21 00.7	26 58.3
24 Su	0 06 22	3 29 33	5♊22 32	12♊17 41	21 37.3	21 35.4	6 33.0	23 38.8	21 29.4	15 17.8	17 18.5	2 38.6	21 00.4	26 58.6
25 M	0 10 18	4 28 59	19 15 35	26 16 07	21R 38.1	22 52.7	7 46.6	24 10.0	21 37.2	15 19.2	17 24.8	2 40.7	21 00.2	26 58.9
26 Tu	0 14 15	5 28 22	3♋19 07	10♋24 25	21 38.2	24 04.0	9 00.2	24 41.4	21 45.3	15 20.4	17 31.2	2 42.7	20 59.9	26 59.3
27 W	0 18 11	6 27 43	17 31 44	24 40 46	21 37.6	25 09.0	10 13.7	25 12.9	21 53.8	15 21.5	17 37.7	2 44.7	20 59.8	26 59.6
28 Th	0 22 08	7 27 01	1♌51 10	9♌02 30	21 36.3	26 07.6	11 27.3	25 44.5	22 02.7	15 22.3	17 44.2	2 46.7	20 59.6	27 00.0
29 F	0 26 05	8 26 17	16 14 16	23 25 55	21 34.7	26 59.4	12 40.9	26 16.2	22 11.9	15 23.0	17 50.7	2 48.7	20 59.5	27 00.4
30 Sa	0 30 01	9 25 31	0♍36 53	7♍46 34	21 33.1	27 44.3	13 54.5	26 48.0	22 21.4	15 23.4	17 57.3	2 50.5	20 59.4	27 00.8
31 Su	0 33 58	10 24 42	14 54 20	21 59 37	21 31.8	28 22.2	15 08.1	27 19.9	22 31.3	15 23.7	18 04.0	2 52.4	20 59.3	27 01.2

April 1912 — LONGITUDE

Day	Sid.Time	☉	0 hr ☽	Noon ☽	True ☊	☿	♀	♂	⚳	♃	♄	♅	♆	♇
1 M	0 37 54	11♈23 52	29♍01 49	6♎00 26	21♈30.9	28♈52.9	16♓21.7	27♊51.9	22♋41.4	15♐23.8	18♉10.7	2♒54.2	20♋59.3	27♊01.7
2 Tu	0 41 51	12 22 59	12♎55 00	19 45 09	21D 30.6	29 16.5	17 35.3	28 23.9	22 51.9	15R 23.7	18 17.5	2 56.0	20D 59.3	27 02.2
3 W	0 45 47	13 22 04	26 30 34	3♏11 06	21 30.7	29 33.0	18 48.8	28 56.1	23 02.8	15 23.4	18 24.3	2 57.7	20 59.4	27 02.7
4 Th	0 49 44	14 21 07	9♏46 37	16 17 08	21 31.2	29R 42.3	20 02.4	29 28.3	23 13.9	15 23.0	18 31.1	2 59.3	20 59.5	27 03.2
5 F	0 53 40	15 20 09	22 42 43	29 03 34	21 31.9	29 44.7	21 16.0	0♋00.7	23 25.3	15 22.3	18 38.0	3 01.0	20 59.6	27 03.8
6 Sa	0 57 37	16 19 09	5♐19 56	11♐32 10	21 32.5	29 40.4	22 29.6	0 33.1	23 37.0	15 21.5	18 44.9	3 02.5	20 59.7	27 04.3
7 Su	1 01 33	17 18 07	17 40 37	23 45 46	21 33.0	29 29.6	23 43.3	1 05.6	23 49.1	15 20.5	18 51.9	3 04.1	20 59.9	27 04.9
8 M	1 05 30	18 17 03	29 48 05	5♑48 06	21 33.2	29 12.7	24 56.9	1 38.1	24 01.4	15 19.3	18 58.9	3 05.6	21 00.1	27 05.5
9 Tu	1 09 27	19 15 57	11♑46 23	17 43 29	21R 33.3	28 50.2	26 10.5	2 10.8	24 14.0	15 17.9	19 06.0	3 07.0	21 00.4	27 06.1
10 W	1 13 23	20 14 50	23 40 00	29 36 30	21 33.3	28 22.5	27 24.1	2 43.5	24 26.9	15 16.3	19 13.1	3 08.4	21 00.6	27 06.8
11 Th	1 17 20	21 13 41	5♒33 34	11♒31 46	21D 33.3	27 50.3	28 37.7	3 16.3	24 40.0	15 14.5	19 20.2	3 09.8	21 01.0	27 07.5
12 F	1 21 16	22 12 30	17 31 38	23 33 43	21 33.3	27 14.3	29 51.3	3 49.2	24 53.5	15 12.5	19 27.4	3 11.1	21 01.3	27 08.2
13 Sa	1 25 13	23 11 17	29 38 30	5♓46 24	21 33.4	26 35.2	1♈04.9	4 22.2	25 07.2	15 10.4	19 34.6	3 12.3	21 01.7	27 08.9
14 Su	1 29 09	24 10 03	11♓57 49	18 13 07	21 33.7	25 53.8	2 18.5	4 55.2	25 21.1	15 08.1	19 41.9	3 13.5	21 02.1	27 09.6
15 M	1 33 06	25 08 46	24 32 33	0♈56 21	21 33.9	25 10.9	3 32.2	5 28.4	25 35.4	15 05.6	19 49.2	3 14.7	21 02.5	27 10.3
16 Tu	1 37 02	26 07 28	7♈24 38	13 57 27	21R 34.1	24 27.3	4 45.8	6 01.5	25 49.9	15 02.9	19 56.5	3 15.8	21 03.0	27 11.1
17 W	1 40 59	27 06 08	20 34 49	27 16 36	21 34.2	23 43.9	5 59.4	6 34.8	26 04.6	15 00.0	20 03.8	3 16.8	21 03.5	27 11.9
18 Th	1 44 56	28 04 46	4♉02 39	10♉52 43	21 33.9	23 01.4	7 13.0	7 08.1	26 19.6	14 57.0	20 11.2	3 17.8	21 04.1	27 12.7
19 F	1 48 52	29 03 22	17 46 29	24 43 35	21 33.2	22 20.5	8 26.6	7 41.5	26 34.8	14 53.8	20 18.6	3 18.8	21 04.7	27 13.5
20 Sa	1 52 49	0♉01 56	1♊43 38	8♊46 10	21 32.3	21 42.1	9 40.2	8 15.0	26 50.3	14 50.4	20 26.0	3 19.7	21 05.3	27 14.4
21 Su	1 56 45	1 00 28	15 50 44	22 56 53	21 31.2	21 06.5	10 53.8	8 48.5	27 06.0	14 46.8	20 33.5	3 20.6	21 05.9	27 15.2
22 M	2 00 42	1 58 58	0♋04 08	7♋12 02	21 30.2	20 34.4	12 07.4	9 22.1	27 22.0	14 43.1	20 41.0	3 21.4	21 06.6	27 16.1
23 Tu	2 04 38	2 57 26	14 20 11	21 28 11	21D 29.5	20 06.2	13 21.0	9 55.8	27 38.2	14 39.2	20 48.5	3 22.1	21 07.3	27 17.0
24 W	2 08 35	3 55 51	28 35 40	5♌42 18	21 29.3	19 42.3	14 34.6	10 29.5	27 54.6	14 35.1	20 56.0	3 22.9	21 08.1	27 17.9
25 Th	2 12 31	4 54 15	12♌47 47	19 51 52	21 29.7	19 22.8	15 48.1	11 03.3	28 11.2	14 30.9	21 03.5	3 23.5	21 08.8	27 18.9
26 F	2 16 28	5 52 36	26 54 18	3♍54 50	21 30.6	19 08.0	17 01.7	11 37.1	28 28.0	14 26.5	21 11.1	3 24.1	21 09.6	27 19.8
27 Sa	2 20 25	6 50 55	10♍53 17	17 49 25	21 31.7	18 58.1	18 15.3	12 11.0	28 45.1	14 22.0	21 18.7	3 24.7	21 10.5	27 20.8
28 Su	2 24 21	7 49 11	24 43 05	1♎34 04	21 32.8	18D 53.0	19 28.8	12 45.0	29 02.3	14 17.3	21 26.3	3 25.2	21 11.3	27 21.8
29 M	2 28 18	8 47 26	8♎22 12	15 07 18	21R 33.5	18 52.8	20 42.4	13 18.9	29 19.8	14 12.4	21 33.9	3 25.7	21 12.2	27 22.8
30 Tu	2 32 14	9 45 39	21 49 12	28 27 46	21 33.5	18 57.5	21 55.9	13 53.0	29 37.4	14 07.4	21 41.6	3 26.1	21 13.1	27 23.8

Astro Data

	Dy Hr Mn
☽0S	4 22:16
⚳D	5 11:57
♇D	11 12:46
☿0N	12 15:28
☽0N	19 8:56
☉0N	20 23:30
☽0S	1 8:04
♃R	1 12:12
♆D	1 16:37
☿R	5 8:25
♀0N	15 12:29
☽0N	15 17:12
♄✶♆	26 6:46
☽0S	28 15:48
☿D	29 0:52

Planet Ingress

	Dy Hr Mn
☿ ♈	12 1:26
♀ ♓	19 3:49
☉ ♈	20 23:29
♂ ♋	5 11:31
☿ ♈	12 14:50
☉ ♉	20 11:12

Last Aspect / ☽ Ingress

Last Aspect Dy Hr Mn		☽ Ingress Dy Hr Mn
2 9:18 ♇ ✶	♍	2 14:14
4 10:45 ♇ □	♎	4 15:53
6 14:55 ♇ △	♏	6 20:25
8 15:55 ☿ △	♐	9 4:43
11 14:23 ☿ □	♑	11 16:12
13 13:59 ☉ ✶	♒	14 4:50
16 10:29 ♇ △	♓	16 16:28
18 22:08 ☉ ☌	♈	19 1:59
21 3:46 ♇ ✶	♉	21 9:16
22 22:49 ♆ ✶	♊	23 14:37
25 13:13 ♇ ☌	♋	25 18:22
27 12:51 ♆ □	♌	27 20:54
29 18:17 ♆ △	♍	29 22:58

Last Aspect / ☽ Ingress

Last Aspect Dy Hr Mn		☽ Ingress Dy Hr Mn
31 21:27 ♂ □	♎	1 1:40
3 5:20 ☿ ☍	♏	3 6:15
4 20:46 ♆ △	♐	5 13:47
7 23:09 ☿ △	♑	8 0:24
10 9:37 ☿ □	♒	10 12:47
12 19:04 ♇ △	♓	13 0:42
15 4:57 ♇ □	♈	15 10:15
17 11:52 ♇ ✶	♉	17 16:51
19 5:42 ♆ ✶	♊	19 21:03
21 19:16 ♇ ☌	♋	21 23:53
23 11:25 ♆ ☌	♌	24 2:22
26 0:43 ♇ ✶	♍	26 5:18
28 4:37 ♇ □	♎	28 9:15
30 10:04 ♇ △	♏	30 14:47

☽ Phases & Eclipses

Dy Hr Mn	
3 10:42	○ 12♍31
10 19:55	☾ 19♐54
18 22:08	● 27♓57
26 3:02	☽ 5♋06
1 22:04	○ 11♎49
1 22:14	☍ P 0.182
9 15:23	☾ 19♑24
17 11:40	● 27♈05
17 11:34:08	● AT00'02"
24 8:47	☽ 3♌48

Astro Data

1 March 1912
Julian Day # 4443
SVP 6♓29'16"
GC 25♐36.8 ⚴ 27♉32.7
Eris 26♓01.4 ⚵ 20♐24.0
⚷ 6♓54.2 ⚶ 23♌33.1R
☽ Mean ☊ 23♈54.4

1 April 1912
Julian Day # 4474
SVP 6♓29'13"
GC 25♐36.8 ⚴ 13♊17.5
Eris 26♓25.4 ⚵ 24♐33.6
⚷ 8♓49.4 ⚶ 19♌11.7R
☽ Mean ☊ 22♈15.9

LONGITUDE — May 1912

Day	Sid.Time	☉	0 hr ☽	Noon☽	True☊	☿	♀	♂	⚳	♃	♄	♅	♆	♇
1 W	2 36 11	10♉43 51	5♏02 53	11♏34 26	21♈32.5	19♈07.0	23♈09.5	14♋27.1	29♋55.3	14♐02.3	21♉49.2	3♒26.4	21♋14.1	27♊24.8
2 Th	2 40 07	11 42 00	18 02 21	24 26 37	21R30.6	19 21.1	24 23.0	15 01.2	0♌13.3	13R57.0	21 56.9	3 26.8	21 15.1	27 25.8
3 F	2 44 04	12 40 08	0♐47 15	7♐04 19	21 27.7	19 39.9	25 36.6	15 35.4	0 31.5	13 51.6	22 04.6	3 27.0	21 16.1	27 26.9
4 Sa	2 48 00	13 38 15	13 17 55	19 28 14	21 24.3	20 03.1	26 50.2	16 09.7	0 49.9	13 46.0	22 12.3	3 27.2	21 17.2	27 28.0
5 Su	2 51 57	14 36 19	25 35 30	1♑39 59	21 20.7	20 30.6	28 03.7	16 44.0	1 08.5	13 40.3	22 20.0	3 27.4	21 18.2	27 29.1
6 M	2 55 54	15 34 23	7♑42 02	13 42 01	21 17.3	21 02.3	29 17.3	17 18.3	1 27.3	13 34.5	22 27.7	3 27.5	21 19.3	27 30.2
7 Tu	2 59 50	16 32 25	19 40 22	25 37 33	21 14.7	21 38.0	0♉30.8	17 52.7	1 46.3	13 28.5	22 35.4	3R27.6	21 20.5	27 31.3
8 W	3 03 47	17 30 25	1♒34 05	7♒30 30	21D13.1	22 17.6	1 44.4	18 27.2	2 05.4	13 22.5	22 43.1	3 27.6	21 21.6	27 32.4
9 Th	3 07 43	18 28 25	13 27 22	19 25 17	21 12.6	23 00.9	2 57.9	19 01.6	2 24.7	13 16.3	22 50.9	3 27.6	21 22.8	27 33.6
10 F	3 11 40	19 26 23	25 24 49	1♓26 35	21 13.2	23 47.8	4 11.5	19 36.2	2 44.1	13 09.9	22 58.6	3 27.5	21 24.1	27 34.7
11 Sa	3 15 36	20 24 19	7♓31 11	13 39 11	21 14.6	24 38.1	5 25.0	20 10.8	3 03.7	13 03.5	23 06.4	3 27.3	21 25.3	27 35.9
12 Su	3 19 33	21 22 14	19 51 07	26 07 31	21 16.2	25 31.8	6 38.6	20 45.4	3 23.5	12 57.0	23 14.1	3 27.2	21 26.6	27 37.1
13 M	3 23 29	22 20 08	2♈28 50	8♈55 28	21R17.6	26 28.7	7 52.2	21 20.1	3 43.5	12 50.4	23 21.9	3 26.9	21 27.9	27 38.3
14 Tu	3 27 26	23 18 01	15 27 41	22 05 44	21 18.1	27 28.7	9 05.7	21 54.8	4 03.6	12 43.6	23 29.6	3 26.6	21 29.2	27 39.5
15 W	3 31 23	24 15 52	28 49 40	5♉39 29	21 17.3	28 31.8	10 19.3	22 29.6	4 23.8	12 36.8	23 37.4	3 26.3	21 30.6	27 40.7
16 Th	3 35 19	25 13 42	12♉34 59	19 35 52	21 14.9	29 37.7	11 32.8	23 04.4	4 44.2	12 29.9	23 45.2	3 25.9	21 31.9	27 42.0
17 F	3 39 16	26 11 31	26 41 42	3♊51 52	21 11.1	0♉46.5	12 46.4	23 39.3	5 04.8	12 22.9	23 52.9	3 25.5	21 33.3	27 43.2
18 Sa	3 43 12	27 09 18	11♊05 42	18 22 23	21 06.1	1 58.0	13 59.9	24 14.2	5 25.5	12 15.8	24 00.7	3 25.0	21 34.8	27 44.5
19 Su	3 47 09	28 07 04	25 41 04	3♋00 52	21 00.6	3 12.2	15 13.5	24 49.1	5 46.3	12 08.6	24 08.4	3 24.5	21 36.2	27 45.7
20 M	3 51 05	29 04 48	10♋20 53	17 40 16	20 55.5	4 29.0	16 27.0	25 24.1	6 07.3	12 01.4	24 16.2	3 23.9	21 37.7	27 47.0
21 Tu	3 55 02	0♊02 31	24 58 14	2♌14 06	20 51.4	5 48.5	17 40.6	25 59.2	6 28.5	11 54.1	24 23.9	3 23.3	21 39.2	27 48.3
22 W	3 58 58	1 00 12	9♌27 16	16 37 17	20 48.9	7 10.4	18 54.1	26 34.3	6 49.7	11 46.8	24 31.6	3 22.7	21 40.8	27 49.6
23 Th	4 02 55	1 57 51	23 43 48	0♍46 35	20D48.0	8 34.9	20 07.7	27 09.4	7 11.1	11 39.4	24 39.4	3 21.9	21 42.3	27 50.9
24 F	4 06 52	2 55 29	7♍45 30	14 40 29	20 48.5	10 01.8	21 21.2	27 44.5	7 32.7	11 32.0	24 47.1	3 21.2	21 43.9	27 52.2
25 Sa	4 10 48	3 53 06	21 31 36	28 18 54	20 49.7	11 31.2	22 34.8	28 19.7	7 54.3	11 24.5	24 54.8	3 20.4	21 45.5	27 53.6
26 Su	4 14 45	4 50 40	5♎02 31	11♎42 34	20R50.9	13 03.1	23 48.3	28 54.9	8 16.1	11 16.9	25 02.5	3 19.5	21 47.1	27 54.9
27 M	4 18 41	5 48 14	18 19 13	24 52 35	20 51.1	14 37.3	25 01.8	29 30.2	8 38.0	11 09.4	25 10.1	3 18.6	21 48.8	27 56.2
28 Tu	4 22 38	6 45 46	1♏22 50	7♏50 04	20 49.7	16 14.0	26 15.4	0♌05.5	9 00.0	11 01.8	25 17.8	3 17.7	21 50.5	27 57.6
29 W	4 26 34	7 43 17	14 14 23	20 35 53	20 46.2	17 53.1	27 28.9	0 40.8	9 22.1	10 54.2	25 25.4	3 16.7	21 52.1	27 59.0
30 Th	4 30 31	8 40 46	26 54 39	3♐10 44	20 40.6	19 34.6	28 42.4	1 16.2	9 44.4	10 46.6	25 33.1	3 15.7	21 53.9	28 00.3
31 F	4 34 27	9 38 15	9♐24 13	15 35 10	20 33.0	21 18.4	29 56.0	1 51.6	10 06.7	10 38.9	25 40.7	3 14.6	21 55.6	28 01.7

LONGITUDE — June 1912

Day	Sid.Time	☉	0 hr ☽	Noon☽	True☊	☿	♀	♂	⚳	♃	♄	♅	♆	♇
1 Sa	4 38 24	10♊35 43	21♐43 41	27♐49 51	20♈24.2	23♉04.7	1♊09.5	2♌27.0	10♌29.2	10♐31.3	25♉48.3	3♒13.5	21♋57.3	28♊03.1
2 Su	4 42 21	11 33 10	3♑53 50	9♑55 48	20R14.8	24 53.3	2 23.1	3 02.5	10 51.8	10R23.7	25 55.9	3R12.3	21 59.1	28 04.5
3 M	4 46 17	12 30 36	15 55 56	21 54 31	20 05.7	26 44.3	3 36.6	3 38.0	11 14.5	10 16.0	26 03.4	3 11.1	22 00.9	28 05.9
4 Tu	4 50 14	13 28 01	27 51 50	3♒48 15	19 57.9	28 37.6	4 50.2	4 13.6	11 37.2	10 08.4	26 11.0	3 09.9	22 02.7	28 07.3
5 W	4 54 10	14 25 25	9♒44 08	15 39 57	19 51.9	0♊33.1	6 03.7	4 49.2	12 00.1	10 00.8	26 18.5	3 08.6	22 04.6	28 08.7
6 Th	4 58 07	15 22 49	21 36 11	27 33 21	19 48.0	2 30.9	7 17.3	5 24.8	12 23.1	9 53.2	26 26.0	3 07.3	22 06.4	28 10.1
7 F	5 02 03	16 20 12	3♓32 01	9♓32 47	19D46.2	4 30.8	8 30.9	6 00.4	12 46.2	9 45.6	26 33.5	3 05.9	22 08.3	28 11.5
8 Sa	5 06 00	17 17 34	15 36 16	21 43 04	19 46.0	6 32.7	9 44.5	6 36.1	13 09.4	9 38.1	26 40.9	3 04.5	22 10.2	28 12.9
9 Su	5 09 57	18 14 56	27 53 51	4♈09 14	19 46.7	8 36.6	10 58.0	7 11.8	13 32.7	9 30.6	26 48.4	3 03.1	22 12.1	28 14.3
10 M	5 13 53	19 12 18	10♈29 47	16 56 03	19R47.3	10 42.2	12 11.6	7 47.6	13 56.1	9 23.1	26 55.8	3 01.6	22 14.0	28 15.7
11 Tu	5 17 50	20 09 38	23 28 31	0♉07 35	19 46.9	12 49.4	13 25.2	8 23.4	14 19.6	9 15.7	27 03.1	3 00.1	22 15.9	28 17.2
12 W	5 21 46	21 06 59	6♉53 29	13 46 23	19 44.6	14 58.0	14 38.8	8 59.2	14 43.2	9 08.3	27 10.5	2 58.5	22 17.9	28 18.6
13 Th	5 25 43	22 04 19	20 46 14	27 52 49	19 40.0	17 07.8	15 52.5	9 35.1	15 06.9	9 01.0	27 17.8	2 56.9	22 19.8	28 20.0
14 F	5 29 39	23 01 39	5♊05 43	12♊24 19	19 33.0	19 18.5	17 06.1	10 11.0	15 30.7	8 53.7	27 25.1	2 55.3	22 21.8	28 21.5
15 Sa	5 33 36	23 58 58	19 47 47	27 15 10	19 24.3	21 29.8	18 19.7	10 47.0	15 54.5	8 46.5	27 32.3	2 53.6	22 23.8	28 22.9
16 Su	5 37 32	24 56 16	4♋45 18	12♋17 00	19 14.7	23 41.6	19 33.3	11 22.9	16 18.5	8 39.4	27 39.5	2 51.9	22 25.8	28 24.3
17 M	5 41 29	25 53 34	19 49 00	27 20 05	19 05.5	25 53.4	20 47.0	11 59.0	16 42.5	8 32.4	27 46.7	2 50.2	22 27.9	28 25.8
18 Tu	5 45 26	26 50 51	4♌49 03	12♌14 54	18 57.7	28 05.1	22 00.6	12 35.0	17 06.6	8 25.4	27 53.9	2 48.4	22 29.9	28 27.2
19 W	5 49 22	27 48 08	19 36 44	26 53 52	18 52.2	0♋16.4	23 14.3	13 11.1	17 30.8	8 18.5	28 01.0	2 46.6	22 32.0	28 28.7
20 Th	5 53 19	28 45 23	4♍05 47	11♍12 09	18 49.0	2 27.0	24 27.9	13 47.2	17 55.1	8 11.8	28 08.0	2 44.8	22 34.0	28 30.1
21 F	5 57 15	29 42 38	18 12 50	25 07 49	18D47.9	4 36.6	25 41.6	14 23.3	18 19.4	8 05.1	28 15.1	2 42.9	22 36.1	28 31.6
22 Sa	6 01 12	0♋39 52	1♎57 14	8♎41 18	18R48.0	6 45.1	26 55.2	14 59.5	18 43.9	7 58.5	28 22.1	2 41.1	22 38.2	28 33.0
23 Su	6 05 08	1 37 05	15 20 18	21 54 34	18 48.1	8 52.3	28 08.9	15 35.7	19 08.4	7 52.0	28 29.0	2 39.1	22 40.3	28 34.4
24 M	6 09 05	2 34 18	28 24 29	4♏50 24	18 47.1	10 58.0	29 22.5	16 12.0	19 33.0	7 45.6	28 35.9	2 37.2	22 42.4	28 35.9
25 Tu	6 13 01	3 31 30	11♏12 42	17 31 43	18 44.1	13 02.1	0♋36.2	16 48.2	19 57.6	7 39.4	28 42.8	2 35.2	22 44.5	28 37.3
26 W	6 16 58	4 28 42	23 47 45	0♐01 07	18 38.5	15 04.4	1 49.9	17 24.5	20 22.3	7 33.2	28 49.6	2 33.2	22 46.6	28 38.8
27 Th	6 20 55	5 25 54	6♐12 03	12 20 46	18 30.0	17 04.9	3 03.6	18 00.9	20 47.1	7 27.2	28 56.4	2 31.2	22 48.8	28 40.2
28 F	6 24 51	6 23 05	18 27 29	24 32 21	18 19.1	19 03.5	4 17.3	18 37.2	21 12.0	7 21.3	29 03.1	2 29.1	22 50.9	28 41.6
29 Sa	6 28 48	7 20 16	0♑35 32	6♑37 09	18 06.4	21 00.2	5 31.0	19 13.6	21 36.9	7 15.5	29 09.8	2 27.0	22 53.1	28 43.1
30 Su	6 32 44	8 17 27	12 37 21	18 36 16	17 53.0	22 54.9	6 44.7	19 50.0	22 01.9	7 09.9	29 16.5	2 24.9	22 55.2	28 44.5

Astro Data

	Dy Hr Mn
♅R	8 7:34
☽0N	13 2:12
☽0S	25 21:20
☽0N	9 10:27
☽0S	22 2:08
♄⚺♇	24 11:48
♃⚼♆	24 21:17

Planet Ingress

	Dy Hr Mn
⚳ ♌	1 18:19
♀ ♉	7 1:57
☿ ♉	16 19:54
☉ ♊	21 10:57
♂ ♌	28 8:16
♀ ♊	31 13:19
☿ ♊	5 5:10
☿ ♋	19 9:00
☉ ♋	21 19:17
♀ ♋	25 0:12

Last Aspect / ☽ Ingress (May)

Last Aspect Dy Hr Mn		☽ Ingress Dy Hr Mn
2 7:16 ♄ ☍	♐	2 22:30
5 4:04 ♀ △	♑	5 8:42
7 5:49 ♄ △	♒	7 20:50
10 4:18 ♇ △	♓	10 9:08
12 14:50 ♇ □	♈	12 19:20
14 22:24 ☿ ☌	♉	15 2:04
16 22:13 ☉ ☌	♊	17 5:33
19 3:23 ♇ ☌	♋	19 7:04
21 8:07 ☉ ⚹	♌	21 8:18
23 7:00 ♇ ⚹	♍	23 10:40
25 12:02 ♂ ⚹	♎	25 15:00
27 20:56 ♂ □	♏	27 21:27
30 2:30 ♀ ☍	♐	30 5:54

Last Aspect / ☽ Ingress (June)

Last Aspect Dy Hr Mn		☽ Ingress Dy Hr Mn
1 12:26 ♇ ☍	♑	1 16:17
3 23:33 ☿ △	♒	4 4:19
6 13:14 ♇ △	♓	6 16:55
9 0:38 ♇ □	♈	9 4:03
11 8:42 ♇ ⚹	♉	11 11:46
13 11:01 ♄ ☌	♊	13 15:33
15 13:49 ♇ ☌	♋	15 16:24
17 12:43 ♄ ⚹	♌	17 16:16
19 14:38 ♇ ⚹	♍	19 17:09
21 17:58 ♇ □	♎	21 20:33
24 0:44 ♀ △	♏	24 2:58
26 9:40 ♄ ☍	♐	26 11:58
28 20:15 ♇ ☍	♑	28 22:49

☽ Phases & Eclipses

Dy Hr Mn	
1 10:19	○ 10♏40
9 9:56	☾ 18♒23
16 22:13	● 25♉38
23 14:11	☽ 2♍03
30 23:29	○ 9♐08
8 2:35	☾ 16♓55
15 6:23	● 23♊46
21 20:39	☽ 0♎03
29 13:33	○ 7♑24

Astro Data

1 May 1912
Julian Day # 4504
SVP 6♓29'09"
GC 25♐36.9 ⚴ 0♋00.8
Eris 26♓45.9 ⚵ 24♐10.7R
⚷ 10♓16.6 ⚶ 21♌51.8
☽ Mean ☊ 20♈40.6

1 June 1912
Julian Day # 4535
SVP 6♓29'04"
GC 25♐37.0 ⚴ 17♋38.6
Eris 26♓59.4 ⚵ 18♐59.0R
⚷ 11♓04.4 ⚶ 0♍04.9
☽ Mean ☊ 19♈02.1

July 1912 LONGITUDE

Day	Sid.Time	☉	0 hr ☽	Noon ☽	True ☊	☿	♀	♂	⚳	♃	♄	♅	♆	♇
1 M	6 36 41	9♋14 38	24♑34 05	0♒30 58	17♈39.9	24♋47.5	7♋58.4	20♌26.5	22♌26.9	7♐04.4	29♉23.0	2♒22.8	22♋57.4	28♊45.9
2 Tu	6 40 37	10 11 49	6♒27 08	12 22 49	17R 28.3	26 38.1	9 12.1	21 03.0	22 52.0	6R 59.0	29 29.6	2R 20.7	22 59.6	28 47.3
3 W	6 44 34	11 08 59	18 18 19	24 13 58	17 18.9	28 26.7	10 25.8	21 39.5	23 17.2	6 53.8	29 36.1	2 18.5	23 01.8	28 48.7
4 Th	6 48 30	12 06 10	0♓10 07	6♓07 14	17 12.1	0♌13.2	11 39.6	22 16.0	23 42.4	6 48.7	29 42.5	2 16.3	23 04.0	28 50.2
5 F	6 52 27	13 03 21	12 05 46	18 06 13	17 08.1	1 57.6	12 53.3	22 52.6	24 07.7	6 43.7	29 48.9	2 14.1	23 06.2	28 51.6
6 Sa	6 56 24	14 00 33	24 09 10	0♈15 11	17 06.3	3 40.0	14 07.1	23 29.2	24 33.1	6 38.9	29 55.2	2 11.9	23 08.4	28 53.0
7 Su	7 00 20	14 57 45	6♈24 53	12 38 54	17 05.9	5 20.3	15 20.9	24 05.9	24 58.5	6 34.2	0♊01.5	2 09.6	23 10.6	28 54.4
8 M	7 04 17	15 54 57	18 57 50	25 22 19	17 05.8	6 58.6	16 34.7	24 42.6	25 24.0	6 29.7	0 07.7	2 07.4	23 12.8	28 55.8
9 Tu	7 08 13	16 52 09	1♉52 54	8♉30 05	17 04.9	8 34.8	17 48.4	25 19.3	25 49.5	6 25.4	0 13.9	2 05.1	23 15.0	28 57.1
10 W	7 12 10	17 49 23	15 14 17	22 05 47	17 02.1	10 08.9	19 02.3	25 56.1	26 15.1	6 21.2	0 20.0	2 02.8	23 17.2	28 58.5
11 Th	7 16 06	18 46 36	29 04 45	6♊11 07	16 57.0	11 40.9	20 16.1	26 32.8	26 40.7	6 17.2	0 26.1	2 00.5	23 19.4	28 59.9
12 F	7 20 03	19 43 51	13♊24 37	20 44 49	16 49.3	13 10.8	21 29.9	27 09.7	27 06.5	6 13.3	0 32.1	1 58.2	23 21.7	29 01.3
13 Sa	7 24 00	20 41 05	28 10 57	5♋42 07	16 39.5	14 38.6	22 43.8	27 46.5	27 32.2	6 09.6	0 38.0	1 55.8	23 23.9	29 02.6
14 Su	7 27 56	21 38 20	13♋17 09	20 54 46	16 28.7	16 04.3	23 57.6	28 23.4	27 58.0	6 06.1	0 43.9	1 53.5	23 26.1	29 04.0
15 M	7 31 53	22 35 36	28 33 32	6♌12 02	16 18.2	17 27.8	25 11.5	29 00.4	28 23.9	6 02.8	0 49.7	1 51.1	23 28.4	29 05.3
16 Tu	7 35 49	23 32 51	13♌48 50	21 22 38	16 09.2	18 49.1	26 25.3	29 37.3	28 49.8	5 59.6	0 55.4	1 48.8	23 30.6	29 06.7
17 W	7 39 46	24 30 07	28 52 17	6♍16 48	16 02.5	20 08.2	27 39.2	0♍14.3	29 15.7	5 56.6	1 01.1	1 46.4	23 32.8	29 08.0
18 Th	7 43 42	25 27 23	13♍35 26	20 47 41	15 58.5	21 25.0	28 53.1	0 51.4	29 41.7	5 53.7	1 06.7	1 44.0	23 35.0	29 09.3
19 F	7 47 39	26 24 39	27 53 13	4♎51 58	15D 56.7	22 39.4	0♌07.0	1 28.4	0♍07.8	5 51.1	1 12.2	1 41.6	23 37.3	29 10.6
20 Sa	7 51 35	27 21 56	11♎43 57	18 29 25	15R 56.5	23 51.4	1 20.9	2 05.5	0 33.9	5 48.6	1 17.7	1 39.2	23 39.5	29 11.9
21 Su	7 55 32	28 19 12	25 08 40	1♏42 06	15 56.5	25 01.0	2 34.8	2 42.6	1 00.0	5 46.3	1 23.1	1 36.8	23 41.7	29 13.2
22 M	7 59 29	29 16 29	8♏10 10	14 33 22	15 55.7	26 08.0	3 48.7	3 19.8	1 26.2	5 44.2	1 28.4	1 34.4	23 43.9	29 14.5
23 Tu	8 03 25	0♌13 47	20 52 11	27 07 07	15 53.0	27 12.4	5 02.6	3 57.0	1 52.4	5 42.2	1 33.7	1 32.0	23 46.1	29 15.8
24 W	8 07 22	1 11 04	3♐18 38	9♐27 11	15 47.8	28 14.0	6 16.5	4 34.2	2 18.7	5 40.5	1 38.8	1 29.6	23 48.4	29 17.0
25 Th	8 11 18	2 08 22	15 33 11	21 37 01	15 39.9	29 12.8	7 30.4	5 11.4	2 45.0	5 38.9	1 44.0	1 27.2	23 50.6	29 18.3
26 F	8 15 15	3 05 41	27 39 01	3♑39 28	15 29.7	0♍08.6	8 44.4	5 48.7	3 11.3	5 37.5	1 49.0	1 24.8	23 52.8	29 19.5
27 Sa	8 19 11	4 03 01	9♑38 40	15 36 50	15 17.7	1 01.3	9 58.3	6 26.0	3 37.7	5 36.3	1 54.0	1 22.5	23 55.0	29 20.7
28 Su	8 23 08	5 00 21	21 34 11	27 30 55	15 05.0	1 50.8	11 12.3	7 03.4	4 04.1	5 35.3	1 58.8	1 20.1	23 57.2	29 22.0
29 M	8 27 04	5 57 41	3♒27 12	9♒23 14	14 52.6	2 37.0	12 26.2	7 40.8	4 30.5	5 34.4	2 03.7	1 17.7	23 59.4	29 23.2
30 Tu	8 31 01	6 55 03	15 19 11	21 15 15	14 41.6	3 19.6	13 40.2	8 18.2	4 57.0	5 33.8	2 08.4	1 15.3	24 01.6	29 24.4
31 W	8 34 58	7 52 25	27 11 39	3♓08 37	14 32.6	3 58.6	14 54.1	8 55.6	5 23.5	5 33.3	2 13.0	1 12.9	24 03.7	29 25.5

August 1912 LONGITUDE

Day	Sid.Time	☉	0 hr ☽	Noon ☽	True ☊	☿	♀	♂	⚳	♃	♄	♅	♆	♇
1 Th	8 38 54	8♌49 48	9♓06 27	15♓05 26	14♈26.3	4♍33.7	16♌08.1	9♍33.1	5♍50.1	5♐33.0	2♊17.6	1♒10.5	24♋05.9	29♊26.7
2 F	8 42 51	9 47 13	21 05 55	27 08 19	14R 22.6	5 04.7	17 22.1	10 10.6	6 16.7	5D 32.9	2 22.1	1R 08.2	24 08.1	29 27.8
3 Sa	8 46 47	10 44 38	3♈13 01	9♈20 32	14D 21.1	5 31.6	18 36.1	10 48.2	6 43.3	5 32.9	2 26.5	1 05.8	24 10.2	29 29.0
4 Su	8 50 44	11 42 05	15 31 20	21 45 56	14 21.2	5 53.9	19 50.1	11 25.8	7 10.0	5 33.2	2 30.8	1 03.4	24 12.4	29 30.1
5 M	8 54 40	12 39 32	28 04 54	4♉28 46	14R 21.8	6 11.7	21 04.1	12 03.4	7 36.6	5 33.6	2 35.1	1 01.1	24 14.5	29 31.2
6 Tu	8 58 37	13 37 02	10♉58 03	17 33 15	14 21.9	6 24.7	22 18.1	12 41.1	8 03.4	5 34.3	2 39.2	0 58.8	24 16.7	29 32.3
7 W	9 02 33	14 34 32	24 14 48	1♊03 03	14 20.7	6 32.7	23 32.1	13 18.8	8 30.1	5 35.1	2 43.3	0 56.4	24 18.8	29 33.4
8 Th	9 06 30	15 32 04	7♊58 14	15 00 27	14 17.5	6R 35.5	24 46.2	13 56.5	8 56.9	5 36.1	2 47.3	0 54.1	24 20.9	29 34.5
9 F	9 10 27	16 29 38	22 09 35	29 25 24	14 12.1	6 33.1	26 00.2	14 34.3	9 23.7	5 37.2	2 51.2	0 51.9	24 23.0	29 35.5
10 Sa	9 14 23	17 27 13	6♋47 22	14♋14 48	14 04.9	6 25.2	27 14.3	15 12.1	9 50.6	5 38.6	2 55.0	0 49.6	24 25.1	29 36.6
11 Su	9 18 20	18 24 49	21 46 45	29 22 06	13 56.7	6 11.9	28 28.3	15 49.9	10 17.4	5 40.1	2 58.7	0 47.3	24 27.2	29 37.6
12 M	9 22 16	19 22 26	6♌59 36	14♌37 53	13 48.6	5 53.1	29 42.4	16 27.8	10 44.3	5 41.9	3 02.4	0 45.1	24 29.2	29 38.6
13 Tu	9 26 13	20 20 05	22 15 34	29 51 15	13 41.6	5 28.9	0♍56.4	17 05.8	11 11.3	5 43.8	3 05.9	0 42.9	24 31.3	29 39.6
14 W	9 30 09	21 17 45	7♍23 41	14♍51 44	13 36.6	4 59.4	2 10.5	17 43.7	11 38.2	5 45.8	3 09.3	0 40.7	24 33.3	29 40.6
15 Th	9 34 06	22 15 25	22 14 28	29 31 07	13D 33.7	4 25.0	3 24.6	18 21.7	12 05.2	5 48.1	3 12.7	0 38.5	24 35.4	29 41.5
16 F	9 38 02	23 13 07	6♎41 11	13♎44 19	13 32.9	3 45.8	4 38.7	18 59.7	12 32.2	5 50.5	3 15.9	0 36.3	24 37.4	29 42.5
17 Sa	9 41 59	24 10 50	20 40 26	27 29 33	13 33.5	3 02.4	5 52.7	19 37.8	12 59.2	5 53.2	3 19.1	0 34.2	24 39.4	29 43.4
18 Su	9 45 56	25 08 34	4♏11 53	10♏47 44	13 34.6	2 15.5	7 06.8	20 15.9	13 26.3	5 56.0	3 22.2	0 32.0	24 41.3	29 44.3
19 M	9 49 52	26 06 19	17 17 30	23 41 41	13R 35.4	1 25.7	8 20.9	20 54.1	13 53.3	5 58.9	3 25.1	0 30.0	24 43.3	29 45.2
20 Tu	9 53 49	27 04 06	0♐00 46	6♐15 18	13 34.9	0 33.8	9 35.0	21 32.2	14 20.4	6 02.1	3 28.0	0 27.9	24 45.3	29 46.0
21 W	9 57 45	28 01 53	12 25 50	18 32 55	13 32.7	29♌40.9	10 49.1	22 10.4	14 47.5	6 05.4	3 30.8	0 25.8	24 47.2	29 46.9
22 Th	10 01 42	28 59 42	24 37 04	0♑38 47	13 28.6	28 47.8	12 03.1	22 48.7	15 14.6	6 08.9	3 33.5	0 23.8	24 49.1	29 47.7
23 F	10 05 38	29 57 32	6♑38 32	12 36 47	13 22.8	27 55.8	13 17.2	23 27.0	15 41.8	6 12.6	3 36.0	0 21.8	24 51.0	29 48.6
24 Sa	10 09 35	0♍55 23	18 33 55	24 30 20	13 15.6	27 05.9	14 31.3	24 05.3	16 08.9	6 16.4	3 38.5	0 19.9	24 52.9	29 49.4
25 Su	10 13 31	1 53 16	0♒26 19	6♒22 13	13 07.9	26 19.2	15 45.4	24 43.7	16 36.1	6 20.4	3 40.9	0 17.9	24 54.8	29 50.1
26 M	10 17 28	2 51 10	12 18 17	18 14 46	13 00.3	25 36.6	16 59.5	25 22.0	17 03.3	6 24.6	3 43.2	0 16.0	24 56.6	29 50.9
27 Tu	10 21 25	3 49 05	24 11 53	0♓09 52	12 53.7	24 59.3	18 13.5	26 00.5	17 30.5	6 28.9	3 45.3	0 14.2	24 58.5	29 51.6
28 W	10 25 21	4 47 02	6♓08 54	12 09 12	12 48.4	24 28.1	19 27.6	26 38.9	17 57.7	6 33.4	3 47.4	0 12.3	25 00.3	29 52.4
29 Th	10 29 18	5 45 00	18 10 57	24 14 24	12 45.0	24 03.7	20 41.7	27 17.4	18 24.9	6 38.1	3 49.4	0 10.5	25 02.1	29 53.1
30 F	10 33 14	6 43 01	0♈19 45	6♈27 16	12D 43.3	23 46.7	21 55.8	27 56.0	18 52.2	6 42.9	3 51.3	0 08.7	25 03.8	29 53.7
31 Sa	10 37 11	7 41 02	12 37 12	18 49 52	12 43.3	23D 37.6	23 09.8	28 34.6	19 19.4	6 47.9	3 53.0	0 07.0	25 05.6	29 54.4

Astro Data	Dy Hr Mn
☽ 0N	6 17:06
☽ 0S	19 8:13
♄△♅	23 6:56
♃ D	2 14:56
☽ 0N	2 22:27
☿ R	8 12:59
☽ 0S	15 16:39
☽ 0N	30 3:40

Planet Ingress		Dy Hr Mn
☿	♌	4 9:00
♄	♊	7 6:13
♂	♍	17 2:43
⚳	♍	19 4:50
♀	♌	19 9:44
☉	♌	23 6:14
☿	♍	26 8:13
♀	♍	12 17:43
☿	♌R	21 3:21
☉	♍	23 13:01

Last Aspect Dy Hr Mn			☽ Ingress	Dy Hr Mn
1 9:42	♄	△	♒	1 10:57
3 22:57	♄	□	♓	3 23:40
6 11:21	♄	⚹	♈	6 11:30
8 18:36	♇	⚹	♉	8 20:33
10 18:55	♂	□	♊	11 1:34
13 1:22	♇	☌	♋	13 2:55
14 17:12	♀	☌	♌	15 2:16
17 1:47	♂	☌	♍	17 1:49
19 3:01	♀	⚹	♎	19 3:37
21 7:26	♇	△	♏	21 8:52
23 12:11	☿	□	♐	23 17:34
26 4:24	☿	△	♑	26 4:41
28 4:47	♆	☍	♒	28 17:01
31 4:29	♇	△	♓	31 5:40

Last Aspect Dy Hr Mn			☽ Ingress	Dy Hr Mn
2 16:37	♇	□	♈	2 17:40
5 2:42	♇	⚹	♉	5 3:37
7 0:05	♆	⚹	♊	7 10:10
9 12:16	♇	☌	♋	9 12:57
11 4:13	♆	☌	♌	11 13:00
13 11:42	♇	⚹	♍	13 12:14
15 12:17	♇	□	♎	15 12:48
17 15:59	♇	△	♏	17 16:28
19 16:56	☉	□	♐	19 23:59
22 10:18	♇	☍	♑	22 10:43
24 12:46	♆	☍	♒	24 23:07
27 11:23	♇	△	♓	27 11:40
29 23:08	♇	□	♈	29 23:21

☽ Phases & Eclipses Dy Hr Mn		
7 16:47	☾	15♈09
14 13:13	●	21♋41
21 5:18	☽	28♎03
29 4:28	○	5♒40
6 4:17	☾	13♉19
12 19:57	●	19♌42
19 16:56	☽	26♏18
27 19:58	○	4♓08

Astro Data

1 July 1912
Julian Day # 4565
SVP 6♓28'58"
GC 25♐37.0 ⚶ 4♌25.6
Eris 27♓02.1R ⚵ 12♐31.9R
⚷ 11♓00.8R ⚴ 11♍17.5
☽ Mean ☊ 17♈26.8

1 August 1912
Julian Day # 4596
SVP 6♓28'53"
GC 25♐37.1 ⚶ 21♌11.2
Eris 26♓53.6R ⚵ 9♐21.1R
⚷ 10♓08.5R ⚴ 24♍55.8
☽ Mean ☊ 15♈48.4

LONGITUDE — September 1912

Day	Sid.Time	☉	0 hr ☽	Noon ☽	True ☊	☿	♀	♂	⚳	♃	♄	♅	♆	♇
1 Su	10 41 07	8♍39 06	25♈05 34	1♉24 40	12♈44.4	23♌36.9	24♍23.9	29♍13.2	19♍46.7	6♐53.1	3♊54.7	0♒05.2	25♋07.3	29♊55.0
2 M	10 45 04	9 37 12	7♉47 28	14 14 23	12 46.0	23 44.6	25 38.0	29 51.8	20 14.0	6 58.4	3 56.2	0R 03.6	25 09.0	29 55.7
3 Tu	10 49 00	10 35 20	20 45 43	27 21 52	12 47.4	24 01.0	26 52.1	0♎30.5	20 41.3	7 03.8	3 57.7	0 01.9	25 10.7	29 56.3
4 W	10 52 57	11 33 30	4♊03 05	10♊49 41	12R 48.0	24 26.0	28 06.1	1 09.3	21 08.6	7 09.5	3 59.0	0 00.3	25 12.4	29 56.8
5 Th	10 56 54	12 31 41	17 41 49	24 39 36	12 47.5	24 59.5	29 20.2	1 48.1	21 35.9	7 15.2	4 00.3	29♑58.7	25 14.1	29 57.4
6 F	11 00 50	13 29 55	1♋43 01	8♋51 55	12 45.6	25 41.2	0♎34.3	2 26.9	22 03.3	7 21.2	4 01.4	29 57.2	25 15.7	29 58.0
7 Sa	11 04 47	14 28 11	16 06 00	23 24 49	12 42.6	26 30.9	1 48.4	3 05.8	22 30.6	7 27.3	4 02.4	29 55.7	25 17.3	29 58.5
8 Su	11 08 43	15 26 29	0♌47 44	8♌14 00	12 39.0	27 28.3	3 02.5	3 44.7	22 58.0	7 33.5	4 03.3	29 54.3	25 18.9	29 59.0
9 M	11 12 40	16 24 49	15 42 41	23 12 45	12 35.3	28 32.8	4 16.5	4 23.7	23 25.3	7 39.9	4 04.1	29 52.8	25 20.4	29 59.5
10 Tu	11 16 36	17 23 11	0♍43 08	8♍12 41	12 32.1	29 44.0	5 30.6	5 02.7	23 52.7	7 46.4	4 04.8	29 51.5	25 22.0	29 59.9
11 W	11 20 33	18 21 35	15 40 18	23 04 54	12 29.9	1♍01.4	6 44.7	5 41.7	24 20.1	7 53.1	4 05.4	29 50.1	25 23.5	0♋00.3
12 Th	11 24 29	19 20 00	0♎25 34	7♎41 26	12D 29.0	2 24.3	7 58.8	6 20.8	24 47.5	7 59.9	4 05.9	29 48.8	25 24.9	0 00.8
13 F	11 28 26	20 18 28	14 51 51	21 56 17	12 29.1	3 52.3	9 12.8	6 59.9	25 14.8	8 06.9	4 06.2	29 47.6	25 26.4	0 01.1
14 Sa	11 32 23	21 16 57	28 54 25	5♏46 04	12 30.1	5 24.7	10 26.9	7 39.0	25 42.2	8 14.0	4 06.5	29 46.4	25 27.8	0 01.5
15 Su	11 36 19	22 15 27	12♏31 11	19 09 54	12 31.6	7 01.0	11 41.0	8 18.2	26 09.6	8 21.2	4R 06.7	29 45.2	25 29.2	0 01.9
16 M	11 40 16	23 14 00	25 42 26	2♐09 07	12 32.9	8 40.6	12 55.0	8 57.5	26 37.0	8 28.6	4 06.7	29 44.1	25 30.6	0 02.2
17 Tu	11 44 12	24 12 34	8♐30 21	14 46 36	12R 33.9	10 23.0	14 09.1	9 36.8	27 04.4	8 36.2	4 06.6	29 43.0	25 32.0	0 02.5
18 W	11 48 09	25 11 10	20 58 23	27 06 14	12 34.1	12 07.7	15 23.1	10 16.1	27 31.8	8 43.8	4 06.4	29 41.9	25 33.3	0 02.8
19 Th	11 52 05	26 09 47	3♑10 44	9♑12 25	12 33.6	13 54.2	16 37.2	10 55.5	27 59.2	8 51.6	4 06.2	29 40.9	25 34.6	0 03.0
20 F	11 56 02	27 08 26	15 11 52	21 09 37	12 32.4	15 42.1	17 51.2	11 34.9	28 26.6	8 59.5	4 05.8	29 40.0	25 35.8	0 03.3
21 Sa	11 59 58	28 07 07	27 06 13	3♒02 09	12 30.6	17 31.0	19 05.2	12 14.3	28 54.0	9 07.6	4 05.3	29 39.1	25 37.1	0 03.5
22 Su	12 03 55	29 05 50	8♒57 54	14 53 55	12 28.6	19 20.7	20 19.2	12 53.8	29 21.4	9 15.8	4 04.6	29 38.2	25 38.3	0 03.7
23 M	12 07 52	0♎04 34	20 50 36	26 48 20	12 26.6	21 10.8	21 33.2	13 33.3	29 48.7	9 24.1	4 03.9	29 37.4	25 39.5	0 03.8
24 Tu	12 11 48	1 03 20	2♓47 28	8♓48 17	12 24.9	23 01.1	22 47.2	14 12.9	0♎16.1	9 32.5	4 03.1	29 36.7	25 40.6	0 04.0
25 W	12 15 45	2 02 08	14 51 03	20 56 01	12 23.8	24 51.4	24 01.2	14 52.5	0 43.5	9 41.1	4 02.1	29 36.0	25 41.8	0 04.1
26 Th	12 19 41	3 00 58	27 03 24	3♈13 21	12D 23.1	26 41.6	25 15.1	15 32.1	1 10.9	9 49.8	4 01.1	29 35.3	25 42.9	0 04.2
27 F	12 23 38	3 59 50	9♈26 03	15 41 37	12 23.0	28 31.3	26 29.1	16 11.8	1 38.2	9 58.6	3 59.9	29 34.7	25 43.9	0 04.3
28 Sa	12 27 34	4 58 44	22 00 11	28 21 52	12 23.3	0♎20.7	27 43.1	16 51.6	2 05.6	10 07.5	3 58.7	29 34.1	25 45.0	0 04.3
29 Su	12 31 31	5 57 40	4♉46 45	11♉14 56	12 23.8	2 09.5	28 57.0	17 31.3	2 32.9	10 16.5	3 57.3	29 33.6	25 46.0	0 04.4
30 M	12 35 27	6 56 39	17 46 30	24 21 31	12 24.4	3 57.7	0♏11.0	18 11.2	3 00.3	10 25.7	3 55.9	29 33.1	25 46.9	0R 04.4

LONGITUDE — October 1912

Day	Sid.Time	☉	0 hr ☽	Noon ☽	True ☊	☿	♀	♂	⚳	♃	♄	♅	♆	♇
1 Tu	12 39 24	7♎55 39	1♊00 05	7♊42 16	12♈24.9	5♎45.3	1♏24.9	18♎51.0	3♎27.6	10♐35.0	3♊54.3	29♑32.7	25♋47.9	0♋04.4
2 W	12 43 20	8 54 43	14 28 05	21 17 36	12 25.2	7 32.1	2 38.8	19 31.0	3 55.0	10 44.3	3R 52.6	29R 32.3	25 48.8	0R 04.3
3 Th	12 47 17	9 53 48	28 10 47	5♋07 37	12R 25.4	9 18.2	3 52.8	20 10.9	4 22.3	10 53.8	3 50.8	29 32.0	25 49.7	0 04.3
4 F	12 51 14	10 52 56	12♋08 00	19 11 48	12 25.4	11 03.5	5 06.7	20 50.9	4 49.6	11 03.4	3 48.9	29 31.7	25 50.6	0 04.2
5 Sa	12 55 10	11 52 06	26 18 48	3♌28 43	12D 25.3	12 48.1	6 20.6	21 31.0	5 16.9	11 13.2	3 47.0	29 31.5	25 51.4	0 04.1
6 Su	12 59 07	12 51 18	10♌41 11	17 55 45	12 25.3	14 31.9	7 34.5	22 11.1	5 44.2	11 23.0	3 44.9	29 31.3	25 52.2	0 04.0
7 M	13 03 03	13 50 33	25 11 55	2♍29 03	12 25.4	16 14.9	8 48.4	22 51.2	6 11.5	11 32.9	3 42.7	29 31.1	25 52.9	0 03.8
8 Tu	13 07 00	14 49 50	9♍46 30	17 03 33	12 25.6	17 57.1	10 02.3	23 31.4	6 38.8	11 42.9	3 40.4	29 31.1	25 53.7	0 03.7
9 W	13 10 56	15 49 09	24 19 29	1♎33 33	12R 25.7	19 38.6	11 16.2	24 11.7	7 06.0	11 53.1	3 38.0	29D 31.0	25 54.4	0 03.5
10 Th	13 14 53	16 48 30	8♎45 02	15 53 14	12 25.8	21 19.3	12 30.1	24 51.9	7 33.3	12 03.3	3 35.5	29 31.1	25 55.0	0 03.3
11 F	13 18 49	17 47 54	22 57 33	29 57 26	12 25.6	22 59.2	13 44.0	25 32.3	8 00.5	12 13.7	3 32.9	29 31.1	25 55.6	0 03.0
12 Sa	13 22 46	18 47 19	6♏52 27	13♏42 15	12 25.1	24 38.4	14 57.9	26 12.7	8 27.7	12 24.1	3 30.2	29 31.3	25 56.2	0 02.8
13 Su	13 26 43	19 46 46	20 26 37	27 05 28	12 24.2	26 17.0	16 11.7	26 53.1	8 54.9	12 34.6	3 27.5	29 31.4	25 56.8	0 02.5
14 M	13 30 39	20 46 16	3♐38 46	10♐06 39	12 23.2	27 54.8	17 25.6	27 33.5	9 22.1	12 45.3	3 24.6	29 31.7	25 57.3	0 02.2
15 Tu	13 34 36	21 45 47	16 29 20	22 47 06	12 22.1	29 31.9	18 39.4	28 14.1	9 49.3	12 56.0	3 21.6	29 31.9	25 57.8	0 01.9
16 W	13 38 32	22 45 20	29 00 19	5♑09 25	12 21.2	1♏08.4	19 53.2	28 54.6	10 16.4	13 06.8	3 18.6	29 32.3	25 58.3	0 01.5
17 Th	13 42 29	23 44 54	11♑14 55	17 17 20	12D 20.6	2 44.2	21 07.1	29 35.2	10 43.5	13 17.7	3 15.5	29 32.7	25 58.7	0 01.2
18 F	13 46 25	24 44 31	23 17 13	29 15 11	12 20.6	4 19.4	22 20.9	0♏15.8	11 10.6	13 28.7	3 12.2	29 33.1	25 59.1	0 00.8
19 Sa	13 50 22	25 44 09	5♒11 47	11♒07 38	12 21.1	5 53.9	23 34.6	0 56.5	11 37.7	13 39.8	3 08.9	29 33.6	25 59.5	0 00.4
20 Su	13 54 18	26 43 49	17 03 20	22 59 27	12 22.1	7 27.9	24 48.4	1 37.3	12 04.7	13 51.0	3 05.5	29 34.1	25 59.8	29♊59.9
21 M	13 58 15	27 43 30	28 56 33	4♓55 09	12 23.5	9 01.3	26 02.2	2 18.0	12 31.7	14 02.2	3 02.1	29 34.7	26 00.1	29 59.5
22 Tu	14 02 12	28 43 14	10♓55 46	16 58 51	12 24.9	10 34.1	27 15.9	2 58.9	12 58.7	14 13.6	2 58.5	29 35.3	26 00.3	29 59.0
23 W	14 06 08	29 42 59	23 04 48	29 14 00	12 26.0	12 06.3	28 29.6	3 39.7	13 25.7	14 25.0	2 54.9	29 36.0	26 00.6	29 58.5
24 Th	14 10 05	0♏42 46	5♈26 45	11♈43 17	12R 26.5	13 38.0	29 43.4	4 20.6	13 52.6	14 36.5	2 51.2	29 36.8	26 00.8	29 58.0
25 F	14 14 01	1 42 34	18 03 47	24 28 23	12 26.0	15 09.2	0♐57.1	5 01.6	14 19.5	14 48.0	2 47.4	29 37.6	26 00.9	29 57.4
26 Sa	14 17 58	2 42 25	0♉57 06	7♉29 55	12 24.6	16 39.8	2 10.7	5 42.6	14 46.4	14 59.7	2 43.6	29 38.4	26 01.0	29 56.9
27 Su	14 21 54	3 42 18	14 06 45	20 47 27	12 22.1	18 09.8	3 24.4	6 23.6	15 13.3	15 11.4	2 39.6	29 39.3	26 01.1	29 56.3
28 M	14 25 51	4 42 13	27 31 49	4♊19 37	12 19.0	19 39.4	4 38.1	7 04.7	15 40.1	15 23.2	2 35.7	29 40.2	26 01.2	29 55.7
29 Tu	14 29 47	5 42 10	11♊10 33	18 04 18	12 15.5	21 08.3	5 51.7	7 45.9	16 06.9	15 35.1	2 31.6	29 41.2	26R 01.2	29 55.1
30 W	14 33 44	6 42 09	25 00 33	1♋59 00	12 12.2	22 36.8	7 05.3	8 27.1	16 33.7	15 47.0	2 27.5	29 42.3	26 01.2	29 54.5
31 Th	14 37 41	7 42 10	8♋59 17	16 01 06	12 09.7	24 04.7	8 18.9	9 08.3	17 00.4	15 59.0	2 23.3	29 43.4	26 01.2	29 53.8

Astro Data

	Dy Hr Mn
☿D	1 2:10
♂0S	5 3:55
♅⊼♇	6 3:21
♀0S	8 3:47
☽0S	12 2:52
♄R	16 8:37
⊙0S	23 10:08
☽0N	26 9:57
☿0S	30 6:28
♇R	30 13:08
♃⚼♆	3 0:31
☽0S	9 13:02
♅D	9 13:43
☽0N	23 17:41
♃∠♅	24 12:43

Planet Ingress

		Dy Hr Mn
♂	♎	2 17:04
♅	♑R	4 16:47
♀	♎	6 0:53
♇	♋	10 16:51
☿	♍	10 17:07
⊙	♎	23 10:08
⚳	♎	23 21:52
☿	♎	28 7:27
♀	♏	30 8:26
☿	♏	15 18:58
♂	♏	18 2:39
♇	♊R	20 7:57
⊙	♏	23 18:50
♀	♐	24 17:25

Last Aspect / ☽ Ingress

Last Aspect Dy Hr Mn		☽ Ingress Dy Hr Mn
1 9:10	♇ ⚹	♉ 1 9:20
3 11:01	♀ △	♊ 3 16:45
5 21:02	♇ ☌	♋ 5 21:06
7 22:35	♅ ☍	♌ 7 22:43
9 22:50	♇ ⚹	♍ 9 22:51
11 23:01	♅ △	♎ 11 23:18
14 1:31	♅ □	♏ 14 1:54
16 7:29	♅ ⚹	♐ 16 7:58
18 7:54	⊙ □	♑ 18 17:42
21 5:10	♅ ☌	♒ 21 5:51
23 0:13	♀ △	♓ 23 18:25
26 4:57	♅ ⚹	♈ 26 5:44
28 14:15	♅ □	♉ 28 15:04
30 21:23	♅ △	♊ 30 22:12

Last Aspect / ☽ Ingress

Last Aspect Dy Hr Mn		☽ Ingress Dy Hr Mn
2 8:44	♂ △	♋ 3 3:09
5 5:23	♅ ☍	♌ 5 6:11
6 19:22	♂ ⚹	♍ 7 7:55
8 8:36	♅ △	♎ 9 9:24
11 11:15	♅ □	♏ 11 12:04
13 16:26	♅ ⚹	♐ 13 17:18
15 23:07	♂ ⚹	♑ 16 1:56
18 12:36	♅ ☌	♒ 18 13:30
21 2:07	♇ △	♓ 21 2:08
23 13:26	♇ □	♈ 23 13:29
25 22:10	♇ ⚹	♉ 25 22:15
28 3:47	♅ △	♊ 28 4:22
30 8:26	♇ ☌	♋ 30 8:36

☽ Phases & Eclipses

Dy Hr Mn	
4 13:23	☾ 11♊37
11 3:48	● 18♍02
18 7:54	☽ 25♐01
26 11:34	○ 3♈00
26 11:45	• P 0.118
3 20:48	☾ 10♋15
10 13:40	● 16♎53
10 13:35:59	• T 01'55"
18 2:06	☽ 24♑20
26 2:30	○ 2♉19

Astro Data

1 September 1912
Julian Day # 4627
SVP 6♓28'49"
GC 25♐37.2 ⚴ 7♍14.7
Eris 26♓36.3R ⚵ 11♐22.9
⚷ 8♓45.4R ⚶ 9♎54.5
☽ Mean ☊ 14♈09.9

1 October 1912
Julian Day # 4657
SVP 6♓28'45"
GC 25♐37.3 ⚴ 22♍03.2
Eris 26♓15.9R ⚵ 17♐20.0
⚷ 7♓24.9R ⚶ 25♎15.0
☽ Mean ☊ 12♈34.5

November 1912 LONGITUDE

Day	Sid.Time	☉	0 hr ☽	Noon☽	True☊	☿	♀	♂	⚳	♃	♄	♅	♆	♇
1 F	14 41 37	8♏42 14	23♋04 10	0♌08 12	12♈08.3	25♏32.0	9♐32.5	9♏49.6	17♎27.1	16♐11.1	2♊19.1	29♑44.5	26♋01.1	29♊53.2
2 Sa	14 45 34	9 42 19	7♌12 56	14 18 07	12D08.1	26 58.7	10 46.1	10 30.9	17 53.8	16 23.2	2R14.8	29 45.7	26R01.0	29R52.5
3 Su	14 49 30	10 42 27	21 23 32	28 28 56	12 09.0	28 24.8	11 59.7	11 12.3	18 20.4	16 35.4	2 10.4	29 46.9	26 00.8	29 51.8
4 M	14 53 27	11 42 37	5♍34 06	12♍38 46	12 10.5	29 50.2	13 13.3	11 53.8	18 47.0	16 47.7	2 06.0	29 48.2	26 00.6	29 51.0
5 Tu	14 57 23	12 42 49	19 42 42	26 45 36	12 11.9	1♐14.9	14 26.8	12 35.2	19 13.6	17 00.1	2 01.5	29 49.5	26 00.4	29 50.3
6 W	15 01 20	13 43 03	3♎47 09	10♎47 03	12R12.6	2 38.9	15 40.3	13 16.8	19 40.1	17 12.5	1 57.0	29 50.9	26 00.2	29 49.5
7 Th	15 05 16	14 43 18	17 44 56	24 40 27	12 12.0	4 02.1	16 53.8	13 58.3	20 06.6	17 24.9	1 52.5	29 52.4	25 59.9	29 48.7
8 F	15 09 13	15 43 36	1♏33 13	8♏22 52	12 09.7	5 24.8	18 07.3	14 40.0	20 33.1	17 37.4	1 47.9	29 53.8	25 59.6	29 47.9
9 Sa	15 13 10	16 43 56	15 09 05	21 51 34	12 05.6	6 45.7	19 20.8	15 21.7	20 59.5	17 50.0	1 43.2	29 55.4	25 59.2	29 47.1
10 Su	15 17 06	17 44 17	28 30 02	5♐04 17	12 00.0	8 06.0	20 34.3	16 03.4	21 25.8	18 02.7	1 38.5	29 56.9	25 58.8	29 46.3
11 M	15 21 03	18 44 40	11♐34 12	17 59 43	11 53.5	9 25.2	21 47.7	16 45.2	21 52.2	18 15.3	1 33.8	29 58.6	25 58.4	29 45.4
12 Tu	15 24 59	19 45 05	24 20 52	0♑37 44	11 46.7	10 43.0	23 01.2	17 27.0	22 18.4	18 28.1	1 29.1	0♒00.2	25 58.0	29 44.6
13 W	15 28 56	20 45 31	6♑50 33	12 59 32	11 40.5	11 59.3	24 14.6	18 08.9	22 44.6	18 40.9	1 24.3	0 01.9	25 57.5	29 43.7
14 Th	15 32 52	21 45 58	19 05 04	25 07 31	11 35.5	13 14.0	25 27.9	18 50.8	23 10.8	18 53.7	1 19.5	0 03.7	25 57.0	29 42.8
15 F	15 36 49	22 46 27	1♒07 24	7♒05 12	11 32.2	14 26.9	26 41.3	19 32.7	23 36.9	19 06.6	1 14.7	0 05.5	25 56.4	29 41.9
16 Sa	15 40 45	23 46 57	13 01 30	18 56 53	11D30.6	15 37.7	27 54.6	20 14.7	24 03.0	19 19.6	1 09.8	0 07.4	25 55.8	29 41.0
17 Su	15 44 42	24 47 28	24 52 00	0♓47 28	11 30.7	16 46.1	29 07.9	20 56.8	24 29.0	19 32.5	1 05.0	0 09.3	25 55.2	29 40.0
18 M	15 48 39	25 48 01	6♓43 57	12 42 06	11 31.9	17 51.9	0♑21.2	21 38.9	24 55.0	19 45.6	1 00.1	0 11.2	25 54.6	29 39.1
19 Tu	15 52 35	26 48 34	18 42 34	24 45 57	11 33.4	18 54.7	1 34.4	22 21.0	25 20.9	19 58.6	0 55.2	0 13.2	25 53.9	29 38.1
20 W	15 56 32	27 49 09	0♈52 51	7♈03 49	11R34.4	19 54.0	2 47.6	23 03.2	25 46.8	20 11.7	0 50.3	0 15.2	25 53.2	29 37.1
21 Th	16 00 28	28 49 46	13 19 18	19 39 34	11 34.2	20 49.5	4 00.8	23 45.4	26 12.6	20 24.9	0 45.4	0 17.3	25 52.5	29 36.1
22 F	16 04 25	29 50 23	26 05 27	2♉36 38	11 32.0	21 40.5	5 14.0	24 27.7	26 38.3	20 38.1	0 40.4	0 19.4	25 51.7	29 35.1
23 Sa	16 08 21	0♐51 02	9♉13 26	15 55 50	11 27.6	22 26.5	6 27.1	25 10.0	27 04.0	20 51.3	0 35.5	0 21.5	25 50.9	29 34.1
24 Su	16 12 18	1 51 43	22 43 40	29 36 40	11 21.0	23 07.0	7 40.1	25 52.4	27 29.6	21 04.6	0 30.6	0 23.7	25 50.1	29 33.1
25 M	16 16 14	2 52 24	6♊34 27	13♊36 29	11 12.8	23 41.0	8 53.2	26 34.8	27 55.2	21 17.9	0 25.7	0 25.9	25 49.2	29 32.0
26 Tu	16 20 11	3 53 07	20 42 09	27 50 45	11 03.8	24 08.0	10 06.2	27 17.3	28 20.7	21 31.2	0 20.8	0 28.2	25 48.3	29 31.0
27 W	16 24 08	4 53 52	5♋01 33	12♋13 46	10 55.2	24 27.1	11 19.2	27 59.8	28 46.2	21 44.5	0 15.9	0 30.5	25 47.4	29 29.9
28 Th	16 28 04	5 54 38	19 26 41	26 39 34	10 48.0	24R37.5	12 32.1	28 42.4	29 11.5	21 57.9	0 11.0	0 32.9	25 46.5	29 28.8
29 F	16 32 01	6 55 25	3♌51 48	11♌02 49	10 42.8	24 38.4	13 45.0	29 25.0	29 36.9	22 11.4	0 06.1	0 35.3	25 45.5	29 27.8
30 Sa	16 35 57	7 56 14	18 12 10	25 19 29	10D40.0	24 29.1	14 57.8	0♐07.7	0♏02.1	22 24.8	0 01.3	0 37.7	25 44.5	29 26.7

December 1912 LONGITUDE

Day	Sid.Time	☉	0 hr ☽	Noon☽	True☊	☿	♀	♂	⚳	♃	♄	♅	♆	♇
1 Su	16 39 54	8♐57 04	2♍24 31	9♍27 06	10♈39.2	24♐09.0	16♑10.6	0♐50.4	0♏27.3	22♐38.3	29♉56.4	0♒40.2	25♋43.5	29♊25.6
2 M	16 43 50	9 57 56	16 27 07	23 24 34	10 39.7	23R37.8	17 23.4	1 33.2	0 52.4	22 51.8	29R51.6	0 42.7	25R42.4	29R24.4
3 Tu	16 47 47	10 58 49	0♎19 25	7♎11 43	10R40.4	22 55.5	18 36.2	2 16.0	1 17.5	23 05.3	29 46.8	0 45.2	25 41.3	29 23.3
4 W	16 51 44	11 59 44	14 01 29	20 48 46	10 40.0	22 02.4	19 48.9	2 58.8	1 42.4	23 18.9	29 42.1	0 47.8	25 40.2	29 22.2
5 Th	16 55 40	13 00 40	27 33 34	4♏15 52	10 37.5	20 59.4	21 01.5	3 41.8	2 07.3	23 32.4	29 37.3	0 50.4	25 39.1	29 21.1
6 F	16 59 37	14 01 37	10♏55 38	17 32 48	10 32.2	19 48.1	22 14.1	4 24.7	2 32.2	23 46.0	29 32.6	0 53.0	25 38.0	29 19.9
7 Sa	17 03 33	15 02 35	24 07 16	0♐38 56	10 24.1	18 30.3	23 26.7	5 07.7	2 56.9	23 59.6	29 28.0	0 55.7	25 36.8	29 18.8
8 Su	17 07 30	16 03 34	7♐07 40	13 33 21	10 13.4	17 08.6	24 39.2	5 50.8	3 21.6	24 13.3	29 23.4	0 58.4	25 35.6	29 17.6
9 M	17 11 26	17 04 35	19 55 53	26 15 11	10 01.0	15 45.5	25 51.7	6 33.9	3 46.2	24 26.9	29 18.8	1 01.2	25 34.3	29 16.4
10 Tu	17 15 23	18 05 36	2♑31 14	8♑44 01	9 48.0	14 24.1	27 04.1	7 17.0	4 10.7	24 40.6	29 14.2	1 04.0	25 33.1	29 15.3
11 W	17 19 19	19 06 38	14 53 37	21 00 09	9 35.5	13 06.9	28 16.4	8 00.2	4 35.1	24 54.3	29 09.8	1 06.8	25 31.8	29 14.1
12 Th	17 23 16	20 07 40	27 03 48	3♒04 50	9 24.7	11 56.3	29 28.7	8 43.5	4 59.4	25 08.0	29 05.3	1 09.6	25 30.5	29 12.9
13 F	17 27 13	21 08 43	9♒03 34	15 00 25	9 16.3	10 54.3	0♒41.0	9 26.8	5 23.7	25 21.6	29 01.0	1 12.5	25 29.2	29 11.7
14 Sa	17 31 09	22 09 47	20 55 48	26 50 16	9 10.7	10 02.1	1 53.1	10 10.1	5 47.8	25 35.4	28 56.6	1 15.4	25 27.8	29 10.6
15 Su	17 35 06	23 10 51	2♓44 20	8♓38 37	9 07.6	9 20.8	3 05.2	10 53.5	6 11.9	25 49.1	28 52.4	1 18.3	25 26.5	29 09.4
16 M	17 39 02	24 11 55	14 33 47	20 30 29	9D06.6	8 50.5	4 17.3	11 36.9	6 35.8	26 02.8	28 48.2	1 21.3	25 25.1	29 08.2
17 Tu	17 42 59	25 13 00	26 29 25	2♈31 16	9R06.7	8 31.2	5 29.2	12 20.3	6 59.7	26 16.5	28 44.0	1 24.3	25 23.7	29 07.0
18 W	17 46 55	26 14 05	8♈36 45	14 46 32	9 06.7	8D22.6	6 41.1	13 03.8	7 23.5	26 30.2	28 39.9	1 27.3	25 22.3	29 05.8
19 Th	17 50 52	27 15 10	21 01 16	27 21 32	9 05.4	8 24.0	7 52.9	13 47.4	7 47.2	26 43.9	28 35.9	1 30.3	25 20.8	29 04.6
20 F	17 54 48	28 16 16	3♉47 51	10♉20 39	9 02.0	8 34.8	9 04.6	14 31.0	8 10.7	26 57.7	28 32.0	1 33.4	25 19.4	29 03.4
21 Sa	17 58 45	29 17 22	17 00 14	23 46 45	8 55.8	8 54.2	10 16.3	15 14.6	8 34.2	27 11.4	28 28.1	1 36.5	25 17.9	29 02.2
22 Su	18 02 42	0♑18 28	0♊40 11	7♊40 22	8 46.9	9 21.3	11 27.8	15 58.3	8 57.6	27 25.1	28 24.3	1 39.6	25 16.4	29 01.0
23 M	18 06 38	1 19 35	14 46 54	21 59 12	8 35.8	9 55.4	12 39.3	16 42.0	9 20.9	27 38.8	28 20.6	1 42.7	25 14.9	28 59.8
24 Tu	18 10 35	2 20 42	29 16 31	6♋37 55	8 23.7	10 35.8	13 50.7	17 25.8	9 44.0	27 52.6	28 16.9	1 45.9	25 13.4	28 58.6
25 W	18 14 31	3 21 49	14♋02 22	21 28 43	8 11.8	11 21.7	15 02.0	18 09.6	10 07.1	28 06.3	28 13.4	1 49.1	25 11.8	28 57.4
26 Th	18 18 28	4 22 57	28 55 51	6♌22 36	8 01.4	12 12.6	16 13.2	18 53.5	10 30.0	28 20.0	28 09.9	1 52.3	25 10.3	28 56.2
27 F	18 22 24	5 24 05	13♌47 55	21 10 52	7 53.7	13 07.9	17 24.2	19 37.4	10 52.9	28 33.7	28 06.5	1 55.5	25 08.7	28 55.0
28 Sa	18 26 21	6 25 14	28 30 39	5♍46 38	7 48.8	14 07.0	18 35.2	20 21.3	11 15.6	28 47.4	28 03.2	1 58.8	25 07.2	28 53.9
29 Su	18 30 18	7 26 23	12♍58 22	20 05 32	7 46.6	15 09.6	19 46.1	21 05.3	11 38.2	29 01.0	28 00.0	2 02.0	25 05.6	28 52.7
30 M	18 34 14	8 27 32	27 08 01	4♎05 46	7 46.1	16 15.2	20 56.9	21 49.4	12 00.7	29 14.7	27 56.8	2 05.3	25 04.0	28 51.5
31 Tu	18 38 11	9 28 42	10♎58 53	17 47 32	7 46.0	17 23.4	22 07.6	22 33.5	12 23.1	29 28.3	27 53.8	2 08.6	25 02.3	28 50.3

Astro Data

	Dy Hr Mn
⚳0S	1 21:43
♅⚻♇	5 20:20
☽0S	5 21:08
☽0N	20 2:09
♄△♅	25 11:10
☿R	29 2:14
☽0S	3 2:36
♄⚺♇	10 4:39
♃⚻♆	14 0:02
☽0N	17 10:03
☿D	18 20:25
♃⚻♄	25 21:55
♃☍♇	28 22:29
☽0S	30 7:11

Planet Ingress

		Dy Hr Mn
☿	♐	4 14:46
♅	♒	12 8:45
♀	♑	18 5:03
☉	♐	22 15:48
♂	♐	30 7:41
⚳	♏	30 9:59
♄	♉R	30 18:18
♀	♒	12 22:23
☉	♑	22 4:45

Last Aspect / ☽ Ingress

Last Aspect Dy Hr Mn			☽ Ingress	Dy Hr Mn
1 11:20	♅	☍	♌	1 11:46
3 14:20	♇	⚹	♍	3 14:34
5 17:15	♇	□	♎	5 17:32
7 21:05	♅	□	♏	7 21:17
10 2:37	♅	⚹	♐	10 2:44
12 10:18	♇	☍	♑	12 10:48
14 13:39	♆	☍	♒	14 21:45
17 9:44	♇	△	♓	17 10:24
19 21:33	♇	□	♈	19 22:17
22 6:28	♇	⚹	♉	22 7:13
24 5:26	♆	⚹	♊	24 12:40
26 14:48	♇	☌	♋	26 15:36
28 15:35	♂	△	♌	28 17:34
30 19:54	♄	□	♍	30 19:55

Last Aspect / ☽ Ingress

Last Aspect Dy Hr Mn			☽ Ingress	Dy Hr Mn
2 23:08	♄	△	♎	2 23:26
5 3:13	♇	△	♏	5 4:22
7 9:50	♄	☍	♐	7 10:48
9 17:46	♇	☍	♑	9 19:10
12 4:05	♄	△	♒	12 5:51
14 16:45	♇	△	♓	14 18:26
17 5:15	♇	□	♈	17 7:00
19 15:13	♇	⚹	♉	19 16:57
21 20:09	♄	☌	♊	21 22:51
23 23:32	♇	☌	♋	24 1:11
25 22:49	♄	⚹	♌	26 1:43
28 0:39	♇	⚹	♍	28 2:27
30 3:29	♃	□	♎	30 4:55

☽ Phases & Eclipses

Dy Hr Mn		
2 3:38	☾	9♌21
9 2:05	●	16♏19
16 22:43	☽	24♒14
24 16:12	○	2♊02
1 11:05	☾	8♍55
8 17:06	●	16♐17
16 20:06	☽	24♓33
24 4:30	○	2♋02
30 20:12	☾	8♎48

Astro Data

1 November 1912
Julian Day # 4688
SVP 6♓28'41"
GC 25♐37.3 ⚵ 6♎28.5
Eris 25♓57.2R ⚶ 26♐15.6
⚷ 6♓32.9R ⚴ 11♏39.2
☽ Mean ☊ 10♈56.0

1 December 1912
Julian Day # 4718
SVP 6♓28'36"
GC 25♐37.4 ⚵ 19♎17.1
Eris 25♓47.0R ⚶ 6♑38.2
⚷ 6♓31.6 ⚴ 27♏46.8
☽ Mean ☊ 9♈20.7

LONGITUDE — January 1913

Day	Sid.Time	☉	0 hr ☽	Noon☽	True☊	☿	♀	♂	⚳	♃	♄	♅	♆	♇
1 W	18 42 07	10♑29 52	24♎31 56	1♏12 20	7♈44.9	18♐34.1	23♒18.1	23♐17.6	12♏45.3	29♐42.0	27♉50.8	2♒12.0	25♋00.7	28♊49.1
2 Th	18 46 04	11 31 02	7♏48 58	14 22 08	7R41.7	19 46.9	24 28.6	24 01.8	13 07.5	29 55.6	27R47.9	2 15.3	24R59.1	28R48.0
3 F	18 50 00	12 32 13	20 52 02	27 18 54	7 35.6	21 01.5	25 38.9	24 46.0	13 29.5	0♑09.2	27 45.2	2 18.7	24 57.4	28 46.8
4 Sa	18 53 57	13 33 24	3♐42 54	10♐04 12	7 26.4	22 17.9	26 49.1	25 30.3	13 51.4	0 22.8	27 42.5	2 22.0	24 55.8	28 45.6
5 Su	18 57 53	14 34 35	16 22 53	22 39 03	7 14.4	23 35.8	27 59.2	26 14.6	14 13.1	0 36.4	27 39.9	2 25.4	24 54.1	28 44.5
6 M	19 01 50	15 35 47	28 52 47	5♑04 06	7 00.4	24 55.0	29 09.2	26 59.0	14 34.7	0 49.9	27 37.4	2 28.8	24 52.5	28 43.4
7 Tu	19 05 47	16 36 58	11♑13 03	17 19 43	6 45.7	26 15.5	0♓19.0	27 43.4	14 56.2	1 03.4	27 35.0	2 32.2	24 50.8	28 42.2
8 W	19 09 43	17 38 08	23 24 08	29 26 25	6 31.5	27 37.1	1 28.7	28 27.8	15 17.5	1 16.9	27 32.8	2 35.7	24 49.1	28 41.1
9 Th	19 13 40	18 39 19	5♒26 40	11♒25 05	6 18.9	28 59.7	2 38.3	29 12.3	15 38.7	1 30.4	27 30.6	2 39.1	24 47.4	28 40.0
10 F	19 17 36	19 40 29	17 21 51	23 17 15	6 08.9	0♑23.3	3 47.7	29 56.8	15 59.7	1 43.8	27 28.5	2 42.6	24 45.7	28 38.9
11 Sa	19 21 33	20 41 38	29 11 37	5♓05 17	6 01.8	1 47.8	4 56.9	0♑41.4	16 20.6	1 57.2	27 26.5	2 46.0	24 44.1	28 37.7
12 Su	19 25 29	21 42 47	10♓58 43	16 52 24	5 57.6	3 13.0	6 06.0	1 26.0	16 41.3	2 10.6	27 24.7	2 49.5	24 42.4	28 36.7
13 M	19 29 26	22 43 56	22 46 51	28 42 39	5D55.9	4 39.1	7 15.0	2 10.6	17 01.9	2 23.9	27 22.9	2 53.0	24 40.7	28 35.6
14 Tu	19 33 22	23 45 03	4♈40 26	10♈40 50	5 55.8	6 05.9	8 23.7	2 55.3	17 22.4	2 37.3	27 21.3	2 56.4	24 39.0	28 34.5
15 W	19 37 19	24 46 10	16 44 32	22 52 14	5R56.1	7 33.4	9 32.3	3 40.0	17 42.6	2 50.5	27 19.8	2 59.9	24 37.3	28 33.4
16 Th	19 41 16	25 47 16	29 04 36	5♉22 19	5 55.7	9 01.5	10 40.7	4 24.8	18 02.8	3 03.8	27 18.3	3 03.4	24 35.6	28 32.4
17 F	19 45 12	26 48 22	11♉46 00	18 16 13	5 53.5	10 30.3	11 48.9	5 09.5	18 22.7	3 17.0	27 17.0	3 06.9	24 33.9	28 31.3
18 Sa	19 49 09	27 49 27	24 53 26	1♊38 02	5 49.1	11 59.8	12 57.0	5 54.4	18 42.5	3 30.1	27 15.8	3 10.4	24 32.2	28 30.3
19 Su	19 53 05	28 50 30	8♊30 12	15 29 59	5 42.1	13 29.9	14 04.8	6 39.2	19 02.1	3 43.2	27 14.7	3 14.0	24 30.5	28 29.3
20 M	19 57 02	29 51 33	22 37 12	29 51 30	5 33.0	15 00.5	15 12.4	7 24.1	19 21.6	3 56.3	27 13.7	3 17.5	24 28.8	28 28.3
21 Tu	20 00 58	0♒52 36	7♋12 14	14♋38 34	5 22.8	16 31.8	16 19.8	8 09.1	19 40.9	4 09.4	27 12.9	3 21.0	24 27.1	28 27.3
22 W	20 04 55	1 53 37	22 09 29	29 43 46	5 12.6	18 03.7	17 27.0	8 54.1	20 00.0	4 22.3	27 12.1	3 24.5	24 25.4	28 26.3
23 Th	20 08 51	2 54 37	7♌20 05	14♌57 05	5 03.7	19 36.3	18 33.9	9 39.1	20 18.9	4 35.3	27 11.5	3 28.0	24 23.8	28 25.3
24 F	20 12 48	3 55 37	22 33 24	0♍07 43	4 57.0	21 09.4	19 40.6	10 24.1	20 37.6	4 48.2	27 10.9	3 31.6	24 22.1	28 24.4
25 Sa	20 16 45	4 56 36	7♍38 54	15 05 56	4 52.9	22 43.2	20 47.1	11 09.2	20 56.2	5 01.0	27 10.5	3 35.1	24 20.4	28 23.4
26 Su	20 20 41	5 57 34	22 28 01	29 44 33	4D51.3	24 17.5	21 53.4	11 54.4	21 14.6	5 13.8	27 10.2	3 38.6	24 18.8	28 22.5
27 M	20 24 38	6 58 32	6♎55 08	13♎59 33	4 51.4	25 52.6	22 59.3	12 39.5	21 32.8	5 26.6	27 10.0	3 42.1	24 17.1	28 21.6
28 Tu	20 28 34	7 59 29	20 57 45	27 49 50	4R52.3	27 28.2	24 05.1	13 24.7	21 50.8	5 39.3	27D09.9	3 45.6	24 15.5	28 20.7
29 W	20 32 31	9 00 25	4♏36 01	11♏16 34	4 52.6	29 04.6	25 10.5	14 10.0	22 08.6	5 51.9	27 09.9	3 49.1	24 13.8	28 19.8
30 Th	20 36 27	10 01 21	17 51 49	24 22 11	4 51.4	0♒41.6	26 15.7	14 55.3	22 26.2	6 04.5	27 10.1	3 52.7	24 12.2	28 19.0
31 F	20 40 24	11 02 16	0♐48 04	7♐09 50	4 48.1	2 19.3	27 20.7	15 40.6	22 43.6	6 17.0	27 10.3	3 56.2	24 10.6	28 18.1

LONGITUDE — February 1913

Day	Sid.Time	☉	0 hr ☽	Noon☽	True☊	☿	♀	♂	⚳	♃	♄	♅	♆	♇
1 Sa	20 44 20	12♒03 11	13♐27 53	19♐42 36	4♈42.4	3♒57.7	28♓25.3	16♑26.0	23♏00.8	6♑29.5	27♉10.7	3♒59.7	24♋09.0	28♊17.3
2 Su	20 48 17	13 04 04	25 54 19	2♑03 20	4R34.5	5 36.8	29 29.6	17 11.4	23 17.8	6 41.9	27 11.2	4 03.2	24R07.4	28R16.5
3 M	20 52 14	14 04 57	8♑09 57	14 14 25	4 25.0	7 16.7	0♈33.7	17 56.8	23 34.5	6 54.2	27 11.8	4 06.6	24 05.8	28 15.7
4 Tu	20 56 10	15 05 48	20 16 57	26 17 45	4 14.9	8 57.3	1 37.4	18 42.2	23 51.1	7 06.5	27 12.5	4 10.1	24 04.2	28 14.9
5 W	21 00 07	16 06 38	2♒17 01	8♒14 56	4 05.1	10 38.7	2 40.8	19 27.7	24 07.4	7 18.7	27 13.3	4 13.6	24 02.7	28 14.2
6 Th	21 04 03	17 07 27	14 11 40	20 07 24	3 56.4	12 20.8	3 43.8	20 13.3	24 23.5	7 30.9	27 14.2	4 17.1	24 01.1	28 13.4
7 F	21 08 00	18 08 15	26 02 20	1♓56 41	3 49.6	14 03.7	4 46.6	20 58.8	24 39.4	7 42.9	27 15.3	4 20.5	23 59.6	28 12.7
8 Sa	21 11 56	19 09 02	7♓50 42	13 44 39	3 45.1	15 47.5	5 48.9	21 44.4	24 55.0	7 55.0	27 16.5	4 23.9	23 58.1	28 12.0
9 Su	21 15 53	20 09 46	19 38 50	25 33 36	3D42.8	17 32.0	6 50.9	22 30.0	25 10.4	8 06.9	27 17.7	4 27.4	23 56.6	28 11.3
10 M	21 19 49	21 10 30	1♈29 21	7♈26 29	3 42.5	19 17.3	7 52.5	23 15.6	25 25.6	8 18.7	27 19.1	4 30.8	23 55.1	28 10.6
11 Tu	21 23 46	22 11 12	13 25 30	19 26 52	3 43.5	21 03.4	8 53.6	24 01.3	25 40.5	8 30.5	27 20.6	4 34.2	23 53.7	28 10.0
12 W	21 27 43	23 11 52	25 31 09	1♉38 54	3 45.1	22 50.4	9 54.4	24 47.0	25 55.1	8 42.2	27 22.2	4 37.6	23 52.2	28 09.3
13 Th	21 31 39	24 12 31	7♉50 42	14 07 08	3R46.5	24 38.1	10 54.8	25 32.7	26 09.6	8 53.9	27 23.9	4 41.0	23 50.8	28 08.7
14 F	21 35 36	25 13 08	20 28 45	26 56 09	3 47.0	26 26.6	11 54.7	26 18.5	26 23.7	9 05.4	27 25.8	4 44.3	23 49.4	28 08.1
15 Sa	21 39 32	26 13 43	3♊29 47	10♊10 06	3 46.0	28 15.9	12 54.1	27 04.3	26 37.6	9 16.9	27 27.7	4 47.7	23 48.0	28 07.6
16 Su	21 43 29	27 14 17	16 57 25	23 51 58	3 43.4	0♓05.9	13 53.0	27 50.1	26 51.3	9 28.3	27 29.8	4 51.0	23 46.6	28 07.0
17 M	21 47 25	28 14 48	0♋53 48	8♋02 46	3 39.3	1 56.5	14 51.5	28 35.9	27 04.7	9 39.6	27 31.9	4 54.3	23 45.3	28 06.5
18 Tu	21 51 22	29 15 18	15 18 33	22 40 38	3 34.3	3 47.8	15 49.4	29 21.8	27 17.8	9 50.8	27 34.2	4 57.6	23 44.0	28 06.0
19 W	21 55 18	0♓15 46	0♌08 17	7♌40 31	3 29.2	5 39.6	16 46.9	0♒07.6	27 30.6	10 01.9	27 36.6	5 00.9	23 42.7	28 05.5
20 Th	21 59 15	1 16 13	15 16 15	22 54 14	3 24.6	7 31.8	17 43.7	0 53.6	27 43.2	10 12.9	27 39.0	5 04.1	23 41.4	28 05.0
21 F	22 03 12	2 16 37	0♍33 07	8♍11 34	3 21.3	9 24.4	18 40.0	1 39.5	27 55.5	10 23.9	27 41.6	5 07.4	23 40.1	28 04.6
22 Sa	22 07 08	3 17 00	15 48 16	23 21 59	3D19.5	11 17.1	19 35.7	2 25.4	28 07.5	10 34.7	27 44.3	5 10.6	23 38.9	28 04.2
23 Su	22 11 05	4 17 22	0♎51 36	8♎16 12	3 19.3	13 09.8	20 30.8	3 11.4	28 19.2	10 45.5	27 47.1	5 13.8	23 37.7	28 03.8
24 M	22 15 01	5 17 41	15 35 04	22 47 37	3 20.2	15 02.3	21 25.2	3 57.4	28 30.6	10 56.2	27 50.0	5 16.9	23 36.5	28 03.4
25 Tu	22 18 58	6 18 00	29 53 32	6♏52 38	3 21.7	16 54.4	22 19.0	4 43.5	28 41.8	11 06.7	27 53.0	5 20.1	23 35.3	28 03.0
26 W	22 22 54	7 18 17	13♏44 55	20 30 29	3 23.2	18 45.8	23 12.2	5 29.5	28 52.6	11 17.2	27 56.0	5 23.2	23 34.2	28 02.7
27 Th	22 26 51	8 18 33	27 09 38	3♐42 39	3R24.0	20 36.1	24 04.6	6 15.6	29 03.1	11 27.6	27 59.2	5 26.3	23 33.1	28 02.4
28 F	22 30 47	9 18 47	10♐09 57	16 32 00	3 23.9	22 24.9	24 56.3	7 01.7	29 13.3	11 37.9	28 02.5	5 29.4	23 32.0	28 02.1

Astro Data	Dy Hr Mn
☽0N	13 16:37
♃⊻♅	16 11:11
☽0S	26 13:49
♄ D	28 18:13
♀0N	2 6:36
☽0N	9 22:17
☽0S	22 23:33
♄⊻♇	28 9:05

Planet Ingress		Dy Hr Mn
♃	♑	2 19:46
♀	♓	7 5:27
☿	♑	10 5:20
♂	♑	10 13:43
☉	♒	20 15:19
☿	♒	30 1:44
♀	♈	2 23:22
☿	♓	16 10:43
☉	♓	19 5:44
♂	♒	19 8:00

Last Aspect Dy Hr Mn			☽ Ingress	Dy Hr Mn
1 9:14	♃	⚹	♏	1 9:49
3 12:49	♄	☍	♐	3 17:01
5 23:43	♇	☍	♑	6 2:10
8 8:14	♄	△	♒	8 13:07
10 22:52	♇	△	♓	11 1:38
13 11:46	♇	□	♈	13 14:36
15 22:59	♇	⚹	♉	16 1:46
18 4:42	☉	△	♊	18 9:07
20 9:43	♇	☌	♋	20 12:14
22 8:00	♄	⚹	♌	22 12:26
24 9:16	♇	⚹	♍	24 11:48
26 9:44	♇	□	♎	26 12:26
28 12:54	♇	△	♏	28 15:50
30 17:12	♄	☍	♐	30 22:30

Last Aspect Dy Hr Mn			☽ Ingress	Dy Hr Mn
2 6:31	♀	□	♑	2 7:59
4 13:50	♄	△	♒	4 19:25
7 4:25	♇	△	♓	7 8:03
9 17:19	♇	□	♈	9 20:59
12 5:11	♇	⚹	♉	12 8:47
14 12:55	♄	☌	♊	14 17:38
16 19:16	♇	☌	♋	16 22:29
18 23:20	♂	☍	♌	18 23:47
20 20:07	♇	⚹	♍	20 23:08
22 19:31	♇	□	♎	22 22:37
24 20:52	♇	△	♏	25 0:11
27 1:28	♄	☍	♐	27 5:11

☽ Phases & Eclipses Dy Hr Mn		
7 10:28	●	16♑33
15 16:01	☽	24♈56
22 15:40	○	2♌03
29 7:34	☾	8♏49
6 5:22	●	16♒51
14 8:33	☽	25♉04
21 2:03	○	1♍52
27 21:15	☾	8♐42

Astro Data

1 January 1913
Julian Day # 4749
SVP 6♓28'30"
GC 25♐37.5 ⚵ 0♏42.9
Eris 25♓48.1 ✱ 18♑27.7
⚷ 7♓23.6 ⚶ 14♐23.3
☽ Mean ☊ 7♈42.3

1 February 1913
Julian Day # 4780
SVP 6♓28'24"
GC 25♐37.5 ⚵ 9♏06.9
Eris 26♓01.0 ✱ 0♒53.3
⚷ 8♓57.7 ⚶ 0♑33.4
☽ Mean ☊ 6♈03.8

March 1913 — LONGITUDE

Day	Sid.Time	☉	0 hr ☽	Noon ☽	True ☊	☿	♀	♂	⚳	♃	♄	♅	♆	♇
1 Sa	22 34 44	10♓19 00	22♐49 16	29♐02 15	3♈22.7	24♓12.0	25♈47.3	7♒47.9	29♏23.2	11♑48.1	28♉05.9	5♒32.5	23♋30.9	28♊01.8
2 Su	22 38 41	11 19 11	5♑11 25	11♑17 17	3R 20.4	25 56.8	26 37.5	8 34.0	29 32.8	11 58.1	28 09.4	5 35.5	23R 29.9	28R 01.6
3 M	22 42 37	12 19 20	17 20 19	23 20 56	3 17.3	27 38.8	27 26.9	9 20.2	29 42.1	12 08.1	28 13.0	5 38.5	23 28.9	28 01.3
4 Tu	22 46 34	13 19 28	29 19 35	5♒16 39	3 13.9	29 17.6	28 15.5	10 06.4	29 51.0	12 17.9	28 16.7	5 41.5	23 27.9	28 01.1
5 W	22 50 30	14 19 34	11♒12 31	17 07 30	3 10.6	0♈52.6	29 03.2	10 52.6	29 59.6	12 27.7	28 20.4	5 44.4	23 26.9	28 01.0
6 Th	22 54 27	15 19 39	23 01 55	28 56 05	3 07.7	2 23.2	29 50.1	11 38.8	0♐07.9	12 37.3	28 24.3	5 47.3	23 26.0	28 00.8
7 F	22 58 23	16 19 41	4♓50 16	10♓44 43	3 05.6	3 49.0	0♉36.0	12 25.1	0 15.8	12 46.8	28 28.3	5 50.2	23 25.1	28 00.7
8 Sa	23 02 20	17 19 42	16 39 41	22 35 27	3D 04.4	5 09.2	1 20.9	13 11.4	0 23.4	12 56.2	28 32.3	5 53.1	23 24.3	28 00.6
9 Su	23 06 16	18 19 40	28 32 14	4♈30 17	3 04.1	6 23.5	2 04.8	13 57.6	0 30.6	13 05.5	28 36.4	5 55.9	23 23.4	28 00.5
10 M	23 10 13	19 19 37	10♈29 54	16 31 21	3 04.5	7 31.4	2 47.7	14 43.9	0 37.5	13 14.7	28 40.7	5 58.7	23 22.6	28 00.4
11 Tu	23 14 10	20 19 32	22 34 56	28 40 57	3 05.5	8 32.2	3 29.5	15 30.2	0 44.0	13 23.7	28 45.0	6 01.5	23 21.8	28 00.3
12 W	23 18 06	21 19 24	4♉49 45	11♉01 41	3 06.6	9 25.7	4 10.1	16 16.5	0 50.2	13 32.6	28 49.4	6 04.2	23 21.1	28D 00.3
13 Th	23 22 03	22 19 15	17 17 07	23 36 26	3 07.7	10 11.5	4 49.6	17 02.9	0 56.0	13 41.4	28 53.9	6 06.9	23 20.3	28 00.3
14 F	23 25 59	23 19 03	0♊00 00	6♊28 13	3 08.5	10 49.3	5 27.8	17 49.2	1 01.4	13 50.1	28 58.5	6 09.6	23 19.7	28 00.4
15 Sa	23 29 56	24 18 49	13 01 25	19 39 56	3R 08.9	11 18.9	6 04.8	18 35.6	1 06.5	13 58.6	29 03.2	6 12.2	23 19.0	28 00.4
16 Su	23 33 52	25 18 33	26 24 02	3♋13 57	3 08.8	11 40.1	6 40.4	19 21.9	1 11.2	14 07.0	29 07.9	6 14.8	23 18.4	28 00.5
17 M	23 37 49	26 18 14	10♋09 46	17 11 31	3 08.5	11 52.9	7 14.7	20 08.3	1 15.5	14 15.3	29 12.8	6 17.4	23 17.8	28 00.6
18 Tu	23 41 45	27 17 53	24 19 06	1♌32 14	3 07.9	11R 57.3	7 47.5	20 54.7	1 19.5	14 23.5	29 17.7	6 19.9	23 17.2	28 00.7
19 W	23 45 42	28 17 30	8♌50 32	16 13 25	3 07.3	11 53.6	8 18.8	21 41.1	1 23.1	14 31.5	29 22.7	6 22.4	23 16.7	28 00.8
20 Th	23 49 39	29 17 05	23 40 11	1♍09 58	3 06.8	11 42.0	8 48.6	22 27.5	1 26.3	14 39.4	29 27.7	6 24.9	23 16.2	28 01.0
21 F	23 53 35	0♈16 37	8♍41 47	16 14 34	3 06.6	11 22.8	9 16.7	23 13.9	1 29.1	14 47.1	29 32.9	6 27.3	23 15.7	28 01.2
22 Sa	23 57 32	1 16 07	23 47 12	1♎18 33	3D 06.5	10 56.7	9 43.2	24 00.3	1 31.5	14 54.7	29 38.1	6 29.7	23 15.3	28 01.4
23 Su	0 01 28	2 15 35	8♎47 30	16 13 01	3R 06.5	10 24.3	10 08.0	24 46.7	1 33.5	15 02.2	29 43.4	6 32.0	23 14.9	28 01.6
24 M	0 05 25	3 15 01	23 34 11	0♏50 12	3 06.5	9 46.4	10 31.0	25 33.1	1 35.2	15 09.5	29 48.8	6 34.3	23 14.5	28 01.9
25 Tu	0 09 21	4 14 26	8♏00 27	15 04 26	3 06.4	9 03.8	10 52.1	26 19.6	1 36.4	15 16.7	29 54.2	6 36.6	23 14.2	28 02.2
26 W	0 13 18	5 13 48	22 01 51	28 52 35	3 06.3	8 17.5	11 11.3	27 06.0	1 37.3	15 23.8	29 59.7	6 38.8	23 13.9	28 02.5
27 Th	0 17 14	6 13 09	5♐36 35	12♐14 02	3 06.0	7 28.5	11 28.6	27 52.5	1R 37.7	15 30.7	0♊05.3	6 41.0	23 13.6	28 02.8
28 F	0 21 11	7 12 28	18 45 10	25 10 19	3 05.8	6 37.9	11 43.8	28 38.9	1 37.8	15 37.4	0 11.0	6 43.2	23 13.4	28 03.1
29 Sa	0 25 08	8 11 45	1♑29 56	7♑44 30	3D 05.6	5 46.7	11 57.0	29 25.4	1 37.5	15 44.0	0 16.7	6 45.3	23 13.2	28 03.5
30 Su	0 29 04	9 11 01	13 54 31	20 00 34	3 05.8	4 56.0	12 08.1	0♓11.9	1 36.7	15 50.5	0 22.5	6 47.4	23 13.0	28 03.9
31 M	0 33 01	10 10 14	26 03 12	2♒03 00	3 06.2	4 06.7	12 16.9	0 58.3	1 35.6	15 56.8	0 28.4	6 49.4	23 12.8	28 04.3

April 1913 — LONGITUDE

Day	Sid.Time	☉	0 hr ☽	Noon ☽	True ☊	☿	♀	♂	⚳	♃	♄	♅	♆	♇
1 Tu	0 36 57	11♈09 26	8♒00 31	13♒56 20	3♈06.9	3♈19.8	12♉23.5	1♓44.8	1♐34.0	16♑02.9	0♊34.3	6♒51.4	23♋12.7	28♊04.7
2 W	0 40 54	12 08 36	19 50 57	25 44 54	3 07.8	2R 35.9	12 27.8	2 31.3	1R 32.0	16 08.9	0 40.3	6 53.3	23R 12.7	28 05.2
3 Th	0 44 50	13 07 44	1♓38 40	7♓32 40	3 08.8	1 55.8	12R 29.8	3 17.7	1 29.7	16 14.8	0 46.4	6 55.2	23D 12.6	28 05.7
4 F	0 48 47	14 06 50	13 27 21	19 23 05	3 09.6	1 20.0	12 29.3	4 04.2	1 26.9	16 20.4	0 52.5	6 57.1	23 12.6	28 06.2
5 Sa	0 52 43	15 05 54	25 20 13	1♈19 04	3R 09.9	0 49.0	12 26.5	4 50.7	1 23.7	16 25.9	0 58.7	6 58.9	23 12.6	28 06.7
6 Su	0 56 40	16 04 57	7♈19 54	13 22 58	3 09.7	0 23.0	12 21.2	5 37.1	1 20.1	16 31.3	1 04.9	7 00.7	23 12.7	28 07.2
7 M	1 00 37	17 03 57	19 28 29	25 36 40	3 08.8	0 02.2	12 13.5	6 23.6	1 16.1	16 36.5	1 11.2	7 02.4	23 12.8	28 07.8
8 Tu	1 04 33	18 02 55	1♉47 39	8♉01 37	3 07.1	29♓46.9	12 03.2	7 10.0	1 11.8	16 41.5	1 17.6	7 04.1	23 12.9	28 08.4
9 W	1 08 30	19 01 51	14 18 41	20 38 59	3 05.0	29 37.0	11 50.6	7 56.5	1 07.0	16 46.3	1 24.0	7 05.7	23 13.1	28 09.0
10 Th	1 12 26	20 00 45	27 02 38	3♊29 45	3 02.5	29D 32.5	11 35.4	8 42.9	1 01.8	16 51.0	1 30.5	7 07.3	23 13.3	28 09.6
11 F	1 16 23	20 59 37	10♊00 25	16 34 46	3 00.1	29 33.4	11 17.9	9 29.3	0 56.3	16 55.5	1 37.0	7 08.8	23 13.5	28 10.2
12 Sa	1 20 19	21 58 27	23 12 52	29 54 49	2 58.2	29 39.5	10 58.0	10 15.7	0 50.3	16 59.9	1 43.6	7 10.3	23 13.8	28 10.9
13 Su	1 24 16	22 57 14	6♋40 40	13♋30 31	2D 57.1	29 50.6	10 35.7	11 02.2	0 44.0	17 04.1	1 50.2	7 11.8	23 14.1	28 11.6
14 M	1 28 12	23 55 59	20 24 20	27 22 08	2 56.9	0♈06.7	10 11.3	11 48.5	0 37.4	17 08.0	1 56.9	7 13.2	23 14.4	28 12.3
15 Tu	1 32 09	24 54 42	4♌23 51	11♌29 20	2 57.5	0 27.5	9 44.7	12 34.9	0 30.3	17 11.9	2 03.6	7 14.6	23 14.8	28 13.0
16 W	1 36 06	25 53 22	18 38 24	25 50 45	2 58.8	0 52.9	9 16.1	13 21.3	0 22.9	17 15.5	2 10.4	7 15.9	23 15.2	28 13.8
17 Th	1 40 02	26 52 00	3♍06 02	10♍23 46	3 00.2	1 22.6	8 45.7	14 07.6	0 15.1	17 19.0	2 17.2	7 17.1	23 15.6	28 14.5
18 F	1 43 59	27 50 36	17 43 24	25 04 15	3R 01.1	1 56.5	8 13.6	14 54.0	0 07.0	17 22.3	2 24.1	7 18.4	23 16.1	28 15.3
19 Sa	1 47 55	28 49 10	2♎25 38	9♎46 43	3 01.1	2 34.3	7 39.9	15 40.3	29♏58.6	17 25.4	2 31.0	7 19.5	23 16.6	28 16.1
20 Su	1 51 52	29 47 41	17 06 41	24 24 41	2 59.9	3 16.0	7 05.0	16 26.6	29 49.8	17 28.3	2 37.9	7 20.6	23 17.1	28 16.9
21 M	1 55 48	0♉46 11	1♏39 55	8♏51 34	2 57.3	4 01.3	6 29.0	17 12.9	29 40.7	17 31.1	2 44.9	7 21.7	23 17.7	28 17.8
22 Tu	1 59 45	1 44 39	15 58 56	23 01 25	2 53.5	4 50.0	5 52.1	17 59.2	29 31.2	17 33.7	2 52.0	7 22.7	23 18.3	28 18.6
23 W	2 03 41	2 43 06	29 58 30	6♐49 50	2 49.0	5 42.1	5 14.7	18 45.5	29 21.5	17 36.1	2 59.1	7 23.7	23 18.9	28 19.5
24 Th	2 07 38	3 41 30	13♐35 11	20 14 27	2 44.4	6 37.3	4 36.9	19 31.7	29 11.5	17 38.3	3 06.2	7 24.6	23 19.6	28 20.4
25 F	2 11 35	4 39 53	26 47 40	3♑14 59	2 40.3	7 35.5	3 59.0	20 18.0	29 01.1	17 40.3	3 13.3	7 25.5	23 20.2	28 21.3
26 Sa	2 15 31	5 38 15	9♑36 42	15 53 09	2 37.2	8 36.7	3 21.2	21 04.2	28 50.5	17 42.2	3 20.5	7 26.4	23 21.0	28 22.3
27 Su	2 19 28	6 36 35	22 04 47	28 12 07	2D 35.4	9 40.6	2 43.8	21 50.4	28 39.6	17 43.8	3 27.8	7 27.1	23 21.7	28 23.2
28 M	2 23 24	7 34 53	4♒15 42	10♒16 09	2 35.1	10 47.2	2 07.1	22 36.6	28 28.5	17 45.3	3 35.0	7 27.9	23 22.5	28 24.2
29 Tu	2 27 21	8 33 10	16 14 03	22 10 04	2 35.9	11 56.5	1 31.3	23 22.8	28 17.1	17 46.6	3 42.3	7 28.6	23 23.3	28 25.2
30 W	2 31 17	9 31 25	28 04 50	3♓58 57	2 37.5	13 08.2	0 56.5	24 08.9	28 05.4	17 47.7	3 49.7	7 29.2	23 24.2	28 26.2

Astro Data	Dy Hr Mn
☿0N	4 7:31
☽0N	9 4:02
♇ D	12 20:19
♃□♄	16 17:55
☿ R	18 12:57
☉0N	21 5:18
☽0S	22 10:47
⚳ R	28 3:30
♀ R	3 19:46
♆ D	4 4:57
☽0N	5 10:28
☿0S	9 0:49
☿ D	10 20:05
♃□♄	18 0:08
☽0S	18 20:54

Planet Ingress	Dy Hr Mn
☿ ♈	4 22:35
⚳ ♐	5 13:06
♀ ♉	6 17:09
☉ ♈	21 5:18
♄ ♊	26 13:07
♂ ♓	30 5:53
☿ ♓R	7 15:02
☿ ♈	14 2:49
⚳ ♏R	19 8:00
☉ ♉	20 17:03
☿0N	23 14:13

Last Aspect Dy Hr Mn		☽ Ingress Dy Hr Mn
1 10:03	♇ ☍	♑ 1 13:52
3 22:01	☿ ⚹	♒ 4 1:21
6 13:57	♀ ⚹	♓ 6 14:10
9 0:04	♄ ⚹	♈ 9 2:57
11 10:40	♇ ⚹	♉ 11 14:35
13 22:00	♄ ☌	♊ 13 24:00
16 2:50	♇ ☌	♋ 16 6:21
18 8:16	♄ ⚹	♌ 18 9:27
20 9:16	♄ □	♍ 20 10:08
22 9:19	♄ △	♎ 22 9:54
24 7:21	♇ △	♏ 24 10:37
26 8:41	♂ □	♐ 26 13:59
28 19:00	♂ ⚹	♑ 28 21:09
30 18:21	♆ ☍	♒ 31 7:53

Last Aspect Dy Hr Mn		☽ Ingress Dy Hr Mn
2 16:46	♇ △	♓ 2 20:39
5 5:34	♇ □	♈ 5 9:22
7 16:54	♇ ⚹	♉ 7 20:32
10 4:41	☿ ⚹	♊ 10 5:31
12 11:32	☿ □	♋ 12 12:09
14 5:39	☉ □	♌ 14 16:30
16 15:57	♇ ⚹	♍ 16 18:53
18 17:12	♇ □	♎ 18 20:02
20 18:24	♇ △	♏ 20 21:14
22 12:29	♆ △	♐ 23 0:03
25 2:53	♇ ☍	♑ 25 5:56
27 2:30	♆ ☍	♒ 27 15:33
30 0:42	♇ △	♓ 30 3:54

☽ Phases & Eclipses Dy Hr Mn	
8 0:22	● 16♓51
15 20:58	☽ 24♊41
22 11:56	○ 1♎16
22 11:58	• T 1.568
29 12:57	☾ 8♑14
6 17:48	● 16♈19
6 17:32:51	• P 0.424
14 5:39	☽ 23♋40
20 21:32	○ 0♏11
28 6:09	☾ 7♒21

Astro Data

1 March 1913
Julian Day # 4808
SVP 6♓28'20"
GC 25♐37.6 ⚴ 12♏24.0
Eris 26♓19.9 ⚵ 12♒15.3
⚷ 10♓41.7 ⚶ 14♑22.6
☽ Mean ☊ 4♈34.8

1 April 1913
Julian Day # 4839
SVP 6♓28'17"
GC 25♐37.7 ⚴ 9♏09.1R
Eris 26♓43.8 ⚵ 24♒36.4
⚷ 12♓36.2 ⚶ 28♑11.3
☽ Mean ☊ 2♈56.3

LONGITUDE — May 1913

Day	Sid.Time	☉	0 hr ☽	Noon ☽	True ☊	☿	♀	♂	⚳	♃	♄	♅	♆	♇
1 Th	2 35 14	10♉29 38	9♓53 04	15♓47 45	2♈39.1	14♈22.3	0♉23.1	24♓55.1	27♏53.6	17♑48.6	3♊57.0	7♒29.8	23♋25.1	28♊27.2
2 F	2 39 10	11 27 50	21 43 34	27 41 03	2R 40.2	15 38.8	29♈51.1	25 41.2	27R 41.5	17 49.3	4 04.4	7 30.3	23 26.0	28 28.2
3 Sa	2 43 07	12 26 01	3♈40 40	9♈42 53	2 40.0	16 57.6	29R 20.8	26 27.2	27 29.2	17 49.9	4 11.8	7 30.8	23 26.9	28 29.2
4 Su	2 47 03	13 24 10	15 48 02	21 56 28	2 38.2	18 18.6	28 52.4	27 13.3	27 16.8	17 50.2	4 19.3	7 31.2	23 27.9	28 30.3
5 M	2 51 00	14 22 17	28 08 26	4♉24 08	2 34.4	19 41.9	28 25.9	27 59.3	27 04.1	17R 50.4	4 26.8	7 31.6	23 28.9	28 31.4
6 Tu	2 54 57	15 20 23	10♉43 41	17 07 09	2 28.9	21 07.3	28 01.5	28 45.3	26 51.4	17 50.3	4 34.3	7 31.9	23 29.9	28 32.5
7 W	2 58 53	16 18 27	23 34 31	0♊05 44	2 21.9	22 34.8	27 39.2	29 31.3	26 38.4	17 50.1	4 41.8	7 32.2	23 31.0	28 33.6
8 Th	3 02 50	17 16 30	6♊40 42	13 19 14	2 14.3	24 04.4	27 19.2	0♈17.2	26 25.4	17 49.7	4 49.3	7 32.4	23 32.1	28 34.7
9 F	3 06 46	18 14 31	20 01 08	26 46 13	2 06.9	25 36.2	27 01.6	1 03.1	26 12.2	17 49.1	4 56.9	7 32.6	23 33.2	28 35.8
10 Sa	3 10 43	19 12 30	3♋34 15	10♋24 58	2 00.5	27 09.9	26 46.2	1 49.0	25 59.0	17 48.3	5 04.5	7 32.8	23 34.3	28 37.0
11 Su	3 14 39	20 10 27	17 18 11	24 13 40	1 55.8	28 45.8	26 33.3	2 34.8	25 45.7	17 47.3	5 12.1	7 32.9	23 35.5	28 38.1
12 M	3 18 36	21 08 22	1♌11 14	8♌10 42	1D 53.1	0♉23.7	26 22.8	3 20.6	25 32.3	17 46.1	5 19.8	7R 32.9	23 36.7	28 39.3
13 Tu	3 22 33	22 06 16	15 11 54	22 14 41	1 52.4	2 03.6	26 14.7	4 06.4	25 18.9	17 44.7	5 27.4	7 32.9	23 38.0	28 40.5
14 W	3 26 29	23 04 08	29 18 54	6♍24 24	1 52.9	3 45.6	26 09.0	4 52.1	25 05.4	17 43.2	5 35.1	7 32.8	23 39.2	28 41.7
15 Th	3 30 26	24 01 57	13♍30 59	20 38 28	1R 53.9	5 29.6	26D 05.7	5 37.8	24 51.9	17 41.5	5 42.8	7 32.7	23 40.5	28 42.9
16 F	3 34 22	24 59 46	27 46 34	4♎55 01	1 54.2	7 15.7	26 04.7	6 23.5	24 38.5	17 39.5	5 50.5	7 32.5	23 41.8	28 44.1
17 Sa	3 38 19	25 57 32	12♎03 25	19 11 23	1 53.0	9 03.8	26 06.1	7 09.1	24 25.0	17 37.4	5 58.2	7 32.3	23 43.2	28 45.4
18 Su	3 42 15	26 55 17	26 18 26	3♏24 04	1 49.5	10 54.0	26 09.8	7 54.7	24 11.6	17 35.1	6 05.9	7 32.1	23 44.5	28 46.6
19 M	3 46 12	27 53 00	10♏27 44	17 28 51	1 43.6	12 46.2	26 15.8	8 40.2	23 58.3	17 32.7	6 13.7	7 31.7	23 45.9	28 47.9
20 Tu	3 50 08	28 50 42	24 26 54	1♐21 21	1 35.6	14 40.4	26 23.9	9 25.7	23 45.0	17 30.0	6 21.4	7 31.4	23 47.3	28 49.1
21 W	3 54 05	29 48 23	8♐11 43	14 57 37	1 26.2	16 36.7	26 34.3	10 11.2	23 31.7	17 27.2	6 29.2	7 31.0	23 48.8	28 50.4
22 Th	3 58 02	0♊46 03	21 38 43	28 14 48	1 16.3	18 34.9	26 46.7	10 56.6	23 18.6	17 24.2	6 36.9	7 30.5	23 50.2	28 51.7
23 F	4 01 58	1 43 41	4♑45 46	11♑11 37	1 07.0	20 35.1	27 01.1	11 42.0	23 05.6	17 21.0	6 44.7	7 30.0	23 51.7	28 53.0
24 Sa	4 05 55	2 41 19	17 32 28	23 48 30	0 59.2	22 37.1	27 17.6	12 27.4	22 52.7	17 17.7	6 52.5	7 29.5	23 53.3	28 54.3
25 Su	4 09 51	3 38 55	0♒00 02	6♒07 28	0 53.4	24 40.9	27 35.9	13 12.7	22 39.9	17 14.2	7 00.3	7 28.9	23 54.8	28 55.7
26 M	4 13 48	4 36 30	12 11 16	18 11 57	0 49.9	26 46.3	27 56.1	13 58.0	22 27.3	17 10.5	7 08.1	7 28.2	23 56.4	28 57.0
27 Tu	4 17 44	5 34 05	24 10 07	0♓06 21	0D 48.5	28 53.3	28 18.1	14 43.2	22 14.9	17 06.6	7 15.9	7 27.6	23 58.0	28 58.3
28 W	4 21 41	6 31 38	6♓01 20	11 55 43	0 48.4	1♊01.7	28 41.8	15 28.4	22 02.6	17 02.6	7 23.7	7 26.8	23 59.6	28 59.7
29 Th	4 25 37	7 29 11	17 50 12	23 45 25	0R 48.9	3 11.3	29 07.2	16 13.5	21 50.5	16 58.4	7 31.4	7 26.0	24 01.2	29 01.0
30 F	4 29 34	8 26 43	29 42 04	5♈40 46	0 49.0	5 21.9	29 34.2	16 58.6	21 38.6	16 54.0	7 39.2	7 25.2	24 02.9	29 02.4
31 Sa	4 33 31	9 24 13	11♈42 08	17 46 44	0 47.6	7 33.2	0♉02.7	17 43.6	21 26.9	16 49.5	7 47.0	7 24.3	24 04.5	29 03.7

LONGITUDE — June 1913

Day	Sid.Time	☉	0 hr ☽	Noon ☽	True ☊	☿	♀	♂	⚳	♃	♄	♅	♆	♇
1 Su	4 37 27	10♊21 44	23♈55 05	0♉07 37	0♈44.1	9♊45.0	0♉32.7	18♈28.6	21♏15.5	16♑44.8	7♊54.8	7♒23.4	24♋06.2	29♊05.1
2 M	4 41 24	11 19 13	6♉24 42	12 46 37	0R 38.1	11 57.1	1 04.2	19 13.6	21R 04.3	16R 39.9	8 02.6	7R 22.5	24 08.0	29 06.5
3 Tu	4 45 20	12 16 41	19 13 33	25 45 33	0 29.6	14 09.2	1 37.0	19 58.5	20 53.3	16 34.9	8 10.4	7 21.4	24 09.7	29 07.9
4 W	4 49 17	13 14 09	2♊22 36	9♊04 33	0 19.2	16 20.9	2 11.1	20 43.3	20 42.6	16 29.8	8 18.2	7 20.4	24 11.5	29 09.3
5 Th	4 53 13	14 11 36	15 51 07	22 41 59	0 07.8	18 32.1	2 46.5	21 28.1	20 32.2	16 24.5	8 26.0	7 19.3	24 13.2	29 10.7
6 F	4 57 10	15 09 02	29 36 41	6♋34 43	29♓56.6	20 42.5	3 23.1	22 12.8	20 22.0	16 19.0	8 33.8	7 18.2	24 15.0	29 12.1
7 Sa	5 01 06	16 06 27	13♋35 32	20 38 34	29 46.7	22 51.8	4 00.8	22 57.5	20 12.2	16 13.5	8 41.5	7 17.0	24 16.9	29 13.5
8 Su	5 05 03	17 03 51	27 43 15	4♌49 04	29 39.1	24 59.7	4 39.7	23 42.1	20 02.6	16 07.8	8 49.3	7 15.8	24 18.7	29 14.9
9 M	5 09 00	18 01 14	11♌55 29	19 02 06	29 34.1	27 06.2	5 19.6	24 26.7	19 53.4	16 01.9	8 57.0	7 14.5	24 20.6	29 16.3
10 Tu	5 12 56	18 58 35	26 08 31	3♍14 28	29 31.7	29 11.0	6 00.6	25 11.1	19 44.5	15 55.9	9 04.8	7 13.2	24 22.4	29 17.8
11 W	5 16 53	19 55 56	10♍19 42	17 24 02	29 31.0	1♋14.0	6 42.6	25 55.6	19 35.9	15 49.8	9 12.5	7 11.9	24 24.3	29 19.2
12 Th	5 20 49	20 53 16	24 27 21	1♎29 32	29 31.0	3 15.0	7 25.5	26 39.9	19 27.6	15 43.6	9 20.2	7 10.5	24 26.2	29 20.6
13 F	5 24 46	21 50 34	8♎30 31	15 30 10	29 30.4	5 13.9	8 09.4	27 24.2	19 19.7	15 37.3	9 27.9	7 09.1	24 28.2	29 22.1
14 Sa	5 28 42	22 47 52	22 28 26	29 25 09	29 28.1	7 10.7	8 54.1	28 08.5	19 12.1	15 30.8	9 35.5	7 07.6	24 30.1	29 23.5
15 Su	5 32 39	23 45 09	6♏20 10	13♏13 18	29 23.2	9 05.3	9 39.7	28 52.7	19 04.9	15 24.3	9 43.2	7 06.1	24 32.1	29 24.9
16 M	5 36 35	24 42 25	20 04 18	26 52 55	29 15.4	10 57.6	10 26.1	29 36.8	18 58.0	15 17.6	9 50.8	7 04.6	24 34.0	29 26.4
17 Tu	5 40 32	25 39 40	3♐38 52	10♐21 52	29 05.1	12 47.7	11 13.4	0♉20.9	18 51.5	15 10.9	9 58.4	7 03.0	24 36.0	29 27.8
18 W	5 44 29	26 36 55	17 01 37	23 37 52	28 53.1	14 35.4	12 01.3	1 04.9	18 45.3	15 04.0	10 06.0	7 01.4	24 38.0	29 29.3
19 Th	5 48 25	27 34 10	0♑10 23	6♑38 59	28 40.5	16 20.8	12 50.1	1 48.8	18 39.5	14 57.1	10 13.6	6 59.7	24 40.1	29 30.7
20 F	5 52 22	28 31 24	13 03 33	19 24 03	28 28.4	18 03.9	13 39.5	2 32.7	18 34.0	14 50.1	10 21.2	6 58.1	24 42.1	29 32.2
21 Sa	5 56 18	29 28 37	25 40 30	1♒53 01	28 17.9	19 44.5	14 29.7	3 16.5	18 29.0	14 43.0	10 28.7	6 56.4	24 44.1	29 33.6
22 Su	6 00 15	0♋25 51	8♒01 49	14 07 09	28 09.7	21 22.8	15 20.5	4 00.2	18 24.2	14 35.8	10 36.2	6 54.6	24 46.2	29 35.1
23 M	6 04 11	1 23 04	20 09 22	26 08 53	28 04.1	22 58.8	16 11.9	4 43.9	18 19.9	14 28.5	10 43.7	6 52.8	24 48.3	29 36.5
24 Tu	6 08 08	2 20 17	2♓06 12	8♓01 50	28 01.1	24 32.3	17 04.0	5 27.5	18 15.9	14 21.2	10 51.2	6 51.0	24 50.3	29 38.0
25 W	6 12 05	3 17 30	13 56 23	19 50 27	27D 59.9	26 03.4	17 56.7	6 11.1	18 12.3	14 13.8	10 58.6	6 49.2	24 52.4	29 39.4
26 Th	6 16 01	4 14 43	25 44 43	1♈39 51	27R 59.8	27 32.1	18 49.9	6 54.5	18 09.1	14 06.4	11 06.0	6 47.3	24 54.5	29 40.8
27 F	6 19 58	5 11 55	7♈36 31	13 35 26	27 59.6	28 58.3	19 43.7	7 37.9	18 06.2	13 58.9	11 13.4	6 45.4	24 56.6	29 42.3
28 Sa	6 23 54	6 09 08	19 37 14	25 42 37	27 58.4	0♌22.0	20 38.0	8 21.3	18 03.7	13 51.3	11 20.7	6 43.5	24 58.8	29 43.7
29 Su	6 27 51	7 06 21	1♉52 11	8♉06 29	27 55.2	1 43.3	21 32.9	9 04.5	18 01.6	13 43.8	11 28.0	6 41.5	25 00.9	29 45.2
30 M	6 31 47	8 03 34	14 26 01	20 51 11	27 49.6	3 02.0	22 28.2	9 47.7	17 59.9	13 36.1	11 35.3	6 39.5	25 03.0	29 46.6

Astro Data	Planet Ingress	Last Aspect	☽ Ingress	Last Aspect	☽ Ingress	☽ Phases & Eclipses	Astro Data
Dy Hr Mn	Dy Hr Mn	Dy Hr Mn	Dy Hr Mn	Dy Hr Mn	Dy Hr Mn	Dy Hr Mn	1 May 1913
☽0N 2 17:34	♀ ♈R 2 5:12	2 13:35 ♇ □	♈ 2 16:39	1 10:00 ♇ ⚹	♉ 1 11:45	6 8:24 ● 15♉12	Julian Day # 4869
♃ R 5 19:02	♂ ♈ 8 3:00	5 0:57 ♀ ☌	♉ 5 3:35	3 9:04 ♆ ⚹	♊ 3 19:42	13 11:45 ☽ 22♌06	SVP 6♓28'13"
♂0N 12 5:32	☿ ♉ 12 6:15	7 10:53 ♂ ⚹	♊ 7 11:49	5 23:16 ♇ ☌	♋ 6 0:40	20 7:18 ○ 28♏39	GC 25♐37.7 ⚴ 0♏34.3R
♅ R 12 16:33	☉ ♊ 21 16:50	9 15:14 ♇ ☌	♋ 9 17:43	7 18:11 ♆ ☌	♌ 8 3:51	28 0:03 ☾ 6♓03	Eris 27♓04.3 ⚵ 5♓52.2
☽0S 16 4:17	☿ ♊ 28 0:30	11 20:51 ☿ □	♌ 11 21:57	10 5:19 ♇ ⚹	♍ 10 6:31		⚷ 14♓05.9 ⚶ 9♒07.0
♀ D 16 9:38	♀ ♉ 31 9:45	13 22:56 ♇ ⚹	♍ 14 1:10	12 8:20 ♇ □	♎ 12 9:27	4 19:57 ● 13♊33	☽ Mean ☊ 1♈21.0
♄△♅ 28 20:53		16 1:36 ♇ □	♎ 16 3:44	14 11:57 ♇ △	♏ 14 13:00	11 16:37 ☽ 20♍07	
☽0N 30 0:53	☊ ♓R 6 4:32	18 4:10 ♇ △	♏ 18 6:14	16 7:54 ♆ △	♐ 16 17:31	18 17:53 ○ 26♐51	1 June 1913
	☿ ♋ 10 21:31	20 7:18 ☉ ☍	♐ 20 9:38	18 22:45 ♇ ☍	♑ 18 23:41	26 17:40 ☾ 4♈28	Julian Day # 4900
☽0S 12 9:19	♂ ♉ 17 0:38	22 13:08 ♇ ☍	♑ 22 15:13	20 22:09 ♆ ☍	♒ 21 8:21		SVP 6♓28'08"
♄∠♆ 13 13:18	☉ ♋ 22 1:10	24 18:54 ♀ □	♒ 24 24:00	23 18:59 ♇ △	♓ 23 19:45		GC 25♐37.8 ⚴ 24♎02.7R
☽0N 26 7:57	☿ ♌ 28 5:37	27 9:42 ♇ △	♓ 27 11:47	26 7:59 ♇ □	♈ 26 8:38		Eris 27♓17.9 ⚵ 16♓05.2
		29 22:39 ♇ □	♈ 30 0:36	28 19:52 ♇ ⚹	♉ 28 20:22		⚷ 14♓59.1 ⚶ 16♒14.4
							☽ Mean ☊ 29♓42.5

July 1913

LONGITUDE

Day	Sid.Time	☉	0 hr ☽	Noon ☽	True ☊	☿	♀	♂	⚳	♃	♄	♅	♆	♇
1 Tu	6 35 44	9♋00 48	27♉22 19	3♊59 33	27♓41.5	4♌18.1	23♉24.0	10♉30.8	17♏58.6	13♑28.5	11♊42.6	6♒37.5	25♋05.2	29♊48.0
2 W	6 39 40	9 58 01	10♊42 58	17 32 27	27R31.5	5 31.5	24 20.3	11 13.8	17R57.6	13R20.8	11 49.8	6R35.5	25 07.3	29 49.5
3 Th	6 43 37	10 55 15	24 27 44	1♋28 25	27 20.3	6 42.3	25 17.0	11 56.8	17 57.0	13 13.1	11 57.0	6 33.4	25 09.5	29 50.9
4 F	6 47 34	11 52 28	8♋33 57	15 43 39	27 09.2	7 50.2	26 14.1	12 39.7	17D56.8	13 05.4	12 04.1	6 31.3	25 11.7	29 52.3
5 Sa	6 51 30	12 49 42	22 56 45	0♌12 24	26 59.4	8 55.3	27 11.7	13 22.5	17 56.9	12 57.7	12 11.2	6 29.2	25 13.9	29 53.8
6 Su	6 55 27	13 46 55	7♌29 44	14 47 53	26 51.9	9 57.5	28 09.6	14 05.2	17 57.4	12 50.0	12 18.3	6 27.1	25 16.1	29 55.2
7 M	6 59 23	14 44 09	22 06 01	29 23 24	26 46.9	10 56.6	29 08.0	14 47.8	17 58.3	12 42.3	12 25.3	6 24.9	25 18.3	29 56.6
8 Tu	7 03 20	15 41 22	6♍39 21	13♍53 19	26D44.6	11 52.6	0♊06.7	15 30.3	17 59.6	12 34.6	12 32.3	6 22.7	25 20.5	29 58.0
9 W	7 07 16	16 38 35	21 04 52	28 13 40	26 44.1	12 45.3	1 05.8	16 12.7	18 01.2	12 26.9	12 39.3	6 20.5	25 22.7	29 59.4
10 Th	7 11 13	17 35 48	5♎19 29	12♎22 12	26R44.3	13 34.6	2 05.2	16 55.1	18 03.1	12 19.2	12 46.2	6 18.3	25 24.9	0♋00.8
11 F	7 15 09	18 33 01	19 21 43	26 18 02	26 44.2	14 20.5	3 04.9	17 37.4	18 05.5	12 11.6	12 53.0	6 16.1	25 27.1	0 02.2
12 Sa	7 19 06	19 30 13	3♏11 11	10♏01 11	26 42.5	15 02.7	4 05.0	18 19.5	18 08.2	12 04.0	12 59.8	6 13.8	25 29.3	0 03.5
13 Su	7 23 03	20 27 26	16 48 06	23 31 58	26 38.6	15 41.1	5 05.4	19 01.6	18 11.2	11 56.4	13 06.6	6 11.6	25 31.5	0 04.9
14 M	7 26 59	21 24 39	0♐12 48	6♐50 38	26 32.2	16 15.7	6 06.2	19 43.6	18 14.6	11 48.9	13 13.3	6 09.3	25 33.7	0 06.3
15 Tu	7 30 56	22 21 52	13 25 28	19 57 15	26 23.5	16 46.1	7 07.2	20 25.5	18 18.3	11 41.4	13 20.0	6 07.0	25 36.0	0 07.7
16 W	7 34 52	23 19 05	26 25 58	2♑51 34	26 13.2	17 12.4	8 08.6	21 07.4	18 22.4	11 34.0	13 26.6	6 04.7	25 38.2	0 09.0
17 Th	7 38 49	24 16 19	9♑14 03	15 33 21	26 02.4	17 34.2	9 10.2	21 49.1	18 26.8	11 26.6	13 33.2	6 02.4	25 40.4	0 10.4
18 F	7 42 45	25 13 33	21 49 29	28 02 30	25 52.0	17 51.6	10 12.1	22 30.8	18 31.6	11 19.3	13 39.7	6 00.0	25 42.6	0 11.7
19 Sa	7 46 42	26 10 47	4♒12 26	10♒19 24	25 42.9	18 04.3	11 14.3	23 12.3	18 36.6	11 12.1	13 46.2	5 57.7	25 44.9	0 13.0
20 Su	7 50 38	27 08 02	16 23 35	22 25 09	25 36.0	18 12.3	12 16.8	23 53.8	18 42.0	11 04.9	13 52.6	5 55.3	25 47.1	0 14.3
21 M	7 54 35	28 05 18	28 24 24	4♓21 39	25 31.3	18R15.4	13 19.5	24 35.1	18 47.7	10 57.8	13 59.0	5 53.0	25 49.3	0 15.6
22 Tu	7 58 32	29 02 34	10♓17 16	16 11 41	25D29.0	18 13.5	14 22.5	25 16.4	18 53.8	10 50.8	14 05.3	5 50.6	25 51.5	0 16.9
23 W	8 02 28	29 59 51	22 05 22	27 58 50	25 28.6	18 06.7	15 25.8	25 57.6	19 00.1	10 43.9	14 11.5	5 48.2	25 53.8	0 18.2
24 Th	8 06 25	0♌57 09	3♈52 40	9♈47 27	25 29.3	17 54.9	16 29.3	26 38.6	19 06.8	10 37.1	14 17.7	5 45.8	25 56.0	0 19.5
25 F	8 10 21	1 54 27	15 43 48	21 42 23	25R30.3	17 38.2	17 33.0	27 19.6	19 13.7	10 30.4	14 23.9	5 43.4	25 58.2	0 20.8
26 Sa	8 14 18	2 51 47	27 43 51	3♉48 51	25 30.8	17 16.7	18 37.0	28 00.5	19 21.0	10 23.7	14 30.0	5 41.0	26 00.4	0 22.0
27 Su	8 18 14	3 49 08	9♉58 02	16 12 01	25 29.9	16 50.6	19 41.2	28 41.3	19 28.6	10 17.2	14 36.0	5 38.7	26 02.6	0 23.3
28 M	8 22 11	4 46 30	22 31 22	28 56 35	25 27.2	16 20.1	20 45.6	29 21.9	19 36.4	10 10.8	14 41.9	5 36.3	26 04.8	0 24.5
29 Tu	8 26 07	5 43 52	5♊28 08	12♊06 19	25 22.6	15 45.7	21 50.2	0♊02.5	19 44.6	10 04.5	14 47.8	5 33.9	26 07.1	0 25.7
30 W	8 30 04	6 41 16	18 51 19	25 43 11	25 16.4	15 07.7	22 55.1	0 43.0	19 53.0	9 58.3	14 53.7	5 31.5	26 09.3	0 27.0
31 Th	8 34 01	7 38 41	2♋41 50	9♋46 56	25 09.2	14 26.7	24 00.1	1 23.3	20 01.8	9 52.2	14 59.4	5 29.1	26 11.5	0 28.2

August 1913

LONGITUDE

Day	Sid.Time	☉	0 hr ☽	Noon ☽	True ☊	☿	♀	♂	⚳	♃	♄	♅	♆	♇
1 F	8 37 57	8♌36 07	16♋58 02	24♋14 29	25♓01.9	13♌43.4	25♊05.4	2♊03.6	20♏10.8	9♑46.3	15♊05.1	5♒26.7	26♋13.6	0♋29.4
2 Sa	8 41 54	9 33 34	1♌35 29	9♌00 05	24R55.4	12R58.3	26 10.8	2 43.7	20 20.1	9R40.5	15 10.8	5R24.3	26 15.8	0 30.5
3 Su	8 45 50	10 31 02	16 27 16	23 55 57	24 50.5	12 12.3	27 16.4	3 23.7	20 29.7	9 34.8	15 16.3	5 21.9	26 18.0	0 31.7
4 M	8 49 47	11 28 31	1♍25 02	8♍53 28	24 47.6	11 26.1	28 22.2	4 03.6	20 39.5	9 29.3	15 21.8	5 19.5	26 20.2	0 32.8
5 Tu	8 53 43	12 26 00	16 20 16	23 44 42	24D46.7	10 40.7	29 28.2	4 43.3	20 49.6	9 23.9	15 27.2	5 17.1	26 22.3	0 34.0
6 W	8 57 40	13 23 30	1♎05 33	8♎22 42	24 47.2	9 56.9	0♋34.3	5 23.0	21 00.0	9 18.6	15 32.6	5 14.8	26 24.5	0 35.1
7 Th	9 01 36	14 21 01	15 35 31	22 43 41	24 48.4	9 15.5	1 40.7	6 02.5	21 10.6	9 13.5	15 37.9	5 12.4	26 26.6	0 36.2
8 F	9 05 33	15 18 33	29 46 59	6♏45 21	24R49.5	8 37.4	2 47.2	6 41.9	21 21.5	9 08.6	15 43.1	5 10.0	26 28.8	0 37.3
9 Sa	9 09 30	16 16 05	13♏38 48	20 27 23	24 49.7	8 03.4	3 53.8	7 21.2	21 32.7	9 03.8	15 48.2	5 07.7	26 30.9	0 38.4
10 Su	9 13 26	17 13 39	27 11 17	3♐50 38	24 48.5	7 34.1	5 00.6	8 00.4	21 44.1	8 59.2	15 53.3	5 05.4	26 33.0	0 39.4
11 M	9 17 23	18 11 13	10♐25 41	16 56 37	24 45.6	7 10.2	6 07.6	8 39.4	21 55.7	8 54.7	15 58.3	5 03.1	26 35.1	0 40.5
12 Tu	9 21 19	19 08 48	23 23 41	29 47 05	24 41.2	6 52.3	7 14.8	9 18.3	22 07.6	8 50.4	16 03.2	5 00.7	26 37.2	0 41.5
13 W	9 25 16	20 06 24	6♑07 03	12♑23 46	24 35.8	6 40.7	8 22.1	9 57.1	22 19.7	8 46.3	16 08.0	4 58.5	26 39.3	0 42.5
14 Th	9 29 12	21 04 02	18 37 26	24 48 16	24 30.0	6D36.0	9 29.5	10 35.7	22 32.0	8 42.3	16 12.7	4 56.2	26 41.4	0 43.5
15 F	9 33 09	22 01 40	0♒56 25	7♒02 04	24 24.5	6 38.3	10 37.1	11 14.3	22 44.6	8 38.5	16 17.4	4 53.9	26 43.4	0 44.5
16 Sa	9 37 06	22 59 20	13 05 24	19 06 38	24 19.7	6 47.9	11 44.9	11 52.6	22 57.4	8 34.9	16 22.0	4 51.7	26 45.5	0 45.5
17 Su	9 41 02	23 57 00	25 05 56	1♓03 33	24 16.2	7 04.9	12 52.8	12 30.9	23 10.4	8 31.4	16 26.5	4 49.4	26 47.5	0 46.4
18 M	9 44 59	24 54 43	6♓59 43	12 54 42	24D14.2	7 29.4	14 00.8	13 09.0	23 23.6	8 28.1	16 30.9	4 47.2	26 49.5	0 47.4
19 Tu	9 48 55	25 52 26	18 48 48	24 42 22	24 13.6	8 01.3	15 09.0	13 47.0	23 37.1	8 25.0	16 35.2	4 45.0	26 51.5	0 48.3
20 W	9 52 52	26 50 11	0♈35 43	6♈29 18	24 14.2	8 40.6	16 17.4	14 24.9	23 50.7	8 22.1	16 39.5	4 42.9	26 53.5	0 49.2
21 Th	9 56 48	27 47 58	12 23 31	18 18 51	24 15.5	9 27.1	17 25.8	15 02.6	24 04.6	8 19.3	16 43.7	4 40.7	26 55.5	0 50.1
22 F	10 00 45	28 45 46	24 15 48	0♉14 53	24 17.3	10 20.7	18 34.5	15 40.2	24 18.7	8 16.7	16 47.7	4 38.6	26 57.5	0 50.9
23 Sa	10 04 41	29 43 36	6♉16 38	12 21 39	24 18.8	11 21.2	19 43.2	16 17.6	24 32.9	8 14.3	16 51.7	4 36.5	26 59.4	0 51.8
24 Su	10 08 38	0♍41 28	18 30 28	24 43 41	24R19.7	12 28.2	20 52.1	16 54.9	24 47.4	8 12.1	16 55.6	4 34.4	27 01.3	0 52.6
25 M	10 12 34	1 39 21	1♊01 51	7♊25 29	24 19.7	13 41.5	22 01.1	17 32.0	25 02.1	8 10.1	16 59.5	4 32.4	27 03.3	0 53.4
26 Tu	10 16 31	2 37 17	13 55 03	20 30 59	24 18.7	15 00.7	23 10.3	18 09.0	25 16.9	8 08.3	17 03.2	4 30.3	27 05.2	0 54.2
27 W	10 20 28	3 35 14	27 13 35	4♋03 04	24 16.9	16 25.3	24 19.6	18 45.9	25 32.0	8 06.6	17 06.8	4 28.3	27 07.0	0 55.0
28 Th	10 24 24	4 33 13	10♋59 31	18 02 51	24 14.5	17 55.1	25 29.0	19 22.5	25 47.2	8 05.2	17 10.4	4 26.4	27 08.9	0 55.7
29 F	10 28 21	5 31 14	25 12 49	2♌29 00	24 12.0	19 29.4	26 38.5	19 59.1	26 02.6	8 03.9	17 13.8	4 24.4	27 10.7	0 56.4
30 Sa	10 32 17	6 29 16	9♌50 47	17 17 23	24 09.8	21 07.8	27 48.2	20 35.4	26 18.2	8 02.8	17 17.2	4 22.5	27 12.6	0 57.2
31 Su	10 36 14	7 27 21	24 47 52	2♍21 09	24 08.2	22 49.9	28 57.9	21 11.6	26 34.0	8 01.9	17 20.4	4 20.6	27 14.4	0 57.9

Astro Data	Planet Ingress	Last Aspect	☽ Ingress	Last Aspect	☽ Ingress	☽ Phases & Eclipses	Astro Data
Dy Hr Mn	Dy Hr Mn	Dy Hr Mn	Dy Hr Mn	Dy Hr Mn	Dy Hr Mn	Dy Hr Mn	
⚳ D 4 14:33	♀ ♊ 8 9:16	30 19:46 ♆ ⚹	♊ 1 4:47	1 15:16 ♆ ☌	♌ 1 21:25	4 5:06 ● 11♋36	1 July 1913
♃⚻♄ 8 15:41	♇ ♋ 9 22:31	3 9:14 ♇ ☌	♋ 3 9:29	3 17:47 ♀ ⚹	♍ 3 21:44	10 21:37 ☽ 17♎59	Julian Day # 4930
☽0S 9 14:03	☉ ♌ 23 12:04	5 6:41 ♀ ⚹	♌ 5 11:40	5 22:06 ♀ □	♎ 5 22:13	18 6:06 ○ 24♑59	SVP 6♓28'03"
☿ R 21 15:04	♂ ♊ 29 10:31	7 12:55 ♇ ⚹	♍ 7 13:00	7 18:19 ♆ □	♏ 8 0:22	26 9:58 ☾ 2♉47	GC 25♐37.9 ⚴ 24♎29.2
☽0N 23 14:32		9 14:59 ♇ □	♎ 9 14:59	9 22:49 ♆ △	♐ 10 5:03		Eris 27♓20.8R ⚵ 23♓27.8
	♀ ♋ 5 23:33	11 10:31 ♆ □	♏ 11 18:26	11 14:29 ☉ △	♑ 12 12:24	2 12:58 ● 9♌36	⚷ 15♓02.4R ⚶ 16♒56.4R
☽0S 5 20:44	☉ ♍ 23 18:48	13 15:35 ♆ △	♐ 13 23:37	14 15:41 ♆ ☍	♒ 14 22:09	9 4:03 ☽ 15♏57	☽ Mean ☊ 28♓07.2
☿ D 14 16:15		15 5:55 ☿ △	♑ 16 6:39	16 20:27 ☉ ☍	♓ 17 9:52	16 20:27 ○ 23♒20	
☽0N 19 20:44		18 7:29 ♆ ☍	♒ 18 15:48	19 16:24 ♆ △	♈ 19 22:47	25 0:17 ☾ 1♊11	1 August 1913
		20 15:08 ♂ □	♓ 21 3:12	22 8:46 ☉ △	♉ 22 11:30	31 20:38 ● 7♍48	Julian Day # 4961
		23 7:44 ♆ △	♈ 23 16:07	24 16:24 ♆ ⚹	♊ 24 22:03	31 20:51:53 ● P 0.151	SVP 6♓27'57"
		25 20:32 ♆ □	♉ 26 4:29	26 7:31 ♂ ☌	♋ 27 4:54		GC 25♐37.9 ⚴ 0♏33.4
		28 12:49 ♂ ☌	♊ 28 13:57	29 3:14 ♆ ☌	♌ 29 7:55		Eris 27♓12.5R ⚵ 26♓32.4R
		30 6:42 ♀ ☌	♋ 30 19:23	30 18:55 ☿ ☌	♍ 31 8:16		⚷ 14♓16.8R ⚶ 11♒00.8R
							☽ Mean ☊ 26♓28.8

LONGITUDE — September 1913

Day	Sid.Time	☉	0 hr ☽	Noon ☽	True ☊	☿	♀	♂	⚳	♃	♄	♅	♆	♇
1 M	10 40 10	8♍25 27	9♍56 07	17♍31 32	24♓07.4	24♌35.1	0♌07.8	21♊47.6	26♏50.0	8♑01.2	17♊23.6	4♒18.7	27♋16.2	0♋58.5
2 Tu	10 44 07	9 23 34	25 06 13	2♎39 01	24D07.4	26 22.9	1 17.8	22 23.5	27 06.1	8R00.7	17 26.6	4R16.9	27 17.9	0 59.2
3 W	10 48 03	10 21 43	10♎08 52	17 34 51	24 08.1	28 13.0	2 27.9	22 59.1	27 22.4	8 00.4	17 29.6	4 15.1	27 19.7	0 59.8
4 Th	10 52 00	11 19 54	24 56 09	2♏12 08	24 09.1	0♍04.8	3 38.1	23 34.6	27 38.9	8D00.3	17 32.5	4 13.3	27 21.4	1 00.4
5 F	10 55 57	12 18 06	9♏22 22	16 26 31	24 10.0	1 58.0	4 48.4	24 09.9	27 55.5	8 00.4	17 35.2	4 11.6	27 23.1	1 01.0
6 Sa	10 59 53	13 16 19	23 24 27	0♐16 08	24 10.7	3 52.2	5 58.8	24 45.0	28 12.3	8 00.6	17 37.9	4 09.9	27 24.8	1 01.6
7 Su	11 03 50	14 14 35	7♐01 40	13 41 16	24R11.0	5 47.0	7 09.3	25 20.0	28 29.3	8 01.1	17 40.5	4 08.3	27 26.4	1 02.1
8 M	11 07 46	15 12 51	20 15 11	26 43 45	24 10.8	7 42.2	8 19.9	25 54.8	28 46.4	8 01.7	17 42.9	4 06.6	27 28.1	1 02.7
9 Tu	11 11 43	16 11 09	3♑07 22	9♑26 24	24 10.2	9 37.5	9 30.7	26 29.3	29 03.6	8 02.6	17 45.3	4 05.1	27 29.7	1 03.2
10 W	11 15 39	17 09 29	15 41 16	21 52 24	24 09.4	11 32.6	10 41.5	27 03.7	29 21.0	8 03.6	17 47.6	4 03.5	27 31.3	1 03.7
11 Th	11 19 36	18 07 50	28 00 12	4♒05 03	24 08.5	13 27.5	11 52.4	27 37.9	29 38.6	8 04.8	17 49.7	4 02.0	27 32.8	1 04.1
12 F	11 23 32	19 06 13	10♒07 22	16 07 31	24 07.8	15 21.8	13 03.4	28 11.9	29 56.3	8 06.3	17 51.8	4 00.5	27 34.4	1 04.6
13 Sa	11 27 29	20 04 38	22 05 49	28 02 38	24 07.3	17 15.6	14 14.5	28 45.7	0♐14.1	8 07.9	17 53.7	3 59.1	27 35.9	1 05.0
14 Su	11 31 26	21 03 04	3♓58 16	9♓53 01	24 07.0	19 08.6	15 25.8	29 19.3	0 32.1	8 09.6	17 55.6	3 57.7	27 37.4	1 05.4
15 M	11 35 22	22 01 32	15 47 10	21 41 01	24D06.9	21 00.9	16 37.1	29 52.7	0 50.3	8 11.6	17 57.3	3 56.3	27 38.8	1 05.8
16 Tu	11 39 19	23 00 02	27 34 50	3♈28 54	24 06.9	22 52.3	17 48.5	0♋25.8	1 08.5	8 13.8	17 58.9	3 55.0	27 40.3	1 06.1
17 W	11 43 15	23 58 34	9♈23 30	15 18 56	24R06.9	24 42.9	19 00.0	0 58.8	1 26.9	8 16.1	18 00.5	3 53.8	27 41.7	1 06.5
18 Th	11 47 12	24 57 08	21 15 29	27 13 29	24 06.9	26 32.5	20 11.6	1 31.6	1 45.4	8 18.7	18 01.9	3 52.5	27 43.1	1 06.8
19 F	11 51 08	25 55 44	3♉13 17	9♉15 13	24 06.7	28 21.1	21 23.3	2 04.1	2 04.1	8 21.4	18 03.2	3 51.3	27 44.5	1 07.1
20 Sa	11 55 05	26 54 22	15 19 40	21 27 01	24 06.4	0♎08.7	22 35.1	2 36.4	2 22.8	8 24.3	18 04.4	3 50.2	27 45.8	1 07.3
21 Su	11 59 01	27 53 02	27 37 41	3♊52 05	24 06.1	1 55.4	23 47.0	3 08.5	2 41.7	8 27.3	18 05.5	3 49.1	27 47.1	1 07.6
22 M	12 02 58	28 51 45	10♊10 38	16 33 45	24 05.8	3 41.1	24 59.0	3 40.4	3 00.8	8 30.6	18 06.5	3 48.0	27 48.4	1 07.8
23 Tu	12 06 55	29 50 30	23 01 52	29 35 20	24D05.6	5 25.9	26 11.0	4 12.0	3 19.9	8 34.1	18 07.3	3 47.0	27 49.6	1 08.0
24 W	12 10 51	0♎49 17	6♋14 30	12♋59 39	24 05.8	7 09.6	27 23.2	4 43.4	3 39.2	8 37.7	18 08.1	3 46.0	27 50.9	1 08.2
25 Th	12 14 48	1 48 07	19 50 58	26 48 34	24 06.2	8 52.4	28 35.4	5 14.5	3 58.6	8 41.5	18 08.8	3 45.1	27 52.1	1 08.3
26 F	12 18 44	2 46 58	3♌52 27	11♌02 26	24 06.9	10 34.3	29 47.7	5 45.4	4 18.1	8 45.5	18 09.3	3 44.3	27 53.3	1 08.5
27 Sa	12 22 41	3 45 52	18 18 14	25 39 23	24 07.7	12 15.2	1♍00.1	6 16.0	4 37.7	8 49.6	18 09.8	3 43.4	27 54.4	1 08.6
28 Su	12 26 37	4 44 49	3♍05 15	10♍35 01	24R08.3	13 55.3	2 12.6	6 46.4	4 57.4	8 54.0	18 10.1	3 42.6	27 55.5	1 08.7
29 M	12 30 34	5 43 47	18 07 47	25 42 28	24 08.5	15 34.4	3 25.2	7 16.4	5 17.3	8 58.5	18 10.3	3 41.9	27 56.6	1 08.7
30 Tu	12 34 30	6 42 47	3♎17 55	10♎52 56	24 08.1	17 12.7	4 37.8	7 46.3	5 37.2	9 03.1	18R10.4	3 41.2	27 57.6	1 08.8

LONGITUDE — October 1913

Day	Sid.Time	☉	0 hr ☽	Noon ☽	True ☊	☿	♀	♂	⚳	♃	♄	♅	♆	♇
1 W	12 38 27	7♎41 49	18♎26 20	25♎56 56	24♓07.1	18♎50.1	5♍50.5	8♋15.8	5♐57.3	9♑08.0	18♊10.4	3♒40.6	27♋58.7	1♋08.8
2 Th	12 42 24	8 40 54	3♏23 42	10♏45 40	24R05.4	20 26.6	7 03.3	8 45.0	6 17.4	9 13.0	18R10.3	3R40.0	27 59.7	1R08.8
3 F	12 46 20	9 40 00	18 02 05	25 12 18	24 03.5	22 02.4	8 16.1	9 14.0	6 37.7	9 18.2	18 10.0	3 39.4	28 00.6	1 08.8
4 Sa	12 50 17	10 39 08	2♐15 55	9♐12 40	24 01.5	23 37.3	9 29.1	9 42.6	6 58.1	9 23.6	18 09.7	3 38.9	28 01.5	1 08.7
5 Su	12 54 13	11 38 18	16 02 29	22 45 25	23 59.9	25 11.4	10 42.0	10 11.0	7 18.5	9 29.1	18 09.3	3 38.5	28 02.4	1 08.6
6 M	12 58 10	12 37 30	29 21 40	5♑51 34	23D59.0	26 44.7	11 55.1	10 39.0	7 39.1	9 34.8	18 08.7	3 38.1	28 03.3	1 08.5
7 Tu	13 02 06	13 36 43	12♑15 32	18 34 00	23 59.0	28 17.3	13 08.2	11 06.8	7 59.8	9 40.7	18 08.0	3 37.7	28 04.2	1 08.4
8 W	13 06 03	14 35 58	24 47 31	0♒56 38	23 59.7	29 49.1	14 21.4	11 34.2	8 20.5	9 46.7	18 07.2	3 37.4	28 05.0	1 08.3
9 Th	13 09 59	15 35 15	7♒01 54	13 03 55	24 01.1	1♏20.1	15 34.7	12 01.3	8 41.3	9 52.9	18 06.3	3 37.2	28 05.7	1 08.1
10 F	13 13 56	16 34 34	19 03 14	25 00 23	24 02.8	2 50.3	16 48.0	12 28.1	9 02.3	9 59.2	18 05.3	3 37.0	28 06.5	1 07.9
11 Sa	13 17 53	17 33 54	0♓55 54	6♓50 18	24 04.4	4 19.8	18 01.3	12 54.5	9 23.3	10 05.7	18 04.2	3 36.8	28 07.2	1 07.7
12 Su	13 21 49	18 33 17	12 44 02	18 37 33	24R05.4	5 48.6	19 14.8	13 20.6	9 44.4	10 12.4	18 03.0	3 36.7	28 07.9	1 07.5
13 M	13 25 46	19 32 41	24 31 13	0♈25 25	24 05.3	7 16.5	20 28.3	13 46.3	10 05.6	10 19.2	18 01.7	3D36.7	28 08.5	1 07.3
14 Tu	13 29 42	20 32 07	6♈20 29	12 16 43	24 04.0	8 43.7	21 41.8	14 11.7	10 26.8	10 26.1	18 00.3	3 36.7	28 09.1	1 07.0
15 W	13 33 39	21 31 35	18 14 22	24 13 41	24 01.2	10 10.1	22 55.4	14 36.8	10 48.2	10 33.2	17 58.7	3 36.7	28 09.7	1 06.7
16 Th	13 37 35	22 31 06	0♉14 53	6♉18 09	23 57.2	11 35.8	24 09.1	15 01.4	11 09.6	10 40.4	17 57.1	3 36.9	28 10.2	1 06.4
17 F	13 41 32	23 30 38	12 23 42	18 31 41	23 52.3	13 00.5	25 22.9	15 25.7	11 31.1	10 47.8	17 55.3	3 37.0	28 10.7	1 06.0
18 Sa	13 45 28	24 30 13	24 42 17	0♊55 40	23 47.0	14 24.5	26 36.7	15 49.6	11 52.7	10 55.4	17 53.5	3 37.2	28 11.2	1 05.7
19 Su	13 49 25	25 29 49	7♊12 02	13 31 34	23 41.8	15 47.5	27 50.5	16 13.2	12 14.4	11 03.1	17 51.5	3 37.5	28 11.7	1 05.3
20 M	13 53 22	26 29 28	19 54 26	26 20 53	23 37.5	17 09.6	29 04.4	16 36.3	12 36.1	11 10.9	17 49.5	3 37.8	28 12.1	1 04.9
21 Tu	13 57 18	27 29 10	2♋51 07	9♋25 22	23 34.5	18 30.8	0♎18.4	16 59.0	12 57.9	11 18.9	17 47.3	3 38.1	28 12.5	1 04.5
22 W	14 01 15	28 28 53	16 03 50	22 46 44	23D33.1	19 50.9	1 32.4	17 21.3	13 19.8	11 27.0	17 45.0	3 38.6	28 12.8	1 04.0
23 Th	14 05 11	29 28 39	29 34 16	6♌26 35	23 33.1	21 09.9	2 46.5	17 43.1	13 41.8	11 35.2	17 42.7	3 39.0	28 13.1	1 03.5
24 F	14 09 08	0♏28 27	13♌23 46	20 25 51	23 34.2	22 27.7	4 00.6	18 04.6	14 03.8	11 43.6	17 40.2	3 39.5	28 13.4	1 03.1
25 Sa	14 13 04	1 28 18	27 32 47	4♍44 24	23 35.6	23 44.2	5 14.8	18 25.5	14 25.9	11 52.1	17 37.7	3 40.1	28 13.6	1 02.5
26 Su	14 17 01	2 28 10	12♍00 24	19 20 22	23R36.6	24 59.3	6 29.0	18 46.0	14 48.0	12 00.7	17 35.0	3 40.7	28 13.8	1 02.0
27 M	14 20 57	3 28 05	26 43 42	4♎09 44	23 36.2	26 12.9	7 43.3	19 06.0	15 10.3	12 09.5	17 32.2	3 41.4	28 14.0	1 01.5
28 Tu	14 24 54	4 28 01	11♎37 35	19 06 18	23 34.0	27 24.8	8 57.6	19 25.6	15 32.6	12 18.4	17 29.4	3 42.1	28 14.2	1 00.9
29 W	14 28 50	5 28 00	26 34 50	4♏02 08	23 29.7	28 34.9	10 12.0	19 44.6	15 54.9	12 27.5	17 26.5	3 42.8	28 14.3	1 00.3
30 Th	14 32 47	6 28 01	11♏27 04	18 48 36	23 23.7	29 43.0	11 26.4	20 03.2	16 17.4	12 36.6	17 23.4	3 43.7	28 14.3	0 59.7
31 F	14 36 44	7 28 04	26 05 47	3♐17 45	23 16.5	0♐48.8	12 40.8	20 21.2	16 39.8	12 45.9	17 20.3	3 44.5	28R14.4	0 59.1

Astro Data (Dy Hr Mn)
☽0S 2 6:08
♃D 4 14:56
☽0N 16 2:49
☿0S 21 21:40
☉0S 23 15:53
☽0S 29 17:10
♄R 30 21:49

♇R 1 19:25
☽0N 13 9:03
♅D 13 23:23
♀0S 24 4:30
☽0S 27 3:30

Planet Ingress (Dy Hr Mn)
♀ ♌ 1 9:20
☿ ♍ 4 10:58
⚳ ♐ 12 16:59
♂ ♋ 15 17:18
☿ ♎ 20 10:03
☉ ♎ 23 15:53
♀ ♍ 26 16:04

☿ ♏ 8 14:53
♀ ♎ 21 6:02
☉ ♏ 24 0:35
☿ ♐ 30 18:07

Last Aspect (Dy Hr Mn) — **☽ Ingress** (Dy Hr Mn)
2 3:28 ♆ ✶ ♎ 2 7:47
4 7:58 ☿ ✶ ♏ 4 8:21
6 6:58 ♆ △ ♐ 6 11:32
8 10:24 ♂ ☍ ♑ 8 18:07
10 23:05 ♆ ☍ ♒ 11 3:56
13 13:31 ♂ △ ♓ 13 15:57
16 0:10 ♆ △ ♈ 16 4:55
18 13:00 ♆ □ ♉ 18 17:34
21 0:17 ♆ ✶ ♊ 21 4:35
23 12:30 ☉ □ ♋ 23 12:45
25 13:49 ♆ ☌ ♌ 25 17:26
26 23:46 ♄ ✶ ♍ 27 19:02
29 15:32 ♆ ✶ ♎ 29 18:47

Last Aspect (Dy Hr Mn) — **☽ Ingress** (Dy Hr Mn)
1 15:16 ♆ □ ♏ 1 18:31
3 16:45 ♆ △ ♐ 3 20:08
5 16:59 ☿ ✶ ♑ 6 1:10
8 9:29 ☿ □ ♒ 8 10:09
9 22:05 ♄ △ ♓ 10 22:07
13 7:22 ♆ △ ♈ 13 11:08
15 19:51 ♆ □ ♉ 15 23:30
18 6:43 ♆ ✶ ♊ 18 10:13
20 17:34 ♀ □ ♋ 20 18:45
22 22:53 ☉ □ ♌ 23 0:45
24 15:47 ☿ □ ♍ 25 4:06
27 2:26 ♆ ✶ ♎ 27 5:17
29 2:40 ♆ □ ♏ 29 5:30
31 3:33 ♆ △ ♐ 31 6:29

☽ Phases & Eclipses (Dy Hr Mn)
7 13:05 ☽ 14♐17
15 12:46 ○ 22♓03
15 12:48 • T 1.430
23 12:30 ☾ 29♊52
30 4:57 ● 6♎25
30 4:45:32 • P 0.825

7 1:46 ☽ 13♑11
15 6:06 ○ 21♈17
22 22:53 ☾ 28♋56
29 14:29 ● 5♏34

Astro Data
1 September 1913
Julian Day # 4992
SVP 6♓27'52"
GC 25♐38.0 ⚴ 10♏03.6
Eris 26♓55.4R ⚵ 23♓04.0R
⚷ 12♓57.5R ⚶ 4♒47.7R
☽ Mean ☊ 24♓50.3

1 October 1913
Julian Day # 5022
SVP 6♓27'49"
GC 25♐38.1 ⚴ 21♏06.9
Eris 26♓35.0R ⚵ 16♓02.9R
⚷ 11♓36.1R ⚶ 4♒53.0
☽ Mean ☊ 23♓14.9

November 1913 — LONGITUDE

Day	Sid.Time	☉	0 hr ☽	Noon ☽	True ☊	☿	♀	♂	⚳	♃	♄	♅	♆	♇
1 Sa	14 40 40	8♏28 08	10♐23 51	17♐23 33	23♓09.2	1♐52.2	13♎55.3	20♋38.7	17♐02.4	12♑55.3	17♊17.1	3♒45.5	28♋14.4	0♋58.4
2 Su	14 44 37	9 28 14	24 16 31	1♑02 36	23R 02.6	2 52.7	15 09.8	20 55.7	17 25.0	13 04.9	17R 13.8	3 46.4	28R 14.3	0R 57.7
3 M	14 48 33	10 28 22	7♑41 49	14 14 19	22 57.5	3 50.1	16 24.4	21 12.1	17 47.7	13 14.5	17 10.4	3 47.5	28 14.3	0 57.1
4 Tu	14 52 30	11 28 31	20 40 24	27 00 29	22 54.3	4 44.1	17 38.9	21 28.0	18 10.4	13 24.3	17 06.9	3 48.5	28 14.2	0 56.4
5 W	14 56 26	12 28 42	3♒15 05	9♒24 45	22D 53.0	5 34.1	18 53.6	21 43.3	18 33.1	13 34.2	17 03.4	3 49.6	28 14.0	0 55.6
6 Th	15 00 23	13 28 54	15 30 07	21 31 49	22 53.3	6 19.8	20 08.2	21 58.0	18 56.0	13 44.2	16 59.8	3 50.8	28 13.9	0 54.9
7 F	15 04 20	14 29 08	27 30 32	3♓26 55	22 54.4	7 00.7	21 22.9	22 12.1	19 18.8	13 54.3	16 56.1	3 52.0	28 13.7	0 54.1
8 Sa	15 08 16	15 29 23	9♓21 39	15 15 22	22R 55.6	7 36.1	22 37.6	22 25.7	19 41.8	14 04.5	16 52.3	3 53.3	28 13.4	0 53.3
9 Su	15 12 13	16 29 40	21 08 42	27 02 12	22 55.7	8 05.4	23 52.4	22 38.6	20 04.7	14 14.8	16 48.4	3 54.6	28 13.2	0 52.5
10 M	15 16 09	17 29 58	2♈56 26	8♈51 54	22 54.2	8 28.0	25 07.1	22 50.9	20 27.7	14 25.3	16 44.5	3 56.0	28 12.9	0 51.7
11 Tu	15 20 06	18 30 18	14 49 02	20 48 13	22 50.3	8 43.2	26 21.9	23 02.6	20 50.8	14 35.8	16 40.5	3 57.4	28 12.5	0 50.9
12 W	15 24 02	19 30 39	26 49 48	2♉54 02	22 43.9	8R 50.3	27 36.8	23 13.7	21 13.9	14 46.4	16 36.4	3 58.8	28 12.2	0 50.1
13 Th	15 27 59	20 31 02	9♉01 10	15 11 20	22 35.2	8 48.6	28 51.6	23 24.1	21 37.1	14 57.2	16 32.3	4 00.3	28 11.8	0 49.2
14 F	15 31 55	21 31 27	21 24 38	27 41 08	22 24.7	8 37.4	0♏06.5	23 33.8	22 00.2	15 08.0	16 28.1	4 01.9	28 11.3	0 48.3
15 Sa	15 35 52	22 31 53	4♊00 50	10♊23 43	22 13.4	8 16.2	1 21.4	23 42.8	22 23.5	15 19.0	16 23.9	4 03.5	28 10.9	0 47.4
16 Su	15 39 49	23 32 21	16 49 43	23 18 45	22 02.4	7 44.7	2 36.4	23 51.2	22 46.8	15 30.0	16 19.5	4 05.2	28 10.4	0 46.5
17 M	15 43 45	24 32 51	29 50 46	6♋25 42	21 52.7	7 02.8	3 51.4	23 58.8	23 10.1	15 41.2	16 15.2	4 06.8	28 09.8	0 45.6
18 Tu	15 47 42	25 33 23	13♋03 27	19 44 01	21 45.1	6 10.7	5 06.4	24 05.8	23 33.4	15 52.4	16 10.8	4 08.6	28 09.3	0 44.7
19 W	15 51 38	26 33 56	26 27 22	3♌13 29	21 40.2	5 09.3	6 21.4	24 12.0	23 56.8	16 03.7	16 06.3	4 10.4	28 08.7	0 43.7
20 Th	15 55 35	27 34 31	10♌02 26	16 54 14	21D 37.8	3 59.7	7 36.5	24 17.4	24 20.3	16 15.1	16 01.8	4 12.2	28 08.0	0 42.7
21 F	15 59 31	28 35 07	23 48 56	0♍46 34	21 37.4	2 43.7	8 51.5	24 22.1	24 43.8	16 26.6	15 57.2	4 14.1	28 07.4	0 41.8
22 Sa	16 03 28	29 35 46	7♍47 10	14 50 43	21R 37.7	1 23.4	10 06.6	24 26.1	25 07.3	16 38.2	15 52.6	4 16.0	28 06.7	0 40.8
23 Su	16 07 24	0♐36 26	21 57 07	29 06 14	21 37.7	0 01.5	11 21.8	24 29.2	25 30.8	16 49.9	15 47.9	4 17.9	28 06.0	0 39.8
24 M	16 11 21	1 37 08	6♎17 48	13♎31 27	21 35.9	28♏40.6	12 36.9	24 31.5	25 54.4	17 01.7	15 43.2	4 19.9	28 05.2	0 38.7
25 Tu	16 15 18	2 37 51	20 46 44	28 03 04	21 31.5	27 23.5	13 52.1	24 33.1	26 18.0	17 13.5	15 38.5	4 22.0	28 04.4	0 37.7
26 W	16 19 14	3 38 36	5♏19 46	12♏36 03	21 24.2	26 12.6	15 07.3	24R 33.8	26 41.6	17 25.5	15 33.7	4 24.1	28 03.6	0 36.7
27 Th	16 23 11	4 39 23	19 51 06	27 04 03	21 14.3	25 10.0	16 22.5	24 33.7	27 05.3	17 37.5	15 28.9	4 26.2	28 02.8	0 35.6
28 F	16 27 07	5 40 11	4♐14 02	11♐20 16	21 02.6	24 17.4	17 37.7	24 32.8	27 29.0	17 49.6	15 24.1	4 28.4	28 01.9	0 34.6
29 Sa	16 31 04	6 41 00	18 22 01	25 18 40	20 50.3	23 35.7	18 52.9	24 31.0	27 52.8	18 01.8	15 19.2	4 30.6	28 01.0	0 33.5
30 Su	16 35 00	7 41 50	2♑09 44	8♑54 51	20 38.7	23 05.5	20 08.2	24 28.4	28 16.5	18 14.0	15 14.4	4 32.9	28 00.1	0 32.4

December 1913 — LONGITUDE

Day	Sid.Time	☉	0 hr ☽	Noon ☽	True ☊	☿	♀	♂	⚳	♃	♄	♅	♆	♇
1 M	16 38 57	8♐42 41	15♑33 53	22♑06 46	20♓29.0	22♏46.9	21♏23.5	24♋25.0	28♐40.3	18♑26.3	15♊09.5	4♒35.2	27♋59.1	0♋31.3
2 Tu	16 42 53	9 43 34	28 33 37	4♒54 41	20R 21.8	22D 39.5	22 38.7	24R 20.7	29 04.1	18 38.7	15R 04.5	4 37.5	27R 58.1	0R 30.2
3 W	16 46 50	10 44 27	11♒10 20	17 21 00	20 17.3	22 42.7	23 54.0	24 15.5	29 28.0	18 51.2	14 59.6	4 39.9	27 57.1	0 29.1
4 Th	16 50 47	11 45 20	23 27 16	29 29 42	20 15.2	22 56.0	25 09.3	24 09.5	29 51.8	19 03.7	14 54.7	4 42.3	27 56.1	0 28.0
5 F	16 54 43	12 46 15	5♓28 58	11♓25 45	20 14.7	23 18.3	26 24.6	24 02.6	0♑15.7	19 16.3	14 49.7	4 44.7	27 55.0	0 26.8
6 Sa	16 58 40	13 47 10	17 20 46	23 14 41	20 14.8	23 48.9	27 39.9	23 54.9	0 39.6	19 29.0	14 44.8	4 47.2	27 53.9	0 25.7
7 Su	17 02 36	14 48 06	29 08 15	5♈02 08	20 14.1	24 27.0	28 55.3	23 46.4	1 03.5	19 41.7	14 39.8	4 49.7	27 52.8	0 24.5
8 M	17 06 33	15 49 03	10♈57 00	16 53 30	20 11.7	25 11.6	0♐10.6	23 37.0	1 27.4	19 54.5	14 34.9	4 52.3	27 51.6	0 23.4
9 Tu	17 10 29	16 50 00	22 52 11	28 53 35	20 06.8	26 02.1	1 25.9	23 26.7	1 51.4	20 07.4	14 29.9	4 54.9	27 50.5	0 22.2
10 W	17 14 26	17 50 59	4♉58 12	11♉06 24	19 59.0	26 57.6	2 41.3	23 15.7	2 15.4	20 20.3	14 25.0	4 57.5	27 49.3	0 21.1
11 Th	17 18 22	18 51 57	17 18 31	23 34 46	19 48.5	27 57.7	3 56.6	23 03.8	2 39.4	20 33.3	14 20.1	5 00.2	27 48.0	0 19.9
12 F	17 22 19	19 52 57	29 55 18	6♊20 10	19 35.8	29 01.7	5 12.0	22 51.1	3 03.4	20 46.3	14 15.1	5 02.9	27 46.8	0 18.7
13 Sa	17 26 16	20 53 58	12♊49 19	19 22 38	19 22.1	0♐09.0	6 27.4	22 37.6	3 27.4	20 59.4	14 10.2	5 05.6	27 45.5	0 17.5
14 Su	17 30 12	21 54 59	25 59 55	2♋40 52	19 08.6	1 19.4	7 42.7	22 23.3	3 51.4	21 12.5	14 05.4	5 08.3	27 44.3	0 16.4
15 M	17 34 09	22 56 01	9♋25 12	16 12 32	18 56.6	2 32.4	8 58.1	22 08.3	4 15.4	21 25.7	14 00.5	5 11.1	27 42.9	0 15.2
16 Tu	17 38 05	23 57 04	23 02 31	29 54 47	18 47.1	3 47.6	10 13.5	21 52.5	4 39.5	21 39.0	13 55.7	5 14.0	27 41.6	0 14.0
17 W	17 42 02	24 58 07	6♌49 00	13♌44 50	18 40.6	5 04.8	11 28.9	21 35.9	5 03.5	21 52.2	13 50.8	5 16.8	27 40.3	0 12.8
18 Th	17 45 58	25 59 11	20 42 02	27 40 23	18 37.1	6 23.8	12 44.3	21 18.7	5 27.6	22 05.6	13 46.1	5 19.7	27 38.9	0 11.6
19 F	17 49 55	27 00 16	4♍39 43	11♍39 54	18D 37.4	7 44.2	13 59.8	21 00.7	5 51.7	22 19.0	13 41.3	5 22.6	27 37.5	0 10.4
20 Sa	17 53 52	28 01 22	18 40 51	25 42 29	18R 35.8	9 06.0	15 15.2	20 42.1	6 15.8	22 32.4	13 36.6	5 25.6	27 36.1	0 09.2
21 Su	17 57 48	29 02 29	2♎44 46	9♎47 37	18 35.5	10 28.9	16 30.6	20 22.8	6 39.9	22 45.9	13 31.9	5 28.5	27 34.7	0 08.0
22 M	18 01 45	0♑03 37	16 50 56	23 54 35	18 33.7	11 52.9	17 46.1	20 02.9	7 04.0	22 59.4	13 27.2	5 31.5	27 33.2	0 06.8
23 Tu	18 05 41	1 04 45	0♏58 21	8♏02 00	18 29.3	13 17.8	19 01.5	19 42.4	7 28.1	23 13.0	13 22.6	5 34.5	27 31.7	0 05.6
24 W	18 09 38	2 05 54	15 05 12	22 07 34	18 22.0	14 43.5	20 17.0	19 21.4	7 52.2	23 26.6	13 18.1	5 37.6	27 30.3	0 04.4
25 Th	18 13 34	3 07 04	29 08 38	6♐07 54	18 12.0	16 09.9	21 32.4	18 59.9	8 16.3	23 40.2	13 13.5	5 40.7	27 28.8	0 03.2
26 F	18 17 31	4 08 14	13♐04 53	19 59 00	18 00.1	17 37.0	22 47.9	18 38.0	8 40.4	23 53.9	13 09.1	5 43.8	27 27.2	0 02.0
27 Sa	18 21 27	5 09 24	26 49 47	3♑36 45	17 47.4	19 04.6	24 03.4	18 15.6	9 04.6	24 07.6	13 04.7	5 46.9	27 25.7	0 00.8
28 Su	18 25 24	6 10 35	10♑19 30	16 57 42	17 35.4	20 32.9	25 18.8	17 52.9	9 28.7	24 21.4	13 00.3	5 50.1	27 24.2	29♊59.6
29 M	18 29 21	7 11 46	23 31 08	29 59 40	17 25.0	22 01.6	26 34.3	17 29.8	9 52.8	24 35.2	12 56.0	5 53.2	27 22.6	29 58.4
30 Tu	18 33 17	8 12 56	6♒23 17	12♒42 05	17 17.2	23 30.9	27 49.8	17 06.4	10 16.9	24 49.0	12 51.8	5 56.4	27 21.0	29 57.2
31 W	18 37 14	9 14 07	18 56 15	25 06 05	17 12.2	25 00.5	29 05.2	16 42.9	10 41.1	25 02.9	12 47.6	5 59.6	27 19.4	29 56.0

Astro Data

	Dy Hr Mn
♆ R	1 3:01
☽ 0N	9 15:34
☿ R	12 19:29
♃⚻♄	19 15:52
☽ 0S	23 11:07
♂ R	26 21:11
☿ D	2 16:26
☽ 0N	6 22:24
☽ 0S	20 16:03

Planet Ingress

		Dy Hr Mn
♀	♏	14 9:55
☉	♐	22 21:35
☿	♏R	23 12:26
⚳	♑	4 20:13
♀	♐	8 8:38
☿	♐	13 8:51
☉	♑	22 10:35
♇	♊R	28 4:10

Last Aspect / ☽ Ingress (November)

Last Aspect Dy Hr Mn			☽ Ingress	Dy Hr Mn
1 11:49	♄	☍	♑	2 10:08
4 14:21	♆	☍	♒	4 17:44
6 8:54	♀	△	♓	7 5:01
9 14:24	♆	△	♈	9 18:02
12 2:44	♆	□	♉	12 6:17
14 12:57	♆	⚹	♊	14 16:24
15 23:08	♄	☌	♋	17 0:17
19 3:00	♆	☌	♌	19 6:18
21 7:56	☉	□	♍	21 10:40
23 13:24	☿	⚹	♎	23 13:30
25 12:02	♆	□	♏	25 15:13
27 13:38	♆	△	♐	27 16:54
28 18:53	♄	☍	♑	29 20:12

Last Aspect / ☽ Ingress (December)

Last Aspect Dy Hr Mn			☽ Ingress	Dy Hr Mn
1 22:55	♆	☍	♒	2 2:42
4 2:22	♀	□	♓	4 13:00
6 22:05	♀	△	♈	7 1:45
9 9:55	♆	□	♉	9 14:12
11 21:03	☿	☍	♊	12 0:09
13 15:00	☉	☍	♋	14 7:12
16 8:08	♆	☌	♌	16 12:09
18 8:52	☉	△	♍	18 16:00
20 16:15	☉	□	♎	20 19:19
22 18:11	♆	□	♏	22 22:21
24 21:11	♆	△	♐	25 1:28
26 17:25	♀	☌	♑	27 5:36
29 7:08	♆	☍	♒	29 12:01
31 21:29	♇	△	♓	31 21:38

☽ Phases & Eclipses

Dy Hr Mn		
5 18:34	☽	12♒45
13 23:11	○	20♉59
21 7:56	☾	28♌25
28 1:41	●	5♐14
5 14:58	☽	12♓54
13 15:00	○	21♊02
20 16:15	☾	28♍12
27 14:59	●	5♑17

Astro Data

1 November 1913
Julian Day # 5053
SVP 6♓27'45"
GC 25♐38.2 ⚴ 3♐34.6
Eris 26♓16.3R ⚵ 13♓10.0
⚷ 10♓38.8R ⚶ 11♒13.2
☽ Mean ☊ 21♓36.4

1 December 1913
Julian Day # 5083
SVP 6♓27'40"
GC 25♐38.2 ⚴ 16♐03.7
Eris 26♓06.0R ⚵ 17♓51.6
⚷ 10♓29.8 ⚶ 21♒11.8
☽ Mean ☊ 20♓01.1

LONGITUDE — January 1914

Day	Sid.Time	☉	0 hr ☽	Noon ☽	True ☊	☿	♀	♂	⚳	♃	♄	♅	♆	♇
1 Th	18 41 10	10♑15 18	1♓11 58	7♓14 21	17♓09.7	26♐30.7	0♑20.7	16♋19.1	11♑05.2	25♑16.7	12♊43.5	6♒02.9	27♋17.8	29♊54.9
2 F	18 45 07	11 16 28	13 13 46	19 10 48	17D 09.3	28 01.2	1 36.1	15R 55.2	11 29.3	25 30.6	12R 39.5	6 06.1	27R 16.2	29R 53.7
3 Sa	18 49 03	12 17 38	25 06 03	1♈00 12	17 09.8	29 32.1	2 51.6	15 31.3	11 53.4	25 44.6	12 35.5	6 09.4	27 14.6	29 52.5
4 Su	18 53 00	13 18 48	6♈53 56	12 47 55	17R 10.2	1♑03.5	4 07.0	15 07.3	12 17.5	25 58.5	12 31.6	6 12.7	27 13.0	29 51.3
5 M	18 56 56	14 19 57	18 42 52	24 39 28	17 09.5	2 35.2	5 22.5	14 43.3	12 41.5	26 12.5	12 27.8	6 16.0	27 11.3	29 50.2
6 Tu	19 00 53	15 21 06	0♉38 23	6♉40 16	17 07.0	4 07.4	6 37.9	14 19.4	13 05.6	26 26.5	12 24.0	6 19.3	27 09.7	29 49.0
7 W	19 04 50	16 22 15	12 45 43	18 55 15	17 02.1	5 40.0	7 53.4	13 55.6	13 29.7	26 40.5	12 20.4	6 22.7	27 08.0	29 47.9
8 Th	19 08 46	17 23 24	25 09 21	1♊28 24	16 54.8	7 12.9	9 08.8	13 32.0	13 53.7	26 54.5	12 16.8	6 26.0	27 06.4	29 46.7
9 F	19 12 43	18 24 32	7♊52 43	14 22 28	16 45.6	8 46.3	10 24.3	13 08.6	14 17.8	27 08.6	12 13.3	6 29.4	27 04.7	29 45.6
10 Sa	19 16 39	19 25 39	20 57 44	27 38 27	16 35.4	10 20.1	11 39.7	12 45.5	14 41.8	27 22.7	12 09.8	6 32.8	27 03.0	29 44.5
11 Su	19 20 36	20 26 46	4♋24 27	11♋15 26	16 25.2	11 54.4	12 55.1	12 22.6	15 05.8	27 36.7	12 06.5	6 36.2	27 01.4	29 43.4
12 M	19 24 32	21 27 53	18 10 59	25 10 36	16 16.1	13 29.1	14 10.6	12 00.1	15 29.8	27 50.8	12 03.3	6 39.6	26 59.7	29 42.2
13 Tu	19 28 29	22 29 00	2♌13 43	9♌19 41	16 08.9	15 04.2	15 26.0	11 38.0	15 53.8	28 05.0	12 00.1	6 43.0	26 58.0	29 41.1
14 W	19 32 26	23 30 06	16 27 51	23 37 32	16 04.3	16 39.9	16 41.4	11 16.3	16 17.8	28 19.1	11 57.0	6 46.5	26 56.3	29 40.1
15 Th	19 36 22	24 31 11	0♍48 08	7♍59 02	16D 02.1	18 16.0	17 56.8	10 55.0	16 41.7	28 33.2	11 54.1	6 49.9	26 54.6	29 39.0
16 F	19 40 19	25 32 17	15 09 44	22 19 45	16 02.0	19 52.6	19 12.2	10 34.3	17 05.7	28 47.3	11 51.2	6 53.4	26 52.9	29 37.9
17 Sa	19 44 15	26 33 22	29 28 44	6♎36 21	16 03.0	21 29.8	20 27.7	10 14.0	17 29.6	29 01.5	11 48.4	6 56.8	26 51.2	29 36.8
18 Su	19 48 12	27 34 27	13♎42 23	20 46 37	16R 04.0	23 07.5	21 43.1	9 54.4	17 53.5	29 15.6	11 45.7	7 00.3	26 49.5	29 35.8
19 M	19 52 08	28 35 31	27 48 57	4♏49 16	16 04.0	24 45.7	22 58.5	9 35.3	18 17.4	29 29.8	11 43.1	7 03.8	26 47.8	29 34.7
20 Tu	19 56 05	29 36 36	11♏47 28	18 43 28	16 02.2	26 24.5	24 13.9	9 16.8	18 41.2	29 43.9	11 40.6	7 07.2	26 46.1	29 33.7
21 W	20 00 01	0♒37 40	25 37 11	2♐28 32	15 58.4	28 03.9	25 29.3	8 59.0	19 05.1	29 58.1	11 38.2	7 10.7	26 44.4	29 32.7
22 Th	20 03 58	1 38 43	9♐17 22	16 03 35	15 52.6	29 43.9	26 44.7	8 41.8	19 28.9	0♒12.3	11 35.9	7 14.2	26 42.7	29 31.7
23 F	20 07 55	2 39 46	22 47 01	29 27 31	15 45.3	1♒24.5	28 00.1	8 25.4	19 52.7	0 26.4	11 33.7	7 17.7	26 41.1	29 30.7
24 Sa	20 11 51	3 40 49	6♑04 56	12♑39 05	15 37.5	3 05.7	29 15.5	8 09.6	20 16.5	0 40.6	11 31.6	7 21.3	26 39.4	29 29.8
25 Su	20 15 48	4 41 51	19 09 51	25 37 06	15 30.0	4 47.6	0♒30.9	7 54.6	20 40.2	0 54.8	11 29.6	7 24.8	26 37.7	29 28.8
26 M	20 19 44	5 42 52	2♒00 46	8♒20 48	15 23.6	6 30.0	1 46.3	7 40.4	21 03.9	1 08.9	11 27.7	7 28.3	26 36.0	29 27.8
27 Tu	20 23 41	6 43 52	14 37 13	20 50 05	15 18.9	8 13.1	3 01.7	7 26.9	21 27.6	1 23.1	11 26.0	7 31.8	26 34.3	29 26.9
28 W	20 27 37	7 44 51	26 59 31	3♓05 43	15 16.2	9 56.7	4 17.1	7 14.2	21 51.3	1 37.2	11 24.3	7 35.3	26 32.7	29 26.0
29 Th	20 31 34	8 45 48	9♓08 56	15 09 28	15D 15.3	11 41.0	5 32.4	7 02.3	22 14.9	1 51.3	11 22.7	7 38.8	26 31.0	29 25.1
30 F	20 35 30	9 46 45	21 07 41	27 04 01	15 16.0	13 25.9	6 47.8	6 51.2	22 38.5	2 05.4	11 21.3	7 42.3	26 29.4	29 24.2
31 Sa	20 39 27	10 47 41	2♈58 56	8♈52 56	15 17.6	15 11.3	8 03.1	6 41.0	23 02.0	2 19.5	11 20.0	7 45.8	26 27.7	29 23.3

LONGITUDE — February 1914

Day	Sid.Time	☉	0 hr ☽	Noon ☽	True ☊	☿	♀	♂	⚳	♃	♄	♅	♆	♇
1 Su	20 43 24	11♒48 35	14♈46 35	20♈40 28	15♓19.5	16♒57.3	9♒18.4	6♋31.5	23♑25.5	2♒33.6	11♊18.7	7♒49.3	26♋26.1	29♊22.5
2 M	20 47 20	12 49 28	26 35 12	2♉31 25	15R 21.0	18 43.7	10 33.8	6R 22.8	23 49.0	2 47.7	11R 17.6	7 52.8	26R 24.5	29R 21.6
3 Tu	20 51 17	13 50 19	8♉29 45	14 30 51	15 21.5	20 30.6	11 49.1	6 15.0	24 12.5	3 01.8	11 16.6	7 56.3	26 22.9	29 20.8
4 W	20 55 13	14 51 09	20 35 21	26 43 52	15 20.7	22 17.8	13 04.4	6 07.9	24 35.9	3 15.8	11 15.7	7 59.8	26 21.3	29 20.0
5 Th	20 59 10	15 51 58	2♊56 58	9♊15 10	15 18.6	24 05.3	14 19.7	6 01.7	24 59.3	3 29.8	11 15.0	8 03.3	26 19.7	29 19.2
6 F	21 03 06	16 52 46	15 38 57	22 08 40	15 15.3	25 52.9	15 34.9	5 56.3	25 22.6	3 43.8	11 14.3	8 06.8	26 18.1	29 18.5
7 Sa	21 07 03	17 53 31	28 44 37	5♋26 56	15 11.2	27 40.5	16 50.2	5 51.7	25 45.9	3 57.8	11 13.7	8 10.3	26 16.6	29 17.7
8 Su	21 10 59	18 54 16	12♋15 39	19 10 40	15 06.9	29 27.9	18 05.4	5 47.9	26 09.1	4 11.8	11 13.3	8 13.8	26 15.0	29 17.0
9 M	21 14 56	19 54 59	26 11 42	3♌18 20	15 03.1	1♓15.0	19 20.7	5 44.8	26 32.4	4 25.7	11 13.0	8 17.2	26 13.5	29 16.3
10 Tu	21 18 53	20 55 40	10♌30 00	17 46 02	15 00.2	3 01.5	20 35.9	5 42.6	26 55.5	4 39.6	11 12.8	8 20.7	26 12.0	29 15.6
11 W	21 22 49	21 56 20	25 05 36	2♍27 51	14D 58.6	4 47.1	21 51.1	5 41.1	27 18.7	4 53.5	11D 12.7	8 24.1	26 10.5	29 14.9
12 Th	21 26 46	22 56 59	9♍51 50	17 16 37	14 58.1	6 31.5	23 06.3	5D 40.3	27 41.7	5 07.3	11 12.7	8 27.5	26 09.0	29 14.3
13 F	21 30 42	23 57 36	24 41 16	2♎04 54	14 58.8	8 14.4	24 21.5	5 40.3	28 04.8	5 21.1	11 12.8	8 31.0	26 07.5	29 13.6
14 Sa	21 34 39	24 58 12	9♎26 45	16 46 04	15 00.0	9 55.3	25 36.7	5 41.1	28 27.7	5 34.9	11 13.1	8 34.4	26 06.1	29 13.0
15 Su	21 38 35	25 58 47	24 02 17	1♏14 54	15 01.4	11 33.7	26 51.9	5 42.6	28 50.7	5 48.7	11 13.4	8 37.8	26 04.6	29 12.4
16 M	21 42 32	26 59 21	8♏23 34	15 28 00	15R 02.4	13 09.2	28 07.0	5 44.8	29 13.6	6 02.4	11 13.9	8 41.1	26 03.2	29 11.8
17 Tu	21 46 28	27 59 54	22 28 02	29 23 37	15 02.7	14 41.3	29 22.2	5 47.7	29 36.4	6 16.1	11 14.5	8 44.5	26 01.8	29 11.3
18 W	21 50 25	29 00 25	6♐14 43	13♐01 24	15 02.2	16 09.2	0♓37.3	5 51.3	29 59.2	6 29.8	11 15.2	8 47.9	26 00.5	29 10.7
19 Th	21 54 22	0♓00 55	19 43 45	26 21 55	15 01.0	17 32.3	1 52.4	5 55.6	0♒22.0	6 43.4	11 16.0	8 51.2	25 59.1	29 10.2
20 F	21 58 18	1 01 24	2♑56 02	9♑26 17	14 59.2	18 50.1	3 07.6	6 00.6	0 44.7	6 57.0	11 16.9	8 54.5	25 57.8	29 09.7
21 Sa	22 02 15	2 01 52	15 52 50	22 15 50	14 57.3	20 01.8	4 22.7	6 06.3	1 07.3	7 10.5	11 17.9	8 57.8	25 56.5	29 09.2
22 Su	22 06 11	3 02 18	28 35 29	4♒51 57	14 55.4	21 06.9	5 37.8	6 12.6	1 29.9	7 24.0	11 19.1	9 01.1	25 55.2	29 08.8
23 M	22 10 08	4 02 42	11♒05 24	17 16 00	14 53.9	22 04.5	6 52.8	6 19.5	1 52.4	7 37.5	11 20.3	9 04.4	25 53.9	29 08.4
24 Tu	22 14 04	5 03 05	23 23 55	29 29 20	14 53.0	22 54.2	8 07.9	6 27.1	2 14.9	7 50.9	11 21.7	9 07.6	25 52.7	29 07.9
25 W	22 18 01	6 03 26	5♓32 27	11♓33 27	14D 52.6	23 35.4	9 22.9	6 35.4	2 37.3	8 04.3	11 23.2	9 10.9	25 51.4	29 07.6
26 Th	22 21 57	7 03 45	17 32 33	23 30 01	14 52.7	24 07.7	10 38.0	6 44.2	2 59.6	8 17.6	11 24.8	9 14.1	25 50.2	29 07.2
27 F	22 25 54	8 04 03	29 26 06	5♈21 06	14 53.1	24 30.7	11 53.0	6 53.6	3 21.9	8 30.9	11 26.5	9 17.3	25 49.0	29 06.8
28 Sa	22 29 51	9 04 18	11♈15 20	17 09 11	14 53.7	24R 44.2	13 08.0	7 03.7	3 44.1	8 44.1	11 28.3	9 20.4	25 47.9	29 06.5

Astro Data

	Dy Hr Mn
☽0N	3 5:32
♃☌♆	9 6:04
♃□♄	9 18:24
♄∠♆	15 1:23
☽0S	16 20:52
♃⊼♇	19 19:50
☽0N	30 12:47
♄∠♆	9 21:29
♄D	11 20:51
♂D	12 23:35
☽0S	13 4:23
☽0N	26 19:48
☿0N	27 4:18

Planet Ingress

	Dy Hr Mn
♀♑	1 5:25
☿♑	3 19:20
☉♒	20 21:12
♃♒	21 15:13
☿♒	22 15:51
♀♒	25 2:09
☿♓	8 19:11
♀♓	18 0:05
⚳♒	18 12:49
☉♓	19 11:38

Last Aspect / ☽ Ingress (January)

Last Aspect Dy Hr Mn		☽ Ingress	Dy Hr Mn
3 9:42	♇ □	♈	3 9:58
5 22:23	♇ ⚹	♉	5 22:43
8 3:44	♆ ⚹	♊	8 9:13
10 15:44	♇ ☌	♋	10 16:12
12 16:38	♃ ☍	♌	12 20:13
14 22:05	♇ ⚹	♍	14 22:40
17 0:15	♇ □	♎	17 0:53
19 3:02	♇ △	♏	19 3:44
21 7:32	♃ ⚹	♐	21 7:40
23 12:06	♇ ☍	♑	23 12:59
25 13:53	♆ ☍	♒	25 20:13
28 4:48	♇ △	♓	28 5:54
30 16:44	♇ □	♈	30 17:57

Last Aspect / ☽ Ingress (February)

Last Aspect Dy Hr Mn		☽ Ingress	Dy Hr Mn
2 5:37	♇ ⚹	♉	2 6:54
4 11:16	♆ ⚹	♊	4 18:20
7 1:00	♇ ☌	♋	7 2:16
9 0:04	♆ ☌	♌	9 6:26
11 6:47	♇ ⚹	♍	11 8:00
13 7:22	♇ □	♎	13 8:37
15 8:36	♇ △	♏	15 9:55
17 11:57	♀ □	♐	17 13:03
19 17:06	♇ ☍	♑	19 18:38
21 18:57	♆ ☍	♒	22 2:41
24 11:18	♇ △	♓	24 13:01
26 23:21	♇ □	♈	27 1:09

☽ Phases & Eclipses

Dy Hr Mn	
4 13:09	☽ 13♈22
12 5:09	○ 21♋10
19 0:30	☾ 28♎06
26 6:34	● 5♒29
3 10:32	☽ 13♉47
10 17:34	○ 21♌10
17 9:23	☾ 27♏53
25 0:02	● 5♓33
25 0:12:43	A 05'35"

Astro Data

1 January 1914
Julian Day # 5114
SVP 6♓27'34"
GC 25♐38.3 ⚴ 28♐54.1
Eris 26♓06.9 ⚵ 28♓35.4
⚷ 11♓13.7 ⚶ 3♓45.2
☽ Mean ☊ 18♓22.7

1 February 1914
Julian Day # 5145
SVP 6♓27'29"
GC 25♐38.4 ⚴ 11♑09.4
Eris 26♓19.5 ⚵ 13♈00.5
⚷ 12♓41.3 ⚶ 17♓31.1
☽ Mean ☊ 16♓44.2

March 1914 — LONGITUDE

Day	Sid.Time	☉	0 hr ☽	Noon ☽	True ☊	☿	♀	♂	⚳	♃	♄	♅	♆	♇
1 Su	22 33 47	10♓04 32	23♈03 02	28♈57 17	14♓54.4	24♓48.2	14♓23.0	7♋14.3	4♒06.2	8♒57.3	11♊30.2	9♒23.6	25♋46.8	29♊06.2
2 M	22 37 44	11 04 44	4♉52 25	10♉48 55	14 54.9	24R 42.6	15 37.9	7 25.4	4 28.3	9 10.4	11 32.3	9 26.7	25R 45.7	29R 05.9
3 Tu	22 41 40	12 04 54	16 47 17	22 48 03	14 55.2	24 27.7	16 52.9	7 37.2	4 50.3	9 23.4	11 34.4	9 29.8	25 44.6	29 05.7
4 W	22 45 37	13 05 01	28 51 47	4♊59 01	14R 55.3	24 04.0	18 07.8	7 49.4	5 12.2	9 36.4	11 36.6	9 32.9	25 43.6	29 05.5
5 Th	22 49 33	14 05 07	11♊10 20	17 26 16	14D 55.4	23 32.1	19 22.7	8 02.2	5 34.1	9 49.4	11 39.0	9 35.9	25 42.5	29 05.3
6 F	22 53 30	15 05 10	23 47 20	0♋14 02	14 55.4	22 52.7	20 37.6	8 15.5	5 55.9	10 02.3	11 41.5	9 39.0	25 41.5	29 05.1
7 Sa	22 57 26	16 05 12	6♋46 46	13 25 55	14 55.4	22 07.0	21 52.4	8 29.3	6 17.6	10 15.1	11 44.0	9 42.0	25 40.6	29 04.9
8 Su	23 01 23	17 05 11	20 11 44	27 04 20	14 55.6	21 16.1	23 07.2	8 43.6	6 39.3	10 27.9	11 46.7	9 44.9	25 39.6	29 04.8
9 M	23 05 20	18 05 08	4♌03 45	11♌09 49	14 55.9	20 21.1	24 22.1	8 58.4	7 00.9	10 40.6	11 49.5	9 47.9	25 38.7	29 04.7
10 Tu	23 09 16	19 05 03	18 22 14	25 40 30	14 56.2	19 23.6	25 36.9	9 13.7	7 22.4	10 53.2	11 52.3	9 50.8	25 37.9	29 04.6
11 W	23 13 13	20 04 55	3♍03 59	10♍31 50	14R 56.3	18 24.7	26 51.6	9 29.3	7 43.8	11 05.8	11 55.3	9 53.7	25 37.0	29 04.5
12 Th	23 17 09	21 04 46	18 03 07	25 36 43	14 56.3	17 25.8	28 06.4	9 45.5	8 05.1	11 18.3	11 58.4	9 56.5	25 36.2	29 04.4
13 F	23 21 06	22 04 35	3♎11 29	10♎46 15	14 55.9	16 28.3	29 21.1	10 02.1	8 26.4	11 30.8	12 01.6	9 59.4	25 35.4	29D 04.4
14 Sa	23 25 02	23 04 22	18 19 49	25 51 03	14 55.1	15 33.2	0♈35.8	10 19.0	8 47.6	11 43.1	12 04.8	10 02.2	25 34.6	29 04.4
15 Su	23 28 59	24 04 07	3♏18 56	10♏42 34	14 54.0	14 41.6	1 50.5	10 36.5	9 08.7	11 55.4	12 08.2	10 04.9	25 33.9	29 04.4
16 M	23 32 55	25 03 50	18 01 13	25 14 17	14 53.0	13 54.3	3 05.1	10 54.3	9 29.7	12 07.7	12 11.7	10 07.7	25 33.2	29 04.5
17 Tu	23 36 52	26 03 32	2♐21 23	9♐22 14	14 52.1	13 12.0	4 19.8	11 12.5	9 50.6	12 19.8	12 15.2	10 10.4	25 32.5	29 04.5
18 W	23 40 48	27 03 12	16 16 47	23 05 04	14D 51.6	12 35.2	5 34.4	11 31.1	10 11.4	12 31.9	12 18.9	10 13.1	25 31.9	29 04.6
19 Th	23 44 45	28 02 51	29 47 13	6♑23 31	14 51.7	12 04.2	6 49.0	11 50.1	10 32.2	12 43.9	12 22.6	10 15.7	25 31.3	29 04.7
20 F	23 48 42	29 02 27	12♑54 16	19 19 51	14 52.4	11 39.3	8 03.6	12 09.4	10 52.9	12 55.8	12 26.5	10 18.3	25 30.7	29 04.9
21 Sa	23 52 38	0♈02 02	25 40 41	1♒57 11	14 53.6	11 20.6	9 18.2	12 29.1	11 13.4	13 07.7	12 30.4	10 20.9	25 30.1	29 05.0
22 Su	23 56 35	1 01 35	8♒09 48	14 18 56	14 55.0	11 08.0	10 32.7	12 49.2	11 33.9	13 19.5	12 34.5	10 23.4	25 29.6	29 05.2
23 M	0 00 31	2 01 06	20 25 02	26 28 29	14 56.3	11D 01.5	11 47.3	13 09.6	11 54.3	13 31.1	12 38.6	10 25.9	25 29.1	29 05.4
24 Tu	0 04 28	3 00 36	2♓29 39	8♓28 55	14R 57.1	11 00.9	13 01.8	13 30.4	12 14.6	13 42.7	12 42.8	10 28.4	25 28.7	29 05.6
25 W	0 08 24	4 00 03	14 26 36	20 23 01	14 57.1	11 06.1	14 16.3	13 51.5	12 34.8	13 54.3	12 47.1	10 30.8	25 28.3	29 05.9
26 Th	0 12 21	4 59 28	26 18 28	2♈13 12	14 56.2	11 16.7	15 30.7	14 12.9	12 54.9	14 05.7	12 51.5	10 33.2	25 27.9	29 06.2
27 F	0 16 17	5 58 51	8♈07 30	14 01 36	14 54.1	11 32.6	16 45.1	14 34.6	13 14.8	14 17.0	12 55.9	10 35.5	25 27.5	29 06.4
28 Sa	0 20 14	6 58 13	19 55 47	25 50 17	14 51.0	11 53.6	17 59.6	14 56.7	13 34.7	14 28.3	13 00.5	10 37.9	25 27.2	29 06.8
29 Su	0 24 11	7 57 32	1♉45 22	7♉41 19	14 47.2	12 19.3	19 13.9	15 19.0	13 54.5	14 39.4	13 05.2	10 40.1	25 26.9	29 07.1
30 M	0 28 07	8 56 49	13 38 25	19 37 00	14 43.1	12 49.5	20 28.3	15 41.7	14 14.2	14 50.5	13 09.9	10 42.4	25 26.7	29 07.5
31 Tu	0 32 04	9 56 03	25 37 22	1♊39 55	14 39.1	13 24.0	21 42.6	16 04.7	14 33.7	15 01.4	13 14.7	10 44.6	25 26.4	29 07.8

April 1914 — LONGITUDE

Day	Sid.Time	☉	0 hr ☽	Noon ☽	True ☊	☿	♀	♂	⚳	♃	♄	♅	♆	♇
1 W	0 36 00	10♈55 16	7♊45 00	13♊53 03	14♓35.8	14♓02.5	22♈56.9	16♋27.9	14♒53.2	15♒12.3	13♊19.6	10♒46.7	25♋26.2	29♊08.3
2 Th	0 39 57	11 54 26	20 04 30	26 19 47	14R 33.5	14 44.9	24 11.2	16 51.4	15 12.5	15 23.0	13 24.6	10 48.8	25R 26.1	29 08.7
3 F	0 43 53	12 53 34	2♋39 21	9♋03 40	14D 32.5	15 30.8	25 25.5	17 15.2	15 31.7	15 33.7	13 29.6	10 50.9	25 26.0	29 09.1
4 Sa	0 47 50	13 52 40	15 33 10	22 08 17	14 32.7	16 20.2	26 39.7	17 39.3	15 50.8	15 44.3	13 34.8	10 53.0	25 25.9	29 09.6
5 Su	0 51 46	14 51 43	28 49 22	5♌36 44	14 33.8	17 12.8	27 53.9	18 03.6	16 09.8	15 54.7	13 40.0	10 55.0	25 25.8	29 10.1
6 M	0 55 43	15 50 44	12♌30 36	19 31 05	14 35.3	18 08.5	29 08.1	18 28.1	16 28.6	16 05.1	13 45.2	10 56.9	25D 25.8	29 10.6
7 Tu	0 59 40	16 49 43	26 38 09	3♍51 38	14R 36.6	19 07.1	0♉22.2	18 53.0	16 47.3	16 15.3	13 50.6	10 58.8	25 25.8	29 11.2
8 W	1 03 36	17 48 39	11♍11 09	18 36 12	14 36.8	20 08.4	1 36.3	19 18.0	17 06.0	16 25.5	13 56.0	11 00.7	25 25.9	29 11.7
9 Th	1 07 33	18 47 33	26 06 00	3♎39 39	14 35.7	21 12.5	2 50.4	19 43.3	17 24.4	16 35.5	14 01.5	11 02.5	25 25.9	29 12.3
10 F	1 11 29	19 46 25	11♎16 05	18 54 04	14 32.8	22 19.0	4 04.4	20 08.8	17 42.8	16 45.4	14 07.1	11 04.3	25 26.1	29 12.9
11 Sa	1 15 26	20 45 15	26 32 17	4♏09 26	14 28.4	23 28.0	5 18.5	20 34.5	18 01.0	16 55.2	14 12.7	11 06.0	25 26.2	29 13.5
12 Su	1 19 22	21 44 03	11♏44 12	19 15 20	14 23.0	24 39.3	6 32.5	21 00.4	18 19.1	17 04.9	14 18.5	11 07.7	25 26.4	29 14.2
13 M	1 23 19	22 42 50	26 41 45	4♐02 31	14 17.4	25 52.8	7 46.4	21 26.6	18 37.1	17 14.5	14 24.2	11 09.4	25 26.6	29 14.8
14 Tu	1 27 15	23 41 34	11♐16 55	18 24 25	14 12.4	27 08.5	9 00.4	21 52.9	18 54.9	17 23.9	14 30.1	11 11.0	25 26.8	29 15.5
15 W	1 31 12	24 40 17	25 24 43	2♑17 42	14 08.7	28 26.3	10 14.3	22 19.5	19 12.6	17 33.3	14 36.0	11 12.5	25 27.1	29 16.2
16 Th	1 35 09	25 38 58	9♑03 26	15 42 06	14D 06.5	29 46.2	11 28.2	22 46.2	19 30.2	17 42.5	14 42.0	11 14.0	25 27.4	29 16.9
17 F	1 39 05	26 37 38	22 14 05	28 39 48	14 06.0	1♈08.0	12 42.1	23 13.2	19 47.6	17 51.6	14 48.0	11 15.5	25 27.8	29 17.7
18 Sa	1 43 02	27 36 16	4♒59 46	11♒14 33	14 06.8	2 31.8	13 55.9	23 40.4	20 04.9	18 00.6	14 54.1	11 16.9	25 28.2	29 18.4
19 Su	1 46 58	28 34 52	17 24 43	23 30 54	14 08.2	3 57.4	15 09.7	24 07.7	20 22.0	18 09.4	15 00.3	11 18.3	25 28.6	29 19.2
20 M	1 50 55	29 33 26	29 33 40	5♓33 38	14R 09.5	5 25.0	16 23.5	24 35.2	20 39.0	18 18.2	15 06.5	11 19.6	25 29.0	29 20.0
21 Tu	1 54 51	0♉31 59	11♓31 20	17 27 18	14 09.7	6 54.3	17 37.3	25 03.0	20 55.8	18 26.8	15 12.8	11 20.9	25 29.5	29 20.8
22 W	1 58 48	1 30 30	23 22 01	29 15 58	14 08.4	8 25.5	18 51.0	25 30.9	21 12.4	18 35.2	15 19.1	11 22.1	25 30.0	29 21.7
23 Th	2 02 44	2 28 59	5♈09 32	11♈03 07	14 04.9	9 58.5	20 04.7	25 58.9	21 28.9	18 43.5	15 25.5	11 23.3	25 30.6	29 22.5
24 F	2 06 41	3 27 26	16 57 01	22 51 33	13 59.1	11 33.2	21 18.4	26 27.2	21 45.3	18 51.7	15 32.0	11 24.4	25 31.1	29 23.4
25 Sa	2 10 38	4 25 52	28 46 58	4♉43 31	13 51.3	13 09.8	22 32.0	26 55.6	22 01.5	18 59.8	15 38.5	11 25.5	25 31.8	29 24.3
26 Su	2 14 34	5 24 16	10♉41 22	16 40 44	13 42.0	14 48.1	23 45.6	27 24.2	22 17.5	19 07.7	15 45.0	11 26.6	25 32.4	29 25.2
27 M	2 18 31	6 22 38	22 41 48	28 44 43	13 31.9	16 28.1	24 59.2	27 52.9	22 33.4	19 15.5	15 51.6	11 27.6	25 33.1	29 26.1
28 Tu	2 22 27	7 20 58	4♊49 41	10♊56 51	13 22.1	18 10.0	26 12.8	28 21.9	22 49.0	19 23.1	15 58.3	11 28.5	25 33.8	29 27.1
29 W	2 26 24	8 19 16	17 06 27	23 18 41	13 13.4	19 53.6	27 26.3	28 50.9	23 04.5	19 30.6	16 05.0	11 29.4	25 34.5	29 28.0
30 Th	2 30 20	9 17 32	29 33 48	5♋52 03	13 06.6	21 39.0	28 39.9	29 20.2	23 19.9	19 38.0	16 11.8	11 30.3	25 35.3	29 29.0

Astro Data	Dy Hr Mn
☿ R	1 9:48
♃☌♅	4 3:24
☿0S	8 5:36
☽0S	12 14:47
♇ D	14 5:00
♀0N	16 9:26
♃△♄	16 23:05
☉0N	21 11:11
☿ D	24 2:24
☽0N	26 2:11
♃☍♇	26 13:01
♆ D	6 14:47
☽0S	9 1:59
☿0N	21 0:27
☽0N	22 7:59

Planet Ingress	Dy Hr Mn
♀ ♈	14 0:30
☉ ♈	21 11:11
♀ ♉	7 4:48
☿ ♈	16 16:06
☉ ♉	20 22:53

Last Aspect Dy Hr Mn		☽ Ingress	Dy Hr Mn
1 12:18	♇ ⚹	♉	1 14:07
3 17:50	♇ ⚹	♊	4 2:14
6 9:52	♆ ☌	♋	6 11:34
8 9:33	♆ ☌	♌	8 17:03
10 17:32	♇ ⚹	♍	10 19:02
12 17:29	♇ □	♎	12 18:57
14 17:10	♇ △	♏	14 18:39
16 12:32	♆ △	♐	16 20:01
18 22:43	♇ ☍	♑	19 0:23
21 8:00	☉ ⚹	♒	21 8:15
23 17:12	♇ △	♓	23 19:01
26 5:40	♇ □	♈	26 7:30
28 18:39	♇ ⚹	♉	28 20:27
30 23:38	♆ ⚹	♊	31 8:42

Last Aspect Dy Hr Mn		☽ Ingress	Dy Hr Mn
2 17:22	♇ ☌	♋	2 18:59
4 20:58	♀ □	♌	5 2:06
7 4:15	♇ ⚹	♍	7 5:37
9 4:56	♇ □	♎	9 6:12
11 4:13	♇ △	♏	11 5:27
12 21:58	♆ △	♐	13 5:23
15 6:42	♇ ☍	♑	15 7:59
17 7:52	☉ □	♒	17 14:31
19 23:32	♇ △	♓	20 0:52
22 12:12	♇ □	♈	22 13:30
25 1:15	♇ ⚹	♉	25 2:28
27 10:13	♂ ⚹	♊	27 14:29
29 23:50	♇ ☌	♋	30 0:50

☽ Phases & Eclipses Dy Hr Mn	
5 5:03	☽ 13♊48
12 4:18	○ 20♍46
12 4:13	☍ P 0.911
18 19:39	☾ 27♐22
26 18:09	● 5♈15
3 19:41	☽ 13♋12
10 13:28	○ 19♎50
17 7:52	☾ 26♑28
25 11:21	● 4♉24

Astro Data

1 March 1914
Julian Day # 5173
SVP 6♓27'25"
GC 25♐38.4 ⚵ 21♑12.9
Eris 26♓38.2 ⚴ 27♈53.9
⚷ 14♓21.8 ⚶ 0♈25.7
☽ Mean ☊ 15♓15.2

1 April 1914
Julian Day # 5204
SVP 6♓27'22"
GC 25♐38.5 ⚵ 0♒28.2
Eris 27♓02.0 ⚴ 15♉30.4
⚷ 16♓15.4 ⚶ 14♈49.6
☽ Mean ☊ 13♓36.7

LONGITUDE — May 1914

Day	Sid.Time	☉	0 hr ☽	Noon ☽	True ☊	☿	♀	♂	⚳	♃	♄	♅	♆	♇
1 F	2 34 17	10♉15 46	12♋13 45	18♋39 13	13♓02.1	23♈26.1	29♉53.3	29♋49.5	23♒35.0	19♒45.2	16♊18.6	11♒31.1	25♋36.1	29♊30.0
2 Sa	2 38 13	11 13 59	25 08 46	1♌42 44	12D59.9	25 15.1	1♊06.8	0♌19.1	23 50.0	19 52.3	16 25.5	11 31.8	25 36.9	29 31.0
3 Su	2 42 10	12 12 09	8♌21 28	15 05 17	12 59.5	27 05.9	2 20.2	0 48.7	24 04.8	19 59.2	16 32.4	11 32.5	25 37.8	29 32.1
4 M	2 46 07	13 10 17	21 54 27	28 49 12	13 00.0	28 58.4	3 33.6	1 18.5	24 19.4	20 05.9	16 39.3	11 33.1	25 38.7	29 33.1
5 Tu	2 50 03	14 08 23	5♍49 40	12♍55 53	13R00.5	0♉52.8	4 46.9	1 48.5	24 33.8	20 12.5	16 46.3	11 33.7	25 39.6	29 34.2
6 W	2 54 00	15 06 27	20 07 44	27 24 57	12 59.7	2 48.9	6 00.2	2 18.6	24 48.0	20 19.0	16 53.3	11 34.3	25 40.6	29 35.2
7 Th	2 57 56	16 04 29	4♎47 08	12♎13 37	12 56.8	4 46.8	7 13.5	2 48.8	25 02.1	20 25.3	17 00.4	11 34.8	25 41.6	29 36.3
8 F	3 01 53	17 02 29	19 43 38	27 16 12	12 51.4	6 46.4	8 26.7	3 19.1	25 15.9	20 31.4	17 07.5	11 35.2	25 42.6	29 37.4
9 Sa	3 05 49	18 00 28	4♏50 10	12♏24 20	12 43.7	8 47.7	9 39.9	3 49.6	25 29.5	20 37.4	17 14.6	11 35.6	25 43.6	29 38.5
10 Su	3 09 46	18 58 25	19 57 24	27 28 06	12 34.3	10 50.7	10 53.1	4 20.2	25 43.0	20 43.3	17 21.8	11 36.0	25 44.7	29 39.7
11 M	3 13 42	19 56 21	4♐55 13	12♐17 39	12 24.3	12 55.2	12 06.2	4 50.9	25 56.2	20 48.9	17 29.0	11 36.3	25 45.8	29 40.8
12 Tu	3 17 39	20 54 15	19 34 28	26 44 54	12 15.0	15 01.2	13 19.3	5 21.7	26 09.3	20 54.4	17 36.3	11 36.6	25 46.9	29 42.0
13 W	3 21 36	21 52 08	3♑48 25	10♑44 41	12 07.3	17 08.5	14 32.4	5 52.6	26 22.1	20 59.8	17 43.6	11 36.8	25 48.1	29 43.2
14 Th	3 25 32	22 49 59	17 33 35	24 15 10	12 01.8	19 17.0	15 45.4	6 23.7	26 34.7	21 05.0	17 50.9	11 36.9	25 49.3	29 44.4
15 F	3 29 29	23 47 50	0♒49 41	7♒17 29	11 58.7	21 26.6	16 58.5	6 54.9	26 47.1	21 10.0	17 58.3	11 37.0	25 50.5	29 45.6
16 Sa	3 33 25	24 45 39	13 39 02	19 54 54	11D57.6	23 36.9	18 11.4	7 26.2	26 59.2	21 14.8	18 05.6	11R37.1	25 51.7	29 46.8
17 Su	3 37 22	25 43 27	26 05 41	2♓12 02	11R57.6	25 47.9	19 24.4	7 57.6	27 11.2	21 19.5	18 13.1	11 37.1	25 53.0	29 48.0
18 M	3 41 18	26 41 13	8♓14 39	14 14 11	11 57.7	27 59.2	20 37.3	8 29.1	27 22.9	21 24.0	18 20.5	11 37.0	25 54.3	29 49.2
19 Tu	3 45 15	27 38 59	20 11 19	26 06 41	11 56.9	0♊10.7	21 50.2	9 00.7	27 34.4	21 28.3	18 28.0	11 36.9	25 55.6	29 50.5
20 W	3 49 11	28 36 43	2♈00 54	7♈54 33	11 54.2	2 21.9	23 03.0	9 32.4	27 45.6	21 32.5	18 35.5	11 36.8	25 57.0	29 51.7
21 Th	3 53 08	29 34 27	13 48 10	19 42 14	11 49.0	4 32.7	24 15.9	10 04.3	27 56.6	21 36.5	18 43.0	11 36.6	25 58.4	29 53.0
22 F	3 57 05	0♊32 09	25 37 12	1♉33 27	11 41.0	6 42.8	25 28.7	10 36.2	28 07.4	21 40.3	18 50.6	11 36.4	25 59.8	29 54.3
23 Sa	4 01 01	1 29 50	7♉31 18	13 31 02	11 30.5	8 51.9	26 41.4	11 08.3	28 17.9	21 43.9	18 58.1	11 36.1	26 01.2	29 55.6
24 Su	4 04 58	2 27 30	19 32 53	25 37 01	11 18.0	10 59.7	27 54.1	11 40.4	28 28.2	21 47.4	19 05.7	11 35.7	26 02.6	29 56.9
25 M	4 08 54	3 25 09	1♊43 34	7♊52 39	11 04.6	13 06.0	29 06.8	12 12.7	28 38.2	21 50.6	19 13.3	11 35.4	26 04.1	29 58.2
26 Tu	4 12 51	4 22 46	14 04 20	20 18 39	10 51.4	15 10.6	0♋19.5	12 45.1	28 48.0	21 53.7	19 21.0	11 34.9	26 05.6	29 59.5
27 W	4 16 47	5 20 22	26 35 39	2♋55 23	10 39.6	17 13.2	1 32.1	13 17.5	28 57.5	21 56.6	19 28.6	11 34.4	26 07.2	0♋00.8
28 Th	4 20 44	6 17 57	9♋17 52	15 43 11	10 30.0	19 13.8	2 44.7	13 50.1	29 06.7	21 59.3	19 36.3	11 33.9	26 08.7	0 02.2
29 F	4 24 40	7 15 31	22 11 25	28 42 39	10 23.2	21 12.1	3 57.3	14 22.7	29 15.7	22 01.9	19 44.0	11 33.3	26 10.3	0 03.5
30 Sa	4 28 37	8 13 04	5♌17 03	11♌54 45	10 19.3	23 08.1	5 09.8	14 55.5	29 24.4	22 04.2	19 51.7	11 32.7	26 11.9	0 04.9
31 Su	4 32 34	9 10 35	18 35 56	25 20 47	10 17.6	25 01.6	6 22.2	15 28.3	29 32.8	22 06.4	19 59.5	11 32.0	26 13.5	0 06.3

LONGITUDE — June 1914

Day	Sid.Time	☉	0 hr ☽	Noon ☽	True ☊	☿	♀	♂	⚳	♃	♄	♅	♆	♇
1 M	4 36 30	10♊08 04	2♍09 30	9♍02 14	10♓17.4	26♊52.6	7♋34.7	16♌01.2	29♒41.0	22♒08.3	20♊07.2	11♒31.3	26♋15.2	0♋07.6
2 Tu	4 40 27	11 05 32	15 59 07	23 00 15	10R17.2	28 41.0	8 47.1	16 34.3	29 48.9	22 10.1	20 14.9	11R30.6	26 16.8	0 09.0
3 W	4 44 23	12 02 59	0♎05 35	7♎15 01	10 15.9	0♋26.7	9 59.4	17 07.3	29 56.5	22 11.7	20 22.7	11 29.8	26 18.5	0 10.4
4 Th	4 48 20	13 00 25	14 28 20	21 45 09	10 12.4	2 09.7	11 11.7	17 40.5	0♓03.8	22 13.1	20 30.5	11 28.9	26 20.2	0 11.8
5 F	4 52 16	13 57 49	29 04 57	6♏27 03	10 06.3	3 50.0	12 24.0	18 13.8	0 10.8	22 14.3	20 38.2	11 28.0	26 22.0	0 13.2
6 Sa	4 56 13	14 55 13	13♏50 39	21 14 51	9 57.7	5 27.6	13 36.2	18 47.1	0 17.5	22 15.4	20 46.0	11 27.1	26 23.7	0 14.6
7 Su	5 00 09	15 52 36	28 38 37	6♐00 56	9 47.2	7 02.4	14 48.3	19 20.6	0 24.0	22 16.2	20 53.8	11 26.1	26 25.5	0 16.0
8 M	5 04 06	16 49 57	13♐20 44	20 37 01	9 36.0	8 34.4	16 00.5	19 54.1	0 30.1	22 16.9	21 01.6	11 25.1	26 27.3	0 17.4
9 Tu	5 08 03	17 47 18	27 48 53	4♑55 34	9 25.3	10 03.5	17 12.6	20 27.7	0 36.0	22 17.3	21 09.4	11 24.0	26 29.1	0 18.8
10 W	5 11 59	18 44 39	11♑56 27	18 51 04	9 16.2	11 29.9	18 24.6	21 01.3	0 41.5	22R17.6	21 17.2	11 22.9	26 30.9	0 20.3
11 Th	5 15 56	19 41 58	25 39 10	2♒20 38	9 09.5	12 53.3	19 36.6	21 35.1	0 46.7	22 17.7	21 25.1	11 21.7	26 32.8	0 21.7
12 F	5 19 52	20 39 17	8♒55 33	15 24 06	9 05.4	14 13.8	20 48.5	22 08.9	0 51.7	22 17.6	21 32.9	11 20.5	26 34.6	0 23.1
13 Sa	5 23 49	21 36 36	21 46 39	28 03 38	9D03.4	15 31.4	22 00.5	22 42.8	0 56.3	22 17.3	21 40.7	11 19.3	26 36.5	0 24.6
14 Su	5 27 45	22 33 54	4♓15 34	10♓23 02	9 03.1	16 46.0	23 12.3	23 16.8	1 00.5	22 16.8	21 48.5	11 18.0	26 38.4	0 26.0
15 M	5 31 42	23 31 12	16 26 41	22 27 10	9R03.2	17 57.6	24 24.1	23 50.9	1 04.5	22 16.1	21 56.3	11 16.7	26 40.3	0 27.4
16 Tu	5 35 39	24 28 29	28 25 10	4♈21 21	9 02.8	19 06.0	25 35.9	24 25.0	1 08.1	22 15.2	22 04.1	11 15.3	26 42.3	0 28.9
17 W	5 39 35	25 25 46	10♈16 23	16 10 56	9 01.0	20 11.2	26 47.6	24 59.2	1 11.4	22 14.1	22 11.9	11 13.9	26 44.2	0 30.3
18 Th	5 43 32	26 23 03	22 05 36	28 00 59	8 56.9	21 13.3	27 59.3	25 33.5	1 14.4	22 12.8	22 19.7	11 12.5	26 46.2	0 31.8
19 F	5 47 28	27 20 19	3♉57 36	9♉55 58	8 50.3	22 11.9	29 11.0	26 07.8	1 17.0	22 11.4	22 27.5	11 11.0	26 48.1	0 33.2
20 Sa	5 51 25	28 17 36	15 56 30	21 59 34	8 41.3	23 07.2	0♌22.6	26 42.3	1 19.3	22 09.7	22 35.3	11 09.5	26 50.1	0 34.7
21 Su	5 55 21	29 14 52	28 05 29	4♊14 30	8 30.5	23 59.0	1 34.1	27 16.8	1 21.3	22 07.9	22 43.1	11 07.9	26 52.1	0 36.1
22 M	5 59 18	0♋12 07	10♊26 48	16 42 28	8 18.8	24 47.1	2 45.6	27 51.4	1 22.9	22 05.9	22 50.9	11 06.3	26 54.2	0 37.6
23 Tu	6 03 14	1 09 23	23 01 35	29 24 08	8 07.2	25 31.6	3 57.1	28 26.1	1 24.2	22 03.6	22 58.7	11 04.7	26 56.2	0 39.0
24 W	6 07 11	2 06 38	5♋50 04	12♋19 18	7 56.8	26 12.2	5 08.5	29 00.8	1 25.1	22 01.2	23 06.5	11 03.0	26 58.3	0 40.5
25 Th	6 11 08	3 03 53	18 51 42	25 27 10	7 48.4	26 48.8	6 19.8	29 35.6	1 25.7	21 58.6	23 14.2	11 01.4	27 00.3	0 42.0
26 F	6 15 04	4 01 07	2♌05 33	8♌46 44	7 42.6	27 21.4	7 31.1	0♍10.5	1R25.9	21 55.9	23 22.0	10 59.6	27 02.4	0 43.4
27 Sa	6 19 01	4 58 21	15 30 35	22 17 00	7 39.5	27 49.9	8 42.4	0 45.4	1 25.8	21 52.9	23 29.7	10 57.9	27 04.5	0 44.9
28 Su	6 22 57	5 55 35	29 05 56	5♍57 20	7D38.5	28 14.0	9 53.5	1 20.4	1 25.3	21 49.8	23 37.4	10 56.1	27 06.6	0 46.3
29 M	6 26 54	6 52 48	12♍51 09	19 47 22	7 38.8	28 33.7	11 04.7	1 55.5	1 24.5	21 46.4	23 45.1	10 54.2	27 08.7	0 47.8
30 Tu	6 30 50	7 50 00	26 45 57	3♎46 52	7R39.4	28 48.9	12 15.7	2 30.7	1 23.3	21 42.9	23 52.8	10 52.4	27 10.8	0 49.2

Astro Data

	Dy Hr Mn
☽ 0S	6 11:31
♅ R	17 2:40
☽ 0N	19 13:45
☽ 0S	2 18:17
♃ R	11 9:56
☽ 0N	15 20:07
♃ △ ♄	17 17:47
⚳ R	26 15:09
☽ 0S	29 23:06

Planet Ingress

		Dy Hr Mn
♀	♊	1 14:11
♂	♌	1 20:31
☿	♉	5 0:58
☿	♊	19 10:03
☉	♊	21 22:38
♀	♋	26 5:34
♇	♋	26 20:50
☿	♋	3 5:53
⚳	♓	3 23:29
♀	♌	20 4:26
☉	♋	22 6:55
♂	♍	26 4:48

Last Aspect / ☽ Ingress (May)

Last Aspect Dy Hr Mn			☽ Ingress	Dy Hr Mn
2 0:51	♆	☌	♌	2 8:53
4 13:16	♇	⚹	♍	4 14:02
6 15:33	♇	□	♎	6 16:13
8 15:44	♇	△	♏	8 16:20
10 9:14	♆	△	♐	10 16:04
12 17:00	♇	☍	♑	12 17:30
14 14:51	♆	☍	♒	14 22:29
17 7:15	♇	△	♓	17 7:40
19 19:35	♇	□	♈	19 19:54
22 8:39	♇	⚹	♉	22 8:51
24 12:51	♆	⚹	♊	24 20:37
26 15:03	♃	△	♋	27 6:28
29 7:20	♆	☌	♌	29 14:22
31 11:21	☿	⚹	♍	31 20:13

Last Aspect / ☽ Ingress (June)

Last Aspect Dy Hr Mn			☽ Ingress	Dy Hr Mn
2 23:00	☿	□	♎	2 23:51
4 19:32	♆	□	♏	5 1:30
6 20:22	♆	△	♐	7 2:12
8 14:46	♃	⚹	♑	9 3:40
11 1:34	♆	☍	♒	11 7:46
13 1:18	♂	☍	♓	13 15:44
15 20:30	♆	△	♈	16 3:11
18 11:56	♀	□	♉	18 16:01
20 21:44	♂	□	♊	21 3:44
23 10:06	♂	⚹	♋	23 13:07
25 14:49	♆	☌	♌	25 20:14
27 14:10	♄	⚹	♍	28 1:35
30 3:22	☿	⚹	♎	30 5:32

☽ Phases & Eclipses

Dy Hr Mn		
3 6:29	☽	11♌59
9 21:30	○	18♏23
16 22:12	☾	25♒10
25 2:34	●	3♊03
1 14:03	☽	10♍13
8 5:18	○	16♐34
15 14:20	☾	23♓37
23 15:33	●	1♋18
30 19:24	☽	8♎08

Astro Data

1 May 1914
Julian Day # 5234
SVP 6♓27'17"
GC 25♐38.6 ⚴ 6♒26.7
Eris 27♓22.6 ⚵ 3♊00.9
⚷ 17♓47.3 ⚶ 28♈34.0
☽ Mean ☊ 12♓01.4

1 June 1914
Julian Day # 5265
SVP 6♓27'12"
GC 25♐38.6 ⚴ 7♒54.6R
Eris 27♓36.4 ⚵ 21♊04.7
⚷ 18♓45.5 ⚶ 12♉17.1
☽ Mean ☊ 10♓22.9

July 1914 LONGITUDE

Day	Sid.Time	☉	0 hr ☽	Noon ☽	True ☊	☿	♀	♂	⚳	♃	♄	♅	♆	♇
1 W	6 34 47	8♋47 12	10♎50 03	17♎55 21	7♓39.1	28♋59.6	13♌26.7	3♍05.9	1♓21.7	21♒39.3	24♊00.4	10♒50.5	27♋12.9	0♋50.6
2 Th	6 38 43	9 44 24	25 02 38	2♏11 37	7R 37.1	29R 05.6	14 37.7	3 41.2	1R 19.8	21R 35.4	24 08.1	10R 48.6	27 15.1	0 52.1
3 F	6 42 40	10 41 35	9♏21 59	16 33 18	7 32.9	29 07.0	15 48.5	4 16.5	1 17.6	21 31.4	24 15.7	10 46.6	27 17.2	0 53.5
4 Sa	6 46 37	11 38 46	23 45 03	0♐56 41	7 26.6	29 03.7	16 59.4	4 51.9	1 15.0	21 27.2	24 23.3	10 44.7	27 19.4	0 55.0
5 Su	6 50 33	12 35 58	8♐07 33	15 16 57	7 18.8	28 55.7	18 10.1	5 27.4	1 12.0	21 22.8	24 30.9	10 42.7	27 21.5	0 56.4
6 M	6 54 30	13 33 08	22 24 12	29 28 36	7 10.3	28 43.2	19 20.8	6 02.9	1 08.7	21 18.3	24 38.4	10 40.6	27 23.7	0 57.8
7 Tu	6 58 26	14 30 19	6♑29 31	13♑26 21	7 02.2	28 26.3	20 31.4	6 38.5	1 05.0	21 13.6	24 46.0	10 38.6	27 25.9	0 59.2
8 W	7 02 23	15 27 30	20 18 38	27 05 57	6 55.3	28 05.2	21 41.9	7 14.2	1 01.0	21 08.8	24 53.5	10 36.5	27 28.1	1 00.7
9 Th	7 06 19	16 24 42	3♒48 02	10♒24 44	6 50.3	27 40.2	22 52.4	7 49.9	0 56.6	21 03.8	25 00.9	10 34.4	27 30.2	1 02.1
10 F	7 10 16	17 21 53	16 56 01	23 21 59	6 47.4	27 11.5	24 02.8	8 25.7	0 51.9	20 58.7	25 08.4	10 32.3	27 32.4	1 03.5
11 Sa	7 14 13	18 19 05	29 42 48	5♓58 47	6D 46.5	26 39.5	25 13.1	9 01.5	0 46.8	20 53.4	25 15.8	10 30.2	27 34.6	1 04.9
12 Su	7 18 09	19 16 17	12♓10 18	18 17 48	6 47.0	26 04.8	26 23.3	9 37.4	0 41.4	20 47.9	25 23.2	10 28.0	27 36.8	1 06.3
13 M	7 22 06	20 13 30	24 21 48	0♈22 52	6 48.3	25 27.9	27 33.5	10 13.4	0 35.6	20 42.3	25 30.6	10 25.8	27 39.1	1 07.7
14 Tu	7 26 02	21 10 43	6♈21 34	12 18 32	6R 49.5	24 49.2	28 43.6	10 49.4	0 29.5	20 36.6	25 37.9	10 23.6	27 41.3	1 09.0
15 W	7 29 59	22 07 56	18 14 24	24 09 49	6 49.8	24 09.6	29 53.7	11 25.5	0 23.0	20 30.7	25 45.2	10 21.4	27 43.5	1 10.4
16 Th	7 33 55	23 05 11	0♉05 25	6♉01 48	6 48.8	23 29.5	1♍03.6	12 01.7	0 16.2	20 24.7	25 52.5	10 19.1	27 45.7	1 11.8
17 F	7 37 52	24 02 26	11 59 35	17 59 21	6 46.1	22 49.8	2 13.5	12 37.9	0 09.1	20 18.5	25 59.7	10 16.9	27 47.9	1 13.2
18 Sa	7 41 48	24 59 42	24 01 36	0♊06 50	6 41.7	22 11.2	3 23.3	13 14.2	0 01.7	20 12.3	26 06.9	10 14.6	27 50.1	1 14.5
19 Su	7 45 45	25 56 58	6♊15 29	12 27 53	6 35.9	21 34.3	4 33.0	13 50.5	29♒53.9	20 05.9	26 14.1	10 12.3	27 52.4	1 15.9
20 M	7 49 42	26 54 16	18 44 22	25 05 07	6 29.3	20 59.7	5 42.7	14 27.0	29 45.8	19 59.4	26 21.2	10 10.0	27 54.6	1 17.2
21 Tu	7 53 38	27 51 33	1♋30 17	7♋59 55	6 22.7	20 28.2	6 52.3	15 03.4	29 37.4	19 52.7	26 28.3	10 07.7	27 56.8	1 18.5
22 W	7 57 35	28 48 52	14 33 59	21 12 22	6 16.8	20 00.3	8 01.7	15 40.0	29 28.6	19 46.0	26 35.4	10 05.4	27 59.1	1 19.8
23 Th	8 01 31	29 46 11	27 54 55	4♌41 22	6 12.2	19 36.6	9 11.1	16 16.6	29 19.6	19 39.2	26 42.4	10 03.0	28 01.3	1 21.2
24 F	8 05 28	0♌43 31	11♌31 25	18 24 44	6 09.2	19 17.6	10 20.4	16 53.2	29 10.3	19 32.2	26 49.4	10 00.7	28 03.5	1 22.5
25 Sa	8 09 24	1 40 51	25 20 57	2♍19 42	6D 08.1	19 03.5	11 29.7	17 30.0	29 00.7	19 25.2	26 56.3	9 58.3	28 05.7	1 23.7
26 Su	8 13 21	2 38 12	9♍20 35	16 23 15	6 08.3	18 54.9	12 38.8	18 06.7	28 50.8	19 18.1	27 03.2	9 56.0	28 08.0	1 25.0
27 M	8 17 17	3 35 33	23 27 19	0♎32 29	6 09.5	18D 51.9	13 47.8	18 43.6	28 40.7	19 10.8	27 10.0	9 53.6	28 10.2	1 26.3
28 Tu	8 21 14	4 32 54	7♎38 24	14 44 47	6 10.9	18 54.9	14 56.8	19 20.5	28 30.2	19 03.5	27 16.8	9 51.2	28 12.4	1 27.5
29 W	8 25 11	5 30 17	21 51 23	28 57 54	6R 11.9	19 03.9	16 05.6	19 57.4	28 19.6	18 56.2	27 23.5	9 48.8	28 14.6	1 28.8
30 Th	8 29 07	6 27 39	6♏04 07	13♏09 45	6 11.9	19 19.1	17 14.3	20 34.5	28 08.7	18 48.8	27 30.2	9 46.4	28 16.8	1 30.0
31 F	8 33 04	7 25 02	20 14 33	27 18 14	6 10.6	19 40.6	18 22.9	21 11.5	27 57.6	18 41.3	27 36.9	9 44.1	28 19.0	1 31.2

August 1914 LONGITUDE

Day	Sid.Time	☉	0 hr ☽	Noon ☽	True ☊	☿	♀	♂	⚳	♃	♄	♅	♆	♇
1 Sa	8 37 00	8♌22 26	4♐20 32	11♐21 08	6♓08.1	20♋08.4	19♍31.4	21♍48.7	27♒46.2	18♒33.7	27♊43.5	9♒41.7	28♋21.2	1♋32.4
2 Su	8 40 57	9 19 51	18 19 44	25 16 02	6R 04.7	20 42.5	20 39.8	22 25.9	27R 34.7	18R 26.1	27 50.0	9R 39.3	28 23.4	1 33.6
3 M	8 44 53	10 17 16	2♑09 41	9♑00 23	6 01.0	21 22.9	21 48.1	23 03.1	27 22.9	18 18.5	27 56.5	9 36.9	28 25.6	1 34.8
4 Tu	8 48 50	11 14 42	15 47 51	22 31 49	5 57.3	22 09.6	22 56.3	23 40.4	27 11.0	18 10.8	28 02.9	9 34.5	28 27.8	1 36.0
5 W	8 52 46	12 12 09	29 12 03	5♒48 23	5 54.3	23 02.4	24 04.3	24 17.8	26 58.8	18 03.0	28 09.3	9 32.1	28 30.0	1 37.2
6 Th	8 56 43	13 09 36	12♒20 40	18 48 50	5 52.3	24 01.2	25 12.2	24 55.2	26 46.6	17 55.3	28 15.7	9 29.7	28 32.2	1 38.3
7 F	9 00 40	14 07 05	25 12 53	1♓32 51	5D 51.4	25 05.9	26 20.0	25 32.7	26 34.1	17 47.5	28 21.9	9 27.3	28 34.3	1 39.4
8 Sa	9 04 36	15 04 35	7♓48 54	14 01 11	5 51.6	26 16.4	27 27.7	26 10.2	26 21.5	17 39.7	28 28.1	9 24.9	28 36.5	1 40.6
9 Su	9 08 33	16 02 06	20 09 58	26 15 33	5 52.5	27 32.4	28 35.2	26 47.8	26 08.8	17 31.9	28 34.3	9 22.6	28 38.6	1 41.7
10 M	9 12 29	16 59 38	2♈18 18	8♈18 38	5 53.9	28 53.8	29 42.6	27 25.4	25 56.0	17 24.0	28 40.4	9 20.2	28 40.8	1 42.7
11 Tu	9 16 26	17 57 12	14 17 01	20 13 55	5 55.4	0♌20.2	0♎49.9	28 03.1	25 43.1	17 16.2	28 46.4	9 17.8	28 42.9	1 43.8
12 W	9 20 22	18 54 47	26 09 53	2♉05 28	5 56.6	1 51.5	1 57.1	28 40.9	25 30.0	17 08.3	28 52.4	9 15.5	28 45.0	1 44.9
13 Th	9 24 19	19 52 23	8♉01 14	13 57 47	5R 57.3	3 27.2	3 04.1	29 18.7	25 16.9	17 00.5	28 58.3	9 13.1	28 47.1	1 45.9
14 F	9 28 15	20 50 01	19 55 41	25 55 33	5 57.4	5 07.1	4 10.9	29 56.6	25 03.7	16 52.7	29 04.1	9 10.8	28 49.2	1 46.9
15 Sa	9 32 12	21 47 41	1♊57 57	8♊03 26	5 56.7	6 50.8	5 17.7	0♎34.5	24 50.5	16 44.9	29 09.9	9 08.5	28 51.3	1 47.9
16 Su	9 36 09	22 45 22	14 12 32	20 25 45	5 55.6	8 37.8	6 24.2	1 12.5	24 37.3	16 37.1	29 15.6	9 06.2	28 53.4	1 48.9
17 M	9 40 05	23 43 05	26 43 30	3♋06 10	5 54.1	10 27.8	7 30.7	1 50.6	24 24.0	16 29.4	29 21.3	9 03.9	28 55.5	1 49.9
18 Tu	9 44 02	24 40 49	9♋34 03	16 07 21	5 52.5	12 20.4	8 37.0	2 28.7	24 10.7	16 21.7	29 26.9	9 01.6	28 57.5	1 50.9
19 W	9 47 58	25 38 35	22 46 11	29 30 33	5 51.2	14 15.1	9 43.1	3 06.9	23 57.4	16 14.1	29 32.4	8 59.3	28 59.6	1 51.8
20 Th	9 51 55	26 36 22	6♌20 23	13♌15 25	5 50.2	16 11.6	10 49.1	3 45.1	23 44.2	16 06.4	29 37.8	8 57.1	29 01.6	1 52.8
21 F	9 55 51	27 34 11	20 15 21	27 19 45	5D 49.7	18 09.4	11 54.9	4 23.4	23 30.9	15 58.9	29 43.2	8 54.8	29 03.6	1 53.7
22 Sa	9 59 48	28 32 01	4♍28 05	11♍39 43	5 49.7	20 08.2	13 00.5	5 01.8	23 17.8	15 51.4	29 48.5	8 52.6	29 05.6	1 54.6
23 Su	10 03 44	29 29 52	18 54 01	26 10 13	5 50.0	22 07.6	14 06.0	5 40.2	23 04.7	15 44.0	29 53.7	8 50.4	29 07.6	1 55.4
24 M	10 07 41	0♍27 45	3♎27 37	10♎45 29	5 50.4	24 07.4	15 11.2	6 18.7	22 51.6	15 36.6	29 58.8	8 48.2	29 09.6	1 56.3
25 Tu	10 11 38	1 25 39	18 03 05	25 19 47	5 50.9	26 07.2	16 16.3	6 57.2	22 38.7	15 29.3	0♋03.9	8 46.1	29 11.5	1 57.1
26 W	10 15 34	2 23 34	2♏34 58	9♏48 05	5 51.2	28 06.9	17 21.2	7 35.8	22 25.9	15 22.1	0 08.9	8 43.9	29 13.5	1 57.9
27 Th	10 19 31	3 21 31	16 58 42	24 06 25	5R 51.4	0♍06.1	18 26.0	8 14.5	22 13.1	15 15.0	0 13.8	8 41.8	29 15.4	1 58.7
28 F	10 23 27	4 19 29	1♐10 57	8♐12 03	5 51.4	2 04.8	19 30.5	8 53.2	22 00.6	15 08.0	0 18.6	8 39.7	29 17.3	1 59.5
29 Sa	10 27 24	5 17 28	15 09 35	22 03 25	5D 51.4	4 02.8	20 34.7	9 31.9	21 48.2	15 01.1	0 23.4	8 37.7	29 19.2	2 00.3
30 Su	10 31 20	6 15 28	28 53 31	5♑39 52	5 51.4	6 00.0	21 38.8	10 10.8	21 35.9	14 54.3	0 28.1	8 35.6	29 21.0	2 01.0
31 M	10 35 17	7 13 30	12♑22 28	19 01 22	5 51.5	7 56.2	22 42.7	10 49.6	21 23.8	14 47.6	0 32.7	8 33.6	29 22.9	2 01.7

Astro Data

	Dy Hr Mn
☿R	3 6:58
♄⚼♅	13 0:00
☽0N	13 3:23
☽0S	27 4:11
☿D	27 12:10
☽0N	9 11:11
♄⚺♆	10 14:25
♀0S	11 2:45
♃⚼♇	15 3:44
♂0S	16 13:47
☽0S	23 11:26
♃⚼♄	27 14:26

Planet Ingress

	Dy Hr Mn
♀ ♍	15 14:10
⚳ ♒R	18 17:12
☉ ♌	23 17:47
♀ ♎	10 18:11
☿ ♌	11 6:30
♂ ♎	14 14:10
☉ ♍	24 0:30
♄ ♋	24 17:28
☿ ♍	27 10:46

Last Aspect / ☽ Ingress (July)

Last Aspect Dy Hr Mn		☽ Ingress Dy Hr Mn
2 6:47	☿ □	♏ 2 8:19
4 8:53	☿ △	♐ 4 10:25
6 3:43	♄ ☍	♑ 6 12:53
8 13:43	☿ ☍	♒ 8 17:11
10 15:22	♄ △	♓ 11 0:33
13 6:32	♆ △	♈ 13 11:14
15 19:14	♆ □	♉ 15 23:49
18 7:30	♆ ⚹	♊ 18 11:47
20 14:24	♄ ☌	♋ 20 21:12
23 2:38	☉ ☌	♌ 23 3:42
25 2:40	♄ ⚹	♍ 25 8:00
27 7:59	♆ ⚹	♎ 27 11:05
29 10:47	♆ □	♏ 29 13:45
31 13:44	♆ △	♐ 31 16:35

Last Aspect / ☽ Ingress (August)

Last Aspect Dy Hr Mn		☽ Ingress Dy Hr Mn
2 16:30	♄ ☍	♑ 2 20:14
4 22:42	♆ ☍	♒ 5 1:27
7 5:54	♄ △	♓ 7 9:03
9 17:05	♀ ☍	♈ 9 19:25
12 5:26	♄ ⚹	♉ 12 7:46
14 17:47	♆ ⚹	♊ 14 20:06
17 4:55	♄ ☌	♋ 17 6:11
19 11:05	♆ ☌	♌ 19 12:52
21 16:03	♄ ⚹	♍ 21 16:30
23 18:10	♄ □	♎ 23 18:18
25 18:24	♆ □	♏ 25 19:43
27 20:45	♆ △	♐ 27 21:59
29 9:12	♀ ⚹	♑ 30 1:57

☽ Phases & Eclipses

Dy Hr Mn		
7 13:59	○	14♑35
15 7:31	☾	21♈57
23 2:38	●	29♋24
29 23:51	☽	5♏59
6 0:40	○	12♒42
14 0:56	☾	20♉23
21 12:26	●	27♌35
21 12:34:09	●	T 02'15"
28 4:52	☽	4♐02

Astro Data

1 July 1914
Julian Day # 5295
SVP 6♓27'07"
GC 25♐38.7 ⚴ 3♒36.7R
Eris 27♓39.4R ⚵ 8♋09.9
⚷ 18♓55.3R ⚶ 24♉47.7
☽ Mean ☊ 8♓47.6

1 August 1914
Julian Day # 5326
SVP 6♓27'01"
GC 25♐38.8 ⚴ 25♑34.7R
Eris 27♓31.4R ⚵ 25♋07.1
⚷ 18♓16.2R ⚶ 6♊28.3
☽ Mean ☊ 7♓09.2

LONGITUDE — September 1914

Day	Sid.Time	☉	0 hr ☽	Noon ☽	True ☊	☿	♀	♂	⚳	♃	♄	♅	♆	♇
1 Tu	10 39 13	8♍11 34	25♑36 37	2♒08 19	5♓51.7	9♍51.4	23♎46.3	11♎28.6	21♒11.9	14♒41.0	0♋37.2	8♒31.6	29♋24.7	2♋02.4
2 W	10 43 10	9 09 38	8♒36 30	15 01 18	5 51.9	11 45.6	24 49.6	12 07.6	21R 00.2	14R 34.5	0 41.6	8R 29.7	29 26.5	2 03.1
3 Th	10 47 07	10 07 44	21 22 47	27 41 05	5R 52.1	13 38.6	25 52.8	12 46.6	20 48.7	14 28.1	0 45.9	8 27.7	29 28.3	2 03.8
4 F	10 51 03	11 05 52	3♓56 18	10♓08 34	5 52.1	15 30.5	26 55.6	13 25.7	20 37.4	14 21.9	0 50.2	8 25.8	29 30.1	2 04.4
5 Sa	10 55 00	12 04 02	16 18 03	22 24 53	5 51.9	17 21.3	27 58.3	14 04.8	20 26.3	14 15.8	0 54.3	8 24.0	29 31.9	2 05.1
6 Su	10 58 56	13 02 13	28 29 18	4♈31 31	5 51.3	19 10.8	29 00.6	14 44.1	20 15.5	14 09.8	0 58.4	8 22.1	29 33.6	2 05.7
7 M	11 02 53	14 00 26	10♈31 45	16 30 18	5 50.3	20 59.2	0♏02.7	15 23.3	20 04.9	14 04.0	1 02.4	8 20.3	29 35.3	2 06.2
8 Tu	11 06 49	14 58 41	22 27 30	28 23 40	5 49.1	22 46.5	1 04.5	16 02.6	19 54.6	13 58.3	1 06.3	8 18.5	29 37.0	2 06.8
9 W	11 10 46	15 56 58	4♉19 12	10♉14 31	5 47.7	24 32.6	2 06.0	16 42.0	19 44.5	13 52.7	1 10.1	8 16.8	29 38.7	2 07.3
10 Th	11 14 42	16 55 17	16 10 03	22 06 19	5 46.5	26 17.5	3 07.2	17 21.5	19 34.7	13 47.3	1 13.8	8 15.1	29 40.3	2 07.9
11 F	11 18 39	17 53 38	28 03 47	4♊02 59	5 45.5	28 01.3	4 08.1	18 01.0	19 25.2	13 42.0	1 17.5	8 13.4	29 41.9	2 08.3
12 Sa	11 22 36	18 52 02	10♊04 30	16 08 51	5D 45.1	29 43.9	5 08.7	18 40.6	19 16.0	13 36.9	1 21.0	8 11.8	29 43.5	2 08.8
13 Su	11 26 32	19 50 27	22 16 37	28 28 21	5 45.3	1♎25.5	6 09.0	19 20.2	19 07.0	13 32.0	1 24.4	8 10.2	29 45.1	2 09.3
14 M	11 30 29	20 48 55	4♋44 36	11♋05 51	5 46.0	3 06.0	7 08.9	19 59.9	18 58.4	13 27.2	1 27.8	8 08.6	29 46.7	2 09.7
15 Tu	11 34 25	21 47 24	17 32 35	24 05 12	5 47.1	4 45.4	8 08.5	20 39.6	18 50.1	13 22.6	1 31.0	8 07.1	29 48.2	2 10.1
16 W	11 38 22	22 45 56	0♌44 01	7♌29 15	5 48.4	6 23.8	9 07.7	21 19.4	18 42.1	13 18.1	1 34.2	8 05.6	29 49.7	2 10.5
17 Th	11 42 18	23 44 30	14 21 02	21 19 17	5 49.5	8 01.1	10 06.6	21 59.3	18 34.4	13 13.8	1 37.2	8 04.1	29 51.2	2 10.9
18 F	11 46 15	24 43 06	28 23 52	5♍34 26	5R 49.9	9 37.3	11 05.1	22 39.2	18 27.1	13 09.7	1 40.2	8 02.7	29 52.7	2 11.2
19 Sa	11 50 11	25 41 44	12♍50 27	20 11 17	5 49.4	11 12.6	12 03.2	23 19.2	18 20.1	13 05.8	1 43.0	8 01.4	29 54.1	2 11.5
20 Su	11 54 08	26 40 24	27 36 04	5♎03 53	5 47.9	12 46.9	13 00.9	23 59.3	18 13.4	13 02.0	1 45.8	8 00.0	29 55.5	2 11.8
21 M	11 58 04	27 39 05	12♎33 40	20 04 20	5 45.5	14 20.2	13 58.2	24 39.4	18 07.1	12 58.5	1 48.4	7 58.7	29 56.9	2 12.1
22 Tu	12 02 01	28 37 49	27 34 43	5♏03 46	5 42.5	15 52.5	14 55.0	25 19.5	18 01.1	12 55.1	1 51.0	7 57.5	29 58.2	2 12.4
23 W	12 05 58	29 36 35	12♏30 25	19 53 47	5 39.4	17 23.8	15 51.4	25 59.7	17 55.5	12 51.9	1 53.4	7 56.3	29 59.5	2 12.6
24 Th	12 09 54	0♎35 22	27 13 03	4♐27 37	5 36.8	18 54.1	16 47.3	26 40.0	17 50.3	12 48.8	1 55.8	7 55.1	0♌00.8	2 12.8
25 F	12 13 51	1 34 11	11♐36 59	18 40 52	5D 35.1	20 23.5	17 42.7	27 20.4	17 45.4	12 46.0	1 58.0	7 54.0	0 02.1	2 13.0
26 Sa	12 17 47	2 33 02	25 39 06	2♑31 39	5 34.5	21 51.9	18 37.6	28 00.8	17 40.8	12 43.4	2 00.1	7 52.9	0 03.4	2 13.2
27 Su	12 21 44	3 31 54	9♑18 35	16 00 07	5 35.0	23 19.3	19 31.9	28 41.2	17 36.7	12 40.9	2 02.2	7 51.9	0 04.6	2 13.3
28 M	12 25 40	4 30 48	22 36 30	29 08 00	5 36.4	24 45.6	20 25.7	29 21.7	17 32.8	12 38.7	2 04.1	7 50.9	0 05.8	2 13.4
29 Tu	12 29 37	5 29 44	5♒35 00	11♒57 50	5 38.0	26 11.0	21 19.0	0♏02.3	17 29.4	12 36.6	2 05.9	7 50.0	0 06.9	2 13.5
30 W	12 33 33	6 28 41	18 16 52	24 32 28	5R 39.4	27 35.3	22 11.6	0 42.9	17 26.3	12 34.8	2 07.6	7 49.1	0 08.0	2 13.6

LONGITUDE — October 1914

Day	Sid.Time	☉	0 hr ☽	Noon ☽	True ☊	☿	♀	♂	⚳	♃	♄	♅	♆	♇
1 Th	12 37 30	7♎27 41	0♓44 57	6♓54 39	5♓39.9	28♎58.6	23♏03.6	1♏23.6	17♒23.6	12♒33.1	2♋09.2	7♒48.2	0♌09.1	2♋13.7
2 F	12 41 27	8 26 42	13 01 53	19 06 55	5R 39.0	0♏20.8	23 54.9	2 04.3	17R 21.3	12R 31.6	2 10.7	7R 47.4	0 10.2	2R 13.7
3 Sa	12 45 23	9 25 45	25 10 00	1♈11 23	5 36.4	1 41.8	24 45.6	2 45.1	17 19.3	12 30.3	2 12.1	7 46.7	0 11.2	2 13.7
4 Su	12 49 20	10 24 50	7♈11 16	13 09 54	5 32.2	3 01.7	25 35.5	3 26.0	17 17.7	12 29.3	2 13.3	7 46.0	0 12.2	2 13.7
5 M	12 53 16	11 23 57	19 07 27	25 04 09	5 26.4	4 20.4	26 24.8	4 06.9	17 16.4	12 28.4	2 14.5	7 45.3	0 13.2	2 13.6
6 Tu	12 57 13	12 23 06	1♉00 13	6♉55 51	5 19.6	5 37.7	27 13.3	4 47.9	17 15.5	12 27.7	2 15.6	7 44.7	0 14.2	2 13.6
7 W	13 01 09	13 22 18	12 51 20	18 46 54	5 12.4	6 53.7	28 01.0	5 28.9	17D 15.0	12 27.2	2 16.5	7 44.1	0 15.1	2 13.5
8 Th	13 05 06	14 21 33	24 42 53	0♊39 35	5 05.6	8 08.3	28 47.8	6 10.0	17 14.8	12D 26.9	2 17.3	7 43.6	0 16.0	2 13.4
9 F	13 09 02	15 20 48	6♊37 24	12 36 42	4 59.8	9 21.4	29 33.9	6 51.1	17 15.0	12 26.8	2 18.1	7 43.1	0 16.8	2 13.2
10 Sa	13 12 59	16 20 06	18 37 57	24 41 36	4 55.6	10 32.7	0♐19.0	7 32.3	17 15.6	12 27.0	2 18.7	7 42.7	0 17.6	2 13.1
11 Su	13 16 56	17 19 27	0♋48 09	6♋58 08	4D 53.2	11 42.4	1 03.3	8 13.6	17 16.5	12 27.3	2 19.2	7 42.3	0 18.4	2 12.9
12 M	13 20 52	18 18 49	13 12 05	19 30 33	4 52.6	12 50.1	1 46.6	8 55.0	17 17.8	12 27.8	2 19.6	7 42.0	0 19.2	2 12.7
13 Tu	13 24 49	19 18 15	25 54 05	2♌23 12	4 53.3	13 55.8	2 28.9	9 36.3	17 19.4	12 28.5	2 19.9	7 41.8	0 19.9	2 12.5
14 W	13 28 45	20 17 42	8♌58 23	15 40 03	4 54.6	14 59.2	3 10.2	10 17.8	17 21.4	12 29.4	2R 20.0	7 41.5	0 20.6	2 12.3
15 Th	13 32 42	21 17 12	22 28 31	29 24 02	4R 55.6	16 00.1	3 50.4	10 59.3	17 23.7	12 30.5	2 20.1	7 41.4	0 21.3	2 12.0
16 F	13 36 38	22 16 44	6♍26 38	13♍36 14	4 55.4	16 58.3	4 29.6	11 40.9	17 26.4	12 31.8	2 20.0	7 41.2	0 21.9	2 11.7
17 Sa	13 40 35	23 16 18	20 52 34	28 15 07	4 53.3	17 53.6	5 07.5	12 22.5	17 29.4	12 33.3	2 19.9	7D 41.2	0 22.5	2 11.4
18 Su	13 44 31	24 15 54	5♎43 10	13♎15 48	4 48.9	18 45.6	5 44.3	13 04.2	17 32.8	12 35.0	2 19.6	7 41.1	0 23.0	2 11.0
19 M	13 48 28	25 15 33	20 51 53	28 30 09	4 42.5	19 34.1	6 19.8	13 46.0	17 36.5	12 36.9	2 19.2	7 41.2	0 23.6	2 10.7
20 Tu	13 52 25	26 15 13	6♏09 13	13♏47 41	4 34.7	20 18.5	6 54.0	14 27.8	17 40.5	12 39.0	2 18.7	7 41.3	0 24.1	2 10.3
21 W	13 56 21	27 14 56	21 24 09	28 57 18	4 26.6	20 58.6	7 26.9	15 09.6	17 44.9	12 41.3	2 18.1	7 41.4	0 24.5	2 09.9
22 Th	14 00 18	28 14 40	6♐25 59	13♐49 13	4 19.1	21 33.9	7 58.3	15 51.6	17 49.6	12 43.8	2 17.3	7 41.6	0 25.0	2 09.5
23 F	14 04 14	29 14 26	21 06 15	28 16 32	4 13.3	22 03.8	8 28.2	16 33.6	17 54.7	12 46.5	2 16.5	7 41.8	0 25.4	2 09.1
24 Sa	14 08 11	0♏14 14	5♑19 45	12♑15 49	4 09.6	22 27.8	8 56.6	17 15.6	18 00.1	12 49.4	2 15.5	7 42.1	0 25.7	2 08.6
25 Su	14 12 07	1 14 03	19 04 47	25 46 53	4D 08.0	22 45.4	9 23.5	17 57.7	18 05.8	12 52.5	2 14.5	7 42.5	0 26.0	2 08.1
26 M	14 16 04	2 13 54	2♒22 27	8♒51 57	4 08.1	22R 56.0	9 48.6	18 39.9	18 11.8	12 55.7	2 13.3	7 42.9	0 26.3	2 07.6
27 Tu	14 20 00	3 13 47	15 15 52	21 34 46	4 08.9	22 58.9	10 12.0	19 22.1	18 18.1	12 59.2	2 12.0	7 43.3	0 26.6	2 07.1
28 W	14 23 57	4 13 41	27 49 10	3♓59 40	4R 09.4	22 53.6	10 33.6	20 04.4	18 24.8	13 02.8	2 10.6	7 43.8	0 26.8	2 06.5
29 Th	14 27 54	5 13 37	10♓06 48	16 11 05	4 08.6	22 39.6	10 53.3	20 46.7	18 31.8	13 06.7	2 09.1	7 44.3	0 27.0	2 06.0
30 F	14 31 50	6 13 35	22 13 01	28 13 03	4 05.6	22 16.4	11 11.2	21 29.1	18 39.0	13 10.7	2 07.5	7 44.9	0 27.2	2 05.4
31 Sa	14 35 47	7 13 34	4♈11 34	10♈08 58	4 00.0	21 43.7	11 27.0	22 11.5	18 46.6	13 14.9	2 05.8	7 45.6	0 27.3	2 04.8

Astro Data

	Dy Hr Mn
☽ 0N	5 18:44
☿ 0S	13 13:53
☽ 0S	19 21:10
☉ 0S	23 21:33
☽ 0N	3 1:21
♇ R	3 3:15
♄☌♇	4 18:26
⚳ D	8 10:53
♃ D	9 10:25
♄ R	15 11:41
☽ 0S	17 7:59
♅ D	18 9:40
☿ R	27 8:47
☽ 0N	30 6:55

Planet Ingress

		Dy Hr Mn
♀	♏	7 10:58
☿	♎	12 15:47
♆	♌	23 20:24
☉	♎	23 21:34
♂	♏	29 10:38
☿	♏	2 5:54
♀	♐	10 1:49
☉	♏	24 6:17

Last Aspect / ☽ Ingress (September)

Last Aspect Dy Hr Mn			☽ Ingress	Dy Hr Mn
1 6:58	♆	☍	♒	1 8:03
3 8:14	♀	△	♓	3 16:26
6 2:06	♆	△	♈	6 3:00
8 14:29	♆	□	♉	8 15:15
11 3:16	♆	⚹	♊	11 3:53
12 17:48	☉	□	♋	13 14:56
15 22:21	♆	☌	♌	15 22:41
17 13:12	♂	⚹	♍	18 2:42
20 3:44	♆	⚹	♎	20 3:52
22 3:49	♆	□	♏	22 3:53
23 4:59	♀	☌	♐	24 4:36
26 3:42	♂	⚹	♑	26 7:34
28 12:27	♂	□	♒	28 13:36
30 18:37	☿	△	♓	30 22:33

Last Aspect / ☽ Ingress (October)

Last Aspect Dy Hr Mn			☽ Ingress	Dy Hr Mn
2 22:14	♀	△	♈	3 9:38
4 10:38	♃	⚹	♉	5 21:58
8 7:59	♀	☍	♊	8 10:40
9 17:57	☉	△	♋	10 22:26
12 9:33	☉	□	♌	13 7:36
14 20:49	☉	⚹	♍	15 13:02
16 17:58	☿	⚹	♎	17 14:49
19 6:33	☉	☌	♏	19 14:21
20 22:46	☿	☌	♐	21 13:40
23 13:45	☉	⚹	♑	23 14:55
25 6:27	☿	⚹	♒	25 19:39
27 14:41	☿	□	♓	28 4:13
30 0:31	☿	△	♈	30 15:35

☽ Phases & Eclipses

Dy Hr Mn	
4 14:01	○ 11♓11
4 13:55	P 0.859
12 17:48	☾ 19♊06
19 21:33	● 26♍05
26 12:03	☽ 2♑33
4 5:59	○ 10♈10
12 9:33	☾ 18♋13
19 6:33	● 25♎02
25 22:44	☽ 1♒41

Astro Data

1 September 1914
Julian Day # 5357
SVP 6♓26'57"
GC 25♐38.9 ⚴ 20♑02.7R
Eris 27♓14.4R ⚵ 11♌05.3
⚷ 17♓00.9R ⚶ 16♊04.1
☽ Mean ☊ 5♓30.7

1 October 1914
Julian Day # 5387
SVP 6♓26'53"
GC 25♐38.9 ⚴ 20♑05.0
Eris 26♓54.1R ⚵ 25♌17.3
⚷ 15♓39.2R ⚶ 22♊01.4
☽ Mean ☊ 3♓55.4

November 1914 — LONGITUDE

Day	Sid.Time	☉	0 hr ☽	Noon ☽	True ☊	☿	♀	♂	⚳	♃	♄	♅	♆	♇
1 Su	14 39 43	8♏13 35	16♈05 33	22♈01 37	3♓51.6	21♏01.7	11♐40.8	22♏54.0	18♒54.4	13♒19.3	2♋04.0	7♒46.3	0♌27.4	2♋04.2
2 M	14 43 40	9 13 38	27 57 24	3♉53 07	3R 40.8	20R 10.4	11 52.4	23 36.6	19 02.6	13 23.8	2R 02.1	7 47.0	0 27.4	2R 03.5
3 Tu	14 47 36	10 13 43	9♉48 59	15 45 09	3 28.3	19 10.5	12 01.9	24 19.2	19 11.0	13 28.6	2 00.1	7 47.8	0R 27.4	2 02.8
4 W	14 51 33	11 13 50	21 41 47	27 39 03	3 15.0	18 03.2	12 09.2	25 01.9	19 19.7	13 33.5	1 57.9	7 48.7	0 27.4	2 02.2
5 Th	14 55 29	12 13 58	3♊37 08	9♊36 14	3 02.1	16 49.8	12 14.2	25 44.6	19 28.7	13 38.6	1 55.7	7 49.6	0 27.4	2 01.5
6 F	14 59 26	13 14 09	15 36 31	21 38 16	2 50.8	15 32.4	12R 16.9	26 27.4	19 38.0	13 43.9	1 53.4	7 50.5	0 27.3	2 00.7
7 Sa	15 03 23	14 14 21	27 41 45	3♋47 16	2 41.7	14 13.1	12 17.2	27 10.2	19 47.6	13 49.3	1 50.9	7 51.5	0 27.2	2 00.0
8 Su	15 07 19	15 14 36	9♋55 11	16 05 53	2 35.4	12 54.6	12 15.1	27 53.1	19 57.4	13 55.0	1 48.4	7 52.6	0 27.0	1 59.3
9 M	15 11 16	16 14 52	22 19 48	28 37 25	2 31.8	11 39.3	12 10.6	28 36.1	20 07.5	14 00.7	1 45.8	7 53.7	0 26.8	1 58.5
10 Tu	15 15 12	17 15 11	4♌59 11	11♌25 38	2D 30.5	10 29.6	12 03.7	29 19.1	20 17.8	14 06.7	1 43.1	7 54.8	0 26.6	1 57.7
11 W	15 19 09	18 15 31	17 57 16	24 34 32	2R 30.4	9 27.8	11 54.3	0♐02.2	20 28.5	14 12.8	1 40.2	7 56.0	0 26.4	1 56.9
12 Th	15 23 05	19 15 54	1♍17 53	8♍07 42	2 30.4	8 35.5	11 42.5	0 45.3	20 39.3	14 19.1	1 37.3	7 57.2	0 26.1	1 56.1
13 F	15 27 02	20 16 18	15 04 13	22 07 36	2 29.2	7 53.9	11 28.3	1 28.5	20 50.4	14 25.6	1 34.3	7 58.5	0 25.8	1 55.2
14 Sa	15 30 58	21 16 44	29 17 48	6♎34 36	2 25.8	7 23.8	11 11.8	2 11.8	21 01.8	14 32.2	1 31.2	7 59.9	0 25.4	1 54.3
15 Su	15 34 55	22 17 12	13♎57 35	21 26 04	2 19.5	7 05.4	10 52.9	2 55.1	21 13.4	14 39.0	1 28.0	8 01.3	0 25.0	1 53.5
16 M	15 38 52	23 17 42	28 59 10	6♏35 46	2 10.5	6D 58.6	10 31.7	3 38.5	21 25.3	14 46.0	1 24.7	8 02.7	0 24.6	1 52.6
17 Tu	15 42 48	24 18 14	14♏14 34	21 54 11	1 59.5	7 02.9	10 08.4	4 21.9	21 37.4	14 53.1	1 21.4	8 04.2	0 24.1	1 51.7
18 W	15 46 45	25 18 47	29 33 07	7♐09 54	1 47.8	7 17.7	9 43.0	5 05.4	21 49.8	15 00.4	1 17.9	8 05.7	0 23.7	1 50.8
19 Th	15 50 41	26 19 22	14♐43 08	22 11 37	1 36.8	7 42.2	9 15.7	5 48.9	22 02.4	15 07.8	1 14.4	8 07.3	0 23.1	1 49.8
20 F	15 54 38	27 19 58	29 34 16	6♑50 16	1 27.6	8 15.6	8 46.6	6 32.5	22 15.2	15 15.4	1 10.8	8 08.9	0 22.6	1 48.9
21 Sa	15 58 34	28 20 35	13♑59 04	21 00 18	1 21.1	8 56.8	8 15.8	7 16.2	22 28.2	15 23.1	1 07.1	8 10.6	0 22.0	1 47.9
22 Su	16 02 31	29 21 14	27 53 53	4♒39 53	1 17.3	9 45.0	7 43.5	7 59.9	22 41.5	15 31.0	1 03.3	8 12.3	0 21.4	1 46.9
23 M	16 06 27	0♐21 53	11♒18 35	17 50 22	1 15.8	10 39.5	7 09.9	8 43.7	22 55.0	15 39.1	0 59.5	8 14.1	0 20.8	1 45.9
24 Tu	16 10 24	1 22 34	24 15 45	0♓35 18	1 15.5	11 39.3	6 35.3	9 27.5	23 08.7	15 47.2	0 55.6	8 15.9	0 20.1	1 44.9
25 W	16 14 21	2 23 16	6♓49 38	12 59 26	1 15.3	12 43.9	5 59.8	10 11.3	23 22.6	15 55.6	0 51.6	8 17.8	0 19.4	1 43.9
26 Th	16 18 17	3 23 59	19 05 20	25 07 59	1 14.0	13 52.6	5 23.7	10 55.3	23 36.7	16 04.0	0 47.5	8 19.7	0 18.6	1 42.9
27 F	16 22 14	4 24 42	1♈08 02	7♈06 03	1 10.5	15 04.7	4 47.3	11 39.2	23 51.0	16 12.6	0 43.4	8 21.6	0 17.9	1 41.8
28 Sa	16 26 10	5 25 27	13 02 37	18 58 14	1 04.2	16 19.9	4 10.8	12 23.3	24 05.5	16 21.4	0 39.2	8 23.6	0 17.1	1 40.8
29 Su	16 30 07	6 26 13	24 53 21	0♉48 24	0 54.9	17 37.7	3 34.5	13 07.3	24 20.2	16 30.3	0 34.9	8 25.6	0 16.2	1 39.7
30 M	16 34 03	7 27 00	6♉43 44	12 39 39	0 42.9	18 57.7	2 58.5	13 51.5	24 35.1	16 39.3	0 30.6	8 27.7	0 15.4	1 38.6

December 1914 — LONGITUDE

Day	Sid.Time	☉	0 hr ☽	Noon ☽	True ☊	☿	♀	♂	⚳	♃	♄	♅	♆	♇
1 Tu	16 38 00	8♐27 49	18♉36 24	24♉34 14	0♓29.0	20♏19.6	2♐23.3	14♐35.6	24♒50.2	16♒48.4	0♋26.3	8♒29.8	0♌14.5	1♋37.6
2 W	16 41 56	9 28 38	0♊33 18	6♊33 45	0R 14.2	21 43.1	1R 49.0	15 19.9	25 05.5	16 57.7	0R 21.8	8 32.0	0R 13.6	1R 36.5
3 Th	16 45 53	10 29 29	12 35 43	18 39 17	29♒59.9	23 07.9	1 15.8	16 04.2	25 21.0	17 07.1	0 17.4	8 34.1	0 12.6	1 35.4
4 F	16 49 50	11 30 20	24 44 35	0♋51 42	29 47.0	24 33.9	0 43.9	16 48.5	25 36.7	17 16.7	0 12.8	8 36.4	0 11.6	1 34.2
5 Sa	16 53 46	12 31 13	7♋00 46	13 11 54	29 36.7	26 00.9	0 13.7	17 32.9	25 52.5	17 26.3	0 08.3	8 38.7	0 10.6	1 33.1
6 Su	16 57 43	13 32 07	19 25 17	25 41 08	29 29.3	27 28.8	29♏45.2	18 17.3	26 08.5	17 36.1	0 03.6	8 41.0	0 09.6	1 32.0
7 M	17 01 39	14 33 02	1♌59 39	8♌21 09	29 25.0	28 57.3	29 18.6	19 01.8	26 24.7	17 46.0	29♊59.0	8 43.3	0 08.6	1 30.9
8 Tu	17 05 36	15 33 59	14 45 54	21 14 16	29D 23.2	0♐26.5	28 54.0	19 46.4	26 41.1	17 56.0	29 54.3	8 45.7	0 07.5	1 29.7
9 W	17 09 32	16 34 56	27 46 35	4♍23 15	29R 23.0	1 56.1	28 31.7	20 31.0	26 57.6	18 06.2	29 49.6	8 48.1	0 06.4	1 28.6
10 Th	17 13 29	17 35 55	11♍04 35	17 50 56	29 23.3	3 26.3	28 11.6	21 15.6	27 14.3	18 16.5	29 44.8	8 50.6	0 05.2	1 27.4
11 F	17 17 26	18 36 55	24 42 34	1♎39 42	29 22.6	4 56.8	27 53.8	22 00.3	27 31.1	18 26.8	29 40.0	8 53.1	0 04.1	1 26.2
12 Sa	17 21 22	19 37 56	8♎42 24	15 50 39	29 20.0	6 27.6	27 38.5	22 45.1	27 48.1	18 37.3	29 35.1	8 55.7	0 02.9	1 25.1
13 Su	17 25 19	20 38 58	23 04 14	0♏22 48	29 14.8	7 58.8	27 25.7	23 29.9	28 05.3	18 47.9	29 30.3	8 58.2	0 01.7	1 23.9
14 M	17 29 15	21 40 01	7♏45 47	15 12 24	29 07.1	9 30.2	27 15.3	24 14.8	28 22.6	18 58.7	29 25.4	9 00.8	0 00.4	1 22.7
15 Tu	17 33 12	22 41 05	22 41 45	0♐12 43	28 57.4	11 01.9	27 07.4	24 59.7	28 40.1	19 09.5	29 20.5	9 03.5	29♋59.2	1 21.5
16 W	17 37 08	23 42 10	7♐44 09	15 14 45	28 46.8	12 33.8	27 02.0	25 44.7	28 57.8	19 20.4	29 15.6	9 06.2	29 57.9	1 20.3
17 Th	17 41 05	24 43 16	22 43 17	0♑08 32	28 36.7	14 05.8	26D 59.1	26 29.7	29 15.6	19 31.5	29 10.6	9 08.9	29 56.6	1 19.1
18 F	17 45 01	25 44 22	7♑29 26	14 45 02	28 28.2	15 38.1	26 58.7	27 14.7	29 33.5	19 42.6	29 05.7	9 11.6	29 55.3	1 17.9
19 Sa	17 48 58	26 45 29	21 54 35	28 57 32	28 22.0	17 10.6	27 00.6	27 59.8	29 51.6	19 53.9	29 00.7	9 14.4	29 54.0	1 16.7
20 Su	17 52 55	27 46 36	5♒53 32	12♒42 28	28 18.5	18 43.3	27 05.0	28 45.0	0♓09.8	20 05.2	28 55.8	9 17.2	29 52.6	1 15.5
21 M	17 56 51	28 47 44	19 24 20	25 59 21	28D 17.3	20 16.1	27 11.6	29 30.2	0 28.2	20 16.7	28 50.8	9 20.1	29 51.2	1 14.3
22 Tu	18 00 48	29 48 51	2♓27 52	8♓50 17	28 17.7	21 49.2	27 20.6	0♑15.4	0 46.6	20 28.2	28 45.8	9 22.9	29 49.8	1 13.1
23 W	18 04 44	0♑49 59	15 07 11	21 19 06	28R 18.6	23 22.4	27 31.8	1 00.7	1 05.3	20 39.9	28 40.9	9 25.8	29 48.4	1 11.9
24 Th	18 08 41	1 51 07	27 26 43	3♈30 39	28 18.9	24 55.9	27 45.1	1 46.1	1 24.0	20 51.6	28 35.9	9 28.8	29 46.9	1 10.7
25 F	18 12 37	2 52 15	9♈31 35	15 30 09	28 17.9	26 29.6	28 00.6	2 31.4	1 42.9	21 03.4	28 30.9	9 31.7	29 45.5	1 09.5
26 Sa	18 16 34	3 53 23	21 27 01	27 22 47	28 14.7	28 03.5	28 18.1	3 16.9	2 01.9	21 15.3	28 26.0	9 34.7	29 44.0	1 08.3
27 Su	18 20 30	4 54 31	3♉18 02	9♉13 18	28 09.2	29 37.7	28 37.7	4 02.3	2 21.0	21 27.3	28 21.1	9 37.7	29 42.5	1 07.1
28 M	18 24 27	5 55 39	15 09 05	21 05 49	28 01.6	1♑12.1	28 59.1	4 47.8	2 40.3	21 39.4	28 16.2	9 40.7	29 41.0	1 05.9
29 Tu	18 28 24	6 56 48	27 03 55	3♊03 43	27 52.4	2 46.8	29 22.5	5 33.4	2 59.6	21 51.6	28 11.3	9 43.8	29 39.5	1 04.7
30 W	18 32 20	7 57 56	9♊05 29	15 09 29	27 42.3	4 21.8	29 47.6	6 19.0	3 19.1	22 03.9	28 06.4	9 46.9	29 37.9	1 03.5
31 Th	18 36 17	8 59 04	21 15 51	27 24 46	27 32.5	5 57.1	0♐14.5	7 04.6	3 38.7	22 16.2	28 01.6	9 50.0	29 36.4	1 02.3

Astro Data	Dy Hr Mn
♄☌♇	1 9:01
♆ R	3 13:17
♀ R	7 3:10
☽ 0S	13 17:35
☿ D	16 14:28
♃⚼♄	25 4:15
☽ 0N	26 12:15
♃⚼♇	30 10:30
♄⚺♆	4 20:02
☽ 0S	11 0:25
♀ D	18 4:29
☽ 0N	23 18:41

Planet Ingress	Dy Hr Mn
♂ ♐	11 10:47
☉ ♐	23 3:20
☊ ♒R	3 11:47
♀ ♏R	5 23:20
♄ ♊R	7 6:48
☿ ♐	8 4:53
♆ ♋R	14 20:38
⚳ ♓	19 23:07
♂ ♑	22 3:49
☉ ♑	22 16:22
☿ ♑	27 17:40
♀ ♐	30 23:15

Last Aspect Dy Hr Mn		☽ Ingress Dy Hr Mn
31 18:17	♃ ⚹	♉ 2 4:08
4 6:23	♂ ☍	♊ 4 16:44
5 20:08	♃ △	♋ 7 4:33
9 11:57	♂ △	♌ 9 14:36
10 23:36	☉ □	♍ 11 21:42
13 8:37	☉ ⚹	♎ 14 1:10
15 1:02	♃ △	♏ 16 1:36
17 16:02	☉ ☌	♐ 18 0:42
19 0:34	♃ ⚹	♑ 20 0:42
22 1:48	☉ ⚹	♒ 22 3:42
23 7:55	♃ ☌	♓ 24 10:53
25 11:27	☿ △	♈ 26 21:44
28 6:38	♃ ⚹	♉ 29 10:22

Last Aspect Dy Hr Mn		☽ Ingress Dy Hr Mn
1 2:21	☿ ☍	♊ 1 22:53
3 8:55	♃ △	♋ 4 10:19
6 19:29	♀ △	♌ 6 20:13
9 3:47	♄ ⚹	♍ 9 4:03
11 8:35	♄ □	♎ 11 9:09
13 10:35	♄ △	♏ 13 11:23
15 11:38	♆ △	♐ 15 11:40
17 10:27	♄ ☍	♑ 17 11:46
19 13:37	♆ ☍	♒ 19 13:47
21 18:53	♂ ⚹	♓ 21 19:25
24 4:37	♆ △	♈ 24 5:02
26 16:46	♆ □	♉ 26 17:19
29 5:13	♆ ⚹	♊ 29 5:53
31 13:11	♄ ☌	♋ 31 17:01

☽ Phases & Eclipses Dy Hr Mn	
2 23:48	○ 9♉43
10 23:36	☾ 17♌44
17 16:02	● 24♏28
24 13:38	☽ 1♓27
2 18:20	○ 9♊45
10 11:31	☾ 17♍35
17 2:35	● 24♐19
24 8:24	☽ 1♈42

Astro Data

1 November 1914
Julian Day # 5418
SVP 6♓26'50"
GC 25♐39.0 ⚴ 24♑45.9
Eris 26♓35.4R ⚵ 8♍09.0
⚷ 14♓37.2R ⚶ 22♊38.9R
☽ Mean ☊ 2♓16.8

1 December 1914
Julian Day # 5448
SVP 6♓26'45"
GC 25♐39.1 ⚴ 2♒09.3
Eris 26♓24.9R ⚵ 17♍58.8
⚷ 14♓21.2 ⚶ 17♊02.3R
☽ Mean ☊ 0♓41.5

LONGITUDE — January 1915

Day	Sid.Time	☉	0 hr ☽	Noon ☽	True ☊	☿	♀	♂	⚳	♃	♄	♅	♆	♇
1 F	18 40 13	10♑00 13	3♋36 19	9♋50 32	27♒23.8	7♑32.7	0♐43.1	7♑50.3	3♓58.4	22♒28.6	27♊56.8	9♒53.1	29♋34.8	1♋01.1
2 Sa	18 44 10	11 01 21	16 07 29	22 27 11	27R16.8	9 08.7	1 13.3	8 36.0	4 18.2	22 41.1	27R52.0	9 56.3	29R33.2	0R59.9
3 Su	18 48 06	12 02 30	28 49 38	5♌14 51	27 12.2	10 45.0	1 45.1	9 21.8	4 38.1	22 53.6	27 47.3	9 59.5	29 31.7	0 58.8
4 M	18 52 03	13 03 38	11♌42 50	18 13 38	27D09.9	12 21.7	2 18.4	10 07.6	4 58.2	23 06.3	27 42.6	10 02.7	29 30.1	0 57.6
5 Tu	18 56 00	14 04 47	24 47 18	1♍23 53	27 09.6	13 58.7	2 53.1	10 53.4	5 18.3	23 19.0	27 37.9	10 05.9	29 28.4	0 56.4
6 W	18 59 56	15 05 56	8♍03 28	14 46 10	27 10.6	15 36.1	3 29.2	11 39.3	5 38.5	23 31.8	27 33.3	10 09.1	29 26.8	0 55.2
7 Th	19 03 53	16 07 05	21 32 05	28 21 19	27 12.0	17 14.0	4 06.7	12 25.2	5 58.9	23 44.6	27 28.7	10 12.4	29 25.2	0 54.1
8 F	19 07 49	17 08 14	5♎13 58	12♎10 04	27R13.1	18 52.2	4 45.5	13 11.2	6 19.3	23 57.5	27 24.2	10 15.6	29 23.5	0 52.9
9 Sa	19 11 46	18 09 23	19 09 38	26 12 37	27 12.9	20 30.9	5 25.5	13 57.2	6 39.8	24 10.5	27 19.7	10 18.9	29 21.9	0 51.8
10 Su	19 15 42	19 10 32	3♏18 53	10♏28 12	27 11.0	22 10.0	6 06.7	14 43.2	7 00.4	24 23.6	27 15.3	10 22.2	29 20.2	0 50.6
11 M	19 19 39	20 11 41	17 40 14	24 54 32	27 07.5	23 49.5	6 49.0	15 29.3	7 21.2	24 36.7	27 10.9	10 25.6	29 18.6	0 49.5
12 Tu	19 23 35	21 12 51	2♐10 33	9♐27 37	27 02.5	25 29.5	7 32.4	16 15.4	7 42.0	24 49.9	27 06.6	10 28.9	29 16.9	0 48.4
13 W	19 27 32	22 14 00	16 45 00	24 01 54	26 57.0	27 09.9	8 16.9	17 01.6	8 02.9	25 03.1	27 02.3	10 32.3	29 15.2	0 47.3
14 Th	19 31 29	23 15 09	1♑17 27	8♑30 50	26 51.5	28 50.7	9 02.4	17 47.8	8 23.9	25 16.4	26 58.1	10 35.7	29 13.5	0 46.2
15 F	19 35 25	24 16 17	15 41 15	22 47 57	26 46.9	0♒31.8	9 48.8	18 34.0	8 45.0	25 29.8	26 54.0	10 39.1	29 11.8	0 45.1
16 Sa	19 39 22	25 17 26	29 50 16	6♒47 40	26 43.8	2 13.3	10 36.1	19 20.3	9 06.1	25 43.2	26 49.9	10 42.5	29 10.2	0 44.0
17 Su	19 43 18	26 18 33	13♒39 44	20 26 11	26D42.3	3 55.2	11 24.3	20 06.6	9 27.4	25 56.7	26 46.0	10 45.9	29 08.5	0 42.9
18 M	19 47 15	27 19 40	27 06 52	3♓41 46	26 42.3	5 37.3	12 13.4	20 53.0	9 48.7	26 10.2	26 42.0	10 49.3	29 06.8	0 41.8
19 Tu	19 51 11	28 20 46	10♓11 01	16 34 48	26 43.5	7 19.6	13 03.3	21 39.3	10 10.1	26 23.8	26 38.2	10 52.7	29 05.1	0 40.8
20 W	19 55 08	29 21 51	22 53 28	29 07 23	26 45.2	9 02.0	13 53.9	22 25.7	10 31.6	26 37.4	26 34.4	10 56.2	29 03.4	0 39.7
21 Th	19 59 04	0♒22 55	5♈17 03	11♈22 58	26 47.0	10 44.5	14 45.3	23 12.1	10 53.2	26 51.1	26 30.7	10 59.6	29 01.7	0 38.7
22 F	20 03 01	1 23 58	17 25 41	23 25 49	26R48.2	12 27.0	15 37.5	23 58.6	11 14.8	27 04.8	26 27.1	11 03.1	29 00.0	0 37.7
23 Sa	20 06 58	2 25 01	29 23 59	5♉20 46	26 48.4	14 09.2	16 30.3	24 45.1	11 36.5	27 18.6	26 23.6	11 06.5	28 58.3	0 36.7
24 Su	20 10 54	3 26 02	11♉16 49	17 12 42	26 47.5	15 51.0	17 23.8	25 31.6	11 58.3	27 32.4	26 20.1	11 10.0	28 56.6	0 35.7
25 M	20 14 51	4 27 02	23 09 02	29 06 23	26 45.6	17 32.3	18 17.9	26 18.1	12 20.2	27 46.2	26 16.8	11 13.5	28 54.9	0 34.7
26 Tu	20 18 47	5 28 01	5♊05 15	11♊06 08	26 42.8	19 12.8	19 12.6	27 04.7	12 42.1	28 00.1	26 13.5	11 17.0	28 53.2	0 33.7
27 W	20 22 44	6 29 00	17 09 30	23 15 43	26 39.5	20 52.3	20 08.0	27 51.3	13 04.1	28 14.0	26 10.3	11 20.5	28 51.5	0 32.8
28 Th	20 26 40	7 29 57	29 25 08	5♋38 02	26 36.2	22 30.3	21 03.9	28 37.9	13 26.1	28 28.0	26 07.2	11 24.0	28 49.9	0 31.8
29 F	20 30 37	8 30 53	11♋54 37	18 15 04	26 33.4	24 06.6	22 00.4	29 24.6	13 48.2	28 42.0	26 04.2	11 27.5	28 48.2	0 30.9
30 Sa	20 34 33	9 31 48	24 39 26	1♌07 47	26 31.2	25 40.7	22 57.4	0♒11.3	14 10.4	28 56.0	26 01.3	11 31.0	28 46.5	0 30.0
31 Su	20 38 30	10 32 42	7♌40 03	14 16 09	26D29.9	27 12.2	23 54.9	0 58.0	14 32.6	29 10.1	25 58.5	11 34.5	28 44.9	0 29.1

LONGITUDE — February 1915

Day	Sid.Time	☉	0 hr ☽	Noon ☽	True ☊	☿	♀	♂	⚳	♃	♄	♅	♆	♇
1 M	20 42 27	11♒33 35	20♌55 57	27♌39 17	26♒29.6	28♒40.5	24♐53.0	1♒44.7	14♓54.9	29♒24.2	25♊55.8	11♒38.0	28♋43.2	0♋28.2
2 Tu	20 46 23	12 34 26	4♍25 55	11♍15 37	26 30.0	0♓05.0	25 51.5	2 31.5	15 17.2	29 38.3	25R53.1	11 41.5	28R41.6	0R27.4
3 W	20 50 20	13 35 17	18 08 08	25 03 12	26 30.9	1 25.1	26 50.5	3 18.2	15 39.6	29 52.5	25 50.6	11 45.0	28 40.0	0 26.5
4 Th	20 54 16	14 36 07	2♎00 32	8♎59 53	26 32.0	2 40.1	27 49.9	4 05.0	16 02.1	0♓06.7	25 48.2	11 48.4	28 38.3	0 25.7
5 F	20 58 13	15 36 56	16 00 58	23 03 32	26 32.9	3 49.2	28 49.8	4 51.9	16 24.6	0 20.9	25 45.9	11 51.9	28 36.7	0 24.9
6 Sa	21 02 09	16 37 44	0♏07 20	7♏12 05	26R33.5	4 51.7	29 50.0	5 38.7	16 47.2	0 35.1	25 43.6	11 55.4	28 35.1	0 24.1
7 Su	21 06 06	17 38 31	14 17 32	21 23 25	26 33.6	5 46.7	0♑50.7	6 25.6	17 09.8	0 49.4	25 41.5	11 58.9	28 33.5	0 23.3
8 M	21 10 02	18 39 18	28 29 28	5♐35 23	26 33.3	6 33.7	1 51.8	7 12.5	17 32.5	1 03.7	25 39.5	12 02.4	28 32.0	0 22.6
9 Tu	21 13 59	19 40 03	12♐40 51	19 45 34	26 32.7	7 11.8	2 53.2	7 59.4	17 55.2	1 18.0	25 37.6	12 05.9	28 30.4	0 21.8
10 W	21 17 56	20 40 48	26 49 10	3♑51 17	26 31.9	7 40.3	3 55.0	8 46.4	18 17.9	1 32.3	25 35.8	12 09.4	28 28.8	0 21.1
11 Th	21 21 52	21 41 31	10♑51 34	17 49 38	26 31.3	7 58.8	4 57.1	9 33.3	18 40.8	1 46.7	25 34.1	12 12.8	28 27.3	0 20.4
12 F	21 25 49	22 42 13	24 45 07	1♒37 40	26 30.8	8R07.0	5 59.6	10 20.3	19 03.6	2 01.1	25 32.5	12 16.3	28 25.8	0 19.7
13 Sa	21 29 45	23 42 54	8♒26 56	15 12 38	26D30.6	8 04.5	7 02.3	11 07.3	19 26.5	2 15.5	25 31.0	12 19.8	28 24.3	0 19.0
14 Su	21 33 42	24 43 33	21 54 31	28 32 22	26 30.5	7 51.4	8 05.4	11 54.3	19 49.5	2 29.9	25 29.7	12 23.2	28 22.8	0 18.4
15 M	21 37 38	25 44 11	5♓06 03	11♓35 30	26R30.6	7 28.0	9 08.7	12 41.3	20 12.5	2 44.3	25 28.4	12 26.6	28 21.3	0 17.8
16 Tu	21 41 35	26 44 47	18 00 41	24 21 41	26 30.6	6 54.9	10 12.4	13 28.4	20 35.5	2 58.7	25 27.3	12 30.1	28 19.8	0 17.2
17 W	21 45 31	27 45 21	0♈38 38	6♈51 42	26 30.5	6 12.9	11 16.3	14 15.4	20 58.6	3 13.1	25 26.2	12 33.5	28 18.4	0 16.6
18 Th	21 49 28	28 45 54	13 01 11	19 07 25	26 30.3	5 23.0	12 20.4	15 02.5	21 21.7	3 27.6	25 25.3	12 36.9	28 17.0	0 16.0
19 F	21 53 25	29 46 25	25 10 44	1♉11 37	26 29.9	4 26.6	13 24.8	15 49.6	21 44.8	3 42.0	25 24.5	12 40.3	28 15.6	0 15.5
20 Sa	21 57 21	0♓46 55	7♉10 30	13 07 56	26 29.5	3 25.3	14 29.5	16 36.7	22 08.0	3 56.5	25 23.8	12 43.6	28 14.2	0 14.9
21 Su	22 01 18	1 47 22	19 04 26	25 00 34	26D29.3	2 20.7	15 34.4	17 23.7	22 31.2	4 11.0	25 23.2	12 47.0	28 12.8	0 14.4
22 M	22 05 14	2 47 48	0♊56 56	6♊54 07	26 29.3	1 14.5	16 39.5	18 10.9	22 54.5	4 25.4	25 22.8	12 50.4	28 11.5	0 14.0
23 Tu	22 09 11	3 48 12	12 52 42	18 53 17	26 29.6	0 08.4	17 44.8	18 58.0	23 17.8	4 39.9	25 22.4	12 53.7	28 10.2	0 13.5
24 W	22 13 07	4 48 34	24 56 25	1♋02 40	26 30.2	29♒03.9	18 50.4	19 45.1	23 41.1	4 54.4	25 22.2	12 57.0	28 08.9	0 13.1
25 Th	22 17 04	5 48 54	7♋12 33	13 26 31	26 31.1	28 02.5	19 56.2	20 32.2	24 04.4	5 08.8	25D22.0	13 00.3	28 07.6	0 12.7
26 F	22 21 00	6 49 12	19 44 59	26 08 17	26 32.1	27 05.4	21 02.1	21 19.4	24 27.8	5 23.3	25 22.0	13 03.6	28 06.3	0 12.3
27 Sa	22 24 57	7 49 28	2♌36 43	9♌10 27	26 32.9	26 13.6	22 08.3	22 06.5	24 51.2	5 37.8	25 22.1	13 06.9	28 05.1	0 11.9
28 Su	22 28 54	8 49 42	15 49 33	22 34 01	26R33.4	25 27.8	23 14.6	22 53.6	25 14.6	5 52.2	25 22.3	13 10.1	28 03.9	0 11.5

Astro Data	Planet Ingress	Last Aspect	☽ Ingress	Last Aspect	☽ Ingress	☽ Phases & Eclipses	Astro Data
Dy Hr Mn	Dy Hr Mn	Dy Hr Mn	Dy Hr Mn	Dy Hr Mn	Dy Hr Mn	Dy Hr Mn	1 January 1915
☽0S 7 5:14	☿ ♒ 15 4:28	3 1:20 ♆ ☌	♌ 3 2:12	1 15:10 ♃ ☍	♍ 1 16:10	1 12:20 ○ 10♋01	Julian Day # 5479
☽0N 20 2:51	☉ ♒ 21 3:00	5 5:13 ♄ ⚹	♍ 5 9:28	3 18:14 ♆ ⚹	♎ 3 20:32	8 21:12 ☾ 17♎32	SVP 6♓26'39"
♃△♄ 20 7:52	♂ ♒ 30 6:12	7 13:52 ♆ ⚹	♎ 7 14:53	5 22:33 ♀ □	♏ 5 23:48	15 14:42 ● 24♑23	GC 25♐39.1 ⚴ 11♒28.4
♄⚼♅ 25 23:32		9 17:20 ♆ □	♏ 9 18:25	8 0:06 ♆ △	♐ 8 2:33	23 5:32 ☽ 2♉09	Eris 26♓25.6 ⚵ 23♍55.7
♃⚻♆ 29 21:30	☿ ♓ 2 10:33	11 19:15 ♆ △	♐ 11 20:25	9 21:57 ♄ ☍	♑ 10 5:25	31 4:41 ○ 10♌14	⚷ 14♓57.3 ⚶ 9♊37.6R
	♃ ♓ 4 0:44	13 16:56 ♄ ☍	♑ 13 21:52	12 6:25 ♆ ☍	♒ 12 9:09	31 4:57 • A 0.045	☽Mean ☊ 29♒03.1
☽0S 3 10:42	♀ ♑ 6 15:57	15 22:53 ♆ ☍	♒ 16 0:17	14 6:29 ♄ △	♓ 14 14:40		
♃△♇ 5 18:23	☉ ♓ 19 17:23	17 23:19 ♄ △	♓ 18 5:14	16 19:33 ♆ △	♈ 16 22:46	7 5:11 ☾ 17♏21	1 February 1915
☿R 12 18:25	☿ ♒R 23 15:04	20 12:31 ☉ ⚹	♈ 20 13:42	19 8:54 ☉ ⚹	♉ 19 9:37	14 4:31 ● 24♒25	Julian Day # 5510
☽0N 16 11:53		22 23:10 ♆ □	♉ 23 1:13	21 18:28 ♆ ⚹	♊ 21 22:05	14 4:33:02 • A 02'03"	SVP 6♓26'33"
♄D 26 3:25		25 11:37 ♆ ⚹	♊ 25 13:48	24 8:26 ♆ △	♋ 24 9:57	22 2:58 ☽ 2♊25	GC 25♐39.2 ⚴ 21♒37.1
		27 21:53 ♃ △	♋ 28 1:08	26 15:39 ♆ ☌	♌ 26 19:11		Eris 26♓38.0 ⚵ 23♍39.9R
		30 7:40 ♆ ☌	♌ 30 9:55				⚷ 16♓18.7 ⚶ 7♊38.3
							☽Mean ☊ 27♒24.6

March 1915 LONGITUDE

Day	Sid.Time	☉	0 hr ☽	Noon ☽	True ☊	☿	♀	♂	⚳	♃	♄	♅	♆	♇
1 M	22 32 50	9♓49 54	29♌23 42	6♍18 22	26♒33.2	24♒48.6	24♑21.2	23♒40.8	25♓38.0	6♓06.7	25♊22.6	13♒13.3	28♋02.7	0♋11.2
2 Tu	22 36 47	10 50 04	13♍17 39	20 21 06	26R 32.3	24R 16.2	25 27.9	24 27.9	26 01.5	6 21.2	25 23.1	13 16.5	28R 01.6	0R 10.9
3 W	22 40 43	11 50 13	27 28 10	4♎38 13	26 30.8	23 50.8	26 34.8	25 15.1	26 25.0	6 35.6	25 23.6	13 19.7	28 00.4	0 10.6
4 Th	22 44 40	12 50 20	11♎50 35	19 04 34	26 28.7	23 32.4	27 41.9	26 02.3	26 48.5	6 50.0	25 24.3	13 22.9	27 59.3	0 10.3
5 F	22 48 36	13 50 25	26 19 25	3♏34 26	26 26.4	23 20.9	28 49.1	26 49.4	27 12.0	7 04.5	25 25.0	13 26.0	27 58.2	0 10.1
6 Sa	22 52 33	14 50 29	10♏48 58	18 02 25	26 24.4	23D 16.1	29 56.5	27 36.6	27 35.6	7 18.9	25 25.9	13 29.1	27 57.2	0 09.9
7 Su	22 56 29	15 50 31	25 14 13	2♐23 55	26 23.0	23 17.8	1♒04.0	28 23.8	27 59.2	7 33.3	25 26.9	13 32.2	27 56.1	0 09.7
8 M	23 00 26	16 50 32	9♐31 09	16 35 37	26D 22.5	23 25.6	2 11.8	29 11.0	28 22.8	7 47.7	25 28.0	13 35.3	27 55.1	0 09.5
9 Tu	23 04 23	17 50 31	23 37 07	0♑35 29	26 23.0	23 39.2	3 19.6	29 58.2	28 46.4	8 02.0	25 29.2	13 38.4	27 54.2	0 09.4
10 W	23 08 19	18 50 28	7♑30 39	14 22 33	26 24.2	23 58.3	4 27.6	0♓45.3	29 10.0	8 16.4	25 30.6	13 41.4	27 53.2	0 09.3
11 Th	23 12 16	19 50 24	21 11 11	27 56 34	26 25.7	24 22.6	5 35.7	1 32.5	29 33.7	8 30.8	25 32.0	13 44.4	27 52.3	0 09.2
12 F	23 16 12	20 50 18	4♒38 44	11♒17 43	26 27.1	24 51.8	6 44.0	2 19.7	29 57.4	8 45.1	25 33.6	13 47.4	27 51.4	0 09.1
13 Sa	23 20 09	21 50 10	17 53 33	24 26 15	26R 27.8	25 25.4	7 52.4	3 06.9	0♈21.1	8 59.4	25 35.2	13 50.3	27 50.5	0 09.0
14 Su	23 24 05	22 50 01	0♓55 52	7♓22 25	26 27.3	26 03.3	9 00.9	3 54.1	0 44.8	9 13.7	25 37.0	13 53.2	27 49.7	0 09.0
15 M	23 28 02	23 49 49	13 45 56	20 06 25	26 25.5	26 45.2	10 09.5	4 41.2	1 08.5	9 27.9	25 38.9	13 56.1	27 48.9	0D 09.0
16 Tu	23 31 58	24 49 36	26 23 57	2♈38 34	26 22.1	27 30.8	11 18.2	5 28.4	1 32.2	9 42.2	25 40.8	13 59.0	27 48.1	0 09.0
17 W	23 35 55	25 49 20	8♈50 20	14 59 23	26 17.5	28 19.9	12 27.0	6 15.5	1 55.9	9 56.4	25 42.9	14 01.8	27 47.4	0 09.0
18 Th	23 39 52	26 49 02	21 05 50	27 09 52	26 12.1	29 12.2	13 36.0	7 02.7	2 19.7	10 10.6	25 45.1	14 04.6	27 46.6	0 09.1
19 F	23 43 48	27 48 43	3♉11 43	9♉11 38	26 06.4	0♓07.7	14 45.0	7 49.8	2 43.5	10 24.7	25 47.4	14 07.4	27 45.9	0 09.2
20 Sa	23 47 45	28 48 21	15 09 57	21 07 01	26 01.1	1 05.9	15 54.1	8 36.9	3 07.2	10 38.8	25 49.8	14 10.1	27 45.3	0 09.3
21 Su	23 51 41	29 47 57	27 03 13	2♊59 01	25 56.8	2 06.9	17 03.3	9 24.0	3 31.0	10 52.9	25 52.4	14 12.8	27 44.7	0 09.4
22 M	23 55 38	0♈47 31	8♊54 55	14 51 25	25 53.8	3 10.5	18 12.7	10 11.1	3 54.8	11 07.0	25 55.0	14 15.5	27 44.1	0 09.5
23 Tu	23 59 34	1 47 02	20 49 06	26 48 32	25D 52.4	4 16.5	19 22.1	10 58.2	4 18.5	11 21.0	25 57.7	14 18.1	27 43.5	0 09.7
24 W	0 03 31	2 46 31	2♋50 19	8♋55 03	25 52.5	5 24.8	20 31.5	11 45.3	4 42.3	11 35.0	26 00.5	14 20.7	27 43.0	0 09.9
25 Th	0 07 27	3 45 58	15 03 23	21 15 53	25 53.6	6 35.4	21 41.1	12 32.4	5 06.1	11 49.0	26 03.5	14 23.3	27 42.5	0 10.1
26 F	0 11 24	4 45 22	27 33 08	3♌55 40	25 55.2	7 48.0	22 50.8	13 19.4	5 29.9	12 02.9	26 06.5	14 25.8	27 42.0	0 10.4
27 Sa	0 15 21	5 44 45	10♌23 58	16 58 25	25R 56.5	9 02.6	24 00.5	14 06.4	5 53.7	12 16.8	26 09.6	14 28.4	27 41.6	0 10.7
28 Su	0 19 17	6 44 04	23 39 19	0♍26 51	25 56.7	10 19.2	25 10.3	14 53.5	6 17.5	12 30.6	26 12.8	14 30.8	27 41.2	0 10.9
29 M	0 23 14	7 43 22	7♍21 03	14 21 47	25 55.2	11 37.6	26 20.2	15 40.5	6 41.3	12 44.4	26 16.2	14 33.2	27 40.8	0 11.3
30 Tu	0 27 10	8 42 37	21 28 47	28 41 32	25 51.9	12 57.9	27 30.2	16 27.4	7 05.1	12 58.2	26 19.6	14 35.6	27 40.5	0 11.6
31 W	0 31 07	9 41 50	5♎59 25	13♎21 35	25 46.6	14 19.9	28 40.2	17 14.4	7 28.8	13 11.9	26 23.1	14 38.0	27 40.2	0 11.9

April 1915 LONGITUDE

Day	Sid.Time	☉	0 hr ☽	Noon ☽	True ☊	☿	♀	♂	⚳	♃	♄	♅	♆	♇
1 Th	0 35 03	10♈41 02	20♎47 06	28♎14 52	25♒40.0	15♓43.6	29♒50.3	18♓01.3	7♈52.6	13♓25.6	26♊26.7	14♒40.3	27♋39.9	0♋12.3
2 F	0 39 00	11 40 11	5♏43 47	13♏12 41	25R 33.0	17 09.0	1♓00.5	18 48.3	8 16.4	13 39.2	26 30.4	14 42.6	27R 39.7	0 12.7
3 Sa	0 42 56	12 39 19	20 40 26	28 06 02	25 26.4	18 36.1	2 10.8	19 35.2	8 40.2	13 52.8	26 34.2	14 44.8	27 39.5	0 13.1
4 Su	0 46 53	13 38 24	5♐28 32	12♐47 10	25 21.1	20 04.7	3 21.1	20 22.1	9 04.0	14 06.3	26 38.1	14 47.0	27 39.3	0 13.6
5 M	0 50 49	14 37 28	20 01 20	27 10 36	25 17.7	21 35.0	4 31.5	21 09.0	9 27.7	14 19.8	26 42.1	14 49.2	27 39.2	0 14.1
6 Tu	0 54 46	15 36 31	4♑14 41	11♑13 28	25D 16.3	23 06.8	5 42.0	21 55.8	9 51.5	14 33.3	26 46.1	14 51.3	27 39.1	0 14.6
7 W	0 58 43	16 35 31	18 06 57	24 55 16	25 16.5	24 40.2	6 52.5	22 42.7	10 15.3	14 46.6	26 50.3	14 53.4	27 39.0	0 15.1
8 Th	1 02 39	17 34 30	1♒38 35	8♒17 11	25 17.4	26 15.1	8 03.1	23 29.5	10 39.0	15 00.0	26 54.5	14 55.5	27D 39.0	0 15.6
9 F	1 06 36	18 33 27	14 51 23	21 21 28	25R 18.3	27 51.6	9 13.7	24 16.3	11 02.8	15 13.2	26 58.9	14 57.5	27 38.9	0 16.2
10 Sa	1 10 32	19 32 22	27 47 47	4♓10 38	25 17.9	29 29.6	10 24.4	25 03.0	11 26.5	15 26.5	27 03.3	14 59.4	27 39.0	0 16.7
11 Su	1 14 29	20 31 15	10♓30 20	16 47 08	25 15.6	1♈09.2	11 35.2	25 49.8	11 50.2	15 39.6	27 07.8	15 01.4	27 39.0	0 17.3
12 M	1 18 25	21 30 07	23 01 18	29 13 02	25 10.8	2 50.3	12 46.0	26 36.5	12 13.9	15 52.7	27 12.4	15 03.2	27 39.1	0 17.9
13 Tu	1 22 22	22 28 56	5♈22 32	11♈29 56	25 03.5	4 32.9	13 56.8	27 23.2	12 37.6	16 05.8	27 17.1	15 05.1	27 39.3	0 18.6
14 W	1 26 18	23 27 44	17 35 26	23 39 07	24 53.9	6 17.1	15 07.7	28 09.9	13 01.3	16 18.8	27 21.8	15 06.8	27 39.4	0 19.2
15 Th	1 30 15	24 26 30	29 41 09	5♉41 39	24 42.8	8 02.8	16 18.6	28 56.5	13 25.0	16 31.7	27 26.7	15 08.6	27 39.6	0 19.9
16 F	1 34 12	25 25 13	11♉40 48	17 38 43	24 31.0	9 50.2	17 29.6	29 43.1	13 48.7	16 44.5	27 31.6	15 10.3	27 39.8	0 20.6
17 Sa	1 38 08	26 23 55	23 35 39	29 31 48	24 19.7	11 39.1	18 40.6	0♈29.7	14 12.3	16 57.3	27 36.6	15 12.0	27 40.1	0 21.3
18 Su	1 42 05	27 22 34	5♊27 27	11♊22 55	24 09.8	13 29.5	19 51.7	1 16.2	14 35.9	17 10.0	27 41.7	15 13.6	27 40.4	0 22.1
19 M	1 46 01	28 21 12	17 18 34	23 14 47	24 02.0	15 21.6	21 02.8	2 02.8	14 59.6	17 22.7	27 46.8	15 15.1	27 40.7	0 22.8
20 Tu	1 49 58	29 19 47	29 12 02	5♋10 48	23 56.7	17 15.3	22 14.0	2 49.2	15 23.2	17 35.3	27 52.1	15 16.7	27 41.1	0 23.6
21 W	1 53 54	0♉18 20	11♋11 38	17 15 07	23 53.8	19 10.6	23 25.1	3 35.7	15 46.7	17 47.8	27 57.4	15 18.1	27 41.5	0 24.4
22 Th	1 57 51	1 16 51	23 21 50	29 32 24	23D 53.0	21 07.4	24 36.3	4 22.1	16 10.3	18 00.2	28 02.8	15 19.6	27 41.9	0 25.2
23 F	2 01 47	2 15 20	5♌47 27	12♌07 36	23R 53.2	23 05.8	25 47.6	5 08.5	16 33.8	18 12.6	28 08.2	15 21.0	27 42.4	0 26.1
24 Sa	2 05 44	3 13 47	18 33 26	25 05 31	23 53.5	25 05.8	26 58.9	5 54.8	16 57.3	18 24.9	28 13.7	15 22.3	27 42.9	0 26.9
25 Su	2 09 41	4 12 11	1♍44 19	8♍30 11	23 52.7	27 07.2	28 10.2	6 41.1	17 20.8	18 37.1	28 19.3	15 23.6	27 43.4	0 27.8
26 M	2 13 37	5 10 33	15 23 24	22 24 02	23 49.9	29 10.1	29 21.5	7 27.4	17 44.3	18 49.2	28 25.0	15 24.8	27 44.0	0 28.7
27 Tu	2 17 34	6 08 53	29 31 59	6♎46 57	23 44.5	1♉14.3	0♈32.9	8 13.6	18 07.7	19 01.2	28 30.7	15 26.0	27 44.6	0 29.6
28 W	2 21 30	7 07 11	14♎08 23	21 35 32	23 36.7	3 19.9	1 44.3	8 59.8	18 31.1	19 13.2	28 36.5	15 27.2	27 45.2	0 30.5
29 Th	2 25 27	8 05 28	29 07 24	6♏42 48	23 27.0	5 26.5	2 55.8	9 46.0	18 54.5	19 25.1	28 42.4	15 28.3	27 45.9	0 31.4
30 F	2 29 23	9 03 42	14♏20 27	21 58 53	23 16.5	7 34.2	4 07.3	10 32.1	19 17.9	19 36.9	28 48.3	15 29.3	27 46.6	0 32.4

Astro Data

	Dy Hr Mn
☽0S	2 18:42
☿D	6 17:42
♇D	15 12:30
☽0N	15 20:04
☉0N	21 16:51
♃⚻♆	29 5:52
☽0S	30 4:45
♃⚺♅	8 2:26
♆D	9 3:32
☽0N	12 2:25
☿0N	13 23:42
♄⚺♆	18 5:41
♂0N	19 23:49
⚳0N	26 5:39
☽0S	26 14:53

Planet Ingress

	Dy Hr Mn
♀ ♒	6 13:15
♂ ♓	9 12:56
⚳ ♈	12 14:39
☿ ♓	19 8:46
☉ ♈	21 16:51
♀ ♓	1 15:19
☿ ♈	10 19:22
♂ ♈	16 20:42
☉ ♉	21 4:29
☿ ♉	26 21:40
♀ ♈	27 0:56
♀0N30 3:24	

Last Aspect / ☽ Ingress

Last Aspect Dy Hr Mn		☽ Ingress Dy Hr Mn
28 16:57	♄ ⚹	♍ 1 1:03
3 0:55	♆ ⚹	♎ 3 4:15
5 3:28	♀ □	♏ 5 6:05
7 4:54	♂ □	♐ 7 7:58
9 10:52	♂ ⚹	♑ 9 10:59
11 11:52	♆ ☍	♒ 11 15:40
13 14:07	♄ △	♓ 13 22:16
16 2:42	♆ △	♈ 16 6:55
18 16:23	☿ ⚹	♉ 18 17:38
21 4:58	☉ ⚹	♊ 21 5:58
23 10:18	♄ ☌	♋ 23 18:22
26 0:17	♆ ☌	♌ 26 4:38
28 4:31	♄ ⚹	♍ 28 11:13
30 10:19	♆ ⚹	♎ 30 14:10

Last Aspect / ☽ Ingress

Last Aspect Dy Hr Mn		☽ Ingress Dy Hr Mn
1 14:46	♀ △	♏ 1 14:49
3 11:17	♆ △	♐ 3 15:05
5 11:12	♄ ☍	♑ 5 16:47
7 16:51	♆ ☍	♒ 7 21:03
9 22:32	♄ △	♓ 10 4:08
12 8:58	♆ △	♈ 12 13:31
14 19:58	♆ □	♉ 15 0:38
17 8:14	♆ ⚹	♊ 17 12:57
19 23:13	☉ ⚹	♋ 20 1:36
22 8:26	♆ ☌	♌ 22 12:53
24 17:44	♄ ⚹	♍ 24 20:53
27 0:46	♀ ☍	♎ 27 0:47
28 23:15	♄ △	♏ 29 1:23

☽ Phases & Eclipses

Dy Hr Mn	
1 18:32	○ 10♍06
1 18:19	⊶ A 0.555
8 12:27	☾ 16♐52
15 19:42	● 24♓09
23 22:48	☽ 2♋14
31 5:37	○ 9♎26
6 20:12	☾ 15♑57
14 11:35	● 23♈27
22 15:39	☽ 1♌26
29 14:19	○ 8♏11

Astro Data

1 March 1915
Julian Day # 5538
SVP 6♓26'29"
GC 25♐39.3 ⚴ 0♓57.0
Eris 26♓56.5 ⚵ 18♍05.6R
⚷ 17♓55.7 ⚶ 11♊26.0
☽ Mean ☊ 25♒55.6

1 April 1915
Julian Day # 5569
SVP 6♓26'26"
GC 25♐39.3 ⚴ 10♓57.6
Eris 27♓20.3 ⚵ 11♍07.4R
⚷ 19♓48.3 ⚶ 19♊50.5
☽ Mean ☊ 24♒17.1

LONGITUDE

May 1915

Day	Sid.Time	☉	0 hr ☽	Noon ☽	True ☊	☿	♀	♂	⚳	♃	♄	♅	♆	♇
1 Sa	2 33 20	10♉01 55	29♏36 43	7♐12 32	23♒06.4	9♉42.8	5♈18.8	11♈18.2	19♈41.2	19♓48.6	28♊54.3	15♒30.3	27♋47.3	0♋33.4
2 Su	2 37 16	11 00 07	14♐45 04	22 13 12	22R 57.9	11 52.0	6 30.4	12 04.3	20 04.5	20 00.2	29 00.3	15 31.3	27 48.0	0 34.4
3 M	2 41 13	11 58 17	29 36 02	6♑52 52	22 51.8	14 01.7	7 42.0	12 50.3	20 27.8	20 11.8	29 06.4	15 32.2	27 48.8	0 35.4
4 Tu	2 45 10	12 56 25	14♑03 15	21 06 55	22 48.3	16 11.5	8 53.6	13 36.3	20 51.1	20 23.2	29 12.6	15 33.1	27 49.6	0 36.4
5 W	2 49 06	13 54 32	28 03 49	4♒54 02	22D 46.9	18 21.3	10 05.2	14 22.2	21 14.3	20 34.6	29 18.8	15 33.9	27 50.5	0 37.5
6 Th	2 53 03	14 52 38	11♒37 51	18 15 34	22R 46.8	20 30.7	11 16.9	15 08.1	21 37.5	20 45.9	29 25.1	15 34.6	27 51.4	0 38.5
7 F	2 56 59	15 50 42	24 47 39	1♓14 32	22 46.6	22 39.6	12 28.6	15 54.0	22 00.7	20 57.1	29 31.5	15 35.4	27 52.3	0 39.6
8 Sa	3 00 56	16 48 44	7♓36 43	13 54 42	22 45.3	24 47.4	13 40.4	16 39.8	22 23.8	21 08.1	29 37.9	15 36.0	27 53.2	0 40.7
9 Su	3 04 52	17 46 46	20 08 58	26 19 59	22 41.9	26 54.1	14 52.1	17 25.6	22 46.9	21 19.1	29 44.3	15 36.6	27 54.2	0 41.8
10 M	3 08 49	18 44 45	2♈28 12	8♈33 58	22 35.7	28 59.2	16 03.9	18 11.3	23 10.0	21 30.0	29 50.9	15 37.2	27 55.2	0 42.9
11 Tu	3 12 45	19 42 44	14 37 41	20 39 39	22 26.6	1♊02.6	17 15.8	18 57.0	23 33.0	21 40.8	29 57.4	15 37.7	27 56.2	0 44.0
12 W	3 16 42	20 40 41	26 40 08	2♉39 23	22 14.9	3 04.0	18 27.6	19 42.6	23 56.0	21 51.5	0♋04.0	15 38.2	27 57.3	0 45.2
13 Th	3 20 39	21 38 37	8♉37 37	14 35 01	22 01.4	5 03.1	19 39.5	20 28.2	24 19.0	22 02.1	0 10.7	15 38.6	27 58.4	0 46.3
14 F	3 24 35	22 36 31	20 31 45	26 28 00	21 47.1	6 59.8	20 51.4	21 13.8	24 41.9	22 12.5	0 17.4	15 39.0	27 59.5	0 47.5
15 Sa	3 28 32	23 34 24	2♊23 56	8♊19 42	21 33.3	8 53.8	22 03.3	21 59.3	25 04.8	22 22.9	0 24.2	15 39.3	28 00.6	0 48.7
16 Su	3 32 28	24 32 15	14 15 30	20 11 34	21 20.9	10 45.1	23 15.2	22 44.8	25 27.7	22 33.1	0 31.0	15 39.6	28 01.8	0 49.9
17 M	3 36 25	25 30 04	26 08 09	2♋05 31	21 11.0	12 33.6	24 27.2	23 30.2	25 50.5	22 43.3	0 37.9	15 39.8	28 03.0	0 51.1
18 Tu	3 40 21	26 27 52	8♋04 01	14 04 01	21 03.8	14 19.0	25 39.1	24 15.6	26 13.2	22 53.3	0 44.8	15 40.0	28 04.2	0 52.4
19 W	3 44 18	27 25 39	20 05 55	26 10 11	20 59.5	16 01.4	26 51.1	25 00.9	26 35.9	23 03.2	0 51.7	15 40.1	28 05.5	0 53.6
20 Th	3 48 14	28 23 24	2♌17 19	8♌27 52	20D 57.6	17 40.7	28 03.1	25 46.1	26 58.6	23 13.0	0 58.7	15R 40.2	28 06.8	0 54.9
21 F	3 52 11	29 21 07	14 42 22	21 01 24	20R 57.2	19 16.7	29 15.2	26 31.3	27 21.2	23 22.7	1 05.7	15 40.2	28 08.1	0 56.1
22 Sa	3 56 08	0♊18 48	27 25 33	3♍55 22	20 57.2	20 49.5	0♉27.2	27 16.5	27 43.8	23 32.3	1 12.8	15 40.2	28 09.4	0 57.4
23 Su	4 00 04	1 16 28	10♍31 22	17 14 01	20 56.5	22 18.9	1 39.3	28 01.6	28 06.3	23 41.7	1 19.9	15 40.1	28 10.8	0 58.7
24 M	4 04 01	2 14 07	24 03 39	1♎00 31	20 53.9	23 45.1	2 51.4	28 46.6	28 28.8	23 51.1	1 27.1	15 39.9	28 12.2	1 00.0
25 Tu	4 07 57	3 11 43	8♎04 42	15 16 04	20 49.0	25 07.8	4 03.5	29 31.6	28 51.2	24 00.3	1 34.3	15 39.8	28 13.6	1 01.3
26 W	4 11 54	4 09 19	22 34 19	29 58 53	20 41.7	26 27.1	5 15.6	0♉16.6	29 13.6	24 09.3	1 41.5	15 39.6	28 15.0	1 02.6
27 Th	4 15 50	5 06 53	7♏28 58	15♏03 33	20 32.4	27 43.0	6 27.7	1 01.5	29 36.0	24 18.3	1 48.7	15 39.3	28 16.5	1 03.9
28 F	4 19 47	6 04 26	22 41 26	0♐21 15	20 22.2	28 55.3	7 39.9	1 46.3	29 58.2	24 27.1	1 56.0	15 39.0	28 18.0	1 05.2
29 Sa	4 23 43	7 01 57	8♐01 32	15 40 49	20 12.3	0♋04.0	8 52.1	2 31.1	0♉20.5	24 35.8	2 03.3	15 38.6	28 19.5	1 06.6
30 Su	4 27 40	7 59 28	23 17 41	0♑50 49	20 03.9	1 09.1	10 04.3	3 15.9	0 42.7	24 44.4	2 10.7	15 38.2	28 21.0	1 07.9
31 M	4 31 37	8 56 58	8♑19 05	15 41 33	19 57.7	2 10.5	11 16.5	4 00.6	1 04.8	24 52.8	2 18.1	15 37.7	28 22.6	1 09.3

LONGITUDE

June 1915

Day	Sid.Time	☉	0 hr ☽	Noon ☽	True ☊	☿	♀	♂	⚳	♃	♄	♅	♆	♇
1 Tu	4 35 33	9♊54 27	22♑57 31	0♒06 30	19♒54.1	3♋08.2	12♉28.8	4♉45.2	1♉26.8	25♓01.1	2♋25.5	15♒37.2	28♋24.2	1♋10.7
2 W	4 39 30	10 51 55	7♒08 17	14 02 47	19D 52.7	4 02.0	13 41.1	5 29.8	1 48.9	25 09.3	2 32.9	15R 36.7	28 25.8	1 12.0
3 Th	4 43 26	11 49 22	20 50 10	27 30 40	19 52.7	4 51.9	14 53.4	6 14.3	2 10.8	25 17.3	2 40.4	15 36.1	28 27.4	1 13.4
4 F	4 47 23	12 46 48	4♓04 40	10♓32 40	19R 53.1	5 37.8	16 05.7	6 58.8	2 32.7	25 25.2	2 47.9	15 35.4	28 29.1	1 14.8
5 Sa	4 51 19	13 44 14	16 55 09	23 12 40	19 52.7	6 19.6	17 18.0	7 43.2	2 54.5	25 33.0	2 55.4	15 34.7	28 30.8	1 16.2
6 Su	4 55 16	14 41 39	29 25 49	5♈35 09	19 50.6	6 57.2	18 30.4	8 27.6	3 16.3	25 40.6	3 03.0	15 34.0	28 32.5	1 17.6
7 M	4 59 13	15 39 04	11♈41 12	17 44 31	19 46.3	7 30.6	19 42.8	9 11.9	3 38.0	25 48.1	3 10.5	15 33.2	28 34.2	1 19.0
8 Tu	5 03 09	16 36 27	23 45 34	29 44 50	19 39.4	7 59.7	20 55.2	9 56.1	3 59.7	25 55.4	3 18.1	15 32.4	28 35.9	1 20.4
9 W	5 07 06	17 33 51	5♉42 42	11♉39 33	19 30.4	8 24.4	22 07.6	10 40.3	4 21.3	26 02.5	3 25.7	15 31.5	28 37.7	1 21.8
10 Th	5 11 02	18 31 13	17 35 44	23 31 31	19 19.7	8 44.6	23 20.1	11 24.5	4 42.8	26 09.6	3 33.4	15 30.6	28 39.5	1 23.3
11 F	5 14 59	19 28 35	29 27 12	5♊22 59	19 08.4	9 00.3	24 32.6	12 08.6	5 04.2	26 16.4	3 41.0	15 29.6	28 41.3	1 24.7
12 Sa	5 18 55	20 25 57	11♊19 07	17 15 45	18 57.3	9 11.4	25 45.0	12 52.6	5 25.6	26 23.2	3 48.7	15 28.6	28 43.1	1 26.1
13 Su	5 22 52	21 23 18	23 13 06	29 11 21	18 47.5	9R 18.0	26 57.6	13 36.5	5 46.9	26 29.7	3 56.4	15 27.5	28 44.9	1 27.6
14 M	5 26 48	22 20 38	5♋10 40	11♋11 17	18 39.7	9 20.0	28 10.1	14 20.4	6 08.2	26 36.1	4 04.1	15 26.4	28 46.8	1 29.0
15 Tu	5 30 45	23 17 57	17 13 25	23 17 18	18 34.3	9 17.5	29 22.6	15 04.3	6 29.3	26 42.4	4 11.8	15 25.3	28 48.6	1 30.4
16 W	5 34 42	24 15 15	29 23 15	5♌31 32	18 31.3	9 10.5	0♊35.2	15 48.0	6 50.4	26 48.4	4 19.6	15 24.1	28 50.5	1 31.9
17 Th	5 38 38	25 12 33	11♌42 32	17 56 36	18D 30.4	8 59.3	1 47.8	16 31.7	7 11.4	26 54.4	4 27.3	15 22.9	28 52.4	1 33.3
18 F	5 42 35	26 09 50	24 14 09	0♍35 36	18 30.9	8 44.0	3 00.4	17 15.4	7 32.4	27 00.1	4 35.1	15 21.6	28 54.4	1 34.8
19 Sa	5 46 31	27 07 06	7♍01 23	13 31 57	18 31.9	8 24.8	4 13.0	17 59.0	7 53.2	27 05.7	4 42.8	15 20.3	28 56.3	1 36.3
20 Su	5 50 28	28 04 21	20 07 41	26 49 00	18R 32.6	8 02.0	5 25.7	18 42.5	8 14.0	27 11.2	4 50.6	15 19.0	28 58.3	1 37.7
21 M	5 54 24	29 01 36	3♎36 11	10♎29 30	18 31.9	7 35.9	6 38.3	19 25.9	8 34.7	27 16.4	4 58.4	15 17.6	29 00.2	1 39.2
22 Tu	5 58 21	29 58 50	17 29 03	24 34 50	18 29.6	7 07.0	7 51.0	20 09.3	8 55.3	27 21.5	5 06.2	15 16.2	29 02.2	1 40.6
23 W	6 02 17	0♋56 03	1♏46 41	9♏04 14	18 25.3	6 35.7	9 03.7	20 52.6	9 15.8	27 26.4	5 14.0	15 14.7	29 04.2	1 42.1
24 Th	6 06 14	1 53 16	16 26 56	23 54 04	18 19.6	6 02.6	10 16.4	21 35.9	9 36.2	27 31.2	5 21.8	15 13.2	29 06.2	1 43.5
25 F	6 10 11	2 50 28	1♐24 42	8♐57 47	18 13.0	5 28.0	11 29.1	22 19.1	9 56.6	27 35.8	5 29.6	15 11.7	29 08.3	1 45.0
26 Sa	6 14 07	3 47 40	16 32 06	24 06 24	18 06.6	4 52.7	12 41.9	23 02.0	10 16.8	27 40.2	5 37.4	15 10.1	29 10.3	1 46.5
27 Su	6 18 04	4 44 51	1♑39 26	9♑09 56	18 01.1	4 17.2	13 54.7	23 45.3	10 37.0	27 44.4	5 45.2	15 08.5	29 12.4	1 47.9
28 M	6 22 00	5 42 03	16 36 48	23 59 01	17 57.3	3 42.2	15 07.5	24 28.3	10 57.1	27 48.5	5 53.0	15 06.9	29 14.4	1 49.4
29 Tu	6 25 57	6 39 14	1♒15 46	8♒26 23	17D 55.3	3 08.2	16 20.3	25 11.2	11 17.0	27 52.4	6 00.9	15 05.2	29 16.5	1 50.8
30 W	6 29 53	7 36 25	15 30 28	22 27 43	17 55.0	2 35.9	17 33.2	25 54.1	11 36.9	27 56.1	6 08.7	15 03.5	29 18.6	1 52.3

Astro Data	Planet Ingress	Last Aspect	☽ Ingress	Last Aspect	☽ Ingress	☽ Phases & Eclipses	Astro Data
Dy Hr Mn	Dy Hr Mn	Dy Hr Mn	Dy Hr Mn	Dy Hr Mn	Dy Hr Mn	Dy Hr Mn	1 May 1915
☽0N 9 7:24	☿ ♊ 10 23:47	30 21:07 ♆ △	♐ 1 0:37	1 9:07 ♆ ☍	♒ 1 11:49	6 5:22 ☾ 14♒37	Julian Day # 5599
♄⚼♅ 17 18:53	♄ ♋ 11 21:23	2 23:06 ♄ ☍	♑ 3 0:39	2 14:45 ♅ ☌	♓ 3 16:32	14 3:31 ● 22♉16	SVP 6♓26'22"
♄☌♇ 19 19:52	♀ ♉ 22 2:56	4 23:36 ♆ ☍	♒ 5 3:23	5 22:15 ♆ △	♈ 6 1:06	22 4:49 ☽ 0♍02	GC 25♐39.4 ⚴ 19♓48.5
♅R 21 10:48	☉ ♊ 22 4:10	7 8:46 ♄ △	♓ 7 9:41	8 9:41 ♆ □	♉ 8 12:30	28 21:33 ○ 6♐27	Eris 27♓40.9 ⚵ 9♍03.8
☽0S 23 23:21	♂ ♉ 26 3:08	9 18:43 ♄ □	♈ 9 19:10	10 22:25 ♆ ⚹	♊ 11 1:06		⚷ 21♓22.2 ⚶ 0♋29.5
	⚳ ♉ 28 13:54	12 2:34 ♆ □	♉ 12 6:40	13 6:32 ♃ □	♋ 13 13:38	4 16:32 ☾ 12♓58	☽ Mean ☊ 22♒41.8
☽0N 5 12:33	☿ ♋ 29 10:34	14 15:05 ♆ ⚹	♊ 14 19:09	15 22:54 ♆ ☌	♌ 16 1:12	12 18:57 ● 20♊43	
☿R 14 10:38		16 18:53 ♀ ⚹	♋ 17 7:47	18 2:58 ☉ ⚹	♍ 18 10:53	20 14:24 ☽ 28♍10	1 June 1915
☽0S 20 5:35	♀ ♊ 16 0:21	19 15:47 ♆ ☌	♌ 19 19:31	20 15:50 ♆ ⚹	♎ 20 17:39	27 4:27 ○ 4♑27	Julian Day # 5630
	☉ ♋ 22 12:29	21 22:57 ♂ △	♍ 22 4:47	22 19:28 ♆ □	♏ 22 21:03		SVP 6♓26'17"
		24 7:10 ♆ ⚹	♎ 24 10:16	24 20:20 ♆ △	♐ 24 21:45		GC 25♐39.5 ⚴ 27♓23.1
		26 9:12 ♆ □	♏ 26 12:02	26 17:41 ♃ □	♑ 26 21:22		Eris 27♓54.8 ⚵ 12♍20.9
		28 8:47 ♆ △	♐ 28 11:27	28 20:40 ♆ ☍	♒ 28 21:54		⚷ 22♓25.1 ⚶ 13♋00.0
		30 2:12 ♃ □	♑ 30 10:39				☽ Mean ☊ 21♒03.3

July 1915 LONGITUDE

Day	Sid.Time	☉	0 hr ☽	Noon ☽	True ☊	☿	♀	♂	⚳	♃	♄	♅	♆	♇
1 Th	6 33 50	8♋33 36	29♒18 05	6♓01 37	17♒55.9	2♋05.8	18♊46.1	26♉36.9	11♉56.7	27♓59.6	6♋16.5	15♒01.7	29♋20.7	1♋53.7
2 F	6 37 46	9 30 47	12♓38 34	19 09 15	17 57.4	1R 38.4	19 59.0	27 19.6	12 16.4	28 02.9	6 24.3	15R 00.0	29 22.8	1 55.2
3 Sa	6 41 43	10 27 58	25 34 05	1♈53 32	17R 58.6	1 14.2	21 11.9	28 02.3	12 36.0	28 06.1	6 32.1	14 58.1	29 24.9	1 56.6
4 Su	6 45 40	11 25 10	8♈08 08	14 18 28	17 58.9	0 53.6	22 24.9	28 44.9	12 55.5	28 09.1	6 39.9	14 56.3	29 27.0	1 58.1
5 M	6 49 36	12 22 22	20 25 04	26 28 32	17 57.8	0 37.1	23 37.9	29 27.5	13 14.9	28 11.8	6 47.7	14 54.4	29 29.2	1 59.5
6 Tu	6 53 33	13 19 34	2♉29 25	8♉28 17	17 55.3	0 25.0	24 50.9	0♊09.9	13 34.2	28 14.4	6 55.5	14 52.5	29 31.3	2 01.0
7 W	6 57 29	14 16 47	14 25 38	20 21 58	17 51.3	0 17.4	26 03.9	0 52.3	13 53.4	28 16.8	7 03.3	14 50.6	29 33.5	2 02.4
8 Th	7 01 26	15 14 00	26 17 44	2♊13 23	17 46.3	0D 14.7	27 17.0	1 34.7	14 12.4	28 19.1	7 11.0	14 48.6	29 35.7	2 03.8
9 F	7 05 22	16 11 13	8♊09 17	14 05 48	17 40.8	0 17.0	28 30.1	2 17.0	14 31.4	28 21.1	7 18.8	14 46.7	29 37.8	2 05.3
10 Sa	7 09 19	17 08 26	20 03 14	26 01 52	17 35.4	0 24.5	29 43.2	2 59.2	14 50.2	28 22.9	7 26.6	14 44.7	29 40.0	2 06.7
11 Su	7 13 16	18 05 40	2♋01 58	8♋03 45	17 30.6	0 37.2	0♋56.4	3 41.3	15 08.9	28 24.6	7 34.3	14 42.6	29 42.2	2 08.1
12 M	7 17 12	19 02 54	14 07 24	20 13 08	17 27.0	0 55.1	2 09.5	4 23.4	15 27.5	28 26.0	7 42.0	14 40.6	29 44.4	2 09.5
13 Tu	7 21 09	20 00 09	26 21 06	2♌31 28	17 24.7	1 18.4	3 22.7	5 05.3	15 46.0	28 27.3	7 49.7	14 38.5	29 46.6	2 10.9
14 W	7 25 05	20 57 23	8♌44 24	15 00 05	17D 23.9	1 47.1	4 35.9	5 47.3	16 04.4	28 28.3	7 57.4	14 36.4	29 48.8	2 12.3
15 Th	7 29 02	21 54 38	21 18 40	27 40 20	17 24.2	2 21.0	5 49.2	6 29.1	16 22.6	28 29.2	8 05.1	14 34.2	29 51.0	2 13.7
16 F	7 32 58	22 51 53	4♍05 17	10♍33 43	17 25.3	3 00.3	7 02.4	7 10.9	16 40.7	28 29.9	8 12.8	14 32.1	29 53.2	2 15.1
17 Sa	7 36 55	23 49 07	17 05 49	23 41 47	17 26.8	3 44.8	8 15.7	7 52.5	16 58.6	28 30.4	8 20.4	14 29.9	29 55.4	2 16.5
18 Su	7 40 51	24 46 23	0♎21 49	7♎06 05	17 28.2	4 34.5	9 29.0	8 34.2	17 16.5	28R 30.6	8 28.0	14 27.7	29 57.6	2 17.8
19 M	7 44 48	25 43 38	13 54 44	20 47 49	17R 28.9	5 29.4	10 42.3	9 15.7	17 34.2	28 30.7	8 35.6	14 25.5	29 59.9	2 19.2
20 Tu	7 48 45	26 40 53	27 45 24	4♏47 25	17 28.8	6 29.3	11 55.7	9 57.2	17 51.7	28 30.6	8 43.2	14 23.2	0♌02.1	2 20.5
21 W	7 52 41	27 38 09	11♏53 42	19 04 02	17 27.8	7 34.3	13 09.1	10 38.5	18 09.2	28 30.3	8 50.8	14 21.0	0 04.3	2 21.9
22 Th	7 56 38	28 35 25	26 18 02	3♐35 14	17 26.0	8 44.2	14 22.5	11 19.8	18 26.4	28 29.8	8 58.3	14 18.7	0 06.5	2 23.2
23 F	8 00 34	29 32 42	10♐55 01	18 16 41	17 23.9	9 59.0	15 35.9	12 01.1	18 43.6	28 29.1	9 05.8	14 16.5	0 08.8	2 24.6
24 Sa	8 04 31	0♌29 59	25 39 26	3♑02 24	17 21.7	11 18.5	16 49.4	12 42.2	19 00.6	28 28.2	9 13.3	14 14.2	0 11.0	2 25.9
25 Su	8 08 27	1 27 16	10♑24 41	17 45 24	17 19.9	12 42.6	18 02.8	13 23.3	19 17.4	28 27.1	9 20.8	14 11.9	0 13.2	2 27.2
26 M	8 12 24	2 24 34	25 03 38	2♒18 33	17 18.8	14 11.2	19 16.3	14 04.3	19 34.1	28 25.8	9 28.2	14 09.6	0 15.4	2 28.5
27 Tu	8 16 20	3 21 52	9♒29 27	16 35 39	17D 18.4	15 44.1	20 29.9	14 45.3	19 50.7	28 24.3	9 35.6	14 07.2	0 17.7	2 29.8
28 W	8 20 17	4 19 11	23 36 41	0♓32 08	17 18.7	17 21.2	21 43.4	15 26.1	20 07.0	28 22.7	9 43.0	14 04.9	0 19.9	2 31.1
29 Th	8 24 14	5 16 31	7♓21 45	14 05 27	17 19.4	19 02.1	22 57.0	16 06.9	20 23.3	28 20.8	9 50.3	14 02.5	0 22.1	2 32.3
30 F	8 28 10	6 13 53	20 43 14	27 15 12	17 20.4	20 46.8	24 10.6	16 47.6	20 39.3	28 18.7	9 57.6	14 00.2	0 24.3	2 33.6
31 Sa	8 32 07	7 11 15	3♈41 37	10♈02 47	17 21.4	22 34.8	25 24.3	17 28.2	20 55.2	28 16.5	10 04.9	13 57.8	0 26.5	2 34.8

August 1915 LONGITUDE

Day	Sid.Time	☉	0 hr ☽	Noon ☽	True ☊	☿	♀	♂	⚳	♃	♄	♅	♆	♇
1 Su	8 36 03	8♌08 38	16♈19 05	22♈30 59	17♒22.1	24♋26.0	26♋37.9	18♊08.8	21♉11.0	28♓14.0	10♋12.1	13♒55.4	0♌28.8	2♋36.0
2 M	8 40 00	9 06 02	28 38 57	4♉43 33	17R 22.4	26 20.0	27 51.6	18 49.3	21 26.5	28R 11.4	10 19.3	13R 53.0	0 31.0	2 37.3
3 Tu	8 43 56	10 03 28	10♉45 19	16 44 50	17 22.4	28 16.4	29 05.3	19 29.7	21 41.9	28 08.6	10 26.5	13 50.7	0 33.2	2 38.5
4 W	8 47 53	11 00 54	22 42 39	28 39 20	17 22.0	0♌15.0	0♌19.1	20 10.0	21 57.1	28 05.6	10 33.6	13 48.3	0 35.4	2 39.7
5 Th	8 51 49	11 58 22	4♊35 37	10♊31 33	17 21.5	2 15.2	1 32.9	20 50.2	22 12.2	28 02.3	10 40.7	13 45.9	0 37.6	2 40.8
6 F	8 55 46	12 55 52	16 28 07	22 25 39	17 20.9	4 16.9	2 46.7	21 30.4	22 27.0	27 59.0	10 47.8	13 43.5	0 39.8	2 42.0
7 Sa	8 59 43	13 53 22	28 24 36	4♋25 23	17 20.4	6 19.5	4 00.5	22 10.5	22 41.7	27 55.4	10 54.8	13 41.1	0 41.9	2 43.2
8 Su	9 03 39	14 50 54	10♋28 23	16 33 55	17 20.1	8 22.9	5 14.4	22 50.5	22 56.2	27 51.6	11 01.7	13 38.7	0 44.1	2 44.3
9 M	9 07 36	15 48 27	22 42 18	28 53 45	17 19.9	10 26.7	6 28.3	23 30.4	23 10.4	27 47.7	11 08.7	13 36.3	0 46.3	2 45.4
10 Tu	9 11 32	16 46 01	5♌08 28	11♌26 37	17 19.8	12 30.5	7 42.2	24 10.2	23 24.5	27 43.6	11 15.6	13 33.9	0 48.5	2 46.6
11 W	9 15 29	17 43 36	17 48 18	24 13 35	17 19.8	14 34.2	8 56.2	24 49.9	23 38.4	27 39.3	11 22.4	13 31.5	0 50.6	2 47.7
12 Th	9 19 25	18 41 12	0♍42 29	7♍15 01	17 19.8	16 37.4	10 10.1	25 29.6	23 52.1	27 34.8	11 29.2	13 29.1	0 52.7	2 48.7
13 F	9 23 22	19 38 50	13 51 07	20 30 42	17 19.6	18 40.1	11 24.1	26 09.1	24 05.5	27 30.2	11 35.9	13 26.8	0 54.9	2 49.8
14 Sa	9 27 18	20 36 28	27 13 42	4♎00 00	17 19.3	20 41.9	12 38.1	26 48.6	24 18.8	27 25.4	11 42.6	13 24.4	0 57.0	2 50.9
15 Su	9 31 15	21 34 07	10♎49 27	17 41 54	17 18.9	22 42.9	13 52.2	27 28.0	24 31.8	27 20.4	11 49.3	13 22.0	0 59.1	2 51.9
16 M	9 35 12	22 31 48	24 37 11	1♏35 07	17 18.5	24 42.8	15 06.2	28 07.3	24 44.6	27 15.3	11 55.9	13 19.7	1 01.2	2 52.9
17 Tu	9 39 08	23 29 29	8♏35 31	15 38 09	17D 18.2	26 41.6	16 20.3	28 46.5	24 57.2	27 10.0	12 02.4	13 17.3	1 03.3	2 53.9
18 W	9 43 05	24 27 12	22 42 48	29 49 10	17 18.2	28 39.2	17 34.4	29 25.6	25 09.6	27 04.6	12 08.9	13 15.0	1 05.4	2 54.9
19 Th	9 47 01	25 24 56	6♐56 59	14♐05 56	17 18.5	0♍35.6	18 48.5	0♋04.6	25 21.7	26 59.0	12 15.3	13 12.7	1 07.5	2 55.9
20 F	9 50 58	26 22 40	21 15 39	28 25 44	17 19.1	2 30.6	20 02.7	0 43.5	25 33.6	26 53.2	12 21.7	13 10.3	1 09.5	2 56.8
21 Sa	9 54 54	27 20 26	5♑35 45	12♑45 17	17 19.9	4 24.3	21 16.8	1 22.4	25 45.3	26 47.3	12 28.0	13 08.0	1 11.6	2 57.8
22 Su	9 58 51	28 18 13	19 53 50	27 00 53	17 20.7	6 16.7	22 31.0	2 01.1	25 56.7	26 41.3	12 34.3	13 05.8	1 13.6	2 58.7
23 M	10 02 47	29 16 02	4♒05 59	11♒08 35	17R 21.2	8 07.7	23 45.2	2 39.8	26 07.9	26 35.2	12 40.5	13 03.5	1 15.7	2 59.6
24 Tu	10 06 44	0♍13 51	18 08 15	25 04 32	17 21.1	9 57.3	24 59.5	3 18.3	26 18.9	26 28.9	12 46.7	13 01.2	1 17.7	3 00.5
25 W	10 10 41	1 11 42	1♓57 01	8♓45 21	17 20.4	11 45.7	26 13.7	3 56.8	26 29.6	26 22.4	12 52.8	12 59.0	1 19.6	3 01.3
26 Th	10 14 37	2 09 35	15 29 18	22 08 37	17 19.0	13 32.6	27 28.0	4 35.2	26 40.0	26 15.9	12 58.8	12 56.8	1 21.6	3 02.2
27 F	10 18 34	3 07 29	28 43 13	5♈13 04	17 16.9	15 18.3	28 42.3	5 13.5	26 50.2	26 09.2	13 04.7	12 54.6	1 23.6	3 03.0
28 Sa	10 22 30	4 05 25	11♈38 11	17 58 44	17 14.6	17 02.6	29 56.6	5 51.7	27 00.1	26 02.4	13 10.6	12 52.4	1 25.5	3 03.8
29 Su	10 26 27	5 03 22	24 14 54	0♉27 00	17 12.2	18 45.6	1♍10.9	6 29.8	27 09.8	25 55.5	13 16.5	12 50.2	1 27.5	3 04.6
30 M	10 30 23	6 01 22	6♉35 22	12 40 25	17 10.1	20 27.3	2 25.3	7 07.8	27 19.2	25 48.5	13 22.3	12 48.1	1 29.4	3 05.4
31 Tu	10 34 20	6 59 23	18 42 36	24 42 27	17 08.7	22 07.8	3 39.7	7 45.7	27 28.3	25 41.4	13 28.0	12 45.9	1 31.3	3 06.1

Astro Data	Dy Hr Mn
☽ 0N	2 19:20
☿ D	8 13:04
☽ 0S	17 10:38
♃ R	19 9:49
☽ 0N	30 3:58
☽ 0S	13 16:15
♄⚻♅	26 6:08
☽ 0N	26 13:23

Planet Ingress		Dy Hr Mn
♂	♊	6 6:23
♀	♋	10 17:31
♆	♌	19 13:33
☉	♌	23 23:26
♀	♌	4 5:47
☿	♌	4 9:00
☿	♍	19 4:38
♂	♋	19 9:10
☉	♍	24 6:15
♀	♍	28 13:06

Last Aspect Dy Hr Mn			☽ Ingress	Dy Hr Mn
30 18:21	♂	□	♓	1 1:14
3 7:16	♆	△	♈	3 8:24
5 18:01	♆	□	♉	5 19:01
8 6:40	♆	⚹	♊	8 7:30
10 16:43	♃	□	♋	10 19:56
13 6:39	♆	☌	♌	13 7:06
14 11:15	♅	☍	♍	15 16:22
17 23:15	♆	⚹	♎	17 23:21
19 21:08	☉	□	♏	20 3:50
22 3:38	♃	△	♐	22 6:06
24 4:35	♃	□	♑	24 7:03
26 5:35	♃	⚹	♒	26 8:10
27 8:43	♂	△	♓	28 11:04
30 13:57	♃	☌	♈	30 17:06

Last Aspect Dy Hr Mn			☽ Ingress	Dy Hr Mn
1 20:56	♀	□	♉	2 2:40
4 10:52	♃	⚹	♊	4 14:43
6 23:05	♃	□	♋	7 3:11
9 9:53	♃	△	♌	9 14:08
11 13:11	♂	⚹	♍	11 22:42
14 0:25	♃	☍	♎	14 4:55
16 5:45	♂	△	♏	16 9:17
18 9:43	☿	□	♐	18 12:18
20 9:26	♃	□	♑	20 14:38
22 11:27	♃	⚹	♒	22 17:03
24 11:50	♀	☍	♓	24 20:35
26 19:26	♃	☌	♈	27 2:21
28 2:50	♄	□	♉	29 11:08
31 13:57	♃	⚹	♊	31 22:38

☽ Phases & Eclipses Dy Hr Mn	
4 5:54	☾ 11♈11
12 9:30	● 18♋57
19 21:08	☽ 26♎05
26 12:11	○ 2♒25
26 12:24	• A 0.354
2 21:27	☾ 9♉29
10 22:52	● 17♌12
10 22:52:07	• A 01'33"
18 2:17	☽ 24♏04
24 21:40	○ 0♓37
24 21:27	• A 0.575

Astro Data

1 July 1915
Julian Day # 5660
SVP 6♓26'11"
GC 25♐39.6 ⚴ 2♈12.1
Eris 27♓58.0R ⚵ 19♍02.4
⚷ 22♓41.0R ⚶ 25♋58.8
☽ Mean ☊ 19♒28.0

1 August 1915
Julian Day # 5691
SVP 6♓26'06"
GC 25♐39.6 ⚴ 3♈04.3R
Eris 27♓50.2R ⚵ 28♍04.0
⚷ 22♓08.3R ⚶ 9♌56.4
☽ Mean ☊ 17♒49.6

LONGITUDE — September 1915

Day	Sid.Time	☉	0 hr ☽	Noon ☽	True ☊	☿	♀	♂	⚳	♃	♄	♅	♆	♇
1 W	10 38 16	7♍57 26	0♊40 30	6♊37 19	17♒08.1	23♍47.0	4♍54.1	8♋23.5	27♉37.1	25♓34.2	13♋33.6	12♒43.8	1♌33.1	3♋06.9
2 Th	10 42 13	8 55 32	12 33 28	18 29 35	17D 08.4	25 25.0	6 08.5	9 01.2	27 45.6	25R 26.9	13 39.2	12R 41.8	1 35.0	3 07.6
3 F	10 46 10	9 53 39	24 26 15	0♋24 03	17 09.5	27 01.7	7 23.0	9 38.8	27 53.9	25 19.6	13 44.7	12 39.7	1 36.9	3 08.3
4 Sa	10 50 06	10 51 48	6♋23 34	12 25 23	17 11.1	28 37.3	8 37.4	10 16.3	28 01.9	25 12.1	13 50.1	12 37.7	1 38.7	3 09.0
5 Su	10 54 03	11 49 59	18 30 00	24 37 55	17 12.8	0♎11.6	9 51.9	10 53.7	28 09.5	25 04.5	13 55.5	12 35.7	1 40.5	3 09.6
6 M	10 57 59	12 48 12	0♌49 35	7♌05 22	17R 14.0	1 44.7	11 06.4	11 31.0	28 16.9	24 56.9	14 00.8	12 33.7	1 42.3	3 10.2
7 Tu	11 01 56	13 46 27	13 25 35	19 50 29	17 14.3	3 16.6	12 21.0	12 08.2	28 23.9	24 49.3	14 06.0	12 31.8	1 44.0	3 10.9
8 W	11 05 52	14 44 44	26 20 12	2♍54 49	17 13.4	4 47.3	13 35.5	12 45.3	28 30.7	24 41.5	14 11.1	12 29.9	1 45.8	3 11.4
9 Th	11 09 49	15 43 02	9♍34 18	16 18 30	17 11.1	6 16.8	14 50.1	13 22.3	28 37.1	24 33.7	14 16.2	12 28.0	1 47.5	3 12.0
10 F	11 13 45	16 41 23	23 07 13	0♎00 07	17 07.6	7 45.1	16 04.7	13 59.1	28 43.2	24 25.9	14 21.1	12 26.1	1 49.2	3 12.6
11 Sa	11 17 42	17 39 45	6♎56 49	13 56 52	17 03.1	9 12.2	17 19.3	14 35.9	28 48.9	24 18.0	14 26.0	12 24.3	1 50.9	3 13.1
12 Su	11 21 38	18 38 08	20 59 43	28 04 51	16 58.4	10 38.1	18 33.9	15 12.5	28 54.4	24 10.1	14 30.9	12 22.5	1 52.5	3 13.6
13 M	11 25 35	19 36 34	5♏11 41	12♏19 41	16 54.1	12 02.7	19 48.5	15 49.0	28 59.5	24 02.1	14 35.6	12 20.8	1 54.2	3 14.1
14 Tu	11 29 32	20 35 01	19 28 18	26 37 04	16 50.7	13 26.0	21 03.1	16 25.4	29 04.3	23 54.1	14 40.3	12 19.0	1 55.8	3 14.5
15 W	11 33 28	21 33 30	3♐45 30	10♐53 14	16D 48.8	14 48.1	22 17.8	17 01.7	29 08.7	23 46.2	14 44.8	12 17.4	1 57.4	3 15.0
16 Th	11 37 25	22 32 00	17 59 56	25 05 20	16 48.4	16 08.8	23 32.5	17 37.8	29 12.8	23 38.2	14 49.3	12 15.7	1 59.0	3 15.4
17 F	11 41 21	23 30 32	2♑09 12	9♑11 21	16 49.2	17 28.1	24 47.1	18 13.9	29 16.6	23 30.2	14 53.7	12 14.1	2 00.5	3 15.8
18 Sa	11 45 18	24 29 06	16 11 38	23 09 55	16 50.6	18 46.0	26 01.8	18 49.8	29 20.0	23 22.2	14 58.0	12 12.5	2 02.0	3 16.2
19 Su	11 49 14	25 27 41	0♒06 05	7♒00 02	16R 51.8	20 02.5	27 16.5	19 25.6	29 23.0	23 14.2	15 02.3	12 11.0	2 03.5	3 16.5
20 M	11 53 11	26 26 18	13 51 37	20 40 45	16 52.1	21 17.3	28 31.2	20 01.3	29 25.7	23 06.2	15 06.4	12 09.5	2 05.0	3 16.9
21 Tu	11 57 08	27 24 57	27 27 14	4♓10 58	16 50.8	22 30.6	29 45.9	20 36.9	29 28.1	22 58.2	15 10.5	12 08.0	2 06.4	3 17.2
22 W	12 01 04	28 23 37	10♓51 46	17 29 28	16 47.4	23 42.1	1♎00.7	21 12.3	29 30.0	22 50.3	15 14.4	12 06.6	2 07.8	3 17.5
23 Th	12 05 01	29 22 19	24 03 56	0♈35 00	16 42.1	24 51.9	2 15.4	21 47.6	29 31.6	22 42.4	15 18.3	12 05.2	2 09.2	3 17.7
24 F	12 08 57	0♎21 03	7♈02 35	13 26 36	16 35.1	25 59.7	3 30.2	22 22.8	29 32.9	22 34.5	15 22.1	12 03.8	2 10.6	3 18.0
25 Sa	12 12 54	1 19 50	19 47 01	26 03 51	16 27.1	27 05.5	4 44.9	22 57.8	29 33.8	22 26.7	15 25.8	12 02.5	2 11.9	3 18.2
26 Su	12 16 50	2 18 38	2♉17 10	8♉27 08	16 18.8	28 09.1	5 59.7	23 32.8	29R 34.3	22 18.9	15 29.4	12 01.3	2 13.2	3 18.4
27 M	12 20 47	3 17 29	14 33 55	20 37 48	16 11.1	29 10.4	7 14.5	24 07.6	29 34.4	22 11.2	15 32.9	12 00.0	2 14.5	3 18.6
28 Tu	12 24 43	4 16 22	26 39 07	2♊38 14	16 04.8	0♏09.2	8 29.3	24 42.2	29 34.1	22 03.6	15 36.3	11 58.9	2 15.8	3 18.7
29 W	12 28 40	5 15 17	8♊35 38	14 31 46	16 00.4	1 05.2	9 44.1	25 16.7	29 33.5	21 56.0	15 39.6	11 57.7	2 17.0	3 18.8
30 Th	12 32 36	6 14 15	20 27 13	26 22 31	15D 57.9	1 58.4	10 58.9	25 51.1	29 32.5	21 48.5	15 42.8	11 56.6	2 18.2	3 19.0

LONGITUDE — October 1915

Day	Sid.Time	☉	0 hr ☽	Noon ☽	True ☊	☿	♀	♂	⚳	♃	♄	♅	♆	♇
1 F	12 36 33	7♎13 14	2♋18 19	8♋15 14	15♒57.3	2♏48.3	12♎13.7	26♋25.4	29♉31.1	21♓41.0	15♋45.9	11♒55.6	2♌19.4	3♋19.0
2 Sa	12 40 30	8 12 16	14 13 55	20 15 01	15 57.9	3 34.7	13 28.6	26 59.5	29R 29.3	21R 33.6	15 49.0	11R 54.6	2 20.5	3 19.1
3 Su	12 44 26	9 11 21	26 19 12	2♌27 05	15 59.0	4 17.4	14 43.4	27 33.5	29 27.1	21 26.4	15 51.9	11 53.6	2 21.6	3 19.1
4 M	12 48 23	10 10 27	8♌39 16	14 56 18	15R 59.7	4 56.0	15 58.3	28 07.3	29 24.5	21 19.2	15 54.7	11 52.7	2 22.7	3R 19.2
5 Tu	12 52 19	11 09 36	21 18 41	27 46 50	15 59.0	5 30.1	17 13.1	28 41.0	29 21.5	21 12.1	15 57.4	11 51.8	2 23.8	3 19.1
6 W	12 56 16	12 08 47	4♍21 02	11♍01 30	15 56.2	5 59.3	18 28.0	29 14.5	29 18.2	21 05.1	16 00.0	11 51.0	2 24.8	3 19.1
7 Th	13 00 12	13 08 00	17 48 16	24 41 14	15 51.1	6 23.3	19 42.9	29 47.8	29 14.4	20 58.3	16 02.5	11 50.2	2 25.8	3 19.1
8 F	13 04 09	14 07 16	1♎40 10	8♎44 37	15 43.6	6 41.4	20 57.8	0♌21.0	29 10.3	20 51.5	16 04.9	11 49.5	2 26.7	3 19.0
9 Sa	13 08 05	15 06 33	15 54 00	23 07 37	15 34.6	6 53.3	22 12.7	0 54.0	29 05.7	20 44.9	16 07.2	11 48.8	2 27.7	3 18.9
10 Su	13 12 02	16 05 53	0♏24 36	7♏44 02	15 24.8	6R 58.4	23 27.6	1 26.9	29 00.8	20 38.4	16 09.4	11 48.2	2 28.6	3 18.7
11 M	13 15 59	17 05 14	15 04 56	22 26 19	15 15.6	6 56.4	24 42.5	1 59.6	28 55.5	20 32.0	16 11.5	11 47.6	2 29.4	3 18.6
12 Tu	13 19 55	18 04 37	29 47 14	7♐06 50	15 08.0	6 46.7	25 57.4	2 32.1	28 49.8	20 25.7	16 13.5	11 47.1	2 30.3	3 18.4
13 W	13 23 52	19 04 03	14♐24 20	21 39 07	15 02.7	6 28.9	27 12.4	3 04.5	28 43.8	20 19.6	16 15.4	11 46.6	2 31.1	3 18.2
14 Th	13 27 48	20 03 30	28 50 40	5♑58 38	14 59.9	6 02.8	28 27.3	3 36.7	28 37.3	20 13.7	16 17.1	11 46.2	2 31.9	3 18.0
15 F	13 31 45	21 02 58	13♑02 47	20 03 01	14D 59.1	5 28.2	29 42.2	4 08.7	28 30.5	20 07.9	16 18.8	11 45.8	2 32.6	3 17.8
16 Sa	13 35 41	22 02 29	26 59 18	3♒51 43	14R 59.4	4 45.2	0♏57.1	4 40.5	28 23.3	20 02.2	16 20.4	11 45.4	2 33.3	3 17.5
17 Su	13 39 38	23 02 01	10♒40 22	17 25 25	14 59.6	3 54.2	2 12.1	5 12.2	28 15.8	19 56.7	16 21.8	11 45.1	2 34.0	3 17.3
18 M	13 43 34	24 01 35	24 07 02	0♓45 24	14 58.6	2 55.6	3 27.0	5 43.6	28 07.9	19 51.4	16 23.1	11 44.9	2 34.6	3 17.0
19 Tu	13 47 31	25 01 10	7♓20 39	13 52 58	14 55.3	1 50.5	4 41.9	6 14.9	27 59.6	19 46.2	16 24.3	11 44.7	2 35.2	3 16.6
20 W	13 51 28	26 00 47	20 22 26	26 49 09	14 49.1	0 40.3	5 56.8	6 46.0	27 51.0	19 41.2	16 25.4	11 44.6	2 35.8	3 16.3
21 Th	13 55 24	27 00 26	3♈13 10	9♈34 31	14 40.1	29♎26.6	7 11.8	7 16.9	27 42.0	19 36.3	16 26.4	11 44.5	2 36.4	3 15.9
22 F	13 59 21	28 00 08	15 53 14	22 09 19	14 28.6	28 11.4	8 26.7	7 47.6	27 32.8	19 31.7	16 27.3	11D 44.4	2 36.9	3 15.5
23 Sa	14 03 17	28 59 51	28 22 47	4♉33 39	14 15.5	26 56.9	9 41.6	8 18.1	27 23.2	19 27.2	16 28.1	11 44.5	2 37.3	3 15.1
24 Su	14 07 14	29 59 36	10♉41 58	16 47 48	14 01.9	25 45.4	10 56.5	8 48.4	27 13.2	19 22.8	16 28.8	11 44.5	2 37.8	3 14.7
25 M	14 11 10	0♏59 23	22 51 17	28 52 33	13 48.9	24 39.0	12 11.5	9 18.5	27 03.0	19 18.7	16 29.3	11 44.6	2 38.2	3 14.2
26 Tu	14 15 07	1 59 12	4♊51 48	10♊49 19	13 37.6	23 39.8	13 26.4	9 48.4	26 52.5	19 14.7	16 29.8	11 44.8	2 38.6	3 13.7
27 W	14 19 03	2 59 04	16 45 25	22 40 27	13 28.8	22 49.4	14 41.4	10 18.1	26 41.6	19 11.0	16 30.1	11 45.0	2 38.9	3 13.2
28 Th	14 23 00	3 58 57	28 34 53	4♋29 11	13 22.8	22 09.2	15 56.3	10 47.6	26 30.5	19 07.4	16 30.3	11 45.3	2 39.2	3 12.7
29 F	14 26 57	4 58 53	10♋23 53	16 19 34	13 19.5	21 40.1	17 11.3	11 16.8	26 19.1	19 04.0	16R 30.4	11 45.6	2 39.5	3 12.2
30 Sa	14 30 53	5 58 51	22 16 52	28 16 24	13D 18.2	21 22.3	18 26.2	11 45.8	26 07.4	19 00.8	16 30.4	11 46.0	2 39.7	3 11.6
31 Su	14 34 50	6 58 51	4♌18 53	10♌24 59	13R 18.1	21D 16.2	19 41.2	12 14.6	25 55.5	18 57.7	16 30.3	11 46.4	2 39.9	3 11.0

Astro Data

	Dy Hr Mn
☿0S	5 12:25
☽0S	9 23:42
☽0N	22 21:58
♀0S	24 3:21
☉0S	24 3:24
⚳R	27 7:53
♇R	4 14:45
☽0S	7 8:54
☿R	10 17:22
☽0N	20 4:33
♅D	22 18:11
♄R	29 22:58
☿D	31 13:00

Planet Ingress

		Dy Hr Mn
☿	♎	5 9:02
♀	♎	21 16:31
☉	♎	24 3:24
☿	♏	28 8:11
♂	♌	7 20:48
♀	♏	15 17:42
☿	♎R	21 1:13
☉	♏	24 12:10

Last Aspect / ☽ Ingress

Last Aspect Dy Hr Mn			☽ Ingress	Dy Hr Mn
3 4:10	☿	□	♋	3 11:12
5 12:51	♃	△	♌	5 22:24
6 22:21	♅	☍	♍	8 6:42
10 2:23	♃	☍	♎	10 12:00
11 13:10	♂	□	♏	12 15:14
14 7:29	♃	△	♐	14 17:41
16 9:34	♃	□	♑	16 20:20
18 17:26	♀	△	♒	18 23:49
20 13:11	☿	△	♓	21 4:32
23 9:35	☉	☍	♈	23 10:55
25 14:10	☿	☍	♉	25 19:35
27 19:19	♂	⚹	♊	28 6:42
30 2:50	♃	□	♋	30 19:20

Last Aspect / ☽ Ingress

Last Aspect Dy Hr Mn			☽ Ingress	Dy Hr Mn
3 1:58	♂	☌	♌	3 7:13
4 14:10	♀	⚹	♍	5 16:04
7 5:36	♃	☍	♎	7 21:09
9 10:21	♀	☌	♏	9 23:20
11 8:55	♃	△	♐	12 0:21
13 22:08	♀	⚹	♑	14 1:56
15 13:51	☉	□	♒	16 5:15
17 22:51	☉	△	♓	18 10:38
19 22:49	♃	☌	♈	20 17:57
23 0:15	☉	☍	♉	23 3:08
24 17:05	♃	⚹	♊	25 14:15
27 12:17	☿	△	♋	28 2:53
29 22:28	☿	□	♌	30 15:26

☽ Phases & Eclipses

Dy Hr Mn		
1 14:56	☾	8♊05
9 10:52	●	15♍40
16 7:21	☽	22♐21
23 9:35	○	29♓16
1 9:44	☾	7♋08
8 21:42	●	14♎31
15 13:51	☽	21♑08
23 0:15	○	28♈31
31 4:39	☾	6♌40

Astro Data

1 September 1915
Julian Day # 5722
SVP 6♓26'02"
GC 25♐39.7 ⚴ 28♓30.5R
Eris 27♓33.4R ⚵ 8♎17.0
⚷ 20♓57.1R ⚶ 24♌12.1
☽ Mean ☊ 16♒11.1

1 October 1915
Julian Day # 5752
SVP 6♓25'59"
GC 25♐39.8 ⚴ 20♓45.5R
Eris 27♓13.2R ⚵ 18♎43.3
⚷ 19♓35.7R ⚶ 8♍03.6
☽ Mean ☊ 14♒35.7

November 1915 — LONGITUDE

Day	Sid.Time	☉	0 hr ☽	Noon ☽	True ☊	☿	♀	♂	⚳	♃	♄	♅	♆	♇
1 M	14 38 46	7♏58 53	16♌35 23	22♌50 46	13♒17.9	21♎21.3	20♏56.1	12♌43.2	25♉43.4	18♓54.9	16♋30.1	11♒46.9	2♌40.1	3♋10.4
2 Tu	14 42 43	8 58 58	29 11 45	5♍38 54	13R 16.5	21 37.1	22 11.1	13 11.5	25R 31.0	18R 52.3	16R 29.7	11 47.4	2 40.3	3R 09.8
3 W	14 46 39	9 59 04	12♍12 44	18 53 37	13 13.0	22 03.1	23 26.1	13 39.5	25 18.4	18 49.9	16 29.3	11 48.0	2 40.4	3 09.2
4 Th	14 50 36	10 59 12	25 41 48	2♎37 21	13 06.7	22 38.3	24 41.0	14 07.3	25 05.6	18 47.6	16 28.7	11 48.6	2 40.4	3 08.5
5 F	14 54 32	11 59 23	9♎40 11	16 49 59	12 57.7	23 21.9	25 56.0	14 34.9	24 52.6	18 45.6	16 28.0	11 49.3	2R 40.5	3 07.8
6 Sa	14 58 29	12 59 35	24 06 11	1♏28 04	12 46.7	24 13.1	27 11.0	15 02.2	24 39.4	18 43.8	16 27.2	11 50.0	2 40.5	3 07.1
7 Su	15 02 26	13 59 50	8♏54 39	16 24 50	12 34.8	25 10.9	28 25.9	15 29.2	24 26.1	18 42.2	16 26.3	11 50.8	2 40.4	3 06.4
8 M	15 06 22	15 00 06	23 57 21	1♐30 54	12 23.3	26 14.5	29 40.9	15 56.0	24 12.6	18 40.7	16 25.3	11 51.6	2 40.4	3 05.7
9 Tu	15 10 19	16 00 24	9♐04 10	16 35 54	12 13.5	27 23.2	0♐55.9	16 22.4	23 59.0	18 39.5	16 24.2	11 52.5	2 40.3	3 04.9
10 W	15 14 15	17 00 43	24 04 57	1♑30 20	12 06.4	28 36.2	2 10.9	16 48.6	23 45.3	18 38.5	16 22.9	11 53.4	2 40.1	3 04.2
11 Th	15 18 12	18 01 04	8♑51 15	16 07 05	12 02.2	29 53.0	3 25.8	17 14.5	23 31.5	18 37.8	16 21.6	11 54.4	2 40.0	3 03.4
12 F	15 22 08	19 01 27	23 17 26	0♒22 05	12D 00.5	1♏13.0	4 40.8	17 40.1	23 17.6	18 37.2	16 20.1	11 55.4	2 39.8	3 02.6
13 Sa	15 26 05	20 01 50	7♒20 58	14 14 10	12R 00.2	2 35.6	5 55.8	18 05.4	23 03.7	18 36.8	16 18.6	11 56.5	2 39.5	3 01.8
14 Su	15 30 01	21 02 15	21 01 53	27 44 22	12 00.1	4 00.5	7 10.7	18 30.4	22 49.7	18D 36.6	16 16.9	11 57.6	2 39.2	3 00.9
15 M	15 33 58	22 02 41	4♓21 58	10♓55 02	11 58.9	5 27.2	8 25.7	18 55.0	22 35.7	18 36.7	16 15.1	11 58.8	2 38.9	3 00.1
16 Tu	15 37 55	23 03 09	17 23 56	23 49 02	11 55.5	6 55.5	9 40.6	19 19.4	22 21.7	18 36.9	16 13.2	12 00.0	2 38.6	2 59.2
17 W	15 41 51	24 03 38	0♈10 40	6♈29 11	11 49.3	8 25.1	10 55.6	19 43.4	22 07.7	18 37.4	16 11.2	12 01.3	2 38.2	2 58.3
18 Th	15 45 48	25 04 08	12 44 50	18 57 54	11 40.1	9 55.7	12 10.5	20 07.1	21 53.7	18 38.0	16 09.1	12 02.6	2 37.8	2 57.4
19 F	15 49 44	26 04 39	25 08 35	1♉17 04	11 28.4	11 27.2	13 25.4	20 30.5	21 39.7	18 38.9	16 06.9	12 04.0	2 37.4	2 56.5
20 Sa	15 53 41	27 05 13	7♉23 31	13 28 04	11 15.0	12 59.3	14 40.4	20 53.5	21 25.8	18 40.0	16 04.6	12 05.4	2 36.9	2 55.5
21 Su	15 57 37	28 05 47	19 30 50	25 31 56	11 01.0	14 32.0	15 55.3	21 16.2	21 12.0	18 41.2	16 02.2	12 06.9	2 36.4	2 54.6
22 M	16 01 34	29 06 23	1♊31 31	7♊29 42	10 47.6	16 05.1	17 10.2	21 38.5	20 58.2	18 42.7	15 59.7	12 08.4	2 35.9	2 53.6
23 Tu	16 05 30	0♐07 01	13 26 38	19 22 31	10 35.9	17 38.5	18 25.2	22 00.5	20 44.6	18 44.4	15 57.1	12 10.0	2 35.3	2 52.6
24 W	16 09 27	1 07 40	25 17 34	1♋12 03	10 26.7	19 12.2	19 40.1	22 22.1	20 31.0	18 46.3	15 54.4	12 11.6	2 34.7	2 51.7
25 Th	16 13 24	2 08 20	7♋06 16	13 00 34	10 20.3	20 46.1	20 55.0	22 43.3	20 17.6	18 48.4	15 51.6	12 13.3	2 34.1	2 50.7
26 F	16 17 20	3 09 02	18 55 23	24 51 09	10 16.7	22 20.0	22 09.9	23 04.1	20 04.4	18 50.7	15 48.8	12 15.0	2 33.4	2 49.6
27 Sa	16 21 17	4 09 46	0♌48 22	6♌47 35	10D 15.4	23 54.1	23 24.8	23 24.6	19 51.3	18 53.2	15 45.8	12 16.7	2 32.7	2 48.6
28 Su	16 25 13	5 10 31	12 49 24	18 54 25	10 15.6	25 28.2	24 39.7	23 44.6	19 38.4	18 55.9	15 42.7	12 18.5	2 32.0	2 47.6
29 M	16 29 10	6 11 17	25 03 16	1♍16 37	10R 16.2	27 02.3	25 54.6	24 04.2	19 25.6	18 58.7	15 39.5	12 20.3	2 31.3	2 46.5
30 Tu	16 33 06	7 12 05	7♍35 06	13 59 20	10 16.0	28 36.5	27 09.5	24 23.3	19 13.1	19 01.8	15 36.3	12 22.2	2 30.5	2 45.5

December 1915 — LONGITUDE

Day	Sid.Time	☉	0 hr ☽	Noon ☽	True ☊	☿	♀	♂	⚳	♃	♄	♅	♆	♇
1 W	16 37 03	8♐12 55	20♍29 53	27♍07 17	10♒14.3	0♐10.6	28♐24.4	24♌42.1	19♉00.8	19♓05.1	15♋32.9	12♒24.1	2♌29.6	2♋44.4
2 Th	16 40 59	9 13 45	3♎51 55	10♎44 03	10R 10.2	1 44.7	29 39.3	25 00.4	18R 48.7	19 08.6	15R 29.5	12 26.1	2R 28.8	2R 43.3
3 F	16 44 56	10 14 38	17 43 49	24 51 07	10 03.8	3 18.8	0♑54.2	25 18.2	18 36.9	19 12.3	15 26.0	12 28.1	2 27.9	2 42.2
4 Sa	16 48 53	11 15 32	2♏05 40	9♏26 57	9 55.5	4 52.9	2 09.1	25 35.5	18 25.3	19 16.1	15 22.4	12 30.2	2 27.0	2 41.1
5 Su	16 52 49	12 16 27	16 54 11	24 26 24	9 46.2	6 27.0	3 24.0	25 52.4	18 14.1	19 20.2	15 18.7	12 32.2	2 26.1	2 40.0
6 M	16 56 46	13 17 23	2♐02 24	9♐40 53	9 37.1	8 01.0	4 38.8	26 08.8	18 03.1	19 24.4	15 15.0	12 34.4	2 25.1	2 38.9
7 Tu	17 00 42	14 18 20	17 20 25	24 59 34	9 29.4	9 35.1	5 53.7	26 24.7	17 52.3	19 28.9	15 11.2	12 36.6	2 24.1	2 37.7
8 W	17 04 39	15 19 19	2♑36 56	10♑11 13	9 23.8	11 09.2	7 08.6	26 40.1	17 41.9	19 33.5	15 07.3	12 38.8	2 23.1	2 36.6
9 Th	17 08 35	16 20 18	17 41 19	25 06 15	9D 20.6	12 43.2	8 23.5	26 55.0	17 31.9	19 38.3	15 03.3	12 41.1	2 22.1	2 35.4
10 F	17 12 32	17 21 17	2♒25 20	9♒38 02	9 19.8	14 17.4	9 38.3	27 09.3	17 22.1	19 43.3	14 59.2	12 43.4	2 21.0	2 34.3
11 Sa	17 16 29	18 22 18	16 44 03	23 43 18	9 20.4	15 51.5	10 53.2	27 23.1	17 12.7	19 48.5	14 55.1	12 45.7	2 19.9	2 33.1
12 Su	17 20 25	19 23 18	0♓35 48	7♓21 46	9R 21.5	17 25.7	12 08.0	27 36.3	17 03.6	19 53.9	14 51.0	12 48.1	2 18.8	2 32.0
13 M	17 24 22	20 24 20	14 01 30	20 35 22	9 22.1	19 00.0	13 22.8	27 49.0	16 54.9	19 59.4	14 46.7	12 50.5	2 17.6	2 30.8
14 Tu	17 28 18	21 25 21	27 03 48	3♈27 16	9 21.2	20 34.3	14 37.6	28 01.1	16 46.5	20 05.1	14 42.4	12 52.9	2 16.5	2 29.6
15 W	17 32 15	22 26 24	9♈46 16	16 01 14	9 18.4	22 08.8	15 52.4	28 12.7	16 38.5	20 11.0	14 38.1	12 55.4	2 15.3	2 28.4
16 Th	17 36 11	23 27 26	22 12 40	28 21 00	9 13.3	23 43.3	17 07.2	28 23.6	16 30.9	20 17.1	14 33.6	12 57.9	2 14.1	2 27.2
17 F	17 40 08	24 28 29	4♉26 38	10♉29 58	9 06.5	25 18.0	18 21.9	28 33.9	16 23.7	20 23.3	14 29.2	13 00.5	2 12.8	2 26.0
18 Sa	17 44 04	25 29 33	16 31 21	22 31 05	8 58.3	26 52.9	19 36.7	28 43.7	16 16.8	20 29.8	14 24.7	13 03.1	2 11.5	2 24.8
19 Su	17 48 01	26 30 37	28 29 28	4♊26 45	8 49.6	28 27.9	20 51.4	28 52.8	16 10.4	20 36.3	14 20.1	13 05.7	2 10.3	2 23.6
20 M	17 51 58	27 31 42	10♊23 10	16 18 56	8 41.3	0♑03.0	22 06.1	29 01.3	16 04.3	20 43.1	14 15.5	13 08.4	2 08.9	2 22.4
21 Tu	17 55 54	28 32 47	22 14 16	28 09 22	8 34.1	1 38.4	23 20.8	29 09.1	15 58.6	20 50.0	14 10.8	13 11.1	2 07.6	2 21.2
22 W	17 59 51	29 33 52	4♋04 26	9♋59 41	8 28.6	3 14.0	24 35.5	29 16.3	15 53.3	20 57.1	14 06.2	13 13.8	2 06.3	2 20.0
23 Th	18 03 47	0♑34 58	15 55 21	21 51 41	8 25.1	4 49.7	25 50.2	29 22.8	15 48.4	21 04.3	14 01.4	13 16.6	2 04.9	2 18.8
24 F	18 07 44	1 36 05	27 48 58	3♌47 31	8D 23.5	6 25.7	27 04.8	29 28.6	15 43.9	21 11.7	13 56.7	13 19.4	2 03.5	2 17.6
25 Sa	18 11 40	2 37 12	9♌47 39	15 49 45	8 23.7	8 01.9	28 19.4	29 33.8	15 39.8	21 19.3	13 51.9	13 22.2	2 02.1	2 16.4
26 Su	18 15 37	3 38 19	21 54 15	28 01 34	8 25.0	9 38.3	29 34.1	29 38.2	15 36.1	21 27.0	13 47.1	13 25.0	2 00.6	2 15.2
27 M	18 19 33	4 39 27	4♍12 11	10♍26 35	8 26.8	11 15.0	0♒48.7	29 41.9	15 32.9	21 34.8	13 42.2	13 27.9	1 59.2	2 14.0
28 Tu	18 23 30	5 40 36	16 45 16	23 08 44	8 28.3	12 51.8	2 03.2	29 44.9	15 30.0	21 42.8	13 37.3	13 30.8	1 57.7	2 12.8
29 W	18 27 27	6 41 45	29 37 28	6♎11 56	8R 29.0	14 28.9	3 17.8	29 47.1	15 27.5	21 51.0	13 32.4	13 33.8	1 56.2	2 11.6
30 Th	18 31 23	7 42 54	12♎52 32	19 39 34	8 28.3	16 06.1	4 32.4	29 48.6	15 25.5	21 59.3	13 27.5	13 36.7	1 54.7	2 10.4
31 F	18 35 20	8 44 04	26 33 17	3♏33 44	8 26.3	17 43.5	5 46.9	29R 49.3	15 23.8	22 07.7	13 22.6	13 39.7	1 53.2	2 09.2

Astro Data
Dy Hr Mn
☽0S 3 18:35
♆R 5 23:53
♃D 14 19:30
☽0N 16 9:24

☽0S 1 2:58
☽0N 13 14:29
☽0S 28 9:18
♄⊼♅ 29 7:53
♂R 31 22:29

Planet Ingress
Dy Hr Mn
♀ ♐ 8 18:07
☿ ♏ 11 14:08
☉ ♐ 23 9:14

☿ ♐ 1 9:18
♀ ♑ 2 18:38
☿ ♑ 20 11:14
☉ ♑ 22 22:16
♀ ♒ 26 20:21

Last Aspect / ☽ Ingress

Last Aspect Dy Hr Mn	☽ Ingress Dy Hr Mn
1 9:07 ☿ ⚹	♍ 2 1:30
3 20:51 ♀ ⚹	♎ 4 7:29
5 23:26 ☿ ☌	♏ 6 9:37
8 8:50 ♀ ☌	♐ 8 9:36
10 6:52 ☿ ⚹	♑ 10 9:33
11 16:11 ♃ ⚹	♒ 12 11:22
13 23:03 ☉ □	♓ 14 16:05
16 10:26 ☉ △	♈ 16 23:40
18 14:19 ♂ △	♉ 19 9:29
21 17:36 ☉ ☍	♊ 21 20:56
23 17:30 ♂ ⚹	♋ 24 9:34
26 6:08 ☿ △	♌ 26 22:23
29 2:40 ☿ □	♍ 29 9:33

Last Aspect Dy Hr Mn	☽ Ingress Dy Hr Mn
1 14:32 ♀ □	♎ 1 17:09
3 12:46 ♂ ⚹	♏ 3 20:33
5 14:19 ♂ □	♐ 5 20:47
7 14:16 ♂ △	♑ 7 19:53
9 3:06 ♃ ⚹	♒ 9 20:01
11 18:29 ♂ ☍	♓ 11 22:57
13 11:38 ☉ □	♈ 14 5:30
16 12:05 ♂ △	♉ 16 15:14
19 0:38 ♂ ☍	♊ 19 3:02
21 14:02 ♂ ⚹	♋ 21 15:44
23 20:57 ♀ ☍	♌ 24 4:23
26 15:09 ♂ ☌	♍ 26 15:51
28 9:18 ♃ ☍	♎ 29 0:41
31 5:37 ♂ ⚹	♏ 31 5:55

☽ Phases & Eclipses
Dy Hr Mn
7 7:52 ● 13♏49
13 23:03 ☽ 20♒30
21 17:36 ○ 28♉20
29 22:10 ☾ 6♍37

6 18:03 ● 13♐33
13 11:38 ☽ 20♓23
21 12:52 ○ 28♊35
29 12:58 ☾ 6♎44

Astro Data
1 November 1915
Julian Day # 5783
SVP 6♓25'55"
GC 25♐39.8 ⚴ 15♓08.7R
Eris 26♓54.4R ✱ 29♎37.1
⚷ 18♓29.6R ⚶ 22♍07.3
☽ Mean ☊ 12♒57.2

1 December 1915
Julian Day # 5813
SVP 6♓25'50"
GC 25♐39.9 ⚴ 15♓22.2
Eris 26♓43.7R ✱ 9♏49.3
⚷ 18♓06.9 ⚶ 4♎59.6
☽ Mean ☊ 11♒21.9

LONGITUDE — January 1916

Day	Sid.Time	☉	0 hr ☽	Noon ☽	True ☊	☿	♀	♂	⚳	♃	♄	♅	♆	♇
1 Sa	18 39 16	9♑45 14	10♏40 53	17♏54 30	8♒23.1	19♑21.1	7♒01.4	29♌49.3	15♉22.6	22♓16.3	13♋17.6	13♒42.8	1♌51.7	2♋08.0
2 Su	18 43 13	10 46 25	25 14 07	2♐39 08	8R 19.1	20 58.7	8 15.9	29R 48.4	15R 21.7	22 25.1	13R 12.7	13 45.8	1R 50.1	2R 06.8
3 M	18 47 09	11 47 36	10♐08 43	17 41 52	8 15.1	22 36.4	9 30.4	29 46.8	15D 21.3	22 34.0	13 07.7	13 48.9	1 48.6	2 05.6
4 Tu	18 51 06	12 48 48	25 17 28	2♑54 14	8 11.7	24 14.1	10 44.8	29 44.4	15 21.3	22 43.0	13 02.8	13 52.0	1 47.0	2 04.4
5 W	18 55 02	13 49 59	10♑30 54	18 06 11	8 09.3	25 51.7	11 59.2	29 41.2	15 21.7	22 52.1	12 57.8	13 55.1	1 45.4	2 03.2
6 Th	18 58 59	14 51 10	25 38 49	3♒07 42	8D 08.3	27 29.0	13 13.7	29 37.1	15 22.5	23 01.4	12 52.8	13 58.2	1 43.8	2 02.0
7 F	19 02 56	15 52 21	10♒31 50	17 50 25	8 08.4	29 06.1	14 28.0	29 32.3	15 23.7	23 10.9	12 47.9	14 01.4	1 42.2	2 00.9
8 Sa	19 06 52	16 53 31	25 02 50	2♓08 39	8 09.5	0♒42.7	15 42.4	29 26.7	15 25.3	23 20.4	12 42.9	14 04.6	1 40.6	1 59.7
9 Su	19 10 49	17 54 41	9♓07 37	15 59 40	8 11.0	2 18.8	16 56.7	29 20.2	15 27.3	23 30.1	12 38.0	14 07.8	1 39.0	1 58.5
10 M	19 14 45	18 55 51	22 44 52	29 23 26	8 12.4	3 54.0	18 11.0	29 12.9	15 29.7	23 39.9	12 33.1	14 11.0	1 37.3	1 57.4
11 Tu	19 18 42	19 56 59	5♈55 41	12♈22 01	8R 13.3	5 28.1	19 25.2	29 04.8	15 32.5	23 49.9	12 28.2	14 14.3	1 35.7	1 56.2
12 W	19 22 38	20 58 08	18 42 54	24 58 49	8 13.4	7 01.0	20 39.4	28 55.9	15 35.6	23 59.9	12 23.3	14 17.5	1 34.0	1 55.1
13 Th	19 26 35	21 59 15	1♉10 19	7♉17 56	8 12.7	8 32.2	21 53.6	28 46.2	15 39.2	24 10.1	12 18.4	14 20.8	1 32.4	1 54.0
14 F	19 30 31	23 00 23	13 22 13	19 23 42	8 11.2	10 01.4	23 07.8	28 35.7	15 43.1	24 20.4	12 13.6	14 24.1	1 30.7	1 52.8
15 Sa	19 34 28	24 01 29	25 22 54	1♊20 19	8 09.3	11 28.2	24 21.9	28 24.4	15 47.4	24 30.8	12 08.8	14 27.4	1 29.0	1 51.7
16 Su	19 38 25	25 02 35	7♊16 24	13 11 37	8 07.2	12 52.1	25 35.9	28 12.4	15 52.1	24 41.4	12 04.0	14 30.8	1 27.4	1 50.6
17 M	19 42 21	26 03 40	19 06 20	25 00 58	8 05.1	14 12.5	26 50.0	27 59.5	15 57.1	24 52.0	11 59.2	14 34.1	1 25.7	1 49.5
18 Tu	19 46 18	27 04 44	0♋55 49	6♋51 14	8 03.5	15 28.9	28 03.9	27 45.9	16 02.5	25 02.8	11 54.5	14 37.5	1 24.0	1 48.5
19 W	19 50 14	28 05 48	12 47 30	18 44 52	8 02.3	16 40.5	29 17.9	27 31.5	16 08.3	25 13.6	11 49.9	14 40.8	1 22.3	1 47.4
20 Th	19 54 11	29 06 51	24 43 34	0♌43 52	8D 01.7	17 46.6	0♓31.8	27 16.4	16 14.4	25 24.6	11 45.2	14 44.2	1 20.6	1 46.3
21 F	19 58 07	0♒07 54	6♌45 56	12 50 01	8 01.7	18 46.4	1 45.6	27 00.6	16 20.9	25 35.7	11 40.7	14 47.6	1 18.9	1 45.3
22 Sa	20 02 04	1 08 56	18 56 19	25 05 02	8 02.0	19 39.1	2 59.4	26 44.0	16 27.7	25 46.9	11 36.1	14 51.0	1 17.2	1 44.2
23 Su	20 06 01	2 09 57	1♍16 22	7♍30 34	8 02.6	20 23.7	4 13.2	26 26.8	16 34.9	25 58.1	11 31.6	14 54.5	1 15.5	1 43.2
24 M	20 09 57	3 10 57	13 47 51	20 08 28	8 03.2	20 59.5	5 26.9	26 08.9	16 42.3	26 09.5	11 27.2	14 57.9	1 13.8	1 42.2
25 Tu	20 13 54	4 11 57	26 32 39	3♎00 38	8 03.7	21 25.7	6 40.6	25 50.4	16 50.2	26 21.0	11 22.8	15 01.3	1 12.1	1 41.2
26 W	20 17 50	5 12 57	9♎32 42	16 09 03	8 04.0	21R 41.5	7 54.2	25 31.2	16 58.3	26 32.6	11 18.5	15 04.8	1 10.4	1 40.2
27 Th	20 21 47	6 13 56	22 49 56	29 35 30	8R 04.1	21 46.4	9 07.8	25 11.4	17 06.8	26 44.2	11 14.2	15 08.2	1 08.8	1 39.2
28 F	20 25 43	7 14 54	6♏25 55	13♏21 14	8D 04.1	21 40.0	10 21.3	24 51.1	17 15.6	26 56.0	11 10.0	15 11.7	1 07.1	1 38.3
29 Sa	20 29 40	8 15 52	20 21 28	27 26 31	8 04.1	21 22.2	11 34.8	24 30.3	17 24.7	27 07.9	11 05.9	15 15.2	1 05.4	1 37.3
30 Su	20 33 36	9 16 49	4♐36 12	11♐50 11	8 04.2	20 53.2	12 48.2	24 08.9	17 34.2	27 19.8	11 01.8	15 18.6	1 03.7	1 36.4
31 M	20 37 33	10 17 45	19 08 02	26 29 11	8 04.3	20 13.7	14 01.6	23 47.1	17 43.9	27 31.9	10 57.8	15 22.1	1 02.0	1 35.5

LONGITUDE — February 1916

Day	Sid.Time	☉	0 hr ☽	Noon ☽	True ☊	☿	♀	♂	⚳	♃	♄	♅	♆	♇
1 Tu	20 41 30	11♒18 41	3♑52 56	11♑18 30	8♒04.6	19♒24.5	15♓14.9	23♌24.9	17♉53.9	27♓44.0	10♋53.9	15♒25.6	1♌00.4	1♋34.6
2 W	20 45 26	12 19 36	18 45 00	26 11 28	8R 04.9	18R 26.9	16 28.2	23R 02.3	18 04.3	27 56.2	10R 50.0	15 29.1	0R 58.7	1R 33.7
3 Th	20 49 23	13 20 30	3♒36 56	11♒00 25	8 04.9	17 22.6	17 41.4	22 39.3	18 14.9	28 08.5	10 46.2	15 32.6	0 57.1	1 32.8
4 F	20 53 19	14 21 22	18 20 59	25 37 45	8 04.7	16 13.4	18 54.5	22 16.1	18 25.9	28 20.9	10 42.5	15 36.1	0 55.4	1 32.0
5 Sa	20 57 16	15 22 13	2♓49 57	9♓56 56	8 04.1	15 01.4	20 07.6	21 52.6	18 37.1	28 33.3	10 38.9	15 39.6	0 53.8	1 31.1
6 Su	21 01 12	16 23 03	16 58 12	23 53 22	8 03.1	13 48.7	21 20.6	21 28.9	18 48.6	28 45.9	10 35.3	15 43.0	0 52.2	1 30.3
7 M	21 05 09	17 23 52	0♈42 15	7♈24 45	8 02.0	12 37.2	22 33.6	21 05.1	19 00.4	28 58.5	10 31.8	15 46.5	0 50.5	1 29.5
8 Tu	21 09 05	18 24 39	14 00 58	20 31 03	8 00.7	11 28.8	23 46.4	20 41.0	19 12.5	29 11.2	10 28.5	15 50.0	0 48.9	1 28.7
9 W	21 13 02	19 25 24	26 55 19	3♉14 08	7 59.8	10 25.0	24 59.2	20 17.1	19 24.8	29 23.9	10 25.2	15 53.5	0 47.3	1 28.0
10 Th	21 16 59	20 26 08	9♉27 58	15 37 20	7D 59.2	9 27.1	26 12.0	19 53.1	19 37.4	29 36.7	10 22.0	15 57.0	0 45.8	1 27.2
11 F	21 20 55	21 26 51	21 42 46	27 44 52	7 59.3	8 36.0	27 24.6	19 29.2	19 50.3	29 49.6	10 18.8	16 00.5	0 44.2	1 26.5
12 Sa	21 24 52	22 27 32	3♊44 13	9♊41 26	8 00.0	7 52.3	28 37.2	19 05.3	20 03.4	0♈02.6	10 15.8	16 04.0	0 42.6	1 25.8
13 Su	21 28 48	23 28 11	15 37 07	21 31 50	8 01.2	7 16.5	29 49.7	18 41.5	20 16.8	0 15.6	10 12.9	16 07.4	0 41.1	1 25.1
14 M	21 32 45	24 28 48	27 26 11	3♋20 41	8 02.7	6 48.6	1♈02.2	18 17.9	20 30.4	0 28.7	10 10.1	16 10.9	0 39.6	1 24.4
15 Tu	21 36 41	25 29 24	9♋15 52	15 12 12	8 04.1	6 28.7	2 14.5	17 54.6	20 44.3	0 41.9	10 07.3	16 14.4	0 38.1	1 23.8
16 W	21 40 38	26 29 59	21 10 07	27 10 02	8R 05.2	6 16.4	3 26.8	17 31.4	20 58.4	0 55.1	10 04.7	16 17.8	0 36.6	1 23.1
17 Th	21 44 34	27 30 31	3♌12 17	9♌17 11	8 05.6	6D 11.6	4 38.9	17 08.6	21 12.7	1 08.4	10 02.1	16 21.3	0 35.1	1 22.5
18 F	21 48 31	28 31 02	15 24 59	21 35 54	8 05.0	6 13.8	5 51.0	16 46.2	21 27.3	1 21.7	9 59.7	16 24.7	0 33.6	1 21.9
19 Sa	21 52 28	29 31 32	27 50 05	4♍07 39	8 03.2	6 22.7	7 03.0	16 24.1	21 42.1	1 35.1	9 57.3	16 28.1	0 32.2	1 21.3
20 Su	21 56 24	0♓31 59	10♍28 41	16 53 12	8 00.5	6 37.9	8 14.9	16 02.4	21 57.1	1 48.6	9 55.1	16 31.5	0 30.8	1 20.8
21 M	22 00 21	1 32 26	23 21 12	29 52 40	7 56.9	6 58.9	9 26.7	15 41.2	22 12.3	2 02.0	9 52.9	16 34.9	0 29.3	1 20.3
22 Tu	22 04 17	2 32 50	6♎27 31	13♎05 42	7 53.0	7 25.2	10 38.4	15 20.4	22 27.8	2 15.6	9 50.9	16 38.3	0 27.9	1 19.7
23 W	22 08 14	3 33 14	19 47 08	26 31 42	7 49.3	7 56.7	11 50.0	15 00.2	22 43.4	2 29.2	9 48.9	16 41.7	0 26.6	1 19.3
24 Th	22 12 10	4 33 36	3♏19 18	10♏09 52	7 46.3	8 32.7	13 01.5	14 40.5	22 59.3	2 42.9	9 47.1	16 45.1	0 25.2	1 18.8
25 F	22 16 07	5 33 56	17 03 16	23 59 24	7D 44.5	9 13.1	14 12.9	14 21.4	23 15.4	2 56.6	9 45.4	16 48.4	0 23.9	1 18.3
26 Sa	22 20 03	6 34 15	0♐58 10	7♐59 27	7 44.0	9 57.4	15 24.2	14 02.9	23 31.7	3 10.3	9 43.8	16 51.8	0 22.6	1 17.9
27 Su	22 24 00	7 34 33	15 03 04	22 08 53	7 44.7	10 45.5	16 35.4	13 45.0	23 48.2	3 24.1	9 42.2	16 55.1	0 21.3	1 17.5
28 M	22 27 57	8 34 50	29 16 39	6♑26 08	7 46.1	11 36.9	17 46.6	13 27.8	24 04.9	3 37.9	9 40.8	16 58.4	0 20.0	1 17.1
29 Tu	22 31 53	9 35 05	13♑37 00	20 48 52	7 47.6	12 31.5	18 57.6	13 11.2	24 21.7	3 51.8	9 39.6	17 01.7	0 18.8	1 16.8

Astro Data	Dy Hr Mn
⚳ D	4 0:44
☽ 0N	9 21:57
☽ 0S	24 14:38
☿ R	27 10:28
☽ 0N	6 7:56
♀0N	14 22:37
♃△♆	15 5:45
☿ D	17 16:11
♅♇	17 19:29
♃□♇	18 12:20
♃∠♅	18 19:10
☽ 0S	20 20:47
♃0N	23 21:34

Planet Ingress		Dy Hr Mn
☿	♒	8 1:22
♀	♓	20 1:41
☉	♒	21 8:54
♃	♈	12 7:11
♀	♈	13 15:24
☉	♓	19 23:18

Last Aspect Dy Hr Mn			☽ Ingress	Dy Hr Mn
2 7:25	♂	□	♐	2 7:43
4 7:02	♂	△	♑	4 7:25
6 1:50	☿	☌	♒	6 6:58
8 7:27	♂	☍	♓	8 8:21
10 1:31	♃	☌	♈	10 13:07
12 19:33	♂	△	♉	12 21:43
15 6:11	♂	□	♊	15 9:18
17 17:56	♂	⚹	♋	17 22:07
20 8:29	☉	☍	♌	20 10:33
22 15:08	♂	☌	♍	22 21:32
24 23:27	♃	☍	♎	25 6:26
27 4:23	♂	⚹	♏	27 12:43
29 11:28	♃	△	♐	29 16:18
31 13:43	♃	□	♑	31 17:43

Last Aspect Dy Hr Mn			☽ Ingress	Dy Hr Mn
2 14:51	♃	⚹	♒	2 18:09
4 6:35	♂	☍	♓	4 19:16
6 20:42	♃	☌	♈	6 22:45
8 12:18	♂	△	♉	9 5:50
11 16:14	♃	⚹	♊	11 16:30
13 16:18	☉	△	♋	14 5:13
15 1:46	♄	☌	♌	16 17:38
19 2:28	☉	☍	♍	19 4:08
19 22:59	♄	⚹	♎	21 12:13
22 18:24	♅	△	♏	23 18:09
24 23:31	♅	□	♐	25 22:20
27 3:08	♅	⚹	♑	28 1:13

☽ Phases & Eclipses Dy Hr Mn	
5 4:45	● 13♑32
12 3:37	☽ 20♈37
20 8:29	○ 28♋58
20 8:39	☍ P 0.133
28 0:35	☾ 6♏46
3 16:05	● 13♒31
3 16:00:03	● T 02'36"
10 22:20	☽ 20♉52
19 2:28	○ 29♌08
26 9:24	☾ 6♐28

Astro Data

1 January 1916
Julian Day # 5844
SVP 6♓25'45"
GC 25♐40.0 ⚵ 20♓47.3
Eris 26♓44.1 ⚹ 19♏25.9
⚷ 18♓35.7 ⚶ 16♎40.6
☽ Mean ☊ 9♒43.5

1 February 1916
Julian Day # 5875
SVP 6♓25'39"
GC 25♐40.0 ⚵ 29♓47.9
Eris 26♓56.3 ⚹ 27♏15.4
⚷ 19♓51.0 ⚶ 25♎11.8
☽ Mean ☊ 8♒05.0

March 1916 — LONGITUDE

Day	Sid.Time	☉	0 hr ☽	Noon ☽	True ☊	☿	♀	♂	⚳	♃	♄	♅	♆	♇
1 W	22 35 50	10♓35 18	28♑01 19	5♒13 50	7♒48.4	13♒29.1	20♈08.5	12♌55.4	24♉38.8	4♈05.7	9♋38.4	17♒05.0	0♌17.6	1♋16.4
2 Th	22 39 46	11 35 30	12♒25 51	19 36 47	7R47.9	14 29.4	21 19.3	12R40.2	24 56.1	4 19.7	9R37.3	17 08.3	0R16.4	1R16.1
3 F	22 43 43	12 35 40	26 46 00	3♓52 51	7 45.6	15 32.3	22 29.9	12 25.8	25 13.5	4 33.7	9 36.3	17 11.5	0 15.2	1 15.8
4 Sa	22 47 39	13 35 48	10♓56 42	17 56 58	7 41.6	16 37.6	23 40.5	12 12.2	25 31.1	4 47.7	9 35.5	17 14.7	0 14.1	1 15.6
5 Su	22 51 36	14 35 54	24 53 06	1♈44 39	7 36.0	17 45.1	24 50.9	11 59.3	25 48.9	5 01.8	9 34.7	17 17.9	0 12.9	1 15.3
6 M	22 55 32	15 35 59	8♈31 14	15 12 35	7 29.5	18 54.8	26 01.2	11 47.1	26 06.9	5 15.9	9 34.1	17 21.1	0 11.8	1 15.1
7 Tu	22 59 29	16 36 01	21 48 34	28 19 08	7 22.9	20 06.4	27 11.4	11 35.8	26 25.1	5 30.1	9 33.6	17 24.3	0 10.8	1 14.9
8 W	23 03 25	17 36 01	4♉44 21	11♉04 25	7 16.8	21 20.0	28 21.5	11 25.2	26 43.4	5 44.2	9 33.2	17 27.4	0 09.7	1 14.7
9 Th	23 07 22	18 35 59	17 19 37	23 30 19	7 12.1	22 35.4	29 31.4	11 15.5	27 01.9	5 58.4	9 32.9	17 30.5	0 08.7	1 14.6
10 F	23 11 19	19 35 56	29 36 57	5♊40 03	7 09.1	23 52.6	0♉41.2	11 06.5	27 20.5	6 12.7	9 32.7	17 33.6	0 07.7	1 14.4
11 Sa	23 15 15	20 35 49	11♊40 09	17 37 53	7D07.9	25 11.4	1 50.9	10 58.3	27 39.3	6 26.9	9D32.6	17 36.7	0 06.8	1 14.3
12 Su	23 19 12	21 35 41	23 33 52	29 28 45	7 08.2	26 31.8	3 00.4	10 50.9	27 58.3	6 41.2	9 32.7	17 39.7	0 05.8	1 14.2
13 M	23 23 08	22 35 31	5♋23 11	11♋17 50	7 09.4	27 53.8	4 09.8	10 44.3	28 17.4	6 55.5	9 32.8	17 42.8	0 04.9	1 14.2
14 Tu	23 27 05	23 35 18	17 13 21	23 10 20	7 10.9	29 17.2	5 19.0	10 38.6	28 36.6	7 09.8	9 33.1	17 45.8	0 04.1	1 14.1
15 W	23 31 01	24 35 03	29 09 24	5♌11 06	7R11.7	0♓42.2	6 28.0	10 33.5	28 56.1	7 24.1	9 33.5	17 48.7	0 03.2	1D14.1
16 Th	23 34 58	25 34 45	11♌15 57	17 24 23	7 11.2	2 08.5	7 36.9	10 29.3	29 15.6	7 38.5	9 34.0	17 51.7	0 02.4	1 14.1
17 F	23 38 54	26 34 26	23 36 49	29 53 32	7 08.6	3 36.3	8 45.6	10 25.8	29 35.3	7 52.9	9 34.6	17 54.6	0 01.6	1 14.1
18 Sa	23 42 51	27 34 04	6♍14 46	12♍40 40	7 03.8	5 05.5	9 54.2	10 23.1	29 55.1	8 07.3	9 35.3	17 57.5	0 00.8	1 14.2
19 Su	23 46 48	28 33 41	19 11 17	25 46 33	6 56.9	6 36.0	11 02.6	10 21.2	0♊15.1	8 21.7	9 36.1	18 00.3	0 00.1	1 14.3
20 M	23 50 44	29 33 15	2♎26 19	9♎10 22	6 48.4	8 07.9	12 10.8	10 20.0	0 35.2	8 36.1	9 37.1	18 03.1	29♋59.4	1 14.4
21 Tu	23 54 41	0♈32 47	15 58 23	22 49 59	6 39.1	9 41.1	13 18.9	10D19.6	0 55.4	8 50.6	9 38.1	18 05.9	29 58.7	1 14.5
22 W	23 58 37	1 32 18	29 44 44	6♏42 10	6 30.2	11 15.6	14 26.7	10 19.9	1 15.8	9 05.0	9 39.3	18 08.7	29 58.1	1 14.6
23 Th	0 02 34	2 31 46	13♏41 49	20 43 13	6 22.5	12 51.5	15 34.4	10 20.9	1 36.3	9 19.5	9 40.5	18 11.5	29 57.5	1 14.8
24 F	0 06 30	3 31 13	27 45 55	4♐49 31	6 16.9	14 28.7	16 41.9	10 22.6	1 56.9	9 34.0	9 41.9	18 14.2	29 56.9	1 15.0
25 Sa	0 10 27	4 30 38	11♐53 40	18 58 02	6 13.7	16 07.3	17 49.2	10 25.0	2 17.6	9 48.5	9 43.4	18 16.8	29 56.4	1 15.2
26 Su	0 14 23	5 30 02	26 02 24	3♑06 32	6D12.6	17 47.2	18 56.3	10 28.1	2 38.5	10 02.9	9 45.0	18 19.5	29 55.9	1 15.5
27 M	0 18 20	6 29 23	10♑10 17	17 13 31	6 12.9	19 28.4	20 03.3	10 31.9	2 59.5	10 17.5	9 46.7	18 22.1	29 55.4	1 15.7
28 Tu	0 22 17	7 28 43	24 16 07	1♒17 57	6R13.5	21 11.0	21 10.0	10 36.4	3 20.6	10 32.0	9 48.5	18 24.7	29 54.9	1 16.0
29 W	0 26 13	8 28 01	8♒18 55	15 18 50	6 13.3	22 55.0	22 16.5	10 41.5	3 41.8	10 46.5	9 50.4	18 27.2	29 54.5	1 16.3
30 Th	0 30 10	9 27 18	22 17 31	29 14 46	6 11.1	24 40.3	23 22.8	10 47.3	4 03.1	11 01.0	9 52.5	18 29.7	29 54.1	1 16.6
31 F	0 34 06	10 26 32	6♓10 17	13♓03 48	6 06.3	26 27.0	24 28.9	10 53.7	4 24.6	11 15.5	9 54.6	18 32.2	29 53.8	1 17.0

April 1916 — LONGITUDE

Day	Sid.Time	☉	0 hr ☽	Noon ☽	True ☊	☿	♀	♂	⚳	♃	♄	♅	♆	♇
1 Sa	0 38 03	11♈25 44	19♓54 58	26♓43 27	5♒58.8	28♓15.1	25♉34.8	11♌00.8	4♊46.1	11♈30.0	9♋56.8	18♒34.6	29♋53.4	1♋17.4
2 Su	0 41 59	12 24 55	3♈28 54	10♈10 58	5R48.9	0♈04.6	26 40.4	11 08.5	5 07.8	11 44.5	9 59.2	18 37.0	29R53.2	1 17.7
3 M	0 45 56	13 24 03	16 49 21	23 23 48	5 37.4	1 55.5	27 45.8	11 16.8	5 29.6	11 59.0	10 01.6	18 39.4	29 52.9	1 18.2
4 Tu	0 49 52	14 23 10	29 54 07	6♉20 10	5 25.3	3 47.9	28 51.0	11 25.8	5 51.4	12 13.6	10 04.2	18 41.7	29 52.7	1 18.6
5 W	0 53 49	15 22 14	12♉41 55	18 59 24	5 14.0	5 41.6	29 55.9	11 35.3	6 13.4	12 28.1	10 06.8	18 44.0	29 52.5	1 19.1
6 Th	0 57 46	16 21 16	25 12 45	1♊22 10	5 04.3	7 36.8	1♊00.6	11 45.4	6 35.5	12 42.6	10 09.6	18 46.3	29 52.3	1 19.6
7 F	1 01 42	17 20 16	7♊27 59	13 30 33	4 57.0	9 33.4	2 05.0	11 56.0	6 57.7	12 57.1	10 12.4	18 48.5	29 52.2	1 20.1
8 Sa	1 05 39	18 19 14	19 30 19	25 27 49	4 52.3	11 31.3	3 09.1	12 07.2	7 20.0	13 11.5	10 15.4	18 50.6	29 52.1	1 20.6
9 Su	1 09 35	19 18 09	1♋23 36	7♋18 16	4 50.0	13 30.6	4 12.9	12 19.0	7 42.3	13 26.0	10 18.4	18 52.8	29 52.1	1 21.1
10 M	1 13 32	20 17 02	13 12 29	19 06 54	4D49.3	15 31.3	5 16.5	12 31.3	8 04.8	13 40.5	10 21.6	18 54.9	29D52.1	1 21.7
11 Tu	1 17 28	21 15 53	25 02 13	0♌59 06	4R49.5	17 33.2	6 19.8	12 44.1	8 27.3	13 54.9	10 24.8	18 56.9	29 52.1	1 22.3
12 W	1 21 25	22 14 42	6♌58 16	13 00 22	4 49.3	19 36.3	7 22.7	12 57.5	8 50.0	14 09.4	10 28.2	18 58.9	29 52.1	1 22.9
13 Th	1 25 21	23 13 28	19 06 03	25 15 55	4 47.8	21 40.4	8 25.3	13 11.3	9 12.7	14 23.8	10 31.6	19 00.9	29 52.2	1 23.6
14 F	1 29 18	24 12 12	1♍30 29	7♍50 14	4 44.0	23 45.6	9 27.7	13 25.6	9 35.5	14 38.2	10 35.2	19 02.8	29 52.3	1 24.2
15 Sa	1 33 15	25 10 54	14 15 32	20 46 39	4 37.6	25 51.6	10 29.6	13 40.4	9 58.4	14 52.6	10 38.8	19 04.7	29 52.5	1 24.9
16 Su	1 37 11	26 09 33	27 23 44	4♎06 46	4 28.7	27 58.2	11 31.3	13 55.7	10 21.4	15 06.9	10 42.5	19 06.5	29 52.7	1 25.6
17 M	1 41 08	27 08 11	10♎55 39	17 50 04	4 17.8	0♉05.3	12 32.5	14 11.4	10 44.4	15 21.3	10 46.3	19 08.3	29 52.9	1 26.3
18 Tu	1 45 04	28 06 47	24 49 35	1♏53 40	4 05.9	2 12.7	13 33.4	14 27.5	11 07.5	15 35.6	10 50.2	19 10.1	29 53.1	1 27.0
19 W	1 49 01	29 05 20	9♏01 38	16 12 43	3 54.3	4 20.1	14 34.0	14 44.1	11 30.7	15 49.9	10 54.2	19 11.8	29 53.4	1 27.8
20 Th	1 52 57	0♉03 52	23 26 06	0♐40 57	3 44.1	6 27.2	15 34.1	15 01.1	11 54.0	16 04.2	10 58.3	19 13.5	29 53.7	1 28.6
21 F	1 56 54	1 02 23	7♐56 27	15 11 50	3 36.4	8 33.8	16 33.8	15 18.6	12 17.4	16 18.4	11 02.5	19 15.1	29 54.1	1 29.3
22 Sa	2 00 50	2 00 51	22 26 25	29 39 37	3 31.5	10 39.4	17 33.2	15 36.4	12 40.8	16 32.7	11 06.7	19 16.7	29 54.4	1 30.2
23 Su	2 04 47	2 59 18	6♑50 55	13♑59 58	3 29.1	12 43.9	18 32.1	15 54.7	13 04.3	16 46.9	11 11.1	19 18.2	29 54.9	1 31.0
24 M	2 08 44	3 57 44	21 06 30	28 10 20	3 28.5	14 46.9	19 30.6	16 13.3	13 27.9	17 01.1	11 15.5	19 19.7	29 55.3	1 31.8
25 Tu	2 12 40	4 56 08	5♒11 23	12♒09 37	3 28.4	16 48.1	20 28.6	16 32.3	13 51.6	17 15.2	11 20.0	19 21.1	29 55.8	1 32.7
26 W	2 16 37	5 54 30	19 05 02	25 57 41	3 27.6	18 47.1	21 26.2	16 51.7	14 15.3	17 29.4	11 24.6	19 22.5	29 56.3	1 33.6
27 Th	2 20 33	6 52 51	2♓47 37	9♓34 52	3 24.8	20 43.8	22 23.3	17 11.5	14 39.1	17 43.5	11 29.3	19 23.9	29 56.8	1 34.5
28 F	2 24 30	7 51 10	16 19 27	23 01 23	3 19.4	22 37.7	23 20.0	17 31.6	15 03.0	17 57.5	11 34.1	19 25.2	29 57.4	1 35.4
29 Sa	2 28 26	8 49 27	29 40 38	6♈17 08	3 11.0	24 28.8	24 16.1	17 52.1	15 26.9	18 11.6	11 38.9	19 26.4	29 58.0	1 36.4
30 Su	2 32 23	9 47 43	12♈50 48	19 21 34	3 00.1	26 16.7	25 11.7	18 12.9	15 50.9	18 25.5	11 43.8	19 27.7	29 58.7	1 37.3

Astro Data Dy Hr Mn	Planet Ingress Dy Hr Mn	Last Aspect Dy Hr Mn	☽ Ingress Dy Hr Mn	Last Aspect Dy Hr Mn	☽ Ingress Dy Hr Mn	☽ Phases & Eclipses Dy Hr Mn	Astro Data
☽0N 4 18:23	♀ ♉ 9 21:49	29 8:38 ♀ □	♒ 1 3:18	1 17:37 ♆ △	♈ 1 17:48	4 3:57 ● 13♓16	1 March 1916
♄ D 11 13:51	☿ ♓ 15 0:08	2 15:07 ♀ ⚹	♓ 3 5:27	3 23:58 ♆ □	♉ 4 0:11	11 18:33 ☽ 20♊52	Julian Day # 5904
♇ D 15 16:58	⚳ ♊ 18 17:52	4 3:57 ☉ ☌	♈ 5 8:56	6 9:04 ♆ ⚹	♊ 6 9:19	19 17:26 ○ 28♍47	SVP 6♓25'35"
☽0S 19 4:32	♆ ♋R 19 15:24	7 9:42 ♀ ☌	♉ 7 15:08	7 22:38 ♅ △	♋ 8 21:11	26 16:22 ☾ 5♑41	GC 25♐40.1 ⚴ 10♈21.9
☉0N 20 22:47	☉ ♈ 20 22:47	9 10:01 ☿ □	♊ 10 0:46	11 9:45 ♆ ☌	♌ 11 10:01		Eris 27♓15.5 ⚵ 1♐53.6
♂ D 21 14:43		12 5:15 ☿ △	♋ 12 13:03	13 7:42 ☉ △	♍ 13 21:07	2 16:21 ● 12♈36	⚷ 21♓28.2 ⚶ 28♎10.4R
♃□♄ 25 2:41	☿ ♈ 2 11:00	14 12:55 ☉ △	♌ 15 1:41	16 4:27 ♆ ⚹	♎ 16 4:40	10 14:35 ☽ 20♋23	☽ Mean ☊ 6♒32.8
	♀ ♊ 5 13:31	16 12:53 ♅ ☍	♍ 17 12:12	18 8:36 ♆ □	♏ 18 8:48	18 5:07 ○ 27♎50	
☽0N 1 3:00	☿ ♉ 17 11:00	19 19:37 ♆ ⚹	♎ 19 19:37	20 10:42 ♆ △	♐ 20 10:52	24 22:38 ☾ 4♒24	1 April 1916
☿0N 4 20:01	☉ ♉ 20 10:25	22 0:24 ♆ □	♏ 22 0:26	21 18:44 ♅ ⚹	♑ 22 12:34		Julian Day # 5935
♆ D 10 13:12		24 3:43 ♆ △	♐ 24 3:48	24 14:59 ♆ ☍	♒ 24 15:07		SVP 6♓25'32"
☽0S 15 13:18		25 10:50 ♅ ⚹	♑ 26 6:43	26 3:30 ♀ △	♓ 26 19:05		GC 25♐40.2 ⚴ 23♈14.2
☽0N 28 8:59		28 9:38 ♆ ☍	♒ 28 9:47	29 0:31 ♆ △	♈ 29 0:35		Eris 27♓39.1 ⚵ 2♐34.6R
		30 1:00 ♀ □	♓ 30 13:18				⚷ 23♓19.6 ⚶ 24♎13.3R
							☽ Mean ☊ 4♒54.3

LONGITUDE

May 1916

Day	Sid.Time	☉	0 hr ☽	Noon☽	True☊	☿	♀	♂	⚳	♃	♄	♅	♆	♇
1 M	2 36 19	10♉45 57	25♈49 18	2♉13 56	2♒47.4	28♉01.4	26♊06.8	18♌34.1	16♊14.9	18♈39.5	11♋48.8	19♒28.8	29♋59.3	1♋38.3
2 Tu	2 40 16	11 44 10	8♉35 22	14 53 32	2R34.1	29 42.6	27 01.3	18 55.6	16 39.1	18 53.4	11 53.9	19 29.9	0♌00.0	1 39.3
3 W	2 44 13	12 42 21	21 08 27	27 20 07	2 21.5	1♊20.1	27 55.2	19 17.4	17 03.2	19 07.3	11 59.1	19 31.0	0 00.8	1 40.3
4 Th	2 48 09	13 40 30	3♊28 38	9♊34 08	2 10.5	2 54.0	28 48.5	19 39.6	17 27.5	19 21.2	12 04.3	19 32.0	0 01.5	1 41.3
5 F	2 52 06	14 38 37	15 36 49	21 36 57	2 01.9	4 24.0	29 41.2	20 02.1	17 51.8	19 35.0	12 09.6	19 33.0	0 02.3	1 42.4
6 Sa	2 56 02	15 36 43	27 34 53	3♋30 59	1 56.1	5 50.1	0♋33.3	20 24.9	18 16.2	19 48.7	12 15.0	19 33.9	0 03.2	1 43.4
7 Su	2 59 59	16 34 46	9♋25 44	15 19 36	1 52.9	7 12.3	1 24.7	20 48.0	18 40.6	20 02.5	12 20.4	19 34.8	0 04.0	1 44.5
8 M	3 03 55	17 32 48	21 13 11	27 07 02	1D51.7	8 30.3	2 15.4	21 11.4	19 05.1	20 16.1	12 25.9	19 35.6	0 04.9	1 45.6
9 Tu	3 07 52	18 30 48	3♌01 49	8♌58 11	1R51.8	9 44.2	3 05.3	21 35.0	19 29.6	20 29.8	12 31.5	19 36.4	0 05.9	1 46.7
10 W	3 11 48	19 28 46	14 56 49	20 58 23	1 51.9	10 53.9	3 54.6	21 59.0	19 54.2	20 43.3	12 37.2	19 37.1	0 06.8	1 47.8
11 Th	3 15 45	20 26 42	27 03 35	3♍13 05	1 51.2	11 59.4	4 43.0	22 23.2	20 18.8	20 56.9	12 42.9	19 37.8	0 07.8	1 49.0
12 F	3 19 42	21 24 36	9♍27 31	15 47 26	1 48.7	13 00.5	5 30.6	22 47.7	20 43.5	21 10.3	12 48.7	19 38.4	0 08.8	1 50.1
13 Sa	3 23 38	22 22 29	22 13 22	28 45 44	1 43.9	13 57.3	6 17.4	23 12.5	21 08.2	21 23.8	12 54.5	19 39.0	0 09.9	1 51.3
14 Su	3 27 35	23 20 20	5♎24 48	12♎10 45	1 36.8	14 49.6	7 03.3	23 37.5	21 33.0	21 37.1	13 00.4	19 39.5	0 10.9	1 52.4
15 M	3 31 31	24 18 09	19 03 35	26 03 06	1 27.8	15 37.3	7 48.3	24 02.8	21 57.8	21 50.5	13 06.4	19 40.0	0 12.0	1 53.6
16 Tu	3 35 28	25 15 56	3♏08 58	10♏20 37	1 17.9	16 20.5	8 32.4	24 28.3	22 22.6	22 03.7	13 12.4	19 40.5	0 13.2	1 54.8
17 W	3 39 24	26 13 42	17 37 22	24 58 19	1 08.0	16 59.0	9 15.5	24 54.0	22 47.5	22 16.9	13 18.5	19 40.9	0 14.3	1 56.0
18 Th	3 43 21	27 11 27	2♐22 29	9♐48 49	0 59.4	17 32.9	9 57.5	25 20.0	23 12.5	22 30.1	13 24.7	19 41.2	0 15.5	1 57.3
19 F	3 47 17	28 09 11	17 16 13	24 43 34	0 52.8	18 02.0	10 38.6	25 46.3	23 37.5	22 43.2	13 30.9	19 41.5	0 16.7	1 58.5
20 Sa	3 51 14	29 06 53	2♑09 53	9♑34 12	0 48.8	18 26.3	11 18.5	26 12.7	24 02.6	22 56.2	13 37.2	19 41.7	0 18.0	1 59.8
21 Su	3 55 11	0♊04 34	16 55 45	24 13 52	0D47.2	18 45.9	11 57.3	26 39.4	24 27.7	23 09.2	13 43.5	19 41.9	0 19.2	2 01.0
22 M	3 59 07	1 02 14	1♒28 03	8♒37 55	0 47.2	19 00.6	12 34.9	27 06.3	24 52.8	23 22.1	13 49.9	19 42.1	0 20.5	2 02.3
23 Tu	4 03 04	1 59 53	15 43 16	22 43 59	0R47.9	19 10.5	13 11.3	27 33.4	25 18.0	23 35.0	13 56.4	19 42.1	0 21.9	2 03.6
24 W	4 07 00	2 57 31	29 40 04	6♓31 35	0 48.1	19R15.7	13 46.5	28 00.7	25 43.2	23 47.8	14 02.9	19R42.2	0 23.2	2 04.9
25 Th	4 10 57	3 55 08	13♓18 41	20 01 31	0 46.8	19 16.2	14 20.4	28 28.3	26 08.4	24 00.5	14 09.4	19 42.2	0 24.6	2 06.2
26 F	4 14 53	4 52 44	26 40 17	3♈15 11	0 43.5	19 12.1	14 52.9	28 56.0	26 33.7	24 13.2	14 16.0	19 42.1	0 26.0	2 07.5
27 Sa	4 18 50	5 50 19	9♈46 25	16 14 10	0 37.9	19 03.6	15 24.0	29 24.0	26 59.1	24 25.8	14 22.6	19 42.0	0 27.4	2 08.8
28 Su	4 22 46	6 47 54	22 38 36	28 59 53	0 30.3	18 50.9	15 53.6	29 52.1	27 24.4	24 38.3	14 29.3	19 41.9	0 28.9	2 10.2
29 M	4 26 43	7 45 27	5♉18 09	11♉33 31	0 21.2	18 34.3	16 21.7	0♍20.5	27 49.8	24 50.7	14 36.1	19 41.7	0 30.3	2 11.5
30 Tu	4 30 40	8 42 59	17 46 06	23 56 02	0 11.7	18 14.0	16 48.3	0 49.0	28 15.3	25 03.1	14 42.9	19 41.4	0 31.8	2 12.9
31 W	4 34 36	9 40 31	0♊03 24	6♊08 21	0 02.6	17 50.4	17 13.3	1 17.7	28 40.8	25 15.4	14 49.7	19 41.1	0 33.4	2 14.2

LONGITUDE

June 1916

Day	Sid.Time	☉	0 hr ☽	Noon☽	True☊	☿	♀	♂	⚳	♃	♄	♅	♆	♇
1 Th	4 38 33	10♊38 01	12♊11 01	18♊11 33	29♑54.7	17♊23.9	17♋36.5	1♍46.7	29♊06.3	25♈27.6	14♋56.6	19♒40.8	0♌34.9	2♋15.6
2 F	4 42 29	11 35 31	24 10 10	0♋07 05	29R48.7	16R54.9	17 58.1	2 15.8	29 31.9	25 39.8	15 03.5	19R40.4	0 36.5	2 17.0
3 Sa	4 46 26	12 32 59	6♋02 34	11 56 56	29 44.8	16 24.0	18 17.8	2 45.1	29 57.4	25 51.8	15 10.5	19 39.9	0 38.1	2 18.4
4 Su	4 50 22	13 30 26	17 50 31	23 43 43	29D43.0	15 51.6	18 35.6	3 14.5	0♋23.1	26 03.8	15 17.5	19 39.4	0 39.7	2 19.7
5 M	4 54 19	14 27 52	29 36 59	5♌30 46	29 43.0	15 18.4	18 51.5	3 44.2	0 48.7	26 15.7	15 24.6	19 38.9	0 41.4	2 21.1
6 Tu	4 58 15	15 25 17	11♌25 37	17 22 05	29 44.1	14 44.8	19 05.4	4 14.0	1 14.4	26 27.6	15 31.6	19 38.3	0 43.0	2 22.6
7 W	5 02 12	16 22 41	23 20 44	29 22 10	29 45.5	14 11.6	19 17.3	4 44.0	1 40.1	26 39.3	15 38.8	19 37.7	0 44.7	2 24.0
8 Th	5 06 09	17 20 04	5♍27 02	11♍35 57	29R46.6	13 39.1	19 27.1	5 14.1	2 05.8	26 50.9	15 45.9	19 37.0	0 46.4	2 25.4
9 F	5 10 05	18 17 25	17 49 31	24 08 21	29 46.5	13 08.1	19 34.6	5 44.5	2 31.6	27 02.5	15 53.1	19 36.3	0 48.1	2 26.8
10 Sa	5 14 02	19 14 46	0♎32 58	7♎03 54	29 45.0	12 38.9	19 40.0	6 14.9	2 57.4	27 14.0	16 00.4	19 35.5	0 49.9	2 28.2
11 Su	5 17 58	20 12 05	13 41 31	20 26 07	29 41.9	12 12.2	19R43.1	6 45.6	3 23.2	27 25.3	16 07.6	19 34.7	0 51.6	2 29.7
12 M	5 21 55	21 09 24	27 17 53	4♏16 49	29 37.4	11 48.3	19 43.8	7 16.3	3 49.0	27 36.6	16 14.9	19 33.8	0 53.4	2 31.1
13 Tu	5 25 51	22 06 42	11♏22 44	18 35 16	29 32.1	11 27.7	19 42.2	7 47.3	4 14.9	27 47.8	16 22.2	19 32.9	0 55.2	2 32.5
14 W	5 29 48	23 03 59	25 53 54	3♐17 52	29 26.7	11 10.7	19 38.3	8 18.4	4 40.8	27 58.9	16 29.6	19 32.0	0 57.1	2 34.0
15 Th	5 33 44	24 01 15	10♐46 15	18 18 00	29 22.0	10 57.6	19 31.9	8 49.6	5 06.7	28 09.9	16 37.0	19 31.0	0 58.9	2 35.4
16 F	5 37 41	24 58 31	25 51 57	3♑26 54	29 18.6	10 48.6	19 23.1	9 21.0	5 32.6	28 20.9	16 44.4	19 30.0	1 00.8	2 36.9
17 Sa	5 41 38	25 55 46	11♑01 37	18 34 55	29D16.7	10D43.9	19 11.8	9 52.5	5 58.6	28 31.7	16 51.9	19 28.9	1 02.7	2 38.4
18 Su	5 45 34	26 53 01	26 05 43	3♒33 03	29 16.4	10 43.7	18 58.2	10 24.1	6 24.6	28 42.4	16 59.3	19 27.8	1 04.6	2 39.8
19 M	5 49 31	27 50 15	10♒56 07	18 14 14	29 17.3	10 48.1	18 42.2	10 55.9	6 50.6	28 53.0	17 06.8	19 26.6	1 06.5	2 41.3
20 Tu	5 53 27	28 47 29	25 26 56	2♓33 59	29 18.7	10 57.1	18 23.9	11 27.8	7 16.6	29 03.5	17 14.4	19 25.4	1 08.4	2 42.7
21 W	5 57 24	29 44 43	9♓34 56	16 30 01	29 20.0	11 10.9	18 03.3	11 59.9	7 42.7	29 13.9	17 21.9	19 24.2	1 10.3	2 44.2
22 Th	6 01 20	0♋41 57	23 19 13	0♈02 42	29R20.6	11 29.3	17 40.6	12 32.1	8 08.7	29 24.2	17 29.5	19 22.9	1 12.3	2 45.7
23 F	6 05 17	1 39 11	6♈40 42	13 13 30	29 20.0	11 52.4	17 15.7	13 04.4	8 34.8	29 34.4	17 37.0	19 21.5	1 14.3	2 47.1
24 Sa	6 09 13	2 36 24	19 41 27	26 04 51	29 18.3	12 20.2	16 48.8	13 36.9	9 00.9	29 44.5	17 44.7	19 20.2	1 16.3	2 48.6
25 Su	6 13 10	3 33 38	2♉24 06	8♉39 32	29 15.4	12 52.6	16 20.0	14 09.5	9 27.0	29 54.4	17 52.3	19 18.8	1 18.3	2 50.1
26 M	6 17 07	4 30 52	14 51 30	21 00 21	29 11.9	13 29.6	15 49.5	14 42.2	9 53.2	0♉04.3	17 59.9	19 17.3	1 20.3	2 51.5
27 Tu	6 21 03	5 28 05	27 06 24	3♊09 57	29 08.0	14 11.0	15 17.5	15 15.1	10 19.4	0 14.0	18 07.6	19 15.9	1 22.3	2 53.0
28 W	6 25 00	6 25 19	9♊11 18	15 10 44	29 04.2	14 57.0	14 44.0	15 48.1	10 45.5	0 23.6	18 15.3	19 14.3	1 24.4	2 54.5
29 Th	6 28 56	7 22 32	21 08 31	27 04 54	29 01.1	15 47.3	14 09.3	16 21.2	11 11.7	0 33.1	18 23.0	19 12.8	1 26.4	2 55.9
30 F	6 32 53	8 19 46	3♋00 10	8♋54 34	28 58.9	16 42.0	13 33.6	16 54.4	11 38.0	0 42.5	18 30.7	19 11.2	1 28.5	2 57.4

Astro Data	Dy Hr Mn
♃✶♅	5 8:18
☽0S	12 21:54
♅R	24 20:13
☿R	25 2:32
☽0N	25 13:35
☽0S	9 5:24
♀R	12 7:48
☿D	18 1:01
☽0N	21 19:05

Planet Ingress		Dy Hr Mn
♆	♌	2 10:48
☿	♊	2 16:14
♀	♋	5 20:37
☉	♊	21 10:06
♂	♍	28 18:42
☊	♑R	31 19:18
⚳	♋	3 14:23
☉	♋	21 18:24
♃	♉	26 1:32

Last Aspect Dy Hr Mn			☽ Ingress	Dy Hr Mn
1 7:47	♆	□	♉	1 7:49
2 20:51	♅	□	♊	3 17:12
5 8:44	♂	✶	♋	6 4:53
7 21:47	♃	□	♌	8 17:51
10 14:04	♂	☌	♍	11 5:45
12 23:20	☉	△	♎	13 14:15
15 8:28	♂	✶	♏	15 18:42
17 14:11	☉	☍	♐	17 20:09
19 13:44	♂	△	♑	19 20:30
21 10:12	♃	□	♒	21 21:33
23 20:37	♂	☍	♓	24 0:35
25 10:39	☿	□	♈	26 6:03
28 13:43	♂	△	♉	28 13:54
30 3:44	♅	□	♊	30 23:53

Last Aspect Dy Hr Mn			☽ Ingress	Dy Hr Mn
2 2:51	♃	✶	♋	2 11:46
4 16:51	♃	□	♌	5 0:47
7 6:31	♃	△	♍	7 13:15
9 3:16	♀	✶	♎	9 22:59
12 0:23	♃	☍	♏	12 4:40
13 13:50	♀	△	♐	14 6:40
16 3:50	♃	△	♑	16 6:33
18 4:06	♃	□	♒	18 6:16
20 6:00	♃	✶	♓	20 7:39
21 14:39	♀	△	♈	22 11:55
24 19:02	♃	☌	♉	24 19:26
26 8:39	♅	□	♊	27 5:43
28 20:09	♅	△	♋	29 17:55

☽ Phases & Eclipses Dy Hr Mn	
2 5:29	● 11♉28
10 8:47	☽ 19♌21
17 14:11	○ 26♏19
24 5:16	☾ 2♓41
31 19:37	● 9♊59
8 23:58	☽ 17♍49
15 21:41	○ 24♐24
22 13:16	☾ 0♈45
30 10:43	● 8♋17

Astro Data

1 May 1916
Julian Day # 5965
SVP 6♓25'28"
GC 25♐40.3 ⚴ 6♉51.7
Eris 27♓59.6 ⚵ 28♏25.1R
⚷ 24♓54.5 ⚶ 17♎07.3R
☽ Mean ☊ 3♒19.0

1 June 1916
Julian Day # 5996
SVP 6♓25'23"
GC 25♐40.3 ⚴ 21♉56.2
Eris 28♓13.3 ⚵ 21♏40.6R
⚷ 26♓00.5 ⚶ 14♎48.5
☽ Mean ☊ 1♒40.5

July 1916 — LONGITUDE

Day	Sid.Time	☉	0 hr ☽	Noon ☽	True ☊	☿	♀	♂	⚳	♃	♄	♅	♆	♇
1 Sa	6 36 49	9♋16 59	14♋48 21	20♋41 49	28♑57.7	17♊40.9	12♋57.2	17♍27.8	12♋04.2	0♉51.8	18♋38.4	19♒09.6	1♌30.6	2♋58.8
2 Su	6 40 46	10 14 12	26 35 16	2♌28 59	28D 57.5	18 44.1	12R 20.1	18 01.3	12 30.4	1 00.9	18 46.1	19R 07.9	1 32.7	3 00.3
3 M	6 44 43	11 11 25	8♌23 19	14 18 37	28 58.2	19 51.4	11 42.8	18 34.9	12 56.7	1 09.9	18 53.9	19 06.2	1 34.8	3 01.8
4 Tu	6 48 39	12 08 38	20 15 16	26 13 42	28 59.3	21 02.9	11 05.3	19 08.6	13 23.0	1 18.8	19 01.6	19 04.5	1 36.9	3 03.2
5 W	6 52 36	13 05 51	2♍14 19	8♍17 35	29 00.7	22 18.3	10 27.9	19 42.4	13 49.2	1 27.6	19 09.4	19 02.7	1 39.0	3 04.7
6 Th	6 56 32	14 03 03	14 24 00	20 34 02	29 02.0	23 37.8	9 51.0	20 16.4	14 15.5	1 36.2	19 17.2	19 00.9	1 41.2	3 06.1
7 F	7 00 29	15 00 15	26 48 11	3♎06 57	29R 02.8	25 01.3	9 14.6	20 50.5	14 41.8	1 44.7	19 25.0	18 59.1	1 43.3	3 07.5
8 Sa	7 04 25	15 57 27	9♎30 48	16 00 12	29 03.1	26 28.6	8 39.1	21 24.6	15 08.1	1 53.0	19 32.7	18 57.2	1 45.5	3 09.0
9 Su	7 08 22	16 54 39	22 35 33	29 17 11	29 02.8	27 59.7	8 04.6	21 58.9	15 34.4	2 01.2	19 40.5	18 55.3	1 47.6	3 10.4
10 M	7 12 18	17 51 51	6♏05 20	13♏00 10	29 02.0	29 34.5	7 31.4	22 33.3	16 00.8	2 09.3	19 48.3	18 53.4	1 49.8	3 11.8
11 Tu	7 16 15	18 49 03	20 01 41	27 09 45	29 01.0	1♋13.0	6 59.6	23 07.8	16 27.1	2 17.2	19 56.1	18 51.5	1 52.0	3 13.3
12 W	7 20 12	19 46 15	4♐24 03	11♐44 08	28 59.9	2 55.0	6 29.4	23 42.4	16 53.5	2 25.0	20 03.9	18 49.5	1 54.1	3 14.7
13 Th	7 24 08	20 43 27	19 09 20	26 38 51	28 59.0	4 40.4	6 01.0	24 17.2	17 19.8	2 32.7	20 11.7	18 47.5	1 56.3	3 16.1
14 F	7 28 05	21 40 39	4♑11 42	11♑46 49	28 58.4	6 29.1	5 34.5	24 52.0	17 46.2	2 40.2	20 19.5	18 45.5	1 58.5	3 17.5
15 Sa	7 32 01	22 37 52	19 23 03	26 59 09	28D 58.2	8 20.8	5 10.1	25 26.9	18 12.5	2 47.6	20 27.3	18 43.4	2 00.7	3 18.9
16 Su	7 35 58	23 35 04	4♒33 57	12♒06 17	28 58.3	10 15.3	4 47.8	26 01.9	18 38.9	2 54.8	20 35.0	18 41.4	2 02.9	3 20.3
17 M	7 39 54	24 32 18	19 35 06	26 59 28	28 58.6	12 12.4	4 27.8	26 37.0	19 05.3	3 01.9	20 42.8	18 39.3	2 05.1	3 21.7
18 Tu	7 43 51	25 29 31	4♓18 35	11♓31 52	28 58.9	14 11.8	4 10.0	27 12.2	19 31.6	3 08.8	20 50.6	18 37.1	2 07.4	3 23.1
19 W	7 47 47	26 26 46	18 38 52	25 39 18	28 59.2	16 13.3	3 54.6	27 47.6	19 58.0	3 15.6	20 58.4	18 35.0	2 09.6	3 24.4
20 Th	7 51 44	27 24 01	2♈33 02	9♈20 08	28 59.4	18 16.5	3 41.6	28 23.0	20 24.4	3 22.2	21 06.1	18 32.8	2 11.8	3 25.8
21 F	7 55 41	28 21 17	16 00 42	22 35 02	28 59.4	20 21.1	3 31.0	28 58.5	20 50.8	3 28.7	21 13.9	18 30.6	2 14.0	3 27.2
22 Sa	7 59 37	29 18 34	29 03 28	5♉26 22	28 59.4	22 26.8	3 22.8	29 34.1	21 17.2	3 35.0	21 21.6	18 28.4	2 16.2	3 28.5
23 Su	8 03 34	0♌15 52	11♉44 13	17 57 30	28 59.5	24 33.3	3 17.1	0♎09.9	21 43.6	3 41.1	21 29.4	18 26.2	2 18.5	3 29.8
24 M	8 07 30	1 13 11	24 06 41	0♊12 18	28 59.6	26 40.3	3D 13.7	0 45.7	22 10.0	3 47.1	21 37.1	18 24.0	2 20.7	3 31.2
25 Tu	8 11 27	2 10 31	6♊14 49	12 14 46	28 59.9	28 47.4	3 12.6	1 21.6	22 36.4	3 53.0	21 44.8	18 21.7	2 22.9	3 32.5
26 W	8 15 23	3 07 51	18 12 34	24 08 42	29 00.3	0♌54.5	3 13.9	1 57.6	23 02.8	3 58.6	21 52.5	18 19.5	2 25.1	3 33.8
27 Th	8 19 20	4 05 13	0♋03 35	5♋57 37	29 00.8	3 01.1	3 17.4	2 33.7	23 29.2	4 04.1	22 00.2	18 17.2	2 27.4	3 35.1
28 F	8 23 16	5 02 35	11 51 11	17 44 37	29R 01.2	5 07.2	3 23.2	3 10.0	23 55.6	4 09.4	22 07.9	18 14.9	2 29.6	3 36.4
29 Sa	8 27 13	5 59 58	23 38 16	29 32 26	29 01.3	7 12.5	3 31.2	3 46.3	24 22.0	4 14.6	22 15.6	18 12.6	2 31.8	3 37.7
30 Su	8 31 10	6 57 22	5♌27 24	11♌23 28	29 01.1	9 16.8	3 41.2	4 22.7	24 48.4	4 19.6	22 23.2	18 10.2	2 34.0	3 38.9
31 M	8 35 06	7 54 47	17 20 54	23 19 56	29 00.5	11 20.0	3 53.4	4 59.2	25 14.8	4 24.4	22 30.8	18 07.9	2 36.3	3 40.2

August 1916 — LONGITUDE

Day	Sid.Time	☉	0 hr ☽	Noon ☽	True ☊	☿	♀	♂	⚳	♃	♄	♅	♆	♇
1 Tu	8 39 03	8♌52 13	29♌20 52	5♍23 57	28♑59.4	13♌22.0	4♋07.5	5♎35.8	25♋41.2	4♉29.0	22♋38.4	18♒05.5	2♌38.5	3♋41.4
2 W	8 42 59	9 49 39	11♍29 26	17 37 37	28R 58.0	15 22.8	4 23.7	6 12.5	26 07.6	4 33.5	22 46.0	18R 03.2	2 40.7	3 42.6
3 Th	8 46 56	10 47 06	23 48 45	0♎03 10	28 56.4	17 22.1	4 41.7	6 49.3	26 33.9	4 37.7	22 53.6	18 00.8	2 42.9	3 43.9
4 F	8 50 52	11 44 34	6♎21 08	12 42 57	28 54.9	19 20.0	5 01.5	7 26.1	27 00.3	4 41.8	23 01.1	17 58.4	2 45.1	3 45.1
5 Sa	8 54 49	12 42 02	19 08 56	25 39 23	28 53.8	21 16.4	5 23.1	8 03.1	27 26.7	4 45.8	23 08.6	17 56.1	2 47.3	3 46.3
6 Su	8 58 45	13 39 32	2♏14 34	8♏54 45	28D 53.2	23 11.4	5 46.4	8 40.2	27 53.0	4 49.5	23 16.1	17 53.7	2 49.5	3 47.4
7 M	9 02 42	14 37 02	15 40 08	22 30 53	28 53.3	25 04.8	6 11.4	9 17.3	28 19.4	4 53.0	23 23.6	17 51.3	2 51.7	3 48.6
8 Tu	9 06 39	15 34 33	29 27 07	6♐28 49	28 54.0	26 56.6	6 38.0	9 54.5	28 45.7	4 56.4	23 31.0	17 48.9	2 53.9	3 49.7
9 W	9 10 35	16 32 05	13♐35 53	20 48 07	28 55.1	28 47.0	7 06.1	10 31.9	29 12.0	4 59.6	23 38.4	17 46.5	2 56.1	3 50.9
10 Th	9 14 32	17 29 38	28 05 11	5♑26 34	28 56.3	0♍35.8	7 35.7	11 09.3	29 38.4	5 02.6	23 45.8	17 44.1	2 58.2	3 52.0
11 F	9 18 28	18 27 11	12♑51 40	20 19 42	28R 57.1	2 23.1	8 06.8	11 46.7	0♌04.7	5 05.4	23 53.1	17 41.7	3 00.4	3 53.1
12 Sa	9 22 25	19 24 46	27 49 49	5♒21 00	28 57.2	4 08.8	8 39.3	12 24.3	0 31.0	5 08.0	24 00.5	17 39.4	3 02.6	3 54.2
13 Su	9 26 21	20 22 22	12♒52 12	20 22 21	28 56.2	5 53.1	9 13.1	13 02.0	0 57.2	5 10.5	24 07.7	17 37.0	3 04.7	3 55.3
14 M	9 30 18	21 19 58	27 50 21	5♓15 09	28 54.2	7 35.9	9 48.2	13 39.7	1 23.5	5 12.7	24 15.0	17 34.6	3 06.9	3 56.4
15 Tu	9 34 14	22 17 37	12♓35 49	19 51 31	28 51.4	9 17.2	10 24.6	14 17.5	1 49.8	5 14.8	24 22.2	17 32.2	3 09.0	3 57.4
16 W	9 38 11	23 15 16	27 01 32	4♈05 21	28 48.0	10 57.1	11 02.1	14 55.4	2 16.0	5 16.6	24 29.4	17 29.8	3 11.1	3 58.4
17 Th	9 42 08	24 12 57	11♈02 36	17 53 06	28 44.7	12 35.5	11 40.9	15 33.4	2 42.2	5 18.3	24 36.5	17 27.4	3 13.2	3 59.4
18 F	9 46 04	25 10 40	24 36 48	1♉13 49	28 42.0	14 12.4	12 20.7	16 11.5	3 08.5	5 19.8	24 43.6	17 25.1	3 15.3	4 00.4
19 Sa	9 50 01	26 08 24	7♉44 23	14 08 51	28 40.2	15 47.9	13 01.7	16 49.7	3 34.7	5 21.0	24 50.7	17 22.7	3 17.4	4 01.4
20 Su	9 53 57	27 06 11	20 27 38	26 41 15	28D 39.5	17 22.0	13 43.7	17 27.9	4 00.8	5 22.1	24 57.7	17 20.4	3 19.5	4 02.4
21 M	9 57 54	28 03 58	2♊50 15	8♊55 13	28 40.0	18 54.7	14 26.7	18 06.3	4 27.0	5 23.0	25 04.7	17 18.0	3 21.6	4 03.3
22 Tu	10 01 50	29 01 48	14 56 45	20 55 29	28 41.4	20 26.0	15 10.6	18 44.7	4 53.2	5 23.7	25 11.7	17 15.7	3 23.6	4 04.3
23 W	10 05 47	29 59 39	26 52 01	2♋46 55	28 43.1	21 55.8	15 55.5	19 23.2	5 19.3	5 24.2	25 18.6	17 13.4	3 25.7	4 05.2
24 Th	10 09 43	0♍57 32	8♋40 48	14 34 11	28 44.7	23 24.2	16 41.3	20 01.8	5 45.4	5R 24.5	25 25.4	17 11.1	3 27.7	4 06.1
25 F	10 13 40	1 55 27	20 27 36	26 21 31	28R 45.5	24 51.1	17 27.9	20 40.4	6 11.5	5 24.5	25 32.3	17 08.8	3 29.7	4 07.0
26 Sa	10 17 37	2 53 23	2♌16 23	8♌12 35	28 45.1	26 16.5	18 15.4	21 19.2	6 37.6	5 24.4	25 39.0	17 06.5	3 31.7	4 07.8
27 Su	10 21 33	3 51 21	14 10 30	20 10 25	28 43.1	27 40.5	19 03.7	21 58.0	7 03.6	5 24.1	25 45.7	17 04.2	3 33.7	4 08.7
28 M	10 25 30	4 49 20	26 12 37	2♍17 19	28 39.3	29 03.0	19 52.7	22 37.0	7 29.7	5 23.6	25 52.4	17 02.0	3 35.7	4 09.5
29 Tu	10 29 26	5 47 22	8♍24 43	14 34 57	28 34.0	0♎23.9	20 42.4	23 16.0	7 55.7	5 22.8	25 59.0	16 59.7	3 37.6	4 10.3
30 W	10 33 23	6 45 24	20 48 09	27 04 25	28 27.6	1 43.2	21 32.9	23 55.1	8 21.6	5 21.9	26 05.6	16 57.5	3 39.5	4 11.1
31 Th	10 37 19	7 43 28	3♎23 49	9♎46 25	28 20.8	3 00.9	22 24.1	24 34.2	8 47.6	5 20.8	26 12.1	16 55.3	3 41.5	4 11.8

Astro Data (Dy Hr Mn)

♄⚻♅ 4 19:07
☽0S 6 11:42
♃□♆ 7 6:52
☽0N 19 2:58
♃✶♇ 21 4:45
♅Q♇ 22 11:39
♂0S 24 18:24
♀ D 25 10:48

☽0S 2 17:25
☽0N 15 13:00
♃ R 25 9:34
☿0S 28 0:48
☽0S 29 23:29

Planet Ingress (Dy Hr Mn)

☿ ♋ 10 18:17
☉ ♌ 23 5:21
♂ ♎ 23 5:23
☿ ♌ 26 1:42

☿ ♍ 10 4:04
⚳ ♌ 11 7:44
☉ ♍ 23 12:09
☿ ♎ 29 4:52

Last Aspect Dy Hr Mn		☽ Ingress Dy Hr Mn
1 7:46	♄☌	♌ 2 6:57
4 0:25	☿✶	♍ 4 19:32
6 18:38	☿□	♎ 7 6:06
9 9:24	☿△	♏ 9 13:16
11 4:57	♂✶	♐ 11 16:43
13 8:05	♂□	♑ 13 17:20
15 9:28	♂△	♒ 15 16:46
16 22:32	♅☌	♓ 17 16:55
19 15:52	♂☍	♈ 19 19:32
21 23:33	☉□	♉ 22 1:46
24 3:34	☿✶	♊ 24 11:36
26 0:16	♅△	♋ 26 23:53
28 21:02	♄☌	♌ 29 12:56

Last Aspect Dy Hr Mn		☽ Ingress Dy Hr Mn
31 1:36	♅☍	♍ 1 1:18
2 22:05	♄✶	♎ 3 11:54
5 7:20	♄□	♏ 5 19:56
7 17:09	☿□	♐ 8 0:56
10 3:00	☿△	♑ 10 3:08
11 17:44	♄☍	♒ 12 3:28
13 12:00	☉☍	♓ 14 3:29
15 19:36	♄△	♈ 16 5:02
18 0:10	☉△	♉ 18 9:45
20 12:52	☉□	♊ 20 18:27
23 5:50	☉✶	♋ 23 6:21
25 10:19	♄☌	♌ 25 19:24
27 15:47	♂✶	♍ 28 7:30
30 10:07	♄✶	♎ 30 17:34

☽ Phases & Eclipses (Dy Hr Mn)

8 11:54 ☽ 15♎57
15 4:40 ○ 22♑20
15 4:46 • P 0.794
21 23:33 ☾ 28♈49
30 2:15 ● 6♌34
30 2:05:52 • A 06'24"

6 21:05 ☽ 14♏01
13 12:00 ○ 20♒22
20 12:52 ☾ 27♉08
28 17:24 ● 5♍02

Astro Data

1 July 1916
Julian Day # 6026
SVP 6♓25'17"
GC 25♐40.4 ⚴ 7♊21.2
Eris 28♓16.3R ⚵ 17♏33.3R
⚷ 26♓20.8R ⚶ 19♎32.8
☽ Mean ☊ 0♒05.2

1 August 1916
Julian Day # 6057
SVP 6♓25'12"
GC 25♐40.5 ⚴ 23♊56.9
Eris 28♓08.4R ⚵ 18♏10.5
⚷ 25♓52.8R ⚶ 29♎27.2
☽ Mean ☊ 28♑26.8

LONGITUDE — September 1916

Day	Sid.Time	☉	0 hr ☽	Noon ☽	True ☊	☿	♀	♂	⚳	♃	♄	♅	♆	♇
1 F	10 41 16	8♍41 34	16♎12 15	22♎41 23	28♑14.3	4♎16.9	23♋15.9	25♎13.5	9♌13.5	5♉19.4	26♋18.6	16♒53.2	3♌43.4	4♋12.6
2 Sa	10 45 12	9 39 41	29 13 52	5♏49 43	28R 08.8	5 31.1	24 08.4	25 52.8	9 39.4	5R 17.9	26 25.0	16R 51.0	3 45.3	4 13.3
3 Su	10 49 09	10 37 50	12♏29 02	19 11 51	28 05.0	6 43.6	25 01.5	26 32.2	10 05.2	5 16.2	26 31.3	16 48.9	3 47.1	4 14.0
4 M	10 53 06	11 36 00	25 58 15	2♐48 17	28D 03.0	7 54.1	25 55.1	27 11.7	10 31.1	5 14.3	26 37.6	16 46.8	3 49.0	4 14.7
5 Tu	10 57 02	12 34 12	9♐42 00	16 39 25	28 02.8	9 02.6	26 49.4	27 51.3	10 56.9	5 12.1	26 43.9	16 44.7	3 50.8	4 15.4
6 W	11 00 59	13 32 25	23 40 31	0♑45 15	28 03.6	10 09.1	27 44.3	28 31.0	11 22.6	5 09.8	26 50.1	16 42.6	3 52.6	4 16.0
7 Th	11 04 55	14 30 40	7♑53 27	15 04 56	28R 04.8	11 13.4	28 39.6	29 10.7	11 48.4	5 07.3	26 56.2	16 40.6	3 54.4	4 16.6
8 F	11 08 52	15 28 56	22 19 23	29 36 23	28 05.3	12 15.3	29 35.5	29 50.5	12 14.1	5 04.6	27 02.2	16 38.6	3 56.2	4 17.2
9 Sa	11 12 48	16 27 13	6♒55 24	14♒15 49	28 04.2	13 14.7	0♌32.0	0♏30.4	12 39.7	5 01.7	27 08.2	16 36.6	3 58.0	4 17.8
10 Su	11 16 45	17 25 33	21 36 53	28 57 49	28 01.0	14 11.5	1 28.9	1 10.3	13 05.4	4 58.6	27 14.2	16 34.7	3 59.7	4 18.4
11 M	11 20 41	18 23 54	6♓17 43	13♓35 43	27 55.6	15 05.5	2 26.3	1 50.3	13 30.9	4 55.3	27 20.1	16 32.7	4 01.4	4 18.9
12 Tu	11 24 38	19 22 16	20 50 54	28 02 26	27 48.3	15 56.5	3 24.2	2 30.5	13 56.5	4 51.9	27 25.9	16 30.8	4 03.1	4 19.4
13 W	11 28 35	20 20 41	5♈09 33	12♈11 35	27 39.9	16 44.3	4 22.6	3 10.6	14 22.0	4 48.2	27 31.6	16 29.0	4 04.8	4 19.9
14 Th	11 32 31	21 19 07	19 08 00	25 58 25	27 31.2	17 28.6	5 21.4	3 50.9	14 47.5	4 44.4	27 37.3	16 27.1	4 06.4	4 20.4
15 F	11 36 28	22 17 36	2♉42 36	9♉20 28	27 23.4	18 09.2	6 20.6	4 31.2	15 12.9	4 40.3	27 42.9	16 25.3	4 08.0	4 20.8
16 Sa	11 40 24	23 16 07	15 52 05	22 17 40	27 17.2	18 45.8	7 20.3	5 11.6	15 38.3	4 36.1	27 48.4	16 23.6	4 09.6	4 21.3
17 Su	11 44 21	24 14 40	28 37 30	4♊52 01	27 13.1	19 18.1	8 20.3	5 52.1	16 03.7	4 31.7	27 53.9	16 21.8	4 11.2	4 21.7
18 M	11 48 17	25 13 15	11♊01 43	17 07 09	27D 11.0	19 45.7	9 20.8	6 32.7	16 29.0	4 27.2	27 59.3	16 20.1	4 12.8	4 22.1
19 Tu	11 52 14	26 11 53	23 08 58	29 07 40	27 10.7	20 08.4	10 21.7	7 13.3	16 54.2	4 22.5	28 04.6	16 18.5	4 14.3	4 22.4
20 W	11 56 10	27 10 32	5♋04 18	10♋59 10	27 11.3	20 25.7	11 22.9	7 54.1	17 19.5	4 17.5	28 09.8	16 16.8	4 15.8	4 22.8
21 Th	12 00 07	28 09 14	16 53 05	22 46 42	27R 12.0	20 37.3	12 24.5	8 34.9	17 44.6	4 12.5	28 15.0	16 15.2	4 17.3	4 23.1
22 F	12 04 04	29 07 58	28 40 39	4♌35 34	27 11.8	20R 42.8	13 26.5	9 15.7	18 09.8	4 07.2	28 20.1	16 13.7	4 18.8	4 23.4
23 Sa	12 08 00	0♎06 45	10♌31 59	16 30 28	27 09.8	20 41.8	14 28.8	9 56.7	18 34.8	4 01.8	28 25.1	16 12.2	4 20.2	4 23.7
24 Su	12 11 57	1 05 33	22 31 28	28 35 23	27 05.5	20 34.0	15 31.4	10 37.7	18 59.9	3 56.2	28 30.1	16 10.7	4 21.6	4 23.9
25 M	12 15 53	2 04 23	4♍42 34	10♍53 19	26 58.5	20 19.0	16 34.3	11 18.8	19 24.8	3 50.5	28 34.9	16 09.2	4 23.0	4 24.2
26 Tu	12 19 50	3 03 16	17 07 48	23 26 08	26 49.2	19 56.7	17 37.6	12 00.0	19 49.7	3 44.6	28 39.7	16 07.8	4 24.3	4 24.4
27 W	12 23 46	4 02 11	29 48 24	6♎14 33	26 38.0	19 26.9	18 41.2	12 41.3	20 14.6	3 38.6	28 44.4	16 06.5	4 25.6	4 24.5
28 Th	12 27 43	5 01 07	12♎44 30	19 18 06	26 26.2	18 49.7	19 45.0	13 22.6	20 39.4	3 32.4	28 49.0	16 05.1	4 26.9	4 24.7
29 F	12 31 39	6 00 06	25 55 10	2♏35 28	26 14.7	18 05.2	20 49.2	14 04.0	21 04.1	3 26.1	28 53.5	16 03.8	4 28.2	4 24.8
30 Sa	12 35 36	6 59 07	9♏18 45	16 04 47	26 04.7	17 13.9	21 53.6	14 45.5	21 28.8	3 19.6	28 58.0	16 02.6	4 29.5	4 25.0

LONGITUDE — October 1916

Day	Sid.Time	☉	0 hr ☽	Noon ☽	True ☊	☿	♀	♂	⚳	♃	♄	♅	♆	♇
1 Su	12 39 32	7♎58 09	22♏53 19	29♏44 08	25♑57.1	16♎16.4	22♌58.3	15♏27.1	21♌53.4	3♉13.1	29♋02.3	16♒01.4	4♌30.7	4♋25.0
2 M	12 43 29	8 57 13	6♐37 01	13♐31 49	25R 52.3	15R 13.6	24 03.2	16 08.7	22 18.0	3R 06.4	29 06.6	16R 00.3	4 31.9	4 25.1
3 Tu	12 47 26	9 56 20	20 28 25	27 26 43	25D 50.0	14 06.9	25 08.5	16 50.4	22 42.5	2 59.5	29 10.8	15 59.1	4 33.0	4 25.2
4 W	12 51 22	10 55 27	4♑26 37	11♑28 04	25 49.5	12 57.8	26 13.9	17 32.2	23 06.9	2 52.6	29 14.9	15 58.1	4 34.1	4R 25.2
5 Th	12 55 19	11 54 37	18 30 59	25 35 18	25R 49.6	11 47.8	27 19.7	18 14.1	23 31.2	2 45.5	29 18.9	15 57.1	4 35.2	4 25.2
6 F	12 59 15	12 53 48	2♒40 53	9♒47 35	25 49.1	10 38.9	28 25.6	18 56.0	23 55.5	2 38.4	29 22.8	15 56.1	4 36.3	4 25.2
7 Sa	13 03 12	13 53 01	16 55 08	24 03 15	25 46.7	9 33.1	29 31.8	19 38.0	24 19.7	2 31.1	29 26.6	15 55.2	4 37.3	4 25.1
8 Su	13 07 08	14 52 16	1♓11 32	8♓19 33	25 41.6	8 32.2	0♍38.3	20 20.0	24 43.9	2 23.7	29 30.3	15 54.3	4 38.3	4 25.1
9 M	13 11 05	15 51 32	15 26 46	22 32 35	25 33.6	7 37.9	1 44.9	21 02.2	25 07.9	2 16.3	29 34.0	15 53.4	4 39.3	4 25.0
10 Tu	13 15 01	16 50 51	29 36 23	6♈37 32	25 23.1	6 51.8	2 51.8	21 44.4	25 31.9	2 08.7	29 37.5	15 52.6	4 40.3	4 24.8
11 W	13 18 58	17 50 11	13♈35 26	20 29 29	25 10.9	6 15.0	3 58.9	22 26.6	25 55.8	2 01.1	29 41.0	15 51.9	4 41.2	4 24.7
12 Th	13 22 55	18 49 34	27 19 12	4♉04 09	24 58.3	5 48.6	5 06.2	23 09.0	26 19.6	1 53.4	29 44.3	15 51.2	4 42.1	4 24.5
13 F	13 26 51	19 48 59	10♉44 02	17 18 37	24 46.5	5D 32.9	6 13.7	23 51.4	26 43.4	1 45.6	29 47.6	15 50.5	4 42.9	4 24.4
14 Sa	13 30 48	20 48 26	23 47 52	0♊11 49	24 36.7	5 28.3	7 21.5	24 33.8	27 07.1	1 37.8	29 50.7	15 49.9	4 43.7	4 24.2
15 Su	13 34 44	21 47 55	6♊30 36	12 44 32	24 29.3	5 34.7	8 29.4	25 16.4	27 30.7	1 29.9	29 53.8	15 49.4	4 44.5	4 23.9
16 M	13 38 41	22 47 26	18 53 57	24 59 20	24 24.7	5 51.7	9 37.6	25 59.0	27 54.2	1 22.0	29 56.7	15 48.9	4 45.3	4 23.7
17 Tu	13 42 37	23 47 00	1♋01 11	7♋00 06	24 22.5	6 18.9	10 45.9	26 41.7	28 17.6	1 14.0	29 59.6	15 48.4	4 46.0	4 23.4
18 W	13 46 34	24 46 36	12 56 42	18 51 40	24 21.8	6 55.5	11 54.4	27 24.5	28 40.9	1 06.0	0♌02.3	15 48.0	4 46.7	4 23.1
19 Th	13 50 30	25 46 14	24 45 41	0♌39 28	24 21.8	7 40.9	13 03.1	28 07.3	29 04.1	0 57.9	0 05.0	15 47.7	4 47.4	4 22.8
20 F	13 54 27	26 45 55	6♌33 41	12 29 03	24 21.2	8 34.2	14 12.0	28 50.2	29 27.3	0 49.8	0 07.5	15 47.4	4 48.0	4 22.5
21 Sa	13 58 24	27 45 38	18 26 14	24 25 53	24 19.0	9 34.6	15 21.1	29 33.2	29 50.3	0 41.7	0 10.0	15 47.1	4 48.6	4 22.1
22 Su	14 02 20	28 45 23	0♍28 35	6♍34 53	24 14.4	10 41.3	16 30.3	0♐16.2	0♍13.3	0 33.5	0 12.3	15 46.9	4 49.1	4 21.7
23 M	14 06 17	29 45 10	12 45 16	19 00 08	24 07.0	11 53.5	17 39.7	0 59.3	0 36.1	0 25.4	0 14.5	15 46.7	4 49.7	4 21.3
24 Tu	14 10 13	0♏44 59	25 19 46	1♎44 25	23 57.0	13 10.4	18 49.2	1 42.5	0 58.9	0 17.3	0 16.7	15 46.6	4 50.2	4 20.9
25 W	14 14 10	1 44 50	8♎14 09	14 48 58	23 45.0	14 31.3	19 58.9	2 25.8	1 21.5	0 09.1	0 18.7	15D 46.6	4 50.6	4 20.4
26 Th	14 18 06	2 44 44	21 28 45	28 13 14	23 32.1	15 55.8	21 08.8	3 09.1	1 44.0	0 01.0	0 20.6	15 46.6	4 51.0	4 19.9
27 F	14 22 03	3 44 39	5♏02 06	11♏54 55	23 19.5	17 23.1	22 18.8	3 52.5	2 06.5	29♈52.9	0 22.4	15 46.6	4 51.4	4 19.5
28 Sa	14 25 59	4 44 37	18 51 11	25 50 22	23 08.6	18 52.8	23 28.9	4 35.9	2 28.8	29 44.8	0 24.1	15 46.7	4 51.8	4 18.9
29 Su	14 29 56	5 44 36	2♐51 53	9♐55 13	23 00.1	20 24.5	24 39.2	5 19.5	2 51.0	29 36.7	0 25.7	15 46.8	4 52.1	4 18.4
30 M	14 33 53	6 44 37	16 59 47	24 05 08	22 54.6	21 57.7	25 49.6	6 03.1	3 13.0	29 28.7	0 27.2	15 47.0	4 52.4	4 17.9
31 Tu	14 37 49	7 44 40	1♑10 48	8♑16 28	22 51.9	23 32.3	27 00.2	6 46.7	3 35.0	29 20.7	0 28.5	15 47.3	4 52.7	4 17.3

Astro Data

Astro Data	Dy Hr Mn
☽0N	11 23:31
♃✶♇	19 12:03
♃□♆	20 18:21
☿R	22 20:28
⊙0S	23 9:15
☽0S	26 6:31
♆⊻♇	26 12:49
♇R	5 1:21
☽0N	9 8:29
☿D	14 10:00
☽0S	23 14:29
♃□♄	24 13:22
♅D	26 3:18

Planet Ingress

Planet Ingress	Dy Hr Mn
♂ ♏	8 17:44
♀ ♌	8 22:26
⊙ ♎	23 9:15
♀ ♍	7 22:11
♄ ♌	17 15:36
⚳ ♍	21 22:06
♂ ♐	22 2:58
⊙ ♏	23 17:57
♃ ♈R	26 14:53

Last Aspect / ☽ Ingress (September)

Last Aspect Dy Hr Mn		☽ Ingress	Dy Hr Mn
1 18:43	♄ □	♏	2 1:24
4 1:04	♄ △	♐	4 7:05
6 8:02	♂ ✶	♑	6 10:44
8 12:24	♂ □	♒	8 12:39
9 15:49	♅ ☌	♓	10 13:42
12 10:58	♄ △	♈	12 15:17
14 14:56	♄ □	♉	14 19:09
16 22:31	♄ ✶	♊	17 2:38
19 5:35	⊙ □	♋	19 13:45
21 23:55	⊙ ✶	♌	22 2:41
23 20:18	☿ ✶	♍	24 14:47
26 21:55	♄ ✶	♎	27 0:22
29 5:19	♄ □	♏	29 7:21

Last Aspect / ☽ Ingress (October)

Last Aspect Dy Hr Mn		☽ Ingress	Dy Hr Mn
1 10:47	♄ △	♐	1 12:28
3 7:42	♀ △	♑	3 16:23
5 18:20	♄ ☍	♒	5 19:28
7 21:59	♀ ☍	♓	7 22:00
9 23:59	♄ △	♈	10 0:40
12 4:15	♄ □	♉	12 4:45
14 11:20	♄ ✶	♊	14 11:38
16 7:16	⊙ △	♋	16 21:58
19 6:30	♂ △	♌	19 10:40
21 22:49	♂ □	♍	21 23:04
23 9:10	♀ ☌	♎	24 8:45
26 15:09	♃ ☍	♏	26 15:09
28 7:35	♀ ✶	♐	28 19:07
30 21:02	♃ △	♑	30 22:00

☽ Phases & Eclipses

Dy Hr Mn		
5 4:26	☽	12♐16
11 20:30	○	18♓45
19 5:35	☾	25♊56
27 7:34	●	3♎51
4 11:00	☽	10♑53
11 7:01	○	17♈38
19 1:08	☾	25♋19
26 20:37	●	3♏06

Astro Data

1 September 1916
Julian Day # 6088
SVP 6♓25'08"
GC 25♐40.5 ⚴ 10♋49.4
Eris 27♓51.5R ⚵ 23♏04.1
⚷ 24♓44.9R ⚶ 12♏22.9
☽Mean ☊ 26♑48.3

1 October 1916
Julian Day # 6118
SVP 6♓25'05"
GC 25♐40.6 ⚴ 26♋39.4
Eris 27♓31.4R ⚵ 0♐34.7
⚷ 23♓23.9R ⚶ 26♏35.7
☽Mean ☊ 25♑12.9

November 1916 LONGITUDE

Day	Sid.Time	☉	0 hr ☽	Noon ☽	True ☊	☿	♀	♂	⚳	♃	♄	♅	♆	♇
1 W	14 41 46	8♏44 44	15♑21 48	22♑26 36	22♑51.3	25♎07.8	28♍10.8	7♐30.4	3♍56.8	29♈12.8	0♌29.8	15♒47.6	4♌52.9	4♋16.7
2 Th	14 45 42	9 44 50	29 30 40	6♒33 55	22R51.5	26 44.1	29 21.6	8 14.2	4 18.5	29R04.9	0 30.9	15 48.0	4 53.1	4R16.1
3 F	14 49 39	10 44 57	13♒36 13	20 37 30	22 51.2	28 21.0	0♎32.6	8 58.1	4 40.1	28 57.1	0 32.0	15 48.4	4 53.2	4 15.4
4 Sa	14 53 35	11 45 06	27 37 41	4♓36 40	22 49.2	29 58.3	1 43.6	9 42.0	5 01.5	28 49.3	0 32.9	15 48.8	4 53.4	4 14.8
5 Su	14 57 32	12 45 16	11♓34 20	18 30 31	22 44.7	1♏35.8	2 54.8	10 25.9	5 22.8	28 41.7	0 33.7	15 49.3	4 53.4	4 14.1
6 M	15 01 28	13 45 27	25 25 01	2♈17 36	22 37.4	3 13.5	4 06.0	11 10.0	5 44.0	28 34.1	0 34.4	15 49.9	4R53.5	4 13.4
7 Tu	15 05 25	14 45 41	9♈07 59	15 55 52	22 27.7	4 51.3	5 17.4	11 54.1	6 05.0	28 26.6	0 35.0	15 50.5	4 53.5	4 12.7
8 W	15 09 22	15 45 56	22 40 57	29 22 56	22 16.5	6 29.0	6 28.9	12 38.2	6 25.9	28 19.1	0 35.4	15 51.1	4 53.5	4 12.0
9 Th	15 13 18	16 46 12	6♉01 29	12♉36 22	22 04.7	8 06.6	7 40.6	13 22.4	6 46.7	28 11.8	0 35.8	15 51.9	4 53.4	4 11.2
10 F	15 17 15	17 46 31	19 07 22	25 34 19	21 53.6	9 44.2	8 52.3	14 06.7	7 07.3	28 04.6	0 36.0	15 52.6	4 53.3	4 10.5
11 Sa	15 21 11	18 46 51	1♊57 08	8♊15 48	21 44.3	11 21.5	10 04.1	14 51.0	7 27.8	27 57.5	0R36.2	15 53.4	4 53.2	4 09.7
12 Su	15 25 08	19 47 13	14 30 25	20 41 06	21 37.3	12 58.7	11 16.1	15 35.4	7 48.1	27 50.5	0 36.2	15 54.3	4 53.1	4 08.9
13 M	15 29 04	20 47 37	26 48 06	2♋51 45	21 32.9	14 35.6	12 28.1	16 19.9	8 08.3	27 43.6	0 36.1	15 55.2	4 52.9	4 08.1
14 Tu	15 33 01	21 48 02	8♋52 24	14 50 31	21D30.9	16 12.4	13 40.3	17 04.4	8 28.3	27 36.8	0 35.9	15 56.2	4 52.7	4 07.2
15 W	15 36 57	22 48 30	20 46 36	26 41 13	21 30.8	17 48.9	14 52.5	17 49.0	8 48.1	27 30.2	0 35.6	15 57.2	4 52.4	4 06.4
16 Th	15 40 54	23 48 59	2♌34 58	8♌28 29	21 31.7	19 25.2	16 04.9	18 33.6	9 07.8	27 23.7	0 35.2	15 58.2	4 52.1	4 05.5
17 F	15 44 51	24 49 30	14 22 26	20 17 29	21R32.5	21 01.2	17 17.3	19 18.3	9 27.3	27 17.3	0 34.6	15 59.3	4 51.8	4 04.6
18 Sa	15 48 47	25 50 02	26 14 20	2♍13 39	21 32.4	22 37.0	18 29.8	20 03.1	9 46.7	27 11.1	0 34.0	16 00.5	4 51.5	4 03.7
19 Su	15 52 44	26 50 37	8♍16 07	14 22 22	21 30.5	24 12.6	19 42.4	20 47.9	10 05.9	27 05.0	0 33.2	16 01.7	4 51.1	4 02.8
20 M	15 56 40	27 51 13	20 32 59	26 48 32	21 26.5	25 48.0	20 55.1	21 32.8	10 24.9	26 59.0	0 32.3	16 03.0	4 50.6	4 01.9
21 Tu	16 00 37	28 51 51	3♎09 28	9♎36 08	21 20.4	27 23.1	22 07.9	22 17.7	10 43.7	26 53.2	0 31.3	16 04.3	4 50.2	4 00.9
22 W	16 04 33	29 52 30	16 08 51	22 47 43	21 12.5	28 58.1	23 20.7	23 02.7	11 02.3	26 47.6	0 30.2	16 05.6	4 49.7	3 59.9
23 Th	16 08 30	0♐53 12	29 32 46	6♏23 51	21 03.8	0♐32.9	24 33.7	23 47.8	11 20.7	26 42.1	0 29.0	16 07.0	4 49.2	3 59.0
24 F	16 12 26	1 53 54	13♏20 41	20 22 50	20 55.1	2 07.6	25 46.7	24 32.9	11 39.0	26 36.8	0 27.7	16 08.5	4 48.6	3 58.0
25 Sa	16 16 23	2 54 39	27 29 43	4♐40 40	20 47.5	3 42.1	26 59.7	25 18.1	11 57.0	26 31.7	0 26.3	16 10.0	4 48.0	3 57.0
26 Su	16 20 20	3 55 24	11♐54 54	19 11 35	20 41.8	5 16.4	28 12.9	26 03.3	12 14.9	26 26.7	0 24.7	16 11.5	4 47.4	3 56.0
27 M	16 24 16	4 56 11	26 29 52	3♑48 54	20 38.3	6 50.7	29 26.1	26 48.6	12 32.5	26 21.9	0 23.1	16 13.1	4 46.8	3 54.9
28 Tu	16 28 13	5 56 59	11♑07 52	18 26 01	20D37.1	8 24.8	0♏39.3	27 33.9	12 49.9	26 17.3	0 21.3	16 14.8	4 46.1	3 53.9
29 W	16 32 09	6 57 48	25 42 43	2♒57 23	20 37.6	9 58.9	1 52.7	28 19.3	13 07.1	26 12.9	0 19.5	16 16.5	4 45.4	3 52.8
30 Th	16 36 06	7 58 38	10♒09 35	17 18 57	20 38.9	11 32.8	3 06.1	29 04.7	13 24.1	26 08.7	0 17.5	16 18.2	4 44.7	3 51.8

December 1916 LONGITUDE

Day	Sid.Time	☉	0 hr ☽	Noon ☽	True ☊	☿	♀	♂	⚳	♃	♄	♅	♆	♇
1 F	16 40 02	8♐59 28	24♒25 15	1♓28 17	20♑40.0	13♐06.7	4♏19.5	29♐50.2	13♍40.9	26♈04.6	0♌15.4	16♒20.0	4♌43.9	3♋50.7
2 Sa	16 43 59	10 00 20	8♓27 58	15 24 15	20R40.1	14 40.6	5 33.0	0♑35.7	13 57.4	26R00.7	0R13.2	16 21.8	4R43.1	3R49.6
3 Su	16 47 55	11 01 12	22 17 07	29 06 35	20 38.6	16 14.4	6 46.5	1 21.3	14 13.8	25 57.1	0 11.0	16 23.6	4 42.2	3 48.5
4 M	16 51 52	12 02 05	5♈52 42	12♈35 29	20 35.2	17 48.2	8 00.1	2 07.0	14 29.8	25 53.6	0 08.6	16 25.6	4 41.4	3 47.4
5 Tu	16 55 49	13 02 59	19 14 59	25 51 13	20 30.1	19 22.0	9 13.8	2 52.6	14 45.7	25 50.3	0 06.1	16 27.5	4 40.5	3 46.3
6 W	16 59 45	14 03 53	2♉24 14	8♉54 01	20 24.0	20 55.8	10 27.5	3 38.4	15 01.3	25 47.2	0 03.5	16 29.5	4 39.6	3 45.2
7 Th	17 03 42	15 04 49	15 20 37	21 44 00	20 17.4	22 29.6	11 41.3	4 24.1	15 16.7	25 44.4	0 00.8	16 31.5	4 38.6	3 44.0
8 F	17 07 38	16 05 45	28 04 14	4♊21 18	20 11.3	24 03.4	12 55.1	5 10.0	15 31.8	25 41.7	29♋58.1	16 33.6	4 37.6	3 42.9
9 Sa	17 11 35	17 06 42	10♊35 17	16 46 15	20 06.2	25 37.2	14 08.9	5 55.8	15 46.7	25 39.2	29 55.2	16 35.7	4 36.6	3 41.8
10 Su	17 15 31	18 07 40	22 54 18	28 59 35	20 02.6	27 11.0	15 22.8	6 41.8	16 01.3	25 36.9	29 52.2	16 37.9	4 35.6	3 40.6
11 M	17 19 28	19 08 40	5♋02 17	11♋02 36	20D00.6	28 44.9	16 36.8	7 27.7	16 15.6	25 34.9	29 49.2	16 40.1	4 34.6	3 39.4
12 Tu	17 23 25	20 09 39	17 00 50	22 57 16	20 00.2	0♑18.7	17 50.8	8 13.7	16 29.7	25 33.0	29 46.1	16 42.3	4 33.5	3 38.3
13 W	17 27 21	21 10 40	28 52 18	4♌46 19	20 01.1	1 52.5	19 04.8	8 59.8	16 43.5	25 31.3	29 42.8	16 44.6	4 32.4	3 37.1
14 Th	17 31 18	22 11 42	10♌39 46	16 33 08	20 02.8	3 26.2	20 18.9	9 45.9	16 57.1	25 29.9	29 39.5	16 46.9	4 31.2	3 35.9
15 F	17 35 14	23 12 44	22 26 59	28 21 50	20 04.7	4 59.9	21 33.0	10 32.0	17 10.3	25 28.6	29 36.1	16 49.3	4 30.1	3 34.7
16 Sa	17 39 11	24 13 48	4♍18 17	10♍16 56	20 06.3	6 33.5	22 47.2	11 18.2	17 23.3	25 27.6	29 32.6	16 51.7	4 28.9	3 33.5
17 Su	17 43 07	25 14 52	16 18 26	22 23 23	20R07.1	8 07.0	24 01.4	12 04.5	17 35.9	25 26.7	29 29.0	16 54.1	4 27.7	3 32.3
18 M	17 47 04	26 15 57	28 32 23	4♎46 04	20 06.8	9 40.2	25 15.6	12 50.7	17 48.3	25 26.1	29 25.4	16 56.6	4 26.4	3 31.1
19 Tu	17 51 00	27 17 03	11♎04 57	17 29 34	20 05.4	11 13.2	26 29.9	13 37.1	18 00.4	25 25.7	29 21.7	16 59.1	4 25.2	3 29.9
20 W	17 54 57	28 18 10	24 00 21	0♏37 38	20 03.1	12 45.8	27 44.2	14 23.4	18 12.1	25D25.5	29 17.9	17 01.7	4 23.9	3 28.7
21 Th	17 58 54	29 19 18	7♏21 39	14 12 29	20 00.2	14 17.9	28 58.6	15 09.8	18 23.6	25 25.5	29 14.0	17 04.2	4 22.6	3 27.5
22 F	18 02 50	0♑20 26	21 10 08	28 14 20	19 57.2	15 49.5	0♐12.9	15 56.3	18 34.7	25 25.7	29 10.0	17 06.9	4 21.3	3 26.3
23 Sa	18 06 47	1 21 35	5♐24 44	12♐40 46	19 54.6	17 20.3	1 27.3	16 42.8	18 45.5	25 26.1	29 06.0	17 09.5	4 19.9	3 25.1
24 Su	18 10 43	2 22 45	20 01 44	27 26 46	19 52.8	18 50.3	2 41.8	17 29.3	18 56.0	25 26.8	29 01.9	17 12.2	4 18.6	3 23.9
25 M	18 14 40	3 23 55	4♑54 53	12♑25 02	19D51.8	20 19.2	3 56.2	18 15.9	19 06.2	25 27.6	28 57.8	17 14.9	4 17.2	3 22.7
26 Tu	18 18 36	4 25 05	19 56 06	27 27 01	19 51.8	21 46.7	5 10.7	19 02.5	19 16.0	25 28.7	28 53.5	17 17.7	4 15.8	3 21.5
27 W	18 22 33	5 26 15	4♒56 41	12♒24 08	19 52.5	23 12.7	6 25.2	19 49.1	19 25.4	25 29.9	28 49.3	17 20.4	4 14.4	3 20.3
28 Th	18 26 29	6 27 25	19 48 30	27 09 02	19 53.6	24 36.7	7 39.7	20 35.8	19 34.5	25 31.4	28 44.9	17 23.2	4 12.9	3 19.1
29 F	18 30 26	7 28 36	4♓25 06	11♓36 16	19 54.7	25 58.4	8 54.3	21 22.5	19 43.3	25 33.1	28 40.5	17 26.1	4 11.5	3 17.8
30 Sa	18 34 23	8 29 45	18 42 13	25 42 44	19 55.4	27 17.4	10 08.8	22 09.2	19 51.7	25 35.0	28 36.1	17 29.0	4 10.0	3 16.6
31 Su	18 38 19	9 30 55	2♈37 47	9♈27 24	19R55.7	28 33.2	11 23.4	22 56.0	19 59.7	25 37.0	28 31.6	17 31.9	4 08.5	3 15.4

Astro Data

	Dy Hr Mn
☽0N	5 14:48
♀0S	6 3:16
♆ R	7 10:37
♄ R	12 5:10
☽0S	19 22:40
☽0N	2 19:26
☽0S	17 6:17
♃ D	20 23:37
☽0N	30 1:11

Planet Ingress

		Dy Hr Mn
♀	♎	3 0:59
☿	♏	4 12:25
☉	♐	22 14:58
☿	♐	23 3:40
♀	♏	27 23:07
♂	♑	1 17:10
♄	♋R	7 19:21
☿	♑	12 7:13
☉	♑	22 3:59
♀	♐	22 7:50

Last Aspect / ☽ Ingress (November)

Last Aspect Dy Hr Mn			☽ Ingress	Dy Hr Mn
1 23:23	♃	□	♒	2 0:50
4 2:59	☿	△	♓	4 4:04
5 1:16	☉	△	♈	6 7:59
8 10:06	♃	☌	♉	8 13:07
9 20:18	☉	☍	♊	10 20:19
13 1:55	♃	⚹	♋	13 6:19
15 13:39	♃	□	♌	15 18:44
18 1:59	♃	△	♍	18 7:33
20 14:09	☉	⚹	♎	20 18:03
22 19:05	♃	☍	♏	23 0:48
24 4:46	♅	□	♐	25 4:12
27 4:10	♀	⚹	♑	27 5:45
29 0:53	♃	□	♒	29 7:06

Last Aspect / ☽ Ingress (December)

Last Aspect Dy Hr Mn			☽ Ingress	Dy Hr Mn
1 9:03	♂	⚹	♓	1 9:29
2 10:35	☿	□	♈	3 13:34
5 11:58	♃	☌	♉	5 19:35
8 3:39	♄	⚹	♊	8 3:40
10 7:54	☿	☍	♋	10 14:00
13 1:45	♄	☌	♌	13 2:18
15 6:09	♃	△	♍	15 15:19
18 1:46	♄	⚹	♎	18 2:50
20 9:37	♄	□	♏	20 10:52
22 13:33	♄	△	♐	22 14:58
24 8:46	♃	△	♑	24 16:07
26 14:18	♄	☍	♒	26 16:05
28 9:20	♃	⚹	♓	28 16:41
30 16:58	♄	△	♈	30 19:25

☽ Phases & Eclipses

Dy Hr Mn		
2 17:50	☽	9♒59
9 20:18	○	17♉07
17 22:00	☾	25♌15
25 8:50	●	2♐47
2 1:55	☽	9♓35
9 12:43	○	17♊09
17 18:06	☾	25♍30
24 20:31	●	2♑44
24 20:45:56	●	P 0.012
31 12:07	☽	9♈31

Astro Data

1 November 1916
Julian Day # 6149
SVP 6♓25'01"
GC 25♐40.7 ⚳ 11♌03.1
Eris 27♓12.7R ⚵ 10♐09.4
⚷ 22♓15.3R ⚶ 12♐19.6
☽ Mean ☊ 23♑34.4

1 December 1916
Julian Day # 6179
SVP 6♓24'56"
GC 25♐40.7 ⚳ 20♌37.4
Eris 27♓02.2R ⚵ 20♐28.8
⚷ 21♓48.0R ⚶ 28♐06.8
☽ Mean ☊ 21♑59.1

LONGITUDE January 1917

Day	Sid.Time	☉	0 hr ☽	Noon ☽	True ☊	☿	♀	♂	⚳	♃	♄	♅	♆	♇
1 M	18 42 16	10♑32 04	16♈11 41	22♈50 50	19♑55.4	29♑45.2	12♐38.0	23♑42.8	20♍07.3	25♈39.3	28♋27.0	17♒34.8	4♌07.0	3♋14.2
2 Tu	18 46 12	11 33 14	29 25 06	5♉54 44	19R 54.8	0♒52.8	13 52.6	24 29.6	20 14.6	25 41.8	28R 22.5	17 37.7	4R 05.5	3R 13.0
3 W	18 50 09	12 34 23	12♉20 03	18 41 21	19 53.9	1 55.3	15 07.2	25 16.5	20 21.5	25 44.5	28 17.8	17 40.7	4 03.9	3 11.8
4 Th	18 54 05	13 35 31	24 58 56	1♊13 07	19 52.9	2 51.9	16 21.8	26 03.4	20 28.1	25 47.4	28 13.2	17 43.7	4 02.4	3 10.6
5 F	18 58 02	14 36 40	7♊24 11	13 32 26	19 52.1	3 41.8	17 36.5	26 50.3	20 34.2	25 50.5	28 08.4	17 46.8	4 00.8	3 09.4
6 Sa	19 01 58	15 37 48	19 38 07	25 41 30	19 51.6	4 24.1	18 51.2	27 37.2	20 40.0	25 53.8	28 03.7	17 49.8	3 59.2	3 08.3
7 Su	19 05 55	16 38 56	1♋42 50	7♋42 22	19 51.3	4 57.9	20 05.9	28 24.2	20 45.4	25 57.3	27 58.9	17 52.9	3 57.6	3 07.1
8 M	19 09 52	17 40 04	13 40 20	19 36 58	19D 51.2	5 22.3	21 20.6	29 11.2	20 50.3	26 00.9	27 54.1	17 56.0	3 56.0	3 05.9
9 Tu	19 13 48	18 41 12	25 32 32	1♌27 16	19 51.2	5R 36.5	22 35.3	29 58.2	20 54.9	26 04.8	27 49.3	17 59.1	3 54.4	3 04.7
10 W	19 17 45	19 42 19	7♌21 26	13 15 20	19R 51.3	5 39.7	23 50.0	0♒45.2	20 59.1	26 08.9	27 44.5	18 02.3	3 52.8	3 03.6
11 Th	19 21 41	20 43 26	19 09 16	25 03 34	19 51.3	5 31.4	25 04.7	1 32.3	21 02.8	26 13.1	27 39.6	18 05.5	3 51.2	3 02.4
12 F	19 25 38	21 44 33	0♍58 35	6♍54 42	19 51.1	5 11.3	26 19.5	2 19.4	21 06.1	26 17.5	27 34.7	18 08.6	3 49.5	3 01.3
13 Sa	19 29 34	22 45 39	12 52 21	18 51 57	19 50.7	4 39.5	27 34.3	3 06.5	21 09.1	26 22.1	27 29.8	18 11.9	3 47.9	3 00.2
14 Su	19 33 31	23 46 46	24 53 58	0♎58 54	19 50.4	3 56.4	28 49.1	3 53.7	21 11.6	26 26.9	27 24.8	18 15.1	3 46.2	2 59.0
15 M	19 37 27	24 47 52	7♎07 15	13 19 31	19D 50.0	3 02.9	0♑03.9	4 40.8	21 13.6	26 31.9	27 19.9	18 18.3	3 44.6	2 57.9
16 Tu	19 41 24	25 48 58	19 36 14	25 57 54	19 49.9	2 00.5	1 18.7	5 28.0	21 15.3	26 37.1	27 15.0	18 21.6	3 42.9	2 56.8
17 W	19 45 21	26 50 04	2♏24 59	8♏57 56	19 50.1	0 50.9	2 33.5	6 15.2	21 16.5	26 42.4	27 10.0	18 24.9	3 41.2	2 55.7
18 Th	19 49 17	27 51 09	15 37 07	22 22 52	19 50.6	29♑36.2	3 48.3	7 02.5	21 17.2	26 48.0	27 05.1	18 28.2	3 39.5	2 54.6
19 F	19 53 14	28 52 14	29 15 21	6♐14 39	19 51.4	28 18.9	5 03.2	7 49.7	21R 17.6	26 53.7	27 00.1	18 31.5	3 37.8	2 53.5
20 Sa	19 57 10	29 53 19	13♐20 44	20 33 20	19 52.2	27 01.2	6 18.0	8 37.0	21 17.4	26 59.5	26 55.2	18 34.8	3 36.2	2 52.5
21 Su	20 01 07	0♒54 24	27 52 03	5♑16 19	19R 52.9	25 45.7	7 32.9	9 24.3	21 16.9	27 05.6	26 50.3	18 38.2	3 34.5	2 51.4
22 M	20 05 03	1 55 28	12♑45 20	20 18 11	19 53.2	24 34.2	8 47.7	10 11.6	21 15.9	27 11.8	26 45.4	18 41.6	3 32.8	2 50.3
23 Tu	20 09 00	2 56 31	27 53 45	5♒30 53	19 52.9	23 28.5	10 02.6	10 58.9	21 14.5	27 18.2	26 40.4	18 44.9	3 31.1	2 49.3
24 W	20 12 57	3 57 33	13♒08 17	20 44 43	19 51.8	22 30.0	11 17.5	11 46.3	21 12.6	27 24.8	26 35.6	18 48.3	3 29.4	2 48.3
25 Th	20 16 53	4 58 35	28 18 54	5♓49 42	19 50.0	21 39.6	12 32.3	12 33.6	21 10.2	27 31.5	26 30.7	18 51.7	3 27.7	2 47.3
26 F	20 20 50	5 59 35	13♓16 06	20 37 12	19 47.9	20 57.9	13 47.2	13 21.0	21 07.4	27 38.4	26 25.8	18 55.1	3 26.0	2 46.3
27 Sa	20 24 46	7 00 34	27 52 20	5♈01 00	19 45.8	20 25.1	15 02.1	14 08.4	21 04.2	27 45.4	26 21.0	18 58.6	3 24.3	2 45.3
28 Su	20 28 43	8 01 32	12♈02 54	18 57 53	19 44.1	20 01.2	16 16.9	14 55.7	21 00.6	27 52.6	26 16.2	19 02.0	3 22.6	2 44.3
29 M	20 32 39	9 02 29	25 45 59	2♉27 23	19D 43.2	19 46.0	17 31.8	15 43.1	20 56.5	28 00.0	26 11.4	19 05.4	3 20.9	2 43.4
30 Tu	20 36 36	10 03 24	9♉02 21	15 31 16	19 43.1	19D 39.2	18 46.7	16 30.5	20 51.9	28 07.5	26 06.7	19 08.9	3 19.3	2 42.4
31 W	20 40 32	11 04 18	21 54 34	28 12 44	19 44.0	19 40.2	20 01.6	17 17.9	20 47.0	28 15.2	26 02.0	19 12.3	3 17.6	2 41.5

LONGITUDE February 1917

Day	Sid.Time	☉	0 hr ☽	Noon ☽	True ☊	☿	♀	♂	⚳	♃	♄	♅	♆	♇
1 Th	20 44 29	12♒05 11	4♊26 18	10♊35 47	19♑45.5	19♑48.6	21♑16.4	18♒05.4	20♍41.6	28♈23.0	25♋57.4	19♒15.8	3♌15.9	2♋40.6
2 F	20 48 26	13 06 03	16 41 42	22 44 35	19 47.2	20 03.9	22 31.3	18 52.8	20R 35.8	28 31.0	25R 52.7	19 19.2	3R 14.2	2R 39.7
3 Sa	20 52 22	14 06 53	28 44 54	4♋43 10	19 48.8	20 25.5	23 46.2	19 40.2	20 29.6	28 39.1	25 48.2	19 22.7	3 12.6	2 38.8
4 Su	20 56 19	15 07 42	10♋39 47	16 35 10	19R 49.6	20 52.9	25 01.0	20 27.6	20 22.9	28 47.4	25 43.6	19 26.2	3 10.9	2 38.0
5 M	21 00 15	16 08 30	22 29 43	28 23 46	19 49.3	21 25.6	26 15.9	21 15.1	20 15.9	28 55.8	25 39.2	19 29.7	3 09.3	2 37.1
6 Tu	21 04 12	17 09 16	4♌17 37	10♌11 35	19 47.6	22 03.3	27 30.8	22 02.5	20 08.4	29 04.3	25 34.7	19 33.1	3 07.7	2 36.3
7 W	21 08 08	18 10 01	16 05 55	22 00 53	19 44.5	22 45.4	28 45.6	22 49.9	20 00.6	29 13.0	25 30.4	19 36.6	3 06.0	2 35.5
8 Th	21 12 05	19 10 45	27 56 41	3♍53 34	19 40.0	23 31.6	0♒00.5	23 37.4	19 52.3	29 21.8	25 26.1	19 40.1	3 04.4	2 34.7
9 F	21 16 01	20 11 27	9♍51 44	15 51 26	19 34.5	24 21.6	1 15.4	24 24.8	19 43.7	29 30.8	25 21.8	19 43.6	3 02.8	2 33.9
10 Sa	21 19 58	21 12 08	21 52 53	27 56 20	19 28.6	25 15.0	2 30.2	25 12.3	19 34.7	29 39.9	25 17.6	19 47.0	3 01.2	2 33.2
11 Su	21 23 55	22 12 48	4♎02 03	10♎10 18	19 23.0	26 11.5	3 45.1	25 59.7	19 25.3	29 49.1	25 13.5	19 50.5	2 59.6	2 32.4
12 M	21 27 51	23 13 27	16 21 24	22 35 40	19 18.3	27 10.9	4 59.9	26 47.2	19 15.6	29 58.4	25 09.4	19 54.0	2 58.0	2 31.7
13 Tu	21 31 48	24 14 05	28 53 27	5♏15 08	19 14.9	28 13.0	6 14.8	27 34.6	19 05.5	0♉07.9	25 05.4	19 57.5	2 56.5	2 31.0
14 W	21 35 44	25 14 41	11♏41 04	18 11 39	19D 13.2	29 17.5	7 29.7	28 22.0	18 55.1	0 17.5	25 01.5	20 00.9	2 54.9	2 30.3
15 Th	21 39 41	26 15 17	24 47 13	1♐28 08	19 13.1	0♒24.4	8 44.5	29 09.5	18 44.4	0 27.2	24 57.6	20 04.4	2 53.4	2 29.7
16 F	21 43 37	27 15 51	8♐14 42	15 07 09	19 14.1	1 33.3	9 59.4	29 56.9	18 33.4	0 37.1	24 53.8	20 07.9	2 51.9	2 29.0
17 Sa	21 47 34	28 16 24	22 05 39	29 10 13	19 15.6	2 44.2	11 14.3	0♓44.4	18 22.0	0 47.1	24 50.1	20 11.3	2 50.4	2 28.4
18 Su	21 51 30	29 16 56	6♑20 48	13♑37 08	19R 16.6	3 57.0	12 29.1	1 31.8	18 10.4	0 57.1	24 46.5	20 14.8	2 48.9	2 27.8
19 M	21 55 27	0♓17 27	20 58 49	28 25 15	19 16.4	5 11.5	13 44.0	2 19.2	17 58.5	1 07.3	24 42.9	20 18.2	2 47.4	2 27.2
20 Tu	21 59 24	1 17 56	5♒55 40	13♒29 06	19 14.4	6 27.7	14 58.8	3 06.7	17 46.3	1 17.7	24 39.4	20 21.7	2 46.0	2 26.7
21 W	22 03 20	2 18 23	21 04 27	28 40 30	19 10.2	7 45.5	16 13.7	3 54.1	17 33.9	1 28.1	24 36.0	20 25.1	2 44.5	2 26.1
22 Th	22 07 17	3 18 49	6♓15 57	13♓49 32	19 04.2	9 04.7	17 28.5	4 41.5	17 21.3	1 38.6	24 32.7	20 28.5	2 43.1	2 25.6
23 F	22 11 13	4 19 13	21 19 58	28 46 06	18 57.0	10 25.3	18 43.3	5 28.9	17 08.4	1 49.3	24 29.5	20 31.9	2 41.7	2 25.1
24 Sa	22 15 10	5 19 35	6♈06 56	13♈21 38	18 49.6	11 47.3	19 58.2	6 16.3	16 55.4	2 00.0	24 26.4	20 35.3	2 40.3	2 24.6
25 Su	22 19 06	6 19 55	20 29 34	27 30 20	18 43.0	13 10.6	21 13.0	7 03.6	16 42.2	2 10.9	24 23.3	20 38.7	2 39.0	2 24.2
26 M	22 23 03	7 20 14	4♉23 42	11♉09 41	18 37.9	14 35.2	22 27.8	7 51.0	16 28.8	2 21.8	24 20.4	20 42.1	2 37.6	2 23.8
27 Tu	22 26 59	8 20 30	17 48 26	24 20 15	18 34.8	16 01.0	23 42.6	8 38.3	16 15.3	2 32.9	24 17.5	20 45.5	2 36.3	2 23.4
28 W	22 30 56	9 20 45	0♊45 33	7♊04 50	18D 33.7	17 28.0	24 57.4	9 25.7	16 01.7	2 44.1	24 14.8	20 48.8	2 35.0	2 23.0

Astro Data

	Dy Hr Mn
☿ R	10 6:48
♅□♇	10 19:16
☽ 0S	13 13:02
⚳ R	19 17:59
♃□♄	20 2:25
☽ 0N	26 10:02
☿ D	30 20:44
☽ 0S	9 19:19
☽ 0N	22 21:11
♃✶♇	26 16:01
♃□♆	27 18:36

Planet Ingress

		Dy Hr Mn
☿	♒	1 17:07
♂	♒	9 12:55
♀	♑	15 10:46
☿	♑R	18 4:29
☉	♒	20 14:37
♀	♒	8 11:51
♃	♉	12 15:58
☿	♒	15 3:21
♂	♓	16 13:33
☉	♓	19 5:05

Last Aspect / ☽ Ingress (January)

Last Aspect Dy Hr Mn			☽ Ingress	Dy Hr Mn
1 22:10	♄	□	♉	2 1:04
4 6:15	♄	✶	♊	4 9:39
6 12:25	♃	✶	♋	6 20:35
9 8:46	♂	☍	♌	9 9:03
11 14:22	♃	△	♍	11 22:01
14 7:15	♀	□	♎	14 10:04
16 14:23	♄	□	♏	16 19:32
18 23:32	☿	✶	♐	19 1:17
20 22:39	♃	△	♑	21 3:28
22 22:58	♃	□	♒	23 3:19
24 22:39	♃	✶	♓	25 2:41
26 21:33	♄	△	♈	27 3:33
29 3:55	♃	☌	♉	29 7:34
31 7:52	♄	✶	♊	31 15:26

Last Aspect / ☽ Ingress (February)

Last Aspect Dy Hr Mn			☽ Ingress	Dy Hr Mn
2 23:40	♃	✶	♋	3 2:31
5 13:06	♃	□	♌	5 15:16
8 2:45	♃	△	♍	8 4:09
10 6:48	♄	✶	♎	10 16:04
12 21:32	☿	□	♏	13 2:06
15 7:37	♂	□	♐	15 9:23
17 10:22	☉	✶	♑	17 13:24
19 6:04	♄	☍	♒	19 14:32
20 22:55	♅	☌	♓	21 14:06
23 5:06	♄	△	♈	23 14:00
25 6:40	♄	□	♉	25 16:19
27 11:55	♄	✶	♊	27 22:34

☽ Phases & Eclipses

Dy Hr Mn		
8 7:42	○	17♋29
8 7:44	☍	T 1.364
16 11:42	☾	25♎48
23 7:40	●	2♒45
23 7:28:13	☌	P 0.726
30 1:01	☽	9♉36
7 3:28	○	17♌48
15 1:53	☾	25♏50
21 18:09	●	2♓34
28 16:43	☽	9♊33

Astro Data

1 January 1917
Julian Day # 6210
SVP 6♓24'51"
GC 25♐40.8 ⚵ 22♌05.0R
Eris 27♓02.8 ⚶ 1♑40.2
⚷ 22♓11.4 ⚴ 14♑38.3
☽ Mean ☊ 20♑20.6

1 February 1917
Julian Day # 6241
SVP 6♓24'46"
GC 25♐40.9 ⚵ 13♌43.0R
Eris 27♓15.1 ⚶ 12♑52.4
⚷ 23♓22.1 ⚴ 1♒02.8
☽ Mean ☊ 18♑42.2

March 1917 — LONGITUDE

Day	Sid.Time	☉	0 hr ☽	Noon ☽	True ☊	☿	♀	♂	⚳	♃	♄	♅	♆	♇
1 Th	22 34 53	10♓20 57	13♊18 42	19♊27 47	18♑34.1	18♒56.2	26♒12.1	10♓13.0	15♍48.0	2♉55.3	24♋12.1	20♒52.2	2♌33.8	2♋22.6
2 F	22 38 49	11 21 08	25 32 42	1♋34 07	18 35.2	20 25.6	27 26.9	11 00.3	15R 34.1	3 06.7	24R 09.6	20 55.5	2R 32.5	2R 22.3
3 Sa	22 42 46	12 21 16	7♋32 42	13 29 05	18R 36.2	21 56.1	28 41.7	11 47.5	15 20.3	3 18.1	24 07.1	20 58.8	2 31.3	2 21.9
4 Su	22 46 42	13 21 22	19 23 51	25 17 36	18 36.0	23 27.7	29 56.4	12 34.8	15 06.4	3 29.7	24 04.7	21 02.1	2 30.1	2 21.6
5 M	22 50 39	14 21 26	1♌10 51	7♌04 07	18 34.0	25 00.5	1♓11.1	13 22.0	14 52.4	3 41.3	24 02.4	21 05.3	2 28.9	2 21.4
6 Tu	22 54 35	15 21 28	12 57 49	18 52 21	18 29.6	26 34.4	2 25.9	14 09.3	14 38.5	3 53.0	24 00.3	21 08.6	2 27.7	2 21.1
7 W	22 58 32	16 21 28	24 48 05	0♍45 18	18 22.6	28 09.5	3 40.6	14 56.5	14 24.6	4 04.8	23 58.2	21 11.8	2 26.6	2 20.9
8 Th	23 02 28	17 21 26	6♍44 15	12 45 09	18 13.3	29 45.6	4 55.3	15 43.7	14 10.6	4 16.7	23 56.2	21 15.1	2 25.5	2 20.7
9 F	23 06 25	18 21 23	18 48 09	24 53 25	18 02.3	1♓22.9	6 10.0	16 30.8	13 56.8	4 28.6	23 54.4	21 18.3	2 24.4	2 20.5
10 Sa	23 10 21	19 21 17	1♎01 03	7♎11 07	17 50.6	3 01.4	7 24.7	17 17.9	13 43.0	4 40.7	23 52.6	21 21.4	2 23.4	2 20.3
11 Su	23 14 18	20 21 09	13 23 44	19 38 57	17 39.1	4 41.0	8 39.4	18 05.1	13 29.3	4 52.8	23 51.0	21 24.6	2 22.3	2 20.2
12 M	23 18 15	21 21 00	25 56 53	2♏17 36	17 29.0	6 21.7	9 54.0	18 52.2	13 15.7	5 05.0	23 49.4	21 27.7	2 21.3	2 20.0
13 Tu	23 22 11	22 20 49	8♏41 14	15 07 55	17 21.1	8 03.6	11 08.7	19 39.2	13 02.2	5 17.3	23 48.0	21 30.8	2 20.4	2 20.0
14 W	23 26 08	23 20 36	21 37 49	28 11 07	17 15.8	9 46.8	12 23.3	20 26.3	12 48.8	5 29.6	23 46.7	21 33.9	2 19.4	2 19.9
15 Th	23 30 04	24 20 21	4♐48 02	11♐28 48	17 13.0	11 31.1	13 38.0	21 13.3	12 35.6	5 42.0	23 45.4	21 37.0	2 18.5	2 19.8
16 F	23 34 01	25 20 05	18 13 37	25 02 42	17D 12.3	13 16.6	14 52.6	22 00.3	12 22.5	5 54.5	23 44.3	21 40.0	2 17.6	2D 19.8
17 Sa	23 37 57	26 19 48	1♑56 16	8♑54 24	17R 12.6	15 03.3	16 07.3	22 47.3	12 09.7	6 07.1	23 43.3	21 43.1	2 16.7	2 19.8
18 Su	23 41 54	27 19 28	15 57 13	23 04 39	17 12.6	16 51.3	17 21.9	23 34.3	11 57.0	6 19.8	23 42.4	21 46.1	2 15.9	2 19.8
19 M	23 45 50	28 19 07	0♒16 34	7♒32 40	17 11.2	18 40.5	18 36.5	24 21.2	11 44.6	6 32.5	23 41.6	21 49.0	2 15.1	2 19.9
20 Tu	23 49 47	29 18 44	14 52 32	22 15 33	17 07.3	20 31.0	19 51.1	25 08.1	11 32.4	6 45.2	23 41.0	21 52.0	2 14.3	2 20.0
21 W	23 53 44	0♈18 19	29 40 59	7♓07 54	17 00.7	22 22.7	21 05.7	25 55.0	11 20.4	6 58.1	23 40.4	21 54.9	2 13.6	2 20.0
22 Th	23 57 40	1 17 52	14♓35 18	22 02 05	16 51.4	24 15.7	22 20.3	26 41.9	11 08.7	7 11.0	23 39.9	21 57.8	2 12.9	2 20.2
23 F	0 01 37	2 17 23	29 27 07	6♈49 16	16 40.4	26 09.9	23 34.9	27 28.7	10 57.3	7 23.9	23 39.6	22 00.6	2 12.2	2 20.3
24 Sa	0 05 33	3 16 52	14♈07 31	21 20 55	16 28.9	28 05.4	24 49.4	28 15.5	10 46.2	7 36.9	23 39.4	22 03.5	2 11.5	2 20.5
25 Su	0 09 30	4 16 19	28 28 40	5♉30 10	16 18.1	0♈02.0	26 04.0	29 02.2	10 35.4	7 50.0	23D 39.2	22 06.3	2 10.9	2 20.6
26 M	0 13 26	5 15 44	12♉24 59	19 12 54	16 09.2	1 59.9	27 18.5	29 49.0	10 24.9	8 03.1	23 39.2	22 09.0	2 10.3	2 20.9
27 Tu	0 17 23	6 15 07	25 53 51	2♊27 58	16 02.7	3 58.9	28 33.0	0♈35.7	10 14.7	8 16.3	23 39.3	22 11.8	2 09.8	2 21.1
28 W	0 21 19	7 14 27	8♊55 31	15 16 54	15 58.9	5 59.0	29 47.5	1 22.3	10 04.9	8 29.6	23 39.6	22 14.5	2 09.2	2 21.3
29 Th	0 25 16	8 13 45	21 32 36	27 43 13	15D 57.3	8 00.0	1♈02.0	2 09.0	9 55.4	8 42.8	23 39.9	22 17.2	2 08.8	2 21.6
30 F	0 29 13	9 13 01	3♋49 21	9♋51 42	15R 57.0	10 02.0	2 16.5	2 55.6	9 46.3	8 56.2	23 40.3	22 19.8	2 08.3	2 21.9
31 Sa	0 33 09	10 12 15	15 50 56	21 47 45	15 56.9	12 04.8	3 30.9	3 42.1	9 37.6	9 09.6	23 40.9	22 22.4	2 07.9	2 22.2

April 1917 — LONGITUDE

Day	Sid.Time	☉	0 hr ☽	Noon ☽	True ☊	☿	♀	♂	⚳	♃	♄	♅	♆	♇
1 Su	0 37 06	11♈11 26	27♋42 52	3♌36 56	15♑56.0	14♈08.1	4♈45.4	4♈28.6	9♍29.2	9♉23.0	23♋41.5	22♒25.0	2♌07.5	2♋22.6
2 M	0 41 02	12 10 35	9♌30 36	15 24 30	15R 53.2	16 12.0	5 59.8	5 15.1	9R 21.2	9 36.5	23 42.3	22 27.5	2R 07.1	2 23.0
3 Tu	0 44 59	13 09 41	21 19 10	27 15 09	15 47.9	18 16.1	7 14.2	6 01.5	9 13.6	9 50.0	23 43.2	22 30.0	2 06.8	2 23.3
4 W	0 48 55	14 08 45	3♍12 54	9♍12 51	15 39.7	20 20.2	8 28.6	6 47.9	9 06.4	10 03.6	23 44.1	22 32.5	2 06.5	2 23.8
5 Th	0 52 52	15 07 47	15 15 18	21 20 34	15 29.0	22 24.1	9 43.0	7 34.3	8 59.6	10 17.2	23 45.2	22 35.0	2 06.2	2 24.2
6 F	0 56 48	16 06 47	27 28 51	3♎40 18	15 16.3	24 27.5	10 57.4	8 20.6	8 53.2	10 30.8	23 46.4	22 37.4	2 06.0	2 24.6
7 Sa	1 00 45	17 05 45	9♎55 00	16 12 58	15 02.7	26 30.0	12 11.7	9 06.9	8 47.2	10 44.5	23 47.8	22 39.7	2 05.8	2 25.1
8 Su	1 04 42	18 04 41	22 34 13	28 58 39	14 49.3	28 31.4	13 26.0	9 53.2	8 41.6	10 58.2	23 49.2	22 42.0	2 05.6	2 25.6
9 M	1 08 38	19 03 35	5♏26 12	11♏56 46	14 37.4	0♉31.2	14 40.4	10 39.4	8 36.5	11 11.9	23 50.7	22 44.3	2 05.4	2 26.1
10 Tu	1 12 35	20 02 27	18 30 13	25 06 28	14 28.0	2 29.2	15 54.7	11 25.5	8 31.7	11 25.7	23 52.3	22 46.6	2 05.3	2 26.7
11 W	1 16 31	21 01 17	1♐45 25	8♐26 59	14 21.4	4 24.9	17 09.0	12 11.7	8 27.4	11 39.6	23 54.1	22 48.8	2 05.3	2 27.3
12 Th	1 20 28	22 00 05	15 11 09	21 57 53	14 17.7	6 18.0	18 23.3	12 57.8	8 23.5	11 53.4	23 55.9	22 51.0	2D 05.2	2 27.8
13 F	1 24 24	22 58 52	28 47 12	5♑39 09	14D 16.3	8 08.2	19 37.5	13 43.8	8 20.0	12 07.3	23 57.9	22 53.1	2 05.2	2 28.5
14 Sa	1 28 21	23 57 37	12♑33 46	19 31 05	14R 16.2	9 55.2	20 51.8	14 29.9	8 16.9	12 21.2	23 59.9	22 55.2	2 05.3	2 29.1
15 Su	1 32 17	24 56 21	26 31 08	3♒33 54	14 16.0	11 38.6	22 06.1	15 15.8	8 14.3	12 35.2	24 02.1	22 57.3	2 05.3	2 29.7
16 M	1 36 14	25 55 02	10♒39 18	17 47 12	14 14.6	13 18.3	23 20.3	16 01.8	8 12.1	12 49.1	24 04.3	22 59.3	2 05.4	2 30.4
17 Tu	1 40 11	26 53 42	24 57 20	2♓09 23	14 10.9	14 53.9	24 34.5	16 47.7	8 10.3	13 03.1	24 06.7	23 01.3	2 05.6	2 31.1
18 W	1 44 07	27 52 21	9♓22 54	16 37 18	14 04.5	16 25.2	25 48.7	17 33.5	8 08.9	13 17.2	24 09.2	23 03.2	2 05.7	2 31.8
19 Th	1 48 04	28 50 57	23 51 58	1♈06 09	13 55.6	17 52.1	27 03.0	18 19.3	8 08.0	13 31.2	24 11.7	23 05.1	2 05.9	2 32.5
20 F	1 52 00	29 49 32	8♈19 04	15 29 53	13 44.9	19 14.4	28 17.1	19 05.1	8D 07.4	13 45.3	24 14.4	23 07.0	2 06.1	2 33.3
21 Sa	1 55 57	0♉48 05	22 37 49	29 42 07	13 33.5	20 31.9	29 31.3	19 50.8	8 07.4	13 59.4	24 17.2	23 08.8	2 06.4	2 34.1
22 Su	1 59 53	1 46 36	6♉42 05	13♉37 09	13 22.8	21 44.5	0♉45.5	20 36.5	8 07.7	14 13.5	24 20.0	23 10.5	2 06.7	2 34.9
23 M	2 03 50	2 45 05	20 26 52	27 10 56	13 13.7	22 52.2	1 59.6	21 22.1	8 08.4	14 27.6	24 23.0	23 12.3	2 07.0	2 35.7
24 Tu	2 07 46	3 43 32	3♊49 09	10♊21 31	13 07.0	23 54.8	3 13.8	22 07.7	8 09.6	14 41.7	24 26.1	23 13.9	2 07.4	2 36.5
25 W	2 11 43	4 41 58	16 48 08	23 09 14	13 02.9	24 52.2	4 27.9	22 53.2	8 11.2	14 55.9	24 29.2	23 15.6	2 07.8	2 37.3
26 Th	2 15 40	5 40 21	29 25 09	5♋36 19	13D 01.1	25 44.3	5 42.0	23 38.7	8 13.2	15 10.1	24 32.5	23 17.2	2 08.2	2 38.2
27 F	2 19 36	6 38 42	11♋43 15	17 46 31	13 00.9	26 31.1	6 56.1	24 24.1	8 15.6	15 24.3	24 35.9	23 18.7	2 08.7	2 39.1
28 Sa	2 23 33	7 37 01	23 46 43	29 44 31	13R 01.5	27 12.5	8 10.2	25 09.5	8 18.4	15 38.5	24 39.3	23 20.2	2 09.2	2 40.0
29 Su	2 27 29	8 35 18	5♌40 35	11♌35 34	13 01.6	27 48.4	9 24.2	25 54.9	8 21.6	15 52.7	24 42.8	23 21.6	2 09.7	2 40.9
30 M	2 31 26	9 33 33	17 30 11	23 25 04	13 00.5	28 18.9	10 38.3	26 40.1	8 25.3	16 06.9	24 46.5	23 23.1	2 10.3	2 41.9

Astro Data Dy Hr Mn	Planet Ingress Dy Hr Mn	Last Aspect Dy Hr Mn	☽ Ingress Dy Hr Mn	Last Aspect Dy Hr Mn	☽ Ingress Dy Hr Mn	☽ Phases & Eclipses Dy Hr Mn	Astro Data
☽0S 9 1:41	♀ ♓ 4 13:09	2 2:50 ♀ △	♋ 2 8:52	31 15:49 ♄ ☌	♌ 1 4:39	8 21:58 ○ 17♍46	1 March 1917
♆⊻♇ 13 23:07	☿ ♓ 8 15:34	4 9:32 ♄ ☌	♌ 4 21:36	3 2:22 ♅ ☍	♍ 3 17:32	16 12:33 ☾ 25♐21	Julian Day # 6269
♇ D 16 23:12	☉ ♈ 21 4:37	7 5:58 ☿ ☍	♍ 7 10:29	5 16:44 ♄ ⚹	♎ 6 4:54	23 4:05 ● 1♈58	SVP 6♓24'42"
☉0N 21 4:37	☿ ♈ 25 11:35	9 10:04 ♄ ⚹	♎ 9 22:01	8 11:00 ☿ ☍	♏ 8 13:54	30 10:36 ☽ 9♋10	GC 25♐40.9 ⚴ 6♌17.4R
☽0N 22 8:06	♂ ♈ 26 17:40	11 20:00 ♄ □	♏ 12 7:40	10 9:45 ♄ △	♐ 10 20:50		Eris 27♓33.5 ⚵ 22♑32.3
♄ D 26 1:53	♀ ♈ 28 16:01	14 3:57 ♄ △	♐ 14 15:18	12 13:34 ♅ ⚹	♑ 13 2:08	7 13:48 ○ 17♎10	⚷ 24♓52.9 ⚶ 15♒29.8
☿0N 27 4:18		16 12:33 ☉ □	♑ 16 20:38	14 20:12 ☉ □	♒ 15 5:56	14 20:12 ☾ 24♑18	☽ Mean ☊ 17♑13.2
♂0N 29 5:43	☿ ♉ 9 5:43	18 19:37 ☉ ⚹	♒ 18 23:33	17 2:36 ☉ ⚹	♓ 17 8:25	21 14:01 ● 0♉53	
♀0N 31 7:44	☉ ♉ 20 16:17	20 11:22 ♅ ☌	♓ 21 0:31	19 0:31 ♄ △	♈ 19 10:10	29 5:21 ☽ 8♌19	1 April 1917
	♀ ♉ 21 21:17	22 19:57 ♂ ☌	♈ 23 0:53	21 11:40 ♀ ☌	♉ 21 12:31		Julian Day # 6300
☽0S 5 8:27		24 15:52 ♄ □	♉ 25 2:35	23 6:58 ♄ ⚹	♊ 23 17:04		SVP 6♓24'39"
♆ D 13 1:02		27 4:05 ♀ ⚹	♊ 27 7:28	25 12:12 ♅ △	♋ 26 1:07		GC 25♐41.0 ⚴ 6♌21.9
☽0N 18 16:34		29 1:24 ♅ △	♋ 29 16:28	28 6:36 ☿ ⚹	♌ 28 12:31		Eris 27♓57.1 ⚵ 2♒06.3
⚳ D 21 5:13							⚷ 26♓43.3 ⚶ 0♓45.6
							☽ Mean ☊ 15♑34.7

LONGITUDE — May 1917

Day	Sid.Time	☉	0 hr ☽	Noon ☽	True ☊	☿	♀	♂	⚳	♃	♄	♅	♆	♇
1 Tu	2 35 22	10♉31 45	29♌20 52	5♍18 11	12♑57.4	28♉44.0	11♉52.3	27♈25.4	8♍29.3	16♉21.1	24♋50.2	23♒24.4	2♌10.9	2♋42.8
2 W	2 39 19	11 29 56	11♍17 36	17 19 37	12R52.1	29 03.5	13 06.3	28 10.6	8 33.7	16 35.4	24 54.0	23 25.7	2 11.5	2 43.8
3 Th	2 43 15	12 28 05	23 24 42	29 33 16	12 44.5	29 17.6	14 20.3	28 55.7	8 38.4	16 49.6	24 57.9	23 27.0	2 12.2	2 44.8
4 F	2 47 12	13 26 12	5♎45 37	12♎02 00	12 35.2	29 26.3	15 34.3	29 40.8	8 43.6	17 03.8	25 01.9	23 28.2	2 12.8	2 45.8
5 Sa	2 51 08	14 24 17	18 22 36	24 47 29	12 25.1	29R29.7	16 48.3	0♉25.8	8 49.1	17 18.1	25 06.0	23 29.4	2 13.6	2 46.8
6 Su	2 55 05	15 22 20	1♏16 40	7♏50 02	12 15.1	29 28.0	18 02.2	1 10.8	8 55.0	17 32.3	25 10.2	23 30.5	2 14.3	2 47.9
7 M	2 59 02	16 20 22	14 27 27	21 08 42	12 06.2	29 21.3	19 16.2	1 55.7	9 01.3	17 46.6	25 14.4	23 31.6	2 15.1	2 48.9
8 Tu	3 02 58	17 18 22	27 53 30	4♐41 34	11 59.2	29 09.8	20 30.1	2 40.6	9 07.9	18 00.8	25 18.8	23 32.6	2 15.9	2 50.0
9 W	3 06 55	18 16 21	11♐32 33	18 26 07	11 54.6	28 53.9	21 44.0	3 25.4	9 14.9	18 15.1	25 23.2	23 33.6	2 16.8	2 51.1
10 Th	3 10 51	19 14 19	25 21 57	2♑19 43	11D52.3	28 33.9	22 57.9	4 10.2	9 22.2	18 29.3	25 27.7	23 34.6	2 17.6	2 52.2
11 F	3 14 48	20 12 14	9♑19 08	16 19 57	11 52.0	28 10.1	24 11.8	4 55.0	9 29.9	18 43.6	25 32.3	23 35.5	2 18.6	2 53.3
12 Sa	3 18 44	21 10 09	23 21 56	0♒24 52	11 52.9	27 43.1	25 25.7	5 39.7	9 37.9	18 57.8	25 36.9	23 36.3	2 19.5	2 54.4
13 Su	3 22 41	22 08 02	7♒28 36	14 32 57	11R53.8	27 13.4	26 39.5	6 24.3	9 46.3	19 12.0	25 41.7	23 37.1	2 20.5	2 55.6
14 M	3 26 38	23 05 55	21 37 45	28 42 49	11 53.9	26 41.4	27 53.4	7 08.9	9 55.0	19 26.3	25 46.5	23 37.8	2 21.5	2 56.7
15 Tu	3 30 34	24 03 45	5♓47 57	12♓52 55	11 52.3	26 07.7	29 07.3	7 53.4	10 04.0	19 40.5	25 51.4	23 38.5	2 22.5	2 57.9
16 W	3 34 31	25 01 35	19 57 28	27 01 17	11 48.9	25 33.0	0♊21.1	8 37.9	10 13.3	19 54.7	25 56.4	23 39.2	2 23.5	2 59.1
17 Th	3 38 27	25 59 24	4♈04 00	11♈05 15	11 43.5	24 57.9	1 34.9	9 22.3	10 23.0	20 08.9	26 01.4	23 39.8	2 24.6	3 00.3
18 F	3 42 24	26 57 11	18 04 37	25 01 39	11 36.8	24 23.0	2 48.8	10 06.7	10 33.0	20 23.1	26 06.6	23 40.3	2 25.7	3 01.5
19 Sa	3 46 20	27 54 57	1♉55 57	8♉47 05	11 29.6	23 48.8	4 02.6	10 51.0	10 43.3	20 37.3	26 11.8	23 40.8	2 26.9	3 02.7
20 Su	3 50 17	28 52 42	15 34 39	22 18 19	11 22.8	23 16.1	5 16.4	11 35.3	10 53.9	20 51.4	26 17.1	23 41.3	2 28.0	3 04.0
21 M	3 54 13	29 50 26	28 57 49	5♊32 56	11 17.0	22 45.2	6 30.2	12 19.5	11 04.8	21 05.6	26 22.4	23 41.7	2 29.2	3 05.2
22 Tu	3 58 10	0♊48 09	12♊03 32	18 29 36	11 12.9	22 16.8	7 44.0	13 03.7	11 16.0	21 19.7	26 27.8	23 42.0	2 30.5	3 06.5
23 W	4 02 07	1 45 50	24 51 09	1♋08 19	11D10.7	21 51.1	8 57.7	13 47.8	11 27.5	21 33.9	26 33.3	23 42.3	2 31.7	3 07.8
24 Th	4 06 03	2 43 29	7♋21 20	13 30 29	11 10.2	21 28.8	10 11.5	14 31.9	11 39.3	21 48.0	26 38.9	23 42.6	2 33.0	3 09.1
25 F	4 10 00	3 41 08	19 36 08	25 38 41	11 11.1	21 10.0	11 25.3	15 15.9	11 51.3	22 02.1	26 44.5	23 42.8	2 34.3	3 10.4
26 Sa	4 13 56	4 38 44	1♌38 38	7♌36 30	11 12.7	20 55.1	12 39.0	15 59.8	12 03.7	22 16.1	26 50.2	23 43.0	2 35.7	3 11.7
27 Su	4 17 53	5 36 20	13 32 50	19 28 14	11 14.3	20 44.2	13 52.7	16 43.7	12 16.3	22 30.2	26 56.0	23 43.1	2 37.0	3 13.0
28 M	4 21 49	6 33 53	25 23 19	1♍18 41	11R15.3	20 37.6	15 06.4	17 27.5	12 29.2	22 44.2	27 01.8	23 43.1	2 38.4	3 14.3
29 Tu	4 25 46	7 31 26	7♍14 59	13 12 49	11 15.3	20D35.4	16 20.1	18 11.3	12 42.3	22 58.2	27 07.7	23R43.1	2 39.8	3 15.7
30 W	4 29 42	8 28 57	19 12 49	25 15 32	11 13.9	20 37.6	17 33.8	18 55.0	12 55.7	23 12.1	27 13.6	23 43.1	2 41.3	3 17.0
31 Th	4 33 39	9 26 27	1♎21 33	7♎31 22	11 11.2	20 44.2	18 47.5	19 38.7	13 09.4	23 26.1	27 19.6	23 43.0	2 42.7	3 18.4

LONGITUDE — June 1917

Day	Sid.Time	☉	0 hr ☽	Noon ☽	True ☊	☿	♀	♂	⚳	♃	♄	♅	♆	♇
1 F	4 37 36	10♊23 55	13♎45 26	20♎04 07	11♑07.3	20♉55.4	20♊01.1	20♉22.3	13♍23.3	23♉40.0	27♋25.7	23♒42.9	2♌44.2	3♋19.7
2 Sa	4 41 32	11 21 23	26 27 45	2♏56 33	11R02.9	21 11.1	21 14.8	21 05.8	13 37.5	23 53.9	27 31.8	23R42.7	2 45.7	3 21.1
3 Su	4 45 29	12 18 49	9♏30 38	16 10 01	10 58.3	21 31.1	22 28.4	21 49.3	13 51.9	24 07.7	27 38.0	23 42.4	2 47.3	3 22.5
4 M	4 49 25	13 16 14	22 54 38	29 44 18	10 54.3	21 55.6	23 42.0	22 32.7	14 06.5	24 21.5	27 44.3	23 42.2	2 48.8	3 23.9
5 Tu	4 53 22	14 13 38	6♐38 43	13♐37 29	10 51.3	22 24.3	24 55.7	23 16.1	14 21.4	24 35.3	27 50.6	23 41.8	2 50.4	3 25.3
6 W	4 57 18	15 11 02	20 40 09	27 46 11	10D49.5	22 57.3	26 09.3	23 59.4	14 36.5	24 49.1	27 56.9	23 41.5	2 52.0	3 26.7
7 Th	5 01 15	16 08 24	4♑55 00	12♑05 59	10 49.0	23 34.4	27 22.9	24 42.7	14 51.8	25 02.8	28 03.3	23 41.0	2 53.6	3 28.1
8 F	5 05 11	17 05 46	19 18 30	26 31 56	10 49.6	24 15.5	28 36.4	25 25.9	15 07.4	25 16.5	28 09.8	23 40.6	2 55.3	3 29.5
9 Sa	5 09 08	18 03 07	3♒45 43	10♒59 16	10 50.8	25 00.7	29 50.0	26 09.1	15 23.1	25 30.2	28 16.3	23 40.0	2 57.0	3 30.9
10 Su	5 13 05	19 00 28	18 12 06	25 23 44	10 52.1	25 49.7	1♋03.6	26 52.2	15 39.1	25 43.8	28 22.9	23 39.5	2 58.7	3 32.3
11 M	5 17 01	19 57 48	2♓33 47	9♓41 54	10R53.1	26 42.5	2 17.1	27 35.2	15 55.3	25 57.4	28 29.5	23 38.9	3 00.4	3 33.8
12 Tu	5 20 58	20 55 07	16 47 48	23 51 13	10 53.3	27 39.0	3 30.7	28 18.2	16 11.7	26 10.9	28 36.1	23 38.2	3 02.1	3 35.2
13 W	5 24 54	21 52 27	0♈51 58	7♈49 51	10 52.7	28 39.1	4 44.2	29 01.1	16 28.3	26 24.4	28 42.8	23 37.5	3 03.9	3 36.6
14 Th	5 28 51	22 49 46	14 44 44	21 36 29	10 51.2	29 42.9	5 57.8	29 44.0	16 45.0	26 37.9	28 49.6	23 36.7	3 05.6	3 38.1
15 F	5 32 47	23 47 04	28 25 01	5♉10 13	10 49.2	0♊50.1	7 11.3	0♊26.8	17 02.0	26 51.3	28 56.4	23 36.0	3 07.4	3 39.5
16 Sa	5 36 44	24 44 23	11♉52 02	18 30 23	10 47.0	2 00.8	8 24.8	1 09.6	17 19.2	27 04.6	29 03.2	23 35.1	3 09.3	3 41.0
17 Su	5 40 40	25 41 40	25 05 13	1♊36 32	10 44.9	3 14.9	9 38.3	1 52.3	17 36.6	27 18.0	29 10.1	23 34.2	3 11.1	3 42.5
18 M	5 44 37	26 38 58	8♊04 17	14 28 29	10 43.2	4 32.3	10 51.9	2 35.0	17 54.2	27 31.2	29 17.0	23 33.3	3 12.9	3 43.9
19 Tu	5 48 34	27 36 15	20 49 12	27 06 29	10 42.2	5 53.1	12 05.4	3 17.6	18 11.9	27 44.5	29 24.0	23 32.3	3 14.8	3 45.4
20 W	5 52 30	28 33 32	3♋20 26	9♋31 12	10D41.8	7 17.2	13 18.9	4 00.1	18 29.8	27 57.7	29 31.0	23 31.3	3 16.7	3 46.9
21 Th	5 56 27	29 30 48	15 38 57	21 43 54	10 42.0	8 44.5	14 32.3	4 42.6	18 47.9	28 10.8	29 38.1	23 30.2	3 18.6	3 48.3
22 F	6 00 23	0♋28 03	27 46 20	3♌46 32	10 42.7	10 15.1	15 45.8	5 25.0	19 06.2	28 23.9	29 45.2	23 29.1	3 20.5	3 49.8
23 Sa	6 04 20	1 25 18	9♌44 51	15 41 39	10 43.6	11 48.8	16 59.3	6 07.4	19 24.7	28 36.9	29 52.3	23 28.0	3 22.5	3 51.3
24 Su	6 08 16	2 22 33	21 37 22	27 32 27	10 44.5	13 25.7	18 12.7	6 49.7	19 43.3	28 49.8	29 59.4	23 26.8	3 24.4	3 52.7
25 M	6 12 13	3 19 47	3♍27 23	9♍22 42	10 45.3	15 05.6	19 26.1	7 31.9	20 02.1	29 02.7	0♌06.6	23 25.6	3 26.4	3 54.2
26 Tu	6 16 09	4 17 00	15 18 55	21 16 35	10 45.7	16 48.7	20 39.6	8 14.1	20 21.0	29 15.6	0 13.9	23 24.3	3 28.4	3 55.7
27 W	6 20 06	5 14 13	27 16 17	3♎18 36	10R45.9	18 34.7	21 53.0	8 56.3	20 40.1	29 28.4	0 21.1	23 23.0	3 30.4	3 57.1
28 Th	6 24 03	6 11 25	9♎24 04	15 33 17	10 45.8	20 23.7	23 06.4	9 38.3	20 59.4	29 41.1	0 28.4	23 21.6	3 32.4	3 58.6
29 F	6 27 59	7 08 37	21 46 44	28 04 57	10 45.6	22 15.4	24 19.8	10 20.3	21 18.8	29 53.8	0 35.7	23 20.2	3 34.4	4 00.1
30 Sa	6 31 56	8 05 49	4♏28 23	10♏57 23	10 45.3	24 09.9	25 33.1	11 02.3	21 38.3	0♊06.4	0 43.1	23 18.8	3 36.4	4 01.6

Astro Data

	Dy Hr Mn
☽0S	2 15:40
☿R	5 15:48
♃∠♇	7 16:16
☽0N	15 22:21
♅R	29 3:26
☿D	29 12:11
☽0S	29 23:10
♃□♅	1 16:54
☽0N	12 3:12
☽0S	26 6:38

Planet Ingress

		Dy Hr Mn
♂	♉	4 22:14
♀	♊	16 5:08
☉	♊	21 15:59
♀	♋	9 15:15
☿	♊	14 18:14
♂	♊	14 20:58
☉	♋	22 0:14
♄	♌	24 13:54
♃	♊	29 23:51

Last Aspect / ☽ Ingress (May)

Last Aspect Dy Hr Mn			☽ Ingress	Dy Hr Mn
30 22:18	☿	□	♍	1 1:19
3 11:29	☿	△	♎	3 12:52
5 12:35	♄	□	♏	5 21:39
8 2:24	☿	☍	♐	8 3:44
9 20:53	♅	⚹	♑	10 8:00
12 7:34	☿	△	♒	12 11:18
14 10:28	♀	□	♓	14 14:11
16 10:09	♄	△	♈	16 17:04
18 13:53	♄	□	♉	18 20:38
21 0:46	☉	☌	♊	21 1:53
22 21:49	♅	△	♋	23 9:49
25 14:12	♄	☌	♌	25 20:42
27 20:37	♅	☍	♍	28 9:21
30 15:55	♄	⚹	♎	30 21:20

Last Aspect / ☽ Ingress (June)

Last Aspect Dy Hr Mn			☽ Ingress	Dy Hr Mn
2 1:55	♄	□	♏	2 6:34
4 8:28	♄	△	♐	4 12:27
6 9:01	♀	☍	♑	6 15:45
8 14:44	♄	☍	♒	8 17:45
10 14:36	♂	□	♓	10 19:42
12 20:11	♄	△	♈	12 22:31
15 0:50	♄	□	♉	15 2:48
17 7:27	♄	⚹	♊	17 9:02
19 13:02	☉	☌	♋	19 17:33
22 3:52	♄	☌	♌	22 4:27
24 14:40	♃	□	♍	24 16:59
27 4:15	♃	△	♎	27 5:26
29 4:06	♀	□	♏	29 15:37

☽ Phases & Eclipses

Dy Hr Mn		
7 2:43	○	15♏58
14 1:48	☾	22♒41
21 0:46	●	29♉23
28 23:33	☽	7♍02
5 13:06	○	14♐16
12 6:38	☾	20♓42
19 13:02	●	27♊39
19 13:15:56	●	P 0.473
27 16:08	☽	5♎24

Astro Data

1 May 1917
Julian Day # 6330
SVP 6♓24'35"
GC 25♐41.1 ⚵ 12♌56.6
Eris 28♓17.6 ⚴ 9♒19.9
⚷ 28♓19.9 ⚶ 14♓24.2
☽ Mean ☊ 13♑59.4

1 June 1917
Julian Day # 6361
SVP 6♓24'31"
GC 25♐41.2 ⚵ 23♌15.5
Eris 28♓31.4 ⚴ 13♒15.6
⚷ 29♓30.2 ⚶ 26♓43.5
☽ Mean ☊ 12♑20.9

July 1917 — LONGITUDE

Day	Sid.Time	☉	0 hr ☽	Noon ☽	True ☊	☿	♀	♂	⚳	♃	♄	♅	♆	♇
1 Su	6 35 52	9♋03 00	17♏32 17	24♏13 16	10♑45.1	26♊06.9	26♋46.5	11♊44.2	21♍58.0	0♊18.9	0♌50.4	23♒17.3	3♌38.5	4♋03.0
2 M	6 39 49	10 00 11	1♐00 28	7♐53 50	10D45.0	28 06.3	27 59.8	12 26.0	22 17.9	0 31.4	0 57.8	23R15.8	3 40.6	4 04.5
3 Tu	6 43 45	10 57 22	14 53 14	21 58 22	10 45.0	0♋07.9	29 13.2	13 07.8	22 37.9	0 43.8	1 05.3	23 14.3	3 42.6	4 06.0
4 W	6 47 42	11 54 33	29 08 48	6♑23 57	10R45.0	2 11.4	0♌26.5	13 49.5	22 58.0	0 56.1	1 12.7	23 12.7	3 44.7	4 07.4
5 Th	6 51 38	12 51 44	13♑43 08	21 05 32	10 45.0	4 16.7	1 39.8	14 31.2	23 18.2	1 08.4	1 20.2	23 11.1	3 46.8	4 08.9
6 F	6 55 35	13 48 54	28 30 17	5♒56 25	10 44.8	6 23.4	2 53.1	15 12.8	23 38.6	1 20.6	1 27.7	23 09.5	3 48.9	4 10.4
7 Sa	6 59 32	14 46 05	13♒22 58	20 49 00	10 44.5	8 31.3	4 06.3	15 54.3	23 59.1	1 32.7	1 35.2	23 07.8	3 51.1	4 11.8
8 Su	7 03 28	15 43 16	28 13 35	5♓35 54	10 44.0	10 40.1	5 19.6	16 35.8	24 19.8	1 44.8	1 42.8	23 06.1	3 53.2	4 13.3
9 M	7 07 25	16 40 28	12♓55 12	20 10 51	10 43.5	12 49.4	6 32.8	17 17.2	24 40.6	1 56.8	1 50.3	23 04.3	3 55.3	4 14.7
10 Tu	7 11 21	17 37 40	27 22 20	4♈29 17	10 43.1	14 59.0	7 46.1	17 58.6	25 01.5	2 08.7	1 57.9	23 02.5	3 57.5	4 16.1
11 W	7 15 18	18 34 52	11♈31 25	18 28 37	10D42.9	17 08.6	8 59.3	18 39.9	25 22.5	2 20.5	2 05.5	23 00.7	3 59.6	4 17.6
12 Th	7 19 14	19 32 05	25 20 48	2♉08 02	10 43.1	19 17.9	10 12.5	19 21.2	25 43.6	2 32.2	2 13.1	22 58.9	4 01.8	4 19.0
13 F	7 23 11	20 29 19	8♉50 24	15 28 05	10 43.7	21 26.7	11 25.7	20 02.4	26 04.9	2 43.9	2 20.8	22 57.0	4 04.0	4 20.4
14 Sa	7 27 07	21 26 33	22 01 16	28 30 13	10 44.6	23 34.7	12 38.9	20 43.5	26 26.2	2 55.5	2 28.4	22 55.1	4 06.1	4 21.9
15 Su	7 31 04	22 23 48	4♊55 10	11♊16 22	10 45.6	25 41.9	13 52.1	21 24.6	26 47.7	3 07.0	2 36.1	22 53.2	4 08.3	4 23.3
16 M	7 35 01	23 21 04	17 34 06	23 48 37	10 46.5	27 47.9	15 05.3	22 05.7	27 09.3	3 18.4	2 43.8	22 51.2	4 10.5	4 24.7
17 Tu	7 38 57	24 18 19	0♋00 09	6♋08 57	10R47.0	29 52.6	16 18.5	22 46.6	27 31.1	3 29.8	2 51.5	22 49.2	4 12.7	4 26.1
18 W	7 42 54	25 15 36	12 15 16	18 19 20	10 46.9	1♌56.0	17 31.6	23 27.6	27 52.9	3 41.0	2 59.2	22 47.2	4 14.9	4 27.5
19 Th	7 46 50	26 12 53	24 21 22	0♌21 35	10 46.0	3 57.8	18 44.8	24 08.4	28 14.8	3 52.1	3 06.9	22 45.2	4 17.1	4 28.9
20 F	7 50 47	27 10 10	6♌20 15	12 17 35	10 44.4	5 58.2	19 57.9	24 49.2	28 36.9	4 03.2	3 14.6	22 43.1	4 19.3	4 30.3
21 Sa	7 54 43	28 07 28	18 13 51	24 09 19	10 42.1	7 56.9	21 11.0	25 30.0	28 59.0	4 14.2	3 22.3	22 41.0	4 21.5	4 31.6
22 Su	7 58 40	29 04 46	0♍04 18	5♍59 05	10 39.3	9 54.0	22 24.1	26 10.6	29 21.2	4 25.0	3 30.1	22 38.9	4 23.8	4 33.0
23 M	8 02 37	0♌02 05	11 54 02	17 49 32	10 36.3	11 49.4	23 37.1	26 51.3	29 43.6	4 35.8	3 37.8	22 36.8	4 26.0	4 34.3
24 Tu	8 06 33	0 59 23	23 45 57	29 43 45	10 33.6	13 43.1	24 50.2	27 31.8	0♎06.0	4 46.5	3 45.6	22 34.6	4 28.2	4 35.7
25 W	8 10 30	1 56 43	5♎43 23	11♎45 20	10 31.4	15 35.1	26 03.2	28 12.3	0 28.5	4 57.1	3 53.3	22 32.4	4 30.4	4 37.0
26 Th	8 14 26	2 54 03	17 50 05	23 58 11	10D30.2	17 25.3	27 16.2	28 52.7	0 51.2	5 07.5	4 01.1	22 30.2	4 32.6	4 38.4
27 F	8 18 23	3 51 23	0♏10 09	6♏26 31	10 29.9	19 13.9	28 29.2	29 33.1	1 13.9	5 17.9	4 08.8	22 28.0	4 34.9	4 39.7
28 Sa	8 22 19	4 48 44	12 47 47	19 14 27	10 30.6	21 00.7	29 42.2	0♋13.4	1 36.7	5 28.2	4 16.5	22 25.8	4 37.1	4 41.0
29 Su	8 26 16	5 46 05	25 46 58	2♐25 42	10 31.9	22 45.9	0♍55.1	0 53.7	1 59.6	5 38.3	4 24.3	22 23.5	4 39.3	4 42.3
30 M	8 30 12	6 43 27	9♐10 58	16 02 57	10 33.3	24 29.3	2 08.1	1 33.9	2 22.5	5 48.4	4 32.0	22 21.3	4 41.5	4 43.6
31 Tu	8 34 09	7 40 50	23 01 45	0♑07 16	10R34.5	26 11.1	3 21.0	2 14.0	2 45.6	5 58.3	4 39.8	22 19.0	4 43.8	4 44.8

August 1917 — LONGITUDE

Day	Sid.Time	☉	0 hr ☽	Noon ☽	True ☊	☿	♀	♂	⚳	♃	♄	♅	♆	♇
1 W	8 38 06	8♌38 13	7♑19 15	14♑37 19	10♑34.7	27♌51.1	4♍33.8	2♋54.1	3♎08.7	6♊08.2	4♌47.5	22♒16.7	4♌46.0	4♋46.1
2 Th	8 42 02	9 35 37	22 00 50	29 29 02	10R33.7	29 29.5	5 46.7	3 34.1	3 32.0	6 17.9	4 55.3	22R14.4	4 48.2	4 47.4
3 F	8 45 59	10 33 02	7♒00 56	14♒35 26	10 31.3	1♍06.3	6 59.5	4 14.0	3 55.3	6 27.5	5 03.0	22 12.1	4 50.4	4 48.6
4 Sa	8 49 55	11 30 28	22 11 21	29 47 25	10 27.7	2 41.3	8 12.3	4 53.9	4 18.6	6 37.0	5 10.7	22 09.8	4 52.7	4 49.8
5 Su	8 53 52	12 27 54	7♓22 21	14♓54 57	10 23.3	4 14.7	9 25.1	5 33.8	4 42.1	6 46.4	5 18.4	22 07.4	4 54.9	4 51.0
6 M	8 57 48	13 25 22	22 24 04	29 48 45	10 18.9	5 46.5	10 37.9	6 13.5	5 05.6	6 55.7	5 26.1	22 05.1	4 57.1	4 52.2
7 Tu	9 01 45	14 22 51	7♈08 10	14♈21 41	10 15.1	7 16.5	11 50.6	6 53.3	5 29.2	7 04.8	5 33.8	22 02.7	4 59.3	4 53.4
8 W	9 05 41	15 20 22	21 28 54	28 29 32	10 12.5	8 44.9	13 03.3	7 32.9	5 52.9	7 13.8	5 41.5	22 00.3	5 01.5	4 54.6
9 Th	9 09 38	16 17 54	5♉23 32	12♉10 58	10D11.4	10 11.6	14 16.0	8 12.5	6 16.6	7 22.7	5 49.2	21 58.0	5 03.7	4 55.8
10 F	9 13 35	17 15 27	18 52 02	25 27 04	10 11.5	11 36.5	15 28.7	8 52.1	6 40.4	7 31.5	5 56.8	21 55.6	5 05.9	4 56.9
11 Sa	9 17 31	18 13 02	1♊56 25	8♊20 32	10 12.7	12 59.7	16 41.4	9 31.6	7 04.3	7 40.1	6 04.5	21 53.2	5 08.0	4 58.0
12 Su	9 21 28	19 10 38	14 39 53	20 54 57	10 14.3	14 21.1	17 54.0	10 11.0	7 28.3	7 48.7	6 12.1	21 50.8	5 10.2	4 59.2
13 M	9 25 24	20 08 16	27 06 13	3♋14 10	10R15.4	15 40.8	19 06.6	10 50.4	7 52.3	7 57.0	6 19.7	21 48.4	5 12.4	5 00.3
14 Tu	9 29 21	21 05 55	9♋19 15	15 21 53	10 15.5	16 58.5	20 19.2	11 29.7	8 16.4	8 05.3	6 27.3	21 46.0	5 14.6	5 01.4
15 W	9 33 17	22 03 36	21 22 29	27 21 24	10 14.0	18 14.4	21 31.8	12 08.9	8 40.6	8 13.4	6 34.9	21 43.6	5 16.7	5 02.4
16 Th	9 37 14	23 01 18	3♌18 59	9♌15 32	10 10.4	19 28.3	22 44.3	12 48.1	9 04.8	8 21.4	6 42.5	21 41.2	5 18.9	5 03.5
17 F	9 41 10	23 59 01	15 11 20	21 06 37	10 04.8	20 40.1	23 56.9	13 27.2	9 29.1	8 29.2	6 50.0	21 38.8	5 21.0	5 04.5
18 Sa	9 45 07	24 56 45	27 01 37	2♍56 36	9 57.5	21 49.8	25 09.3	14 06.3	9 53.4	8 36.9	6 57.5	21 36.4	5 23.1	5 05.6
19 Su	9 49 04	25 54 31	8♍51 44	14 47 16	9 49.0	22 57.4	26 21.8	14 45.3	10 17.8	8 44.5	7 05.0	21 34.1	5 25.2	5 06.6
20 M	9 53 00	26 52 18	20 43 25	26 40 25	9 40.1	24 02.6	27 34.2	15 24.2	10 42.3	8 51.9	7 12.5	21 31.7	5 27.3	5 07.6
21 Tu	9 56 57	27 50 07	2♎38 31	8♎38 02	9 31.7	25 05.5	28 46.7	16 03.1	11 06.8	8 59.1	7 19.9	21 29.3	5 29.4	5 08.5
22 W	10 00 53	28 47 56	14 39 14	20 42 29	9 24.4	26 05.8	29 59.0	16 41.9	11 31.4	9 06.3	7 27.3	21 26.9	5 31.5	5 09.5
23 Th	10 04 50	29 45 47	26 48 10	2♏56 40	9 19.0	27 03.5	1♎11.4	17 20.6	11 56.0	9 13.2	7 34.7	21 24.6	5 33.6	5 10.4
24 F	10 08 46	0♍43 39	9♏08 26	15 23 55	9 15.7	27 58.3	2 23.7	17 59.3	12 20.7	9 20.0	7 42.1	21 22.2	5 35.7	5 11.4
25 Sa	10 12 43	1 41 33	21 43 36	28 07 59	9D14.4	28 50.3	3 36.0	18 37.9	12 45.4	9 26.7	7 49.4	21 19.9	5 37.7	5 12.3
26 Su	10 16 39	2 39 28	4♐37 31	11♐12 41	9 14.7	29 39.1	4 48.2	19 16.4	13 10.2	9 33.2	7 56.7	21 17.5	5 39.7	5 13.2
27 M	10 20 36	3 37 24	17 53 53	24 41 30	9 15.6	0♎24.5	6 00.5	19 54.9	13 35.0	9 39.6	8 04.0	21 15.2	5 41.8	5 14.0
28 Tu	10 24 33	4 35 21	1♑35 46	8♑36 51	9R16.1	1 06.4	7 12.6	20 33.3	13 59.9	9 45.8	8 11.2	21 12.9	5 43.8	5 14.9
29 W	10 28 29	5 33 20	15 44 44	22 59 16	9 15.4	1 44.6	8 24.8	21 11.7	14 24.8	9 51.8	8 18.4	21 10.6	5 45.8	5 15.7
30 Th	10 32 26	6 31 20	0♒20 03	7♒46 33	9 12.6	2 18.7	9 36.9	21 50.0	14 49.8	9 57.7	8 25.6	21 08.3	5 47.8	5 16.5
31 F	10 36 22	7 29 21	15 17 56	22 53 12	9 07.4	2 48.6	10 49.0	22 28.2	15 14.8	10 03.4	8 32.7	21 06.0	5 49.7	5 17.3

Astro Data Dy Hr Mn	Planet Ingress Dy Hr Mn	Last Aspect Dy Hr Mn	☽ Ingress Dy Hr Mn	Last Aspect Dy Hr Mn	☽ Ingress Dy Hr Mn	☽ Phases & Eclipses Dy Hr Mn	Astro Data
♃⚹♄ 8 1:18	☿ ♋ 3 10:27	1 16:59 ♀ △	♐ 1 22:14	31 19:44 ♇ ☍	♒ 2 12:50	4 21:40 ○ 12♑18	1 July 1917
☽0N 9 9:24	♀ ♌ 4 3:20	3 14:07 ♅ ⚹	♑ 4 1:25	3 23:59 ♅ ☌	♓ 4 12:20	4 21:39 ☍ T 1.618	Julian Day # 6391
♃⚹♆ 22 8:24	☿ ♌ 17 13:26	4 21:40 ☉ ☍	♒ 6 2:25	5 2:29 ♀ ☍	♈ 6 12:18	11 12:12 ☾ 18♈35	SVP 6♓24'25"
♃⊻♇ 23 8:14	☉ ♌ 23 11:08	7 15:44 ♅ ☌	♓ 8 2:53	8 0:55 ♅ ⚹	♉ 8 14:36	19 3:00 ● 25♋51	GC 25♐41.2 ⚴ 4♍57.8
☽0S 23 13:43	⚳ ♎ 24 5:35	9 6:58 ♂ □	♈ 10 4:25	10 5:34 ♅ □	♊ 10 20:24	19 2:42:23 ☌ P 0.086	Eris 28♓34.6R ⚵ 11♒59.9R
	♂ ♋ 28 4:00	11 19:53 ♅ ⚹	♉ 12 8:13	12 13:48 ♅ △	♋ 13 5:39	27 6:40 ☽ 3♏39	⚷ 29♓56.1 ⚶ 5♈57.3
♄☌♆ 1 5:20	♀ ♍ 28 17:52	14 1:41 ♅ □	♊ 14 14:47	14 23:00 ♀ ⚹	♌ 15 17:19		☽ Mean ☊ 10♑45.6
♄⊻♇ 1 6:44		16 10:10 ♅ △	♋ 16 24:00	17 18:21 ☉ ☌	♍ 18 6:02	3 5:11 ○ 10♒17	
♆⊻♇ 1 14:40	☿ ♍ 2 19:31	19 3:00 ☉ ☌	♌ 19 11:17	20 14:01 ♀ ☌	♎ 20 18:42	9 19:56 ☾ 16♉37	1 August 1917
☽0N 5 18:08	♀ ♎ 22 12:19	21 14:53 ♂ ⚹	♍ 21 23:51	23 5:16 ☉ ⚹	♏ 23 6:16	17 18:21 ● 24♌14	Julian Day # 6422
☽0S 19 20:16	☉ ♍ 23 17:54	24 7:19 ♂ □	♎ 24 12:33	25 13:24 ☿ ⚹	♐ 25 15:28	25 19:08 ☽ 1♐59	SVP 6♓24'20"
☿0S 21 23:22	☿ ♎ 26 22:50	26 22:03 ♂ △	♏ 26 23:40	27 5:58 ♅ ⚹	♑ 27 21:15		GC 25♐41.3 ⚴ 17♍59.8
♀0S 24 2:12		28 17:51 ♅ □	♐ 29 7:38	29 8:54 ♂ ☍	♒ 29 23:27		Eris 28♓26.9R ⚵ 5♒38.6R
⚳0S 31 17:15		31 4:28 ☿ △	♑ 31 11:48	31 9:11 ♅ ☌	♓ 31 23:11		⚷ 29♓34.3R ⚶ 10♈59.9
							☽ Mean ☊ 9♑07.1

LONGITUDE — September 1917

Day	Sid.Time	☉	0 hr ☽	Noon ☽	True ☊	☿	♀	♂	⚳	♃	♄	♅	♆	♇
1 Sa	10 40 19	8♍27 24	0♓31 11	8♓10 34	9♑00.1	3♎14.0	12♎01.0	23♋06.3	15♎39.9	10♊08.9	8♌39.8	21♒03.8	5♌51.7	5♋18.1
2 Su	10 44 15	9 25 28	15 49 55	23 27 49	8R51.3	3 34.5	13 13.0	23 44.4	16 05.0	10 14.3	8 46.9	21R01.5	5 53.6	5 18.9
3 M	10 48 12	10 23 35	1♈02 54	8♈33 52	8 42.3	3 49.9	14 24.9	24 22.5	16 30.1	10 19.5	8 53.9	20 59.3	5 55.5	5 19.6
4 Tu	10 52 08	11 21 43	15 59 38	23 19 16	8 34.1	4 00.0	15 36.9	25 00.4	16 55.3	10 24.6	9 00.9	20 57.1	5 57.4	5 20.3
5 W	10 56 05	12 19 53	0♉32 07	7♉37 43	8 27.6	4R04.3	16 48.7	25 38.3	17 20.6	10 29.4	9 07.8	20 54.9	5 59.3	5 21.0
6 Th	11 00 01	13 18 05	14 35 51	21 26 29	8 23.3	4 02.7	18 00.6	26 16.1	17 45.8	10 34.1	9 14.7	20 52.8	6 01.1	5 21.7
7 F	11 03 58	14 16 19	28 09 46	4♊46 01	8D21.3	3 54.9	19 12.4	26 53.9	18 11.1	10 38.7	9 21.6	20 50.6	6 03.0	5 22.3
8 Sa	11 07 55	15 14 36	11♊15 40	17 39 12	8 20.9	3 40.6	20 24.2	27 31.6	18 36.5	10 43.0	9 28.4	20 48.5	6 04.8	5 23.0
9 Su	11 11 51	16 12 54	23 57 13	0♋10 18	8R21.3	3 19.8	21 35.9	28 09.3	19 01.9	10 47.2	9 35.1	20 46.4	6 06.6	5 23.6
10 M	11 15 48	17 11 15	6♋19 06	12 24 13	8 21.4	2 52.5	22 47.6	28 46.8	19 27.3	10 51.2	9 41.9	20 44.4	6 08.4	5 24.2
11 Tu	11 19 44	18 09 37	18 26 16	24 25 50	8 20.2	2 18.6	23 59.3	29 24.3	19 52.8	10 55.0	9 48.5	20 42.3	6 10.2	5 24.8
12 W	11 23 41	19 08 02	0♌23 28	6♌19 40	8 16.7	1 38.3	25 10.9	0♌01.8	20 18.3	10 58.6	9 55.1	20 40.3	6 11.9	5 25.3
13 Th	11 27 37	20 06 28	12 14 56	18 09 39	8 10.6	0 52.1	26 22.5	0 39.1	20 43.8	11 02.1	10 01.7	20 38.3	6 13.6	5 25.8
14 F	11 31 34	21 04 57	24 04 12	29 58 55	8 01.6	0 00.5	27 34.1	1 16.4	21 09.4	11 05.3	10 08.2	20 36.3	6 15.4	5 26.3
15 Sa	11 35 30	22 03 27	5♍54 05	11♍49 55	7 50.3	29♍04.2	28 45.6	1 53.6	21 35.0	11 08.4	10 14.7	20 34.4	6 17.0	5 26.8
16 Su	11 39 27	23 02 00	17 46 40	23 44 29	7 37.2	28 04.2	29 57.0	2 30.8	22 00.6	11 11.3	10 21.1	20 32.5	6 18.7	5 27.3
17 M	11 43 24	24 00 34	29 43 33	5♎43 59	7 23.4	27 01.6	1♏08.5	3 07.8	22 26.3	11 14.0	10 27.4	20 30.6	6 20.3	5 27.7
18 Tu	11 47 20	24 59 10	11♎45 58	17 49 36	7 10.1	25 57.9	2 19.8	3 44.8	22 52.0	11 16.5	10 33.7	20 28.8	6 21.9	5 28.2
19 W	11 51 17	25 57 48	23 55 05	0♏02 35	6 58.5	24 54.5	3 31.2	4 21.8	23 17.7	11 18.8	10 40.0	20 26.9	6 23.5	5 28.5
20 Th	11 55 13	26 56 28	6♏12 18	12 24 28	6 49.2	23 52.9	4 42.5	4 58.6	23 43.5	11 20.9	10 46.2	20 25.2	6 25.1	5 28.9
21 F	11 59 10	27 55 10	18 39 22	24 57 19	6 42.9	22 54.7	5 53.7	5 35.4	24 09.2	11 22.8	10 52.3	20 23.4	6 26.6	5 29.3
22 Sa	12 03 06	28 53 53	1♐18 38	7♐43 42	6 39.3	22 01.5	7 04.9	6 12.1	24 35.0	11 24.5	10 58.3	20 21.7	6 28.2	5 29.6
23 Su	12 07 03	29 52 39	14 12 54	20 46 38	6D38.0	21 14.6	8 16.1	6 48.7	25 00.9	11 26.1	11 04.3	20 20.0	6 29.7	5 29.9
24 M	12 10 59	0♎51 26	27 25 17	4♑09 15	6R37.8	20 35.3	9 27.1	7 25.2	25 26.7	11 27.4	11 10.3	20 18.4	6 31.1	5 30.2
25 Tu	12 14 56	1 50 14	10♑58 50	17 54 16	6 37.6	20 04.6	10 38.2	8 01.7	25 52.6	11 28.5	11 16.2	20 16.8	6 32.6	5 30.5
26 W	12 18 53	2 49 05	24 55 44	2♒03 14	6 36.1	19 43.2	11 49.2	8 38.1	26 18.5	11 29.4	11 22.0	20 15.2	6 34.0	5 30.7
27 Th	12 22 49	3 47 57	9♒16 38	16 35 37	6 32.3	19D31.8	13 00.1	9 14.4	26 44.4	11 30.2	11 27.7	20 13.7	6 35.4	5 30.9
28 F	12 26 46	4 46 50	23 59 38	1♓28 00	6 25.8	19 30.5	14 10.9	9 50.6	27 10.4	11 30.7	11 33.4	20 12.2	6 36.7	5 31.1
29 Sa	12 30 42	5 45 46	8♓59 46	16 33 50	6 16.7	19 39.5	15 21.7	10 26.7	27 36.3	11 31.0	11 39.0	20 10.7	6 38.1	5 31.3
30 Su	12 34 39	6 44 43	24 08 59	1♈43 51	6 05.8	19 58.6	16 32.5	11 02.8	28 02.3	11R31.2	11 44.5	20 09.3	6 39.4	5 31.4

LONGITUDE — October 1917

Day	Sid.Time	☉	0 hr ☽	Noon ☽	True ☊	☿	♀	♂	⚳	♃	♄	♅	♆	♇
1 M	12 38 35	7♎43 42	9♈17 07	16♈47 27	5♑54.3	20♍27.5	17♏43.1	11♌38.8	28♎28.3	11♊31.1	11♌50.0	20♒07.9	6♌40.7	5♋31.6
2 Tu	12 42 32	8 42 44	24 13 38	1♉34 37	5R43.7	21 05.7	18 53.7	12 14.7	28 54.3	11R30.9	11 55.4	20R06.6	6 41.9	5 31.7
3 W	12 46 28	9 41 48	8♉49 30	15 57 39	5 34.9	21 52.7	20 04.3	12 50.5	29 20.4	11 30.4	12 00.7	20 05.3	6 43.2	5 31.7
4 Th	12 50 25	10 40 54	22 58 38	29 52 12	5 28.7	22 47.7	21 14.8	13 26.2	29 46.4	11 29.7	12 05.9	20 04.0	6 44.4	5 31.8
5 F	12 54 22	11 40 02	6♊38 22	13♊17 17	5 25.2	23 50.1	22 25.2	14 01.9	0♏12.5	11 28.9	12 11.1	20 02.8	6 45.5	5 31.8
6 Sa	12 58 18	12 39 13	19 49 16	26 14 45	5D23.8	24 59.1	23 35.5	14 37.5	0 38.6	11 27.8	12 16.2	20 01.6	6 46.7	5R31.8
7 Su	13 02 15	13 38 25	2♋34 16	8♋48 25	5R23.6	26 14.0	24 45.8	15 13.0	1 04.7	11 26.5	12 21.2	20 00.5	6 47.8	5 31.8
8 M	13 06 11	14 37 41	14 57 51	21 03 12	5 23.5	27 34.0	25 56.1	15 48.4	1 30.8	11 25.0	12 26.2	19 59.4	6 48.9	5 31.8
9 Tu	13 10 08	15 36 58	27 05 11	3♌04 27	5 22.4	28 58.5	27 06.2	16 23.7	1 56.9	11 23.4	12 31.0	19 58.4	6 49.9	5 31.7
10 W	13 14 04	16 36 18	9♌01 39	14 57 25	5 19.2	0♎26.9	28 16.3	16 58.9	2 23.1	11 21.5	12 35.8	19 57.4	6 51.0	5 31.7
11 Th	13 18 01	17 35 40	20 52 18	26 46 53	5 13.4	1 58.4	29 26.3	17 34.1	2 49.2	11 19.4	12 40.5	19 56.5	6 51.9	5 31.5
12 F	13 21 57	18 35 04	2♍41 38	8♍37 00	5 04.8	3 32.6	0♐36.3	18 09.1	3 15.4	11 17.1	12 45.1	19 55.6	6 52.9	5 31.4
13 Sa	13 25 54	19 34 31	14 33 22	20 31 04	4 53.7	5 09.0	1 46.1	18 44.1	3 41.6	11 14.6	12 49.7	19 54.7	6 53.8	5 31.3
14 Su	13 29 50	20 33 59	26 30 22	2♎31 31	4 40.9	6 47.2	2 55.9	19 18.9	4 07.7	11 12.0	12 54.1	19 53.9	6 54.7	5 31.1
15 M	13 33 47	21 33 30	8♎34 42	14 40 01	4 27.3	8 26.7	4 05.6	19 53.7	4 33.9	11 09.1	12 58.5	19 53.1	6 55.6	5 30.9
16 Tu	13 37 44	22 33 03	20 47 36	26 57 31	4 14.1	10 07.3	5 15.3	20 28.4	5 00.1	11 06.0	13 02.8	19 52.4	6 56.4	5 30.7
17 W	13 41 40	23 32 38	3♏09 49	9♏24 33	4 02.6	11 48.6	6 24.8	21 02.9	5 26.4	11 02.8	13 07.0	19 51.7	6 57.2	5 30.4
18 Th	13 45 37	24 32 15	15 41 45	22 01 29	3 53.4	13 30.5	7 34.3	21 37.4	5 52.6	10 59.3	13 11.0	19 51.1	6 58.0	5 30.2
19 F	13 49 33	25 31 54	28 23 50	4♐48 52	3 47.1	15 12.7	8 43.6	22 11.8	6 18.8	10 55.7	13 15.1	19 50.5	6 58.8	5 29.9
20 Sa	13 53 30	26 31 34	11♐16 44	17 47 35	3 43.7	16 55.1	9 52.9	22 46.0	6 45.0	10 51.8	13 19.0	19 50.0	6 59.5	5 29.6
21 Su	13 57 26	27 31 17	24 21 36	0♑58 59	3D42.6	18 37.5	11 02.1	23 20.2	7 11.3	10 47.8	13 22.8	19 49.5	7 00.1	5 29.2
22 M	14 01 23	28 31 01	7♑39 57	14 24 44	3 42.8	20 19.8	12 11.2	23 54.2	7 37.5	10 43.6	13 26.5	19 49.1	7 00.8	5 28.9
23 Tu	14 05 19	29 30 47	21 13 32	28 06 32	3R43.2	22 01.9	13 20.2	24 28.1	8 03.8	10 39.2	13 30.2	19 48.8	7 01.4	5 28.5
24 W	14 09 16	0♏30 35	5♒03 51	12♒05 34	3 42.7	23 43.8	14 29.0	25 02.0	8 30.0	10 34.7	13 33.7	19 48.4	7 02.0	5 28.1
25 Th	14 13 13	1 30 24	19 11 36	26 21 49	3 40.2	25 25.3	15 37.8	25 35.7	8 56.2	10 29.9	13 37.2	19 48.2	7 02.5	5 27.7
26 F	14 17 09	2 30 14	3♓35 54	10♓53 24	3 35.3	27 06.5	16 46.4	26 09.3	9 22.5	10 25.0	13 40.5	19 47.9	7 03.0	5 27.2
27 Sa	14 21 06	3 30 07	18 13 45	25 36 10	3 28.1	28 47.2	17 54.9	26 42.8	9 48.7	10 20.0	13 43.8	19 47.8	7 03.5	5 26.8
28 Su	14 25 02	4 30 01	2♈59 48	10♈23 42	3 19.3	0♏27.6	19 03.3	27 16.2	10 14.9	10 14.7	13 46.9	19 47.6	7 03.9	5 26.3
29 M	14 28 59	5 29 57	17 46 48	25 08 05	3 09.9	2 07.5	20 11.5	27 49.4	10 41.2	10 09.3	13 50.0	19D47.6	7 04.3	5 25.8
30 Tu	14 32 55	6 29 55	2♉26 30	9♉41 07	3 01.0	3 47.0	21 19.7	28 22.6	11 07.4	10 03.7	13 52.9	19 47.5	7 04.7	5 25.2
31 W	14 36 52	7 29 54	16 51 05	23 55 42	2 53.7	5 26.0	22 27.6	28 55.6	11 33.6	9 58.0	13 55.8	19 47.6	7 05.1	5 24.7

Astro Data

	Dy Hr Mn
☽0N	2 4:51
☿R	5 17:38
☽0S	16 2:24
♅⚼♇	18 18:34
☿0N	20 11:17
☉0S	23 15:00
♃✱♄	27 23:38
☿D	28 2:54
☽0N	29 15:41
♃R	30 16:05
♇R	6 12:13
☿0S	13 3:23
☽0S	13 8:32
☽0N	27 0:36
♅D	30 10:31

Planet Ingress

		Dy Hr Mn
♂	♌	12 10:52
☿	♍R	14 12:12
♀	♏	16 13:00
☉	♎	23 15:00
⚳	♏	5 0:31
☿	♎	10 4:48
♀	♐	11 23:33
☉	♏	23 23:44
☿	♏	28 5:23

Last Aspect / ☽ Ingress

Last Aspect Dy Hr Mn			☽ Ingress	Dy Hr Mn
2 12:27	♂	△	♈	2 22:20
4 14:55	♂	□	♉	4 23:06
6 21:01	♂	✱	♊	7 3:19
8 17:58	♅	△	♋	9 11:40
11 22:34	♂	☌	♌	11 23:13
14 6:33	♀	✱	♍	14 12:02
16 20:00	☿	☌	♎	17 0:33
18 17:13	♅	△	♏	19 11:55
21 18:05	☉	✱	♐	21 21:32
23 12:48	☿	□	♑	24 4:37
25 15:37	☿	△	♒	26 8:33
27 17:54	♅	☌	♓	28 9:39
29 16:59	☿	☍	♈	30 9:15

Last Aspect / ☽ Ingress

Last Aspect Dy Hr Mn			☽ Ingress	Dy Hr Mn
1 17:22	♅	✱	♉	2 9:25
3 22:47	☿	△	♊	4 12:14
6 9:23	☿	□	♋	6 19:06
9 2:40	☿	✱	♌	9 5:50
11 17:59	♀	□	♍	11 18:32
12 17:23	♃	□	♎	14 6:58
16 2:41	☉	☌	♏	16 17:53
18 11:12	♂	□	♐	19 3:00
21 5:14	☉	✱	♑	21 10:14
23 14:37	☉	□	♒	23 15:17
25 10:40	♂	☍	♓	25 18:03
26 22:26	♀	□	♈	27 19:08
29 16:35	♂	△	♉	29 19:59
31 20:56	♂	□	♊	31 22:26

☽ Phases & Eclipses

Dy Hr Mn		
1 12:28	○	8♓29
8 7:05	☾	15♊03
16 10:27	●	22♍58
24 5:41	☽	0♑36
30 20:31	○	7♈06
7 22:14	☾	14♋04
16 2:41	●	22♎10
23 14:37	☽	29♑37
30 6:19	○	6♉16

Astro Data

1 September 1917
Julian Day # 6453
SVP 6♓24'16"
GC 25♐41.4 ⚴ 1♎33.2
Eris 28♓10.2R ⚵ 29♑22.7R
⚷ 28♓30.8R ⚶ 9♈23.7R
☽ Mean ☊ 7♑28.6

1 October 1917
Julian Day # 6483
SVP 6♓24'13"
GC 25♐41.4 ⚴ 14♎55.2
Eris 27♓50.1R ⚵ 28♑41.3
⚷ 27♓10.5R ⚶ 2♈27.4R
☽ Mean ☊ 5♑53.3

November 1917 — LONGITUDE

Day	Sid.Time	☉	0 hr ☽	Noon ☽	True ☊	☿	♀	♂	⚳	♃	♄	♅	♆	♇
1 Th	14 40 48	8♏29 56	0♊54 26	7♊46 55	2♑48.6	7♏04.5	23♐35.5	29♌28.6	11♏59.8	9♊52.1	13♌58.5	19♒47.6	7♌05.4	5♋24.1
2 F	14 44 45	9 30 00	14 32 56	21 12 29	2D 45.9	8 42.7	24 43.2	0♍01.4	12 26.0	9R 46.1	14 01.2	19 47.8	7 05.6	5R 23.5
3 Sa	14 48 42	10 30 06	27 45 39	4♋12 42	2 45.2	10 20.3	25 50.8	0 34.0	12 52.2	9 39.9	14 03.7	19 48.0	7 05.9	5 22.9
4 Su	14 52 38	11 30 14	10♋34 00	16 49 59	2 45.9	11 57.6	26 58.2	1 06.6	13 18.5	9 33.6	14 06.2	19 48.2	7 06.1	5 22.3
5 M	14 56 35	12 30 24	23 01 12	29 08 13	2 47.2	13 34.4	28 05.4	1 39.0	13 44.7	9 27.2	14 08.5	19 48.5	7 06.3	5 21.7
6 Tu	15 00 31	13 30 36	5♌11 40	11♌12 11	2R 48.0	15 10.9	29 12.5	2 11.3	14 10.8	9 20.6	14 10.8	19 48.8	7 06.4	5 21.0
7 W	15 04 28	14 30 50	17 10 25	23 07 03	2 47.5	16 46.9	0♑19.5	2 43.5	14 37.0	9 13.8	14 12.9	19 49.2	7 06.5	5 20.3
8 Th	15 08 24	15 31 06	29 02 41	4♍57 58	2 45.3	18 22.6	1 26.2	3 15.5	15 03.2	9 07.0	14 14.9	19 49.6	7 06.6	5 19.6
9 F	15 12 21	16 31 24	10♍53 29	16 49 46	2 40.9	19 57.9	2 32.8	3 47.4	15 29.4	9 00.0	14 16.8	19 50.1	7R 06.6	5 18.9
10 Sa	15 16 17	17 31 44	22 47 22	28 46 43	2 34.8	21 32.9	3 39.3	4 19.2	15 55.5	8 52.9	14 18.6	19 50.7	7 06.6	5 18.1
11 Su	15 20 14	18 32 06	4♎48 14	10♎52 17	2 27.2	23 07.5	4 45.5	4 50.8	16 21.6	8 45.7	14 20.3	19 51.2	7 06.6	5 17.4
12 M	15 24 11	19 32 30	16 59 09	23 09 03	2 18.9	24 41.8	5 51.6	5 22.3	16 47.8	8 38.4	14 21.9	19 51.9	7 06.5	5 16.6
13 Tu	15 28 07	20 32 55	29 22 11	5♏38 38	2 10.8	26 15.9	6 57.4	5 53.6	17 13.9	8 31.0	14 23.4	19 52.6	7 06.4	5 15.8
14 W	15 32 04	21 33 22	11♏58 28	18 21 42	2 03.7	27 49.6	8 03.1	6 24.7	17 40.0	8 23.5	14 24.8	19 53.3	7 06.2	5 15.0
15 Th	15 36 00	22 33 51	24 48 17	1♐18 08	1 58.3	29 23.1	9 08.5	6 55.8	18 06.1	8 16.0	14 26.0	19 54.1	7 06.1	5 14.1
16 F	15 39 57	23 34 22	7♐51 11	14 27 17	1 54.9	0♐56.4	10 13.7	7 26.6	18 32.2	8 08.3	14 27.2	19 55.0	7 05.9	5 13.3
17 Sa	15 43 53	24 34 54	21 06 21	27 48 14	1D 53.5	2 29.4	11 18.7	7 57.3	18 58.2	8 00.6	14 28.2	19 55.9	7 05.6	5 12.4
18 Su	15 47 50	25 35 28	4♑32 51	11♑20 05	1 53.7	4 02.2	12 23.5	8 27.8	19 24.2	7 52.7	14 29.1	19 56.8	7 05.4	5 11.5
19 M	15 51 46	26 36 02	18 09 51	25 02 05	1 55.1	5 34.8	13 28.0	8 58.2	19 50.3	7 44.9	14 29.9	19 57.8	7 05.1	5 10.6
20 Tu	15 55 43	27 36 38	1♒56 43	8♒53 40	1 56.6	7 07.1	14 32.2	9 28.4	20 16.3	7 36.9	14 30.6	19 58.9	7 04.7	5 09.7
21 W	15 59 40	28 37 15	15 52 52	22 54 14	1R 57.7	8 39.2	15 36.2	9 58.4	20 42.2	7 28.9	14 31.2	19 59.9	7 04.3	5 08.8
22 Th	16 03 36	29 37 53	29 57 38	7♓02 53	1 57.5	10 11.2	16 39.9	10 28.3	21 08.2	7 20.9	14 31.7	20 01.1	7 03.9	5 07.8
23 F	16 07 33	0♐38 33	14♓09 46	21 18 00	1 56.0	11 42.9	17 43.3	10 57.9	21 34.1	7 12.8	14 32.0	20 02.3	7 03.5	5 06.9
24 Sa	16 11 29	1 39 13	28 27 14	5♈37 02	1 53.0	13 14.4	18 46.4	11 27.4	22 00.0	7 04.7	14 32.3	20 03.5	7 03.0	5 05.9
25 Su	16 15 26	2 39 54	12♈46 55	19 56 21	1 49.1	14 45.8	19 49.2	11 56.8	22 25.9	6 56.6	14R 32.4	20 04.8	7 02.5	5 04.9
26 M	16 19 22	3 40 37	27 04 44	4♉11 29	1 44.6	16 16.9	20 51.6	12 25.9	22 51.7	6 48.4	14 32.4	20 06.2	7 02.0	5 03.9
27 Tu	16 23 19	4 41 21	11♉15 58	18 17 35	1 40.5	17 47.7	21 53.7	12 54.8	23 17.5	6 40.3	14 32.4	20 07.5	7 01.4	5 02.9
28 W	16 27 15	5 42 06	25 15 48	2♊10 07	1 37.1	19 18.3	22 55.5	13 23.6	23 43.3	6 32.1	14 32.2	20 09.0	7 00.8	5 01.9
29 Th	16 31 12	6 42 52	9♊00 05	15 45 25	1 34.9	20 48.6	23 56.9	13 52.1	24 09.1	6 23.9	14 31.8	20 10.5	7 00.2	5 00.8
30 F	16 35 09	7 43 39	22 25 50	29 01 14	1D 34.0	22 18.6	24 57.9	14 20.5	24 34.8	6 15.7	14 31.4	20 12.0	6 59.5	4 59.8

December 1917 — LONGITUDE

Day	Sid.Time	☉	0 hr ☽	Noon ☽	True ☊	☿	♀	♂	⚳	♃	♄	♅	♆	♇
1 Sa	16 39 05	8♐44 28	5♋31 35	11♋56 56	1♑34.4	23♐48.3	25♑58.6	14♍48.7	25♏00.5	6♊07.5	14♌30.9	20♒13.6	6♌58.8	4♋58.7
2 Su	16 43 02	9 45 18	18 17 29	24 33 27	1 35.6	25 17.5	26 58.8	15 16.6	25 26.2	5R 59.4	14R 30.2	20 15.2	6R 58.1	4R 57.6
3 M	16 46 58	10 46 10	0♌45 12	6♌53 06	1 37.2	26 46.3	27 58.6	15 44.4	25 51.9	5 51.3	14 29.5	20 16.9	6 57.3	4 56.6
4 Tu	16 50 55	11 47 02	12 57 38	18 59 18	1 38.8	28 14.5	28 58.0	16 11.9	26 17.5	5 43.2	14 28.6	20 18.6	6 56.5	4 55.5
5 W	16 54 51	12 47 56	24 58 39	0♍56 15	1 40.1	29 42.1	29 57.0	16 39.2	26 43.1	5 35.1	14 27.6	20 20.3	6 55.7	4 54.4
6 Th	16 58 48	13 48 51	6♍52 42	12 48 35	1R 40.6	1♑08.9	0♒55.5	17 06.3	27 08.6	5 27.1	14 26.5	20 22.1	6 54.9	4 53.2
7 F	17 02 45	14 49 48	18 44 33	24 41 11	1 40.2	2 34.8	1 53.5	17 33.2	27 34.2	5 19.1	14 25.3	20 24.0	6 54.0	4 52.1
8 Sa	17 06 41	15 50 45	0♎39 05	6♎38 49	1 39.1	3 59.7	2 51.0	17 59.8	27 59.6	5 11.1	14 24.0	20 25.9	6 53.1	4 51.0
9 Su	17 10 38	16 51 44	12 40 55	18 45 54	1 37.4	5 23.5	3 48.0	18 26.2	28 25.1	5 03.3	14 22.6	20 27.8	6 52.2	4 49.8
10 M	17 14 34	17 52 44	24 54 13	1♏06 17	1 35.4	6 45.8	4 44.4	18 52.3	28 50.5	4 55.5	14 21.0	20 29.8	6 51.2	4 48.7
11 Tu	17 18 31	18 53 45	7♏22 27	13 42 57	1 33.3	8 06.4	5 40.4	19 18.2	29 15.9	4 47.7	14 19.4	20 31.8	6 50.2	4 47.5
12 W	17 22 27	19 54 47	20 08 01	26 37 44	1 31.6	9 25.1	6 35.7	19 43.8	29 41.2	4 40.1	14 17.6	20 33.9	6 49.2	4 46.4
13 Th	17 26 24	20 55 50	3♐12 10	9♐51 14	1 30.4	10 41.6	7 30.4	20 09.2	0♐06.5	4 32.5	14 15.8	20 36.0	6 48.1	4 45.2
14 F	17 30 20	21 56 54	16 34 48	23 22 40	1D 29.8	11 55.4	8 24.5	20 34.3	0 31.8	4 25.0	14 13.8	20 38.1	6 47.1	4 44.0
15 Sa	17 34 17	22 57 59	0♑14 31	7♑10 01	1 29.8	13 06.1	9 18.0	20 59.1	0 57.0	4 17.6	14 11.8	20 40.3	6 46.0	4 42.8
16 Su	17 38 14	23 59 04	14 08 44	21 10 15	1 30.1	14 13.3	10 10.7	21 23.6	1 22.1	4 10.4	14 09.6	20 42.6	6 44.9	4 41.7
17 M	17 42 10	25 00 10	28 14 04	5♒19 44	1 30.7	15 16.3	11 02.8	21 47.9	1 47.3	4 03.2	14 07.3	20 44.8	6 43.7	4 40.5
18 Tu	17 46 07	26 01 16	12♒26 45	19 34 39	1 31.3	16 14.5	11 54.1	22 11.8	2 12.3	3 56.1	14 05.0	20 47.1	6 42.5	4 39.3
19 W	17 50 03	27 02 22	26 42 58	3♓51 20	1 31.8	17 07.3	12 44.7	22 35.5	2 37.3	3 49.2	14 02.5	20 49.5	6 41.3	4 38.1
20 Th	17 54 00	28 03 29	10♓59 19	18 06 35	1R 32.0	17 53.8	13 34.4	22 58.9	3 02.3	3 42.3	13 59.9	20 51.9	6 40.1	4 36.9
21 F	17 57 56	29 04 35	25 12 50	2♈17 46	1 32.1	18 33.2	14 23.3	23 21.9	3 27.2	3 35.6	13 57.2	20 54.3	6 38.9	4 35.6
22 Sa	18 01 53	0♑05 42	9♈21 09	16 22 43	1 32.0	19 04.6	15 11.3	23 44.6	3 52.1	3 29.1	13 54.5	20 56.7	6 37.6	4 34.4
23 Su	18 05 49	1 06 49	23 22 18	0♉19 41	1D 31.9	19 27.1	15 58.4	24 07.0	4 16.9	3 22.7	13 51.6	20 59.2	6 36.3	4 33.2
24 M	18 09 46	2 07 56	7♉14 41	14 07 06	1 31.9	19R 39.9	16 44.6	24 29.1	4 41.6	3 16.4	13 48.7	21 01.8	6 35.0	4 32.0
25 Tu	18 13 43	3 09 03	20 56 48	27 43 36	1 32.1	19 42.0	17 29.7	24 50.9	5 06.4	3 10.2	13 45.6	21 04.3	6 33.7	4 30.8
26 W	18 17 39	4 10 11	4♊27 20	11♊07 53	1 32.3	19 32.9	18 13.9	25 12.3	5 31.0	3 04.2	13 42.5	21 06.9	6 32.3	4 29.6
27 Th	18 21 36	5 11 18	17 45 06	24 18 53	1R 32.5	19 12.1	18 56.9	25 33.3	5 55.6	2 58.4	13 39.3	21 09.6	6 30.9	4 28.4
28 F	18 25 32	6 12 26	0♋49 08	7♋15 50	1 32.5	18 39.4	19 38.8	25 54.1	6 20.1	2 52.7	13 36.0	21 12.2	6 29.5	4 27.1
29 Sa	18 29 29	7 13 34	13 38 56	19 58 29	1 32.2	17 55.1	20 19.6	26 14.4	6 44.6	2 47.2	13 32.6	21 14.9	6 28.1	4 25.9
30 Su	18 33 25	8 14 42	26 14 33	2♌27 14	1 31.6	17 00.0	20 59.1	26 34.4	7 09.0	2 41.8	13 29.1	21 17.7	6 26.7	4 24.7
31 M	18 37 22	9 15 50	8♌36 44	14 43 14	1 30.6	15 55.4	21 37.4	26 54.0	7 33.4	2 36.7	13 25.6	21 20.4	6 25.2	4 23.5

Astro Data (Dy Hr Mn)

- ☽0S 9 15:12
- ♆R 9 22:27
- ☽0N 23 6:49
- ♃✱♆ 24 17:21
- ♅⚼♇ 25 12:59
- ♄R 26 4:38

- ☽0S 6 22:40
- ♃⊻♇ 11 12:44
- ☽0N 20 11:52
- ☿R 25 4:42

Planet Ingress (Dy Hr Mn)

- ♂ ♍ 2 11:00
- ♀ ♑ 7 5:01
- ☿ ♐ 15 21:29
- ☉ ♐ 22 20:45

- ♀ ♒ 5 13:14
- ☿ ♑ 5 16:57
- ⚳ ♐ 13 5:49
- ☉ ♑ 22 9:46

Last Aspect Dy Hr Mn		☽ Ingress Dy Hr Mn	Last Aspect Dy Hr Mn		☽ Ingress Dy Hr Mn
2 19:01	♀ ☍	♋ 3 4:09	2 17:05	♀ ☍	♌ 2 22:32
4 1:17	☿ △	♌ 5 13:42	5 9:10	☿ △	♍ 5 10:07
7 5:20	♅ ☍	♍ 8 1:56	6 21:02	♂ ☌	♎ 7 22:42
9 19:17	☿ ✱	♎ 10 14:26	9 15:20	♅ △	♏ 10 9:52
12 5:37	♅ △	♏ 13 1:13	12 0:46	♅ □	♐ 12 18:10
15 7:59	☿ ☌	♐ 15 9:36	14 9:17	☉ ☌	♑ 14 23:35
16 21:52	♅ ✱	♑ 17 15:55	16 12:23	♂ △	♒ 17 2:59
19 14:56	☉ ✱	♒ 19 20:38	18 23:40	☉ ✱	♓ 19 5:31
21 22:28	☉ □	♓ 22 0:04	21 6:07	☉ □	♈ 21 8:06
23 5:30	♀ ✱	♈ 24 2:35	22 19:51	♅ ✱	♉ 23 11:26
25 12:14	♅ ✱	♉ 26 4:55	25 6:45	♂ △	♊ 25 16:03
27 18:41	♀ △	♊ 28 8:13	27 14:21	♂ □	♋ 27 22:29
29 22:14	☿ ☍	♋ 30 13:48	30 0:20	♂ ✱	♌ 30 7:15

☽ Phases & Eclipses (Dy Hr Mn)

- 6 17:03 ☾ 13♌43
- 14 18:28 ● 21♏50
- 21 22:28 ☽ 29♒04
- 28 18:41 ○ 5♊59

- 6 14:13 ☾ 13♍54
- 14 9:17 ● 21♐50
- 14 9:26:56 ● A 01'16"
- 21 6:07 ☽ 28♓50
- 28 9:51 ○ 6♋07
- 28 9:46 ● T 1.006

Astro Data

1 November 1917
Julian Day # 6514
SVP 6♓24'10"
GC 25♐41.5 ⚴ 28♎44.9
Eris 27♓31.4R ⚵ 4♒01.8
⚷ 25♓58.6R ⚶ 26♓50.6R
☽ Mean ☊ 4♑14.7

1 December 1917
Julian Day # 6544
SVP 6♓24'05"
GC 25♐41.6 ⚴ 11♏51.7
Eris 27♓20.7R ⚵ 13♒25.9
⚷ 25♓25.4R ⚶ 27♓47.1
☽ Mean ☊ 2♑39.4

LONGITUDE — January 1918

Day	Sid.Time	☉	0 hr ☽	Noon ☽	True ☊	☿	♀	♂	⚳	♃	♄	♅	♆	♇
1 Tu	18 41 18	10♑16 59	20♌47 02	26♌48 27	1♑29.4	14♑43.0	22♒14.4	27♍13.2	7♐57.7	2♊31.6	13♌22.0	21♒23.2	6♌23.8	4♋22.3
2 W	18 45 15	11 18 08	2♍47 51	8♍45 38	1R 28.0	13R 25.2	22 50.0	27 32.0	8 21.9	2R 26.8	13R 18.2	21 26.1	6R 22.3	4R 21.1
3 Th	18 49 12	12 19 17	14 42 17	20 38 16	1 26.8	12 04.4	23 24.2	27 50.4	8 46.1	2 22.1	13 14.5	21 28.9	6 20.8	4 19.9
4 F	18 53 08	13 20 26	26 34 07	2♎30 23	1D 26.0	10 43.4	23 56.9	28 08.4	9 10.2	2 17.6	13 10.6	21 31.8	6 19.3	4 18.7
5 Sa	18 57 05	14 21 35	8♎27 40	14 26 31	1 25.7	9 24.6	24 28.1	28 26.0	9 34.2	2 13.3	13 06.7	21 34.7	6 17.7	4 17.5
6 Su	19 01 01	15 22 45	20 27 34	26 31 23	1 26.0	8 10.6	24 57.7	28 43.1	9 58.2	2 09.2	13 02.7	21 37.6	6 16.2	4 16.3
7 M	19 04 58	16 23 54	2♏38 34	8♏49 40	1 26.9	7 03.1	25 25.7	28 59.8	10 22.1	2 05.2	12 58.6	21 40.6	6 14.6	4 15.1
8 Tu	19 08 54	17 25 04	15 05 13	21 25 41	1 28.2	6 03.8	25 52.0	29 16.0	10 45.9	2 01.5	12 54.5	21 43.6	6 13.1	4 13.9
9 W	19 12 51	18 26 14	27 51 29	4♐22 58	1 29.6	5 13.6	26 16.5	29 31.8	11 09.7	1 57.9	12 50.3	21 46.6	6 11.5	4 12.7
10 Th	19 16 47	19 27 24	11♐00 23	17 43 51	1 30.8	4 33.2	26 39.2	29 47.1	11 33.3	1 54.6	12 46.0	21 49.7	6 09.9	4 11.6
11 F	19 20 44	20 28 33	24 33 23	1♑28 51	1R 31.2	4 02.6	26 59.9	0♎01.9	11 56.9	1 51.4	12 41.7	21 52.8	6 08.3	4 10.4
12 Sa	19 24 41	21 29 43	8♑30 01	15 36 27	1 30.7	3 41.8	27 18.8	0 16.2	12 20.5	1 48.4	12 37.3	21 55.8	6 06.7	4 09.2
13 Su	19 28 37	22 30 52	22 47 36	0♒02 48	1 29.1	3D 30.5	27 35.5	0 30.0	12 43.9	1 45.6	12 32.9	21 59.0	6 05.0	4 08.1
14 M	19 32 34	23 32 01	7♒21 15	14 42 04	1 26.5	3 28.1	27 50.2	0 43.2	13 07.3	1 43.1	12 28.5	22 02.1	6 03.4	4 06.9
15 Tu	19 36 30	24 33 09	22 04 20	29 27 06	1 23.2	3 34.1	28 02.8	0 56.0	13 30.6	1 40.7	12 23.9	22 05.3	6 01.8	4 05.8
16 W	19 40 27	25 34 16	6♓49 27	14♓10 29	1 19.8	3 47.9	28 13.1	1 08.2	13 53.8	1 38.5	12 19.4	22 08.4	6 00.1	4 04.7
17 Th	19 44 23	26 35 22	21 29 25	28 45 34	1 16.9	4 08.7	28 21.1	1 19.8	14 16.9	1 36.6	12 14.8	22 11.7	5 58.4	4 03.6
18 F	19 48 20	27 36 28	5♈58 21	13♈07 21	1 14.9	4 36.0	28 26.7	1 30.9	14 39.9	1 34.8	12 10.1	22 14.9	5 56.8	4 02.4
19 Sa	19 52 16	28 37 33	20 12 14	27 12 48	1D 14.2	5 09.2	28R 30.0	1 41.4	15 02.9	1 33.3	12 05.4	22 18.1	5 55.1	4 01.3
20 Su	19 56 13	29 38 36	4♉08 58	11♉00 44	1 14.6	5 47.7	28 30.8	1 51.3	15 25.7	1 31.9	12 00.7	22 21.4	5 53.4	4 00.3
21 M	20 00 10	0♒39 39	17 48 11	24 31 27	1 16.0	6 31.0	28 29.1	2 00.7	15 48.5	1 30.8	11 56.0	22 24.6	5 51.7	3 59.2
22 Tu	20 04 06	1 40 41	1♊10 42	7♊46 07	1 17.7	7 18.7	28 24.9	2 09.4	16 11.1	1 29.9	11 51.2	22 27.9	5 50.1	3 58.1
23 W	20 08 03	2 41 42	14 17 55	20 46 19	1R 19.1	8 10.2	28 18.2	2 17.6	16 33.7	1 29.1	11 46.4	22 31.2	5 48.4	3 57.1
24 Th	20 11 59	3 42 42	27 11 30	3♋33 39	1 19.5	9 05.4	28 08.9	2 25.1	16 56.2	1 28.6	11 41.6	22 34.6	5 46.7	3 56.0
25 F	20 15 56	4 43 41	9♋52 56	16 09 31	1 18.4	10 03.7	27 57.1	2 32.0	17 18.6	1 28.3	11 36.7	22 37.9	5 45.0	3 55.0
26 Sa	20 19 52	5 44 39	22 23 32	28 35 06	1 15.5	11 05.0	27 42.7	2 38.3	17 40.8	1D 28.2	11 31.9	22 41.3	5 43.3	3 54.0
27 Su	20 23 49	6 45 36	4♌44 21	10♌51 23	1 10.8	12 08.9	27 25.9	2 43.9	18 03.0	1 28.3	11 27.0	22 44.6	5 41.6	3 53.0
28 M	20 27 46	7 46 32	16 56 21	22 59 23	1 04.6	13 15.2	27 06.7	2 48.8	18 25.1	1 28.6	11 22.1	22 48.0	5 39.9	3 52.0
29 Tu	20 31 42	8 47 28	29 00 38	5♍00 17	0 57.4	14 23.7	26 45.1	2 53.1	18 47.1	1 29.1	11 17.2	22 51.4	5 38.2	3 51.0
30 W	20 35 39	9 48 22	10♍58 33	16 55 42	0 49.8	15 34.2	26 21.2	2 56.6	19 08.9	1 29.8	11 12.3	22 54.8	5 36.5	3 50.1
31 Th	20 39 35	10 49 16	22 52 00	28 47 48	0 42.7	16 46.6	25 55.2	2 59.5	19 30.7	1 30.7	11 07.4	22 58.2	5 34.9	3 49.1

LONGITUDE — February 1918

Day	Sid.Time	☉	0 hr ☽	Noon ☽	True ☊	☿	♀	♂	⚳	♃	♄	♅	♆	♇
1 F	20 43 32	11♒50 08	4♎43 28	10♎39 27	0♑36.7	18♑00.7	25♒27.2	3♎01.7	19♐52.4	1♊31.8	11♌02.5	23♒01.6	5♌33.2	3♋48.2
2 Sa	20 47 28	12 51 00	16 36 10	22 34 09	0R 32.5	19 16.4	24R 57.3	3 03.1	20 13.9	1 33.1	10R 57.6	23 05.0	5R 31.5	3R 47.3
3 Su	20 51 25	13 51 51	28 33 56	4♏36 06	0D 30.1	20 33.6	24 25.8	3R 03.8	20 35.4	1 34.6	10 52.7	23 08.5	5 29.8	3 46.3
4 M	20 55 21	14 52 41	10♏41 13	16 49 54	0 29.6	21 52.2	23 52.7	3 03.8	20 56.7	1 36.3	10 47.8	23 11.9	5 28.2	3 45.5
5 Tu	20 59 18	15 53 30	23 02 46	29 20 26	0 30.4	23 12.2	23 18.4	3 03.0	21 17.9	1 38.3	10 42.9	23 15.3	5 26.5	3 44.6
6 W	21 03 15	16 54 19	5♐43 27	12♐12 23	0 31.8	24 33.3	22 43.0	3 01.5	21 39.0	1 40.4	10 38.0	23 18.8	5 24.8	3 43.7
7 Th	21 07 11	17 55 06	18 47 41	25 29 44	0R 32.8	25 55.7	22 06.7	2 59.2	22 00.0	1 42.7	10 33.2	23 22.3	5 23.2	3 42.9
8 F	21 11 08	18 55 53	2♑18 48	9♑15 01	0 32.6	27 19.1	21 29.9	2 56.1	22 20.8	1 45.2	10 28.3	23 25.7	5 21.6	3 42.1
9 Sa	21 15 04	19 56 38	16 18 19	23 28 30	0 30.4	28 43.7	20 52.8	2 52.2	22 41.6	1 47.9	10 23.5	23 29.2	5 19.9	3 41.3
10 Su	21 19 01	20 57 22	0♒45 06	8♒07 28	0 25.8	0♒09.3	20 15.5	2 47.6	23 02.2	1 50.8	10 18.7	23 32.7	5 18.3	3 40.5
11 M	21 22 57	21 58 05	15 34 46	23 05 56	0 19.2	1 35.9	19 38.4	2 42.1	23 22.6	1 53.9	10 13.9	23 36.1	5 16.7	3 39.7
12 Tu	21 26 54	22 58 46	0♓39 48	8♓15 04	0 11.0	3 03.6	19 01.8	2 35.9	23 43.0	1 57.2	10 09.2	23 39.6	5 15.1	3 39.0
13 W	21 30 50	23 59 26	15 50 23	23 24 25	0 02.4	4 32.1	18 25.8	2 28.9	24 03.2	2 00.7	10 04.5	23 43.1	5 13.5	3 38.3
14 Th	21 34 47	25 00 04	0♈55 57	8♈23 51	29♐54.5	6 01.7	17 50.6	2 21.1	24 23.2	2 04.3	9 59.8	23 46.5	5 11.9	3 37.6
15 F	21 38 44	26 00 41	15 47 09	23 05 08	29 48.2	7 32.2	17 16.6	2 12.5	24 43.2	2 08.2	9 55.2	23 50.0	5 10.3	3 36.9
16 Sa	21 42 40	27 01 16	0♉17 14	7♉23 07	29 44.2	9 03.6	16 44.0	2 03.1	25 03.0	2 12.2	9 50.6	23 53.5	5 08.8	3 36.2
17 Su	21 46 37	28 01 49	14 22 38	21 15 48	29D 42.4	10 35.9	16 12.9	1 52.9	25 22.6	2 16.5	9 46.1	23 57.0	5 07.3	3 35.6
18 M	21 50 33	29 02 20	28 02 47	4♊43 51	29 42.3	12 09.2	15 43.4	1 42.0	25 42.1	2 20.9	9 41.6	24 00.4	5 05.7	3 34.9
19 Tu	21 54 30	0♓02 49	11♊19 21	17 49 43	29R 43.1	13 43.3	15 15.9	1 30.3	26 01.5	2 25.5	9 37.1	24 03.9	5 04.2	3 34.3
20 W	21 58 26	1 03 17	24 15 22	0♋36 46	29 43.5	15 18.5	14 50.3	1 17.9	26 20.7	2 30.2	9 32.7	24 07.3	5 02.7	3 33.7
21 Th	22 02 23	2 03 43	6♋54 23	13 08 38	29 42.5	16 54.5	14 27.0	1 04.7	26 39.7	2 35.2	9 28.4	24 10.8	5 01.3	3 33.2
22 F	22 06 19	3 04 07	19 19 57	25 28 40	29 39.3	18 31.5	14 05.8	0 50.8	26 58.6	2 40.3	9 24.1	24 14.2	4 59.8	3 32.6
23 Sa	22 10 16	4 04 29	1♌35 10	7♌39 44	29 33.4	20 09.5	13 47.0	0 36.2	27 17.4	2 45.6	9 19.8	24 17.7	4 58.4	3 32.1
24 Su	22 14 13	5 04 49	13 42 37	19 44 03	29 24.6	21 48.4	13 30.6	0 20.8	27 36.0	2 51.0	9 15.7	24 21.1	4 56.9	3 31.6
25 M	22 18 09	6 05 07	25 44 15	1♍43 23	29 13.4	23 28.3	13 16.6	0 04.8	27 54.4	2 56.7	9 11.6	24 24.5	4 55.5	3 31.1
26 Tu	22 22 06	7 05 24	7♍41 36	13 39 04	29 00.5	25 09.2	13 05.1	29♍48.1	28 12.7	3 02.4	9 07.5	24 27.9	4 54.2	3 30.6
27 W	22 26 02	8 05 39	19 35 55	25 32 20	28 47.0	26 51.1	12 56.1	29 30.7	28 30.8	3 08.4	9 03.5	24 31.3	4 52.8	3 30.2
28 Th	22 29 59	9 05 52	1♎28 30	7♎24 36	28 34.1	28 34.0	12 49.6	29 12.7	28 48.7	3 14.5	8 59.6	24 34.7	4 51.4	3 29.8

Astro Data

	Dy Hr Mn
☽ 0S	3 6:46
☿ D	14 6:33
☽ 0N	16 18:30
♀ R	20 7:51
♃ D	26 12:48
☽ 0S	30 14:44
♂ R	3 23:02
☽ 0N	13 4:02
☽ 0S	26 21:48

Planet Ingress

	Dy Hr Mn
♂ ♎	11 8:55
☉ ♒	20 20:25
☿ ♒	10 9:24
☊ ♐R	13 18:58
☉ ♓	19 10:53
♂ ♍R	25 19:00

Last Aspect / ☽ Ingress (January)

Last Aspect Dy Hr Mn		☽ Ingress	Dy Hr Mn
1 2:25	♀ ☍	♍	1 18:23
4 2:57	♂ ☌	♎	4 6:56
6 8:48	♀ △	♏	6 18:50
9 2:55	♂ ⚹	♐	9 3:58
11 4:04	♀ ⚹	♑	11 9:27
12 22:35	☉ ☌	♒	13 11:55
15 9:41	♀ ☌	♓	15 12:54
17 8:08	☉ ⚹	♈	17 14:03
19 14:38	☉ □	♉	19 16:48
21 19:06	♀ □	♊	21 21:52
24 1:56	♀ △	♋	24 5:17
24 23:21	☿ ☍	♌	26 14:45
28 19:59	♀ ☍	♍	29 1:59
30 8:57	☿ △	♎	31 14:26

Last Aspect / ☽ Ingress (February)

Last Aspect Dy Hr Mn		☽ Ingress	Dy Hr Mn
2 16:35	♀ △	♏	3 2:52
5 1:00	♀ □	♐	5 13:15
7 8:12	♅ ⚹	♑	7 19:57
9 21:37	☿ ☌	♒	9 22:46
11 12:48	♅ ☌	♓	11 22:57
12 4:44	♇ △	♈	13 22:31
15 17:13	☉ ⚹	♉	15 23:31
18 0:56	☉ □	♊	18 3:29
19 23:42	♅ △	♋	20 10:50
20 17:36	♇ ☌	♌	22 20:53
24 21:16	♅ ☍	♍	25 8:33
27 19:50	♂ ☌	♎	27 21:01

☽ Phases & Eclipses

Dy Hr Mn	
5 11:49	☾ 14♎21
12 22:35	● 21♑57
19 14:38	☽ 28♈44
27 3:14	○ 6♌23
4 7:51	☾ 14♏42
11 10:04	● 21♒53
18 0:56	☽ 28♉34
25 21:34	○ 6♍29

Astro Data

1 January 1918
Julian Day # 6575
SVP 6♓23'59"
GC 25♐41.6 ⚵ 24♏41.2
Eris 27♓21.1 ⚴ 26♒01.9
⚷ 25♓42.0 ⚶ 4♈26.3
☽ Mean ☊ 1♑01.0

1 February 1918
Julian Day # 6606
SVP 6♓23'54"
GC 25♐41.7 ⚵ 6♐04.1
Eris 27♓33.1 ⚴ 10♓35.3
⚷ 26♓46.9 ⚶ 14♈36.2
☽ Mean ☊ 29♐22.5

March 1918 LONGITUDE

Day	Sid.Time	☉	0 hr ☽	Noon ☽	True ☊	☿	♀	♂	⚳	♃	♄	♅	♆	♇
1 F	22 33 55	10♓06 03	13♎20 52	19♎17 36	28♐22.6	0♓17.9	12♒45.5	28♍54.1	29♐06.5	3♊20.8	8♌55.8	24♒38.1	4♌50.1	3♋29.4
2 Sa	22 37 52	11 06 13	25 15 07	1♏13 45	28R13.6	2 02.9	12D44.0	28R35.0	29 24.1	3 27.2	8R52.0	24 41.5	4R48.8	3R29.0
3 Su	22 41 48	12 06 22	7♏13 55	13 16 06	28 07.3	3 49.0	12 44.8	28 15.2	29 41.6	3 33.9	8 48.3	24 44.8	4 47.5	3 28.6
4 M	22 45 45	13 06 29	19 20 45	25 28 26	28 03.8	5 36.1	12 48.1	27 55.0	29 58.8	3 40.6	8 44.7	24 48.2	4 46.3	3 28.3
5 Tu	22 49 41	14 06 34	1♐39 42	7♐55 09	28D02.5	7 24.4	12 53.7	27 34.2	0♑15.9	3 47.5	8 41.1	24 51.5	4 45.0	3 28.0
6 W	22 53 38	15 06 38	14 15 23	20 40 58	28R02.4	9 13.7	13 01.6	27 13.0	0 32.8	3 54.6	8 37.7	24 54.8	4 43.8	3 27.7
7 Th	22 57 35	16 06 40	27 12 29	3♑50 26	28 02.4	11 04.1	13 11.7	26 51.3	0 49.5	4 01.8	8 34.3	24 58.1	4 42.6	3 27.5
8 F	23 01 31	17 06 41	10♑35 17	17 27 20	28 01.2	12 55.5	13 24.0	26 29.3	1 06.0	4 09.2	8 31.0	25 01.4	4 41.5	3 27.2
9 Sa	23 05 28	18 06 40	24 26 48	1♒33 40	27 57.9	14 48.1	13 38.4	26 06.9	1 22.3	4 16.7	8 27.8	25 04.7	4 40.3	3 27.0
10 Su	23 09 24	19 06 37	8♒47 47	16 08 43	27 51.8	16 41.7	13 54.9	25 44.2	1 38.5	4 24.3	8 24.7	25 07.9	4 39.2	3 26.8
11 M	23 13 21	20 06 32	23 35 49	1♓08 12	27 43.0	18 36.4	14 13.3	25 21.2	1 54.4	4 32.1	8 21.6	25 11.2	4 38.1	3 26.6
12 Tu	23 17 17	21 06 26	8♓44 43	16 24 05	27 32.3	20 32.0	14 33.6	24 58.1	2 10.1	4 40.1	8 18.7	25 14.4	4 37.0	3 26.5
13 W	23 21 14	22 06 18	24 04 50	1♈45 29	27 20.8	22 28.6	14 55.8	24 34.7	2 25.6	4 48.2	8 15.8	25 17.6	4 36.0	3 26.4
14 Th	23 25 10	23 06 07	9♈24 30	17 00 29	27 09.9	24 26.1	15 19.7	24 11.2	2 40.9	4 56.4	8 13.0	25 20.8	4 35.0	3 26.3
15 F	23 29 07	24 05 55	24 32 09	1♉58 25	27 00.9	26 24.4	15 45.4	23 47.6	2 56.0	5 04.7	8 10.4	25 23.9	4 34.0	3 26.2
16 Sa	23 33 04	25 05 40	9♉18 26	16 31 35	26 54.5	28 23.4	16 12.7	23 24.0	3 10.9	5 13.2	8 07.8	25 27.0	4 33.0	3 26.1
17 Su	23 37 00	26 05 24	23 37 31	0♊36 05	26 50.8	0♈22.9	16 41.5	23 00.4	3 25.6	5 21.8	8 05.3	25 30.2	4 32.1	3D26.1
18 M	23 40 57	27 05 05	7♊27 20	14 11 29	26D49.4	2 22.8	17 11.9	22 36.9	3 40.0	5 30.6	8 02.9	25 33.3	4 31.2	3 26.1
19 Tu	23 44 53	28 04 43	20 48 54	27 20 00	26R49.2	4 23.0	17 43.8	22 13.4	3 54.3	5 39.5	8 00.7	25 36.3	4 30.3	3 26.1
20 W	23 48 50	29 04 20	3♋45 20	10♋05 27	26 49.0	6 23.1	18 17.0	21 50.2	4 08.3	5 48.5	7 58.5	25 39.4	4 29.5	3 26.1
21 Th	23 52 46	0♈03 54	16 20 56	22 32 21	26 47.5	8 23.0	18 51.6	21 27.1	4 22.0	5 57.6	7 56.4	25 42.4	4 28.7	3 26.2
22 F	23 56 43	1 03 26	28 40 18	4♌45 18	26 43.9	10 22.4	19 27.6	21 04.2	4 35.6	6 06.9	7 54.4	25 45.4	4 27.9	3 26.3
23 Sa	0 00 39	2 02 55	10♌47 52	16 48 28	26 37.5	12 20.9	20 04.7	20 41.6	4 48.8	6 16.2	7 52.5	25 48.3	4 27.1	3 26.4
24 Su	0 04 36	3 02 23	22 47 31	28 45 24	26 28.2	14 18.3	20 43.1	20 19.4	5 01.9	6 25.7	7 50.8	25 51.3	4 26.4	3 26.5
25 M	0 08 33	4 01 48	4♍42 27	10♍38 57	26 16.3	16 14.0	21 22.7	19 57.5	5 14.7	6 35.3	7 49.1	25 54.2	4 25.7	3 26.7
26 Tu	0 12 29	5 01 11	16 35 09	22 31 17	26 02.6	18 07.9	22 03.3	19 36.0	5 27.3	6 45.0	7 47.5	25 57.1	4 25.0	3 26.9
27 W	0 16 26	6 00 31	28 27 31	4♎24 01	25 48.3	19 59.3	22 45.1	19 14.9	5 39.6	6 54.8	7 46.1	25 59.9	4 24.4	3 27.1
28 Th	0 20 22	6 59 50	10♎20 58	16 18 31	25 34.4	21 48.0	23 27.9	18 54.2	5 51.7	7 04.8	7 44.7	26 02.8	4 23.8	3 27.3
29 F	0 24 19	7 59 07	22 16 49	28 16 03	25 22.1	23 33.4	24 11.6	18 34.1	6 03.5	7 14.8	7 43.5	26 05.6	4 23.2	3 27.5
30 Sa	0 28 15	8 58 22	4♏16 25	10♏18 09	25 12.2	25 15.3	24 56.4	18 14.5	6 15.1	7 24.9	7 42.3	26 08.3	4 22.7	3 27.8
31 Su	0 32 12	9 57 35	16 21 30	22 26 46	25 05.3	26 53.2	25 42.0	17 55.4	6 26.4	7 35.2	7 41.3	26 11.1	4 22.2	3 28.1

April 1918 LONGITUDE

Day	Sid.Time	☉	0 hr ☽	Noon ☽	True ☊	☿	♀	♂	⚳	♃	♄	♅	♆	♇
1 M	0 36 08	10♈56 46	28♏34 19	4♐44 30	25♐01.2	28♈26.7	26♒28.6	17♍37.0	6♑37.4	7♊45.5	7♌40.4	26♒13.8	4♌21.7	3♋28.4
2 Tu	0 40 05	11 55 56	10♐57 45	17 14 32	24D59.5	29 55.5	27 16.0	17R19.1	6 48.1	7 56.0	7R39.5	26 16.5	4R21.3	3 28.8
3 W	0 44 02	12 55 03	23 35 18	0♑00 34	24 59.3	1♉19.3	28 04.2	17 01.9	6 58.6	8 06.5	7 38.8	26 19.1	4 20.8	3 29.1
4 Th	0 47 58	13 54 09	6♑30 49	13 06 32	24R59.6	2 37.8	28 53.1	16 45.3	7 08.8	8 17.2	7 38.2	26 21.7	4 20.5	3 29.5
5 F	0 51 55	14 53 13	19 48 08	26 36 00	24 59.1	3 50.8	29 42.9	16 29.4	7 18.8	8 27.9	7 37.7	26 24.3	4 20.1	3 29.9
6 Sa	0 55 51	15 52 16	3♒30 24	10♒31 29	24 56.8	4 58.0	0♓33.3	16 14.2	7 28.4	8 38.8	7 37.3	26 26.9	4 19.8	3 30.3
7 Su	0 59 48	16 51 16	17 39 15	24 53 30	24 52.1	5 59.2	1 24.5	15 59.7	7 37.8	8 49.7	7 37.1	26 29.4	4 19.5	3 30.8
8 M	1 03 44	17 50 15	2♓13 50	9♓39 38	24 45.0	6 54.3	2 16.3	15 45.9	7 46.8	9 00.7	7 36.9	26 31.8	4 19.3	3 31.3
9 Tu	1 07 41	18 49 12	17 10 05	24 44 07	24 36.1	7 43.1	3 08.7	15 32.9	7 55.6	9 11.9	7D36.8	26 34.3	4 19.0	3 31.8
10 W	1 11 37	19 48 07	2♈20 33	9♈58 03	24 26.3	8 25.6	4 01.8	15 20.6	8 04.0	9 23.1	7 36.9	26 36.7	4 18.8	3 32.3
11 Th	1 15 34	20 47 00	17 35 12	25 10 37	24 16.8	9 01.7	4 55.4	15 09.1	8 12.2	9 34.3	7 37.0	26 39.1	4 18.7	3 32.8
12 F	1 19 30	21 45 51	2♉42 58	10♉11 03	24 08.9	9 31.3	5 49.6	14 58.4	8 20.0	9 45.7	7 37.3	26 41.4	4 18.6	3 33.4
13 Sa	1 23 27	22 44 41	17 33 51	24 50 31	24 03.3	9 54.4	6 44.3	14 48.4	8 27.5	9 57.2	7 37.7	26 43.7	4 18.5	3 34.0
14 Su	1 27 24	23 43 28	2♊00 27	9♊03 18	24 00.2	10 11.0	7 39.6	14 39.3	8 34.7	10 08.7	7 38.2	26 46.0	4D18.4	3 34.6
15 M	1 31 20	24 42 13	15 58 52	22 47 11	23D59.2	10 21.2	8 35.4	14 31.0	8 41.6	10 20.3	7 38.8	26 48.2	4 18.4	3 35.2
16 Tu	1 35 17	25 40 55	29 28 26	6♋02 57	23 59.6	10R25.2	9 31.6	14 23.4	8 48.2	10 32.0	7 39.5	26 50.4	4 18.4	3 35.8
17 W	1 39 13	26 39 36	12♋31 08	18 53 30	24R00.5	10 23.1	10 28.3	14 16.7	8 54.5	10 43.8	7 40.3	26 52.5	4 18.5	3 36.5
18 Th	1 43 10	27 38 14	25 10 37	1♌23 04	24 00.6	10 15.1	11 25.4	14 10.7	9 00.4	10 55.7	7 41.2	26 54.6	4 18.6	3 37.2
19 F	1 47 06	28 36 50	7♌31 27	13 36 24	23 59.3	10 01.5	12 23.0	14 05.6	9 06.0	11 07.6	7 42.2	26 56.7	4 18.7	3 37.9
20 Sa	1 51 03	29 35 23	19 38 29	25 38 18	23 55.9	9 42.7	13 21.0	14 01.2	9 11.2	11 19.6	7 43.4	26 58.7	4 18.8	3 38.6
21 Su	1 54 59	0♉33 55	1♍36 21	7♍33 11	23 50.2	9 19.1	14 19.4	13 57.6	9 16.1	11 31.6	7 44.6	27 00.7	4 19.0	3 39.4
22 M	1 58 56	1 32 24	13 29 14	19 24 56	23 42.6	8 51.3	15 18.2	13 54.8	9 20.7	11 43.7	7 46.0	27 02.6	4 19.2	3 40.1
23 Tu	2 02 53	2 30 51	25 20 40	1♎16 46	23 33.6	8 19.7	16 17.4	13 52.8	9 24.9	11 55.9	7 47.4	27 04.5	4 19.5	3 40.9
24 W	2 06 49	3 29 17	7♎13 32	13 11 13	23 23.9	7 45.1	17 17.0	13 51.5	9 28.8	12 08.2	7 49.0	27 06.4	4 19.8	3 41.7
25 Th	2 10 46	4 27 40	19 10 03	25 10 13	23 14.6	7 08.1	18 16.9	13D51.0	9 32.4	12 20.5	7 50.7	27 08.2	4 20.1	3 42.6
26 F	2 14 42	5 26 02	1♏11 54	7♏15 16	23 06.3	6 29.4	19 17.1	13 51.2	9 35.5	12 32.9	7 52.4	27 10.0	4 20.4	3 43.4
27 Sa	2 18 39	6 24 21	13 20 27	19 27 36	22 59.8	5 49.7	20 17.7	13 52.2	9 38.4	12 45.3	7 54.3	27 11.7	4 20.8	3 44.3
28 Su	2 22 35	7 22 40	25 36 54	1♐48 29	22 55.5	5 09.7	21 18.6	13 53.9	9 40.9	12 57.8	7 56.3	27 13.4	4 21.2	3 45.2
29 M	2 26 32	8 20 56	8♐02 33	14 19 18	22D53.4	4 30.3	22 19.8	13 56.3	9 43.0	13 10.4	7 58.4	27 15.0	4 21.7	3 46.1
30 Tu	2 30 28	9 19 11	20 38 57	27 01 47	22 53.1	3 52.0	23 21.4	13 59.4	9 44.8	13 23.0	8 00.6	27 16.6	4 22.1	3 47.0

Astro Data	Dy Hr Mn
♀ D	2 15:24
♃⊻♇	2 18:04
♃✶♆	12 3:56
☽ 0N	12 15:17
♇ D	18 6:18
☿ 0N	18 8:07
☉ 0N	21 10:26
☽ 0S	26 3:50
♃✶♄	1 0:58
☽ 0N	9 1:51
♄ D	9 13:34
♆ D	15 11:59
☿ R	16 15:29
☽ 0S	22 9:31
♂ D	25 16:44

Planet Ingress		Dy Hr Mn
☿	♓	1 7:52
⚳	♑	4 13:40
☿	♈	17 7:24
☉	♈	21 10:26
☿	♉	2 13:15
♀	♓	5 20:11
☉	♉	20 22:05

Last Aspect Dy Hr Mn			☽ Ingress	Dy Hr Mn
1 22:49	♅	△	♏	2 9:32
4 16:37	♂	✶	♐	4 20:47
6 23:42	♂	□	♑	7 5:05
9 3:04	♂	△	♒	9 9:23
11 2:30	♅	☌	♓	11 10:12
13 1:03	♂	☍	♈	13 9:15
15 1:21	♅	✶	♉	15 8:48
17 3:37	☉	✶	♊	17 10:57
19 13:30	☉	□	♋	19 16:58
21 9:57	♂	✶	♌	22 2:37
24 6:08	♅	☍	♍	24 14:30
26 6:16	♂	☌	♎	27 3:07
29 7:38	♅	△	♏	29 15:28

Last Aspect Dy Hr Mn			☽ Ingress	Dy Hr Mn
31 19:22	♅	□	♐	1 2:47
3 8:09	♀	✶	♑	3 11:59
4 18:26	♂	△	♒	5 17:56
7 14:38	♅	☌	♓	7 20:22
8 21:37	♂	☍	♈	9 20:19
11 14:21	♅	✶	♉	11 19:40
13 15:09	♅	□	♊	13 20:37
15 19:12	♅	△	♋	16 0:57
18 4:07	☉	□	♌	18 9:19
20 20:39	☉	△	♍	20 20:46
22 2:55	♀	☍	♎	23 9:25
25 15:56	♅	△	♏	25 21:37
28 3:06	♅	□	♐	28 8:30
30 12:28	♅	✶	♑	30 17:33

☽ Phases & Eclipses Dy Hr Mn		
6 0:43	☾	14♐38
12 19:52	●	21♓26
19 13:30	☽	28♊08
27 15:32	○	6♎09
4 13:33	☾	13♑58
11 4:34	●	20♈29
18 4:07	☽	27♋19
26 8:05	○	5♏17

Astro Data

1 March 1918
Julian Day # 6634
SVP 6♓23'51"
GC 25♐41.8 ⚵ 14♐09.3
Eris 27♓51.4 ⚴ 24♓54.0
⚷ 28♓14.4 ⚶ 25♈28.0
☽ Mean ☊ 27♐53.5

1 April 1918
Julian Day # 6665
SVP 6♓23'48"
GC 25♐41.9 ⚵ 18♐59.0
Eris 28♓14.9 ⚴ 11♈39.1
⚷ 0♈03.7 ⚶ 8♉27.8
☽ Mean ☊ 26♐15.0

LONGITUDE — May 1918

Day	Sid.Time	☉	0 hr ☽	Noon ☽	True ☊	☿	♀	♂	⚳	♃	♄	♅	♆	♇
1 W	2 34 25	10♉17 24	3♑28 02	9♑58 00	22♐54.0	3♉15.5	24♓23.2	14♍03.2	9♑46.2	13♊35.6	8♌02.8	27♒18.2	4♌22.6	3♋47.9
2 Th	2 38 22	11 15 36	16 31 59	23 10 15	22 55.4	2R 41.4	25 25.3	14 07.7	9 47.2	13 48.4	8 05.2	27 19.7	4 23.2	3 48.9
3 F	2 42 18	12 13 46	29 53 04	6♒40 41	22R 56.4	2 10.3	26 27.7	14 12.9	9 47.9	14 01.1	8 07.7	27 21.2	4 23.8	3 49.8
4 Sa	2 46 15	13 11 55	13♒33 15	20 30 54	22 56.3	1 42.5	27 30.3	14 18.8	9R 48.1	14 14.0	8 10.3	27 22.6	4 24.4	3 50.8
5 Su	2 50 11	14 10 02	27 33 36	4♓41 14	22 54.7	1 18.5	28 33.2	14 25.3	9 48.1	14 26.8	8 13.0	27 23.9	4 25.0	3 51.8
6 M	2 54 08	15 08 08	11♓53 35	19 10 13	22 51.4	0 58.6	29 36.4	14 32.4	9 47.6	14 39.8	8 15.8	27 25.3	4 25.7	3 52.9
7 Tu	2 58 04	16 06 13	26 30 37	3♈54 03	22 46.9	0 43.0	0♈39.7	14 40.2	9 46.8	14 52.7	8 18.6	27 26.6	4 26.4	3 53.9
8 W	3 02 01	17 04 16	11♈19 41	18 46 35	22 41.7	0 31.8	1 43.4	14 48.7	9 45.6	15 05.7	8 21.6	27 27.8	4 27.1	3 54.9
9 Th	3 05 57	18 02 18	26 13 42	3♉39 59	22 36.6	0D 25.3	2 47.2	14 57.8	9 44.0	15 18.8	8 24.7	27 29.0	4 27.9	3 56.0
10 F	3 09 54	19 00 18	11♉04 22	18 25 49	22 32.4	0 23.4	3 51.2	15 07.4	9 42.0	15 31.9	8 27.8	27 30.1	4 28.7	3 57.1
11 Sa	3 13 51	19 58 17	25 43 24	2♊56 20	22 29.5	0 26.1	4 55.5	15 17.7	9 39.7	15 45.1	8 31.1	27 31.2	4 29.5	3 58.2
12 Su	3 17 47	20 56 14	10♊03 55	17 05 40	22D 28.3	0 33.6	5 59.9	15 28.6	9 37.0	15 58.2	8 34.5	27 32.3	4 30.4	3 59.3
13 M	3 21 44	21 54 10	24 01 14	0♋50 26	22 28.4	0 45.6	7 04.6	15 40.1	9 33.9	16 11.5	8 37.9	27 33.3	4 31.3	4 00.5
14 Tu	3 25 40	22 52 04	7♋33 15	14 09 46	22 29.5	1 02.1	8 09.4	15 52.1	9 30.5	16 24.7	8 41.5	27 34.2	4 32.2	4 01.6
15 W	3 29 37	23 49 56	20 40 15	27 05 00	22 31.1	1 23.0	9 14.4	16 04.7	9 26.6	16 38.0	8 45.1	27 35.1	4 33.2	4 02.8
16 Th	3 33 33	24 47 46	3♌24 26	9♌39 02	22 32.6	1 48.3	10 19.6	16 17.9	9 22.4	16 51.4	8 48.8	27 36.0	4 34.1	4 04.0
17 F	3 37 30	25 45 35	15 49 20	21 55 53	22R 33.4	2 17.7	11 24.9	16 31.6	9 17.9	17 04.7	8 52.6	27 36.8	4 35.1	4 05.1
18 Sa	3 41 26	26 43 22	27 59 15	4♍00 02	22 33.2	2 51.3	12 30.5	16 45.8	9 12.9	17 18.1	8 56.5	27 37.5	4 36.2	4 06.3
19 Su	3 45 23	27 41 07	9♍58 48	15 56 09	22 31.9	3 28.8	13 36.1	17 00.5	9 07.6	17 31.5	9 00.5	27 38.2	4 37.3	4 07.6
20 M	3 49 20	28 38 51	21 52 36	27 48 42	22 29.6	4 10.1	14 42.0	17 15.7	9 02.0	17 45.0	9 04.6	27 38.9	4 38.4	4 08.8
21 Tu	3 53 16	29 36 33	3♎44 57	9♎41 49	22 26.5	4 55.1	15 48.0	17 31.4	8 56.0	17 58.5	9 08.8	27 39.5	4 39.5	4 10.0
22 W	3 57 13	0♊34 13	15 39 43	21 39 03	22 23.0	5 43.7	16 54.1	17 47.6	8 49.7	18 12.0	9 13.0	27 40.1	4 40.6	4 11.3
23 Th	4 01 09	1 31 52	27 40 09	3♏43 21	22 19.6	6 35.8	18 00.4	18 04.3	8 43.0	18 25.5	9 17.3	27 40.6	4 41.8	4 12.5
24 F	4 05 06	2 29 30	9♏48 53	15 57 01	22 16.6	7 31.3	19 06.8	18 21.4	8 35.9	18 39.1	9 21.7	27 41.0	4 43.0	4 13.8
25 Sa	4 09 02	3 27 07	22 07 54	28 21 42	22 14.4	8 30.1	20 13.4	18 39.0	8 28.5	18 52.7	9 26.2	27 41.5	4 44.3	4 15.1
26 Su	4 12 59	4 24 42	4♐38 32	10♐58 30	22D 13.2	9 32.1	21 20.1	18 57.0	8 20.8	19 06.3	9 30.8	27 41.8	4 45.5	4 16.4
27 M	4 16 55	5 22 16	17 21 40	23 48 05	22 12.9	10 37.2	22 27.0	19 15.5	8 12.8	19 19.9	9 35.4	27 42.2	4 46.8	4 17.7
28 Tu	4 20 52	6 19 49	0♑17 47	6♑50 48	22 13.3	11 45.3	23 34.0	19 34.4	8 04.5	19 33.6	9 40.2	27 42.4	4 48.2	4 19.0
29 W	4 24 49	7 17 22	13 27 08	20 06 48	22 14.3	12 56.4	24 41.1	19 53.7	7 55.8	19 47.2	9 45.0	27 42.7	4 49.5	4 20.4
30 Th	4 28 45	8 14 53	26 49 48	3♒36 08	22 15.4	14 10.4	25 48.3	20 13.4	7 46.8	20 00.9	9 49.9	27 42.8	4 50.9	4 21.7
31 F	4 32 42	9 12 23	10♒25 46	17 18 39	22 16.4	15 27.3	26 55.7	20 33.5	7 37.6	20 14.6	9 54.8	27 43.0	4 52.3	4 23.1

LONGITUDE — June 1918

Day	Sid.Time	☉	0 hr ☽	Noon ☽	True ☊	☿	♀	♂	⚳	♃	♄	♅	♆	♇
1 Sa	4 36 38	10♊09 53	24♒14 44	1♓13 54	22♐17.1	16♉47.0	28♈03.2	20♍54.0	7♑28.0	20♊28.3	9♌59.8	27♒43.0	4♌53.7	4♋24.4
2 Su	4 40 35	11 07 21	8♓16 01	15 20 54	22R 17.2	18 09.5	29 10.8	21 14.9	7R 18.1	20 42.0	10 05.0	27R 43.1	4 55.2	4 25.8
3 M	4 44 31	12 04 49	22 28 18	29 37 54	22 16.8	19 34.7	0♉18.5	21 36.1	7 08.0	20 55.8	10 10.1	27 43.0	4 56.6	4 27.2
4 Tu	4 48 28	13 02 17	6♈49 19	14♈02 08	22 16.0	21 02.6	1 26.3	21 57.8	6 57.6	21 09.6	10 15.4	27 43.0	4 58.1	4 28.5
5 W	4 52 24	13 59 44	21 15 49	28 29 49	22 15.1	22 33.3	2 34.3	22 19.8	6 46.9	21 23.3	10 20.7	27 42.8	4 59.6	4 29.9
6 Th	4 56 21	14 57 10	5♉43 32	12♉56 19	22 14.2	24 06.6	3 42.3	22 42.1	6 36.0	21 37.1	10 26.1	27 42.7	5 01.2	4 31.3
7 F	5 00 18	15 54 35	20 07 31	27 16 29	22 13.5	25 42.6	4 50.5	23 04.9	6 24.8	21 50.9	10 31.5	27 42.5	5 02.8	4 32.7
8 Sa	5 04 14	16 52 00	4♊22 37	11♊25 20	22D 13.2	27 21.2	5 58.7	23 27.9	6 13.5	22 04.7	10 37.1	27 42.2	5 04.4	4 34.1
9 Su	5 08 11	17 49 24	18 24 07	25 18 33	22 13.1	29 02.5	7 07.0	23 51.4	6 01.9	22 18.5	10 42.7	27 41.9	5 06.0	4 35.6
10 M	5 12 07	18 46 48	2♋08 16	8♋53 03	22 13.2	0♊46.4	8 15.5	24 15.1	5 50.1	22 32.3	10 48.3	27 41.5	5 07.6	4 37.0
11 Tu	5 16 04	19 44 10	15 32 43	22 07 13	22 13.5	2 32.8	9 24.0	24 39.2	5 38.1	22 46.1	10 54.1	27 41.1	5 09.3	4 38.4
12 W	5 20 00	20 41 31	28 36 38	5♌01 04	22 13.7	4 21.9	10 32.6	25 03.6	5 25.9	22 59.9	10 59.9	27 40.7	5 11.0	4 39.9
13 Th	5 23 57	21 38 52	11♌20 46	17 36 02	22R 13.8	6 13.4	11 41.3	25 28.3	5 13.6	23 13.8	11 05.7	27 40.2	5 12.7	4 41.3
14 F	5 27 54	22 36 12	23 47 13	29 54 45	22 13.8	8 07.4	12 50.0	25 53.4	5 01.1	23 27.6	11 11.6	27 39.6	5 14.4	4 42.8
15 Sa	5 31 50	23 33 30	5♍59 06	12♍00 47	22 13.8	10 03.8	13 58.9	26 18.7	4 48.4	23 41.4	11 17.6	27 39.0	5 16.1	4 44.2
16 Su	5 35 47	24 30 48	18 00 20	23 58 18	22D 13.7	12 02.5	15 07.8	26 44.3	4 35.7	23 55.2	11 23.6	27 38.4	5 17.9	4 45.7
17 M	5 39 43	25 28 05	29 55 16	5♎51 49	22 13.8	14 03.4	16 16.8	27 10.2	4 22.8	24 09.0	11 29.7	27 37.7	5 19.7	4 47.1
18 Tu	5 43 40	26 25 21	11♎48 30	17 45 53	22 14.0	16 06.3	17 25.9	27 36.4	4 09.9	24 22.8	11 35.9	27 36.9	5 21.5	4 48.6
19 W	5 47 36	27 22 37	23 44 32	29 44 56	22 14.5	18 11.0	18 35.1	28 02.9	3 56.8	24 36.6	11 42.1	27 36.1	5 23.3	4 50.0
20 Th	5 51 33	28 19 51	5♏47 35	11♏52 58	22 15.1	20 17.5	19 44.4	28 29.7	3 43.7	24 50.4	11 48.3	27 35.3	5 25.2	4 51.5
21 F	5 55 29	29 17 06	18 01 27	24 13 25	22 15.7	22 25.4	20 53.7	28 56.7	3 30.5	25 04.2	11 54.6	27 34.4	5 27.0	4 53.0
22 Sa	5 59 26	0♋14 19	0♐29 11	6♐48 58	22 16.3	24 34.5	22 03.1	29 24.0	3 17.3	25 18.0	12 01.0	27 33.5	5 28.9	4 54.5
23 Su	6 03 23	1 11 32	13 12 58	19 41 17	22R 16.5	26 44.6	23 12.6	29 51.5	3 04.1	25 31.7	12 07.4	27 32.6	5 30.8	4 55.9
24 M	6 07 19	2 08 45	26 13 57	2♑50 58	22 16.4	28 55.3	24 22.1	0♎19.3	2 50.8	25 45.5	12 13.9	27 31.6	5 32.7	4 57.4
25 Tu	6 11 16	3 05 58	9♑32 12	16 17 31	22 15.8	1♋06.5	25 31.8	0 47.4	2 37.6	25 59.2	12 20.4	27 30.5	5 34.6	4 58.9
26 W	6 15 12	4 03 10	23 06 39	29 59 20	22 14.6	3 17.8	26 41.5	1 15.7	2 24.4	26 13.0	12 27.0	27 29.5	5 36.6	5 00.4
27 Th	6 19 09	5 00 22	6♒55 14	13♒53 59	22 13.1	5 28.9	27 51.3	1 44.2	2 11.1	26 26.7	12 33.6	27 28.3	5 38.5	5 01.9
28 F	6 23 05	5 57 34	20 55 12	27 58 27	22 11.5	7 39.6	29 01.1	2 13.0	1 58.0	26 40.4	12 40.2	27 27.1	5 40.5	5 03.3
29 Sa	6 27 02	6 54 46	5♓03 20	12♓09 26	22 10.1	9 49.7	0♊11.1	2 42.0	1 44.9	26 54.1	12 46.9	27 25.9	5 42.5	5 04.8
30 Su	6 30 58	7 51 58	19 16 21	26 23 43	22D 09.2	11 58.8	1 21.1	3 11.2	1 31.8	27 07.7	12 53.7	27 24.7	5 44.5	5 06.3

Astro Data	Planet Ingress	Last Aspect	☽ Ingress	Last Aspect	☽ Ingress	☽ Phases & Eclipses	Astro Data
Dy Hr Mn	Dy Hr Mn	Dy Hr Mn	Dy Hr Mn	Dy Hr Mn	Dy Hr Mn	Dy Hr Mn	
⚳R 4 18:55	♀ ♈ 6 20:58	2 16:23 ♀ ⚹	♒ 3 0:12	1 6:04 ♀ ⚹	♓ 1 9:53	3 22:26 ☾ 12♒39	1 May 1918
☽0N 6 10:04	☉ ♊ 21 21:46	4 23:42 ♅ ☌	♓ 5 4:07	2 22:12 ♂ ☍	♈ 3 12:37	10 13:01 ● 19♉03	Julian Day # 6695
♀0N 9 18:53		6 4:53 ☉ ⚹	♈ 7 5:41	5 10:42 ♅ ⚹	♉ 5 14:30	17 20:14 ☽ 26♌05	SVP 6♓23'44"
☿D 10 9:46	♀ ♉ 3 5:27	9 2:01 ♅ ⚹	♉ 9 6:05	7 12:44 ♅ □	♊ 7 16:36	25 22:32 ○ 3♐52	GC 25♐41.9 ⚴ 17♐25.4R
☽0S 19 15:53	☿ ♊ 10 1:22	11 2:58 ♅ □	♊ 11 7:06	9 16:11 ♅ △	♋ 9 20:14		Eris 28♓35.4 ⚵ 28♈29.7
♃∠♆ 29 16:28	☉ ♋ 22 6:00	13 6:11 ♅ △	♋ 13 10:31	11 16:49 ♂ ⚹	♌ 12 2:35	2 4:20 ☾ 10♓49	⚷ 1♈41.9 ⚶ 21♉28.8
	♂ ♎ 23 19:19	15 5:24 ☉ ⚹	♌ 15 17:31	14 7:35 ♅ ☍	♍ 14 12:10	8 22:02 ● 17♊16	☽ Mean ☊ 24♐39.7
♅R 2 12:30	☿ ♋ 24 23:50	17 23:16 ♅ ☍	♍ 18 4:00	16 17:47 ♂ ☌	♎ 17 0:10	8 22:07:21 ● T 02'23"	
☽0N 2 16:04	♀ ♊ 29 8:12	20 13:50 ☉ △	♎ 20 16:25	19 7:43 ♅ △	♏ 19 12:30	16 13:11 ☽ 24♍34	1 June 1918
☽0S 15 23:27		23 0:00 ♅ △	♏ 23 4:38	21 21:24 ♂ ⚹	♐ 21 23:04	24 10:38 ○ 2♑05	Julian Day # 6726
♂0S 25 9:25		25 10:43 ♅ □	♐ 25 15:08	24 3:29 ♅ □	♑ 24 6:51	24 10:28 ● P 0.130	SVP 6♓23'40"
☽0N 29 21:29		27 19:13 ♅ ⚹	♑ 27 23:27	26 5:44 ♀ △	♒ 26 12:01		GC 25♐42.0 ⚴ 9♐33.2R
		29 20:55 ♀ □	♒ 30 5:38	28 13:56 ♀ □	♓ 28 15:26		Eris 28♓49.3 ⚵ 16♉17.2
				30 13:15 ♃ □	♈ 30 18:04		⚷ 2♈56.3 ⚶ 5♊01.3
							☽ Mean ☊ 23♐01.2

July 1918

LONGITUDE

Day	Sid.Time	☉	0 hr ☽	Noon ☽	True ☊	☿	♀	♂	⚳	♃	♄	♅	♆	♇
1 M	6 34 55	8♋49 10	3♈31 11	10♈38 23	22♐08.9	14♋06.9	2♊31.1	3♎40.6	1♑18.8	27♊21.4	13♌00.5	27♒23.4	5♌46.5	5♋07.8
2 Tu	6 38 52	9 46 23	17 45 02	24 50 50	22 09.3	16 13.7	3 41.3	4 10.3	1R06.0	27 35.0	13 07.3	27R22.0	5 48.5	5 09.2
3 W	6 42 48	10 43 35	1♉55 30	8♉58 47	22 10.4	18 19.1	4 51.5	4 40.2	0 53.2	27 48.6	13 14.2	27 20.7	5 50.6	5 10.7
4 Th	6 46 45	11 40 48	16 00 24	23 00 08	22 11.7	20 22.9	6 01.8	5 10.4	0 40.6	28 02.2	13 21.1	27 19.3	5 52.6	5 12.2
5 F	6 50 41	12 38 02	29 57 43	6♊52 54	22 12.8	22 25.1	7 12.1	5 40.7	0 28.1	28 15.8	13 28.1	27 17.8	5 54.7	5 13.7
6 Sa	6 54 38	13 35 15	13♊45 27	20 35 07	22R13.3	24 25.5	8 22.5	6 11.2	0 15.7	28 29.3	13 35.1	27 16.3	5 56.8	5 15.1
7 Su	6 58 34	14 32 29	27 21 40	4♋04 55	22 12.9	26 24.2	9 33.0	6 42.0	0 03.5	28 42.9	13 42.1	27 14.8	5 58.9	5 16.6
8 M	7 02 31	15 29 43	10♋44 38	17 20 41	22 11.4	28 21.0	10 43.5	7 13.0	29♐51.5	28 56.4	13 49.2	27 13.2	6 01.0	5 18.1
9 Tu	7 06 27	16 26 57	23 52 57	0♌21 20	22 08.7	0♌16.0	11 54.1	7 44.2	29 39.7	29 09.8	13 56.3	27 11.6	6 03.1	5 19.5
10 W	7 10 24	17 24 11	6♌45 48	13 06 24	22 05.1	2 09.0	13 04.8	8 15.6	29 28.1	29 23.3	14 03.4	27 10.0	6 05.2	5 21.0
11 Th	7 14 21	18 21 25	19 23 12	25 36 22	22 00.9	4 00.2	14 15.5	8 47.1	29 16.7	29 36.7	14 10.6	27 08.3	6 07.4	5 22.4
12 F	7 18 17	19 18 39	1♍46 06	7♍52 39	21 56.7	5 49.4	15 26.3	9 18.9	29 05.5	29 50.0	14 17.8	27 06.6	6 09.5	5 23.9
13 Sa	7 22 14	20 15 54	13 56 23	19 57 40	21 53.0	7 36.7	16 37.1	9 50.9	28 54.6	0♋03.4	14 25.0	27 04.9	6 11.7	5 25.3
14 Su	7 26 10	21 13 08	25 56 55	1♎54 38	21 50.2	9 22.1	17 48.0	10 23.0	28 43.9	0 16.7	14 32.3	27 03.1	6 13.8	5 26.7
15 M	7 30 07	22 10 22	7♎51 20	13 47 32	21D48.6	11 05.5	18 58.9	10 55.4	28 33.4	0 30.0	14 39.6	27 01.3	6 16.0	5 28.2
16 Tu	7 34 03	23 07 36	19 43 51	25 40 50	21 48.3	12 47.0	20 09.9	11 27.9	28 23.2	0 43.2	14 46.9	26 59.5	6 18.2	5 29.6
17 W	7 38 00	24 04 51	1♏39 08	7♏39 19	21 49.1	14 26.7	21 21.0	12 00.6	28 13.3	0 56.4	14 54.3	26 57.6	6 20.3	5 31.0
18 Th	7 41 56	25 02 06	13 42 00	19 47 47	21 50.6	16 04.4	22 32.1	12 33.5	28 03.7	1 09.6	15 01.7	26 55.7	6 22.5	5 32.4
19 F	7 45 53	25 59 21	25 57 11	2♐10 46	21 52.2	17 40.2	23 43.3	13 06.5	27 54.4	1 22.7	15 09.1	26 53.8	6 24.7	5 33.8
20 Sa	7 49 50	26 56 36	8♐28 58	14 52 13	21R53.3	19 14.0	24 54.5	13 39.7	27 45.3	1 35.8	15 16.5	26 51.8	6 26.9	5 35.2
21 Su	7 53 46	27 53 52	21 20 48	27 54 59	21 53.3	20 46.0	26 05.8	14 13.1	27 36.6	1 48.8	15 23.9	26 49.9	6 29.1	5 36.6
22 M	7 57 43	28 51 08	4♑34 52	11♑20 29	21 51.9	22 15.9	27 17.1	14 46.7	27 28.1	2 01.8	15 31.4	26 47.9	6 31.3	5 38.0
23 Tu	8 01 39	29 48 24	18 11 41	25 08 13	21 48.7	23 44.0	28 28.5	15 20.4	27 20.0	2 14.7	15 38.9	26 45.8	6 33.5	5 39.4
24 W	8 05 36	0♌45 41	2♒09 42	9♒15 37	21 44.0	25 10.0	29 40.0	15 54.3	27 12.2	2 27.6	15 46.4	26 43.8	6 35.8	5 40.7
25 Th	8 09 32	1 42 59	16 25 21	23 38 11	21 38.2	26 34.1	0♋51.5	16 28.3	27 04.8	2 40.5	15 53.9	26 41.7	6 38.0	5 42.1
26 F	8 13 29	2 40 17	0♓53 19	8♓09 57	21 32.1	27 56.1	2 03.1	17 02.5	26 57.6	2 53.3	16 01.5	26 39.6	6 40.2	5 43.4
27 Sa	8 17 25	3 37 37	15 27 14	22 44 24	21 26.6	29 16.1	3 14.7	17 36.8	26 50.8	3 06.0	16 09.0	26 37.5	6 42.4	5 44.8
28 Su	8 21 22	4 34 57	0♈00 42	7♈15 28	21 22.3	0♍33.9	4 26.4	18 11.3	26 44.3	3 18.8	16 16.6	26 35.3	6 44.6	5 46.1
29 M	8 25 19	5 32 18	14 28 07	21 38 13	21 19.7	1 49.6	5 38.1	18 46.0	26 38.2	3 31.4	16 24.2	26 33.2	6 46.9	5 47.4
30 Tu	8 29 15	6 29 41	28 45 25	5♉49 27	21D18.8	3 03.1	6 49.9	19 20.8	26 32.4	3 44.0	16 31.8	26 31.0	6 49.1	5 48.7
31 W	8 33 12	7 27 04	12♉50 09	19 47 27	21 19.3	4 14.3	8 01.8	19 55.7	26 26.9	3 56.6	16 39.4	26 28.8	6 51.3	5 50.0

August 1918

LONGITUDE

Day	Sid.Time	☉	0 hr ☽	Noon ☽	True ☊	☿	♀	♂	⚳	♃	♄	♅	♆	♇
1 Th	8 37 08	8♌24 29	26♉41 20	3♊31 49	21♐20.5	5♍23.2	9♋13.7	20♎30.8	26♐21.8	4♋09.1	16♌47.1	26♒26.5	6♌53.5	5♋51.3
2 F	8 41 05	9 21 55	10♊18 59	17 02 54	21R21.4	6 29.6	10 25.7	21 06.1	26R17.1	4 21.5	16 54.7	26R24.3	6 55.8	5 52.6
3 Sa	8 45 01	10 19 22	23 43 40	0♋21 20	21 21.1	7 33.5	11 37.8	21 41.5	26 12.7	4 33.9	17 02.4	26 22.0	6 58.0	5 53.9
4 Su	8 48 58	11 16 50	6♋55 58	13 27 39	21 18.9	8 34.7	12 49.9	22 17.1	26 08.7	4 46.2	17 10.0	26 19.8	7 00.2	5 55.1
5 M	8 52 54	12 14 20	19 56 23	26 22 12	21 14.4	9 33.3	14 02.0	22 52.8	26 05.0	4 58.5	17 17.7	26 17.5	7 02.4	5 56.4
6 Tu	8 56 51	13 11 50	2♌45 08	9♌05 09	21 07.6	10 28.9	15 14.2	23 28.6	26 01.7	5 10.7	17 25.4	26 15.2	7 04.7	5 57.6
7 W	9 00 48	14 09 21	15 22 19	21 36 37	20 59.0	11 21.6	16 26.5	24 04.6	25 58.8	5 22.8	17 33.1	26 12.9	7 06.9	5 58.8
8 Th	9 04 44	15 06 54	27 48 07	3♍56 54	20 49.2	12 11.0	17 38.8	24 40.8	25 56.2	5 34.8	17 40.8	26 10.5	7 09.1	6 00.0
9 F	9 08 41	16 04 27	10♍03 05	16 06 49	20 39.1	12 57.2	18 51.1	25 17.0	25 54.0	5 46.8	17 48.4	26 08.2	7 11.3	6 01.2
10 Sa	9 12 37	17 02 01	22 08 19	28 07 49	20 29.7	13 39.9	20 03.5	25 53.5	25 52.1	5 58.8	17 56.1	26 05.8	7 13.5	6 02.4
11 Su	9 16 34	17 59 36	4♎05 39	10♎02 11	20 21.7	14 18.9	21 16.0	26 30.0	25 50.6	6 10.6	18 03.8	26 03.5	7 15.7	6 03.5
12 M	9 20 30	18 57 12	15 57 49	21 53 01	20 15.9	14 54.1	22 28.5	27 06.7	25 49.5	6 22.4	18 11.5	26 01.1	7 17.9	6 04.7
13 Tu	9 24 27	19 54 50	27 48 17	3♏44 12	20 12.3	15 25.2	23 41.0	27 43.5	25 48.8	6 34.1	18 19.2	25 58.7	7 20.1	6 05.8
14 W	9 28 23	20 52 28	9♏41 19	15 40 17	20D10.8	15 51.9	24 53.6	28 20.4	25D48.4	6 45.7	18 26.9	25 56.3	7 22.2	6 06.9
15 Th	9 32 20	21 50 07	21 41 43	27 46 17	20 10.9	16 14.2	26 06.3	28 57.5	25 48.3	6 57.3	18 34.6	25 54.0	7 24.4	6 08.0
16 F	9 36 17	22 47 47	3♐54 37	10♐07 22	20R11.5	16 31.7	27 19.0	29 34.7	25 48.6	7 08.8	18 42.3	25 51.6	7 26.6	6 09.1
17 Sa	9 40 13	23 45 28	16 25 09	22 48 30	20 11.8	16 44.2	28 31.7	0♏12.0	25 49.3	7 20.2	18 49.9	25 49.2	7 28.7	6 10.2
18 Su	9 44 10	24 43 11	29 17 56	5♑53 51	20 10.7	16R51.6	29 44.5	0 49.5	25 50.4	7 31.5	18 57.6	25 46.8	7 30.9	6 11.2
19 M	9 48 06	25 40 54	12♑36 33	19 26 10	20 07.5	16 53.6	0♌57.4	1 27.1	25 51.7	7 42.7	19 05.3	25 44.4	7 33.0	6 12.2
20 Tu	9 52 03	26 38 39	26 22 43	3♒25 59	20 01.9	16 49.9	2 10.3	2 04.8	25 53.5	7 53.9	19 12.9	25 42.0	7 35.2	6 13.3
21 W	9 55 59	27 36 24	10♒35 37	17 51 01	19 53.9	16 40.6	3 23.2	2 42.6	25 55.5	8 05.0	19 20.6	25 39.6	7 37.3	6 14.3
22 Th	9 59 56	28 34 12	25 11 27	2♓35 57	19 44.4	16 25.4	4 36.2	3 20.5	25 57.9	8 16.0	19 28.2	25 37.2	7 39.4	6 15.3
23 F	10 03 52	29 32 00	10♓03 27	17 32 49	19 34.2	16 04.4	5 49.3	3 58.5	26 00.7	8 26.9	19 35.8	25 34.8	7 41.5	6 16.2
24 Sa	10 07 49	0♍29 50	25 02 49	2♈32 16	19 24.7	15 37.6	7 02.4	4 36.7	26 03.8	8 37.7	19 43.4	25 32.5	7 43.6	6 17.2
25 Su	10 11 46	1 27 42	10♈00 04	17 25 10	19 16.9	15 05.1	8 15.5	5 15.0	26 07.2	8 48.4	19 51.0	25 30.1	7 45.7	6 18.1
26 M	10 15 42	2 25 35	24 46 44	2♉04 04	19 11.5	14 27.2	9 28.7	5 53.4	26 10.9	8 59.0	19 58.6	25 27.7	7 47.7	6 19.0
27 Tu	10 19 39	3 23 31	9♉16 40	16 24 10	19 08.5	13 44.3	10 42.0	6 31.9	26 15.0	9 09.5	20 06.1	25 25.3	7 49.8	6 19.9
28 W	10 23 35	4 21 28	23 26 24	0♊23 21	19D07.6	12 57.0	11 55.3	7 10.5	26 19.4	9 20.0	20 13.7	25 23.0	7 51.8	6 20.8
29 Th	10 27 32	5 19 27	7♊15 06	14 01 50	19R07.6	12 05.8	13 08.6	7 49.3	26 24.1	9 30.3	20 21.2	25 20.6	7 53.9	6 21.7
30 F	10 31 28	6 17 28	20 43 47	27 21 14	19 07.5	11 11.7	14 22.0	8 28.2	26 29.2	9 40.6	20 28.7	25 18.3	7 55.9	6 22.5
31 Sa	10 35 25	7 15 31	3♋54 32	10♋23 59	19 06.0	10 15.5	15 35.5	9 07.1	26 34.5	9 50.7	20 36.2	25 16.0	7 57.9	6 23.4

Astro Data	Dy Hr Mn
♃△♅	1 15:13
♃∠♄	7 9:09
☽0S	13 7:52
☽0N	27 4:14
☽0S	9 16:07
♃☌♇	10 20:02
⚳ D	15 2:32
♃⚺♆	18 10:24
☿ R	19 8:32
☽0N	23 13:11

Planet Ingress		Dy Hr Mn
⚳	♐R	7 19:02
☿	♌	9 8:39
♃	♋	13 5:54
☉	♌	23 16:51
♀	♋	24 18:44
☿	♍	28 1:27
♂	♏	17 4:16
♀	♌	18 17:06
☉	♍	23 23:37

Last Aspect Dy Hr Mn		☽ Ingress	Dy Hr Mn
2 16:43	♃ ⚹	♉	2 20:44
4 19:26	♅ □	♊	5 0:04
7 2:15	♃ ☌	♋	7 4:42
8 8:22	☉ ☌	♌	9 11:20
11 19:56	♃ ⚹	♍	11 20:33
13 12:40	☉ ⚹	♎	14 8:09
16 14:38	♅ △	♏	16 20:41
19 1:51	♅ □	♐	19 7:49
21 10:02	♅ ⚹	♑	21 15:46
22 18:18	♂ □	♒	23 20:19
25 17:22	☿ ☍	♓	25 22:32
26 7:58	♇ △	♈	27 23:59
29 20:15	♅ ⚹	♉	30 2:06

Last Aspect Dy Hr Mn		☽ Ingress	Dy Hr Mn
31 23:36	♅ □	♊	1 5:48
3 4:47	♅ △	♋	3 11:21
5 5:10	♂ □	♌	5 18:49
7 20:53	♅ ☍	♍	8 4:17
9 18:03	♀ ⚹	♎	10 15:45
12 23:10	♂ ☌	♏	13 4:27
15 8:21	♀ △	♐	15 16:22
17 17:34	♅ ⚹	♑	18 1:17
19 7:33	☿ △	♒	20 6:11
22 5:02	☉ ☍	♓	22 7:48
23 9:42	☿ ☍	♈	24 7:56
26 1:09	♅ ⚹	♉	26 8:35
28 3:22	♅ □	♊	28 11:19
30 8:17	♅ △	♋	30 16:50

☽ Phases & Eclipses Dy Hr Mn	
1 8:43	☾ 8♈41
8 8:22	● 15♋21
16 6:24	☽ 22♎54
23 20:34	○ 0♒09
30 13:14	☾ 6♉33
6 20:29	● 13♌32
14 23:16	☽ 21♏20
22 5:02	○ 28♒17
28 19:27	☾ 4♊39

Astro Data

1 July 1918
Julian Day # 6756
SVP 6♓23'35"
GC 25♐42.1 ⚴ 2♐10.9R
Eris 28♓52.7R ⚵ 3♊35.8
⚷ 3♈27.8 ⚶ 17♊56.9
☽ Mean ☊ 21♐25.9

1 August 1918
Julian Day # 6787
SVP 6♓23'30"
GC 25♐42.1 ⚴ 0♐47.1
Eris 28♓45.2R ⚵ 21♊10.7
⚷ 3♈12.1R ⚶ 0♋50.3
☽ Mean ☊ 19♐47.4

LONGITUDE — September 1918

Day	Sid.Time	☉	0 hr ☽	Noon ☽	True ☊	☿	♀	♂	⚳	♃	♄	♅	♆	♇
1 Su	10 39 21	8♍13 36	16♋49 52	23♋12 31	19♐02.1	9♍18.5	16♌49.0	9♏46.2	26♐40.2	10♋00.8	20♌43.7	25♒13.6	7♌59.9	6♋24.2
2 M	10 43 18	9 11 43	29 32 11	5♌49 04	18R55.4	8R21.7	18 02.6	10 25.4	26 46.2	10 10.7	20 51.2	25R11.3	8 01.9	6 25.0
3 Tu	10 47 15	10 09 51	12♌03 24	18 15 20	18 45.8	7 26.5	19 16.1	11 04.8	26 52.5	10 20.5	20 58.6	25 09.0	8 03.8	6 25.7
4 W	10 51 11	11 08 02	24 25 01	0♍32 35	18 33.7	6 34.0	20 29.8	11 44.2	26 59.1	10 30.2	21 06.0	25 06.8	8 05.7	6 26.5
5 Th	10 55 08	12 06 13	6♍38 07	12 41 44	18 20.1	5 45.6	21 43.5	12 23.7	27 06.0	10 39.9	21 13.4	25 04.5	8 07.7	6 27.2
6 F	10 59 04	13 04 27	18 43 34	24 43 42	18 06.0	5 02.2	22 57.2	13 03.4	27 13.2	10 49.4	21 20.7	25 02.3	8 09.6	6 27.9
7 Sa	11 03 01	14 02 42	0♎42 19	6♎39 35	17 52.7	4 25.1	24 10.9	13 43.2	27 20.7	10 58.7	21 28.0	25 00.0	8 11.5	6 28.6
8 Su	11 06 57	15 00 59	12 35 43	18 30 58	17 41.2	3 55.1	25 24.8	14 23.0	27 28.5	11 08.0	21 35.3	24 57.8	8 13.3	6 29.2
9 M	11 10 54	15 59 18	24 25 38	0♏20 05	17 32.1	3 33.0	26 38.6	15 03.0	27 36.5	11 17.2	21 42.6	24 55.6	8 15.2	6 29.9
10 Tu	11 14 50	16 57 38	6♏14 43	12 09 58	17 25.9	3 19.4	27 52.5	15 43.1	27 44.9	11 26.2	21 49.8	24 53.4	8 17.0	6 30.5
11 W	11 18 47	17 56 00	18 06 22	24 04 26	17 22.5	3D14.6	29 06.4	16 23.3	27 53.5	11 35.1	21 57.0	24 51.3	8 18.8	6 31.1
12 Th	11 22 43	18 54 24	0♐04 47	6♐08 00	17D21.1	3 19.1	0♍20.4	17 03.6	28 02.5	11 43.9	22 04.2	24 49.2	8 20.6	6 31.7
13 F	11 26 40	19 52 49	12 14 46	18 25 43	17R20.9	3 32.7	1 34.4	17 44.0	28 11.6	11 52.6	22 11.3	24 47.1	8 22.4	6 32.3
14 Sa	11 30 37	20 51 16	24 41 31	1♑02 48	17 20.7	3 55.6	2 48.4	18 24.5	28 21.1	12 01.1	22 18.4	24 45.0	8 24.2	6 32.8
15 Su	11 34 33	21 49 44	7♑30 10	14 04 10	17 19.4	4 27.5	4 02.5	19 05.1	28 30.8	12 09.5	22 25.5	24 42.9	8 25.9	6 33.3
16 M	11 38 30	22 48 14	20 45 14	27 33 42	17 16.1	5 08.1	5 16.6	19 45.8	28 40.8	12 17.8	22 32.5	24 40.9	8 27.6	6 33.8
17 Tu	11 42 26	23 46 46	4♒29 44	11♒33 21	17 10.2	5 57.0	6 30.8	20 26.6	28 51.0	12 26.0	22 39.5	24 38.9	8 29.3	6 34.3
18 W	11 46 23	24 45 19	18 44 20	26 02 15	17 01.8	6 53.9	7 44.9	21 07.5	29 01.5	12 34.0	22 46.4	24 36.9	8 31.0	6 34.8
19 Th	11 50 19	25 43 54	3♓26 25	10♓55 55	16 51.5	7 58.0	8 59.2	21 48.4	29 12.2	12 41.9	22 53.3	24 35.0	8 32.6	6 35.2
20 F	11 54 16	26 42 31	18 29 41	26 06 25	16 40.5	9 08.8	10 13.4	22 29.5	29 23.2	12 49.6	23 00.1	24 33.1	8 34.3	6 35.6
21 Sa	11 58 12	27 41 10	3♈44 43	11♈23 11	16 30.0	10 25.8	11 27.7	23 10.7	29 34.4	12 57.2	23 07.0	24 31.2	8 35.9	6 36.0
22 Su	12 02 09	28 39 50	19 00 23	26 34 59	16 21.3	11 48.2	12 42.0	23 51.9	29 45.9	13 04.7	23 13.7	24 29.3	8 37.4	6 36.3
23 M	12 06 06	29 38 33	4♉05 50	11♉31 55	16 15.2	13 15.4	13 56.4	24 33.3	29 57.6	13 12.1	23 20.4	24 27.5	8 39.0	6 36.7
24 Tu	12 10 02	0♎37 19	18 52 27	26 06 54	16 11.7	14 46.9	15 10.8	25 14.8	0♑09.5	13 19.3	23 27.1	24 25.7	8 40.5	6 37.0
25 W	12 13 59	1 36 06	3♊14 53	10♊16 17	16D10.4	16 21.9	16 25.2	25 56.3	0 21.7	13 26.3	23 33.8	24 23.9	8 42.0	6 37.3
26 Th	12 17 55	2 34 56	17 11 06	23 59 30	16R10.4	18 00.0	17 39.7	26 37.9	0 34.0	13 33.2	23 40.3	24 22.2	8 43.5	6 37.6
27 F	12 21 52	3 33 48	0♋41 47	7♋18 18	16 10.5	19 40.6	18 54.2	27 19.7	0 46.6	13 40.0	23 46.9	24 20.5	8 45.0	6 37.8
28 Sa	12 25 48	4 32 42	13 49 27	20 15 43	16 09.4	21 23.2	20 08.8	28 01.5	0 59.5	13 46.6	23 53.4	24 18.9	8 46.4	6 38.1
29 Su	12 29 45	5 31 39	26 37 32	2♌55 23	16 06.3	23 07.5	21 23.4	28 43.4	1 12.5	13 53.0	23 59.8	24 17.3	8 47.8	6 38.3
30 M	12 33 41	6 30 38	9♌09 41	15 20 52	16 00.5	24 52.9	22 38.0	29 25.4	1 25.7	13 59.3	24 06.2	24 15.7	8 49.2	6 38.4

LONGITUDE — October 1918

Day	Sid.Time	☉	0 hr ☽	Noon ☽	True ☊	☿	♀	♂	⚳	♃	♄	♅	♆	♇
1 Tu	12 37 38	7♎29 39	21♌29 18	27♌35 21	15♐52.1	26♍39.3	23♍52.6	0♐07.6	1♑39.2	14♋05.5	24♌12.5	24♒14.1	8♌50.5	6♋38.6
2 W	12 41 35	8 28 42	3♍39 19	9♍41 28	15R41.3	28 26.2	25 07.3	0 49.8	1 52.9	14 11.5	24 18.7	24R12.6	8 51.9	6 38.7
3 Th	12 45 31	9 27 47	15 42 03	21 41 17	15 29.0	0♎13.5	26 22.0	1 32.0	2 06.7	14 17.3	24 24.9	24 11.1	8 53.2	6 38.8
4 F	12 49 28	10 26 55	27 39 22	3♎36 28	15 16.2	2 00.9	27 36.7	2 14.4	2 20.8	14 22.9	24 31.1	24 09.7	8 54.4	6 38.9
5 Sa	12 53 24	11 26 04	9♎32 45	15 28 23	15 04.1	3 48.3	28 51.5	2 56.9	2 35.1	14 28.4	24 37.2	24 08.3	8 55.7	6 39.0
6 Su	12 57 21	12 25 16	21 23 35	27 18 31	14 53.6	5 35.5	0♎06.2	3 39.5	2 49.5	14 33.8	24 43.2	24 06.9	8 56.9	6 39.0
7 M	13 01 17	13 24 30	3♏13 26	9♏08 33	14 45.5	7 22.4	1 21.1	4 22.1	3 04.2	14 38.9	24 49.2	24 05.6	8 58.1	6R39.1
8 Tu	13 05 14	14 23 45	15 04 12	21 00 41	14 40.0	9 08.9	2 35.9	5 04.8	3 19.1	14 43.9	24 55.1	24 04.4	8 59.2	6 39.1
9 W	13 09 10	15 23 03	26 58 22	2♐57 42	14D37.1	10 54.9	3 50.7	5 47.6	3 34.1	14 48.7	25 00.9	24 03.1	9 00.4	6 39.0
10 Th	13 13 07	16 22 22	8♐59 07	15 03 06	14 36.4	12 40.4	5 05.6	6 30.6	3 49.3	14 53.4	25 06.7	24 01.9	9 01.5	6 39.0
11 F	13 17 04	17 21 43	21 10 13	27 21 00	14 36.9	14 25.3	6 20.5	7 13.5	4 04.7	14 57.9	25 12.4	24 00.8	9 02.5	6 38.9
12 Sa	13 21 00	18 21 06	3♑36 02	9♑55 54	14R37.8	16 09.6	7 35.4	7 56.6	4 20.3	15 02.2	25 18.0	23 59.7	9 03.6	6 38.8
13 Su	13 24 57	19 20 31	16 21 10	22 52 23	14 38.0	17 53.3	8 50.4	8 39.8	4 36.0	15 06.3	25 23.6	23 58.7	9 04.6	6 38.7
14 M	13 28 53	20 19 58	29 30 03	6♒14 33	14 36.7	19 36.3	10 05.3	9 23.0	4 52.0	15 10.2	25 29.1	23 57.7	9 05.5	6 38.5
15 Tu	13 32 50	21 19 26	13♒06 12	20 05 09	14 33.4	21 18.6	11 20.3	10 06.3	5 08.1	15 14.0	25 34.5	23 56.7	9 06.5	6 38.4
16 W	13 36 46	22 18 56	27 11 23	4♓24 43	14 28.0	23 00.2	12 35.3	10 49.7	5 24.3	15 17.6	25 39.9	23 55.8	9 07.4	6 38.2
17 Th	13 40 43	23 18 27	11♓44 42	19 10 43	14 21.0	24 41.2	13 50.3	11 33.1	5 40.7	15 21.0	25 45.2	23 54.9	9 08.3	6 38.0
18 F	13 44 39	24 18 01	26 41 52	4♈17 05	14 13.2	26 21.6	15 05.3	12 16.7	5 57.3	15 24.2	25 50.4	23 54.1	9 09.1	6 37.7
19 Sa	13 48 36	25 17 36	11♈55 08	19 34 39	14 05.7	28 01.2	16 20.4	13 00.3	6 14.0	15 27.2	25 55.5	23 53.3	9 10.0	6 37.5
20 Su	13 52 32	26 17 13	27 14 13	4♉52 25	13 59.5	29 40.3	17 35.5	13 44.0	6 30.9	15 30.1	26 00.6	23 52.6	9 10.7	6 37.2
21 M	13 56 29	27 16 53	12♉27 55	19 59 30	13 55.2	1♏18.7	18 50.5	14 27.7	6 47.9	15 32.7	26 05.6	23 51.9	9 11.5	6 36.9
22 Tu	14 00 26	28 16 34	27 26 07	4♊46 58	13D53.1	2 56.6	20 05.6	15 11.6	7 05.1	15 35.2	26 10.5	23 51.3	9 12.2	6 36.6
23 W	14 04 22	29 16 18	12♊01 24	19 09 00	13 52.9	4 33.8	21 20.8	15 55.5	7 22.5	15 37.5	26 15.3	23 50.7	9 12.9	6 36.2
24 Th	14 08 19	0♏16 04	26 09 35	3♋03 07	13 53.9	6 10.5	22 35.9	16 39.4	7 39.9	15 39.6	26 20.1	23 50.1	9 13.6	6 35.9
25 F	14 12 15	1 15 53	9♋49 43	16 29 40	13 55.3	7 46.6	23 51.1	17 23.5	7 57.5	15 41.5	26 24.7	23 49.6	9 14.2	6 35.5
26 Sa	14 16 12	2 15 43	23 03 18	29 31 03	13R56.1	9 22.2	25 06.3	18 07.6	8 15.3	15 43.2	26 29.3	23 49.2	9 14.8	6 35.1
27 Su	14 20 08	3 15 36	5♌53 26	12♌10 57	13 55.7	10 57.3	26 21.5	18 51.8	8 33.2	15 44.7	26 33.8	23 48.8	9 15.4	6 34.6
28 M	14 24 05	4 15 31	18 24 07	24 33 29	13 53.6	12 31.8	27 36.7	19 36.1	8 51.2	15 46.0	26 38.2	23 48.5	9 15.9	6 34.2
29 Tu	14 28 02	5 15 28	0♍39 34	6♍42 52	13 49.7	14 05.9	28 51.9	20 20.5	9 09.4	15 47.1	26 42.5	23 48.2	9 16.4	6 33.7
30 W	14 31 58	6 15 27	12 43 51	18 42 57	13 44.2	15 39.5	0♏07.1	21 04.9	9 27.7	15 48.0	26 46.8	23 47.9	9 16.8	6 33.2
31 Th	14 35 55	7 15 28	24 40 35	0♎37 07	13 37.6	17 12.6	1 22.4	21 49.4	9 46.1	15 48.7	26 50.9	23 47.7	9 17.3	6 32.7

Astro Data

	Dy Hr Mn
♃□♅	2 13:16
☽0S	5 23:18
♄∠♇	7 14:00
☿ D	11 12:30
☽0N	19 23:45
☉0S	23 20:46
♄☍♅	1 17:02
☽0S	3 5:12
☿0S	5 14:44
♇ R	7 19:12
♀0S	9 2:56
☽0N	17 10:17
☽0S	30 10:32

Planet Ingress

		Dy Hr Mn
♀	♍	12 5:23
⚳	♑	23 16:54
☉	♎	23 20:46
♂	♐	1 7:42
☿	♎	3 8:59
♀	♎	6 10:00
☿	♏	20 16:47
☉	♏	24 5:33
♀	♏	30 9:43

Last Aspect / ☽ Ingress (September)

Last Aspect Dy Hr Mn		☽ Ingress Dy Hr Mn
31 11:45	☿ ⚹	♌ 2 0:53
4 1:24	♅ ☍	♍ 4 10:56
5 11:22	♂ ⚹	♎ 6 22:35
9 3:38	♀ ⚹	♏ 9 11:19
11 23:13	♀ □	♐ 11 23:50
14 0:09	♅ ⚹	♑ 14 10:02
16 2:59	☉ △	♒ 16 16:15
18 9:41	♅ ☌	♓ 18 18:27
20 13:01	☉ ☍	♈ 20 18:07
22 8:41	♅ ⚹	♉ 22 17:27
24 10:29	♂ ☍	♊ 24 18:31
26 12:40	♅ △	♋ 26 22:45
29 3:31	♂ △	♌ 29 6:25

Last Aspect / ☽ Ingress (October)

Last Aspect Dy Hr Mn		☽ Ingress Dy Hr Mn
1 5:24	♅ ☍	♍ 1 16:46
3 22:30	♀ ☌	♎ 4 4:43
6 6:42	♄ ⚹	♏ 6 17:28
8 19:56	♄ □	♐ 9 6:04
11 7:49	♄ △	♑ 11 17:06
13 4:59	☉ □	♒ 14 0:54
15 21:21	♄ ☍	♓ 16 4:42
17 5:49	♃ △	♈ 18 5:14
20 2:50	☿ ☍	♉ 20 4:20
21 21:53	♄ □	♊ 22 4:10
24 0:14	♄ ⚹	♋ 24 6:40
26 2:54	♀ □	♌ 26 12:54
28 18:41	♀ ⚹	♍ 28 22:42
30 17:04	♂ □	♎ 31 10:45

☽ Phases & Eclipses

Dy Hr Mn	
5 10:43	● 12♍03
13 15:02	☽ 20♐00
20 13:01	○ 26♓45
27 4:38	☾ 3♋16
5 3:05	● 11♎04
13 4:59	☽ 19♑03
19 21:34	○ 25♈41
26 17:35	☾ 2♌30

Astro Data

1 September 1918
Julian Day # 6818
SVP 6♓23'26"
GC 25♐42.2 ⚵ 5♐21.4
Eris 28♓28.7R ⚶ 7♋52.0
⚷ 2♈13.0R ⚴ 12♋50.7
☽ Mean ☊ 18♐08.9

1 October 1918
Julian Day # 6848
SVP 6♓23'23"
GC 25♐42.3 ⚵ 13♐20.3
Eris 28♓08.6R ⚶ 22♋19.1
⚷ 0♈53.8R ⚴ 22♋58.0
☽ Mean ☊ 16♐33.6

November 1918 LONGITUDE

Day	Sid.Time	☉	0 hr ☽	Noon ☽	True ☊	☿	♀	♂	⚳	♃	♄	♅	♆	♇
1 F	14 39 51	8♏15 32	6♎32 54	12♎28 13	13♐30.7	18♏45.3	2♏37.7	22♐34.0	10♑04.7	15♋49.3	26♌55.0	23♒47.6	9♌17.6	6♋32.1
2 Sa	14 43 48	9 15 37	18 23 22	24 18 36	13R 24.0	20 17.6	3 52.9	23 18.6	10 23.4	15 49.6	26 59.0	23R 47.5	9 18.0	6R 31.6
3 Su	14 47 44	10 15 44	0♏14 09	6♏10 14	13 18.4	21 49.4	5 08.2	24 03.3	10 42.2	15R 49.7	27 02.9	23D 47.5	9 18.3	6 31.0
4 M	14 51 41	11 15 53	12 07 03	18 04 51	13 14.2	23 20.8	6 23.5	24 48.1	11 01.1	15 49.6	27 06.6	23 47.5	9 18.6	6 30.4
5 Tu	14 55 37	12 16 04	24 03 48	0♐04 11	13 11.7	24 51.8	7 38.9	25 32.9	11 20.2	15 49.3	27 10.3	23 47.5	9 18.9	6 29.7
6 W	14 59 34	13 16 17	6♐06 12	12 10 08	13D 10.8	26 22.4	8 54.2	26 17.9	11 39.4	15 48.8	27 13.9	23 47.7	9 19.1	6 29.1
7 Th	15 03 30	14 16 31	18 16 16	24 24 55	13 11.3	27 52.6	10 09.5	27 02.8	11 58.7	15 48.1	27 17.5	23 47.8	9 19.3	6 28.4
8 F	15 07 27	15 16 47	0♑36 25	6♑51 08	13 12.7	29 22.4	11 24.9	27 47.9	12 18.1	15 47.3	27 20.9	23 48.0	9 19.4	6 27.7
9 Sa	15 11 24	16 17 05	13 09 27	19 31 45	13 14.5	0♐51.7	12 40.2	28 33.0	12 37.6	15 46.2	27 24.2	23 48.3	9 19.5	6 27.0
10 Su	15 15 20	17 17 24	25 58 26	2♒29 53	13 16.0	2 20.6	13 55.6	29 18.1	12 57.2	15 44.9	27 27.4	23 48.6	9 19.6	6 26.3
11 M	15 19 17	18 17 44	9♒06 28	15 48 30	13R 16.7	3 49.0	15 10.9	0♑03.4	13 16.9	15 43.4	27 30.5	23 49.0	9R 19.7	6 25.6
12 Tu	15 23 13	19 18 06	22 36 16	29 29 56	13 16.3	5 16.9	16 26.3	0 48.6	13 36.8	15 41.7	27 33.5	23 49.4	9 19.7	6 24.8
13 W	15 27 10	20 18 29	6♓29 34	13♓35 08	13 14.9	6 44.4	17 41.7	1 34.0	13 56.7	15 39.8	27 36.4	23 49.9	9 19.7	6 24.0
14 Th	15 31 06	21 18 53	20 46 26	28 03 05	13 12.6	8 11.3	18 57.0	2 19.4	14 16.7	15 37.7	27 39.3	23 50.4	9 19.6	6 23.2
15 F	15 35 03	22 19 19	5♈24 36	12♈50 15	13 09.7	9 37.6	20 12.4	3 04.8	14 36.8	15 35.4	27 42.0	23 51.0	9 19.5	6 22.4
16 Sa	15 38 59	23 19 46	20 19 11	27 50 26	13 07.0	11 03.3	21 27.8	3 50.3	14 57.1	15 33.0	27 44.6	23 51.6	9 19.4	6 21.6
17 Su	15 42 56	24 20 15	5♉22 54	12♉55 25	13 04.7	12 28.3	22 43.2	4 35.9	15 17.4	15 30.3	27 47.1	23 52.3	9 19.2	6 20.8
18 M	15 46 53	25 20 45	20 26 49	27 55 58	13 03.3	13 52.6	23 58.6	5 21.5	15 37.8	15 27.4	27 49.5	23 53.0	9 19.1	6 19.9
19 Tu	15 50 49	26 21 17	5♊21 47	12♊43 19	13D 02.8	15 16.0	25 14.0	6 07.2	15 58.3	15 24.4	27 51.8	23 53.8	9 18.8	6 19.0
20 W	15 54 46	27 21 50	19 59 44	27 10 24	13 03.2	16 38.4	26 29.4	6 52.9	16 18.9	15 21.1	27 54.0	23 54.6	9 18.6	6 18.1
21 Th	15 58 42	28 22 25	4♋14 50	11♋12 42	13 04.1	17 59.8	27 44.8	7 38.7	16 39.6	15 17.7	27 56.1	23 55.5	9 18.3	6 17.2
22 F	16 02 39	29 23 02	18 03 53	24 48 22	13 05.4	19 20.0	29 00.2	8 24.5	17 00.4	15 14.1	27 58.1	23 56.5	9 18.0	6 16.3
23 Sa	16 06 35	0♐23 40	1♌26 18	7♌57 56	13 06.5	20 38.8	0♐15.6	9 10.4	17 21.2	15 10.3	28 00.0	23 57.4	9 17.6	6 15.3
24 Su	16 10 32	1 24 20	14 23 39	20 43 50	13R 07.2	21 56.1	1 31.0	9 56.3	17 42.2	15 06.3	28 01.7	23 58.5	9 17.2	6 14.4
25 M	16 14 29	2 25 01	26 59 01	3♍09 43	13 07.5	23 11.5	2 46.5	10 42.3	18 03.2	15 02.1	28 03.4	23 59.5	9 16.8	6 13.4
26 Tu	16 18 25	3 25 44	9♍16 29	15 19 53	13 07.2	24 25.0	4 01.9	11 28.3	18 24.3	14 57.7	28 05.0	24 00.7	9 16.3	6 12.4
27 W	16 22 22	4 26 29	21 20 30	27 18 54	13 06.5	25 36.1	5 17.4	12 14.4	18 45.5	14 53.2	28 06.4	24 01.9	9 15.9	6 11.4
28 Th	16 26 18	5 27 15	3♎15 37	9♎11 11	13 05.5	26 44.6	6 32.8	13 00.5	19 06.8	14 48.5	28 07.7	24 03.1	9 15.3	6 10.4
29 F	16 30 15	6 28 03	15 06 08	21 00 53	13 04.5	27 50.1	7 48.3	13 46.7	19 28.1	14 43.6	28 09.0	24 04.4	9 14.8	6 09.4
30 Sa	16 34 11	7 28 52	26 55 56	2♏51 38	13 03.6	28 52.1	9 03.7	14 32.9	19 49.5	14 38.5	28 10.1	24 05.7	9 14.2	6 08.3

December 1918 LONGITUDE

Day	Sid.Time	☉	0 hr ☽	Noon ☽	True ☊	☿	♀	♂	⚳	♃	♄	♅	♆	♇
1 Su	16 38 08	8♐29 43	8♏48 24	14♏46 31	13♐03.0	29♐50.0	10♐19.2	15♑19.2	20♑11.0	14♋33.3	28♌11.1	24♒07.0	9♌13.6	6♋07.3
2 M	16 42 04	9 30 34	20 46 20	26 48 04	13R 02.6	0♑43.5	11 34.6	16 05.5	20 32.6	14R 27.9	28 12.0	24 08.5	9R 12.9	6R 06.2
3 Tu	16 46 01	10 31 27	2♐51 59	8♐58 15	13D 02.4	1 31.8	12 50.1	16 51.9	20 54.3	14 22.4	28 12.7	24 09.9	9 12.2	6 05.2
4 W	16 49 58	11 32 22	15 07 05	21 18 37	13 02.4	2 14.2	14 05.6	17 38.3	21 16.0	14 16.7	28 13.4	24 11.5	9 11.5	6 04.1
5 Th	16 53 54	12 33 17	27 33 00	3♑50 21	13R 02.5	2 49.9	15 21.0	18 24.7	21 37.8	14 10.8	28 14.0	24 13.0	9 10.8	6 03.0
6 F	16 57 51	13 34 13	10♑10 48	16 34 27	13 02.5	3 18.3	16 36.5	19 11.2	21 59.6	14 04.8	28 14.4	24 14.6	9 10.0	6 01.9
7 Sa	17 01 47	14 35 10	23 01 24	29 31 45	13 02.4	3 38.3	17 52.0	19 57.7	22 21.5	13 58.7	28 14.7	24 16.3	9 09.2	6 00.7
8 Su	17 05 44	15 36 08	6♒05 38	12♒43 06	13 02.1	3R 49.1	19 07.5	20 44.3	22 43.5	13 52.4	28 14.9	24 18.0	9 08.4	5 59.6
9 M	17 09 40	16 37 06	19 24 17	26 09 14	13 01.9	3 50.0	20 22.9	21 30.9	23 05.5	13 46.0	28R 15.0	24 19.7	9 07.5	5 58.5
10 Tu	17 13 37	17 38 05	2♓58 01	9♓50 40	13D 01.6	3 40.2	21 38.4	22 17.6	23 27.6	13 39.4	28 15.0	24 21.5	9 06.6	5 57.3
11 W	17 17 33	18 39 05	16 47 09	23 47 25	13 01.6	3 19.1	22 53.8	23 04.2	23 49.8	13 32.7	28 14.9	24 23.4	9 05.7	5 56.2
12 Th	17 21 30	19 40 05	0♈51 21	7♈58 45	13 01.9	2 46.5	24 09.3	23 50.9	24 12.0	13 25.9	28 14.7	24 25.2	9 04.7	5 55.0
13 F	17 25 27	20 41 05	15 09 20	22 24 59	13 02.4	2 02.5	25 24.7	24 37.7	24 34.3	13 19.0	28 14.3	24 27.2	9 03.8	5 53.9
14 Sa	17 29 23	21 42 06	29 38 34	6♉56 14	13 03.2	1 07.7	26 40.2	25 24.5	24 56.6	13 11.9	28 13.9	24 29.1	9 02.8	5 52.7
15 Su	17 33 20	22 43 08	14♉15 06	21 34 30	13 04.0	0 03.0	27 55.6	26 11.3	25 19.0	13 04.8	28 13.3	24 31.1	9 01.7	5 51.5
16 M	17 37 16	23 44 10	28 53 41	6♊11 51	13R 04.4	28♐50.3	29 11.1	26 58.1	25 41.4	12 57.6	28 12.6	24 33.2	9 00.7	5 50.3
17 Tu	17 41 13	24 45 13	13♊28 12	20 41 59	13 04.4	27 31.5	0♑26.5	27 44.9	26 03.9	12 50.2	28 11.8	24 35.3	8 59.6	5 49.1
18 W	17 45 09	25 46 16	27 52 25	4♋58 51	13 03.7	26 09.3	1 42.0	28 31.8	26 26.4	12 42.8	28 10.9	24 37.4	8 58.5	5 47.9
19 Th	17 49 06	26 47 20	12♋00 42	18 57 27	13 02.3	24 46.4	2 57.4	29 18.8	26 49.0	12 35.3	28 09.9	24 39.6	8 57.3	5 46.7
20 F	17 53 02	27 48 25	25 48 46	2♌34 23	13 00.4	23 25.7	4 12.8	0♒05.7	27 11.6	12 27.7	28 08.8	24 41.8	8 56.2	5 45.5
21 Sa	17 56 59	28 49 30	9♌14 11	15 48 11	12 58.1	22 09.7	5 28.3	0 52.7	27 34.3	12 20.0	28 07.6	24 44.1	8 55.0	5 44.3
22 Su	18 00 56	29 50 36	22 16 29	28 39 18	12 55.9	21 00.7	6 43.7	1 39.7	27 57.0	12 12.3	28 06.2	24 46.4	8 53.8	5 43.1
23 M	18 04 52	0♑51 42	4♍56 59	11♍09 54	12 54.0	20 00.3	7 59.1	2 26.7	28 19.7	12 04.4	28 04.8	24 48.7	8 52.5	5 41.9
24 Tu	18 08 49	1 52 50	17 18 33	23 23 25	12D 52.9	19 09.7	9 14.5	3 13.7	28 42.5	11 56.6	28 03.2	24 51.1	8 51.3	5 40.7
25 W	18 12 45	2 53 57	29 25 05	5♎24 07	12 52.6	18 29.6	10 30.0	4 00.8	29 05.4	11 48.6	28 01.6	24 53.5	8 50.0	5 39.5
26 Th	18 16 42	3 55 06	11♎21 10	17 16 50	12 53.2	18 00.3	11 45.4	4 47.9	29 28.2	11 40.7	27 59.8	24 55.9	8 48.7	5 38.2
27 F	18 20 38	4 56 15	23 11 43	29 06 28	12 54.6	17 41.6	13 00.8	5 35.0	29 51.2	11 32.6	27 57.9	24 58.4	8 47.4	5 37.0
28 Sa	18 24 35	5 57 24	5♏01 39	10♏57 51	12 56.4	17D 33.0	14 16.2	6 22.1	0♒14.1	11 24.6	27 56.0	25 00.9	8 46.0	5 35.8
29 Su	18 28 31	6 58 34	16 55 36	22 55 24	12 58.1	17 34.1	15 31.6	7 09.3	0 37.1	11 16.5	27 53.9	25 03.5	8 44.7	5 34.6
30 M	18 32 28	7 59 45	28 57 43	5♐02 57	12R 59.3	17 44.1	16 47.1	7 56.5	1 00.2	11 08.4	27 51.7	25 06.1	8 43.3	5 33.4
31 Tu	18 36 25	9 00 55	11♐11 28	17 23 32	12 59.5	18 02.3	18 02.5	8 43.7	1 23.3	11 00.3	27 49.4	25 08.7	8 41.9	5 32.1

Astro Data	Planet Ingress	Last Aspect	☽ Ingress	Last Aspect	☽ Ingress	☽ Phases & Eclipses	Astro Data
Dy Hr Mn	Dy Hr Mn	Dy Hr Mn	Dy Hr Mn	Dy Hr Mn	Dy Hr Mn	Dy Hr Mn	1 November 1918
♃ R 3 13:52	☿ ♐ 8 22:06	2 17:27 ♄ ⚹	♏ 2 23:31	2 14:47 ♄ □	♐ 2 18:20	3 21:01 ● 10♏38	Julian Day # 6879
♅ D 3 18:27	♂ ♑ 11 10:13	5 6:11 ♄ □	♐ 5 11:52	5 1:18 ♄ △	♑ 5 4:41	11 16:46 ☽ 18♒30	SVP 6♓23'20"
♆ R 12 9:18	☉ ♐ 23 2:38	7 17:37 ♄ △	♑ 7 22:50	6 17:11 ♂ ☌	♒ 7 12:52	18 7:33 ○ 25♉10	GC 25♐42.3 ⚴ 23♐39.1
☽ 0N 13 19:04	♀ ♐ 23 7:02	9 5:23 ☉ ⚹	♒ 10 7:25	9 15:42 ♄ ☍	♓ 9 18:47	25 10:25 ☾ 2♍21	Eris 27♓49.8R ⚵ 4♌04.5
☽ 0S 26 16:47		12 8:38 ♄ ☍	♓ 12 12:52	11 10:42 ♂ ⚹	♈ 11 22:33		⚷ 29♓39.0R ⚶ 0♌39.7
	☿ ♑ 1 16:19	14 0:04 ☉ △	♈ 14 15:11	13 21:41 ♄ △	♉ 14 0:35	3 15:19 ● 10♐40	☽ Mean ☊ 14♐55.1
☿ R 9 2:04	☿ ♐R 15 13:03	16 11:51 ♄ △	♉ 16 15:26	15 22:53 ♄ □	♊ 16 1:49	3 15:21:40 • A 07'06"	
♄ R 9 21:31	♀ ♑ 17 3:34	18 11:50 ♄ □	♊ 18 15:20	18 0:32 ♄ ⚹	♋ 18 3:35	11 2:31 ☽ 18♓15	1 December 1918
☽ 0N 11 1:36	♂ ♒ 20 9:05	20 13:14 ♄ ⚹	♋ 20 16:46	20 7:19 ♂ ☍	♌ 20 7:25	17 19:17 ○ 25♊04	Julian Day # 6909
♃∠♄ 14 5:00	☉ ♑ 22 15:42	22 20:57 ☉ △	♌ 22 21:23	22 14:27 ☉ △	♍ 22 14:33	17 19:06 • A 0.834	SVP 6♓23'16"
☽ 0S 24 0:55	⚳ ♒ 27 21:14	25 2:03 ♄ ☌	♍ 25 5:50	24 4:09 ☿ □	♎ 25 1:10	25 6:30 ☾ 2♎40	GC 25♐42.4 ⚴ 4♑40.3
☿ D 28 21:11		27 8:11 ☿ □	♎ 27 17:25	27 9:41 ♄ ⚹	♏ 27 13:49		Eris 27♓39.1R ⚵ 10♌11.4
		30 3:10 ☿ ⚹	♏ 30 6:13	29 21:52 ♄ □	♐ 30 2:03		⚷ 29♓00.3R ⚶ 3♌31.0R
							☽ Mean ☊ 13♐19.7

LONGITUDE — January 1919

Day	Sid.Time	☉	0 hr ☽	Noon ☽	True ☊	☿	♀	♂	⚳	♃	♄	♅	♆	♇
1 W	18 40 21	10♑02 06	23♐39 24	29♐59 13	12♐58.3	18♐27.9	19♑17.9	9♒30.9	1♒46.4	10♋52.2	27♌47.1	25♒11.3	8♌40.5	5♋30.9
2 Th	18 44 18	11 03 17	6♑23 05	12♑51 00	12R 55.7	19 00.2	20 33.3	10 18.2	2 09.5	10R 44.0	27R 44.6	25 14.0	8R 39.0	5R 29.7
3 F	18 48 14	12 04 28	19 22 57	25 58 47	12 51.7	19 38.6	21 48.7	11 05.4	2 32.7	10 35.9	27 42.0	25 16.7	8 37.6	5 28.5
4 Sa	18 52 11	13 05 39	2♒38 23	9♒21 30	12 46.8	20 22.4	23 04.1	11 52.7	2 55.9	10 27.8	27 39.3	25 19.5	8 36.1	5 27.3
5 Su	18 56 07	14 06 50	16 07 54	22 57 19	12 41.6	21 10.9	24 19.4	12 40.0	3 19.1	10 19.7	27 36.6	25 22.3	8 34.6	5 26.1
6 M	19 00 04	15 08 00	29 49 27	6♓44 00	12 36.8	22 03.8	25 34.8	13 27.3	3 42.4	10 11.6	27 33.7	25 25.1	8 33.1	5 24.9
7 Tu	19 04 00	16 09 10	13♓40 41	20 39 13	12 33.0	23 00.5	26 50.2	14 14.6	4 05.7	10 03.5	27 30.7	25 27.9	8 31.6	5 23.7
8 W	19 07 57	17 10 20	27 39 21	4♈40 52	12D 30.7	24 00.6	28 05.5	15 01.9	4 29.0	9 55.5	27 27.7	25 30.8	8 30.0	5 22.5
9 Th	19 11 54	18 11 29	11♈43 30	18 47 06	12 30.0	25 03.7	29 20.9	15 49.2	4 52.3	9 47.6	27 24.6	25 33.7	8 28.5	5 21.3
10 F	19 15 50	19 12 37	25 51 26	2♉56 21	12 30.7	26 09.6	0♒36.2	16 36.5	5 15.7	9 39.6	27 21.3	25 36.6	8 26.9	5 20.1
11 Sa	19 19 47	20 13 45	10♉01 38	17 07 06	12 32.1	27 17.9	1 51.5	17 23.9	5 39.1	9 31.8	27 18.0	25 39.6	8 25.3	5 18.9
12 Su	19 23 43	21 14 52	24 12 28	1♊17 31	12R 33.5	28 28.4	3 06.8	18 11.2	6 02.5	9 23.9	27 14.7	25 42.6	8 23.7	5 17.7
13 M	19 27 40	22 15 59	8♊21 54	15 25 18	12 33.9	29 40.9	4 22.1	18 58.5	6 25.9	9 16.2	27 11.2	25 45.6	8 22.1	5 16.6
14 Tu	19 31 36	23 17 05	22 27 19	29 27 33	12 32.6	0♑55.2	5 37.4	19 45.9	6 49.3	9 08.5	27 07.6	25 48.6	8 20.5	5 15.4
15 W	19 35 33	24 18 11	6♋25 34	13♋20 54	12 29.3	2 11.1	6 52.6	20 33.2	7 12.8	9 00.9	27 04.0	25 51.7	8 18.9	5 14.3
16 Th	19 39 30	25 19 16	20 13 08	27 01 51	12 23.8	3 28.5	8 07.9	21 20.6	7 36.3	8 53.4	27 00.3	25 54.8	8 17.3	5 13.1
17 F	19 43 26	26 20 20	3♌46 39	10♌27 15	12 16.6	4 47.2	9 23.1	22 07.9	7 59.8	8 46.0	26 56.6	25 57.9	8 15.6	5 12.0
18 Sa	19 47 23	27 21 24	17 03 24	23 34 56	12 08.3	6 07.2	10 38.4	22 55.2	8 23.3	8 38.6	26 52.7	26 01.0	8 14.0	5 10.9
19 Su	19 51 19	28 22 28	0♍01 46	6♍23 56	11 59.9	7 28.3	11 53.6	23 42.6	8 46.8	8 31.4	26 48.8	26 04.2	8 12.3	5 09.8
20 M	19 55 16	29 23 31	12 41 33	18 54 48	11 52.2	8 50.5	13 08.8	24 29.9	9 10.3	8 24.2	26 44.8	26 07.3	8 10.7	5 08.7
21 Tu	19 59 12	0♒24 33	25 04 00	1♎09 31	11 46.0	10 13.7	14 24.0	25 17.3	9 33.9	8 17.2	26 40.8	26 10.5	8 09.0	5 07.6
22 W	20 03 09	1 25 35	7♎11 48	13 11 20	11 41.8	11 37.9	15 39.1	26 04.6	9 57.4	8 10.3	26 36.7	26 13.7	8 07.3	5 06.5
23 Th	20 07 05	2 26 37	19 08 42	25 04 30	11D 39.7	13 03.0	16 54.3	26 52.0	10 21.0	8 03.4	26 32.5	26 16.9	8 05.6	5 05.4
24 F	20 11 02	3 27 38	0♏59 20	6♏53 54	11 39.4	14 28.9	18 09.5	27 39.3	10 44.6	7 56.7	26 28.3	26 20.2	8 04.0	5 04.3
25 Sa	20 14 58	4 28 39	12 48 50	18 44 51	11 40.3	15 55.7	19 24.6	28 26.6	11 08.2	7 50.2	26 24.0	26 23.5	8 02.3	5 03.3
26 Su	20 18 55	5 29 39	24 42 34	0♐42 40	11R 41.4	17 23.3	20 39.7	29 14.0	11 31.8	7 43.8	26 19.6	26 26.7	8 00.6	5 02.3
27 M	20 22 52	6 30 38	6♐45 46	12 52 27	11 41.9	18 51.6	21 54.8	0♓01.3	11 55.4	7 37.5	26 15.2	26 30.0	7 58.9	5 01.2
28 Tu	20 26 48	7 31 37	19 03 15	25 18 38	11 40.9	20 20.7	23 09.9	0 48.6	12 19.0	7 31.3	26 10.8	26 33.3	7 57.2	5 00.2
29 W	20 30 45	8 32 35	1♑38 58	8♑04 33	11 37.6	21 50.6	24 25.0	1 35.9	12 42.6	7 25.3	26 06.3	26 36.7	7 55.5	4 59.2
30 Th	20 34 41	9 33 33	14 35 34	21 12 05	11 31.7	23 21.2	25 40.1	2 23.2	13 06.2	7 19.4	26 01.8	26 40.0	7 53.8	4 58.2
31 F	20 38 38	10 34 29	27 54 03	4♒41 16	11 23.5	24 52.5	26 55.1	3 10.5	13 29.9	7 13.7	25 57.2	26 43.4	7 52.1	4 57.3

LONGITUDE — February 1919

Day	Sid.Time	☉	0 hr ☽	Noon ☽	True ☊	☿	♀	♂	⚳	♃	♄	♅	♆	♇
1 Sa	20 42 34	11♒35 24	11♒33 26	18♒30 07	11♐13.6	26♑24.6	28♒10.2	3♓57.8	13♒53.5	7♋08.1	25♌52.6	26♒46.7	7♌50.5	4♋56.3
2 Su	20 46 31	12 36 19	25 30 46	2♓34 47	11R 03.0	27 57.3	29 25.2	4 45.1	14 17.1	7R 02.7	25R 47.9	26 50.1	7R 48.8	4R 55.4
3 M	20 50 28	13 37 11	9♓41 28	16 50 07	10 52.9	29 30.8	0♓40.2	5 32.4	14 40.8	6 57.5	25 43.2	26 53.5	7 47.1	4 54.4
4 Tu	20 54 24	14 38 03	24 00 02	1♈10 31	10 44.4	1♒05.1	1 55.1	6 19.6	15 04.4	6 52.4	25 38.5	26 56.9	7 45.4	4 53.5
5 W	20 58 21	15 38 53	8♈20 57	15 30 48	10 38.3	2 40.1	3 10.1	7 06.9	15 28.0	6 47.5	25 33.8	27 00.3	7 43.7	4 52.6
6 Th	21 02 17	16 39 42	22 39 35	29 46 56	10 34.8	4 15.8	4 25.0	7 54.1	15 51.6	6 42.8	25 29.0	27 03.7	7 42.1	4 51.8
7 F	21 06 14	17 40 29	6♉52 35	13♉56 20	10D 33.6	5 52.3	5 39.9	8 41.3	16 15.2	6 38.2	25 24.2	27 07.2	7 40.4	4 50.9
8 Sa	21 10 10	18 41 15	20 58 03	27 57 41	10R 33.8	7 29.5	6 54.8	9 28.5	16 38.9	6 33.9	25 19.4	27 10.6	7 38.7	4 50.1
9 Su	21 14 07	19 41 59	4♊55 12	11♊50 36	10 34.1	9 07.6	8 09.6	10 15.6	17 02.5	6 29.7	25 14.6	27 14.0	7 37.1	4 49.2
10 M	21 18 03	20 42 42	18 43 53	25 35 04	10 33.2	10 46.4	9 24.4	11 02.8	17 26.1	6 25.7	25 09.8	27 17.5	7 35.4	4 48.4
11 Tu	21 22 00	21 43 23	2♋24 05	9♋10 55	10 30.1	12 26.0	10 39.2	11 49.9	17 49.6	6 21.8	25 04.9	27 20.9	7 33.8	4 47.6
12 W	21 25 57	22 44 02	15 55 28	22 37 36	10 24.1	14 06.5	11 54.0	12 37.0	18 13.2	6 18.2	25 00.1	27 24.4	7 32.2	4 46.9
13 Th	21 29 53	23 44 40	29 17 12	5♌54 04	10 15.1	15 47.8	13 08.7	13 24.1	18 36.8	6 14.7	24 55.2	27 27.8	7 30.6	4 46.1
14 F	21 33 50	24 45 16	12♌28 02	18 58 55	10 03.7	17 30.0	14 23.4	14 11.1	19 00.3	6 11.5	24 50.3	27 31.3	7 29.0	4 45.4
15 Sa	21 37 46	25 45 51	25 26 34	1♍50 49	9 50.6	19 13.0	15 38.1	14 58.2	19 23.9	6 08.4	24 45.5	27 34.8	7 27.4	4 44.7
16 Su	21 41 43	26 46 24	8♍11 35	14 28 49	9 37.0	20 57.0	16 52.7	15 45.2	19 47.4	6 05.5	24 40.6	27 38.2	7 25.8	4 44.0
17 M	21 45 39	27 46 56	20 42 32	26 52 48	9 24.3	22 41.8	18 07.3	16 32.1	20 10.9	6 02.8	24 35.8	27 41.7	7 24.2	4 43.3
18 Tu	21 49 36	28 47 27	2♎59 47	9♎03 43	9 13.4	24 27.5	19 21.9	17 19.1	20 34.4	6 00.3	24 30.9	27 45.1	7 22.7	4 42.6
19 W	21 53 32	29 47 56	15 04 52	21 03 36	9 05.0	26 14.2	20 36.5	18 06.0	20 57.9	5 58.0	24 26.1	27 48.6	7 21.1	4 42.0
20 Th	21 57 29	0♓48 23	27 00 23	2♏55 40	8 59.5	28 01.7	21 51.0	18 52.9	21 21.4	5 55.8	24 21.2	27 52.1	7 19.6	4 41.4
21 F	22 01 25	1 48 50	8♏50 02	14 44 03	8 56.5	29 50.2	23 05.5	19 39.8	21 44.8	5 53.9	24 16.4	27 55.5	7 18.1	4 40.8
22 Sa	22 05 22	2 49 15	20 38 22	26 33 38	8D 55.5	1♓39.6	24 20.0	20 26.7	22 08.3	5 52.2	24 11.6	27 59.0	7 16.6	4 40.2
23 Su	22 09 19	3 49 38	2♐30 34	8♐29 50	8R 55.4	3 29.8	25 34.4	21 13.5	22 31.7	5 50.7	24 06.9	28 02.4	7 15.1	4 39.6
24 M	22 13 15	4 50 01	14 32 10	20 38 14	8 55.1	5 21.0	26 48.8	22 00.3	22 55.1	5 49.3	24 02.1	28 05.9	7 13.6	4 39.1
25 Tu	22 17 12	5 50 22	26 48 43	3♑04 12	8 53.5	7 13.0	28 03.2	22 47.1	23 18.5	5 48.2	23 57.4	28 09.3	7 12.2	4 38.6
26 W	22 21 08	6 50 41	9♑25 16	15 52 23	8 49.6	9 05.7	29 17.5	23 33.9	23 41.9	5 47.3	23 52.7	28 12.8	7 10.8	4 38.1
27 Th	22 25 05	7 50 59	22 25 54	29 06 04	8 42.9	10 59.3	0♈31.8	24 20.6	24 05.2	5 46.5	23 48.1	28 16.2	7 09.4	4 37.6
28 F	22 29 01	8 51 15	5♒52 57	12♒46 30	8 33.6	12 53.4	1 46.1	25 07.3	24 28.5	5 46.0	23 43.4	28 19.6	7 08.0	4 37.2

Astro Data (Dy Hr Mn)

	Dy Hr Mn
♃⚼♅	5 6:16
☽0N	7 7:20
☽0S	20 10:28
♃⚺♆	23 1:37
♄☍♅	25 13:38
☽0N	3 14:29
☽0S	16 19:41

Planet Ingress (Dy Hr Mn)

		Dy Hr Mn
♀	♒	10 0:28
☿	♑	13 18:13
☉	♒	21 2:21
♂	♓	27 11:20
♀	♓	2 23:08
☿	♒	3 19:27
☉	♓	19 16:48
☿	♓	21 14:10
♀	♈	27 1:43

Last Aspect / ☽ Ingress (January)

Last Aspect Dy Hr Mn			☽ Ingress	Dy Hr Mn
1 7:51	♄	△	♑	1 12:01
3 3:38	♀	☌	♒	3 19:15
5 20:07	♄	☍	♓	6 0:18
7 23:38	♀	⚹	♈	8 4:00
10 2:35	♄	△	♉	10 7:01
12 5:10	♄	□	♊	12 9:49
14 8:01	♄	⚹	♋	14 12:56
16 8:44	☉	☍	♌	16 17:16
18 18:05	♄	☌	♍	18 23:57
19 16:00	♃	⚹	♎	21 9:43
23 15:54	♂	△	♏	23 22:00
26 8:51	♂	□	♐	26 10:35
28 14:23	♅	⚹	♑	28 20:54
30 16:22	☿	☌	♒	31 3:44

Last Aspect / ☽ Ingress (February)

Last Aspect Dy Hr Mn			☽ Ingress	Dy Hr Mn
2 6:08	♀	☌	♓	2 7:38
2 19:30	♃	△	♈	4 10:02
6 7:24	♅	⚹	♉	6 12:22
8 10:39	♅	□	♊	8 15:31
10 15:01	♅	△	♋	10 19:46
11 17:00	♂	△	♌	13 1:17
15 3:57	♅	☍	♍	15 8:32
16 17:07	♀	☍	♎	17 18:06
20 1:42	♅	△	♏	20 6:04
22 14:53	♅	□	♐	22 18:57
25 2:33	♅	⚹	♑	25 6:08
27 2:56	♂	⚹	♒	27 13:36

☽ Phases & Eclipses (Dy Hr Mn)

Dy Hr Mn	
2 8:24	● 10♑54
9 10:55	☽ 18♈09
16 8:44	○ 25♋11
24 4:22	☾ 3♏08
31 23:07	● 11♒03
7 18:52	☽ 17♉58
14 23:38	○ 25♌15
23 1:47	☾ 3♐24

Astro Data

1 January 1919
Julian Day # 6940
SVP 6♓23'10"
GC 25♐42.5 ⚴ 16♑26.9
Eris 27♓39.2 ⚵ 8♌34.3R
⚷ 29♓10.2 ⚶ 29♋49.0R
☽ Mean ☊ 11♐41.3

1 February 1919
Julian Day # 6971
SVP 6♓23'05"
GC 25♐42.6 ⚴ 28♑03.7
Eris 27♓51.0 ⚵ 1♌08.1R
⚷ 0♈09.4 ⚶ 21♋59.9R
☽ Mean ☊ 10♐02.8

March 1919 — LONGITUDE

Day	Sid.Time	☉	0 hr ☽	Noon ☽	True ☊	☿	♀	♂	⚳	♃	♄	♅	♆	♇
1 Sa	22 32 58	9♓51 30	19♒46 27	26♒52 21	8♐22.2	14♓48.2	3♈00.3	25♓54.0	24♒51.8	5♋45.7	23♌38.9	28♒23.0	7♌06.6	4♋36.7
2 Su	22 36 54	10 51 43	4♓03 36	11♓19 24	8R 09.9	16 43.3	4 14.5	26 40.6	25 15.1	5D 45.5	23R 34.3	28 26.5	7R 05.2	4R 36.3
3 M	22 40 51	11 51 54	18 38 51	26 00 55	7 58.0	18 38.8	5 28.7	27 27.2	25 38.3	5 45.6	23 29.8	28 29.8	7 03.9	4 35.9
4 Tu	22 44 48	12 52 03	3♈24 35	10♈48 44	7 47.8	20 34.4	6 42.8	28 13.8	26 01.5	5 45.8	23 25.3	28 33.2	7 02.6	4 35.6
5 W	22 48 44	13 52 10	18 12 23	25 34 35	7 40.3	22 29.9	7 56.9	29 00.3	26 24.7	5 46.3	23 20.9	28 36.6	7 01.3	4 35.2
6 Th	22 52 41	14 52 16	2♉54 31	10♉11 30	7 35.7	24 25.2	9 11.0	29 46.8	26 47.9	5 47.0	23 16.6	28 40.0	7 00.0	4 34.9
7 F	22 56 37	15 52 19	17 25 01	24 34 41	7D 33.6	26 19.8	10 25.0	0♈33.3	27 11.0	5 47.8	23 12.3	28 43.3	6 58.8	4 34.6
8 Sa	23 00 34	16 52 20	1♊40 16	8♊41 40	7R 33.2	28 13.5	11 38.9	1 19.7	27 34.1	5 48.9	23 08.0	28 46.7	6 57.5	4 34.4
9 Su	23 04 30	17 52 18	15 38 52	22 31 56	7 33.2	0♈06.0	12 52.9	2 06.1	27 57.1	5 50.1	23 03.8	28 50.0	6 56.3	4 34.1
10 M	23 08 27	18 52 15	29 21 01	6♋06 18	7 32.3	1 56.9	14 06.7	2 52.5	28 20.1	5 51.6	22 59.7	28 53.3	6 55.2	4 33.9
11 Tu	23 12 23	19 52 09	12♋47 57	19 26 10	7 29.2	3 45.7	15 20.6	3 38.8	28 43.1	5 53.2	22 55.6	28 56.6	6 54.0	4 33.7
12 W	23 16 20	20 52 01	26 01 08	2♌33 00	7 23.5	5 32.0	16 34.3	4 25.1	29 06.1	5 55.0	22 51.6	28 59.9	6 52.9	4 33.5
13 Th	23 20 17	21 51 51	9♌01 54	15 27 58	7 14.8	7 15.3	17 48.1	5 11.3	29 29.0	5 57.0	22 47.7	29 03.2	6 51.8	4 33.3
14 F	23 24 13	22 51 39	21 51 14	28 11 47	7 03.7	8 55.1	19 01.7	5 57.5	29 51.9	5 59.3	22 43.8	29 06.4	6 50.7	4 33.2
15 Sa	23 28 10	23 51 25	4♍29 39	10♍44 51	6 51.0	10 31.0	20 15.4	6 43.7	0♓14.7	6 01.6	22 40.0	29 09.6	6 49.7	4 33.1
16 Su	23 32 06	24 51 08	16 57 25	23 07 24	6 37.7	12 02.4	21 29.0	7 29.8	0 37.5	6 04.2	22 36.2	29 12.8	6 48.6	4 33.0
17 M	23 36 03	25 50 50	29 14 50	5♎19 49	6 25.2	13 28.8	22 42.5	8 15.8	1 00.2	6 07.0	22 32.6	29 16.0	6 47.6	4 33.0
18 Tu	23 39 59	26 50 29	11♎22 28	17 22 56	6 14.3	14 49.8	23 56.0	9 01.9	1 23.0	6 09.9	22 29.0	29 19.2	6 46.7	4 32.9
19 W	23 43 56	27 50 07	23 21 26	29 18 14	6 05.9	16 05.0	25 09.4	9 47.9	1 45.6	6 13.1	22 25.5	29 22.3	6 45.7	4D 32.9
20 Th	23 47 52	28 49 43	5♏13 37	11♏07 59	6 00.3	17 14.0	26 22.8	10 33.8	2 08.3	6 16.4	22 22.0	29 25.5	6 44.8	4 32.9
21 F	23 51 49	29 49 17	17 01 45	22 55 22	5 57.2	18 16.3	27 36.1	11 19.7	2 30.8	6 19.9	22 18.7	29 28.6	6 43.9	4 32.9
22 Sa	23 55 46	0♈48 49	28 49 22	4♐44 18	5D 56.3	19 11.7	28 49.4	12 05.6	2 53.4	6 23.6	22 15.4	29 31.7	6 43.1	4 33.0
23 Su	23 59 42	1 48 20	10♐40 48	16 39 30	5 56.7	19 59.9	0♉02.7	12 51.4	3 15.9	6 27.4	22 12.2	29 34.7	6 42.2	4 33.1
24 M	0 03 39	2 47 49	22 41 02	28 46 05	5R 57.2	20 40.8	1 15.8	13 37.2	3 38.3	6 31.4	22 09.1	29 37.8	6 41.4	4 33.2
25 Tu	0 07 35	3 47 16	4♑55 19	11♑09 25	5 57.0	21 14.0	2 29.0	14 22.9	4 00.8	6 35.6	22 06.1	29 40.8	6 40.7	4 33.3
26 W	0 11 32	4 46 41	17 28 38	23 54 36	5 55.2	21 39.7	3 42.1	15 08.6	4 23.1	6 40.0	22 03.2	29 43.8	6 39.9	4 33.4
27 Th	0 15 28	5 46 04	0♒26 45	7♒05 52	5 51.2	21 57.6	4 55.1	15 54.3	4 45.4	6 44.5	22 00.3	29 46.8	6 39.2	4 33.6
28 F	0 19 25	6 45 26	13 52 11	20 45 50	5 44.9	22R 07.9	6 08.1	16 39.9	5 07.7	6 49.3	21 57.6	29 49.7	6 38.5	4 33.8
29 Sa	0 23 21	7 44 46	27 46 44	4♓54 40	5 36.8	22 10.7	7 21.0	17 25.5	5 29.9	6 54.1	21 54.9	29 52.6	6 37.9	4 34.0
30 Su	0 27 18	8 44 04	12♓09 07	19 29 27	5 27.8	22 06.2	8 33.9	18 11.0	5 52.0	6 59.2	21 52.4	29 55.5	6 37.3	4 34.3
31 M	0 31 14	9 43 19	26 54 47	4♈24 04	5 18.9	21 54.6	9 46.7	18 56.5	6 14.1	7 04.4	21 49.9	29 58.4	6 36.7	4 34.5

April 1919 — LONGITUDE

Day	Sid.Time	☉	0 hr ☽	Noon ☽	True ☊	☿	♀	♂	⚳	♃	♄	♅	♆	♇
1 Tu	0 35 11	10♈42 33	11♈56 09	19♈29 47	5♐11.3	21♈36.4	10♉59.5	19♈42.0	6♓36.1	7♋09.8	21♌47.5	0♓01.2	6♌36.1	4♋34.8
2 W	0 39 08	11 41 45	27 03 42	4♉36 40	5R 05.8	21R 12.1	12 12.2	20 27.4	6 58.1	7 15.3	21R 45.2	0 04.0	6R 35.6	4 35.1
3 Th	0 43 04	12 40 55	12♉07 31	19 35 15	5 02.6	20 42.2	13 24.8	21 12.7	7 20.0	7 21.0	21 43.1	0 06.8	6 35.1	4 35.4
4 F	0 47 01	13 40 03	26 59 00	4♊18 04	5D 01.6	20 07.4	14 37.4	21 58.0	7 41.9	7 26.9	21 41.0	0 09.5	6 34.6	4 35.8
5 Sa	0 50 57	14 39 08	11♊31 58	18 40 21	5 02.2	19 28.5	15 49.9	22 43.3	8 03.7	7 32.9	21 39.0	0 12.2	6 34.2	4 36.2
6 Su	0 54 54	15 38 11	25 43 04	2♋40 03	5 03.2	18 46.3	17 02.4	23 28.5	8 25.4	7 39.1	21 37.1	0 14.9	6 33.8	4 36.6
7 M	0 58 50	16 37 12	9♋31 24	16 17 18	5R 03.8	18 01.6	18 14.8	24 13.6	8 47.1	7 45.4	21 35.3	0 17.6	6 33.5	4 37.0
8 Tu	1 02 47	17 36 10	22 58 00	29 33 46	5 03.1	17 15.5	19 27.1	24 58.7	9 08.7	7 51.9	21 33.7	0 20.2	6 33.1	4 37.5
9 W	1 06 43	18 35 06	6♌04 56	12♌31 49	5 00.4	16 28.7	20 39.3	25 43.8	9 30.2	7 58.5	21 32.1	0 22.8	6 32.8	4 37.9
10 Th	1 10 40	19 33 59	18 54 46	25 14 06	4 55.7	15 42.3	21 51.5	26 28.8	9 51.7	8 05.3	21 30.6	0 25.3	6 32.6	4 38.4
11 F	1 14 37	20 32 51	1♍30 06	7♍43 05	4 49.3	14 57.0	23 03.6	27 13.7	10 13.1	8 12.2	21 29.3	0 27.8	6 32.3	4 38.9
12 Sa	1 18 33	21 31 40	13 53 17	20 00 58	4 41.7	14 13.6	24 15.7	27 58.6	10 34.4	8 19.2	21 28.0	0 30.3	6 32.1	4 39.5
13 Su	1 22 30	22 30 27	26 06 21	2♎09 38	4 33.7	13 32.9	25 27.6	28 43.5	10 55.7	8 26.4	21 26.8	0 32.8	6 31.9	4 40.0
14 M	1 26 26	23 29 12	8♎11 00	14 10 40	4 26.0	12 55.6	26 39.5	29 28.3	11 16.8	8 33.7	21 25.8	0 35.2	6 31.8	4 40.6
15 Tu	1 30 23	24 27 55	20 08 49	26 05 40	4 19.5	12 22.0	27 51.4	0♉13.0	11 37.9	8 41.2	21 24.8	0 37.5	6 31.7	4 41.2
16 W	1 34 19	25 26 36	2♏01 24	7♏56 16	4 14.7	11 52.7	29 03.1	0 57.7	11 59.0	8 48.8	21 24.0	0 39.9	6 31.6	4 41.8
17 Th	1 38 16	26 25 15	13 50 31	19 44 27	4 11.7	11 28.0	0♊14.8	1 42.4	12 19.9	8 56.5	21 23.3	0 42.2	6D 31.6	4 42.5
18 F	1 42 12	27 23 52	25 38 22	1♐32 39	4D 10.5	11 08.1	1 26.4	2 27.0	12 40.8	9 04.4	21 22.6	0 44.4	6 31.6	4 43.1
19 Sa	1 46 09	28 22 28	7♐27 39	13 23 50	4 10.9	10 53.3	2 37.9	3 11.6	13 01.6	9 12.4	21 22.1	0 46.7	6 31.6	4 43.8
20 Su	1 50 06	29 21 02	19 21 37	25 21 32	4 12.2	10 43.5	3 49.4	3 56.1	13 22.4	9 20.5	21 21.7	0 48.9	6 31.7	4 44.5
21 M	1 54 02	0♉19 34	1♑24 06	7♑29 51	4 14.0	10D 38.8	5 00.7	4 40.5	13 43.0	9 28.8	21 21.4	0 51.0	6 31.8	4 45.2
22 Tu	1 57 59	1 18 04	13 39 21	19 53 10	4R 15.4	10 39.3	6 12.0	5 24.9	14 03.6	9 37.2	21 21.2	0 53.1	6 31.9	4 46.0
23 W	2 01 55	2 16 33	26 11 53	2♒36 01	4 15.9	10 44.7	7 23.3	6 09.3	14 24.1	9 45.6	21D 21.1	0 55.2	6 32.1	4 46.7
24 Th	2 05 52	3 15 00	9♒06 04	15 42 29	4 15.3	10 55.1	8 34.4	6 53.6	14 44.5	9 54.3	21 21.1	0 57.2	6 32.3	4 47.5
25 F	2 09 48	4 13 26	22 25 37	29 15 41	4 13.3	11 10.2	9 45.5	7 37.9	15 04.8	10 03.0	21 21.2	0 59.2	6 32.5	4 48.3
26 Sa	2 13 45	5 11 50	6♓12 50	13♓17 00	4 10.1	11 30.0	10 56.5	8 22.1	15 25.0	10 11.9	21 21.5	1 01.2	6 32.8	4 49.1
27 Su	2 17 41	6 10 12	20 27 57	27 45 17	4 06.3	11 54.3	12 07.4	9 06.2	15 45.1	10 20.8	21 21.8	1 03.1	6 33.1	4 50.0
28 M	2 21 38	7 08 33	5♈08 22	12♈36 25	4 02.5	12 22.9	13 18.2	9 50.3	16 05.2	10 29.9	21 22.2	1 04.9	6 33.4	4 50.8
29 Tu	2 25 35	8 06 52	20 08 27	27 43 21	3 59.1	12 55.7	14 28.9	10 34.4	16 25.1	10 39.1	21 22.8	1 06.8	6 33.8	4 51.7
30 W	2 29 31	9 05 10	5♉19 54	12♉56 51	3 56.8	13 32.4	15 39.6	11 18.4	16 45.0	10 48.4	21 23.4	1 08.5	6 34.2	4 52.6

Astro Data

	Dy Hr Mn
♀0N	1 1:09
♃ D	2 16:35
☽ 0N	2 23:50
♂0N	8 18:50
☿0N	9 15:22
☽ 0S	16 3:08
♇ D	19 17:34
☉0N	21 16:19
♃⊻♆	26 11:40
☿ R	29 9:00
♃∠♄	29 14:29
☽ 0N	30 10:19
☽ 0S	12 8:46
♆ D	18 1:28
☿ D	21 21:58

Planet Ingress

		Dy Hr Mn
♂	♈	6 18:48
☿	♈	9 10:42
⚳	♓	14 20:33
☉	♈	21 16:19
♀	♉	23 11:08
♅	♓	1 1:48
♂	♉	15 5:00
♀	♊	17 7:03
☉	♉	21 3:59

♄ D23 21:10
☽ 0N26 20:13

Last Aspect / ☽ Ingress (March)

Last Aspect Dy Hr Mn			☽ Ingress	Dy Hr Mn
1 14:33	♅	☌	♓	1 17:14
3 14:28	♂	☌	♈	3 18:28
5 16:59	♅	⚹	♉	5 19:14
7 19:02	♅	□	♊	7 21:10
9 23:08	♅	△	♋	10 1:09
11 12:51	☉	△	♌	12 7:18
14 13:44	♅	☍	♍	14 15:26
16 15:41	☉	☍	♎	17 1:29
19 12:08	♅	△	♏	19 13:24
22 1:23	♅	□	♐	22 2:23
24 13:42	♅	⚹	♑	24 14:25
26 7:42	☿	□	♒	26 23:11
29 3:31	♅	☌	♓	29 3:45
29 16:26	♀	⚹	♈	31 4:57

Last Aspect / ☽ Ingress (April)

Last Aspect Dy Hr Mn			☽ Ingress	Dy Hr Mn
1 15:38	♄	△	♉	2 4:40
3 15:26	♄	□	♊	4 4:56
5 19:16	♂	⚹	♋	6 7:22
8 3:09	♂	□	♌	8 12:48
10 14:32	♂	△	♍	10 21:07
12 21:16	♀	△	♎	13 7:43
15 8:25	☉	☍	♏	15 19:54
17 15:21	♄	□	♐	18 8:52
20 20:38	☉	△	♑	20 21:14
21 18:09	☿	□	♒	23 7:09
24 22:06	♄	☍	♓	25 13:17
26 7:41	♀	□	♈	27 15:40
29 1:58	♄	△	♉	29 15:36

☽ Phases & Eclipses

Dy Hr Mn		
2 11:11	●	10♓50
9 3:14	☽	17♊30
16 15:41	○	25♍00
24 20:34	☾	3♑09
31 21:04	●	10♈06
7 12:38	☽	16♋39
15 8:25	○	24♎19
23 11:21	☾	2♒15
30 5:30	●	8♉49

Astro Data

1 March 1919
Julian Day # 6999
SVP 6♓23'01"
GC 25♐42.6 ⚴ 7♒57.7
Eris 28♓09.1 ⚵ 26♋59.1R
⚷ 1♈33.6 ⚶ 18♋02.5R
☽ Mean ☊ 8♐33.8

1 April 1919
Julian Day # 7030
SVP 6♓22'59"
GC 25♐42.7 ⚴ 17♒41.8
Eris 28♓32.5 ⚵ 29♋05.3
⚷ 3♈21.9 ⚶ 20♋19.8
☽ Mean ☊ 6♐55.3

LONGITUDE May 1919

Day	Sid.Time	☉	0 hr ☽	Noon ☽	True ☊	☿	♀	♂	⚳	♃	♄	♅	♆	♇
1 Th	2 33 28	10♉03 26	20♉32 54	28♉06 53	3♐55.8	14♈13.0	16♊50.1	12♉02.4	17♓04.7	10♋57.8	21♌24.2	1♓10.3	6♌34.6	4♋53.5
2 F	2 37 24	11 01 40	5♊37 39	13♊04 14	3D55.9	14 57.2	18 00.6	12 46.3	17 24.4	11 07.4	21 25.1	1 12.0	6 35.1	4 54.5
3 Sa	2 41 21	11 59 52	20 25 49	27 41 45	3 56.9	15 45.0	19 11.0	13 30.1	17 44.0	11 17.0	21 26.1	1 13.6	6 35.6	4 55.4
4 Su	2 45 17	12 58 02	4♋51 36	11♋55 03	3 58.2	16 36.1	20 21.3	14 13.9	18 03.4	11 26.7	21 27.2	1 15.2	6 36.1	4 56.4
5 M	2 49 14	13 56 10	18 51 59	25 42 26	3 59.5	17 30.5	21 31.5	14 57.7	18 22.8	11 36.6	21 28.3	1 16.8	6 36.6	4 57.4
6 Tu	2 53 10	14 54 16	2♌26 31	9♌04 28	4R00.2	18 28.0	22 41.6	15 41.4	18 42.0	11 46.5	21 29.6	1 18.3	6 37.2	4 58.4
7 W	2 57 07	15 52 20	15 36 36	22 03 19	4 00.2	19 28.5	23 51.5	16 25.0	19 01.1	11 56.6	21 31.0	1 19.8	6 37.9	4 59.4
8 Th	3 01 04	16 50 22	28 25 01	4♍42 08	3 59.4	20 31.9	25 01.4	17 08.6	19 20.1	12 06.7	21 32.5	1 21.2	6 38.5	5 00.5
9 F	3 05 00	17 48 23	10♍55 07	17 04 26	3 57.8	21 38.1	26 11.2	17 52.2	19 39.1	12 16.9	21 34.1	1 22.6	6 39.2	5 01.5
10 Sa	3 08 57	18 46 21	23 10 32	29 13 50	3 55.8	22 47.0	27 20.8	18 35.6	19 57.9	12 27.2	21 35.9	1 23.9	6 39.9	5 02.6
11 Su	3 12 53	19 44 18	5♎14 45	11♎13 41	3 53.6	23 58.6	28 30.4	19 19.0	20 16.5	12 37.6	21 37.7	1 25.2	6 40.7	5 03.7
12 M	3 16 50	20 42 13	17 11 00	23 07 03	3 51.6	25 12.7	29 39.8	20 02.4	20 35.1	12 48.1	21 39.6	1 26.5	6 41.5	5 04.8
13 Tu	3 20 46	21 40 06	29 02 10	4♏56 40	3 50.0	26 29.3	0♋49.2	20 45.7	20 53.6	12 58.7	21 41.6	1 27.7	6 42.3	5 05.9
14 W	3 24 43	22 37 58	10♏50 50	16 44 58	3 48.8	27 48.4	1 58.4	21 29.0	21 11.9	13 09.4	21 43.7	1 28.8	6 43.1	5 07.0
15 Th	3 28 39	23 35 48	22 39 20	28 34 12	3D48.3	29 09.9	3 07.4	22 12.2	21 30.1	13 20.1	21 45.9	1 29.9	6 44.0	5 08.2
16 F	3 32 36	24 33 37	4♐29 52	10♐26 35	3 48.4	0♉33.7	4 16.4	22 55.4	21 48.2	13 31.0	21 48.2	1 31.0	6 44.9	5 09.3
17 Sa	3 36 33	25 31 24	16 24 40	22 24 23	3 48.8	1 59.9	5 25.3	23 38.5	22 06.2	13 41.9	21 50.7	1 32.0	6 45.8	5 10.5
18 Su	3 40 29	26 29 11	28 26 05	4♑30 04	3 49.5	3 28.4	6 34.0	24 21.5	22 24.0	13 52.9	21 53.2	1 33.0	6 46.8	5 11.7
19 M	3 44 26	27 26 56	10♑36 41	16 46 19	3 50.2	4 59.2	7 42.6	25 04.5	22 41.7	14 04.0	21 55.8	1 33.9	6 47.8	5 12.9
20 Tu	3 48 22	28 24 40	22 59 19	29 16 04	3 50.8	6 32.3	8 51.0	25 47.5	22 59.3	14 15.1	21 58.5	1 34.8	6 48.8	5 14.1
21 W	3 52 19	29 22 22	5♒36 59	12♒02 24	3 51.2	8 07.6	9 59.4	26 30.4	23 16.8	14 26.4	22 01.3	1 35.6	6 49.9	5 15.3
22 Th	3 56 15	0♊20 04	18 32 44	25 08 17	3R51.3	9 45.2	11 07.6	27 13.3	23 34.1	14 37.7	22 04.2	1 36.4	6 51.0	5 16.6
23 F	4 00 12	1 17 44	1♓49 21	8♓36 11	3 51.3	11 25.0	12 15.6	27 56.1	23 51.2	14 49.1	22 07.2	1 37.1	6 52.1	5 17.8
24 Sa	4 04 08	2 15 24	15 28 56	22 27 39	3 51.2	13 07.0	13 23.6	28 38.8	24 08.3	15 00.5	22 10.3	1 37.8	6 53.2	5 19.1
25 Su	4 08 05	3 13 03	29 32 17	6♈42 39	3D51.2	14 51.3	14 31.4	29 21.5	24 25.2	15 12.0	22 13.4	1 38.4	6 54.4	5 20.4
26 M	4 12 02	4 10 40	13♈58 25	21 19 05	3 51.1	16 37.9	15 39.0	0♊04.2	24 41.9	15 23.6	22 16.7	1 39.0	6 55.6	5 21.7
27 Tu	4 15 58	5 08 17	28 44 02	6♉12 28	3 51.2	18 26.6	16 46.5	0 46.8	24 58.5	15 35.3	22 20.1	1 39.5	6 56.8	5 23.0
28 W	4 19 55	6 05 53	13♉43 29	21 16 02	3R51.3	20 17.6	17 53.9	1 29.4	25 15.0	15 47.0	22 23.5	1 40.0	6 58.0	5 24.3
29 Th	4 23 51	7 03 28	28 49 04	6♊21 26	3 51.4	22 10.8	19 01.1	2 11.9	25 31.3	15 58.8	22 27.1	1 40.4	6 59.3	5 25.6
30 F	4 27 48	8 01 01	13♊52 01	21 19 45	3 51.2	24 06.1	20 08.2	2 54.4	25 47.4	16 10.7	22 30.7	1 40.8	7 00.6	5 26.9
31 Sa	4 31 44	8 58 34	28 43 40	6♋02 53	3 50.9	26 03.6	21 15.1	3 36.8	26 03.4	16 22.6	22 34.4	1 41.1	7 02.0	5 28.3

LONGITUDE June 1919

Day	Sid.Time	☉	0 hr ☽	Noon ☽	True ☊	☿	♀	♂	⚳	♃	♄	♅	♆	♇
1 Su	4 35 41	9♊56 05	13♋16 41	20♋24 31	3♐50.3	28♉03.1	22♋21.8	4♊19.1	26♓19.2	16♋34.6	22♌38.3	1♓41.4	7♌03.3	5♋29.6
2 M	4 39 37	10 53 36	27 25 58	4♌20 48	3R49.5	0♊04.6	23 28.4	5 01.4	26 34.9	16 46.6	22 42.2	1 41.7	7 04.7	5 31.0
3 Tu	4 43 34	11 51 04	11♌08 58	17 50 30	3 48.8	2 07.9	24 34.7	5 43.7	26 50.4	16 58.7	22 46.1	1 41.8	7 06.1	5 32.4
4 W	4 47 31	12 48 32	24 25 36	0♍54 33	3 48.2	4 13.1	25 41.0	6 25.9	27 05.7	17 10.9	22 50.2	1 42.0	7 07.6	5 33.7
5 Th	4 51 27	13 45 58	7♍17 44	13 35 36	3D48.0	6 19.8	26 47.0	7 08.0	27 20.8	17 23.1	22 54.4	1 42.1	7 09.0	5 35.1
6 F	4 55 24	14 43 23	19 48 38	25 57 23	3 48.3	8 28.0	27 52.8	7 50.1	27 35.8	17 35.3	22 58.6	1R42.1	7 10.5	5 36.5
7 Sa	4 59 20	15 40 47	2♎02 23	8♎04 12	3 49.0	10 37.4	28 58.4	8 32.1	27 50.6	17 47.6	23 02.9	1 42.1	7 12.0	5 37.9
8 Su	5 03 17	16 38 10	14 03 24	20 00 30	3 50.0	12 47.9	0♌03.9	9 14.1	28 05.2	18 00.0	23 07.3	1 42.0	7 13.5	5 39.3
9 M	5 07 13	17 35 32	25 56 03	1♏50 34	3 51.3	14 59.2	1 09.1	9 56.1	28 19.7	18 12.4	23 11.8	1 41.9	7 15.1	5 40.7
10 Tu	5 11 10	18 32 53	7♏44 32	13 38 23	3 52.4	17 10.9	2 14.1	10 37.9	28 33.9	18 24.9	23 16.3	1 41.8	7 16.7	5 42.2
11 W	5 15 06	19 30 13	19 32 32	25 27 25	3R53.2	19 23.0	3 18.9	11 19.8	28 48.0	18 37.4	23 21.0	1 41.6	7 18.3	5 43.6
12 Th	5 19 03	20 27 32	1♐23 21	7♐20 40	3 53.3	21 35.0	4 23.4	12 01.6	29 01.9	18 49.9	23 25.7	1 41.3	7 19.9	5 45.0
13 F	5 23 00	21 24 51	13 19 41	19 20 38	3 52.7	23 46.7	5 27.8	12 43.3	29 15.6	19 02.5	23 30.5	1 41.0	7 21.6	5 46.5
14 Sa	5 26 56	22 22 08	25 23 48	1♑29 22	3 51.1	25 57.9	6 31.9	13 25.0	29 29.0	19 15.1	23 35.3	1 40.7	7 23.2	5 47.9
15 Su	5 30 53	23 19 26	7♑37 33	13 48 31	3 48.8	28 08.2	7 35.8	14 06.6	29 42.3	19 27.8	23 40.3	1 40.3	7 24.9	5 49.4
16 M	5 34 49	24 16 42	20 02 26	26 19 29	3 45.9	0♋17.5	8 39.4	14 48.2	29 55.4	19 40.5	23 45.3	1 39.9	7 26.6	5 50.8
17 Tu	5 38 46	25 13 59	2♒39 46	9♒03 29	3 42.7	2 25.6	9 42.8	15 29.7	0♈08.3	19 53.3	23 50.4	1 39.4	7 28.4	5 52.3
18 W	5 42 42	26 11 14	15 30 45	22 01 42	3 39.8	4 32.2	10 45.9	16 11.2	0 21.0	20 06.1	23 55.5	1 38.8	7 30.1	5 53.7
19 Th	5 46 39	27 08 30	28 36 28	5♓15 12	3 37.5	6 37.2	11 48.7	16 52.7	0 33.5	20 18.9	24 00.8	1 38.3	7 31.9	5 55.2
20 F	5 50 35	28 05 45	11♓58 00	18 44 58	3D36.2	8 40.4	12 51.3	17 34.1	0 45.8	20 31.7	24 06.0	1 37.6	7 33.7	5 56.7
21 Sa	5 54 32	29 03 00	25 36 11	2♈31 40	3 35.9	10 41.9	13 53.6	18 15.4	0 57.8	20 44.6	24 11.4	1 37.0	7 35.5	5 58.2
22 Su	5 58 29	0♋00 15	9♈31 24	16 35 18	3 36.6	12 41.4	14 55.6	18 56.7	1 09.6	20 57.6	24 16.8	1 36.2	7 37.3	5 59.6
23 M	6 02 25	0 57 30	23 43 14	0♉54 57	3 37.9	14 38.9	15 57.3	19 38.0	1 21.2	21 10.5	24 22.3	1 35.5	7 39.2	6 01.1
24 Tu	6 06 22	1 54 45	8♉10 06	15 28 15	3 39.3	16 34.3	16 58.8	20 19.2	1 32.6	21 23.5	24 27.9	1 34.7	7 41.0	6 02.6
25 W	6 10 18	2 52 00	22 48 51	0♊11 15	3R40.1	18 27.6	17 59.9	21 00.4	1 43.7	21 36.6	24 33.5	1 33.8	7 42.9	6 04.1
26 Th	6 14 15	3 49 15	7♊34 42	14 58 22	3 39.7	20 18.8	19 00.7	21 41.5	1 54.6	21 49.6	24 39.2	1 32.9	7 44.8	6 05.6
27 F	6 18 11	4 46 29	22 21 22	29 42 49	3 37.9	22 07.9	20 01.2	22 22.6	2 05.3	22 02.7	24 45.0	1 32.0	7 46.8	6 07.1
28 Sa	6 22 08	5 43 44	7♋01 47	14♋17 24	3 34.6	23 54.8	21 01.3	23 03.6	2 15.7	22 15.8	24 50.8	1 31.0	7 48.7	6 08.5
29 Su	6 26 04	6 40 58	21 28 54	28 35 34	3 30.1	25 39.5	22 01.1	23 44.6	2 25.9	22 29.0	24 56.7	1 30.0	7 50.6	6 10.0
30 M	6 30 01	7 38 12	5♌36 50	12♌32 15	3 25.0	27 22.0	23 00.5	24 25.5	2 35.8	22 42.1	25 02.6	1 28.9	7 52.6	6 11.5

Astro Data

	Dy Hr Mn
☽0S	9 14:01
☽0N	24 4:25
♃□♅	2 1:55
☽0S	5 20:36
♅ R	6 19:12
☽0N	20 10:59

Planet Ingress

		Dy Hr Mn
♀	♋	12 18:59
☿	♉	16 2:25
☉	♊	22 3:39
♂	♊	26 9:38
☿	♊	2 11:06
♀	♌	8 10:35
☿	♋	16 8:44
⚳	♈	16 20:26
☉	♋	22 11:54

Last Aspect / ☽ Ingress (May)

Last Aspect Dy Hr Mn		☽ Ingress	Dy Hr Mn
1 1:21	♄ □	♊	1 15:00
3 1:38	♄ ⚹	♋	3 15:50
4 20:37	☿ □	♌	5 19:38
7 15:44	♀ ⚹	♍	8 3:01
10 7:52	♀ □	♎	10 13:32
12 16:45	☿ ☍	♏	13 1:57
15 1:01	☉ ☍	♐	15 14:54
17 10:52	♄ △	♑	18 3:06
20 10:14	☉ △	♒	20 13:23
22 15:58	♂ □	♓	22 20:45
24 23:03	♂ ⚹	♈	25 0:47
26 13:34	♄ △	♉	27 2:02
28 13:48	♄ □	♊	29 1:53
30 13:55	♄ ⚹	♋	31 2:05

Last Aspect / ☽ Ingress (June)

Last Aspect Dy Hr Mn		☽ Ingress	Dy Hr Mn
2 3:17	☿ ⚹	♌	2 4:26
3 21:00	♄ ☌	♍	4 10:18
6 16:09	♀ ⚹	♎	6 19:58
8 18:20	♄ ⚹	♏	9 8:15
11 7:42	♄ □	♐	11 21:12
13 22:44	☿ ☍	♑	14 9:04
15 23:05	♃ ☍	♒	16 18:58
18 20:12	☉ △	♓	19 2:31
21 5:33	☉ □	♈	21 7:38
23 1:01	♄ △	♉	23 10:29
25 2:47	♄ □	♊	25 11:42
27 3:51	♄ ⚹	♋	27 12:28
29 6:20	☿ ☌	♌	29 14:24

☽ Phases & Eclipses

Dy Hr Mn	
6 23:33	☽ 15♌22
15 1:01	○ 23♏09
15 1:14	A 0.910
22 22:04	☾ 0♓44
29 13:12	● 7♊06
29 13:08:34	T 06'51"
5 12:22	☽ 13♍47
13 16:28	○ 21♐36
21 5:33	☾ 28♓48
27 20:52	● 5♋08

Astro Data

1 May 1919
Julian Day # 7060
SVP 6♓22'56"
GC 25♐42.8 ⚴ 25♒08.6
Eris 28♓53.0 ⚵ 6♌01.2
⚷ 5♈01.6 ⚶ 27♋41.3
☽ Mean ☊ 5♐20.0

1 June 1919
Julian Day # 7091
SVP 6♓22'51"
GC 25♐42.8 ⚴ 29♒38.0
Eris 29♓07.1 ⚵ 15♌56.0
⚷ 6♈19.8 ⚶ 8♌32.8
☽ Mean ☊ 3♐41.5

July 1919 — LONGITUDE

Day	Sid.Time	☉	0 hr ☽	Noon ☽	True ☊	☿	♀	♂	⚳	♃	♄	♅	♆	♇
1 Tu	6 33 58	8♋35 25	19♌21 32	26♌04 32	3♐19.9	29♋02.3	23♌59.6	25♊06.4	2♈45.4	22♋55.3	25♌08.6	1♓27.8	7♌54.6	6♋13.0
2 W	6 37 54	9 32 39	2♍41 15	9♍11 49	3R 15.5	0♌40.5	24 58.3	25 47.2	2 54.8	23 08.5	25 14.7	1R 26.6	7 56.6	6 14.5
3 Th	6 41 51	10 29 51	15 36 29	21 55 35	3 12.4	2 16.4	25 56.5	26 28.0	3 04.0	23 21.7	25 20.8	1 25.4	7 58.6	6 16.0
4 F	6 45 47	11 27 04	28 09 34	4♎18 57	3D 10.7	3 50.2	26 54.4	27 08.7	3 12.8	23 34.9	25 26.9	1 24.2	8 00.6	6 17.5
5 Sa	6 49 44	12 24 16	10♎24 16	16 26 08	3 10.5	5 21.7	27 51.8	27 49.4	3 21.5	23 48.2	25 33.1	1 22.9	8 02.7	6 18.9
6 Su	6 53 40	13 21 28	22 25 10	28 22 01	3 11.5	6 51.0	28 48.8	28 30.0	3 29.8	24 01.5	25 39.4	1 21.6	8 04.7	6 20.4
7 M	6 57 37	14 18 40	4♏17 17	10♏11 36	3 13.0	8 18.0	29 45.3	29 10.6	3 37.9	24 14.8	25 45.7	1 20.2	8 06.8	6 21.9
8 Tu	7 01 33	15 15 52	16 05 37	21 59 52	3R 14.4	9 42.7	0♍41.3	29 51.2	3 45.6	24 28.0	25 52.1	1 18.8	8 08.8	6 23.4
9 W	7 05 30	16 13 03	27 54 57	3♐51 22	3 15.0	11 05.1	1 36.9	0♋31.7	3 53.2	24 41.4	25 58.5	1 17.4	8 10.9	6 24.8
10 Th	7 09 27	17 10 15	9♐49 35	15 50 03	3 14.1	12 25.2	2 31.9	1 12.1	4 00.4	24 54.7	26 05.0	1 15.9	8 13.0	6 26.3
11 F	7 13 23	18 07 27	21 53 08	27 59 09	3 11.3	13 42.8	3 26.4	1 52.5	4 07.3	25 08.0	26 11.5	1 14.4	8 15.1	6 27.8
12 Sa	7 17 20	19 04 39	4♑08 22	10♑21 00	3 06.6	14 58.1	4 20.4	2 32.9	4 14.0	25 21.4	26 18.1	1 12.8	8 17.3	6 29.2
13 Su	7 21 16	20 01 51	16 37 10	22 56 59	3 00.0	16 10.8	5 13.8	3 13.2	4 20.3	25 34.7	26 24.7	1 11.2	8 19.4	6 30.7
14 M	7 25 13	20 59 03	29 20 27	5♒47 33	2 52.2	17 20.9	6 06.6	3 53.5	4 26.4	25 48.1	26 31.4	1 09.6	8 21.5	6 32.1
15 Tu	7 29 09	21 56 16	12♒18 14	18 52 23	2 44.0	18 28.5	6 58.8	4 33.7	4 32.1	26 01.4	26 38.1	1 08.0	8 23.7	6 33.6
16 W	7 33 06	22 53 29	25 29 52	2♓10 33	2 36.1	19 33.2	7 50.4	5 13.9	4 37.6	26 14.8	26 44.8	1 06.3	8 25.8	6 35.0
17 Th	7 37 02	23 50 43	8♓54 17	15 40 54	2 29.5	20 35.2	8 41.3	5 54.0	4 42.7	26 28.2	26 51.6	1 04.6	8 28.0	6 36.4
18 F	7 40 59	24 47 57	22 30 15	29 22 12	2 24.7	21 34.3	9 31.6	6 34.1	4 47.5	26 41.6	26 58.4	1 02.8	8 30.1	6 37.9
19 Sa	7 44 56	25 45 12	6♈16 38	13♈13 26	2D 22.1	22 30.3	10 21.2	7 14.1	4 52.0	26 54.9	27 05.3	1 01.0	8 32.3	6 39.3
20 Su	7 48 52	26 42 28	20 12 30	27 13 45	2 21.4	23 23.3	11 10.0	7 54.2	4 56.2	27 08.3	27 12.2	0 59.2	8 34.5	6 40.7
21 M	7 52 49	27 39 45	4♉17 03	11♉22 18	2 21.9	24 12.9	11 58.2	8 34.1	5 00.1	27 21.7	27 19.1	0 57.3	8 36.7	6 42.1
22 Tu	7 56 45	28 37 02	18 29 18	25 37 54	2R 22.7	24 59.2	12 45.5	9 14.1	5 03.6	27 35.1	27 26.1	0 55.5	8 38.9	6 43.5
23 W	8 00 42	29 34 21	2♊47 47	9♊58 39	2 22.6	25 41.9	13 32.1	9 53.9	5 06.8	27 48.4	27 33.1	0 53.5	8 41.1	6 44.9
24 Th	8 04 38	0♌31 40	17 10 05	24 21 37	2 20.8	26 20.9	14 17.9	10 33.8	5 09.6	28 01.8	27 40.2	0 51.6	8 43.3	6 46.3
25 F	8 08 35	1 29 00	1♋32 43	8♋42 45	2 16.5	26 56.1	15 02.8	11 13.6	5 12.2	28 15.2	27 47.3	0 49.6	8 45.5	6 47.7
26 Sa	8 12 32	2 26 21	15 51 06	22 57 06	2 09.8	27 27.3	15 46.8	11 53.3	5 14.4	28 28.6	27 54.4	0 47.6	8 47.7	6 49.0
27 Su	8 16 28	3 23 43	0♌00 05	6♌59 27	2 01.0	27 54.2	16 29.9	12 33.1	5 16.2	28 41.9	28 01.5	0 45.6	8 49.9	6 50.4
28 M	8 20 25	4 21 05	13 54 37	20 45 07	1 51.0	28 16.8	17 12.1	13 12.7	5 17.7	28 55.3	28 08.7	0 43.6	8 52.2	6 51.7
29 Tu	8 24 21	5 18 28	27 30 33	4♍10 40	1 40.8	28 34.8	17 53.2	13 52.4	5 18.8	29 08.6	28 15.9	0 41.5	8 54.4	6 53.1
30 W	8 28 18	6 15 51	10♍45 19	17 14 29	1 31.5	28 48.1	18 33.3	14 31.9	5 19.6	29 22.0	28 23.2	0 39.4	8 56.6	6 54.4
31 Th	8 32 14	7 13 15	23 38 15	29 56 50	1 23.9	28 56.5	19 12.3	15 11.5	5R 20.0	29 35.3	28 30.4	0 37.3	8 58.8	6 55.7

August 1919 — LONGITUDE

Day	Sid.Time	☉	0 hr ☽	Noon ☽	True ☊	☿	♀	♂	⚳	♃	♄	♅	♆	♇
1 F	8 36 11	8♌10 40	6♎10 33	12♎19 49	1♐18.6	29♌00.0	19♍50.2	15♋51.0	5♈20.1	29♋48.6	28♌37.7	0♓35.1	9♌01.1	6♋57.0
2 Sa	8 40 07	9 08 06	18 25 05	24 26 55	1R 15.6	28R 58.2	20 27.0	16 30.4	5R 19.8	0♌01.9	28 45.1	0R 33.0	9 03.2	6 58.3
3 Su	8 44 04	10 05 32	0♏25 56	6♏22 43	1D 14.5	28 51.3	21 02.5	17 09.8	5 19.2	0 15.1	28 52.4	0 30.8	9 05.5	6 59.6
4 M	8 48 00	11 02 58	12 17 59	18 12 22	1 14.6	28 39.1	21 36.7	17 49.2	5 18.2	0 28.4	28 59.8	0 28.6	9 07.7	7 00.9
5 Tu	8 51 57	12 00 26	24 06 34	0♐01 15	1R 14.9	28 21.7	22 09.6	18 28.5	5 16.9	0 41.6	29 07.2	0 26.4	9 09.9	7 02.1
6 W	8 55 54	12 57 54	5♐57 06	11 54 43	1 14.4	27 59.1	22 41.2	19 07.8	5 15.2	0 54.8	29 14.6	0 24.1	9 12.2	7 03.4
7 Th	8 59 50	13 55 23	17 54 43	23 57 39	1 12.3	27 31.5	23 11.3	19 47.0	5 13.1	1 08.0	29 22.0	0 21.9	9 14.4	7 04.6
8 F	9 03 47	14 52 53	0♑04 01	6♑14 14	1 07.7	26 59.2	23 39.9	20 26.2	5 10.7	1 21.2	29 29.5	0 19.6	9 16.6	7 05.8
9 Sa	9 07 43	15 50 24	12 28 40	18 47 36	1 00.6	26 22.4	24 07.1	21 05.3	5 07.9	1 34.4	29 36.9	0 17.3	9 18.8	7 07.1
10 Su	9 11 40	16 47 56	25 11 11	1♒39 30	0 51.2	25 41.7	24 32.6	21 44.4	5 04.8	1 47.5	29 44.4	0 15.0	9 21.0	7 08.3
11 M	9 15 36	17 45 29	8♒12 33	14 50 13	0 40.0	24 57.5	24 56.5	22 23.5	5 01.3	2 00.6	29 51.9	0 12.7	9 23.2	7 09.4
12 Tu	9 19 33	18 43 02	21 32 16	28 18 24	0 28.1	24 10.7	25 18.6	23 02.5	4 57.4	2 13.7	29 59.4	0 10.4	9 25.5	7 10.6
13 W	9 23 29	19 40 37	5♓08 16	12♓01 25	0 16.6	23 21.8	25 39.0	23 41.5	4 53.2	2 26.7	0♍06.9	0 08.1	9 27.7	7 11.8
14 Th	9 27 26	20 38 14	18 57 25	25 55 46	0 06.8	22 31.9	25 57.6	24 20.4	4 48.6	2 39.8	0 14.5	0 05.7	9 29.8	7 12.9
15 F	9 31 23	21 35 51	2♈56 01	9♈57 44	29♏59.4	21 41.7	26 14.3	24 59.3	4 43.6	2 52.7	0 22.0	0 03.4	9 32.0	7 14.0
16 Sa	9 35 19	22 33 31	17 00 29	24 03 57	29 54.8	20 52.4	26 29.1	25 38.2	4 38.3	3 05.7	0 29.6	0 01.0	9 34.2	7 15.1
17 Su	9 39 16	23 31 12	1♉07 48	8♉11 49	29 52.6	20 04.8	26 41.9	26 17.0	4 32.7	3 18.6	0 37.2	29♒58.6	9 36.4	7 16.2
18 M	9 43 12	24 28 54	15 15 48	22 19 37	29 52.1	19 19.9	26 52.6	26 55.8	4 26.7	3 31.5	0 44.8	29 56.2	9 38.6	7 17.3
19 Tu	9 47 09	25 26 38	29 23 07	6♊26 13	29 52.1	18 38.8	27 01.3	27 34.6	4 20.3	3 44.4	0 52.4	29 53.9	9 40.7	7 18.4
20 W	9 51 05	26 24 24	13♊28 48	20 30 45	29 51.2	18 02.3	27 07.8	28 13.3	4 13.6	3 57.3	1 00.0	29 51.5	9 42.9	7 19.4
21 Th	9 55 02	27 22 12	27 31 55	4♋32 07	29 48.3	17 31.1	27 12.1	28 52.0	4 06.6	4 10.1	1 07.6	29 49.1	9 45.0	7 20.5
22 F	9 58 58	28 20 01	11♋31 05	18 28 35	29 42.7	17 06.1	27R 14.2	29 30.6	3 59.2	4 22.8	1 15.2	29 46.7	9 47.2	7 21.5
23 Sa	10 02 55	29 17 52	25 24 15	2♌17 45	29 34.3	16 47.8	27 14.0	0♌09.2	3 51.4	4 35.5	1 22.8	29 44.3	9 49.3	7 22.5
24 Su	10 06 52	0♍15 44	9♌08 42	15 56 42	29 23.4	16D 36.7	27 11.5	0 47.7	3 43.4	4 48.2	1 30.4	29 41.9	9 51.4	7 23.5
25 M	10 10 48	1 13 38	22 41 24	29 22 25	29 11.0	16 33.2	27 06.6	1 26.2	3 35.0	5 00.9	1 38.0	29 39.5	9 53.5	7 24.4
26 Tu	10 14 45	2 11 34	5♍59 28	12♍32 18	28 58.3	16 37.5	26 59.3	2 04.7	3 26.3	5 13.4	1 45.7	29 37.1	9 55.6	7 25.4
27 W	10 18 41	3 09 31	19 00 46	25 24 47	28 46.4	16 49.9	26 49.7	2 43.1	3 17.3	5 26.0	1 53.3	29 34.7	9 57.7	7 26.3
28 Th	10 22 38	4 07 29	1♎44 22	7♎59 36	28 36.5	17 10.5	26 37.7	3 21.5	3 08.0	5 38.5	2 00.9	29 32.3	9 59.8	7 27.2
29 F	10 26 34	5 05 29	14 10 42	20 17 56	28 29.1	17 39.1	26 23.4	3 59.8	2 58.3	5 50.9	2 08.5	29 29.9	10 01.8	7 28.1
30 Sa	10 30 31	6 03 30	26 21 40	2♏22 21	28 24.3	18 15.7	26 06.7	4 38.1	2 48.4	6 03.4	2 16.1	29 27.6	10 03.9	7 29.0
31 Su	10 34 27	7 01 32	8♏20 28	14 16 35	28 22.0	19 00.2	25 47.6	5 16.4	2 38.2	6 15.7	2 23.7	29 25.2	10 05.9	7 29.9

Astro Data Dy Hr Mn	Planet Ingress Dy Hr Mn	Last Aspect Dy Hr Mn	☽ Ingress Dy Hr Mn	Last Aspect Dy Hr Mn	☽ Ingress Dy Hr Mn	☽ Phases & Eclipses Dy Hr Mn
☽0S 3 5:08	☿ ♌ 2 2:02	1 10:19 ♄ ☌	♍ 1 19:06	2 21:00 ☿ ⚹	♏ 2 23:08	5 3:17 ☽ 12♎03
☽0N 17 17:03	♀ ♍ 7 18:17	3 21:14 ♂ □	♎ 4 3:34	5 10:09 ♄ □	♐ 5 11:57	13 6:02 ○ 19♑48
♃⚺♄ 21 2:25	♂ ♋ 8 17:14	6 12:59 ♀ ⚹	♏ 6 15:18	7 22:44 ♄ △	♑ 7 23:52	20 11:03 ☾ 26♈40
☽0S 30 14:48	☉ ♌ 23 22:45	8 19:55 ♄ □	♐ 9 4:13	9 22:21 ♀ △	♒ 10 8:56	27 5:22 ● 3♌08
		11 8:27 ♄ △	♑ 11 15:56	12 5:06 ☿ ☍	♓ 12 14:59	
⚳ R 1 5:29	♃ ♌ 2 8:39	13 17:02 ♃ ☍	♒ 14 1:14	14 12:03 ♀ ☍	♈ 14 18:59	3 20:11 ☽ 10♏25
☿ R 1 16:02	♄ ♍ 12 13:52	16 2:10 ♄ ☍	♓ 16 8:06	16 14:48 ♂ □	♉ 16 22:05	11 17:39 ○ 17♒59
♃⚻♅ 4 12:19	☊ ♏R 15 9:53	18 7:15 ♃ △	♈ 18 13:06	19 0:54 ♅ □	♊ 19 1:03	18 15:56 ☾ 24♉38
♀0S 6 18:33	♅ ♒R 16 22:06	20 11:57 ♄ △	♉ 20 16:43	21 3:56 ♅ △	♋ 21 4:14	25 15:37 ● 1♍22
♄☍♅ 13 14:43	♂ ♌ 23 6:17	22 17:22 ☉ ⚹	♊ 22 19:19	23 3:11 ♀ ⚹	♌ 23 8:00	
☽0N 13 23:58	☉ ♍ 24 5:28	24 17:34 ♄ ⚹	♋ 24 21:25	25 12:31 ♅ ☍	♍ 25 13:08	
♀ R 22 21:51		26 21:33 ♃ ☌	♌ 26 24:00	27 14:38 ♀ ☌	♎ 27 20:41	
☿ D 25 10:48		29 1:42 ☿ ☌	♍ 29 4:28	30 6:12 ♅ △	♏ 30 7:15	
☽0S 27 0:05		31 11:18 ♃ ⚹	♎ 31 12:06			

Astro Data

1 July 1919
Julian Day # 7121
SVP 6♓22'46"
GC 25♐42.9 ⚳ 29♒27.2R
Eris 29♓10.6R ⚵ 26♌52.1
⚷ 6♈56.9 ⚶ 20♌58.0
☽ Mean ☊ 2♐06.2

1 August 1919
Julian Day # 7152
SVP 6♓22'41"
GC 25♐43.0 ⚳ 23♒59.4R
Eris 29♓03.3R ⚵ 8♍48.4
⚷ 6♈47.2R ⚶ 5♍03.6
☽ Mean ☊ 0♐27.7

LONGITUDE — September 1919

Day	Sid.Time	☉	0 hr ☽	Noon ☽	True ☊	☿	♀	♂	ʔ	♃	♄	♅	♆	♇
1 M	10 38 24	7♍59 36	20♏11 18	26♏05 16	28♏21.4	19♌52.2	25♍26.4	5♌54.6	2♈27.8	6♌28.0	2♍31.3	29♒22.8	10♌07.9	7♋30.7
2 Tu	10 42 21	8 57 42	1♐59 08	7♐53 35	28R 21.4	20 51.5	25R 03.0	6 32.8	2R 17.1	6 40.3	2 38.9	29R 20.5	10 10.0	7 31.5
3 W	10 46 17	9 55 48	13 49 20	19 47 04	28 21.1	21 57.7	24 37.5	7 10.9	2 06.1	6 52.5	2 46.5	29 18.1	10 12.0	7 32.3
4 Th	10 50 14	10 53 57	25 47 26	1♑51 07	28 19.4	23 10.5	24 10.0	7 49.0	1 54.9	7 04.6	2 54.1	29 15.8	10 13.9	7 33.1
5 F	10 54 10	11 52 06	7♑58 42	14 10 45	28 15.5	24 29.2	23 40.7	8 27.0	1 43.5	7 16.7	3 01.6	29 13.5	10 15.9	7 33.8
6 Sa	10 58 07	12 50 18	20 27 45	26 50 07	28 09.2	25 53.4	23 09.7	9 05.1	1 31.8	7 28.7	3 09.2	29 11.2	10 17.8	7 34.6
7 Su	11 02 03	13 48 30	3♒18 07	9♒51 57	28 00.4	27 22.7	22 37.2	9 43.0	1 19.9	7 40.7	3 16.7	29 08.9	10 19.8	7 35.3
8 M	11 06 00	14 46 45	16 31 41	23 17 14	27 49.9	28 56.5	22 03.3	10 20.9	1 07.8	7 52.6	3 24.3	29 06.6	10 21.7	7 36.0
9 Tu	11 09 56	15 45 00	0♓08 22	7♓04 43	27 38.6	0♍34.2	21 28.4	10 58.8	0 55.6	8 04.4	3 31.8	29 04.3	10 23.6	7 36.7
10 W	11 13 53	16 43 18	14 05 50	21 11 04	27 27.7	2 15.2	20 52.5	11 36.7	0 43.1	8 16.2	3 39.3	29 02.1	10 25.5	7 37.3
11 Th	11 17 50	17 41 37	28 19 46	5♈31 09	27 18.3	3 59.2	20 16.0	12 14.5	0 30.5	8 27.9	3 46.7	28 59.8	10 27.3	7 38.0
12 F	11 21 46	18 39 59	12♈44 27	19 58 54	27 11.3	5 45.6	19 39.0	12 52.2	0 17.8	8 39.5	3 54.2	28 57.6	10 29.2	7 38.6
13 Sa	11 25 43	19 38 22	27 13 45	4♉28 19	27 07.0	7 33.9	19 01.8	13 29.9	0 04.9	8 51.1	4 01.6	28 55.4	10 31.0	7 39.2
14 Su	11 29 39	20 36 48	11♉42 00	18 54 17	27D 05.1	9 23.7	18 24.7	14 07.6	29♓51.9	9 02.6	4 09.1	28 53.2	10 32.8	7 39.8
15 M	11 33 36	21 35 16	26 04 47	3♊13 09	27 05.0	11 14.7	17 47.9	14 45.3	29 38.7	9 14.0	4 16.5	28 51.1	10 34.6	7 40.3
16 Tu	11 37 32	22 33 46	10♊19 10	17 22 42	27R 05.5	13 06.4	17 11.7	15 22.9	29 25.5	9 25.4	4 23.9	28 49.0	10 36.4	7 40.8
17 W	11 41 29	23 32 18	24 23 37	1♋21 53	27 05.3	14 58.7	16 36.3	16 00.4	29 12.2	9 36.7	4 31.2	28 46.8	10 38.1	7 41.4
18 Th	11 45 25	24 30 52	8♋17 29	15 10 23	27 03.5	16 51.1	16 01.8	16 38.0	28 58.8	9 47.9	4 38.6	28 44.8	10 39.8	7 41.8
19 F	11 49 22	25 29 29	22 00 36	28 48 04	26 59.3	18 43.6	15 28.6	17 15.5	28 45.3	9 59.1	4 45.9	28 42.7	10 41.5	7 42.3
20 Sa	11 53 19	26 28 07	5♌32 48	12♌14 41	26 52.7	20 35.9	14 56.8	17 52.9	28 31.8	10 10.1	4 53.2	28 40.7	10 43.2	7 42.8
21 Su	11 57 15	27 26 48	18 53 41	25 29 42	26 43.9	22 27.8	14 26.5	18 30.3	28 18.3	10 21.1	5 00.4	28 38.6	10 44.9	7 43.2
22 M	12 01 12	28 25 31	2♍02 37	8♍32 20	26 33.8	24 19.2	13 58.0	19 07.7	28 04.8	10 32.0	5 07.6	28 36.7	10 46.5	7 43.6
23 Tu	12 05 08	29 24 16	14 58 46	21 21 49	26 23.3	26 10.1	13 31.4	19 45.0	27 51.2	10 42.8	5 14.8	28 34.7	10 48.1	7 43.9
24 W	12 09 05	0♎23 03	27 41 29	3♎57 42	26 13.5	28 00.3	13 06.9	20 22.2	27 37.7	10 53.5	5 22.0	28 32.8	10 49.7	7 44.3
25 Th	12 13 01	1 21 52	10♎10 33	16 20 05	26 05.3	29 49.7	12 44.4	20 59.5	27 24.2	11 04.2	5 29.1	28 30.9	10 51.3	7 44.6
26 F	12 16 58	2 20 43	22 26 28	28 29 53	25 59.3	1♎38.4	12 24.2	21 36.6	27 10.8	11 14.7	5 36.2	28 29.0	10 52.8	7 44.9
27 Sa	12 20 54	3 19 36	4♏30 37	10♏28 58	25 55.7	3 26.3	12 06.2	22 13.8	26 57.4	11 25.2	5 43.3	28 27.1	10 54.4	7 45.2
28 Su	12 24 51	4 18 30	16 25 20	22 20 08	25D 54.2	5 13.3	11 50.6	22 50.9	26 44.1	11 35.5	5 50.3	28 25.3	10 55.9	7 45.5
29 M	12 28 47	5 17 27	28 13 52	4♐07 03	25 54.5	6 59.4	11 37.4	23 27.9	26 30.9	11 45.8	5 57.3	28 23.6	10 57.3	7 45.7
30 Tu	12 32 44	6 16 25	10♐00 16	15 54 07	25 55.6	8 44.7	11 26.5	24 04.9	26 17.8	11 56.0	6 04.3	28 21.8	10 58.8	7 45.9

LONGITUDE — October 1919

Day	Sid.Time	☉	0 hr ☽	Noon ☽	True ☊	☿	♀	♂	ʔ	♃	♄	♅	♆	♇
1 W	12 36 41	7♎15 25	21♐49 15	27♐46 18	25♏56.9	10♎29.2	11♍18.1	24♌41.9	26♓04.9	12♌06.1	6♍11.2	28♒20.1	11♌00.2	7♋46.1
2 Th	12 40 37	8 14 27	3♑45 57	9♑48 51	25R 57.3	12 12.7	11R 12.1	25 18.8	25R 52.0	12 16.0	6 18.1	28R 18.5	11 01.6	7 46.3
3 F	12 44 34	9 13 31	15 55 39	22 06 59	25 56.3	13 55.4	11D 08.6	25 55.6	25 39.4	12 25.9	6 24.9	28 16.8	11 02.9	7 46.4
4 Sa	12 48 30	10 12 36	28 23 26	4♒45 31	25 53.4	15 37.2	11 07.4	26 32.5	25 26.8	12 35.7	6 31.7	28 15.2	11 04.3	7 46.6
5 Su	12 52 27	11 11 43	11♒13 41	17 48 17	25 48.8	17 18.2	11 08.6	27 09.2	25 14.5	12 45.4	6 38.5	28 13.7	11 05.6	7 46.7
6 M	12 56 23	12 10 52	24 29 33	1♓17 33	25 42.7	18 58.4	11 12.2	27 45.9	25 02.4	12 54.9	6 45.2	28 12.1	11 06.9	7 46.7
7 Tu	13 00 20	13 10 03	8♓12 15	15 13 23	25 35.9	20 37.8	11 18.0	28 22.6	24 50.4	13 04.4	6 51.8	28 10.7	11 08.1	7 46.8
8 W	13 04 16	14 09 16	22 20 35	29 33 16	25 29.1	22 16.4	11 26.1	28 59.2	24 38.7	13 13.7	6 58.4	28 09.2	11 09.4	7R 46.8
9 Th	13 08 13	15 08 30	6♈50 42	14♈12 04	25 23.4	23 54.2	11 36.4	29 35.8	24 27.2	13 23.0	7 05.0	28 07.8	11 10.6	7 46.8
10 F	13 12 10	16 07 47	21 36 22	29 02 38	25 19.2	25 31.2	11 48.9	0♍12.4	24 15.9	13 32.1	7 11.5	28 06.4	11 11.7	7 46.8
11 Sa	13 16 06	17 07 05	6♉29 47	13♉56 50	25D 17.0	27 07.5	12 03.5	0 48.8	24 04.8	13 41.1	7 18.0	28 05.1	11 12.9	7 46.7
12 Su	13 20 03	18 06 27	21 22 49	28 46 50	25 16.6	28 43.1	12 20.1	1 25.3	23 54.0	13 50.0	7 24.4	28 03.8	11 14.0	7 46.7
13 M	13 23 59	19 05 50	6♊08 09	13♊26 07	25 17.5	0♏18.1	12 38.8	2 01.7	23 43.5	13 58.8	7 30.7	28 02.6	11 15.1	7 46.6
14 Tu	13 27 56	20 05 16	20 40 15	27 50 08	25 18.9	1 52.3	12 59.3	2 38.0	23 33.3	14 07.5	7 37.0	28 01.4	11 16.1	7 46.5
15 W	13 31 52	21 04 44	4♋55 34	11♋56 22	25R 20.1	3 25.8	13 21.8	3 14.4	23 23.3	14 16.0	7 43.3	28 00.2	11 17.1	7 46.4
16 Th	13 35 49	22 04 14	18 52 30	25 44 00	25 20.4	4 58.7	13 46.0	3 50.6	23 13.6	14 24.4	7 49.5	27 59.1	11 18.1	7 46.2
17 F	13 39 45	23 03 47	2♌30 57	9♌13 29	25 19.3	6 31.0	14 12.0	4 26.8	23 04.3	14 32.7	7 55.6	27 58.1	11 19.1	7 46.0
18 Sa	13 43 42	24 03 21	15 51 46	22 25 57	25 16.6	8 02.6	14 39.6	5 03.0	22 55.2	14 40.9	8 01.7	27 57.0	11 20.0	7 45.8
19 Su	13 47 39	25 02 59	28 56 16	5♍22 52	25 12.7	9 33.5	15 08.9	5 39.1	22 46.4	14 48.9	8 07.7	27 56.1	11 20.9	7 45.6
20 M	13 51 35	26 02 38	11♍45 56	18 05 40	25 08.0	11 03.9	15 39.8	6 15.1	22 38.0	14 56.8	8 13.7	27 55.1	11 21.8	7 45.3
21 Tu	13 55 32	27 02 19	24 22 13	0♎35 46	25 03.0	12 33.6	16 12.1	6 51.2	22 29.9	15 04.6	8 19.6	27 54.2	11 22.6	7 45.1
22 W	13 59 28	28 02 03	6♎46 27	12 54 26	24 58.3	14 02.7	16 45.9	7 27.1	22 22.2	15 12.2	8 25.4	27 53.4	11 23.4	7 44.8
23 Th	14 03 25	29 01 49	18 59 53	25 02 59	24 54.6	15 31.1	17 21.1	8 03.0	22 14.7	15 19.7	8 31.2	27 52.6	11 24.2	7 44.5
24 F	14 07 21	0♏01 36	1♏03 53	7♏02 50	24 52.0	16 58.9	17 57.6	8 38.8	22 07.7	15 27.1	8 36.9	27 51.9	11 24.9	7 44.1
25 Sa	14 11 18	1 01 26	13 00 03	18 55 46	24D 50.8	18 26.1	18 35.4	9 14.6	22 01.0	15 34.3	8 42.6	27 51.2	11 25.6	7 43.7
26 Su	14 15 14	2 01 18	24 50 17	0♐43 55	24 50.7	19 52.6	19 14.4	9 50.4	21 54.6	15 41.4	8 48.1	27 50.5	11 26.3	7 43.4
27 M	14 19 11	3 01 11	6♐37 02	12 30 01	24 51.7	21 18.4	19 54.7	10 26.0	21 48.6	15 48.3	8 53.6	27 49.9	11 27.0	7 43.0
28 Tu	14 23 08	4 01 06	18 23 18	24 17 20	24 53.3	22 43.4	20 36.1	11 01.6	21 43.0	15 55.1	8 59.1	27 49.4	11 27.6	7 42.5
29 W	14 27 04	5 01 03	0♑12 38	6♑09 41	24 54.9	24 07.7	21 18.6	11 37.2	21 37.8	16 01.8	9 04.4	27 48.9	11 28.1	7 42.1
30 Th	14 31 01	6 01 02	12 09 05	18 11 22	24 56.4	25 31.2	22 02.1	12 12.7	21 32.9	16 08.2	9 09.7	27 48.4	11 28.7	7 41.6
31 F	14 34 57	7 01 02	24 17 09	0♒26 59	24R 57.2	26 53.8	22 46.7	12 48.1	21 28.4	16 14.6	9 14.9	27 48.0	11 29.2	7 41.1

Astro Data

	Dy Hr Mn
♃⚻♇	7 0:34
☽0N	10 8:29
☽0S	23 7:43
♃☌♆	24 1:59
☉0S	24 2:35
♀0N	26 1:48
☿0S	27 8:38
♀ D	4 11:46
☽0N	7 18:21
♇ R	9 4:02
♄⚹♇	15 23:32
☽0S	20 13:31

Planet Ingress

	Dy Hr Mn
☿ ♍	9 3:43
ʔ ♓R	13 21:01
☉ ♎	24 2:35
☿ ♎	25 14:16
♂ ♍	10 3:53
☿ ♏	13 7:25
☉ ♏	24 11:21

Last Aspect / ☽ Ingress (September)

Last Aspect Dy Hr Mn		☽ Ingress	Dy Hr Mn
1 18:41	♅ □	♐	1 19:58
4 6:54	♅ ⚹	♑	4 8:21
6 5:23	♀ △	♒	6 17:54
8 23:14	☿ ☍	♓	8 23:45
10 11:30	♀ ☍	♈	11 2:48
13 2:50	♅ ⚹	♉	13 4:35
15 4:40	♅ □	♊	15 6:35
17 7:33	♅ △	♋	17 9:39
19 5:41	☉ ⚹	♌	19 14:08
21 17:45	♅ ☍	♍	21 20:15
23 22:39	☿ ☌	♎	24 4:24
26 11:58	♅ △	♏	26 14:59
29 0:22	♅ □	♐	29 3:36

Last Aspect / ☽ Ingress (October)

Last Aspect Dy Hr Mn		☽ Ingress	Dy Hr Mn
1 13:08	♅ ⚹	♑	1 16:28
2 17:30	☿ □	♒	4 3:03
6 6:35	♅ ☌	♓	6 9:44
7 5:16	♀ ☍	♈	8 12:44
10 10:30	♅ ⚹	♉	10 13:32
12 10:50	♅ □	♊	12 13:59
14 12:19	♅ △	♋	14 15:39
16 5:04	☉ □	♌	16 19:32
18 22:10	♅ ☍	♍	19 1:58
20 7:11	♀ ☌	♎	21 10:51
23 20:39	☉ ☌	♏	23 21:52
26 6:07	♅ □	♐	26 10:31
28 19:10	♅ ⚹	♑	28 23:34
31 4:14	☿ ⚹	♒	31 11:08

☽ Phases & Eclipses

Dy Hr Mn	
2 14:22	☽ 9♐03
10 3:54	○ 16♓24
16 21:31	☾ 22♊57
24 4:34	● 0♎05
2 8:37	☽ 8♑06
9 13:38	○ 15♈13
16 5:04	☾ 21♋47
23 20:39	● 29♎23

Astro Data

1 September 1919
Julian Day # 7183
SVP 6♓22'38"
GC 25♐43.0 ⚳ 16♒18.1R
Eris 28♓46.9R ⚵ 20♍56.9
⚷ 5♈52.7R ⚶ 20♍00.8
☽ Mean ☊ 28♏49.2

1 October 1919
Julian Day # 7213
SVP 6♓22'35"
GC 25♐43.1 ⚳ 12♒00.1R
Eris 28♓26.9R ⚵ 2♎34.2
⚷ 4♈34.9R ⚶ 5♎02.0
☽ Mean ☊ 27♏13.8

November 1919 LONGITUDE

Day	Sid.Time	☉	0 hr ☽	Noon ☽	True ☊	☿	♀	♂	⚳	♃	♄	♅	♆	♇
1 Sa	14 38 54	8♏01 04	6♒41 28	13♒01 08	24♏57.3	28♏15.6	23♍32.3	13♍23.5	21♓24.3	16♌20.8	9♍20.1	27♒47.6	11♌29.7	7♋40.6
2 Su	14 42 50	9 01 07	19 26 31	25 58 04	24R56.5	29 36.3	24 18.8	13 58.8	21R20.5	16 26.8	9 25.1	27R47.3	11 30.1	7R40.1
3 M	14 46 47	10 01 12	2♓36 10	9♓21 06	24 55.2	0♐55.9	25 06.3	14 34.0	21 17.2	16 32.7	9 30.1	27 47.1	11 30.5	7 39.5
4 Tu	14 50 43	11 01 19	16 13 01	23 11 57	24 53.4	2 14.4	25 54.6	15 09.2	21 14.2	16 38.4	9 35.0	27 46.9	11 30.9	7 38.9
5 W	14 54 40	12 01 27	0♈17 45	7♈30 07	24 51.7	3 31.6	26 43.8	15 44.3	21 11.6	16 43.9	9 39.9	27 46.7	11 31.2	7 38.3
6 Th	14 58 36	13 01 37	14 48 31	22 12 18	24 50.2	4 47.4	27 33.8	16 19.4	21 09.4	16 49.3	9 44.6	27 46.6	11 31.5	7 37.7
7 F	15 02 33	14 01 48	29 40 38	7♉12 30	24 49.3	6 01.6	28 24.6	16 54.4	21 07.5	16 54.6	9 49.3	27D46.6	11 31.8	7 37.1
8 Sa	15 06 30	15 02 01	14♉46 48	22 22 21	24D48.9	7 14.1	29 16.2	17 29.3	21 06.0	16 59.6	9 53.9	27 46.6	11 32.0	7 36.4
9 Su	15 10 26	16 02 17	29 57 57	7♊32 25	24 49.0	8 24.6	0♎08.6	18 04.2	21 05.0	17 04.5	9 58.4	27 46.6	11 32.2	7 35.7
10 M	15 14 23	17 02 34	15♊04 35	22 33 28	24 49.6	9 33.0	1 01.7	18 39.0	21 04.2	17 09.3	10 02.8	27 46.7	11 32.4	7 35.0
11 Tu	15 18 19	18 02 52	29 58 08	7♋17 51	24 50.2	10 38.9	1 55.4	19 13.8	21D03.9	17 13.8	10 07.1	27 46.9	11 32.5	7 34.3
12 W	15 22 16	19 03 13	14♋32 03	21 40 18	24 50.8	11 42.1	2 49.9	19 48.5	21 03.9	17 18.2	10 11.4	27 47.1	11 32.6	7 33.6
13 Th	15 26 12	20 03 36	28 42 22	5♌38 09	24 51.2	12 42.2	3 45.0	20 23.1	21 04.3	17 22.5	10 15.6	27 47.3	11 32.7	7 32.8
14 F	15 30 09	21 04 01	12♌27 40	19 11 04	24R51.3	13 38.8	4 40.7	20 57.6	21 05.1	17 26.5	10 19.6	27 47.6	11R32.7	7 32.1
15 Sa	15 34 06	22 04 27	25 48 35	2♍20 31	24 51.3	14 31.5	5 37.0	21 32.1	21 06.3	17 30.4	10 23.6	27 48.0	11 32.7	7 31.3
16 Su	15 38 02	23 04 56	8♍47 14	15 09 06	24 51.1	15 19.8	6 33.9	22 06.5	21 07.8	17 34.1	10 27.5	27 48.4	11 32.7	7 30.5
17 M	15 41 59	24 05 26	21 26 33	27 40 00	24D51.0	16 03.0	7 31.4	22 40.8	21 09.7	17 37.6	10 31.3	27 48.8	11 32.6	7 29.6
18 Tu	15 45 55	25 05 58	3♎49 52	9♎56 33	24 51.0	16 40.7	8 29.4	23 15.1	21 11.9	17 40.9	10 35.0	27 49.4	11 32.5	7 28.8
19 W	15 49 52	26 06 32	16 00 27	22 01 56	24 51.1	17 12.1	9 27.9	23 49.3	21 14.5	17 44.0	10 38.7	27 49.9	11 32.4	7 27.9
20 Th	15 53 48	27 07 07	28 01 23	3♏59 06	24 51.3	17 36.6	10 26.9	24 23.4	21 17.5	17 47.0	10 42.2	27 50.5	11 32.2	7 27.0
21 F	15 57 45	28 07 44	9♏55 25	15 50 38	24R51.4	17 53.2	11 26.4	24 57.4	21 20.8	17 49.8	10 45.6	27 51.2	11 32.0	7 26.1
22 Sa	16 01 41	29 08 23	21 45 02	27 38 53	24 51.5	18R01.4	12 26.4	25 31.3	21 24.5	17 52.4	10 49.0	27 51.9	11 31.8	7 25.2
23 Su	16 05 38	0♐09 03	3♐32 27	9♐26 00	24 51.3	18 00.2	13 26.8	26 05.2	21 28.6	17 54.8	10 52.2	27 52.7	11 31.5	7 24.3
24 M	16 09 34	1 09 44	15 19 48	21 14 08	24 50.8	17 49.1	14 27.6	26 39.0	21 33.0	17 57.0	10 55.3	27 53.5	11 31.2	7 23.4
25 Tu	16 13 31	2 10 27	27 09 16	3♑05 32	24 49.9	17 27.5	15 28.8	27 12.7	21 37.7	17 59.0	10 58.4	27 54.4	11 30.8	7 22.4
26 W	16 17 28	3 11 11	9♑03 13	15 02 42	24 48.7	16 55.1	16 30.5	27 46.3	21 42.8	18 00.8	11 01.3	27 55.3	11 30.5	7 21.4
27 Th	16 21 24	4 11 56	21 04 18	27 08 27	24 47.4	16 11.8	17 32.6	28 19.8	21 48.2	18 02.5	11 04.2	27 56.2	11 30.0	7 20.5
28 F	16 25 21	5 12 43	3♒15 32	9♒25 59	24 46.2	15 18.0	18 35.0	28 53.2	21 54.0	18 03.9	11 06.9	27 57.3	11 29.6	7 19.5
29 Sa	16 29 17	6 13 30	15 40 14	21 58 45	24 45.3	14 14.7	19 37.8	29 26.5	22 00.0	18 05.2	11 09.5	27 58.3	11 29.1	7 18.4
30 Su	16 33 14	7 14 18	28 21 57	4♓50 18	24D44.9	13 03.2	20 40.9	29 59.8	22 06.4	18 06.2	11 12.1	27 59.4	11 28.6	7 17.4

December 1919 LONGITUDE

Day	Sid.Time	☉	0 hr ☽	Noon ☽	True ☊	☿	♀	♂	⚳	♃	♄	♅	♆	♇
1 M	16 37 10	8♐15 07	11♓24 11	18♓03 58	24♏45.1	11♐45.4	21♎44.4	0♎32.9	22♓13.2	18♌07.1	11♍14.5	28♒00.6	11♌28.1	7♋16.4
2 Tu	16 41 07	9 15 57	24 49 57	1♈42 21	24 45.8	10R23.7	22 48.2	1 06.0	22 20.2	18 07.7	11 16.8	28 01.8	11R27.5	7R15.3
3 W	16 45 03	10 16 47	8♈41 17	15 46 43	24 47.0	9 00.9	23 52.3	1 38.9	22 27.6	18 08.2	11 19.1	28 03.1	11 26.9	7 14.3
4 Th	16 49 00	11 17 39	22 58 31	0♉16 20	24 48.2	7 39.7	24 56.8	2 11.8	22 35.3	18R08.5	11 21.2	28 04.4	11 26.3	7 13.2
5 F	16 52 57	12 18 31	7♉39 40	15 07 51	24R49.1	6 22.9	26 01.5	2 44.5	22 43.3	18 08.5	11 23.2	28 05.8	11 25.6	7 12.1
6 Sa	16 56 53	13 19 25	22 40 01	0♊15 08	24 49.2	5 12.9	27 06.6	3 17.2	22 51.6	18 08.4	11 25.1	28 07.2	11 24.9	7 11.0
7 Su	17 00 50	14 20 19	7♊52 06	15 29 39	24 48.3	4 11.5	28 11.9	3 49.8	23 00.2	18 08.1	11 26.9	28 08.6	11 24.2	7 09.9
8 M	17 04 46	15 21 15	23 06 32	0♋41 27	24 46.4	3 20.2	29 17.5	4 22.3	23 09.0	18 07.6	11 28.6	28 10.1	11 23.4	7 08.8
9 Tu	17 08 43	16 22 11	8♋13 12	15 40 42	24 43.6	2 40.0	0♏23.4	4 54.6	23 18.2	18 06.9	11 30.2	28 11.7	11 22.6	7 07.7
10 W	17 12 39	17 23 09	23 02 59	0♌19 15	24 40.4	2 11.0	1 29.6	5 26.9	23 27.7	18 06.0	11 31.7	28 13.3	11 21.8	7 06.5
11 Th	17 16 36	18 24 07	7♌28 56	14 31 38	24 37.3	1 53.3	2 36.0	5 59.0	23 37.4	18 04.9	11 33.0	28 14.9	11 21.0	7 05.4
12 F	17 20 33	19 25 07	21 27 09	28 15 27	24 34.8	1D46.5	3 42.6	6 31.1	23 47.4	18 03.6	11 34.3	28 16.6	11 20.1	7 04.2
13 Sa	17 24 29	20 26 07	4♍56 41	11♍31 07	24D33.3	1 50.0	4 49.6	7 03.0	23 57.7	18 02.1	11 35.4	28 18.3	11 19.2	7 03.1
14 Su	17 28 26	21 27 09	17 59 07	24 21 09	24 33.0	2 03.0	5 56.7	7 34.9	24 08.3	18 00.4	11 36.5	28 20.1	11 18.2	7 01.9
15 M	17 32 22	22 28 12	0♎37 44	6♎49 26	24 33.8	2 24.7	7 04.0	8 06.6	24 19.1	17 58.5	11 37.4	28 21.9	11 17.3	7 00.7
16 Tu	17 36 19	23 29 16	12 56 51	19 00 34	24 35.4	2 54.3	8 11.6	8 38.1	24 30.2	17 56.4	11 38.2	28 23.8	11 16.3	6 59.5
17 W	17 40 15	24 30 20	25 01 11	0♏59 16	24 37.3	3 31.0	9 19.4	9 09.6	24 41.6	17 54.2	11 38.9	28 25.7	11 15.3	6 58.4
18 Th	17 44 12	25 31 26	6♏55 22	12 50 01	24 38.9	4 13.9	10 27.4	9 41.0	24 53.2	17 51.7	11 39.5	28 27.7	11 14.2	6 57.2
19 F	17 48 08	26 32 32	18 43 42	24 36 52	24R39.5	5 02.5	11 35.5	10 12.2	25 05.0	17 49.0	11 40.0	28 29.7	11 13.1	6 56.0
20 Sa	17 52 05	27 33 39	0♐29 55	6♐23 16	24 38.7	5 56.0	12 43.9	10 43.3	25 17.2	17 46.2	11 40.4	28 31.7	11 12.0	6 54.8
21 Su	17 56 02	28 34 47	12 17 12	18 12 04	24 36.2	6 53.8	13 52.4	11 14.2	25 29.5	17 43.1	11 40.6	28 33.8	11 10.9	6 53.5
22 M	17 59 58	29 35 55	24 08 05	0♑05 31	24 31.9	7 55.4	15 01.2	11 45.0	25 42.2	17 39.9	11R40.8	28 35.9	11 09.8	6 52.3
23 Tu	18 03 55	0♑37 04	6♑04 34	12 05 25	24 26.0	9 00.4	16 10.0	12 15.7	25 55.0	17 36.5	11 40.8	28 38.1	11 08.6	6 51.1
24 W	18 07 51	1 38 13	18 08 16	24 13 15	24 19.0	10 08.4	17 19.1	12 46.2	26 08.1	17 32.9	11 40.8	28 40.3	11 07.4	6 49.9
25 Th	18 11 48	2 39 22	0♒20 33	6♒30 21	24 11.6	11 18.9	18 28.3	13 16.6	26 21.4	17 29.1	11 40.6	28 42.5	11 06.2	6 48.7
26 F	18 15 44	3 40 32	12 42 48	18 58 08	24 04.6	12 31.8	19 37.6	13 46.9	26 35.0	17 25.1	11 40.3	28 44.8	11 04.9	6 47.5
27 Sa	18 19 41	4 41 41	25 16 31	1♓38 13	23 58.8	13 46.6	20 47.1	14 17.0	26 48.7	17 21.0	11 39.9	28 47.1	11 03.6	6 46.2
28 Su	18 23 37	5 42 51	8♓03 29	14 32 33	23 54.6	15 03.3	21 56.8	14 46.9	27 02.7	17 16.6	11 39.3	28 49.5	11 02.3	6 45.0
29 M	18 27 34	6 44 00	21 05 44	27 43 17	23D52.4	16 21.5	23 06.5	15 16.7	27 16.9	17 12.1	11 38.7	28 51.9	11 01.0	6 43.8
30 Tu	18 31 31	7 45 09	4♈25 28	11♈12 33	23 52.1	17 41.1	24 16.4	15 46.3	27 31.4	17 07.5	11 38.0	28 54.3	10 59.7	6 42.5
31 W	18 35 27	8 46 18	18 04 44	25 02 09	23 53.0	19 02.0	25 26.5	16 15.8	27 46.0	17 02.6	11 37.1	28 56.8	10 58.3	6 41.3

Astro Data

	Dy Hr Mn
☽0N	4 4:23
♅D	8 0:34
♀0S	10 16:04
⚳D	11 21:41
♆R	14 21:40
☽0S	16 18:47
☿R	22 21:13
☽0N	1 13:14
♃R	5 9:36
♄⊻♆	6 10:09
♂0S	7 23:27
☿D	12 15:40
☽0S	14 1:38
♄R	23 8:07
☽0N	28 20:24

Planet Ingress

	Dy Hr Mn
☿ ♐	2 19:07
♀ ♎	9 8:05
☉ ♐	23 8:25
♂ ♎	30 12:10
♀ ♏	9 3:29
☉ ♑	22 21:27

Last Aspect / ☽ Ingress

Last Aspect Dy Hr Mn	☽ Ingress Dy Hr Mn
2 15:19 ♅ ☌	♓ 2 19:19
4 16:53 ♀ ☍	♈ 4 23:30
6 20:57 ♅ ⚹	♉ 7 0:31
8 23:34 ♀ △	♊ 9 0:03
10 20:27 ♅ △	♋ 11 0:03
12 8:43 ♂ ⚹	♌ 13 2:14
15 3:38 ♅ ☍	♍ 15 7:41
17 4:29 ☉ ⚹	♎ 17 16:32
19 23:38 ♅ △	♏ 20 3:58
22 15:19 ☉ ☌	♐ 22 16:47
25 1:30 ♅ ⚹	♑ 25 5:45
27 14:27 ♂ △	♒ 27 17:37
29 23:17 ♅ ☌	♓ 30 3:03

Last Aspect / ☽ Ingress

Last Aspect Dy Hr Mn	☽ Ingress Dy Hr Mn
1 1:40 ☿ □	♈ 2 9:02
4 8:24 ♅ ⚹	♉ 4 11:33
6 8:38 ♅ □	♊ 6 11:36
8 9:37 ♀ △	♋ 8 10:54
9 5:15 ♄ ⚹	♌ 10 11:28
12 12:02 ♅ ☍	♍ 12 15:06
14 6:02 ☉ □	♎ 14 22:47
17 6:50 ♅ △	♏ 17 10:01
19 19:56 ♅ □	♐ 19 22:59
22 10:55 ☉ ☌	♑ 22 11:49
23 20:57 ♀ ⚹	♒ 24 23:20
27 6:37 ♀ □	♓ 27 8:55
29 2:51 ♀ △	♈ 29 16:06
31 18:42 ♅ ⚹	♉ 31 20:28

☽ Phases & Eclipses

Dy Hr Mn	
1 1:43	☽ 7♒35
7 23:35	○ 14♉31
7 23:44	☍ P 0.178
14 15:40	☾ 21♌13
22 15:19	● 29♏17
22 15:13:51	● A 11'36"
30 16:47	☽ 7♓26
7 10:03	○ 14♊15
14 6:02	☾ 21♍12
22 10:55	● 29♐33
30 5:25	☽ 7♈28

Astro Data

1 November 1919
Julian Day # 7244
SVP 6♓22'32"
GC 25♐43.2 ⚴ 12♒52.8
Eris 28♓08.1R ⚵ 14♎06.1
⚷ 3♈17.7R ⚶ 20♎52.3
☽ Mean ☊ 25♏35.3

1 December 1919
Julian Day # 7274
SVP 6♓22'28"
GC 25♐43.3 ⚴ 17♒51.2
Eris 27♓57.2R ⚵ 24♎21.0
⚷ 2♈33.6R ⚶ 6♏14.1
☽ Mean ☊ 24♏00.0

LONGITUDE — January 1920

Day	Sid.Time	☉	0 hr ☽	Noon ☽	True ☊	☿	♀	♂	⚳	♃	♄	♅	♆	♇
1 Th	18 39 24	9♑47 27	2♉04 53	9♉12 53	23♏54.3	20♐24.0	26♏36.6	16♎45.1	28♓00.8	16♌57.6	11♍36.2	28♒59.3	10♌57.0	6♋40.1
2 F	18 43 20	10 48 36	16 25 59	23 43 53	23R54.9	21 47.0	27 46.9	17 14.2	28 15.9	16R52.5	11R35.1	29 01.8	10R55.6	6R38.9
3 Sa	18 47 17	11 49 45	1♊06 06	8♊32 01	23 54.0	23 11.0	28 57.3	17 43.2	28 31.1	16 47.2	11 33.9	29 04.4	10 54.2	6 37.7
4 Su	18 51 13	12 50 54	16 00 51	23 31 38	23 50.9	24 35.8	0♐07.8	18 12.0	28 46.5	16 41.7	11 32.6	29 07.0	10 52.7	6 36.4
5 M	18 55 10	13 52 02	1♋03 17	8♋34 41	23 45.5	26 01.3	1 18.5	18 40.6	29 02.2	16 36.1	11 31.3	29 09.7	10 51.3	6 35.2
6 Tu	18 59 06	14 53 10	16 04 36	23 31 52	23 38.0	27 27.6	2 29.2	19 09.1	29 18.0	16 30.3	11 29.8	29 12.3	10 49.8	6 34.0
7 W	19 03 03	15 54 18	0♌55 21	8♌14 02	23 29.4	28 54.6	3 40.1	19 37.4	29 34.0	16 24.4	11 28.2	29 15.1	10 48.3	6 32.8
8 Th	19 07 00	16 55 26	15 27 03	22 33 44	23 20.6	0♑22.3	4 51.1	20 05.5	29 50.1	16 18.3	11 26.5	29 17.8	10 46.8	6 31.6
9 F	19 10 56	17 56 34	29 33 34	6♍26 16	23 12.7	1 50.5	6 02.1	20 33.4	0♈06.5	16 12.2	11 24.7	29 20.6	10 45.3	6 30.4
10 Sa	19 14 53	18 57 42	13♍11 45	19 50 04	23 06.6	3 19.3	7 13.3	21 01.1	0 23.0	16 05.8	11 22.7	29 23.4	10 43.8	6 29.2
11 Su	19 18 49	19 58 50	26 21 28	2♎46 18	23 02.8	4 48.7	8 24.6	21 28.6	0 39.7	15 59.4	11 20.7	29 26.2	10 42.2	6 28.0
12 M	19 22 46	20 59 58	9♎05 05	15 18 20	23D01.0	6 18.6	9 35.9	21 55.9	0 56.6	15 52.8	11 18.6	29 29.1	10 40.7	6 26.8
13 Tu	19 26 42	22 01 06	21 26 41	27 30 47	23 01.0	7 49.1	10 47.4	22 23.0	1 13.6	15 46.1	11 16.4	29 31.9	10 39.1	6 25.6
14 W	19 30 39	23 02 13	3♏31 21	9♏29 02	23 01.8	9 20.0	11 58.9	22 49.9	1 30.9	15 39.3	11 14.1	29 34.9	10 37.5	6 24.5
15 Th	19 34 35	24 03 21	15 24 33	21 18 33	23R02.4	10 51.6	13 10.5	23 16.6	1 48.2	15 32.4	11 11.7	29 37.8	10 35.9	6 23.3
16 F	19 38 32	25 04 28	27 11 40	3♐04 32	23 01.8	12 23.6	14 22.2	23 43.1	2 05.8	15 25.3	11 09.2	29 40.8	10 34.3	6 22.1
17 Sa	19 42 29	26 05 36	8♐57 42	14 51 42	22 59.2	13 56.2	15 34.0	24 09.3	2 23.5	15 18.2	11 06.6	29 43.8	10 32.7	6 21.0
18 Su	19 46 25	27 06 42	20 46 58	26 43 57	22 53.9	15 29.3	16 45.8	24 35.3	2 41.3	15 11.0	11 03.9	29 46.8	10 31.1	6 19.8
19 M	19 50 22	28 07 49	2♑42 59	8♑44 23	22 45.8	17 02.9	17 57.8	25 01.0	2 59.3	15 03.6	11 01.1	29 49.9	10 29.4	6 18.7
20 Tu	19 54 18	29 08 54	14 48 21	20 55 05	22 35.3	18 37.1	19 09.8	25 26.6	3 17.5	14 56.2	10 58.2	29 52.9	10 27.8	6 17.6
21 W	19 58 15	0♒10 00	27 04 42	3♒17 17	22 22.9	20 11.8	20 21.8	25 51.8	3 35.8	14 48.7	10 55.2	29 56.0	10 26.1	6 16.5
22 Th	20 02 11	1 11 04	9♒32 50	15 51 23	22 09.8	21 47.1	21 33.9	26 16.8	3 54.2	14 41.2	10 52.2	29 59.1	10 24.5	6 15.4
23 F	20 06 08	2 12 08	22 12 54	28 37 20	21 57.2	23 23.0	22 46.1	26 41.6	4 12.8	14 33.6	10 49.0	0♓02.3	10 22.8	6 14.3
24 Sa	20 10 04	3 13 10	5♓04 38	11♓34 46	21 46.2	24 59.5	23 58.3	27 06.1	4 31.5	14 25.9	10 45.8	0 05.4	10 21.1	6 13.2
25 Su	20 14 01	4 14 12	18 07 44	24 43 30	21 37.7	26 36.5	25 10.6	27 30.3	4 50.4	14 18.1	10 42.4	0 08.6	10 19.5	6 12.1
26 M	20 17 58	5 15 13	1♈22 07	8♈03 38	21 32.2	28 14.2	26 23.0	27 54.2	5 09.4	14 10.3	10 39.0	0 11.8	10 17.8	6 11.1
27 Tu	20 21 54	6 16 12	14 48 08	21 35 43	21 29.4	29 52.5	27 35.3	28 17.8	5 28.5	14 02.5	10 35.6	0 15.0	10 16.1	6 10.0
28 W	20 25 51	7 17 11	28 26 30	5♉20 36	21D28.6	1♒31.5	28 47.8	28 41.2	5 47.7	13 54.6	10 32.0	0 18.3	10 14.4	6 09.0
29 Th	20 29 47	8 18 08	12♉18 05	19 19 01	21R28.7	3 11.1	0♑00.3	29 04.3	6 07.1	13 46.7	10 28.4	0 21.5	10 12.7	6 08.0
30 F	20 33 44	9 19 04	26 23 23	3♊31 06	21 28.3	4 51.4	1 12.8	29 27.0	6 26.6	13 38.7	10 24.7	0 24.8	10 11.0	6 07.0
31 Sa	20 37 40	10 19 58	10♊42 00	17 55 46	21 26.2	6 32.4	2 25.4	29 49.5	6 46.2	13 30.8	10 20.9	0 28.1	10 09.4	6 06.0

LONGITUDE — February 1920

Day	Sid.Time	☉	0 hr ☽	Noon ☽	True ☊	☿	♀	♂	⚳	♃	♄	♅	♆	♇
1 Su	20 41 37	11♒20 52	25♊11 58	2♋30 03	21♏21.4	8♒14.1	3♑38.0	0♏11.7	7♈06.0	13♌22.8	10♍17.1	0♓31.4	10♌07.7	6♋05.0
2 M	20 45 34	12 21 44	9♋49 19	17 09 00	21R13.6	9 56.5	4 50.7	0 33.5	7 25.8	13R14.8	10R13.2	0 34.7	10R06.0	6R04.0
3 Tu	20 49 30	13 22 35	24 28 11	1♌45 58	21 03.2	11 39.6	6 03.4	0 55.0	7 45.8	13 06.8	10 09.2	0 38.1	10 04.3	6 03.1
4 W	20 53 27	14 23 24	9♌01 22	16 13 29	20 51.1	13 23.5	7 16.1	1 16.2	8 05.9	12 58.8	10 05.2	0 41.4	10 02.6	6 02.2
5 Th	20 57 23	15 24 13	23 21 27	0♍24 32	20 38.6	15 08.0	8 28.9	1 37.1	8 26.1	12 50.9	10 01.1	0 44.8	10 00.9	6 01.2
6 F	21 01 20	16 25 00	7♍22 07	14 13 43	20 27.0	16 53.3	9 41.8	1 57.6	8 46.4	12 42.9	9 56.9	0 48.1	9 59.2	6 00.3
7 Sa	21 05 16	17 25 46	20 59 03	27 38 00	20 17.4	18 39.4	10 54.6	2 17.8	9 06.8	12 34.9	9 52.7	0 51.5	9 57.6	5 59.4
8 Su	21 09 13	18 26 31	4♎10 34	10♎36 57	20 10.4	20 26.1	12 07.6	2 37.6	9 27.3	12 27.0	9 48.4	0 54.9	9 55.9	5 58.6
9 M	21 13 09	19 27 15	16 57 27	23 12 28	20 06.2	22 13.5	13 20.5	2 57.0	9 47.9	12 19.1	9 44.1	0 58.3	9 54.2	5 57.7
10 Tu	21 17 06	20 27 59	29 22 31	5♏28 11	20 04.3	24 01.6	14 33.5	3 16.0	10 08.6	12 11.3	9 39.7	1 01.7	9 52.6	5 56.9
11 W	21 21 02	21 28 41	11♏30 07	17 28 58	20 03.9	25 50.3	15 46.5	3 34.7	10 29.4	12 03.5	9 35.3	1 05.1	9 50.9	5 56.1
12 Th	21 24 59	22 29 21	23 25 27	29 20 16	20 03.8	27 39.6	16 59.6	3 52.9	10 50.3	11 55.7	9 30.9	1 08.5	9 49.3	5 55.3
13 F	21 28 56	23 30 01	5♐14 07	11♐07 43	20 03.0	29 29.3	18 12.7	4 10.8	11 11.3	11 48.0	9 26.3	1 12.0	9 47.6	5 54.5
14 Sa	21 32 52	24 30 40	17 01 43	22 56 45	20 00.2	1♓19.5	19 25.8	4 28.2	11 32.4	11 40.3	9 21.8	1 15.4	9 46.0	5 53.7
15 Su	21 36 49	25 31 18	28 53 27	4♑52 19	19 54.9	3 09.9	20 39.0	4 45.2	11 53.6	11 32.7	9 17.2	1 18.8	9 44.4	5 53.0
16 M	21 40 45	26 31 54	10♑53 53	16 58 32	19 46.7	5 00.5	21 52.2	5 01.7	12 14.9	11 25.2	9 12.6	1 22.3	9 42.8	5 52.2
17 Tu	21 44 42	27 32 29	23 06 39	29 18 29	19 35.9	6 51.1	23 05.4	5 17.8	12 36.2	11 17.8	9 08.0	1 25.7	9 41.2	5 51.5
18 W	21 48 38	28 33 02	5♒34 13	11♒53 59	19 23.1	8 41.5	24 18.6	5 33.5	12 57.7	11 10.4	9 03.3	1 29.2	9 39.6	5 50.9
19 Th	21 52 35	29 33 34	18 17 48	24 45 35	19 09.5	10 31.5	25 31.9	5 48.7	13 19.2	11 03.1	8 58.6	1 32.7	9 38.0	5 50.2
20 F	21 56 31	0♓34 04	1♓17 13	7♓52 32	18 56.2	12 20.7	26 45.2	6 03.3	13 40.9	10 56.0	8 53.9	1 36.1	9 36.5	5 49.5
21 Sa	22 00 28	1 34 33	14 31 16	21 13 10	18 44.6	14 09.0	27 58.5	6 17.5	14 02.6	10 48.9	8 49.1	1 39.6	9 34.9	5 48.9
22 Su	22 04 25	2 35 00	27 57 56	4♈45 17	18 35.6	15 55.9	29 11.8	6 31.2	14 24.4	10 41.9	8 44.3	1 43.0	9 33.4	5 48.3
23 M	22 08 21	3 35 25	11♈34 56	18 26 39	18 29.5	17 41.1	0♒25.1	6 44.4	14 46.2	10 35.0	8 39.6	1 46.5	9 31.9	5 47.7
24 Tu	22 12 18	4 35 48	25 20 11	2♉15 24	18 26.4	19 24.1	1 38.5	6 57.1	15 08.2	10 28.2	8 34.8	1 49.9	9 30.4	5 47.1
25 W	22 16 14	5 36 10	9♉12 08	16 10 17	18D25.5	21 04.4	2 51.8	7 09.3	15 30.2	10 21.6	8 30.0	1 53.4	9 28.9	5 46.6
26 Th	22 20 11	6 36 29	23 09 47	0♊10 34	18R25.7	22 41.5	4 05.2	7 20.9	15 52.3	10 15.1	8 25.2	1 56.8	9 27.4	5 46.1
27 F	22 24 07	7 36 47	7♊12 35	14 15 46	18 25.6	24 14.9	5 18.6	7 31.9	16 14.4	10 08.7	8 20.3	2 00.3	9 25.9	5 45.6
28 Sa	22 28 04	8 37 02	21 20 01	28 25 09	18 24.1	25 43.9	6 32.0	7 42.4	16 36.7	10 02.4	8 15.5	2 03.7	9 24.5	5 45.1
29 Su	22 32 00	9 37 15	5♋30 59	12♋37 14	18 20.2	27 08.0	7 45.4	7 52.4	16 59.0	9 56.3	8 10.7	2 07.2	9 23.1	5 44.6

Astro Data Dy Hr Mn	Planet Ingress Dy Hr Mn
☽0S 10 11:06	♀ ♐ 4 9:20
☽0N 25 2:47	☿ ♑ 8 5:55
	⚳ ♈ 9 2:29
♄⊻♆ 5 13:17	☉ ♒ 21 8:04
♄0S 6 21:58	♅ ♓ 22 18:33
☽0N 21 9:53	☿ ♒ 27 13:49
⚳0N 26 11:14	♀ ♑ 29 11:55
☿0N 29 21:20	♂ ♏ 31 23:18
	☿ ♓ 13 18:41
	☉ ♓ 19 22:29
	♀ ♒ 23 3:47

Last Aspect Dy Hr Mn	☽ Ingress Dy Hr Mn	Last Aspect Dy Hr Mn	☽ Ingress Dy Hr Mn
2 20:40 ♅ □	♊ 2 22:13	31 4:45 ♃ ✱	♋ 1 7:54
4 20:56 ♅ △	♋ 4 22:19	2 0:42 ♄ ✱	♌ 3 9:05
6 4:43 ♂ □	♌ 6 22:30	4 8:42 ☉ ☍	♍ 5 11:18
8 23:35 ♅ ☍	♍ 9 0:46	6 4:32 ♄ ☌	♎ 7 16:19
10 10:17 ☉ △	♎ 11 6:47	9 9:47 ☿ △	♏ 10 1:13
13 16:02 ♅ △	♏ 13 16:57	12 7:58 ☿ □	♐ 12 13:21
16 5:02 ♅ □	♐ 16 5:43	14 15:28 ☉ ✱	♑ 15 2:14
18 18:09 ♅ ✱	♑ 18 18:34	16 22:38 ♀ ☌	♒ 17 13:20
21 5:27 ☉ ☌	♒ 21 5:39	19 21:34 ☉ ☌	♓ 19 21:39
23 8:17 ♂ △	♓ 23 14:34	22 1:12 ♀ ✱	♈ 22 3:36
25 15:53 ♀ ✱	♈ 25 21:32	22 22:22 ♃ △	♉ 24 8:06
28 0:05 ♂ ☍	♉ 28 2:43	25 21:32 ♀ ✱	♊ 26 11:42
29 2:37 ♃ □	♊ 30 6:05	28 6:56 ☿ □	♋ 28 14:40

☽ Phases & Eclipses Dy Hr Mn	
5 21:05	○ 14♋15
13 0:08	☾ 21♎31
21 5:27	● 29♑53
28 15:38	☽ 7♉26
4 8:42	○ 14♌15
11 20:49	☾ 21♏51
19 21:34	● 29♒58
26 23:49	☽ 7♊06

Astro Data

1 January 1920
Julian Day # 7305
SVP 6♓22'23"
GC 25♐43.3 ⚴ 25♒43.2
Eris 27♓57.1 ⚵ 3♏17.6
⚷ 2♈37.0 ⚶ 21♏45.8
☽ Mean ☊ 22♏21.5

1 February 1920
Julian Day # 7336
SVP 6♓22'17"
GC 25♐43.4 ⚴ 5♓11.8
Eris 28♓08.7 ⚵ 9♏27.7
⚷ 3♈30.7 ⚶ 6♐22.3
☽ Mean ☊ 20♏43.1

March 1920 — LONGITUDE

Day	Sid.Time	☉	0 hr ☽	Noon ☽	True ☊	☿	♀	♂	⚳	♃	♄	♅	♆	♇
1 M	22 35 57	10♓37 27	19♋43 32	26♋49 29	18♏13.7	28♓26.5	8♒58.9	8♏01.7	17♈21.3	9♌50.3	8♍05.9	2♓10.6	9♌21.7	5♋44.2
2 Tu	22 39 54	11 37 36	3♌54 34	10♌58 14	18R 04.7	29 39.0	10 12.3	8 10.5	17 43.8	9R 44.4	8R 01.1	2 14.0	9R 20.3	5R 43.8
3 W	22 43 50	12 37 43	17 59 56	24 59 04	17 54.2	0♈44.7	11 25.8	8 18.7	18 06.2	9 38.7	7 56.3	2 17.4	9 18.9	5 43.4
4 Th	22 47 47	13 37 48	1♍55 04	8♍47 23	17 43.1	1 43.2	12 39.2	8 26.3	18 28.8	9 33.2	7 51.5	2 20.8	9 17.6	5 43.0
5 F	22 51 43	14 37 51	15 35 34	22 19 12	17 32.7	2 34.0	13 52.7	8 33.2	18 51.4	9 27.8	7 46.8	2 24.2	9 16.3	5 42.7
6 Sa	22 55 40	15 37 53	28 58 00	5♎31 48	17 24.1	3 16.7	15 06.2	8 39.5	19 14.1	9 22.5	7 42.0	2 27.6	9 15.0	5 42.3
7 Su	22 59 36	16 37 53	12♎00 29	18 24 07	17 17.8	3 50.9	16 19.7	8 45.2	19 36.8	9 17.4	7 37.3	2 31.0	9 13.7	5 42.0
8 M	23 03 33	17 37 50	24 42 51	0♏56 54	17 14.0	4 16.3	17 33.3	8 50.2	19 59.6	9 12.4	7 32.6	2 34.4	9 12.4	5 41.8
9 Tu	23 07 29	18 37 47	7♏06 39	13 12 29	17D 12.6	4 32.9	18 46.8	8 54.5	20 22.4	9 07.6	7 27.9	2 37.7	9 11.2	5 41.5
10 W	23 11 26	19 37 41	19 14 55	25 14 29	17 12.8	4R 40.6	20 00.4	8 58.2	20 45.3	9 03.0	7 23.2	2 41.1	9 10.0	5 41.3
11 Th	23 15 23	20 37 34	1♐11 46	7♐07 26	17 13.7	4 39.5	21 13.9	9 01.1	21 08.3	8 58.6	7 18.6	2 44.4	9 08.8	5 41.0
12 F	23 19 19	21 37 25	13 02 07	18 56 29	17R 14.4	4 29.7	22 27.5	9 03.4	21 31.3	8 54.3	7 14.0	2 47.7	9 07.6	5 40.9
13 Sa	23 23 16	22 37 15	24 51 13	0♑46 59	17 14.1	4 11.8	23 41.1	9 05.0	21 54.3	8 50.2	7 09.5	2 51.1	9 06.5	5 40.7
14 Su	23 27 12	23 37 03	6♑44 26	12 44 13	17 11.9	3 46.1	24 54.7	9R 05.8	22 17.4	8 46.2	7 04.9	2 54.4	9 05.4	5 40.6
15 M	23 31 09	24 36 49	18 46 54	24 53 03	17 07.6	3 13.3	26 08.3	9 05.9	22 40.6	8 42.5	7 00.4	2 57.6	9 04.3	5 40.4
16 Tu	23 35 05	25 36 33	1♒03 08	7♒17 35	17 01.3	2 34.3	27 21.9	9 05.2	23 03.8	8 38.9	6 56.0	3 00.9	9 03.2	5 40.3
17 W	23 39 02	26 36 16	13 36 44	20 00 49	16 53.3	1 50.0	28 35.6	9 03.8	23 27.1	8 35.5	6 51.6	3 04.1	9 02.2	5 40.3
18 Th	23 42 58	27 35 56	26 29 59	3♓04 17	16 44.6	1 01.5	29 49.2	9 01.7	23 50.4	8 32.3	6 47.3	3 07.4	9 01.2	5 40.2
19 F	23 46 55	28 35 35	9♓43 37	16 27 51	16 35.9	0 09.8	1♓02.8	8 58.8	24 13.7	8 29.2	6 42.9	3 10.6	9 00.2	5D 40.2
20 Sa	23 50 51	29 35 12	23 16 41	0♈09 44	16 28.3	29♓16.1	2 16.5	8 55.1	24 37.1	8 26.4	6 38.7	3 13.8	8 59.3	5 40.2
21 Su	23 54 48	0♈34 47	7♈06 35	14 06 43	16 22.6	28 21.7	3 30.1	8 50.6	25 00.5	8 23.7	6 34.5	3 16.9	8 58.3	5 40.2
22 M	23 58 45	1 34 19	21 09 37	28 14 41	16 19.0	27 27.6	4 43.8	8 45.4	25 24.0	8 21.2	6 30.4	3 20.1	8 57.4	5 40.3
23 Tu	0 02 41	2 33 50	5♉21 25	12♉29 15	16D 17.6	26 34.9	5 57.4	8 39.4	25 47.5	8 18.9	6 26.3	3 23.2	8 56.6	5 40.3
24 W	0 06 38	3 33 18	19 37 43	26 46 22	16 17.9	25 44.7	7 11.1	8 32.6	26 11.1	8 16.8	6 22.3	3 26.3	8 55.7	5 40.4
25 Th	0 10 34	4 32 44	3♊54 48	11♊02 42	16 19.1	24 57.7	8 24.7	8 25.1	26 34.7	8 14.9	6 18.3	3 29.4	8 54.9	5 40.5
26 F	0 14 31	5 32 08	18 09 45	25 15 44	16R 20.3	24 14.7	9 38.3	8 16.7	26 58.3	8 13.2	6 14.4	3 32.5	8 54.1	5 40.7
27 Sa	0 18 27	6 31 29	2♋20 27	9♋23 41	16 20.7	23 36.3	10 52.0	8 07.7	27 21.9	8 11.6	6 10.6	3 35.5	8 53.4	5 40.8
28 Su	0 22 24	7 30 48	16 25 18	23 25 08	16 19.5	23 02.9	12 05.6	7 57.8	27 45.6	8 10.3	6 06.8	3 38.5	8 52.6	5 41.0
29 M	0 26 20	8 30 05	0♌23 01	7♌18 47	16 16.7	22 35.0	13 19.3	7 47.2	28 09.4	8 09.1	6 03.2	3 41.5	8 52.0	5 41.2
30 Tu	0 30 17	9 29 19	14 12 15	21 03 13	16 12.3	22 12.6	14 32.9	7 35.9	28 33.1	8 08.2	5 59.6	3 44.5	8 51.3	5 41.5
31 W	0 34 14	10 28 31	27 51 30	4♍36 52	16 06.8	21 55.9	15 46.6	7 23.8	28 56.9	8 07.4	5 56.0	3 47.4	8 50.7	5 41.7

April 1920 — LONGITUDE

Day	Sid.Time	☉	0 hr ☽	Noon ☽	True ☊	☿	♀	♂	⚳	♃	♄	♅	♆	♇
1 Th	0 38 10	11♈27 41	11♍19 09	17♍58 07	16♏00.9	21♓44.9	17♓00.2	7♏11.0	29♈20.7	8♌06.8	5♍52.6	3♓50.3	8♌50.1	5♋42.0
2 F	0 42 07	12 26 48	24 33 38	1♎05 32	15R 55.4	21D 39.7	18 13.8	6R 57.5	29 44.5	8R 06.4	5R 49.2	3 53.2	8R 49.5	5 42.3
3 Sa	0 46 03	13 25 54	7♎33 43	13 58 06	15 50.9	21 40.0	19 27.5	6 43.3	0♉08.4	8D 06.2	5 45.9	3 56.1	8 48.9	5 42.6
4 Su	0 50 00	14 24 57	20 18 43	26 35 35	15 47.8	21 45.7	20 41.1	6 28.4	0 32.3	8 06.2	5 42.6	3 58.9	8 48.4	5 43.0
5 M	0 53 56	15 23 58	2♏48 49	8♏58 34	15D 46.2	21 56.7	21 54.8	6 12.8	0 56.2	8 06.4	5 39.5	4 01.7	8 48.0	5 43.4
6 Tu	0 57 53	16 22 58	15 05 05	21 08 39	15 46.1	22 12.8	23 08.4	5 56.6	1 20.2	8 06.8	5 36.4	4 04.5	8 47.5	5 43.8
7 W	1 01 49	17 21 56	27 09 35	3♐08 19	15 47.2	22 33.7	24 22.1	5 39.8	1 44.2	8 07.3	5 33.5	4 07.2	8 47.1	5 44.2
8 Th	1 05 46	18 20 52	9♐05 16	15 00 55	15 48.9	22 59.3	25 35.7	5 22.3	2 08.2	8 08.1	5 30.6	4 10.0	8 46.7	5 44.6
9 F	1 09 43	19 19 46	20 55 48	26 50 28	15 50.6	23 29.3	26 49.4	5 04.2	2 32.2	8 09.0	5 27.8	4 12.6	8 46.4	5 45.1
10 Sa	1 13 39	20 18 38	2♑45 30	8♑41 31	15 52.0	24 03.5	28 03.0	4 45.6	2 56.3	8 10.1	5 25.1	4 15.3	8 46.1	5 45.6
11 Su	1 17 36	21 17 29	14 39 06	20 38 52	15R 52.6	24 41.7	29 16.7	4 26.4	3 20.3	8 11.4	5 22.4	4 17.9	8 45.8	5 46.1
12 M	1 21 32	22 16 17	26 41 27	2♒47 25	15 52.1	25 23.7	0♈30.3	4 06.8	3 44.4	8 12.9	5 19.9	4 20.5	8 45.5	5 46.6
13 Tu	1 25 29	23 15 04	8♒57 21	15 11 46	15 50.6	26 09.4	1 44.0	3 46.6	4 08.5	8 14.6	5 17.5	4 23.1	8 45.3	5 47.1
14 W	1 29 25	24 13 50	21 31 07	27 55 50	15 48.3	26 58.4	2 57.7	3 26.1	4 32.7	8 16.4	5 15.1	4 25.6	8 45.1	5 47.7
15 Th	1 33 22	25 12 33	4♓26 14	11♓02 32	15 45.4	27 50.8	4 11.3	3 05.1	4 56.8	8 18.4	5 12.9	4 28.1	8 45.0	5 48.3
16 F	1 37 18	26 11 15	17 44 50	24 33 08	15 42.5	28 46.2	5 25.0	2 43.8	5 21.0	8 20.7	5 10.7	4 30.5	8 44.8	5 48.9
17 Sa	1 41 15	27 09 55	1♈27 18	8♈27 03	15 39.9	29 44.7	6 38.6	2 22.1	5 45.2	8 23.0	5 08.6	4 32.9	8 44.8	5 49.6
18 Su	1 45 11	28 08 33	15 32 00	22 41 36	15 38.1	0♈46.0	7 52.3	2 00.2	6 09.4	8 25.6	5 06.7	4 35.3	8 44.7	5 50.2
19 M	1 49 08	29 07 09	29 55 13	7♉12 08	15D 37.1	1 50.0	9 05.9	1 38.0	6 33.6	8 28.4	5 04.8	4 37.7	8D 44.7	5 50.9
20 Tu	1 53 05	0♉05 44	14♉31 32	21 52 35	15 37.1	2 56.6	10 19.6	1 15.7	6 57.9	8 31.3	5 03.1	4 40.0	8 44.7	5 51.6
21 W	1 57 01	1 04 16	29 14 27	6♊36 17	15 37.7	4 05.7	11 33.2	0 53.2	7 22.1	8 34.4	5 01.4	4 42.2	8 44.7	5 52.3
22 Th	2 00 58	2 02 46	13♊57 18	21 16 45	15 38.7	5 17.2	12 46.8	0 30.6	7 46.4	8 37.7	4 59.8	4 44.5	8 44.8	5 53.1
23 F	2 04 54	3 01 14	28 34 00	5♋48 30	15 39.7	6 31.1	14 00.5	0 08.0	8 10.7	8 41.2	4 58.4	4 46.7	8 44.9	5 53.8
24 Sa	2 08 51	3 59 40	12♋59 47	20 07 28	15 40.4	7 47.2	15 14.1	29♎45.4	8 35.0	8 44.8	4 57.0	4 48.8	8 45.1	5 54.6
25 Su	2 12 47	4 58 04	27 11 18	4♌11 06	15R 40.7	9 05.5	16 27.7	29 22.8	8 59.3	8 48.6	4 55.8	4 50.9	8 45.3	5 55.4
26 M	2 16 44	5 56 26	11♌06 45	17 58 11	15 40.5	10 26.0	17 41.3	29 00.3	9 23.6	8 52.6	4 54.6	4 53.0	8 45.5	5 56.2
27 Tu	2 20 40	6 54 45	24 45 27	1♍28 35	15 39.9	11 48.6	18 54.9	28 38.0	9 47.9	8 56.7	4 53.6	4 55.1	8 45.7	5 57.1
28 W	2 24 37	7 53 03	8♍07 40	14 42 48	15 39.0	13 13.2	20 08.5	28 15.9	10 12.2	9 01.0	4 52.6	4 57.1	8 46.0	5 57.9
29 Th	2 28 34	8 51 18	21 14 08	27 41 47	15 38.1	14 39.8	21 22.1	27 53.9	10 36.5	9 05.5	4 51.8	4 59.0	8 46.3	5 58.8
30 F	2 32 30	9 49 31	4♎05 54	10♎26 38	15 37.3	16 08.5	22 35.7	27 32.3	11 00.8	9 10.1	4 51.1	5 00.9	8 46.7	5 59.7

Astro Data

	Dy Hr Mn
☽0S	5 8:01
♃☌♆	8 11:58
☿R	10 20:52
♂R	15 3:04
☽0N	19 18:22
♇D	20 2:47
☉0N	20 21:59
☿0S	25 18:47
☽0S	1 15:42
☿D	2 22:40
♃D	4 1:36
♄⚹♇	4 9:35
♀0N	14 23:35
☽0N	16 3:48
♆D	19 13:37

Planet Ingress

		Dy Hr Mn
☿	♈	2 19:25
♀	♓	18 15:31
☿	♓R	19 16:26
☉	♈	20 21:59
⚳	♉	3 3:32
♀	♈	12 2:07
☿	♈	17 18:06
☉	♉	20 9:39
♂	♎R	23 20:29

☿0N23 8:57
♃☌☌24 13:52
♄☍☍27 0:25
☽0S28 21:25

Last Aspect / ☽ Ingress (March)

Dy Hr Mn	Aspect	☽ Ingress	Dy Hr Mn
1 15:00	☿ △	♌	1 17:22
2 10:34	♀ ☍	♍	3 20:40
4 21:12	☉ ☍	♎	6 1:53
7 7:41	♀ △	♏	8 10:10
10 0:19	♀ □	♐	10 21:35
12 19:58	♀ ⚹	♑	13 10:25
15 11:25	☉ ⚹	♒	15 21:58
18 5:28	♀ ☌	♓	18 6:25
20 10:55	☉ ☌	♈	20 11:43
21 3:13	♆ △	♉	22 14:58
24 10:22	☿ ⚹	♊	24 17:25
26 10:21	☿ □	♋	26 20:02
28 11:23	☿ △	♌	28 23:20
29 14:42	♆ ☌	♍	31 3:48

Last Aspect / ☽ Ingress (April)

Dy Hr Mn	Aspect	☽ Ingress	Dy Hr Mn
1 18:48	☿ ☍	♎	2 9:59
3 10:54	☉ ☍	♏	4 18:33
6 16:25	♀ △	♐	7 5:42
9 11:58	♀ □	♑	9 18:25
11 20:32	☿ ⚹	♒	12 6:32
14 4:31	☉ ⚹	♓	14 15:50
16 19:54	☿ ☌	♈	16 21:29
18 21:43	☉ ☌	♉	19 0:08
19 14:32	♆ □	♊	21 1:14
21 20:49	♀ ⚹	♋	23 2:22
25 3:58	♂ □	♌	25 4:48
27 7:03	♂ ⚹	♍	27 9:21
27 22:34	☉ △	♎	29 16:18

☽ Phases & Eclipses

Dy Hr Mn		
4 21:12	○	14♍01
12 17:57	☾	21♐52
20 10:55	●	29♓33
27 6:45	☽	6♋18
3 10:54	○	13♎23
11 13:24	☾	21♑21
18 21:43	●	28♈32
25 13:27	☽	5♌02

Astro Data

1 March 1920
Julian Day # 7365
SVP 6♓22'14"
GC 25♐43.5 ⚴ 14♓48.8
Eris 28♓27.3 ⚵ 11♏23.0R
⚷ 4♈54.8 ⚶ 18♐26.2
☽ Mean ☊ 19♏10.9

1 April 1920
Julian Day # 7396
SVP 6♓22'11"
GC 25♐43.5 ⚴ 25♓21.0
Eris 28♓50.7 ⚵ 8♏15.7R
⚷ 6♈42.1 ⚶ 28♐17.0
☽ Mean ☊ 17♏32.4

LONGITUDE May 1920

Day	Sid.Time	☉	0 hr ☽	Noon ☽	True ☊	☿	♀	♂	⚳	♃	♄	♅	♆	♇
1 Sa	2 36 27	10♉47 43	16♎44 08	22♎58 34	15♏36.8	17♈39.1	23♈49.3	27♎10.9	11♉25.2	9♌14.9	4♍50.4	5♓02.8	8♌47.1	6♋00.6
2 Su	2 40 23	11 45 52	29 10 05	5♏18 52	15D36.5	19 11.6	25 02.9	26R49.9	11 49.5	9 19.8	4R49.9	5 04.6	8 47.5	6 01.5
3 M	2 44 20	12 44 00	11♏25 06	17 28 58	15 36.4	20 46.1	26 16.5	26 29.3	12 13.9	9 24.9	4 49.5	5 06.4	8 47.9	6 02.5
4 Tu	2 48 16	13 42 07	23 30 42	29 30 31	15 36.5	22 22.5	27 30.0	26 09.1	12 38.2	9 30.2	4 49.2	5 08.2	8 48.4	6 03.4
5 W	2 52 13	14 40 11	5♐28 42	11♐25 32	15R36.6	24 00.9	28 43.6	25 49.4	13 02.6	9 35.6	4 49.0	5 09.9	8 48.9	6 04.4
6 Th	2 56 09	15 38 14	17 21 19	23 16 24	15 36.7	25 41.2	29 57.2	25 30.1	13 26.9	9 41.2	4D48.9	5 11.5	8 49.4	6 05.4
7 F	3 00 06	16 36 16	29 11 10	5♑06 01	15 36.6	27 23.4	1♉10.8	25 11.4	13 51.3	9 46.9	4 48.9	5 13.2	8 50.0	6 06.5
8 Sa	3 04 03	17 34 16	11♑01 23	16 57 44	15 36.4	29 07.5	2 24.4	24 53.2	14 15.6	9 52.7	4 49.0	5 14.7	8 50.6	6 07.5
9 Su	3 07 59	18 32 15	22 55 34	28 55 24	15 36.2	0♉53.6	3 37.9	24 35.6	14 40.0	9 58.8	4 49.2	5 16.3	8 51.3	6 08.5
10 M	3 11 56	19 30 13	4♒57 44	11♒03 08	15D36.0	2 41.6	4 51.5	24 18.6	15 04.4	10 04.9	4 49.5	5 17.7	8 51.9	6 09.6
11 Tu	3 15 52	20 28 09	17 12 08	23 25 16	15 36.0	4 31.6	6 05.1	24 02.3	15 28.7	10 11.2	4 49.9	5 19.2	8 52.6	6 10.7
12 W	3 19 49	21 26 04	29 43 05	6♓06 02	15 36.2	6 23.5	7 18.7	23 46.6	15 53.1	10 17.6	4 50.4	5 20.6	8 53.4	6 11.8
13 Th	3 23 45	22 23 57	12♓34 36	19 09 09	15 36.6	8 17.3	8 32.3	23 31.6	16 17.4	10 24.2	4 51.1	5 21.9	8 54.1	6 12.9
14 F	3 27 42	23 21 50	25 49 59	2♈37 19	15 37.3	10 13.0	9 45.8	23 17.3	16 41.8	10 30.9	4 51.8	5 23.2	8 54.9	6 14.0
15 Sa	3 31 38	24 19 41	9♈31 14	16 31 41	15 38.0	12 10.7	10 59.4	23 03.7	17 06.1	10 37.8	4 52.6	5 24.5	8 55.8	6 15.2
16 Su	3 35 35	25 17 31	23 38 29	0♉51 16	15 38.6	14 10.1	12 13.0	22 50.9	17 30.5	10 44.8	4 53.6	5 25.7	8 56.6	6 16.3
17 M	3 39 32	26 15 19	8♉09 31	15 32 32	15R38.8	16 11.4	13 26.6	22 38.9	17 54.8	10 51.9	4 54.6	5 26.9	8 57.5	6 17.5
18 Tu	3 43 28	27 13 07	22 59 30	0♊29 27	15 38.5	18 14.4	14 40.2	22 27.6	18 19.2	10 59.2	4 55.8	5 28.0	8 58.4	6 18.7
19 W	3 47 25	28 10 53	8♊01 19	15 33 58	15 37.7	20 19.1	15 53.7	22 17.1	18 43.5	11 06.6	4 57.0	5 29.1	8 59.4	6 19.9
20 Th	3 51 21	29 08 37	23 06 17	0♋37 08	15 36.3	22 25.3	17 07.3	22 07.4	19 07.8	11 14.1	4 58.4	5 30.1	9 00.4	6 21.1
21 F	3 55 18	0♊06 20	8♋05 28	15 30 20	15 34.6	24 33.0	18 20.9	21 58.5	19 32.2	11 21.8	4 59.8	5 31.1	9 01.4	6 22.4
22 Sa	3 59 14	1 04 02	22 50 55	0♌06 33	15 32.9	26 41.9	19 34.5	21 50.5	19 56.5	11 29.5	5 01.4	5 32.0	9 02.4	6 23.6
23 Su	4 03 11	2 01 42	7♌16 45	14 21 10	15 31.6	28 51.8	20 48.0	21 43.2	20 20.8	11 37.4	5 03.1	5 32.9	9 03.5	6 24.9
24 M	4 07 07	2 59 20	21 19 35	28 12 00	15D31.0	1♊02.6	22 01.6	21 36.8	20 45.0	11 45.5	5 04.8	5 33.7	9 04.6	6 26.1
25 Tu	4 11 04	3 56 57	4♍58 27	11♍39 07	15 31.1	3 14.0	23 15.2	21 31.2	21 09.3	11 53.6	5 06.7	5 34.5	9 05.7	6 27.4
26 W	4 15 01	4 54 32	18 14 16	24 44 13	15 31.9	5 25.9	24 28.7	21 26.4	21 33.6	12 01.9	5 08.7	5 35.2	9 06.8	6 28.7
27 Th	4 18 57	5 52 06	1♎09 19	7♎29 58	15 33.2	7 37.8	25 42.3	21 22.5	21 57.8	12 10.2	5 10.7	5 35.9	9 08.0	6 30.0
28 F	4 22 54	6 49 38	13 46 33	19 59 30	15 34.7	9 49.5	26 55.8	21 19.3	22 22.0	12 18.7	5 12.9	5 36.6	9 09.2	6 31.3
29 Sa	4 26 50	7 47 09	26 09 10	2♏15 58	15 36.0	12 00.8	28 09.4	21 17.0	22 46.2	12 27.3	5 15.2	5 37.1	9 10.5	6 32.6
30 Su	4 30 47	8 44 39	8♏20 14	14 22 21	15R36.6	14 11.4	29 23.0	21 15.5	23 10.4	12 36.1	5 17.5	5 37.7	9 11.7	6 34.0
31 M	4 34 43	9 42 08	20 22 36	26 21 18	15 36.1	16 21.1	0♊36.5	21D14.7	23 34.6	12 44.9	5 20.0	5 38.2	9 13.0	6 35.3

LONGITUDE June 1920

Day	Sid.Time	☉	0 hr ☽	Noon ☽	True ☊	☿	♀	♂	⚳	♃	♄	♅	♆	♇
1 Tu	4 38 40	10♊39 36	2♐18 45	8♐15 11	15♏34.4	18♊29.5	1♊50.1	21♎14.8	23♉58.8	12♌53.8	5♍22.5	5♓38.6	9♌14.3	6♋36.7
2 W	4 42 36	11 37 03	14 10 53	20 06 06	15R31.5	20 36.5	3 03.6	21 15.6	24 23.0	13 02.9	5 25.2	5 39.0	9 15.7	6 38.0
3 Th	4 46 33	12 34 28	26 01 05	1♑56 04	15 27.6	22 41.8	4 17.2	21 17.2	24 47.1	13 12.0	5 27.9	5 39.4	9 17.1	6 39.4
4 F	4 50 30	13 31 53	7♑51 21	13 47 10	15 22.9	24 45.3	5 30.8	21 19.6	25 11.2	13 21.2	5 30.8	5 39.7	9 18.5	6 40.8
5 Sa	4 54 26	14 29 18	19 43 50	25 41 40	15 18.0	26 46.9	6 44.4	21 22.7	25 35.3	13 30.6	5 33.7	5 39.9	9 19.9	6 42.2
6 Su	4 58 23	15 26 41	1♒40 59	7♒42 10	15 13.5	28 46.3	7 57.9	21 26.6	25 59.4	13 40.1	5 36.7	5 40.1	9 21.3	6 43.6
7 M	5 02 19	16 24 04	13 45 36	19 51 42	15 09.8	0♋43.6	9 11.5	21 31.2	26 23.5	13 49.6	5 39.8	5 40.3	9 22.8	6 45.0
8 Tu	5 06 16	17 21 26	26 00 54	2♓13 40	15 07.3	2 38.6	10 25.1	21 36.5	26 47.5	13 59.2	5 43.0	5 40.4	9 24.3	6 46.4
9 W	5 10 12	18 18 47	8♓30 27	14 51 45	15D06.2	4 31.2	11 38.7	21 42.6	27 11.5	14 09.0	5 46.3	5R40.5	9 25.8	6 47.8
10 Th	5 14 09	19 16 08	21 18 01	27 49 42	15 06.4	6 21.4	12 52.3	21 49.4	27 35.5	14 18.8	5 49.7	5 40.5	9 27.4	6 49.2
11 F	5 18 05	20 13 29	4♈27 12	11♈10 53	15 07.6	8 09.2	14 05.9	21 56.9	27 59.5	14 28.8	5 53.2	5 40.4	9 28.9	6 50.7
12 Sa	5 22 02	21 10 49	18 01 01	24 57 46	15 09.0	9 54.6	15 19.6	22 05.0	28 23.5	14 38.8	5 56.8	5 40.3	9 30.5	6 52.1
13 Su	5 25 59	22 08 09	2♉01 11	9♉11 10	15R10.0	11 37.4	16 33.2	22 13.9	28 47.4	14 48.9	6 00.4	5 40.2	9 32.1	6 53.6
14 M	5 29 55	23 05 28	16 27 25	23 49 30	15 09.9	13 17.8	17 46.8	22 23.4	29 11.3	14 59.1	6 04.2	5 40.0	9 33.8	6 55.0
15 Tu	5 33 52	24 02 47	1♊16 43	8♊48 15	15 08.1	14 55.6	19 00.5	22 33.7	29 35.2	15 09.4	6 08.0	5 39.8	9 35.4	6 56.5
16 W	5 37 48	25 00 06	16 23 03	23 59 58	15 04.5	16 30.9	20 14.1	22 44.5	29 59.1	15 19.8	6 11.9	5 39.5	9 37.1	6 57.9
17 Th	5 41 45	25 57 24	1♋37 42	9♋14 57	14 59.4	18 03.6	21 27.8	22 56.0	0♊22.9	15 30.2	6 15.9	5 39.2	9 38.8	6 59.4
18 F	5 45 41	26 54 41	16 50 21	24 22 40	14 53.4	19 33.8	22 41.4	23 08.2	0 46.7	15 40.8	6 20.0	5 38.8	9 40.5	7 00.9
19 Sa	5 49 38	27 51 58	1♌50 46	9♌13 38	14 47.3	21 01.4	23 55.1	23 21.0	1 10.5	15 51.4	6 24.1	5 38.4	9 42.3	7 02.3
20 Su	5 53 35	28 49 14	16 30 30	23 40 47	14 42.0	22 26.3	25 08.7	23 34.4	1 34.2	16 02.1	6 28.4	5 37.9	9 44.0	7 03.8
21 M	5 57 31	29 46 29	0♍44 06	7♍40 16	14 38.2	23 48.6	26 22.4	23 48.4	1 57.9	16 12.9	6 32.7	5 37.4	9 45.8	7 05.3
22 Tu	6 01 28	0♋43 44	14 29 18	21 11 22	14D36.1	25 08.2	27 36.1	24 02.9	2 21.6	16 23.7	6 37.1	5 36.8	9 47.6	7 06.8
23 W	6 05 24	1 40 58	27 46 45	4♎15 51	14 35.7	26 25.0	28 49.7	24 18.1	2 45.2	16 34.7	6 41.6	5 36.2	9 49.4	7 08.3
24 Th	6 09 21	2 38 11	10♎39 10	16 57 12	14 36.5	27 39.1	0♋03.4	24 33.8	3 08.8	16 45.7	6 46.1	5 35.6	9 51.3	7 09.8
25 F	6 13 17	3 35 24	23 10 32	29 19 44	14 37.7	28 50.3	1 17.1	24 50.1	3 32.3	16 56.7	6 50.8	5 34.9	9 53.1	7 11.2
26 Sa	6 17 14	4 32 36	5♏25 22	11♏27 59	14R38.6	29 58.6	2 30.8	25 07.0	3 55.9	17 07.9	6 55.5	5 34.1	9 55.0	7 12.7
27 Su	6 21 10	5 29 48	17 28 08	23 26 19	14 38.2	1♌03.9	3 44.5	25 24.3	4 19.4	17 19.1	7 00.3	5 33.3	9 56.9	7 14.2
28 M	6 25 07	6 26 59	29 23 01	5♐18 39	14 35.9	2 06.2	4 58.2	25 42.2	4 42.8	17 30.4	7 05.1	5 32.5	9 58.8	7 15.7
29 Tu	6 29 04	7 24 11	11♐13 36	17 08 15	14 31.5	3 05.3	6 11.9	26 00.6	5 06.2	17 41.7	7 10.1	5 31.6	10 00.7	7 17.2
30 W	6 33 00	8 21 22	23 02 53	28 57 49	14 24.7	4 01.1	7 25.6	26 19.5	5 29.6	17 53.2	7 15.1	5 30.7	10 02.7	7 18.7

Astro Data

	Dy Hr Mn
♄ D	7 0:04
☽ 0N	13 13:13
☽ 0S	26 3:02
♂ D	31 22:25
♄☍♅	7 15:37
☽ 0N	9 21:44
♅ R	10 4:07
☽ 0S	22 10:20

Planet Ingress

	Dy Hr Mn
♀ ♉	6 12:55
☿ ♉	8 23:55
☉ ♊	21 9:22
☿ ♊	24 0:32
♀ ♊	31 0:05
☿ ♋	7 3:02
⚳ ♊	16 12:57
☉ ♋	21 17:40
♀ ♋	24 10:53
☿ ♌	26 12:30

Last Aspect / ☽ Ingress (May)

Last Aspect Dy Hr Mn		☽ Ingress Dy Hr Mn
1 19:55	♂ ☌	♏ 2 1:37
3 1:47	☉ ☍	♐ 4 12:59
6 17:43	☿ △	♑ 7 1:39
9 3:33	♂ □	♒ 9 14:09
11 13:09	♂ △	♓ 12 0:32
13 18:19	☉ ⚹	♈ 14 7:23
15 22:52	♂ ☍	♉ 16 10:35
18 6:25	☉ ☌	♊ 18 11:13
19 22:35	♂ △	♋ 20 11:01
22 5:22	☿ ⚹	♌ 22 11:49
24 0:35	♂ ⚹	♍ 24 15:10
26 11:28	♀ △	♎ 26 21:50
28 14:34	♂ ☌	♏ 29 7:32
30 8:26	♃ □	♐ 31 19:20

Last Aspect / ☽ Ingress (June)

Last Aspect Dy Hr Mn		☽ Ingress Dy Hr Mn
2 14:21	♂ ⚹	♑ 3 8:05
5 3:17	♂ □	♒ 5 20:38
7 15:16	♂ △	♓ 8 7:43
9 18:58	☉ □	♈ 10 15:57
12 7:00	♂ ☍	♉ 12 20:35
13 21:25	♃ □	♊ 14 21:57
16 13:41	☉ ☌	♋ 16 21:26
18 9:59	♂ □	♌ 18 21:01
20 21:22	☉ ⚹	♍ 20 22:44
23 0:53	♀ □	♎ 23 4:05
25 10:56	☿ □	♏ 25 13:19
26 23:30	♃ □	♐ 28 1:15
30 6:30	♂ ⚹	♑ 30 14:06

☽ Phases & Eclipses

Dy Hr Mn	
3 1:47	○ 12♏19
3 1:51	• T 1.220
11 5:51	☾ 20♒13
18 6:25	● 27♉00
18 6:14:34	• P 0.974
24 21:07	☽ 3♍21
1 17:18	○ 10♐52
9 18:58	☾ 18♓35
16 13:41	● 25♊04
23 6:49	☽ 1♎29

Astro Data

1 May 1920
Julian Day # 7426
SVP 6♓22'09"
GC 25♐43.6 ⚴ 5♈21.9
Eris 29♓11.1 ⚵ 1♏45.8R
⚷ 8♈22.8 ⚶ 2♑46.3
☽ Mean ☊ 15♏57.0

1 June 1920
Julian Day # 7457
SVP 6♓22'04"
GC 25♐43.7 ⚴ 15♈02.7
Eris 29♓24.9 ⚵ 26♎29.5R
⚷ 9♈43.9 ⚶ 0♑10.6R
☽ Mean ☊ 14♏18.5

July 1920

LONGITUDE

Day	Sid.Time	☉	0 hr ☽	Noon ☽	True ☊	☿	♀	♂	⚳	♃	♄	♅	♆	♇
1 Th	6 36 57	9♋18 32	4♑53 16	10♑49 29	14♏16.0	4♌53.6	8♋39.3	26♎38.9	5♊53.0	18♌04.6	7♍20.1	5♓29.7	10♌04.6	7♋20.2
2 F	6 40 53	10 15 43	16 46 40	22 45 00	14R 05.9	5 42.7	9 53.1	26 58.7	6 16.2	18 16.2	7 25.3	5R 28.7	10 06.6	7 21.7
3 Sa	6 44 50	11 12 54	28 44 41	4♒45 53	13 55.4	6 28.2	11 06.8	27 19.1	6 39.5	18 27.8	7 30.5	5 27.6	10 08.6	7 23.2
4 Su	6 48 46	12 10 05	10♒48 49	16 53 40	13 45.4	7 09.9	12 20.5	27 39.9	7 02.7	18 39.4	7 35.8	5 26.5	10 10.6	7 24.7
5 M	6 52 43	13 07 16	23 00 41	29 10 07	13 36.7	7 47.9	13 34.3	28 01.1	7 25.9	18 51.1	7 41.1	5 25.4	10 12.6	7 26.2
6 Tu	6 56 39	14 04 27	5♓22 13	11♓37 20	13 30.1	8 21.9	14 48.1	28 22.8	7 49.0	19 02.9	7 46.5	5 24.2	10 14.6	7 27.6
7 W	7 00 36	15 01 38	17 55 46	24 17 54	13 25.8	8 51.7	16 01.8	28 44.9	8 12.1	19 14.7	7 52.0	5 23.0	10 16.7	7 29.1
8 Th	7 04 33	15 58 50	0♈44 06	7♈14 46	13D 23.8	9 17.4	17 15.6	29 07.5	8 35.1	19 26.6	7 57.5	5 21.7	10 18.7	7 30.6
9 F	7 08 29	16 56 03	13 50 17	20 31 01	13 23.5	9 38.7	18 29.4	29 30.5	8 58.1	19 38.6	8 03.1	5 20.4	10 20.8	7 32.1
10 Sa	7 12 26	17 53 15	27 17 18	4♉09 25	13R 24.0	9 55.6	19 43.2	29 53.9	9 21.1	19 50.6	8 08.8	5 19.1	10 22.9	7 33.6
11 Su	7 16 22	18 50 29	11♉07 32	18 11 45	13 24.1	10 07.8	20 57.0	0♏17.7	9 44.0	20 02.6	8 14.5	5 17.7	10 25.0	7 35.0
12 M	7 20 19	19 47 43	25 22 01	2♊38 05	13 22.8	10 15.4	22 10.9	0 41.9	10 06.8	20 14.7	8 20.3	5 16.2	10 27.1	7 36.5
13 Tu	7 24 15	20 44 57	9♊59 33	17 25 51	13 19.2	10R 18.2	23 24.7	1 06.5	10 29.6	20 26.8	8 26.2	5 14.8	10 29.2	7 38.0
14 W	7 28 12	21 42 12	24 56 08	2♋29 27	13 13.1	10 16.2	24 38.6	1 31.5	10 52.3	20 39.0	8 32.1	5 13.3	10 31.3	7 39.4
15 Th	7 32 08	22 39 28	10♋04 38	17 40 26	13 04.7	10 09.4	25 52.4	1 56.8	11 15.0	20 51.3	8 38.1	5 11.7	10 33.4	7 40.9
16 F	7 36 05	23 36 44	25 15 31	2♌48 32	12 54.9	9 57.8	27 06.3	2 22.6	11 37.6	21 03.6	8 44.1	5 10.2	10 35.6	7 42.3
17 Sa	7 40 02	24 34 00	10♌18 13	17 43 25	12 44.8	9 41.5	28 20.2	2 48.7	12 00.2	21 15.9	8 50.2	5 08.6	10 37.7	7 43.8
18 Su	7 43 58	25 31 16	25 03 07	2♍16 31	12 35.6	9 20.7	29 34.1	3 15.2	12 22.7	21 28.2	8 56.3	5 06.9	10 39.9	7 45.2
19 M	7 47 55	26 28 33	9♍23 02	16 22 19	12 28.2	8 55.5	0♌48.0	3 42.0	12 45.2	21 40.7	9 02.5	5 05.2	10 42.0	7 46.6
20 Tu	7 51 51	27 25 50	23 14 11	29 58 42	12 23.3	8 26.2	2 01.8	4 09.2	13 07.5	21 53.1	9 08.7	5 03.5	10 44.2	7 48.1
21 W	7 55 48	28 23 07	6♎36 04	13♎06 37	12 20.6	7 53.3	3 15.7	4 36.7	13 29.9	22 05.6	9 15.0	5 01.8	10 46.4	7 49.5
22 Th	7 59 44	29 20 25	19 30 50	25 49 15	12D 19.8	7 17.0	4 29.7	5 04.6	13 52.1	22 18.1	9 21.3	5 00.0	10 48.6	7 50.9
23 F	8 03 41	0♌17 42	2♏02 28	8♏11 07	12R 19.8	6 38.0	5 43.6	5 32.8	14 14.3	22 30.7	9 27.7	4 58.2	10 50.8	7 52.3
24 Sa	8 07 37	1 15 01	14 15 53	20 17 23	12 19.7	5 56.9	6 57.5	6 01.3	14 36.4	22 43.2	9 34.2	4 56.3	10 53.0	7 53.7
25 Su	8 11 34	2 12 19	26 16 18	2♐13 15	12 18.3	5 14.3	8 11.4	6 30.1	14 58.5	22 55.9	9 40.6	4 54.5	10 55.2	7 55.1
26 M	8 15 31	3 09 39	8♐08 49	14 03 33	12 14.7	4 30.9	9 25.3	6 59.2	15 20.5	23 08.5	9 47.2	4 52.6	10 57.4	7 56.4
27 Tu	8 19 27	4 06 58	19 57 58	25 52 32	12 08.6	3 47.5	10 39.3	7 28.7	15 42.4	23 21.2	9 53.8	4 50.6	10 59.6	7 57.8
28 W	8 23 24	5 04 19	1♑47 39	7♑43 41	11 59.7	3 04.9	11 53.2	7 58.4	16 04.2	23 33.9	10 00.4	4 48.7	11 01.8	7 59.2
29 Th	8 27 20	6 01 40	13 40 57	19 39 42	11 48.4	2 23.8	13 07.2	8 28.4	16 26.0	23 46.7	10 07.0	4 46.7	11 04.0	8 00.5
30 F	8 31 17	6 59 01	25 40 10	1♒42 31	11 35.4	1 45.1	14 21.1	8 58.7	16 47.7	23 59.4	10 13.7	4 44.7	11 06.2	8 01.9
31 Sa	8 35 13	7 56 24	7♒46 53	13 53 23	11 21.9	1 09.4	15 35.1	9 29.3	17 09.3	24 12.2	10 20.5	4 42.6	11 08.5	8 03.2

August 1920

LONGITUDE

Day	Sid.Time	☉	0 hr ☽	Noon ☽	True ☊	☿	♀	♂	⚳	♃	♄	♅	♆	♇
1 Su	8 39 10	8♌53 47	20♒02 07	26♒13 09	11♏08.9	0♌37.6	16♌49.0	10♏00.1	17♊30.9	24♌25.1	10♍27.3	4♓40.6	11♌10.7	8♋04.5
2 M	8 43 06	9 51 11	2♓26 35	8♓42 29	10R 57.5	0R 10.1	18 03.0	10 31.2	17 52.3	24 37.9	10 34.1	4R 38.5	11 12.9	8 05.8
3 Tu	8 47 03	10 48 36	15 00 58	21 22 08	10 48.6	29♋47.7	19 17.0	11 02.6	18 13.7	24 50.8	10 40.9	4 36.4	11 15.1	8 07.1
4 W	8 51 00	11 46 03	27 46 10	4♈13 12	10 42.5	29 30.8	20 31.0	11 34.3	18 35.0	25 03.7	10 47.8	4 34.3	11 17.3	8 08.4
5 Th	8 54 56	12 43 30	10♈43 28	17 17 11	10 39.1	29 19.8	21 45.0	12 06.2	18 56.3	25 16.6	10 54.8	4 32.1	11 19.6	8 09.6
6 F	8 58 53	13 40 59	23 54 37	0♉36 00	10D 37.8	29D 15.0	22 59.0	12 38.3	19 17.4	25 29.5	11 01.7	4 29.9	11 21.8	8 10.9
7 Sa	9 02 49	14 38 30	7♉21 36	14 11 38	10R 37.7	29 16.8	24 13.0	13 10.7	19 38.5	25 42.4	11 08.7	4 27.7	11 24.0	8 12.2
8 Su	9 06 46	15 36 02	21 06 18	28 05 44	10 37.4	29 25.3	25 27.0	13 43.4	19 59.5	25 55.4	11 15.8	4 25.5	11 26.2	8 13.4
9 M	9 10 42	16 33 35	5♊09 57	12♊18 52	10 35.8	29 40.6	26 41.0	14 16.3	20 20.3	26 08.4	11 22.8	4 23.3	11 28.5	8 14.6
10 Tu	9 14 39	17 31 09	19 32 16	26 49 48	10 31.9	0♌02.9	27 55.0	14 49.4	20 41.1	26 21.4	11 29.9	4 21.0	11 30.7	8 15.8
11 W	9 18 35	18 28 45	4♋10 55	11♋34 56	10 25.3	0 32.2	29 09.1	15 22.8	21 01.8	26 34.4	11 37.1	4 18.8	11 32.9	8 17.0
12 Th	9 22 32	19 26 23	19 00 59	26 28 05	10 16.3	1 08.4	0♍23.1	15 56.4	21 22.4	26 47.4	11 44.2	4 16.5	11 35.1	8 18.2
13 F	9 26 29	20 24 02	3♌55 10	11♌21 06	10 05.7	1 51.5	1 37.2	16 30.3	21 42.9	27 00.5	11 51.4	4 14.2	11 37.3	8 19.4
14 Sa	9 30 25	21 21 41	18 44 44	26 05 00	9 54.6	2 41.4	2 51.2	17 04.3	22 03.3	27 13.5	11 58.6	4 11.9	11 39.5	8 20.5
15 Su	9 34 22	22 19 23	3♍20 54	10♍31 36	9 44.4	3 37.9	4 05.3	17 38.7	22 23.6	27 26.6	12 05.9	4 09.6	11 41.7	8 21.7
16 M	9 38 18	23 17 05	17 36 25	24 34 50	9 36.0	4 40.8	5 19.3	18 13.2	22 43.8	27 39.7	12 13.1	4 07.2	11 43.9	8 22.8
17 Tu	9 42 15	24 14 48	1♎26 33	8♎11 27	9 30.2	5 49.8	6 33.4	18 47.9	23 03.9	27 52.7	12 20.4	4 04.9	11 46.1	8 23.9
18 W	9 46 11	25 12 33	14 49 35	21 21 08	9 26.8	7 04.9	7 47.5	19 22.9	23 23.9	28 05.8	12 27.7	4 02.5	11 48.3	8 25.0
19 Th	9 50 08	26 10 19	27 46 28	4♏06 00	9D 25.6	8 25.5	9 01.5	19 58.1	23 43.8	28 18.9	12 35.0	4 00.2	11 50.5	8 26.1
20 F	9 54 04	27 08 05	10♏20 15	16 29 50	9R 25.6	9 51.5	10 15.6	20 33.4	24 03.5	28 32.0	12 42.4	3 57.8	11 52.6	8 27.1
21 Sa	9 58 01	28 05 54	22 35 22	28 37 30	9 25.8	11 22.4	11 29.6	21 09.0	24 23.1	28 45.1	12 49.8	3 55.4	11 54.8	8 28.2
22 Su	10 01 58	29 03 43	4♐36 54	10♐34 16	9 25.2	12 57.8	12 43.7	21 44.8	24 42.7	28 58.1	12 57.1	3 53.0	11 56.9	8 29.2
23 M	10 05 54	0♍01 33	16 30 14	22 25 25	9 22.8	14 37.4	13 57.8	22 20.8	25 02.1	29 11.2	13 04.6	3 50.6	11 59.1	8 30.2
24 Tu	10 09 51	0 59 25	28 20 26	4♑15 52	9 18.1	16 20.6	15 11.8	22 56.9	25 21.4	29 24.3	13 12.0	3 48.3	12 01.2	8 31.2
25 W	10 13 47	1 57 18	10♑12 12	16 09 54	9 10.9	18 07.0	16 25.9	23 33.3	25 40.5	29 37.4	13 19.4	3 45.9	12 03.3	8 32.2
26 Th	10 17 44	2 55 12	22 09 25	28 11 04	9 01.5	19 56.1	17 39.9	24 09.8	25 59.5	29 50.5	13 26.9	3 43.5	12 05.4	8 33.2
27 F	10 21 40	3 53 08	4♒15 10	10♒21 57	8 50.6	21 47.6	18 54.0	24 46.6	26 18.4	0♍03.5	13 34.3	3 41.1	12 07.5	8 34.1
28 Sa	10 25 37	4 51 05	16 31 35	22 44 12	8 39.0	23 41.0	20 08.0	25 23.5	26 37.2	0 16.6	13 41.8	3 38.7	12 09.6	8 35.0
29 Su	10 29 33	5 49 04	28 59 52	5♓18 36	8 27.9	25 35.8	21 22.1	26 00.5	26 55.9	0 29.7	13 49.3	3 36.3	12 11.7	8 35.9
30 M	10 33 30	6 47 04	11♓40 24	18 05 13	8 18.2	27 31.7	22 36.1	26 37.8	27 14.4	0 42.7	13 56.8	3 33.9	12 13.8	8 36.8
31 Tu	10 37 26	7 45 06	24 33 01	1♈03 43	8 10.7	29 28.4	23 50.2	27 15.2	27 32.7	0 55.7	14 04.3	3 31.5	12 15.8	8 37.7

Astro Data

	Dy Hr Mn
♄⚹♇	1 12:25
☽0N	7 5:01
☿R	13 14:06
☽0S	19 19:45
♃∠♇	25 10:16
☽0N	3 11:32
☿D	6 17:37
♄⊻♆	10 15:42
☽0S	16 6:18
☽0N	30 18:12

Planet Ingress

	Dy Hr Mn
♂ ♏	10 18:14
♀ ♌	18 20:26
☉ ♌	23 4:35
☿ ♋R	2 22:10
☿ ♌	10 9:13
♀ ♍	12 4:31
☉ ♍	23 11:21
♃ ♍	27 5:29
☿ ♍	31 18:29

Last Aspect / ☽ Ingress (July)

Last Aspect Dy Hr Mn		☽ Ingress Dy Hr Mn
2 20:43	♂ □	♒ 3 2:30
5 9:42	♂ △	♓ 5 13:37
6 18:43	♀ △	♈ 7 22:38
10 4:22	♂ ☍	♉ 10 4:45
11 17:04	♀ ⚹	♊ 12 7:40
13 16:54	♃ ⚹	♋ 14 8:03
16 2:07	♀ ☌	♌ 16 7:32
17 17:52	♃ ☌	♍ 18 8:12
20 7:06	☉ ⚹	♎ 20 12:02
22 19:20	☉ □	♏ 22 20:03
24 16:57	♃ □	♐ 25 7:31
27 6:47	♃ △	♑ 27 20:22
28 16:38	♄ △	♒ 30 8:37

Last Aspect / ☽ Ingress (August)

Last Aspect Dy Hr Mn		☽ Ingress Dy Hr Mn
1 8:27	♃ ☍	♓ 1 19:18
4 3:25	☿ △	♈ 4 4:10
6 9:36	☿ □	♉ 6 10:56
8 14:18	☿ ⚹	♊ 8 15:15
10 13:57	♀ ⚹	♋ 10 17:11
11 18:22	♂ △	♌ 12 17:41
14 13:54	♃ ☌	♍ 14 18:27
16 0:35	♂ ⚹	♎ 16 21:28
19 0:50	♃ ⚹	♏ 19 4:12
21 12:15	♃ □	♐ 21 14:45
24 1:58	♃ △	♑ 24 3:22
26 3:35	♂ ⚹	♒ 26 15:36
28 17:22	♂ □	♓ 29 1:55
31 4:38	♂ △	♈ 31 10:03

☽ Phases & Eclipses

Dy Hr Mn	
1 8:40	○ 9♑11
9 5:05	☾ 16♈40
15 20:25	● 23♋00
22 19:20	☽ 29♎38
30 23:19	○ 7♒26
7 12:50	☾ 14♉41
14 3:44	● 21♌02
21 10:51	☽ 28♏03
29 13:02	○ 5♓52

Astro Data

1 July 1920
Julian Day # 7487
SVP 6♓21'59"
GC 25♐43.7 ⚵ 23♈07.9
Eris 29♓28.3R ⚴ 25♎57.9
⚷ 10♈25.0 ⚶ 23♐20.6R
☽ Mean ☊ 12♏43.2

1 August 1920
Julian Day # 7518
SVP 6♓21'54"
GC 25♐43.8 ⚵ 29♈03.2
Eris 29♓20.8R ⚴ 29♎52.0
⚷ 10♈19.8R ⚶ 20♐05.9
☽ Mean ☊ 11♏04.8

LONGITUDE — September 1920

Day	Sid.Time	☉	0 hr ☽	Noon ☽	True ☊	☿	♀	♂	⚳	♃	♄	♅	♆	♇
1 W	10 41 23	8♍43 09	7♈37 16	14♈13 36	8♏05.7	1♍25.5	25♍04.2	27♏52.8	27♊51.0	1♍08.8	14♍11.8	3♓29.1	12♌17.9	8♋38.5
2 Th	10 45 20	9 41 15	20 52 42	27 34 32	8D 03.3	3 22.8	26 18.2	28 30.5	28 09.1	1 21.8	14 19.3	3R 26.7	12 19.9	8 39.4
3 F	10 49 16	10 39 22	4♉19 08	11♉06 30	8 02.9	5 20.0	27 32.3	29 08.5	28 27.0	1 34.8	14 26.8	3 24.4	12 21.9	8 40.2
4 Sa	10 53 13	11 37 32	17 56 41	24 49 44	8 03.5	7 16.9	28 46.3	29 46.6	28 44.8	1 47.8	14 34.4	3 22.0	12 23.9	8 41.0
5 Su	10 57 09	12 35 43	1♊45 41	8♊44 31	8R 04.2	9 13.3	0♎00.4	0♐24.8	29 02.5	2 00.8	14 41.9	3 19.6	12 25.9	8 41.7
6 M	11 01 06	13 33 57	15 46 14	22 50 44	8 03.9	11 09.1	1 14.4	1 03.2	29 20.0	2 13.7	14 49.4	3 17.3	12 27.9	8 42.5
7 Tu	11 05 02	14 32 12	29 57 51	7♋07 22	8 01.8	13 04.2	2 28.4	1 41.8	29 37.3	2 26.7	14 57.0	3 15.0	12 29.8	8 43.2
8 W	11 08 59	15 30 30	14♋18 55	21 32 04	7 57.6	14 58.5	3 42.5	2 20.5	29 54.5	2 39.6	15 04.5	3 12.6	12 31.8	8 43.9
9 Th	11 12 55	16 28 50	28 46 17	6♌00 56	7 51.4	16 51.9	4 56.5	2 59.4	0♋11.5	2 52.5	15 12.1	3 10.3	12 33.7	8 44.6
10 F	11 16 52	17 27 12	13♌15 18	20 28 37	7 43.8	18 44.3	6 10.6	3 38.5	0 28.3	3 05.4	15 19.6	3 08.0	12 35.6	8 45.3
11 Sa	11 20 49	18 25 35	27 40 07	4♍49 02	7 35.8	20 35.7	7 24.6	4 17.7	0 45.0	3 18.2	15 27.1	3 05.7	12 37.5	8 45.9
12 Su	11 24 45	19 24 01	11♍54 36	18 56 11	7 28.3	22 26.1	8 38.6	4 57.0	1 01.5	3 31.1	15 34.7	3 03.4	12 39.4	8 46.6
13 M	11 28 42	20 22 28	25 53 10	2♎45 07	7 22.2	24 15.4	9 52.7	5 36.5	1 17.8	3 43.9	15 42.2	3 01.2	12 41.2	8 47.2
14 Tu	11 32 38	21 20 58	9♎31 42	16 12 41	7 18.1	26 03.7	11 06.7	6 16.2	1 34.0	3 56.7	15 49.7	2 58.9	12 43.1	8 47.8
15 W	11 36 35	22 19 29	22 48 01	29 17 44	7D 16.1	27 50.9	12 20.7	6 56.0	1 49.9	4 09.4	15 57.2	2 56.7	12 44.9	8 48.3
16 Th	11 40 31	23 18 01	5♏42 01	12♏01 09	7 15.9	29 37.1	13 34.7	7 35.9	2 05.7	4 22.1	16 04.7	2 54.5	12 46.7	8 48.9
17 F	11 44 28	24 16 36	18 15 29	24 25 28	7 16.9	1♎22.1	14 48.7	8 16.0	2 21.3	4 34.8	16 12.2	2 52.3	12 48.5	8 49.4
18 Sa	11 48 24	25 15 12	0♐31 37	6♐34 29	7 18.4	3 06.2	16 02.7	8 56.2	2 36.6	4 47.5	16 19.7	2 50.1	12 50.2	8 49.9
19 Su	11 52 21	26 13 50	12 34 39	18 32 44	7R 19.7	4 49.2	17 16.7	9 36.6	2 51.8	5 00.1	16 27.2	2 48.0	12 52.0	8 50.4
20 M	11 56 18	27 12 30	24 29 24	0♑25 15	7 19.9	6 31.2	18 30.7	10 17.1	3 06.8	5 12.7	16 34.7	2 45.9	12 53.7	8 50.8
21 Tu	12 00 14	28 11 11	6♑20 55	12 17 02	7 18.7	8 12.2	19 44.7	10 57.7	3 21.6	5 25.2	16 42.1	2 43.8	12 55.4	8 51.2
22 W	12 04 11	29 09 54	18 14 11	24 12 55	7 15.8	9 52.2	20 58.7	11 38.4	3 36.1	5 37.8	16 49.5	2 41.7	12 57.0	8 51.7
23 Th	12 08 07	0♎08 39	0♒13 47	6♒17 14	7 11.4	11 31.2	22 12.6	12 19.3	3 50.5	5 50.2	16 57.0	2 39.7	12 58.7	8 52.0
24 F	12 12 04	1 07 25	12 23 43	18 33 35	7 05.9	13 09.3	23 26.6	13 00.3	4 04.6	6 02.7	17 04.4	2 37.6	13 00.3	8 52.4
25 Sa	12 16 00	2 06 13	24 47 08	1♓04 35	6 59.8	14 46.5	24 40.5	13 41.4	4 18.6	6 15.1	17 11.7	2 35.7	13 01.9	8 52.7
26 Su	12 19 57	3 05 03	7♓26 07	13 51 48	6 53.9	16 22.7	25 54.4	14 22.6	4 32.3	6 27.4	17 19.1	2 33.7	13 03.5	8 53.1
27 M	12 23 53	4 03 55	20 21 38	26 55 35	6 48.8	17 58.0	27 08.3	15 04.0	4 45.7	6 39.7	17 26.5	2 31.7	13 05.0	8 53.4
28 Tu	12 27 50	5 02 49	3♈33 30	10♈15 13	6 45.0	19 32.4	28 22.2	15 45.4	4 59.0	6 52.0	17 33.8	2 29.8	13 06.6	8 53.6
29 W	12 31 46	6 01 45	17 00 30	23 49 05	6D 42.8	21 06.0	29 36.1	16 27.0	5 12.0	7 04.2	17 41.1	2 28.0	13 08.1	8 53.9
30 Th	12 35 43	7 00 43	0♉40 41	7♉34 59	6 42.2	22 38.7	0♏50.0	17 08.7	5 24.7	7 16.4	17 48.3	2 26.1	13 09.6	8 54.1

LONGITUDE — October 1920

Day	Sid.Time	☉	0 hr ☽	Noon ☽	True ☊	☿	♀	♂	⚳	♃	♄	♅	♆	♇
1 F	12 39 40	7♎59 44	14♉31 40	21♉30 27	6♏42.8	24♎10.5	2♏03.9	17♐50.5	5♋37.3	7♍28.5	17♍55.6	2♓24.3	13♌11.0	8♋54.3
2 Sa	12 43 36	8 58 46	28 31 02	5♊33 07	6 44.2	25 41.5	3 17.8	18 32.4	5 49.5	7 40.6	18 02.8	2R 22.5	13 12.4	8 54.5
3 Su	12 47 33	9 57 51	12♊36 27	19 40 46	6 45.7	27 11.6	4 31.7	19 14.5	6 01.6	7 52.6	18 10.0	2 20.8	13 13.9	8 54.6
4 M	12 51 29	10 56 59	26 45 49	3♋51 23	6R 46.7	28 40.9	5 45.5	19 56.6	6 13.3	8 04.5	18 17.2	2 19.0	13 15.2	8 54.8
5 Tu	12 55 26	11 56 08	10♋57 11	18 02 59	6 46.7	0♏09.4	6 59.4	20 38.9	6 24.9	8 16.5	18 24.3	2 17.4	13 16.6	8 54.9
6 W	12 59 22	12 55 20	25 08 32	2♌13 32	6 45.6	1 37.0	8 13.2	21 21.2	6 36.1	8 28.3	18 31.5	2 15.7	13 17.9	8 55.0
7 Th	13 03 19	13 54 35	9♌17 40	16 20 38	6 43.5	3 03.7	9 27.1	22 03.7	6 47.1	8 40.1	18 38.5	2 14.1	13 19.2	8 55.0
8 F	13 07 15	14 53 51	23 22 04	0♍21 36	6 40.7	4 29.5	10 40.9	22 46.3	6 57.8	8 51.8	18 45.6	2 12.5	13 20.5	8 55.1
9 Sa	13 11 12	15 53 10	7♍18 53	14 13 33	6 37.6	5 54.5	11 54.7	23 28.9	7 08.2	9 03.5	18 52.6	2 11.0	13 21.7	8R 55.1
10 Su	13 15 09	16 52 31	21 05 14	27 53 37	6 34.7	7 18.5	13 08.6	24 11.7	7 18.3	9 15.1	18 59.6	2 09.5	13 22.9	8 55.1
11 M	13 19 05	17 51 54	4♎38 23	11♎19 17	6 32.5	8 41.6	14 22.4	24 54.6	7 28.1	9 26.7	19 06.5	2 08.0	13 24.1	8 55.0
12 Tu	13 23 02	18 51 19	17 56 08	24 28 47	6D 31.2	10 03.6	15 36.2	25 37.6	7 37.7	9 38.2	19 13.4	2 06.6	13 25.3	8 55.0
13 W	13 26 58	19 50 47	0♏57 10	7♏21 18	6 30.8	11 24.7	16 50.0	26 20.7	7 46.9	9 49.6	19 20.3	2 05.2	13 26.4	8 54.9
14 Th	13 30 55	20 50 16	13 41 14	19 57 08	6 31.2	12 44.6	18 03.8	27 03.9	7 55.8	10 00.9	19 27.1	2 03.9	13 27.5	8 54.8
15 F	13 34 51	21 49 47	26 09 11	2♐17 41	6 32.2	14 03.4	19 17.5	27 47.1	8 04.4	10 12.2	19 33.9	2 02.6	13 28.6	8 54.7
16 Sa	13 38 48	22 49 20	8♐22 58	14 25 25	6 33.5	15 21.0	20 31.3	28 30.5	8 12.7	10 23.4	19 40.7	2 01.3	13 29.6	8 54.5
17 Su	13 42 44	23 48 55	20 25 29	26 23 39	6 34.8	16 37.3	21 45.1	29 14.0	8 20.7	10 34.5	19 47.4	2 00.1	13 30.6	8 54.4
18 M	13 46 41	24 48 32	2♑20 26	8♑16 23	6 35.8	17 52.1	22 58.8	29 57.5	8 28.4	10 45.6	19 54.1	1 59.0	13 31.6	8 54.2
19 Tu	13 50 38	25 48 10	14 12 05	20 08 06	6R 36.3	19 05.5	24 12.5	0♑41.2	8 35.7	10 56.5	20 00.7	1 57.8	13 32.5	8 53.9
20 W	13 54 34	26 47 50	26 05 02	2♒03 30	6 36.3	20 17.2	25 26.2	1 24.9	8 42.7	11 07.4	20 07.2	1 56.8	13 33.4	8 53.7
21 Th	13 58 31	27 47 32	8♒04 04	14 07 18	6 35.9	21 27.1	26 39.9	2 08.7	8 49.4	11 18.3	20 13.8	1 55.7	13 34.3	8 53.4
22 F	14 02 27	28 47 16	20 13 45	26 23 56	6 35.1	22 35.0	27 53.6	2 52.6	8 55.7	11 29.0	20 20.2	1 54.7	13 35.2	8 53.2
23 Sa	14 06 24	29 47 01	2♓38 19	8♓57 18	6 34.3	23 40.9	29 07.3	3 36.6	9 01.7	11 39.6	20 26.7	1 53.8	13 36.0	8 52.8
24 Su	14 10 20	0♏46 48	15 21 12	21 50 19	6 33.4	24 44.3	0♐20.9	4 20.6	9 07.3	11 50.2	20 33.0	1 52.9	13 36.8	8 52.5
25 M	14 14 17	1 46 37	28 24 46	5♈04 40	6 32.8	25 45.1	1 34.5	5 04.7	9 12.6	12 00.7	20 39.3	1 52.0	13 37.5	8 52.2
26 Tu	14 18 13	2 46 28	11♈49 57	18 40 29	6 32.4	26 43.0	2 48.1	5 48.9	9 17.6	12 11.1	20 45.6	1 51.2	13 38.3	8 51.8
27 W	14 22 10	3 46 20	25 36 01	2♉36 11	6D 32.3	27 37.8	4 01.7	6 33.2	9 22.1	12 21.4	20 51.8	1 50.5	13 38.9	8 51.4
28 Th	14 26 07	4 46 14	9♉40 32	16 48 30	6 32.3	28 28.9	5 15.3	7 17.6	9 26.3	12 31.6	20 58.0	1 49.8	13 39.6	8 51.0
29 F	14 30 03	5 46 11	23 59 29	1♊12 48	6R 32.4	29 16.1	6 28.9	8 02.0	9 30.2	12 41.7	21 04.1	1 49.1	13 40.2	8 50.5
30 Sa	14 34 00	6 46 10	8♊27 46	15 43 39	6 32.4	29 58.9	7 42.4	8 46.5	9 33.6	12 51.7	21 10.1	1 48.5	13 40.8	8 50.0
31 Su	14 37 56	7 46 10	22 59 45	0♋15 26	6 32.3	0♐36.8	8 56.0	9 31.0	9 36.7	13 01.6	21 16.1	1 47.9	13 41.4	8 49.6

Astro Data

	Dy Hr Mn
♀0S	7 14:32
♃☍♅	10 16:10
☽0S	12 16:19
☿0S	17 23:38
☉0S	23 8:29
☽0N	27 1:56
♃⚹♇	8 18:38
♇R	9 14:24
☽0S	10 0:28
☽0N	24 10:59

Planet Ingress

		Dy Hr Mn
♂	♐	4 20:27
♀	♎	5 11:53
⚳	♋	8 19:45
☿	♎	16 17:13
☉	♎	23 8:28
♀	♏	29 19:45
☿	♏	5 9:27
♂	♑	18 13:22
☉	♏	23 17:13
♀	♐	24 5:11
☿	♐	30 12:40

Last Aspect / ☽ Ingress (September)

Last Aspect Dy Hr Mn			☽ Ingress	Dy Hr Mn
1 8:30	♆	△	♉	2 16:19
4 19:30	♀	△	♊	4 20:58
5 22:16	♄	□	♋	7 0:04
8 1:16	☉	⚹	♌	9 2:02
9 22:52	♆	☌	♍	11 3:54
12 18:56	☿	☌	♎	13 7:10
14 5:42	♆	⚹	♏	15 13:19
17 11:41	☉	⚹	♐	17 22:58
20 4:55	☉	□	♑	20 11:09
22 22:45	☉	△	♒	22 23:33
24 22:27	♀	△	♓	25 9:57
26 18:27	♄	☍	♈	27 17:35
29 6:36	☿	☍	♉	29 22:49

Last Aspect / ☽ Ingress (October)

Last Aspect Dy Hr Mn			☽ Ingress	Dy Hr Mn
1 5:48	♄	△	♊	2 2:32
4 2:13	☿	△	♋	4 5:29
5 12:36	♄	⚹	♌	6 8:14
7 22:17	♂	△	♍	8 11:23
10 5:06	♂	□	♎	10 15:44
12 14:14	♂	⚹	♏	12 22:14
14 11:02	♄	⚹	♐	15 7:30
17 18:06	♂	☌	♑	17 19:16
20 0:28	☉	□	♒	20 7:52
22 17:01	☉	△	♓	22 18:57
24 17:46	☿	△	♈	25 2:52
26 3:10	♆	△	♉	27 7:33
29 8:36	☿	☍	♊	29 9:59
30 21:03	♄	□	♋	31 11:34

☽ Phases & Eclipses

Dy Hr Mn		
5 19:05	☾	12♊53
12 12:51	●	19♍26
20 4:55	☽	26♐55
28 1:56	○	4♈38
5 0:53	☾	11♋29
12 0:50	●	18♎24
20 0:28	☽	26♑19
27 14:09	○	3♉52
27 14:11	☍	T 1.398

Astro Data

1 September 1920
Julian Day # 7549
SVP 6♓21'51"
GC 25♐43.9 ⚴ 0♉36.8R
Eris 29♓04.4R ⚵ 6♏52.6
⚷ 9♈28.9R ⚶ 24♐02.0
☽ Mean ☊ 9♏26.2

1 October 1920
Julian Day # 7579
SVP 6♓21'49"
GC 25♐44.0 ⚴ 26♈00.4R
Eris 28♓44.4R ⚵ 15♏30.6
⚷ 8♈12.3R ⚶ 2♑52.1
☽ Mean ☊ 7♏50.9

November 1920 — LONGITUDE

Day	Sid.Time	☉	0 hr ☽	Noon ☽	True ☊	☿	♀	♂	⚳	♃	♄	♅	♆	♇
1 M	14 41 53	8♏46 13	7♋30 03	14♋43 04	6♏32.2	1♐09.2	10♐09.5	10♑15.7	9♋39.4	13♍11.5	21♍22.0	1♓47.4	13♌41.9	8♋49.1
2 Tu	14 45 49	9 46 18	21 54 00	29 02 27	6D32.0	1 35.6	11 23.0	11 00.4	9 41.7	13 21.2	21 27.9	1R46.9	13 42.4	8R48.5
3 W	14 49 46	10 46 25	6♌08 05	13♌10 39	6 32.0	1 55.4	12 36.5	11 45.1	9 43.6	13 30.8	21 33.7	1 46.5	13 42.9	8 48.0
4 Th	14 53 42	11 46 34	20 09 58	27 05 54	6 32.1	2 07.8	13 49.9	12 30.0	9 45.2	13 40.4	21 39.4	1 46.1	13 43.3	8 47.4
5 F	14 57 39	12 46 45	3♍58 24	10♍47 24	6 32.5	2R12.3	15 03.4	13 14.9	9 46.3	13 49.8	21 45.1	1 45.8	13 43.7	8 46.8
6 Sa	15 01 36	13 46 59	17 32 54	24 14 56	6 33.2	2 08.2	16 16.8	13 59.8	9 47.0	13 59.1	21 50.7	1 45.6	13 44.0	8 46.2
7 Su	15 05 32	14 47 14	0♎53 32	7♎28 42	6 34.0	1 54.9	17 30.2	14 44.9	9R47.3	14 08.3	21 56.2	1 45.3	13 44.3	8 45.6
8 M	15 09 29	15 47 31	14 00 32	20 29 03	6 34.7	1 31.9	18 43.6	15 30.0	9 47.2	14 17.4	22 01.7	1 45.2	13 44.6	8 44.9
9 Tu	15 13 25	16 47 50	26 54 19	3♏16 24	6R35.0	0 58.9	19 57.0	16 15.1	9 46.7	14 26.4	22 07.1	1 45.0	13 44.9	8 44.2
10 W	15 17 22	17 48 11	9♏35 22	15 51 18	6 34.9	0 16.0	21 10.4	17 00.3	9 45.8	14 35.2	22 12.4	1D45.0	13 45.1	8 43.5
11 Th	15 21 18	18 48 34	22 04 18	28 14 28	6 34.1	29♏23.3	22 23.7	17 45.6	9 44.5	14 44.0	22 17.7	1 45.0	13 45.3	8 42.8
12 F	15 25 15	19 48 58	4♐21 58	10♐26 58	6 32.6	28 21.7	23 37.1	18 31.0	9 42.7	14 52.6	22 22.9	1 45.0	13 45.4	8 42.1
13 Sa	15 29 11	20 49 24	16 29 40	22 30 18	6 30.6	27 12.3	24 50.4	19 16.4	9 40.6	15 01.1	22 28.0	1 45.1	13 45.5	8 41.3
14 Su	15 33 08	21 49 52	28 29 09	4♑26 32	6 28.1	25 56.8	26 03.6	20 01.8	9 38.0	15 09.5	22 33.0	1 45.2	13 45.6	8 40.6
15 M	15 37 05	22 50 20	10♑22 49	16 18 23	6 25.6	24 37.3	27 16.9	20 47.3	9 35.0	15 17.7	22 38.0	1 45.4	13R45.7	8 39.8
16 Tu	15 41 01	23 50 51	22 13 41	28 09 11	6 23.4	23 16.3	28 30.1	21 32.9	9 31.6	15 25.9	22 42.9	1 45.7	13 45.7	8 39.0
17 W	15 44 58	24 51 22	4♒05 23	10♒02 49	6 21.8	21 56.5	29 43.3	22 18.5	9 27.8	15 33.9	22 47.7	1 45.9	13 45.7	8 38.2
18 Th	15 48 54	25 51 55	16 02 03	22 03 39	6D21.1	20 40.5	0♑56.5	23 04.1	9 23.6	15 41.8	22 52.4	1 46.3	13 45.6	8 37.3
19 F	15 52 51	26 52 29	28 08 13	4♓16 20	6 21.2	19 30.7	2 09.6	23 49.8	9 18.9	15 49.5	22 57.1	1 46.7	13 45.5	8 36.5
20 Sa	15 56 47	27 53 04	10♓28 34	16 45 29	6 22.2	18 29.2	3 22.7	24 35.6	9 13.9	15 57.1	23 01.6	1 47.1	13 45.4	8 35.6
21 Su	16 00 44	28 53 40	23 07 36	29 35 23	6 23.7	17 37.7	4 35.8	25 21.4	9 08.4	16 04.6	23 06.1	1 47.6	13 45.2	8 34.7
22 M	16 04 40	29 54 18	6♈09 14	12♈49 27	6 25.3	16 57.2	5 48.8	26 07.2	9 02.6	16 11.9	23 10.5	1 48.2	13 45.0	8 33.8
23 Tu	16 08 37	0♐54 56	19 36 15	26 29 41	6R26.4	16 28.2	7 01.8	26 53.0	8 56.3	16 19.1	23 14.8	1 48.8	13 44.8	8 32.9
24 W	16 12 33	1 55 36	3♉29 42	10♉36 01	6 26.7	16 10.9	8 14.8	27 38.9	8 49.6	16 26.2	23 19.0	1 49.4	13 44.5	8 31.9
25 Th	16 16 30	2 56 18	17 48 16	25 05 50	6 25.6	16D05.0	9 27.7	28 24.9	8 42.6	16 33.1	23 23.2	1 50.1	13 44.2	8 31.0
26 F	16 20 27	3 57 00	2♊27 59	9♊53 49	6 23.2	16 09.9	10 40.6	29 10.9	8 35.2	16 39.9	23 27.2	1 50.9	13 43.9	8 30.0
27 Sa	16 24 23	4 57 44	17 22 18	24 52 20	6 19.6	16 25.0	11 53.4	29 56.9	8 27.3	16 46.5	23 31.2	1 51.7	13 43.6	8 29.0
28 Su	16 28 20	5 58 30	2♋22 47	9♋52 29	6 15.2	16 49.4	13 06.2	0♒42.9	8 19.1	16 53.0	23 35.0	1 52.5	13 43.2	8 28.0
29 M	16 32 16	6 59 16	17 20 22	24 45 25	6 10.9	17 22.1	14 19.0	1 29.0	8 10.6	16 59.4	23 38.8	1 53.4	13 42.7	8 27.0
30 Tu	16 36 13	8 00 04	2♌06 48	9♌23 47	6 07.2	18 02.4	15 31.7	2 15.1	8 01.6	17 05.6	23 42.5	1 54.4	13 42.3	8 26.0

December 1920 — LONGITUDE

Day	Sid.Time	☉	0 hr ☽	Noon ☽	True ☊	☿	♀	♂	⚳	♃	♄	♅	♆	♇
1 W	16 40 09	9♐00 54	16♌35 50	23♌42 35	6♏04.7	18♏49.4	16♑44.4	3♒01.3	7♋52.3	17♍11.6	23♍46.1	1♓55.4	13♌41.8	8♋24.9
2 Th	16 44 06	10 01 45	0♍43 47	7♍39 22	6D03.7	19 42.2	17 57.0	3 47.4	7R42.7	17 17.5	23 49.6	1 56.5	13R41.3	8R23.9
3 F	16 48 03	11 02 37	14 29 25	21 14 03	6 04.0	20 40.3	19 09.6	4 33.6	7 32.7	17 23.2	23 53.0	1 57.6	13 40.7	8 22.8
4 Sa	16 51 59	12 03 31	27 53 32	4♎28 08	6 05.4	21 42.8	20 22.2	5 19.9	7 22.3	17 28.8	23 56.4	1 58.7	13 40.1	8 21.8
5 Su	16 55 56	13 04 26	10♎58 12	17 24 05	6 07.1	22 49.2	21 34.7	6 06.1	7 11.6	17 34.2	23 59.6	1 59.9	13 39.5	8 20.7
6 M	16 59 52	14 05 23	23 46 08	0♏04 43	6R08.3	23 59.1	22 47.1	6 52.4	7 00.7	17 39.4	24 02.7	2 01.2	13 38.8	8 19.6
7 Tu	17 03 49	15 06 20	6♏20 08	12 32 43	6 08.2	25 11.8	23 59.5	7 38.8	6 49.4	17 44.5	24 05.7	2 02.5	13 38.2	8 18.5
8 W	17 07 45	16 07 19	18 42 44	24 50 27	6 06.3	26 27.2	25 11.9	8 25.1	6 37.8	17 49.4	24 08.7	2 03.8	13 37.4	8 17.3
9 Th	17 11 42	17 08 19	0♐56 06	6♐59 54	6 02.4	27 44.7	26 24.2	9 11.5	6 25.9	17 54.2	24 11.5	2 05.2	13 36.7	8 16.2
10 F	17 15 38	18 09 19	13 02 01	19 02 38	5 56.3	29 04.1	27 36.4	9 57.9	6 13.8	17 58.8	24 14.2	2 06.6	13 35.9	8 15.1
11 Sa	17 19 35	19 10 21	25 01 55	1♑00 03	5 48.4	0♐25.1	28 48.6	10 44.3	6 01.4	18 03.2	24 16.8	2 08.1	13 35.1	8 13.9
12 Su	17 23 32	20 11 23	6♑57 11	12 53 32	5 39.5	1 47.6	0♒00.7	11 30.8	5 48.8	18 07.4	24 19.4	2 09.7	13 34.3	8 12.8
13 M	17 27 28	21 12 26	18 49 19	24 44 45	5 30.2	3 11.2	1 12.8	12 17.3	5 36.0	18 11.5	24 21.8	2 11.3	13 33.4	8 11.6
14 Tu	17 31 25	22 13 30	0♒40 08	6♒35 47	5 21.6	4 36.0	2 24.8	13 03.8	5 22.9	18 15.4	24 24.1	2 12.9	13 32.5	8 10.4
15 W	17 35 21	23 14 34	12 32 01	18 29 16	5 14.3	6 01.6	3 36.7	13 50.3	5 09.6	18 19.1	24 26.3	2 14.6	13 31.6	8 09.3
16 Th	17 39 18	24 15 38	24 27 58	0♓28 34	5 09.0	7 28.1	4 48.5	14 36.8	4 56.2	18 22.7	24 28.4	2 16.3	13 30.6	8 08.1
17 F	17 43 14	25 16 43	6♓31 37	12 37 38	5 06.0	8 55.3	6 00.3	15 23.3	4 42.6	18 26.0	24 30.4	2 18.1	13 29.7	8 06.9
18 Sa	17 47 11	26 17 48	18 47 13	25 00 56	5D04.9	10 23.1	7 12.0	16 09.9	4 28.9	18 29.2	24 32.3	2 19.9	13 28.7	8 05.7
19 Su	17 51 07	27 18 54	1♈19 24	7♈43 11	5 05.4	11 51.4	8 23.6	16 56.4	4 15.1	18 32.2	24 34.1	2 21.7	13 27.6	8 04.5
20 M	17 55 04	28 19 59	14 12 51	20 48 54	5 06.5	13 20.3	9 35.1	17 43.0	4 01.1	18 35.0	24 35.8	2 23.6	13 26.6	8 03.3
21 Tu	17 59 01	29 21 05	27 31 46	4♉21 46	5R07.1	14 49.6	10 46.6	18 29.5	3 47.0	18 37.6	24 37.4	2 25.6	13 25.5	8 02.1
22 W	18 02 57	0♑22 12	11♉19 07	18 23 50	5 06.3	16 19.3	11 57.9	19 16.1	3 32.9	18 40.1	24 38.8	2 27.6	13 24.3	8 00.8
23 Th	18 06 54	1 23 18	25 35 46	2♊54 33	5 03.3	17 49.4	13 09.2	20 02.7	3 18.7	18 42.4	24 40.2	2 29.6	13 23.2	7 59.6
24 F	18 10 50	2 24 25	10♊19 34	17 50 01	4 57.8	19 19.9	14 20.3	20 49.3	3 04.5	18 44.4	24 41.5	2 31.7	13 22.0	7 58.4
25 Sa	18 14 47	3 25 32	25 24 50	3♋02 47	4 50.1	20 50.7	15 31.4	21 35.9	2 50.3	18 46.3	24 42.6	2 33.8	13 20.9	7 57.2
26 Su	18 18 43	4 26 39	10♋42 30	18 22 32	4 40.8	22 21.9	16 42.3	22 22.5	2 36.1	18 48.1	24 43.6	2 35.9	13 19.7	7 56.0
27 M	18 22 40	5 27 46	26 01 24	3♌37 42	4 31.3	23 53.4	17 53.2	23 09.1	2 21.8	18 49.6	24 44.6	2 38.1	13 18.4	7 54.7
28 Tu	18 26 36	6 28 54	11♌10 08	18 37 37	4 22.6	25 25.2	19 03.9	23 55.7	2 07.6	18 50.9	24 45.4	2 40.3	13 17.2	7 53.5
29 W	18 30 33	7 30 03	25 59 13	3♍14 18	4 15.8	26 57.3	20 14.5	24 42.3	1 53.5	18 52.0	24 46.1	2 42.6	13 15.9	7 52.3
30 Th	18 34 30	8 31 11	10♍22 24	17 23 20	4 11.5	28 29.7	21 25.0	25 28.9	1 39.4	18 53.0	24 46.7	2 44.9	13 14.6	7 51.0
31 F	18 38 26	9 32 20	24 17 06	1♎03 49	4D09.5	0♑02.4	22 35.4	26 15.4	1 25.4	18 53.7	24 47.2	2 47.3	13 13.2	7 49.8

Astro Data	Dy Hr Mn
♃⊻♆	4 19:45
☿ R	5 12:47
☽ 0S	6 6:40
⚳ R	7 18:32
♅ D	11 7:15
♆ R	16 8:24
☽ 0N	20 20:43
☿ D	25 12:50
☽ 0S	3 12:31
☽ 0N	18 5:55
☽ 0S	30 20:12

Planet Ingress		Dy Hr Mn
☿	♏R	10 19:45
♀	♑	17 17:28
☉	♐	22 14:15
♂	♒	27 13:38
☿	♐	11 4:37
♀	♒	12 11:46
☉	♑	22 3:17
☿	♑	31 11:22

Last Aspect Dy Hr Mn			☽ Ingress	Dy Hr Mn
1 23:11	♄	⚹	♌	2 13:37
3 12:55	♆	☌	♍	4 17:03
6 7:39	♄	☌	♎	6 22:23
8 8:24	♀	⚹	♏	9 5:49
11 14:05	☿	☌	♐	11 15:26
13 17:13	♀	☌	♑	14 3:03
16 3:08	☿	⚹	♒	16 15:44
18 20:12	☉	□	♓	19 3:39
21 10:37	☉	△	♈	21 12:45
23 12:43	♂	□	♉	23 18:02
25 17:43	♂	△	♊	25 20:00
27 9:50	♄	□	♋	27 20:12
29 10:12	♄	⚹	♌	29 20:32

Last Aspect Dy Hr Mn			☽ Ingress	Dy Hr Mn
1 3:14	☿	□	♍	1 22:45
3 16:47	♄	☌	♎	4 3:50
5 20:41	♀	□	♏	6 11:51
8 15:32	☿	☌	♐	8 22:09
10 22:27	♄	□	♑	11 9:59
13 11:13	♄	△	♒	13 22:39
15 22:26	☉	⚹	♓	16 11:03
18 14:40	☉	□	♈	18 21:30
21 2:31	☉	△	♉	21 4:22
22 22:27	♄	△	♊	23 7:15
24 22:52	♄	□	♋	25 7:13
26 21:58	♄	⚹	♌	27 6:16
29 0:22	☿	△	♍	29 6:37
31 9:56	☿	□	♎	31 10:06

☽ Phases & Eclipses Dy Hr Mn		
3 7:35	☾	10♌35
10 16:05	●	17♏58
10 15:51:53	●	P 0.742
18 20:12	☽	26♒13
26 1:42	○	3♊31
2 16:29	☾	10♍13
10 10:04	●	18♐04
18 14:40	☽	26♓25
25 12:38	○	3♋27

Astro Data

1 November 1920
Julian Day # 7610
SVP 6♓21'46"
GC 25♐44.0 ⚴ 16♈53.7R
Eris 28♓25.7R ⚵ 25♏33.4
⚷ 6♈53.4R ⚶ 15♑04.2
☽ Mean ☊ 6♏12.4

1 December 1920
Julian Day # 7640
SVP 6♓21'41"
GC 25♐44.1 ⚴ 11♈31.9R
Eris 28♓15.0R ⚵ 5♐48.2
⚷ 6♈05.6R ⚶ 28♑34.6
☽ Mean ☊ 4♏37.1

LONGITUDE — January 1921

Day	Sid.Time	☉	0 hr ☽	Noon ☽	True ☊	☿	♀	♂	⚳	♃	♄	♅	♆	♇
1 Sa	18 42 23	10♑33 30	7♎43 49	14♎17 30	4♏09.2	1♑35.5	23♒45.7	27♒02.0	1♋11.5	18♍54.3	24♍47.6	2♓49.7	13♌11.9	7♋48.6
2 Su	18 46 19	11 34 39	20 45 21	27 07 54	4R09.6	3 08.9	24 55.9	27 48.6	0R57.7	18 54.7	24 47.8	2 52.1	13R10.5	7R47.3
3 M	18 50 16	12 35 50	3♏25 41	9♏39 17	4 09.7	4 42.7	26 05.9	28 35.2	0 44.0	18R54.8	24R48.0	2 54.5	13 09.1	7 46.1
4 Tu	18 54 12	13 37 00	15 49 15	21 56 06	4 08.1	6 16.8	27 15.8	29 21.8	0 30.5	18 54.8	24 48.1	2 57.0	13 07.7	7 44.9
5 W	18 58 09	14 38 10	28 00 19	4♐02 23	4 04.0	7 51.3	28 25.6	0♓08.4	0 17.2	18 54.6	24 48.0	2 59.6	13 06.3	7 43.7
6 Th	19 02 05	15 39 21	10♐02 40	16 01 34	3 57.0	9 26.1	29 35.2	0 55.0	0 04.1	18 54.2	24 47.8	3 02.1	13 04.9	7 42.5
7 F	19 06 02	16 40 32	21 59 23	27 56 23	3 47.0	11 01.4	0♓44.7	1 41.6	29♊51.1	18 53.6	24 47.5	3 04.7	13 03.4	7 41.2
8 Sa	19 09 59	17 41 42	3♑52 50	9♑48 55	3 34.5	12 37.1	1 54.1	2 28.2	29 38.4	18 52.8	24 47.2	3 07.4	13 01.9	7 40.0
9 Su	19 13 55	18 42 52	15 44 49	21 40 43	3 20.2	14 13.1	3 03.3	3 14.8	29 25.9	18 51.8	24 46.7	3 10.0	13 00.4	7 38.8
10 M	19 17 52	19 44 02	27 36 44	3♒33 03	3 05.4	15 49.7	4 12.4	4 01.3	29 13.7	18 50.6	24 46.0	3 12.7	12 58.9	7 37.6
11 Tu	19 21 48	20 45 12	9♒29 48	15 27 12	2 51.2	17 26.6	5 21.2	4 47.9	29 01.7	18 49.2	24 45.3	3 15.5	12 57.4	7 36.4
12 W	19 25 45	21 46 21	21 25 26	27 24 44	2 38.9	19 04.1	6 30.0	5 34.4	28 50.1	18 47.7	24 44.5	3 18.2	12 55.9	7 35.2
13 Th	19 29 41	22 47 29	3♓25 23	9♓27 42	2 29.2	20 42.0	7 38.5	6 21.0	28 38.7	18 45.9	24 43.6	3 21.0	12 54.3	7 34.0
14 F	19 33 38	23 48 37	15 32 02	21 38 49	2 22.5	22 20.4	8 46.9	7 07.5	28 27.6	18 43.9	24 42.5	3 23.8	12 52.7	7 32.8
15 Sa	19 37 34	24 49 44	27 48 29	4♈01 31	2 18.8	23 59.3	9 55.1	7 54.0	28 16.8	18 41.8	24 41.4	3 26.7	12 51.2	7 31.7
16 Su	19 41 31	25 50 51	10♈18 27	16 39 49	2D17.3	25 38.7	11 03.1	8 40.5	28 06.4	18 39.5	24 40.1	3 29.6	12 49.6	7 30.5
17 M	19 45 28	26 51 56	23 06 10	29 38 02	2R17.1	27 18.7	12 10.8	9 26.9	27 56.3	18 36.9	24 38.7	3 32.5	12 48.0	7 29.3
18 Tu	19 49 24	27 53 01	6♉15 55	13♉00 18	2 16.9	28 59.1	13 18.4	10 13.4	27 46.5	18 34.2	24 37.3	3 35.4	12 46.4	7 28.2
19 W	19 53 21	28 54 05	19 51 31	26 49 50	2 15.4	0♒40.2	14 25.8	10 59.8	27 37.1	18 31.3	24 35.7	3 38.4	12 44.7	7 27.1
20 Th	19 57 17	29 55 08	3♊55 19	11♊07 55	2 11.6	2 21.7	15 33.0	11 46.2	27 28.1	18 28.2	24 34.0	3 41.4	12 43.1	7 25.9
21 F	20 01 14	0♒56 10	18 27 18	25 52 56	2 04.9	4 03.8	16 39.9	12 32.6	27 19.5	18 25.0	24 32.2	3 44.4	12 41.5	7 24.8
22 Sa	20 05 10	1 57 12	3♋24 02	10♋59 37	1 55.6	5 46.4	17 46.6	13 19.0	27 11.2	18 21.6	24 30.4	3 47.4	12 39.8	7 23.7
23 Su	20 09 07	2 58 12	18 38 25	26 19 04	1 44.4	7 29.5	18 53.0	14 05.3	27 03.3	18 17.9	24 28.4	3 50.5	12 38.2	7 22.6
24 M	20 13 04	3 59 12	4♌00 04	11♌39 54	1 32.7	9 13.1	19 59.2	14 51.6	26 55.8	18 14.1	24 26.3	3 53.6	12 36.5	7 21.5
25 Tu	20 17 00	5 00 10	19 17 05	26 50 14	1 21.7	10 57.1	21 05.2	15 37.9	26 48.7	18 10.2	24 24.1	3 56.7	12 34.9	7 20.4
26 W	20 20 57	6 01 08	4♍18 10	11♍39 56	1 12.7	12 41.6	22 10.8	16 24.2	26 42.0	18 06.0	24 21.9	3 59.8	12 33.2	7 19.4
27 Th	20 24 53	7 02 05	18 54 46	26 02 12	1 06.4	14 26.4	23 16.2	17 10.5	26 35.7	18 01.7	24 19.5	4 03.0	12 31.5	7 18.3
28 F	20 28 50	8 03 02	3♎01 59	9♎54 06	1 02.9	16 11.5	24 21.4	17 56.7	26 29.9	17 57.3	24 17.0	4 06.1	12 29.8	7 17.3
29 Sa	20 32 46	9 03 58	16 38 43	23 16 07	1D01.6	17 56.8	25 26.2	18 42.9	26 24.4	17 52.6	24 14.5	4 09.3	12 28.1	7 16.2
30 Su	20 36 43	10 04 53	29 46 46	6♏11 12	1R01.5	19 42.3	26 30.8	19 29.1	26 19.4	17 47.8	24 11.8	4 12.5	12 26.5	7 15.2
31 M	20 40 39	11 05 47	12♏30 00	18 43 47	1 01.3	21 27.6	27 35.0	20 15.2	26 14.7	17 42.8	24 09.1	4 15.8	12 24.8	7 14.2

LONGITUDE — February 1921

Day	Sid.Time	☉	0 hr ☽	Noon ☽	True ☊	☿	♀	♂	⚳	♃	♄	♅	♆	♇
1 Tu	20 44 36	12♒06 41	24♏53 13	0♐58 55	0♏59.9	23♒12.8	28♓39.0	21♓01.3	26♊10.6	17♍37.7	24♍06.2	4♓19.0	12♌23.1	7♋13.2
2 W	20 48 32	13 07 34	7♐01 32	13 01 39	0R56.3	24 57.7	29 42.6	21 47.4	26R06.8	17R32.4	24R03.3	4 22.3	12R21.4	7R12.3
3 Th	20 52 29	14 08 26	18 59 50	24 56 35	0 49.9	26 41.9	0♈45.9	22 33.5	26 03.5	17 27.0	24 00.3	4 25.5	12 19.7	7 11.3
4 F	20 56 26	15 09 17	0♑52 24	6♑47 41	0 40.5	28 25.3	1 48.9	23 19.6	26 00.5	17 21.4	23 57.2	4 28.8	12 18.0	7 10.4
5 Sa	21 00 22	16 10 07	12 42 49	18 38 07	0 28.6	0♓07.5	2 51.5	24 05.6	25 58.1	17 15.7	23 54.0	4 32.2	12 16.3	7 09.4
6 Su	21 04 19	17 10 56	24 33 51	0♒30 16	0 15.0	1 48.2	3 53.7	24 51.6	25 56.0	17 09.9	23 50.8	4 35.5	12 14.6	7 08.5
7 M	21 08 15	18 11 44	6♒27 33	12 25 53	0 00.8	3 27.0	4 55.6	25 37.6	25 54.4	17 03.9	23 47.4	4 38.8	12 13.0	7 07.6
8 Tu	21 12 12	19 12 30	18 25 25	24 26 15	29♎47.2	5 03.5	5 57.1	26 23.5	25 53.2	16 57.7	23 44.0	4 42.2	12 11.3	7 06.7
9 W	21 16 08	20 13 15	0♓28 31	6♓32 22	29 35.2	6 37.0	6 58.2	27 09.4	25 52.5	16 51.5	23 40.5	4 45.5	12 09.6	7 05.9
10 Th	21 20 05	21 13 59	12 37 56	18 45 23	29 25.8	8 07.2	7 58.9	27 55.3	25D52.2	16 45.1	23 36.9	4 48.9	12 07.9	7 05.0
11 F	21 24 01	22 14 41	24 54 53	1♈06 42	29 19.3	9 33.2	8 59.1	28 41.1	25 52.3	16 38.6	23 33.3	4 52.3	12 06.3	7 04.2
12 Sa	21 27 58	23 15 22	7♈21 03	13 38 16	29 15.7	10 54.6	9 58.9	29 26.9	25 52.8	16 32.0	23 29.5	4 55.7	12 04.6	7 03.4
13 Su	21 31 55	24 16 01	19 58 39	26 22 36	29D14.5	12 10.7	10 58.3	0♈12.7	25 53.8	16 25.2	23 25.8	4 59.1	12 03.0	7 02.6
14 M	21 35 51	25 16 38	2♉50 28	9♉22 40	29 14.8	13 20.6	11 57.1	0 58.4	25 55.2	16 18.4	23 21.9	5 02.5	12 01.3	7 01.8
15 Tu	21 39 48	26 17 14	15 59 35	22 41 37	29R15.3	14 23.7	12 55.5	1 44.1	25 57.0	16 11.5	23 18.0	5 05.9	11 59.7	7 01.1
16 W	21 43 44	27 17 48	29 29 03	6♊22 11	29 15.0	15 19.4	13 53.3	2 29.8	25 59.2	16 04.5	23 14.0	5 09.3	11 58.1	7 00.3
17 Th	21 47 41	28 18 20	13♊21 09	20 26 01	29 12.9	16 06.8	14 50.6	3 15.4	26 01.8	15 57.3	23 10.0	5 12.7	11 56.5	6 59.6
18 F	21 51 37	29 18 50	27 36 39	4♋52 48	29 08.4	16 45.5	15 47.4	4 01.0	26 04.9	15 50.1	23 05.9	5 16.2	11 54.9	6 58.9
19 Sa	21 55 34	0♓19 19	12♋13 57	19 39 29	29 01.7	17 14.9	16 43.6	4 46.5	26 08.3	15 42.9	23 01.7	5 19.6	11 53.3	6 58.2
20 Su	21 59 30	1 19 45	27 08 30	4♌40 00	28 53.3	17 34.6	17 39.1	5 32.0	26 12.1	15 35.5	22 57.5	5 23.1	11 51.7	6 57.6
21 M	22 03 27	2 20 10	12♌12 48	19 45 40	28 44.2	17R44.3	18 34.1	6 17.5	26 16.4	15 28.1	22 53.3	5 26.5	11 50.1	6 57.0
22 Tu	22 07 24	3 20 33	27 17 19	4♍46 30	28 35.6	17 44.0	19 28.4	7 02.9	26 21.0	15 20.6	22 49.0	5 30.0	11 48.6	6 56.3
23 W	22 11 20	4 20 55	12♍12 01	19 32 51	28 28.5	17 33.7	20 22.1	7 48.3	26 26.0	15 13.1	22 44.6	5 33.4	11 47.1	6 55.7
24 Th	22 15 17	5 21 14	26 48 07	3♎57 08	28 23.6	17 13.7	21 15.0	8 33.6	26 31.4	15 05.5	22 40.2	5 36.9	11 45.5	6 55.2
25 F	22 19 13	6 21 32	10♎59 26	17 54 44	28D21.1	16 44.6	22 07.3	9 18.9	26 37.2	14 57.8	22 35.8	5 40.3	11 44.0	6 54.6
26 Sa	22 23 10	7 21 49	24 43 57	1♏24 12	28 20.6	16 07.0	22 58.8	10 04.2	26 43.3	14 50.1	22 31.3	5 43.7	11 42.5	6 54.1
27 Su	22 27 06	8 22 04	7♏58 41	14 26 46	28 21.5	15 22.1	23 49.6	10 49.4	26 49.8	14 42.4	22 26.8	5 47.2	11 41.0	6 53.6
28 M	22 31 03	9 22 18	20 48 55	27 05 40	28 22.7	14 30.8	24 39.6	11 34.6	26 56.7	14 34.6	22 22.2	5 50.6	11 39.6	6 53.1

Astro Data

	Dy Hr Mn
♃ R	3 21:37
♄ R	4 10:52
☽ 0N	14 13:44
☽ 0S	27 6:30
♀ 0N	1 22:32
⚳ D	10 17:51
☽ 0N	10 20:26
♂ 0N	14 18:16
☿ R	21 23:14
☽ 0S	23 17:59

Planet Ingress

	Dy Hr Mn
♂ ♓	5 7:39
⚳ ♊R	6 19:30
♀ ♓	6 20:33
☿ ♒	19 2:28
☉ ♒	20 13:55
♀ ♈	2 18:35
☿ ♓	5 10:14
☊ ♎R	7 13:22
♂ ♈	13 5:21
☉ ♓	19 4:20

Last Aspect / ☽ Ingress (January)

Last Aspect Dy Hr Mn		☽ Ingress Dy Hr Mn
2 13:22	♂ △	♏ 2 17:27
5 3:42	♂ □	♐ 5 3:58
7 5:39	♄ □	♑ 7 16:10
9 18:16	♄ △	♒ 10 4:50
11 6:59	♆ ☍	♓ 12 17:10
14 17:58	♄ ☍	♈ 15 4:15
17 7:08	☿ □	♉ 17 12:40
19 15:48	☉ △	♊ 19 17:23
21 9:50	♄ □	♋ 21 18:35
23 9:08	♄ ⚹	♌ 23 17:45
24 13:29	♆ ☌	♍ 25 17:04
27 9:06	♄ ☌	♎ 27 18:46
29 0:53	☿ △	♏ 30 0:25

Last Aspect / ☽ Ingress (February)

Last Aspect Dy Hr Mn		☽ Ingress Dy Hr Mn
1 6:57	♀ △	♐ 1 10:04
3 16:09	☿ ⚹	♑ 3 22:14
5 23:49	♂ ⚹	♒ 6 10:59
8 0:36	☉ ☌	♓ 8 23:03
11 7:00	♂ ☌	♈ 11 9:51
13 7:43	☉ ⚹	♉ 13 18:45
15 18:53	☉ □	♊ 16 0:54
18 2:08	☉ △	♋ 18 3:58
19 17:23	♄ ⚹	♌ 20 4:34
21 9:59	♀ △	♍ 22 4:20
23 17:15	♄ ☌	♎ 24 5:21
25 19:54	♀ ☍	♏ 26 9:28
28 3:01	♄ ⚹	♐ 28 17:36

☽ Phases & Eclipses

Dy Hr Mn	
1 4:34	☾ 10♎15
9 5:26	● 18♑26
17 6:30	☽ 26♈38
23 23:07	○ 3♌26
30 20:02	☾ 10♏25
8 0:36	● 18♒44
15 18:53	☽ 26♉35
22 9:32	○ 3♍14

Astro Data

1 January 1921
Julian Day # 7671
SVP 6♓21'36"
GC 25♐44.2 ⚴ 13♈47.9
Eris 28♓15.0 ✱ 16♐24.5
⚷ 6♈04.3 ⚵ 13♒28.5
☽ Mean ☊ 2♏58.6

1 February 1921
Julian Day # 7702
SVP 6♓21'32"
GC 25♐44.2 ⚴ 22♈29.4
Eris 28♓26.7 ✱ 26♐26.6
⚷ 6♈53.8 ⚵ 28♒47.2
☽ Mean ☊ 1♏20.1

March 1921

LONGITUDE

Day	Sid.Time	☉	0 hr ☽	Noon ☽	True ☊	☿	♀	♂	⚳	♃	♄	♅	♆	♇
1 Tu	22 34 59	10♓22 30	3♐17 35	9♐25 17	28♎23.4	13♓34.6	25♈28.7	12♈19.8	27♊04.0	14♍26.8	22♍17.7	5♓54.1	11♌38.1	6♋52.6
2 W	22 38 56	11 22 41	15 29 25	21 30 35	28R 22.8	12R 35.0	26 17.0	13 04.9	27 11.5	14R 19.0	22R 13.1	5 57.5	11R 36.7	6R 52.1
3 Th	22 42 53	12 22 50	27 29 27	3♑26 35	28 20.3	11 33.3	27 04.5	13 49.9	27 19.5	14 11.2	22 08.4	6 01.0	11 35.3	6 51.7
4 F	22 46 49	13 22 58	9♑22 36	15 18 00	28 15.7	10 31.1	27 51.0	14 34.9	27 27.8	14 03.3	22 03.8	6 04.4	11 33.9	6 51.3
5 Sa	22 50 46	14 23 04	21 13 19	27 09 01	28 09.4	9 29.8	28 36.6	15 19.9	27 36.4	13 55.5	21 59.1	6 07.8	11 32.5	6 50.9
6 Su	22 54 42	15 23 08	3♒05 30	9♒03 08	28 01.7	8 30.8	29 21.2	16 04.9	27 45.4	13 47.6	21 54.4	6 11.2	11 31.2	6 50.6
7 M	22 58 39	16 23 11	15 02 15	21 03 07	27 53.6	7 35.2	0♉04.8	16 49.8	27 54.7	13 39.8	21 49.7	6 14.7	11 29.9	6 50.2
8 Tu	23 02 35	17 23 12	27 05 58	3♓11 00	27 45.6	6 43.9	0 47.4	17 34.6	28 04.4	13 32.0	21 44.9	6 18.1	11 28.5	6 49.9
9 W	23 06 32	18 23 11	9♓18 21	15 28 08	27 38.7	5 57.8	1 28.8	18 19.4	28 14.4	13 24.2	21 40.2	6 21.5	11 27.3	6 49.6
10 Th	23 10 28	19 23 07	21 40 29	27 55 26	27 33.5	5 17.4	2 09.1	19 04.2	28 24.7	13 16.4	21 35.4	6 24.9	11 26.0	6 49.4
11 F	23 14 25	20 23 02	4♈13 06	10♈33 31	27 30.2	4 43.2	2 48.2	19 48.9	28 35.3	13 08.6	21 30.7	6 28.2	11 24.7	6 49.1
12 Sa	23 18 21	21 22 55	16 56 46	23 22 57	27D 28.8	4 15.3	3 26.1	20 33.6	28 46.2	13 00.9	21 25.9	6 31.6	11 23.5	6 48.9
13 Su	23 22 18	22 22 46	29 52 08	6♉24 26	27 29.0	3 54.0	4 02.7	21 18.3	28 57.4	12 53.2	21 21.1	6 35.0	11 22.3	6 48.7
14 M	23 26 15	23 22 35	12♉59 58	19 38 52	27 30.3	3 39.1	4 37.9	22 02.9	29 09.0	12 45.6	21 16.4	6 38.3	11 21.1	6 48.5
15 Tu	23 30 11	24 22 22	26 21 16	3♊07 18	27 31.9	3D 30.6	5 11.8	22 47.4	29 20.8	12 38.0	21 11.6	6 41.6	11 20.0	6 48.4
16 W	23 34 08	25 22 06	9♊57 04	16 50 38	27R 33.1	3 28.4	5 44.2	23 31.9	29 33.0	12 30.5	21 06.9	6 45.0	11 18.9	6 48.3
17 Th	23 38 04	26 21 48	23 48 03	0♋49 18	27 33.3	3 32.1	6 15.1	24 16.4	29 45.4	12 23.1	21 02.2	6 48.3	11 17.8	6 48.2
18 F	23 42 01	27 21 28	7♋54 14	15 02 41	27 32.1	3 41.6	6 44.4	25 00.8	29 58.1	12 15.7	20 57.4	6 51.5	11 16.7	6 48.1
19 Sa	23 45 57	28 21 05	22 14 20	29 28 46	27 29.6	3 56.5	7 12.1	25 45.1	0♋11.1	12 08.4	20 52.7	6 54.8	11 15.7	6 48.0
20 Su	23 49 54	29 20 40	6♌45 27	14♌03 46	27 26.1	4 16.7	7 38.1	26 29.4	0 24.3	12 01.1	20 48.1	6 58.1	11 14.6	6D 48.0
21 M	23 53 50	0♈20 13	21 22 58	28 42 16	27 22.2	4 41.8	8 02.4	27 13.7	0 37.8	11 54.0	20 43.4	7 01.3	11 13.6	6 48.0
22 Tu	23 57 47	1 19 43	6♍00 49	13♍17 46	27 18.4	5 11.5	8 24.8	27 57.9	0 51.6	11 46.9	20 38.8	7 04.5	11 12.7	6 48.0
23 W	0 01 44	2 19 12	20 32 16	27 43 31	27 15.4	5 45.6	8 45.4	28 42.0	1 05.6	11 40.0	20 34.1	7 07.8	11 11.7	6 48.0
24 Th	0 05 40	3 18 38	4♎50 49	11♎53 31	27 13.4	6 23.8	9 04.0	29 26.2	1 19.9	11 33.1	20 29.6	7 10.9	11 10.8	6 48.1
25 F	0 09 37	4 18 02	18 51 09	25 43 20	27D 12.7	7 06.0	9 20.6	0♉10.2	1 34.5	11 26.3	20 25.0	7 14.1	11 09.9	6 48.2
26 Sa	0 13 33	5 17 25	2♏29 50	9♏10 32	27 13.1	7 51.7	9 35.2	0 54.2	1 49.3	11 19.7	20 20.5	7 17.3	11 09.1	6 48.3
27 Su	0 17 30	6 16 45	15 45 28	22 14 45	27 14.3	8 40.9	9 47.7	1 38.2	2 04.3	11 13.1	20 16.0	7 20.4	11 08.3	6 48.4
28 M	0 21 26	7 16 04	28 38 39	4♐57 27	27 15.8	9 33.4	9 58.0	2 22.1	2 19.6	11 06.7	20 11.6	7 23.5	11 07.5	6 48.6
29 Tu	0 25 23	8 15 21	11♐11 36	17 21 32	27 17.2	10 29.0	10 06.1	3 06.0	2 35.1	11 00.4	20 07.1	7 26.6	11 06.7	6 48.8
30 W	0 29 19	9 14 36	23 27 46	29 30 52	27R 18.3	11 27.4	10 11.9	3 49.8	2 50.8	10 54.2	20 02.8	7 29.6	11 06.0	6 49.0
31 Th	0 33 16	10 13 49	5♑31 24	11♑29 57	27 18.6	12 28.6	10R 15.4	4 33.6	3 06.8	10 48.1	19 58.5	7 32.7	11 05.2	6 49.2

April 1921

LONGITUDE

Day	Sid.Time	☉	0 hr ☽	Noon ☽	True ☊	☿	♀	♂	⚳	♃	♄	♅	♆	♇
1 F	0 37 13	11♈13 01	17♑27 06	23♑23 28	27♎18.1	13♓32.4	10♉16.5	5♉17.3	3♋22.9	10♍42.1	19♍54.2	7♓35.7	11♌04.6	6♋49.4
2 Sa	0 41 09	12 12 11	29 19 36	5♒16 04	27R 16.9	14 38.7	10R 15.2	6 01.0	3 39.3	10R 36.3	19R 50.0	7 38.7	11R 03.9	6 49.7
3 Su	0 45 06	13 11 19	11♒13 25	17 12 09	27 15.2	15 47.4	10 11.5	6 44.7	3 56.0	10 30.6	19 45.8	7 41.7	11 03.3	6 50.0
4 M	0 49 02	14 10 25	23 12 43	29 15 34	27 13.3	16 58.4	10 05.4	7 28.3	4 12.8	10 25.1	19 41.7	7 44.6	11 02.7	6 50.3
5 Tu	0 52 59	15 09 29	5♓21 03	11♓29 32	27 11.4	18 11.5	9 56.7	8 11.8	4 29.8	10 19.7	19 37.6	7 47.5	11 02.2	6 50.7
6 W	0 56 55	16 08 31	17 41 16	23 56 29	27 09.8	19 26.7	9 45.7	8 55.3	4 47.1	10 14.5	19 33.6	7 50.4	11 01.6	6 51.0
7 Th	1 00 52	17 07 32	0♈15 21	6♈37 58	27 08.7	20 44.0	9 32.1	9 38.8	5 04.5	10 09.4	19 29.6	7 53.3	11 01.1	6 51.4
8 F	1 04 48	18 06 30	13 04 24	19 34 39	27D 08.2	22 03.2	9 16.2	10 22.2	5 22.2	10 04.4	19 25.7	7 56.1	11 00.7	6 51.8
9 Sa	1 08 45	19 05 26	26 08 40	2♉46 23	27 08.2	23 24.3	8 57.8	11 05.6	5 40.0	9 59.6	19 21.9	7 58.9	11 00.2	6 52.2
10 Su	1 12 41	20 04 21	9♉27 39	16 12 19	27 08.5	24 47.3	8 37.1	11 48.9	5 58.1	9 55.0	19 18.2	8 01.7	10 59.8	6 52.7
11 M	1 16 38	21 03 13	23 00 12	29 51 06	27 09.0	26 12.1	8 14.2	12 32.1	6 16.3	9 50.6	19 14.5	8 04.4	10 59.5	6 53.2
12 Tu	1 20 35	22 02 03	6♊44 48	13♊41 03	27 09.6	27 38.6	7 49.0	13 15.4	6 34.7	9 46.3	19 10.9	8 07.2	10 59.2	6 53.7
13 W	1 24 31	23 00 51	20 39 37	27 40 16	27 10.0	29 06.9	7 21.8	13 58.5	6 53.3	9 42.1	19 07.3	8 09.8	10 58.9	6 54.2
14 Th	1 28 28	23 59 37	4♋42 44	11♋46 46	27R 10.2	0♈37.0	6 52.7	14 41.7	7 12.1	9 38.2	19 03.9	8 12.5	10 58.6	6 54.8
15 F	1 32 24	24 58 20	18 52 06	25 58 26	27 10.3	2 08.7	6 21.7	15 24.7	7 31.1	9 34.4	19 00.5	8 15.1	10 58.4	6 55.3
16 Sa	1 36 21	25 57 01	3♌05 28	10♌12 55	27 10.3	3 42.1	5 49.1	16 07.7	7 50.2	9 30.7	18 57.2	8 17.7	10 58.2	6 55.9
17 Su	1 40 17	26 55 40	17 20 26	24 27 39	27D 10.2	5 17.1	5 15.1	16 50.7	8 09.5	9 27.3	18 53.9	8 20.3	10 58.0	6 56.5
18 M	1 44 14	27 54 16	1♍34 12	8♍39 43	27 10.2	6 53.9	4 39.8	17 33.6	8 28.9	9 24.0	18 50.8	8 22.8	10 57.9	6 57.2
19 Tu	1 48 10	28 52 50	15 43 45	22 45 56	27 10.4	8 32.3	4 03.5	18 16.5	8 48.5	9 20.9	18 47.7	8 25.3	10 57.8	6 57.8
20 W	1 52 07	29 51 22	29 45 51	6♎43 04	27 10.6	10 12.3	3 26.4	18 59.3	9 08.3	9 18.0	18 44.7	8 27.7	10 57.7	6 58.5
21 Th	1 56 04	0♉49 52	13♎37 15	20 28 02	27R 10.7	11 54.1	2 48.8	19 42.1	9 28.2	9 15.2	18 41.8	8 30.2	10D 57.7	6 59.2
22 F	2 00 00	1 48 21	27 15 07	3♏58 14	27 10.7	13 37.5	2 10.9	20 24.8	9 48.3	9 12.7	18 38.9	8 32.5	10 57.6	6 59.9
23 Sa	2 03 57	2 46 47	10♏37 12	17 11 51	27 10.4	15 22.6	1 33.0	21 07.5	10 08.6	9 10.3	18 36.2	8 34.9	10 57.7	7 00.6
24 Su	2 07 53	3 45 11	23 42 09	0♐08 06	27 09.8	17 09.4	0 55.2	21 50.1	10 28.9	9 08.1	18 33.5	8 37.2	10 57.7	7 01.4
25 M	2 11 50	4 43 34	6♐29 45	12 47 16	27 08.9	18 57.9	0 18.0	22 32.7	10 49.5	9 06.0	18 31.0	8 39.5	10 57.8	7 02.2
26 Tu	2 15 46	5 41 55	19 00 52	25 10 49	27 07.9	20 48.1	29♈41.5	23 15.2	11 10.1	9 04.2	18 28.5	8 41.7	10 58.0	7 02.9
27 W	2 19 43	6 40 15	1♑17 28	7♑21 12	27 06.7	22 40.0	29 05.9	23 57.7	11 30.9	9 02.5	18 26.1	8 43.9	10 58.1	7 03.8
28 Th	2 23 39	7 38 33	13 22 28	19 21 45	27 05.8	24 33.6	28 31.5	24 40.1	11 51.9	9 01.0	18 23.8	8 46.1	10 58.3	7 04.6
29 F	2 27 36	8 36 49	25 19 34	1♒16 28	27D 05.2	26 28.9	27 58.5	25 22.5	12 13.0	8 59.7	18 21.6	8 48.2	10 58.6	7 05.5
30 Sa	2 31 33	9 35 04	7♒13 00	13 09 46	27 05.1	28 25.9	27 27.1	26 04.8	12 34.2	8 58.6	18 19.5	8 50.3	10 58.8	7 06.3

Astro Data	Planet Ingress	Last Aspect	☽ Ingress	Last Aspect	☽ Ingress	☽ Phases & Eclipses	Astro Data
Dy Hr Mn	Dy Hr Mn	Dy Hr Mn	Dy Hr Mn	Dy Hr Mn	Dy Hr Mn	Dy Hr Mn	1 March 1921
☽0N 10 3:02	♀ ♉ 7 9:18	2 22:15 ♀ △	♑ 3 5:03	1 5:00 ♄ △	♒ 2 1:22	1 14:03 ☾ 10♐28	Julian Day # 7730
☿D 16 8:55	⚳ ♋ 18 15:35	5 15:09 ♀ □	♒ 5 17:46	3 3:14 ☉ ⚹	♓ 4 13:28	9 18:09 ● 18♓39	SVP 6♓21'28"
♅△♇ 17 11:18	☉ ♈ 21 3:51	7 3:01 ♂ ⚹	♓ 8 5:44	6 3:39 ♄ ☍	♈ 6 23:31	17 3:49 ☽ 26♊01	GC 25♐44.3 ⚴ 3♉59.2
☉0N 21 3:52	♂ ♉ 25 6:26	9 23:55 ♄ ☍	♈ 10 15:58	8 9:05 ☉ ☌	♉ 9 7:00	23 20:18 ○ 2♎40	Eris 28♓44.7 ⚵ 4♑24.4
♇D 21 10:01		12 6:26 ♂ ☌	♉ 13 0:15	11 4:52 ☿ ⚹	♊ 11 12:16	31 9:13 ☾ 10♑07	⚷ 8♈12.2 ⚶ 12♓38.1
☽0S 23 4:28	☿ ♈ 14 2:12	14 19:13 ☉ ⚹	♊ 15 6:29	13 14:45 ☿ □	♋ 13 15:58		☽ Mean ☊ 29♎51.1
♃⚺♆ 28 8:39	☉ ♉ 20 15:32	17 3:49 ☉ □	♋ 17 10:36	15 10:11 ☉ □	♌ 15 18:47	8 9:05 ● 17♈59	
	♀ ♈R 25 23:46	19 10:00 ☉ △	♌ 19 12:52	17 16:28 ☉ △	♍ 17 21:21	8 9:14:38 ● A 01'50"	1 April 1921
♀R 1 11:19		21 9:27 ♂ △	♍ 21 14:07	19 5:15 ♄ ☌	♎ 20 0:24	15 10:11 ☽ 24♋54	Julian Day # 7761
☽0N 6 10:32		23 0:07 ♄ ☌	♎ 23 15:49	20 19:22 ♆ ⚹	♏ 22 4:54	22 7:49 ○ 1♏38	SVP 6♓21'26"
☿0N 17 21:01		24 10:47 ♆ ⚹	♏ 25 19:33	23 19:39 ♂ ☍	♐ 24 11:45	22 7:44 ● T 1.068	GC 25♐44.4 ⚴ 19♉21.6
☽0S 19 12:39		27 8:21 ♄ ⚹	♐ 28 2:34	26 20:26 ♀ △	♑ 26 21:27	30 4:08 ☾ 9♒16	Eris 29♓07.9 ⚵ 11♑03.6
♆D 22 2:06		29 17:23 ♄ □	♑ 30 12:58	29 5:38 ♀ □	♒ 29 9:26		⚷ 9♈58.4 ⚶ 27♓41.1
							☽ Mean ☊ 28♎12.6

LONGITUDE — May 1921

Day	Sid.Time	☉	0 hr ☽	Noon ☽	True ☊	☿	♀	♂	⚳	♃	♄	♅	♆	♇
1 Su	2 35 29	10♉33 18	19♒07 19	25♒06 16	27♎05.5	0♉24.6	26♈57.4	26♉47.1	12♋55.5	8♍57.7	18♍17.5	8♓52.4	10♌59.1	7♋07.2
2 M	2 39 26	11 31 29	1♓07 11	7♓10 37	27 06.5	2 24.9	26R 29.6	27 29.4	13 17.0	8R 56.9	18R 15.6	8 54.4	10 59.4	7 08.1
3 Tu	2 43 22	12 29 40	13 17 06	19 27 06	27 07.8	4 26.9	26 03.8	28 11.6	13 38.6	8 56.4	18 13.8	8 56.3	10 59.8	7 09.1
4 W	2 47 19	13 27 48	25 41 06	1♈59 29	27 09.1	6 30.3	25 40.2	28 53.8	14 00.4	8 56.0	18 12.0	8 58.3	11 00.2	7 10.0
5 Th	2 51 15	14 25 56	8♈22 33	14 50 34	27R 10.1	8 35.2	25 18.7	29 35.9	14 22.2	8D 55.8	18 10.4	9 00.1	11 00.6	7 11.0
6 F	2 55 12	15 24 02	21 23 41	28 01 59	27 10.4	10 41.5	24 59.6	0♊18.0	14 44.2	8 55.8	18 08.9	9 02.0	11 01.1	7 11.9
7 Sa	2 59 08	16 22 06	4♉45 25	11♉33 51	27 09.9	12 49.0	24 42.8	1 00.0	15 06.3	8 55.9	18 07.5	9 03.8	11 01.6	7 12.9
8 Su	3 03 05	17 20 09	18 27 02	25 24 37	27 08.4	14 57.6	24 28.4	1 42.0	15 28.5	8 56.3	18 06.1	9 05.5	11 02.1	7 14.0
9 M	3 07 02	18 18 10	2♊26 10	9♊31 10	27 06.0	17 07.1	24 16.4	2 23.9	15 50.9	8 56.8	18 04.9	9 07.3	11 02.7	7 15.0
10 Tu	3 10 58	19 16 09	16 39 02	23 49 07	27 03.1	19 17.3	24 06.8	3 05.8	16 13.3	8 57.6	18 03.8	9 08.9	11 03.3	7 16.1
11 W	3 14 55	20 14 07	1♋00 46	8♋13 19	27 00.0	21 27.9	23 59.6	3 47.7	16 35.9	8 58.5	18 02.8	9 10.6	11 03.9	7 17.1
12 Th	3 18 51	21 12 03	15 26 09	22 38 40	26 57.4	23 38.8	23 54.8	4 29.5	16 58.6	8 59.6	18 01.9	9 12.1	11 04.5	7 18.2
13 F	3 22 48	22 09 57	29 50 17	7♌00 33	26 55.6	25 49.6	23D 52.4	5 11.2	17 21.3	9 00.8	18 01.0	9 13.7	11 05.2	7 19.3
14 Sa	3 26 44	23 07 49	14♌09 02	21 15 25	26D 54.8	28 00.1	23 52.4	5 52.9	17 44.2	9 02.3	18 00.3	9 15.2	11 05.9	7 20.4
15 Su	3 30 41	24 05 40	28 19 26	5♍20 51	26 55.2	0♊10.0	23 54.7	6 34.6	18 07.2	9 03.9	17 59.7	9 16.6	11 06.7	7 21.6
16 M	3 34 37	25 03 28	12♍19 32	19 15 24	26 56.4	2 19.0	23 59.2	7 16.2	18 30.3	9 05.7	17 59.2	9 18.0	11 07.5	7 22.7
17 Tu	3 38 34	26 01 15	26 08 20	2♎58 20	26 57.9	4 26.8	24 06.0	7 57.8	18 53.5	9 07.7	17 58.8	9 19.4	11 08.3	7 23.9
18 W	3 42 31	26 59 00	9♎45 21	16 29 21	26R 59.1	6 33.2	24 14.9	8 39.3	19 16.7	9 09.8	17 58.5	9 20.7	11 09.1	7 25.0
19 Th	3 46 27	27 56 44	23 10 19	29 48 13	26 59.5	8 37.9	24 26.0	9 20.7	19 40.1	9 12.2	17 58.3	9 22.0	11 10.0	7 26.2
20 F	3 50 24	28 54 26	6♏23 03	12♏54 46	26 58.4	10 40.8	24 39.1	10 02.2	20 03.6	9 14.7	17D 58.2	9 23.2	11 10.9	7 27.4
21 Sa	3 54 20	29 52 07	19 23 21	25 48 46	26 55.8	12 41.5	24 54.3	10 43.6	20 27.1	9 17.4	17 58.2	9 24.4	11 11.8	7 28.6
22 Su	3 58 17	0♊49 47	2♐11 02	8♐30 09	26 51.6	14 40.0	25 11.4	11 24.9	20 50.8	9 20.2	17 58.3	9 25.5	11 12.8	7 29.9
23 M	4 02 13	1 47 25	14 46 10	20 59 09	26 46.2	16 36.0	25 30.4	12 06.2	21 14.5	9 23.2	17 58.6	9 26.6	11 13.8	7 31.1
24 Tu	4 06 10	2 45 02	27 09 11	3♑16 28	26 39.9	18 29.5	25 51.3	12 47.4	21 38.3	9 26.4	17 58.9	9 27.6	11 14.8	7 32.4
25 W	4 10 06	3 42 38	9♑21 10	15 23 32	26 33.6	20 20.4	26 13.9	13 28.7	22 02.2	9 29.8	17 59.3	9 28.6	11 15.9	7 33.6
26 Th	4 14 03	4 40 13	21 23 52	27 22 31	26 27.9	22 08.5	26 38.2	14 09.8	22 26.2	9 33.3	17 59.8	9 29.6	11 16.9	7 34.9
27 F	4 18 00	5 37 47	3♒19 52	9♒16 23	26 23.3	23 53.8	27 04.1	14 51.0	22 50.3	9 37.0	18 00.5	9 30.5	11 18.0	7 36.2
28 Sa	4 21 56	6 35 20	15 12 31	21 08 48	26 20.2	25 36.3	27 31.7	15 32.0	23 14.4	9 40.8	18 01.2	9 31.3	11 19.2	7 37.5
29 Su	4 25 53	7 32 53	27 05 48	3♓04 06	26D 18.8	27 15.9	28 00.7	16 13.1	23 38.7	9 44.8	18 02.0	9 32.1	11 20.3	7 38.8
30 M	4 29 49	8 30 24	9♓04 17	15 06 58	26 18.9	28 52.5	28 31.3	16 54.1	24 03.0	9 49.0	18 03.0	9 32.9	11 21.5	7 40.1
31 Tu	4 33 46	9 27 55	21 12 47	27 22 19	26 20.0	0♋26.2	29 03.2	17 35.1	24 27.4	9 53.3	18 04.0	9 33.6	11 22.8	7 41.5

LONGITUDE — June 1921

Day	Sid.Time	☉	0 hr ☽	Noon ☽	True ☊	☿	♀	♂	⚳	♃	♄	♅	♆	♇
1 W	4 37 42	10♊25 24	3♈36 10	9♈54 54	26♎21.4	1♋56.9	29♈36.6	18♊16.0	24♋51.9	9♍57.8	18♍05.1	9♓34.2	11♌24.0	7♋42.8
2 Th	4 41 39	11 22 53	16 18 59	22 48 51	26R 22.3	3 24.6	0♉11.2	18 56.9	25 16.4	10 02.4	18 06.4	9 34.8	11 25.3	7 44.2
3 F	4 45 35	12 20 22	29 24 51	6♉07 12	26 21.9	4 49.2	0 47.0	19 37.7	25 41.0	10 07.2	18 07.7	9 35.4	11 26.6	7 45.5
4 Sa	4 49 32	13 17 49	12♉56 00	19 51 12	26 19.7	6 10.7	1 24.1	20 18.5	26 05.7	10 12.2	18 09.2	9 35.9	11 27.9	7 46.9
5 Su	4 53 29	14 15 16	26 52 35	3♊59 47	26 15.5	7 29.1	2 02.3	20 59.3	26 30.5	10 17.3	18 10.7	9 36.4	11 29.3	7 48.3
6 M	4 57 25	15 12 42	11♊12 14	18 29 15	26 09.4	8 44.4	2 41.7	21 40.0	26 55.4	10 22.6	18 12.3	9 36.8	11 30.7	7 49.7
7 Tu	5 01 22	16 10 07	25 49 56	3♋13 22	26 02.0	9 56.4	3 22.1	22 20.7	27 20.3	10 28.0	18 14.1	9 37.1	11 32.1	7 51.1
8 W	5 05 18	17 07 31	10♋38 29	18 04 14	25 54.4	11 05.1	4 03.5	23 01.4	27 45.3	10 33.5	18 15.9	9 37.5	11 33.5	7 52.5
9 Th	5 09 15	18 04 55	25 29 32	2♌53 25	25 47.4	12 10.4	4 45.8	23 42.0	28 10.3	10 39.3	18 17.9	9 37.7	11 35.0	7 53.9
10 F	5 13 11	19 02 17	10♌14 59	17 33 27	25 42.0	13 12.4	5 29.2	24 22.5	28 35.4	10 45.1	18 19.9	9 38.0	11 36.4	7 55.4
11 Sa	5 17 08	19 59 38	24 48 11	1♍58 44	25 38.6	14 10.8	6 13.4	25 03.1	29 00.6	10 51.1	18 22.1	9 38.1	11 38.0	7 56.8
12 Su	5 21 04	20 56 58	9♍04 45	16 06 05	25D 37.2	15 05.7	6 58.5	25 43.6	29 25.8	10 57.2	18 24.3	9 38.2	11 39.5	7 58.2
13 M	5 25 01	21 54 17	23 02 40	29 54 32	25 37.3	15 56.9	7 44.4	26 24.0	29 51.1	11 03.5	18 26.6	9R 38.3	11 41.0	7 59.7
14 Tu	5 28 58	22 51 35	6♎41 49	13♎24 43	25R 38.1	16 44.3	8 31.2	27 04.4	0♌16.5	11 09.9	18 29.1	9 38.3	11 42.6	8 01.1
15 W	5 32 54	23 48 52	20 03 28	26 38 18	25 38.5	17 27.9	9 18.7	27 44.8	0 41.9	11 16.5	18 31.6	9 38.3	11 44.2	8 02.6
16 Th	5 36 51	24 46 09	3♏09 30	9♏37 17	25 37.6	18 07.5	10 07.0	28 25.1	1 07.4	11 23.2	18 34.2	9 38.2	11 45.8	8 04.0
17 F	5 40 47	25 43 24	16 01 54	22 23 34	25 34.6	18 43.0	10 56.0	29 05.4	1 32.9	11 30.0	18 36.9	9 38.1	11 47.5	8 05.5
18 Sa	5 44 44	26 40 39	28 42 28	4♐58 45	25 29.0	19 14.4	11 45.7	29 45.6	1 58.5	11 37.0	18 39.7	9 37.9	11 49.1	8 07.0
19 Su	5 48 40	27 37 54	11♐12 34	17 24 02	25 20.9	19 41.5	12 36.1	0♋25.8	2 24.1	11 44.0	18 42.6	9 37.7	11 50.8	8 08.4
20 M	5 52 37	28 35 08	23 33 16	29 40 22	25 10.7	20 04.3	13 27.1	1 06.0	2 49.8	11 51.2	18 45.6	9 37.5	11 52.5	8 09.9
21 Tu	5 56 33	29 32 21	5♑45 26	11♑48 35	24 59.3	20 22.6	14 18.8	1 46.2	3 15.6	11 58.6	18 48.7	9 37.2	11 54.3	8 11.4
22 W	6 00 30	0♋29 34	17 49 58	23 49 45	24 47.5	20 36.5	15 11.1	2 26.3	3 41.4	12 06.0	18 51.8	9 36.8	11 56.0	8 12.9
23 Th	6 04 27	1 26 47	29 48 06	5♒45 17	24 36.5	20 45.7	16 03.9	3 06.3	4 07.2	12 13.6	18 55.1	9 36.4	11 57.8	8 14.4
24 F	6 08 23	2 24 00	11♒41 34	17 37 16	24 27.0	20R 50.4	16 57.4	3 46.4	4 33.1	12 21.3	18 58.4	9 35.9	11 59.6	8 15.9
25 Sa	6 12 20	3 21 13	23 32 47	29 28 30	24 19.8	20 50.5	17 51.3	4 26.4	4 59.0	12 29.2	19 01.9	9 35.4	12 01.4	8 17.4
26 Su	6 16 16	4 18 25	5♓24 55	11♓22 31	24 15.1	20 46.0	18 45.8	5 06.3	5 25.0	12 37.1	19 05.4	9 34.9	12 03.2	8 18.9
27 M	6 20 13	5 15 37	17 21 52	23 23 34	24 12.7	20 37.1	19 40.9	5 46.3	5 51.1	12 45.2	19 09.0	9 34.3	12 05.1	8 20.4
28 Tu	6 24 09	6 12 50	29 28 12	5♈36 26	24D 12.1	20 23.8	20 36.4	6 26.1	6 17.2	12 53.4	19 12.7	9 33.6	12 06.9	8 21.9
29 W	6 28 06	7 10 02	11♈48 53	18 06 11	24R 12.3	20 06.3	21 32.4	7 06.0	6 43.3	13 01.7	19 16.4	9 33.0	12 08.8	8 23.4
30 Th	6 32 02	8 07 15	24 28 57	0♉57 43	24 12.2	19 44.9	22 28.8	7 45.8	7 09.5	13 10.1	19 20.3	9 32.2	12 10.7	8 24.9

Astro Data

Astro Data	Dy Hr Mn
♃☍♅	3 12:18
☽0N	3 19:11
♃D	6 1:47
♀D	14 0:27
☽0S	16 19:00
♄D	20 21:37
♃☍♅	25 0:45
☽0N	31 4:29
☽0S	13 1:13
♅R	14 10:55
♃⚻♆	20 17:36
☿R	25 0:25
☽0N	27 13:27

Planet Ingress

Planet Ingress	Dy Hr Mn
☿ ♉	1 7:03
♂ ♊	6 1:45
☿ ♊	15 10:09
☉ ♊	21 15:17
☿ ♋	31 5:12
♀ ♉	2 4:21
⚳ ♌	13 20:24
♂ ♋	18 20:34
☉ ♋	21 23:36

Last Aspect / ☽ Ingress

Last Aspect Dy Hr Mn		☽ Ingress Dy Hr Mn
1 15:34 ♂ □	♓	1 21:46
4 5:47 ♂ ⚹	♈	4 8:14
6 6:39 ♀ ☌	♉	6 15:32
7 23:25 ♄ △	♊	8 19:51
10 12:29 ♀ ⚹	♋	10 22:19
12 14:06 ♀ □	♌	13 0:16
15 1:32 ☿ □	♍	15 2:51
16 22:52 ☉ △	♎	17 6:46
19 2:08 ♀ ☍	♏	19 12:21
20 21:22 ♄ ⚹	♐	21 19:53
23 21:02 ♀ △	♑	24 5:34
26 10:28 ♀ □	♒	26 17:17
29 1:24 ♀ ⚹	♓	29 5:50
30 17:48 ♄ ☍	♈	31 17:05

Last Aspect Dy Hr Mn		☽ Ingress Dy Hr Mn
2 4:29 ♂ ⚹	♉	3 1:03
4 9:04 ♄ △	♊	5 5:17
6 17:27 ♂ ☌	♋	7 6:46
8 12:19 ♄ ⚹	♌	9 7:18
10 23:51 ♂ ⚹	♍	11 8:41
13 5:32 ♂ □	♎	13 12:10
15 14:08 ♂ △	♏	15 18:10
17 4:50 ♄ ⚹	♐	18 2:28
20 9:41 ☉ ☍	♑	20 12:39
22 5:26 ☿ ☍	♒	23 0:24
24 10:33 ♀ □	♓	25 13:04
27 6:34 ☿ △	♈	28 1:02
29 15:41 ☿ □	♉	30 10:14

☽ Phases & Eclipses

Dy Hr Mn		
7 21:01	●	16♉44
14 15:24	☽	23♌16
21 20:15	○	0♐12
29 21:44	☾	7♓56
6 6:14	●	14♊59
12 20:59	☽	21♍18
20 9:41	○	28♐30
28 13:17	☾	6♈16

Astro Data

1 May 1921
Julian Day # 7791
SVP 6♓21'23"
GC 25♐44.4 ⚴ 5♊59.0
Eris 29♓28.4 ⚵ 14♑01.9
⚷ 11♈40.5 ⚶ 11♈41.9
☽ Mean ☊ 26♎37.3

1 June 1921
Julian Day # 7822
SVP 6♓21'19"
GC 25♐44.5 ⚴ 24♊12.7
Eris 29♓42.3 ⚵ 12♑06.2R
⚷ 13♈05.5 ⚶ 25♈17.2
☽ Mean ☊ 24♎58.8

July 1921 LONGITUDE

Day	Sid.Time	☉	0 hr ☽	Noon ☽	True ☊	☿	♀	♂	⚳	♃	♄	♅	♆	♇
1 F	6 35 59	9♋04 28	7♉33 01	14♉15 12	24♎10.8	19♋19.8	23♉25.7	8♋25.6	7♌35.7	13♍18.6	19♍24.2	9♓31.4	12♌12.6	8♋26.4
2 Sa	6 39 56	10 01 41	21 04 35	28 01 15	24R 07.3	18R 51.4	24 23.0	9 05.4	8 02.0	13 27.2	19 28.3	9R 30.6	12 14.6	8 27.9
3 Su	6 43 52	10 58 54	5♊05 10	12♊16 04	24 01.2	18 20.1	25 20.7	9 45.1	8 28.4	13 36.0	19 32.4	9 29.8	12 16.5	8 29.4
4 M	6 47 49	11 56 08	19 33 29	26 56 43	23 52.8	17 46.4	26 18.9	10 24.9	8 54.7	13 44.8	19 36.6	9 28.8	12 18.5	8 30.9
5 Tu	6 51 45	12 53 22	4♋24 51	11♋56 47	23 42.6	17 10.8	27 17.4	11 04.5	9 21.1	13 53.8	19 40.8	9 27.9	12 20.4	8 32.4
6 W	6 55 42	13 50 35	19 31 17	27 07 01	23 32.0	16 33.9	28 16.2	11 44.2	9 47.6	14 02.8	19 45.2	9 26.9	12 22.4	8 33.9
7 Th	6 59 38	14 47 49	4♌42 36	12♌16 44	23 22.0	15 56.2	29 15.5	12 23.8	10 14.1	14 12.0	19 49.6	9 25.9	12 24.5	8 35.4
8 F	7 03 35	15 45 02	19 48 10	27 15 48	23 13.9	15 18.5	0♊15.0	13 03.4	10 40.6	14 21.3	19 54.1	9 24.8	12 26.5	8 36.8
9 Sa	7 07 32	16 42 16	4♍38 45	11♍56 18	23 08.3	14 41.3	1 14.9	13 42.9	11 07.2	14 30.6	19 58.7	9 23.6	12 28.5	8 38.3
10 Su	7 11 28	17 39 29	19 07 58	26 13 27	23 05.2	14 05.4	2 15.2	14 22.4	11 33.8	14 40.1	20 03.3	9 22.5	12 30.6	8 39.8
11 M	7 15 25	18 36 42	3♎12 40	10♎05 38	23 04.2	13 31.3	3 15.7	15 01.9	12 00.4	14 49.7	20 08.1	9 21.2	12 32.6	8 41.3
12 Tu	7 19 21	19 33 55	16 52 35	23 33 45	23 04.1	12 59.7	4 16.6	15 41.3	12 27.1	14 59.3	20 12.9	9 20.0	12 34.7	8 42.8
13 W	7 23 18	20 31 08	0♏09 32	6♏40 19	23 03.7	12 31.2	5 17.7	16 20.7	12 53.8	15 09.1	20 17.7	9 18.7	12 36.8	8 44.3
14 Th	7 27 14	21 28 22	13 06 32	19 28 37	23 02.0	12 06.2	6 19.2	17 00.1	13 20.5	15 18.9	20 22.7	9 17.4	12 38.9	8 45.7
15 F	7 31 11	22 25 35	25 46 59	2♐02 04	22 58.0	11 45.2	7 20.9	17 39.4	13 47.3	15 28.8	20 27.7	9 16.0	12 41.0	8 47.2
16 Sa	7 35 07	23 22 49	8♐14 12	14 23 46	22 51.2	11 28.7	8 22.9	18 18.7	14 14.1	15 38.8	20 32.8	9 14.6	12 43.1	8 48.7
17 Su	7 39 04	24 20 02	20 31 02	26 36 18	22 41.6	11 17.0	9 25.2	18 58.0	14 40.9	15 48.9	20 37.9	9 13.1	12 45.2	8 50.1
18 M	7 43 01	25 17 16	2♑39 47	8♑41 42	22 29.7	11D 10.3	10 27.7	19 37.3	15 07.8	15 59.1	20 43.1	9 11.6	12 47.3	8 51.6
19 Tu	7 46 57	26 14 31	14 42 14	20 41 32	22 16.4	11 09.1	11 30.5	20 16.5	15 34.7	16 09.4	20 48.4	9 10.1	12 49.5	8 53.0
20 W	7 50 54	27 11 46	26 39 47	2♒37 08	22 02.6	11 13.4	12 33.6	20 55.7	16 01.6	16 19.7	20 53.8	9 08.6	12 51.6	8 54.5
21 Th	7 54 50	28 09 01	8♒33 44	14 29 46	21 49.6	11 23.3	13 36.9	21 34.9	16 28.6	16 30.2	20 59.2	9 07.0	12 53.8	8 55.9
22 F	7 58 47	29 06 17	20 25 28	26 21 02	21 38.3	11 39.1	14 40.5	22 14.0	16 55.5	16 40.7	21 04.7	9 05.3	12 56.0	8 57.3
23 Sa	8 02 43	0♌03 34	2♓16 46	8♓12 58	21 29.5	12 00.7	15 44.2	22 53.1	17 22.5	16 51.3	21 10.2	9 03.7	12 58.1	8 58.7
24 Su	8 06 40	1 00 52	14 10 00	20 08 15	21 23.4	12 28.1	16 48.3	23 32.2	17 49.6	17 02.0	21 15.8	9 02.0	13 00.3	9 00.1
25 M	8 10 36	1 58 10	26 08 10	2♈10 15	21 20.0	13 01.4	17 52.5	24 11.2	18 16.6	17 12.7	21 21.5	9 00.2	13 02.5	9 01.5
26 Tu	8 14 33	2 55 29	8♈15 01	14 23 02	21D 18.8	13 40.6	18 57.0	24 50.3	18 43.7	17 23.5	21 27.2	8 58.5	13 04.7	9 02.9
27 W	8 18 29	3 52 49	20 34 53	26 51 10	21R 18.7	14 25.7	20 01.6	25 29.3	19 10.8	17 34.4	21 33.0	8 56.7	13 06.9	9 04.3
28 Th	8 22 26	4 50 11	3♉12 30	9♉39 26	21 18.7	15 16.4	21 06.5	26 08.2	19 38.0	17 45.4	21 38.8	8 54.8	13 09.1	9 05.7
29 F	8 26 23	5 47 33	16 12 32	22 52 17	21 17.7	16 12.9	22 11.6	26 47.2	20 05.1	17 56.4	21 44.7	8 53.0	13 11.3	9 07.1
30 Sa	8 30 19	6 44 57	29 39 03	6♊33 06	21 14.8	17 15.0	23 16.9	27 26.1	20 32.3	18 07.5	21 50.7	8 51.1	13 13.5	9 08.4
31 Su	8 34 16	7 42 21	13♊34 33	20 43 18	21 09.4	18 22.5	24 22.4	28 05.0	20 59.5	18 18.7	21 56.7	8 49.2	13 15.7	9 09.8

August 1921 LONGITUDE

Day	Sid.Time	☉	0 hr ☽	Noon ☽	True ☊	☿	♀	♂	⚳	♃	♄	♅	♆	♇
1 M	8 38 12	8♌39 47	27♊59 05	5♋21 22	21♎01.8	19♋35.4	25♊28.1	28♋43.9	21♌26.8	18♍30.0	22♍02.7	8♓47.2	13♌18.0	9♋11.1
2 Tu	8 42 09	9 37 14	12♋49 24	20 22 12	20R 52.4	20 53.4	26 33.9	29 22.8	21 54.0	18 41.3	22 08.9	8R 45.2	13 20.2	9 12.5
3 W	8 46 05	10 34 42	27 58 37	5♌37 18	20 42.4	22 16.5	27 39.9	0♌01.6	22 21.3	18 52.6	22 15.0	8 43.2	13 22.4	9 13.8
4 Th	8 50 02	11 32 11	13♌16 50	20 55 46	20 32.9	23 44.4	28 46.2	0 40.4	22 48.6	19 04.1	22 21.3	8 41.2	13 24.6	9 15.1
5 F	8 53 59	12 29 40	28 32 42	6♍06 18	20 25.2	25 16.9	29 52.5	1 19.2	23 15.9	19 15.6	22 27.5	8 39.1	13 26.9	9 16.4
6 Sa	8 57 55	13 27 11	13♍35 27	20 59 12	20 19.8	26 53.6	0♋59.1	1 57.9	23 43.3	19 27.1	22 33.8	8 37.1	13 29.1	9 17.7
7 Su	9 01 52	14 24 42	28 16 49	5♎27 49	20 16.9	28 34.5	2 05.8	2 36.6	24 10.6	19 38.8	22 40.2	8 34.9	13 31.3	9 18.9
8 M	9 05 48	15 22 14	12♎31 54	19 28 58	20D 16.1	0♌19.0	3 12.6	3 15.3	24 38.0	19 50.4	22 46.6	8 32.8	13 33.5	9 20.2
9 Tu	9 09 45	16 19 47	26 19 08	3♏02 36	20 16.5	2 06.9	4 19.6	3 54.0	25 05.4	20 02.2	22 53.1	8 30.7	13 35.7	9 21.4
10 W	9 13 41	17 17 21	9♏39 43	16 10 54	20R 16.9	3 57.9	5 26.8	4 32.7	25 32.8	20 14.0	22 59.6	8 28.5	13 38.0	9 22.7
11 Th	9 17 38	18 14 56	22 36 37	28 57 22	20 16.3	5 51.4	6 34.1	5 11.3	26 00.2	20 25.8	23 06.1	8 26.3	13 40.2	9 23.9
12 F	9 21 34	19 12 32	5♐13 42	11♐26 08	20 13.9	7 47.2	7 41.6	5 49.9	26 27.6	20 37.7	23 12.7	8 24.1	13 42.4	9 25.1
13 Sa	9 25 31	20 10 08	17 35 09	23 41 15	20 09.2	9 44.9	8 49.2	6 28.4	26 55.1	20 49.6	23 19.4	8 21.9	13 44.6	9 26.3
14 Su	9 29 27	21 07 46	29 44 54	5♑46 29	20 02.2	11 44.0	9 57.0	7 07.0	27 22.5	21 01.6	23 26.0	8 19.6	13 46.8	9 27.5
15 M	9 33 24	22 05 25	11♑46 24	17 44 59	19 53.1	13 44.3	11 04.9	7 45.5	27 50.0	21 13.7	23 32.8	8 17.4	13 49.0	9 28.6
16 Tu	9 37 21	23 03 04	23 42 33	29 39 23	19 42.8	15 45.3	12 12.9	8 24.0	28 17.5	21 25.7	23 39.5	8 15.1	13 51.3	9 29.8
17 W	9 41 17	24 00 45	5♒35 43	11♒31 46	19 32.1	17 46.7	13 21.1	9 02.5	28 44.9	21 37.9	23 46.3	8 12.8	13 53.5	9 30.9
18 Th	9 45 14	24 58 28	17 27 45	23 23 53	19 22.0	19 48.3	14 29.5	9 40.9	29 12.4	21 50.1	23 53.1	8 10.5	13 55.6	9 32.0
19 F	9 49 10	25 56 11	29 20 19	5♓17 17	19 13.4	21 49.8	15 37.9	10 19.3	29 40.0	22 02.3	24 00.0	8 08.2	13 57.8	9 33.2
20 Sa	9 53 07	26 53 56	11♓14 59	17 13 39	19 06.7	23 51.0	16 46.5	10 57.8	0♍07.5	22 14.5	24 06.9	8 05.9	14 00.0	9 34.2
21 Su	9 57 03	27 51 43	23 13 32	29 14 54	19 02.4	25 51.6	17 55.3	11 36.1	0 35.0	22 26.8	24 13.8	8 03.5	14 02.2	9 35.3
22 M	10 01 00	28 49 31	5♈18 05	11♈23 26	19D 00.4	27 51.5	19 04.1	12 14.5	1 02.5	22 39.2	24 20.8	8 01.2	14 04.4	9 36.4
23 Tu	10 04 56	29 47 20	17 31 19	23 42 08	19 00.1	29 50.6	20 13.1	12 52.8	1 30.1	22 51.5	24 27.7	7 58.8	14 06.5	9 37.4
24 W	10 08 53	0♍45 12	29 56 22	6♉14 26	19 01.1	1♍48.8	21 22.3	13 31.2	1 57.6	23 04.0	24 34.8	7 56.4	14 08.7	9 38.4
25 Th	10 12 50	1 43 05	12♉36 50	19 04 02	19 02.3	3 45.9	22 31.5	14 09.5	2 25.2	23 16.4	24 41.8	7 54.1	14 10.8	9 39.4
26 F	10 16 46	2 41 00	25 36 29	2♊14 37	19R 02.9	5 41.9	23 40.9	14 47.8	2 52.8	23 28.9	24 48.9	7 51.7	14 13.0	9 40.4
27 Sa	10 20 43	3 38 57	8♊58 47	15 49 15	19 02.2	7 36.8	24 50.4	15 26.0	3 20.3	23 41.4	24 56.0	7 49.3	14 15.1	9 41.4
28 Su	10 24 39	4 36 56	22 46 13	29 49 42	18 59.8	9 30.4	26 00.1	16 04.3	3 47.9	23 54.0	25 03.2	7 46.9	14 17.2	9 42.4
29 M	10 28 36	5 34 56	6♋59 35	14♋15 34	18 55.6	11 22.9	27 09.8	16 42.5	4 15.5	24 06.6	25 10.3	7 44.5	14 19.3	9 43.3
30 Tu	10 32 32	6 32 59	21 37 07	29 03 33	18 50.0	13 14.1	28 19.7	17 20.7	4 43.1	24 19.2	25 17.5	7 42.1	14 21.4	9 44.2
31 W	10 36 29	7 31 03	6♌33 59	14♌07 21	18 43.9	15 04.0	29 29.7	17 58.9	5 10.7	24 31.9	25 24.7	7 39.7	14 23.5	9 45.1

Astro Data

	Dy Hr Mn
☽0S	10 8:55
☿D	19 5:32
☽0N	24 21:18
♅△♇	25 1:57
☽0S	6 18:34
☽0N	21 3:57

Planet Ingress

		Dy Hr Mn
♀	♊	8 5:57
☉	♌	23 10:30
♂	♌	3 11:01
♀	♋	5 14:42
☿	♌	8 7:42
⚳	♍	20 5:29
☿	♍	23 13:54
☉	♍	23 17:15
♀	♌	31 22:24

Last Aspect / ☽ Ingress (July)

Last Aspect Dy Hr Mn			☽ Ingress	Dy Hr Mn
2 5:17	♀	☌	♊	2 15:23
4 0:02	♄	□	♋	4 16:55
6 13:57	♀	⚹	♌	6 16:33
7 12:12	♆	☌	♍	8 16:26
10 1:30	♄	☌	♎	10 18:28
12 4:15	☉	□	♏	12 23:43
14 16:06	☉	△	♐	15 8:05
17 0:09	♄	□	♑	17 18:43
20 0:07	☉	☍	♒	20 6:43
21 10:03	♀	△	♓	22 19:23
24 19:12	♂	△	♈	25 7:42
27 9:16	♂	□	♉	27 17:58
29 19:18	♂	⚹	♊	30 0:37

Last Aspect / ☽ Ingress (August)

Last Aspect Dy Hr Mn			☽ Ingress	Dy Hr Mn
31 18:33	♀	☌	♋	1 3:18
3 2:50	♂	☌	♌	3 3:11
5 1:20	♀	⚹	♍	5 2:18
6 22:58	☿	⚹	♎	7 2:51
8 4:21	☉	⚹	♏	9 6:33
11 0:50	♄	⚹	♐	11 13:59
13 11:16	♄	□	♑	14 0:30
15 23:47	♄	△	♒	16 12:42
18 15:28	☉	☍	♓	19 1:20
21 1:54	♄	☍	♈	21 13:30
23 4:33	♀	□	♉	24 0:07
25 22:26	♄	△	♊	26 7:58
28 3:50	♄	□	♋	28 12:17
30 10:43	♀	☌	♌	30 13:31

☽ Phases & Eclipses

Dy Hr Mn		
5 13:36	●	12♋57
12 4:15	☽	19♎15
20 0:07	○	26♑43
28 2:20	☾	4♉27
3 20:17	●	10♌55
10 14:13	☽	17♏23
18 15:28	○	25♒07
26 12:51	☾	2♊43

Astro Data

1 July 1921
Julian Day # 7852
SVP 6♓21'14"
GC 25♐44.6 ⚴ 12♋13.9
Eris 29♓45.9R ⚵ 5♑58.1R
⚷ 13♈52.0 ⚶ 7♉08.2
☽ Mean ☊ 23♎23.5

1 August 1921
Julian Day # 7883
SVP 6♓21'09"
GC 25♐44.6 ⚴ 0♌38.6
Eris 29♓38.6R ⚵ 29♐53.3R
⚷ 13♈53.0R ⚶ 17♉16.6
☽ Mean ☊ 21♎45.0

LONGITUDE — September 1921

Day	Sid.Time	☉	0 hr ☽	Noon ☽	True ☊	☿	♀	♂	⚳	♃	♄	♅	♆	♇
1 Th	10 40 25	8♍29 09	21♌42 28	29♌18 03	18♎38.0	16♍52.7	0♌39.7	18♌37.1	5♍38.3	24♍44.5	25♍32.0	7♓37.3	14♌25.6	9♋46.0
2 F	10 44 22	9 27 17	6♍52 50	14♍25 31	18R33.3	18 40.2	1 49.9	19 15.2	6 05.9	24 57.2	25 39.2	7R34.9	14 27.6	9 46.9
3 Sa	10 48 19	10 25 26	21 54 56	29 20 02	18 30.1	20 26.4	3 00.2	19 53.3	6 33.5	25 10.0	25 46.5	7 32.5	14 29.7	9 47.7
4 Su	10 52 15	11 23 37	6♎39 54	13♎53 52	18D28.8	22 11.4	4 10.6	20 31.4	7 01.1	25 22.7	25 53.8	7 30.1	14 31.7	9 48.5
5 M	10 56 12	12 21 50	21 01 24	28 02 11	18 29.0	23 55.2	5 21.2	21 09.5	7 28.7	25 35.5	26 01.1	7 27.7	14 33.8	9 49.3
6 Tu	11 00 08	13 20 04	4♏56 06	11♏43 11	18 30.3	25 37.8	6 31.8	21 47.6	7 56.3	25 48.3	26 08.4	7 25.4	14 35.8	9 50.1
7 W	11 04 05	14 18 19	18 23 35	24 57 36	18 31.8	27 19.3	7 42.5	22 25.6	8 23.9	26 01.1	26 15.8	7 23.0	14 37.8	9 50.9
8 Th	11 08 01	15 16 37	1♐25 37	7♐48 05	18R32.9	28 59.5	8 53.3	23 03.6	8 51.5	26 14.0	26 23.2	7 20.6	14 39.7	9 51.6
9 F	11 11 58	16 14 55	14 05 30	20 18 25	18 33.1	0♎38.6	10 04.2	23 41.6	9 19.1	26 26.8	26 30.5	7 18.2	14 41.7	9 52.3
10 Sa	11 15 54	17 13 15	26 27 23	2♑32 56	18 31.9	2 16.6	11 15.2	24 19.6	9 46.6	26 39.7	26 37.9	7 15.9	14 43.7	9 53.0
11 Su	11 19 51	18 11 37	8♑35 37	14 36 00	18 29.4	3 53.4	12 26.3	24 57.6	10 14.2	26 52.6	26 45.3	7 13.5	14 45.6	9 53.7
12 M	11 23 48	19 10 01	20 34 32	26 31 45	18 25.6	5 29.1	13 37.5	25 35.5	10 41.8	27 05.5	26 52.7	7 11.2	14 47.5	9 54.4
13 Tu	11 27 44	20 08 26	2♒28 04	8♒23 55	18 21.1	7 03.8	14 48.8	26 13.4	11 09.3	27 18.4	27 00.1	7 08.9	14 49.4	9 55.0
14 W	11 31 41	21 06 52	14 19 40	20 15 40	18 16.3	8 37.3	16 00.1	26 51.3	11 36.9	27 31.3	27 07.6	7 06.6	14 51.3	9 55.7
15 Th	11 35 37	22 05 21	26 12 14	2♓09 39	18 11.7	10 09.8	17 11.6	27 29.2	12 04.4	27 44.3	27 15.0	7 04.3	14 53.1	9 56.2
16 F	11 39 34	23 03 51	8♓08 10	14 08 02	18 07.8	11 41.2	18 23.2	28 07.1	12 32.0	27 57.2	27 22.4	7 02.0	14 55.0	9 56.8
17 Sa	11 43 30	24 02 23	20 09 27	26 12 37	18 05.1	13 11.5	19 34.8	28 44.9	12 59.5	28 10.2	27 29.9	6 59.7	14 56.8	9 57.4
18 Su	11 47 27	25 00 57	2♈17 44	8♈25 00	18D03.6	14 40.8	20 46.6	29 22.7	13 27.0	28 23.1	27 37.3	6 57.5	14 58.6	9 57.9
19 M	11 51 23	25 59 33	14 34 35	20 46 41	18 03.3	16 08.9	21 58.4	0♍00.5	13 54.5	28 36.1	27 44.8	6 55.3	15 00.4	9 58.4
20 Tu	11 55 20	26 58 11	27 01 32	3♉19 19	18 03.9	17 36.0	23 10.3	0 38.3	14 22.0	28 49.1	27 52.3	6 53.1	15 02.2	9 58.9
21 W	11 59 16	27 56 51	9♉40 16	16 04 38	18 05.2	19 02.0	24 22.4	1 16.1	14 49.5	29 02.0	27 59.7	6 50.9	15 03.9	9 59.4
22 Th	12 03 13	28 55 33	22 32 38	29 04 32	18 06.7	20 26.9	25 34.5	1 53.8	15 17.0	29 15.0	28 07.2	6 48.7	15 05.6	9 59.8
23 F	12 07 10	29 54 18	5♊40 34	12♊20 57	18 07.9	21 50.6	26 46.6	2 31.6	15 44.4	29 28.0	28 14.6	6 46.5	15 07.3	10 00.2
24 Sa	12 11 06	0♎53 05	19 05 52	25 55 28	18R08.6	23 13.2	27 58.9	3 09.3	16 11.9	29 41.0	28 22.1	6 44.4	15 09.0	10 00.6
25 Su	12 15 03	1 51 54	2♋49 51	9♋49 01	18 08.5	24 34.6	29 11.3	3 47.0	16 39.3	29 54.0	28 29.5	6 42.3	15 10.7	10 01.0
26 M	12 18 59	2 50 45	16 52 54	24 01 18	18 07.7	25 54.8	0♍23.7	4 24.7	17 06.7	0♎06.9	28 37.0	6 40.2	15 12.3	10 01.4
27 Tu	12 22 56	3 49 41	1♌13 55	8♌30 20	18 06.3	27 13.7	1 36.3	5 02.4	17 34.1	0 19.9	28 44.4	6 38.2	15 13.9	10 01.7
28 W	12 26 52	4 48 35	15 49 59	23 12 12	18 04.7	28 31.2	2 48.9	5 40.0	18 01.5	0 32.9	28 51.9	6 36.1	15 15.5	10 02.0
29 Th	12 30 49	5 47 33	0♍36 11	8♍01 05	18 03.1	29 47.4	4 01.5	6 17.7	18 28.9	0 45.9	28 59.3	6 34.1	15 17.1	10 02.3
30 F	12 34 45	6 46 34	15 25 57	22 49 50	18 01.9	1♏02.1	5 14.3	6 55.3	18 56.3	0 58.8	29 06.7	6 32.1	15 18.6	10 02.5

LONGITUDE — October 1921

Day	Sid.Time	☉	0 hr ☽	Noon ☽	True ☊	☿	♀	♂	⚳	♃	♄	♅	♆	♇
1 Sa	12 38 42	7♎45 36	0♎11 47	7♎30 52	18♎01.2	2♏15.2	6♍27.1	7♍32.9	19♍23.6	1♎11.8	29♍14.1	6♓30.2	15♌20.2	10♋02.8
2 Su	12 42 39	8 44 41	14 46 17	21 57 16	18D01.1	3 26.7	7 40.0	8 10.5	19 50.9	1 24.7	29 21.5	6R28.3	15 21.7	10 03.0
3 M	12 46 35	9 43 47	29 03 12	6♏03 36	18 01.4	4 36.4	8 53.0	8 48.0	20 18.2	1 37.7	29 28.9	6 26.4	15 23.1	10 03.2
4 Tu	12 50 32	10 42 56	12♏58 09	19 46 37	18 02.0	5 44.2	10 06.0	9 25.6	20 45.5	1 50.6	29 36.3	6 24.5	15 24.6	10 03.3
5 W	12 54 28	11 42 06	26 28 58	3♐05 15	18 02.7	6 50.0	11 19.1	10 03.1	21 12.7	2 03.5	29 43.7	6 22.7	15 26.0	10 03.5
6 Th	12 58 25	12 41 18	9♐35 39	16 00 26	18 03.3	7 53.6	12 32.3	10 40.6	21 39.9	2 16.4	29 51.0	6 20.9	15 27.4	10 03.6
7 F	13 02 21	13 40 32	22 19 58	28 34 42	18 03.7	8 54.7	13 45.5	11 18.1	22 07.1	2 29.2	29 58.4	6 19.1	15 28.8	10 03.7
8 Sa	13 06 18	14 39 48	4♑45 06	10♑51 43	18R03.8	9 53.3	14 58.8	11 55.5	22 34.3	2 42.1	0♎05.7	6 17.4	15 30.1	10 03.8
9 Su	13 10 14	15 39 05	16 55 04	22 55 45	18 03.8	10 49.1	16 12.1	12 33.0	23 01.4	2 54.9	0 13.0	6 15.7	15 31.4	10 03.8
10 M	13 14 11	16 38 25	28 54 20	4♒51 24	18 03.7	11 41.8	17 25.5	13 10.4	23 28.5	3 07.8	0 20.2	6 14.1	15 32.7	10R03.9
11 Tu	13 18 08	17 37 46	10♒47 30	16 43 11	18D03.6	12 31.1	18 39.0	13 47.8	23 55.6	3 20.5	0 27.5	6 12.4	15 33.9	10 03.9
12 W	13 22 04	18 37 09	22 38 59	28 35 24	18 03.7	13 16.7	19 52.5	14 25.2	24 22.6	3 33.3	0 34.7	6 10.9	15 35.2	10 03.8
13 Th	13 26 01	19 36 33	4♓32 53	10♓31 52	18 03.8	13 58.2	21 06.1	15 02.5	24 49.6	3 46.1	0 41.9	6 09.3	15 36.4	10 03.8
14 F	13 29 57	20 36 00	16 32 45	22 35 52	18 04.0	14 35.2	22 19.7	15 39.9	25 16.6	3 58.8	0 49.1	6 07.8	15 37.5	10 03.7
15 Sa	13 33 54	21 35 28	28 41 33	4♈50 01	18 04.2	15 07.3	23 33.4	16 17.2	25 43.6	4 11.5	0 56.3	6 06.3	15 38.7	10 03.6
16 Su	13 37 50	22 34 58	11♈01 32	17 16 14	18R04.3	15 34.1	24 47.2	16 54.5	26 10.5	4 24.1	1 03.4	6 04.9	15 39.8	10 03.5
17 M	13 41 47	23 34 31	23 34 16	29 55 43	18 04.2	15 54.9	26 01.0	17 31.8	26 37.4	4 36.8	1 10.5	6 03.5	15 40.9	10 03.4
18 Tu	13 45 43	24 34 05	6♉20 38	12♉49 02	18 03.8	16 09.4	27 14.9	18 09.0	27 04.2	4 49.4	1 17.6	6 02.2	15 41.9	10 03.2
19 W	13 49 40	25 33 42	19 20 55	25 56 15	18 03.0	16R16.9	28 28.8	18 46.3	27 31.0	5 02.0	1 24.6	6 00.9	15 42.9	10 03.0
20 Th	13 53 36	26 33 20	2♊34 57	9♊16 57	18 02.0	16 16.9	29 42.8	19 23.5	27 57.8	5 14.5	1 31.6	5 59.6	15 43.9	10 02.8
21 F	13 57 33	27 33 01	16 02 09	22 50 28	18 00.9	16 08.8	0♎56.8	20 00.8	28 24.5	5 27.0	1 38.6	5 58.4	15 44.9	10 02.6
22 Sa	14 01 30	28 32 45	29 41 47	6♋35 57	17 59.9	15 52.3	2 10.9	20 38.0	28 51.2	5 39.5	1 45.6	5 57.2	15 45.8	10 02.3
23 Su	14 05 26	29 32 30	13♋32 51	20 32 19	17D59.2	15 26.9	3 25.1	21 15.1	29 17.9	5 51.9	1 52.5	5 56.1	15 46.7	10 02.0
24 M	14 09 23	0♏32 18	27 34 11	4♌38 14	17 59.1	14 52.6	4 39.2	21 52.3	29 44.5	6 04.3	1 59.4	5 55.0	15 47.6	10 01.7
25 Tu	14 13 19	1 32 08	11♌44 17	18 52 02	17 59.6	14 09.2	5 53.5	22 29.4	0♎11.1	6 16.7	2 06.2	5 53.9	15 48.4	10 01.4
26 W	14 17 16	2 32 00	26 01 11	3♍11 24	18 00.5	13 17.2	7 07.8	23 06.6	0 37.6	6 29.0	2 13.0	5 52.9	15 49.2	10 01.1
27 Th	14 21 12	3 31 54	10♍22 16	17 33 22	18 01.7	12 17.1	8 22.1	23 43.7	1 04.1	6 41.3	2 19.8	5 51.9	15 50.0	10 00.7
28 F	14 25 09	4 31 51	24 44 12	1♎54 15	18 02.8	11 10.1	9 36.5	24 20.8	1 30.5	6 53.5	2 26.5	5 51.0	15 50.7	10 00.3
29 Sa	14 29 05	5 31 49	9♎02 58	16 09 47	18R03.3	9 57.5	10 50.9	24 57.8	1 56.9	7 05.7	2 33.2	5 50.2	15 51.4	9 59.9
30 Su	14 33 02	6 31 50	23 14 10	0♏15 32	18 02.9	8 41.3	12 05.4	25 34.9	2 23.3	7 17.8	2 39.8	5 49.3	15 52.1	9 59.5
31 M	14 36 59	7 31 53	7♏13 25	14 07 19	18 01.5	7 23.7	13 19.9	26 11.9	2 49.6	7 29.9	2 46.4	5 48.6	15 52.7	9 59.0

Astro Data	Dy Hr Mn
☽0S	3 5:25
☿0S	9 17:50
♃☌♄	10 4:14
☽0N	17 10:13
☉0S	23 14:19
♃∠♆	26 23:23
☽0S	30 15:59
♃0S	7 16:30
♇R	11 1:05
♄∠♆	12 13:45
☽0N	14 17:14
☿R	20 0:00
♀0S	23 15:52
♃⚻♅	23 19:20
☽0S	28 0:54

Planet Ingress		Dy Hr Mn
☿	♎	9 2:37
♂	♍	19 11:40
☉	♎	23 14:20
♃	♎	25 23:10
♀	♍	26 4:08
☿	♏	29 16:01
♄	♎	7 17:22
♀	♎	20 17:35
☉	♏	23 23:02
⚳	♎	25 1:59

Last Aspect Dy Hr Mn			☽ Ingress	Dy Hr Mn
31 18:23	♂	☌	♍	1 13:06
3 6:11	♄	☌	♎	3 13:05
4 23:41	♂	⚹	♏	5 15:24
7 17:01	☿	⚹	♐	7 21:20
10 0:14	♄	□	♑	10 6:58
12 13:09	♃	△	♒	12 19:01
15 2:04	♂	☍	♓	15 7:39
17 15:56	♃	☍	♈	17 19:29
19 14:33	♀	△	♉	20 5:41
22 12:19	♃	△	♊	22 13:41
24 18:39	♃	□	♋	24 19:06
26 19:44	♄	⚹	♌	26 21:57
28 21:26	☿	⚹	♍	28 23:01
30 22:19	♄	☌	♎	30 23:41

Last Aspect Dy Hr Mn			☽ Ingress	Dy Hr Mn
2 0:58	♆	⚹	♏	3 1:37
5 5:49	♄	⚹	♐	5 6:22
7 14:44	♄	□	♑	7 14:45
8 21:04	♀	△	♒	10 2:12
11 14:01	☉	△	♓	12 14:51
14 11:24	♀	☍	♈	15 2:34
16 22:59	☉	☍	♉	17 12:08
19 17:04	♀	△	♊	19 19:21
21 20:54	☉	△	♋	22 0:32
23 13:17	♂	⚹	♌	24 4:08
25 6:51	♆	☌	♍	26 6:40
27 22:47	♂	☌	♎	28 8:49
29 11:29	♆	⚹	♏	30 11:33

☽ Phases & Eclipses Dy Hr Mn		
2 3:33	●	9♍07
9 3:29	☽	15♐54
17 7:20	○	23♓51
24 21:17	☾	1♋16
1 12:26	●	7♎47
1 12:35:35	●	T 01'52"
8 20:11	☽	15♑00
16 22:59	○	23♈02
16 22:54	●	P 0.931
24 4:31	☾	0♌14
30 23:38	●	7♏01

Astro Data

1 September 1921
Julian Day # 7914
SVP 6♓21'06"
GC 25♐44.7 ⚴ 18♌20.5
Eris 29♓22.3R ⚵ 28♐41.9
⚷ 13♈07.0R ⚶ 23♉55.0
☽ Mean ☊ 20♎06.5

1 October 1921
Julian Day # 7944
SVP 6♓21'04"
GC 25♐44.8 ⚴ 4♍24.1
Eris 29♓02.4R ⚵ 2♑40.8
⚷ 11♈52.3R ⚶ 25♉02.9R
☽ Mean ☊ 18♎31.1

November 1921 — LONGITUDE

Day	Sid.Time	☉	0 hr ☽	Noon ☽	True ☊	☿	♀	♂	⚳	♃	♄	♅	♆	♇
1 Tu	14 40 55	8♏31 57	20♏56 52	27♏41 46	17♎59.1	6♏07.0	14♎34.4	26♍48.9	3♎15.8	7♎41.9	2♎53.0	5♓47.8	15♌53.3	9♋58.5
2 W	14 44 52	9 32 03	4♐21 46	10♐56 45	17R 55.9	4R 53.6	15 49.0	27 25.9	3 42.0	7 53.9	2 59.5	5R 47.2	15 53.9	9R 58.0
3 Th	14 48 48	10 32 11	17 26 40	23 51 37	17 52.4	3 45.9	17 03.6	28 02.8	4 08.1	8 05.9	3 06.0	5 46.5	15 54.5	9 57.5
4 F	14 52 45	11 32 21	0♑11 45	6♑27 18	17 48.9	2 45.9	18 18.2	28 39.7	4 34.2	8 17.7	3 12.4	5 46.0	15 55.0	9 56.9
5 Sa	14 56 41	12 32 32	12 38 36	18 46 03	17 46.0	1 55.3	19 32.9	29 16.6	5 00.2	8 29.6	3 18.7	5 45.4	15 55.4	9 56.4
6 Su	15 00 38	13 32 45	24 50 06	0♒51 16	17 44.0	1 15.3	20 47.6	29 53.5	5 26.2	8 41.3	3 25.0	5 45.0	15 55.9	9 55.8
7 M	15 04 34	14 32 59	6♒50 07	12 47 13	17D 43.3	0 46.7	22 02.3	0♎30.4	5 52.1	8 53.0	3 31.3	5 44.5	15 56.3	9 55.2
8 Tu	15 08 31	15 33 15	18 43 11	24 38 38	17 43.6	0D 29.8	23 17.1	1 07.2	6 17.9	9 04.7	3 37.5	5 44.1	15 56.6	9 54.6
9 W	15 12 28	16 33 32	0♓34 11	6♓30 27	17 45.0	0 24.4	24 31.9	1 44.0	6 43.7	9 16.2	3 43.6	5 43.8	15 57.0	9 53.9
10 Th	15 16 24	17 33 51	12 28 04	18 27 36	17 46.8	0 30.2	25 46.7	2 20.8	7 09.4	9 27.7	3 49.7	5 43.5	15 57.3	9 53.2
11 F	15 20 21	18 34 11	24 29 36	0♈34 36	17 48.5	0 46.7	27 01.6	2 57.5	7 35.0	9 39.2	3 55.8	5 43.3	15 57.5	9 52.5
12 Sa	15 24 17	19 34 32	6♈43 04	12 55 25	17R 49.5	1 12.8	28 16.4	3 34.3	8 00.6	9 50.6	4 01.7	5 43.1	15 57.8	9 51.8
13 Su	15 28 14	20 34 55	19 11 59	25 33 03	17 49.4	1 48.0	29 31.3	4 11.0	8 26.1	10 01.9	4 07.7	5 43.0	15 58.0	9 51.1
14 M	15 32 10	21 35 20	1♉58 48	8♉29 20	17 47.6	2 31.1	0♏46.3	4 47.6	8 51.5	10 13.1	4 13.5	5 42.9	15 58.1	9 50.4
15 Tu	15 36 07	22 35 46	15 04 39	21 44 40	17 44.1	3 21.4	2 01.2	5 24.3	9 16.9	10 24.3	4 19.3	5D 42.9	15 58.3	9 49.6
16 W	15 40 03	23 36 13	28 29 11	5♊17 57	17 39.1	4 18.0	3 16.2	6 00.9	9 42.2	10 35.4	4 25.0	5 42.9	15 58.4	9 48.8
17 Th	15 44 00	24 36 43	12♊10 34	19 06 39	17 33.2	5 20.1	4 31.2	6 37.5	10 07.4	10 46.4	4 30.7	5 43.0	15 58.4	9 48.0
18 F	15 47 57	25 37 14	26 05 42	3♋07 13	17 26.9	6 27.0	5 46.2	7 14.1	10 32.6	10 57.3	4 36.3	5 43.1	15R 58.5	9 47.2
19 Sa	15 51 53	26 37 47	10♋10 40	17 15 33	17 21.3	7 38.0	7 01.3	7 50.7	10 57.6	11 08.2	4 41.9	5 43.3	15 58.5	9 46.4
20 Su	15 55 50	27 38 21	24 21 22	1♌27 38	17 16.9	8 52.5	8 16.4	8 27.2	11 22.6	11 19.0	4 47.4	5 43.5	15 58.4	9 45.5
21 M	15 59 46	28 38 58	8♌33 59	15 40 02	17D 14.3	10 10.1	9 31.5	9 03.7	11 47.6	11 29.7	4 52.8	5 43.8	15 58.3	9 44.6
22 Tu	16 03 43	29 39 35	22 45 31	29 50 09	17 13.5	11 30.2	10 46.6	9 40.2	12 12.4	11 40.3	4 58.1	5 44.1	15 58.2	9 43.7
23 W	16 07 39	0♐40 15	6♍53 46	13♍56 13	17 14.1	12 52.6	12 01.8	10 16.7	12 37.1	11 50.9	5 03.4	5 44.5	15 58.1	9 42.8
24 Th	16 11 36	1 40 56	20 57 20	27 57 02	17 15.5	14 16.7	13 16.9	10 53.1	13 01.8	12 01.3	5 08.6	5 44.9	15 57.9	9 41.9
25 F	16 15 32	2 41 39	4♎55 11	11♎51 40	17R 16.5	15 42.4	14 32.1	11 29.5	13 26.4	12 11.7	5 13.7	5 45.4	15 57.7	9 41.0
26 Sa	16 19 29	3 42 24	18 46 19	25 39 01	17 16.3	17 09.4	15 47.3	12 05.9	13 50.9	12 22.0	5 18.8	5 46.0	15 57.5	9 40.0
27 Su	16 23 26	4 43 10	2♏29 31	9♏17 39	17 14.1	18 37.5	17 02.6	12 42.2	14 15.3	12 32.1	5 23.7	5 46.5	15 57.2	9 39.1
28 M	16 27 22	5 43 57	16 03 11	22 45 50	17 09.5	20 06.4	18 17.8	13 18.5	14 39.6	12 42.2	5 28.6	5 47.2	15 56.9	9 38.1
29 Tu	16 31 19	6 44 46	29 25 24	6♐01 37	17 02.5	21 36.2	19 33.1	13 54.8	15 03.8	12 52.2	5 33.5	5 47.9	15 56.5	9 37.1
30 W	16 35 15	7 45 36	12♐34 19	19 03 17	16 53.7	23 06.5	20 48.4	14 31.1	15 27.9	13 02.1	5 38.2	5 48.6	15 56.1	9 36.1

December 1921 — LONGITUDE

Day	Sid.Time	☉	0 hr ☽	Noon ☽	True ☊	☿	♀	♂	⚳	♃	♄	♅	♆	♇
1 Th	16 39 12	8♐46 27	25♐28 26	1♑49 42	16♎43.7	24♏37.4	22♏03.6	15♎07.3	15♎52.0	13♎11.9	5♎42.9	5♓49.4	15♌55.7	9♋35.0
2 F	16 43 08	9 47 20	8♑07 05	14 20 40	16R 33.7	26 08.6	23 18.9	15 43.5	16 15.9	13 21.6	5 47.5	5 50.2	15R 55.3	9R 34.0
3 Sa	16 47 05	10 48 13	20 30 37	26 37 08	16 24.5	27 40.3	24 34.3	16 19.6	16 39.7	13 31.2	5 52.0	5 51.1	15 54.8	9 33.0
4 Su	16 51 01	11 49 07	2♒40 33	8♒41 14	16 17.1	29 12.2	25 49.6	16 55.7	17 03.4	13 40.7	5 56.4	5 52.1	15 54.3	9 31.9
5 M	16 54 58	12 50 02	14 39 37	20 36 12	16 11.9	0♐44.3	27 04.9	17 31.8	17 27.0	13 50.1	6 00.7	5 53.1	15 53.7	9 30.8
6 Tu	16 58 55	13 50 57	26 31 31	2♓26 12	16 09.1	2 16.7	28 20.2	18 07.8	17 50.5	13 59.4	6 05.0	5 54.1	15 53.2	9 29.7
7 W	17 02 51	14 51 54	8♓20 50	14 16 06	16D 08.2	3 49.2	29 35.6	18 43.8	18 13.8	14 08.5	6 09.1	5 55.2	15 52.6	9 28.6
8 Th	17 06 48	15 52 51	20 12 40	26 11 13	16 08.7	5 21.8	0♐50.9	19 19.8	18 37.1	14 17.6	6 13.2	5 56.4	15 51.9	9 27.5
9 F	17 10 44	16 53 48	2♈12 25	8♈16 56	16R 09.5	6 54.6	2 06.3	19 55.7	19 00.3	14 26.5	6 17.2	5 57.5	15 51.2	9 26.4
10 Sa	17 14 41	17 54 47	14 25 25	20 38 27	16 09.6	8 27.4	3 21.7	20 31.6	19 23.3	14 35.3	6 21.1	5 58.8	15 50.5	9 25.3
11 Su	17 18 37	18 55 45	26 56 34	3♉20 13	16 08.1	10 00.4	4 37.0	21 07.4	19 46.2	14 44.0	6 24.9	6 00.1	15 49.8	9 24.1
12 M	17 22 34	19 56 45	9♉49 48	16 25 31	16 04.2	11 33.5	5 52.4	21 43.2	20 09.0	14 52.6	6 28.6	6 01.4	15 49.0	9 23.0
13 Tu	17 26 30	20 57 45	23 07 31	29 55 45	15 57.7	13 06.7	7 07.8	22 19.0	20 31.6	15 01.1	6 32.3	6 02.8	15 48.3	9 21.8
14 W	17 30 27	21 58 46	6♊50 03	13♊50 04	15 48.8	14 40.0	8 23.2	22 54.7	20 54.2	15 09.4	6 35.8	6 04.2	15 47.4	9 20.7
15 Th	17 34 24	22 59 48	20 55 16	28 05 01	15 38.1	16 13.4	9 38.6	23 30.4	21 16.6	15 17.6	6 39.3	6 05.7	15 46.6	9 19.5
16 F	17 38 20	24 00 50	5♋18 32	12♋34 55	15 27.0	17 46.9	10 54.0	24 06.1	21 38.9	15 25.7	6 42.6	6 07.2	15 45.7	9 18.3
17 Sa	17 42 17	25 01 53	19 53 15	27 12 35	15 16.5	19 20.6	12 09.4	24 41.7	22 01.0	15 33.7	6 45.9	6 08.8	15 44.8	9 17.1
18 Su	17 46 13	26 02 57	4♌31 58	11♌50 33	15 07.9	20 54.4	13 24.8	25 17.2	22 23.0	15 41.6	6 49.1	6 10.4	15 43.9	9 15.9
19 M	17 50 10	27 04 01	19 07 33	26 22 20	15 01.9	22 28.3	14 40.3	25 52.8	22 44.9	15 49.3	6 52.1	6 12.1	15 42.9	9 14.7
20 Tu	17 54 06	28 05 06	3♍34 21	10♍43 14	14 58.6	24 02.4	15 55.7	26 28.3	23 06.7	15 56.9	6 55.1	6 13.8	15 41.9	9 13.5
21 W	17 58 03	29 06 13	17 48 43	24 50 39	14D 57.5	25 36.7	17 11.1	27 03.7	23 28.3	16 04.3	6 58.0	6 15.6	15 40.9	9 12.3
22 Th	18 01 59	0♑07 19	1♎49 01	8♎43 49	14R 57.5	27 11.2	18 26.6	27 39.1	23 49.7	16 11.6	7 00.8	6 17.4	15 39.8	9 11.1
23 F	18 05 56	1 08 27	15 35 11	22 23 13	14 57.4	28 45.9	19 42.0	28 14.5	24 11.0	16 18.8	7 03.4	6 19.2	15 38.7	9 09.9
24 Sa	18 09 53	2 09 35	29 08 05	5♏49 54	14 55.9	0♑20.8	20 57.5	28 49.8	24 32.2	16 25.8	7 06.0	6 21.1	15 37.6	9 08.7
25 Su	18 13 49	3 10 44	12♏28 50	19 04 58	14 51.8	1 56.0	22 12.9	29 25.1	24 53.2	16 32.7	7 08.5	6 23.0	15 36.5	9 07.4
26 M	18 17 46	4 11 54	25 38 23	2♐09 08	14 44.7	3 31.4	23 28.4	0♏00.3	25 14.0	16 39.5	7 10.9	6 25.0	15 35.4	9 06.2
27 Tu	18 21 42	5 13 03	8♐37 14	15 02 39	14 34.5	5 07.0	24 43.9	0 35.5	25 34.7	16 46.1	7 13.1	6 27.0	15 34.2	9 05.0
28 W	18 25 39	6 14 14	21 25 23	27 45 21	14 21.7	6 43.0	25 59.4	1 10.6	25 55.2	16 52.5	7 15.3	6 29.1	15 33.0	9 03.7
29 Th	18 29 35	7 15 24	4♑02 33	10♑16 56	14 07.4	8 19.2	27 14.8	1 45.6	26 15.5	16 58.8	7 17.4	6 31.2	15 31.7	9 02.5
30 F	18 33 32	8 16 35	16 28 30	22 37 17	13 52.8	9 55.8	28 30.3	2 20.6	26 35.7	17 05.0	7 19.3	6 33.3	15 30.5	9 01.3
31 Sa	18 37 29	9 17 45	28 43 20	4♒46 48	13 39.1	11 32.7	29 45.8	2 55.6	26 55.7	17 11.0	7 21.2	6 35.5	15 29.2	9 00.0

Astro Data Dy Hr Mn	Planet Ingress Dy Hr Mn	Last Aspect Dy Hr Mn	☽ Ingress Dy Hr Mn	Last Aspect Dy Hr Mn	☽ Ingress Dy Hr Mn	☽ Phases & Eclipses Dy Hr Mn
☿ D 9 11:17	♂ ♎ 6 16:13	1 10:21 ♂ ⚹	♐ 1 16:08	30 6:13 ♆ △	♑ 1 8:32	7 15:54 ☽ 14♒43
☽0N 11 1:46	♀ ♏ 13 21:11	3 20:19 ♂ □	♑ 3 23:38	3 14:23 ♆ ⚹	♒ 3 18:41	15 13:39 ○ 22♉40
♂0S 11 15:54	☉ ♐ 22 20:05	6 9:58 ♂ △	♒ 6 10:17	6 2:41 ♀ □	♓ 6 7:03	22 11:41 ☾ 29♌39
♃□♇ 12 14:32		8 8:55 ♀ △	♓ 8 22:51	7 13:19 ☉ □	♈ 8 19:37	29 13:25 ● 6♐48
♅ D 15 12:50	☿ ♐ 5 0:28	10 10:03 ☉ △	♈ 11 10:52	10 11:46 ♂ ☍	♉ 11 5:46	
♆ R 18 20:57	♀ ♐ 7 19:47	13 20:14 ♀ ☍	♉ 13 20:19	12 10:54 ♅ □	♊ 13 12:07	7 13:19 ☽ 14♓55
♄0S 23 1:06	☉ ♑ 22 9:07	15 13:39 ☉ ☍	♊ 16 2:41	15 4:01 ♂ △	♋ 15 15:12	15 2:50 ○ 22♊36
☽0S 24 7:56	☿ ♑ 24 6:45	17 6:35 ♆ ⚹	♋ 18 6:41	17 7:42 ♂ □	♌ 17 16:34	21 19:54 ☾ 29♍26
	♂ ♏ 26 11:48	20 5:03 ☉ △	♌ 20 9:32	19 13:15 ☉ △	♍ 19 18:02	29 5:39 ● 6♑59
♄⊼♅ 3 6:29	♀ ♑ 31 16:31	22 11:41 ☉ □	♍ 22 12:17	21 19:54 ☉ □	♎ 21 20:52	
☽0N 8 11:27		23 9:59 ☿ ⚹	♎ 24 15:31	24 0:51 ☿ ⚹	♏ 24 1:33	
⚳0S 18 12:59		25 19:07 ♆ ⚹	♏ 26 19:37	25 5:41 ♆ □	♐ 26 8:02	
♃⚹♆ 18 18:17		28 6:39 ☿ ☌	♐ 29 1:03	28 8:16 ♀ ☌	♑ 28 16:16	
☽0S 21 14:25				30 1:06 ♃ □	♒ 31 2:31	

Astro Data

1 November 1921
Julian Day # 7975
SVP 6♓21'01"
GC 25♐44.9 ⚳ 19♍29.6
Eris 28♓43.7R ⚵ 10♑41.2
⚷ 10♈31.5R ⚶ 19♉40.6R
☽ Mean ☊ 16♎52.6

1 December 1921
Julian Day # 8005
SVP 6♓20'57"
GC 25♐44.9 ⚳ 2♎04.6
Eris 28♓32.8R ⚵ 20♑56.7
⚷ 9♈38.7R ⚶ 12♉23.4R
☽ Mean ☊ 15♎17.3

LONGITUDE — January 1922

Day	Sid.Time	☉	0 hr ☽	Noon ☽	True ☊	☿	♀	♂	⚳	♃	♄	♅	♆	♇
1 Su	18 41 25	10♑18 56	10♒47 50	16♒46 42	13♎27.4	13♑09.9	1♑01.2	3♏30.5	27♎15.5	17♎16.8	7♎23.0	6♓37.7	15♌27.9	8♋58.8
2 M	18 45 22	11 20 06	22 43 40	28 39 07	13R 18.5	14 47.4	2 16.7	4 05.3	27 35.2	17 22.5	7 24.6	6 40.0	15R 26.6	8R 57.6
3 Tu	18 49 18	12 21 17	4♓33 28	10♓27 12	13 12.6	16 25.2	3 32.2	4 40.1	27 54.6	17 28.0	7 26.1	6 42.3	15 25.3	8 56.3
4 W	18 53 15	13 22 27	16 20 51	22 15 00	13 09.4	18 03.4	4 47.6	5 14.8	28 13.9	17 33.4	7 27.6	6 44.6	15 23.9	8 55.1
5 Th	18 57 11	14 23 36	28 10 16	4♈07 19	13 08.3	19 41.9	6 03.1	5 49.4	28 33.0	17 38.6	7 28.9	6 47.0	15 22.5	8 53.9
6 F	19 01 08	15 24 45	10♈06 50	16 09 32	13 08.1	21 20.8	7 18.6	6 24.0	28 51.9	17 43.7	7 30.1	6 49.4	15 21.1	8 52.6
7 Sa	19 05 04	16 25 54	22 16 06	28 27 14	13 07.8	23 00.0	8 34.0	6 58.5	29 10.6	17 48.5	7 31.2	6 51.9	15 19.7	8 51.4
8 Su	19 09 01	17 27 03	4♉43 36	11♉05 49	13 06.1	24 39.4	9 49.5	7 33.0	29 29.1	17 53.2	7 32.2	6 54.4	15 18.3	8 50.2
9 M	19 12 58	18 28 11	17 34 26	24 09 53	13 02.2	26 19.1	11 04.9	8 07.4	29 47.4	17 57.8	7 33.1	6 56.9	15 16.8	8 49.0
10 Tu	19 16 54	19 29 18	0♊52 30	7♊42 28	12 55.5	27 59.1	12 20.3	8 41.8	0♏05.4	18 02.2	7 33.9	6 59.4	15 15.4	8 47.7
11 W	19 20 51	20 30 25	14 39 46	21 44 12	12 46.3	29 39.3	13 35.8	9 16.0	0 23.3	18 06.4	7 34.6	7 02.0	15 13.9	8 46.5
12 Th	19 24 47	21 31 32	28 55 21	6♋12 37	12 35.1	1♒19.5	14 51.2	9 50.2	0 41.0	18 10.4	7 35.1	7 04.7	15 12.4	8 45.3
13 F	19 28 44	22 32 38	13♋35 09	21 01 56	12 23.1	2 59.9	16 06.6	10 24.4	0 58.5	18 14.3	7 35.6	7 07.3	15 10.9	8 44.1
14 Sa	19 32 40	23 33 43	28 31 50	6♌03 36	12 11.8	4 40.2	17 22.1	10 58.5	1 15.7	18 18.0	7 36.0	7 10.0	15 09.3	8 42.9
15 Su	19 36 37	24 34 49	13♌35 56	21 07 37	12 02.3	6 20.4	18 37.5	11 32.5	1 32.7	18 21.5	7 36.2	7 12.7	15 07.8	8 41.7
16 M	19 40 33	25 35 53	28 37 26	6♍04 23	11 55.5	8 00.4	19 52.9	12 06.4	1 49.5	18 24.9	7R 36.3	7 15.5	15 06.2	8 40.6
17 Tu	19 44 30	26 36 58	13♍27 33	20 46 15	11 51.5	9 39.9	21 08.3	12 40.3	2 06.1	18 28.1	7 36.4	7 18.3	15 04.7	8 39.4
18 W	19 48 27	27 38 02	27 59 59	5♎08 24	11D 50.1	11 18.8	22 23.7	13 14.1	2 22.4	18 31.1	7 36.3	7 21.1	15 03.1	8 38.2
19 Th	19 52 23	28 39 06	12♎11 23	19 08 53	11R 50.0	12 57.0	23 39.1	13 47.8	2 38.5	18 33.9	7 36.1	7 23.9	15 01.5	8 37.1
20 F	19 56 20	29 40 09	26 01 01	2♏48 00	11 50.1	14 34.0	24 54.6	14 21.4	2 54.4	18 36.5	7 35.8	7 26.8	14 59.9	8 35.9
21 Sa	20 00 16	0♒41 13	9♏30 05	16 07 34	11 49.1	16 09.7	26 10.0	14 55.0	3 10.0	18 38.9	7 35.4	7 29.7	14 58.3	8 34.8
22 Su	20 04 13	1 42 16	22 40 46	29 10 02	11 45.9	17 43.7	27 25.4	15 28.5	3 25.3	18 41.2	7 34.9	7 32.6	14 56.6	8 33.7
23 M	20 08 09	2 43 18	5♐35 41	11♐57 59	11 40.0	19 15.5	28 40.8	16 01.9	3 40.4	18 43.3	7 34.3	7 35.6	14 55.0	8 32.5
24 Tu	20 12 06	3 44 20	18 17 14	24 33 39	11 31.2	20 44.7	29 56.2	16 35.2	3 55.2	18 45.2	7 33.5	7 38.5	14 53.4	8 31.4
25 W	20 16 02	4 45 21	0♑47 27	6♑58 47	11 20.0	22 10.9	1♒11.6	17 08.4	4 09.8	18 46.9	7 32.7	7 41.6	14 51.7	8 30.3
26 Th	20 19 59	5 46 22	13 07 50	19 14 42	11 07.4	23 33.3	2 26.9	17 41.6	4 24.1	18 48.4	7 31.7	7 44.6	14 50.0	8 29.2
27 F	20 23 56	6 47 21	25 19 30	1♒22 22	10 54.4	24 51.4	3 42.3	18 14.6	4 38.1	18 49.7	7 30.7	7 47.6	14 48.4	8 28.2
28 Sa	20 27 52	7 48 20	7♒23 24	13 22 44	10 42.2	26 04.4	4 57.7	18 47.6	4 51.9	18 50.9	7 29.5	7 50.7	14 46.7	8 27.1
29 Su	20 31 49	8 49 18	19 20 31	25 16 56	10 31.7	27 11.7	6 13.1	19 20.4	5 05.4	18 51.8	7 28.3	7 53.8	14 45.0	8 26.0
30 M	20 35 45	9 50 15	1♓12 11	7♓06 32	10 23.8	28 12.3	7 28.4	19 53.2	5 18.5	18 52.6	7 26.9	7 56.9	14 43.4	8 25.0
31 Tu	20 39 42	10 51 10	13 00 18	18 53 48	10 18.5	29 05.6	8 43.8	20 25.8	5 31.4	18 53.2	7 25.4	8 00.1	14 41.7	8 24.0

LONGITUDE — February 1922

Day	Sid.Time	☉	0 hr ☽	Noon ☽	True ☊	☿	♀	♂	⚳	♃	♄	♅	♆	♇
1 W	20 43 38	11♒52 04	24♓47 28	0♈41 42	10♎15.9	29♒50.6	9♒59.1	20♏58.4	5♏44.0	18♎53.5	7♎23.9	8♓03.2	14♌40.0	8♋23.0
2 Th	20 47 35	12 52 57	6♈37 02	12 33 59	10D 15.4	0♓26.6	11 14.4	21 30.8	5 56.3	18R 53.7	7R 22.2	8 06.4	14R 38.3	8R 22.0
3 F	20 51 31	13 53 49	18 33 08	24 35 05	10 16.1	0 52.9	12 29.7	22 03.2	6 08.3	18 53.7	7 20.4	8 09.6	14 36.6	8 21.0
4 Sa	20 55 28	14 54 39	0♉40 29	6♉49 59	10R 17.1	1R 08.9	13 45.0	22 35.4	6 20.0	18 53.5	7 18.5	8 12.8	14 34.9	8 20.0
5 Su	20 59 25	15 55 28	13 04 13	19 23 50	10 17.3	1 14.2	15 00.3	23 07.6	6 31.3	18 53.1	7 16.6	8 16.1	14 33.2	8 19.1
6 M	21 03 21	16 56 16	25 49 25	2♊21 32	10 16.0	1 08.5	16 15.6	23 39.6	6 42.4	18 52.6	7 14.5	8 19.3	14 31.5	8 18.1
7 Tu	21 07 18	17 57 02	9♊00 37	15 47 01	10 12.6	0 51.8	17 30.9	24 11.5	6 53.1	18 51.8	7 12.3	8 22.6	14 29.9	8 17.2
8 W	21 11 14	18 57 46	22 40 58	29 42 28	10 07.1	0 24.5	18 46.1	24 43.3	7 03.5	18 50.8	7 10.1	8 25.9	14 28.2	8 16.3
9 Th	21 15 11	19 58 29	6♋51 23	14♋07 20	10 00.0	29♒47.2	20 01.3	25 15.0	7 13.6	18 49.7	7 07.7	8 29.2	14 26.5	8 15.4
10 F	21 19 07	20 59 11	21 29 43	28 57 42	9 52.1	29 00.6	21 16.6	25 46.5	7 23.4	18 48.4	7 05.3	8 32.5	14 24.8	8 14.5
11 Sa	21 23 04	21 59 50	6♌30 17	14♌06 16	9 44.5	28 06.2	22 31.8	26 18.0	7 32.8	18 46.9	7 02.7	8 35.8	14 23.2	8 13.7
12 Su	21 27 00	23 00 29	21 44 19	29 23 05	9 38.1	27 05.5	23 47.0	26 49.3	7 41.9	18 45.2	7 00.1	8 39.2	14 21.5	8 12.9
13 M	21 30 57	24 01 06	7♍01 09	14♍37 14	9 33.6	26 00.0	25 02.2	27 20.5	7 50.6	18 43.3	6 57.4	8 42.5	14 19.8	8 12.0
14 Tu	21 34 54	25 01 42	22 10 07	29 38 45	9D 31.3	24 51.7	26 17.3	27 51.6	7 59.0	18 41.2	6 54.6	8 45.9	14 18.2	8 11.2
15 W	21 38 50	26 02 16	7♎02 17	14♎20 02	9 31.0	23 42.4	27 32.5	28 22.6	8 07.0	18 38.9	6 51.7	8 49.3	14 16.5	8 10.4
16 Th	21 42 47	27 02 49	21 31 35	28 36 39	9 32.0	22 33.9	28 47.7	28 53.4	8 14.7	18 36.5	6 48.7	8 52.7	14 14.9	8 09.7
17 F	21 46 43	28 03 21	5♏35 08	12♏27 07	9 33.4	21 28.0	0♓02.8	29 24.1	8 22.0	18 33.8	6 45.6	8 56.0	14 13.2	8 08.9
18 Sa	21 50 40	29 03 52	19 12 46	25 52 21	9R 34.3	20 26.0	1 17.9	29 54.6	8 28.9	18 31.0	6 42.5	8 59.4	14 11.6	8 08.2
19 Su	21 54 36	0♓04 22	2♐26 15	8♐54 50	9 34.0	19 29.1	2 33.1	0♐25.0	8 35.5	18 28.0	6 39.3	9 02.9	14 10.0	8 07.5
20 M	21 58 33	1 04 50	15 18 33	21 37 50	9 31.9	18 38.3	3 48.2	0 55.3	8 41.7	18 24.9	6 36.0	9 06.3	14 08.4	8 06.8
21 Tu	22 02 29	2 05 17	27 53 07	4♑04 50	9 28.0	17 54.3	5 03.3	1 25.4	8 47.5	18 21.5	6 32.6	9 09.7	14 06.8	8 06.1
22 W	22 06 26	3 05 42	10♑13 24	16 19 12	9 22.7	17 17.4	6 18.3	1 55.3	8 52.9	18 18.0	6 29.1	9 13.1	14 05.2	8 05.5
23 Th	22 10 22	4 06 06	22 22 36	28 23 54	9 16.3	16 47.8	7 33.4	2 25.1	8 57.9	18 14.3	6 25.6	9 16.6	14 03.6	8 04.9
24 F	22 14 19	5 06 29	4♒23 27	10♒21 30	9 09.6	16 25.7	8 48.5	2 54.7	9 02.6	18 10.4	6 22.0	9 20.0	14 02.1	8 04.3
25 Sa	22 18 16	6 06 50	16 18 19	22 14 09	9 03.3	16 10.9	10 03.5	3 24.2	9 06.8	18 06.4	6 18.3	9 23.4	14 00.5	8 03.7
26 Su	22 22 12	7 07 09	28 09 13	4♓03 46	8 58.0	16D 03.2	11 18.5	3 53.5	9 10.6	18 02.2	6 14.6	9 26.9	13 59.0	8 03.1
27 M	22 26 09	8 07 27	9♓58 00	15 52 10	8 54.2	16 02.3	12 33.5	4 22.6	9 14.1	17 57.8	6 10.8	9 30.3	13 57.5	8 02.6
28 Tu	22 30 05	9 07 42	21 46 30	27 41 16	8D 52.0	16 07.9	13 48.5	4 51.5	9 17.1	17 53.2	6 06.9	9 33.8	13 56.0	8 02.0

Astro Data	Dy Hr Mn
☽ 0N	4 21:01
♄ R	17 5:56
☽ 0S	17 22:21
♄⚻♅	23 3:16
☽ 0N	1 5:14
♃ R	2 23:30
☿ R	5 11:35
♅△♇	6 5:03
☽ 0S	14 8:35
☿ D	27 3:11
☽ 0N	28 11:55

Planet Ingress	Dy Hr Mn
⚳ ♏	10 4:45
☿ ♒	11 16:58
☉ ♒	20 19:48
♀ ♒	24 13:13
☿ ♓	1 17:43
☿ ♒R	9 4:25
♀ ♓	17 11:06
♂ ♐	18 16:15
☉ ♓	19 10:16

Last Aspect Dy Hr Mn		☽ Ingress Dy Hr Mn
1 13:01	♃ △	♓ 2 14:44
4 2:06	☿ ⚹	♈ 5 3:42
6 23:47	☿ □	♉ 7 14:58
9 16:25	☿ △	♊ 9 22:27
11 5:50	♃ △	♋ 12 1:47
13 14:36	☉ ☍	♌ 14 2:21
15 7:34	♃ ⚹	♍ 16 2:13
17 22:26	☉ △	♎ 18 3:21
20 6:00	☉ □	♏ 20 7:02
22 8:25	♀ ⚹	♐ 22 13:33
24 3:43	☿ ⚹	♑ 24 22:28
26 11:08	♃ □	♒ 27 9:16
29 16:15	☿ ☌	♓ 29 21:34

Last Aspect Dy Hr Mn		☽ Ingress Dy Hr Mn
31 15:17	♂ △	♈ 1 10:35
3 0:41	♃ ☍	♉ 3 22:41
5 19:17	♂ ☍	♊ 6 7:42
7 17:23	♃ △	♋ 8 12:30
10 6:43	♂ △	♌ 10 13:39
12 8:38	☿ ☍	♍ 12 12:58
14 9:01	♂ ⚹	♎ 14 12:34
16 12:21	♀ △	♏ 16 14:23
18 18:18	☉ □	♐ 18 19:31
20 6:39	☿ ⚹	♑ 21 4:05
22 15:54	♃ □	♒ 23 15:12
25 3:41	♃ △	♓ 26 3:45
27 4:28	♀ ☌	♈ 28 16:41

☽ Phases & Eclipses Dy Hr Mn	
6 10:23	☽ 15♈21
13 14:36	○ 22♋39
20 6:00	☾ 29♎25
27 23:48	● 7♒17
5 4:52	☽ 15♉37
12 1:17	○ 22♌33
18 18:18	☾ 29♏20
26 18:47	● 7♓24

Astro Data

1 January 1922
Julian Day # 8036
SVP 6♓20'51"
GC 25♐45.0 ⚴ 11♎55.5
Eris 28♓32.6 ⚵ 3♒14.4
⚷ 9♈31.1 ⚶ 9♉53.7
☽ Mean ☊ 13♎38.8

1 February 1922
Julian Day # 8067
SVP 6♓20'47"
GC 25♐45.1 ⚴ 16♎37.7
Eris 28♓44.1 ⚵ 16♒38.8
⚷ 10♈15.0 ⚶ 13♉56.1
☽ Mean ☊ 12♎00.3

March 1922 — LONGITUDE

Day	Sid.Time	☉	0 hr ☽	Noon ☽	True ☊	☿	♀	♂	⚳	♃	♄	♅	♆	♇
1 W	22 34 02	10♓07 56	3♈36 47	9♈33 19	8♎51.3	16♒19.6	15♓03.5	5♐20.3	9♏19.7	17♎48.5	6♎02.9	9♓37.2	13♌54.5	8♋01.5
2 Th	22 37 58	11 08 08	15 31 15	21 30 55	8 52.0	16 37.1	16 18.5	5 48.9	9 21.9	17R43.7	5R59.0	9 40.7	13R53.0	8R01.1
3 F	22 41 55	12 08 18	27 32 46	3♉37 12	8 53.5	17 00.0	17 33.4	6 17.2	9 23.7	17 38.7	5 54.9	9 44.1	13 51.6	8 00.6
4 Sa	22 45 51	13 08 26	9♉44 41	15 55 43	8 55.2	17 28.0	18 48.3	6 45.4	9 25.0	17 33.5	5 50.8	9 47.5	13 50.1	8 00.2
5 Su	22 49 48	14 08 32	22 10 46	28 30 21	8 56.7	18 00.7	20 03.2	7 13.4	9 26.0	17 28.2	5 46.6	9 51.0	13 48.7	7 59.7
6 M	22 53 45	15 08 36	4♊54 58	11♊25 05	8R57.5	18 37.8	21 18.1	7 41.2	9R26.5	17 22.8	5 42.4	9 54.4	13 47.3	7 59.4
7 Tu	22 57 41	16 08 37	18 01 06	24 43 23	8 57.3	19 19.0	22 32.9	8 08.8	9 26.6	17 17.2	5 38.2	9 57.8	13 45.9	7 59.0
8 W	23 01 38	17 08 37	1♋32 14	8♋27 47	8 56.1	20 04.0	23 47.8	8 36.2	9 26.3	17 11.4	5 33.9	10 01.3	13 44.6	7 58.6
9 Th	23 05 34	18 08 34	15 30 06	22 39 01	8 54.0	20 52.5	25 02.6	9 03.3	9 25.6	17 05.6	5 29.6	10 04.7	13 43.3	7 58.3
10 F	23 09 31	19 08 29	29 54 15	7♌15 20	8 51.4	21 44.4	26 17.4	9 30.3	9 24.5	16 59.6	5 25.2	10 08.1	13 41.9	7 58.0
11 Sa	23 13 27	20 08 22	14♌41 33	22 12 05	8 48.8	22 39.3	27 32.1	9 57.0	9 22.9	16 53.5	5 20.8	10 11.5	13 40.6	7 57.8
12 Su	23 17 24	21 08 13	29 45 53	7♍21 51	8 46.7	23 37.2	28 46.9	10 23.5	9 20.9	16 47.3	5 16.3	10 14.9	13 39.4	7 57.5
13 M	23 21 20	22 08 02	14♍58 44	22 35 16	8 45.3	24 37.8	0♈01.6	10 49.8	9 18.5	16 40.9	5 11.8	10 18.3	13 38.1	7 57.3
14 Tu	23 25 17	23 07 48	0♎10 12	7♎42 22	8D44.9	25 41.0	1 16.3	11 15.9	9 15.7	16 34.5	5 07.3	10 21.7	13 36.9	7 57.1
15 W	23 29 14	24 07 33	15 10 41	22 34 13	8 45.2	26 46.5	2 30.9	11 41.7	9 12.5	16 27.9	5 02.7	10 25.1	13 35.7	7 56.9
16 Th	23 33 10	25 07 16	29 52 11	7♏04 01	8 46.0	27 54.4	3 45.6	12 07.2	9 08.8	16 21.2	4 58.2	10 28.4	13 34.5	7 56.7
17 F	23 37 07	26 06 58	14♏09 17	21 07 47	8 47.1	29 04.5	5 00.2	12 32.5	9 04.7	16 14.4	4 53.6	10 31.8	13 33.3	7 56.6
18 Sa	23 41 03	27 06 37	27 59 26	4♐44 18	8 48.1	0♓16.6	6 14.8	12 57.6	9 00.2	16 07.6	4 48.9	10 35.1	13 32.2	7 56.5
19 Su	23 45 00	28 06 15	11♐22 36	17 54 38	8R48.8	1 30.7	7 29.4	13 22.4	8 55.3	16 00.6	4 44.3	10 38.5	13 31.1	7 56.4
20 M	23 48 56	29 05 52	24 20 47	0♑41 30	8 48.9	2 46.7	8 44.0	13 46.9	8 50.0	15 53.6	4 39.7	10 41.8	13 30.0	7 56.3
21 Tu	23 52 53	0♈05 26	6♑57 15	13 08 34	8 48.7	4 04.6	9 58.5	14 11.1	8 44.3	15 46.4	4 35.0	10 45.1	13 28.9	7 56.3
22 W	23 56 49	1 04 59	19 15 59	25 20 00	8 48.0	5 24.1	11 13.1	14 35.1	8 38.2	15 39.2	4 30.3	10 48.4	13 27.9	7D56.3
23 Th	0 00 46	2 04 30	1♒21 10	7♒20 00	8 47.2	6 45.4	12 27.6	14 58.7	8 31.7	15 32.0	4 25.6	10 51.6	13 26.9	7 56.3
24 F	0 04 43	3 03 59	13 16 57	19 12 30	8 46.3	8 08.3	13 42.1	15 22.0	8 24.7	15 24.6	4 20.9	10 54.9	13 25.9	7 56.3
25 Sa	0 08 39	4 03 26	25 07 05	1♓01 06	8 45.6	9 32.8	14 56.5	15 45.1	8 17.4	15 17.2	4 16.2	10 58.1	13 25.0	7 56.3
26 Su	0 12 36	5 02 51	6♓54 56	12 48 57	8 45.1	10 58.9	16 11.0	16 07.8	8 09.8	15 09.7	4 11.5	11 01.4	13 24.0	7 56.4
27 M	0 16 32	6 02 14	18 43 27	24 38 45	8 44.8	12 26.5	17 25.4	16 30.2	8 01.7	15 02.2	4 06.8	11 04.6	13 23.1	7 56.5
28 Tu	0 20 29	7 01 36	0♈35 07	6♈32 49	8D44.7	13 55.6	18 39.8	16 52.2	7 53.3	14 54.6	4 02.1	11 07.8	13 22.3	7 56.6
29 W	0 24 25	8 00 55	12 32 06	18 33 13	8R44.7	15 26.2	19 54.1	17 13.9	7 44.5	14 47.0	3 57.4	11 10.9	13 21.4	7 56.8
30 Th	0 28 22	9 00 12	24 36 23	0♉41 50	8 44.7	16 58.3	21 08.5	17 35.3	7 35.4	14 39.4	3 52.7	11 14.1	13 20.6	7 57.0
31 F	0 32 18	9 59 27	6♉49 49	13 00 34	8 44.7	18 31.8	22 22.8	17 56.2	7 25.9	14 31.7	3 48.1	11 17.2	13 19.8	7 57.1

April 1922 — LONGITUDE

Day	Sid.Time	☉	0 hr ☽	Noon ☽	True ☊	☿	♀	♂	⚳	♃	♄	♅	♆	♇
1 Sa	0 36 15	10♈58 40	19♉14 20	25♉31 20	8♎44.4	20♓06.8	23♈37.1	18♐16.9	7♏16.1	14♎24.1	3♎43.4	11♓20.3	13♌19.1	7♋57.4
2 Su	0 40 11	11 57 51	1♊51 52	8♊16 11	8R44.1	21 43.3	24 51.4	18 37.1	7R06.0	14R16.4	3R38.8	11 23.4	13R18.4	7 57.6
3 M	0 44 08	12 56 59	14 44 31	21 17 09	8 43.8	23 21.1	26 05.6	18 57.0	6 55.6	14 08.6	3 34.2	11 26.5	13 17.7	7 57.9
4 Tu	0 48 05	13 56 06	27 54 19	4♋36 13	8D43.5	25 00.4	27 19.8	19 16.5	6 44.9	14 00.9	3 29.6	11 29.5	13 17.0	7 58.2
5 W	0 52 01	14 55 09	11♋23 01	18 14 52	8 43.4	26 41.2	28 34.0	19 35.6	6 33.9	13 53.2	3 25.0	11 32.5	13 16.4	7 58.5
6 Th	0 55 58	15 54 11	25 11 48	2♌13 47	8 43.7	28 23.4	29 48.1	19 54.3	6 22.6	13 45.5	3 20.5	11 35.5	13 15.8	7 58.8
7 F	0 59 54	16 53 10	9♌20 43	16 32 21	8 44.2	0♈07.1	1♉02.3	20 12.5	6 11.1	13 37.8	3 16.0	11 38.5	13 15.2	7 59.2
8 Sa	1 03 51	17 52 07	23 48 20	1♍08 10	8 45.0	1 52.3	2 16.3	20 30.4	5 59.4	13 30.1	3 11.5	11 41.4	13 14.7	7 59.6
9 Su	1 07 47	18 51 01	8♍31 16	15 56 53	8 45.7	3 38.9	3 30.4	20 47.8	5 47.4	13 22.4	3 07.1	11 44.3	13 14.2	8 00.0
10 M	1 11 44	19 49 54	23 24 12	0♎52 17	8R46.2	5 27.0	4 44.4	21 04.8	5 35.2	13 14.8	3 02.7	11 47.2	13 13.7	8 00.4
11 Tu	1 15 40	20 48 44	8♎20 10	15 46 50	8 46.2	7 16.7	5 58.4	21 21.4	5 22.8	13 07.2	2 58.3	11 50.1	13 13.2	8 00.8
12 W	1 19 37	21 47 32	23 11 18	0♏32 37	8 45.6	9 07.8	7 12.4	21 37.4	5 10.2	12 59.6	2 54.0	11 52.9	13 12.8	8 01.3
13 Th	1 23 34	22 46 18	7♏49 54	15 02 23	8 44.3	11 00.5	8 26.3	21 53.1	4 57.4	12 52.1	2 49.7	11 55.7	13 12.4	8 01.8
14 F	1 27 30	23 45 02	22 09 27	29 10 36	8 42.4	12 54.7	9 40.2	22 08.2	4 44.5	12 44.6	2 45.5	11 58.5	13 12.1	8 02.3
15 Sa	1 31 27	24 43 45	6♐05 30	12♐53 56	8 40.3	14 50.4	10 54.1	22 22.8	4 31.4	12 37.1	2 41.3	12 01.3	13 11.8	8 02.9
16 Su	1 35 23	25 42 26	19 35 53	26 11 27	8 38.3	16 47.6	12 08.0	22 37.0	4 18.2	12 29.8	2 37.2	12 04.0	13 11.5	8 03.4
17 M	1 39 20	26 41 05	2♑40 49	9♑04 20	8 36.7	18 46.3	13 21.8	22 50.6	4 04.9	12 22.5	2 33.1	12 06.7	13 11.3	8 04.0
18 Tu	1 43 16	27 39 43	15 22 23	21 35 26	8D35.9	20 46.5	14 35.6	23 03.7	3 51.5	12 15.2	2 29.0	12 09.3	13 11.0	8 04.6
19 W	1 47 13	28 38 19	27 44 02	3♒48 43	8 35.8	22 48.0	15 49.4	23 16.2	3 38.0	12 08.0	2 25.1	12 12.0	13 10.8	8 05.2
20 Th	1 51 09	29 36 53	9♒50 07	15 48 48	8 36.6	24 51.0	17 03.1	23 28.2	3 24.5	12 00.9	2 21.1	12 14.6	13 10.7	8 05.9
21 F	1 55 06	0♉35 25	21 45 23	27 40 28	8 38.0	26 55.2	18 16.9	23 39.6	3 10.9	11 53.9	2 17.3	12 17.1	13 10.6	8 06.5
22 Sa	1 59 03	1 33 56	3♓34 37	9♓28 25	8 39.7	29 00.5	19 30.6	23 50.5	2 57.2	11 47.0	2 13.5	12 19.7	13 10.5	8 07.2
23 Su	2 02 59	2 32 25	15 22 23	21 17 02	8 41.3	1♉06.9	20 44.2	24 00.7	2 43.6	11 40.1	2 09.8	12 22.2	13 10.4	8 07.9
24 M	2 06 56	3 30 52	27 12 49	3♈10 10	8R42.2	3 14.3	21 57.9	24 10.3	2 30.0	11 33.3	2 06.1	12 24.6	13D10.4	8 08.7
25 Tu	2 10 52	4 29 18	9♈09 29	15 11 05	8 42.2	5 22.3	23 11.5	24 19.4	2 16.4	11 26.7	2 02.5	12 27.1	13 10.4	8 09.4
26 W	2 14 49	5 27 42	21 15 16	27 22 16	8 40.8	7 30.9	24 25.1	24 27.8	2 02.8	11 20.1	1 59.0	12 29.4	13 10.5	8 10.2
27 Th	2 18 45	6 26 04	3♉32 19	9♉45 34	8 38.2	9 39.8	25 38.6	24 35.5	1 49.3	11 13.7	1 55.5	12 31.8	13 10.6	8 11.0
28 F	2 22 42	7 24 24	16 02 07	22 22 03	8 34.3	11 48.7	26 52.2	24 42.6	1 35.8	11 07.4	1 52.1	12 34.1	13 10.7	8 11.8
29 Sa	2 26 38	8 22 43	28 45 26	5♊12 16	8 29.6	13 57.4	28 05.7	24 49.1	1 22.5	11 01.2	1 48.8	12 36.4	13 10.8	8 12.6
30 Su	2 30 35	9 21 00	11♊42 33	18 16 15	8 24.6	16 05.6	29 19.1	24 54.9	1 09.3	10 55.1	1 45.6	12 38.7	13 11.0	8 13.5

Astro Data

	Dy Hr Mn
♄0N	2 8:52
⚳R	7 6:43
☽0S	13 20:00
♀0N	15 20:14
☉0N	21 9:48
♇D	22 18:40
☽0N	27 18:03
☿0N	10 6:05
☽0S	10 6:48
♃✱♆	10 15:42
♃⚻♅	19 2:17
☽0N	24 0:56
♆D	24 15:22

Planet Ingress

		Dy Hr Mn
♀	♈	13 11:30
☿	♓	18 6:32
☉	♈	21 9:49
♀	♉	6 15:50
☿	♈	7 10:22
☉	♉	20 21:29
☿	♉	22 23:19

Last Aspect / ☽ Ingress (March)

Last Aspect Dy Hr Mn		☽ Ingress Dy Hr Mn
2 4:29	♃ ☍	♉ 3 4:52
4 18:09	♀ ✱	♊ 5 14:49
7 7:44	♀ □	♋ 7 21:19
9 16:21	♀ △	♌ 10 0:09
11 12:46	☿ ☍	♍ 12 0:22
13 11:14	☉ ☍	♎ 13 23:44
15 19:28	☿ △	♏ 16 0:13
18 3:16	☿ □	♐ 18 3:33
20 8:43	☉ □	♑ 20 10:41
21 17:06	♃ □	♒ 22 21:18
24 4:23	♃ △	♓ 25 9:56
26 18:57	♂ □	♈ 27 22:49
29 14:59	♀ ☌	♉ 30 10:38

Last Aspect / ☽ Ingress (April)

Last Aspect Dy Hr Mn		☽ Ingress Dy Hr Mn
1 0:11	☿ ✱	♊ 1 20:29
3 21:38	♀ ✱	♋ 4 3:46
6 7:29	♀ □	♌ 6 8:13
7 18:12	♂ △	♍ 8 10:09
9 19:58	♂ □	♎ 10 10:36
11 21:12	♂ ✱	♏ 12 11:07
13 8:56	♆ □	♐ 14 13:25
16 11:03	☉ △	♑ 16 19:01
19 0:53	☉ □	♒ 19 4:28
21 10:08	☿ ✱	♓ 21 16:44
23 17:36	♂ □	♈ 24 5:37
26 6:15	♂ △	♉ 26 17:08
28 21:22	♀ ☌	♊ 29 2:19

☽ Phases & Eclipses

Dy Hr Mn	
6 19:21	☽ 15♊27
13 11:14	○ 22♍06
13 11:28	A 0.132
20 8:43	☾ 28♐58
28 13:03	● 7♈04
28 13:05:03	A 07'50"
5 5:45	☽ 14♋40
11 20:43	○ 21♎10
11 20:32	A 0.781
19 0:53	☾ 28♑11
27 5:03	● 6♉09

Astro Data

1 March 1922
Julian Day # 8095
SVP 6♓20'44"
GC 25♐45.1 ⚴ 14♎23.5R
Eris 29♓01.9 ⚵ 29♒21.1
⚷ 11♈30.1 ⚶ 21♉27.0
☽ Mean ☊ 10♎31.4

1 April 1922
Julian Day # 8126
SVP 6♓20'41"
GC 25♐45.2 ⚴ 5♎38.5R
Eris 29♓25.1 ⚵ 13♓46.6
⚷ 13♈15.1 ⚶ 2♊16.0
☽ Mean ☊ 8♎52.8

LONGITUDE — May 1922

Day	Sid.Time	☉	0 hr ☽	Noon ☽	True ☊	☿	♀	♂	⚳	♃	♄	♅	♆	♇
1 M	2 34 31	10♉19 14	24♊53 21	1♋33 47	8♎20.1	18♉13.0	0♊32.6	25♐00.0	0♏56.2	10♎49.1	1♎42.4	12♓40.9	13♌11.2	8♋14.3
2 Tu	2 38 28	11 17 27	8♋17 31	15 04 29	8R16.4	20 19.3	1 46.0	25 04.4	0R43.2	10R43.3	1R39.3	12 43.0	13 11.5	8 15.2
3 W	2 42 25	12 15 38	21 54 40	28 47 58	8 14.2	22 24.1	2 59.3	25 08.2	0 30.4	10 37.6	1 36.3	12 45.2	13 11.7	8 16.1
4 Th	2 46 21	13 13 46	5♌44 20	12♌43 41	8D13.4	24 27.3	4 12.7	25 11.2	0 17.8	10 32.0	1 33.4	12 47.3	13 12.1	8 17.1
5 F	2 50 18	14 11 53	19 45 55	26 50 53	8 14.0	26 28.4	5 26.0	25 13.6	0 05.3	10 26.5	1 30.6	12 49.3	13 12.4	8 18.0
6 Sa	2 54 14	15 09 58	3♍58 25	11♍08 16	8 15.3	28 27.4	6 39.2	25 15.2	29♎53.1	10 21.3	1 27.8	12 51.3	13 12.8	8 19.0
7 Su	2 58 11	16 08 00	18 20 08	25 33 40	8R16.5	0♊23.8	7 52.4	25R16.1	29 41.0	10 16.1	1 25.2	12 53.3	13 13.2	8 20.0
8 M	3 02 07	17 06 01	2♎48 23	10♎03 49	8 17.0	2 17.6	9 05.6	25 16.3	29 29.2	10 11.1	1 22.6	12 55.2	13 13.6	8 21.0
9 Tu	3 06 04	18 04 00	17 19 19	24 34 17	8 16.0	4 08.5	10 18.8	25 15.8	29 17.7	10 06.2	1 20.1	12 57.1	13 14.1	8 22.0
10 W	3 10 00	19 01 57	1♏48 01	8♏59 46	8 13.1	5 56.4	11 31.9	25 14.5	29 06.4	10 01.5	1 17.7	12 59.0	13 14.6	8 23.0
11 Th	3 13 57	19 59 53	16 08 52	23 14 36	8 08.3	7 41.1	12 45.0	25 12.5	28 55.3	9 57.0	1 15.4	13 00.8	13 15.1	8 24.1
12 F	3 17 54	20 57 47	0♐16 20	7♐13 31	8 02.0	9 22.6	13 58.0	25 09.7	28 44.5	9 52.6	1 13.2	13 02.6	13 15.7	8 25.1
13 Sa	3 21 50	21 55 40	14 05 41	20 52 29	7 54.9	11 00.8	15 11.1	25 06.2	28 34.0	9 48.4	1 11.1	13 04.3	13 16.3	8 26.2
14 Su	3 25 47	22 53 31	27 33 42	4♑09 13	7 47.7	12 35.5	16 24.0	25 01.9	28 23.8	9 44.3	1 09.0	13 06.0	13 17.0	8 27.3
15 M	3 29 43	23 51 21	10♑39 03	17 03 22	7 41.4	14 06.8	17 37.0	24 56.9	28 13.9	9 40.4	1 07.1	13 07.6	13 17.6	8 28.4
16 Tu	3 33 40	24 49 10	23 22 23	29 36 27	7 36.6	15 34.4	18 49.9	24 51.0	28 04.3	9 36.6	1 05.2	13 09.2	13 18.3	8 29.5
17 W	3 37 36	25 46 58	5♒46 01	11♒51 34	7 33.6	16 58.5	20 02.8	24 44.5	27 55.1	9 33.0	1 03.5	13 10.8	13 19.1	8 30.7
18 Th	3 41 33	26 44 44	17 53 39	23 52 52	7D32.4	18 18.9	21 15.7	24 37.2	27 46.1	9 29.6	1 01.8	13 12.3	13 19.8	8 31.8
19 F	3 45 29	27 42 30	29 49 51	5♓45 15	7 32.7	19 35.6	22 28.5	24 29.1	27 37.5	9 26.4	1 00.3	13 13.7	13 20.6	8 33.0
20 Sa	3 49 26	28 40 14	11♓39 43	17 33 55	7 33.7	20 48.6	23 41.3	24 20.3	27 29.2	9 23.3	0 58.8	13 15.2	13 21.4	8 34.2
21 Su	3 53 23	29 37 57	23 28 30	29 24 05	7R34.8	21 57.7	24 54.0	24 10.7	27 21.3	9 20.4	0 57.4	13 16.5	13 22.3	8 35.4
22 M	3 57 19	0♊35 39	5♈21 16	11♈20 37	7 35.0	23 03.0	26 06.7	24 00.4	27 13.8	9 17.7	0 56.2	13 17.9	13 23.2	8 36.6
23 Tu	4 01 16	1 33 20	17 22 39	23 27 49	7 33.6	24 04.3	27 19.4	23 49.4	27 06.5	9 15.1	0 55.0	13 19.1	13 24.1	8 37.9
24 W	4 05 12	2 31 00	29 36 33	5♉49 09	7 30.1	25 01.7	28 32.1	23 37.6	26 59.7	9 12.7	0 53.9	13 20.4	13 25.0	8 39.1
25 Th	4 09 09	3 28 38	12♉05 54	18 26 57	7 24.3	25 54.9	29 44.7	23 25.2	26 53.2	9 10.5	0 53.0	13 21.6	13 26.0	8 40.4
26 F	4 13 05	4 26 16	24 52 25	1♊22 17	7 16.3	26 44.1	0♋57.3	23 12.1	26 47.2	9 08.5	0 52.1	13 22.7	13 27.0	8 41.6
27 Sa	4 17 02	5 23 52	7♊56 28	14 34 50	7 07.0	27 29.0	2 09.8	22 58.4	26 41.5	9 06.6	0 51.3	13 23.8	13 28.1	8 42.9
28 Su	4 20 58	6 21 28	21 17 08	28 03 05	6 57.1	28 09.6	3 22.3	22 44.0	26 36.1	9 05.0	0 50.7	13 24.9	13 29.1	8 44.2
29 M	4 24 55	7 19 02	4♋52 21	11♋44 33	6 47.7	28 45.9	4 34.8	22 29.1	26 31.2	9 03.5	0 50.1	13 25.9	13 30.2	8 45.5
30 Tu	4 28 52	8 16 35	18 39 19	25 36 17	6 39.9	29 17.7	5 47.2	22 13.6	26 26.7	9 02.2	0 49.6	13 26.8	13 31.3	8 46.8
31 W	4 32 48	9 14 06	2♌35 04	9♌35 21	6 34.3	29 45.1	6 59.6	21 57.5	26 22.5	9 01.1	0 49.3	13 27.7	13 32.5	8 48.2

LONGITUDE — June 1922

Day	Sid.Time	☉	0 hr ☽	Noon ☽	True ☊	☿	♀	♂	⚳	♃	♄	♅	♆	♇
1 Th	4 36 45	10♊11 36	16♌36 50	23♌39 16	6♎31.1	0♋07.9	8♋12.0	21♐40.9	26♎18.8	9♎00.1	0♎49.0	13♓28.6	13♌33.7	8♋49.5
2 F	4 40 41	11 09 05	0♍42 26	7♍46 09	6D30.0	0 26.1	9 24.3	21R23.9	26R15.4	8R59.4	0R48.9	13 29.4	13 34.9	8 50.8
3 Sa	4 44 38	12 06 33	14 50 15	21 54 36	6 30.2	0 39.6	10 36.6	21 06.4	26 12.5	8 58.8	0D48.8	13 30.2	13 36.1	8 52.2
4 Su	4 48 34	13 03 59	28 59 04	6♎03 29	6R30.5	0 48.5	11 48.8	20 48.6	26 09.9	8 58.4	0 48.8	13 30.9	13 37.4	8 53.6
5 M	4 52 31	14 01 24	13♎07 42	20 11 29	6 29.8	0R52.8	13 00.9	20 30.3	26 07.7	8D58.2	0 49.0	13 31.6	13 38.7	8 54.9
6 Tu	4 56 27	14 58 47	27 14 34	4♏16 40	6 27.2	0 52.6	14 13.1	20 11.8	26 06.0	8 58.1	0 49.2	13 32.2	13 40.0	8 56.3
7 W	5 00 24	15 56 10	11♏17 26	18 16 27	6 21.9	0 47.9	15 25.2	19 53.0	26 04.6	8 58.3	0 49.6	13 32.8	13 41.3	8 57.7
8 Th	5 04 21	16 53 32	25 13 20	2♐07 36	6 14.0	0 38.8	16 37.2	19 33.9	26 03.6	8 58.6	0 50.1	13 33.3	13 42.7	8 59.1
9 F	5 08 17	17 50 53	8♐58 51	15 46 38	6 03.9	0 25.6	17 49.2	19 14.6	26 03.0	8 59.1	0 50.6	13 33.8	13 44.1	9 00.5
10 Sa	5 12 14	18 48 13	22 30 34	29 10 20	5 52.5	0 08.4	19 01.1	18 55.1	26D02.8	8 59.8	0 51.3	13 34.2	13 45.5	9 02.0
11 Su	5 16 10	19 45 33	5♑45 40	12♑16 24	5 40.9	29♊47.6	20 13.0	18 35.6	26 02.9	9 00.6	0 52.0	13 34.6	13 46.9	9 03.4
12 M	5 20 07	20 42 52	18 42 27	25 03 51	5 30.2	29 23.5	21 24.9	18 15.9	26 03.5	9 01.7	0 52.9	13 34.9	13 48.4	9 04.8
13 Tu	5 24 03	21 40 10	1♒20 42	7♒33 13	5 21.3	28 56.5	22 36.7	17 56.2	26 04.4	9 02.9	0 53.8	13 35.2	13 49.9	9 06.3
14 W	5 28 00	22 37 28	13 41 42	19 46 31	5 14.9	28 26.9	23 48.4	17 36.5	26 05.7	9 04.3	0 54.9	13 35.4	13 51.4	9 07.7
15 Th	5 31 57	23 34 45	25 48 09	1♓47 05	5 10.9	27 55.4	25 00.1	17 16.9	26 07.4	9 05.8	0 56.0	13 35.6	13 53.0	9 09.2
16 F	5 35 53	24 32 02	7♓43 54	13 39 14	5 09.1	27 22.4	26 11.8	16 57.4	26 09.4	9 07.6	0 57.3	13 35.8	13 54.5	9 10.6
17 Sa	5 39 50	25 29 19	19 33 42	25 27 59	5 08.7	26 48.5	27 23.4	16 38.0	26 11.8	9 09.5	0 58.7	13 35.8	13 56.1	9 12.1
18 Su	5 43 46	26 26 35	1♈22 46	7♈18 44	5 08.7	26 14.3	28 35.0	16 18.8	26 14.6	9 11.6	1 00.1	13R35.9	13 57.7	9 13.6
19 M	5 47 43	27 23 51	13 16 34	19 16 55	5 08.1	25 40.3	29 46.5	15 59.8	26 17.8	9 13.8	1 01.7	13 35.9	13 59.4	9 15.0
20 Tu	5 51 39	28 21 07	25 20 26	1♉27 41	5 05.9	25 07.1	0♌58.0	15 41.1	26 21.3	9 16.3	1 03.3	13 35.8	14 01.0	9 16.5
21 W	5 55 36	29 18 23	7♉39 12	13 55 26	5 01.4	24 35.4	2 09.4	15 22.8	26 25.1	9 18.9	1 05.1	13 35.7	14 02.7	9 18.0
22 Th	5 59 32	0♋15 38	20 16 47	26 43 30	4 54.3	24 05.5	3 20.7	15 04.8	26 29.4	9 21.7	1 06.9	13 35.6	14 04.4	9 19.5
23 F	6 03 29	1 12 54	3♊15 46	9♊53 36	4 44.8	23 38.2	4 32.1	14 47.2	26 33.9	9 24.6	1 08.9	13 35.4	14 06.1	9 21.0
24 Sa	6 07 25	2 10 09	16 36 55	23 25 31	4 33.5	23 13.7	5 43.3	14 30.1	26 38.9	9 27.7	1 10.9	13 35.1	14 07.8	9 22.5
25 Su	6 11 22	3 07 24	0♋19 03	7♋17 02	4 21.5	22 52.6	6 54.6	14 13.5	26 44.1	9 31.0	1 13.0	13 34.8	14 09.6	9 24.0
26 M	6 15 19	4 04 38	14 18 55	21 24 04	4 10.2	22 35.2	8 05.7	13 57.4	26 49.8	9 34.4	1 15.3	13 34.5	14 11.4	9 25.5
27 Tu	6 19 15	5 01 52	28 31 48	5♌41 24	4 00.5	22 21.8	9 16.8	13 41.9	26 55.7	9 38.1	1 17.6	13 34.1	14 13.2	9 27.0
28 W	6 23 12	5 59 06	12♌52 10	20 03 27	3 53.3	22 12.8	10 27.9	13 26.9	27 02.0	9 41.8	1 20.0	13 33.6	14 15.0	9 28.5
29 Th	6 27 08	6 56 20	27 14 38	4♍25 13	3 48.9	22D08.2	11 38.8	13 12.7	27 08.6	9 45.8	1 22.6	13 33.2	14 16.8	9 30.0
30 F	6 31 05	7 53 32	11♍34 46	18 42 55	3 47.0	22 08.3	12 49.8	12 59.1	27 15.6	9 49.9	1 25.2	13 32.6	14 18.7	9 31.5

Astro Data

	Dy Hr Mn
☽0S	7 15:44
♂R	8 6:09
☽0N	21 9:13
♄D	3 13:07
☽0S	3 22:53
☿R	5 22:39
♃D	6 4:49
♃□♇	7 23:43
⚳D	10 13:48
☽0N	17 18:32
♅R	18 19:50
♃□♇	20 17:33
☿D	29 23:29

Planet Ingress

		Dy Hr Mn
♀	♊	1 1:22
⚳	♎R	5 22:23
☿	♊	7 7:03
☉	♊	21 21:10
♀	♋	25 17:04
☿	♋	1 3:08
☿	♊R	10 22:13
♀	♌	19 16:32
☉	♋	22 5:27

Last Aspect / ☽ Ingress (May)

Dy Hr Mn	Aspect	☽ Ingress	Dy Hr Mn
1 0:08	♂ ☍	♋	1 9:12
2 22:52	☿ ⚹	♌	3 14:05
5 11:16	☿ □	♍	5 17:19
7 11:31	♂ □	♎	7 19:21
9 13:09	♂ ⚹	♏	9 21:00
11 6:06	☉ ☍	♐	11 23:32
13 19:32	♂ ☌	♑	14 4:25
16 2:00	☉ △	♒	16 12:46
18 18:17	☉ □	♓	19 0:21
21 12:30	☉ ⚹	♈	21 13:13
23 20:23	♀ ⚹	♉	24 0:46
25 2:31	♆ □	♊	26 9:29
28 12:12	☿ ☌	♋	28 15:26
29 14:56	♅ △	♌	30 19:34

Last Aspect / ☽ Ingress (June)

Dy Hr Mn	Aspect	☽ Ingress	Dy Hr Mn
1 8:42	♂ △	♍	1 22:48
3 10:40	♂ □	♎	4 1:43
5 12:31	♂ ⚹	♏	6 4:42
7 6:38	♀ △	♐	8 8:18
9 18:01	♂ ☌	♑	10 13:30
12 4:23	♀ ☍	♒	12 21:25
15 4:35	☿ △	♓	15 8:25
17 16:21	♀ △	♈	17 21:12
20 5:24	☉ ⚹	♉	20 9:09
21 12:14	♆ □	♊	22 18:02
24 11:40	☿ ☌	♋	24 23:27
25 22:45	♅ △	♌	27 2:28
28 15:34	☿ ⚹	♍	29 4:36

☽ Phases & Eclipses

Dy Hr Mn		
4 12:55	☽	13♌16
11 6:06	○	19♏46
18 18:17	☾	27♒00
26 18:04	●	4♊41
2 18:10	☽	11♍24
9 15:58	○	18♐00
17 12:03	☾	25♓29
25 4:19	●	2♋49

Astro Data

1 May 1922
Julian Day # 8156
SVP 6♓20'38"
GC 25♐45.3 ⚴ 28♍33.6R
Eris 29♓45.5 ⚵ 27♓50.8
⚷ 14♈58.7 ⚶ 14♊08.8
☽ Mean ☊ 7♎17.5

1 June 1922
Julian Day # 8187
SVP 6♓20'34"
GC 25♐45.3 ⚴ 28♍20.6
Eris 29♓59.6 ⚵ 12♈13.0
⚷ 16♈27.5 ⚶ 27♊13.0
☽ Mean ☊ 5♎39.0

July 1922

LONGITUDE

Day	Sid.Time	☉	0 hr ☽	Noon ☽	True ☊	☿	♀	♂	⚳	♃	♄	♅	♆	♇
1 Sa	6 35 01	8♋50 45	25♍49 25	2♎54 04	3♎46.6	22♊13.2	14♌00.6	12♐46.2	27♎22.8	9♎54.1	1♎27.9	13♓32.0	14♌20.6	9♋33.0
2 Su	6 38 58	9 47 57	9♎56 46	16 57 25	3R 46.5	22 23.0	15 11.4	12R 34.0	27 30.4	9 58.6	1 30.7	13R 31.4	14 22.4	9 34.5
3 M	6 42 55	10 45 09	23 55 58	0♏52 23	3 45.5	22 37.8	16 22.1	12 22.5	27 38.3	10 03.1	1 33.6	13 30.7	14 24.4	9 36.0
4 Tu	6 46 51	11 42 20	7♏46 39	14 38 41	3 42.5	22 57.6	17 32.8	12 11.8	27 46.5	10 07.9	1 36.5	13 30.0	14 26.3	9 37.5
5 W	6 50 48	12 39 31	21 28 25	28 15 46	3 36.8	23 22.4	18 43.4	12 01.9	27 55.0	10 12.7	1 39.6	13 29.3	14 28.2	9 39.0
6 Th	6 54 44	13 36 42	5♐00 36	11♐42 45	3 28.4	23 52.2	19 53.9	11 52.8	28 03.8	10 17.8	1 42.8	13 28.4	14 30.2	9 40.5
7 F	6 58 41	14 33 53	18 22 04	24 58 21	3 17.8	24 27.0	21 04.3	11 44.4	28 12.9	10 23.0	1 46.0	13 27.6	14 32.1	9 42.0
8 Sa	7 02 37	15 31 04	1♑31 27	8♑01 11	3 05.8	25 06.7	22 14.7	11 36.9	28 22.2	10 28.3	1 49.3	13 26.7	14 34.1	9 43.5
9 Su	7 06 34	16 28 15	14 27 25	20 50 03	2 53.5	25 51.3	23 25.0	11 30.2	28 31.9	10 33.8	1 52.8	13 25.8	14 36.1	9 45.0
10 M	7 10 30	17 25 27	27 09 02	3♒24 24	2 42.1	26 40.7	24 35.2	11 24.3	28 41.9	10 39.4	1 56.3	13 24.8	14 38.1	9 46.5
11 Tu	7 14 27	18 22 38	9♒36 11	15 44 33	2 32.5	27 34.9	25 45.3	11 19.2	28 52.1	10 45.2	1 59.8	13 23.8	14 40.2	9 48.0
12 W	7 18 24	19 19 50	21 49 42	27 51 55	2 25.4	28 33.9	26 55.4	11 14.9	29 02.6	10 51.1	2 03.5	13 22.7	14 42.2	9 49.5
13 Th	7 22 20	20 17 02	3♓51 31	9♓48 57	2 20.8	29 37.6	28 05.4	11 11.5	29 13.3	10 57.1	2 07.3	13 21.6	14 44.3	9 51.0
14 F	7 26 17	21 14 15	15 44 39	21 39 09	2D 18.6	0♋45.9	29 15.3	11 08.9	29 24.3	11 03.3	2 11.1	13 20.4	14 46.3	9 52.5
15 Sa	7 30 13	22 11 28	27 33 00	3♈26 50	2 18.1	1 58.7	0♍25.1	11 07.2	29 35.6	11 09.7	2 15.0	13 19.2	14 48.4	9 54.0
16 Su	7 34 10	23 08 42	9♈21 16	15 16 58	2R 18.4	3 16.0	1 34.8	11D 06.3	29 47.1	11 16.1	2 19.0	13 18.0	14 50.5	9 55.5
17 M	7 38 06	24 05 57	21 14 36	27 14 52	2 18.6	4 37.6	2 44.5	11 06.2	29 58.9	11 22.7	2 23.1	13 16.7	14 52.6	9 56.9
18 Tu	7 42 03	25 03 12	3♉18 25	9♉25 56	2 17.6	6 03.6	3 54.1	11 07.0	0♏10.9	11 29.5	2 27.3	13 15.4	14 54.7	9 58.4
19 W	7 45 59	26 00 28	15 38 00	21 55 12	2 14.7	7 33.8	5 03.6	11 08.5	0 23.2	11 36.4	2 31.5	13 14.0	14 56.8	9 59.9
20 Th	7 49 56	26 57 45	28 18 01	4♊46 53	2 09.5	9 08.0	6 13.0	11 11.0	0 35.8	11 43.4	2 35.8	13 12.6	14 58.9	10 01.3
21 F	7 53 53	27 55 02	11♊22 04	18 03 46	2 02.1	10 46.1	7 22.3	11 14.2	0 48.5	11 50.5	2 40.2	13 11.2	15 01.1	10 02.8
22 Sa	7 57 49	28 52 21	24 51 58	1♋46 35	1 53.2	12 28.0	8 31.6	11 18.3	1 01.5	11 57.8	2 44.7	13 09.7	15 03.2	10 04.2
23 Su	8 01 46	29 49 40	8♋47 17	15 53 36	1 43.4	14 13.4	9 40.8	11 23.2	1 14.8	12 05.2	2 49.2	13 08.2	15 05.4	10 05.7
24 M	8 05 42	0♌46 59	23 04 55	0♌20 29	1 34.1	16 02.2	10 49.8	11 28.9	1 28.2	12 12.7	2 53.9	13 06.6	15 07.5	10 07.1
25 Tu	8 09 39	1 44 20	7♌39 26	15 00 48	1 26.2	17 54.0	11 58.8	11 35.4	1 41.9	12 20.4	2 58.6	13 05.1	15 09.7	10 08.5
26 W	8 13 35	2 41 41	22 23 38	29 46 57	1 20.4	19 48.7	13 07.7	11 42.7	1 55.8	12 28.1	3 03.3	13 03.4	15 11.9	10 09.9
27 Th	8 17 32	3 39 02	7♍09 49	14♍31 24	1 17.2	21 45.8	14 16.4	11 50.8	2 09.9	12 36.0	3 08.2	13 01.8	15 14.1	10 11.3
28 F	8 21 28	4 36 24	21 50 58	29 07 52	1D 16.1	23 45.1	15 25.1	11 59.6	2 24.3	12 44.1	3 13.1	13 00.1	15 16.3	10 12.7
29 Sa	8 25 25	5 33 46	6♎21 37	13♎31 51	1 16.4	25 46.2	16 33.7	12 09.3	2 38.8	12 52.2	3 18.1	12 58.4	15 18.5	10 14.1
30 Su	8 29 22	6 31 09	20 38 19	27 40 51	1R 17.2	27 48.8	17 42.1	12 19.7	2 53.6	13 00.4	3 23.1	12 56.6	15 20.7	10 15.5
31 M	8 33 18	7 28 33	4♏39 24	11♏33 57	1 17.4	29 52.6	18 50.5	12 30.8	3 08.5	13 08.8	3 28.2	12 54.8	15 22.9	10 16.9

August 1922

LONGITUDE

Day	Sid.Time	☉	0 hr ☽	Noon ☽	True ☊	☿	♀	♂	⚳	♃	♄	♅	♆	♇
1 Tu	8 37 15	8♌25 57	18♏24 35	25♏11 22	1♎16.1	1♌57.2	19♍58.7	12♐42.7	3♏23.7	13♎17.3	3♎33.4	12♓53.0	15♌25.1	10♋18.2
2 W	8 41 11	9 23 21	1♐54 24	8♐33 49	1R 12.7	4 02.3	21 06.8	12 55.3	3 39.0	13 25.9	3 38.7	12R 51.1	15 27.3	10 19.6
3 Th	8 45 08	10 20 47	15 09 44	21 42 14	1 07.2	6 07.7	22 14.8	13 08.5	3 54.5	13 34.6	3 44.0	12 49.3	15 29.5	10 20.9
4 F	8 49 04	11 18 13	28 11 26	4♑37 24	1 00.0	8 12.9	23 22.6	13 22.5	4 10.3	13 43.4	3 49.4	12 47.3	15 31.7	10 22.2
5 Sa	8 53 01	12 15 40	11♑00 13	17 19 57	0 51.6	10 17.8	24 30.3	13 37.2	4 26.2	13 52.3	3 54.8	12 45.4	15 33.9	10 23.6
6 Su	8 56 57	13 13 07	23 36 40	29 50 25	0 43.0	12 22.2	25 37.9	13 52.5	4 42.3	14 01.3	4 00.3	12 43.4	15 36.2	10 24.9
7 M	9 00 54	14 10 36	6♒01 19	12♒09 27	0 35.1	14 25.8	26 45.4	14 08.4	4 58.5	14 10.4	4 05.9	12 41.4	15 38.4	10 26.2
8 Tu	9 04 51	15 08 06	18 14 56	24 17 57	0 28.4	16 28.5	27 52.7	14 25.0	5 15.0	14 19.6	4 11.5	12 39.4	15 40.6	10 27.4
9 W	9 08 47	16 05 37	0♓18 39	6♓17 18	0 23.7	18 30.3	28 59.9	14 42.2	5 31.6	14 29.0	4 17.2	12 37.4	15 42.8	10 28.7
10 Th	9 12 44	17 03 09	12 14 10	18 09 32	0 20.9	20 30.8	0♎07.0	15 00.0	5 48.4	14 38.4	4 22.9	12 35.3	15 45.1	10 30.0
11 F	9 16 40	18 00 42	24 03 48	29 57 22	0D 20.1	22 30.2	1 13.9	15 18.5	6 05.3	14 47.9	4 28.7	12 33.2	15 47.3	10 31.2
12 Sa	9 20 37	18 58 16	5♈50 39	11♈44 11	0 20.7	24 28.2	2 20.7	15 37.5	6 22.4	14 57.5	4 34.5	12 31.1	15 49.5	10 32.5
13 Su	9 24 33	19 55 52	17 38 28	23 34 03	0 22.1	26 25.0	3 27.3	15 57.1	6 39.7	15 07.2	4 40.5	12 28.9	15 51.7	10 33.7
14 M	9 28 30	20 53 30	29 31 34	5♉31 35	0 23.6	28 20.3	4 33.8	16 17.2	6 57.1	15 17.0	4 46.4	12 26.8	15 53.9	10 34.9
15 Tu	9 32 26	21 51 09	11♉34 45	17 41 40	0R 24.6	0♍14.2	5 40.1	16 37.9	7 14.7	15 26.9	4 52.4	12 24.6	15 56.2	10 36.1
16 W	9 36 23	22 48 50	23 52 59	0♊09 16	0 24.4	2 06.8	6 46.2	16 59.2	7 32.4	15 36.9	4 58.5	12 22.4	15 58.4	10 37.2
17 Th	9 40 19	23 46 32	6♊31 05	12 58 56	0 22.8	3 57.9	7 52.2	17 21.0	7 50.3	15 47.0	5 04.6	12 20.2	16 00.6	10 38.4
18 F	9 44 16	24 44 16	19 33 13	26 14 15	0 19.6	5 47.5	8 58.1	17 43.3	8 08.4	15 57.2	5 10.8	12 17.9	16 02.8	10 39.6
19 Sa	9 48 13	25 42 01	3♋02 14	9♋57 13	0 15.3	7 35.8	10 03.7	18 06.2	8 26.6	16 07.5	5 17.0	12 15.7	16 05.0	10 40.7
20 Su	9 52 09	26 39 48	16 59 03	24 07 28	0 10.4	9 22.6	11 09.2	18 29.5	8 44.9	16 17.8	5 23.3	12 13.4	16 07.2	10 41.8
21 M	9 56 06	27 37 37	1♌21 59	8♌41 56	0 05.6	11 08.1	12 14.6	18 53.4	9 03.4	16 28.2	5 29.6	12 11.1	16 09.4	10 42.9
22 Tu	10 00 02	28 35 27	16 06 30	23 34 43	0 01.5	12 52.1	13 19.7	19 17.7	9 22.0	16 38.7	5 36.0	12 08.8	16 11.6	10 44.0
23 W	10 03 59	29 33 18	1♍05 31	8♍37 46	29♍58.7	14 34.8	14 24.7	19 42.6	9 40.8	16 49.3	5 42.4	12 06.5	16 13.8	10 45.1
24 Th	10 07 55	0♍31 11	16 10 18	23 42 00	29D 57.4	16 16.1	15 29.5	20 07.9	9 59.7	17 00.0	5 48.8	12 04.2	16 15.9	10 46.1
25 F	10 11 52	1 29 05	1♎11 48	8♎38 45	29 57.5	17 56.1	16 34.0	20 33.6	10 18.7	17 10.8	5 55.3	12 01.8	16 18.1	10 47.2
26 Sa	10 15 48	2 27 01	16 02 02	23 20 58	29 58.6	19 34.7	17 38.4	20 59.9	10 37.8	17 21.6	6 01.9	11 59.5	16 20.3	10 48.2
27 Su	10 19 45	3 24 58	0♏35 01	7♏43 49	29 60.0	21 12.1	18 42.5	21 26.5	10 57.1	17 32.5	6 08.5	11 57.1	16 22.4	10 49.2
28 M	10 23 42	4 22 56	14 47 08	21 44 53	0♎01.2	22 48.0	19 46.5	21 53.7	11 16.5	17 43.5	6 15.1	11 54.7	16 24.5	10 50.2
29 Tu	10 27 38	5 20 55	28 37 03	5♐23 44	0R 01.7	24 22.7	20 50.2	22 21.2	11 36.1	17 54.6	6 21.8	11 52.4	16 26.7	10 51.1
30 W	10 31 35	6 18 56	12♐05 07	18 41 26	0 01.1	25 56.1	21 53.7	22 49.1	11 55.7	18 05.7	6 28.5	11 50.0	16 28.8	10 52.1
31 Th	10 35 31	7 16 58	25 12 57	1♑39 58	29♍59.5	27 28.2	22 56.9	23 17.5	12 15.5	18 16.9	6 35.2	11 47.6	16 30.9	10 53.0

Astro Data Dy Hr Mn	Planet Ingress Dy Hr Mn	Last Aspect Dy Hr Mn	☽ Ingress Dy Hr Mn	Last Aspect Dy Hr Mn	☽ Ingress Dy Hr Mn	☽ Phases & Eclipses Dy Hr Mn	Astro Data
☽0S 1 5:26	☿ ♋ 13 20:04	30 17:48 ☿ □	♎ 1 7:04	1 1:55 ♀ ⚹	♐ 1 20:35	1 22:51 ☽ 9♎17	1 July 1922
☽0N 15 3:47	♀ ♍ 15 3:22	2 21:29 ☿ △	♏ 3 10:29	3 13:06 ♀ □	♑ 4 3:22	9 3:07 ○ 16♑07	Julian Day # 8217
♂ D 17 2:12	⚳ ♏ 17 14:11	4 17:34 ♀ □	♐ 5 15:05	6 3:05 ♀ △	♒ 6 12:19	17 5:11 ☾ 23♈50	SVP 6♓20'29"
☽0S 28 12:54	☉ ♌ 23 16:20	7 11:00 ☿ ☍	♑ 7 21:12	7 18:52 ♆ ☍	♓ 8 23:23	24 12:47 ● 0♌49	GC 25♐45.4 ⚴ 3♎53.2
♃⚻♅ 30 2:51	☿ ♌ 31 13:25	9 3:07 ☉ ☍	♒ 10 5:27	10 5:26 ♂ □	♈ 11 12:05	31 4:21 ☽ 7♏10	Eris 0♈03.4R ⚵ 25♈33.6
		12 13:32 ☿ △	♓ 12 16:16	13 18:51 ☿ △	♉ 14 0:57		⚷ 17♈19.4 ⚶ 10♋15.3
♀0S 10 16:30	♀ ♎ 10 9:30	14 11:05 ☉ △	♈ 15 4:59	15 20:45 ☉ □	♊ 16 11:42	7 16:18 ○ 14♒21	☽ Mean ☊ 4♎03.7
☽0N 11 11:55	☿ ♍ 15 8:59	17 5:11 ☉ □	♉ 17 17:28	18 9:07 ☉ ⚹	♋ 18 18:40	15 20:45 ☾ 22♉12	
♄0S 18 11:19	☊ ♍R 22 23:24	19 20:20 ☉ ⚹	♊ 20 3:10	19 22:40 ♃ □	♌ 20 21:45	22 20:34 ● 28♌56	1 August 1922
♃⚹♆ 19 4:43	☉ ♍ 23 23:04	21 6:33 ♆ ⚹	♋ 22 8:56	22 20:34 ☉ ☌	♍ 22 22:16	29 11:55 ☽ 5♐21	Julian Day # 8248
☽0S 24 22:06	☊ ♎ 27 12:17	23 8:47 ☿ ☌	♌ 24 11:26	24 6:09 ♂ □	♎ 24 22:05		SVP 6♓20'25"
	☊ ♍R 31 6:06	25 12:15 ♆ ☌	♍ 26 12:21	26 8:01 ♂ ⚹	♏ 26 23:02		GC 25♐45.5 ⚴ 13♎12.7
		28 1:43 ☿ ⚹	♎ 28 13:26	28 14:04 ☿ ⚹	♐ 29 2:26		Eris 29♓56.3R ⚵ 8♉01.5
		30 12:16 ☿ □	♏ 30 15:59	31 3:08 ☿ □	♑ 31 8:53		⚷ 17♈26.8R ⚶ 23♋51.6
							☽ Mean ☊ 2♎25.2

LONGITUDE — September 1922

Day	Sid.Time	☉	0 hr ☽	Noon☽	True☊	☿	♀	♂	⚳	♃	♄	♅	♆	♇
1 F	10 39 28	8♍15 02	8♑02 46	14♑21 41	29♍57.0	28♍59.0	23♎59.9	23♐46.2	12♏35.4	18♎28.1	6♎42.0	11♓45.2	16♌33.0	10♋53.9
2 Sa	10 43 24	9 13 07	20 37 01	26 49 04	29R54.0	0♎28.5	25 02.6	24 15.4	12 55.4	18 39.5	6 48.8	11R42.8	16 35.1	10 54.8
3 Su	10 47 21	10 11 13	2♒58 08	9♒04 30	29 50.8	1 56.6	26 05.1	24 44.9	13 15.5	18 50.9	6 55.6	11 40.4	16 37.2	10 55.7
4 M	10 51 17	11 09 21	15 08 25	21 10 10	29 47.9	3 23.5	27 07.3	25 14.7	13 35.7	19 02.3	7 02.5	11 38.0	16 39.3	10 56.6
5 Tu	10 55 14	12 07 31	27 09 58	3♓08 07	29 45.6	4 49.0	28 09.2	25 44.9	13 56.1	19 13.9	7 09.4	11 35.6	16 41.3	10 57.4
6 W	10 59 11	13 05 42	9♓04 49	15 00 21	29 44.1	6 13.1	29 10.8	26 15.5	14 16.5	19 25.4	7 16.3	11 33.2	16 43.4	10 58.2
7 Th	11 03 07	14 03 55	20 54 57	26 48 56	29D43.5	7 35.9	0♏12.1	26 46.4	14 37.0	19 37.1	7 23.3	11 30.8	16 45.4	10 59.0
8 F	11 07 04	15 02 10	2♈42 33	8♈36 08	29 43.6	8 57.3	1 13.1	27 17.6	14 57.7	19 48.8	7 30.3	11 28.4	16 47.4	10 59.8
9 Sa	11 11 00	16 00 27	14 30 00	20 24 32	29 44.4	10 17.2	2 13.8	27 49.2	15 18.4	20 00.6	7 37.3	11 26.1	16 49.4	11 00.5
10 Su	11 14 57	16 58 46	26 20 06	2♉17 08	29 45.5	11 35.6	3 14.2	28 21.1	15 39.3	20 12.4	7 44.4	11 23.7	16 51.4	11 01.3
11 M	11 18 53	17 57 06	8♉16 03	14 17 20	29 46.7	12 52.5	4 14.2	28 53.3	16 00.2	20 24.3	7 51.4	11 21.3	16 53.4	11 02.0
12 Tu	11 22 50	18 55 29	20 21 27	26 28 55	29 47.7	14 07.8	5 13.9	29 25.8	16 21.2	20 36.2	7 58.5	11 18.9	16 55.3	11 02.7
13 W	11 26 46	19 53 54	2♊40 14	8♊55 55	29R48.4	15 21.5	6 13.3	29 58.6	16 42.4	20 48.2	8 05.7	11 16.5	16 57.3	11 03.4
14 Th	11 30 43	20 52 21	15 16 28	21 42 22	29 48.6	16 33.4	7 12.3	0♑31.7	17 03.6	21 00.2	8 12.8	11 14.2	16 59.2	11 04.0
15 F	11 34 40	21 50 51	28 14 03	4♋51 54	29 48.3	17 43.4	8 10.9	1 05.1	17 24.9	21 12.3	8 20.0	11 11.8	17 01.1	11 04.6
16 Sa	11 38 36	22 49 22	11♋36 13	18 27 12	29 47.8	18 51.6	9 09.1	1 38.7	17 46.3	21 24.4	8 27.2	11 09.5	17 03.0	11 05.3
17 Su	11 42 33	23 47 56	25 24 56	2♌29 22	29 47.2	19 57.7	10 06.9	2 12.7	18 07.8	21 36.6	8 34.4	11 07.2	17 04.9	11 05.8
18 M	11 46 29	24 46 32	9♌40 17	16 57 17	29 46.6	21 01.6	11 04.3	2 46.9	18 29.4	21 48.9	8 41.6	11 04.9	17 06.7	11 06.4
19 Tu	11 50 26	25 45 09	24 19 49	1♍47 09	29 46.1	22 03.2	12 01.3	3 21.4	18 51.1	22 01.1	8 48.9	11 02.6	17 08.6	11 07.0
20 W	11 54 22	26 43 49	9♍18 23	16 52 29	29D45.9	23 02.4	12 57.8	3 56.2	19 12.8	22 13.5	8 56.2	11 00.3	17 10.4	11 07.5
21 Th	11 58 19	27 42 31	24 28 19	2♎04 40	29 45.8	23 58.9	13 53.9	4 31.2	19 34.7	22 25.8	9 03.4	10 58.0	17 12.2	11 08.0
22 F	12 02 15	28 41 15	9♎40 19	17 14 06	29 45.9	24 52.6	14 49.5	5 06.5	19 56.6	22 38.3	9 10.7	10 55.7	17 13.9	11 08.5
23 Sa	12 06 12	29 40 01	24 44 53	2♏11 39	29R45.9	25 43.1	15 44.6	5 42.1	20 18.6	22 50.7	9 18.0	10 53.5	17 15.7	11 08.9
24 Su	12 10 08	0♎38 48	9♏33 34	16 49 55	29 45.9	26 30.4	16 39.1	6 17.8	20 40.7	23 03.2	9 25.4	10 51.3	17 17.4	11 09.3
25 M	12 14 05	1 37 38	24 00 10	1♐03 58	29 45.7	27 14.0	17 33.2	6 53.9	21 02.8	23 15.7	9 32.7	10 49.1	17 19.1	11 09.7
26 Tu	12 18 02	2 36 29	8♐01 09	14 51 39	29 45.5	27 53.8	18 26.7	7 30.1	21 25.0	23 28.3	9 40.0	10 46.9	17 20.8	11 10.1
27 W	12 21 58	3 35 22	21 35 36	28 13 12	29D45.4	28 29.3	19 19.5	8 06.6	21 47.3	23 40.9	9 47.4	10 44.7	17 22.5	11 10.5
28 Th	12 25 55	4 34 16	4♑44 45	11♑10 38	29 45.4	29 00.2	20 11.8	8 43.3	22 09.7	23 53.5	9 54.8	10 42.6	17 24.2	11 10.8
29 F	12 29 51	5 33 13	17 31 17	23 47 10	29 45.7	29 26.1	21 03.5	9 20.2	22 32.2	24 06.2	10 02.1	10 40.5	17 25.8	11 11.2
30 Sa	12 33 48	6 32 11	29 58 47	6♒06 36	29 46.2	29 46.7	21 54.4	9 57.4	22 54.7	24 18.9	10 09.5	10 38.4	17 27.4	11 11.5

LONGITUDE — October 1922

Day	Sid.Time	☉	0 hr ☽	Noon☽	True☊	☿	♀	♂	⚳	♃	♄	♅	♆	♇
1 Su	12 37 44	7♎31 11	12♒11 08	18♒12 51	29♍47.0	0♏01.4	22♏44.7	10♑34.7	23♏17.3	24♎31.6	10♎16.9	10♓36.3	17♌29.0	11♋11.7
2 M	12 41 41	8 30 12	24 12 13	0♓09 42	29 47.9	0R09.9	23 34.3	11 12.2	23 39.9	24 44.4	10 24.2	10R34.3	17 30.5	11 12.0
3 Tu	12 45 37	9 29 16	6♓05 41	12 00 36	29 48.6	0 11.7	24 23.1	11 49.9	24 02.6	24 57.2	10 31.6	10 32.3	17 32.1	11 12.2
4 W	12 49 34	10 28 21	17 54 47	23 48 35	29R49.1	0 06.4	25 11.2	12 27.8	24 25.4	25 10.0	10 39.0	10 30.3	17 33.6	11 12.4
5 Th	12 53 31	11 27 28	29 42 20	5♈36 20	29 49.1	29♎53.6	25 58.4	13 05.9	24 48.2	25 22.8	10 46.4	10 28.3	17 35.0	11 12.6
6 F	12 57 27	12 26 38	11♈30 51	17 26 10	29 48.5	29 33.0	26 44.9	13 44.2	25 11.1	25 35.7	10 53.8	10 26.4	17 36.5	11 12.7
7 Sa	13 01 24	13 25 49	23 22 32	29 20 13	29 47.2	29 04.5	27 30.4	14 22.6	25 34.0	25 48.5	11 01.1	10 24.5	17 37.9	11 12.9
8 Su	13 05 20	14 25 03	5♉19 28	11♉20 32	29 45.3	28 27.8	28 15.1	15 01.2	25 57.1	26 01.4	11 08.5	10 22.6	17 39.3	11 13.0
9 M	13 09 17	15 24 18	17 23 41	23 29 13	29 42.9	27 43.3	28 58.8	15 40.0	26 20.1	26 14.4	11 15.9	10 20.8	17 40.7	11 13.0
10 Tu	13 13 13	16 23 36	29 37 23	5♊48 30	29 40.5	26 51.3	29 41.5	16 19.0	26 43.2	26 27.3	11 23.2	10 19.0	17 42.1	11 13.1
11 W	13 17 10	17 22 57	12♊02 53	18 20 52	29 38.2	25 52.4	0♐23.3	16 58.1	27 06.4	26 40.3	11 30.6	10 17.2	17 43.4	11 13.1
12 Th	13 21 06	18 22 19	24 42 46	1♋08 56	29 36.5	24 47.7	1 03.9	17 37.3	27 29.7	26 53.2	11 38.0	10 15.5	17 44.7	11R13.2
13 F	13 25 03	19 21 44	7♋39 42	14 15 22	29D35.7	23 38.5	1 43.5	18 16.7	27 53.0	27 06.2	11 45.3	10 13.8	17 46.0	11 13.1
14 Sa	13 29 00	20 21 11	20 56 15	27 42 34	29 35.8	22 26.4	2 22.0	18 56.3	28 16.3	27 19.2	11 52.6	10 12.1	17 47.2	11 13.1
15 Su	13 32 56	21 20 41	4♌34 32	11♌32 13	29 36.7	21 13.3	2 59.3	19 36.0	28 39.7	27 32.3	12 00.0	10 10.5	17 48.4	11 13.1
16 M	13 36 53	22 20 13	18 35 40	25 44 46	29 38.0	20 01.3	3 35.3	20 15.9	29 03.1	27 45.3	12 07.3	10 08.9	17 49.6	11 13.0
17 Tu	13 40 49	23 19 47	2♍59 15	10♍18 45	29 39.4	18 52.5	4 10.1	20 55.9	29 26.6	27 58.4	12 14.6	10 07.3	17 50.7	11 12.9
18 W	13 44 46	24 19 23	17 42 43	25 10 27	29R40.2	17 49.0	4 43.5	21 36.1	29 50.2	28 11.4	12 21.9	10 05.8	17 51.9	11 12.7
19 Th	13 48 42	25 19 02	2♎41 05	10♎13 38	29 39.9	16 52.5	5 15.6	22 16.4	0♐13.8	28 24.5	12 29.2	10 04.3	17 53.0	11 12.6
20 F	13 52 39	26 18 42	17 47 01	25 20 05	29 38.3	16 04.8	5 46.2	22 56.8	0 37.4	28 37.5	12 36.4	10 02.9	17 54.0	11 12.4
21 Sa	13 56 35	27 18 25	2♏51 38	10♏20 32	29 35.4	15 27.0	6 15.4	23 37.4	1 01.1	28 50.6	12 43.6	10 01.5	17 55.1	11 12.2
22 Su	14 00 32	28 18 10	17 45 42	25 06 09	29 31.4	15 00.0	6 42.9	24 18.1	1 24.8	29 03.7	12 50.9	10 00.1	17 56.1	11 12.0
23 M	14 04 28	29 17 56	2♐21 04	9♐29 48	29 26.9	14D44.3	7 08.9	24 58.9	1 48.6	29 16.8	12 58.1	9 58.8	17 57.0	11 11.7
24 Tu	14 08 25	0♏17 44	16 31 52	23 26 59	29 22.7	14 39.9	7 33.2	25 39.9	2 12.4	29 29.9	13 05.3	9 57.5	17 58.0	11 11.5
25 W	14 12 22	1 17 34	0♑15 04	6♑56 08	29 19.2	14 46.7	7 55.7	26 21.0	2 36.3	29 43.0	13 12.4	9 56.3	17 58.9	11 11.2
26 Th	14 16 18	2 17 26	13 30 26	19 58 15	29 17.0	15 04.2	8 16.4	27 02.2	3 00.2	29 56.0	13 19.5	9 55.1	17 59.8	11 10.9
27 F	14 20 15	3 17 19	26 20 01	2♒36 16	29D16.2	15 31.8	8 35.2	27 43.5	3 24.1	0♏09.1	13 26.7	9 53.9	18 00.6	11 10.5
28 Sa	14 24 11	4 17 14	8♒47 32	14 54 25	29 16.7	16 08.6	8 52.1	28 24.9	3 48.1	0 22.2	13 33.7	9 52.8	18 01.4	11 10.2
29 Su	14 28 08	5 17 11	20 57 33	26 57 33	29 18.2	16 53.9	9 06.9	29 06.4	4 12.1	0 35.3	13 40.8	9 51.8	18 02.2	11 09.8
30 M	14 32 04	6 17 09	2♓55 03	8♓50 39	29 20.0	17 46.9	9 19.7	29 48.0	4 36.1	0 48.3	13 47.8	9 50.8	18 03.0	11 09.4
31 Tu	14 36 01	7 17 09	14 44 56	20 38 29	29R21.4	18 46.5	9 30.3	0♒29.7	5 00.2	1 01.4	13 54.8	9 49.8	18 03.7	11 08.9

Astro Data

	Dy Hr Mn
☿0S	1 20:57
☽0N	7 18:38
♅△♇	17 23:03
☽0S	21 8:49
☉0S	23 20:10
☿R	3 6:17
♄⊼♅	3 13:42
☽0N	5 0:42
♃□♆	5 20:59
♄□♇	9 2:41
♇R	12 14:08
☽0S	18 19:51
☿D	24 9:17

Planet Ingress

		Dy Hr Mn
☿	♎	2 4:20
♀	♏	7 7:15
♂	♑	13 13:02
☉	♎	23 20:10
☿	♏	1 9:14
☿	♎R	5 1:45
♀	♐	10 22:33
⚳	♐	18 22:00
☉	♏	24 4:53
♃	♏	26 19:16
♂	♒	30 18:55

Last Aspect / ☽ Ingress

Last Aspect Dy Hr Mn		☽ Ingress Dy Hr Mn	Last Aspect Dy Hr Mn		☽ Ingress Dy Hr Mn
2 8:14	♀ □	♒ 2 18:12	2 0:53	♃ △	♓ 2 11:40
5 1:02	♀ △	♓ 5 5:41	4 15:00	♀ △	♈ 5 0:36
7 11:55	♂ □	♈ 7 18:29	7 11:30	☿ ☍	♉ 7 13:20
10 3:42	♂ △	♉ 10 7:24	9 23:25	♀ ☍	♊ 10 0:44
11 19:53	☉ △	♊ 12 18:50	12 3:56	♃ △	♋ 12 9:52
14 10:41	♃ △	♋ 15 3:13	14 11:18	♃ □	♌ 14 16:01
16 20:07	☉ ✶	♌ 17 7:48	16 15:24	♃ ✶	♍ 16 19:04
18 20:02	♃ ✶	♍ 19 9:08	18 6:00	♂ △	♎ 18 19:43
21 4:38	☉ ☌	♎ 21 8:43	20 17:19	♃ ☌	♏ 20 19:26
23 0:57	☿ ☌	♏ 23 8:27	22 10:37	♂ ✶	♐ 22 20:05
24 12:46	♆ □	♐ 25 10:11	24 22:50	♃ ✶	♑ 24 23:33
27 12:31	☿ ✶	♑ 27 15:15	27 2:06	♂ ☌	♒ 27 7:00
29 23:17	☿ □	♒ 30 0:02	28 18:10	♆ ☍	♓ 29 18:07

☽ Phases & Eclipses

Dy Hr Mn	
6 7:47	○ 12♓55
14 10:20	☾ 20♊48
21 4:38	● 27♍24
21 4:40:08	• T 05'59"
27 22:40	☽ 4♑02
6 0:58	○ 11♈59
6 0:43	• A 0.636
13 21:55	☾ 19♋46
20 13:40	● 26♎23
27 13:26	☽ 3♒21

Astro Data

1 September 1922
Julian Day # 8279
SVP 6♓20'21"
GC 25♐45.6 ⚴ 24♎39.1
Eris 29♓40.2R ⚵ 17♉40.6
⚷ 16♈46.0R ⚶ 7♌20.4
☽ Mean ☊ 0♎46.7

1 October 1922
Julian Day # 8309
SVP 6♓20'19"
GC 25♐45.6 ⚴ 6♏53.0
Eris 29♓20.3R ⚵ 21♉52.1
⚷ 15♈33.5R ⚶ 19♌56.8
☽ Mean ☊ 29♍11.3

November 1922 — LONGITUDE

Day	Sid.Time	☉	0 hr ☽	Noon ☽	True ☊	☿	♀	♂	⚳	♃	♄	♅	♆	♇
1 W	14 39 57	8♏17 10	26♓31 47	2♈25 20	29♍21.7	19♎52.1	9♐38.7	1♒11.5	5♐24.3	1♏14.4	14♎01.8	9♓48.9	18♌04.4	11♋08.5
2 Th	14 43 54	9 17 14	8♈19 34	14 14 54	29R 20.4	21 02.9	9 44.9	1 53.4	5 48.4	1 27.5	14 08.7	9R 48.0	18 05.0	11R 08.0
3 F	14 47 51	10 17 19	20 11 39	26 10 09	29 17.1	22 18.1	9 48.8	2 35.4	6 12.6	1 40.5	14 15.6	9 47.2	18 05.7	11 07.5
4 Sa	14 51 47	11 17 25	2♉10 39	8♉13 22	29 11.9	23 37.1	9R 50.3	3 17.5	6 36.7	1 53.5	14 22.5	9 46.4	18 06.2	11 07.0
5 Su	14 55 44	12 17 34	14 18 29	20 26 08	29 04.9	24 59.3	9 49.4	3 59.6	7 01.0	2 06.5	14 29.3	9 45.6	18 06.8	11 06.5
6 M	14 59 40	13 17 45	26 36 28	2♊49 32	28 56.7	26 24.2	9 46.1	4 41.9	7 25.2	2 19.5	14 36.1	9 45.0	18 07.3	11 05.9
7 Tu	15 03 37	14 17 57	9♊05 27	15 24 16	28 48.2	27 51.4	9 40.4	5 24.2	7 49.5	2 32.4	14 42.9	9 44.3	18 07.8	11 05.3
8 W	15 07 33	15 18 11	21 46 04	28 10 55	28 40.2	29 20.5	9 32.3	6 06.6	8 13.8	2 45.4	14 49.6	9 43.7	18 08.3	11 04.7
9 Th	15 11 30	16 18 28	4♋38 53	11♋10 04	28 33.6	0♏51.0	9 21.7	6 49.1	8 38.1	2 58.3	14 56.3	9 43.2	18 08.7	11 04.1
10 F	15 15 26	17 18 46	17 44 35	24 22 34	28 29.0	2 22.8	9 08.6	7 31.6	9 02.5	3 11.2	15 02.9	9 42.7	18 09.1	11 03.4
11 Sa	15 19 23	18 19 06	1♌04 07	7♌49 25	28D 26.5	3 55.6	8 53.2	8 14.2	9 26.9	3 24.1	15 09.6	9 42.3	18 09.4	11 02.8
12 Su	15 23 20	19 19 28	14 38 35	21 31 43	28 26.0	5 29.2	8 35.4	8 56.9	9 51.3	3 37.0	15 16.1	9 41.9	18 09.7	11 02.1
13 M	15 27 16	20 19 52	28 28 56	5♍30 15	28 26.7	7 03.4	8 15.4	9 39.7	10 15.7	3 49.8	15 22.6	9 41.5	18 10.0	11 01.4
14 Tu	15 31 13	21 20 18	12♍35 38	19 44 58	28R 27.6	8 38.1	7 53.1	10 22.5	10 40.1	4 02.6	15 29.1	9 41.2	18 10.3	11 00.7
15 W	15 35 09	22 20 46	26 58 03	4♎14 30	28 27.7	10 13.1	7 28.7	11 05.4	11 04.6	4 15.4	15 35.5	9 41.0	18 10.5	10 59.9
16 Th	15 39 06	23 21 16	11♎33 52	18 55 33	28 26.0	11 48.3	7 02.3	11 48.4	11 29.1	4 28.2	15 41.9	9 40.8	18 10.7	10 59.2
17 F	15 43 02	24 21 47	26 18 47	3♏42 44	28 21.8	13 23.7	6 34.1	12 31.4	11 53.6	4 40.9	15 48.2	9 40.6	18 10.8	10 58.4
18 Sa	15 46 59	25 22 21	11♏06 27	18 28 56	28 15.0	14 59.2	6 04.1	13 14.5	12 18.1	4 53.6	15 54.5	9 40.5	18 10.9	10 57.6
19 Su	15 50 55	26 22 56	25 49 11	3♐06 13	28 06.2	16 34.7	5 32.6	13 57.7	12 42.7	5 06.3	16 00.8	9D 40.5	18 11.0	10 56.8
20 M	15 54 52	27 23 32	10♐19 05	17 27 01	27 56.2	18 10.2	4 59.7	14 40.9	13 07.3	5 18.9	16 06.9	9 40.5	18R 11.0	10 55.9
21 Tu	15 58 49	28 24 10	24 29 19	1♑25 28	27 46.2	19 45.6	4 25.7	15 24.2	13 31.8	5 31.5	16 13.1	9 40.6	18 11.1	10 55.1
22 W	16 02 45	29 24 49	8♑15 09	14 58 11	27 37.2	21 21.0	3 50.7	16 07.5	13 56.4	5 44.0	16 19.1	9 40.7	18 11.0	10 54.2
23 Th	16 06 42	0♐25 29	21 34 35	28 04 28	27 30.3	22 56.2	3 15.0	16 50.9	14 21.0	5 56.6	16 25.2	9 40.9	18 11.0	10 53.3
24 F	16 10 38	1 26 10	4♒28 09	10♒46 02	27 25.7	24 31.4	2 38.8	17 34.3	14 45.6	6 09.0	16 31.1	9 41.1	18 10.9	10 52.4
25 Sa	16 14 35	2 26 53	16 58 37	23 06 27	27D 23.5	26 06.5	2 02.4	18 17.8	15 10.3	6 21.5	16 37.0	9 41.4	18 10.8	10 51.5
26 Su	16 18 31	3 27 36	29 10 11	5♓10 29	27 23.0	27 41.4	1 26.0	19 01.3	15 34.9	6 33.8	16 42.8	9 41.7	18 10.6	10 50.6
27 M	16 22 28	4 28 20	11♓08 02	17 03 31	27R 23.5	29 16.2	0 49.9	19 44.8	15 59.5	6 46.2	16 48.6	9 42.0	18 10.4	10 49.6
28 Tu	16 26 24	5 29 06	22 57 40	28 51 07	27 23.8	0♐50.9	0 14.3	20 28.4	16 24.2	6 58.5	16 54.3	9 42.5	18 10.2	10 48.7
29 W	16 30 21	6 29 52	4♈44 34	10♈38 37	27 22.9	2 25.5	29♏39.5	21 12.1	16 48.8	7 10.7	17 00.0	9 42.9	18 09.9	10 47.7
30 Th	16 34 18	7 30 40	16 33 50	22 30 47	27 19.8	4 00.1	29 05.7	21 55.7	17 13.5	7 22.9	17 05.6	9 43.5	18 09.6	10 46.7

December 1922 — LONGITUDE

Day	Sid.Time	☉	0 hr ☽	Noon ☽	True ☊	☿	♀	♂	⚳	♃	♄	♅	♆	♇
1 F	16 38 14	8♐31 28	28♈29 56	4♉31 43	27♍14.1	5♐34.5	28♏33.1	22♒39.4	17♐38.2	7♏35.1	17♎11.1	9♓44.0	18♌09.3	10♋45.7
2 Sa	16 42 11	9 32 18	10♉36 27	16 44 27	27R 05.6	7 08.9	28R 02.0	23 23.2	18 02.8	7 47.1	17 16.6	9 44.7	18R 08.9	10R 44.6
3 Su	16 46 07	10 33 09	22 55 54	29 10 57	26 54.5	8 43.2	27 32.5	24 06.9	18 27.5	7 59.2	17 21.9	9 45.3	18 08.5	10 43.6
4 M	16 50 04	11 34 00	5♊29 40	11♊52 02	26 41.8	10 17.4	27 04.8	24 50.7	18 52.2	8 11.2	17 27.3	9 46.1	18 08.1	10 42.6
5 Tu	16 54 00	12 34 53	18 17 59	24 47 25	26 28.5	11 51.7	26 39.1	25 34.5	19 16.9	8 23.1	17 32.5	9 46.9	18 07.6	10 41.5
6 W	16 57 57	13 35 47	1♋20 09	7♋56 01	26 15.8	13 25.9	26 15.5	26 18.4	19 41.5	8 35.0	17 37.7	9 47.7	18 07.1	10 40.4
7 Th	17 01 53	14 36 42	14 34 47	21 16 16	26 04.9	15 00.1	25 54.1	27 02.2	20 06.2	8 46.8	17 42.8	9 48.6	18 06.6	10 39.3
8 F	17 05 50	15 37 38	28 00 17	4♌46 39	25 56.7	16 34.3	25 35.0	27 46.1	20 30.9	8 58.5	17 47.9	9 49.5	18 06.0	10 38.2
9 Sa	17 09 47	16 38 35	11♌35 14	18 25 55	25 51.4	18 08.6	25 18.4	28 30.0	20 55.6	9 10.2	17 52.8	9 50.5	18 05.4	10 37.1
10 Su	17 13 43	17 39 34	25 18 39	2♍13 24	25 48.9	19 42.9	25 04.1	29 13.9	21 20.3	9 21.8	17 57.7	9 51.5	18 04.8	10 36.0
11 M	17 17 40	18 40 33	9♍10 08	16 08 51	25 48.3	21 17.3	24 52.4	29 57.9	21 44.9	9 33.4	18 02.5	9 52.6	18 04.1	10 34.9
12 Tu	17 21 36	19 41 34	23 09 33	0♎12 12	25 48.3	22 51.8	24 43.1	0♓41.8	22 09.6	9 44.9	18 07.3	9 53.7	18 03.5	10 33.7
13 W	17 25 33	20 42 35	7♎16 44	14 23 02	25 47.5	24 26.4	24 36.4	1 25.8	22 34.3	9 56.3	18 11.9	9 54.9	18 02.7	10 32.6
14 Th	17 29 29	21 43 38	21 30 55	28 40 04	25 44.6	26 01.0	24 32.1	2 09.8	22 59.0	10 07.7	18 16.5	9 56.1	18 02.0	10 31.4
15 F	17 33 26	22 44 42	5♏50 08	13♏00 38	25 38.9	27 35.8	24D 30.4	2 53.8	23 23.6	10 18.9	18 21.0	9 57.4	18 01.2	10 30.3
16 Sa	17 37 22	23 45 47	20 11 00	27 20 37	25 30.2	29 10.7	24 31.1	3 37.9	23 48.3	10 30.1	18 25.4	9 58.7	18 00.4	10 29.1
17 Su	17 41 19	24 46 53	4♐28 47	11♐34 46	25 18.9	0♑45.7	24 34.2	4 21.9	24 12.9	10 41.3	18 29.8	10 00.1	17 59.6	10 27.9
18 M	17 45 16	25 47 59	18 37 52	25 37 22	25 06.0	2 20.9	24 39.7	5 06.0	24 37.6	10 52.3	18 34.0	10 01.5	17 58.7	10 26.7
19 Tu	17 49 12	26 49 06	2♑32 41	9♑23 15	24 52.8	3 56.2	24 47.5	5 50.1	25 02.2	11 03.3	18 38.2	10 03.0	17 57.8	10 25.5
20 W	17 53 09	27 50 13	16 08 40	22 48 33	24 40.8	5 31.6	24 57.5	6 34.2	25 26.8	11 14.2	18 42.3	10 04.5	17 56.9	10 24.3
21 Th	17 57 05	28 51 21	29 22 59	5♒51 42	24 30.9	7 07.2	25 09.8	7 18.3	25 51.4	11 25.0	18 46.3	10 06.1	17 55.9	10 23.1
22 F	18 01 02	29 52 29	12♒14 54	18 32 48	24 23.8	8 42.8	25 24.2	8 02.4	26 16.0	11 35.7	18 50.2	10 07.7	17 54.9	10 21.9
23 Sa	18 04 58	0♑53 37	24 45 43	0♓54 07	24 19.5	10 18.6	25 40.7	8 46.5	26 40.6	11 46.4	18 54.0	10 09.4	17 53.9	10 20.7
24 Su	18 08 55	1 54 46	6♓58 30	12 59 26	24D 17.6	11 54.4	25 59.2	9 30.7	27 05.1	11 56.9	18 57.8	10 11.1	17 52.9	10 19.5
25 M	18 12 52	2 55 54	18 57 33	24 53 32	24R 17.2	13 30.2	26 19.7	10 14.8	27 29.7	12 07.4	19 01.4	10 12.8	17 51.8	10 18.2
26 Tu	18 16 48	3 57 03	0♈48 04	6♈41 51	24 17.3	15 06.1	26 42.0	10 58.9	27 54.2	12 17.7	19 05.0	10 14.6	17 50.7	10 17.0
27 W	18 20 45	4 58 11	12 35 37	18 30 02	24 16.5	16 41.9	27 06.2	11 43.0	28 18.7	12 28.0	19 08.4	10 16.4	17 49.6	10 15.8
28 Th	18 24 41	5 59 20	24 25 48	0♉23 33	24 14.0	18 17.6	27 32.2	12 27.2	28 43.2	12 38.2	19 11.8	10 18.3	17 48.4	10 14.5
29 F	18 28 38	7 00 28	6♉23 55	12 27 28	24 09.0	19 53.2	27 59.9	13 11.3	29 07.7	12 48.2	19 15.1	10 20.2	17 47.3	10 13.3
30 Sa	18 32 34	8 01 37	18 34 40	24 45 57	24 01.3	21 28.4	28 29.2	13 55.4	29 32.1	12 58.2	19 18.2	10 22.2	17 46.1	10 12.0
31 Su	18 36 31	9 02 45	1♊01 40	7♊22 04	23 51.0	23 03.3	29 00.1	14 39.5	29 56.5	13 08.1	19 21.3	10 24.2	17 44.9	10 10.8

Astro Data (Dy Hr Mn)
☽0N 1 7:25
♀R 4 15:21
☽0S 15 5:40
♅D 19 18:06
♆R 21 6:47
☽0N 28 15:42

♄✱♆ 11 19:03
☽0S 12 13:28
♃△♅ 13 8:42
♀D 15 17:08
♃△♇ 16 9:56
☽0N 26 1:21
♅△♇ 27 6:41

Planet Ingress (Dy Hr Mn)
☿ ♏ 8 22:32
☉ ♐ 23 1:55
☿ ♐ 27 23:05
♀ ♏R 28 21:47

♂ ♓ 11 13:10
☿ ♑ 17 0:27
☉ ♑ 22 14:57
⚳ ♑ 31 15:25

Last Aspect Dy Hr Mn		☽ Ingress Dy Hr Mn
30 16:41	♇ △	♈ 1 7:04
3 3:19	♀ ☍	♉ 3 19:40
5 7:28	♆ □	♊ 6 6:33
8 14:27	☿ △	♋ 8 15:23
9 22:10	☉ △	♌ 10 22:05
12 7:52	☉ □	♍ 13 2:36
14 14:51	☉ ✱	♎ 15 5:01
16 10:47	♆ ✱	♏ 17 5:59
19 0:06	☉ ☌	♐ 19 6:52
20 13:15	♆ △	♑ 21 9:31
23 1:11	☿ ✱	♒ 23 15:36
25 18:49	☿ □	♓ 26 1:39
26 23:24	♇ △	♈ 28 14:20

Last Aspect Dy Hr Mn		☽ Ingress Dy Hr Mn
30 10:45	♂ ✱	♉ 1 3:00
3 8:59	♀ ☍	♊ 3 13:34
5 13:32	♂ △	♋ 5 21:34
7 20:04	♀ △	♌ 8 3:33
10 6:31	♂ ☍	♍ 10 8:09
12 2:45	♀ ✱	♎ 12 11:39
14 7:00	☿ ✱	♏ 14 14:14
16 7:15	♀ ☌	♐ 16 16:28
18 12:20	☉ ☌	♑ 18 19:34
20 15:58	♀ ✱	♒ 21 1:08
23 1:32	♀ □	♓ 23 10:14
25 15:00	♀ △	♈ 25 22:22
27 13:18	♄ ☍	♉ 28 11:13
30 19:27	♀ ☍	♊ 30 22:02

☽ Phases & Eclipses (Dy Hr Mn)
4 18:36 ○ 11♉34
12 7:52 ☾ 19♌09
19 0:06 ● 25♏53
26 8:15 ☽ 3♓18

4 11:23 ○ 11♊32
11 16:40 ☾ 18♍52
18 12:20 ● 25♐49
26 5:53 ☽ 3♈41

Astro Data
1 November 1922
Julian Day # 8340
SVP 6♓20'16"
GC 25♐45.7 ⚴ 20♏09.7
Eris 29♓01.6R ⚵ 18♉35.6R
⚷ 14♈11.1R ⚶ 1♍58.5
☽ Mean ☊ 27♍32.8

1 December 1922
Julian Day # 8370
SVP 6♓20'12"
GC 25♐45.8 ⚴ 3♐11.9
Eris 28♓50.5R ⚵ 12♉30.3R
⚷ 13♈13.6R ⚶ 11♍43.8
☽ Mean ☊ 25♍57.5

LONGITUDE — January 1923

Day	Sid.Time	☉	0 hr ☽	Noon ☽	True ☊	☿	♀	♂	⚳	♃	♄	♅	♆	♇
1 M	18 40 27	10♑03 54	13♊47 17	20♊17 22	23♍39.0	24♑37.6	29♏32.6	15♓23.6	0♑20.9	13♏17.9	19♎24.3	10♓26.3	17♌43.6	10♋09.6
2 Tu	18 44 24	11 05 02	26 52 15	3♋31 46	23R 26.2	26 11.3	0♐06.5	16 07.7	0 45.3	13 27.6	19 27.2	10 28.4	17R 42.4	10R 08.3
3 W	18 48 21	12 06 10	10♋15 39	17 03 33	23 14.0	27 44.1	0 41.9	16 51.8	1 09.7	13 37.2	19 30.0	10 30.5	17 41.1	10 07.1
4 Th	18 52 17	13 07 19	23 55 04	0♌49 43	23 03.5	29 15.9	1 18.6	17 35.9	1 34.0	13 46.6	19 32.7	10 32.7	17 39.8	10 05.8
5 F	18 56 14	14 08 27	7♌47 00	14 46 27	22 55.6	0♒46.3	1 56.7	18 20.0	1 58.3	13 56.0	19 35.3	10 34.9	17 38.5	10 04.6
6 Sa	19 00 10	15 09 36	21 47 34	28 49 54	22 50.6	2 15.0	2 36.0	19 04.0	2 22.6	14 05.2	19 37.8	10 37.1	17 37.1	10 03.4
7 Su	19 04 07	16 10 44	5♍53 03	12♍56 42	22D 48.3	3 41.8	3 16.6	19 48.1	2 46.8	14 14.4	19 40.2	10 39.4	17 35.7	10 02.1
8 M	19 08 03	17 11 52	20 00 32	27 04 20	22 48.0	5 06.2	3 58.3	20 32.1	3 11.0	14 23.4	19 42.5	10 41.7	17 34.3	10 00.9
9 Tu	19 12 00	18 13 01	4♎07 56	11♎11 12	22R 48.5	6 27.7	4 41.1	21 16.1	3 35.2	14 32.3	19 44.7	10 44.1	17 32.9	9 59.7
10 W	19 15 56	19 14 10	18 14 01	25 16 17	22 48.5	7 45.7	5 25.0	22 00.1	3 59.4	14 41.1	19 46.8	10 46.5	17 31.5	9 58.4
11 Th	19 19 53	20 15 18	2♏17 55	9♏18 48	22 46.9	8 59.8	6 10.0	22 44.1	4 23.5	14 49.8	19 48.8	10 49.0	17 30.1	9 57.2
12 F	19 23 50	21 16 27	16 18 46	23 17 39	22 42.8	10 09.3	6 55.9	23 28.1	4 47.6	14 58.4	19 50.7	10 51.4	17 28.6	9 56.0
13 Sa	19 27 46	22 17 36	0♐15 12	7♐11 11	22 36.2	11 13.3	7 42.8	24 12.1	5 11.7	15 06.8	19 52.5	10 53.9	17 27.1	9 54.8
14 Su	19 31 43	23 18 44	14 05 17	20 57 08	22 27.3	12 11.1	8 30.6	24 56.1	5 35.7	15 15.1	19 54.1	10 56.5	17 25.6	9 53.6
15 M	19 35 39	24 19 53	27 46 24	4♑32 42	22 17.0	13 01.8	9 19.3	25 40.0	5 59.7	15 23.3	19 55.7	10 59.1	17 24.1	9 52.4
16 Tu	19 39 36	25 21 01	11♑15 43	17 55 07	22 06.4	13 44.6	10 08.8	26 24.0	6 23.7	15 31.4	19 57.2	11 01.7	17 22.6	9 51.2
17 W	19 43 32	26 22 08	24 30 37	1♒02 00	21 56.6	14 18.6	10 59.1	27 07.9	6 47.6	15 39.3	19 58.6	11 04.4	17 21.1	9 50.0
18 Th	19 47 29	27 23 15	7♒29 09	13 51 59	21 48.5	14 42.9	11 50.2	27 51.8	7 11.5	15 47.1	19 59.8	11 07.0	17 19.5	9 48.8
19 F	19 51 25	28 24 21	20 10 32	26 24 55	21 42.8	14R 56.8	12 42.0	28 35.7	7 35.3	15 54.8	20 01.0	11 09.8	17 17.9	9 47.6
20 Sa	19 55 22	29 25 26	2♓35 18	8♓41 58	21 39.5	14 59.6	13 34.5	29 19.6	7 59.1	16 02.3	20 02.0	11 12.5	17 16.4	9 46.5
21 Su	19 59 19	0♒26 31	14 45 16	20 45 38	21D 38.5	14 51.0	14 27.7	0♈03.4	8 22.9	16 09.7	20 02.9	11 15.3	17 14.8	9 45.3
22 M	20 03 15	1 27 34	26 43 32	2♈39 30	21 39.0	14 30.7	15 21.5	0 47.3	8 46.6	16 16.9	20 03.8	11 18.1	17 13.2	9 44.2
23 Tu	20 07 12	2 28 37	8♈34 07	14 28 00	21 40.4	13 59.0	16 16.0	1 31.1	9 10.3	16 24.0	20 04.5	11 20.9	17 11.5	9 43.0
24 W	20 11 08	3 29 38	20 21 48	26 16 11	21R 41.5	13 16.4	17 11.1	2 14.9	9 33.9	16 31.0	20 05.1	11 23.8	17 09.9	9 41.9
25 Th	20 15 05	4 30 39	2♉11 48	8♉09 20	21 41.7	12 24.0	18 06.8	2 58.6	9 57.5	16 37.8	20 05.6	11 26.7	17 08.3	9 40.8
26 F	20 19 01	5 31 38	14 09 28	20 12 49	21 40.3	11 23.1	19 03.0	3 42.4	10 21.0	16 44.5	20 06.0	11 29.6	17 06.7	9 39.7
27 Sa	20 22 58	6 32 37	26 19 59	2♊31 33	21 37.0	10 15.5	19 59.8	4 26.1	10 44.5	16 51.1	20 06.3	11 32.5	17 05.0	9 38.6
28 Su	20 26 54	7 33 34	8♊47 59	15 09 44	21 31.8	9 03.2	20 57.0	5 09.8	11 07.9	16 57.4	20 06.5	11 35.5	17 03.4	9 37.5
29 M	20 30 51	8 34 30	21 37 05	28 10 17	21 25.2	7 48.5	21 54.8	5 53.5	11 31.3	17 03.7	20R 06.6	11 38.5	17 01.7	9 36.4
30 Tu	20 34 48	9 35 25	4♋49 26	11♋34 28	21 17.9	6 33.5	22 53.1	6 37.1	11 54.6	17 09.8	20 06.6	11 41.5	17 00.0	9 35.4
31 W	20 38 44	10 36 19	18 25 16	25 21 30	21 10.8	5 20.4	23 51.9	7 20.7	12 17.8	17 15.7	20 06.4	11 44.6	16 58.4	9 34.3

LONGITUDE — February 1923

Day	Sid.Time	☉	0 hr ☽	Noon ☽	True ☊	☿	♀	♂	⚳	♃	♄	♅	♆	♇
1 Th	20 42 41	11♒37 11	2♌22 44	9♌28 26	21♍04.7	4♒11.1	24♐51.1	8♈04.3	12♑41.1	17♏21.5	20♎06.2	11♓47.6	16♌56.7	9♋33.3
2 F	20 46 37	12 38 03	16 37 57	23 50 34	21R 00.2	3R 07.0	25 50.7	8 47.8	13 04.2	17 27.1	20R 05.9	11 50.7	16R 55.0	9R 32.3
3 Sa	20 50 34	13 38 53	1♍05 31	8♍22 00	20D 57.7	2 09.6	26 50.8	9 31.3	13 27.3	17 32.6	20 05.4	11 53.8	16 53.3	9 31.2
4 Su	20 54 30	14 39 43	15 39 15	22 56 32	20 57.1	1 19.7	27 51.3	10 14.8	13 50.4	17 37.9	20 04.9	11 57.0	16 51.6	9 30.3
5 M	20 58 27	15 40 31	0♎13 11	7♎28 34	20 57.9	0 37.8	28 52.2	10 58.3	14 13.3	17 43.0	20 04.2	12 00.1	16 50.0	9 29.3
6 Tu	21 02 23	16 41 19	14 42 11	21 53 35	20 59.4	0 04.3	29 53.4	11 41.7	14 36.3	17 48.0	20 03.4	12 03.3	16 48.3	9 28.3
7 W	21 06 20	17 42 05	29 02 27	6♏08 30	21R 00.7	29♑39.2	0♑55.1	12 25.1	14 59.1	17 52.8	20 02.6	12 06.5	16 46.6	9 27.4
8 Th	21 10 17	18 42 51	13♏11 33	20 11 27	21 01.2	29 22.3	1 57.0	13 08.5	15 21.9	17 57.5	20 01.6	12 09.7	16 44.9	9 26.4
9 F	21 14 13	19 43 36	27 08 08	4♐01 33	21 00.3	29D 13.4	2 59.4	13 51.8	15 44.7	18 02.0	20 00.5	12 12.9	16 43.2	9 25.5
10 Sa	21 18 10	20 44 20	10♐51 40	17 38 29	20 58.0	29 12.0	4 02.0	14 35.2	16 07.4	18 06.3	19 59.3	12 16.2	16 41.5	9 24.6
11 Su	21 22 06	21 45 02	24 22 00	1♑02 12	20 54.3	29 17.8	5 05.0	15 18.4	16 30.0	18 10.4	19 58.0	12 19.5	16 39.8	9 23.7
12 M	21 26 03	22 45 44	7♑39 06	14 12 42	20 49.8	29 30.3	6 08.2	16 01.7	16 52.5	18 14.4	19 56.6	12 22.7	16 38.2	9 22.9
13 Tu	21 29 59	23 46 24	20 42 59	27 09 58	20 45.1	29 49.1	7 11.8	16 44.9	17 15.0	18 18.2	19 55.2	12 26.0	16 36.5	9 22.0
14 W	21 33 56	24 47 03	3♒33 40	9♒54 05	20 40.8	0♒13.6	8 15.6	17 28.1	17 37.4	18 21.9	19 53.6	12 29.3	16 34.8	9 21.2
15 Th	21 37 52	25 47 41	16 11 17	22 25 18	20 37.3	0 43.4	9 19.7	18 11.3	17 59.8	18 25.3	19 51.9	12 32.7	16 33.2	9 20.4
16 F	21 41 49	26 48 17	28 36 15	4♓44 15	20 35.0	1 18.1	10 24.1	18 54.5	18 22.0	18 28.6	19 50.1	12 36.0	16 31.5	9 19.6
17 Sa	21 45 46	27 48 51	10♓49 27	16 52 04	20D 34.1	1 57.3	11 28.7	19 37.6	18 44.2	18 31.7	19 48.2	12 39.3	16 29.8	9 18.8
18 Su	21 49 42	28 49 24	22 52 21	28 50 35	20 34.2	2 40.7	12 33.5	20 20.7	19 06.3	18 34.6	19 46.2	12 42.7	16 28.2	9 18.0
19 M	21 53 39	29 49 56	4♈47 05	10♈42 16	20 35.3	3 28.0	13 38.6	21 03.7	19 28.4	18 37.3	19 44.1	12 46.1	16 26.6	9 17.3
20 Tu	21 57 35	0♓50 25	16 36 30	22 30 18	20 36.9	4 18.7	14 43.9	21 46.7	19 50.3	18 39.9	19 41.9	12 49.4	16 24.9	9 16.6
21 W	22 01 32	1 50 53	28 24 07	4♉18 30	20 38.6	5 12.7	15 49.4	22 29.7	20 12.2	18 42.3	19 39.7	12 52.8	16 23.3	9 15.9
22 Th	22 05 28	2 51 19	10♉14 00	16 11 13	20 40.0	6 09.8	16 55.1	23 12.6	20 34.0	18 44.4	19 37.3	12 56.2	16 21.7	9 15.2
23 F	22 09 25	3 51 43	22 10 43	28 13 08	20R 40.7	7 09.6	18 01.0	23 55.5	20 55.7	18 46.5	19 34.8	12 59.6	16 20.1	9 14.6
24 Sa	22 13 21	4 52 05	4♊19 03	10♊29 04	20 40.7	8 12.0	19 07.2	24 38.4	21 17.3	18 48.3	19 32.3	13 03.0	16 18.5	9 13.9
25 Su	22 17 18	5 52 25	16 43 44	23 03 36	20 40.0	9 16.9	20 13.5	25 21.3	21 38.8	18 49.9	19 29.7	13 06.5	16 16.9	9 13.3
26 M	22 21 14	6 52 43	29 29 08	6♋00 43	20 38.7	10 23.9	21 20.0	26 04.1	22 00.3	18 51.4	19 27.0	13 09.9	16 15.4	9 12.7
27 Tu	22 25 11	7 52 59	12♋38 41	19 23 13	20 37.0	11 33.2	22 26.6	26 46.8	22 21.6	18 52.6	19 24.1	13 13.3	16 13.8	9 12.1
28 W	22 29 08	8 53 13	26 14 23	3♌12 07	20 35.4	12 44.4	23 33.5	27 29.5	22 42.9	18 53.7	19 21.3	13 16.7	16 12.3	9 11.6

Astro Data

	Dy Hr Mn
☽0S	8 20:07
☿R	20 5:57
☽0N	22 11:02
♂0N	22 12:02
♃□♆	29 5:56
♄R	29 18:45
☽0S	5 3:35
☿D	10 4:20
☽0N	18 19:25

Planet Ingress

		Dy Hr Mn
♀	♐	2 7:27
☿	♒	4 23:40
☉	♒	21 1:35
♂	♈	21 10:07
♀	♑	6 14:34
☿	♑R	6 15:36
☿	♒	13 23:24
☉	♓	19 16:00

Last Aspect / ☽ Ingress

Last Aspect Dy Hr Mn			☽ Ingress	Dy Hr Mn
1 10:22	♄	△	♋	2 5:39
4 8:57	☿	☍	♌	4 10:34
5 20:16	♄	✶	♍	6 13:59
8 0:17	♂	☍	♎	8 16:59
10 2:37	♄	☌	♏	10 20:04
12 12:19	♂	△	♐	12 23:34
14 19:24	♂	□	♑	15 3:56
17 4:23	♂	✶	♒	17 10:05
18 23:41	♄	△	♓	19 18:57
21 2:43	♃	△	♈	22 6:37
23 23:25	♄	☍	♉	24 19:34
26 5:53	♆	□	♊	27 7:07
28 23:38	♀	☍	♋	29 15:19
31 2:56	♄	□	♌	31 19:57

Last Aspect Dy Hr Mn			☽ Ingress	Dy Hr Mn
2 15:34	♀	△	♍	2 22:12
4 20:42	♀	□	♎	4 23:38
7 1:19	☿	□	♏	7 1:37
9 3:41	☿	✶	♐	9 4:59
10 17:58	☉	✶	♑	11 10:08
13 17:07	☿	☌	♒	13 17:18
15 19:07	☉	☌	♓	16 2:43
17 15:19	♃	△	♈	18 14:20
20 10:26	♂	☌	♉	21 3:15
22 17:08	♃	☍	♊	23 15:31
25 16:34	♂	✶	♋	26 0:57
28 1:38	♂	□	♌	28 6:30

☽ Phases & Eclipses

Dy Hr Mn		
3 2:33	○	11♋42
10 0:54	☾	18♎46
17 2:41	●	25♑58
25 3:59	☽	4♉10
1 15:53	○	11♌47
8 9:16	☾	18♏36
15 19:07	●	26♒06
24 0:06	☽	4♊22

Astro Data

1 January 1923
Julian Day # 8401
SVP 6♓20'07"
GC 25♐45.8 ⚴ 16♐24.3
Eris 28♓50.2 ⚵ 12♉37.8
⚷ 12♈59.6 ⚶ 18♍10.9
☽ Mean ☊ 24♍19.0

1 February 1923
Julian Day # 8432
SVP 6♓20'02"
GC 25♐45.9 ⚴ 28♐47.9
Eris 29♓01.4 ⚵ 20♉32.6
⚷ 13♈37.8 ⚶ 18♍29.2R
☽ Mean ☊ 22♍40.5

March 1923 — LONGITUDE

Day	Sid.Time	☉	0 hr ☽	Noon ☽	True ☊	☿	♀	♂	⚳	♃	♄	♅	♆	♇
1 Th	22 33 04	9♓53 25	10♌16 13	17♌26 16	20♍34.0	13♒57.5	24♑40.5	28♈12.2	23♑04.1	18♏54.6	19♎18.3	13♓20.2	16♌10.8	9♋11.0
2 F	22 37 01	10 53 36	24 41 46	2♍01 59	20R 33.1	15 12.3	25 47.7	28 54.9	23 25.1	18 55.3	19R 15.2	13 23.6	16R 09.3	9R 10.5
3 Sa	22 40 57	11 53 44	9♍26 07	16 53 13	20D 32.8	16 28.9	26 55.0	29 37.5	23 46.1	18 55.9	19 12.1	13 27.0	16 07.8	9 10.0
4 Su	22 44 54	12 53 51	24 22 17	1♎52 16	20 32.9	17 47.1	28 02.5	0♉20.1	24 07.0	18 56.2	19 08.9	13 30.5	16 06.3	9 09.6
5 M	22 48 50	13 53 55	9♎22 05	16 50 43	20 33.3	19 06.9	29 10.2	1 02.6	24 27.8	18R 56.3	19 05.6	13 33.9	16 04.8	9 09.1
6 Tu	22 52 47	14 53 58	24 17 14	1♏40 45	20 33.8	20 28.2	0♒18.0	1 45.1	24 48.5	18 56.3	19 02.2	13 37.4	16 03.4	9 08.7
7 W	22 56 43	15 54 00	9♏00 33	16 16 02	20 34.3	21 50.9	1 26.0	2 27.5	25 09.1	18 56.1	18 58.8	13 40.8	16 02.0	9 08.3
8 Th	23 00 40	16 54 00	23 26 42	0♐32 16	20 34.6	23 15.0	2 34.1	3 10.0	25 29.6	18 55.7	18 55.3	13 44.2	16 00.6	9 07.9
9 F	23 04 37	17 53 59	7♐32 31	14 27 21	20R 34.7	24 40.5	3 42.3	3 52.3	25 50.0	18 55.1	18 51.7	13 47.7	15 59.2	9 07.6
10 Sa	23 08 33	18 53 55	21 16 49	28 01 01	20 34.7	26 07.4	4 50.7	4 34.7	26 10.3	18 54.3	18 48.1	13 51.1	15 57.8	9 07.2
11 Su	23 12 30	19 53 51	4♑40 07	11♑14 21	20D 34.7	27 35.5	5 59.2	5 17.0	26 30.5	18 53.3	18 44.4	13 54.5	15 56.5	9 06.9
12 M	23 16 26	20 53 44	17 43 59	24 09 17	20 34.7	29 04.9	7 07.8	5 59.3	26 50.6	18 52.1	18 40.6	13 58.0	15 55.1	9 06.6
13 Tu	23 20 23	21 53 36	0♒30 35	6♒48 11	20 34.8	0♓35.7	8 16.5	6 41.5	27 10.5	18 50.8	18 36.8	14 01.4	15 53.8	9 06.4
14 W	23 24 19	22 53 26	13 02 21	19 13 25	20 35.0	2 07.6	9 25.3	7 23.8	27 30.4	18 49.2	18 32.9	14 04.8	15 52.5	9 06.1
15 Th	23 28 16	23 53 14	25 21 39	1♓27 19	20 35.2	3 40.8	10 34.3	8 05.9	27 50.1	18 47.5	18 28.9	14 08.2	15 51.3	9 05.9
16 F	23 32 12	24 53 01	7♓30 41	13 32 01	20R 35.4	5 15.3	11 43.3	8 48.1	28 09.7	18 45.6	18 24.9	14 11.6	15 50.0	9 05.7
17 Sa	23 36 09	25 52 45	19 31 33	25 29 32	20 35.5	6 51.0	12 52.5	9 30.2	28 29.2	18 43.5	18 20.8	14 15.0	15 48.8	9 05.6
18 Su	23 40 06	26 52 27	1♈26 12	7♈21 48	20 35.2	8 28.0	14 01.7	10 12.2	28 48.6	18 41.2	18 16.7	14 18.4	15 47.6	9 05.4
19 M	23 44 02	27 52 07	13 16 37	19 10 55	20 34.5	10 06.2	15 11.1	10 54.3	29 07.9	18 38.7	18 12.5	14 21.7	15 46.4	9 05.3
20 Tu	23 47 59	28 51 46	25 04 58	0♉59 07	20 33.5	11 45.6	16 20.5	11 36.3	29 27.0	18 36.0	18 08.3	14 25.1	15 45.3	9 05.2
21 W	23 51 55	29 51 22	6♉53 40	12 49 01	20 32.2	13 26.3	17 30.0	12 18.2	29 46.0	18 33.2	18 04.1	14 28.4	15 44.2	9 05.1
22 Th	23 55 52	0♈50 56	18 45 32	24 43 38	20 30.7	15 08.3	18 39.6	13 00.1	0♒04.9	18 30.2	17 59.8	14 31.8	15 43.1	9 05.1
23 F	23 59 48	1 50 27	0♊43 47	6♊46 27	20 29.4	16 51.5	19 49.3	13 42.0	0 23.6	18 27.0	17 55.4	14 35.1	15 42.0	9D 05.0
24 Sa	0 03 45	2 49 57	12 52 06	19 01 15	20 28.5	18 36.1	20 59.0	14 23.8	0 42.2	18 23.7	17 51.1	14 38.4	15 41.0	9 05.0
25 Su	0 07 41	3 49 24	25 14 25	1♋32 06	20D 28.0	20 21.9	22 08.9	15 05.7	1 00.7	18 20.1	17 46.6	14 41.7	15 39.9	9 05.1
26 M	0 11 38	4 48 49	7♋54 48	14 23 00	20 28.2	22 09.0	23 18.8	15 47.4	1 19.0	18 16.4	17 42.2	14 45.0	15 38.9	9 05.1
27 Tu	0 15 35	5 48 11	20 57 07	27 37 32	20 29.0	23 57.5	24 28.8	16 29.1	1 37.2	18 12.6	17 37.7	14 48.3	15 38.0	9 05.2
28 W	0 19 31	6 47 31	4♌24 30	11♌18 12	20 30.2	25 47.3	25 38.8	17 10.8	1 55.2	18 08.5	17 33.2	14 51.6	15 37.0	9 05.3
29 Th	0 23 28	7 46 49	18 18 43	25 25 56	20 31.4	27 38.5	26 49.0	17 52.5	2 13.1	18 04.4	17 28.7	14 54.8	15 36.1	9 05.4
30 F	0 27 24	8 46 05	2♍39 36	9♍59 17	20R 32.3	29 30.9	27 59.2	18 34.1	2 30.9	18 00.0	17 24.2	14 58.0	15 35.3	9 05.5
31 Sa	0 31 21	9 45 18	17 24 22	24 54 03	20 32.5	1♈24.8	29 09.4	19 15.6	2 48.5	17 55.5	17 19.6	15 01.2	15 34.4	9 05.7

April 1923 — LONGITUDE

Day	Sid.Time	☉	0 hr ☽	Noon ☽	True ☊	☿	♀	♂	⚳	♃	♄	♅	♆	♇
1 Su	0 35 17	10♈44 29	2♎27 21	10♎03 11	20♍31.7	3♈20.0	0♓19.8	19♉57.1	3♒06.0	17♏50.8	17♎15.0	15♓04.4	15♌33.6	9♋05.9
2 M	0 39 14	11 43 38	17 40 21	25 17 33	20R 29.9	5 16.5	1 30.1	20 38.6	3 23.3	17R 46.0	17R 10.4	15 07.6	15R 32.8	9 06.1
3 Tu	0 43 10	12 42 45	2♏53 32	10♏27 04	20 27.2	7 14.3	2 40.6	21 20.1	3 40.5	17 41.0	17 05.8	15 10.7	15 32.0	9 06.3
4 W	0 47 07	13 41 50	17 57 00	25 22 21	20 24.1	9 13.4	3 51.1	22 01.5	3 57.5	17 35.9	17 01.2	15 13.8	15 31.3	9 06.6
5 Th	0 51 03	14 40 54	2♐42 16	9♐56 07	20 21.1	11 13.7	5 01.7	22 42.8	4 14.3	17 30.7	16 56.6	15 17.0	15 30.6	9 06.9
6 F	0 55 00	15 39 56	17 03 26	24 03 57	20 18.7	13 15.2	6 12.4	23 24.2	4 31.0	17 25.2	16 51.9	15 20.0	15 29.9	9 07.2
7 Sa	0 58 57	16 38 56	0♑57 34	7♑44 22	20D 17.2	15 17.8	7 23.1	24 05.5	4 47.5	17 19.7	16 47.3	15 23.1	15 29.2	9 07.5
8 Su	1 02 53	17 37 54	14 24 32	20 58 23	20 17.0	17 21.4	8 33.9	24 46.7	5 03.9	17 14.0	16 42.6	15 26.2	15 28.6	9 07.8
9 M	1 06 50	18 36 51	27 26 18	3♒48 45	20 17.8	19 25.9	9 44.7	25 27.9	5 20.1	17 08.2	16 38.0	15 29.2	15 28.0	9 08.2
10 Tu	1 10 46	19 35 45	10♒06 12	16 19 11	20 19.3	21 31.1	10 55.6	26 09.1	5 36.1	17 02.3	16 33.4	15 32.2	15 27.5	9 08.6
11 W	1 14 43	20 34 38	22 28 14	28 33 51	20 21.0	23 36.8	12 06.5	26 50.3	5 51.9	16 56.2	16 28.7	15 35.1	15 27.0	9 09.0
12 Th	1 18 39	21 33 30	4♓36 32	10♓36 46	20R 22.4	25 42.8	13 17.5	27 31.4	6 07.6	16 50.0	16 24.1	15 38.1	15 26.5	9 09.5
13 F	1 22 36	22 32 19	16 35 01	22 31 42	20 22.8	27 49.0	14 28.5	28 12.5	6 23.1	16 43.7	16 19.5	15 41.0	15 26.0	9 09.9
14 Sa	1 26 32	23 31 06	28 27 11	4♈21 51	20 21.8	29 54.9	15 39.5	28 53.5	6 38.4	16 37.3	16 14.9	15 43.9	15 25.6	9 10.4
15 Su	1 30 29	24 29 52	10♈16 01	16 09 59	20 19.1	2♉00.5	16 50.7	29 34.5	6 53.5	16 30.8	16 10.3	15 46.8	15 25.2	9 10.9
16 M	1 34 26	25 28 35	22 04 01	27 58 23	20 14.7	4 05.3	18 01.8	0♊15.5	7 08.4	16 24.2	16 05.8	15 49.6	15 24.8	9 11.5
17 Tu	1 38 22	26 27 17	3♉53 18	9♉49 02	20 08.8	6 09.0	19 13.0	0 56.5	7 23.2	16 17.4	16 01.2	15 52.4	15 24.5	9 12.0
18 W	1 42 19	27 25 57	15 45 46	21 43 46	20 02.0	8 11.3	20 24.2	1 37.4	7 37.7	16 10.6	15 56.7	15 55.2	15 24.2	9 12.6
19 Th	1 46 15	28 24 34	27 43 15	3♊44 28	19 54.9	10 11.8	21 35.5	2 18.2	7 52.0	16 03.7	15 52.3	15 58.0	15 23.9	9 13.2
20 F	1 50 12	29 23 10	9♊47 41	15 53 11	19 48.3	12 10.3	22 46.8	2 59.1	8 06.2	15 56.7	15 47.8	16 00.7	15 23.7	9 13.8
21 Sa	1 54 08	0♉21 44	22 01 18	28 12 22	19 42.8	14 06.4	23 58.1	3 39.9	8 20.1	15 49.7	15 43.4	16 03.4	15 23.5	9 14.5
22 Su	1 58 05	1 20 15	4♋26 45	10♋44 49	19 38.9	15 59.8	25 09.5	4 20.6	8 33.8	15 42.5	15 39.0	16 06.1	15 23.3	9 15.1
23 M	2 02 01	2 18 44	17 06 58	23 33 38	19D 36.9	17 50.2	26 20.9	5 01.4	8 47.3	15 35.3	15 34.6	16 08.7	15 23.2	9 15.8
24 Tu	2 05 58	3 17 11	0♌05 12	6♌42 03	19 36.5	19 37.5	27 32.3	5 42.1	9 00.6	15 28.0	15 30.3	16 11.3	15 23.1	9 16.5
25 W	2 09 55	4 15 36	13 24 33	20 13 01	19 37.4	21 21.2	28 43.7	6 22.7	9 13.7	15 20.7	15 26.0	16 13.9	15 23.0	9 17.2
26 Th	2 13 51	5 13 59	27 07 39	4♍08 35	19 38.6	23 01.3	29 55.2	7 03.3	9 26.6	15 13.3	15 21.8	16 16.4	15D 23.0	9 18.0
27 F	2 17 48	6 12 19	11♍15 50	18 29 14	19R 39.3	24 37.6	1♈06.7	7 43.9	9 39.2	15 05.9	15 17.6	16 18.9	15 23.0	9 18.8
28 Sa	2 21 44	7 10 38	25 48 29	3♎13 04	19 38.6	26 10.0	2 18.3	8 24.4	9 51.7	14 58.4	15 13.5	16 21.4	15 23.0	9 19.5
29 Su	2 25 41	8 08 54	10♎42 17	18 15 15	19 35.9	27 38.2	3 29.8	9 04.9	10 03.9	14 50.9	15 09.4	16 23.8	15 23.1	9 20.3
30 M	2 29 37	9 07 09	25 50 54	3♏28 02	19 31.0	29 02.2	4 41.5	9 45.4	10 15.8	14 43.3	15 05.4	16 26.2	15 23.2	9 21.2

Astro Data

	Dy Hr Mn
☽0S	4 13:05
♃R	5 18:50
♃⊻♄	8 9:10
☽0N	18 2:13
☉0N	21 15:29
♇D	24 2:06
☽0S	1 0:07
☿0N	1 20:13
♅⊼♆	9 4:26
☽0N	14 8:18
♄⊼♅	18 17:01
♃△♅	20 2:13
♃⊻♄	23 17:35
♃□♆	25 4:21
♄✶♆	26 5:16

Planet Ingress

	Dy Hr Mn
♂ ♉	4 0:42
♀ ♒	6 5:38
☿ ♓	13 2:36
☉ ♈	21 15:29
⚳ ♒	22 5:48
☿ ♈	30 18:09
♀ ♓	1 5:16
☿ ♉	14 12:58
♂ ♊	16 2:54
☉ ♉	21 3:06
♀ ♈	26 13:36
♆ D	27 2:19
☽ 0S	28 11:08
♀0N	29 15:54

Last Aspect / ☽ Ingress (March)

Last Aspect Dy Hr Mn		☽ Ingress Dy Hr Mn
2 6:39	♂ △	♍ 2 8:41
4 5:23	♀ △	♎ 4 9:00
5 16:01	☿ △	♏ 6 9:16
7 22:20	☿ □	♐ 8 11:05
10 8:12	☿ ✶	♑ 10 15:34
12 5:23	☉ ✶	♒ 12 23:02
14 11:13	♃ □	♓ 15 9:08
17 12:51	☉ ☌	♈ 17 21:06
19 10:02	♄ ☍	♉ 20 10:00
21 23:32	♃ ☍	♊ 22 22:33
24 16:12	♀ △	♋ 25 9:05
27 4:24	♀ △	♌ 27 16:13
29 14:31	♀ ☍	♍ 29 19:36
31 2:32	♂ △	♎ 31 20:06

Last Aspect / ☽ Ingress (April)

Last Aspect Dy Hr Mn		☽ Ingress Dy Hr Mn
1 23:17	♄ ☌	♏ 2 19:26
4 6:18	♂ ☍	♐ 4 19:33
5 23:44	♄ ✶	♑ 6 22:19
8 19:26	♂ △	♒ 9 4:48
11 8:23	♂ □	♓ 11 14:51
14 0:13	♂ ✶	♈ 14 3:08
16 6:28	☉ ☌	♉ 16 16:07
18 9:03	♀ ✶	♊ 19 4:33
21 2:55	♀ □	♋ 21 15:28
23 17:40	♀ △	♌ 23 23:51
25 14:16	☿ □	♍ 26 4:56
27 23:16	☿ △	♎ 28 6:48
29 7:27	♆ ✶	♏ 30 6:32

☽ Phases & Eclipses

Dy Hr Mn	
3 3:23	○ 11♍32
3 3:32	• P 0.370
9 18:31	☾ 18♐10
17 12:51	● 25♓55
17 12:44:34	● A 07'51"
25 16:41	☽ 4♋01
1 13:10	○ 10♎47
8 5:22	☾ 17♑22
16 6:28	● 25♈15
24 5:20	☽ 3♌01
30 21:30	○ 9♏30

Astro Data

1 March 1923
Julian Day # 8460
SVP 6♓19'59"
GC 25♐46.0 ⚴ 8♑40.7
Eris 29♓19.1 ⚵ 1♊43.4
⚷ 14♈49.6 ⚶ 12♍52.0R
☽Mean ☊ 21♍11.6

1 April 1923
Julian Day # 8491
SVP 6♓19'57"
GC 25♐46.0 ⚴ 17♑10.3
Eris 29♓42.1 ⚵ 16♊15.1
⚷ 16♈33.3 ⚶ 5♍52.0R
☽Mean ☊ 19♍33.0

LONGITUDE — May 1923

Day	Sid.Time	☉	0 hr ☽	Noon ☽	True ☊	☿	♀	♂	⚳	♃	♄	♅	♆	♇
1 Tu	2 33 34	10♉05 21	11♏05 21	18♏41 30	19♍24.3	0♊21.8	5♈53.1	10♊25.8	10♒27.6	14♏35.7	15♎01.4	16♓28.6	15♌23.3	9♋22.0
2 W	2 37 30	11 03 33	26 15 11	3♐45 07	19R16.6	1 37.1	7 04.8	11 06.2	10 39.1	14R28.1	14R57.4	16 30.9	15 23.5	9 22.9
3 Th	2 41 27	12 01 42	11♐10 14	18 29 33	19 08.8	2 47.8	8 16.5	11 46.6	10 50.4	14 20.5	14 53.6	16 33.2	15 23.7	9 23.8
4 F	2 45 24	12 59 50	25 42 21	2♑48 06	19 01.9	3 54.0	9 28.2	12 26.9	11 01.4	14 12.9	14 49.8	16 35.4	15 23.9	9 24.7
5 Sa	2 49 20	13 57 57	9♑46 30	16 37 26	18 56.7	4 55.6	10 40.0	13 07.2	11 12.2	14 05.2	14 46.0	16 37.7	15 24.2	9 25.6
6 Su	2 53 17	14 56 02	23 21 00	29 57 25	18 53.6	5 52.5	11 51.7	13 47.5	11 22.7	13 57.6	14 42.3	16 39.8	15 24.5	9 26.5
7 M	2 57 13	15 54 06	6♒27 03	12♒50 24	18D52.4	6 44.6	13 03.6	14 27.7	11 33.0	13 49.9	14 38.7	16 42.0	15 24.8	9 27.5
8 Tu	3 01 10	16 52 08	19 08 00	25 20 27	18 52.6	7 31.8	14 15.4	15 07.9	11 43.0	13 42.3	14 35.1	16 44.1	15 25.1	9 28.5
9 W	3 05 06	17 50 09	1♓28 23	7♓32 26	18R53.5	8 14.2	15 27.3	15 48.1	11 52.7	13 34.7	14 31.6	16 46.2	15 25.5	9 29.5
10 Th	3 09 03	18 48 09	13 33 16	19 31 30	18 53.9	8 51.6	16 39.2	16 28.2	12 02.2	13 27.1	14 28.2	16 48.2	15 26.0	9 30.5
11 F	3 12 59	19 46 07	25 27 43	1♈22 31	18 53.0	9 24.1	17 51.1	17 08.3	12 11.4	13 19.5	14 24.8	16 50.2	15 26.4	9 31.5
12 Sa	3 16 56	20 44 04	7♈16 25	13 09 55	18 50.1	9 51.6	19 03.0	17 48.4	12 20.4	13 11.9	14 21.5	16 52.1	15 26.9	9 32.6
13 Su	3 20 52	21 41 59	19 03 27	24 57 25	18 44.6	10 14.0	20 15.0	18 28.5	12 29.1	13 04.4	14 18.3	16 54.0	15 27.4	9 33.6
14 M	3 24 49	22 39 53	0♉52 10	6♉48 00	18 36.6	10 31.4	21 27.0	19 08.5	12 37.5	12 56.9	14 15.2	16 55.9	15 28.0	9 34.7
15 Tu	3 28 46	23 37 46	12 45 11	18 43 57	18 26.4	10 43.8	22 39.0	19 48.5	12 45.6	12 49.5	14 12.1	16 57.7	15 28.6	9 35.8
16 W	3 32 42	24 35 37	24 44 27	0♊46 53	18 14.6	10 51.2	23 51.0	20 28.4	12 53.4	12 42.1	14 09.1	16 59.5	15 29.2	9 36.9
17 Th	3 36 39	25 33 27	6♊51 22	12 58 01	18 02.3	10R53.7	25 03.1	21 08.4	13 00.9	12 34.8	14 06.2	17 01.2	15 29.8	9 38.0
18 F	3 40 35	26 31 15	19 06 58	25 18 53	17 50.7	10 51.4	26 15.2	21 48.3	13 08.2	12 27.5	14 03.4	17 02.9	15 30.5	9 39.2
19 Sa	3 44 32	27 29 02	1♋32 13	7♋48 48	17 40.6	10 44.5	27 27.2	22 28.1	13 15.1	12 20.3	14 00.7	17 04.6	15 31.2	9 40.4
20 Su	3 48 28	28 26 48	14 08 15	20 30 44	17 32.8	10 33.2	28 39.4	23 08.0	13 21.7	12 13.2	13 58.0	17 06.2	15 32.0	9 41.5
21 M	3 52 25	29 24 31	26 56 30	3♌25 46	17 27.7	10 17.7	29 51.5	23 47.8	13 28.1	12 06.1	13 55.5	17 07.7	15 32.8	9 42.7
22 Tu	3 56 21	0♊22 13	9♌58 49	16 35 55	17 25.2	9 58.4	1♉03.6	24 27.6	13 34.1	11 59.1	13 53.0	17 09.3	15 33.6	9 43.9
23 W	4 00 18	1 19 54	23 17 22	0♍03 26	17D24.5	9 35.5	2 15.8	25 07.3	13 39.8	11 52.3	13 50.6	17 10.7	15 34.4	9 45.1
24 Th	4 04 15	2 17 33	6♍54 20	13 50 16	17R24.7	9 09.6	3 27.9	25 47.0	13 45.2	11 45.5	13 48.3	17 12.2	15 35.3	9 46.4
25 F	4 08 11	3 15 10	20 51 22	27 57 36	17 24.4	8 40.9	4 40.1	26 26.7	13 50.3	11 38.7	13 46.1	17 13.5	15 36.2	9 47.6
26 Sa	4 12 08	4 12 46	5♎08 54	12♎25 00	17 22.6	8 10.2	5 52.3	27 06.4	13 55.1	11 32.1	13 44.0	17 14.9	15 37.1	9 48.9
27 Su	4 16 04	5 10 20	19 45 27	27 09 41	17 18.3	7 37.8	7 04.5	27 46.0	13 59.6	11 25.6	13 41.9	17 16.2	15 38.1	9 50.1
28 M	4 20 01	6 07 53	4♏36 56	12♏06 16	17 11.4	7 04.4	8 16.8	28 25.6	14 03.7	11 19.2	13 40.0	17 17.4	15 39.1	9 51.4
29 Tu	4 23 57	7 05 25	19 36 37	27 06 50	17 02.2	6 30.6	9 29.0	29 05.1	14 07.5	11 12.9	13 38.1	17 18.6	15 40.1	9 52.7
30 W	4 27 54	8 02 55	4♐35 43	12♐02 05	16 51.5	5 56.9	10 41.3	29 44.7	14 11.0	11 06.8	13 36.4	17 19.8	15 41.1	9 54.0
31 Th	4 31 50	9 00 25	19 24 46	26 42 46	16 40.5	5 23.9	11 53.6	0♋24.2	14 14.2	11 00.7	13 34.7	17 20.9	15 42.2	9 55.3

LONGITUDE — June 1923

Day	Sid.Time	☉	0 hr ☽	Noon ☽	True ☊	☿	♀	♂	⚳	♃	♄	♅	♆	♇
1 F	4 35 47	9♊57 54	3♑55 13	11♑01 26	16♍30.5	4♊52.2	13♉06.0	1♋03.7	14♒17.0	10♏54.8	13♎33.2	17♓22.0	15♌43.3	9♋56.7
2 Sa	4 39 44	10 55 21	18 00 54	24 53 20	16R22.4	4R22.4	14 18.3	1 43.1	14 19.5	10R49.0	13R31.7	17 23.0	15 44.5	9 58.0
3 Su	4 43 40	11 52 48	1♒38 40	8♒16 57	16 16.9	3 54.8	15 30.7	2 22.5	14 21.6	10 43.3	13 30.3	17 24.0	15 45.6	9 59.4
4 M	4 47 37	12 50 14	14 48 26	21 13 29	16 13.7	3 30.0	16 43.1	3 01.9	14 23.4	10 37.7	13 29.0	17 24.9	15 46.8	10 00.7
5 Tu	4 51 33	13 47 40	27 32 34	3♓46 16	16D12.5	3 08.4	17 55.5	3 41.3	14 24.9	10 32.3	13 27.8	17 25.8	15 48.0	10 02.1
6 W	4 55 30	14 45 04	9♓55 10	15 59 56	16R12.4	2 50.3	19 07.9	4 20.7	14 26.0	10 27.0	13 26.8	17 26.6	15 49.3	10 03.5
7 Th	4 59 26	15 42 29	22 01 16	27 59 49	16 12.1	2 35.9	20 20.4	5 00.0	14 26.7	10 21.9	13 25.8	17 27.4	15 50.5	10 04.9
8 F	5 03 23	16 39 52	3♈56 16	9♈51 18	16 10.8	2 25.7	21 32.8	5 39.3	14R27.1	10 16.9	13 24.9	17 28.1	15 51.8	10 06.3
9 Sa	5 07 19	17 37 15	15 45 31	21 39 32	16 07.4	2D19.6	22 45.3	6 18.6	14 27.2	10 12.0	13 24.1	17 28.8	15 53.2	10 07.7
10 Su	5 11 16	18 34 37	27 33 53	3♉29 05	16 01.5	2 17.9	23 57.8	6 57.8	14 26.9	10 07.3	13 23.4	17 29.4	15 54.5	10 09.1
11 M	5 15 13	19 31 59	9♉25 36	15 23 49	15 52.8	2 20.7	25 10.4	7 37.1	14 26.2	10 02.7	13 22.8	17 30.0	15 55.9	10 10.5
12 Tu	5 19 09	20 29 20	21 24 04	27 26 39	15 41.7	2 28.0	26 22.9	8 16.3	14 25.2	9 58.3	13 22.3	17 30.6	15 57.3	10 11.9
13 W	5 23 06	21 26 41	3♊31 47	9♊39 37	15 29.0	2 39.8	27 35.5	8 55.5	14 23.8	9 54.1	13 21.9	17 31.1	15 58.7	10 13.4
14 Th	5 27 02	22 24 01	15 50 18	22 03 52	15 15.7	2 56.2	28 48.1	9 34.6	14 22.1	9 50.0	13 21.6	17 31.5	16 00.2	10 14.8
15 F	5 30 59	23 21 21	28 20 23	4♋39 49	15 03.0	3 17.1	0♊00.7	10 13.8	14 20.0	9 46.1	13 21.4	17 31.9	16 01.7	10 16.3
16 Sa	5 34 55	24 18 39	11♋02 10	17 27 24	14 52.0	3 42.5	1 13.4	10 52.9	14 17.5	9 42.3	13D21.3	17 32.2	16 03.2	10 17.7
17 Su	5 38 52	25 15 58	23 55 29	0♌26 25	14 43.4	4 12.4	2 26.0	11 32.0	14 14.7	9 38.7	13 21.3	17 32.5	16 04.7	10 19.2
18 M	5 42 49	26 13 15	7♌00 11	13 36 48	14 37.7	4 46.6	3 38.7	12 11.1	14 11.5	9 35.3	13 21.4	17 32.8	16 06.3	10 20.7
19 Tu	5 46 45	27 10 31	20 16 20	26 58 50	14 34.6	5 25.2	4 51.4	12 50.1	14 07.9	9 32.1	13 21.6	17 33.0	16 07.8	10 22.2
20 W	5 50 42	28 07 47	3♍44 24	10♍33 08	14D33.7	6 08.0	6 04.1	13 29.2	14 04.0	9 29.0	13 22.0	17 33.1	16 09.4	10 23.6
21 Th	5 54 38	29 05 02	17 25 08	24 20 30	14R33.7	6 54.9	7 16.8	14 08.2	13 59.8	9 26.1	13 22.4	17 33.2	16 11.1	10 25.1
22 F	5 58 35	0♋02 16	1♎19 18	8♎21 31	14 33.6	7 46.0	8 29.5	14 47.1	13 55.2	9 23.3	13 22.9	17R33.3	16 12.7	10 26.6
23 Sa	6 02 31	0 59 30	15 27 07	22 35 56	14 32.1	8 41.1	9 42.3	15 26.1	13 50.2	9 20.8	13 23.5	17 33.3	16 14.4	10 28.1
24 Su	6 06 28	1 56 43	29 47 43	7♏02 05	14 28.3	9 40.2	10 55.0	16 05.0	13 44.9	9 18.4	13 24.2	17 33.3	16 16.0	10 29.6
25 M	6 10 24	2 53 55	14♏18 34	21 36 31	14 22.1	10 43.2	12 07.8	16 43.9	13 39.3	9 16.2	13 25.0	17 33.2	16 17.7	10 31.1
26 Tu	6 14 21	3 51 07	28 55 14	6♐13 52	14 13.6	11 50.1	13 20.6	17 22.8	13 33.3	9 14.1	13 25.9	17 33.0	16 19.5	10 32.6
27 W	6 18 18	4 48 19	13♐31 34	20 47 25	14 03.7	13 00.8	14 33.5	18 01.7	13 27.0	9 12.3	13 26.9	17 32.9	16 21.2	10 34.1
28 Th	6 22 14	5 45 30	28 00 31	5♑10 02	13 53.4	14 15.3	15 46.3	18 40.6	13 20.3	9 10.6	13 28.0	17 32.6	16 23.0	10 35.6
29 F	6 26 11	6 42 41	12♑15 12	19 15 22	13 44.0	15 33.5	16 59.2	19 19.4	13 13.3	9 09.1	13 29.3	17 32.3	16 24.8	10 37.1
30 Sa	6 30 07	7 39 52	26 10 02	2♒58 50	13 36.3	16 55.4	18 12.1	19 58.2	13 06.0	9 07.8	13 30.6	17 32.0	16 26.6	10 38.6

Astro Data

	Dy Hr Mn
☽0N	11 14:59
☿R	17 12:31
☽0S	25 20:43
☽0N	7 23:03
⚳R	9 3:13
♃△♇	10 4:57
☿D	10 9:10
♄D	16 21:41
☽0S	22 4:21
♅R	23 2:41

Planet Ingress

	Dy Hr Mn
☿ ♊	1 5:18
♀ ♉	21 14:50
☉ ♊	22 2:45
♂ ♋	30 21:19
♀ ♊	15 11:46
☉ ♋	22 11:03

Last Aspect / ☽ Ingress (May)

Last Aspect Dy Hr Mn		☽ Ingress Dy Hr Mn
1 8:29	♅ △	♐ 2 5:59
3 8:48	♅ □	♑ 4 7:14
5 12:00	♅ ✶	♒ 6 12:05
7 18:18	☉ □	♓ 8 21:06
10 10:25	☉ ✶	♈ 11 9:12
13 1:21	♀ ☌	♉ 13 22:14
15 22:38	☉ ☌	♊ 16 10:27
18 14:02	♀ ✶	♋ 18 21:03
21 4:44	♀ □	♌ 21 5:40
23 2:49	♂ ✶	♍ 23 11:54
25 9:20	♂ □	♎ 25 15:25
27 13:01	♂ △	♏ 27 16:35
28 20:18	♅ △	♐ 29 16:37
30 20:37	♅ □	♑ 31 17:27

Last Aspect / ☽ Ingress (June)

Last Aspect Dy Hr Mn		☽ Ingress Dy Hr Mn
1 22:54	♅ ✶	♒ 2 21:04
4 2:41	♀ □	♓ 5 4:43
6 18:55	♀ ✶	♈ 7 16:02
9 3:04	☉ ✶	♉ 10 4:56
12 9:40	♀ ☌	♊ 12 17:03
14 12:42	☉ ☌	♋ 15 3:10
16 12:09	♅ △	♌ 17 11:12
19 12:22	☉ ✶	♍ 19 17:22
21 20:46	☉ □	♎ 21 21:44
23 1:18	♆ ✶	♏ 24 0:20
25 5:20	♅ △	♐ 26 1:46
27 6:38	♅ □	♑ 28 3:20
29 12:07	♂ ☍	♒ 30 6:44

☽ Phases & Eclipses

Dy Hr Mn	
7 18:18	☾ 16♒09
15 22:38	● 24♉03
23 14:25	☽ 1♍26
30 5:07	○ 7♐46
6 9:19	☾ 14♓39
14 12:42	● 22♊26
21 20:46	☽ 29♍26
28 13:04	○ 5♑48

Astro Data

1 May 1923
Julian Day # 8521
SVP 6♓19'54"
GC 25♐46.1 ⚴ 21♑28.1
Eris 0♈02.6 ⚵ 1♋10.4
⚷ 18♈18.2 ⚶ 5♍08.4
☽ Mean ☊ 17♍57.7

1 June 1923
Julian Day # 8552
SVP 6♓19'50"
GC 25♐46.2 ⚴ 19♑58.4R
Eris 0♈16.8 ⚵ 16♋44.7
⚷ 19♈50.9 ⚶ 11♍05.0
☽ Mean ☊ 16♍19.2

July 1923 — LONGITUDE

Day	Sid.Time	☉	0 hr ☽	Noon ☽	True ☊	☿	♀	♂	⚳	♃	♄	♅	♆	♇
1 Su	6 34 04	8♋37 03	9♒41 34	16♒18 11	13♍30.9	18♊20.9	19♊25.1	20♋37.0	12♒58.4	9♏06.7	13♎32.0	17♓31.6	16♌28.4	10♋40.2
2 M	6 38 00	9 34 14	22 48 45	29 13 31	13R28.0	19 50.0	20 38.0	21 15.8	12R50.4	9R05.7	13 33.5	17R31.2	16 30.3	10 41.7
3 Tu	6 41 57	10 31 25	5♓32 47	11♓47 00	13D27.0	21 22.6	21 51.0	21 54.5	12 42.2	9 04.9	13 35.1	17 30.7	16 32.1	10 43.2
4 W	6 45 53	11 28 36	17 56 38	24 02 17	13 27.3	22 58.8	23 04.0	22 33.3	12 33.6	9 04.3	13 36.7	17 30.2	16 34.0	10 44.7
5 Th	6 49 50	12 25 47	0♈04 33	6♈04 03	13R28.0	24 38.3	24 17.0	23 12.0	12 24.7	9 03.9	13 38.5	17 29.7	16 35.9	10 46.2
6 F	6 53 47	13 22 59	12 01 27	17 57 26	13 28.1	26 21.1	25 30.1	23 50.7	12 15.5	9D03.6	13 40.4	17 29.1	16 37.8	10 47.7
7 Sa	6 57 43	14 20 11	23 52 38	29 47 42	13 26.7	28 07.2	26 43.2	24 29.4	12 06.0	9 03.6	13 42.4	17 28.4	16 39.7	10 49.2
8 Su	7 01 40	15 17 23	5♉43 15	11♉39 52	13 23.3	29 56.4	27 56.3	25 08.1	11 56.3	9 03.7	13 44.5	17 27.7	16 41.7	10 50.8
9 M	7 05 36	16 14 36	17 38 07	23 38 28	13 17.7	1♋48.5	29 09.4	25 46.7	11 46.3	9 04.0	13 46.6	17 27.0	16 43.6	10 52.3
10 Tu	7 09 33	17 11 49	29 41 24	5♊47 18	13 10.2	3 43.4	0♋22.6	26 25.4	11 36.0	9 04.5	13 48.9	17 26.2	16 45.6	10 53.8
11 W	7 13 29	18 09 03	11♊56 28	18 09 10	13 01.2	5 40.8	1 35.7	27 04.0	11 25.4	9 05.1	13 51.3	17 25.3	16 47.6	10 55.3
12 Th	7 17 26	19 06 17	24 25 34	0♋45 48	12 51.6	7 40.6	2 49.0	27 42.6	11 14.6	9 06.0	13 53.7	17 24.4	16 49.6	10 56.8
13 F	7 21 22	20 03 31	7♋09 54	13 37 50	12 42.4	9 42.5	4 02.2	28 21.3	11 03.6	9 07.0	13 56.3	17 23.5	16 51.6	10 58.3
14 Sa	7 25 19	21 00 46	20 09 31	26 44 48	12 34.5	11 46.2	5 15.4	28 59.8	10 52.3	9 08.2	13 58.9	17 22.5	16 53.7	10 59.8
15 Su	7 29 16	21 58 01	3♌23 33	10♌05 31	12 28.5	13 51.5	6 28.7	29 38.4	10 40.9	9 09.6	14 01.6	17 21.5	16 55.7	11 01.3
16 M	7 33 12	22 55 16	16 50 31	23 38 18	12 24.8	15 58.0	7 42.0	0♌17.0	10 29.2	9 11.1	14 04.5	17 20.5	16 57.8	11 02.8
17 Tu	7 37 09	23 52 31	0♍28 39	7♍21 22	12D23.2	18 05.3	8 55.4	0 55.5	10 17.3	9 12.9	14 07.4	17 19.4	16 59.8	11 04.3
18 W	7 41 05	24 49 46	14 16 16	21 13 09	12 23.4	20 13.3	10 08.7	1 34.1	10 05.3	9 14.8	14 10.4	17 18.2	17 01.9	11 05.7
19 Th	7 45 02	25 47 02	28 11 53	5♎12 19	12 24.4	22 21.5	11 22.1	2 12.6	9 53.1	9 16.9	14 13.4	17 17.0	17 04.0	11 07.2
20 F	7 48 58	26 44 18	12♎14 19	19 17 44	12R25.4	24 29.8	12 35.5	2 51.1	9 40.7	9 19.2	14 16.6	17 15.8	17 06.1	11 08.7
21 Sa	7 52 55	27 41 34	26 22 25	3♏28 11	12 25.5	26 37.8	13 48.9	3 29.6	9 28.2	9 21.6	14 19.9	17 14.5	17 08.2	11 10.2
22 Su	7 56 51	28 38 50	10♏34 49	17 42 01	12 24.0	28 45.3	15 02.3	4 08.0	9 15.5	9 24.2	14 23.2	17 13.2	17 10.3	11 11.6
23 M	8 00 48	29 36 07	24 49 30	1♐56 52	12 20.7	0♌52.1	16 15.8	4 46.5	9 02.8	9 27.0	14 26.7	17 11.9	17 12.5	11 13.1
24 Tu	8 04 45	0♌33 24	9♐03 42	16 09 32	12 15.7	2 58.0	17 29.3	5 24.9	8 49.9	9 29.9	14 30.2	17 10.5	17 14.6	11 14.5
25 W	8 08 41	1 30 41	23 13 51	0♑16 07	12 09.8	5 02.8	18 42.8	6 03.4	8 36.9	9 33.1	14 33.8	17 09.1	17 16.8	11 16.0
26 Th	8 12 38	2 27 59	7♑15 49	14 12 27	12 03.5	7 06.4	19 56.3	6 41.8	8 23.9	9 36.4	14 37.5	17 07.6	17 18.9	11 17.4
27 F	8 16 34	3 25 17	21 05 32	27 54 39	11 57.7	9 08.7	21 09.9	7 20.2	8 10.8	9 39.8	14 41.2	17 06.1	17 21.1	11 18.8
28 Sa	8 20 31	4 22 37	4♒39 28	11♒19 43	11 53.1	11 09.6	22 23.5	7 58.6	7 57.7	9 43.5	14 45.1	17 04.6	17 23.3	11 20.2
29 Su	8 24 27	5 19 56	17 55 13	24 25 53	11 50.1	13 09.1	23 37.1	8 37.0	7 44.5	9 47.2	14 49.0	17 03.0	17 25.5	11 21.6
30 M	8 28 24	6 17 17	0♓51 45	7♓12 56	11D48.8	15 07.0	24 50.7	9 15.3	7 31.3	9 51.2	14 53.0	17 01.4	17 27.6	11 23.0
31 Tu	8 32 20	7 14 39	13 29 36	19 42 03	11 49.0	17 03.3	26 04.4	9 53.7	7 18.1	9 55.3	14 57.1	16 59.8	17 29.8	11 24.4

August 1923 — LONGITUDE

Day	Sid.Time	☉	0 hr ☽	Noon ☽	True ☊	☿	♀	♂	⚳	♃	♄	♅	♆	♇
1 W	8 36 17	8♌12 01	25♓50 38	1♈55 47	11♍50.2	18♌58.1	27♋18.1	10♌32.0	7♒04.8	9♏59.6	15♎01.3	16♓58.1	17♌32.0	11♋25.8
2 Th	8 40 14	9 09 25	7♈57 56	13 57 38	11 51.8	20 51.3	28 31.8	11 10.4	6R51.6	10 04.0	15 05.5	16R56.4	17 34.2	11 27.2
3 F	8 44 10	10 06 50	19 55 26	25 51 54	11 53.4	22 42.9	29 45.5	11 48.7	6 38.4	10 08.6	15 09.8	16 54.6	17 36.4	11 28.5
4 Sa	8 48 07	11 04 16	1♉47 40	7♉43 18	11R54.2	24 32.9	0♌59.3	12 27.1	6 25.3	10 13.4	15 14.2	16 52.8	17 38.6	11 29.9
5 Su	8 52 03	12 01 44	13 39 27	19 36 44	11 54.0	26 21.3	2 13.1	13 05.4	6 12.2	10 18.3	15 18.7	16 51.0	17 40.8	11 31.2
6 M	8 56 00	12 59 12	25 35 42	1♊36 58	11 52.5	28 08.0	3 26.9	13 43.7	5 59.2	10 23.3	15 23.3	16 49.2	17 43.1	11 32.6
7 Tu	8 59 56	13 56 42	7♊41 03	13 48 28	11 49.9	29 53.2	4 40.8	14 22.0	5 46.3	10 28.6	15 27.9	16 47.3	17 45.3	11 33.9
8 W	9 03 53	14 54 13	19 59 39	26 14 59	11 46.3	1♍36.9	5 54.7	15 00.3	5 33.5	10 33.9	15 32.6	16 45.4	17 47.5	11 35.2
9 Th	9 07 49	15 51 46	2♋34 48	8♋59 19	11 42.3	3 18.9	7 08.6	15 38.6	5 20.7	10 39.5	15 37.3	16 43.5	17 49.7	11 36.5
10 F	9 11 46	16 49 20	15 28 43	22 03 04	11 38.4	4 59.5	8 22.5	16 16.9	5 08.1	10 45.1	15 42.2	16 41.5	17 52.0	11 37.8
11 Sa	9 15 43	17 46 55	28 42 19	5♌26 21	11 35.1	6 38.4	9 36.5	16 55.2	4 55.7	10 51.0	15 47.1	16 39.5	17 54.2	11 39.1
12 Su	9 19 39	18 44 31	12♌14 58	19 07 53	11 32.7	8 15.9	10 50.5	17 33.4	4 43.4	10 56.9	15 52.0	16 37.5	17 56.4	11 40.3
13 M	9 23 36	19 42 09	26 04 43	3♍05 03	11D31.5	9 51.8	12 04.5	18 11.7	4 31.2	11 03.1	15 57.1	16 35.5	17 58.6	11 41.6
14 Tu	9 27 32	20 39 47	10♍08 24	17 14 15	11 31.4	11 26.2	13 18.5	18 50.0	4 19.3	11 09.3	16 02.2	16 33.4	18 00.9	11 42.8
15 W	9 31 29	21 37 27	24 22 05	1♎31 22	11 32.2	12 59.0	14 32.6	19 28.2	4 07.5	11 15.7	16 07.4	16 31.3	18 03.1	11 44.0
16 Th	9 35 25	22 35 07	8♎41 36	15 52 17	11 33.4	14 30.3	15 46.7	20 06.5	3 55.9	11 22.3	16 12.6	16 29.2	18 05.3	11 45.2
17 F	9 39 22	23 32 49	23 02 56	0♏13 09	11 34.6	16 00.1	17 00.8	20 44.7	3 44.6	11 29.0	16 17.9	16 27.1	18 07.5	11 46.4
18 Sa	9 43 18	24 30 32	7♏22 32	14 30 44	11R35.4	17 28.3	18 14.9	21 22.9	3 33.5	11 35.8	16 23.3	16 24.9	18 09.7	11 47.6
19 Su	9 47 15	25 28 15	21 37 26	28 42 21	11 35.6	18 55.0	19 29.0	22 01.2	3 22.6	11 42.7	16 28.7	16 22.7	18 11.9	11 48.7
20 M	9 51 12	26 26 00	5♐45 15	12♐45 53	11 35.1	20 20.1	20 43.2	22 39.4	3 11.9	11 49.8	16 34.2	16 20.5	18 14.2	11 49.9
21 Tu	9 55 08	27 23 46	19 44 03	26 39 34	11 33.9	21 43.6	21 57.4	23 17.6	3 01.5	11 57.1	16 39.8	16 18.3	18 16.4	11 51.0
22 W	9 59 05	28 21 34	3♑32 14	10♑21 56	11 32.4	23 05.4	23 11.6	23 55.8	2 51.4	12 04.4	16 45.4	16 16.1	18 18.6	11 52.1
23 Th	10 03 01	29 19 22	17 08 28	23 51 43	11 30.7	24 25.6	24 25.8	24 34.0	2 41.5	12 11.9	16 51.0	16 13.8	18 20.8	11 53.2
24 F	10 06 58	0♍17 12	0♒31 35	7♒07 56	11 29.2	25 44.1	25 40.0	25 12.2	2 31.9	12 19.6	16 56.8	16 11.6	18 22.9	11 54.3
25 Sa	10 10 54	1 15 03	13 40 42	20 09 51	11 28.2	27 00.8	26 54.3	25 50.4	2 22.6	12 27.3	17 02.5	16 09.3	18 25.1	11 55.4
26 Su	10 14 51	2 12 55	26 35 21	2♓57 14	11D27.6	28 15.7	28 08.6	26 28.5	2 13.6	12 35.2	17 08.4	16 07.0	18 27.3	11 56.4
27 M	10 18 47	3 10 49	9♓15 33	15 30 25	11 27.5	29 28.7	29 22.9	27 06.7	2 04.8	12 43.2	17 14.3	16 04.7	18 29.5	11 57.5
28 Tu	10 22 44	4 08 45	21 41 57	27 50 22	11 27.8	0♎39.7	0♍37.2	27 44.9	1 56.4	12 51.3	17 20.2	16 02.3	18 31.6	11 58.5
29 W	10 26 40	5 06 42	3♈55 53	9♈58 48	11 28.4	1 48.8	1 51.5	28 23.1	1 48.3	12 59.5	17 26.2	16 00.0	18 33.8	11 59.5
30 Th	10 30 37	6 04 41	15 59 27	21 58 10	11 29.0	2 55.7	3 05.9	29 01.2	1 40.5	13 07.9	17 32.3	15 57.7	18 35.9	12 00.4
31 F	10 34 34	7 02 42	27 55 23	3♉51 33	11 29.5	4 00.4	4 20.3	29 39.4	1 33.1	13 16.3	17 38.4	15 55.3	18 38.1	12 01.4

Astro Data

	Dy Hr Mn
☽0N	5 8:12
♃ D	7 8:21
☽0S	19 10:46
♅⊼♆	23 7:59
☽0N	1 17:28
☽0S	15 17:30
♄⊼♅	18 17:08
♃△♇	20 12:08
☿0S	25 19:32
☽0N	29 1:50

Planet Ingress

		Dy Hr Mn
☿	♋	8 12:47
♀	♋	10 4:36
♂	♌	16 1:26
☿	♌	23 2:07
☉	♌	23 22:01
♀	♌	3 16:42
☿	♍	7 13:33
☉	♍	24 4:52
☿	♎	27 22:30
♀	♍	27 23:59

Last Aspect / ☽ Ingress (July)

Last Aspect Dy Hr Mn			☽ Ingress	Dy Hr Mn
1 18:19	♀	△	♓	2 13:28
4 9:52	♀	□	♈	4 23:51
7 8:00	☿	⚹	♉	7 12:25
9 16:29	♂	⚹	♊	10 0:37
11 10:36	♅	□	♋	12 10:34
14 16:17	♂	☌	♌	14 17:53
16 0:11	♆	☌	♍	16 23:10
18 18:40	☉	⚹	♎	19 3:05
21 1:32	☉	□	♏	21 6:08
23 7:46	☉	△	♐	23 8:43
24 13:51	♆	△	♑	25 11:32
26 22:58	♀	☍	♒	27 15:42
28 23:03	♆	☍	♓	29 22:23

Last Aspect / ☽ Ingress (August)

Last Aspect Dy Hr Mn			☽ Ingress	Dy Hr Mn
1 1:50	♀	△	♈	1 8:11
3 4:28	☿	△	♉	3 20:22
6 3:52	☿	□	♊	6 8:47
7 19:42	♆	⚹	♋	8 19:08
10 2:15	♅	△	♌	11 2:19
12 11:16	☉	☌	♍	13 6:44
14 10:51	♅	☍	♎	15 9:27
17 0:02	☉	⚹	♏	17 11:38
19 6:07	☉	□	♐	19 14:12
21 13:23	☉	△	♑	21 17:49
23 13:07	☿	△	♒	23 23:03
26 1:57	♀	☍	♓	26 6:25
27 13:06	♅	☌	♈	28 16:15
31 3:01	♂	△	♉	31 4:12

☽ Phases & Eclipses

Dy Hr Mn		
6 1:56	☾	12♈59
14 0:45	●	20♋34
21 1:32	☽	27♎17
27 22:32	○	3♒50
4 19:22	☾	11♉22
12 11:16	●	18♌43
19 6:07	☽	25♏14
26 10:29	○	2♓09
26 10:39	☊	P 0.163

Astro Data

1 July 1923
Julian Day # 8582
SVP 6♓19'45"
GC 25♐46.3 ⚵ 12♑54.9R
Eris 0♈20.8R ⚶ 1♌35.5
⚷ 20♈48.4 ⚴ 21♍05.8
☽ Mean ☊ 14♍43.9

1 August 1923
Julian Day # 8613
SVP 6♓19'40"
GC 25♐46.3 ⚵ 5♑16.9R
Eris 0♈13.9R ⚶ 16♌29.0
⚷ 21♈02.2R ⚴ 4♎05.7
☽ Mean ☊ 13♍05.4

LONGITUDE — September 1923

Day	Sid.Time	☉	0 hr ☽	Noon ☽	True ☊	☿	♀	♂	⚳	♃	♄	♅	♆	♇
1 Sa	10 38 30	8♍00 44	9♉47 09	15♉42 41	11♍29.9	5♎02.7	5♍34.7	0♍17.6	1♒25.9	13♏24.9	17♎44.5	15♓52.9	18♌40.2	12♋02.4
2 Su	10 42 27	8 58 49	21 38 41	27 35 42	11 30.1	6 02.6	6 49.1	0 55.7	1R 19.1	13 33.6	17 50.7	15R 50.6	18 42.3	12 03.3
3 M	10 46 23	9 56 55	3♊34 19	9♊35 06	11R 30.2	6 59.8	8 03.6	1 33.9	1 12.6	13 42.5	17 56.9	15 48.2	18 44.4	12 04.2
4 Tu	10 50 20	10 55 04	15 38 37	21 45 27	11D 30.2	7 54.3	9 18.0	2 12.1	1 06.5	13 51.4	18 03.2	15 45.8	18 46.5	12 05.1
5 W	10 54 16	11 53 14	27 56 08	4♋11 10	11 30.2	8 45.8	10 32.5	2 50.2	1 00.7	14 00.4	18 09.6	15 43.4	18 48.6	12 05.9
6 Th	10 58 13	12 51 27	10♋31 02	16 56 08	11 30.3	9 34.1	11 47.0	3 28.4	0 55.3	14 09.6	18 16.0	15 41.0	18 50.7	12 06.8
7 F	11 02 09	13 49 42	23 26 50	0♌03 21	11 30.5	10 19.1	13 01.6	4 06.6	0 50.2	14 18.9	18 22.4	15 38.6	18 52.7	12 07.6
8 Sa	11 06 06	14 47 58	6♌45 51	13 34 23	11 30.8	11 00.5	14 16.1	4 44.8	0 45.4	14 28.2	18 28.9	15 36.2	18 54.8	12 08.4
9 Su	11 10 03	15 46 16	20 28 52	27 29 04	11R 31.0	11 38.0	15 30.7	5 22.9	0 41.0	14 37.7	18 35.4	15 33.8	18 56.8	12 09.2
10 M	11 13 59	16 44 37	4♍34 38	11♍45 05	11 31.1	12 11.4	16 45.3	6 01.1	0 37.0	14 47.3	18 41.9	15 31.4	18 58.9	12 10.0
11 Tu	11 17 56	17 42 59	18 59 49	26 18 05	11 31.0	12 40.4	17 59.9	6 39.3	0 33.3	14 57.0	18 48.5	15 29.0	19 00.9	12 10.7
12 W	11 21 52	18 41 23	3♎39 05	11♎01 57	11 30.5	13 04.6	19 14.5	7 17.4	0 30.0	15 06.8	18 55.1	15 26.6	19 02.9	12 11.5
13 Th	11 25 49	19 39 48	18 25 44	25 49 34	11 29.7	13 23.7	20 29.1	7 55.6	0 27.1	15 16.6	19 01.8	15 24.2	19 04.8	12 12.2
14 F	11 29 45	20 38 15	3♏12 31	10♏33 47	11 28.7	13 37.4	21 43.8	8 33.7	0 24.5	15 26.6	19 08.5	15 21.8	19 06.8	12 12.9
15 Sa	11 33 42	21 36 44	17 52 37	25 08 23	11 27.7	13R 45.4	22 58.4	9 11.9	0 22.3	15 36.7	19 15.2	15 19.4	19 08.8	12 13.5
16 Su	11 37 38	22 35 15	2♐20 31	9♐28 38	11D 27.0	13 47.3	24 13.1	9 50.1	0 20.5	15 46.9	19 22.0	15 17.1	19 10.7	12 14.2
17 M	11 41 35	23 33 47	16 32 26	23 31 43	11 26.7	13 42.7	25 27.7	10 28.2	0 19.0	15 57.1	19 28.8	15 14.7	19 12.6	12 14.8
18 Tu	11 45 32	24 32 21	0♑26 23	7♑16 28	11 27.0	13 31.5	26 42.4	11 06.4	0 17.9	16 07.5	19 35.7	15 12.3	19 14.5	12 15.4
19 W	11 49 28	25 30 57	14 01 59	20 43 05	11 27.8	13 13.3	27 57.1	11 44.5	0 17.1	16 17.9	19 42.5	15 10.0	19 16.4	12 16.0
20 Th	11 53 25	26 29 34	27 19 55	3♒52 40	11 29.0	12 48.0	29 11.8	12 22.7	0D 16.7	16 28.5	19 49.4	15 07.6	19 18.2	12 16.5
21 F	11 57 21	27 28 13	10♒21 34	16 46 48	11 30.2	12 15.6	0♎26.5	13 00.9	0 16.7	16 39.1	19 56.4	15 05.3	19 20.1	12 17.1
22 Sa	12 01 18	28 26 53	23 08 36	29 27 10	11R 31.2	11 36.3	1 41.3	13 39.0	0 17.0	16 49.8	20 03.3	15 03.0	19 21.9	12 17.6
23 Su	12 05 14	29 25 36	5♓42 42	11♓55 26	11 31.6	10 50.2	2 56.0	14 17.2	0 17.7	17 00.6	20 10.3	15 00.7	19 23.7	12 18.1
24 M	12 09 11	0♎24 20	18 05 31	24 13 10	11 31.1	9 58.0	4 10.7	14 55.3	0 18.7	17 11.5	20 17.3	14 58.4	19 25.5	12 18.5
25 Tu	12 13 07	1 23 06	0♈18 33	6♈21 52	11 29.6	9 00.3	5 25.5	15 33.5	0 20.1	17 22.4	20 24.3	14 56.1	19 27.3	12 19.0
26 W	12 17 04	2 21 54	12 23 19	18 23 06	11 27.0	7 58.1	6 40.2	16 11.7	0 21.8	17 33.4	20 31.4	14 53.8	19 29.0	12 19.4
27 Th	12 21 00	3 20 45	24 21 27	0♉18 36	11 23.7	6 52.7	7 55.0	16 49.8	0 23.9	17 44.5	20 38.5	14 51.6	19 30.7	12 19.8
28 F	12 24 57	4 19 37	6♉14 50	12 10 28	11 19.9	5 45.5	9 09.8	17 28.0	0 26.3	17 55.7	20 45.6	14 49.4	19 32.4	12 20.2
29 Sa	12 28 54	5 18 32	18 05 48	24 01 12	11 16.0	4 38.2	10 24.6	18 06.2	0 29.0	18 07.0	20 52.7	14 47.2	19 34.1	12 20.5
30 Su	12 32 50	6 17 29	29 57 05	5♊53 53	11 12.5	3 32.5	11 39.4	18 44.3	0 32.1	18 18.3	20 59.8	14 45.0	19 35.8	12 20.9

LONGITUDE — October 1923

Day	Sid.Time	☉	0 hr ☽	Noon ☽	True ☊	☿	♀	♂	⚳	♃	♄	♅	♆	♇
1 M	12 36 47	7♎16 28	11♊52 03	17♊52 05	11♍09.9	2♎30.1	12♎54.2	19♍22.5	0♒35.6	18♏29.7	21♎07.0	14♓42.8	19♌37.4	12♋21.2
2 Tu	12 40 43	8 15 30	23 54 30	29 59 51	11D 08.4	1R 32.9	14 09.0	20 00.7	0 39.3	18 41.2	21 14.2	14R 40.7	19 39.0	12 21.5
3 W	12 44 40	9 14 33	6♋08 40	12♋21 33	11 08.1	0 42.3	15 23.8	20 38.9	0 43.4	18 52.8	21 21.4	14 38.6	19 40.6	12 21.7
4 Th	12 48 36	10 13 40	18 39 01	25 01 37	11 08.9	29♍59.8	16 38.7	21 17.1	0 47.8	19 04.4	21 28.6	14 36.5	19 42.2	12 22.0
5 F	12 52 33	11 12 48	1♌29 50	8♌04 08	11 10.4	29 26.5	17 53.5	21 55.3	0 52.6	19 16.1	21 35.8	14 34.4	19 43.7	12 22.2
6 Sa	12 56 29	12 11 59	14 44 52	21 32 20	11 11.9	29 03.1	19 08.4	22 33.5	0 57.7	19 27.8	21 43.1	14 32.3	19 45.3	12 22.4
7 Su	13 00 26	13 11 12	28 26 39	5♍27 51	11R 12.9	28D 50.2	20 23.3	23 11.7	1 03.0	19 39.6	21 50.3	14 30.3	19 46.8	12 22.5
8 M	13 04 23	14 10 27	12♍35 46	19 50 04	11 12.8	28 48.1	21 38.1	23 49.9	1 08.8	19 51.5	21 57.6	14 28.3	19 48.2	12 22.7
9 Tu	13 08 19	15 09 44	27 10 14	4♎35 32	11 11.1	28 56.6	22 53.0	24 28.2	1 14.8	20 03.5	22 04.8	14 26.3	19 49.7	12 22.8
10 W	13 12 16	16 09 04	12♎05 03	19 37 45	11 07.7	29 15.6	24 07.9	25 06.4	1 21.1	20 15.5	22 12.1	14 24.4	19 51.1	12 22.9
11 Th	13 16 12	17 08 26	27 12 26	4♏47 49	11 02.9	29 44.5	25 22.8	25 44.6	1 27.7	20 27.5	22 19.4	14 22.5	19 52.5	12 23.0
12 F	13 20 09	18 07 49	12♏22 39	19 55 40	10 57.4	0♎22.9	26 37.7	26 22.8	1 34.7	20 39.7	22 26.7	14 20.6	19 53.8	12 23.0
13 Sa	13 24 05	19 07 15	27 25 42	4♐51 42	10 51.9	1 09.9	27 52.6	27 01.1	1 41.9	20 51.9	22 34.0	14 18.8	19 55.2	12R 23.0
14 Su	13 28 02	20 06 42	12♐12 49	19 28 22	10 47.4	2 04.8	29 07.5	27 39.3	1 49.5	21 04.1	22 41.3	14 16.9	19 56.5	12 23.0
15 M	13 31 58	21 06 11	26 37 51	3♑40 59	10 44.3	3 06.9	0♏22.4	28 17.6	1 57.3	21 16.4	22 48.6	14 15.2	19 57.8	12 23.0
16 Tu	13 35 55	22 05 42	10♑37 38	17 27 53	10D 42.9	4 15.3	1 37.4	28 55.8	2 05.5	21 28.7	22 55.9	14 13.4	19 59.0	12 23.0
17 W	13 39 52	23 05 15	24 11 52	0♒49 53	10 43.1	5 29.3	2 52.3	29 34.0	2 13.9	21 41.1	23 03.3	14 11.7	20 00.3	12 22.9
18 Th	13 43 48	24 04 49	7♒22 18	13 49 30	10 44.3	6 48.1	4 07.2	0♎12.3	2 22.6	21 53.6	23 10.6	14 10.0	20 01.4	12 22.8
19 F	13 47 45	25 04 25	20 11 59	26 30 10	10 45.7	8 11.1	5 22.1	0 50.5	2 31.6	22 06.1	23 17.9	14 08.4	20 02.6	12 22.7
20 Sa	13 51 41	26 04 03	2♓44 32	8♓55 33	10R 46.5	9 37.6	6 37.0	1 28.8	2 40.8	22 18.6	23 25.2	14 06.8	20 03.8	12 22.5
21 Su	13 55 38	27 03 42	15 03 38	21 09 11	10 45.9	11 07.1	7 51.9	2 07.0	2 50.3	22 31.2	23 32.5	14 05.2	20 04.9	12 22.3
22 M	13 59 34	28 03 24	27 12 34	3♈14 08	10 43.3	12 39.0	9 06.8	2 45.3	3 00.1	22 43.8	23 39.8	14 03.7	20 05.9	12 22.2
23 Tu	14 03 31	29 03 07	9♈14 10	15 12 58	10 38.3	14 12.9	10 21.7	3 23.6	3 10.1	22 56.5	23 47.1	14 02.2	20 07.0	12 21.9
24 W	14 07 27	0♏02 52	21 10 44	27 07 44	10 31.1	15 48.4	11 36.6	4 01.8	3 20.4	23 09.2	23 54.4	14 00.7	20 08.0	12 21.7
25 Th	14 11 24	1 02 39	3♉04 08	9♉00 08	10 22.1	17 25.2	12 51.6	4 40.1	3 31.0	23 21.9	24 01.6	13 59.3	20 09.0	12 21.4
26 F	14 15 20	2 02 28	14 55 56	20 51 43	10 11.9	19 03.0	14 06.5	5 18.4	3 41.8	23 34.7	24 08.9	13 58.0	20 09.9	12 21.2
27 Sa	14 19 17	3 02 20	26 47 42	2♊44 05	10 01.4	20 41.5	15 21.4	5 56.7	3 52.9	23 47.6	24 16.2	13 56.6	20 10.9	12 20.8
28 Su	14 23 14	4 02 13	8♊41 08	14 39 08	9 51.7	22 20.5	16 36.3	6 35.0	4 04.2	24 00.4	24 23.4	13 55.3	20 11.8	12 20.5
29 M	14 27 10	5 02 09	20 38 22	26 39 12	9 43.4	23 59.8	17 51.2	7 13.3	4 15.7	24 13.3	24 30.7	13 54.1	20 12.6	12 20.2
30 Tu	14 31 07	6 02 06	2♋42 02	8♋47 17	9 37.4	25 39.4	19 06.2	7 51.6	4 27.5	24 26.3	24 37.9	13 52.9	20 13.5	12 19.8
31 W	14 35 03	7 02 06	14 55 24	21 06 54	9 33.7	27 19.1	20 21.1	8 29.9	4 39.5	24 39.2	24 45.1	13 51.7	20 14.3	12 19.4

Astro Data

	Dy Hr Mn
☽0S	12 1:56
♃△♅	14 2:43
♄⚹♆	14 3:23
☿ R	16 7:09
⚳ D	21 2:28
♀0S	23 14:08
☉0S	24 2:03
☽0N	25 8:55
☿0N	5 20:49
♃□♆	8 4:26
☿ D	8 4:46
☽0S	9 12:22
♇ R	14 0:00
☿0S	16 13:38
♂0S	22 1:37

Planet Ingress

		Dy Hr Mn
♂	♍	1 0:57
♀	♎	21 3:29
☉	♎	24 2:04
☿	♍R	4 11:53
☿	♎	11 22:23
♀	♏	15 4:49
♂	♎	18 4:18
☉	♏	24 10:51

☽0N22 15:15

Last Aspect / ☽ Ingress (September)

Last Aspect Dy Hr Mn			☽ Ingress	Dy Hr Mn
1 18:00	♆	□	♊	2 16:50
4 6:09	♆	⚹	♋	5 3:59
6 14:29	♄	□	♌	7 11:54
8 21:19	♆	☌	♍	9 16:16
10 21:04	♀	☌	♎	11 18:03
13 1:02	♆	⚹	♏	13 18:47
15 8:05	♀	⚹	♐	15 20:05
17 15:41	♀	□	♑	17 23:14
20 2:30	♀	△	♒	20 4:53
21 18:00	♄	△	♓	22 13:03
23 22:02	♃	△	♈	24 23:23
26 16:20	♄	☍	♉	27 11:22
29 2:58	♆	□	♊	30 0:06

Last Aspect / ☽ Ingress (October)

Last Aspect Dy Hr Mn			☽ Ingress	Dy Hr Mn
1 18:32	♄	△	♋	2 12:00
4 20:49	☿	⚹	♌	4 21:14
6 12:19	♄	⚹	♍	7 2:41
9 2:45	☿	☌	♎	9 4:35
10 19:46	♀	☌	♏	11 4:25
12 22:47	♂	⚹	♐	13 4:08
15 2:23	♂	□	♑	15 5:43
17 9:35	♂	△	♒	17 10:29
19 9:02	☉	△	♓	19 18:43
21 14:45	♃	△	♈	22 5:33
24 5:26	♄	☍	♉	24 17:48
26 17:36	♃	☍	♊	27 6:29
29 7:41	♄	△	♋	29 18:39

☽ Phases & Eclipses

Dy Hr Mn		
3 12:47	☾	9♊59
10 20:52	●	17♍06
10 20:47:05	●	T 03'37"
17 12:04	☽	23♐34
25 1:16	○	0♈57
3 5:29	☾	8♋59
10 6:05	●	15♎54
16 20:53	☽	22♑28
24 18:26	○	0♉19

Astro Data

1 September 1923
Julian Day # 8644
SVP 6♓19'37"
GC 25♐46.4 ⚵ 3♑00.1
Eris 29♓57.9R ⚴ 0♍45.2
⚷ 20♈26.9R ⚶ 18♎45.8
☽ Mean ☊ 11♍26.9

1 October 1923
Julian Day # 8674
SVP 6♓19'35"
GC 25♐46.5 ⚵ 6♑11.0
Eris 29♓38.2R ⚴ 13♍46.4
⚷ 19♈17.1R ⚶ 3♏58.6
☽ Mean ☊ 9♍51.6

November 1923 — LONGITUDE

Day	Sid.Time	☉	0 hr ☽	Noon ☽	True ☊	☿	♀	♂	⚳	♃	♄	♅	♆	♇
1 Th	14 39 00	8♏02 08	27♋22 18	3♌42 07	9♍32.3	28♎58.7	21♏36.0	9♎08.2	4♒51.7	24♏52.2	24♎52.3	13♓50.6	20♌15.0	12♋19.0
2 F	14 42 56	9 02 12	10♌06 55	16 37 13	9D 32.4	0♏38.2	22 51.0	9 46.5	5 04.2	25 05.3	24 59.5	13R 49.5	20 15.8	12R 18.5
3 Sa	14 46 53	10 02 18	23 13 31	29 56 15	9R 33.1	2 17.6	24 05.9	10 24.9	5 16.9	25 18.3	25 06.6	13 48.5	20 16.5	12 18.1
4 Su	14 50 49	11 02 26	6♍45 47	13♍42 21	9 33.3	3 56.8	25 20.9	11 03.2	5 29.8	25 31.4	25 13.8	13 47.5	20 17.1	12 17.6
5 M	14 54 46	12 02 37	20 46 05	27 56 53	9 31.9	5 35.7	26 35.8	11 41.6	5 43.0	25 44.5	25 20.9	13 46.6	20 17.8	12 17.1
6 Tu	14 58 43	13 02 49	5♎14 30	12♎38 26	9 28.1	7 14.3	27 50.7	12 19.9	5 56.3	25 57.7	25 28.0	13 45.7	20 18.4	12 16.5
7 W	15 02 39	14 03 04	20 07 58	27 42 09	9 21.7	8 52.6	29 05.7	12 58.3	6 09.9	26 10.8	25 35.1	13 44.9	20 18.9	12 16.0
8 Th	15 06 36	15 03 20	5♏19 50	12♏59 41	9 12.9	10 30.6	0♐20.6	13 36.7	6 23.7	26 24.0	25 42.1	13 44.1	20 19.5	12 15.4
9 F	15 10 32	16 03 38	20 40 15	28 20 04	9 02.8	12 08.3	1 35.6	14 15.0	6 37.7	26 37.2	25 49.2	13 43.3	20 20.0	12 14.8
10 Sa	15 14 29	17 03 58	5♐57 39	13♐31 38	8 52.5	13 45.7	2 50.5	14 53.4	6 51.9	26 50.5	25 56.2	13 42.6	20 20.5	12 14.2
11 Su	15 18 25	18 04 19	21 00 48	28 24 08	8 43.3	15 22.7	4 05.5	15 31.8	7 06.3	27 03.7	26 03.1	13 42.0	20 20.9	12 13.6
12 M	15 22 22	19 04 42	5♑40 52	12♑50 26	8 36.2	16 59.4	5 20.4	16 10.2	7 20.8	27 17.0	26 10.1	13 41.4	20 21.3	12 12.9
13 Tu	15 26 18	20 05 07	19 52 33	26 47 08	8 31.6	18 35.8	6 35.4	16 48.5	7 35.6	27 30.3	26 17.0	13 40.8	20 21.7	12 12.2
14 W	15 30 15	21 05 32	3♒34 17	10♒14 16	8D 29.5	20 11.9	7 50.3	17 26.9	7 50.6	27 43.5	26 23.9	13 40.3	20 22.0	12 11.5
15 Th	15 34 12	22 05 59	16 47 30	23 14 27	8 29.0	21 47.6	9 05.3	18 05.3	8 05.8	27 56.8	26 30.8	13 39.9	20 22.3	12 10.8
16 F	15 38 08	23 06 28	29 35 41	5♓51 49	8R 29.2	23 23.2	10 20.2	18 43.7	8 21.1	28 10.2	26 37.6	13 39.5	20 22.6	12 10.1
17 Sa	15 42 05	24 06 57	12♓03 27	18 11 13	8 28.9	24 58.4	11 35.1	19 22.1	8 36.6	28 23.5	26 44.4	13 39.1	20 22.8	12 09.3
18 Su	15 46 01	25 07 28	24 15 42	0♈17 30	8 26.9	26 33.3	12 50.0	20 00.5	8 52.4	28 36.8	26 51.1	13 38.8	20 23.0	12 08.5
19 M	15 49 58	26 08 00	6♈17 09	12 15 08	8 22.4	28 08.1	14 04.9	20 38.9	9 08.2	28 50.2	26 57.8	13 38.5	20 23.1	12 07.7
20 Tu	15 53 54	27 08 34	18 11 56	24 07 56	8 14.9	29 42.6	15 19.8	21 17.3	9 24.3	29 03.5	27 04.5	13 38.3	20 23.3	12 06.9
21 W	15 57 51	28 09 08	0♉03 29	5♉58 55	8 04.5	1♐16.9	16 34.7	21 55.8	9 40.5	29 16.9	27 11.1	13 38.2	20 23.4	12 06.1
22 Th	16 01 47	29 09 45	11 54 30	17 50 26	7 51.6	2 51.0	17 49.6	22 34.2	9 56.9	29 30.2	27 17.7	13 38.1	20 23.4	12 05.2
23 F	16 05 44	0♐10 22	23 46 55	29 44 08	7 37.1	4 24.9	19 04.5	23 12.6	10 13.4	29 43.6	27 24.3	13D 38.0	20R 23.4	12 04.4
24 Sa	16 09 41	1 11 01	5♊42 13	11♊41 19	7 22.3	5 58.7	20 19.4	23 51.0	10 30.1	29 56.9	27 30.8	13 38.0	20 23.4	12 03.5
25 Su	16 13 37	2 11 42	17 41 33	23 43 05	7 08.2	7 32.3	21 34.3	24 29.5	10 47.0	0♐10.3	27 37.3	13 38.1	20 23.4	12 02.6
26 M	16 17 34	3 12 24	29 46 04	5♋50 42	6 56.0	9 05.8	22 49.2	25 07.9	11 04.0	0 23.6	27 43.7	13 38.2	20 23.3	12 01.7
27 Tu	16 21 30	4 13 07	11♋57 11	18 05 46	6 46.5	10 39.2	24 04.1	25 46.4	11 21.2	0 37.0	27 50.1	13 38.3	20 23.2	12 00.7
28 W	16 25 27	5 13 52	24 16 46	0♌30 31	6 40.1	12 12.5	25 19.0	26 24.8	11 38.5	0 50.4	27 56.4	13 38.6	20 23.0	11 59.8
29 Th	16 29 23	6 14 39	6♌47 22	13 07 45	6 36.6	13 45.7	26 33.8	27 03.3	11 56.0	1 03.7	28 02.7	13 38.8	20 22.9	11 58.8
30 F	16 33 20	7 15 27	19 32 05	26 00 50	6 35.3	15 18.8	27 48.7	27 41.8	12 13.6	1 17.0	28 09.0	13 39.1	20 22.6	11 57.9

December 1923 — LONGITUDE

Day	Sid.Time	☉	0 hr ☽	Noon ☽	True ☊	☿	♀	♂	⚳	♃	♄	♅	♆	♇
1 Sa	16 37 16	8♐16 16	2♍34 28	9♍13 24	6♍35.1	16♐51.8	29♐03.6	28♎20.3	12♒31.4	1♐30.4	28♎15.1	13♓39.5	20♌22.4	11♋56.9
2 Su	16 41 13	9 17 07	15 58 04	22 48 46	6R 34.8	18 24.7	0♑18.4	28 58.8	12 49.3	1 43.7	28 21.3	13 39.9	20R 22.1	11R 55.9
3 M	16 45 10	10 17 59	29 45 47	6♎49 14	6 33.0	19 57.6	1 33.3	29 37.3	13 07.3	1 57.0	28 27.4	13 40.3	20 21.8	11 54.8
4 Tu	16 49 06	11 18 53	13♎59 05	21 15 06	6 28.8	21 30.4	2 48.1	0♏15.8	13 25.5	2 10.3	28 33.4	13 40.9	20 21.4	11 53.8
5 W	16 53 03	12 19 48	28 36 54	6♏03 49	6 21.7	23 03.1	4 03.0	0 54.3	13 43.8	2 23.6	28 39.4	13 41.4	20 21.1	11 52.7
6 Th	16 56 59	13 20 44	13♏35 00	21 09 24	6 12.1	24 35.7	5 17.8	1 32.8	14 02.2	2 36.9	28 45.3	13 42.0	20 20.6	11 51.7
7 F	17 00 56	14 21 42	28 45 46	6♐22 45	6 00.7	26 08.2	6 32.7	2 11.3	14 20.8	2 50.2	28 51.1	13 42.7	20 20.2	11 50.6
8 Sa	17 04 52	15 22 40	13♐58 56	21 32 55	5 48.9	27 40.6	7 47.5	2 49.8	14 39.5	3 03.4	28 57.0	13 43.4	20 19.7	11 49.5
9 Su	17 08 49	16 23 40	29 03 23	6♑29 07	5 38.1	29 12.8	9 02.3	3 28.3	14 58.4	3 16.6	29 02.7	13 44.2	20 19.2	11 48.4
10 M	17 12 46	17 24 40	13♑49 07	21 02 35	5 29.5	0♑44.8	10 17.1	4 06.8	15 17.3	3 29.8	29 08.4	13 45.0	20 18.7	11 47.3
11 Tu	17 16 42	18 25 41	28 08 59	5♒07 58	5 23.6	2 16.6	11 31.9	4 45.3	15 36.4	3 43.0	29 14.0	13 45.9	20 18.1	11 46.2
12 W	17 20 39	19 26 43	11♒59 25	18 43 26	5 20.5	3 48.1	12 46.7	5 23.9	15 55.6	3 56.2	29 19.6	13 46.8	20 17.5	11 45.1
13 Th	17 24 35	20 27 45	25 20 16	1♓50 18	5D 19.4	5 19.2	14 01.5	6 02.4	16 14.9	4 09.3	29 25.0	13 47.8	20 16.8	11 43.9
14 F	17 28 32	21 28 47	8♓14 02	14 32 02	5R 19.5	6 49.8	15 16.3	6 40.9	16 34.4	4 22.4	29 30.5	13 48.8	20 16.1	11 42.8
15 Sa	17 32 28	22 29 50	20 44 55	26 53 21	5 19.6	8 19.9	16 31.0	7 19.4	16 53.9	4 35.5	29 35.8	13 49.9	20 15.4	11 41.6
16 Su	17 36 25	23 30 53	2♈58 01	8♈59 33	5 18.4	9 49.3	17 45.8	7 58.0	17 13.6	4 48.5	29 41.1	13 51.0	20 14.7	11 40.4
17 M	17 40 21	24 31 57	14 58 37	20 55 50	5 15.0	11 18.0	19 00.5	8 36.5	17 33.3	5 01.5	29 46.3	13 52.2	20 13.9	11 39.3
18 Tu	17 44 18	25 33 01	26 51 48	2♉47 02	5 09.0	12 45.6	20 15.2	9 15.0	17 53.2	5 14.5	29 51.5	13 53.4	20 13.1	11 38.1
19 W	17 48 15	26 34 06	8♉42 02	14 37 16	5 00.2	14 12.1	21 29.9	9 53.5	18 13.2	5 27.5	29 56.6	13 54.7	20 12.3	11 36.9
20 Th	17 52 11	27 35 11	20 33 06	26 29 54	4 49.2	15 37.2	22 44.6	10 32.1	18 33.2	5 40.4	0♏01.6	13 56.0	20 11.4	11 35.7
21 F	17 56 08	28 36 16	2♊27 55	8♊27 26	4 36.6	17 00.7	23 59.3	11 10.6	18 53.4	5 53.3	0 06.5	13 57.4	20 10.6	11 34.5
22 Sa	18 00 04	29 37 22	14 28 36	20 31 36	4 23.5	18 22.2	25 13.9	11 49.1	19 13.7	6 06.1	0 11.4	13 58.8	20 09.6	11 33.3
23 Su	18 04 01	0♑38 29	26 36 33	2♋43 32	4 11.1	19 41.4	26 28.5	12 27.7	19 34.0	6 18.9	0 16.2	14 00.2	20 08.7	11 32.0
24 M	18 07 57	1 39 35	8♋52 38	15 03 55	4 00.4	20 57.8	27 43.1	13 06.2	19 54.5	6 31.7	0 20.9	14 01.7	20 07.7	11 30.8
25 Tu	18 11 54	2 40 42	21 17 27	27 33 20	3 52.2	22 11.0	28 57.7	13 44.8	20 15.0	6 44.4	0 25.5	14 03.3	20 06.7	11 29.6
26 W	18 15 50	3 41 50	3♌51 39	10♌12 33	3 46.8	23 20.6	0♒12.3	14 23.3	20 35.7	6 57.1	0 30.1	14 04.9	20 05.7	11 28.4
27 Th	18 19 47	4 42 58	16 36 09	23 02 40	3D 44.1	24 25.7	1 26.8	15 01.9	20 56.4	7 09.7	0 34.5	14 06.5	20 04.6	11 27.1
28 F	18 23 44	5 44 06	29 32 18	6♍05 17	3 43.5	25 25.8	2 41.4	15 40.5	21 17.2	7 22.3	0 38.9	14 08.2	20 03.6	11 25.9
29 Sa	18 27 40	6 45 15	12♍41 53	19 22 22	3 44.2	26 20.2	3 55.9	16 19.0	21 38.1	7 34.8	0 43.3	14 10.0	20 02.5	11 24.7
30 Su	18 31 37	7 46 24	26 06 58	2♎55 56	3R 45.0	27 07.9	5 10.4	16 57.6	21 59.1	7 47.3	0 47.5	14 11.7	20 01.3	11 23.4
31 M	18 35 33	8 47 34	9♎49 27	16 47 39	3 44.8	27 48.1	6 24.8	17 36.2	22 20.1	7 59.8	0 51.6	14 13.6	20 00.2	11 22.2

Astro Data

	Dy Hr Mn
♃⚺♄	1 12:16
☽0S	5 23:43
♃□♇	12 4:59
☽0N	18 21:57
♆R	23 16:52
♅D	23 23:29
☽0S	3 10:03
♄□♅	5 21:15
☽0N	16 5:58
☽0S	30 18:02

Planet Ingress

	Dy Hr Mn
☿ ♏	2 2:47
♀ ♐	8 5:23
☿ ♐	20 16:26
☉ ♐	23 7:54
♃ ♐	24 17:31
♀ ♑	2 6:06
♂ ♏	4 2:11
☿ ♑	10 0:18
♄ ♏	20 4:25
☉ ♑	22 20:53
♀ ♒	26 8:03

Last Aspect / ☽ Ingress

Last Aspect Dy Hr Mn		☽ Ingress Dy Hr Mn
1 1:42	☿ □	♌ 1 5:00
3 3:36	♃ □	♍ 3 12:07
5 9:32	♀ ⚹	♎ 5 15:24
7 8:38	♄ ☌	♏ 7 15:37
9 9:16	♃ ☌	♐ 9 14:37
11 8:08	♄ ⚹	♑ 11 14:37
13 13:17	♃ ⚹	♒ 13 17:39
15 21:02	♃ □	♓ 16 0:46
18 8:35	♃ △	♈ 18 11:25
20 18:01	♄ ☍	♉ 20 23:53
23 11:59	♃ ☍	♊ 23 12:32
25 19:49	♄ △	♋ 26 0:28
28 7:01	♄ △	♌ 28 11:01
30 15:57	♄ ⚹	♍ 30 19:19

Last Aspect / ☽ Ingress

Last Aspect Dy Hr Mn		☽ Ingress Dy Hr Mn
2 3:19	☿ □	♎ 3 0:24
4 23:59	♄ ☌	♏ 5 2:14
6 10:43	♆ □	♐ 7 1:57
8 23:54	♄ ⚹	♑ 9 1:31
11 1:47	☿ ☌	♒ 11 3:10
13 7:29	♄ △	♓ 13 8:35
15 2:38	☉ □	♈ 15 18:08
18 6:01	♄ ☍	♉ 18 6:21
20 3:32	♀ △	♊ 20 19:03
22 11:17	♆ ⚹	♋ 23 6:40
25 14:59	♀ ☍	♌ 25 16:40
27 6:30	♆ ☌	♍ 28 0:51
30 1:11	☿ △	♎ 30 6:51

☽ Phases & Eclipses

Dy Hr Mn		
1 20:49	☾	8♌24
8 15:27	●	15♏12
15 9:41	☽	22♒00
23 12:58	○	0♊13
1 10:09	☾	8♍12
8 1:30	●	14♐56
15 2:38	☽	22♓06
23 7:33	○	0♋27
30 21:07	☾	8♎10

Astro Data

1 November 1923
Julian Day # 8705
SVP 6♓19'32"
GC 25♐46.5 ⚴ 13♑10.6
Eris 29♓19.4R ⚵ 26♍04.6
⚷ 17♈53.3R ⚶ 20♏21.3
☽ Mean ☊ 8♍13.0

1 December 1923
Julian Day # 8735
SVP 6♓19'28"
GC 25♐46.6 ⚴ 22♑02.1
Eris 29♓08.2R ⚵ 6♎18.6
⚷ 16♈51.2R ⚶ 6♐32.2
☽ Mean ☊ 6♍37.7

LONGITUDE — January 1924

Day	Sid.Time	☉	0 hr ☽	Noon ☽	True ☊	☿	♀	♂	⚳	♃	♄	♅	♆	♇
1 Tu	18 39 30	9♑48 44	23♎50 32	0♏58 02	3♍42.7	28♑20.0	7♒39.3	18♏14.7	22♒41.3	8♐12.1	0♏55.7	14♓15.4	19♌59.0	11♋20.9
2 W	18 43 26	10 49 55	8♏09 56	15 25 51	3R38.4	28 42.6	8 53.7	18 53.3	23 02.5	8 24.5	0 59.7	14 17.4	19R57.8	11R19.7
3 Th	18 47 23	11 51 06	22 45 17	0♐07 32	3 32.0	28R55.0	10 08.1	19 31.9	23 23.8	8 36.8	1 03.6	14 19.3	19 56.6	11 18.4
4 F	18 51 19	12 52 17	7♐31 48	14 57 06	3 24.2	28 56.5	11 22.5	20 10.4	23 45.2	8 49.0	1 07.4	14 21.3	19 55.3	11 17.2
5 Sa	18 55 16	13 53 28	22 22 26	29 46 43	3 15.8	28 46.5	12 36.9	20 49.0	24 06.7	9 01.2	1 11.1	14 23.4	19 54.0	11 15.9
6 Su	18 59 13	14 54 40	7♑08 51	14♑27 49	3 08.1	28 24.7	13 51.2	21 27.6	24 28.2	9 13.3	1 14.7	14 25.4	19 52.7	11 14.7
7 M	19 03 09	15 55 51	21 42 40	28 52 36	3 01.9	27 51.0	15 05.6	22 06.1	24 49.9	9 25.3	1 18.3	14 27.6	19 51.4	11 13.4
8 Tu	19 07 06	16 57 02	5♒56 57	12♒55 13	2 57.8	27 06.0	16 19.8	22 44.7	25 11.5	9 37.3	1 21.7	14 29.7	19 50.1	11 12.2
9 W	19 11 02	17 58 12	19 47 06	26 32 27	2D55.9	26 10.5	17 34.1	23 23.3	25 33.3	9 49.2	1 25.1	14 31.9	19 48.7	11 11.0
10 Th	19 14 59	18 59 22	3♓11 17	9♓43 45	2 55.9	25 05.9	18 48.3	24 01.8	25 55.1	10 01.1	1 28.3	14 34.2	19 47.3	11 09.7
11 F	19 18 55	20 00 32	16 10 10	22 30 53	2 57.1	23 54.2	20 02.5	24 40.4	26 17.0	10 12.9	1 31.5	14 36.5	19 45.9	11 08.5
12 Sa	19 22 52	21 01 41	28 46 25	4♈57 17	2 58.7	22 37.5	21 16.7	25 18.9	26 38.9	10 24.6	1 34.6	14 38.8	19 44.5	11 07.3
13 Su	19 26 48	22 02 49	11♈04 04	17 07 25	2R59.8	21 18.3	22 30.8	25 57.5	27 00.9	10 36.2	1 37.6	14 41.1	19 43.1	11 06.0
14 M	19 30 45	23 03 57	23 07 56	29 06 17	2 59.7	19 59.1	23 44.8	26 36.0	27 23.0	10 47.8	1 40.4	14 43.5	19 41.6	11 04.8
15 Tu	19 34 42	24 05 04	5♉03 04	10♉58 57	2 57.9	18 42.4	24 58.9	27 14.5	27 45.1	10 59.3	1 43.2	14 46.0	19 40.1	11 03.6
16 W	19 38 38	25 06 10	16 54 29	22 50 15	2 54.4	17 30.4	26 12.9	27 53.0	28 07.3	11 10.7	1 45.9	14 48.4	19 38.7	11 02.4
17 Th	19 42 35	26 07 16	28 46 47	4♊44 33	2 49.4	16 24.7	27 26.8	28 31.6	28 29.6	11 22.0	1 48.5	14 51.0	19 37.2	11 01.2
18 F	19 46 31	27 08 21	10♊43 59	16 45 28	2 43.2	15 26.7	28 40.7	29 10.1	28 51.9	11 33.3	1 51.0	14 53.5	19 35.6	11 00.0
19 Sa	19 50 28	28 09 25	22 49 20	28 55 52	2 36.6	14 37.4	29 54.6	29 48.6	29 14.2	11 44.5	1 53.4	14 56.1	19 34.1	10 58.8
20 Su	19 54 24	29 10 28	5♋05 17	11♋17 44	2 30.3	13 57.4	1♓08.4	0♐27.1	29 36.6	11 55.6	1 55.7	14 58.7	19 32.6	10 57.6
21 M	19 58 21	0♒11 31	17 33 21	23 52 11	2 24.9	13 26.6	2 22.2	1 05.6	29 59.1	12 06.6	1 57.9	15 01.3	19 31.0	10 56.4
22 Tu	20 02 17	1 12 33	0♌14 16	6♌39 36	2 20.9	13 05.2	3 35.9	1 44.2	0♓21.6	12 17.5	2 00.0	15 04.0	19 29.4	10 55.3
23 W	20 06 14	2 13 34	13 08 08	19 39 49	2D18.6	12D52.7	4 49.6	2 22.7	0 44.1	12 28.4	2 02.0	15 06.7	19 27.8	10 54.1
24 Th	20 10 11	3 14 34	26 14 35	2♍52 20	2 17.9	12 48.8	6 03.2	3 01.2	1 06.7	12 39.1	2 03.9	15 09.4	19 26.2	10 53.0
25 F	20 14 07	4 15 34	9♍33 02	16 16 35	2 18.6	12 52.9	7 16.8	3 39.7	1 29.4	12 49.8	2 05.7	15 12.2	19 24.6	10 51.8
26 Sa	20 18 04	5 16 33	23 02 56	29 52 02	2 20.0	13 04.5	8 30.3	4 18.2	1 52.0	13 00.4	2 07.4	15 15.0	19 23.0	10 50.7
27 Su	20 22 00	6 17 32	6♎43 48	13♎38 12	2 21.6	13 23.0	9 43.8	4 56.7	2 14.8	13 10.8	2 09.0	15 17.8	19 21.4	10 49.6
28 M	20 25 57	7 18 30	20 35 10	27 34 37	2R22.8	13 47.9	10 57.2	5 35.2	2 37.6	13 21.2	2 10.5	15 20.7	19 19.8	10 48.5
29 Tu	20 29 53	8 19 27	4♏36 26	11♏40 28	2 23.1	14 18.5	12 10.6	6 13.6	3 00.4	13 31.5	2 11.8	15 23.6	19 18.1	10 47.4
30 W	20 33 50	9 20 24	18 46 30	25 54 17	2 22.2	14 54.4	13 23.9	6 52.1	3 23.2	13 41.7	2 13.1	15 26.5	19 16.5	10 46.3
31 Th	20 37 46	10 21 20	3♐03 30	10♐13 45	2 20.3	15 35.1	14 37.1	7 30.6	3 46.1	13 51.8	2 14.3	15 29.4	19 14.8	10 45.2

LONGITUDE — February 1924

Day	Sid.Time	☉	0 hr ☽	Noon ☽	True ☊	☿	♀	♂	⚳	♃	♄	♅	♆	♇
1 F	20 41 43	11♒22 15	17♐24 34	24♐35 27	2♍17.7	16♑20.1	15♓50.3	8♐09.1	4♓09.1	14♐01.8	2♏15.4	15♓32.4	19♌13.1	10♋44.2
2 Sa	20 45 40	12 23 10	1♑45 48	8♑55 03	2R14.7	17 09.2	17 03.5	8 47.5	4 32.1	14 11.7	2 16.3	15 35.4	19R11.5	10R43.1
3 Su	20 49 36	13 24 04	16 02 33	23 07 41	2 12.0	18 01.8	18 16.6	9 26.0	4 55.1	14 21.5	2 17.2	15 38.4	19 09.8	10 42.1
4 M	20 53 33	14 24 56	0♒09 53	7♒08 35	2 09.9	18 57.7	19 29.6	10 04.4	5 18.1	14 31.2	2 17.9	15 41.4	19 08.1	10 41.1
5 Tu	20 57 29	15 25 48	14 03 17	20 53 36	2D08.7	19 56.7	20 42.5	10 42.9	5 41.2	14 40.7	2 18.6	15 44.5	19 06.4	10 40.1
6 W	21 01 26	16 26 38	27 39 12	4♓19 52	2 08.4	20 58.3	21 55.4	11 21.3	6 04.3	14 50.2	2 19.1	15 47.6	19 04.8	10 39.1
7 Th	21 05 22	17 27 27	10♓55 30	17 26 03	2 08.9	22 02.5	23 08.3	11 59.7	6 27.5	14 59.5	2 19.5	15 50.7	19 03.1	10 38.1
8 F	21 09 19	18 28 14	23 51 37	0♈12 23	2 09.9	23 09.1	24 21.0	12 38.1	6 50.7	15 08.8	2 19.9	15 53.8	19 01.4	10 37.2
9 Sa	21 13 15	19 29 00	6♈28 36	12 40 36	2 11.2	24 17.7	25 33.7	13 16.4	7 13.9	15 17.9	2 20.1	15 57.0	18 59.7	10 36.2
10 Su	21 17 12	20 29 44	18 48 47	24 53 36	2 12.3	25 28.4	26 46.3	13 54.8	7 37.1	15 26.9	2R20.2	16 00.1	18 58.0	10 35.3
11 M	21 21 09	21 30 27	0♉55 35	6♉55 14	2 13.2	26 40.8	27 58.8	14 33.1	8 00.4	15 35.7	2 20.2	16 03.3	18 56.3	10 34.4
12 Tu	21 25 05	22 31 08	12 53 09	18 49 54	2R13.6	27 55.1	29 11.3	15 11.5	8 23.7	15 44.5	2 20.1	16 06.5	18 54.6	10 33.5
13 W	21 29 02	23 31 48	24 46 05	0♊42 18	2 13.5	29 10.9	0♈23.6	15 49.8	8 47.0	15 53.1	2 19.9	16 09.7	18 53.0	10 32.6
14 Th	21 32 58	24 32 26	6♊39 08	12 37 11	2 13.1	0♒28.2	1 35.9	16 28.1	9 10.3	16 01.6	2 19.6	16 13.0	18 51.3	10 31.8
15 F	21 36 55	25 33 02	18 36 59	24 39 05	2 12.4	1 47.0	2 48.1	17 06.4	9 33.7	16 10.0	2 19.2	16 16.2	18 49.6	10 30.9
16 Sa	21 40 51	26 33 37	0♋43 57	6♋52 03	2 11.6	3 07.2	4 00.2	17 44.7	9 57.0	16 18.3	2 18.6	16 19.5	18 47.9	10 30.1
17 Su	21 44 48	27 34 09	13 03 47	19 19 29	2 10.9	4 28.7	5 12.2	18 22.9	10 20.4	16 26.4	2 18.0	16 22.8	18 46.3	10 29.3
18 M	21 48 44	28 34 41	25 39 25	2♌03 47	2 10.4	5 51.4	6 24.1	19 01.2	10 43.9	16 34.4	2 17.3	16 26.1	18 44.6	10 28.5
19 Tu	21 52 41	29 35 10	8♌32 42	15 06 14	2 10.1	7 15.3	7 36.0	19 39.4	11 07.3	16 42.3	2 16.5	16 29.4	18 42.9	10 27.7
20 W	21 56 38	0♓35 38	21 44 20	28 26 53	2D10.0	8 40.5	8 47.7	20 17.6	11 30.7	16 50.0	2 15.5	16 32.7	18 41.3	10 27.0
21 Th	22 00 34	1 36 04	5♍13 41	12♍04 30	2R10.0	10 06.7	9 59.3	20 55.8	11 54.2	16 57.6	2 14.5	16 36.1	18 39.7	10 26.3
22 F	22 04 31	2 36 28	18 58 58	25 56 44	2 10.0	11 34.1	11 10.8	21 34.0	12 17.7	17 05.0	2 13.4	16 39.4	18 38.0	10 25.6
23 Sa	22 08 27	3 36 51	2♎57 21	10♎00 23	2 09.9	13 02.6	12 22.3	22 12.2	12 41.2	17 12.3	2 12.1	16 42.8	18 36.4	10 24.9
24 Su	22 12 24	4 37 13	17 05 21	24 11 48	2 09.7	14 32.1	13 33.6	22 50.4	13 04.7	17 19.5	2 10.8	16 46.2	18 34.8	10 24.2
25 M	22 16 20	5 37 33	1♏19 15	8♏27 15	2 09.4	16 02.7	14 44.8	23 28.5	13 28.2	17 26.6	2 09.4	16 49.5	18 33.2	10 23.5
26 Tu	22 20 17	6 37 52	15 35 23	22 43 17	2 09.1	17 34.4	15 55.9	24 06.7	13 51.7	17 33.4	2 07.8	16 52.9	18 31.6	10 22.9
27 W	22 24 13	7 38 09	29 50 33	6♐56 54	2D09.0	19 07.1	17 06.9	24 44.8	14 15.3	17 40.2	2 06.2	16 56.3	18 30.0	10 22.3
28 Th	22 28 10	8 38 25	14♐02 02	21 05 41	2 09.1	20 40.9	18 17.8	25 22.9	14 38.9	17 46.8	2 04.5	16 59.7	18 28.4	10 21.7
29 F	22 32 07	9 38 39	28 07 36	5♑07 36	2 09.6	22 15.7	19 28.6	26 00.9	15 02.4	17 53.2	2 02.7	17 03.2	18 26.9	10 21.2

Astro Data Dy Hr Mn	Planet Ingress Dy Hr Mn	Last Aspect Dy Hr Mn	☽ Ingress Dy Hr Mn	Last Aspect Dy Hr Mn	☽ Ingress Dy Hr Mn	☽ Phases & Eclipses Dy Hr Mn
☿R 4 3:12	♀ ♓ 19 13:45	1 7:26 ☿ ☐	♏ 1 10:23	1 3:02 ♆ △	♑ 1 21:03	6 12:48 ● 14♑57
☽0N 12 15:19	♂ ♐ 19 19:06	3 10:01 ☿ ✶	♐ 3 11:48	3 3:00 ♀ ✶	♒ 3 23:43	13 22:44 ☽ 22♈30
♃⚻♇ 15 20:12	☉ ♒ 21 7:28	4 20:01 ♆ △	♑ 5 12:22	5 8:52 ♆ ☍	♓ 6 4:12	22 0:57 ○ 0♌44
☿D 24 11:24	⚳ ♓ 21 13:00	7 10:21 ☿ ☌	♒ 7 13:54	7 23:46 ♀ ☌	♈ 8 11:36	29 5:53 ☾ 8♏04
☽0S 27 0:16		9 6:06 ♂ ☐	♓ 9 18:13	10 13:16 ☿ ☐	♉ 10 22:09	
	♀ ♈ 13 4:10	11 16:21 ♂ △	♈ 12 2:22	13 8:33 ☿ △	♊ 13 10:35	5 1:38 ● 15♒00
☽0N 9 0:58	☿ ♒ 14 3:18	13 24:00 ♀ ✶	♉ 14 13:48	15 13:57 ☉ △	♋ 15 22:34	12 20:09 ☽ 22♉52
♄R 11 1:16	☉ ♓ 19 21:51	16 22:47 ♂ ☍	♊ 17 2:28	17 6:21 ♅ △	♌ 18 8:09	20 16:07 ○ 0♍46
♀0N 14 10:42		18 17:37 ♆ ✶	♋ 19 14:05	19 20:40 ♂ △	♍ 20 14:45	20 16:09 • T 1.599
♃☐♅ 16 18:07		20 19:06 ♅ △	♌ 21 23:33	22 4:06 ♂ ☐	♎ 22 18:57	27 13:15 ☾ 7♐41
☽0S 23 6:53		23 11:38 ♆ ☌	♍ 24 6:49	24 9:36 ♂ ✶	♏ 24 21:47	
♃∠♄ 23 11:27		25 10:05 ♅ ☍	♎ 26 12:14	26 4:57 ♆ ☐	♐ 27 0:16	
♄⚼♅ 29 9:45		27 21:52 ♆ ✶	♏ 28 16:09	28 19:39 ♂ ☌	♑ 29 3:12	
		30 0:52 ♆ ☐	♐ 30 18:52			

Astro Data

1 January 1924
Julian Day # 8766
SVP 6♓19'23"
GC 25♐46.7 ⚵ 2♒18.7
Eris 29♓07.6 ⚴ 14♎10.2
⚷ 16♈30.9 ⚶ 23♐17.0
☽ Mean ☊ 4♍59.2

1 February 1924
Julian Day # 8797
SVP 6♓19'18"
GC 25♐46.7 ⚵ 13♒00.0
Eris 29♓18.7 ⚴ 17♎44.1
⚷ 17♈03.3 ⚶ 9♑42.6
☽ Mean ☊ 3♍20.8

March 1924 — LONGITUDE

Day	Sid.Time	☉	0 hr ☽	Noon ☽	True ☊	☿	♀	♂	⚳	♃	♄	♅	♆	♇
1 Sa	22 36 03	10♓38 52	12♑05 27	19♑00 59	2♍10.3	23♒51.6	20♈39.3	26♐39.0	15♓26.0	17♐59.5	2♏00.7	17♓06.6	18♌25.4	10♋20.6
2 Su	22 40 00	11 39 04	25 54 01	2♒44 21	2 11.2	25 28.5	21 49.8	27 17.0	15 49.6	18 05.7	1R58.7	17 10.0	18R23.8	10R20.1
3 M	22 43 56	12 39 13	9♒31 50	16 16 18	2 11.9	27 06.5	23 00.3	27 55.0	16 13.2	18 11.7	1 56.6	17 13.4	18 22.3	10 19.6
4 Tu	22 47 53	13 39 21	22 57 35	29 35 34	2R12.3	28 45.5	24 10.6	28 33.0	16 36.8	18 17.5	1 54.4	17 16.9	18 20.8	10 19.1
5 W	22 51 49	14 39 28	6♓10 07	12♓41 09	2 12.1	0♓25.6	25 20.8	29 11.0	17 00.4	18 23.2	1 52.1	17 20.3	18 19.3	10 18.7
6 Th	22 55 46	15 39 32	19 08 35	25 32 25	2 11.1	2 06.8	26 30.8	29 48.9	17 24.0	18 28.7	1 49.7	17 23.7	18 17.9	10 18.2
7 F	22 59 42	16 39 34	1♈52 39	8♈09 21	2 09.5	3 49.1	27 40.8	0♑26.8	17 47.6	18 34.1	1 47.2	17 27.2	18 16.4	10 17.8
8 Sa	23 03 39	17 39 35	14 22 37	20 32 38	2 07.3	5 32.6	28 50.6	1 04.6	18 11.2	18 39.3	1 44.7	17 30.6	18 15.0	10 17.4
9 Su	23 07 35	18 39 33	26 39 37	2♉43 51	2 04.7	7 17.1	0♉00.2	1 42.5	18 34.8	18 44.3	1 42.0	17 34.0	18 13.6	10 17.1
10 M	23 11 32	19 39 29	8♉45 38	14 45 21	2 02.1	9 02.8	1 09.8	2 20.3	18 58.4	18 49.2	1 39.3	17 37.5	18 12.2	10 16.7
11 Tu	23 15 29	20 39 23	20 43 26	26 40 20	1 59.9	10 49.6	2 19.1	2 58.0	19 22.1	18 53.9	1 36.5	17 40.9	18 10.8	10 16.4
12 W	23 19 25	21 39 15	2♊36 33	8♊32 37	1 58.3	12 37.6	3 28.4	3 35.8	19 45.7	18 58.4	1 33.6	17 44.3	18 09.4	10 16.1
13 Th	23 23 22	22 39 05	14 29 06	20 26 35	1D57.7	14 26.8	4 37.4	4 13.5	20 09.3	19 02.7	1 30.6	17 47.8	18 08.1	10 15.8
14 F	23 27 18	23 38 52	26 25 40	2♋26 56	1 57.9	16 17.2	5 46.3	4 51.2	20 32.9	19 06.9	1 27.5	17 51.2	18 06.8	10 15.6
15 Sa	23 31 15	24 38 38	8♋30 58	14 38 23	1 59.0	18 08.7	6 55.1	5 28.8	20 56.4	19 11.0	1 24.4	17 54.6	18 05.5	10 15.4
16 Su	23 35 11	25 38 21	20 49 43	27 05 30	2 00.6	20 01.4	8 03.7	6 06.4	21 20.0	19 14.8	1 21.2	17 58.0	18 04.2	10 15.2
17 M	23 39 08	26 38 01	3♌26 12	9♌52 12	2 02.2	21 55.3	9 12.1	6 44.0	21 43.6	19 18.5	1 17.9	18 01.4	18 03.0	10 15.0
18 Tu	23 43 04	27 37 40	16 23 52	23 01 24	2R03.4	23 50.3	10 20.3	7 21.5	22 07.2	19 22.0	1 14.5	18 04.8	18 01.7	10 14.8
19 W	23 47 01	28 37 16	29 44 55	6♍34 27	2 03.6	25 46.5	11 28.4	7 59.0	22 30.7	19 25.3	1 11.1	18 08.2	18 00.5	10 14.7
20 Th	23 50 58	29 36 50	13♍29 49	20 30 45	2 02.5	27 43.7	12 36.2	8 36.5	22 54.3	19 28.5	1 07.6	18 11.6	17 59.3	10 14.6
21 F	23 54 54	0♈36 22	27 36 50	4♎47 30	2 00.0	29 42.1	13 43.9	9 13.9	23 17.8	19 31.4	1 04.0	18 15.0	17 58.2	10 14.5
22 Sa	23 58 51	1 35 52	12♎02 04	19 19 44	1 56.3	1♈41.3	14 51.4	9 51.3	23 41.4	19 34.2	1 00.4	18 18.4	17 57.1	10 14.4
23 Su	0 02 47	2 35 20	26 39 38	4♏00 50	1 51.8	3 41.5	15 58.7	10 28.7	24 04.9	19 36.8	0 56.7	18 21.7	17 55.9	10 14.4
24 M	0 06 44	3 34 47	11♏22 26	18 43 31	1 47.3	5 42.5	17 05.8	11 06.0	24 28.4	19 39.3	0 52.9	18 25.1	17 54.9	10D14.4
25 Tu	0 10 40	4 34 11	26 03 16	3♐20 54	1 43.4	7 44.1	18 12.7	11 43.3	24 51.9	19 41.5	0 49.1	18 28.4	17 53.8	10 14.4
26 W	0 14 37	5 33 34	10♐35 47	17 47 23	1 40.7	9 46.2	19 19.4	12 20.5	25 15.4	19 43.6	0 45.2	18 31.7	17 52.8	10 14.4
27 Th	0 18 33	6 32 55	24 55 19	1♑59 18	1D39.4	11 48.7	20 25.9	12 57.7	25 38.8	19 45.5	0 41.3	18 35.0	17 51.8	10 14.5
28 F	0 22 30	7 32 14	8♑59 09	15 54 50	1 39.6	13 51.2	21 32.2	13 34.9	26 02.3	19 47.2	0 37.3	18 38.4	17 50.8	10 14.6
29 Sa	0 26 27	8 31 32	22 46 20	29 33 44	1 40.8	15 53.6	22 38.2	14 12.0	26 25.7	19 48.7	0 33.3	18 41.6	17 49.9	10 14.7
30 Su	0 30 23	9 30 48	6♒17 12	12♒56 51	1 42.3	17 55.6	23 44.1	14 49.0	26 49.1	19 50.0	0 29.2	18 44.9	17 48.9	10 14.8
31 M	0 34 20	10 30 02	19 32 53	26 05 28	1R43.4	19 56.9	24 49.7	15 26.1	27 12.6	19 51.2	0 25.1	18 48.2	17 48.0	10 15.0

April 1924 — LONGITUDE

Day	Sid.Time	☉	0 hr ☽	Noon ☽	True ☊	☿	♀	♂	⚳	♃	♄	♅	♆	♇
1 Tu	0 38 16	11♈29 14	2♓34 47	9♓00 59	1♍43.3	21♈57.0	25♉55.0	16♑03.0	27♓35.9	19♐52.1	0♏20.9	18♓51.4	17♌47.2	10♋15.1
2 W	0 42 13	12 28 24	15 24 14	21 44 39	1R41.4	23 55.8	27 00.1	16 39.9	27 59.3	19 52.9	0R16.7	18 54.6	17R46.3	10 15.3
3 Th	0 46 09	13 27 32	28 02 21	4♈17 27	1 37.4	25 52.8	28 05.0	17 16.7	28 22.6	19 53.5	0 12.4	18 57.8	17 45.5	10 15.6
4 F	0 50 06	14 26 38	10♈30 01	16 40 09	1 31.4	27 47.6	29 09.6	17 53.5	28 46.0	19 53.9	0 08.1	19 01.0	17 44.7	10 15.8
5 Sa	0 54 02	15 25 42	22 47 58	28 53 34	1 23.8	29 39.8	0♊14.0	18 30.2	29 09.3	19R54.1	0 03.7	19 04.2	17 44.0	10 16.1
6 Su	0 57 59	16 24 44	4♉57 05	10♉58 41	1 15.2	1♉29.2	1 18.1	19 06.9	29 32.5	19 54.1	29♎59.4	19 07.4	17 43.3	10 16.4
7 M	1 01 55	17 23 44	16 58 34	22 56 57	1 06.5	3 15.2	2 21.9	19 43.4	29 55.8	19 53.9	29 55.0	19 10.5	17 42.6	10 16.7
8 Tu	1 05 52	18 22 42	28 54 06	4♊50 22	0 58.4	4 57.6	3 25.4	20 20.0	0♈19.0	19 53.5	29 50.5	19 13.6	17 41.9	10 17.1
9 W	1 09 49	19 21 38	10♊46 05	16 41 40	0 51.8	6 36.1	4 28.6	20 56.4	0 42.2	19 53.0	29 46.1	19 16.7	17 41.3	10 17.4
10 Th	1 13 45	20 20 31	22 37 35	28 34 20	0 47.1	8 10.4	5 31.6	21 32.8	1 05.4	19 52.2	29 41.6	19 19.8	17 40.7	10 17.8
11 F	1 17 42	21 19 22	4♋32 26	10♋32 22	0D44.5	9 40.1	6 34.2	22 09.1	1 28.5	19 51.3	29 37.1	19 22.8	17 40.1	10 18.2
12 Sa	1 21 38	22 18 11	16 35 02	22 40 45	0 43.8	11 05.1	7 36.4	22 45.3	1 51.6	19 50.2	29 32.6	19 25.8	17 39.6	10 18.7
13 Su	1 25 35	23 16 58	28 50 14	5♌04 06	0 44.4	12 25.2	8 38.4	23 21.5	2 14.7	19 48.9	29 28.0	19 28.8	17 39.1	10 19.1
14 M	1 29 31	24 15 42	11♌22 58	17 47 23	0R45.5	13 40.2	9 40.0	23 57.6	2 37.8	19 47.4	29 23.5	19 31.8	17 38.6	10 19.6
15 Tu	1 33 28	25 14 24	24 17 53	0♍54 54	0 46.0	14 49.8	10 41.2	24 33.6	3 00.8	19 45.8	29 18.9	19 34.7	17 38.2	10 20.1
16 W	1 37 24	26 13 04	7♍38 44	14 29 38	0 45.2	15 54.1	11 42.0	25 09.5	3 23.7	19 43.9	29 14.4	19 37.7	17 37.7	10 20.6
17 Th	1 41 21	27 11 42	21 27 37	28 32 35	0 42.2	16 52.8	12 42.5	25 45.4	3 46.7	19 41.9	29 09.8	19 40.6	17 37.4	10 21.2
18 F	1 45 18	28 10 17	5♎44 11	13♎01 55	0 36.9	17 45.9	13 42.6	26 21.2	4 09.6	19 39.6	29 05.2	19 43.4	17 37.0	10 21.8
19 Sa	1 49 14	29 08 51	20 25 02	27 52 37	0 29.5	18 33.2	14 42.3	26 56.9	4 32.5	19 37.2	29 00.6	19 46.3	17 36.7	10 22.3
20 Su	1 53 11	0♉07 22	5♏23 35	12♏56 42	0 20.8	19 14.8	15 41.5	27 32.5	4 55.3	19 34.7	28 56.0	19 49.1	17 36.4	10 23.0
21 M	1 57 07	1 05 52	20 30 42	28 04 15	0 11.7	19 50.5	16 40.4	28 08.1	5 18.1	19 31.9	28 51.5	19 51.9	17 36.2	10 23.6
22 Tu	2 01 04	2 04 20	5♐36 08	13♐05 11	0 03.5	20 20.3	17 38.7	28 43.5	5 40.9	19 29.0	28 46.9	19 54.6	17 36.0	10 24.3
23 W	2 05 00	3 02 47	20 30 23	27 50 56	29♌57.0	20 44.3	18 36.7	29 18.9	6 03.6	19 25.9	28 42.3	19 57.4	17 35.8	10 24.9
24 Th	2 08 57	4 01 12	5♑06 09	12♑15 38	29 52.9	21 02.4	19 34.1	29 54.2	6 26.3	19 22.6	28 37.7	20 00.1	17 35.6	10 25.6
25 F	2 12 53	4 59 35	19 19 09	26 16 35	29D51.0	21 14.8	20 31.1	0♒29.3	6 49.0	19 19.2	28 33.2	20 02.8	17 35.5	10 26.4
26 Sa	2 16 50	5 57 57	3♒08 02	9♒53 41	29 50.7	21R21.4	21 27.6	1 04.4	7 11.6	19 15.5	28 28.7	20 05.4	17 35.4	10 27.1
27 Su	2 20 47	6 56 17	16 33 50	23 08 49	29R51.1	21 22.4	22 23.6	1 39.4	7 34.1	19 11.7	28 24.2	20 08.0	17 35.4	10 27.9
28 M	2 24 43	7 54 35	29 39 02	6♓04 54	29 51.1	21 18.0	23 19.1	2 14.2	7 56.7	19 07.8	28 19.7	20 10.6	17D35.3	10 28.6
29 Tu	2 28 40	8 52 52	12♓26 48	18 45 10	29 49.5	21 08.5	24 14.0	2 49.0	8 19.2	19 03.7	28 15.2	20 13.1	17 35.4	10 29.4
30 W	2 32 36	9 51 08	25 00 21	1♈12 43	29 45.6	20 54.0	25 08.3	3 23.6	8 41.6	18 59.4	28 10.7	20 15.6	17 35.4	10 30.3

Astro Data Dy Hr Mn	Planet Ingress Dy Hr Mn	Last Aspect Dy Hr Mn	☽ Ingress Dy Hr Mn	Last Aspect Dy Hr Mn	☽ Ingress Dy Hr Mn	☽ Phases & Eclipses Dy Hr Mn	Astro Data
♃△♆ 4 22:57	☿ ♓ 5 5:53	1 15:07 ♀ □	♒ 2 7:11	2 22:58 ♀ ⚹	♈ 3 3:45	5 15:58 ● 14♓49	1 March 1924
☽0N 7 9:43	♂ ♑ 6 19:02	4 10:16 ☿ ☌	♓ 4 12:44	5 13:48 ☿ ☌	♉ 5 14:11	5 15:43:56 ◐ P 0.582	Julian Day # 8826
♅⚻♆ 17 19:55	♀ ♉ 9 11:55	5 22:40 ♃ □	♈ 6 20:26	7 5:10 ♂ △	♊ 8 2:13	13 16:50 ☽ 22♊51	SVP 6♓19'14"
☉0N 20 21:20	☉ ♈ 20 21:20	9 6:02 ♀ ☌	♉ 9 6:35	10 14:15 ♄ ☍	♋ 10 14:53	21 4:30 ○ 0♎18	GC 25♐46.8 ⚴ 22♒51.1
☽0S 21 15:32	☿ ♈ 21 15:37	10 22:45 ☉ ⚹	♊ 11 18:43	13 1:17 ♄ □	♌ 13 2:15	27 20:24 ☾ 6♑54	Eris 29♓36.9 ⚵ 15♎49.4R
☿0N 23 1:49		13 16:50 ☉ □	♋ 14 7:08	15 9:08 ♄ ⚹	♍ 15 10:21		⚷ 18♈14.4 ⚶ 24♑25.4
♇ D 24 12:42	♀ ♊ 5 6:46	16 8:59 ☉ △	♌ 16 17:31	17 7:06 ♂ △	♎ 17 14:27	4 7:17 ● 14♈15	☽ Mean ☊ 1♍48.6
	☿ ♉ 5 16:23	18 5:22 ♃ △	♍ 19 0:27	19 14:10 ☉ ☍	♏ 19 15:24	12 11:12 ☽ 22♋16	
☽0N 3 17:01	♄ ♎R 6 8:35	21 2:08 ☿ ☍	♎ 21 4:00	21 12:06 ♂ ⚹	♐ 21 15:04	19 14:10 ○ 29♎14	1 April 1924
♃R 6 1:27	⚳ ♈ 7 16:21	22 12:24 ♃ ⚹	♏ 23 5:27	23 13:24 ♄ ⚹	♑ 23 15:33	26 4:28 ☾ 5♒40	Julian Day # 8857
♃□♅ 17 18:10	☉ ♉ 20 8:59	24 11:30 ♅ △	♐ 25 6:29	25 15:57 ♄ □	♒ 25 18:30		SVP 6♓19'12"
☽0S 18 2:04	☊ ♌R 22 23:55	26 15:15 ♃ ☌	♑ 27 8:37	27 21:38 ♄ △	♓ 28 0:39		GC 25♐46.9 ⚴ 2♓42.0
☿R 27 4:27	♂ ♒ 24 15:58	28 22:41 ♀ △	♒ 29 12:47	29 23:20 ♀ □	♈ 30 9:39		Eris 29♓59.9 ⚵ 9♎12.2R
♆D 28 15:25		31 9:28 ♀ □	♓ 31 19:13				⚷ 19♈57.4 ⚶ 8♒57.5
☽0N 30 23:27							☽ Mean ☊ 0♍10.1

LONGITUDE — May 1924

Day	Sid.Time	☉	0 hr ☽	Noon ☽	True ☊	☿	♀	♂	⚳	♃	♄	♅	♆	♇
1 Th	2 36 33	10♉49 22	7♈22 35	13♈30 13	29♌38.8	20♉35.0	26♊02.1	3♒58.1	9♈04.0	18♐54.9	28♎06.3	20♓18.1	17♌35.5	10♋31.1
2 F	2 40 29	11 47 34	19 35 51	25 39 43	29R 29.3	20R 11.9	26 55.2	4 32.5	9 26.3	18R 50.3	28R 01.9	20 20.6	17 35.6	10 32.0
3 Sa	2 44 26	12 45 45	1♉41 59	7♉42 50	29 17.5	19 45.1	27 47.8	5 06.8	9 48.6	18 45.5	27 57.5	20 23.0	17 35.7	10 32.9
4 Su	2 48 22	13 43 54	13 42 25	19 40 52	29 04.3	19 15.1	28 39.6	5 40.9	10 10.9	18 40.6	27 53.2	20 25.3	17 35.9	10 33.8
5 M	2 52 19	14 42 01	25 38 21	1♊35 02	28 50.8	18 42.5	29 30.8	6 14.9	10 33.0	18 35.6	27 48.9	20 27.7	17 36.1	10 34.7
6 Tu	2 56 16	15 40 06	7♊31 06	13 26 45	28 38.0	18 07.9	0♋21.4	6 48.7	10 55.2	18 30.3	27 44.6	20 30.0	17 36.4	10 35.6
7 W	3 00 12	16 38 10	19 22 16	25 17 54	28 27.0	17 31.9	1 11.1	7 22.4	11 17.3	18 25.0	27 40.4	20 32.2	17 36.6	10 36.6
8 Th	3 04 09	17 36 12	1♋14 00	7♋10 57	28 18.6	16 55.2	2 00.2	7 56.0	11 39.3	18 19.5	27 36.2	20 34.5	17 37.0	10 37.6
9 F	3 08 05	18 34 13	13 09 10	19 09 07	28 12.9	16 18.4	2 48.4	8 29.4	12 01.3	18 13.9	27 32.1	20 36.7	17 37.3	10 38.5
10 Sa	3 12 02	19 32 11	25 11 18	1♌16 18	28 09.8	15 42.2	3 35.8	9 02.7	12 23.2	18 08.1	27 28.0	20 38.8	17 37.7	10 39.6
11 Su	3 15 58	20 30 07	7♌24 41	13 37 02	28D 08.7	15 07.3	4 22.4	9 35.8	12 45.0	18 02.2	27 24.0	20 40.9	17 38.1	10 40.6
12 M	3 19 55	21 28 02	19 54 00	26 16 10	28R 08.6	14 34.1	5 08.1	10 08.7	13 06.8	17 56.2	27 20.0	20 43.0	17 38.5	10 41.6
13 Tu	3 23 51	22 25 55	2♍44 09	9♍18 27	28 08.4	14 03.2	5 52.9	10 41.5	13 28.6	17 50.1	27 16.0	20 45.0	17 39.0	10 42.7
14 W	3 27 48	23 23 46	15 59 34	22 47 51	28 06.9	13 35.1	6 36.7	11 14.1	13 50.2	17 43.8	27 12.2	20 47.0	17 39.5	10 43.8
15 Th	3 31 45	24 21 35	29 43 34	6♎46 46	28 03.1	13 10.2	7 19.5	11 46.6	14 11.8	17 37.5	27 08.3	20 49.0	17 40.1	10 44.9
16 F	3 35 41	25 19 23	13♎57 19	21 14 55	27 56.8	12 48.9	8 01.3	12 18.9	14 33.4	17 31.0	27 04.6	20 50.9	17 40.6	10 46.0
17 Sa	3 39 38	26 17 09	28 38 58	6♏08 39	27 48.1	12 31.5	8 42.1	12 51.0	14 54.9	17 24.4	27 00.9	20 52.8	17 41.2	10 47.1
18 Su	3 43 34	27 14 54	13♏42 57	21 20 36	27 37.7	12 18.2	9 21.7	13 23.0	15 16.3	17 17.8	26 57.2	20 54.6	17 41.9	10 48.3
19 M	3 47 31	28 12 37	29 00 15	6♐40 25	27 26.8	12 09.2	10 00.2	13 54.7	15 37.6	17 11.0	26 53.6	20 56.4	17 42.5	10 49.4
20 Tu	3 51 27	29 10 19	14♐19 39	21 56 29	27 16.8	12D 04.7	10 37.5	14 26.3	15 58.9	17 04.2	26 50.1	20 58.1	17 43.2	10 50.6
21 W	3 55 24	0♊07 59	29 29 40	6♑58 03	27 08.6	12 04.6	11 13.5	14 57.7	16 20.1	16 57.2	26 46.7	20 59.8	17 44.0	10 51.8
22 Th	3 59 20	1 05 39	14♑20 43	21 37 02	27 03.0	12 09.1	11 48.3	15 28.8	16 41.3	16 50.2	26 43.3	21 01.5	17 44.7	10 53.0
23 F	4 03 17	2 03 18	28 46 30	5♒48 56	27 00.0	12 18.1	12 21.7	15 59.8	17 02.4	16 43.1	26 40.0	21 03.1	17 45.5	10 54.2
24 Sa	4 07 14	3 00 55	12♒44 16	19 32 41	26D 58.9	12 31.6	12 53.8	16 30.6	17 23.4	16 35.9	26 36.7	21 04.7	17 46.3	10 55.4
25 Su	4 11 10	3 58 32	26 14 25	2♓49 53	26R 58.8	12 49.6	13 24.4	17 01.1	17 44.3	16 28.7	26 33.6	21 06.2	17 47.2	10 56.7
26 M	4 15 07	4 56 07	9♓19 31	15 43 49	26 58.5	13 11.9	13 53.6	17 31.4	18 05.1	16 21.4	26 30.5	21 07.7	17 48.1	10 57.9
27 Tu	4 19 03	5 53 42	22 03 20	28 18 36	26 56.9	13 38.6	14 21.2	18 01.5	18 25.9	16 14.0	26 27.4	21 09.2	17 49.0	10 59.2
28 W	4 23 00	6 51 16	4♈30 07	10♈38 25	26 53.0	14 09.4	14 47.3	18 31.3	18 46.6	16 06.6	26 24.5	21 10.6	17 49.9	11 00.5
29 Th	4 26 56	7 48 49	16 43 57	22 47 10	26 46.4	14 44.3	15 11.7	19 00.8	19 07.2	15 59.1	26 21.6	21 11.9	17 50.9	11 01.8
30 F	4 30 53	8 46 21	28 48 28	4♉48 12	26 37.1	15 23.3	15 34.4	19 30.1	19 27.8	15 51.6	26 18.8	21 13.2	17 51.9	11 03.1
31 Sa	4 34 49	9 43 52	10♉46 41	16 44 11	26 25.5	16 06.1	15 55.3	19 59.2	19 48.2	15 44.1	26 16.1	21 14.5	17 52.9	11 04.4

LONGITUDE — June 1924

Day	Sid.Time	☉	0 hr ☽	Noon ☽	True ☊	☿	♀	♂	⚳	♃	♄	♅	♆	♇
1 Su	4 38 46	10♊41 22	22♉40 58	28♉37 14	26♌12.4	16♉52.7	16♋14.5	20♒27.9	20♈08.6	15♐36.5	26♎13.5	21♓15.7	17♌54.0	11♋05.7
2 M	4 42 43	11 38 51	4♊33 11	10♊29 00	25R 59.0	17 43.0	16 31.7	20 56.4	20 28.9	15R 28.9	26R 11.0	21 16.9	17 55.1	11 07.1
3 Tu	4 46 39	12 36 20	16 24 52	22 20 57	25 46.3	18 36.8	16 47.0	21 24.6	20 49.1	15 21.3	26 08.5	21 18.0	17 56.2	11 08.4
4 W	4 50 36	13 33 47	28 17 27	4♋14 34	25 35.4	19 34.2	17 00.3	21 52.5	21 09.2	15 13.6	26 06.1	21 19.1	17 57.4	11 09.8
5 Th	4 54 32	14 31 13	10♋12 33	16 11 39	25 26.9	20 35.0	17 11.5	22 20.1	21 29.2	15 06.0	26 03.8	21 20.1	17 58.5	11 11.2
6 F	4 58 29	15 28 39	22 12 10	28 14 27	25 21.2	21 39.2	17 20.6	22 47.4	21 49.1	14 58.3	26 01.7	21 21.1	17 59.7	11 12.6
7 Sa	5 02 25	16 26 03	4♌18 52	10♌25 51	25 18.1	22 46.6	17 27.6	23 14.4	22 08.9	14 50.7	25 59.6	21 22.1	18 01.0	11 14.0
8 Su	5 06 22	17 23 26	16 35 51	22 49 22	25D 17.1	23 57.3	17 32.3	23 41.0	22 28.7	14 43.1	25 57.5	21 23.0	18 02.2	11 15.4
9 M	5 10 18	18 20 48	29 06 54	5♍28 58	25 17.3	25 11.1	17R 34.7	24 07.3	22 48.3	14 35.4	25 55.6	21 23.8	18 03.5	11 16.8
10 Tu	5 14 15	19 18 09	11♍56 07	18 28 49	25R 17.7	26 28.1	17 34.7	24 33.3	23 07.8	14 27.8	25 53.8	21 24.6	18 04.8	11 18.2
11 W	5 18 12	20 15 29	25 07 35	1♎52 46	25 17.1	27 48.1	17 32.5	24 58.9	23 27.2	14 20.2	25 52.0	21 25.3	18 06.2	11 19.6
12 Th	5 22 08	21 12 48	8♎44 41	15 43 31	25 14.8	29 11.2	17 27.8	25 24.1	23 46.6	14 12.7	25 50.4	21 26.0	18 07.5	11 21.0
13 F	5 26 05	22 10 06	22 49 18	0♏01 52	25 10.2	0♊37.3	17 20.7	25 49.0	24 05.8	14 05.1	25 48.8	21 26.7	18 08.9	11 22.5
14 Sa	5 30 01	23 07 23	7♏20 52	14 45 42	25 03.5	2 06.5	17 11.2	26 13.6	24 24.9	13 57.6	25 47.4	21 27.3	18 10.3	11 23.9
15 Su	5 33 58	24 04 39	22 15 34	29 49 29	24 55.3	3 38.5	16 59.2	26 37.7	24 43.9	13 50.2	25 46.0	21 27.9	18 11.8	11 25.4
16 M	5 37 54	25 01 55	7♐26 14	15♐04 31	24 46.6	5 13.6	16 44.9	27 01.5	25 02.8	13 42.8	25 44.7	21 28.4	18 13.2	11 26.9
17 Tu	5 41 51	25 59 10	22 42 55	0♑20 04	24 38.4	6 51.5	16 28.1	27 24.9	25 21.6	13 35.5	25 43.6	21 28.8	18 14.7	11 28.3
18 W	5 45 47	26 56 25	7♑54 35	15 25 15	24 31.8	8 32.4	16 09.1	27 47.8	25 40.3	13 28.2	25 42.5	21 29.2	18 16.2	11 29.8
19 Th	5 49 44	27 53 39	22 50 59	0♒10 55	24 27.3	10 16.1	15 47.7	28 10.4	25 58.8	13 21.0	25 41.5	21 29.6	18 17.8	11 31.3
20 F	5 53 41	28 50 53	7♒24 24	14 30 59	24D 25.1	12 02.7	15 24.2	28 32.5	26 17.3	13 13.8	25 40.6	21 29.9	18 19.3	11 32.8
21 Sa	5 57 37	29 48 06	21 30 27	28 22 44	24 24.8	13 52.0	14 58.6	28 54.1	26 35.6	13 06.7	25 39.8	21 30.2	18 20.9	11 34.3
22 Su	6 01 34	0♋45 19	5♓07 59	11♓46 27	24 25.5	15 44.0	14 31.1	29 15.3	26 53.8	12 59.7	25 39.1	21 30.4	18 22.5	11 35.8
23 M	6 05 30	1 42 33	18 18 31	24 44 38	24R 26.4	17 38.6	14 01.7	29 36.1	27 11.9	12 52.8	25 38.5	21 30.6	18 24.2	11 37.3
24 Tu	6 09 27	2 39 46	1♈05 19	7♈21 06	24 26.5	19 35.7	13 30.6	29 56.3	27 29.8	12 46.0	25 38.0	21 30.7	18 25.8	11 38.8
25 W	6 13 23	3 36 59	13 32 34	19 40 17	24 25.1	21 35.1	12 58.0	0♓16.0	27 47.7	12 39.2	25 37.6	21 30.8	18 27.5	11 40.3
26 Th	6 17 20	4 34 12	25 44 49	1♉46 42	24 21.7	23 36.8	12 24.0	0 35.3	28 05.4	12 32.6	25 37.3	21R 30.8	18 29.2	11 41.8
27 F	6 21 16	5 31 25	7♉46 27	13 44 34	24 16.2	25 40.4	11 49.0	0 54.0	28 22.9	12 26.0	25 37.1	21 30.8	18 30.9	11 43.3
28 Sa	6 25 13	6 28 39	19 41 28	25 37 34	24 09.0	27 45.8	11 13.0	1 12.1	28 40.4	12 19.6	25D 37.0	21 30.7	18 32.6	11 44.8
29 Su	6 29 10	7 25 52	1♊33 15	7♊28 51	24 00.7	29 52.7	10 36.2	1 29.7	28 57.7	12 13.2	25 37.0	21 30.6	18 34.4	11 46.3
30 M	6 33 06	8 23 05	13 24 38	19 20 54	23 52.1	2♋00.9	9 59.1	1 46.8	29 14.8	12 07.0	25 37.1	21 30.4	18 36.2	11 47.9

Astro Data

	Dy Hr Mn
♃△♆	15 3:05
☽0S	15 13:00
☿ D	21 0:20
☽0N	28 6:03
⚳0N	3 10:29
♀ R	10 0:50
☽0S	11 22:41
☽0N	24 13:42
♅ R	26 12:03
♄ D	29 0:43

Planet Ingress

		Dy Hr Mn
♀	♋	6 1:49
☉	♊	21 8:40
☿	♊	13 1:42
☉	♋	21 16:59
♂	♓	24 16:27
☿	♋	29 13:22

Last Aspect / ☽ Ingress

Last Aspect Dy Hr Mn		☽ Ingress	Dy Hr Mn
2 16:40	♄ ☍	♉	2 20:37
4 13:30	♅ ✶	♊	5 8:48
7 16:47	♄ △	♋	7 21:30
10 4:33	♄ □	♌	10 9:30
12 13:59	♄ ✶	♍	12 18:57
14 13:07	☉ △	♎	15 0:28
16 21:25	♄ ☌	♏	17 2:10
18 21:52	☉ ☍	♐	19 1:33
20 19:44	♄ ✶	♑	21 0:48
22 20:30	♄ □	♒	23 2:04
25 0:37	♄ △	♓	25 6:49
26 22:15	♅ ☌	♈	27 15:16
29 19:05	♄ ☍	♉	30 2:23

Last Aspect / ☽ Ingress

Last Aspect Dy Hr Mn		☽ Ingress	Dy Hr Mn
31 21:06	♅ ✶	♊	1 14:47
3 19:38	♄ △	♋	4 3:27
6 7:37	♄ □	♌	6 15:29
8 17:59	♄ ✶	♍	9 1:41
11 3:58	☿ △	♎	11 8:41
13 5:01	♄ ☌	♏	13 11:57
15 6:48	♂ □	♐	15 12:17
17 7:17	♂ ✶	♑	17 11:28
19 4:38	♄ □	♒	19 11:42
21 14:42	☉ △	♓	21 14:52
23 5:57	♅ ☌	♈	23 21:56
25 23:45	♄ ☍	♉	26 8:27
28 3:41	♅ ✶	♊	28 20:51

☽ Phases & Eclipses

Dy Hr Mn	
3 23:00	● 13♉12
12 2:13	☽ 21♌04
18 21:52	○ 27♏39
25 14:16	☾ 4♓04
2 14:34	● 11♊45
10 13:37	☽ 19♍22
17 4:41	○ 25♐42
24 2:16	☾ 2♈17

Astro Data

1 May 1924
Julian Day # 8887
SVP 6♓19'09"
GC 25♐47.0 ⚴ 10♓58.2
Eris 0♈20.3 ⚵ 3♎20.9R
⚷ 21♈43.6 ⚶ 21♒08.5
☽ Mean ☊ 28♌34.7

1 June 1924
Julian Day # 8918
SVP 6♓19'05"
GC 25♐47.0 ⚴ 17♓21.4
Eris 0♈34.3 ⚵ 2♎08.5
⚷ 23♈19.4 ⚶ 0♓34.7
☽ Mean ☊ 26♌56.2

July 1924 LONGITUDE

Day	Sid.Time	☉	0 hr ☽	Noon ☽	True ☊	☿	♀	♂	⚳	♃	♄	♅	♆	♇
1 Tu	6 37 03	9♋20 18	25♊17 52	1♋15 46	23♌43.9	4♋10.1	9♋21.6	2♓03.2	29♈31.8	12♐00.9	25♎37.3	21♓30.2	18♌38.0	11♋49.4
2 W	6 40 59	10 17 31	7♋14 48	13 15 08	23R 36.9	6 20.0	8R 44.2	2 19.1	29 48.7	11R 54.9	25 37.6	21R 29.9	18 39.8	11 50.9
3 Th	6 44 56	11 14 45	19 16 59	25 20 32	23 31.7	8 30.3	8 07.0	2 34.4	0♉05.4	11 49.1	25 38.0	21 29.6	18 41.6	11 52.4
4 F	6 48 52	12 11 58	1♌25 59	7♌33 33	23 28.5	10 40.8	7 30.2	2 49.1	0 22.0	11 43.3	25 38.5	21 29.3	18 43.5	11 53.9
5 Sa	6 52 49	13 09 10	13 43 29	19 56 02	23D 27.2	12 51.1	6 54.1	3 03.1	0 38.4	11 37.7	25 39.1	21 28.9	18 45.3	11 55.5
6 Su	6 56 45	14 06 23	26 11 29	2♍30 08	23 27.5	15 01.0	6 19.0	3 16.5	0 54.7	11 32.3	25 39.8	21 28.4	18 47.2	11 57.0
7 M	7 00 42	15 03 36	8♍52 19	15 18 23	23 28.7	17 10.3	5 44.9	3 29.3	1 10.8	11 27.0	25 40.6	21 27.9	18 49.1	11 58.5
8 Tu	7 04 39	16 00 48	21 48 39	28 23 28	23 30.2	19 18.6	5 12.2	3 41.4	1 26.7	11 21.8	25 41.5	21 27.3	18 51.0	12 00.0
9 W	7 08 35	16 58 00	5♎03 08	11♎47 57	23R 31.1	21 26.0	4 41.0	3 52.8	1 42.5	11 16.7	25 42.5	21 26.8	18 53.0	12 01.6
10 Th	7 12 32	17 55 13	18 38 07	25 33 47	23 31.0	23 32.1	4 11.4	4 03.6	1 58.1	11 11.9	25 43.6	21 26.1	18 54.9	12 03.1
11 F	7 16 28	18 52 25	2♏34 59	9♏41 37	23 29.4	25 36.8	3 43.6	4 13.7	2 13.6	11 07.1	25 44.7	21 25.4	18 56.9	12 04.6
12 Sa	7 20 25	19 49 37	16 53 29	24 10 11	23 26.5	27 40.0	3 17.8	4 23.1	2 28.8	11 02.5	25 46.0	21 24.7	18 58.9	12 06.1
13 Su	7 24 21	20 46 49	1♐31 12	8♐55 48	23 22.5	29 41.7	2 54.1	4 31.8	2 43.9	10 58.1	25 47.4	21 23.9	19 00.9	12 07.6
14 M	7 28 18	21 44 01	16 23 09	23 52 17	23 18.1	1♌41.8	2 32.5	4 39.8	2 58.9	10 53.9	25 48.9	21 23.1	19 02.9	12 09.1
15 Tu	7 32 14	22 41 14	1♑22 08	8♑51 35	23 14.0	3 40.1	2 13.1	4 47.1	3 13.6	10 49.8	25 50.5	21 22.2	19 04.9	12 10.6
16 W	7 36 11	23 38 27	16 19 31	23 44 52	23 10.7	5 36.7	1 56.1	4 53.7	3 28.2	10 45.8	25 52.1	21 21.3	19 07.0	12 12.1
17 Th	7 40 08	24 35 40	1♒06 38	8♒23 55	23 08.6	7 31.5	1 41.4	4 59.5	3 42.6	10 42.0	25 53.9	21 20.4	19 09.0	12 13.6
18 F	7 44 04	25 32 53	15 36 00	22 42 18	23D 08.0	9 24.6	1 29.1	5 04.5	3 56.8	10 38.4	25 55.7	21 19.4	19 11.1	12 15.1
19 Sa	7 48 01	26 30 08	29 42 26	6♓36 08	23 08.5	11 15.8	1 19.2	5 08.8	4 10.8	10 35.0	25 57.7	21 18.3	19 13.1	12 16.6
20 Su	7 51 57	27 27 22	13♓23 19	20 04 03	23 09.7	13 05.3	1 11.7	5 12.4	4 24.6	10 31.7	25 59.7	21 17.2	19 15.2	12 18.1
21 M	7 55 54	28 24 38	26 38 32	3♈07 02	23 11.3	14 52.9	1 06.6	5 15.1	4 38.2	10 28.6	26 01.9	21 16.1	19 17.3	12 19.6
22 Tu	7 59 50	29 21 54	9♈29 57	15 47 43	23 12.5	16 38.8	1D 03.9	5 17.1	4 51.6	10 25.7	26 04.1	21 14.9	19 19.4	12 21.0
23 W	8 03 47	0♌19 12	22 00 50	28 09 51	23R 13.2	18 22.9	1 03.6	5R 18.2	5 04.8	10 22.9	26 06.4	21 13.7	19 21.5	12 22.5
24 Th	8 07 43	1 16 30	4♉15 19	10♉17 48	23 12.9	20 05.2	1 05.6	5 18.6	5 17.8	10 20.3	26 08.8	21 12.5	19 23.7	12 23.9
25 F	8 11 40	2 13 49	16 17 51	22 16 04	23 11.6	21 45.7	1 09.8	5 18.2	5 30.6	10 17.9	26 11.4	21 11.2	19 25.8	12 25.4
26 Sa	8 15 37	3 11 09	28 12 57	4♊09 03	23 09.5	23 24.5	1 16.3	5 16.9	5 43.2	10 15.7	26 14.0	21 09.8	19 27.9	12 26.8
27 Su	8 19 33	4 08 30	10♊04 51	16 00 48	23 06.9	25 01.5	1 24.9	5 14.9	5 55.6	10 13.6	26 16.6	21 08.5	19 30.1	12 28.3
28 M	8 23 30	5 05 52	21 57 20	27 54 52	23 04.0	26 36.7	1 35.7	5 12.1	6 07.7	10 11.8	26 19.4	21 07.1	19 32.3	12 29.7
29 Tu	8 27 26	6 03 15	3♋53 43	9♋54 14	23 01.4	28 10.2	1 48.5	5 08.5	6 19.6	10 10.1	26 22.3	21 05.6	19 34.4	12 31.1
30 W	8 31 23	7 00 39	15 56 41	22 01 19	22 59.2	29 41.9	2 03.3	5 04.1	6 31.3	10 08.6	26 25.3	21 04.1	19 36.6	12 32.5
31 Th	8 35 19	7 58 04	28 08 22	4♌18 00	22 57.6	1♍11.8	2 20.0	4 58.9	6 42.8	10 07.3	26 28.3	21 02.6	19 38.8	12 33.9

August 1924 LONGITUDE

Day	Sid.Time	☉	0 hr ☽	Noon ☽	True ☊	☿	♀	♂	⚳	♃	♄	♅	♆	♇
1 F	8 39 16	8♌55 30	10♌30 23	16♌45 40	22♌56.9	2♍39.9	2♋38.7	4♓52.9	6♉54.0	10♐06.1	26♎31.4	21♓01.0	19♌41.0	12♋35.3
2 Sa	8 43 12	9 52 56	23 03 57	29 25 21	22D 56.9	4 06.2	2 59.1	4R 46.2	7 04.9	10R 05.2	26 34.7	20R 59.4	19 43.2	12 36.7
3 Su	8 47 09	10 50 23	5♍49 59	12♍17 54	22 57.5	5 30.6	3 21.3	4 38.8	7 15.6	10 04.4	26 38.0	20 57.8	19 45.4	12 38.1
4 M	8 51 06	11 47 51	18 49 13	25 24 00	22 58.4	6 53.2	3 45.2	4 30.7	7 26.1	10 03.9	26 41.4	20 56.1	19 47.6	12 39.5
5 Tu	8 55 02	12 45 20	2♎02 18	8♎44 12	22 59.3	8 13.9	4 10.7	4 21.8	7 36.3	10 03.5	26 44.9	20 54.4	19 49.8	12 40.8
6 W	8 58 59	13 42 50	15 29 44	22 18 55	23 00.1	9 32.6	4 37.8	4 12.3	7 46.3	10D 03.3	26 48.4	20 52.7	19 52.0	12 42.2
7 Th	9 02 55	14 40 20	29 11 47	6♏08 15	23R 00.5	10 49.4	5 06.4	4 02.2	7 56.0	10 03.3	26 52.1	20 50.9	19 54.2	12 43.5
8 F	9 06 52	15 37 51	13♏08 15	20 11 39	23 00.6	12 04.1	5 36.5	3 51.5	8 05.4	10 03.4	26 55.8	20 49.1	19 56.4	12 44.8
9 Sa	9 10 48	16 35 23	27 18 13	4♐27 41	23 00.3	13 16.7	6 08.0	3 40.1	8 14.6	10 03.8	26 59.6	20 47.3	19 58.7	12 46.1
10 Su	9 14 45	17 32 56	11♐39 42	18 53 48	22 59.8	14 27.1	6 40.9	3 28.2	8 23.5	10 04.3	27 03.5	20 45.4	20 00.9	12 47.4
11 M	9 18 41	18 30 30	26 09 30	3♑26 11	22 59.3	15 35.2	7 15.1	3 15.8	8 32.1	10 05.0	27 07.5	20 43.5	20 03.1	12 48.7
12 Tu	9 22 38	19 28 05	10♑43 13	17 59 54	22 58.9	16 41.0	7 50.5	3 02.9	8 40.5	10 06.0	27 11.5	20 41.6	20 05.3	12 50.0
13 W	9 26 35	20 25 41	25 15 30	2♒29 19	22 58.7	17 44.3	8 27.2	2 49.5	8 48.5	10 07.1	27 15.6	20 39.6	20 07.5	12 51.2
14 Th	9 30 31	21 23 17	9♒40 38	16 48 47	22D 58.6	18 45.1	9 05.1	2 35.7	8 56.3	10 08.3	27 19.8	20 37.7	20 09.8	12 52.5
15 F	9 34 28	22 20 56	23 53 10	0♓53 14	22R 58.6	19 43.2	9 44.2	2 21.5	9 03.8	10 09.8	27 24.1	20 35.7	20 12.0	12 53.7
16 Sa	9 38 24	23 18 35	7♓48 35	14 38 51	22 58.6	20 38.5	10 24.3	2 07.0	9 11.0	10 11.4	27 28.5	20 33.6	20 14.2	12 54.9
17 Su	9 42 21	24 16 16	21 23 49	28 03 22	22 58.5	21 30.8	11 05.5	1 52.1	9 17.9	10 13.2	27 32.9	20 31.6	20 16.4	12 56.1
18 M	9 46 17	25 13 58	4♈37 31	11♈06 19	22 58.3	22 20.0	11 47.8	1 36.9	9 24.5	10 15.2	27 37.4	20 29.5	20 18.7	12 57.3
19 Tu	9 50 14	26 11 42	17 29 59	23 48 47	22 58.0	23 05.9	12 31.0	1 21.5	9 30.8	10 17.4	27 42.0	20 27.4	20 20.9	12 58.5
20 W	9 54 10	27 09 27	0♉03 04	6♉13 14	22 57.6	23 48.3	13 15.2	1 05.9	9 36.8	10 19.8	27 46.6	20 25.3	20 23.1	12 59.6
21 Th	9 58 07	28 07 14	12 19 45	18 23 08	22D 57.3	24 27.0	14 00.3	0 50.1	9 42.5	10 22.3	27 51.3	20 23.1	20 25.3	13 00.8
22 F	10 02 04	29 05 03	24 23 55	0♊22 40	22 57.2	25 01.8	14 46.3	0 34.3	9 47.8	10 25.0	27 56.1	20 20.9	20 27.5	13 01.9
23 Sa	10 06 00	0♍02 54	6♊19 56	12 16 19	22 57.4	25 32.4	15 33.2	0 18.3	9 52.9	10 27.9	28 01.0	20 18.7	20 29.7	13 03.0
24 Su	10 09 57	1 00 46	18 12 24	24 08 45	22 57.9	25 58.7	16 20.9	0 02.4	9 57.6	10 31.0	28 05.9	20 16.5	20 31.9	13 04.1
25 M	10 13 53	1 58 40	0♋05 54	6♋04 24	22 58.7	26 20.3	17 09.3	29♒46.5	10 01.9	10 34.2	28 10.9	20 14.3	20 34.1	13 05.2
26 Tu	10 17 50	2 56 36	12 04 45	18 07 24	22 59.7	26 37.0	17 58.6	29 30.7	10 06.0	10 37.6	28 16.0	20 12.0	20 36.3	13 06.3
27 W	10 21 46	3 54 34	24 12 47	0♌21 17	23 00.6	26 48.5	18 48.5	29 15.0	10 09.7	10 41.2	28 21.1	20 09.8	20 38.5	13 07.3
28 Th	10 25 43	4 52 33	6♌33 12	12 48 49	23R 01.3	26R 54.6	19 39.2	28 59.5	10 13.0	10 45.0	28 26.3	20 07.5	20 40.6	13 08.3
29 F	10 29 39	5 50 34	19 08 21	25 31 56	23 01.5	26 55.1	20 30.5	28 44.2	10 16.0	10 48.9	28 31.5	20 05.2	20 42.8	13 09.4
30 Sa	10 33 36	6 48 36	1♍59 39	8♍31 30	23 01.0	26 49.6	21 22.5	28 29.2	10 18.7	10 53.0	28 36.9	20 02.9	20 45.0	13 10.4
31 Su	10 37 33	7 46 41	15 07 27	21 47 23	22 59.8	26 38.1	22 15.2	28 14.5	10 21.0	10 57.3	28 42.2	20 00.6	20 47.1	13 11.3

Astro Data

	Dy Hr Mn
♃⊼♇	3 1:03
☽0S	9 6:12
♃∠♄	15 9:01
☽0N	21 22:27
♀D	23 3:33
♂R	24 11:01
☽0S	5 12:05
♃D	7 2:10
☽0N	18 7:43
☿0S	20 6:33
♅⊼♆	20 23:57
☿R	29 1:49

Planet Ingress

	Dy Hr Mn
⚳ ♉	3 4:10
☿ ♌	13 15:38
☉ ♌	23 3:58
☿ ♍	30 16:48
☉ ♍	23 10:48
♂ ♒R	24 15:38

Last Aspect / ☽ Ingress

Last Aspect Dy Hr Mn		☽ Ingress Dy Hr Mn
1 0:39	♄△	♋ 1 9:28
3 12:35	♄□	♌ 3 21:11
5 22:59	♄⚹	♍ 6 7:15
7 23:21	♅☍	♎ 8 14:55
10 12:17	♄☌	♏ 10 19:36
12 18:39	☿△	♐ 12 21:32
14 15:07	♄⚹	♑ 14 21:49
16 15:27	♄□	♒ 16 22:11
18 17:31	♄△	♓ 19 0:30
21 2:34	☉△	♈ 21 6:12
23 7:58	♄☍	♉ 23 15:36
25 10:49	☿□	♊ 26 3:36
28 8:59	☿⚹	♋ 28 16:11
30 20:40	♄□	♌ 31 3:38

Last Aspect Dy Hr Mn		☽ Ingress Dy Hr Mn
2 6:37	♄⚹	♍ 2 13:05
4 3:53	♅☍	♎ 4 20:20
6 19:53	♄☌	♏ 7 1:24
8 13:03	♅△	♐ 9 4:32
11 1:33	♄⚹	♑ 11 6:20
13 3:17	♄□	♒ 13 7:52
15 5:59	♄△	♓ 15 10:28
16 23:24	☿☍	♈ 17 15:32
19 19:30	♄☍	♉ 19 23:54
22 9:10	☉□	♊ 22 11:14
24 23:37	♂△	♋ 24 23:48
27 8:04	♄□	♌ 27 11:19
29 17:51	♂☍	♍ 29 20:19

☽ Phases & Eclipses

Dy Hr Mn	
2 5:35	● 10♋02
9 21:46	☽ 17♎21
16 11:49	○ 23♑38
23 16:36	☾ 0♉30
31 19:42	● 8♌16
31 19:57:58	● P 0.192
8 3:41	☽ 15♏18
14 20:19	○ 21♒43
14 20:20	• T 1.652
22 9:10	☾ 28♉58
30 8:37	● 6♍40
30 8:22:36	● P 0.425

Astro Data

1 July 1924
Julian Day # 8948
SVP 6♓19'00"
GC 25♐47.1 ⚴ 20♓15.0
Eris 0♈38.1R ⚵ 5♎36.9
⚷ 24♈21.3 ⚶ 4♓48.0
☽ Mean ☊ 25♌20.9

1 August 1924
Julian Day # 8979
SVP 6♓18'55"
GC 25♐47.2 ⚴ 18♓23.6R
Eris 0♈31.0R ⚵ 12♎26.8
⚷ 24♈40.1R ⚶ 2♓09.9R
☽ Mean ☊ 23♌42.5

LONGITUDE September 1924

Day	Sid.Time	☉	0 hr ☽	Noon ☽	True ☊	☿	♀	♂	⚳	♃	♄	♅	♆	♇
1 M	10 41 29	8♍44 46	28♍31 07	5♎18 28	22♌58.0	26♍20.3	23♋08.4	28♒00.2	10♉22.9	11♐01.7	28♎47.7	19♓58.2	20♌49.3	13♋12.3
2 Tu	10 45 26	9 42 54	12♎09 08	19 02 52	22R 55.8	25R 56.3	24 02.3	27R 46.3	10 24.5	11 06.3	28 53.2	19R 55.9	20 51.4	13 13.2
3 W	10 49 22	10 41 02	25 59 19	2♏58 10	22 53.6	25 26.1	24 56.7	27 32.9	10 25.8	11 11.1	28 58.8	19 53.5	20 53.5	13 14.1
4 Th	10 53 19	11 39 13	9♏59 05	17 01 43	22 51.7	24 49.7	25 51.7	27 19.9	10 26.6	11 16.0	29 04.4	19 51.2	20 55.6	13 15.0
5 F	10 57 15	12 37 25	24 05 44	1♐10 50	22D 50.4	24 07.7	26 47.2	27 07.5	10R 27.1	11 21.1	29 10.1	19 48.8	20 57.7	13 15.9
6 Sa	11 01 12	13 35 38	8♐16 42	15 23 02	22 50.1	23 20.2	27 43.2	26 55.7	10 27.3	11 26.4	29 15.8	19 46.4	20 59.8	13 16.8
7 Su	11 05 08	14 33 53	22 29 34	29 36 00	22 50.7	22 28.1	28 39.7	26 44.4	10 27.0	11 31.8	29 21.6	19 44.0	21 01.9	13 17.6
8 M	11 09 05	15 32 09	6♑42 04	13♑47 29	22 51.9	21 32.2	29 36.8	26 33.8	10 26.4	11 37.3	29 27.4	19 41.6	21 04.0	13 18.5
9 Tu	11 13 02	16 30 27	20 51 58	27 55 13	22 53.3	20 33.3	0♌34.3	26 23.8	10 25.5	11 43.1	29 33.3	19 39.2	21 06.0	13 19.3
10 W	11 16 58	17 28 46	4♒56 56	11♒56 48	22R 54.4	19 32.7	1 32.2	26 14.5	10 24.1	11 49.0	29 39.3	19 36.8	21 08.1	13 20.0
11 Th	11 20 55	18 27 07	18 54 29	25 49 40	22 54.7	18 31.7	2 30.7	26 05.8	10 22.4	11 55.0	29 45.3	19 34.4	21 10.1	13 20.8
12 F	11 24 51	19 25 30	2♓42 00	9♓31 11	22 53.8	17 31.6	3 29.5	25 57.9	10 20.3	12 01.2	29 51.3	19 32.0	21 12.1	13 21.6
13 Sa	11 28 48	20 23 54	16 16 54	22 58 56	22 51.5	16 33.9	4 28.8	25 50.7	10 17.9	12 07.5	29 57.4	19 29.6	21 14.1	13 22.3
14 Su	11 32 44	21 22 20	29 37 01	6♈11 01	22 47.9	15 40.0	5 28.5	25 44.2	10 15.0	12 14.0	0♏03.6	19 27.2	21 16.1	13 23.0
15 M	11 36 41	22 20 49	12♈40 48	19 06 21	22 43.3	14 51.4	6 28.6	25 38.5	10 11.8	12 20.6	0 09.8	19 24.8	21 18.1	13 23.6
16 Tu	11 40 37	23 19 29	25 27 41	1♉44 54	22 38.2	14 09.1	7 29.1	25 33.5	10 08.2	12 27.4	0 16.0	19 22.4	21 20.0	13 24.3
17 W	11 44 34	24 17 51	7♉58 12	14 07 48	22 33.3	13 34.3	8 30.0	25 29.2	10 04.2	12 34.3	0 22.3	19 20.0	21 22.0	13 24.9
18 Th	11 48 30	25 16 26	20 14 02	26 17 17	22 29.0	13 07.9	9 31.3	25 25.8	9 59.9	12 41.4	0 28.6	19 17.7	21 23.9	13 25.6
19 F	11 52 27	26 15 03	2♊17 58	8♊16 36	22 25.9	12 50.6	10 32.9	25 23.1	9 55.2	12 48.6	0 35.0	19 15.3	21 25.8	13 26.2
20 Sa	11 56 24	27 13 42	14 13 41	20 09 47	22D 24.3	12D 42.9	11 34.9	25 21.2	9 50.1	12 55.9	0 41.4	19 12.9	21 27.7	13 26.7
21 Su	12 00 20	28 12 23	26 05 30	2♋01 28	22 24.1	12 44.9	12 37.2	25D 20.1	9 44.6	13 03.4	0 47.9	19 10.5	21 29.6	13 27.3
22 M	12 04 17	29 11 06	7♋58 16	13 56 33	22 25.0	12 56.8	13 39.8	25 19.8	9 38.7	13 11.0	0 54.4	19 08.2	21 31.4	13 27.8
23 Tu	12 08 13	0♎09 52	19 56 57	26 00 02	22 26.6	13 18.4	14 42.8	25 20.3	9 32.5	13 18.8	1 00.9	19 05.8	21 33.3	13 28.3
24 W	12 12 10	1 08 40	2♌06 26	8♌16 38	22 28.1	13 49.5	15 46.1	25 21.6	9 26.0	13 26.6	1 07.5	19 03.5	21 35.1	13 28.8
25 Th	12 16 06	2 07 30	14 31 10	20 50 26	22R 28.9	14 29.7	16 49.7	25 23.7	9 19.0	13 34.7	1 14.1	19 01.2	21 36.9	13 29.2
26 F	12 20 03	3 06 22	27 14 49	3♍44 32	22 28.3	15 18.4	17 53.6	25 26.6	9 11.7	13 42.8	1 20.8	18 58.8	21 38.6	13 29.7
27 Sa	12 23 59	4 05 17	10♍19 46	17 00 33	22 25.9	16 15.1	18 57.8	25 30.2	9 04.0	13 51.1	1 27.5	18 56.5	21 40.4	13 30.1
28 Su	12 27 56	5 04 13	23 46 48	0♎38 19	22 21.5	17 19.0	20 02.2	25 34.7	8 56.0	13 59.5	1 34.2	18 54.3	21 42.1	13 30.5
29 M	12 31 53	6 03 12	7♎34 46	14 35 41	22 15.4	18 29.6	21 06.9	25 39.9	8 47.7	14 08.0	1 41.0	18 52.0	21 43.9	13 30.8
30 Tu	12 35 49	7 02 12	21 40 31	28 48 36	22 08.3	19 46.1	22 11.9	25 46.0	8 39.0	14 16.7	1 47.8	18 49.7	21 45.5	13 31.2

LONGITUDE October 1924

Day	Sid.Time	☉	0 hr ☽	Noon ☽	True ☊	☿	♀	♂	⚳	♃	♄	♅	♆	♇
1 W	12 39 46	8♎01 15	5♏59 15	13♏11 41	22♌01.0	21♍07.8	23♌17.2	25♒52.8	8♉30.0	14♐25.5	1♏54.6	18♓47.5	21♌47.2	13♋31.5
2 Th	12 43 42	9 00 19	20 25 10	27 38 58	21R 54.5	22 34.1	24 22.7	26 00.4	8R 20.6	14 34.4	2 01.4	18R 45.3	21 48.9	13 31.8
3 F	12 47 39	9 59 25	4♐52 25	12♐04 52	21 49.6	24 04.3	25 28.4	26 08.7	8 11.0	14 43.4	2 08.3	18 43.1	21 50.5	13 32.1
4 Sa	12 51 35	10 58 33	19 15 50	26 24 52	21 46.7	25 37.8	26 34.4	26 17.8	8 01.0	14 52.5	2 15.2	18 40.9	21 52.1	13 32.3
5 Su	12 55 32	11 57 43	3♑31 39	10♑35 56	21D 45.7	27 14.0	27 40.6	26 27.6	7 50.7	15 01.8	2 22.1	18 38.8	21 53.7	13 32.6
6 M	12 59 28	12 56 55	17 37 33	24 36 26	21 46.1	28 52.5	28 47.0	26 38.2	7 40.2	15 11.2	2 29.1	18 36.6	21 55.2	13 32.8
7 Tu	13 03 25	13 56 08	1♒32 31	8♒25 49	21R 47.2	0♎32.8	29 53.7	26 49.4	7 29.3	15 20.7	2 36.1	18 34.5	21 56.8	13 32.9
8 W	13 07 22	14 55 23	15 16 21	22 04 08	21 47.7	2 14.5	1♍00.6	27 01.4	7 18.2	15 30.3	2 43.1	18 32.5	21 58.3	13 33.1
9 Th	13 11 18	15 54 40	28 49 13	5♓31 35	21 46.8	3 57.2	2 07.6	27 14.0	7 06.9	15 40.0	2 50.1	18 30.4	21 59.7	13 33.2
10 F	13 15 15	16 53 58	12♓11 13	18 48 07	21 43.7	5 40.8	3 15.0	27 27.3	6 55.3	15 49.8	2 57.2	18 28.4	22 01.2	13 33.3
11 Sa	13 19 11	17 53 19	25 22 13	1♈53 27	21 38.0	7 24.8	4 22.5	27 41.2	6 43.4	15 59.7	3 04.2	18 26.4	22 02.6	13 33.4
12 Su	13 23 08	18 52 41	8♈21 45	14 47 03	21 29.9	9 09.2	5 30.2	27 55.8	6 31.3	16 09.7	3 11.3	18 24.4	22 04.0	13 33.5
13 M	13 27 04	19 52 05	21 09 15	27 28 21	21 19.8	10 53.7	6 38.1	28 11.0	6 19.1	16 19.8	3 18.4	18 22.4	22 05.4	13R 33.5
14 Tu	13 31 01	20 51 32	3♉44 17	9♉57 07	21 08.6	12 38.2	7 46.2	28 26.9	6 06.6	16 30.0	3 25.5	18 20.5	22 06.7	13 33.5
15 W	13 34 57	21 51 01	16 06 54	22 13 45	20 57.4	14 22.5	8 54.5	28 43.3	5 53.9	16 40.4	3 32.7	18 18.6	22 08.1	13 33.5
16 Th	13 38 54	22 50 32	28 17 52	4♊19 27	20 47.2	16 06.5	10 03.0	29 00.3	5 41.0	16 50.8	3 39.8	18 16.8	22 09.4	13 33.4
17 F	13 42 50	23 50 05	10♊18 50	16 16 23	20 38.8	17 50.3	11 11.7	29 17.9	5 28.0	17 01.3	3 47.0	18 15.0	22 10.6	13 33.4
18 Sa	13 46 47	24 49 40	22 12 29	28 07 39	20 32.8	19 33.6	12 20.5	29 36.0	5 14.8	17 11.9	3 54.2	18 13.2	22 11.9	13 33.3
19 Su	13 50 44	25 49 18	4♋02 22	9♋57 15	20 29.2	21 16.5	13 29.5	29 54.7	5 01.5	17 22.6	4 01.4	18 11.4	22 13.1	13 33.2
20 M	13 54 40	26 48 58	15 52 52	21 49 53	20D 27.7	22 58.9	14 38.7	0♓13.9	4 48.1	17 33.5	4 08.6	18 09.7	22 14.3	13 33.1
21 Tu	13 58 37	27 48 40	27 48 57	3♌50 45	20 27.7	24 40.9	15 48.1	0 33.7	4 34.5	17 44.4	4 15.8	18 08.0	22 15.4	13 32.9
22 W	14 02 33	28 48 25	9♌55 58	16 05 15	20R 28.2	26 22.3	16 57.6	0 53.9	4 20.9	17 55.3	4 23.0	18 06.3	22 16.5	13 32.7
23 Th	14 06 30	29 48 11	22 19 16	28 38 35	20 28.0	28 03.1	18 07.3	1 14.7	4 07.2	18 06.4	4 30.2	18 04.7	22 17.6	13 32.5
24 F	14 10 26	0♏48 00	5♍03 44	11♍35 11	20 26.1	29 43.4	19 17.1	1 36.0	3 53.4	18 17.6	4 37.5	18 03.1	22 18.7	13 32.3
25 Sa	14 14 23	1 47 51	18 13 15	24 58 09	20 21.8	1♏23.2	20 27.1	1 57.8	3 39.6	18 28.8	4 44.7	18 01.6	22 19.7	13 32.0
26 Su	14 18 19	2 47 44	1♎49 56	8♎48 27	20 14.8	3 02.4	21 37.3	2 20.0	3 25.7	18 40.2	4 52.0	18 00.1	22 20.7	13 31.8
27 M	14 22 16	3 47 40	15 53 25	23 04 18	20 05.3	4 41.2	22 47.5	2 42.7	3 11.8	18 51.6	4 59.2	17 58.6	22 21.7	13 31.5
28 Tu	14 26 13	4 47 37	0♏20 26	7♏40 55	19 54.3	6 19.3	23 57.9	3 05.9	2 57.9	19 03.1	5 06.5	17 57.2	22 22.6	13 31.1
29 W	14 30 09	5 47 36	15 04 47	22 30 54	19 42.8	7 57.0	25 08.5	3 29.5	2 44.1	19 14.7	5 13.7	17 55.8	22 23.6	13 30.8
30 Th	14 34 06	6 47 37	29 58 08	7♐25 19	19 32.3	9 34.2	26 19.2	3 53.6	2 30.3	19 26.3	5 21.0	17 54.5	22 24.4	13 30.4
31 F	14 38 02	7 47 40	14♐51 23	22 15 19	19 23.9	11 10.9	27 30.0	4 18.1	2 16.5	19 38.1	5 28.2	17 53.2	22 25.3	13 30.0

Astro Data	Dy Hr Mn
☽0S	1 18:02
⚳R	6 9:04
☿0N	9 4:05
☽0N	14 16:36
☿D	20 19:05
♂D	22 9:15
☉0S	23 7:58
♃⊼♇	24 18:51
☽0S	29 1:48
☿0S	9 18:05
☽0N	12 0:30
♄□♅	13 22:40
♇R	14 9:40
♃□♅	23 8:48
☽0S	26 11:53

Planet Ingress		Dy Hr Mn
♀	♌	8 21:43
♄	♏	13 21:59
☉	♎	23 7:58
☿	♎	7 4:12
♀	♍	7 14:16
♂	♓	19 18:42
☉	♏	23 16:44
☿	♏	24 15:59

Last Aspect Dy Hr Mn		☽ Ingress	Dy Hr Mn
31 20:29	☿ ☌	♎	1 2:38
3 5:06	♄ ☌	♏	3 6:54
5 5:14	♂ □	♐	5 10:00
7 11:36	♄ ⚹	♑	7 12:41
9 14:48	♄ □	♒	9 15:33
11 18:54	♄ △	♓	11 19:17
13 7:00	☉ ☍	♈	14 0:42
16 0:15	♂ ⚹	♉	16 8:39
18 10:18	♂ □	♊	18 19:24
21 3:35	☉ □	♋	21 7:54
22 22:21	♅ △	♌	23 19:52
25 20:35	♂ ☍	♍	26 5:06
27 15:26	♅ ☍	♎	28 10:53
30 6:51	♂ △	♏	30 14:00

Last Aspect Dy Hr Mn		☽ Ingress	Dy Hr Mn
2 9:15	♂ □	♐	2 15:54
4 12:17	♀ △	♑	4 18:02
6 20:23	☿ △	♒	6 21:19
8 20:56	♂ ☌	♓	9 2:06
10 11:24	♅ ☌	♈	11 8:31
13 13:23	♂ ⚹	♉	13 16:50
16 1:09	♂ □	♊	16 3:23
18 15:04	♂ △	♋	18 15:48
20 22:54	☉ □	♌	21 4:21
23 14:22	☉ ⚹	♍	23 14:33
25 3:14	♀ ☌	♎	25 20:49
27 10:49	♆ ⚹	♏	27 23:26
29 16:36	♀ ⚹	♐	30 0:03

☽ Phases & Eclipses Dy Hr Mn	
6 8:45	☽ 13♐28
13 7:00	○ 20♓12
21 3:35	☾ 27♊52
28 20:16	● 5♎25
5 14:30	☽ 12♑04
12 20:21	○ 19♈13
20 22:54	☾ 27♋16
28 6:57	● 4♏35

Astro Data

1 September 1924
Julian Day # 9010
SVP 6♓18'52"
GC 25♐47.2 ⚵ 11♓42.5R
Eris 0♈15.0R ⚴ 21♎16.5
⚷ 24♈09.2R ⚶ 24♒51.2R
☽ Mean ☊ 22♌03.9

1 October 1924
Julian Day # 9040
SVP 6♓18'50"
GC 25♐47.3 ⚵ 4♓39.5R
Eris 29♓55.3R ⚴ 0♏54.4
⚷ 23♈01.4R ⚶ 20♒56.5R
☽ Mean ☊ 20♌28.6

November 1924 — LONGITUDE

Day	Sid.Time	☉	0 hr ☽	Noon ☽	True ☊	☿	♀	♂	⚳	♃	♄	♅	♆	♇
1 Sa	14 41 59	8♏47 45	29♐36 17	6♑53 34	19♌18.2	12♏47.2	28♍40.9	4♓43.0	2♉02.8	19♐49.9	5♏35.5	17♓51.9	22♌26.1	13♋29.6
2 Su	14 45 55	9 47 51	14♑06 38	21 15 10	19R15.2	14 22.9	29 51.9	5 08.3	1R49.2	20 01.8	5 42.7	17R50.7	22 26.9	13R29.2
3 M	14 49 52	10 47 59	28 18 55	5♒17 50	19D14.2	15 58.3	1♎03.1	5 34.0	1 35.7	20 13.7	5 49.9	17 49.5	22 27.6	13 28.7
4 Tu	14 53 48	11 48 08	12♒11 59	19 01 30	19R14.2	17 33.2	2 14.3	6 00.1	1 22.3	20 25.8	5 57.2	17 48.4	22 28.3	13 28.3
5 W	14 57 45	12 48 18	25 46 36	2♓27 31	19 13.7	19 07.8	3 25.7	6 26.5	1 09.1	20 37.8	6 04.4	17 47.3	22 29.0	13 27.8
6 Th	15 01 42	13 48 30	9♓04 32	15 37 55	19 11.7	20 41.9	4 37.2	6 53.3	0 56.0	20 50.0	6 11.6	17 46.3	22 29.7	13 27.2
7 F	15 05 38	14 48 44	22 07 56	28 34 48	19 07.1	22 15.7	5 48.8	7 20.5	0 43.0	21 02.2	6 18.8	17 45.3	22 30.3	13 26.7
8 Sa	15 09 35	15 48 59	4♈58 45	11♈19 57	18 59.4	23 49.1	7 00.5	7 48.0	0 30.3	21 14.5	6 26.0	17 44.4	22 30.9	13 26.1
9 Su	15 13 31	16 49 16	17 38 33	23 54 39	18 48.7	25 22.2	8 12.3	8 15.8	0 17.7	21 26.9	6 33.2	17 43.5	22 31.4	13 25.5
10 M	15 17 28	17 49 34	0♉08 21	6♉19 43	18 35.7	26 54.9	9 24.3	8 44.0	0 05.3	21 39.3	6 40.3	17 42.6	22 31.9	13 24.9
11 Tu	15 21 24	18 49 54	12 28 48	18 35 41	18 21.3	28 27.4	10 36.3	9 12.4	29♈53.1	21 51.8	6 47.5	17 41.8	22 32.4	13 24.3
12 W	15 25 21	19 50 16	24 40 25	0♊43 06	18 06.7	29 59.5	11 48.4	9 41.2	29 41.2	22 04.3	6 54.6	17 41.0	22 32.9	13 23.6
13 Th	15 29 17	20 50 40	6♊43 51	12 42 49	17 53.2	1♐31.3	13 00.6	10 10.2	29 29.5	22 16.9	7 01.7	17 40.3	22 33.3	13 23.0
14 F	15 33 14	21 51 05	18 40 12	24 36 14	17 41.7	3 02.9	14 12.9	10 39.6	29 18.0	22 29.5	7 08.8	17 39.7	22 33.7	13 22.3
15 Sa	15 37 11	22 51 32	0♋31 14	6♋25 32	17 32.9	4 34.1	15 25.3	11 09.2	29 06.8	22 42.2	7 15.9	17 39.1	22 34.0	13 21.6
16 Su	15 41 07	23 52 01	12 19 32	18 13 43	17 27.2	6 05.1	16 37.8	11 39.1	28 55.9	22 55.0	7 23.0	17 38.5	22 34.3	13 20.8
17 M	15 45 04	24 52 32	24 08 34	0♌04 38	17 24.1	7 35.8	17 50.4	12 09.2	28 45.3	23 07.8	7 30.0	17 38.0	22 34.6	13 20.1
18 Tu	15 49 00	25 53 04	6♌02 33	12 02 55	17D23.1	9 06.1	19 03.1	12 39.6	28 34.9	23 20.7	7 37.0	17 37.5	22 34.9	13 19.3
19 W	15 52 57	26 53 38	18 06 25	24 13 44	17R23.1	10 36.2	20 15.8	13 10.3	28 24.9	23 33.6	7 44.0	17 37.1	22 35.1	13 18.5
20 Th	15 56 53	27 54 14	0♍25 32	6♍42 29	17 22.9	12 05.9	21 28.7	13 41.2	28 15.1	23 46.5	7 51.0	17 36.7	22 35.3	13 17.7
21 F	16 00 50	28 54 52	13 05 15	19 34 24	17 21.3	13 35.3	22 41.6	14 12.4	28 05.7	23 59.5	7 57.9	17 36.4	22 35.4	13 16.9
22 Sa	16 04 46	29 55 31	26 10 26	2♎53 44	17 17.5	15 04.3	23 54.6	14 43.7	27 56.6	24 12.6	8 04.9	17 36.1	22 35.5	13 16.0
23 Su	16 08 43	0♐56 12	9♎44 35	16 43 04	17 11.1	16 32.9	25 07.7	15 15.4	27 47.9	24 25.7	8 11.8	17 35.9	22 35.6	13 15.2
24 M	16 12 40	1 56 54	23 49 03	1♏02 13	17 02.1	18 01.1	26 20.8	15 47.2	27 39.5	24 38.8	8 18.6	17 35.8	22R35.6	13 14.3
25 Tu	16 16 36	2 57 39	8♏22 00	15 47 36	16 51.4	19 28.7	27 34.0	16 19.3	27 31.4	24 52.0	8 25.5	17 35.6	22 35.6	13 13.4
26 W	16 20 33	3 58 24	23 18 02	0♐52 04	16 40.2	20 55.8	28 47.3	16 51.6	27 23.7	25 05.2	8 32.3	17D35.6	22 35.6	13 12.5
27 Th	16 24 29	4 59 11	8♐28 25	16 05 40	16 29.6	22 22.2	0♏00.6	17 24.1	27 16.4	25 18.5	8 39.0	17 35.6	22 35.5	13 11.5
28 F	16 28 26	6 00 00	23 42 26	1♑17 21	16 21.1	23 47.9	1 14.0	17 56.8	27 09.4	25 31.8	8 45.8	17 35.6	22 35.4	13 10.6
29 Sa	16 32 22	7 00 49	8♑49 14	16 17 01	16 15.2	25 12.8	2 27.5	18 29.7	27 02.9	25 45.1	8 52.5	17 35.7	22 35.3	13 09.6
30 Su	16 36 19	8 01 40	23 39 50	0♒57 03	16 12.1	26 36.7	3 41.0	19 02.8	26 56.7	25 58.5	8 59.1	17 35.9	22 35.1	13 08.7

December 1924 — LONGITUDE

Day	Sid.Time	☉	0 hr ☽	Noon ☽	True ☊	☿	♀	♂	⚳	♃	♄	♅	♆	♇
1 M	16 40 15	9♐02 31	8♒08 14	15♒13 10	16♌11.2	27♐59.4	4♏54.5	19♓36.1	26♈50.9	26♐11.9	9♏05.8	17♓36.1	22♌34.9	13♋07.7
2 Tu	16 44 12	10 03 23	22 11 46	29 04 08	16R11.5	29 20.9	6 08.2	20 09.5	26R45.5	26 25.3	9 12.3	17 36.3	22R34.7	13R06.7
3 W	16 48 09	11 04 16	5♓50 28	12♓31 06	16 11.8	0♑40.8	7 21.8	20 43.2	26 40.4	26 38.7	9 18.9	17 36.6	22 34.4	13 05.6
4 Th	16 52 05	12 05 09	19 06 23	25 36 43	16 10.9	1 59.1	8 35.5	21 17.0	26 35.8	26 52.2	9 25.4	17 37.0	22 34.1	13 04.6
5 F	16 56 02	13 06 04	2♈02 31	8♈24 14	16 07.8	3 15.3	9 49.3	21 51.0	26 31.6	27 05.7	9 31.9	17 37.4	22 33.8	13 03.6
6 Sa	16 59 58	14 06 59	14 42 15	20 56 58	16 02.1	4 29.2	11 03.1	22 25.1	26 27.7	27 19.3	9 38.3	17 37.8	22 33.4	13 02.5
7 Su	17 03 55	15 07 55	27 08 45	3♉17 55	15 53.8	5 40.4	12 17.0	22 59.4	26 24.3	27 32.8	9 44.6	17 38.3	22 33.0	13 01.4
8 M	17 07 51	16 08 51	9♉24 45	15 29 31	15 43.5	6 48.5	13 30.9	23 33.8	26 21.2	27 46.4	9 51.0	17 38.9	22 32.6	13 00.3
9 Tu	17 11 48	17 09 49	21 32 27	27 33 45	15 31.9	7 53.0	14 44.8	24 08.4	26 18.6	28 00.0	9 57.3	17 39.5	22 32.1	12 59.2
10 W	17 15 44	18 10 47	3♊33 35	9♊32 08	15 20.0	8 53.4	15 58.8	24 43.1	26 16.3	28 13.6	10 03.5	17 40.1	22 31.6	12 58.1
11 Th	17 19 41	19 11 46	15 29 32	21 25 59	15 09.1	9 49.1	17 12.9	25 18.0	26 14.5	28 27.3	10 09.7	17 40.9	22 31.1	12 57.0
12 F	17 23 38	20 12 46	27 21 39	3♋16 43	14 59.8	10 39.3	18 26.9	25 53.0	26 13.0	28 40.9	10 15.8	17 41.6	22 30.5	12 55.9
13 Sa	17 27 34	21 13 47	9♋11 24	15 05 58	14 52.9	11 23.4	19 41.1	26 28.1	26 12.0	28 54.6	10 21.9	17 42.4	22 29.9	12 54.7
14 Su	17 31 31	22 14 49	21 00 40	26 55 52	14 48.5	12 00.4	20 55.2	27 03.3	26 11.3	29 08.3	10 27.9	17 43.3	22 29.3	12 53.6
15 M	17 35 27	23 15 52	2♌51 54	8♌49 12	14D46.6	12 29.7	22 09.4	27 38.7	26D11.1	29 22.0	10 33.9	17 44.2	22 28.6	12 52.4
16 Tu	17 39 24	24 16 55	14 48 12	20 49 25	14 46.6	12 50.1	23 23.7	28 14.2	26 11.2	29 35.7	10 39.8	17 45.2	22 27.9	12 51.2
17 W	17 43 20	25 17 59	26 53 22	3♍00 36	14 47.7	13R01.0	24 38.0	28 49.8	26 11.7	29 49.5	10 45.7	17 46.2	22 27.2	12 50.1
18 Th	17 47 17	26 19 04	9♍11 43	15 27 19	14R48.9	13 01.4	25 52.3	29 25.5	26 12.6	0♑03.2	10 51.5	17 47.2	22 26.4	12 48.9
19 F	17 51 13	27 20 10	21 47 59	28 14 17	14 49.5	12 50.7	27 06.6	0♈01.3	26 13.9	0 16.9	10 57.3	17 48.3	22 25.7	12 47.7
20 Sa	17 55 10	28 21 17	4♎46 45	11♎25 52	14 48.5	12 28.4	28 21.0	0 37.2	26 15.6	0 30.7	11 03.0	17 49.5	22 24.8	12 46.5
21 Su	17 59 07	29 22 24	18 11 58	25 05 20	14 45.7	11 54.4	29 35.4	1 13.2	26 17.6	0 44.5	11 08.6	17 50.7	22 24.0	12 45.3
22 M	18 03 03	0♑23 33	2♏06 04	9♏14 04	14 40.9	11 08.9	0♐49.9	1 49.3	26 20.1	0 58.2	11 14.2	17 52.0	22 23.1	12 44.1
23 Tu	18 07 00	1 24 42	16 29 04	23 50 33	14 34.8	10 12.6	2 04.3	2 25.5	26 22.9	1 12.0	11 19.7	17 53.3	22 22.2	12 42.8
24 W	18 10 56	2 25 51	1♐17 49	8♐49 55	14 27.9	9 06.8	3 18.8	3 01.9	26 26.1	1 25.8	11 25.1	17 54.6	22 21.3	12 41.6
25 Th	18 14 53	3 27 01	16 25 43	24 03 58	14 21.5	7 53.4	4 33.4	3 38.3	26 29.7	1 39.5	11 30.5	17 56.0	22 20.3	12 40.4
26 F	18 18 49	4 28 12	1♑43 16	9♑22 15	14 16.2	6 34.5	5 47.9	4 14.8	26 33.6	1 53.3	11 35.8	17 57.5	22 19.3	12 39.1
27 Sa	18 22 46	5 29 23	16 59 32	24 33 49	14 12.8	5 12.7	7 02.5	4 51.4	26 37.9	2 07.1	11 41.1	17 59.0	22 18.3	12 37.9
28 Su	18 26 43	6 30 34	2♒03 59	9♒29 03	14D11.3	3 50.9	8 17.1	5 28.1	26 42.6	2 20.9	11 46.2	18 00.5	22 17.3	12 36.7
29 M	18 30 39	7 31 44	16 48 16	24 01 04	14 11.6	2 31.6	9 31.7	6 04.9	26 47.7	2 34.6	11 51.3	18 02.1	22 16.2	12 35.4
30 Tu	18 34 36	8 32 55	1♓07 07	8♓06 14	14 12.9	1 17.3	10 46.3	6 41.8	26 53.0	2 48.4	11 56.4	18 03.8	22 15.1	12 34.2
31 W	18 38 32	9 34 06	14 58 27	21 43 55	14 14.5	0 10.1	12 00.9	7 18.7	26 58.8	3 02.1	12 01.3	18 05.5	22 14.0	12 32.9

Astro Data Dy Hr Mn	Planet Ingress Dy Hr Mn	Last Aspect Dy Hr Mn	☽ Ingress Dy Hr Mn	Last Aspect Dy Hr Mn	☽ Ingress Dy Hr Mn	☽ Phases & Eclipses Dy Hr Mn
♀0S 5 16:53	♀ ♎ 2 14:44	31 21:18 ♀ □	♑ 1 0:39	2 12:33 ☿ ⚹	♓ 2 13:38	3 22:18 ☽ 11♒14
☽0N 8 7:23	⚳ ♈R 10 22:23	2 6:16 ♅ ⚹	♒ 3 2:53	4 14:23 ♃ □	♈ 4 20:10	11 12:31 ○ 18♉51
♃∠♄ 10 16:40	☿ ♐ 12 12:08	4 18:07 ♆ ☍	♓ 5 7:34	7 0:34 ♃ △	♉ 7 5:33	19 17:38 ☾ 27♌08
♃△♆ 14 20:04	☉ ♐ 22 13:46	6 22:38 ☿ △	♈ 7 14:39	9 4:50 ♂ ⚹	♊ 9 16:52	26 17:15 ● 4♐12
☽0S 22 23:04	♀ ♏ 27 11:48	9 9:20 ♆ △	♉ 9 23:44	12 2:30 ♃ ☍	♋ 12 5:21	
♆R 25 2:49		12 10:21 ☿ ☍	♊ 12 10:34	14 12:16 ♂ △	♌ 14 18:13	3 9:10 ☽ 10♓57
♅D 27 4:02	☿ ♑ 2 23:41	14 7:52 ♆ ⚹	♋ 14 22:57	17 5:39 ♃ △	♍ 17 6:07	11 7:03 ○ 18♊59
	♃ ♑ 18 6:25	17 0:30 ☉ △	♌ 17 11:51	19 10:11 ☉ □	♎ 19 15:15	19 10:11 ☾ 27♍16
☽0N 5 13:59	♂ ♈ 19 11:09	19 17:38 ☉ □	♍ 19 23:11	21 19:56 ☉ ⚹	♏ 21 20:26	26 3:46 ● 4♑07
⚳D 15 16:20	♀ ♐ 21 19:56	22 6:18 ☉ ⚹	♎ 22 6:51	23 9:37 ♆ □	♐ 23 21:55	
☿R 18 0:58	☉ ♑ 22 2:46	24 3:30 ♀ ☌	♏ 24 10:17	25 9:18 ♆ △	♑ 25 21:18	
☽0S 20 9:06	☿ ♐R 31 15:52	25 22:52 ♆ □	♐ 26 10:38	27 1:33 ♅ ⚹	♒ 27 20:41	
♂0N 20 12:22		28 2:45 ♃ ☌	♑ 28 9:57	29 9:05 ♆ ☍	♓ 29 22:06	
		29 15:43 ♂ ⚹	♒ 30 10:25			

Astro Data

1 November 1924
Julian Day # 9071
SVP 6♓18'46"
GC 25♐47.4 ⚵ 1♓46.6
Eris 29♓36.6R ⚴ 11♏24.1
⚷ 21♈36.7R ⚶ 23♒46.7
☽ Mean ☊ 18♌50.1

1 December 1924
Julian Day # 9101
SVP 6♓18'42"
GC 25♐47.4 ⚵ 4♓12.4
Eris 29♓25.6R ⚴ 21♏36.0
⚷ 20♈31.2R ⚶ 1♓36.3
☽ Mean ☊ 17♌14.8

LONGITUDE — January 1925

Day	Sid.Time	☉	0 hr ☽	Noon ☽	True ☊	☿	♀	♂	⚳	♃	♄	♅	♆	♇
1 Th	18 42 29	10♑35 16	28♓22 53	4♈55 43	14♌15.6	29♐11.3	13♐15.6	7♈55.7	27♈04.9	3♑15.8	12♏06.2	18♓07.2	22♌12.8	12♋31.7
2 F	18 46 25	11 36 26	11♈22 52	17 44 47	14R 15.5	28R 22.1	14 30.3	8 32.8	27 11.3	3 29.6	12 11.1	18 09.0	22R 11.7	12R 30.4
3 Sa	18 50 22	12 37 35	24 01 58	0♉14 56	14 14.0	27 43.1	15 44.9	9 10.0	27 18.1	3 43.3	12 15.8	18 10.8	22 10.5	12 29.2
4 Su	18 54 18	13 38 45	6♉24 12	12 30 14	14 11.0	27 14.2	16 59.6	9 47.2	27 25.2	3 57.0	12 20.5	18 12.6	22 09.3	12 27.9
5 M	18 58 15	14 39 54	18 33 32	24 34 32	14 06.7	26 55.5	18 14.3	10 24.5	27 32.7	4 10.7	12 25.0	18 14.5	22 08.0	12 26.7
6 Tu	19 02 12	15 41 03	0♊33 39	6♊31 17	14 01.7	26D 46.6	19 29.1	11 01.8	27 40.4	4 24.3	12 29.6	18 16.5	22 06.7	12 25.4
7 W	19 06 08	16 42 11	12 27 47	18 23 28	13 56.4	26 46.7	20 43.8	11 39.3	27 48.5	4 38.0	12 34.0	18 18.5	22 05.5	12 24.2
8 Th	19 10 05	17 43 20	24 18 39	0♋13 35	13 51.6	26 55.4	21 58.6	12 16.7	27 56.9	4 51.6	12 38.3	18 20.5	22 04.2	12 22.9
9 F	19 14 01	18 44 28	6♋08 32	12 03 45	13 47.6	27 12.0	23 13.3	12 54.2	28 05.7	5 05.2	12 42.6	18 22.6	22 02.8	12 21.7
10 Sa	19 17 58	19 45 35	17 59 26	23 55 51	13 44.9	27 35.7	24 28.1	13 31.8	28 14.7	5 18.8	12 46.8	18 24.7	22 01.5	12 20.4
11 Su	19 21 54	20 46 43	29 53 12	5♌51 43	13D 43.4	28 05.9	25 42.9	14 09.4	28 24.0	5 32.3	12 50.9	18 26.9	22 00.1	12 19.2
12 M	19 25 51	21 47 50	11♌51 40	17 53 18	13 43.2	28 42.0	26 57.7	14 47.1	28 33.7	5 45.9	12 55.0	18 29.1	21 58.7	12 17.9
13 Tu	19 29 47	22 48 56	23 56 54	0♍02 47	13 44.0	29 23.3	28 12.5	15 24.8	28 43.6	5 59.4	12 58.9	18 31.3	21 57.3	12 16.7
14 W	19 33 44	23 50 03	6♍11 17	12 22 45	13 45.5	0♑09.5	29 27.3	16 02.6	28 53.8	6 12.9	13 02.8	18 33.6	21 55.9	12 15.5
15 Th	19 37 41	24 51 09	18 37 33	24 56 04	13 47.1	0 59.8	0♑42.2	16 40.4	29 04.3	6 26.3	13 06.5	18 35.9	21 54.4	12 14.3
16 F	19 41 37	25 52 15	1♎18 42	7♎45 51	13 48.4	1 54.1	1 57.0	17 18.2	29 15.1	6 39.8	13 10.2	18 38.2	21 53.0	12 13.0
17 Sa	19 45 34	26 53 20	14 17 53	20 55 11	13R 49.2	2 51.7	3 11.9	17 56.1	29 26.2	6 53.2	13 13.8	18 40.6	21 51.5	12 11.8
18 Su	19 49 30	27 54 26	27 38 01	4♏26 39	13 49.2	3 52.5	4 26.8	18 34.0	29 37.5	7 06.5	13 17.3	18 43.1	21 50.0	12 10.6
19 M	19 53 27	28 55 31	11♏21 14	18 21 49	13 48.4	4 56.1	5 41.6	19 12.0	29 49.1	7 19.8	13 20.7	18 45.5	21 48.5	12 09.4
20 Tu	19 57 23	29 56 36	25 28 19	2♐40 31	13 47.1	6 02.1	6 56.5	19 50.0	0♉01.0	7 33.1	13 24.1	18 48.0	21 46.9	12 08.2
21 W	20 01 20	0♒57 40	9♐58 01	17 20 16	13 45.4	7 10.5	8 11.4	20 28.1	0 13.2	7 46.4	13 27.3	18 50.5	21 45.4	12 07.1
22 Th	20 05 16	1 58 44	24 46 35	2♑16 04	13 43.9	8 21.0	9 26.3	21 06.2	0 25.6	7 59.6	13 30.4	18 53.1	21 43.9	12 05.9
23 F	20 09 13	2 59 48	9♑47 44	17 20 30	13 42.7	9 33.3	10 41.2	21 44.3	0 38.2	8 12.8	13 33.5	18 55.7	21 42.3	12 04.7
24 Sa	20 13 10	4 00 51	24 53 14	2♒24 44	13D 42.0	10 47.4	11 56.1	22 22.5	0 51.2	8 26.0	13 36.5	18 58.4	21 40.7	12 03.6
25 Su	20 17 06	5 01 52	9♒53 53	17 19 38	13 41.9	12 03.1	13 11.1	23 00.7	1 04.3	8 39.1	13 39.3	19 01.0	21 39.1	12 02.4
26 M	20 21 03	6 02 53	24 41 03	1♓57 18	13 42.2	13 20.3	14 26.0	23 38.9	1 17.7	8 52.1	13 42.1	19 03.7	21 37.5	12 01.3
27 Tu	20 24 59	7 03 53	9♓07 45	16 11 56	13 42.7	14 38.8	15 40.9	24 17.2	1 31.4	9 05.1	13 44.7	19 06.5	21 35.9	12 00.2
28 W	20 28 56	8 04 52	23 09 33	0♈00 26	13 43.4	15 58.6	16 55.8	24 55.5	1 45.3	9 18.1	13 47.3	19 09.2	21 34.3	11 59.0
29 Th	20 32 52	9 05 49	6♈44 37	13 22 14	13 43.9	17 19.6	18 10.7	25 33.8	1 59.4	9 31.0	13 49.8	19 12.0	21 32.6	11 57.9
30 F	20 36 49	10 06 46	19 53 33	26 18 55	13 44.2	18 41.8	19 25.6	26 12.2	2 13.8	9 43.8	13 52.2	19 14.8	21 31.0	11 56.8
31 Sa	20 40 45	11 07 40	2♉38 46	8♉53 36	13R 44.3	20 05.0	20 40.5	26 50.5	2 28.4	9 56.6	13 54.4	19 17.7	21 29.4	11 55.8

LONGITUDE — February 1925

Day	Sid.Time	☉	0 hr ☽	Noon ☽	True ☊	☿	♀	♂	⚳	♃	♄	♅	♆	♇
1 Su	20 44 42	12♒08 34	15♉03 57	21♉10 21	13♌44.3	21♑29.2	21♑55.4	27♈28.9	2♉43.2	10♑09.4	13♏56.6	19♓20.5	21♌27.7	11♋54.7
2 M	20 48 39	13 09 26	27 13 23	3♊13 37	13D 44.2	22 54.4	23 10.3	28 07.4	2 58.2	10 22.1	13 58.7	19 23.5	21R 26.0	11R 53.6
3 Tu	20 52 35	14 10 17	9♊11 37	15 07 57	13 44.2	24 20.6	24 25.3	28 45.8	3 13.4	10 34.7	14 00.7	19 26.4	21 24.4	11 52.6
4 W	20 56 32	15 11 07	21 03 07	26 57 38	13 44.3	25 47.7	25 40.2	29 24.3	3 28.9	10 47.3	14 02.6	19 29.3	21 22.7	11 51.6
5 Th	21 00 28	16 11 55	2♋51 58	8♋46 34	13 44.6	27 15.7	26 55.1	0♉02.7	3 44.5	10 59.8	14 04.3	19 32.3	21 21.0	11 50.6
6 F	21 04 25	17 12 42	14 41 50	20 38 08	13 44.9	28 44.5	28 10.0	0 41.2	4 00.3	11 12.3	14 06.0	19 35.3	21 19.4	11 49.6
7 Sa	21 08 21	18 13 27	26 35 48	2♌35 10	13R 45.2	0♒14.2	29 24.9	1 19.7	4 16.4	11 24.7	14 07.6	19 38.4	21 17.7	11 48.6
8 Su	21 12 18	19 14 11	8♌36 27	14 39 56	13 45.3	1 44.8	0♒39.7	1 58.3	4 32.6	11 37.0	14 09.1	19 41.4	21 16.0	11 47.6
9 M	21 16 14	20 14 54	20 45 49	26 54 16	13 45.1	3 16.2	1 54.6	2 36.8	4 49.1	11 49.3	14 10.4	19 44.5	21 14.3	11 46.7
10 Tu	21 20 11	21 15 35	3♍05 27	9♍19 32	13 44.6	4 48.5	3 09.5	3 15.3	5 05.7	12 01.5	14 11.7	19 47.6	21 12.6	11 45.7
11 W	21 24 08	22 16 16	15 36 38	21 56 52	13 43.6	6 21.6	4 24.4	3 53.9	5 22.5	12 13.7	14 12.9	19 50.7	21 10.9	11 44.8
12 Th	21 28 04	23 16 54	28 20 21	4♎47 12	13 42.3	7 55.6	5 39.3	4 32.4	5 39.5	12 25.7	14 13.9	19 53.9	21 09.2	11 43.9
13 F	21 32 01	24 17 32	11♎17 31	17 51 23	13 40.9	9 30.4	6 54.2	5 11.0	5 56.6	12 37.7	14 14.9	19 57.0	21 07.6	11 43.0
14 Sa	21 35 57	25 18 08	24 28 56	1♏10 13	13 39.7	11 06.0	8 09.1	5 49.6	6 13.9	12 49.7	14 15.7	20 00.2	21 05.9	11 42.1
15 Su	21 39 54	26 18 43	7♏55 20	14 44 21	13D 38.8	12 42.6	9 24.0	6 28.2	6 31.5	13 01.5	14 16.5	20 03.4	21 04.2	11 41.3
16 M	21 43 50	27 19 18	21 37 15	28 34 04	13 38.6	14 20.0	10 38.9	7 06.8	6 49.1	13 13.3	14 17.1	20 06.6	21 02.5	11 40.5
17 Tu	21 47 47	28 19 50	5♐34 43	12♐39 06	13 39.0	15 58.3	11 53.7	7 45.4	7 07.0	13 25.0	14 17.7	20 09.9	21 00.8	11 39.6
18 W	21 51 43	29 20 22	19 47 01	26 58 12	13 39.9	17 37.5	13 08.6	8 24.0	7 25.0	13 36.7	14 18.1	20 13.1	20 59.2	11 38.8
19 Th	21 55 40	0♓20 53	4♑12 18	11♑28 51	13 41.2	19 17.6	14 23.5	9 02.6	7 43.2	13 48.2	14 18.5	20 16.4	20 57.5	11 38.1
20 F	21 59 37	1 21 22	18 47 20	26 07 05	13 42.3	20 58.7	15 38.4	9 41.3	8 01.5	13 59.7	14 18.7	20 19.7	20 55.9	11 37.3
21 Sa	22 03 33	2 21 49	3♒27 26	10♒47 35	13R 42.9	22 40.7	16 53.3	10 19.9	8 20.0	14 11.1	14R 18.8	20 23.0	20 54.2	11 36.6
22 Su	22 07 30	3 22 15	18 06 44	25 24 04	13 42.6	24 23.6	18 08.1	10 58.6	8 38.7	14 22.4	14 18.9	20 26.3	20 52.6	11 35.9
23 M	22 11 26	4 22 40	2♓38 46	9♓50 03	13 41.2	26 07.5	19 23.0	11 37.3	8 57.5	14 33.6	14 18.8	20 29.6	20 50.9	11 35.2
24 Tu	22 15 23	5 23 02	16 57 15	23 59 43	13 38.7	27 52.4	20 37.8	12 15.9	9 16.4	14 44.7	14 18.6	20 32.9	20 49.3	11 34.5
25 W	22 19 19	6 23 23	0♈56 57	7♈48 35	13 35.4	29 38.3	21 52.7	12 54.6	9 35.5	14 55.7	14 18.3	20 36.3	20 47.7	11 33.8
26 Th	22 23 16	7 23 42	14 34 22	21 14 12	13 31.7	1♓25.2	23 07.5	13 33.3	9 54.8	15 06.7	14 17.9	20 39.6	20 46.1	11 33.2
27 F	22 27 12	8 23 59	27 48 03	4♉16 06	13 28.2	3 13.1	24 22.3	14 12.0	10 14.1	15 17.5	14 17.4	20 43.0	20 44.5	11 32.6
28 Sa	22 31 09	9 24 14	10♉38 34	16 55 48	13 25.3	5 02.0	25 37.1	14 50.7	10 33.7	15 28.3	14 16.8	20 46.4	20 42.9	11 32.0

Astro Data

	Dy Hr Mn
☽ 0N	1 21:27
♄△♇	5 18:38
☿ D	6 23:28
☽ 0S	16 16:31
♃☐♆	17 9:18
☽ 0N	29 6:22
♃☍♇	9 7:10
☽ 0S	12 22:05
♃✱♄	22 4:32
♄ R	22 4:51
☽ 0N	25 16:11
♅⚻♆	27 19:09

Planet Ingress

	Dy Hr Mn
☿ ♑	14 7:16
♀ ♑	14 22:28
⚳ ♉	20 10:00
☉ ♒	20 13:20
♂ ♉	5 10:17
☿ ♒	7 8:12
♀ ♒	7 23:16
☉ ♓	19 3:43
☿ ♓	25 16:53

Last Aspect / ☽ Ingress (January)

Last Aspect Dy Hr Mn		☽ Ingress Dy Hr Mn
1 2:10	☿ ☐	♈ 1 2:57
3 7:19	☿ △	♉ 3 11:31
5 7:08	♆ ☐	♊ 5 22:52
8 5:11	☿ ☍	♋ 8 11:32
10 2:47	☉ ☍	♌ 11 0:14
13 10:38	☿ △	♍ 13 11:55
15 11:50	☉ △	♎ 15 21:33
17 23:33	☉ ☐	♏ 18 4:11
20 7:07	☉ ✱	♐ 20 7:34
21 19:08	♆ △	♑ 22 8:22
23 19:18	♂ ☐	♒ 24 8:09
25 21:41	♂ ✱	♓ 26 8:46
27 17:01	♅ ☌	♈ 28 11:59
30 11:47	♂ ☌	♉ 30 18:58

Last Aspect / ☽ Ingress (February)

Last Aspect Dy Hr Mn		☽ Ingress Dy Hr Mn
1 13:39	♀ △	♊ 2 5:32
4 17:15	♂ ✱	♋ 4 18:11
7 6:38	☿ ☍	♌ 7 6:50
9 0:57	♆ ☌	♍ 9 18:01
11 8:01	♅ ☍	♎ 12 3:06
14 0:37	☉ △	♏ 14 9:54
16 9:41	☉ ☐	♐ 16 14:28
18 16:14	☉ ✱	♑ 18 17:02
20 2:29	♅ ✱	♒ 20 18:21
22 10:07	☿ ☌	♓ 22 19:36
24 6:05	♅ ☌	♈ 24 22:21
26 15:48	♀ ✱	♉ 27 4:04

☽ Phases & Eclipses

Dy Hr Mn	
1 23:25	☽ 11♈04
10 2:47	○ 19♋22
17 23:33	☾ 27♎23
24 14:45	● 4♒08
24 14:53:41	● T 02'32"
31 16:43	☽ 11♉20
8 21:49	○ 19♌39
8 21:42	● P 0.730
16 9:41	☾ 27♏13
23 2:12	● 3♓58

Astro Data

1 January 1925
Julian Day # 9132
SVP 6♓18'37"
GC 25♐47.5 ⚴ 10♓44.1
Eris 29♓25.2 ⚵ 1♐38.4
⚷ 20♈06.1 ⚶ 12♓47.8
☽ Mean ☊ 15♌36.3

1 February 1925
Julian Day # 9163
SVP 6♓18'32"
GC 25♐47.6 ⚴ 19♓53.2
Eris 29♓36.4 ⚵ 10♐28.4
⚷ 20♈34.2 ⚶ 25♓42.6
☽ Mean ☊ 13♌57.8

March 1925

LONGITUDE

Day	Sid.Time	☉	0 hr ☽	Noon ☽	True ☊	☿	♀	♂	⚳	♃	♄	♅	♆	♇
1 Su	22 35 05	10♓24 27	23♉08 12	29♉16 17	13♌23.5	6♓51.9	26♒51.9	15♉29.4	10♉53.3	15♑38.9	14♏16.1	20♓49.8	20♌41.3	11♋31.4
2 M	22 39 02	11 24 38	5♊20 35	11♊21 40	13D 22.9	8 42.8	28 06.7	16 08.1	11 13.1	15 49.5	14R 15.3	20 53.2	20R 39.8	11R 30.8
3 Tu	22 42 59	12 24 47	17 20 10	23 16 41	13 23.5	10 34.7	29 21.5	16 46.7	11 33.0	15 59.9	14 14.4	20 56.6	20 38.2	11 30.3
4 W	22 46 55	13 24 54	29 11 52	5♋06 21	13 24.9	12 27.6	0♓36.3	17 25.4	11 53.1	16 10.3	14 13.4	21 00.0	20 36.7	11 29.8
5 Th	22 50 52	14 24 58	11♋00 43	16 55 35	13 26.8	14 21.4	1 51.0	18 04.1	12 13.2	16 20.6	14 12.3	21 03.4	20 35.2	11 29.3
6 F	22 54 48	15 25 01	22 51 32	28 49 04	13 28.4	16 16.2	3 05.8	18 42.8	12 33.5	16 30.7	14 11.1	21 06.8	20 33.7	11 28.8
7 Sa	22 58 45	16 25 02	4♌48 42	10♌50 53	13R 29.3	18 11.7	4 20.5	19 21.5	12 53.9	16 40.7	14 09.8	21 10.2	20 32.2	11 28.4
8 Su	23 02 41	17 25 00	16 56 00	23 04 23	13 28.9	20 08.1	5 35.2	20 00.1	13 14.5	16 50.7	14 08.3	21 13.6	20 30.7	11 28.0
9 M	23 06 38	18 24 56	29 16 20	5♍32 03	13 26.8	22 05.0	6 50.0	20 38.8	13 35.1	17 00.5	14 06.8	21 17.1	20 29.2	11 27.6
10 Tu	23 10 34	19 24 51	11♍51 40	18 15 16	13 23.0	24 02.6	8 04.7	21 17.5	13 55.9	17 10.2	14 05.3	21 20.5	20 27.8	11 27.2
11 W	23 14 31	20 24 43	24 42 51	1♎14 23	13 17.6	26 00.6	9 19.4	21 56.1	14 16.7	17 19.8	14 03.6	21 23.9	20 26.4	11 26.8
12 Th	23 18 28	21 24 34	7♎49 44	14 28 45	13 11.3	27 58.8	10 34.0	22 34.8	14 37.7	17 29.3	14 01.8	21 27.4	20 25.0	11 26.5
13 F	23 22 24	22 24 22	21 11 12	27 56 53	13 04.7	29 57.0	11 48.7	23 13.4	14 58.8	17 38.7	13 59.9	21 30.8	20 23.6	11 26.2
14 Sa	23 26 21	23 24 09	4♏45 32	11♏36 52	12 58.5	1♈55.1	13 03.4	23 52.0	15 20.0	17 48.0	13 57.9	21 34.2	20 22.2	11 25.9
15 Su	23 30 17	24 23 54	18 30 38	25 26 35	12 53.7	3 52.8	14 18.0	24 30.7	15 41.3	17 57.1	13 55.8	21 37.7	20 20.9	11 25.7
16 M	23 34 14	25 23 38	2♐24 28	9♐24 05	12 50.7	5 49.6	15 32.7	25 09.3	16 02.7	18 06.1	13 53.7	21 41.1	20 19.6	11 25.4
17 Tu	23 38 10	26 23 20	16 25 13	23 27 36	12D 49.5	7 45.4	16 47.3	25 47.9	16 24.2	18 15.1	13 51.4	21 44.5	20 18.3	11 25.2
18 W	23 42 07	27 23 00	0♑31 22	7♑36 02	12 49.8	9 39.7	18 02.0	26 26.5	16 45.8	18 23.8	13 49.1	21 47.9	20 17.0	11 25.0
19 Th	23 46 03	28 22 38	14 41 33	21 47 42	12 51.0	11 32.2	19 16.6	27 05.2	17 07.5	18 32.5	13 46.7	21 51.4	20 15.7	11 24.9
20 F	23 50 00	29 22 15	28 54 17	6♒01 02	12R 52.0	13 22.4	20 31.2	27 43.8	17 29.3	18 41.0	13 44.2	21 54.8	20 14.5	11 24.7
21 Sa	23 53 57	0♈21 50	13♒07 38	20 13 46	12 51.9	15 09.8	21 45.8	28 22.4	17 51.2	18 49.4	13 41.6	21 58.2	20 13.3	11 24.6
22 Su	23 57 53	1 21 23	27 19 00	4♓22 53	12 50.0	16 54.1	23 00.4	29 01.0	18 13.1	18 57.7	13 38.9	22 01.6	20 12.1	11 24.5
23 M	0 01 50	2 20 54	11♓24 58	18 24 44	12 45.7	18 34.8	24 15.0	29 39.6	18 35.2	19 05.8	13 36.1	22 05.0	20 10.9	11 24.4
24 Tu	0 05 46	3 20 23	25 21 40	2♈15 17	12 39.1	20 11.4	25 29.6	0♊18.2	18 57.4	19 13.8	13 33.3	22 08.4	20 09.8	11 24.4
25 W	0 09 43	4 19 50	9♈05 08	15 50 49	12 30.7	21 43.6	26 44.1	0 56.8	19 19.6	19 21.7	13 30.3	22 11.7	20 08.6	11D 24.4
26 Th	0 13 39	5 19 15	22 32 00	29 08 26	12 21.3	23 10.8	27 58.7	1 35.3	19 42.0	19 29.4	13 27.3	22 15.1	20 07.5	11 24.4
27 F	0 17 36	6 18 38	5♉39 58	12♉06 35	12 11.9	24 32.8	29 13.2	2 13.9	20 04.4	19 37.0	13 24.3	22 18.5	20 06.5	11 24.4
28 Sa	0 21 32	7 17 59	18 28 18	24 45 19	12 03.5	25 49.3	0♈27.7	2 52.5	20 26.9	19 44.4	13 21.1	22 21.8	20 05.4	11 24.4
29 Su	0 25 29	8 17 17	0♊57 52	7♊06 17	11 56.9	26 59.8	1 42.2	3 31.0	20 49.5	19 51.8	13 17.9	22 25.2	20 04.4	11 24.5
30 M	0 29 26	9 16 34	13 11 00	19 12 30	11 52.4	28 04.1	2 56.7	4 09.6	21 12.1	19 58.9	13 14.6	22 28.5	20 03.4	11 24.6
31 Tu	0 33 22	10 15 48	25 11 20	1♋08 06	11D 50.1	29 02.1	4 11.2	4 48.1	21 34.9	20 05.9	13 11.2	22 31.8	20 02.5	11 24.7

April 1925

LONGITUDE

Day	Sid.Time	☉	0 hr ☽	Noon ☽	True ☊	☿	♀	♂	⚳	♃	♄	♅	♆	♇
1 W	0 37 19	11♈14 59	7♋03 25	12♋57 57	11♌49.6	29♈53.4	5♈25.6	5♊26.7	21♉57.7	20♑12.8	13♏07.7	22♓35.1	20♌01.5	11♋24.9
2 Th	0 41 15	12 14 08	18 52 21	24 47 20	11 50.2	0♉37.9	6 40.1	6 05.2	22 20.6	20 19.5	13R 04.2	22 38.4	20R 00.6	11 25.1
3 F	0 45 12	13 13 15	0♌43 32	6♌41 38	11R 50.9	1 15.6	7 54.5	6 43.7	22 43.5	20 26.1	13 00.7	22 41.7	19 59.7	11 25.3
4 Sa	0 49 08	14 12 20	12 42 15	18 45 59	11 50.8	1 46.4	9 08.9	7 22.2	23 06.6	20 32.5	12 57.0	22 44.9	19 58.9	11 25.5
5 Su	0 53 05	15 11 22	24 53 24	1♍04 58	11 48.9	2 10.1	10 23.3	8 00.7	23 29.7	20 38.8	12 53.3	22 48.2	19 58.1	11 25.7
6 M	0 57 01	16 10 22	7♍21 06	13 42 09	11 44.7	2 26.8	11 37.7	8 39.1	23 52.8	20 44.9	12 49.6	22 51.4	19 57.3	11 26.0
7 Tu	1 00 58	17 09 20	20 08 21	26 39 49	11 38.0	2R 36.7	12 52.0	9 17.6	24 16.1	20 50.8	12 45.8	22 54.6	19 56.5	11 26.3
8 W	1 04 54	18 08 16	3♎16 33	9♎58 29	11 29.0	2 39.7	14 06.4	9 56.1	24 39.4	20 56.6	12 41.9	22 57.8	19 55.8	11 26.6
9 Th	1 08 51	19 07 10	16 45 22	23 36 52	11 18.4	2 36.2	15 20.7	10 34.5	25 02.7	21 02.3	12 38.0	23 01.0	19 55.1	11 26.9
10 F	1 12 48	20 06 01	0♏32 32	7♏31 52	11 07.3	2 26.4	16 35.0	11 12.9	25 26.1	21 07.7	12 34.0	23 04.1	19 54.4	11 27.3
11 Sa	1 16 44	21 04 51	14 34 15	21 39 05	10 56.9	2 10.6	17 49.3	11 51.3	25 49.6	21 13.0	12 30.0	23 07.2	19 53.7	11 27.6
12 Su	1 20 41	22 03 39	28 45 43	5♐53 31	10 48.2	1 49.3	19 03.6	12 29.7	26 13.2	21 18.2	12 25.9	23 10.4	19 53.1	11 28.1
13 M	1 24 37	23 02 26	13♐01 55	20 10 22	10 42.1	1 22.9	20 17.9	13 08.1	26 36.8	21 23.2	12 21.8	23 13.4	19 52.5	11 28.5
14 Tu	1 28 34	24 01 10	27 18 26	4♑25 43	10 38.5	0 52.0	21 32.1	13 46.5	27 00.4	21 28.0	12 17.6	23 16.5	19 52.0	11 28.9
15 W	1 32 30	24 59 53	11♑31 56	18 36 52	10D 37.2	0 17.3	22 46.4	14 24.9	27 24.2	21 32.7	12 13.4	23 19.6	19 51.5	11 29.4
16 Th	1 36 27	25 58 34	25 40 20	2♒42 15	10R 37.2	29♈39.5	24 00.6	15 03.2	27 48.0	21 37.2	12 09.2	23 22.6	19 51.0	11 29.9
17 F	1 40 23	26 57 14	9♒42 33	16 41 10	10 37.2	28 59.3	25 14.9	15 41.6	28 11.8	21 41.5	12 04.9	23 25.6	19 50.5	11 30.4
18 Sa	1 44 20	27 55 52	23 38 03	0♓33 09	10 35.9	28 17.6	26 29.1	16 19.9	28 35.7	21 45.6	12 00.6	23 28.6	19 50.1	11 31.0
19 Su	1 48 17	28 54 28	7♓26 22	14 17 37	10 32.4	27 35.1	27 43.3	16 58.3	28 59.6	21 49.6	11 56.3	23 31.5	19 49.7	11 31.5
20 M	1 52 13	29 53 02	21 06 44	27 53 33	10 26.0	26 52.6	28 57.5	17 36.6	29 23.6	21 53.4	11 51.9	23 34.5	19 49.3	11 32.1
21 Tu	1 56 10	0♉51 35	4♈37 51	11♈19 25	10 16.8	26 10.9	0♉11.6	18 14.9	29 47.7	21 57.0	11 47.5	23 37.4	19 49.0	11 32.7
22 W	2 00 06	1 50 06	17 58 00	24 33 22	10 05.2	25 30.7	1 25.8	18 53.2	0♊11.8	22 00.5	11 43.1	23 40.3	19 48.7	11 33.4
23 Th	2 04 03	2 48 35	1♉05 19	7♉33 40	9 52.2	24 52.6	2 40.0	19 31.5	0 35.9	22 03.7	11 38.6	23 43.1	19 48.4	11 34.0
24 F	2 07 59	3 47 02	13 58 16	20 19 03	9 39.1	24 17.4	3 54.1	20 09.8	1 00.2	22 06.8	11 34.2	23 45.9	19 48.2	11 34.7
25 Sa	2 11 56	4 45 27	26 36 00	2♊49 11	9 27.0	23 45.4	5 08.2	20 48.1	1 24.4	22 09.7	11 29.7	23 48.7	19 48.0	11 35.4
26 Su	2 15 52	5 43 51	8♊58 44	15 04 52	9 16.9	23 17.1	6 22.3	21 26.4	1 48.7	22 12.4	11 25.2	23 51.5	19 47.8	11 36.1
27 M	2 19 49	6 42 12	21 07 52	27 08 06	9 09.4	22 53.0	7 36.4	22 04.7	2 13.0	22 15.0	11 20.7	23 54.2	19 47.7	11 36.8
28 Tu	2 23 46	7 40 31	3♋06 00	9♋02 04	9 04.7	22 33.2	8 50.5	22 42.9	2 37.4	22 17.3	11 16.2	23 56.9	19 47.6	11 37.6
29 W	2 27 42	8 38 49	14 56 49	20 50 53	9 02.3	22 18.1	10 04.6	23 21.2	3 01.9	22 19.5	11 11.6	23 59.6	19 47.5	11 38.4
30 Th	2 31 39	9 37 04	26 44 51	2♌39 26	9 01.6	22 07.6	11 18.6	23 59.4	3 26.3	22 21.5	11 07.1	24 02.3	19D 47.5	11 39.2

Astro Data	Planet Ingress	Last Aspect	☽ Ingress	Last Aspect	☽ Ingress	☽ Phases & Eclipses
Dy Hr Mn	Dy Hr Mn	Dy Hr Mn	Dy Hr Mn	Dy Hr Mn	Dy Hr Mn	Dy Hr Mn
☽0S 12 4:02	♀ ♓ 4 0:21	1 6:45 ♀ □	♊ 1 13:26	2 7:37 ♅ △	♌ 2 22:32	2 12:06 ☽ 11♊25
☿0N 14 5:54	☿ ♈ 13 12:36	3 7:15 ♅ □	♋ 4 1:38	4 14:23 ♆ ☌	♍ 5 9:55	10 14:21 ○ 19♍31
☉0N 21 3:12	☉ ♈ 21 3:12	5 20:24 ♅ △	♌ 6 14:22	7 5:05 ♅ ☍	♎ 7 18:04	17 17:21 ☾ 26♐37
☽0N 25 1:38	♂ ♊ 24 0:42	8 7:01 ♆ ☌	♍ 9 1:24	9 7:28 ♃ □	♏ 9 23:04	24 14:03 ● 3♈25
♇ D 25 23:08	♀ ♈ 28 3:04	11 0:41 ☿ ☍	♎ 11 9:44	11 14:30 ♅ △	♐ 12 2:05	
♀0N 30 18:37		12 22:36 ♆ ✶	♏ 13 15:37	13 17:11 ☉ △	♑ 14 4:32	1 8:12 ☽ 11♋06
♃⊼♆ 31 1:30	☿ ♉ 1 15:21	15 10:19 ♂ ☍	♐ 15 19:51	16 7:02 ☿ □	♒ 16 7:23	9 3:33 ○ 18♎46
	☿ ♈R 15 23:12	17 17:21 ☉ □	♑ 17 23:07	18 8:16 ☿ ✶	♓ 18 11:02	15 23:40 ☾ 25♑28
☿ R 8 11:02	☉ ♉ 20 14:51	19 23:57 ☉ ✶	♒ 20 1:51	20 4:19 ♅ ☌	♈ 20 15:45	23 2:28 ● 2♉25
☽0S 8 12:03	♀ ♉ 21 8:14	22 2:27 ♂ □	♓ 22 4:33	22 13:40 ♅ ☌	♉ 22 22:00	
☽0N 21 9:45	⚳ ♊ 22 0:16	23 23:04 ♀ ☌	♈ 24 8:04	24 18:36 ♅ ✶	♊ 25 6:33	
♄△♇ 24 9:34		25 23:52 ☿ ☌	♉ 26 13:34	27 5:30 ♅ □	♋ 27 17:45	
		28 7:24 ♅ ✶	♊ 28 22:08	29 18:25 ♅ △	♌ 30 6:36	
		31 7:24 ☿ ✶	♋ 31 9:42			

Astro Data

1 March 1925
Julian Day # 9191
SVP 6♓18'29"
GC 25♐47.6 ⚳ 29♓33.9
Eris 29♓54.0 ⚴ 16♐36.0
⚷ 21♈39.9 ⚵ 8♈07.4
☽ Mean ☊ 12♌28.8

1 April 1925
Julian Day # 9222
SVP 6♓18'26"
GC 25♐47.7 ⚳ 11♈15.6
Eris 0♈16.9 ⚴ 20♐05.2
⚷ 23♈21.4 ⚵ 22♈10.8
☽ Mean ☊ 10♌50.3

LONGITUDE — May 1925

Day	Sid.Time	☉	0 hr ☽	Noon ☽	True ☊	☿	♀	♂	⚳	♃	♄	♅	♆	♇
1 F	2 35 35	10♉35 17	8♌35 16	14♌33 04	9♌01.5	22♈01.9	12♉32.6	24♊37.6	3♊50.8	22♑23.3	11♏02.5	24♓04.9	19♌47.5	11♋40.0
2 Sa	2 39 32	11 33 28	20 33 32	26 37 20	9R01.0	22D01.1	13 46.6	25 15.8	4 15.4	22 24.9	10R58.0	24 07.5	19 47.5	11 40.8
3 Su	2 43 28	12 31 37	2♍45 07	8♍57 30	8 59.0	22 05.0	15 00.6	25 54.0	4 40.0	22 26.4	10 53.5	24 10.0	19 47.6	11 41.7
4 M	2 47 25	13 29 44	15 15 03	21 38 14	8 54.8	22 13.7	16 14.6	26 32.2	5 04.6	22 27.6	10 48.9	24 12.5	19 47.7	11 42.6
5 Tu	2 51 21	14 27 50	28 07 26	4♎42 55	8 48.0	22 27.1	17 28.6	27 10.4	5 29.2	22 28.7	10 44.4	24 15.0	19 47.8	11 43.5
6 W	2 55 18	15 25 53	11♎24 49	18 13 08	8 38.7	22 45.0	18 42.5	27 48.6	5 53.9	22 29.5	10 39.9	24 17.5	19 48.0	11 44.4
7 Th	2 59 15	16 23 55	25 07 40	2♏08 06	8 27.8	23 07.4	19 56.5	28 26.7	6 18.7	22 30.2	10 35.4	24 19.9	19 48.2	11 45.3
8 F	3 03 11	17 21 54	9♏13 54	16 24 26	8 16.3	23 34.1	21 10.4	29 04.8	6 43.4	22 30.7	10 30.9	24 22.3	19 48.4	11 46.3
9 Sa	3 07 08	18 19 53	23 38 54	0♐56 26	8 05.3	24 05.0	22 24.3	29 43.0	7 08.2	22 31.0	10 26.4	24 24.6	19 48.7	11 47.3
10 Su	3 11 04	19 17 50	8♐16 05	15 36 54	7 56.2	24 39.9	23 38.2	0♋21.1	7 33.1	22R31.1	10 22.0	24 26.9	19 49.0	11 48.2
11 M	3 15 01	20 15 45	22 57 56	0♑18 18	7 49.5	25 18.7	24 52.1	0 59.2	7 57.9	22 31.1	10 17.5	24 29.2	19 49.3	11 49.3
12 Tu	3 18 57	21 13 39	7♑37 15	14 54 04	7 45.6	26 01.3	26 05.9	1 37.3	8 22.8	22 30.8	10 13.1	24 31.4	19 49.7	11 50.3
13 W	3 22 54	22 11 32	22 08 13	29 19 18	7D44.1	26 47.6	27 19.8	2 15.4	8 47.7	22 30.4	10 08.7	24 33.6	19 50.0	11 51.3
14 Th	3 26 50	23 09 24	6♒27 00	13♒31 09	7R44.0	27 37.3	28 33.7	2 53.4	9 12.7	22 29.7	10 04.3	24 35.8	19 50.5	11 52.4
15 F	3 30 47	24 07 14	20 31 40	27 28 32	7 44.1	28 30.4	29 47.5	3 31.5	9 37.7	22 28.9	10 00.0	24 37.9	19 50.9	11 53.5
16 Sa	3 34 44	25 05 04	4♓21 47	11♓11 32	7 43.1	29 26.8	1♊01.3	4 09.6	10 02.7	22 27.9	9 55.7	24 40.0	19 51.4	11 54.6
17 Su	3 38 40	26 02 52	17 57 51	24 40 53	7 40.2	0♉26.3	2 15.2	4 47.6	10 27.8	22 26.7	9 51.4	24 42.1	19 51.9	11 55.7
18 M	3 42 37	27 00 38	1♈20 42	7♈57 24	7 34.6	1 28.9	3 29.0	5 25.7	10 52.8	22 25.3	9 47.2	24 44.1	19 52.5	11 56.8
19 Tu	3 46 33	27 58 24	14 31 04	21 01 43	7 26.4	2 34.5	4 42.8	6 03.7	11 17.9	22 23.7	9 43.0	24 46.0	19 53.1	11 57.9
20 W	3 50 30	28 56 09	27 29 23	3♉54 05	7 16.1	3 42.9	5 56.6	6 41.8	11 43.1	22 21.9	9 38.8	24 48.0	19 53.7	11 59.1
21 Th	3 54 26	29 53 52	10♉15 49	16 34 34	7 04.5	4 54.2	7 10.3	7 19.8	12 08.2	22 20.0	9 34.7	24 49.8	19 54.3	12 00.3
22 F	3 58 23	0♊51 34	22 50 22	29 03 13	6 52.7	6 08.2	8 24.1	7 57.8	12 33.4	22 17.8	9 30.6	24 51.7	19 55.0	12 01.5
23 Sa	4 02 19	1 49 15	5♊13 11	11♊20 20	6 41.7	7 24.9	9 37.9	8 35.8	12 58.6	22 15.5	9 26.5	24 53.5	19 55.7	12 02.7
24 Su	4 06 16	2 46 55	17 24 48	23 26 44	6 32.6	8 44.2	10 51.6	9 13.8	13 23.9	22 13.0	9 22.6	24 55.3	19 56.5	12 03.9
25 M	4 10 13	3 44 33	29 26 23	5♋24 01	6 25.8	10 06.2	12 05.4	9 51.8	13 49.1	22 10.3	9 18.6	24 57.0	19 57.3	12 05.1
26 Tu	4 14 09	4 42 10	11♋19 57	17 14 33	6 21.5	11 30.7	13 19.1	10 29.8	14 14.4	22 07.5	9 14.7	24 58.7	19 58.1	12 06.4
27 W	4 18 06	5 39 46	23 08 17	29 01 36	6D19.6	12 57.7	14 32.8	11 07.8	14 39.7	22 04.4	9 10.9	25 00.3	19 58.9	12 07.6
28 Th	4 22 02	6 37 20	4♌55 03	10♌49 12	6 19.4	14 27.3	15 46.5	11 45.8	15 05.0	22 01.2	9 07.1	25 01.9	19 59.8	12 08.9
29 F	4 25 59	7 34 53	16 44 40	22 42 03	6 20.1	15 59.3	17 00.2	12 23.8	15 30.3	21 57.8	9 03.4	25 03.4	20 00.7	12 10.2
30 Sa	4 29 55	8 32 24	28 42 02	4♍45 17	6R20.8	17 33.8	18 13.9	13 01.7	15 55.7	21 54.2	8 59.8	25 04.9	20 01.6	12 11.5
31 Su	4 33 52	9 29 54	10♍52 26	17 04 09	6 20.5	19 10.8	19 27.5	13 39.7	16 21.0	21 50.5	8 56.2	25 06.4	20 02.6	12 12.8

LONGITUDE — June 1925

Day	Sid.Time	☉	0 hr ☽	Noon ☽	True ☊	☿	♀	♂	⚳	♃	♄	♅	♆	♇
1 M	4 37 48	10♊27 23	23♍21 04	29♍43 43	6♌18.6	20♉50.3	20♊41.2	14♋17.6	16♊46.4	21♑46.6	8♏52.7	25♓07.8	20♌03.5	12♋14.1
2 Tu	4 41 45	11 24 51	6♎12 37	12♎48 09	6R14.7	22 32.2	21 54.8	14 55.6	17 11.8	21R42.5	8R49.2	25 09.2	20 04.6	12 15.4
3 W	4 45 42	12 22 17	19 30 37	26 20 10	6 08.9	24 16.6	23 08.4	15 33.5	17 37.2	21 38.2	8 45.8	25 10.5	20 05.6	12 16.8
4 Th	4 49 38	13 19 42	3♏16 46	10♏20 14	6 01.6	26 03.3	24 22.0	16 11.4	18 02.6	21 33.8	8 42.5	25 11.8	20 06.7	12 18.1
5 F	4 53 35	14 17 06	17 30 10	24 46 00	5 53.6	27 52.5	25 35.6	16 49.3	18 28.1	21 29.3	8 39.2	25 13.0	20 07.8	12 19.5
6 Sa	4 57 31	15 14 29	2♐06 59	9♐32 11	5 46.0	29 44.1	26 49.2	17 27.2	18 53.5	21 24.5	8 36.0	25 14.2	20 08.9	12 20.9
7 Su	5 01 28	16 11 51	17 00 34	24 31 00	5 39.7	1♊38.0	28 02.8	18 05.1	19 19.0	21 19.7	8 32.9	25 15.3	20 10.1	12 22.3
8 M	5 05 24	17 09 13	2♑02 20	9♑33 24	5 35.2	3 34.2	29 16.4	18 43.0	19 44.5	21 14.7	8 29.8	25 16.4	20 11.3	12 23.7
9 Tu	5 09 21	18 06 34	17 03 07	24 30 28	5D32.9	5 32.7	0♋29.9	19 20.9	20 10.0	21 09.5	8 26.9	25 17.5	20 12.5	12 25.1
10 W	5 13 17	19 03 54	1♒54 37	9♒14 51	5 32.5	7 33.2	1 43.5	19 58.8	20 35.5	21 04.2	8 24.0	25 18.5	20 13.7	12 26.5
11 Th	5 17 14	20 01 14	16 30 36	23 41 28	5 33.4	9 35.8	2 57.0	20 36.7	21 01.0	20 58.7	8 21.2	25 19.4	20 15.0	12 27.9
12 F	5 21 11	20 58 33	0♓47 12	7♓47 40	5 34.5	11 40.3	4 10.5	21 14.5	21 26.5	20 53.1	8 18.4	25 20.3	20 16.3	12 29.3
13 Sa	5 25 07	21 55 51	14 42 53	21 32 55	5R35.1	13 46.5	5 24.0	21 52.4	21 52.1	20 47.4	8 15.8	25 21.2	20 17.6	12 30.8
14 Su	5 29 04	22 53 10	28 17 55	4♈58 06	5 34.4	15 54.2	6 37.5	22 30.3	22 17.6	20 41.5	8 13.2	25 22.0	20 19.0	12 32.2
15 M	5 33 00	23 50 28	11♈33 42	18 04 57	5 32.0	18 03.2	7 51.0	23 08.1	22 43.2	20 35.5	8 10.7	25 22.8	20 20.3	12 33.7
16 Tu	5 36 57	24 47 46	24 32 09	0♉55 33	5 27.8	20 13.3	9 04.5	23 46.0	23 08.8	20 29.4	8 08.3	25 23.5	20 21.7	12 35.1
17 W	5 40 53	25 45 03	7♉15 24	13 31 57	5 22.1	22 24.2	10 18.0	24 23.8	23 34.3	20 23.1	8 05.9	25 24.2	20 23.2	12 36.6
18 Th	5 44 50	26 42 20	19 45 25	25 56 02	5 15.5	24 35.6	11 31.5	25 01.7	23 59.9	20 16.8	8 03.7	25 24.8	20 24.6	12 38.1
19 F	5 48 46	27 39 37	2♊04 00	8♊09 30	5 08.7	26 47.4	12 45.0	25 39.6	24 25.5	20 10.3	8 01.5	25 25.4	20 26.1	12 39.6
20 Sa	5 52 43	28 36 53	14 12 44	20 13 54	5 02.5	28 59.1	13 58.4	26 17.4	24 51.1	20 03.7	7 59.5	25 25.9	20 27.6	12 41.1
21 Su	5 56 40	29 34 09	26 13 11	2♋10 49	4 57.4	1♋10.5	15 11.9	26 55.3	25 16.7	19 57.0	7 57.5	25 26.4	20 29.1	12 42.6
22 M	6 00 36	0♋31 25	8♋07 00	14 02 00	4 53.8	3 21.4	16 25.3	27 33.1	25 42.4	19 50.2	7 55.6	25 26.8	20 30.7	12 44.1
23 Tu	6 04 33	1 28 40	19 56 05	25 49 33	4D51.8	5 31.4	17 38.8	28 11.0	26 08.0	19 43.3	7 53.8	25 27.2	20 32.3	12 45.6
24 W	6 08 29	2 25 55	1♌42 46	7♌36 05	4 51.5	7 40.5	18 52.2	28 48.8	26 33.6	19 36.4	7 52.1	25 27.5	20 33.8	12 47.1
25 Th	6 12 26	3 23 09	13 29 54	19 24 41	4 52.3	9 48.4	20 05.6	29 26.7	26 59.2	19 29.3	7 50.5	25 27.8	20 35.5	12 48.6
26 F	6 16 22	4 20 22	25 20 54	1♍19 03	4 53.8	11 54.8	21 19.0	0♌04.5	27 24.8	19 22.1	7 48.9	25 28.0	20 37.1	12 50.1
27 Sa	6 20 19	5 17 36	7♍19 40	13 23 20	4 55.5	13 59.8	22 32.4	0 42.4	27 50.5	19 14.9	7 47.5	25 28.2	20 38.8	12 51.6
28 Su	6 24 15	6 14 48	19 30 35	25 42 01	4R56.8	16 03.0	23 45.7	1 20.2	28 16.1	19 07.6	7 46.2	25 28.3	20 40.4	12 53.1
29 M	6 28 12	7 12 01	1♎58 12	8♎19 40	4 57.2	18 04.6	24 59.1	1 58.0	28 41.7	19 00.3	7 44.9	25 28.4	20 42.2	12 54.6
30 Tu	6 32 09	8 09 12	14 46 56	21 20 27	4 56.5	20 04.2	26 12.4	2 35.9	29 07.3	18 52.9	7 43.8	25R28.5	20 43.9	12 56.2

Astro Data (Dy Hr Mn)

♆D 1 1:21
☿D 2 4:14
☽0S 5 21:57
♃R 10 15:30
☽0N 18 16:32
♄⚼♅ 19 0:01

☽0S 2 8:15
☽0N 14 22:51
♃⊼♆ 17 11:51
☽0S 29 17:18
♅R 30 19:13

Planet Ingress (Dy Hr Mn)

♂ ♋ 9 22:44
♀ ♊ 15 16:04
☿ ♉ 17 1:32
☉ ♊ 21 14:33

☿ ♊ 6 15:23
♀ ♋ 9 2:14
☿ ♋ 20 23:07
☉ ♋ 21 22:50
♂ ♌ 26 9:08

Last Aspect (Dy Hr Mn) — **☽ Ingress** (Dy Hr Mn)

2 9:10 ♂ ⚹ ♍ 2 18:38
4 21:33 ♂ □ ♎ 5 3:26
7 5:24 ♂ △ ♏ 7 8:22
9 1:14 ♅ △ ♐ 9 10:27
11 3:27 ☿ △ ♑ 11 11:30
13 8:21 ♀ △ ♒ 13 13:08
15 13:55 ☿ ⚹ ♓ 15 16:23
17 14:39 ☉ ⚹ ♈ 17 21:34
19 14:31 ♃ □ ♉ 20 4:41
22 3:52 ♅ ⚹ ♊ 22 13:50
24 14:57 ♅ □ ♋ 25 1:08
27 3:47 ♅ △ ♌ 27 13:59
29 6:35 ♆ ☌ ♍ 30 2:35

Last Aspect (Dy Hr Mn) — **☽ Ingress** (Dy Hr Mn)

1 3:21 ♅ ☍ ♎ 1 12:30
3 5:51 ♀ △ ♏ 3 18:21
5 17:49 ☿ ☍ ♐ 5 20:33
7 18:08 ♀ ☍ ♑ 7 20:45
9 13:16 ♅ ⚹ ♒ 9 20:54
11 6:14 ♆ ☍ ♓ 11 22:40
13 18:45 ♅ ☌ ♈ 14 3:03
15 23:34 ☉ ⚹ ♉ 16 10:15
18 10:59 ♅ ⚹ ♊ 18 19:57
21 6:17 ☉ ☌ ♋ 21 7:36
23 17:05 ♂ ☌ ♌ 23 20:31
25 14:24 ♆ ☌ ♍ 26 9:21
28 11:34 ♅ ☍ ♎ 28 20:15

☽ Phases & Eclipses (Dy Hr Mn)

1 3:20 ☽ 10♌14
8 13:42 ○ 17♏26
15 5:46 ☾ 23♒52
22 15:48 ● 1♊01
30 20:04 ☽ 8♍52

6 21:48 ○ 15♐38
13 12:44 ☾ 21♓58
21 6:17 ● 29♊21
29 9:43 ☽ 7♎07

Astro Data

1 May 1925
Julian Day # 9252
SVP 6♓18'23"
GC 25♐47.8 ⚴ 23♈11.6
Eris 0♈37.3 ⚵ 18♐52.5R
⚷ 25♈09.1 ⚶ 5♉45.2
☽ Mean ☊ 9♌15.0

1 June 1925
Julian Day # 9283
SVP 6♓18'19"
GC 25♐47.9 ⚴ 5♉54.4
Eris 0♈51.5 ⚵ 13♐06.8R
⚷ 26♈48.9 ⚶ 19♉27.9
☽ Mean ☊ 7♌36.5

July 1925 — LONGITUDE

Day	Sid.Time	☉	0 hr ☽	Noon ☽	True ☊	☿	♀	♂	⚳	♃	♄	♅	♆	♇
1 W	6 36 05	9♋06 24	28♎00 35	4♏47 36	4♌54.7	22♋02.0	27♋25.7	3♌13.7	29♊32.9	18♑45.4	7♏42.7	25♓28.5	20♌45.6	12♋57.7
2 Th	6 40 02	10 03 35	11♏41 38	18 42 41	4R52.1	23 57.9	28 39.0	3 51.5	29 58.6	18R37.9	7R41.8	25R28.4	20 47.4	12 59.2
3 F	6 43 58	11 00 46	25 50 36	3♐05 00	4 49.0	25 51.7	29 52.3	4 29.4	0♋24.2	18 30.4	7 40.9	25 28.3	20 49.2	13 00.8
4 Sa	6 47 55	11 57 57	10♐25 20	17 50 55	4 45.9	27 43.6	1♌05.6	5 07.2	0 49.8	18 22.8	7 40.2	25 28.2	20 51.0	13 02.3
5 Su	6 51 51	12 55 07	25 20 49	2♑54 01	4 43.4	29 33.5	2 18.9	5 45.0	1 15.4	18 15.1	7 39.5	25 28.0	20 52.8	13 03.8
6 M	6 55 48	13 52 18	10♑29 21	18 05 37	4 41.8	1♌21.3	3 32.1	6 22.9	1 41.0	18 07.5	7 38.9	25 27.7	20 54.6	13 05.3
7 Tu	6 59 44	14 49 29	25 41 35	3♒16 04	4D41.2	3 07.1	4 45.4	7 00.7	2 06.6	17 59.8	7 38.5	25 27.4	20 56.5	13 06.9
8 W	7 03 41	15 46 40	10♒47 56	18 16 10	4 41.5	4 50.9	5 58.6	7 38.5	2 32.2	17 52.1	7 38.1	25 27.1	20 58.4	13 08.4
9 Th	7 07 38	16 43 51	25 39 56	2♓58 30	4 42.5	6 32.7	7 11.8	8 16.3	2 57.8	17 44.4	7 37.8	25 26.7	21 00.3	13 09.9
10 F	7 11 34	17 41 02	10♓11 22	17 18 08	4 43.7	8 12.4	8 25.0	8 54.2	3 23.4	17 36.7	7 37.6	25 26.2	21 02.2	13 11.5
11 Sa	7 15 31	18 38 14	24 18 37	1♈12 45	4 44.7	9 50.1	9 38.1	9 32.0	3 48.9	17 29.0	7D37.5	25 25.8	21 04.1	13 13.0
12 Su	7 19 27	19 35 26	8♈00 35	14 42 18	4R45.3	11 25.8	10 51.3	10 09.8	4 14.5	17 21.3	7 37.5	25 25.2	21 06.0	13 14.5
13 M	7 23 24	20 32 40	21 18 09	27 48 27	4 45.2	12 59.4	12 04.5	10 47.7	4 40.1	17 13.6	7 37.6	25 24.7	21 08.0	13 16.0
14 Tu	7 27 20	21 29 53	4♉13 33	10♉33 53	4 44.6	14 31.0	13 17.6	11 25.5	5 05.6	17 05.9	7 37.9	25 24.0	21 10.0	13 17.6
15 W	7 31 17	22 27 07	16 49 52	23 01 53	4 43.4	16 00.6	14 30.7	12 03.4	5 31.2	16 58.2	7 38.2	25 23.4	21 12.0	13 19.1
16 Th	7 35 13	23 24 22	29 10 24	5♊15 49	4 41.9	17 28.1	15 43.9	12 41.2	5 56.7	16 50.5	7 38.6	25 22.6	21 14.0	13 20.6
17 F	7 39 10	24 21 38	11♊18 32	17 18 55	4 40.4	18 53.4	16 57.0	13 19.1	6 22.3	16 42.9	7 39.1	25 21.9	21 16.0	13 22.1
18 Sa	7 43 07	25 18 54	23 17 22	29 14 12	4 39.0	20 16.7	18 10.1	13 57.0	6 47.8	16 35.4	7 39.7	25 21.1	21 18.0	13 23.6
19 Su	7 47 03	26 16 11	5♋09 46	11♋04 22	4 38.0	21 37.8	19 23.1	14 34.8	7 13.3	16 27.8	7 40.4	25 20.2	21 20.1	13 25.1
20 M	7 51 00	27 13 28	16 58 19	22 51 54	4D37.4	22 56.7	20 36.2	15 12.7	7 38.8	16 20.3	7 41.2	25 19.3	21 22.1	13 26.6
21 Tu	7 54 56	28 10 46	28 45 24	4♌39 06	4 37.3	24 13.3	21 49.2	15 50.6	8 04.3	16 12.9	7 42.1	25 18.4	21 24.2	13 28.1
22 W	7 58 53	29 08 04	10♌33 17	16 28 16	4 37.4	25 27.7	23 02.3	16 28.5	8 29.7	16 05.5	7 43.1	25 17.4	21 26.3	13 29.6
23 Th	8 02 49	0♌05 23	22 24 20	28 21 49	4 37.8	26 39.6	24 15.3	17 06.4	8 55.2	15 58.2	7 44.2	25 16.4	21 28.4	13 31.1
24 F	8 06 46	1 02 42	4♍21 02	10♍22 20	4 38.2	27 49.2	25 28.3	17 44.3	9 20.6	15 51.0	7 45.4	25 15.3	21 30.5	13 32.6
25 Sa	8 10 43	2 00 02	16 26 06	22 32 43	4 38.5	28 56.2	26 41.2	18 22.2	9 46.0	15 43.8	7 46.6	25 14.2	21 32.6	13 34.0
26 Su	8 14 39	2 57 22	28 42 34	4♎56 05	4 38.7	0♍00.6	27 54.2	19 00.1	10 11.4	15 36.7	7 48.0	25 13.0	21 34.7	13 35.5
27 M	8 18 36	3 54 42	11♎13 41	17 35 45	4R38.8	1 02.3	29 07.1	19 38.0	10 36.8	15 29.7	7 49.5	25 11.8	21 36.8	13 36.9
28 Tu	8 22 32	4 52 03	24 02 43	0♏34 58	4D38.8	2 01.3	0♍20.0	20 15.9	11 02.1	15 22.8	7 51.1	25 10.6	21 39.0	13 38.4
29 W	8 26 29	5 49 25	7♏12 48	13 56 33	4 38.9	2 57.2	1 32.9	20 53.8	11 27.5	15 16.0	7 52.7	25 09.3	21 41.1	13 39.8
30 Th	8 30 25	6 46 47	20 46 23	27 42 26	4 39.0	3 50.2	2 45.8	21 31.8	11 52.8	15 09.3	7 54.5	25 08.0	21 43.3	13 41.3
31 F	8 34 22	7 44 10	4♐44 43	11♐53 05	4 39.2	4 39.9	3 58.6	22 09.7	12 18.1	15 02.7	7 56.4	25 06.6	21 45.4	13 42.7

August 1925 — LONGITUDE

Day	Sid.Time	☉	0 hr ☽	Noon ☽	True ☊	☿	♀	♂	⚳	♃	♄	♅	♆	♇
1 Sa	8 38 18	8♌41 33	19♐07 16	26♐26 51	4♌39.5	5♍26.3	5♍11.4	22♌47.6	12♋43.4	14♑56.2	7♏58.3	25♓05.2	21♌47.6	13♋44.1
2 Su	8 42 15	9 38 57	3♑51 13	11♑19 39	4 39.9	6 09.2	6 24.2	23 25.6	13 08.6	14R49.8	8 00.4	25R03.8	21 49.8	13 45.5
3 M	8 46 12	10 36 22	18 51 15	26 25 00	4R40.1	6 48.4	7 37.0	24 03.5	13 33.8	14 43.5	8 02.5	25 02.3	21 52.0	13 46.9
4 Tu	8 50 08	11 33 48	3♒59 48	11♒34 29	4 40.2	7 23.8	8 49.7	24 41.5	13 59.0	14 37.4	8 04.8	25 00.8	21 54.2	13 48.3
5 W	8 54 05	12 31 14	19 07 53	26 38 52	4 39.8	7 55.1	10 02.4	25 19.4	14 24.2	14 31.3	8 07.1	24 59.2	21 56.4	13 49.7
6 Th	8 58 01	13 28 42	4♓06 23	11♓29 27	4 39.1	8 22.2	11 15.1	25 57.4	14 49.4	14 25.4	8 09.5	24 57.7	21 58.6	13 51.0
7 F	9 01 58	14 26 10	18 47 18	25 59 15	4 38.0	8 44.9	12 27.7	26 35.4	15 14.5	14 19.7	8 12.0	24 56.0	22 00.8	13 52.4
8 Sa	9 05 54	15 23 40	3♈04 50	10♈03 44	4 36.8	9 02.9	13 40.4	27 13.4	15 39.6	14 14.0	8 14.6	24 54.4	22 03.0	13 53.7
9 Su	9 09 51	16 21 12	16 55 49	23 41 06	4 35.7	9 16.1	14 53.0	27 51.4	16 04.7	14 08.5	8 17.3	24 52.7	22 05.2	13 55.1
10 M	9 13 47	17 18 45	0♉19 42	6♉51 54	4D34.9	9 24.3	16 05.6	28 29.4	16 29.7	14 03.2	8 20.1	24 51.0	22 07.4	13 56.4
11 Tu	9 17 44	18 16 19	13 18 04	19 38 36	4 34.7	9R27.2	17 18.2	29 07.4	16 54.7	13 58.0	8 22.9	24 49.2	22 09.6	13 57.7
12 W	9 21 40	19 13 54	25 54 00	2♊04 47	4 35.1	9 24.9	18 30.7	29 45.4	17 19.7	13 52.9	8 25.9	24 47.4	22 11.8	13 59.0
13 Th	9 25 37	20 11 32	8♊11 32	14 14 45	4 36.0	9 17.0	19 43.2	0♍23.5	17 44.7	13 48.0	8 28.9	24 45.6	22 14.1	14 00.3
14 F	9 29 34	21 09 10	20 15 03	26 12 56	4 37.4	9 03.6	20 55.7	1 01.5	18 09.6	13 43.2	8 32.0	24 43.7	22 16.3	14 01.5
15 Sa	9 33 30	22 06 50	2♋08 58	8♋03 38	4 38.8	8 44.7	22 08.2	1 39.6	18 34.5	13 38.6	8 35.3	24 41.8	22 18.5	14 02.8
16 Su	9 37 27	23 04 32	13 57 25	19 50 48	4 40.0	8 20.2	23 20.6	2 17.7	18 59.4	13 34.2	8 38.6	24 39.9	22 20.7	14 04.1
17 M	9 41 23	24 02 15	25 44 10	1♌37 55	4R40.7	7 50.4	24 33.0	2 55.8	19 24.2	13 29.9	8 41.9	24 38.0	22 23.0	14 05.3
18 Tu	9 45 20	24 59 59	7♌32 25	13 27 59	4 40.4	7 15.4	25 45.4	3 33.9	19 49.0	13 25.8	8 45.4	24 36.0	22 25.2	14 06.5
19 W	9 49 16	25 57 45	19 24 56	25 23 30	4 39.1	6 35.7	26 57.8	4 12.0	20 13.7	13 21.8	8 49.0	24 34.0	22 27.4	14 07.7
20 Th	9 53 13	26 55 32	1♍23 57	7♍26 31	4 36.8	5 51.6	28 10.1	4 50.1	20 38.4	13 18.1	8 52.6	24 32.0	22 29.6	14 08.9
21 F	9 57 09	27 53 21	13 31 23	19 38 46	4 33.6	5 03.9	29 22.4	5 28.3	21 03.1	13 14.5	8 56.3	24 29.9	22 31.8	14 10.1
22 Sa	10 01 06	28 51 10	25 48 52	2♎01 51	4 29.7	4 13.2	0♎34.7	6 06.4	21 27.7	13 11.1	9 00.1	24 27.8	22 34.1	14 11.2
23 Su	10 05 03	29 49 01	8♎17 55	14 37 14	4 25.8	3 20.3	1 47.0	6 44.6	21 52.3	13 07.8	9 04.0	24 25.7	22 36.3	14 12.4
24 M	10 08 59	0♍46 54	21 00 00	27 26 26	4 22.3	2 26.4	2 59.2	7 22.8	22 16.8	13 04.7	9 07.9	24 23.6	22 38.5	14 13.5
25 Tu	10 12 56	1 44 47	3♏56 42	10♏31 01	4 19.6	1 32.4	4 11.4	8 01.0	22 41.3	13 01.9	9 12.0	24 21.5	22 40.7	14 14.6
26 W	10 16 52	2 42 42	17 09 34	23 52 31	4D18.1	0 39.4	5 23.5	8 39.2	23 05.8	12 59.2	9 16.1	24 19.3	22 42.9	14 15.7
27 Th	10 20 49	3 40 39	0♐40 02	7♐32 14	4 17.9	29♌48.5	6 35.6	9 17.4	23 30.2	12 56.6	9 20.3	24 17.1	22 45.1	14 16.8
28 F	10 24 45	4 38 36	14 29 10	21 30 51	4 18.7	29 01.0	7 47.7	9 55.6	23 54.5	12 54.3	9 24.6	24 14.9	22 47.3	14 17.8
29 Sa	10 28 42	5 36 35	28 37 11	5♑48 01	4 20.1	28 17.8	8 59.7	10 33.8	24 18.8	12 52.2	9 28.9	24 12.7	22 49.5	14 18.9
30 Su	10 32 38	6 34 35	13♑03 02	20 21 51	4R21.4	27 40.0	10 11.7	11 12.1	24 43.1	12 50.2	9 33.3	24 10.4	22 51.6	14 19.9
31 M	10 36 35	7 32 37	27 43 54	5♒08 32	4 21.9	27 08.5	11 23.7	11 50.4	25 07.3	12 48.5	9 37.8	24 08.2	22 53.8	14 20.9

Astro Data Dy Hr Mn	Planet Ingress Dy Hr Mn	Last Aspect Dy Hr Mn	☽ Ingress Dy Hr Mn	Last Aspect Dy Hr Mn	☽ Ingress Dy Hr Mn	☽ Phases & Eclipses Dy Hr Mn
♄ D 11 21:18	⚳ ♋ 2 13:21	30 21:39 ♀ □	♏ 1 3:33	1 9:47 ♅ □	♑ 1 17:46	6 4:54 ○ 13♑35
☽ 0N 12 5:49	♀ ♌ 3 14:31	3 6:13 ♀ △	♐ 3 6:55	3 9:49 ♅ ⚹	♒ 3 17:40	12 21:34 ☾ 19♈58
☽ 0S 27 0:11	☿ ♌ 5 17:52	5 0:12 ♅ □	♑ 5 7:24	5 9:47 ♂ ☍	♓ 5 17:23	20 21:40 ● 27♋37
	☉ ♌ 23 9:45	6 23:38 ♅ ⚹	♒ 7 6:49	7 10:14 ♅ ☌	♈ 7 18:46	20 21:48:19 ● A 07'14"
☽ 0N 8 14:09	☿ ♍ 26 11:46	8 16:23 ♆ ☍	♓ 9 7:06	9 19:53 ♂ △	♉ 9 23:24	28 20:23 ☽ 5♏12
♃☍♇ 11 12:59	♀ ♍ 28 5:25	11 1:56 ♅ ☌	♈ 11 9:53	12 7:14 ♂ □	♊ 12 7:57	
☿ R 11 13:28		12 23:40 ♆ △	♉ 13 16:05	14 9:01 ♅ □	♋ 14 19:39	4 11:59 ○ 11♒34
☽ 0S 23 5:30	♂ ♍ 12 21:12	15 16:35 ♅ ⚹	♊ 16 1:37	16 21:48 ♅ △	♌ 17 8:41	4 11:53 ☍ P 0.746
♀0S 23 13:52	♀ ♎ 22 0:28	18 4:10 ♅ □	♋ 18 13:33	19 13:15 ☉ ☌	♍ 19 21:13	11 9:11 ☾ 18♉10
♄⊡♅ 27 0:06	☉ ♍ 23 16:33	20 21:40 ☉ ☌	♌ 21 2:32	21 21:25 ♅ ☍	♎ 22 8:05	19 13:15 ● 26♌01
	☿ ♌R 27 6:28	23 8:12 ☿ ☌	♍ 23 15:17	24 3:03 ♆ ⚹	♏ 24 16:44	27 4:46 ☽ 3♐23
		25 17:15 ♅ ☍	♎ 26 2:30	26 12:47 ♅ △	♐ 26 22:50	
		27 19:31 ♆ ⚹	♏ 28 10:56	29 0:03 ☿ △	♑ 29 2:19	
		30 7:34 ♅ △	♐ 30 15:56	30 18:12 ♅ ⚹	♒ 31 3:41	

Astro Data

1 July 1925
Julian Day # 9313
SVP 6♓18'14"
GC 25♐47.9 ⚴ 18♉21.9
Eris 0♈55.4R ⚵ 6♐56.8R
⚷ 27♈56.6 ⚶ 2♊09.3
☽ Mean ☊ 6♌01.2

1 August 1925
Julian Day # 9344
SVP 6♓18'09"
GC 25♐48.0 ⚴ 1♊05.1
Eris 0♈48.6R ⚵ 4♐33.9
⚷ 28♈22.4 ⚶ 14♊17.0
☽ Mean ☊ 4♌22.7

LONGITUDE — September 1925

Day	Sid.Time	☉	0 hr ☽	Noon ☽	True ☊	☿	♀	♂	⚳	♃	♄	♅	♆	♇
1 Tu	10 40 32	8♍30 39	12♒34 58	20♒02 19	4♌21.1	26♌44.0	12♎35.6	12♍28.6	25♋31.4	12♑46.9	9♏42.4	24♓05.9	22♌56.0	14♋21.9
2 W	10 44 28	9 28 44	27 29 37	4♓55 51	4R 18.6	26R 27.1	13 47.4	13 06.9	25 55.5	12R 45.5	9 47.0	24R 03.6	22 58.1	14 22.9
3 Th	10 48 25	10 26 50	12♓20 00	19 41 04	4 14.5	26D 18.4	14 59.3	13 45.2	26 19.6	12 44.3	9 51.7	24 01.3	23 00.3	14 23.8
4 F	10 52 21	11 24 58	26 58 08	4♈10 22	4 09.1	26 18.2	16 11.1	14 23.5	26 43.5	12 43.3	9 56.5	23 59.0	23 02.4	14 24.8
5 Sa	10 56 18	12 23 07	11♈17 06	18 17 47	4 03.2	26 26.7	17 22.8	15 01.9	27 07.5	12 42.4	10 01.3	23 56.6	23 04.5	14 25.7
6 Su	11 00 14	13 21 19	25 12 03	1♉59 41	3 57.6	26 44.1	18 34.5	15 40.2	27 31.3	12 41.8	10 06.2	23 54.3	23 06.6	14 26.6
7 M	11 04 11	14 19 32	8♉40 37	15 15 00	3 52.9	27 10.1	19 46.2	16 18.6	27 55.1	12 41.4	10 11.2	23 51.9	23 08.8	14 27.4
8 Tu	11 08 07	15 17 48	21 43 01	28 05 03	3 49.6	27 44.8	20 57.8	16 57.0	28 18.9	12D 41.1	10 16.2	23 49.6	23 10.9	14 28.3
9 W	11 12 04	16 16 06	4♊21 31	10♊32 57	3D 48.0	28 27.8	22 09.4	17 35.4	28 42.6	12 41.1	10 21.4	23 47.2	23 12.9	14 29.1
10 Th	11 16 01	17 14 26	16 39 55	22 43 02	3 48.0	29 18.8	23 21.0	18 13.8	29 06.2	12 41.2	10 26.5	23 44.8	23 15.0	14 30.0
11 F	11 19 57	18 12 48	28 42 57	4♋40 18	3 49.0	0♍17.5	24 32.5	18 52.3	29 29.8	12 41.5	10 31.8	23 42.4	23 17.1	14 30.8
12 Sa	11 23 54	19 11 12	10♋35 44	16 29 53	3 50.5	1 23.3	25 44.0	19 30.7	29 53.3	12 42.0	10 37.1	23 40.0	23 19.1	14 31.5
13 Su	11 27 50	20 09 38	22 23 24	28 16 50	3R 51.6	2 35.6	26 55.4	20 09.2	0♌16.7	12 42.7	10 42.4	23 37.7	23 21.2	14 32.3
14 M	11 31 47	21 08 06	4♌10 47	10♌05 44	3 51.5	3 54.1	28 06.8	20 47.7	0 40.1	12 43.6	10 47.9	23 35.3	23 23.2	14 33.0
15 Tu	11 35 43	22 06 36	16 02 10	22 00 31	3 49.7	5 17.9	29 18.2	21 26.2	1 03.4	12 44.7	10 53.4	23 32.8	23 25.2	14 33.8
16 W	11 39 40	23 05 08	28 01 09	4♍04 24	3 45.7	6 46.7	0♏29.5	22 04.8	1 26.6	12 46.0	10 58.9	23 30.4	23 27.2	14 34.4
17 Th	11 43 36	24 03 42	10♍10 29	16 19 39	3 39.4	8 19.7	1 40.7	22 43.3	1 49.7	12 47.5	11 04.5	23 28.0	23 29.2	14 35.1
18 F	11 47 33	25 02 18	22 32 01	28 47 42	3 31.3	9 56.4	2 51.9	23 21.9	2 12.8	12 49.2	11 10.2	23 25.6	23 31.1	14 35.8
19 Sa	11 51 29	26 00 56	5♎06 43	11♎29 06	3 22.0	11 36.2	4 03.1	24 00.5	2 35.8	12 51.0	11 15.9	23 23.2	23 33.1	14 36.4
20 Su	11 55 26	26 59 36	17 54 48	24 23 46	3 12.4	13 18.7	5 14.2	24 39.1	2 58.6	12 53.1	11 21.6	23 20.8	23 35.0	14 37.0
21 M	11 59 23	27 58 18	0♏55 56	7♏31 13	3 03.5	15 03.2	6 25.3	25 17.7	3 21.5	12 55.3	11 27.5	23 18.4	23 36.9	14 37.6
22 Tu	12 03 19	28 57 01	14 09 32	20 50 49	2 56.1	16 49.5	7 36.3	25 56.4	3 44.2	12 57.7	11 33.3	23 16.0	23 38.8	14 38.1
23 W	12 07 16	29 55 47	27 35 00	4♐22 02	2 51.0	18 37.0	8 47.3	26 35.1	4 06.8	13 00.3	11 39.3	23 13.6	23 40.7	14 38.7
24 Th	12 11 12	0♎54 34	11♐11 55	18 04 36	2D 48.3	20 25.5	9 58.2	27 13.7	4 29.4	13 03.1	11 45.3	23 11.3	23 42.6	14 39.2
25 F	12 15 09	1 53 23	25 00 07	1♑58 26	2 47.5	22 14.6	11 09.0	27 52.5	4 51.8	13 06.1	11 51.3	23 08.9	23 44.4	14 39.7
26 Sa	12 19 05	2 52 13	8♑59 31	16 03 19	2 48.0	24 04.0	12 19.8	28 31.2	5 14.2	13 09.3	11 57.4	23 06.5	23 46.2	14 40.2
27 Su	12 23 02	3 51 05	23 09 44	0♒18 36	2R 48.5	25 53.6	13 30.6	29 09.9	5 36.5	13 12.7	12 03.5	23 04.2	23 48.1	14 40.6
28 M	12 26 58	4 49 59	7♒29 40	14 42 36	2 48.0	27 43.1	14 41.2	29 48.7	5 58.7	13 16.2	12 09.7	23 01.8	23 49.8	14 41.0
29 Tu	12 30 55	5 48 55	21 56 58	29 12 14	2 45.4	29 32.4	15 51.8	0♎27.4	6 20.7	13 19.9	12 15.9	22 59.5	23 51.6	14 41.5
30 W	12 34 52	6 47 52	6♓27 49	13♓42 58	2 40.3	1♎21.3	17 02.4	1 06.2	6 42.7	13 23.8	12 22.2	22 57.2	23 53.4	14 41.8

LONGITUDE — October 1925

Day	Sid.Time	☉	0 hr ☽	Noon ☽	True ☊	☿	♀	♂	⚳	♃	♄	♅	♆	♇
1 Th	12 38 48	7♎46 51	20♓56 58	28♓09 00	2♌32.5	3♎09.8	18♏12.9	1♎45.1	7♌04.6	13♑27.9	12♏28.5	22♓54.9	23♌55.1	14♋42.2
2 F	12 42 45	8 45 53	5♈18 17	12♈24 03	2R 22.7	4 57.8	19 23.3	2 23.9	7 26.4	13 32.1	12 34.8	22R 52.6	23 56.8	14 42.5
3 Sa	12 46 41	9 44 56	19 25 37	26 22 22	2 11.7	6 45.2	20 33.6	3 02.8	7 48.0	13 36.5	12 41.2	22 50.3	23 58.5	14 42.8
4 Su	12 50 38	10 44 01	3♉13 48	9♉59 35	2 00.9	8 31.9	21 43.8	3 41.6	8 09.6	13 41.1	12 47.6	22 48.1	24 00.1	14 43.1
5 M	12 54 34	11 43 09	16 39 29	23 13 25	1 51.2	10 17.9	22 54.0	4 20.5	8 31.1	13 45.9	12 54.1	22 45.8	24 01.8	14 43.4
6 Tu	12 58 31	12 42 19	29 41 28	6♊03 49	1 43.6	12 03.2	24 04.2	4 59.5	8 52.4	13 50.8	13 00.6	22 43.6	24 03.4	14 43.6
7 W	13 02 27	13 41 31	12♊20 46	18 32 44	1 38.4	13 47.7	25 14.2	5 38.4	9 13.7	13 55.9	13 07.2	22 41.4	24 05.0	14 43.8
8 Th	13 06 24	14 40 46	24 40 12	0♋43 45	1 35.6	15 31.5	26 24.2	6 17.4	9 34.8	14 01.2	13 13.8	22 39.2	24 06.5	14 44.0
9 F	13 10 21	15 40 02	6♋43 59	12 41 33	1D 34.7	17 14.6	27 34.1	6 56.4	9 55.8	14 06.6	13 20.4	22 37.1	24 08.1	14 44.2
10 Sa	13 14 17	16 39 22	18 37 09	24 31 29	1R 34.8	18 56.9	28 43.9	7 35.4	10 16.6	14 12.2	13 27.0	22 34.9	24 09.6	14 44.3
11 Su	13 18 14	17 38 43	0♌25 13	6♌19 03	1 34.8	20 38.5	29 53.7	8 14.5	10 37.4	14 18.0	13 33.7	22 32.8	24 11.1	14 44.4
12 M	13 22 10	18 38 07	12 13 39	18 09 41	1 33.7	22 19.3	1♐03.4	8 53.5	10 58.0	14 23.9	13 40.5	22 30.7	24 12.5	14 44.5
13 Tu	13 26 07	19 37 33	24 07 43	0♍08 19	1 30.5	23 59.4	2 13.0	9 32.6	11 18.5	14 30.0	13 47.2	22 28.6	24 14.0	14 44.6
14 W	13 30 03	20 37 01	6♍12 00	12 19 11	1 24.6	25 38.8	3 22.5	10 11.8	11 38.9	14 36.3	13 54.0	22 26.6	24 15.4	14 44.7
15 Th	13 34 00	21 36 31	18 30 13	24 45 24	1 16.0	27 17.5	4 31.9	10 50.9	11 59.1	14 42.7	14 00.8	22 24.6	24 16.8	14R 44.7
16 F	13 37 56	22 36 04	1♎04 54	7♎28 48	1 04.9	28 55.6	5 41.2	11 30.1	12 19.2	14 49.3	14 07.7	22 22.6	24 18.2	14 44.7
17 Sa	13 41 53	23 35 39	13 57 08	20 29 47	0 52.2	0♏32.9	6 50.5	12 09.3	12 39.1	14 56.0	14 14.5	22 20.6	24 19.5	14 44.6
18 Su	13 45 50	24 35 15	27 06 36	3♏47 19	0 39.0	2 09.7	7 59.7	12 48.5	12 58.9	15 02.9	14 21.4	22 18.7	24 20.8	14 44.6
19 M	13 49 46	25 34 54	10♏31 38	17 19 11	0 26.6	3 45.8	9 08.7	13 27.7	13 18.5	15 09.9	14 28.4	22 16.8	24 22.1	14 44.5
20 Tu	13 53 43	26 34 35	24 09 36	1♐02 29	0 16.2	5 21.3	10 17.7	14 07.0	13 38.0	15 17.1	14 35.3	22 14.9	24 23.3	14 44.4
21 W	13 57 39	27 34 17	7♐57 28	14 54 11	0 08.6	6 56.2	11 26.6	14 46.3	13 57.4	15 24.5	14 42.3	22 13.1	24 24.6	14 44.3
22 Th	14 01 36	28 34 02	21 52 20	28 51 38	0 03.9	8 30.5	12 35.3	15 25.6	14 16.5	15 32.0	14 49.3	22 11.3	24 25.8	14 44.2
23 F	14 05 32	29 33 48	5♑51 53	12♑52 54	0 01.9	10 04.3	13 44.0	16 04.9	14 35.6	15 39.6	14 56.3	22 09.5	24 26.9	14 44.0
24 Sa	14 09 29	0♏33 36	19 54 33	26 56 46	0 01.4	11 37.5	14 52.5	16 44.3	14 54.4	15 47.4	15 03.3	22 07.8	24 28.1	14 43.8
25 Su	14 13 25	1 33 25	3♒59 25	11♒02 28	0 01.3	13 10.1	16 00.9	17 23.6	15 13.1	15 55.3	15 10.4	22 06.1	24 29.2	14 43.6
26 M	14 17 22	2 33 16	18 05 48	25 09 18	0 00.2	14 42.2	17 09.2	18 03.0	15 31.6	16 03.3	15 17.4	22 04.5	24 30.2	14 43.3
27 Tu	14 21 19	3 33 08	2♓12 47	9♓16 03	29♋56.9	16 13.9	18 17.3	18 42.5	15 49.9	16 11.5	15 24.5	22 02.8	24 31.3	14 43.1
28 W	14 25 15	4 33 03	16 18 47	23 20 38	29 50.7	17 44.9	19 25.3	19 21.9	16 08.1	16 19.9	15 31.6	22 01.2	24 32.3	14 42.8
29 Th	14 29 12	5 32 59	0♈21 14	7♈20 05	29 41.7	19 15.5	20 33.2	20 01.4	16 26.1	16 28.3	15 38.7	21 59.7	24 33.3	14 42.5
30 F	14 33 08	6 32 56	14 16 44	21 10 40	29 30.3	20 45.6	21 40.9	20 40.9	16 43.9	16 36.9	15 45.8	21 58.2	24 34.2	14 42.1
31 Sa	14 37 05	7 32 56	28 01 23	4♉48 28	29 17.6	22 15.2	22 48.5	21 20.4	17 01.5	16 45.7	15 53.0	21 56.7	24 35.2	14 41.8

Astro Data

	Dy Hr Mn
☿ D	4 0:32
☽ 0N	4 23:41
♃ D	9 7:17
♅⚻♆	17 5:45
☽ 0S	19 11:02
☉ 0S	23 13:44
☿ 0S	1 18:56
♂ 0S	1 23:33
☽ 0N	2 9:31
♃☍♇	15 19:15
♇ R	15 20:16
☽ 0S	16 18:26
♄△♇	21 18:48
☽ 0N	29 18:25

Planet Ingress

		Dy Hr Mn
☿	♍	11 5:09
⚳	♌	12 18:52
♀	♏	16 2:05
☉	♎	23 13:43
♂	♎	28 19:01
☿	♎	29 18:04
♀	♐	11 14:10
☿	♏	17 3:52
☉	♏	23 22:31
☊	♋R	26 13:52

Last Aspect / ☽ Ingress (September)

Last Aspect Dy Hr Mn			☽ Ingress	Dy Hr Mn
1 22:33	☿	☍	♓	2 4:02
3 19:07	♅	☌	♈	4 5:02
6 2:28	☿	△	♉	6 8:27
8 11:20	☿	□	♊	8 15:39
11 2:21	☿	⚹	♋	11 2:35
13 8:56	♀	□	♌	13 15:30
15 14:50	♆	☌	♍	16 3:56
18 4:12	☉	☌	♎	18 14:18
20 10:30	♆	⚹	♏	20 22:18
23 3:33	☉	⚹	♐	23 4:17
25 4:37	♂	□	♑	25 8:37
27 9:59	♂	△	♒	27 11:29
29 3:09	♆	☍	♓	29 13:19

Last Aspect / ☽ Ingress (October)

Last Aspect Dy Hr Mn			☽ Ingress	Dy Hr Mn
1 3:18	♅	☌	♈	1 15:06
3 7:50	♆	△	♉	3 18:20
5 13:29	♆	□	♊	6 0:35
7 22:52	♆	⚹	♋	8 10:33
10 21:30	♀	△	♌	10 23:09
13 0:11	♆	☌	♍	13 11:43
15 7:31	♅	☍	♎	15 21:57
17 18:58	♆	⚹	♏	18 5:12
20 0:23	♆	□	♐	20 10:11
22 11:28	☉	⚹	♑	22 13:57
24 3:48	♅	⚹	♒	24 17:12
26 10:53	♆	☍	♓	26 20:14
28 9:45	♅	☌	♈	28 23:24
30 17:57	♆	△	♉	31 3:29

☽ Phases & Eclipses

Dy Hr Mn		
2 19:53	○	9♓48
10 0:11	☾	16♊46
18 4:12	●	24♍43
25 11:51	☽	1♑53
2 5:23	○	8♈30
9 18:34	☾	15♋56
17 18:06	●	23♎51
24 18:38	☽	0♒50
31 17:16	○	7♉46

Astro Data

1 September 1925
Julian Day # 9375
SVP 6♓18'05"
GC 25♐48.1 ⚴ 13♊01.3
Eris 0♈32.7R ⚵ 7♐15.9
⚷ 27♈57.7R ⚶ 24♊45.6
☽ Mean ☊ 2♌44.2

1 October 1925
Julian Day # 9405
SVP 6♓18'03"
GC 25♐48.1 ⚴ 22♊30.3
Eris 0♈13.1R ⚵ 13♐35.3
⚷ 26♈53.3R ⚶ 2♋13.5
☽ Mean ☊ 1♌08.9

November 1925 LONGITUDE

Day	Sid.Time	☉	0 hr ☽	Noon ☽	True ☊	☿	♀	♂	⚳	♃	♄	♅	♆	♇
1 Su	14 41 01	8♏32 57	11♉31 29	18♉10 06	29♋04.8	23♏44.2	23♐55.9	21♎59.9	17♌18.9	16♑54.5	16♏00.1	21♓55.3	24♌36.0	14♋41.4
2 M	14 44 58	9 33 01	24 44 04	1♊13 16	28R 53.2	25 12.8	25 03.2	22 39.5	17 36.2	17 03.5	16 07.3	21R 53.9	24 36.9	14R 41.0
3 Tu	14 48 54	10 33 06	7♊37 37	13 57 11	28 43.7	26 40.8	26 10.3	23 19.1	17 53.2	17 12.7	16 14.4	21 52.5	24 37.7	14 40.6
4 W	14 52 51	11 33 13	20 12 09	26 22 45	28 36.9	28 08.2	27 17.3	23 58.7	18 10.0	17 21.9	16 21.6	21 51.2	24 38.5	14 40.1
5 Th	14 56 47	12 33 23	2♋29 22	8♋32 24	28 32.9	29 35.1	28 24.1	24 38.4	18 26.7	17 31.3	16 28.8	21 49.9	24 39.3	14 39.6
6 F	15 00 44	13 33 34	14 32 21	20 29 48	28D 31.2	1♐01.4	29 30.7	25 18.1	18 43.1	17 40.8	16 36.0	21 48.7	24 40.0	14 39.1
7 Sa	15 04 41	14 33 48	26 25 21	2♌19 39	28 31.0	2 27.1	0♑37.2	25 57.8	18 59.3	17 50.4	16 43.2	21 47.5	24 40.7	14 38.6
8 Su	15 08 37	15 34 03	8♌13 22	14 07 12	28R 31.3	3 52.0	1 43.4	26 37.5	19 15.3	18 00.1	16 50.4	21 46.4	24 41.4	14 38.1
9 M	15 12 34	16 34 21	20 01 51	25 58 00	28 30.8	5 16.3	2 49.5	27 17.3	19 31.1	18 09.9	16 57.5	21 45.3	24 42.0	14 37.5
10 Tu	15 16 30	17 34 40	1♍56 21	7♍57 33	28 28.8	6 39.8	3 55.4	27 57.1	19 46.6	18 19.9	17 04.7	21 44.2	24 42.6	14 36.9
11 W	15 20 27	18 35 01	14 02 13	20 10 56	28 24.5	8 02.4	5 01.0	28 36.9	20 02.0	18 30.0	17 11.9	21 43.2	24 43.2	14 36.3
12 Th	15 24 23	19 35 25	26 24 11	2♎42 23	28 17.5	9 24.0	6 06.5	29 16.7	20 17.0	18 40.2	17 19.1	21 42.3	24 43.7	14 35.7
13 F	15 28 20	20 35 50	9♎05 53	15 34 53	28 08.2	10 44.6	7 11.8	29 56.6	20 31.9	18 50.5	17 26.3	21 41.4	24 44.2	14 35.1
14 Sa	15 32 16	21 36 17	22 09 30	28 49 42	27 57.3	12 04.1	8 16.8	0♏36.5	20 46.5	19 00.9	17 33.5	21 40.5	24 44.7	14 34.4
15 Su	15 36 13	22 36 46	5♏35 19	12♏26 06	27 45.8	13 22.2	9 21.6	1 16.5	21 00.8	19 11.4	17 40.7	21 39.7	24 45.1	14 33.7
16 M	15 40 10	23 37 16	19 21 36	26 21 20	27 34.9	14 38.9	10 26.2	1 56.4	21 14.9	19 22.0	17 47.9	21 38.9	24 45.5	14 33.0
17 Tu	15 44 06	24 37 48	3♐24 42	10♐31 02	27 25.8	15 54.0	11 30.5	2 36.4	21 28.7	19 32.7	17 55.0	21 38.2	24 45.9	14 32.3
18 W	15 48 03	25 38 22	17 39 39	24 49 50	27 19.2	17 07.1	12 34.6	3 16.4	21 42.3	19 43.6	18 02.2	21 37.5	24 46.2	14 31.5
19 Th	15 51 59	26 38 57	2♑00 56	9♑12 19	27 15.4	18 18.2	13 38.4	3 56.5	21 55.5	19 54.5	18 09.3	21 36.9	24 46.5	14 30.8
20 F	15 55 56	27 39 33	16 23 26	23 33 47	27D 14.0	19 26.8	14 41.9	4 36.5	22 08.6	20 05.5	18 16.5	21 36.3	24 46.8	14 30.0
21 Sa	15 59 52	28 40 10	0♒43 00	7♒50 44	27 14.2	20 32.8	15 45.1	5 16.6	22 21.3	20 16.7	18 23.6	21 35.8	24 47.0	14 29.2
22 Su	16 03 49	29 40 49	14 56 47	22 00 57	27R 15.0	21 35.6	16 48.1	5 56.7	22 33.8	20 27.9	18 30.7	21 35.3	24 47.2	14 28.4
23 M	16 07 46	0♐41 28	29 03 08	6♓03 14	27 15.1	22 34.9	17 50.7	6 36.9	22 45.9	20 39.2	18 37.8	21 34.9	24 47.3	14 27.5
24 Tu	16 11 42	1 42 09	13♓01 12	19 56 59	27 13.4	23 30.2	18 53.0	7 17.0	22 57.8	20 50.6	18 44.9	21 34.5	24 47.5	14 26.7
25 W	16 15 39	2 42 51	26 50 30	3♈41 42	27 09.5	24 20.9	19 54.9	7 57.2	23 09.4	21 02.1	18 52.0	21 34.2	24 47.5	14 25.8
26 Th	16 19 35	3 43 33	10♈30 29	17 16 44	27 03.3	25 06.5	20 56.5	8 37.4	23 20.7	21 13.7	18 59.0	21 33.9	24 47.6	14 24.9
27 F	16 23 32	4 44 17	24 00 18	0♉41 03	26 55.1	25 46.2	21 57.7	9 17.7	23 31.6	21 25.4	19 06.0	21 33.7	24R 47.6	14 24.0
28 Sa	16 27 28	5 45 02	7♉18 49	13 53 27	26 45.8	26 19.4	22 58.5	9 58.0	23 42.3	21 37.1	19 13.0	21 33.5	24 47.6	14 23.0
29 Su	16 31 25	6 45 48	20 24 46	26 52 38	26 36.4	26 45.2	23 59.0	10 38.3	23 52.6	21 49.0	19 20.0	21 33.4	24 47.6	14 22.1
30 M	16 35 21	7 46 36	3♊16 58	9♊37 42	26 27.8	27 02.9	24 59.0	11 18.6	24 02.7	22 00.9	19 27.0	21D 33.3	24 47.5	14 21.1

December 1925 LONGITUDE

Day	Sid.Time	☉	0 hr ☽	Noon ☽	True ☊	☿	♀	♂	⚳	♃	♄	♅	♆	♇
1 Tu	16 39 18	8♐47 25	15♊54 49	22♊08 22	26♋20.9	27♐11.6	25♑58.6	11♏58.9	24♌12.4	22♑12.9	19♏33.9	21♓33.3	24♌47.4	14♋20.2
2 W	16 43 15	9 48 14	28 18 27	4♋25 13	26R 16.1	27R 10.5	26 57.8	12 39.3	24 21.8	22 25.0	19 40.8	21 33.3	24R 47.2	14R 19.2
3 Th	16 47 11	10 49 06	10♋28 55	16 29 50	26D 13.5	26 58.9	27 56.5	13 19.7	24 30.8	22 37.2	19 47.7	21 33.4	24 47.0	14 18.2
4 F	16 51 08	11 49 58	22 28 20	28 24 49	26 13.0	26 36.4	28 54.7	14 00.2	24 39.5	22 49.4	19 54.6	21 33.6	24 46.8	14 17.2
5 Sa	16 55 04	12 50 51	4♌19 46	10♌13 40	26 13.9	26 02.6	29 52.5	14 40.7	24 47.9	23 01.7	20 01.4	21 33.7	24 46.5	14 16.1
6 Su	16 59 01	13 51 46	16 07 07	22 00 40	26 15.5	25 17.6	0♒49.7	15 21.2	24 55.9	23 14.1	20 08.2	21 34.0	24 46.3	14 15.1
7 M	17 02 57	14 52 42	27 54 58	3♍50 39	26 17.0	24 22.0	1 46.4	16 01.7	25 03.5	23 26.6	20 15.0	21 34.3	24 45.9	14 14.0
8 Tu	17 06 54	15 53 40	9♍48 23	15 48 49	26R 17.6	23 16.7	2 42.6	16 42.3	25 10.8	23 39.1	20 21.8	21 34.6	24 45.6	14 12.9
9 W	17 10 50	16 54 38	21 52 36	28 00 23	26 16.9	22 03.5	3 38.2	17 22.9	25 17.7	23 51.7	20 28.5	21 35.0	24 45.2	14 11.9
10 Th	17 14 47	17 55 37	4♎12 46	10♎30 17	26 14.4	20 44.5	4 33.2	18 03.5	25 24.3	24 04.3	20 35.2	21 35.4	24 44.8	14 10.8
11 F	17 18 44	18 56 38	16 53 26	23 22 36	26 10.3	19 22.1	5 27.6	18 44.2	25 30.4	24 17.1	20 41.8	21 35.9	24 44.3	14 09.6
12 Sa	17 22 40	19 57 40	29 58 06	6♏40 05	26 05.0	17 59.2	6 21.4	19 24.8	25 36.2	24 29.9	20 48.4	21 36.5	24 43.8	14 08.5
13 Su	17 26 37	20 58 43	13♏28 37	20 23 33	25 59.1	16 38.5	7 14.5	20 05.6	25 41.6	24 42.7	20 55.0	21 37.1	24 43.3	14 07.4
14 M	17 30 33	21 59 47	27 24 38	4♐31 27	25 53.4	15 22.8	8 06.9	20 46.3	25 46.6	24 55.7	21 01.5	21 37.7	24 42.8	14 06.2
15 Tu	17 34 30	23 00 51	11♐43 22	18 59 43	25 48.7	14 14.2	8 58.6	21 27.1	25 51.2	25 08.7	21 08.0	21 38.4	24 42.2	14 05.1
16 W	17 38 26	24 01 57	26 19 37	3♑42 11	25 45.4	13 14.5	9 49.5	22 07.9	25 55.4	25 21.7	21 14.5	21 39.2	24 41.6	14 03.9
17 Th	17 42 23	25 03 03	11♑06 27	18 31 25	25D 43.8	12 24.8	10 39.7	22 48.7	25 59.2	25 34.8	21 20.9	21 40.0	24 40.9	14 02.8
18 F	17 46 19	26 04 09	25 56 11	3♒19 49	25 43.8	11 46.0	11 29.1	23 29.6	26 02.6	25 48.0	21 27.2	21 40.8	24 40.2	14 01.6
19 Sa	17 50 16	27 05 16	10♒41 32	18 00 38	25 45.0	11 18.2	12 17.6	24 10.4	26 05.5	26 01.2	21 33.6	21 41.7	24 39.5	14 00.4
20 Su	17 54 13	28 06 23	25 16 33	2♓28 50	25 46.5	11 01.2	13 05.3	24 51.3	26 08.1	26 14.4	21 39.8	21 42.7	24 38.8	13 59.2
21 M	17 58 09	29 07 31	9♓37 06	16 41 10	25R 47.8	10D 54.7	13 52.0	25 32.3	26 10.2	26 27.7	21 46.1	21 43.7	24 38.0	13 58.0
22 Tu	18 02 06	0♑08 38	23 40 52	0♈36 10	25 48.3	10 58.0	14 37.7	26 13.2	26 11.9	26 41.1	21 52.2	21 44.8	24 37.2	13 56.8
23 W	18 06 02	1 09 45	7♈27 04	14 13 40	25 47.7	11 10.3	15 22.5	26 54.2	26 13.2	26 54.5	21 58.4	21 45.9	24 36.4	13 55.6
24 Th	18 09 59	2 10 53	20 56 03	27 34 22	25 45.8	11 31.0	16 06.2	27 35.2	26 14.0	27 08.0	22 04.4	21 47.0	24 35.5	13 54.3
25 F	18 13 55	3 12 01	4♉08 45	10♉39 23	25 43.0	11 59.2	16 48.8	28 16.3	26R 14.5	27 21.5	22 10.5	21 48.2	24 34.6	13 53.1
26 Sa	18 17 52	4 13 08	17 06 25	23 30 00	25 39.6	12 34.2	17 30.2	28 57.3	26 14.5	27 35.0	22 16.4	21 49.5	24 33.7	13 51.9
27 Su	18 21 48	5 14 16	29 50 17	6♊07 26	25 36.1	13 15.2	18 10.5	29 38.4	26 14.0	27 48.6	22 22.4	21 50.8	24 32.7	13 50.6
28 M	18 25 45	6 15 24	12♊21 35	18 32 53	25 33.0	14 01.6	18 49.5	0♐19.5	26 13.2	28 02.2	22 28.2	21 52.1	24 31.8	13 49.4
29 Tu	18 29 42	7 16 33	24 41 29	0♋47 32	25 30.6	14 52.7	19 27.3	1 00.7	26 11.9	28 15.9	22 34.0	21 53.5	24 30.8	13 48.1
30 W	18 33 38	8 17 41	6♋51 13	12 52 43	25 29.1	15 48.2	20 03.7	1 41.9	26 10.1	28 29.6	22 39.8	21 55.0	24 29.7	13 46.9
31 Th	18 37 35	9 18 49	18 52 14	24 50 00	25D 28.6	16 47.4	20 38.7	2 23.1	26 08.0	28 43.3	22 45.5	21 56.4	24 28.7	13 45.7

Astro Data Dy Hr Mn	Planet Ingress Dy Hr Mn	Last Aspect Dy Hr Mn	☽ Ingress Dy Hr Mn	Last Aspect Dy Hr Mn	☽ Ingress Dy Hr Mn	☽ Phases & Eclipses Dy Hr Mn	Astro Data
☽0S 13 4:00	☿ ♐ 5 18:54	1 23:46 ♆ □	♊ 2 9:44	1 21:51 ☿ ☍	♋ 2 3:19	8 15:13 ☾ 15♌42	1 November 1925
☽0N 26 1:39	♀ ♑ 6 22:34	4 13:57 ♀ ☍	♋ 4 19:06	4 13:06 ♀ ☍	♌ 4 15:13	16 6:58 ● 23♏25	Julian Day # 9436
♆R 27 12:22	♂ ♏ 13 14:02	6 22:18 ♂ □	♌ 7 7:16	6 18:13 ☿ △	♍ 7 4:13	23 2:05 ☽ 0♓16	SVP 6♓18'00"
♃✶♅ 28 4:45	☉ ♐ 22 19:35	9 14:49 ♂ ✶	♍ 9 20:07	9 3:46 ♃ △	♎ 9 15:52	30 8:11 ○ 7♊37	GC 25♐48.2 ⚴ 27♊15.3
		11 14:59 ♅ ☍	♎ 12 6:52	11 14:30 ♆ ✶	♏ 12 0:03		Eris 29♓54.4R ⚵ 22♐40.4
♅D 1 9:02	♀ ♒ 5 15:09	14 4:40 ♆ ✶	♏ 14 14:05	13 19:31 ♃ ✶	♐ 14 4:23	8 12:11 ☾ 15♍54	⚷ 25♈27.9R ⚶ 5♋17.0R
☿R 1 21:31	☉ ♑ 22 8:37	16 9:16 ♆ □	♐ 16 18:13	15 21:21 ♆ △	♑ 16 5:59	15 19:05 ● 23♐19	☽ Mean ☊ 29♋30.3
☽0S 10 14:16	♂ ♐ 28 0:36	18 11:54 ♆ △	♑ 18 20:38	17 23:36 ♃ ☌	♒ 18 6:35	22 11:08 ☽ 0♈06	
♃⊼♆ 13 13:01		20 19:23 ☉ ✶	♒ 20 22:48	20 4:09 ☉ ✶	♓ 20 7:51	30 2:01 ○ 7♋52	1 December 1925
♄△♅ 21 1:06		22 16:43 ♆ ☍	♓ 23 1:37	22 5:05 ♃ ✶	♈ 22 10:57		Julian Day # 9466
☿D 21 15:44		24 18:36 ♆ □	♈ 25 5:31	24 11:11 ♃ □	♉ 24 16:25		SVP 6♓17'56"
☽0N 23 7:48		27 2:44 ☿ △	♉ 27 10:46	26 22:55 ♂ ☍	♊ 27 0:18		GC 25♐48.3 ⚴ 23♊05.2R
⚳R 25 23:53		29 8:07 ♆ □	♊ 29 17:50	28 23:40 ♆ ✶	♋ 29 10:26		Eris 29♓43.2R ⚵ 3♑02.5
				31 20:00 ♃ ☍	♌ 31 22:26		⚷ 24♈17.9R ⚶ 1♋56.7R
							☽ Mean ☊ 27♋55.0

LONGITUDE — January 1926

Day	Sid.Time	☉	0 hr ☽	Noon ☽	True ☊	☿	♀	♂	⚳	♃	♄	♅	♆	♇
1 F	18 41 31	10♑19 58	0♌46 16	6♌41 21	25♋29.0	17♐49.9	21♒12.3	3♐04.3	26♌05.4	28♑57.1	22♏51.1	21♓58.0	24♌27.6	13♋44.4
2 Sa	18 45 28	11 21 07	12 35 34	18 29 16	25 30.0	18 55.4	21 44.4	3 45.6	26R 02.3	29 10.9	22 56.7	21 59.6	24R 26.5	13R 43.1
3 Su	18 49 24	12 22 16	24 22 50	0♍16 44	25 31.3	20 03.6	22 14.9	4 26.9	25 58.8	29 24.7	23 02.2	22 01.2	24 25.4	13 41.9
4 M	18 53 21	13 23 25	6♍11 24	12 07 21	25 32.6	21 14.1	22 43.8	5 08.3	25 54.9	29 38.6	23 07.7	22 02.9	24 24.2	13 40.6
5 Tu	18 57 17	14 24 34	18 05 06	24 05 11	25 33.6	22 26.6	23 11.0	5 49.6	25 50.5	29 52.5	23 13.1	22 04.6	24 23.0	13 39.4
6 W	19 01 14	15 25 43	0♎08 12	6♎14 41	25R 34.3	23 41.1	23 36.5	6 31.0	25 45.7	0♒06.4	23 18.4	22 06.3	24 21.8	13 38.1
7 Th	19 05 11	16 26 53	12 25 14	18 40 24	25 34.4	24 57.2	24 00.2	7 12.4	25 40.5	0 20.3	23 23.6	22 08.2	24 20.6	13 36.8
8 F	19 09 07	17 28 02	25 00 44	1♏26 44	25 34.1	26 14.8	24 22.0	7 53.9	25 34.9	0 34.3	23 28.8	22 10.0	24 19.3	13 35.6
9 Sa	19 13 04	18 29 12	7♏58 51	14 37 26	25 33.5	27 33.8	24 41.9	8 35.4	25 28.8	0 48.3	23 34.0	22 11.9	24 18.0	13 34.3
10 Su	19 17 00	19 30 22	21 22 45	28 14 58	25 32.8	28 54.1	24 59.9	9 16.9	25 22.3	1 02.3	23 39.0	22 13.8	24 16.7	13 33.1
11 M	19 20 57	20 31 31	5♐14 04	12♐19 54	25 32.1	0♑15.5	25 15.7	9 58.4	25 15.3	1 16.4	23 44.0	22 15.8	24 15.4	13 31.8
12 Tu	19 24 53	21 32 41	19 32 09	26 50 20	25 31.7	1 37.9	25 29.5	10 40.0	25 08.0	1 30.4	23 48.9	22 17.9	24 14.1	13 30.6
13 W	19 28 50	22 33 50	4♑13 45	11♑41 35	25D 31.4	3 01.4	25 41.1	11 21.6	25 00.3	1 44.5	23 53.8	22 19.9	24 12.7	13 29.3
14 Th	19 32 47	23 35 00	19 12 50	26 46 25	25 31.3	4 25.7	25 50.4	12 03.2	24 52.1	1 58.6	23 58.5	22 22.0	24 11.3	13 28.1
15 F	19 36 43	24 36 08	4♒21 11	11♒55 54	25R 31.4	5 50.8	25 57.4	12 44.9	24 43.6	2 12.8	24 03.2	22 24.2	24 09.9	13 26.9
16 Sa	19 40 40	25 37 16	19 29 25	27 00 36	25 31.4	7 16.8	26 02.1	13 26.6	24 34.7	2 26.9	24 07.8	22 26.4	24 08.5	13 25.6
17 Su	19 44 36	26 38 23	4♓28 26	11♓52 03	25 31.3	8 43.5	26R 04.4	14 08.3	24 25.4	2 41.0	24 12.4	22 28.6	24 07.1	13 24.4
18 M	19 48 33	27 39 30	19 10 42	26 23 49	25 31.2	10 10.9	26 04.2	14 50.0	24 15.7	2 55.2	24 16.8	22 30.9	24 05.6	13 23.2
19 Tu	19 52 29	28 40 35	3♈31 02	10♈32 05	25 30.9	11 39.1	26 01.5	15 31.7	24 05.7	3 09.4	24 21.2	22 33.2	24 04.1	13 22.0
20 W	19 56 26	29 41 40	17 26 53	24 15 29	25D 30.8	13 07.9	25 56.3	16 13.5	23 55.3	3 23.5	24 25.5	22 35.5	24 02.6	13 20.8
21 Th	20 00 22	0♒42 43	0♉58 02	7♉34 47	25 30.8	14 37.4	25 48.5	16 55.3	23 44.7	3 37.7	24 29.7	22 37.9	24 01.1	13 19.6
22 F	20 04 19	1 43 46	14 06 02	20 32 10	25 31.1	16 07.5	25 38.3	17 37.1	23 33.7	3 51.9	24 33.9	22 40.3	23 59.6	13 18.4
23 Sa	20 08 15	2 44 47	26 53 34	3♊10 39	25 31.7	17 38.3	25 25.4	18 19.0	23 22.4	4 06.1	24 37.9	22 42.8	23 58.1	13 17.2
24 Su	20 12 12	3 45 48	9♊23 50	15 33 33	25 32.6	19 09.7	25 10.1	19 00.9	23 10.8	4 20.3	24 41.9	22 45.3	23 56.5	13 16.0
25 M	20 16 09	4 46 48	21 40 11	27 44 09	25 33.5	20 41.7	24 52.3	19 42.8	22 58.9	4 34.5	24 45.8	22 47.8	23 55.0	13 14.9
26 Tu	20 20 05	5 47 47	3♋45 48	9♋45 29	25 34.3	22 14.4	24 32.1	20 24.7	22 46.8	4 48.7	24 49.6	22 50.4	23 53.4	13 13.7
27 W	20 24 02	6 48 44	15 43 33	21 40 16	25R 34.7	23 47.8	24 09.6	21 06.7	22 34.4	5 02.9	24 53.3	22 53.0	23 51.8	13 12.6
28 Th	20 27 58	7 49 41	27 35 57	3♌30 53	25 34.6	25 21.8	23 44.8	21 48.7	22 21.8	5 17.1	24 57.0	22 55.6	23 50.2	13 11.4
29 F	20 31 55	8 50 37	9♌25 17	15 19 27	25 33.8	26 56.4	23 18.0	22 30.7	22 08.9	5 31.3	25 00.5	22 58.2	23 48.6	13 10.3
30 Sa	20 35 51	9 51 31	21 13 37	27 08 03	25 32.3	28 31.7	22 49.1	23 12.8	21 55.9	5 45.4	25 04.0	23 00.9	23 47.0	13 09.2
31 Su	20 39 48	10 52 25	3♍03 01	8♍58 47	25 30.1	0♒07.7	22 18.5	23 54.9	21 42.6	5 59.6	25 07.4	23 03.7	23 45.4	13 08.1

LONGITUDE — February 1926

Day	Sid.Time	☉	0 hr ☽	Noon ☽	True ☊	☿	♀	♂	⚳	♃	♄	♅	♆	♇
1 M	20 43 45	11♒53 18	14♍55 38	20♍53 55	25♋27.4	1♒44.4	21♒46.3	24♐37.0	21♌29.2	6♒13.8	25♏10.6	23♓06.4	23♌43.7	13♋07.0
2 Tu	20 47 41	12 54 10	26 53 56	2♎56 04	25R 24.7	3 21.8	21R 12.6	25 19.1	21R 15.7	6 27.9	25 13.8	23 09.2	23R 42.1	13R 05.9
3 W	20 51 38	13 55 01	9♎00 41	15 08 12	25 22.2	4 59.9	20 37.7	26 01.3	21 02.0	6 42.1	25 16.9	23 12.0	23 40.4	13 04.9
4 Th	20 55 34	14 55 51	21 19 03	27 33 40	25 20.3	6 38.8	20 01.9	26 43.5	20 48.1	6 56.2	25 19.9	23 14.8	23 38.8	13 03.8
5 F	20 59 31	15 56 40	3♏52 30	10♏16 01	25D 19.3	8 18.4	19 25.4	27 25.7	20 34.2	7 10.4	25 22.9	23 17.7	23 37.1	13 02.8
6 Sa	21 03 27	16 57 28	16 44 39	23 18 49	25 19.3	9 58.8	18 48.3	28 07.9	20 20.2	7 24.5	25 25.7	23 20.6	23 35.5	13 01.8
7 Su	21 07 24	17 58 16	29 58 53	6♐45 10	25 20.2	11 39.9	18 11.1	28 50.2	20 06.1	7 38.6	25 28.4	23 23.5	23 33.8	13 00.7
8 M	21 11 20	18 59 02	13♐37 54	20 37 12	25 21.7	13 21.9	17 33.9	29 32.5	19 52.0	7 52.7	25 31.1	23 26.5	23 32.1	12 59.8
9 Tu	21 15 17	19 59 48	27 43 03	4♑55 17	25 23.2	15 04.7	16 56.9	0♑14.9	19 37.9	8 06.8	25 33.6	23 29.5	23 30.4	12 58.8
10 W	21 19 14	21 00 32	12♑13 36	19 37 27	25R 24.1	16 48.2	16 20.6	0 57.2	19 23.7	8 20.8	25 36.0	23 32.5	23 28.7	12 57.8
11 Th	21 23 10	22 01 16	27 06 10	4♒38 51	25 23.9	18 32.6	15 45.0	1 39.6	19 09.6	8 34.9	25 38.4	23 35.5	23 27.1	12 56.9
12 F	21 27 07	23 01 57	12♒14 27	19 51 48	25 22.4	20 17.9	15 10.4	2 22.0	18 55.5	8 48.9	25 40.6	23 38.5	23 25.4	12 55.9
13 Sa	21 31 03	24 02 38	27 29 38	5♓06 37	25 19.4	22 04.0	14 37.1	3 04.5	18 41.5	9 02.9	25 42.8	23 41.6	23 23.7	12 55.0
14 Su	21 35 00	25 03 17	12♓41 28	20 12 57	25 15.3	23 50.9	14 05.2	3 46.9	18 27.5	9 16.8	25 44.8	23 44.7	23 22.0	12 54.1
15 M	21 38 56	26 03 54	27 39 57	5♈01 32	25 10.6	25 38.6	13 34.9	4 29.4	18 13.6	9 30.7	25 46.8	23 47.8	23 20.3	12 53.2
16 Tu	21 42 53	27 04 30	12♈16 56	19 25 34	25 06.2	27 27.2	13 06.4	5 11.9	17 59.8	9 44.7	25 48.6	23 51.0	23 18.6	12 52.4
17 W	21 46 49	28 05 04	26 27 06	3♉21 23	25 02.6	29 16.5	12 39.8	5 54.4	17 46.2	9 58.5	25 50.4	23 54.1	23 17.0	12 51.5
18 Th	21 50 46	29 05 36	10♉08 24	16 48 22	25 00.3	1♓06.6	12 15.3	6 36.9	17 32.7	10 12.4	25 52.0	23 57.3	23 15.3	12 50.7
19 F	21 54 42	0♓06 06	23 21 35	29 48 26	24D 59.6	2 57.5	11 53.0	7 19.5	17 19.4	10 26.2	25 53.6	24 00.5	23 13.6	12 49.9
20 Sa	21 58 39	1 06 34	6♊09 27	12♊25 09	25 00.2	4 49.0	11 33.0	8 02.1	17 06.3	10 40.0	25 55.0	24 03.7	23 11.9	12 49.1
21 Su	22 02 36	2 07 01	18 36 08	24 42 58	25 01.7	6 41.1	11 15.3	8 44.7	16 53.3	10 53.7	25 56.4	24 06.9	23 10.3	12 48.3
22 M	22 06 32	3 07 26	0♋46 17	6♋46 39	25 03.4	8 33.8	11 00.0	9 27.3	16 40.6	11 07.4	25 57.6	24 10.2	23 08.6	12 47.6
23 Tu	22 10 29	4 07 49	12 44 39	18 40 49	25R 04.7	10 26.9	10 47.2	10 10.0	16 28.1	11 21.1	25 58.8	24 13.4	23 07.0	12 46.9
24 W	22 14 25	5 08 09	24 35 40	0♌29 39	25 04.7	12 20.2	10 36.8	10 52.7	16 15.9	11 34.8	25 59.8	24 16.7	23 05.3	12 46.2
25 Th	22 18 22	6 08 29	6♌23 12	12 16 43	25 03.0	14 13.7	10 28.9	11 35.4	16 03.9	11 48.4	26 00.8	24 20.0	23 03.7	12 45.5
26 F	22 22 18	7 08 46	18 10 34	24 05 01	24 59.2	16 07.2	10 23.5	12 18.1	15 52.3	12 01.9	26 01.6	24 23.3	23 02.1	12 44.8
27 Sa	22 26 15	8 09 01	0♍00 23	5♍56 54	24 53.4	18 00.3	10D 20.6	13 00.8	15 40.8	12 15.4	26 02.3	24 26.6	23 00.4	12 44.2
28 Su	22 30 11	9 09 15	11 54 46	17 54 11	24 45.9	19 53.0	10 20.1	13 43.6	15 29.7	12 28.9	26 03.0	24 30.0	22 58.8	12 43.5

Astro Data

	Dy Hr Mn
☽0S	6 23:10
♄□♆	16 14:42
♀R	17 22:11
☽0N	19 14:33
☽0S	3 5:43
♅⊼♆	9 16:58
♃∠♅	11 13:24
☽0N	15 23:14
♀D	28 4:47

Planet Ingress

	Dy Hr Mn
♃ ♒	6 1:01
☿ ♑	11 7:27
☉ ♒	20 19:12
☿ ♒	31 10:04
♂ ♑	9 3:35
☿ ♓	17 21:30
☉ ♓	19 9:35

Last Aspect / ☽ Ingress (January)

Last Aspect Dy Hr Mn		☽ Ingress Dy Hr Mn
3 0:06	♆ ☌	♍ 3 11:26
5 23:42	♃ △	♎ 5 23:44
8 1:13	☿ ⚹	♏ 8 9:19
10 6:13	♀ □	♐ 10 15:02
12 9:46	♀ ⚹	♑ 12 17:09
14 7:32	♄ ⚹	♒ 14 17:07
16 10:26	♀ ☌	♓ 16 16:48
18 14:17	☉ ⚹	♈ 18 18:03
20 14:58	♀ ⚹	♉ 20 22:16
22 21:28	♀ □	♊ 23 5:55
25 6:28	♀ △	♋ 25 16:30
27 18:33	♄ △	♌ 28 4:52
30 7:47	♄ □	♍ 30 17:49

Last Aspect / ☽ Ingress (February)

Last Aspect Dy Hr Mn		☽ Ingress Dy Hr Mn
1 20:36	♄ ⚹	♎ 2 6:11
4 10:18	♂ ⚹	♏ 4 16:39
6 15:50	♄ ☌	♐ 7 0:02
8 16:56	☿ △	♑ 9 3:49
10 21:37	♄ ⚹	♒ 11 4:37
12 21:10	♄ □	♓ 13 3:57
14 20:55	♄ △	♈ 15 3:47
17 3:48	☿ ⚹	♉ 17 6:08
19 4:41	♄ ☍	♊ 19 12:22
21 10:49	♅ □	♋ 21 22:28
24 2:50	♄ △	♌ 24 11:00
26 15:57	♄ □	♍ 26 23:59

☽ Phases & Eclipses

Dy Hr Mn		
7 7:22	☾	16♎15
14 6:35	●	23♑21
14 6:36:34	●	T 04'11"
20 22:31	☽	0♉08
28 21:35	○	8♌14
28 21:20	●	A 0.555
5 23:25	☾	16♏26
12 17:20	●	23♒15
19 12:36	☽	0♊08
27 16:51	○	8♍21

Astro Data

1 January 1926
Julian Day # 9497
SVP 6♓17'50"
GC 25♐48.4 ⚴ 13♊29.8R
Eris 29♓42.7 ⚵ 14♑43.9
⚷ 23♈46.2R ⚶ 24♊11.4R
☽ Mean ☊ 26♋16.6

1 February 1926
Julian Day # 9528
SVP 6♓17'45"
GC 25♐48.4 ⚴ 11♊56.8
Eris 29♓53.6 ⚵ 26♑53.8
⚷ 24♈08.2 ⚶ 19♊38.2R
☽ Mean ☊ 24♋38.1

March 1926 — LONGITUDE

Day	Sid.Time	☉	0 hr ☽	Noon ☽	True ☊	☿	♀	♂	⚳	♃	♄	♅	♆	♇
1 M	22 34 08	10♓09 27	23♍55 20	29♍58 23	24♋37.2	21♓44.8	10♒22.0	14♑26.4	15♌19.0	12♒42.3	26♏03.5	24♓33.3	22♌57.2	12♋42.9
2 Tu	22 38 05	11 09 37	6♎03 30	12♎10 51	24R 28.2	23 35.4	10 26.3	15 09.2	15R 08.5	12 55.7	26 03.9	24 36.7	22R 55.6	12R 42.3
3 W	22 42 01	12 09 45	18 20 36	24 32 57	24 19.7	25 24.5	10 33.0	15 52.1	14 58.3	13 09.0	26 04.3	24 40.0	22 54.1	12 41.8
4 Th	22 45 58	13 09 52	0♏48 08	7♏06 22	24 12.7	27 11.6	10 41.9	16 35.0	14 48.6	13 22.3	26 04.5	24 43.4	22 52.5	12 41.2
5 F	22 49 54	14 09 57	13 27 54	19 53 02	24 07.6	28 56.2	10 53.0	17 17.9	14 39.1	13 35.6	26R 04.6	24 46.8	22 50.9	12 40.7
6 Sa	22 53 51	15 10 01	26 22 04	2♐55 18	24D 04.8	0♈38.0	11 06.2	18 00.8	14 30.1	13 48.7	26 04.6	24 50.2	22 49.4	12 40.2
7 Su	22 57 47	16 10 03	9♐33 03	16 15 37	24 04.0	2 16.4	11 21.6	18 43.7	14 21.4	14 01.9	26 04.5	24 53.6	22 47.9	12 39.7
8 M	23 01 44	17 10 04	23 03 17	29 56 15	24 04.6	3 50.8	11 39.0	19 26.7	14 13.1	14 15.0	26 04.4	24 57.0	22 46.4	12 39.3
9 Tu	23 05 40	18 10 03	6♑54 41	13♑58 39	24R 05.5	5 20.7	11 58.3	20 09.7	14 05.1	14 28.0	26 04.1	25 00.4	22 44.9	12 38.8
10 W	23 09 37	19 10 00	21 08 06	28 22 50	24 05.7	6 45.6	12 19.5	20 52.7	13 57.6	14 41.0	26 03.7	25 03.8	22 43.4	12 38.4
11 Th	23 13 34	20 09 56	5♒42 30	13♒06 34	24 04.3	8 04.9	12 42.6	21 35.7	13 50.5	14 53.9	26 03.2	25 07.2	22 41.9	12 38.0
12 F	23 17 30	21 09 50	20 34 19	28 04 53	24 00.4	9 18.2	13 07.3	22 18.8	13 43.8	15 06.7	26 02.6	25 10.6	22 40.5	12 37.7
13 Sa	23 21 27	22 09 42	5♓37 13	13♓10 11	23 54.0	10 25.0	13 33.8	23 01.8	13 37.5	15 19.5	26 01.9	25 14.1	22 39.0	12 37.3
14 Su	23 25 23	23 09 32	20 42 33	28 13 04	23 45.6	11 24.8	14 01.9	23 44.9	13 31.6	15 32.2	26 01.1	25 17.5	22 37.6	12 37.0
15 M	23 29 20	24 09 20	5♈40 30	13♈03 43	23 35.9	12 17.3	14 31.6	24 28.0	13 26.2	15 44.9	26 00.2	25 20.9	22 36.2	12 36.7
16 Tu	23 33 16	25 09 06	20 21 44	27 33 44	23 26.3	13 02.1	15 02.7	25 11.1	13 21.2	15 57.5	25 59.2	25 24.4	22 34.9	12 36.4
17 W	23 37 13	26 08 50	4♉39 04	11♉37 20	23 17.8	13 39.1	15 35.3	25 54.2	13 16.6	16 10.0	25 58.1	25 27.8	22 33.5	12 36.2
18 Th	23 41 09	27 08 32	18 28 20	25 12 01	23 11.3	14 08.0	16 09.3	26 37.3	13 12.5	16 22.5	25 56.9	25 31.2	22 32.2	12 36.0
19 F	23 45 06	28 08 12	1♊48 34	8♊18 15	23 07.1	14 28.6	16 44.6	27 20.5	13 08.8	16 34.9	25 55.6	25 34.6	22 30.9	12 35.8
20 Sa	23 49 03	29 07 49	14 41 32	20 58 54	23D 05.2	14 41.1	17 21.1	28 03.7	13 05.5	16 47.2	25 54.3	25 38.1	22 29.6	12 35.6
21 Su	23 52 59	0♈07 24	27 10 58	3♋18 23	23 04.9	14R 45.4	17 58.9	28 46.8	13 02.7	16 59.4	25 52.8	25 41.5	22 28.3	12 35.5
22 M	23 56 56	1 06 56	9♋21 47	15 21 53	23R 05.4	14 41.8	18 37.9	29 30.0	13 00.3	17 11.6	25 51.2	25 44.9	22 27.1	12 35.3
23 Tu	0 00 52	2 06 27	21 19 21	27 14 52	23 05.5	14 30.5	19 18.0	0♒13.2	12 58.3	17 23.7	25 49.5	25 48.3	22 25.8	12 35.2
24 W	0 04 49	3 05 55	3♌09 04	9♌02 33	23 04.2	14 11.9	19 59.3	0 56.4	12 56.8	17 35.7	25 47.8	25 51.8	22 24.6	12 35.1
25 Th	0 08 45	4 05 21	14 55 54	20 49 39	23 00.7	13 46.5	20 41.5	1 39.7	12 55.8	17 47.6	25 45.9	25 55.2	22 23.5	12 35.1
26 F	0 12 42	5 04 44	26 44 16	2♍40 10	22 54.5	13 14.9	21 24.8	2 22.9	12D 55.1	17 59.5	25 43.9	25 58.6	22 22.3	12D 35.1
27 Sa	0 16 38	6 04 05	8♍37 44	14 37 17	22 45.6	12 38.0	22 09.0	3 06.2	12 54.9	18 11.2	25 41.9	26 02.0	22 21.2	12 35.1
28 Su	0 20 35	7 03 25	20 39 03	26 43 14	22 34.3	11 56.5	22 54.2	3 49.5	12 55.1	18 22.9	25 39.8	26 05.3	22 20.1	12 35.1
29 M	0 24 31	8 02 42	2♎50 01	8♎59 29	22 21.4	11 11.4	23 40.3	4 32.8	12 55.8	18 34.5	25 37.5	26 08.7	22 19.0	12 35.1
30 Tu	0 28 28	9 01 57	15 11 41	21 26 42	22 08.0	10 23.6	24 27.2	5 16.1	12 56.9	18 46.0	25 35.2	26 12.1	22 17.9	12 35.2
31 W	0 32 25	10 01 10	27 44 30	4♏05 07	21 55.4	9 34.2	25 15.0	5 59.4	12 58.3	18 57.5	25 32.8	26 15.4	22 16.9	12 35.3

April 1926 — LONGITUDE

Day	Sid.Time	☉	0 hr ☽	Noon ☽	True ☊	☿	♀	♂	⚳	♃	♄	♅	♆	♇
1 Th	0 36 21	11♈00 21	10♏28 32	16♏54 45	21♋44.4	8♈44.1	26♒03.6	6♒42.7	13♌00.3	19♒08.8	25♏30.4	26♓18.8	22♌15.9	12♋35.4
2 F	0 40 18	11 59 30	23 23 49	29 55 45	21R 36.1	7R 54.5	26 53.0	7 26.0	13 02.6	19 20.1	25R 27.8	26 22.1	22R 14.9	12 35.5
3 Sa	0 44 14	12 58 37	6♐30 38	13♐08 33	21 30.7	7 06.1	27 43.0	8 09.4	13 05.3	19 31.2	25 25.2	26 25.5	22 14.0	12 35.7
4 Su	0 48 11	13 57 43	19 49 39	26 34 02	21 27.9	6 20.0	28 33.9	8 52.8	13 08.5	19 42.3	25 22.4	26 28.8	22 13.1	12 35.9
5 M	0 52 07	14 56 47	3♑21 54	10♑13 21	21 27.1	5 36.8	29 25.3	9 36.2	13 12.1	19 53.3	25 19.6	26 32.1	22 12.2	12 36.1
6 Tu	0 56 04	15 55 49	17 08 32	24 07 33	21 27.1	4 57.3	0♓17.5	10 19.5	13 16.0	20 04.1	25 16.7	26 35.4	22 11.3	12 36.3
7 W	1 00 00	16 54 50	1♒10 25	8♒17 06	21 26.5	4 21.9	1 10.3	11 02.9	13 20.4	20 14.9	25 13.8	26 38.6	22 10.5	12 36.6
8 Th	1 03 57	17 53 49	15 27 27	22 41 10	21 24.2	3 51.1	2 03.7	11 46.3	13 25.2	20 25.6	25 10.7	26 41.9	22 09.7	12 36.8
9 F	1 07 54	18 52 46	29 57 53	7♓17 02	21 19.2	3 25.2	2 57.6	12 29.8	13 30.3	20 36.2	25 07.6	26 45.2	22 08.9	12 37.1
10 Sa	1 11 50	19 51 41	14♓37 57	21 59 48	21 11.4	3 04.5	3 52.1	13 13.2	13 35.8	20 46.7	25 04.4	26 48.4	22 08.1	12 37.5
11 Su	1 15 47	20 50 34	29 21 43	6♈42 41	21 01.2	2 49.0	4 47.2	13 56.6	13 41.8	20 57.0	25 01.2	26 51.6	22 07.4	12 37.8
12 M	1 19 43	21 49 25	14♈01 42	21 17 48	20 49.5	2 38.9	5 42.8	14 40.0	13 48.1	21 07.3	24 57.8	26 54.8	22 06.7	12 38.2
13 Tu	1 23 40	22 48 15	28 30 03	5♉37 36	20 37.6	2D 34.2	6 38.8	15 23.4	13 54.8	21 17.4	24 54.4	26 58.0	22 06.1	12 38.6
14 W	1 27 36	23 47 02	12♉39 47	19 36 02	20 26.7	2 34.7	7 35.4	16 06.8	14 01.8	21 27.5	24 51.0	27 01.1	22 05.4	12 39.0
15 Th	1 31 33	24 45 47	26 26 00	3♊09 30	20 18.0	2 40.4	8 32.3	16 50.2	14 09.2	21 37.4	24 47.4	27 04.3	22 04.8	12 39.5
16 F	1 35 29	25 44 30	9♊46 28	16 17 03	20 11.9	2 51.1	9 29.8	17 33.6	14 17.0	21 47.2	24 43.9	27 07.4	22 04.3	12 39.9
17 Sa	1 39 26	26 43 11	22 41 31	29 00 14	20 08.5	3 06.8	10 27.6	18 17.1	14 25.2	21 56.9	24 40.2	27 10.5	22 03.7	12 40.4
18 Su	1 43 23	27 41 50	5♋13 41	11♋22 25	20D 07.1	3 27.1	11 25.9	19 00.5	14 33.7	22 06.5	24 36.5	27 13.6	22 03.2	12 40.9
19 M	1 47 19	28 40 27	17 27 04	23 28 16	20R 06.9	3 52.0	12 24.5	19 43.9	14 42.5	22 16.0	24 32.7	27 16.6	22 02.8	12 41.5
20 Tu	1 51 16	29 39 01	29 26 42	5♌23 05	20 06.9	4 21.2	13 23.6	20 27.3	14 51.7	22 25.3	24 28.9	27 19.6	22 02.3	12 42.0
21 W	1 55 12	0♉37 33	11♌18 04	17 12 21	20 05.8	4 54.6	14 23.0	21 10.6	15 01.2	22 34.5	24 25.0	27 22.6	22 01.9	12 42.6
22 Th	1 59 09	1 36 03	23 06 36	29 01 24	20 02.9	5 32.0	15 22.7	21 54.0	15 11.0	22 43.6	24 21.1	27 25.6	22 01.5	12 43.2
23 F	2 03 05	2 34 31	4♍57 23	10♍55 03	19 57.5	6 13.2	16 22.9	22 37.4	15 21.2	22 52.6	24 17.1	27 28.6	22 01.2	12 43.8
24 Sa	2 07 02	3 32 56	16 54 55	22 57 23	19 49.4	6 58.0	17 23.3	23 20.8	15 31.7	23 01.5	24 13.1	27 31.5	22 00.9	12 44.5
25 Su	2 10 58	4 31 20	29 02 49	5♎11 31	19 39.1	7 46.3	18 24.1	24 04.2	15 42.5	23 10.2	24 09.0	27 34.4	22 00.6	12 45.2
26 M	2 14 55	5 29 42	11♎23 41	17 39 29	19 27.1	8 37.9	19 25.2	24 47.5	15 53.6	23 18.8	24 04.9	27 37.3	22 00.3	12 45.9
27 Tu	2 18 52	6 28 01	23 58 58	0♏22 08	19 14.6	9 32.8	20 26.5	25 30.9	16 05.0	23 27.2	24 00.8	27 40.2	22 00.1	12 46.6
28 W	2 22 48	7 26 19	6♏48 57	13 19 18	19 02.7	10 30.6	21 28.2	26 14.2	16 16.7	23 35.6	23 56.6	27 43.0	21 59.9	12 47.3
29 Th	2 26 45	8 24 35	19 53 02	26 29 58	18 52.5	11 31.5	22 30.2	26 57.6	16 28.7	23 43.8	23 52.4	27 45.8	21 59.8	12 48.0
30 F	2 30 41	9 22 50	3♐09 54	9♐52 38	18 44.8	12 35.1	23 32.5	27 40.9	16 41.0	23 51.8	23 48.1	27 48.6	21 59.7	12 48.8

Astro Data

	Dy Hr Mn
♃⚻♇	1 13:01
☽0S	2 10:56
☿0N	5 18:47
♄ R	6 4:53
☽0N	15 9:32
☉0N	21 9:02
☿ R	21 12:55
♄△♅	23 17:30
♇ D	27 8:09
⚳ D	27 11:34
☽0S	29 16:47
☽0N	11 19:50
☿ D	13 21:36
♃☍♆	18 4:12
☽0S	26 0:21

Planet Ingress

		Dy Hr Mn
☿	♈	6 2:57
☉	♈	21 9:01
♂	♒	23 4:39
♀	♓	6 3:59
☉	♉	20 20:36
♃□□		30 4:43

Last Aspect / ☽ Ingress

Last Aspect Dy Hr Mn			☽ Ingress	Dy Hr Mn
1 4:14	♄	⚹	♎	1 12:03
3 8:50	♆	⚹	♏	3 22:28
5 23:28	♄	☌	♐	6 6:40
8 3:17	♅	□	♑	8 12:07
10 8:10	♄	⚹	♒	10 14:40
12 8:45	♄	□	♓	12 15:03
14 8:29	♄	△	♈	14 14:52
16 7:49	♂	□	♉	16 16:06
18 15:47	☉	⚹	♊	18 20:42
21 5:12	☉	□	♋	21 5:30
23 9:07	♄	△	♌	23 17:35
25 22:00	♄	□	♍	26 6:36
28 10:45	♅	☍	♎	28 18:27
30 18:08	♀	△	♏	31 4:17

Last Aspect / ☽ Ingress

Last Aspect Dy Hr Mn			☽ Ingress	Dy Hr Mn
2 6:02	♀	□	♐	2 12:08
4 15:46	♀	⚹	♑	4 18:04
6 16:13	♅	⚹	♒	6 22:01
8 16:06	♄	□	♓	9 0:03
10 19:52	♅	☌	♈	11 1:02
12 13:21	♆	△	♉	13 2:31
15 1:05	♅	⚹	♊	15 6:20
17 8:29	♅	□	♋	17 13:55
19 23:23	☉	□	♌	20 1:07
22 2:34	♄	□	♍	22 13:59
24 21:03	♅	☍	♎	25 1:52
27 2:20	♂	△	♏	27 11:19
29 14:17	♅	△	♐	29 18:19

☽ Phases & Eclipses

Dy Hr Mn		
7 11:49	☾	16♐10
14 3:20	●	22♓48
21 5:12	☽	29♊51
29 10:00	○	7♎58
5 20:50	☾	15♑19
12 12:56	●	21♈52
19 23:23	☽	29♋08
28 0:16	○	6♏58

Astro Data

1 March 1926
Julian Day # 9556
SVP 6♓17'42"
GC 25♐48.5 ⚴ 18♊56.2
Eris 0♈11.0 ⚵ 7♒54.6
⚷ 25♈10.1 ⚶ 21♊23.4
☽ Mean ☊ 23♋09.1

1 April 1926
Julian Day # 9587
SVP 6♓17'39"
GC 25♐48.6 ⚴ 1♋37.5
Eris 0♈33.9 ⚵ 19♒41.6
⚷ 26♈50.1 ⚶ 28♊24.9
☽ Mean ☊ 21♋30.6

LONGITUDE — May 1926

Day	Sid.Time	☉	0 hr ☽	Noon ☽	True ☊	☿	♀	♂	⚳	♃	♄	♅	♆	♇
1 Sa	2 34 38	10♉21 03	16♐37 59	23♐25 46	18♋39.8	13♈41.5	24♓35.0	28♒24.2	16♌53.6	23♒59.8	23♏43.8	27♓51.3	21♌59.6	12♋49.6
2 Su	2 38 34	11 19 14	0♑15 50	7♑08 04	18D37.4	14 50.5	25 37.8	29 07.6	17 06.5	24 07.6	23R39.5	27 54.0	21R59.5	12 50.4
3 M	2 42 31	12 17 24	14 02 22	20 58 40	18 36.9	16 02.0	26 40.8	29 50.9	17 19.6	24 15.2	23 35.2	27 56.7	21D59.5	12 51.3
4 Tu	2 46 27	13 15 33	27 56 55	4♒57 03	18R37.3	17 16.0	27 44.1	0♓34.2	17 33.0	24 22.7	23 30.8	27 59.4	21 59.5	12 52.1
5 W	2 50 24	14 13 40	11♒59 00	19 02 43	18 37.4	18 32.4	28 47.7	1 17.4	17 46.7	24 30.1	23 26.4	28 02.0	21 59.6	12 53.0
6 Th	2 54 21	15 11 46	26 08 03	3♓14 49	18 36.1	19 51.2	29 51.4	2 00.7	18 00.6	24 37.3	23 22.0	28 04.6	21 59.7	12 53.9
7 F	2 58 17	16 09 50	10♓22 47	17 31 37	18 32.6	21 12.2	0♈55.4	2 43.9	18 14.8	24 44.4	23 17.5	28 07.2	21 59.8	12 54.8
8 Sa	3 02 14	17 07 53	24 40 56	1♈50 14	18 26.7	22 35.5	1 59.6	3 27.2	18 29.3	24 51.3	23 13.1	28 09.7	21 59.9	12 55.7
9 Su	3 06 10	18 05 54	8♈58 59	16 06 35	18 18.7	24 00.9	3 04.0	4 10.4	18 44.0	24 58.1	23 08.6	28 12.2	22 00.1	12 56.7
10 M	3 10 07	19 03 54	23 12 23	0♉15 45	18 09.4	25 28.6	4 08.6	4 53.5	18 58.9	25 04.7	23 04.1	28 14.6	22 00.3	12 57.7
11 Tu	3 14 03	20 01 53	7♉16 02	14 12 41	17 59.8	26 58.4	5 13.4	5 36.7	19 14.1	25 11.2	22 59.6	28 17.1	22 00.6	12 58.7
12 W	3 18 00	20 59 50	21 05 09	27 52 59	17 51.1	28 30.3	6 18.4	6 19.8	19 29.5	25 17.5	22 55.1	28 19.5	22 00.8	12 59.7
13 Th	3 21 56	21 57 46	4♊35 54	11♊13 38	17 44.1	0♉04.4	7 23.5	7 02.9	19 45.2	25 23.7	22 50.6	28 21.8	22 01.1	13 00.7
14 F	3 25 53	22 55 40	17 46 06	24 13 19	17 39.2	1 40.5	8 28.8	7 45.9	20 01.1	25 29.7	22 46.1	28 24.1	22 01.5	13 01.7
15 Sa	3 29 50	23 53 32	0♋35 25	6♋52 36	17D36.7	3 18.8	9 34.3	8 28.9	20 17.2	25 35.5	22 41.6	28 26.4	22 01.9	13 02.8
16 Su	3 33 46	24 51 23	13 05 14	19 13 41	17 36.1	4 59.1	10 40.0	9 11.9	20 33.6	25 41.2	22 37.1	28 28.7	22 02.3	13 03.9
17 M	3 37 43	25 49 12	25 18 28	1♌20 05	17 36.8	6 41.6	11 45.8	9 54.9	20 50.1	25 46.7	22 32.7	28 30.9	22 02.7	13 05.0
18 Tu	3 41 39	26 46 59	7♌19 07	13 16 12	17 37.9	8 26.1	12 51.7	10 37.8	21 06.9	25 52.0	22 28.2	28 33.1	22 03.2	13 06.1
19 W	3 45 36	27 44 45	19 11 58	25 07 03	17R38.7	10 12.8	13 57.9	11 20.7	21 23.9	25 57.2	22 23.7	28 35.2	22 03.7	13 07.2
20 Th	3 49 32	28 42 29	1♍02 06	6♍57 47	17 38.3	12 01.5	15 04.1	12 03.5	21 41.1	26 02.2	22 19.2	28 37.3	22 04.2	13 08.3
21 F	3 53 29	29 40 11	12 54 43	18 53 31	17 36.2	13 52.3	16 10.5	12 46.3	21 58.5	26 07.1	22 14.8	28 39.4	22 04.8	13 09.5
22 Sa	3 57 25	0♊37 52	24 54 45	0♎58 57	17 32.3	15 45.1	17 17.0	13 29.0	22 16.1	26 11.7	22 10.3	28 41.4	22 05.4	13 10.7
23 Su	4 01 22	1 35 31	7♎06 35	13 18 05	17 26.6	17 40.1	18 23.7	14 11.8	22 33.9	26 16.2	22 05.9	28 43.4	22 06.0	13 11.9
24 M	4 05 19	2 33 09	19 33 46	25 53 54	17 19.6	19 37.0	19 30.5	14 54.4	22 51.9	26 20.6	22 01.5	28 45.3	22 06.7	13 13.1
25 Tu	4 09 15	3 30 46	2♏18 41	8♏48 11	17 12.2	21 36.0	20 37.4	15 37.1	23 10.0	26 24.7	21 57.2	28 47.2	22 07.4	13 14.3
26 W	4 13 12	4 28 21	15 22 24	22 01 14	17 05.0	23 36.9	21 44.5	16 19.6	23 28.4	26 28.7	21 52.8	28 49.0	22 08.1	13 15.5
27 Th	4 17 08	5 25 55	28 44 32	5♐32 00	16 58.8	25 39.6	22 51.7	17 02.2	23 46.9	26 32.5	21 48.5	28 50.9	22 08.9	13 16.8
28 F	4 21 05	6 23 28	12♐23 20	19 18 08	16 54.4	27 44.1	23 59.0	17 44.7	24 05.6	26 36.1	21 44.2	28 52.6	22 09.7	13 18.0
29 Sa	4 25 01	7 20 59	26 15 59	3♑16 28	16D51.8	29 50.2	25 06.5	18 27.1	24 24.5	26 39.6	21 40.0	28 54.4	22 10.5	13 19.3
30 Su	4 28 58	8 18 30	10♑19 06	17 23 27	16 51.1	1♊57.8	26 14.0	19 09.6	24 43.5	26 42.9	21 35.8	28 56.1	22 11.4	13 20.6
31 M	4 32 54	9 16 00	24 29 07	1♒35 40	16 51.7	4 06.7	27 21.7	19 51.9	25 02.7	26 46.0	21 31.6	28 57.7	22 12.2	13 21.9

LONGITUDE — June 1926

Day	Sid.Time	☉	0 hr ☽	Noon ☽	True ☊	☿	♀	♂	⚳	♃	♄	♅	♆	♇
1 Tu	4 36 51	10♊13 29	8♒42 46	15♒50 04	16♋53.1	6♊16.8	28♈29.5	20♓34.2	25♌22.1	26♒48.9	21♏27.4	28♓59.3	22♌13.1	13♋23.2
2 W	4 40 48	11 10 57	22 57 17	0♓04 08	16R54.3	8 27.7	29 37.4	21 16.4	25 41.7	26 51.6	21R23.3	29 00.9	22 14.1	13 24.5
3 Th	4 44 44	12 08 25	7♓10 22	14 15 45	16 54.7	10 39.3	0♉45.4	21 58.6	26 01.4	26 54.2	21 19.3	29 02.4	22 15.1	13 25.9
4 F	4 48 41	13 05 52	21 20 03	28 23 03	16 53.8	12 51.3	1 53.5	22 40.8	26 21.2	26 56.5	21 15.2	29 03.9	22 16.1	13 27.2
5 Sa	4 52 37	14 03 18	5♈24 31	12♈24 10	16 51.4	15 03.4	3 01.7	23 22.8	26 41.2	26 58.7	21 11.3	29 05.3	22 17.1	13 28.6
6 Su	4 56 34	15 00 44	19 21 47	26 17 05	16 47.7	17 15.4	4 10.0	24 04.8	27 01.4	27 00.7	21 07.3	29 06.7	22 18.1	13 29.9
7 M	5 00 30	15 58 09	3♉09 48	9♉59 39	16 43.3	19 27.0	5 18.4	24 46.7	27 21.7	27 02.5	21 03.5	29 08.0	22 19.2	13 31.3
8 Tu	5 04 27	16 55 33	16 46 24	23 29 47	16 38.6	21 37.8	6 26.9	25 28.6	27 42.2	27 04.1	20 59.6	29 09.3	22 20.4	13 32.7
9 W	5 08 23	17 52 57	0♊09 36	6♊45 38	16 34.3	23 47.8	7 35.5	26 10.3	28 02.8	27 05.5	20 55.9	29 10.6	22 21.5	13 34.1
10 Th	5 12 20	18 50 20	13 17 47	19 45 57	16 31.0	25 56.5	8 44.2	26 52.0	28 23.5	27 06.7	20 52.1	29 11.8	22 22.7	13 35.5
11 F	5 16 17	19 47 42	26 10 06	2♋30 16	16 29.0	28 03.9	9 52.9	27 33.6	28 44.4	27 07.8	20 48.5	29 12.9	22 23.9	13 36.9
12 Sa	5 20 13	20 45 04	8♋46 32	14 59 05	16D28.2	0♋09.7	11 01.8	28 15.1	29 05.4	27 08.6	20 44.9	29 14.1	22 25.1	13 38.4
13 Su	5 24 10	21 42 24	21 08 08	27 13 56	16 28.6	2 13.8	12 10.7	28 56.6	29 26.6	27 09.2	20 41.4	29 15.1	22 26.4	13 39.8
14 M	5 28 06	22 39 44	3♌16 52	9♌17 17	16 29.8	4 16.0	13 19.7	29 37.9	29 47.9	27 09.7	20 37.9	29 16.1	22 27.7	13 41.2
15 Tu	5 32 03	23 37 03	15 15 38	21 12 24	16 31.5	6 16.3	14 28.8	0♈19.2	0♍09.3	27R10.0	20 34.5	29 17.1	22 29.0	13 42.7
16 W	5 35 59	24 34 21	27 08 06	3♍03 16	16 33.0	8 14.5	15 38.0	1 00.3	0 30.9	27 10.0	20 31.1	29 18.0	22 30.3	13 44.1
17 Th	5 39 56	25 31 38	8♍58 30	14 54 21	16R34.1	10 10.5	16 47.2	1 41.4	0 52.5	27 09.9	20 27.9	29 18.9	22 31.7	13 45.6
18 F	5 43 52	26 28 55	20 51 26	26 50 20	16 34.5	12 04.4	17 56.5	2 22.4	1 14.3	27 09.6	20 24.7	29 19.7	22 33.0	13 47.1
19 Sa	5 47 49	27 26 10	2♎51 40	8♎56 00	16 34.1	13 56.0	19 05.9	3 03.3	1 36.2	27 09.1	20 21.5	29 20.5	22 34.5	13 48.6
20 Su	5 51 46	28 23 25	15 03 53	21 15 49	16 32.8	15 45.4	20 15.3	3 44.0	1 58.2	27 08.4	20 18.5	29 21.2	22 35.9	13 50.1
21 M	5 55 42	29 20 39	27 32 18	3♏53 43	16 30.9	17 32.5	21 24.8	4 24.7	2 20.4	27 07.5	20 15.5	29 21.9	22 37.4	13 51.5
22 Tu	5 59 39	0♋17 53	10♏20 25	16 52 38	16 28.8	19 17.2	22 34.4	5 05.3	2 42.6	27 06.4	20 12.6	29 22.6	22 38.8	13 53.0
23 W	6 03 35	1 15 06	23 30 31	0♐14 08	16 26.7	20 59.7	23 44.1	5 45.7	3 05.0	27 05.1	20 09.7	29 23.2	22 40.4	13 54.5
24 Th	6 07 32	2 12 18	7♐03 25	13 58 09	16 24.9	22 39.9	24 53.8	6 26.1	3 27.4	27 03.7	20 07.0	29 23.7	22 41.9	13 56.1
25 F	6 11 28	3 09 31	20 58 02	28 02 40	16 23.7	24 17.7	26 03.6	7 06.4	3 50.0	27 02.0	20 04.3	29 24.2	22 43.5	13 57.6
26 Sa	6 15 25	4 06 43	5♑11 31	12♑23 57	16D23.3	25 53.2	27 13.5	7 46.5	4 12.7	27 00.2	20 01.7	29 24.6	22 45.0	13 59.1
27 Su	6 19 21	5 03 54	19 39 18	26 56 49	16 23.4	27 26.3	28 23.5	8 26.5	4 35.5	26 58.2	19 59.2	29 25.0	22 46.6	14 00.6
28 M	6 23 18	6 01 06	4♒15 44	11♒35 16	16 23.9	28 57.1	29 33.5	9 06.4	4 58.3	26 56.0	19 56.7	29 25.4	22 48.3	14 02.1
29 Tu	6 27 15	6 58 17	18 54 41	26 13 16	16 24.7	0♌25.5	0♊43.6	9 46.2	5 21.3	26 53.6	19 54.4	29 25.7	22 49.9	14 03.7
30 W	6 31 11	7 55 29	3♓30 22	10♓45 23	16 25.4	1 51.4	1 53.8	10 25.9	5 44.4	26 51.0	19 52.1	29 25.9	22 51.6	14 05.2

Astro Data	Dy Hr Mn
♆ D	3 13:12
☽ 0N	9 4:37
♀ 0N	9 13:50
☽ 0S	23 9:19
♄□♆	23 11:31
☽ 0N	5 11:26
♃ R	16 8:35
☽ 0S	19 18:27
♂ 0N	23 12:37

Planet Ingress		Dy Hr Mn
♂	♓	3 17:03
♀	♈	6 15:13
☿	♉	13 10:53
☉	♊	21 20:15
☿	♊	29 13:51
♀	♉	2 19:59
☿	♋	12 10:08
♂	♈	15 0:50
⚳	♍	15 1:35
☉	♋	22 4:30
♀	♊	28 21:05
☿	♌	29 5:01

Last Aspect Dy Hr Mn		☽ Ingress	Dy Hr Mn
1 21:14	♂ ✶	♑	1 23:32
4 0:02	♅ ✶	♒	4 3:31
5 21:19	♃ ☌	♓	6 6:32
8 5:49	♅ ☌	♈	8 8:55
10 3:06	♃ ✶	♉	10 11:33
12 12:47	♅ ✶	♊	12 15:46
14 19:53	♅ □	♋	14 22:53
17 6:21	♅ △	♌	17 9:20
19 17:48	☉ □	♍	19 21:54
22 7:28	♅ ☍	♎	22 10:04
24 12:50	♃ △	♏	24 19:42
27 0:10	♅ △	♐	27 2:14
29 4:31	♅ □	♑	29 6:24
31 7:33	♅ ✶	♒	31 9:19

Last Aspect Dy Hr Mn		☽ Ingress	Dy Hr Mn
2 11:11	♀ ✶	♓	2 11:53
4 13:10	♅ ☌	♈	4 14:45
6 13:16	♃ ✶	♉	6 18:28
8 22:12	♅ ✶	♊	8 23:43
11 5:45	♅ □	♋	11 7:15
13 16:00	♅ △	♌	13 17:29
16 0:04	♃ ☍	♍	16 5:48
18 16:59	♅ ☍	♎	18 18:19
21 2:44	☉ △	♏	21 4:40
23 10:29	♅ △	♐	23 11:35
25 14:17	♅ □	♑	25 15:18
27 16:03	♅ ✶	♒	27 17:01
29 13:06	♃ ☌	♓	29 18:13

☽ Phases & Eclipses Dy Hr Mn		
5 3:13	☾	13♒52
11 22:55	●	20♉28
19 17:48	☽	27♌59
27 11:48	○	5♐25
3 8:09	☾	11♓59
10 10:08	●	18♊46
18 11:13	☽	26♍27
25 21:13	○	3♑31
25 21:25	•	A 0.675

Astro Data
1 May 1926
Julian Day # 9617
SVP 6♓17'36"
GC 25♐48.6 ⚴ 15♋58.8
Eris 0♈54.3 ⚵ 0♓09.1
⚷ 28♈39.0 ⚶ 8♋21.1
☽ Mean ☊ 19♋55.2

1 June 1926
Julian Day # 9648
SVP 6♓17'31"
GC 25♐48.7 ⚴ 1♌28.3
Eris 1♈08.6 ⚵ 9♓07.1
⚷ 0♉23.0 ⚶ 20♋31.3
☽ Mean ☊ 18♋16.8

July 1926 — LONGITUDE

Day	Sid.Time	☉	0 hr ☽	Noon ☽	True ☊	☿	♀	♂	⚳	♃	♄	♅	♆	♇
1 Th	6 35 08	8♋52 41	17♓57 50	25♓07 18	16♋25.9	3♌15.0	3♊04.0	11♈05.4	6♍07.5	26♒48.2	19♏49.9	29♓26.1	22♌53.3	14♋06.7
2 F	6 39 04	9 49 52	2♈13 27	9♈16 00	16R 26.1	4 36.1	4 14.3	11 44.8	6 30.8	26R 45.2	19R 47.8	29 26.3	22 55.0	14 08.3
3 Sa	6 43 01	10 47 04	16 14 48	23 09 43	16 26.0	5 54.6	5 24.6	12 24.1	6 54.1	26 42.1	19 45.8	29 26.4	22 56.7	14 09.8
4 Su	6 46 57	11 44 17	0♉00 42	6♉47 43	16 25.6	7 10.7	6 35.1	13 03.2	7 17.6	26 38.8	19 43.9	29R 26.5	22 58.5	14 11.3
5 M	6 50 54	12 41 30	13 30 49	20 10 02	16 25.2	8 24.1	7 45.6	13 42.2	7 41.1	26 35.3	19 42.0	29 26.5	23 00.3	14 12.9
6 Tu	6 54 50	13 38 43	26 45 26	3♊17 06	16 24.9	9 34.9	8 56.1	14 21.0	8 04.7	26 31.6	19 40.3	29 26.4	23 02.0	14 14.4
7 W	6 58 47	14 35 56	9♊45 10	16 09 43	16 24.6	10 42.9	10 06.7	14 59.7	8 28.4	26 27.7	19 38.6	29 26.4	23 03.9	14 16.0
8 Th	7 02 44	15 33 09	22 30 52	28 48 46	16D 24.5	11 48.1	11 17.4	15 38.2	8 52.2	26 23.7	19 37.0	29 26.2	23 05.7	14 17.5
9 F	7 06 40	16 30 23	5♋03 32	11♋15 20	16R 24.5	12 50.4	12 28.1	16 16.5	9 16.1	26 19.5	19 35.6	29 26.0	23 07.5	14 19.0
10 Sa	7 10 37	17 27 37	17 24 19	23 30 40	16 24.5	13 49.8	13 38.9	16 54.7	9 40.1	26 15.1	19 34.2	29 25.8	23 09.4	14 20.6
11 Su	7 14 33	18 24 51	29 34 36	5♌36 19	16 24.4	14 46.0	14 49.8	17 32.7	10 04.1	26 10.6	19 32.9	29 25.5	23 11.3	14 22.1
12 M	7 18 30	19 22 05	11♌36 06	17 34 12	16 24.2	15 39.0	16 00.7	18 10.5	10 28.2	26 05.9	19 31.7	29 25.2	23 13.2	14 23.7
13 Tu	7 22 26	20 19 20	23 30 57	29 26 42	16 23.7	16 28.7	17 11.7	18 48.2	10 52.4	26 01.0	19 30.6	29 24.8	23 15.1	14 25.2
14 W	7 26 23	21 16 34	5♍21 48	11♍16 40	16 23.2	17 14.9	18 22.7	19 25.6	11 16.7	25 56.0	19 29.6	29 24.4	23 17.1	14 26.7
15 Th	7 30 20	22 13 48	17 11 44	23 07 28	16 22.5	17 57.6	19 33.7	20 02.9	11 41.0	25 50.8	19 28.7	29 23.9	23 19.0	14 28.3
16 F	7 34 16	23 11 03	29 04 23	5♎02 58	16 21.9	18 36.5	20 44.9	20 40.0	12 05.5	25 45.5	19 27.9	29 23.4	23 21.0	14 29.8
17 Sa	7 38 13	24 08 18	11♎03 47	17 07 21	16D 21.6	19 11.5	21 56.0	21 16.8	12 30.0	25 40.0	19 27.1	29 22.8	23 23.0	14 31.3
18 Su	7 42 09	25 05 33	23 14 14	29 24 59	16 21.5	19 42.4	23 07.3	21 53.5	12 54.5	25 34.4	19 26.5	29 22.2	23 24.9	14 32.8
19 M	7 46 06	26 02 48	5♏40 08	12♏00 11	16 21.9	20 09.2	24 18.6	22 30.0	13 19.1	25 28.6	19 26.0	29 21.6	23 27.0	14 34.3
20 Tu	7 50 02	27 00 03	18 25 36	24 56 49	16 22.6	20 31.6	25 29.9	23 06.3	13 43.8	25 22.7	19 25.6	29 20.9	23 29.0	14 35.8
21 W	7 53 59	27 57 19	1♐34 08	8♐17 50	16 23.5	20 49.4	26 41.3	23 42.3	14 08.6	25 16.7	19 25.2	29 20.1	23 31.0	14 37.4
22 Th	7 57 55	28 54 35	15 08 01	22 04 44	16 24.5	21 02.7	27 52.7	24 18.2	14 33.4	25 10.6	19 25.0	29 19.3	23 33.1	14 38.9
23 F	8 01 52	29 51 51	29 07 50	6♑17 02	16R 25.1	21 11.1	29 04.2	24 53.8	14 58.3	25 04.3	19D 24.9	29 18.5	23 35.1	14 40.4
24 Sa	8 05 49	0♌49 08	13♑31 52	20 51 46	16 25.3	21R 14.7	0♋15.8	25 29.2	15 23.2	24 57.9	19 24.8	29 17.6	23 37.2	14 41.9
25 Su	8 09 45	1 46 26	28 15 56	5♒43 29	16 24.7	21 13.2	1 27.4	26 04.4	15 48.2	24 51.4	19 24.9	29 16.7	23 39.3	14 43.3
26 M	8 13 42	2 43 44	13♒13 25	20 44 39	16 23.4	21 06.7	2 39.1	26 39.4	16 13.3	24 44.7	19 25.0	29 15.7	23 41.4	14 44.8
27 Tu	8 17 38	3 41 03	28 16 04	5♓46 33	16 21.4	20 55.2	3 50.8	27 14.1	16 38.4	24 38.0	19 25.3	29 14.7	23 43.5	14 46.3
28 W	8 21 35	4 38 22	13♓15 04	20 40 37	16 19.2	20 38.7	5 02.6	27 48.6	17 03.5	24 31.1	19 25.6	29 13.7	23 45.6	14 47.8
29 Th	8 25 31	5 35 43	28 02 22	5♈19 36	16 17.1	20 17.2	6 14.5	28 22.8	17 28.8	24 24.2	19 26.1	29 12.6	23 47.7	14 49.2
30 F	8 29 28	6 33 05	12♈31 46	19 38 29	16 15.6	19 51.1	7 26.4	28 56.7	17 54.1	24 17.1	19 26.6	29 11.4	23 49.9	14 50.7
31 Sa	8 33 24	7 30 27	26 39 29	3♉34 41	16D 14.8	19 20.5	8 38.3	29 30.4	18 19.4	24 10.0	19 27.2	29 10.2	23 52.0	14 52.1

August 1926 — LONGITUDE

Day	Sid.Time	☉	0 hr ☽	Noon ☽	True ☊	☿	♀	♂	⚳	♃	♄	♅	♆	♇
1 Su	8 37 21	8♌27 52	10♉24 05	17♉07 51	16♋15.0	18♌45.7	9♋50.3	0♉03.8	18♍44.8	24♒02.8	19♏28.0	29♓09.0	23♌54.2	14♋53.6
2 M	8 41 18	9 25 17	23 46 10	0♊19 19	16 16.0	18R 07.3	11 02.4	0 37.0	19 10.2	23R 55.5	19 28.8	29R 07.7	23 56.3	14 55.0
3 Tu	8 45 14	10 22 43	6♊47 38	13 11 28	16 17.5	17 25.7	12 14.5	1 09.8	19 35.7	23 48.1	19 29.7	29 06.4	23 58.5	14 56.4
4 W	8 49 11	11 20 11	19 31 11	25 47 10	16 19.0	16 41.6	13 26.7	1 42.4	20 01.3	23 40.6	19 30.8	29 05.1	24 00.7	14 57.8
5 Th	8 53 07	12 17 40	1♋59 46	8♋09 21	16R 20.1	15 55.7	14 38.9	2 14.6	20 26.9	23 33.1	19 31.9	29 03.7	24 02.8	14 59.2
6 F	8 57 04	13 15 10	14 16 14	20 20 45	16 20.3	15 08.8	15 51.2	2 46.5	20 52.5	23 25.6	19 33.1	29 02.3	24 05.0	15 00.6
7 Sa	9 01 00	14 12 41	26 23 12	2♌23 50	16 19.2	14 21.6	17 03.6	3 18.1	21 18.2	23 17.9	19 34.4	29 00.8	24 07.2	15 02.0
8 Su	9 04 57	15 10 13	8♌22 56	14 20 44	16 16.7	13 35.1	18 16.0	3 49.4	21 44.0	23 10.2	19 35.9	28 59.3	24 09.4	15 03.4
9 M	9 08 53	16 07 46	20 17 29	26 13 25	16 12.8	12 50.2	19 28.4	4 20.4	22 09.8	23 02.5	19 37.4	28 57.8	24 11.6	15 04.7
10 Tu	9 12 50	17 05 21	2♍08 46	8♍03 46	16 07.8	12 07.7	20 40.9	4 51.0	22 35.6	22 54.8	19 39.0	28 56.2	24 13.8	15 06.1
11 W	9 16 47	18 02 56	13 58 42	19 53 49	16 02.2	11 28.5	21 53.4	5 21.2	23 01.5	22 47.0	19 40.7	28 54.6	24 16.1	15 07.4
12 Th	9 20 43	19 00 32	25 49 25	1♎45 51	15 56.5	10 53.4	23 06.0	5 51.1	23 27.4	22 39.1	19 42.5	28 52.9	24 18.3	15 08.7
13 F	9 24 40	19 58 09	7♎43 26	13 42 34	15 51.4	10 23.2	24 18.7	6 20.6	23 53.4	22 31.3	19 44.4	28 51.2	24 20.5	15 10.0
14 Sa	9 28 36	20 55 48	19 43 40	25 47 09	15 47.4	9 58.5	25 31.3	6 49.8	24 19.4	22 23.5	19 46.3	28 49.5	24 22.7	15 11.3
15 Su	9 32 33	21 53 27	1♏53 31	8♏03 14	15 44.8	9 39.9	26 44.1	7 18.5	24 45.4	22 15.6	19 48.4	28 47.8	24 24.9	15 12.6
16 M	9 36 29	22 51 07	14 16 49	20 34 48	15D 43.8	9 27.9	27 56.8	7 46.9	25 11.5	22 07.7	19 50.6	28 46.0	24 27.1	15 13.9
17 Tu	9 40 26	23 48 49	26 57 40	3♐25 56	15 44.2	9D 22.8	29 09.7	8 14.9	25 37.6	21 59.9	19 52.8	28 44.2	24 29.4	15 15.1
18 W	9 44 22	24 46 31	10♐00 02	16 40 24	15 45.4	9 25.0	0♌22.5	8 42.5	26 03.7	21 52.0	19 55.2	28 42.3	24 31.6	15 16.4
19 Th	9 48 19	25 44 15	23 27 22	0♑21 08	15 46.8	9 34.7	1 35.5	9 09.7	26 29.9	21 44.2	19 57.6	28 40.4	24 33.8	15 17.6
20 F	9 52 15	26 41 59	7♑21 50	14 29 24	15R 47.5	9 51.9	2 48.4	9 36.4	26 56.1	21 36.4	20 00.2	28 38.5	24 36.0	15 18.8
21 Sa	9 56 12	27 39 45	21 43 37	29 04 05	15 46.9	10 16.7	4 01.5	10 02.8	27 22.4	21 28.6	20 02.8	28 36.6	24 38.3	15 20.0
22 Su	10 00 09	28 37 32	6♒30 09	14♒01 01	15 44.4	10 49.2	5 14.5	10 28.7	27 48.7	21 20.9	20 05.5	28 34.6	24 40.5	15 21.2
23 M	10 04 05	29 35 21	21 35 39	29 12 54	15 40.0	11 29.1	6 27.6	10 54.1	28 15.0	21 13.2	20 08.3	28 32.6	24 42.7	15 22.4
24 Tu	10 08 02	0♍33 11	6♓51 27	14♓29 57	15 34.0	12 16.5	7 40.8	11 19.1	28 41.3	21 05.5	20 11.2	28 30.6	24 44.9	15 23.6
25 W	10 11 58	1 31 02	22 07 01	29 41 23	15 27.3	13 11.0	8 54.0	11 43.6	29 07.7	20 57.9	20 14.2	28 28.6	24 47.1	15 24.7
26 Th	10 15 55	2 28 55	7♈11 43	14♈37 06	15 20.7	14 12.4	10 07.3	12 07.6	29 34.1	20 50.4	20 17.3	28 26.5	24 49.3	15 25.8
27 F	10 19 51	3 26 49	21 56 38	29 09 42	15 15.1	15 20.5	11 20.6	12 31.2	0♎00.6	20 42.9	20 20.4	28 24.4	24 51.5	15 26.9
28 Sa	10 23 48	4 24 46	6♉15 51	13♉14 54	15 11.2	16 34.8	12 33.9	12 54.2	0 27.0	20 35.4	20 23.6	28 22.3	24 53.8	15 28.0
29 Su	10 27 44	5 22 45	20 06 47	26 51 41	15D 09.2	17 54.9	13 47.3	13 16.7	0 53.5	20 28.1	20 27.0	28 20.1	24 55.9	15 29.1
30 M	10 31 41	6 20 45	3♊29 50	10♊01 39	15 08.9	19 20.5	15 00.8	13 38.7	1 20.0	20 20.8	20 30.4	28 18.0	24 58.1	15 30.1
31 Tu	10 35 38	7 18 47	16 27 35	22 48 08	15 09.7	20 51.0	16 14.3	14 00.2	1 46.6	20 13.6	20 33.8	28 15.8	25 00.3	15 31.2

Astro Data	Dy Hr Mn
☽ 0N	2 17:10
♅ R	5 5:02
☽ 0S	17 2:25
♄ D	24 9:37
☿ R	24 17:05
☽ 0N	29 23:28
♃☍♆	2 9:53
☽ 0S	13 8:41
☿ D	17 16:55
☽ 0N	26 7:39
♃□♄	29 14:29

Planet Ingress		Dy Hr Mn
☉	♌	23 15:25
♀	♋	24 6:42
♂	♉	1 9:14
♀	♌	18 4:35
☉	♍	23 22:14
⚳	♎	27 11:30

Last Aspect Dy Hr Mn			☽ Ingress	Dy Hr Mn
1 19:17	♅	☌	♈	1 20:14
3 18:10	♃	⚹	♉	3 23:59
6 4:55	♅	⚹	♊	6 5:57
8 13:12	♅	□	♋	8 14:16
10 23:42	♅	△	♌	11 0:50
13 5:06	♃	☍	♍	13 13:07
16 0:39	♅	☍	♎	16 1:52
18 4:37	♃	△	♏	18 13:08
20 19:59	♅	△	♐	20 21:10
23 0:19	♅	□	♑	23 1:28
25 1:39	♅	⚹	♒	25 2:48
26 21:48	♂	⚹	♓	27 2:46
29 1:56	♅	☌	♈	29 3:13
31 4:37	♂	☌	♉	31 5:46

Last Aspect Dy Hr Mn			☽ Ingress	Dy Hr Mn
2 9:48	♅	⚹	♊	2 11:24
4 18:21	♅	□	♋	4 20:08
7 5:15	♅	△	♌	7 7:12
9 7:53	♆	☌	♍	9 19:39
12 6:12	♅	☍	♎	12 8:26
14 11:25	♀	□	♏	14 20:18
17 3:20	♅	△	♐	17 5:39
19 9:06	♅	□	♑	19 11:24
21 11:15	♅	⚹	♒	21 13:31
23 12:38	☉	☍	♓	23 13:14
25 10:05	♅	☌	♈	25 12:30
27 4:48	♆	△	♉	27 13:24
29 14:39	♅	⚹	♊	29 17:39

☽ Phases & Eclipses Dy Hr Mn		
2 13:02	☾	9♈52
9 23:06	●	16♋57
9 23:05:38	☉	A 03'39"
18 2:55	☽	24♎44
25 5:13	○	1♒30
25 5:00	☊	A 0.354
31 19:25	☾	7♉48
8 13:48	●	15♌15
16 16:38	☽	23♏02
23 12:38	○	29♒37
30 4:40	☾	6♊03

Astro Data

1 July 1926
Julian Day # 9678
SVP 6♓17'26"
GC 25♐48.8 ⚵ 16♌29.5
Eris 1♈12.7R ⚶ 14♓38.8
⚷ 1♉36.7 ⚸ 3♌25.2
☽ Mean ☊ 16♋41.5

1 August 1926
Julian Day # 9709
SVP 6♓17'21"
GC 25♐48.8 ⚵ 1♍47.6
Eris 1♈06.1R ⚶ 15♓02.6R
⚷ 2♉09.8 ⚸ 17♌28.7
☽ Mean ☊ 15♋03.0

LONGITUDE — September 1926

Day	Sid.Time	☉	0 hr ☽	Noon☽	True☊	☿	♀	♂	⚳	♃	♄	♅	♆	♇
1 W	10 39 34	8♍16 52	29♊03 53	5♋15 21	15♋10.7	22♌26.1	17♌27.9	14♉21.1	2♎13.2	20♒06.4	20♏37.4	28♓13.6	25♌02.5	15♋32.2
2 Th	10 43 31	9 14 58	11♋23 08	17 27 46	15R 11.1	24 05.1	18 41.5	14 41.4	2 39.8	19R 59.4	20 41.1	28R 11.4	25 04.7	15 33.2
3 F	10 47 27	10 13 06	23 29 45	29 29 34	15 09.9	25 47.6	19 55.1	15 01.1	3 06.4	19 52.5	20 44.8	28 09.1	25 06.9	15 34.2
4 Sa	10 51 24	11 11 16	5♌27 41	11♌24 30	15 06.5	27 33.0	21 08.8	15 20.2	3 33.0	19 45.6	20 48.6	28 06.9	25 09.0	15 35.2
5 Su	10 55 20	12 09 27	17 20 23	23 15 40	15 00.7	29 21.0	22 22.5	15 38.7	3 59.7	19 38.9	20 52.5	28 04.6	25 11.2	15 36.1
6 M	10 59 17	13 07 41	29 10 38	5♍05 32	14 52.4	1♍11.0	23 36.3	15 56.6	4 26.4	19 32.3	20 56.5	28 02.3	25 13.3	15 37.1
7 Tu	11 03 13	14 05 56	11♍00 38	16 56 07	14 42.1	3 02.7	24 50.1	16 13.8	4 53.1	19 25.8	21 00.5	28 00.0	25 15.4	15 38.0
8 W	11 07 10	15 04 13	22 52 10	28 48 59	14 30.6	4 55.5	26 04.0	16 30.4	5 19.9	19 19.4	21 04.7	27 57.7	25 17.6	15 38.9
9 Th	11 11 07	16 02 31	4♎46 45	10♎45 40	14 18.9	6 49.3	27 17.9	16 46.3	5 46.6	19 13.2	21 08.9	27 55.3	25 19.7	15 39.7
10 F	11 15 03	17 00 52	16 45 56	22 47 47	14 08.0	8 43.5	28 31.8	17 01.6	6 13.4	19 07.1	21 13.2	27 53.0	25 21.8	15 40.6
11 Sa	11 19 00	17 59 14	28 51 27	4♏57 16	13 58.9	10 38.0	29 45.8	17 16.1	6 40.2	19 01.1	21 17.5	27 50.6	25 23.9	15 41.4
12 Su	11 22 56	18 57 37	11♏05 30	17 16 33	13 52.1	12 32.6	0♍59.8	17 30.0	7 07.0	18 55.2	21 22.0	27 48.3	25 25.9	15 42.2
13 M	11 26 53	19 56 03	23 30 47	29 48 38	13 47.9	14 26.9	2 13.8	17 43.1	7 33.8	18 49.5	21 26.5	27 45.9	25 28.0	15 43.0
14 Tu	11 30 49	20 54 30	6♐10 33	12♐36 58	13D 46.0	16 21.0	3 27.9	17 55.5	8 00.7	18 44.0	21 31.0	27 43.5	25 30.1	15 43.8
15 W	11 34 46	21 52 58	19 08 21	25 45 10	13 45.8	18 14.5	4 42.0	18 07.2	8 27.6	18 38.6	21 35.7	27 41.1	25 32.1	15 44.5
16 Th	11 38 42	22 51 29	2♑27 49	9♑16 38	13R 46.1	20 07.3	5 56.2	18 18.2	8 54.4	18 33.4	21 40.4	27 38.7	25 34.2	15 45.3
17 F	11 42 39	23 50 00	16 11 54	23 13 47	13 45.9	21 59.5	7 10.4	18 28.3	9 21.3	18 28.3	21 45.2	27 36.3	25 36.2	15 46.0
18 Sa	11 46 36	24 48 34	0♒22 16	7♒37 12	13 44.0	23 50.9	8 24.6	18 37.8	9 48.2	18 23.3	21 50.1	27 33.9	25 38.2	15 46.7
19 Su	11 50 32	25 47 09	14 58 12	22 24 43	13 39.6	25 41.4	9 38.9	18 46.4	10 15.1	18 18.6	21 55.0	27 31.5	25 40.2	15 47.3
20 M	11 54 29	26 45 46	29 55 57	7♓30 53	13 32.6	27 31.0	10 53.2	18 54.2	10 42.0	18 14.0	22 00.0	27 29.1	25 42.1	15 48.0
21 Tu	11 58 25	27 44 24	15♓08 21	22 46 59	13 23.3	29 19.7	12 07.5	19 01.3	11 08.9	18 09.5	22 05.0	27 26.7	25 44.1	15 48.6
22 W	12 02 22	28 43 05	0♈25 25	8♈02 11	13 12.7	1♎07.5	13 21.8	19 07.5	11 35.9	18 05.3	22 10.2	27 24.3	25 46.0	15 49.2
23 Th	12 06 18	29 41 47	15 35 54	23 05 20	13 02.2	2 54.3	14 36.2	19 12.9	12 02.8	18 01.2	22 15.3	27 21.9	25 47.9	15 49.8
24 F	12 10 15	0♎40 32	0♉29 21	7♉47 04	12 52.8	4 40.2	15 50.7	19 17.5	12 29.8	17 57.3	22 20.6	27 19.5	25 49.8	15 50.3
25 Sa	12 14 11	1 39 18	14 57 50	22 01 13	12 45.5	6 25.1	17 05.1	19 21.2	12 56.7	17 53.5	22 25.9	27 17.1	25 51.7	15 50.9
26 Su	12 18 08	2 38 08	28 57 01	5♊45 14	12 40.8	8 09.1	18 19.6	19 24.1	13 23.7	17 50.0	22 31.3	27 14.7	25 53.6	15 51.4
27 M	12 22 05	3 36 59	12♊26 04	18 59 50	12 38.5	9 52.2	19 34.2	19 26.1	13 50.7	17 46.6	22 36.7	27 12.3	25 55.5	15 51.9
28 Tu	12 26 01	4 35 53	25 27 00	1♋48 06	12 37.8	11 34.3	20 48.7	19R 27.2	14 17.7	17 43.4	22 42.2	27 09.9	25 57.3	15 52.3
29 W	12 29 58	5 34 49	8♋03 45	14 14 35	12 37.8	13 15.5	22 03.3	19 27.4	14 44.7	17 40.4	22 47.8	27 07.5	25 59.1	15 52.8
30 Th	12 33 54	6 33 47	20 21 15	26 24 25	12 37.3	14 55.9	23 18.0	19 26.7	15 11.7	17 37.6	22 53.4	27 05.2	26 00.9	15 53.2

LONGITUDE — October 1926

Day	Sid.Time	☉	0 hr ☽	Noon☽	True☊	☿	♀	♂	⚳	♃	♄	♅	♆	♇
1 F	12 37 51	7♎32 48	2♌24 44	8♌22 48	12♋35.2	16♎35.3	24♍32.6	19♉25.1	15♎38.7	17♒35.0	22♏59.0	27♓02.8	26♌02.7	15♋53.6
2 Sa	12 41 47	8 31 50	14 19 12	20 14 29	12R 30.6	18 13.9	25 47.3	19R 22.6	16 05.7	17R 32.6	23 04.7	27R 00.5	26 04.5	15 53.9
3 Su	12 45 44	9 30 55	26 09 10	2♍03 39	12 23.1	19 51.7	27 02.1	19 19.2	16 32.7	17 30.3	23 10.5	26 58.1	26 06.2	15 54.3
4 M	12 49 40	10 30 02	7♍58 22	13 53 39	12 12.8	21 28.6	28 16.8	19 14.9	16 59.7	17 28.3	23 16.3	26 55.8	26 07.9	15 54.6
5 Tu	12 53 37	11 29 12	19 49 48	25 47 04	12 00.0	23 04.8	29 31.6	19 09.7	17 26.7	17 26.4	23 22.2	26 53.5	26 09.6	15 54.9
6 W	12 57 33	12 28 23	1♎45 38	7♎45 42	11 45.9	24 40.1	0♎46.4	19 03.6	17 53.7	17 24.8	23 28.2	26 51.2	26 11.3	15 55.2
7 Th	13 01 30	13 27 36	13 47 23	19 50 49	11 31.4	26 14.7	2 01.2	18 56.6	18 20.8	17 23.3	23 34.1	26 48.9	26 12.9	15 55.4
8 F	13 05 27	14 26 52	25 56 06	2♏03 20	11 17.7	27 48.5	3 16.1	18 48.7	18 47.8	17 22.1	23 40.2	26 46.6	26 14.5	15 55.7
9 Sa	13 09 23	15 26 09	8♏12 38	14 24 06	11 06.1	29 21.6	4 30.9	18 39.9	19 14.8	17 21.0	23 46.3	26 44.4	26 16.1	15 55.9
10 Su	13 13 20	16 25 29	20 37 54	26 54 12	10 57.2	0♏53.9	5 45.8	18 30.3	19 41.8	17 20.2	23 52.4	26 42.2	26 17.7	15 56.0
11 M	13 17 16	17 24 50	3♐13 12	9♐35 08	10 51.4	2 25.5	7 00.7	18 19.8	20 08.8	17 19.5	23 58.6	26 39.9	26 19.3	15 56.2
12 Tu	13 21 13	18 24 13	16 00 17	22 28 57	10 48.3	3 56.3	8 15.7	18 08.5	20 35.8	17 19.1	24 04.8	26 37.8	26 20.8	15 56.3
13 W	13 25 09	19 23 38	29 01 27	5♑38 08	10D 47.4	5 26.4	9 30.6	17 56.4	21 02.8	17D 18.9	24 11.1	26 35.6	26 22.3	15 56.4
14 Th	13 29 06	20 23 05	12♑19 19	19 05 20	10R 47.4	6 55.8	10 45.6	17 43.6	21 29.8	17 18.8	24 17.4	26 33.4	26 23.8	15 56.5
15 F	13 33 02	21 22 33	25 56 27	2♒52 52	10 47.0	8 24.5	12 00.6	17 29.9	21 56.8	17 19.0	24 23.7	26 31.3	26 25.2	15 56.6
16 Sa	13 36 59	22 22 03	9♒54 41	17 01 55	10 45.1	9 52.5	13 15.6	17 15.6	22 23.7	17 19.3	24 30.1	26 29.2	26 26.7	15R 56.6
17 Su	13 40 56	23 21 35	24 14 24	1♓31 48	10 40.9	11 19.6	14 30.7	17 00.5	22 50.7	17 19.9	24 36.5	26 27.1	26 28.1	15 56.6
18 M	13 44 52	24 21 08	8♓53 38	16 19 11	10 33.9	12 46.1	15 45.7	16 44.7	23 17.7	17 20.7	24 43.0	26 25.1	26 29.4	15 56.6
19 Tu	13 48 49	25 20 44	23 47 36	1♈17 51	10 24.6	14 11.7	17 00.8	16 28.3	23 44.6	17 21.6	24 49.5	26 23.1	26 30.8	15 56.6
20 W	13 52 45	26 20 21	8♈48 47	16 19 11	10 13.8	15 36.6	18 15.8	16 11.3	24 11.5	17 22.8	24 56.1	26 21.1	26 32.1	15 56.5
21 Th	13 56 42	27 20 00	23 47 48	1♉13 25	10 02.9	17 00.6	19 30.9	15 53.8	24 38.4	17 24.1	25 02.6	26 19.1	26 33.4	15 56.4
22 F	14 00 38	28 19 41	8♉34 56	15 51 22	9 53.0	18 23.8	20 46.0	15 35.6	25 05.4	17 25.7	25 09.2	26 17.2	26 34.7	15 56.3
23 Sa	14 04 35	29 19 24	23 01 56	0♊06 01	9 45.2	19 46.1	22 01.2	15 17.0	25 32.3	17 27.5	25 15.9	26 15.3	26 35.9	15 56.2
24 Su	14 08 31	0♏19 10	7♊03 14	13 53 22	9 40.1	21 07.4	23 16.3	14 57.9	25 59.1	17 29.4	25 22.6	26 13.4	26 37.1	15 56.0
25 M	14 12 28	1 18 57	20 36 26	27 12 34	9D 37.4	22 27.6	24 31.5	14 38.4	26 26.0	17 31.6	25 29.3	26 11.6	26 38.3	15 55.8
26 Tu	14 16 25	2 18 47	3♋42 05	10♋05 23	9 36.8	23 46.8	25 46.6	14 18.5	26 52.9	17 33.9	25 36.0	26 09.7	26 39.4	15 55.6
27 W	14 20 21	3 18 39	16 23 00	22 35 31	9R 37.2	25 04.8	27 01.8	13 58.3	27 19.7	17 36.4	25 42.8	26 08.0	26 40.6	15 55.4
28 Th	14 24 18	4 18 34	28 43 33	4♌47 45	9 37.5	26 21.6	28 17.1	13 37.8	27 46.6	17 39.2	25 49.6	26 06.2	26 41.7	15 55.1
29 F	14 28 14	5 18 30	10♌48 48	16 47 23	9 36.8	27 36.9	29 32.3	13 17.0	28 13.4	17 42.1	25 56.4	26 04.5	26 42.7	15 54.9
30 Sa	14 32 11	6 18 29	22 44 07	28 39 41	9 34.1	28 50.8	0♏47.5	12 56.1	28 40.2	17 45.2	26 03.3	26 02.8	26 43.7	15 54.6
31 Su	14 36 07	7 18 29	4♍34 38	10♍29 34	9 28.9	0♐02.9	2 02.8	12 35.0	29 07.0	17 48.5	26 10.2	26 01.2	26 44.7	15 54.2

Astro Data

	Dy Hr Mn
☽0S	9 13:58
☽0N	22 17:46
☿0S	23 10:34
☉0S	23 19:26
♂R	29 5:42
⚳0S	2 3:26
☽0S	6 19:40
♀0S	8 13:53
♃D	14 4:48
♅⚻♆	17 5:37
♇R	17 8:50
☽0N	20 4:35
♄△♅	30 10:44

Planet Ingress

		Dy Hr Mn
☿	♍	5 20:33
♀	♍	11 16:37
☿	♎	21 20:57
☉	♎	23 19:27
♀	♎	5 21:07
☿	♏	9 21:58
☉	♏	24 4:18
♀	♏	29 20:50
☿	♐	31 11:01

Last Aspect / ☽ Ingress (September)

Last Aspect Dy Hr Mn			☽ Ingress	Dy Hr Mn
31 22:26	♅	□	♋	1 1:48
3 9:19	♅	△	♌	3 13:01
5 15:55	♆	☌	♍	6 1:40
8 10:17	♅	☍	♎	8 14:23
11 0:38	♀	⚹	♏	11 2:15
13 8:08	♅	△	♐	13 12:22
15 15:28	♅	□	♑	15 19:37
17 19:21	♅	⚹	♒	17 23:23
19 17:13	♆	☍	♓	20 0:06
21 20:19	☉	☍	♈	21 23:20
23 16:23	♆	△	♉	23 23:12
25 21:04	♅	⚹	♊	26 1:50
28 3:15	♅	□	♋	28 8:35
30 13:21	♅	△	♌	30 19:10

Last Aspect / ☽ Ingress (October)

Last Aspect Dy Hr Mn			☽ Ingress	Dy Hr Mn
2 23:52	♆	☌	♍	3 7:49
5 20:24	♀	☌	♎	5 20:28
8 2:28	☿	☌	♏	8 7:59
10 11:37	♅	△	♐	10 17:54
12 19:36	♅	□	♑	13 1:47
15 1:02	♅	⚹	♒	15 7:02
17 3:40	♆	☍	♓	17 9:30
19 4:10	♅	☌	♈	19 9:56
21 5:15	☉	☍	♉	21 10:01
23 6:01	♆	□	♊	23 11:50
25 10:57	♆	⚹	♋	25 17:08
27 21:40	♀	□	♌	28 2:31
30 12:25	☿	□	♍	30 14:43

☽ Phases & Eclipses

Dy Hr Mn		
7 5:45	●	13♍51
15 4:26	☽	21♐35
21 20:19	○	28♓05
28 17:48	☾	4♋50
6 22:13	●	12♎54
14 14:28	☽	20♑29
21 5:15	○	27♈03
28 10:57	☾	4♌16

Astro Data

1 September 1926
Julian Day # 9740
SVP 6♓17'18"
GC 25♐48.9 ⚵ 16♍47.1
Eris 0♈50.4R ⚴ 9♓17.5R
⚷ 1♉51.9R ⚶ 2♍00.3
☽ Mean ☊ 13♋24.5

1 October 1926
Julian Day # 9770
SVP 6♓17'15"
GC 25♐49.0 ⚵ 0♎56.1
Eris 0♈30.9R ⚴ 2♓51.6R
⚷ 0♉51.2R ⚶ 16♍16.9
☽ Mean ☊ 11♋49.1

November 1926 LONGITUDE

Day	Sid.Time	☉	0 hr ☽	Noon ☽	True ☊	☿	♀	♂	⚳	♃	♄	♅	♆	♇
1 M	14 40 04	8♏18 32	16♍24 59	22♍21 22	9♋21.3	1♐13.2	3♏18.1	12♉13.8	29♎33.7	17♒52.0	26♏17.1	25♓59.6	26♌45.7	15♋53.9
2 Tu	14 44 00	9 18 37	28 19 07	4♎18 35	9R11.6	2 21.5	4 33.3	11R52.7	0♏00.5	17 55.7	26 24.0	25R58.0	26 46.6	15R53.5
3 W	14 47 57	10 18 44	10♎20 06	16 23 54	9 00.5	3 27.5	5 48.6	11 31.5	0 27.2	17 59.6	26 30.9	25 56.5	26 47.6	15 53.1
4 Th	14 51 54	11 18 52	22 30 09	28 39 01	8 49.0	4 31.0	7 03.9	11 10.4	0 53.9	18 03.6	26 37.9	25 55.0	26 48.4	15 52.7
5 F	14 55 50	12 19 03	4♏50 36	11♏04 56	8 38.2	5 31.6	8 19.2	10 49.5	1 20.6	18 07.9	26 44.9	25 53.6	26 49.3	15 52.3
6 Sa	14 59 47	13 19 16	17 22 03	23 41 58	8 29.1	6 29.1	9 34.6	10 28.7	1 47.2	18 12.3	26 51.9	25 52.2	26 50.1	15 51.8
7 Su	15 03 43	14 19 30	0♐04 39	6♐30 06	8 22.2	7 23.0	10 49.9	10 08.2	2 13.9	18 17.0	26 58.9	25 50.8	26 50.9	15 51.3
8 M	15 07 40	15 19 46	12 58 19	19 29 18	8 18.0	8 12.9	12 05.2	9 48.0	2 40.5	18 21.8	27 06.0	25 49.5	26 51.6	15 50.8
9 Tu	15 11 36	16 20 04	26 03 05	2♑39 42	8D16.2	8 58.4	13 20.6	9 28.1	3 07.0	18 26.7	27 13.0	25 48.2	26 52.3	15 50.3
10 W	15 15 33	17 20 23	9♑19 15	16 01 47	8 16.3	9 38.9	14 36.0	9 08.6	3 33.6	18 31.9	27 20.1	25 47.0	26 53.0	15 49.7
11 Th	15 19 29	18 20 43	22 47 27	29 36 19	8 17.3	10 13.7	15 51.3	8 49.6	4 00.1	18 37.3	27 27.2	25 45.8	26 53.6	15 49.1
12 F	15 23 26	19 21 05	6♒28 30	13♒24 05	8R18.3	10 42.4	17 06.7	8 31.0	4 26.6	18 42.8	27 34.3	25 44.6	26 54.3	15 48.5
13 Sa	15 27 23	20 21 29	20 23 05	27 25 30	8 18.2	11 04.1	18 22.0	8 12.9	4 53.1	18 48.5	27 41.4	25 43.5	26 54.8	15 47.9
14 Su	15 31 19	21 21 53	4♓31 11	11♓39 59	8 16.4	11 18.1	19 37.4	7 55.4	5 19.5	18 54.3	27 48.5	25 42.5	26 55.4	15 47.3
15 M	15 35 16	22 22 19	18 51 35	26 05 33	8 12.5	11R23.8	20 52.8	7 38.4	5 45.9	19 00.4	27 55.6	25 41.4	26 55.9	15 46.6
16 Tu	15 39 12	23 22 46	3♈21 22	10♈38 23	8 06.8	11 20.4	22 08.2	7 22.1	6 12.2	19 06.5	28 02.8	25 40.5	26 56.4	15 45.9
17 W	15 43 09	24 23 15	17 55 52	25 13 02	8 00.0	11 07.3	23 23.5	7 06.4	6 38.6	19 12.9	28 09.9	25 39.6	26 56.8	15 45.2
18 Th	15 47 05	25 23 45	2♉29 00	9♉42 56	7 52.9	10 44.0	24 38.9	6 51.3	7 04.9	19 19.4	28 17.0	25 38.7	26 57.2	15 44.5
19 F	15 51 02	26 24 16	16 53 59	24 01 23	7 46.5	10 10.2	25 54.3	6 37.0	7 31.1	19 26.1	28 24.2	25 37.9	26 57.6	15 43.8
20 Sa	15 54 58	27 24 49	1♊04 26	8♊02 35	7 41.5	9 25.9	27 09.7	6 23.4	7 57.3	19 33.0	28 31.3	25 37.1	26 58.0	15 43.0
21 Su	15 58 55	28 25 24	14 55 22	21 42 29	7 38.4	8 31.4	28 25.1	6 10.5	8 23.5	19 40.0	28 38.5	25 36.3	26 58.3	15 42.2
22 M	16 02 52	29 26 00	28 23 45	4♋59 10	7D37.2	7 27.8	29 40.5	5 58.3	8 49.7	19 47.2	28 45.6	25 35.7	26 58.5	15 41.5
23 Tu	16 06 48	0♐26 38	11♋28 49	17 52 55	7 37.6	6 16.2	0♐55.9	5 46.9	9 15.8	19 54.5	28 52.8	25 35.0	26 58.8	15 40.6
24 W	16 10 45	1 27 17	24 11 46	0♌25 48	7 39.0	4 58.7	2 11.4	5 36.3	9 41.8	20 02.0	28 59.9	25 34.4	26 59.0	15 39.8
25 Th	16 14 41	2 27 58	6♌35 29	12 41 20	7 40.8	3 37.5	3 26.8	5 26.4	10 07.9	20 09.6	29 07.1	25 33.9	26 59.2	15 38.9
26 F	16 18 38	3 28 41	18 43 56	24 43 53	7R42.2	2 15.2	4 42.2	5 17.3	10 33.9	20 17.4	29 14.2	25 33.4	26 59.3	15 38.1
27 Sa	16 22 34	4 29 25	0♍41 49	6♍38 22	7 42.6	0 54.7	5 57.6	5 09.1	10 59.8	20 25.4	29 21.3	25 33.0	26 59.4	15 37.2
28 Su	16 26 31	5 30 10	12 34 09	18 29 48	7 41.6	29♏38.7	7 13.1	5 01.6	11 25.7	20 33.4	29 28.5	25 32.6	26 59.5	15 36.3
29 M	16 30 27	6 30 57	24 25 55	0♎23 03	7 39.1	28 29.5	8 28.5	4 55.0	11 51.6	20 41.7	29 35.6	25 32.2	26R59.5	15 35.4
30 Tu	16 34 24	7 31 46	6♎21 47	12 22 34	7 35.3	27 29.1	9 44.0	4 49.2	12 17.4	20 50.0	29 42.7	25 32.0	26 59.5	15 34.4

December 1926 LONGITUDE

Day	Sid.Time	☉	0 hr ☽	Noon ☽	True ☊	☿	♀	♂	⚳	♃	♄	♅	♆	♇
1 W	16 38 21	8♐32 36	18♎25 53	24♎32 07	7♋30.6	26♏38.9	10♐59.4	4♉44.2	12♏43.1	20♒58.6	29♏49.8	25♓31.7	26♌59.5	15♋33.5
2 Th	16 42 17	9 33 27	0♏41 36	6♏54 36	7R25.6	25R59.8	12 14.9	4R40.0	13 08.9	21 07.2	29 56.9	25R31.5	26R59.4	15R32.5
3 F	16 46 14	10 34 20	13 11 21	19 31 59	7 20.8	25 32.3	13 30.3	4 36.7	13 34.5	21 16.0	0♐04.0	25 31.4	26 59.3	15 31.5
4 Sa	16 50 10	11 35 14	25 56 33	2♐25 04	7 16.8	25D16.1	14 45.8	4 34.1	14 00.1	21 25.0	0 11.0	25 31.3	26 59.2	15 30.5
5 Su	16 54 07	12 36 09	8♐57 29	15 33 41	7 14.0	25 11.0	16 01.2	4 32.4	14 25.7	21 34.0	0 18.1	25D31.3	26 59.0	15 29.5
6 M	16 58 03	13 37 05	22 13 31	28 56 46	7D12.6	25 16.4	17 16.7	4D31.5	14 51.2	21 43.3	0 25.1	25 31.3	26 58.8	15 28.4
7 Tu	17 02 00	14 38 02	5♑43 14	12♑32 40	7 12.4	25 31.5	18 32.2	4 31.5	15 16.7	21 52.6	0 32.1	25 31.4	26 58.5	15 27.4
8 W	17 05 56	15 39 00	19 24 48	26 19 22	7 13.3	25 55.4	19 47.6	4 32.2	15 42.1	22 02.1	0 39.1	25 31.5	26 58.3	15 26.3
9 Th	17 09 53	16 39 59	3♒16 08	10♒14 50	7 14.7	26 27.3	21 03.1	4 33.7	16 07.4	22 11.7	0 46.1	25 31.7	26 58.0	15 25.3
10 F	17 13 50	17 40 58	17 15 15	24 17 07	7 16.1	27 06.4	22 18.5	4 36.0	16 32.7	22 21.4	0 53.1	25 31.9	26 57.6	15 24.2
11 Sa	17 17 46	18 41 58	1♓20 14	8♓24 23	7R17.1	27 51.8	23 34.0	4 39.1	16 57.9	22 31.3	1 00.0	25 32.2	26 57.3	15 23.1
12 Su	17 21 43	19 42 58	15 29 19	22 34 47	7 17.3	28 42.8	24 49.4	4 42.9	17 23.1	22 41.2	1 06.9	25 32.5	26 56.8	15 22.0
13 M	17 25 39	20 43 59	29 40 34	6♈46 22	7 16.7	29 38.8	26 04.9	4 47.5	17 48.2	22 51.3	1 13.8	25 32.9	26 56.4	15 20.8
14 Tu	17 29 36	21 45 00	13♈51 52	20 56 46	7 15.4	0♐39.1	27 20.3	4 52.8	18 13.2	23 01.5	1 20.7	25 33.3	26 55.9	15 19.7
15 W	17 33 32	22 46 02	28 00 42	5♉03 16	7 13.6	1 43.2	28 35.7	4 58.9	18 38.2	23 11.9	1 27.5	25 33.8	26 55.4	15 18.6
16 Th	17 37 29	23 47 04	12♉04 06	19 02 48	7 11.6	2 50.5	29 51.2	5 05.6	19 03.0	23 22.3	1 34.3	25 34.4	26 54.9	15 17.4
17 F	17 41 25	24 48 07	25 58 57	2♊52 10	7 09.9	4 00.8	1♑06.6	5 13.1	19 27.9	23 32.9	1 41.1	25 35.0	26 54.3	15 16.3
18 Sa	17 45 22	25 49 10	9♊42 06	16 28 26	7 08.7	5 13.6	2 22.0	5 21.2	19 52.6	23 43.5	1 47.9	25 35.6	26 53.7	15 15.1
19 Su	17 49 19	26 50 14	23 10 52	29 49 12	7D08.1	6 28.6	3 37.5	5 30.0	20 17.3	23 54.3	1 54.6	25 36.3	26 53.1	15 13.9
20 M	17 53 15	27 51 19	6♋23 17	12♋53 02	7 08.1	7 45.5	4 52.9	5 39.5	20 42.0	24 05.2	2 01.3	25 37.0	26 52.4	15 12.7
21 Tu	17 57 12	28 52 24	19 18 26	25 39 34	7 08.5	9 04.2	6 08.3	5 49.6	21 06.5	24 16.2	2 08.0	25 37.8	26 51.7	15 11.5
22 W	18 01 08	29 53 30	1♌56 33	8♌09 36	7 09.2	10 24.3	7 23.7	6 00.3	21 31.0	24 27.3	2 14.6	25 38.7	26 51.0	15 10.3
23 Th	18 05 05	0♑54 36	14 19 00	20 25 05	7 10.0	11 45.7	8 39.1	6 11.6	21 55.4	24 38.5	2 21.2	25 39.6	26 50.2	15 09.1
24 F	18 09 01	1 55 43	26 28 14	2♍28 55	7 10.6	13 08.3	9 54.5	6 23.5	22 19.7	24 49.8	2 27.7	25 40.5	26 49.4	15 07.9
25 Sa	18 12 58	2 56 50	8♍27 36	14 24 49	7 11.1	14 31.9	11 09.9	6 36.0	22 44.0	25 01.2	2 34.2	25 41.5	26 48.6	15 06.7
26 Su	18 16 55	3 57 58	20 21 06	26 17 03	7R11.3	15 56.5	12 25.4	6 49.1	23 08.2	25 12.7	2 40.7	25 42.5	26 47.8	15 05.4
27 M	18 20 51	4 59 06	2♎13 14	8♎10 16	7 11.3	17 21.9	13 40.8	7 02.8	23 32.3	25 24.2	2 47.1	25 43.6	26 46.9	15 04.2
28 Tu	18 24 48	6 00 15	14 08 44	20 09 14	7 11.3	18 48.0	14 56.2	7 17.0	23 56.3	25 35.9	2 53.5	25 44.8	26 46.0	15 02.9
29 W	18 28 44	7 01 25	26 12 19	2♏18 32	7D11.2	20 14.8	16 11.6	7 31.8	24 20.2	25 47.7	2 59.9	25 46.0	26 45.1	15 01.7
30 Th	18 32 41	8 02 35	8♏28 25	14 42 24	7 11.3	21 42.2	17 27.0	7 47.0	24 44.1	25 59.6	3 06.2	25 47.2	26 44.1	15 00.4
31 F	18 36 37	9 03 45	21 00 53	27 24 14	7 11.4	23 10.2	18 42.4	8 02.8	25 07.8	26 11.5	3 12.5	25 48.5	26 43.1	14 59.2

Astro Data

	Dy Hr Mn
☽0S	3 2:51
♄□♆	6 4:57
☿R	15 15:19
☽0N	16 14:08
♆R	29 23:02
☽0S	30 11:26
☿D	5 11:22
♅D	5 13:51
♄□♇	6 21:53
♂D	7 2:25
☽0N	13 21:12
☽0S	27 20:14
♃⚺♅	29 8:04

Planet Ingress

		Dy Hr Mn
⚳	♏	2 11:35
♀	♐	22 18:12
☉	♐	23 1:28
☿	♏R	28 5:05
♄	♐	2 22:35
☿	♐	13 20:38
♀	♑	16 14:48
☉	♑	22 14:33

Last Aspect / ☽ Ingress (November)

Last Aspect Dy Hr Mn		☽ Ingress Dy Hr Mn
1 19:59	♄ ⚹	♎ 2 3:22
4 8:24	♆ ⚹	♏ 4 14:37
6 18:01	♄ ☌	♐ 6 23:51
9 1:29	♆ △	♑ 9 7:11
11 8:11	♄ ⚹	♒ 11 12:42
13 12:27	♄ □	♓ 13 16:22
15 15:04	♄ △	♈ 15 18:28
17 14:51	♆ △	♉ 17 19:54
19 19:30	♄ ☍	♊ 19 22:10
21 21:26	♆ ⚹	♋ 22 2:54
24 9:12	♄ △	♌ 24 11:10
26 21:09	♄ □	♍ 26 22:36
29 10:23	♄ ⚹	♎ 29 11:14

Last Aspect / ☽ Ingress (December)

Last Aspect Dy Hr Mn		☽ Ingress Dy Hr Mn
1 16:48	♆ ⚹	♏ 1 22:39
4 1:57	♆ □	♐ 4 7:32
6 8:30	♆ △	♑ 6 13:52
8 11:17	☿ ⚹	♒ 8 18:22
10 17:04	☿ □	♓ 10 21:44
12 23:05	☿ △	♈ 13 0:33
14 23:55	♀ △	♉ 15 3:23
17 1:37	♆ □	♊ 17 6:59
19 6:41	♆ ⚹	♋ 19 12:20
21 11:57	♅ △	♌ 21 20:17
24 0:43	♆ ☌	♍ 24 7:02
26 10:50	♅ ☍	♎ 26 19:31
29 1:05	♆ ⚹	♏ 29 7:28
31 10:43	♆ □	♐ 31 16:50

☽ Phases & Eclipses

Dy Hr Mn	
5 14:34	● 12♏26
12 23:01	☽ 19♒49
19 16:21	○ 26♉35
27 7:15	☾ 4♍17
5 6:11	● 12♐21
12 6:47	☽ 19♓30
19 6:09	○ 26♊35
19 6:20	A 1.026
27 4:59	☾ 4♎41

Astro Data

1 November 1926
Julian Day # 9801
SVP 6♓17'11"
GC 25♐49.0 ⚵ 15♎03.7
Eris 0♈12.1R ⚶ 2♓23.0
⚷ 29♈25.6R ⚴ 0♎59.4
☽ Mean ☊ 10♋10.6

1 December 1926
Julian Day # 9831
SVP 6♓17'07"
GC 25♐49.1 ⚵ 27♎59.5
Eris 0♈00.9R ⚶ 8♓46.4
⚷ 28♈11.2R ⚴ 14♎47.8
☽ Mean ☊ 8♋35.3

LONGITUDE — January 1927

Day	Sid.Time	☉	0 hr ☽	Noon ☽	True ☊	☿	♀	♂	⚳	♃	♄	♅	♆	♇
1 Sa	18 40 34	10♑04 56	3♐52 41	10♐26 25	7♋11.7	24♐38.8	19♑57.7	8♉19.2	25♏31.5	26♒23.6	3♐18.7	25♓49.8	26♌42.1	14♋57.9
2 Su	18 44 30	11 06 07	17 05 28	23 49 51	7R12.0	26 07.8	21 13.1	8 36.0	25 55.1	26 35.7	3 24.9	25 51.2	26R41.0	14R56.7
3 M	18 48 27	12 07 18	0♑39 23	7♑33 50	7 12.1	27 37.4	22 28.5	8 53.3	26 18.6	26 47.9	3 31.0	25 52.7	26 40.0	14 55.4
4 Tu	18 52 24	13 08 29	14 32 50	21 35 55	7 11.9	29 07.4	23 43.9	9 11.0	26 42.0	27 00.2	3 37.1	25 54.1	26 38.9	14 54.2
5 W	18 56 20	14 09 40	28 42 34	5♒52 10	7 11.4	0♑37.9	24 59.3	9 29.3	27 05.3	27 12.6	3 43.1	25 55.7	26 37.7	14 52.9
6 Th	19 00 17	15 10 51	13♒04 02	20 17 29	7 10.6	2 08.8	26 14.6	9 48.0	27 28.5	27 25.1	3 49.1	25 57.2	26 36.6	14 51.6
7 F	19 04 13	16 12 01	27 31 51	4♓46 25	7 09.5	3 40.1	27 30.0	10 07.1	27 51.6	27 37.6	3 55.0	25 58.9	26 35.4	14 50.4
8 Sa	19 08 10	17 13 11	12♓00 33	19 13 40	7 08.4	5 11.9	28 45.3	10 26.7	28 14.6	27 50.2	4 00.9	26 00.5	26 34.2	14 49.1
9 Su	19 12 06	18 14 21	26 25 15	3♈34 50	7 07.6	6 44.1	0♒00.6	10 46.7	28 37.5	28 02.9	4 06.7	26 02.2	26 33.0	14 47.8
10 M	19 16 03	19 15 29	10♈42 03	17 46 36	7D07.2	8 16.7	1 16.0	11 07.1	29 00.3	28 15.7	4 12.4	26 04.0	26 31.7	14 46.6
11 Tu	19 19 59	20 16 38	24 48 16	1♉46 53	7 07.5	9 49.8	2 31.3	11 27.9	29 23.0	28 28.5	4 18.1	26 05.8	26 30.5	14 45.3
12 W	19 23 56	21 17 45	8♉42 22	15 34 37	7 08.3	11 23.3	3 46.5	11 49.1	29 45.5	28 41.4	4 23.7	26 07.7	26 29.2	14 44.1
13 Th	19 27 53	22 18 53	22 23 37	29 09 23	7 09.5	12 57.3	5 01.8	12 10.7	0♐08.0	28 54.4	4 29.3	26 09.5	26 27.9	14 42.8
14 F	19 31 49	23 19 59	5♊51 55	12♊31 14	7 10.8	14 31.7	6 17.1	12 32.6	0 30.4	29 07.4	4 34.8	26 11.5	26 26.5	14 41.5
15 Sa	19 35 46	24 21 05	19 07 21	25 40 19	7R11.8	16 06.6	7 32.3	12 54.9	0 52.6	29 20.5	4 40.3	26 13.5	26 25.2	14 40.3
16 Su	19 39 42	25 22 10	2♋10 08	8♋36 51	7 12.2	17 42.1	8 47.6	13 17.5	1 14.7	29 33.7	4 45.7	26 15.5	26 23.8	14 39.1
17 M	19 43 39	26 23 15	15 00 28	21 21 02	7 11.5	19 18.0	10 02.8	13 40.5	1 36.7	29 46.9	4 51.0	26 17.5	26 22.4	14 37.8
18 Tu	19 47 35	27 24 19	27 38 36	3♌53 13	7 09.8	20 54.5	11 18.0	14 03.8	1 58.6	0♓00.2	4 56.3	26 19.6	26 21.0	14 36.6
19 W	19 51 32	28 25 23	10♌04 59	16 14 01	7 07.0	22 31.4	12 33.2	14 27.4	2 20.4	0 13.5	5 01.5	26 21.8	26 19.6	14 35.4
20 Th	19 55 28	29 26 26	22 20 27	28 24 29	7 03.4	24 09.0	13 48.4	14 51.3	2 42.1	0 26.9	5 06.6	26 24.0	26 18.1	14 34.2
21 F	19 59 25	0♒27 28	4♍26 20	10♍26 15	6 59.3	25 47.1	15 03.6	15 15.6	3 03.6	0 40.3	5 11.7	26 26.2	26 16.7	14 32.9
22 Sa	20 03 22	1 28 30	16 24 34	22 21 37	6 55.3	27 25.8	16 18.7	15 40.1	3 25.0	0 53.8	5 16.7	26 28.4	26 15.2	14 31.7
23 Su	20 07 18	2 29 32	28 17 50	4♎13 37	6 51.7	29 05.1	17 33.9	16 04.9	3 46.3	1 07.4	5 21.6	26 30.7	26 13.7	14 30.5
24 M	20 11 15	3 30 33	10♎09 29	16 05 55	6 49.0	0♒45.0	18 49.0	16 30.0	4 07.4	1 21.0	5 26.4	26 33.1	26 12.2	14 29.3
25 Tu	20 15 11	4 31 33	22 03 30	28 02 46	6D47.6	2 25.5	20 04.1	16 55.4	4 28.4	1 34.6	5 31.2	26 35.4	26 10.7	14 28.2
26 W	20 19 08	5 32 33	4♏04 20	10♏08 49	6 47.5	4 06.7	21 19.2	17 21.0	4 49.3	1 48.3	5 35.9	26 37.8	26 09.1	14 27.0
27 Th	20 23 04	6 33 32	16 16 47	22 28 51	6 48.5	5 48.5	22 34.3	17 46.9	5 10.0	2 02.1	5 40.6	26 40.3	26 07.6	14 25.8
28 F	20 27 01	7 34 31	28 45 36	5♐07 32	6 50.1	7 31.0	23 49.4	18 13.0	5 30.6	2 15.9	5 45.1	26 42.8	26 06.0	14 24.7
29 Sa	20 30 57	8 35 29	11♐35 10	18 08 52	6 51.8	9 14.1	25 04.4	18 39.4	5 51.1	2 29.7	5 49.6	26 45.3	26 04.4	14 23.5
30 Su	20 34 54	9 36 26	24 48 57	1♑35 38	6R52.9	10 57.8	26 19.5	19 06.1	6 11.4	2 43.6	5 54.0	26 47.9	26 02.8	14 22.4
31 M	20 38 51	10 37 23	8♑28 57	15 28 48	6 52.7	12 42.2	27 34.5	19 33.0	6 31.6	2 57.5	5 58.4	26 50.4	26 01.2	14 21.3

LONGITUDE — February 1927

Day	Sid.Time	☉	0 hr ☽	Noon ☽	True ☊	☿	♀	♂	⚳	♃	♄	♅	♆	♇
1 Tu	20 42 47	11♒38 18	22♑34 57	29♑46 56	6♋50.8	14♒27.3	28♒49.5	20♉00.1	6♐51.6	3♓11.5	6♐02.6	26♓53.1	25♌59.6	14♋20.2
2 W	20 46 44	12 39 13	7♒04 08	14♒25 47	6R47.2	16 12.9	0♓04.5	20 27.5	7 11.5	3 25.5	6 06.8	26 55.7	25R58.0	14R19.1
3 Th	20 50 40	13 40 06	21 50 55	29 18 31	6 42.1	17 59.2	1 19.5	20 55.1	7 31.2	3 39.5	6 10.9	26 58.4	25 56.4	14 18.0
4 F	20 54 37	14 40 59	6♓47 28	14♓16 35	6 36.2	19 45.9	2 34.4	21 22.9	7 50.7	3 53.6	6 14.9	27 01.1	25 54.7	14 16.9
5 Sa	20 58 33	15 41 50	21 44 47	29 10 59	6 30.3	21 33.2	3 49.3	21 50.9	8 10.1	4 07.7	6 18.8	27 03.9	25 53.1	14 15.8
6 Su	21 02 30	16 42 39	6♈34 14	13♈53 45	6 25.3	23 20.9	5 04.2	22 19.1	8 29.3	4 21.8	6 22.7	27 06.6	25 51.4	14 14.8
7 M	21 06 26	17 43 27	21 08 51	28 19 04	6 21.8	25 08.9	6 19.1	22 47.6	8 48.4	4 36.0	6 26.4	27 09.5	25 49.8	14 13.8
8 Tu	21 10 23	18 44 13	5♉24 05	12♉23 44	6D20.1	26 57.2	7 34.0	23 16.2	9 07.2	4 50.2	6 30.1	27 12.3	25 48.1	14 12.7
9 W	21 14 20	19 44 58	19 18 01	26 07 00	6 20.1	28 45.6	8 48.8	23 45.0	9 26.0	5 04.4	6 33.7	27 15.2	25 46.4	14 11.7
10 Th	21 18 16	20 45 42	2♊50 52	9♊29 53	6 21.2	0♓34.0	10 03.6	24 14.0	9 44.5	5 18.6	6 37.2	27 18.1	25 44.7	14 10.7
11 F	21 22 13	21 46 23	16 04 20	22 34 34	6 22.6	2 22.2	11 18.3	24 43.2	10 02.9	5 32.9	6 40.6	27 21.0	25 43.1	14 09.8
12 Sa	21 26 09	22 47 03	29 00 54	5♋23 40	6R23.3	4 09.9	12 33.1	25 12.5	10 21.0	5 47.2	6 43.9	27 23.9	25 41.4	14 08.8
13 Su	21 30 06	23 47 42	11♋43 12	17 59 47	6 22.6	5 57.0	13 47.8	25 42.0	10 39.0	6 01.5	6 47.1	27 26.9	25 39.7	14 07.9
14 M	21 34 02	24 48 19	24 13 40	0♌25 08	6 19.7	7 43.1	15 02.4	26 11.7	10 56.9	6 15.8	6 50.3	27 29.9	25 38.0	14 07.0
15 Tu	21 37 59	25 48 54	6♌34 22	12 41 33	6 14.4	9 27.9	16 17.1	26 41.6	11 14.5	6 30.2	6 53.3	27 32.9	25 36.3	14 06.0
16 W	21 41 55	26 49 28	18 46 52	24 50 28	6 06.8	11 11.0	17 31.7	27 11.5	11 32.0	6 44.6	6 56.3	27 36.0	25 34.7	14 05.2
17 Th	21 45 52	27 50 00	0♍52 28	6♍53 02	5 57.3	12 52.0	18 46.3	27 41.7	11 49.2	6 59.0	6 59.2	27 39.0	25 33.0	14 04.3
18 F	21 49 49	28 50 31	12 52 18	18 50 27	5 46.7	14 30.4	20 00.8	28 12.0	12 06.3	7 13.4	7 01.9	27 42.1	25 31.3	14 03.4
19 Sa	21 53 45	29 51 00	24 47 39	0♎44 07	5 35.9	16 05.7	21 15.3	28 42.4	12 23.1	7 27.8	7 04.6	27 45.2	25 29.6	14 02.6
20 Su	21 57 42	0♓51 28	6♎40 06	12 35 53	5 25.9	17 37.3	22 29.8	29 13.0	12 39.8	7 42.2	7 07.2	27 48.3	25 27.9	14 01.8
21 M	22 01 38	1 51 54	18 31 49	24 28 15	5 17.6	19 04.6	23 44.3	29 43.7	12 56.2	7 56.6	7 09.7	27 51.5	25 26.3	14 01.0
22 Tu	22 05 35	2 52 19	0♏25 37	6♏24 23	5 11.5	20 27.0	24 58.7	0♊14.5	13 12.5	8 11.1	7 12.1	27 54.7	25 24.6	14 00.2
23 W	22 09 31	3 52 43	12 25 03	18 28 11	5 07.9	21 43.8	26 13.1	0 45.5	13 28.5	8 25.6	7 14.4	27 57.8	25 22.9	13 59.4
24 Th	22 13 28	4 53 05	24 34 20	0♐44 07	5D06.4	22 54.4	27 27.5	1 16.6	13 44.4	8 40.0	7 16.6	28 01.1	25 21.3	13 58.7
25 F	22 17 24	5 53 26	6♐58 08	13 17 01	5 06.6	23 58.2	28 41.8	1 47.8	14 00.0	8 54.5	7 18.7	28 04.3	25 19.6	13 58.0
26 Sa	22 21 21	6 53 45	19 41 21	26 11 42	5R07.3	24 54.5	29 56.1	2 19.2	14 15.3	9 09.0	7 20.7	28 07.5	25 18.0	13 57.3
27 Su	22 25 18	7 54 03	2♑48 34	9♑32 22	5 07.4	25 42.8	1♈10.3	2 50.7	14 30.5	9 23.5	7 22.7	28 10.8	25 16.3	13 56.6
28 M	22 29 14	8 54 20	16 23 24	23 21 49	5 06.0	26 22.7	2 24.6	3 22.3	14 45.4	9 38.0	7 24.5	28 14.1	25 14.7	13 55.9

Astro Data	Planet Ingress	Last Aspect	☽ Ingress	Last Aspect	☽ Ingress	☽ Phases & Eclipses	Astro Data
Dy Hr Mn	Dy Hr Mn	Dy Hr Mn	Dy Hr Mn	Dy Hr Mn	Dy Hr Mn	Dy Hr Mn	1 January 1927
♃☍♆ 2 21:39	☿ ♑ 5 1:58	2 17:02 ♆ △	♑ 2 22:51	1 7:10 ♅ ✶	♒ 1 12:22	3 20:28 ● 12♑29	Julian Day # 9862
☽0N 10 2:36	♀ ♒ 9 11:48	4 19:17 ♅ ✶	♒ 5 2:10	3 6:36 ♆ ☍	♓ 3 13:07	3 20:22:28 ● A 00'02"	SVP 6♓17'02"
♃□♇ 16 20:59	⚳ ♐ 13 3:27	6 23:59 ♃ ☌	♓ 7 4:05	5 8:34 ♅ ☌	♈ 5 13:19	10 14:43 ☽ 19♈22	GC 25♐49.2 ⚴ 10♏04.6
♅⊼♆ 18 21:22	♃ ♓ 18 11:44	9 5:26 ♀ ✶	♈ 9 5:59	7 7:50 ♆ △	♉ 7 14:50	17 22:27 ○ 26♋50	Eris 0♈00.1 ⚵ 20♓19.3
☽0S 24 3:58	☉ ♒ 21 1:12	11 6:13 ♃ ✶	♉ 11 8:56	9 17:25 ♅ □	♊ 9 18:54	26 2:05 ☾ 5♏07	⚷ 27♈32.9R ⚶ 27♎58.9
	☿ ♒ 24 1:13	13 11:33 ♃ □	♊ 13 13:30	11 20:55 ♅ □	♋ 12 1:51		☽ Mean ☊ 6♋56.8
☽0N 6 8:50		15 18:53 ♃ △	♋ 15 19:59	14 6:18 ♅ △	♌ 14 11:11	2 8:54 ● 12♒31	
♃□♄ 17 12:25	♀ ♓ 2 10:33	17 22:27 ☉ ☍	♌ 18 4:31	16 16:52 ♂ □	♍ 16 22:15	8 23:54 ☽ 19♉14	1 February 1927
☽0S 20 10:18	☿ ♓ 10 4:28	20 7:50 ♆ ☌	♍ 20 15:10	19 7:43 ♂ △	♎ 19 10:31	16 16:18 ○ 27♌00	Julian Day # 9893
☿0N 27 9:37	☉ ♓ 19 15:34	22 23:54 ♅ △	♎ 23 3:27	21 13:57 ♅ ✶	♏ 21 23:08	24 20:42 ☾ 5♐15	SVP 6♓16'56"
♀0N 28 12:23	♂ ♊ 22 0:43	25 8:16 ♆ ✶	♏ 25 15:54	24 6:42 ♅ △	♐ 24 10:35		GC 25♐49.3 ⚴ 19♏55.3
	♀ ♈ 26 13:16	27 20:03 ♅ △	♐ 28 2:21	26 15:32 ♅ □	♑ 26 18:56		Eris 0♈10.8 ⚵ 5♈01.1
		30 3:30 ♅ □	♑ 30 9:12	28 20:17 ♅ ✶	♒ 28 23:14		⚷ 27♈48.3 ⚶ 8♏57.3
							☽ Mean ☊ 5♋18.4

March 1927 LONGITUDE

Day	Sid.Time	☉	0 hr ☽	Noon ☽	True ☊	☿	♀	♂	⚳	♃	♄	♅	♆	♇
1 Tu	22 33 11	9♓54 35	0♒27 36	7♒40 32	5♋02.2	26♓53.6	3♈38.8	3♊54.0	15♐00.1	9♓52.5	7♐26.2	28♓17.3	25♌13.1	13♋55.3
2 W	22 37 07	10 54 49	15 00 10	22 25 49	4R 55.8	27 15.4	4 52.9	4 25.8	15 14.6	10 07.0	7 27.8	28 20.7	25R 11.5	13R 54.7
3 Th	22 41 04	11 55 00	29 56 35	7♓31 21	4 47.0	27R 27.7	6 07.0	4 57.7	15 28.8	10 21.4	7 29.3	28 24.0	25 09.9	13 54.1
4 F	22 45 00	12 55 10	15♓08 50	22 47 39	4 36.8	27 30.7	7 21.1	5 29.8	15 42.8	10 35.9	7 30.8	28 27.3	25 08.3	13 53.5
5 Sa	22 48 57	13 55 18	0♈26 19	8♈03 26	4 26.3	27 24.3	8 35.2	6 01.9	15 56.5	10 50.4	7 32.1	28 30.6	25 06.7	13 52.9
6 Su	22 52 53	14 55 24	15 37 37	23 07 42	4 17.0	27 09.0	9 49.2	6 34.2	16 10.0	11 04.9	7 33.3	28 34.0	25 05.1	13 52.4
7 M	22 56 50	15 55 28	0♉32 38	7♉51 40	4 09.7	26 45.0	11 03.1	7 06.6	16 23.2	11 19.4	7 34.4	28 37.3	25 03.5	13 51.9
8 Tu	23 00 47	16 55 29	15 04 12	22 09 55	4 05.0	26 13.1	12 17.0	7 39.0	16 36.2	11 33.8	7 35.4	28 40.7	25 02.0	13 51.4
9 W	23 04 43	17 55 29	29 08 42	6♊00 35	4D 02.8	25 34.1	13 30.9	8 11.6	16 48.9	11 48.3	7 36.3	28 44.1	25 00.5	13 50.9
10 Th	23 08 40	18 55 26	12♊45 47	19 24 38	4 02.3	24 49.0	14 44.7	8 44.2	17 01.3	12 02.7	7 37.2	28 47.5	24 59.0	13 50.5
11 F	23 12 36	19 55 22	25 57 33	2♋25 01	4R 02.4	23 58.8	15 58.5	9 17.0	17 13.5	12 17.2	7 37.9	28 50.9	24 57.5	13 50.1
12 Sa	23 16 33	20 55 15	8♋47 32	15 05 38	4 02.0	23 04.8	17 12.2	9 49.8	17 25.4	12 31.6	7 38.5	28 54.3	24 56.0	13 49.7
13 Su	23 20 29	21 55 06	21 19 51	27 30 40	3 59.9	22 08.2	18 25.9	10 22.7	17 37.0	12 46.0	7 39.0	28 57.7	24 54.5	13 49.3
14 M	23 24 26	22 54 54	3♌38 34	9♌43 59	3 55.3	21 10.5	19 39.5	10 55.7	17 48.4	13 00.4	7 39.4	29 01.1	24 53.1	13 49.0
15 Tu	23 28 22	23 54 41	15 47 20	21 48 57	3 47.6	20 12.8	20 53.1	11 28.8	17 59.4	13 14.7	7 39.7	29 04.5	24 51.6	13 48.6
16 W	23 32 19	24 54 25	27 49 09	3♍48 13	3 37.1	19 16.5	22 06.6	12 01.9	18 10.2	13 29.1	7 39.9	29 07.9	24 50.2	13 48.3
17 Th	23 36 16	25 54 07	9♍46 22	15 43 49	3 24.2	18 22.5	23 20.1	12 35.1	18 20.7	13 43.4	7R 40.0	29 11.4	24 48.8	13 48.0
18 F	23 40 12	26 53 47	21 40 45	27 37 20	3 09.9	17 31.9	24 33.5	13 08.4	18 30.9	13 57.7	7 40.0	29 14.8	24 47.4	13 47.8
19 Sa	23 44 09	27 53 25	3♎33 42	9♎30 01	2 55.3	16 45.5	25 46.9	13 41.8	18 40.8	14 12.0	7 39.9	29 18.2	24 46.1	13 47.5
20 Su	23 48 05	28 53 01	15 26 28	21 23 12	2 41.5	16 03.9	27 00.2	14 15.2	18 50.4	14 26.3	7 39.7	29 21.6	24 44.7	13 47.3
21 M	23 52 02	29 52 36	27 20 28	3♏18 28	2 29.7	15 27.8	28 13.4	14 48.7	18 59.7	14 40.5	7 39.4	29 25.1	24 43.4	13 47.2
22 Tu	23 55 58	0♈52 08	9♏17 31	15 17 56	2 20.6	14 57.3	29 26.7	15 22.3	19 08.7	14 54.7	7 39.0	29 28.5	24 42.1	13 47.0
23 W	23 59 55	1 51 39	21 20 03	27 24 19	2 14.4	14 32.8	0♉39.8	15 55.9	19 17.3	15 08.9	7 38.5	29 31.9	24 40.8	13 46.8
24 Th	0 03 51	2 51 07	3♐31 10	9♐41 06	2 11.1	14 14.3	1 52.9	16 29.6	19 25.7	15 23.1	7 37.9	29 35.3	24 39.6	13 46.7
25 F	0 07 48	3 50 34	15 54 39	22 12 22	2 09.9	14 01.8	3 06.0	17 03.4	19 33.7	15 37.2	7 37.2	29 38.8	24 38.3	13 46.6
26 Sa	0 11 44	4 50 00	28 34 48	5♑02 31	2 09.7	13D 55.4	4 19.0	17 37.2	19 41.4	15 51.3	7 36.5	29 42.2	24 37.1	13 46.6
27 Su	0 15 41	5 49 23	11♑36 04	18 15 55	2 09.4	13 54.8	5 31.9	18 11.1	19 48.8	16 05.4	7 35.6	29 45.6	24 35.9	13 46.5
28 M	0 19 38	6 48 45	25 02 30	1♒56 07	2 07.8	13 59.8	6 44.8	18 45.1	19 55.9	16 19.5	7 34.6	29 49.0	24 34.8	13D 46.5
29 Tu	0 23 34	7 48 05	8♒56 56	16 04 58	2 03.9	14 10.3	7 57.6	19 19.1	20 02.6	16 33.5	7 33.5	29 52.4	24 33.6	13 46.5
30 W	0 27 31	8 47 23	23 20 01	0♓41 38	1 57.3	14 26.1	9 10.4	19 53.2	20 09.0	16 47.4	7 32.3	29 55.8	24 32.5	13 46.6
31 Th	0 31 27	9 46 40	8♓09 11	15 41 45	1 48.2	14 46.8	10 23.2	20 27.3	20 15.0	17 01.4	7 31.0	29 59.2	24 31.4	13 46.6

April 1927 LONGITUDE

Day	Sid.Time	☉	0 hr ☽	Noon ☽	True ☊	☿	♀	♂	⚳	♃	♄	♅	♆	♇
1 F	0 35 24	10♈45 54	23♓18 14	0♈57 20	1♋37.5	15♓12.2	11♉35.8	21♊01.5	20♐20.7	17♓15.3	7♐29.6	0♈02.6	24♌30.4	13♋46.7
2 Sa	0 39 20	11 45 06	8♈37 36	16 17 33	1R 26.3	15 42.2	12 48.4	21 35.8	20 26.0	17 29.1	7R 28.2	0 06.0	24R 29.3	13 46.8
3 Su	0 43 17	12 44 17	23 55 43	1♉30 41	1 16.1	16 16.4	14 01.0	22 10.1	20 31.0	17 43.0	7 26.6	0 09.4	24 28.3	13 46.9
4 M	0 47 13	13 43 25	9♉01 12	16 26 13	1 08.0	16 54.7	15 13.5	22 44.4	20 35.6	17 56.7	7 24.9	0 12.7	24 27.3	13 47.1
5 Tu	0 51 10	14 42 31	23 44 54	0♊56 39	1 02.5	17 36.8	16 25.9	23 18.8	20 39.8	18 10.5	7 23.2	0 16.1	24 26.3	13 47.3
6 W	0 55 07	15 41 35	8♊01 07	14 58 09	0 59.6	18 22.5	17 38.2	23 53.3	20 43.7	18 24.2	7 21.3	0 19.4	24 25.4	13 47.5
7 Th	0 59 03	16 40 36	21 47 49	28 30 21	0D 58.7	19 11.7	18 50.5	24 27.8	20 47.2	18 37.8	7 19.4	0 22.8	24 24.5	13 47.7
8 F	1 03 00	17 39 36	5♋06 05	11♋35 29	0R 58.9	20 04.1	20 02.7	25 02.4	20 50.4	18 51.4	7 17.3	0 26.1	24 23.6	13 47.9
9 Sa	1 06 56	18 38 32	17 59 04	24 17 25	0 58.8	20 59.5	21 14.9	25 37.0	20 53.2	19 04.9	7 15.2	0 29.4	24 22.8	13 48.2
10 Su	1 10 53	19 37 27	0♌31 07	6♌40 47	0 57.5	21 57.9	22 27.0	26 11.6	20 55.6	19 18.4	7 13.0	0 32.7	24 22.0	13 48.5
11 M	1 14 49	20 36 19	12 47 00	18 50 20	0 54.0	22 59.1	23 39.0	26 46.3	20 57.6	19 31.9	7 10.7	0 36.0	24 21.2	13 48.8
12 Tu	1 18 46	21 35 09	24 51 19	0♍50 27	0 47.9	24 03.0	24 50.9	27 21.1	20 59.3	19 45.3	7 08.4	0 39.2	24 20.4	13 49.2
13 W	1 22 42	22 33 57	6♍48 12	12 44 59	0 39.2	25 09.4	26 02.8	27 55.8	21 00.6	19 58.6	7 05.9	0 42.5	24 19.7	13 49.5
14 Th	1 26 39	23 32 42	18 41 08	24 37 01	0 28.4	26 18.3	27 14.5	28 30.6	21 01.5	20 11.9	7 03.4	0 45.7	24 19.0	13 49.9
15 F	1 30 36	24 31 26	0♎32 55	6♎29 03	0 16.2	27 29.5	28 26.2	29 05.5	21R 02.0	20 25.1	7 00.7	0 48.9	24 18.3	13 50.3
16 Sa	1 34 32	25 30 07	12 25 39	18 22 55	0 03.8	28 43.0	29 37.9	29 40.4	21 02.2	20 38.3	6 58.0	0 52.1	24 17.7	13 50.8
17 Su	1 38 29	26 28 47	24 21 00	0♏20 05	29♊52.0	29 58.7	0♊49.4	0♋15.3	21 01.9	20 51.4	6 55.2	0 55.3	24 17.1	13 51.2
18 M	1 42 25	27 27 24	6♏20 19	12 21 52	29 42.0	1♈16.5	2 00.9	0 50.3	21 01.3	21 04.4	6 52.4	0 58.4	24 16.5	13 51.7
19 Tu	1 46 22	28 26 00	18 24 55	24 29 40	29 34.3	2 36.4	3 12.3	1 25.3	21 00.3	21 17.4	6 49.4	1 01.6	24 15.9	13 52.2
20 W	1 50 18	29 24 34	0♐36 20	6♐45 11	29 29.3	3 58.3	4 23.6	2 00.3	20 58.9	21 30.3	6 46.4	1 04.7	24 15.4	13 52.8
21 Th	1 54 15	0♉23 06	12 56 30	19 10 37	29D 26.8	5 22.2	5 34.8	2 35.4	20 57.1	21 43.2	6 43.3	1 07.8	24 14.9	13 53.3
22 F	1 58 11	1 21 36	25 27 53	1♑48 40	29 26.3	6 48.0	6 45.9	3 10.5	20 54.9	21 56.0	6 40.2	1 10.9	24 14.5	13 53.9
23 Sa	2 02 08	2 20 05	8♑13 24	14 42 29	29 26.9	8 15.7	7 57.0	3 45.6	20 52.4	22 08.7	6 37.0	1 14.0	24 14.0	13 54.5
24 Su	2 06 05	3 18 32	21 16 20	27 55 20	29R 27.7	9 45.3	9 08.0	4 20.8	20 49.4	22 21.4	6 33.7	1 17.0	24 13.7	13 55.1
25 M	2 10 01	4 16 58	4♒39 50	11♒30 07	29 27.6	11 16.7	10 18.9	4 56.0	20 46.1	22 34.0	6 30.3	1 20.0	24 13.3	13 55.8
26 Tu	2 13 58	5 15 22	18 26 23	25 28 43	29 25.8	12 50.0	11 29.7	5 31.3	20 42.4	22 46.5	6 26.9	1 23.0	24 13.0	13 56.4
27 W	2 17 54	6 13 45	2♓37 02	9♓51 06	29 21.9	14 25.1	12 40.4	6 06.6	20 38.3	22 59.0	6 23.4	1 26.0	24 12.7	13 57.1
28 Th	2 21 51	7 12 05	17 10 31	24 34 40	29 16.1	16 02.0	13 51.1	6 41.9	20 33.8	23 11.3	6 19.8	1 28.9	24 12.4	13 57.8
29 F	2 25 47	8 10 25	2♈02 44	9♈33 45	29 08.8	17 40.7	15 01.7	7 17.2	20 28.9	23 23.7	6 16.2	1 31.8	24 12.2	13 58.5
30 Sa	2 29 44	9 08 42	17 06 37	24 40 06	29 01.1	19 21.2	16 12.1	7 52.6	20 23.7	23 35.9	6 12.5	1 34.7	24 12.0	13 59.3

Astro Data

	Dy Hr Mn
☿R	4 7:33
☽0N	5 17:39
☿0S	13 18:42
♃△♇	17 19:37
♄R	18 0:48
☽0S	19 16:00
☉0N	21 14:59
☿D	27 2:32
♇D	28 16:01
☽0N	2 4:27
☽0S	15 22:06
⚳R	16 8:59
☿0N	22 3:11
☽0N	29 15:15

Planet Ingress

	Dy Hr Mn
☉ ♈	21 14:59
♀ ♉	22 22:56
♅ ♈	31 17:26
♀ ♊	16 19:25
☊ ♊R	16 19:27
♂ ♋	17 1:29
☿ ♈	17 12:24
☉ ♉	21 2:32

Last Aspect / ☽ Ingress

Last Aspect Dy Hr Mn		☽ Ingress Dy Hr Mn
2 16:25 ♆ ☍	♓	3 0:05
4 20:55 ♅ ☌	♈	4 23:19
6 15:09 ♅ △	♉	6 23:07
8 23:14 ♅ ✶	♊	9 1:29
11 5:19 ♅ □	♋	11 7:29
13 14:51 ♅ △	♌	13 16:52
15 18:04 ♆ ☌	♍	16 4:22
18 15:18 ♅ ☍	♎	18 16:48
21 0:37 ♀ ☍	♏	21 5:21
23 16:12 ♅ △	♐	23 17:06
26 2:03 ♅ □	♑	26 2:39
28 8:19 ♅ ✶	♒	28 8:39
30 2:00 ♆ ☍	♓	30 10:53

Last Aspect Dy Hr Mn		☽ Ingress Dy Hr Mn
31 19:48 ♂ □	♈	1 10:30
3 0:52 ♆ △	♉	3 9:36
5 1:09 ♆ □	♊	5 10:25
7 4:39 ♆ ✶	♋	7 14:42
9 5:35 ♀ ✶	♌	9 23:00
12 4:38 ♂ ✶	♍	12 10:19
14 20:17 ♂ □	♎	14 22:53
17 3:35 ☉ ☍	♏	17 11:20
19 11:33 ♆ □	♐	19 22:49
21 21:41 ♆ △	♑	22 8:35
24 1:48 ♃ ✶	♒	24 15:43
26 9:52 ♆ ☍	♓	26 19:37
28 9:43 ♃ ☌	♈	28 20:43
30 11:15 ♆ △	♉	30 20:28

☽ Phases & Eclipses

Dy Hr Mn		
3 19:25	●	12♓14
10 11:03	☽	18♊53
18 10:24	○	26♍50
26 11:35	☾	4♑49
2 4:24	●	11♈26
9 0:21	☽	18♋10
17 3:35	○	26♎08
24 22:21	☾	3♒44

Astro Data

1 March 1927
Julian Day # 9921
SVP 6♓16'53"
GC 25♐49.3 ⚴ 25♏32.1
Eris 0♈28.1 ⚵ 19♈58.0
⚷ 28♈46.2 ⚶ 15♏25.0
☽ Mean ☊ 3♋49.4

1 April 1927
Julian Day # 9952
SVP 6♓16'50"
GC 25♐49.4 ⚴ 25♏55.1R
Eris 0♈50.9 ⚵ 7♉36.4
⚷ 0♉24.5 ⚶ 16♏22.5R
☽ Mean ☊ 2♋10.9

LONGITUDE May 1927

Day	Sid.Time	☉	0 hr ☽	Noon ☽	True ☊	☿	♀	♂	⚳	♃	♄	♅	♆	♇
1 Su	2 33 40	10♉06 58	2♉12 56	9♉43 52	28♊54.0	21♈03.5	17♊22.5	8♋28.0	20♐18.0	23♓48.0	6♐08.8	1♈37.6	24♌11.8	14♋00.1
2 M	2 37 37	11 05 13	17 11 41	24 35 20	28R 48.3	22 47.7	18 32.8	9 03.5	20R 12.1	24 00.1	6R 05.0	1 40.4	24R 11.7	14 00.8
3 Tu	2 41 33	12 03 25	1♊53 52	9♊06 33	28 44.7	24 33.6	19 43.0	9 39.0	20 05.7	24 12.1	6 01.2	1 43.2	24 11.6	14 01.7
4 W	2 45 30	13 01 36	16 12 49	23 12 20	28D 43.1	26 21.4	20 53.1	10 14.5	19 59.0	24 24.0	5 57.3	1 46.0	24 11.5	14 02.5
5 Th	2 49 27	13 59 45	0♋04 56	6♋50 38	28 43.2	28 11.0	22 03.1	10 50.1	19 51.9	24 35.8	5 53.3	1 48.8	24D 11.5	14 03.3
6 F	2 53 23	14 57 51	13 29 34	20 02 04	28 44.4	0♉02.5	23 12.9	11 25.6	19 44.5	24 47.5	5 49.3	1 51.5	24 11.5	14 04.2
7 Sa	2 57 20	15 55 56	26 28 29	2♌49 19	28 45.7	1 55.7	24 22.7	12 01.2	19 36.7	24 59.2	5 45.3	1 54.2	24 11.5	14 05.1
8 Su	3 01 16	16 53 59	9♌05 05	15 16 21	28R 46.4	3 50.8	25 32.4	12 36.9	19 28.6	25 10.7	5 41.2	1 56.9	24 11.6	14 06.0
9 M	3 05 13	17 52 00	21 23 43	27 27 46	28 45.9	5 47.7	26 42.0	13 12.5	19 20.2	25 22.2	5 37.1	1 59.5	24 11.7	14 07.0
10 Tu	3 09 09	18 49 59	3♍29 05	9♍28 16	28 43.7	7 46.4	27 51.4	13 48.2	19 11.4	25 33.6	5 33.0	2 02.1	24 11.8	14 07.9
11 W	3 13 06	19 47 56	15 25 52	21 22 24	28 39.9	9 46.8	29 00.7	14 23.9	19 02.3	25 44.9	5 28.8	2 04.7	24 12.0	14 08.9
12 Th	3 17 03	20 45 52	27 18 21	3♎14 11	28 34.5	11 48.9	0♋09.9	14 59.6	18 53.0	25 56.0	5 24.5	2 07.2	24 12.1	14 09.9
13 F	3 20 59	21 43 46	9♎10 19	15 07 07	28 28.3	13 52.6	1 19.0	15 35.4	18 43.3	26 07.1	5 20.3	2 09.7	24 12.4	14 10.9
14 Sa	3 24 56	22 41 38	21 04 55	27 04 01	28 21.7	15 57.9	2 28.0	16 11.2	18 33.3	26 18.1	5 16.0	2 12.2	24 12.6	14 11.9
15 Su	3 28 52	23 39 28	3♏04 40	9♏07 06	28 15.6	18 04.6	3 36.8	16 47.0	18 23.1	26 29.0	5 11.7	2 14.6	24 12.9	14 12.9
16 M	3 32 49	24 37 17	15 11 30	21 18 03	28 10.4	20 12.6	4 45.5	17 22.8	18 12.6	26 39.8	5 07.4	2 17.0	24 13.3	14 14.0
17 Tu	3 36 45	25 35 05	27 26 53	3♐38 09	28 06.6	22 21.7	5 54.1	17 58.6	18 01.8	26 50.5	5 03.0	2 19.4	24 13.6	14 15.1
18 W	3 40 42	26 32 51	9♐51 59	16 08 30	28D 04.4	24 31.8	7 02.6	18 34.5	17 50.8	27 01.1	4 58.6	2 21.7	24 14.0	14 16.1
19 Th	3 44 38	27 30 36	22 27 50	28 50 08	28 03.8	26 42.6	8 10.9	19 10.4	17 39.5	27 11.6	4 54.2	2 24.0	24 14.4	14 17.3
20 F	3 48 35	28 28 19	5♑15 32	11♑44 12	28 04.4	28 53.9	9 19.0	19 46.3	17 28.0	27 22.0	4 49.8	2 26.3	24 14.9	14 18.4
21 Sa	3 52 32	29 26 02	18 16 17	24 51 58	28 05.8	1♊05.5	10 27.1	20 22.2	17 16.3	27 32.2	4 45.4	2 28.5	24 15.4	14 19.5
22 Su	3 56 28	0♊23 43	1♒31 24	8♒14 46	28 07.3	3 17.0	11 35.0	20 58.2	17 04.4	27 42.4	4 40.9	2 30.7	24 15.9	14 20.7
23 M	4 00 25	1 21 24	15 02 10	21 53 44	28R 08.5	5 28.3	12 42.7	21 34.2	16 52.3	27 52.5	4 36.5	2 32.8	24 16.5	14 21.9
24 Tu	4 04 21	2 19 03	28 49 29	5♓49 26	28 08.7	7 39.0	13 50.4	22 10.2	16 40.0	28 02.4	4 32.0	2 34.9	24 17.0	14 23.0
25 W	4 08 18	3 16 41	12♓53 28	20 01 24	28 07.9	9 48.8	14 57.8	22 46.3	16 27.5	28 12.2	4 27.6	2 37.0	24 17.7	14 24.2
26 Th	4 12 14	4 14 18	27 12 56	4♈27 40	28 06.0	11 57.5	16 05.1	23 22.3	16 14.9	28 21.9	4 23.1	2 39.1	24 18.3	14 25.5
27 F	4 16 11	5 11 55	11♈45 05	19 04 32	28 03.3	14 04.9	17 12.3	23 58.4	16 02.1	28 31.5	4 18.6	2 41.0	24 19.0	14 26.7
28 Sa	4 20 07	6 09 30	26 25 19	3♉46 35	28 00.4	16 10.6	18 19.3	24 34.5	15 49.2	28 41.0	4 14.2	2 43.0	24 19.7	14 27.9
29 Su	4 24 04	7 07 05	11♉07 31	18 27 13	27 57.6	18 14.6	19 26.1	25 10.6	15 36.2	28 50.4	4 09.7	2 44.9	24 20.4	14 29.2
30 M	4 28 01	8 04 39	25 44 48	2♊59 26	27 55.6	20 16.6	20 32.8	25 46.8	15 23.1	28 59.6	4 05.2	2 46.8	24 21.2	14 30.5
31 Tu	4 31 57	9 02 11	10♊10 22	17 16 56	27D 54.4	22 16.5	21 39.3	26 23.0	15 09.9	29 08.7	4 00.8	2 48.6	24 22.0	14 31.8

LONGITUDE June 1927

Day	Sid.Time	☉	0 hr ☽	Noon ☽	True ☊	☿	♀	♂	⚳	♃	♄	♅	♆	♇
1 W	4 35 54	9♊59 43	24♊18 34	1♋14 50	27♊54.1	24♊14.1	22♋45.7	26♋59.2	14♐56.6	29♓17.7	3♐56.3	2♈50.4	24♌22.9	14♋33.1
2 Th	4 39 50	10 57 13	8♋05 28	14 50 17	27 54.7	26 09.4	23 51.8	27 35.5	14R 43.3	29 26.5	3R 51.9	2 52.2	24 23.7	14 34.4
3 F	4 43 47	11 54 43	21 29 15	28 02 27	27 55.8	28 02.2	24 57.8	28 11.7	14 30.0	29 35.2	3 47.5	2 53.9	24 24.6	14 35.7
4 Sa	4 47 43	12 52 11	4♌30 06	10♌52 27	27 57.1	29 52.6	26 03.6	28 48.0	14 16.6	29 43.8	3 43.1	2 55.5	24 25.5	14 37.1
5 Su	4 51 40	13 49 37	17 09 54	23 22 51	27 58.2	1♋40.3	27 09.2	29 24.3	14 03.2	29 52.3	3 38.7	2 57.2	24 26.5	14 38.4
6 M	4 55 36	14 47 03	29 31 48	5♍37 16	27R 58.9	3 25.5	28 14.6	0♌00.6	13 49.9	0♈00.6	3 34.4	2 58.7	24 27.5	14 39.8
7 Tu	4 59 33	15 44 27	11♍39 49	17 39 59	27 59.1	5 08.0	29 19.8	0 36.9	13 36.5	0 08.8	3 30.1	3 00.3	24 28.5	14 41.1
8 W	5 03 30	16 41 51	23 38 21	29 35 30	27 58.7	6 47.8	0♌24.7	1 13.3	13 23.3	0 16.8	3 25.8	3 01.7	24 29.6	14 42.5
9 Th	5 07 26	17 39 13	5♎32 00	11♎28 23	27 57.9	8 24.9	1 29.5	1 49.7	13 10.0	0 24.7	3 21.5	3 03.2	24 30.6	14 43.9
10 F	5 11 23	18 36 34	17 25 10	23 22 53	27 56.8	9 59.3	2 34.0	2 26.1	12 56.8	0 32.5	3 17.3	3 04.6	24 31.7	14 45.3
11 Sa	5 15 19	19 33 54	29 21 59	5♏22 53	27 55.6	11 31.0	3 38.3	3 02.5	12 43.8	0 40.1	3 13.1	3 05.9	24 32.9	14 46.7
12 Su	5 19 16	20 31 13	11♏26 00	17 31 40	27 54.6	12 59.9	4 42.3	3 38.9	12 30.8	0 47.6	3 08.9	3 07.3	24 34.0	14 48.1
13 M	5 23 12	21 28 32	23 40 12	29 51 51	27 53.8	14 26.1	5 46.1	4 15.4	12 17.9	0 54.9	3 04.8	3 08.5	24 35.2	14 49.6
14 Tu	5 27 09	22 25 49	6♐06 48	12♐25 15	27 53.3	15 49.4	6 49.7	4 51.9	12 05.1	1 02.1	3 00.7	3 09.7	24 36.4	14 51.0
15 W	5 31 05	23 23 06	18 47 18	25 13 01	27D 53.1	17 09.9	7 53.0	5 28.4	11 52.5	1 09.2	2 56.6	3 10.9	24 37.7	14 52.5
16 Th	5 35 02	24 20 23	1♑42 24	8♑15 28	27 53.2	18 27.4	8 56.0	6 04.9	11 40.1	1 16.1	2 52.6	3 12.0	24 38.9	14 53.9
17 F	5 38 59	25 17 39	14 52 09	21 32 22	27 53.4	19 42.1	9 58.8	6 41.4	11 27.8	1 22.8	2 48.7	3 13.1	24 40.2	14 55.4
18 Sa	5 42 55	26 14 54	28 16 00	5♒02 55	27 53.6	20 53.7	11 01.3	7 18.0	11 15.6	1 29.4	2 44.8	3 14.2	24 41.6	14 56.9
19 Su	5 46 52	27 12 09	11♒52 58	18 45 57	27R 53.7	22 02.3	12 03.5	7 54.6	11 03.7	1 35.8	2 40.9	3 15.2	24 42.9	14 58.3
20 M	5 50 48	28 09 24	25 41 42	2♓40 01	27 53.7	23 07.8	13 05.4	8 31.2	10 52.0	1 42.1	2 37.1	3 16.1	24 44.3	14 59.8
21 Tu	5 54 45	29 06 39	9♓40 39	16 43 22	27D 53.7	24 10.1	14 07.0	9 07.8	10 40.4	1 48.2	2 33.3	3 17.0	24 45.7	15 01.3
22 W	5 58 41	0♋03 53	23 47 56	0♈54 04	27 53.6	25 09.1	15 08.3	9 44.4	10 29.1	1 54.1	2 29.6	3 17.8	24 47.1	15 02.8
23 Th	6 02 38	1 01 08	8♈01 28	15 09 49	27 53.7	26 04.7	16 09.3	10 21.1	10 18.0	1 59.9	2 25.9	3 18.6	24 48.5	15 04.3
24 F	6 06 34	1 58 22	22 18 46	29 27 56	27 53.9	26 57.0	17 10.0	10 57.8	10 07.2	2 05.6	2 22.3	3 19.4	24 50.0	15 05.8
25 Sa	6 10 31	2 55 36	6♉36 56	13♉45 19	27 54.4	27 45.6	18 10.3	11 34.5	9 56.6	2 11.0	2 18.8	3 20.1	24 51.5	15 07.3
26 Su	6 14 28	3 52 50	20 52 38	27 58 27	27 54.9	28 30.6	19 10.3	12 11.3	9 46.3	2 16.3	2 15.3	3 20.7	24 53.0	15 08.9
27 M	6 18 24	4 50 05	5♊02 18	12♊03 43	27 55.3	29 11.8	20 09.9	12 48.0	9 36.3	2 21.5	2 11.9	3 21.4	24 54.6	15 10.4
28 Tu	6 22 21	5 47 19	19 02 15	25 57 31	27R 55.5	29 49.1	21 09.2	13 24.8	9 26.5	2 26.4	2 08.6	3 21.9	24 56.2	15 11.9
29 W	6 26 17	6 44 33	2♋49 08	9♋36 47	27 55.4	0♌22.4	22 08.1	14 01.6	9 17.0	2 31.2	2 05.3	3 22.4	24 57.8	15 13.5
30 Th	6 30 14	7 41 47	16 20 11	22 59 11	27 54.7	0 51.5	23 06.6	14 38.5	9 07.9	2 35.8	2 02.1	3 22.9	24 59.4	15 15.0

Astro Data	Dy Hr Mn
♅0N	1 22:27
♃⚻♆	3 10:58
♆ D	5 23:54
☽0S	13 5:07
☽0N	27 0:08
☽0S	9 12:53
♄△♅	12 19:18
☽0N	23 6:34
♃△♄	26 9:14

Planet Ingress		Dy Hr Mn
☿	♉	6 11:28
♀	♋	12 8:33
☿	♊	21 0:03
☉	♊	22 2:08
☿	♋	4 13:38
♃	♈	6 10:14
♂	♌	6 11:36
♀	♌	8 2:51
☉	♋	22 10:22
☿	♌	28 19:33

Last Aspect Dy Hr Mn			☽ Ingress	Dy Hr Mn
2 11:22	♆	□	♊	2 20:52
4 18:18	☿	⚹	♋	4 23:51
6 20:59	♃	△	♌	7 6:39
9 10:19	♀	⚹	♍	9 17:03
12 5:07	♀	□	♎	12 5:27
14 6:17	♆	⚹	♏	14 17:52
16 22:38	♃	△	♐	17 4:58
19 8:52	♃	□	♑	19 14:11
21 20:53	☉	△	♒	21 21:16
23 16:08	♆	☍	♓	24 2:01
26 1:48	♃	☌	♈	26 4:37
27 20:34	♆	△	♉	28 5:50
30 5:18	♃	⚹	♊	30 7:02

Last Aspect Dy Hr Mn			☽ Ingress	Dy Hr Mn
1 8:34	♃	□	♋	1 9:50
3 14:53	♃	△	♌	3 15:37
5 14:04	♆	☌	♍	6 0:55
7 7:49	☉	□	♎	8 12:49
10 14:18	♆	⚹	♏	11 1:16
13 1:46	♆	□	♐	13 12:16
15 10:54	♆	△	♑	15 20:51
17 8:22	☿	☍	♒	18 3:05
20 3:40	☉	△	♓	20 7:25
22 1:35	☿	△	♈	22 10:29
24 7:31	☿	□	♉	24 12:54
26 12:57	☿	⚹	♊	26 15:26
28 10:13	♆	⚹	♋	28 19:03

☽ Phases & Eclipses Dy Hr Mn	
1 12:40	● 10♉09
8 15:27	☽ 17♌02
16 19:03	○ 24♏54
24 5:34	☾ 2♓04
30 21:06	● 8♊26
7 7:49	☽ 15♍34
15 8:19	○ 23♐14
15 8:24	☍ T 1.012
22 10:29	☾ 0♈00
29 6:32	● 6♋32
29 6:23:01	☌ T 00'50"

Astro Data

1 May 1927
Julian Day # 9982
SVP 6♓16'47"
GC 25♐49.5 ⚴ 19♏25.6R
Eris 1♈11.3 ⚵ 25♉12.8
⚷ 2♉14.8 ⚶ 10♏40.1R
☽ Mean ☊ 0♋35.5

1 June 1927
Julian Day # 10013
SVP 6♓16'42"
GC 25♐49.5 ⚴ 10♏46.9R
Eris 1♈25.7 ⚵ 13♊29.5
⚷ 4♉02.9 ⚶ 4♏29.9R
☽ Mean ☊ 28♊57.0

July 1927 — LONGITUDE

Day	Sid.Time	☉	0 hr ☽	Noon ☽	True ☊	☿	♀	♂	⚳	♃	♄	♅	♆	♇
1 F	6 34 10	8♋39 00	29♋33 38	6♌03 30	27♊53.6	1♌16.4	24♌04.8	15♌15.3	8♐59.0	2♈40.2	1♐58.9	3♈23.3	25♌01.0	15♋16.5
2 Sa	6 38 07	9 36 14	12♌28 49	18 49 42	27R52.2	1 36.9	25 02.5	15 52.2	8R50.5	2 44.5	1R55.9	3 23.7	25 02.7	15 18.1
3 Su	6 42 04	10 33 27	25 06 21	1♍19 01	27 50.5	1 52.9	25 59.7	16 29.1	8 42.2	2 48.6	1 52.9	3 24.0	25 04.4	15 19.6
4 M	6 46 00	11 30 39	7♍28 01	13 33 45	27 48.9	2 04.4	26 56.5	17 06.0	8 34.3	2 52.5	1 49.9	3 24.3	25 06.1	15 21.2
5 Tu	6 49 57	12 27 52	19 36 38	25 37 09	27 47.6	2R11.2	27 52.9	17 43.0	8 26.8	2 56.2	1 47.1	3 24.5	25 07.8	15 22.7
6 W	6 53 53	13 25 04	1♎35 50	7♎33 12	27D46.9	2 13.3	28 48.8	18 20.0	8 19.6	2 59.7	1 44.3	3 24.6	25 09.5	15 24.3
7 Th	6 57 50	14 22 16	13 29 50	19 26 19	27 46.9	2 10.7	29 44.2	18 56.9	8 12.7	3 03.1	1 41.6	3 24.8	25 11.3	15 25.8
8 F	7 01 46	15 19 28	25 23 13	1♏21 07	27 47.6	2 03.5	0♍39.0	19 34.0	8 06.2	3 06.2	1 39.0	3 24.8	25 13.1	15 27.4
9 Sa	7 05 43	16 16 39	7♏20 36	13 22 14	27 48.8	1 51.6	1 33.3	20 11.0	8 00.0	3 09.2	1 36.5	3R24.9	25 14.9	15 28.9
10 Su	7 09 39	17 13 51	19 26 33	25 34 02	27 50.2	1 35.2	2 27.1	20 48.0	7 54.2	3 12.0	1 34.0	3 24.8	25 16.7	15 30.4
11 M	7 13 36	18 11 03	1♐45 09	8♐00 18	27 51.6	1 14.5	3 20.3	21 25.1	7 48.7	3 14.6	1 31.6	3 24.8	25 18.5	15 32.0
12 Tu	7 17 32	19 08 15	14 19 50	20 44 01	27R52.5	0 49.7	4 12.9	22 02.2	7 43.6	3 17.1	1 29.3	3 24.7	25 20.4	15 33.5
13 W	7 21 29	20 05 27	27 13 03	3♑47 02	27 52.5	0 21.1	5 04.9	22 39.3	7 38.8	3 19.3	1 27.1	3 24.5	25 22.3	15 35.1
14 Th	7 25 26	21 02 39	10♑25 59	17 09 48	27 51.5	29♋49.2	5 56.3	23 16.5	7 34.4	3 21.3	1 25.0	3 24.3	25 24.2	15 36.6
15 F	7 29 22	21 59 51	23 58 20	0♒51 17	27 49.4	29 14.3	6 47.0	23 53.6	7 30.4	3 23.2	1 23.0	3 24.0	25 26.1	15 38.2
16 Sa	7 33 19	22 57 04	7♒48 18	14 48 56	27 46.3	28 36.9	7 37.0	24 30.8	7 26.7	3 24.9	1 21.0	3 23.7	25 28.0	15 39.7
17 Su	7 37 15	23 54 17	21 52 41	28 58 58	27 42.8	27 57.8	8 26.3	25 08.0	7 23.4	3 26.4	1 19.2	3 23.4	25 29.9	15 41.3
18 M	7 41 12	24 51 31	6♓07 13	13♓16 51	27 39.2	27 17.4	9 14.9	25 45.2	7 20.5	3 27.6	1 17.4	3 22.9	25 31.9	15 42.8
19 Tu	7 45 08	25 48 45	20 27 15	27 37 53	27 36.1	26 36.5	10 02.7	26 22.5	7 17.9	3 28.7	1 15.7	3 22.5	25 33.9	15 44.3
20 W	7 49 05	26 46 00	4♈48 13	11♈57 48	27 34.1	25 55.8	10 49.7	26 59.8	7 15.7	3 29.6	1 14.1	3 22.0	25 35.8	15 45.9
21 Th	7 53 02	27 43 16	19 06 14	26 13 10	27D33.3	25 16.0	11 35.9	27 37.1	7 13.9	3 30.3	1 12.6	3 21.4	25 37.8	15 47.4
22 F	7 56 58	28 40 33	3♉18 19	10♉21 28	27 33.7	24 37.9	12 21.3	28 14.4	7 12.4	3 30.8	1 11.2	3 20.9	25 39.9	15 48.9
23 Sa	8 00 55	29 37 51	17 22 26	24 21 04	27 35.0	24 02.1	13 05.8	28 51.8	7 11.3	3 31.1	1 09.9	3 20.2	25 41.9	15 50.4
24 Su	8 04 51	0♌35 09	1♊17 14	8♊10 52	27 36.4	23 29.2	13 49.5	29 29.1	7 10.5	3R31.2	1 08.7	3 19.5	25 43.9	15 51.9
25 M	8 08 48	1 32 29	15 01 51	21 50 07	27R37.4	23 00.1	14 32.2	0♍06.6	7D10.2	3 31.1	1 07.5	3 18.8	25 46.0	15 53.4
26 Tu	8 12 44	2 29 49	28 35 33	5♋18 04	27 37.3	22 35.0	15 13.9	0 44.0	7 10.1	3 30.8	1 06.5	3 18.0	25 48.1	15 54.9
27 W	8 16 41	3 27 10	11♋57 34	18 33 57	27 35.6	22 14.7	15 54.6	1 21.5	7 10.5	3 30.4	1 05.5	3 17.2	25 50.1	15 56.4
28 Th	8 20 37	4 24 32	25 07 08	1♌37 00	27 32.1	21 59.5	16 34.3	1 59.0	7 11.2	3 29.7	1 04.7	3 16.3	25 52.2	15 57.9
29 F	8 24 34	5 21 55	8♌03 31	14 26 38	27 27.0	21 49.8	17 12.8	2 36.5	7 12.2	3 28.8	1 03.9	3 15.4	25 54.3	15 59.4
30 Sa	8 28 31	6 19 19	20 46 19	27 02 38	27 20.6	21D45.9	17 50.2	3 14.0	7 13.7	3 27.7	1 03.3	3 14.5	25 56.4	16 00.9
31 Su	8 32 27	7 16 43	3♍15 38	9♍25 29	27 13.6	21 48.0	18 26.5	3 51.6	7 15.4	3 26.4	1 02.7	3 13.5	25 58.6	16 02.3

August 1927 — LONGITUDE

Day	Sid.Time	☉	0 hr ☽	Noon ☽	True ☊	☿	♀	♂	⚳	♃	♄	♅	♆	♇
1 M	8 36 24	8♌14 07	15♍32 20	21♍36 26	27♊06.7	21♋56.3	19♍01.5	4♍29.2	7♐17.6	3♈25.0	1♐02.3	3♈12.4	26♌00.7	16♋03.8
2 Tu	8 40 20	9 11 33	27 38 05	3♎37 39	27R00.6	22 11.0	19 35.2	5 06.8	7 20.0	3R23.3	1R01.9	3R11.3	26 02.8	16 05.2
3 W	8 44 17	10 08 59	9♎35 31	15 32 09	26 56.0	22 32.2	20 07.6	5 44.5	7 22.8	3 21.4	1 01.6	3 10.2	26 05.0	16 06.7
4 Th	8 48 13	11 06 26	21 28 04	27 23 47	26 53.0	22 59.8	20 38.7	6 22.1	7 26.0	3 19.4	1 01.4	3 09.0	26 07.1	16 08.1
5 F	8 52 10	12 03 53	3♏19 52	9♏16 56	26D51.9	23 33.8	21 08.2	6 59.8	7 29.5	3 17.1	1D01.4	3 07.8	26 09.3	16 09.5
6 Sa	8 56 06	13 01 22	15 15 36	21 16 30	26 52.2	24 14.4	21 36.3	7 37.6	7 33.4	3 14.7	1 01.4	3 06.6	26 11.5	16 10.9
7 Su	9 00 03	13 58 51	27 20 16	3♐27 30	26 53.4	25 01.3	22 02.8	8 15.3	7 37.5	3 12.0	1 01.5	3 05.3	26 13.7	16 12.3
8 M	9 04 00	14 56 21	9♐38 48	15 54 45	26R54.6	25 54.4	22 27.8	8 53.1	7 42.0	3 09.2	1 01.7	3 03.9	26 15.8	16 13.7
9 Tu	9 07 56	15 53 52	22 15 52	28 42 33	26 55.0	26 53.8	22 51.0	9 30.9	7 46.9	3 06.2	1 02.0	3 02.5	26 18.0	16 15.1
10 W	9 11 53	16 51 23	5♑15 11	11♑54 01	26 54.0	27 59.1	23 12.5	10 08.7	7 52.0	3 03.0	1 02.4	3 01.1	26 20.2	16 16.5
11 Th	9 15 49	17 48 56	18 39 09	25 30 35	26 50.9	29 10.3	23 32.2	10 46.6	7 57.5	2 59.6	1 02.9	2 59.7	26 22.4	16 17.8
12 F	9 19 46	18 46 30	2♒28 09	9♒31 29	26 45.6	0♌27.1	23 50.1	11 24.5	8 03.3	2 56.0	1 03.6	2 58.2	26 24.6	16 19.2
13 Sa	9 23 42	19 44 04	16 40 07	23 53 23	26 38.6	1 49.3	24 06.1	12 02.4	8 09.4	2 52.3	1 04.3	2 56.7	26 26.8	16 20.5
14 Su	9 27 39	20 41 40	1♓10 29	8♓30 33	26 30.5	3 16.6	24 20.1	12 40.3	8 15.8	2 48.4	1 05.0	2 55.1	26 29.1	16 21.9
15 M	9 31 35	21 39 17	15 52 35	23 15 35	26 22.2	4 48.6	24 32.0	13 18.3	8 22.5	2 44.3	1 05.9	2 53.5	26 31.3	16 23.2
16 Tu	9 35 32	22 36 56	0♈38 34	8♈00 34	26 14.9	6 25.1	24 41.9	13 56.3	8 29.4	2 40.0	1 06.9	2 51.9	26 33.5	16 24.5
17 W	9 39 29	23 34 36	15 20 45	22 38 21	26 09.4	8 05.6	24 49.7	14 34.3	8 36.7	2 35.5	1 08.0	2 50.2	26 35.7	16 25.8
18 Th	9 43 25	24 32 18	29 52 47	7♉03 33	26 06.0	9 49.9	24 55.3	15 12.3	8 44.3	2 30.9	1 09.2	2 48.5	26 37.9	16 27.0
19 F	9 47 22	25 30 01	14♉10 21	21 12 58	26D04.7	11 37.4	24R58.7	15 50.4	8 52.2	2 26.1	1 10.5	2 46.7	26 40.2	16 28.3
20 Sa	9 51 18	26 27 47	28 11 19	5♊05 26	26 04.8	13 27.7	24 59.8	16 28.5	9 00.4	2 21.1	1 11.8	2 45.0	26 42.4	16 29.5
21 Su	9 55 15	27 25 33	11♊55 23	18 41 19	26R05.5	15 20.5	24 58.6	17 06.7	9 08.8	2 16.0	1 13.3	2 43.2	26 44.6	16 30.8
22 M	9 59 11	28 23 22	25 23 26	2♋01 54	26 05.5	17 15.2	24 55.1	17 44.9	9 17.5	2 10.7	1 14.9	2 41.3	26 46.8	16 32.0
23 Tu	10 03 08	29 21 12	8♋36 56	15 08 43	26 03.9	19 11.6	24 49.2	18 23.1	9 26.5	2 05.3	1 16.5	2 39.4	26 49.0	16 33.2
24 W	10 07 04	0♍19 04	21 37 25	28 03 11	25 59.8	21 09.2	24 41.0	19 01.3	9 35.8	1 59.7	1 18.3	2 37.5	26 51.3	16 34.4
25 Th	10 11 01	1 16 58	4♌26 09	10♌46 23	25 53.1	23 07.6	24 30.4	19 39.6	9 45.4	1 54.0	1 20.1	2 35.6	26 53.5	16 35.6
26 F	10 14 58	2 14 53	17 03 59	23 19 01	25 43.8	25 06.5	24 17.5	20 17.9	9 55.2	1 48.1	1 22.1	2 33.7	26 55.7	16 36.7
27 Sa	10 18 54	3 12 49	29 31 31	5♍41 34	25 32.4	27 05.7	24 02.2	20 56.2	10 05.3	1 42.0	1 24.1	2 31.7	26 57.9	16 37.9
28 Su	10 22 51	4 10 48	11♍49 14	17 54 35	25 20.0	29 04.9	23 44.5	21 34.6	10 15.6	1 35.8	1 26.3	2 29.7	27 00.1	16 39.0
29 M	10 26 47	5 08 47	23 57 45	29 58 53	25 07.6	1♍03.8	23 24.6	22 13.0	10 26.2	1 29.5	1 28.5	2 27.6	27 02.4	16 40.1
30 Tu	10 30 44	6 06 48	5♎58 10	11♎55 50	24 56.2	3 02.2	23 02.6	22 51.4	10 37.0	1 23.1	1 30.8	2 25.5	27 04.6	16 41.2
31 W	10 34 40	7 04 51	17 52 12	23 47 35	24 46.8	5 00.1	22 38.3	23 29.9	10 48.1	1 16.5	1 33.2	2 23.4	27 06.8	16 42.2

Astro Data	Dy Hr Mn
☿R	6 10:50
☽0S	6 20:44
♃0N	7 11:54
♅R	9 12:31
♃☌♅	15 21:37
☽0N	20 11:41
♃R	24 13:10
⚳D	26 1:17
☿D	30 15:42
♄□♇	31 16:43
☽0S	3 4:03
♃0S	3 9:35
♄D	5 18:58
♀0S	7 9:48
♃☌♅	11 11:02

Planet Ingress	Dy Hr Mn
♀ ♍	7 18:55
☿ ♋R	14 4:08
☉ ♌	23 21:17
♂ ♍	25 7:47
☿ ♌	12 3:43
☉ ♍	24 4:05
☿ ♍	28 23:07
☽0N	16 17:35
♀R	20 11:42
♃△△	29 14:53
☽0S	30 10:35

Last Aspect Dy Hr Mn		☽ Ingress	Dy Hr Mn
29 22:02	♇ ☌	♌	1 0:48
3 0:52	♀ ☌	♍	3 9:27
4 15:33	♇ ⚹	♎	5 20:47
7 23:38	♆ ⚹	♏	8 9:17
10 11:26	♆ □	♐	10 20:37
12 20:34	♆ △	♑	13 5:06
15 9:18	☿ ☍	♒	15 10:31
17 6:07	♆ ☍	♓	17 13:43
19 10:22	☿ △	♈	19 15:58
21 14:43	☉ □	♉	21 18:24
23 20:10	♂ □	♊	23 21:46
25 18:59	♆ ⚹	♋	26 2:31
27 18:35	☿ ☌	♌	28 9:00
30 9:53	♆ ☌	♍	30 17:42

Last Aspect Dy Hr Mn		☽ Ingress	Dy Hr Mn
1 12:40	☿ ⚹	♎	2 4:44
4 9:24	♆ ⚹	♏	4 17:16
6 21:46	♆ □	♐	7 5:14
9 7:31	♆ △	♑	9 14:23
11 18:58	☿ ☍	♒	11 19:46
13 16:14	♆ ☍	♓	13 22:04
15 14:06	♀ ☍	♈	15 22:57
17 18:34	♆ △	♉	18 0:12
19 21:24	♆ □	♊	20 3:08
22 4:53	☉ ⚹	♋	22 8:19
24 5:46	♀ ⚹	♌	24 15:39
26 19:00	♆ ☌	♍	27 0:55
28 23:16	♀ ☌	♎	29 12:02

☽ Phases & Eclipses Dy Hr Mn	
7 0:52	☽ 13♎56
14 19:22	○ 21♑20
21 14:43	☾ 27♈50
28 17:36	● 4♌38
5 18:05	☽ 12♏18
13 4:37	○ 19♒26
19 19:54	☾ 25♉49
27 6:45	● 3♍00

Astro Data

1 July 1927
Julian Day # 10043
SVP 6♓16'36"
GC 25♐49.6 ⚴ 7♏48.4
Eris 1♈30.0R ⚵ 0♋53.0
⚷ 5♉22.9 ⚶ 4♏57.8
☽ Mean ☊ 27♊21.8

1 August 1927
Julian Day # 10074
SVP 6♓16'31"
GC 25♐49.7 ⚴ 11♏19.5
Eris 1♈23.6R ⚵ 18♋12.3
⚷ 6♉03.7 ⚶ 11♏58.5
☽ Mean ☊ 25♊43.3

LONGITUDE — September 1927

Day	Sid.Time	☉	0 hr ☽	Noon ☽	True ☊	☿	♀	♂	⚳	♃	♄	♅	♆	♇
1 Th	10 38 37	8♍02 55	29♎42 23	5♏37 03	24♊39.8	6♍57.1	22♍12.1	24♍08.4	10♐59.4	1♈09.8	1♐35.7	2♈21.3	27♌08.9	16♋43.3
2 F	10 42 33	9 01 00	11♏32 05	17 28 00	24R35.5	8 53.4	21R43.9	24 46.9	11 11.0	1R03.0	1 38.3	2R19.2	27 11.1	16 44.3
3 Sa	10 46 30	9 59 07	23 25 25	29 24 55	24D33.5	10 48.7	21 14.0	25 25.5	11 22.8	0 56.1	1 41.0	2 17.0	27 13.3	16 45.4
4 Su	10 50 26	10 57 16	5♐27 10	11♐32 49	24 33.1	12 43.0	20 42.5	26 04.1	11 34.9	0 49.1	1 43.7	2 14.8	27 15.5	16 46.4
5 M	10 54 23	11 55 26	17 42 32	23 56 59	24R33.2	14 36.2	20 09.5	26 42.7	11 47.1	0 41.9	1 46.6	2 12.6	27 17.7	16 47.3
6 Tu	10 58 20	12 53 37	0♑16 47	6♑42 31	24 32.8	16 28.3	19 35.2	27 21.3	11 59.6	0 34.7	1 49.5	2 10.4	27 19.8	16 48.3
7 W	11 02 16	13 51 50	13 14 43	19 53 48	24 30.7	18 19.3	18 59.9	28 00.0	12 12.3	0 27.4	1 52.6	2 08.2	27 22.0	16 49.3
8 Th	11 06 13	14 50 04	26 40 04	3♒33 40	24 26.3	20 09.2	18 23.8	28 38.7	12 25.3	0 20.0	1 55.7	2 05.9	27 24.1	16 50.2
9 F	11 10 09	15 48 20	10♒34 35	17 42 34	24 19.3	21 57.9	17 47.0	29 17.5	12 38.4	0 12.5	1 58.9	2 03.7	27 26.3	16 51.1
10 Sa	11 14 06	16 46 37	24 57 13	2♓17 51	24 09.9	23 45.5	17 09.9	29 56.3	12 51.8	0 05.0	2 02.2	2 01.4	27 28.4	16 52.0
11 Su	11 18 02	17 44 57	9♓43 36	17 13 26	23 59.1	25 31.9	16 32.7	0♎35.1	13 05.4	29♓57.4	2 05.5	1 59.1	27 30.5	16 52.8
12 M	11 21 59	18 43 18	24 46 07	2♈20 23	23 48.0	27 17.2	15 55.6	1 13.9	13 19.1	29 49.7	2 09.0	1 56.7	27 32.6	16 53.7
13 Tu	11 25 55	19 41 40	9♈54 53	17 28 19	23 37.9	29 01.4	15 18.9	1 52.8	13 33.1	29 41.9	2 12.5	1 54.4	27 34.7	16 54.5
14 W	11 29 52	20 40 05	24 59 27	2♉27 13	23 29.9	0♎44.5	14 42.9	2 31.7	13 47.3	29 34.1	2 16.1	1 52.1	27 36.8	16 55.3
15 Th	11 33 49	21 38 32	9♉50 42	17 09 11	23 24.6	2 26.4	14 07.7	3 10.6	14 01.6	29 26.3	2 19.8	1 49.7	27 38.9	16 56.1
16 F	11 37 45	22 37 02	24 22 10	1♊29 20	23 21.9	4 07.4	13 33.6	3 49.6	14 16.2	29 18.4	2 23.6	1 47.3	27 40.9	16 56.9
17 Sa	11 41 42	23 35 33	8♊30 32	15 25 49	23 21.0	5 47.2	13 00.8	4 28.6	14 30.9	29 10.4	2 27.5	1 45.0	27 43.0	16 57.6
18 Su	11 45 38	24 34 07	22 15 18	28 59 15	23 21.0	7 26.1	12 29.4	5 07.7	14 45.9	29 02.5	2 31.4	1 42.6	27 45.0	16 58.4
19 M	11 49 35	25 32 43	5♋37 58	12♋11 50	23 20.4	9 03.9	11 59.8	5 46.8	15 01.0	28 54.5	2 35.4	1 40.2	27 47.1	16 59.1
20 Tu	11 53 31	26 31 21	18 41 14	25 06 32	23 18.2	10 40.7	11 31.9	6 25.9	15 16.3	28 46.5	2 39.5	1 37.8	27 49.1	16 59.7
21 W	11 57 28	27 30 01	1♌28 09	7♌46 26	23 13.4	12 16.5	11 06.0	7 05.1	15 31.8	28 38.5	2 43.7	1 35.4	27 51.1	17 00.4
22 Th	12 01 24	28 28 44	14 01 43	20 14 16	23 05.6	13 51.4	10 42.2	7 44.3	15 47.4	28 30.4	2 48.0	1 33.0	27 53.1	17 01.0
23 F	12 05 21	29 27 28	26 24 23	2♍32 16	22 55.1	15 25.3	10 20.5	8 23.6	16 03.3	28 22.4	2 52.3	1 30.6	27 55.0	17 01.6
24 Sa	12 09 18	0♎26 15	8♍38 08	14 42 09	22 42.3	16 58.2	10 01.1	9 02.8	16 19.3	28 14.4	2 56.7	1 28.2	27 57.0	17 02.2
25 Su	12 13 14	1 25 04	20 44 27	26 45 11	22 28.3	18 30.2	9 44.0	9 42.2	16 35.4	28 06.4	3 01.2	1 25.8	27 58.9	17 02.8
26 M	12 17 11	2 23 54	2♎44 29	8♎42 29	22 14.2	20 01.2	9 29.3	10 21.5	16 51.8	27 58.4	3 05.7	1 23.3	28 00.8	17 03.4
27 Tu	12 21 07	3 22 47	14 39 21	20 35 16	22 01.1	21 31.3	9 17.0	11 00.9	17 08.3	27 50.4	3 10.3	1 20.9	28 02.7	17 03.9
28 W	12 25 04	4 21 42	26 30 26	2♏25 05	21 50.2	23 00.4	9 07.1	11 40.3	17 24.9	27 42.5	3 15.0	1 18.5	28 04.6	17 04.4
29 Th	12 29 00	5 20 38	8♏19 32	14 14 04	21 41.9	24 28.6	8 59.6	12 19.8	17 41.8	27 34.6	3 19.8	1 16.1	28 06.4	17 04.9
30 F	12 32 57	6 19 37	20 09 06	26 05 03	21 36.6	25 55.9	8 54.5	12 59.3	17 58.7	27 26.7	3 24.6	1 13.7	28 08.3	17 05.3

LONGITUDE — October 1927

Day	Sid.Time	☉	0 hr ☽	Noon ☽	True ☊	☿	♀	♂	⚳	♃	♄	♅	♆	♇
1 Sa	12 36 53	7♎18 37	2♐02 22	8♐01 36	21♊33.9	27♎22.2	8♍51.8	13♎38.8	18♐15.9	27♓18.9	3♐29.5	1♈11.3	28♌10.1	17♋05.7
2 Su	12 40 50	8 17 39	14 03 18	20 08 04	21D33.1	28 47.4	8D51.6	14 18.4	18 33.1	27R11.2	3 34.5	1R08.9	28 11.9	17 06.1
3 M	12 44 47	9 16 43	26 16 31	2♑29 17	21R33.3	0♏11.7	8 53.6	14 58.0	18 50.6	27 03.5	3 39.5	1 06.5	28 13.7	17 06.5
4 Tu	12 48 43	10 15 49	8♑47 00	15 10 18	21 33.3	1 35.0	8 58.0	15 37.7	19 08.1	26 55.9	3 44.6	1 04.2	28 15.5	17 06.9
5 W	12 52 40	11 14 56	21 39 45	28 15 54	21 32.1	2 57.2	9 04.7	16 17.3	19 25.9	26 48.4	3 49.8	1 01.8	28 17.2	17 07.2
6 Th	12 56 36	12 14 05	4♒59 11	11♒49 53	21 28.8	4 18.3	9 13.6	16 57.1	19 43.7	26 40.9	3 55.0	0 59.4	28 19.0	17 07.5
7 F	13 00 33	13 13 16	18 48 12	25 54 05	21 23.0	5 38.2	9 24.6	17 36.8	20 01.7	26 33.5	4 00.3	0 57.1	28 20.7	17 07.8
8 Sa	13 04 29	14 12 29	3♓07 20	10♓27 27	21 15.1	6 57.0	9 37.8	18 16.6	20 19.8	26 26.3	4 05.6	0 54.8	28 22.3	17 08.1
9 Su	13 08 26	15 11 43	17 53 47	25 25 22	21 05.6	8 14.4	9 53.1	18 56.4	20 38.1	26 19.1	4 11.0	0 52.5	28 24.0	17 08.3
10 M	13 12 22	16 11 00	3♈01 06	10♈39 38	20 55.7	9 30.5	10 10.3	19 36.3	20 56.5	26 12.0	4 16.5	0 50.1	28 25.6	17 08.6
11 Tu	13 16 19	17 10 18	18 19 36	25 59 30	20 46.6	10 45.2	10 29.6	20 16.2	21 15.0	26 05.0	4 22.0	0 47.9	28 27.2	17 08.7
12 W	13 20 15	18 09 39	3♉37 56	11♉13 31	20 39.4	11 58.4	10 50.7	20 56.1	21 33.6	25 58.1	4 27.6	0 45.6	28 28.8	17 08.9
13 Th	13 24 12	19 09 01	18 45 05	26 11 37	20 34.7	13 10.0	11 13.7	21 36.1	21 52.4	25 51.4	4 33.2	0 43.3	28 30.4	17 09.1
14 F	13 28 09	20 08 26	3♊32 19	10♊46 37	20D32.5	14 19.8	11 38.5	22 16.2	22 11.2	25 44.7	4 38.9	0 41.1	28 31.9	17 09.2
15 Sa	13 32 05	21 07 54	17 54 10	24 54 48	20 32.2	15 27.6	12 05.0	22 56.2	22 30.2	25 38.2	4 44.7	0 38.9	28 33.4	17 09.3
16 Su	13 36 02	22 07 24	1♋48 34	8♋35 38	20 32.8	16 33.4	12 33.1	23 36.3	22 49.4	25 31.8	4 50.5	0 36.7	28 34.9	17 09.4
17 M	13 39 58	23 06 56	15 16 17	21 50 54	20R33.4	17 37.0	13 02.9	24 16.5	23 08.6	25 25.6	4 56.4	0 34.5	28 36.4	17 09.4
18 Tu	13 43 55	24 06 30	28 19 55	4♌43 48	20 32.8	18 38.1	13 34.2	24 56.7	23 27.9	25 19.5	5 02.3	0 32.3	28 37.9	17R09.4
19 W	13 47 51	25 06 07	11♌03 05	17 18 15	20 30.3	19 36.4	14 07.0	25 36.9	23 47.4	25 13.5	5 08.2	0 30.2	28 39.3	17 09.4
20 Th	13 51 48	26 05 45	23 29 46	29 38 30	20 25.4	20 31.8	14 41.3	26 17.2	24 07.0	25 07.7	5 14.2	0 28.1	28 40.7	17 09.4
21 F	13 55 44	27 05 26	5♍43 43	11♍47 00	20 18.2	21 23.8	15 16.9	26 57.5	24 26.7	25 02.0	5 20.3	0 26.0	28 42.0	17 09.4
22 Sa	13 59 41	28 05 10	17 48 18	23 47 59	20 09.2	22 12.2	15 53.8	27 37.9	24 46.5	24 56.5	5 26.4	0 23.9	28 43.3	17 09.3
23 Su	14 03 38	29 04 55	29 46 19	5♎43 34	19 59.1	22 56.5	16 32.0	28 18.3	25 06.3	24 51.1	5 32.5	0 21.9	28 44.7	17 09.2
24 M	14 07 34	0♏04 42	11♎39 59	17 35 48	19 48.9	23 36.4	17 11.5	28 58.7	25 26.4	24 45.9	5 38.7	0 19.9	28 45.9	17 09.0
25 Tu	14 11 31	1 04 32	23 31 11	29 26 22	19 39.5	24 11.3	17 52.1	29 39.2	25 46.5	24 40.9	5 45.0	0 17.9	28 47.2	17 08.9
26 W	14 15 27	2 04 23	5♏21 32	11♏16 52	19 31.7	24 40.8	18 33.9	0♏19.7	26 06.7	24 36.0	5 51.3	0 16.0	28 48.4	17 08.7
27 Th	14 19 24	3 04 17	17 12 37	23 09 00	19 26.0	25 04.3	19 16.7	1 00.3	26 27.0	24 31.3	5 57.6	0 14.1	28 49.6	17 08.5
28 F	14 23 20	4 04 12	29 06 17	5♐04 47	19 22.7	25 21.1	20 00.6	1 40.9	26 47.4	24 26.8	6 04.0	0 12.2	28 50.8	17 08.3
29 Sa	14 27 17	5 04 09	11♐04 48	17 06 43	19D21.4	25R30.8	20 45.5	2 21.5	27 07.9	24 22.5	6 10.4	0 10.3	28 51.9	17 08.1
30 Su	14 31 13	6 04 08	23 10 56	29 17 53	19 21.9	25 32.6	21 31.4	3 02.2	27 28.5	24 18.4	6 16.8	0 08.5	28 53.0	17 07.8
31 M	14 35 10	7 04 08	5♑28 03	11♑41 54	19 23.2	25 25.9	22 18.2	3 42.9	27 49.1	24 14.4	6 23.3	0 06.7	28 54.1	17 07.5

Astro Data

	Dy Hr Mn
♄□♇	5 21:20
♄△♅	10 8:35
☽0N	13 1:54
♂0S	13 5:52
☿0S	15 2:16
♅0S	16 14:03
♀0N	21 2:16
☉0S	24 1:18
♃⊼♆	26 6:08
☽0S	26 16:38
♀ D	2 2:50
☽0N	10 12:35
♇ R	18 23:13
☽0S	23 22:47
☿ R	30 5:19

Planet Ingress

	Dy Hr Mn
♂ ♎	10 14:19
♃ ♓R	11 3:43
☿ ♎	14 1:37
☉ ♎	24 1:17
☿ ♏	3 8:38
☉ ♏	24 10:07
♂ ♏	26 0:20

Last Aspect / ☽ Ingress

Last Aspect Dy Hr Mn		☽ Ingress Dy Hr Mn
31 18:45	♆ ⚹	♏ 1 0:36
3 7:36	♆ □	♐ 3 13:10
5 18:23	♆ △	♑ 5 23:28
8 3:03	♂ △	♒ 8 5:50
10 4:07	♆ ☍	♓ 10 8:16
12 8:03	♃ ☌	♈ 12 8:18
14 4:11	♆ △	♉ 14 8:03
16 8:20	♃ ⚹	♊ 16 9:29
18 12:06	♃ □	♋ 18 13:49
20 18:50	♃ △	♌ 20 21:13
23 2:56	♆ ☌	♍ 23 7:01
25 14:41	♃ ☍	♎ 25 18:30
28 3:10	♆ ⚹	♏ 28 7:05
30 16:09	♆ □	♐ 30 19:54

Last Aspect Dy Hr Mn		☽ Ingress Dy Hr Mn
3 7:02	☿ ⚹	♑ 3 7:13
5 9:23	♃ ⚹	♒ 5 15:07
7 16:05	♆ ☍	♓ 7 18:50
9 13:24	♃ ☌	♈ 9 19:15
11 15:52	♆ △	♉ 11 18:17
13 15:46	♆ □	♊ 13 18:12
15 18:20	♆ ⚹	♋ 15 20:50
17 18:33	♃ △	♌ 18 3:07
20 10:07	♆ ☌	♍ 20 12:43
22 14:16	♃ ☍	♎ 23 0:28
25 12:28	♂ ☌	♏ 25 13:08
27 23:28	♆ □	♐ 28 1:48
30 11:11	♆ △	♑ 30 13:22

☽ Phases & Eclipses

Dy Hr Mn	
4 10:44	☽ 10♐54
11 12:54	○ 17♓47
18 3:29	☾ 24♊13
25 22:11	● 1♎50
4 2:01	☽ 9♑51
10 21:14	○ 16♈34
17 14:32	☾ 23♋13
25 15:37	● 1♏14

Astro Data

1 September 1927
Julian Day # 10105
SVP 6♓16'28"
GC 25♐49.7 ⚴ 19♏16.1
Eris 1♈08.1R ⚵ 4♌31.7
⚷ 5♉52.9R ⚶ 23♏11.3
☽ Mean ☊ 24♊04.8

1 October 1927
Julian Day # 10135
SVP 6♓16'25"
GC 25♐49.8 ⚴ 29♏22.1
Eris 0♈48.7R ⚵ 18♌58.4
⚷ 4♉56.8R ⚶ 6♐22.3
☽ Mean ☊ 22♊29.4

November 1927 — LONGITUDE

Day	Sid.Time	☉	0 hr ☽	Noon ☽	True ☊	☿	♀	♂	⚳	♃	♄	♅	♆	♇
1 Tu	14 39 07	8♏04 11	17♑59 57	24♑22 43	19♊24.7	25♏10.3	23♍06.0	4♏23.7	28♐09.9	24♓10.6	6♐29.8	0♈04.9	28♌55.1	17♋07.2
2 W	14 43 03	9 04 14	0♒50 43	7♒24 23	19R 25.5	24R 45.4	23 54.6	5 04.5	28 30.8	24R 07.0	6 36.4	0R 03.2	28 56.1	17R 06.9
3 Th	14 47 00	10 04 20	14 04 11	20 50 26	19 24.9	24 10.9	24 44.0	5 45.3	28 51.7	24 03.7	6 43.0	0 01.5	28 57.1	17 06.5
4 F	14 50 56	11 04 26	27 43 24	4♓43 11	19 22.7	23 26.7	25 34.3	6 26.2	29 12.7	24 00.5	6 49.6	29♓59.9	28 58.1	17 06.1
5 Sa	14 54 53	12 04 35	11♓49 47	19 02 57	19 18.9	22 33.4	26 25.3	7 07.2	29 33.8	23 57.4	6 56.3	29 58.3	28 59.0	17 05.7
6 Su	14 58 49	13 04 44	26 22 18	3♈47 12	19 13.9	21 31.5	27 17.1	7 48.1	29 55.0	23 54.6	7 03.0	29 56.7	28 59.9	17 05.3
7 M	15 02 46	14 04 56	11♈16 51	18 50 15	19 08.5	20 22.3	28 09.6	8 29.1	0♑16.3	23 52.0	7 09.7	29 55.2	29 00.7	17 04.8
8 Tu	15 06 42	15 05 09	26 26 14	4♉03 32	19 03.5	19 07.3	29 02.8	9 10.2	0 37.6	23 49.6	7 16.4	29 53.7	29 01.6	17 04.3
9 W	15 10 39	16 05 24	11♉40 50	19 16 48	18 59.6	17 48.8	29 56.8	9 51.3	0 59.0	23 47.4	7 23.2	29 52.2	29 02.3	17 03.8
10 Th	15 14 36	17 05 40	26 50 10	4♊19 47	18D 57.3	16 28.9	0♎51.3	10 32.4	1 20.5	23 45.4	7 30.0	29 50.8	29 03.1	17 03.3
11 F	15 18 32	18 05 59	11♊44 38	19 03 53	18 56.5	15 10.4	1 46.6	11 13.6	1 42.1	23 43.6	7 36.8	29 49.4	29 03.8	17 02.8
12 Sa	15 22 29	19 06 19	26 16 53	3♋23 14	18 57.2	13 55.8	2 42.4	11 54.8	2 03.7	23 42.0	7 43.7	29 48.1	29 04.5	17 02.2
13 Su	15 26 25	20 06 41	10♋22 39	17 15 06	18 58.6	12 47.5	3 38.9	12 36.0	2 25.5	23 40.6	7 50.6	29 46.8	29 05.2	17 01.6
14 M	15 30 22	21 07 05	24 00 38	0♌39 29	19 00.2	11 47.4	4 35.9	13 17.4	2 47.2	23 39.4	7 57.5	29 45.6	29 05.8	17 01.0
15 Tu	15 34 18	22 07 31	7♌11 58	13 38 31	19R 01.4	10 57.3	5 33.5	13 58.7	3 09.1	23 38.4	8 04.4	29 44.4	29 06.4	17 00.4
16 W	15 38 15	23 07 59	19 59 35	26 15 41	19 01.7	10 18.2	6 31.6	14 40.1	3 31.0	23 37.6	8 11.3	29 43.2	29 07.0	16 59.7
17 Th	15 42 11	24 08 29	2♍27 22	8♍35 11	19 00.7	9 50.6	7 30.2	15 21.5	3 53.0	23 37.1	8 18.3	29 42.1	29 07.5	16 59.1
18 F	15 46 08	25 09 00	14 39 40	20 41 22	18 58.6	9D 34.8	8 29.4	16 03.0	4 15.0	23 36.7	8 25.3	29 41.0	29 08.0	16 58.4
19 Sa	15 50 05	26 09 33	26 40 48	2♎38 27	18 55.6	9 30.5	9 29.0	16 44.6	4 37.1	23D 36.5	8 32.3	29 40.0	29 08.5	16 57.6
20 Su	15 54 01	27 10 08	8♎34 48	14 30 16	18 52.0	9 37.1	10 29.0	17 26.1	4 59.3	23 36.6	8 39.3	29 39.0	29 08.9	16 56.9
21 M	15 57 58	28 10 45	20 25 15	26 20 08	18 48.2	9 54.0	11 29.6	18 07.8	5 21.5	23 36.8	8 46.3	29 38.1	29 09.3	16 56.2
22 Tu	16 01 54	29 11 23	2♏15 13	8♏10 50	18 44.8	10 20.3	12 30.5	18 49.4	5 43.8	23 37.3	8 53.4	29 37.2	29 09.6	16 55.4
23 W	16 05 51	0♐12 03	14 07 14	20 04 42	18 42.1	10 55.1	13 31.9	19 31.1	6 06.2	23 38.0	9 00.4	29 36.3	29 10.0	16 54.6
24 Th	16 09 47	1 12 44	26 03 26	2♐03 40	18 40.3	11 37.5	14 33.7	20 12.9	6 28.6	23 38.8	9 07.5	29 35.5	29 10.3	16 53.8
25 F	16 13 44	2 13 27	8♐05 36	14 09 26	18D 39.5	12 26.8	15 35.8	20 54.7	6 51.1	23 39.9	9 14.6	29 34.8	29 10.5	16 52.9
26 Sa	16 17 40	3 14 11	20 15 24	26 23 40	18 39.6	13 22.0	16 38.4	21 36.5	7 13.6	23 41.2	9 21.7	29 34.1	29 10.7	16 52.1
27 Su	16 21 37	4 14 56	2♑34 29	8♑48 04	18 40.4	14 22.3	17 41.3	22 18.4	7 36.2	23 42.7	9 28.8	29 33.5	29 10.9	16 51.2
28 M	16 25 34	5 15 43	15 04 40	21 24 31	18 41.5	15 27.3	18 44.5	23 00.3	7 58.8	23 44.4	9 35.9	29 32.9	29 11.1	16 50.3
29 Tu	16 29 30	6 16 30	27 47 55	4♒15 06	18 42.8	16 36.1	19 48.1	23 42.3	8 21.5	23 46.4	9 43.0	29 32.3	29 11.2	16 49.4
30 W	16 33 27	7 17 19	10♒46 22	17 21 57	18 43.8	17 48.3	20 52.0	24 24.3	8 44.2	23 48.5	9 50.1	29 31.8	29 11.3	16 48.5

December 1927 — LONGITUDE

Day	Sid.Time	☉	0 hr ☽	Noon ☽	True ☊	☿	♀	♂	⚳	♃	♄	♅	♆	♇
1 Th	16 37 23	8♐18 08	24♒02 07	0♓47 04	18♊44.3	19♏03.4	21♎56.2	25♏06.3	9♑07.0	23♓50.8	9♐57.2	29♓31.4	29♌11.3	16♋47.6
2 F	16 41 20	9 18 58	7♓36 57	14 31 53	18R 44.4	20 21.0	23 00.7	25 48.4	9 29.8	23 53.3	10 04.3	29R 31.0	29R 11.3	16R 46.6
3 Sa	16 45 16	10 19 49	21 31 52	28 36 50	18 44.0	21 40.7	24 05.6	26 30.5	9 52.6	23 56.0	10 11.4	29 30.6	29 11.3	16 45.7
4 Su	16 49 13	11 20 41	5♈46 33	13♈00 43	18 43.3	23 02.3	25 10.7	27 12.7	10 15.5	23 59.0	10 18.5	29 30.3	29 11.3	16 44.7
5 M	16 53 09	12 21 33	20 18 52	27 40 26	18 42.5	24 25.4	26 16.1	27 54.9	10 38.5	24 02.1	10 25.7	29 30.1	29 11.2	16 43.7
6 Tu	16 57 06	13 22 27	5♉04 40	12♉30 46	18 41.8	25 49.8	27 21.8	28 37.1	11 01.5	24 05.4	10 32.8	29 29.9	29 11.1	16 42.7
7 W	17 01 03	14 23 21	19 57 48	27 24 48	18 41.4	27 15.4	28 27.7	29 19.4	11 24.5	24 08.9	10 39.9	29 29.7	29 10.9	16 41.6
8 Th	17 04 59	15 24 16	4♊50 45	12♊14 40	18D 41.2	28 42.0	29 33.9	0♐01.7	11 47.6	24 12.6	10 47.0	29 29.6	29 10.7	16 40.6
9 F	17 08 56	16 25 12	19 35 35	26 52 39	18 41.2	0♐09.4	0♏40.4	0 44.1	12 10.7	24 16.5	10 54.1	29D 29.6	29 10.5	16 39.5
10 Sa	17 12 52	17 26 10	4♋05 05	11♋12 15	18 41.3	1 37.5	1 47.1	1 26.5	12 33.8	24 20.6	11 01.2	29 29.6	29 10.2	16 38.5
11 Su	17 16 49	18 27 08	18 13 39	25 08 56	18R 41.4	3 06.2	2 54.0	2 09.0	12 57.0	24 24.9	11 08.3	29 29.7	29 09.9	16 37.4
12 M	17 20 45	19 28 07	1♌57 55	8♌40 32	18 41.3	4 35.5	4 01.2	2 51.5	13 20.2	24 29.3	11 15.3	29 29.8	29 09.6	16 36.3
13 Tu	17 24 42	20 29 07	15 16 52	21 47 06	18 41.2	6 05.2	5 08.6	3 34.1	13 43.4	24 34.0	11 22.4	29 30.0	29 09.3	16 35.2
14 W	17 28 39	21 30 08	28 11 33	4♍30 35	18 41.0	7 35.4	6 16.2	4 16.7	14 06.7	24 38.8	11 29.5	29 30.2	29 08.9	16 34.1
15 Th	17 32 35	22 31 10	10♍44 41	16 54 19	18D 40.8	9 05.9	7 24.0	4 59.3	14 30.0	24 43.8	11 36.5	29 30.4	29 08.4	16 32.9
16 F	17 36 32	23 32 14	23 00 04	29 02 30	18 40.8	10 36.7	8 32.1	5 42.0	14 53.4	24 49.0	11 43.5	29 30.8	29 08.0	16 31.8
17 Sa	17 40 28	24 33 18	5♎02 13	10♎59 47	18 41.1	12 07.8	9 40.3	6 24.7	15 16.7	24 54.4	11 50.5	29 31.1	29 07.5	16 30.6
18 Su	17 44 25	25 34 22	16 55 49	22 50 53	18 41.7	13 39.2	10 48.7	7 07.5	15 40.1	25 00.0	11 57.5	29 31.6	29 07.0	16 29.5
19 M	17 48 21	26 35 28	28 45 32	4♏40 19	18 42.5	15 10.8	11 57.3	7 50.3	16 03.6	25 05.7	12 04.5	29 32.0	29 06.4	16 28.3
20 Tu	17 52 18	27 36 35	10♏35 44	16 32 14	18 43.4	16 42.7	13 06.1	8 33.2	16 27.0	25 11.6	12 11.5	29 32.5	29 05.8	16 27.1
21 W	17 56 14	28 37 42	22 30 16	28 30 13	18 44.3	18 14.8	14 15.0	9 16.1	16 50.5	25 17.7	12 18.4	29 33.1	29 05.2	16 25.9
22 Th	18 00 11	29 38 50	4♐32 25	10♐37 11	18R 44.9	19 47.1	15 24.2	9 59.1	17 14.0	25 24.0	12 25.4	29 33.8	29 04.5	16 24.7
23 F	18 04 08	0♑39 59	16 44 45	22 55 20	18 45.0	21 19.7	16 33.4	10 42.1	17 37.5	25 30.4	12 32.3	29 34.4	29 03.9	16 23.5
24 Sa	18 08 04	1 41 08	29 09 06	5♑26 10	18 44.5	22 52.5	17 42.8	11 25.1	18 01.1	25 37.0	12 39.1	29 35.2	29 03.1	16 22.3
25 Su	18 12 01	2 42 17	11♑46 37	18 10 29	18 43.2	24 25.5	18 52.4	12 08.2	18 24.7	25 43.8	12 46.0	29 36.0	29 02.4	16 21.1
26 M	18 15 57	3 43 27	24 37 47	1♒08 30	18 41.2	25 58.7	20 02.1	12 51.3	18 48.3	25 50.7	12 52.8	29 36.8	29 01.6	16 19.8
27 Tu	18 19 54	4 44 36	7♒42 36	14 20 02	18 38.9	27 32.2	21 12.0	13 34.5	19 11.9	25 57.8	12 59.6	29 37.7	29 00.8	16 18.6
28 W	18 23 50	5 45 46	21 00 44	27 44 37	18 36.5	29 06.0	22 21.9	14 17.7	19 35.5	26 05.1	13 06.4	29 38.6	29 00.0	16 17.4
29 Th	18 27 47	6 46 56	4♓31 37	11♓21 38	18 34.4	0♑40.0	23 32.0	15 00.9	19 59.2	26 12.5	13 13.1	29 39.6	28 59.1	16 16.1
30 F	18 31 43	7 48 06	18 14 35	25 10 22	18D 33.0	2 14.3	24 42.3	15 44.2	20 22.9	26 20.1	13 19.8	29 40.6	28 58.2	16 14.9
31 Sa	18 35 40	8 49 15	2♈08 53	9♈09 58	18 32.6	3 48.9	25 52.6	16 27.5	20 46.5	26 27.8	13 26.5	29 41.7	28 57.3	16 13.6

Astro Data

	Dy Hr Mn
☽0N	6 23:51
♀0S	11 5:11
☿D	19 9:16
♃D	19 18:48
☽0S	20 5:27
♆R	2 8:53
☽0N	4 9:16
♅D	9 18:15
☽0S	17 12:45
☽0N	31 15:36

Planet Ingress

		Dy Hr Mn
♅	♓R	4 10:30
⚳	♑	6 17:37
♀	♎	9 13:26
☉	♐	23 7:14
♂	♐	8 11:01
♀	♏	8 21:26
☿	♐	9 9:26
☉	♑	22 20:19
☿	♑	29 1:48

Last Aspect / ☽ Ingress

Last Aspect Dy Hr Mn		☽ Ingress	Dy Hr Mn
1 13:27	☿ ⚹	♒	1 22:26
4 2:08	♆ ☍	♓	4 3:56
6 5:49	♅ ☌	♈	6 5:53
8 4:04	♆ △	♉	8 5:37
10 4:49	♅ ⚹	♊	10 5:03
12 5:56	♅ □	♋	12 6:15
14 10:22	♅ △	♌	14 10:48
16 17:31	♆ ☌	♍	16 19:14
19 6:01	♅ ☍	♎	19 6:41
21 17:43	♆ ⚹	♏	21 19:26
24 7:05	♅ △	♐	24 7:53
26 18:10	♅ □	♑	26 19:01
29 3:15	♅ ⚹	♒	29 4:06

Last Aspect / ☽ Ingress

Last Aspect Dy Hr Mn		☽ Ingress	Dy Hr Mn
1 9:11	♆ ☍	♓	1 10:37
3 13:30	♅ ☌	♈	3 14:20
5 14:27	♆ △	♉	5 15:47
7 15:21	♅ ⚹	♊	7 16:10
9 16:20	♅ □	♋	9 17:11
11 19:38	♅ △	♌	11 20:31
14 1:49	♆ ☌	♍	14 3:25
16 12:56	♅ ☍	♎	16 13:55
19 0:43	♆ ⚹	♏	19 2:31
21 14:05	♅ △	♐	21 14:59
24 0:49	♅ □	♑	24 1:38
26 9:11	♅ ⚹	♒	26 9:54
28 14:43	☿ ⚹	♓	28 16:00
30 19:46	♅ ☌	♈	30 20:19

☽ Phases & Eclipses

Dy Hr Mn		
2 15:16	☽	9♒12
9 6:36	○	15♉52
16 5:28	☾	22♌52
24 10:09	●	1♐08
2 2:15	☽	8♓54
8 17:32	○	15♊38
8 17:35	☍	T 1.351
16 0:04	☾	23♍02
24 4:13	●	1♑21
24 3:59:15	☌	P 0.549
31 11:22	☽	8♈48

Astro Data

1 November 1927
Julian Day # 10166
SVP 6♓16'21"
GC 25♐49.9 ⚳ 11♐10.1
Eris 0♈29.9R ⚵ 1♍52.6
⚷ 3♉31.3R ⚶ 21♐24.3
☽ Mean ☊ 20♊50.9

1 December 1927
Julian Day # 10196
SVP 6♓16'16"
GC 25♐50.0 ⚳ 23♐12.3
Eris 0♈18.5R ⚵ 11♍22.8
⚷ 2♉12.8R ⚶ 6♑43.5
☽ Mean ☊ 19♊15.6

LONGITUDE — January 1928

Day	Sid.Time	☉	0 hr ☽	Noon ☽	True ☊	☿	♀	♂	⚳	♃	♄	♅	♆	♇
1 Su	18 39 37	9♑50 24	16♈13 30	23♈19 17	18♊33.1	5♑23.8	27♏03.1	17♐10.9	21♑10.2	26♓35.7	13♐33.2	29♓42.9	28♌56.3	16♋12.3
2 M	18 43 33	10 51 33	0♉27 04	7♉36 36	18 34.3	6 59.0	28 13.7	17 54.3	21 33.9	26 43.8	13 39.8	29 44.0	28R 55.4	16R 11.1
3 Tu	18 47 30	11 52 42	14 47 31	21 59 27	18 35.8	8 34.5	29 24.3	18 37.7	21 57.7	26 52.0	13 46.3	29 45.3	28 54.4	16 09.8
4 W	18 51 26	12 53 51	29 11 57	6♊24 29	18R 37.0	10 10.4	0♐35.1	19 21.2	22 21.4	27 00.3	13 52.9	29 46.6	28 53.3	16 08.6
5 Th	18 55 23	13 54 59	13♊36 30	20 47 25	18 37.4	11 46.7	1 46.0	20 04.7	22 45.1	27 08.8	13 59.4	29 47.9	28 52.3	16 07.3
6 F	18 59 19	14 56 08	27 56 36	5♋03 25	18 36.5	13 23.3	2 57.0	20 48.3	23 08.9	27 17.4	14 05.9	29 49.3	28 51.2	16 06.0
7 Sa	19 03 16	15 57 16	12♋07 16	19 07 33	18 34.2	15 00.4	4 08.2	21 31.9	23 32.6	27 26.2	14 12.3	29 50.7	28 50.1	16 04.8
8 Su	19 07 13	16 58 24	26 03 46	2♌55 27	18 30.5	16 37.8	5 19.4	22 15.5	23 56.4	27 35.1	14 18.7	29 52.2	28 48.9	16 03.5
9 M	19 11 09	17 59 31	9♌42 15	16 23 54	18 25.7	18 15.7	6 30.7	22 59.2	24 20.2	27 44.1	14 25.0	29 53.7	28 47.8	16 02.2
10 Tu	19 15 06	19 00 39	23 00 15	29 31 16	18 20.5	19 54.0	7 42.1	23 42.9	24 43.9	27 53.3	14 31.3	29 55.3	28 46.6	16 01.0
11 W	19 19 02	20 01 46	5♍57 00	12♍17 38	18 15.6	21 32.8	8 53.6	24 26.7	25 07.7	28 02.6	14 37.6	29 56.9	28 45.4	15 59.7
12 Th	19 22 59	21 02 54	18 33 25	24 44 43	18 11.4	23 12.0	10 05.1	25 10.5	25 31.5	28 12.0	14 43.8	29 58.5	28 44.1	15 58.4
13 F	19 26 55	22 04 01	0♎51 58	6♎55 38	18 08.5	24 51.6	11 16.8	25 54.3	25 55.3	28 21.6	14 49.9	0♈00.2	28 42.9	15 57.2
14 Sa	19 30 52	23 05 08	12 56 17	18 54 30	18D 07.2	26 31.8	12 28.5	26 38.2	26 19.1	28 31.3	14 56.1	0 02.0	28 41.6	15 55.9
15 Su	19 34 48	24 06 15	24 50 54	0♏46 06	18 07.4	28 12.3	13 40.4	27 22.2	26 42.9	28 41.1	15 02.1	0 03.8	28 40.3	15 54.6
16 M	19 38 45	25 07 22	6♏40 47	12 35 34	18 08.6	29 53.3	14 52.3	28 06.1	27 06.7	28 51.1	15 08.2	0 05.6	28 39.0	15 53.4
17 Tu	19 42 42	26 08 29	18 31 05	24 28 00	18 10.4	1♒34.8	16 04.2	28 50.2	27 30.5	29 01.2	15 14.1	0 07.5	28 37.6	15 52.1
18 W	19 46 38	27 09 35	0♐26 52	6♐28 16	18R 12.0	3 16.6	17 16.3	29 34.2	27 54.3	29 11.4	15 20.1	0 09.4	28 36.3	15 50.9
19 Th	19 50 35	28 10 41	12 32 43	18 40 41	18 12.6	4 58.9	18 28.4	0♑18.3	28 18.0	29 21.7	15 25.9	0 11.4	28 34.9	15 49.7
20 F	19 54 31	29 11 47	24 52 33	1♑08 40	18 11.7	6 41.4	19 40.6	1 02.4	28 41.8	29 32.1	15 31.7	0 13.4	28 33.5	15 48.4
21 Sa	19 58 28	0♒12 52	7♑29 16	13 54 31	18 08.7	8 24.3	20 52.8	1 46.6	29 05.6	29 42.7	15 37.5	0 15.4	28 32.1	15 47.2
22 Su	20 02 24	1 13 57	20 24 28	26 59 07	18 03.7	10 07.4	22 05.1	2 30.8	29 29.4	29 53.3	15 43.2	0 17.5	28 30.6	15 46.0
23 M	20 06 21	2 15 00	3♒38 19	10♒21 52	17 57.0	11 50.6	23 17.5	3 15.1	29 53.2	0♈04.1	15 48.8	0 19.7	28 29.2	15 44.8
24 Tu	20 10 17	3 16 03	17 09 29	24 00 46	17 49.1	13 33.8	24 29.9	3 59.4	0♒16.9	0 15.0	15 54.4	0 21.9	28 27.7	15 43.5
25 W	20 14 14	4 17 05	0♓55 19	7♓52 39	17 41.0	15 17.0	25 42.3	4 43.7	0 40.7	0 26.0	16 00.0	0 24.1	28 26.2	15 42.3
26 Th	20 18 11	5 18 06	14 52 17	21 53 46	17 33.7	17 00.0	26 54.9	5 28.0	1 04.4	0 37.1	16 05.4	0 26.3	28 24.7	15 41.2
27 F	20 22 07	6 19 06	28 56 36	6♈00 21	17 28.0	18 42.5	28 07.4	6 12.4	1 28.2	0 48.3	16 10.8	0 28.6	28 23.2	15 40.0
28 Sa	20 26 04	7 20 05	13♈04 39	20 09 10	17 24.4	20 24.4	29 20.0	6 56.8	1 51.9	0 59.6	16 16.2	0 30.9	28 21.6	15 38.8
29 Su	20 30 00	8 21 03	27 13 36	4♉17 44	17D 23.0	22 05.5	0♑32.6	7 41.3	2 15.6	1 11.0	16 21.4	0 33.3	28 20.1	15 37.6
30 M	20 33 57	9 21 59	11♉21 24	18 24 25	17 23.2	23 45.4	1 45.3	8 25.8	2 39.3	1 22.5	16 26.6	0 35.7	28 18.5	15 36.5
31 Tu	20 37 53	10 22 54	25 26 41	2♊28 04	17 24.2	25 23.8	2 58.1	9 10.3	3 02.9	1 34.1	16 31.8	0 38.2	28 17.0	15 35.3

LONGITUDE — February 1928

Day	Sid.Time	☉	0 hr ☽	Noon ☽	True ☊	☿	♀	♂	⚳	♃	♄	♅	♆	♇
1 W	20 41 50	11♒23 48	9♊28 28	16♊27 45	17♊24.9	27♒00.4	4♑10.8	9♑54.9	3♒26.6	1♈45.8	16♐36.9	0♈40.6	28♌15.4	15♋34.2
2 Th	20 45 46	12 24 41	23 25 45	0♋22 17	17R 24.1	28 34.7	5 23.6	10 39.4	3 50.2	1 57.5	16 41.9	0 43.2	28R 13.8	15R 33.1
3 F	20 49 43	13 25 32	7♋17 07	14 09 59	17 21.1	0♓06.1	6 36.5	11 24.1	4 13.8	2 09.4	16 46.8	0 45.7	28 12.2	15 32.0
4 Sa	20 53 40	14 26 22	21 00 37	27 48 41	17 15.4	1 34.2	7 49.4	12 08.7	4 37.4	2 21.4	16 51.7	0 48.3	28 10.6	15 30.9
5 Su	20 57 36	15 27 10	4♌33 52	11♌15 51	17 07.2	2 58.3	9 02.3	12 53.4	5 01.0	2 33.4	16 56.5	0 50.9	28 08.9	15 29.8
6 M	21 01 33	16 27 58	17 54 21	24 29 06	16 57.0	4 17.8	10 15.3	13 38.2	5 24.6	2 45.5	17 01.2	0 53.5	28 07.3	15 28.7
7 Tu	21 05 29	17 28 44	0♍59 53	7♍26 35	16 45.7	5 31.9	11 28.3	14 22.9	5 48.1	2 57.8	17 05.8	0 56.2	28 05.7	15 27.7
8 W	21 09 26	18 29 29	13 49 06	20 07 28	16 34.4	6 40.0	12 41.3	15 07.7	6 11.6	3 10.1	17 10.4	0 58.9	28 04.0	15 26.6
9 Th	21 13 22	19 30 13	26 21 45	2♎32 09	16 24.3	7 41.2	13 54.4	15 52.6	6 35.1	3 22.4	17 14.9	1 01.7	28 02.4	15 25.6
10 F	21 17 19	20 30 56	8♎38 56	14 42 25	16 16.2	8 34.9	15 07.5	16 37.4	6 58.6	3 34.9	17 19.4	1 04.4	28 00.7	15 24.6
11 Sa	21 21 15	21 31 37	20 43 01	26 41 13	16 10.5	9 20.2	16 20.6	17 22.3	7 22.1	3 47.4	17 23.7	1 07.2	27 59.0	15 23.6
12 Su	21 25 12	22 32 18	2♏37 33	8♏32 37	16 07.2	9 56.5	17 33.8	18 07.3	7 45.5	4 00.0	17 28.0	1 10.1	27 57.4	15 22.6
13 M	21 29 09	23 32 57	14 27 01	20 21 25	16D 06.1	10 23.3	18 47.0	18 52.2	8 08.9	4 12.7	17 32.2	1 12.9	27 55.7	15 21.6
14 Tu	21 33 05	24 33 36	26 16 30	2♐12 57	16 06.2	10 40.0	20 00.2	19 37.2	8 32.3	4 25.5	17 36.3	1 15.8	27 54.0	15 20.7
15 W	21 37 02	25 34 13	8♐11 28	14 12 44	16R 06.6	10R 46.4	21 13.5	20 22.3	8 55.6	4 38.3	17 40.3	1 18.7	27 52.3	15 19.8
16 Th	21 40 58	26 34 49	20 17 24	26 26 06	16 06.1	10 42.3	22 26.8	21 07.4	9 18.9	4 51.2	17 44.3	1 21.7	27 50.6	15 18.8
17 F	21 44 55	27 35 24	2♑39 24	8♑57 48	16 03.8	10 27.8	23 40.1	21 52.5	9 42.2	5 04.2	17 48.2	1 24.6	27 49.0	15 17.9
18 Sa	21 48 51	28 35 58	15 21 44	21 51 31	15 59.0	10 03.2	24 53.4	22 37.6	10 05.5	5 17.2	17 52.0	1 27.6	27 47.3	15 17.1
19 Su	21 52 48	29 36 30	28 27 20	5♒09 16	15 51.4	9 29.2	26 06.8	23 22.8	10 28.7	5 30.3	17 55.7	1 30.6	27 45.6	15 16.2
20 M	21 56 44	0♓37 00	11♒57 13	18 50 57	15 41.4	8 46.6	27 20.2	24 07.9	10 51.9	5 43.4	17 59.3	1 33.7	27 43.9	15 15.3
21 Tu	22 00 41	1 37 29	25 50 04	2♓54 02	15 29.7	7 56.6	28 33.6	24 53.2	11 15.0	5 56.7	18 02.8	1 36.7	27 42.2	15 14.5
22 W	22 04 38	2 37 57	10♓02 11	17 13 44	15 17.6	7 00.4	29 47.0	25 38.4	11 38.1	6 09.9	18 06.3	1 39.8	27 40.6	15 13.7
23 Th	22 08 34	3 38 23	24 27 51	1♈43 40	15 06.4	5 59.6	1♒00.4	26 23.7	12 01.2	6 23.3	18 09.6	1 42.9	27 38.9	15 12.9
24 F	22 12 31	4 38 46	9♈00 16	16 16 51	14 57.3	4 55.7	2 13.9	27 09.0	12 24.2	6 36.7	18 12.9	1 46.1	27 37.2	15 12.1
25 Sa	22 16 27	5 39 08	23 32 38	0♉46 57	14 50.9	3 50.5	3 27.3	27 54.3	12 47.2	6 50.1	18 16.1	1 49.2	27 35.5	15 11.4
26 Su	22 20 24	6 39 28	7♉59 16	15 09 08	14 47.4	2 45.5	4 40.8	28 39.6	13 10.2	7 03.6	18 19.2	1 52.4	27 33.9	15 10.6
27 M	22 24 20	7 39 46	22 16 16	29 20 26	14D 46.1	1 42.4	5 54.3	29 25.0	13 33.1	7 17.2	18 22.2	1 55.6	27 32.2	15 09.9
28 Tu	22 28 17	8 40 03	6♊21 34	13♊19 37	14R 46.0	0 42.3	7 07.8	0♒10.4	13 56.0	7 30.8	18 25.1	1 58.8	27 30.6	15 09.2
29 W	22 32 13	9 40 17	20 14 38	27 06 40	14 45.7	29♒46.5	8 21.3	0 55.8	14 18.8	7 44.5	18 27.9	2 02.0	27 28.9	15 08.6

Astro Data

	Dy Hr Mn
☽0S	13 20:25
♃⚻♆	15 10:13
♄⚻♇	22 21:40
♃☌♅	25 6:49
☽0N	27 20:22
♃0N	6 2:31
☽0S	10 4:06
☿R	15 14:36
♅0N	21 12:04
☽0N	24 2:31

Planet Ingress

		Dy Hr Mn
♀	♐	4 0:06
♅	♈	13 8:47
☿	♒	16 13:35
♂	♑	19 2:02
☉	♒	21 6:57
♃	♈	23 2:54
⚳	♒	23 18:54
♀	♑	29 1:13
☿	♓	3 10:22
☉	♓	19 21:19
♀	♒	22 16:15
♂	♒	28 6:30
☿	♒R	29 6:00

Last Aspect / ☽ Ingress (January)

Last Aspect Dy Hr Mn			☽ Ingress	Dy Hr Mn
1 21:27	♆	△	♉	1 23:15
4 0:57	♅	⚹	♊	4 1:20
6 3:09	♅	□	♋	6 3:28
8 6:38	♅	△	♌	8 6:52
10 10:37	♆	☌	♍	10 12:53
12 22:16	♅	☍	♎	12 22:18
15 7:45	♆	⚹	♏	15 10:26
17 21:16	♃	△	♐	17 23:06
20 8:53	♃	□	♑	20 9:49
22 17:19	♃	⚹	♒	22 17:27
24 19:43	♆	☍	♓	24 22:24
26 21:21	♀	□	♈	27 1:48
29 1:54	♆	△	♉	29 4:42
31 4:52	♆	□	♊	31 7:47

Last Aspect / ☽ Ingress (February)

Last Aspect Dy Hr Mn			☽ Ingress	Dy Hr Mn
2 8:30	☿	△	♋	2 11:21
3 14:23	♇	☌	♌	4 15:53
6 18:40	♆	☌	♍	6 22:09
8 6:20	♄	□	♎	9 7:03
11 14:37	♆	⚹	♏	11 18:41
14 3:19	♆	□	♐	14 7:32
16 14:43	♆	△	♑	16 18:54
18 18:06	♀	☌	♒	19 2:47
21 3:12	♆	☍	♓	21 7:05
23 2:43	♂	⚹	♈	23 9:09
25 6:58	♂	□	♉	25 10:42
27 12:08	♂	△	♊	27 13:07
29 16:24	☿	△	♋	29 17:04

☽ Phases & Eclipses

Dy Hr Mn		
7 6:08	○	15♋42
14 21:14	☾	23♎29
22 20:19	●	1♒35
29 19:25	☽	8♉40
5 20:11	○	15♌48
13 19:05	☾	23♏51
21 9:41	●	1♓32
28 3:21	☽	8♊18

Astro Data

1 January 1928
Julian Day # 10227
SVP 6♓16'11"
GC 25♐50.0 ⚴ 5♑43.8
Eris 0♈17.5 ⚵ 16♍22.4
⚷ 1♉27.5R ⚶ 22♑55.2
☽ Mean ☊ 17♊37.1

1 February 1928
Julian Day # 10258
SVP 6♓16'06"
GC 25♐50.1 ⚴ 17♑49.5
Eris 0♈28.0 ⚵ 14♍32.7R
⚷ 1♉36.1 ⚶ 9♒07.5
☽ Mean ☊ 15♊58.7

March 1928 LONGITUDE

Day	Sid.Time	☉	0 hr ☽	Noon ☽	True ☊	☿	♀	♂	⚳	♃	♄	♅	♆	♇
1 Th	22 36 10	10♓40 29	3♋55 50	10♋42 12	14♊43.9	28♒55.9	9♒34.8	1♒41.3	14♒41.6	7♈58.2	18♐30.7	2♈05.2	27♌27.3	15♋07.9
2 F	22 40 07	11 40 38	17 25 52	24 06 52	14R 39.6	28R 11.2	10 48.3	2 26.7	15 04.3	8 11.9	18 33.3	2 08.5	27R 25.7	15R 07.3
3 Sa	22 44 03	12 40 46	0♌45 14	7♌20 58	14 32.3	27 33.0	12 01.9	3 12.2	15 27.0	8 25.7	18 35.8	2 11.8	27 24.1	15 06.7
4 Su	22 48 00	13 40 52	13 54 03	20 24 24	14 22.1	27 01.4	13 15.4	3 57.7	15 49.6	8 39.5	18 38.3	2 15.0	27 22.5	15 06.1
5 M	22 51 56	14 40 56	26 51 56	3♍16 36	14 09.5	26 36.8	14 29.0	4 43.3	16 12.2	8 53.4	18 40.6	2 18.3	27 20.9	15 05.5
6 Tu	22 55 53	15 40 58	9♍38 18	15 56 58	13 55.6	26 18.9	15 42.6	5 28.8	16 34.8	9 07.3	18 42.9	2 21.6	27 19.3	15 05.0
7 W	22 59 49	16 40 58	22 12 34	28 25 06	13 41.7	26 07.9	16 56.2	6 14.4	16 57.3	9 21.3	18 45.1	2 25.0	27 17.7	15 04.5
8 Th	23 03 46	17 40 56	4♎34 35	10♎41 08	13 28.8	26D 03.5	18 09.8	7 00.0	17 19.7	9 35.2	18 47.1	2 28.3	27 16.2	15 04.0
9 F	23 07 42	18 40 52	16 44 54	22 46 06	13 18.1	26 05.3	19 23.4	7 45.6	17 42.1	9 49.3	18 49.1	2 31.6	27 14.6	15 03.5
10 Sa	23 11 39	19 40 47	28 45 01	4♏42 00	13 10.1	26 13.3	20 37.0	8 31.3	18 04.4	10 03.3	18 51.0	2 35.0	27 13.1	15 03.0
11 Su	23 15 35	20 40 39	10♏37 27	16 31 49	13 04.9	26 27.0	21 50.6	9 16.9	18 26.7	10 17.4	18 52.8	2 38.4	27 11.5	15 02.6
12 M	23 19 32	21 40 31	22 25 39	28 19 30	13 02.4	26 46.1	23 04.3	10 02.6	18 48.9	10 31.5	18 54.5	2 41.7	27 10.0	15 02.2
13 Tu	23 23 29	22 40 20	4♐13 59	10♐09 45	13D 01.6	27 10.3	24 17.9	10 48.3	19 11.1	10 45.7	18 56.0	2 45.1	27 08.5	15 01.8
14 W	23 27 25	23 40 08	16 07 28	22 07 50	13R 01.7	27 39.4	25 31.6	11 34.1	19 33.2	10 59.9	18 57.5	2 48.5	27 07.1	15 01.4
15 Th	23 31 22	24 39 54	28 11 32	4♑19 15	13 01.4	28 12.9	26 45.3	12 19.8	19 55.2	11 14.1	18 58.9	2 51.9	27 05.6	15 01.1
16 F	23 35 18	25 39 38	10♑31 41	16 49 26	12 59.7	28 50.7	27 58.9	13 05.6	20 17.2	11 28.3	19 00.2	2 55.3	27 04.2	15 00.8
17 Sa	23 39 15	26 39 21	23 13 04	29 43 04	12 55.7	29 32.5	29 12.6	13 51.4	20 39.2	11 42.6	19 01.4	2 58.7	27 02.8	15 00.5
18 Su	23 43 11	27 39 02	6♒19 49	13♒03 33	12 49.2	0♓18.0	0♓26.3	14 37.2	21 01.0	11 56.9	19 02.5	3 02.1	27 01.3	15 00.2
19 M	23 47 08	28 38 41	19 54 22	26 52 11	12 40.2	1 06.9	1 40.0	15 23.0	21 22.8	12 11.2	19 03.5	3 05.6	27 00.0	15 00.0
20 Tu	23 51 04	29 38 18	3♓56 41	11♓07 26	12 29.6	1 59.1	2 53.7	16 08.8	21 44.6	12 25.6	19 04.4	3 09.0	26 58.6	14 59.8
21 W	23 55 01	0♈37 53	18 23 44	25 44 45	12 18.4	2 54.4	4 07.4	16 54.7	22 06.2	12 39.9	19 05.2	3 12.4	26 57.2	14 59.6
22 Th	23 58 58	1 37 26	3♈09 30	10♈36 50	12 07.9	3 52.6	5 21.1	17 40.5	22 27.8	12 54.3	19 05.8	3 15.8	26 55.9	14 59.4
23 F	0 02 54	2 36 58	18 05 38	25 34 42	11 59.3	4 53.5	6 34.9	18 26.4	22 49.4	13 08.7	19 06.4	3 19.3	26 54.6	14 59.2
24 Sa	0 06 51	3 36 27	3♉02 56	10♉29 17	11 53.3	5 57.0	7 48.6	19 12.3	23 10.8	13 23.1	19 06.9	3 22.7	26 53.3	14 59.1
25 Su	0 10 47	4 35 53	17 52 51	25 12 54	11 50.0	7 03.0	9 02.3	19 58.2	23 32.2	13 37.5	19 07.3	3 26.1	26 52.0	14 59.0
26 M	0 14 44	5 35 18	2♊28 49	9♊40 12	11D 49.0	8 11.3	10 16.0	20 44.1	23 53.5	13 51.9	19 07.6	3 29.6	26 50.8	14 58.9
27 Tu	0 18 40	6 34 40	16 46 47	23 48 27	11R 49.2	9 21.8	11 29.7	21 30.0	24 14.7	14 06.4	19 07.8	3 33.0	26 49.6	14 58.9
28 W	0 22 37	7 34 00	0♋45 11	7♋37 05	11 49.6	10 34.4	12 43.4	22 15.9	24 35.9	14 20.9	19R 07.9	3 36.4	26 48.4	14D 58.9
29 Th	0 26 33	8 33 18	14 24 19	21 07 04	11 48.9	11 49.1	13 57.1	23 01.8	24 57.0	14 35.3	19 07.8	3 39.8	26 47.2	14 58.9
30 F	0 30 30	9 32 33	27 45 36	4♌20 10	11 46.1	13 05.7	15 10.8	23 47.7	25 17.9	14 49.8	19 07.7	3 43.3	26 46.1	14 58.9
31 Sa	0 34 27	10 31 46	10♌51 01	17 18 23	11 40.9	14 24.3	16 24.5	24 33.6	25 38.9	15 04.3	19 07.5	3 46.7	26 44.9	14 58.9

April 1928 LONGITUDE

Day	Sid.Time	☉	0 hr ☽	Noon ☽	True ☊	☿	♀	♂	⚳	♃	♄	♅	♆	♇
1 Su	0 38 23	11♈30 56	23♌42 28	0♍03 30	11♊33.2	15♓44.6	17♓38.2	25♒19.6	25♒59.7	15♈18.8	19♐07.2	3♈50.1	26♌43.8	14♋59.0
2 M	0 42 20	12 30 05	6♍21 38	12 37 01	11R 23.6	17 06.8	18 51.9	26 05.5	26 20.4	15 33.3	19R 06.8	3 53.5	26R 42.8	14 59.1
3 Tu	0 46 16	13 29 11	18 49 47	25 00 03	11 12.8	18 30.7	20 05.6	26 51.5	26 41.1	15 47.8	19 06.3	3 56.9	26 41.7	14 59.2
4 W	0 50 13	14 28 15	1♎07 55	7♎13 31	11 01.9	19 56.2	21 19.3	27 37.4	27 01.7	16 02.3	19 05.7	4 00.3	26 40.7	14 59.4
5 Th	0 54 09	15 27 16	13 16 58	19 18 23	10 51.9	21 23.5	22 33.0	28 23.4	27 22.1	16 16.7	19 05.0	4 03.6	26 39.7	14 59.5
6 F	0 58 06	16 26 16	25 17 56	1♏15 48	10 43.5	22 52.4	23 46.6	29 09.3	27 42.5	16 31.2	19 04.1	4 07.0	26 38.7	14 59.7
7 Sa	1 02 02	17 25 14	7♏12 13	13 07 26	10 37.4	24 22.9	25 00.3	29 55.3	28 02.9	16 45.7	19 03.2	4 10.4	26 37.8	14 59.9
8 Su	1 05 59	18 24 10	19 01 45	24 55 32	10 33.8	25 55.0	26 14.0	0♓41.3	28 23.1	17 00.2	19 02.2	4 13.7	26 36.9	15 00.2
9 M	1 09 56	19 23 04	0♐49 11	6♐43 07	10D 32.3	27 28.7	27 27.7	1 27.3	28 43.2	17 14.7	19 01.2	4 17.1	26 36.0	15 00.4
10 Tu	1 13 52	20 21 57	12 37 49	18 33 50	10 32.5	29 04.0	28 41.4	2 13.3	29 03.2	17 29.2	19 00.0	4 20.4	26 35.1	15 00.7
11 W	1 17 49	21 20 47	24 31 43	0♑32 04	10 33.7	0♈40.9	29 55.1	2 59.2	29 23.2	17 43.7	18 58.7	4 23.7	26 34.3	15 01.0
12 Th	1 21 45	22 19 36	6♑35 29	12 42 37	10R 34.9	2 19.3	1♈08.8	3 45.2	29 43.0	17 58.2	18 57.3	4 27.0	26 33.5	15 01.4
13 F	1 25 42	23 18 23	18 54 05	25 10 31	10 35.3	3 59.3	2 22.5	4 31.2	0♓02.7	18 12.6	18 55.8	4 30.3	26 32.7	15 01.7
14 Sa	1 29 38	24 17 09	1♒32 30	8♒00 34	10 34.3	5 40.9	3 36.2	5 17.2	0 22.4	18 27.1	18 54.3	4 33.6	26 32.0	15 02.1
15 Su	1 33 35	25 15 53	14 35 13	21 16 47	10 31.4	7 24.1	4 49.9	6 03.2	0 41.9	18 41.5	18 52.6	4 36.9	26 31.2	15 02.5
16 M	1 37 31	26 14 35	28 05 34	5♓01 37	10 26.8	9 08.9	6 03.6	6 49.1	1 01.3	18 56.0	18 50.9	4 40.1	26 30.6	15 03.0
17 Tu	1 41 28	27 13 15	12♓04 54	19 15 09	10 20.9	10 55.2	7 17.3	7 35.1	1 20.7	19 10.4	18 49.0	4 43.4	26 29.9	15 03.4
18 W	1 45 25	28 11 53	26 31 54	3♈54 28	10 14.3	12 43.2	8 31.0	8 21.1	1 39.9	19 24.8	18 47.1	4 46.6	26 29.3	15 03.9
19 Th	1 49 21	29 10 30	11♈21 59	18 53 26	10 08.1	14 32.8	9 44.7	9 07.0	1 59.0	19 39.2	18 45.1	4 49.8	26 28.7	15 04.4
20 F	1 53 18	0♉09 05	26 27 39	4♉03 22	10 03.0	16 24.0	10 58.4	9 53.0	2 18.0	19 53.6	18 42.9	4 53.0	26 28.1	15 04.9
21 Sa	1 57 14	1 07 38	11♉39 18	19 14 12	9 59.7	18 16.8	12 12.1	10 38.9	2 36.8	20 08.0	18 40.7	4 56.1	26 27.6	15 05.5
22 Su	2 01 11	2 06 09	26 46 53	4♊16 18	9D 58.2	20 11.2	13 25.7	11 24.8	2 55.6	20 22.3	18 38.5	4 59.3	26 27.1	15 06.0
23 M	2 05 07	3 04 38	11♊41 31	19 01 49	9 58.3	22 07.3	14 39.4	12 10.8	3 14.2	20 36.6	18 36.1	5 02.4	26 26.6	15 06.6
24 Tu	2 09 04	4 03 05	26 16 38	3♋25 35	9 59.5	24 04.9	15 53.1	12 56.7	3 32.7	20 50.9	18 33.6	5 05.5	26 26.2	15 07.2
25 W	2 13 00	5 01 29	10♋28 28	17 25 12	10 00.9	26 04.2	17 06.7	13 42.5	3 51.1	21 05.2	18 31.1	5 08.6	26 25.8	15 07.9
26 Th	2 16 57	5 59 52	24 15 53	1♌00 38	10R 01.9	28 05.0	18 20.4	14 28.4	4 09.4	21 19.4	18 28.5	5 11.7	26 25.4	15 08.5
27 F	2 20 54	6 58 13	7♌39 44	14 13 29	10 01.8	0♉07.2	19 34.0	15 14.3	4 27.5	21 33.7	18 25.8	5 14.7	26 25.0	15 09.2
28 Sa	2 24 50	7 56 31	20 42 13	27 06 19	10 00.2	2 11.0	20 47.7	16 00.1	4 45.5	21 47.9	18 23.0	5 17.8	26 24.7	15 09.9
29 Su	2 28 47	8 54 47	3♍26 11	9♍42 10	9 57.2	4 16.0	22 01.3	16 45.9	5 03.4	22 02.0	18 20.2	5 20.8	26 24.5	15 10.6
30 M	2 32 43	9 53 01	15 54 40	22 04 01	9 53.1	6 22.3	23 14.9	17 31.7	5 21.2	22 16.2	18 17.3	5 23.7	26 24.2	15 11.4

Astro Data	Dy Hr Mn
☽0S	8 11:23
☿D	8 16:44
♃♇♆	18 18:48
☉0N	20 20:45
☽0N	22 11:31
♄R	28 20:37
♇D	28 23:45
♃□♇	31 3:07
☽0S	4 18:04
☿0N	14 9:58
♀0N	14 10:53
♃△♄	16 4:25
☽0N	18 22:24

Planet Ingress		Dy Hr Mn
☿	♓	18 2:45
♀	♓	18 3:25
☉	♈	20 20:44
♂	♓	7 14:27
☿	♈	11 1:55
♀	♈	11 13:35
⚳	♓	13 8:39
☉	♉	20 8:17
☿	♉	27 10:35

Last Aspect Dy Hr Mn			☽ Ingress	Dy Hr Mn
1 19:53	♇	☌	♌	2 22:38
5 0:55	♆	☌	♍	5 5:51
6 17:18	♄	□	♎	7 15:04
9 20:57	♆	⚹	♏	10 2:31
12 9:39	♆	□	♐	12 15:24
14 23:27	☿	⚹	♑	15 3:33
17 5:54	☉	⚹	♒	17 12:31
19 12:13	♆	☍	♓	19 17:20
21 1:07	♄	□	♈	21 18:54
23 14:08	♆	△	♉	23 19:06
25 14:43	♆	□	♊	25 19:53
27 17:11	♆	⚹	♋	27 22:42
29 1:01	♇	☌	♌	30 4:04

Last Aspect Dy Hr Mn			☽ Ingress	Dy Hr Mn
1 5:43	♆	☌	♍	1 11:53
3 1:24	♀	☍	♎	3 21:47
6 7:28	♂	△	♏	6 9:27
8 15:26	♆	□	♐	8 22:20
11 10:38	♀	□	♑	11 10:56
13 8:09	☉	□	♒	13 21:07
15 21:14	♆	☍	♓	16 3:19
17 11:17	♄	□	♈	18 5:40
20 5:25	☉	☌	♉	20 5:36
21 23:29	♆	□	♊	22 5:09
24 0:16	♆	⚹	♋	24 6:14
26 5:51	☿	□	♌	26 10:11
28 10:42	♆	☌	♍	28 17:28

☽ Phases & Eclipses Dy Hr Mn		
6 11:27	○	15♍40
14 15:20	☾	23♐48
21 20:29	●	0♈59
28 11:54	☽	7♋34
5 3:38	○	15♎07
13 8:09	☾	23♑09
20 5:25	●	29♈53
26 21:42	☽	6♌23

Astro Data

1 March 1928
Julian Day # 10287
SVP 6♓16'02"
GC 25♐50.2 ⚴ 28♑14.7
Eris 0♈45.9 ⚵ 7♍50.1R
⚷ 2♉32.1 ⚶ 24♒00.5
☽ Mean ☊ 14♊26.5

1 April 1928
Julian Day # 10318
SVP 6♓15'58"
GC 25♐50.2 ⚴ 7♒44.4
Eris 1♈08.6 ⚵ 1♍55.0R
⚷ 4♉09.5 ⚶ 9♓19.0
☽ Mean ☊ 12♊48.0

LONGITUDE — May 1928

Day	Sid.Time	☉	0 hr ☽	Noon ☽	True ☊	☿	♀	♂	⚳	♃	♄	♅	♆	♇
1 Tu	2 36 40	10♉51 13	28♍10 36	4♎14 42	9♊48.3	8♉29.7	24♈28.6	18♓17.5	5♓38.8	22♈30.3	18♐14.3	5♈26.7	26♌24.0	15♋12.2
2 W	2 40 36	11 49 23	10♎16 38	16 16 42	9R 43.3	10 38.1	25 42.2	19 03.3	5 56.2	22 44.4	18R 11.2	5 29.6	26R 23.8	15 12.9
3 Th	2 44 33	12 47 32	22 15 08	28 12 14	9 38.8	12 47.2	26 55.8	19 49.0	6 13.6	22 58.4	18 08.1	5 32.5	26 23.7	15 13.7
4 F	2 48 29	13 45 39	4♏08 13	10♏03 20	9 35.2	14 57.0	28 09.4	20 34.8	6 30.8	23 12.4	18 04.8	5 35.4	26 23.5	15 14.6
5 Sa	2 52 26	14 43 44	15 57 51	21 52 00	9 32.8	17 07.0	29 23.0	21 20.5	6 47.8	23 26.4	18 01.6	5 38.2	26 23.5	15 15.4
6 Su	2 56 22	15 41 47	27 46 04	3♐40 20	9D 31.6	19 17.2	0♉36.6	22 06.2	7 04.8	23 40.3	17 58.2	5 41.0	26 23.4	15 16.3
7 M	3 00 19	16 39 49	9♐35 06	15 30 41	9 31.6	21 27.1	1 50.2	22 51.8	7 21.5	23 54.2	17 54.8	5 43.8	26D 23.4	15 17.2
8 Tu	3 04 16	17 37 49	21 27 28	27 25 48	9 32.5	23 36.6	3 03.8	23 37.5	7 38.1	24 08.1	17 51.3	5 46.6	26 23.4	15 18.1
9 W	3 08 12	18 35 48	3♑26 07	9♑28 50	9 33.9	25 45.3	4 17.5	24 23.1	7 54.6	24 21.9	17 47.8	5 49.3	26 23.5	15 19.0
10 Th	3 12 09	19 33 46	15 34 25	21 43 20	9 35.5	27 53.0	5 31.1	25 08.7	8 10.9	24 35.7	17 44.2	5 52.0	26 23.5	15 20.0
11 F	3 16 05	20 31 42	27 56 05	4♒13 10	9 36.8	29 59.3	6 44.7	25 54.3	8 27.1	24 49.5	17 40.6	5 54.7	26 23.7	15 20.9
12 Sa	3 20 02	21 29 37	10♒35 03	17 02 12	9R 37.4	2♊04.1	7 58.3	26 39.9	8 43.1	25 03.2	17 36.9	5 57.4	26 23.8	15 21.9
13 Su	3 23 58	22 27 31	23 35 03	0♓13 59	9 37.3	4 07.0	9 11.9	27 25.4	8 58.9	25 16.9	17 33.1	6 00.0	26 24.0	15 22.9
14 M	3 27 55	23 25 23	6♓59 17	13 51 10	9 36.5	6 07.8	10 25.5	28 10.9	9 14.6	25 30.5	17 29.3	6 02.5	26 24.2	15 23.9
15 Tu	3 31 52	24 23 14	20 49 41	27 54 48	9 35.0	8 06.3	11 39.1	28 56.4	9 30.1	25 44.0	17 25.4	6 05.1	26 24.4	15 25.0
16 W	3 35 48	25 21 04	5♈06 17	12♈23 43	9 33.3	10 02.3	12 52.7	29 41.9	9 45.5	25 57.6	17 21.5	6 07.6	26 24.7	15 26.0
17 Th	3 39 45	26 18 53	19 46 34	27 14 04	9 31.7	11 55.7	14 06.3	0♈27.3	10 00.6	26 11.0	17 17.5	6 10.1	26 25.0	15 27.1
18 F	3 43 41	27 16 40	4♉45 18	12♉19 15	9 30.4	13 46.4	15 19.9	1 12.7	10 15.6	26 24.5	17 13.5	6 12.5	26 25.4	15 28.2
19 Sa	3 47 38	28 14 27	19 54 46	27 30 38	9D 29.6	15 34.2	16 33.5	1 58.0	10 30.4	26 37.8	17 09.5	6 15.0	26 25.7	15 29.3
20 Su	3 51 34	29 12 12	5♊05 38	12♊38 37	9 29.5	17 19.0	17 47.1	2 43.3	10 45.1	26 51.2	17 05.4	6 17.3	26 26.1	15 30.4
21 M	3 55 31	0♊09 56	20 08 28	27 34 12	9 29.8	19 00.9	19 00.7	3 28.6	10 59.5	27 04.4	17 01.3	6 19.7	26 26.6	15 31.6
22 Tu	3 59 27	1 07 38	4♋54 58	12♋10 07	9 30.4	20 39.6	20 14.3	4 13.8	11 13.8	27 17.7	16 57.1	6 22.0	26 27.1	15 32.7
23 W	4 03 24	2 05 18	19 19 07	26 21 40	9 31.1	22 15.2	21 27.9	4 59.0	11 27.8	27 30.8	16 52.9	6 24.3	26 27.6	15 33.9
24 Th	4 07 21	3 02 58	3♌17 34	10♌06 49	9 31.7	23 47.7	22 41.5	5 44.2	11 41.7	27 43.9	16 48.7	6 26.5	26 28.1	15 35.1
25 F	4 11 17	4 00 35	16 49 31	23 25 55	9R 32.1	25 16.8	23 55.1	6 29.3	11 55.4	27 56.9	16 44.4	6 28.7	26 28.7	15 36.3
26 Sa	4 15 14	4 58 11	29 56 17	6♍21 02	9 32.1	26 42.8	25 08.7	7 14.3	12 08.8	28 09.9	16 40.1	6 30.9	26 29.3	15 37.5
27 Su	4 19 10	5 55 46	12♍40 37	18 55 28	9 32.0	28 05.4	26 22.3	7 59.3	12 22.1	28 22.8	16 35.8	6 33.0	26 29.9	15 38.7
28 M	4 23 07	6 53 19	25 06 06	1♎13 01	9 31.8	29 24.7	27 35.9	8 44.3	12 35.2	28 35.7	16 31.5	6 35.1	26 30.6	15 40.0
29 Tu	4 27 03	7 50 51	7♎16 43	13 17 42	9 31.6	0♋40.5	28 49.5	9 29.2	12 48.0	28 48.4	16 27.1	6 37.1	26 31.3	15 41.3
30 W	4 31 00	8 48 21	19 16 26	25 13 24	9D 31.4	1 53.0	0♊03.1	10 14.1	13 00.7	29 01.1	16 22.7	6 39.1	26 32.0	15 42.5
31 Th	4 34 56	9 45 50	1♏09 00	7♏03 41	9 31.4	3 01.9	1 16.6	10 58.9	13 13.1	29 13.8	16 18.3	6 41.1	26 32.8	15 43.8

LONGITUDE — June 1928

Day	Sid.Time	☉	0 hr ☽	Noon ☽	True ☊	☿	♀	♂	⚳	♃	♄	♅	♆	♇
1 F	4 38 53	10♊43 18	12♏57 48	18♏51 44	9♊31.5	4♋07.3	2♊30.2	11♈43.7	13♓25.4	29♈26.4	16♐13.9	6♈43.0	26♌33.5	15♋45.1
2 Sa	4 42 50	11 40 45	24 45 50	0♐40 24	9R 31.6	5 09.1	3 43.8	12 28.5	13 37.4	29 38.9	16R 09.5	6 44.9	26 34.4	15 46.4
3 Su	4 46 46	12 38 11	6♐35 44	12 32 07	9 31.6	6 07.1	4 57.4	13 13.2	13 49.2	29 51.3	16 05.1	6 46.8	26 35.2	15 47.8
4 M	4 50 43	13 35 36	18 29 49	24 29 07	9 31.5	7 01.5	6 11.0	13 57.8	14 00.7	0♉03.7	16 00.7	6 48.6	26 36.1	15 49.1
5 Tu	4 54 39	14 33 00	0♑30 15	6♑33 29	9 31.1	7 51.9	7 24.6	14 42.4	14 12.1	0 16.0	15 56.2	6 50.3	26 37.0	15 50.5
6 W	4 58 36	15 30 24	12 39 05	18 47 17	9 30.5	8 38.5	8 38.2	15 27.0	14 23.2	0 28.2	15 51.8	6 52.0	26 38.0	15 51.8
7 Th	5 02 32	16 27 47	24 58 22	1♒12 36	9 29.6	9 21.0	9 51.8	16 11.5	14 34.0	0 40.3	15 47.3	6 53.7	26 38.9	15 53.2
8 F	5 06 29	17 25 09	7♒30 17	13 51 39	9 28.7	9 59.5	11 05.4	16 55.9	14 44.7	0 52.4	15 42.9	6 55.4	26 39.9	15 54.6
9 Sa	5 10 25	18 22 30	20 17 02	26 46 41	9 27.9	10 33.7	12 19.0	17 40.3	14 55.1	1 04.4	15 38.5	6 57.0	26 41.0	15 56.0
10 Su	5 14 22	19 19 51	3♓20 51	9♓59 49	9D 27.4	11 03.7	13 32.6	18 24.7	15 05.2	1 16.3	15 34.0	6 58.5	26 42.0	15 57.4
11 M	5 18 19	20 17 11	16 43 45	23 32 49	9 27.2	11 29.3	14 46.2	19 08.9	15 15.1	1 28.1	15 29.6	7 00.0	26 43.1	15 58.8
12 Tu	5 22 15	21 14 31	0♈27 08	7♈26 43	9 27.6	11 50.5	15 59.9	19 53.2	15 24.7	1 39.8	15 25.2	7 01.5	26 44.2	16 00.2
13 W	5 26 12	22 11 50	14 31 29	21 41 16	9 28.4	12 07.2	17 13.5	20 37.3	15 34.1	1 51.5	15 20.8	7 02.9	26 45.4	16 01.7
14 Th	5 30 08	23 09 10	28 55 45	6♉14 32	9 29.4	12 19.3	18 27.2	21 21.4	15 43.2	2 03.1	15 16.4	7 04.3	26 46.5	16 03.1
15 F	5 34 05	24 06 28	13♉37 01	21 02 34	9 30.3	12 26.9	19 40.8	22 05.5	15 52.1	2 14.5	15 12.0	7 05.6	26 47.7	16 04.6
16 Sa	5 38 01	25 03 47	28 30 19	5♊59 25	9R 30.8	12R 30.0	20 54.5	22 49.4	16 00.7	2 25.9	15 07.6	7 06.9	26 49.0	16 06.0
17 Su	5 41 58	26 01 05	13♊28 50	20 57 34	9 30.6	12 28.5	22 08.1	23 33.4	16 09.0	2 37.2	15 03.3	7 08.1	26 50.2	16 07.5
18 M	5 45 54	26 58 23	28 24 34	5♋48 50	9 29.5	12 22.6	23 21.8	24 17.2	16 17.0	2 48.4	14 59.0	7 09.3	26 51.5	16 09.0
19 Tu	5 49 51	27 55 40	13♋09 26	20 25 31	9 27.6	12 12.4	24 35.5	25 01.0	16 24.8	2 59.5	14 54.7	7 10.5	26 52.8	16 10.5
20 W	5 53 48	28 52 56	27 36 22	4♌41 24	9 25.2	11 57.9	25 49.2	25 44.7	16 32.3	3 10.6	14 50.5	7 11.6	26 54.1	16 12.0
21 Th	5 57 44	29 50 12	11♌40 13	18 32 33	9 22.5	11 39.5	27 02.8	26 28.3	16 39.5	3 21.5	14 46.2	7 12.6	26 55.5	16 13.5
22 F	6 01 41	0♋47 27	25 18 18	1♍57 31	9 20.1	11 17.3	28 16.5	27 11.8	16 46.3	3 32.3	14 42.0	7 13.6	26 56.9	16 15.0
23 Sa	6 05 37	1 44 41	8♍30 21	14 57 05	9 18.2	10 51.8	29 30.2	27 55.3	16 52.9	3 43.0	14 37.9	7 14.6	26 58.3	16 16.5
24 Su	6 09 34	2 41 55	21 18 07	27 33 53	9D 17.3	10 23.3	0♋43.9	28 38.7	16 59.3	3 53.6	14 33.8	7 15.5	26 59.7	16 18.0
25 M	6 13 30	3 39 08	3♎44 54	9♎51 44	9 17.3	9 52.2	1 57.6	29 22.0	17 05.3	4 04.1	14 29.7	7 16.3	27 01.2	16 19.5
26 Tu	6 17 27	4 36 21	15 54 57	21 55 08	9 18.3	9 19.1	3 11.3	0♉05.3	17 11.0	4 14.5	14 25.6	7 17.2	27 02.7	16 21.0
27 W	6 21 23	5 33 33	27 52 55	3♏48 51	9 19.8	8 44.4	4 25.0	0 48.5	17 16.4	4 24.8	14 21.6	7 17.9	27 04.2	16 22.6
28 Th	6 25 20	6 30 45	9♏43 33	15 37 34	9 21.5	8 08.7	5 38.7	1 31.5	17 21.5	4 35.0	14 17.7	7 18.6	27 05.7	16 24.1
29 F	6 29 17	7 27 56	21 31 25	27 25 36	9 22.9	7 32.7	6 52.4	2 14.6	17 26.2	4 45.0	14 13.8	7 19.3	27 07.3	16 25.6
30 Sa	6 33 13	8 25 07	3♐20 36	9♐16 49	9R 23.5	6 57.0	8 06.1	2 57.5	17 30.7	4 55.0	14 09.9	7 19.9	27 08.9	16 27.2

Astro Data	Planet Ingress	Last Aspect	☽ Ingress	Last Aspect	☽ Ingress	☽ Phases & Eclipses	Astro Data
Dy Hr Mn	Dy Hr Mn	Dy Hr Mn	Dy Hr Mn	Dy Hr Mn	Dy Hr Mn	Dy Hr Mn	
☽0S 2 0:18	♀ ♉ 6 0:03	30 4:39 ♄ □	♎ 1 3:36	2 3:40 ♆ □	♐ 2 10:38	4 20:12 ○ 14♏05	1 May 1928
♆D 7 12:31	☿ ♊ 11 12:08	3 9:08 ♀ ☍	♏ 3 15:38	4 16:14 ♆ △	♑ 4 23:00	12 20:50 ☾ 21♒51	Julian Day # 10348
☽0N 16 8:55	♂ ♈ 16 21:35	5 21:12 ♆ □	♐ 6 4:32	6 6:17 ♇ ☍	♒ 7 9:41	19 13:14 ● 28♉17	SVP 6♓15'55"
♃△♆ 18 13:38	☉ ♊ 21 7:52	8 9:55 ♆ △	♑ 8 17:09	9 11:49 ♆ ☍	♓ 9 17:54	19 13:23:56 ◒ T non-C	GC 25♐50.3 ⚴ 14♒21.5
♂0N 21 14:30	☿ ♋ 28 23:03	11 2:19 ☿ △	♒ 11 3:58	11 5:51 ☉ □	♈ 11 23:13	26 9:11 ☽ 4♍51	Eris 1♈28.9 ⚵ 1♍46.3
☽0S 29 6:31	♀ ♊ 30 11:00	13 5:06 ♆ ☍	♓ 13 11:35	13 20:25 ♆ △	♉ 14 1:46		⚷ 6♉01.2 ⚶ 23♓12.2
		15 13:49 ♂ ☌	♈ 15 15:30	15 21:16 ♆ □	♊ 16 2:24	3 12:13 ○ 12♐39	☽ Mean ☊ 11♊12.7
♄⊼♇ 6 11:52	♃ ♉ 4 4:51	17 10:41 ♆ △	♉ 17 16:25	17 21:29 ♆ ✶	♋ 18 2:34	3 12:10 ◒ T 1.242	
♃⚼♄ 7 22:11	☉ ♋ 21 16:06	19 13:14 ☉ ☌	♊ 19 15:56	19 20:04 ♂ □	♌ 20 4:02	11 5:51 ☾ 20♓02	1 June 1928
☽0N 12 17:14	♀ ♋ 23 21:42	21 11:11 ♃ ✶	♋ 21 15:57	22 4:39 ♀ ✶	♍ 22 8:27	17 20:42 ● 26♊22	Julian Day # 10379
☿R 16 16:11	♂ ♉ 26 9:04	23 14:01 ♃ □	♌ 23 18:17	23 14:29 ♇ ✶	♎ 24 16:43	17 20:27:02 ◒ P 0.038	SVP 6♓15'50"
☽0S 25 13:10		25 20:27 ♃ △	♍ 26 0:07	26 22:20 ♆ ✶	♏ 27 4:17	24 22:47 ☽ 3♎08	GC 25♐50.4 ⚴ 17♒06.0
		28 8:01 ☿ □	♎ 28 9:36	29 11:23 ♆ □	♐ 29 17:13		Eris 1♈43.2 ⚵ 6♍39.0
		30 19:49 ♃ ☍	♏ 30 21:40				⚷ 7♉53.2 ⚶ 6♈06.5
							☽ Mean ☊ 9♊34.2

July 1928

LONGITUDE

Day	Sid.Time	☉	0 hr ☽	Noon ☽	True ☊	☿	♀	♂	⚳	♃	♄	♅	♆	♇
1 Su	6 37 10	9♋22 18	15♐14 40	21♐14 28	9♊22.8	6♋22.1	9♋19.9	3♉40.3	17♓34.8	5♉04.9	14♐06.1	7♈20.5	27♌10.5	16♋28.7
2 M	6 41 06	10 19 29	27 16 32	3♑21 07	9R 20.8	5R 48.7	10 33.6	4 23.1	17 38.7	5 14.6	14R 02.3	7 21.1	27 12.1	16 30.3
3 Tu	6 45 03	11 16 40	9♑28 26	15 38 41	9 17.2	5 17.4	11 47.4	5 05.8	17 42.2	5 24.2	13 58.6	7 21.5	27 13.8	16 31.8
4 W	6 48 59	12 13 51	21 52 00	28 08 28	9 12.5	4 48.7	13 01.1	5 48.4	17 45.4	5 33.7	13 55.0	7 22.0	27 15.4	16 33.4
5 Th	6 52 56	13 11 01	4♒28 12	10♒51 14	9 07.1	4 23.1	14 14.9	6 30.9	17 48.2	5 43.1	13 51.4	7 22.4	27 17.1	16 34.9
6 F	6 56 53	14 08 12	17 17 37	23 47 23	9 01.5	4 01.2	15 28.6	7 13.4	17 50.7	5 52.4	13 47.9	7 22.7	27 18.8	16 36.5
7 Sa	7 00 49	15 05 23	0♓20 32	6♓57 06	8 56.4	3 43.2	16 42.4	7 55.7	17 52.9	6 01.5	13 44.4	7 23.0	27 20.6	16 38.1
8 Su	7 04 46	16 02 35	13 37 04	20 20 28	8 52.5	3 29.6	17 56.2	8 38.0	17 54.8	6 10.5	13 41.0	7 23.2	27 22.3	16 39.6
9 M	7 08 42	16 59 46	27 07 19	3♈57 35	8 50.2	3 20.6	19 10.0	9 20.2	17 56.3	6 19.4	13 37.6	7 23.4	27 24.1	16 41.2
10 Tu	7 12 39	17 56 59	10♈51 18	17 48 26	8D 49.4	3D 16.5	20 23.8	10 02.2	17 57.4	6 28.2	13 34.4	7 23.5	27 25.9	16 42.7
11 W	7 16 35	18 54 11	24 48 55	1♉52 41	8 50.0	3 17.5	21 37.6	10 44.2	17 58.2	6 36.8	13 31.1	7 23.6	27 27.7	16 44.3
12 Th	7 20 32	19 51 25	8♉59 34	16 09 23	8 51.2	3 23.7	22 51.4	11 26.1	17R 58.7	6 45.3	13 28.0	7R 23.7	27 29.5	16 45.8
13 F	7 24 28	20 48 39	23 21 51	0♊36 36	8R 52.3	3 35.3	24 05.3	12 07.9	17 58.8	6 53.7	13 24.9	7 23.7	27 31.4	16 47.4
14 Sa	7 28 25	21 45 53	7♊53 10	15 11 01	8 52.4	3 52.3	25 19.1	12 49.6	17 58.5	7 01.9	13 21.9	7 23.6	27 33.2	16 49.0
15 Su	7 32 22	22 43 09	22 29 30	29 47 56	8 50.7	4 14.8	26 33.0	13 31.2	17 57.9	7 10.0	13 19.0	7 23.5	27 35.1	16 50.5
16 M	7 36 18	23 40 24	7♋05 31	14♋21 29	8 47.1	4 42.7	27 46.8	14 12.7	17 57.0	7 17.9	13 16.1	7 23.4	27 37.0	16 52.1
17 Tu	7 40 15	24 37 40	21 34 59	28 45 16	8 41.5	5 16.0	29 00.7	14 54.0	17 55.6	7 25.7	13 13.3	7 23.2	27 38.9	16 53.6
18 W	7 44 11	25 34 57	5♌51 36	12♌53 18	8 34.4	5 54.8	0♌14.6	15 35.3	17 54.0	7 33.4	13 10.6	7 22.9	27 40.9	16 55.2
19 Th	7 48 08	26 32 14	19 49 52	26 40 53	8 26.7	6 39.0	1 28.5	16 16.4	17 51.9	7 40.9	13 08.0	7 22.7	27 42.8	16 56.7
20 F	7 52 04	27 29 31	3♍26 02	10♍05 12	8 19.3	7 28.6	2 42.4	16 57.5	17 49.5	7 48.3	13 05.5	7 22.3	27 44.8	16 58.2
21 Sa	7 56 01	28 26 48	16 38 23	23 05 42	8 12.9	8 23.4	3 56.3	17 38.4	17 46.7	7 55.5	13 03.0	7 21.9	27 46.8	16 59.8
22 Su	7 59 57	29 24 06	29 27 22	5♎43 47	8 08.2	9 23.5	5 10.2	18 19.2	17 43.6	8 02.6	13 00.6	7 21.5	27 48.8	17 01.3
23 M	8 03 54	0♌21 24	11♎55 20	18 02 33	8 05.5	10 28.7	6 24.1	18 59.9	17 40.1	8 09.5	12 58.3	7 21.0	27 50.8	17 02.8
24 Tu	8 07 51	1 18 42	24 06 00	0♏06 18	8D 04.6	11 38.9	7 38.0	19 40.5	17 36.3	8 16.3	12 56.1	7 20.5	27 52.8	17 04.4
25 W	8 11 47	2 16 01	6♏04 04	11 59 57	8 05.0	12 54.1	8 51.9	20 20.9	17 32.1	8 22.9	12 53.9	7 19.9	27 54.8	17 05.9
26 Th	8 15 44	3 13 20	17 54 39	23 48 47	8 06.0	14 14.2	10 05.8	21 01.3	17 27.6	8 29.4	12 51.9	7 19.3	27 56.9	17 07.4
27 F	8 19 40	4 10 40	29 43 02	5♐37 59	8R 06.7	15 38.9	11 19.7	21 41.5	17 22.7	8 35.7	12 49.9	7 18.6	27 58.9	17 08.9
28 Sa	8 23 37	5 08 00	11♐34 15	17 32 22	8 06.3	17 08.2	12 33.7	22 21.6	17 17.4	8 41.9	12 48.1	7 17.9	28 01.0	17 10.4
29 Su	8 27 33	6 05 21	23 32 51	29 36 10	8 03.9	18 41.8	13 47.6	23 01.5	17 11.9	8 47.8	12 46.3	7 17.1	28 03.1	17 11.9
30 M	8 31 30	7 02 43	5♑42 41	11♑52 44	7 59.3	20 19.5	15 01.6	23 41.4	17 05.9	8 53.7	12 44.6	7 16.3	28 05.2	17 13.4
31 Tu	8 35 26	8 00 05	18 06 35	24 24 25	7 52.4	22 01.2	16 15.5	24 21.1	16 59.6	8 59.3	12 43.0	7 15.4	28 07.3	17 14.8

August 1928

LONGITUDE

Day	Sid.Time	☉	0 hr ☽	Noon ☽	True ☊	☿	♀	♂	⚳	♃	♄	♅	♆	♇
1 W	8 39 23	8♌57 28	0♒46 18	7♒12 17	7♊43.4	23♋46.5	17♌29.5	25♉00.7	16♓53.0	9♉04.8	12♐41.5	7♈14.6	28♌09.4	17♋16.3
2 Th	8 43 20	9 54 52	13 42 20	20 16 17	7R 33.3	25 35.2	18 43.4	25 40.1	16R 46.1	9 10.2	12R 40.0	7R 13.6	28 11.5	17 17.8
3 F	8 47 16	10 52 17	26 54 00	3♓35 15	7 22.8	27 26.9	19 57.4	26 19.5	16 38.8	9 15.3	12 38.7	7 12.6	28 13.7	17 19.2
4 Sa	8 51 13	11 49 43	10♓19 45	17 07 14	7 13.2	29 21.3	21 11.3	26 58.7	16 31.2	9 20.3	12 37.5	7 11.6	28 15.8	17 20.7
5 Su	8 55 09	12 47 10	23 57 23	0♈49 56	7 05.3	1♌18.0	22 25.3	27 37.7	16 23.3	9 25.1	12 36.3	7 10.5	28 18.0	17 22.1
6 M	8 59 06	13 44 38	7♈44 37	14 41 11	6 59.8	3 16.7	23 39.3	28 16.6	16 15.0	9 29.8	12 35.3	7 09.4	28 20.1	17 23.5
7 Tu	9 03 02	14 42 08	21 39 24	28 39 07	6 56.7	5 17.0	24 53.3	28 55.4	16 06.4	9 34.2	12 34.3	7 08.2	28 22.3	17 24.9
8 W	9 06 59	15 39 38	5♉40 09	12♉42 23	6D 55.7	7 18.6	26 07.2	29 34.1	15 57.5	9 38.5	12 33.4	7 07.0	28 24.5	17 26.4
9 Th	9 10 55	16 37 11	19 45 43	26 50 00	6R 55.9	9 21.0	27 21.2	0♊12.6	15 48.4	9 42.6	12 32.7	7 05.8	28 26.6	17 27.8
10 F	9 14 52	17 34 45	3♊55 08	11♊00 57	6 56.0	11 24.0	28 35.3	0 50.9	15 38.9	9 46.6	12 32.0	7 04.5	28 28.8	17 29.1
11 Sa	9 18 49	18 32 20	18 07 15	25 13 47	6 54.9	13 27.2	29 49.3	1 29.1	15 29.1	9 50.3	12 31.4	7 03.2	28 31.0	17 30.5
12 Su	9 22 45	19 29 57	2♋20 13	9♋26 13	6 51.5	15 30.5	1♍03.3	2 07.1	15 19.1	9 53.9	12 30.9	7 01.8	28 33.2	17 31.9
13 M	9 26 42	20 27 35	16 31 19	23 35 02	6 45.4	17 33.5	2 17.3	2 45.0	15 08.8	9 57.3	12 30.5	7 00.4	28 35.4	17 33.2
14 Tu	9 30 38	21 25 15	0♌36 51	7♌36 13	6 36.7	19 36.0	3 31.3	3 22.7	14 58.2	10 00.5	12 30.2	6 59.0	28 37.6	17 34.6
15 W	9 34 35	22 22 56	14 32 35	21 25 25	6 25.8	21 37.8	4 45.4	4 00.3	14 47.4	10 03.5	12 30.0	6 57.5	28 39.9	17 35.9
16 Th	9 38 31	23 20 38	28 14 16	4♍58 43	6 13.9	23 38.8	5 59.4	4 37.7	14 36.3	10 06.3	12D 29.9	6 56.0	28 42.1	17 37.2
17 F	9 42 28	24 18 21	11♍38 26	18 13 13	6 02.1	25 38.8	7 13.4	5 14.9	14 25.0	10 08.9	12 29.9	6 54.4	28 44.3	17 38.5
18 Sa	9 46 24	25 16 05	24 42 55	1♎07 35	5 51.6	27 37.8	8 27.5	5 51.9	14 13.4	10 11.4	12 30.0	6 52.8	28 46.5	17 39.8
19 Su	9 50 21	26 13 51	7♎27 17	13 42 14	5 43.2	29 35.7	9 41.5	6 28.8	14 01.7	10 13.6	12 30.2	6 51.2	28 48.7	17 41.1
20 M	9 54 18	27 11 38	19 52 46	25 59 15	5 37.3	1♍32.3	10 55.5	7 05.4	13 49.8	10 15.6	12 30.5	6 49.5	28 51.0	17 42.3
21 Tu	9 58 14	28 09 26	2♏02 11	8♏02 05	5 34.0	3 27.7	12 09.6	7 41.9	13 37.6	10 17.5	12 30.9	6 47.8	28 53.2	17 43.6
22 W	10 02 11	29 07 15	13 59 34	19 55 14	5D 32.7	5 21.8	13 23.6	8 18.3	13 25.3	10 19.1	12 31.4	6 46.1	28 55.4	17 44.8
23 Th	10 06 07	0♍05 06	25 49 46	1♐43 51	5R 32.5	7 14.6	14 37.6	8 54.4	13 12.9	10 20.6	12 32.0	6 44.3	28 57.6	17 46.0
24 F	10 10 04	1 02 57	7♐38 10	13 33 24	5 32.4	9 06.1	15 51.7	9 30.3	13 00.3	10 21.9	12 32.7	6 42.5	28 59.8	17 47.2
25 Sa	10 14 00	2 00 50	19 30 15	25 29 21	5 31.3	10 56.3	17 05.7	10 06.1	12 47.5	10 22.9	12 33.5	6 40.7	29 02.1	17 48.4
26 Su	10 17 57	2 58 45	1♑31 19	7♑36 45	5 28.3	12 45.1	18 19.7	10 41.7	12 34.6	10 23.8	12 34.3	6 38.8	29 04.3	17 49.6
27 M	10 21 53	3 56 40	13 46 09	19 59 58	5 22.8	14 32.6	19 33.8	11 17.0	12 21.7	10 24.5	12 35.3	6 36.9	29 06.5	17 50.8
28 Tu	10 25 50	4 54 37	26 18 34	2♒42 13	5 14.7	16 18.8	20 47.8	11 52.2	12 08.6	10 25.0	12 36.4	6 35.0	29 08.7	17 51.9
29 W	10 29 47	5 52 36	9♒11 04	15 45 11	5 04.2	18 03.7	22 01.8	12 27.1	11 55.4	10R 25.2	12 37.6	6 33.1	29 11.0	17 53.0
30 Th	10 33 43	6 50 36	22 24 29	29 08 47	4 52.3	19 47.3	23 15.8	13 01.9	11 42.2	10 25.3	12 38.8	6 31.1	29 13.2	17 54.1
31 F	10 37 40	7 48 37	5♓57 48	12♓51 07	4 40.1	21 29.6	24 29.8	13 36.5	11 28.9	10 25.2	12 40.2	6 29.1	29 15.4	17 55.2

Astro Data	Dy Hr Mn
☽0N	9 23:01
☿D	10 19:22
♅R	12 22:34
⚳R	13 7:08
♃⚺♅	17 4:18
☽0S	22 20:29
☽0N	6 3:42
♄D	17 0:17
☽0S	19 4:17
♃R	30 9:18

Planet Ingress	Dy Hr Mn
♀ ♌	18 7:16
☉ ♌	23 3:02
☿ ♌	4 20:00
♂ ♊	9 4:10
♀ ♍	11 15:29
☿ ♍	19 16:59
☉ ♍	23 9:53

Last Aspect Dy Hr Mn		☽ Ingress Dy Hr Mn
1 23:50	♆ △	♑ 2 5:23
3 13:43	♇ ☍	♒ 4 15:32
6 18:29	♆ ☍	♓ 6 23:23
8 7:17	♀ △	♈ 9 5:04
11 4:29	♆ △	♉ 11 8:49
13 6:53	♆ □	♊ 13 11:00
15 8:21	♆ ⚹	♋ 15 12:20
17 12:28	♀ ☌	♌ 17 14:06
19 13:50	♆ ☌	♍ 19 17:53
21 22:54	☉ ⚹	♎ 22 1:02
24 7:32	♆ ⚹	♏ 24 11:47
26 20:26	♆ □	♐ 27 0:34
29 8:56	♆ △	♑ 29 12:47
31 11:53	♂ △	♒ 31 22:33

Last Aspect Dy Hr Mn		☽ Ingress Dy Hr Mn
3 2:22	♆ ☍	♓ 3 5:35
5 6:08	♂ ⚹	♈ 5 10:33
7 11:31	♆ △	♉ 7 14:18
9 14:44	♆ □	♊ 9 17:22
11 17:34	♆ ⚹	♋ 11 20:03
13 1:44	♇ ☌	♌ 13 22:57
16 0:47	♆ ☌	♍ 16 3:07
17 10:56	♇ ⚹	♎ 18 9:53
20 17:41	♆ ⚹	♏ 20 19:57
23 8:21	☉ □	♐ 23 8:29
25 19:05	♆ △	♑ 25 20:59
27 11:04	♀ △	♒ 28 6:57
30 12:08	♆ ☍	♓ 30 13:31

☽ Phases & Eclipses Dy Hr Mn	
3 2:48	○ 10♑55
10 12:16	☾ 17♈58
17 4:35	● 24♋20
24 14:38	☽ 1♏25
1 15:30	○ 9♒06
8 17:24	☾ 15♉53
15 13:49	● 22♌27
23 8:21	☽ 29♏56
31 2:34	○ 7♓26

Astro Data

1 July 1928
Julian Day # 10409
SVP 6♓15'45"
GC 25♐50.4 ⚴ 14♒23.9R
Eris 1♈47.3R ⚵ 14♍22.3
⚷ 9♉18.6 ⚶ 16♈27.0
☽ Mean ☊ 7♊58.9

1 August 1928
Julian Day # 10440
SVP 6♓15'39"
GC 25♐50.5 ⚴ 7♒00.1R
Eris 1♈40.7R ⚵ 24♍05.5
⚷ 10♉06.1 ⚶ 23♈33.7
☽ Mean ☊ 6♊20.4

LONGITUDE — September 1928

Day	Sid.Time	☉	0 hr ☽	Noon ☽	True ☊	☿	♀	♂	⚳	♃	♄	♅	♆	♇
1 Sa	10 41 36	8♍46 40	19♓48 15	26♓48 38	4♊28.6	23♍10.7	25♍43.8	14♊10.8	11♓15.5	10♉24.9	12♐41.6	6♈27.0	29♌17.6	17♋56.3
2 Su	10 45 33	9 44 45	3♈51 40	10♈56 46	4R 19.2	24 50.5	26 57.8	14 44.9	11R 02.2	10R 24.4	12 43.2	6R 25.0	29 19.8	17 57.3
3 M	10 49 29	10 42 52	18 03 19	25 10 44	4 12.4	26 29.1	28 11.8	15 18.9	10 48.8	10 23.6	12 44.8	6 22.9	29 22.0	17 58.4
4 Tu	10 53 26	11 41 00	2♉18 32	9♉26 16	4 08.5	28 06.5	29 25.8	15 52.5	10 35.4	10 22.7	12 46.6	6 20.8	29 24.1	17 59.4
5 W	10 57 22	12 39 11	16 33 31	23 40 02	4D 06.9	29 42.8	0♎39.8	16 26.0	10 22.0	10 21.6	12 48.4	6 18.6	29 26.3	18 00.4
6 Th	11 01 19	13 37 24	0♊45 34	7♊49 57	4R 06.7	1♎17.8	1 53.8	16 59.2	10 08.7	10 20.3	12 50.3	6 16.5	29 28.5	18 01.4
7 F	11 05 16	14 35 39	14 53 03	21 54 47	4 06.6	2 51.7	3 07.8	17 32.2	9 55.4	10 18.7	12 52.3	6 14.3	29 30.7	18 02.3
8 Sa	11 09 12	15 33 56	28 55 04	5♋53 50	4 05.4	4 24.4	4 21.8	18 05.0	9 42.1	10 17.0	12 54.5	6 12.1	29 32.8	18 03.3
9 Su	11 13 09	16 32 15	12♋50 59	19 46 25	4 02.0	5 55.9	5 35.8	18 37.5	9 28.9	10 15.1	12 56.7	6 09.9	29 35.0	18 04.2
10 M	11 17 05	17 30 36	26 39 59	3♌31 31	3 55.8	7 26.3	6 49.8	19 09.7	9 15.8	10 13.0	12 59.0	6 07.7	29 37.1	18 05.1
11 Tu	11 21 02	18 28 59	10♌20 47	17 07 34	3 46.9	8 55.5	8 03.8	19 41.7	9 02.8	10 10.7	13 01.3	6 05.4	29 39.3	18 06.0
12 W	11 24 58	19 27 24	23 51 35	0♍32 36	3 35.9	10 23.5	9 17.8	20 13.4	8 49.9	10 08.1	13 03.8	6 03.1	29 41.4	18 06.9
13 Th	11 28 55	20 25 51	7♍10 20	13 44 33	3 23.7	11 50.4	10 31.7	20 44.9	8 37.2	10 05.4	13 06.4	6 00.8	29 43.5	18 07.7
14 F	11 32 51	21 24 20	20 15 04	26 41 42	3 11.6	13 16.0	11 45.7	21 16.1	8 24.5	10 02.5	13 09.1	5 58.5	29 45.6	18 08.5
15 Sa	11 36 48	22 22 51	3♎04 22	9♎23 03	3 00.7	14 40.5	12 59.7	21 46.9	8 12.1	9 59.4	13 11.8	5 56.2	29 47.7	18 09.3
16 Su	11 40 44	23 21 23	15 37 48	21 48 43	2 51.9	16 03.7	14 13.7	22 17.5	7 59.8	9 56.1	13 14.7	5 53.9	29 49.8	18 10.1
17 M	11 44 41	24 19 58	27 56 02	4♏00 01	2 45.6	17 25.6	15 27.6	22 47.8	7 47.6	9 52.6	13 17.6	5 51.5	29 51.8	18 10.9
18 Tu	11 48 38	25 18 34	10♏01 01	15 59 27	2 41.9	18 46.2	16 41.6	23 17.9	7 35.7	9 48.9	13 20.6	5 49.2	29 53.9	18 11.6
19 W	11 52 34	26 17 12	21 55 48	27 50 36	2D 40.5	20 05.5	17 55.5	23 47.6	7 24.0	9 45.1	13 23.7	5 46.8	29 55.9	18 12.3
20 Th	11 56 31	27 15 52	3♐44 27	9♐37 56	2 40.6	21 23.4	19 09.5	24 17.0	7 12.4	9 41.0	13 26.9	5 44.4	29 58.0	18 13.0
21 F	12 00 27	28 14 33	15 31 44	21 26 30	2R 41.1	22 39.8	20 23.4	24 46.0	7 01.2	9 36.8	13 30.2	5 42.0	29 60.0	18 13.7
22 Sa	12 04 24	29 13 16	27 22 55	3♑21 41	2 41.2	23 54.7	21 37.3	25 14.8	6 50.1	9 32.4	13 33.5	5 39.6	0♍02.0	18 14.4
23 Su	12 08 20	0♎12 01	9♑23 28	15 28 56	2 39.9	25 08.0	22 51.2	25 43.3	6 39.3	9 27.8	13 37.0	5 37.2	0 04.0	18 15.0
24 M	12 12 17	1 10 48	21 38 41	27 53 18	2 36.6	26 19.6	24 05.1	26 11.4	6 28.8	9 23.0	13 40.5	5 34.8	0 06.0	18 15.6
25 Tu	12 16 13	2 09 36	4♒13 16	10♒39 00	2 31.0	27 29.5	25 19.0	26 39.1	6 18.5	9 18.1	13 44.1	5 32.4	0 07.9	18 16.2
26 W	12 20 10	3 08 26	17 10 49	23 48 54	2 23.3	28 37.4	26 32.9	27 06.6	6 08.5	9 13.0	13 47.8	5 30.0	0 09.9	18 16.7
27 Th	12 24 07	4 07 18	0♓33 18	7♓23 55	2 14.2	29 43.3	27 46.8	27 33.7	5 58.8	9 07.8	13 51.6	5 27.6	0 11.8	18 17.3
28 F	12 28 03	5 06 11	14 20 31	21 22 40	2 04.7	0♏47.0	29 00.6	28 00.4	5 49.4	9 02.3	13 55.5	5 25.2	0 13.7	18 17.8
29 Sa	12 32 00	6 05 07	28 29 50	5♈41 20	1 55.8	1 48.4	0♏14.5	28 26.8	5 40.2	8 56.8	13 59.4	5 22.8	0 15.6	18 18.3
30 Su	12 35 56	7 04 04	12♈56 22	20 14 06	1 48.5	2 47.3	1 28.3	28 52.8	5 31.4	8 51.0	14 03.4	5 20.4	0 17.4	18 18.8

LONGITUDE — October 1928

Day	Sid.Time	☉	0 hr ☽	Noon ☽	True ☊	☿	♀	♂	⚳	♃	♄	♅	♆	♇
1 M	12 39 53	8♎03 04	27♈33 37	4♉54 02	1♊43.4	3♏43.4	2♏42.1	29♊18.4	5♓22.9	8♉45.1	14♐07.5	5♈17.9	0♍19.3	18♋19.2
2 Tu	12 43 49	9 02 06	12♉14 28	19 34 09	1D 40.7	4 36.6	3 55.9	29 43.6	5R 14.7	8R 39.1	14 11.7	5R 15.5	0 21.1	18 19.6
3 W	12 47 46	10 01 10	26 52 21	4♊08 28	1 40.2	5 26.6	5 09.8	0♋08.5	5 06.9	8 32.9	14 15.9	5 13.1	0 22.9	18 20.0
4 Th	12 51 42	11 00 17	11♊22 00	18 32 34	1 40.9	6 13.1	6 23.6	0 32.9	4 59.4	8 26.6	14 20.2	5 10.7	0 24.7	18 20.4
5 F	12 55 39	11 59 26	25 39 54	2♋43 49	1R 41.9	6 55.7	7 37.3	0 57.0	4 52.2	8 20.2	14 24.6	5 08.3	0 26.5	18 20.8
6 Sa	12 59 36	12 58 37	9♋44 11	16 40 59	1 42.2	7 34.2	8 51.1	1 20.6	4 45.3	8 13.6	14 29.1	5 05.9	0 28.3	18 21.1
7 Su	13 03 32	13 57 51	23 34 13	0♌23 56	1 40.9	8 08.1	10 04.9	1 43.7	4 38.8	8 06.8	14 33.6	5 03.6	0 30.0	18 21.4
8 M	13 07 29	14 57 07	7♌10 09	13 52 58	1 37.5	8 37.1	11 18.7	2 06.5	4 32.6	8 00.0	14 38.2	5 01.2	0 31.7	18 21.7
9 Tu	13 11 25	15 56 25	20 32 25	27 08 34	1 32.1	9 00.7	12 32.5	2 28.7	4 26.8	7 53.0	14 42.9	4 58.8	0 33.4	18 21.9
10 W	13 15 22	16 55 46	3♍41 27	10♍11 07	1 25.1	9 18.3	13 46.2	2 50.5	4 21.4	7 46.0	14 47.7	4 56.5	0 35.1	18 22.2
11 Th	13 19 18	17 55 09	16 37 34	23 00 50	1 17.3	9 29.6	15 00.0	3 11.8	4 16.3	7 38.8	14 52.5	4 54.1	0 36.7	18 22.4
12 F	13 23 15	18 54 33	29 20 57	5♎37 56	1 09.4	9R 34.0	16 13.7	3 32.7	4 11.6	7 31.5	14 57.4	4 51.8	0 38.4	18 22.6
13 Sa	13 27 11	19 54 00	11♎51 50	18 02 44	1 02.3	9 31.0	17 27.4	3 53.0	4 07.2	7 24.1	15 02.4	4 49.5	0 40.0	18 22.7
14 Su	13 31 08	20 53 29	24 10 43	0♏15 55	0 56.6	9 20.2	18 41.1	4 12.8	4 03.3	7 16.6	15 07.4	4 47.2	0 41.5	18 22.8
15 M	13 35 05	21 53 00	6♏18 30	12 18 42	0 52.9	9 01.1	19 54.8	4 32.2	3 59.7	7 09.0	15 12.5	4 44.9	0 43.1	18 23.0
16 Tu	13 39 01	22 52 33	18 16 47	24 13 01	0D 51.0	8 33.6	21 08.5	4 50.9	3 56.4	7 01.4	15 17.6	4 42.6	0 44.6	18 23.0
17 W	13 42 58	23 52 08	0♐07 48	6♐01 30	0 50.9	7 57.4	22 22.2	5 09.2	3 53.6	6 53.7	15 22.9	4 40.4	0 46.1	18 23.1
18 Th	13 46 54	24 51 45	11 54 36	17 47 34	0 52.1	7 12.8	23 35.9	5 26.9	3 51.1	6 45.9	15 28.1	4 38.1	0 47.6	18 23.1
19 F	13 50 51	25 51 24	23 40 56	29 35 16	0 53.8	6 19.9	24 49.6	5 44.0	3 49.0	6 38.0	15 33.5	4 35.9	0 49.1	18R 23.2
20 Sa	13 54 47	26 51 04	5♑31 10	11♑29 14	0 55.5	5 19.6	26 03.2	6 00.6	3 47.2	6 30.1	15 38.9	4 33.7	0 50.5	18 23.1
21 Su	13 58 44	27 50 46	17 30 06	23 34 25	0R 56.5	4 12.9	27 16.8	6 16.6	3 45.9	6 22.1	15 44.4	4 31.6	0 51.9	18 23.1
22 M	14 02 40	28 50 30	29 42 48	5♒55 51	0 56.3	3 01.3	28 30.4	6 32.0	3 44.9	6 14.1	15 49.9	4 29.4	0 53.3	18 23.0
23 Tu	14 06 37	29 50 16	12♒14 10	18 38 16	0 54.8	1 46.4	29 44.0	6 46.8	3 44.3	6 06.1	15 55.5	4 27.3	0 54.6	18 23.0
24 W	14 10 34	0♏50 03	25 08 35	1♓45 29	0 51.9	0 30.5	0♐57.6	7 00.9	3D 44.1	5 58.0	16 01.1	4 25.2	0 55.9	18 22.8
25 Th	14 14 30	1 49 52	8♓29 13	15 19 54	0 48.1	29♎15.8	2 11.2	7 14.5	3 44.2	5 49.9	16 06.8	4 23.1	0 57.2	18 22.7
26 F	14 18 27	2 49 42	22 17 29	29 21 46	0 43.8	28 04.6	3 24.7	7 27.4	3 44.7	5 41.8	16 12.6	4 21.1	0 58.5	18 22.5
27 Sa	14 22 23	3 49 35	6♈32 21	13♈48 41	0 39.7	26 59.0	4 38.2	7 39.7	3 45.5	5 33.6	16 18.4	4 19.1	0 59.7	18 22.4
28 Su	14 26 20	4 49 29	21 10 03	28 35 33	0 36.5	26 01.2	5 51.7	7 51.3	3 46.8	5 25.5	16 24.2	4 17.1	1 00.9	18 22.1
29 M	14 30 16	5 49 25	6♉04 12	13♉34 56	0 34.4	25 12.6	7 05.2	8 02.2	3 48.3	5 17.3	16 30.1	4 15.1	1 02.1	18 21.9
30 Tu	14 34 13	6 49 23	21 06 37	28 38 07	0D 33.6	24 34.5	8 18.7	8 12.5	3 50.3	5 09.2	16 36.1	4 13.2	1 03.2	18 21.7
31 W	14 38 09	7 49 23	6♊08 23	13♊36 26	0 34.0	24 07.7	9 32.1	8 22.1	3 52.6	5 01.0	16 42.1	4 11.3	1 04.4	18 21.4

Astro Data

	Dy Hr Mn
☽0N	2 9:36
☿0S	5 23:24
♀0S	7 1:29
☽0S	15 12:04
☉0S	23 7:05
☽0N	29 18:08
☿R	12 14:32
☽0S	12 19:14
♇R	19 12:07
⚳D	24 15:43
☽0N	27 4:51

Planet Ingress

	Dy Hr Mn
♀ ♎	4 23:05
☿ ♎	5 16:20
♆ ♍	21 12:05
☉ ♎	23 7:06
☿ ♏	27 18:12
♀ ♏	29 7:18
♂ ♋	3 3:46
☉ ♏	23 15:55
♀ ♐	23 17:12
☿ ♎R	24 21:43

Last Aspect / ☽ Ingress

Last Aspect Dy Hr Mn		☽ Ingress Dy Hr Mn
1 9:59	♀ ☍	♈ 1 17:26
3 19:04	♆ △	♉ 3 20:07
5 21:47	♆ □	♊ 5 22:43
8 1:03	♆ ⚹	♋ 8 1:51
9 9:02	♇ ☌	♌ 10 5:49
12 10:28	♆ ☌	♍ 12 11:01
14 1:28	♂ □	♎ 14 18:12
17 3:47	♆ ⚹	♏ 17 4:05
19 16:16	♆ □	♐ 19 16:23
22 2:58	☉ □	♑ 22 5:16
24 8:42	♆ □	♒ 24 16:01
26 21:21	☿ △	♓ 26 23:01
28 23:32	♂ □	♈ 29 2:31

Last Aspect / ☽ Ingress

Last Aspect Dy Hr Mn		☽ Ingress Dy Hr Mn
1 2:35	♂ ⚹	♉ 1 3:59
2 9:58	♇ ⚹	♊ 3 5:09
4 4:55	♄ ☍	♋ 5 7:21
6 14:54	♇ ☌	♌ 7 11:18
8 14:04	☉ ⚹	♍ 9 17:13
11 3:16	♇ ⚹	♎ 12 1:14
13 15:56	☉ ☌	♏ 14 11:29
16 5:04	♀ ☌	♐ 16 23:44
19 3:44	☉ ⚹	♑ 19 12:50
21 21:06	☉ □	♒ 22 0:33
23 6:54	♄ ⚹	♓ 24 8:50
25 17:17	♇ △	♈ 26 13:04
28 8:05	☿ ☍	♉ 28 14:16
29 19:37	♇ ⚹	♊ 30 14:11

☽ Phases & Eclipses

Dy Hr Mn	
6 22:35	☾ 14♊03
14 1:20	● 20♍58
22 2:58	☽ 28♐51
29 12:42	○ 6♈07
6 5:06	☾ 12♋42
13 15:56	● 20♎04
21 21:06	☽ 28♑13
28 22:43	○ 5♉16

Astro Data

1 September 1928
Julian Day # 10471
SVP 6♓15'36"
GC 25♐50.6 ⚴ 0♒15.1R
Eris 1♈25.2R ⚵ 4♎45.1
⚷ 10♉01.4R ⚶ 24♈57.9R
☽ Mean ☊ 4♊41.9

1 October 1928
Julian Day # 10501
SVP 6♓15'33"
GC 25♐50.7 ⚴ 28♑35.5
Eris 1♈05.7R ⚵ 15♎27.2
⚷ 9♉09.0R ⚶ 19♈51.2R
☽ Mean ☊ 3♊06.6

November 1928 LONGITUDE

Day	Sid.Time	☉	0 hr ☽	Noon ☽	True ☊	☿	♀	♂	⚳	♃	♄	♅	♆	♇
1 Th	14 42 06	8♏49 26	21♊01 21	28♊22 24	0♊35.1	23♎52.4	10♐45.5	8♋30.9	3♓55.2	4♉52.9	16♐48.1	4♈09.4	1♍05.5	18♋21.1
2 F	14 46 03	9 49 30	5♋38 59	12♋50 39	0 36.5	23D 48.6	11 59.0	8 39.0	3 58.2	4R 44.8	16 54.2	4R 07.6	1 06.5	18R 20.8
3 Sa	14 49 59	10 49 37	19 57 05	26 58 06	0 37.7	23 56.1	13 12.4	8 46.4	4 01.6	4 36.8	17 00.4	4 05.8	1 07.5	18 20.4
4 Su	14 53 56	11 49 45	3♌53 38	10♌43 44	0R 38.2	24 14.2	14 25.7	8 53.0	4 05.3	4 28.7	17 06.6	4 04.1	1 08.5	18 20.0
5 M	14 57 52	12 49 56	17 28 31	24 08 11	0 37.8	24 42.1	15 39.1	8 58.9	4 09.3	4 20.8	17 12.8	4 02.3	1 09.5	18 19.6
6 Tu	15 01 49	13 50 09	0♍42 56	7♍13 04	0 36.6	25 19.0	16 52.4	9 04.0	4 13.7	4 12.8	17 19.1	4 00.6	1 10.4	18 19.2
7 W	15 05 45	14 50 24	13 38 52	20 00 38	0 34.8	26 04.1	18 05.8	9 08.2	4 18.4	4 04.9	17 25.4	3 59.0	1 11.3	18 18.8
8 Th	15 09 42	15 50 40	26 18 38	2♎33 12	0 32.5	26 56.4	19 19.1	9 11.7	4 23.4	3 57.1	17 31.8	3 57.3	1 12.2	18 18.3
9 F	15 13 38	16 50 59	8♎44 37	14 53 07	0 30.3	27 55.2	20 32.3	9 14.4	4 28.8	3 49.3	17 38.2	3 55.7	1 13.1	18 17.8
10 Sa	15 17 35	17 51 19	20 59 00	27 02 31	0 28.4	28 59.5	21 45.6	9 16.2	4 34.5	3 41.6	17 44.6	3 54.2	1 13.9	18 17.3
11 Su	15 21 32	18 51 42	3♏03 53	9♏03 22	0 27.0	0♏08.6	22 58.9	9R 17.2	4 40.5	3 34.0	17 51.1	3 52.7	1 14.6	18 16.8
12 M	15 25 28	19 52 06	15 01 11	20 57 35	0D 26.2	1 21.9	24 12.1	9 17.3	4 46.9	3 26.5	17 57.6	3 51.2	1 15.4	18 16.2
13 Tu	15 29 25	20 52 32	26 52 48	2♐47 07	0 26.1	2 38.8	25 25.3	9 16.6	4 53.6	3 19.1	18 04.2	3 49.8	1 16.1	18 15.6
14 W	15 33 21	21 52 59	8♐40 47	14 34 06	0 26.4	3 58.7	26 38.5	9 15.1	5 00.6	3 11.7	18 10.8	3 48.4	1 16.8	18 15.0
15 Th	15 37 18	22 53 28	20 27 24	26 21 00	0 27.0	5 21.2	27 51.6	9 12.7	5 07.9	3 04.5	18 17.4	3 47.0	1 17.4	18 14.4
16 F	15 41 14	23 53 58	2♑15 18	8♑10 41	0 27.8	6 45.8	29 04.7	9 09.4	5 15.5	2 57.4	18 24.1	3 45.7	1 18.0	18 13.8
17 Sa	15 45 11	24 54 30	14 07 34	20 06 26	0 28.5	8 12.2	0♑17.8	9 05.2	5 23.4	2 50.4	18 30.8	3 44.5	1 18.6	18 13.1
18 Su	15 49 07	25 55 03	26 07 45	2♒12 02	0 29.0	9 40.1	1 30.9	9 00.2	5 31.6	2 43.5	18 37.5	3 43.3	1 19.2	18 12.4
19 M	15 53 04	26 55 38	8♒19 47	14 31 32	0 29.4	11 09.3	2 43.9	8 54.3	5 40.1	2 36.7	18 44.2	3 42.1	1 19.7	18 11.7
20 Tu	15 57 01	27 56 13	20 47 49	27 09 09	0R 29.4	12 39.4	3 56.9	8 47.5	5 48.9	2 30.0	18 51.0	3 41.0	1 20.1	18 11.0
21 W	16 00 57	28 56 50	3♓36 01	10♓08 51	0 29.4	14 10.4	5 09.9	8 39.9	5 58.0	2 23.5	18 57.8	3 39.9	1 20.6	18 10.2
22 Th	16 04 54	29 57 28	16 48 02	23 33 52	0D 29.3	15 42.0	6 22.8	8 31.4	6 07.4	2 17.2	19 04.6	3 38.8	1 21.0	18 09.4
23 F	16 08 50	0♐58 07	0♈26 32	7♈26 06	0 29.3	17 14.1	7 35.7	8 22.1	6 17.0	2 10.9	19 11.5	3 37.9	1 21.4	18 08.7
24 Sa	16 12 47	1 58 47	14 32 28	21 45 24	0 29.4	18 46.7	8 48.5	8 11.9	6 26.9	2 04.9	19 18.3	3 36.9	1 21.7	18 07.9
25 Su	16 16 43	2 59 28	29 04 28	6♉29 03	0 29.6	20 19.6	10 01.3	8 00.8	6 37.1	1 58.9	19 25.2	3 36.0	1 22.0	18 07.0
26 M	16 20 40	4 00 10	13♉58 22	21 31 27	0R 29.8	21 52.8	11 14.1	7 48.9	6 47.6	1 53.2	19 32.1	3 35.2	1 22.3	18 06.2
27 Tu	16 24 36	5 00 54	29 07 13	6♊44 29	0 29.8	23 26.1	12 26.8	7 36.3	6 58.3	1 47.5	19 39.1	3 34.4	1 22.5	18 05.3
28 W	16 28 33	6 01 39	14♊22 00	21 58 30	0 29.6	24 59.6	13 39.5	7 22.8	7 09.3	1 42.1	19 46.0	3 33.6	1 22.7	18 04.4
29 Th	16 32 30	7 02 26	29 32 46	7♋03 40	0 29.0	26 33.2	14 52.1	7 08.5	7 20.6	1 36.8	19 53.0	3 32.9	1 22.9	18 03.6
30 F	16 36 26	8 03 13	14♋30 12	21 51 30	0 28.2	28 06.9	16 04.7	6 53.4	7 32.0	1 31.7	20 00.0	3 32.2	1 23.0	18 02.6

December 1928 LONGITUDE

Day	Sid.Time	☉	0 hr ☽	Noon ☽	True ☊	☿	♀	♂	⚳	♃	♄	♅	♆	♇
1 Sa	16 40 23	9♐04 02	29♋06 55	6♌15 57	0♊27.2	29♏40.6	17♑17.2	6♋37.5	7♓43.8	1♉26.7	20♐07.0	3♈31.6	1♍23.1	18♋01.7
2 Su	16 44 19	10 04 53	13♌18 18	20 13 48	0R 26.4	1♐14.4	18 29.7	6R 20.9	7 55.8	1R 22.0	20 14.0	3R 31.1	1 23.2	18R 00.8
3 M	16 48 16	11 05 45	27 02 30	3♍44 32	0D 25.8	2 48.2	19 42.1	6 03.6	8 08.0	1 17.4	20 21.0	3 30.6	1R 23.2	17 59.8
4 Tu	16 52 12	12 06 38	10♍20 11	16 49 47	0 25.8	4 22.0	20 54.5	5 45.6	8 20.5	1 12.9	20 28.1	3 30.1	1 23.2	17 58.8
5 W	16 56 09	13 07 33	23 13 45	29 32 35	0 26.3	5 55.8	22 06.9	5 26.9	8 33.2	1 08.7	20 35.1	3 29.7	1 23.2	17 57.8
6 Th	17 00 05	14 08 28	5♎46 45	11♎56 46	0 27.3	7 29.7	23 19.1	5 07.6	8 46.1	1 04.6	20 42.2	3 29.3	1 23.1	17 56.8
7 F	17 04 02	15 09 25	18 03 10	24 06 25	0 28.7	9 03.5	24 31.4	4 47.7	8 59.2	1 00.8	20 49.3	3 29.0	1 23.0	17 55.8
8 Sa	17 07 59	16 10 24	0♏07 02	6♏05 28	0 30.1	10 37.4	25 43.6	4 27.2	9 12.6	0 57.1	20 56.4	3 28.7	1 22.9	17 54.7
9 Su	17 11 55	17 11 23	12 02 08	17 57 29	0 31.2	12 11.3	26 55.7	4 06.2	9 26.2	0 53.6	21 03.4	3 28.5	1 22.7	17 53.7
10 M	17 15 52	18 12 24	23 51 52	29 45 39	0R 31.7	13 45.2	28 07.7	3 44.7	9 40.1	0 50.4	21 10.5	3 28.4	1 22.5	17 52.6
11 Tu	17 19 48	19 13 25	5♐39 08	11♐32 38	0 31.2	15 19.2	29 19.8	3 22.8	9 54.1	0 47.3	21 17.6	3 28.3	1 22.2	17 51.5
12 W	17 23 45	20 14 27	17 26 24	23 20 44	0 29.7	16 53.3	0♒31.7	3 00.5	10 08.4	0 44.4	21 24.7	3D 28.2	1 21.9	17 50.4
13 Th	17 27 41	21 15 30	29 15 51	5♑12 00	0 27.2	18 27.4	1 43.6	2 37.8	10 22.8	0 41.7	21 31.8	3 28.2	1 21.6	17 49.3
14 F	17 31 38	22 16 34	11♑09 24	17 08 20	0 23.7	20 01.7	2 55.4	2 14.8	10 37.5	0 39.3	21 38.9	3 28.3	1 21.3	17 48.2
15 Sa	17 35 34	23 17 38	23 09 00	29 11 42	0 19.8	21 36.0	4 07.1	1 51.6	10 52.4	0 37.0	21 46.0	3 28.4	1 20.9	17 47.1
16 Su	17 39 31	24 18 43	5♒16 41	11♒24 16	0 15.7	23 10.5	5 18.8	1 28.2	11 07.4	0 34.9	21 53.1	3 28.5	1 20.5	17 45.9
17 M	17 43 28	25 19 48	17 34 45	23 48 28	0 12.1	24 45.1	6 30.3	1 04.6	11 22.7	0 33.1	22 00.2	3 28.7	1 20.1	17 44.8
18 Tu	17 47 24	26 20 54	0♓05 47	6♓27 03	0 09.4	26 19.8	7 41.8	0 40.9	11 38.2	0 31.4	22 07.3	3 29.0	1 19.6	17 43.6
19 W	17 51 21	27 22 00	12 52 40	19 22 58	0D 07.9	27 54.7	8 53.2	0 17.2	11 53.8	0 30.0	22 14.4	3 29.3	1 19.1	17 42.4
20 Th	17 55 17	28 23 06	25 58 21	2♈39 06	0 07.7	29 29.8	10 04.5	29♊53.5	12 09.6	0 28.8	22 21.5	3 29.7	1 18.5	17 41.2
21 F	17 59 14	29 24 12	9♈25 33	16 17 54	0 08.6	1♑05.1	11 15.8	29 29.8	12 25.7	0 27.8	22 28.6	3 30.1	1 17.9	17 40.0
22 Sa	18 03 10	0♑25 18	23 16 17	0♉20 45	0 10.1	2 40.5	12 26.9	29 06.3	12 41.8	0 27.0	22 35.6	3 30.6	1 17.3	17 38.8
23 Su	18 07 07	1 26 25	7♉31 11	14 47 22	0 11.6	4 16.2	13 37.9	28 42.9	12 58.2	0 26.4	22 42.7	3 31.1	1 16.7	17 37.6
24 M	18 11 04	2 27 32	22 08 51	29 35 03	0R 12.2	5 52.1	14 48.8	28 19.7	13 14.7	0 26.0	22 49.7	3 31.6	1 16.0	17 36.4
25 Tu	18 15 00	3 28 39	7♊05 14	14♊38 27	0 11.5	7 28.3	15 59.6	27 56.7	13 31.5	0D 25.8	22 56.8	3 32.3	1 15.3	17 35.2
26 W	18 18 57	4 29 46	22 13 36	29 49 32	0 09.1	9 04.7	17 10.3	27 34.1	13 48.3	0 25.8	23 03.8	3 32.9	1 14.6	17 34.0
27 Th	18 22 53	5 30 53	7♋24 59	14♋58 40	0 04.9	10 41.4	18 20.9	27 11.7	14 05.4	0 26.1	23 10.8	3 33.7	1 13.8	17 32.7
28 F	18 26 50	6 32 01	22 29 22	29 55 55	29♉59.5	12 18.3	19 31.4	26 49.8	14 22.6	0 26.5	23 17.8	3 34.4	1 13.1	17 31.5
29 Sa	18 30 46	7 33 09	7♌17 20	14♌32 45	29 53.5	13 55.4	20 41.7	26 28.3	14 39.9	0 27.1	23 24.7	3 35.3	1 12.2	17 30.2
30 Su	18 34 43	8 34 17	21 41 33	28 43 17	29 47.8	15 32.8	21 52.0	26 07.2	14 57.4	0 28.0	23 31.7	3 36.1	1 11.4	17 29.0
31 M	18 38 39	9 35 26	5♍37 42	12♍24 46	29 43.1	17 10.4	23 02.1	25 46.6	15 15.1	0 29.1	23 38.6	3 37.1	1 10.5	17 27.7

Astro Data

	Dy Hr Mn
☿ D	2 7:51
♃⚺♅	8 11:05
☽ 0S	9 1:31
♂ R	12 4:13
♃⚼♄	14 13:38
♄⚻♇	15 2:03
☽ 0N	23 15:36
♃△♆	2 5:46
♆ R	3 20:48
☽ 0S	6 7:18
♅ D	12 23:57
☽ 0N	20 23:59
♃ D	25 20:33

Planet Ingress

		Dy Hr Mn
☿	♏	11 9:05
♀	♑	17 6:09
☉	♐	22 13:00
☿	♐	1 16:57
♀	♒	12 1:25
♂	♊R	20 5:23
☿	♑	20 19:37
☉	♑	22 2:04
☊	♉R	28 9:48

Last Aspect / ☽ Ingress (November)

Last Aspect Dy Hr Mn			☽ Ingress	Dy Hr Mn
1 4:44	☿	△	♋	1 14:40
3 6:43	☿	□	♌	3 17:14
5 13:04	☿	⚹	♍	5 22:41
7 8:47	♇	⚹	♎	8 7:05
10 16:16	☿	☌	♏	10 17:53
12 9:35	☉	☌	♐	13 6:20
15 15:26	♀	☌	♑	15 19:25
17 22:27	☉	⚹	♒	18 7:40
20 13:36	☉	□	♓	20 17:19
22 4:00	♄	□	♈	22 23:14
24 7:55	♄	△	♉	25 1:30
26 12:38	☿	☍	♊	27 1:23
28 8:29	♄	☍	♋	29 0:43

Last Aspect / ☽ Ingress (December)

Last Aspect Dy Hr Mn			☽ Ingress	Dy Hr Mn
30 23:35	☿	△	♌	1 1:28
2 12:00	♄	△	♍	3 5:16
4 20:26	♀	△	♎	5 12:52
7 12:55	♀	□	♏	7 23:46
10 8:18	♀	⚹	♐	10 12:29
12 8:02	♄	☌	♑	13 1:29
14 13:20	♇	☍	♒	15 13:36
17 15:10	☉	⚹	♓	17 23:49
20 7:12	♂	□	♈	20 7:15
22 9:58	♂	⚹	♉	22 11:25
23 16:38	♇	⚹	♊	24 12:40
26 8:31	♂	☌	♋	26 12:17
27 16:05	♇	☌	♌	28 12:07
30 7:39	♂	⚹	♍	30 14:12

☽ Phases & Eclipses

Dy Hr Mn		
4 14:06	☾	11♌55
12 9:35	●	19♏46
12 9:48:02	☀	P 0.808
20 13:36	☽	28♒00
27 9:05	○	4♊54
27 9:01	☽	T 1.149
4 2:31	☾	11♍43
12 5:06	●	19♐57
20 3:43	☽	28♓02
26 19:55	○	4♋50

Astro Data

1 November 1928
Julian Day # 10532
SVP 6♓15'29"
GC 25♐50.7 ⚴ 1♒54.9
Eris 0♈47.0R ⚵ 26♎29.1
⚷ 7♉43.7R ⚶ 12♈27.9R
☽ Mean ☊ 1♊28.1

1 December 1928
Julian Day # 10562
SVP 6♓15'24"
GC 25♐50.8 ⚴ 8♒27.1
Eris 0♈35.8R ⚵ 6♏41.3
⚷ 6♉21.8R ⚶ 10♈16.0
☽ Mean ☊ 29♉52.8

LONGITUDE — January 1929

Day	Sid.Time	☉	0 hr ☽	Noon ☽	True ☊	☿	♀	♂	⚳	♃	♄	♅	♆	♇
1 Tu	18 42 36	10♑36 35	19♍04 35	25♍37 26	29♉40.1	18♑48.2	24♒12.1	25♊26.5	15♓32.9	0♉30.3	23♐45.5	3♈38.0	1♍09.6	17♋26.5
2 W	18 46 33	11 37 44	2♎03 43	8♎23 54	29D 38.8	20 26.3	25 21.9	25R 07.0	15 50.8	0 31.8	23 52.4	3 39.1	1R 08.7	17R 25.2
3 Th	18 50 29	12 38 54	14 38 33	20 48 16	29 39.1	22 04.4	26 31.6	24 48.1	16 08.9	0 33.5	23 59.3	3 40.1	1 07.7	17 23.9
4 F	18 54 26	13 40 03	26 53 42	2♏55 30	29 40.4	23 42.7	27 41.2	24 29.8	16 27.2	0 35.4	24 06.1	3 41.3	1 06.7	17 22.7
5 Sa	18 58 22	14 41 13	8♏54 18	14 50 45	29 42.0	25 21.1	28 50.7	24 12.1	16 45.6	0 37.5	24 12.9	3 42.4	1 05.7	17 21.4
6 Su	19 02 19	15 42 23	20 45 28	26 39 02	29R 42.9	26 59.4	29 59.9	23 55.2	17 04.1	0 39.8	24 19.7	3 43.6	1 04.6	17 20.1
7 M	19 06 15	16 43 34	2♐31 59	8♐24 50	29 42.5	28 37.7	1♓09.1	23 38.9	17 22.7	0 42.3	24 26.5	3 44.9	1 03.6	17 18.8
8 Tu	19 10 12	17 44 44	14 18 02	20 12 01	29 40.1	0♒15.7	2 18.1	23 23.4	17 41.5	0 44.9	24 33.2	3 46.2	1 02.5	17 17.6
9 W	19 14 08	18 45 54	26 07 08	2♑03 42	29 35.2	1 53.5	3 26.9	23 08.6	18 00.5	0 47.8	24 39.9	3 47.6	1 01.3	17 16.3
10 Th	19 18 05	19 47 04	8♑02 00	14 02 15	29 28.1	3 30.7	4 35.6	22 54.5	18 19.5	0 50.9	24 46.6	3 49.0	1 00.2	17 15.0
11 F	19 22 02	20 48 13	20 04 38	26 09 18	29 18.9	5 07.4	5 44.1	22 41.3	18 38.7	0 54.2	24 53.3	3 50.5	0 59.0	17 13.7
12 Sa	19 25 58	21 49 23	2♒16 23	8♒25 58	29 08.6	6 43.2	6 52.4	22 28.8	18 58.0	0 57.7	24 59.9	3 52.0	0 57.8	17 12.5
13 Su	19 29 55	22 50 31	14 38 09	20 52 59	28 58.0	8 17.9	8 00.5	22 17.1	19 17.5	1 01.4	25 06.5	3 53.6	0 56.6	17 11.2
14 M	19 33 51	23 51 40	27 10 35	3♓31 00	28 48.2	9 51.2	9 08.5	22 06.3	19 37.0	1 05.3	25 13.0	3 55.2	0 55.3	17 09.9
15 Tu	19 37 48	24 52 47	9♓54 22	16 20 47	28 40.0	11 22.7	10 16.2	21 56.2	19 56.7	1 09.4	25 19.5	3 56.8	0 54.1	17 08.7
16 W	19 41 44	25 53 54	22 50 25	29 23 25	28 34.3	12 52.2	11 23.8	21 47.0	20 16.5	1 13.6	25 26.0	3 58.5	0 52.8	17 07.4
17 Th	19 45 41	26 55 00	5♈59 58	12♈40 17	28 31.0	14 19.1	12 31.1	21 38.6	20 36.4	1 18.1	25 32.4	4 00.3	0 51.5	17 06.2
18 F	19 49 37	27 56 05	19 24 34	26 13 01	28D 30.0	15 43.0	13 38.2	21 31.0	20 56.4	1 22.7	25 38.8	4 02.1	0 50.1	17 04.9
19 Sa	19 53 34	28 57 09	3♉05 49	10♉03 05	28 30.3	17 03.2	14 45.1	21 24.3	21 16.5	1 27.5	25 45.1	4 03.9	0 48.8	17 03.6
20 Su	19 57 31	29 58 12	17 04 53	24 11 14	28R 31.0	18 19.1	15 51.8	21 18.4	21 36.7	1 32.5	25 51.4	4 05.8	0 47.4	17 02.4
21 M	20 01 27	0♒59 15	1♊22 00	8♊36 55	28 30.6	19 30.1	16 58.2	21 13.2	21 57.0	1 37.7	25 57.7	4 07.7	0 46.0	17 01.2
22 Tu	20 05 24	2 00 16	15 55 38	23 17 34	28 28.3	20 35.3	18 04.4	21 08.9	22 17.5	1 43.1	26 03.9	4 09.6	0 44.6	16 59.9
23 W	20 09 20	3 01 17	0♋42 02	8♋08 13	28 23.3	21 34.0	19 10.3	21 05.4	22 38.0	1 48.6	26 10.1	4 11.6	0 43.2	16 58.7
24 Th	20 13 17	4 02 17	15 35 07	23 01 42	28 15.5	22 25.3	20 15.9	21 02.7	22 58.6	1 54.3	26 16.2	4 13.7	0 41.7	16 57.5
25 F	20 17 13	5 03 15	0♌26 51	7♌49 28	28 05.6	23 08.3	21 21.3	21 00.8	23 19.3	2 00.2	26 22.3	4 15.8	0 40.3	16 56.3
26 Sa	20 21 10	6 04 13	15 08 30	22 22 58	27 54.5	23 42.3	22 26.3	20 59.7	23 40.2	2 06.3	26 28.3	4 17.9	0 38.8	16 55.1
27 Su	20 25 07	7 05 10	29 32 03	6♍35 04	27 43.6	24 06.5	23 31.1	20D 59.3	24 01.1	2 12.5	26 34.3	4 20.1	0 37.3	16 53.9
28 M	20 29 03	8 06 06	13♍31 33	20 21 11	27 33.9	24R 20.1	24 35.6	20 59.7	24 22.1	2 18.9	26 40.2	4 22.3	0 35.8	16 52.7
29 Tu	20 33 00	9 07 02	27 03 52	3♎39 40	27 26.5	24 22.8	25 39.8	21 00.8	24 43.1	2 25.4	26 46.1	4 24.5	0 34.2	16 51.6
30 W	20 36 56	10 07 56	10♎08 47	16 31 35	27 21.6	24 14.3	26 43.7	21 02.7	25 04.3	2 32.1	26 51.9	4 26.8	0 32.7	16 50.4
31 Th	20 40 53	11 08 50	22 48 31	29 00 08	27 19.1	23 54.4	27 47.2	21 05.2	25 25.6	2 39.0	26 57.7	4 29.1	0 31.1	16 49.2

LONGITUDE — February 1929

Day	Sid.Time	☉	0 hr ☽	Noon ☽	True ☊	☿	♀	♂	⚳	♃	♄	♅	♆	♇
1 F	20 44 49	12♒09 43	5♏07 04	11♏09 58	27♉18.4	23♒23.6	28♓50.4	21♊08.5	25♓46.9	2♉46.1	27♐03.4	4♈31.5	0♍29.6	16♋48.1
2 Sa	20 48 46	13 10 36	17 09 31	23 06 27	27R 18.6	22R 42.5	29 53.3	21 12.6	26 08.3	2 53.3	27 09.0	4 33.9	0R 28.0	16R 47.0
3 Su	20 52 42	14 11 27	29 01 26	4♐55 12	27 18.4	21 52.2	0♈55.8	21 17.3	26 29.8	3 00.6	27 14.6	4 36.3	0 26.4	16 45.9
4 M	20 56 39	15 12 18	10♐48 24	16 41 41	27 16.8	20 53.8	1 58.0	21 22.7	26 51.4	3 08.1	27 20.2	4 38.8	0 24.8	16 44.7
5 Tu	21 00 36	16 13 08	22 35 39	28 30 51	27 12.9	19 49.2	2 59.7	21 28.7	27 13.1	3 15.8	27 25.6	4 41.3	0 23.2	16 43.7
6 W	21 04 32	17 13 57	4♑27 47	10♑26 53	27 06.1	18 40.3	4 01.1	21 35.4	27 34.8	3 23.6	27 31.1	4 43.8	0 21.6	16 42.6
7 Th	21 08 29	18 14 44	16 28 34	22 33 06	26 56.5	17 28.9	5 02.1	21 42.8	27 56.7	3 31.6	27 36.4	4 46.4	0 19.9	16 41.5
8 F	21 12 25	19 15 31	28 40 45	4♒51 41	26 44.3	16 17.1	6 02.7	21 50.8	28 18.6	3 39.7	27 41.7	4 49.0	0 18.3	16 40.5
9 Sa	21 16 22	20 16 16	11♒06 00	17 23 44	26 30.6	15 06.8	7 02.8	21 59.5	28 40.5	3 47.9	27 46.9	4 51.7	0 16.7	16 39.4
10 Su	21 20 18	21 17 00	23 44 53	0♓09 22	26 16.4	13 59.8	8 02.5	22 08.8	29 02.6	3 56.3	27 52.1	4 54.3	0 15.0	16 38.4
11 M	21 24 15	22 17 43	6♓37 04	13 07 52	26 03.1	12 57.6	9 01.7	22 18.6	29 24.7	4 04.9	27 57.2	4 57.0	0 13.4	16 37.4
12 Tu	21 28 11	23 18 24	19 41 37	26 18 10	25 51.9	12 01.2	10 00.5	22 29.1	29 46.8	4 13.6	28 02.2	4 59.8	0 11.7	16 36.4
13 W	21 32 08	24 19 03	2♈57 22	9♈39 07	25 43.4	11 11.6	10 58.7	22 40.1	0♈09.1	4 22.4	28 07.2	5 02.5	0 10.0	16 35.4
14 Th	21 36 04	25 19 41	16 23 19	23 09 55	25 38.1	10 29.4	11 56.4	22 51.7	0 31.4	4 31.3	28 12.1	5 05.3	0 08.3	16 34.4
15 F	21 40 01	26 20 17	29 58 54	6♉50 16	25 35.6	9 54.9	12 53.6	23 03.9	0 53.7	4 40.4	28 16.9	5 08.2	0 06.7	16 33.5
16 Sa	21 43 58	27 20 51	13♉44 03	20 40 18	25 34.9	9 28.1	13 50.3	23 16.6	1 16.2	4 49.6	28 21.6	5 11.0	0 05.0	16 32.6
17 Su	21 47 54	28 21 24	27 39 01	4♊40 15	25 34.9	9 09.2	14 46.3	23 29.9	1 38.7	4 59.0	28 26.3	5 13.9	0 03.3	16 31.6
18 M	21 51 51	29 21 54	11♊43 56	18 50 01	25 34.0	8 57.8	15 41.8	23 43.6	2 01.2	5 08.5	28 30.9	5 16.8	0 01.6	16 30.8
19 Tu	21 55 47	0♓22 23	25 58 17	3♋08 30	25 31.2	8D 53.6	16 36.6	23 57.9	2 23.8	5 18.1	28 35.5	5 19.7	29♌60.0	16 29.9
20 W	21 59 44	1 22 50	10♋20 18	17 33 12	25 25.6	8 56.4	17 30.8	24 12.6	2 46.5	5 27.8	28 39.9	5 22.7	29 58.3	16 29.0
21 Th	22 03 40	2 23 15	24 46 37	1♌59 53	25 17.1	9 05.8	18 24.3	24 27.8	3 09.2	5 37.6	28 44.3	5 25.7	29 56.6	16 28.2
22 F	22 07 37	3 23 39	9♌12 17	16 23 00	25 06.3	9 21.2	19 17.1	24 43.5	3 31.9	5 47.6	28 48.6	5 28.7	29 54.9	16 27.4
23 Sa	22 11 34	4 24 00	23 31 15	0♍36 16	24 54.1	9 42.4	20 09.2	24 59.7	3 54.7	5 57.6	28 52.8	5 31.7	29 53.2	16 26.6
24 Su	22 15 30	5 24 20	7♍37 20	14 33 49	24 41.8	10 09.0	21 00.6	25 16.2	4 17.6	6 07.8	28 57.0	5 34.8	29 51.6	16 25.8
25 M	22 19 27	6 24 38	21 25 12	28 11 05	24 30.7	10 40.4	21 51.1	25 33.3	4 40.5	6 18.1	29 01.0	5 37.9	29 49.9	16 25.0
26 Tu	22 23 23	7 24 55	4♎51 14	11♎25 33	24 21.9	11 16.5	22 40.9	25 50.7	5 03.4	6 28.5	29 05.0	5 41.0	29 48.2	16 24.3
27 W	22 27 20	8 25 10	17 54 03	24 16 56	24 15.7	11 56.9	23 29.8	26 08.5	5 26.4	6 39.0	29 08.9	5 44.1	29 46.6	16 23.5
28 Th	22 31 16	9 25 23	0♏34 27	6♏47 00	24 12.2	12 41.2	24 17.9	26 26.8	5 49.5	6 49.7	29 12.8	5 47.2	29 44.9	16 22.8

Astro Data

	Dy Hr Mn
☽0S	2 13:41
♃△♆	12 12:23
☽0N	17 5:25
♂ D	27 12:02
☿ R	29 5:46
☽0S	29 21:30
♀0N	1 14:57
☽0N	13 10:00
☿ D	19 14:07
♃⚺♅	19 18:00
☽0S	26 6:26

Planet Ingress

	Dy Hr Mn
♀ ♓	6 12:01
☿ ♒	8 8:09
☉ ♒	20 12:42
♀ ♈	2 14:34
⚳ ♈	13 2:12
☉ ♓	19 3:07
♆ ♌R	19 11:23

Last Aspect / ☽ Ingress

Last Aspect Dy Hr Mn		☽ Ingress	Dy Hr Mn
1 11:40	♂ □	♎	1 20:08
4 0:28	♀ △	♏	4 6:10
6 12:48	☿ ⚹	♐	6 18:50
8 20:55	♄ ☌	♑	9 7:51
11 0:28	☉ ☌	♒	11 19:33
13 20:08	♄ ⚹	♓	14 5:21
16 5:05	☉ ⚹	♈	16 13:07
18 15:15	☉ □	♉	18 18:37
20 1:09	☿ □	♊	20 21:43
22 16:32	♄ ☍	♋	22 22:52
24 7:11	♀ △	♌	24 23:16
26 18:53	♄ △	♍	27 0:47
28 23:22	♄ □	♎	29 5:19
31 8:00	♄ ⚹	♏	31 13:57

Last Aspect / ☽ Ingress

Last Aspect Dy Hr Mn		☽ Ingress	Dy Hr Mn
2 11:15	☿ □	♐	3 1:59
5 9:47	♄ ☌	♑	5 15:00
7 0:27	♇ ☍	♒	8 2:34
10 7:42	♄ ⚹	♓	10 11:43
12 15:09	♄ □	♈	12 18:41
14 20:56	♄ △	♉	15 0:02
17 0:22	☉ □	♊	17 4:01
19 4:21	♄ ☍	♋	19 6:45
20 11:56	♀ □	♌	21 8:41
23 10:47	♆ ☌	♍	23 10:58
25 13:30	♄ □	♎	25 15:15
27 22:27	♆ ⚹	♏	27 22:54

☽ Phases & Eclipses

Dy Hr Mn	
2 18:44	☾ 11♎55
11 0:28	● 20♑19
18 15:15	☽ 28♈04
25 7:09	○ 4♌51
1 14:10	☾ 12♏15
9 17:55	● 20♒31
17 0:22	☽ 27♉52
23 18:59	○ 4♍42

Astro Data

1 January 1929
Julian Day # 10593
SVP 6♓15'18"
GC 25♐50.9 ⚴ 17♒14.6
Eris 0♈35.0 ⚵ 16♏08.1
⚷ 5♉30.9R ⚶ 14♈29.6
☽ Mean ☊ 28♉14.3

1 February 1929
Julian Day # 10624
SVP 6♓15'13"
GC 25♐50.9 ⚴ 27♒07.7
Eris 0♈45.7 ⚵ 23♏34.4
⚷ 5♉34.0 ⚶ 23♈11.3
☽ Mean ☊ 26♉35.8

March 1929 LONGITUDE

Day	Sid.Time	☉	0 hr ☽	Noon ☽	True ☊	☿	♀	♂	⚳	♃	♄	♅	♆	♇
1 F	22 35 13	10♓25 35	12♏55 03	18♏59 11	24♉10.9	13♒29.1	25♈05.1	26♊45.4	6♈12.5	7♉00.4	29♐16.5	5♈50.4	29♌43.3	16♋22.1
2 Sa	22 39 09	11 25 45	24 59 58	0♐58 03	24R 10.9	14 20.5	25 51.3	27 04.5	6 35.7	7 11.2	29 20.2	5 53.6	29R 41.6	16R 21.5
3 Su	22 43 06	12 25 54	6♐54 07	12 48 52	24 11.2	15 15.0	26 36.6	27 23.9	6 58.9	7 22.2	29 23.8	5 56.8	29 40.0	16 20.8
4 M	22 47 02	13 26 02	18 42 59	24 37 10	24 10.5	16 12.5	27 20.9	27 43.6	7 22.1	7 33.2	29 27.2	6 00.0	29 38.4	16 20.2
5 Tu	22 50 59	14 26 07	0♑32 05	6♑28 22	24 08.1	17 12.7	28 04.2	28 03.8	7 45.3	7 44.3	29 30.7	6 03.2	29 36.8	16 19.6
6 W	22 54 56	15 26 11	12 26 40	18 27 31	24 03.3	18 15.6	28 46.4	28 24.3	8 08.6	7 55.6	29 34.0	6 06.5	29 35.1	16 19.0
7 Th	22 58 52	16 26 14	24 31 26	0♒38 53	23 55.9	19 20.8	29 27.5	28 45.1	8 32.0	8 06.9	29 37.2	6 09.7	29 33.5	16 18.5
8 F	23 02 49	17 26 15	6♒50 13	13 05 44	23 46.2	20 28.3	0♉07.4	29 06.3	8 55.4	8 18.3	29 40.4	6 13.0	29 32.0	16 18.0
9 Sa	23 06 45	18 26 14	19 25 38	25 50 01	23 35.0	21 37.9	0 46.1	29 27.8	9 18.8	8 29.8	29 43.4	6 16.3	29 30.4	16 17.4
10 Su	23 10 42	19 26 11	2♓18 56	8♓52 17	23 23.3	22 49.6	1 23.6	29 49.6	9 42.2	8 41.4	29 46.4	6 19.6	29 28.8	16 17.0
11 M	23 14 38	20 26 06	15 29 54	22 11 34	23 12.3	24 03.2	1 59.8	0♋11.8	10 05.7	8 53.1	29 49.2	6 22.9	29 27.3	16 16.5
12 Tu	23 18 35	21 25 59	28 56 57	5♈45 43	23 02.9	25 18.7	2 34.6	0 34.2	10 29.2	9 04.9	29 52.0	6 26.3	29 25.7	16 16.0
13 W	23 22 31	22 25 51	12♈37 28	19 31 49	22 56.0	26 35.9	3 08.0	0 57.0	10 52.8	9 16.7	29 54.7	6 29.6	29 24.2	16 15.6
14 Th	23 26 28	23 25 40	26 28 22	3♉26 44	22 51.9	27 54.8	3 40.0	1 20.0	11 16.3	9 28.7	29 57.3	6 33.0	29 22.7	16 15.2
15 F	23 30 25	24 25 27	10♉26 35	17 27 36	22D 50.3	29 15.3	4 10.4	1 43.4	11 39.9	9 40.7	29 59.8	6 36.3	29 21.2	16 14.9
16 Sa	23 34 21	25 25 12	24 29 31	1♊32 07	22 50.4	0♓37.4	4 39.3	2 07.0	12 03.6	9 52.8	0♑02.2	6 39.7	29 19.7	16 14.5
17 Su	23 38 18	26 24 54	8♊35 14	15 38 41	22R 51.2	2 01.1	5 06.5	2 30.9	12 27.2	10 05.0	0 04.5	6 43.1	29 18.2	16 14.2
18 M	23 42 14	27 24 35	22 42 21	29 46 06	22 51.5	3 26.2	5 32.0	2 55.0	12 50.9	10 17.3	0 06.8	6 46.5	29 16.8	16 13.9
19 Tu	23 46 11	28 24 13	6♋49 47	13♋53 14	22 50.4	4 52.8	5 55.8	3 19.5	13 14.6	10 29.6	0 08.9	6 49.9	29 15.4	16 13.6
20 W	23 50 07	29 23 49	20 56 16	27 58 38	22 47.1	6 20.8	6 17.7	3 44.1	13 38.3	10 42.0	0 10.9	6 53.3	29 14.0	16 13.3
21 Th	23 54 04	0♈23 22	5♌00 04	12♌00 14	22 41.7	7 50.2	6 37.7	4 09.1	14 02.1	10 54.5	0 12.9	6 56.7	29 12.6	16 13.1
22 F	23 58 00	1 22 53	18 58 47	25 55 19	22 34.3	9 21.0	6 55.7	4 34.2	14 25.9	11 07.0	0 14.7	7 00.1	29 11.2	16 12.9
23 Sa	0 01 57	2 22 22	2♍49 25	9♍40 41	22 25.9	10 53.2	7 11.8	4 59.6	14 49.7	11 19.6	0 16.5	7 03.5	29 09.8	16 12.7
24 Su	0 05 54	3 21 49	16 28 42	23 13 08	22 17.3	12 26.8	7 25.7	5 25.2	15 13.5	11 32.3	0 18.1	7 07.0	29 08.5	16 12.6
25 M	0 09 50	4 21 13	29 53 39	6♎30 00	22 09.5	14 01.7	7 37.5	5 51.0	15 37.3	11 45.0	0 19.7	7 10.4	29 07.2	16 12.4
26 Tu	0 13 47	5 20 36	13♎01 59	19 29 31	22 03.4	15 38.0	7 47.1	6 17.1	16 01.1	11 57.8	0 21.1	7 13.8	29 05.9	16 12.3
27 W	0 17 43	6 19 56	25 52 36	2♏11 16	21 59.2	17 15.7	7 54.4	6 43.4	16 25.0	12 10.7	0 22.5	7 17.2	29 04.6	16 12.2
28 Th	0 21 40	7 19 15	8♏25 42	14 36 08	21D 57.2	18 54.7	7 59.5	7 09.8	16 48.9	12 23.6	0 23.7	7 20.6	29 03.4	16 12.2
29 F	0 25 36	8 18 32	20 42 54	26 46 22	21 57.0	20 35.0	8R 02.1	7 36.5	17 12.8	12 36.6	0 24.9	7 24.1	29 02.1	16D 12.1
30 Sa	0 29 33	9 17 47	2♐47 00	8♐45 18	21 58.1	22 16.8	8 02.4	8 03.4	17 36.7	12 49.6	0 26.0	7 27.5	29 00.9	16 12.1
31 Su	0 33 29	10 17 00	14 41 48	20 37 07	21 59.7	24 00.0	8 00.3	8 30.4	18 00.6	13 02.7	0 26.9	7 30.9	28 59.7	16 12.1

April 1929 LONGITUDE

Day	Sid.Time	☉	0 hr ☽	Noon ☽	True ☊	☿	♀	♂	⚳	♃	♄	♅	♆	♇
1 M	0 37 26	11♈16 12	26♐31 49	2♑26 35	22♉01.1	25♓44.5	7♉55.8	8♋57.7	18♈24.6	13♉15.8	0♑27.8	7♈34.4	28♌58.6	16♋12.2
2 Tu	0 41 23	12 15 21	8♑22 01	14 18 48	22R 01.5	27 30.4	7R 48.7	9 25.1	18 48.6	13 29.0	0 28.6	7 37.8	28R 57.4	16 12.2
3 W	0 45 19	13 14 29	20 17 32	26 18 52	22 00.4	29 17.8	7 39.3	9 52.7	19 12.5	13 42.3	0 29.2	7 41.2	28 56.3	16 12.3
4 Th	0 49 16	14 13 35	2♒23 24	8♒31 39	21 57.8	1♈06.6	7 27.3	10 20.5	19 36.5	13 55.6	0 29.8	7 44.6	28 55.2	16 12.4
5 F	0 53 12	15 12 40	14 44 08	21 01 18	21 53.6	2 56.8	7 12.9	10 48.5	20 00.5	14 09.0	0 30.3	7 48.0	28 54.2	16 12.6
6 Sa	0 57 09	16 11 42	27 23 30	3♓50 59	21 48.3	4 48.5	6 56.1	11 16.7	20 24.5	14 22.3	0 30.6	7 51.4	28 53.1	16 12.7
7 Su	1 01 05	17 10 43	10♓23 57	17 02 27	21 42.5	6 41.6	6 36.9	11 45.0	20 48.5	14 35.8	0 30.9	7 54.8	28 52.1	16 12.9
8 M	1 05 02	18 09 41	23 46 25	0♈35 42	21 37.0	8 36.1	6 15.4	12 13.5	21 12.6	14 49.3	0 31.1	7 58.2	28 51.2	16 13.1
9 Tu	1 08 58	19 08 38	7♈30 00	14 28 55	21 32.3	10 32.1	5 51.7	12 42.2	21 36.6	15 02.8	0R 31.1	8 01.6	28 50.2	16 13.3
10 W	1 12 55	20 07 33	21 31 57	28 38 34	21 29.1	12 29.6	5 25.8	13 11.0	22 00.6	15 16.4	0 31.1	8 05.0	28 49.3	16 13.6
11 Th	1 16 51	21 06 26	5♉48 06	12♉59 54	21D 27.4	14 28.4	4 58.0	13 40.0	22 24.7	15 30.0	0 31.0	8 08.3	28 48.4	16 13.9
12 F	1 20 48	22 05 16	20 13 17	27 27 36	21 27.3	16 28.6	4 28.2	14 09.1	22 48.7	15 43.6	0 30.7	8 11.7	28 47.5	16 14.2
13 Sa	1 24 45	23 04 05	4♊42 11	11♊56 27	21 28.3	18 30.1	3 56.7	14 38.4	23 12.8	15 57.3	0 30.4	8 15.1	28 46.6	16 14.5
14 Su	1 28 41	24 02 51	19 09 53	26 21 59	21 29.7	20 32.8	3 23.7	15 07.8	23 36.8	16 11.1	0 30.0	8 18.4	28 45.8	16 14.9
15 M	1 32 38	25 01 36	3♋32 21	10♋40 39	21 31.0	22 36.8	2 49.3	15 37.4	24 00.9	16 24.8	0 29.5	8 21.7	28 45.1	16 15.2
16 Tu	1 36 34	26 00 17	17 46 36	24 49 59	21R 31.6	24 41.8	2 13.7	16 07.1	24 24.9	16 38.6	0 28.8	8 25.0	28 44.3	16 15.6
17 W	1 40 31	26 58 57	1♌50 36	8♌48 19	21 31.1	26 47.7	1 37.2	16 37.0	24 49.0	16 52.4	0 28.1	8 28.3	28 43.6	16 16.1
18 Th	1 44 27	27 57 34	15 43 02	22 34 39	21 29.5	28 54.4	0 59.9	17 06.9	25 13.0	17 06.3	0 27.3	8 31.6	28 42.9	16 16.5
19 F	1 48 24	28 56 09	29 23 04	6♍08 15	21 27.0	1♉01.7	0 22.2	17 37.0	25 37.1	17 20.2	0 26.4	8 34.9	28 42.2	16 17.0
20 Sa	1 52 21	29 54 42	12♍50 08	19 28 39	21 24.0	3 09.3	29♈44.3	18 07.3	26 01.1	17 34.1	0 25.4	8 38.1	28 41.6	16 17.5
21 Su	1 56 17	0♉53 13	26 03 47	2♎35 29	21 20.8	5 17.2	29 06.4	18 37.6	26 25.2	17 48.0	0 24.3	8 41.4	28 41.0	16 18.0
22 M	2 00 14	1 51 41	9♎03 45	15 28 35	21 18.0	7 24.9	28 28.9	19 08.1	26 49.2	18 02.0	0 23.1	8 44.6	28 40.4	16 18.5
23 Tu	2 04 10	2 50 08	21 49 59	28 08 02	21 15.9	9 32.2	27 51.8	19 38.7	27 13.2	18 15.9	0 21.8	8 47.8	28 39.8	16 19.1
24 W	2 08 07	3 48 33	4♏22 47	10♏34 22	21D 14.6	11 38.9	27 15.6	20 09.4	27 37.3	18 29.9	0 20.4	8 51.0	28 39.3	16 19.7
25 Th	2 12 03	4 46 56	16 42 55	22 48 39	21 14.3	13 44.5	26 40.4	20 40.2	28 01.3	18 44.0	0 18.9	8 54.2	28 38.8	16 20.3
26 F	2 16 00	5 45 18	28 51 47	4♐52 36	21 14.8	15 48.8	26 06.4	21 11.2	28 25.3	18 58.0	0 17.4	8 57.3	28 38.4	16 20.9
27 Sa	2 19 56	6 43 37	10♐51 25	16 48 36	21 15.8	17 51.6	25 33.9	21 42.2	28 49.3	19 12.1	0 15.7	9 00.5	28 38.0	16 21.6
28 Su	2 23 53	7 41 55	22 44 31	28 39 38	21 17.1	19 52.3	25 03.0	22 13.4	29 13.3	19 26.2	0 13.9	9 03.6	28 37.6	16 22.2
29 M	2 27 49	8 40 12	4♑34 25	10♑29 22	21 18.3	21 50.9	24 33.8	22 44.7	29 37.3	19 40.3	0 12.1	9 06.7	28 37.2	16 22.9
30 Tu	2 31 46	9 38 27	16 25 01	22 21 54	21 19.3	23 47.0	24 06.7	23 16.0	0♉01.3	19 54.4	0 10.2	9 09.8	28 36.9	16 23.6

Astro Data	Planet Ingress	Last Aspect	☽ Ingress	Last Aspect	☽ Ingress	☽ Phases & Eclipses	Astro Data
Dy Hr Mn	Dy Hr Mn	Dy Hr Mn	Dy Hr Mn	Dy Hr Mn	Dy Hr Mn	Dy Hr Mn	1 March 1929
♄△♆ 6 17:45	♀ ♉ 8 7:29	2 9:26 ♆ □	♐ 2 10:03	1 4:59 ♆ △	♑ 1 7:03	3 11:09 ☾ 12♐24	Julian Day # 10652
☽0N 12 16:24	♂ ♋ 10 23:18	4 22:10 ♆ △	♑ 4 22:55	3 18:56 ☿ ⚹	♒ 3 19:18	11 8:36 ● 20♓18	SVP 6♓15'09"
☉0N 21 2:35	♄ ♑ 15 13:49	7 9:33 ♀ □	♒ 7 10:44	6 2:48 ♆ ☍	♓ 6 4:52	18 7:41 ☽ 27♊14	GC 25♐51.0 ⚴ 6♓25.0
☽0S 25 15:11	☿ ♓ 16 1:07	9 19:15 ♄ ⚹	♓ 9 19:44	7 10:31 ♇ △	♈ 8 10:58	25 7:46 ○ 4♎11	Eris 1♈02.8 ⚵ 27♏30.0
⚳0N 27 5:25	☉ ♈ 21 2:35	12 1:35 ♄ □	♈ 12 1:51	10 12:18 ♆ △	♉ 10 14:17		⚷ 6♉24.1 ⚶ 3♉14.9
♀R 30 3:02		14 5:59 ♄ △	♉ 14 6:05	12 14:12 ♆ □	♊ 12 16:13	2 7:29 ☾ 12♑04	☽ Mean ☊ 25♉06.9
♇D 30 11:51	☿ ♈ 3 21:21	16 8:15 ♆ □	♊ 16 9:23	14 16:00 ♆ ⚹	♋ 14 18:04	9 20:32 ● 19♈30	
	☿ ♉ 19 0:23	18 11:10 ♆ ⚹	♋ 18 12:24	16 14:09 ☉ □	♌ 16 20:50	16 14:09 ☽ 26♋06	1 April 1929
☿0N 6 9:17	♀ ♈R 20 2:05	20 14:36 ☉ △	♌ 20 15:27	18 22:48 ♆ ☌	♍ 19 1:05	23 21:47 ○ 3♏14	Julian Day # 10683
☽0N 9 1:20	☉ ♉ 20 14:10	22 17:39 ♆ ☌	♍ 22 19:05	20 9:27 ♂ ⚹	♎ 21 7:13		SVP 6♓15'06"
♄R 9 16:01	⚳ ♉ 30 10:41	23 23:32 ♇ ⚹	♎ 25 0:11	23 13:01 ♆ ⚹	♏ 23 15:34		GC 25♐51.1 ⚴ 16♓35.1
♃⚼♄ 11 13:41		27 6:05 ♆ ⚹	♏ 27 7:49	25 23:34 ♆ □	♐ 26 2:16		Eris 1♈25.5 ⚵ 27♏23.5R
♃⚹♇ 14 18:49		29 16:30 ♆ □	♐ 29 18:26	28 11:56 ♆ △	♑ 28 14:43		⚷ 7♉59.3 ⚶ 15♉42.8
☽0S 21 22:35							☽ Mean ☊ 23♉28.4

LONGITUDE — May 1929

Day	Sid.Time	☉	0 hr ☽	Noon ☽	True ☊	☿	♀	♂	⚵	♃	♄	♅	♆	♇
1 W	2 35 43	10♉36 40	28♑20 37	4♒21 43	21♉19.8	25♉40.4	23♈41.6	23♋47.5	0♉25.3	20♉08.5	0♑08.2	9♈12.8	28♌36.6	16♋24.4
2 Th	2 39 39	11 34 52	10♒25 48	16 33 26	21R 19.8	27 30.8	23R 18.7	24 19.1	0 49.3	20 22.7	0R 06.1	9 15.8	28R 36.3	16 25.1
3 F	2 43 36	12 33 03	22 45 11	29 01 32	21 19.4	29 18.1	22 58.0	24 50.8	1 13.2	20 36.8	0 03.9	9 18.8	28 36.1	16 25.9
4 Sa	2 47 32	13 31 11	5♓23 00	11♓50 00	21 18.7	1♊02.1	22 39.7	25 22.5	1 37.2	20 51.0	0 01.6	9 21.8	28 35.9	16 26.7
5 Su	2 51 29	14 29 19	18 22 52	25 01 51	21 17.9	2 42.7	22 23.7	25 54.4	2 01.1	21 05.2	29♐59.2	9 24.8	28 35.7	16 27.6
6 M	2 55 25	15 27 25	1♈47 07	8♈38 42	21 17.1	4 19.7	22 10.2	26 26.4	2 25.0	21 19.4	29 56.8	9 27.7	28 35.6	16 28.4
7 Tu	2 59 22	16 25 30	15 36 27	22 40 10	21 16.6	5 53.1	21 59.1	26 58.5	2 48.9	21 33.6	29 54.3	9 30.6	28 35.5	16 29.3
8 W	3 03 18	17 23 33	29 49 25	7♉03 41	21D 16.3	7 22.7	21 50.4	27 30.6	3 12.8	21 47.8	29 51.7	9 33.5	28 35.4	16 30.1
9 Th	3 07 15	18 21 34	14♉22 16	21 44 24	21 16.2	8 48.4	21 44.2	28 02.9	3 36.7	22 02.0	29 49.0	9 36.4	28D 35.4	16 31.0
10 F	3 11 12	19 19 34	29 09 12	6♊35 42	21 16.2	10 10.3	21 40.3	28 35.3	4 00.6	22 16.2	29 46.2	9 39.2	28 35.4	16 32.0
11 Sa	3 15 08	20 17 33	14♊02 55	21 29 53	21 16.3	11 28.2	21D 38.8	29 07.7	4 24.4	22 30.4	29 43.4	9 42.0	28 35.4	16 32.9
12 Su	3 19 05	21 15 30	28 55 40	6♋19 21	21R 16.4	12 42.1	21 39.7	29 40.2	4 48.2	22 44.6	29 40.5	9 44.8	28 35.5	16 33.9
13 M	3 23 01	22 13 25	13♋40 12	20 57 30	21 16.3	13 51.9	21 42.9	0♌12.9	5 12.0	22 58.9	29 37.5	9 47.5	28 35.6	16 34.9
14 Tu	3 26 58	23 11 18	28 10 43	5♌19 25	21 16.2	14 57.5	21 48.3	0 45.6	5 35.8	23 13.1	29 34.4	9 50.2	28 35.7	16 35.9
15 W	3 30 54	24 09 09	12♌23 18	19 22 12	21D 16.2	15 58.9	21 55.9	1 18.4	5 59.6	23 27.3	29 31.3	9 52.9	28 35.9	16 36.9
16 Th	3 34 51	25 06 59	26 16 01	3♍04 46	21 16.2	16 56.1	22 05.7	1 51.2	6 23.3	23 41.5	29 28.1	9 55.6	28 36.1	16 37.9
17 F	3 38 48	26 04 47	9♍48 33	16 27 31	21 16.4	17 48.8	22 17.6	2 24.2	6 47.0	23 55.7	29 24.8	9 58.2	28 36.3	16 39.0
18 Sa	3 42 44	27 02 33	23 01 52	29 31 50	21 16.9	18 37.2	22 31.5	2 57.2	7 10.7	24 09.9	29 21.5	10 00.8	28 36.6	16 40.0
19 Su	3 46 41	28 00 17	5♎57 41	12♎19 40	21 17.5	19 21.1	22 47.4	3 30.3	7 34.4	24 24.1	29 18.1	10 03.4	28 36.9	16 41.1
20 M	3 50 37	28 58 00	18 38 03	24 53 07	21 18.2	20 00.5	23 05.2	4 03.5	7 58.0	24 38.3	29 14.6	10 05.9	28 37.2	16 42.2
21 Tu	3 54 34	29 55 41	1♏05 08	7♏14 21	21 18.7	20 35.2	23 24.8	4 36.7	8 21.6	24 52.4	29 11.1	10 08.4	28 37.6	16 43.4
22 W	3 58 30	0♊53 21	13 21 01	19 25 23	21R 19.0	21 05.3	23 46.3	5 10.0	8 45.2	25 06.6	29 07.5	10 10.8	28 37.9	16 44.5
23 Th	4 02 27	1 51 00	25 27 41	1♐28 09	21 18.8	21 30.7	24 09.5	5 43.4	9 08.8	25 20.8	29 03.9	10 13.3	28 38.4	16 45.7
24 F	4 06 23	2 48 38	7♐27 03	13 24 36	21 18.1	21 51.4	24 34.4	6 16.9	9 32.3	25 34.9	29 00.2	10 15.7	28 38.8	16 46.8
25 Sa	4 10 20	3 46 14	19 21 04	25 16 44	21 16.8	22 07.3	25 01.0	6 50.4	9 55.8	25 49.0	28 56.4	10 18.0	28 39.3	16 48.0
26 Su	4 14 17	4 43 49	1♑11 51	7♑06 45	21 15.0	22 18.5	25 29.1	7 24.0	10 19.3	26 03.1	28 52.6	10 20.3	28 39.8	16 49.2
27 M	4 18 13	5 41 24	13 01 46	18 57 14	21 12.9	22R 24.9	25 58.7	7 57.7	10 42.7	26 17.2	28 48.8	10 22.6	28 40.4	16 50.4
28 Tu	4 22 10	6 38 57	24 53 33	0♒51 07	21 10.7	22 26.7	26 29.7	8 31.4	11 06.1	26 31.3	28 44.9	10 24.9	28 41.0	16 51.7
29 W	4 26 06	7 36 29	6♒50 23	12 51 48	21 08.9	22 23.9	27 02.2	9 05.2	11 29.5	26 45.4	28 41.0	10 27.1	28 41.6	16 52.9
30 Th	4 30 03	8 34 01	18 55 50	25 03 01	21 07.6	22 16.7	27 36.0	9 39.1	11 52.9	26 59.4	28 37.0	10 29.3	28 42.2	16 54.2
31 F	4 33 59	9 31 31	1♓13 50	7♓28 49	21D 07.0	22 05.2	28 11.1	10 13.1	12 16.2	27 13.4	28 32.9	10 31.4	28 42.9	16 55.5

LONGITUDE — June 1929

Day	Sid.Time	☉	0 hr ☽	Noon ☽	True ☊	☿	♀	♂	⚵	♃	♄	♅	♆	♇
1 Sa	4 37 56	10♊29 01	13♓48 27	20♓13 14	21♉07.3	21♊49.8	28♈47.4	10♌47.1	12♉39.5	27♉27.5	28♐28.9	10♈33.5	28♌43.6	16♋56.8
2 Su	4 41 52	11 26 30	26 43 37	3♈20 00	21 08.2	21R 30.5	29 24.9	11 21.1	13 02.7	27 41.4	28R 24.7	10 35.6	28 44.4	16 58.1
3 M	4 45 49	12 23 58	10♈02 42	16 51 58	21 09.5	21 07.9	0♉03.6	11 55.3	13 25.9	27 55.4	28 20.6	10 37.6	28 45.1	16 59.4
4 Tu	4 49 46	13 21 26	23 47 55	0♉50 32	21 10.9	20 42.2	0 43.4	12 29.5	13 49.1	28 09.3	28 16.4	10 39.6	28 46.0	17 00.7
5 W	4 53 42	14 18 53	7♉59 40	15 14 58	21R 11.7	20 14.0	1 24.2	13 03.8	14 12.2	28 23.2	28 12.2	10 41.5	28 46.8	17 02.0
6 Th	4 57 39	15 16 19	22 35 55	0♊01 50	21 11.6	19 43.6	2 06.0	13 38.1	14 35.3	28 37.1	28 07.9	10 43.4	28 47.7	17 03.4
7 F	5 01 35	16 13 45	7♊31 52	15 04 58	21 10.3	19 11.6	2 48.8	14 12.5	14 58.4	28 51.0	28 03.7	10 45.3	28 48.6	17 04.8
8 Sa	5 05 32	17 11 09	22 40 01	0♋15 47	21 07.8	18 38.6	3 32.5	14 47.0	15 21.4	29 04.8	27 59.4	10 47.1	28 49.5	17 06.1
9 Su	5 09 28	18 08 33	7♋51 02	15 24 32	21 04.5	18 05.0	4 17.2	15 21.5	15 44.4	29 18.6	27 55.1	10 48.9	28 50.4	17 07.5
10 M	5 13 25	19 05 56	22 55 07	0♌21 44	21 00.7	17 31.5	5 02.6	15 56.1	16 07.3	29 32.4	27 50.7	10 50.6	28 51.4	17 08.9
11 Tu	5 17 21	20 03 18	7♌43 31	14 59 43	20 57.2	16 58.7	5 48.9	16 30.8	16 30.2	29 46.1	27 46.3	10 52.3	28 52.4	17 10.4
12 W	5 21 18	21 00 39	22 09 49	29 13 27	20 54.5	16 27.1	6 36.0	17 05.5	16 53.1	29 59.8	27 42.0	10 54.0	28 53.5	17 11.8
13 Th	5 25 15	21 57 59	6♍10 29	13♍00 53	20D 52.9	15 57.2	7 23.9	17 40.3	17 15.9	0♊13.5	27 37.6	10 55.6	28 54.6	17 13.2
14 F	5 29 11	22 55 18	19 44 48	26 22 28	20 52.6	15 29.6	8 12.5	18 15.1	17 38.6	0 27.1	27 33.2	10 57.2	28 55.7	17 14.6
15 Sa	5 33 08	23 52 36	2♎54 14	9♎20 29	20 53.5	15 04.7	9 01.7	18 50.0	18 01.3	0 40.7	27 28.7	10 58.7	28 56.8	17 16.1
16 Su	5 37 04	24 49 53	15 41 42	21 58 20	20 55.0	14 42.9	9 51.7	19 24.9	18 24.0	0 54.2	27 24.3	11 00.2	28 57.9	17 17.6
17 M	5 41 01	25 47 09	28 10 53	4♏19 51	20 56.5	14 24.6	10 42.4	19 59.9	18 46.5	1 07.7	27 19.9	11 01.6	28 59.1	17 19.0
18 Tu	5 44 57	26 44 25	10♏25 42	16 28 53	20R 57.5	14 10.1	11 33.7	20 34.9	19 09.1	1 21.2	27 15.5	11 03.0	29 00.3	17 20.5
19 W	5 48 54	27 41 40	22 29 51	28 28 59	20 57.3	13 59.8	12 25.6	21 10.0	19 31.6	1 34.6	27 11.0	11 04.3	29 01.6	17 22.0
20 Th	5 52 50	28 38 54	4♐26 39	10♐23 13	20 55.5	13D 53.7	13 18.1	21 45.2	19 54.0	1 48.0	27 06.6	11 05.6	29 02.9	17 23.5
21 F	5 56 47	29 36 08	16 18 59	22 14 13	20 51.9	13 52.1	14 11.1	22 20.4	20 16.4	2 01.3	27 02.2	11 06.9	29 04.2	17 25.0
22 Sa	6 00 44	0♋33 21	28 09 12	4♑04 12	20 46.5	13 55.1	15 04.8	22 55.7	20 38.7	2 14.6	26 57.7	11 08.1	29 05.5	17 26.5
23 Su	6 04 40	1 30 34	9♑59 24	15 55 05	20 39.8	14 02.7	15 58.9	23 31.0	21 01.0	2 27.8	26 53.3	11 09.3	29 06.8	17 28.0
24 M	6 08 37	2 27 47	21 51 26	27 48 42	20 32.2	14 15.2	16 53.6	24 06.3	21 23.2	2 41.0	26 48.9	11 10.4	29 08.2	17 29.5
25 Tu	6 12 33	3 25 00	3♒47 08	9♒46 59	20 24.6	14 32.3	17 48.8	24 41.8	21 45.4	2 54.2	26 44.5	11 11.4	29 09.6	17 31.0
26 W	6 16 30	4 22 12	15 48 33	21 52 07	20 17.6	14 54.3	18 44.5	25 17.2	22 07.5	3 07.3	26 40.2	11 12.5	29 11.0	17 32.6
27 Th	6 20 26	5 19 24	27 58 02	4♓06 39	20 11.9	15 20.9	19 40.7	25 52.8	22 29.6	3 20.3	26 35.8	11 13.4	29 12.5	17 34.1
28 F	6 24 23	6 16 37	10♓18 22	16 33 35	20 08.1	15 52.3	20 37.3	26 28.3	22 51.5	3 33.3	26 31.4	11 14.4	29 13.9	17 35.6
29 Sa	6 28 19	7 13 49	22 52 44	29 16 16	20D 06.1	16 28.4	21 34.3	27 04.0	23 13.5	3 46.2	26 27.1	11 15.3	29 15.4	17 37.2
30 Su	6 32 16	8 11 01	5♈44 37	12♈18 13	20 05.9	17 09.1	22 31.8	27 39.6	23 35.3	3 59.1	26 22.8	11 16.1	29 17.0	17 38.7

Astro Data	Planet Ingress	Last Aspect	☽ Ingress	Last Aspect	☽ Ingress	☽ Phases & Eclipses	Astro Data
Dy Hr Mn	Dy Hr Mn	Dy Hr Mn	Dy Hr Mn	Dy Hr Mn	Dy Hr Mn	Dy Hr Mn	
☽0N 6 11:29	☿ ♊ 3 21:34	30 15:24 ☿ △	♒ 1 3:19	2 3:08 ♄ □	♈ 2 5:58	2 1:25 ☾ 11♒09	1 May 1929
♆ D 9 23:44	♄ ♐R 5 4:18	3 12:37 ☿ □	♓ 3 13:51	4 8:29 ♆ △	♉ 4 10:34	9 6:07 ● 18♉07	Julian Day # 10713
♀ D 11 15:01	♂ ♌ 13 2:33	5 20:48 ♄ □	♈ 5 20:51	6 10:01 ♆ □	♊ 6 11:57	9 6:10:10 ● T 05'07"	SVP 6♓15'02"
☽0S 19 4:30	☉ ♊ 21 13:48	8 0:06 ♄ △	♉ 8 0:18	8 9:44 ♆ ⚹	♋ 8 11:35	15 20:56 ☽ 24♌31	GC 25♐51.1 ⚳ 25♓49.8
♃∠♅ 22 20:41		9 23:05 ♆ □	♊ 10 1:22	10 10:39 ♃ ⚹	♌ 10 11:25	23 12:50 ○ 1♐53	Eris 1♈45.9 ⚴ 22♏34.0R
☿ R 28 9:17	♀ ♉ 3 9:48	12 1:15 ♄ ☍	♋ 12 1:44	12 11:26 ♆ ☌	♍ 12 13:20	23 12:37 ● A 0.937	⚷ 9♉52.3 ⚶ 28♉27.1
♄△♆ 29 8:36	♃ ♊ 12 12:20	13 15:24 ♃ ⚹	♌ 14 3:03	14 14:08 ♄ □	♎ 14 18:38	31 16:13 ☾ 9♓42	☽ Mean ☊ 21♉53.0
	☉ ♋ 21 22:01	16 5:39 ♄ △	♍ 16 6:33	17 1:33 ♆ ⚹	♏ 17 3:32		
☽0N 2 20:54		18 11:41 ♄ □	♎ 18 12:52	19 13:06 ♆ □	♐ 19 15:03	7 13:56 ● 16♊18	1 June 1929
♃⚻♄ 4 21:22		20 20:23 ♄ ⚹	♏ 20 21:54	22 1:53 ♆ △	♑ 22 3:45	14 5:14 ☽ 22♍39	Julian Day # 10744
♃□♆ 7 7:29		23 6:20 ♆ □	♐ 23 9:04	23 15:08 ♇ ☍	♒ 24 16:24	22 4:15 ○ 0♑15	SVP 6♓14'57"
☽0S 15 9:53		25 19:23 ♄ ☌	♑ 25 21:34	27 2:25 ♆ ☍	♓ 27 3:59	30 3:54 ☾ 7♈52	GC 25♐51.2 ⚳ 4♈09.3
☿ D 21 8:28		28 3:07 ♃ △	♒ 28 10:17	29 6:45 ♄ □	♈ 29 13:22		Eris 2♈00.2 ⚴ 15♏54.1R
♃∠♇ 23 12:19		30 19:07 ♆ ☍	♓ 30 21:37				⚷ 11♉48.8 ⚶ 11♊53.2
☽0N 30 4:09							☽ Mean ☊ 20♉14.6

July 1929

LONGITUDE

Day	Sid.Time	☉	0 hr ☽	Noon ☽	True ☊	☿	♀	♂	⚳	♃	♄	♅	♆	♇
1 M	6 36 13	9♋08 14	18♈57 28	25♈42 43	20♉06.7	17♊54.4	23♉29.7	28♌15.4	23♉57.1	4♊11.9	26♐18.5	11♈16.9	29♌18.5	17♋40.3
2 Tu	6 40 09	10 05 27	2♉34 16	9♉32 16	20R 07.7	18 44.1	24 28.0	28 51.2	24 18.8	4 24.7	26R 14.3	11 17.6	29 20.1	17 41.8
3 W	6 44 06	11 02 40	16 36 48	23 47 46	20 08.0	19 38.4	25 26.6	29 27.0	24 40.5	4 37.4	26 10.1	11 18.3	29 21.7	17 43.4
4 Th	6 48 02	11 59 54	1♊04 53	8♊27 44	20 06.7	20 37.0	26 25.6	0♍02.9	25 02.1	4 50.0	26 05.9	11 19.0	29 23.3	17 44.9
5 F	6 51 59	12 57 07	15 55 39	23 27 45	20 03.3	21 40.0	27 25.0	0 38.9	25 23.6	5 02.6	26 01.7	11 19.6	29 24.9	17 46.5
6 Sa	6 55 55	13 54 21	1♋03 00	8♋40 14	19 57.7	22 47.2	28 24.8	1 14.9	25 45.0	5 15.1	25 57.6	11 20.1	29 26.6	17 48.1
7 Su	6 59 52	14 51 35	16 18 06	23 55 15	19 50.3	23 58.7	29 24.8	1 50.9	26 06.4	5 27.6	25 53.5	11 20.6	29 28.3	17 49.6
8 M	7 03 49	15 48 49	1♌30 21	9♌02 04	19 42.0	25 14.4	0♊25.2	2 27.1	26 27.7	5 40.0	25 49.5	11 21.1	29 30.0	17 51.2
9 Tu	7 07 45	16 46 03	16 29 16	23 50 57	19 33.9	26 34.1	1 25.9	3 03.2	26 48.9	5 52.3	25 45.5	11 21.5	29 31.7	17 52.8
10 W	7 11 42	17 43 17	1♍06 19	8♍14 48	19 27.0	27 57.9	2 26.9	3 39.4	27 10.0	6 04.5	25 41.5	11 21.8	29 33.4	17 54.3
11 Th	7 15 38	18 40 30	15 16 02	22 09 54	19 22.0	29 25.6	3 28.2	4 15.7	27 31.1	6 16.7	25 37.6	11 22.1	29 35.2	17 55.9
12 F	7 19 35	19 37 44	28 56 25	5♎35 48	19 19.2	0♋57.3	4 29.7	4 52.0	27 52.1	6 28.8	25 33.8	11 22.4	29 37.0	17 57.5
13 Sa	7 23 31	20 34 58	12♎08 24	18 34 40	19D 18.2	2 32.7	5 31.6	5 28.4	28 12.9	6 40.8	25 29.9	11 22.6	29 38.8	17 59.0
14 Su	7 27 28	21 32 11	24 55 07	1♏10 20	19 18.5	4 11.8	6 33.7	6 04.8	28 33.7	6 52.8	25 26.2	11 22.7	29 40.6	18 00.6
15 M	7 31 24	22 29 25	7♏20 55	13 27 31	19R 19.1	5 54.5	7 36.0	6 41.2	28 54.5	7 04.6	25 22.5	11 22.8	29 42.4	18 02.2
16 Tu	7 35 21	23 26 39	19 30 44	25 31 10	19 19.1	7 40.6	8 38.7	7 17.7	29 15.1	7 16.4	25 18.8	11R 22.9	29 44.3	18 03.7
17 W	7 39 18	24 23 53	1♐29 24	7♐25 59	19 17.4	9 29.9	9 41.6	7 54.3	29 35.6	7 28.1	25 15.2	11 22.9	29 46.2	18 05.3
18 Th	7 43 14	25 21 08	13 21 26	19 16 11	19 13.5	11 22.2	10 44.7	8 30.9	29 56.0	7 39.8	25 11.7	11 22.9	29 48.1	18 06.9
19 F	7 47 11	26 18 22	25 10 40	1♑05 16	19 07.0	13 17.3	11 48.1	9 07.5	0♊16.4	7 51.3	25 08.2	11 22.8	29 50.0	18 08.4
20 Sa	7 51 07	27 15 37	7♑00 18	12 56 04	18 58.0	15 14.9	12 51.7	9 44.2	0 36.7	8 02.8	25 04.8	11 22.7	29 51.9	18 10.0
21 Su	7 55 04	28 12 53	18 52 47	24 50 42	18 46.9	17 14.7	13 55.5	10 21.0	0 56.8	8 14.2	25 01.5	11 22.5	29 53.8	18 11.5
22 M	7 59 00	29 10 09	0♒49 59	6♒50 48	18 34.6	19 16.5	14 59.6	10 57.7	1 16.9	8 25.5	24 58.2	11 22.3	29 55.8	18 13.1
23 Tu	8 02 57	0♌07 26	12 53 17	18 57 36	18 22.1	21 19.9	16 03.9	11 34.6	1 36.8	8 36.7	24 55.0	11 22.0	29 57.8	18 14.6
24 W	8 06 53	1 04 43	25 03 52	1♓12 15	18 10.4	23 24.6	17 08.4	12 11.5	1 56.7	8 47.8	24 51.8	11 21.7	29 59.7	18 16.2
25 Th	8 10 50	2 02 01	7♓22 56	13 36 05	18 00.6	25 30.2	18 13.1	12 48.4	2 16.5	8 58.8	24 48.8	11 21.3	0♍01.7	18 17.7
26 F	8 14 47	2 59 20	19 51 55	26 10 42	17 53.3	27 36.5	19 18.0	13 25.4	2 36.1	9 09.8	24 45.7	11 20.9	0 03.8	18 19.2
27 Sa	8 18 43	3 56 39	2♈32 42	8♈58 14	17 48.7	29 43.2	20 23.2	14 02.4	2 55.7	9 20.6	24 42.8	11 20.4	0 05.8	18 20.7
28 Su	8 22 40	4 54 00	15 27 36	22 01 10	17 46.5	1♌49.8	21 28.5	14 39.5	3 15.1	9 31.4	24 39.9	11 19.9	0 07.8	18 22.3
29 M	8 26 36	5 51 22	28 39 16	5♉22 14	17 45.9	3 56.3	22 34.0	15 16.6	3 34.5	9 42.0	24 37.2	11 19.3	0 09.9	18 23.8
30 Tu	8 30 33	6 48 45	12♉10 22	19 03 54	17 46.0	6 02.2	23 39.7	15 53.8	3 53.7	9 52.6	24 34.4	11 18.7	0 11.9	18 25.3
31 W	8 34 29	7 46 09	26 03 01	3♊07 46	17 45.4	8 07.6	24 45.6	16 31.0	4 12.8	10 03.0	24 31.8	11 18.1	0 14.0	18 26.8

August 1929

LONGITUDE

Day	Sid.Time	☉	0 hr ☽	Noon ☽	True ☊	☿	♀	♂	⚳	♃	♄	♅	♆	♇
1 Th	8 38 26	8♌43 34	10♊18 06	17♊33 45	17♉43.0	10♌12.0	25♊51.7	17♍08.3	4♊31.8	10♊13.4	24♐29.3	11♈17.4	0♍16.1	18♋28.3
2 F	8 42 22	9 41 01	24 54 20	2♋19 15	17R 38.2	12 15.5	26 57.9	17 45.6	4 50.6	10 23.6	24R 26.8	11R 16.6	0 18.2	18 29.8
3 Sa	8 46 19	10 38 29	9♋47 42	17 18 46	17 30.6	14 17.9	28 04.3	18 23.0	5 09.4	10 33.8	24 24.4	11 15.8	0 20.3	18 31.2
4 Su	8 50 16	11 35 57	24 51 18	2♌24 06	17 20.9	16 19.0	29 10.9	19 00.5	5 28.0	10 43.8	24 22.1	11 15.0	0 22.5	18 32.7
5 M	8 54 12	12 33 27	9♌55 53	17 25 23	17 09.9	18 18.8	0♋17.7	19 37.9	5 46.5	10 53.7	24 19.9	11 14.1	0 24.6	18 34.2
6 Tu	8 58 09	13 30 58	24 51 24	2♍12 49	16 58.9	20 17.2	1 24.6	20 15.5	6 04.8	11 03.5	24 17.7	11 13.2	0 26.7	18 35.6
7 W	9 02 05	14 28 29	9♍28 43	16 38 21	16 49.2	22 14.1	2 31.6	20 53.1	6 23.1	11 13.2	24 15.7	11 12.2	0 28.9	18 37.1
8 Th	9 06 02	15 26 01	23 41 10	0♎36 52	16 41.7	24 09.6	3 38.8	21 30.7	6 41.2	11 22.8	24 13.7	11 11.2	0 31.0	18 38.5
9 F	9 09 58	16 23 34	7♎25 20	14 06 36	16 36.8	26 03.6	4 46.2	22 08.4	6 59.1	11 32.3	24 11.8	11 10.1	0 33.2	18 39.9
10 Sa	9 13 55	17 21 09	20 40 56	27 08 40	16 34.3	27 56.2	5 53.7	22 46.1	7 16.9	11 41.6	24 10.0	11 09.0	0 35.4	18 41.3
11 Su	9 17 51	18 18 43	3♏30 17	9♏46 20	16 33.5	29 47.2	7 01.3	23 23.9	7 34.6	11 50.9	24 08.3	11 07.9	0 37.5	18 42.7
12 M	9 21 48	19 16 19	15 57 26	22 04 14	16 33.5	1♍36.7	8 09.1	24 01.7	7 52.1	12 00.0	24 06.7	11 06.7	0 39.7	18 44.1
13 Tu	9 25 45	20 13 56	28 07 24	4♐07 36	16 33.0	3 24.7	9 17.0	24 39.6	8 09.5	12 08.9	24 05.2	11 05.4	0 41.9	18 45.5
14 W	9 29 41	21 11 34	10♐05 30	16 01 45	16 31.1	5 11.2	10 25.1	25 17.5	8 26.7	12 17.8	24 03.7	11 04.2	0 44.1	18 46.8
15 Th	9 33 38	22 09 13	21 56 56	27 51 38	16 27.0	6 56.2	11 33.3	25 55.5	8 43.8	12 26.5	24 02.4	11 02.8	0 46.3	18 48.2
16 F	9 37 34	23 06 53	3♑46 24	9♑41 41	16 20.1	8 39.8	12 41.6	26 33.5	9 00.7	12 35.2	24 01.2	11 01.5	0 48.5	18 49.5
17 Sa	9 41 31	24 04 34	15 37 56	21 35 31	16 10.7	10 21.9	13 50.1	27 11.5	9 17.4	12 43.6	24 00.0	11 00.1	0 50.7	18 50.9
18 Su	9 45 27	25 02 16	27 34 45	3♒35 54	15 59.0	12 02.6	14 58.7	27 49.7	9 34.0	12 52.0	23 59.0	10 58.7	0 53.0	18 52.2
19 M	9 49 24	25 59 59	9♒39 12	15 44 47	15 46.0	13 41.9	16 07.4	28 27.8	9 50.5	13 00.2	23 58.0	10 57.2	0 55.2	18 53.5
20 Tu	9 53 20	26 57 44	21 52 48	28 03 18	15 32.8	15 19.7	17 16.2	29 06.0	10 06.8	13 08.3	23 57.1	10 55.7	0 57.4	18 54.8
21 W	9 57 17	27 55 30	4♓16 23	10♓32 03	15 20.4	16 56.1	18 25.2	29 44.3	10 22.9	13 16.2	23 56.3	10 54.1	0 59.6	18 56.1
22 Th	10 01 14	28 53 18	16 50 21	23 11 18	15 10.0	18 31.1	19 34.3	0♎22.6	10 38.8	13 24.0	23 55.7	10 52.6	1 01.8	18 57.3
23 F	10 05 10	29 51 07	29 34 55	6♈01 17	15 02.2	20 04.7	20 43.6	1 00.9	10 54.5	13 31.7	23 55.1	10 50.9	1 04.1	18 58.6
24 Sa	10 09 07	0♍48 57	12♈30 26	19 02 30	14 57.2	21 37.0	21 52.9	1 39.3	11 10.1	13 39.2	23 54.6	10 49.3	1 06.3	18 59.8
25 Su	10 13 03	1 46 50	25 37 34	2♉15 49	14D 54.8	23 07.8	23 02.4	2 17.8	11 25.5	13 46.6	23 54.2	10 47.6	1 08.5	19 01.0
26 M	10 17 00	2 44 44	8♉57 24	15 42 30	14 54.2	24 37.2	24 12.0	2 56.3	11 40.7	13 53.8	23 53.9	10 45.9	1 10.7	19 02.2
27 Tu	10 20 56	3 42 40	22 31 16	29 23 53	14R 54.5	26 05.2	25 21.7	3 34.8	11 55.8	14 00.9	23 53.7	10 44.1	1 12.9	19 03.4
28 W	10 24 53	4 40 38	6♊20 28	13♊21 03	14 54.3	27 31.9	26 31.6	4 13.4	12 10.6	14 07.9	23D 53.6	10 42.3	1 15.2	19 04.6
29 Th	10 28 49	5 38 38	20 25 39	27 34 06	14 52.5	28 57.0	27 41.5	4 52.1	12 25.2	14 14.7	23 53.6	10 40.5	1 17.4	19 05.7
30 F	10 32 46	6 36 40	4♋46 12	12♋01 34	14 48.5	0♎20.8	28 51.6	5 30.8	12 39.7	14 21.3	23 53.7	10 38.6	1 19.6	19 06.9
31 Sa	10 36 43	7 34 44	19 19 41	26 39 53	14 42.0	1 43.0	0♌01.8	6 09.6	12 53.9	14 27.8	23 53.9	10 36.8	1 21.8	19 08.0

Astro Data

	Dy Hr Mn
☽0S	12 16:05
♅R	17 6:26
☽0N	27 9:21
♃⚹♅	7 9:39
☽0S	8 23:55
☽0N	23 14:06
♂0S	24 1:59
♄D	29 0:57
☿0S	29 8:43

Planet Ingress

	Dy Hr Mn
♂ ♍	4 10:03
♀ ♊	8 2:00
☿ ♋	11 21:07
⚳ ♊	18 16:39
☉ ♌	23 8:53
♆ ♍	24 15:04
☿ ♌	27 15:12
♀ ♋	5 5:39
☿ ♍	11 14:48
♂ ♎	21 21:52
☉ ♍	23 15:41
☿ ♎	30 6:01
♀ ♌	31 11:24

Last Aspect / ☽ Ingress

Last Aspect Dy Hr Mn		☽ Ingress Dy Hr Mn
1 18:20 ♆ △	♉	1 19:31
3 21:43 ♂ □	♊	3 22:14
5 21:26 ♆ ⚹	♋	5 22:21
7 21:18 ♀ ⚹	♌	7 21:37
9 21:24 ♆ ☌	♍	9 22:10
11 18:05 ♄ □	♎	12 1:54
14 9:07 ♆ ⚹	♏	14 9:44
16 20:30 ♆ □	♐	16 21:00
19 9:27 ♆ △	♑	19 9:48
21 19:21 ☉ ☍	♒	21 22:20
24 9:38 ♆ ☍	♓	24 9:39
26 15:15 ☿ △	♈	26 19:13
28 16:47 ♄ △	♉	29 2:25
30 10:53 ♇ ⚹	♊	31 6:43

Last Aspect Dy Hr Mn		☽ Ingress Dy Hr Mn
2 2:39 ♀ ☌	♋	2 8:15
3 13:56 ♇ ☌	♌	4 8:11
5 23:07 ♄ △	♍	6 8:22
8 0:57 ♄ □	♎	8 10:56
10 13:44 ☿ ⚹	♏	10 17:22
12 16:05 ♂ ⚹	♐	13 3:44
15 7:51 ♂ □	♑	15 16:21
17 23:51 ♂ △	♒	18 4:50
20 9:42 ☉ ☍	♓	20 15:46
22 13:23 ♄ □	♈	23 0:47
24 20:53 ♄ △	♉	25 7:55
27 5:33 ☿ △	♊	27 13:03
29 14:34 ☿ □	♋	29 16:04
30 23:40 ♇ ☌	♌	31 17:27

☽ Phases & Eclipses

Dy Hr Mn	
6 20:47	● 14♋15
13 16:05	☽ 20♎45
21 19:21	○ 28♑30
29 12:56	☾ 5♉54
5 3:40	● 12♌13
12 6:01	☽ 19♏02
20 9:42	○ 26♒52
27 20:02	☾ 4♊02

Astro Data

1 July 1929
Julian Day # 10774
SVP 6♓14'52"
GC 25♐51.3 ⚵ 10♈08.9
Eris 2♈04.5R ⚶ 12♏30.4R
⚷ 13♉21.1 ⚴ 24♊52.0
☽ Mean ☊ 18♉39.3

1 August 1929
Julian Day # 10805
SVP 6♓14'46"
GC 25♐51.4 ⚵ 12♈46.9
Eris 1♈58.1R ⚶ 13♏53.7
⚷ 14♉17.2 ⚴ 7♋59.7
☽ Mean ☊ 17♉00.8

LONGITUDE — September 1929

Day	Sid.Time	☉	0 hr ☽	Noon ☽	True ☊	☿	♀	♂	⚳	♃	♄	♅	♆	♇
1 Su	10 40 39	8♍32 49	4♌01 25	11♌23 23	14♉33.4	3♎03.7	1♌12.1	6♎48.4	13♊07.9	14♊34.1	23♐54.2	10♈34.8	1♍24.1	19♋09.1
2 M	10 44 36	9 30 57	18 44 50	26 04 46	14R 23.5	4 22.9	2 22.4	7 27.3	13 21.7	14 40.3	23 54.5	10R 32.9	1 26.3	19 10.2
3 Tu	10 48 32	10 29 06	3♍22 11	10♍36 10	14 13.6	5 40.5	3 32.9	8 06.2	13 35.3	14 46.3	23 55.0	10 30.9	1 28.5	19 11.3
4 W	10 52 29	11 27 16	17 45 51	24 50 31	14 04.8	6 56.4	4 43.5	8 45.1	13 48.7	14 52.1	23 55.6	10 28.9	1 30.7	19 12.3
5 Th	10 56 25	12 25 29	1♎49 35	8♎42 37	13 57.9	8 10.6	5 54.2	9 24.2	14 01.9	14 57.8	23 56.3	10 26.9	1 32.9	19 13.4
6 F	11 00 22	13 23 43	15 29 24	22 09 50	13 53.4	9 22.9	7 05.0	10 03.2	14 14.8	15 03.3	23 57.1	10 24.8	1 35.1	19 14.4
7 Sa	11 04 18	14 21 58	28 43 57	5♏11 59	13D 51.3	10 33.5	8 15.9	10 42.4	14 27.5	15 08.6	23 57.9	10 22.7	1 37.2	19 15.4
8 Su	11 08 15	15 20 15	11♏34 15	17 51 10	13 51.0	11 42.0	9 26.9	11 21.5	14 39.9	15 13.8	23 58.9	10 20.6	1 39.4	19 16.4
9 M	11 12 12	16 18 34	24 03 14	0♐11 00	13 51.7	12 48.5	10 37.9	12 00.8	14 52.2	15 18.8	24 00.0	10 18.5	1 41.6	19 17.3
10 Tu	11 16 08	17 16 54	6♐15 06	12 16 09	13R 52.5	13 52.8	11 49.1	12 40.0	15 04.1	15 23.6	24 01.1	10 16.3	1 43.8	19 18.3
11 W	11 20 05	18 15 16	18 14 49	24 11 45	13 52.4	14 54.8	13 00.4	13 19.4	15 15.9	15 28.3	24 02.4	10 14.1	1 45.9	19 19.2
12 Th	11 24 01	19 13 39	0♑07 36	6♑03 00	13 50.7	15 54.4	14 11.7	13 58.7	15 27.4	15 32.8	24 03.8	10 11.9	1 48.1	19 20.1
13 F	11 27 58	20 12 04	11 58 33	17 54 50	13 46.9	16 51.3	15 23.2	14 38.2	15 38.6	15 37.1	24 05.2	10 09.7	1 50.2	19 21.0
14 Sa	11 31 54	21 10 31	23 52 24	29 51 42	13 41.0	17 45.4	16 34.7	15 17.6	15 49.6	15 41.2	24 06.8	10 07.5	1 52.3	19 21.8
15 Su	11 35 51	22 08 59	5♒53 12	11♒57 15	13 33.3	18 36.4	17 46.3	15 57.2	16 00.3	15 45.2	24 08.4	10 05.2	1 54.5	19 22.7
16 M	11 39 47	23 07 29	18 04 12	24 14 16	13 24.5	19 24.3	18 58.0	16 36.7	16 10.7	15 48.9	24 10.2	10 03.0	1 56.6	19 23.5
17 Tu	11 43 44	24 06 01	0♓27 39	6♓44 29	13 15.3	20 08.7	20 09.8	17 16.3	16 20.9	15 52.5	24 12.0	10 00.7	1 58.7	19 24.3
18 W	11 47 41	25 04 35	13 04 50	19 28 41	13 06.8	20 49.3	21 21.7	17 56.0	16 30.8	15 55.9	24 14.0	9 58.4	2 00.7	19 25.1
19 Th	11 51 37	26 03 10	25 56 00	2♈26 43	12 59.6	21 25.9	22 33.7	18 35.7	16 40.4	15 59.1	24 16.0	9 56.0	2 02.8	19 25.8
20 F	11 55 34	27 01 47	9♈00 43	15 37 50	12 54.5	21 58.1	23 45.7	19 15.5	16 49.8	16 02.2	24 18.1	9 53.7	2 04.9	19 26.5
21 Sa	11 59 30	28 00 27	22 17 57	29 00 54	12 51.6	22 25.7	24 57.8	19 55.3	16 58.9	16 05.0	24 20.3	9 51.4	2 06.9	19 27.3
22 Su	12 03 27	28 59 08	5♉46 33	12♉34 46	12D 50.7	22 48.1	26 10.1	20 35.2	17 07.6	16 07.6	24 22.6	9 49.0	2 09.0	19 27.9
23 M	12 07 23	29 57 52	19 25 25	26 18 25	12 51.3	23 05.2	27 22.4	21 15.2	17 16.1	16 10.1	24 25.0	9 46.6	2 11.0	19 28.6
24 Tu	12 11 20	0♎56 38	3♊13 40	10♊11 05	12 52.6	23 16.4	28 34.8	21 55.1	17 24.3	16 12.4	24 27.5	9 44.2	2 13.0	19 29.3
25 W	12 15 16	1 55 26	17 10 34	24 12 03	12R 53.7	23R 21.4	29 47.2	22 35.2	17 32.1	16 14.5	24 30.1	9 41.9	2 15.0	19 29.9
26 Th	12 19 13	2 54 17	1♋15 23	8♋20 25	12 53.8	23 19.9	0♍59.8	23 15.3	17 39.7	16 16.3	24 32.8	9 39.5	2 17.0	19 30.5
27 F	12 23 10	3 53 10	15 26 56	22 34 41	12 52.3	23 11.3	2 12.4	23 55.4	17 46.9	16 18.0	24 35.5	9 37.1	2 18.9	19 31.1
28 Sa	12 27 06	4 52 06	29 43 21	6♌52 30	12 49.2	22 55.5	3 25.1	24 35.6	17 53.9	16 19.5	24 38.4	9 34.7	2 20.9	19 31.6
29 Su	12 31 03	5 51 03	14♌01 43	21 10 29	12 44.6	22 32.2	4 37.9	25 15.9	18 00.5	16 20.8	24 41.3	9 32.2	2 22.8	19 32.2
30 M	12 34 59	6 50 03	28 18 12	5♍24 19	12 39.1	22 01.2	5 50.8	25 56.2	18 06.7	16 21.9	24 44.3	9 29.8	2 24.7	19 32.7

LONGITUDE — October 1929

Day	Sid.Time	☉	0 hr ☽	Noon ☽	True ☊	☿	♀	♂	⚳	♃	♄	♅	♆	♇
1 Tu	12 38 56	7♎49 05	12♍28 14	19♍29 20	12♉33.5	21♎22.7	7♍03.7	26♎36.6	18♊12.6	16♊22.8	24♐47.4	9♈27.4	2♍26.6	19♋33.2
2 W	12 42 52	8 48 09	26 27 06	3♎21 00	12R 28.5	20R 36.8	8 16.7	27 17.0	18 18.2	16 23.5	24 50.6	9R 25.0	2 28.5	19 33.6
3 Th	12 46 49	9 47 15	10♎10 38	16 55 40	12 24.8	19 44.0	9 29.8	27 57.5	18 23.5	16 24.0	24 53.9	9 22.6	2 30.4	19 34.1
4 F	12 50 45	10 46 23	23 35 49	0♏10 59	12D 22.5	18 45.0	10 42.9	28 38.0	18 28.4	16R 24.3	24 57.3	9 20.1	2 32.2	19 34.5
5 Sa	12 54 42	11 45 33	6♏41 07	13 06 17	12 21.9	17 40.9	11 56.1	29 18.6	18 32.9	16 24.3	25 00.8	9 17.7	2 34.1	19 34.9
6 Su	12 58 38	12 44 45	19 26 38	25 42 26	12 22.6	16 32.9	13 09.3	29 59.2	18 37.1	16 24.2	25 04.3	9 15.3	2 35.9	19 35.2
7 M	13 02 35	13 43 59	1♐54 00	8♐01 45	12 24.1	15 22.7	14 22.7	0♏39.9	18 40.9	16 23.9	25 07.9	9 12.9	2 37.7	19 35.6
8 Tu	13 06 32	14 43 14	14 06 07	20 07 38	12 25.9	14 12.0	15 36.0	1 20.7	18 44.4	16 23.4	25 11.6	9 10.5	2 39.4	19 35.9
9 W	13 10 28	15 42 32	26 06 50	2♑04 19	12 27.4	13 02.7	16 49.5	2 01.5	18 47.5	16 22.7	25 15.4	9 08.1	2 41.2	19 36.2
10 Th	13 14 25	16 41 51	8♑00 39	13 56 28	12R 28.1	11 56.9	18 03.0	2 42.3	18 50.2	16 21.7	25 19.3	9 05.7	2 42.9	19 36.5
11 F	13 18 21	17 41 12	19 52 23	25 49 00	12 27.8	10 56.4	19 16.5	3 23.2	18 52.6	16 20.6	25 23.2	9 03.3	2 44.6	19 36.7
12 Sa	13 22 18	18 40 35	1♒46 56	7♒46 43	12 26.4	10 03.0	20 30.1	4 04.2	18 54.6	16 19.3	25 27.3	9 00.9	2 46.3	19 36.9
13 Su	13 26 14	19 40 00	13 48 56	19 54 04	12 24.1	9 18.2	21 43.8	4 45.2	18 56.2	16 17.7	25 31.4	8 58.5	2 47.9	19 37.1
14 M	13 30 11	20 39 26	26 02 36	2♓14 55	12 21.0	8 43.1	22 57.5	5 26.2	18 57.4	16 16.0	25 35.6	8 56.2	2 49.6	19 37.3
15 Tu	13 34 07	21 38 54	8♓31 21	14 52 12	12 17.7	8 18.5	24 11.3	6 07.3	18 58.3	16 14.1	25 39.8	8 53.8	2 51.2	19 37.5
16 W	13 38 04	22 38 25	21 17 38	27 47 46	12 14.6	8D 04.9	25 25.1	6 48.5	18R 58.7	16 12.0	25 44.2	8 51.5	2 52.8	19 37.6
17 Th	13 42 01	23 37 56	4♈22 37	11♈02 07	12 12.1	8 02.5	26 39.0	7 29.7	18 58.8	16 09.6	25 48.6	8 49.1	2 54.3	19 37.7
18 F	13 45 57	24 37 30	17 46 08	24 34 27	12 10.4	8 11.0	27 52.9	8 11.0	18 58.5	16 07.1	25 53.1	8 46.8	2 55.9	19 37.7
19 Sa	13 49 54	25 37 06	1♉26 45	8♉22 40	12D 09.7	8 30.2	29 06.9	8 52.3	18 57.8	16 04.4	25 57.6	8 44.5	2 57.4	19 37.8
20 Su	13 53 50	26 36 44	15 21 49	22 23 45	12 09.9	8 59.3	0♎21.0	9 33.7	18 56.7	16 01.5	26 02.2	8 42.3	2 58.9	19R 37.8
21 M	13 57 47	27 36 25	29 27 58	6♊34 02	12 10.7	9 37.8	1 35.1	10 15.1	18 55.2	15 58.4	26 06.9	8 40.0	3 00.3	19 37.8
22 Tu	14 01 43	28 36 07	13♊41 26	20 49 44	12 11.8	10 24.8	2 49.2	10 56.6	18 53.3	15 55.1	26 11.7	8 37.8	3 01.8	19 37.8
23 W	14 05 40	29 35 52	27 58 28	5♋07 15	12 12.8	11 19.5	4 03.4	11 38.1	18 51.0	15 51.6	26 16.6	8 35.6	3 03.2	19 37.8
24 Th	14 09 36	0♏35 39	12♋15 41	19 23 25	12R 13.5	12 21.0	5 17.7	12 19.7	18 48.3	15 47.9	26 21.5	8 33.4	3 04.6	19 37.7
25 F	14 13 33	1 35 28	26 30 08	3♌35 34	12 13.7	13 28.5	6 32.0	13 01.4	18 45.2	15 44.0	26 26.4	8 31.2	3 05.9	19 37.6
26 Sa	14 17 30	2 35 20	10♌39 26	17 41 30	12 13.4	14 41.4	7 46.3	13 43.1	18 41.7	15 40.0	26 31.5	8 29.0	3 07.3	19 37.5
27 Su	14 21 26	3 35 13	24 41 33	1♍39 21	12 12.7	15 58.7	9 00.7	14 24.9	18 37.7	15 35.7	26 36.6	8 26.9	3 08.6	19 37.3
28 M	14 25 23	4 35 09	8♍34 42	15 27 26	12 11.8	17 19.9	10 15.1	15 06.7	18 33.4	15 31.3	26 41.8	8 24.8	3 09.9	19 37.1
29 Tu	14 29 19	5 35 07	22 17 20	29 04 15	12 10.8	18 44.4	11 29.6	15 48.5	18 28.7	15 26.7	26 47.0	8 22.7	3 11.1	19 36.9
30 W	14 33 16	6 35 07	5♎48 00	12♎28 26	12 10.1	20 11.6	12 44.1	16 30.5	18 23.6	15 21.9	26 52.3	8 20.6	3 12.3	19 36.7
31 Th	14 37 12	7 35 09	19 05 25	25 38 52	12 09.7	21 41.1	13 58.6	17 12.5	18 18.1	15 17.0	26 57.7	8 18.6	3 13.5	19 36.5

Astro Data

	Dy Hr Mn
☽0S	5 9:06
☽0N	19 20:18
☉0S	23 12:52
☿ R	25 18:24
☽0S	2 18:22
♃ R	5 9:56
⚳ R	17 4:25
☽0N	17 4:46
☿ D	17 5:14
♇ R	21 2:07
♀0S	23 3:18
☽0S	30 2:13

Planet Ingress

	Dy Hr Mn
☉ ♎	23 12:52
♀ ♍	25 16:13
♂ ♏	6 12:27
♀ ♎	20 5:12
☉ ♏	23 21:41

Last Aspect / ☽ Ingress (September)

Last Aspect Dy Hr Mn		☽ Ingress Dy Hr Mn
2 8:26	♄ △	♍ 2 18:27
4 10:26	♄ □	♎ 4 20:51
6 15:15	♄ ⚹	♏ 7 2:20
8 14:44	♇ △	♐ 9 11:38
11 11:41	♄ ☌	♑ 11 23:45
13 17:01	☉ △	♒ 14 12:17
16 11:52	♄ ⚹	♓ 16 23:07
18 23:16	☉ ☍	♈ 19 7:30
21 4:04	♀ △	♉ 21 13:45
23 14:02	♀ □	♊ 23 18:25
25 12:31	♄ ☍	♋ 25 21:52
27 14:22	♂ □	♌ 28 0:28
29 19:13	♂ ⚹	♍ 30 2:52

Last Aspect / ☽ Ingress (October)

Last Aspect Dy Hr Mn		☽ Ingress Dy Hr Mn
1 21:10	♄ □	♎ 2 6:09
4 9:01	♂ ☌	♏ 4 11:40
6 0:16	♇ △	♐ 6 20:18
8 22:12	♄ ☌	♑ 9 7:49
10 23:28	♇ ☍	♒ 11 20:25
13 23:03	♄ ⚹	♓ 14 7:40
16 8:12	♄ □	♈ 16 16:02
18 14:19	♄ △	♉ 18 21:29
20 7:17	♇ ⚹	♊ 21 0:54
23 2:02	☉ △	♋ 23 3:24
24 12:24	♇ ☌	♌ 25 5:55
27 3:15	♄ △	♍ 27 9:08
29 7:55	♄ □	♎ 29 13:39
31 14:26	♄ ⚹	♏ 31 20:02

☽ Phases & Eclipses

Dy Hr Mn	
3 11:47	● 10♍29
10 22:57	☽ 17♐44
18 23:16	○ 25♓32
26 2:07	☾ 2♋30
2 22:19	● 9♎14
10 18:05	☽ 16♑57
18 12:06	○ 24♈38
25 8:21	☾ 1♌26

Astro Data

1 September 1929
Julian Day # 10836
SVP 6♓14'42"
GC 25♐51.4 ⚴ 10♈03.2R
Eris 1♈42.7R ⚵ 19♏18.4
⚷ 14♉21.2R ⚶ 20♋29.4
☽ Mean ☊ 15♉22.3

1 October 1929
Julian Day # 10866
SVP 6♓14'39"
GC 25♐51.5 ⚴ 2♈36.2R
Eris 1♈23.4R ⚵ 27♏05.7
⚷ 13♉34.6R ⚶ 1♌26.9
☽ Mean ☊ 13♉47.0

November 1929 LONGITUDE

Day	Sid.Time	☉	0 hr ☽	Noon☽	True☊	☿	♀	♂	⚳	♃	♄	♅	♆	♇
1 F	14 41 09	8♏35 13	2♏08 41	8♏34 50	12♉09.5	23♎12.4	15♎13.2	17♏54.5	18♊12.1	15♊11.9	27♐03.1	8♈16.6	3♍14.7	19♋36.2
2 Sa	14 45 05	9 35 19	14 57 19	21 16 11	12D 09.5	24 45.3	16 27.8	18 36.6	18R 05.8	15R 06.6	27 08.6	8R 14.6	3 15.8	19R 35.9
3 Su	14 49 02	10 35 27	27 31 30	3♐43 26	12 09.7	26 19.3	17 42.5	19 18.8	17 59.1	15 01.1	27 14.1	8 12.7	3 16.9	19 35.6
4 M	14 52 59	11 35 37	9♐52 09	15 57 55	12R 09.8	27 54.3	18 57.2	20 01.0	17 52.1	14 55.5	27 19.7	8 10.8	3 18.0	19 35.3
5 Tu	14 56 55	12 35 48	22 00 59	28 01 43	12 09.8	29 30.0	20 11.9	20 43.2	17 44.6	14 49.7	27 25.4	8 08.9	3 19.0	19 34.9
6 W	15 00 52	13 36 01	4♑00 30	9♑57 45	12 09.7	1♏06.3	21 26.7	21 25.5	17 36.8	14 43.8	27 31.1	8 07.1	3 20.0	19 34.5
7 Th	15 04 48	14 36 15	15 53 56	21 49 33	12 09.4	2 43.0	22 41.4	22 07.9	17 28.6	14 37.7	27 36.9	8 05.2	3 21.0	19 34.1
8 F	15 08 45	15 36 31	27 45 09	3♒41 16	12 09.2	4 19.9	23 56.3	22 50.3	17 20.0	14 31.5	27 42.7	8 03.5	3 22.0	19 33.7
9 Sa	15 12 41	16 36 48	9♒38 29	15 37 23	12D 09.1	5 56.9	25 11.1	23 32.8	17 11.1	14 25.1	27 48.6	8 01.7	3 22.9	19 33.2
10 Su	15 16 38	17 37 07	21 38 33	27 42 34	12 09.2	7 34.1	26 26.0	24 15.3	17 01.8	14 18.6	27 54.5	8 00.0	3 23.8	19 32.7
11 M	15 20 34	18 37 27	3♓50 01	10♓01 26	12 09.6	9 11.2	27 40.8	24 57.9	16 52.2	14 12.0	28 00.5	7 58.3	3 24.6	19 32.2
12 Tu	15 24 31	19 37 49	16 17 20	22 38 11	12 10.3	10 48.2	28 55.8	25 40.5	16 42.3	14 05.2	28 06.5	7 56.7	3 25.5	19 31.7
13 W	15 28 28	20 38 12	29 04 22	5♈36 12	12 11.1	12 25.2	0♏10.7	26 23.2	16 32.0	13 58.4	28 12.6	7 55.1	3 26.2	19 31.1
14 Th	15 32 24	21 38 36	12♈13 56	18 57 40	12 11.9	14 02.0	1 25.7	27 05.9	16 21.5	13 51.4	28 18.7	7 53.5	3 27.0	19 30.6
15 F	15 36 21	22 39 02	25 47 25	2♉43 02	12R 12.4	15 38.6	2 40.6	27 48.7	16 10.6	13 44.3	28 24.9	7 52.0	3 27.7	19 30.0
16 Sa	15 40 17	23 39 30	9♉44 16	16 50 43	12 12.5	17 15.0	3 55.6	28 31.5	15 59.4	13 37.0	28 31.1	7 50.5	3 28.4	19 29.4
17 Su	15 44 14	24 39 59	24 01 51	1♊16 59	12 12.0	18 51.3	5 10.7	29 14.4	15 48.0	13 29.7	28 37.3	7 49.1	3 29.1	19 28.7
18 M	15 48 10	25 40 29	8♊35 22	15 56 10	12 10.8	20 27.4	6 25.7	29 57.3	15 36.3	13 22.3	28 43.6	7 47.7	3 29.7	19 28.1
19 Tu	15 52 07	26 41 02	23 18 27	0♋41 20	12 09.1	22 03.2	7 40.8	0♐40.3	15 24.3	13 14.8	28 50.0	7 46.3	3 30.3	19 27.4
20 W	15 56 03	27 41 36	8♋03 54	15 25 16	12 07.1	23 38.9	8 55.9	1 23.4	15 12.1	13 07.2	28 56.3	7 45.0	3 30.9	19 26.7
21 Th	16 00 00	28 42 11	22 44 40	0♌01 24	12 05.3	25 14.3	10 11.1	2 06.5	14 59.6	12 59.5	29 02.8	7 43.8	3 31.4	19 26.0
22 F	16 03 57	29 42 49	7♌14 54	14 24 40	12 03.9	26 49.6	11 26.2	2 49.6	14 47.0	12 51.8	29 09.2	7 42.5	3 31.9	19 25.2
23 Sa	16 07 53	0♐43 28	21 30 24	28 31 50	12D 03.3	28 24.7	12 41.4	3 32.9	14 34.1	12 44.0	29 15.7	7 41.3	3 32.3	19 24.5
24 Su	16 11 50	1 44 09	5♍28 53	12♍21 29	12 03.6	29 59.6	13 56.6	4 16.1	14 21.0	12 36.1	29 22.2	7 40.2	3 32.8	19 23.7
25 M	16 15 46	2 44 51	19 09 41	25 53 37	12 04.6	1♐34.4	15 11.8	4 59.4	14 07.7	12 28.1	29 28.8	7 39.1	3 33.2	19 22.9
26 Tu	16 19 43	3 45 35	2♎33 24	9♎09 13	12 06.2	3 09.0	16 27.0	5 42.8	13 54.3	12 20.1	29 35.4	7 38.0	3 33.5	19 22.1
27 W	16 23 39	4 46 20	15 41 16	22 09 45	12 07.7	4 43.5	17 42.3	6 26.2	13 40.7	12 12.1	29 42.0	7 37.0	3 33.8	19 21.2
28 Th	16 27 36	5 47 07	28 34 51	4♏56 46	12R 08.7	6 17.9	18 57.6	7 09.7	13 27.0	12 04.0	29 48.7	7 36.1	3 34.1	19 20.4
29 F	16 31 32	6 47 56	11♏15 41	17 31 45	12 08.8	7 52.2	20 12.8	7 53.3	13 13.1	11 55.8	29 55.4	7 35.2	3 34.4	19 19.5
30 Sa	16 35 29	7 48 46	23 45 09	29 56 00	12 07.6	9 26.4	21 28.1	8 36.9	12 59.2	11 47.7	0♑02.1	7 34.3	3 34.6	19 18.6

December 1929 LONGITUDE

Day	Sid.Time	☉	0 hr ☽	Noon☽	True☊	☿	♀	♂	⚳	♃	♄	♅	♆	♇
1 Su	16 39 26	8♐49 37	6♐04 28	12♐10 40	12♉04.9	11♐00.5	22♏43.4	9♐20.5	12♊45.2	11♊39.5	0♑08.9	7♈33.5	3♍34.8	19♋17.7
2 M	16 43 22	9 50 29	18 14 47	24 16 57	12R 00.9	12 34.6	23 58.8	10 04.2	12R 31.1	11R 31.3	0 15.7	7R 32.7	3 34.9	19R 16.8
3 Tu	16 47 19	10 51 22	0♑17 22	6♑16 14	11 55.8	14 08.6	25 14.1	10 47.9	12 17.0	11 23.2	0 22.5	7 32.0	3 35.0	19 15.8
4 W	16 51 15	11 52 16	12 13 46	18 10 14	11 50.1	15 42.6	26 29.4	11 31.7	12 02.8	11 15.0	0 29.3	7 31.3	3 35.1	19 14.9
5 Th	16 55 12	12 53 12	24 05 58	0♒01 16	11 44.6	17 16.6	27 44.8	12 15.6	11 48.6	11 06.8	0 36.2	7 30.7	3R 35.2	19 13.9
6 F	16 59 08	13 54 07	5♒56 33	11 52 12	11 39.7	18 50.7	29 00.2	12 59.5	11 34.5	10 58.6	0 43.1	7 30.1	3 35.2	19 12.9
7 Sa	17 03 05	14 55 04	17 48 42	23 46 33	11 36.0	20 24.7	0♐15.5	13 43.4	11 20.4	10 50.4	0 50.0	7 29.6	3 35.1	19 11.9
8 Su	17 07 02	15 56 02	29 46 16	5♓48 25	11D 33.8	21 58.7	1 30.9	14 27.4	11 06.3	10 42.3	0 56.9	7 29.1	3 35.1	19 10.9
9 M	17 10 58	16 56 59	11♓53 34	18 02 19	11 33.3	23 32.8	2 46.3	15 11.4	10 52.2	10 34.2	1 03.9	7 28.7	3 35.0	19 09.8
10 Tu	17 14 55	17 57 58	24 15 17	0♈33 01	11 34.0	25 06.9	4 01.7	15 55.5	10 38.3	10 26.2	1 10.8	7 28.3	3 34.9	19 08.8
11 W	17 18 51	18 58 57	6♈56 07	13 25 04	11 35.5	26 41.0	5 17.0	16 39.7	10 24.4	10 18.1	1 17.8	7 28.0	3 34.7	19 07.7
12 Th	17 22 48	19 59 57	20 00 20	26 42 19	11 37.0	28 15.2	6 32.4	17 23.8	10 10.7	10 10.2	1 24.8	7 27.8	3 34.5	19 06.6
13 F	17 26 44	21 00 57	3♉31 14	10♉27 15	11R 37.8	29 49.4	7 47.8	18 08.1	9 57.1	10 02.3	1 31.8	7 27.5	3 34.3	19 05.5
14 Sa	17 30 41	22 01 58	17 30 18	24 40 12	11 37.1	1♑23.7	9 03.2	18 52.3	9 43.6	9 54.4	1 38.8	7 27.4	3 34.0	19 04.4
15 Su	17 34 37	23 03 00	1♊56 31	9♊18 39	11 34.4	2 57.9	10 18.7	19 36.7	9 30.3	9 46.6	1 45.9	7 27.3	3 33.7	19 03.3
16 M	17 38 34	24 04 02	16 45 45	24 16 51	11 29.8	4 32.2	11 34.1	20 21.0	9 17.1	9 38.9	1 52.9	7D 27.2	3 33.4	19 02.2
17 Tu	17 42 31	25 05 05	1♋50 47	9♋26 17	11 23.5	6 06.5	12 49.5	21 05.5	9 04.2	9 31.3	2 00.0	7 27.2	3 33.0	19 01.0
18 W	17 46 27	26 06 08	17 02 01	24 36 41	11 16.5	7 40.7	14 04.9	21 49.9	8 51.4	9 23.8	2 07.0	7 27.2	3 32.6	18 59.9
19 Th	17 50 24	27 07 13	2♌09 01	9♌37 53	11 09.5	9 14.8	15 20.4	22 34.5	8 38.9	9 16.3	2 14.1	7 27.3	3 32.2	18 58.7
20 F	17 54 20	28 08 18	17 02 17	24 21 27	11 03.7	10 48.8	16 35.8	23 19.0	8 26.6	9 09.0	2 21.2	7 27.5	3 31.8	18 57.5
21 Sa	17 58 17	29 09 23	1♍34 46	8♍41 52	10 59.7	12 22.6	17 51.3	24 03.7	8 14.5	9 01.7	2 28.3	7 27.7	3 31.3	18 56.4
22 Su	18 02 13	0♑10 30	15 42 32	22 36 45	10D 57.7	13 56.2	19 06.7	24 48.3	8 02.7	8 54.6	2 35.4	7 27.9	3 30.7	18 55.2
23 M	18 06 10	1 11 37	29 24 39	6♎06 29	10 57.5	15 29.3	20 22.2	25 33.0	7 51.2	8 47.5	2 42.4	7 28.2	3 30.2	18 54.0
24 Tu	18 10 06	2 12 44	12♎42 34	19 13 18	10 58.5	17 02.1	21 37.6	26 17.8	7 40.0	8 40.6	2 49.5	7 28.5	3 29.6	18 52.7
25 W	18 14 03	3 13 53	25 39 09	2♏00 34	10R 59.6	18 34.2	22 53.1	27 02.6	7 29.0	8 33.8	2 56.6	7 28.9	3 28.9	18 51.5
26 Th	18 18 00	4 15 02	8♏18 00	14 31 56	10 59.9	20 05.6	24 08.6	27 47.5	7 18.4	8 27.2	3 03.7	7 29.4	3 28.3	18 50.3
27 F	18 21 56	5 16 11	20 42 46	26 50 55	10 58.4	21 36.1	25 24.1	28 32.4	7 08.0	8 20.6	3 10.8	7 29.9	3 27.6	18 49.1
28 Sa	18 25 53	6 17 21	2♐56 44	9♐00 33	10 54.4	23 05.5	26 39.6	29 17.3	6 58.0	8 14.2	3 17.9	7 30.5	3 26.9	18 47.8
29 Su	18 29 49	7 18 32	15 02 40	21 03 19	10 47.8	24 33.5	27 55.0	0♑02.3	6 48.4	8 07.9	3 25.0	7 31.1	3 26.1	18 46.6
30 M	18 33 46	8 19 42	27 02 44	3♑01 07	10 38.6	25 59.8	29 10.5	0 47.4	6 39.1	8 01.8	3 32.1	7 31.7	3 25.4	18 45.3
31 Tu	18 37 42	9 20 53	8♑58 38	14 55 27	10 27.4	27 24.1	0♑26.0	1 32.5	6 30.1	7 55.9	3 39.2	7 32.5	3 24.6	18 44.1

Astro Data Dy Hr Mn	Planet Ingress Dy Hr Mn	Last Aspect Dy Hr Mn	☽ Ingress Dy Hr Mn	Last Aspect Dy Hr Mn	☽ Ingress Dy Hr Mn	☽ Phases & Eclipses Dy Hr Mn	Astro Data
☽0N 13 14:37	☿ ♏ 5 19:29	2 8:49 ♇ △	♐ 3 4:47	1 10:59 ♃ ☍	♑ 2 23:25	1 12:01 ● 8♏35	1 November 1929
☽0S 26 8:05	♀ ♏ 13 8:35	5 15:24 ☿ ⚹	♑ 5 15:57	5 6:51 ♀ ⚹	♒ 5 11:57	1 12:04:46 ● A 03'54"	Julian Day # 10897
	♂ ♐ 18 13:29	7 13:57 ♀ □	♒ 8 4:33	7 4:13 ☿ ⚹	♓ 8 0:27	9 14:10 ☽ 16♒42	SVP 6♓14'35"
♆R 6 7:27	☉ ♐ 22 18:48	10 12:24 ♄ ⚹	♓ 10 16:30	10 0:10 ☿ □	♈ 10 10:57	17 0:14 ○ 24♉10	GC 25♐51.6 ⚳ 25♓20.5R
☽0N 10 23:51	☿ ♐ 24 12:06	12 22:18 ♄ □	♈ 13 1:43	12 15:06 ☿ △	♉ 12 17:50	17 0:03 ● A 0.846	Eris 1♈04.6R ⚵ 6♐47.7
♅D 17 4:19	♄ ♑ 30 4:22	15 4:31 ♄ △	♉ 15 7:19	14 2:39 ♇ ⚹	♊ 14 20:49	23 16:04 ☾ 0♍54	⚷ 12♉10.6R ⚶ 10♌38.0
☽0S 23 13:04		17 8:27 ♂ ☍	♊ 17 9:53	16 11:38 ☉ ☍	♋ 16 21:05		☽ Mean ☊ 12♉08.5
♄△♆ 29 15:26	♀ ♐ 7 7:03	19 8:58 ♄ ☍	♋ 19 10:53	18 3:07 ♇ ☌	♌ 18 20:34	1 4:48 ● 8♐31	
	☿ ♑ 13 14:42	21 9:39 ☉ △	♌ 21 11:58	20 18:44 ☉ △	♍ 20 21:22	9 9:42 ☽ 16♓51	1 December 1929
	☉ ♑ 22 7:53	23 13:16 ♄ △	♍ 23 14:32	22 16:04 ♂ □	♎ 23 1:03	16 11:38 ○ 24♊03	Julian Day # 10927
	♂ ♑ 29 10:45	25 18:30 ♄ □	♎ 25 19:23	25 2:02 ♂ ⚹	♏ 25 8:12	23 2:27 ☾ 0♎47	SVP 6♓14'30"
	♀ ♑ 31 3:44	28 2:14 ♄ ⚹	♏ 28 2:40	27 0:18 ☿ ⚹	♐ 27 18:12	30 23:42 ● 8♑50	GC 25♐51.6 ⚳ 23♓55.4
		29 17:45 ♀ ☌	♐ 30 12:08	30 3:22 ♀ ☌	♑ 30 5:56		Eris 0♈53.3R ⚵ 17♐06.8
							⚷ 10♉44.8R ⚶ 15♌49.4
							☽ Mean ☊ 10♉33.2

LONGITUDE — January 1930

Day	Sid.Time	☉	0 hr ☽	Noon ☽	True ☊	☿	♀	♂	⚳	♃	♄	♅	♆	♇
1 W	18 41 39	10♑22 04	20♑51 44	26♑47 39	10♉15.1	28♑46.0	1♑41.5	2♑17.6	6♊21.5	7♊50.1	3♑46.3	7♈33.2	3♍23.7	18♋42.8
2 Th	18 45 36	11 23 15	2♒43 22	8♒39 07	10R 02.6	0♒05.1	2 57.0	3 02.8	6R 13.3	7R 44.4	3 53.3	7 34.0	3R 22.9	18R 41.5
3 F	18 49 32	12 24 25	14 35 05	20 31 34	9 51.1	1 20.8	4 12.5	3 48.0	6 05.5	7 38.9	4 00.4	7 34.9	3 22.0	18 40.3
4 Sa	18 53 29	13 25 35	26 28 51	2♓27 17	9 41.6	2 32.6	5 27.9	4 33.3	5 58.1	7 33.6	4 07.4	7 35.8	3 21.0	18 39.0
5 Su	18 57 25	14 26 46	8♓27 15	14 29 11	9 34.6	3 39.7	6 43.4	5 18.6	5 51.0	7 28.4	4 14.5	7 36.8	3 20.1	18 37.7
6 M	19 01 22	15 27 55	20 33 35	26 40 55	9 30.3	4 41.5	7 58.9	6 03.9	5 44.4	7 23.5	4 21.5	7 37.8	3 19.1	18 36.4
7 Tu	19 05 18	16 29 04	2♈51 47	9♈06 43	9D 28.4	5 37.2	9 14.3	6 49.3	5 38.1	7 18.6	4 28.5	7 38.9	3 18.1	18 35.2
8 W	19 09 15	17 30 13	15 26 20	21 51 11	9 28.2	6 25.9	10 29.8	7 34.7	5 32.3	7 14.0	4 35.5	7 40.0	3 17.0	18 33.9
9 Th	19 13 11	18 31 22	28 21 52	4♉58 53	9R 28.6	7 06.7	11 45.2	8 20.1	5 26.9	7 09.6	4 42.4	7 41.1	3 16.0	18 32.6
10 F	19 17 08	19 32 29	11♉42 42	18 33 40	9 28.4	7 38.8	13 00.7	9 05.6	5 21.8	7 05.3	4 49.4	7 42.4	3 14.9	18 31.3
11 Sa	19 21 04	20 33 37	25 32 01	2♊37 48	9 26.4	8 01.2	14 16.1	9 51.2	5 17.2	7 01.2	4 56.3	7 43.6	3 13.8	18 30.0
12 Su	19 25 01	21 34 44	9♊50 54	17 10 58	9 21.8	8R 13.1	15 31.6	10 36.7	5 13.1	6 57.3	5 03.2	7 44.9	3 12.6	18 28.8
13 M	19 28 58	22 35 50	24 37 24	2♋09 22	9 14.5	8 13.9	16 47.0	11 22.4	5 09.3	6 53.7	5 10.1	7 46.3	3 11.5	18 27.5
14 Tu	19 32 54	23 36 56	9♋45 48	17 25 26	9 04.8	8 03.2	18 02.4	12 08.0	5 06.0	6 50.1	5 17.0	7 47.7	3 10.3	18 26.2
15 W	19 36 51	24 38 01	25 06 51	2♌48 30	8 53.7	7 40.6	19 17.9	12 53.7	5 03.0	6 46.8	5 23.9	7 49.2	3 09.1	18 24.9
16 Th	19 40 47	25 39 06	10♌28 53	18 06 30	8 42.6	7 06.4	20 33.3	13 39.4	5 00.5	6 43.7	5 30.7	7 50.7	3 07.9	18 23.7
17 F	19 44 44	26 40 10	25 40 01	3♍08 17	8 32.7	6 21.2	21 48.7	14 25.2	4 58.4	6 40.8	5 37.5	7 52.2	3 06.6	18 22.4
18 Sa	19 48 40	27 41 14	10♍30 20	17 45 30	8 25.2	5 26.0	23 04.1	15 11.0	4 56.7	6 38.1	5 44.2	7 53.8	3 05.3	18 21.1
19 Su	19 52 37	28 42 17	24 53 19	1♎53 37	8 20.3	4 22.3	24 19.5	15 56.8	4 55.5	6 35.5	5 51.0	7 55.5	3 04.0	18 19.9
20 M	19 56 34	29 43 20	8♎46 22	15 31 45	8 18.0	3 12.0	25 35.0	16 42.7	4 54.6	6 33.2	5 57.7	7 57.1	3 02.7	18 18.6
21 Tu	20 00 30	0♒44 23	22 10 08	28 41 56	8 17.4	1 57.1	26 50.4	17 28.6	4D 54.2	6 31.1	6 04.4	7 58.9	3 01.3	18 17.4
22 W	20 04 27	1 45 25	5♏07 41	11♏27 57	8 17.4	0 40.1	28 05.8	18 14.6	4 54.2	6 29.1	6 11.0	8 00.7	3 00.0	18 16.1
23 Th	20 08 23	2 46 27	17 43 21	23 54 30	8 16.7	29♑23.4	29 21.2	19 00.5	4 54.6	6 27.4	6 17.7	8 02.5	2 58.6	18 14.9
24 F	20 12 20	3 47 29	0♐01 59	6♐06 23	8 14.2	28 09.1	0♒36.6	19 46.6	4 55.4	6 25.9	6 24.2	8 04.3	2 57.2	18 13.7
25 Sa	20 16 16	4 48 30	12 08 15	18 08 05	8 09.0	26 59.1	1 52.0	20 32.6	4 56.6	6 24.6	6 30.8	8 06.3	2 55.8	18 12.4
26 Su	20 20 13	5 49 30	24 06 21	0♑03 28	8 00.6	25 55.2	3 07.3	21 18.7	4 58.3	6 23.5	6 37.3	8 08.2	2 54.3	18 11.2
27 M	20 24 09	6 50 30	5♑59 46	11 55 35	7 49.3	24 58.5	4 22.7	22 04.9	5 00.3	6 22.6	6 43.8	8 10.2	2 52.9	18 10.0
28 Tu	20 28 06	7 51 29	17 51 12	23 46 49	7 35.6	24 10.0	5 38.1	22 51.0	5 02.8	6 21.9	6 50.2	8 12.2	2 51.4	18 08.8
29 W	20 32 03	8 52 27	29 42 39	5♒38 53	7 20.5	23 30.0	6 53.5	23 37.2	5 05.6	6 21.4	6 56.6	8 14.3	2 49.9	18 07.6
30 Th	20 35 59	9 53 23	11♒35 38	17 33 05	7 05.2	22 58.8	8 08.8	24 23.4	5 08.8	6D 21.1	7 03.0	8 16.4	2 48.4	18 06.4
31 F	20 39 56	10 54 19	23 31 20	29 30 35	6 50.9	22 36.4	9 24.2	25 09.7	5 12.5	6 21.0	7 09.3	8 18.6	2 46.9	18 05.3

LONGITUDE — February 1930

Day	Sid.Time	☉	0 hr ☽	Noon ☽	True ☊	☿	♀	♂	⚳	♃	♄	♅	♆	♇
1 Sa	20 43 52	11♒55 14	5♓30 58	11♓32 41	6♉38.8	22♑22.5	10♒39.5	25♑55.9	5♊16.5	6♊21.1	7♑15.6	8♈20.8	2♍45.4	18♋04.1
2 Su	20 47 49	12 56 07	17 35 58	23 41 05	6R 29.5	22D 16.8	11 54.8	26 42.3	5 20.9	6 21.5	7 21.8	8 23.0	2R 43.8	18R 02.9
3 M	20 51 45	13 56 59	29 48 21	5♈58 06	6 23.4	22 18.7	13 10.2	27 28.6	5 25.7	6 22.0	7 28.0	8 25.3	2 42.2	18 01.8
4 Tu	20 55 42	14 57 50	12♈10 44	18 26 41	6 20.2	22 27.9	14 25.5	28 14.9	5 30.9	6 22.7	7 34.1	8 27.6	2 40.7	18 00.7
5 W	20 59 38	15 58 40	24 46 25	1♉10 24	6D 19.1	22 43.8	15 40.8	29 01.3	5 36.4	6 23.7	7 40.2	8 30.0	2 39.1	17 59.5
6 Th	21 03 35	16 59 27	7♉39 09	14 13 09	6R 19.1	23 05.8	16 56.0	29 47.7	5 42.4	6 24.8	7 46.3	8 32.4	2 37.5	17 58.4
7 F	21 07 32	18 00 14	20 52 51	27 38 40	6 18.9	23 33.6	18 11.3	0♒34.2	5 48.6	6 26.2	7 52.3	8 34.8	2 35.9	17 57.4
8 Sa	21 11 28	19 00 59	4♊30 55	11♊29 50	6 17.2	24 06.6	19 26.6	1 20.6	5 55.3	6 27.8	7 58.2	8 37.3	2 34.3	17 56.3
9 Su	21 15 25	20 01 42	18 35 29	25 47 45	6 13.1	24 44.4	20 41.8	2 07.1	6 02.3	6 29.5	8 04.1	8 39.8	2 32.7	17 55.2
10 M	21 19 21	21 02 24	3♋06 21	10♋30 46	6 06.3	25 26.7	21 57.0	2 53.6	6 09.7	6 31.5	8 10.0	8 42.3	2 31.0	17 54.2
11 Tu	21 23 18	22 03 04	18 00 13	25 33 46	5 57.2	26 12.9	23 12.3	3 40.1	6 17.4	6 33.6	8 15.7	8 44.9	2 29.4	17 53.1
12 W	21 27 14	23 03 43	3♌10 14	10♌48 18	5 46.6	27 02.9	24 27.5	4 26.7	6 25.4	6 36.0	8 21.5	8 47.5	2 27.7	17 52.1
13 Th	21 31 11	24 04 20	18 26 33	26 03 33	5 35.7	27 56.2	25 42.6	5 13.3	6 33.8	6 38.5	8 27.1	8 50.1	2 26.1	17 51.1
14 F	21 35 07	25 04 56	3♍37 53	11♍08 16	5 25.8	28 52.7	26 57.8	5 59.9	6 42.5	6 41.2	8 32.8	8 52.8	2 24.4	17 50.1
15 Sa	21 39 04	26 05 30	18 33 33	25 52 49	5 18.1	29 52.0	28 13.0	6 46.5	6 51.5	6 44.2	8 38.3	8 55.5	2 22.8	17 49.1
16 Su	21 43 01	27 06 03	3♎05 20	10♎10 39	5 13.1	0♒54.0	29 28.1	7 33.1	7 00.9	6 47.3	8 43.8	8 58.2	2 21.1	17 48.2
17 M	21 46 57	28 06 34	17 08 31	23 58 53	5D 10.6	1 58.5	0♓43.2	8 19.8	7 10.5	6 50.6	8 49.3	9 01.0	2 19.4	17 47.2
18 Tu	21 50 54	29 07 05	0♏41 54	7♏17 51	5 10.1	3 05.2	1 58.4	9 06.5	7 20.5	6 54.1	8 54.6	9 03.7	2 17.8	17 46.3
19 W	21 54 50	0♓07 34	13 47 09	20 10 20	5R 10.6	4 14.1	3 13.5	9 53.2	7 30.8	6 57.7	9 00.0	9 06.6	2 16.1	17 45.4
20 Th	21 58 47	1 08 02	26 27 57	2♐40 39	5 10.9	5 25.0	4 28.6	10 39.9	7 41.4	7 01.6	9 05.2	9 09.4	2 14.4	17 44.5
21 F	22 02 43	2 08 28	8♐49 02	14 53 45	5 10.0	6 37.7	5 43.7	11 26.6	7 52.3	7 05.6	9 10.4	9 12.3	2 12.7	17 43.6
22 Sa	22 06 40	3 08 54	20 55 28	26 54 46	5 07.0	7 52.2	6 58.7	12 13.4	8 03.5	7 09.9	9 15.6	9 15.2	2 11.0	17 42.8
23 Su	22 10 36	4 09 18	2♑52 15	8♑48 27	5 01.5	9 08.4	8 13.8	13 00.2	8 15.0	7 14.3	9 20.6	9 18.1	2 09.4	17 42.0
24 M	22 14 33	5 09 40	14 43 53	20 38 59	4 53.5	10 26.2	9 28.9	13 47.0	8 26.8	7 18.9	9 25.6	9 21.1	2 07.7	17 41.1
25 Tu	22 18 30	6 10 01	26 34 11	2♒29 50	4 43.5	11 45.4	10 43.9	14 33.8	8 38.8	7 23.7	9 30.5	9 24.1	2 06.0	17 40.4
26 W	22 22 26	7 10 20	8♒26 15	14 23 42	4 32.2	13 06.1	11 58.9	15 20.6	8 51.2	7 28.6	9 35.4	9 27.1	2 04.3	17 39.6
27 Th	22 26 23	8 10 38	20 22 25	26 22 35	4 20.6	14 28.2	13 13.9	16 07.5	9 03.8	7 33.7	9 40.2	9 30.1	2 02.7	17 38.8
28 F	22 30 19	9 10 54	2♓24 22	8♓27 53	4 09.9	15 51.6	14 28.9	16 54.3	9 16.7	7 39.0	9 44.9	9 33.2	2 01.0	17 38.1

Astro Data (Dy Hr Mn)
- ♃⚹♅ 4 3:25
- ☽0N 7 6:49
- ☿R 13 1:43
- ☽0S 19 19:29
- ⚳D 22 0:47
- ♃⚻♄ 24 16:59
- ♃D 31 9:17

- ☿D 2 17:43
- ☽0N 3 11:52
- ☽0S 16 4:29
- ♄□♅ 22 8:04

Planet Ingress (Dy Hr Mn)
- ☿ ♒ 2 10:25
- ☉ ♒ 20 18:33
- ☿ ♑R 23 0:30
- ♀ ♒ 24 0:22

- ♂ ♒ 6 18:21
- ☿ ♒ 15 15:08
- ♀ ♓ 16 22:11
- ☉ ♓ 19 9:00

Last Aspect / ☽ Ingress (Dy Hr Mn)

Last Aspect Dy Hr Mn			☽ Ingress	Dy Hr Mn
1 16:30	☿	☌	♒	1 18:29
2 10:10	♃	△	♓	4 7:04
5 20:11	♇	△	♈	6 18:27
8 5:53	♇	□	♉	9 2:59
10 13:50	☉	△	♊	11 7:35
11 21:08	☿	△	♋	13 8:35
14 22:21	☉	☍	♌	15 7:37
15 19:51	♅	△	♍	17 6:56
19 6:05	☉	△	♎	19 8:44
21 8:12	♀	□	♏	21 14:25
23 23:53	♀	⚹	♐	23 23:56
24 15:55	♅	△	♑	26 11:53
28 12:44	☿	☌	♒	29 0:35
29 19:07	☉	☌	♓	31 12:59

Last Aspect Dy Hr Mn			☽ Ingress	Dy Hr Mn
2 18:20	♂	⚹	♈	3 0:23
5 7:43	♂	□	♉	5 9:49
7 4:30	☿	△	♊	7 16:08
9 2:43	♀	△	♋	9 18:55
11 13:05	☿	☍	♌	11 19:00
13 11:24	♀	☍	♍	13 18:14
14 22:49	♇	⚹	♎	15 18:50
17 19:57	☉	△	♏	17 22:45
19 7:27	♇	△	♐	20 6:49
21 4:42	♂	⚹	♑	22 18:13
24 6:00	♇	☍	♒	25 6:57
26 14:02	♂	☌	♓	27 19:13

☽ Phases & Eclipses (Dy Hr Mn)
- 8 3:11 ☽ 17♈08
- 14 22:21 ○ 24♋03
- 21 16:07 ☾ 0♏55
- 29 19:07 ● 9♒11

- 6 17:26 ☽ 17♉13
- 13 8:39 ○ 23♌56
- 20 8:44 ☾ 1♐00
- 28 13:33 ● 9♓15

Astro Data

1 January 1930
Julian Day # 10958
SVP 6♓14'24"
GC 25♐51.7 ⚴ 28♓33.6
Eris 0♈52.3 ⚵ 28♐11.1
⚷ 9♉46.4R ⚶ 15♌04.6R
☽ Mean ☊ 8♉54.7

1 February 1930
Julian Day # 10989
SVP 6♓14'18"
GC 25♐51.8 ⚴ 7♈36.1
Eris 1♈02.7 ⚵ 9♑08.6
⚷ 9♉41.7 ⚶ 8♌07.9R
☽ Mean ☊ 7♉16.2

March 1930 — LONGITUDE

Day	Sid.Time	☉	0 hr ☽	Noon ☽	True ☊	☿	♀	♂	⚳	♃	♄	♅	♆	♇
1 Sa	22 34 16	10♓11 08	14♓33 17	20♓40 39	4♉00.8	17♒16.4	15♓43.9	17♒41.2	9♊29.9	7♊44.5	9♑49.5	9♈36.2	1♍59.3	17♋37.4
2 Su	22 38 12	11 11 20	26 50 08	3♈01 50	3R54.0	18 42.3	16 58.8	18 28.1	9 43.3	7 50.1	9 54.1	9 39.3	1R57.7	17R36.7
3 M	22 42 09	12 11 30	9♈15 53	15 32 28	3 49.8	20 09.6	18 13.7	19 14.9	9 57.0	7 55.9	9 58.6	9 42.4	1 56.0	17 36.0
4 Tu	22 46 05	13 11 38	21 51 46	28 14 00	3D48.0	21 38.0	19 28.6	20 01.8	10 10.9	8 01.9	10 03.0	9 45.6	1 54.4	17 35.3
5 W	22 50 02	14 11 45	4♉39 25	11♉08 15	3 48.0	23 07.6	20 43.5	20 48.7	10 25.1	8 08.0	10 07.4	9 48.7	1 52.7	17 34.7
6 Th	22 53 59	15 11 49	17 40 49	24 17 24	3 49.1	24 38.4	21 58.4	21 35.6	10 39.5	8 14.3	10 11.6	9 51.9	1 51.1	17 34.1
7 F	22 57 55	16 11 51	0♊58 17	7♊43 43	3R50.2	26 10.4	23 13.2	22 22.6	10 54.2	8 20.7	10 15.8	9 55.1	1 49.5	17 33.5
8 Sa	23 01 52	17 11 51	14 33 57	21 29 06	3 50.4	27 43.5	24 28.1	23 09.5	11 09.1	8 27.4	10 19.9	9 58.3	1 47.9	17 32.9
9 Su	23 05 48	18 11 49	28 29 17	5♋34 27	3 49.0	29 17.8	25 42.9	23 56.4	11 24.3	8 34.1	10 24.0	10 01.6	1 46.3	17 32.4
10 M	23 09 45	19 11 45	12♋44 26	19 58 56	3 45.7	0♓53.2	26 57.6	24 43.3	11 39.6	8 41.0	10 27.9	10 04.8	1 44.7	17 31.9
11 Tu	23 13 41	20 11 38	27 17 29	4♌39 29	3 40.6	2 29.8	28 12.4	25 30.3	11 55.2	8 48.1	10 31.8	10 08.1	1 43.1	17 31.4
12 W	23 17 38	21 11 30	12♌04 08	19 30 32	3 34.4	4 07.6	29 27.1	26 17.2	12 11.1	8 55.3	10 35.6	10 11.4	1 41.6	17 30.9
13 Th	23 21 34	22 11 19	26 57 41	4♍24 29	3 27.8	5 46.5	0♈41.8	27 04.1	12 27.1	9 02.7	10 39.3	10 14.6	1 40.0	17 30.4
14 F	23 25 31	23 11 05	11♍49 52	19 12 45	3 21.8	7 26.6	1 56.5	27 51.1	12 43.3	9 10.2	10 42.9	10 17.9	1 38.5	17 30.0
15 Sa	23 29 28	24 10 50	26 32 07	3♎47 04	3 17.2	9 07.9	3 11.2	28 38.0	12 59.8	9 17.8	10 46.5	10 21.3	1 36.9	17 29.6
16 Su	23 33 24	25 10 33	10♎56 52	18 00 55	3 14.4	10 50.4	4 25.8	29 25.0	13 16.4	9 25.6	10 49.9	10 24.6	1 35.4	17 29.2
17 M	23 37 21	26 10 14	24 58 47	1♏50 12	3D13.4	12 34.1	5 40.4	0♓11.9	13 33.3	9 33.6	10 53.3	10 27.9	1 33.9	17 28.8
18 Tu	23 41 17	27 09 54	8♏35 06	15 13 32	3 13.9	14 19.0	6 55.0	0 58.9	13 50.3	9 41.6	10 56.6	10 31.3	1 32.4	17 28.5
19 W	23 45 14	28 09 32	21 45 42	28 11 54	3 15.3	16 05.2	8 09.6	1 45.8	14 07.6	9 49.8	10 59.8	10 34.6	1 31.0	17 28.2
20 Th	23 49 10	29 09 07	4♐32 32	10♐48 04	3 17.0	17 52.6	9 24.1	2 32.8	14 25.0	9 58.2	11 02.9	10 38.0	1 29.5	17 27.9
21 F	23 53 07	0♈08 42	16 59 04	23 06 05	3R18.2	19 41.3	10 38.7	3 19.7	14 42.7	10 06.6	11 05.9	10 41.4	1 28.1	17 27.6
22 Sa	23 57 03	1 08 14	29 09 42	5♑10 33	3 18.4	21 31.3	11 53.2	4 06.7	15 00.5	10 15.2	11 08.9	10 44.8	1 26.7	17 27.4
23 Su	0 01 00	2 07 45	11♑09 14	17 06 22	3 17.2	23 22.5	13 07.7	4 53.6	15 18.5	10 24.0	11 11.7	10 48.2	1 25.3	17 27.2
24 M	0 04 57	3 07 14	23 02 30	28 58 14	3 14.6	25 15.0	14 22.1	5 40.6	15 36.7	10 32.8	11 14.5	10 51.6	1 23.9	17 27.0
25 Tu	0 08 53	4 06 41	4♒54 04	10♒50 30	3 10.8	27 08.8	15 36.6	6 27.5	15 55.0	10 41.8	11 17.1	10 55.0	1 22.5	17 26.8
26 W	0 12 50	5 06 06	16 48 00	22 46 58	3 06.2	29 03.9	16 51.0	7 14.5	16 13.5	10 50.9	11 19.7	10 58.4	1 21.2	17 26.7
27 Th	0 16 46	6 05 29	28 47 46	4♓50 43	3 01.4	1♈00.2	18 05.4	8 01.4	16 32.3	11 00.1	11 22.2	11 01.8	1 19.8	17 26.5
28 F	0 20 43	7 04 51	10♓56 06	17 04 07	2 56.8	2 57.8	19 19.8	8 48.3	16 51.1	11 09.5	11 24.6	11 05.3	1 18.5	17 26.4
29 Sa	0 24 39	8 04 10	23 14 59	29 28 48	2 53.1	4 56.5	20 34.1	9 35.2	17 10.2	11 18.9	11 26.9	11 08.7	1 17.2	17 26.4
30 Su	0 28 36	9 03 28	5♈45 42	12♈05 43	2 50.5	6 56.4	21 48.4	10 22.1	17 29.4	11 28.5	11 29.1	11 12.1	1 16.0	17 26.3
31 M	0 32 32	10 02 43	18 28 56	24 55 20	2D49.1	8 57.4	23 02.7	11 09.0	17 48.7	11 38.2	11 31.2	11 15.5	1 14.7	17D26.3

April 1930 — LONGITUDE

Day	Sid.Time	☉	0 hr ☽	Noon ☽	True ☊	☿	♀	♂	⚳	♃	♄	♅	♆	♇
1 Tu	0 36 29	11♈01 56	1♉24 57	7♉57 45	2♉49.0	10♈59.3	24♈17.0	11♓55.9	18♊08.2	11♊48.0	11♑33.2	11♈19.0	1♍13.5	17♋26.3
2 W	0 40 25	12 01 07	14 33 44	21 12 54	2 49.8	13 02.1	25 31.2	12 42.8	18 27.9	11 57.9	11 35.1	11 22.4	1R12.3	17 26.3
3 Th	0 44 22	13 00 16	27 55 12	4♊40 39	2 51.1	15 05.6	26 45.5	13 29.6	18 47.7	12 07.9	11 36.9	11 25.8	1 11.2	17 26.4
4 F	0 48 19	13 59 23	11♊29 12	18 20 51	2 52.5	17 09.8	27 59.6	14 16.5	19 07.7	12 18.1	11 38.6	11 29.3	1 10.0	17 26.5
5 Sa	0 52 15	14 58 28	25 15 31	2♋13 09	2R53.5	19 14.3	29 13.8	15 03.3	19 27.8	12 28.3	11 40.3	11 32.7	1 08.9	17 26.6
6 Su	0 56 12	15 57 30	9♋13 38	16 16 50	2 53.9	21 19.0	0♉27.9	15 50.1	19 48.1	12 38.6	11 41.8	11 36.1	1 07.8	17 26.7
7 M	1 00 08	16 56 30	23 22 33	0♌30 31	2 53.5	23 23.6	1 42.0	16 36.9	20 08.5	12 49.1	11 43.2	11 39.5	1 06.7	17 26.8
8 Tu	1 04 05	17 55 27	7♌40 25	14 51 51	2 52.4	25 27.9	2 56.1	17 23.7	20 29.0	12 59.6	11 44.5	11 42.9	1 05.7	17 27.0
9 W	1 08 01	18 54 22	22 04 22	29 17 26	2 50.8	27 31.5	4 10.1	18 10.5	20 49.7	13 10.2	11 45.8	11 46.4	1 04.7	17 27.2
10 Th	1 11 58	19 53 15	6♍30 28	13♍42 52	2 49.1	29 34.2	5 24.1	18 57.2	21 10.5	13 20.9	11 46.9	11 49.8	1 03.7	17 27.4
11 F	1 15 54	20 52 06	20 53 58	28 03 08	2 47.6	1♉35.5	6 38.1	19 43.9	21 31.4	13 31.7	11 48.0	11 53.2	1 02.7	17 27.7
12 Sa	1 19 51	21 50 54	5♎09 44	12♎13 10	2 46.6	3 35.2	7 52.1	20 30.6	21 52.5	13 42.6	11 48.9	11 56.6	1 01.8	17 27.9
13 Su	1 23 48	22 49 40	19 12 54	26 08 26	2D46.0	5 32.9	9 06.0	21 17.3	22 13.7	13 53.6	11 49.8	11 59.9	1 00.9	17 28.2
14 M	1 27 44	23 48 25	2♏59 26	9♏45 34	2 46.0	7 28.2	10 19.8	22 04.0	22 35.0	14 04.7	11 50.5	12 03.3	1 00.0	17 28.6
15 Tu	1 31 41	24 47 08	16 26 39	23 02 37	2 46.4	9 20.9	11 33.7	22 50.6	22 56.4	14 15.9	11 51.1	12 06.7	0 59.1	17 28.9
16 W	1 35 37	25 45 48	29 33 28	5♐59 17	2 47.1	11 10.6	12 47.5	23 37.2	23 17.9	14 27.1	11 51.7	12 10.0	0 58.3	17 29.3
17 Th	1 39 34	26 44 28	12♐20 18	18 36 45	2 47.8	12 56.9	14 01.3	24 23.8	23 39.6	14 38.5	11 52.2	12 13.4	0 57.5	17 29.7
18 F	1 43 30	27 43 05	24 49 01	0♑57 29	2 48.3	14 39.7	15 15.1	25 10.4	24 01.3	14 49.9	11 52.5	12 16.7	0 56.7	17 30.1
19 Sa	1 47 27	28 41 41	7♑02 37	13 04 55	2 48.7	16 18.7	16 28.8	25 57.0	24 23.2	15 01.4	11 52.8	12 20.1	0 56.0	17 30.5
20 Su	1 51 23	29 40 15	19 04 56	25 03 11	2R48.9	17 53.6	17 42.6	26 43.5	24 45.2	15 13.0	11 52.9	12 23.4	0 55.3	17 31.0
21 M	1 55 20	0♉38 47	1♒00 17	6♒56 47	2 48.9	19 24.3	18 56.2	27 30.1	25 07.3	15 24.6	11R53.0	12 26.7	0 54.6	17 31.5
22 Tu	1 59 17	1 37 18	12 53 17	18 50 21	2 48.8	20 50.7	20 09.9	28 16.6	25 29.6	15 36.3	11 53.0	12 30.0	0 53.9	17 32.0
23 W	2 03 13	2 35 47	24 48 33	0♓48 24	2D48.7	22 12.5	21 23.5	29 03.0	25 51.9	15 48.1	11 52.8	12 33.3	0 53.3	17 32.5
24 Th	2 07 10	3 34 14	6♓50 26	12 55 05	2 48.8	23 29.6	22 37.1	29 49.5	26 14.3	16 00.0	11 52.6	12 36.5	0 52.7	17 33.0
25 F	2 11 06	4 32 40	19 02 49	25 14 00	2 48.9	24 41.9	23 50.7	0♈35.9	26 36.8	16 12.0	11 52.2	12 39.8	0 52.2	17 33.6
26 Sa	2 15 03	5 31 04	1♈28 58	7♈47 58	2 49.1	25 49.4	25 04.2	1 22.3	26 59.5	16 24.0	11 51.8	12 43.0	0 51.6	17 34.2
27 Su	2 18 59	6 29 26	14 11 12	20 38 48	2R49.3	26 51.9	26 17.8	2 08.6	27 22.2	16 36.1	11 51.3	12 46.2	0 51.1	17 34.8
28 M	2 22 56	7 27 47	27 10 49	3♉47 15	2 49.4	27 49.4	27 31.2	2 54.9	27 45.0	16 48.2	11 50.6	12 49.4	0 50.7	17 35.5
29 Tu	2 26 52	8 26 06	10♉27 59	17 12 51	2 49.3	28 41.7	28 44.7	3 41.2	28 07.9	17 00.4	11 49.9	12 52.6	0 50.2	17 36.2
30 W	2 30 49	9 24 23	24 01 39	0♊54 05	2 48.8	29 28.9	29 58.1	4 27.5	28 31.0	17 12.7	11 49.1	12 55.8	0 49.8	17 36.8

Astro Data	Dy Hr Mn
☽ 0N	2 16:57
♀0N	15 7:05
☽ 0S	15 14:58
☉0N	21 8:30
♃✶♅	27 18:58
☿0N	28 18:58
☽ 0N	29 23:36
♃⚻♄	30 13:47
♇ D	31 23:40
♄□♅	9 5:46
☽ 0S	12 0:42
♄ R	21 14:31
☽ 0N	26 7:49
♂0N	28 4:12

Planet Ingress		Dy Hr Mn
☿	♓	9 22:39
♀	♈	12 22:34
♂	♓	17 5:55
☉	♈	21 8:30
☿	♈	26 23:36
♀	♉	6 2:57
☿	♉	10 17:05
☉	♉	20 20:06
♂	♈	24 17:27
♀	♊	30 12:37

Last Aspect Dy Hr Mn			☽ Ingress	Dy Hr Mn
1 6:02	♇	△	♈	2 6:08
3 21:56	☿	✶	♉	4 15:19
6 12:43	☿	□	♊	6 22:16
9 0:02	☿	△	♋	9 2:34
11 0:31	♀	△	♌	11 4:25
12 23:31	♂	☍	♍	13 4:54
14 18:58	☉	☍	♎	15 5:43
16 11:06	♇	□	♏	17 8:46
19 11:55	☉	△	♐	19 15:23
21 4:07	☿	□	♑	22 1:40
24 3:03	☿	✶	♒	24 14:05
25 22:43	♀	✶	♓	27 2:24
28 12:43	♇	△	♈	29 13:00
31 8:09	♀	☌	♉	31 21:24

Last Aspect Dy Hr Mn			☽ Ingress	Dy Hr Mn
2 5:12	♇	✶	♊	3 3:42
5 6:21	♀	✶	♋	5 8:11
6 21:59	☿	□	♌	7 11:09
9 8:35	☿	△	♍	9 13:11
10 21:15	♂	☍	♎	11 15:17
13 5:48	☉	☍	♏	13 18:45
15 11:37	♂	△	♐	16 0:49
18 5:06	☉	△	♑	18 10:07
20 15:36	♂	✶	♒	20 21:58
22 16:34	☿	□	♓	23 10:23
25 10:52	☿	✶	♈	25 21:10
27 6:19	♇	□	♉	28 5:08
30 10:13	♀	☌	♊	30 10:26

☽ Phases & Eclipses Dy Hr Mn	
8 4:00	☽ 16♊52
14 18:58	○ 23♍28
22 3:13	☾ 0♑46
30 5:46	● 8♈48
6 11:25	☽ 15♋56
13 5:48	○ 22♎35
13 5:58	☍ P 0.106
20 22:08	☾ 0♒05
28 19:08	● 7♉45
28 19:03:09	● AT00'02"

Astro Data

1 March 1930
Julian Day # 11017
SVP 6♓14'15"
GC 25♐51.8 ⚳ 18♈18.5
Eris 1♈19.7 ✱ 18♑27.2
⚷ 10♉26.5 ⚵ 2♌06.1R
☽ Mean ☊ 5♉47.3

1 April 1930
Julian Day # 11048
SVP 6♓14'12"
GC 25♐51.9 ⚳ 2♉08.4
Eris 1♈42.3 ✱ 27♑24.9
⚷ 11♉59.1 ⚵ 1♌40.4
☽ Mean ☊ 4♉08.7

LONGITUDE — May 1930

Day	Sid.Time	☉	0 hr ☽	Noon ☽	True ☊	☿	♀	♂	⚳	♃	♄	♅	♆	♇
1 Th	2 34 46	10♉22 38	7♊49 49	14♊48 28	2♉48.0	0♊10.8	1♊11.5	5♈13.7	28♊54.1	17♊25.1	11♑48.2	12♈58.9	0♍49.4	17♋37.6
2 F	2 38 42	11 20 52	21 49 39	28 52 56	2R 47.1	0 47.4	2 24.9	5 59.9	29 17.3	17 37.5	11R 47.2	13 02.0	0R 49.1	17 38.3
3 Sa	2 42 39	12 19 03	5♋57 54	13♋04 06	2 46.1	1 18.7	3 38.2	6 46.1	29 40.6	17 49.9	11 46.1	13 05.1	0 48.8	17 39.1
4 Su	2 46 35	13 17 13	20 11 08	27 18 37	2 45.3	1 44.7	4 51.5	7 32.2	0♋04.0	18 02.5	11 44.9	13 08.2	0 48.5	17 39.8
5 M	2 50 32	14 15 20	4♌26 11	11♌33 27	2D 45.0	2 05.3	6 04.8	8 18.3	0 27.4	18 15.0	11 43.6	13 11.3	0 48.3	17 40.6
6 Tu	2 54 28	15 13 26	18 40 08	25 45 54	2 45.1	2 20.5	7 18.0	9 04.3	0 51.0	18 27.7	11 42.2	13 14.3	0 48.1	17 41.5
7 W	2 58 25	16 11 29	2♍50 30	9♍53 39	2 45.8	2 30.5	8 31.2	9 50.3	1 14.6	18 40.4	11 40.7	13 17.3	0 47.9	17 42.3
8 Th	3 02 21	17 09 30	16 55 06	23 54 38	2 46.9	2R 35.2	9 44.3	10 36.3	1 38.3	18 53.1	11 39.1	13 20.3	0 47.7	17 43.1
9 F	3 06 18	18 07 30	0♎51 59	7♎46 57	2 48.0	2 34.9	10 57.4	11 22.2	2 02.1	19 05.9	11 37.5	13 23.3	0 47.6	17 44.0
10 Sa	3 10 15	19 05 28	14 39 18	21 28 48	2R 48.8	2 29.6	12 10.5	12 08.1	2 25.9	19 18.7	11 35.7	13 26.2	0 47.5	17 44.9
11 Su	3 14 11	20 03 24	28 15 16	4♏58 30	2 49.1	2 19.6	13 23.5	12 53.9	2 49.9	19 31.6	11 33.9	13 29.1	0D 47.5	17 45.8
12 M	3 18 08	21 01 18	11♏38 19	18 14 35	2 48.5	2 05.1	14 36.5	13 39.7	3 13.9	19 44.5	11 31.9	13 32.0	0 47.5	17 46.8
13 Tu	3 22 04	21 59 11	24 47 10	1♐16 01	2 47.0	1 46.5	15 49.5	14 25.5	3 37.9	19 57.5	11 29.9	13 34.9	0 47.5	17 47.7
14 W	3 26 01	22 57 03	7♐41 04	14 02 21	2 44.5	1 24.1	17 02.4	15 11.2	4 02.1	20 10.5	11 27.8	13 37.7	0 47.5	17 48.7
15 Th	3 29 57	23 54 53	20 19 57	26 33 58	2 41.4	0 58.4	18 15.3	15 56.9	4 26.3	20 23.5	11 25.6	13 40.6	0 47.6	17 49.7
16 F	3 33 54	24 52 42	2♑44 36	8♑52 06	2 38.0	0 29.8	19 28.2	16 42.5	4 50.6	20 36.6	11 23.4	13 43.3	0 47.7	17 50.7
17 Sa	3 37 50	25 50 30	14 56 44	20 58 52	2 34.7	29♉58.8	20 41.0	17 28.1	5 15.0	20 49.8	11 21.0	13 46.1	0 47.9	17 51.8
18 Su	3 41 47	26 48 17	26 58 54	2♒57 16	2 31.9	29 26.0	21 53.8	18 13.7	5 39.4	21 02.9	11 18.6	13 48.8	0 48.1	17 52.8
19 M	3 45 44	27 46 02	8♒54 28	14 51 01	2 30.1	28 52.0	23 06.6	18 59.2	6 03.9	21 16.1	11 16.1	13 51.5	0 48.3	17 53.9
20 Tu	3 49 40	28 43 46	20 47 28	26 44 23	2D 29.3	28 17.4	24 19.3	19 44.7	6 28.5	21 29.4	11 13.5	13 54.2	0 48.5	17 55.0
21 W	3 53 37	29 41 29	2♓42 22	8♓42 00	2 29.6	27 42.8	25 32.0	20 30.1	6 53.1	21 42.7	11 10.8	13 56.8	0 48.8	17 56.1
22 Th	3 57 33	0♊39 11	14 43 54	20 48 38	2 30.8	27 08.7	26 44.6	21 15.5	7 17.8	21 56.0	11 08.0	13 59.4	0 49.1	17 57.2
23 F	4 01 30	1 36 52	26 56 47	3♈08 52	2 32.4	26 35.9	27 57.2	22 00.9	7 42.5	22 09.3	11 05.2	14 02.0	0 49.5	17 58.3
24 Sa	4 05 26	2 34 32	9♈25 24	15 46 49	2 34.0	26 04.7	29 09.8	22 46.2	8 07.3	22 22.7	11 02.3	14 04.6	0 49.8	17 59.5
25 Su	4 09 23	3 32 11	22 13 28	28 45 39	2R 34.8	25 35.8	0♋22.3	23 31.4	8 32.2	22 36.1	10 59.3	14 07.1	0 50.2	18 00.7
26 M	4 13 19	4 29 48	5♉23 32	12♉07 12	2 34.5	25 09.6	1 34.9	24 16.6	8 57.2	22 49.6	10 56.2	14 09.5	0 50.7	18 01.9
27 Tu	4 17 16	5 27 25	18 56 35	25 51 31	2 32.7	24 46.5	2 47.3	25 01.8	9 22.2	23 03.0	10 53.1	14 12.0	0 51.2	18 03.1
28 W	4 21 13	6 25 01	2♊51 39	9♊56 34	2 29.4	24 26.9	3 59.8	25 46.9	9 47.2	23 16.5	10 49.9	14 14.4	0 51.7	18 04.3
29 Th	4 25 09	7 22 36	17 05 39	24 18 15	2 24.9	24 11.0	5 12.2	26 31.9	10 12.3	23 30.1	10 46.7	14 16.8	0 52.2	18 05.5
30 F	4 29 06	8 20 10	1♋33 35	8♋50 49	2 19.6	23 59.1	6 24.5	27 16.9	10 37.5	23 43.6	10 43.3	14 19.1	0 52.8	18 06.8
31 Sa	4 33 02	9 17 42	16 09 07	23 27 37	2 14.4	23 51.3	7 36.8	28 01.8	11 02.7	23 57.2	10 39.9	14 21.4	0 53.4	18 08.0

LONGITUDE — June 1930

Day	Sid.Time	☉	0 hr ☽	Noon ☽	True ☊	☿	♀	♂	⚳	♃	♄	♅	♆	♇
1 Su	4 36 59	10♊15 13	0♌45 32	8♌02 09	2♉10.0	23♉47.9	8♋49.1	28♈46.7	11♋28.0	24♊10.8	10♑36.5	14♈23.7	0♍54.0	18♋09.3
2 M	4 40 55	11 12 42	15 16 46	22 28 53	2R 07.0	23D 48.9	10 01.3	29 31.5	11 53.3	24 24.4	10R 33.0	14 25.9	0 54.7	18 10.6
3 Tu	4 44 52	12 10 11	29 38 03	6♍43 57	2D 05.6	23 54.4	11 13.5	0♉16.3	12 18.7	24 38.0	10 29.4	14 28.1	0 55.4	18 11.9
4 W	4 48 49	13 07 38	13♍46 21	20 45 08	2 05.7	24 04.3	12 25.7	1 01.0	12 44.1	24 51.6	10 25.8	14 30.3	0 56.1	18 13.2
5 Th	4 52 45	14 05 03	27 40 15	4♎31 42	2 06.8	24 18.8	13 37.8	1 45.7	13 09.6	25 05.3	10 22.1	14 32.4	0 56.9	18 14.6
6 F	4 56 42	15 02 28	11♎19 34	18 03 55	2 08.1	24 37.6	14 49.8	2 30.3	13 35.1	25 19.0	10 18.3	14 34.4	0 57.6	18 15.9
7 Sa	5 00 38	15 59 51	24 44 52	1♏22 33	2R 08.8	25 00.9	16 01.8	3 14.8	14 00.6	25 32.7	10 14.5	14 36.5	0 58.5	18 17.3
8 Su	5 04 35	16 57 14	7♏57 02	14 28 27	2 08.0	25 28.6	17 13.7	3 59.3	14 26.2	25 46.3	10 10.7	14 38.5	0 59.3	18 18.6
9 M	5 08 31	17 54 35	20 56 52	27 22 22	2 05.4	26 00.5	18 25.6	4 43.7	14 51.9	26 00.1	10 06.8	14 40.4	1 00.2	18 20.0
10 Tu	5 12 28	18 51 56	3♐45 00	10♐04 49	2 00.6	26 36.6	19 37.5	5 28.1	15 17.6	26 13.8	10 02.9	14 42.4	1 01.1	18 21.4
11 W	5 16 24	19 49 16	16 21 53	22 36 13	1 53.8	27 16.8	20 49.3	6 12.4	15 43.3	26 27.5	9 58.9	14 44.2	1 02.0	18 22.8
12 Th	5 20 21	20 46 35	28 47 55	4♑57 03	1 45.5	28 01.1	22 01.0	6 56.6	16 09.1	26 41.2	9 54.9	14 46.1	1 03.0	18 24.2
13 F	5 24 18	21 43 54	11♑03 44	17 08 06	1 36.4	28 49.3	23 12.7	7 40.8	16 34.9	26 55.0	9 50.8	14 47.9	1 04.0	18 25.6
14 Sa	5 28 14	22 41 12	23 10 20	29 10 39	1 27.3	29 41.4	24 24.4	8 25.0	17 00.8	27 08.7	9 46.7	14 49.6	1 05.0	18 27.1
15 Su	5 32 11	23 38 29	5♒09 20	11♒06 42	1 19.3	0♊37.3	25 36.0	9 09.1	17 26.7	27 22.5	9 42.6	14 51.3	1 06.1	18 28.5
16 M	5 36 07	24 35 46	17 03 07	22 58 59	1 12.8	1 37.0	26 47.5	9 53.1	17 52.6	27 36.3	9 38.4	14 53.0	1 07.2	18 30.0
17 Tu	5 40 04	25 33 03	28 54 47	4♓51 00	1 08.4	2 40.3	27 59.0	10 37.0	18 18.6	27 50.0	9 34.2	14 54.6	1 08.3	18 31.4
18 W	5 44 00	26 30 19	10♓48 11	16 46 56	1D 06.0	3 47.2	29 10.5	11 20.9	18 44.6	28 03.8	9 30.0	14 56.2	1 09.4	18 32.9
19 Th	5 47 57	27 27 35	22 47 50	28 51 31	1 05.5	4 57.6	0♌21.9	12 04.8	19 10.7	28 17.6	9 25.7	14 57.8	1 10.6	18 34.4
20 F	5 51 53	28 24 51	4♈58 36	11♈09 44	1 06.0	6 11.5	1 33.2	12 48.6	19 36.8	28 31.3	9 21.4	14 59.3	1 11.8	18 35.9
21 Sa	5 55 50	29 22 07	17 25 30	23 46 32	1R 06.8	7 29.0	2 44.5	13 32.3	20 02.9	28 45.1	9 17.1	15 00.7	1 13.0	18 37.4
22 Su	5 59 47	0♋19 22	0♉13 18	6♉46 18	1 06.9	8 49.8	3 55.7	14 15.9	20 29.0	28 58.8	9 12.7	15 02.1	1 14.3	18 38.9
23 M	6 03 43	1 16 38	13 25 53	20 12 17	1 05.3	10 14.0	5 06.9	14 59.5	20 55.3	29 12.6	9 08.4	15 03.5	1 15.6	18 40.4
24 Tu	6 07 40	2 13 53	27 05 35	4♊05 44	1 01.5	11 41.5	6 18.1	15 43.0	21 21.5	29 26.4	9 04.0	15 04.8	1 16.9	18 41.9
25 W	6 11 36	3 11 08	11♊12 28	18 25 21	0 55.4	13 12.4	7 29.1	16 26.5	21 47.8	29 40.1	8 59.6	15 06.1	1 18.2	18 43.4
26 Th	6 15 33	4 08 23	25 43 42	3♋06 44	0 47.2	14 46.5	8 40.2	17 09.9	22 14.1	29 53.9	8 55.2	15 07.3	1 19.6	18 45.0
27 F	6 19 29	5 05 38	10♋33 24	18 02 38	0 37.9	16 23.8	9 51.1	17 53.2	22 40.4	0♋07.6	8 50.8	15 08.5	1 21.0	18 46.5
28 Sa	6 23 26	6 02 53	25 33 12	3♌03 54	0 28.5	18 04.3	11 02.0	18 36.4	23 06.8	0 21.3	8 46.4	15 09.6	1 22.4	18 48.0
29 Su	6 27 22	7 00 07	10♌33 33	18 01 01	0 20.2	19 48.0	12 12.9	19 19.6	23 33.2	0 35.1	8 41.9	15 10.7	1 23.8	18 49.6
30 M	6 31 19	7 57 20	25 25 20	2♍45 40	0 13.9	21 34.6	13 23.6	20 02.7	23 59.6	0 48.8	8 37.5	15 11.8	1 25.3	18 51.1

Astro Data

	Dy Hr Mn
♃⚺♇	2 13:40
☿ R	8 22:20
☽ 0S	9 8:10
♆ D	12 11:55
☽ 0N	23 16:31
☿ D	1 18:39
☽ 0S	5 13:30
☽ 0N	20 0:23

Planet Ingress

		Dy Hr Mn
☿	♊	1 5:31
⚳	♋	4 7:57
☿	♉R	17 11:06
☉	♊	21 19:42
♀	♋	25 4:36
♂	♉	3 3:15
☿	♊	14 20:09
♀	♌	19 4:39
☉	♋	22 3:53
♃	♋	26 22:42

Last Aspect / ☽ Ingress (May)

Last Aspect Dy Hr Mn			☽ Ingress	Dy Hr Mn
1 16:32	♃	☌	♋	2 13:54
3 19:44	♇	☌	♌	4 16:32
5 23:28	♃	⚹	♍	6 19:11
8 3:14	♃	□	♎	8 22:30
10 8:07	♃	△	♏	11 3:06
12 17:29	☉	☍	♐	13 9:39
14 23:54	♃	☍	♑	15 18:39
18 5:14	☿	△	♒	18 6:03
20 16:21	☉	□	♓	20 18:34
23 0:52	♀	□	♈	23 5:56
25 1:48	♂	☌	♉	25 14:15
27 10:11	☿	☌	♊	27 19:07
29 15:54	♂	⚹	♋	29 21:26
31 19:55	♂	□	♌	31 22:45

Last Aspect / ☽ Ingress (June)

Last Aspect Dy Hr Mn			☽ Ingress	Dy Hr Mn
3 0:28	♂	△	♍	3 0:37
4 19:14	♃	□	♎	5 4:04
7 1:15	♃	△	♏	7 9:30
9 9:20	☿	☍	♐	9 16:56
11 19:36	♃	☍	♑	12 2:20
14 13:07	☿	△	♒	14 13:39
16 21:32	♃	△	♓	17 2:12
19 10:52	♃	□	♈	19 14:15
21 23:15	☉	⚹	♉	21 23:35
23 9:18	♇	⚹	♊	24 5:00
26 6:42	♃	☌	♋	26 6:57
27 13:10	♇	☌	♌	28 7:06
29 15:16	☿	⚹	♍	30 7:28

☽ Phases & Eclipses

Dy Hr Mn		
5 16:53	☽	14♌27
12 17:29	○	21♏15
20 16:21	☾	28♒54
28 5:36	●	6♊10
3 21:56	☽	12♍34
11 6:12	○	19♐35
19 9:00	☾	27♓20
26 13:46	●	4♋13

Astro Data

1 May 1930
Julian Day # 11078
SVP 6♓14'08"
GC 25♐52.0 ⚴ 17♉02.3
Eris 2♈02.7 ⚵ 3♒44.5
⚷ 13♉53.2 ⚶ 7♌21.2
☽ Mean ☊ 2♉33.4

1 June 1930
Julian Day # 11109
SVP 6♓14'02"
GC 25♐52.0 ⚴ 3♊41.0
Eris 2♈17.1 ⚵ 6♒19.4R
⚷ 15♉54.3 ⚶ 17♌17.8
☽ Mean ☊ 0♉54.9

July 1930

LONGITUDE

Day	Sid.Time	☉	0 hr ☽	Noon ☽	True ☊	☿	♀	♂	⚳	♃	♄	♅	♆	♇
1 Tu	6 35 16	8♋54 34	10♍01 24	17♍12 03	0♉10.0	23♊24.2	14♌34.3	20♉45.7	24♋26.1	1♋02.5	8♑33.1	15♈12.8	1♍26.8	18♋52.7
2 W	6 39 12	9 51 46	24 17 19	1♎17 07	0D 08.3	25 16.6	15 45.0	21 28.7	24 52.5	1 16.1	8R 28.6	15 13.7	1 28.3	18 54.3
3 Th	6 43 09	10 48 59	8♎11 26	15 00 24	0 08.1	27 11.8	16 55.5	22 11.6	25 19.0	1 29.8	8 24.2	15 14.6	1 29.8	18 55.8
4 F	6 47 05	11 46 11	21 44 15	28 23 15	0R 08.3	29 09.4	18 06.0	22 54.4	25 45.6	1 43.4	8 19.8	15 15.4	1 31.4	18 57.4
5 Sa	6 51 02	12 43 23	4♏57 44	11♏28 01	0 07.9	1♋09.4	19 16.5	23 37.1	26 12.1	1 57.0	8 15.4	15 16.3	1 32.9	18 58.9
6 Su	6 54 58	13 40 34	17 54 29	24 17 26	0 05.7	3 11.5	20 26.8	24 19.8	26 38.7	2 10.6	8 11.0	15 17.0	1 34.5	19 00.5
7 M	6 58 55	14 37 46	0♐37 12	6♐54 04	0 01.0	5 15.5	21 37.1	25 02.4	27 05.3	2 24.2	8 06.6	15 17.7	1 36.2	19 02.1
8 Tu	7 02 51	15 34 58	13 08 16	19 20 03	29♈53.6	7 21.1	22 47.3	25 44.9	27 31.9	2 37.8	8 02.2	15 18.4	1 37.8	19 03.7
9 W	7 06 48	16 32 09	25 29 35	1♑37 04	29 43.5	9 28.1	23 57.4	26 27.3	27 58.6	2 51.3	7 57.8	15 19.0	1 39.5	19 05.2
10 Th	7 10 45	17 29 21	7♑42 37	13 46 23	29 31.3	11 36.0	25 07.4	27 09.7	28 25.3	3 04.9	7 53.5	15 19.6	1 41.2	19 06.8
11 F	7 14 41	18 26 33	19 48 15	25 49 04	29 18.1	13 44.8	26 17.4	27 52.0	28 51.9	3 18.4	7 49.2	15 20.1	1 42.9	19 08.4
12 Sa	7 18 38	19 23 45	1♒48 15	7♒46 14	29 04.9	15 53.9	27 27.2	28 34.2	29 18.7	3 31.8	7 44.9	15 20.6	1 44.6	19 09.9
13 Su	7 22 34	20 20 57	13 43 10	19 39 18	28 52.8	18 03.2	28 37.0	29 16.3	29 45.4	3 45.3	7 40.6	15 21.0	1 46.4	19 11.5
14 M	7 26 31	21 18 10	25 34 53	1♓30 14	28 42.6	20 12.4	29 46.7	29 58.4	0♌12.1	3 58.7	7 36.3	15 21.3	1 48.1	19 13.1
15 Tu	7 30 27	22 15 23	7♓25 42	13 21 40	28 35.0	22 21.2	0♍56.4	0♊40.4	0 38.9	4 12.1	7 32.1	15 21.7	1 49.9	19 14.7
16 W	7 34 24	23 12 37	19 18 36	25 17 00	28 30.2	24 29.4	2 05.9	1 22.3	1 05.7	4 25.4	7 27.9	15 21.9	1 51.7	19 16.3
17 Th	7 38 21	24 09 51	1♈17 22	7♈20 19	28 27.7	26 36.7	3 15.3	2 04.2	1 32.5	4 38.7	7 23.8	15 22.2	1 53.6	19 17.9
18 F	7 42 17	25 07 06	13 26 26	19 36 20	28 27.0	28 43.0	4 24.7	2 45.9	1 59.4	4 52.0	7 19.6	15 22.3	1 55.4	19 19.4
19 Sa	7 46 14	26 04 22	25 50 40	2♉10 03	28 27.0	0♌48.2	5 34.0	3 27.6	2 26.2	5 05.3	7 15.6	15 22.5	1 57.3	19 21.0
20 Su	7 50 10	27 01 38	8♉35 06	15 06 22	28 26.5	2 52.1	6 43.1	4 09.2	2 53.1	5 18.5	7 11.5	15 22.6	1 59.2	19 22.6
21 M	7 54 07	27 58 56	21 44 21	28 29 25	28 24.4	4 54.5	7 52.2	4 50.8	3 20.0	5 31.7	7 07.5	15R 22.6	2 01.1	19 24.1
22 Tu	7 58 03	28 56 14	5♊21 52	12♊21 46	28 20.0	6 55.5	9 01.2	5 32.2	3 46.9	5 44.9	7 03.6	15 22.6	2 03.0	19 25.7
23 W	8 02 00	29 53 33	19 29 02	26 43 24	28 13.1	8 54.9	10 10.1	6 13.6	4 13.8	5 58.0	6 59.6	15 22.5	2 04.9	19 27.3
24 Th	8 05 56	0♌50 53	4♋04 18	11♋31 00	28 03.9	10 52.8	11 18.9	6 54.9	4 40.7	6 11.1	6 55.8	15 22.4	2 06.9	19 28.8
25 F	8 09 53	1 48 14	19 02 31	26 37 39	27 53.3	12 48.9	12 27.7	7 36.1	5 07.7	6 24.1	6 52.0	15 22.2	2 08.8	19 30.4
26 Sa	8 13 50	2 45 35	4♌15 06	11♌53 27	27 42.5	14 43.4	13 36.3	8 17.2	5 34.7	6 37.1	6 48.2	15 22.0	2 10.8	19 31.9
27 Su	8 17 46	3 42 57	19 31 17	27 07 12	27 32.7	16 36.3	14 44.8	8 58.2	6 01.6	6 50.1	6 44.5	15 21.8	2 12.8	19 33.5
28 M	8 21 43	4 40 19	4♍39 56	12♍08 23	27 25.2	18 27.4	15 53.2	9 39.1	6 28.6	7 03.0	6 40.8	15 21.4	2 14.8	19 35.0
29 Tu	8 25 39	5 37 42	19 31 37	26 48 59	27 20.2	20 16.9	17 01.4	10 19.9	6 55.6	7 15.8	6 37.2	15 21.1	2 16.8	19 36.5
30 W	8 29 36	6 35 05	3♎59 58	11♎04 20	27 17.7	22 04.7	18 09.6	11 00.7	7 22.6	7 28.7	6 33.7	15 20.7	2 18.9	19 38.1
31 Th	8 33 32	7 32 29	18 02 01	24 53 06	27D 17.0	23 50.8	19 17.6	11 41.3	7 49.7	7 41.4	6 30.2	15 20.2	2 20.9	19 39.6

August 1930

LONGITUDE

Day	Sid.Time	☉	0 hr ☽	Noon ☽	True ☊	☿	♀	♂	⚳	♃	♄	♅	♆	♇
1 F	8 37 29	8♌29 54	1♏37 49	8♏16 29	27♈17.1	25♌35.2	20♍25.6	12♊21.9	8♌16.7	7♋54.1	6♑26.8	15♈19.7	2♍23.0	19♋41.1
2 Sa	8 41 25	9 27 19	14 49 31	21 17 22	27R 16.7	27 18.0	21 33.4	13 02.4	8 43.7	8 06.8	6R 23.4	15R 19.2	2 25.1	19 42.6
3 Su	8 45 22	10 24 45	27 40 29	3♐59 23	27 14.6	28 59.1	22 41.0	13 42.8	9 10.7	8 19.4	6 20.1	15 18.6	2 27.1	19 44.1
4 M	8 49 19	11 22 12	10♐14 30	16 26 19	27 10.3	0♍38.6	23 48.6	14 23.1	9 37.8	8 31.9	6 16.9	15 17.9	2 29.2	19 45.6
5 Tu	8 53 15	12 19 39	22 35 14	28 41 40	27 03.2	2 16.4	24 56.0	15 03.3	10 04.8	8 44.4	6 13.8	15 17.3	2 31.3	19 47.1
6 W	8 57 12	13 17 07	4♑45 56	10♑48 22	26 53.5	3 52.6	26 03.2	15 43.4	10 31.9	8 56.9	6 10.7	15 16.5	2 33.5	19 48.5
7 Th	9 01 08	14 14 36	16 49 14	22 48 48	26 41.9	5 27.2	27 10.4	16 23.4	10 59.0	9 09.3	6 07.7	15 15.8	2 35.6	19 50.0
8 F	9 05 05	15 12 06	28 47 16	4♒44 50	26 29.2	7 00.1	28 17.3	17 03.3	11 26.0	9 21.6	6 04.7	15 14.9	2 37.7	19 51.5
9 Sa	9 09 01	16 09 37	10♒41 41	16 38 00	26 16.4	8 31.5	29 24.2	17 43.1	11 53.1	9 33.9	6 01.9	15 14.1	2 39.9	19 52.9
10 Su	9 12 58	17 07 09	22 33 58	28 29 45	26 04.7	10 01.1	0♎30.8	18 22.9	12 20.2	9 46.1	5 59.1	15 13.1	2 42.0	19 54.3
11 M	9 16 54	18 04 42	4♓25 33	10♓21 37	25 54.9	11 29.1	1 37.4	19 02.5	12 47.3	9 58.2	5 56.4	15 12.2	2 44.2	19 55.8
12 Tu	9 20 51	19 02 16	16 18 12	22 15 35	25 47.6	12 55.5	2 43.7	19 42.1	13 14.3	10 10.3	5 53.7	15 11.2	2 46.3	19 57.2
13 W	9 24 48	19 59 52	28 14 06	4♈14 08	25 43.0	14 20.1	3 49.9	20 21.5	13 41.4	10 22.3	5 51.2	15 10.1	2 48.5	19 58.6
14 Th	9 28 44	20 57 29	10♈16 05	16 20 25	25D 40.8	15 43.0	4 56.0	21 00.9	14 08.5	10 34.2	5 48.7	15 09.0	2 50.7	20 00.0
15 F	9 32 41	21 55 07	22 27 36	28 38 11	25 40.4	17 04.2	6 01.9	21 40.1	14 35.6	10 46.1	5 46.3	15 07.9	2 52.9	20 01.3
16 Sa	9 36 37	22 52 48	4♉52 42	11♉11 42	25R 40.9	18 23.6	7 07.6	22 19.3	15 02.7	10 57.9	5 44.0	15 06.7	2 55.1	20 02.7
17 Su	9 40 34	23 50 29	17 35 45	24 05 23	25 41.3	19 41.2	8 13.1	22 58.3	15 29.8	11 09.6	5 41.7	15 05.5	2 57.3	20 04.1
18 M	9 44 30	24 48 13	0♊41 06	7♊23 20	25 40.6	20 56.9	9 18.5	23 37.3	15 56.9	11 21.3	5 39.6	15 04.3	2 59.5	20 05.4
19 Tu	9 48 27	25 45 58	14 12 24	21 08 33	25 38.0	22 10.6	10 23.7	24 16.1	16 24.0	11 32.9	5 37.5	15 03.0	3 01.7	20 06.8
20 W	9 52 23	26 43 44	28 11 50	5♋22 08	25 33.2	23 22.4	11 28.7	24 54.9	16 51.1	11 44.4	5 35.5	15 01.6	3 03.9	20 08.1
21 Th	9 56 20	27 41 33	12♋39 08	20 02 17	25 26.4	24 32.1	12 33.5	25 33.5	17 18.2	11 55.9	5 33.7	15 00.2	3 06.1	20 09.4
22 F	10 00 17	28 39 23	27 30 50	5♌03 47	25 18.3	25 39.6	13 38.1	26 12.1	17 45.3	12 07.2	5 31.9	14 58.8	3 08.4	20 10.7
23 Sa	10 04 13	29 37 14	12♌39 59	20 18 08	25 09.9	26 44.8	14 42.5	26 50.5	18 12.3	12 18.5	5 30.2	14 57.4	3 10.6	20 12.0
24 Su	10 08 10	0♍35 07	27 56 52	5♍34 44	25 02.3	27 47.7	15 46.8	27 28.8	18 39.4	12 29.7	5 28.5	14 55.9	3 12.8	20 13.2
25 M	10 12 06	1 33 01	13♍10 24	20 42 36	24 56.4	28 48.1	16 50.8	28 07.0	19 06.5	12 40.8	5 27.0	14 54.3	3 15.0	20 14.5
26 Tu	10 16 03	2 30 57	28 10 14	5♎32 23	24 52.7	29 45.8	17 54.5	28 45.1	19 33.6	12 51.8	5 25.6	14 52.7	3 17.2	20 15.7
27 W	10 19 59	3 28 54	12♎48 21	19 57 39	24D 51.2	0♎40.8	18 58.1	29 23.0	20 00.6	13 02.7	5 24.2	14 51.1	3 19.5	20 16.9
28 Th	10 23 56	4 26 52	27 00 00	3♏55 20	24 51.4	1 32.8	20 01.4	0♋00.9	20 27.7	13 13.6	5 23.0	14 49.5	3 21.7	20 18.1
29 F	10 27 52	5 24 52	10♏43 42	17 25 20	24 52.4	2 21.7	21 04.5	0 38.6	20 54.7	13 24.3	5 21.8	14 47.8	3 23.9	20 19.3
30 Sa	10 31 49	6 22 53	24 00 34	0♐29 50	24R 53.3	3 07.3	22 07.3	1 16.2	21 21.7	13 35.0	5 20.8	14 46.1	3 26.1	20 20.5
31 Su	10 35 46	7 20 56	6♐53 35	13 12 21	24 53.3	3 49.3	23 09.9	1 53.7	21 48.8	13 45.6	5 19.8	14 44.3	3 28.4	20 21.7

Astro Data (Dy Hr Mn)

☽0S 2 18:24
♃✶♆ 3 12:03
☽0N 17 6:46
♅R 21 16:09
♃☍♄ 27 3:55
☽0S 30 0:52

♀0S 10 6:16
☽0N 13 12:06
♅0S 22 22:51
☽0S 26 9:47

Planet Ingress (Dy Hr Mn)

☿ ♋ 4 22:10
☊ ♈R 7 15:55
⚳ ♌ 14 1:06
♂ ♊ 14 12:54
♀ ♍ 14 16:34
☿ ♌ 19 2:44
☉ ♌ 23 14:42

☿ ♍ 4 2:38
♀ ♎ 10 0:54
☉ ♍ 23 21:26
☿ ♎ 26 18:04
♂ ♋ 28 11:27

Last Aspect Dy Hr Mn	☽ Ingress Dy Hr Mn	Last Aspect Dy Hr Mn	☽ Ingress Dy Hr Mn
2 0:05 ☿ □	♎ 2 9:47	3 1:02 ☿ □	♐ 3 4:24
4 13:39 ☿ △	♏ 4 14:56	5 3:51 ♀ □	♑ 5 14:35
6 12:05 ♂ ☍	♐ 6 22:49	7 21:39 ♀ △	♒ 8 2:26
8 19:26 ♀ △	♑ 9 8:49	9 14:20 ♂ △	♓ 10 15:03
11 16:21 ♂ △	♒ 11 20:23	12 7:21 ♇ △	♈ 13 3:32
14 8:42 ♂ □	♓ 14 8:57	14 21:50 ☉ △	♉ 15 14:38
16 10:04 ☿ △	♈ 16 21:26	17 11:30 ☉ □	♊ 17 22:46
18 23:29 ☉ □	♉ 19 7:54	19 20:28 ☉ ✶	♋ 20 3:02
21 11:02 ☉ ✶	♊ 21 14:39	21 19:50 ♀ ✶	♌ 22 3:58
22 17:06 ♅ ✶	♋ 23 17:22	23 22:43 ♂ ✶	♍ 24 3:13
25 0:43 ♇ ☌	♌ 25 17:19	26 1:56 ☿ ☌	♎ 26 2:58
26 17:28 ♅ △	♍ 27 16:34	28 4:53 ♂ △	♏ 28 5:11
29 0:07 ♇ ✶	♎ 29 17:18	29 17:16 ♇ △	♐ 30 11:04
31 9:54 ☿ ✶	♏ 31 21:05		

☽ Phases & Eclipses (Dy Hr Mn)

3 4:03 ☽ 10♎30
10 20:01 ○ 17♑48
18 23:29 ☾ 25♈34
25 20:42 ● 2♌09

1 12:26 ☽ 8♏31
9 10:58 ○ 16♒07
17 11:30 ☾ 23♉49
24 3:37 ● 0♍15
30 23:57 ☽ 6♐52

Astro Data

1 July 1930
Julian Day # 11139
SVP 6♓13'57"
GC 25♐52.1 ⚴ 20♊43.6
Eris 2♈21.6R ⚵ 3♒35.1R
⚷ 17♉33.9 ⚶ 29♌18.5
☽ Mean ☊ 29♈19.7

1 August 1930
Julian Day # 11170
SVP 6♓13'52"
GC 25♐52.2 ⚴ 8♋55.1
Eris 2♈15.4R ⚵ 26♑39.3R
⚷ 18♉39.3 ⚶ 13♍16.2
☽ Mean ☊ 27♈41.2

LONGITUDE — September 1930

Day	Sid.Time	☉	0 hr ☽	Noon ☽	True ☊	☿	♀	♂	⚳	♃	♄	♅	♆	♇
1 M	10 39 42	8♍19 00	19♐26 40	25♐37 04	24♈51.6	4♎27.6	24♎12.2	2♋31.0	22♌15.8	13♋56.1	5♑18.9	14♈42.5	3♍30.6	20♋22.8
2 Tu	10 43 39	9 17 05	1♑44 05	7♑48 14	24R48.0	5 01.8	25 14.3	3 08.3	22 42.8	14 06.4	5R18.2	14R40.7	3 32.8	20 23.9
3 W	10 47 35	10 15 12	13 50 00	19 49 50	24 42.6	5 31.8	26 16.0	3 45.4	23 09.7	14 16.7	5 17.5	14 38.9	3 35.0	20 25.0
4 Th	10 51 32	11 13 20	25 48 11	1♒45 24	24 35.6	5 57.2	27 17.4	4 22.4	23 36.7	14 26.9	5 16.9	14 37.0	3 37.2	20 26.1
5 F	10 55 28	12 11 29	7♒41 51	13 37 51	24 27.8	6 17.7	28 18.6	4 59.3	24 03.7	14 37.0	5 16.4	14 35.1	3 39.4	20 27.2
6 Sa	10 59 25	13 09 40	19 33 42	25 29 39	24 19.9	6 33.1	29 19.4	5 36.0	24 30.6	14 46.9	5 16.0	14 33.1	3 41.6	20 28.2
7 Su	11 03 21	14 07 53	1♓25 56	7♓22 46	24 12.6	6 43.0	0♏19.9	6 12.7	24 57.5	14 56.8	5 15.7	14 31.1	3 43.8	20 29.3
8 M	11 07 18	15 06 08	13 20 22	19 18 56	24 06.7	6R47.1	1 20.1	6 49.1	25 24.4	15 06.6	5 15.6	14 29.1	3 46.0	20 30.3
9 Tu	11 11 15	16 04 24	25 18 40	1♈19 48	24 02.5	6 45.2	2 19.9	7 25.5	25 51.3	15 16.2	5D15.5	14 27.1	3 48.2	20 31.3
10 W	11 15 11	17 02 42	7♈22 33	13 27 10	24D00.2	6 37.0	3 19.4	8 01.7	26 18.2	15 25.8	5 15.5	14 25.1	3 50.4	20 32.2
11 Th	11 19 08	18 01 02	19 33 55	25 43 05	23 59.7	6 22.2	4 18.5	8 37.9	26 45.1	15 35.2	5 15.6	14 23.0	3 52.6	20 33.2
12 F	11 23 04	18 59 25	1♉55 00	8♉09 59	24 00.4	6 00.8	5 17.2	9 13.8	27 11.9	15 44.5	5 15.7	14 20.9	3 54.7	20 34.1
13 Sa	11 27 01	19 57 49	14 28 26	20 50 41	24 01.9	5 32.6	6 15.5	9 49.7	27 38.7	15 53.7	5 16.0	14 18.7	3 56.9	20 35.1
14 Su	11 30 57	20 56 15	27 17 09	3♊48 12	24 03.5	4 57.8	7 13.5	10 25.4	28 05.5	16 02.8	5 16.4	14 16.6	3 59.1	20 36.0
15 M	11 34 54	21 54 44	10♊24 12	17 05 28	24R04.4	4 16.5	8 11.0	11 00.9	28 32.3	16 11.8	5 16.9	14 14.4	4 01.2	20 36.8
16 Tu	11 38 50	22 53 15	23 52 16	0♋44 49	24 04.3	3 29.2	9 08.1	11 36.3	28 59.1	16 20.7	5 17.5	14 12.2	4 03.3	20 37.7
17 W	11 42 47	23 51 48	7♋43 12	14 47 23	24 02.8	2 36.3	10 04.8	12 11.6	29 25.8	16 29.4	5 18.2	14 10.0	4 05.5	20 38.5
18 Th	11 46 44	24 50 23	21 57 14	29 12 24	24 00.1	1 38.8	11 01.0	12 46.7	29 52.6	16 38.0	5 19.0	14 07.8	4 07.6	20 39.4
19 F	11 50 40	25 49 00	6♌32 24	13♌56 34	23 56.5	0 37.6	11 56.7	13 21.7	0♍19.2	16 46.5	5 19.9	14 05.5	4 09.7	20 40.2
20 Sa	11 54 37	26 47 40	21 24 07	28 54 04	23 52.6	29♍34.0	12 52.0	13 56.5	0 45.9	16 54.9	5 20.9	14 03.2	4 11.8	20 40.9
21 Su	11 58 33	27 46 21	6♍25 21	13♍56 51	23 49.1	28 29.2	13 46.7	14 31.2	1 12.6	17 03.1	5 22.0	14 00.9	4 13.9	20 41.7
22 M	12 02 30	28 45 05	21 27 23	28 55 50	23 46.5	27 25.0	14 40.9	15 05.7	1 39.2	17 11.2	5 23.1	13 58.6	4 15.9	20 42.4
23 Tu	12 06 26	29 43 50	6♎21 06	13♎42 15	23D45.0	26 22.9	15 34.6	15 40.0	2 05.8	17 19.1	5 24.4	13 56.3	4 18.0	20 43.1
24 W	12 10 23	0♎42 38	20 58 27	28 09 02	23 44.8	25 24.4	16 27.7	16 14.2	2 32.3	17 27.0	5 25.8	13 54.0	4 20.0	20 43.8
25 Th	12 14 19	1 41 27	5♏13 31	12♏11 34	23 45.6	24 31.3	17 20.3	16 48.2	2 58.8	17 34.6	5 27.3	13 51.6	4 22.1	20 44.5
26 F	12 18 16	2 40 18	19 03 01	25 47 54	23 46.9	23 44.8	18 12.2	17 22.0	3 25.3	17 42.2	5 28.8	13 49.2	4 24.1	20 45.1
27 Sa	12 22 12	3 39 11	2♐26 19	8♐58 31	23 48.4	23 06.2	19 03.4	17 55.7	3 51.8	17 49.6	5 30.5	13 46.9	4 26.1	20 45.7
28 Su	12 26 09	4 38 06	15 24 52	21 45 46	23 49.5	22 36.6	19 54.0	18 29.2	4 18.2	17 56.9	5 32.3	13 44.5	4 28.1	20 46.3
29 M	12 30 06	5 37 02	28 01 43	4♑13 13	23R50.0	22 16.5	20 43.9	19 02.5	4 44.6	18 04.0	5 34.1	13 42.1	4 30.1	20 46.9
30 Tu	12 34 02	6 36 00	10♑20 50	16 25 06	23 49.7	22D06.7	21 33.1	19 35.7	5 10.9	18 11.0	5 36.1	13 39.7	4 32.0	20 47.4

LONGITUDE — October 1930

Day	Sid.Time	☉	0 hr ☽	Noon ☽	True ☊	☿	♀	♂	⚳	♃	♄	♅	♆	♇
1 W	12 37 59	7♎35 00	22♑26 37	28♑25 54	23♈48.6	22♍07.2	22♏21.5	20♋08.6	5♍37.3	18♋17.8	5♑38.1	13♈37.3	4♍34.0	20♋48.0
2 Th	12 41 55	8 34 02	4♒23 32	10♒20 00	23R46.9	22 18.0	23 09.1	20 41.4	6 03.5	18 24.4	5 40.3	13R34.9	4 35.9	20 48.5
3 F	12 45 52	9 33 05	16 15 49	22 11 26	23 44.8	22 39.0	23 55.9	21 14.0	6 29.8	18 31.0	5 42.5	13 32.5	4 37.8	20 49.0
4 Sa	12 49 48	10 32 10	28 07 17	4♓03 46	23 42.7	23 09.7	24 41.9	21 46.4	6 56.0	18 37.3	5 44.8	13 30.0	4 39.7	20 49.4
5 Su	12 53 45	11 31 17	10♓01 15	16 00 04	23 40.8	23 49.7	25 27.0	22 18.6	7 22.1	18 43.5	5 47.3	13 27.6	4 41.6	20 49.8
6 M	12 57 41	12 30 26	22 00 29	28 02 48	23 39.3	24 38.3	26 11.1	22 50.6	7 48.2	18 49.6	5 49.8	13 25.2	4 43.4	20 50.2
7 Tu	13 01 38	13 29 37	4♈07 13	10♈13 57	23 38.5	25 34.8	26 54.3	23 22.4	8 14.3	18 55.5	5 52.4	13 22.8	4 45.2	20 50.6
8 W	13 05 35	14 28 50	16 23 10	22 35 03	23D38.2	26 38.4	27 36.5	23 54.1	8 40.3	19 01.2	5 55.1	13 20.3	4 47.0	20 51.0
9 Th	13 09 31	15 28 05	28 49 43	5♉07 20	23 38.3	27 48.5	28 17.6	24 25.5	9 06.3	19 06.8	5 57.8	13 17.9	4 48.8	20 51.3
10 F	13 13 28	16 27 22	11♉27 59	17 51 49	23 38.8	29 04.2	28 57.7	24 56.7	9 32.2	19 12.2	6 00.7	13 15.5	4 50.6	20 51.6
11 Sa	13 17 24	17 26 42	24 18 56	0♊49 27	23 39.5	0♎24.9	29 36.6	25 27.7	9 58.1	19 17.5	6 03.7	13 13.0	4 52.4	20 51.9
12 Su	13 21 21	18 26 04	7♊23 29	14 01 06	23 40.1	1 49.8	0♐14.4	25 58.5	10 23.9	19 22.6	6 06.7	13 10.6	4 54.1	20 52.2
13 M	13 25 17	19 25 28	20 42 26	27 27 33	23 40.5	3 18.3	0 51.0	26 29.1	10 49.7	19 27.5	6 09.9	13 08.2	4 55.8	20 52.4
14 Tu	13 29 14	20 24 54	4♋16 29	11♋09 16	23R40.7	4 49.9	1 26.3	26 59.5	11 15.5	19 32.2	6 13.1	13 05.8	4 57.5	20 52.6
15 W	13 33 10	21 24 23	18 05 54	25 06 17	23 40.8	6 24.0	2 00.4	27 29.6	11 41.2	19 36.8	6 16.4	13 03.4	4 59.2	20 52.8
16 Th	13 37 07	22 23 54	2♌10 18	9♌17 44	23 40.7	8 00.1	2 33.0	27 59.5	12 06.8	19 41.2	6 19.8	13 01.0	5 00.8	20 53.0
17 F	13 41 04	23 23 27	16 28 18	23 41 36	23D40.6	9 37.9	3 04.3	28 29.2	12 32.4	19 45.4	6 23.3	12 58.6	5 02.5	20 53.1
18 Sa	13 45 00	24 23 03	0♍57 12	8♍14 31	23 40.7	11 17.0	3 34.1	28 58.6	12 57.9	19 49.5	6 26.9	12 56.3	5 04.1	20 53.2
19 Su	13 48 57	25 22 41	15 32 55	22 51 44	23 40.8	12 57.0	4 02.3	29 27.8	13 23.4	19 53.3	6 30.5	12 53.9	5 05.6	20 53.3
20 M	13 52 53	26 22 21	0♎10 12	7♎27 32	23 40.9	14 37.7	4 29.0	29 56.7	13 48.8	19 57.0	6 34.2	12 51.6	5 07.2	20 53.4
21 Tu	13 56 50	27 22 03	14 42 58	21 55 44	23R41.0	16 18.9	4 54.1	0♌25.4	14 14.1	20 00.5	6 38.1	12 49.2	5 08.7	20 53.4
22 W	14 00 46	28 21 47	29 05 08	6♏10 31	23 40.9	18 00.4	5 17.4	0 53.8	14 39.4	20 03.8	6 42.0	12 46.9	5 10.2	20R53.4
23 Th	14 04 43	29 21 33	13♏11 20	20 07 08	23 40.6	19 42.1	5 39.0	1 21.9	15 04.6	20 07.0	6 45.9	12 44.6	5 11.7	20 53.4
24 F	14 08 39	0♏21 21	26 57 34	3♐42 26	23 39.9	21 23.8	5 58.7	1 49.8	15 29.8	20 09.9	6 50.0	12 42.3	5 13.2	20 53.4
25 Sa	14 12 36	1 21 11	10♐21 37	16 55 09	23 38.9	23 05.4	6 16.6	2 17.4	15 54.9	20 12.7	6 54.2	12 40.0	5 14.6	20 53.3
26 Su	14 16 33	2 21 02	23 23 10	29 45 52	23 37.9	24 46.8	6 32.4	2 44.7	16 19.9	20 15.2	6 58.4	12 37.8	5 16.0	20 53.3
27 M	14 20 29	3 20 56	6♑03 35	12♑16 42	23 36.9	26 27.9	6 46.3	3 11.7	16 44.8	20 17.6	7 02.7	12 35.6	5 17.4	20 53.1
28 Tu	14 24 26	4 20 51	18 25 41	24 31 01	23D36.2	28 08.7	6 58.0	3 38.4	17 09.7	20 19.8	7 07.0	12 33.4	5 18.7	20 53.0
29 W	14 28 22	5 20 47	0♒33 15	6♒32 58	23 36.0	29 49.2	7 07.6	4 04.8	17 34.5	20 21.8	7 11.5	12 31.2	5 20.0	20 52.9
30 Th	14 32 19	6 20 46	12 30 44	18 27 10	23 36.4	1♏29.4	7 14.9	4 30.9	17 59.2	20 23.6	7 16.0	12 29.0	5 21.3	20 52.7
31 F	14 36 15	7 20 45	24 22 52	0♓18 24	23 37.3	3 09.1	7 20.0	4 56.7	18 23.8	20 25.2	7 20.6	12 26.9	5 22.6	20 52.5

Astro Data	Planet Ingress	Last Aspect	☽ Ingress	Last Aspect	☽ Ingress	☽ Phases & Eclipses
Dy Hr Mn	Dy Hr Mn	Dy Hr Mn	Dy Hr Mn	Dy Hr Mn	Dy Hr Mn	Dy Hr Mn
♃□♅ 5 8:10	♀ ♏ 7 4:05	1 8:59 ♀ ⚹	♑ 1 20:35	30 23:18 ☿ △	♒ 1 15:09	8 2:48 ○ 14♓44
☿ R 8 16:32	⚳ ♍ 18 18:42	4 2:09 ♀ □	♒ 4 8:27	3 15:46 ♀ □	♓ 4 3:48	15 21:13 ☾ 22♊17
☽ 0N 9 17:29	☿ ♍R 20 2:16	6 20:28 ♀ △	♓ 6 21:06	6 8:04 ♀ △	♈ 6 15:52	22 11:42 ● 28♍44
♄ D 9 23:54	☉ ♎ 23 18:36	8 14:23 ♇ △	♈ 9 9:21	8 14:39 ♂ □	♉ 9 2:14	29 14:58 ☽ 5♑44
☽ 0S 22 20:19		11 1:55 ♇ □	♉ 11 20:18	11 9:39 ♀ ☍	♊ 11 10:29	
☉0S 23 18:36	☿ ♎ 11 4:45	13 11:31 ♇ ⚹	♊ 14 5:01	12 20:34 ☉ △	♋ 13 16:29	7 18:55 ○ 13♈47
☿0N 24 16:08	♀ ♐ 12 2:45	15 21:13 ☉ □	♋ 16 10:42	15 16:13 ♂ ☌	♌ 15 20:19	7 19:07 ☍ P 0.025
☿ D 30 22:55	♂ ♌ 20 14:43	18 4:16 ☉ ⚹	♌ 18 13:18	17 11:28 ☉ ⚹	♍ 17 22:26	15 5:12 ☾ 21♋08
	☉ ♏ 24 3:26	19 12:14 ♅ △	♍ 20 13:45	19 23:13 ♂ ⚹	♎ 19 23:43	21 21:48 ● 27♎46
☽ 0N 6 23:56	☿ ♏ 29 14:35	22 11:42 ☉ ☌	♎ 22 13:43	21 21:48 ☉ ☌	♏ 22 1:32	21 21:43:29 ☌ T 01'55"
☿0S 14 8:16		23 23:35 ♇ □	♏ 24 15:07	23 13:21 ♇ △	♐ 24 5:23	29 9:22 ☽ 5♒14
☽ 0S 20 6:28		26 8:31 ☿ ⚹	♐ 26 19:34	26 1:11 ☿ ⚹	♑ 26 12:27	
♇ R 22 13:32		28 13:34 ☿ □	♑ 29 3:48	28 20:22 ☿ □	♒ 28 22:54	
♃∠♆ 27 6:03				29 23:59 ♅ ⚹	♓ 31 11:23	

Astro Data

1 September 1930
Julian Day # 11201
SVP 6♓13'47"
GC 25♐52.3 ⚳ 27♋06.9
Eris 2♈00.2R ✱ 21♑25.5R
⚷ 18♉52.7R ⚶ 28♍16.8
☽ Mean ☊ 26♈02.7

1 October 1930
Julian Day # 11231
SVP 6♓13'44"
GC 25♐52.3 ⚳ 13♌58.4
Eris 1♈40.9R ✱ 22♑02.0
⚷ 18♉13.0R ⚶ 13♎28.7
☽ Mean ☊ 24♈27.4

November 1930 LONGITUDE

Day	Sid.Time	☉	0 hr ☽	Noon ☽	True ☊	☿	♀	♂	⚳	♃	♄	♅	♆	♇
1 Sa	14 40 12	8♏20 47	6♓14 21	12♓11 16	23♈38.6	4♏48.4	7♐22.7	5♌22.2	18♍48.4	20♋26.6	7♑25.3	12♈24.7	5♍23.8	20♋52.2
2 Su	14 44 08	9 20 50	18 09 41	24 10 05	23 40.0	6 27.3	7R 23.1	5 47.4	19 12.8	20 27.8	7 30.0	12R 22.6	5 25.0	20R 52.0
3 M	14 48 05	10 20 55	0♈12 54	6♈18 33	23 41.2	8 05.7	7 21.1	6 12.2	19 37.2	20 28.8	7 34.8	12 20.6	5 26.2	20 51.7
4 Tu	14 52 02	11 21 01	12 27 22	18 39 40	23R41.9	9 43.8	7 16.6	6 36.8	20 01.5	20 29.6	7 39.7	12 18.5	5 27.3	20 51.4
5 W	14 55 58	12 21 09	24 55 40	1♉15 32	23 41.8	11 21.4	7 09.7	7 00.9	20 25.8	20 30.2	7 44.6	12 16.5	5 28.4	20 51.1
6 Th	14 59 55	13 21 19	7♉39 22	14 07 14	23 40.7	12 58.7	7 00.4	7 24.8	20 49.9	20 30.7	7 49.6	12 14.5	5 29.5	20 50.7
7 F	15 03 51	14 21 31	20 39 05	27 14 51	23 38.6	14 35.5	6 48.6	7 48.2	21 14.0	20R30.9	7 54.7	12 12.6	5 30.6	20 50.3
8 Sa	15 07 48	15 21 44	3♊54 24	10♊37 32	23 35.7	16 11.9	6 34.3	8 11.3	21 37.9	20 30.9	7 59.9	12 10.7	5 31.6	20 49.9
9 Su	15 11 44	16 22 00	17 24 03	24 13 39	23 32.3	17 48.0	6 17.7	8 34.1	22 01.8	20 30.7	8 05.1	12 08.8	5 32.6	20 49.5
10 M	15 15 41	17 22 18	1♋06 06	8♋01 05	23 28.9	19 23.8	5 58.8	8 56.5	22 25.6	20 30.4	8 10.3	12 06.9	5 33.6	20 49.1
11 Tu	15 19 37	18 22 37	14 58 19	21 57 30	23 26.0	20 59.1	5 37.5	9 18.5	22 49.2	20 29.8	8 15.7	12 05.1	5 34.5	20 48.6
12 W	15 23 34	19 22 58	28 58 23	6♌00 40	23 24.2	22 34.2	5 14.2	9 40.0	23 12.8	20 29.0	8 21.1	12 03.3	5 35.4	20 48.1
13 Th	15 27 31	20 23 22	13♌04 07	20 08 29	23D23.5	24 09.0	4 48.7	10 01.2	23 36.3	20 28.0	8 26.5	12 01.5	5 36.3	20 47.6
14 F	15 31 27	21 23 47	27 13 33	4♍19 05	23 24.0	25 43.4	4 21.3	10 22.0	23 59.7	20 26.9	8 32.1	11 59.8	5 37.1	20 47.0
15 Sa	15 35 24	22 24 14	11♍24 51	18 30 37	23 25.4	27 17.6	3 52.2	10 42.3	24 23.0	20 25.5	8 37.6	11 58.1	5 37.9	20 46.5
16 Su	15 39 20	23 24 43	25 36 07	2♎41 04	23 26.9	28 51.6	3 21.4	11 02.3	24 46.1	20 23.9	8 43.3	11 56.5	5 38.7	20 45.9
17 M	15 43 17	24 25 14	9♎45 09	16 48 02	23R28.0	0♐25.3	2 49.1	11 21.7	25 09.2	20 22.1	8 49.0	11 54.9	5 39.4	20 45.3
18 Tu	15 47 13	25 25 46	23 49 21	0♏48 43	23 27.9	1 58.8	2 15.6	11 40.7	25 32.1	20 20.2	8 54.7	11 53.3	5 40.1	20 44.7
19 W	15 51 10	26 26 21	7♏45 42	14 39 56	23 26.3	3 32.0	1 41.1	11 59.3	25 55.0	20 18.0	9 00.5	11 51.7	5 40.8	20 44.0
20 Th	15 55 06	27 26 57	21 31 00	28 18 33	23 22.8	5 05.1	1 05.7	12 17.4	26 17.7	20 15.6	9 06.4	11 50.3	5 41.5	20 43.3
21 F	15 59 03	28 27 34	5♐02 13	11♐41 45	23 17.7	6 37.9	0 29.8	12 35.0	26 40.3	20 13.0	9 12.3	11 48.8	5 42.1	20 42.6
22 Sa	16 03 00	29 28 13	18 16 56	24 47 38	23 11.5	8 10.6	29♏53.5	12 52.0	27 02.7	20 10.3	9 18.2	11 47.4	5 42.6	20 41.9
23 Su	16 06 56	0♐28 53	1♑13 47	7♑35 25	23 04.8	9 43.1	29 17.2	13 08.6	27 25.1	20 07.3	9 24.3	11 46.0	5 43.2	20 41.2
24 M	16 10 53	1 29 34	13 52 39	20 05 42	22 58.3	11 15.4	28 40.9	13 24.7	27 47.3	20 04.2	9 30.3	11 44.7	5 43.7	20 40.5
25 Tu	16 14 49	2 30 17	26 14 50	2♒20 25	22 52.9	12 47.6	28 05.1	13 40.3	28 09.4	20 00.8	9 36.4	11 43.4	5 44.2	20 39.7
26 W	16 18 46	3 31 01	8♒22 53	14 22 43	22 49.0	14 19.6	27 29.9	13 55.3	28 31.3	19 57.3	9 42.6	11 42.2	5 44.6	20 38.9
27 Th	16 22 42	4 31 45	20 20 26	26 16 38	22D46.9	15 51.4	26 55.6	14 09.8	28 53.1	19 53.6	9 48.8	11 41.0	5 45.0	20 38.1
28 F	16 26 39	5 32 31	2♓11 55	8♓06 56	22 46.5	17 23.0	26 22.4	14 23.7	29 14.8	19 49.7	9 55.0	11 39.8	5 45.4	20 37.2
29 Sa	16 30 35	6 33 17	14 02 19	19 58 43	22 47.3	18 54.4	25 50.6	14 37.1	29 36.3	19 45.6	10 01.3	11 38.7	5 45.7	20 36.4
30 Su	16 34 32	7 34 05	25 56 48	1♈57 12	22 48.9	20 25.7	25 20.2	14 49.8	29 57.7	19 41.3	10 07.7	11 37.6	5 46.0	20 35.5

December 1930 LONGITUDE

Day	Sid.Time	☉	0 hr ☽	Noon ☽	True ☊	☿	♀	♂	⚳	♃	♄	♅	♆	♇
1 M	16 38 29	8♐34 53	8♈00 32	14♈07 22	22♈50.2	21♐56.6	24♏51.6	15♌02.0	0♎19.0	19♋36.9	10♑14.0	11♈36.6	5♍46.3	20♋34.6
2 Tu	16 42 25	9 35 43	20 18 13	26 33 35	22R50.5	23 27.4	24R 24.8	15 13.6	0 40.1	19R 32.2	10 20.4	11R 35.6	5 46.5	20R 33.7
3 W	16 46 22	10 36 33	2♉53 50	9♉19 17	22 49.0	24 57.8	24 00.1	15 24.7	1 01.0	19 27.5	10 26.9	11 34.7	5 46.7	20 32.8
4 Th	16 50 18	11 37 25	15 50 07	22 26 27	22 45.3	26 27.9	23 37.4	15 35.0	1 21.8	19 22.5	10 33.4	11 33.8	5 46.9	20 31.8
5 F	16 54 15	12 38 17	29 08 15	5♊55 22	22 39.4	27 57.6	23 17.1	15 44.8	1 42.4	19 17.4	10 39.9	11 33.0	5 47.0	20 30.9
6 Sa	16 58 11	13 39 11	12♊47 30	19 44 16	22 31.6	29 26.8	22 59.1	15 53.9	2 02.9	19 12.1	10 46.5	11 32.2	5 47.1	20 29.9
7 Su	17 02 08	14 40 05	26 45 08	3♋49 31	22 22.8	0♑55.5	22 43.4	16 02.4	2 23.2	19 06.6	10 53.1	11 31.5	5 47.2	20 28.9
8 M	17 06 05	15 41 01	10♋56 44	18 06 05	22 13.8	2 23.6	22 30.3	16 10.2	2 43.4	19 01.0	10 59.7	11 30.8	5R 47.2	20 27.9
9 Tu	17 10 01	16 41 58	25 16 51	2♌28 17	22 05.9	3 50.9	22 19.6	16 17.3	3 03.4	18 55.3	11 06.4	11 30.2	5 47.2	20 26.9
10 W	17 13 58	17 42 55	9♌39 46	16 50 42	21 59.9	5 17.3	22 11.5	16 23.7	3 23.2	18 49.4	11 13.1	11 29.6	5 47.2	20 25.9
11 Th	17 17 54	18 43 54	24 00 33	1♍08 54	21 56.2	6 42.7	22 05.8	16 29.4	3 42.8	18 43.3	11 19.8	11 29.1	5 47.1	20 24.8
12 F	17 21 51	19 44 54	8♍15 27	15 19 56	21D54.7	8 06.9	22D02.7	16 34.4	4 02.3	18 37.1	11 26.5	11 28.6	5 47.0	20 23.8
13 Sa	17 25 47	20 45 55	22 22 13	29 22 12	21 54.9	9 29.6	22 02.0	16 38.7	4 21.6	18 30.8	11 33.3	11 28.2	5 46.8	20 22.7
14 Su	17 29 44	21 46 58	6♎19 50	13♎15 08	21R55.6	10 50.6	22 03.8	16 42.3	4 40.7	18 24.3	11 40.1	11 27.8	5 46.6	20 21.6
15 M	17 33 40	22 48 01	20 08 06	26 58 44	21 55.7	12 09.6	22 08.0	16 45.0	4 59.6	18 17.7	11 47.0	11 27.4	5 46.4	20 20.5
16 Tu	17 37 37	23 49 05	3♏47 03	10♏33 01	21 54.1	13 26.2	22 14.6	16 47.0	5 18.3	18 11.0	11 53.8	11 27.1	5 46.2	20 19.4
17 W	17 41 34	24 50 10	17 16 35	23 57 42	21 49.9	14 40.2	22 23.4	16 48.3	5 36.8	18 04.1	12 00.7	11 26.9	5 45.9	20 18.2
18 Th	17 45 30	25 51 16	0♐36 13	7♐12 02	21 42.8	15 50.9	22 34.6	16R48.7	5 55.1	17 57.1	12 07.6	11 26.7	5 45.6	20 17.1
19 F	17 49 27	26 52 23	13 44 59	20 14 57	21 33.0	16 57.9	22 47.9	16 48.4	6 13.2	17 50.0	12 14.5	11 26.6	5 45.2	20 15.9
20 Sa	17 53 23	27 53 30	26 41 46	3♑05 19	21 21.1	18 00.6	23 03.3	16 47.2	6 31.1	17 42.9	12 21.5	11D26.5	5 44.9	20 14.8
21 Su	17 57 20	28 54 38	9♑25 30	15 42 18	21 08.2	18 58.3	23 20.8	16 45.3	6 48.8	17 35.6	12 28.5	11 26.5	5 44.4	20 13.6
22 M	18 01 16	29 55 46	21 55 42	28 05 47	20 55.5	19 50.3	23 40.3	16 42.5	7 06.3	17 28.2	12 35.5	11 26.5	5 44.0	20 12.4
23 Tu	18 05 13	0♑56 55	4♒12 41	10♒16 36	20 44.1	20 35.8	24 01.7	16 39.0	7 23.5	17 20.7	12 42.5	11 26.6	5 43.5	20 11.2
24 W	18 09 09	1 58 03	16 17 48	22 16 38	20 34.8	21 14.0	24 24.9	16 34.6	7 40.5	17 13.2	12 49.5	11 26.8	5 43.0	20 10.0
25 Th	18 13 06	2 59 12	28 13 31	4♓08 54	20 28.3	21 43.8	24 50.0	16 29.3	7 57.3	17 05.5	12 56.5	11 26.9	5 42.5	20 08.8
26 F	18 17 03	4 00 21	10♓03 20	15 57 23	20 24.4	22 04.5	25 16.8	16 23.3	8 13.9	16 57.8	13 03.5	11 27.2	5 41.9	20 07.6
27 Sa	18 20 59	5 01 30	21 51 39	27 46 48	20D22.8	22R15.2	25 45.3	16 16.4	8 30.2	16 50.0	13 10.6	11 27.5	5 41.3	20 06.3
28 Su	18 24 56	6 02 39	3♈43 32	9♈42 31	20R22.6	22 15.0	26 15.4	16 08.7	8 46.3	16 42.2	13 17.7	11 27.8	5 40.6	20 05.1
29 M	18 28 52	7 03 47	15 44 28	21 50 04	20 22.8	22 03.3	26 47.0	16 00.2	9 02.1	16 34.3	13 24.7	11 28.2	5 39.9	20 03.8
30 Tu	18 32 49	8 04 56	28 00 01	4♉14 54	20 22.0	21 39.9	27 20.2	15 50.9	9 17.7	16 26.4	13 31.8	11 28.6	5 39.2	20 02.6
31 W	18 36 45	9 06 05	10♉35 21	17 01 49	20 19.4	21 04.6	27 54.8	15 40.7	9 33.0	16 18.4	13 38.9	11 29.1	5 38.5	20 01.3

Astro Data	Dy Hr Mn
♀R	2 3:50
☽0N	3 7:38
♃∠♆	7 19:29
♃R	8 3:21
☽0S	16 14:16
♆∠♇	21 22:45
☽0N	30 15:49
♆R	8 20:17
♄□♅	12 18:48
♀D	13 6:23
☽0S	13 19:26
♂R	18 13:45
♅D	21 10:18
☽0N	27 23:22
☿R	27 23:40

Planet Ingress		Dy Hr Mn
☿	♐	17 5:31
♀	♏R	22 7:44
☉	♐	23 0:35
⚳	♎	30 14:34
☿	♑	6 20:57
☉	♑	22 13:40

Last Aspect Dy Hr Mn		☽ Ingress Dy Hr Mn
2 5:25	♇ △	♈ 2 23:34
4 16:13	♇ □	♉ 5 9:37
7 0:21	♇ ⚹	♊ 7 16:58
8 14:45	♅ ⚹	♋ 9 22:05
11 10:07	☿ △	♌ 12 1:45
13 19:38	☿ □	♍ 14 4:42
16 4:43	☿ ⚹	♎ 16 7:27
17 18:45	♇ □	♏ 18 10:36
20 10:21	☉ ☌	♐ 20 15:00
21 13:39	♂ △	♑ 22 21:42
25 4:00	♀ ⚹	♒ 25 7:23
27 13:15	♀ □	♓ 27 19:33
29 23:18	♀ △	♈ 30 8:06

Last Aspect Dy Hr Mn		☽ Ingress Dy Hr Mn
2 5:15	☿ △	♉ 2 18:32
4 14:04	♀ ☍	♊ 5 1:32
6 5:19	♂ ⚹	♋ 7 5:31
8 19:16	♀ △	♌ 9 7:53
10 20:53	♀ □	♍ 11 10:04
12 23:26	♀ ⚹	♎ 13 13:05
15 4:05	☉ ⚹	♏ 15 17:19
17 9:08	♀ ☌	♐ 17 22:54
20 1:24	☉ ☌	♑ 20 6:11
22 3:08	♀ ⚹	♒ 22 15:43
24 16:28	♀ □	♓ 25 3:35
27 7:43	♀ △	♈ 27 16:29
29 12:25	☿ □	♉ 30 3:52

☽ Phases & Eclipses Dy Hr Mn	
6 10:28	○ 13♉17
13 12:27	☾ 20♌25
20 10:21	● 27♏23
28 6:18	☽ 5♓18
6 0:40	○ 13♊10
12 20:07	☾ 20♍06
20 1:24	● 27♐26
28 3:59	☽ 5♈42

Astro Data

1 November 1930
Julian Day # 11262
SVP 6♓13'40"
GC 25♐52.4 ⚴ 29♌35.5
Eris 1♈22.1R ⚵ 28♑10.7
⚷ 16♉51.1R ⚶ 29♎36.8
☽ Mean ☊ 22♈48.9

1 December 1930
Julian Day # 11292
SVP 6♓13'35"
GC 25♐52.5 ⚴ 11♍35.0
Eris 1♈10.6R ⚵ 7♒51.4
⚷ 15♉21.7R ⚶ 15♏22.6
☽ Mean ☊ 21♈13.5

LONGITUDE — January 1931

Day	Sid.Time	☉	0 hr ☽	Noon ☽	True ☊	☿	♀	♂	⚳	♃	♄	♅	♆	♇
1 Th	18 40 42	10♑07 13	23♉34 44	0♊14 22	20♈14.2	20♑17.8	28♏30.8	15♌29.8	9♎48.1	16♋10.4	13♑46.0	11♈29.7	5♍37.7	20♋00.1
2 F	18 44 38	11 08 22	7♊00 50	13 54 07	20R 06.2	19R 20.6	29 08.1	15R 18.0	10 02.9	16R 02.3	13 53.1	11 30.3	5R 36.9	19R 58.8
3 Sa	18 48 35	12 09 30	20 54 00	28 00 04	19 55.8	18 14.2	29 46.8	15 05.5	10 17.5	15 54.3	14 00.2	11 30.9	5 36.1	19 57.6
4 Su	18 52 32	13 10 39	5♋11 45	12♋28 15	19 43.8	17 00.7	0♐26.6	14 52.1	10 31.8	15 46.2	14 07.3	11 31.6	5 35.3	19 56.3
5 M	18 56 28	14 11 47	19 48 40	27 11 58	19 31.6	15 42.3	1 07.7	14 38.0	10 45.8	15 38.1	14 14.4	11 32.4	5 34.4	19 55.0
6 Tu	19 00 25	15 12 55	4♌37 03	12♌02 48	19 20.5	14 21.6	1 49.9	14 23.2	10 59.5	15 30.0	14 21.5	11 33.2	5 33.5	19 53.7
7 W	19 04 21	16 14 03	19 28 08	26 52 01	19 11.6	13 01.2	2 33.2	14 07.6	11 13.0	15 21.9	14 28.6	11 34.1	5 32.5	19 52.5
8 Th	19 08 18	17 15 12	4♍13 35	11♍32 05	19 05.7	11 43.7	3 17.6	13 51.2	11 26.2	15 13.7	14 35.7	11 35.0	5 31.6	19 51.2
9 F	19 12 14	18 16 20	18 46 54	25 57 39	19 02.5	10 31.3	4 03.0	13 34.2	11 39.0	15 05.7	14 42.8	11 35.9	5 30.6	19 49.9
10 Sa	19 16 11	19 17 28	3♎04 02	10♎05 56	19 01.5	9 25.8	4 49.4	13 16.4	11 51.6	14 57.6	14 49.9	11 36.9	5 29.5	19 48.6
11 Su	19 20 08	20 18 36	17 03 21	23 56 21	19 01.4	8 28.5	5 36.7	12 58.0	12 03.9	14 49.5	14 57.0	11 38.0	5 28.5	19 47.3
12 M	19 24 04	21 19 44	0♏45 06	7♏29 48	19 00.9	7 40.5	6 25.0	12 39.0	12 15.9	14 41.5	15 04.1	11 39.1	5 27.4	19 46.0
13 Tu	19 28 01	22 20 53	14 10 41	20 47 59	18 58.6	7 02.1	7 14.1	12 19.3	12 27.5	14 33.5	15 11.2	11 40.2	5 26.3	19 44.7
14 W	19 31 57	23 22 01	27 21 57	3♐52 45	18 53.7	6 33.4	8 04.0	11 59.1	12 38.8	14 25.6	15 18.3	11 41.4	5 25.2	19 43.4
15 Th	19 35 54	24 23 09	10♐20 36	16 45 38	18 45.6	6 14.4	8 54.7	11 38.3	12 49.9	14 17.7	15 25.3	11 42.7	5 24.0	19 42.2
16 F	19 39 50	25 24 17	23 07 57	29 27 40	18 34.6	6D 04.6	9 46.2	11 17.0	13 00.5	14 09.8	15 32.4	11 44.0	5 22.9	19 40.9
17 Sa	19 43 47	26 25 24	5♑44 48	11♑59 26	18 21.2	6 03.6	10 38.4	10 55.3	13 10.9	14 02.0	15 39.4	11 45.4	5 21.7	19 39.6
18 Su	19 47 43	27 26 31	18 11 35	24 21 16	18 06.7	6 10.7	11 31.3	10 33.1	13 20.9	13 54.3	15 46.4	11 46.8	5 20.4	19 38.3
19 M	19 51 40	28 27 37	0♒28 32	6♒33 28	17 52.2	6 25.4	12 24.8	10 10.5	13 30.6	13 46.7	15 53.4	11 48.2	5 19.2	19 37.1
20 Tu	19 55 37	29 28 43	12 36 08	18 36 42	17 39.0	6 47.0	13 19.0	9 47.5	13 39.9	13 39.1	16 00.4	11 49.7	5 17.9	19 35.8
21 W	19 59 33	0♒29 48	24 35 18	0♓32 11	17 28.1	7 14.9	14 13.9	9 24.3	13 48.9	13 31.6	16 07.4	11 51.2	5 16.6	19 34.5
22 Th	20 03 30	1 30 52	6♓27 38	12 21 59	17 20.0	7 48.6	15 09.3	9 00.8	13 57.5	13 24.2	16 14.3	11 52.8	5 15.3	19 33.3
23 F	20 07 26	2 31 55	18 15 37	24 09 00	17 15.0	8 27.4	16 05.3	8 37.1	14 05.7	13 16.9	16 21.3	11 54.5	5 14.0	19 32.0
24 Sa	20 11 23	3 32 57	0♈02 37	5♈57 01	17D 12.5	9 11.0	17 01.8	8 13.2	14 13.6	13 09.7	16 28.2	11 56.1	5 12.6	19 30.8
25 Su	20 15 19	4 33 58	11 52 49	17 50 38	17 11.9	9 58.8	17 58.9	7 49.2	14 21.1	13 02.6	16 35.1	11 57.9	5 11.2	19 29.5
26 M	20 19 16	5 34 58	23 51 08	29 55 00	17R 12.2	10 50.4	18 56.5	7 25.2	14 28.2	12 55.7	16 42.0	11 59.6	5 09.9	19 28.3
27 Tu	20 23 12	6 35 56	6♉02 55	12♉15 34	17 12.2	11 45.6	19 54.5	7 01.1	14 35.0	12 48.8	16 48.8	12 01.5	5 08.4	19 27.1
28 W	20 27 09	7 36 54	18 33 38	24 57 42	17 10.7	12 43.9	20 53.1	6 37.1	14 41.4	12 42.0	16 55.6	12 03.3	5 07.0	19 25.8
29 Th	20 31 06	8 37 51	1♊28 21	8♊06 01	17 07.1	13 45.1	21 52.1	6 13.1	14 47.3	12 35.4	17 02.4	12 05.2	5 05.6	19 24.6
30 F	20 35 02	9 38 46	14 51 03	21 43 38	17 01.0	14 48.9	22 51.6	5 49.3	14 53.0	12 28.9	17 09.2	12 07.2	5 04.1	19 23.4
31 Sa	20 38 59	10 39 40	28 43 45	5♋51 13	16 52.6	15 55.1	23 51.4	5 25.6	14 58.2	12 22.6	17 15.9	12 09.2	5 02.6	19 22.2

LONGITUDE — February 1931

Day	Sid.Time	☉	0 hr ☽	Noon ☽	True ☊	☿	♀	♂	⚳	♃	♄	♅	♆	♇
1 Su	20 42 55	11♒40 33	13♋05 37	20♋26 18	16♈42.6	17♑03.5	24♐51.7	5♌02.2	15♎03.0	12♋16.4	17♑22.6	12♈11.2	5♍01.1	19♋21.1
2 M	20 46 52	12 41 25	27 52 26	5♌22 56	16R 32.3	18 13.9	25 52.4	4R 39.0	15 07.4	12R 10.3	17 29.3	12 13.3	4R 59.6	19R 19.9
3 Tu	20 50 48	13 42 15	12♌56 38	20 32 11	16 22.7	19 26.2	26 53.5	4 16.1	15 11.4	12 04.4	17 35.9	12 15.4	4 58.1	19 18.7
4 W	20 54 45	14 43 05	28 08 16	5♍43 33	16 15.1	20 40.2	27 55.0	3 53.5	15 15.0	11 58.6	17 42.5	12 17.5	4 56.6	19 17.6
5 Th	20 58 41	15 43 53	13♍16 46	20 46 48	16 10.1	21 55.9	28 56.8	3 31.3	15 18.2	11 52.9	17 49.1	12 19.7	4 55.0	19 16.4
6 F	21 02 38	16 44 40	28 12 43	5♎33 44	16D 07.6	23 13.0	29 58.9	3 09.5	15 20.9	11 47.4	17 55.7	12 21.9	4 53.4	19 15.3
7 Sa	21 06 35	17 45 26	12♎49 17	19 59 00	16 07.2	24 31.5	1♑01.4	2 48.2	15 23.3	11 42.1	18 02.2	12 24.2	4 51.9	19 14.2
8 Su	21 10 31	18 46 12	27 02 43	4♏00 23	16 07.9	25 51.4	2 04.3	2 27.3	15 25.2	11 37.0	18 08.6	12 26.5	4 50.3	19 13.1
9 M	21 14 28	19 46 56	10♏52 06	17 38 05	16R 08.5	27 12.5	3 07.4	2 07.0	15 26.7	11 32.0	18 15.1	12 28.9	4 48.7	19 12.0
10 Tu	21 18 24	20 47 40	24 18 35	0♐53 58	16 08.0	28 34.9	4 10.9	1 47.2	15 27.8	11 27.1	18 21.4	12 31.3	4 47.1	19 10.9
11 W	21 22 21	21 48 22	7♐24 36	13 50 50	16 05.5	29 58.4	5 14.6	1 28.0	15R 28.4	11 22.5	18 27.8	12 33.7	4 45.4	19 09.9
12 Th	21 26 17	22 49 03	20 13 05	26 31 41	16 00.7	1♒23.0	6 18.6	1 09.4	15 28.6	11 18.0	18 34.1	12 36.1	4 43.8	19 08.8
13 F	21 30 14	23 49 44	2♑46 59	8♑59 19	15 53.5	2 48.7	7 22.9	0 51.4	15 28.4	11 13.7	18 40.4	12 38.6	4 42.2	19 07.8
14 Sa	21 34 10	24 50 23	15 08 58	21 16 10	15 44.6	4 15.5	8 27.5	0 34.1	15 27.7	11 09.6	18 46.6	12 41.2	4 40.6	19 06.8
15 Su	21 38 07	25 51 00	27 21 11	3♒24 13	15 34.6	5 43.2	9 32.2	0 17.5	15 26.6	11 05.6	18 52.8	12 43.7	4 38.9	19 05.8
16 M	21 42 04	26 51 36	9♒25 28	15 25 05	15 24.6	7 12.0	10 37.3	0 01.6	15 25.1	11 01.8	18 58.9	12 46.3	4 37.2	19 04.8
17 Tu	21 46 00	27 52 11	21 23 16	27 20 10	15 15.5	8 41.7	11 42.5	29♋46.4	15 23.1	10 58.3	19 05.0	12 48.9	4 35.6	19 03.8
18 W	21 49 57	28 52 44	3♓16 00	9♓10 57	15 08.1	10 12.4	12 48.0	29 31.9	15 20.7	10 54.9	19 11.0	12 51.6	4 33.9	19 02.8
19 Th	21 53 53	29 53 16	15 05 15	20 59 08	15 02.8	11 44.1	13 53.7	29 18.2	15 17.8	10 51.7	19 17.0	12 54.3	4 32.3	19 01.9
20 F	21 57 50	0♓53 46	26 52 54	2♈46 53	14 59.7	13 16.7	14 59.6	29 05.3	15 14.5	10 48.6	19 22.9	12 57.0	4 30.6	19 01.0
21 Sa	22 01 46	1 54 14	8♈41 26	14 36 57	14D 58.8	14 50.3	16 05.7	28 53.2	15 10.8	10 45.8	19 28.8	12 59.8	4 28.9	19 00.1
22 Su	22 05 43	2 54 40	20 33 54	26 32 44	14 59.4	16 24.9	17 12.0	28 41.8	15 06.6	10 43.2	19 34.6	13 02.6	4 27.2	18 59.2
23 M	22 09 39	3 55 05	2♉34 00	8♉38 14	15 00.9	18 00.4	18 18.5	28 31.2	15 02.0	10 40.8	19 40.4	13 05.4	4 25.5	18 58.3
24 Tu	22 13 36	4 55 27	14 46 01	20 57 56	15 02.5	19 36.8	19 25.1	28 21.5	14 57.0	10 38.5	19 46.1	13 08.2	4 23.9	18 57.5
25 W	22 17 33	5 55 48	27 14 35	3♊36 32	15R 03.3	21 14.3	20 31.9	28 12.5	14 51.6	10 36.5	19 51.7	13 11.1	4 22.2	18 56.7
26 Th	22 21 29	6 56 07	10♊04 20	16 38 28	15 02.9	22 52.7	21 38.9	28 04.3	14 45.8	10 34.7	19 57.3	13 14.0	4 20.5	18 55.8
27 F	22 25 26	7 56 23	23 19 23	0♋07 22	15 00.8	24 32.1	22 46.1	27 57.0	14 39.5	10 33.0	20 02.9	13 16.9	4 18.8	18 55.1
28 Sa	22 29 22	8 56 38	7♋02 36	14 05 09	14 57.2	26 12.6	23 53.4	27 50.4	14 32.9	10 31.6	20 08.4	13 19.9	4 17.2	18 54.3

Astro Data

	Dy Hr Mn
☽0S	10 0:11
♃☍♄	11 0:07
☿D	17 2:51
☽0N	24 5:47
♃□♅	2 3:12
☽0S	6 7:22
⚳R	12 11:17
♄☍♇	17 8:00
☽0N	20 11:34
♄⚼♆	21 12:22

Planet Ingress

	Dy Hr Mn
♀ ♐	3 20:03
☉ ♒	21 0:18
♀ ♑	6 12:25
☿ ♒	11 12:27
♂ ♋R	16 14:27
☉ ♓	19 14:40

Last Aspect / ☽ Ingress (January)

Last Aspect Dy Hr Mn		☽ Ingress Dy Hr Mn
1 8:46	♀ ☍	♊ 1 11:34
2 14:23	♂ ⚹	♋ 3 15:21
5 0:11	♇ ☌	♌ 5 16:32
6 15:43	♂ ☌	♍ 7 17:06
9 1:46	♇ ⚹	♎ 9 18:48
11 5:09	☉ □	♏ 11 22:40
13 15:03	☉ ⚹	♐ 14 4:51
15 2:40	♂ △	♑ 16 13:02
18 18:36	☉ ☌	♒ 18 23:04
20 0:34	♀ ⚹	♓ 21 10:55
23 2:37	♇ △	♈ 23 23:55
25 15:18	♇ □	♉ 26 12:10
28 1:40	♇ ⚹	♊ 28 21:18
30 14:06	♀ ☍	♋ 31 2:09

Last Aspect / ☽ Ingress (February)

Last Aspect Dy Hr Mn		☽ Ingress Dy Hr Mn
1 10:14	♇ ☌	♌ 2 3:25
3 22:45	♀ △	♍ 4 2:56
6 2:11	♀ □	♎ 6 2:54
7 20:30	☿ □	♏ 8 5:04
10 7:16	☿ ⚹	♐ 10 10:21
12 4:19	☉ ⚹	♑ 12 18:39
14 7:46	♇ ☍	♒ 15 5:15
17 13:11	☉ ☌	♓ 17 17:23
20 4:37	♂ △	♈ 20 6:21
22 16:14	♂ □	♉ 22 18:54
25 1:57	♂ ⚹	♊ 25 5:13
27 0:46	☿ △	♋ 27 11:47

☽ Phases & Eclipses

Dy Hr Mn	
4 13:15	○ 13♋14
11 5:09	☾ 20♎01
18 18:36	● 27♑43
27 0:05	☽ 6♉06
3 0:26	○ 13♌13
9 16:10	☾ 19♏57
17 13:11	● 27♒55
25 16:42	☽ 6♊08

Astro Data

1 January 1931
Julian Day # 11323
SVP 6♓13'29"
GC 25♐52.5 ⚵ 18♍29.6
Eris 1♈09.4 ✱ 20♒24.2
⚷ 14♉15.6R ⚶ 1♐28.7
☽ Mean ☊ 19♈35.1

1 February 1931
Julian Day # 11354
SVP 6♓13'23"
GC 25♐52.6 ⚵ 16♍49.5R
Eris 1♈19.7 ✱ 4♓40.7
⚷ 14♉02.4 ⚶ 16♐55.8
☽ Mean ☊ 17♈56.6

March 1931 — LONGITUDE

Day	Sid.Time	☉	0 hr ☽	Noon ☽	True ☊	☿	♀	♂	⚳	♃	♄	♅	♆	♇
1 Su	22 33 19	9♓56 51	21♋14 49	28♋31 16	14♈52.4	27♒54.0	25♑00.9	27♋44.6	14♎25.8	10♋30.3	20♑13.8	13♈22.9	4♍15.5	18♋53.5
2 M	22 37 15	10 57 01	5♌53 56	13♌22 03	14R 47.2	29 36.5	26 08.5	27R 39.6	14R 18.4	10R 29.3	20 19.2	13 25.9	4R 13.8	18R 52.8
3 Tu	22 41 12	11 57 10	20 54 38	28 30 34	14 42.4	1♓20.1	27 16.3	27 35.4	14 10.5	10 28.4	20 24.5	13 28.9	4 12.2	18 52.1
4 W	22 45 08	12 57 17	6♍08 34	13♍47 20	14 38.5	3 04.6	28 24.2	27 32.0	14 02.3	10 27.7	20 29.7	13 31.9	4 10.5	18 51.4
5 Th	22 49 05	13 57 21	21 25 29	29 01 46	14 36.2	4 50.3	29 32.3	27 29.3	13 53.7	10 27.3	20 34.9	13 35.0	4 08.9	18 50.8
6 F	22 53 02	14 57 24	6♎34 56	14♎03 56	14D 35.4	6 37.1	0♒40.5	27 27.4	13 44.8	10D 27.0	20 40.0	13 38.1	4 07.2	18 50.1
7 Sa	22 56 58	15 57 26	21 27 52	28 46 02	14 35.9	8 25.0	1 48.8	27 26.2	13 35.5	10 26.9	20 45.0	13 41.2	4 05.6	18 49.5
8 Su	23 00 55	16 57 26	5♏57 55	13♏03 12	14 37.3	10 13.9	2 57.3	27D 25.8	13 25.8	10 27.1	20 50.0	13 44.3	4 04.0	18 48.9
9 M	23 04 51	17 57 24	20 01 43	26 53 30	14 38.8	12 04.0	4 05.9	27 26.1	13 15.9	10 27.4	20 54.9	13 47.5	4 02.3	18 48.3
10 Tu	23 08 48	18 57 20	3♐38 41	10♐17 30	14R 40.0	13 55.2	5 14.6	27 27.1	13 05.6	10 27.9	20 59.7	13 50.7	4 00.7	18 47.7
11 W	23 12 44	19 57 15	16 50 19	23 17 30	14 40.2	15 47.6	6 23.4	27 28.9	12 54.9	10 28.6	21 04.5	13 53.9	3 59.1	18 47.2
12 Th	23 16 41	20 57 09	29 39 31	5♑56 50	14 39.3	17 41.0	7 32.4	27 31.3	12 44.0	10 29.5	21 09.2	13 57.1	3 57.5	18 46.7
13 F	23 20 37	21 57 00	12♑09 55	18 19 16	14 37.3	19 35.5	8 41.4	27 34.5	12 32.8	10 30.6	21 13.8	14 00.3	3 55.9	18 46.2
14 Sa	23 24 34	22 56 50	24 25 19	0♒28 33	14 34.5	21 31.0	9 50.6	27 38.3	12 21.3	10 31.9	21 18.4	14 03.5	3 54.4	18 45.7
15 Su	23 28 31	23 56 38	6♒29 24	12 28 15	14 31.1	23 27.5	10 59.9	27 42.9	12 09.5	10 33.4	21 22.9	14 06.8	3 52.8	18 45.3
16 M	23 32 27	24 56 24	18 25 30	24 21 30	14 27.7	25 25.0	12 09.2	27 48.0	11 57.5	10 35.1	21 27.3	14 10.1	3 51.3	18 44.9
17 Tu	23 36 24	25 56 09	0♓16 34	6♓11 01	14 24.6	27 23.4	13 18.7	27 53.9	11 45.2	10 37.0	21 31.6	14 13.4	3 49.7	18 44.5
18 W	23 40 20	26 55 51	12 05 08	17 59 11	14 22.2	29 22.5	14 28.2	28 00.4	11 32.7	10 39.0	21 35.9	14 16.7	3 48.2	18 44.1
19 Th	23 44 17	27 55 32	23 53 27	29 48 10	14 20.6	1♈22.3	15 37.9	28 07.5	11 20.0	10 41.3	21 40.0	14 20.0	3 46.7	18 43.7
20 F	23 48 13	28 55 10	5♈43 36	11♈40 00	14D 20.0	3 22.6	16 47.6	28 15.3	11 07.2	10 43.7	21 44.1	14 23.3	3 45.2	18 43.4
21 Sa	23 52 10	29 54 46	17 37 38	23 36 47	14 20.2	5 23.3	17 57.4	28 23.6	10 54.1	10 46.3	21 48.1	14 26.7	3 43.7	18 43.1
22 Su	23 56 06	0♈54 21	29 37 44	5♉40 50	14 21.0	7 24.1	19 07.2	28 32.6	10 40.9	10 49.2	21 52.1	14 30.0	3 42.3	18 42.8
23 M	0 00 03	1 53 53	11♉46 23	17 54 45	14 22.1	9 24.9	20 17.2	28 42.2	10 27.6	10 52.2	21 55.9	14 33.4	3 40.8	18 42.6
24 Tu	0 04 00	2 53 23	24 06 18	0♊21 26	14 23.3	11 25.3	21 27.2	28 52.3	10 14.1	10 55.3	21 59.7	14 36.7	3 39.4	18 42.3
25 W	0 07 56	3 52 50	6♊40 32	13 04 00	14 24.2	13 25.0	22 37.3	29 03.0	10 00.6	10 58.7	22 03.4	14 40.1	3 38.0	18 42.1
26 Th	0 11 53	4 52 16	19 32 13	26 05 34	14R 24.8	15 23.8	23 47.5	29 14.3	9 46.9	11 02.2	22 07.0	14 43.5	3 36.6	18 42.0
27 F	0 15 49	5 51 39	2♋44 22	9♋28 54	14 24.9	17 21.3	24 57.7	29 26.1	9 33.2	11 06.0	22 10.5	14 46.9	3 35.2	18 41.8
28 Sa	0 19 46	6 51 00	16 19 22	23 15 53	14 24.6	19 17.1	26 08.0	29 38.4	9 19.5	11 09.9	22 14.0	14 50.3	3 33.9	18 41.7
29 Su	0 23 42	7 50 18	0♌18 27	7♌26 55	14 24.0	21 10.7	27 18.4	29 51.3	9 05.7	11 13.9	22 17.3	14 53.7	3 32.6	18 41.6
30 M	0 27 39	8 49 34	14 41 02	22 00 21	14 23.4	23 01.9	28 28.8	0♌04.6	8 51.9	11 18.2	22 20.6	14 57.1	3 31.3	18 41.5
31 Tu	0 31 35	9 48 48	29 24 16	6♍52 03	14 22.8	24 50.2	29 39.3	0 18.5	8 38.2	11 22.6	22 23.8	15 00.6	3 30.0	18 41.4

April 1931 — LONGITUDE

Day	Sid.Time	☉	0 hr ☽	Noon ☽	True ☊	☿	♀	♂	⚳	♃	♄	♅	♆	♇
1 W	0 35 32	10♈47 59	14♍22 47	21♍55 28	14♈22.4	26♈35.1	0♓49.8	0♌32.8	8♎24.4	11♋27.2	22♑26.9	15♈04.0	3♍28.7	18♋41.4
2 Th	0 39 29	11 47 08	29 29 00	7♎02 14	14D 22.3	28 16.4	2 00.4	0 47.6	8R 10.7	11 31.9	22 29.9	15 07.4	3R 27.4	18D 41.4
3 F	0 43 25	12 46 15	14♎34 03	22 02 18	14 22.3	29 53.6	3 11.1	1 02.8	7 57.1	11 36.8	22 32.8	15 10.8	3 26.2	18 41.4
4 Sa	0 47 22	13 45 21	29 28 59	6♏50 10	14R 22.3	1♉26.4	4 21.8	1 18.5	7 43.5	11 41.9	22 35.6	15 14.3	3 25.0	18 41.4
5 Su	0 51 18	14 44 24	14♏06 05	21 16 06	14 22.3	2 54.5	5 32.6	1 34.7	7 30.0	11 47.1	22 38.4	15 17.7	3 23.8	18 41.5
6 M	0 55 15	15 43 26	28 19 47	5♐16 52	14 22.2	4 17.5	6 43.4	1 51.3	7 16.6	11 52.6	22 41.0	15 21.1	3 22.7	18 41.6
7 Tu	0 59 11	16 42 25	12♐07 11	18 50 48	14 22.0	5 35.4	7 54.3	2 08.3	7 03.4	11 58.1	22 43.6	15 24.5	3 21.6	18 41.7
8 W	1 03 08	17 41 23	25 27 50	1♑58 35	14 21.8	6 47.7	9 05.2	2 25.7	6 50.3	12 03.8	22 46.1	15 28.0	3 20.5	18 41.8
9 Th	1 07 04	18 40 20	8♑23 24	14 42 42	14D 21.7	7 54.3	10 16.2	2 43.5	6 37.3	12 09.7	22 48.4	15 31.4	3 19.4	18 42.0
10 F	1 11 01	19 39 14	20 57 00	27 06 49	14 21.7	8 55.2	11 27.3	3 01.7	6 24.6	12 15.7	22 50.7	15 34.8	3 18.3	18 42.2
11 Sa	1 14 58	20 38 07	3♒12 41	9♒15 12	14 22.0	9 50.0	12 38.4	3 20.3	6 12.0	12 21.9	22 52.9	15 38.3	3 17.3	18 42.4
12 Su	1 18 54	21 36 58	15 14 54	21 12 22	14 22.6	10 38.7	13 49.5	3 39.3	5 59.6	12 28.2	22 55.0	15 41.7	3 16.3	18 42.6
13 M	1 22 51	22 35 47	27 08 07	3♓02 42	14 23.5	11 21.2	15 00.7	3 58.6	5 47.4	12 34.7	22 57.0	15 45.1	3 15.3	18 42.9
14 Tu	1 26 47	23 34 35	8♓56 35	14 50 16	14 24.4	11 57.4	16 11.9	4 18.3	5 35.5	12 41.4	22 58.9	15 48.5	3 14.3	18 43.2
15 W	1 30 44	24 33 20	20 44 09	26 38 40	14 25.2	12 27.3	17 23.2	4 38.4	5 23.8	12 48.1	23 00.7	15 51.9	3 13.4	18 43.5
16 Th	1 34 40	25 32 04	2♈34 11	8♈31 01	14R 25.7	12 50.9	18 34.5	4 58.8	5 12.4	12 55.0	23 02.4	15 55.3	3 12.5	18 43.8
17 F	1 38 37	26 30 45	14 29 30	20 29 53	14 25.7	13 08.2	19 45.8	5 19.6	5 01.2	13 02.1	23 04.1	15 58.7	3 11.7	18 44.2
18 Sa	1 42 33	27 29 25	26 32 25	2♉37 20	14 25.0	13 19.3	20 57.2	5 40.7	4 50.4	13 09.3	23 05.6	16 02.1	3 10.8	18 44.6
19 Su	1 46 30	28 28 03	8♉44 50	14 55 05	14 23.7	13R 24.3	22 08.6	6 02.1	4 39.8	13 16.6	23 07.0	16 05.5	3 10.0	18 45.0
20 M	1 50 26	29 26 39	21 08 16	27 24 31	14 21.8	13 23.2	23 20.1	6 23.9	4 29.6	13 24.1	23 08.3	16 08.8	3 09.2	18 45.4
21 Tu	1 54 23	0♉25 13	3♊43 59	10♊06 49	14 19.5	13 16.5	24 31.5	6 46.0	4 19.7	13 31.7	23 09.6	16 12.2	3 08.5	18 45.8
22 W	1 58 20	1 23 45	16 33 09	23 03 06	14 17.1	13 04.3	25 43.1	7 08.4	4 10.1	13 39.5	23 10.7	16 15.5	3 07.7	18 46.3
23 Th	2 02 16	2 22 15	29 36 48	6♋14 23	14 15.1	12 46.9	26 54.6	7 31.0	4 00.8	13 47.4	23 11.7	16 18.9	3 07.0	18 46.8
24 F	2 06 13	3 20 43	12♋55 57	19 41 36	14 13.7	12 24.8	28 06.2	7 54.0	3 51.9	13 55.4	23 12.7	16 22.2	3 06.4	18 47.4
25 Sa	2 10 09	4 19 08	26 31 23	3♌25 22	14D 13.2	11 58.4	29 17.7	8 17.3	3 43.4	14 03.5	23 13.5	16 25.5	3 05.7	18 47.9
26 Su	2 14 06	5 17 31	10♌23 31	17 25 47	14 13.6	11 28.3	0♈29.4	8 40.8	3 35.2	14 11.8	23 14.3	16 28.8	3 05.1	18 48.5
27 M	2 18 02	6 15 53	24 32 02	1♍42 02	14 14.7	10 55.1	1 41.0	9 04.7	3 27.4	14 20.1	23 14.9	16 32.1	3 04.6	18 49.1
28 Tu	2 21 59	7 14 12	8♍55 30	16 12 01	14 16.0	10 19.4	2 52.7	9 28.8	3 20.0	14 28.6	23 15.4	16 35.4	3 04.0	18 49.7
29 W	2 25 55	8 12 28	23 31 06	0♎52 08	14R 17.2	9 41.8	4 04.4	9 53.1	3 12.9	14 37.3	23 15.9	16 38.6	3 03.5	18 50.3
30 Th	2 29 52	9 10 43	8♎14 25	15 37 12	14 17.6	9 03.1	5 16.1	10 17.7	3 06.3	14 46.0	23 16.2	16 41.8	3 03.0	18 51.0

Astro Data

	Dy Hr Mn
☽ 0S	5 17:33
♃ D	7 8:40
♂ D	8 13:52
☽ 0N	19 17:28
☿ 0N	19 23:02
☉ 0N	21 14:06
♆∠♇	22 0:44
☽ 0S	2 4:49
♇ D	2 11:24
☽ 0N	15 23:54
☿ R	19 19:52
♀ 0N	29 4:15
☽ 0S	29 14:38

Planet Ingress

		Dy Hr Mn
☿	♓	2 17:28
♀	♒	5 21:46
☿	♈	18 19:31
☉	♈	21 14:06
♂	♌	30 3:48
♀	♓	31 19:04
☿	♉	3 13:38
☉	♉	21 1:40
♀	♈	26 2:10

Last Aspect / ☽ Ingress

Last Aspect Dy Hr Mn		☽ Ingress	Dy Hr Mn
1 10:44	♂ ☌	♌	1 14:25
2 12:06	♅ △	♍	3 14:21
5 12:52	♀ △	♎	5 13:32
7 9:48	♂ □	♏	7 14:03
9 12:58	♂ △	♐	9 17:30
11 5:15	☉ □	♑	12 0:39
14 6:20	♂ ☍	♒	14 11:03
15 15:19	♅ ⚹	♓	16 23:26
19 8:34	♂ △	♈	19 12:24
21 21:40	♂ □	♉	22 0:44
24 9:07	♂ ⚹	♊	24 11:19
26 7:24	♀ △	♋	26 19:04
28 23:02	♂ ☌	♌	28 23:29
30 23:24	♀ ☍	♍	31 0:58

Last Aspect / ☽ Ingress

Last Aspect Dy Hr Mn		☽ Ingress	Dy Hr Mn
1 12:50	♄ △	♎	2 0:49
3 12:48	♄ □	♏	4 0:50
5 14:19	♄ ⚹	♐	6 2:52
7 7:52	☉ △	♑	8 8:20
10 3:39	♄ ☌	♒	10 17:40
12 12:54	☉ ⚹	♓	13 5:49
15 4:36	♄ ⚹	♈	15 18:48
18 1:00	☉ ☌	♉	18 6:50
20 3:50	♄ △	♊	20 16:56
22 17:23	♀ □	♋	23 0:42
25 4:09	♀ △	♌	25 6:04
26 10:23	♅ △	♍	27 9:10
28 23:35	♄ △	♎	29 10:35

☽ Phases & Eclipses

Dy Hr Mn		
4 10:36	○	12♍54
11 5:15	☾	19♐40
19 7:51	●	27♓45
27 5:04	☽	5♋34
2 20:05	○	12♎07
2 20:08	•	T 1.502
9 20:15	☾	19♑01
18 1:00	●	27♈03
18 0:45:10	•	P 0.511
25 13:40	☽	4♌23

Astro Data

1 March 1931
Julian Day # 11382
SVP 6♓13'19"
GC 25♐52.7 ⚴ 8♍32.5R
Eris 1♈36.5 ⚵ 18♓36.0
⚷ 14♉41.3 ⚶ 29♐46.7
☽ Mean ☊ 16♈27.7

1 April 1931
Julian Day # 11413
SVP 6♓13'16"
GC 25♐52.7 ⚴ 0♍56.1R
Eris 1♈59.0 ⚵ 4♈48.6
⚷ 16♉11.0 ⚶ 11♑50.9
☽ Mean ☊ 14♈49.1

LONGITUDE May 1931

Day	Sid.Time	☉	0 hr ☽	Noon ☽	True ☊	☿	♀	♂	⚳	♃	♄	♅	♆	♇
1 F	2 33 49	10♉08 56	22♎59 37	0♏20 50	14♈16.9	8♉24.1	6♈27.8	10♌42.5	3♎00.0	14♋54.8	23♑16.5	16♈45.1	3♍02.6	18♋51.7
2 Sa	2 37 45	11 07 07	7♏39 57	14 56 07	14R 14.8	7R 45.3	7 39.6	11 07.6	2R 54.1	15 03.8	23 16.6	16 48.3	3R 02.2	18 52.4
3 Su	2 41 42	12 05 17	22 08 32	29 16 29	14 11.5	7 07.5	8 51.4	11 33.0	2 48.6	15 12.9	23R 16.7	16 51.5	3 01.8	18 53.1
4 M	2 45 38	13 03 25	6♐19 22	13♐16 41	14 07.4	6 31.3	10 03.3	11 58.5	2 43.5	15 22.1	23 16.7	16 54.6	3 01.4	18 53.8
5 Tu	2 49 35	14 01 32	20 08 06	26 53 23	14 02.9	5 57.3	11 15.1	12 24.3	2 38.9	15 31.4	23 16.5	16 57.8	3 01.1	18 54.6
6 W	2 53 31	14 59 37	3♑32 29	10♑05 27	13 58.7	5 26.1	12 27.0	12 50.3	2 34.6	15 40.8	23 16.3	17 00.9	3 00.8	18 55.4
7 Th	2 57 28	15 57 40	16 32 28	22 53 50	13 55.4	4 58.1	13 38.9	13 16.6	2 30.7	15 50.3	23 16.0	17 04.0	3 00.5	18 56.2
8 F	3 01 25	16 55 42	29 09 56	5♒21 13	13 53.3	4 33.7	14 50.9	13 43.0	2 27.2	15 59.9	23 15.5	17 07.1	3 00.3	18 57.1
9 Sa	3 05 21	17 53 43	11♒28 14	17 31 31	13D 52.6	4 13.2	16 02.9	14 09.7	2 24.2	16 09.6	23 15.0	17 10.2	3 00.1	18 57.9
10 Su	3 09 18	18 51 43	23 31 42	29 29 24	13 53.1	3 56.9	17 14.9	14 36.5	2 21.5	16 19.4	23 14.4	17 13.2	3 00.0	18 58.8
11 M	3 13 14	19 49 41	5♓25 14	11♓19 51	13 54.5	3 45.0	18 26.9	15 03.6	2 19.2	16 29.4	23 13.7	17 16.3	2 59.8	18 59.7
12 Tu	3 17 11	20 47 37	17 13 52	23 07 53	13 56.2	3 37.6	19 38.9	15 30.9	2 17.4	16 39.4	23 12.8	17 19.3	2 59.7	19 00.6
13 W	3 21 07	21 45 33	29 02 28	4♈58 12	13R 57.5	3D 34.8	20 51.0	15 58.4	2 16.0	16 49.5	23 11.9	17 22.2	2 59.7	19 01.5
14 Th	3 25 04	22 43 27	10♈55 34	16 55 01	13 57.9	3 36.6	22 03.1	16 26.1	2 14.9	16 59.7	23 10.9	17 25.2	2D 59.6	19 02.5
15 F	3 29 00	23 41 19	22 57 00	29 01 52	13 56.7	3 43.1	23 15.2	16 54.0	2 14.3	17 10.0	23 09.8	17 28.1	2 59.6	19 03.5
16 Sa	3 32 57	24 39 11	5♉09 55	11♉21 24	13 53.6	3 54.1	24 27.3	17 22.0	2D 14.1	17 20.4	23 08.6	17 31.0	2 59.7	19 04.4
17 Su	3 36 53	25 37 01	17 36 30	23 55 19	13 48.7	4 09.7	25 39.4	17 50.3	2 14.3	17 30.9	23 07.3	17 33.9	2 59.7	19 05.5
18 M	3 40 50	26 34 49	0♊17 57	6♊44 22	13 42.3	4 29.6	26 51.6	18 18.7	2 14.9	17 41.4	23 05.9	17 36.8	2 59.8	19 06.5
19 Tu	3 44 47	27 32 37	13 14 32	19 48 20	13 34.9	4 54.0	28 03.8	18 47.3	2 15.9	17 52.1	23 04.5	17 39.6	2 59.9	19 07.5
20 W	3 48 43	28 30 23	26 25 40	3♋06 20	13 27.5	5 22.5	29 16.0	19 16.1	2 17.3	18 02.8	23 02.9	17 42.4	3 00.1	19 08.6
21 Th	3 52 40	29 28 07	9♋50 11	16 37 00	13 20.8	5 55.1	0♉28.2	19 45.1	2 19.1	18 13.7	23 01.2	17 45.2	3 00.3	19 09.7
22 F	3 56 36	0♊25 50	23 26 36	0♌18 48	13 15.5	6 31.8	1 40.4	20 14.2	2 21.3	18 24.6	22 59.5	17 47.9	3 00.5	19 10.8
23 Sa	4 00 33	1 23 31	7♌13 26	14 10 20	13 12.2	7 12.3	2 52.6	20 43.6	2 23.8	18 35.6	22 57.7	17 50.6	3 00.8	19 11.9
24 Su	4 04 29	2 21 10	21 09 21	28 10 21	13D 10.9	7 56.6	4 04.9	21 13.0	2 26.8	18 46.6	22 55.7	17 53.3	3 01.1	19 13.1
25 M	4 08 26	3 18 48	5♍13 11	12♍17 44	13 11.1	8 44.5	5 17.2	21 42.6	2 30.1	18 57.8	22 53.7	17 55.9	3 01.4	19 14.2
26 Tu	4 12 23	4 16 25	19 23 49	26 31 14	13 12.1	9 35.9	6 29.5	22 12.4	2 33.9	19 09.0	22 51.6	17 58.6	3 01.8	19 15.4
27 W	4 16 19	5 14 00	3♎39 47	10♎49 10	13R 12.7	10 30.8	7 41.8	22 42.4	2 38.0	19 20.3	22 49.4	18 01.1	3 02.2	19 16.6
28 Th	4 20 16	6 11 33	17 59 02	25 09 00	13 12.2	11 29.0	8 54.1	23 12.4	2 42.4	19 31.6	22 47.2	18 03.7	3 02.6	19 17.8
29 F	4 24 12	7 09 05	2♏18 35	9♏27 18	13 09.6	12 30.5	10 06.4	23 42.7	2 47.2	19 43.1	22 44.8	18 06.2	3 03.1	19 19.0
30 Sa	4 28 09	8 06 36	16 34 32	23 39 45	13 04.7	13 35.1	11 18.8	24 13.0	2 52.4	19 54.6	22 42.4	18 08.7	3 03.6	19 20.2
31 Su	4 32 05	9 04 06	0♐42 18	7♐41 38	12 57.6	14 42.8	12 31.1	24 43.6	2 58.0	20 06.1	22 39.9	18 11.2	3 04.1	19 21.5

LONGITUDE June 1931

Day	Sid.Time	☉	0 hr ☽	Noon ☽	True ☊	☿	♀	♂	⚳	♃	♄	♅	♆	♇
1 M	4 36 02	10♊01 35	14♐37 10	21♐28 27	12♈48.7	15♉53.6	13♉43.5	25♌14.2	3♎03.9	20♋17.8	22♑37.3	18♈13.6	3♍04.6	19♋22.7
2 Tu	4 39 58	10 59 03	28 15 04	4♑56 42	12R 39.1	17 07.4	14 55.9	25 45.0	3 10.1	20 29.5	22R 34.6	18 16.0	3 05.2	19 24.0
3 W	4 43 55	11 56 30	11♑33 08	18 04 18	12 29.7	18 24.1	16 08.4	26 15.9	3 16.7	20 41.2	22 31.9	18 18.3	3 05.8	19 25.3
4 Th	4 47 52	12 53 56	24 30 12	0♒50 59	12 21.6	19 43.6	17 20.8	26 47.0	3 23.6	20 53.1	22 29.0	18 20.7	3 06.5	19 26.6
5 F	4 51 48	13 51 21	7♒06 52	13 18 13	12 15.3	21 06.1	18 33.3	27 18.2	3 30.9	21 04.9	22 26.1	18 22.9	3 07.2	19 27.9
6 Sa	4 55 45	14 48 46	19 25 25	25 28 58	12 11.2	22 31.3	19 45.8	27 49.5	3 38.4	21 16.9	22 23.2	18 25.2	3 07.9	19 29.3
7 Su	4 59 41	15 46 10	1♓29 26	7♓27 23	12D 09.2	23 59.3	20 58.3	28 20.9	3 46.3	21 28.9	22 20.1	18 27.4	3 08.6	19 30.6
8 M	5 03 38	16 43 33	13 23 27	19 18 19	12 08.9	25 30.1	22 10.8	28 52.5	3 54.6	21 41.0	22 17.0	18 29.6	3 09.4	19 32.0
9 Tu	5 07 34	17 40 56	25 12 38	1♈07 04	12R 09.4	27 03.7	23 23.4	29 24.2	4 03.1	21 53.1	22 13.8	18 31.7	3 10.2	19 33.4
10 W	5 11 31	18 38 18	7♈02 19	12 59 01	12 09.7	28 40.0	24 36.0	29 56.1	4 11.9	22 05.2	22 10.6	18 33.8	3 11.0	19 34.7
11 Th	5 15 27	19 35 40	18 57 48	24 59 15	12 08.9	0♊19.0	25 48.6	0♍28.0	4 21.1	22 17.5	22 07.2	18 35.8	3 11.9	19 36.1
12 F	5 19 24	20 33 01	1♉03 55	7♉12 18	12 06.2	2 00.7	27 01.2	1 00.1	4 30.6	22 29.7	22 03.8	18 37.9	3 12.8	19 37.5
13 Sa	5 23 21	21 30 22	13 24 48	19 41 47	12 01.0	3 45.1	28 13.8	1 32.3	4 40.3	22 42.1	22 00.4	18 39.8	3 13.7	19 39.0
14 Su	5 27 17	22 27 42	26 03 29	2♊30 03	11 53.3	5 32.1	29 26.5	2 04.6	4 50.4	22 54.4	21 56.9	18 41.8	3 14.7	19 40.4
15 M	5 31 14	23 25 02	9♊01 33	15 37 55	11 43.5	7 21.8	0♊39.2	2 37.1	5 00.8	23 06.9	21 53.3	18 43.7	3 15.6	19 41.8
16 Tu	5 35 10	24 22 21	22 19 01	29 04 34	11 32.4	9 13.9	1 51.9	3 09.6	5 11.4	23 19.4	21 49.7	18 45.5	3 16.7	19 43.3
17 W	5 39 07	25 19 40	5♋54 13	12♋47 35	11 21.0	11 08.6	3 04.6	3 42.3	5 22.4	23 31.9	21 46.0	18 47.3	3 17.7	19 44.7
18 Th	5 43 03	26 16 58	19 44 09	26 43 25	11 10.6	13 05.7	4 17.3	4 15.1	5 33.6	23 44.4	21 42.3	18 49.1	3 18.8	19 46.2
19 F	5 47 00	27 14 15	3♌44 52	10♌47 58	11 02.1	15 05.0	5 30.0	4 48.0	5 45.1	23 57.1	21 38.5	18 50.8	3 19.9	19 47.7
20 Sa	5 50 56	28 11 32	17 52 15	24 57 17	10 56.2	17 06.5	6 42.8	5 21.0	5 56.8	24 09.7	21 34.6	18 52.5	3 21.0	19 49.2
21 Su	5 54 53	29 08 47	2♍02 39	9♍08 02	10 53.0	19 10.0	7 55.6	5 54.1	6 08.8	24 22.4	21 30.7	18 54.2	3 22.2	19 50.7
22 M	5 58 50	0♋06 02	16 13 11	23 17 53	10D 51.8	21 15.3	9 08.4	6 27.4	6 21.1	24 35.1	21 26.8	18 55.8	3 23.4	19 52.2
23 Tu	6 02 46	1 03 17	0♎21 59	7♎25 21	10R 51.8	23 22.2	10 21.2	7 00.7	6 33.7	24 47.9	21 22.8	18 57.3	3 24.6	19 53.7
24 W	6 06 43	2 00 30	14 27 53	21 29 28	10 51.6	25 30.5	11 34.0	7 34.1	6 46.5	25 00.7	21 18.8	18 58.8	3 25.8	19 55.2
25 Th	6 10 39	2 57 43	28 30 00	5♏29 20	10 50.0	27 39.9	12 46.9	8 07.7	6 59.5	25 13.5	21 14.7	19 00.3	3 27.1	19 56.7
26 F	6 14 36	3 54 56	12♏27 20	19 23 45	10 46.0	29 50.1	13 59.7	8 41.3	7 12.8	25 26.4	21 10.6	19 01.7	3 28.4	19 58.2
27 Sa	6 18 32	4 52 08	26 18 22	3♐10 55	10 39.3	2♋00.9	15 12.6	9 15.1	7 26.3	25 39.3	21 06.5	19 03.1	3 29.7	19 59.8
28 Su	6 22 29	5 49 20	10♐01 03	16 48 29	10 29.9	4 12.0	16 25.5	9 48.9	7 40.1	25 52.2	21 02.3	19 04.5	3 31.0	20 01.3
29 M	6 26 26	6 46 31	23 32 52	0♑13 53	10 18.5	6 23.0	17 38.5	10 22.8	7 54.0	26 05.1	20 58.1	19 05.8	3 32.4	20 02.9
30 Tu	6 30 22	7 43 42	6♑51 15	13 24 43	10 06.0	8 33.8	18 51.4	10 56.8	8 08.3	26 18.1	20 53.8	19 07.0	3 33.8	20 04.4

Astro Data

	Dy Hr Mn
♄ R	3 14:28
☽ 0N	13 6:49
☿ D	13 14:33
♆ D	15 1:10
⚳ D	16 12:37
♃□♅	17 21:31
♃∠♆	20 5:50
☽ 0S	26 21:38
♃☌♇	27 3:14
♅⚻♆	27 23:37
☽ 0N	9 13:55
♃☍♄	10 20:13
☽ 0S	23 2:29

Planet Ingress

		Dy Hr Mn
♀	♉	21 2:38
☉	♊	22 1:15
♂	♍	10 14:58
☿	♊	11 7:27
♀	♊	14 23:04
☉	♋	22 9:28
☿	♋	26 13:49

Last Aspect / ☽ Ingress (May)

Last Aspect Dy Hr Mn		☽ Ingress Dy Hr Mn
1 0:27	♄ □	♏ 1 11:26
3 1:54	♄ ⚹	♐ 3 13:14
4 18:22	♅ △	♑ 5 17:35
7 12:42	♄ ☌	♒ 8 1:37
9 12:48	☉ □	♓ 10 13:02
12 12:10	♄ ⚹	♈ 13 1:57
15 0:26	♄ □	♉ 15 13:54
17 15:28	☉ ☌	♊ 17 23:26
20 4:26	♀ ⚹	♋ 20 6:26
21 23:14	♄ ☍	♌ 22 11:27
23 23:40	♂ ☌	♍ 24 15:07
26 5:51	♄ △	♎ 26 17:51
28 8:38	♂ ⚹	♏ 28 20:08
30 12:59	♂ □	♐ 30 22:48

Last Aspect / ☽ Ingress (June)

Last Aspect Dy Hr Mn		☽ Ingress Dy Hr Mn
1 18:54	♂ △	♑ 2 3:07
3 20:16	♄ ☌	♒ 4 10:23
6 16:53	♂ ☍	♓ 6 21:01
9 2:30	☿ ⚹	♈ 9 9:44
11 6:33	♃ □	♉ 11 21:54
14 5:44	♀ ☌	♊ 14 7:22
16 3:02	☉ ☌	♋ 16 13:38
18 6:48	♃ ☌	♌ 18 17:36
20 17:53	☉ ⚹	♍ 20 20:32
22 14:13	♃ ⚹	♎ 22 23:23
24 20:07	☿ △	♏ 25 2:34
26 22:39	♃ △	♐ 27 6:26
28 16:02	♅ △	♑ 29 11:35

☽ Phases & Eclipses

Dy Hr Mn	
2 5:14	○ 10♏51
9 12:48	☾ 17♒56
17 15:28	● 25♉45
24 19:39	☽ 2♍40
31 14:33	○ 9♐10
8 6:18	☾ 16♓30
16 3:02	● 24♊01
23 0:23	☽ 0♎36
30 0:47	○ 7♑17

Astro Data

1 May 1931
Julian Day # 11443
SVP 6♓13'12"
GC 25♐52.8 ⚴ 1♍02.2
Eris 2♈19.4 ⚵ 21♈03.4
⚷ 18♉06.0 ⚶ 19♑53.7
☽ Mean ☊ 13♈13.8

1 June 1931
Julian Day # 11474
SVP 6♓13'07"
GC 25♐52.9 ⚴ 7♍12.7
Eris 2♈33.9 ⚵ 8♉11.9
⚷ 20♉11.7 ⚶ 22♑09.4R
☽ Mean ☊ 11♈35.3

July 1931 — LONGITUDE

Day	Sid.Time	☉	0 hr ☽	Noon ☽	True ☊	☿	♀	♂	⚳	♃	♄	♅	♆	♇
1 W	6 34 19	8♋40 53	19♑54 06	26♑19 18	9♈53.7	10♋44.1	20♊04.4	11♍31.0	8♎22.7	26♋31.2	20♑49.6	19♈08.2	3♍35.2	20♋06.0
2 Th	6 38 15	9 38 04	2♒40 15	8♒57 02	9R42.7	12 53.5	21 17.4	12 05.2	8 37.3	26 44.2	20R45.3	19 09.4	3 36.7	20 07.5
3 F	6 42 12	10 35 15	15 09 44	21 18 37	9 33.7	15 02.0	22 30.4	12 39.5	8 52.2	26 57.3	20 41.0	19 10.5	3 38.2	20 09.1
4 Sa	6 46 08	11 32 27	27 23 57	3♓26 07	9 27.4	17 09.4	23 43.5	13 13.9	9 07.3	27 10.3	20 36.6	19 11.5	3 39.6	20 10.7
5 Su	6 50 05	12 29 38	9♓25 34	15 22 47	9 23.6	19 15.4	24 56.5	13 48.4	9 22.5	27 23.5	20 32.3	19 12.5	3 41.2	20 12.2
6 M	6 54 01	13 26 50	21 18 21	27 12 51	9 22.0	21 19.9	26 09.6	14 23.0	9 38.0	27 36.6	20 27.9	19 13.5	3 42.7	20 13.8
7 Tu	6 57 58	14 24 01	3♈06 55	9♈01 14	9 21.7	23 22.9	27 22.8	14 57.6	9 53.7	27 49.8	20 23.5	19 14.4	3 44.3	20 15.4
8 W	7 01 55	15 21 14	14 56 28	20 53 19	9 21.6	25 24.2	28 35.9	15 32.4	10 09.6	28 02.9	20 19.1	19 15.3	3 45.9	20 17.0
9 Th	7 05 51	16 18 26	26 52 27	2♉54 33	9 20.8	27 23.7	29 49.1	16 07.3	10 25.7	28 16.1	20 14.7	19 16.1	3 47.5	20 18.6
10 F	7 09 48	17 15 39	9♉00 16	15 10 10	9 18.2	29 21.5	1♋02.3	16 42.2	10 42.0	28 29.3	20 10.2	19 16.9	3 49.1	20 20.2
11 Sa	7 13 44	18 12 53	21 24 49	27 44 41	9 13.4	1♌17.5	2 15.5	17 17.3	10 58.4	28 42.6	20 05.8	19 17.6	3 50.8	20 21.7
12 Su	7 17 41	19 10 07	4♊10 08	10♊41 27	9 06.0	3 11.6	3 28.8	17 52.4	11 15.1	28 55.8	20 01.4	19 18.3	3 52.4	20 23.3
13 M	7 21 37	20 07 21	17 18 47	24 02 07	8 56.3	5 03.8	4 42.0	18 27.6	11 31.9	29 09.1	19 56.9	19 19.0	3 54.1	20 24.9
14 Tu	7 25 34	21 04 36	0♋51 21	7♋46 11	8 45.3	6 54.1	5 55.3	19 03.0	11 48.9	29 22.4	19 52.5	19 19.5	3 55.9	20 26.5
15 W	7 29 30	22 01 52	14 46 13	21 50 52	8 33.9	8 42.6	7 08.7	19 38.4	12 06.1	29 35.7	19 48.1	19 20.1	3 57.6	20 28.1
16 Th	7 33 27	22 59 07	28 59 28	6♌11 16	8 23.4	10 29.2	8 22.0	20 13.9	12 23.5	29 49.0	19 43.6	19 20.6	3 59.4	20 29.7
17 F	7 37 24	23 56 23	13♌25 28	20 41 13	8 14.9	12 13.9	9 35.4	20 49.4	12 41.0	0♌02.3	19 39.2	19 21.0	4 01.2	20 31.3
18 Sa	7 41 20	24 53 39	27 57 43	5♍14 10	8 09.0	13 56.7	10 48.8	21 25.1	12 58.7	0 15.6	19 34.8	19 21.4	4 03.0	20 32.9
19 Su	7 45 17	25 50 56	12♍29 54	19 44 18	8 05.7	15 37.6	12 02.2	22 00.9	13 16.6	0 28.9	19 30.4	19 21.7	4 04.8	20 34.4
20 M	7 49 13	26 48 12	26 56 52	4♎07 12	8D04.6	17 16.6	13 15.6	22 36.7	13 34.6	0 42.3	19 26.0	19 22.0	4 06.6	20 36.0
21 Tu	7 53 10	27 45 29	11♎15 01	18 20 05	8R04.7	18 53.8	14 29.1	23 12.6	13 52.8	0 55.6	19 21.6	19 22.3	4 08.5	20 37.6
22 W	7 57 06	28 42 46	25 22 19	2♏21 37	8 04.8	20 29.1	15 42.6	23 48.6	14 11.2	1 08.9	19 17.2	19 22.5	4 10.3	20 39.2
23 Th	8 01 03	29 40 03	9♏17 59	16 11 25	8 03.8	22 02.5	16 56.1	24 24.7	14 29.7	1 22.3	19 12.9	19 22.6	4 12.2	20 40.8
24 F	8 04 59	0♌37 21	23 01 57	29 49 35	8 00.6	23 34.0	18 09.6	25 00.8	14 48.3	1 35.6	19 08.6	19 22.7	4 14.1	20 42.3
25 Sa	8 08 56	1 34 39	6♐34 20	13♐16 11	7 55.0	25 03.6	19 23.1	25 37.1	15 07.1	1 49.0	19 04.3	19R22.7	4 16.1	20 43.9
26 Su	8 12 53	2 31 57	19 55 06	26 31 04	7 47.0	26 31.3	20 36.7	26 13.4	15 26.1	2 02.3	19 00.0	19 22.7	4 18.0	20 45.5
27 M	8 16 49	3 29 16	3♑04 01	9♑33 51	7 37.1	27 57.1	21 50.3	26 49.8	15 45.1	2 15.6	18 55.8	19 22.7	4 20.0	20 47.0
28 Tu	8 20 46	4 26 36	16 00 32	22 24 00	7 26.2	29 20.9	23 03.9	27 26.3	16 04.4	2 29.0	18 51.6	19 22.6	4 21.9	20 48.6
29 W	8 24 42	5 23 56	28 44 12	5♒01 07	7 15.4	0♍42.7	24 17.6	28 02.8	16 23.7	2 42.3	18 47.4	19 22.5	4 23.9	20 50.1
30 Th	8 28 39	6 21 17	11♒14 46	17 25 14	7 05.8	2 02.4	25 31.2	28 39.4	16 43.2	2 55.6	18 43.3	19 22.3	4 25.9	20 51.7
31 F	8 32 35	7 18 39	23 32 37	29 37 05	6 58.0	3 20.1	26 44.9	29 16.1	17 02.8	3 09.0	18 39.2	19 22.0	4 27.9	20 53.2

August 1931 — LONGITUDE

Day	Sid.Time	☉	0 hr ☽	Noon ☽	True ☊	☿	♀	♂	⚳	♃	♄	♅	♆	♇
1 Sa	8 36 32	8♌16 02	5♓38 52	11♓38 14	6♈52.5	4♍35.7	27♋58.6	29♍52.9	17♎22.6	3♌22.3	18♑35.2	19♈21.7	4♍30.0	20♋54.7
2 Su	8 40 28	9 13 25	17 35 33	23 31 10	6R49.5	5 49.0	29 12.4	0♎29.8	17 42.4	3 35.6	18R31.1	19R21.4	4 32.0	20 56.3
3 M	8 44 25	10 10 50	29 25 35	5♈19 15	6D48.4	7 00.1	0♌26.2	1 06.7	18 02.4	3 48.9	18 27.2	19 21.0	4 34.1	20 57.8
4 Tu	8 48 22	11 08 16	11♈12 43	17 06 35	6 48.8	8 08.9	1 40.0	1 43.7	18 22.5	4 02.1	18 23.2	19 20.6	4 36.1	20 59.3
5 W	8 52 18	12 05 43	23 01 27	28 57 57	6 49.8	9 15.3	2 53.8	2 20.8	18 42.8	4 15.4	18 19.4	19 20.1	4 38.2	21 00.8
6 Th	8 56 15	13 03 11	4♉56 45	10♉58 30	6R50.5	10 19.2	4 07.6	2 57.9	19 03.1	4 28.7	18 15.5	19 19.6	4 40.3	21 02.3
7 F	9 00 11	14 00 41	17 03 51	23 13 28	6 50.1	11 20.5	5 21.5	3 35.2	19 23.6	4 41.9	18 11.8	19 19.0	4 42.4	21 03.8
8 Sa	9 04 08	14 58 12	29 27 56	5♊47 49	6 47.9	12 19.1	6 35.4	4 12.5	19 44.2	4 55.1	18 08.0	19 18.4	4 44.5	21 05.3
9 Su	9 08 04	15 55 45	12♊13 37	18 45 45	6 43.8	13 14.8	7 49.4	4 49.9	20 04.9	5 08.4	18 04.4	19 17.7	4 46.6	21 06.7
10 M	9 12 01	16 53 18	25 24 29	2♋09 59	6 37.8	14 07.6	9 03.3	5 27.4	20 25.7	5 21.6	18 00.7	19 17.0	4 48.8	21 08.2
11 Tu	9 15 57	17 50 54	9♋02 16	16 01 12	6 30.7	14 57.2	10 17.3	6 04.9	20 46.7	5 34.7	17 57.2	19 16.2	4 50.9	21 09.6
12 W	9 19 54	18 48 30	23 06 26	0♌17 29	6 23.1	15 43.5	11 31.3	6 42.6	21 07.7	5 47.9	17 53.7	19 15.4	4 53.1	21 11.1
13 Th	9 23 51	19 46 08	7♌33 41	14 54 12	6 16.0	16 26.4	12 45.4	7 20.3	21 28.8	6 01.1	17 50.3	19 14.5	4 55.2	21 12.5
14 F	9 27 47	20 43 47	22 18 07	29 44 24	6 10.4	17 05.6	13 59.4	7 58.1	21 50.1	6 14.2	17 46.9	19 13.6	4 57.4	21 13.9
15 Sa	9 31 44	21 41 27	7♍12 00	14♍39 51	6 06.7	17 40.9	15 13.5	8 35.9	22 11.4	6 27.3	17 43.6	19 12.7	4 59.6	21 15.4
16 Su	9 35 40	22 39 08	22 06 56	29 32 19	6D05.0	18 12.2	16 27.6	9 13.9	22 32.9	6 40.3	17 40.3	19 11.7	5 01.7	21 16.7
17 M	9 39 37	23 36 50	6♎55 11	14♎14 50	6 05.1	18 39.2	17 41.7	9 51.9	22 54.4	6 53.4	17 37.2	19 10.7	5 03.9	21 18.1
18 Tu	9 43 33	24 34 33	21 30 41	28 42 20	6 06.1	19 01.6	18 55.9	10 29.9	23 16.1	7 06.4	17 34.1	19 09.6	5 06.1	21 19.5
19 W	9 47 30	25 32 18	5♏49 29	12♏51 57	6R07.4	19 19.3	20 10.0	11 08.1	23 37.8	7 19.4	17 31.1	19 08.5	5 08.3	21 20.9
20 Th	9 51 26	26 30 03	19 49 40	26 42 40	6 07.9	19 32.0	21 24.2	11 46.3	23 59.7	7 32.3	17 28.1	19 07.3	5 10.5	21 22.2
21 F	9 55 23	27 27 50	3♐31 01	10♐14 50	6 07.2	19R39.4	22 38.4	12 24.6	24 21.6	7 45.2	17 25.2	19 06.1	5 12.7	21 23.6
22 Sa	9 59 20	28 25 38	16 54 19	23 29 37	6 04.7	19 41.4	23 52.6	13 03.0	24 43.6	7 58.1	17 22.4	19 04.8	5 14.9	21 24.9
23 Su	10 03 16	29 23 26	0♑00 58	6♑28 32	6 00.7	19 37.7	25 06.9	13 41.4	25 05.7	8 11.0	17 19.7	19 03.6	5 17.1	21 26.2
24 M	10 07 13	0♍21 17	12 52 31	19 13 07	5 55.5	19 28.2	26 21.1	14 19.9	25 27.9	8 23.8	17 17.1	19 02.2	5 19.4	21 27.5
25 Tu	10 11 09	1 19 08	25 30 30	1♒44 51	5 49.6	19 12.9	27 35.4	14 58.5	25 50.2	8 36.6	17 14.5	19 00.9	5 21.6	21 28.8
26 W	10 15 06	2 17 01	7♒56 19	14 05 04	5 43.7	18 51.5	28 49.7	15 37.2	26 12.5	8 49.3	17 12.0	18 59.4	5 23.8	21 30.0
27 Th	10 19 02	3 14 55	20 11 16	26 15 05	5 38.5	18 24.2	0♍04.0	16 15.9	26 34.9	9 02.0	17 09.6	18 58.0	5 26.0	21 31.3
28 F	10 22 59	4 12 51	2♓16 43	8♓16 21	5 34.4	17 51.2	1 18.3	16 54.7	26 57.4	9 14.7	17 07.3	18 56.5	5 28.3	21 32.5
29 Sa	10 26 55	5 10 48	14 14 12	20 10 31	5 31.8	17 12.6	2 32.7	17 33.5	27 20.0	9 27.3	17 05.1	18 55.0	5 30.5	21 33.7
30 Su	10 30 52	6 08 46	26 05 36	1♈59 43	5D30.7	16 28.9	3 47.1	18 12.5	27 42.7	9 39.9	17 02.9	18 53.4	5 32.7	21 34.9
31 M	10 34 49	7 06 47	7♈53 15	13 46 33	5 30.9	15 40.6	5 01.5	18 51.5	28 05.4	9 52.4	17 00.8	18 51.8	5 34.9	21 36.1

Astro Data	Planet Ingress	Last Aspect	☽ Ingress	Last Aspect	☽ Ingress	☽ Phases & Eclipses	Astro Data
Dy Hr Mn	Dy Hr Mn	Dy Hr Mn	Dy Hr Mn	Dy Hr Mn	Dy Hr Mn	Dy Hr Mn	
☽0N 6 20:53	♀ ♋ 9 15:35	1 12:23 ♃ ☍	♒ 1 18:56	3 0:54 ♀ △	♈ 3 1:10	7 23:52 ☾ 14♈52	1 July 1931
♄☍♇ 8 20:27	☿ ♌ 10 19:56	3 14:37 ♀ △	♓ 4 5:10	4 19:53 ♇ □	♉ 5 14:05	15 12:20 ● 22♋03	Julian Day # 11504
☽0S 20 7:23	♃ ♌ 17 7:52	6 12:49 ♃ △	♈ 6 17:40	7 7:48 ♇ ⚹	♊ 8 1:01	22 5:16 ☽ 28♎27	SVP 6♓13'01"
♄□♅ 21 8:28	☉ ♌ 23 20:21	9 5:11 ♀ ⚹	♉ 9 6:14	9 12:58 ♅ ⚹	♋ 10 8:11	29 12:47 ○ 5♒26	GC 25♐53.0 ⚵ 16♍33.0
♄⚼♆ 23 14:32	☿ ♍ 28 23:24	11 13:51 ♃ ⚹	♊ 11 16:14	11 20:44 ♇ ☌	♌ 12 11:31		Eris 2♈38.6R ⚶ 24♉52.6
♅ R 26 0:36		13 3:35 ♅ ⚹	♋ 13 22:30	13 20:27 ☉ ☌	♍ 14 12:25	6 16:28 ☾ 13♉14	⚷ 21♉58.9 ⚴ 17♑27.6R
♅⚼♆ 28 19:29	♂ ♎ 1 16:38	16 1:13 ♃ ☌	♌ 16 1:41	15 22:38 ♇ ⚹	♎ 16 12:45	13 20:27 ● 20♌06	☽ Mean ☊ 10♈00.1
⚳0S 29 1:01	♀ ♌ 3 3:29	17 9:48 ♅ △	♍ 18 3:22	18 4:36 ☉ ⚹	♏ 18 14:10	20 11:36 ☽ 26♏29	
	☉ ♍ 24 3:10	19 22:53 ☉ ⚹	♎ 20 5:06	20 11:36 ☉ □	♐ 20 17:47	28 3:09 ○ 3♓51	1 August 1931
☽0N 3 3:32	♀ ♍ 27 10:42	22 5:16 ☉ □	♏ 22 7:56	22 21:47 ☉ △	♑ 22 23:58		Julian Day # 11535
♂0S 3 9:52		24 3:06 ♂ ⚹	♐ 24 12:18	24 16:16 ♇ ☍	♒ 25 8:38		SVP 6♓12'56"
♃⚺♆ 7 13:02		26 12:01 ☿ △	♑ 26 18:22	26 21:37 ♅ ⚹	♓ 27 19:27		GC 25♐53.0 ⚵ 28♍07.6
☽0S 16 14:27		28 22:01 ♂ △	♒ 29 2:24	29 14:49 ♇ △	♈ 30 7:56		Eris 2♈32.6R ⚶ 11♊49.0
☿ R 22 8:33		30 15:49 ♅ ⚹	♓ 31 12:45				⚷ 23♉14.4 ⚴ 10♑45.6R
☽0N 30 9:54							☽ Mean ☊ 8♈21.6

LONGITUDE — September 1931

Day	Sid.Time	☉	0 hr ☽	Noon ☽	True ☊	☿	♀	♂	⚳	♃	♄	♅	♆	♇
1 Tu	10 38 45	8♍04 49	19♈40 02	25♈34 10	5♈32.1	14♍48.5	6♍15.9	19♎30.5	28♎28.2	10♌04.9	16♑58.9	18♈50.2	5♍37.1	21♋37.3
2 W	10 42 42	9 02 54	1♉29 25	7♉26 18	5 33.8	13R53.3	7 30.3	20 09.7	28 51.1	10 17.4	16R57.0	18R48.5	5 39.4	21 38.5
3 Th	10 46 38	10 01 00	13 25 21	19 27 09	5 35.5	12 56.0	8 44.8	20 48.9	29 14.1	10 29.8	16 55.2	18 46.8	5 41.6	21 39.6
4 F	10 50 35	10 59 08	25 32 16	1♊41 17	5R36.6	11 57.9	9 59.2	21 28.2	29 37.1	10 42.1	16 53.4	18 45.0	5 43.8	21 40.7
5 Sa	10 54 31	11 57 18	7♊54 46	14 13 17	5 36.9	11 00.2	11 13.7	22 07.5	0♏00.2	10 54.4	16 51.8	18 43.2	5 46.0	21 41.8
6 Su	10 58 28	12 55 30	20 37 21	27 07 27	5 36.2	10 04.0	12 28.2	22 47.0	0 23.3	11 06.7	16 50.3	18 41.4	5 48.2	21 42.9
7 M	11 02 24	13 53 44	3♋43 58	10♋27 13	5 34.6	9 10.8	13 42.8	23 26.5	0 46.6	11 18.9	16 48.9	18 39.6	5 50.5	21 44.0
8 Tu	11 06 21	14 52 01	17 17 24	24 14 33	5 32.2	8 21.9	14 57.3	24 06.1	1 09.9	11 31.0	16 47.5	18 37.7	5 52.7	21 45.0
9 W	11 10 18	15 50 19	1♌18 34	8♌29 10	5 29.5	7 38.2	16 11.9	24 45.7	1 33.2	11 43.1	16 46.3	18 35.8	5 54.9	21 46.1
10 Th	11 14 14	16 48 39	15 45 54	23 08 07	5 27.0	7 01.1	17 26.5	25 25.4	1 56.7	11 55.1	16 45.1	18 33.9	5 57.1	21 47.1
11 F	11 18 11	17 47 01	0♍35 01	8♍05 39	5 25.1	6 31.3	18 41.1	26 05.2	2 20.2	12 07.1	16 44.1	18 31.9	5 59.3	21 48.1
12 Sa	11 22 07	18 45 25	15 38 54	23 13 39	5D23.9	6 09.7	19 55.7	26 45.1	2 43.7	12 19.0	16 43.1	18 29.9	6 01.4	21 49.1
13 Su	11 26 04	19 43 51	0♎48 41	8♎22 49	5 23.7	5D56.8	21 10.3	27 25.0	3 07.3	12 30.9	16 42.2	18 27.9	6 03.6	21 50.0
14 M	11 30 00	20 42 18	15 54 56	23 23 59	5 24.2	5 53.1	22 24.9	28 05.1	3 31.0	12 42.6	16 41.4	18 25.8	6 05.8	21 50.9
15 Tu	11 33 57	21 40 47	0♏49 04	8♏09 27	5 25.1	5 58.6	23 39.6	28 45.1	3 54.7	12 54.4	16 40.8	18 23.7	6 08.0	21 51.9
16 W	11 37 53	22 39 18	15 24 30	22 33 49	5 26.1	6 13.6	24 54.2	29 25.3	4 18.5	13 06.0	16 40.2	18 21.6	6 10.1	21 52.8
17 Th	11 41 50	23 37 51	29 37 07	6♐34 15	5 27.0	6 38.0	26 08.9	0♏05.5	4 42.3	13 17.6	16 39.7	18 19.5	6 12.3	21 53.6
18 F	11 45 47	24 36 25	13♐25 15	20 10 12	5R27.4	7 11.4	27 23.6	0 45.8	5 06.2	13 29.1	16 39.3	18 17.3	6 14.4	21 54.5
19 Sa	11 49 43	25 35 01	26 49 20	3♑22 54	5 27.3	7 53.5	28 38.3	1 26.1	5 30.2	13 40.6	16 39.1	18 15.2	6 16.5	21 55.3
20 Su	11 53 40	26 33 38	9♑51 15	16 14 43	5 26.8	8 44.0	29 53.0	2 06.6	5 54.2	13 51.9	16 38.9	18 13.0	6 18.7	21 56.1
21 M	11 57 36	27 32 18	22 33 44	28 48 40	5 26.0	9 42.2	1♎07.7	2 47.1	6 18.2	14 03.2	16D38.8	18 10.8	6 20.8	21 56.9
22 Tu	12 01 33	28 30 58	4♒59 56	11♒07 55	5 25.1	10 47.6	2 22.4	3 27.6	6 42.3	14 14.5	16 38.8	18 08.5	6 22.9	21 57.7
23 W	12 05 29	29 29 41	17 13 01	23 15 35	5 24.2	11 59.7	3 37.2	4 08.2	7 06.4	14 25.6	16 38.9	18 06.3	6 25.0	21 58.4
24 Th	12 09 26	0♎28 25	29 15 59	5♓14 32	5 23.5	13 17.6	4 51.9	4 48.9	7 30.6	14 36.7	16 39.2	18 04.0	6 27.0	21 59.2
25 F	12 13 22	1 27 11	11♓11 34	17 07 23	5 23.1	14 40.9	6 06.6	5 29.7	7 54.8	14 47.7	16 39.5	18 01.7	6 29.1	21 59.9
26 Sa	12 17 19	2 26 00	23 02 16	28 56 30	5D22.9	16 08.8	7 21.4	6 10.5	8 19.1	14 58.6	16 39.9	17 59.4	6 31.2	22 00.5
27 Su	12 21 16	3 24 50	4♈50 22	10♈44 08	5 22.9	17 40.6	8 36.1	6 51.4	8 43.4	15 09.4	16 40.4	17 57.1	6 33.2	22 01.2
28 M	12 25 12	4 23 42	16 38 05	22 32 30	5R22.9	19 15.9	9 50.9	7 32.3	9 07.7	15 20.1	16 41.0	17 54.7	6 35.2	22 01.8
29 Tu	12 29 09	5 22 36	28 27 42	4♉23 58	5 23.0	20 54.1	11 05.7	8 13.4	9 32.1	15 30.8	16 41.7	17 52.4	6 37.2	22 02.4
30 W	12 33 05	6 21 32	10♉21 40	16 21 06	5 22.9	22 34.5	12 20.5	8 54.4	9 56.6	15 41.3	16 42.5	17 50.0	6 39.2	22 03.0

LONGITUDE — October 1931

Day	Sid.Time	☉	0 hr ☽	Noon ☽	True ☊	☿	♀	♂	⚳	♃	♄	♅	♆	♇
1 Th	12 37 02	7♎20 31	22♉22 41	28♉26 47	5♈22.7	24♍16.9	13♎35.2	9♏35.6	10♏21.0	15♌51.8	16♑43.4	17♈47.6	6♍41.2	22♋03.6
2 F	12 40 58	8 19 32	4♊33 49	10♊44 12	5R22.4	26 00.8	14 50.1	10 16.8	10 45.6	16 02.2	16 44.4	17R45.2	6 43.2	22 04.1
3 Sa	12 44 55	9 18 35	16 58 22	23 16 46	5 22.1	27 45.7	16 04.9	10 58.1	11 10.1	16 12.5	16 45.5	17 42.8	6 45.1	22 04.7
4 Su	12 48 51	10 17 41	29 39 51	6♋08 00	5D22.0	29 31.5	17 19.7	11 39.5	11 34.7	16 22.7	16 46.7	17 40.4	6 47.0	22 05.2
5 M	12 52 48	11 16 49	12♋41 38	19 21 05	5 22.0	1♎17.8	18 34.5	12 20.9	11 59.3	16 32.8	16 48.0	17 38.0	6 49.0	22 05.6
6 Tu	12 56 45	12 15 59	26 06 38	2♌58 29	5 22.3	3 04.3	19 49.4	13 02.5	12 24.0	16 42.8	16 49.4	17 35.6	6 50.9	22 06.1
7 W	13 00 41	13 15 11	9♌56 44	17 01 22	5 22.9	4 51.0	21 04.2	13 44.0	12 48.7	16 52.7	16 50.9	17 33.2	6 52.8	22 06.5
8 Th	13 04 38	14 14 26	24 12 11	1♍28 53	5 23.7	6 37.6	22 19.1	14 25.7	13 13.4	17 02.5	16 52.5	17 30.8	6 54.6	22 06.9
9 F	13 08 34	15 13 43	8♍50 57	16 17 44	5 24.4	8 24.0	23 33.9	15 07.4	13 38.2	17 12.2	16 54.2	17 28.3	6 56.5	22 07.3
10 Sa	13 12 31	16 13 02	23 48 24	1♎21 59	5R24.7	10 10.1	24 48.8	15 49.2	14 03.0	17 21.8	16 56.0	17 25.9	6 58.3	22 07.6
11 Su	13 16 27	17 12 23	8♎57 23	16 33 24	5 24.6	11 55.8	26 03.7	16 31.0	14 27.8	17 31.3	16 57.9	17 23.4	7 00.1	22 08.0
12 M	13 20 24	18 11 47	24 08 51	1♏42 31	5 23.8	13 41.0	27 18.5	17 12.9	14 52.7	17 40.7	16 59.8	17 21.0	7 01.9	22 08.3
13 Tu	13 24 20	19 11 12	9♏13 13	16 39 55	5 22.4	15 25.7	28 33.4	17 54.9	15 17.6	17 50.0	17 01.9	17 18.6	7 03.6	22 08.5
14 W	13 28 17	20 10 39	24 01 41	1♐17 45	5 20.6	17 09.9	29 48.3	18 37.0	15 42.5	17 59.1	17 04.1	17 16.1	7 05.4	22 08.8
15 Th	13 32 14	21 10 09	8♐27 32	15 30 37	5 18.6	18 53.4	1♏03.2	19 19.1	16 07.5	18 08.2	17 06.4	17 13.7	7 07.1	22 09.0
16 F	13 36 10	22 09 40	22 26 48	29 16 01	5 16.9	20 36.4	2 18.1	20 01.3	16 32.4	18 17.1	17 08.7	17 11.3	7 08.8	22 09.2
17 Sa	13 40 07	23 09 12	5♑58 22	12♑34 04	5D15.8	22 18.7	3 33.0	20 43.6	16 57.4	18 25.9	17 11.2	17 08.9	7 10.5	22 09.4
18 Su	13 44 03	24 08 47	19 03 27	25 26 56	5 15.5	24 00.3	4 47.9	21 25.9	17 22.5	18 34.6	17 13.7	17 06.4	7 12.2	22 09.6
19 M	13 48 00	25 08 23	1♒45 01	7♒58 12	5 16.0	25 41.4	6 02.8	22 08.3	17 47.5	18 43.2	17 16.4	17 04.0	7 13.8	22 09.7
20 Tu	13 51 56	26 08 01	14 07 03	20 12 08	5 17.2	27 21.7	7 17.7	22 50.7	18 12.6	18 51.6	17 19.1	17 01.6	7 15.4	22 09.8
21 W	13 55 53	27 07 40	26 14 01	2♓13 15	5 18.9	29 01.5	8 32.6	23 33.2	18 37.7	18 59.9	17 21.9	16 59.3	7 17.0	22 09.9
22 Th	13 59 49	28 07 22	8♓10 22	14 05 53	5 20.5	0♏40.7	9 47.5	24 15.8	19 02.8	19 08.1	17 24.8	16 56.9	7 18.6	22 09.9
23 F	14 03 46	29 07 05	20 00 17	25 54 01	5R21.7	2 19.2	11 02.3	24 58.4	19 27.9	19 16.2	17 27.8	16 54.5	7 20.1	22R10.0
24 Sa	14 07 42	0♏06 50	1♈47 31	7♈41 09	5 22.0	3 57.2	12 17.2	25 41.1	19 53.0	19 24.1	17 30.9	16 52.1	7 21.6	22 10.0
25 Su	14 11 39	1 06 36	13 35 17	19 30 13	5 21.2	5 34.6	13 32.1	26 23.9	20 18.2	19 31.9	17 34.1	16 49.8	7 23.1	22 09.9
26 M	14 15 36	2 06 25	25 26 14	1♉23 37	5 18.9	7 11.4	14 47.0	27 06.7	20 43.4	19 39.6	17 37.4	16 47.5	7 24.6	22 09.9
27 Tu	14 19 32	3 06 16	7♉22 35	13 23 21	5 15.3	8 47.8	16 01.9	27 49.6	21 08.6	19 47.1	17 40.7	16 45.2	7 26.0	22 09.8
28 W	14 23 29	4 06 09	19 26 07	25 31 04	5 10.7	10 23.5	17 16.8	28 32.5	21 33.8	19 54.5	17 44.2	16 42.9	7 27.4	22 09.7
29 Th	14 27 25	5 06 03	1♊38 24	7♊48 18	5 05.4	11 58.8	18 31.7	29 15.5	21 59.0	20 01.8	17 47.7	16 40.6	7 28.8	22 09.6
30 F	14 31 22	6 06 00	14 00 57	20 16 33	5 00.1	13 33.6	19 46.6	29 58.6	22 24.3	20 08.9	17 51.3	16 38.3	7 30.2	22 09.5
31 Sa	14 35 18	7 05 59	26 35 18	2♋57 27	4 55.5	15 08.0	21 01.5	0♐41.8	22 49.5	20 15.9	17 55.0	16 36.1	7 31.5	22 09.3

Astro Data

Astro Data	Dy Hr Mn
☽ 0S	13 0:13
☿ D	14 9:43
♄ D	21 19:53
♀ 0S	23 0:42
☉ 0S	24 0:23
☽ 0N	26 16:05
☿ 0S	7 2:13
♃⚻♄	7 6:49
☽ 0S	10 11:20
♃△♅	10 20:10
♆∠♇	16 18:41
♄□♅	17 0:38
☽ 0N	23 22:16
♇ R	24 1:48

Planet Ingress

Planet Ingress		Dy Hr Mn
⚳	♏	5 11:49
♂	♏	17 8:43
♀	♎	20 14:15
☉	♎	24 0:23
☿	♎	4 18:27
♀	♏	14 15:45
☿	♏	22 2:08
☉	♏	24 9:16
♂	♐	30 12:46

Last Aspect / ☽ Ingress (September)

Last Aspect Dy Hr Mn			☽ Ingress	Dy Hr Mn
1 3:58	♇	□	♉	1 20:59
3 16:22	♇	✱	♊	4 8:43
6 3:35	♂	△	♋	6 17:15
8 11:45	♂	□	♌	8 21:47
10 15:52	♂	✱	♍	10 23:04
12 9:46	♇	✱	♎	12 22:43
14 19:55	♂	☌	♏	14 22:40
16 16:21	♀	✱	♐	17 0:39
19 2:24	♀	□	♑	19 5:48
21 9:20	☉	△	♒	21 14:18
23 1:47	♅	✱	♓	24 1:28
25 21:54	♇	△	♈	26 14:09
28 10:58	♇	□	♉	29 3:07

Last Aspect / ☽ Ingress (October)

Last Aspect Dy Hr Mn			☽ Ingress	Dy Hr Mn
1 2:25	☿	△	♊	1 15:03
3 21:47	☿	□	♋	4 0:38
5 16:54	♇	☌	♌	6 6:49
7 19:26	♀	✱	♍	8 9:34
9 21:19	♇	✱	♎	10 9:50
12 4:23	♀	☌	♏	12 9:17
13 20:55	♇	△	♐	14 9:51
15 22:32	☉	✱	♑	16 13:18
18 9:20	☉	□	♒	18 20:39
21 4:33	☿	△	♓	21 7:32
23 9:59	♂	△	♈	23 20:21
25 17:23	♇	□	♉	26 9:12
28 18:18	♂	☍	♊	28 20:48
30 11:45	♃	✱	♋	31 6:26

☽ Phases & Eclipses

Dy Hr Mn		
5 7:21	☾	11♊46
12 4:26	●	18♍27
12 4:40:58	☄	P 0.047
18 20:37	☽	24♐57
26 19:45	○	2♈45
26 19:48	☄	T 1.321
4 20:15	☾	10♋38
11 13:06	●	17♎15
11 12:55:15	☄	P 0.901
18 9:20	☽	24♑02
26 13:34	○	2♉10

Astro Data

1 September 1931
Julian Day # 11566
SVP 6♓12'52"
GC 25♐53.1 ⚵ 10♎50.2
Eris 2♈17.5R ⚴ 27♊48.6
⚷ 23♉38.3R ⚶ 9♑51.9
☽ Mean ☊ 6♈43.1

1 October 1931
Julian Day # 11596
SVP 6♓12'48"
GC 25♐53.2 ⚵ 23♎45.5
Eris 1♈58.3R ⚴ 11♋20.6
⚷ 23♉06.6R ⚶ 15♑25.9
☽ Mean ☊ 5♈07.7

November 1931 LONGITUDE

Day	Sid.Time	☉	0 hr ☽	Noon ☽	True ☊	☿	♀	♂	⚳	♃	♄	♅	♆	♇
1 Su	14 39 15	8♏06 00	9♋23 13	15♋52 51	4♈52.0	16♏41.9	22♏16.4	1♐25.0	23♏14.8	20♌22.7	17♑58.8	16♈33.9	7♍32.8	22♋09.1
2 M	14 43 12	9 06 04	22 26 35	29 04 41	4D 50.0	18 15.3	23 31.3	2 08.2	23 40.1	20 29.4	18 02.7	16R 31.7	7 34.1	22R 08.9
3 Tu	14 47 08	10 06 09	5♌47 22	12♌34 51	4 49.5	19 48.3	24 46.2	2 51.6	24 05.4	20 35.9	18 06.6	16 29.5	7 35.3	22 08.6
4 W	14 51 05	11 06 17	19 27 17	26 24 48	4 50.3	21 20.9	26 01.1	3 35.0	24 30.7	20 42.3	18 10.6	16 27.3	7 36.5	22 08.4
5 Th	14 55 01	12 06 26	3♍27 25	10♍35 04	4 51.7	22 53.1	27 16.0	4 18.4	24 56.0	20 48.5	18 14.7	16 25.2	7 37.7	22 08.1
6 F	14 58 58	13 06 38	17 47 34	25 04 38	4R 53.0	24 24.9	28 30.9	5 02.0	25 21.3	20 54.6	18 18.9	16 23.1	7 38.9	22 07.8
7 Sa	15 02 54	14 06 51	2♎25 46	9♎50 24	4 53.2	25 56.4	29 45.8	5 45.6	25 46.6	21 00.5	18 23.2	16 21.0	7 40.0	22 07.4
8 Su	15 06 51	15 07 07	17 17 45	24 46 56	4 51.7	27 27.4	1♐00.8	6 29.2	26 12.0	21 06.3	18 27.5	16 18.9	7 41.1	22 07.1
9 M	15 10 47	16 07 25	2♏16 57	9♏46 43	4 48.2	28 58.1	2 15.7	7 12.9	26 37.3	21 11.9	18 31.9	16 16.9	7 42.2	22 06.7
10 Tu	15 14 44	17 07 44	17 15 05	24 40 57	4 42.7	0♐28.4	3 30.6	7 56.7	27 02.7	21 17.4	18 36.4	16 14.9	7 43.2	22 06.3
11 W	15 18 40	18 08 05	2♐03 15	9♐21 00	4 35.9	1 58.3	4 45.5	8 40.6	27 28.1	21 22.6	18 41.0	16 12.9	7 44.2	22 05.8
12 Th	15 22 37	19 08 28	16 33 22	23 39 40	4 28.6	3 27.8	6 00.4	9 24.5	27 53.4	21 27.8	18 45.6	16 11.0	7 45.2	22 05.4
13 F	15 26 34	20 08 52	0♑39 24	7♑32 17	4 21.6	4 56.9	7 15.3	10 08.4	28 18.8	21 32.7	18 50.3	16 09.1	7 46.2	22 04.9
14 Sa	15 30 30	21 09 18	14 18 09	20 57 04	4 16.0	6 25.6	8 30.3	10 52.5	28 44.2	21 37.5	18 55.1	16 07.2	7 47.1	22 04.4
15 Su	15 34 27	22 09 45	27 29 13	3♒54 55	4 12.1	7 53.8	9 45.2	11 36.5	29 09.6	21 42.1	19 00.0	16 05.4	7 48.0	22 03.8
16 M	15 38 23	23 10 13	10♒14 38	16 28 51	4D 10.3	9 21.6	11 00.1	12 20.7	29 34.9	21 46.5	19 04.9	16 03.6	7 48.8	22 03.3
17 Tu	15 42 20	24 10 43	22 38 09	28 43 12	4 10.1	10 48.8	12 15.0	13 04.9	0♐00.3	21 50.8	19 09.9	16 01.8	7 49.6	22 02.7
18 W	15 46 16	25 11 14	4♓44 38	10♓43 07	4 11.1	12 15.5	13 29.8	13 49.1	0 25.7	21 54.9	19 15.0	16 00.1	7 50.4	22 02.1
19 Th	15 50 13	26 11 46	16 39 19	22 33 55	4R 12.3	13 41.5	14 44.7	14 33.4	0 51.0	21 58.8	19 20.1	15 58.4	7 51.2	22 01.5
20 F	15 54 10	27 12 19	28 27 31	4♈20 45	4 12.9	15 06.9	15 59.6	15 17.8	1 16.4	22 02.5	19 25.3	15 56.7	7 51.9	22 00.9
21 Sa	15 58 06	28 12 54	10♈14 11	16 08 20	4 12.0	16 31.6	17 14.5	16 02.2	1 41.7	22 06.1	19 30.6	15 55.1	7 52.6	22 00.2
22 Su	16 02 03	29 13 30	22 03 41	28 00 40	4 08.9	17 55.4	18 29.3	16 46.7	2 07.1	22 09.5	19 35.9	15 53.5	7 53.2	21 59.5
23 M	16 05 59	0♐14 07	3♉59 39	10♉00 57	4 03.4	19 18.2	19 44.2	17 31.2	2 32.4	22 12.7	19 41.3	15 52.0	7 53.9	21 58.8
24 Tu	16 09 56	1 14 46	16 04 51	22 11 31	3 55.3	20 40.0	20 59.1	18 15.8	2 57.7	22 15.7	19 46.7	15 50.5	7 54.4	21 58.1
25 W	16 13 52	2 15 26	28 21 07	4♊33 45	3 45.3	22 00.6	22 13.9	19 00.5	3 23.1	22 18.5	19 52.2	15 49.0	7 55.0	21 57.3
26 Th	16 17 49	3 16 07	10♊49 28	17 08 16	3 34.1	23 19.8	23 28.7	19 45.2	3 48.4	22 21.2	19 57.8	15 47.6	7 55.5	21 56.6
27 F	16 21 45	4 16 50	23 30 08	29 55 03	3 22.7	24 37.4	24 43.6	20 29.9	4 13.7	22 23.6	20 03.4	15 46.2	7 56.0	21 55.8
28 Sa	16 25 42	5 17 34	6♋22 57	12♋53 47	3 12.3	25 53.2	25 58.4	21 14.7	4 39.0	22 25.9	20 09.1	15 44.8	7 56.5	21 55.0
29 Su	16 29 39	6 18 20	19 27 31	26 04 06	3 03.8	27 06.9	27 13.3	21 59.6	5 04.3	22 28.0	20 14.8	15 43.5	7 56.9	21 54.1
30 M	16 33 35	7 19 07	2♌43 33	9♌25 53	2 57.9	28 18.2	28 28.1	22 44.5	5 29.6	22 29.9	20 20.6	15 42.3	7 57.3	21 53.3

December 1931 LONGITUDE

Day	Sid.Time	☉	0 hr ☽	Noon ☽	True ☊	☿	♀	♂	⚳	♃	♄	♅	♆	♇
1 Tu	16 37 32	8♐19 56	16♌11 07	22♌59 20	2♈54.6	29♐26.8	29♐42.9	23♐29.5	5♐54.9	22♌31.6	20♑26.5	15♈41.1	7♍57.6	21♋52.4
2 W	16 41 28	9 20 45	29 50 36	6♍45 00	2D 53.5	0♑32.3	0♑57.7	24 14.5	6 20.1	22 33.1	20 32.4	15R 39.9	7 58.0	21R 51.6
3 Th	16 45 25	10 21 37	13♍42 34	20 43 20	2R 53.7	1 34.2	2 12.5	24 59.6	6 45.4	22 34.4	20 38.3	15 38.8	7 58.2	21 50.7
4 F	16 49 21	11 22 30	27 47 19	4♎54 24	2 54.0	2 31.9	3 27.3	25 44.7	7 10.6	22 35.5	20 44.3	15 37.7	7 58.5	21 49.7
5 Sa	16 53 18	12 23 24	12♎04 25	19 17 06	2 53.0	3 25.0	4 42.1	26 29.9	7 35.8	22 36.5	20 50.4	15 36.7	7 58.7	21 48.8
6 Su	16 57 14	13 24 19	26 32 03	3♏48 46	2 49.7	4 12.7	5 56.9	27 15.2	8 01.0	22 37.2	20 56.5	15 35.7	7 58.9	21 47.8
7 M	17 01 11	14 25 16	11♏06 38	18 24 54	2 43.5	4 54.3	7 11.7	28 00.5	8 26.2	22 37.7	21 02.7	15 34.7	7 59.0	21 46.9
8 Tu	17 05 08	15 26 14	25 42 45	2♐59 19	2 34.5	5 29.0	8 26.5	28 45.9	8 51.4	22 38.1	21 08.9	15 33.8	7 59.1	21 45.9
9 W	17 09 04	16 27 13	10♐13 40	17 24 56	2 23.3	5 56.0	9 41.3	29 31.3	9 16.5	22R 38.2	21 15.1	15 33.0	7 59.2	21 44.9
10 Th	17 13 01	17 28 13	24 32 17	1♑34 58	2 11.0	6 14.4	10 56.1	0♑16.7	9 41.7	22 38.2	21 21.4	15 32.2	7R 59.3	21 43.9
11 F	17 16 57	18 29 14	8♑32 22	15 24 00	1 59.1	6R 23.4	12 10.9	1 02.2	10 06.8	22 37.9	21 27.8	15 31.5	7 59.3	21 42.8
12 Sa	17 20 54	19 30 16	22 09 31	28 48 48	1 48.6	6 22.1	13 25.6	1 47.8	10 31.9	22 37.5	21 34.1	15 30.8	7 59.2	21 41.8
13 Su	17 24 50	20 31 18	5♒21 48	11♒48 40	1 40.5	6 09.9	14 40.4	2 33.4	10 56.9	22 36.8	21 40.6	15 30.1	7 59.2	21 40.7
14 M	17 28 47	21 32 20	18 09 40	24 25 11	1 35.2	5 46.3	15 55.1	3 19.0	11 22.0	22 36.0	21 47.0	15 29.5	7 59.1	21 39.6
15 Tu	17 32 43	22 33 24	0♓35 43	6♓41 48	1 32.4	5 11.1	17 09.8	4 04.7	11 47.0	22 34.9	21 53.5	15 29.0	7 59.0	21 38.5
16 W	17 36 40	23 34 27	12 44 05	18 43 12	1D 31.5	4 24.5	18 24.5	4 50.5	12 12.0	22 33.7	22 00.1	15 28.5	7 58.8	21 37.4
17 Th	17 40 37	24 35 31	24 39 51	0♈34 45	1R 31.4	3 27.2	19 39.2	5 36.3	12 36.9	22 32.2	22 06.6	15 28.0	7 58.6	21 36.3
18 F	17 44 33	25 36 35	6♈28 37	12 22 07	1 31.1	2 20.5	20 53.8	6 22.1	13 01.8	22 30.6	22 13.2	15 27.6	7 58.4	21 35.2
19 Sa	17 48 30	26 37 40	18 15 59	24 10 50	1 29.4	1 06.1	22 08.5	7 08.0	13 26.7	22 28.8	22 19.9	15 27.3	7 58.1	21 34.0
20 Su	17 52 26	27 38 44	0♉07 17	6♉05 55	1 25.4	29♐46.4	23 23.1	7 53.9	13 51.6	22 26.8	22 26.5	15 27.0	7 57.8	21 32.9
21 M	17 56 23	28 39 50	12 07 15	18 11 43	1 18.5	28 23.9	24 37.7	8 39.8	14 16.4	22 24.6	22 33.3	15 26.8	7 57.4	21 31.7
22 Tu	18 00 19	29 40 55	24 19 43	0♊31 31	1 08.8	27 01.5	25 52.3	9 25.8	14 41.2	22 22.1	22 40.0	15 26.6	7 57.1	21 30.5
23 W	18 04 16	0♑42 01	6♊47 21	13 07 20	0 56.7	25 41.8	27 06.9	10 11.9	15 06.0	22 19.6	22 46.8	15 26.4	7 56.7	21 29.4
24 Th	18 08 13	1 43 08	19 31 30	25 59 49	0 43.1	24 27.5	28 21.5	10 58.0	15 30.8	22 16.8	22 53.6	15 26.4	7 56.3	21 28.2
25 F	18 12 09	2 44 15	2♋32 09	9♋08 18	0 29.3	23 20.4	29 36.0	11 44.1	15 55.5	22 13.8	23 00.4	15D 26.3	7 55.8	21 27.0
26 Sa	18 16 06	3 45 22	15 48 01	22 30 59	0 16.5	22 22.3	0♒50.5	12 30.3	16 20.1	22 10.6	23 07.2	15 26.3	7 55.3	21 25.7
27 Su	18 20 02	4 46 29	29 16 53	6♌05 23	0 05.9	21 34.1	2 05.0	13 16.5	16 44.8	22 07.3	23 14.1	15 26.4	7 54.8	21 24.5
28 M	18 23 59	5 47 37	12♌56 10	19 48 55	29♓58.2	20 56.4	3 19.5	14 02.7	17 09.4	22 03.8	23 21.0	15 26.5	7 54.2	21 23.3
29 Tu	18 27 55	6 48 45	26 43 23	3♍39 20	29 53.6	20 29.3	4 33.9	14 49.0	17 33.9	22 00.1	23 27.9	15 26.7	7 53.6	21 22.1
30 W	18 31 52	7 49 54	10♍36 35	17 35 01	29D 51.6	20 12.6	5 48.4	15 35.3	17 58.5	21 56.2	23 34.9	15 26.9	7 53.0	21 20.8
31 Th	18 35 48	8 51 03	24 34 32	1♎35 03	29R 51.2	20D 05.9	7 02.8	16 21.7	18 22.9	21 52.1	23 41.8	15 27.2	7 52.3	21 19.6

Astro Data	Dy Hr Mn
☽ 0S	6 21:25
♃⊻♇	20 2:40
☽ 0N	20 4:37
☽ 0S	4 4:34
♃ R	9 17:30
♆ R	11 6:18
☿ R	11 21:12
♄☍♇	13 12:30
☽ 0N	17 11:21
♃⊼♄	20 12:36
♄⚼♆	24 20:55
♅ D	25 15:29
☽ 0S	31 9:15
☿ D	31 16:55

Planet Ingress		Dy Hr Mn
♀	♐	7 16:32
☿	♐	10 4:27
⚳	♐	17 11:44
☉	♐	23 6:25
♀	♑	1 17:29
☿	♑	2 0:00
♂	♑	10 3:11
☿	♐R	20 7:59
☉	♑	22 19:30
♀	♒	25 19:44
☊	♓R	28 5:25

Last Aspect Dy Hr Mn		☽ Ingress	Dy Hr Mn
2 0:55	♀ △	♌	2 13:39
4 11:15	♀ □	♍	4 18:08
6 18:09	♀ ⚹	♎	6 20:03
8 7:44	♇ □	♏	8 20:21
10 7:50	♇ △	♐	10 20:39
12 8:15	♃ △	♑	12 22:52
14 14:03	♇ ☍	♒	15 4:40
17 2:13	☉ □	♓	17 14:32
19 20:05	☉ △	♈	20 3:08
22 0:08	♃ △	♉	22 16:00
24 12:08	♃ □	♊	25 3:12
27 1:15	♀ ☍	♋	27 12:09
29 4:27	♇ ☌	♌	29 19:06

Last Aspect Dy Hr Mn		☽ Ingress	Dy Hr Mn
1 12:56	♂ △	♍	2 0:16
3 19:40	♂ □	♎	4 3:44
6 0:36	♂ ⚹	♏	6 5:43
7 18:56	♃ □	♐	8 7:04
9 20:47	♃ △	♑	10 9:17
11 23:11	♇ ☍	♒	12 14:10
14 8:30	♃ ☍	♓	14 22:50
16 22:43	☉ □	♈	17 10:49
19 17:25	☉ △	♉	19 23:45
22 2:00	♀ △	♊	22 10:59
24 9:24	☿ ☍	♋	24 19:22
26 13:05	♄ ☍	♌	27 1:16
28 15:54	♃ ☌	♍	29 5:41
30 22:23	♄ △	♎	31 9:17

☽ Phases & Eclipses Dy Hr Mn		
3 7:17	☾	9♌54
9 22:55	●	16♏35
17 2:13	☽	23♒46
25 7:10	○	2♊03
2 16:50	☾	9♍33
9 10:16	●	16♐23
16 22:43	☽	24♓02
24 23:23	○	2♋12

Astro Data

1 November 1931
Julian Day # 11627
SVP 6♓12'44"
GC 25♐53.2 ⚵ 7♏24.2
Eris 1♈39.5R ⚶ 21♋27.6
⚷ 21♉48.0R ⚴ 25♑33.6
☽ Mean ☊ 3♈29.3

1 December 1931
Julian Day # 11657
SVP 6♓12'39"
GC 25♐53.3 ⚵ 20♏33.4
Eris 1♈27.9R ⚶ 24♋47.2R
⚷ 20♉15.5R ⚴ 7♒48.9
☽ Mean ☊ 1♈54.0

LONGITUDE

January 1932

Day	Sid.Time	☉	0 hr ☽	Noon ☽	True ☊	☿	♀	♂	⚳	♃	♄	♅	♆	♇
1 F	18 39 45	9♑52 12	8♎36 32	15♎38 55	29♓51.2	20♐08.6	8♒17.2	17♑08.1	18♐47.4	21♌47.8	23♑48.8	15♈27.5	7♍51.6	21♋18.3
2 Sa	18 43 42	10 53 22	22 42 08	29 46 04	29R50.1	20 19.9	9 31.5	17 54.6	19 11.8	21R43.4	23 55.8	15 27.9	7R50.9	21R17.0
3 Su	18 47 38	11 54 32	6♏50 35	13♏55 25	29 46.8	20 39.2	10 45.9	18 41.0	19 36.1	21 38.8	24 02.8	15 28.3	7 50.2	21 15.8
4 M	18 51 35	12 55 43	21 00 19	28 04 54	29 40.6	21 05.8	12 00.2	19 27.6	20 00.5	21 34.1	24 09.9	15 28.8	7 49.4	21 14.5
5 Tu	18 55 31	13 56 54	5♐08 43	12♐11 18	29 31.6	21 38.8	13 14.5	20 14.1	20 24.7	21 29.1	24 16.9	15 29.4	7 48.6	21 13.2
6 W	18 59 28	14 58 05	19 12 05	26 10 32	29 20.3	22 17.7	14 28.8	21 00.7	20 49.0	21 24.0	24 24.0	15 29.9	7 47.7	21 11.9
7 Th	19 03 24	15 59 16	3♑06 03	9♑58 07	29 07.8	23 01.9	15 43.0	21 47.4	21 13.2	21 18.8	24 31.0	15 30.6	7 46.9	21 10.6
8 F	19 07 21	17 00 27	16 46 15	23 30 00	28 55.5	23 50.7	16 57.2	22 34.1	21 37.3	21 13.4	24 38.1	15 31.3	7 46.0	21 09.4
9 Sa	19 11 17	18 01 37	0♒09 04	6♒43 13	28 44.5	24 43.8	18 11.4	23 20.8	22 01.4	21 07.8	24 45.2	15 32.0	7 45.0	21 08.1
10 Su	19 15 14	19 02 47	13 12 19	19 36 23	28 35.8	25 40.6	19 25.6	24 07.5	22 25.4	21 02.1	24 52.3	15 32.8	7 44.1	21 06.8
11 M	19 19 11	20 03 57	25 55 30	2♓09 55	28 29.8	26 40.7	20 39.7	24 54.2	22 49.4	20 56.2	24 59.5	15 33.7	7 43.1	21 05.5
12 Tu	19 23 07	21 05 06	8♓19 55	14 25 54	28 26.6	27 43.8	21 53.8	25 41.0	23 13.3	20 50.2	25 06.6	15 34.6	7 42.1	21 04.2
13 W	19 27 04	22 06 15	20 28 21	26 27 49	28D25.5	28 49.6	23 07.8	26 27.9	23 37.1	20 44.1	25 13.7	15 35.5	7 41.0	21 02.9
14 Th	19 31 00	23 07 23	2♈24 53	8♈20 12	28 25.8	29 57.8	24 21.8	27 14.7	24 00.9	20 37.8	25 20.8	15 36.5	7 40.0	21 01.6
15 F	19 34 57	24 08 30	14 14 24	20 08 12	28R26.4	1♑08.1	25 35.8	28 01.6	24 24.7	20 31.4	25 28.0	15 37.6	7 38.9	21 00.3
16 Sa	19 38 53	25 09 37	26 02 17	1♉57 21	28 26.2	2 20.4	26 49.7	28 48.5	24 48.4	20 24.9	25 35.1	15 38.7	7 37.8	20 59.0
17 Su	19 42 50	26 10 42	7♉54 04	13 53 07	28 24.3	3 34.5	28 03.6	29 35.4	25 12.0	20 18.2	25 42.2	15 39.8	7 36.6	20 57.7
18 M	19 46 46	27 11 48	19 55 06	26 00 38	28 20.2	4 50.3	29 17.4	0♒22.4	25 35.6	20 11.5	25 49.3	15 41.0	7 35.5	20 56.4
19 Tu	19 50 43	28 12 52	2♊10 12	8♊24 17	28 13.6	6 07.5	0♓31.2	1 09.3	25 59.1	20 04.6	25 56.5	15 42.2	7 34.3	20 55.2
20 W	19 54 40	29 13 55	14 43 14	21 07 20	28 05.0	7 26.0	1 44.9	1 56.3	26 22.5	19 57.6	26 03.6	15 43.5	7 33.1	20 53.9
21 Th	19 58 36	0♒14 58	27 36 44	4♋11 30	27 55.0	8 45.9	2 58.6	2 43.3	26 45.9	19 50.5	26 10.7	15 44.9	7 31.8	20 52.6
22 F	20 02 33	1 16 00	10♋51 35	17 36 46	27 44.6	10 06.9	4 12.2	3 30.4	27 09.2	19 43.4	26 17.9	15 46.3	7 30.6	20 51.3
23 Sa	20 06 29	2 17 01	24 26 46	1♌21 11	27 34.9	11 29.0	5 25.8	4 17.5	27 32.4	19 36.1	26 25.0	15 47.7	7 29.3	20 50.1
24 Su	20 10 26	3 18 02	8♌19 32	15 21 15	27 26.9	12 52.1	6 39.3	5 04.5	27 55.6	19 28.8	26 32.1	15 49.2	7 28.0	20 48.8
25 M	20 14 22	4 19 01	22 25 43	29 32 20	27 21.3	14 16.2	7 52.8	5 51.6	28 18.7	19 21.3	26 39.2	15 50.7	7 26.7	20 47.6
26 Tu	20 18 19	5 20 00	6♍40 29	13♍49 35	27D18.3	15 41.2	9 06.2	6 38.8	28 41.8	19 13.8	26 46.3	15 52.3	7 25.3	20 46.3
27 W	20 22 16	6 20 58	20 59 03	28 08 27	27 17.4	17 07.1	10 19.6	7 25.9	29 04.7	19 06.2	26 53.3	15 53.9	7 23.9	20 45.1
28 Th	20 26 12	7 21 56	5♎17 20	12♎25 22	27 18.1	18 33.9	11 32.9	8 13.1	29 27.6	18 58.6	27 00.4	15 55.6	7 22.6	20 43.8
29 F	20 30 09	8 22 52	19 32 16	26 37 49	27R19.2	20 01.4	12 46.2	9 00.3	29 50.4	18 50.9	27 07.4	15 57.3	7 21.2	20 42.6
30 Sa	20 34 05	9 23 49	3♏41 50	10♏44 11	27 19.7	21 29.8	13 59.4	9 47.5	0♑13.2	18 43.1	27 14.5	15 59.1	7 19.7	20 41.4
31 Su	20 38 02	10 24 44	17 44 44	24 43 25	27 18.7	22 59.0	15 12.5	10 34.7	0 35.8	18 35.3	27 21.5	16 00.9	7 18.3	20 40.2

LONGITUDE

February 1932

Day	Sid.Time	☉	0 hr ☽	Noon ☽	True ☊	☿	♀	♂	⚳	♃	♄	♅	♆	♇
1 M	20 41 58	11♒25 39	1♐40 06	8♐34 41	27♓15.7	24♑29.0	16♓25.6	11♒22.0	0♑58.4	18♌27.5	27♑28.5	16♈02.7	7♍16.8	20♋39.0
2 Tu	20 45 55	12 26 34	15 27 01	22 16 58	27R10.6	25 59.7	17 38.6	12 09.2	1 21.0	18R19.6	27 35.5	16 04.6	7R15.4	20R37.8
3 W	20 49 51	13 27 27	29 04 22	5♑49 02	27 03.8	27 31.2	18 51.6	12 56.5	1 43.4	18 11.7	27 42.5	16 06.6	7 13.9	20 36.6
4 Th	20 53 48	14 28 20	12♑30 47	19 09 24	26 56.2	29 03.5	20 04.5	13 43.8	2 05.7	18 03.7	27 49.4	16 08.6	7 12.4	20 35.4
5 F	20 57 45	15 29 11	25 44 43	2♒16 34	26 48.5	0♒36.5	21 17.3	14 31.1	2 28.0	17 55.8	27 56.4	16 10.6	7 10.9	20 34.2
6 Sa	21 01 41	16 30 01	8♒44 49	15 09 23	26 41.7	2 10.3	22 30.0	15 18.4	2 50.2	17 47.8	28 03.3	16 12.6	7 09.3	20 33.1
7 Su	21 05 38	17 30 50	21 30 12	27 47 19	26 36.4	3 44.8	23 42.7	16 05.8	3 12.3	17 39.8	28 10.1	16 14.8	7 07.8	20 32.0
8 M	21 09 34	18 31 38	4♓00 45	10♓10 41	26 33.0	5 20.1	24 55.4	16 53.1	3 34.3	17 31.8	28 17.0	16 16.9	7 06.2	20 30.8
9 Tu	21 13 31	19 32 24	16 17 17	22 20 49	26D31.5	6 56.2	26 07.9	17 40.5	3 56.2	17 23.9	28 23.8	16 19.1	7 04.7	20 29.7
10 W	21 17 27	20 33 09	28 21 37	4♈20 03	26 31.7	8 33.1	27 20.4	18 27.8	4 18.0	17 15.9	28 30.6	16 21.3	7 03.1	20 28.6
11 Th	21 21 24	21 33 52	10♈16 34	16 11 38	26 33.1	10 10.8	28 32.7	19 15.2	4 39.7	17 08.0	28 37.4	16 23.6	7 01.5	20 27.5
12 F	21 25 20	22 34 34	22 05 48	27 59 36	26 34.9	11 49.3	29 45.0	20 02.6	5 01.3	17 00.0	28 44.2	16 25.9	6 59.9	20 26.4
13 Sa	21 29 17	23 35 14	3♉53 40	9♉48 35	26 36.6	13 28.6	0♈57.3	20 49.9	5 22.8	16 52.1	28 50.9	16 28.2	6 58.3	20 25.4
14 Su	21 33 14	24 35 52	15 45 00	21 43 34	26R37.5	15 08.8	2 09.4	21 37.3	5 44.3	16 44.3	28 57.6	16 30.6	6 56.6	20 24.3
15 M	21 37 10	25 36 29	27 44 55	3♊49 40	26 37.1	16 49.8	3 21.4	22 24.7	6 05.6	16 36.5	29 04.2	16 33.0	6 55.0	20 23.3
16 Tu	21 41 07	26 37 04	9♊58 26	16 11 47	26 35.4	18 31.7	4 33.4	23 12.1	6 26.8	16 28.7	29 10.8	16 35.5	6 53.4	20 22.3
17 W	21 45 03	27 37 37	22 30 12	28 54 09	26 32.4	20 14.5	5 45.2	23 59.5	6 47.9	16 21.0	29 17.4	16 38.0	6 51.7	20 21.3
18 Th	21 49 00	28 38 09	5♋23 59	11♋59 57	26 28.5	21 58.2	6 57.0	24 46.9	7 08.9	16 13.3	29 24.0	16 40.5	6 50.1	20 20.3
19 F	21 52 56	29 38 39	18 42 12	25 30 43	26 24.3	23 42.8	8 08.6	25 34.2	7 29.8	16 05.8	29 30.5	16 43.0	6 48.4	20 19.3
20 Sa	21 56 53	0♓39 07	2♌25 23	9♌25 55	26 20.2	25 28.3	9 20.2	26 21.6	7 50.6	15 58.2	29 36.9	16 45.6	6 46.8	20 18.4
21 Su	22 00 49	1 39 33	16 31 53	23 42 44	26 16.9	27 14.8	10 31.6	27 09.0	8 11.3	15 50.8	29 43.4	16 48.2	6 45.1	20 17.5
22 M	22 04 46	2 39 58	0♍57 47	8♍16 16	26 14.7	29 02.2	11 43.0	27 56.4	8 31.8	15 43.4	29 49.8	16 50.9	6 43.4	20 16.6
23 Tu	22 08 43	3 40 21	15 37 17	22 59 59	26D13.9	0♓50.5	12 54.2	28 43.8	8 52.3	15 36.1	29 56.1	16 53.6	6 41.8	20 15.7
24 W	22 12 39	4 40 42	0♎23 26	7♎46 46	26 14.2	2 39.8	14 05.3	29 31.2	9 12.6	15 28.9	0♒02.4	16 56.3	6 40.1	20 14.8
25 Th	22 16 36	5 41 02	15 09 07	22 29 45	26 15.2	4 30.0	15 16.3	0♓18.5	9 32.9	15 21.8	0 08.7	16 59.0	6 38.4	20 13.9
26 F	22 20 32	6 41 20	29 47 59	7♏03 16	26 16.6	6 21.1	16 27.2	1 05.9	9 53.0	15 14.8	0 14.9	17 01.8	6 36.7	20 13.1
27 Sa	22 24 29	7 41 37	14♏15 07	21 23 11	26 17.8	8 13.1	17 38.0	1 53.3	10 13.0	15 07.9	0 21.1	17 04.6	6 35.1	20 12.2
28 Su	22 28 25	8 41 53	28 27 13	5♐27 03	26R18.3	10 06.0	18 48.7	2 40.7	10 32.8	15 01.2	0 27.2	17 07.5	6 33.4	20 11.4
29 M	22 32 22	9 42 07	12♐22 37	19 13 53	26 18.2	11 59.6	19 59.2	3 28.1	10 52.6	14 54.5	0 33.3	17 10.3	6 31.7	20 10.7

Astro Data

	Dy Hr Mn
♃⊻♇	9 10:33
☽0N	13 18:35
☽0S	27 14:20
☽0N	10 2:05
♀0N	13 22:49
♃△♅	15 20:08
☽0S	23 22:18

Planet Ingress

	Dy Hr Mn
☿ ♑	14 12:47
♂ ♒	18 0:35
♀ ♓	19 1:52
☉ ♒	21 6:07
⚳ ♑	29 22:05
☿ ♒	5 2:36
♀ ♈	12 16:58
☉ ♓	19 20:28
☿ ♓	23 0:50
♄ ♒	24 2:47
♂ ♓	25 2:36

Last Aspect / ☽ Ingress

Last Aspect Dy Hr Mn		☽ Ingress Dy Hr Mn
2 2:00	♄ □	♏ 2 12:24
4 5:18	♄ ⚹	♐ 4 15:15
6 4:58	♀ ⚹	♑ 6 18:37
8 14:03	♄ ☌	♒ 8 23:44
11 0:31	☿ ⚹	♓ 11 7:49
13 17:15	☿ □	♈ 13 19:07
16 5:10	♂ □	♉ 16 8:02
18 19:07	♀ □	♊ 18 19:47
20 9:51	♃ ⚹	♋ 21 4:22
23 3:22	♀ ☍	♌ 23 9:40
24 18:57	♃ ☌	♍ 25 12:47
27 9:53	♄ △	♎ 27 15:07
29 12:51	♄ □	♏ 29 17:43
31 16:35	♄ ⚹	♐ 31 21:07

Last Aspect / ☽ Ingress

Last Aspect Dy Hr Mn		☽ Ingress Dy Hr Mn
2 5:07	♃ △	♑ 3 1:39
5 3:57	♄ ☌	♒ 5 7:48
6 16:56	♃ ☍	♓ 7 16:15
10 0:11	☿ ⚹	♈ 10 3:17
12 13:32	♄ □	♉ 12 16:05
15 2:32	♄ △	♊ 15 4:28
17 9:25	☉ △	♋ 17 14:02
19 19:01	♄ ☍	♌ 19 19:49
21 18:41	☿ ☍	♍ 21 22:25
23 23:20	♄ △	♎ 23 23:22
25 8:18	♇ □	♏ 26 0:20
27 10:00	♇ △	♐ 28 2:39

☽ Phases & Eclipses

Dy Hr Mn		
1 1:23	☾	9♎25
7 23:29	●	16♑29
15 20:55	☽	24♈31
23 13:44	○	2♌21
30 9:32	☾	9♏18
6 14:45	●	16♒37
14 18:16	☽	24♉52
22 2:07	○	2♍15
28 18:03	☾	8♐57

Astro Data

1 January 1932
Julian Day # 11688
SVP 6♓12'33"
GC 25♐53.4 ⚴ 3♐39.7
Eris 1♈26.4 ⚵ 20♋00.8R
⚷ 19♉01.3R ⚶ 21♒52.6
☽ Mean ☊ 0♈15.5

1 February 1932
Julian Day # 11719
SVP 6♓12'28"
GC 25♐53.4 ⚴ 15♐39.2
Eris 1♈36.5 ⚵ 13♋16.0R
⚷ 18♉38.8 ⚶ 6♓38.2
☽ Mean ☊ 28♓37.0

March 1932 — LONGITUDE

Day	Sid.Time	☉	0 hr ☽	Noon ☽	True ☊	☿	♀	♂	⚳	♃	♄	♅	♆	♇
1 Tu	22 36 18	10♓42 20	26♐00 54	2♑43 44	26♓17.2	13♓54.0	21♈09.7	4♓15.4	11♑12.2	14♌47.9	0♒39.3	17♈13.2	6♍30.0	20♋09.9
2 W	22 40 15	11 42 31	9♑22 30	15 57 20	26R15.6	15 49.0	22 20.0	5 02.8	11 31.7	14R41.5	0 45.3	17 16.2	6R28.4	20R09.2
3 Th	22 44 12	12 42 41	22 28 21	28 55 43	26 13.6	17 44.6	23 30.2	5 50.1	11 51.0	14 35.2	0 51.3	17 19.1	6 26.7	20 08.4
4 F	22 48 08	13 42 49	5♒19 35	11♒40 06	26 11.7	19 40.6	24 40.3	6 37.5	12 10.2	14 29.0	0 57.1	17 22.1	6 25.1	20 07.7
5 Sa	22 52 05	14 42 55	17 57 24	24 11 39	26 10.1	21 36.8	25 50.2	7 24.8	12 29.3	14 22.9	1 03.0	17 25.1	6 23.4	20 07.1
6 Su	22 56 01	15 42 59	0♓23 00	6♓31 36	26 08.9	23 33.1	27 00.0	8 12.1	12 48.2	14 17.0	1 08.7	17 28.1	6 21.7	20 06.4
7 M	22 59 58	16 43 02	12 37 39	18 41 18	26D08.3	25 29.3	28 09.7	8 59.5	13 07.0	14 11.2	1 14.5	17 31.1	6 20.1	20 05.8
8 Tu	23 03 54	17 43 03	24 42 46	0♈42 16	26 08.2	27 25.1	29 19.2	9 46.8	13 25.7	14 05.6	1 20.1	17 34.2	6 18.5	20 05.1
9 W	23 07 51	18 43 01	6♈40 03	12 36 24	26 08.6	29 20.2	0♉28.6	10 34.1	13 44.2	14 00.1	1 25.7	17 37.3	6 16.8	20 04.5
10 Th	23 11 47	19 42 58	18 31 36	24 26 00	26 09.2	1♈14.3	1 37.8	11 21.3	14 02.5	13 54.8	1 31.3	17 40.4	6 15.2	20 04.0
11 F	23 15 44	20 42 52	0♉19 59	6♉13 56	26 09.8	3 07.0	2 46.9	12 08.6	14 20.7	13 49.6	1 36.8	17 43.5	6 13.6	20 03.4
12 Sa	23 19 40	21 42 45	12 08 18	18 03 32	26 10.4	4 57.9	3 55.8	12 55.8	14 38.8	13 44.6	1 42.2	17 46.7	6 12.0	20 02.9
13 Su	23 23 37	22 42 35	24 00 08	29 58 39	26 10.8	6 46.7	5 04.6	13 43.0	14 56.7	13 39.8	1 47.5	17 49.9	6 10.4	20 02.4
14 M	23 27 34	23 42 23	5♊59 35	12♊03 31	26 11.0	8 32.8	6 13.1	14 30.3	15 14.4	13 35.1	1 52.8	17 53.1	6 08.8	20 01.9
15 Tu	23 31 30	24 42 09	18 11 00	24 22 36	26R11.1	10 15.7	7 21.6	15 17.4	15 32.0	13 30.6	1 58.1	17 56.3	6 07.2	20 01.4
16 W	23 35 27	25 41 53	0♋38 52	7♋00 18	26D11.1	11 55.0	8 29.8	16 04.6	15 49.4	13 26.2	2 03.3	17 59.5	6 05.6	20 01.0
17 Th	23 39 23	26 41 34	13 27 23	20 00 32	26 11.1	13 30.3	9 37.9	16 51.8	16 06.6	13 22.1	2 08.4	18 02.7	6 04.1	20 00.6
18 F	23 43 20	27 41 13	26 40 05	3♌26 16	26 11.2	15 01.0	10 45.8	17 38.9	16 23.7	13 18.1	2 13.4	18 06.0	6 02.6	20 00.2
19 Sa	23 47 16	28 40 50	10♌19 13	17 18 54	26 11.4	16 26.6	11 53.5	18 26.0	16 40.6	13 14.2	2 18.4	18 09.3	6 01.0	19 59.9
20 Su	23 51 13	29 40 25	24 25 10	1♍37 41	26 11.7	17 46.7	13 01.0	19 13.1	16 57.4	13 10.6	2 23.3	18 12.6	5 59.5	19 59.5
21 M	23 55 09	0♈39 57	8♍55 55	16 19 14	26R11.9	19 01.0	14 08.3	20 00.1	17 14.0	13 07.1	2 28.1	18 15.9	5 58.0	19 59.2
22 Tu	23 59 06	1 39 27	23 46 46	1♎17 34	26 11.9	20 09.1	15 15.4	20 47.1	17 30.3	13 03.8	2 32.9	18 19.2	5 56.5	19 58.9
23 W	0 03 03	2 38 55	8♎50 33	16 24 35	26 11.7	21 10.6	16 22.3	21 34.2	17 46.6	13 00.7	2 37.6	18 22.5	5 55.1	19 58.6
24 Th	0 06 59	3 38 22	23 58 29	1♏31 07	26 11.1	22 05.2	17 29.0	22 21.1	18 02.6	12 57.8	2 42.2	18 25.8	5 53.6	19 58.4
25 F	0 10 56	4 37 46	9♏01 22	16 28 15	26 10.2	22 52.8	18 35.4	23 08.1	18 18.4	12 55.0	2 46.8	18 29.2	5 52.2	19 58.2
26 Sa	0 14 52	5 37 09	23 50 53	1♐08 36	26 09.1	23 33.1	19 41.7	23 55.0	18 34.1	12 52.4	2 51.3	18 32.6	5 50.8	19 58.0
27 Su	0 18 49	6 36 30	8♐20 48	15 27 08	26 08.2	24 06.0	20 47.7	24 42.0	18 49.6	12 50.1	2 55.7	18 35.9	5 49.4	19 57.8
28 M	0 22 45	7 35 49	22 27 21	29 21 23	26D07.6	24 31.4	21 53.5	25 28.9	19 04.9	12 47.9	3 00.0	18 39.3	5 48.0	19 57.7
29 Tu	0 26 42	8 35 06	6♑09 18	12♑51 14	26 07.5	24 49.3	22 59.1	26 15.7	19 20.0	12 45.9	3 04.3	18 42.7	5 46.7	19 57.5
30 W	0 30 38	9 34 22	19 27 26	25 58 14	26 08.0	24R59.7	24 04.4	27 02.6	19 34.9	12 44.0	3 08.4	18 46.1	5 45.3	19 57.5
31 Th	0 34 35	10 33 36	2♒23 58	8♒45 04	26 09.0	25 02.9	25 09.5	27 49.4	19 49.5	12 42.4	3 12.5	18 49.5	5 44.0	19 57.4

April 1932 — LONGITUDE

Day	Sid.Time	☉	0 hr ☽	Noon ☽	True ☊	☿	♀	♂	⚳	♃	♄	♅	♆	♇
1 F	0 38 32	11♈32 47	15♒01 55	21♒14 56	26♓10.3	24♈58.9	26♉14.3	28♓36.2	20♑04.0	12♌41.0	3♒16.6	18♈52.9	5♍42.7	19♋57.3
2 Sa	0 42 28	12 31 58	27 24 33	3♓31 08	26 11.6	24R48.1	27 18.9	29 22.9	20 18.3	12R39.7	3 20.5	18 56.3	5R41.4	19D57.3
3 Su	0 46 25	13 31 06	9♓35 05	15 36 46	26R12.6	24 30.8	28 23.2	0♈09.7	20 32.3	12 38.6	3 24.4	18 59.7	5 40.2	19 57.3
4 M	0 50 21	14 30 12	21 36 30	27 34 38	26 12.9	24 07.5	29 27.2	0 56.4	20 46.2	12 37.8	3 28.2	19 03.2	5 38.9	19 57.3
5 Tu	0 54 18	15 29 16	3♈31 26	9♈27 13	26 12.3	23 38.7	0♊31.0	1 43.0	20 59.8	12 37.1	3 31.9	19 06.6	5 37.7	19 57.4
6 W	0 58 14	16 28 18	15 22 13	21 16 42	26 10.7	23 05.2	1 34.5	2 29.7	21 13.2	12 36.6	3 35.5	19 10.0	5 36.5	19 57.5
7 Th	1 02 11	17 27 19	27 10 57	3♉05 11	26 08.0	22 27.6	2 37.6	3 16.3	21 26.4	12 36.3	3 39.0	19 13.5	5 35.4	19 57.6
8 F	1 06 07	18 26 17	8♉59 41	14 54 43	26 04.5	21 46.7	3 40.5	4 02.8	21 39.3	12D36.2	3 42.4	19 16.9	5 34.2	19 57.7
9 Sa	1 10 04	19 25 13	20 50 33	26 47 32	26 00.6	21 03.4	4 43.1	4 49.4	21 52.0	12 36.2	3 45.8	19 20.3	5 33.1	19 57.8
10 Su	1 14 01	20 24 07	2♊45 57	8♊46 10	25 56.6	20 18.5	5 45.3	5 35.9	22 04.5	12 36.5	3 49.1	19 23.8	5 32.0	19 58.0
11 M	1 17 57	21 22 59	14 48 34	20 53 33	25 53.2	19 32.9	6 47.2	6 22.3	22 16.7	12 37.0	3 52.3	19 27.2	5 30.9	19 58.2
12 Tu	1 21 54	22 21 48	27 01 33	3♋13 00	25 50.6	18 47.5	7 48.7	7 08.8	22 28.7	12 37.6	3 55.4	19 30.6	5 29.9	19 58.5
13 W	1 25 50	23 20 35	9♋28 21	15 48 05	25D49.2	18 03.1	8 49.9	7 55.1	22 40.5	12 38.4	3 58.4	19 34.1	5 28.9	19 58.7
14 Th	1 29 47	24 19 20	22 12 40	28 42 33	25 49.0	17 20.5	9 50.7	8 41.5	22 52.0	12 39.5	4 01.3	19 37.5	5 27.9	19 59.0
15 F	1 33 43	25 18 03	5♌18 08	11♌59 47	25 49.9	16 40.4	10 51.2	9 27.8	23 03.2	12 40.7	4 04.2	19 40.9	5 26.9	19 59.3
16 Sa	1 37 40	26 16 43	18 47 49	25 42 26	25 51.4	16 03.4	11 51.2	10 14.1	23 14.2	12 42.1	4 06.9	19 44.3	5 26.0	19 59.6
17 Su	1 41 36	27 15 22	2♍43 43	9♍51 37	25 52.8	15 30.0	12 50.8	11 00.3	23 24.9	12 43.6	4 09.6	19 47.7	5 25.1	20 00.0
18 M	1 45 33	28 13 57	17 05 56	24 26 16	25R53.5	15 00.8	13 50.0	11 46.5	23 35.4	12 45.4	4 12.1	19 51.2	5 24.2	20 00.3
19 Tu	1 49 30	29 12 31	1♎52 02	9♎22 28	25 52.9	14 36.0	14 48.8	12 32.6	23 45.6	12 47.3	4 14.6	19 54.6	5 23.4	20 00.7
20 W	1 53 26	0♉11 03	16 56 38	24 33 23	25 50.7	14 15.9	15 47.1	13 18.7	23 55.6	12 49.5	4 17.0	19 57.9	5 22.5	20 01.1
21 Th	1 57 23	1 09 33	2♏11 31	9♏49 42	25 46.9	14 00.7	16 44.9	14 04.8	24 05.3	12 51.7	4 19.3	20 01.3	5 21.7	20 01.6
22 F	2 01 19	2 08 01	17 26 36	25 00 56	25 41.9	13 50.5	17 42.3	14 50.8	24 14.7	12 54.2	4 21.5	20 04.7	5 21.0	20 02.1
23 Sa	2 05 16	3 06 27	2♐31 30	9♐57 12	25 36.4	13D45.3	18 39.2	15 36.8	24 23.8	12 56.9	4 23.6	20 08.1	5 20.2	20 02.5
24 Su	2 09 12	4 04 52	17 17 10	24 30 43	25 31.3	13 45.1	19 35.5	16 22.7	24 32.7	12 59.7	4 25.6	20 11.5	5 19.5	20 03.1
25 M	2 13 09	5 03 15	1♑37 21	8♑36 47	25 27.2	13 49.9	20 31.4	17 08.6	24 41.2	13 02.7	4 27.5	20 14.8	5 18.9	20 03.6
26 Tu	2 17 05	6 01 37	15 28 58	22 13 57	25 24.6	13 59.6	21 26.7	17 54.5	24 49.5	13 05.9	4 29.3	20 18.1	5 18.2	20 04.2
27 W	2 21 02	6 59 57	28 52 00	5♒23 27	25D23.6	14 14.1	22 21.5	18 40.3	24 57.5	13 09.2	4 31.1	20 21.5	5 17.6	20 04.8
28 Th	2 24 59	7 58 15	11♒48 46	18 08 26	25 24.0	14 33.2	23 15.6	19 26.1	25 05.2	13 12.8	4 32.7	20 24.8	5 17.0	20 05.4
29 F	2 28 55	8 56 32	24 23 02	0♓33 08	25 25.3	14 56.8	24 09.2	20 11.8	25 12.6	13 16.4	4 34.2	20 28.1	5 16.4	20 06.0
30 Sa	2 32 52	9 54 47	6♓39 19	12 42 12	25 26.7	15 24.7	25 02.2	20 57.5	25 19.6	13 20.3	4 35.7	20 31.4	5 15.9	20 06.6

Astro Data

	Dy Hr Mn
☽0N	8 9:14
☿0N	10 5:02
☉0N	20 19:53
☽0S	22 8:52
☿ R	31 10:26
♇ D	2 22:58
☽0N	4 15:33
♂0N	6 0:25
♃ D	8 14:10
☽0S	18 19:51
♅□♇	21 14:04
☿ D	24 0:44
♅⚼♆	26 12:20

Planet Ingress

		Dy Hr Mn
♀	♉	9 2:07
☿	♈	9 20:21
☉	♈	20 19:54
♂	♈	3 7:02
♀	♊	5 0:19
☉	♉	20 7:28

Last Aspect / ☽ Ingress (March)

Last Aspect Dy Hr Mn			☽ Ingress	Dy Hr Mn
29 13:27	♀	△	♑	1 7:06
3 0:54	♀	□	♒	3 14:00
5 15:30	♀	⚹	♓	5 23:15
8 4:09	☿	☌	♈	8 10:35
10 3:08	♇	□	♉	10 23:19
12 20:04	☉	⚹	♊	13 12:03
15 12:41	☉	□	♋	15 22:46
18 1:00	☉	△	♌	18 5:56
19 13:26	♅	△	♍	20 9:18
21 18:16	♂	☍	♎	22 9:56
23 20:04	☿	☍	♏	24 9:35
25 23:27	♂	△	♐	26 10:07
28 4:50	♂	□	♑	28 13:08
30 14:07	♂	⚹	♒	30 19:30

Last Aspect / ☽ Ingress (April)

Last Aspect Dy Hr Mn			☽ Ingress	Dy Hr Mn
1 22:39	♀	□	♓	2 5:05
4 16:09	♀	⚹	♈	4 16:53
6 15:30	☿	☌	♉	7 5:44
8 22:13	♇	⚹	♊	9 18:27
11 13:03	☉	⚹	♋	12 5:47
14 3:15	☉	□	♌	14 14:22
16 13:03	☉	△	♍	16 19:22
18 4:46	♇	⚹	♎	18 21:00
20 4:51	♇	□	♏	20 20:33
22 4:06	♇	△	♐	22 19:57
24 4:46	♅	△	♑	24 21:15
26 8:32	♅	□	♒	27 2:04
28 22:36	♀	△	♓	29 10:55

☽ Phases & Eclipses

Dy Hr Mn	
7 7:44	● 16♓32
7 7:55:25	● A 05'19"
15 12:41	☽ 24♊44
22 12:37	○ 1♎41
22 12:32	● P 0.966
29 3:43	☾ 8♑15
6 1:21	● 16♈02
14 3:15	☽ 23♋58
20 21:27	○ 0♏34
27 15:14	☾ 7♒08

Astro Data

1 March 1932
Julian Day # 11748
SVP 6♓12'23"
GC 25♐53.5 ⚴ 25♐02.0
Eris 1♈53.9 ⚵ 12♋44.7
⚷ 19♉13.1 ⚶ 20♓38.4
☽ Mean ☊ 27♓04.9

1 April 1932
Julian Day # 11779
SVP 6♓12'20"
GC 25♐53.6 ⚴ 1♑42.1
Eris 2♈16.3 ⚵ 18♋33.1
⚷ 20♉40.5 ⚶ 5♈28.5
☽ Mean ☊ 25♓26.4

LONGITUDE — May 1932

Day	Sid.Time	☉	0 hr ☽	Noon ☽	True ☊	☿	♀	♂	⚳	♃	♄	♅	♆	♇
1 Su	2 36 48	10♉53 01	18♓42 19	24♓40 13	25♓27.4	15♈56.8	25♊54.5	21♈43.1	25♑26.4	13♌24.3	4♒37.0	20♈34.7	5♍15.4	20♋07.3
2 M	2 40 45	11 51 13	0♈36 25	6♈31 23	25R 26.7	16 32.9	26 46.2	22 28.7	25 32.9	13 28.5	4 38.3	20 37.9	5R 14.9	20 08.0
3 Tu	2 44 41	12 49 24	12 25 34	18 19 20	25 24.0	17 12.8	27 37.2	23 14.3	25 39.0	13 32.9	4 39.4	20 41.2	5 14.5	20 08.7
4 W	2 48 38	13 47 33	24 13 04	0♉07 03	25 19.1	17 56.5	28 27.5	23 59.8	25 44.9	13 37.4	4 40.5	20 44.4	5 14.1	20 09.5
5 Th	2 52 34	14 45 40	6♉01 36	11 56 58	25 12.1	18 43.7	29 17.1	24 45.3	25 50.4	13 42.0	4 41.4	20 47.6	5 13.7	20 10.2
6 F	2 56 31	15 43 46	17 53 21	23 50 58	25 03.3	19 34.3	0♋05.9	25 30.7	25 55.6	13 46.9	4 42.3	20 50.8	5 13.4	20 11.0
7 Sa	3 00 28	16 41 50	29 50 01	5♊50 40	24 53.6	20 28.2	0 53.9	26 16.0	26 00.4	13 51.9	4 43.0	20 54.0	5 13.1	20 11.8
8 Su	3 04 24	17 39 52	11♊53 07	17 57 33	24 43.7	21 25.3	1 41.1	27 01.3	26 04.9	13 57.0	4 43.7	20 57.2	5 12.8	20 12.7
9 M	3 08 21	18 37 53	24 04 11	0♋13 12	24 34.7	22 25.4	2 27.5	27 46.6	26 09.1	14 02.4	4 44.3	21 00.3	5 12.6	20 13.5
10 Tu	3 12 17	19 35 52	6♋24 53	12 39 29	24 27.4	23 28.4	3 13.0	28 31.8	26 13.0	14 07.8	4 44.7	21 03.4	5 12.4	20 14.4
11 W	3 16 14	20 33 49	18 57 18	25 18 39	24 22.2	24 34.3	3 57.5	29 17.0	26 16.5	14 13.4	4 45.1	21 06.5	5 12.2	20 15.3
12 Th	3 20 10	21 31 45	1♌43 53	8♌13 20	24 19.3	25 42.9	4 41.1	0♉02.1	26 19.7	14 19.2	4 45.4	21 09.6	5 12.0	20 16.2
13 F	3 24 07	22 29 38	14 47 22	21 26 21	24D 18.4	26 54.3	5 23.7	0 47.1	26 22.5	14 25.1	4 45.5	21 12.7	5 11.9	20 17.1
14 Sa	3 28 03	23 27 30	28 10 36	5♍00 23	24 18.8	28 08.2	6 05.2	1 32.2	26 25.0	14 31.2	4R 45.6	21 15.7	5 11.8	20 18.1
15 Su	3 32 00	24 25 20	11♍55 57	18 57 24	24R 19.4	29 24.7	6 45.7	2 17.1	26 27.1	14 37.4	4 45.6	21 18.7	5 11.8	20 19.0
16 M	3 35 57	25 23 08	26 04 45	3♎17 51	24 19.2	0♉43.7	7 25.0	3 02.0	26 28.9	14 43.7	4 45.4	21 21.7	5D 11.8	20 20.0
17 Tu	3 39 53	26 20 54	10♎36 26	18 00 00	24 17.2	2 05.1	8 03.2	3 46.8	26 30.3	14 50.2	4 45.2	21 24.7	5 11.8	20 21.0
18 W	3 43 50	27 18 39	25 27 52	2♏59 11	24 12.8	3 28.9	8 40.2	4 31.6	26 31.4	14 56.8	4 44.9	21 27.6	5 11.8	20 22.1
19 Th	3 47 46	28 16 22	10♏32 56	18 07 57	24 05.9	4 55.2	9 15.9	5 16.4	26 32.2	15 03.6	4 44.5	21 30.5	5 11.9	20 23.1
20 F	3 51 43	29 14 04	25 42 56	3♐16 36	23 57.2	6 23.8	9 50.3	6 01.1	26R 32.6	15 10.5	4 44.0	21 33.4	5 12.0	20 24.2
21 Sa	3 55 39	0♊11 45	10♐47 40	18 14 54	23 47.4	7 54.7	10 23.3	6 45.7	26 32.6	15 17.5	4 43.4	21 36.3	5 12.2	20 25.3
22 Su	3 59 36	1 09 25	25 37 13	2♑53 42	23 37.9	9 28.0	10 55.0	7 30.3	26 32.2	15 24.7	4 42.7	21 39.1	5 12.4	20 26.4
23 M	4 03 32	2 07 03	10♑03 39	17 06 34	23 29.8	11 03.6	11 25.2	8 14.8	26 31.5	15 32.0	4 41.9	21 41.9	5 12.6	20 27.5
24 Tu	4 07 29	3 04 40	24 02 08	0♒50 18	23 23.6	12 41.4	11 53.9	8 59.3	26 30.5	15 39.4	4 41.0	21 44.7	5 12.8	20 28.6
25 W	4 11 26	4 02 17	7♒31 09	14 04 57	23 19.9	14 21.6	12 21.0	9 43.7	26 29.1	15 46.9	4 40.0	21 47.5	5 13.1	20 29.8
26 Th	4 15 22	4 59 52	20 32 05	26 53 03	23D 18.2	16 04.1	12 46.5	10 28.1	26 27.3	15 54.6	4 38.9	21 50.2	5 13.4	20 30.9
27 F	4 19 19	5 57 27	3♓08 25	9♓18 47	23 18.0	17 48.9	13 10.4	11 12.4	26 25.1	16 02.4	4 37.7	21 52.9	5 13.8	20 32.1
28 Sa	4 23 15	6 55 00	15 24 50	21 27 14	23R 18.2	19 35.9	13 32.5	11 56.7	26 22.6	16 10.3	4 36.4	21 55.6	5 14.1	20 33.3
29 Su	4 27 12	7 52 33	27 26 38	3♈23 43	23 17.8	21 25.3	13 52.9	12 40.9	26 19.7	16 18.4	4 35.1	21 58.2	5 14.5	20 34.5
30 M	4 31 08	8 50 04	9♈19 05	15 13 21	23 15.8	23 16.8	14 11.4	13 25.1	26 16.4	16 26.5	4 33.6	22 00.8	5 15.0	20 35.8
31 Tu	4 35 05	9 47 35	21 07 04	27 00 46	23 11.5	25 10.6	14 28.0	14 09.2	26 12.8	16 34.8	4 32.1	22 03.4	5 15.4	20 37.0

LONGITUDE — June 1932

Day	Sid.Time	☉	0 hr ☽	Noon ☽	True ☊	☿	♀	♂	⚳	♃	♄	♅	♆	♇
1 W	4 39 01	10♊45 06	2♉54 54	8♉49 53	23♓04.5	27♉06.6	14♋42.6	14♉53.2	26♑08.8	16♌43.2	4♒30.4	22♈05.9	5♍16.0	20♋38.3
2 Th	4 42 58	11 42 35	14 46 05	20 43 50	22R 54.7	29 04.8	14 55.3	15 37.2	26R 04.5	16 51.7	4R 28.7	22 08.4	5 16.5	20 39.6
3 F	4 46 55	12 40 03	26 43 21	2♊44 53	22 42.9	1♊05.0	15 05.8	16 21.2	25 59.8	17 00.3	4 26.9	22 10.9	5 17.1	20 40.9
4 Sa	4 50 51	13 37 31	8♊48 35	14 54 36	22 29.7	3 07.1	15 14.2	17 05.1	25 54.7	17 09.1	4 24.9	22 13.3	5 17.7	20 42.2
5 Su	4 54 48	14 34 58	21 03 01	27 13 55	22 16.4	5 11.2	15 20.5	17 48.9	25 49.3	17 17.9	4 22.9	22 15.7	5 18.3	20 43.5
6 M	4 58 44	15 32 23	3♋27 22	9♋43 26	22 04.0	7 17.0	15 24.4	18 32.6	25 43.5	17 26.9	4 20.9	22 18.1	5 19.0	20 44.8
7 Tu	5 02 41	16 29 48	16 02 09	22 23 37	21 53.6	9 24.3	15R 26.2	19 16.4	25 37.4	17 36.0	4 18.7	22 20.4	5 19.7	20 46.2
8 W	5 06 37	17 27 12	28 47 56	5♌15 11	21 45.9	11 33.0	15 25.5	20 00.0	25 31.0	17 45.1	4 16.4	22 22.7	5 20.4	20 47.5
9 Th	5 10 34	18 24 34	11♌45 33	18 19 10	21 41.0	13 42.9	15 22.5	20 43.6	25 24.2	17 54.4	4 14.1	22 25.0	5 21.1	20 48.9
10 F	5 14 31	19 21 56	24 56 15	1♍37 00	21 38.7	15 53.7	15 17.1	21 27.1	25 17.0	18 03.8	4 11.7	22 27.2	5 21.9	20 50.3
11 Sa	5 18 27	20 19 17	8♍21 38	15 10 22	21 38.1	18 05.1	15 09.3	22 10.6	25 09.6	18 13.2	4 09.2	22 29.4	5 22.7	20 51.7
12 Su	5 22 24	21 16 36	22 03 22	29 00 47	21 38.0	20 17.0	14 59.1	22 54.0	25 01.8	18 22.8	4 06.6	22 31.6	5 23.6	20 53.1
13 M	5 26 20	22 13 55	6♎02 41	13♎09 02	21 37.3	22 29.0	14 46.4	23 37.3	24 53.7	18 32.5	4 03.9	22 33.7	5 24.5	20 54.5
14 Tu	5 30 17	23 11 12	20 19 43	27 34 26	21 34.6	24 40.9	14 31.4	24 20.6	24 45.3	18 42.2	4 01.2	22 35.7	5 25.4	20 56.0
15 W	5 34 13	24 08 29	4♏52 49	12♏14 15	21 29.5	26 52.3	14 13.9	25 03.8	24 36.5	18 52.1	3 58.3	22 37.8	5 26.3	20 57.4
16 Th	5 38 10	25 05 45	19 38 02	27 03 17	21 21.7	29 03.1	13 54.2	25 47.0	24 27.5	19 02.0	3 55.5	22 39.8	5 27.3	20 58.9
17 F	5 42 06	26 03 00	4♐29 02	11♐54 14	21 11.8	1♋12.9	13 32.2	26 30.1	24 18.2	19 12.1	3 52.5	22 41.7	5 28.3	21 00.3
18 Sa	5 46 03	27 00 15	19 17 47	26 38 37	21 00.8	3 21.6	13 08.0	27 13.2	24 08.6	19 22.2	3 49.5	22 43.6	5 29.3	21 01.8
19 Su	5 50 00	27 57 29	3♑55 42	11♑08 08	20 49.9	5 29.0	12 41.7	27 56.2	23 58.8	19 32.4	3 46.4	22 45.5	5 30.4	21 03.3
20 M	5 53 56	28 54 43	18 15 09	25 16 09	20 40.2	7 34.9	12 13.5	28 39.1	23 48.6	19 42.7	3 43.2	22 47.3	5 31.5	21 04.8
21 Tu	5 57 53	29 51 57	2♒10 42	8♒58 35	20 32.7	9 39.2	11 43.5	29 22.0	23 38.3	19 53.1	3 39.9	22 49.1	5 32.6	21 06.3
22 W	6 01 49	0♋49 10	15 39 44	22 14 14	20 27.7	11 41.6	11 11.8	0♊04.8	23 27.6	20 03.5	3 36.6	22 50.9	5 33.7	21 07.8
23 Th	6 05 46	1 46 23	28 42 21	5♓04 26	20 25.2	13 42.2	10 38.7	0 47.5	23 16.7	20 14.1	3 33.2	22 52.6	5 34.9	21 09.3
24 F	6 09 42	2 43 36	11♓20 58	17 32 29	20D 24.4	15 40.9	10 04.3	1 30.2	23 05.6	20 24.7	3 29.8	22 54.3	5 36.1	21 10.8
25 Sa	6 13 39	3 40 49	23 39 36	29 42 57	20R 24.5	17 37.6	9 28.8	2 12.9	22 54.3	20 35.4	3 26.3	22 55.9	5 37.3	21 12.3
26 Su	6 17 35	4 38 02	5♈43 12	11♈41 01	20 24.3	19 32.2	8 52.5	2 55.4	22 42.7	20 46.2	3 22.7	22 57.5	5 38.6	21 13.9
27 M	6 21 32	5 35 15	17 37 07	23 32 06	20 23.0	21 24.7	8 15.5	3 38.0	22 30.9	20 57.0	3 19.1	22 59.0	5 39.8	21 15.4
28 Tu	6 25 29	6 32 28	29 26 39	5♉21 22	20 19.5	23 15.2	7 38.2	4 20.4	22 19.0	21 08.0	3 15.4	23 00.5	5 41.1	21 17.0
29 W	6 29 25	7 29 41	11♉16 47	17 13 27	20 13.7	25 03.5	7 00.7	5 02.8	22 06.9	21 19.0	3 11.7	23 01.9	5 42.5	21 18.5
30 Th	6 33 22	8 26 54	23 11 49	29 12 18	20 05.3	26 49.7	6 23.2	5 45.2	21 54.6	21 30.0	3 07.9	23 03.3	5 43.8	21 20.1

Astro Data Dy Hr Mn	Planet Ingress Dy Hr Mn
☽0N 1 21:11	♀ ♋ 6 9:04
♆∠♇ 8 15:03	♂ ♉ 12 10:53
♄R 14 16:46	☿ ♉ 15 22:49
☽0S 16 4:56	☉ ♊ 21 7:07
♆D 16 12:31	
⚳R 21 1:34	☿ ♊ 2 23:05
☽0N 29 2:52	☿ ♋ 16 22:30
	☉ ♋ 21 15:23
♀R 7 17:36	♂ ♊ 22 9:19
☽0S 12 11:16	
☽0N 25 9:21	
♃∠♇ 29 10:50	

Last Aspect Dy Hr Mn		☽ Ingress Dy Hr Mn
1 14:42 ♀ □	♈	1 22:46
4 8:22 ♀ ⚹	♉	4 11:46
6 4:37 ♇ ⚹	♊	7 0:20
9 6:56 ♂ ⚹	♋	9 11:34
11 19:54 ♂ □	♌	11 20:47
13 22:43 ☿ △	♍	14 3:13
15 21:53 ☉ △	♎	16 6:32
17 17:31 ♅ ☍	♏	18 7:15
20 5:09 ☉ ☍	♐	20 6:48
21 17:28 ♅ △	♑	22 7:12
23 19:57 ♅ □	♒	24 10:31
26 2:25 ♅ ⚹	♓	26 17:57
28 10:12 ♇ △	♈	29 5:09
31 1:52 ♅ ☌	♉	31 18:05

Last Aspect Dy Hr Mn		☽ Ingress Dy Hr Mn
2 11:51 ♇ ⚹	♊	3 6:32
5 2:20 ♅ ⚹	♋	5 17:21
7 11:54 ♅ □	♌	8 2:14
9 19:28 ♅ △	♍	10 9:06
12 0:53 ♂ △	♎	12 13:42
14 6:22 ☿ △	♏	14 16:00
16 9:50 ♂ ☍	♐	16 16:45
18 12:38 ☉ ☍	♑	18 17:31
20 18:10 ♂ △	♒	20 20:12
22 13:08 ♅ ⚹	♓	23 2:25
24 19:08 ♇ △	♈	25 12:34
27 10:53 ♅ ☌	♉	28 1:08
30 6:27 ♅ ⚹	♊	30 13:35

☽ Phases & Eclipses Dy Hr Mn	
5 18:11	● 15♉01
13 14:02	☽ 22♌35
20 5:09	○ 28♏58
27 4:54	☾ 5♓40
4 9:16	● 13♊31
11 21:39	☽ 20♍42
18 12:38	○ 27♐02
25 20:36	☾ 4♈01

Astro Data

1 May 1932
Julian Day # 11809
SVP 6♓12'16"
GC 25♐53.7 ⚵ 2♑53.2R
Eris 2♈36.6 ✱ 27♋50.7
⚷ 22♉36.8 ⚶ 19♈25.4
☽ Mean ☊ 23♓51.0

1 June 1932
Julian Day # 11840
SVP 6♓12'11"
GC 25♐53.7 ⚵ 27♐19.9R
Eris 2♈51.0 ✱ 9♌19.8
⚷ 24♉47.3 ⚶ 3♉07.3
☽ Mean ☊ 22♓12.6

July 1932 — LONGITUDE

Day	Sid.Time	☉	0 hr ☽	Noon ☽	True ☊	☿	♀	♂	⚳	♃	♄	♅	♆	♇
1 F	6 37 18	9♋24 07	5♊15 15	11♊20 58	19♓54.9	28♋33.8	5♋46.1	6♊27.4	21♑42.1	21♌41.2	3♒04.0	23♈04.7	5♍45.2	21♋21.6
2 Sa	6 41 15	10 21 21	17 29 40	23 41 30	19R 43.2	0♌15.7	5R 09.6	7 09.7	21R 29.5	21 52.4	3R 00.1	23 06.0	5 46.6	21 23.2
3 Su	6 45 11	11 18 34	29 56 35	6♋14 57	19 31.2	1 55.5	4 33.8	7 51.8	21 16.8	22 03.7	2 56.2	23 07.3	5 48.1	21 24.8
4 M	6 49 08	12 15 47	12♋36 36	19 01 30	19 20.1	3 33.1	3 59.0	8 33.9	21 04.0	22 15.1	2 52.2	23 08.5	5 49.5	21 26.4
5 Tu	6 53 04	13 13 01	25 29 35	2♌00 44	19 10.9	5 08.6	3 25.4	9 15.9	20 51.1	22 26.5	2 48.2	23 09.7	5 51.0	21 27.9
6 W	6 57 01	14 10 14	8♌34 52	15 11 53	19 04.1	6 41.9	2 53.2	9 57.9	20 38.1	22 38.0	2 44.1	23 10.8	5 52.5	21 29.5
7 Th	7 00 58	15 07 27	21 51 41	28 34 11	19 00.0	8 13.1	2 22.5	10 39.8	20 25.0	22 49.5	2 40.0	23 11.9	5 54.1	21 31.1
8 F	7 04 54	16 04 40	5♍19 22	12♍07 10	18D 58.3	9 42.0	1 53.6	11 21.6	20 11.9	23 01.1	2 35.8	23 12.9	5 55.6	21 32.7
9 Sa	7 08 51	17 01 53	18 57 36	25 50 39	18 58.2	11 08.7	1 26.5	12 03.4	19 58.7	23 12.8	2 31.7	23 13.9	5 57.2	21 34.3
10 Su	7 12 47	17 59 06	2♎46 20	9♎44 39	18R 58.8	12 33.2	1 01.4	12 45.1	19 45.5	23 24.5	2 27.4	23 14.8	5 58.8	21 35.9
11 M	7 16 44	18 56 19	16 45 33	23 49 00	18 58.9	13 55.5	0 38.4	13 26.7	19 32.3	23 36.3	2 23.2	23 15.7	6 00.4	21 37.5
12 Tu	7 20 40	19 53 32	0♏54 52	8♏02 57	18 57.5	15 15.4	0 17.5	14 08.3	19 19.0	23 48.1	2 18.9	23 16.6	6 02.1	21 39.1
13 W	7 24 37	20 50 44	15 12 59	22 24 36	18 54.1	16 32.9	29♊58.9	14 49.8	19 05.8	24 00.0	2 14.6	23 17.4	6 03.7	21 40.7
14 Th	7 28 33	21 47 57	29 37 19	6♐50 37	18 48.4	17 48.1	29 42.7	15 31.3	18 52.7	24 11.9	2 10.3	23 18.1	6 05.4	21 42.3
15 F	7 32 30	22 45 10	14♐03 51	21 16 18	18 41.0	19 00.8	29 28.7	16 12.7	18 39.6	24 23.9	2 05.9	23 18.8	6 07.1	21 43.9
16 Sa	7 36 27	23 42 23	28 27 16	5♑36 00	18 32.5	20 10.9	29 17.2	16 54.0	18 26.5	24 35.9	2 01.6	23 19.5	6 08.9	21 45.5
17 Su	7 40 23	24 39 37	12♑41 46	19 43 53	18 24.0	21 18.5	29 08.0	17 35.2	18 13.5	24 48.0	1 57.2	23 20.1	6 10.6	21 47.1
18 M	7 44 20	25 36 51	26 41 46	3♒34 53	18 16.6	22 23.3	29 01.3	18 16.4	18 00.6	25 00.2	1 52.8	23 20.6	6 12.4	21 48.7
19 Tu	7 48 16	26 34 05	10♒22 52	17 05 27	18 10.8	23 25.4	28 56.9	18 57.5	17 47.8	25 12.3	1 48.4	23 21.1	6 14.2	21 50.3
20 W	7 52 13	27 31 20	23 42 30	0♓13 59	18 07.2	24 24.6	28D 54.9	19 38.6	17 35.0	25 24.6	1 43.9	23 21.6	6 16.0	21 51.9
21 Th	7 56 09	28 28 36	6♓40 02	13 00 51	18D 05.6	25 20.9	28 55.3	20 19.6	17 22.4	25 36.8	1 39.5	23 22.0	6 17.8	21 53.5
22 F	8 00 06	29 25 52	19 16 46	25 28 11	18 05.7	26 14.0	28 57.9	21 00.5	17 10.0	25 49.1	1 35.0	23 22.4	6 19.7	21 55.1
23 Sa	8 04 03	0♌23 09	1♈35 33	7♈39 25	18 06.8	27 03.9	29 02.9	21 41.4	16 57.7	26 01.5	1 30.6	23 22.7	6 21.5	21 56.6
24 Su	8 07 59	1 20 27	13 40 21	19 38 58	18 08.1	27 50.4	29 10.0	22 22.2	16 45.5	26 13.9	1 26.1	23 22.9	6 23.4	21 58.2
25 M	8 11 56	2 17 46	25 35 53	1♉31 45	18R 08.7	28 33.4	29 19.3	23 03.0	16 33.5	26 26.3	1 21.7	23 23.2	6 25.3	21 59.8
26 Tu	8 15 52	3 15 06	7♉27 11	13 22 50	18 08.1	29 12.7	29 30.7	23 43.7	16 21.7	26 38.8	1 17.2	23 23.3	6 27.2	22 01.4
27 W	8 19 49	4 12 27	19 19 19	25 17 13	18 05.8	29 48.2	29 44.2	24 24.3	16 10.1	26 51.3	1 12.7	23 23.4	6 29.1	22 03.0
28 Th	8 23 45	5 09 49	1♊17 05	7♊19 27	18 01.7	0♍19.7	29 59.6	25 04.8	15 58.7	27 03.8	1 08.3	23R 23.5	6 31.1	22 04.5
29 F	8 27 42	6 07 12	13 24 45	19 33 25	17 56.1	0 47.0	0♋17.0	25 45.3	15 47.5	27 16.4	1 03.9	23 23.5	6 33.1	22 06.1
30 Sa	8 31 38	7 04 36	25 45 46	2♋02 05	17 49.5	1 09.9	0 36.2	26 25.8	15 36.5	27 29.0	0 59.4	23 23.5	6 35.0	22 07.6
31 Su	8 35 35	8 02 01	8♋22 34	14 47 20	17 42.6	1 28.3	0 57.2	27 06.1	15 25.8	27 41.7	0 55.0	23 23.4	6 37.0	22 09.2

August 1932 — LONGITUDE

Day	Sid.Time	☉	0 hr ☽	Noon ☽	True ☊	☿	♀	♂	⚳	♃	♄	♅	♆	♇
1 M	8 39 32	8♌59 27	21♋16 24	27♋49 45	17♓36.2	1♍41.9	1♋20.0	27♊46.4	15♑15.3	27♌54.3	0♒50.6	23♈23.3	6♍39.0	22♋10.7
2 Tu	8 43 28	9 56 54	4♌27 17	11♌08 47	17R 30.9	1 50.6	1 44.4	28 26.6	15R 05.1	28 07.1	0R 46.2	23R 23.1	6 41.1	22 12.3
3 W	8 47 25	10 54 21	17 54 03	24 42 47	17 27.2	1R 54.3	2 10.5	29 06.8	14 55.1	28 19.8	0 41.9	23 22.9	6 43.1	22 13.8
4 Th	8 51 21	11 51 50	1♍34 42	8♍29 26	17D 25.4	1 52.9	2 38.1	29 46.9	14 45.4	28 32.6	0 37.5	23 22.6	6 45.1	22 15.3
5 F	8 55 18	12 49 19	15 26 40	22 26 03	17 25.2	1 46.1	3 07.3	0♋26.9	14 36.0	28 45.3	0 33.2	23 22.3	6 47.2	22 16.9
6 Sa	8 59 14	13 46 50	29 27 16	6♎30 00	17 26.1	1 34.0	3 37.8	1 06.8	14 26.9	28 58.2	0 28.9	23 21.9	6 49.3	22 18.4
7 Su	9 03 11	14 44 21	13♎33 56	20 38 50	17 27.5	1 16.6	4 09.8	1 46.7	14 18.1	29 11.0	0 24.7	23 21.5	6 51.4	22 19.9
8 M	9 07 07	15 41 53	27 44 24	4♏50 24	17R 28.7	0 54.0	4 43.1	2 26.5	14 09.6	29 23.8	0 20.4	23 21.0	6 53.5	22 21.4
9 Tu	9 11 04	16 39 25	11♏56 35	19 02 42	17 29.1	0 26.2	5 17.7	3 06.2	14 01.4	29 36.7	0 16.3	23 20.5	6 55.6	22 22.8
10 W	9 15 01	17 36 59	26 08 30	3♐13 43	17 28.2	29♌53.6	5 53.6	3 45.9	13 53.6	29 49.6	0 12.1	23 20.0	6 57.7	22 24.3
11 Th	9 18 57	18 34 33	10♐18 02	17 21 11	17 26.0	29 16.4	6 30.7	4 25.5	13 46.0	0♍02.5	0 08.0	23 19.4	6 59.8	22 25.8
12 F	9 22 54	19 32 09	24 22 48	1♑22 32	17 22.8	28 35.1	7 08.9	5 05.0	13 38.8	0 15.5	0 03.9	23 18.7	7 01.9	22 27.3
13 Sa	9 26 50	20 29 45	8♑20 04	15 15 01	17 18.9	27 50.3	7 48.3	5 44.5	13 31.9	0 28.4	29♑59.9	23 18.0	7 04.1	22 28.7
14 Su	9 30 47	21 27 22	22 07 02	28 55 48	17 15.1	27 02.6	8 28.7	6 23.8	13 25.4	0 41.4	29 55.9	23 17.3	7 06.2	22 30.1
15 M	9 34 43	22 25 01	5♒41 00	12♒22 24	17 11.7	26 12.9	9 10.2	7 03.1	13 19.2	0 54.4	29 51.9	23 16.5	7 08.4	22 31.6
16 Tu	9 38 40	23 22 41	18 59 48	25 33 03	17 09.2	25 21.9	9 52.7	7 42.4	13 13.3	1 07.4	29 48.0	23 15.6	7 10.6	22 33.0
17 W	9 42 36	24 20 21	2♓02 03	8♓26 49	17D 07.9	24 30.7	10 36.2	8 21.6	13 07.8	1 20.4	29 44.2	23 14.7	7 12.8	22 34.4
18 Th	9 46 33	25 18 04	14 47 23	21 03 54	17 07.7	23 40.3	11 20.7	9 00.7	13 02.6	1 33.4	29 40.4	23 13.8	7 14.9	22 35.8
19 F	9 50 30	26 15 48	27 16 34	3♈25 38	17 08.4	22 51.6	12 06.0	9 39.7	12 57.8	1 46.4	29 36.6	23 12.8	7 17.1	22 37.1
20 Sa	9 54 26	27 13 33	9♈31 26	15 34 21	17 09.8	22 05.8	12 52.2	10 18.6	12 53.3	1 59.4	29 32.9	23 11.8	7 19.3	22 38.5
21 Su	9 58 23	28 11 20	21 34 48	27 33 15	17 11.3	21 23.7	13 39.3	10 57.5	12 49.2	2 12.5	29 29.3	23 10.7	7 21.5	22 39.9
22 M	10 02 19	29 09 08	3♉30 13	9♉26 15	17 12.7	20 46.4	14 27.1	11 36.4	12 45.4	2 25.5	29 25.7	23 09.6	7 23.7	22 41.2
23 Tu	10 06 16	0♍06 59	15 21 55	21 17 46	17R 13.6	20 14.6	15 15.8	12 15.1	12 42.0	2 38.6	29 22.2	23 08.5	7 25.9	22 42.5
24 W	10 10 12	1 04 51	27 14 26	3♊12 29	17 13.8	19 49.1	16 05.2	12 53.8	12 39.0	2 51.6	29 18.7	23 07.3	7 28.1	22 43.8
25 Th	10 14 09	2 02 45	9♊12 30	15 15 05	17 13.3	19 30.5	16 55.4	13 32.4	12 36.3	3 04.7	29 15.4	23 06.0	7 30.4	22 45.1
26 F	10 18 05	3 00 41	21 20 46	27 30 04	17 12.2	19D 19.3	17 46.2	14 10.9	12 34.0	3 17.8	29 12.0	23 04.8	7 32.6	22 46.4
27 Sa	10 22 02	3 58 38	3♋43 28	10♋01 23	17 10.7	19 16.0	18 37.8	14 49.4	12 32.0	3 30.8	29 08.8	23 03.5	7 34.8	22 47.7
28 Su	10 25 59	4 56 38	16 24 10	22 52 05	17 09.0	19 20.7	19 29.9	15 27.8	12 30.4	3 43.9	29 05.6	23 02.1	7 37.0	22 48.9
29 M	10 29 55	5 54 39	29 25 21	6♌04 03	17 07.4	19 33.7	20 22.8	16 06.1	12 29.2	3 57.0	29 02.5	23 00.7	7 39.2	22 50.2
30 Tu	10 33 52	6 52 42	12♌48 09	19 37 33	17 06.2	19 55.0	21 16.2	16 44.3	12 28.3	4 10.0	28 59.4	22 59.3	7 41.5	22 51.4
31 W	10 37 48	7 50 46	26 32 02	3♍31 14	17D 05.5	20 24.5	22 10.2	17 22.5	12D 27.7	4 23.1	28 56.4	22 57.8	7 43.7	22 52.6

Astro Data (Dy Hr Mn)	Planet Ingress (Dy Hr Mn)
♃△♅ 9 14:32	☿ ♌ 2 8:16
☽0S 9 15:58	♀ ♊R 13 10:33
♀D 20 20:23	☉ ♌ 23 2:18
☽0N 22 16:52	☿ ♍ 27 20:38
♅R 29 10:14	♀ ♋ 28 12:36
☿R 3 17:13	♂ ♋ 4 19:52
☽0S 5 21:13	☿ ♌R 10 7:32
♃⊼♄ 11 19:40	♃ ♍ 11 7:16
☽0N 19 0:56	♄ ♑R 13 11:14
☿D 27 10:02	☉ ♍ 23 9:06

Last Aspect (Dy Hr Mn)	☽ Ingress (Dy Hr Mn)	Last Aspect (Dy Hr Mn)	☽ Ingress (Dy Hr Mn)
2 10:51 ♅ ⚹	♋ 3 0:07	1 3:53 ♅ □	♌ 1 15:57
4 19:40 ♅ □	♌ 5 8:18	3 20:06 ♂ ⚹	♍ 3 21:15
7 2:23 ♅ △	♍ 7 14:33	5 11:44 ♇ ⚹	♎ 6 0:56
9 4:33 ♇ ⚹	♎ 9 19:12	8 2:40 ♃ ⚹	♏ 8 3:49
11 11:38 ♃ ⚹	♏ 11 22:27	10 6:09 ♃ □	♐ 10 6:32
13 14:41 ♃ □	♐ 14 0:38	12 7:26 ☿ △	♑ 12 9:38
16 1:32 ♀ ☍	♑ 16 2:35	14 13:46 ♄ ☌	♒ 14 13:54
17 21:06 ☉ ☍	♒ 18 5:44	16 11:41 ☿ ☍	♓ 16 20:13
20 9:34 ♀ △	♓ 20 11:34	19 4:35 ♄ ⚹	♈ 19 5:18
22 20:24 ☉ △	♈ 22 20:52	21 15:53 ♄ □	♉ 21 16:56
25 7:28 ♀ ⚹	♉ 25 8:54	24 4:13 ♄ △	♊ 24 5:33
27 15:12 ♃ □	♊ 27 21:26	26 3:24 ♅ ⚹	♋ 26 16:50
30 3:09 ♃ ⚹	♋ 30 8:07	28 23:21 ♄ ☍	♌ 29 1:03
		30 17:51 ♅ △	♍ 31 5:58

☽ Phases & Eclipses (Dy Hr Mn)	Astro Data
3 22:20 ● 11♋43	1 July 1932
11 3:07 ☽ 18♎35	Julian Day # 11870
17 21:06 ○ 25♑01	SVP 6♓12'05"
25 13:41 ☾ 2♉22	GC 25♐53.8 ⚴ 18♐57.5R
	Eris 2♈55.4R ⚵ 21♌17.0
2 9:42 ● 9♌51	⚷ 26♉41.8 ⚶ 15♉19.5
9 7:40 ☽ 16♏29	☽ Mean ☊ 20♓37.3
16 7:42 ○ 23♒12	
24 7:21 ☾ 0♊54	1 August 1932
31 19:54 ● 8♍10	Julian Day # 11901
31 20:03:16 ● T 01'45"	SVP 6♓12'00"
	GC 25♐53.9 ⚴ 14♐30.0R
	Eris 2♈49.3R ⚵ 3♍56.9
	⚷ 28♉06.9 ⚶ 26♉14.3
	☽ Mean ☊ 18♓58.8

LONGITUDE — September 1932

Day	Sid.Time	☉	0 hr ☽	Noon ☽	True ☊	☿	♀	♂	⚳	♃	♄	♅	♆	♇
1 Th	10 41 45	8♍48 52	10♍34 45	17♍42 03	17♓05.3	21♌02.2	23♋04.8	18♋00.5	12♑27.6	4♍36.1	28♑53.5	22♈56.2	7♍45.9	22♋53.8
2 F	10 45 41	9 47 00	24 52 31	2♎05 31	17 05.5	21 47.8	23 59.9	18 38.5	12 27.8	4 49.2	28R 50.7	22R 54.7	7 48.1	22 55.0
3 Sa	10 49 38	10 45 09	9♎20 22	16 36 22	17 06.0	22 41.0	24 55.5	19 16.5	12 28.3	5 02.2	28 48.0	22 53.1	7 50.4	22 56.1
4 Su	10 53 34	11 43 20	23 52 49	1♏09 03	17 06.5	23 41.5	25 51.7	19 54.3	12 29.2	5 15.2	28 45.3	22 51.5	7 52.6	22 57.3
5 M	10 57 31	12 41 32	8♏24 26	15 38 26	17 06.9	24 48.9	26 48.4	20 32.0	12 30.5	5 28.3	28 42.7	22 49.8	7 54.8	22 58.4
6 Tu	11 01 28	13 39 46	22 50 31	0♐00 15	17 07.2	26 02.8	27 45.5	21 09.7	12 32.1	5 41.3	28 40.2	22 48.1	7 57.0	22 59.5
7 W	11 05 24	14 38 02	7♐07 18	14 11 22	17R 07.3	27 22.6	28 43.1	21 47.3	12 34.0	5 54.3	28 37.8	22 46.3	7 59.3	23 00.6
8 Th	11 09 21	15 36 19	21 12 13	28 09 42	17 07.2	28 47.8	29 41.2	22 24.8	12 36.3	6 07.2	28 35.5	22 44.6	8 01.5	23 01.7
9 F	11 13 17	16 34 37	5♑03 43	11♑54 10	17D 07.2	0♍17.9	0♌39.7	23 02.2	12 39.0	6 20.2	28 33.2	22 42.8	8 03.7	23 02.7
10 Sa	11 17 14	17 32 57	18 41 02	25 24 19	17 07.2	1 52.3	1 38.6	23 39.5	12 41.9	6 33.1	28 31.1	22 40.9	8 05.9	23 03.7
11 Su	11 21 10	18 31 18	2♒04 00	8♒40 09	17 07.3	3 30.4	2 38.0	24 16.8	12 45.3	6 46.1	28 29.0	22 39.0	8 08.1	23 04.8
12 M	11 25 07	19 29 41	15 12 47	21 41 58	17 07.4	5 11.8	3 37.7	24 54.0	12 48.9	6 59.0	28 27.0	22 37.1	8 10.3	23 05.7
13 Tu	11 29 03	20 28 06	28 07 45	4♓30 13	17 07.6	6 55.9	4 37.9	25 31.1	12 52.9	7 11.9	28 25.1	22 35.2	8 12.5	23 06.7
14 W	11 33 00	21 26 33	10♓49 26	17 05 32	17R 07.7	8 42.3	5 38.4	26 08.1	12 57.2	7 24.7	28 23.3	22 33.2	8 14.7	23 07.7
15 Th	11 36 57	22 25 01	23 18 36	29 28 48	17 07.6	10 30.4	6 39.3	26 45.0	13 01.8	7 37.6	28 21.6	22 31.3	8 16.8	23 08.6
16 F	11 40 53	23 23 31	5♈36 17	11♈41 14	17 07.2	12 19.9	7 40.6	27 21.8	13 06.8	7 50.4	28 19.9	22 29.2	8 19.0	23 09.5
17 Sa	11 44 50	24 22 04	17 43 53	23 44 29	17 06.4	14 10.4	8 42.3	27 58.5	13 12.0	8 03.2	28 18.4	22 27.2	8 21.2	23 10.4
18 Su	11 48 46	25 20 38	29 43 19	5♉40 43	17 05.3	16 01.5	9 44.3	28 35.2	13 17.6	8 15.9	28 17.0	22 25.1	8 23.3	23 11.3
19 M	11 52 43	26 19 14	11♉37 02	17 32 40	17 04.0	17 53.1	10 46.6	29 11.8	13 23.5	8 28.7	28 15.6	22 23.0	8 25.5	23 12.1
20 Tu	11 56 39	27 17 53	23 28 03	29 23 38	17 02.8	19 44.8	11 49.3	29 48.3	13 29.7	8 41.4	28 14.4	22 20.9	8 27.6	23 13.0
21 W	12 00 36	28 16 34	5♊19 55	11♊17 26	17 01.8	21 36.5	12 52.3	0♌24.7	13 36.2	8 54.1	28 13.2	22 18.7	8 29.7	23 13.8
22 Th	12 04 32	29 15 17	17 16 42	23 18 18	17D 01.2	23 28.0	13 55.6	1 01.0	13 43.0	9 06.7	28 12.1	22 16.6	8 31.8	23 14.6
23 F	12 08 29	0♎14 03	29 22 46	5♋30 42	17 01.2	25 19.0	14 59.2	1 37.2	13 50.1	9 19.4	28 11.2	22 14.4	8 33.9	23 15.3
24 Sa	12 12 25	1 12 50	11♋42 38	17 59 07	17 01.8	27 09.6	16 03.1	2 13.3	13 57.5	9 31.9	28 10.3	22 12.1	8 36.0	23 16.1
25 Su	12 16 22	2 11 40	24 20 39	0♌47 42	17 02.8	28 59.6	17 07.3	2 49.4	14 05.2	9 44.5	28 09.5	22 09.9	8 38.1	23 16.8
26 M	12 20 19	3 10 32	7♌20 38	13 59 46	17 04.1	0♎48.9	18 11.8	3 25.3	14 13.1	9 57.0	28 08.9	22 07.6	8 40.2	23 17.5
27 Tu	12 24 15	4 09 27	20 45 18	27 37 19	17 05.3	2 37.5	19 16.6	4 01.1	14 21.4	10 09.5	28 08.3	22 05.4	8 42.3	23 18.2
28 W	12 28 12	5 08 23	4♍35 46	11♍40 27	17R 05.9	4 25.3	20 21.6	4 36.9	14 29.9	10 21.9	28 07.8	22 03.1	8 44.3	23 18.8
29 Th	12 32 08	6 07 22	18 50 59	26 06 50	17 05.8	6 12.4	21 26.8	5 12.5	14 38.7	10 34.3	28 07.4	22 00.8	8 46.3	23 19.5
30 F	12 36 05	7 06 22	3♎27 21	10♎51 39	17 04.7	7 58.6	22 32.4	5 48.1	14 47.8	10 46.7	28 07.2	21 58.4	8 48.3	23 20.1

LONGITUDE — October 1932

Day	Sid.Time	☉	0 hr ☽	Noon ☽	True ☊	☿	♀	♂	⚳	♃	♄	♅	♆	♇
1 Sa	12 40 01	8♎05 25	18♎18 49	25♎47 49	17♓02.6	9♎43.9	23♌38.1	6♌23.5	14♑57.2	10♍59.0	28♑07.0	21♈56.1	8♍50.3	23♋20.6
2 Su	12 43 58	9 04 30	3♏17 31	10♏46 51	16R 59.8	11 28.5	24 44.1	6 58.8	15 06.8	11 11.3	28D 06.9	21R 53.7	8 52.3	23 21.2
3 M	12 47 54	10 03 36	18 14 44	25 40 12	16 56.7	13 12.2	25 50.4	7 34.0	15 16.7	11 23.5	28 06.9	21 51.4	8 54.3	23 21.7
4 Tu	12 51 51	11 02 45	3♐02 21	10♐20 27	16 53.9	14 55.1	26 56.8	8 09.2	15 26.9	11 35.7	28 07.1	21 49.0	8 56.3	23 22.3
5 W	12 55 48	12 01 55	17 33 54	24 42 16	16 51.9	16 37.1	28 03.5	8 44.2	15 37.3	11 47.8	28 07.3	21 46.6	8 58.2	23 22.7
6 Th	12 59 44	13 01 07	1♑45 17	8♑42 47	16D 50.9	18 18.3	29 10.4	9 19.1	15 48.0	11 59.9	28 07.6	21 44.2	9 00.1	23 23.2
7 F	13 03 41	14 00 21	15 34 47	22 21 21	16 51.1	19 58.7	0♍17.5	9 53.9	15 58.9	12 11.9	28 08.1	21 41.8	9 02.1	23 23.7
8 Sa	13 07 37	14 59 36	29 02 41	5♒39 01	16 52.2	21 38.4	1 24.8	10 28.5	16 10.1	12 23.8	28 08.6	21 39.4	9 03.9	23 24.1
9 Su	13 11 34	15 58 53	12♒10 40	18 37 56	16 53.9	23 17.2	2 32.3	11 03.1	16 21.5	12 35.7	28 09.2	21 36.9	9 05.8	23 24.5
10 M	13 15 30	16 58 12	25 01 10	1♓20 43	16 55.4	24 55.3	3 40.0	11 37.5	16 33.1	12 47.6	28 10.0	21 34.5	9 07.7	23 24.8
11 Tu	13 19 27	17 57 33	7♓36 54	13 50 02	16R 56.3	26 32.7	4 47.9	12 11.9	16 45.0	12 59.4	28 10.8	21 32.1	9 09.5	23 25.2
12 W	13 23 23	18 56 55	20 00 25	26 08 20	16 55.9	28 09.4	5 55.9	12 46.1	16 57.1	13 11.1	28 11.7	21 29.6	9 11.3	23 25.5
13 Th	13 27 20	19 56 20	2♈14 03	8♈17 47	16 53.9	29 45.3	7 04.2	13 20.2	17 09.4	13 22.8	28 12.7	21 27.2	9 13.1	23 25.8
14 F	13 31 17	20 55 46	14 19 46	20 20 12	16 50.2	1♏20.6	8 12.7	13 54.2	17 22.0	13 34.4	28 13.9	21 24.7	9 14.9	23 26.0
15 Sa	13 35 13	21 55 15	26 19 17	2♉17 13	16 45.0	2 55.2	9 21.3	14 28.1	17 34.8	13 45.9	28 15.1	21 22.3	9 16.6	23 26.3
16 Su	13 39 10	22 54 45	8♉14 12	14 10 28	16 38.5	4 29.1	10 30.1	15 01.8	17 47.8	13 57.4	28 16.4	21 19.9	9 18.4	23 26.5
17 M	13 43 06	23 54 18	20 06 13	26 01 43	16 31.4	6 02.4	11 39.1	15 35.4	18 01.0	14 08.8	28 17.9	21 17.4	9 20.1	23 26.7
18 Tu	13 47 03	24 53 53	1♊57 15	7♊53 07	16 24.4	7 35.1	12 48.3	16 08.9	18 14.4	14 20.2	28 19.4	21 15.0	9 21.8	23 26.9
19 W	13 50 59	25 53 31	13 49 41	19 47 19	16 18.2	9 07.2	13 57.6	16 42.3	18 28.0	14 31.5	28 21.0	21 12.5	9 23.4	23 27.0
20 Th	13 54 56	26 53 10	25 46 26	1♋47 29	16 13.5	10 38.7	15 07.1	17 15.6	18 41.9	14 42.7	28 22.7	21 10.1	9 25.1	23 27.1
21 F	13 58 52	27 52 52	7♋50 59	13 57 25	16 10.5	12 09.5	16 16.8	17 48.7	18 55.9	14 53.8	28 24.5	21 07.7	9 26.7	23 27.2
22 Sa	14 02 49	28 52 36	20 07 20	26 21 18	16D 09.3	13 39.8	17 26.6	18 21.7	19 10.1	15 04.9	28 26.5	21 05.3	9 28.3	23 27.3
23 Su	14 06 46	29 52 22	2♌39 52	9♌03 35	16 09.7	15 09.5	18 36.6	18 54.6	19 24.6	15 15.9	28 28.5	21 02.9	9 29.9	23 27.4
24 M	14 10 42	0♏52 10	15 32 59	22 08 33	16 10.9	16 38.5	19 46.7	19 27.3	19 39.2	15 26.8	28 30.6	21 00.5	9 31.4	23R 27.4
25 Tu	14 14 39	1 52 01	28 50 41	5♍39 42	16R 12.1	18 07.0	20 56.9	19 59.9	19 54.0	15 37.6	28 32.8	20 58.1	9 33.0	23 27.4
26 W	14 18 35	2 51 54	12♍35 48	19 39 03	16 12.5	19 34.9	22 07.3	20 32.3	20 09.0	15 48.4	28 35.1	20 55.7	9 34.5	23 27.3
27 Th	14 22 32	3 51 48	26 49 19	4♎06 17	16 11.1	21 02.1	23 17.9	21 04.6	20 24.2	15 59.0	28 37.5	20 53.3	9 36.0	23 27.3
28 F	14 26 28	4 51 45	11♎29 24	18 57 56	16 07.6	22 28.7	24 28.5	21 36.7	20 39.6	16 09.6	28 40.0	20 51.0	9 37.4	23 27.2
29 Sa	14 30 25	5 51 44	26 30 54	4♏07 10	16 01.8	23 54.6	25 39.3	22 08.7	20 55.1	16 20.1	28 42.6	20 48.6	9 38.8	23 27.1
30 Su	14 34 21	6 51 46	11♏45 26	19 24 19	15 54.4	25 19.9	26 50.2	22 40.5	21 10.8	16 30.5	28 45.2	20 46.3	9 40.2	23 27.0
31 M	14 38 18	7 51 48	27 02 25	4♐38 19	15 46.2	26 44.4	28 01.3	23 12.2	21 26.8	16 40.8	28 48.0	20 44.0	9 41.6	23 26.8

Astro Data

	Dy Hr Mn
⚳ D	1 11:26
☽ 0S	2 4:46
♅□♇	2 9:27
♅⚼♆	4 4:54
♆∠♇	8 15:51
♃⚼♅	15 1:47
☽ 0N	15 8:38
♃∠♇	18 2:35
♃☌♆	19 4:41
☉0S	23 6:16
☿0S	27 21:27
☽ 0S	29 14:41
♄ D	2 17:39
♃⚼♄	12 13:20
☽ 0N	12 15:09

Planet Ingress

		Dy Hr Mn
♀	♌	8 19:45
☿	♍	9 7:20
♂	♌	20 19:43
☉	♎	23 6:16
☿	♎	26 1:15
♀	♍	7 5:46
☿	♏	13 15:41
☉	♏	23 15:04

♇ R24 17:45
☽ 0S27 1:22

Last Aspect / ☽ Ingress (September)

Last Aspect Dy Hr Mn			☽ Ingress	Dy Hr Mn
2 6:38	♄	△	♎	2 8:32
4 8:03	♄	□	♏	4 10:06
6 9:46	♄	⚹	♐	6 12:00
8 13:14	☿	△	♑	8 15:11
10 17:35	♄	☌	♒	10 20:16
12 13:42	♅	⚹	♓	13 3:31
15 9:49	♄	⚹	♈	15 13:01
17 21:08	♄	□	♉	18 0:34
20 12:53	♂	⚹	♊	20 13:14
23 0:47	☉	□	♋	23 1:13
25 8:07	☿	⚹	♌	25 10:32
27 2:22	♅	△	♍	27 16:07
29 15:18	♄	△	♎	29 18:22

Last Aspect / ☽ Ingress (October)

Last Aspect Dy Hr Mn			☽ Ingress	Dy Hr Mn
1 15:43	♄	□	♏	1 18:44
3 15:58	♄	⚹	♐	3 19:02
5 18:11	♀	△	♑	5 21:00
7 22:22	♄	☌	♒	8 1:44
9 22:01	☿	△	♓	10 9:26
12 16:03	♄	⚹	♈	12 19:36
15 3:52	♄	□	♉	15 7:24
17 16:36	♄	△	♊	17 20:03
20 1:20	☉	△	♋	20 8:26
22 17:14	☉	□	♌	22 18:57
24 9:57	♅	△	♍	25 2:03
27 2:58	♄	△	♎	27 5:15
29 3:27	♄	□	♏	29 5:30
31 2:45	♄	⚹	♐	31 4:40

☽ Phases & Eclipses

Dy Hr Mn	
7 12:49	☽ 14♐40
14 21:06	○ 21♓49
14 21:01	☍ P 0.975
23 0:47	☾ 29♊47
30 5:30	● 6♎50
6 20:05	☽ 13♑21
14 13:18	○ 20♈59
22 17:14	☾ 29♋06
29 14:56	● 5♏59

Astro Data

1 September 1932
Julian Day # 11932
SVP 6♓11'55"
GC 25♐53.9 ⚴ 16♐27.0
Eris 2♈34.1R ⚵ 16♍35.4
⚷ 28♉40.7 ⚶ 4♊20.1
☽ Mean ☊ 17♓20.3

1 October 1932
Julian Day # 11962
SVP 6♓11'52"
GC 25♐54.0 ⚴ 22♐42.6
Eris 2♈14.9R ⚵ 28♍31.5
⚷ 28♉16.6R ⚶ 7♊45.2
☽ Mean ☊ 15♓45.0

November 1932 LONGITUDE

Day	Sid.Time	☉	0 hr ☽	Noon ☽	True ☊	☿	♀	♂	⚳	♃	♄	♅	♆	♇
1 Tu	14 42 15	8♏51 53	12♐10 45	19♐38 37	15♓38.4	28♏08.1	29♍12.4	23♌43.7	21♑42.8	16♍51.1	28♑50.9	20♈41.7	9♍42.9	23♋26.6
2 W	14 46 11	9 52 00	27 00 56	4♑17 01	15R 31.9	29 31.0	0♎23.7	24 15.1	21 59.1	17 01.2	28 53.8	20R 39.4	9 44.3	23R 26.4
3 Th	14 50 08	10 52 08	11♑26 21	18 28 40	15 27.4	0♐53.0	1 35.1	24 46.3	22 15.5	17 11.2	28 56.9	20 37.2	9 45.6	23 26.2
4 F	14 54 04	11 52 17	25 23 54	2♒12 08	15D 25.1	2 14.0	2 46.6	25 17.3	22 32.1	17 21.2	29 00.0	20 34.9	9 46.8	23 25.9
5 Sa	14 58 01	12 52 28	8♒53 36	15 28 42	15 24.7	3 33.9	3 58.2	25 48.1	22 48.8	17 31.0	29 03.3	20 32.7	9 48.0	23 25.6
6 Su	15 01 57	13 52 40	21 57 50	28 21 32	15 25.4	4 52.7	5 09.9	26 18.8	23 05.7	17 40.7	29 06.6	20 30.5	9 49.2	23 25.3
7 M	15 05 54	14 52 54	4♓40 20	10♓54 47	15R 26.1	6 10.3	6 21.7	26 49.3	23 22.7	17 50.4	29 10.0	20 28.4	9 50.4	23 25.0
8 Tu	15 09 50	15 53 09	17 05 25	23 12 47	15 25.9	7 26.4	7 33.6	27 19.6	23 39.9	17 59.9	29 13.5	20 26.2	9 51.6	23 24.7
9 W	15 13 47	16 53 26	29 17 23	5♈19 40	15 23.7	8 40.9	8 45.6	27 49.8	23 57.3	18 09.3	29 17.0	20 24.1	9 52.7	23 24.3
10 Th	15 17 44	17 53 44	11♈20 04	17 19 00	15 19.0	9 53.7	9 57.6	28 19.7	24 14.8	18 18.6	29 20.7	20 22.0	9 53.8	23 23.9
11 F	15 21 40	18 54 04	23 16 47	29 13 43	15 11.6	11 04.5	11 09.8	28 49.5	24 32.4	18 27.9	29 24.5	20 19.9	9 54.8	23 23.4
12 Sa	15 25 37	19 54 26	5♉10 05	11♉06 06	15 01.5	12 13.1	12 22.1	29 19.1	24 50.2	18 37.0	29 28.3	20 17.9	9 55.8	23 23.0
13 Su	15 29 33	20 54 49	17 01 59	22 57 54	14 49.3	13 19.2	13 34.5	29 48.5	25 08.1	18 45.9	29 32.2	20 15.9	9 56.8	23 22.5
14 M	15 33 30	21 55 14	28 54 02	4♊50 32	14 36.1	14 22.5	14 47.0	0♍17.7	25 26.1	18 54.8	29 36.2	20 13.9	9 57.8	23 22.0
15 Tu	15 37 26	22 55 40	10♊47 36	16 45 22	14 22.9	15 22.6	15 59.5	0 46.7	25 44.3	19 03.6	29 40.3	20 12.0	9 58.7	23 21.5
16 W	15 41 23	23 56 09	22 44 04	28 43 55	14 10.8	16 19.2	17 12.2	1 15.5	26 02.6	19 12.2	29 44.4	20 10.1	9 59.6	23 21.0
17 Th	15 45 19	24 56 39	4♋45 10	10♋48 07	14 00.8	17 11.7	18 24.9	1 44.1	26 21.1	19 20.8	29 48.7	20 08.2	10 00.5	23 20.4
18 F	15 49 16	25 57 10	16 53 06	23 00 30	13 53.5	17 59.7	19 37.7	2 12.5	26 39.6	19 29.2	29 53.0	20 06.3	10 01.3	23 19.8
19 Sa	15 53 13	26 57 44	29 10 44	5♌24 15	13 49.0	18 42.5	20 50.6	2 40.7	26 58.3	19 37.4	29 57.4	20 04.5	10 02.1	23 19.2
20 Su	15 57 09	27 58 19	11♌41 32	18 03 06	13D 46.9	19 19.5	22 03.6	3 08.7	27 17.1	19 45.6	0♒01.8	20 02.7	10 02.9	23 18.6
21 M	16 01 06	28 58 56	24 29 28	1♍01 09	13R 46.6	19 50.1	23 16.6	3 36.4	27 36.1	19 53.6	0 06.4	20 01.0	10 03.6	23 17.9
22 Tu	16 05 02	29 59 34	7♍38 37	14 22 21	13 46.7	20 13.4	24 29.8	4 03.9	27 55.1	20 01.5	0 11.0	19 59.2	10 04.3	23 17.2
23 W	16 08 59	1♐00 15	21 12 41	28 09 53	13 46.1	20 28.7	25 43.0	4 31.1	28 14.3	20 09.3	0 15.7	19 57.6	10 05.0	23 16.5
24 Th	16 12 55	2 00 56	5♎14 04	12♎25 11	13 43.5	20R 35.2	26 56.2	4 58.2	28 33.6	20 16.9	0 20.5	19 55.9	10 05.6	23 15.8
25 F	16 16 52	3 01 40	19 42 59	27 07 00	13 38.3	20 32.2	28 09.6	5 24.9	28 53.0	20 24.5	0 25.3	19 54.3	10 06.2	23 15.1
26 Sa	16 20 48	4 02 25	4♏36 31	12♏10 36	13 30.2	20 19.0	29 23.0	5 51.5	29 12.6	20 31.8	0 30.2	19 52.8	10 06.8	23 14.3
27 Su	16 24 45	5 03 12	19 48 05	27 27 39	13 19.7	19 55.0	0♏36.4	6 17.7	29 32.2	20 39.1	0 35.2	19 51.2	10 07.4	23 13.5
28 M	16 28 42	6 04 00	5♐07 51	12♐47 10	13 08.1	19 20.1	1 49.9	6 43.7	29 52.0	20 46.1	0 40.3	19 49.8	10 07.9	23 12.7
29 Tu	16 32 38	7 04 49	20 24 09	27 57 24	12 56.6	18 34.3	3 03.5	7 09.5	0♒11.8	20 53.1	0 45.4	19 48.3	10 08.3	23 11.9
30 W	16 36 35	8 05 39	5♑25 42	12♑48 01	12 46.6	17 38.1	4 17.1	7 34.9	0 31.8	20 59.9	0 50.6	19 46.9	10 08.8	23 11.1

December 1932 LONGITUDE

Day	Sid.Time	☉	0 hr ☽	Noon ☽	True ☊	☿	♀	♂	⚳	♃	♄	♅	♆	♇
1 Th	16 40 31	9♐06 31	20♑03 35	27♑11 51	12♓39.1	16♐32.6	5♏30.8	8♍00.1	0♒51.9	21♍06.6	0♒55.8	19♈45.6	10♍09.2	23♋10.2
2 F	16 44 28	10 07 23	4♒12 31	11♒05 31	12R 34.4	15R 19.2	6 44.5	8 25.0	1 12.0	21 13.1	1 01.2	19R 44.3	10 09.5	23R 09.4
3 Sa	16 48 24	11 08 16	17 50 57	24 29 08	12 32.1	14 00.1	7 58.3	8 49.6	1 32.3	21 19.4	1 06.5	19 43.0	10 09.9	23 08.5
4 Su	16 52 21	12 09 10	1♓00 28	7♓25 27	12 31.6	12 37.8	9 12.1	9 13.9	1 52.6	21 25.6	1 12.0	19 41.8	10 10.2	23 07.5
5 M	16 56 18	13 10 04	13 44 42	19 58 50	12 31.5	11 15.0	10 26.0	9 37.9	2 13.1	21 31.7	1 17.5	19 40.6	10 10.4	23 06.6
6 Tu	17 00 14	14 10 59	26 08 29	2♈14 20	12 30.7	9 54.6	11 39.9	10 01.6	2 33.6	21 37.6	1 23.1	19 39.4	10 10.7	23 05.7
7 W	17 04 11	15 11 55	8♈17 01	14 17 08	12 28.0	8 39.2	12 53.8	10 25.0	2 54.3	21 43.3	1 28.7	19 38.3	10 10.8	23 04.7
8 Th	17 08 07	16 12 51	20 15 17	26 11 59	12 22.7	7 31.1	14 07.8	10 48.1	3 15.0	21 48.9	1 34.4	19 37.3	10 11.0	23 03.7
9 F	17 12 04	17 13 49	2♉07 45	8♉03 00	12 14.3	6 32.0	15 21.9	11 10.8	3 35.8	21 54.4	1 40.1	19 36.3	10 11.1	23 02.7
10 Sa	17 16 00	18 14 47	13 58 09	19 53 32	12 03.1	5 43.3	16 36.0	11 33.2	3 56.7	21 59.6	1 45.9	19 35.4	10 11.2	23 01.7
11 Su	17 19 57	19 15 46	25 49 26	1♊46 07	11 49.7	5 05.5	17 50.1	11 55.3	4 17.7	22 04.7	1 51.8	19 34.5	10 11.3	23 00.7
12 M	17 23 53	20 16 45	7♊43 45	13 42 32	11 35.0	4 39.1	19 04.2	12 17.0	4 38.7	22 09.7	1 57.7	19 33.6	10R 11.3	22 59.6
13 Tu	17 27 50	21 17 46	19 42 36	25 44 04	11 20.2	4D 23.8	20 18.4	12 38.4	4 59.9	22 14.5	2 03.6	19 32.8	10 11.3	22 58.5
14 W	17 31 47	22 18 47	1♋47 03	7♋51 39	11 06.6	4 19.1	21 32.7	12 59.5	5 21.1	22 19.1	2 09.7	19 32.0	10 11.2	22 57.5
15 Th	17 35 43	23 19 49	13 58 00	20 06 14	10 55.2	4 24.4	22 46.9	13 20.1	5 42.4	22 23.5	2 15.7	19 31.3	10 11.2	22 56.4
16 F	17 39 40	24 20 52	26 16 31	2♌29 01	10 46.7	4 39.1	24 01.3	13 40.4	6 03.8	22 27.8	2 21.8	19 30.7	10 11.1	22 55.3
17 Sa	17 43 36	25 21 55	8♌43 58	15 01 39	10 41.3	5 02.1	25 15.6	14 00.3	6 25.2	22 31.9	2 28.0	19 30.1	10 10.9	22 54.2
18 Su	17 47 33	26 23 00	21 22 21	27 46 25	10D 38.7	5 32.8	26 30.0	14 19.8	6 46.7	22 35.8	2 34.2	19 29.5	10 10.7	22 53.0
19 M	17 51 29	27 24 05	4♍14 12	10♍46 06	10 38.1	6 10.3	27 44.4	14 38.9	7 08.3	22 39.6	2 40.5	19 29.0	10 10.5	22 51.9
20 Tu	17 55 26	28 25 11	17 22 29	24 03 44	10R 38.3	6 53.9	28 58.8	14 57.6	7 30.0	22 43.2	2 46.8	19 28.5	10 10.3	22 50.7
21 W	17 59 22	29 26 17	0♎50 11	7♎42 08	10 38.1	7 43.0	0♐13.3	15 15.9	7 51.7	22 46.6	2 53.1	19 28.1	10 10.0	22 49.6
22 Th	18 03 19	0♑27 25	14 39 45	21 43 10	10 36.3	8 36.8	1 27.8	15 33.7	8 13.5	22 49.8	2 59.5	19 27.8	10 09.6	22 48.4
23 F	18 07 16	1 28 33	28 52 17	6♏06 55	10 32.1	9 34.8	2 42.3	15 51.1	8 35.4	22 52.8	3 05.9	19 27.4	10 09.3	22 47.2
24 Sa	18 11 12	2 29 42	13♏26 37	20 50 50	10 25.3	10 36.5	3 56.9	16 08.0	8 57.3	22 55.7	3 12.4	19 27.2	10 08.9	22 46.0
25 Su	18 15 09	3 30 51	28 18 43	5♐49 20	10 16.2	11 41.5	5 11.5	16 24.5	9 19.3	22 58.4	3 18.9	19 27.0	10 08.5	22 44.8
26 M	18 19 05	4 32 01	13♐21 31	20 54 04	10 05.8	12 49.3	6 26.1	16 40.5	9 41.4	23 00.9	3 25.5	19 26.8	10 08.0	22 43.6
27 Tu	18 23 02	5 33 12	28 25 40	5♑55 02	9 55.4	13 59.8	7 40.7	16 56.0	10 03.5	23 03.2	3 32.1	19 26.7	10 07.6	22 42.4
28 W	18 26 58	6 34 23	13♑20 58	20 42 22	9 46.1	15 12.4	8 55.4	17 11.1	10 25.7	23 05.3	3 38.7	19D 26.7	10 07.0	22 41.1
29 Th	18 30 55	7 35 33	27 58 19	5♒08 04	9 39.1	16 27.0	10 10.0	17 25.6	10 47.9	23 07.2	3 45.4	19 26.7	10 06.5	22 39.9
30 F	18 34 51	8 36 44	12♒11 05	19 07 03	9 34.7	17 43.4	11 24.7	17 39.6	11 10.2	23 09.0	3 52.1	19 26.8	10 05.9	22 38.6
31 Sa	18 38 48	9 37 54	25 55 52	2♓37 35	9D 32.7	19 01.4	12 39.4	17 53.1	11 32.6	23 10.5	3 58.8	19 26.9	10 05.3	22 37.4

Astro Data	Planet Ingress	Last Aspect	☽ Ingress	Last Aspect	☽ Ingress	☽ Phases & Eclipses	Astro Data
Dy Hr Mn	Dy Hr Mn	Dy Hr Mn	Dy Hr Mn	Dy Hr Mn	Dy Hr Mn	Dy Hr Mn	
♀0S 5 6:01	♀ ♎ 2 4:01	1 18:53 ♂ △	♑ 2 4:54	1 5:13 ♇ ☍	♒ 1 16:46	5 6:50 ☽ 12♒40	1 November 1932
☽0N 8 20:31	☿ ♐ 2 20:28	4 6:18 ♄ ☌	♒ 4 8:06	3 3:22 ♅ ⚹	♓ 3 22:08	13 7:28 ○ 20♉43	Julian Day # 11993
♃⚻♅ 22 6:14	♂ ♍ 13 21:25	6 7:59 ♂ ☍	♓ 6 15:06	5 18:04 ♇ △	♈ 6 7:35	21 7:58 ☾ 28♌49	SVP 6♓11'48"
☽0S 23 10:28	♄ ♒ 20 2:10	8 23:56 ♄ ⚹	♈ 9 1:24	8 5:40 ♇ □	♉ 8 19:41	28 0:43 ● 5♐35	GC 25♐54.1 ⚴ 1♑49.7
☿ R 24 16:40	☉ ♐ 22 12:10	11 12:22 ♄ □	♉ 11 13:33	10 18:20 ♇ ⚹	♊ 11 8:26		Eris 1♈56.2R ⚵ 10♎13.1
	♀ ♏ 27 0:06	14 1:22 ♄ △	♊ 14 2:13	13 5:00 ♃ □	♋ 13 20:28	4 21:45 ☽ 12♓34	⚷ 27♉01.2R ⚶ 4♊49.5R
☽0N 6 1:50	⚳ ♒ 28 21:44	15 18:54 ♅ ⚹	♋ 16 14:32	15 17:48 ♀ △	♌ 16 7:13	13 2:21 ○ 20♊53	☽ Mean ☊ 14♓06.5
♆ R 12 16:30		19 1:27 ♄ ☍	♌ 19 1:35	18 9:22 ♀ □	♍ 18 16:09	20 20:22 ☾ 28♍46	
☿ D 14 10:54	♀ ♐ 21 7:43	21 7:58 ☉ □	♍ 21 10:08	20 21:36 ♀ ⚹	♎ 20 22:32	27 11:22 ● 5♑32	1 December 1932
☽0S 20 16:47	☉ ♑ 22 1:14	23 3:35 ♇ ⚹	♎ 23 15:08	22 13:50 ♇ □	♏ 23 1:53		Julian Day # 12023
♃⚹♇ 22 4:17		25 13:50 ♀ ☌	♏ 25 16:38	24 15:22 ♃ ⚹	♐ 25 2:42		SVP 6♓11'43"
♅ D 28 21:01		27 5:22 ♇ △	♐ 27 15:58	26 15:22 ♃ □	♑ 27 2:31		GC 25♐54.1 ⚴ 12♑02.7
		29 0:41 ♃ □	♑ 29 15:16	28 15:56 ♃ △	♒ 29 3:23		Eris 1♈44.7R ⚵ 20♎26.8
				30 12:35 ♅ ⚹	♓ 31 7:16		⚷ 25♉26.2R ⚶ 27♉25.3R
							☽ Mean ☊ 12♓31.2

LONGITUDE — January 1933

Day	Sid.Time	☉	0 hr ☽	Noon☽	True☊	☿	♀	♂	⚳	♃	♄	♅	♆	♇
1 Su	18 42 45	10♑39 05	9♓12 25	15♓40 44	9♓32.6	20♐20.8	13♐54.1	18♍06.0	11♒55.0	23♍11.9	4♒05.6	19♈27.0	10♍04.7	22♋36.1
2 M	18 46 41	11 40 15	22 02 59	28 19 42	9 33.5	21 41.4	15 08.8	18 18.4	12 17.4	23 13.0	4 12.4	19 27.2	10R 04.0	22R 34.8
3 Tu	18 50 38	12 41 24	4♈31 30	10♈39 01	9R 34.1	23 03.1	16 23.6	18 30.3	12 40.0	23 14.0	4 19.2	19 27.5	10 03.3	22 33.6
4 W	18 54 34	13 42 34	16 42 54	22 43 48	9 33.6	24 25.9	17 38.3	18 41.6	13 02.5	23 14.8	4 26.0	19 27.8	10 02.5	22 32.3
5 Th	18 58 31	14 43 43	28 42 22	4♉39 15	9 31.2	25 49.6	18 53.1	18 52.3	13 25.1	23 15.4	4 32.9	19 28.2	10 01.8	22 31.0
6 F	19 02 27	15 44 52	10♉35 03	16 30 33	9 26.5	27 14.2	20 07.9	19 02.4	13 47.8	23 15.8	4 39.8	19 28.6	10 01.0	22 29.7
7 Sa	19 06 24	16 46 00	22 25 34	28 21 19	9 19.5	28 39.6	21 22.6	19 12.0	14 10.5	23R 16.0	4 46.7	19 29.1	10 00.1	22 28.4
8 Su	19 10 20	17 47 09	4♊17 58	10♊15 55	9 10.7	0♑05.7	22 37.4	19 20.9	14 33.2	23 16.0	4 53.7	19 29.6	9 59.3	22 27.1
9 M	19 14 17	18 48 16	16 15 28	22 16 55	9 00.8	1 32.6	23 52.2	19 29.2	14 56.0	23 15.8	5 00.6	19 30.2	9 58.4	22 25.8
10 Tu	19 18 14	19 49 24	28 20 28	4♋26 18	8 50.8	3 00.0	25 07.1	19 36.9	15 18.8	23 15.5	5 07.6	19 30.8	9 57.5	22 24.6
11 W	19 22 10	20 50 31	10♋34 33	16 45 19	8 41.5	4 28.2	26 21.9	19 44.0	15 41.7	23 14.9	5 14.6	19 31.5	9 56.5	22 23.3
12 Th	19 26 07	21 51 37	22 58 40	29 14 38	8 33.9	5 56.9	27 36.7	19 50.4	16 04.6	23 14.2	5 21.7	19 32.3	9 55.6	22 22.0
13 F	19 30 03	22 52 44	5♌33 16	11♌54 36	8 28.3	7 26.2	28 51.6	19 56.1	16 27.5	23 13.2	5 28.7	19 33.0	9 54.6	22 20.7
14 Sa	19 34 00	23 53 50	18 18 38	24 45 27	8 25.2	8 56.1	0♑06.4	20 01.2	16 50.5	23 12.1	5 35.8	19 33.9	9 53.5	22 19.4
15 Su	19 37 56	24 54 55	1♍15 06	7♍47 38	8D 24.2	10 26.6	1 21.3	20 05.6	17 13.5	23 10.8	5 42.9	19 34.8	9 52.5	22 18.1
16 M	19 41 53	25 56 00	14 23 11	21 01 50	8 24.8	11 57.6	2 36.2	20 09.3	17 36.5	23 09.2	5 49.9	19 35.7	9 51.4	22 16.8
17 Tu	19 45 50	26 57 05	27 43 45	4♎29 02	8 26.2	13 29.2	3 51.1	20 12.3	17 59.6	23 07.5	5 57.0	19 36.7	9 50.3	22 15.5
18 W	19 49 46	27 58 10	11♎17 49	18 10 12	8R 27.5	15 01.3	5 06.0	20 14.6	18 22.7	23 05.6	6 04.2	19 37.7	9 49.2	22 14.2
19 Th	19 53 43	28 59 14	25 06 16	2♏06 02	8 27.9	16 34.0	6 20.9	20 16.1	18 45.9	23 03.5	6 11.3	19 38.8	9 48.0	22 12.9
20 F	19 57 39	0♒00 18	9♏09 26	16 16 19	8 26.7	18 07.2	7 35.8	20R 16.9	19 09.1	23 01.2	6 18.4	19 39.9	9 46.8	22 11.6
21 Sa	20 01 36	1 01 22	23 26 27	0♐39 29	8 23.7	19 41.1	8 50.7	20 16.9	19 32.3	22 58.8	6 25.6	19 41.1	9 45.6	22 10.3
22 Su	20 05 32	2 02 26	7♐54 55	15 12 11	8 19.3	21 15.5	10 05.7	20 16.2	19 55.5	22 56.1	6 32.7	19 42.4	9 44.4	22 09.0
23 M	20 09 29	3 03 29	22 30 34	29 49 18	8 13.9	22 50.5	11 20.6	20 14.7	20 18.8	22 53.3	6 39.9	19 43.7	9 43.2	22 07.7
24 Tu	20 13 25	4 04 31	7♑07 31	14♑24 23	8 08.3	24 26.1	12 35.6	20 12.5	20 42.1	22 50.2	6 47.1	19 45.0	9 41.9	22 06.5
25 W	20 17 22	5 05 33	21 39 00	28 50 32	8 03.4	26 02.3	13 50.5	20 09.4	21 05.4	22 47.0	6 54.2	19 46.4	9 40.6	22 05.2
26 Th	20 21 19	6 06 34	5♒58 14	13♒01 26	7 59.7	27 39.1	15 05.4	20 05.6	21 28.8	22 43.6	7 01.4	19 47.8	9 39.3	22 03.9
27 F	20 25 15	7 07 33	19 59 35	26 52 16	7D 57.6	29 16.5	16 20.4	20 01.0	21 52.2	22 40.1	7 08.6	19 49.3	9 38.0	22 02.7
28 Sa	20 29 12	8 08 32	3♓39 13	10♓20 18	7 57.1	0♒54.7	17 35.3	19 55.6	22 15.6	22 36.3	7 15.8	19 50.8	9 36.6	22 01.4
29 Su	20 33 08	9 09 30	16 55 30	23 24 58	7 58.0	2 33.4	18 50.3	19 49.3	22 39.0	22 32.4	7 22.9	19 52.4	9 35.2	22 00.2
30 M	20 37 05	10 10 26	29 48 55	6♈07 42	7 59.6	4 12.9	20 05.2	19 42.3	23 02.4	22 28.3	7 30.1	19 54.0	9 33.8	21 59.0
31 Tu	20 41 01	11 11 21	12♈21 42	18 31 25	8 01.3	5 53.0	21 20.2	19 34.5	23 25.9	22 24.0	7 37.3	19 55.7	9 32.4	21 57.7

LONGITUDE — February 1933

Day	Sid.Time	☉	0 hr ☽	Noon☽	True☊	☿	♀	♂	⚳	♃	♄	♅	♆	♇
1 W	20 44 58	12♒12 15	24♈37 22	0♉40 08	8♓02.7	7♒33.9	22♑35.1	19♍25.9	23♒49.3	22♍19.6	7♒44.4	19♈57.4	9♍31.0	21♋56.5
2 Th	20 48 54	13 13 08	6♉40 19	12 38 30	8R 03.3	9 15.5	23 50.0	19R 16.6	24 12.8	22R 15.0	7 51.6	19 59.1	9R 29.5	21R 55.3
3 F	20 52 51	14 13 59	18 35 20	24 31 24	8 02.8	10 57.8	25 05.0	19 06.4	24 36.3	22 10.2	7 58.7	20 00.9	9 28.1	21 54.1
4 Sa	20 56 48	15 14 49	0♊27 18	6♊23 38	8 01.2	12 40.8	26 19.9	18 55.4	24 59.8	22 05.3	8 05.9	20 02.8	9 26.6	21 52.9
5 Su	21 00 44	16 15 37	12 20 56	18 19 44	7 58.6	14 24.6	27 34.8	18 43.7	25 23.4	22 00.2	8 13.0	20 04.7	9 25.1	21 51.8
6 M	21 04 41	17 16 24	24 20 29	0♋23 38	7 55.5	16 09.2	28 49.8	18 31.3	25 46.9	21 55.0	8 20.1	20 06.6	9 23.6	21 50.6
7 Tu	21 08 37	18 17 10	6♋29 34	12 38 36	7 52.1	17 54.5	0♒04.7	18 18.0	26 10.5	21 49.6	8 27.2	20 08.6	9 22.1	21 49.5
8 W	21 12 34	19 17 54	18 51 01	25 07 00	7 49.0	19 40.6	1 19.6	18 04.0	26 34.0	21 44.1	8 34.3	20 10.6	9 20.5	21 48.3
9 Th	21 16 30	20 18 36	1♌26 43	7♌50 15	7 46.6	21 27.4	2 34.5	17 49.3	26 57.6	21 38.4	8 41.4	20 12.6	9 19.0	21 47.2
10 F	21 20 27	21 19 18	14 17 38	20 48 50	7 45.0	23 14.9	3 49.4	17 33.9	27 21.2	21 32.6	8 48.5	20 14.7	9 17.4	21 46.1
11 Sa	21 24 23	22 19 58	27 23 47	4♍02 20	7D 44.3	25 03.2	5 04.4	17 17.8	27 44.8	21 26.7	8 55.5	20 16.9	9 15.8	21 45.0
12 Su	21 28 20	23 20 36	10♍44 22	17 29 40	7 44.4	26 52.1	6 19.3	17 01.0	28 08.4	21 20.6	9 02.6	20 19.0	9 14.2	21 43.9
13 M	21 32 17	24 21 13	24 18 02	1♎09 15	7 45.2	28 41.6	7 34.2	16 43.5	28 32.0	21 14.4	9 09.6	20 21.3	9 12.6	21 42.8
14 Tu	21 36 13	25 21 49	8♎03 04	14 59 16	7 46.3	0♓31.7	8 49.1	16 25.4	28 55.6	21 08.0	9 16.6	20 23.5	9 11.0	21 41.8
15 W	21 40 10	26 22 24	21 57 36	28 57 50	7 47.3	2 22.2	10 04.0	16 06.7	29 19.2	21 01.6	9 23.6	20 25.8	9 09.4	21 40.7
16 Th	21 44 06	27 22 57	5♏59 44	13♏03 03	7 48.0	4 13.2	11 18.9	15 47.4	29 42.8	20 55.0	9 30.5	20 28.1	9 07.8	21 39.7
17 F	21 48 03	28 23 30	20 07 33	27 12 59	7R 48.3	6 04.4	12 33.8	15 27.5	0♓06.4	20 48.4	9 37.4	20 30.5	9 06.2	21 38.7
18 Sa	21 51 59	29 24 01	4♐19 04	11♐25 32	7 48.1	7 55.8	13 48.7	15 07.1	0 30.0	20 41.6	9 44.4	20 32.9	9 04.5	21 37.7
19 Su	21 55 56	0♓24 31	18 32 05	25 38 23	7 47.6	9 47.1	15 03.6	14 46.2	0 53.7	20 34.7	9 51.2	20 35.4	9 02.9	21 36.7
20 M	21 59 52	1 25 00	2♑44 04	9♑48 46	7 46.9	11 38.2	16 18.5	14 24.8	1 17.3	20 27.7	9 58.1	20 37.8	9 01.2	21 35.7
21 Tu	22 03 49	2 25 27	16 52 07	23 53 41	7 46.2	13 28.7	17 33.4	14 02.9	1 40.9	20 20.6	10 04.9	20 40.4	8 59.6	21 34.8
22 W	22 07 46	3 25 53	0♒53 05	7♒49 54	7 45.6	15 18.5	18 48.3	13 40.7	2 04.6	20 13.5	10 11.8	20 42.9	8 57.9	21 33.9
23 Th	22 11 42	4 26 18	14 43 45	21 34 16	7 45.3	17 07.1	20 03.1	13 18.2	2 28.2	20 06.2	10 18.5	20 45.5	8 56.2	21 33.0
24 F	22 15 39	5 26 40	28 21 09	5♓04 06	7D 45.2	18 54.3	21 18.0	12 55.3	2 51.8	19 58.9	10 25.3	20 48.1	8 54.6	21 32.1
25 Sa	22 19 35	6 27 01	11♓42 57	18 17 30	7 45.2	20 39.6	22 32.9	12 32.1	3 15.4	19 51.5	10 32.0	20 50.8	8 52.9	21 31.2
26 Su	22 23 32	7 27 20	24 47 42	1♈13 33	7R 45.3	22 22.6	23 47.7	12 08.7	3 39.0	19 44.0	10 38.7	20 53.5	8 51.2	21 30.3
27 M	22 27 28	8 27 37	7♈35 06	13 52 29	7 45.2	24 02.7	25 02.6	11 45.2	4 02.6	19 36.5	10 45.3	20 56.2	8 49.6	21 29.5
28 Tu	22 31 25	9 27 53	20 05 56	26 15 43	7 45.1	25 39.5	26 17.4	11 21.5	4 26.2	19 28.9	10 51.9	20 58.9	8 47.9	21 28.7

Astro Data

	Dy Hr Mn
☽0N	2 8:35
♃R	8 2:22
☽0S	16 21:29
♂R	21 1:28
☽0N	29 17:14
♃□♄	30 8:09
♃⚹♇	7 12:43
☽0S	13 3:15
♄⚻♆	13 20:32
♃⚻♅	19 10:18
☽0N	26 2:31

Planet Ingress

		Dy Hr Mn
☿	♑	8 10:25
♀	♑	14 9:56
☉	♒	20 11:53
☿	♒	27 22:39
♀	♒	7 10:30
☿	♓	14 5:06
⚳	♓	17 5:29
☉	♓	19 2:16

Last Aspect / ☽ Ingress

Last Aspect Dy Hr Mn		☽ Ingress Dy Hr Mn
2 2:12 ♃ ☍	♈	2 15:13
4 15:51 ☿ △	♉	5 2:36
7 1:42 ♃ △	♊	7 15:19
9 15:31 ♀ ☍	♋	10 3:16
12 0:31 ♃ ⚹	♌	12 13:27
14 2:20 ♅ △	♍	14 21:42
16 21:31 ☉ △	♎	17 4:03
19 6:15 ☉ □	♏	19 8:24
20 23:16 ♃ ⚹	♐	21 10:55
23 0:40 ♃ □	♑	23 12:18
25 6:43 ☿ ☌	♒	25 13:56
26 23:41 ♅ ⚹	♓	27 17:31
29 10:23 ♃ ☍	♈	30 0:21

Last Aspect / ☽ Ingress

Last Aspect Dy Hr Mn		☽ Ingress Dy Hr Mn
31 18:44 ♇ □	♉	1 10:40
3 13:16 ♀ △	♊	3 23:05
5 19:17 ♃ □	♋	6 11:13
8 5:41 ♇ ☌	♌	8 21:16
10 17:09 ☿ ☍	♍	11 4:43
12 19:28 ♇ ⚹	♎	13 9:59
15 7:13 ☉ △	♏	15 13:46
17 14:08 ☉ □	♐	17 16:42
19 3:31 ♃ □	♑	19 19:22
21 8:03 ♇ ☍	♒	21 22:29
23 10:34 ♅ ⚹	♓	24 2:56
25 17:56 ♇ △	♈	26 9:42
28 12:04 ♀ ⚹	♉	28 19:20

☽ Phases & Eclipses

Dy Hr Mn		
3 16:24	☽	12♈53
11 20:36	○	21♋12
19 6:15	☾	28♎45
25 23:20	●	5♒34
2 13:16	☽	13♉16
10 13:00	○	21♌22
10 13:17	☍	A 0.018
17 14:08	☾	28♏29
24 12:44	●	5♓29
24 12:46:15	☌	A 01'31"

Astro Data

1 January 1933
Julian Day # 12054
SVP 6♓11'37"
GC 25♐54.2 ⚵ 23♑14.5
Eris 1♈43.5 ⚶ 29♎07.5
⚷ 24♉04.9R ⚴ 22♉19.9R
☽ Mean ☊ 10♓52.7

1 February 1933
Julian Day # 12085
SVP 6♓11'32"
GC 25♐54.3 ⚵ 4♒28.8
Eris 1♈53.7 ⚶ 4♏40.9
⚷ 23♉34.1 ⚴ 23♉56.4
☽ Mean ☊ 9♓14.2

March 1933 LONGITUDE

Day	Sid.Time	☉	0 hr ☽	Noon ☽	True ☊	☿	♀	♂	⚳	♃	♄	♅	♆	♇
1 W	22 35 21	10♓28 06	2♉22 10	8♉25 40	7♓44.8	27♓12.4	27♒32.2	10♍57.7	4♓49.8	19♍21.3	10♒58.5	21♈01.7	8♍46.2	21♋27.9
2 Th	22 39 18	11 28 17	14 26 42	20 25 42	7R 44.4	28 40.7	28 47.0	10R 34.0	5 13.3	19R 13.6	11 05.0	21 04.5	8R 44.5	21R 27.1
3 F	22 43 15	12 28 27	26 23 14	2♊19 49	7D 44.2	0♈04.0	0♓01.8	10 10.2	5 36.9	19 05.9	11 11.5	21 07.3	8 42.9	21 26.3
4 Sa	22 47 11	13 28 34	8♊16 02	14 12 29	7 44.1	1 21.6	1 16.6	9 46.4	6 00.4	18 58.2	11 18.0	21 10.2	8 41.2	21 25.6
5 Su	22 51 08	14 28 39	20 09 43	26 08 22	7 44.2	2 33.0	2 31.4	9 22.8	6 24.0	18 50.4	11 24.4	21 13.1	8 39.5	21 24.9
6 M	22 55 04	15 28 43	2♋08 59	8♋12 09	7 44.7	3 37.6	3 46.2	8 59.3	6 47.5	18 42.6	11 30.8	21 16.0	8 37.9	21 24.2
7 Tu	22 59 01	16 28 44	14 18 23	20 28 13	7 45.5	4 34.9	5 00.9	8 36.0	7 11.0	18 34.8	11 37.1	21 18.9	8 36.2	21 23.5
8 W	23 02 57	17 28 42	26 42 04	3♌00 21	7 46.5	5 24.5	6 15.7	8 13.0	7 34.5	18 27.0	11 43.4	21 21.9	8 34.6	21 22.9
9 Th	23 06 54	18 28 39	9♌23 24	15 51 28	7 47.4	6 06.1	7 30.4	7 50.2	7 58.0	18 19.2	11 49.7	21 24.9	8 32.9	21 22.3
10 F	23 10 50	19 28 34	22 24 42	29 03 13	7R 48.0	6 39.3	8 45.2	7 27.7	8 21.4	18 11.4	11 55.9	21 27.9	8 31.3	21 21.6
11 Sa	23 14 47	20 28 26	5♍46 57	12♍35 46	7 48.1	7 03.8	9 59.9	7 05.6	8 44.8	18 03.5	12 02.0	21 31.0	8 29.6	21 21.1
12 Su	23 18 44	21 28 17	19 29 27	26 27 37	7 47.5	7 19.7	11 14.6	6 43.9	9 08.2	17 55.7	12 08.1	21 34.0	8 28.0	21 20.5
13 M	23 22 40	22 28 05	3♎29 51	10♎35 37	7 46.2	7R 26.8	12 29.3	6 22.6	9 31.6	17 47.9	12 14.2	21 37.1	8 26.4	21 19.9
14 Tu	23 26 37	23 27 52	17 44 19	24 55 18	7 44.3	7 25.2	13 43.9	6 01.7	9 55.0	17 40.2	12 20.2	21 40.2	8 24.8	21 19.4
15 W	23 30 33	24 27 37	2♏07 54	9♏21 25	7 42.1	7 15.3	14 58.6	5 41.4	10 18.4	17 32.4	12 26.1	21 43.3	8 23.2	21 18.9
16 Th	23 34 30	25 27 20	16 35 12	23 48 37	7 40.0	6 57.4	16 13.3	5 21.5	10 41.7	17 24.7	12 32.0	21 46.5	8 21.6	21 18.5
17 F	23 38 26	26 27 02	1♐01 06	8♐12 07	7 38.4	6 32.0	17 27.9	5 02.2	11 05.0	17 17.1	12 37.9	21 49.7	8 20.0	21 18.0
18 Sa	23 42 23	27 26 42	15 21 16	22 28 09	7D 37.6	5 59.8	18 42.6	4 43.5	11 28.3	17 09.5	12 43.7	21 52.9	8 18.4	21 17.6
19 Su	23 46 19	28 26 20	29 32 29	6♑34 05	7 37.7	5 21.5	19 57.2	4 25.4	11 51.6	17 01.9	12 49.4	21 56.1	8 16.9	21 17.2
20 M	23 50 16	29 25 56	13♑32 47	20 28 27	7 38.6	4 38.1	21 11.8	4 08.0	12 14.8	16 54.4	12 55.1	21 59.3	8 15.3	21 16.8
21 Tu	23 54 13	0♈25 31	27 21 04	4♒10 34	7 40.1	3 50.6	22 26.5	3 51.1	12 38.0	16 46.9	13 00.8	22 02.5	8 13.8	21 16.5
22 W	23 58 09	1 25 04	10♒56 57	17 40 13	7 41.6	3 00.0	23 41.1	3 35.0	13 01.2	16 39.5	13 06.3	22 05.8	8 12.3	21 16.1
23 Th	0 02 06	2 24 35	24 20 22	0♓57 24	7R 42.5	2 07.5	24 55.7	3 19.6	13 24.4	16 32.2	13 11.8	22 09.1	8 10.8	21 15.8
24 F	0 06 02	3 24 04	7♓31 20	14 02 09	7 42.5	1 14.3	26 10.2	3 04.8	13 47.5	16 25.0	13 17.3	22 12.3	8 09.3	21 15.5
25 Sa	0 09 59	4 23 31	20 29 51	26 54 27	7 41.2	0 21.3	27 24.8	2 50.8	14 10.6	16 17.8	13 22.7	22 15.6	8 07.8	21 15.3
26 Su	0 13 55	5 22 57	3♈15 57	9♈34 23	7 38.5	29♓29.7	28 39.4	2 37.6	14 33.7	16 10.7	13 28.0	22 19.0	8 06.4	21 15.1
27 M	0 17 52	6 22 20	15 49 48	22 02 16	7 34.4	28 40.4	29 53.9	2 25.1	14 56.7	16 03.7	13 33.3	22 22.3	8 04.9	21 14.8
28 Tu	0 21 48	7 21 41	28 11 54	4♉18 50	7 29.3	27 54.3	1♈08.4	2 13.4	15 19.7	15 56.8	13 38.5	22 25.6	8 03.5	21 14.7
29 W	0 25 45	8 20 59	10♉23 15	16 25 24	7 23.8	27 12.1	2 23.0	2 02.5	15 42.7	15 50.0	13 43.6	22 29.0	8 02.1	21 14.5
30 Th	0 29 41	9 20 16	22 25 33	28 24 02	7 18.5	26 34.2	3 37.5	1 52.3	16 05.6	15 43.3	13 48.7	22 32.3	8 00.7	21 14.4
31 F	0 33 38	10 19 31	4♊21 13	10♊17 31	7 13.9	26 01.3	4 51.9	1 42.9	16 28.5	15 36.8	13 53.7	22 35.7	7 59.4	21 14.3

April 1933 LONGITUDE

Day	Sid.Time	☉	0 hr ☽	Noon ☽	True ☊	☿	♀	♂	⚳	♃	♄	♅	♆	♇
1 Sa	0 37 35	11♈18 43	16♊13 24	22♊09 22	7♓10.5	25♓33.7	6♈06.4	1♍34.4	16♓51.4	15♍30.3	13♒58.6	22♈39.1	7♍58.0	21♋14.2
2 Su	0 41 31	12 17 53	28 05 58	4♋03 45	7D 08.7	25R 11.5	7 20.9	1R 26.6	17 14.2	15R 24.0	14 03.5	22 42.5	7R 56.7	21R 14.1
3 M	0 45 28	13 17 00	10♋03 18	16 05 15	7 08.3	24 54.9	8 35.3	1 19.6	17 36.9	15 17.7	14 08.3	22 45.9	7 55.4	21D 14.1
4 Tu	0 49 24	14 16 06	22 10 11	28 18 43	7 09.2	24 43.9	9 49.7	1 13.4	17 59.7	15 11.6	14 13.0	22 49.3	7 54.1	21 14.1
5 W	0 53 21	15 15 09	4♌31 28	10♌48 58	7 10.7	24D 38.4	11 04.1	1 08.0	18 22.4	15 05.7	14 17.7	22 52.7	7 52.8	21 14.1
6 Th	0 57 17	16 14 09	17 11 45	23 40 17	7 12.2	24 38.5	12 18.5	1 03.4	18 45.0	14 59.8	14 22.2	22 56.1	7 51.6	21 14.1
7 F	1 01 14	17 13 08	0♍14 56	6♍55 58	7R 12.9	24 44.0	13 32.9	0 59.5	19 07.6	14 54.1	14 26.8	22 59.5	7 50.4	21 14.2
8 Sa	1 05 10	18 12 04	13 43 32	20 37 40	7 12.1	24 54.7	14 47.2	0 56.5	19 30.2	14 48.6	14 31.2	23 03.0	7 49.2	21 14.3
9 Su	1 09 07	19 10 58	27 38 13	4♎44 50	7 09.4	25 10.3	16 01.5	0 54.2	19 52.7	14 43.1	14 35.5	23 06.4	7 48.0	21 14.4
10 M	1 13 04	20 09 49	11♎57 04	19 14 14	7 04.9	25 30.9	17 15.9	0 52.6	20 15.1	14 37.9	14 39.8	23 09.8	7 46.8	21 14.5
11 Tu	1 17 00	21 08 39	26 35 32	3♏59 59	6 58.8	25 56.0	18 30.2	0D 51.8	20 37.6	14 32.7	14 44.0	23 13.3	7 45.7	21 14.7
12 W	1 20 57	22 07 27	11♏26 34	18 54 09	6 51.9	26 25.6	19 44.5	0 51.7	20 59.9	14 27.8	14 48.2	23 16.7	7 44.6	21 14.9
13 Th	1 24 53	23 06 13	26 21 39	3♐48 00	6 45.1	26 59.4	20 58.7	0 52.4	21 22.3	14 22.9	14 52.2	23 20.1	7 43.5	21 15.1
14 F	1 28 50	24 04 58	11♐12 11	18 33 20	6 39.4	27 37.1	22 13.0	0 53.8	21 44.5	14 18.3	14 56.2	23 23.6	7 42.5	21 15.4
15 Sa	1 32 46	25 03 41	25 50 45	3♑03 50	6 35.4	28 18.8	23 27.3	0 55.8	22 06.8	14 13.8	15 00.1	23 27.0	7 41.5	21 15.6
16 Su	1 36 43	26 02 22	10♑12 12	17 15 36	6D 33.4	29 04.0	24 41.5	0 58.6	22 29.0	14 09.4	15 03.9	23 30.4	7 40.5	21 15.9
17 M	1 40 39	27 01 01	24 13 54	1♒07 08	6 33.1	29 52.7	25 55.7	1 02.1	22 51.1	14 05.2	15 07.6	23 33.9	7 39.5	21 16.2
18 Tu	1 44 36	27 59 39	7♒55 24	14 38 53	6 33.9	0♈44.7	27 10.0	1 06.3	23 13.1	14 01.2	15 11.3	23 37.3	7 38.5	21 16.6
19 W	1 48 33	28 58 15	21 17 52	27 52 35	6R 34.9	1 39.9	28 24.2	1 11.2	23 35.2	13 57.4	15 14.8	23 40.7	7 37.6	21 16.9
20 Th	1 52 29	29 56 49	4♓23 21	10♓50 28	6 35.1	2 38.0	29 38.4	1 16.7	23 57.1	13 53.7	15 18.3	23 44.2	7 36.7	21 17.3
21 F	1 56 26	0♉55 21	17 14 13	23 34 51	6 33.6	3 39.1	0♉52.5	1 22.9	24 19.0	13 50.1	15 21.7	23 47.6	7 35.9	21 17.7
22 Sa	2 00 22	1 53 52	29 52 38	6♈07 46	6 29.8	4 42.9	2 06.7	1 29.7	24 40.9	13 46.8	15 25.0	23 51.0	7 35.0	21 18.2
23 Su	2 04 19	2 52 21	12♈20 26	18 30 49	6 23.4	5 49.3	3 20.9	1 37.1	25 02.6	13 43.6	15 28.2	23 54.4	7 34.2	21 18.6
24 M	2 08 15	3 50 49	24 39 03	0♉45 16	6 14.7	6 58.2	4 35.0	1 45.2	25 24.4	13 40.6	15 31.4	23 57.8	7 33.4	21 19.1
25 Tu	2 12 12	4 49 14	6♉49 35	12 52 08	6 04.2	8 09.6	5 49.1	1 53.9	25 46.0	13 37.8	15 34.4	24 01.2	7 32.7	21 19.6
26 W	2 16 08	5 47 38	18 53 04	24 52 50	5 52.8	9 23.4	7 03.2	2 03.3	26 07.6	13 35.2	15 37.4	24 04.6	7 31.9	21 20.1
27 Th	2 20 05	6 45 59	0♊50 39	6♊47 42	5 41.4	10 39.5	8 17.3	2 13.2	26 29.1	13 32.7	15 40.3	24 08.0	7 31.3	21 20.7
28 F	2 24 02	7 44 19	12 43 55	18 39 34	5 31.2	11 57.8	9 31.4	2 23.7	26 50.6	13 30.5	15 43.0	24 11.3	7 30.6	21 21.3
29 Sa	2 27 58	8 42 37	24 34 59	0♋30 34	5 22.8	13 18.3	10 45.5	2 34.7	27 12.0	13 28.4	15 45.7	24 14.7	7 30.0	21 21.9
30 Su	2 31 55	9 40 53	6♋26 44	12 23 57	5 16.8	14 41.0	11 59.5	2 46.4	27 33.3	13 26.4	15 48.3	24 18.1	7 29.4	21 22.5

Astro Data	Dy Hr Mn
☿0N	2 4:33
♅□♇	8 18:25
☽0S	12 11:29
☿ R	13 19:44
☉0N	21 1:43
☽0N	25 10:37
♀0N	30 5:18
☿0S	30 21:39
♇ D	4 7:29
♅⚼♆	5 12:39
☿ D	5 23:36
☽0S	8 21:26
♃⚻♄	10 7:04
♂ D	12 2:17
☽0N	21 16:43

Planet Ingress	Dy Hr Mn
☿ ♈	3 10:49
♀ ♓	3 11:24
☉ ♈	21 1:43
☿ ♓R	25 21:49
♀ ♈	27 13:58
☿ ♈	17 15:27
☉ ♉	20 13:18
♀ ♉	20 19:00
☿0N	23 21:29

Last Aspect Dy Hr Mn		☽ Ingress	Dy Hr Mn
3 6:50	☿ ⚹	♊	3 7:18
5 2:05	♅ ⚹	♋	5 19:43
7 13:47	♇ ☌	♌	8 6:18
9 22:13	♅ △	♍	10 13:42
12 3:12	♇ ⚹	♎	12 18:03
14 6:33	♅ ☍	♏	14 20:27
16 14:56	☉ △	♐	16 22:18
18 21:04	☉ □	♑	19 0:47
20 14:39	♅ □	♒	21 4:39
22 19:59	♅ ⚹	♓	23 10:16
25 13:03	♀ ☌	♈	25 17:49
27 12:39	♅ ☌	♉	28 3:32
30 8:30	☿ ⚹	♊	30 15:13

Last Aspect Dy Hr Mn		☽ Ingress	Dy Hr Mn
1 18:39	☿ □	♋	2 3:50
4 5:06	☿ △	♌	4 15:16
6 10:38	♅ △	♍	6 23:33
8 19:29	☿ ☍	♎	9 4:00
10 18:27	♅ ☍	♏	11 5:32
13 0:34	☿ △	♐	13 5:52
15 3:41	☿ □	♑	15 6:53
17 9:41	☿ ⚹	♒	17 10:02
19 14:10	☉ ⚹	♓	19 15:54
21 7:40	♇ △	♈	22 0:14
23 22:35	♅ ☌	♉	24 10:31
26 4:54	♇ ⚹	♊	26 22:18
28 23:15	♅ ⚹	♋	29 10:58

☽ Phases & Eclipses Dy Hr Mn	
4 10:23	☽ 13♊25
12 2:46	○ 21♍05
12 2:33	☊ A 0.592
18 21:04	☾ 27♐49
26 3:20	● 5♈01
3 5:56	☽ 13♋02
10 13:37	○ 20♎14
17 4:17	☾ 26♑42
24 18:38	● 4♉07

Astro Data

1 March 1933
Julian Day # 12113
SVP 6♓11'28"
GC 25♐54.4 ⚵ 14♒12.4
Eris 2♈10.4 ⚶ 5♏42.3R
⚷ 24♉00.7 ⚴ 0♊03.0
☽ Mean ☊ 7♓45.3

1 April 1933
Julian Day # 12144
SVP 6♓11'24"
GC 25♐54.4 ⚵ 23♒58.3
Eris 2♈32.8 ⚶ 1♏39.7R
⚷ 25♉23.7 ⚴ 9♊57.5
☽ Mean ☊ 6♓06.8

LONGITUDE — May 1933

Day	Sid.Time	☉	0 hr ☽	Noon ☽	True ☊	☿	♀	♂	⚳	♃	♄	♅	♆	♇
1 M	2 35 51	10♉39 07	18♋22 44	24♋23 39	5♓13.3	16♈05.7	13♉13.5	2♍58.6	27♓54.5	13♍24.7	15♒50.9	24♈21.4	7♍28.8	21♋23.1
2 Tu	2 39 48	11 37 19	0♌27 16	6♌34 12	5D 11.9	17 32.5	14 27.6	3 11.3	28 15.7	13R 23.2	15 53.3	24 24.7	7R 28.2	21 23.8
3 W	2 43 44	12 35 28	12 45 04	19 00 31	5 12.0	19 01.3	15 41.6	3 24.5	28 36.8	13 21.8	15 55.6	24 28.0	7 27.7	21 24.5
4 Th	2 47 41	13 33 36	25 21 10	1♍47 35	5R 12.4	20 32.1	16 55.5	3 38.3	28 57.8	13 20.6	15 57.8	24 31.3	7 27.3	21 25.2
5 F	2 51 37	14 31 42	8♍20 19	14 59 48	5 12.0	22 04.9	18 09.5	3 52.6	29 18.8	13 19.6	16 00.0	24 34.6	7 26.8	21 25.9
6 Sa	2 55 34	15 29 46	21 46 24	28 40 20	5 10.0	23 39.7	19 23.5	4 07.4	29 39.6	13 18.8	16 02.0	24 37.9	7 26.4	21 26.7
7 Su	2 59 31	16 27 48	5♎41 38	12♎50 11	5 05.6	25 16.4	20 37.4	4 22.6	0♈00.4	13 18.2	16 04.0	24 41.1	7 26.0	21 27.5
8 M	3 03 27	17 25 48	20 05 37	27 27 22	4 58.7	26 55.1	21 51.3	4 38.3	0 21.1	13 17.7	16 05.8	24 44.4	7 25.6	21 28.3
9 Tu	3 07 24	18 23 46	4♏54 37	12♏26 21	4 49.6	28 35.8	23 05.2	4 54.5	0 41.8	13D 17.5	16 07.6	24 47.6	7 25.3	21 29.1
10 W	3 11 20	19 21 43	20 01 24	27 38 26	4 39.3	0♉18.5	24 19.1	5 11.1	1 02.3	13 17.4	16 09.2	24 50.8	7 25.0	21 29.9
11 Th	3 15 17	20 19 39	5♐16 02	12♐52 50	4 29.1	2 03.1	25 33.0	5 28.2	1 22.8	13 17.5	16 10.8	24 54.0	7 24.8	21 30.8
12 F	3 19 13	21 17 33	20 27 27	27 58 41	4 20.1	3 49.8	26 46.8	5 45.7	1 43.2	13 17.8	16 12.3	24 57.2	7 24.5	21 31.7
13 Sa	3 23 10	22 15 25	5♑25 27	12♑46 56	4 13.2	5 38.3	28 00.7	6 03.7	2 03.5	13 18.3	16 13.7	25 00.3	7 24.4	21 32.6
14 Su	3 27 06	23 13 17	20 02 27	27 11 37	4 08.8	7 28.9	29 14.5	6 22.0	2 23.7	13 18.9	16 15.0	25 03.5	7 24.2	21 33.5
15 M	3 31 03	24 11 07	4♒14 13	11♒10 12	4 06.8	9 21.5	0♊28.4	6 40.8	2 43.8	13 19.7	16 16.2	25 06.6	7 24.1	21 34.5
16 Tu	3 35 00	25 08 56	17 59 43	24 42 59	4 06.4	11 15.9	1 42.2	6 59.9	3 03.9	13 20.7	16 17.2	25 09.7	7 24.0	21 35.4
17 W	3 38 56	26 06 44	1♓20 23	7♓52 19	4 06.4	13 12.4	2 56.0	7 19.5	3 23.8	13 21.9	16 18.2	25 12.7	7 23.9	21 36.4
18 Th	3 42 53	27 04 30	14 19 14	20 41 37	4 05.6	15 10.7	4 09.8	7 39.4	3 43.7	13 23.3	16 19.1	25 15.8	7D 23.9	21 37.4
19 F	3 46 49	28 02 16	26 59 55	3♈14 38	4 03.0	17 11.0	5 23.6	7 59.7	4 03.4	13 24.8	16 19.9	25 18.8	7 23.9	21 38.5
20 Sa	3 50 46	29 00 00	9♈26 11	15 34 58	3 57.8	19 13.0	6 37.4	8 20.4	4 23.1	13 26.5	16 20.6	25 21.8	7 23.9	21 39.5
21 Su	3 54 42	29 57 43	21 41 22	27 45 41	3 49.8	21 16.7	7 51.1	8 41.4	4 42.6	13 28.4	16 21.2	25 24.8	7 24.0	21 40.6
22 M	3 58 39	0♊55 25	3♉48 14	9♉49 16	3 38.9	23 22.1	9 04.9	9 02.9	5 02.1	13 30.5	16 21.7	25 27.8	7 24.1	21 41.6
23 Tu	4 02 35	1 53 06	15 49 00	21 47 38	3 26.0	25 29.0	10 18.6	9 24.6	5 21.5	13 32.8	16 22.1	25 30.7	7 24.2	21 42.7
24 W	4 06 32	2 50 46	27 45 20	3♊42 17	3 12.0	27 37.3	11 32.4	9 46.8	5 40.7	13 35.2	16 22.4	25 33.6	7 24.4	21 43.9
25 Th	4 10 29	3 48 25	9♊38 38	15 34 33	2 58.0	29 46.7	12 46.1	10 09.2	5 59.8	13 37.8	16 22.6	25 36.5	7 24.6	21 45.0
26 F	4 14 25	4 46 02	21 30 14	27 25 52	2 45.1	1♊57.2	13 59.8	10 32.0	6 18.9	13 40.6	16R 22.7	25 39.3	7 24.8	21 46.1
27 Sa	4 18 22	5 43 38	3♋21 42	9♋17 59	2 34.4	4 08.4	15 13.5	10 55.1	6 37.8	13 43.5	16 22.8	25 42.2	7 25.0	21 47.3
28 Su	4 22 18	6 41 13	15 15 03	21 13 14	2 26.3	6 20.1	16 27.2	11 18.5	6 56.6	13 46.6	16 22.7	25 45.0	7 25.3	21 48.5
29 M	4 26 15	7 38 46	27 12 56	3♌14 35	2 21.2	8 32.1	17 40.9	11 42.3	7 15.3	13 49.9	16 22.5	25 47.7	7 25.7	21 49.7
30 Tu	4 30 11	8 36 18	9♌18 41	15 25 44	2 18.6	10 44.1	18 54.5	12 06.3	7 33.9	13 53.3	16 22.2	25 50.5	7 26.0	21 50.9
31 W	4 34 08	9 33 49	21 36 18	27 50 58	2 17.8	12 55.8	20 08.2	12 30.7	7 52.3	13 57.0	16 21.8	25 53.2	7 26.4	21 52.2

LONGITUDE — June 1933

Day	Sid.Time	☉	0 hr ☽	Noon ☽	True ☊	☿	♀	♂	⚳	♃	♄	♅	♆	♇
1 Th	4 38 05	10♊31 18	4♍10 18	10♍34 54	2♓17.8	15♊06.9	21♊21.8	12♍55.3	8♈10.7	14♍00.7	16♒21.3	25♈55.8	7♍26.8	21♋53.4
2 F	4 42 01	11 28 46	17 05 20	23 42 05	2R 17.4	17 17.2	22 35.4	13 20.3	8 28.9	14 04.7	16R 20.7	25 58.5	7 27.3	21 54.7
3 Sa	4 45 58	12 26 13	0♎25 37	7♎16 16	2 15.5	19 26.4	23 49.1	13 45.5	8 47.0	14 08.8	16 20.1	26 01.1	7 27.8	21 55.9
4 Su	4 49 54	13 23 38	14 14 15	21 19 35	2 11.4	21 34.3	25 02.6	14 11.0	9 04.9	14 13.0	16 19.3	26 03.7	7 28.3	21 57.2
5 M	4 53 51	14 21 03	28 32 08	5♏51 32	2 04.9	23 40.7	26 16.2	14 36.7	9 22.8	14 17.5	16 18.4	26 06.2	7 28.9	21 58.5
6 Tu	4 57 47	15 18 26	13♏17 08	20 48 08	1 56.1	25 45.4	27 29.8	15 02.7	9 40.5	14 22.0	16 17.5	26 08.8	7 29.4	21 59.9
7 W	5 01 44	16 15 48	28 23 26	6♐01 48	1 46.1	27 48.2	28 43.3	15 29.0	9 58.1	14 26.8	16 16.4	26 11.3	7 30.1	22 01.2
8 Th	5 05 40	17 13 10	13♐41 51	21 22 06	1 35.9	29 49.0	29 56.9	15 55.5	10 15.5	14 31.7	16 15.3	26 13.7	7 30.7	22 02.6
9 F	5 09 37	18 10 31	29 01 06	6♑37 26	1 26.9	1♋47.8	1♋10.4	16 22.3	10 32.8	14 36.7	16 14.0	26 16.1	7 31.4	22 03.9
10 Sa	5 13 34	19 07 51	14♑09 50	21 37 11	1 19.9	3 44.3	2 23.9	16 49.3	10 50.0	14 41.9	16 12.7	26 18.5	7 32.1	22 05.3
11 Su	5 17 30	20 05 10	28 58 39	6♒13 32	1 15.4	5 38.5	3 37.4	17 16.6	11 07.1	14 47.2	16 11.3	26 20.9	7 32.8	22 06.7
12 M	5 21 27	21 02 29	13♒21 27	20 22 11	1D 13.3	7 30.4	4 50.9	17 44.1	11 23.9	14 52.7	16 09.8	26 23.2	7 33.6	22 08.1
13 Tu	5 25 23	21 59 48	27 15 43	4♓02 13	1 12.9	9 20.0	6 04.4	18 11.8	11 40.7	14 58.3	16 08.1	26 25.5	7 34.4	22 09.5
14 W	5 29 20	22 57 06	10♓41 58	17 15 21	1R 13.3	11 07.1	7 17.9	18 39.8	11 57.3	15 04.1	16 06.4	26 27.7	7 35.2	22 10.9
15 Th	5 33 16	23 54 23	23 42 52	0♈05 01	1 13.2	12 51.8	8 31.4	19 07.9	12 13.8	15 10.0	16 04.7	26 29.9	7 36.1	22 12.3
16 F	5 37 13	24 51 41	6♈22 21	12 35 25	1 11.7	14 34.1	9 44.8	19 36.3	12 30.1	15 16.1	16 02.8	26 32.1	7 37.0	22 13.8
17 Sa	5 41 09	25 48 58	18 44 46	24 50 56	1 08.1	16 14.0	10 58.3	20 05.0	12 46.2	15 22.3	16 00.8	26 34.2	7 37.9	22 15.2
18 Su	5 45 06	26 46 15	0♉54 26	6♉55 42	1 02.0	17 51.3	12 11.7	20 33.8	13 02.2	15 28.6	15 58.7	26 36.3	7 38.9	22 16.7
19 M	5 49 03	27 43 31	12 55 12	18 53 19	0 53.5	19 26.2	13 25.2	21 02.9	13 18.0	15 35.1	15 56.6	26 38.4	7 39.9	22 18.2
20 Tu	5 52 59	28 40 47	24 50 23	0♊46 45	0 43.1	20 58.6	14 38.6	21 32.1	13 33.7	15 41.7	15 54.4	26 40.4	7 40.9	22 19.7
21 W	5 56 56	29 38 03	6♊42 39	12 38 22	0 31.8	22 28.4	15 52.0	22 01.6	13 49.2	15 48.5	15 52.0	26 42.4	7 41.9	22 21.2
22 Th	6 00 52	0♋35 19	18 34 07	24 30 05	0 20.4	23 55.7	17 05.4	22 31.3	14 04.5	15 55.3	15 49.6	26 44.3	7 43.0	22 22.7
23 F	6 04 49	1 32 34	0♋26 29	6♋23 30	0 10.0	25 20.5	18 18.8	23 01.2	14 19.7	16 02.4	15 47.2	26 46.2	7 44.1	22 24.2
24 Sa	6 08 45	2 29 49	12 21 19	18 20 08	0 01.4	26 42.6	19 32.2	23 31.2	14 34.6	16 09.5	15 44.6	26 48.1	7 45.2	22 25.7
25 Su	6 12 42	3 27 04	24 20 11	0♌21 42	29♒55.1	28 02.1	20 45.6	24 01.5	14 49.4	16 16.8	15 41.9	26 49.9	7 46.4	22 27.2
26 M	6 16 38	4 24 18	6♌24 57	12 30 15	29 51.2	29 18.9	21 59.0	24 32.0	15 04.1	16 24.2	15 39.2	26 51.6	7 47.6	22 28.8
27 Tu	6 20 35	5 21 32	18 37 56	24 48 23	29D 49.7	0♌33.0	23 12.3	25 02.6	15 18.5	16 31.7	15 36.4	26 53.4	7 48.8	22 30.3
28 W	6 24 32	6 18 45	1♍01 59	7♍19 10	29 49.7	1 44.3	24 25.6	25 33.5	15 32.7	16 39.4	15 33.5	26 55.0	7 50.0	22 31.9
29 Th	6 28 28	7 15 58	13 40 23	20 06 06	29 50.7	2 52.8	25 39.0	26 04.5	15 46.8	16 47.1	15 30.6	26 56.7	7 51.3	22 33.4
30 F	6 32 25	8 13 10	26 36 46	3♎12 48	29R 51.5	3 58.3	26 52.3	26 35.7	16 00.7	16 55.0	15 27.5	26 58.3	7 52.6	22 35.0

Astro Data	Dy Hr Mn
☽0S	6 7:09
♃ D	10 10:21
☽0N	18 21:32
♆ D	19 1:36
♄ R	27 2:19
☽0S	2 15:05
☽0N	15 2:50
♃⚻♄	21 21:19
☽0S	29 20:58

Planet Ingress		Dy Hr Mn
⚳	♈	7 11:30
☿	♉	10 7:42
♀	♊	15 2:47
☉	♊	21 12:57
☿	♊	25 14:27
♀	♋	8 13:01
☿	♋	8 14:12
☉	♋	21 21:12
☊	♒R	24 16:36
☿	♌	27 1:12

Last Aspect Dy Hr Mn			☽ Ingress	Dy Hr Mn
1 11:56	♅	□	♌	1 23:06
3 22:23	♅	△	♍	4 8:41
5 23:25	♇	⚹	♎	6 14:17
8 11:01	☿	☍	♏	8 16:07
10 6:19	♀	☍	♐	10 15:43
12 7:09	♅	△	♑	12 15:15
14 15:48	♀	△	♒	14 16:46
16 12:50	☉	□	♓	16 21:34
19 1:09	☉	⚹	♈	19 5:45
21 7:20	♅	☌	♉	21 16:26
23 21:02	☿	☌	♊	24 4:31
26 8:23	♅	⚹	♋	26 17:12
28 21:06	♅	□	♌	29 5:33
31 8:14	♅	△	♍	31 16:06

Last Aspect Dy Hr Mn			☽ Ingress	Dy Hr Mn
2 9:48	♀	□	♎	2 23:15
4 19:56	♅	☍	♏	5 2:25
6 13:54	♇	△	♐	7 2:32
8 19:38	♅	△	♑	9 1:33
10 19:39	♅	□	♒	11 1:41
12 22:30	♅	⚹	♓	13 4:50
14 23:25	☉	□	♈	15 11:50
17 15:25	♅	☌	♉	17 22:12
19 18:54	♇	⚹	♊	20 10:25
22 16:32	♅	⚹	♋	22 23:07
25 6:49	☿	☌	♌	25 11:17
27 16:02	♅	△	♍	27 22:01
29 23:28	♂	☌	♎	30 6:11

☽ Phases & Eclipses Dy Hr Mn	
2 22:39	☽ 12♌03
9 22:04	○ 18♏48
16 12:50	☾ 25♒11
24 10:07	● 2♊46
1 11:53	☽ 10♍31
8 5:05	○ 16♐57
14 23:25	☾ 23♓24
23 1:22	● 1♋07
30 21:40	☽ 8♎36

Astro Data

1 May 1933
Julian Day # 12174
SVP 6♓11'20"
GC 25♐54.5 ⚴ 1♓44.6
Eris 2♈53.1 ⚵ 24♎58.3R
⚷ 27♉20.4 ⚶ 21♊22.1
☽ Mean ☊ 4♓31.4

1 June 1933
Julian Day # 12205
SVP 6♓11'15"
GC 25♐54.6 ⚴ 7♓00.6
Eris 3♈07.6 ⚵ 20♎28.0R
⚷ 29♉35.8 ⚶ 4♋13.2
☽ Mean ☊ 2♓53.0

July 1933

LONGITUDE

Day	Sid.Time	☉	0 hr ☽	Noon ☽	True ☊	☿	♀	♂	⚳	♃	♄	♅	♆	♇
1 Sa	6 36 21	9♋10 22	9♎54 36	16♎42 28	29♒51.3	5♌00.7	28♋05.6	27♍07.1	16♈14.3	17♍03.0	15♒24.4	26♈59.8	7♍53.9	22♋36.5
2 Su	6 40 18	10 07 33	23 36 39	0♏37 14	29R 49.5	6 00.1	29 18.8	27 38.6	16 27.8	17 11.2	15R 21.3	27 01.3	7 55.2	22 38.1
3 M	6 44 14	11 04 45	7♏44 13	14 57 21	29 45.8	6 56.3	0♌32.1	28 10.3	16 41.1	17 19.4	15 18.0	27 02.8	7 56.6	22 39.7
4 Tu	6 48 11	12 01 56	22 16 17	29 40 23	29 40.4	7 49.2	1 45.3	28 42.2	16 54.1	17 27.8	15 14.7	27 04.2	7 58.0	22 41.3
5 W	6 52 07	12 59 07	7♐08 53	14♐40 49	29 33.9	8 38.7	2 58.5	29 14.3	17 07.0	17 36.2	15 11.4	27 05.6	7 59.4	22 42.9
6 Th	6 56 04	13 56 18	22 15 04	29 50 23	29 27.2	9 24.6	4 11.8	29 46.5	17 19.6	17 44.8	15 07.9	27 06.9	8 00.9	22 44.5
7 F	7 00 01	14 53 28	7♑25 29	14♑59 05	29 21.2	10 06.8	5 24.9	0♎18.8	17 32.1	17 53.5	15 04.4	27 08.2	8 02.3	22 46.1
8 Sa	7 03 57	15 50 39	22 29 56	29 56 55	29 16.7	10 45.3	6 38.1	0 51.4	17 44.3	18 02.3	15 00.9	27 09.5	8 03.8	22 47.7
9 Su	7 07 54	16 47 50	7♒19 03	14♒35 32	29 14.0	11 19.8	7 51.3	1 24.0	17 56.3	18 11.2	14 57.2	27 10.7	8 05.3	22 49.3
10 M	7 11 50	17 45 02	21 45 46	28 49 19	29D 13.1	11 50.2	9 04.4	1 56.9	18 08.1	18 20.2	14 53.6	27 11.8	8 06.9	22 50.9
11 Tu	7 15 47	18 42 13	5♓45 59	12♓35 43	29 13.7	12 16.5	10 17.6	2 29.8	18 19.7	18 29.3	14 49.8	27 12.9	8 08.5	22 52.5
12 W	7 19 43	19 39 25	19 18 38	25 54 58	29 15.1	12 38.4	11 30.7	3 03.0	18 31.0	18 38.5	14 46.0	27 14.0	8 10.0	22 54.1
13 Th	7 23 40	20 36 38	2♈25 04	8♈49 23	29 16.4	12 55.8	12 43.8	3 36.3	18 42.1	18 47.8	14 42.2	27 15.0	8 11.6	22 55.7
14 F	7 27 37	21 33 51	15 08 23	21 22 38	29R 17.0	13 08.6	13 56.9	4 09.7	18 52.9	18 57.2	14 38.3	27 15.9	8 13.3	22 57.3
15 Sa	7 31 33	22 31 05	27 32 39	3♉39 02	29 16.3	13 16.8	15 09.9	4 43.3	19 03.5	19 06.7	14 34.4	27 16.9	8 14.9	22 58.9
16 Su	7 35 30	23 28 20	9♉42 21	15 43 08	29 14.1	13R 20.1	16 23.0	5 17.0	19 13.9	19 16.3	14 30.4	27 17.7	8 16.6	23 00.5
17 M	7 39 26	24 25 35	21 41 56	27 39 14	29 10.4	13 18.6	17 36.0	5 50.9	19 24.0	19 26.0	14 26.3	27 18.6	8 18.3	23 02.1
18 Tu	7 43 23	25 22 51	3♊35 33	9♊31 18	29 05.5	13 12.3	18 49.1	6 24.9	19 33.9	19 35.8	14 22.3	27 19.3	8 20.0	23 03.7
19 W	7 47 19	26 20 08	15 26 54	21 22 42	28 59.9	13 01.0	20 02.1	6 59.0	19 43.5	19 45.6	14 18.1	27 20.0	8 21.8	23 05.3
20 Th	7 51 16	27 17 25	27 19 04	3♋16 17	28 54.2	12 45.1	21 15.1	7 33.3	19 52.8	19 55.6	14 14.0	27 20.7	8 23.5	23 06.9
21 F	7 55 12	28 14 43	9♋14 37	15 14 19	28 49.0	12 24.4	22 28.1	8 07.8	20 01.9	20 05.7	14 09.8	27 21.4	8 25.3	23 08.5
22 Sa	7 59 09	29 12 01	21 15 37	27 18 41	28 44.8	11 59.3	23 41.0	8 42.3	20 10.7	20 15.8	14 05.6	27 21.9	8 27.1	23 10.1
23 Su	8 03 06	0♌09 20	3♌23 44	9♌30 57	28 42.0	11 30.1	24 54.0	9 17.1	20 19.2	20 26.0	14 01.3	27 22.5	8 28.9	23 11.7
24 M	8 07 02	1 06 40	15 40 29	21 52 32	28D 40.6	10 56.9	26 06.9	9 51.9	20 27.4	20 36.4	13 57.0	27 22.9	8 30.8	23 13.3
25 Tu	8 10 59	2 04 00	28 07 16	4♍24 54	28 40.5	10 20.4	27 19.8	10 26.9	20 35.4	20 46.7	13 52.7	27 23.4	8 32.6	23 14.9
26 W	8 14 55	3 01 20	10♍45 38	17 09 42	28 41.5	9 41.0	28 32.7	11 02.0	20 43.1	20 57.2	13 48.3	27 23.7	8 34.5	23 16.5
27 Th	8 18 52	3 58 41	23 37 17	0♎08 39	28 42.9	8 59.3	29 45.6	11 37.2	20 50.5	21 07.8	13 43.9	27 24.1	8 36.4	23 18.1
28 F	8 22 48	4 56 03	6♎44 01	13 23 36	28 44.4	8 16.0	0♍58.4	12 12.6	20 57.6	21 18.4	13 39.5	27 24.4	8 38.3	23 19.7
29 Sa	8 26 45	5 53 25	20 07 36	26 56 09	28R 45.4	7 31.7	2 11.2	12 48.1	21 04.4	21 29.1	13 35.1	27 24.6	8 40.2	23 21.3
30 Su	8 30 41	6 50 48	3♏49 23	10♏47 18	28 45.6	6 47.4	3 24.0	13 23.7	21 10.9	21 39.9	13 30.7	27 24.8	8 42.2	23 22.9
31 M	8 34 38	7 48 11	17 49 52	24 56 56	28 44.8	6 03.7	4 36.8	13 59.5	21 17.1	21 50.8	13 26.3	27 24.9	8 44.1	23 24.4

August 1933

LONGITUDE

Day	Sid.Time	☉	0 hr ☽	Noon ☽	True ☊	☿	♀	♂	⚳	♃	♄	♅	♆	♇
1 Tu	8 38 35	8♌45 35	2♐08 14	9♐23 23	28♒43.2	5♌21.5	5♍49.6	14♎35.3	21♈23.0	22♍01.7	13♒21.8	27♈25.0	8♍46.1	23♋26.0
2 W	8 42 31	9 42 59	16 41 51	24 03 00	28R 41.0	4R 41.6	7 02.3	15 11.3	21 28.6	22 12.7	13R 17.3	27R 25.0	8 48.1	23 27.6
3 Th	8 46 28	10 40 25	1♑26 06	8♑50 18	28 38.7	4 04.7	8 15.0	15 47.4	21 33.9	22 23.8	13 12.9	27 25.0	8 50.1	23 29.1
4 F	8 50 24	11 37 51	16 14 41	23 38 18	28 36.6	3 31.7	9 27.6	16 23.6	21 38.8	22 34.9	13 08.4	27 25.0	8 52.1	23 30.7
5 Sa	8 54 21	12 35 17	1♒00 14	8♒19 33	28 35.2	3 03.1	10 40.3	17 00.0	21 43.5	22 46.1	13 03.9	27 24.9	8 54.1	23 32.2
6 Su	8 58 17	13 32 45	15 35 25	22 47 03	28D 34.5	2 39.7	11 52.9	17 36.4	21 47.8	22 57.4	12 59.4	27 24.7	8 56.2	23 33.7
7 M	9 02 14	14 30 14	29 53 50	6♓55 16	28 34.5	2 21.8	13 05.5	18 13.0	21 51.8	23 08.7	12 54.9	27 24.5	8 58.2	23 35.3
8 Tu	9 06 10	15 27 44	13♓50 58	20 40 42	28 35.2	2 10.0	14 18.0	18 49.6	21 55.5	23 20.1	12 50.5	27 24.2	9 00.3	23 36.8
9 W	9 10 07	16 25 15	27 24 23	4♈02 03	28 36.2	2D 04.5	15 30.5	19 26.4	21 58.8	23 31.6	12 46.0	27 23.9	9 02.4	23 38.3
10 Th	9 14 04	17 22 47	10♈33 50	17 00 00	28 37.2	2 05.8	16 43.0	20 03.3	22 01.8	23 43.1	12 41.5	27 23.6	9 04.4	23 39.8
11 F	9 18 00	18 20 21	23 20 53	29 36 53	28 38.0	2 14.0	17 55.5	20 40.3	22 04.5	23 54.7	12 37.1	27 23.2	9 06.5	23 41.3
12 Sa	9 21 57	19 17 57	5♉48 29	11♉56 11	28R 38.5	2 29.2	19 08.0	21 17.5	22 06.8	24 06.3	12 32.6	27 22.7	9 08.7	23 42.8
13 Su	9 25 53	20 15 33	18 00 32	24 02 04	28 38.6	2 51.6	20 20.4	21 54.7	22 08.7	24 18.0	12 28.2	27 22.2	9 10.8	23 44.2
14 M	9 29 50	21 13 12	0♊01 22	5♊59 01	28 38.3	3 21.0	21 32.8	22 32.1	22 10.4	24 29.8	12 23.8	27 21.7	9 12.9	23 45.7
15 Tu	9 33 46	22 10 52	11 55 33	17 51 32	28 37.7	3 57.6	22 45.2	23 09.5	22 11.6	24 41.6	12 19.4	27 21.1	9 15.0	23 47.1
16 W	9 37 43	23 08 33	23 47 30	29 43 56	28 37.0	4 41.2	23 57.5	23 47.1	22 12.5	24 53.5	12 15.0	27 20.5	9 17.2	23 48.6
17 Th	9 41 39	24 06 16	5♋41 19	11♋40 06	28 36.4	5 31.8	25 09.8	24 24.8	22R 13.1	25 05.4	12 10.7	27 19.8	9 19.4	23 50.0
18 F	9 45 36	25 04 01	17 40 40	23 43 23	28 35.9	6 29.0	26 22.1	25 02.6	22 13.3	25 17.4	12 06.3	27 19.1	9 21.5	23 51.4
19 Sa	9 49 33	26 01 47	29 48 34	5♌56 30	28 35.6	7 32.8	27 34.4	25 40.5	22 13.1	25 29.4	12 02.1	27 18.3	9 23.7	23 52.8
20 Su	9 53 29	26 59 34	12♌07 25	18 21 30	28D 35.4	8 42.8	28 46.6	26 18.5	22 12.5	25 41.4	11 57.8	27 17.5	9 25.9	23 54.2
21 M	9 57 26	27 57 23	24 38 54	0♍59 44	28R 35.4	9 58.8	29 58.8	26 56.6	22 11.6	25 53.5	11 53.6	27 16.6	9 28.1	23 55.6
22 Tu	10 01 22	28 55 13	7♍24 04	13 51 56	28 35.4	11 20.4	1♎11.0	27 34.8	22 10.3	26 05.7	11 49.4	27 15.7	9 30.3	23 57.0
23 W	10 05 19	29 53 04	20 23 20	26 58 16	28 35.3	12 47.3	2 23.2	28 13.1	22 08.7	26 17.9	11 45.2	27 14.7	9 32.5	23 58.3
24 Th	10 09 15	0♍50 57	3♎36 39	10♎18 26	28 35.1	14 19.0	3 35.3	28 51.6	22 06.6	26 30.1	11 41.1	27 13.7	9 34.7	23 59.7
25 F	10 13 12	1 48 51	17 03 33	23 51 52	28 34.8	15 55.2	4 47.3	29 30.1	22 04.3	26 42.4	11 37.0	27 12.6	9 36.9	24 01.0
26 Sa	10 17 08	2 46 47	0♏43 17	7♏37 39	28 34.5	17 35.4	5 59.4	0♏08.8	22 01.5	26 54.8	11 33.0	27 11.5	9 39.1	24 02.3
27 Su	10 21 05	3 44 44	14 34 51	21 34 41	28D 34.2	19 19.1	7 11.4	0 47.5	21 58.4	27 07.1	11 29.0	27 10.4	9 41.3	24 03.6
28 M	10 25 02	4 42 42	28 36 58	5♐41 29	28 34.0	21 05.9	8 23.3	1 26.3	21 54.9	27 19.5	11 25.0	27 09.2	9 43.5	24 04.9
29 Tu	10 28 58	5 40 41	12♐47 58	19 56 09	28 34.2	22 55.3	9 35.3	2 05.3	21 51.0	27 32.0	11 21.1	27 08.0	9 45.7	24 06.2
30 W	10 32 55	6 38 42	27 05 41	4♑16 11	28 34.7	24 46.8	10 47.1	2 44.3	21 46.8	27 44.5	11 17.3	27 06.7	9 48.0	24 07.5
31 Th	10 36 51	7 36 44	11♑27 17	18 38 29	28 35.4	26 40.1	11 59.0	3 23.5	21 42.2	27 57.0	11 13.5	27 05.4	9 50.2	24 08.7

Astro Data (Dy Hr Mn)

♂0S 8 7:33
☽0N 12 10:00
☿R 16 16:37
☽0S 27 1:58

♅R 2 19:43
☽0N 8 19:03
☿D 9 19:33
♃✶♇ 10 4:02
⚳R 18 12:06
♀0S 23 1:17
☽0S 23 7:45
♃⚼♄ 25 4:01
♃⚻♅ 27 17:47

Planet Ingress (Dy Hr Mn)

♀ ♌ 3 1:29
♂ ♎ 6 22:03
☉ ♌ 23 8:05
♀ ♍ 27 16:45

♀ ♎ 21 12:23
☉ ♍ 23 14:52
♂ ♏ 26 6:34

Last Aspect / ☽ Ingress (Dy Hr Mn / Dy Hr Mn)

2 9:34 ♀ □ ♏ 2 10:57
4 10:23 ♂ ✶ ♐ 4 12:32
6 11:54 ♂ □ ♑ 6 12:15
8 7:29 ♅ □ ♒ 8 12:05
10 9:13 ♅ ✶ ♓ 10 14:01
12 6:29 ♇ △ ♈ 12 19:31
14 23:28 ♅ ☌ ♉ 15 4:49
17 4:55 ☉ ✶ ♊ 17 16:44
20 0:03 ♅ ✶ ♋ 20 5:25
22 16:03 ☉ ☌ ♌ 22 17:19
24 22:35 ♅ △ ♍ 25 3:36
26 23:23 ♇ ✶ ♎ 27 11:44
29 12:50 ♅ ☍ ♏ 29 17:21
31 9:24 ♇ △ ♐ 31 20:27

Last Aspect / ☽ Ingress (Dy Hr Mn / Dy Hr Mn)

2 17:29 ♅ △ ♑ 2 21:40
4 18:09 ♅ □ ♒ 4 22:22
6 19:47 ♅ ✶ ♓ 7 0:10
8 17:13 ♇ △ ♈ 9 4:40
11 7:43 ♅ ☌ ♉ 11 12:45
13 12:32 ♃ △ ♊ 13 23:57
16 7:11 ♅ ✶ ♋ 16 12:32
18 19:05 ♅ □ ♌ 19 0:22
21 5:48 ☉ ☌ ♍ 21 10:07
23 10:46 ♃ ☌ ♎ 23 17:29
25 22:21 ♂ ☌ ♏ 25 22:45
27 21:36 ♃ ✶ ♐ 28 2:21
30 0:55 ♃ □ ♑ 30 4:52

☽ Phases & Eclipses (Dy Hr Mn)

7 11:51 ○ 14♑53
14 12:24 ☾ 21♈35
22 16:03 ● 29♋22
30 4:44 ☽ 6♏33

5 19:32 ○ 12♒53
5 19:46 • A 0.232
13 3:49 ☾ 19♉56
21 5:48 ● 27♌42
21 5:48:47 • A 02'03"
28 10:13 ☽ 4♐38

Astro Data

1 July 1933
Julian Day # 12235
SVP 6♓11'10"
GC 25♐54.6 ⚴ 8♓04.7R
Eris 3♈12.2R ⚵ 20♎53.3
⚷ 1♊38.9 ⚶ 17♋14.2
☽ Mean ☊ 1♓17.7

1 August 1933
Julian Day # 12266
SVP 6♓11'04"
GC 25♐54.7 ⚴ 3♓56.8R
Eris 3♈06.2R ⚵ 25♎31.8
⚷ 3♊15.9 ⚶ 0♌59.3
☽ Mean ☊ 29♒39.2

LONGITUDE — September 1933

Day	Sid.Time	☉	0 hr ☽	Noon ☽	True ☊	☿	♀	♂	⚳	♃	♄	♅	♆	♇
1 F	10 40 48	8♍34 48	25♑49 19	2♒59 16	28♒36.2	28♌34.7	13♎10.8	4♏02.7	21♈37.2	28♍09.5	11♒09.8	27♈04.1	9♍52.4	24♋09.9
2 Sa	10 44 44	9 32 52	10♒07 47	17 14 20	28R 36.8	0♍30.2	14 22.5	4 42.0	21R 31.9	28 22.1	11R 06.1	27R 02.7	9 54.6	24 11.1
3 Su	10 48 41	10 30 59	24 18 24	1♓19 27	28 37.0	2 26.4	15 34.2	5 21.4	21 26.2	28 34.7	11 02.5	27 01.2	9 56.9	24 12.3
4 M	10 52 37	11 29 07	8♓17 00	15 10 39	28 36.5	4 22.9	16 45.9	6 00.9	21 20.1	28 47.3	10 59.0	26 59.8	9 59.1	24 13.5
5 Tu	10 56 34	12 27 17	22 00 02	28 44 51	28 35.4	6 19.5	17 57.5	6 40.5	21 13.7	29 00.0	10 55.5	26 58.3	10 01.3	24 14.6
6 W	11 00 31	13 25 28	5♈24 54	12♈00 04	28 33.6	8 15.9	19 09.1	7 20.2	21 07.0	29 12.6	10 52.1	26 56.7	10 03.5	24 15.8
7 Th	11 04 27	14 23 42	18 30 20	24 55 44	28 31.4	10 11.9	20 20.6	8 00.0	20 59.9	29 25.4	10 48.7	26 55.1	10 05.7	24 16.9
8 F	11 08 24	15 21 57	1♉16 27	7♉32 42	28 29.1	12 07.5	21 32.1	8 39.9	20 52.5	29 38.1	10 45.4	26 53.5	10 08.0	24 18.0
9 Sa	11 12 20	16 20 15	13 44 47	19 53 05	28 27.0	14 02.4	22 43.6	9 19.9	20 44.7	29 50.9	10 42.2	26 51.8	10 10.2	24 19.1
10 Su	11 16 17	17 18 34	25 58 01	2♊00 04	28 25.4	15 56.6	23 55.0	9 59.9	20 36.5	0♎03.6	10 39.0	26 50.1	10 12.4	24 20.2
11 M	11 20 13	18 16 56	7♊59 45	13 57 39	28D 24.6	17 49.9	25 06.4	10 40.1	20 28.1	0 16.4	10 35.9	26 48.4	10 14.6	24 21.2
12 Tu	11 24 10	19 15 20	19 54 18	25 50 20	28 24.7	19 42.4	26 17.7	11 20.4	20 19.3	0 29.3	10 32.9	26 46.7	10 16.8	24 22.3
13 W	11 28 06	20 13 46	1♋46 20	7♋42 54	28 25.6	21 33.9	27 29.0	12 00.7	20 10.2	0 42.1	10 30.0	26 44.9	10 19.0	24 23.3
14 Th	11 32 03	21 12 14	13 40 38	19 40 05	28 27.1	23 24.4	28 40.2	12 41.2	20 00.8	0 55.0	10 27.2	26 43.0	10 21.2	24 24.3
15 F	11 36 00	22 10 44	25 41 50	1♌46 23	28 28.8	25 13.9	29 51.4	13 21.7	19 51.1	1 07.9	10 24.4	26 41.2	10 23.4	24 25.2
16 Sa	11 39 56	23 09 16	7♌54 12	14 05 44	28 30.2	27 02.4	1♏02.5	14 02.3	19 41.1	1 20.8	10 21.7	26 39.3	10 25.6	24 26.2
17 Su	11 43 53	24 07 50	20 21 19	26 41 16	28R 30.9	28 49.8	2 13.6	14 43.1	19 30.7	1 33.7	10 19.1	26 37.3	10 27.8	24 27.1
18 M	11 47 49	25 06 27	3♍05 48	9♍35 03	28 30.4	0♎36.2	3 24.7	15 23.9	19 20.2	1 46.6	10 16.5	26 35.4	10 30.0	24 28.0
19 Tu	11 51 46	26 05 05	16 09 05	22 47 49	28 28.6	2 21.6	4 35.7	16 04.8	19 09.3	1 59.5	10 14.1	26 33.4	10 32.1	24 28.9
20 W	11 55 42	27 03 45	29 31 10	6♎18 52	28 25.5	4 06.0	5 46.6	16 45.8	18 58.2	2 12.5	10 11.7	26 31.4	10 34.3	24 29.8
21 Th	11 59 39	28 02 27	13♎10 38	20 06 05	28 21.4	5 49.3	6 57.5	17 26.9	18 46.8	2 25.4	10 09.5	26 29.3	10 36.4	24 30.6
22 F	12 03 35	29 01 11	27 04 46	4♏06 13	28 16.7	7 31.7	8 08.4	18 08.0	18 35.2	2 38.4	10 07.3	26 27.2	10 38.6	24 31.5
23 Sa	12 07 32	29 59 57	11♏09 54	18 15 18	28 12.2	9 13.1	9 19.1	18 49.3	18 23.3	2 51.4	10 05.2	26 25.1	10 40.7	24 32.3
24 Su	12 11 28	0♎58 45	25 21 55	2♐29 15	28 08.5	10 53.5	10 29.9	19 30.6	18 11.3	3 04.4	10 03.2	26 23.0	10 42.8	24 33.1
25 M	12 15 25	1 57 34	9♐36 52	16 44 20	28 06.0	12 32.9	11 40.5	20 12.1	17 59.0	3 17.3	10 01.2	26 20.9	10 44.9	24 33.8
26 Tu	12 19 22	2 56 25	23 51 18	0♑57 28	28D 05.1	14 11.4	12 51.2	20 53.6	17 46.6	3 30.3	9 59.4	26 18.7	10 47.0	24 34.6
27 W	12 23 18	3 55 18	8♑02 34	15 06 24	28 05.5	15 49.0	14 01.7	21 35.2	17 34.0	3 43.3	9 57.7	26 16.5	10 49.1	24 35.3
28 Th	12 27 15	4 54 13	22 08 46	29 09 31	28 06.8	17 25.7	15 12.2	22 16.9	17 21.2	3 56.3	9 56.0	26 14.3	10 51.2	24 36.0
29 F	12 31 11	5 53 09	6♒08 30	13♒05 35	28 08.2	19 01.6	16 22.6	22 58.7	17 08.3	4 09.3	9 54.5	26 12.0	10 53.3	24 36.6
30 Sa	12 35 08	6 52 07	20 00 37	26 53 26	28R 09.0	20 36.5	17 32.9	23 40.5	16 55.2	4 22.2	9 53.0	26 09.8	10 55.3	24 37.3

LONGITUDE — October 1933

Day	Sid.Time	☉	0 hr ☽	Noon ☽	True ☊	☿	♀	♂	⚳	♃	♄	♅	♆	♇
1 Su	12 39 04	7♎51 07	3♓43 52	10♓31 45	28♒08.3	22♎10.6	18♏43.2	24♏22.4	16♈42.0	4♎35.2	9♒51.7	26♈07.5	10♍57.4	24♋37.9
2 M	12 43 01	8 50 08	17 16 53	23 59 04	28R 05.7	23 43.8	19 53.4	25 04.4	16R 28.7	4 48.2	9R 50.4	26R 05.2	10 59.4	24 38.5
3 Tu	12 46 57	9 49 12	0♈38 07	7♈13 50	28 01.1	25 16.2	21 03.5	25 46.5	16 15.3	5 01.1	9 49.3	26 02.9	11 01.4	24 39.1
4 W	12 50 54	10 48 17	13 46 04	20 14 41	27 54.7	26 47.8	22 13.5	26 28.7	16 01.8	5 14.1	9 48.2	26 00.6	11 03.4	24 39.6
5 Th	12 54 51	11 47 25	26 39 35	3♉00 44	27 47.0	28 18.6	23 23.5	27 11.0	15 48.2	5 27.1	9 47.2	25 58.2	11 05.4	24 40.2
6 F	12 58 47	12 46 35	9♉18 10	15 31 57	27 38.8	29 48.5	24 33.4	27 53.3	15 34.6	5 40.0	9 46.4	25 55.9	11 07.3	24 40.7
7 Sa	13 02 44	13 45 47	21 42 14	27 49 14	27 30.9	1♏17.7	25 43.2	28 35.7	15 21.0	5 52.9	9 45.6	25 53.5	11 09.3	24 41.2
8 Su	13 06 40	14 45 01	3♊53 14	9♊54 36	27 24.1	2 46.0	26 52.9	29 18.2	15 07.3	6 05.8	9 44.9	25 51.1	11 11.2	24 41.6
9 M	13 10 37	15 44 18	15 53 42	21 51 02	27 19.0	4 13.5	28 02.6	0♐00.8	14 53.7	6 18.8	9 44.3	25 48.7	11 13.1	24 42.1
10 Tu	13 14 33	16 43 37	27 47 06	3♋42 27	27 16.0	5 40.1	29 12.1	0 43.4	14 40.0	6 31.6	9 43.9	25 46.3	11 15.0	24 42.5
11 W	13 18 30	17 42 58	9♋37 41	15 33 25	27D 14.9	7 05.9	0♐21.6	1 26.1	14 26.3	6 44.5	9 43.5	25 43.9	11 16.9	24 42.9
12 Th	13 22 26	18 42 22	21 30 19	27 29 00	27 15.2	8 30.9	1 31.0	2 08.9	14 12.7	6 57.4	9 43.2	25 41.5	11 18.8	24 43.2
13 F	13 26 23	19 41 47	3♌30 09	9♌34 25	27 16.3	9 54.9	2 40.3	2 51.8	13 59.2	7 10.2	9 43.0	25 39.0	11 20.6	24 43.6
14 Sa	13 30 20	20 41 15	15 42 25	21 54 44	27R 17.2	11 18.0	3 49.6	3 34.8	13 45.7	7 23.1	9D 43.0	25 36.6	11 22.5	24 43.9
15 Su	13 34 16	21 40 46	28 11 55	4♍34 26	27 17.1	12 40.2	4 58.7	4 17.8	13 32.3	7 35.9	9 43.0	25 34.2	11 24.3	24 44.2
16 M	13 38 13	22 40 18	11♍02 40	17 36 56	27 15.1	14 01.3	6 07.7	5 01.0	13 19.0	7 48.6	9 43.1	25 31.7	11 26.0	24 44.4
17 Tu	13 42 09	23 39 53	24 17 21	1♎03 58	27 10.7	15 21.4	7 16.7	5 44.2	13 05.8	8 01.4	9 43.4	25 29.3	11 27.8	24 44.6
18 W	13 46 06	24 39 30	7♎56 40	14 55 09	27 04.0	16 40.4	8 25.5	6 27.5	12 52.7	8 14.1	9 43.7	25 26.8	11 29.6	24 44.9
19 Th	13 50 02	25 39 09	21 59 00	29 07 36	26 55.3	17 58.1	9 34.2	7 10.8	12 39.8	8 26.8	9 44.1	25 24.4	11 31.3	24 45.0
20 F	13 53 59	26 38 50	6♏20 14	13♏36 05	26 45.6	19 14.6	10 42.9	7 54.2	12 27.0	8 39.5	9 44.7	25 21.9	11 33.0	24 45.2
21 Sa	13 57 55	27 38 33	20 54 13	28 13 43	26 36.0	20 29.6	11 51.4	8 37.8	12 14.4	8 52.2	9 45.3	25 19.5	11 34.7	24 45.3
22 Su	14 01 52	28 38 18	5♐33 36	12♐53 01	26 27.7	21 43.2	12 59.8	9 21.3	12 02.0	9 04.8	9 46.1	25 17.0	11 36.3	24 45.4
23 M	14 05 49	29 38 04	20 11 07	27 27 12	26 21.5	22 55.1	14 08.1	10 05.0	11 49.8	9 17.4	9 46.9	25 14.6	11 38.0	24 45.5
24 Tu	14 09 45	0♏37 53	4♑40 40	11♑51 04	26 17.7	24 05.3	15 16.3	10 48.7	11 37.8	9 29.9	9 47.9	25 12.1	11 39.6	24 45.6
25 W	14 13 42	1 37 42	18 58 05	26 01 30	26D 16.2	25 13.5	16 24.3	11 32.5	11 26.1	9 42.5	9 48.9	25 09.7	11 41.2	24R 45.6
26 Th	14 17 38	2 37 34	3♒01 14	9♒57 16	26 16.3	26 19.5	17 32.2	12 16.4	11 14.5	9 55.0	9 50.1	25 07.3	11 42.7	24 45.6
27 F	14 21 35	3 37 27	16 49 39	23 38 32	26R 16.7	27 23.1	18 40.0	13 00.3	11 03.3	10 07.4	9 51.3	25 04.8	11 44.3	24 45.6
28 Sa	14 25 31	4 37 22	0♓24 01	7♓06 16	26 16.2	28 24.1	19 47.6	13 44.3	10 52.2	10 19.8	9 52.7	25 02.4	11 45.8	24 45.6
29 Su	14 29 28	5 37 18	13 45 26	20 21 39	26 13.9	29 22.1	20 55.1	14 28.4	10 41.5	10 32.2	9 54.1	25 00.0	11 47.3	24 45.5
30 M	14 33 24	6 37 16	26 55 00	3♈25 34	26 08.8	0♐16.9	22 02.4	15 12.5	10 31.0	10 44.5	9 55.7	24 57.6	11 48.7	24 45.4
31 Tu	14 37 21	7 37 16	9♈53 26	16 18 35	26 00.7	1 08.0	23 09.6	15 56.7	10 20.8	10 56.8	9 57.3	24 55.3	11 50.2	24 45.3

Astro Data

	Dy Hr Mn
☽0N	5 4:42
♄⚻♆	15 16:42
☿0S	19 12:22
☽0S	19 15:21
♃0S	22 0:03
☉0S	23 12:01
☽0N	2 13:13
♅⚼♆	3 20:17
♄ D	14 17:14
☽0S	17 0:31
♃△♄	26 1:37
♇ R	26 8:09
☽0N	29 19:31

Planet Ingress

		Dy Hr Mn
☿	♍	2 5:44
♃	♎	10 5:11
♀	♏	15 14:54
☿	♎	18 3:48
☉	♎	23 12:01
☿	♏	6 15:04
♂	♐	9 11:35
♀	♐	11 4:32
☉	♏	23 20:48
☿	♐	30 4:27

Last Aspect / ☽ Ingress

Last Aspect Dy Hr Mn		☽ Ingress	Dy Hr Mn
1 3:47	♃ △	♒	1 7:00
3 4:39	♅ ⚹	♓	3 9:44
5 12:28	♃ ☍	♈	5 14:15
7 15:44	♅ ☌	♉	7 21:35
9 20:45	♇ ⚹	♊	10 8:01
12 13:54	♅ ⚹	♋	12 20:25
15 7:49	♀ □	♌	15 8:31
17 11:53	♅ △	♍	17 18:13
19 18:21	☉ ☌	♎	20 0:51
21 22:58	♅ ☍	♏	22 5:00
23 22:37	♇ △	♐	24 7:49
26 4:10	♅ △	♑	26 10:23
28 7:01	♅ □	♒	28 13:27
30 10:44	♅ ⚹	♓	30 17:27

Last Aspect / ☽ Ingress

Last Aspect Dy Hr Mn		☽ Ingress	Dy Hr Mn
2 14:04	♂ △	♈	2 22:51
5 1:55	☿ ☍	♉	5 6:18
7 13:37	♂ ☍	♊	7 16:18
9 19:59	♅ ⚹	♋	10 4:29
12 8:25	♅ □	♌	12 17:02
14 19:03	♅ △	♍	15 3:25
17 0:48	♇ ⚹	♎	17 10:07
19 5:47	♅ ☍	♏	19 13:28
21 6:19	♇ △	♐	21 14:54
23 15:53	☉ ⚹	♑	23 16:13
25 10:32	♅ □	♒	25 18:48
27 19:11	☿ □	♓	27 23:17
29 20:02	♇ △	♈	30 5:40

☽ Phases & Eclipses

Dy Hr Mn	
4 5:04	○ 11♓12
4 4:52	• A 0.696
11 21:30	☾ 18♊40
19 18:21	● 26♍21
26 15:36	☽ 3♑05
3 17:08	○ 10♈02
11 16:45	☾ 17♋55
19 5:45	● 25♎24
25 22:21	☽ 2♒04

Astro Data

1 September 1933
Julian Day # 12297
SVP 6♓11'00"
GC 25♐54.8 ⚴ 26♒20.6R
Eris 2♈51.2R ⚵ 3♏00.1
⚷ 4♊02.8 ⚶ 14♌48.2
☽ Mean ☊ 28♒00.7

1 October 1933
Julian Day # 12327
SVP 6♓10'56"
GC 25♐54.8 ⚴ 20♒47.8R
Eris 2♈32.1R ⚵ 11♏53.4
⚷ 3♊49.9R ⚶ 27♌57.5
☽ Mean ☊ 26♒25.4

November 1933 LONGITUDE

Day	Sid.Time	☉	0 hr ☽	Noon☽	True☊	☿	♀	♂	⚳	♃	♄	♅	♆	♇
1 W	14 41 18	8♏37 18	22♈41 03	29♈00 49	25♒50.0	1♐55.1	24♐16.6	16♐41.0	10♈11.0	11♎09.0	9♒59.1	24♈52.9	11♍51.6	24♋45.2
2 Th	14 45 14	9 37 21	5♉17 52	11♉32 12	25R 37.3	2 37.6	25 23.4	17 25.3	10R 01.4	11 21.2	10 00.9	24R 50.5	11 52.9	24R 45.0
3 F	14 49 11	10 37 26	17 43 49	23 52 45	25 23.7	3 15.1	26 30.0	18 09.8	9 52.1	11 33.3	10 02.9	24 48.2	11 54.3	24 44.8
4 Sa	14 53 07	11 37 34	29 59 06	6♊02 57	25 10.3	3 47.1	27 36.5	18 54.2	9 43.2	11 45.4	10 04.9	24 45.9	11 55.6	24 44.6
5 Su	14 57 04	12 37 43	12♊04 28	18 03 53	24 58.4	4 12.8	28 42.8	19 38.7	9 34.6	11 57.5	10 07.1	24 43.6	11 56.9	24 44.3
6 M	15 01 00	13 37 54	24 01 28	29 57 34	24 48.6	4 31.7	29 48.9	20 23.3	9 26.3	12 09.5	10 09.3	24 41.3	11 58.2	24 44.1
7 Tu	15 04 57	14 38 07	5♋52 34	11♋46 55	24 41.7	4R 43.0	0♑54.8	21 08.0	9 18.4	12 21.4	10 11.7	24 39.0	11 59.5	24 43.8
8 W	15 08 53	15 38 22	17 41 07	23 35 44	24 37.5	4 46.2	2 00.5	21 52.7	9 10.8	12 33.3	10 14.1	24 36.8	12 00.7	24 43.5
9 Th	15 12 50	16 38 39	29 31 21	5♌28 36	24 35.6	4 40.5	3 06.0	22 37.5	9 03.5	12 45.1	10 16.6	24 34.6	12 01.9	24 43.1
10 F	15 16 47	17 38 58	11♌28 10	17 30 43	24 35.3	4 25.3	4 11.3	23 22.4	8 56.7	12 56.9	10 19.3	24 32.4	12 03.0	24 42.8
11 Sa	15 20 43	18 39 19	23 36 58	29 47 34	24 35.2	4 00.3	5 16.4	24 07.3	8 50.1	13 08.6	10 22.0	24 30.2	12 04.1	24 42.4
12 Su	15 24 40	19 39 42	6♍03 13	12♍24 31	24 34.4	3 25.1	6 21.2	24 52.3	8 44.0	13 20.3	10 24.8	24 28.0	12 05.2	24 41.9
13 M	15 28 36	20 40 07	18 52 02	25 26 15	24 31.6	2 39.9	7 25.9	25 37.3	8 38.2	13 31.9	10 27.7	24 25.9	12 06.3	24 41.5
14 Tu	15 32 33	21 40 34	2♎07 32	8♎56 05	24 26.2	1 44.9	8 30.2	26 22.4	8 32.8	13 43.4	10 30.7	24 23.8	12 07.3	24 41.0
15 W	15 36 29	22 41 02	15 51 57	22 55 00	24 18.1	0 41.1	9 34.4	27 07.6	8 27.8	13 54.9	10 33.8	24 21.7	12 08.3	24 40.6
16 Th	15 40 26	23 41 32	0♏04 53	7♏21 03	24 07.6	29♏29.8	10 38.2	27 52.8	8 23.2	14 06.3	10 37.0	24 19.6	12 09.3	24 40.0
17 F	15 44 22	24 42 04	14 42 41	22 08 51	23 55.7	28 12.8	11 41.8	28 38.1	8 18.9	14 17.6	10 40.2	24 17.6	12 10.3	24 39.5
18 Sa	15 48 19	25 42 38	29 38 24	7♐10 06	23 43.7	26 52.4	12 45.2	29 23.5	8 15.0	14 28.9	10 43.6	24 15.6	12 11.2	24 39.0
19 Su	15 52 16	26 43 13	14♐42 40	22 14 48	23 33.1	25 31.1	13 48.2	0♑08.9	8 11.6	14 40.1	10 47.0	24 13.7	12 12.1	24 38.4
20 M	15 56 12	27 43 50	29 45 19	7♑13 05	23 24.9	24 11.6	14 50.9	0 54.4	8 08.5	14 51.2	10 50.6	24 11.7	12 12.9	24 37.8
21 Tu	16 00 09	28 44 28	14♑37 11	21 56 51	23 19.6	22 56.6	15 53.4	1 39.9	8 05.8	15 02.2	10 54.2	24 09.8	12 13.7	24 37.2
22 W	16 04 05	29 45 07	29 11 32	6♒20 51	23 17.0	21 48.5	16 55.5	2 25.5	8 03.5	15 13.2	10 57.9	24 08.0	12 14.5	24 36.5
23 Th	16 08 02	0♐45 47	13♒24 37	20 22 49	23 16.3	20 49.1	17 57.2	3 11.1	8 01.6	15 24.1	11 01.7	24 06.1	12 15.3	24 35.9
24 F	16 11 58	1 46 28	27 15 30	4♓02 54	23 16.3	20 00.0	18 58.6	3 56.8	8 00.1	15 34.9	11 05.6	24 04.3	12 16.0	24 35.2
25 Sa	16 15 55	2 47 10	10♓45 17	17 22 56	23 15.6	19 22.1	19 59.6	4 42.5	7 59.0	15 45.6	11 09.6	24 02.6	12 16.7	24 34.5
26 Su	16 19 51	3 47 53	23 56 14	0♈25 31	23 13.1	18 55.8	21 00.3	5 28.3	7 58.3	15 56.2	11 13.6	24 00.9	12 17.3	24 33.7
27 M	16 23 48	4 48 37	6♈51 08	13 13 23	23 07.9	18D 41.1	22 00.5	6 14.1	7D 57.9	16 06.8	11 17.8	23 59.2	12 17.9	24 33.0
28 Tu	16 27 45	5 49 22	19 32 34	25 48 58	22 59.8	18 37.6	23 00.3	7 00.0	7 58.0	16 17.3	11 22.0	23 57.5	12 18.5	24 32.2
29 W	16 31 41	6 50 08	2♉02 46	8♉14 12	22 48.8	18 44.7	23 59.7	7 45.9	7 58.4	16 27.6	11 26.3	23 55.9	12 19.1	24 31.4
30 Th	16 35 38	7 50 55	14 23 24	20 30 31	22 35.8	19 01.7	24 58.6	8 31.9	7 59.2	16 37.9	11 30.7	23 54.3	12 19.6	24 30.6

December 1933 LONGITUDE

Day	Sid.Time	☉	0 hr ☽	Noon☽	True☊	☿	♀	♂	⚳	♃	♄	♅	♆	♇
1 F	16 39 34	8♐51 44	26♉35 39	2♊38 56	22♒21.8	19♏27.6	25♑57.1	9♑17.9	8♈00.4	16♎48.1	11♒35.1	23♈52.8	12♍20.1	24♋29.7
2 Sa	16 43 31	9 52 34	8♊40 28	14 40 22	22R 08.0	20 01.7	26 55.1	10 04.0	8 01.9	16 58.2	11 39.6	23R 51.3	12 20.5	24R 28.9
3 Su	16 47 27	10 53 24	20 38 46	26 35 49	21 55.6	20 43.1	27 52.6	10 50.1	8 03.9	17 08.2	11 44.2	23 49.8	12 20.9	24 28.0
4 M	16 51 24	11 54 16	2♋31 44	8♋26 44	21 45.4	21 30.9	28 49.5	11 36.2	8 06.2	17 18.1	11 48.9	23 48.4	12 21.3	24 27.1
5 Tu	16 55 21	12 55 10	14 21 06	20 15 09	21 38.0	22 24.3	29 46.0	12 22.5	8 08.9	17 28.0	11 53.7	23 47.1	12 21.7	24 26.2
6 W	16 59 17	13 56 04	26 09 16	2♌03 52	21 33.5	23 22.7	0♒41.8	13 08.7	8 11.9	17 37.7	11 58.5	23 45.7	12 22.0	24 25.3
7 Th	17 03 14	14 56 59	7♌59 25	13 56 27	21D 31.5	24 25.5	1 37.1	13 55.0	8 15.3	17 47.3	12 03.4	23 44.4	12 22.3	24 24.4
8 F	17 07 10	15 57 56	19 55 31	25 57 13	21 31.2	25 32.0	2 31.8	14 41.3	8 19.1	17 56.8	12 08.4	23 43.2	12 22.5	24 23.4
9 Sa	17 11 07	16 58 54	2♍02 12	8♍11 06	21R 31.8	26 41.8	3 25.9	15 27.7	8 23.2	18 06.2	12 13.4	23 42.0	12 22.7	24 22.4
10 Su	17 15 03	17 59 53	14 24 34	20 43 16	21 32.1	27 54.5	4 19.3	16 14.1	8 27.7	18 15.5	12 18.5	23 40.9	12 22.9	24 21.4
11 M	17 19 00	19 00 53	27 07 48	3♎38 46	21 30.9	29 09.6	5 12.0	17 00.6	8 32.5	18 24.7	12 23.7	23 39.7	12 23.0	24 20.4
12 Tu	17 22 56	20 01 54	10♎16 38	17 01 48	21 27.7	0♐26.9	6 04.1	17 47.1	8 37.7	18 33.8	12 28.9	23 38.7	12 23.1	24 19.4
13 W	17 26 53	21 02 56	23 54 30	0♏54 52	21 22.1	1 46.0	6 55.4	18 33.7	8 43.2	18 42.7	12 34.3	23 37.7	12 23.2	24 18.3
14 Th	17 30 50	22 03 59	8♏02 44	15 17 49	21 14.3	3 06.7	7 45.9	19 20.3	8 49.1	18 51.6	12 39.6	23 36.7	12R 23.3	24 17.3
15 F	17 34 46	23 05 04	22 39 33	0♐07 07	21 05.2	4 28.8	8 35.7	20 06.9	8 55.3	19 00.3	12 45.1	23 35.8	12 23.3	24 16.2
16 Sa	17 38 43	24 06 09	7♐39 31	15 15 34	20 55.8	5 52.1	9 24.7	20 53.6	9 01.8	19 08.9	12 50.6	23 34.9	12 23.2	24 15.1
17 Su	17 42 39	25 07 15	22 53 55	0♑33 09	20 47.4	7 16.5	10 12.8	21 40.3	9 08.7	19 17.4	12 56.2	23 34.1	12 23.2	24 14.0
18 M	17 46 36	26 08 21	8♑11 50	15 48 36	20 40.9	8 41.8	11 00.0	22 27.1	9 15.9	19 25.8	13 01.8	23 33.3	12 23.1	24 12.9
19 Tu	17 50 32	27 09 28	23 22 12	0♒51 31	20 36.8	10 07.9	11 46.3	23 13.8	9 23.4	19 34.1	13 07.5	23 32.6	12 22.9	24 11.8
20 W	17 54 29	28 10 35	8♒15 40	15 33 57	20D 35.2	11 34.7	12 31.6	24 00.7	9 31.3	19 42.2	13 13.3	23 31.9	12 22.8	24 10.6
21 Th	17 58 25	29 11 43	22 45 53	29 51 12	20 35.4	13 02.2	13 15.9	24 47.5	9 39.4	19 50.2	13 19.1	23 31.3	12 22.6	24 09.5
22 F	18 02 22	0♑12 50	6♓49 50	13♓41 50	20 36.4	14 30.3	13 59.1	25 34.4	9 47.9	19 58.0	13 24.9	23 30.7	12 22.3	24 08.3
23 Sa	18 06 19	1 13 58	20 27 25	27 06 52	20R 37.3	15 58.8	14 41.2	26 21.3	9 56.7	20 05.8	13 30.8	23 30.2	12 22.0	24 07.1
24 Su	18 10 15	2 15 06	3♈40 35	10♈08 59	20 37.0	17 27.9	15 22.2	27 08.2	10 05.7	20 13.4	13 36.8	23 29.8	12 21.7	24 05.9
25 M	18 14 12	3 16 13	16 32 31	22 51 40	20 34.9	18 57.4	16 01.9	27 55.2	10 15.1	20 20.8	13 42.8	23 29.3	12 21.4	24 04.7
26 Tu	18 18 08	4 17 21	29 06 52	5♉18 35	20 30.6	20 27.3	16 40.4	28 42.2	10 24.8	20 28.2	13 48.9	23 29.0	12 21.0	24 03.5
27 W	18 22 05	5 18 29	11♉27 14	17 33 13	20 24.3	21 57.6	17 17.6	29 29.2	10 34.7	20 35.3	13 55.1	23 28.6	12 20.6	24 02.3
28 Th	18 26 01	6 19 37	23 36 54	29 38 37	20 16.5	23 28.2	17 53.5	0♒16.2	10 45.0	20 42.4	14 01.2	23 28.4	12 20.2	24 01.1
29 F	18 29 58	7 20 45	5♊38 39	11♊37 17	20 07.9	24 59.2	18 27.9	1 03.3	10 55.5	20 49.3	14 07.5	23 28.2	12 19.7	23 59.8
30 Sa	18 33 54	8 21 53	17 34 46	23 31 18	19 59.3	26 30.6	19 00.8	1 50.4	11 06.3	20 56.1	14 13.7	23 28.0	12 19.2	23 58.6
31 Su	18 37 51	9 23 02	29 27 08	5♋22 26	19 51.7	28 02.3	19 32.3	2 37.5	11 17.4	21 02.7	14 20.1	23 27.9	12 18.7	23 57.3

Astro Data	Planet Ingress	Last Aspect	☽ Ingress	Last Aspect	☽ Ingress	☽ Phases & Eclipses	Astro Data
Dy Hr Mn	Dy Hr Mn	Dy Hr Mn	Dy Hr Mn	Dy Hr Mn	Dy Hr Mn	Dy Hr Mn	1 November 1933
♅□♇ 5 3:19	♀ ♑ 6 16:02	1 4:11 ♅ ☌	♉ 1 13:53	30 21:34 ♀ △	♊ 1 6:45	2 7:59 ○ 9♉27	Julian Day # 12358
♃⚺♆ 5 10:46	☿ ♏R 16 2:07	3 13:42 ♇ ⚹	♊ 4 0:02	3 6:26 ♅ ⚹	♋ 3 18:53	10 12:18 ☾ 17♌40	SVP 6♓10'53"
☿ R 8 8:47	♂ ♑ 19 7:18	6 11:41 ♀ ☍	♋ 6 12:05	5 20:30 ♇ ☌	♌ 6 7:49	17 16:24 ● 24♏53	GC 25♐54.9 ⚴ 20♒15.1
☽ 0S 13 9:48	☉ ♐ 22 17:53	8 14:17 ♇ ☌	♌ 9 0:58	8 11:05 ☿ □	♍ 8 20:00	24 7:38 ☽ 1♓35	Eris 2♈13.4R ⚵ 22♏03.1
☽ 0N 26 0:10		11 1:46 ♅ △	♍ 11 12:24	11 2:52 ☿ ⚹	♎ 11 5:19		⚷ 2♊40.6R ⚶ 10♍54.0
⚳ D 27 21:25	♀ ♒ 5 18:00	13 12:21 ♂ □	♎ 13 20:13	13 0:42 ♇ □	♏ 13 10:27	2 1:31 ○ 9♊26	☽ Mean ☊ 24♒46.9
☿ D 28 7:41	☿ ♐ 12 3:43	15 19:28 ♂ ⚹	♏ 15 23:52	15 2:37 ♇ △	♐ 15 11:49	10 6:24 ☾ 17♍46	
	☉ ♑ 22 6:58	17 20:56 ☿ ☌	♐ 18 0:34	17 2:53 ☉ ☌	♑ 17 11:08	17 2:53 ● 24♐44	1 December 1933
☽ 0S 10 17:38	♂ ♒ 28 3:43	19 15:09 ♅ △	♑ 20 0:24	19 1:20 ♇ ☍	♒ 19 10:37	23 20:09 ☽ 1♈35	Julian Day # 12388
♄⚻♆ 11 8:53		22 0:06 ☉ ⚹	♒ 22 1:21	21 10:48 ☉ ⚹	♓ 21 12:15	31 20:54 ○ 9♋46	SVP 6♓10'48"
♆ R 15 3:00		23 18:28 ♅ ⚹	♓ 24 4:50	23 10:32 ♂ ⚹	♈ 23 17:15		GC 25♐55.0 ⚴ 24♒17.7
☽ 0N 23 5:31		26 1:10 ♇ △	♈ 26 11:13	25 22:21 ♂ □	♉ 26 1:43		Eris 2♈01.8R ⚵ 2♐17.5
		28 9:33 ♇ □	♉ 28 20:03	28 0:49 ♇ ⚹	♊ 28 12:43		⚷ 1♊04.0R ⚶ 22♍05.6
				30 18:56 ☿ ☍	♋ 31 1:07		☽ Mean ☊ 23♒11.6

LONGITUDE — January 1934

Day	Sid.Time	☉	0 hr ☽	Noon ☽	True ☊	☿	♀	♂	⚳	♃	♄	♅	♆	♇
1 M	18 41 48	10♑24 10	11♋17 26	17♋12 19	19♒45.5	29♐34.4	20♒02.1	3♒24.7	11♈28.7	21♎09.2	14♒26.4	23♈27.8	12♍18.1	23♋56.1
2 Tu	18 45 44	11 25 18	23 07 19	29 02 40	19R 41.3	1♑06.8	20 30.3	4 11.8	11 40.3	21 15.5	14 32.8	23D 27.8	12R 17.5	23R 54.8
3 W	18 49 41	12 26 27	4♌58 38	10♌55 31	19D 39.1	2 39.5	20 56.8	4 59.0	11 52.2	21 21.7	14 39.3	23 27.9	12 16.9	23 53.6
4 Th	18 53 37	13 27 35	16 53 37	22 53 20	19 38.7	4 12.7	21 21.5	5 46.2	12 04.3	21 27.7	14 45.8	23 28.0	12 16.2	23 52.3
5 F	18 57 34	14 28 44	28 55 01	4♍59 07	19 39.7	5 46.1	21 44.3	6 33.4	12 16.6	21 33.6	14 52.3	23 28.1	12 15.5	23 51.0
6 Sa	19 01 30	15 29 52	11♍06 05	17 16 25	19 41.4	7 20.0	22 05.3	7 20.7	12 29.2	21 39.3	14 58.9	23 28.3	12 14.8	23 49.7
7 Su	19 05 27	16 31 01	23 30 36	29 49 10	19 43.1	8 54.3	22 24.3	8 07.9	12 42.1	21 44.9	15 05.5	23 28.6	12 14.0	23 48.4
8 M	19 09 24	17 32 10	6♎12 38	12♎41 28	19R 44.1	10 28.9	22 41.3	8 55.2	12 55.2	21 50.3	15 12.1	23 28.9	12 13.3	23 47.1
9 Tu	19 13 20	18 33 18	19 16 09	25 57 05	19 44.0	12 04.0	22 56.2	9 42.5	13 08.5	21 55.5	15 18.8	23 29.2	12 12.4	23 45.8
10 W	19 17 17	19 34 27	2♏44 34	9♏38 49	19 42.4	13 39.5	23 08.9	10 29.8	13 22.1	22 00.6	15 25.6	23 29.6	12 11.6	23 44.5
11 Th	19 21 13	20 35 36	16 39 55	23 47 46	19 39.6	15 15.4	23 19.5	11 17.2	13 35.9	22 05.5	15 32.3	23 30.1	12 10.7	23 43.2
12 F	19 25 10	21 36 45	1♐02 08	8♐22 32	19 35.8	16 51.8	23 27.8	12 04.5	13 49.9	22 10.3	15 39.1	23 30.6	12 09.8	23 41.9
13 Sa	19 29 06	22 37 54	15 48 18	23 18 37	19 31.8	18 28.7	23 33.8	12 51.9	14 04.2	22 14.9	15 45.9	23 31.2	12 08.9	23 40.6
14 Su	19 33 03	23 39 03	0♑52 25	8♑28 34	19 28.0	20 06.0	23R 37.4	13 39.3	14 18.6	22 19.3	15 52.8	23 31.8	12 07.9	23 39.3
15 M	19 36 59	24 40 11	16 05 48	23 42 48	19 25.2	21 43.9	23 38.6	14 26.7	14 33.3	22 23.6	15 59.7	23 32.5	12 07.0	23 38.0
16 Tu	19 40 56	25 41 19	1♒18 16	8♒51 00	19D 23.7	23 22.3	23 37.3	15 14.1	14 48.2	22 27.6	16 06.6	23 33.2	12 05.9	23 36.7
17 W	19 44 53	26 42 26	16 19 51	23 43 51	19 23.5	25 01.2	23 33.6	16 01.5	15 03.3	22 31.5	16 13.5	23 34.0	12 04.9	23 35.4
18 Th	19 48 49	27 43 33	1♓02 14	8♓14 24	19 24.2	26 40.6	23 27.3	16 48.9	15 18.7	22 35.3	16 20.5	23 34.8	12 03.8	23 34.1
19 F	19 52 46	28 44 38	15 19 55	22 18 35	19 25.6	28 20.6	23 18.5	17 36.3	15 34.2	22 38.8	16 27.5	23 35.7	12 02.7	23 32.8
20 Sa	19 56 42	29 45 43	29 10 20	5♈55 15	19 27.1	0♒01.1	23 07.2	18 23.8	15 49.9	22 42.2	16 34.5	23 36.6	12 01.6	23 31.5
21 Su	20 00 39	0♒46 46	12♈33 34	19 05 37	19R 28.2	1 42.2	22 53.3	19 11.2	16 05.8	22 45.4	16 41.5	23 37.6	12 00.5	23 30.2
22 M	20 04 35	1 47 49	25 31 47	1♉52 32	19 28.6	3 23.8	22 37.0	19 58.7	16 21.9	22 48.4	16 48.5	23 38.6	11 59.3	23 28.9
23 Tu	20 08 32	2 48 51	8♉08 23	14 19 51	19 28.2	5 06.1	22 18.2	20 46.1	16 38.2	22 51.3	16 55.6	23 39.7	11 58.1	23 27.6
24 W	20 12 28	3 49 52	20 27 28	26 31 46	19 26.9	6 48.8	21 57.1	21 33.5	16 54.7	22 53.9	17 02.7	23 40.8	11 56.9	23 26.3
25 Th	20 16 25	4 50 51	2♊33 18	8♊32 32	19 25.1	8 32.2	21 33.6	22 21.0	17 11.3	22 56.4	17 09.8	23 42.0	11 55.7	23 25.0
26 F	20 20 22	5 51 50	14 29 59	20 26 06	19 23.0	10 16.0	21 08.0	23 08.4	17 28.2	22 58.7	17 16.9	23 43.2	11 54.4	23 23.7
27 Sa	20 24 18	6 52 48	26 21 18	2♋15 58	19 20.9	12 00.4	20 40.4	23 55.9	17 45.2	23 00.8	17 24.1	23 44.5	11 53.1	23 22.5
28 Su	20 28 15	7 53 44	8♋10 30	14 05 12	19 19.1	13 45.2	20 10.8	24 43.3	18 02.4	23 02.7	17 31.2	23 45.8	11 51.8	23 21.2
29 M	20 32 11	8 54 40	20 00 24	25 56 22	19 17.7	15 30.5	19 39.5	25 30.8	18 19.7	23 04.5	17 38.4	23 47.2	11 50.5	23 19.9
30 Tu	20 36 08	9 55 34	1♌53 21	7♌51 38	19D 17.0	17 16.1	19 06.6	26 18.2	18 37.2	23 06.0	17 45.5	23 48.6	11 49.1	23 18.7
31 W	20 40 04	10 56 27	13 51 24	19 52 55	19 16.7	19 02.0	18 32.4	27 05.7	18 54.9	23 07.4	17 52.7	23 50.1	11 47.8	23 17.5

LONGITUDE — February 1934

Day	Sid.Time	☉	0 hr ☽	Noon ☽	True ☊	☿	♀	♂	⚳	♃	♄	♅	♆	♇
1 Th	20 44 01	11♒57 20	25♌56 22	2♍01 59	19♒17.0	20♒48.1	17♒57.1	27♒53.1	19♈12.7	23♎08.6	17♒59.9	23♈51.6	11♍46.4	23♋16.2
2 F	20 47 57	12 58 11	8♍10 00	14 20 38	19 17.5	22 34.3	17R 20.9	28 40.5	19 30.7	23 09.6	18 07.1	23 53.2	11R 45.0	23R 15.0
3 Sa	20 51 54	13 59 01	20 34 07	26 50 43	19 18.1	24 20.4	16 44.0	29 27.9	19 48.9	23 10.4	18 14.3	23 54.8	11 43.6	23 13.8
4 Su	20 55 51	14 59 51	3♎10 40	9♎34 16	19 18.6	26 06.3	16 06.8	0♓15.4	20 07.2	23 11.0	18 21.5	23 56.4	11 42.1	23 12.6
5 M	20 59 47	16 00 39	16 01 45	22 33 24	19 19.0	27 51.7	15 29.5	1 02.8	20 25.6	23 11.4	18 28.7	23 58.1	11 40.7	23 11.4
6 Tu	21 03 44	17 01 27	29 09 29	5♏50 12	19R 19.2	29 36.6	14 52.4	1 50.2	20 44.2	23R 11.7	18 35.9	23 59.9	11 39.2	23 10.2
7 W	21 07 40	18 02 13	12♏35 46	19 26 20	19 19.2	1♓20.4	14 15.6	2 37.6	21 03.0	23 11.7	18 43.2	24 01.7	11 37.7	23 09.0
8 Th	21 11 37	19 02 59	26 21 58	3♐22 40	19D 19.2	3 03.1	13 39.6	3 25.0	21 21.8	23 11.6	18 50.4	24 03.5	11 36.2	23 07.8
9 F	21 15 33	20 03 44	10♐28 21	17 38 47	19 19.2	4 44.1	13 04.4	4 12.4	21 40.9	23 11.3	18 57.6	24 05.4	11 34.7	23 06.7
10 Sa	21 19 30	21 04 28	24 53 39	2♑12 29	19 19.4	6 23.0	12 30.4	4 59.8	22 00.0	23 10.7	19 04.8	24 07.3	11 33.2	23 05.6
11 Su	21 23 26	22 05 11	9♑34 41	16 59 32	19 19.6	7 59.4	11 57.7	5 47.1	22 19.3	23 10.0	19 12.1	24 09.3	11 31.6	23 04.4
12 M	21 27 23	23 05 52	24 26 12	1♒53 47	19 19.9	9 32.8	11 26.5	6 34.5	22 38.8	23 09.1	19 19.3	24 11.3	11 30.1	23 03.3
13 Tu	21 31 20	24 06 33	9♒21 17	16 47 42	19R 20.0	11 02.6	10 57.1	7 21.8	22 58.3	23 08.0	19 26.5	24 13.3	11 28.5	23 02.2
14 W	21 35 16	25 07 11	24 12 02	1♓33 19	19 19.9	12 28.2	10 29.6	8 09.2	23 18.0	23 06.7	19 33.7	24 15.4	11 26.9	23 01.1
15 Th	21 39 13	26 07 49	8♓50 41	16 03 22	19 19.5	13 48.8	10 04.0	8 56.5	23 37.8	23 05.3	19 40.9	24 17.5	11 25.3	23 00.1
16 F	21 43 09	27 08 24	23 10 41	0♈12 11	19 18.6	15 03.9	9 40.6	9 43.8	23 57.8	23 03.6	19 48.1	24 19.7	11 23.7	22 59.0
17 Sa	21 47 06	28 08 58	7♈07 29	13 56 24	19 17.5	16 12.8	9 19.4	10 31.1	24 17.8	23 01.7	19 55.3	24 21.9	11 22.1	22 58.0
18 Su	21 51 02	29 09 30	20 38 52	27 14 59	19 16.4	17 14.6	9 00.5	11 18.4	24 38.0	22 59.7	20 02.5	24 24.2	11 20.5	22 56.9
19 M	21 54 59	0♓10 01	3♉44 56	10♉09 03	19 15.3	18 08.9	8 44.0	12 05.6	24 58.3	22 57.5	20 09.6	24 26.5	11 18.8	22 55.9
20 Tu	21 58 55	1 10 29	16 27 42	22 41 23	19D 14.6	18 54.8	8 29.9	12 52.8	25 18.7	22 55.1	20 16.8	24 28.8	11 17.2	22 54.9
21 W	22 02 52	2 10 56	28 50 35	4♊55 52	19 14.5	19 32.0	8 18.2	13 40.0	25 39.2	22 52.5	20 23.9	24 31.2	11 15.6	22 54.0
22 Th	22 06 49	3 11 21	10♊57 50	16 57 04	19 14.9	19 59.9	8 09.1	14 27.2	25 59.8	22 49.7	20 31.0	24 33.6	11 13.9	22 53.0
23 F	22 10 45	4 11 44	22 54 11	28 49 46	19 16.0	20 18.1	8 02.3	15 14.4	26 20.6	22 46.8	20 38.1	24 36.0	11 12.3	22 52.1
24 Sa	22 14 42	5 12 05	4♋44 23	10♋38 37	19 17.4	20R 26.5	7 58.1	16 01.5	26 41.4	22 43.6	20 45.2	24 38.5	11 10.6	22 51.1
25 Su	22 18 38	6 12 25	16 32 59	22 28 00	19 18.9	20 24.9	7D 56.3	16 48.6	27 02.4	22 40.3	20 52.3	24 41.0	11 08.9	22 50.2
26 M	22 22 35	7 12 42	28 24 08	4♌21 48	19 20.1	20 13.6	7 57.0	17 35.7	27 23.4	22 36.8	20 59.3	24 43.5	11 07.3	22 49.3
27 Tu	22 26 31	8 12 57	10♌21 23	16 23 14	19R 20.8	19 52.9	8 00.0	18 22.8	27 44.5	22 33.2	21 06.3	24 46.1	11 05.6	22 48.5
28 W	22 30 28	9 13 11	22 27 39	28 34 54	19 20.5	19 23.3	8 05.3	19 09.8	28 05.8	22 29.4	21 13.3	24 48.7	11 03.9	22 47.6

Astro Data	Dy Hr Mn
♅D	2 3:05
☽0S	6 23:36
♀R	15 11:45
♅□♇	18 3:48
☽0N	19 13:35
⚳0N	24 3:27
☽0S	3 4:58
♃□♇	5 10:57
♃R	7 6:19
☽0N	15 24:00
♃□♇	20 14:07
☿R	24 20:18
♀D	25 17:43

Planet Ingress	Dy Hr Mn
☿ ♑	1 18:40
☿ ♒	20 11:44
☉ ♒	20 17:37
♂ ♓	4 4:13
☿ ♓	6 17:24
☉ ♓	19 8:02

Last Aspect Dy Hr Mn	☽ Ingress Dy Hr Mn
2 1:37 ♇ ☌	♌ 2 13:56
4 13:09 ♅ △	♍ 5 2:09
7 0:35 ♇ ⚹	♎ 7 12:20
9 8:06 ♇ □	♏ 9 19:11
11 11:52 ♇ △	♐ 11 22:18
13 12:24 ♀ ⚹	♑ 13 22:37
15 13:37 ☉ ☌	♒ 15 21:56
17 11:44 ♅ ⚹	♓ 17 22:17
20 0:09 ☉ ⚹	♈ 20 1:28
21 20:27 ♅ ☌	♉ 22 8:26
24 5:53 ♇ ⚹	♊ 24 18:54
26 18:40 ♅ ⚹	♋ 27 7:24
29 7:38 ♅ □	♌ 29 20:12

Last Aspect Dy Hr Mn	☽ Ingress Dy Hr Mn
1 3:16 ♂ ☍	♍ 1 8:00
3 5:07 ♇ ⚹	♎ 3 18:00
5 23:07 ☿ △	♏ 6 1:31
7 18:26 ♇ △	♐ 8 6:14
9 22:42 ♅ △	♑ 10 8:23
11 23:34 ♅ □	♒ 12 8:57
14 0:43 ☉ ☌	♓ 14 9:27
15 23:41 ♇ △	♈ 16 11:39
18 15:48 ☉ ⚹	♉ 18 17:03
20 12:26 ♇ ⚹	♊ 21 2:16
23 3:24 ♅ ⚹	♋ 23 14:22
25 16:30 ♅ □	♌ 26 3:13
28 4:36 ♅ △	♍ 28 14:46

☽ Phases & Eclipses Dy Hr Mn	
8 21:36	☾ 17♎57
15 13:37	● 24♑44
22 11:50	☽ 1♉47
30 16:31	○ 10♌07
30 16:42	☍ P 0.112
7 9:21	☾ 17♏56
14 0:43	● 24♒39
14 0:38:18	☌ T 02'52"
21 6:05	☽ 1♊56

Astro Data

1 January 1934
Julian Day # 12419
SVP 6♓10'42"
GC 25♐55.1 ⚴ 1♓39.3
Eris 2♈00.3 ⚵ 12♐46.1
⚷ 29♉34.3R ⚶ 0♎59.2
☽ Mean ☊ 21♒33.1

1 February 1934
Julian Day # 12450
SVP 6♓10'36"
GC 25♐55.1 ⚴ 10♓58.7
Eris 2♈10.3 ⚵ 22♐32.0
⚷ 28♉52.3R ⚶ 4♎59.0
☽ Mean ☊ 19♒54.6

March 1934 LONGITUDE

Day	Sid.Time	☉	0 hr ☽	Noon ☽	True ☊	☿	♀	♂	⚳	♃	♄	♅	♆	♇
1 Th	22 34 24	10♓13 22	4♍45 09	10♍58 35	19♒19.2	18♓45.6	8♒13.0	19♓56.9	28♈27.1	22♎25.4	21♒20.3	24♈51.4	11♍02.3	22♋46.8
2 F	22 38 21	11 13 32	17 15 20	23 35 27	19R16.8	18R00.7	8 22.9	20 43.8	28 48.5	22R21.2	21 27.3	24 54.0	11R00.6	22R46.0
3 Sa	22 42 18	12 13 40	29 58 59	6♎25 58	19 13.5	17 09.8	8 34.9	21 30.8	29 10.0	22 16.9	21 34.2	24 56.8	10 58.9	22 45.2
4 Su	22 46 14	13 13 47	12♎56 22	19 30 10	19 09.7	16 14.3	8 49.1	22 17.7	29 31.6	22 12.4	21 41.1	24 59.5	10 57.2	22 44.4
5 M	22 50 11	14 13 51	26 07 19	2♏47 45	19 05.9	15 15.4	9 05.4	23 04.6	29 53.3	22 07.8	21 48.0	25 02.3	10 55.6	22 43.7
6 Tu	22 54 07	15 13 55	9♏31 24	16 18 13	19 02.7	14 14.7	9 23.7	23 51.5	0♉15.1	22 03.0	21 54.8	25 05.1	10 53.9	22 42.9
7 W	22 58 04	16 13 56	23 08 06	0♐01 00	19 00.4	13 13.6	9 43.9	24 38.4	0 37.0	21 58.0	22 01.6	25 07.9	10 52.2	22 42.2
8 Th	23 02 00	17 13 56	6♐56 50	13 55 29	18D59.5	12 13.5	10 05.9	25 25.2	0 58.9	21 52.9	22 08.4	25 10.7	10 50.6	22 41.5
9 F	23 05 57	18 13 55	20 56 52	28 00 49	18 59.8	11 15.7	10 29.8	26 12.0	1 20.9	21 47.7	22 15.2	25 13.6	10 48.9	22 40.9
10 Sa	23 09 53	19 13 52	5♑07 10	12♑15 42	19 00.9	10 21.2	10 55.4	26 58.8	1 43.1	21 42.3	22 21.9	25 16.5	10 47.3	22 40.2
11 Su	23 13 50	20 13 47	19 26 08	26 38 07	19 02.5	9 31.0	11 22.7	27 45.5	2 05.3	21 36.7	22 28.6	25 19.5	10 45.6	22 39.6
12 M	23 17 47	21 13 41	3♒51 15	11♒05 04	19R03.6	8 45.8	11 51.6	28 32.2	2 27.5	21 31.0	22 35.3	25 22.5	10 44.0	22 39.0
13 Tu	23 21 43	22 13 33	18 19 01	25 32 30	19 03.6	8 06.3	12 22.0	29 18.9	2 49.9	21 25.2	22 41.9	25 25.4	10 42.3	22 38.4
14 W	23 25 40	23 13 23	2♓44 53	9♓55 29	19 02.1	7 32.8	12 53.9	0♈05.6	3 12.3	21 19.3	22 48.5	25 28.5	10 40.7	22 37.9
15 Th	23 29 36	24 13 11	17 03 38	24 08 40	18 58.8	7 05.6	13 27.2	0 52.2	3 34.8	21 13.2	22 55.0	25 31.5	10 39.1	22 37.3
16 F	23 33 33	25 12 57	1♈09 58	8♈06 59	18 53.8	6 44.7	14 01.9	1 38.7	3 57.4	21 07.0	23 01.5	25 34.6	10 37.5	22 36.8
17 Sa	23 37 29	26 12 41	14 59 15	21 46 24	18 47.7	6 30.2	14 37.8	2 25.3	4 20.0	21 00.7	23 08.0	25 37.6	10 35.9	22 36.3
18 Su	23 41 26	27 12 23	28 28 10	5♉04 25	18 41.1	6D21.9	15 15.1	3 11.8	4 42.7	20 54.2	23 14.4	25 40.8	10 34.3	22 35.9
19 M	23 45 22	28 12 02	11♉35 09	18 00 25	18 35.0	6 19.8	15 53.5	3 58.3	5 05.5	20 47.7	23 20.8	25 43.9	10 32.7	22 35.4
20 Tu	23 49 19	29 11 40	24 20 28	0♊35 35	18 29.9	6 23.6	16 33.1	4 44.7	5 28.3	20 41.1	23 27.2	25 47.0	10 31.1	22 35.0
21 W	23 53 16	0♈11 15	6♊46 09	12 52 39	18 26.4	6 33.1	17 13.8	5 31.1	5 51.3	20 34.3	23 33.5	25 50.2	10 29.6	22 34.6
22 Th	23 57 12	1 10 48	18 55 36	24 55 34	18D24.7	6 48.0	17 55.6	6 17.4	6 14.2	20 27.5	23 39.7	25 53.4	10 28.0	22 34.3
23 F	0 01 09	2 10 19	0♋53 10	6♋49 03	18 24.6	7 08.1	18 38.4	7 03.8	6 37.3	20 20.5	23 45.9	25 56.6	10 26.5	22 33.9
24 Sa	0 05 05	3 09 48	12 43 51	18 38 13	18 25.6	7 33.0	19 22.1	7 50.0	7 00.3	20 13.5	23 52.1	25 59.8	10 25.0	22 33.6
25 Su	0 09 02	4 09 14	24 32 49	0♌28 17	18 27.1	8 02.6	20 06.9	8 36.3	7 23.5	20 06.4	23 58.2	26 03.1	10 23.5	22 33.3
26 M	0 12 58	5 08 38	6♌25 14	12 24 14	18R28.2	8 36.5	20 52.5	9 22.4	7 46.7	19 59.3	24 04.2	26 06.3	10 22.0	22 33.0
27 Tu	0 16 55	6 07 59	18 25 51	24 30 33	18 28.2	9 14.5	21 39.0	10 08.6	8 09.9	19 52.0	24 10.2	26 09.6	10 20.5	22 32.8
28 W	0 20 51	7 07 19	0♍38 47	6♍50 56	18 26.4	9 56.4	22 26.4	10 54.7	8 33.3	19 44.7	24 16.2	26 12.9	10 19.0	22 32.6
29 Th	0 24 48	8 06 36	13 07 16	19 28 00	18 22.4	10 42.0	23 14.6	11 40.8	8 56.6	19 37.3	24 22.1	26 16.2	10 17.6	22 32.4
30 F	0 28 44	9 05 51	25 53 16	2♎23 07	18 16.2	11 31.0	24 03.5	12 26.8	9 20.0	19 29.9	24 27.9	26 19.5	10 16.2	22 32.2
31 Sa	0 32 41	10 05 04	8♎57 29	15 36 13	18 08.3	12 23.2	24 53.2	13 12.8	9 43.5	19 22.4	24 33.7	26 22.8	10 14.7	22 32.0

April 1934 LONGITUDE

Day	Sid.Time	☉	0 hr ☽	Noon ☽	True ☊	☿	♀	♂	⚳	♃	♄	♅	♆	♇
1 Su	0 36 38	11♈04 15	22♎19 06	29♎05 50	17♒59.3	13♓18.6	25♒43.7	13♈58.7	10♉07.0	19♎14.9	24♒39.4	26♈26.1	10♍13.3	22♋31.9
2 M	0 40 34	12 03 24	5♏56 04	12♏49 24	17R50.2	14 16.9	26 34.8	14 44.6	10 30.6	19R07.3	24 45.1	26 29.5	10R12.0	22R31.8
3 Tu	0 44 31	13 02 31	19 45 25	26 43 40	17 42.1	15 17.9	27 26.6	15 30.4	10 54.2	18 59.7	24 50.7	26 32.9	10 10.6	22 31.7
4 W	0 48 27	14 01 36	3♐43 44	10♐45 13	17 35.8	16 21.6	28 19.1	16 16.2	11 17.8	18 52.1	24 56.3	26 36.2	10 09.3	22 31.7
5 Th	0 52 24	15 00 40	17 47 44	24 51 00	17 31.7	17 27.8	29 12.2	17 02.0	11 41.6	18 44.4	25 01.8	26 39.6	10 08.0	22D31.7
6 F	0 56 20	15 59 42	1♑54 44	8♑58 41	17D30.0	18 36.4	0♓05.9	17 47.7	12 05.3	18 36.8	25 07.3	26 43.0	10 06.7	22 31.7
7 Sa	1 00 17	16 58 42	16 02 41	23 06 34	17 29.9	19 47.3	1 00.2	18 33.4	12 29.1	18 29.1	25 12.6	26 46.4	10 05.4	22 31.7
8 Su	1 04 13	17 57 41	0♒10 12	7♒13 28	17R30.5	21 00.4	1 55.0	19 19.1	12 53.0	18 21.4	25 18.0	26 49.8	10 04.2	22 31.8
9 M	1 08 10	18 56 37	14 16 12	21 18 16	17 30.7	22 15.7	2 50.3	20 04.7	13 16.8	18 13.6	25 23.2	26 53.2	10 02.9	22 31.8
10 Tu	1 12 07	19 55 32	28 19 28	5♓19 35	17 29.4	23 33.0	3 46.2	20 50.2	13 40.8	18 05.9	25 28.4	26 56.7	10 01.7	22 31.9
11 W	1 16 03	20 54 25	12♓18 20	19 15 24	17 25.7	24 52.3	4 42.6	21 35.7	14 04.7	17 58.2	25 33.5	27 00.1	10 00.5	22 32.1
12 Th	1 20 00	21 53 17	26 10 29	3♈03 10	17 19.3	26 13.5	5 39.4	22 21.2	14 28.7	17 50.5	25 38.6	27 03.5	9 59.4	22 32.2
13 F	1 23 56	22 52 06	9♈53 04	16 39 50	17 10.3	27 36.6	6 36.6	23 06.6	14 52.8	17 42.9	25 43.6	27 06.9	9 58.2	22 32.4
14 Sa	1 27 53	23 50 53	23 23 05	0♉02 30	16 59.4	29 01.5	7 34.3	23 52.0	15 16.9	17 35.2	25 48.5	27 10.4	9 57.1	22 32.6
15 Su	1 31 49	24 49 39	6♉37 49	13 08 50	16 47.7	0♈28.3	8 32.5	24 37.3	15 41.0	17 27.6	25 53.4	27 13.8	9 56.0	22 32.8
16 M	1 35 46	25 48 22	19 35 25	25 57 33	16 36.2	1 56.8	9 31.0	25 22.5	16 05.2	17 20.0	25 58.1	27 17.3	9 55.0	22 33.1
17 Tu	1 39 42	26 47 03	2♊15 17	8♊28 47	16 26.1	3 27.1	10 29.9	26 07.8	16 29.4	17 12.5	26 02.8	27 20.7	9 53.9	22 33.4
18 W	1 43 39	27 45 43	14 38 17	20 44 05	16 18.2	4 59.1	11 29.2	26 52.9	16 53.6	17 05.0	26 07.5	27 24.1	9 52.9	22 33.7
19 Th	1 47 36	28 44 20	26 46 37	2♋46 20	16 12.8	6 32.8	12 28.8	27 38.1	17 17.8	16 57.5	26 12.1	27 27.6	9 51.9	22 34.0
20 F	1 51 32	29 42 55	8♋43 46	14 39 30	16 09.8	8 08.3	13 28.8	28 23.1	17 42.1	16 50.2	26 16.5	27 31.0	9 51.0	22 34.4
21 Sa	1 55 29	0♉41 28	20 34 09	26 28 23	16D08.8	9 45.4	14 29.2	29 08.2	18 06.4	16 42.8	26 21.0	27 34.5	9 50.0	22 34.7
22 Su	1 59 25	1 39 58	2♌22 52	8♌18 17	16R08.8	11 24.3	15 29.8	29 53.1	18 30.8	16 35.6	26 25.3	27 37.9	9 49.1	22 35.1
23 M	2 03 22	2 38 26	14 15 19	20 14 40	16 08.8	13 04.8	16 30.8	0♉38.1	18 55.2	16 28.4	26 29.6	27 41.3	9 48.2	22 35.6
24 Tu	2 07 18	3 36 53	26 16 58	2♍22 52	16 07.9	14 47.0	17 32.1	1 22.9	19 19.6	16 21.3	26 33.7	27 44.8	9 47.4	22 36.0
25 W	2 11 15	4 35 17	8♍32 55	14 47 40	16 04.9	16 31.0	18 33.6	2 07.7	19 44.0	16 14.2	26 37.9	27 48.2	9 46.6	22 36.5
26 Th	2 15 11	5 33 39	21 07 31	27 32 51	15 59.5	18 16.7	19 35.5	2 52.5	20 08.4	16 07.3	26 41.9	27 51.6	9 45.8	22 37.0
27 F	2 19 08	6 31 59	4♎03 53	10♎40 43	15 51.4	20 04.1	20 37.6	3 37.2	20 32.9	16 00.4	26 45.8	27 55.0	9 45.0	22 37.5
28 Sa	2 23 05	7 30 17	17 23 22	24 11 40	15 41.1	21 53.2	21 40.1	4 21.9	20 57.4	15 53.7	26 49.7	27 58.4	9 44.3	22 38.0
29 Su	2 27 01	8 28 33	1♏05 18	8♏03 52	15 29.4	23 44.0	22 42.7	5 06.5	21 21.9	15 47.0	26 53.5	28 01.8	9 43.6	22 38.6
30 M	2 30 58	9 26 47	15 06 47	22 13 24	15 17.6	25 36.6	23 45.7	5 51.0	21 46.5	15 40.4	26 57.2	28 05.2	9 42.9	22 39.2

Astro Data	Dy Hr Mn
☽0S	2 11:17
♃△♄	7 4:37
♄⊼♇	13 0:22
☽0N	15 10:27
♂0N	16 13:43
♅♀♆	17 2:56
☿D	19 8:25
☉0N	21 7:28
☽0S	29 19:01
♇D	5 19:22
☽0N	11 18:44
☿0N	19 3:46
☽0S	26 3:29

Planet Ingress		Dy Hr Mn
⚳	♉	5 19:22
♂	♈	14 9:09
☉	♈	21 7:28
♀	♓	6 9:23
☿	♈	15 4:14
☉	♉	20 19:00
♂	♉	22 15:40

Last Aspect Dy Hr Mn			☽ Ingress	Dy Hr Mn
2 10:27	♇	⚹	♎	3 0:02
4 22:00	♅	☍	♏	5 6:59
7 2:04	♂	△	♐	7 11:58
9 8:45	♂	□	♑	9 15:22
11 13:59	♂	⚹	♒	11 17:36
13 11:48	♅	⚹	♓	13 19:25
15 12:08	☉	☌	♈	15 22:00
17 18:55	♅	☌	♉	18 2:46
20 9:04	☉	⚹	♊	20 10:51
22 13:57	♅	⚹	♋	22 22:13
25 3:01	♅	□	♌	25 11:03
27 15:15	♅	△	♍	27 22:45
29 17:45	♇	⚹	♎	30 7:37

Last Aspect Dy Hr Mn			☽ Ingress	Dy Hr Mn
1 7:17	♅	☍	♏	1 13:35
3 13:19	♀	□	♐	3 17:37
5 19:54	♀	⚹	♑	5 20:45
7 18:15	♅	□	♒	7 23:43
9 21:35	♅	⚹	♓	10 2:52
11 22:47	☿	☌	♈	12 6:40
14 6:48	♅	☌	♉	14 11:55
16 12:01	♄	□	♊	16 19:41
19 3:12	☉	⚹	♋	19 6:26
21 17:47	♂	□	♌	21 19:10
24 2:51	♅	△	♍	24 7:20
26 2:48	♇	⚹	♎	26 16:32
28 18:37	♅	☍	♏	28 22:07

☽ Phases & Eclipses Dy Hr Mn	
1 10:26	○ 10♍09
8 18:06	☾ 17♐29
15 12:08	● 24♓14
23 1:44	☽ 1♋45
31 1:14	○ 9♎39
7 0:48	☾ 16♑31
13 23:57	● 23♈21
21 21:20	☽ 1♌04
29 12:45	○ 8♏30

Astro Data

1 March 1934
Julian Day # 12478
SVP 6♓10'32"
GC 25♐55.2 ⚴ 20♓21.8
Eris 2♈26.9 ⚵ 0♑05.0
⚷ 29♉10.1 ⚶ 2♎27.5R
☽ Mean ☊ 18♒25.7

1 April 1934
Julian Day # 12509
SVP 6♓10'30"
GC 25♐55.3 ⚴ 1♈16.6
Eris 2♈49.2 ⚵ 6♑01.1
⚷ 0♊27.7 ⚶ 24♍56.9R
☽ Mean ☊ 16♒47.2

LONGITUDE — May 1934

Day	Sid.Time	☉	0 hr ☽	Noon ☽	True ☊	☿	♀	♂	⚷	♃	♄	♅	♆	♇
1 Tu	2 34 54	10♉25 00	29♏22 59	6♐34 47	15♒06.9	27♈31.0	24♓48.9	6♉35.5	22♉11.0	15♎34.0	27♒00.8	28♈08.6	9♍42.2	22♋39.8
2 W	2 38 51	11 23 12	13♐47 58	21 01 49	14R 58.3	29 27.1	25 52.3	7 20.0	22 35.6	15R 27.6	27 04.4	28 12.0	9R 41.6	22 40.5
3 Th	2 42 47	12 21 21	28 15 36	5♑28 40	14 52.4	1♉24.8	26 56.0	8 04.4	23 00.2	15 21.4	27 07.8	28 15.4	9 41.0	22 41.1
4 F	2 46 44	13 19 30	12♑40 30	19 50 39	14 49.2	3 24.3	27 59.9	8 48.8	23 24.9	15 15.3	27 11.2	28 18.7	9 40.5	22 41.8
5 Sa	2 50 40	14 17 36	26 58 47	4♒04 39	14 48.1	5 25.4	29 04.0	9 33.1	23 49.5	15 09.3	27 14.5	28 22.1	9 40.0	22 42.5
6 Su	2 54 37	15 15 42	11♒08 06	18 09 02	14 48.0	7 28.2	0♈08.3	10 17.3	24 14.2	15 03.4	27 17.7	28 25.4	9 39.5	22 43.2
7 M	2 58 34	16 13 46	25 07 26	2♓03 17	14 47.5	9 32.4	1 12.9	11 01.5	24 38.9	14 57.7	27 20.8	28 28.7	9 39.0	22 44.0
8 Tu	3 02 30	17 11 49	8♓56 36	15 47 25	14 45.6	11 38.1	2 17.6	11 45.7	25 03.6	14 52.1	27 23.8	28 32.0	9 38.6	22 44.8
9 W	3 06 27	18 09 50	22 35 43	29 21 30	14 41.2	13 45.1	3 22.5	12 29.8	25 28.3	14 46.6	27 26.8	28 35.3	9 38.2	22 45.5
10 Th	3 10 23	19 07 50	6♈04 42	12♈45 17	14 33.9	15 53.3	4 27.6	13 13.8	25 53.1	14 41.2	27 29.6	28 38.6	9 37.8	22 46.4
11 F	3 14 20	20 05 48	19 23 07	25 58 06	14 23.9	18 02.5	5 32.9	13 57.8	26 17.8	14 36.0	27 32.4	28 41.9	9 37.4	22 47.2
12 Sa	3 18 16	21 03 45	2♉30 06	8♉59 00	14 11.8	20 12.5	6 38.4	14 41.8	26 42.6	14 31.0	27 35.0	28 45.1	9 37.1	22 48.1
13 Su	3 22 13	22 01 41	15 24 40	21 47 00	13 58.7	22 23.1	7 44.0	15 25.7	27 07.4	14 26.1	27 37.6	28 48.4	9 36.9	22 48.9
14 M	3 26 09	22 59 35	28 05 57	4♊21 30	13 45.9	24 34.1	8 49.8	16 09.5	27 32.2	14 21.3	27 40.1	28 51.6	9 36.6	22 49.8
15 Tu	3 30 06	23 57 28	10♊33 40	16 42 33	13 34.4	26 45.2	9 55.7	16 53.3	27 57.0	14 16.7	27 42.5	28 54.8	9 36.4	22 50.8
16 W	3 34 03	24 55 19	22 48 18	28 51 09	13 25.0	28 56.2	11 01.8	17 37.1	28 21.8	14 12.3	27 44.8	28 58.0	9 36.2	22 51.7
17 Th	3 37 59	25 53 09	4♋51 23	10♋49 21	13 18.4	1♊06.7	12 08.1	18 20.8	28 46.7	14 08.0	27 47.0	29 01.1	9 36.1	22 52.7
18 F	3 41 56	26 50 57	16 45 28	22 40 13	13 14.4	3 16.5	13 14.5	19 04.4	29 11.5	14 03.9	27 49.1	29 04.3	9 36.0	22 53.7
19 Sa	3 45 52	27 48 43	28 34 06	4♌27 44	13D 12.7	5 25.3	14 21.0	19 48.0	29 36.3	13 59.9	27 51.1	29 07.4	9 35.9	22 54.7
20 Su	3 49 49	28 46 28	10♌21 41	16 16 37	13 12.4	7 32.8	15 27.6	20 31.5	0♊01.2	13 56.1	27 53.0	29 10.5	9D 35.8	22 55.7
21 M	3 53 45	29 44 11	22 13 12	28 12 07	13R 12.6	9 38.7	16 34.4	21 14.9	0 26.1	13 52.5	27 54.8	29 13.6	9 35.8	22 56.7
22 Tu	3 57 42	0♊41 52	4♍14 03	10♍19 40	13 12.3	11 42.9	17 41.3	21 58.3	0 50.9	13 49.0	27 56.6	29 16.7	9 35.8	22 57.8
23 W	4 01 38	1 39 32	16 29 39	22 44 35	13 10.4	13 45.2	18 48.4	22 41.7	1 15.8	13 45.7	27 58.2	29 19.7	9 35.9	22 58.9
24 Th	4 05 35	2 37 10	29 05 03	5♎31 31	13 06.3	15 45.3	19 55.5	23 25.0	1 40.7	13 42.6	27 59.7	29 22.7	9 36.0	22 59.9
25 F	4 09 32	3 34 47	12♎04 22	18 43 52	12 59.9	17 43.1	21 02.8	24 08.2	2 05.6	13 39.7	28 01.2	29 25.7	9 36.1	23 01.1
26 Sa	4 13 28	4 32 22	25 30 09	2♏23 09	12 51.4	19 38.5	22 10.2	24 51.4	2 30.5	13 36.9	28 02.5	29 28.7	9 36.2	23 02.2
27 Su	4 17 25	5 29 56	9♏22 41	16 28 21	12 41.5	21 31.3	23 17.7	25 34.5	2 55.4	13 34.3	28 03.8	29 31.6	9 36.4	23 03.3
28 M	4 21 21	6 27 29	23 39 36	0♐55 41	12 31.4	23 21.5	24 25.3	26 17.6	3 20.3	13 31.9	28 04.9	29 34.5	9 36.6	23 04.5
29 Tu	4 25 18	7 25 01	8♐15 45	15 38 49	12 22.1	25 09.0	25 33.1	27 00.7	3 45.2	13 29.6	28 06.0	29 37.4	9 36.9	23 05.7
30 W	4 29 14	8 22 32	23 03 51	0♑29 47	12 14.8	26 53.8	26 41.0	27 43.6	4 10.1	13 27.5	28 06.9	29 40.3	9 37.2	23 06.9
31 Th	4 33 11	9 20 02	7♑55 35	15 20 17	12 09.8	28 35.7	27 48.9	28 26.6	4 35.0	13 25.6	28 07.8	29 43.1	9 37.5	23 08.1

LONGITUDE — June 1934

Day	Sid.Time	☉	0 hr ☽	Noon ☽	True ☊	☿	♀	♂	⚷	♃	♄	♅	♆	♇
1 F	4 37 08	10♊17 30	22♑43 01	0♒03 02	12♒07.3	0♋14.8	28♈57.0	29♉09.4	4♊59.9	13♎23.9	28♒08.6	29♈46.0	9♍37.8	23♋09.3
2 Sa	4 41 04	11 14 59	7♒19 44	14 32 39	12D 06.8	1 51.0	0♉05.2	29 52.2	5 24.8	13R 22.4	28 09.2	29 48.7	9 38.2	23 10.6
3 Su	4 45 01	12 12 26	21 41 27	28 45 57	12 07.4	3 24.4	1 13.4	0♊35.0	5 49.7	13 21.0	28 09.8	29 51.5	9 38.6	23 11.9
4 M	4 48 57	13 09 52	5♓46 04	12♓41 47	12R 07.8	4 54.8	2 21.8	1 17.7	6 14.6	13 19.8	28 10.3	29 54.2	9 39.0	23 13.1
5 Tu	4 52 54	14 07 18	19 33 10	26 20 21	12 07.2	6 22.2	3 30.3	2 00.4	6 39.5	13 18.8	28 10.6	29 56.9	9 39.5	23 14.4
6 W	4 56 50	15 04 44	3♈03 28	9♈42 43	12 04.6	7 46.6	4 38.9	2 43.0	7 04.4	13 18.0	28 10.9	29 59.6	9 40.0	23 15.7
7 Th	5 00 47	16 02 08	16 18 14	22 50 12	11 59.7	9 08.1	5 47.5	3 25.6	7 29.3	13 17.3	28 11.1	0♉02.2	9 40.5	23 17.0
8 F	5 04 43	16 59 32	29 18 47	5♉44 06	11 52.6	10 26.4	6 56.3	4 08.1	7 54.2	13 16.9	28R 11.1	0 04.8	9 41.1	23 18.4
9 Sa	5 08 40	17 56 56	12♉06 16	18 25 25	11 43.9	11 41.7	8 05.1	4 50.5	8 19.1	13 16.6	28 11.1	0 07.4	9 41.7	23 19.7
10 Su	5 12 37	18 54 19	24 41 39	0♊55 02	11 34.3	12 53.8	9 14.0	5 32.9	8 44.0	13D 16.5	28 11.0	0 10.0	9 42.3	23 21.1
11 M	5 16 33	19 51 41	7♊05 40	13 13 40	11 24.9	14 02.7	10 23.0	6 15.3	9 08.9	13 16.5	28 10.8	0 12.5	9 43.0	23 22.5
12 Tu	5 20 30	20 49 03	19 19 08	25 22 13	11 16.5	15 08.3	11 32.1	6 57.6	9 33.8	13 16.8	28 10.4	0 14.9	9 43.7	23 23.9
13 W	5 24 26	21 46 24	1♋23 05	7♋21 56	11 09.7	16 10.6	12 41.2	7 39.8	9 58.7	13 17.2	28 10.0	0 17.4	9 44.4	23 25.3
14 Th	5 28 23	22 43 44	13 18 59	19 14 33	11 05.1	17 09.4	13 50.5	8 22.0	10 23.5	13 17.9	28 09.5	0 19.8	9 45.2	23 26.7
15 F	5 32 19	23 41 03	25 08 56	1♌02 30	11D 02.7	18 04.8	14 59.8	9 04.2	10 48.4	13 18.7	28 08.9	0 22.2	9 46.0	23 28.1
16 Sa	5 36 16	24 38 22	6♌55 41	12 48 55	11 02.1	18 56.5	16 09.2	9 46.2	11 13.2	13 19.6	28 08.2	0 24.5	9 46.8	23 29.6
17 Su	5 40 12	25 35 39	18 42 42	24 37 35	11 02.9	19 44.5	17 18.6	10 28.3	11 38.1	13 20.8	28 07.3	0 26.8	9 47.6	23 31.0
18 M	5 44 09	26 32 56	0♍34 08	6♍32 56	11 04.3	20 28.8	18 28.1	11 10.2	12 02.9	13 22.1	28 06.4	0 29.1	9 48.5	23 32.5
19 Tu	5 48 06	27 30 12	12 34 37	18 39 49	11R 05.5	21 09.1	19 37.7	11 52.2	12 27.7	13 23.6	28 05.4	0 31.3	9 49.4	23 33.9
20 W	5 52 02	28 27 28	24 49 09	1♎03 14	11 05.8	21 45.4	20 47.3	12 34.0	12 52.5	13 25.3	28 04.3	0 33.5	9 50.4	23 35.4
21 Th	5 55 59	29 24 42	7♎22 40	13 47 59	11 04.7	22 17.6	21 57.1	13 15.8	13 17.3	13 27.2	28 03.1	0 35.6	9 51.3	23 36.9
22 F	5 59 55	0♋21 56	20 19 39	26 58 03	11 02.0	22 45.6	23 06.8	13 57.6	13 42.1	13 29.2	28 01.8	0 37.7	9 52.3	23 38.4
23 Sa	6 03 52	1 19 10	3♏43 27	10♏35 59	10 57.8	23 09.3	24 16.7	14 39.3	14 06.8	13 31.4	28 00.4	0 39.8	9 53.3	23 39.9
24 Su	6 07 48	2 16 23	17 35 38	24 42 10	10 52.5	23 28.5	25 26.6	15 20.9	14 31.6	13 33.8	27 59.0	0 41.8	9 54.4	23 41.4
25 M	6 11 45	3 13 35	1♐55 12	9♐14 08	10 46.9	23 43.2	26 36.6	16 02.5	14 56.3	13 36.4	27 57.4	0 43.8	9 55.5	23 43.0
26 Tu	6 15 41	4 10 47	16 38 13	24 06 30	10 41.8	23 53.4	27 46.6	16 44.1	15 21.0	13 39.1	27 55.7	0 45.8	9 56.6	23 44.5
27 W	6 19 38	5 07 59	1♑37 56	9♑11 20	10 37.7	23R 59.0	28 56.8	17 25.6	15 45.7	13 42.0	27 54.0	0 47.7	9 57.7	23 46.0
28 Th	6 23 35	6 05 10	16 45 31	24 19 18	10 35.3	23 59.9	0♊06.9	18 07.0	16 10.4	13 45.0	27 52.2	0 49.6	9 58.9	23 47.6
29 F	6 27 31	7 02 22	1♒51 31	9♒21 08	10D 34.4	23 56.3	1 17.2	18 48.4	16 35.1	13 48.3	27 50.2	0 51.4	10 00.1	23 49.1
30 Sa	6 31 28	7 59 33	16 47 13	24 09 01	10 34.9	23 48.1	2 27.5	19 29.7	16 59.7	13 51.7	27 48.2	0 53.2	10 01.3	23 50.7

Astro Data

	Dy Hr Mn
☽0N	9 0:23
♀0N	9 8:02
♆ D	21 11:52
☽0S	23 11:38
☽0N	5 4:57
♄ R	8 17:06
♃ D	10 13:41
☽0S	19 18:44
☿ R	28 4:56

Planet Ingress

		Dy Hr Mn
☿	♉	2 18:45
♀	♈	6 8:54
☿	♊	16 23:43
⚷	♊	20 10:50
☉	♊	21 18:35
☿	♋	1 8:22
♀	♉	2 10:11
♂	♊	2 16:21
♅	♉	6 15:41
☉	♋	22 2:48
♀	♊	28 9:38

Last Aspect / ☽ Ingress (May)

Last Aspect Dy Hr Mn			☽ Ingress	Dy Hr Mn
30 19:58	♄	□	♐	1 1:02
2 23:57	♅	△	♑	3 2:53
5 2:50	♀	⚹	♒	5 5:06
7 5:46	♅	⚹	♓	7 8:26
9 0:17	♇	△	♈	9 13:09
11 17:01	♅	☌	♉	11 19:24
13 23:08	♄	□	♊	14 3:38
16 12:14	♅	⚹	♋	16 14:17
19 1:05	♅	□	♌	19 2:55
21 15:20	☉	□	♍	21 15:35
23 12:27	♇	⚹	♎	24 1:43
26 6:56	♅	☍	♏	26 7:52
28 7:19	♄	□	♐	28 10:28
30 10:40	♅	△	♑	30 11:12

Last Aspect / ☽ Ingress (June)

Last Aspect Dy Hr Mn			☽ Ingress	Dy Hr Mn
1 11:32	♅	□	♒	1 11:55
3 13:52	♅	⚹	♓	3 14:06
5 6:30	♇	△	♈	5 18:31
7 21:54	♄	⚹	♉	8 1:17
10 6:43	♄	□	♊	10 10:14
12 17:35	♄	△	♋	12 21:14
14 20:33	♇	☌	♌	15 9:53
17 19:04	♄	☍	♍	17 22:51
20 6:37	☉	□	♎	20 9:59
22 13:54	♄	△	♏	22 17:25
24 17:28	♄	□	♐	24 20:49
26 18:05	♄	⚹	♑	26 21:24
28 11:29	☿	☍	♒	28 21:02
30 17:59	♄	☌	♓	30 21:38

☽ Phases & Eclipses

Dy Hr Mn	
6 6:41	☾ 15♒03
13 12:30	● 22♉03
21 15:20	☽ 29♌52
28 21:41	○ 6♐51
4 12:53	☾ 13♓12
12 2:11	● 20♊26
20 6:37	☽ 28♍15
27 5:08	○ 4♑52

Astro Data

1 May 1934
Julian Day # 12539
SVP 6♓10'26"
GC 25♐55.3 ⚳ 11♈57.8
Eris 3♈09.5 ⚵ 7♑58.9R
⚷ 2♊24.1 ⚶ 20♍47.4R
☽ Mean ☊ 15♒11.8

1 June 1934
Julian Day # 12570
SVP 6♓10'20"
GC 25♐55.4 ⚳ 22♈44.9
Eris 3♈24.1 ⚵ 4♑55.0R
⚷ 4♊44.4 ⚶ 23♍47.4
☽ Mean ☊ 13♒33.4

July 1934 — LONGITUDE

Day	Sid.Time	☉	0 hr ☽	Noon ☽	True ☊	☿	♀	♂	⚳	♃	♄	♅	♆	♇
1 Su	6 35 24	8♋56 44	1♓25 55	8♓37 28	10♒36.2	23♋35.5	3♊37.9	20♊11.0	17♊24.3	13♎55.2	27♒46.1	0♉54.9	10♍02.6	23♋52.3
2 M	6 39 21	9 53 56	15 43 24	22 43 32	10 37.6	23R 18.6	4 48.3	20 52.3	17 48.9	13 58.9	27R 43.9	0 56.7	10 03.9	23 53.8
3 Tu	6 43 17	10 51 07	29 37 52	6♈26 28	10R 38.4	22 57.7	5 58.8	21 33.5	18 13.5	14 02.8	27 41.6	0 58.3	10 05.2	23 55.4
4 W	6 47 14	11 48 19	13♈09 31	19 47 15	10 38.2	22 32.9	7 09.4	22 14.6	18 38.1	14 06.8	27 39.3	0 59.9	10 06.5	23 57.0
5 Th	6 51 10	12 45 32	26 19 56	2♉47 53	10 36.8	22 04.7	8 20.0	22 55.7	19 02.7	14 11.0	27 36.8	1 01.5	10 07.8	23 58.6
6 F	6 55 07	13 42 44	9♉11 26	15 30 55	10 34.2	21 33.5	9 30.7	23 36.7	19 27.2	14 15.4	27 34.3	1 03.0	10 09.2	24 00.2
7 Sa	6 59 04	14 39 57	21 46 40	27 59 01	10 30.7	20 59.7	10 41.5	24 17.7	19 51.7	14 19.9	27 31.7	1 04.5	10 10.6	24 01.8
8 Su	7 03 00	15 37 10	4♊08 16	10♊14 44	10 26.7	20 23.8	11 52.3	24 58.7	20 16.2	14 24.6	27 29.0	1 06.0	10 12.1	24 03.4
9 M	7 06 57	16 34 24	16 18 42	22 20 26	10 22.7	19 46.4	13 03.2	25 39.6	20 40.6	14 29.4	27 26.2	1 07.4	10 13.5	24 05.0
10 Tu	7 10 53	17 31 38	28 20 13	4♋18 17	10 19.2	19 08.2	14 14.1	26 20.4	21 05.1	14 34.4	27 23.4	1 08.7	10 15.0	24 06.6
11 W	7 14 50	18 28 52	10♋14 55	16 10 20	10 16.6	18 29.7	15 25.1	27 01.2	21 29.5	14 39.5	27 20.4	1 10.1	10 16.5	24 08.2
12 Th	7 18 46	19 26 06	22 04 49	27 58 38	10 15.0	17 51.6	16 36.1	27 42.0	21 53.9	14 44.8	27 17.4	1 11.3	10 18.0	24 09.8
13 F	7 22 43	20 23 21	3♌52 03	9♌45 23	10D 14.4	17 14.6	17 47.2	28 22.6	22 18.2	14 50.2	27 14.3	1 12.5	10 19.6	24 11.5
14 Sa	7 26 40	21 20 35	15 38 57	21 33 06	10 14.8	16 39.4	18 58.4	29 03.3	22 42.5	14 55.8	27 11.2	1 13.7	10 21.2	24 13.1
15 Su	7 30 36	22 17 50	27 28 12	3♍24 39	10 15.9	16 06.5	20 09.6	29 43.9	23 06.8	15 01.5	27 08.0	1 14.8	10 22.8	24 14.7
16 M	7 34 33	23 15 05	9♍22 52	15 23 20	10 17.3	15 36.6	21 20.8	0♋24.4	23 31.1	15 07.4	27 04.7	1 15.9	10 24.4	24 16.3
17 Tu	7 38 29	24 12 20	21 26 29	27 32 51	10 18.6	15 10.3	22 32.1	1 04.9	23 55.3	15 13.4	27 01.3	1 16.9	10 26.0	24 17.9
18 W	7 42 26	25 09 36	3♎42 56	9♎57 13	10 19.7	14 48.0	23 43.5	1 45.3	24 19.5	15 19.6	26 57.9	1 17.9	10 27.7	24 19.5
19 Th	7 46 22	26 06 51	16 16 13	22 40 27	10R 20.2	14 30.1	24 54.9	2 25.7	24 43.6	15 25.9	26 54.4	1 18.9	10 29.4	24 21.2
20 F	7 50 19	27 04 07	29 10 20	5♏46 16	10 20.0	14 17.1	26 06.3	3 06.0	25 07.7	15 32.3	26 50.8	1 19.7	10 31.1	24 22.8
21 Sa	7 54 15	28 01 23	12♏28 37	19 17 35	10 19.3	14D 09.3	27 17.8	3 46.3	25 31.8	15 38.9	26 47.2	1 20.6	10 32.8	24 24.4
22 Su	7 58 12	28 58 39	26 13 18	3♐15 46	10 18.3	14 06.9	28 29.4	4 26.5	25 55.9	15 45.6	26 43.5	1 21.4	10 34.6	24 26.0
23 M	8 02 09	29 55 56	10♐24 48	17 40 04	10 17.0	14 10.1	29 41.0	5 06.7	26 19.9	15 52.4	26 39.8	1 22.1	10 36.4	24 27.6
24 Tu	8 06 05	0♌53 13	25 01 04	2♑27 07	10 15.9	14 19.2	0♋52.7	5 46.8	26 43.8	15 59.4	26 36.0	1 22.8	10 38.1	24 29.3
25 W	8 10 02	1 50 31	9♑57 21	17 30 48	10 15.2	14 34.1	2 04.4	6 26.9	27 07.8	16 06.5	26 32.2	1 23.5	10 40.0	24 30.9
26 Th	8 13 58	2 47 49	25 06 20	2♒42 46	10D 14.8	14 55.0	3 16.2	7 06.9	27 31.6	16 13.8	26 28.3	1 24.1	10 41.8	24 32.5
27 F	8 17 55	3 45 08	10♒18 54	17 53 31	10 14.8	15 22.0	4 28.0	7 46.9	27 55.5	16 21.1	26 24.3	1 24.6	10 43.6	24 34.1
28 Sa	8 21 51	4 42 27	25 25 30	2♓53 48	10 15.0	15 55.0	5 39.9	8 26.8	28 19.3	16 28.6	26 20.4	1 25.1	10 45.5	24 35.7
29 Su	8 25 48	5 39 48	10♓17 31	17 35 54	10 15.4	16 34.0	6 51.8	9 06.7	28 43.1	16 36.2	26 16.3	1 25.6	10 47.4	24 37.3
30 M	8 29 44	6 37 09	24 48 22	1♈54 31	10 15.8	17 19.0	8 03.8	9 46.5	29 06.8	16 43.9	26 12.2	1 26.0	10 49.3	24 38.9
31 Tu	8 33 41	7 34 31	8♈54 06	15 47 01	10 16.1	18 09.8	9 15.9	10 26.3	29 30.5	16 51.8	26 08.1	1 26.3	10 51.2	24 40.5

August 1934 — LONGITUDE

Day	Sid.Time	☉	0 hr ☽	Noon ☽	True ☊	☿	♀	♂	⚳	♃	♄	♅	♆	♇
1 W	8 37 38	8♌31 55	22♈33 20	29♈13 14	10♒16.2	19♋06.5	10♋28.0	11♋06.0	29♊54.1	16♎59.8	26♒03.9	1♉26.6	10♍53.1	24♋42.0
2 Th	8 41 34	9 29 20	5♉46 57	12♉14 51	10D 16.2	20 09.0	11 40.1	11 45.7	0♋17.7	17 07.9	25R 59.7	1 26.9	10 55.1	24 43.6
3 F	8 45 31	10 26 46	18 37 21	24 54 52	10 16.2	21 17.0	12 52.3	12 25.4	0 41.2	17 16.1	25 55.5	1 27.1	10 57.0	24 45.2
4 Sa	8 49 27	11 24 13	1♊07 55	7♊16 58	10 16.3	22 30.4	14 04.6	13 05.0	1 04.7	17 24.4	25 51.2	1 27.3	10 59.0	24 46.8
5 Su	8 53 24	12 21 42	13 22 30	19 25 01	10 16.5	23 49.2	15 16.9	13 44.5	1 28.2	17 32.8	25 46.9	1 27.4	11 01.0	24 48.3
6 M	8 57 20	13 19 11	25 24 59	1♋22 51	10 16.8	25 13.0	16 29.3	14 24.0	1 51.6	17 41.4	25 42.6	1R 27.4	11 03.0	24 49.9
7 Tu	9 01 17	14 16 42	7♋19 04	13 14 01	10 17.2	26 41.6	17 41.7	15 03.5	2 14.9	17 50.1	25 38.2	1 27.4	11 05.0	24 51.4
8 W	9 05 13	15 14 14	19 08 07	25 01 42	10 17.5	28 14.9	18 54.2	15 42.9	2 38.2	17 58.8	25 33.8	1 27.4	11 07.1	24 53.0
9 Th	9 09 10	16 11 47	0♌55 07	6♌48 41	10R 17.7	29 52.4	20 06.7	16 22.3	3 01.4	18 07.7	25 29.4	1 27.3	11 09.1	24 54.5
10 F	9 13 07	17 09 22	12 42 43	18 37 29	10 17.6	1♌34.0	21 19.3	17 01.6	3 24.6	18 16.7	25 24.9	1 27.2	11 11.2	24 56.0
11 Sa	9 17 03	18 06 57	24 33 17	0♍30 22	10 17.2	3 19.2	22 31.9	17 40.8	3 47.7	18 25.8	25 20.5	1 27.0	11 13.2	24 57.6
12 Su	9 21 00	19 04 34	6♍29 01	12 29 30	10 16.3	5 07.6	23 44.6	18 20.0	4 10.8	18 35.0	25 16.0	1 26.7	11 15.3	24 59.1
13 M	9 24 56	20 02 11	18 32 04	24 37 02	10 15.1	6 59.0	24 57.3	18 59.2	4 33.8	18 44.3	25 11.5	1 26.5	11 17.4	25 00.6
14 Tu	9 28 53	20 59 50	0♎44 41	6♎55 18	10 13.7	8 52.9	26 10.1	19 38.3	4 56.7	18 53.7	25 07.0	1 26.1	11 19.5	25 02.0
15 W	9 32 49	21 57 29	13 09 12	19 26 43	10 12.2	10 48.8	27 22.9	20 17.4	5 19.6	19 03.2	25 02.5	1 25.7	11 21.6	25 03.5
16 Th	9 36 46	22 55 10	25 48 09	2♏13 52	10 11.0	12 46.5	28 35.7	20 56.4	5 42.4	19 12.8	24 58.0	1 25.3	11 23.8	25 05.0
17 F	9 40 42	23 52 52	8♏44 08	15 19 17	10D 10.3	14 45.5	29 48.6	21 35.3	6 05.1	19 22.5	24 53.5	1 24.8	11 25.9	25 06.4
18 Sa	9 44 39	24 50 35	21 59 35	28 45 15	10 10.2	16 45.5	1♌01.6	22 14.2	6 27.7	19 32.3	24 48.9	1 24.3	11 28.0	25 07.9
19 Su	9 48 36	25 48 19	5♐36 27	12♐33 18	10 10.7	18 46.1	2 14.6	22 53.1	6 50.3	19 42.2	24 44.4	1 23.7	11 30.2	25 09.3
20 M	9 52 32	26 46 04	19 35 47	26 43 47	10 11.7	20 47.1	3 27.6	23 31.9	7 12.9	19 52.2	24 39.9	1 23.1	11 32.4	25 10.8
21 Tu	9 56 29	27 43 50	3♑57 05	11♑15 19	10 12.9	22 48.0	4 40.7	24 10.6	7 35.3	20 02.3	24 35.4	1 22.4	11 34.5	25 12.2
22 W	10 00 25	28 41 38	18 37 57	26 04 19	10R 13.9	24 48.8	5 53.8	24 49.3	7 57.7	20 12.4	24 30.9	1 21.7	11 36.7	25 13.6
23 Th	10 04 22	29 39 26	3♒33 37	11♒04 55	10 14.3	26 49.2	7 07.0	25 28.0	8 20.0	20 22.7	24 26.4	1 21.0	11 38.9	25 15.0
24 F	10 08 18	0♍37 16	18 37 13	26 09 23	10 13.7	28 49.0	8 20.2	26 06.6	8 42.2	20 33.0	24 21.9	1 20.1	11 41.1	25 16.3
25 Sa	10 12 15	1 35 07	3♓40 20	11♓08 56	10 12.1	0♍48.0	9 33.5	26 45.2	9 04.4	20 43.4	24 17.4	1 19.3	11 43.3	25 17.7
26 Su	10 16 11	2 33 00	18 34 09	25 55 02	10 09.6	2 46.2	10 46.8	27 23.7	9 26.5	20 53.9	24 13.0	1 18.4	11 45.5	25 19.0
27 M	10 20 08	3 30 55	3♈10 45	10♈20 36	10 06.5	4 43.4	12 00.2	28 02.1	9 48.5	21 04.5	24 08.5	1 17.4	11 47.7	25 20.4
28 Tu	10 24 05	4 28 51	17 24 07	24 20 57	10 03.2	6 39.5	13 13.6	28 40.6	10 10.4	21 15.1	24 04.1	1 16.5	11 49.9	25 21.7
29 W	10 28 01	5 26 49	1♉10 56	7♉54 03	10 00.3	8 34.6	14 27.0	29 18.9	10 32.2	21 25.9	23 59.7	1 15.4	11 52.1	25 23.0
30 Th	10 31 58	6 24 49	14 30 27	21 00 24	9 58.3	10 28.5	15 40.6	29 57.3	10 53.9	21 36.7	23 55.4	1 14.3	11 54.3	25 24.3
31 F	10 35 54	7 22 51	27 24 16	3♊42 30	9D 57.3	12 21.2	16 54.1	0♌35.5	11 15.6	21 47.6	23 51.0	1 13.2	11 56.5	25 25.6

Astro Data	Planet Ingress
Dy Hr Mn	Dy Hr Mn
☽0N 2 10:44	♂ ♋ 15 21:33
☽0S 17 0:51	☉ ♌ 23 13:42
☿D 22 10:21	♀ ♋ 23 18:22
☽0N 29 19:03	
	⚳ ♋ 1 18:00
♅R 7 5:24	☿ ♌ 9 13:49
☽0S 13 6:35	♀ ♌ 17 15:45
♄⊼♇ 15 7:53	☉ ♍ 23 20:32
☽0N 26 5:25	☿ ♍ 25 2:18
	♂ ♌ 30 13:43

Last Aspect	☽ Ingress	Last Aspect	☽ Ingress
Dy Hr Mn	Dy Hr Mn	Dy Hr Mn	Dy Hr Mn
2 14:02 ♇ △	♈ 3 0:39	1 6:20 ♄ ✶	♉ 1 13:25
5 2:24 ♄ ✶	♉ 5 6:47	3 13:56 ♄ □	♊ 3 21:48
7 11:07 ♄ □	♊ 7 15:55	6 0:39 ♄ △	♋ 6 9:13
9 22:09 ♄ △	♋ 10 3:20	8 19:36 ☿ ☌	♌ 8 22:08
12 4:13 ♇ ☌	♌ 12 16:07	11 1:39 ♄ ☍	♍ 11 10:59
15 4:08 ♂ ✶	♍ 15 5:07	13 12:46 ♇ ✶	♎ 13 22:33
17 5:37 ♇ ✶	♎ 17 16:47	16 4:31 ♀ □	♏ 16 7:51
19 19:48 ♄ △	♏ 20 1:31	18 5:35 ♇ △	♐ 18 14:12
22 4:11 ☉ △	♐ 22 6:28	20 12:04 ☉ △	♑ 20 17:27
24 2:36 ♄ ✶	♑ 24 8:03	22 10:38 ♇ ☍	♒ 22 18:18
25 23:05 ♇ ☍	♒ 26 7:43	24 16:53 ☿ ☍	♓ 24 18:08
28 1:31 ♄ ☌	♓ 28 7:20	26 14:33 ♂ △	♈ 26 18:44
29 23:43 ♇ △	♈ 30 8:45	28 19:57 ♂ □	♉ 28 21:55
		30 20:15 ♇ ✶	♊ 31 4:55

☽ Phases & Eclipses	Astro Data
Dy Hr Mn	1 July 1934
3 20:28 ☾ 11♈11	Julian Day # 12600
11 17:06 ● 18♋41	SVP 6♓10'15"
19 18:53 ☽ 26♎23	GC 25♐55.5 ⚴ 2♉28.8
26 12:09 ○ 2♒48	Eris 3♈28.8R ⚵ 28♐24.3R
26 12:15 • P 0.661	⚷ 6♊56.6 ⚶ 2♎08.9
	☽ Mean ☊ 11♒58.1
2 6:27 ☾ 9♉16	
10 8:46 ● 17♌02	1 August 1934
10 8:37:24 • A 06'33"	Julian Day # 12631
18 4:33 ☽ 24♏33	SVP 6♓10'10"
24 19:37 ○ 0♓56	GC 25♐55.5 ⚴ 11♉01.3
31 19:40 ☾ 7♊41	Eris 3♈23.1R ⚵ 23♐06.1R
	⚷ 8♊46.5 ⚶ 14♎13.0
	☽ Mean ☊ 10♒19.6

LONGITUDE — September 1934

Day	Sid.Time	☉	0 hr ☽	Noon☽	True☊	☿	♀	♂	⚳	♃	♄	♅	♆	♇
1 Sa	10 39 51	8♍20 55	9♊55 37	16♊04 10	9♒57.5	14♍12.7	18♌07.7	1♌13.8	11♋37.2	21♎58.5	23♒46.7	1♉12.0	11♍58.8	25♋26.8
2 Su	10 43 47	9 19 01	22 08 46	28 10 00	9 58.6	16 03.0	19 21.4	1 51.9	11 58.7	22 09.6	23R 42.4	1R 10.8	12 01.0	25 28.1
3 M	10 47 44	10 17 08	4♋08 29	10♋04 49	10 00.3	17 52.1	20 35.1	2 30.1	12 20.0	22 20.7	23 38.2	1 09.6	12 03.2	25 29.3
4 Tu	10 51 40	11 15 18	15 59 35	21 53 22	10 02.0	19 40.0	21 48.8	3 08.2	12 41.3	22 31.9	23 34.0	1 08.3	12 05.4	25 30.5
5 W	10 55 37	12 13 29	27 46 40	3♌40 00	10R 03.2	21 26.6	23 02.6	3 46.2	13 02.5	22 43.1	23 29.8	1 06.9	12 07.7	25 31.7
6 Th	10 59 34	13 11 43	9♌33 50	15 28 35	10 03.2	23 12.1	24 16.4	4 24.2	13 23.6	22 54.5	23 25.7	1 05.6	12 09.9	25 32.9
7 F	11 03 30	14 09 58	21 24 38	27 22 20	10 01.7	24 56.3	25 30.3	5 02.1	13 44.6	23 05.9	23 21.6	1 04.1	12 12.1	25 34.0
8 Sa	11 07 27	15 08 15	3♍21 58	9♍23 47	9 58.6	26 39.4	26 44.2	5 40.0	14 05.5	23 17.3	23 17.5	1 02.7	12 14.3	25 35.2
9 Su	11 11 23	16 06 34	15 28 02	21 34 52	9 53.8	28 21.4	27 58.1	6 17.8	14 26.3	23 28.9	23 13.6	1 01.2	12 16.6	25 36.3
10 M	11 15 20	17 04 54	27 44 27	3♎56 54	9 47.8	0♎02.1	29 12.1	6 55.6	14 46.9	23 40.4	23 09.6	0 59.6	12 18.8	25 37.4
11 Tu	11 19 16	18 03 17	10♎12 20	16 30 50	9 41.1	1 41.8	0♍26.1	7 33.3	15 07.5	23 52.1	23 05.7	0 58.1	12 21.0	25 38.5
12 W	11 23 13	19 01 41	22 52 28	29 17 19	9 34.4	3 20.3	1 40.2	8 11.0	15 27.9	24 03.8	23 01.9	0 56.4	12 23.2	25 39.5
13 Th	11 27 09	20 00 07	5♏45 28	12♏16 58	9 28.5	4 57.8	2 54.3	8 48.6	15 48.3	24 15.6	22 58.1	0 54.8	12 25.4	25 40.6
14 F	11 31 06	20 58 34	18 51 56	25 30 26	9 24.1	6 34.1	4 08.4	9 26.2	16 08.5	24 27.4	22 54.4	0 53.1	12 27.6	25 41.6
15 Sa	11 35 02	21 57 03	2♐12 34	8♐58 27	9 21.5	8 09.4	5 22.6	10 03.7	16 28.6	24 39.3	22 50.7	0 51.4	12 29.9	25 42.6
16 Su	11 38 59	22 55 34	15 48 09	22 41 44	9D 20.7	9 43.6	6 36.8	10 41.2	16 48.5	24 51.2	22 47.1	0 49.6	12 32.1	25 43.6
17 M	11 42 56	23 54 06	29 39 14	6♑40 41	9 21.3	11 16.8	7 51.0	11 18.6	17 08.4	25 03.2	22 43.6	0 47.8	12 34.3	25 44.6
18 Tu	11 46 52	24 52 40	13♑45 59	20 55 00	9 22.5	12 48.9	9 05.3	11 55.9	17 28.1	25 15.3	22 40.1	0 46.0	12 36.4	25 45.6
19 W	11 50 49	25 51 16	28 07 31	5♒23 11	9R 23.4	14 20.0	10 19.6	12 33.2	17 47.7	25 27.4	22 36.7	0 44.1	12 38.6	25 46.5
20 Th	11 54 45	26 49 53	12♒41 34	20 02 05	9 23.0	15 50.1	11 33.9	13 10.5	18 07.1	25 39.5	22 33.4	0 42.2	12 40.8	25 47.4
21 F	11 58 42	27 48 32	27 24 03	4♓46 43	9 20.6	17 19.1	12 48.2	13 47.6	18 26.4	25 51.7	22 30.1	0 40.3	12 43.0	25 48.3
22 Sa	12 02 38	28 47 13	12♓09 11	19 30 33	9 16.0	18 47.0	14 02.6	14 24.8	18 45.6	26 03.9	22 26.9	0 38.4	12 45.1	25 49.1
23 Su	12 06 35	29 45 55	26 49 52	4♈06 13	9 09.4	20 13.9	15 17.1	15 01.9	19 04.7	26 16.2	22 23.8	0 36.4	12 47.3	25 50.0
24 M	12 10 31	0♎44 40	11♈18 43	18 26 36	9 01.3	21 39.7	16 31.5	15 38.9	19 23.6	26 28.5	22 20.7	0 34.4	12 49.4	25 50.8
25 Tu	12 14 28	1 43 27	25 29 11	2♉25 57	8 52.7	23 04.5	17 46.0	16 15.9	19 42.3	26 40.9	22 17.7	0 32.3	12 51.6	25 51.6
26 W	12 18 25	2 42 15	9♉16 32	16 00 44	8 44.6	24 28.1	19 00.5	16 52.8	20 01.0	26 53.3	22 14.9	0 30.3	12 53.7	25 52.4
27 Th	12 22 21	3 41 07	22 38 28	29 09 50	8 37.8	25 50.6	20 15.1	17 29.7	20 19.4	27 05.8	22 12.0	0 28.2	12 55.8	25 53.2
28 F	12 26 18	4 40 00	5♊35 05	11♊54 33	8 33.0	27 12.0	21 29.7	18 06.5	20 37.7	27 18.3	22 09.3	0 26.0	12 57.9	25 53.9
29 Sa	12 30 14	5 38 56	18 08 40	24 17 59	8 30.4	28 32.1	22 44.3	18 43.2	20 55.9	27 30.8	22 06.6	0 23.9	13 00.0	25 54.6
30 Su	12 34 11	6 37 54	0♋23 03	6♋24 31	8D 29.6	29 51.0	23 59.0	19 20.0	21 13.9	27 43.4	22 04.1	0 21.7	13 02.1	25 55.3

LONGITUDE — October 1934

Day	Sid.Time	☉	0 hr ☽	Noon☽	True☊	☿	♀	♂	⚳	♃	♄	♅	♆	♇
1 M	12 38 07	7♎36 54	12♋23 02	18♋19 17	8♒30.0	1♏08.6	25♍13.7	19♌56.6	21♋31.7	27♎56.0	22♒01.6	0♉19.5	13♍04.2	25♋56.0
2 Tu	12 42 04	8 35 57	24 13 58	0♌07 43	8R 30.9	2 24.8	26 28.4	20 33.2	21 49.4	28 08.6	21R 59.2	0R 17.3	13 06.2	25 56.6
3 W	12 46 00	9 35 01	6♌01 13	11 55 05	8 31.1	3 39.5	27 43.1	21 09.8	22 06.9	28 21.3	21 56.9	0 15.1	13 08.3	25 57.2
4 Th	12 49 57	10 34 08	17 49 55	23 46 17	8 29.8	4 52.7	28 57.9	21 46.2	22 24.2	28 34.0	21 54.7	0 12.8	13 10.3	25 57.8
5 F	12 53 54	11 33 18	29 44 41	5♍45 34	8 26.2	6 04.3	0♎12.7	22 22.7	22 41.4	28 46.8	21 52.5	0 10.5	13 12.3	25 58.4
6 Sa	12 57 50	12 32 29	11♍49 19	17 56 17	8 20.0	7 14.1	1 27.5	22 59.0	22 58.3	28 59.5	21 50.5	0 08.2	13 14.3	25 59.0
7 Su	13 01 47	13 31 43	24 06 41	0♎20 43	8 11.3	8 22.0	2 42.4	23 35.3	23 15.1	29 12.3	21 48.5	0 05.9	13 16.3	25 59.5
8 M	13 05 43	14 30 58	6♎38 29	13 00 02	8 00.6	9 27.9	3 57.2	24 11.6	23 31.7	29 25.2	21 46.6	0 03.6	13 18.3	26 00.0
9 Tu	13 09 40	15 30 16	19 25 20	25 54 17	7 48.8	10 31.7	5 12.1	24 47.7	23 48.1	29 38.0	21 44.9	0 01.2	13 20.2	26 00.5
10 W	13 13 36	16 29 36	2♏26 46	9♏02 36	7 36.9	11 33.0	6 27.0	25 23.8	24 04.3	29 50.9	21 43.2	29♈58.9	13 22.2	26 00.9
11 Th	13 17 33	17 28 58	15 41 35	22 23 29	7 26.2	12 31.7	7 42.0	25 59.9	24 20.3	0♏03.8	21 41.6	29 56.5	13 24.1	26 01.3
12 F	13 21 29	18 28 21	29 08 07	5♐55 15	7 17.6	13 27.6	8 56.9	26 35.9	24 36.1	0 16.7	21 40.2	29 54.1	13 26.0	26 01.7
13 Sa	13 25 26	19 27 47	12♐44 44	19 36 23	7 11.7	14 20.3	10 11.9	27 11.8	24 51.7	0 29.7	21 38.8	29 51.7	13 27.9	26 02.1
14 Su	13 29 23	20 27 14	26 30 06	3♑25 47	7 08.5	15 09.6	11 26.9	27 47.7	25 07.1	0 42.7	21 37.5	29 49.3	13 29.8	26 02.5
15 M	13 33 19	21 26 43	10♑23 23	17 22 50	7D 07.5	15 55.2	12 41.9	28 23.4	25 22.3	0 55.6	21 36.3	29 46.9	13 31.6	26 02.8
16 Tu	13 37 16	22 26 14	24 24 06	1♒27 07	7R 07.6	16 36.6	13 57.0	28 59.2	25 37.2	1 08.6	21 35.2	29 44.5	13 33.5	26 03.1
17 W	13 41 12	23 25 47	8♒31 48	15 38 02	7 07.4	17 13.5	15 12.0	29 34.8	25 51.9	1 21.7	21 34.2	29 42.0	13 35.3	26 03.4
18 Th	13 45 09	24 25 21	22 45 37	29 54 18	7 05.8	17 45.3	16 27.1	0♍10.4	26 06.4	1 34.7	21 33.4	29 39.6	13 37.1	26 03.6
19 F	13 49 05	25 24 57	7♓03 44	14♓13 30	7 01.8	18 11.6	17 42.1	0 45.9	26 20.7	1 47.7	21 32.6	29 37.1	13 38.9	26 03.9
20 Sa	13 53 02	26 24 34	21 23 05	28 31 55	6 54.8	18 32.0	18 57.2	1 21.4	26 34.8	2 00.8	21 31.9	29 34.7	13 40.6	26 04.1
21 Su	13 56 58	27 24 14	5♈39 21	12♈44 44	6 45.1	18 45.7	20 12.3	1 56.7	26 48.6	2 13.8	21 31.3	29 32.2	13 42.3	26 04.2
22 M	14 00 55	28 23 55	19 47 22	26 46 37	6 33.3	18R 52.3	21 27.4	2 32.0	27 02.1	2 26.9	21 30.8	29 29.8	13 44.0	26 04.4
23 Tu	14 04 52	29 23 38	3♉41 53	10♉32 37	6 20.7	18 51.2	22 42.6	3 07.3	27 15.4	2 40.0	21 30.4	29 27.3	13 45.7	26 04.5
24 W	14 08 48	0♏23 24	17 18 24	23 58 56	6 08.5	18 41.9	23 57.7	3 42.5	27 28.5	2 53.1	21 30.1	29 24.9	13 47.4	26 04.6
25 Th	14 12 45	1 23 11	0♊34 01	7♊03 35	5 57.9	18 23.9	25 12.9	4 17.6	27 41.3	3 06.2	21 30.0	29 22.4	13 49.0	26 04.7
26 F	14 16 41	2 23 01	13 27 43	19 46 35	5 49.7	17 56.8	26 28.1	4 52.6	27 53.9	3 19.3	21D 29.9	29 20.0	13 50.7	26 04.7
27 Sa	14 20 38	3 22 53	26 00 30	2♋09 50	5 44.1	17 20.6	27 43.3	5 27.6	28 06.2	3 32.4	21 29.9	29 17.5	13 52.3	26R 04.8
28 Su	14 24 34	4 22 47	8♋15 05	14 16 48	5 41.2	16 35.3	28 58.5	6 02.4	28 18.2	3 45.5	21 30.1	29 15.1	13 53.8	26 04.8
29 M	14 28 31	5 22 43	20 15 34	26 12 02	5 40.1	15 41.2	0♏13.7	6 37.3	28 30.0	3 58.6	21 30.3	29 12.6	13 55.4	26 04.7
30 Tu	14 32 27	6 22 42	2♌06 54	8♌00 50	5 40.0	14 39.2	1 29.0	7 12.0	28 41.4	4 11.7	21 30.6	29 10.2	13 56.9	26 04.7
31 W	14 36 24	7 22 42	13 54 34	19 48 46	5 39.7	13 30.3	2 44.2	7 46.7	28 52.6	4 24.8	21 31.1	29 07.8	13 58.4	26 04.6

Astro Data

	Dy Hr Mn
♃△♄	8 12:20
☽0S	9 12:43
☿0S	11 5:37
♃□♇	21 4:46
☽0N	22 15:59
☉0S	23 17:46
♃∠♆	2 6:32
☽0S	6 19:43
♀0S	8 0:31
♃☍♅	11 0:32
☽0N	20 0:40
☿ R	22 20:44
♄ D	26 17:18
♇ R	28 0:33

Planet Ingress

		Dy Hr Mn
☿	♎	10 11:29
♀	♍	11 3:32
☉	♎	23 17:45
☿	♏	30 14:46
♀	♎	5 7:56
♅	♈R	10 0:37
♃	♏	11 4:55
♂	♍	18 4:59
☉	♏	24 2:36
♀	♏	29 7:37

Last Aspect / ☽ Ingress (September)

Last Aspect Dy Hr Mn			☽ Ingress	Dy Hr Mn
2 3:09	♄	△	♋	2 15:40
4 19:23	♇	☌	♌	5 4:32
7 7:49	♀	☌	♍	7 17:16
10 3:16	☿	☌	♎	10 4:23
12 5:13	♇	□	♏	12 13:19
14 12:20	♇	△	♐	14 20:03
16 15:47	♃	⚹	♑	17 0:36
18 20:05	♇	☍	♒	19 3:06
20 21:17	♃	△	♓	21 4:14
23 4:19	☉	☍	♈	23 5:13
25 1:54	♃	☍	♉	25 7:47
27 5:56	♇	⚹	♊	27 13:33
29 21:22	☿	△	♋	29 23:14

Last Aspect / ☽ Ingress (October)

Last Aspect Dy Hr Mn			☽ Ingress	Dy Hr Mn
2 7:53	♃	□	♌	2 11:44
4 21:49	♃	⚹	♍	5 0:31
7 3:38	♇	⚹	♎	7 11:20
9 18:58	♃	☌	♏	9 19:31
11 18:44	♂	□	♐	12 1:32
14 5:47	♅	△	♑	14 6:04
16 9:06	♅	□	♒	16 9:32
18 11:35	♅	⚹	♓	18 12:10
20 7:51	♇	△	♈	20 14:28
22 16:41	♅	☌	♉	22 17:34
24 15:48	♇	⚹	♊	24 22:58
27 6:24	♅	⚹	♋	27 7:46
29 18:05	♅	□	♌	29 19:42

☽ Phases & Eclipses

Dy Hr Mn		
9 0:20	●	15♍38
16 12:26	☽	22♐57
23 4:19	○	29♓27
30 12:29	☾	6♋39
8 15:05	●	14♎39
15 19:29	☽	21♑45
22 15:01	○	28♈31
30 8:22	☾	6♌14

Astro Data

1 September 1934
Julian Day # 12662
SVP 6♓10'05"
GC 25♐55.6 ⚴ 16♉31.7
Eris 3♈08.2R ⚵ 22♐58.5
⚷ 9♊48.3 ⚶ 28♎23.1
☽ Mean ☊ 8♒41.1

1 October 1934
Julian Day # 12692
SVP 6♓10'02"
GC 25♐55.7 ⚴ 16♉30.8R
Eris 2♈49.2R ⚵ 27♐38.2
⚷ 9♊48.6R ⚶ 13♏20.0
☽ Mean ☊ 7♒05.8

November 1934 — LONGITUDE

Day	Sid.Time	☉	0 hr ☽	Noon ☽	True ☊	☿	♀	♂	ʔ	♃	♄	♅	♆	♇
1 Th	14 40 21	8♏22 45	25♌44 10	1♍41 24	5♒38.1	12♏16.2	3♏59.5	8♍21.2	29♋03.5	4♏37.9	21♒31.6	29♈05.3	13♍59.9	26♋04.5
2 F	14 44 17	9 22 50	7♍41 06	13 43 51	5R 34.3	10R 58.9	5 14.8	8 55.7	29 14.1	4 51.0	21 32.2	29R 02.9	14 01.3	26R 04.4
3 Sa	14 48 14	10 22 56	19 50 11	26 00 33	5 27.7	9 40.7	6 30.1	9 30.2	29 24.4	5 04.1	21 33.0	29 00.5	14 02.8	26 04.2
4 Su	14 52 10	11 23 05	2♎15 20	8♎34 48	5 18.4	8 23.9	7 45.4	10 04.5	29 34.4	5 17.2	21 33.8	28 58.1	14 04.2	26 04.0
5 M	14 56 07	12 23 16	14 59 10	21 28 29	5 06.8	7 11.2	9 00.7	10 38.7	29 44.1	5 30.2	21 34.8	28 55.7	14 05.5	26 03.8
6 Tu	15 00 03	13 23 29	28 02 44	4♏41 46	4 53.9	6 04.6	10 16.0	11 12.9	29 53.5	5 43.3	21 35.9	28 53.4	14 06.9	26 03.6
7 W	15 04 00	14 23 43	11♏25 21	18 13 09	4 40.9	5 06.4	11 31.4	11 47.0	0♌02.5	5 56.4	21 37.0	28 51.0	14 08.2	26 03.4
8 Th	15 07 56	15 24 00	25 04 44	1♐59 38	4 29.1	4 17.9	12 46.7	12 21.0	0 11.2	6 09.4	21 38.3	28 48.7	14 09.5	26 03.1
9 F	15 11 53	16 24 18	8♐57 20	15 57 18	4 19.5	3 40.3	14 02.1	12 54.9	0 19.6	6 22.4	21 39.7	28 46.4	14 10.7	26 02.8
10 Sa	15 15 50	17 24 38	22 59 02	0♑02 02	4 12.8	3 14.3	15 17.4	13 28.7	0 27.7	6 35.5	21 41.1	28 44.1	14 12.0	26 02.4
11 Su	15 19 46	18 24 59	7♑05 52	14 10 09	4 09.1	3D 00.0	16 32.8	14 02.4	0 35.4	6 48.5	21 42.7	28 41.8	14 13.2	26 02.1
12 M	15 23 43	19 25 22	21 14 33	28 18 50	4D 07.8	2 57.2	17 48.2	14 36.0	0 42.8	7 01.4	21 44.4	28 39.6	14 14.3	26 01.7
13 Tu	15 27 39	20 25 46	5♒22 47	12♒26 16	4R 07.8	3 05.4	19 03.5	15 09.5	0 49.8	7 14.4	21 46.2	28 37.3	14 15.5	26 01.3
14 W	15 31 36	21 26 11	19 29 10	26 31 25	4 07.8	3 23.9	20 18.9	15 43.0	0 56.5	7 27.3	21 48.0	28 35.1	14 16.6	26 00.9
15 Th	15 35 32	22 26 37	3♓32 54	10♓33 33	4 06.6	3 52.0	21 34.3	16 16.3	1 02.8	7 40.2	21 50.0	28 32.9	14 17.7	26 00.4
16 F	15 39 29	23 27 05	17 33 14	24 31 48	4 03.0	4 28.7	22 49.7	16 49.5	1 08.8	7 53.1	21 52.1	28 30.7	14 18.7	26 00.0
17 Sa	15 43 25	24 27 34	1♈29 04	8♈24 47	3 56.7	5 13.2	24 05.1	17 22.6	1 14.4	8 06.0	21 54.3	28 28.6	14 19.7	25 59.5
18 Su	15 47 22	25 28 05	15 18 41	22 10 27	3 47.8	6 04.5	25 20.4	17 55.6	1 19.6	8 18.8	21 56.5	28 26.5	14 20.7	25 58.9
19 M	15 51 19	26 28 36	28 59 43	5♉46 11	3 37.0	7 01.9	26 35.8	18 28.6	1 24.5	8 31.6	21 58.9	28 24.4	14 21.7	25 58.4
20 Tu	15 55 15	27 29 10	12♉29 27	19 09 14	3 25.2	8 04.5	27 51.2	19 01.4	1 28.9	8 44.4	22 01.4	28 22.3	14 22.6	25 57.8
21 W	15 59 12	28 29 44	25 45 14	2♊17 13	3 13.7	9 11.8	29 06.6	19 34.1	1 33.0	8 57.2	22 03.9	28 20.3	14 23.5	25 57.2
22 Th	16 03 08	29 30 21	8♊45 02	15 08 34	3 03.6	10 22.9	0♐22.0	20 06.7	1 36.7	9 09.9	22 06.6	28 18.3	14 24.4	25 56.6
23 F	16 07 05	0♐30 58	21 27 50	27 42 54	2 55.8	11 37.5	1 37.4	20 39.2	1 40.1	9 22.6	22 09.4	28 16.3	14 25.2	25 56.0
24 Sa	16 11 01	1 31 38	3♋53 57	10♋01 14	2 50.5	12 55.0	2 52.9	21 11.6	1 43.0	9 35.3	22 12.2	28 14.4	14 26.0	25 55.3
25 Su	16 14 58	2 32 19	16 05 03	22 05 50	2D 47.8	14 14.9	4 08.3	21 43.9	1 45.5	9 47.9	22 15.2	28 12.4	14 26.8	25 54.6
26 M	16 18 54	3 33 01	28 04 02	4♌00 10	2 47.1	15 36.9	5 23.7	22 16.1	1 47.6	10 00.5	22 18.2	28 10.6	14 27.5	25 53.9
27 Tu	16 22 51	4 33 45	9♌54 50	15 48 38	2 47.7	17 00.7	6 39.1	22 48.1	1 49.3	10 13.0	22 21.3	28 08.7	14 28.2	25 53.2
28 W	16 26 48	5 34 30	21 42 13	27 36 14	2R 48.7	18 26.0	7 54.5	23 20.0	1 50.6	10 25.5	22 24.5	28 06.9	14 28.9	25 52.5
29 Th	16 30 44	6 35 17	3♍31 24	9♍28 22	2 48.9	19 52.6	9 10.0	23 51.8	1 51.5	10 38.0	22 27.9	28 05.1	14 29.5	25 51.7
30 F	16 34 41	7 36 05	15 27 51	21 30 29	2 47.7	21 20.2	10 25.4	24 23.5	1R 52.0	10 50.4	22 31.3	28 03.4	14 30.1	25 50.9

December 1934 — LONGITUDE

Day	Sid.Time	☉	0 hr ☽	Noon ☽	True ☊	☿	♀	♂	ʔ	♃	♄	♅	♆	♇
1 Sa	16 38 37	8♐36 55	27♍36 55	3♎47 43	2♒44.4	22♏48.7	11♐40.8	24♍55.1	1♌52.0	11♏02.8	22♒34.8	28♈01.7	14♍30.7	25♋50.1
2 Su	16 42 34	9 37 46	10♎03 24	16 24 27	2R 38.9	24 17.9	12 56.3	25 26.5	1R 51.7	11 15.1	22 38.3	28R 00.0	14 31.2	25R 49.3
3 M	16 46 30	10 38 39	22 51 11	29 23 51	2 31.4	25 47.8	14 11.7	25 57.8	1 50.9	11 27.4	22 42.0	27 58.4	14 31.7	25 48.4
4 Tu	16 50 27	11 39 33	6♏02 35	12♏47 21	2 22.8	27 18.2	15 27.2	26 29.0	1 49.6	11 39.6	22 45.8	27 56.8	14 32.1	25 47.6
5 W	16 54 23	12 40 28	19 38 01	26 34 16	2 13.8	28 49.0	16 42.6	27 00.0	1 48.0	11 51.8	22 49.6	27 55.2	14 32.6	25 46.7
6 Th	16 58 20	13 41 24	3♐35 39	10♐41 37	2 05.6	0♐20.2	17 58.1	27 30.9	1 45.9	12 03.9	22 53.5	27 53.7	14 33.0	25 45.8
7 F	17 02 17	14 42 22	17 51 30	25 04 31	1 59.0	1 51.7	19 13.5	28 01.6	1 43.4	12 16.0	22 57.6	27 52.3	14 33.3	25 44.9
8 Sa	17 06 13	15 43 20	2♑19 53	9♑36 46	1 54.7	3 23.5	20 29.0	28 32.2	1 40.4	12 28.1	23 01.7	27 50.8	14 33.7	25 43.9
9 Su	17 10 10	16 44 19	16 54 21	24 11 53	1D 52.7	4 55.4	21 44.5	29 02.7	1 37.0	12 40.0	23 05.9	27 49.4	14 34.0	25 43.0
10 M	17 14 06	17 45 19	1♒28 40	8♒44 05	1 52.6	6 27.6	22 59.9	29 33.0	1 33.2	12 51.9	23 10.1	27 48.1	14 34.2	25 42.0
11 Tu	17 18 03	18 46 19	15 57 36	23 08 48	1 53.7	7 59.9	24 15.4	0♎03.1	1 29.0	13 03.8	23 14.5	27 46.8	14 34.5	25 41.0
12 W	17 21 59	19 47 20	0♓17 22	7♓23 04	1R 55.0	9 32.4	25 30.8	0 33.1	1 24.4	13 15.6	23 18.9	27 45.6	14 34.6	25 40.0
13 Th	17 25 56	20 48 22	14 25 43	21 25 14	1 55.6	11 05.1	26 46.2	1 02.9	1 19.3	13 27.3	23 23.4	27 44.3	14 34.8	25 39.0
14 F	17 29 52	21 49 23	28 21 33	5♈14 40	1 54.7	12 37.8	28 01.7	1 32.5	1 13.8	13 38.9	23 28.0	27 43.2	14 34.9	25 37.9
15 Sa	17 33 49	22 50 25	12♈04 34	18 51 16	1 52.0	14 10.7	29 17.1	2 02.0	1 07.9	13 50.5	23 32.7	27 42.1	14 35.0	25 36.9
16 Su	17 37 46	23 51 28	25 34 47	2♉15 08	1 47.5	15 43.7	0♑32.5	2 31.4	1 01.6	14 02.0	23 37.4	27 41.0	14R 35.0	25 35.8
17 M	17 41 42	24 52 31	8♉52 17	15 26 16	1 41.6	17 16.9	1 48.0	3 00.5	0 54.8	14 13.5	23 42.2	27 40.0	14 35.1	25 34.7
18 Tu	17 45 39	25 53 35	21 57 03	28 24 38	1 35.2	18 50.2	3 03.4	3 29.5	0 47.7	14 24.9	23 47.1	27 39.0	14 35.0	25 33.6
19 W	17 49 35	26 54 39	4♊48 59	11♊10 07	1 28.8	20 23.7	4 18.8	3 58.3	0 40.2	14 36.2	23 52.1	27 38.1	14 35.0	25 32.5
20 Th	17 53 32	27 55 43	17 28 03	23 42 49	1 23.2	21 57.3	5 34.2	4 26.9	0 32.3	14 47.4	23 57.1	27 37.2	14 34.9	25 31.4
21 F	17 57 28	28 56 49	29 54 28	6♋03 07	1 19.1	23 31.1	6 49.6	4 55.4	0 24.0	14 58.6	24 02.2	27 36.3	14 34.8	25 30.2
22 Sa	18 01 25	29 57 54	12♋08 55	18 12 02	1 16.5	25 05.1	8 05.0	5 23.6	0 15.3	15 09.7	24 07.4	27 35.6	14 34.6	25 29.1
23 Su	18 05 22	0♑59 00	24 12 43	0♌11 13	1D 15.6	26 39.2	9 20.4	5 51.7	0 06.3	15 20.7	24 12.6	27 34.8	14 34.4	25 27.9
24 M	18 09 18	2 00 07	6♌07 53	12 03 05	1 16.2	28 13.6	10 35.8	6 19.6	29♋56.8	15 31.6	24 17.9	27 34.1	14 34.2	25 26.7
25 Tu	18 13 15	3 01 14	17 57 14	23 50 48	1 17.6	29 48.2	11 51.2	6 47.3	29 47.1	15 42.4	24 23.3	27 33.5	14 34.0	25 25.5
26 W	18 17 11	4 02 21	29 44 16	5♍38 12	1 19.5	1♑23.1	13 06.6	7 14.8	29 36.9	15 53.2	24 28.7	27 32.9	14 33.7	25 24.3
27 Th	18 21 08	5 03 29	11♍33 08	17 29 42	1 21.3	2 58.2	14 22.0	7 42.0	29 26.5	16 03.9	24 34.2	27 32.4	14 33.4	25 23.1
28 F	18 25 04	6 04 38	23 28 30	29 30 09	1R 22.4	4 33.5	15 37.4	8 09.1	29 15.7	16 14.5	24 39.8	27 31.9	14 33.0	25 21.9
29 Sa	18 29 01	7 05 47	5♎35 16	11♎44 29	1 22.5	6 09.2	16 52.7	8 35.9	29 04.6	16 25.0	24 45.4	27 31.4	14 32.6	25 20.7
30 Su	18 32 57	8 06 56	17 58 23	24 17 31	1 21.5	7 45.2	18 08.1	9 02.6	28 53.2	16 35.4	24 51.1	27 31.1	14 32.2	25 19.4
31 M	18 36 54	9 08 06	0♏42 23	7♏13 23	1 19.4	9 21.5	19 23.5	9 29.0	28 41.5	16 45.7	24 56.9	27 30.7	14 31.7	25 18.2

Astro Data

	Dy Hr Mn
♅□♆	2 21:49
☽0S	3 3:26
☿D	12 5:57
☽0N	16 6:35
☽0S	30 11:14
ʔR	1 2:36
☽0N	13 11:09
♆R	17 11:49
♃⚹♆	19 9:28
♂0S	21 7:17
☽0S	27 18:31

Planet Ingress

		Dy Hr Mn
ʔ	♌	7 5:14
♀	♐	22 4:59
☉	♐	22 23:44
☿	♐	6 6:42
♂	♎	11 9:32
♀	♑	16 1:39
☉	♑	22 12:49
ʔ	♋R	24 4:02
☿	♑	25 14:59

Last Aspect / ☽ Ingress

Last Aspect Dy Hr Mn			☽ Ingress	Dy Hr Mn
1 6:47	♅	△	♍	1 8:36
3 12:07	♇	⚹	♎	3 19:41
6 1:34	♅	☍	♏	6 3:32
8 1:42	♇	△	♐	8 8:33
10 9:48	♅	△	♑	10 11:57
12 12:35	♅	□	♒	12 14:52
14 15:31	♅	⚹	♓	14 17:56
16 14:32	♇	△	♈	16 21:26
18 23:00	♅	☌	♉	19 1:46
21 5:32	♀	☍	♊	21 7:47
23 13:04	♅	⚹	♋	23 16:25
26 0:15	♅	□	♌	26 3:54
28 13:02	♅	△	♍	28 16:52

Last Aspect / ☽ Ingress

Last Aspect Dy Hr Mn			☽ Ingress	Dy Hr Mn
30 20:32	♇	⚹	♎	1 4:39
3 9:24	♅	☍	♏	3 13:06
5 16:19	☿	☌	♐	5 17:53
7 17:04	♂	□	♑	7 20:09
9 20:16	♂	△	♒	9 21:34
11 19:46	♅	⚹	♓	11 23:31
13 22:10	♀	□	♈	14 2:51
16 3:47	♅	☌	♉	16 7:56
18 6:42	♇	⚹	♊	18 14:58
20 20:53	☉	☍	♋	21 0:11
23 6:46	♅	□	♌	23 11:37
25 19:33	♅	△	♍	26 0:32
28 3:47	♇	⚹	♎	28 12:59
30 18:03	♅	☍	♏	30 22:41

☽ Phases & Eclipses

Dy Hr Mn	
7 4:44	● 14♏05
14 2:39	☽ 21♒03
21 4:26	○ 28♉11
29 5:39	☾ 6♍19
6 17:25	● 13♐55
13 10:52	☽ 20♓45
20 20:53	○ 28♊18
29 2:08	☾ 6♎41

Astro Data

1 November 1934
Julian Day # 12723
SVP 6♓09'58"
GC 25♐55.8 ⚳ 9♉07.3R
Eris 2♈30.4R ⚵ 5♑57.8
⚷ 8♊47.8R ⚶ 29♏34.0
☽ Mean ☊ 5♒27.3

1 December 1934
Julian Day # 12753
SVP 6♓09'54"
GC 25♐55.8 ⚳ 0♉19.2R
Eris 2♈18.7R ⚵ 16♑15.9
⚷ 7♊11.1R ⚶ 15♐41.1
☽ Mean ☊ 3♒51.9

LONGITUDE

January 1935

Day	Sid.Time	☉	0 hr ☽	Noon☽	True☊	☿	♀	♂	⚳	♃	♄	♅	♆	♇
1 Tu	18 40 51	10♑09 17	13♏50 52	20♏35 02	1♒16.7	10♑58.1	20♑38.9	9♎55.1	28♋29.5	16♏55.9	25♒02.7	27♈30.4	14♍31.2	25♋16.9
2 W	18 44 47	11 10 27	27 25 58	4♐23 36	1R13.6	12 35.0	21 54.2	10 21.1	28R17.2	17 06.0	25 08.5	27R30.2	14R30.7	25R15.7
3 Th	18 48 44	12 11 38	11♐27 42	18 37 53	1 10.8	14 12.3	23 09.6	10 46.7	28 04.7	17 16.1	25 14.5	27 30.0	14 30.2	25 14.4
4 F	18 52 40	13 12 50	25 53 34	3♑14 02	1 08.6	15 50.0	24 25.0	11 12.2	27 52.0	17 26.0	25 20.5	27 29.9	14 29.6	25 13.1
5 Sa	18 56 37	14 14 01	10♑38 27	18 05 49	1D07.3	17 28.0	25 40.3	11 37.3	27 39.0	17 35.8	25 26.5	27D29.9	14 29.0	25 11.8
6 Su	19 00 33	15 15 12	25 35 06	3♒05 15	1 07.0	19 06.4	26 55.7	12 02.3	27 25.9	17 45.6	25 32.6	27 29.8	14 28.3	25 10.6
7 M	19 04 30	16 16 22	10♒35 09	18 03 48	1 07.4	20 45.2	28 11.0	12 26.9	27 12.5	17 55.2	25 38.7	27 29.9	14 27.6	25 09.3
8 Tu	19 08 26	17 17 33	25 30 14	2♓53 37	1 08.4	22 24.3	29 26.3	12 51.3	26 59.0	18 04.7	25 44.9	27 30.0	14 26.9	25 08.0
9 W	19 12 23	18 18 42	10♓13 13	17 28 28	1 09.5	24 03.7	0♒41.7	13 15.4	26 45.3	18 14.1	25 51.2	27 30.1	14 26.2	25 06.7
10 Th	19 16 20	19 19 51	24 38 56	1♈44 18	1 10.4	25 43.6	1 57.0	13 39.2	26 31.5	18 23.4	25 57.5	27 30.3	14 25.4	25 05.4
11 F	19 20 16	20 21 00	8♈44 23	15 39 09	1R10.9	27 23.7	3 12.2	14 02.7	26 17.6	18 32.6	26 03.8	27 30.5	14 24.6	25 04.0
12 Sa	19 24 13	21 22 08	22 28 37	29 12 54	1 10.8	29 04.1	4 27.5	14 25.9	26 03.5	18 41.7	26 10.2	27 30.8	14 23.8	25 02.7
13 Su	19 28 09	22 23 15	5♉52 10	12♉26 41	1 10.3	0♒44.8	5 42.8	14 48.9	25 49.4	18 50.6	26 16.6	27 31.2	14 22.9	25 01.4
14 M	19 32 06	23 24 22	18 56 40	25 22 25	1 09.5	2 25.7	6 58.0	15 11.5	25 35.3	18 59.4	26 23.1	27 31.6	14 22.0	25 00.1
15 Tu	19 36 02	24 25 28	1♊44 14	8♊02 22	1 08.5	4 06.7	8 13.3	15 33.8	25 21.1	19 08.2	26 29.6	27 32.0	14 21.1	24 58.8
16 W	19 39 59	25 26 34	14 17 08	20 28 48	1 07.6	5 47.8	9 28.5	15 55.8	25 06.9	19 16.8	26 36.2	27 32.5	14 20.1	24 57.5
17 Th	19 43 55	26 27 39	26 37 38	2♋43 54	1 07.0	7 28.8	10 43.7	16 17.5	24 52.6	19 25.2	26 42.8	27 33.1	14 19.2	24 56.2
18 F	19 47 52	27 28 43	8♋47 50	14 49 40	1 06.6	9 09.8	11 58.9	16 38.9	24 38.4	19 33.6	26 49.4	27 33.7	14 18.2	24 54.9
19 Sa	19 51 49	28 29 46	20 49 39	26 48 00	1D06.4	10 50.4	13 14.1	16 59.9	24 24.2	19 41.8	26 56.1	27 34.3	14 17.1	24 53.6
20 Su	19 55 45	29 30 49	2♌44 58	8♌40 47	1 06.5	12 30.6	14 29.2	17 20.5	24 10.1	19 49.9	27 02.8	27 35.1	14 16.1	24 52.2
21 M	19 59 42	0♒31 51	14 35 43	20 30 01	1R06.5	14 10.2	15 44.4	17 40.9	23 56.0	19 57.9	27 09.6	27 35.8	14 15.0	24 50.9
22 Tu	20 03 38	1 32 53	26 24 00	2♍17 58	1 06.5	15 48.9	16 59.5	18 00.8	23 42.0	20 05.8	27 16.4	27 36.6	14 13.9	24 49.6
23 W	20 07 35	2 33 54	8♍12 16	14 07 15	1 06.4	17 26.4	18 14.6	18 20.4	23 28.1	20 13.5	27 23.2	27 37.5	14 12.8	24 48.3
24 Th	20 11 31	3 34 54	20 03 19	26 00 54	1 06.1	19 02.5	19 29.7	18 39.6	23 14.4	20 21.0	27 30.0	27 38.4	14 11.6	24 47.0
25 F	20 15 28	4 35 54	2♎00 27	8♎02 26	1 05.8	20 36.7	20 44.8	18 58.4	23 00.8	20 28.5	27 36.9	27 39.4	14 10.4	24 45.7
26 Sa	20 19 24	5 36 53	14 07 22	20 15 44	1 05.4	22 08.7	21 59.9	19 16.9	22 47.3	20 35.8	27 43.8	27 40.4	14 09.2	24 44.4
27 Su	20 23 21	6 37 52	26 28 05	2♏44 55	1D05.2	23 37.9	23 15.0	19 34.9	22 34.0	20 43.0	27 50.7	27 41.5	14 08.0	24 43.1
28 M	20 27 18	7 38 50	9♏06 45	15 34 03	1 05.2	25 03.9	24 30.0	19 52.5	22 20.9	20 50.0	27 57.7	27 42.6	14 06.7	24 41.9
29 Tu	20 31 14	8 39 47	22 07 17	28 46 48	1 05.6	26 26.0	25 45.0	20 09.7	22 07.9	20 56.9	28 04.7	27 43.7	14 05.5	24 40.6
30 W	20 35 11	9 40 44	5♐32 55	12♐25 47	1 06.3	27 43.5	27 00.0	20 26.4	21 55.3	21 03.6	28 11.7	27 45.0	14 04.2	24 39.3
31 Th	20 39 07	10 41 40	19 25 30	26 31 59	1 07.2	28 55.7	28 15.0	20 42.7	21 42.8	21 10.2	28 18.8	27 46.2	14 02.9	24 38.1

LONGITUDE

February 1935

Day	Sid.Time	☉	0 hr ☽	Noon☽	True☊	☿	♀	♂	⚳	♃	♄	♅	♆	♇
1 F	20 43 04	11♒42 36	3♑44 57	11♑04 00	1♒08.0	0♓01.9	29♒30.0	20♎58.6	21♋30.6	21♏16.7	28♒25.9	27♈47.5	14♍01.5	24♋36.8
2 Sa	20 47 00	12 43 30	18 28 31	25 57 42	1R08.4	1 01.3	0♓45.0	21 13.9	21R18.7	21 23.0	28 33.0	27 48.9	14R00.2	24R35.6
3 Su	20 50 57	13 44 23	3♒30 37	11♒06 09	1 08.3	1 53.1	1 59.9	21 28.8	21 07.0	21 29.1	28 40.1	27 50.3	13 58.8	24 34.3
4 M	20 54 54	14 45 16	18 43 06	26 20 14	1 07.5	2 36.4	3 14.8	21 43.2	20 55.7	21 35.1	28 47.2	27 51.8	13 57.4	24 33.1
5 Tu	20 58 50	15 46 07	3♓56 15	11♓29 57	1 06.0	3 10.7	4 29.7	21 57.1	20 44.6	21 40.9	28 54.4	27 53.3	13 56.0	24 31.9
6 W	21 02 47	16 46 56	19 00 11	26 25 57	1 04.0	3 35.1	5 44.6	22 10.5	20 33.9	21 46.6	29 01.5	27 54.8	13 54.6	24 30.7
7 Th	21 06 43	17 47 44	3♈46 24	11♈00 54	1 01.9	3R49.1	6 59.4	22 23.4	20 23.5	21 52.1	29 08.7	27 56.4	13 53.1	24 29.5
8 F	21 10 40	18 48 31	18 08 56	25 10 15	1 00.0	3 52.5	8 14.2	22 35.8	20 13.5	21 57.5	29 15.9	27 58.1	13 51.6	24 28.3
9 Sa	21 14 36	19 49 16	2♉04 43	8♉52 24	0D58.8	3 44.9	9 29.0	22 47.6	20 03.8	22 02.7	29 23.1	27 59.8	13 50.2	24 27.1
10 Su	21 18 33	20 49 59	15 33 26	22 08 09	0 58.4	3 26.6	10 43.8	22 58.9	19 54.5	22 07.7	29 30.3	28 01.5	13 48.7	24 25.9
11 M	21 22 29	21 50 41	28 36 55	5♊00 09	0 59.0	2 57.9	11 58.5	23 09.6	19 45.6	22 12.6	29 37.6	28 03.3	13 47.1	24 24.8
12 Tu	21 26 26	22 51 22	11♊18 21	17 32 01	1 00.3	2 19.4	13 13.2	23 19.8	19 37.0	22 17.3	29 44.8	28 05.1	13 45.6	24 23.6
13 W	21 30 23	23 52 00	23 41 40	29 47 48	1 02.0	1 32.2	14 27.9	23 29.4	19 28.8	22 21.8	29 52.1	28 07.0	13 44.1	24 22.5
14 Th	21 34 19	24 52 37	5♋50 57	11♋51 34	1 03.7	0 37.4	15 42.5	23 38.4	19 21.1	22 26.2	29 59.4	28 08.9	13 42.5	24 21.4
15 F	21 38 16	25 53 13	17 50 07	23 47 02	1R04.8	29♒36.7	16 57.1	23 46.8	19 13.7	22 30.4	0♓06.6	28 10.9	13 41.0	24 20.3
16 Sa	21 42 12	26 53 46	29 42 42	5♌37 30	1 04.9	28 31.6	18 11.7	23 54.6	19 06.7	22 34.4	0 13.9	28 12.9	13 39.4	24 19.2
17 Su	21 46 09	27 54 18	11♌31 45	17 25 45	1 03.7	27 24.0	19 26.2	24 01.7	19 00.2	22 38.3	0 21.2	28 14.9	13 37.8	24 18.2
18 M	21 50 05	28 54 49	23 19 48	29 14 09	1 01.1	26 15.7	20 40.7	24 08.3	18 54.0	22 42.0	0 28.5	28 17.0	13 36.2	24 17.1
19 Tu	21 54 02	29 55 18	5♍09 03	11♍04 44	0 57.0	25 08.5	21 55.2	24 14.2	18 48.3	22 45.5	0 35.7	28 19.1	13 34.6	24 16.1
20 W	21 57 58	0♓55 45	17 01 26	22 59 21	0 51.9	24 03.8	23 09.7	24 19.4	18 43.0	22 48.8	0 43.0	28 21.3	13 33.0	24 15.0
21 Th	22 01 55	1 56 11	28 58 44	4♎59 50	0 46.2	23 03.1	24 24.1	24 24.0	18 38.1	22 52.0	0 50.3	28 23.5	13 31.4	24 14.0
22 F	22 05 51	2 56 35	11♎02 55	17 08 14	0 40.5	22 07.6	25 38.4	24 27.9	18 33.7	22 55.0	0 57.6	28 25.7	13 29.7	24 13.0
23 Sa	22 09 48	3 56 58	23 16 06	29 26 50	0 35.4	21 18.1	26 52.8	24 31.2	18 29.7	22 57.8	1 04.9	28 28.0	13 28.1	24 12.1
24 Su	22 13 45	4 57 20	5♏40 47	11♏58 19	0 31.6	20 35.2	28 07.1	24 33.7	18 26.1	23 00.4	1 12.1	28 30.3	13 26.4	24 11.1
25 M	22 17 41	5 57 40	18 19 49	24 45 40	0D29.3	19 59.4	29 21.4	24 35.5	18 22.9	23 02.9	1 19.4	28 32.7	13 24.8	24 10.2
26 Tu	22 21 38	6 57 59	1♐16 16	7♐51 59	0 28.7	19 30.8	0♈35.6	24 36.6	18 20.2	23 05.1	1 26.7	28 35.1	13 23.1	24 09.2
27 W	22 25 34	7 58 16	14 33 11	21 20 09	0 29.4	19 09.5	1 49.8	24R37.0	18 17.9	23 07.2	1 33.9	28 37.5	13 21.5	24 08.3
28 Th	22 29 31	8 58 32	28 13 08	5♑12 16	0 30.8	18 55.4	3 04.0	24 36.6	18 16.1	23 09.1	1 41.2	28 40.0	13 19.8	24 07.5

Astro Data

	Dy Hr Mn
♄⚻♇	3 11:45
♅ D	6 8:35
☽ 0N	9 17:19
☽ 0S	24 1:11
♄✶♅	25 22:05
☽ 0N	6 2:41
☿ R	8 7:24
☽ 0S	20 7:30
♅□♆	23 12:31
♂ R	27 12:11
♀0N	27 23:18

Planet Ingress

		Dy Hr Mn
♀	♒	8 22:44
☿	♒	13 1:20
☉	♒	20 23:28
☿	♓	1 11:16
♀	♓	1 21:36
♄	♓	14 14:08
☿	♒R	15 3:02
☉	♓	19 13:52
♀	♈	26 0:30

Last Aspect / ☽ Ingress

Last Aspect Dy Hr Mn			☽ Ingress	Dy Hr Mn
1 20:14	♇	△	♐	2 4:27
4 2:38	♅	△	♑	4 6:44
6 3:04	♅	□	♒	6 7:04
8 3:14	♅	✶	♓	8 7:17
10 0:46	♇	△	♈	10 9:03
12 11:42	☿	□	♉	12 13:24
14 13:55	♄	□	♊	14 20:43
17 1:48	♅	✶	♋	17 6:37
19 15:44	☉	☍	♌	19 18:27
22 2:27	♅	△	♍	22 7:19
24 9:32	♇	✶	♎	24 19:59
27 2:33	♄	△	♏	27 6:46
29 10:44	♄	□	♐	29 14:11
31 16:21	☿	✶	♑	31 17:47

Last Aspect / ☽ Ingress

Last Aspect Dy Hr Mn			☽ Ingress	Dy Hr Mn
2 14:57	♅	□	♒	2 18:26
4 15:54	♄	☌	♓	4 17:47
6 8:53	♇	△	♈	6 17:49
8 19:09	♄	✶	♉	8 20:22
11 1:48	♄	□	♊	11 2:35
13 12:09	♄	△	♋	13 12:24
15 20:55	♅	□	♌	16 0:35
18 11:17	☉	☍	♍	18 13:33
20 14:32	♇	✶	♎	21 2:02
23 10:06	♅	☍	♏	23 13:04
25 21:22	♀	△	♐	25 21:40
28 0:44	♅	△	♑	28 3:05

☽ Phases & Eclipses

Dy Hr Mn		
5 5:20	●	13♑57
5 5:35:15	●	P 0.001
11 20:55	☽	20♈44
19 15:44	○	28♋39
19 15:47	○	T 1.350
27 19:59	☾	6♏58
3 16:27	●	13♒56
3 16:15:57	●	P 0.739
10 9:25	☽	20♉43
18 11:17	○	28♌53
26 10:14	☾	6♐54

Astro Data

1 January 1935
Julian Day # 12784
SVP 6♓09'48"
GC 25♐55.9 ⚴ 29♈00.3
Eris 2♈17.1 ⚵ 28♑24.2
⚷ 5♊33.0R ⚶ 2♑26.4
☽ Mean ☊ 2♒13.5

1 February 1935
Julian Day # 12815
SVP 6♓09'42"
GC 25♐56.0 ⚴ 6♉24.5
Eris 2♈26.8 ⚵ 11♒29.4
⚷ 4♊38.5R ⚶ 18♑58.1
☽ Mean ☊ 0♒35.0

March 1935 LONGITUDE

Day	Sid.Time	☉	0 hr ☽	Noon ☽	True ☊	☿	♀	♂	⚳	♃	♄	♅	♆	♇
1 F	22 33 27	9♓58 47	12♑17 37	19♑29 02	0♒32.1	18♒48.2	4♈18.1	24♎35.5	18♋14.7	23♏10.8	1♓48.4	28♈42.5	13♍18.2	24♋06.6
2 Sa	22 37 24	10 59 00	26 46 17	4♒08 54	0R 32.4	18D 47.7	5 32.2	24R 33.6	18R 13.7	23 12.4	1 55.7	28 45.0	13R 16.5	24R 05.7
3 Su	22 41 20	11 59 11	11♒36 16	19 07 35	0 31.1	18 53.7	6 46.3	24 31.0	18D 13.2	23 13.7	2 02.9	28 47.6	13 14.8	24 04.9
4 M	22 45 17	12 59 21	26 41 49	4♓17 52	0 27.7	19 05.7	8 00.3	24 27.6	18 13.0	23 14.9	2 10.1	28 50.2	13 13.1	24 04.1
5 Tu	22 49 14	13 59 29	11♓54 29	19 30 20	0 22.4	19 23.4	9 14.3	24 23.4	18 13.4	23 15.8	2 17.3	28 52.9	13 11.5	24 03.3
6 W	22 53 10	14 59 34	27 04 08	4♈34 37	0 15.6	19 46.4	10 28.2	24 18.5	18 14.1	23 16.6	2 24.5	28 55.5	13 09.8	24 02.6
7 Th	22 57 07	15 59 38	12♈00 38	19 21 13	0 08.3	20 14.4	11 42.1	24 12.7	18 15.3	23 17.2	2 31.7	28 58.2	13 08.1	24 01.8
8 F	23 01 03	16 59 40	26 35 32	3♉43 00	0 01.5	20 47.1	12 55.9	24 06.2	18 16.9	23 17.6	2 38.8	29 01.0	13 06.5	24 01.1
9 Sa	23 05 00	17 59 40	10♉43 15	17 36 06	29♑55.9	21 24.2	14 09.8	23 58.9	18 18.9	23R 17.8	2 45.9	29 03.7	13 04.8	24 00.4
10 Su	23 08 56	18 59 38	24 21 32	0♊59 47	29 52.2	22 05.3	15 23.5	23 50.8	18 21.4	23 17.8	2 53.1	29 06.5	13 03.1	23 59.7
11 M	23 12 53	19 59 33	7♊31 08	13 56 02	29D 50.4	22 50.2	16 37.2	23 42.0	18 24.3	23 17.6	3 00.1	29 09.4	13 01.5	23 59.0
12 Tu	23 16 49	20 59 26	20 15 00	26 28 37	29 50.4	23 38.7	17 50.9	23 32.4	18 27.6	23 17.3	3 07.2	29 12.2	12 59.8	23 58.4
13 W	23 20 46	21 59 17	2♋37 31	8♋42 20	29 51.4	24 30.5	19 04.5	23 22.0	18 31.2	23 16.7	3 14.3	29 15.1	12 58.2	23 57.8
14 Th	23 24 43	22 59 06	14 43 44	20 42 20	29R 52.5	25 25.4	20 18.1	23 10.9	18 35.3	23 16.0	3 21.3	29 18.0	12 56.5	23 57.2
15 F	23 28 39	23 58 53	26 38 47	2♌33 40	29 52.8	26 23.2	21 31.6	22 59.1	18 39.8	23 15.1	3 28.3	29 20.9	12 54.9	23 56.6
16 Sa	23 32 36	24 58 37	8♌27 31	14 20 54	29 51.5	27 23.7	22 45.0	22 46.5	18 44.7	23 14.0	3 35.2	29 23.9	12 53.3	23 56.1
17 Su	23 36 32	25 58 19	20 14 10	26 08 00	29 48.0	28 26.8	23 58.4	22 33.1	18 50.0	23 12.7	3 42.2	29 26.9	12 51.6	23 55.6
18 M	23 40 29	26 57 59	2♍02 33	7♍58 12	29 41.9	29 32.3	25 11.8	22 19.1	18 55.6	23 11.2	3 49.1	29 29.9	12 50.0	23 55.1
19 Tu	23 44 25	27 57 37	13 55 16	19 53 59	29 33.5	0♓40.2	26 25.1	22 04.3	19 01.7	23 09.6	3 56.0	29 32.9	12 48.4	23 54.6
20 W	23 48 22	28 57 13	25 54 33	1♎57 08	29 23.1	1 50.2	27 38.3	21 48.9	19 08.1	23 07.7	4 02.8	29 36.0	12 46.8	23 54.1
21 Th	23 52 18	29 56 47	8♎01 52	14 08 52	29 11.6	3 02.3	28 51.5	21 32.7	19 14.9	23 05.7	4 09.7	29 39.1	12 45.2	23 53.7
22 F	23 56 15	0♈56 19	20 18 14	26 30 05	29 00.0	4 16.4	0♉04.6	21 16.0	19 22.0	23 03.5	4 16.4	29 42.2	12 43.6	23 53.3
23 Sa	0 00 12	1 55 49	2♏44 30	9♏01 35	28 49.4	5 32.5	1 17.7	20 58.6	19 29.5	23 01.1	4 23.2	29 45.3	12 42.1	23 52.9
24 Su	0 04 08	2 55 17	15 21 28	21 44 18	28 40.7	6 50.4	2 30.7	20 40.6	19 37.4	22 58.5	4 29.9	29 48.4	12 40.5	23 52.5
25 M	0 08 05	3 54 44	28 10 15	4♐39 31	28 34.6	8 10.0	3 43.6	20 22.0	19 45.6	22 55.8	4 36.6	29 51.6	12 39.0	23 52.2
26 Tu	0 12 01	4 54 09	11♐12 18	17 48 51	28 31.0	9 31.4	4 56.6	20 02.8	19 54.2	22 52.9	4 43.3	29 54.8	12 37.5	23 51.9
27 W	0 15 58	5 53 32	24 29 25	1♑14 14	28D 29.7	10 54.5	6 09.4	19 43.1	20 03.1	22 49.7	4 49.9	29 58.0	12 35.9	23 51.6
28 Th	0 19 54	6 52 53	8♑03 31	14 57 30	28R 29.7	12 19.2	7 22.2	19 22.9	20 12.4	22 46.5	4 56.5	0♉01.2	12 34.5	23 51.4
29 F	0 23 51	7 52 12	21 56 16	28 59 55	28 30.0	13 45.5	8 34.9	19 02.3	20 21.9	22 43.0	5 03.0	0 04.5	12 33.0	23 51.1
30 Sa	0 27 47	8 51 30	6♒08 23	13♒21 30	28 29.3	15 13.3	9 47.6	18 41.2	20 31.8	22 39.4	5 09.5	0 07.7	12 31.5	23 50.9
31 Su	0 31 44	9 50 46	20 38 56	28 00 12	28 26.4	16 42.7	11 00.2	18 19.7	20 42.1	22 35.6	5 16.0	0 11.0	12 30.0	23 50.7

April 1935 LONGITUDE

Day	Sid.Time	☉	0 hr ☽	Noon ☽	True ☊	☿	♀	♂	⚳	♃	♄	♅	♆	♇
1 M	0 35 41	10♈50 00	5♓24 40	12♓51 32	28♑20.9	18♓13.6	12♉12.8	17♎57.8	20♋52.6	22♏31.6	5♓22.4	0♉14.3	12♍28.6	23♋50.6
2 Tu	0 39 37	11 49 12	20 19 49	27 48 29	28R 12.6	19 46.1	13 25.3	17R 35.6	21 03.5	22R 27.5	5 28.7	0 17.6	12R 27.2	23R 50.4
3 W	0 43 34	12 48 22	5♈16 22	12♈42 20	28 02.3	21 19.9	14 37.7	17 13.2	21 14.7	22 23.2	5 35.1	0 20.9	12 25.8	23 50.3
4 Th	0 47 30	13 47 30	20 05 13	27 23 58	27 51.0	22 55.3	15 50.1	16 50.5	21 26.2	22 18.7	5 41.3	0 24.2	12 24.4	23 50.2
5 F	0 51 27	14 46 37	4♉37 39	11♉45 31	27 40.0	24 32.2	17 02.4	16 27.7	21 38.0	22 14.1	5 47.6	0 27.6	12 23.0	23 50.2
6 Sa	0 55 23	15 45 40	18 46 57	25 41 34	27 30.5	26 10.5	18 14.7	16 04.7	21 50.1	22 09.4	5 53.7	0 30.9	12 21.7	23D 50.1
7 Su	0 59 20	16 44 42	2♊29 11	9♊09 46	27 23.3	27 50.3	19 26.8	15 41.6	22 02.5	22 04.5	5 59.9	0 34.3	12 20.4	23 50.1
8 M	1 03 16	17 43 42	15 43 28	22 10 36	27 18.7	29 31.6	20 38.9	15 18.5	22 15.2	21 59.4	6 06.0	0 37.7	12 19.1	23 50.1
9 Tu	1 07 13	18 42 39	28 31 35	4♋46 55	27 16.4	1♈14.4	21 51.0	14 55.4	22 28.1	21 54.2	6 12.0	0 41.0	12 17.8	23 50.2
10 W	1 11 10	19 41 34	10♋57 13	17 03 06	27 15.8	2 58.7	23 02.9	14 32.3	22 41.4	21 48.8	6 18.0	0 44.4	12 16.5	23 50.2
11 Th	1 15 06	20 40 27	23 05 15	29 04 22	27 15.8	4 44.5	24 14.8	14 09.4	22 54.9	21 43.3	6 23.9	0 47.8	12 15.3	23 50.3
12 F	1 19 03	21 39 17	5♌01 07	10♌56 13	27 15.3	6 31.7	25 26.6	13 46.6	23 08.7	21 37.7	6 29.8	0 51.2	12 14.1	23 50.5
13 Sa	1 22 59	22 38 05	16 50 19	22 44 02	27 13.2	8 20.6	26 38.3	13 23.9	23 22.7	21 31.9	6 35.6	0 54.7	12 12.9	23 50.6
14 Su	1 26 56	23 36 51	28 37 59	4♍32 43	27 08.8	10 10.9	27 50.0	13 01.5	23 37.0	21 26.1	6 41.3	0 58.1	12 11.7	23 50.8
15 M	1 30 52	24 35 34	10♍28 43	16 26 27	27 01.6	12 02.8	29 01.6	12 39.4	23 51.6	21 20.1	6 47.0	1 01.5	12 10.6	23 50.9
16 Tu	1 34 49	25 34 16	22 26 17	28 28 34	26 51.7	13 56.2	0♊13.1	12 17.5	24 06.4	21 13.9	6 52.7	1 04.9	12 09.4	23 51.2
17 W	1 38 45	26 32 55	4♎33 32	10♎41 24	26 39.6	15 51.2	1 24.5	11 56.0	24 21.4	21 07.7	6 58.2	1 08.4	12 08.3	23 51.4
18 Th	1 42 42	27 31 33	16 52 18	23 06 18	26 26.2	17 47.7	2 35.8	11 34.9	24 36.7	21 01.3	7 03.7	1 11.8	12 07.3	23 51.7
19 F	1 46 38	28 30 08	29 23 28	5♏43 45	26 12.7	19 45.8	3 47.0	11 14.2	24 52.2	20 54.9	7 09.2	1 15.3	12 06.2	23 52.0
20 Sa	1 50 35	29 28 42	12♏07 08	18 33 32	26 00.2	21 45.3	4 58.2	10 54.0	25 08.0	20 48.3	7 14.6	1 18.7	12 05.2	23 52.3
21 Su	1 54 32	0♉27 13	25 02 52	1♐35 04	25 49.9	23 46.3	6 09.3	10 34.2	25 23.9	20 41.6	7 19.9	1 22.1	12 04.2	23 52.6
22 M	1 58 28	1 25 44	8♐10 03	14 47 46	25 42.3	25 48.7	7 20.2	10 15.0	25 40.1	20 34.9	7 25.2	1 25.6	12 03.2	23 53.0
23 Tu	2 02 25	2 24 12	21 28 12	28 11 20	25 37.6	27 52.5	8 31.1	9 56.3	25 56.6	20 28.0	7 30.4	1 29.0	12 02.3	23 53.4
24 W	2 06 21	3 22 39	4♑57 12	11♑45 50	25 35.5	29 57.5	9 42.0	9 38.2	26 13.2	20 21.1	7 35.6	1 32.5	12 01.3	23 53.8
25 Th	2 10 18	4 21 04	18 37 20	25 31 44	25 35.0	2♉03.6	10 52.7	9 20.7	26 30.1	20 14.0	7 40.6	1 35.9	12 00.5	23 54.2
26 F	2 14 14	5 19 28	2♒29 07	9♒29 29	25 35.1	4 10.8	12 03.3	9 03.9	26 47.1	20 06.9	7 45.6	1 39.4	11 59.6	23 54.7
27 Sa	2 18 11	6 17 50	16 32 50	23 39 04	25 34.2	6 18.7	13 13.9	8 47.7	27 04.4	19 59.8	7 50.6	1 42.8	11 58.8	23 55.2
28 Su	2 22 07	7 16 10	0♓48 02	7♓59 27	25 31.4	8 27.4	14 24.3	8 32.1	27 21.9	19 52.5	7 55.5	1 46.3	11 57.9	23 55.7
29 M	2 26 04	8 14 29	15 12 57	22 28 01	25 26.1	10 36.5	15 34.7	8 17.3	27 39.6	19 45.2	8 00.3	1 49.7	11 57.2	23 56.2
30 Tu	2 30 01	9 12 46	29 44 03	7♈00 21	25 18.1	12 45.7	16 45.0	8 03.2	27 57.4	19 37.8	8 05.0	1 53.1	11 56.4	23 56.8

Astro Data

	Dy Hr Mn
☿ D	2 1:36
⚳ D	4 6:09
☽ 0N	5 14:01
♃ R	10 2:47
☽ 0S	19 13:49
☉ 0N	21 13:18
☽ 0N	2 0:39
♇ D	7 7:55
☿ 0N	11 17:38
☽ 0S	15 20:23
☽ 0N	29 8:38

Planet Ingress

	Dy Hr Mn
☊ ♑R	8 17:40
☿ ♓	18 21:53
☉ ♈	21 13:18
♀ ♉	22 10:29
♅ ♉	28 2:57
☿ ♈	8 18:40
♀ ♊	16 7:37
☉ ♉	21 0:50
☿ ♉	24 12:29

Last Aspect / ☽ Ingress (March)

Last Aspect Dy Hr Mn		☽ Ingress Dy Hr Mn
2 3:12	♅ □	♒ 2 5:16
4 3:21	♅ ⚹	♓ 4 5:13
5 19:12	♇ △	♈ 6 4:40
8 4:02	♅ ☌	♉ 8 5:43
9 23:22	♇ ⚹	♊ 10 10:11
12 17:19	♅ ⚹	♋ 12 18:52
15 5:27	♅ □	♌ 15 6:48
17 18:46	♅ △	♍ 17 19:51
20 5:31	☉ ☍	♎ 20 8:08
22 18:12	♅ ☍	♏ 22 18:44
24 16:00	♇ △	♐ 25 3:24
27 9:44	♅ △	♑ 27 9:49
29 3:16	♇ ☍	♒ 29 13:41
31 3:13	♃ □	♓ 31 15:15

Last Aspect / ☽ Ingress (April)

Last Aspect Dy Hr Mn		☽ Ingress Dy Hr Mn
2 5:38	♇ △	♈ 2 15:31
4 6:08	♇ □	♉ 4 16:18
6 12:58	☿ ⚹	♊ 6 19:35
8 3:01	☉ ⚹	♋ 9 2:49
11 1:30	♇ ☌	♌ 11 13:52
13 20:50	♀ □	♍ 14 2:47
16 2:49	♇ ⚹	♎ 16 15:01
18 21:10	☉ ☍	♏ 19 1:09
20 21:50	♇ △	♐ 21 9:06
23 11:20	☿ △	♑ 23 15:13
25 9:11	♇ ☍	♒ 25 19:43
27 5:53	♃ □	♓ 27 22:40
29 14:26	♇ △	♈ 30 0:26

☽ Phases & Eclipses

Dy Hr Mn	
5 2:40	● 13♓36
12 0:30	☽ 20♊31
20 5:31	○ 28♍41
27 20:51	☾ 6♑15
3 12:11	● 12♈49
10 17:42	☽ 19♋56
18 21:10	○ 27♎54
26 4:20	☾ 5♒01

Astro Data

1 March 1935
Julian Day # 12843
SVP 6♓09'39"
GC 25♐56.0 ⚴ 17♉58.7
Eris 2♈43.3 ⚵ 23♒45.9
⚷ 4♊46.2 ⚶ 3♒23.9
☽ Mean ☊ 29♑06.0

1 April 1935
Julian Day # 12874
SVP 6♓09'35"
GC 25♐56.1 ⚴ 3♊53.4
Eris 3♈05.5 ⚵ 7♓32.6
⚷ 5♊56.9 ⚶ 18♒25.8
☽ Mean ☊ 27♑27.5

LONGITUDE — May 1935

Day	Sid.Time	☉	0 hr ☽	Noon ☽	True ☊	☿	♀	♂	⚳	♃	♄	♅	♆	♇
1 W	2 33 57	10♉11 02	14♈16 07	21♈30 31	25♑07.9	14♉55.0	17♊55.1	7♎49.8	28♋15.5	19♏30.4	8♓09.6	1♉56.5	11♍55.7	23♋57.4
2 Th	2 37 54	11 09 16	28 42 42	5♉51 50	24R 56.8	17 03.8	19 05.2	7R 37.2	28 33.8	19R 22.9	8 14.2	2 00.0	11R 55.0	23 58.0
3 F	2 41 50	12 07 29	12♉57 08	19 57 55	24 45.8	19 12.1	20 15.2	7 25.3	28 52.2	19 15.4	8 18.7	2 03.4	11 54.3	23 58.6
4 Sa	2 45 47	13 05 40	26 53 36	3♊43 45	24 36.1	21 19.4	21 25.1	7 14.3	29 10.9	19 07.9	8 23.1	2 06.8	11 53.7	23 59.3
5 Su	2 49 43	14 03 49	10♊28 04	17 06 24	24 28.6	23 25.5	22 34.9	7 04.0	29 29.7	19 00.3	8 27.5	2 10.2	11 53.1	23 59.9
6 M	2 53 40	15 01 56	23 38 46	0♋05 18	24 23.7	25 30.0	23 44.5	6 54.5	29 48.7	18 52.7	8 31.8	2 13.6	11 52.5	24 00.6
7 Tu	2 57 36	16 00 01	6♋26 16	12 42 00	24D 21.2	27 32.8	24 54.1	6 45.8	0♌07.8	18 45.1	8 36.0	2 16.9	11 52.0	24 01.4
8 W	3 01 33	16 58 05	18 52 59	24 59 44	24 20.6	29 33.5	26 03.6	6 37.9	0 27.2	18 37.5	8 40.1	2 20.3	11 51.5	24 02.1
9 Th	3 05 30	17 56 06	1♌02 51	7♌02 56	24R 21.0	1♊31.9	27 12.9	6 30.9	0 46.7	18 29.8	8 44.1	2 23.7	11 51.0	24 02.9
10 F	3 09 26	18 54 06	13 00 40	18 56 43	24 21.4	3 27.7	28 22.1	6 24.6	1 06.3	18 22.2	8 48.1	2 27.0	11 50.6	24 03.7
11 Sa	3 13 23	19 52 03	24 51 45	0♍46 26	24 20.7	5 20.9	29 31.2	6 19.2	1 26.2	18 14.5	8 52.0	2 30.3	11 50.1	24 04.5
12 Su	3 17 19	20 49 59	6♍41 26	12 37 21	24 18.2	7 11.2	0♋40.1	6 14.5	1 46.1	18 06.9	8 55.8	2 33.7	11 49.8	24 05.3
13 M	3 21 16	21 47 53	18 34 48	24 34 20	24 13.5	8 58.5	1 49.0	6 10.7	2 06.3	17 59.3	8 59.5	2 37.0	11 49.4	24 06.1
14 Tu	3 25 12	22 45 46	0♎36 26	6♎41 33	24 06.5	10 42.6	2 57.7	6 07.6	2 26.6	17 51.7	9 03.1	2 40.3	11 49.1	24 07.0
15 W	3 29 09	23 43 36	12 50 03	19 02 14	23 57.7	12 23.6	4 06.3	6 05.4	2 47.0	17 44.1	9 06.7	2 43.5	11 48.8	24 07.9
16 Th	3 33 05	24 41 25	25 18 20	1♏38 31	23 47.6	14 01.3	5 14.7	6 03.9	3 07.6	17 36.5	9 10.1	2 46.8	11 48.5	24 08.8
17 F	3 37 02	25 39 13	8♏02 49	14 31 14	23 37.3	15 35.6	6 23.0	6D 03.2	3 28.3	17 29.0	9 13.5	2 50.0	11 48.3	24 09.8
18 Sa	3 40 59	26 36 59	21 03 41	27 40 01	23 27.9	17 06.4	7 31.2	6 03.3	3 49.2	17 21.5	9 16.8	2 53.3	11 48.1	24 10.7
19 Su	3 44 55	27 34 44	4♐20 03	11♐03 30	23 20.1	18 33.8	8 39.2	6 04.1	4 10.2	17 14.1	9 20.0	2 56.5	11 47.9	24 11.7
20 M	3 48 52	28 32 27	17 50 06	24 39 35	23 14.6	19 57.7	9 47.1	6 05.7	4 31.3	17 06.7	9 23.1	2 59.7	11 47.8	24 12.7
21 Tu	3 52 48	29 30 10	1♑31 37	8♑25 57	23 11.5	21 18.0	10 54.8	6 08.0	4 52.6	16 59.3	9 26.1	3 02.9	11 47.7	24 13.7
22 W	3 56 45	0♊27 51	15 22 17	22 20 23	23D 10.5	22 34.7	12 02.4	6 11.1	5 14.0	16 52.1	9 29.1	3 06.0	11 47.7	24 14.8
23 Th	4 00 41	1 25 31	29 20 03	6♒21 04	23 11.0	23 47.7	13 09.8	6 14.9	5 35.5	16 44.8	9 31.9	3 09.2	11D 47.6	24 15.8
24 F	4 04 38	2 23 10	13♒23 17	20 26 33	23R 12.0	24 57.0	14 17.1	6 19.4	5 57.2	16 37.7	9 34.7	3 12.3	11 47.6	24 16.9
25 Sa	4 08 35	3 20 48	27 30 41	4♓35 34	23 12.4	26 02.5	15 24.2	6 24.6	6 18.9	16 30.6	9 37.4	3 15.4	11 47.7	24 18.0
26 Su	4 12 31	4 18 25	11♓40 58	18 46 42	23 11.5	27 04.1	16 31.1	6 30.5	6 40.8	16 23.6	9 40.0	3 18.5	11 47.7	24 19.1
27 M	4 16 28	5 16 01	25 52 31	2♈58 07	23 08.7	28 01.9	17 37.9	6 37.1	7 02.9	16 16.7	9 42.4	3 21.5	11 47.8	24 20.2
28 Tu	4 20 24	6 13 36	10♈03 09	17 07 13	23 03.9	28 55.7	18 44.5	6 44.4	7 25.0	16 09.8	9 44.8	3 24.5	11 47.9	24 21.3
29 W	4 24 21	7 11 10	24 09 53	1♉10 43	22 57.6	29 45.4	19 51.0	6 52.3	7 47.3	16 03.1	9 47.1	3 27.6	11 48.1	24 22.5
30 Th	4 28 17	8 08 44	8♉09 12	15 04 54	22 50.4	0♋31.0	20 57.3	7 01.0	8 09.7	15 56.4	9 49.4	3 30.5	11 48.3	24 23.7
31 F	4 32 14	9 06 16	21 57 21	28 46 08	22 43.3	1 12.5	22 03.4	7 10.2	8 32.2	15 49.9	9 51.5	3 33.5	11 48.5	24 24.9

LONGITUDE — June 1935

Day	Sid.Time	☉	0 hr ☽	Noon ☽	True ☊	☿	♀	♂	⚳	♃	♄	♅	♆	♇
1 Sa	4 36 10	10♊03 48	5♊30 53	12♊11 19	22♑37.0	1♋49.6	23♋09.3	7♎20.2	8♌54.8	15♏43.4	9♓53.5	3♉36.4	11♍48.8	24♋26.1
2 Su	4 40 07	11 01 19	18 47 14	25 18 29	22R 32.3	2 22.4	24 15.0	7 30.7	9 17.5	15R 37.1	9 55.4	3 39.4	11 49.1	24 27.3
3 M	4 44 04	11 58 48	1♋45 03	8♋06 59	22 29.4	2 50.7	25 20.6	7 41.9	9 40.3	15 30.9	9 57.2	3 42.2	11 49.4	24 28.6
4 Tu	4 48 00	12 56 16	14 24 26	20 37 39	22D 28.4	3 14.6	26 25.9	7 53.7	10 03.2	15 24.7	9 59.0	3 45.1	11 49.8	24 29.9
5 W	4 51 57	13 53 44	26 46 56	2♌52 39	22 28.8	3 33.9	27 31.1	8 06.1	10 26.3	15 18.8	10 00.6	3 47.9	11 50.2	24 31.1
6 Th	4 55 53	14 51 10	8♌55 16	14 55 15	22 30.2	3 48.7	28 36.0	8 19.1	10 49.4	15 12.9	10 02.1	3 50.7	11 50.6	24 32.4
7 F	4 59 50	15 48 35	20 53 10	26 49 34	22 31.9	3 58.8	29 40.7	8 32.6	11 12.6	15 07.2	10 03.6	3 53.5	11 51.1	24 33.7
8 Sa	5 03 46	16 45 58	2♍45 04	8♍40 16	22R 33.1	4R 04.3	0♌45.1	8 46.7	11 36.0	15 01.5	10 04.9	3 56.3	11 51.5	24 35.1
9 Su	5 07 43	17 43 21	14 35 49	20 32 19	22 33.4	4 05.3	1 49.4	9 01.4	11 59.4	14 56.1	10 06.2	3 59.0	11 52.1	24 36.4
10 M	5 11 39	18 40 42	26 30 23	2♎30 38	22 32.4	4 01.8	2 53.4	9 16.6	12 22.9	14 50.7	10 07.3	4 01.6	11 52.6	24 37.8
11 Tu	5 15 36	19 38 03	8♎33 38	14 39 54	22 29.9	3 53.9	3 57.1	9 32.4	12 46.5	14 45.5	10 08.4	4 04.3	11 53.2	24 39.1
12 W	5 19 33	20 35 23	20 49 57	27 04 12	22 26.3	3 41.7	5 00.6	9 48.7	13 10.2	14 40.5	10 09.3	4 06.9	11 53.8	24 40.5
13 Th	5 23 29	21 32 41	3♏23 01	9♏46 41	22 21.8	3 25.6	6 03.8	10 05.5	13 34.0	14 35.6	10 10.2	4 09.5	11 54.4	24 41.9
14 F	5 27 26	22 29 59	16 15 23	22 49 15	22 17.1	3 05.7	7 06.8	10 22.7	13 57.9	14 30.8	10 10.9	4 12.1	11 55.1	24 43.3
15 Sa	5 31 22	23 27 16	29 28 16	6♐12 20	22 12.7	2 42.3	8 09.5	10 40.5	14 21.8	14 26.2	10 11.6	4 14.6	11 55.8	24 44.7
16 Su	5 35 19	24 24 33	13♐01 16	19 54 46	22 09.1	2 15.9	9 11.9	10 58.8	14 45.9	14 21.8	10 12.1	4 17.1	11 56.6	24 46.1
17 M	5 39 15	25 21 49	26 52 28	3♑53 55	22 06.8	1 46.8	10 14.0	11 17.5	15 10.0	14 17.5	10 12.6	4 19.6	11 57.3	24 47.6
18 Tu	5 43 12	26 19 04	10♑58 35	18 05 56	22D 05.8	1 15.5	11 15.8	11 36.7	15 34.2	14 13.3	10 12.9	4 22.0	11 58.2	24 49.0
19 W	5 47 08	27 16 19	25 15 24	2♒26 22	22 06.1	0 42.6	12 17.4	11 56.3	15 58.4	14 09.4	10 13.2	4 24.4	11 59.0	24 50.5
20 Th	5 51 05	28 13 34	9♒38 18	16 50 38	22 07.1	0 08.6	13 18.5	12 16.4	16 22.8	14 05.6	10 13.4	4 26.7	11 59.8	24 52.0
21 F	5 55 02	29 10 48	24 02 52	1♓14 31	22 08.5	29♊34.0	14 19.4	12 36.9	16 47.2	14 01.9	10R 13.4	4 29.1	12 00.7	24 53.5
22 Sa	5 58 58	0♋08 02	8♓25 11	15 34 28	22 09.6	28 59.5	15 20.0	12 57.8	17 11.7	13 58.4	10 13.4	4 31.3	12 01.7	24 54.9
23 Su	6 02 55	1 05 16	22 42 03	29 47 39	22R 10.1	28 25.6	16 20.2	13 19.1	17 36.3	13 55.1	10 13.2	4 33.6	12 02.6	24 56.4
24 M	6 06 51	2 02 30	6♈51 00	13♈51 55	22 09.8	27 53.0	17 20.0	13 40.9	18 01.0	13 51.9	10 13.0	4 35.8	12 03.6	24 58.0
25 Tu	6 10 48	2 59 44	20 50 12	27 45 40	22 08.5	27 22.1	18 19.5	14 03.0	18 25.7	13 48.9	10 12.7	4 38.0	12 04.6	24 59.5
26 W	6 14 44	3 56 58	4♉38 11	11♉27 36	22 06.6	26 53.6	19 18.6	14 25.6	18 50.5	13 46.1	10 12.2	4 40.1	12 05.6	25 01.0
27 Th	6 18 41	4 54 12	18 13 48	24 56 41	22 04.3	26 27.9	20 17.4	14 48.6	19 15.4	13 43.5	10 11.7	4 42.2	12 06.7	25 02.6
28 F	6 22 37	5 51 25	1♊36 08	8♊12 05	22 02.0	26 05.4	21 15.7	15 11.9	19 40.3	13 41.0	10 11.1	4 44.3	12 07.8	25 04.1
29 Sa	6 26 34	6 48 39	14 44 29	21 13 16	22 00.0	25 46.6	22 13.7	15 35.6	20 05.3	13 38.7	10 10.3	4 46.3	12 08.9	25 05.7
30 Su	6 30 31	7 45 53	27 38 27	4♋00 03	21 58.7	25 31.8	23 11.2	15 59.7	20 30.4	13 36.6	10 09.5	4 48.3	12 10.1	25 07.2

Astro Data (Dy Hr Mn)

☽0S 13 3:18
♄□♇ 15 23:42
♂D 17 21:37
♆D 24 0:16
☽0N 26 14:05

☿R 9 5:06
☽0S 9 10:33
♄R 21 14:27
☽0N 22 18:56

Planet Ingress (Dy Hr Mn)

⚳ ♌ 7 2:14
☿ ♊ 8 17:20
♀ ♋ 11 22:01
☉ ♊ 22 0:25
☿ ♋ 29 19:26

♀ ♌ 7 19:11
☿ ♊R 20 17:58
☉ ♋ 22 8:38

Last Aspect / ☽ Ingress (May)

Last Aspect Dy Hr Mn			☽ Ingress	Dy Hr Mn
1 16:04	♇	□	♉	2 2:09
3 18:56	♇	⚹	♊	4 5:26
5 23:01	♀	☌	♋	6 11:50
8 10:06	♇	☌	♌	8 21:55
11 9:11	♀	⚹	♍	11 10:26
13 11:04	♇	⚹	♎	13 22:48
15 21:46	♇	□	♏	16 8:54
18 9:57	☉	☍	♐	18 16:13
20 2:49	☿	☍	♑	20 21:20
22 15:17	♇	☍	♒	23 1:08
24 20:18	☿	△	♓	25 4:13
27 3:03	☿	□	♈	27 6:59
29 9:25	☿	⚹	♉	29 9:59
31 4:18	♇	⚹	♊	31 14:11

Last Aspect / ☽ Ingress (June)

Last Aspect Dy Hr Mn			☽ Ingress	Dy Hr Mn
1 11:19	♆	□	♋	2 20:43
5 0:25	♀	☌	♌	5 6:19
6 12:35	♃	□	♍	7 18:26
9 20:12	♇	⚹	♎	10 7:00
12 7:24	♇	□	♏	12 17:35
14 15:27	♇	△	♐	15 0:57
16 20:20	☉	☍	♑	17 5:21
18 23:17	♇	☍	♒	19 7:56
21 9:19	☿	△	♓	21 9:56
23 9:46	☿	□	♈	23 12:21
25 11:20	☿	⚹	♉	25 15:54
27 12:11	♇	⚹	♊	27 21:06
29 20:20	☿	☌	♋	30 4:26

☽ Phases & Eclipses (Dy Hr Mn)

2 21:36 ● 11♉33
10 11:54 ☽ 18♌54
18 9:57 ○ 26♏32
25 9:44 ☾ 3♓15

1 7:52 ● 9♊54
9 5:49 ☽ 17♍29
16 20:20 ○ 24♐44
23 14:21 ☾ 1♈11
30 19:44 ● 8♋04
30 19:59:17 ● P 0.338

Astro Data

1 May 1935
Julian Day # 12904
SVP 6♓09'32"
GC 25♐56.2 ⚴ 20♊54.1
Eris 3♈25.8 ⚵ 20♓46.0
⚷ 7♊52.2 ⚶ 1♓30.4
☽ Mean ☊ 25♑52.2

1 June 1935
Julian Day # 12935
SVP 6♓09'27"
GC 25♐56.2 ⚴ 9♋03.7
Eris 3♈40.5 ⚵ 3♈56.2
⚷ 10♊17.1 ⚶ 12♓37.0
☽ Mean ☊ 24♑13.7

July 1935 — LONGITUDE

Day	Sid.Time	☉	0 hr ☽	Noon☽	True☊	☿	♀	♂	⚳	♃	♄	♅	♆	♇
1 M	6 34 27	8♋43 07	10♋18 08	16♋32 47	21♑58.1	25♊21.3	24♌08.3	16♎24.2	20♌55.5	13♏34.7	10♓08.6	4♉50.2	12♍11.3	25♋08.8
2 Tu	6 38 24	9 40 20	22 44 09	28 52 24	21D58.1	25D15.3	25 05.0	16 49.0	21 20.8	13R32.9	10R07.6	4 52.1	12 12.5	25 10.4
3 W	6 42 20	10 37 34	4♌57 47	11♌00 33	21 58.7	25 14.0	26 01.1	17 14.2	21 46.0	13 31.4	10 06.4	4 54.0	12 13.7	25 12.0
4 Th	6 46 17	11 34 47	17 01 00	22 59 32	21 59.6	25 17.6	26 56.8	17 39.7	22 11.3	13 30.0	10 05.2	4 55.8	12 15.0	25 13.5
5 F	6 50 13	12 31 59	28 56 30	4♍52 22	22 00.6	25 26.2	27 52.0	18 05.5	22 36.7	13 28.8	10 03.9	4 57.5	12 16.3	25 15.1
6 Sa	6 54 10	13 29 12	10♍47 35	16 42 40	22 01.4	25 39.8	28 46.7	18 31.7	23 02.2	13 27.7	10 02.5	4 59.3	12 17.6	25 16.7
7 Su	6 58 06	14 26 24	22 38 07	28 34 31	22 02.1	25 58.5	29 40.8	18 58.2	23 27.7	13 26.9	10 01.0	5 00.9	12 18.9	25 18.3
8 M	7 02 03	15 23 37	4♎32 24	10♎32 21	22R02.3	26 22.2	0♍34.4	19 25.1	23 53.2	13 26.2	9 59.4	5 02.6	12 20.3	25 19.9
9 Tu	7 06 00	16 20 49	16 34 56	22 40 44	22 02.3	26 51.1	1 27.4	19 52.2	24 18.8	13 25.8	9 57.7	5 04.2	12 21.7	25 21.5
10 W	7 09 56	17 18 01	28 50 18	5♏04 09	22 02.1	27 25.1	2 19.8	20 19.7	24 44.5	13 25.4	9 55.9	5 05.7	12 23.1	25 23.2
11 Th	7 13 53	18 15 13	11♏22 46	17 46 35	22 01.7	28 04.2	3 11.6	20 47.4	25 10.2	13D25.3	9 54.0	5 07.3	12 24.5	25 24.8
12 F	7 17 49	19 12 25	24 15 57	0♐51 11	22 01.4	28 48.3	4 02.7	21 15.5	25 36.0	13 25.4	9 52.1	5 08.7	12 26.0	25 26.4
13 Sa	7 21 46	20 09 37	7♐32 27	14 19 50	22 01.1	29 37.3	4 53.2	21 43.8	26 01.8	13 25.6	9 50.0	5 10.1	12 27.5	25 28.0
14 Su	7 25 42	21 06 49	21 13 16	28 12 35	22D01.0	0♋31.3	5 43.0	22 12.4	26 27.7	13 26.1	9 47.9	5 11.5	12 29.0	25 29.7
15 M	7 29 39	22 04 02	5♑17 29	12♑27 31	22R01.0	1 30.1	6 32.0	22 41.3	26 53.6	13 26.7	9 45.7	5 12.9	12 30.6	25 31.3
16 Tu	7 33 36	23 01 14	19 42 05	27 00 30	22 01.0	2 33.7	7 20.3	23 10.5	27 19.5	13 27.5	9 43.4	5 14.1	12 32.1	25 32.9
17 W	7 37 32	23 58 27	4♒21 58	11♒45 38	22 00.9	3 42.1	8 07.9	23 39.9	27 45.6	13 28.4	9 41.0	5 15.4	12 33.7	25 34.5
18 Th	7 41 29	24 55 41	19 10 32	26 35 47	22 00.7	4 55.1	8 54.6	24 09.6	28 11.6	13 29.6	9 38.5	5 16.6	12 35.3	25 36.2
19 F	7 45 25	25 52 55	4♓00 27	11♓23 40	22 00.4	6 12.8	9 40.5	24 39.5	28 37.7	13 30.9	9 35.9	5 17.7	12 37.0	25 37.8
20 Sa	7 49 22	26 50 10	18 44 38	26 02 38	21 59.9	7 34.8	10 25.5	25 09.7	29 03.8	13 32.4	9 33.3	5 18.8	12 38.6	25 39.4
21 Su	7 53 18	27 47 25	3♈17 07	10♈27 34	21 59.5	9 01.3	11 09.7	25 40.2	29 30.0	13 34.0	9 30.5	5 19.9	12 40.3	25 41.1
22 M	7 57 15	28 44 41	17 33 39	24 35 07	21D59.3	10 32.1	11 52.9	26 10.9	29 56.2	13 35.9	9 27.7	5 20.9	12 42.0	25 42.7
23 Tu	8 01 11	29 41 59	1♉31 49	8♉23 42	21 59.4	12 06.9	12 35.2	26 41.8	0♍22.5	13 37.9	9 24.8	5 21.9	12 43.7	25 44.3
24 W	8 05 08	0♌39 17	15 10 50	21 53 17	21 59.8	13 45.7	13 16.4	27 13.0	0 48.8	13 40.1	9 21.9	5 22.8	12 45.4	25 46.0
25 Th	8 09 05	1 36 36	28 31 13	5♊04 49	22 00.5	15 28.3	13 56.7	27 44.4	1 15.2	13 42.5	9 18.8	5 23.6	12 47.2	25 47.6
26 F	8 13 01	2 33 56	11♊34 17	17 59 51	22 01.5	17 14.4	14 35.9	28 16.1	1 41.6	13 45.0	9 15.7	5 24.5	12 49.0	25 49.2
27 Sa	8 16 58	3 31 17	24 21 45	0♋40 13	22 02.4	19 03.7	15 14.0	28 48.0	2 08.0	13 47.8	9 12.5	5 25.2	12 50.8	25 50.8
28 Su	8 20 54	4 28 39	6♋55 30	13 07 48	22R03.0	20 56.1	15 50.9	29 20.1	2 34.5	13 50.6	9 09.3	5 25.9	12 52.6	25 52.5
29 M	8 24 51	5 26 01	19 17 22	25 24 23	22 03.1	22 51.3	16 26.7	29 52.5	3 01.0	13 53.7	9 05.9	5 26.6	12 54.4	25 54.1
30 Tu	8 28 47	6 23 25	1♌29 06	7♌31 43	22 02.6	24 48.8	17 01.2	0♏25.1	3 27.6	13 56.9	9 02.5	5 27.2	12 56.3	25 55.7
31 W	8 32 44	7 20 49	13 32 27	19 31 33	22 01.3	26 48.3	17 34.4	0 57.9	3 54.2	14 00.4	8 59.1	5 27.8	12 58.2	25 57.3

August 1935 — LONGITUDE

Day	Sid.Time	☉	0 hr ☽	Noon☽	True☊	☿	♀	♂	⚳	♃	♄	♅	♆	♇
1 Th	8 36 40	8♌18 14	25♌29 14	1♍25 46	21♑59.3	28♋49.6	18♍06.2	1♏30.9	4♍20.8	14♏03.9	8♓55.5	5♉28.3	13♍00.1	25♋58.9
2 F	8 40 37	9 15 39	7♍21 26	13 16 32	21R56.7	0♌52.3	18 36.7	2 04.1	4 47.4	14 07.7	8R51.9	5 28.8	13 02.0	26 00.5
3 Sa	8 44 34	10 13 06	19 11 24	25 06 24	21 53.9	2 55.9	19 05.7	2 37.6	5 14.1	14 11.6	8 48.3	5 29.2	13 03.9	26 02.1
4 Su	8 48 30	11 10 33	1♎01 54	6♎58 20	21 51.2	5 00.3	19 33.1	3 11.2	5 40.8	14 15.6	8 44.5	5 29.6	13 05.8	26 03.7
5 M	8 52 27	12 08 01	12 56 08	18 55 48	21 49.0	7 05.0	19 59.1	3 45.1	6 07.6	14 19.9	8 40.7	5 29.9	13 07.8	26 05.3
6 Tu	8 56 23	13 05 29	24 57 48	1♏02 41	21 47.5	9 09.8	20 23.4	4 19.2	6 34.4	14 24.3	8 36.9	5 30.2	13 09.7	26 06.8
7 W	9 00 20	14 02 59	7♏10 57	13 23 10	21D47.0	11 14.5	20 46.0	4 53.4	7 01.2	14 28.8	8 33.0	5 30.4	13 11.7	26 08.4
8 Th	9 04 16	15 00 29	19 39 52	26 01 32	21 47.4	13 18.7	21 06.8	5 27.9	7 28.0	14 33.5	8 29.1	5 30.6	13 13.7	26 10.0
9 F	9 08 13	15 58 00	2♐28 41	9♐01 44	21 48.5	15 22.3	21 25.8	6 02.5	7 54.9	14 38.4	8 25.1	5 30.7	13 15.7	26 11.5
10 Sa	9 12 09	16 55 32	15 41 05	22 26 59	21 50.0	17 25.1	21 43.0	6 37.3	8 21.8	14 43.5	8 21.0	5 30.8	13 17.8	26 13.1
11 Su	9 16 06	17 53 05	29 19 38	6♑19 04	21 51.3	19 26.9	21 58.2	7 12.3	8 48.7	14 48.6	8 16.9	5R30.9	13 19.8	26 14.6
12 M	9 20 03	18 50 39	13♑25 12	20 37 44	21R51.9	21 27.7	22 11.5	7 47.5	9 15.6	14 54.0	8 12.8	5 30.8	13 21.9	26 16.1
13 Tu	9 23 59	19 48 13	27 56 14	5♒20 02	21 51.4	23 27.4	22 22.7	8 22.9	9 42.6	14 59.5	8 08.6	5 30.8	13 23.9	26 17.7
14 W	9 27 56	20 45 49	12♒48 21	20 20 10	21 49.5	25 25.8	22 31.7	8 58.4	10 09.6	15 05.1	8 04.4	5 30.7	13 26.0	26 19.2
15 Th	9 31 52	21 43 26	27 54 24	5♓29 50	21 46.3	27 22.9	22 38.6	9 34.1	10 36.6	15 10.9	8 00.2	5 30.5	13 28.1	26 20.7
16 F	9 35 49	22 41 05	13♓05 13	20 39 17	21 42.3	29 18.6	22 43.3	10 10.0	11 03.6	15 16.8	7 55.9	5 30.3	13 30.2	26 22.2
17 Sa	9 39 45	23 38 44	28 10 52	5♈38 52	21 37.9	1♍13.0	22R45.8	10 46.0	11 30.7	15 22.9	7 51.6	5 30.0	13 32.3	26 23.7
18 Su	9 43 42	24 36 26	13♈02 21	20 20 33	21 33.9	3 06.0	22 45.9	11 22.2	11 57.7	15 29.1	7 47.2	5 29.7	13 34.4	26 25.1
19 M	9 47 38	25 34 08	27 32 53	4♉38 57	21 31.0	4 57.6	22 43.8	11 58.6	12 24.8	15 35.5	7 42.8	5 29.3	13 36.6	26 26.6
20 Tu	9 51 35	26 31 53	11♉38 34	18 31 39	21D29.3	6 47.8	22 39.3	12 35.2	12 52.0	15 42.0	7 38.4	5 28.9	13 38.7	26 28.0
21 W	9 55 32	27 29 39	25 18 19	1♊58 47	21 29.1	8 36.6	22 32.4	13 11.9	13 19.1	15 48.7	7 34.0	5 28.5	13 40.9	26 29.5
22 Th	9 59 28	28 27 27	8♊33 22	15 02 26	21 30.1	10 24.1	22 23.2	13 48.7	13 46.3	15 55.4	7 29.5	5 28.0	13 43.0	26 30.9
23 F	10 03 25	29 25 17	21 26 25	27 45 47	21 31.6	12 10.1	22 11.6	14 25.8	14 13.5	16 02.4	7 25.0	5 27.4	13 45.2	26 32.3
24 Sa	10 07 21	0♍23 09	4♋01 00	10♋12 31	21R33.0	13 54.8	21 57.7	15 03.0	14 40.7	16 09.4	7 20.5	5 26.8	13 47.3	26 33.7
25 Su	10 11 18	1 21 02	16 20 49	22 26 18	21 33.5	15 38.1	21 41.4	15 40.3	15 07.9	16 16.6	7 16.0	5 26.2	13 49.5	26 35.1
26 M	10 15 14	2 18 57	28 29 24	4♌30 28	21 32.6	17 20.1	21 22.8	16 17.8	15 35.1	16 24.0	7 11.4	5 25.5	13 51.7	26 36.5
27 Tu	10 19 11	3 16 53	10♌29 52	16 27 53	21 29.8	19 00.8	21 02.0	16 55.5	16 02.4	16 31.4	7 06.9	5 24.7	13 53.9	26 37.9
28 W	10 23 07	4 14 51	22 24 51	28 20 59	21 24.9	20 40.2	20 39.1	17 33.3	16 29.7	16 39.0	7 02.3	5 23.9	13 56.1	26 39.2
29 Th	10 27 04	5 12 51	4♍16 32	10♍11 45	21 18.2	22 18.2	20 14.0	18 11.3	16 56.9	16 46.8	6 57.8	5 23.1	13 58.3	26 40.6
30 F	10 31 01	6 10 52	16 06 50	22 01 59	21 10.1	23 55.0	19 47.0	18 49.4	17 24.2	16 54.6	6 53.2	5 22.2	14 00.5	26 41.9
31 Sa	10 34 57	7 08 54	27 57 27	3♎53 27	21 01.3	25 30.5	19 18.2	19 27.7	17 51.6	17 02.6	6 48.6	5 21.3	14 02.7	26 43.2

Astro Data	Dy Hr Mn
♄⚼♇	1 9:58
☿ D	3 6:24
☽0S	6 17:54
♃ D	11 15:39
☽0N	20 1:27
☽0S	3 0:59
♀0S	8 6:21
♅ R	11 15:49
☽0N	16 10:33
♀ R	18 1:41
☽0S	30 7:31

Planet Ingress		Dy Hr Mn
♀	♍	7 20:33
☿	♋	13 22:22
⚳	♍	22 15:26
☉	♌	23 19:33
♂	♏	29 17:32
☿	♌	2 1:48
☿	♍	16 20:39
☉	♍	24 2:24

Last Aspect Dy Hr Mn			☽ Ingress	Dy Hr Mn
2 4:44	♇	☌	♌	2 14:13
4 20:39	♀	☌	♍	5 2:08
7 6:36	☿	□	♎	7 14:52
9 20:31	☿	△	♏	10 2:15
12 2:08	♇	△	♐	12 10:27
14 1:20	♂	⚹	♑	14 15:03
16 9:36	♇	☍	♒	16 16:53
18 7:55	♂	△	♓	18 17:30
20 13:24	☉	△	♈	20 18:33
22 19:42	☉	□	♉	22 21:21
24 19:01	♇	⚹	♊	25 2:42
27 8:16	♂	△	♋	27 10:43
29 12:59	♇	☌	♌	29 21:04

Last Aspect Dy Hr Mn			☽ Ingress	Dy Hr Mn
31 0:53	♃	□	♍	1 9:07
3 13:53	♇	⚹	♎	3 21:55
6 2:15	♇	□	♏	6 9:57
8 12:16	♇	△	♐	8 19:25
10 10:41	♀	□	♑	11 1:10
12 21:17	♇	☍	♒	13 3:22
14 21:17	☿	☍	♓	15 3:19
16 21:07	♇	△	♈	17 2:55
18 22:08	♇	□	♉	19 4:07
21 3:17	☉	□	♊	21 8:25
23 15:26	☉	⚹	♋	23 16:17
25 20:14	♇	☌	♌	26 3:00
27 12:59	♂	□	♍	28 15:20
30 21:28	♇	⚹	♎	31 4:08

☽ Phases & Eclipses Dy Hr Mn		
8 22:28	☽	15♎49
16 5:00	○	22♑45
16 5:00	•	T 1.754
22 19:42	☾	29♈03
30 9:32	●	6♌18
30 9:16:04	•	P 0.232
7 13:23	☽	14♏06
14 12:43	○	20♒48
21 3:17	☾	27♉09
29 1:00	●	4♍46

Astro Data

1 July 1935
Julian Day # 12965
SVP 6♓09'21"
GC 25♐56.3 ⚴ 26♋30.4
Eris 3♈45.4R ⚵ 15♈38.0
⚷ 12♊38.8 ⚶ 19♓37.8
☽ Mean ☊ 22♑38.4

1 August 1935
Julian Day # 12996
SVP 6♓09'16"
GC 25♐56.4 ⚴ 13♌58.1
Eris 3♈39.9R ⚵ 25♈33.1
⚷ 14♊42.8 ⚶ 20♓52.2R
☽ Mean ☊ 20♑59.9

LONGITUDE — September 1935

Day	Sid.Time	☉	0 hr ☽	Noon ☽	True ☊	☿	♀	♂	⚳	♃	♄	♅	♆	♇
1 Su	10 38 54	8♍06 59	9♎50 15	15♎48 05	20♑52.7	27♍04.7	18♍47.6	20♏06.1	18♍18.9	17♏10.7	6♓44.1	5♉20.3	14♍04.9	26♋44.5
2 M	10 42 50	9 05 04	21 47 17	27 48 10	20R 45.0	28 37.6	18R 15.5	20 44.6	18 46.2	17 18.9	6R 39.5	5R 19.3	14 07.2	26 45.8
3 Tu	10 46 47	10 03 12	3♏51 06	9♏56 28	20 39.0	0♎09.3	17 42.1	21 23.3	19 13.6	17 27.3	6 34.9	5 18.2	14 09.4	26 47.0
4 W	10 50 43	11 01 20	16 04 43	22 16 18	20 35.1	1 39.7	17 07.4	22 02.2	19 40.9	17 35.7	6 30.4	5 17.1	14 11.6	26 48.3
5 Th	10 54 40	11 59 31	28 31 41	4♐51 23	20D 33.2	3 08.9	16 31.8	22 41.1	20 08.3	17 44.3	6 25.8	5 15.9	14 13.8	26 49.5
6 F	10 58 36	12 57 42	11♐15 53	17 45 42	20 33.0	4 36.8	15 55.5	23 20.3	20 35.6	17 53.0	6 21.3	5 14.7	14 16.1	26 50.7
7 Sa	11 02 33	13 55 55	24 21 17	1♑03 03	20 33.9	6 03.4	15 18.6	23 59.5	21 03.0	18 01.8	6 16.8	5 13.5	14 18.3	26 51.9
8 Su	11 06 30	14 54 10	7♑51 22	14 46 28	20R 34.7	7 28.6	14 41.5	24 38.9	21 30.4	18 10.8	6 12.3	5 12.2	14 20.5	26 53.1
9 M	11 10 26	15 52 26	21 48 30	28 57 25	20 34.5	8 52.6	14 04.3	25 18.4	21 57.8	18 19.8	6 07.9	5 10.9	14 22.7	26 54.3
10 Tu	11 14 23	16 50 44	6♒13 01	13♒34 54	20 32.5	10 15.2	13 27.3	25 58.0	22 25.2	18 29.0	6 03.4	5 09.5	14 25.0	26 55.4
11 W	11 18 19	17 49 03	21 02 26	28 34 46	20 28.2	11 36.4	12 50.8	26 37.8	22 52.6	18 38.2	5 59.0	5 08.1	14 27.2	26 56.5
12 Th	11 22 16	18 47 24	6♓10 51	13♓49 28	20 21.6	12 56.2	12 15.0	27 17.6	23 20.0	18 47.6	5 54.6	5 06.7	14 29.4	26 57.6
13 F	11 26 12	19 45 47	21 29 15	29 08 48	20 13.3	14 14.6	11 40.1	27 57.6	23 47.4	18 57.0	5 50.2	5 05.2	14 31.6	26 58.7
14 Sa	11 30 09	20 44 11	6♈46 38	14♈21 25	20 04.2	15 31.4	11 06.4	28 37.7	24 14.8	19 06.6	5 45.9	5 03.6	14 33.8	26 59.8
15 Su	11 34 05	21 42 38	21 51 54	29 16 59	19 55.6	16 46.6	10 34.0	29 18.0	24 42.2	19 16.3	5 41.6	5 02.1	14 36.1	27 00.8
16 M	11 38 02	22 41 07	6♉35 49	13♉47 45	19 48.5	18 00.3	10 03.2	29 58.3	25 09.7	19 26.1	5 37.3	5 00.5	14 38.3	27 01.9
17 Tu	11 41 58	23 39 38	20 52 24	27 49 34	19 43.5	19 12.2	9 34.1	0♐38.8	25 37.1	19 35.9	5 33.1	4 58.8	14 40.5	27 02.9
18 W	11 45 55	24 38 11	4♊39 16	11♊21 42	19 40.7	20 22.2	9 06.9	1 19.4	26 04.5	19 45.9	5 28.9	4 57.2	14 42.7	27 03.9
19 Th	11 49 52	25 36 47	17 57 11	24 26 10	19D 39.9	21 30.4	8 41.7	2 00.1	26 31.9	19 56.0	5 24.7	4 55.4	14 44.9	27 04.8
20 F	11 53 48	26 35 24	0♋49 10	7♋06 46	19 40.2	22 36.6	8 18.6	2 41.0	26 59.4	20 06.1	5 20.6	4 53.7	14 47.1	27 05.8
21 Sa	11 57 45	27 34 04	13 19 34	19 28 11	19R 40.5	23 40.6	7 57.7	3 21.9	27 26.8	20 16.4	5 16.6	4 51.9	14 49.3	27 06.7
22 Su	12 01 41	28 32 46	25 33 14	1♌35 19	19 39.9	24 42.3	7 39.1	4 03.0	27 54.2	20 26.8	5 12.6	4 50.1	14 51.4	27 07.6
23 M	12 05 38	29 31 31	7♌34 59	13 32 47	19 37.2	25 41.5	7 22.9	4 44.2	28 21.6	20 37.2	5 08.6	4 48.2	14 53.6	27 08.5
24 Tu	12 09 34	0♎30 17	19 29 12	25 24 40	19 32.0	26 38.1	7 09.0	5 25.5	28 49.1	20 47.7	5 04.7	4 46.3	14 55.8	27 09.4
25 W	12 13 31	1 29 05	1♍19 35	7♍14 18	19 23.9	27 31.8	6 57.6	6 06.9	29 16.5	20 58.4	5 00.8	4 44.4	14 57.9	27 10.2
26 Th	12 17 27	2 27 56	13 09 09	19 04 22	19 13.2	28 22.4	6 48.6	6 48.4	29 43.9	21 09.1	4 57.0	4 42.5	15 00.1	27 11.0
27 F	12 21 24	3 26 49	25 00 11	0♎56 48	19 00.5	29 09.7	6 42.0	7 30.1	0♎11.3	21 19.9	4 53.3	4 40.5	15 02.2	27 11.8
28 Sa	12 25 21	4 25 43	6♎54 24	12 53 08	18 46.7	29 53.3	6 37.8	8 11.8	0 38.7	21 30.8	4 49.6	4 38.5	15 04.4	27 12.6
29 Su	12 29 17	5 24 40	18 53 10	24 54 37	18 33.0	0♏33.0	6D 36.1	8 53.7	1 06.1	21 41.7	4 46.0	4 36.4	15 06.5	27 13.4
30 M	12 33 14	6 23 38	0♏57 39	7♏02 27	18 20.6	1 08.5	6 36.7	9 35.6	1 33.5	21 52.8	4 42.5	4 34.4	15 08.6	27 14.1

LONGITUDE — October 1935

Day	Sid.Time	☉	0 hr ☽	Noon ☽	True ☊	☿	♀	♂	⚳	♃	♄	♅	♆	♇
1 Tu	12 37 10	7♎22 39	13♏09 14	19♏18 12	18♑10.4	1♏39.2	6♍39.6	10♐17.7	2♎00.9	22♏03.9	4♓39.0	4♉32.3	15♍10.7	27♋14.8
2 W	12 41 07	8 21 42	25 29 37	1♐43 48	18R 03.0	2 04.9	6 44.9	10 59.9	2 28.3	22 15.1	4R 35.6	4R 30.2	15 12.8	27 15.5
3 Th	12 45 03	9 20 46	8♐01 05	14 21 49	17 58.5	2 25.2	6 52.3	11 42.1	2 55.6	22 26.4	4 32.3	4 28.0	15 14.9	27 16.2
4 F	12 49 00	10 19 52	20 46 25	27 15 18	17 56.5	2 39.5	7 02.0	12 24.5	3 23.0	22 37.7	4 29.0	4 25.8	15 16.9	27 16.8
5 Sa	12 52 56	11 19 00	3♑48 53	10♑27 35	17 56.0	2R 47.5	7 13.9	13 07.0	3 50.3	22 49.2	4 25.8	4 23.7	15 19.0	27 17.4
6 Su	12 56 53	12 18 10	17 11 46	24 01 48	17 56.0	2 48.6	7 27.8	13 49.5	4 17.6	23 00.7	4 22.7	4 21.4	15 21.0	27 18.0
7 M	13 00 50	13 17 21	0♒57 53	8♒00 12	17 55.1	2 42.5	7 43.8	14 32.2	4 44.9	23 12.3	4 19.7	4 19.2	15 23.0	27 18.6
8 Tu	13 04 46	14 16 34	15 08 44	22 23 19	17 52.2	2 28.7	8 01.7	15 15.0	5 12.2	23 23.9	4 16.7	4 16.9	15 25.1	27 19.1
9 W	13 08 43	15 15 49	29 43 36	7♓09 00	17 46.6	2 07.0	8 21.6	15 57.8	5 39.5	23 35.6	4 13.8	4 14.7	15 27.1	27 19.6
10 Th	13 12 39	16 15 05	14♓38 46	22 11 54	17 38.3	1 37.1	8 43.4	16 40.7	6 06.8	23 47.4	4 11.0	4 12.4	15 29.0	27 20.1
11 F	13 16 36	17 14 24	29 47 15	7♈23 32	17 27.8	0 59.0	9 06.9	17 23.7	6 34.0	23 59.2	4 08.3	4 10.0	15 31.0	27 20.6
12 Sa	13 20 32	18 13 44	14♈59 22	22 33 23	17 16.4	0 12.8	9 32.2	18 06.9	7 01.2	24 11.1	4 05.7	4 07.7	15 32.9	27 21.1
13 Su	13 24 29	19 13 07	0♉04 15	7♉30 44	17 05.2	29♎19.2	9 59.2	18 50.1	7 28.5	24 23.1	4 03.2	4 05.4	15 34.9	27 21.5
14 M	13 28 25	20 12 32	14 51 48	22 06 35	16 55.6	28 18.6	10 27.9	19 33.3	7 55.6	24 35.1	4 00.7	4 03.0	15 36.8	27 21.9
15 Tu	13 32 22	21 11 59	29 14 29	6♊15 03	16 48.5	27 12.4	10 58.1	20 16.7	8 22.8	24 47.2	3 58.3	4 00.6	15 38.7	27 22.2
16 W	13 36 19	22 11 29	13♊08 09	19 53 47	16 44.0	26 01.8	11 29.9	21 00.2	8 50.0	24 59.3	3 56.1	3 58.2	15 40.6	27 22.6
17 Th	13 40 15	23 11 00	26 32 09	3♋03 35	16 42.0	24 48.5	12 03.1	21 43.7	9 17.1	25 11.5	3 53.9	3 55.8	15 42.4	27 22.9
18 F	13 44 12	24 10 34	9♋28 34	15 47 37	16 41.5	23 34.7	12 37.8	22 27.4	9 44.2	25 23.8	3 51.8	3 53.4	15 44.3	27 23.2
19 Sa	13 48 08	25 10 11	22 01 23	28 10 28	16 41.5	22 22.4	13 13.8	23 11.1	10 11.3	25 36.1	3 49.8	3 51.0	15 46.1	27 23.5
20 Su	13 52 05	26 09 49	4♌15 35	10♌17 24	16 40.8	21 13.8	13 51.2	23 54.9	10 38.4	25 48.5	3 47.9	3 48.6	15 47.9	27 23.7
21 M	13 56 01	27 09 30	16 16 33	22 13 42	16 38.4	20 11.0	14 29.8	24 38.8	11 05.5	26 00.9	3 46.1	3 46.1	15 49.7	27 24.0
22 Tu	13 59 58	28 09 13	28 09 27	4♍04 21	16 33.4	19 15.7	15 09.6	25 22.7	11 32.5	26 13.4	3 44.3	3 43.7	15 51.5	27 24.1
23 W	14 03 54	29 08 58	9♍58 58	15 53 44	16 25.6	18 29.6	15 50.6	26 06.8	11 59.5	26 25.9	3 42.7	3 41.2	15 53.2	27 24.3
24 Th	14 07 51	0♏08 45	21 49 05	27 45 23	16 15.1	17 53.8	16 32.7	26 50.9	12 26.5	26 38.4	3 41.2	3 38.8	15 54.9	27 24.5
25 F	14 11 47	1 08 35	3♎42 58	9♎42 05	16 02.5	17 29.0	17 15.9	27 35.1	12 53.4	26 51.1	3 39.8	3 36.3	15 56.6	27 24.6
26 Sa	14 15 44	2 08 26	15 42 56	21 45 42	15 48.9	17D 15.7	18 00.1	28 19.4	13 20.4	27 03.7	3 38.4	3 33.8	15 58.3	27 24.7
27 Su	14 19 41	3 08 20	27 50 30	3♏57 26	15 35.2	17 13.7	18 45.4	29 03.8	13 47.2	27 16.4	3 37.2	3 31.4	16 00.0	27 24.7
28 M	14 23 37	4 08 15	10♏06 36	16 18 02	15 22.8	17 22.8	19 31.6	29 48.2	14 14.1	27 29.2	3 36.1	3 28.9	16 01.6	27 24.8
29 Tu	14 27 34	5 08 13	22 31 48	28 47 58	15 12.6	17 42.5	20 18.7	0♑32.7	14 40.9	27 42.0	3 35.0	3 26.4	16 03.2	27R 24.8
30 W	14 31 30	6 08 12	5♐06 36	11♐27 49	15 05.2	18 12.1	21 06.7	1 17.3	15 07.7	27 54.8	3 34.1	3 24.0	16 04.8	27 24.8
31 Th	14 35 27	7 08 13	17 51 44	24 18 31	15 00.7	18 50.7	21 55.6	2 02.0	15 34.5	28 07.7	3 33.3	3 21.5	16 06.3	27 24.7

Astro Data

	Dy Hr Mn
☿0S	3 6:47
☽0N	12 21:25
♀0N	16 1:21
☉0S	23 23:38
☽0S	26 13:33
♀D	29 17:46
☿R	6 3:53
♄✶♅	8 4:00
☽0N	10 8:04
♄✶♅	21 14:44
☽0S	23 19:29
☿D	27 4:09
♃△♇	28 3:41
♇R	29 14:18

Planet Ingress

		Dy Hr Mn
☿	♎	3 9:33
♂	♐	16 12:59
☉	♎	23 23:38
⚳	♎	27 2:06
☿	♏	28 15:52
☿	♎R	12 18:03
☉	♏	24 8:29
♂	♑	28 18:22

Last Aspect / ☽ Ingress (September)

Last Aspect Dy Hr Mn			☽ Ingress	Dy Hr Mn
2 9:56	♇	□	♏	2 16:22
4 20:43	♇	△	♐	5 2:48
6 8:46	♀	□	♑	7 10:08
9 8:34	♇	☍	♒	9 13:44
11 8:46	♂	□	♓	11 14:15
13 10:03	♂	△	♈	13 13:20
15 8:19	♇	□	♉	15 13:10
17 10:39	♇	✶	♊	17 15:48
19 14:23	☉	□	♋	19 22:27
22 5:24	☉	✶	♌	22 8:50
24 14:41	☿	✶	♍	24 21:18
27 4:26	♇	✶	♎	27 10:05
29 16:36	♇	□	♏	29 22:06

Last Aspect / ☽ Ingress (October)

Last Aspect Dy Hr Mn			☽ Ingress	Dy Hr Mn
2 3:24	♇	△	♐	2 8:41
3 13:40	♆	□	♑	4 17:02
6 17:41	♇	☍	♒	6 22:20
8 13:41	♃	□	♓	9 0:27
10 20:08	♇	△	♈	11 0:20
12 23:34	☿	☍	♉	12 23:53
14 20:50	♇	✶	♊	15 1:17
16 22:09	☿	△	♋	17 6:21
19 10:28	♇	☌	♌	19 15:35
21 22:53	☉	✶	♍	22 3:44
24 11:18	♇	✶	♎	24 16:31
27 1:47	♂	✶	♏	27 4:15
29 9:52	♃	☌	♐	29 14:17
31 7:17	♀	□	♑	31 22:31

☽ Phases & Eclipses

Dy Hr Mn		
6 2:26	☽	12♐35
12 20:18	○	19♓08
19 14:23	☾	25♊43
27 17:29	●	3♎40
5 13:39	☽	11♑23
12 4:39	○	17♈56
19 5:36	☾	24♋54
27 10:15	●	3♏04

Astro Data

1 September 1935
Julian Day # 13027
SVP 6♓09'13"
GC 25♐56.4 ⚴ 0♍37.5
Eris 3♈25.1R ⚵ 1♉14.2
⚷ 16♊01.4 ⚶ 15♓15.6R
☽ Mean ☊ 19♑21.4

1 October 1935
Julian Day # 13057
SVP 6♓09'10"
GC 25♐56.5 ⚴ 15♍50.7
Eris 3♈06.2R ⚵ 0♉10.7R
⚷ 16♊17.5R ⚶ 8♓31.6R
☽ Mean ☊ 17♑46.1

November 1935 — LONGITUDE

Day	Sid.Time	☉	0 hr ☽	Noon ☽	True ☊	☿	♀	♂	⚳	♃	♄	♅	♆	♇
1 F	14 39 23	8♏08 16	0♑48 21	7♑21 26	14♑58.8	19♎37.6	22♍45.3	2♑46.7	16♎01.2	28♏20.6	3♓32.6	3♉19.1	16♍07.9	27♋24.7
2 Sa	14 43 20	9 08 20	13 58 01	20 38 21	14D 58.7	20 31.8	23 35.8	3 31.5	16 27.9	28 33.5	3R 32.0	3R 16.6	16 09.4	27R 24.6
3 Su	14 47 17	10 08 26	27 22 41	4♒11 15	14R 59.2	21 32.5	24 27.0	4 16.4	16 54.6	28 46.5	3 31.5	3 14.2	16 10.9	27 24.5
4 M	14 51 13	11 08 34	11♒04 15	18 01 48	14 59.1	22 38.9	25 19.0	5 01.3	17 21.2	28 59.5	3 31.1	3 11.7	16 12.3	27 24.3
5 Tu	14 55 10	12 08 43	25 03 59	2♓10 43	14 57.3	23 50.1	26 11.8	5 46.3	17 47.8	29 12.5	3 30.7	3 09.3	16 13.8	27 24.2
6 W	14 59 06	13 08 53	9♓21 51	16 37 02	14 53.3	25 05.7	27 05.2	6 31.4	18 14.3	29 25.6	3 30.5	3 06.9	16 15.2	27 24.0
7 Th	15 03 03	14 09 05	23 55 49	1♈17 32	14 46.9	26 24.8	27 59.3	7 16.5	18 40.8	29 38.7	3D 30.5	3 04.5	16 16.6	27 23.8
8 F	15 06 59	15 09 18	8♈41 24	16 06 30	14 38.5	27 47.0	28 54.0	8 01.7	19 07.2	29 51.8	3 30.5	3 02.1	16 17.9	27 23.5
9 Sa	15 10 56	16 09 33	23 31 50	0♉56 19	14 29.1	29 11.7	29 49.4	8 46.9	19 33.6	0♐05.0	3 30.6	2 59.7	16 19.2	27 23.2
10 Su	15 14 52	17 09 50	8♉18 51	15 38 23	14 19.8	0♏38.6	0♎45.4	9 32.2	20 00.0	0 18.1	3 30.8	2 57.3	16 20.5	27 23.0
11 M	15 18 49	18 10 09	22 53 57	0♊04 42	14 11.8	2 07.3	1 41.9	10 17.6	20 26.3	0 31.3	3 31.1	2 55.0	16 21.8	27 22.6
12 Tu	15 22 45	19 10 29	7♊09 56	14 09 07	14 05.8	3 37.4	2 39.1	11 03.0	20 52.6	0 44.6	3 31.6	2 52.6	16 23.0	27 22.3
13 W	15 26 42	20 10 51	21 01 54	27 48 06	14 02.2	5 08.7	3 36.8	11 48.5	21 18.8	0 57.8	3 32.1	2 50.3	16 24.3	27 21.9
14 Th	15 30 39	21 11 15	4♋27 42	11♋00 51	14D 00.9	6 41.0	4 35.0	12 34.0	21 45.0	1 11.1	3 32.7	2 48.0	16 25.4	27 21.6
15 F	15 34 35	22 11 41	17 27 50	23 49 00	14 01.2	8 14.0	5 33.7	13 19.6	22 11.2	1 24.4	3 33.5	2 45.7	16 26.6	27 21.1
16 Sa	15 38 32	23 12 09	0♌04 51	6♌15 56	14 02.4	9 47.6	6 33.0	14 05.2	22 37.2	1 37.7	3 34.3	2 43.4	16 27.7	27 20.7
17 Su	15 42 28	24 12 38	12 22 49	18 26 09	14R 03.4	11 21.7	7 32.7	14 50.9	23 03.3	1 51.0	3 35.3	2 41.2	16 28.8	27 20.2
18 M	15 46 25	25 13 10	24 26 34	0♍24 45	14 03.5	12 56.1	8 32.9	15 36.6	23 29.3	2 04.3	3 36.3	2 38.9	16 29.9	27 19.8
19 Tu	15 50 21	26 13 43	6♍21 19	12 16 55	14 01.8	14 30.8	9 33.5	16 22.4	23 55.2	2 17.7	3 37.5	2 36.7	16 30.9	27 19.2
20 W	15 54 18	27 14 17	18 12 11	24 07 39	13 58.1	16 05.6	10 34.6	17 08.2	24 21.1	2 31.0	3 38.7	2 34.5	16 31.9	27 18.7
21 Th	15 58 15	28 14 54	0♎03 54	6♎01 25	13 52.4	17 40.5	11 36.1	17 54.1	24 46.9	2 44.4	3 40.1	2 32.4	16 32.9	27 18.1
22 F	16 02 11	29 15 32	12 00 39	18 01 59	13 45.1	19 15.5	12 37.9	18 40.1	25 12.7	2 57.8	3 41.6	2 30.2	16 33.8	27 17.6
23 Sa	16 06 08	0♐16 12	24 05 46	0♏12 17	13 36.8	20 50.5	13 40.2	19 26.1	25 38.4	3 11.2	3 43.2	2 28.1	16 34.7	27 17.0
24 Su	16 10 04	1 16 54	6♏21 44	12 34 17	13 28.4	22 25.4	14 42.8	20 12.1	26 04.0	3 24.6	3 44.8	2 26.1	16 35.6	27 16.3
25 M	16 14 01	2 17 37	18 50 03	25 09 04	13 20.8	24 00.4	15 45.8	20 58.2	26 29.6	3 38.0	3 46.6	2 24.0	16 36.5	27 15.7
26 Tu	16 17 57	3 18 21	1♐31 22	7♐56 53	13 14.7	25 35.2	16 49.2	21 44.4	26 55.1	3 51.4	3 48.5	2 22.0	16 37.3	27 15.0
27 W	16 21 54	4 19 07	14 25 35	20 57 23	13 10.5	27 10.0	17 52.9	22 30.5	27 20.6	4 04.8	3 50.5	2 20.0	16 38.0	27 14.3
28 Th	16 25 50	5 19 54	27 32 12	4♑09 55	13D 08.3	28 44.7	18 56.9	23 16.8	27 46.0	4 18.2	3 52.6	2 18.0	16 38.8	27 13.6
29 F	16 29 47	6 20 42	10♑50 28	17 33 47	13 08.0	0♐19.4	20 01.2	24 03.0	28 11.3	4 31.6	3 54.8	2 16.1	16 39.5	27 12.9
30 Sa	16 33 44	7 21 31	24 19 46	1♒08 23	13 09.0	1 53.9	21 05.9	24 49.3	28 36.6	4 45.0	3 57.1	2 14.2	16 40.2	27 12.1

December 1935 — LONGITUDE

Day	Sid.Time	☉	0 hr ☽	Noon ☽	True ☊	☿	♀	♂	⚳	♃	♄	♅	♆	♇
1 Su	16 37 40	8♐22 21	7♒59 36	14♒53 22	13♑10.6	3♐28.4	22♎10.8	25♑35.7	29♎01.7	4♐58.4	3♓59.4	2♉12.4	16♍40.8	27♋11.3
2 M	16 41 37	9 23 12	21 49 40	28 48 24	13R 11.9	5 02.8	23 16.0	26 22.1	29 26.8	5 11.8	4 01.9	2R 10.5	16 41.5	27R 10.5
3 Tu	16 45 33	10 24 04	5♓49 32	12♓52 55	13 12.3	6 37.1	24 21.5	27 08.5	29 51.9	5 25.2	4 04.5	2 08.7	16 42.0	27 09.7
4 W	16 49 30	11 24 56	19 58 25	27 05 46	13 11.3	8 11.4	25 27.2	27 54.9	0♏16.8	5 38.6	4 07.2	2 07.0	16 42.6	27 08.9
5 Th	16 53 26	12 25 49	4♈14 40	11♈24 47	13 08.8	9 45.6	26 33.2	28 41.4	0 41.7	5 52.0	4 10.0	2 05.3	16 43.1	27 08.0
6 F	16 57 23	13 26 43	18 35 37	25 46 41	13 05.2	11 19.8	27 39.5	29 27.9	1 06.5	6 05.4	4 12.9	2 03.6	16 43.6	27 07.1
7 Sa	17 01 19	14 27 38	2♉57 24	10♉07 08	13 00.8	12 54.0	28 46.0	0♒14.4	1 31.2	6 18.7	4 15.8	2 01.9	16 44.0	27 06.2
8 Su	17 05 16	15 28 34	17 15 15	24 21 06	12 56.4	14 28.3	29 52.8	1 01.0	1 55.9	6 32.1	4 18.9	2 00.3	16 44.4	27 05.3
9 M	17 09 13	16 29 31	1♊24 03	8♊23 31	12 52.7	16 02.5	0♏59.8	1 47.6	2 20.5	6 45.4	4 22.1	1 58.8	16 44.8	27 04.4
10 Tu	17 13 09	17 30 28	15 18 59	22 10 01	12 50.1	17 36.8	2 07.0	2 34.2	2 44.9	6 58.7	4 25.3	1 57.2	16 45.1	27 03.4
11 W	17 17 06	18 31 26	28 56 17	5♋37 31	12D 48.7	19 11.1	3 14.4	3 20.9	3 09.3	7 12.0	4 28.7	1 55.8	16 45.4	27 02.5
12 Th	17 21 02	19 32 26	12♋13 37	18 44 32	12 48.7	20 45.5	4 22.1	4 07.5	3 33.7	7 25.3	4 32.1	1 54.3	16 45.7	27 01.5
13 F	17 24 59	20 33 26	25 10 23	1♌31 18	12 49.6	22 19.9	5 30.0	4 54.2	3 57.9	7 38.6	4 35.6	1 52.9	16 46.0	27 00.5
14 Sa	17 28 55	21 34 27	7♌47 34	13 59 33	12 51.2	23 54.5	6 38.0	5 40.9	4 22.0	7 51.9	4 39.2	1 51.6	16 46.2	26 59.4
15 Su	17 32 52	22 35 29	20 07 38	26 12 18	12 52.9	25 29.2	7 46.3	6 27.7	4 46.1	8 05.1	4 42.9	1 50.3	16 46.3	26 58.4
16 M	17 36 48	23 36 32	2♍14 04	8♍13 29	12 54.3	27 04.0	8 54.8	7 14.4	5 10.0	8 18.3	4 46.7	1 49.0	16 46.5	26 57.4
17 Tu	17 40 45	24 37 36	14 11 08	20 07 38	12R 55.0	28 38.9	10 03.4	8 01.2	5 33.9	8 31.5	4 50.6	1 47.8	16 46.6	26 56.3
18 W	17 44 42	25 38 41	26 03 33	1♎59 32	12 54.9	0♑14.0	11 12.3	8 48.0	5 57.7	8 44.6	4 54.6	1 46.6	16 46.6	26 55.2
19 Th	17 48 38	26 39 46	7♎56 11	13 54 04	12 54.0	1 49.2	12 21.3	9 34.9	6 21.3	8 57.8	4 58.6	1 45.4	16R 46.7	26 54.1
20 F	17 52 35	27 40 53	19 53 45	25 55 47	12 52.5	3 24.6	13 30.4	10 21.7	6 44.9	9 10.9	5 02.8	1 44.4	16 46.7	26 53.0
21 Sa	17 56 31	28 42 00	2♏00 39	8♏08 48	12 50.5	5 00.2	14 39.8	11 08.6	7 08.4	9 23.9	5 07.0	1 43.3	16 46.6	26 51.9
22 Su	18 00 28	29 43 08	14 20 37	20 36 27	12 48.4	6 35.9	15 49.3	11 55.5	7 31.7	9 37.0	5 11.3	1 42.3	16 46.6	26 50.7
23 M	18 04 24	0♑44 17	26 56 32	3♐21 04	12 46.5	8 11.8	16 58.9	12 42.4	7 55.0	9 50.0	5 15.7	1 41.4	16 46.4	26 49.6
24 Tu	18 08 21	1 45 26	9♐50 09	16 23 48	12 45.1	9 47.8	18 08.7	13 29.3	8 18.1	10 03.0	5 20.2	1 40.5	16 46.3	26 48.4
25 W	18 12 17	2 46 36	23 01 59	29 44 34	12D 44.3	11 24.0	19 18.6	14 16.3	8 41.2	10 15.9	5 24.7	1 39.6	16 46.1	26 47.2
26 Th	18 16 14	3 47 46	6♑31 18	13♑21 57	12 44.0	13 00.3	20 28.6	15 03.2	9 04.1	10 28.8	5 29.4	1 38.8	16 45.9	26 46.0
27 F	18 20 11	4 48 56	20 16 10	27 13 33	12 44.3	14 36.7	21 38.8	15 50.2	9 26.9	10 41.7	5 34.1	1 38.1	16 45.7	26 44.8
28 Sa	18 24 07	5 50 07	4♒13 42	11♒16 10	12 44.8	16 13.2	22 49.1	16 37.1	9 49.6	10 54.5	5 38.8	1 37.4	16 45.4	26 43.6
29 Su	18 28 04	6 51 17	18 20 31	25 26 17	12 45.5	17 49.7	23 59.5	17 24.1	10 12.2	11 07.3	5 43.7	1 36.7	16 45.1	26 42.4
30 M	18 32 00	7 52 28	2♓33 03	9♓40 23	12 46.0	19 26.2	25 10.1	18 11.1	10 34.6	11 20.0	5 48.6	1 36.1	16 44.8	26 41.2
31 Tu	18 35 57	8 53 38	16 47 54	23 55 15	12 46.3	21 02.5	26 20.7	18 58.1	10 56.9	11 32.7	5 53.7	1 35.6	16 44.4	26 39.9

Astro Data Dy Hr Mn	Planet Ingress Dy Hr Mn	Last Aspect Dy Hr Mn	☽ Ingress Dy Hr Mn	Last Aspect Dy Hr Mn	☽ Ingress Dy Hr Mn	☽ Phases & Eclipses Dy Hr Mn	Astro Data
⚳0S 5 14:34	♃ ♐ 9 2:56	3 2:19 ♃ ✶	♒ 3 4:38	2 1:40 ♀ △	♓ 2 14:03	3 23:12 ☽ 10♒36	1 November 1935
☽0N 6 16:30	♀ ♎ 9 16:34	5 6:56 ♃ □	♓ 5 8:20	4 13:27 ♂ ✶	♈ 4 16:53	10 14:42 ○ 17♉17	Julian Day # 13088
♄ D 7 21:59	☿ ♏ 10 1:24	7 9:17 ♃ △	♈ 7 9:54	6 18:31 ♂ □	♉ 6 19:03	18 0:36 ☾ 24♌44	SVP 6♓09'06"
♀0S 11 14:07	☉ ♐ 23 5:35	9 8:52 ☿ ☍	♉ 9 10:29	8 16:39 ♇ ✶	♊ 8 21:36	26 2:36 ● 2♐55	GC 25♐56.6 ⚴ 0♎28.0
☽0S 20 1:56	☿ ♐ 29 7:05	11 7:28 ♇ ✶	♊ 11 11:52	10 3:10 ☉ ☍	♋ 11 1:54		Eris 2♈47.4R ⚵ 23♈35.1R
♃⚻♅ 20 17:27		12 15:53 ♆ □	♋ 13 15:56	13 3:28 ♇ ☌	♌ 13 9:07	3 7:28 ☽ 10♓13	⚷ 15♊28.2R ⚶ 7♓18.7
♃□♄ 26 5:59	⚳ ♏ 3 19:48	15 18:45 ♇ ☌	♌ 15 23:51	15 10:22 ☿ △	♍ 15 19:33	10 3:10 ○ 17♊08	☽ Mean ☊ 16♑07.6
	♂ ♒ 7 4:34	18 0:36 ☉ □	♍ 18 11:10	18 7:54 ☿ □	♎ 18 7:58	17 21:57 ☾ 25♍03	
☽0N 3 22:17	♀ ♏ 8 14:36	20 18:53 ☉ ✶	♎ 20 23:52	20 15:47 ☉ ✶	♏ 20 20:03	25 17:49 ● 3♑01	1 December 1935
☽0S 17 9:22	☿ ♑ 18 8:28	23 6:17 ♇ □	♏ 23 11:36	22 23:48 ♇ △	♐ 23 5:45	25 17:59:25 ● A 01'30"	Julian Day # 13118
♅Q♆ 18 10:55	☉ ♑ 22 18:37	25 15:59 ♇ △	♐ 25 21:08	24 12:41 ♆ □	♑ 25 12:27		SVP 6♓09'01"
♆ R 19 21:24		27 5:52 ♀ ✶	♑ 28 4:28	27 11:11 ♇ ☍	♒ 27 16:46		GC 25♐56.7 ⚴ 13♎12.1
☽0N 31 3:19		30 5:05 ♇ ☍	♒ 30 10:00	29 9:20 ♀ □	♓ 29 19:42		Eris 2♈35.6R ⚵ 20♈27.9
				31 16:37 ♇ △	♈ 31 22:15		⚷ 13♊53.6R ⚶ 12♓21.7
							☽ Mean ☊ 14♑32.3

LONGITUDE — January 1936

Day	Sid.Time	☉	0 hr ☽	Noon ☽	True ☊	☿	♀	♂	⚳	♃	♄	♅	♆	♇
1 W	18 39 53	9♑54 48	1♈02 04	8♈08 05	12♑46.4	22♑38.7	27♏31.5	19♒45.1	11♏19.1	11♐45.4	5♓58.7	1♉35.1	16♍44.0	26♋38.7
2 Th	18 43 50	10 55 57	15 13 01	22 16 35	12R46.4	24 14.6	28 42.3	20 32.1	11 41.2	11 58.0	6 03.9	1R34.6	16R43.5	26R37.4
3 F	18 47 46	11 57 07	29 18 35	6♉18 45	12D46.3	25 50.2	29 53.3	21 19.1	12 03.1	12 10.5	6 09.1	1 34.2	16 43.0	26 36.1
4 Sa	18 51 43	12 58 16	13♉16 54	20 12 49	12 46.3	27 25.2	1♐04.3	22 06.1	12 24.9	12 23.0	6 14.4	1 33.9	16 42.5	26 34.9
5 Su	18 55 40	13 59 25	27 06 17	3♊57 06	12 46.4	28 59.4	2 15.5	22 53.2	12 46.6	12 35.5	6 19.8	1 33.6	16 42.0	26 33.6
6 M	18 59 36	15 00 34	10♊45 06	17 30 04	12 46.5	0♒32.8	3 26.8	23 40.2	13 08.1	12 47.8	6 25.2	1 33.4	16 41.4	26 32.3
7 Tu	19 03 33	16 01 42	24 11 50	0♋50 16	12R46.7	2 05.1	4 38.1	24 27.2	13 29.5	13 00.2	6 30.7	1 33.2	16 40.8	26 31.0
8 W	19 07 29	17 02 51	7♋25 12	13 56 34	12 46.8	3 36.0	5 49.6	25 14.2	13 50.8	13 12.5	6 36.3	1 33.0	16 40.2	26 29.7
9 Th	19 11 26	18 03 59	20 24 17	26 48 20	12 46.7	5 05.1	7 01.1	26 01.2	14 11.9	13 24.7	6 41.9	1 33.0	16 39.5	26 28.4
10 F	19 15 22	19 05 06	3♌08 43	9♌25 31	12 46.2	6 32.1	8 12.7	26 48.2	14 32.9	13 36.9	6 47.6	1D32.9	16 38.8	26 27.1
11 Sa	19 19 19	20 06 14	15 38 51	21 48 53	12 45.3	7 56.6	9 24.4	27 35.2	14 53.7	13 49.0	6 53.3	1 32.9	16 38.1	26 25.8
12 Su	19 23 16	21 07 21	27 55 51	4♍00 01	12 44.2	9 18.1	10 36.2	28 22.2	15 14.4	14 01.0	6 59.1	1 33.0	16 37.3	26 24.5
13 M	19 27 12	22 08 28	10♍01 43	16 01 21	12 42.9	10 36.0	11 48.1	29 09.1	15 34.9	14 13.0	7 05.0	1 33.1	16 36.5	26 23.2
14 Tu	19 31 09	23 09 35	21 59 19	27 56 06	12 41.6	11 49.7	13 00.0	29 56.1	15 55.3	14 24.9	7 10.9	1 33.3	16 35.7	26 21.9
15 W	19 35 05	24 10 42	3♎52 11	9♎48 07	12 40.6	12 58.5	14 12.0	0♓43.1	16 15.5	14 36.7	7 16.9	1 33.5	16 34.9	26 20.5
16 Th	19 39 02	25 11 49	15 44 28	21 41 48	12D40.1	14 01.6	15 24.1	1 30.0	16 35.5	14 48.5	7 22.9	1 33.8	16 34.0	26 19.2
17 F	19 42 58	26 12 55	27 40 42	3♏41 47	12 40.2	14 58.3	16 36.3	2 17.0	16 55.4	15 00.2	7 29.0	1 34.1	16 33.1	26 17.9
18 Sa	19 46 55	27 14 01	9♏45 38	15 52 50	12 41.0	15 47.7	17 48.5	3 03.9	17 15.1	15 11.9	7 35.2	1 34.5	16 32.1	26 16.6
19 Su	19 50 51	28 15 07	22 03 57	28 19 28	12 42.2	16 28.9	19 00.8	3 50.9	17 34.7	15 23.4	7 41.4	1 35.0	16 31.2	26 15.2
20 M	19 54 48	29 16 12	4♐39 52	11♐05 34	12 43.6	17 01.0	20 13.2	4 37.8	17 54.1	15 34.9	7 47.6	1 35.5	16 30.2	26 13.9
21 Tu	19 58 45	0♒17 18	17 36 53	24 14 03	12 44.9	17 23.2	21 25.6	5 24.8	18 13.3	15 46.3	7 53.9	1 36.0	16 29.2	26 12.6
22 W	20 02 41	1 18 22	0♑57 11	7♑46 16	12R45.6	17R34.9	22 38.1	6 11.7	18 32.3	15 57.7	8 00.3	1 36.6	16 28.1	26 11.3
23 Th	20 06 38	2 19 26	14 41 11	21 41 40	12 45.5	17 35.4	23 50.6	6 58.6	18 51.1	16 08.9	8 06.7	1 37.3	16 27.1	26 10.0
24 F	20 10 34	3 20 30	28 47 18	5♒57 32	12 44.3	17 24.4	25 03.2	7 45.5	19 09.8	16 20.1	8 13.2	1 38.0	16 26.0	26 08.7
25 Sa	20 14 31	4 21 32	13♒11 41	20 29 00	12 42.0	17 01.9	26 15.8	8 32.3	19 28.2	16 31.2	8 19.6	1 38.7	16 24.8	26 07.4
26 Su	20 18 27	5 22 34	27 48 37	5♓09 37	12 38.9	16 28.2	27 28.5	9 19.2	19 46.5	16 42.2	8 26.2	1 39.5	16 23.7	26 06.0
27 M	20 22 24	6 23 34	12♓31 07	19 52 13	12 35.5	15 43.9	28 41.2	10 06.0	20 04.6	16 53.1	8 32.8	1 40.4	16 22.5	26 04.7
28 Tu	20 26 20	7 24 33	27 12 03	4♈29 53	12 32.4	14 50.1	29 53.9	10 52.8	20 22.4	17 04.0	8 39.4	1 41.3	16 21.3	26 03.4
29 W	20 30 17	8 25 31	11♈45 04	18 57 02	12 30.0	13 48.4	1♑06.7	11 39.6	20 40.1	17 14.7	8 46.1	1 42.2	16 20.1	26 02.2
30 Th	20 34 14	9 26 28	26 05 23	3♉09 49	12D28.7	12 40.4	2 19.6	12 26.4	20 57.5	17 25.3	8 52.8	1 43.2	16 18.9	26 00.9
31 F	20 38 10	10 27 24	10♉10 08	17 06 15	12 28.8	11 28.3	3 32.4	13 13.2	21 14.8	17 35.9	8 59.5	1 44.3	16 17.6	25 59.6

LONGITUDE — February 1936

Day	Sid.Time	☉	0 hr ☽	Noon ☽	True ☊	☿	♀	♂	⚳	♃	♄	♅	♆	♇
1 Sa	20 42 07	11♒28 18	23♉58 10	0♊45 57	12♑29.8	10♒14.2	4♑45.3	13♓59.9	21♏31.8	17♐46.3	9♓06.3	1♉45.4	16♍16.3	25♋58.3
2 Su	20 46 03	12 29 11	7♊29 42	14 09 36	12 31.5	9R00.2	5 58.3	14 46.6	21 48.7	17 56.7	9 13.1	1 46.6	16R15.0	25R57.1
3 M	20 50 00	13 30 03	20 45 48	27 18 29	12 33.0	7 48.3	7 11.3	15 33.3	22 05.3	18 07.0	9 19.9	1 47.8	16 13.7	25 55.8
4 Tu	20 53 56	14 30 53	3♋47 50	10♋14 01	12R33.9	6 40.5	8 24.3	16 20.0	22 21.7	18 17.1	9 26.8	1 49.0	16 12.3	25 54.6
5 W	20 57 53	15 31 42	16 37 12	22 57 32	12 33.4	5 38.1	9 37.3	17 06.6	22 37.8	18 27.2	9 33.8	1 50.3	16 11.0	25 53.3
6 Th	21 01 49	16 32 30	29 15 08	5♌30 06	12 31.2	4 42.3	10 50.4	17 53.2	22 53.8	18 37.2	9 40.7	1 51.7	16 09.6	25 52.1
7 F	21 05 46	17 33 16	11♌42 35	17 52 39	12 27.1	3 54.0	12 03.5	18 39.8	23 09.5	18 47.0	9 47.7	1 53.1	16 08.2	25 50.9
8 Sa	21 09 43	18 34 01	24 00 26	0♍06 03	12 21.5	3 13.7	13 16.7	19 26.4	23 25.0	18 56.8	9 54.7	1 54.5	16 06.8	25 49.7
9 Su	21 13 39	19 34 45	6♍09 38	12 11 19	12 14.6	2 41.6	14 29.9	20 12.9	23 40.2	19 06.4	10 01.7	1 56.0	16 05.3	25 48.5
10 M	21 17 36	20 35 27	18 11 20	24 09 53	12 07.1	2 17.6	15 43.1	20 59.4	23 55.2	19 15.9	10 08.8	1 57.6	16 03.9	25 47.3
11 Tu	21 21 32	21 36 09	0♎07 13	6♎03 39	11 59.8	2 01.8	16 56.3	21 45.8	24 09.9	19 25.4	10 15.9	1 59.2	16 02.4	25 46.1
12 W	21 25 29	22 36 49	11 59 32	17 55 15	11 53.5	1D53.8	18 09.6	22 32.3	24 24.4	19 34.7	10 23.0	2 00.8	16 00.9	25 44.9
13 Th	21 29 25	23 37 28	23 51 14	29 47 58	11 48.7	1 53.2	19 22.9	23 18.7	24 38.7	19 43.9	10 30.1	2 02.5	15 59.4	25 43.8
14 F	21 33 22	24 38 06	5♏45 58	11♏45 47	11 45.7	1 59.6	20 36.2	24 05.1	24 52.7	19 52.9	10 37.3	2 04.2	15 57.9	25 42.6
15 Sa	21 37 18	25 38 42	17 47 59	23 53 11	11D44.6	2 12.6	21 49.6	24 51.4	25 06.4	20 01.9	10 44.4	2 06.0	15 56.3	25 41.5
16 Su	21 41 15	26 39 18	0♐02 00	6♐15 02	11 45.1	2 31.7	23 03.0	25 37.8	25 19.9	20 10.8	10 51.6	2 07.8	15 54.8	25 40.4
17 M	21 45 12	27 39 52	12 32 54	18 56 10	11 46.3	2 56.4	24 16.4	26 24.1	25 33.1	20 19.5	10 58.8	2 09.7	15 53.2	25 39.3
18 Tu	21 49 08	28 40 26	25 25 21	2♑00 55	11R47.6	3 26.5	25 29.8	27 10.3	25 46.0	20 28.1	11 06.1	2 11.6	15 51.7	25 38.2
19 W	21 53 05	29 40 58	8♑43 14	15 32 32	11 47.9	4 01.3	26 43.3	27 56.6	25 58.6	20 36.6	11 13.3	2 13.5	15 50.1	25 37.1
20 Th	21 57 01	0♓41 28	22 28 56	29 32 21	11 46.5	4 40.6	27 56.8	28 42.8	26 11.0	20 44.9	11 20.6	2 15.5	15 48.5	25 36.1
21 F	22 00 58	1 41 57	6♒42 32	13♒59 01	11 42.8	5 24.1	29 10.3	29 28.9	26 23.0	20 53.1	11 27.9	2 17.5	15 46.9	25 35.0
22 Sa	22 04 54	2 42 24	21 21 07	28 47 59	11 36.9	6 11.3	0♒23.8	0♈15.1	26 34.8	21 01.2	11 35.2	2 19.6	15 45.3	25 34.0
23 Su	22 08 51	3 42 50	6♓18 34	13♓51 41	11 29.2	7 02.1	1 37.3	1 01.2	26 46.3	21 09.2	11 42.5	2 21.7	15 43.7	25 33.0
24 M	22 12 47	4 43 14	21 26 02	29 00 19	11 20.7	7 56.1	2 50.8	1 47.3	26 57.5	21 17.0	11 49.8	2 23.9	15 42.0	25 32.0
25 Tu	22 16 44	5 43 36	6♈33 15	14♈03 36	11 12.5	8 53.0	4 04.4	2 33.3	27 08.3	21 24.7	11 57.1	2 26.1	15 40.4	25 31.0
26 W	22 20 41	6 43 57	21 30 19	28 52 30	11 05.6	9 52.8	5 17.9	3 19.3	27 18.9	21 32.2	12 04.5	2 28.3	15 38.7	25 30.1
27 Th	22 24 37	7 44 15	6♉09 25	13♉20 34	11 00.8	10 55.2	6 31.5	4 05.2	27 29.1	21 39.6	12 11.8	2 30.6	15 37.1	25 29.1
28 F	22 28 34	8 44 32	20 25 38	27 24 31	10D58.2	12 00.0	7 45.1	4 51.2	27 39.1	21 46.9	12 19.1	2 32.9	15 35.4	25 28.2
29 Sa	22 32 30	9 44 46	4♊17 13	11♊03 55	10 57.6	13 07.1	8 58.7	5 37.0	27 48.7	21 54.0	12 26.5	2 35.3	15 33.8	25 27.3

Astro Data

	Dy Hr Mn
♃⏍♇	1 0:25
♅ D	10 15:20
☽ 0S	13 17:33
♅⏍♆	16 15:29
☿ R	23 1:02
♃□♆	24 23:29
♃⏍♅	26 5:37
☽ 0N	27 10:21
☽ 0S	10 1:34
☿ D	13 1:57
♄⏍♇	15 3:31
☽ 0N	23 20:12
♂ 0N	23 21:30

Planet Ingress

		Dy Hr Mn
♀	♐	3 14:16
☿	♒	6 3:32
♂	♓	14 13:59
☉	♒	21 5:12
♀	♑	28 14:00
☉	♓	19 19:33
♂	♈	22 4:09
♀	♒	22 4:14

Last Aspect / ☽ Ingress

Last Aspect Dy Hr Mn		☽ Ingress	Dy Hr Mn
2 19:24	♇ □	♉	3 1:11
5 2:11	☿ △	♊	5 5:04
6 23:44	♂ △	♋	7 10:29
9 11:23	♇ ☌	♌	9 18:02
12 0:06	♂ ☍	♍	12 4:05
14 8:50	♇ ⚹	♎	14 16:10
16 21:16	♇ □	♏	17 4:38
19 11:51	☉ ⚹	♐	19 15:11
21 6:25	♀ ☌	♑	21 22:19
23 19:34	♇ ☍	♒	24 2:02
25 22:19	♀ ⚹	♓	26 3:35
28 3:45	♀ □	♈	28 4:36
29 23:53	♇ □	♉	30 6:37

Last Aspect / ☽ Ingress

Last Aspect Dy Hr Mn		☽ Ingress	Dy Hr Mn
1 3:32	♇ ⚹	♊	1 10:39
2 18:57	♃ ☍	♋	3 16:58
5 17:34	♇ ☌	♌	6 1:26
7 13:48	♃ △	♍	8 11:48
10 15:16	♇ ⚹	♎	10 23:45
13 3:48	♇ □	♏	13 12:24
15 15:45	☉ □	♐	15 23:56
18 5:26	☉ ⚹	♑	18 8:21
20 10:31	♂ ⚹	♒	20 12:47
21 23:21	♃ ⚹	♓	22 13:55
24 6:30	♇ △	♈	24 13:35
26 6:30	♇ □	♉	26 13:51
28 8:39	♇ ⚹	♊	28 16:30

☽ Phases & Eclipses

Dy Hr Mn	
1 15:15	☽ 10♈03
8 18:15	○ 17♋19
8 18:10	T 1.017
16 19:41	☾ 25♎31
24 7:18	● 3♒09
30 23:36	☽ 9♉56
7 11:19	○ 17♌32
15 15:45	☾ 25♏48
22 18:42	● 2♓59
29 9:28	☽ 9♊38

Astro Data

1 January 1936
Julian Day # 13149
SVP 6♓08'55"
GC 25♐56.7 ⚴ 24♎10.3
Eris 2♈33.7 ⚵ 25♈31.3
⚷ 12♊07.6R ⚶ 21♓47.6
☽ Mean ☊ 12♑53.8

1 February 1936
Julian Day # 13180
SVP 6♓08'50"
GC 25♐56.8 ⚴ 1♏31.5
Eris 2♈43.3 ⚵ 6♉48.7
⚷ 10♊59.5R ⚶ 3♈38.6
☽ Mean ☊ 11♑15.4

March 1936

LONGITUDE

Day	Sid.Time	☉	0 hr ☽	Noon ☽	True ☊	☿	♀	♂	⚳	♃	♄	♅	♆	♇
1 Su	22 36 27	10♓44 58	17♊44 54	24♊20 28	10♑58.2	14♒16.2	10♒12.3	6♈22.9	27♏58.0	22♐01.0	12♓33.9	2♉37.7	15♍32.1	25♋26.5
2 M	22 40 23	11 45 08	0♋51 04	7♋17 06	10R58.9	15 27.5	11 25.9	7 08.7	28 06.9	22 07.8	12 41.2	2 40.1	15R30.5	25R25.6
3 Tu	22 44 20	12 45 17	13 39 01	19 57 14	10 58.5	16 40.6	12 39.5	7 54.4	28 15.6	22 14.5	12 48.6	2 42.5	15 28.8	25 24.8
4 W	22 48 16	13 45 23	26 12 10	2♌24 12	10 56.2	17 55.5	13 53.1	8 40.2	28 23.9	22 21.1	12 55.9	2 45.0	15 27.1	25 23.9
5 Th	22 52 13	14 45 26	8♌33 41	14 40 56	10 51.3	19 12.1	15 06.8	9 25.8	28 31.8	22 27.4	13 03.3	2 47.6	15 25.5	25 23.1
6 F	22 56 10	15 45 28	20 46 14	26 49 49	10 43.6	20 30.3	16 20.4	10 11.4	28 39.5	22 33.7	13 10.6	2 50.1	15 23.8	25 22.3
7 Sa	23 00 06	16 45 28	2♍51 54	8♍52 39	10 33.3	21 50.2	17 34.1	10 57.0	28 46.7	22 39.8	13 18.0	2 52.7	15 22.1	25 21.6
8 Su	23 04 03	17 45 26	14 52 15	20 50 50	10 21.0	23 11.6	18 47.7	11 42.6	28 53.7	22 45.7	13 25.3	2 55.4	15 20.5	25 20.8
9 M	23 07 59	18 45 22	26 48 35	2♎45 37	10 07.7	24 34.4	20 01.4	12 28.1	29 00.2	22 51.5	13 32.7	2 58.0	15 18.8	25 20.1
10 Tu	23 11 56	19 45 16	8♎42 06	14 38 16	9 54.6	25 58.7	21 15.1	13 13.5	29 06.4	22 57.1	13 40.0	3 00.7	15 17.1	25 19.4
11 W	23 15 52	20 45 09	20 34 17	26 30 25	9 42.7	27 24.4	22 28.8	13 58.9	29 12.3	23 02.6	13 47.3	3 03.5	15 15.4	25 18.8
12 Th	23 19 49	21 44 59	2♏26 59	8♏24 17	9 32.9	28 51.4	23 42.5	14 44.3	29 17.8	23 07.9	13 54.6	3 06.2	15 13.8	25 18.1
13 F	23 23 45	22 44 48	14 22 44	20 22 44	9 25.8	0♓19.8	24 56.2	15 29.6	29 22.9	23 13.0	14 01.9	3 09.0	15 12.1	25 17.5
14 Sa	23 27 42	23 44 35	26 24 45	2♐29 19	9 21.4	1 49.5	26 09.9	16 14.9	29 27.6	23 18.0	14 09.2	3 11.8	15 10.5	25 16.9
15 Su	23 31 38	24 44 21	8♐37 00	14 48 20	9D19.4	3 20.5	27 23.6	17 00.2	29 32.0	23 22.8	14 16.5	3 14.7	15 08.8	25 16.3
16 M	23 35 35	25 44 05	21 03 57	27 24 27	9R19.1	4 52.7	28 37.4	17 45.4	29 36.0	23 27.4	14 23.8	3 17.6	15 07.2	25 15.7
17 Tu	23 39 32	26 43 47	3♑50 25	10♑22 26	9 19.2	6 26.3	29 51.1	18 30.5	29 39.6	23 31.9	14 31.1	3 20.5	15 05.6	25 15.2
18 W	23 43 28	27 43 27	17 00 58	23 46 29	9 18.6	8 01.2	1♓04.9	19 15.6	29 42.8	23 36.2	14 38.3	3 23.4	15 03.9	25 14.7
19 Th	23 47 25	28 43 06	0♒39 16	7♒39 30	9 16.1	9 37.3	2 18.6	20 00.7	29 45.7	23 40.4	14 45.5	3 26.4	15 02.3	25 14.2
20 F	23 51 21	29 42 42	14 47 08	22 01 59	9 11.0	11 14.7	3 32.4	20 45.7	29 48.1	23 44.3	14 52.7	3 29.3	15 00.7	25 13.7
21 Sa	23 55 18	0♈42 17	29 23 34	6♓51 12	9 03.3	12 53.4	4 46.1	21 30.7	29 50.1	23 48.1	14 59.9	3 32.4	14 59.1	25 13.2
22 Su	23 59 14	1 41 50	14♓23 57	22 00 39	8 53.2	14 33.3	5 59.9	22 15.6	29 51.8	23 51.7	15 07.1	3 35.4	14 57.5	25 12.8
23 M	0 03 11	2 41 21	29 40 00	7♈20 31	8 41.9	16 14.5	7 13.7	23 00.5	29 53.0	23 55.2	15 14.2	3 38.4	14 55.9	25 12.4
24 Tu	0 07 07	3 40 50	15♈00 42	22 39 05	8 30.8	17 57.1	8 27.4	23 45.4	29 53.9	23 58.4	15 21.4	3 41.5	14 54.4	25 12.0
25 W	0 11 04	4 40 17	0♉14 16	7♉45 01	8 21.1	19 40.9	9 41.2	24 30.2	29R54.3	24 01.5	15 28.5	3 44.6	14 52.8	25 11.7
26 Th	0 15 01	5 39 42	15 10 18	22 29 19	8 13.8	21 26.1	10 55.0	25 14.9	29 54.3	24 04.4	15 35.6	3 47.8	14 51.3	25 11.4
27 F	0 18 57	6 39 04	29 41 29	6♊46 29	8 09.2	23 12.6	12 08.7	25 59.6	29 54.0	24 07.1	15 42.6	3 50.9	14 49.7	25 11.1
28 Sa	0 22 54	7 38 24	13♊44 13	20 34 45	8 07.1	25 00.5	13 22.5	26 44.3	29 53.2	24 09.7	15 49.6	3 54.1	14 48.2	25 10.8
29 Su	0 26 50	8 37 42	27 18 19	3♋55 18	8 06.6	26 49.7	14 36.2	27 28.9	29 52.0	24 12.0	15 56.6	3 57.3	14 46.7	25 10.6
30 M	0 30 47	9 36 58	10♋26 07	16 51 19	8 06.5	28 40.2	15 50.0	28 13.5	29 50.4	24 14.2	16 03.6	4 00.5	14 45.2	25 10.3
31 Tu	0 34 43	10 36 11	23 11 26	29 27 02	8 05.7	0♈32.2	17 03.7	28 58.0	29 48.4	24 16.2	16 10.6	4 03.7	14 43.8	25 10.1

April 1936

LONGITUDE

Day	Sid.Time	☉	0 hr ☽	Noon ☽	True ☊	☿	♀	♂	⚳	♃	♄	♅	♆	♇
1 W	0 38 40	11♈35 21	5♌38 42	11♌46 57	8♑02.9	2♈25.5	18♓17.5	29♈42.4	29♏46.0	24♐18.0	16♓17.5	4♉06.9	14♍42.3	25♋10.0
2 Th	0 42 36	12 34 30	17 52 20	23 55 20	7R57.5	4 20.1	19 31.2	0♉26.8	29R43.2	24 19.6	16 24.3	4 10.2	14R40.9	25R09.8
3 F	0 46 33	13 33 36	29 56 22	5♍55 51	7 49.2	6 16.1	20 44.9	1 11.2	29 40.0	24 21.1	16 31.2	4 13.4	14 39.4	25 09.7
4 Sa	0 50 30	14 32 40	11♍54 08	17 51 33	7 38.2	8 13.5	21 58.7	1 55.5	29 36.5	24 22.3	16 38.0	4 16.7	14 38.0	25 09.6
5 Su	0 54 26	15 31 41	23 48 20	29 44 45	7 25.1	10 12.2	23 12.4	2 39.7	29 32.5	24 23.4	16 44.8	4 20.0	14 36.6	25 09.5
6 M	0 58 23	16 30 41	5♎40 59	11♎37 14	7 10.9	12 12.2	24 26.1	3 23.9	29 28.1	24 24.3	16 51.5	4 23.3	14 35.3	25 09.5
7 Tu	1 02 19	17 29 39	17 33 39	23 30 25	6 56.9	14 13.4	25 39.9	4 08.1	29 23.3	24 25.0	16 58.2	4 26.7	14 33.9	25D09.4
8 W	1 06 16	18 28 34	29 27 41	5♏25 37	6 44.0	16 15.7	26 53.6	4 52.2	29 18.1	24 25.5	17 04.9	4 30.0	14 32.6	25 09.4
9 Th	1 10 12	19 27 28	11♏24 25	17 24 18	6 33.3	18 19.1	28 07.3	5 36.2	29 12.6	24 25.8	17 11.5	4 33.4	14 31.3	25 09.5
10 F	1 14 09	20 26 20	23 25 31	29 28 21	6 25.4	20 23.5	29 21.1	6 20.3	29 06.6	24R26.0	17 18.1	4 36.7	14 30.0	25 09.5
11 Sa	1 18 05	21 25 10	5♐33 07	11♐40 12	6 20.4	22 28.7	0♈34.8	7 04.2	29 00.3	24 25.9	17 24.6	4 40.1	14 28.7	25 09.6
12 Su	1 22 02	22 23 58	17 50 00	24 02 57	6D17.9	24 34.6	1 48.5	7 48.1	28 53.6	24 25.7	17 31.1	4 43.5	14 27.4	25 09.7
13 M	1 25 59	23 22 45	0♑19 32	6♑40 15	6 17.4	26 40.9	3 02.2	8 32.0	28 46.6	24 25.3	17 37.6	4 46.9	14 26.2	25 09.8
14 Tu	1 29 55	24 21 30	13 05 37	19 36 08	6R17.6	28 47.5	4 16.0	9 15.8	28 39.1	24 24.7	17 44.0	4 50.3	14 25.0	25 10.0
15 W	1 33 52	25 20 13	26 12 16	2♒54 29	6 17.5	0♉54.0	5 29.7	9 59.6	28 31.3	24 23.9	17 50.4	4 53.7	14 23.8	25 10.2
16 Th	1 37 48	26 18 54	9♒43 07	16 38 26	6 15.9	3 00.3	6 43.4	10 43.3	28 23.2	24 22.9	17 56.7	4 57.1	14 22.7	25 10.4
17 F	1 41 45	27 17 34	23 40 33	0♓49 27	6 12.1	5 06.0	7 57.2	11 26.9	28 14.7	24 21.7	18 03.0	5 00.5	14 21.5	25 10.6
18 Sa	1 45 41	28 16 12	8♓04 53	15 26 25	6 05.8	7 10.9	9 10.9	12 10.6	28 05.8	24 20.3	18 09.2	5 04.0	14 20.4	25 10.8
19 Su	1 49 38	29 14 48	22 53 23	0♈24 54	5 57.4	9 14.5	10 24.6	12 54.1	27 56.7	24 18.8	18 15.4	5 07.4	14 19.3	25 11.1
20 M	1 53 34	0♉13 22	7♈59 53	15 37 05	5 47.8	11 16.7	11 38.3	13 37.7	27 47.2	24 17.0	18 21.5	5 10.9	14 18.3	25 11.4
21 Tu	1 57 31	1 11 55	23 15 08	0♉52 38	5 38.2	13 16.9	12 52.0	14 21.1	27 37.4	24 15.1	18 27.6	5 14.3	14 17.2	25 11.7
22 W	2 01 28	2 10 26	8♉28 10	16 00 25	5 29.7	15 15.0	14 05.7	15 04.6	27 27.3	24 13.0	18 33.6	5 17.7	14 16.2	25 12.1
23 Th	2 05 24	3 08 55	23 28 13	0♊50 34	5 23.2	17 10.6	15 19.5	15 47.9	27 16.8	24 10.7	18 39.6	5 21.2	14 15.2	25 12.5
24 F	2 09 21	4 07 22	8♊06 40	15 15 57	5 19.3	19 03.5	16 33.2	16 31.3	27 06.2	24 08.2	18 45.5	5 24.7	14 14.3	25 12.9
25 Sa	2 13 17	5 05 47	22 18 07	29 13 00	5D17.6	20 53.4	17 46.8	17 14.5	26 55.2	24 05.6	18 51.4	5 28.1	14 13.4	25 13.3
26 Su	2 17 14	6 04 10	6♋00 39	12♋41 18	5 17.6	22 40.0	19 00.5	17 57.8	26 44.0	24 02.8	18 57.2	5 31.6	14 12.5	25 13.8
27 M	2 21 10	7 02 31	19 15 17	25 43 02	5R18.4	24 23.1	20 14.2	18 40.9	26 32.6	23 59.8	19 02.9	5 35.0	14 11.6	25 14.3
28 Tu	2 25 07	8 00 49	2♌05 04	8♌21 56	5 18.9	26 02.6	21 27.9	19 24.1	26 20.9	23 56.6	19 08.6	5 38.5	14 10.7	25 14.8
29 W	2 29 03	8 59 06	14 34 14	20 42 34	5 18.0	27 38.4	22 41.6	20 07.1	26 09.0	23 53.2	19 14.2	5 41.9	14 09.9	25 15.3
30 Th	2 33 00	9 57 20	26 47 31	2♍49 41	5 15.3	29 10.2	23 55.2	20 50.1	25 56.9	23 49.7	19 19.8	5 45.4	14 09.1	25 15.8

Astro Data	Dy Hr Mn
☽0S	8 8:30
⊙0N	20 18:58
♄☍♆	21 9:47
☽0N	22 7:20
⚳R	26 1:51
☿0N	2 9:58
☽0S	4 14:16
♇D	7 23:25
♃R	10 17:49
♀0N	13 21:47
☽0N	18 17:25

Planet Ingress		Dy Hr Mn
☿	♓	13 6:40
♀	♓	17 14:53
⊙	♈	20 18:58
☿	♈	31 5:08
♂	♉	1 21:30
♀	♈	11 0:41
☿	♉	15 1:45
⊙	♉	20 6:31

Last Aspect Dy Hr Mn			☽ Ingress	Dy Hr Mn
1 7:43	♃	☍	♋	1 22:25
3 22:28	♇	☌	♌	4 7:20
6 3:28	♃	△	♍	6 18:18
8 21:03	♇	⚹	♎	9 6:26
11 14:04	☿	△	♏	11 19:03
13 22:06	♀	□	♐	14 7:06
16 14:31	♀	⚹	♑	16 16:51
18 19:27	⊙	⚹	♒	18 22:52
20 14:48	♃	⚹	♓	21 0:59
22 17:01	♇	△	♈	23 0:31
24 16:01	♇	□	♉	24 23:37
26 16:29	♇	⚹	♊	27 0:31
28 23:38	♂	⚹	♋	29 4:52
31 11:00	♂	□	♌	31 13:04

Last Aspect Dy Hr Mn			☽ Ingress	Dy Hr Mn
2 12:48	♃	△	♍	3 0:07
5 2:44	♇	⚹	♎	5 12:31
7 15:20	♇	□	♏	8 1:05
10 11:44	♀	△	♐	10 13:03
12 13:13	☿	△	♑	12 23:23
14 22:08	♇	☍	♒	15 6:49
17 5:40	⊙	⚹	♓	17 10:38
19 3:40	♇	△	♈	19 11:20
21 3:03	♇	□	♉	21 10:37
23 2:49	♇	⚹	♊	23 10:37
25 3:07	♃	☍	♋	25 13:22
27 11:06	♇	☌	♌	27 20:03
30 3:41	☿	□	♍	30 6:22

☽ Phases & Eclipses Dy Hr Mn		
8 5:14	○	17♍29
16 8:35	☾	25♐36
23 4:14	●	2♈22
29 21:22	☽	9♋01
6 22:46	○	16♎57
14 21:21	☾	24♑44
21 12:33	●	1♉13
28 11:16	☽	7♌59

Astro Data

1 March 1936
Julian Day # 13209
SVP 6♓08'46"
GC 25♐56.9 ⚵ 3♏06.6R
Eris 3♈00.3 ⚶ 20♉26.9
⚷ 10♊56.1 ⚴ 15♈53.0
☽ Mean ☊ 9♑43.2

1 April 1936
Julian Day # 13240
SVP 6♓08'43"
GC 25♐56.9 ⚵ 27♎29.6R
Eris 3♈22.5 ⚶ 6♊33.7
⚷ 12♊00.1 ⚴ 29♈32.5
☽ Mean ☊ 8♑04.7

LONGITUDE — May 1936

Day	Sid.Time	☉	0 hr ☽	Noon ☽	True ☊	☿	♀	♂	⚳	♃	♄	♅	♆	♇
1 F	2 36 57	10♉55 32	8♍49 37	14♍47 49	5♑10.4	0♊37.9	25♈08.9	21♉33.1	25♏44.5	23♐46.0	19♓25.3	5♉48.8	14♍08.4	25♋16.4
2 Sa	2 40 53	11 53 43	20 44 47	26 40 59	5R 03.3	2 01.6	26 22.5	22 16.0	25R 32.1	23R 42.1	19 30.8	5 52.2	14R 07.6	25 17.0
3 Su	2 44 50	12 51 51	2♎36 47	8♎32 34	4 54.6	3 20.9	27 36.2	22 58.9	25 19.4	23 38.1	19 36.1	5 55.7	14 06.9	25 17.6
4 M	2 48 46	13 49 58	14 28 39	20 25 19	4 45.0	4 36.0	28 49.8	23 41.7	25 06.6	23 33.9	19 41.4	5 59.1	14 06.2	25 18.3
5 Tu	2 52 43	14 48 03	26 22 48	2♏21 20	4 35.3	5 46.7	0♉03.4	24 24.5	24 53.7	23 29.6	19 46.7	6 02.5	14 05.6	25 18.9
6 W	2 56 39	15 46 06	8♏21 06	14 22 17	4 26.6	6 53.0	1 17.1	25 07.2	24 40.7	23 25.1	19 51.9	6 06.0	14 05.0	25 19.6
7 Th	3 00 36	16 44 07	20 25 03	26 29 32	4 19.4	7 54.7	2 30.7	25 49.8	24 27.5	23 20.4	19 57.0	6 09.4	14 04.4	25 20.3
8 F	3 04 32	17 42 07	2♐35 56	8♐44 24	4 14.3	8 51.8	3 44.3	26 32.4	24 14.3	23 15.6	20 02.1	6 12.8	14 03.8	25 21.1
9 Sa	3 08 29	18 40 06	14 55 08	21 08 20	4 11.4	9 44.3	4 57.9	27 15.0	24 00.9	23 10.6	20 07.0	6 16.2	14 03.3	25 21.8
10 Su	3 12 26	19 38 03	27 24 15	3♑43 07	4D 10.5	10 32.1	6 11.6	27 57.5	23 47.5	23 05.5	20 11.9	6 19.6	14 02.8	25 22.6
11 M	3 16 22	20 35 59	10♑05 13	16 30 52	4 11.1	11 15.1	7 25.2	28 40.0	23 34.1	23 00.3	20 16.8	6 22.9	14 02.3	25 23.4
12 Tu	3 20 19	21 33 53	23 00 22	29 34 01	4 12.4	11 53.3	8 38.8	29 22.4	23 20.7	22 54.9	20 21.6	6 26.3	14 01.9	25 24.2
13 W	3 24 15	22 31 46	6♒12 09	12♒55 02	4R 13.6	12 26.6	9 52.5	0♊04.8	23 07.2	22 49.3	20 26.3	6 29.7	14 01.5	25 25.1
14 Th	3 28 12	23 29 38	19 42 55	26 35 58	4 13.9	12 55.0	11 06.1	0 47.1	22 53.7	22 43.7	20 30.9	6 33.0	14 01.1	25 26.0
15 F	3 32 08	24 27 29	3♓34 17	10♓37 52	4 12.8	13 18.5	12 19.7	1 29.4	22 40.2	22 37.9	20 35.4	6 36.3	14 00.8	25 26.8
16 Sa	3 36 05	25 25 18	17 46 34	25 00 07	4 10.0	13 37.0	13 33.3	2 11.6	22 26.8	22 31.9	20 39.9	6 39.7	14 00.5	25 27.7
17 Su	3 40 01	26 23 06	2♈18 04	9♈39 50	4 05.8	13 50.6	14 47.0	2 53.8	22 13.4	22 25.9	20 44.3	6 43.0	14 00.2	25 28.7
18 M	3 43 58	27 20 53	17 04 41	24 31 42	4 00.7	13 59.3	16 00.6	3 36.0	22 00.1	22 19.7	20 48.6	6 46.2	14 00.0	25 29.6
19 Tu	3 47 55	28 18 39	1♉59 54	9♉28 13	3 55.4	14R 03.2	17 14.2	4 18.1	21 46.9	22 13.4	20 52.9	6 49.5	13 59.8	25 30.6
20 W	3 51 51	29 16 24	16 55 32	24 20 47	3 50.8	14 02.3	18 27.8	5 00.1	21 33.7	22 07.0	20 57.0	6 52.8	13 59.6	25 31.6
21 Th	3 55 48	0♊14 08	1♊42 55	9♊01 00	3 47.4	13 56.8	19 41.5	5 42.1	21 20.7	22 00.5	21 01.1	6 56.0	13 59.4	25 32.6
22 F	3 59 44	1 11 50	16 14 14	23 21 59	3D 45.5	13 46.9	20 55.1	6 24.1	21 07.8	21 53.8	21 05.1	6 59.3	13 59.3	25 33.6
23 Sa	4 03 41	2 09 31	0♋23 44	7♋19 10	3 45.2	13 32.7	22 08.7	7 06.0	20 55.0	21 47.1	21 09.1	7 02.5	13 59.3	25 34.7
24 Su	4 07 37	3 07 10	14 08 10	20 50 42	3 46.0	13 14.7	23 22.3	7 47.8	20 42.4	21 40.3	21 12.9	7 05.7	13D 59.2	25 35.8
25 M	4 11 34	4 04 48	27 26 55	3♌57 04	3 47.5	12 53.1	24 36.0	8 29.7	20 30.0	21 33.4	21 16.7	7 08.9	13 59.2	25 36.9
26 Tu	4 15 30	5 02 25	10♌21 29	16 40 37	3 49.1	12 28.2	25 49.6	9 11.4	20 17.7	21 26.4	21 20.3	7 12.0	13 59.2	25 38.0
27 W	4 19 27	5 59 59	22 54 58	29 05 02	3R 50.1	12 00.6	27 03.2	9 53.1	20 05.7	21 19.4	21 23.9	7 15.1	13 59.3	25 39.1
28 Th	4 23 24	6 57 33	5♍11 24	11♍14 38	3 50.2	11 30.6	28 16.8	10 34.8	19 53.9	21 12.2	21 27.4	7 18.3	13 59.3	25 40.2
29 F	4 27 20	7 55 05	17 15 19	23 14 02	3 49.2	10 58.9	29 30.4	11 16.4	19 42.3	21 05.0	21 30.8	7 21.3	13 59.5	25 41.4
30 Sa	4 31 17	8 52 36	29 11 21	5♎07 47	3 47.1	10 26.0	0♊44.0	11 58.0	19 30.9	20 57.8	21 34.2	7 24.4	13 59.6	25 42.6
31 Su	4 35 13	9 50 05	11♎03 52	17 00 05	3 44.1	9 52.4	1 57.6	12 39.5	19 19.7	20 50.4	21 37.4	7 27.5	13 59.8	25 43.8

LONGITUDE — June 1936

Day	Sid.Time	☉	0 hr ☽	Noon ☽	True ☊	☿	♀	♂	⚳	♃	♄	♅	♆	♇
1 M	4 39 10	10♊47 33	22♎56 53	28♎54 40	3♑40.5	9♊18.8	3♊11.2	13♊21.0	19♏08.9	20♐43.0	21♓40.6	7♉30.5	14♍00.0	25♋45.0
2 Tu	4 43 06	11 45 00	4♏53 50	10♏54 41	3R 36.9	8R 45.7	4 24.8	14 02.4	18R 58.3	20R 35.6	21 43.6	7 33.5	14 00.2	25 46.2
3 W	4 47 03	12 42 26	16 57 32	23 02 39	3 33.6	8 13.6	5 38.4	14 43.8	18 47.9	20 28.1	21 46.6	7 36.5	14 00.5	25 47.5
4 Th	4 50 59	13 39 51	29 10 13	5♐20 27	3 31.1	7 43.2	6 52.0	15 25.1	18 37.9	20 20.6	21 49.5	7 39.4	14 00.8	25 48.7
5 F	4 54 56	14 37 15	11♐33 29	17 49 27	3 29.4	7 14.9	8 05.6	16 06.4	18 28.1	20 13.1	21 52.3	7 42.3	14 01.2	25 50.0
6 Sa	4 58 53	15 34 38	24 08 27	0♑30 34	3D 28.7	6 49.2	9 19.2	16 47.7	18 18.7	20 05.5	21 55.0	7 45.2	14 01.5	25 51.3
7 Su	5 02 49	16 32 01	6♑55 54	13 24 28	3 29.0	6 26.6	10 32.8	17 28.9	18 09.5	19 57.9	21 57.6	7 48.1	14 01.9	25 52.6
8 M	5 06 46	17 29 22	19 56 20	26 31 33	3 29.8	6 07.3	11 46.5	18 10.0	18 00.7	19 50.2	22 00.2	7 51.0	14 02.4	25 53.9
9 Tu	5 10 42	18 26 43	3♒10 10	9♒52 12	3 31.0	5 51.7	13 00.1	18 51.2	17 52.2	19 42.6	22 02.6	7 53.8	14 02.9	25 55.3
10 W	5 14 39	19 24 04	16 37 41	23 26 36	3 32.1	5 40.1	14 13.7	19 32.2	17 44.0	19 35.0	22 04.9	7 56.6	14 03.4	25 56.6
11 Th	5 18 35	20 21 24	0♓18 58	7♓14 43	3 32.9	5 32.7	15 27.3	20 13.3	17 36.2	19 27.3	22 07.2	7 59.4	14 03.9	25 58.0
12 F	5 22 32	21 18 43	14 13 47	21 16 01	3R 33.2	5D 29.7	16 41.0	20 54.2	17 28.7	19 19.7	22 09.3	8 02.1	14 04.5	25 59.4
13 Sa	5 26 28	22 16 02	28 21 16	5♈29 14	3 32.9	5 31.0	17 54.6	21 35.2	17 21.5	19 12.0	22 11.4	8 04.8	14 05.1	26 00.8
14 Su	5 30 25	23 13 21	12♈39 38	19 52 03	3 32.2	5 37.0	19 08.3	22 16.1	17 14.7	19 04.4	22 13.3	8 07.5	14 05.7	26 02.2
15 M	5 34 22	24 10 39	27 06 01	4♉20 59	3 31.2	5 47.5	20 21.9	22 57.0	17 08.3	18 56.8	22 15.2	8 10.1	14 06.3	26 03.6
16 Tu	5 38 18	25 07 57	11♉36 22	18 51 31	3 30.2	6 02.6	21 35.6	23 37.8	17 02.2	18 49.2	22 17.0	8 12.7	14 07.0	26 05.0
17 W	5 42 15	26 05 15	26 05 44	3♊18 20	3 29.4	6 22.3	22 49.3	24 18.6	16 56.5	18 41.6	22 18.6	8 15.3	14 07.8	26 06.5
18 Th	5 46 11	27 02 33	10♊28 39	17 36 01	3 28.9	6 46.6	24 03.0	24 59.3	16 51.1	18 34.1	22 20.2	8 17.9	14 08.5	26 07.9
19 F	5 50 08	27 59 50	24 39 51	1♋39 37	3D 28.7	7 15.3	25 16.7	25 40.0	16 46.1	18 26.6	22 21.7	8 20.4	14 09.3	26 09.4
20 Sa	5 54 04	28 57 06	8♋34 52	15 25 15	3 28.8	7 48.6	26 30.3	26 20.7	16 41.5	18 19.2	22 23.1	8 22.9	14 10.1	26 10.9
21 Su	5 58 01	29 54 22	22 10 33	28 50 36	3 29.0	8 26.2	27 44.0	27 01.3	16 37.3	18 11.8	22 24.3	8 25.3	14 11.0	26 12.3
22 M	6 01 57	0♋51 37	5♌25 22	11♌54 55	3 29.3	9 08.2	28 57.7	27 41.9	16 33.5	18 04.4	22 25.5	8 27.7	14 11.8	26 13.8
23 Tu	6 05 54	1 48 52	18 19 25	24 39 05	3 29.6	9 54.4	0♋11.4	28 22.4	16 30.0	17 57.2	22 26.6	8 30.1	14 12.7	26 15.4
24 W	6 09 51	2 46 06	0♍54 17	7♍05 22	3R 29.7	10 44.9	1 25.1	29 02.9	16 26.9	17 50.0	22 27.6	8 32.4	14 13.7	26 16.9
25 Th	6 13 47	3 43 20	13 12 46	19 17 00	3 29.7	11 39.4	2 38.9	29 43.3	16 24.2	17 42.8	22 28.4	8 34.8	14 14.6	26 18.4
26 F	6 17 44	4 40 33	25 18 34	1♎18 01	3D 29.7	12 38.1	3 52.6	0♋23.8	16 21.9	17 35.8	22 29.2	8 37.0	14 15.6	26 19.9
27 Sa	6 21 40	5 37 45	7♎15 54	13 12 49	3 29.7	13 40.8	5 06.3	1 04.1	16 19.9	17 28.8	22 29.9	8 39.2	14 16.7	26 21.5
28 Su	6 25 37	6 34 57	19 09 19	25 05 58	3 29.8	14 47.5	6 20.0	1 44.4	16 18.3	17 21.9	22 30.5	8 41.4	14 17.7	26 23.0
29 M	6 29 33	7 32 09	1♏03 20	7♏01 57	3 30.2	15 58.1	7 33.7	2 24.7	16 17.1	17 15.1	22 30.9	8 43.6	14 18.8	26 24.6
30 Tu	6 33 30	8 29 20	13 02 19	19 04 54	3 30.6	17 12.5	8 47.5	3 05.0	16 16.3	17 08.4	22 31.3	8 45.7	14 19.9	26 26.2

Astro Data

	Dy Hr Mn
☽0S	1 19:44
☽0N	16 1:04
☿R	19 19:26
♃□♅	21 22:49
♆D	25 11:08
♃□♄	27 1:45
☽0S	29 2:03
☽0N	12 6:43
☿D	12 16:36
☽0S	25 9:44

Planet Ingress

		Dy Hr Mn
☿	♊	1 1:30
♀	♉	5 10:53
♂	♊	13 9:17
☉	♊	21 6:07
♀	♊	29 21:39
☉	♋	21 14:22
♀	♋	23 8:16
♂	♋	25 21:53

Last Aspect / ☽ Ingress

Last Aspect Dy Hr Mn			☽ Ingress	Dy Hr Mn
2 9:10	♇	⚹	♎	2 18:43
5 6:52	♀	☍	♏	5 7:16
7 10:37	♂	☍	♐	7 18:54
9 15:53	♃	☌	♑	10 4:57
12 11:38	♂	△	♒	12 12:47
14 6:12	☉	□	♓	14 17:52
16 12:46	♇	△	♈	16 20:14
18 13:33	♇	□	♉	18 20:47
20 20:34	☉	☌	♊	20 21:12
22 9:32	♃	☍	♋	22 23:19
24 20:38	♇	☌	♌	25 4:41
27 7:36	♀	□	♍	27 13:48
29 16:57	♇	⚹	♎	30 1:38

Last Aspect / ☽ Ingress

Last Aspect Dy Hr Mn			☽ Ingress	Dy Hr Mn
1 5:38	♇	□	♏	1 14:11
3 17:24	♇	△	♐	4 1:37
5 19:44	♄	□	♑	6 11:03
8 10:52	♇	☍	♒	8 18:17
10 5:17	♃	⚹	♓	10 23:27
12 20:01	♇	△	♈	13 2:47
14 22:15	♇	□	♉	15 4:48
16 24:00	♇	⚹	♊	17 6:29
19 5:14	☉	☌	♋	19 9:08
21 7:14	♇	☌	♌	21 14:06
23 19:32	♂	⚹	♍	23 22:15
26 2:01	♇	⚹	♎	26 9:23
28 14:36	♇	□	♏	28 21:53

☽ Phases & Eclipses

Dy Hr Mn		
6 15:01	○	15♏53
14 6:12	☾	23♒16
20 20:34	●	29♉37
28 2:46	☽	6♍35
5 5:22	○	14♐21
12 12:05	☾	21♓19
19 5:14	●	27♊44
19 5:20:06	●	T 02'32"
26 19:23	☽	4♎58

Astro Data

1 May 1936
Julian Day # 13270
SVP 6♓08'40"
GC 25♐57.0 ⚴ 18♎38.9R
Eris 3♈42.6 ⚵ 22♊40.5
⚷ 13♊54.4 ⚶ 12♉54.4
☽ Mean ☊ 6♑29.4

1 June 1936
Julian Day # 13301
SVP 6♓08'35"
GC 25♐57.1 ⚴ 14♎16.6R
Eris 3♈57.2 ⚵ 9♋15.6
⚷ 16♊24.0 ⚶ 26♉33.9
☽ Mean ☊ 4♑50.9

July 1936 — LONGITUDE

Day	Sid.Time	☉	0 hr ☽	Noon ☽	True ☊	☿	♀	♂	⚳	♃	♄	♅	♆	♇
1 W	6 37 26	9♋26 32	25♏10 10	1♐18 29	3♑31.2	18♊30.8	10♋01.2	3♋45.2	16♏15.9	17♐01.8	22♓31.6	8♉47.8	14♍21.0	26♋27.7
2 Th	6 41 23	10 23 42	7♐30 12	13 45 37	3 31.8	19 52.8	11 14.9	4 25.3	16D15.8	16R55.3	22 31.8	8 49.8	14 22.2	26 29.3
3 F	6 45 20	11 20 53	20 04 58	26 28 24	3R32.1	21 18.6	12 28.7	5 05.4	16 16.1	16 48.9	22R31.8	8 51.8	14 23.4	26 30.9
4 Sa	6 49 16	12 18 04	2♑56 01	9♑27 53	3 32.1	22 48.1	13 42.4	5 45.5	16 16.8	16 42.6	22 31.8	8 53.8	14 24.6	26 32.5
5 Su	6 53 13	13 15 14	16 03 57	22 44 07	3 31.7	24 21.2	14 56.2	6 25.6	16 17.8	16 36.4	22 31.7	8 55.7	14 25.9	26 34.1
6 M	6 57 09	14 12 25	29 28 15	6♒16 07	3 30.8	25 57.8	16 10.0	7 05.6	16 19.2	16 30.4	22 31.5	8 57.6	14 27.2	26 35.7
7 Tu	7 01 06	15 09 36	13♒07 28	20 02 01	3 29.5	27 37.9	17 23.7	7 45.5	16 21.0	16 24.4	22 31.2	8 59.4	14 28.5	26 37.3
8 W	7 05 02	16 06 47	26 59 24	3♓59 16	3 28.0	29 21.3	18 37.5	8 25.5	16 23.1	16 18.6	22 30.7	9 01.2	14 29.8	26 38.9
9 Th	7 08 59	17 03 58	11♓01 16	18 05 01	3 26.6	1♋08.0	19 51.3	9 05.4	16 25.6	16 13.0	22 30.2	9 03.0	14 31.1	26 40.6
10 F	7 12 56	18 01 10	25 10 08	2♈16 16	3 25.5	2 57.8	21 05.1	9 45.2	16 28.4	16 07.4	22 29.6	9 04.7	14 32.5	26 42.2
11 Sa	7 16 52	18 58 22	9♈23 03	16 30 10	3D25.0	4 50.5	22 18.9	10 25.0	16 31.5	16 02.0	22 28.9	9 06.4	14 33.9	26 43.8
12 Su	7 20 49	19 55 35	23 37 16	0♉44 04	3 25.3	6 46.0	23 32.7	11 04.8	16 35.0	15 56.7	22 28.0	9 08.0	14 35.4	26 45.4
13 M	7 24 45	20 52 49	7♉50 16	14 55 34	3 26.1	8 44.0	24 46.6	11 44.6	16 38.9	15 51.6	22 27.1	9 09.6	14 36.8	26 47.1
14 Tu	7 28 42	21 50 03	21 59 41	29 02 20	3 27.3	10 44.3	26 00.4	12 24.3	16 43.1	15 46.6	22 26.1	9 11.1	14 38.3	26 48.7
15 W	7 32 38	22 47 18	6♊03 14	13♊02 06	3 28.5	12 46.6	27 14.3	13 04.0	16 47.6	15 41.8	22 25.0	9 12.6	14 39.8	26 50.4
16 Th	7 36 35	23 44 33	19 58 40	26 52 37	3R29.3	14 50.6	28 28.1	13 43.7	16 52.5	15 37.1	22 23.8	9 14.1	14 41.3	26 52.0
17 F	7 40 31	24 41 49	3♋43 41	10♋31 37	3 29.3	16 56.0	29 42.0	14 23.3	16 57.7	15 32.6	22 22.5	9 15.5	14 42.9	26 53.6
18 Sa	7 44 28	25 39 05	17 16 09	23 57 04	3 28.2	19 02.5	0♌55.9	15 02.9	17 03.3	15 28.2	22 21.1	9 16.8	14 44.5	26 55.3
19 Su	7 48 25	26 36 22	0♌34 12	7♌07 25	3 26.0	21 09.8	2 09.8	15 42.4	17 09.1	15 24.0	22 19.6	9 18.1	14 46.1	26 56.9
20 M	7 52 21	27 33 39	13 36 36	20 01 45	3 22.8	23 17.5	3 23.6	16 21.9	17 15.3	15 20.0	22 18.0	9 19.4	14 47.7	26 58.6
21 Tu	7 56 18	28 30 57	26 22 52	2♍40 05	3 18.9	25 25.4	4 37.5	17 01.4	17 21.8	15 16.1	22 16.3	9 20.6	14 49.3	27 00.2
22 W	8 00 14	29 28 15	8♍53 32	15 03 27	3 14.8	27 33.2	5 51.4	17 40.8	17 28.6	15 12.4	22 14.5	9 21.8	14 51.0	27 01.9
23 Th	8 04 11	0♌25 33	21 10 07	27 13 53	3 11.1	29 40.6	7 05.3	18 20.2	17 35.7	15 08.8	22 12.6	9 22.9	14 52.7	27 03.5
24 F	8 08 07	1 22 52	3♎15 10	9♎14 24	3 08.1	1♌47.5	8 19.3	18 59.6	17 43.2	15 05.4	22 10.7	9 24.0	14 54.4	27 05.1
25 Sa	8 12 04	2 20 11	15 12 04	21 08 43	3 06.2	3 53.5	9 33.2	19 38.9	17 50.9	15 02.2	22 08.6	9 25.0	14 56.1	27 06.8
26 Su	8 16 00	3 17 31	27 04 54	3♏01 13	3D05.6	5 58.6	10 47.1	20 18.2	17 58.9	14 59.2	22 06.4	9 26.0	14 57.9	27 08.4
27 M	8 19 57	4 14 51	8♏58 14	14 56 36	3 06.1	8 02.6	12 01.0	20 57.5	18 07.2	14 56.4	22 04.2	9 27.0	14 59.6	27 10.0
28 Tu	8 23 54	5 12 11	20 56 53	26 59 42	3 07.4	10 05.3	13 14.9	21 36.7	18 15.9	14 53.7	22 01.9	9 27.8	15 01.4	27 11.7
29 W	8 27 50	6 09 33	3♐05 36	9♐15 10	3 09.1	12 06.7	14 28.9	22 15.9	18 24.8	14 51.2	21 59.5	9 28.7	15 03.2	27 13.3
30 Th	8 31 47	7 06 54	15 28 53	21 47 12	3R10.5	14 06.7	15 42.8	22 55.1	18 33.9	14 48.9	21 57.0	9 29.5	15 05.0	27 14.9
31 F	8 35 43	8 04 17	28 10 30	4♑39 05	3 10.9	16 05.2	16 56.7	23 34.2	18 43.4	14 46.8	21 54.4	9 30.2	15 06.9	27 16.6

August 1936 — LONGITUDE

Day	Sid.Time	☉	0 hr ☽	Noon ☽	True ☊	☿	♀	♂	⚳	♃	♄	♅	♆	♇
1 Sa	8 39 40	9♌01 40	11♑13 10	17♑52 50	3♑10.0	18♌02.2	18♌10.7	24♋13.3	18♏53.1	14♐44.8	21♓51.7	9♉30.9	15♍08.8	27♋18.2
2 Su	8 43 36	9 59 04	24 38 04	1♒28 44	3R07.5	19 57.7	19 24.6	24 52.3	19 03.1	14R43.0	21R49.0	9 31.6	15 10.6	27 19.8
3 M	8 47 33	10 56 29	8♒24 34	15 25 11	3 03.3	21 51.5	20 38.5	25 31.4	19 13.4	14 41.4	21 46.1	9 32.2	15 12.5	27 21.4
4 Tu	8 51 29	11 53 54	22 30 03	29 38 34	2 57.9	23 43.8	21 52.5	26 10.4	19 23.9	14 40.0	21 43.2	9 32.7	15 14.4	27 23.0
5 W	8 55 26	12 51 21	6♓50 02	14♓03 42	2 51.9	25 34.5	23 06.4	26 49.3	19 34.6	14 38.8	21 40.2	9 33.2	15 16.4	27 24.6
6 Th	8 59 23	13 48 49	21 18 48	28 34 31	2 46.2	27 23.7	24 20.4	27 28.3	19 45.7	14 37.8	21 37.2	9 33.7	15 18.3	27 26.2
7 F	9 03 19	14 46 18	5♈50 09	13♈04 58	2 41.4	29 11.3	25 34.4	28 07.2	19 56.9	14 36.9	21 34.0	9 34.1	15 20.3	27 27.8
8 Sa	9 07 16	15 43 48	20 18 23	27 29 52	2 38.3	0♍57.3	26 48.3	28 46.0	20 08.4	14 36.2	21 30.8	9 34.4	15 22.3	27 29.3
9 Su	9 11 12	16 41 20	4♉38 59	11♉45 25	2D36.9	2 41.7	28 02.3	29 24.9	20 20.2	14 35.7	21 27.5	9 34.7	15 24.2	27 30.9
10 M	9 15 09	17 38 53	18 48 57	25 49 24	2 37.0	4 24.7	29 16.3	0♌03.7	20 32.2	14 35.4	21 24.1	9 35.0	15 26.3	27 32.5
11 Tu	9 19 05	18 36 28	2♊46 43	9♊40 51	2 38.1	6 06.1	0♍30.3	0 42.5	20 44.4	14D35.3	21 20.7	9 35.2	15 28.3	27 34.0
12 W	9 23 02	19 34 05	16 31 51	23 19 49	2R39.2	7 45.9	1 44.3	1 21.2	20 56.9	14 35.4	21 17.2	9 35.3	15 30.3	27 35.6
13 Th	9 26 58	20 31 42	0♋04 31	6♋46 17	2 39.4	9 24.3	2 58.3	2 00.0	21 09.6	14 35.7	21 13.6	9 35.4	15 32.4	27 37.1
14 F	9 30 55	21 29 22	13 25 05	20 00 56	2 38.0	11 01.2	4 12.3	2 38.7	21 22.5	14 36.1	21 10.0	9R35.5	15 34.4	27 38.7
15 Sa	9 34 52	22 27 02	26 33 51	3♌03 49	2 34.4	12 36.6	5 26.3	3 17.4	21 35.6	14 36.7	21 06.3	9 35.5	15 36.5	27 40.2
16 Su	9 38 48	23 24 44	9♌30 50	15 54 54	2 28.5	14 10.5	6 40.3	3 56.0	21 49.0	14 37.5	21 02.6	9 35.5	15 38.6	27 41.7
17 M	9 42 45	24 22 27	22 15 58	28 34 03	2 20.5	15 42.9	7 54.3	4 34.6	22 02.6	14 38.5	20 58.7	9 35.4	15 40.7	27 43.2
18 Tu	9 46 41	25 20 12	4♍49 10	11♍01 21	2 11.1	17 13.8	9 08.3	5 13.2	22 16.4	14 39.7	20 54.9	9 35.2	15 42.8	27 44.7
19 W	9 50 38	26 17 58	17 10 41	23 17 17	2 01.1	18 43.2	10 22.3	5 51.7	22 30.4	14 41.1	20 50.9	9 35.0	15 44.9	27 46.2
20 Th	9 54 34	27 15 45	29 21 20	5♎23 01	1 51.5	20 11.1	11 36.3	6 30.3	22 44.6	14 42.6	20 46.9	9 34.8	15 47.0	27 47.6
21 F	9 58 31	28 13 33	11♎22 39	17 20 32	1 43.1	21 37.4	12 50.3	7 08.7	22 59.0	14 44.4	20 42.9	9 34.5	15 49.2	27 49.1
22 Sa	10 02 27	29 11 22	23 17 03	29 12 39	1 36.7	23 02.2	14 04.3	7 47.2	23 13.6	14 46.3	20 38.8	9 34.1	15 51.3	27 50.5
23 Su	10 06 24	0♍09 13	5♏07 49	11♏03 04	1 32.5	24 25.5	15 18.3	8 25.6	23 28.4	14 48.4	20 34.7	9 33.7	15 53.4	27 52.0
24 M	10 10 21	1 07 05	16 58 58	22 56 08	1D30.4	25 47.1	16 32.3	9 04.0	23 43.4	14 50.7	20 30.5	9 33.3	15 55.6	27 53.4
25 Tu	10 14 17	2 04 58	28 55 12	4♐56 47	1 30.1	27 07.1	17 46.3	9 42.4	23 58.6	14 53.1	20 26.3	9 32.8	15 57.8	27 54.8
26 W	10 18 14	3 02 53	11♐01 35	17 10 13	1 30.7	28 25.4	19 00.3	10 20.7	24 14.0	14 55.8	20 22.0	9 32.3	16 00.0	27 56.2
27 Th	10 22 10	4 00 49	23 23 19	29 41 30	1R31.2	29 42.0	20 14.3	10 59.0	24 29.5	14 58.6	20 17.7	9 31.7	16 02.1	27 57.6
28 F	10 26 07	4 58 46	6♑05 18	12♑35 12	1 30.7	0♎56.8	21 28.3	11 37.3	24 45.2	15 01.6	20 13.4	9 31.1	16 04.3	27 59.0
29 Sa	10 30 03	5 56 45	19 11 35	25 54 42	1 28.3	2 09.8	22 42.3	12 15.6	25 01.2	15 04.8	20 09.0	9 30.4	16 06.5	28 00.3
30 Su	10 34 00	6 54 45	2♒44 40	9♒41 27	1 23.5	3 20.8	23 56.3	12 53.8	25 17.2	15 08.1	20 04.6	9 29.7	16 08.7	28 01.7
31 M	10 37 56	7 52 46	16 44 50	23 54 23	1 16.2	4 29.8	25 10.2	13 32.0	25 33.5	15 11.7	20 00.1	9 28.9	16 10.9	28 03.0

Astro Data	Planet Ingress	Last Aspect	☽ Ingress	Last Aspect	☽ Ingress	☽ Phases & Eclipses
Dy Hr Mn	Dy Hr Mn	Dy Hr Mn	Dy Hr Mn	Dy Hr Mn	Dy Hr Mn	Dy Hr Mn
⚳ D 2 4:24	☿ ♋ 8 20:47	1 2:31 ♇ △	♐ 1 9:27	2 4:44 ♇ ☍	♒ 2 9:25	4 17:34 ○ 12♑31
♄ R 3 18:52	♀ ♌ 17 17:51	3 4:37 ♄ □	♑ 3 18:34	4 0:35 ☿ ☍	♓ 4 12:36	4 17:25 • P 0.267
☽0N 9 12:10	☉ ♌ 23 1:18	5 18:51 ♇ ☍	♒ 6 0:56	6 10:07 ♇ △	♈ 6 14:21	11 16:28 ☾ 19♈09
☽0S 22 18:17	☿ ♌ 23 15:39	8 2:56 ☿ △	♓ 8 5:10	8 14:14 ♂ □	♉ 8 16:11	18 15:19 ● 25♋47
♃□♆ 26 19:00		10 2:35 ♇ △	♈ 10 8:10	10 18:31 ♀ □	♊ 10 19:12	26 12:36 ☽ 3♏19
	☿ ♍ 7 22:59	12 5:17 ♇ □	♉ 12 10:46	12 8:24 ♄ □	♋ 12 23:52	
☽0N 5 19:09	♂ ♌ 10 9:43	14 8:12 ♇ ⚹	♊ 14 13:38	15 2:01 ♇ ☌	♌ 15 6:20	3 3:47 ○ 10♒37
♃ D 11 14:59	♀ ♍ 11 2:11	16 4:13 ♄ □	♋ 16 17:28	17 3:21 ☉ ☌	♍ 17 14:44	9 20:59 ☾ 17♉03
♅ R 15 2:35	☉ ♍ 23 8:11	18 17:23 ♇ ☌	♌ 18 22:58	19 20:52 ♇ ⚹	♎ 20 1:17	17 3:21 ● 24♌02
☽0S 19 2:35	☿ ♎ 27 17:43	20 3:15 ♃ △	♍ 21 6:54	22 11:57 ☉ ⚹	♏ 22 13:36	25 5:49 ☽ 1♐50
☿0S 26 0:59		23 11:39 ♇ ⚹	♎ 23 17:30	24 21:58 ♇ △	♐ 25 2:09	
		26 0:05 ♇ □	♏ 26 5:54	27 12:01 ☿ □	♑ 27 12:35	
		28 12:24 ♇ △	♐ 28 17:56	29 15:42 ♇ ☍	♒ 29 19:12	
		30 12:18 ♄ □	♑ 31 3:24	30 21:19 ♃ ⚹	♓ 31 22:06	

Astro Data

1 July 1936
Julian Day # 13331
SVP 6♓08'30"
GC 25♐57.1 ⚴ 16♎47.5
Eris 4♈01.9R ⚵ 24♋55.6
⚷ 18♊55.3 ⚶ 9♊22.5
☽Mean ☊ 3♑15.6

1 August 1936
Julian Day # 13362
SVP 6♓08'25"
GC 25♐57.2 ⚴ 24♎14.2
Eris 3♈56.2R ⚵ 10♌30.8
⚷ 21♊13.6 ⚶ 21♊51.5
☽Mean ☊ 1♑37.1

LONGITUDE — September 1936

Day	Sid.Time	☉	0 hr ☽	Noon ☽	True ☊	☿	♀	♂	⚳	♃	♄	♅	♆	♇
1 Tu	10 41 53	8♍50 49	1♓09 31	8♓29 26	1♑07.1	5♎36.7	26♍24.2	14♌10.1	25♏49.9	15♐15.4	19♓55.7	9♉28.1	16♍13.1	28♋04.3
2 W	10 45 50	9 48 53	15 53 13	23 19 46	0R 57.0	6 41.4	27 38.2	14 48.3	26 06.5	15 19.2	19R 51.2	9R 27.2	16 15.4	28 05.6
3 Th	10 49 46	10 47 00	0♈47 59	8♈16 39	0 47.1	7 43.8	28 52.1	15 26.4	26 23.2	15 23.3	19 46.7	9 26.3	16 17.6	28 06.9
4 F	10 53 43	11 45 08	15 44 38	23 10 53	0 38.5	8 43.7	0♎06.1	16 04.5	26 40.1	15 27.5	19 42.1	9 25.3	16 19.8	28 08.1
5 Sa	10 57 39	12 43 18	0♉34 26	7♉54 28	0 32.2	9 41.0	1 20.0	16 42.5	26 57.2	15 31.8	19 37.6	9 24.3	16 22.0	28 09.4
6 Su	11 01 36	13 41 30	15 10 21	22 21 37	0 28.4	10 35.5	2 34.0	17 20.5	27 14.4	15 36.4	19 33.0	9 23.3	16 24.2	28 10.6
7 M	11 05 32	14 39 45	29 27 59	6♊29 17	0D 26.9	11 27.1	3 47.9	17 58.6	27 31.7	15 41.1	19 28.4	9 22.2	16 26.5	28 11.8
8 Tu	11 09 29	15 38 01	13♊25 31	20 16 47	0R 26.7	12 15.5	5 01.9	18 36.5	27 49.2	15 46.0	19 23.8	9 21.0	16 28.7	28 13.0
9 W	11 13 25	16 36 20	27 03 15	3♋45 11	0 26.8	13 00.6	6 15.8	19 14.5	28 06.9	15 51.0	19 19.2	9 19.9	16 30.9	28 14.2
10 Th	11 17 22	17 34 40	10♋22 50	16 56 30	0 25.9	13 42.0	7 29.8	19 52.4	28 24.7	15 56.2	19 14.6	9 18.6	16 33.1	28 15.4
11 F	11 21 19	18 33 03	23 26 29	29 53 04	0 22.9	14 19.5	8 43.7	20 30.3	28 42.7	16 01.5	19 10.0	9 17.4	16 35.4	28 16.5
12 Sa	11 25 15	19 31 28	6♌16 30	12♌37 01	0 17.2	14 52.9	9 57.6	21 08.2	29 00.8	16 07.1	19 05.4	9 16.1	16 37.6	28 17.7
13 Su	11 29 12	20 29 54	18 54 48	25 10 02	0 08.5	15 21.8	11 11.6	21 46.1	29 19.0	16 12.7	19 00.8	9 14.7	16 39.8	28 18.8
14 M	11 33 08	21 28 23	1♍22 51	7♍33 23	29♐57.2	15 45.9	12 25.5	22 23.9	29 37.4	16 18.6	18 56.1	9 13.3	16 42.0	28 19.9
15 Tu	11 37 05	22 26 54	13 41 41	19 47 54	29 43.9	16 04.9	13 39.4	23 01.7	29 55.9	16 24.5	18 51.5	9 11.9	16 44.3	28 20.9
16 W	11 41 01	23 25 26	25 52 05	1♎54 22	29 29.8	16 18.4	14 53.3	23 39.4	0♐14.5	16 30.7	18 46.9	9 10.4	16 46.5	28 22.0
17 Th	11 44 58	24 24 00	7♎54 52	13 53 43	29 16.1	16R 26.1	16 07.3	24 17.2	0 33.3	16 37.0	18 42.3	9 08.9	16 48.7	28 23.0
18 F	11 48 54	25 22 37	19 51 06	25 47 16	29 03.8	16 27.6	17 21.2	24 54.9	0 52.1	16 43.4	18 37.7	9 07.3	16 50.9	28 24.0
19 Sa	11 52 51	26 21 15	1♏42 29	7♏37 03	28 53.9	16 22.5	18 35.1	25 32.6	1 11.2	16 50.0	18 33.2	9 05.7	16 53.1	28 25.0
20 Su	11 56 47	27 19 54	13 31 21	19 25 50	28 46.7	16 10.6	19 49.0	26 10.2	1 30.3	16 56.8	18 28.6	9 04.1	16 55.3	28 26.0
21 M	12 00 44	28 18 36	25 20 56	1♐17 12	28 42.4	15 51.7	21 02.8	26 47.9	1 49.6	17 03.6	18 24.1	9 02.4	16 57.5	28 26.9
22 Tu	12 04 41	29 17 20	7♐15 11	13 15 30	28 40.4	15 25.5	22 16.7	27 25.5	2 09.0	17 10.7	18 19.6	9 00.7	16 59.7	28 27.8
23 W	12 08 37	0♎16 05	19 18 46	25 25 41	28 39.9	14 52.2	23 30.6	28 03.0	2 28.5	17 17.9	18 15.1	8 59.0	17 01.9	28 28.8
24 Th	12 12 34	1 14 52	1♑36 52	7♑53 01	28 39.9	14 11.7	24 44.4	28 40.6	2 48.1	17 25.2	18 10.7	8 57.2	17 04.1	28 29.6
25 F	12 16 30	2 13 40	14 14 45	20 42 41	28 39.0	13 24.4	25 58.3	29 18.1	3 07.8	17 32.6	18 06.3	8 55.4	17 06.2	28 30.5
26 Sa	12 20 27	3 12 30	27 17 19	3♒59 05	28 36.4	12 30.8	27 12.1	29 55.5	3 27.6	17 40.2	18 01.9	8 53.5	17 08.4	28 31.4
27 Su	12 24 23	4 11 22	10♒48 18	17 45 07	28 31.3	11 31.8	28 25.9	0♍33.0	3 47.6	17 48.0	17 57.6	8 51.7	17 10.5	28 32.2
28 M	12 28 20	5 10 16	24 49 28	2♓01 07	28 23.6	10 28.3	29 39.7	1 10.4	4 07.6	17 55.8	17 53.3	8 49.7	17 12.7	28 33.0
29 Tu	12 32 16	6 09 12	9♓19 35	16 44 09	28 13.8	9 21.7	0♏53.5	1 47.8	4 27.8	18 03.8	17 49.0	8 47.8	17 14.8	28 33.7
30 W	12 36 13	7 08 09	24 13 52	1♈47 38	28 02.7	8 13.5	2 07.3	2 25.2	4 48.0	18 11.9	17 44.8	8 45.8	17 16.9	28 34.5

LONGITUDE — October 1936

Day	Sid.Time	☉	0 hr ☽	Noon ☽	True ☊	☿	♀	♂	⚳	♃	♄	♅	♆	♇
1 Th	12 40 10	8♎07 09	9♈24 07	17♈01 57	27♐51.8	7♎05.4	3♏21.0	3♍02.5	5♐08.4	18♐20.2	17♓40.6	8♉43.8	17♍19.1	28♋35.2
2 F	12 44 06	9 06 10	24 39 43	2♉16 01	27R 42.2	5R 59.2	4 34.8	3 39.8	5 28.8	18 28.6	17R 36.4	8R 41.8	17 21.2	28 35.9
3 Sa	12 48 03	10 05 14	9♉49 35	17 19 16	27 35.0	4 56.7	5 48.5	4 17.1	5 49.4	18 37.1	17 32.4	8 39.7	17 23.3	28 36.6
4 Su	12 51 59	11 04 20	24 44 07	2♊03 26	27 30.5	3 59.8	7 02.3	4 54.4	6 10.0	18 45.7	17 28.3	8 37.6	17 25.3	28 37.3
5 M	12 55 56	12 03 29	9♊16 41	16 23 33	27D 28.5	3 09.9	8 16.0	5 31.6	6 30.7	18 54.5	17 24.3	8 35.5	17 27.4	28 37.9
6 Tu	12 59 52	13 02 39	23 23 57	0♋17 54	27 28.2	2 28.5	9 29.7	6 08.8	6 51.6	19 03.4	17 20.4	8 33.4	17 29.5	28 38.5
7 W	13 03 49	14 01 53	7♋05 37	13 47 22	27R 28.4	1 56.5	10 43.4	6 46.0	7 12.5	19 12.4	17 16.5	8 31.2	17 31.5	28 39.1
8 Th	13 07 45	15 01 08	20 23 31	26 54 29	27 27.8	1 34.8	11 57.1	7 23.2	7 33.5	19 21.5	17 12.7	8 29.0	17 33.6	28 39.7
9 F	13 11 42	16 00 26	3♌20 43	9♌42 38	27 25.5	1D 23.8	13 10.8	8 00.3	7 54.6	19 30.7	17 09.0	8 26.8	17 35.6	28 40.2
10 Sa	13 15 39	16 59 46	16 00 43	22 15 21	27 20.6	1 23.7	14 24.5	8 37.4	8 15.8	19 40.1	17 05.3	8 24.6	17 37.6	28 40.7
11 Su	13 19 35	17 59 08	28 26 56	4♍35 50	27 12.9	1 34.3	15 38.2	9 14.5	8 37.1	19 49.6	17 01.6	8 22.3	17 39.6	28 41.2
12 M	13 23 32	18 58 32	10♍42 22	16 46 49	27 02.7	1 55.3	16 51.9	9 51.5	8 58.4	19 59.2	16 58.1	8 20.0	17 41.5	28 41.7
13 Tu	13 27 28	19 57 59	22 49 26	28 50 27	26 50.6	2 26.2	18 05.5	10 28.5	9 19.9	20 08.9	16 54.6	8 17.7	17 43.5	28 42.1
14 W	13 31 25	20 57 28	4♎50 03	10♎48 25	26 37.8	3 06.4	19 19.2	11 05.5	9 41.4	20 18.7	16 51.2	8 15.4	17 45.4	28 42.5
15 Th	13 35 21	21 56 59	16 45 43	22 42 07	26 25.1	3 55.0	20 32.8	11 42.5	10 03.0	20 28.6	16 47.8	8 13.1	17 47.4	28 42.9
16 F	13 39 18	22 56 32	28 37 47	4♏32 55	26 13.9	4 51.4	21 46.4	12 19.4	10 24.7	20 38.6	16 44.5	8 10.7	17 49.3	28 43.3
17 Sa	13 43 14	23 56 07	10♏27 41	16 22 22	26 04.8	5 54.7	23 00.0	12 56.3	10 46.5	20 48.7	16 41.3	8 08.4	17 51.1	28 43.6
18 Su	13 47 11	24 55 44	22 17 12	28 12 29	25 58.3	7 04.1	24 13.7	13 33.2	11 08.3	20 59.0	16 38.2	8 06.0	17 53.0	28 43.9
19 M	13 51 07	25 55 23	4♐08 36	10♐05 54	25 54.5	8 18.8	25 27.2	14 10.0	11 30.2	21 09.3	16 35.2	8 03.6	17 54.9	28 44.2
20 Tu	13 55 04	26 55 03	16 04 51	22 05 55	25D 53.1	9 38.2	26 40.8	14 46.8	11 52.2	21 19.7	16 32.2	8 01.2	17 56.7	28 44.5
21 W	13 59 01	27 54 46	28 09 37	4♑16 30	25 53.3	11 01.4	27 54.4	15 23.6	12 14.2	21 30.3	16 29.3	7 58.8	17 58.5	28 44.7
22 Th	14 02 57	28 54 30	10♑27 08	16 42 09	25 54.2	12 28.1	29 07.9	16 00.3	12 36.4	21 40.9	16 26.6	7 56.4	18 00.3	28 45.0
23 F	14 06 54	29 54 16	23 02 06	29 27 35	25R 54.7	13 57.5	0♐21.4	16 37.0	12 58.6	21 51.6	16 23.8	7 53.9	18 02.1	28 45.1
24 Sa	14 10 50	0♏54 04	5♒59 10	12♒37 18	25 54.0	15 29.2	1 34.9	17 13.6	13 20.8	22 02.5	16 21.2	7 51.5	18 03.8	28 45.3
25 Su	14 14 47	1 53 53	19 22 25	26 14 47	25 51.3	17 02.8	2 48.4	17 50.3	13 43.1	22 13.4	16 18.7	7 49.0	18 05.6	28 45.4
26 M	14 18 43	2 53 44	3♓14 33	10♓21 40	25 46.5	18 37.9	4 01.9	18 26.9	14 05.5	22 24.4	16 16.3	7 46.6	18 07.3	28 45.5
27 Tu	14 22 40	3 53 36	17 35 55	24 56 49	25 39.9	20 14.2	5 15.3	19 03.4	14 27.9	22 35.5	16 13.9	7 44.1	18 09.0	28 45.6
28 W	14 26 36	4 53 30	2♈23 41	9♈55 37	25 32.2	21 51.3	6 28.8	19 39.9	14 50.4	22 46.6	16 11.6	7 41.6	18 10.6	28 45.7
29 Th	14 30 33	5 53 26	17 31 30	25 10 04	25 24.3	23 29.2	7 42.2	20 16.4	15 13.0	22 57.9	16 09.5	7 39.2	18 12.3	28R 45.7
30 F	14 34 30	6 53 24	2♉49 55	10♉29 38	25 17.4	25 07.6	8 55.5	20 52.9	15 35.6	23 09.3	16 07.4	7 36.7	18 13.9	28 45.7
31 Sa	14 38 26	7 53 24	18 07 48	25 43 05	25 12.3	26 46.3	10 08.9	21 29.3	15 58.3	23 20.7	16 05.4	7 34.2	18 15.5	28 45.7

Astro Data

	Dy Hr Mn
☽0N	2 4:19
♀0S	6 12:11
☽0S	15 9:38
☿R	18 5:32
♃□♆	20 4:25
☉0S	23 5:26
♃□♄	28 6:58
☽0N	29 14:50
♄☍♆	4 23:47
☿D	10 0:14
☿0N	10 6:46
☽0S	12 15:15
☿0S	15 6:31
☽0N	27 0:59
♃⚼♅	28 3:12

Planet Ingress

	Dy Hr Mn
♀ ♎	4 10:02
☊ ♐R	14 6:30
⚳ ♐	15 17:21
☉ ♎	23 5:26
♂ ♍	26 14:51
♀ ♏	28 18:36
♀ ♐	23 5:00
☉ ♏	23 14:18
♇ R	30 5:21

Last Aspect / ☽ Ingress (September)

Last Aspect Dy Hr Mn		☽ Ingress Dy Hr Mn
2 19:40	♇ △	♈ 2 22:43
4 20:03	♇ □	♉ 4 23:04
6 21:50	♇ ⚹	♊ 7 0:54
8 10:27	♄ □	♋ 9 5:16
11 8:59	♇ ☌	♌ 11 12:13
13 5:07	♂ ☌	♍ 13 21:20
16 4:57	♇ ⚹	♎ 16 8:12
18 17:18	♇ □	♏ 18 20:32
21 6:16	♇ △	♐ 21 9:24
23 17:23	♂ △	♑ 23 20:53
26 2:13	♇ ☍	♒ 26 4:53
28 7:43	♀ △	♓ 28 8:39
30 6:54	♇ △	♈ 30 9:10

Last Aspect / ☽ Ingress (October)

Last Aspect Dy Hr Mn		☽ Ingress Dy Hr Mn
2 6:12	♇ □	♉ 2 8:25
4 6:21	♇ ⚹	♊ 4 8:37
5 16:20	♃ ☍	♋ 6 11:29
8 15:15	♇ ☌	♌ 8 17:45
10 6:57	♃ △	♍ 11 3:01
13 11:43	♇ ⚹	♎ 13 14:19
16 0:11	♇ □	♏ 16 2:47
18 13:04	♇ △	♐ 18 15:38
20 22:24	☉ ⚹	♑ 21 3:37
23 12:53	☉ □	♒ 23 13:00
25 4:54	♃ ⚹	♓ 25 18:28
27 18:10	♇ △	♈ 27 20:09
29 17:38	♇ □	♉ 29 19:34
31 16:51	♇ ⚹	♊ 31 18:49

☽ Phases & Eclipses

Dy Hr Mn	
1 12:37	○ 8♓52
8 3:14	☾ 15♊17
15 17:41	● 22♍41
23 22:12	☽ 0♑41
30 21:01	○ 7♈30
7 12:28	☾ 14♋03
15 10:20	● 21♎53
23 12:53	☽ 29♑56
30 5:58	○ 6♉38

Astro Data

1 September 1936
Julian Day # 13393
SVP 6♓08'21"
GC 25♐57.3 ⚴ 4♏34.3
Eris 3♈41.4R ⚵ 25♌19.1
⚷ 22♊49.4 ⚶ 3♋02.8
☽ Mean ☊ 29♐58.6

1 October 1936
Julian Day # 13423
SVP 6♓08'18"
GC 25♐57.4 ⚴ 16♏08.5
Eris 3♈22.5R ⚵ 8♍41.5
⚷ 23♊22.3R ⚶ 11♋45.0
☽ Mean ☊ 28♐23.3

November 1936 — LONGITUDE

Day	Sid.Time	☉	0 hr ☽	Noon ☽	True ☊	☿	♀	♂	⚳	♃	♄	♅	♆	♇
1 Su	14 42 23	8♏53 26	3♊14 18	10♊40 27	25♐09.4	28♎25.2	11♐22.2	22♍05.7	16♐21.0	23♐32.2	16♓03.5	7♉31.7	18♍17.1	28♋45.7
2 M	14 46 19	9 53 30	18 00 43	25 14 31	25D 08.5	0♏04.1	12 35.6	22 42.1	16 43.8	23 43.8	16R 01.8	7R 29.3	18 18.6	28R 45.6
3 Tu	14 50 16	10 53 37	2♋21 28	9♋21 24	25 09.2	1 43.1	13 48.9	23 18.4	17 06.6	23 55.5	16 00.1	7 26.8	18 20.1	28 45.5
4 W	14 54 12	11 53 45	16 14 19	23 00 21	25 10.5	3 22.0	15 02.2	23 54.7	17 29.5	24 07.2	15 58.5	7 24.4	18 21.6	28 45.4
5 Th	14 58 09	12 53 55	29 39 48	6♌13 01	25R 11.7	5 00.7	16 15.4	24 31.0	17 52.5	24 19.0	15 57.0	7 21.9	18 23.1	28 45.2
6 F	15 02 05	13 54 07	12♌40 27	19 02 36	25 11.7	6 39.2	17 28.7	25 07.2	18 15.5	24 30.9	15 55.6	7 19.4	18 24.6	28 45.0
7 Sa	15 06 02	14 54 22	25 19 57	1♍33 03	25 10.2	8 17.5	18 41.9	25 43.4	18 38.5	24 42.9	15 54.3	7 17.0	18 26.0	28 44.8
8 Su	15 09 59	15 54 38	7♍42 24	13 48 32	25 06.8	9 55.5	19 55.1	26 19.6	19 01.6	24 55.0	15 53.1	7 14.5	18 27.4	28 44.6
9 M	15 13 55	16 54 56	19 51 55	25 53 00	25 01.7	11 33.3	21 08.3	26 55.7	19 24.8	25 07.1	15 52.0	7 12.1	18 28.7	28 44.4
10 Tu	15 17 52	17 55 17	1♎52 13	7♎49 58	24 55.3	13 10.8	22 21.5	27 31.8	19 47.9	25 19.3	15 51.0	7 09.7	18 30.1	28 44.1
11 W	15 21 48	18 55 39	13 46 35	19 42 25	24 48.3	14 48.0	23 34.6	28 07.8	20 11.2	25 31.5	15 50.2	7 07.3	18 31.4	28 43.8
12 Th	15 25 45	19 56 03	25 37 45	1♏32 50	24 41.4	16 24.9	24 47.7	28 43.8	20 34.5	25 43.8	15 49.4	7 04.9	18 32.7	28 43.5
13 F	15 29 41	20 56 29	7♏27 56	13 23 16	24 35.3	18 01.5	26 00.8	29 19.8	20 57.8	25 56.2	15 48.7	7 02.5	18 33.9	28 43.1
14 Sa	15 33 38	21 56 56	19 19 04	25 15 31	24 30.5	19 37.8	27 13.9	29 55.7	21 21.1	26 08.7	15 48.1	7 00.1	18 35.1	28 42.7
15 Su	15 37 34	22 57 25	1♐12 52	7♐11 19	24 27.3	21 13.8	28 26.9	0♎31.6	21 44.6	26 21.2	15 47.7	6 57.8	18 36.3	28 42.3
16 M	15 41 31	23 57 56	13 11 07	19 12 31	24D 25.9	22 49.6	29 39.9	1 07.4	22 08.0	26 33.8	15 47.3	6 55.4	18 37.5	28 41.9
17 Tu	15 45 28	24 58 28	25 15 48	1♑21 16	24 26.0	24 25.1	0♑52.9	1 43.2	22 31.5	26 46.4	15 47.1	6 53.1	18 38.6	28 41.5
18 W	15 49 24	25 59 02	7♑29 16	13 40 08	24 27.1	26 00.3	2 05.9	2 18.9	22 55.0	26 59.1	15D 46.9	6 50.8	18 39.7	28 41.0
19 Th	15 53 21	26 59 37	19 54 16	26 12 03	24 28.9	27 35.3	3 18.8	2 54.6	23 18.6	27 11.8	15 46.9	6 48.5	18 40.8	28 40.5
20 F	15 57 17	28 00 13	2♒33 55	9♒00 16	24 30.5	29 10.1	4 31.7	3 30.3	23 42.2	27 24.6	15 47.0	6 46.3	18 41.9	28 40.0
21 Sa	16 01 14	29 00 50	15 31 30	22 08 01	24R 31.6	0♐44.7	5 44.5	4 05.9	24 05.8	27 37.5	15 47.2	6 44.0	18 42.9	28 39.4
22 Su	16 05 10	0♐01 28	28 50 08	5♓38 07	24 31.6	2 19.1	6 57.3	4 41.5	24 29.4	27 50.4	15 47.5	6 41.8	18 43.9	28 38.8
23 M	16 09 07	1 02 08	12♓32 10	19 32 21	24 30.5	3 53.3	8 10.1	5 17.0	24 53.1	28 03.3	15 47.9	6 39.6	18 44.8	28 38.2
24 Tu	16 13 03	2 02 48	26 38 35	3♈50 41	24 28.4	5 27.4	9 22.8	5 52.4	25 16.8	28 16.3	15 48.4	6 37.4	18 45.7	28 37.6
25 W	16 17 00	3 03 30	11♈08 15	18 30 44	24 25.7	7 01.3	10 35.5	6 27.8	25 40.6	28 29.4	15 49.0	6 35.3	18 46.6	28 37.0
26 Th	16 20 57	4 04 13	25 57 25	3♉27 24	24 22.8	8 35.1	11 48.1	7 03.2	26 04.4	28 42.5	15 49.7	6 33.2	18 47.5	28 36.3
27 F	16 24 53	5 04 57	10♉59 40	18 33 06	24 20.3	10 08.8	13 00.7	7 38.5	26 28.2	28 55.6	15 50.5	6 31.1	18 48.3	28 35.6
28 Sa	16 28 50	6 05 42	26 06 30	3♊38 41	24 18.5	11 42.4	14 13.3	8 13.8	26 52.0	29 08.8	15 51.4	6 29.0	18 49.1	28 34.9
29 Su	16 32 46	7 06 28	11♊08 29	18 34 49	24D 17.7	13 15.9	15 25.8	8 49.0	27 15.8	29 22.0	15 52.5	6 27.0	18 49.9	28 34.2
30 M	16 36 43	8 07 16	25 56 45	3♋13 26	24 17.8	14 49.3	16 38.2	9 24.2	27 39.7	29 35.2	15 53.6	6 25.0	18 50.6	28 33.5

December 1936 — LONGITUDE

Day	Sid.Time	☉	0 hr ☽	Noon ☽	True ☊	☿	♀	♂	⚳	♃	♄	♅	♆	♇
1 Tu	16 40 39	9♐08 05	10♋24 15	17♋28 43	24♐18.6	16♐22.7	17♑50.6	9♎59.3	28♐03.6	29♐48.5	15♓54.9	6♉23.0	18♍51.3	28♋32.7
2 W	16 44 36	10 08 55	24 26 33	1♌17 37	24 19.7	17 56.0	19 02.9	10 34.4	28 27.5	0♑01.9	15 56.2	6R 21.1	18 52.0	28R 31.9
3 Th	16 48 33	11 09 47	8♌01 56	14 39 41	24 20.9	19 29.3	20 15.2	11 09.4	28 51.5	0 15.2	15 57.7	6 19.1	18 52.6	28 31.1
4 F	16 52 29	12 10 40	21 11 07	27 36 36	24 21.8	21 02.5	21 27.4	11 44.4	29 15.4	0 28.6	15 59.2	6 17.3	18 53.2	28 30.3
5 Sa	16 56 26	13 11 34	3♍56 36	10♍11 35	24R 22.3	22 35.7	22 39.6	12 19.3	29 39.4	0 42.1	16 00.9	6 15.4	18 53.7	28 29.4
6 Su	17 00 22	14 12 30	16 22 06	22 28 42	24 22.2	24 08.8	23 51.7	12 54.2	0♑03.4	0 55.5	16 02.6	6 13.6	18 54.3	28 28.5
7 M	17 04 19	15 13 27	28 31 58	4♎32 28	24 21.6	25 41.9	25 03.8	13 29.0	0 27.5	1 09.0	16 04.5	6 11.8	18 54.8	28 27.6
8 Tu	17 08 15	16 14 25	10♎30 45	16 27 22	24 20.6	27 14.9	26 15.8	14 03.8	0 51.5	1 22.6	16 06.5	6 10.1	18 55.2	28 26.7
9 W	17 12 12	17 15 24	22 22 50	28 17 39	24 19.6	28 47.8	27 27.8	14 38.5	1 15.6	1 36.1	16 08.6	6 08.4	18 55.6	28 25.8
10 Th	17 16 08	18 16 25	4♏12 16	10♏07 07	24 18.6	0♑20.6	28 39.6	15 13.1	1 39.6	1 49.7	16 10.7	6 06.7	18 56.0	28 24.8
11 F	17 20 05	19 17 26	16 02 36	21 59 05	24 17.9	1 53.3	29 51.5	15 47.7	2 03.7	2 03.3	16 13.0	6 05.1	18 56.4	28 23.9
12 Sa	17 24 02	20 18 28	27 56 52	3♐56 15	24 17.4	3 25.8	1♒03.2	16 22.2	2 27.8	2 17.0	16 15.4	6 03.5	18 56.7	28 22.9
13 Su	17 27 58	21 19 32	9♐57 30	16 00 51	24D 17.1	4 58.1	2 14.9	16 56.6	2 52.0	2 30.6	16 17.9	6 02.0	18 57.0	28 21.9
14 M	17 31 55	22 20 36	22 06 29	28 14 35	24 17.1	6 30.1	3 26.5	17 31.0	3 16.1	2 44.3	16 20.5	6 00.5	18 57.3	28 20.9
15 Tu	17 35 51	23 21 41	4♑25 19	10♑38 51	24R 17.2	8 01.8	4 38.0	18 05.3	3 40.2	2 58.0	16 23.2	5 59.0	18 57.5	28 19.8
16 W	17 39 48	24 22 46	16 55 18	23 14 48	24 17.2	9 33.0	5 49.5	18 39.5	4 04.4	3 11.7	16 25.9	5 57.6	18 57.7	28 18.8
17 Th	17 43 44	25 23 52	29 37 30	6♒03 30	24 17.1	11 03.7	7 00.8	19 13.7	4 28.6	3 25.5	16 28.8	5 56.3	18 57.8	28 17.7
18 F	17 47 41	26 24 58	12♒32 56	19 05 56	24 17.0	12 33.6	8 12.1	19 47.8	4 52.7	3 39.2	16 31.8	5 54.9	18 57.9	28 16.6
19 Sa	17 51 37	27 26 05	25 42 38	2♓23 07	24 16.7	14 02.8	9 23.3	20 21.8	5 16.9	3 53.0	16 34.9	5 53.7	18 58.0	28 15.5
20 Su	17 55 34	28 27 11	9♓07 30	15 55 51	24D 16.4	15 31.0	10 34.4	20 55.8	5 41.1	4 06.8	16 38.0	5 52.4	18R 58.0	28 14.4
21 M	17 59 31	29 28 18	22 48 14	29 44 38	24 16.3	16 58.0	11 45.4	21 29.6	6 05.2	4 20.6	16 41.3	5 51.2	18 58.1	28 13.3
22 Tu	18 03 27	0♑29 26	6♈45 00	13♈49 14	24 16.5	18 23.6	12 56.3	22 03.4	6 29.4	4 34.3	16 44.7	5 50.1	18 58.0	28 12.2
23 W	18 07 24	1 30 33	20 57 07	28 08 23	24 16.9	19 47.4	14 07.1	22 37.2	6 53.6	4 48.2	16 48.1	5 49.0	18 58.0	28 11.0
24 Th	18 11 20	2 31 40	5♉22 39	12♉39 27	24 17.6	21 09.2	15 17.8	23 10.8	7 17.8	5 02.0	16 51.7	5 47.9	18 57.9	28 09.8
25 F	18 15 17	3 32 48	19 58 14	27 18 19	24 18.4	22 28.6	16 28.3	23 44.4	7 42.0	5 15.8	16 55.3	5 46.9	18 57.7	28 08.7
26 Sa	18 19 13	4 33 55	4♊39 00	11♊59 28	24R 19.0	23 45.1	17 38.8	24 17.9	8 06.2	5 29.6	16 59.0	5 45.9	18 57.6	28 07.5
27 Su	18 23 10	5 35 03	19 18 56	26 36 33	24 19.2	24 58.3	18 49.1	24 51.3	8 30.3	5 43.5	17 02.8	5 45.0	18 57.4	28 06.3
28 M	18 27 06	6 36 11	3♋51 30	11♋03 01	24 18.8	26 07.6	19 59.3	25 24.6	8 54.5	5 57.2	17 06.7	5 44.2	18 57.2	28 05.1
29 Tu	18 31 03	7 37 20	18 10 25	25 13 05	24 17.6	27 12.3	21 09.4	25 57.9	9 18.7	6 11.1	17 10.7	5 43.4	18 56.9	28 03.8
30 W	18 35 00	8 38 28	2♌10 32	9♌02 25	24 15.9	28 11.8	22 19.3	26 31.1	9 42.9	6 24.9	17 14.8	5 42.6	18 56.6	28 02.6
31 Th	18 38 56	9 39 37	15 48 28	22 28 35	24 13.7	29 05.2	23 29.1	27 04.1	10 07.0	6 38.7	17 19.0	5 41.9	18 56.3	28 01.4

Astro Data Dy Hr Mn	Planet Ingress Dy Hr Mn	Last Aspect Dy Hr Mn	☽ Ingress Dy Hr Mn	Last Aspect Dy Hr Mn	☽ Ingress Dy Hr Mn	☽ Phases & Eclipses Dy Hr Mn
☽0S 8 20:24	☿ ♏ 2 11:00	2 9:27 ♃ ☍	♋ 2 20:00	2 7:09 ♇ ☌	♌ 2 9:43	6 1:29 ☾ 13♌28
♄ D 19 7:07	♂ ♎ 14 14:52	4 22:21 ♇ ☌	♌ 5 0:37	3 22:04 ☿ △	♍ 4 16:31	14 4:42 ● 21♏39
♂0S 20 6:32	♀ ♑ 16 18:36	6 22:36 ♃ △	♍ 7 9:00	6 23:52 ♇ ⚹	♎ 7 2:55	22 1:19 ☽ 29♒34
☽0N 23 9:07	☿ ♐ 21 0:39	9 17:43 ♇ ⚹	♎ 9 20:15	9 13:10 ☿ ⚹	♏ 9 15:28	28 16:12 ○ 6♊16
♃⊼♇ 26 1:19	☉ ♐ 22 11:25	12 6:17 ♇ □	♏ 12 8:52	12 0:53 ♇ △	♐ 12 4:07	
		14 18:58 ♇ △	♐ 14 21:33	13 23:25 ☉ ☌	♑ 14 15:25	5 18:20 ☾ 13♍28
☽0S 6 2:45	♃ ♑ 2 8:39	17 2:49 ♃ ☌	♑ 17 9:20	16 21:32 ♇ ☍	♒ 17 0:42	13 23:25 ● 21♐49
☽0N 20 15:11	⚳ ♑ 6 8:34	19 16:41 ♇ ☍	♒ 19 19:11	19 2:22 ☉ ⚹	♓ 19 7:44	13 23:27:47 A 07'07"
♆R 21 5:56	☿ ♑ 10 6:40	22 1:19 ☉ □	♓ 22 2:04	21 11:30 ☉ □	♈ 21 12:26	21 11:30 ☽ 29♓27
♃△♅ 27 14:39	♀ ♒ 11 14:51	24 3:20 ♇ △	♈ 24 5:37	23 12:04 ♇ □	♉ 23 15:06	28 4:00 ○ 6♋16
	☉ ♑ 22 0:27	26 4:18 ♃ △	♉ 26 6:29	25 13:22 ♇ ⚹	♊ 25 16:24	28 3:49 A 0.845
		28 3:56 ♇ ⚹	♊ 28 6:11	27 9:00 ♂ △	♋ 27 17:36	
		30 5:54 ♃ ☍	♋ 30 6:40	29 16:53 ♇ ☍	♌ 29 20:14	

Astro Data

1 November 1936
Julian Day # 13454
SVP 6♓08'15"
GC 25♐57.4 ⚴ 28♏58.2
Eris 3♈03.8R ⚵ 21♍09.2
⚷ 22♊45.9R ⚶ 16♋56.6
☽ Mean ☊ 26♐44.7

1 December 1936
Julian Day # 13484
SVP 6♓08'10"
GC 25♐57.5 ⚴ 11♐42.9
Eris 2♈52.1R ⚵ 1♎16.2
⚷ 21♊15.2R ⚶ 16♋12.0R
☽ Mean ☊ 25♐09.4

LONGITUDE — January 1937

Day	Sid.Time	☉	0 hr ☽	Noon ☽	True ☊	☿	♀	♂	⚳	♃	♄	♅	♆	♇
1 F	18 42 53	10♑40 46	29♌02 46	5♍31 11	24♐11.4	29♑51.8	24♒38.8	27♎37.2	10♑31.2	6♑52.6	17♓23.2	5♉41.2	18♍55.9	28♋00.1
2 Sa	18 46 49	11 41 55	11♍54 03	18 11 42	24R 09.4	0♒30.6	25 48.3	28 10.1	10 55.4	7 06.4	17 27.5	5R 40.6	18R 55.5	27R 58.9
3 Su	18 50 46	12 43 04	24 24 33	0♎33 05	24 08.0	1 00.7	26 57.7	28 42.9	11 19.5	7 20.2	17 32.0	5 40.0	18 55.1	27 57.6
4 M	18 54 42	13 44 14	6♎37 49	12 39 21	24D 07.4	1 21.3	28 07.0	29 15.6	11 43.7	7 34.0	17 36.4	5 39.5	18 54.6	27 56.3
5 Tu	18 58 39	14 45 24	18 38 15	24 35 09	24 07.8	1R 31.5	29 16.0	29 48.3	12 07.8	7 47.8	17 41.0	5 39.0	18 54.1	27 55.0
6 W	19 02 35	15 46 34	0♏30 39	6♏25 24	24 09.0	1 30.5	0♓25.0	0♏20.8	12 31.9	8 01.6	17 45.7	5 38.6	18 53.6	27 53.7
7 Th	19 06 32	16 47 44	12 19 59	18 15 00	24 10.7	1 17.9	1 33.8	0 53.2	12 56.0	8 15.3	17 50.4	5 38.3	18 53.0	27 52.4
8 F	19 10 29	17 48 54	24 11 01	0♐08 33	24 12.5	0 53.5	2 42.4	1 25.6	13 20.2	8 29.1	17 55.2	5 38.0	18 52.5	27 51.1
9 Sa	19 14 25	18 50 04	6♐08 06	12 10 07	24R 13.9	0 17.4	3 50.8	1 57.8	13 44.3	8 42.9	18 00.1	5 37.7	18 51.8	27 49.8
10 Su	19 18 22	19 51 15	18 14 59	24 23 03	24 14.5	29♑30.1	4 59.1	2 29.9	14 08.3	8 56.6	18 05.1	5 37.5	18 51.2	27 48.5
11 M	19 22 18	20 52 25	0♑34 36	6♑49 52	24 13.8	28 32.7	6 07.2	3 02.0	14 32.4	9 10.3	18 10.1	5 37.4	18 50.5	27 47.2
12 Tu	19 26 15	21 53 34	13 08 58	19 32 00	24 11.6	27 26.7	7 15.1	3 33.9	14 56.5	9 24.0	18 15.3	5 37.3	18 49.8	27 45.9
13 W	19 30 11	22 54 44	25 59 00	2♒29 56	24 08.1	26 14.1	8 22.8	4 05.7	15 20.5	9 37.7	18 20.5	5D 37.2	18 49.0	27 44.6
14 Th	19 34 08	23 55 53	9♒04 40	15 43 05	24 03.5	24 57.2	9 30.3	4 37.3	15 44.5	9 51.4	18 25.7	5 37.2	18 48.3	27 43.2
15 F	19 38 05	24 57 01	22 24 59	29 10 08	23 58.3	23 38.4	10 37.6	5 08.9	16 08.5	10 05.0	18 31.0	5 37.3	18 47.4	27 41.9
16 Sa	19 42 01	25 58 08	5♓58 17	12♓49 12	23 53.2	22 20.1	11 44.6	5 40.3	16 32.5	10 18.6	18 36.4	5 37.4	18 46.6	27 40.6
17 Su	19 45 58	26 59 15	19 42 36	26 38 14	23 49.0	21 04.8	12 51.5	6 11.6	16 56.4	10 32.2	18 41.9	5 37.5	18 45.7	27 39.3
18 M	19 49 54	28 00 21	3♈35 51	10♈35 15	23 46.0	19 54.4	13 58.1	6 42.8	17 20.4	10 45.8	18 47.5	5 37.8	18 44.8	27 37.9
19 Tu	19 53 51	29 01 26	17 36 11	24 38 29	23D 44.8	18 50.6	15 04.5	7 13.9	17 44.3	10 59.3	18 53.1	5 38.0	18 43.9	27 36.6
20 W	19 57 47	0♒02 30	1♉41 58	8♉46 25	23 45.0	17 54.7	16 10.6	7 44.8	18 08.2	11 12.8	18 58.7	5 38.3	18 43.0	27 35.3
21 Th	20 01 44	1 03 33	15 51 42	22 57 34	23 46.2	17 07.4	17 16.5	8 15.6	18 32.0	11 26.3	19 04.5	5 38.7	18 42.0	27 33.9
22 F	20 05 40	2 04 35	0♊03 50	7♊10 12	23 47.7	16 29.2	18 22.1	8 46.3	18 55.8	11 39.7	19 10.2	5 39.2	18 41.0	27 32.6
23 Sa	20 09 37	3 05 37	14 16 25	21 22 07	23R 48.5	16 00.2	19 27.4	9 16.8	19 19.6	11 53.1	19 16.1	5 39.6	18 39.9	27 31.3
24 Su	20 13 34	4 06 37	28 26 56	5♋30 26	23 48.0	15 40.3	20 32.5	9 47.2	19 43.4	12 06.5	19 22.0	5 40.2	18 38.9	27 30.0
25 M	20 17 30	5 07 36	12♋32 09	19 31 38	23 45.4	15D 29.2	21 37.2	10 17.5	20 07.2	12 19.8	19 28.0	5 40.8	18 37.8	27 28.7
26 Tu	20 21 27	6 08 35	26 28 24	3♌21 57	23 40.8	15 26.4	22 41.7	10 47.6	20 30.9	12 33.1	19 34.0	5 41.4	18 36.7	27 27.3
27 W	20 25 23	7 09 32	10♌11 53	16 57 47	23 34.2	15 31.5	23 45.8	11 17.5	20 54.6	12 46.3	19 40.1	5 42.1	18 35.6	27 26.0
28 Th	20 29 20	8 10 28	23 39 20	0♍16 17	23 26.2	15 43.9	24 49.6	11 47.4	21 18.2	12 59.5	19 46.2	5 42.8	18 34.4	27 24.7
29 F	20 33 16	9 11 24	6♍48 28	13 15 48	23 17.9	16 03.0	25 53.1	12 17.0	21 41.8	13 12.7	19 52.4	5 43.6	18 33.2	27 23.4
30 Sa	20 37 13	10 12 19	19 38 21	25 56 14	23 09.9	16 28.3	26 56.2	12 46.6	22 05.4	13 25.8	19 58.7	5 44.4	18 32.0	27 22.1
31 Su	20 41 09	11 13 12	2♎09 39	8♎18 56	23 03.2	16 59.3	27 59.0	13 15.9	22 29.0	13 38.9	20 05.0	5 45.3	18 30.8	27 20.8

LONGITUDE — February 1937

Day	Sid.Time	☉	0 hr ☽	Noon ☽	True ☊	☿	♀	♂	⚳	♃	♄	♅	♆	♇
1 M	20 45 06	12♒14 05	14♎24 29	20♎26 45	22♐58.4	17♑35.5	29♓01.4	13♏45.1	22♑52.5	13♑52.0	20♓11.3	5♉46.3	18♍29.5	27♋19.5
2 Tu	20 49 03	13 14 58	26 26 14	2♏23 32	22R 55.6	18 16.3	0♈03.5	14 14.2	23 16.0	14 05.0	20 17.7	5 47.3	18R 28.2	27R 18.3
3 W	20 52 59	14 15 49	8♏19 16	14 14 02	22D 54.8	19 01.5	1 05.1	14 43.0	23 39.4	14 17.9	20 24.2	5 48.3	18 26.9	27 17.0
4 Th	20 56 56	15 16 40	20 08 33	26 03 27	22 55.4	19 50.5	2 06.4	15 11.7	24 02.9	14 30.8	20 30.7	5 49.4	18 25.6	27 15.7
5 F	21 00 52	16 17 29	1♐59 24	7♐57 06	22 56.6	20 43.2	3 07.3	15 40.2	24 26.2	14 43.6	20 37.2	5 50.5	18 24.3	27 14.5
6 Sa	21 04 49	17 18 18	13 57 10	20 00 14	22R 57.4	21 39.1	4 07.7	16 08.6	24 49.6	14 56.4	20 43.8	5 51.7	18 22.9	27 13.2
7 Su	21 08 45	18 19 06	26 06 50	2♑17 31	22 57.0	22 38.0	5 07.7	16 36.7	25 12.9	15 09.2	20 50.5	5 53.0	18 21.6	27 12.0
8 M	21 12 42	19 19 53	8♑32 43	14 52 47	22 54.5	23 39.6	6 07.3	17 04.6	25 36.1	15 21.8	20 57.1	5 54.3	18 20.2	27 10.8
9 Tu	21 16 38	20 20 38	21 18 01	27 48 33	22 49.5	24 43.7	7 06.4	17 32.4	25 59.3	15 34.5	21 03.9	5 55.6	18 18.7	27 09.6
10 W	21 20 35	21 21 22	4♒24 28	11♒05 41	22 42.1	25 50.2	8 05.0	18 00.0	26 22.5	15 47.0	21 10.6	5 57.0	18 17.3	27 08.4
11 Th	21 24 32	22 22 05	17 52 01	24 43 08	22 32.7	26 58.8	9 03.1	18 27.3	26 45.6	15 59.5	21 17.4	5 58.5	18 15.9	27 07.2
12 F	21 28 28	23 22 47	1♓38 37	8♓37 57	22 22.2	28 09.4	10 00.7	18 54.4	27 08.7	16 11.9	21 24.3	5 59.9	18 14.4	27 06.0
13 Sa	21 32 25	24 23 27	15 40 33	22 45 45	22 11.8	29 21.8	10 57.8	19 21.3	27 31.7	16 24.3	21 31.1	6 01.5	18 12.9	27 04.8
14 Su	21 36 21	25 24 05	29 52 54	7♈01 19	22 02.6	0♒36.0	11 54.3	19 48.0	27 54.7	16 36.6	21 38.0	6 03.1	18 11.4	27 03.7
15 M	21 40 18	26 24 42	14♈10 22	21 19 29	21 55.6	1 51.8	12 50.2	20 14.5	28 17.6	16 48.9	21 45.0	6 04.7	18 09.9	27 02.5
16 Tu	21 44 14	27 25 17	28 28 09	5♉35 57	21 51.2	3 09.1	13 45.6	20 40.7	28 40.4	17 01.0	21 52.0	6 06.4	18 08.4	27 01.4
17 W	21 48 11	28 25 50	12♉42 32	19 47 39	21D 49.2	4 27.9	14 40.2	21 06.8	29 03.2	17 13.1	21 59.0	6 08.1	18 06.8	27 00.3
18 Th	21 52 07	29 26 21	26 51 07	3♊52 50	21 49.0	5 48.1	15 34.3	21 32.5	29 26.0	17 25.1	22 06.0	6 09.8	18 05.3	26 59.2
19 F	21 56 04	0♓26 51	10♊52 43	17 50 44	21R 49.4	7 09.7	16 27.7	21 58.1	29 48.7	17 37.1	22 13.1	6 11.7	18 03.7	26 58.1
20 Sa	22 00 01	1 27 19	24 46 53	1♋41 07	21 49.1	8 32.5	17 20.3	22 23.4	0♒11.3	17 49.0	22 20.2	6 13.5	18 02.1	26 57.0
21 Su	22 03 57	2 27 44	8♋33 24	15 23 41	21 46.9	9 56.5	18 12.3	22 48.4	0 33.9	18 00.8	22 27.3	6 15.4	18 00.6	26 56.0
22 M	22 07 54	3 28 08	22 11 52	28 57 49	21 42.1	11 21.8	19 03.4	23 13.2	0 56.4	18 12.5	22 34.5	6 17.3	17 59.0	26 55.0
23 Tu	22 11 50	4 28 30	5♌41 24	12♌22 24	21 34.3	12 48.2	19 53.8	23 37.7	1 18.9	18 24.1	22 41.6	6 19.3	17 57.4	26 53.9
24 W	22 15 47	5 28 51	19 00 39	25 35 54	21 23.8	14 15.7	20 43.4	24 02.0	1 41.3	18 35.7	22 48.8	6 21.4	17 55.7	26 52.9
25 Th	22 19 43	6 29 09	2♍07 57	8♍36 39	21 11.3	15 44.4	21 32.1	24 25.9	2 03.6	18 47.2	22 56.0	6 23.4	17 54.1	26 51.9
26 F	22 23 40	7 29 25	15 01 49	21 27 48	20 57.9	17 14.2	22 19.9	24 49.7	2 25.9	18 58.6	23 03.3	6 25.5	17 52.5	26 51.0
27 Sa	22 27 36	8 29 40	27 41 13	3♎55 26	20 45.0	18 45.0	23 06.9	25 13.1	2 48.1	19 09.9	23 10.5	6 27.7	17 50.8	26 50.0
28 Su	22 31 33	9 29 54	10♎06 05	16 13 20	20 33.5	20 17.0	23 52.9	25 36.2	3 10.3	19 21.1	23 17.8	6 29.9	17 49.2	26 49.1

Astro Data

	Dy Hr Mn
☽0S	2 11:15
☿R	5 22:05
♅D	13 21:32
☽0N	16 20:57
♄☍♆	18 2:18
☿D	26 8:10
☽0S	29 21:05
♀0N	1 7:15
♄∠♅	7 23:16
☽0N	13 4:22
♃△♆	21 11:36
☽0S	26 6:15

Planet Ingress

	Dy Hr Mn
☿ ♒	1 16:41
♂ ♏	5 20:39
♀ ♓	6 3:18
☿ ♑R	9 21:28
☉ ♒	20 11:01
♀ ♈	2 10:39
☿ ♒	14 0:26
☉ ♓	19 1:21
⚳ ♒	19 23:59

Last Aspect / ☽ Ingress (January)

Last Aspect Dy Hr Mn		☽ Ingress Dy Hr Mn
31 20:44	♂ ⚹	♍ 1 1:45
3 6:56	♇ ⚹	♎ 3 10:55
5 22:30	♀ △	♏ 5 22:58
8 7:24	♇ △	♐ 8 11:43
10 1:12	♆ □	♑ 10 22:53
13 3:16	♇ ☍	♒ 13 7:25
13 17:42	♅ □	♓ 15 13:28
17 13:45	♇ △	♈ 17 17:48
19 20:02	☉ □	♉ 19 21:07
21 19:46	♇ ⚹	♊ 21 23:54
23 8:30	♀ □	♋ 24 2:38
26 1:43	♇ ☌	♌ 26 6:08
27 1:33	♂ □	♍ 28 11:30
30 14:45	♇ ⚹	♎ 30 19:49

Last Aspect / ☽ Ingress (February)

Last Aspect Dy Hr Mn		☽ Ingress Dy Hr Mn
2 1:46	♇ □	♏ 2 7:10
4 14:26	♇ △	♐ 4 19:59
6 13:27	♄ □	♑ 7 7:34
9 10:49	♇ ☍	♒ 9 16:00
11 7:34	☉ ☌	♓ 11 21:10
14 0:11	☿ ⚹	♈ 14 0:12
15 21:35	♇ □	♉ 16 2:34
18 3:50	☉ □	♊ 18 5:22
19 19:37	♄ □	♋ 20 9:04
22 8:22	♇ ☌	♌ 22 13:51
24 9:03	♂ □	♍ 24 20:04
26 22:23	♇ ⚹	♎ 27 4:26

☽ Phases & Eclipses

Dy Hr Mn	
4 14:22	☾ 13♎50
12 16:47	● 22♑06
19 20:02	☽ 29♈22
26 17:15	○ 6♌22
3 12:04	☾ 14♏16
11 7:34	● 22♒11
18 3:50	☽ 29♉06
25 7:43	○ 6♍18

Astro Data

1 January 1937
Julian Day # 13515
SVP 6♓08'04"
GC 25♐57.6 ⚴ 24♐44.6
Eris 2♈50.5 ⚵ 8♎35.4
⚷ 19♊22.9R ⚶ 9♋24.0R
☽ Mean ☊ 23♐31.0

1 February 1937
Julian Day # 13546
SVP 6♓07'59"
GC 25♐57.6 ⚴ 7♑06.0
Eris 3♈00.2 ⚵ 11♎02.3R
⚷ 18♊01.7R ⚶ 2♋45.8R
☽ Mean ☊ 21♐52.5

March 1937 — LONGITUDE

Day	Sid.Time	☉	0 hr ☽	Noon ☽	True ☊	☿	♀	♂	⚳	♃	♄	♅	♆	♇
1 M	22 35 29	10♓30 05	22♎17 27	28♎18 42	20♐24.3	21♒50.0	24♈37.9	25♏59.0	3♒32.4	19♑32.2	23♓25.1	6♉32.1	17♍47.5	26♋48.2
2 Tu	22 39 26	11 30 16	4♏17 31	10♏14 19	20R 18.0	23 24.1	25 21.9	26 21.6	3 54.4	19 43.3	23 32.4	6 34.3	17R 45.9	26R 47.3
3 W	22 43 23	12 30 24	16 09 37	22 03 59	20 14.3	24 59.3	26 04.8	26 43.8	4 16.3	19 54.3	23 39.8	6 36.7	17 44.2	26 46.4
4 Th	22 47 19	13 30 31	27 58 03	3♐52 25	20D 12.7	26 35.5	26 46.7	27 05.7	4 38.2	20 05.1	23 47.1	6 39.0	17 42.6	26 45.5
5 F	22 51 16	14 30 37	9♐47 47	15 44 51	20R 12.5	28 12.9	27 27.4	27 27.2	5 00.0	20 15.9	23 54.5	6 41.4	17 40.9	26 44.7
6 Sa	22 55 12	15 30 41	21 44 17	27 46 49	20 12.4	29 51.3	28 06.9	27 48.4	5 21.7	20 26.6	24 01.8	6 43.8	17 39.2	26 43.9
7 Su	22 59 09	16 30 43	3♑53 08	10♑03 50	20 11.3	1♓30.9	28 45.3	28 09.3	5 43.4	20 37.2	24 09.2	6 46.3	17 37.6	26 43.1
8 M	23 03 05	17 30 44	16 19 34	22 40 51	20 08.2	3 11.5	29 22.3	28 29.8	6 05.0	20 47.6	24 16.6	6 48.7	17 35.9	26 42.3
9 Tu	23 07 02	18 30 42	29 08 08	5♒41 45	20 02.5	4 53.3	29 58.1	28 50.0	6 26.5	20 58.0	24 24.0	6 51.3	17 34.2	26 41.6
10 W	23 10 58	19 30 40	12♒21 54	19 08 40	19 54.1	6 36.2	0♉32.4	29 09.7	6 47.9	21 08.3	24 31.4	6 53.8	17 32.6	26 40.8
11 Th	23 14 55	20 30 35	26 01 55	3♓01 24	19 43.4	8 20.2	1 05.4	29 29.1	7 09.3	21 18.5	24 38.9	6 56.4	17 30.9	26 40.1
12 F	23 18 52	21 30 28	10♓06 38	17 17 00	19 31.3	10 05.4	1 36.9	29 48.1	7 30.5	21 28.5	24 46.3	6 59.1	17 29.2	26 39.4
13 Sa	23 22 48	22 30 20	24 31 45	1♈49 57	19 19.1	11 51.8	2 06.8	0♐06.7	7 51.7	21 38.5	24 53.7	7 01.7	17 27.6	26 38.7
14 Su	23 26 45	23 30 09	9♈10 39	16 32 48	19 08.2	13 39.4	2 35.2	0 24.9	8 12.8	21 48.3	25 01.2	7 04.4	17 25.9	26 38.1
15 M	23 30 41	24 29 57	23 55 24	1♉17 28	18 59.7	15 28.1	3 01.9	0 42.7	8 33.8	21 58.0	25 08.6	7 07.1	17 24.2	26 37.5
16 Tu	23 34 38	25 29 42	8♉38 08	15 56 38	18 54.0	17 18.1	3 26.9	1 00.0	8 54.7	22 07.7	25 16.0	7 09.9	17 22.6	26 36.9
17 W	23 38 34	26 29 25	23 12 19	0♊24 43	18 51.1	19 09.2	3 50.1	1 16.9	9 15.5	22 17.2	25 23.5	7 12.7	17 20.9	26 36.3
18 Th	23 42 31	27 29 06	7♊33 30	14 38 25	18 50.3	21 01.6	4 11.4	1 33.3	9 36.3	22 26.6	25 30.9	7 15.5	17 19.3	26 35.7
19 F	23 46 27	28 28 45	21 39 24	28 36 26	18 50.3	22 55.2	4 30.9	1 49.3	9 56.9	22 35.8	25 38.3	7 18.4	17 17.7	26 35.2
20 Sa	23 50 24	29 28 21	5♋29 36	12♋19 01	18 49.8	24 49.9	4 48.3	2 04.9	10 17.5	22 45.0	25 45.8	7 21.2	17 16.0	26 34.7
21 Su	23 54 21	0♈27 55	19 04 49	25 47 11	18 47.7	26 45.8	5 03.7	2 19.9	10 37.9	22 54.0	25 53.2	7 24.1	17 14.4	26 34.2
22 M	23 58 17	1 27 26	2♌26 16	9♌02 13	18 43.0	28 42.9	5 17.0	2 34.5	10 58.3	23 02.9	26 00.6	7 27.1	17 12.8	26 33.8
23 Tu	0 02 14	2 26 55	15 35 10	22 05 11	18 35.4	0♈41.1	5 28.2	2 48.6	11 18.5	23 11.7	26 08.0	7 30.0	17 11.2	26 33.3
24 W	0 06 10	3 26 22	28 32 23	4♍56 46	18 25.1	2 40.2	5 37.1	3 02.2	11 38.7	23 20.3	26 15.4	7 33.0	17 09.6	26 32.9
25 Th	0 10 07	4 25 47	11♍18 23	17 37 15	18 13.0	4 40.4	5 43.7	3 15.3	11 58.7	23 28.9	26 22.8	7 36.0	17 08.0	26 32.5
26 F	0 14 03	5 25 10	23 53 21	0♎06 44	17 59.9	6 41.4	5 48.0	3 27.9	12 18.7	23 37.3	26 30.2	7 39.0	17 06.4	26 32.1
27 Sa	0 18 00	6 24 30	6♎17 24	12 25 24	17 47.1	8 43.2	5R 49.9	3 39.9	12 38.5	23 45.5	26 37.5	7 42.1	17 04.9	26 31.8
28 Su	0 21 56	7 23 49	18 30 50	24 33 50	17 35.7	10 45.6	5 49.4	3 51.4	12 58.2	23 53.7	26 44.9	7 45.2	17 03.3	26 31.5
29 M	0 25 53	8 23 05	0♏34 33	6♏33 12	17 26.5	12 48.4	5 46.5	4 02.4	13 17.9	24 01.7	26 52.2	7 48.2	17 01.8	26 31.2
30 Tu	0 29 49	9 22 20	12 30 05	18 25 32	17 20.0	14 51.5	5 41.1	4 12.8	13 37.4	24 09.6	26 59.6	7 51.4	17 00.3	26 30.9
31 W	0 33 46	10 21 33	24 19 54	0♐13 40	17 16.2	16 54.6	5 33.2	4 22.6	13 56.8	24 17.3	27 06.9	7 54.5	16 58.8	26 30.7

April 1937 — LONGITUDE

Day	Sid.Time	☉	0 hr ☽	Noon ☽	True ☊	☿	♀	♂	⚳	♃	♄	♅	♆	♇
1 Th	0 37 43	11♈20 44	6♐07 17	12♐01 19	17♐14.7	18♈57.4	5♉22.8	4♐31.8	14♒16.1	24♑24.9	27♓14.2	7♉57.7	16♍57.3	26♋30.5
2 F	0 41 39	12 19 53	17 56 20	23 52 58	17D 14.7	20 59.7	5R 10.0	4 40.4	14 35.3	24 32.3	27 21.4	8 00.9	16R 55.8	26R 30.3
3 Sa	0 45 36	13 19 00	29 51 50	5♑53 38	17R 15.3	23 01.2	4 54.7	4 48.3	14 54.3	24 39.7	27 28.7	8 04.1	16 54.3	26 30.1
4 Su	0 49 32	14 18 06	11♑59 01	18 08 39	17 15.4	25 01.4	4 37.0	4 55.7	15 13.3	24 46.8	27 36.0	8 07.3	16 52.9	26 30.0
5 M	0 53 29	15 17 10	24 23 13	0♒43 17	17 14.2	27 00.1	4 17.0	5 02.4	15 32.1	24 53.9	27 43.2	8 10.5	16 51.4	26 29.9
6 Tu	0 57 25	16 16 12	7♒09 27	13 42 11	17 10.9	28 56.9	3 54.7	5 08.4	15 50.8	25 00.7	27 50.4	8 13.8	16 50.0	26 29.8
7 W	1 01 22	17 15 12	20 21 50	27 08 40	17 05.3	0♉51.4	3 30.1	5 13.8	16 09.4	25 07.5	27 57.5	8 17.0	16 48.6	26 29.7
8 Th	1 05 18	18 14 11	4♓02 45	11♓03 59	16 57.8	2 43.3	3 03.6	5 18.5	16 27.8	25 14.0	28 04.7	8 20.3	16 47.2	26 29.7
9 F	1 09 15	19 13 07	18 12 04	25 26 31	16 48.9	4 32.1	2 35.0	5 22.6	16 46.1	25 20.5	28 11.8	8 23.6	16 45.9	26D 29.7
10 Sa	1 13 12	20 12 02	2♈46 39	10♈11 33	16 39.9	6 17.5	2 04.6	5 25.9	17 04.3	25 26.7	28 18.9	8 27.0	16 44.5	26 29.7
11 Su	1 17 08	21 10 55	17 40 12	25 11 26	16 31.7	7 59.3	1 32.6	5 28.5	17 22.4	25 32.9	28 26.0	8 30.3	16 43.2	26 29.7
12 M	1 21 05	22 09 45	2♉44 02	10♉16 46	16 25.3	9 37.1	0 59.1	5 30.4	17 40.3	25 38.8	28 33.0	8 33.6	16 41.9	26 29.8
13 Tu	1 25 01	23 08 34	17 48 26	25 17 57	16 21.2	11 10.7	0 24.3	5 31.6	17 58.1	25 44.6	28 40.1	8 37.0	16 40.6	26 29.9
14 W	1 28 58	24 07 21	2♊44 20	10♊06 46	16D 19.5	12 39.8	29♈48.4	5R 32.0	18 15.7	25 50.3	28 47.0	8 40.4	16 39.4	26 30.0
15 Th	1 32 54	25 06 05	17 24 38	24 37 27	16 19.6	14 04.2	29 11.7	5 31.7	18 33.2	25 55.7	28 54.0	8 43.7	16 38.1	26 30.1
16 F	1 36 51	26 04 47	1♋44 54	8♋46 51	16 20.6	15 23.8	28 34.3	5 30.7	18 50.5	26 01.0	29 00.9	8 47.1	16 36.9	26 30.3
17 Sa	1 40 47	27 03 27	15 43 18	22 34 18	16R 21.4	16 38.3	27 56.6	5 28.9	19 07.7	26 06.2	29 07.8	8 50.5	16 35.7	26 30.5
18 Su	1 44 44	28 02 05	29 20 02	6♌00 45	16 21.2	17 47.6	27 18.7	5 26.4	19 24.8	26 11.2	29 14.6	8 53.9	16 34.6	26 30.7
19 M	1 48 41	29 00 40	12♌36 42	19 08 12	16 19.2	18 51.6	26 41.0	5 23.2	19 41.7	26 16.0	29 21.5	8 57.4	16 33.4	26 30.9
20 Tu	1 52 37	29 59 13	25 35 33	1♍59 03	16 15.2	19 50.3	26 03.6	5 19.1	19 58.4	26 20.6	29 28.2	9 00.8	16 32.3	26 31.2
21 W	1 56 34	0♉57 44	8♍19 00	14 35 41	16 09.3	20 43.4	25 26.9	5 14.4	20 15.0	26 25.1	29 35.0	9 04.2	16 31.2	26 31.5
22 Th	2 00 30	1 56 13	20 49 21	27 00 14	16 02.0	21 30.9	24 51.0	5 08.8	20 31.4	26 29.4	29 41.7	9 07.6	16 30.1	26 31.8
23 F	2 04 27	2 54 40	3♎08 34	9♎14 32	15 54.0	22 12.8	24 16.1	5 02.5	20 47.7	26 33.6	29 48.3	9 11.1	16 29.1	26 32.2
24 Sa	2 08 23	3 53 04	15 18 21	21 20 11	15 46.1	22 49.0	23 42.6	4 55.5	21 03.8	26 37.5	29 54.9	9 14.5	16 28.1	26 32.5
25 Su	2 12 20	4 51 27	27 20 13	3♏18 39	15 39.1	23 19.5	23 10.6	4 47.7	21 19.7	26 41.3	0♈01.5	9 18.0	16 27.1	26 32.9
26 M	2 16 16	5 49 48	9♏15 41	15 11 32	15 33.7	23 44.2	22 40.3	4 39.1	21 35.5	26 44.9	0 08.0	9 21.4	16 26.1	26 33.3
27 Tu	2 20 13	6 48 08	21 06 26	27 00 39	15 30.0	24 03.2	22 11.8	4 29.8	21 51.1	26 48.4	0 14.5	9 24.9	16 25.2	26 33.8
28 W	2 24 10	7 46 25	2♐54 30	8♐48 19	15D 28.3	24 16.6	21 45.3	4 19.8	22 06.5	26 51.7	0 21.0	9 28.3	16 24.2	26 34.2
29 Th	2 28 06	8 44 41	14 42 27	20 37 19	15 28.2	24R 24.3	21 20.9	4 09.0	22 21.7	26 54.7	0 27.4	9 31.8	16 23.3	26 34.7
30 F	2 32 03	9 42 56	26 33 22	2♑31 05	15 29.2	24 26.6	20 58.7	3 57.5	22 36.8	26 57.7	0 33.7	9 35.2	16 22.5	26 35.3

Astro Data

	Dy Hr Mn
☽0N	12 13:46
☉0N	21 0:45
☿0N	24 16:34
☽0S	25 13:20
♄△♇	26 18:10
♀R	27 19:07
☽0N	8 23:56
♇D	9 13:47
♂R	14 14:42
☽0S	21 18:37
♃☍♇	23 2:56
☿R	30 10:03

Planet Ingress

		Dy Hr Mn
☿	♓	6 14:06
♀	♉	9 13:19
♂	♐	13 3:16
☉	♈	21 0:45
☿	♈	23 3:41
☿	♉	7 1:09
♀	♈R	14 4:19
☉	♉	20 12:19
♄	♈	25 6:29

Last Aspect / ☽ Ingress (March)

Last Aspect Dy Hr Mn			☽ Ingress	Dy Hr Mn
1 8:59	♇	□	♏	1 15:23
3 21:47	♂	☌	♐	4 4:08
6 12:42	♀	△	♑	6 16:23
9 1:02	♀	□	♒	9 1:36
11 5:48	♂	□	♓	11 6:50
13 3:30	♇	△	♈	13 9:00
15 4:24	♇	□	♉	15 9:54
17 5:39	♇	⚹	♊	17 11:19
19 11:46	☉	□	♋	19 14:25
21 14:03	☿	△	♌	21 19:35
22 9:06	♅	□	♍	24 2:44
26 5:06	♇	⚹	♎	26 11:47
28 15:54	♇	□	♏	28 22:51
31 5:36	♄	△	♐	31 11:32

Last Aspect / ☽ Ingress (April)

Last Aspect Dy Hr Mn			☽ Ingress	Dy Hr Mn
2 19:03	♄	□	♑	3 0:16
5 6:17	♄	⚹	♒	5 10:39
6 17:01	☉	⚹	♓	7 16:59
9 16:34	♄	☌	♈	9 19:28
11 14:05	♇	□	♉	11 19:39
13 17:28	♄	⚹	♊	13 19:34
15 19:22	♀	⚹	♋	15 21:02
17 23:44	♄	△	♌	18 1:11
20 7:56	☉	△	♍	20 8:16
22 17:18	♄	☍	♎	22 17:51
24 22:38	♃	□	♏	25 5:21
27 11:35	♃	⚹	♐	27 18:05
29 13:25	♀	△	♑	30 6:56

☽ Phases & Eclipses

Dy Hr Mn		
5 9:17	☾	14♐24
12 19:32	●	21♓49
19 11:46	☽	28♊28
26 23:12	○	5♎53
4 3:53	☾	13♑58
11 5:10	●	20♈54
17 20:34	☽	27♋24
25 15:24	○	5♏00

Astro Data

1 March 1937
Julian Day # 13574
SVP 6♓07'56"
GC 25♐57.7 ⚵ 17♑08.5
Eris 3♈16.5 ⚴ 7♎58.3R
⚷ 17♊45.2 ⚶ 2♋11.6
☽ Mean ☊ 20♐23.5

1 April 1937
Julian Day # 13605
SVP 6♓07'53"
GC 25♐57.8 ⚵ 26♑11.1
Eris 3♈38.6 ⚴ 0♎50.2R
⚷ 18♊38.0 ⚶ 7♋30.1
☽ Mean ☊ 18♐45.0

LONGITUDE — May 1937

Day	Sid.Time	☉	0 hr ☽	Noon ☽	True ☊	☿	♀	♂	⚳	♃	♄	♅	♆	♇
1 Sa	2 35 59	10♉41 08	8♑30 58	14♑33 34	15♐30.9	24♉23.5	20♈38.8	3♐45.2	22♒51.7	27♑00.4	0♈40.0	9♉38.7	16♍21.7	26♋35.8
2 Su	2 39 56	11 39 20	20 39 26	26 49 09	15 32.5	24R 15.3	20R 21.3	3R 32.3	23 06.4	27 02.9	0 46.3	9 42.2	16R 20.8	26 36.4
3 M	2 43 52	12 37 30	3♒03 17	9♒22 24	15R 33.3	24 02.3	20 06.1	3 18.6	23 20.9	27 05.3	0 52.5	9 45.6	16 20.1	26 36.9
4 Tu	2 47 49	13 35 38	15 47 03	22 17 43	15 33.0	23 44.7	19 53.4	3 04.3	23 35.3	27 07.5	0 58.6	9 49.1	16 19.3	26 37.6
5 W	2 51 45	14 33 45	28 54 50	5♓38 43	15 31.4	23 23.0	19 43.2	2 49.3	23 49.4	27 09.5	1 04.7	9 52.5	16 18.6	26 38.2
6 Th	2 55 42	15 31 50	12♓29 37	19 27 35	15 28.6	22 57.5	19 35.4	2 33.7	24 03.3	27 11.3	1 10.8	9 56.0	16 17.9	26 38.8
7 F	2 59 39	16 29 55	26 32 34	3♈44 17	15 24.8	22 28.9	19 30.0	2 17.4	24 17.1	27 12.9	1 16.8	9 59.4	16 17.2	26 39.5
8 Sa	3 03 35	17 27 57	11♈02 17	18 25 56	15 20.8	21 57.5	19D 27.0	2 00.6	24 30.6	27 14.3	1 22.7	10 02.9	16 16.6	26 40.2
9 Su	3 07 32	18 25 59	25 54 22	3♉26 38	15 17.2	21 24.0	19 26.4	1 43.2	24 44.0	27 15.5	1 28.6	10 06.3	16 16.0	26 41.0
10 M	3 11 28	19 23 58	11♉01 33	18 37 56	15 14.4	20 49.0	19 28.2	1 25.3	24 57.1	27 16.6	1 34.4	10 09.7	16 15.4	26 41.7
11 Tu	3 15 25	20 21 57	26 14 31	3♊50 02	15D 12.9	20 13.1	19 32.2	1 06.9	25 10.0	27 17.5	1 40.2	10 13.2	16 14.9	26 42.5
12 W	3 19 21	21 19 54	11♊23 19	18 53 17	15 12.6	19 36.9	19 38.5	0 48.0	25 22.7	27 18.1	1 45.9	10 16.6	16 14.4	26 43.3
13 Th	3 23 18	22 17 49	26 18 59	3♋39 38	15 13.3	19 01.2	19 47.0	0 28.7	25 35.2	27 18.6	1 51.5	10 20.0	16 13.9	26 44.1
14 F	3 27 14	23 15 42	10♋54 39	18 03 36	15 14.6	18 26.4	19 57.6	0 09.0	25 47.4	27 18.9	1 57.1	10 23.4	16 13.5	26 44.9
15 Sa	3 31 11	24 13 34	25 06 14	2♌02 25	15 15.9	17 53.3	20 10.3	29♏49.0	25 59.4	27R 19.0	2 02.6	10 26.8	16 13.1	26 45.8
16 Su	3 35 08	25 11 23	8♌52 13	15 35 46	15R 16.9	17 22.2	20 24.9	29 28.7	26 11.2	27 18.9	2 08.1	10 30.2	16 12.7	26 46.7
17 M	3 39 04	26 09 11	22 13 18	28 45 09	15 17.1	16 53.8	20 41.6	29 08.1	26 22.8	27 18.7	2 13.5	10 33.5	16 12.3	26 47.6
18 Tu	3 43 01	27 06 58	5♍11 42	11♍33 19	15 16.5	16 28.5	21 00.1	28 47.3	26 34.1	27 18.2	2 18.8	10 36.9	16 12.0	26 48.5
19 W	3 46 57	28 04 42	17 50 28	24 03 34	15 15.1	16 06.5	21 20.5	28 26.4	26 45.2	27 17.5	2 24.0	10 40.2	16 11.7	26 49.5
20 Th	3 50 54	29 02 25	0♎13 03	6♎19 21	15 13.1	15 48.4	21 42.6	28 05.3	26 56.1	27 16.7	2 29.2	10 43.6	16 11.4	26 50.4
21 F	3 54 50	0♊00 07	12 22 54	18 24 04	15 10.9	15 34.2	22 06.4	27 44.2	27 06.7	27 15.7	2 34.4	10 46.9	16 11.2	26 51.4
22 Sa	3 58 47	0 57 47	24 23 14	0♏20 46	15 08.6	15 24.2	22 31.9	27 23.0	27 17.1	27 14.4	2 39.4	10 50.2	16 11.0	26 52.4
23 Su	4 02 43	1 55 25	6♏17 00	12 12 15	15 06.8	15D 18.6	22 59.0	27 01.8	27 27.2	27 13.0	2 44.4	10 53.5	16 10.9	26 53.4
24 M	4 06 40	2 53 03	18 06 49	24 01 00	15 05.4	15 17.4	23 27.7	26 40.7	27 37.1	27 11.4	2 49.3	10 56.7	16 10.7	26 54.5
25 Tu	4 10 37	3 50 39	29 55 04	5♐49 18	15D 04.6	15 20.8	23 57.8	26 19.6	27 46.7	27 09.7	2 54.2	11 00.0	16 10.6	26 55.6
26 W	4 14 33	4 48 14	11♐43 58	17 39 22	15 04.5	15 28.6	24 29.4	25 58.7	27 56.0	27 07.7	2 58.9	11 03.2	16 10.6	26 56.6
27 Th	4 18 30	5 45 48	23 35 46	29 33 29	15 04.8	15 41.0	25 02.3	25 38.0	28 05.1	27 05.6	3 03.6	11 06.5	16D 10.5	26 57.8
28 F	4 22 26	6 43 20	5♑32 50	11♑34 08	15 05.5	15 57.8	25 36.5	25 17.5	28 13.9	27 03.2	3 08.3	11 09.7	16 10.5	26 58.9
29 Sa	4 26 23	7 40 52	17 37 43	23 43 59	15 06.2	16 19.0	26 12.1	24 57.3	28 22.5	27 00.7	3 12.8	11 12.9	16 10.6	27 00.0
30 Su	4 30 19	8 38 23	29 53 17	6♒06 02	15 07.0	16 44.5	26 48.8	24 37.4	28 30.8	26 58.0	3 17.3	11 16.0	16 10.6	27 01.2
31 M	4 34 16	9 35 53	12♒22 38	18 43 28	15 07.5	17 14.3	27 26.8	24 17.8	28 38.8	26 55.2	3 21.7	11 19.2	16 10.7	27 02.4

LONGITUDE — June 1937

Day	Sid.Time	☉	0 hr ☽	Noon ☽	True ☊	☿	♀	♂	⚳	♃	♄	♅	♆	♇
1 Tu	4 38 12	10♊33 22	25♒08 57	1♓39 27	15♐07.8	17♉48.2	28♈05.9	23♏58.6	28♒46.5	26♑52.1	3♈26.0	11♉22.3	16♍10.9	27♋03.5
2 W	4 42 09	11 30 50	8♓15 19	14 56 51	15R 07.8	18 26.2	28 46.0	23R 39.9	28 53.9	26R 48.9	3 30.2	11 25.4	16 11.0	27 04.8
3 Th	4 46 06	12 28 18	21 44 17	28 37 46	15 07.7	19 08.2	29 27.2	23 21.6	29 01.1	26 45.5	3 34.4	11 28.5	16 11.2	27 06.0
4 F	4 50 02	13 25 45	5♈37 20	12♈42 56	15 07.5	19 53.9	0♉09.4	23 03.8	29 07.9	26 41.9	3 38.5	11 31.6	16 11.4	27 07.2
5 Sa	4 53 59	14 23 12	19 54 20	27 11 11	15D 07.4	20 43.5	0 52.6	22 46.6	29 14.5	26 38.1	3 42.5	11 34.6	16 11.7	27 08.5
6 Su	4 57 55	15 20 37	4♉32 57	11♉58 57	15 07.4	21 36.7	1 36.7	22 29.9	29 20.8	26 34.2	3 46.4	11 37.6	16 12.0	27 09.8
7 M	5 01 52	16 18 03	19 28 24	27 00 18	15 07.5	22 33.5	2 21.7	22 13.9	29 26.7	26 30.1	3 50.2	11 40.6	16 12.3	27 11.1
8 Tu	5 05 48	17 15 27	4♊33 39	12♊07 17	15R 07.5	23 32.8	3 07.5	21 58.5	29 32.4	26 25.8	3 54.0	11 43.6	16 12.7	27 12.4
9 W	5 09 45	18 12 51	19 40 05	27 10 56	15 07.5	24 37.5	3 54.2	21 43.7	29 37.7	26 21.4	3 57.7	11 46.6	16 13.1	27 13.7
10 Th	5 13 41	19 10 14	4♋38 44	12♋02 33	15 07.3	25 44.6	4 41.6	21 29.7	29 42.7	26 16.8	4 01.3	11 49.5	16 13.5	27 15.0
11 F	5 17 38	20 07 36	19 21 30	26 34 55	15 06.8	26 55.0	5 29.8	21 16.3	29 47.4	26 12.1	4 04.8	11 52.4	16 14.0	27 16.4
12 Sa	5 21 35	21 04 57	3♌42 15	10♌43 09	15 06.2	28 08.7	6 18.7	21 03.8	29 51.8	26 07.2	4 08.2	11 55.3	16 14.4	27 17.8
13 Su	5 25 31	22 02 17	17 37 23	24 24 55	15 05.5	29 25.5	7 08.3	20 52.0	29 55.9	26 02.1	4 11.5	11 58.1	16 15.0	27 19.2
14 M	5 29 28	22 59 36	1♍05 50	7♍40 21	15 05.0	0♊45.5	7 58.5	20 40.9	29 59.6	25 56.9	4 14.7	12 00.9	16 15.5	27 20.5
15 Tu	5 33 24	23 56 54	14 08 46	20 31 28	15D 04.7	2 08.7	8 49.4	20 30.7	0♓03.0	25 51.6	4 17.8	12 03.7	16 16.1	27 22.0
16 W	5 37 21	24 54 11	26 48 56	3♎01 38	15 04.8	3 34.9	9 41.0	20 21.2	0 06.1	25 46.1	4 20.9	12 06.5	16 16.7	27 23.4
17 Th	5 41 17	25 51 28	9♎10 07	15 14 55	15 05.3	5 04.2	10 33.1	20 12.6	0 08.9	25 40.5	4 23.9	12 09.2	16 17.3	27 24.8
18 F	5 45 14	26 48 44	21 16 36	27 15 42	15 06.2	6 36.6	11 25.8	20 04.8	0 11.3	25 34.7	4 26.7	12 11.9	16 18.0	27 26.3
19 Sa	5 49 10	27 45 59	3♏12 46	9♏08 18	15 07.4	8 12.0	12 19.1	19 57.8	0 13.3	25 28.8	4 29.5	12 14.5	16 18.7	27 27.7
20 Su	5 53 07	28 43 13	15 02 48	20 56 44	15 08.5	9 50.4	13 13.0	19 51.7	0 15.1	25 22.8	4 32.2	12 17.2	16 19.5	27 29.2
21 M	5 57 04	29 40 27	26 50 33	2♐44 38	15 09.4	11 31.7	14 07.3	19 46.4	0 16.5	25 16.7	4 34.8	12 19.8	16 20.2	27 30.7
22 Tu	6 01 00	0♋37 40	8♐39 23	14 35 08	15R 09.8	13 16.0	15 02.2	19 41.9	0 17.5	25 10.4	4 37.3	12 22.4	16 21.0	27 32.2
23 W	6 04 57	1 34 53	20 32 13	26 30 54	15 09.5	15 03.1	15 57.6	19 38.2	0 18.2	25 04.0	4 39.7	12 24.9	16 21.9	27 33.7
24 Th	6 08 53	2 32 06	2♑31 28	8♑34 08	15 08.3	16 53.0	16 53.4	19 35.4	0R 18.6	24 57.5	4 42.0	12 27.4	16 22.7	27 35.2
25 F	6 12 50	3 29 18	14 39 08	20 46 41	15 06.3	18 45.7	17 49.7	19 33.4	0 18.6	24 50.9	4 44.2	12 29.9	16 23.6	27 36.7
26 Sa	6 16 46	4 26 30	26 56 57	3♒10 08	15 03.6	20 40.9	18 46.5	19D 32.2	0 18.3	24 44.2	4 46.3	12 32.3	16 24.5	27 38.2
27 Su	6 20 43	5 23 42	9♒26 24	15 45 55	15 00.6	22 38.6	19 43.7	19 31.9	0 17.6	24 37.4	4 48.4	12 34.7	16 25.5	27 39.8
28 M	6 24 40	6 20 53	22 08 52	28 35 25	14 57.7	24 38.7	20 41.3	19 32.4	0 16.6	24 30.5	4 50.3	12 37.1	16 26.5	27 41.3
29 Tu	6 28 36	7 18 05	5♓05 43	11♓39 58	14 55.3	26 40.9	21 39.3	19 33.6	0 15.2	24 23.5	4 52.1	12 39.4	16 27.5	27 42.9
30 W	6 32 33	8 15 17	18 18 17	25 00 49	14 53.7	28 45.0	22 37.7	19 35.7	0 13.4	24 16.5	4 53.9	12 41.7	16 28.5	27 44.4

Astro Data

	Dy Hr Mn
☽ 0N	6 9:13
♀ D	9 5:56
♃ R	15 13:02
☽ 0S	18 23:49
☿ D	24 6:15
♆ D	27 23:14
♃☍♇	29 16:28
☽ 0N	2 16:50
☽ 0S	15 6:38
⚳ R	25 1:03
♂ D	27 10:08
☽ 0N	29 23:04

Planet Ingress

	Dy Hr Mn
♂ ♏R	14 22:52
☉ ♊	21 11:57
♀ ♉	4 6:41
☿ ♊	13 22:28
⚳ ♓	14 14:34
☉ ♋	21 20:12

Last Aspect / ☽ Ingress (May)

Last Aspect Dy Hr Mn		☽ Ingress Dy Hr Mn
2 12:27	♃ ☌	♒ 2 18:08
4 14:35	☿ □	♓ 5 1:57
7 1:06	♃ ⚹	♈ 7 5:47
9 2:09	♃ □	♉ 9 6:32
11 1:39	♃ △	♊ 11 5:56
12 13:13	♀ ⚹	♋ 13 6:00
15 8:14	♂ △	♌ 15 8:27
17 12:41	♂ □	♍ 17 14:19
19 20:29	☉ △	♎ 19 23:34
22 5:45	♃ □	♏ 22 11:18
24 18:26	♃ ⚹	♐ 25 0:10
27 2:28	♀ △	♑ 27 12:53
29 18:24	♇ ☍	♒ 30 0:13

Last Aspect / ☽ Ingress (June)

Last Aspect Dy Hr Mn		☽ Ingress Dy Hr Mn
1 5:06	♀ ⚹	♓ 1 8:58
3 9:21	♇ △	♈ 3 14:22
5 11:55	♇ □	♉ 5 16:36
7 12:17	♇ ⚹	♊ 7 16:46
8 20:43	☉ ☌	♋ 9 16:31
11 13:10	♇ ☌	♌ 11 17:44
13 21:58	☿ □	♍ 13 22:01
16 1:05	♇ ⚹	♎ 16 6:08
18 12:21	♇ □	♏ 18 17:31
21 1:20	♇ △	♐ 21 6:25
22 15:34	♆ □	♑ 23 18:58
26 1:19	♇ ☍	♒ 26 5:54
28 3:18	☿ △	♓ 28 14:37
30 19:50	☿ □	♈ 30 20:50

☽ Phases & Eclipses

Dy Hr Mn		
3 18:36	☾	12♒54
10 13:18	●	19♉27
17 6:49	☽	25♌57
25 7:38	○	3♐40
25 7:51	☍	A 0.770
2 5:23	☾	11♓15
8 20:43	●	17♊36
8 20:40:38	☌	T 07'04"
15 19:03	☽	24♍14
23 23:00	○	2♑01

Astro Data

1 May 1937
Julian Day # 13635
SVP 6♓07'50"
GC 25♐57.8 ⚴ 1♒38.3
Eris 3♈58.8 ⚵ 25♍50.4R
⚷ 20♊28.4 ⚶ 16♋31.8
☽ Mean ☊ 17♐09.7

1 June 1937
Julian Day # 13666
SVP 6♓07'45"
GC 25♐57.9 ⚴ 2♒06.9R
Eris 4♈13.5 ⚵ 25♍58.1
⚷ 23♊01.3 ⚶ 28♋14.6
☽ Mean ☊ 15♐31.2

July 1937 LONGITUDE

Day	Sid.Time	☉	0 hr ☽	Noon ☽	True ☊	☿	♀	♂	⚳	♃	♄	♅	♆	♇
1 Th	6 36 29	9♋12 29	1♈47 42	8♈39 01	14♐53.1	0♋50.8	23♉36.5	19♏38.6	0♓11.3	24♑09.3	4♈55.5	12♉44.0	16♍29.6	27♋46.0
2 F	6 40 26	10 09 41	15 34 48	22 35 03	14D53.5	2 58.0	24 35.7	19 42.3	0R08.8	24R02.1	4 57.0	12 46.2	16 30.7	27 47.6
3 Sa	6 44 22	11 06 54	29 39 40	6♉48 31	14 54.7	5 06.4	25 35.2	19 46.8	0 06.0	23 54.8	4 58.5	12 48.4	16 31.8	27 49.2
4 Su	6 48 19	12 04 07	14♉01 19	21 17 42	14 56.1	7 15.7	26 35.1	19 52.0	0 02.8	23 47.4	4 59.8	12 50.5	16 32.9	27 50.8
5 M	6 52 15	13 01 20	28 37 13	5♊59 14	14R57.1	9 25.6	27 35.2	19 58.1	29♒59.2	23 40.0	5 01.1	12 52.6	16 34.1	27 52.4
6 Tu	6 56 12	13 58 33	13♊23 05	20 47 58	14 57.2	11 35.7	28 35.8	20 04.9	29 55.3	23 32.5	5 02.2	12 54.7	16 35.3	27 54.0
7 W	7 00 09	14 55 47	28 13 00	5♋37 16	14 56.0	13 45.9	29 36.6	20 12.4	29 51.1	23 24.9	5 03.2	12 56.7	16 36.6	27 55.6
8 Th	7 04 05	15 53 01	12♋59 49	20 19 43	14 53.3	15 55.8	0♊37.7	20 20.7	29 46.5	23 17.4	5 04.2	12 58.7	16 37.8	27 57.2
9 F	7 08 02	16 50 15	27 36 05	4♌48 07	14 49.3	18 05.2	1 39.1	20 29.8	29 41.5	23 09.7	5 05.0	13 00.6	16 39.1	27 58.9
10 Sa	7 11 58	17 47 29	11♌55 07	18 56 31	14 44.5	20 13.8	2 40.8	20 39.6	29 36.2	23 02.1	5 05.8	13 02.6	16 40.4	28 00.5
11 Su	7 15 55	18 44 43	25 51 55	2♍41 01	14 39.5	22 21.5	3 42.8	20 50.1	29 30.5	22 54.4	5 06.4	13 04.4	16 41.8	28 02.1
12 M	7 19 51	19 41 57	9♍23 44	16 00 04	14 35.0	24 28.1	4 45.0	21 01.3	29 24.5	22 46.7	5 06.9	13 06.2	16 43.2	28 03.8
13 Tu	7 23 48	20 39 11	22 30 12	28 54 23	14 31.6	26 33.4	5 47.5	21 13.2	29 18.1	22 39.0	5 07.3	13 08.0	16 44.5	28 05.4
14 W	7 27 44	21 36 24	5♎13 01	11♎26 33	14D29.5	28 37.3	6 50.2	21 25.8	29 11.4	22 31.2	5 07.7	13 09.8	16 46.0	28 07.0
15 Th	7 31 41	22 33 38	17 35 30	23 40 26	14 29.0	0♌39.7	7 53.2	21 39.1	29 04.4	22 23.5	5 07.9	13 11.4	16 47.4	28 08.7
16 F	7 35 38	23 30 53	29 41 59	5♏40 45	14 29.7	2 40.5	8 56.4	21 53.0	28 57.0	22 15.8	5R08.0	13 13.1	16 48.9	28 10.3
17 Sa	7 39 34	24 28 07	11♏37 22	17 32 28	14 31.1	4 39.6	9 59.8	22 07.6	28 49.4	22 08.0	5 08.0	13 14.7	16 50.4	28 12.0
18 Su	7 43 31	25 25 22	23 26 41	29 20 36	14 32.7	6 37.1	11 03.5	22 22.8	28 41.4	22 00.3	5 08.0	13 16.3	16 51.9	28 13.6
19 M	7 47 27	26 22 36	5♐14 48	11♐09 49	14R33.6	8 32.8	12 07.4	22 38.7	28 33.1	21 52.6	5 07.8	13 17.8	16 53.4	28 15.3
20 Tu	7 51 24	27 19 51	17 06 10	23 04 17	14 33.3	10 26.8	13 11.5	22 55.1	28 24.5	21 44.9	5 07.5	13 19.3	16 55.0	28 17.0
21 W	7 55 20	28 17 07	29 04 36	5♑07 28	14 31.2	12 19.0	14 15.9	23 12.2	28 15.6	21 37.3	5 07.1	13 20.7	16 56.6	28 18.6
22 Th	7 59 17	29 14 23	11♑13 10	17 21 59	14 27.1	14 09.4	15 20.4	23 29.8	28 06.4	21 29.7	5 06.6	13 22.1	16 58.2	28 20.3
23 F	8 03 13	0♌11 39	23 34 06	29 49 38	14 21.2	15 58.1	16 25.2	23 48.0	27 56.9	21 22.1	5 06.1	13 23.4	16 59.8	28 21.9
24 Sa	8 07 10	1 08 56	6♒08 40	12♒31 15	14 13.8	17 45.0	17 30.2	24 06.7	27 47.1	21 14.6	5 05.4	13 24.7	17 01.5	28 23.6
25 Su	8 11 07	2 06 14	18 57 21	25 26 56	14 05.7	19 30.2	18 35.3	24 26.0	27 37.1	21 07.1	5 04.6	13 26.0	17 03.1	28 25.2
26 M	8 15 03	3 03 32	1♓59 55	8♓36 11	13 57.7	21 13.6	19 40.7	24 45.9	27 26.8	20 59.7	5 03.7	13 27.2	17 04.8	28 26.9
27 Tu	8 19 00	4 00 52	15 15 37	21 58 08	13 50.6	22 55.2	20 46.2	25 06.3	27 16.2	20 52.3	5 02.7	13 28.3	17 06.6	28 28.5
28 W	8 22 56	4 58 12	28 43 34	5♈31 51	13 45.2	24 35.1	21 51.9	25 27.1	27 05.4	20 45.0	5 01.6	13 29.4	17 08.3	28 30.2
29 Th	8 26 53	5 55 33	12♈22 53	19 16 34	13 42.0	26 13.3	22 57.9	25 48.5	26 54.4	20 37.7	5 00.5	13 30.5	17 10.0	28 31.8
30 F	8 30 49	6 52 56	26 12 49	3♉11 35	13D40.7	27 49.8	24 04.0	26 10.4	26 43.1	20 30.6	4 59.2	13 31.5	17 11.8	28 33.5
31 Sa	8 34 46	7 50 19	10♉12 46	17 16 18	13 40.9	29 24.5	25 10.2	26 32.8	26 31.6	20 23.5	4 57.8	13 32.5	17 13.6	28 35.1

August 1937 LONGITUDE

Day	Sid.Time	☉	0 hr ☽	Noon ☽	True ☊	☿	♀	♂	⚳	♃	♄	♅	♆	♇
1 Su	8 38 42	8♌47 44	24♉22 01	1♊29 47	13♐41.7	0♍57.5	26♊16.7	26♏55.7	26♒20.0	20♑16.5	4♈56.3	13♉33.4	17♍15.4	28♋36.7
2 M	8 42 39	9 45 10	8♊39 22	15 50 29	13R42.1	2 28.7	27 23.3	27 19.1	26R08.1	20R09.6	4R54.8	13 34.2	17 17.3	28 38.4
3 Tu	8 46 36	10 42 37	23 02 45	0♋15 43	13 41.0	3 58.2	28 30.1	27 42.9	25 56.0	20 02.7	4 53.1	13 35.1	17 19.1	28 40.0
4 W	8 50 32	11 40 06	7♋28 53	14 41 38	13 37.7	5 26.0	29 37.0	28 07.2	25 43.7	19 56.0	4 51.3	13 35.8	17 21.0	28 41.6
5 Th	8 54 29	12 37 35	21 53 19	29 03 14	13 31.9	6 52.0	0♋44.1	28 31.9	25 31.3	19 49.4	4 49.5	13 36.6	17 22.9	28 43.3
6 F	8 58 25	13 35 05	6♌10 41	13♌14 59	13 23.9	8 16.1	1 51.3	28 57.1	25 18.8	19 42.9	4 47.5	13 37.2	17 24.8	28 44.9
7 Sa	9 02 22	14 32 37	20 15 28	27 11 34	13 14.3	9 38.5	2 58.7	29 22.7	25 06.1	19 36.5	4 45.5	13 37.9	17 26.7	28 46.5
8 Su	9 06 18	15 30 09	4♍02 47	10♍48 45	13 04.1	10 58.9	4 06.3	29 48.8	24 53.3	19 30.2	4 43.3	13 38.4	17 28.7	28 48.1
9 M	9 10 15	16 27 42	17 29 13	24 04 02	12 54.5	12 17.5	5 13.9	0♐15.2	24 40.3	19 24.0	4 41.1	13 39.0	17 30.6	28 49.7
10 Tu	9 14 11	17 25 17	0♎33 13	6♎56 54	12 46.5	13 34.1	6 21.7	0 42.1	24 27.3	19 18.0	4 38.8	13 39.4	17 32.6	28 51.3
11 W	9 18 08	18 22 52	13 15 18	19 28 47	12 40.5	14 48.7	7 29.7	1 09.4	24 14.2	19 12.1	4 36.4	13 39.9	17 34.6	28 52.8
12 Th	9 22 05	19 20 28	25 37 46	1♏42 45	12 36.9	16 01.2	8 37.7	1 37.1	24 01.1	19 06.4	4 33.9	13 40.2	17 36.6	28 54.4
13 F	9 26 01	20 18 05	7♏44 20	13 43 05	12D35.3	17 11.6	9 46.0	2 05.1	23 47.9	19 00.7	4 31.3	13 40.6	17 38.6	28 56.0
14 Sa	9 29 58	21 15 43	19 39 41	25 34 47	12 35.2	18 19.7	10 54.3	2 33.6	23 34.6	18 55.2	4 28.6	13 40.8	17 40.6	28 57.5
15 Su	9 33 54	22 13 22	1♐29 04	7♐23 14	12R35.6	19 25.5	12 02.8	3 02.4	23 21.3	18 49.9	4 25.9	13 41.1	17 42.6	28 59.1
16 M	9 37 51	23 11 02	13 17 55	19 13 48	12 35.5	20 28.9	13 11.4	3 31.6	23 08.1	18 44.7	4 23.0	13 41.2	17 44.7	29 00.6
17 Tu	9 41 47	24 08 44	25 11 29	1♑11 33	12 33.9	21 29.7	14 20.1	4 01.1	22 54.8	18 39.7	4 20.1	13 41.4	17 46.8	29 02.1
18 W	9 45 44	25 06 26	7♑14 33	13 20 56	12 30.2	22 27.9	15 28.9	4 30.9	22 41.5	18 34.8	4 17.1	13 41.4	17 48.8	29 03.7
19 Th	9 49 40	26 04 09	19 31 07	25 45 26	12 23.9	23 23.3	16 37.9	5 01.1	22 28.3	18 30.1	4 14.1	13R41.5	17 50.9	29 05.2
20 F	9 53 37	27 01 54	2♒04 08	8♒27 22	12 15.0	24 15.7	17 47.0	5 31.7	22 15.2	18 25.5	4 10.9	13 41.5	17 53.0	29 06.7
21 Sa	9 57 34	27 59 40	14 55 12	21 27 35	12 04.2	25 05.0	18 56.2	6 02.5	22 02.0	18 21.1	4 07.7	13 41.4	17 55.1	29 08.2
22 Su	10 01 30	28 57 27	28 04 24	4♓45 26	11 52.3	25 51.0	20 05.5	6 33.7	21 49.0	18 16.8	4 04.4	13 41.3	17 57.3	29 09.6
23 M	10 05 27	29 55 16	11♓30 24	18 18 55	11 40.5	26 33.6	21 15.0	7 05.2	21 36.0	18 12.8	4 01.0	13 41.1	17 59.4	29 11.1
24 Tu	10 09 23	0♍53 06	25 10 37	2♈05 04	11 30.0	27 12.4	22 24.6	7 36.9	21 23.2	18 08.8	3 57.5	13 40.9	18 01.5	29 12.6
25 W	10 13 20	1 50 58	9♈01 50	16 00 29	11 21.6	27 47.3	23 34.3	8 09.0	21 10.4	18 05.1	3 54.0	13 40.6	18 03.7	29 14.0
26 Th	10 17 16	2 48 52	23 00 38	0♉01 57	11 16.0	28 18.1	24 44.1	8 41.4	20 57.8	18 01.5	3 50.4	13 40.3	18 05.8	29 15.4
27 F	10 21 13	3 46 47	7♉04 06	14 06 50	11 13.0	28 44.4	25 54.0	9 14.0	20 45.3	17 58.1	3 46.8	13 39.9	18 08.0	29 16.8
28 Sa	10 25 09	4 44 45	21 09 58	28 13 20	11 12.0	29 06.1	27 04.0	9 47.0	20 33.0	17 54.9	3 43.0	13 39.5	18 10.2	29 18.2
29 Su	10 29 06	5 42 44	5♊16 47	12♊20 15	11 12.0	29 22.8	28 14.2	10 20.2	20 20.8	17 51.9	3 39.3	13 39.0	18 12.4	29 19.6
30 M	10 33 03	6 40 45	19 23 35	26 26 42	11 11.5	29 34.3	29 24.5	10 53.7	20 08.8	17 49.1	3 35.4	13 38.5	18 14.5	29 21.0
31 Tu	10 36 59	7 38 49	3♋29 26	10♋31 37	11 09.5	29R40.3	0♌34.8	11 27.4	19 57.0	17 46.4	3 31.5	13 38.0	18 16.7	29 22.4

Astro Data	Dy Hr Mn
☽0S	12 15:30
♄ R	17 5:18
☽0N	27 5:06
☽0S	9 1:23
♅ R	19 13:48
☿0S	20 18:27
☽0N	23 12:09
♃△♆	25 17:55

Planet Ingress		Dy Hr Mn
☿	♋	1 2:21
⚳	♒R	5 7:05
♀	♊	7 21:13
☿	♌	15 4:11
☉	♌	23 7:07
☿	♍	31 21:07
♀	♋	4 20:14
♂	♐	8 22:14
☉	♍	23 13:58
♀	♌	31 0:08

Last Aspect Dy Hr Mn			☽ Ingress	Dy Hr Mn
2 20:52	♇	□	♉	3 0:34
4 22:45	♇	⚹	♊	5 2:15
6 5:11	♆	□	♋	7 2:53
9 0:37	♇	☌	♌	9 3:59
10 15:00	♂	□	♍	11 7:15
13 10:27	♇	⚹	♎	13 14:04
15 20:55	♇	□	♏	16 0:36
18 9:43	♇	△	♐	18 13:20
19 23:36	♆	□	♑	21 1:50
23 9:12	♇	☍	♒	23 12:20
25 10:05	♂	□	♓	25 20:21
27 23:35	♇	△	♈	28 2:15
30 4:01	♇	□	♉	30 6:31

Last Aspect Dy Hr Mn			☽ Ingress	Dy Hr Mn
1 7:09	♇	⚹	♊	1 9:29
3 8:50	♀	☌	♋	3 11:34
5 11:26	♇	☌	♌	5 13:35
7 15:56	♂	□	♍	7 16:54
9 20:49	♇	⚹	♎	9 22:58
12 6:26	♇	□	♏	12 8:37
14 18:53	♇	△	♐	14 20:59
16 20:40	☉	△	♑	17 9:37
19 18:22	♇	☍	♒	19 20:05
22 0:47	☉	☍	♓	22 3:28
24 7:00	♇	△	♈	24 8:23
26 10:40	♇	□	♉	26 11:57
28 13:51	♇	⚹	♊	28 15:01
30 17:23	☿	□	♋	30 18:03

☽ Phases & Eclipses Dy Hr Mn		
1 13:03	☾	9♈15
8 4:13	●	15♋34
15 9:36	☽	22♎28
23 12:45	○	0♒13
30 18:47	☾	7♉09
6 12:37	●	13♌37
14 2:28	☽	20♏53
22 0:47	○	28♒30
28 23:54	☾	5♊14

Astro Data

1 July 1937
Julian Day # 13696
SVP 6♓07'40"
GC 25♐58.0 ⚴ 26♑44.4R
Eris 4♈18.4R ⚵ 0♎27.9
⚷ 25♊42.7 ⚶ 10♌59.2
☽ Mean ☊ 13♐55.9

1 August 1937
Julian Day # 13727
SVP 6♓07'35"
GC 25♐58.1 ⚴ 18♑35.3R
Eris 4♈12.9R ⚵ 8♎00.0
⚷ 28♊17.5 ⚶ 25♌05.4
☽ Mean ☊ 12♐17.4

LONGITUDE September 1937

Day	Sid.Time	☉	0 hr ☽	Noon ☽	True ☊	☿	♀	♂	⚳	♃	♄	♅	♆	♇
1 W	10 40 56	8♍36 54	17♋33 02	24♋33 23	11♐04.9	29♍40.6	1♌45.3	12♐01.5	19♒45.4	17♑43.9	3♈27.6	13♉37.4	18♍18.9	29♋23.7
2 Th	10 44 52	9 35 01	1♌32 22	8♌29 35	10R 57.4	29R 34.9	2 55.9	12 35.8	19R 34.0	17R 41.6	3R 23.5	13R 36.7	18 21.1	29 25.1
3 F	10 48 49	10 33 09	15 24 38	22 17 06	10 47.3	29 23.0	4 06.6	13 10.3	19 22.8	17 39.5	3 19.5	13 36.0	18 23.3	29 26.4
4 Sa	10 52 45	11 31 20	29 06 32	5♍52 33	10 35.2	29 04.8	5 17.3	13 45.1	19 11.9	17 37.6	3 15.3	13 35.2	18 25.6	29 27.7
5 Su	10 56 42	12 29 32	12♍34 45	19 12 50	10 22.4	28 40.2	6 28.2	14 20.2	19 01.2	17 35.8	3 11.2	13 34.4	18 27.8	29 29.0
6 M	11 00 38	13 27 46	25 46 31	2♎15 41	10 10.1	28 09.3	7 39.2	14 55.5	18 50.7	17 34.3	3 06.9	13 33.6	18 30.0	29 30.2
7 Tu	11 04 35	14 26 01	8♎40 13	15 00 10	9 59.4	27 32.2	8 50.2	15 31.0	18 40.5	17 32.9	3 02.7	13 32.7	18 32.2	29 31.5
8 W	11 08 31	15 24 19	21 15 40	27 26 54	9 51.1	26 49.2	10 01.4	16 06.8	18 30.6	17 31.8	2 58.4	13 31.7	18 34.4	29 32.7
9 Th	11 12 28	16 22 37	3♏34 11	9♏37 55	9 45.6	26 00.8	11 12.6	16 42.8	18 21.0	17 30.8	2 54.0	13 30.8	18 36.7	29 33.9
10 F	11 16 25	17 20 58	15 38 32	21 36 35	9 42.5	25 07.7	12 23.9	17 19.1	18 11.7	17 30.0	2 49.6	13 29.7	18 38.9	29 35.1
11 Sa	11 20 21	18 19 20	27 32 38	3♐27 18	9D 41.4	24 10.6	13 35.4	17 55.6	18 02.6	17 29.5	2 45.2	13 28.6	18 41.1	29 36.3
12 Su	11 24 18	19 17 44	9♐21 15	15 15 09	9R 41.4	23 10.7	14 46.9	18 32.2	17 53.9	17 29.1	2 40.7	13 27.5	18 43.3	29 37.5
13 M	11 28 14	20 16 09	21 09 41	27 05 33	9 41.3	22 09.0	15 58.5	19 09.1	17 45.5	17D 28.9	2 36.3	13 26.3	18 45.6	29 38.6
14 Tu	11 32 11	21 14 36	3♑03 27	9♑04 03	9 40.0	21 07.1	17 10.1	19 46.2	17 37.4	17 28.9	2 31.7	13 25.1	18 47.8	29 39.8
15 W	11 36 07	22 13 04	15 07 58	21 15 49	9 36.8	20 06.2	18 21.9	20 23.5	17 29.6	17 29.1	2 27.2	13 23.9	18 50.0	29 40.9
16 Th	11 40 04	23 11 34	27 28 07	3♒45 21	9 31.2	19 07.9	19 33.7	21 01.0	17 22.1	17 29.5	2 22.6	13 22.6	18 52.2	29 42.0
17 F	11 44 00	24 10 06	10♒07 52	16 35 57	9 23.0	18 13.7	20 45.7	21 38.7	17 15.0	17 30.1	2 18.1	13 21.2	18 54.5	29 43.0
18 Sa	11 47 57	25 08 40	23 09 46	29 49 19	9 12.8	17 24.9	21 57.7	22 16.6	17 08.2	17 30.8	2 13.4	13 19.9	18 56.7	29 44.1
19 Su	11 51 54	26 07 15	6♓34 31	13♓25 07	9 01.4	16 42.9	23 09.8	22 54.7	17 01.8	17 31.8	2 08.8	13 18.4	18 58.9	29 45.1
20 M	11 55 50	27 05 52	20 20 46	27 20 56	8 50.0	16 08.6	24 22.0	23 32.9	16 55.7	17 33.0	2 04.2	13 17.0	19 01.1	29 46.1
21 Tu	11 59 47	28 04 31	4♈25 03	11♈32 26	8 39.8	15 43.0	25 34.2	24 11.4	16 50.0	17 34.3	1 59.5	13 15.5	19 03.3	29 47.1
22 W	12 03 43	29 03 12	18 42 21	25 54 05	8 31.7	15 26.8	26 46.6	24 50.0	16 44.6	17 35.9	1 54.9	13 13.9	19 05.5	29 48.1
23 Th	12 07 40	0♎01 55	3♉06 54	10♉20 05	8 26.3	15D 20.3	27 59.0	25 28.7	16 39.5	17 37.6	1 50.2	13 12.3	19 07.7	29 49.0
24 F	12 11 36	1 00 41	17 33 01	24 45 10	8D 23.6	15 23.8	29 11.5	26 07.7	16 34.8	17 39.5	1 45.5	13 10.7	19 09.9	29 50.0
25 Sa	12 15 33	1 59 28	1♊56 03	9♊05 18	8 22.9	15 37.3	0♍24.1	26 46.8	16 30.5	17 41.6	1 40.9	13 09.1	19 12.1	29 50.9
26 Su	12 19 29	2 58 19	16 12 40	23 17 54	8R 23.3	16 00.6	1 36.7	27 26.1	16 26.5	17 43.9	1 36.2	13 07.4	19 14.3	29 51.8
27 M	12 23 26	3 57 11	0♋20 54	7♋21 34	8 23.5	16 33.4	2 49.5	28 05.5	16 22.9	17 46.4	1 31.5	13 05.7	19 16.5	29 52.6
28 Tu	12 27 23	4 56 06	14 19 50	21 15 41	8 22.4	17 15.2	4 02.3	28 45.1	16 19.7	17 49.1	1 26.9	13 03.9	19 18.6	29 53.5
29 W	12 31 19	5 55 03	28 09 04	4♌59 58	8 19.0	18 05.5	5 15.2	29 24.9	16 16.8	17 51.9	1 22.2	13 02.1	19 20.8	29 54.3
30 Th	12 35 16	6 54 02	11♌48 19	18 34 02	8 13.2	19 03.6	6 28.1	0♑04.8	16 14.3	17 55.0	1 17.6	13 00.2	19 22.9	29 55.1

LONGITUDE October 1937

Day	Sid.Time	☉	0 hr ☽	Noon ☽	True ☊	☿	♀	♂	⚳	♃	♄	♅	♆	♇
1 F	12 39 12	7♎53 03	25♌17 02	1♍57 11	8♐04.9	20♍08.8	7♍41.2	0♑44.8	16♒12.1	17♑58.2	1♈12.9	12♉58.4	19♍25.1	29♋55.9
2 Sa	12 43 09	8 52 07	8♍34 23	15 08 29	7R 55.0	21 20.5	8 54.3	1 25.1	16R 10.3	18 01.6	1R 08.3	12R 56.5	19 27.2	29 56.6
3 Su	12 47 05	9 51 13	21 39 21	28 06 51	7 44.4	22 37.9	10 07.4	2 05.4	16 08.9	18 05.2	1 03.7	12 54.5	19 29.3	29 57.3
4 M	12 51 02	10 50 20	4♎30 53	10♎51 25	7 34.2	24 00.3	11 20.6	2 46.0	16 07.8	18 09.0	0 59.1	12 52.6	19 31.4	29 58.0
5 Tu	12 54 58	11 49 30	17 08 24	23 21 53	7 25.3	25 27.1	12 33.9	3 26.6	16 07.2	18 13.0	0 54.6	12 50.6	19 33.5	29 58.7
6 W	12 58 55	12 48 42	29 31 57	5♏38 45	7 18.4	26 57.6	13 47.3	4 07.4	16D 06.8	18 17.1	0 50.0	12 48.5	19 35.6	29 59.4
7 Th	13 02 51	13 47 56	11♏42 29	17 43 27	7 13.9	28 31.1	15 00.7	4 48.4	16 06.9	18 21.4	0 45.5	12 46.5	19 37.7	29 60.0
8 F	13 06 48	14 47 12	23 41 58	29 38 26	7D 11.8	0♎07.3	16 14.2	5 29.4	16 07.3	18 25.9	0 41.1	12 44.4	19 39.8	0♌00.6
9 Sa	13 10 45	15 46 30	5♐33 18	11♐27 04	7 11.5	1 45.6	17 27.7	6 10.7	16 08.1	18 30.6	0 36.6	12 42.3	19 41.8	0 01.2
10 Su	13 14 41	16 45 49	17 20 18	23 13 35	7 12.5	3 25.6	18 41.3	6 52.0	16 09.2	18 35.5	0 32.2	12 40.1	19 43.9	0 01.8
11 M	13 18 38	17 45 10	29 07 31	5♑02 45	7 13.8	5 06.8	19 54.9	7 33.5	16 10.7	18 40.5	0 27.9	12 38.0	19 45.9	0 02.3
12 Tu	13 22 34	18 44 34	10♑59 58	16 59 49	7R 14.5	6 49.1	21 08.6	8 15.1	16 12.5	18 45.7	0 23.6	12 35.8	19 47.9	0 02.8
13 W	13 26 31	19 43 58	23 02 58	29 10 04	7 14.0	8 32.0	22 22.4	8 56.8	16 14.7	18 51.0	0 19.3	12 33.6	19 49.9	0 03.3
14 Th	13 30 27	20 43 25	5♒21 44	11♒38 33	7 11.7	10 15.4	23 36.2	9 38.6	16 17.3	18 56.6	0 15.0	12 31.3	19 51.9	0 03.7
15 F	13 34 24	21 42 53	18 01 01	24 29 33	7 07.5	11 59.1	24 50.0	10 20.5	16 20.2	19 02.3	0 10.9	12 29.1	19 53.8	0 04.2
16 Sa	13 38 20	22 42 24	1♓04 29	7♓46 01	7 01.7	13 42.8	26 03.9	11 02.6	16 23.4	19 08.1	0 06.7	12 26.8	19 55.8	0 04.6
17 Su	13 42 17	23 41 55	14 34 13	21 28 59	6 54.8	15 26.5	27 17.9	11 44.7	16 27.0	19 14.2	0 02.6	12 24.5	19 57.7	0 05.0
18 M	13 46 14	24 41 29	28 30 04	5♈37 02	6 47.8	17 10.0	28 31.9	12 27.0	16 30.9	19 20.3	29♓58.6	12 22.2	19 59.6	0 05.3
19 Tu	13 50 10	25 41 05	12♈49 19	20 06 10	6 41.5	18 53.3	29 45.9	13 09.3	16 35.1	19 26.7	29 54.6	12 19.9	20 01.5	0 05.7
20 W	13 54 07	26 40 43	27 26 45	4♉50 07	6 36.6	20 36.3	1♎00.0	13 51.8	16 39.7	19 33.2	29 50.7	12 17.5	20 03.4	0 06.0
21 Th	13 58 03	27 40 22	12♉15 17	19 41 14	6 33.6	22 18.9	2 14.2	14 34.3	16 44.6	19 39.8	29 46.9	12 15.1	20 05.2	0 06.3
22 F	14 02 00	28 40 04	27 06 59	4♊31 37	6D 32.5	24 01.0	3 28.4	15 17.0	16 49.8	19 46.7	29 43.1	12 12.8	20 07.1	0 06.5
23 Sa	14 05 56	29 39 48	11♊54 18	19 14 20	6 33.0	25 42.7	4 42.6	15 59.7	16 55.4	19 53.6	29 39.4	12 10.4	20 08.9	0 06.7
24 Su	14 09 53	0♏39 35	26 31 05	3♋44 07	6 34.3	27 24.0	5 56.9	16 42.6	17 01.3	20 00.7	29 35.7	12 08.0	20 10.7	0 07.0
25 M	14 13 49	1 39 24	10♋53 04	17 57 43	6 35.7	29 04.7	7 11.3	17 25.5	17 07.4	20 08.0	29 32.1	12 05.5	20 12.5	0 07.1
26 Tu	14 17 46	2 39 14	24 57 56	1♌53 41	6R 36.4	0♏44.9	8 25.7	18 08.5	17 13.9	20 15.4	29 28.6	12 03.1	20 14.3	0 07.3
27 W	14 21 43	3 39 08	8♌44 58	15 31 54	6 35.8	2 24.6	9 40.1	18 51.7	17 20.7	20 23.0	29 25.1	12 00.7	20 16.0	0 07.4
28 Th	14 25 39	4 39 03	22 14 34	28 53 09	6 33.6	4 03.8	10 54.6	19 34.8	17 27.8	20 30.7	29 21.7	11 58.2	20 17.7	0 07.5
29 F	14 29 36	5 39 00	5♍27 46	11♍58 37	6 30.1	5 42.5	12 09.1	20 18.1	17 35.2	20 38.6	29 18.4	11 55.8	20 19.4	0 07.6
30 Sa	14 33 32	6 39 00	18 25 51	24 49 36	6 25.5	7 20.8	13 23.7	21 01.5	17 43.0	20 46.6	29 15.2	11 53.3	20 21.1	0 07.6
31 Su	14 37 29	7 39 01	1♎10 04	7♎27 21	6 20.4	8 58.5	14 38.3	21 45.0	17 51.0	20 54.7	29 12.1	11 50.8	20 22.8	0R 07.7

Astro Data

	Dy Hr Mn
☿ R	1 1:07
☽ 0S	5 10:38
☿ 0N	13 17:02
♃ D	13 23:18
☽ 0N	19 20:43
☉ 0S	23 11:13
☿ D	23 15:39
☽ 0S	2 17:58
⚳ D	6 20:58
☿ 0S	11 2:55
♄ △ ♇	16 23:25
☽ 0N	17 6:21
♀ 0S	22 14:29
♃ △ ♆	26 7:09
☽ 0S	29 23:23

Planet Ingress

	Dy Hr Mn
☉ ♎	23 11:13
♀ ♍	25 4:03
♂ ♑	30 9:08
♇ ♌	7 12:08
☿ ♎	8 10:12
♄ ♓R	18 3:41
♀ ♎	19 16:33
☉ ♏	23 20:07
☿ ♏	26 1:14
♇ R	31 20:07

Last Aspect / ☽ Ingress

Last Aspect Dy Hr Mn		☽ Ingress Dy Hr Mn
1 20:45	☿ ⚹	♌ 1 21:21
2 20:52	♅ □	♍ 4 1:34
6 6:52	♇ ⚹	♎ 6 7:48
8 16:06	♇ □	♏ 8 16:59
11 4:10	♇ △	♐ 11 4:59
13 2:48	☿ □	♑ 13 17:52
16 4:16	♇ ☍	♒ 16 4:51
17 21:42	♂ ⚹	♓ 18 12:19
20 16:07	♇ △	♈ 20 16:31
22 18:30	♇ □	♉ 22 18:49
24 20:30	♇ ⚹	♊ 24 20:46
26 19:23	♂ ☍	♋ 26 23:24
29 3:03	♇ ☌	♌ 29 3:14

Last Aspect / ☽ Ingress

Last Aspect Dy Hr Mn		☽ Ingress Dy Hr Mn
30 2:09	♅ □	♍ 1 8:29
3 15:27	♇ ⚹	♎ 3 15:31
6 0:53	♇ □	♏ 6 0:55
7 15:50	♆ ⚹	♐ 8 12:44
10 4:51	♆ □	♑ 11 1:47
12 21:10	♀ △	♒ 13 13:37
15 6:27	☉ △	♓ 15 22:03
17 22:54	♀ ☍	♈ 18 2:32
19 21:47	☉ ☍	♉ 20 4:09
22 4:15	♄ ⚹	♊ 22 4:40
24 5:08	♄ □	♋ 24 5:47
26 7:49	♄ △	♌ 26 8:42
27 5:46	♅ □	♍ 28 14:01
30 20:20	♄ ☍	♎ 30 21:47

☽ Phases & Eclipses

Dy Hr Mn	
4 22:53	● 11♍58
12 20:57	☽ 19♐40
20 11:32	○ 27♓05
27 5:43	☾ 3♋42
4 11:58	● 10♎50
12 15:47	☽ 18♑54
19 21:47	○ 26♈05
26 13:26	☾ 2♌43

Astro Data

1 September 1937
Julian Day # 13758
SVP 6♓07'31"
GC 25♐58.1 ⚴ 14♑07.6R
Eris 3♈58.2R ⚵ 17♎16.2
⚷ 0♋14.7 ⚶ 9♍49.3
☽ Mean ☊ 10♐38.9

1 October 1937
Julian Day # 13788
SVP 6♓07'29"
GC 25♐58.2 ⚴ 15♑20.2
Eris 3♈39.4R ⚵ 27♎09.4
⚷ 1♋10.0 ⚶ 24♍26.7
☽ Mean ☊ 9♐03.6

November 1937 LONGITUDE

Day	Sid.Time	☉	0 hr ☽	Noon ☽	True ☊	☿	♀	♂	⚳	♃	♄	♅	♆	♇
1 M	14 41 25	8♏39 05	13♎41 37	19♎53 00	6♐15.5	10♏35.7	15♎52.9	22♑28.5	17♒59.2	21♑03.0	29♓09.0	11♉48.4	20♍24.4	0♌07.7
2 Tu	14 45 22	9 39 11	26 01 39	2♏07 41	6R 11.3	12 12.5	17 07.6	23 12.1	18 07.8	21 11.4	29R 06.0	11R 45.9	20 26.0	0R 07.6
3 W	14 49 18	10 39 18	8♏11 19	14 12 41	6 08.2	13 48.9	18 22.3	23 55.8	18 16.7	21 20.0	29 03.1	11 43.4	20 27.6	0 07.6
4 Th	14 53 15	11 39 28	20 12 00	26 09 30	6D 06.5	15 24.8	19 37.0	24 39.6	18 25.9	21 28.6	29 00.3	11 40.9	20 29.1	0 07.5
5 F	14 57 12	12 39 39	2♐05 27	8♐00 08	6 06.1	17 00.3	20 51.8	25 23.4	18 35.3	21 37.5	28 57.6	11 38.4	20 30.7	0 07.4
6 Sa	15 01 08	13 39 52	13 53 52	19 47 02	6 06.8	18 35.4	22 06.6	26 07.4	18 45.0	21 46.4	28 55.0	11 36.0	20 32.2	0 07.3
7 Su	15 05 05	14 40 07	25 40 02	1♑33 18	6 08.2	20 10.1	23 21.4	26 51.4	18 55.0	21 55.5	28 52.4	11 33.5	20 33.7	0 07.1
8 M	15 09 01	15 40 23	7♑27 19	13 22 35	6 09.9	21 44.5	24 36.3	27 35.4	19 05.2	22 04.7	28 50.0	11 31.0	20 35.1	0 06.9
9 Tu	15 12 58	16 40 40	19 19 39	25 19 04	6 11.5	23 18.5	25 51.1	28 19.6	19 15.7	22 14.1	28 47.6	11 28.5	20 36.6	0 06.7
10 W	15 16 54	17 40 59	1♒21 25	7♒27 17	6R 12.6	24 52.2	27 06.0	29 03.7	19 26.5	22 23.5	28 45.3	11 26.1	20 38.0	0 06.5
11 Th	15 20 51	18 41 20	13 37 16	19 51 57	6 12.9	26 25.6	28 21.0	29 48.0	19 37.5	22 33.1	28 43.2	11 23.6	20 39.3	0 06.2
12 F	15 24 47	19 41 42	26 11 53	2♓37 34	6 12.4	27 58.6	29 35.9	0♒32.3	19 48.8	22 42.8	28 41.1	11 21.2	20 40.7	0 05.9
13 Sa	15 28 44	20 42 05	9♓09 28	15 47 57	6 11.2	29 31.4	0♏50.9	1 16.6	20 00.3	22 52.6	28 39.1	11 18.7	20 42.0	0 05.6
14 Su	15 32 41	21 42 30	22 33 17	29 25 37	6 09.5	1♐03.8	2 05.9	2 01.1	20 12.0	23 02.6	28 37.2	11 16.3	20 43.3	0 05.3
15 M	15 36 37	22 42 56	6♈24 56	13♈31 05	6 07.7	2 36.0	3 20.9	2 45.5	20 24.0	23 12.6	28 35.5	11 13.9	20 44.6	0 04.9
16 Tu	15 40 34	23 43 23	20 43 43	28 02 19	6 06.0	4 08.0	4 35.9	3 30.0	20 36.3	23 22.8	28 33.8	11 11.5	20 45.8	0 04.5
17 W	15 44 30	24 43 52	5♉26 12	12♉54 30	6 04.8	5 39.6	5 51.0	4 14.6	20 48.7	23 33.1	28 32.2	11 09.1	20 47.0	0 04.1
18 Th	15 48 27	25 44 22	20 26 12	28 00 12	6D 04.2	7 11.0	7 06.1	4 59.2	21 01.4	23 43.5	28 30.7	11 06.7	20 48.2	0 03.7
19 F	15 52 23	26 44 54	5♊35 20	13♊10 24	6 04.2	8 42.2	8 21.2	5 43.8	21 14.3	23 54.0	28 29.3	11 04.3	20 49.3	0 03.2
20 Sa	15 56 20	27 45 28	20 44 13	28 15 40	6 04.6	10 13.0	9 36.3	6 28.5	21 27.5	24 04.6	28 28.1	11 02.0	20 50.5	0 02.7
21 Su	16 00 16	28 46 03	5♋43 45	13♋07 37	6 05.3	11 43.7	10 51.5	7 13.3	21 40.8	24 15.3	28 26.9	10 59.6	20 51.5	0 02.2
22 M	16 04 13	29 46 40	20 26 31	27 39 56	6 05.9	13 14.0	12 06.7	7 58.0	21 54.4	24 26.1	28 25.8	10 57.3	20 52.6	0 01.7
23 Tu	16 08 10	0♐47 19	4♌47 28	11♌48 53	6 06.4	14 44.0	13 21.9	8 42.9	22 08.2	24 37.0	28 24.9	10 55.0	20 53.6	0 01.1
24 W	16 12 06	1 47 59	18 44 06	25 33 09	6R 06.6	16 13.7	14 37.1	9 27.7	22 22.2	24 48.0	28 24.0	10 52.8	20 54.6	0 00.5
25 Th	16 16 03	2 48 41	2♍16 12	8♍53 29	6 06.7	17 43.1	15 52.3	10 12.6	22 36.4	24 59.1	28 23.3	10 50.5	20 55.6	29♋59.9
26 F	16 19 59	3 49 24	15 25 17	21 51 57	6 06.5	19 12.0	17 07.6	10 57.5	22 50.8	25 10.3	28 22.6	10 48.3	20 56.5	29 59.3
27 Sa	16 23 56	4 50 10	28 13 54	4♎31 29	6 06.4	20 40.6	18 22.8	11 42.5	23 05.4	25 21.6	28 22.1	10 46.1	20 57.4	29 58.6
28 Su	16 27 52	5 50 56	10♎45 09	16 55 17	6D 06.3	22 08.6	19 38.1	12 27.5	23 20.2	25 33.0	28 21.7	10 43.9	20 58.3	29 58.0
29 M	16 31 49	6 51 44	23 02 17	29 06 32	6 06.3	23 36.1	20 53.4	13 12.5	23 35.2	25 44.5	28 21.3	10 41.7	20 59.1	29 57.3
30 Tu	16 35 45	7 52 34	5♏08 22	11♏08 09	6 06.5	25 03.0	22 08.7	13 57.6	23 50.4	25 56.1	28 21.1	10 39.6	20 59.9	29 56.6

December 1937 LONGITUDE

Day	Sid.Time	☉	0 hr ☽	Noon ☽	True ☊	☿	♀	♂	⚳	♃	♄	♅	♆	♇
1 W	16 39 42	8♐53 25	17♏06 12	23♏02 49	6♐06.6	26♐29.1	23♏24.1	14♒42.7	24♒05.7	26♑07.8	28♓21.0	10♉37.5	21♍00.7	29♋55.8
2 Th	16 43 39	9 54 17	28 58 18	4♐52 53	6R 06.7	27 54.4	24 39.4	15 27.9	24 21.3	26 19.5	28D 21.0	10R 35.4	21 01.5	29R 55.1
3 F	16 47 35	10 55 10	10♐46 53	16 40 32	6 06.6	29 18.8	25 54.7	16 13.0	24 37.0	26 31.4	28 21.1	10 33.3	21 02.2	29 54.3
4 Sa	16 51 32	11 56 04	22 34 06	28 27 52	6 06.2	0♑42.0	27 10.1	16 58.2	24 53.0	26 43.3	28 21.4	10 31.3	21 02.9	29 53.5
5 Su	16 55 28	12 57 00	4♑22 05	10♑17 04	6 05.5	2 03.8	28 25.5	17 43.4	25 09.1	26 55.3	28 21.7	10 29.3	21 03.5	29 52.6
6 M	16 59 25	13 57 56	16 13 07	22 10 34	6 04.4	3 24.2	29 40.9	18 28.7	25 25.4	27 07.4	28 22.1	10 27.4	21 04.1	29 51.8
7 Tu	17 03 21	14 58 53	28 09 47	4♒11 07	6 03.2	4 42.8	0♐56.2	19 14.0	25 41.8	27 19.6	28 22.7	10 25.4	21 04.7	29 50.9
8 W	17 07 18	15 59 51	10♒14 59	16 21 48	6 01.9	5 59.3	2 11.6	19 59.2	25 58.4	27 31.8	28 23.3	10 23.5	21 05.2	29 50.0
9 Th	17 11 14	17 00 49	22 32 02	28 46 06	6 00.9	7 13.4	3 27.0	20 44.6	26 15.2	27 44.2	28 24.1	10 21.7	21 05.7	29 49.1
10 F	17 15 11	18 01 48	5♓04 29	11♓27 38	6D 00.2	8 24.8	4 42.4	21 29.9	26 32.1	27 56.6	28 25.0	10 19.9	21 06.2	29 48.2
11 Sa	17 19 08	19 02 48	17 56 01	24 30 01	6 00.2	9 32.9	5 57.8	22 15.2	26 49.2	28 09.0	28 26.0	10 18.1	21 06.6	29 47.3
12 Su	17 23 04	20 03 48	1♈10 01	7♈56 18	6 00.8	10 37.3	7 13.3	23 00.6	27 06.5	28 21.6	28 27.1	10 16.3	21 07.0	29 46.3
13 M	17 27 01	21 04 49	14 49 07	21 48 32	6 01.9	11 37.4	8 28.7	23 45.9	27 23.9	28 34.2	28 28.3	10 14.6	21 07.4	29 45.3
14 Tu	17 30 57	22 05 50	28 54 32	6♉06 57	6 03.1	12 32.6	9 44.1	24 31.3	27 41.4	28 46.9	28 29.6	10 12.9	21 07.7	29 44.3
15 W	17 34 54	23 06 52	13♉25 25	20 49 26	6 04.1	13 22.1	10 59.5	25 16.7	27 59.1	28 59.6	28 31.0	10 11.3	21 08.0	29 43.3
16 Th	17 38 50	24 07 54	28 18 16	5♊51 03	6R 04.6	14 05.3	12 15.0	26 02.1	28 17.0	29 12.4	28 32.5	10 09.7	21 08.3	29 42.3
17 F	17 42 47	25 08 57	13♊26 44	21 04 09	6 04.1	14 41.1	13 30.4	26 47.5	28 35.0	29 25.3	28 34.1	10 08.2	21 08.5	29 41.2
18 Sa	17 46 43	26 10 01	28 42 02	6♋19 08	6 02.6	15 08.9	14 45.8	27 32.9	28 53.1	29 38.3	28 35.8	10 06.7	21 08.7	29 40.2
19 Su	17 50 40	27 11 05	13♋54 08	21 25 51	6 00.1	15 27.6	16 01.3	28 18.3	29 11.3	29 51.3	28 37.7	10 05.2	21 08.9	29 39.1
20 M	17 54 37	28 12 10	28 53 11	6♌15 11	5 57.0	15R 36.4	17 16.7	29 03.7	29 29.7	0♒04.3	28 39.6	10 03.8	21 09.0	29 38.0
21 Tu	17 58 33	29 13 15	13♌31 06	20 40 22	5 53.8	15 34.5	18 32.2	29 49.1	29 48.3	0 17.4	28 41.7	10 02.4	21 09.1	29 36.9
22 W	18 02 30	0♑14 21	27 42 36	4♍37 39	5 51.0	15 21.2	19 47.6	0♓34.5	0♓06.9	0 30.6	28 43.8	10 01.0	21 09.2	29 35.8
23 Th	18 06 26	1 15 28	11♍25 30	18 06 17	5 49.1	14 56.3	21 03.1	1 19.9	0 25.7	0 43.8	28 46.1	9 59.7	21R 09.2	29 34.6
24 F	18 10 23	2 16 36	24 40 19	1♎07 58	5D 48.4	14 19.6	22 18.6	2 05.3	0 44.6	0 57.1	28 48.4	9 58.5	21 09.2	29 33.5
25 Sa	18 14 19	3 17 44	7♎29 43	13 46 06	5 48.9	13 31.5	23 34.1	2 50.7	1 03.7	1 10.4	28 50.9	9 57.2	21 09.2	29 32.3
26 Su	18 18 16	4 18 53	19 57 39	26 04 59	5 50.2	12 32.9	24 49.5	3 36.2	1 22.8	1 23.8	28 53.4	9 56.1	21 09.1	29 31.1
27 M	18 22 13	5 20 02	2♏08 40	8♏09 18	5 52.1	11 25.3	26 05.0	4 21.6	1 42.1	1 37.2	28 56.1	9 55.0	21 09.0	29 30.0
28 Tu	18 26 09	6 21 12	14 07 27	20 03 38	5 53.8	10 10.4	27 20.5	5 07.0	2 01.5	1 50.7	28 58.8	9 53.9	21 08.8	29 28.8
29 W	18 30 06	7 22 22	25 58 23	1♐52 09	5R 54.9	8 50.9	28 36.0	5 52.4	2 21.0	2 04.2	29 01.7	9 52.9	21 08.6	29 27.5
30 Th	18 34 02	8 23 33	7♐45 24	13 38 32	5 54.6	7 29.1	29 51.5	6 37.8	2 40.7	2 17.8	29 04.6	9 51.9	21 08.4	29 26.3
31 F	18 37 59	9 24 43	19 31 53	25 25 47	5 52.7	6 08.0	1♑07.0	7 23.3	3 00.4	2 31.4	29 07.7	9 51.0	21 08.2	29 25.1

Astro Data	Planet Ingress	Last Aspect	☽ Ingress	Last Aspect	☽ Ingress	☽ Phases & Eclipses	Astro Data
Dy Hr Mn	Dy Hr Mn	Dy Hr Mn	Dy Hr Mn	Dy Hr Mn	Dy Hr Mn	Dy Hr Mn	1 November 1937
☽0N 13 15:51	♂ ♒ 11 18:31	1 17:22 ♂ □	♏ 2 7:48	2 1:56 ♇ △	♐ 2 2:05	3 4:16 ● 10♏20	Julian Day # 13819
☽0S 26 4:37	♀ ♏ 12 19:43	4 17:44 ♄ △	♐ 4 19:46	4 11:47 ♄ □	♑ 4 15:07	11 9:33 ☽ 18♒35	SVP 6♓07'26"
	☿ ♐ 13 19:25	7 6:33 ♄ □	♑ 7 8:50	7 3:23 ♇ ☍	♒ 7 3:40	18 8:09 ○ 25♉35	GC 25♐58.3 ⚴ 20♑54.1
♄D 1 23:03	☉ ♐ 22 17:17	9 18:54 ♄ ✶	♒ 9 21:19	8 19:31 ♂ ☌	♓ 9 14:21	18 8:19 • P 0.144	Eris 3♈20.7R ⚵ 7♏46.4
☽0N 11 0:01	♇ ♋R 25 9:13	12 5:46 ♀ △	♓ 12 7:07	11 21:31 ♇ △	♈ 11 21:55	25 0:04 ☾ 2♍19	⚷ 0♋53.5R ⚶ 9♎41.2
♃✶♄ 12 23:29		14 10:36 ♄ ☌	♈ 14 12:59	14 1:24 ♇ □	♉ 14 1:50		☽ Mean ☊ 7♐25.0
♃☍♇ 18 15:18	☿ ♑ 3 23:51	16 4:17 ♃ □	♉ 16 15:12	16 2:15 ♇ ✶	♊ 16 2:42	2 23:11 ● 10♐23	
☿R 20 19:56	♀ ♐ 6 18:06	18 12:48 ♄ ✶	♊ 18 15:10	17 23:49 ♄ □	♋ 18 2:03	2 23:05:22 • A 11'13"	1 December 1937
☽0S 23 11:53	♃ ♒ 20 4:06	20 12:20 ♄ □	♋ 20 14:47	20 1:46 ♃ ☍	♌ 20 1:48	11 1:12 ☽ 18♓35	Julian Day # 13849
♆R 23 16:58	♂ ♓ 21 17:46	22 15:49 ☉ △	♌ 22 15:55	22 3:46 ☉ △	♍ 22 3:57	17 18:52 ○ 25♊26	SVP 6♓07'21"
	⚳ ♓ 22 3:06	23 17:39 ☿ △	♍ 24 19:56	24 9:04 ♇ ✶	♎ 24 9:53	24 14:20 ☾ 2♎23	GC 25♐58.3 ⚴ 28♑51.2
	☉ ♑ 22 6:22	27 3:19 ♇ ✶	♎ 27 3:22	26 18:47 ♇ □	♏ 26 19:45		Eris 3♈08.9R ⚵ 17♏58.3
	♀ ♑ 30 14:42	29 13:41 ♇ □	♏ 29 13:46	29 7:06 ♇ △	♐ 29 8:12		⚷ 29♊32.2R ⚶ 24♎14.7
				31 19:33 ♄ □	♑ 31 21:17		☽ Mean ☊ 5♐49.7

LONGITUDE January 1938

Day	Sid.Time	☉	0 hr ☽	Noon ☽	True ☊	☿	♀	♂	⚳	♃	♄	♅	♆	♇
1 Sa	18 41 55	10♑25 54	1♑20 32	7♑16 23	5♐49.0	4♑49.9	2♑22.5	8♓08.7	3♓20.3	2♒45.1	29♓10.8	9♉50.1	21♍07.9	29♋23.8
2 Su	18 45 52	11 27 06	13 13 34	19 12 18	5R 43.6	3R 37.4	3 38.0	8 54.1	3 40.3	2 58.8	29 14.1	9R 49.2	21R 07.6	29R 22.6
3 M	18 49 48	12 28 17	25 12 44	1♒15 06	5 36.9	2 32.2	4 53.5	9 39.5	4 00.3	3 12.5	29 17.4	9 48.5	21 07.2	29 21.3
4 Tu	18 53 45	13 29 27	7♒19 32	13 26 14	5 29.5	1 35.7	6 08.9	10 24.9	4 20.5	3 26.3	29 20.9	9 47.7	21 06.9	29 20.1
5 W	18 57 42	14 30 38	19 35 23	25 47 10	5 22.3	0 48.8	7 24.4	11 10.2	4 40.8	3 40.1	29 24.4	9 47.1	21 06.4	29 18.8
6 Th	19 01 38	15 31 48	2♓01 49	8♓19 33	5 15.9	0 11.9	8 39.9	11 55.6	5 01.2	3 53.9	29 28.0	9 46.4	21 06.0	29 17.5
7 F	19 05 35	16 32 58	14 40 38	21 05 20	5 11.1	29♐45.2	9 55.4	12 41.0	5 21.6	4 07.8	29 31.7	9 45.8	21 05.5	29 16.2
8 Sa	19 09 31	17 34 08	27 33 56	4♈06 45	5 08.2	29 28.4	11 10.9	13 26.3	5 42.2	4 21.7	29 35.6	9 45.3	21 05.0	29 14.9
9 Su	19 13 28	18 35 17	10♈44 03	17 26 10	5D 07.2	29D 21.1	12 26.3	14 11.6	6 02.9	4 35.7	29 39.5	9 44.8	21 04.4	29 13.6
10 M	19 17 24	19 36 26	24 13 19	1♉05 44	5 07.7	29 22.7	13 41.8	14 56.9	6 23.6	4 49.6	29 43.4	9 44.4	21 03.9	29 12.3
11 Tu	19 21 21	20 37 34	8♉03 35	15 06 54	5 09.0	29 32.6	14 57.2	15 42.2	6 44.5	5 03.6	29 47.5	9 44.0	21 03.2	29 11.0
12 W	19 25 17	21 38 41	22 15 39	29 29 39	5R 10.0	29 50.1	16 12.7	16 27.5	7 05.4	5 17.6	29 51.7	9 43.7	21 02.6	29 09.6
13 Th	19 29 14	22 39 48	6♊48 34	14♊11 54	5 09.8	0♑14.6	17 28.1	17 12.8	7 26.4	5 31.7	29 55.9	9 43.4	21 01.9	29 08.3
14 F	19 33 11	23 40 54	21 39 00	29 09 00	5 07.6	0 45.4	18 43.6	17 58.0	7 47.5	5 45.7	0♈00.3	9 43.2	21 01.2	29 07.0
15 Sa	19 37 07	24 42 00	6♋40 56	14♋13 41	5 03.0	1 21.9	19 59.0	18 43.2	8 08.7	5 59.8	0 04.7	9 43.1	21 00.5	29 05.7
16 Su	19 41 04	25 43 05	21 46 03	29 16 49	4 56.3	2 03.6	21 14.4	19 28.4	8 30.0	6 13.9	0 09.2	9 42.9	20 59.7	29 04.3
17 M	19 45 00	26 44 09	6♌44 46	14♌08 46	4 48.0	2 49.9	22 29.9	20 13.6	8 51.3	6 28.0	0 13.8	9D 42.9	20 58.9	29 03.0
18 Tu	19 48 57	27 45 13	21 27 47	28 40 59	4 39.2	3 40.4	23 45.3	20 58.7	9 12.7	6 42.2	0 18.4	9 42.9	20 58.1	29 01.7
19 W	19 52 53	28 46 17	5♍47 42	12♍47 26	4 31.0	4 34.7	25 00.7	21 43.8	9 34.2	6 56.3	0 23.2	9 42.9	20 57.3	29 00.3
20 Th	19 56 50	29 47 20	19 39 57	26 25 10	4 24.2	5 32.3	26 16.1	22 28.9	9 55.8	7 10.5	0 28.0	9 43.0	20 56.4	28 59.0
21 F	20 00 46	0♒48 23	3♎03 10	9♎34 15	4 19.6	6 33.0	27 31.5	23 14.0	10 17.4	7 24.7	0 32.9	9 43.2	20 55.5	28 57.6
22 Sa	20 04 43	1 49 25	15 58 46	22 17 14	4D 17.2	7 36.5	28 46.9	23 59.1	10 39.1	7 38.9	0 37.9	9 43.4	20 54.5	28 56.3
23 Su	20 08 40	2 50 27	28 30 12	4♏38 19	4 16.6	8 42.5	0♒02.3	24 44.1	11 00.9	7 53.1	0 42.9	9 43.6	20 53.6	28 55.0
24 M	20 12 36	3 51 28	10♏42 15	16 42 39	4 17.3	9 50.7	1 17.7	25 29.1	11 22.8	8 07.3	0 48.1	9 43.9	20 52.6	28 53.6
25 Tu	20 16 33	4 52 29	22 40 15	28 35 42	4R 18.1	11 01.0	2 33.1	26 14.1	11 44.7	8 21.6	0 53.3	9 44.3	20 51.5	28 52.3
26 W	20 20 29	5 53 30	4♐29 40	10♐22 48	4 18.0	12 13.2	3 48.5	26 59.0	12 06.7	8 35.8	0 58.5	9 44.7	20 50.5	28 51.0
27 Th	20 24 26	6 54 29	16 15 39	22 08 48	4 16.1	13 27.2	5 03.9	27 44.0	12 28.8	8 50.1	1 03.9	9 45.1	20 49.4	28 49.7
28 F	20 28 22	7 55 28	28 02 45	3♑57 57	4 11.8	14 42.8	6 19.3	28 28.9	12 50.9	9 04.3	1 09.3	9 45.7	20 48.3	28 48.3
29 Sa	20 32 19	8 56 27	9♑54 48	15 53 37	4 04.7	15 59.8	7 34.6	29 13.8	13 13.1	9 18.6	1 14.8	9 46.2	20 47.2	28 47.0
30 Su	20 36 15	9 57 24	21 54 42	27 58 17	3 54.9	17 18.3	8 50.0	29 58.6	13 35.3	9 32.8	1 20.3	9 46.9	20 46.1	28 45.7
31 M	20 40 12	10 58 20	4♒04 30	10♒13 30	3 43.1	18 38.0	10 05.4	0♈43.5	13 57.6	9 47.1	1 26.0	9 47.5	20 44.9	28 44.4

LONGITUDE February 1938

Day	Sid.Time	☉	0 hr ☽	Noon ☽	True ☊	☿	♀	♂	⚳	♃	♄	♅	♆	♇
1 Tu	20 44 09	11♒59 15	16♒25 21	22♒40 04	3♐30.1	19♑59.0	11♒20.7	1♈28.3	14♓20.0	10♒01.3	1♈31.7	9♉48.3	20♍43.7	28♋43.1
2 W	20 48 05	13 00 10	28 57 41	5♓18 11	3R 17.2	21 21.1	12 36.0	2 13.0	14 42.4	10 15.6	1 37.4	9 49.0	20R 42.5	28R 41.8
3 Th	20 52 02	14 01 02	11♓41 32	18 07 44	3 05.5	22 44.3	13 51.4	2 57.8	15 04.9	10 29.8	1 43.2	9 49.9	20 41.2	28 40.5
4 F	20 55 58	15 01 54	24 36 45	1♈08 37	2 56.0	24 08.5	15 06.7	3 42.5	15 27.4	10 44.1	1 49.1	9 50.7	20 39.9	28 39.2
5 Sa	20 59 55	16 02 44	7♈43 22	14 21 03	2 49.4	25 33.8	16 22.0	4 27.2	15 50.0	10 58.3	1 55.1	9 51.7	20 38.6	28 38.0
6 Su	21 03 51	17 03 33	21 01 46	27 45 37	2 45.6	27 00.0	17 37.3	5 11.8	16 12.6	11 12.5	2 01.1	9 52.6	20 37.3	28 36.7
7 M	21 07 48	18 04 20	4♉32 44	11♉23 16	2D 44.2	28 27.2	18 52.5	5 56.4	16 35.3	11 26.7	2 07.1	9 53.7	20 36.0	28 35.4
8 Tu	21 11 44	19 05 06	18 17 20	25 15 02	2R 44.1	29 55.3	20 07.8	6 41.0	16 58.0	11 41.0	2 13.2	9 54.8	20 34.7	28 34.2
9 W	21 15 41	20 05 50	2♊16 26	9♊21 29	2 44.1	1♒24.3	21 23.1	7 25.6	17 20.8	11 55.1	2 19.4	9 55.9	20 33.3	28 33.0
10 Th	21 19 38	21 06 33	16 30 08	23 42 09	2 42.8	2 54.1	22 38.3	8 10.1	17 43.6	12 09.3	2 25.6	9 57.1	20 31.9	28 31.7
11 F	21 23 34	22 07 14	0♋57 11	8♋14 48	2 39.1	4 24.9	23 53.5	8 54.5	18 06.5	12 23.5	2 31.9	9 58.3	20 30.5	28 30.5
12 Sa	21 27 31	23 07 53	15 34 23	22 55 11	2 32.5	5 56.6	25 08.7	9 39.0	18 29.4	12 37.6	2 38.3	9 59.6	20 29.1	28 29.3
13 Su	21 31 27	24 08 31	0♌16 22	7♌37 01	2 23.1	7 29.1	26 23.9	10 23.4	18 52.3	12 51.8	2 44.6	10 00.9	20 27.6	28 28.1
14 M	21 35 24	25 09 07	14 56 08	22 12 44	2 11.6	9 02.5	27 39.1	11 07.7	19 15.3	13 05.9	2 51.1	10 02.3	20 26.2	28 27.0
15 Tu	21 39 20	26 09 42	29 25 54	6♍34 43	1 59.2	10 36.7	28 54.2	11 52.0	19 38.3	13 20.0	2 57.6	10 03.7	20 24.7	28 25.8
16 W	21 43 17	27 10 15	13♍38 28	20 36 32	1 47.3	12 11.9	0♓09.4	12 36.3	20 01.4	13 34.1	3 04.1	10 05.2	20 23.2	28 24.6
17 Th	21 47 13	28 10 47	27 28 28	4♎13 59	1 37.0	13 47.9	1 24.5	13 20.6	20 24.5	13 48.1	3 10.7	10 06.7	20 21.7	28 23.5
18 F	21 51 10	29 11 17	10♎53 00	17 25 32	1 29.1	15 24.8	2 39.6	14 04.8	20 47.6	14 02.1	3 17.3	10 08.3	20 20.2	28 22.4
19 Sa	21 55 07	0♓11 47	23 51 49	0♏12 10	1 24.1	17 02.7	3 54.7	14 48.9	21 10.8	14 16.1	3 24.0	10 09.9	20 18.6	28 21.2
20 Su	21 59 03	1 12 14	6♏27 01	12 36 54	1 21.5	18 41.4	5 09.8	15 33.1	21 34.0	14 30.1	3 30.7	10 11.6	20 17.1	28 20.1
21 M	22 03 00	2 12 41	18 42 26	24 44 14	1 20.7	20 21.1	6 24.9	16 17.2	21 57.2	14 44.1	3 37.5	10 13.3	20 15.5	28 19.1
22 Tu	22 06 56	3 13 06	0♐43 00	6♐39 25	1 20.7	22 01.8	7 40.0	17 01.2	22 20.5	14 58.0	3 44.3	10 15.0	20 14.0	28 18.0
23 W	22 10 53	4 13 30	12 34 12	18 28 04	1 20.2	23 43.4	8 55.0	17 45.2	22 43.8	15 11.9	3 51.1	10 16.8	20 12.4	28 16.9
24 Th	22 14 49	5 13 52	24 21 41	0♑15 44	1 18.1	25 26.0	10 10.1	18 29.2	23 07.1	15 25.8	3 58.0	10 18.7	20 10.8	28 15.9
25 F	22 18 46	6 14 13	6♑10 48	12 07 30	1 13.7	27 09.5	11 25.1	19 13.2	23 30.5	15 39.6	4 04.9	10 20.6	20 09.2	28 14.9
26 Sa	22 22 42	7 14 33	18 06 21	24 07 49	1 06.5	28 54.1	12 40.1	19 57.1	23 53.9	15 53.4	4 11.8	10 22.5	20 07.6	28 13.9
27 Su	22 26 39	8 14 51	0♒12 19	6♒20 10	0 56.5	0♓39.7	13 55.1	20 40.9	24 17.3	16 07.2	4 18.8	10 24.5	20 06.0	28 12.9
28 M	22 30 36	9 15 07	12 31 37	18 46 51	0 44.3	2 26.3	15 10.1	21 24.8	24 40.7	16 20.9	4 25.9	10 26.5	20 04.3	28 11.9

Astro Data		Planet Ingress		Last Aspect	☽ Ingress	Last Aspect	☽ Ingress	☽ Phases & Eclipses	
	Dy Hr Mn		Dy Hr Mn	Dy Hr Mn	Dy Hr Mn	Dy Hr Mn	Dy Hr Mn	Dy Hr Mn	
♄△♇	4 7:53	☿ ♐R	6 21:37	3 8:15 ♇ ☍	♒ 3 9:31	31 13:35 ☉ ☌	♓ 2 1:58	1 18:58	● 10♑44
☽0N	7 6:45	☿ ♑	12 22:30	4 4:52 ♅ □	♓ 5 20:07	4 7:27 ♇ △	♈ 4 9:54	9 14:13	☽ 18♈41
☿D	9 19:30	♄ ♈	14 10:31	8 3:41 ♄ ☌	♈ 8 4:29	6 13:31 ♇ □	♉ 6 15:58	16 5:53	○ 25♋28
♃♀♆	15 13:06	☉ ♒	20 16:59	10 9:00 ☿ △	♉ 10 10:06	8 17:41 ♇ ⚹	♊ 8 20:08	23 8:09	☾ 2♏41
♅D	18 4:53	♀ ♒	23 11:16	12 12:36 ♄ ⚹	♊ 12 12:50	10 10:04 ♀ △	♋ 10 22:26	31 13:35	● 11♒02
☽0S	19 21:53	♂ ♈	30 12:44	13 23:00 ♆ □	♋ 14 13:21	12 21:05 ♇ ☌	♌ 12 23:33		
♃□♅	31 12:49			16 11:40 ♇ ☌	♌ 16 13:09	14 21:53 ♀ ☍	♍ 15 0:57	8 0:32	☽ 18♉36
♂0N	31 19:03	☿ ♒	8 13:17	17 4:48 ♅ □	♍ 18 14:12	17 1:38 ♇ ⚹	♎ 17 4:28	14 17:14	○ 25♌22
		♀ ♓	16 9:00	20 16:36 ♇ ⚹	♎ 20 18:27	19 8:29 ♇ □	♏ 19 11:37	22 4:24	☾ 2♐54
☽0N	3 13:06	☉ ♓	19 7:20	23 1:58 ♀ □	♏ 23 2:55	21 19:10 ♇ △	♐ 21 22:33		
☽0S	16 8:58	☿ ♓	27 3:01	25 12:34 ♇ △	♐ 25 14:51	24 0:31 ☿ ⚹	♑ 24 11:28		
				28 0:08 ♂ □	♑ 28 3:58	26 20:06 ♇ ☍	♒ 26 23:36		
				30 13:33 ♇ ☍	♒ 30 16:00				

Astro Data

1 January 1938
Julian Day # 13880
SVP 6♓07'16"
GC 25♐58.4 ⚴ 8♒31.8
Eris 3♈07.0 ⚵ 27♏52.7
⚷ 27♊35.3R ⚶ 8♏35.3
☽ Mean ☊ 4♐11.3

1 February 1938
Julian Day # 13911
SVP 6♓07'11"
GC 25♐58.5 ⚴ 18♒52.2
Eris 3♈16.5 ⚵ 6♐24.3
⚷ 25♊58.3R ⚶ 21♏24.4
☽ Mean ☊ 2♐32.8

March 1938 LONGITUDE

Day	Sid.Time	☉	0 hr ☽	Noon ☽	True ☊	☿	♀	♂	⚷	♃	♄	♅	♆	♇
1 Tu	22 34 32	10♓15 22	25♒05 57	1♓28 57	0♐30.9	4♓13.9	16♓25.1	22♈08.6	25♓04.2	16♒34.6	4♈32.9	10♉28.5	20♍02.7	28♋11.0
2 W	22 38 29	11 15 34	7♓55 47	14 26 20	0R17.4	6 02.6	17 40.0	22 52.3	25 27.7	16 48.2	4 40.0	10 30.6	20R01.1	28R10.0
3 Th	22 42 25	12 15 45	21 00 25	27 37 49	0 05.0	7 52.3	18 54.9	23 36.0	25 51.2	17 01.8	4 47.1	10 32.8	19 59.4	28 09.1
4 F	22 46 22	13 15 54	4♈18 18	11♈01 37	29♏55.0	9 43.0	20 09.8	24 19.7	26 14.7	17 15.4	4 54.3	10 35.0	19 57.8	28 08.2
5 Sa	22 50 18	14 16 02	17 47 30	24 35 43	29 47.9	11 34.8	21 24.7	25 03.3	26 38.3	17 28.9	5 01.5	10 37.2	19 56.1	28 07.4
6 Su	22 54 15	15 16 07	1♉26 04	8♉18 23	29 43.7	13 27.6	22 39.6	25 46.9	27 01.9	17 42.4	5 08.7	10 39.4	19 54.4	28 06.5
7 M	22 58 11	16 16 10	15 12 31	22 08 23	29D42.1	15 21.4	23 54.4	26 30.5	27 25.5	17 55.8	5 15.9	10 41.7	19 52.8	28 05.7
8 Tu	23 02 08	17 16 10	29 05 53	6♊05 00	29R42.0	17 16.1	25 09.2	27 14.0	27 49.1	18 09.2	5 23.2	10 44.1	19 51.1	28 04.9
9 W	23 06 04	18 16 09	13♊05 40	20 07 50	29 42.2	19 11.7	26 24.0	27 57.5	28 12.7	18 22.5	5 30.4	10 46.5	19 49.4	28 04.1
10 Th	23 10 01	19 16 06	27 11 27	4♋16 22	29 41.3	21 08.2	27 38.8	28 40.9	28 36.3	18 35.8	5 37.7	10 48.9	19 47.8	28 03.3
11 F	23 13 58	20 16 00	11♋22 26	18 29 24	29 38.4	23 05.4	28 53.6	29 24.3	29 00.0	18 49.0	5 45.1	10 51.3	19 46.1	28 02.5
12 Sa	23 17 54	21 15 52	25 36 57	2♌44 42	29 32.9	25 03.2	0♈08.3	0♉07.6	29 23.7	19 02.2	5 52.4	10 53.8	19 44.4	28 01.8
13 Su	23 21 51	22 15 42	9♌52 10	16 58 48	29 24.9	27 01.6	1 23.0	0 50.9	29 47.3	19 15.3	5 59.8	10 56.3	19 42.8	28 01.1
14 M	23 25 47	23 15 29	24 04 02	1♍07 15	29 14.9	29 00.3	2 37.7	1 34.1	0♈11.0	19 28.4	6 07.1	10 58.9	19 41.1	28 00.4
15 Tu	23 29 44	24 15 15	8♍07 48	15 05 05	29 04.0	0♈59.3	3 52.3	2 17.3	0 34.7	19 41.4	6 14.5	11 01.5	19 39.4	27 59.8
16 W	23 33 40	25 14 58	21 58 33	28 47 43	28 53.3	2 58.2	5 06.9	3 00.5	0 58.4	19 54.3	6 21.9	11 04.1	19 37.8	27 59.1
17 Th	23 37 37	26 14 39	5♎32 12	12♎11 40	28 44.1	4 56.8	6 21.5	3 43.6	1 22.1	20 07.2	6 29.4	11 06.7	19 36.1	27 58.5
18 F	23 41 33	27 14 19	18 45 59	25 15 04	28 37.0	6 54.9	7 36.1	4 26.6	1 45.9	20 20.0	6 36.8	11 09.4	19 34.5	27 57.9
19 Sa	23 45 30	28 13 56	1♏38 59	7♏57 54	28 32.4	8 52.1	8 50.7	5 09.6	2 09.6	20 32.8	6 44.3	11 12.1	19 32.8	27 57.3
20 Su	23 49 27	29 13 32	14 12 05	20 21 53	28D30.3	10 48.0	10 05.2	5 52.6	2 33.3	20 45.5	6 51.7	11 14.9	19 31.2	27 56.8
21 M	23 53 23	0♈13 06	26 27 45	2♐30 12	28 30.0	12 42.4	11 19.7	6 35.6	2 57.1	20 58.1	6 59.2	11 17.7	19 29.5	27 56.3
22 Tu	23 57 20	1 12 39	8♐29 48	14 27 08	28 30.8	14 34.8	12 34.2	7 18.5	3 20.8	21 10.7	7 06.7	11 20.5	19 27.9	27 55.8
23 W	0 01 16	2 12 09	20 22 51	26 17 37	28R31.7	16 24.7	13 48.7	8 01.3	3 44.6	21 23.2	7 14.2	11 23.3	19 26.3	27 55.3
24 Th	0 05 13	3 11 38	2♑12 06	8♑06 59	28 31.7	18 11.8	15 03.1	8 44.1	4 08.4	21 35.6	7 21.7	11 26.2	19 24.7	27 54.8
25 F	0 09 09	4 11 05	14 02 55	20 00 32	28 30.2	19 55.6	16 17.5	9 26.9	4 32.1	21 48.0	7 29.2	11 29.1	19 23.1	27 54.4
26 Sa	0 13 06	5 10 30	26 00 29	2♒03 18	28 26.5	21 35.7	17 31.9	10 09.6	4 55.9	22 00.3	7 36.7	11 32.0	19 21.5	27 54.0
27 Su	0 17 02	6 09 54	8♒09 33	14 19 41	28 20.8	23 11.6	18 46.3	10 52.3	5 19.7	22 12.5	7 44.2	11 35.0	19 19.9	27 53.6
28 M	0 20 59	7 09 15	20 34 05	26 53 05	28 13.3	24 43.0	20 00.7	11 34.9	5 43.4	22 24.6	7 51.7	11 37.9	19 18.3	27 53.3
29 Tu	0 24 56	8 08 35	3♓16 54	9♓45 39	28 04.6	26 09.5	21 15.0	12 17.5	6 07.2	22 36.7	7 59.2	11 40.9	19 16.7	27 52.9
30 W	0 28 52	9 07 52	16 19 21	22 57 57	27 55.8	27 30.7	22 29.3	13 00.1	6 31.0	22 48.7	8 06.7	11 44.0	19 15.2	27 52.6
31 Th	0 32 49	10 07 08	29 41 15	6♈28 58	27 47.7	28 46.3	23 43.6	13 42.6	6 54.7	23 00.6	8 14.2	11 47.0	19 13.6	27 52.3

April 1938 LONGITUDE

Day	Sid.Time	☉	0 hr ☽	Noon ☽	True ☊	☿	♀	♂	⚷	♃	♄	♅	♆	♇
1 F	0 36 45	11♈06 22	13♈20 46	20♈16 14	27♏41.2	29♈56.1	24♈57.8	14♉25.1	7♈18.5	23♒12.4	8♈21.7	11♉50.1	19♍12.1	27♋52.1
2 Sa	0 40 42	12 05 33	27 14 52	4♉16 11	27R36.8	0♉59.8	26 12.0	15 07.5	7 42.2	23 24.1	8 29.2	11 53.2	19R10.6	27R51.8
3 Su	0 44 38	13 04 43	11♉19 41	18 24 50	27D34.6	1 57.2	27 26.2	15 49.9	8 06.0	23 35.8	8 36.8	11 56.3	19 09.1	27 51.6
4 M	0 48 35	14 03 50	25 31 10	2♊38 15	27 34.3	2 48.2	28 40.4	16 32.3	8 29.7	23 47.3	8 44.2	11 59.5	19 07.6	27 51.5
5 Tu	0 52 31	15 02 55	9♊45 40	16 53 03	27 35.3	3 32.5	29 54.5	17 14.6	8 53.5	23 58.8	8 51.7	12 02.6	19 06.1	27 51.3
6 W	0 56 28	16 01 58	24 00 08	1♋06 37	27 36.6	4 10.1	1♉08.6	17 56.8	9 17.2	24 10.2	8 59.2	12 05.8	19 04.7	27 51.2
7 Th	1 00 25	17 00 59	8♋12 18	15 16 57	27R37.3	4 40.9	2 22.7	18 39.1	9 40.9	24 21.5	9 06.7	12 09.0	19 03.2	27 51.1
8 F	1 04 21	17 59 57	22 20 24	29 22 28	27 36.8	5 04.8	3 36.8	19 21.2	10 04.6	24 32.7	9 14.2	12 12.2	19 01.8	27 51.0
9 Sa	1 08 18	18 58 52	6♌22 59	13♌21 44	27 34.5	5 22.0	4 50.8	20 03.3	10 28.3	24 43.8	9 21.6	12 15.5	19 00.4	27 50.9
10 Su	1 12 14	19 57 46	20 18 32	27 13 10	27 30.6	5 32.5	6 04.8	20 45.4	10 52.0	24 54.8	9 29.0	12 18.7	18 59.0	27D50.9
11 M	1 16 11	20 56 37	4♍05 24	10♍54 58	27 25.4	5R36.3	7 18.7	21 27.5	11 15.7	25 05.7	9 36.5	12 22.0	18 57.7	27 50.9
12 Tu	1 20 07	21 55 26	17 41 40	24 25 14	27 19.6	5 33.7	8 32.6	22 09.4	11 39.3	25 16.5	9 43.9	12 25.3	18 56.3	27 50.9
13 W	1 24 04	22 54 12	1♎05 27	7♎42 08	27 13.9	5 24.9	9 46.5	22 51.4	12 03.0	25 27.2	9 51.3	12 28.6	18 55.0	27 51.0
14 Th	1 28 00	23 52 57	14 15 06	20 44 14	27 09.0	5 10.3	11 00.3	23 33.3	12 26.6	25 37.8	9 58.6	12 31.9	18 53.7	27 51.1
15 F	1 31 57	24 51 40	27 09 29	3♏30 49	27 05.3	4 50.2	12 14.2	24 15.1	12 50.2	25 48.4	10 06.0	12 35.2	18 52.4	27 51.2
16 Sa	1 35 53	25 50 21	9♏48 18	16 02 02	27D03.3	4 25.2	13 28.0	24 57.0	13 13.8	25 58.8	10 13.3	12 38.6	18 51.1	27 51.3
17 Su	1 39 50	26 48 59	22 12 12	28 19 03	27 02.7	3 55.7	14 41.7	25 38.7	13 37.4	26 09.1	10 20.7	12 41.9	18 49.9	27 51.4
18 M	1 43 47	27 47 37	4♐22 52	10♐24 01	27 03.4	3 22.4	15 55.5	26 20.5	14 01.0	26 19.3	10 28.0	12 45.3	18 48.6	27 51.6
19 Tu	1 47 43	28 46 12	16 22 55	22 20 01	27 04.9	2 45.9	17 09.2	27 02.1	14 24.5	26 29.3	10 35.3	12 48.7	18 47.4	27 51.8
20 W	1 51 40	29 44 46	28 15 49	4♑10 52	27 06.7	2 07.0	18 22.8	27 43.8	14 48.0	26 39.3	10 42.5	12 52.1	18 46.3	27 52.1
21 Th	1 55 36	0♉43 18	10♑05 42	16 00 56	27 08.2	1 26.4	19 36.5	28 25.4	15 11.6	26 49.2	10 49.7	12 55.5	18 45.1	27 52.3
22 F	1 59 33	1 41 48	21 57 09	27 54 59	27R09.1	0 44.9	20 50.1	29 07.0	15 35.1	26 58.9	10 57.0	12 58.9	18 44.0	27 52.6
23 Sa	2 03 29	2 40 17	3♒55 02	9♒57 54	27 08.9	0 03.3	22 03.7	29 48.5	15 58.5	27 08.6	11 04.1	13 02.3	18 42.9	27 52.9
24 Su	2 07 26	3 38 44	16 04 11	22 14 25	27 07.7	29♈22.3	23 17.2	0♊30.0	16 22.0	27 18.1	11 11.3	13 05.7	18 41.8	27 53.2
25 M	2 11 22	4 37 09	28 29 08	4♓48 45	27 05.5	28 42.7	24 30.8	1 11.4	16 45.4	27 27.5	11 18.4	13 09.2	18 40.7	27 53.6
26 Tu	2 15 19	5 35 33	11♓13 40	17 44 11	27 02.7	28 05.1	25 44.2	1 52.8	17 08.8	27 36.8	11 25.5	13 12.6	18 39.7	27 54.0
27 W	2 19 16	6 33 55	24 20 30	1♈02 43	26 59.6	27 30.0	26 57.7	2 34.2	17 32.2	27 45.9	11 32.6	13 16.0	18 38.7	27 54.4
28 Th	2 23 12	7 32 16	7♈50 47	14 44 33	26 56.8	26 58.1	28 11.2	3 15.5	17 55.5	27 55.0	11 39.6	13 19.5	18 37.7	27 54.8
29 F	2 27 09	8 30 35	21 43 44	28 47 55	26 54.7	26 29.8	29 24.6	3 56.8	18 18.9	28 03.9	11 46.6	13 23.0	18 36.7	27 55.3
30 Sa	2 31 05	9 28 52	5♉56 36	13♉09 09	26D53.3	26 05.5	0♊37.9	4 38.1	18 42.2	28 12.6	11 53.6	13 26.4	18 35.8	27 55.7

Astro Data	Planet Ingress	Last Aspect	☽ Ingress	Last Aspect	☽ Ingress	☽ Phases & Eclipses	Astro Data
Dy Hr Mn	Dy Hr Mn	Dy Hr Mn	Dy Hr Mn	Dy Hr Mn	Dy Hr Mn	Dy Hr Mn	1 March 1938
☽0N 2 20:16	☊ ♏R 3 23:16	28 17:19 ♂ ⚹	♓ 1 9:13	2 1:04 ♇ □	♉ 2 4:43	2 5:40 ● 11♓00	Julian Day # 13939
♄0N 5 14:08	♂ ♉ 12 7:48	3 12:56 ♇ △	♈ 3 16:16	4 3:57 ♇ ⚹	♊ 4 7:33	9 8:35 ☽ 18♊08	SVP 6♓07'07"
♀0N 14 17:40	♀ ♈ 12 9:20	5 18:11 ♇ □	♉ 5 21:29	6 0:07 ♃ △	♋ 6 10:07	16 5:15 ○ 24♍58	GC 25♐58.5 ⚳ 28♒15.7
♃⚻♆ 15 8:50	⚷ ♈ 14 0:50	7 22:16 ♇ ⚹	♊ 8 1:33	8 9:24 ♇ ☌	♌ 8 13:04	24 1:06 ☾ 2♑45	Eris 3♈32.8 ⚴ 12♐02.9
☽0S 15 18:44	☿ ♈ 15 0:02	10 2:01 ♂ ⚹	♋ 10 4:46	10 7:56 ♃ ☍	♍ 10 16:51	31 18:52 ● 10♈24	⚵ 25♊25.0R ⚶ 0♐32.7
☿0N 15 20:28	☉ ♈ 21 6:43	12 7:21 ♂ □	♌ 12 7:23	12 18:09 ♇ ⚹	♎ 12 22:02		☽ Mean ☊ 1♐03.8
☉0N 21 6:43		13 15:54 ♃ ☍	♍ 14 10:05	15 1:18 ♇ □	♏ 15 5:21	7 15:10 ☽ 17♋09	
☽0N 30 4:38	☿ ♉ 1 13:24	16 10:34 ♇ ⚹	♎ 16 14:08	17 11:06 ♇ △	♐ 17 15:19	14 18:21 ○ 24♎08	1 April 1938
♃∠♄ 3 17:45	♀ ♉ 5 13:46	18 17:04 ♇ □	♏ 18 20:53	20 2:12 ☉ △	♑ 20 3:31	22 20:14 ☾ 2♒02	Julian Day # 13970
♇D 11 1:55	☉ ♉ 20 18:15	21 2:56 ♇ △	♐ 21 7:01	22 14:33 ♂ △	♒ 22 16:11	30 5:28 ● 9♉13	SVP 6♓07'05"
☿R 11 14:12	☿ ♈R 23 13:56	23 1:52 ♃ ⚹	♑ 23 19:32	25 1:00 ☿ ⚹	♓ 25 2:53		GC 25♐58.6 ⚳ 8♓12.5
☽0S 12 1:56	♂ ♊ 23 18:39	26 3:46 ♇ ☍	♒ 26 7:56	27 6:24 ♇ △	♈ 27 10:08		Eris 3♈54.8 ⚴ 14♐43.0
☽0N 26 13:39	♀ ♊ 29 23:35	28 7:21 ♃ ⚹	♓ 28 17:52	29 10:45 ♃ ⚹	♉ 29 14:02		⚵ 26♊03.2 ⚶ 5♐57.3
⚷0N 28 3:53		30 20:47 ♇ △	♈ 31 0:33				☽ Mean ☊ 29♏25.3
♃⚻♇ 28 11:33							

LONGITUDE — May 1938

Day	Sid.Time	☉	0 hr ☽	Noon ☽	True ☊	☿	♀	♂	⚳	♃	♄	♅	♆	♇
1 Su	2 35 02	10♉27 07	20♉24 50	27♉42 55	26♏53.0	25♈45.3	1♊51.3	5♊19.3	19♈05.4	28♒21.3	12♈00.6	13♉29.9	18♍34.9	27♋56.2
2 M	2 38 58	11 25 21	5♊02 34	12♊22 59	26 53.4	25R 29.7	3 04.6	6 00.5	19 28.7	28 29.8	12 07.5	13 33.3	18R 34.0	27 56.8
3 Tu	2 42 55	12 23 33	19 43 23	27 03 00	26 54.3	25 18.7	4 17.9	6 41.6	19 51.9	28 38.2	12 14.3	13 36.8	18 33.2	27 57.3
4 W	2 46 51	13 21 43	4♋21 11	11♋37 17	26 55.3	25D 12.3	5 31.1	7 22.7	20 15.1	28 46.4	12 21.2	13 40.3	18 32.4	27 57.9
5 Th	2 50 48	14 19 51	18 50 47	26 01 15	26 56.2	25 10.8	6 44.3	8 03.7	20 38.2	28 54.6	12 27.9	13 43.7	18 31.6	27 58.5
6 F	2 54 45	15 17 56	3♌08 21	10♌11 47	26R 56.7	25 14.0	7 57.5	8 44.8	21 01.3	29 02.5	12 34.7	13 47.2	18 30.8	27 59.1
7 Sa	2 58 41	16 16 00	17 11 25	24 07 05	26 56.7	25 21.9	9 10.6	9 25.7	21 24.4	29 10.4	12 41.4	13 50.7	18 30.1	27 59.8
8 Su	3 02 38	17 14 02	0♍58 46	7♍46 26	26 56.1	25 34.4	10 23.7	10 06.7	21 47.4	29 18.1	12 48.1	13 54.2	18 29.4	28 00.5
9 M	3 06 34	18 12 02	14 30 08	21 09 54	26 55.3	25 51.5	11 36.8	10 47.5	22 10.4	29 25.6	12 54.7	13 57.6	18 28.7	28 01.2
10 Tu	3 10 31	19 10 00	27 45 51	4♎18 02	26 54.3	26 13.0	12 49.8	11 28.4	22 33.4	29 33.0	13 01.3	14 01.1	18 28.1	28 01.9
11 W	3 14 27	20 07 56	10♎46 37	17 11 40	26 53.3	26 38.9	14 02.8	12 09.2	22 56.3	29 40.3	13 07.8	14 04.5	18 27.4	28 02.6
12 Th	3 18 24	21 05 51	23 33 20	29 51 44	26 52.6	27 09.0	15 15.7	12 50.0	23 19.2	29 47.4	13 14.3	14 08.0	18 26.9	28 03.4
13 F	3 22 20	22 03 44	6♏07 01	12♏19 20	26 52.2	27 43.1	16 28.6	13 30.7	23 42.1	29 54.4	13 20.7	14 11.4	18 26.3	28 04.2
14 Sa	3 26 17	23 01 35	18 28 50	24 35 43	26D 52.1	28 21.2	17 41.5	14 11.4	24 04.9	0♓01.2	13 27.1	14 14.9	18 25.8	28 05.0
15 Su	3 30 14	23 59 25	0♐40 08	6♐42 21	26 52.1	29 03.0	18 54.3	14 52.0	24 27.7	0 07.9	13 33.5	14 18.3	18 25.3	28 05.8
16 M	3 34 10	24 57 14	12 42 34	18 41 04	26 52.3	29 48.5	20 07.1	15 32.6	24 50.4	0 14.4	13 39.8	14 21.7	18 24.8	28 06.7
17 Tu	3 38 07	25 55 01	24 38 09	0♑34 08	26 52.4	0♉37.6	21 19.9	16 13.2	25 13.1	0 20.8	13 46.0	14 25.1	18 24.4	28 07.5
18 W	3 42 03	26 52 47	6♑29 23	12 24 16	26R 52.5	1 30.1	22 32.6	16 53.8	25 35.7	0 27.0	13 52.2	14 28.5	18 24.0	28 08.4
19 Th	3 46 00	27 50 32	18 19 14	24 14 43	26 52.4	2 25.9	23 45.3	17 34.3	25 58.4	0 33.0	13 58.3	14 31.9	18 23.6	28 09.4
20 F	3 49 56	28 48 16	0♒11 11	6♒09 10	26 52.3	3 24.9	24 57.9	18 14.7	26 20.9	0 38.9	14 04.4	14 35.3	18 23.3	28 10.3
21 Sa	3 53 53	29 45 58	12 09 09	18 11 43	26 52.1	4 27.1	26 10.5	18 55.2	26 43.4	0 44.6	14 10.5	14 38.7	18 23.0	28 11.3
22 Su	3 57 49	0♊43 39	24 17 22	0♓26 41	26D 52.0	5 32.2	27 23.1	19 35.6	27 05.9	0 50.2	14 16.4	14 42.1	18 22.7	28 12.2
23 M	4 01 46	1 41 20	6♓40 12	12 58 24	26 52.1	6 40.3	28 35.6	20 15.9	27 28.3	0 55.6	14 22.4	14 45.4	18 22.5	28 13.2
24 Tu	4 05 43	2 38 59	19 21 49	25 50 51	26 52.5	7 51.3	29 48.1	20 56.3	27 50.7	1 00.9	14 28.2	14 48.8	18 22.2	28 14.3
25 W	4 09 39	3 36 38	2♈25 53	9♈07 12	26 53.0	9 05.1	1♋00.6	21 36.6	28 13.0	1 05.9	14 34.0	14 52.1	18 22.1	28 15.3
26 Th	4 13 36	4 34 15	15 54 59	22 49 17	26 53.7	10 21.6	2 13.0	22 16.8	28 35.3	1 10.8	14 39.8	14 55.4	18 21.9	28 16.4
27 F	4 17 32	5 31 51	29 50 03	6♉57 04	26 54.3	11 40.9	3 25.4	22 57.1	28 57.5	1 15.6	14 45.5	14 58.8	18 21.8	28 17.4
28 Sa	4 21 29	6 29 27	14♉09 55	21 28 04	26R 54.7	13 02.8	4 37.8	23 37.3	29 19.7	1 20.1	14 51.1	15 02.0	18 21.7	28 18.5
29 Su	4 25 25	7 27 01	28 50 50	6♊17 22	26 54.6	14 27.3	5 50.1	24 17.5	29 41.8	1 24.5	14 56.6	15 05.3	18D 21.7	28 19.7
30 M	4 29 22	8 24 35	13♊46 42	21 17 47	26 54.0	15 54.4	7 02.3	24 57.6	0♉03.8	1 28.7	15 02.1	15 08.6	18 21.7	28 20.8
31 Tu	4 33 18	9 22 07	28 49 30	6♋20 45	26 52.8	17 24.1	8 14.6	25 37.7	0 25.8	1 32.8	15 07.6	15 11.8	18 21.7	28 22.0

LONGITUDE — June 1938

Day	Sid.Time	☉	0 hr ☽	Noon ☽	True ☊	☿	♀	♂	⚳	♃	♄	♅	♆	♇
1 W	4 37 15	10♊19 38	13♋50 27	21♋17 34	26♏51.3	18♉56.4	9♋26.8	26♊17.8	0♉47.8	1♓36.6	15♈12.9	15♉15.1	18♍21.7	28♋23.1
2 Th	4 41 12	11 17 08	28 41 14	6♌00 38	26R 49.7	20 31.2	10 38.9	26 57.8	1 09.6	1 40.3	15 18.2	15 18.3	18 21.8	28 24.3
3 F	4 45 08	12 14 37	13♌15 10	20 24 21	26 48.3	22 08.6	11 51.0	27 37.8	1 31.5	1 43.8	15 23.5	15 21.5	18 21.9	28 25.5
4 Sa	4 49 05	13 12 04	27 27 52	4♍25 34	26D 47.5	23 48.4	13 03.0	28 17.8	1 53.2	1 47.1	15 28.6	15 24.6	18 22.1	28 26.8
5 Su	4 53 01	14 09 30	11♍17 24	18 03 26	26 47.4	25 30.8	14 15.0	28 57.7	2 14.9	1 50.3	15 33.7	15 27.8	18 22.3	28 28.0
6 M	4 56 58	15 06 54	24 43 53	1♎18 57	26 48.0	27 15.6	15 27.0	29 37.6	2 36.5	1 53.2	15 38.7	15 30.9	18 22.5	28 29.3
7 Tu	5 00 54	16 04 18	7♎48 59	14 14 18	26 49.1	29 03.0	16 38.9	0♋17.5	2 58.1	1 56.0	15 43.7	15 34.0	18 22.7	28 30.6
8 W	5 04 51	17 01 41	20 35 17	26 52 18	26 50.6	0♊52.8	17 50.7	0 57.3	3 19.5	1 58.6	15 48.6	15 37.1	18 23.0	28 31.8
9 Th	5 08 47	17 59 02	3♏05 44	9♏15 58	26 51.9	2 45.0	19 02.5	1 37.1	3 41.0	2 01.0	15 53.4	15 40.2	18 23.3	28 33.2
10 F	5 12 44	18 56 23	15 23 20	21 28 13	26R 52.8	4 39.6	20 14.2	2 16.9	4 02.3	2 03.2	15 58.1	15 43.2	18 23.6	28 34.5
11 Sa	5 16 41	19 53 42	27 30 54	3♐31 42	26 52.7	6 36.4	21 25.9	2 56.6	4 23.6	2 05.2	16 02.7	15 46.2	18 24.0	28 35.8
12 Su	5 20 37	20 51 01	9♐30 54	15 28 47	26 51.5	8 35.5	22 37.6	3 36.3	4 44.8	2 07.1	16 07.3	15 49.2	18 24.4	28 37.2
13 M	5 24 34	21 48 19	21 25 36	27 21 36	26 49.1	10 36.8	23 49.2	4 16.0	5 05.9	2 08.7	16 11.8	15 52.2	18 24.9	28 38.5
14 Tu	5 28 30	22 45 37	3♑17 02	9♑12 10	26 45.6	12 40.0	25 00.7	4 55.6	5 27.0	2 10.2	16 16.3	15 55.1	18 25.3	28 39.9
15 W	5 32 27	23 42 54	15 07 13	21 02 29	26 41.3	14 45.0	26 12.2	5 35.3	5 48.0	2 11.5	16 20.6	15 58.0	18 25.8	28 41.3
16 Th	5 36 23	24 40 11	26 58 16	2♒54 50	26 36.6	16 51.8	27 23.6	6 14.8	6 08.9	2 12.6	16 24.9	16 00.9	18 26.4	28 42.7
17 F	5 40 20	25 37 27	8♒52 32	14 51 43	26 32.0	18 59.9	28 35.0	6 54.4	6 29.7	2 13.5	16 29.1	16 03.8	18 26.9	28 44.2
18 Sa	5 44 16	26 34 42	20 52 46	26 56 05	26 28.1	21 09.3	29 46.3	7 33.9	6 50.5	2 14.2	16 33.2	16 06.6	18 27.5	28 45.6
19 Su	5 48 13	27 31 58	3♓02 07	9♓11 19	26 25.4	23 19.6	0♌57.5	8 13.4	7 11.2	2 14.7	16 37.2	16 09.4	18 28.1	28 47.0
20 M	5 52 10	28 29 13	15 24 09	21 41 07	26D 23.9	25 30.7	2 08.7	8 52.9	7 31.7	2 15.0	16 41.1	16 12.2	18 28.8	28 48.5
21 Tu	5 56 06	29 26 28	28 02 40	4♈29 19	26 23.8	27 42.1	3 19.9	9 32.4	7 52.3	2R 15.1	16 45.0	16 15.0	18 29.5	28 50.0
22 W	6 00 03	0♋23 43	11♈01 29	17 39 35	26 24.7	29 53.7	4 31.0	10 11.8	8 12.7	2 15.1	16 48.8	16 17.7	18 30.2	28 51.5
23 Th	6 03 59	1 20 57	24 23 58	1♉14 53	26 26.2	2♋05.2	5 42.0	10 51.2	8 33.0	2 14.8	16 52.5	16 20.4	18 31.0	28 53.0
24 F	6 07 56	2 18 12	8♉12 30	15 16 48	26R 27.4	4 16.3	6 53.0	11 30.6	8 53.3	2 14.3	16 56.1	16 23.0	18 31.8	28 54.5
25 Sa	6 11 52	3 15 27	22 27 41	29 44 48	26 27.7	6 26.7	8 03.9	12 09.9	9 13.4	2 13.7	16 59.6	16 25.7	18 32.6	28 56.0
26 Su	6 15 49	4 12 41	7♊07 40	14♊35 34	26 26.6	8 36.2	9 14.8	12 49.2	9 33.5	2 12.9	17 03.0	16 28.3	18 33.4	28 57.5
27 M	6 19 46	5 09 56	22 07 38	29 42 47	26 23.7	10 44.6	10 25.6	13 28.5	9 53.5	2 11.8	17 06.4	16 30.8	18 34.3	28 59.0
28 Tu	6 23 42	6 07 10	7♋19 50	14♋57 29	26 19.2	12 51.8	11 36.3	14 07.8	10 13.3	2 10.6	17 09.6	16 33.4	18 35.2	29 00.6
29 W	6 27 39	7 04 24	22 34 25	0♌09 18	26 13.6	14 57.5	12 47.0	14 47.1	10 33.1	2 09.2	17 12.8	16 35.9	18 36.1	29 02.2
30 Th	6 31 35	8 01 38	7♌40 55	15 08 08	26 07.6	17 01.6	13 57.6	15 26.3	10 52.8	2 07.5	17 15.8	16 38.3	18 37.1	29 03.7

Astro Data

	Dy Hr Mn
☿ D	5 7:53
☽ 0S	9 7:19
☽ 0N	23 22:29
♆ D	30 10:13
♄⚺♅	2 12:18
☽ 0S	5 12:59
☽ 0N	20 6:28
♃ R	21 15:30
♃∠♄	28 17:12

Planet Ingress

		Dy Hr Mn
♃	♓	14 7:46
☿	♉	16 17:46
☉	♊	21 17:50
♀	♋	24 15:56
⚳	♉	30 7:49
♂	♋	7 1:28
☿	♊	8 0:32
♀	♌	18 16:37
☉	♋	22 2:04
☿	♋	22 13:09

Last Aspect / ☽ Ingress (May)

Last Aspect Dy Hr Mn			☽ Ingress	Dy Hr Mn
1 13:04	♃	□	♊	1 15:45
3 14:38	♃	△	♋	3 16:50
5 15:17	♇	☌	♌	5 18:42
7 20:55	♃	☍	♍	7 22:17
10 0:29	♇	⚹	♎	10 4:06
12 11:52	♃	△	♏	12 12:16
14 18:53	♇	△	♐	14 22:40
16 15:13	♀	☍	♑	17 10:51
19 19:55	♇	☍	♒	19 23:37
22 5:24	♀	△	♓	22 11:08
24 16:23	♇	△	♈	24 19:35
26 21:21	♇	□	♉	27 0:17
28 23:09	♇	⚹	♊	29 1:52
30 18:07	♂	☌	♋	31 1:52

Last Aspect / ☽ Ingress (June)

Last Aspect Dy Hr Mn			☽ Ingress	Dy Hr Mn
1 23:31	♇	☌	♌	2 2:09
4 0:54	♂	⚹	♍	4 4:21
6 8:45	♂	□	♎	6 9:35
8 15:12	♇	□	♏	8 18:01
11 2:08	♇	△	♐	11 4:57
12 23:47	☉	☍	♑	13 17:21
16 3:30	♇	☍	♒	16 6:07
18 11:14	☉	△	♓	18 18:02
21 1:52	☉	□	♈	21 3:40
23 7:52	♇	□	♉	23 9:50
25 10:40	♇	⚹	♊	25 12:25
26 18:20	♆	□	♋	27 12:27
29 10:13	♇	☌	♌	29 11:45

☽ Phases & Eclipses

Dy Hr Mn		
6 21:24	☽	15♌41
14 8:39	○	22♏54
14 8:44	☍	T 1.097
22 12:36	☾	0♓45
29 13:59	●	7♊32
29 13:49:55	☌	T 04'04"
5 4:32	☽	13♍52
12 23:47	○	21♐19
21 1:52	☾	29♓02
27 21:10	●	5♋32

Astro Data

1 May 1938
Julian Day # 14000
SVP 6♓07'02"
GC 25♐58.7 ⚴ 16♓50.8
Eris 4♈15.0 ⚵ 12♐32.9R
⚷ 27♊47.0 ⚶ 4♐19.3R
☽ Mean ☊ 27♏49.9

1 June 1938
Julian Day # 14031
SVP 6♓06'57"
GC 25♐58.8 ⚴ 24♓00.0
Eris 4♈29.7 ⚵ 6♐16.6R
⚷ 0♋21.7 ⚶ 27♏21.6R
☽ Mean ☊ 26♏11.5

July 1938 LONGITUDE

Day	Sid.Time	☉	0 hr ☽	Noon ☽	True ☊	☿	♀	♂	⚷	♃	♄	♅	♆	♇
1 F	6 35 32	8♋58 51	22♌30 03	29♌45 52	26♏02.1	19♋04.1	15♌08.2	16♋05.5	11♉12.4	2♓05.7	17♈18.8	16♉40.7	18♍38.1	29♋05.3
2 Sa	6 39 28	9 56 04	6♍55 05	13♍57 21	25R 57.8	21 04.8	16 18.6	16 44.7	11 31.8	2R 03.7	17 21.7	16 43.1	18 39.1	29 06.9
3 Su	6 43 25	10 53 17	20 52 31	27 40 39	25 55.3	23 03.6	17 29.0	17 23.8	11 51.2	2 01.5	17 24.5	16 45.5	18 40.2	29 08.5
4 M	6 47 21	11 50 29	4♎21 55	10♎56 39	25D 54.4	25 00.6	18 39.4	18 02.9	12 10.4	1 59.2	17 27.2	16 47.8	18 41.2	29 10.1
5 Tu	6 51 18	12 47 41	17 25 14	23 48 10	25 54.9	26 55.6	19 49.6	18 42.0	12 29.6	1 56.6	17 29.8	16 50.1	18 42.4	29 11.7
6 W	6 55 15	13 44 53	0♏05 57	6♏19 10	25 56.1	28 48.7	20 59.8	19 21.1	12 48.6	1 53.9	17 32.3	16 52.3	18 43.5	29 13.3
7 Th	6 59 11	14 42 04	12 28 22	18 34 05	25R 57.2	0♌39.8	22 09.9	20 00.1	13 07.5	1 50.9	17 34.7	16 54.5	18 44.7	29 14.9
8 F	7 03 08	15 39 16	24 36 54	0♐37 18	25 57.3	2 28.9	23 19.9	20 39.2	13 26.3	1 47.8	17 37.0	16 56.7	18 45.9	29 16.5
9 Sa	7 07 04	16 36 27	6♐35 46	12 32 46	25 55.8	4 16.1	24 29.8	21 18.2	13 45.0	1 44.5	17 39.2	16 58.8	18 47.1	29 18.1
10 Su	7 11 01	17 33 39	18 28 42	24 23 57	25 52.1	6 01.2	25 39.6	21 57.1	14 03.6	1 41.1	17 41.4	17 00.9	18 48.3	29 19.8
11 M	7 14 57	18 30 50	0♑18 50	6♑13 39	25 46.1	7 44.4	26 49.4	22 36.1	14 22.1	1 37.4	17 43.4	17 03.0	18 49.6	29 21.4
12 Tu	7 18 54	19 28 02	12 08 41	18 04 10	25 38.1	9 25.5	27 59.0	23 15.0	14 40.4	1 33.6	17 45.3	17 05.0	18 50.9	29 23.1
13 W	7 22 50	20 25 14	24 00 19	29 57 20	25 28.5	11 04.7	29 08.6	23 53.9	14 58.6	1 29.6	17 47.2	17 07.0	18 52.2	29 24.7
14 Th	7 26 47	21 22 26	5♒55 24	11♒54 44	25 18.2	12 41.9	0♍18.1	24 32.8	15 16.7	1 25.4	17 48.9	17 08.9	18 53.6	29 26.4
15 F	7 30 44	22 19 39	17 55 32	23 57 58	25 08.0	14 17.1	1 27.5	25 11.7	15 34.6	1 21.1	17 50.5	17 10.8	18 55.0	29 28.0
16 Sa	7 34 40	23 16 52	0♓02 18	6♓08 46	24 58.9	15 50.3	2 36.8	25 50.5	15 52.5	1 16.6	17 52.1	17 12.7	18 56.4	29 29.7
17 Su	7 38 37	24 14 06	12 17 39	18 29 15	24 51.6	17 21.5	3 46.0	26 29.3	16 10.2	1 11.9	17 53.5	17 14.5	18 57.8	29 31.3
18 M	7 42 33	25 11 20	24 43 54	1♈01 58	24 46.6	18 50.6	4 55.1	27 08.1	16 27.7	1 07.1	17 54.8	17 16.2	18 59.2	29 33.0
19 Tu	7 46 30	26 08 35	7♈23 50	13 49 54	24 44.0	20 17.8	6 04.2	27 46.9	16 45.1	1 02.1	17 56.1	17 17.9	19 00.7	29 34.7
20 W	7 50 26	27 05 51	20 20 36	26 56 18	24D 43.2	21 42.9	7 13.1	28 25.7	17 02.4	0 56.9	17 57.2	17 19.6	19 02.2	29 36.3
21 Th	7 54 23	28 03 08	3♉37 25	10♉24 17	24 43.6	23 05.8	8 21.9	29 04.4	17 19.5	0 51.6	17 58.2	17 21.3	19 03.8	29 38.0
22 F	7 58 19	29 00 25	17 17 09	24 16 13	24R 44.0	24 26.7	9 30.6	29 43.2	17 36.5	0 46.2	17 59.2	17 22.9	19 05.3	29 39.7
23 Sa	8 02 16	29 57 44	1♊21 32	8♊33 01	24 43.3	25 45.4	10 39.3	0♌21.9	17 53.4	0 40.6	18 00.0	17 24.4	19 06.9	29 41.3
24 Su	8 06 13	0♌55 03	15 50 24	23 13 15	24 40.6	27 01.9	11 47.8	1 00.6	18 10.1	0 34.8	18 00.7	17 25.9	19 08.5	29 43.0
25 M	8 10 09	1 52 23	0♋40 54	8♋12 30	24 35.5	28 16.2	12 56.2	1 39.3	18 26.6	0 28.9	18 01.3	17 27.4	19 10.1	29 44.7
26 Tu	8 14 06	2 49 44	15 46 59	23 23 11	24 27.9	29 28.1	14 04.5	2 17.9	18 43.0	0 22.9	18 01.9	17 28.8	19 11.7	29 46.3
27 W	8 18 02	3 47 06	0♌59 47	8♌35 26	24 18.5	0♍37.6	15 12.7	2 56.6	18 59.2	0 16.8	18 02.3	17 30.2	19 13.4	29 48.0
28 Th	8 21 59	4 44 28	16 08 46	23 38 31	24 08.4	1 44.7	16 20.8	3 35.2	19 15.3	0 10.5	18 02.6	17 31.5	19 15.1	29 49.7
29 F	8 25 55	5 41 51	1♍03 32	8♍22 51	23 58.8	2 49.1	17 28.8	4 13.8	19 31.1	0 04.1	18 02.8	17 32.8	19 16.8	29 51.3
30 Sa	8 29 52	6 39 15	15 35 41	22 41 31	23 50.8	3 50.9	18 36.7	4 52.4	19 46.9	29♒57.5	18R 02.9	17 34.0	19 18.5	29 53.0
31 Su	8 33 48	7 36 39	29 40 01	6♎31 05	23 45.1	4 50.0	19 44.4	5 31.0	20 02.4	29 50.9	18 02.9	17 35.2	19 20.3	29 54.6

August 1938 LONGITUDE

Day	Sid.Time	☉	0 hr ☽	Noon ☽	True ☊	☿	♀	♂	⚷	♃	♄	♅	♆	♇
1 M	8 37 45	8♌34 03	13♎14 47	19♎51 21	23♏41.8	5♍46.1	20♍52.0	6♌09.6	20♉17.8	29♒44.1	18♈02.8	17♉36.3	19♍22.0	29♋56.3
2 Tu	8 41 42	9 31 29	26 21 11	2♏44 46	23D 40.5	6 39.2	21 59.5	6 48.1	20 32.9	29R 37.3	18R 02.6	17 37.4	19 23.8	29 57.9
3 W	8 45 38	10 28 55	9♏02 38	15 15 24	23R 40.4	7 29.1	23 06.8	7 26.6	20 48.0	29 30.3	18 02.3	17 38.4	19 25.6	29 59.6
4 Th	8 49 35	11 26 21	21 23 43	27 28 14	23 40.5	8 15.8	24 14.0	8 05.1	21 02.8	29 23.3	18 01.8	17 39.4	19 27.5	0♌01.2
5 F	8 53 31	12 23 49	3♐29 37	9♐28 29	23 39.6	8 58.9	25 21.0	8 43.6	21 17.4	29 16.1	18 01.3	17 40.4	19 29.3	0 02.9
6 Sa	8 57 28	13 21 17	15 25 26	21 21 04	23 36.8	9 38.4	26 27.9	9 22.1	21 31.9	29 08.9	18 00.7	17 41.3	19 31.2	0 04.5
7 Su	9 01 24	14 18 46	27 15 54	3♑10 26	23 31.5	10 14.1	27 34.7	10 00.5	21 46.1	29 01.6	18 00.0	17 42.1	19 33.1	0 06.1
8 M	9 05 21	15 16 16	9♑05 05	15 00 16	23 23.4	10 45.7	28 41.3	10 39.0	22 00.2	28 54.2	17 59.2	17 42.9	19 35.0	0 07.8
9 Tu	9 09 17	16 13 47	20 56 18	26 53 30	23 12.7	11 13.0	29 47.7	11 17.4	22 14.1	28 46.8	17 58.2	17 43.7	19 36.9	0 09.4
10 W	9 13 14	17 11 18	2♒52 06	8♒52 18	23 00.1	11 36.0	0♎54.0	11 55.8	22 27.7	28 39.2	17 57.2	17 44.4	19 38.8	0 11.0
11 Th	9 17 11	18 08 51	14 54 16	20 58 08	22 46.6	11 54.3	2 00.1	12 34.2	22 41.2	28 31.7	17 56.1	17 45.0	19 40.7	0 12.6
12 F	9 21 07	19 06 25	27 04 01	3♓12 01	22 33.2	12 07.7	3 06.1	13 12.6	22 54.4	28 24.0	17 54.9	17 45.6	19 42.7	0 14.2
13 Sa	9 25 04	20 04 00	9♓22 14	15 34 46	22 21.1	12 16.0	4 11.8	13 51.0	23 07.5	28 16.3	17 53.6	17 46.2	19 44.7	0 15.8
14 Su	9 29 00	21 01 37	21 49 42	28 07 11	22 11.2	12R 19.1	5 17.4	14 29.3	23 20.3	28 08.6	17 52.1	17 46.7	19 46.7	0 17.4
15 M	9 32 57	21 59 15	4♈27 22	10♈50 25	22 04.0	12 16.8	6 22.8	15 07.7	23 32.9	28 00.8	17 50.6	17 47.1	19 48.7	0 18.9
16 Tu	9 36 53	22 56 54	17 16 33	23 46 01	21 59.7	12 08.9	7 28.1	15 46.0	23 45.3	27 53.0	17 49.0	17 47.5	19 50.7	0 20.5
17 W	9 40 50	23 54 35	0♉19 05	6♉56 00	21 57.8	11 55.5	8 33.1	16 24.3	23 57.4	27 45.2	17 47.3	17 47.9	19 52.7	0 22.1
18 Th	9 44 46	24 52 18	13 37 06	20 22 37	21 57.4	11 36.3	9 38.0	17 02.6	24 09.4	27 37.3	17 45.5	17 48.2	19 54.8	0 23.6
19 F	9 48 43	25 50 02	27 12 48	4♊07 53	21 57.4	11 11.5	10 42.7	17 40.9	24 21.1	27 29.5	17 43.6	17 48.4	19 56.8	0 25.1
20 Sa	9 52 40	26 47 48	11♊07 57	18 13 04	21 56.3	10 41.3	11 47.1	18 19.2	24 32.5	27 21.6	17 41.6	17 48.6	19 58.9	0 26.7
21 Su	9 56 36	27 45 36	25 23 05	2♋37 48	21 53.3	10 05.8	12 51.4	18 57.5	24 43.7	27 13.7	17 39.5	17 48.8	20 01.0	0 28.2
22 M	10 00 33	28 43 26	9♋56 47	17 19 27	21 47.6	9 25.4	13 55.4	19 35.8	24 54.7	27 05.8	17 37.3	17 48.9	20 03.1	0 29.7
23 Tu	10 04 29	29 41 17	24 45 04	2♌12 42	21 39.3	8 40.6	14 59.3	20 14.1	25 05.4	26 58.0	17 35.0	17R 49.0	20 05.2	0 31.2
24 W	10 08 26	0♍39 09	9♌41 20	17 09 49	21 29.1	7 52.0	16 02.9	20 52.3	25 15.8	26 50.1	17 32.6	17 49.0	20 07.3	0 32.7
25 Th	10 12 22	1 37 04	24 36 58	2♍01 39	21 18.0	7 00.4	17 06.3	21 30.6	25 26.0	26 42.3	17 30.1	17 48.9	20 09.4	0 34.2
26 F	10 16 19	2 34 59	9♍22 43	16 39 12	21 07.2	6 06.6	18 09.5	22 08.8	25 35.9	26 34.4	17 27.6	17 48.8	20 11.6	0 35.6
27 Sa	10 20 15	3 32 56	23 50 15	0♎55 13	20 58.1	5 11.6	19 12.4	22 47.0	25 45.6	26 26.7	17 24.9	17 48.7	20 13.7	0 37.1
28 Su	10 24 12	4 30 55	7♎53 36	14 45 08	20 51.3	4 16.6	20 15.0	23 25.2	25 55.0	26 18.9	17 22.2	17 48.5	20 15.9	0 38.5
29 M	10 28 08	5 28 54	21 29 45	28 07 30	20 47.1	3 22.6	21 17.4	24 03.4	26 04.1	26 11.2	17 19.4	17 48.2	20 18.0	0 39.9
30 Tu	10 32 05	6 26 56	4♏38 39	11♏03 33	20D 45.3	2 30.9	22 19.6	24 41.6	26 12.9	26 03.6	17 16.5	17 47.9	20 20.2	0 41.3
31 W	10 36 02	7 24 58	17 22 39	23 36 31	20 45.0	1 42.6	23 21.4	25 19.8	26 21.4	25 56.0	17 13.5	17 47.6	20 22.4	0 42.7

Astro Data

	Dy Hr Mn
☽0S	2 20:38
☽0N	17 13:26
☽0S	30 6:27
♄ R	30 23:14
♃⊼♇	31 1:13
♀0S	9 20:08
☽0N	13 19:51
☿ R	14 13:51
♄⊻♅	17 5:07
♅ R	24 2:08
☽0S	26 17:11

Planet Ingress

		Dy Hr Mn
☿	♌	7 3:21
♀	♍	14 5:44
♂	♌	22 22:26
☉	♌	23 12:57
☿	♍	26 22:55
♃	♒R	30 3:01
♇	♌	3 17:56
♀	♎	9 16:26
☉	♍	23 19:46

Last Aspect / ☽ Ingress

Last Aspect Dy Hr Mn			☽ Ingress	Dy Hr Mn
30 15:28	♄	△	♍	1 12:24
3 14:37	♇	✶	♎	3 16:09
5 22:17	♇	□	♏	5 23:49
8 9:18	♇	△	♐	8 10:45
10 14:50	♀	△	♑	10 23:22
13 10:54	♇	☍	♒	13 12:05
14 23:48	♄	✶	♓	15 23:55
18 9:11	♇	△	♈	18 10:02
20 16:49	♇	□	♉	20 17:31
22 21:41	♂	✶	♊	22 21:43
24 18:42	☿	✶	♋	24 22:54
26 22:05	♇	☌	♌	26 22:26
28 3:01	♄	△	♍	28 22:17
31 0:24	♇	✶	♎	31 0:35

Last Aspect / ☽ Ingress

Last Aspect Dy Hr Mn			☽ Ingress	Dy Hr Mn
2 6:45	♇	□	♏	2 6:49
4 15:46	♃	□	♐	4 17:02
7 3:40	♃	✶	♑	7 5:33
8 21:17	♆	△	♒	9 18:15
12 2:43	♃	☌	♓	12 5:45
13 20:02	♆	☍	♈	14 15:34
16 19:29	♃	✶	♉	16 23:25
19 0:36	♃	□	♊	19 4:51
21 3:22	☉	✶	♋	21 7:39
22 16:25	♆	✶	♌	23 8:27
25 3:27	♃	☍	♍	25 8:43
26 17:54	♆	☌	♎	27 10:26
29 8:30	♃	△	♏	29 15:26

☽ Phases & Eclipses

Dy Hr Mn		
4 13:47	☽	11♎55
12 15:05	○	19♑35
20 12:19	☾	27♈07
27 3:53	●	3♌28
3 2:00	☽	10♏05
11 5:57	○	17♒54
18 20:30	☾	25♉13
25 11:17	●	1♍35

Astro Data

1 July 1938
Julian Day # 14061
SVP 6♓06'52"
GC 25♐58.8 ⚳ 28♓08.0
Eris 4♈34.8R ⚴ 0♐35.7R
⚵ 3♋12.6 ⚶ 23♏25.9R
☽ Mean ☊ 24♏36.2

1 August 1938
Julian Day # 14092
SVP 6♓06'48"
GC 25♐58.9 ⚳ 28♓00.0R
Eris 4♈29.5R ⚴ 29♏09.2
⚵ 6♋04.8 ⚶ 26♏35.1
☽ Mean ☊ 22♏57.7

LONGITUDE — September 1938

Day	Sid.Time	☉	0 hr ☽	Noon ☽	True ☊	☿	♀	♂	⚷	♃	♄	♅	♆	♇
1 Th	10 39 58	8♍23 02	29♏45 44	5♐50 58	20♏45.2	0♍58.8	24♎23.0	25♌57.9	26♉29.7	25♒48.4	17♈10.4	17♉47.2	20♍24.6	0♌44.1
2 F	10 43 55	9 21 08	11♐52 53	17 52 07	20R44.9	0R20.6	25 24.3	26 36.1	26 37.6	25R41.0	17R07.3	17R46.8	20 26.8	0 45.5
3 Sa	10 47 51	10 19 15	23 49 22	29 45 17	20 43.1	29♌48.9	26 25.2	27 14.2	26 45.3	25 33.6	17 04.0	17 46.3	20 28.9	0 46.8
4 Su	10 51 48	11 17 23	5♑40 27	11♑35 29	20 39.1	29 24.4	27 25.9	27 52.4	26 52.6	25 26.3	17 00.7	17 45.7	20 31.1	0 48.2
5 M	10 55 44	12 15 33	17 30 56	23 27 16	20 32.5	29 07.8	28 26.2	28 30.5	26 59.7	25 19.0	16 57.4	17 45.1	20 33.4	0 49.5
6 Tu	10 59 41	13 13 44	29 24 58	5♒24 24	20 23.6	28D59.6	29 26.2	29 08.6	27 06.5	25 11.9	16 53.9	17 44.5	20 35.6	0 50.8
7 W	11 03 37	14 11 57	11♒25 55	17 29 47	20 12.9	29 00.1	0♏25.8	29 46.7	27 12.9	25 04.8	16 50.4	17 43.8	20 37.8	0 52.1
8 Th	11 07 34	15 10 11	23 36 14	29 45 24	20 01.1	29 09.5	1 25.0	0♍24.8	27 19.0	24 57.9	16 46.8	17 43.1	20 40.0	0 53.4
9 F	11 11 31	16 08 27	5♓57 25	12♓12 21	19 49.5	29 27.9	2 23.9	1 02.9	27 24.8	24 51.0	16 43.1	17 42.3	20 42.2	0 54.6
10 Sa	11 15 27	17 06 45	18 30 14	24 51 02	19 39.0	29 55.1	3 22.4	1 41.0	27 30.3	24 44.3	16 39.4	17 41.5	20 44.4	0 55.8
11 Su	11 19 24	18 05 05	1♈14 44	7♈41 19	19 30.5	0♍31.0	4 20.5	2 19.0	27 35.4	24 37.6	16 35.6	17 40.6	20 46.7	0 57.1
12 M	11 23 20	19 03 27	14 10 43	20 42 55	19 24.6	1 15.4	5 18.2	2 57.1	27 40.3	24 31.1	16 31.8	17 39.7	20 48.9	0 58.3
13 Tu	11 27 17	20 01 50	27 17 55	3♉55 41	19 21.2	2 07.7	6 15.4	3 35.2	27 44.7	24 24.7	16 27.8	17 38.7	20 51.1	0 59.5
14 W	11 31 13	21 00 16	10♉36 17	17 19 43	19D20.1	3 07.7	7 12.2	4 13.2	27 48.9	24 18.5	16 23.9	17 37.7	20 53.3	1 00.6
15 Th	11 35 10	21 58 44	24 06 05	0♊55 27	19 20.5	4 14.7	8 08.6	4 51.3	27 52.7	24 12.3	16 19.8	17 36.6	20 55.6	1 01.8
16 F	11 39 06	22 57 14	7♊47 53	14 43 26	19R21.3	5 28.2	9 04.5	5 29.3	27 56.1	24 06.3	16 15.7	17 35.5	20 57.8	1 02.9
17 Sa	11 43 03	23 55 47	21 42 08	28 43 58	19 21.4	6 47.6	9 59.9	6 07.4	27 59.2	24 00.4	16 11.6	17 34.4	21 00.0	1 04.0
18 Su	11 47 00	24 54 21	5♋48 52	12♋56 38	19 20.0	8 12.4	10 54.8	6 45.4	28 02.0	23 54.7	16 07.4	17 33.2	21 02.2	1 05.1
19 M	11 50 56	25 52 58	20 07 02	27 19 42	19 16.5	9 41.8	11 49.2	7 23.4	28 04.4	23 49.1	16 03.1	17 31.9	21 04.5	1 06.2
20 Tu	11 54 53	26 51 37	4♌34 08	11♌49 45	19 10.8	11 15.3	12 43.1	8 01.4	28 06.4	23 43.7	15 58.8	17 30.7	21 06.7	1 07.3
21 W	11 58 49	27 50 18	19 05 54	26 21 49	19 03.5	12 52.3	13 36.4	8 39.5	28 08.0	23 38.4	15 54.5	17 29.3	21 08.9	1 08.3
22 Th	12 02 46	28 49 01	3♍36 40	10♍49 39	18 55.4	14 32.3	14 29.1	9 17.5	28 09.3	23 33.3	15 50.1	17 28.0	21 11.1	1 09.3
23 F	12 06 42	29 47 46	17 59 56	25 06 46	18 47.5	16 14.7	15 21.2	9 55.5	28 10.2	23 28.3	15 45.7	17 26.6	21 13.3	1 10.3
24 Sa	12 10 39	0♎46 34	2♎09 27	9♎07 23	18 40.8	17 59.1	16 12.7	10 33.5	28R10.7	23 23.5	15 41.2	17 25.1	21 15.5	1 11.3
25 Su	12 14 35	1 45 23	16 00 06	22 47 17	18 35.9	19 45.0	17 03.6	11 11.5	28 10.9	23 18.9	15 36.7	17 23.6	21 17.7	1 12.2
26 M	12 18 32	2 44 14	29 28 44	6♏04 23	18D33.1	21 32.1	17 53.8	11 49.5	28 10.6	23 14.4	15 32.2	17 22.1	21 19.9	1 13.1
27 Tu	12 22 29	3 43 07	12♏34 18	18 58 42	18 32.3	23 20.0	18 43.2	12 27.5	28 10.0	23 10.1	15 27.6	17 20.5	21 22.1	1 14.0
28 W	12 26 25	4 42 02	25 17 52	1♐32 10	18 33.0	25 08.5	19 32.0	13 05.4	28 09.0	23 06.0	15 23.0	17 18.9	21 24.3	1 14.9
29 Th	12 30 22	5 40 58	7♐42 06	13 48 11	18 34.4	26 57.3	20 20.0	13 43.4	28 07.6	23 02.1	15 18.4	17 17.3	21 26.5	1 15.8
30 F	12 34 18	6 39 57	19 50 58	25 51 05	18R35.8	28 46.1	21 07.1	14 21.4	28 05.9	22 58.4	15 13.8	17 15.6	21 28.7	1 16.6

LONGITUDE — October 1938

Day	Sid.Time	☉	0 hr ☽	Noon ☽	True ☊	☿	♀	♂	⚷	♃	♄	♅	♆	♇
1 Sa	12 38 15	7♎38 57	1♑49 08	7♑45 46	18♏36.4	0♎34.8	21♏53.5	14♍59.3	28♉03.7	22♒54.8	15♈09.1	17♉13.9	21♍30.8	1♌17.5
2 Su	12 42 11	8 37 59	13 41 36	19 37 18	18R35.7	2 23.3	22 39.0	15 37.3	28R01.2	22R51.4	15R04.5	17R12.1	21 33.0	1 18.2
3 M	12 46 08	9 37 02	25 33 26	1♒30 37	18 33.2	4 11.4	23 23.6	16 15.2	27 58.3	22 48.2	14 59.8	17 10.3	21 35.1	1 19.0
4 Tu	12 50 04	10 36 08	7♒29 23	13 30 15	18 29.2	5 59.1	24 07.2	16 53.2	27 54.9	22 45.2	14 55.1	17 08.5	21 37.3	1 19.8
5 W	12 54 01	11 35 15	19 33 41	25 40 04	18 23.8	7 46.2	24 49.9	17 31.1	27 51.2	22 42.4	14 50.3	17 06.6	21 39.4	1 20.5
6 Th	12 57 57	12 34 24	1♓49 46	8♓03 04	18 17.6	9 32.7	25 31.5	18 09.0	27 47.2	22 39.8	14 45.6	17 04.7	21 41.5	1 21.2
7 F	13 01 54	13 33 35	14 20 09	20 41 12	18 11.4	11 18.6	26 12.1	18 46.9	27 42.7	22 37.3	14 40.9	17 02.8	21 43.6	1 21.9
8 Sa	13 05 51	14 32 47	27 06 16	3♈35 21	18 05.8	13 03.8	26 51.6	19 24.8	27 37.8	22 35.1	14 36.2	17 00.8	21 45.7	1 22.5
9 Su	13 09 47	15 32 02	10♈08 23	16 45 16	18 01.4	14 48.3	27 29.9	20 02.7	27 32.6	22 33.1	14 31.4	16 58.8	21 47.8	1 23.1
10 M	13 13 44	16 31 19	23 25 48	0♉09 48	17 58.5	16 32.1	28 07.0	20 40.6	27 27.0	22 31.2	14 26.7	16 56.8	21 49.8	1 23.8
11 Tu	13 17 40	17 30 38	6♉57 00	13 47 10	17D57.3	18 15.2	28 42.9	21 18.6	27 21.0	22 29.6	14 22.0	16 54.8	21 51.9	1 24.3
12 W	13 21 37	18 29 59	20 40 00	27 35 14	17 57.6	19 57.6	29 17.5	21 56.5	27 14.6	22 28.1	14 17.3	16 52.7	21 53.9	1 24.9
13 Th	13 25 33	19 29 23	4♊32 36	11♊31 51	17 58.7	21 39.2	29 50.8	22 34.4	27 07.9	22 26.9	14 12.6	16 50.6	21 56.0	1 25.4
14 F	13 29 30	20 28 48	18 32 43	25 35 00	18 00.3	23 20.2	0♐22.7	23 12.3	27 00.8	22 25.8	14 07.9	16 48.5	21 58.0	1 25.9
15 Sa	13 33 26	21 28 17	2♋38 27	9♋42 51	18R01.5	25 00.4	0 53.1	23 50.2	26 53.3	22 25.0	14 03.2	16 46.3	22 00.0	1 26.4
16 Su	13 37 23	22 27 47	16 47 58	23 53 36	18 01.9	26 40.0	1 22.1	24 28.0	26 45.5	22 24.3	13 58.5	16 44.1	22 02.0	1 26.9
17 M	13 41 20	23 27 20	0♌59 28	8♌05 18	18 01.3	28 18.8	1 49.4	25 05.9	26 37.3	22 23.9	13 53.9	16 41.9	22 04.0	1 27.3
18 Tu	13 45 16	24 26 55	15 10 50	22 15 42	17 59.4	29 57.1	2 15.2	25 43.8	26 28.7	22D23.6	13 49.3	16 39.7	22 05.9	1 27.7
19 W	13 49 13	25 26 32	29 19 35	6♍22 05	17 56.7	1♏34.6	2 39.3	26 21.7	26 19.8	22 23.6	13 44.7	16 37.4	22 07.9	1 28.1
20 Th	13 53 09	26 26 12	13♍22 49	20 21 23	17 53.6	3 11.6	3 01.7	26 59.6	26 10.6	22 23.7	13 40.1	16 35.1	22 09.8	1 28.4
21 F	13 57 06	27 25 53	27 17 22	4♎10 22	17 50.5	4 48.0	3 22.3	27 37.5	26 01.0	22 24.1	13 35.6	16 32.8	22 11.7	1 28.8
22 Sa	14 01 02	28 25 37	11♎00 03	17 46 04	17 48.0	6 23.7	3 41.0	28 15.3	25 51.1	22 24.6	13 31.1	16 30.5	22 13.6	1 29.1
23 Su	14 04 59	29 25 23	24 28 09	1♏06 05	17 46.3	7 58.9	3 57.8	28 53.2	25 40.9	22 25.4	13 26.6	16 28.2	22 15.4	1 29.4
24 M	14 08 55	0♏25 11	7♏39 43	14 08 58	17D45.5	9 33.5	4 12.6	29 31.1	25 30.4	22 26.4	13 22.2	16 25.8	22 17.3	1 29.6
25 Tu	14 12 52	1 25 00	20 33 51	26 54 25	17 45.7	11 07.6	4 25.4	0♎08.9	25 19.6	22 27.5	13 17.8	16 23.5	22 19.1	1 29.8
26 W	14 16 49	2 24 52	3♐10 51	9♐23 20	17 46.6	12 41.2	4 36.1	0 46.8	25 08.5	22 28.9	13 13.5	16 21.1	22 20.9	1 30.0
27 Th	14 20 45	3 24 45	15 32 11	21 37 44	17 47.9	14 14.2	4 44.5	1 24.6	24 57.2	22 30.5	13 09.2	16 18.7	22 22.7	1 30.2
28 F	14 24 42	4 24 41	27 40 23	3♑40 37	17 49.2	15 46.8	4 50.8	2 02.5	24 45.5	22 32.3	13 04.9	16 16.3	22 24.5	1 30.3
29 Sa	14 28 38	5 24 38	9♑38 54	15 35 47	17 50.3	17 18.8	4 54.7	2 40.3	24 33.7	22 34.2	13 00.7	16 13.9	22 26.3	1 30.5
30 Su	14 32 35	6 24 36	21 31 49	27 27 35	17R51.0	18 50.4	4R56.4	3 18.2	24 21.5	22 36.4	12 56.6	16 11.4	22 28.0	1 30.6
31 M	14 36 31	7 24 36	3♒23 40	9♒20 40	17 51.2	20 21.4	4 55.6	3 56.0	24 09.2	22 38.8	12 52.5	16 09.0	22 29.7	1 30.6

Astro Data

	Dy Hr Mn
☿ D	6 22:41
☽ 0N	10 2:32
☽ 0S	23 3:03
☉ 0S	23 16:59
⚷ R	25 9:10
☿ 0S	3 7:02
☽ 0N	7 10:12
♃ D	19 5:46
☽ 0S	20 10:46
♂ 0S	29 12:09
♀ R	30 16:22

Planet Ingress

		Dy Hr Mn
☿	♌R	3 2:58
♀	♏	7 1:36
♂	♍	7 20:22
☿	♍	10 15:38
☉	♎	23 17:00
☿	♎	1 4:19
♀	♐	13 18:49
☿	♏	18 12:43
☉	♏	24 1:54
♂	♎	25 6:20

Last Aspect / ☽ Ingress (September)

Last Aspect Dy Hr Mn			☽ Ingress	Dy Hr Mn
31 16:28	♃	□	♐	1 0:28
3 12:07	☿	△	♑	3 12:30
5 22:57	♀	□	♒	6 1:10
8 10:49	☿	☍	♓	8 12:28
10 4:13	♆	☍	♈	10 21:40
12 18:53	♃	⚹	♉	13 4:54
15 0:16	♃	□	♊	15 10:23
17 4:00	♃	△	♋	17 14:09
19 9:25	☉	⚹	♌	19 16:26
21 7:32	♃	☍	♍	21 18:01
23 5:24	♆	☌	♎	23 20:19
25 12:56	♃	△	♏	26 0:57
27 21:38	☿	⚹	♐	28 9:02
30 18:54	☿	□	♑	30 20:20

Last Aspect / ☽ Ingress (October)

Last Aspect Dy Hr Mn			☽ Ingress	Dy Hr Mn
2 18:32	♀	⚹	♒	3 8:58
5 10:16	♀	□	♓	5 20:27
7 22:53	♀	△	♈	8 5:22
9 22:24	♃	⚹	♉	10 11:43
12 15:04	♀	☍	♊	12 16:10
14 7:45	♂	□	♋	14 19:31
16 17:18	☿	□	♌	16 22:19
18 15:59	☉	⚹	♍	19 1:09
21 0:02	♂	☌	♎	21 4:43
23 8:42	☉	☌	♏	23 10:00
25 3:33	♃	□	♐	25 17:54
27 13:45	♃	⚹	♑	28 4:39
30 1:52	♆	△	♒	30 17:08

☽ Phases & Eclipses

Dy Hr Mn		
1 17:28	☽	8♐36
9 20:08	○	16♓28
17 3:12	☾	23♊34
23 20:34	●	0♎09
1 11:45	☽	7♑38
9 9:37	○	15♈26
16 9:24	☾	22♋21
23 8:42	●	29♎17
31 7:45	☽	7♒14

Astro Data

1 September 1938
Julian Day # 14123
SVP 6♓06'44"
GC 25♐59.0 ⚳ 22♓32.5R
Eris 4♈15.0R ⚵ 2♐35.1
⚷ 8♋25.6 ⚶ 5♐25.0
☽ Mean ☊ 21♏19.2

1 October 1938
Julian Day # 14153
SVP 6♓06'41"
GC 25♐59.0 ⚳ 14♓53.3R
Eris 3♈56.2R ⚵ 9♐18.6
⚷ 9♋47.5 ⚶ 17♐12.2
☽ Mean ☊ 19♏43.8

November 1938 LONGITUDE

Day	Sid.Time	☉	0 hr ☽	Noon ☽	True ☊	☿	♀	♂	?	♃	♄	♅	♆	♇
1 Tu	14 40 28	8♏24 38	15♒19 11	21♒19 49	17♏50.9	21♏52.0	4♐52.4	4♎33.8	23♉56.6	22♒41.3	12♈48.5	16♉06.5	22♍31.4	1♌30.7
2 W	14 44 24	9 24 41	27 23 06	3♓29 36	17R50.2	23 22.1	4R46.8	5 11.6	23R43.9	22 44.1	12R44.5	16R04.1	22 33.0	1R30.7
3 Th	14 48 21	10 24 46	9♓39 49	15 54 10	17 49.3	24 51.8	4 38.7	5 49.4	23 30.9	22 47.1	12 40.6	16 01.6	22 34.7	1 30.7
4 F	14 52 18	11 24 52	22 13 05	28 36 51	17 48.3	26 20.9	4 28.2	6 27.2	23 17.8	22 50.2	12 36.7	15 59.1	22 36.3	1 30.6
5 Sa	14 56 14	12 25 00	5♈05 44	11♈39 54	17 47.6	27 49.6	4 15.2	7 05.0	23 04.6	22 53.5	12 33.0	15 56.6	22 37.9	1 30.6
6 Su	15 00 11	13 25 10	18 19 22	25 04 07	17 47.1	29 17.8	3 59.8	7 42.8	22 51.1	22 57.1	12 29.2	15 54.2	22 39.4	1 30.5
7 M	15 04 07	14 25 22	1♉53 59	8♉48 43	17D46.8	0♐45.4	3 42.1	8 20.6	22 37.6	23 00.8	12 25.6	15 51.7	22 41.0	1 30.4
8 Tu	15 08 04	15 25 35	15 47 57	22 51 14	17 46.8	2 12.5	3 22.0	8 58.4	22 24.0	23 04.7	12 22.0	15 49.2	22 42.5	1 30.2
9 W	15 12 00	16 25 50	29 58 02	7♊07 45	17 46.9	3 39.0	2 59.7	9 36.2	22 10.2	23 08.8	12 18.5	15 46.7	22 44.0	1 30.1
10 Th	15 15 57	17 26 07	14♊19 45	21 33 21	17R47.0	5 04.9	2 35.2	10 13.9	21 56.4	23 13.1	12 15.1	15 44.2	22 45.5	1 29.9
11 F	15 19 53	18 26 26	28 47 53	6♋02 40	17 47.0	6 30.2	2 08.7	10 51.7	21 42.5	23 17.5	12 11.8	15 41.7	22 46.9	1 29.6
12 Sa	15 23 50	19 26 47	13♋17 06	20 30 35	17 46.9	7 54.8	1 40.4	11 29.5	21 28.5	23 22.2	12 08.5	15 39.3	22 48.3	1 29.4
13 Su	15 27 47	20 27 09	27 42 36	4♌52 41	17 46.7	9 18.5	1 10.3	12 07.3	21 14.5	23 27.0	12 05.3	15 36.8	22 49.7	1 29.1
14 M	15 31 43	21 27 34	12♌00 29	19 05 40	17D46.6	10 41.5	0 38.7	12 45.0	21 00.5	23 32.0	12 02.2	15 34.3	22 51.1	1 28.8
15 Tu	15 35 40	22 28 01	26 07 59	3♍07 16	17 46.7	12 03.5	0 05.8	13 22.8	20 46.5	23 37.2	11 59.2	15 31.8	22 52.4	1 28.5
16 W	15 39 36	23 28 29	10♍03 22	16 56 13	17 47.0	13 24.4	29♏31.7	14 00.5	20 32.5	23 42.6	11 56.2	15 29.4	22 53.7	1 28.2
17 Th	15 43 33	24 28 59	23 45 46	0♎31 58	17 47.6	14 44.2	28 56.7	14 38.3	20 18.5	23 48.1	11 53.4	15 26.9	22 55.0	1 27.8
18 F	15 47 29	25 29 31	7♎14 49	13 54 20	17 48.3	16 02.7	28 20.9	15 16.1	20 04.6	23 53.8	11 50.6	15 24.5	22 56.3	1 27.4
19 Sa	15 51 26	26 30 05	20 30 32	27 03 25	17 49.0	17 19.7	27 44.8	15 53.8	19 50.7	23 59.7	11 48.0	15 22.0	22 57.5	1 27.0
20 Su	15 55 22	27 30 41	3♏33 01	9♏59 23	17R49.5	18 35.0	27 08.4	16 31.5	19 36.9	24 05.8	11 45.4	15 19.6	22 58.7	1 26.5
21 M	15 59 19	28 31 18	16 22 31	22 42 30	17 49.6	19 48.5	26 32.1	17 09.3	19 23.3	24 12.0	11 42.9	15 17.2	22 59.8	1 26.0
22 Tu	16 03 16	29 31 56	28 59 22	5♐13 14	17 49.0	20 59.8	25 56.1	17 47.0	19 09.7	24 18.4	11 40.5	15 14.8	23 01.0	1 25.5
23 W	16 07 12	0♐32 36	11♐24 12	17 32 23	17 47.8	22 08.6	25 20.5	18 24.7	18 56.3	24 25.0	11 38.2	15 12.4	23 02.1	1 25.0
24 Th	16 11 09	1 33 18	23 37 58	29 41 09	17 46.0	23 14.7	24 45.8	19 02.4	18 43.0	24 31.7	11 36.0	15 10.1	23 03.1	1 24.5
25 F	16 15 05	2 34 00	5♑42 12	11♑41 22	17 43.6	24 17.5	24 12.1	19 40.1	18 29.8	24 38.6	11 33.9	15 07.7	23 04.2	1 23.9
26 Sa	16 19 02	3 34 44	17 39 00	23 35 27	17 41.2	25 16.8	23 39.5	20 17.8	18 16.9	24 45.7	11 31.9	15 05.4	23 05.2	1 23.3
27 Su	16 22 58	4 35 29	29 31 09	5♒26 32	17 38.8	26 11.9	23 08.4	20 55.5	18 04.1	24 52.9	11 30.0	15 03.1	23 06.2	1 22.7
28 M	16 26 55	5 36 15	11♒22 05	17 18 19	17 37.0	27 02.3	22 38.9	21 33.2	17 51.6	25 00.3	11 28.2	15 00.8	23 07.1	1 22.1
29 Tu	16 30 51	6 37 02	23 15 47	29 15 02	17D36.0	27 47.3	22 11.2	22 10.8	17 39.2	25 07.8	11 26.5	14 58.5	23 08.0	1 21.4
30 W	16 34 48	7 37 50	5♓16 41	11♓21 17	17 35.8	28 26.3	21 45.4	22 48.5	17 27.1	25 15.5	11 24.9	14 56.3	23 08.9	1 20.7

December 1938 LONGITUDE

Day	Sid.Time	☉	0 hr ☽	Noon ☽	True ☊	☿	♀	♂	?	♃	♄	♅	♆	♇
1 Th	16 38 45	8♐38 39	17♓29 28	23♓41 47	17♏36.5	28♐58.5	21♏21.7	23♎26.1	17♉15.3	25♒23.3	11♈23.4	14♉54.1	23♍09.8	1♌20.0
2 F	16 42 41	9 39 28	29 58 47	6♈21 00	17 37.9	29 23.2	21R00.1	24 03.8	17R03.7	25 31.3	11R22.0	14R51.9	23 10.6	1R19.3
3 Sa	16 46 38	10 40 19	12♈48 54	19 22 50	17 39.5	29 39.3	20 40.9	24 41.4	16 52.4	25 39.4	11 20.7	14 49.7	23 11.4	1 18.5
4 Su	16 50 34	11 41 10	26 03 08	2♉49 57	17 40.9	29R46.2	20 23.9	25 19.0	16 41.4	25 47.7	11 19.6	14 47.5	23 12.1	1 17.7
5 M	16 54 31	12 42 03	9♉43 21	16 43 14	17R41.5	29 43.1	20 09.4	25 56.6	16 30.6	25 56.1	11 18.5	14 45.4	23 12.8	1 16.9
6 Tu	16 58 27	13 42 56	23 49 21	1♊01 16	17 41.0	29 29.3	19 57.4	26 34.2	16 20.2	26 04.7	11 17.5	14 43.3	23 13.5	1 16.1
7 W	17 02 24	14 43 50	8♊18 23	15 39 57	17 39.0	29 04.2	19 47.8	27 11.8	16 10.1	26 13.4	11 16.7	14 41.3	23 14.2	1 15.3
8 Th	17 06 20	15 44 46	23 05 03	0♋32 42	17 35.8	28 27.8	19 40.8	27 49.4	16 00.3	26 22.2	11 15.9	14 39.2	23 14.8	1 14.4
9 F	17 10 17	16 45 42	8♋01 46	15 31 09	17 31.7	27 40.2	19 36.2	28 27.0	15 50.8	26 31.2	11 15.3	14 37.2	23 15.4	1 13.6
10 Sa	17 14 14	17 46 39	22 59 44	0♌26 28	17 27.2	26 42.1	19D34.2	29 04.6	15 41.7	26 40.3	11 14.8	14 35.3	23 16.0	1 12.7
11 Su	17 18 10	18 47 38	7♌50 24	15 10 41	17 23.2	25 34.7	19 34.6	29 42.1	15 32.9	26 49.6	11 14.3	14 33.3	23 16.5	1 11.8
12 M	17 22 07	19 48 37	22 26 40	29 37 49	17 20.2	24 19.8	19 37.5	0♏19.7	15 24.4	26 59.0	11 14.0	14 31.4	23 17.0	1 10.8
13 Tu	17 26 03	20 49 38	6♍43 47	13♍44 23	17D18.6	22 59.7	19 42.7	0 57.2	15 16.4	27 08.5	11 13.8	14 29.5	23 17.4	1 09.9
14 W	17 30 00	21 50 40	20 39 32	27 29 19	17 18.5	21 36.9	19 50.3	1 34.8	15 08.6	27 18.1	11D13.7	14 27.7	23 17.8	1 08.9
15 Th	17 33 56	22 51 42	4♎13 52	10♎53 25	17 19.6	20 14.3	20 00.2	2 12.3	15 01.3	27 27.9	11 13.7	14 25.9	23 18.2	1 07.9
16 F	17 37 53	23 52 46	17 28 16	23 58 44	17 21.2	18 54.6	20 12.4	2 49.8	14 54.3	27 37.8	11 13.9	14 24.1	23 18.6	1 06.9
17 Sa	17 41 49	24 53 51	0♏25 07	6♏47 48	17R22.7	17 40.4	20 26.6	3 27.3	14 47.8	27 47.8	11 14.1	14 22.4	23 18.9	1 05.9
18 Su	17 45 46	25 54 56	13 07 04	19 23 15	17 23.2	16 33.9	20 43.0	4 04.8	14 41.6	27 57.9	11 14.4	14 20.7	23 19.2	1 04.8
19 M	17 49 43	26 56 03	25 36 38	1♐47 29	17 22.0	15 36.5	21 01.5	4 42.3	14 35.8	28 08.2	11 14.9	14 19.0	23 19.4	1 03.8
20 Tu	17 53 39	27 57 10	7♐56 00	14 02 26	17 18.8	14 49.3	21 21.9	5 19.8	14 30.4	28 18.5	11 15.5	14 17.4	23 19.6	1 02.7
21 W	17 57 36	28 58 18	20 06 57	26 09 44	17 13.4	14 13.0	21 44.2	5 57.2	14 25.4	28 29.0	11 16.1	14 15.9	23 19.8	1 01.6
22 Th	18 01 32	29 59 26	2♑10 56	8♑10 43	17 06.1	13 47.5	22 08.4	6 34.7	14 20.8	28 39.6	11 16.9	14 14.3	23 20.0	1 00.5
23 F	18 05 29	1♑00 34	14 09 14	20 06 42	16 57.5	13D32.8	22 34.3	7 12.1	14 16.6	28 50.3	11 17.8	14 12.8	23 20.1	0 59.4
24 Sa	18 09 25	2 01 43	26 03 16	1♒59 10	16 48.2	13 28.2	23 02.0	7 49.5	14 12.8	29 01.2	11 18.8	14 11.4	23 20.1	0 58.2
25 Su	18 13 22	3 02 52	7♒54 40	13 50 02	16 39.3	13 33.2	23 31.3	8 26.9	14 09.5	29 12.1	11 19.9	14 10.0	23R20.2	0 57.1
26 M	18 17 18	4 04 02	19 45 36	25 41 44	16 31.4	13 47.1	24 02.1	9 04.3	14 06.5	29 23.1	11 21.2	14 08.6	23 20.2	0 55.9
27 Tu	18 21 15	5 05 11	1♓38 51	7♓37 24	16 25.4	14 08.9	24 34.5	9 41.6	14 04.0	29 34.3	11 22.5	14 07.3	23 20.2	0 54.7
28 W	18 25 12	6 06 20	13 37 53	19 40 49	16 21.6	14 38.1	25 08.4	10 19.0	14 01.8	29 45.5	11 23.9	14 06.0	23 20.1	0 53.6
29 Th	18 29 08	7 07 29	25 46 46	1♈56 19	16D19.9	15 13.8	25 43.7	10 56.3	14 00.1	29 56.9	11 25.5	14 04.8	23 20.0	0 52.4
30 F	18 33 05	8 08 39	8♈10 05	14 28 39	16 20.0	15 55.4	26 20.3	11 33.6	13 58.8	0♓08.3	11 27.1	14 03.6	23 19.9	0 51.1
31 Sa	18 37 01	9 09 48	20 52 37	27 22 32	16 20.9	16 42.2	26 58.3	12 10.9	13 57.9	0 19.9	11 28.9	14 02.5	23 19.7	0 49.9

Astro Data Dy Hr Mn	Planet Ingress Dy Hr Mn	Last Aspect Dy Hr Mn	☽ Ingress Dy Hr Mn	Last Aspect Dy Hr Mn	☽ Ingress Dy Hr Mn	☽ Phases & Eclipses Dy Hr Mn	Astro Data
♇R 2 12:20	☿ ♐ 6 23:33	1 14:43 ♃ ☌	♓ 2 5:09	1 22:28 ☿ □	♈ 2 0:02	7 22:23 ○ 14♉51	1 November 1938
☽0N 3 18:57	♀ ♏R 15 16:07	4 7:13 ☿ △	♈ 4 14:35	4 6:35 ☿ △	♉ 4 7:01	7 22:26 ☊ T 1.352	Julian Day # 14184
☽0S 16 16:35	☉ ♐ 22 23:06	6 8:14 ♃ ⚹	♉ 6 20:41	6 3:42 ♃ □	♊ 6 10:18	14 16:20 ☾ 21♌38	SVP 6♓06'38"
		8 12:23 ♃ □	♊ 9 0:03	8 8:48 ☿ ☍	♋ 8 11:08	22 0:05 ● 29♏02	GC 25♐59.1 ⚳ 10♓15.5R
☽0N 1 4:10	♂ ♏ 11 23:25	10 14:46 ♃ △	♋ 11 1:59	10 9:42 ♂ □	♌ 10 11:17	21 23:52:02 ● P 0.778	Eris 3♈37.5R ⚵ 18♐33.8
☿R 4 16:46	☉ ♑ 22 12:13	12 15:50 ♆ ⚹	♌ 13 3:50	12 7:31 ♃ ☍	♍ 12 12:37	30 3:59 ☽ 7♓18	⚷ 9♋56.6R ⚶ 1♑19.0
♃∠♄ 7 20:13	♃ ♓ 29 18:34	14 19:36 ♃ ☍	♍ 15 6:38	14 4:37 ♆ ☌	♎ 14 16:27		☽ Mean ☊ 18♏05.3
♀D 10 19:52		17 9:18 ♀ ⚹	♎ 17 11:03	16 18:53 ♃ △	♏ 16 23:13	7 10:22 ○ 14♊40	1 December 1938
☽0S 13 22:29		19 6:20 ♃ △	♏ 19 17:26	19 4:48 ♃ □	♐ 19 8:31	14 1:17 ☾ 21♍23	Julian Day # 14214
♄D 14 21:34		22 0:05 ☉ ☌	♐ 22 1:56	21 18:07 ☉ ☌	♑ 21 19:39	21 18:07 ● 29♐14	SVP 6♓06'34"
☿D 24 11:09		24 1:41 ♃ ⚹	♑ 24 12:37	23 18:30 ♆ △	♒ 24 7:59	29 22:53 ☽ 7♈35	GC 25♐59.2 ⚳ 11♓20.1
♆R 26 2:27		26 12:08 ♀ ⚹	♒ 27 0:58	26 19:34 ♃ ☌	♓ 26 20:41		Eris 3♈25.6R ⚵ 28♐55.3
☽0N 28 12:49		29 8:54 ☿ ⚹	♓ 29 13:30	28 23:17 ♀ △	♈ 29 8:14		⚷ 8♋50.9R ⚶ 16♑02.4
				30 14:54 ☿ △	♉ 31 16:48		☽ Mean ☊ 16♏30.0

LONGITUDE — January 1939

Day	Sid.Time	☉	0 hr ☽	Noon ☽	True ☊	☿	♀	♂	⚳	♃	♄	♅	♆	♇
1 Su	18 40 58	10♑10 56	3♉58 53	10♉42 07	16♏21.9	17♐33.6	27♏37.5	12♏48.2	13♉57.4	0♓31.5	11♈30.8	14♉01.4	23♍19.5	0♌48.7
2 M	18 44 54	11 12 05	17 32 33	24 30 20	16R21.7	18 29.2	28 17.9	13 25.4	13D57.3	0 43.2	11 32.8	14R00.4	23R19.2	0R47.4
3 Tu	18 48 51	12 13 14	1♊35 29	8♊47 49	16 19.6	19 28.5	28 59.5	14 02.6	13 57.6	0 55.1	11 34.8	13 59.4	23 19.0	0 46.2
4 W	18 52 47	13 14 22	16 06 57	23 32 14	16 15.0	20 31.0	29 42.2	14 39.9	13 58.3	1 07.0	11 37.0	13 58.4	23 18.7	0 44.9
5 Th	18 56 44	14 15 31	1♋02 49	8♋37 38	16 08.0	21 36.4	0♐26.0	15 17.1	13 59.5	1 19.0	11 39.3	13 57.5	23 18.3	0 43.7
6 F	19 00 41	15 16 39	16 15 25	23 54 49	15 59.1	22 44.4	1 10.9	15 54.3	14 01.0	1 31.1	11 41.7	13 56.7	23 18.0	0 42.4
7 Sa	19 04 37	16 17 47	1♌34 21	9♌12 35	15 49.6	23 54.7	1 56.7	16 31.4	14 02.9	1 43.2	11 44.2	13 55.9	23 17.6	0 41.1
8 Su	19 08 34	17 18 55	16 48 08	24 19 43	15 40.4	25 07.1	2 43.5	17 08.6	14 05.2	1 55.5	11 46.8	13 55.1	23 17.1	0 39.8
9 M	19 12 30	18 20 03	1♍46 18	9♍06 59	15 32.9	26 21.3	3 31.3	17 45.7	14 07.8	2 07.8	11 49.5	13 54.4	23 16.7	0 38.5
10 Tu	19 16 27	19 21 11	16 21 11	23 28 28	15 27.6	27 37.2	4 19.9	18 22.8	14 10.9	2 20.2	11 52.3	13 53.8	23 16.2	0 37.2
11 W	19 20 23	20 22 19	0♎28 40	7♎21 47	15 24.8	28 54.6	5 09.4	18 59.9	14 14.3	2 32.7	11 55.2	13 53.2	23 15.6	0 35.9
12 Th	19 24 20	21 23 26	14 08 01	20 47 40	15D24.0	0♑13.4	5 59.7	19 37.0	14 18.1	2 45.3	11 58.2	13 52.6	23 15.1	0 34.5
13 F	19 28 16	22 24 34	27 21 08	3♏48 54	15R24.3	1 33.4	6 50.8	20 14.1	14 22.3	2 57.9	12 01.3	13 52.1	23 14.5	0 33.2
14 Sa	19 32 13	23 25 42	10♏11 30	16 29 28	15 24.6	2 54.6	7 42.6	20 51.1	14 26.9	3 10.7	12 04.5	13 51.7	23 13.8	0 31.9
15 Su	19 36 10	24 26 50	22 43 21	28 53 41	15 23.7	4 16.9	8 35.2	21 28.1	14 31.8	3 23.5	12 07.8	13 51.3	23 13.2	0 30.6
16 M	19 40 06	25 27 57	5♐00 58	11♐05 40	15 20.7	5 40.1	9 28.4	22 05.1	14 37.1	3 36.3	12 11.2	13 51.0	23 12.5	0 29.2
17 Tu	19 44 03	26 29 05	17 08 14	23 09 02	15 14.7	7 04.3	10 22.3	22 42.1	14 42.8	3 49.3	12 14.7	13 50.7	23 11.8	0 27.9
18 W	19 47 59	27 30 12	29 08 26	5♑06 42	15 05.7	8 29.4	11 16.9	23 19.0	14 48.8	4 02.3	12 18.3	13 50.4	23 11.0	0 26.5
19 Th	19 51 56	28 31 18	11♑04 07	17 00 53	14 54.0	9 55.2	12 12.1	23 55.9	14 55.2	4 15.3	12 21.9	13 50.3	23 10.2	0 25.2
20 F	19 55 52	29 32 24	22 57 13	28 53 17	14 40.3	11 21.9	13 07.8	24 32.8	15 01.9	4 28.5	12 25.7	13 50.1	23 09.4	0 23.8
21 Sa	19 59 49	0♒33 29	4♒49 14	10♒45 13	14 25.5	12 49.3	14 04.1	25 09.6	15 08.9	4 41.7	12 29.6	13 50.0	23 08.6	0 22.5
22 Su	20 03 46	1 34 33	16 41 24	22 37 57	14 11.1	14 17.4	15 01.0	25 46.5	15 16.3	4 54.9	12 33.5	13D50.0	23 07.7	0 21.2
23 M	20 07 42	2 35 37	28 35 03	4♓32 55	13 58.0	15 46.3	15 58.4	26 23.3	15 24.1	5 08.3	12 37.6	13 50.0	23 06.8	0 19.8
24 Tu	20 11 39	3 36 39	10♓31 50	16 32 03	13 47.3	17 15.8	16 56.3	27 00.0	15 32.2	5 21.6	12 41.7	13 50.1	23 05.9	0 18.5
25 W	20 15 35	4 37 41	22 33 56	28 37 52	13 39.6	18 46.0	17 54.6	27 36.7	15 40.6	5 35.1	12 45.9	13 50.3	23 04.9	0 17.1
26 Th	20 19 32	5 38 41	4♈44 16	10♈53 37	13 34.9	20 16.9	18 53.5	28 13.4	15 49.3	5 48.6	12 50.2	13 50.4	23 03.9	0 15.8
27 F	20 23 28	6 39 41	17 06 25	23 23 13	13 32.7	21 48.5	19 52.7	28 50.1	15 58.3	6 02.1	12 54.6	13 50.7	23 02.9	0 14.4
28 Sa	20 27 25	7 40 39	29 44 33	6♉11 00	13 32.2	23 20.7	20 52.4	29 26.7	16 07.7	6 15.7	12 59.1	13 51.0	23 01.9	0 13.1
29 Su	20 31 21	8 41 36	12♉43 06	19 21 23	13 32.2	24 53.6	21 52.6	0♐03.3	16 17.4	6 29.3	13 03.6	13 51.3	23 00.8	0 11.8
30 M	20 35 18	9 42 32	26 06 16	2♊58 07	13 31.3	26 27.2	22 53.1	0 39.9	16 27.4	6 43.0	13 08.3	13 51.7	22 59.7	0 10.5
31 Tu	20 39 14	10 43 27	9♊57 10	17 03 29	13 28.4	28 01.4	23 54.0	1 16.4	16 37.6	6 56.8	13 13.0	13 52.2	22 58.6	0 09.1

LONGITUDE — February 1939

Day	Sid.Time	☉	0 hr ☽	Noon ☽	True ☊	☿	♀	♂	⚳	♃	♄	♅	♆	♇
1 W	20 43 11	11♒44 21	24♊16 57	1♋37 14	13♏22.8	29♑36.4	24♐55.3	1♐52.9	16♉48.2	7♓10.5	13♈17.8	13♉52.7	22♍57.5	0♌07.8
2 Th	20 47 08	12 45 13	9♋03 45	16 35 40	13R14.4	1♒12.0	25 57.0	2 29.4	16 59.1	7 24.4	13 22.7	13 53.2	22R56.3	0R06.5
3 F	20 51 04	13 46 04	24 11 57	1♌51 20	13 03.9	2 48.3	26 59.0	3 05.8	17 10.2	7 38.2	13 27.7	13 53.8	22 55.1	0 05.2
4 Sa	20 55 01	14 46 53	9♌32 24	17 13 37	12 52.2	4 25.4	28 01.3	3 42.2	17 21.7	7 52.2	13 32.7	13 54.5	22 53.9	0 03.9
5 Su	20 58 57	15 47 42	24 53 29	2♍30 30	12 40.8	6 03.2	29 04.0	4 18.6	17 33.4	8 06.1	13 37.8	13 55.2	22 52.7	0 02.6
6 M	21 02 54	16 48 29	10♍03 21	17 30 51	12 31.0	7 41.8	0♑07.0	4 54.9	17 45.3	8 20.1	13 43.0	13 56.0	22 51.4	0 01.3
7 Tu	21 06 50	17 49 15	24 52 04	2♎06 18	12 23.8	9 21.1	1 10.3	5 31.2	17 57.6	8 34.1	13 48.3	13 56.8	22 50.2	0 00.1
8 W	21 10 47	18 50 00	9♎13 06	16 12 17	12 19.3	11 01.2	2 14.0	6 07.5	18 10.1	8 48.2	13 53.6	13 57.6	22 48.9	29♋58.8
9 Th	21 14 43	19 50 45	23 03 49	29 47 54	12D17.4	12 42.1	3 17.9	6 43.7	18 22.9	9 02.3	13 59.0	13 58.6	22 47.5	29 57.5
10 F	21 18 40	20 51 28	6♏24 53	12♏55 12	12R17.0	14 23.9	4 22.0	7 19.9	18 35.9	9 16.4	14 04.5	13 59.5	22 46.2	29 56.3
11 Sa	21 22 37	21 52 10	19 19 23	25 38 02	12 17.0	16 06.4	5 26.5	7 56.0	18 49.2	9 30.5	14 10.0	14 00.5	22 44.8	29 55.0
12 Su	21 26 33	22 52 52	1♐51 47	8♐01 15	12 16.1	17 49.8	6 31.2	8 32.1	19 02.7	9 44.7	14 15.7	14 01.6	22 43.5	29 53.8
13 M	21 30 30	23 53 32	14 07 04	20 09 51	12 13.4	19 34.1	7 36.2	9 08.2	19 16.5	9 59.0	14 21.3	14 02.7	22 42.1	29 52.6
14 Tu	21 34 26	24 54 11	26 10 11	2♑08 36	12 08.0	21 19.2	8 41.4	9 44.2	19 30.5	10 13.2	14 27.1	14 03.9	22 40.7	29 51.4
15 W	21 38 23	25 54 48	8♑05 36	14 01 38	11 59.6	23 05.1	9 46.8	10 20.2	19 44.8	10 27.5	14 32.9	14 05.1	22 39.2	29 50.2
16 Th	21 42 19	26 55 25	19 57 06	25 52 22	11 48.5	24 51.9	10 52.5	10 56.1	19 59.3	10 41.8	14 38.8	14 06.4	22 37.8	29 49.0
17 F	21 46 16	27 56 00	1♒47 44	7♒43 28	11 35.4	26 39.6	11 58.3	11 31.9	20 14.0	10 56.1	14 44.7	14 07.7	22 36.3	29 47.8
18 Sa	21 50 12	28 56 33	13 39 46	19 36 51	11 21.3	28 28.2	13 04.4	12 07.7	20 28.9	11 10.5	14 50.7	14 09.1	22 34.8	29 46.7
19 Su	21 54 09	29 57 05	25 34 53	1♓33 59	11 07.4	0♓17.6	14 10.7	12 43.5	20 44.1	11 24.8	14 56.8	14 10.5	22 33.3	29 45.5
20 M	21 58 06	0♓57 36	7♓34 18	13 35 59	10 54.8	2 07.8	15 17.1	13 19.2	20 59.5	11 39.2	15 02.9	14 11.9	22 31.8	29 44.4
21 Tu	22 02 02	1 58 04	19 39 09	25 43 59	10 44.5	3 58.8	16 23.8	13 54.9	21 15.1	11 53.6	15 09.1	14 13.4	22 30.3	29 43.3
22 W	22 05 59	2 58 31	1♈50 39	7♈59 23	10 37.0	5 50.5	17 30.6	14 30.5	21 30.9	12 08.1	15 15.3	14 15.0	22 28.7	29 42.2
23 Th	22 09 55	3 58 57	14 10 25	20 24 03	10 32.4	7 42.9	18 37.6	15 06.0	21 47.0	12 22.5	15 21.6	14 16.6	22 27.2	29 41.1
24 F	22 13 52	4 59 20	26 40 35	3♉00 25	10D30.4	9 35.9	19 44.7	15 41.5	22 03.2	12 36.9	15 28.0	14 18.3	22 25.6	29 40.0
25 Sa	22 17 48	5 59 42	9♉23 54	15 51 28	10 30.3	11 29.4	20 52.0	16 16.9	22 19.6	12 51.4	15 34.4	14 20.0	22 24.0	29 39.0
26 Su	22 21 45	7 00 01	22 23 31	29 00 28	10R30.9	13 23.3	21 59.5	16 52.2	22 36.3	13 05.9	15 40.8	14 21.7	22 22.4	29 38.0
27 M	22 25 41	8 00 19	5♊42 42	12♊30 32	10 31.0	15 17.5	23 07.1	17 27.5	22 53.1	13 20.4	15 47.3	14 23.5	22 20.8	29 36.9
28 Tu	22 29 38	9 00 34	19 24 15	26 24 00	10 29.6	17 11.8	24 14.9	18 02.8	23 10.1	13 34.9	15 53.9	14 25.3	22 19.2	29 35.9

Astro Data

	Dy Hr Mn
⚳ D	2 5:16
♃⊼♇	2 19:44
☽ 0S	10 6:41
♅ D	22 12:05
☽ 0N	24 20:17
☽ 0S	6 17:28
♄⊻♅	9 9:33
☽ 0N	21 2:51

Planet Ingress

	Dy Hr Mn
♀ ♐	4 21:48
☿ ♑	12 7:57
☉ ♒	20 22:51
♂ ♐	29 9:49
☿ ♒	1 17:57
♀ ♑	6 9:20
♇ ♋R	7 13:00
☿ ♓	19 8:09
☉ ♓	19 13:09

Last Aspect / ☽ Ingress (January)

Last Aspect Dy Hr Mn		☽ Ingress Dy Hr Mn
2 18:47	♀ ☍	♊ 2 21:19
4 11:38	♆ □	♋ 4 22:20
6 11:02	♆ ✶	♌ 6 21:32
8 13:23	☿ △	♍ 8 21:08
10 19:48	☿ □	♎ 10 23:11
12 13:11	☉ □	♏ 13 4:54
15 2:34	☉ ✶	♐ 15 14:10
17 12:05	♆ □	♑ 18 1:44
20 13:27	☉ ☌	♒ 20 14:15
22 18:41	♂ □	♓ 23 2:51
25 9:53	♂ △	♈ 25 14:42
27 8:35	☿ □	♉ 28 0:29
29 23:08	☿ △	♊ 30 6:50

Last Aspect / ☽ Ingress (February)

Last Aspect Dy Hr Mn		☽ Ingress Dy Hr Mn
1 0:14	♀ ☍	♋ 1 9:22
2 22:00	♆ ✶	♌ 3 9:06
5 6:10	♀ △	♍ 5 8:02
6 20:41	♆ ☌	♎ 7 8:29
9 12:17	♇ □	♏ 9 12:22
11 20:13	♇ △	♐ 11 20:24
13 20:07	☉ ✶	♑ 14 7:41
16 19:59	♇ ☍	♒ 16 20:22
19 8:28	☉ ☌	♓ 19 8:52
21 19:50	♇ △	♈ 21 20:23
24 5:42	♇ □	♉ 24 6:19
26 13:07	♇ ✶	♊ 26 13:47
28 5:02	♆ □	♋ 28 18:07

☽ Phases & Eclipses

Dy Hr Mn	
5 21:30	○ 14♋40
12 13:11	☾ 21♎26
20 13:27	● 29♑36
28 15:00	☽ 7♉48
4 7:55	○ 14♌37
11 4:12	☾ 21♏32
19 8:28	● 29♒48
27 3:26	☽ 7♊39

Astro Data

1 January 1939
Julian Day # 14245
SVP 6♓06'29"
GC 25♐59.2 ⚵ 17♓10.5
Eris 3♈23.5 ✱ 10♑27.5
⚷ 6♋53.9R ⚶ 1♒48.6
☽ Mean ☊ 14♏51.5

1 February 1939
Julian Day # 14276
SVP 6♓06'24"
GC 25♐59.3 ⚵ 26♓13.4
Eris 3♈32.8 ✱ 22♑19.7
⚷ 5♋01.5R ⚶ 17♒44.0
☽ Mean ☊ 13♏13.0

March 1939 — LONGITUDE

Day	Sid.Time	☉	0 hr ☽	Noon ☽	True ☊	☿	♀	♂	⚳	♃	♄	♅	♆	♇
1 W	22 33 35	10♓00 48	3♋29 48	10♋41 30	10♏26.0	19♓05.9	25♑22.8	18♐37.9	23♉27.3	13♓49.4	16♈00.5	14♉27.2	22♍17.6	29♋35.0
2 Th	22 37 31	11 00 59	17 58 49	25 21 13	10R 20.1	20 59.7	26 30.8	19 13.1	23 44.7	14 03.9	16 07.1	14 29.1	22R 16.0	29R 34.0
3 F	22 41 28	12 01 09	2♌47 59	10♌18 14	10 12.2	22 52.8	27 39.0	19 48.1	24 02.3	14 18.4	16 13.8	14 31.1	22 14.4	29 33.0
4 Sa	22 45 24	13 01 16	17 50 53	25 24 44	10 03.3	24 45.0	28 47.3	20 23.1	24 20.0	14 32.9	16 20.6	14 33.1	22 12.7	29 32.1
5 Su	22 49 21	14 01 21	2♍58 30	10♍30 53	9 54.4	26 35.9	29 55.8	20 58.0	24 38.0	14 47.4	16 27.4	14 35.1	22 11.1	29 31.2
6 M	22 53 17	15 01 24	18 00 36	25 26 30	9 46.8	28 25.1	1♒04.4	21 32.9	24 56.0	15 01.9	16 34.2	14 37.2	22 09.5	29 30.3
7 Tu	22 57 14	16 01 26	2♎47 32	10♎02 50	9 41.1	0♈12.3	2 13.0	22 07.7	25 14.3	15 16.4	16 41.0	14 39.4	22 07.8	29 29.4
8 W	23 01 10	17 01 26	17 11 47	24 13 54	9 37.8	1 56.8	3 21.9	22 42.4	25 32.7	15 30.9	16 47.9	14 41.5	22 06.1	29 28.6
9 Th	23 05 07	18 01 24	1♏08 58	7♏56 54	9D 36.7	3 38.2	4 30.8	23 17.0	25 51.3	15 45.4	16 54.9	14 43.7	22 04.5	29 27.8
10 F	23 09 04	19 01 21	14 37 50	21 12 02	9 37.1	5 16.1	5 39.8	23 51.6	26 10.0	15 59.9	17 01.9	14 46.0	22 02.8	29 27.0
11 Sa	23 13 00	20 01 16	27 39 51	4♐01 46	9 38.3	6 49.9	6 49.0	24 26.1	26 28.9	16 14.4	17 08.9	14 48.3	22 01.2	29 26.2
12 Su	23 16 57	21 01 09	10♐18 19	16 30 06	9R 39.3	8 19.1	7 58.3	25 00.5	26 47.9	16 28.9	17 15.9	14 50.6	21 59.5	29 25.4
13 M	23 20 53	22 01 01	22 37 44	28 41 49	9 39.1	9 43.1	9 07.6	25 34.9	27 07.1	16 43.4	17 23.0	14 53.0	21 57.8	29 24.7
14 Tu	23 24 50	23 00 51	4♑43 00	10♑41 54	9 37.3	11 01.5	10 17.1	26 09.1	27 26.5	16 57.9	17 30.2	14 55.4	21 56.2	29 23.9
15 W	23 28 46	24 00 39	16 39 05	22 35 09	9 33.4	12 13.8	11 26.7	26 43.3	27 46.0	17 12.4	17 37.3	14 57.8	21 54.5	29 23.2
16 Th	23 32 43	25 00 25	28 30 36	4♒25 56	9 27.6	13 19.5	12 36.3	27 17.4	28 05.6	17 26.8	17 44.5	15 00.3	21 52.8	29 22.5
17 F	23 36 39	26 00 10	10♒21 36	16 17 59	9 20.3	14 18.3	13 46.1	27 51.4	28 25.4	17 41.3	17 51.7	15 02.8	21 51.2	29 21.9
18 Sa	23 40 36	26 59 53	22 15 28	28 14 19	9 12.1	15 09.9	14 55.9	28 25.3	28 45.3	17 55.7	17 59.0	15 05.3	21 49.5	29 21.3
19 Su	23 44 33	27 59 33	4♓14 50	10♓17 13	9 04.0	15 53.9	16 05.8	28 59.1	29 05.4	18 10.1	18 06.2	15 07.9	21 47.8	29 20.6
20 M	23 48 29	28 59 12	16 21 40	22 28 20	8 56.7	16 30.1	17 15.8	29 32.8	29 25.6	18 24.5	18 13.5	15 10.5	21 46.2	29 20.0
21 Tu	23 52 26	29 58 49	28 37 19	4♈48 46	8 50.8	16 58.4	18 25.9	0♑06.4	29 45.9	18 38.9	18 20.9	15 13.2	21 44.5	29 19.5
22 W	23 56 22	0♈58 24	11♈02 45	17 19 22	8 46.7	17 18.7	19 36.0	0 39.9	0♊06.3	18 53.3	18 28.2	15 15.9	21 42.9	29 18.9
23 Th	0 00 19	1 57 57	23 38 43	0♉00 52	8D 44.7	17 30.9	20 46.2	1 13.3	0 26.9	19 07.6	18 35.6	15 18.6	21 41.2	29 18.4
24 F	0 04 15	2 57 28	6♉25 58	12 54 06	8 44.4	17R 35.3	21 56.5	1 46.6	0 47.6	19 21.9	18 43.0	15 21.3	21 39.6	29 17.9
25 Sa	0 08 12	3 56 56	19 25 26	26 00 06	8 45.4	17 31.8	23 06.8	2 19.8	1 08.4	19 36.2	18 50.4	15 24.1	21 38.0	29 17.5
26 Su	0 12 08	4 56 22	2♊38 17	9♊20 07	8 46.9	17 20.9	24 17.2	2 52.8	1 29.4	19 50.5	18 57.8	15 26.9	21 36.4	29 17.0
27 M	0 16 05	5 55 46	16 05 46	22 55 20	8 48.3	17 02.9	25 27.7	3 25.8	1 50.5	20 04.7	19 05.3	15 29.7	21 34.7	29 16.6
28 Tu	0 20 01	6 55 08	29 48 57	6♋46 38	8R 48.9	16 38.4	26 38.2	3 58.6	2 11.7	20 19.0	19 12.7	15 32.6	21 33.1	29 16.2
29 W	0 23 58	7 54 27	13♋48 21	20 54 00	8 48.3	16 07.8	27 48.8	4 31.3	2 32.9	20 33.2	19 20.2	15 35.5	21 31.6	29 15.8
30 Th	0 27 55	8 53 44	28 03 20	5♌16 04	8 46.2	15 32.0	28 59.4	5 03.9	2 54.4	20 47.3	19 27.7	15 38.4	21 30.0	29 15.5
31 F	0 31 51	9 52 59	12♌31 42	19 49 43	8 43.0	14 51.7	0♓10.1	5 36.4	3 15.9	21 01.4	19 35.2	15 41.4	21 28.4	29 15.2

April 1939 — LONGITUDE

Day	Sid.Time	☉	0 hr ☽	Noon ☽	True ☊	☿	♀	♂	⚳	♃	♄	♅	♆	♇
1 Sa	0 35 48	10♈52 11	27♌09 24	4♍30 01	8♏39.2	14♈07.8	1♓20.8	6♑08.8	3♊37.5	21♓15.5	19♈42.8	15♉44.4	21♍26.9	29♋14.9
2 Su	0 39 44	11 51 21	11♍50 43	19 10 36	8R 35.2	13R 21.2	2 31.6	6 41.0	3 59.2	21 29.6	19 50.3	15 47.3	21R 25.3	29R 14.6
3 M	0 43 41	12 50 28	26 28 48	3♎44 25	8 31.8	12 33.0	3 42.5	7 13.1	4 21.0	21 43.6	19 57.8	15 50.4	21 23.8	29 14.3
4 Tu	0 47 37	13 49 34	10♎56 40	18 04 48	8 29.5	11 44.2	4 53.4	7 45.1	4 43.0	21 57.6	20 05.4	15 53.4	21 22.2	29 14.1
5 W	0 51 34	14 48 37	25 08 12	2♏06 23	8D 28.3	10 55.6	6 04.4	8 16.9	5 05.0	22 11.6	20 12.9	15 56.5	21 20.7	29 13.9
6 Th	0 55 30	15 47 39	8♏58 58	15 45 45	8 28.3	10 08.2	7 15.4	8 48.7	5 27.1	22 25.5	20 20.5	15 59.6	21 19.3	29 13.8
7 F	0 59 27	16 46 39	22 26 38	29 01 39	8 29.3	9 22.8	8 26.5	9 20.2	5 49.3	22 39.4	20 28.1	16 02.7	21 17.8	29 13.6
8 Sa	1 03 24	17 45 37	5♐30 58	11♐54 49	8 30.7	8 40.3	9 37.6	9 51.7	6 11.6	22 53.2	20 35.7	16 05.8	21 16.3	29 13.5
9 Su	1 07 20	18 44 33	18 13 35	24 27 39	8 32.3	8 01.2	10 48.7	10 22.9	6 34.0	23 07.0	20 43.3	16 09.0	21 14.9	29 13.4
10 M	1 11 17	19 43 28	0♑37 31	6♑43 41	8 33.4	7 26.2	11 59.9	10 54.1	6 56.5	23 20.8	20 50.8	16 12.2	21 13.4	29 13.3
11 Tu	1 15 13	20 42 21	12 46 44	18 47 13	8R 34.0	6 55.5	13 11.2	11 25.0	7 19.1	23 34.5	20 58.4	16 15.4	21 12.0	29 13.3
12 W	1 19 10	21 41 11	24 45 44	0♒42 52	8 33.7	6 29.7	14 22.5	11 55.8	7 41.8	23 48.2	21 06.0	16 18.6	21 10.6	29D 13.3
13 Th	1 23 06	22 40 01	6♒39 13	12 35 20	8 32.7	6 08.9	15 33.8	12 26.5	8 04.6	24 01.8	21 13.6	16 21.8	21 09.3	29 13.3
14 F	1 27 03	23 38 48	18 31 47	24 29 05	8 31.1	5 53.3	16 45.2	12 56.9	8 27.4	24 15.4	21 21.2	16 25.1	21 07.9	29 13.3
15 Sa	1 30 59	24 37 34	0♓27 43	6♓28 08	8 29.1	5 43.0	17 56.6	13 27.2	8 50.3	24 28.9	21 28.8	16 28.4	21 06.6	29 13.4
16 Su	1 34 56	25 36 17	12 30 46	18 35 58	8 27.1	5D 37.9	19 08.1	13 57.3	9 13.4	24 42.4	21 36.4	16 31.7	21 05.2	29 13.5
17 M	1 38 53	26 34 59	24 44 03	0♈55 17	8 25.4	5 38.0	20 19.6	14 27.2	9 36.5	24 55.8	21 43.9	16 35.0	21 03.9	29 13.6
18 Tu	1 42 49	27 33 40	7♈09 54	13 28 02	8 24.0	5 43.2	21 31.1	14 56.9	9 59.6	25 09.2	21 51.5	16 38.3	21 02.7	29 13.7
19 W	1 46 46	28 32 18	19 49 48	26 15 17	8D 23.3	5 53.5	22 42.7	15 26.4	10 22.9	25 22.5	21 59.1	16 41.6	21 01.4	29 13.9
20 Th	1 50 42	29 30 54	2♉44 27	9♉17 19	8 23.1	6 08.6	23 54.3	15 55.7	10 46.2	25 35.8	22 06.6	16 45.0	21 00.2	29 14.1
21 F	1 54 39	0♉29 29	15 53 48	22 33 47	8 23.3	6 28.4	25 05.9	16 24.9	11 09.6	25 49.0	22 14.2	16 48.3	20 59.0	29 14.3
22 Sa	1 58 35	1 28 01	29 17 09	6♊03 44	8 23.8	6 52.8	26 17.5	16 53.7	11 33.1	26 02.1	22 21.7	16 51.7	20 57.8	29 14.5
23 Su	2 02 32	2 26 32	12♊53 23	19 45 55	8 24.4	7 21.5	27 29.2	17 22.4	11 56.7	26 15.2	22 29.2	16 55.1	20 56.6	29 14.8
24 M	2 06 28	3 25 00	26 41 06	3♋38 46	8 24.9	7 54.3	28 40.9	17 50.9	12 20.3	26 28.3	22 36.8	16 58.5	20 55.5	29 15.1
25 Tu	2 10 25	4 23 26	10♋38 42	17 40 38	8 25.3	8 31.2	29 52.6	18 19.1	12 44.0	26 41.2	22 44.2	17 01.9	20 54.3	29 15.4
26 W	2 14 22	5 21 50	24 44 22	1♌49 37	8R 25.4	9 11.9	1♈04.4	18 47.1	13 07.8	26 54.1	22 51.7	17 05.3	20 53.3	29 15.8
27 Th	2 18 18	6 20 12	8♌56 07	16 03 34	8 25.4	9 56.2	2 16.1	19 14.9	13 31.6	27 06.9	22 59.2	17 08.7	20 52.2	29 16.1
28 F	2 22 15	7 18 32	23 11 38	0♍19 59	8 25.3	10 44.1	3 27.9	19 42.4	13 55.5	27 19.7	23 06.6	17 12.2	20 51.1	29 16.5
29 Sa	2 26 11	8 16 49	7♍28 14	14 35 57	8D 25.2	11 35.3	4 39.7	20 09.7	14 19.5	27 32.4	23 14.1	17 15.6	20 50.1	29 16.9
30 Su	2 30 08	9 15 05	21 42 45	28 48 10	8 25.3	12 29.7	5 51.6	20 36.7	14 43.5	27 45.0	23 21.5	17 19.0	20 49.1	29 17.4

Astro Data	Dy Hr Mn
♃⚼♇	4 10:49
♃⚹♅	4 12:25
☽0S	6 5:02
☿0N	7 6:49
♃⚺♄	18 22:56
☽0N	20 9:23
☉0N	21 12:28
☿R	24 13:17
♃☍♆	2 5:23
☽0S	2 15:06
♇D	12 15:17
♄⚻♆	13 0:21
☽0N	16 16:42
☿D	16 23:27
♀0N	28 16:24

Planet Ingress		Dy Hr Mn
♀	♒	5 13:29
☿	♈	7 9:14
♂	♑	21 7:25
☉	♈	21 12:28
⚳	♊	22 4:35
♀	♓	31 8:34
☉	♉	20 23:55
♀	♈	25 14:28

☽0S29 22:44

Last Aspect Dy Hr Mn			☽ Ingress	Dy Hr Mn
2 18:48	♇	☌	♌	2 19:30
4 3:42	♂	△	♍	4 19:17
6 18:37	♇	⚹	♎	6 19:25
8 21:04	♇	□	♏	8 22:00
11 3:20	♇	△	♐	11 4:23
13 5:31	♂	☌	♑	13 14:35
16 1:46	♇	☍	♒	16 3:01
18 12:23	♂	⚹	♓	18 15:31
21 2:27	♂	□	♈	21 2:41
23 10:40	♇	□	♉	23 11:58
25 17:57	♇	⚹	♊	25 19:15
27 16:51	♀	△	♋	28 0:19
30 2:01	♇	☌	♌	30 3:15

Last Aspect Dy Hr Mn			☽ Ingress	Dy Hr Mn
31 11:36	♄	△	♍	1 4:39
3 4:33	♇	⚹	♎	3 5:48
5 7:02	♇	□	♏	5 8:21
7 12:22	♇	△	♐	7 13:47
9 9:21	♃	□	♑	9 22:47
12 8:59	♇	☍	♒	12 10:33
14 10:10	☉	⚹	♓	14 23:04
17 8:43	♇	△	♈	17 10:13
19 17:31	♇	□	♉	19 18:57
21 23:55	♇	⚹	♊	22 1:16
24 2:39	♀	□	♋	24 5:43
26 7:40	♇	☌	♌	26 8:55
27 23:45	♄	△	♍	28 11:26
30 12:50	♇	⚹	♎	30 14:02

☽ Phases & Eclipses Dy Hr Mn		
5 18:00	○	14♍16
12 21:37	☾	21♐25
21 1:49	●	29♓34
28 12:16	☽	6♋56
4 4:18	○	13♎31
11 16:11	☾	20♑53
19 16:35	●	28♈43
19 16:45:28	●	A 01'49"
26 18:25	☽	5♌37

Astro Data

1 March 1939
Julian Day # 14304
SVP 6♓06'21"
GC 25♐59.4 ⚴ 6♈11.3
Eris 3♈48.9 ⚵ 2♒56.0
⚷ 4♋08.4R ⚶ 1♓57.6
☽ Mean ☊ 11♏44.1

1 April 1939
Julian Day # 14335
SVP 6♓06'18"
GC 25♐59.4 ⚴ 18♈33.6
Eris 4♈10.9 ⚵ 14♒03.6
⚷ 4♋27.5 ⚶ 17♓15.2
☽ Mean ☊ 10♏05.5

LONGITUDE May 1939

Day	Sid.Time	☉	0 hr ☽	Noon ☽	True ☊	☿	♀	♂	⚳	♃	♄	♅	♆	♇
1 M	2 34 04	10♉13 18	5♎51 46	12♎53 06	8♏25.4	13♈27.2	7♈03.4	21♑03.5	15♊07.6	27♓57.6	23♈28.9	17♉22.5	20♍48.2	29♋17.8
2 Tu	2 38 01	11 11 30	19 51 43	26 47 14	8R 25.5	14 27.6	8 15.3	21 30.0	15 31.7	28 10.1	23 36.2	17 25.9	20R 47.2	29 18.3
3 W	2 41 57	12 09 40	3♏39 16	10♏27 29	8 25.6	15 31.0	9 27.3	21 56.2	15 55.9	28 22.5	23 43.6	17 29.4	20 46.3	29 18.9
4 Th	2 45 54	13 07 48	17 11 37	23 51 28	8 25.5	16 37.1	10 39.2	22 22.2	16 20.1	28 34.8	23 50.9	17 32.9	20 45.4	29 19.4
5 F	2 49 50	14 05 54	0♐26 53	6♐57 48	8 25.0	17 45.8	11 51.2	22 47.9	16 44.5	28 47.1	23 58.2	17 36.3	20 44.6	29 20.0
6 Sa	2 53 47	15 03 59	13 24 14	19 46 16	8 24.3	18 57.1	13 03.1	23 13.3	17 08.8	28 59.2	24 05.5	17 39.8	20 43.7	29 20.6
7 Su	2 57 44	16 02 03	26 04 04	2♑17 51	8 23.4	20 11.0	14 15.2	23 38.4	17 33.2	29 11.3	24 12.7	17 43.3	20 42.9	29 21.2
8 M	3 01 40	17 00 05	8♑27 56	14 34 39	8 22.4	21 27.3	15 27.2	24 03.2	17 57.7	29 23.4	24 20.0	17 46.8	20 42.1	29 21.8
9 Tu	3 05 37	17 58 05	20 38 26	26 39 42	8 21.4	22 45.9	16 39.3	24 27.7	18 22.3	29 35.3	24 27.2	17 50.2	20 41.4	29 22.5
10 W	3 09 33	18 56 04	2♒38 59	8♒36 48	8D 20.7	24 06.9	17 51.3	24 51.9	18 46.8	29 47.2	24 34.3	17 53.7	20 40.7	29 23.2
11 Th	3 13 30	19 54 02	14 33 41	20 30 14	8 20.5	25 30.2	19 03.5	25 15.7	19 11.5	29 59.0	24 41.5	17 57.2	20 40.0	29 23.9
12 F	3 17 26	20 51 59	26 27 01	2♓24 36	8 20.8	26 55.8	20 15.6	25 39.2	19 36.2	0♈10.6	24 48.6	18 00.7	20 39.3	29 24.6
13 Sa	3 21 23	21 49 54	8♓23 35	14 24 32	8 21.6	28 23.5	21 27.7	26 02.3	20 00.9	0 22.2	24 55.6	18 04.1	20 38.7	29 25.4
14 Su	3 25 19	22 47 47	20 27 59	26 34 28	8 22.8	29 53.5	22 39.9	26 25.1	20 25.7	0 33.8	25 02.7	18 07.6	20 38.1	29 26.1
15 M	3 29 16	23 45 40	2♈44 27	8♈58 21	8 24.1	1♉25.6	23 52.1	26 47.5	20 50.5	0 45.2	25 09.7	18 11.1	20 37.5	29 26.9
16 Tu	3 33 13	24 43 31	15 16 34	21 39 23	8 25.2	3 00.0	25 04.3	27 09.5	21 15.4	0 56.5	25 16.6	18 14.5	20 37.0	29 27.8
17 W	3 37 09	25 41 21	28 07 03	4♉39 42	8R 25.8	4 36.4	26 16.5	27 31.1	21 40.4	1 07.8	25 23.6	18 18.0	20 36.5	29 28.6
18 Th	3 41 06	26 39 10	11♉17 24	18 00 05	8 25.6	6 15.0	27 28.8	27 52.3	22 05.3	1 18.9	25 30.5	18 21.4	20 36.0	29 29.5
19 F	3 45 02	27 36 58	24 47 37	1♊39 46	8 24.4	7 55.8	28 41.1	28 13.1	22 30.4	1 29.9	25 37.3	18 24.9	20 35.6	29 30.4
20 Sa	3 48 59	28 34 44	8♊36 12	15 36 28	8 22.4	9 38.7	29 53.3	28 33.5	22 55.4	1 40.9	25 44.1	18 28.3	20 35.1	29 31.3
21 Su	3 52 55	29 32 28	22 40 06	29 46 32	8 19.7	11 23.7	1♉05.6	28 53.5	23 20.5	1 51.7	25 50.9	18 31.8	20 34.8	29 32.2
22 M	3 56 52	0♊30 11	6♋55 11	14♋05 24	8 16.8	13 10.9	2 17.9	29 13.0	23 45.7	2 02.5	25 57.7	18 35.2	20 34.4	29 33.2
23 Tu	4 00 48	1 27 53	21 16 36	28 28 11	8 14.1	15 00.2	3 30.3	29 32.0	24 10.9	2 13.1	26 04.3	18 38.6	20 34.1	29 34.2
24 W	4 04 45	2 25 33	5♌39 34	12♌50 15	8 12.0	16 51.7	4 42.6	29 50.6	24 36.1	2 23.7	26 11.0	18 42.0	20 33.8	29 35.2
25 Th	4 08 42	3 23 11	19 59 47	27 07 47	8D 10.9	18 45.2	5 55.0	0♒08.8	25 01.4	2 34.1	26 17.6	18 45.4	20 33.5	29 36.2
26 F	4 12 38	4 20 48	4♍13 54	11♍17 54	8 11.0	20 40.9	7 07.3	0 26.4	25 26.7	2 44.4	26 24.1	18 48.8	20 33.3	29 37.2
27 Sa	4 16 35	5 18 24	18 19 34	25 18 44	8 11.9	22 38.5	8 19.7	0 43.6	25 52.0	2 54.6	26 30.6	18 52.2	20 33.1	29 38.3
28 Su	4 20 31	6 15 57	2♎15 16	9♎09 05	8 13.3	24 38.2	9 32.1	1 00.3	26 17.4	3 04.7	26 37.1	18 55.5	20 33.0	29 39.4
29 M	4 24 28	7 13 30	16 00 07	22 48 17	8 14.7	26 39.8	10 44.5	1 16.5	26 42.8	3 14.7	26 43.5	18 58.9	20 32.8	29 40.5
30 Tu	4 28 24	8 11 01	29 33 32	6♏15 48	8R 15.4	28 43.2	11 56.9	1 32.1	27 08.3	3 24.6	26 49.9	19 02.2	20 32.7	29 41.6
31 W	4 32 21	9 08 31	12♏55 01	19 31 09	8 14.9	0♊48.4	13 09.4	1 47.3	27 33.7	3 34.3	26 56.2	19 05.5	20 32.7	29 42.7

LONGITUDE June 1939

Day	Sid.Time	☉	0 hr ☽	Noon ☽	True ☊	☿	♀	♂	⚳	♃	♄	♅	♆	♇
1 Th	4 36 17	10♊06 00	26♏04 07	2♐33 53	8♏13.0	2♊55.2	14♉21.8	2♒01.9	27♊59.2	3♈44.0	27♈02.4	19♉08.8	20♍32.6	29♋43.9
2 F	4 40 14	11 03 27	9♐00 24	15 23 38	8R 09.4	5 03.4	15 34.3	2 15.9	28 24.8	3 53.5	27 08.6	19 12.1	20D 32.7	29 45.0
3 Sa	4 44 11	12 00 54	21 43 36	28 00 20	8 04.5	7 12.8	16 46.8	2 29.4	28 50.4	4 02.9	27 14.8	19 15.4	20 32.7	29 46.2
4 Su	4 48 07	12 58 20	4♑13 55	10♑24 26	7 58.6	9 23.2	17 59.3	2 42.3	29 16.0	4 12.2	27 20.9	19 18.7	20 32.8	29 47.4
5 M	4 52 04	13 55 45	16 32 04	22 37 01	7 52.5	11 34.5	19 11.8	2 54.7	29 41.6	4 21.3	27 26.9	19 21.9	20 32.8	29 48.7
6 Tu	4 56 00	14 53 09	28 39 34	4♒40 00	7 46.7	13 46.3	20 24.4	3 06.4	0♋07.3	4 30.4	27 32.9	19 25.1	20 33.0	29 49.9
7 W	4 59 57	15 50 33	10♒38 42	16 36 05	7 41.9	15 58.4	21 37.0	3 17.5	0 32.9	4 39.3	27 38.8	19 28.3	20 33.1	29 51.2
8 Th	5 03 53	16 47 56	22 32 36	28 28 45	7 38.4	18 10.5	22 49.6	3 28.0	0 58.7	4 48.1	27 44.7	19 31.5	20 33.3	29 52.4
9 F	5 07 50	17 45 18	4♓25 03	10♓22 06	7D 36.6	20 22.3	24 02.2	3 37.8	1 24.4	4 56.7	27 50.5	19 34.7	20 33.6	29 53.7
10 Sa	5 11 46	18 42 40	16 20 29	22 20 48	7 36.4	22 33.5	25 14.8	3 47.0	1 50.2	5 05.2	27 56.2	19 37.8	20 33.8	29 55.0
11 Su	5 15 43	19 40 01	28 23 40	4♈29 41	7 37.3	24 44.0	26 27.4	3 55.5	2 16.0	5 13.6	28 01.9	19 41.0	20 34.1	29 56.4
12 M	5 19 40	20 37 21	10♈39 29	16 53 37	7 38.7	26 53.4	27 40.1	4 03.4	2 41.8	5 21.9	28 07.5	19 44.1	20 34.4	29 57.7
13 Tu	5 23 36	21 34 42	23 12 38	29 37 01	7R 39.8	29 01.6	28 52.8	4 10.5	3 07.7	5 30.0	28 13.1	19 47.2	20 34.8	29 59.0
14 W	5 27 33	22 32 01	6♉07 09	12♉43 22	7 40.0	1♋08.3	0♊05.5	4 16.9	3 33.6	5 38.0	28 18.6	19 50.2	20 35.2	0♌00.4
15 Th	5 31 29	23 29 21	19 25 50	26 14 40	7 38.5	3 13.4	1 18.2	4 22.7	3 59.5	5 45.8	28 24.0	19 53.3	20 35.6	0 01.8
16 F	5 35 26	24 26 40	3♊09 45	10♊10 51	7 35.0	5 16.8	2 31.0	4 27.7	4 25.4	5 53.5	28 29.4	19 56.3	20 36.1	0 03.2
17 Sa	5 39 22	25 23 58	17 17 36	24 29 23	7 29.5	7 18.2	3 43.8	4 32.0	4 51.4	6 01.1	28 34.7	19 59.3	20 36.5	0 04.6
18 Su	5 43 19	26 21 16	1♋45 32	9♋05 11	7 22.7	9 17.7	4 56.5	4 35.5	5 17.4	6 08.5	28 39.9	20 02.2	20 37.1	0 06.0
19 M	5 47 16	27 18 34	16 27 23	23 51 07	7 15.1	11 15.1	6 09.3	4 38.4	5 43.4	6 15.7	28 45.0	20 05.2	20 37.6	0 07.5
20 Tu	5 51 12	28 15 50	1♌15 23	8♌39 10	7 07.9	13 10.4	7 22.2	4 40.4	6 09.4	6 22.8	28 50.1	20 08.1	20 38.2	0 08.9
21 W	5 55 09	29 13 06	16 01 30	23 21 34	7 02.0	15 03.5	8 35.0	4 41.8	6 35.4	6 29.8	28 55.1	20 11.0	20 38.8	0 10.4
22 Th	5 59 05	0♋10 21	0♍38 38	7♍52 08	6 57.9	16 54.4	9 47.8	4R 42.3	7 01.5	6 36.6	29 00.1	20 13.8	20 39.5	0 11.9
23 F	6 03 02	1 07 36	15 01 36	22 06 47	6D 55.9	18 43.1	11 00.7	4 42.2	7 27.6	6 43.2	29 04.9	20 16.7	20 40.1	0 13.4
24 Sa	6 06 58	2 04 50	29 07 29	6♎03 41	6 55.7	20 29.5	12 13.6	4 41.2	7 53.7	6 49.7	29 09.7	20 19.5	20 40.8	0 14.9
25 Su	6 10 55	3 02 03	12♎55 25	19 42 49	6 56.4	22 13.7	13 26.5	4 39.6	8 19.8	6 56.0	29 14.4	20 22.2	20 41.6	0 16.4
26 M	6 14 51	3 59 15	26 26 02	3♏05 18	6R 57.1	23 55.6	14 39.4	4 37.2	8 45.9	7 02.2	29 19.0	20 25.0	20 42.3	0 17.9
27 Tu	6 18 48	4 56 28	9♏40 49	16 12 51	6 56.7	25 35.2	15 52.3	4 34.0	9 12.0	7 08.2	29 23.6	20 27.7	20 43.1	0 19.4
28 W	6 22 45	5 53 39	22 41 34	29 07 12	6 54.5	27 12.6	17 05.3	4 30.1	9 38.2	7 14.1	29 28.1	20 30.4	20 44.0	0 21.0
29 Th	6 26 41	6 50 51	5♐29 54	11♐49 51	6 49.9	28 47.6	18 18.3	4 25.5	10 04.4	7 19.8	29 32.5	20 33.0	20 44.8	0 22.5
30 F	6 30 38	7 48 02	18 07 10	24 21 58	6 42.7	0♌20.3	19 31.3	4 20.2	10 30.6	7 25.3	29 36.8	20 35.7	20 45.7	0 24.1

Astro Data	Dy Hr Mn
♃△♇	8 8:43
☽0N	14 1:02
♃0N	26 0:47
☽0S	27 4:45
♆D	1 22:38
♃∠♅	5 14:17
☽0N	10 9:57
♂R	22 18:34
☽0S	23 11:03

Planet Ingress		Dy Hr Mn
♃	♈	11 14:08
☿	♉	14 13:43
♀	♉	20 14:13
☉	♊	21 23:27
♂	♒	25 0:19
☿	♊	31 2:45
⚳	♋	6 5:13
☿	♋	13 23:01
♇	♌	14 4:46
♀	♊	14 10:11
☉	♋	22 7:39
☿	♌	30 6:41

Last Aspect Dy Hr Mn			☽ Ingress	Dy Hr Mn
2 16:23	♇	□	♏	2 17:36
4 21:57	♇	△	♐	4 23:11
7 5:54	♃	□	♑	7 7:34
9 17:57	♃	⚹	♒	9 18:41
11 23:27	☿	⚹	♓	12 7:09
14 17:35	♇	△	♈	14 18:41
17 2:30	♇	□	♉	17 3:28
19 8:15	♇	⚹	♊	19 9:06
21 5:20	♄	⚹	♋	21 12:23
23 13:50	♇	☌	♌	23 14:33
25 10:35	♄	△	♍	25 16:51
27 19:29	♇	⚹	♎	27 20:06
30 0:13	♇	□	♏	30 0:47

Last Aspect Dy Hr Mn			☽ Ingress	Dy Hr Mn
1 6:45	♇	△	♐	1 7:15
3 10:32	♄	△	♑	3 15:50
6 2:19	♇	☍	♒	6 2:40
8 10:30	♄	⚹	♓	8 15:04
11 3:02	♇	△	♈	11 3:10
13 12:41	♇	□	♉	13 12:43
15 2:03	♆	△	♊	15 18:32
17 18:48	♄	⚹	♋	17 21:06
19 19:59	♄	□	♌	19 21:58
21 22:19	☉	⚹	♍	21 22:56
23 9:33	♆	☌	♎	24 1:30
26 5:09	♄	☍	♏	26 6:25
28 7:55	☿	△	♐	28 13:39
30 22:12	♄	△	♑	30 22:53

☽ Phases & Eclipses Dy Hr Mn		
3 15:15	○	12♏18
3 15:11	•	T 1.177
11 10:40	☾	19♒51
19 4:25	●	27♉19
25 23:20	☽	3♍50
2 3:11	○	10♐42
10 4:07	☾	18♓24
17 13:37	●	25♊28
24 4:35	☽	1♎47

Astro Data

1 May 1939
Julian Day # 14365
SVP 6♓06'15"
GC 25♐59.5 ⚳ 1♉30.6
Eris 4♈31.1 ⚵ 23♒34.1
⚷ 6♋00.7 ⚶ 1♈18.2
☽ Mean ☊ 8♏30.2

1 June 1939
Julian Day # 14396
SVP 6♓06'11"
GC 25♐59.6 ⚳ 15♉41.4
Eris 4♈45.9 ⚵ 1♓02.9
⚷ 8♋34.4 ⚶ 14♈39.2
☽ Mean ☊ 6♏51.7

July 1939 — LONGITUDE

Day	Sid.Time	☉	0 hr ☽	Noon ☽	True☊	☿	♀	♂	⚳	♃	♄	♅	♆	♇
1 Sa	6 34 34	8♋45 13	0♑34 20	6♑44 22	6♏33.3	1♌50.8	20♊44.3	4♒14.1	10♋56.7	7♈30.6	29♈41.0	20♉38.2	20♍46.6	0♌25.7
2 Su	6 38 31	9 42 23	12 52 09	18 57 48	6R 22.4	3 18.9	21 57.3	4R 07.3	11 23.0	7 35.8	29 45.2	20 40.8	20 47.6	0 27.2
3 M	6 42 27	10 39 34	25 01 25	1♒03 08	6 10.8	4 44.6	23 10.4	3 59.7	11 49.2	7 40.9	29 49.3	20 43.3	20 48.6	0 28.8
4 Tu	6 46 24	11 36 45	7♒03 09	13 01 38	5 59.5	6 07.9	24 23.5	3 51.5	12 15.4	7 45.7	29 53.3	20 45.8	20 49.6	0 30.4
5 W	6 50 20	12 33 55	18 58 52	24 55 08	5 49.6	7 28.8	25 36.6	3 42.6	12 41.7	7 50.4	29 57.2	20 48.3	20 50.6	0 32.0
6 Th	6 54 17	13 31 06	0♓50 47	6♓46 13	5 41.8	8 47.3	26 49.7	3 33.0	13 07.9	7 54.9	0♉01.0	20 50.7	20 51.7	0 33.6
7 F	6 58 14	14 28 17	12 41 51	18 38 11	5 36.4	10 03.2	28 02.9	3 22.8	13 34.2	7 59.2	0 04.7	20 53.1	20 52.8	0 35.3
8 Sa	7 02 10	15 25 29	24 35 46	0♈35 09	5 33.4	11 16.6	29 16.0	3 11.9	14 00.5	8 03.4	0 08.4	20 55.4	20 53.9	0 36.9
9 Su	7 06 07	16 22 41	6♈36 57	12 41 46	5D 32.3	12 27.4	0♋29.2	3 00.4	14 26.8	8 07.4	0 11.9	20 57.7	20 55.0	0 38.5
10 M	7 10 03	17 19 53	18 50 16	25 03 05	5R 32.4	13 35.4	1 42.5	2 48.3	14 53.1	8 11.2	0 15.4	21 00.0	20 56.2	0 40.2
11 Tu	7 14 00	18 17 06	1♉20 51	7♉44 10	5 32.6	14 40.8	2 55.7	2 35.6	15 19.4	8 14.8	0 18.8	21 02.2	20 57.4	0 41.8
12 W	7 17 56	19 14 19	14 13 35	20 49 33	5 31.8	15 43.2	4 09.0	2 22.4	15 45.7	8 18.2	0 22.1	21 04.4	20 58.7	0 43.4
13 Th	7 21 53	20 11 33	27 32 27	4♊22 32	5 29.0	16 42.7	5 22.3	2 08.7	16 12.0	8 21.5	0 25.3	21 06.6	20 59.9	0 45.1
14 F	7 25 49	21 08 47	11♊19 53	18 24 24	5 23.8	17 39.1	6 35.7	1 54.5	16 38.4	8 24.5	0 28.4	21 08.7	21 01.2	0 46.8
15 Sa	7 29 46	22 06 02	25 35 46	2♋53 29	5 16.1	18 32.4	7 49.0	1 39.9	17 04.7	8 27.4	0 31.4	21 10.8	21 02.5	0 48.4
16 Su	7 33 43	23 03 18	10♋16 48	17 44 48	5 06.4	19 22.4	9 02.4	1 24.8	17 31.1	8 30.1	0 34.4	21 12.9	21 03.9	0 50.1
17 M	7 37 39	24 00 33	25 16 21	2♌50 13	4 55.8	20 09.0	10 15.8	1 09.4	17 57.4	8 32.6	0 37.2	21 14.9	21 05.2	0 51.8
18 Tu	7 41 36	24 57 49	10♌25 05	17 59 35	4 45.5	20 52.0	11 29.2	0 53.7	18 23.8	8 34.9	0 40.0	21 16.8	21 06.6	0 53.4
19 W	7 45 32	25 55 06	25 32 28	3♍02 31	4 36.6	21 31.2	12 42.7	0 37.7	18 50.1	8 37.0	0 42.6	21 18.7	21 08.0	0 55.1
20 Th	7 49 29	26 52 22	10♍28 43	17 50 13	4 30.1	22 06.7	13 56.2	0 21.5	19 16.5	8 38.9	0 45.1	21 20.6	21 09.5	0 56.8
21 F	7 53 25	27 49 39	25 06 22	2♎16 43	4 26.3	22 38.1	15 09.6	0 05.2	19 42.8	8 40.7	0 47.6	21 22.5	21 11.0	0 58.5
22 Sa	7 57 22	28 46 56	9♎21 03	16 19 16	4D 24.6	23 05.3	16 23.2	29♑48.7	20 09.2	8 42.2	0 49.9	21 24.3	21 12.4	1 00.1
23 Su	8 01 18	29 44 13	23 11 27	29 57 47	4R 24.3	23 28.2	17 36.7	29 32.1	20 35.6	8 43.5	0 52.2	21 26.0	21 14.0	1 01.8
24 M	8 05 15	0♌41 31	6♏38 35	13♏14 11	4 24.2	23 46.5	18 50.2	29 15.4	21 01.9	8 44.7	0 54.3	21 27.7	21 15.5	1 03.5
25 Tu	8 09 12	1 38 49	19 44 58	26 11 22	4 23.1	24 00.2	20 03.8	28 58.8	21 28.3	8 45.6	0 56.4	21 29.4	21 17.1	1 05.2
26 W	8 13 08	2 36 07	2♐33 47	8♐52 38	4 19.9	24 09.1	21 17.4	28 42.3	21 54.6	8 46.4	0 58.4	21 31.0	21 18.7	1 06.9
27 Th	8 17 05	3 33 26	15 08 15	21 21 01	4 14.0	24R 13.0	22 31.0	28 25.8	22 21.0	8 47.0	1 00.2	21 32.6	21 20.3	1 08.5
28 F	8 21 01	4 30 45	27 31 15	3♑39 11	4 05.3	24 11.9	23 44.7	28 09.5	22 47.4	8 47.3	1 02.0	21 34.1	21 21.9	1 10.2
29 Sa	8 24 58	5 28 05	9♑45 06	15 49 12	3 54.1	24 05.8	24 58.4	27 53.4	23 13.7	8R 47.5	1 03.7	21 35.6	21 23.5	1 11.9
30 Su	8 28 54	6 25 26	21 51 39	27 52 39	3 41.1	23 54.5	26 12.0	27 37.5	23 40.0	8 47.5	1 05.2	21 37.0	21 25.2	1 13.6
31 M	8 32 51	7 22 48	3♒52 19	9♒50 50	3 27.3	23 38.1	27 25.8	27 21.9	24 06.4	8 47.3	1 06.7	21 38.4	21 26.9	1 15.2

August 1939 — LONGITUDE

Day	Sid.Time	☉	0 hr ☽	Noon ☽	True☊	☿	♀	♂	⚳	♃	♄	♅	♆	♇
1 Tu	8 36 47	8♌20 10	15♒48 19	21♒44 59	3♏13.9	23♌16.7	28♋39.5	27♑06.6	24♋32.7	8♈46.8	1♉08.0	21♉39.8	21♍28.6	1♌16.9
2 W	8 40 44	9 17 33	27 40 59	3♓36 32	3R 01.9	22R 50.5	29 53.3	26R 51.6	24 59.1	8R 46.2	1 09.3	21 41.1	21 30.4	1 18.6
3 Th	8 44 41	10 14 57	9♓31 54	15 27 23	2 52.2	22 19.6	1♌07.1	26 37.1	25 25.4	8 45.4	1 10.4	21 42.4	21 32.1	1 20.2
4 F	8 48 37	11 12 22	21 23 17	27 20 00	2 45.2	21 44.6	2 20.9	26 22.9	25 51.7	8 44.4	1 11.5	21 43.6	21 33.9	1 21.9
5 Sa	8 52 34	12 09 49	3♈17 57	9♈17 33	2 40.9	21 05.7	3 34.7	26 09.3	26 18.0	8 43.2	1 12.4	21 44.7	21 35.7	1 23.6
6 Su	8 56 30	13 07 16	15 19 30	21 24 09	2D 39.0	20 23.5	4 48.6	25 56.1	26 44.3	8 41.8	1 13.3	21 45.9	21 37.5	1 25.2
7 M	9 00 27	14 04 45	27 32 08	3♉44 05	2R 38.7	19 38.6	6 02.5	25 43.4	27 10.6	8 40.2	1 14.0	21 46.9	21 39.3	1 26.9
8 Tu	9 04 23	15 02 15	10♉00 37	16 22 18	2 38.7	18 51.8	7 16.4	25 31.3	27 36.9	8 38.4	1 14.6	21 47.9	21 41.2	1 28.5
9 W	9 08 20	15 59 47	22 49 46	29 23 31	2 38.2	18 03.9	8 30.3	25 19.8	28 03.2	8 36.4	1 15.2	21 48.9	21 43.1	1 30.2
10 Th	9 12 16	16 57 20	6♊04 03	12♊51 43	2 35.9	17 15.7	9 44.3	25 09.0	28 29.5	8 34.2	1 15.6	21 49.9	21 45.0	1 31.8
11 F	9 16 13	17 54 54	19 46 45	26 49 15	2 31.3	16 28.1	10 58.3	24 58.8	28 55.8	8 31.8	1 15.9	21 50.7	21 46.9	1 33.4
12 Sa	9 20 10	18 52 30	3♋59 04	11♋15 52	2 24.3	15 42.0	12 12.3	24 49.2	29 22.0	8 29.3	1 16.1	21 51.6	21 48.8	1 35.0
13 Su	9 24 06	19 50 08	18 39 06	26 07 57	2 15.3	14 58.4	13 26.4	24 40.4	29 48.3	8 26.5	1R 16.2	21 52.3	21 50.7	1 36.7
14 M	9 28 03	20 47 46	3♌41 24	11♌18 14	2 05.2	14 18.2	14 40.5	24 32.3	0♌14.5	8 23.5	1 16.2	21 53.1	21 52.7	1 38.3
15 Tu	9 31 59	21 45 26	18 57 06	26 36 35	1 55.3	13 42.2	15 54.6	24 25.0	0 40.7	8 20.4	1 16.1	21 53.8	21 54.7	1 39.9
16 W	9 35 56	22 43 07	4♍15 12	11♍51 35	1 46.8	13 11.1	17 08.7	24 18.4	1 06.9	8 17.0	1 15.9	21 54.4	21 56.6	1 41.5
17 Th	9 39 52	23 40 49	19 24 27	26 52 43	1 40.5	12 45.7	18 22.8	24 12.7	1 33.1	8 13.5	1 15.6	21 55.0	21 58.6	1 43.1
18 F	9 43 49	24 38 32	4♎15 28	11♎32 02	1 36.7	12 26.6	19 37.0	24 07.7	1 59.3	8 09.8	1 15.2	21 55.5	22 00.7	1 44.6
19 Sa	9 47 45	25 36 16	18 41 58	25 45 01	1D 35.2	12 14.1	20 51.1	24 03.5	2 25.4	8 05.9	1 14.7	21 56.0	22 02.7	1 46.2
20 Su	9 51 42	26 34 02	2♏41 08	9♏30 26	1 35.3	12D 08.9	22 05.3	24 00.2	2 51.6	8 01.8	1 14.1	21 56.4	22 04.7	1 47.7
21 M	9 55 39	27 31 49	16 13 09	22 49 40	1R 35.8	12 11.0	23 19.6	23 57.7	3 17.7	7 57.6	1 13.3	21 56.8	22 06.8	1 49.3
22 Tu	9 59 35	28 29 36	29 20 22	5♐45 46	1 35.6	12 20.9	24 33.8	23 56.0	3 43.8	7 53.2	1 12.5	21 57.1	22 08.8	1 50.8
23 W	10 03 32	29 27 25	12♐06 20	18 22 36	1 33.8	12 38.4	25 48.0	23D 55.2	4 09.8	7 48.6	1 11.6	21 57.4	22 10.9	1 52.4
24 Th	10 07 28	0♍25 15	24 35 04	0♑44 13	1 29.8	13 03.8	27 02.3	23 55.2	4 35.9	7 43.8	1 10.5	21 57.6	22 13.0	1 53.9
25 F	10 11 25	1 23 07	6♑50 31	12 54 24	1 23.4	13 37.0	28 16.6	23 56.0	5 01.9	7 38.9	1 09.4	21 57.8	22 15.1	1 55.4
26 Sa	10 15 21	2 21 00	18 56 15	24 56 26	1 14.8	14 17.8	29 30.9	23 57.7	5 27.9	7 33.8	1 08.1	21 58.0	22 17.2	1 56.9
27 Su	10 19 18	3 18 54	0♒55 16	6♒53 03	1 04.6	15 06.0	0♍45.2	24 00.2	5 53.9	7 28.5	1 06.8	21 58.0	22 19.3	1 58.4
28 M	10 23 14	4 16 49	12 50 02	18 46 27	0 53.7	16 01.6	1 59.6	24 03.5	6 19.8	7 23.1	1 05.3	21R 58.1	22 21.5	1 59.8
29 Tu	10 27 11	5 14 46	24 42 30	0♓38 24	0 43.1	17 04.0	3 13.9	24 07.6	6 45.8	7 17.6	1 03.8	21 58.0	22 23.6	2 01.3
30 W	10 31 07	6 12 44	6♓34 20	12 30 30	0 33.7	18 13.1	4 28.3	24 12.5	7 11.7	7 11.9	1 02.2	21 58.0	22 25.8	2 02.7
31 Th	10 35 04	7 10 44	18 27 06	24 24 21	0 26.2	19 28.5	5 42.7	24 18.2	7 37.5	7 06.0	1 00.4	21 57.9	22 27.9	2 04.1

Astro Data (Dy Hr Mn)

♅△♆ 7 6:19
☽0N 7 18:34
☽0S 20 19:06
☿R 27 18:54
♃R 29 21:01

☽0N 4 2:10
♄R 14 1:02
♅△♆ 14 19:23
☽0S 17 5:08
☿D 20 17:08
♂D 23 23:58
♅R 28 14:27
☽0N 31 8:42

Planet Ingress (Dy Hr Mn)

♄ ♉ 6 5:45
♀ ♋ 9 2:25
♂ ♑R 21 19:31
☉ ♌ 23 18:37

♀ ♌ 2 14:11
⚳ ♌ 13 22:44
☉ ♍ 24 1:31
♀ ♍ 26 21:24

Last Aspect / ☽ Ingress (Dy Hr Mn)

3 9:32 ♄ □ ♒ 3 9:54
5 22:15 ♄ ✶ ♓ 5 22:17
8 9:04 ♀ □ ♈ 8 10:50
9 19:49 ☉ □ ♉ 10 21:27
12 12:27 ♅ ☌ ♊ 13 4:21
14 16:23 ♆ □ ♋ 15 7:16
16 21:03 ☉ ☌ ♌ 17 7:30
18 17:14 ♅ □ ♍ 19 7:07
21 4:00 ☉ ✶ ♎ 21 8:10
23 11:34 ☉ □ ♏ 23 12:04
25 17:08 ♂ ✶ ♐ 25 19:10
27 17:34 ☿ △ ♑ 28 4:51
30 11:30 ♂ ☌ ♒ 30 16:15

Last Aspect / ☽ Ingress (Dy Hr Mn)

1 14:59 ☿ ☍ ♓ 2 4:41
4 10:07 ♂ ✶ ♈ 4 17:22
6 20:44 ♂ □ ♉ 7 4:47
9 4:42 ♂ △ ♊ 9 13:06
11 3:25 ♅ ☌ ♋ 11 17:21
13 9:41 ♂ ☍ ♌ 13 18:09
15 4:36 ♅ □ ♍ 15 17:19
17 7:44 ♂ △ ♎ 17 17:03
19 11:44 ☉ ✶ ♏ 19 19:20
21 21:21 ☉ □ ♐ 22 1:14
24 3:58 ♀ △ ♑ 24 10:33
26 10:02 ♂ ☌ ♒ 26 22:09
28 18:27 ♅ □ ♓ 29 10:42
31 11:48 ♂ ✶ ♈ 31 23:15

☽ Phases & Eclipses (Dy Hr Mn)

1 16:16 ○ 8♑55
9 19:49 ☾ 16♈41
16 21:03 ● 23♋25
23 11:34 ☽ 29♎43
31 6:37 ○ 7♒10

8 9:18 ☾ 14♉56
15 3:53 ● 21♌26
21 21:21 ☽ 27♏54
29 22:09 ○ 5♓39

Astro Data

1 July 1939
Julian Day # 14426
SVP 6♓06'06"
GC 25♐59.7 ⚴ 0♊03.4
Eris 4♈51.2R ⚵ 4♓25.4
⚷ 11♋33.7 ⚶ 25♈51.8
☽ Mean ☊ 5♏16.4

1 August 1939
Julian Day # 14457
SVP 6♓06'01"
GC 25♐59.7 ⚴ 15♊24.1
Eris 4♈46.0R ⚵ 2♓04.2R
⚷ 14♋43.4 ⚶ 4♉38.7
☽ Mean ☊ 3♏37.9

LONGITUDE September 1939

Day	Sid.Time	☉	0 hr ☽	Noon ☽	True ☊	☿	♀	♂	⚳	♃	♄	♅	♆	♇
1 F	10 39 01	8♍08 46	0♈22 30	6♈21 49	0♏21.0	20♌49.6	6♍57.1	24♑24.7	8♌03.4	7♈00.0	0♉58.6	21♉57.7	22♍30.1	2♌05.6
2 Sa	10 42 57	9 06 50	12 22 36	18 25 11	0D 18.2	22 16.1	8 11.5	24 32.0	8 29.2	6R 53.9	0R 56.6	21R 57.5	22 32.3	2 07.0
3 Su	10 46 54	10 04 55	24 29 56	0♉37 16	0 17.4	23 47.5	9 26.0	24 40.0	8 55.0	6 47.6	0 54.6	21 57.2	22 34.4	2 08.3
4 M	10 50 50	11 03 02	6♉47 37	13 01 26	0 18.0	25 23.1	10 40.4	24 48.8	9 20.7	6 41.2	0 52.5	21 56.9	22 36.6	2 09.7
5 Tu	10 54 47	12 01 12	19 19 13	25 41 28	0 19.2	27 02.7	11 54.9	24 58.4	9 46.5	6 34.6	0 50.3	21 56.5	22 38.8	2 11.1
6 W	10 58 43	12 59 23	2♊08 39	8♊41 16	0R 20.1	28 45.5	13 09.4	25 08.7	10 12.2	6 28.0	0 47.9	21 56.1	22 41.0	2 12.4
7 Th	11 02 40	13 57 37	15 19 43	22 04 23	0 19.9	0♍31.2	14 24.0	25 19.7	10 37.9	6 21.2	0 45.5	21 55.6	22 43.2	2 13.8
8 F	11 06 36	14 55 52	28 55 32	5♋53 20	0 18.0	2 19.2	15 38.5	25 31.5	11 03.5	6 14.3	0 43.0	21 55.1	22 45.4	2 15.1
9 Sa	11 10 33	15 54 10	12♋57 48	20 08 47	0 14.3	4 09.1	16 53.1	25 44.0	11 29.1	6 07.3	0 40.4	21 54.5	22 47.6	2 16.4
10 Su	11 14 30	16 52 29	27 25 55	4♌48 41	0 09.0	6 00.5	18 07.6	25 57.1	11 54.7	6 00.1	0 37.7	21 53.9	22 49.9	2 17.6
11 M	11 18 26	17 50 51	12♌16 20	19 47 55	0 02.8	7 53.0	19 22.2	26 11.0	12 20.2	5 52.9	0 35.0	21 53.3	22 52.1	2 18.9
12 Tu	11 22 23	18 49 14	27 22 20	4♍58 22	29♎56.6	9 46.2	20 36.8	26 25.6	12 45.7	5 45.6	0 32.1	21 52.6	22 54.3	2 20.1
13 W	11 26 19	19 47 40	12♍34 43	20 10 04	29 51.3	11 39.8	21 51.5	26 40.8	13 11.1	5 38.2	0 29.1	21 51.8	22 56.5	2 21.4
14 Th	11 30 16	20 46 07	27 43 08	5♎12 43	29 47.4	13 33.7	23 06.1	26 56.8	13 36.5	5 30.7	0 26.1	21 51.0	22 58.7	2 22.6
15 F	11 34 12	21 44 36	12♎37 48	19 57 31	29D 45.4	15 27.5	24 20.7	27 13.3	14 01.9	5 23.1	0 23.0	21 50.1	23 01.0	2 23.8
16 Sa	11 38 09	22 43 07	27 11 10	4♏18 18	29 45.1	17 21.0	25 35.4	27 30.6	14 27.2	5 15.5	0 19.8	21 49.2	23 03.2	2 24.9
17 Su	11 42 05	23 41 40	11♏18 36	18 12 00	29 46.1	19 14.2	26 50.1	27 48.4	14 52.5	5 07.8	0 16.5	21 48.3	23 05.4	2 26.1
18 M	11 46 02	24 40 14	24 58 32	1♐38 25	29 47.6	21 06.8	28 04.7	28 06.9	15 17.7	5 00.0	0 13.2	21 47.3	23 07.7	2 27.2
19 Tu	11 49 59	25 38 50	8♐11 56	14 39 31	29R 49.0	22 58.8	29 19.4	28 26.0	15 42.9	4 52.2	0 09.7	21 46.2	23 09.9	2 28.4
20 W	11 53 55	26 37 28	21 01 35	27 18 41	29 49.5	24 50.1	0♎34.1	28 45.6	16 08.0	4 44.3	0 06.2	21 45.2	23 12.1	2 29.4
21 Th	11 57 52	27 36 07	3♑31 20	9♑40 06	29 48.7	26 40.6	1 48.8	29 05.9	16 33.1	4 36.4	0 02.6	21 44.0	23 14.3	2 30.5
22 F	12 01 48	28 34 48	15 45 30	21 48 06	29 46.5	28 30.2	3 03.5	29 26.7	16 58.2	4 28.5	29♈59.0	21 42.8	23 16.6	2 31.6
23 Sa	12 05 45	29 33 31	27 48 24	3♒46 55	29 43.0	0♎19.0	4 18.3	29 48.0	17 23.1	4 20.5	29 55.3	21 41.6	23 18.8	2 32.6
24 Su	12 09 41	0♎32 15	9♒44 06	15 40 23	29 38.5	2 06.8	5 33.0	0♒09.9	17 48.1	4 12.5	29 51.5	21 40.4	23 21.0	2 33.6
25 M	12 13 38	1 31 01	21 36 11	27 31 50	29 33.5	3 53.8	6 47.7	0 32.3	18 12.9	4 04.5	29 47.6	21 39.1	23 23.2	2 34.6
26 Tu	12 17 34	2 29 49	3♓27 42	9♓24 03	29 28.6	5 39.8	8 02.5	0 55.2	18 37.7	3 56.5	29 43.7	21 37.7	23 25.4	2 35.6
27 W	12 21 31	3 28 39	15 21 11	21 19 21	29 24.4	7 24.9	9 17.2	1 18.6	19 02.5	3 48.4	29 39.7	21 36.3	23 27.6	2 36.5
28 Th	12 25 27	4 27 31	27 18 46	3♈19 39	29 21.1	9 09.1	10 32.0	1 42.5	19 27.2	3 40.4	29 35.7	21 34.9	23 29.8	2 37.5
29 F	12 29 24	5 26 25	9♈22 12	15 26 37	29 19.1	10 52.4	11 46.7	2 06.8	19 51.8	3 32.3	29 31.6	21 33.4	23 32.0	2 38.4
30 Sa	12 33 21	6 25 21	21 33 06	27 41 51	29D 18.4	12 34.8	13 01.5	2 31.7	20 16.4	3 24.3	29 27.4	21 31.9	23 34.2	2 39.3

LONGITUDE October 1939

Day	Sid.Time	☉	0 hr ☽	Noon ☽	True ☊	☿	♀	♂	⚳	♃	♄	♅	♆	♇
1 Su	12 37 17	7♎24 19	3♉53 05	10♉07 02	29♎18.7	14♎16.2	14♎16.3	2♒56.9	20♌40.9	3♈16.3	29♈23.2	21♉30.3	23♍36.4	2♌40.1
2 M	12 41 14	8 23 19	16 23 55	22 43 59	29 19.9	15 56.9	15 31.0	3 22.6	21 05.4	3R 08.3	29R 18.9	21R 28.7	23 38.5	2 41.0
3 Tu	12 45 10	9 22 22	29 07 31	5♊34 46	29 21.4	17 36.6	16 45.8	3 48.7	21 29.8	3 00.4	29 14.6	21 27.1	23 40.7	2 41.8
4 W	12 49 07	10 21 26	12♊06 00	18 41 29	29 22.8	19 15.5	18 00.6	4 15.3	21 54.1	2 52.5	29 10.3	21 25.4	23 42.9	2 42.6
5 Th	12 53 03	11 20 34	25 21 28	2♋06 09	29R 23.7	20 53.6	19 15.4	4 42.2	22 18.4	2 44.6	29 05.9	21 23.7	23 45.0	2 43.4
6 F	12 57 00	12 19 43	8♋55 42	15 50 14	29 23.9	22 30.9	20 30.3	5 09.6	22 42.6	2 36.7	29 01.4	21 22.0	23 47.2	2 44.1
7 Sa	13 00 56	13 18 55	22 49 44	29 54 09	29 23.3	24 07.4	21 45.1	5 37.3	23 06.7	2 29.0	28 56.9	21 20.2	23 49.3	2 44.8
8 Su	13 04 53	14 18 09	7♌03 17	14♌16 48	29 22.0	25 43.2	22 59.9	6 05.5	23 30.7	2 21.2	28 52.4	21 18.4	23 51.4	2 45.5
9 M	13 08 50	15 17 26	21 34 16	28 55 05	29 20.4	27 18.2	24 14.8	6 34.0	23 54.7	2 13.6	28 47.8	21 16.5	23 53.5	2 46.2
10 Tu	13 12 46	16 16 44	6♍18 33	13♍43 51	29 18.7	28 52.4	25 29.6	7 02.8	24 18.6	2 06.0	28 43.2	21 14.6	23 55.6	2 46.9
11 W	13 16 43	17 16 05	21 10 04	28 36 13	29 17.2	0♏25.9	26 44.5	7 32.1	24 42.4	1 58.5	28 38.6	21 12.7	23 57.7	2 47.5
12 Th	13 20 39	18 15 28	6♎01 19	13♎24 23	29 16.3	1 58.7	27 59.3	8 01.6	25 06.1	1 51.1	28 33.9	21 10.8	23 59.8	2 48.1
13 F	13 24 36	19 14 54	20 44 28	28 00 44	29D 16.0	3 30.8	29 14.2	8 31.6	25 29.8	1 43.7	28 29.3	21 08.8	24 01.9	2 48.7
14 Sa	13 28 32	20 14 21	5♏12 25	12♏18 54	29 16.2	5 02.2	0♏29.1	9 01.8	25 53.3	1 36.5	28 24.6	21 06.8	24 03.9	2 49.2
15 Su	13 32 29	21 13 50	19 19 43	26 14 32	29 16.7	6 32.9	1 43.9	9 32.4	26 16.8	1 29.3	28 19.8	21 04.7	24 05.9	2 49.7
16 M	13 36 25	22 13 21	3♐03 09	9♐45 31	29 17.4	8 03.0	2 58.8	10 03.4	26 40.2	1 22.3	28 15.1	21 02.6	24 08.0	2 50.3
17 Tu	13 40 22	23 12 54	16 21 45	22 52 02	29 18.1	9 32.3	4 13.7	10 34.6	27 03.5	1 15.4	28 10.3	21 00.5	24 10.0	2 50.7
18 W	13 44 19	24 12 29	29 16 39	5♑36 00	29 18.6	11 00.9	5 28.5	11 06.1	27 26.7	1 08.6	28 05.6	20 58.4	24 12.0	2 51.2
19 Th	13 48 15	25 12 05	11♑50 31	18 00 42	29R 18.9	12 28.9	6 43.4	11 38.0	27 49.8	1 01.9	28 00.8	20 56.3	24 14.0	2 51.6
20 F	13 52 12	26 11 43	24 07 05	0♒10 14	29 18.9	13 56.1	7 58.3	12 10.1	28 12.8	0 55.3	27 56.0	20 54.1	24 15.9	2 52.0
21 Sa	13 56 08	27 11 23	6♒10 43	12 09 07	29 18.8	15 22.6	9 13.2	12 42.5	28 35.7	0 48.9	27 51.2	20 51.9	24 17.9	2 52.4
22 Su	14 00 05	28 11 04	18 06 00	24 01 57	29 18.7	16 48.3	10 28.0	13 15.2	28 58.5	0 42.6	27 46.4	20 49.6	24 19.8	2 52.7
23 M	14 04 01	29 10 48	29 57 28	5♓53 06	29D 18.6	18 13.3	11 42.9	13 48.1	29 21.2	0 36.5	27 41.6	20 47.4	24 21.7	2 53.1
24 Tu	14 07 58	0♏10 33	11♓49 19	17 46 35	29 18.6	19 37.4	12 57.8	14 21.3	29 43.8	0 30.5	27 36.9	20 45.1	24 23.6	2 53.4
25 W	14 11 54	1 10 20	23 45 18	29 45 52	29 18.8	21 00.8	14 12.6	14 54.7	0♍06.3	0 24.6	27 32.1	20 42.8	24 25.5	2 53.6
26 Th	14 15 51	2 10 08	5♈48 37	11♈53 50	29 19.0	22 23.2	15 27.5	15 28.3	0 28.7	0 18.9	27 27.3	20 40.5	24 27.3	2 53.9
27 F	14 19 48	3 09 59	18 01 46	24 12 39	29R 19.2	23 44.7	16 42.4	16 02.2	0 51.0	0 13.3	27 22.6	20 38.2	24 29.2	2 54.1
28 Sa	14 23 44	4 09 51	0♉26 37	6♉43 50	29 19.1	25 05.2	17 57.2	16 36.3	1 13.1	0 07.9	27 17.8	20 35.8	24 31.0	2 54.3
29 Su	14 27 41	5 09 46	13 04 22	19 28 17	29 18.8	26 24.6	19 12.1	17 10.7	1 35.2	0 02.7	27 13.1	20 33.5	24 32.8	2 54.4
30 M	14 31 37	6 09 42	25 55 38	2♊26 23	29 18.2	27 42.9	20 27.0	17 45.2	1 57.1	29♓57.6	27 08.4	20 31.1	24 34.6	2 54.6
31 Tu	14 35 34	7 09 40	9♊00 32	15 38 03	29 17.3	28 59.9	21 41.9	18 20.0	2 18.9	29 52.7	27 03.7	20 28.7	24 36.3	2 54.7

Astro Data Dy Hr Mn	Planet Ingress Dy Hr Mn	Last Aspect Dy Hr Mn	☽ Ingress Dy Hr Mn	Last Aspect Dy Hr Mn	☽ Ingress Dy Hr Mn	☽ Phases & Eclipses Dy Hr Mn
♃∠♅ 1 21:25	☿ ♍ 7 4:58	3 0:12 ♂ □	♉ 3 10:47	2 13:43 ♆ △	♊ 3 1:38	6 20:24 ☾ 13♊20
☽0S 13 16:09	☊ ♎R 11 22:47	5 14:55 ♂ □	♊ 5 20:02	5 6:42 ♄ ⚹	♋ 5 8:16	13 11:22 ● 19♍46
♀0S 22 11:19	♀ ♎ 20 1:02	7 13:09 ♆ □	♋ 8 1:52	7 10:24 ♄ □	♌ 7 12:10	20 10:34 ☽ 26♐34
☉0S 23 22:50	♄ ♈R 22 5:18	9 21:21 ♂ ☍	♌ 10 4:12	9 11:48 ♄ △	♍ 9 13:46	28 14:27 ○ 4♈34
☿0S 24 23:22	☿ ♎ 23 7:48	11 15:19 ♅ □	♍ 12 4:09	11 4:29 ♆ ☌	♎ 11 14:15	
☽0N 27 14:54	☉ ♎ 23 22:49	13 22:32 ♂ △	♎ 14 3:39	13 14:14 ♀ ☌	♏ 13 15:18	6 5:27 ☾ 12♋04
♃0S 27 19:49	♂ ♒ 24 1:13	16 0:18 ♂ □	♏ 16 4:43	15 8:15 ♆ ⚹	♐ 15 18:36	12 20:30 ● 18♎37
		18 5:29 ♂ ⚹	♐ 18 9:02	17 21:51 ♄ △	♑ 18 1:22	12 20:39:58 ● T 01'33"
♃△♇ 5 15:24	☿ ♏ 11 5:20	20 10:34 ☉ □	♑ 20 17:11	20 7:35 ♄ □	♒ 20 11:40	20 3:24 ☽ 25♑50
☽0S 11 2:29	♀ ♏ 14 2:41	23 4:17 ☉ □	♒ 23 4:24	22 21:11 ☉ △	♓ 23 0:05	28 6:42 ○ 3♉57
☽0N 24 21:51	☉ ♏ 24 7:46	25 16:33 ♄ ⚹	♓ 25 17:00	25 1:19 ♆ ☍	♈ 25 12:28	28 6:36 ● P 0.987
	⚳ ♍ 25 5:15	27 16:18 ♆ ☍	♈ 28 5:22	27 18:04 ♄ ☌	♉ 27 23:09	
	♃ ♓R 30 0:44	30 15:24 ♄ ☌	♉ 30 16:29	30 7:28 ♃ ⚹	♊ 30 7:31	

Astro Data

1 September 1939
Julian Day # 14488
SVP 6♓05'58"
GC 25♐59.8 ⚴ 0♋53.7
Eris 4♈31.7R ⚵ 24♒58.8R
⚷ 17♋29.9 ⚶ 8♉48.5
☽ Mean ☊ 1♏59.4

1 October 1939
Julian Day # 14518
SVP 6♓05'56"
GC 25♐59.9 ⚴ 15♋15.1
Eris 4♈13.0R ⚵ 20♒08.2R
⚷ 19♋22.2 ⚶ 6♉32.2R
☽ Mean ☊ 0♏24.0

November 1939 LONGITUDE

Day	Sid.Time	☉	0 hr ☽	Noon ☽	True ☊	☿	♀	♂	⚳	♃	♄	♅	♆	♇
1 W	14 39 30	8♏09 41	22♊18 53	29♊02 58	29♎16.2	0♐15.5	22♏56.7	18♒54.9	2♍40.6	29♓48.0	26♈59.1	20♉26.3	24♍38.1	2♌54.8
2 Th	14 43 27	9 09 44	5♋50 14	12♋40 35	29R 15.1	1 29.5	24 11.6	19 30.0	3 02.2	29R 43.5	26R 54.4	20R 23.8	24 39.8	2 54.9
3 F	14 47 23	10 09 49	19 33 56	26 30 10	29 14.3	2 42.0	25 26.5	20 05.4	3 23.6	29 39.1	26 49.8	20 21.4	24 41.5	2R 54.9
4 Sa	14 51 20	11 09 55	3♌29 10	10♌30 45	29D 14.0	3 52.5	26 41.3	20 40.9	3 44.9	29 34.9	26 45.3	20 19.0	24 43.2	2 54.9
5 Su	14 55 17	12 10 04	17 34 46	24 41 00	29 14.3	5 01.0	27 56.2	21 16.6	4 06.1	29 30.9	26 40.7	20 16.5	24 44.8	2 54.9
6 M	14 59 13	13 10 16	1♍49 09	8♍58 57	29 15.1	6 07.2	29 11.1	21 52.5	4 27.2	29 27.1	26 36.2	20 14.0	24 46.5	2 54.8
7 Tu	15 03 10	14 10 29	16 10 00	23 21 55	29 16.2	7 10.8	0♐26.0	22 28.6	4 48.1	29 23.4	26 31.8	20 11.6	24 48.1	2 54.8
8 W	15 07 06	15 10 44	0♎34 12	7♎46 22	29 17.4	8 11.5	1 40.9	23 04.8	5 08.8	29 20.0	26 27.3	20 09.1	24 49.6	2 54.7
9 Th	15 11 03	16 11 01	14 57 49	22 08 00	29R 18.1	9 09.0	2 55.7	23 41.2	5 29.4	29 16.7	26 23.0	20 06.6	24 51.2	2 54.5
10 F	15 14 59	17 11 20	29 16 17	6♏22 06	29 18.1	10 02.9	4 10.6	24 17.8	5 49.9	29 13.7	26 18.6	20 04.1	24 52.7	2 54.4
11 Sa	15 18 56	18 11 41	13♏24 51	20 23 59	29 17.1	10 52.6	5 25.5	24 54.5	6 10.2	29 10.8	26 14.4	20 01.6	24 54.2	2 54.2
12 Su	15 22 52	19 12 04	27 19 04	4♐09 38	29 15.1	11 37.8	6 40.4	25 31.4	6 30.3	29 08.2	26 10.2	19 59.1	24 55.7	2 54.0
13 M	15 26 49	20 12 28	10♐55 24	17 36 08	29 12.2	12 17.9	7 55.3	26 08.5	6 50.3	29 05.7	26 06.0	19 56.6	24 57.2	2 53.8
14 Tu	15 30 45	21 12 54	24 11 41	0♑42 04	29 08.7	12 52.1	9 10.1	26 45.7	7 10.1	29 03.5	26 01.9	19 54.1	24 58.6	2 53.5
15 W	15 34 42	22 13 21	7♑07 19	13 27 38	29 05.2	13 20.0	10 25.0	27 23.0	7 29.8	29 01.4	25 57.8	19 51.6	25 00.0	2 53.3
16 Th	15 38 39	23 13 49	19 43 17	25 54 37	29 02.1	13 40.7	11 39.9	28 00.5	7 49.3	28 59.6	25 53.9	19 49.1	25 01.4	2 52.9
17 F	15 42 35	24 14 19	2♒02 01	8♒05 59	28 59.8	13R 53.5	12 54.8	28 38.2	8 08.6	28 57.9	25 49.9	19 46.6	25 02.7	2 52.6
18 Sa	15 46 32	25 14 50	14 07 03	20 05 46	28D 58.6	13 57.7	14 09.6	29 15.9	8 27.8	28 56.5	25 46.1	19 44.2	25 04.0	2 52.3
19 Su	15 50 28	26 15 23	26 02 43	1♓58 32	28 58.7	13 52.6	15 24.5	29 53.8	8 46.7	28 55.3	25 42.3	19 41.7	25 05.3	2 51.9
20 M	15 54 25	27 15 56	7♓53 50	13 49 15	28 59.7	13 37.5	16 39.3	0♓31.8	9 05.5	28 54.3	25 38.6	19 39.2	25 06.6	2 51.5
21 Tu	15 58 21	28 16 31	19 45 23	25 42 52	29 01.5	13 11.9	17 54.2	1 09.9	9 24.1	28 53.5	25 35.0	19 36.7	25 07.8	2 51.0
22 W	16 02 18	29 17 07	1♈42 15	7♈44 06	29 03.3	12 35.8	19 09.0	1 48.1	9 42.5	28 52.9	25 31.4	19 34.3	25 09.0	2 50.6
23 Th	16 06 14	0♐17 45	13 48 54	19 57 09	29R 04.7	11 49.0	20 23.8	2 26.4	10 00.7	28 52.5	25 27.9	19 31.9	25 10.2	2 50.1
24 F	16 10 11	1 18 23	26 09 12	2♉25 25	29 05.0	10 52.2	21 38.6	3 04.9	10 18.7	28D 52.3	25 24.5	19 29.4	25 11.3	2 49.6
25 Sa	16 14 08	2 19 03	8♉46 02	15 11 14	29 03.8	9 46.3	22 53.5	3 43.4	10 36.6	28 52.3	25 21.2	19 27.0	25 12.4	2 49.0
26 Su	16 18 04	3 19 44	21 41 07	28 15 39	29 00.9	8 32.9	24 08.3	4 22.0	10 54.2	28 52.5	25 17.9	19 24.6	25 13.5	2 48.5
27 M	16 22 01	4 20 27	4♊54 46	11♊38 16	28 56.3	7 14.0	25 23.1	5 00.7	11 11.6	28 53.0	25 14.7	19 22.2	25 14.6	2 47.9
28 Tu	16 25 57	5 21 11	18 25 52	25 17 15	28 50.6	5 52.0	26 37.9	5 39.6	11 28.8	28 53.6	25 11.7	19 19.8	25 15.6	2 47.3
29 W	16 29 54	6 21 56	2♋12 00	9♋09 40	28 44.3	4 29.7	27 52.7	6 18.5	11 45.8	28 54.5	25 08.7	19 17.5	25 16.6	2 46.7
30 Th	16 33 50	7 22 42	16 09 46	23 11 49	28 38.3	3 09.8	29 07.4	6 57.4	12 02.6	28 55.5	25 05.8	19 15.1	25 17.6	2 46.0

December 1939 LONGITUDE

Day	Sid.Time	☉	0 hr ☽	Noon ☽	True ☊	☿	♀	♂	⚳	♃	♄	♅	♆	♇
1 F	16 37 47	8♐23 31	0♌15 21	7♌19 54	28♎33.4	1♐55.1	0♑22.2	7♓36.5	12♍19.2	28♓56.8	25♈02.9	19♉12.8	25♍18.5	2♌45.4
2 Sa	16 41 44	9 24 20	14 25 03	21 30 25	28R 30.1	0R 47.7	1 37.0	8 15.7	12 35.5	28 58.3	25R 00.2	19R 10.5	25 19.4	2R 44.7
3 Su	16 45 40	10 25 11	28 35 42	5♍40 37	28D 28.6	29♏49.5	2 51.8	8 54.9	12 51.6	28 59.9	24 57.6	19 08.2	25 20.3	2 43.9
4 M	16 49 37	11 26 03	12♍44 57	19 48 31	28 28.8	29 01.9	4 06.5	9 34.2	13 07.5	29 01.8	24 55.0	19 06.0	25 21.1	2 43.2
5 Tu	16 53 33	12 26 57	26 51 09	3♎52 43	28 30.0	28 25.4	5 21.3	10 13.6	13 23.1	29 03.9	24 52.6	19 03.7	25 21.9	2 42.4
6 W	16 57 30	13 27 52	10♎53 05	17 52 07	28R 31.2	28 00.4	6 36.0	10 53.0	13 38.5	29 06.2	24 50.2	19 01.5	25 22.7	2 41.7
7 Th	17 01 26	14 28 48	24 49 40	1♏45 34	28 31.6	27D 46.7	7 50.8	11 32.6	13 53.6	29 08.7	24 48.0	18 59.3	25 23.4	2 40.8
8 F	17 05 23	15 29 46	8♏39 36	15 31 32	28 30.2	27 43.9	9 05.5	12 12.2	14 08.5	29 11.3	24 45.8	18 57.1	25 24.1	2 40.0
9 Sa	17 09 19	16 30 44	22 21 08	29 08 06	28 26.5	27 51.3	10 20.3	12 51.8	14 23.1	29 14.2	24 43.8	18 55.0	25 24.8	2 39.2
10 Su	17 13 16	17 31 44	5♐52 12	12♐33 06	28 20.4	28 08.1	11 35.0	13 31.6	14 37.4	29 17.3	24 41.8	18 52.9	25 25.4	2 38.3
11 M	17 17 13	18 32 45	19 10 35	25 44 25	28 12.1	28 33.5	12 49.7	14 11.4	14 51.5	29 20.6	24 40.0	18 50.8	25 26.0	2 37.4
12 Tu	17 21 09	19 33 46	2♑14 24	8♑40 25	28 02.5	29 06.6	14 04.4	14 51.3	15 05.3	29 24.1	24 38.2	18 48.8	25 26.6	2 36.5
13 W	17 25 06	20 34 48	15 02 23	21 20 21	27 52.4	29 46.6	15 19.1	15 31.2	15 18.8	29 27.8	24 36.6	18 46.7	25 27.1	2 35.6
14 Th	17 29 02	21 35 51	27 34 22	3♒44 38	27 42.9	0♐32.8	16 33.8	16 11.2	15 32.0	29 31.7	24 35.1	18 44.8	25 27.6	2 34.6
15 F	17 32 59	22 36 54	9♒51 22	15 54 55	27 34.8	1 24.3	17 48.5	16 51.2	15 45.0	29 35.7	24 33.6	18 42.8	25 28.1	2 33.7
16 Sa	17 36 55	23 37 58	21 55 39	27 54 02	27 28.9	2 20.6	19 03.1	17 31.3	15 57.6	29 40.0	24 32.3	18 40.9	25 28.5	2 32.7
17 Su	17 40 52	24 39 02	3♓50 35	9♓45 52	27 25.3	3 21.1	20 17.8	18 11.5	16 10.0	29 44.4	24 31.1	18 39.0	25 28.9	2 31.7
18 M	17 44 48	25 40 07	15 40 29	21 35 04	27D 23.8	4 25.3	21 32.4	18 51.7	16 22.0	29 49.1	24 30.0	18 37.1	25 29.3	2 30.7
19 Tu	17 48 45	26 41 12	27 30 18	3♈26 51	27 24.0	5 32.6	22 47.0	19 31.9	16 33.8	29 53.9	24 29.0	18 35.3	25 29.6	2 29.6
20 W	17 52 42	27 42 17	9♈25 23	15 26 36	27R 24.8	6 42.8	24 01.6	20 12.2	16 45.2	29 58.9	24 28.1	18 33.5	25 29.9	2 28.6
21 Th	17 56 38	28 43 22	21 31 09	27 39 40	27 25.3	7 55.4	25 16.2	20 52.5	16 56.3	0♈04.1	24 27.3	18 31.8	25 30.2	2 27.5
22 F	18 00 35	29 44 28	3♉52 44	10♉10 51	27 24.4	9 10.2	26 30.7	21 32.9	17 07.1	0 09.5	24 26.6	18 30.1	25 30.4	2 26.4
23 Sa	18 04 31	0♑45 34	16 34 28	23 03 56	27 21.4	10 26.9	27 45.2	22 13.3	17 17.6	0 15.0	24 26.1	18 28.4	25 30.6	2 25.3
24 Su	18 08 28	1 46 41	29 39 28	6♊21 09	27 15.7	11 45.2	28 59.7	22 53.7	17 27.7	0 20.8	24 25.6	18 26.8	25 30.7	2 24.2
25 M	18 12 24	2 47 47	13♊08 58	20 02 41	27 07.5	13 05.1	0♒14.2	23 34.2	17 37.5	0 26.7	24 25.3	18 25.2	25 30.9	2 23.1
26 Tu	18 16 21	3 48 54	27 01 58	4♋06 16	26 57.4	14 26.2	1 28.7	24 14.7	17 47.0	0 32.8	24 25.2	18 23.6	25 31.0	2 21.9
27 W	18 20 17	4 50 01	11♋14 57	18 27 15	26 46.2	15 48.5	2 43.1	24 55.2	17 56.1	0 39.0	24D 25.0	18 22.1	25 31.0	2 20.7
28 Th	18 24 14	5 51 09	25 42 19	2♌59 13	26 35.2	17 11.8	3 57.5	25 35.7	18 04.9	0 45.4	24 25.0	18 20.7	25R 31.0	2 19.6
29 F	18 28 11	6 52 17	10♌17 03	17 34 57	26 25.8	18 36.0	5 11.9	26 16.3	18 13.3	0 52.0	24 25.1	18 19.2	25 31.0	2 18.4
30 Sa	18 32 07	7 53 25	24 52 04	2♍07 42	26 18.7	20 01.1	6 26.3	26 56.9	18 21.4	0 58.8	24 25.3	18 17.9	25 31.0	2 17.2
31 Su	18 36 04	8 54 33	9♍21 14	16 32 11	26 14.4	21 26.9	7 40.6	27 37.5	18 29.1	1 05.7	24 25.6	18 16.5	25 30.9	2 16.0

Astro Data	Planet Ingress	Last Aspect	☽ Ingress	Last Aspect	☽ Ingress	☽ Phases & Eclipses	Astro Data
Dy Hr Mn	Dy Hr Mn	Dy Hr Mn	Dy Hr Mn	Dy Hr Mn	Dy Hr Mn	Dy Hr Mn	
♇ R 4 8:07	☿ ♐ 1 7:03	1 13:19 ♃ □	♋ 1 13:41	2 17:54 ♄ △	♍ 3 2:23	4 13:12 ☾ 11♌13	1 November 1939
☽ 0S 7 10:55	♀ ♐ 7 3:41	3 17:24 ♃ △	♌ 3 18:01	5 3:45 ♃ ☍	♎ 5 5:22	11 7:54 ● 18♏01	Julian Day # 14549
☿ R 18 11:04	♂ ♓ 19 15:56	5 18:00 ♀ □	♍ 5 20:57	6 23:59 ♄ ☍	♏ 7 8:57	18 23:21 ☽ 25♒43	SVP 6♓05'53"
☽ 0N 21 6:12	☉ ♐ 23 4:59	7 22:00 ♃ ☍	♎ 7 23:03	9 12:11 ♃ △	♐ 9 13:32	26 21:54 ○ 3♊45	GC 25♐59.9 ⚴ 27♋42.2
♃ D 24 21:17		9 19:06 ♄ ☍	♏ 10 1:14	11 18:40 ♃ □	♑ 11 19:51		Eris 3♈54.2R ⚵ 22♒00.2
♄⊼♆ 27 12:53	♀ ♑ 1 4:52	12 3:12 ♃ △	♐ 12 4:41	14 3:45 ♃ ⚹	♒ 14 4:42	3 20:40 ☾ 10♍47	⚷ 20♋03.8R ⚶ 29♈06.0R
	☿ ♏R 3 7:22	14 8:58 ♃ □	♑ 14 10:42	16 5:15 ♄ ⚹	♓ 16 16:14	10 21:45 ● 17♐57	☽ Mean ☊ 28♎45.5
☽ 0S 4 17:31	☿ ♐ 13 19:16	16 18:01 ♃ ⚹	♒ 16 20:00	19 4:47 ♃ ☌	♈ 19 5:03	18 21:04 ☽ 26♓03	
☿ D 8 6:22	♃ ♈ 20 17:03	19 7:33 ♂ ☌	♓ 19 8:00	21 14:15 ☉ △	♉ 21 16:32	26 11:28 ○ 3♋48	1 December 1939
☽ 0N 18 15:38	☉ ♑ 22 18:06	21 18:22 ♃ ☌	♈ 21 20:36	23 21:26 ♀ △	♊ 24 0:37		Julian Day # 14579
♄ D 28 1:12	♀ ♒ 25 7:25	23 22:38 ♄ ☌	♉ 24 7:23	25 21:24 ♆ □	♋ 26 5:03		SVP 6♓05'48"
♆ R 28 14:15		26 13:07 ♃ ⚹	♊ 26 15:09	27 23:41 ♆ ⚹	♌ 28 7:05		GC 26♐00.0 ⚴ 4♌12.3
		28 18:17 ♃ □	♋ 28 20:11	29 23:16 ♄ △	♍ 30 8:29		Eris 3♈42.2R ⚵ 29♒46.4
		30 21:45 ♃ △	♌ 30 23:34				⚷ 19♋22.1R ⚶ 23♈54.0R
							☽ Mean ☊ 27♎10.2

LONGITUDE — January 1940

Day	Sid.Time	☉	0 hr ☽	Noon ☽	True ☊	☿	♀	♂	⚳	♃	♄	♅	♆	♇
1 M	18 40 00	9♑55 42	23♍40 11	0♎45 01	26♎12.5	22♐53.5	8♒54.9	28♓18.2	18♍36.4	1♈12.8	24♈26.0	18♉15.2	25♍30.8	2♌14.8
2 Tu	18 43 57	10 56 52	7♎46 32	14 44 44	26R 12.3	24 20.7	10 09.2	28 58.8	18 43.3	1 20.0	24 26.6	18R 14.0	25R 30.6	2R 13.5
3 W	18 47 53	11 58 01	21 39 37	28 31 18	26 12.4	25 48.5	11 23.5	29 39.5	18 49.9	1 27.4	24 27.2	18 12.8	25 30.4	2 12.3
4 Th	18 51 50	12 59 12	5♏19 52	12♏05 27	26 11.6	27 16.9	12 37.8	0♈20.2	18 56.0	1 35.0	24 28.0	18 11.6	25 30.2	2 11.0
5 F	18 55 46	14 00 22	18 48 11	25 28 08	26 08.5	28 45.8	13 52.0	1 00.9	19 01.8	1 42.7	24 28.9	18 10.5	25 30.0	2 09.8
6 Sa	18 59 43	15 01 32	2♐05 25	8♐40 02	26 02.6	0♑15.2	15 06.2	1 41.7	19 07.2	1 50.5	24 29.9	18 09.4	25 29.7	2 08.5
7 Su	19 03 40	16 02 43	15 12 01	21 41 21	25 53.5	1 45.1	16 20.4	2 22.5	19 12.1	1 58.6	24 31.0	18 08.4	25 29.3	2 07.2
8 M	19 07 36	17 03 54	28 07 58	4♑31 50	25 41.6	3 15.5	17 34.5	3 03.3	19 16.7	2 06.7	24 32.2	18 07.5	25 29.0	2 05.9
9 Tu	19 11 33	18 05 04	10♑52 52	17 11 00	25 27.8	4 46.4	18 48.6	3 44.1	19 20.9	2 15.1	24 33.5	18 06.6	25 28.6	2 04.6
10 W	19 15 29	19 06 14	23 26 13	29 38 30	25 13.2	6 17.7	20 02.7	4 24.9	19 24.6	2 23.5	24 35.0	18 05.7	25 28.2	2 03.3
11 Th	19 19 26	20 07 24	5♒47 51	11♒54 22	24 59.1	7 49.5	21 16.7	5 05.8	19 27.9	2 32.1	24 36.5	18 04.9	25 27.7	2 02.0
12 F	19 23 22	21 08 34	17 58 11	23 59 28	24 46.7	9 21.8	22 30.7	5 46.6	19 30.8	2 40.9	24 38.2	18 04.1	25 27.2	2 00.7
13 Sa	19 27 19	22 09 42	29 58 29	5♓55 33	24 36.8	10 54.5	23 44.7	6 27.5	19 33.3	2 49.8	24 39.9	18 03.4	25 26.7	1 59.3
14 Su	19 31 15	23 10 51	11♓51 02	17 45 23	24 29.9	12 27.7	24 58.6	7 08.4	19 35.3	2 58.8	24 41.8	18 02.7	25 26.2	1 58.0
15 M	19 35 12	24 11 58	23 39 06	29 32 44	24 25.9	14 01.4	26 12.5	7 49.2	19 36.9	3 08.0	24 43.8	18 02.1	25 25.6	1 56.7
16 Tu	19 39 09	25 13 05	5♈26 53	11♈22 10	24 24.2	15 35.6	27 26.3	8 30.1	19 38.1	3 17.3	24 45.9	18 01.5	25 25.0	1 55.3
17 W	19 43 05	26 14 12	17 19 17	23 18 55	24 23.8	17 10.3	28 40.1	9 11.0	19 38.9	3 26.7	24 48.1	18 01.0	25 24.3	1 54.0
18 Th	19 47 02	27 15 17	29 21 45	5♉28 32	24 23.7	18 45.5	29 53.9	9 51.9	19R 39.2	3 36.3	24 50.4	18 00.6	25 23.6	1 52.6
19 F	19 50 58	28 16 22	11♉39 54	17 56 33	24 22.6	20 21.2	1♓07.6	10 32.8	19 39.1	3 46.0	24 52.8	18 00.2	25 22.9	1 51.3
20 Sa	19 54 55	29 17 26	24 19 04	0♊47 59	24 19.5	21 57.4	2 21.2	11 13.7	19 38.5	3 55.8	24 55.3	17 59.8	25 22.2	1 50.0
21 Su	19 58 51	0♒18 29	7♊23 43	14 06 34	24 13.8	23 34.2	3 34.8	11 54.7	19 37.5	4 05.8	24 57.9	17 59.5	25 21.4	1 48.6
22 M	20 02 48	1 19 31	20 56 41	27 54 02	24 05.4	25 11.6	4 48.3	12 35.6	19 36.1	4 15.8	25 00.6	17 59.2	25 20.6	1 47.3
23 Tu	20 06 44	2 20 32	4♋58 24	12♋09 19	23 54.8	26 49.6	6 01.8	13 16.5	19 34.2	4 26.0	25 03.4	17 59.0	25 19.8	1 45.9
24 W	20 10 41	3 21 32	19 26 10	26 48 06	23 42.9	28 28.1	7 15.3	13 57.4	19 31.9	4 36.3	25 06.3	17 58.9	25 18.9	1 44.6
25 Th	20 14 38	4 22 32	4♌14 07	11♌43 03	23 31.1	0♒07.3	8 28.6	14 38.3	19 29.1	4 46.7	25 09.3	17 58.8	25 18.1	1 43.2
26 F	20 18 34	5 23 31	19 13 42	26 44 48	23 20.8	1 47.1	9 42.0	15 19.2	19 25.9	4 57.3	25 12.4	17D 58.8	25 17.1	1 41.9
27 Sa	20 22 31	6 24 28	4♍15 10	11♍43 39	23 13.0	3 27.5	10 55.2	16 00.0	19 22.3	5 07.9	25 15.7	17 58.8	25 16.2	1 40.5
28 Su	20 26 27	7 25 26	19 09 15	26 31 10	23 08.0	5 08.6	12 08.4	16 40.9	19 18.2	5 18.7	25 19.0	17 58.8	25 15.2	1 39.2
29 M	20 30 24	8 26 22	3♎48 43	11♎01 26	23D 05.7	6 50.4	13 21.5	17 21.8	19 13.7	5 29.5	25 22.4	17 58.9	25 14.2	1 37.8
30 Tu	20 34 20	9 27 18	18 09 02	25 11 22	23 05.3	8 32.8	14 34.6	18 02.7	19 08.8	5 40.5	25 25.9	17 59.1	25 13.2	1 36.5
31 W	20 38 17	10 28 13	2♏08 26	9♏00 21	23R 05.5	10 16.0	15 47.6	18 43.5	19 03.4	5 51.6	25 29.5	17 59.3	25 12.1	1 35.1

LONGITUDE — February 1940

Day	Sid.Time	☉	0 hr ☽	Noon ☽	True ☊	☿	♀	♂	⚳	♃	♄	♅	♆	♇
1 Th	20 42 13	11♒29 08	15♏47 19	22♏29 34	23♎05.0	11♒59.8	17♓00.6	19♈24.4	18♍57.6	6♈02.7	25♈33.1	17♉59.6	25♍11.1	1♌33.8
2 F	20 46 10	12 30 02	29 07 23	5♐41 06	23R 02.7	13 44.2	18 13.5	20 05.2	18R 51.3	6 14.0	25 36.9	17 59.9	25R 10.0	1R 32.5
3 Sa	20 50 07	13 30 55	12♐11 00	18 37 22	22 57.8	15 29.4	19 26.3	20 46.1	18 44.7	6 25.4	25 40.8	18 00.3	25 08.8	1 31.2
4 Su	20 54 03	14 31 47	25 00 28	1♑20 34	22 50.1	17 15.2	20 39.1	21 26.9	18 37.6	6 36.9	25 44.8	18 00.7	25 07.7	1 29.8
5 M	20 58 00	15 32 38	7♑37 51	13 52 29	22 39.7	19 01.6	21 51.8	22 07.8	18 30.1	6 48.5	25 48.8	18 01.2	25 06.5	1 28.5
6 Tu	21 01 56	16 33 29	20 04 38	26 14 26	22 27.6	20 48.7	23 04.4	22 48.6	18 22.3	7 00.1	25 53.0	18 01.8	25 05.3	1 27.2
7 W	21 05 53	17 34 18	2♒21 59	8♒27 24	22 14.7	22 36.3	24 16.9	23 29.4	18 14.0	7 11.9	25 57.2	18 02.3	25 04.1	1 25.9
8 Th	21 09 49	18 35 05	14 30 46	20 32 12	22 02.1	24 24.4	25 29.4	24 10.3	18 05.3	7 23.8	26 01.6	18 03.0	25 02.8	1 24.6
9 F	21 13 46	19 35 52	26 31 50	2♓29 49	21 51.0	26 12.9	26 41.8	24 51.1	17 56.3	7 35.7	26 06.0	18 03.7	25 01.6	1 23.4
10 Sa	21 17 42	20 36 37	8♓26 21	14 21 39	21 42.2	28 01.7	27 54.1	25 31.9	17 46.9	7 47.7	26 10.5	18 04.4	25 00.3	1 22.1
11 Su	21 21 39	21 37 21	20 15 59	26 09 41	21 36.1	29 50.8	29 06.4	26 12.7	17 37.1	7 59.9	26 15.1	18 05.2	24 59.0	1 20.8
12 M	21 25 36	22 38 03	2♈03 05	7♈56 38	21 32.7	1♓40.0	0♈18.5	26 53.4	17 27.0	8 12.1	26 19.7	18 06.1	24 57.6	1 19.6
13 Tu	21 29 32	23 38 44	13 50 46	19 46 01	21D 31.5	3 29.2	1 30.6	27 34.2	17 16.6	8 24.4	26 24.5	18 07.0	24 56.3	1 18.3
14 W	21 33 29	24 39 23	25 42 55	1♉42 05	21 31.9	5 18.0	2 42.5	28 15.0	17 05.8	8 36.7	26 29.3	18 07.9	24 54.9	1 17.1
15 Th	21 37 25	25 40 00	7♉44 06	13 49 39	21 32.9	7 06.4	3 54.4	28 55.7	16 54.7	8 49.2	26 34.2	18 08.9	24 53.5	1 15.9
16 F	21 41 22	26 40 36	19 59 22	26 13 54	21R 33.5	8 54.0	5 06.2	29 36.4	16 43.4	9 01.7	26 39.2	18 10.0	24 52.1	1 14.7
17 Sa	21 45 18	27 41 09	2♊33 54	8♊59 57	21 32.7	10 40.6	6 17.9	0♉17.1	16 31.7	9 14.3	26 44.3	18 11.1	24 50.7	1 13.5
18 Su	21 49 15	28 41 42	15 32 34	22 12 13	21 30.1	12 25.7	7 29.5	0 57.8	16 19.8	9 27.0	26 49.4	18 12.2	24 49.2	1 12.3
19 M	21 53 11	29 42 12	28 59 12	5♋53 43	21 25.3	14 09.1	8 40.9	1 38.5	16 07.6	9 39.7	26 54.6	18 13.5	24 47.8	1 11.1
20 Tu	21 57 08	0♓42 41	12♋55 45	20 05 08	21 18.7	15 50.1	9 52.3	2 19.2	15 55.2	9 52.5	26 59.9	18 14.7	24 46.3	1 10.0
21 W	22 01 05	1 43 07	27 21 27	4♌44 04	21 11.0	17 28.4	11 03.6	2 59.8	15 42.6	10 05.4	27 05.3	18 16.0	24 44.8	1 08.8
22 Th	22 05 01	2 43 32	12♌12 09	19 44 38	21 03.1	19 03.4	12 14.7	3 40.4	15 29.8	10 18.4	27 10.7	18 17.4	24 43.3	1 07.7
23 F	22 08 58	3 43 55	27 20 20	4♍57 57	20 56.1	20 34.6	13 25.7	4 21.0	15 16.8	10 31.4	27 16.3	18 18.8	24 41.8	1 06.6
24 Sa	22 12 54	4 44 17	12♍36 05	20 13 25	20 50.9	22 01.2	14 36.7	5 01.6	15 03.6	10 44.4	27 21.8	18 20.2	24 40.3	1 05.5
25 Su	22 16 51	5 44 37	27 48 38	5♎20 35	20 47.8	23 22.8	15 47.5	5 42.2	14 50.2	10 57.6	27 27.5	18 21.7	24 38.7	1 04.4
26 M	22 20 47	6 44 55	12♎48 15	20 10 50	20D 46.9	24 38.6	16 58.1	6 22.7	14 36.7	11 10.8	27 33.2	18 23.2	24 37.2	1 03.3
27 Tu	22 24 44	7 45 12	27 27 42	4♏38 26	20 47.5	25 48.1	18 08.7	7 03.2	14 23.1	11 24.0	27 39.0	18 24.8	24 35.6	1 02.3
28 W	22 28 40	8 45 27	11♏42 48	18 40 42	20 48.8	26 50.6	19 19.1	7 43.7	14 09.4	11 37.3	27 44.8	18 26.5	24 34.0	1 01.2
29 Th	22 32 37	9 45 41	25 32 14	2♐17 34	20R 50.0	27 45.6	20 29.5	8 24.2	13 55.5	11 50.7	27 50.7	18 28.2	24 32.4	1 00.2

Astro Data

	Dy Hr Mn
☽0S	1 0:04
♂0N	4 21:25
♃△♇	8 9:54
♃0N	13 18:35
♃∠♅	14 21:34
☽0N	15 0:56
⚳R	18 17:13
♅D	26 20:25
♄⊼♆	27 15:05
☽0S	28 8:31
☽0N	11 8:57
♀0N	13 10:59
☽0S	24 19:10
☿0N	28 5:00

Planet Ingress

		Dy Hr Mn
♂	♈	4 0:05
☿	♑	6 7:56
♀	♓	18 14:00
☉	♒	21 4:44
☿	♒	25 10:14
☿	♓	11 14:01
♀	♈	12 5:51
♂	♉	17 1:54
☉	♓	19 19:04

Last Aspect / ☽ Ingress

Last Aspect Dy Hr Mn			☽ Ingress	Dy Hr Mn
1 7:38	♂	☍	♎	1 10:43
3 6:40	☿	⚹	♏	3 14:36
5 12:03	♆	⚹	♐	5 20:12
7 19:04	♆	□	♑	8 3:30
10 3:56	♆	△	♒	10 12:42
12 13:18	♄	⚹	♓	13 0:03
15 3:37	♆	☍	♈	15 12:55
17 23:50	♀	⚹	♉	18 1:15
20 8:59	☉	△	♊	20 10:32
22 7:37	♆	□	♋	22 15:35
24 15:02	☿	☍	♌	24 17:10
26 9:32	♄	△	♍	26 17:12
28 9:56	♆	☌	♎	28 17:43
30 12:25	♄	☍	♏	30 20:17

Last Aspect / ☽ Ingress

Last Aspect Dy Hr Mn			☽ Ingress	Dy Hr Mn
1 16:51	♆	⚹	♐	2 1:36
4 1:20	♄	△	♑	4 9:27
6 11:18	♄	□	♒	6 19:21
8 23:03	♄	⚹	♓	9 6:58
11 18:41	♀	☌	♈	11 19:49
14 4:40	♂	☌	♉	14 8:36
16 12:55	☉	□	♊	16 19:10
19 0:24	☉	△	♋	19 1:46
20 23:29	♄	□	♌	21 4:19
22 23:49	♄	△	♍	23 4:11
24 19:01	♆	☌	♎	25 3:29
27 0:14	♄	☍	♏	27 4:13
29 3:22	☿	△	♐	29 7:54

☽ Phases & Eclipses

Dy Hr Mn		
2 4:56	☾	10♎39
9 13:53	●	18♑10
17 18:21	☽	26♈30
24 23:22	○	3♌50
31 14:47	☾	10♏35
8 7:45	●	18♒24
16 12:55	☽	26♉43
23 9:55	○	3♍39

Astro Data

1 January 1940
Julian Day # 14610
SVP 6♓05'43"
GC 26♐00.1 ⚴ 0♌49.4R
Eris 3♈40.0 ⚵ 11♓56.0
⚷ 17♋32.4R ⚶ 25♈07.5
☽ Mean ☊ 25♎31.7

1 February 1940
Julian Day # 14641
SVP 6♓05'39"
GC 26♐00.1 ⚴ 21♋05.3R
Eris 3♈49.1 ⚵ 26♓47.2
⚷ 15♋26.8R ⚶ 1♉53.5
☽ Mean ☊ 23♎53.3

March 1940 LONGITUDE

Day	Sid.Time	☉	0 hr ☽	Noon ☽	True ☊	☿	♀	♂	⚳	♃	♄	♅	♆	♇
1 F	22 36 34	10♓45 54	8♐57 00	15♐30 51	20♎50.1	28♓32.5	21♈39.7	9♉04.7	13♍41.7	12♈04.1	27♈56.7	18♉29.9	24♍30.8	0♌59.2
2 Sa	22 40 30	11 46 05	21 59 31	28 23 25	20R 48.7	29 11.0	22 49.7	9 45.1	13R 27.7	12 17.6	28 02.7	18 31.7	24R 29.2	0R 58.2
3 Su	22 44 27	12 46 15	4♑42 59	10♑58 36	20 45.4	29 40.7	23 59.7	10 25.5	13 13.8	12 31.2	28 08.8	18 33.5	24 27.6	0 57.3
4 M	22 48 23	13 46 22	17 10 43	23 19 43	20 40.5	0♈01.3	25 09.5	11 06.0	12 59.8	12 44.7	28 15.0	18 35.3	24 26.0	0 56.3
5 Tu	22 52 20	14 46 29	29 25 56	5♒29 45	20 34.4	0R 12.6	26 19.1	11 46.4	12 45.8	12 58.4	28 21.2	18 37.2	24 24.3	0 55.4
6 W	22 56 16	15 46 33	11♒31 27	17 31 21	20 27.8	0 14.7	27 28.6	12 26.7	12 31.8	13 12.1	28 27.5	18 39.2	24 22.7	0 54.5
7 Th	23 00 13	16 46 36	23 29 42	29 26 44	20 21.3	0 07.8	28 38.0	13 07.1	12 17.9	13 25.8	28 33.8	18 41.2	24 21.1	0 53.6
8 F	23 04 09	17 46 37	5♓22 43	11♓17 52	20 15.6	29♓52.0	29 47.3	13 47.4	12 04.1	13 39.6	28 40.2	18 43.2	24 19.4	0 52.7
9 Sa	23 08 06	18 46 36	17 12 23	23 06 32	20 11.2	29 27.9	0♉56.3	14 27.8	11 50.3	13 53.4	28 46.6	18 45.3	24 17.7	0 51.9
10 Su	23 12 02	19 46 33	29 00 33	4♈54 40	20 08.4	28 56.2	2 05.3	15 08.1	11 36.7	14 07.2	28 53.1	18 47.4	24 16.1	0 51.1
11 M	23 15 59	20 46 28	10♈49 11	16 44 23	20D 07.3	28 17.6	3 14.0	15 48.3	11 23.2	14 21.1	28 59.7	18 49.6	24 14.4	0 50.3
12 Tu	23 19 56	21 46 21	22 40 37	28 38 13	20 07.5	27 33.1	4 22.6	16 28.6	11 09.8	14 35.1	29 06.3	18 51.8	24 12.8	0 49.5
13 W	23 23 52	22 46 12	4♉37 35	10♉39 08	20 08.8	26 43.7	5 31.1	17 08.8	10 56.5	14 49.0	29 12.9	18 54.0	24 11.1	0 48.7
14 Th	23 27 49	23 46 01	16 43 21	22 50 40	20 10.5	25 50.7	6 39.3	17 49.1	10 43.5	15 03.1	29 19.6	18 56.3	24 09.4	0 48.0
15 F	23 31 45	24 45 48	29 01 37	5♊16 41	20 12.2	24 55.3	7 47.4	18 29.3	10 30.6	15 17.1	29 26.3	18 58.6	24 07.8	0 47.3
16 Sa	23 35 42	25 45 32	11♊36 24	18 01 14	20R 13.3	23 58.8	8 55.3	19 09.4	10 18.0	15 31.2	29 33.1	19 01.0	24 06.1	0 46.6
17 Su	23 39 38	26 45 15	24 31 41	1♋08 10	20 13.4	23 02.3	10 03.1	19 49.6	10 05.6	15 45.3	29 39.9	19 03.4	24 04.4	0 45.9
18 M	23 43 35	27 44 55	7♋51 02	14 40 33	20 12.5	22 07.1	11 10.6	20 29.7	9 53.4	15 59.4	29 46.8	19 05.8	24 02.8	0 45.2
19 Tu	23 47 31	28 44 32	21 36 51	28 39 58	20 10.6	21 14.2	12 17.9	21 09.8	9 41.5	16 13.6	29 53.7	19 08.3	24 01.1	0 44.6
20 W	23 51 28	29 44 08	5♌49 45	13♌05 50	20 08.2	20 24.6	13 25.0	21 49.9	9 29.8	16 27.8	0♉00.7	19 10.8	23 59.4	0 44.0
21 Th	23 55 25	0♈43 41	20 27 43	27 54 43	20 05.5	19 39.1	14 31.9	22 30.0	9 18.4	16 42.0	0 07.7	19 13.3	23 57.8	0 43.4
22 F	23 59 21	1 43 11	5♍25 54	13♍00 16	20 03.1	18 58.3	15 38.6	23 10.0	9 07.3	16 56.3	0 14.7	19 15.9	23 56.1	0 42.9
23 Sa	0 03 18	2 42 40	20 36 38	28 13 47	20 01.4	18 22.7	16 45.1	23 50.0	8 56.5	17 10.5	0 21.8	19 18.5	23 54.5	0 42.3
24 Su	0 07 14	3 42 06	5♎50 25	13♎25 19	20D 00.6	17 52.7	17 51.3	24 30.0	8 46.1	17 24.8	0 28.9	19 21.1	23 52.9	0 41.8
25 M	0 11 11	4 41 31	20 57 18	28 25 19	20 00.7	17 28.4	18 57.4	25 09.9	8 35.9	17 39.1	0 36.0	19 23.8	23 51.2	0 41.3
26 Tu	0 15 07	5 40 54	5♏48 26	13♏05 56	20 01.4	17 10.2	20 03.1	25 49.8	8 26.1	17 53.4	0 43.2	19 26.5	23 49.6	0 40.9
27 W	0 19 04	6 40 15	20 17 15	27 21 59	20 02.4	16 57.8	21 08.7	26 29.7	8 16.7	18 07.8	0 50.4	19 29.3	23 48.0	0 40.4
28 Th	0 23 00	7 39 34	4♐19 58	11♐11 07	20 03.5	16D 51.3	22 14.0	27 09.6	8 07.6	18 22.2	0 57.6	19 32.0	23 46.4	0 40.0
29 F	0 26 57	8 38 51	17 55 32	24 33 26	20 04.3	16 50.6	23 19.0	27 49.5	7 58.8	18 36.6	1 04.9	19 34.8	23 44.8	0 39.6
30 Sa	0 30 54	9 38 07	1♑05 09	7♑31 02	20R 04.6	16 55.5	24 23.8	28 29.3	7 50.5	18 51.0	1 12.1	19 37.7	23 43.2	0 39.3
31 Su	0 34 50	10 37 21	13 51 33	20 07 11	20 04.5	17 05.8	25 28.4	29 09.1	7 42.5	19 05.4	1 19.5	19 40.5	23 41.6	0 38.9

April 1940 LONGITUDE

Day	Sid.Time	☉	0 hr ☽	Noon ☽	True ☊	☿	♀	♂	⚳	♃	♄	♅	♆	♇
1 M	0 38 47	11♈36 33	26♑18 27	2♒25 51	20♎03.9	17♓21.3	26♉32.6	29♉48.9	7♍34.9	19♈19.8	1♉26.8	19♉43.4	23♍40.0	0♌38.6
2 Tu	0 42 43	12 35 43	8♒29 54	14 31 08	20R 03.1	17 41.8	27 36.6	0♊28.7	7R 27.7	19 34.2	1 34.2	19 46.3	23R 38.4	0R 38.3
3 W	0 46 40	13 34 51	20 30 01	26 27 02	20 02.2	18 06.9	28 40.3	1 08.4	7 20.9	19 48.7	1 41.6	19 49.3	23 36.9	0 38.1
4 Th	0 50 36	14 33 58	2♓22 39	8♓17 16	20 01.3	18 36.6	29 43.8	1 48.2	7 14.5	20 03.1	1 49.0	19 52.2	23 35.4	0 37.8
5 F	0 54 33	15 33 02	14 11 17	20 05 04	20 00.7	19 10.5	0♊46.9	2 27.9	7 08.5	20 17.6	1 56.5	19 55.2	23 33.8	0 37.6
6 Sa	0 58 29	16 32 05	25 58 57	1♈53 16	20 00.3	19 48.5	1 49.7	3 07.6	7 02.9	20 32.1	2 03.9	19 58.2	23 32.3	0 37.4
7 Su	1 02 26	17 31 06	7♈48 19	13 44 21	20D 00.1	20 30.3	2 52.2	3 47.2	6 57.7	20 46.6	2 11.4	20 01.3	23 30.8	0 37.2
8 M	1 06 22	18 30 04	19 41 40	25 40 29	20 00.1	21 15.7	3 54.4	4 26.9	6 53.0	21 01.0	2 18.9	20 04.3	23 29.3	0 37.1
9 Tu	1 10 19	19 29 01	1♉41 05	7♉43 41	20R 00.1	22 04.6	4 56.2	5 06.5	6 48.7	21 15.5	2 26.4	20 07.4	23 27.9	0 37.0
10 W	1 14 16	20 27 55	13 48 32	19 55 54	20 00.1	22 56.8	5 57.7	5 46.1	6 44.8	21 30.0	2 34.0	20 10.6	23 26.4	0 36.9
11 Th	1 18 12	21 26 48	26 06 01	2♊19 10	20 00.0	23 52.0	6 58.8	6 25.7	6 41.3	21 44.5	2 41.6	20 13.7	23 25.0	0 36.9
12 F	1 22 09	22 25 38	8♊35 37	14 55 38	19 59.8	24 50.2	7 59.6	7 05.2	6 38.3	21 59.0	2 49.1	20 16.9	23 23.6	0D 36.8
13 Sa	1 26 05	23 24 26	21 19 31	27 47 33	19 59.5	25 51.2	9 00.0	7 44.8	6 35.7	22 13.5	2 56.7	20 20.0	23 22.2	0 36.8
14 Su	1 30 02	24 23 12	4♋19 59	10♋57 05	19 59.2	26 55.0	9 59.9	8 24.3	6 33.6	22 28.0	3 04.3	20 23.2	23 20.8	0 36.9
15 M	1 33 58	25 21 56	17 39 05	24 26 09	19D 59.1	28 01.3	10 59.5	9 03.8	6 31.8	22 42.4	3 11.9	20 26.5	23 19.4	0 36.9
16 Tu	1 37 55	26 20 37	1♌18 25	8♌15 56	19 59.2	29 10.0	11 58.7	9 43.2	6 30.5	22 56.9	3 19.5	20 29.7	23 18.1	0 37.0
17 W	1 41 51	27 19 16	15 18 41	22 26 30	19 59.6	0♈21.2	12 57.4	10 22.7	6 29.7	23 11.4	3 27.2	20 33.0	23 16.7	0 37.1
18 Th	1 45 48	28 17 53	29 39 09	6♍56 15	20 00.3	1 34.6	13 55.6	11 02.1	6D 29.2	23 25.8	3 34.8	20 36.2	23 15.4	0 37.2
19 F	1 49 45	29 16 28	14♍17 17	21 41 36	20 01.0	2 50.3	14 53.4	11 41.4	6 29.2	23 40.2	3 42.4	20 39.5	23 14.2	0 37.3
20 Sa	1 53 41	0♉15 00	29 08 26	6♎36 55	20R 01.6	4 08.1	15 50.7	12 20.8	6 29.6	23 54.7	3 50.1	20 42.8	23 12.9	0 37.5
21 Su	1 57 38	1 13 30	14♎06 06	21 34 57	20 01.8	5 28.0	16 47.5	13 00.1	6 30.4	24 09.1	3 57.7	20 46.1	23 11.6	0 37.7
22 M	2 01 34	2 11 59	29 02 28	6♏27 37	20 01.4	6 50.0	17 43.8	13 39.4	6 31.6	24 23.5	4 05.4	20 49.5	23 10.4	0 38.0
23 Tu	2 05 31	3 10 25	13♏49 27	21 07 05	20 00.4	8 13.9	18 39.5	14 18.7	6 33.3	24 37.9	4 13.0	20 52.8	23 09.2	0 38.2
24 W	2 09 27	4 08 50	28 19 46	5♐26 52	19 58.8	9 39.9	19 34.7	14 58.0	6 35.3	24 52.2	4 20.7	20 56.2	23 08.1	0 38.5
25 Th	2 13 24	5 07 14	12♐27 56	19 22 37	19 56.9	11 07.7	20 29.3	15 37.2	6 37.8	25 06.6	4 28.4	20 59.6	23 06.9	0 38.8
26 F	2 17 20	6 05 35	26 10 47	2♑52 23	19 54.9	12 37.5	21 23.4	16 16.5	6 40.6	25 20.9	4 36.0	21 02.9	23 05.8	0 39.1
27 Sa	2 21 17	7 03 55	9♑27 34	15 56 33	19 53.3	14 09.2	22 16.8	16 55.7	6 43.9	25 35.3	4 43.7	21 06.3	23 04.7	0 39.5
28 Su	2 25 14	8 02 14	22 19 40	28 37 21	19D 52.2	15 42.7	23 09.6	17 34.8	6 47.5	25 49.6	4 51.3	21 09.8	23 03.6	0 39.9
29 M	2 29 10	9 00 30	4♒50 04	10♒58 21	19 51.9	17 18.1	24 01.8	18 14.0	6 51.6	26 03.9	4 59.0	21 13.2	23 02.5	0 40.3
30 Tu	2 33 07	9 58 46	17 02 48	23 03 58	19 52.5	18 55.4	24 53.3	18 53.1	6 56.0	26 18.1	5 06.6	21 16.6	23 01.5	0 40.7

Astro Data	Planet Ingress	Last Aspect	☽ Ingress	Last Aspect	☽ Ingress	☽ Phases & Eclipses	Astro Data
Dy Hr Mn	Dy Hr Mn	Dy Hr Mn	Dy Hr Mn	Dy Hr Mn	Dy Hr Mn	Dy Hr Mn	1 March 1940
☿ R 6 5:30	☿ ♈ 4 10:09	2 13:34 ☿ □	♑ 2 15:02	1 6:34 ♂ △	♒ 1 7:13	1 2:35 ☾ 10♐22	Julian Day # 14670
☽ 0N 9 15:30	☿ ♓R 8 1:25	4 21:45 ♄ □	♒ 5 1:07	3 16:56 ♀ □	♓ 3 19:11	9 2:23 ● 18♓23	SVP 6♓05'35"
☿ 0S 17 20:29	♀ ♉ 8 16:25	7 10:12 ♄ ✶	♓ 7 13:07	5 19:04 ♆ ☍	♈ 6 8:10	17 3:25 ☽ 26♊24	GC 26♐00.2 ⚵ 18♋11.6
☉ 0N 20 18:24	♄ ♉ 20 9:40	10 0:24 ☿ ☌	♈ 10 2:01	8 2:28 ♃ ☌	♉ 8 20:39	23 19:33 ○ 3♎01	Eris 4♈05.7 ✱ 12♈15.6
☽ 0S 23 6:36	☉ ♈ 20 18:24	12 12:57 ♄ ☌	♉ 12 14:44	10 18:49 ♆ △	♊ 11 7:32	23 19:48 ☍ A 0.079	⚷ 14♋09.7R ⚶ 11♉15.6
♄□♇ 26 4:48		14 17:26 ☿ ✶	♊ 15 1:53	13 8:06 ☿ □	♋ 13 16:04	30 16:20 ☾ 9♑49	☽ Mean ☊ 22♎21.1
☿ D 29 2:56	♂ ♊ 1 18:41	17 9:19 ♄ ✶	♋ 17 9:57	15 18:51 ☿ △	♌ 15 21:44		
	♀ ♊ 4 18:10	19 14:05 ♄ □	♌ 19 14:15	17 20:43 ☉ △	♍ 18 0:34	7 20:18 ● 17♈52	1 April 1940
♃⚺♅ 3 13:11	☿ ♈ 17 4:56	21 2:53 ♂ □	♍ 21 15:21	19 14:29 ♆ ☌	♎ 20 1:23	7 20:20:56 ☌ A 07'30"	Julian Day # 14701
☽ 0N 5 21:33	☉ ♉ 20 5:51	23 5:12 ♆ ☌	♎ 23 14:47	21 16:12 ♃ ☍	♏ 22 1:33	15 13:45 ☽ 25♋26	SVP 6♓05'33"
♇ D 13 3:15		24 18:27 ♃ ☍	♏ 25 14:33	23 15:22 ♆ ✶	♐ 24 2:48	22 4:37 ○ 1♏54	GC 26♐00.3 ⚵ 23♋37.4
♃⚻♆ 17 20:13		27 10:26 ♂ ☍	♐ 27 16:31	25 22:17 ♃ △	♑ 26 6:50	22 4:26 ☍ A 0.868	Eris 4♈27.6 ✱ 29♈51.8
⚳ D 19 1:24		29 10:32 ♆ □	♑ 29 21:59	28 6:33 ♃ □	♒ 28 14:39	29 7:49 ☾ 8♒50	⚷ 14♋06.9 ⚶ 23♉04.7
☽ 0S 19 16:58							☽ Mean ☊ 20♎42.6
☿ 0N 22 3:14							

LONGITUDE — May 1940

Day	Sid.Time	☉	0 hr ☽	Noon☽	True☊	☿	♀	♂	⚳	♃	♄	♅	♆	♇
1 W	2 37 03	10♉57 00	29♒02 29	4♓58 55	19♎53.7	20♈34.5	25♊44.1	19♊32.3	7♍00.8	26♈32.4	5♉14.3	21♉20.0	23♍00.5	0♌41.2
2 Th	2 41 00	11 55 12	10♓53 53	16 47 57	19 55.3	22 15.4	26 34.2	20 11.4	7 06.0	26 46.6	5 21.9	21 23.5	22R 59.5	0 41.6
3 F	2 44 56	12 53 22	22 41 39	28 35 31	19 56.9	23 58.2	27 23.5	20 50.4	7 11.5	27 00.8	5 29.5	21 26.9	22 58.6	0 42.1
4 Sa	2 48 53	13 51 32	4♈30 02	10♈25 39	19R 58.1	25 42.9	28 12.1	21 29.5	7 17.5	27 14.9	5 37.1	21 30.4	22 57.6	0 42.7
5 Su	2 52 49	14 49 39	16 22 47	22 21 49	19 58.4	27 29.4	28 59.9	22 08.5	7 23.8	27 29.1	5 44.7	21 33.8	22 56.7	0 43.2
6 M	2 56 46	15 47 45	28 23 03	4♉26 47	19 57.6	29 17.8	29 46.9	22 47.6	7 30.5	27 43.2	5 52.3	21 37.3	22 55.9	0 43.8
7 Tu	3 00 43	16 45 50	10♉33 16	16 42 41	19 55.4	1♉08.1	0♋33.0	23 26.6	7 37.5	27 57.2	5 59.9	21 40.8	22 55.0	0 44.4
8 W	3 04 39	17 43 53	22 55 12	29 10 56	19 52.0	3 00.2	1 18.2	24 05.6	7 44.9	28 11.3	6 07.5	21 44.3	22 54.2	0 45.0
9 Th	3 08 36	18 41 54	5♊29 59	11♊52 25	19 47.7	4 54.2	2 02.5	24 44.5	7 52.6	28 25.3	6 15.0	21 47.8	22 53.4	0 45.7
10 F	3 12 32	19 39 54	18 18 15	24 47 31	19 42.9	6 50.0	2 45.8	25 23.5	8 00.7	28 39.3	6 22.6	21 51.2	22 52.6	0 46.4
11 Sa	3 16 29	20 37 52	1♋20 12	7♋56 20	19 38.2	8 47.6	3 28.1	26 02.4	8 09.2	28 53.2	6 30.1	21 54.7	22 51.9	0 47.1
12 Su	3 20 25	21 35 48	14 35 52	21 18 48	19 34.3	10 47.1	4 09.4	26 41.3	8 17.9	29 07.1	6 37.6	21 58.2	22 51.2	0 47.8
13 M	3 24 22	22 33 42	28 05 07	4♌54 48	19 31.6	12 48.3	4 49.6	27 20.2	8 27.0	29 21.0	6 45.1	22 01.7	22 50.5	0 48.6
14 Tu	3 28 18	23 31 35	11♌47 47	18 44 04	19D 30.4	14 51.2	5 28.7	27 59.1	8 36.5	29 34.8	6 52.6	22 05.2	22 49.9	0 49.3
15 W	3 32 15	24 29 25	25 43 33	2♍46 09	19 30.6	16 55.7	6 06.6	28 37.9	8 46.2	29 48.6	7 00.0	22 08.7	22 49.3	0 50.1
16 Th	3 36 12	25 27 14	9♍51 44	17 00 05	19 31.7	19 01.7	6 43.2	29 16.7	8 56.3	0♉02.3	7 07.4	22 12.1	22 48.7	0 50.9
17 F	3 40 08	26 25 01	24 10 58	1♎24 04	19 33.1	21 09.1	7 18.6	29 55.5	9 06.7	0 16.0	7 14.8	22 15.6	22 48.2	0 51.8
18 Sa	3 44 05	27 22 47	8♎38 58	15 55 11	19R 33.9	23 17.7	7 52.7	0♋34.3	9 17.3	0 29.7	7 22.2	22 19.1	22 47.6	0 52.6
19 Su	3 48 01	28 20 30	23 12 09	0♏29 14	19 33.5	25 27.4	8 25.3	1 13.1	9 28.3	0 43.3	7 29.5	22 22.6	22 47.1	0 53.5
20 M	3 51 58	29 18 13	7♏45 45	15 00 56	19 31.4	27 38.0	8 56.6	1 51.8	9 39.6	0 56.9	7 36.8	22 26.0	22 46.7	0 54.4
21 Tu	3 55 54	0♊15 54	22 14 03	29 24 21	19 27.3	29 49.2	9 26.4	2 30.6	9 51.1	1 10.4	7 44.1	22 29.5	22 46.3	0 55.4
22 W	3 59 51	1 13 34	6♐31 06	13♐33 41	19 21.7	2♊00.8	9 54.7	3 09.3	10 03.0	1 23.8	7 51.4	22 33.0	22 45.9	0 56.3
23 Th	4 03 47	2 11 12	20 31 31	27 24 08	19 14.9	4 12.5	10 21.3	3 48.0	10 15.1	1 37.3	7 58.6	22 36.4	22 45.5	0 57.3
24 F	4 07 44	3 08 49	4♑11 13	10♑52 32	19 07.9	6 24.1	10 46.4	4 26.6	10 27.5	1 50.6	8 05.8	22 39.9	22 45.2	0 58.3
25 Sa	4 11 41	4 06 26	17 28 01	23 57 44	19 01.5	8 35.2	11 09.7	5 05.3	10 40.2	2 03.9	8 13.0	22 43.3	22 44.9	0 59.3
26 Su	4 15 37	5 04 01	0♒21 49	6♒40 33	18 56.3	10 45.7	11 31.3	5 43.9	10 53.1	2 17.2	8 20.2	22 46.7	22 44.6	1 00.3
27 M	4 19 34	6 01 35	12 54 19	19 03 33	18 52.8	12 55.2	11 51.1	6 22.5	11 06.3	2 30.4	8 27.3	22 50.1	22 44.3	1 01.4
28 Tu	4 23 30	6 59 09	25 08 47	1♓10 34	18D 51.2	15 03.5	12 09.0	7 01.1	11 19.8	2 43.6	8 34.4	22 53.6	22 44.1	1 02.4
29 W	4 27 27	7 56 41	7♓09 32	13 06 19	18 51.1	17 10.3	12 25.0	7 39.7	11 33.5	2 56.7	8 41.4	22 57.0	22 44.0	1 03.5
30 Th	4 31 23	8 54 13	19 01 33	24 55 54	18 52.1	19 15.5	12 39.0	8 18.3	11 47.5	3 09.7	8 48.4	23 00.3	22 43.8	1 04.6
31 F	4 35 20	9 51 44	0♈50 01	6♈44 33	18 53.3	21 18.8	12 50.9	8 56.9	12 01.7	3 22.7	8 55.4	23 03.7	22 43.7	1 05.8

LONGITUDE — June 1940

Day	Sid.Time	☉	0 hr ☽	Noon☽	True☊	☿	♀	♂	⚳	♃	♄	♅	♆	♇
1 Sa	4 39 16	10♊49 14	12♈40 05	18♈37 15	18♎53.9	23♊20.1	13♋00.8	9♋35.4	12♍16.1	3♉35.6	9♉02.3	23♉07.1	22♍43.6	1♌06.9
2 Su	4 43 13	11 46 43	24 36 33	0♉38 31	18R 53.1	25 19.3	13 08.5	10 14.0	12 30.8	3 48.5	9 09.2	23 10.4	22D 43.6	1 08.1
3 M	4 47 10	12 44 11	6♉43 34	12 52 05	18 50.3	27 16.2	13 14.0	10 52.5	12 45.8	4 01.2	9 16.0	23 13.8	22 43.5	1 09.3
4 Tu	4 51 06	13 41 39	19 04 24	25 20 45	18 45.3	29 10.8	13R 17.3	11 31.0	13 00.9	4 14.0	9 22.8	23 17.1	22 43.6	1 10.5
5 W	4 55 03	14 39 06	1♊41 17	8♊06 04	18 38.1	1♋02.9	13 18.3	12 09.5	13 16.3	4 26.6	9 29.6	23 20.4	22 43.6	1 11.7
6 Th	4 58 59	15 36 32	14 35 07	21 08 21	18 29.2	2 52.5	13 16.9	12 48.0	13 31.9	4 39.2	9 36.3	23 23.7	22 43.7	1 13.0
7 F	5 02 56	16 33 57	27 45 37	4♋26 42	18 19.5	4 39.7	13 13.2	13 26.5	13 47.8	4 51.7	9 43.0	23 27.0	22 43.8	1 14.2
8 Sa	5 06 52	17 31 21	11♋11 20	17 59 11	18 09.9	6 24.2	13 07.1	14 04.9	14 03.8	5 04.2	9 49.6	23 30.3	22 44.0	1 15.5
9 Su	5 10 49	18 28 44	24 49 58	1♌43 19	18 01.6	8 06.2	12 58.5	14 43.4	14 20.1	5 16.6	9 56.2	23 33.5	22 44.1	1 16.8
10 M	5 14 45	19 26 06	8♌38 55	15 36 26	17 55.2	9 45.5	12 47.6	15 21.8	14 36.6	5 28.9	10 02.8	23 36.7	22 44.4	1 18.1
11 Tu	5 18 42	20 23 27	22 35 35	29 36 08	17 51.3	11 22.2	12 34.2	16 00.2	14 53.2	5 41.1	10 09.2	23 39.9	22 44.6	1 19.4
12 W	5 22 39	21 20 47	6♍37 51	13♍40 33	17D 49.5	12 56.3	12 18.5	16 38.6	15 10.1	5 53.2	10 15.7	23 43.1	22 44.9	1 20.8
13 Th	5 26 35	22 18 06	20 44 04	27 48 16	17 49.4	14 27.6	12 00.4	17 17.0	15 27.2	6 05.3	10 22.1	23 46.3	22 45.2	1 22.1
14 F	5 30 32	23 15 24	4♎53 00	11♎58 07	17R 49.8	15 56.3	11 40.0	17 55.4	15 44.4	6 17.3	10 28.4	23 49.5	22 45.5	1 23.5
15 Sa	5 34 28	24 12 42	19 03 27	26 08 48	17 49.7	17 22.2	11 17.3	18 33.7	16 01.9	6 29.2	10 34.7	23 52.6	22 45.9	1 24.9
16 Su	5 38 25	25 09 58	3♏13 54	10♏18 29	17 47.9	18 45.4	10 52.5	19 12.1	16 19.5	6 41.0	10 40.9	23 55.7	22 46.3	1 26.3
17 M	5 42 21	26 07 14	17 22 10	24 24 34	17 43.6	20 05.8	10 25.7	19 50.4	16 37.4	6 52.8	10 47.1	23 58.8	22 46.7	1 27.7
18 Tu	5 46 18	27 04 28	1♐25 14	8♐23 41	17 36.7	21 23.3	9 56.9	20 28.7	16 55.3	7 04.4	10 53.2	24 01.8	22 47.2	1 29.1
19 W	5 50 14	28 01 43	15 19 28	22 12 04	17 27.4	22 38.0	9 26.3	21 07.0	17 13.5	7 16.0	10 59.2	24 04.9	22 47.7	1 30.6
20 Th	5 54 11	28 58 57	29 01 04	5♑46 02	17 16.5	23 49.7	8 54.2	21 45.3	17 31.9	7 27.5	11 05.2	24 07.9	22 48.3	1 32.0
21 F	5 58 08	29 56 10	12♑26 39	19 02 39	17 05.0	24 58.5	8 20.6	22 23.6	17 50.4	7 38.9	11 11.2	24 10.9	22 48.8	1 33.5
22 Sa	6 02 04	0♋53 23	25 33 52	2♒00 15	16 54.1	26 04.2	7 45.8	23 01.9	18 09.0	7 50.2	11 17.1	24 13.8	22 49.4	1 35.0
23 Su	6 06 01	1 50 36	8♒21 49	14 38 43	16 44.7	27 06.7	7 09.9	23 40.1	18 27.9	8 01.4	11 22.9	24 16.8	22 50.0	1 36.5
24 M	6 09 57	2 47 49	20 51 12	26 59 34	16 37.6	28 06.0	6 33.3	24 18.4	18 46.9	8 12.6	11 28.6	24 19.7	22 50.7	1 38.0
25 Tu	6 13 54	3 45 01	3♓04 14	9♓05 41	16 33.0	29 02.0	5 56.1	24 56.6	19 06.0	8 23.6	11 34.3	24 22.6	22 51.4	1 39.5
26 W	6 17 50	4 42 13	15 04 28	21 01 08	16 30.6	29 54.6	5 18.6	25 34.9	19 25.3	8 34.5	11 40.0	24 25.4	22 52.1	1 41.0
27 Th	6 21 47	5 39 26	26 56 21	2♈50 45	16D 29.9	0♌43.7	4 41.0	26 13.1	19 44.8	8 45.3	11 45.5	24 28.2	22 52.9	1 42.5
28 F	6 25 43	6 36 38	8♈45 02	14 39 52	16R 29.9	1 29.2	4 03.6	26 51.3	20 04.4	8 56.1	11 51.0	24 31.0	22 53.6	1 44.1
29 Sa	6 29 40	7 33 51	20 35 56	26 33 54	16 29.6	2 10.9	3 26.6	27 29.5	20 24.1	9 06.7	11 56.5	24 33.8	22 54.5	1 45.6
30 Su	6 33 37	8 31 04	2♉34 26	8♉38 09	16 28.0	2 48.8	2 50.2	28 07.7	20 44.0	9 17.2	12 01.8	24 36.6	22 55.3	1 47.2

Astro Data	Planet Ingress	Last Aspect	☽ Ingress	Last Aspect	☽ Ingress	☽ Phases & Eclipses	Astro Data
Dy Hr Mn	Dy Hr Mn	Dy Hr Mn	Dy Hr Mn	Dy Hr Mn	Dy Hr Mn	Dy Hr Mn	
☽0N 3 4:20	♀ ♋ 6 18:47	30 18:37 ♃ ⚹	♓ 1 1:56	1 23:20 ☿ ⚹	♉ 2 10:44	7 12:07 ● 16♉46	1 May 1940
☽0S 17 1:21	☿ ♉ 6 21:14	3 9:23 ♀ □	♈ 3 14:52	4 8:03 ♅ ☌	♊ 4 20:49	14 20:51 ☽ 23♌53	Julian Day # 14731
♃□♇ 20 7:24	♃ ♉ 16 7:54	6 2:08 ♀ ⚹	♉ 6 3:12	6 14:53 ♆ □	♋ 7 4:02	21 13:33 ○ 0♐20	SVP 6♓05'30"
♄⚼♆ 21 18:37	♂ ♋ 17 14:45	7 23:59 ♆ △	♊ 8 13:34	8 21:43 ♅ ⚹	♌ 9 9:00	29 0:40 ☾ 7♓30	GC 26♐00.4 ⚴ 3♌29.6
♅△♆ 25 22:03	☉ ♊ 21 5:23	10 19:13 ♃ ⚹	♋ 10 21:33	11 1:48 ♅ □	♍ 11 12:41		Eris 4♈47.7 ⚵ 17♉29.2
☽0N 30 12:34	☿ ♊ 21 13:59	13 2:04 ♃ □	♌ 13 3:22	13 5:08 ♅ △	♎ 13 15:43	6 1:05 ● 15♊10	⚷ 15♋26.6 ⚶ 5♊28.1
		15 6:53 ♃ △	♍ 15 7:18	15 8:29 ☉ △	♏ 15 18:32	13 1:59 ☽ 21♍54	☽ Mean ☊ 19♎07.2
♆ D 3 11:47	☿ ♋ 4 22:29	17 9:26 ♂ □	♎ 17 9:40	17 11:16 ♅ ☍	♐ 17 21:34	19 23:02 ○ 28♐28	
♀ R 5 10:05	☉ ♋ 21 13:36	17 22:11 ♀ □	♏ 19 11:12	19 23:02 ☉ ☍	♑ 20 1:44	27 18:13 ☾ 5♈54	1 June 1940
☽0S 13 8:09	☿ ♌ 26 14:32	21 12:49 ☿ ☍	♐ 21 13:00	21 23:56 ☿ ☍	♒ 22 8:15		Julian Day # 14762
♃⚼♆ 22 10:12		23 3:53 ♆ □	♑ 23 16:35	24 6:45 ♅ □	♓ 24 17:55		SVP 6♓05'26"
☽0N 26 21:50		25 9:45 ♆ △	♒ 25 23:19	26 21:46 ♂ △	♈ 27 6:13		GC 26♐00.4 ⚴ 15♌52.5
		27 19:28 ♅ □	♓ 28 9:39	29 13:58 ♂ □	♉ 29 18:52		Eris 5♈02.4 ⚵ 5♊53.6
		30 8:04 ♅ ⚹	♈ 30 22:18				⚷ 17♋56.5 ⚶ 18♊44.8
							☽ Mean ☊ 17♎28.7

July 1940 LONGITUDE

Day	Sid.Time	☉	0 hr ☽	Noon ☽	True ☊	☿	♀	♂	⚳	♃	♄	♅	♆	♇
1 M	6 37 33	9♋28 16	14♉45 36	20♉57 17	16♎24.3	3♌22.7	2♋14.6	28♋46.0	21♍04.1	9♉27.7	12♉07.1	24♉39.3	22♍56.2	1♌48.8
2 Tu	6 41 30	10 25 29	27 13 39	3♊35 03	16R 18.0	3 52.5	1R 40.2	29 24.2	21 24.3	9 38.0	12 12.4	24 42.0	22 57.1	1 50.4
3 W	6 45 26	11 22 43	10♊01 43	16 33 46	16 09.2	4 18.0	1 07.0	0♌02.3	21 44.6	9 48.2	12 17.5	24 44.6	22 58.0	1 52.0
4 Th	6 49 23	12 19 56	23 11 16	29 54 03	15 58.3	4 39.2	0 35.3	0 40.5	22 05.0	9 58.3	12 22.6	24 47.2	22 59.0	1 53.6
5 F	6 53 19	13 17 09	6♋41 55	13♋34 31	15 46.4	4 55.9	0 05.2	1 18.7	22 25.6	10 08.3	12 27.6	24 49.8	23 00.0	1 55.2
6 Sa	6 57 16	14 14 23	20 31 23	27 31 58	15 34.6	5 08.1	29♊36.9	1 56.9	22 46.4	10 18.2	12 32.6	24 52.4	23 01.0	1 56.8
7 Su	7 01 12	15 11 36	4♌35 39	11♌41 48	15 24.2	5 15.6	29 10.4	2 35.1	23 07.2	10 27.9	12 37.4	24 54.9	23 02.0	1 58.4
8 M	7 05 09	16 08 49	18 49 44	25 58 50	15 16.0	5R 18.5	28 46.0	3 13.2	23 28.2	10 37.6	12 42.2	24 57.4	23 03.1	2 00.1
9 Tu	7 09 06	17 06 02	3♍08 28	10♍18 06	15 10.7	5 16.5	28 23.8	3 51.4	23 49.3	10 47.1	12 46.9	24 59.8	23 04.2	2 01.7
10 W	7 13 02	18 03 15	17 27 16	24 35 35	15 07.9	5 09.9	28 03.7	4 29.5	24 10.5	10 56.5	12 51.6	25 02.2	23 05.4	2 03.4
11 Th	7 16 59	19 00 28	1♎42 44	8♎48 29	15 07.1	4 58.5	27 45.9	5 07.7	24 31.8	11 05.8	12 56.1	25 04.6	23 06.5	2 05.0
12 F	7 20 55	19 57 41	15 52 41	22 55 12	15 07.1	4 42.6	27 30.4	5 45.8	24 53.3	11 15.0	13 00.6	25 06.9	23 07.7	2 06.7
13 Sa	7 24 52	20 54 54	29 55 57	6♏54 54	15 06.5	4 22.3	27 17.2	6 23.9	25 14.9	11 24.0	13 05.0	25 09.2	23 09.0	2 08.3
14 Su	7 28 48	21 52 07	13♏51 57	20 47 04	15 04.3	3 57.7	27 06.4	7 02.0	25 36.5	11 32.9	13 09.3	25 11.5	23 10.2	2 10.0
15 M	7 32 45	22 49 20	27 40 10	4♐31 07	14 59.6	3 29.3	26 58.0	7 40.2	25 58.3	11 41.7	13 13.5	25 13.7	23 11.5	2 11.7
16 Tu	7 36 41	23 46 33	11♐19 46	18 05 58	14 52.1	2 57.3	26 52.0	8 18.3	26 20.2	11 50.3	13 17.7	25 15.9	23 12.8	2 13.3
17 W	7 40 38	24 43 47	24 49 31	1♑30 12	14 42.1	2 22.2	26 48.4	8 56.4	26 42.2	11 58.9	13 21.8	25 18.1	23 14.1	2 15.0
18 Th	7 44 35	25 41 01	8♑07 47	14 42 05	14 30.5	1 44.5	26D 47.1	9 34.5	27 04.3	12 07.3	13 25.7	25 20.2	23 15.5	2 16.7
19 F	7 48 31	26 38 15	21 12 54	27 40 06	14 18.1	1 04.8	26 48.2	10 12.6	27 26.5	12 15.5	13 29.6	25 22.3	23 16.8	2 18.4
20 Sa	7 52 28	27 35 29	4♒03 32	10♒23 11	14 06.3	0 23.7	26 51.5	10 50.7	27 48.8	12 23.6	13 33.4	25 24.3	23 18.2	2 20.1
21 Su	7 56 24	28 32 45	16 39 03	22 51 13	13 56.1	29♋42.0	26 57.1	11 28.8	28 11.2	12 31.6	13 37.2	25 26.3	23 19.7	2 21.8
22 M	8 00 21	29 30 00	28 59 51	5♓05 09	13 48.1	29 00.3	27 04.8	12 06.8	28 33.6	12 39.5	13 40.8	25 28.2	23 21.1	2 23.5
23 Tu	8 04 17	0♌27 17	11♓07 26	17 07 03	13 42.7	28 19.4	27 14.7	12 44.9	28 56.2	12 47.2	13 44.3	25 30.1	23 22.6	2 25.1
24 W	8 08 14	1 24 34	23 04 28	29 00 08	13 39.8	27 40.0	27 26.7	13 23.0	29 18.9	12 54.7	13 47.8	25 32.0	23 24.1	2 26.8
25 Th	8 12 10	2 21 52	4♈54 36	10♈48 12	13D 38.8	27 03.0	27 40.8	14 01.1	29 41.7	13 02.1	13 51.1	25 33.8	23 25.6	2 28.5
26 F	8 16 07	3 19 12	16 42 19	22 36 50	13R 39.0	26 28.8	27 56.8	14 39.2	0♎04.5	13 09.4	13 54.4	25 35.6	23 27.2	2 30.2
27 Sa	8 20 04	4 16 32	28 32 41	4♉30 33	13 39.2	25 58.3	28 14.7	15 17.3	0 27.4	13 16.5	13 57.6	25 37.4	23 28.8	2 31.9
28 Su	8 24 00	5 13 53	10♉31 05	16 34 59	13 38.6	25 32.1	28 34.5	15 55.4	0 50.5	13 23.5	14 00.7	25 39.1	23 30.4	2 33.6
29 M	8 27 57	6 11 15	22 42 53	28 55 24	13 36.3	25 10.5	28 56.1	16 33.4	1 13.6	13 30.3	14 03.7	25 40.7	23 32.0	2 35.3
30 Tu	8 31 53	7 08 38	5♊13 03	11♊36 19	13 31.7	24 54.2	29 19.4	17 11.5	1 36.8	13 37.0	14 06.6	25 42.3	23 33.6	2 37.0
31 W	8 35 50	8 06 03	18 05 36	24 41 09	13 24.9	24 43.5	29 44.3	17 49.6	2 00.1	13 43.5	14 09.4	25 43.9	23 35.3	2 38.7

August 1940 LONGITUDE

Day	Sid.Time	☉	0 hr ☽	Noon ☽	True ☊	☿	♀	♂	⚳	♃	♄	♅	♆	♇
1 Th	8 39 46	9♌03 28	1♋23 06	8♋11 26	13♎16.2	24♋38.7	0♋10.9	18♌27.7	2♎23.4	13♉49.8	14♉12.1	25♉45.4	23♍37.0	2♌40.4
2 F	8 43 43	10 00 55	15 06 01	22 06 29	13R 06.4	24D 40.1	0 39.0	19 05.8	2 46.9	13 56.0	14 14.7	25 46.9	23 38.7	2 42.1
3 Sa	8 47 39	10 58 22	29 12 22	6♌23 01	12 56.6	24 47.9	1 08.6	19 43.9	3 10.4	14 02.1	14 17.2	25 48.3	23 40.4	2 43.7
4 Su	8 51 36	11 55 51	13♌37 42	20 55 33	12 48.0	25 02.2	1 39.7	20 22.0	3 34.0	14 07.9	14 19.6	25 49.7	23 42.2	2 45.4
5 M	8 55 33	12 53 20	28 15 39	5♍37 02	12 41.3	25 23.0	2 12.1	21 00.1	3 57.7	14 13.6	14 22.0	25 51.0	23 43.9	2 47.1
6 Tu	8 59 29	13 50 50	12♍58 49	20 20 06	12 37.0	25 50.6	2 45.8	21 38.2	4 21.4	14 19.1	14 24.2	25 52.3	23 45.7	2 48.8
7 W	9 03 26	14 48 21	27 40 06	4♎58 07	12D 35.2	26 24.7	3 20.9	22 16.3	4 45.2	14 24.5	14 26.3	25 53.6	23 47.5	2 50.4
8 Th	9 07 22	15 45 53	12♎13 36	19 26 04	12 35.1	27 05.5	3 57.1	22 54.4	5 09.1	14 29.7	14 28.3	25 54.8	23 49.3	2 52.1
9 F	9 11 19	16 43 26	26 35 13	3♏40 48	12R 35.9	27 52.8	4 34.6	23 32.5	5 33.1	14 34.7	14 30.2	25 55.9	23 51.2	2 53.8
10 Sa	9 15 15	17 40 59	10♏42 41	17 40 49	12 36.3	28 46.5	5 13.1	24 10.6	5 57.1	14 39.6	14 32.0	25 57.0	23 53.1	2 55.4
11 Su	9 19 12	18 38 34	24 35 12	1♐25 53	12 35.6	29 46.5	5 52.8	24 48.8	6 21.2	14 44.2	14 33.7	25 58.1	23 54.9	2 57.1
12 M	9 23 08	19 36 09	8♐12 56	14 56 26	12 32.9	0♌52.6	6 33.6	25 26.9	6 45.3	14 48.7	14 35.3	25 59.1	23 56.8	2 58.7
13 Tu	9 27 05	20 33 45	21 36 28	28 13 07	12 28.0	2 04.6	7 15.4	26 05.0	7 09.6	14 53.1	14 36.8	26 00.0	23 58.7	3 00.3
14 W	9 31 02	21 31 22	4♑46 28	11♑16 34	12 21.1	3 22.2	7 58.2	26 43.1	7 33.8	14 57.2	14 38.3	26 00.9	24 00.7	3 02.0
15 Th	9 34 58	22 29 01	17 43 29	24 07 13	12 12.9	4 45.2	8 41.9	27 21.2	7 58.2	15 01.2	14 39.5	26 01.8	24 02.6	3 03.6
16 F	9 38 55	23 26 40	0♒27 51	6♒45 25	12 04.1	6 13.4	9 26.6	27 59.3	8 22.6	15 05.0	14 40.7	26 02.6	24 04.6	3 05.2
17 Sa	9 42 51	24 24 21	12 59 57	19 11 33	11 55.7	7 46.2	10 12.1	28 37.4	8 47.0	15 08.6	14 41.8	26 03.4	24 06.6	3 06.8
18 Su	9 46 48	25 22 03	25 20 16	1♓26 15	11 48.5	9 23.5	10 58.5	29 15.6	9 11.5	15 12.0	14 42.8	26 04.1	24 08.6	3 08.4
19 M	9 50 44	26 19 46	7♓29 38	13 30 38	11 43.0	11 04.7	11 45.8	29 53.7	9 36.1	15 15.2	14 43.7	26 04.8	24 10.6	3 10.0
20 Tu	9 54 41	27 17 31	19 29 29	25 26 28	11 39.5	12 49.5	12 33.8	0♍31.8	10 00.7	15 18.3	14 44.5	26 05.4	24 12.6	3 11.5
21 W	9 58 37	28 15 17	1♈21 55	7♈16 12	11D 38.0	14 37.4	13 22.6	1 10.0	10 25.4	15 21.1	14 45.1	26 05.9	24 14.6	3 13.1
22 Th	10 02 34	29 13 05	13 09 45	19 03 01	11 38.2	16 28.0	14 12.2	1 48.1	10 50.1	15 23.8	14 45.7	26 06.4	24 16.7	3 14.7
23 F	10 06 31	0♍10 54	24 56 31	0♉50 49	11 39.4	18 20.9	15 02.5	2 26.3	11 14.9	15 26.3	14 46.2	26 06.9	24 18.7	3 16.2
24 Sa	10 10 27	1 08 45	6♉46 27	12 44 03	11 41.0	20 15.7	15 53.5	3 04.4	11 39.7	15 28.6	14 46.5	26 07.3	24 20.8	3 17.7
25 Su	10 14 24	2 06 38	18 44 14	24 47 38	11R 42.2	22 11.8	16 45.2	3 42.6	12 04.6	15 30.7	14 46.8	26 07.7	24 22.9	3 19.3
26 M	10 18 20	3 04 33	0♊54 52	7♊06 33	11 42.4	24 09.1	17 37.5	4 20.8	12 29.5	15 32.6	14R 46.9	26 08.0	24 25.0	3 20.8
27 Tu	10 22 17	4 02 30	13 23 18	19 45 38	11 41.1	26 07.1	18 30.5	4 59.0	12 54.5	15 34.3	14 46.9	26 08.3	24 27.1	3 22.3
28 W	10 26 13	5 00 28	26 14 03	2♋48 57	11 38.4	28 05.5	19 24.0	5 37.2	13 19.5	15 35.8	14 46.9	26 08.5	24 29.2	3 23.8
29 Th	10 30 10	5 58 29	9♋30 36	16 19 11	11 34.3	0♍04.0	20 18.2	6 15.4	13 44.6	15 37.1	14 46.7	26 08.6	24 31.3	3 25.3
30 F	10 34 06	6 56 31	23 14 42	0♌17 01	11 29.3	2 02.5	21 12.9	6 53.6	14 09.7	15 38.2	14 46.4	26 08.7	24 33.5	3 26.7
31 Sa	10 38 03	7 54 35	7♌25 47	14 40 30	11 24.2	4 00.6	22 08.1	7 31.8	14 34.9	15 39.1	14 46.0	26R 08.8	24 35.6	3 28.2

Astro Data Dy Hr Mn	Planet Ingress Dy Hr Mn	Last Aspect Dy Hr Mn	☽ Ingress Dy Hr Mn	Last Aspect Dy Hr Mn	☽ Ingress Dy Hr Mn	☽ Phases & Eclipses Dy Hr Mn
☿R 8 14:17	♂ ♌ 3 10:32	2 3:42 ♂ ✶	♊ 2 5:15	2 18:14 ♅ ✶	♌ 3 1:20	5 11:28 ● 13♋16
☽0S 10 14:44	♀ ♊R 5 16:17	3 23:37 ♆ □	♋ 4 12:11	4 20:02 ♅ □	♍ 5 2:50	12 6:35 ☽ 19♎45
♀D 18 13:13	☿ ♋R 21 1:39	6 7:27 ♅ ✶	♌ 6 16:12	6 21:21 ☿ ✶	♎ 7 3:50	19 9:55 ○ 26♑33
☽0N 24 7:02	☉ ♌ 23 0:34	8 16:33 ♀ ✶	♍ 8 18:44	9 1:35 ☿ □	♏ 9 5:46	27 11:29 ☾ 4♉15
	⚳ ♎ 26 7:17	10 17:43 ♀ □	♎ 10 21:07	11 8:51 ☿ △	♐ 11 9:29	
☿D 1 18:43		12 19:43 ♀ △	♏ 13 0:07	13 7:55 ♂ △	♑ 13 15:15	3 20:09 ● 11♌18
☽0S 6 22:33	♀ ♋ 1 2:20	14 19:42 ♅ ☍	♐ 15 4:05	15 15:36 ♅ △	♒ 15 23:07	10 12:00 ☽ 17♏41
♃☌♄ 8 1:24	☿ ♌ 11 17:06	17 3:35 ♀ ☍	♑ 17 9:17	18 7:28 ♂ ☍	♓ 18 9:10	17 23:02 ○ 24♒51
☽0N 20 15:06	♂ ♍ 19 15:58	19 9:55 ☉ ☍	♒ 19 16:22	20 13:19 ♅ ✶	♈ 20 21:14	26 3:33 ☾ 2♊44
♄R 27 7:43	☉ ♍ 23 7:29	21 20:04 ♀ △	♓ 22 1:58	22 5:45 ☿ △	♉ 23 10:17	
	☿ ♍ 29 11:11	24 9:26 ☿ △	♈ 24 14:01	25 14:38 ♅ ☌	♊ 25 22:13	
		26 23:04 ♀ ✶	♉ 27 2:56	28 1:53 ☿ ✶	♋ 28 6:53	
		29 5:44 ♅ ☌	♊ 29 14:04	30 4:58 ♅ ✶	♌ 30 11:31	
		31 21:22 ♀ ☌	♋ 31 21:32			

Astro Data

1 July 1940
Julian Day # 14792
SVP 6♓05'21"
GC 26♐00.5 ⚴ 28♌49.5
Eris 5♈07.5R ⚵ 23♊31.2
⚷ 21♋02.3 ⚶ 1♋44.7
☽ Mean ☊ 15♎53.4

1 August 1940
Julian Day # 14823
SVP 6♓05'16"
GC 26♐00.6 ⚴ 12♍40.4
Eris 5♈02.2R ⚵ 11♋09.6
⚷ 24♋28.7 ⚶ 15♋04.2
☽ Mean ☊ 14♎14.9

LONGITUDE — September 1940

Day	Sid.Time	☉	0 hr ☽	Noon ☽	True ☊	☿	♀	♂	⚳	♃	♄	♅	♆	♇
1 Su	10 42 00	8♍52 41	22♌00 29	29♌24 53	11♎19.6	5♍58.2	23♋03.9	8♍10.1	15♎00.1	15♉39.9	14♉45.5	26♉08.8	24♍37.8	3♌29.6
2 M	10 45 56	9 50 48	6♍52 45	14♍23 00	11R 16.2	7 55.1	24 00.2	8 48.3	15 25.4	15 40.4	14R 44.9	26R 08.8	24 39.9	3 31.0
3 Tu	10 49 53	10 48 57	21 54 30	29 26 08	11D 14.3	9 51.3	24 57.0	9 26.6	15 50.7	15 40.7	14 44.2	26 08.7	24 42.1	3 32.4
4 W	10 53 49	11 47 08	6♎56 48	14♎25 28	11 13.9	11 46.6	25 54.2	10 04.8	16 16.0	15R 40.8	14 43.4	26 08.5	24 44.3	3 33.8
5 Th	10 57 46	12 45 20	21 51 15	29 13 20	11 14.7	13 41.0	26 51.9	10 43.1	16 41.4	15 40.7	14 42.4	26 08.3	24 46.5	3 35.2
6 F	11 01 42	13 43 34	6♏31 06	13♏44 04	11 16.1	15 34.4	27 50.1	11 21.4	17 06.8	15 40.4	14 41.4	26 08.1	24 48.6	3 36.6
7 Sa	11 05 39	14 41 49	20 51 53	27 54 20	11 17.4	17 26.7	28 48.7	11 59.7	17 32.2	15 39.9	14 40.3	26 07.8	24 50.8	3 37.9
8 Su	11 09 35	15 40 06	4♐51 21	11♐42 57	11R 18.2	19 17.9	29 47.7	12 38.0	17 57.7	15 39.2	14 39.0	26 07.5	24 53.0	3 39.3
9 M	11 13 32	16 38 24	18 29 14	25 10 22	11 18.0	21 08.0	0♌47.1	13 16.3	18 23.3	15 38.3	14 37.7	26 07.1	24 55.3	3 40.6
10 Tu	11 17 29	17 36 44	1♑46 35	8♑18 07	11 16.7	22 57.0	1 46.9	13 54.6	18 48.8	15 37.2	14 36.2	26 06.6	24 57.5	3 41.9
11 W	11 21 25	18 35 06	14 45 17	21 08 21	11 14.3	24 44.9	2 47.1	14 32.9	19 14.4	15 35.9	14 34.7	26 06.1	24 59.7	3 43.2
12 Th	11 25 22	19 33 29	27 27 36	3♒43 21	11 11.3	26 31.7	3 47.7	15 11.2	19 40.0	15 34.4	14 33.0	26 05.6	25 01.9	3 44.4
13 F	11 29 18	20 31 53	9♒55 51	16 05 23	11 08.0	28 17.3	4 48.7	15 49.6	20 05.7	15 32.7	14 31.3	26 05.0	25 04.1	3 45.7
14 Sa	11 33 15	21 30 19	22 12 13	28 16 35	11 04.8	0♎01.9	5 50.0	16 27.9	20 31.3	15 30.8	14 29.4	26 04.4	25 06.3	3 46.9
15 Su	11 37 11	22 28 48	4♓18 44	10♓18 55	11 02.2	1 45.4	6 51.7	17 06.3	20 57.1	15 28.8	14 27.5	26 03.7	25 08.6	3 48.1
16 M	11 41 08	23 27 17	16 17 22	22 14 19	11 00.3	3 27.8	7 53.7	17 44.6	21 22.8	15 26.5	14 25.5	26 02.9	25 10.8	3 49.3
17 Tu	11 45 04	24 25 49	28 10 02	4♈04 45	10D 59.4	5 09.1	8 56.1	18 23.0	21 48.6	15 24.0	14 23.3	26 02.1	25 13.0	3 50.5
18 W	11 49 01	25 24 23	9♈58 45	15 52 21	10 59.3	6 49.4	9 58.7	19 01.4	22 14.4	15 21.3	14 21.1	26 01.3	25 15.2	3 51.7
19 Th	11 52 57	26 22 59	21 45 51	27 39 36	10 59.9	8 28.7	11 01.7	19 39.8	22 40.2	15 18.4	14 18.7	26 00.4	25 17.5	3 52.8
20 F	11 56 54	27 21 37	3♉33 58	9♉29 22	11 01.0	10 07.0	12 05.0	20 18.2	23 06.0	15 15.4	14 16.3	25 59.5	25 19.7	3 53.9
21 Sa	12 00 51	28 20 17	15 26 12	21 24 56	11 02.2	11 44.3	13 08.6	20 56.6	23 31.9	15 12.1	14 13.8	25 58.5	25 21.9	3 55.0
22 Su	12 04 47	29 18 59	27 26 04	3♊30 05	11 03.4	13 20.6	14 12.6	21 35.1	23 57.8	15 08.7	14 11.2	25 57.5	25 24.2	3 56.1
23 M	12 08 44	0♎17 43	9♊37 29	15 48 49	11 04.2	14 56.0	15 16.8	22 13.5	24 23.7	15 05.0	14 08.5	25 56.4	25 26.4	3 57.2
24 Tu	12 12 40	1 16 30	22 04 36	28 25 21	11R 04.5	16 30.5	16 21.2	22 52.0	24 49.7	15 01.2	14 05.7	25 55.3	25 28.6	3 58.2
25 W	12 16 37	2 15 19	4♋51 31	11♋23 35	11 04.4	18 04.0	17 26.0	23 30.5	25 15.6	14 57.2	14 02.8	25 54.2	25 30.8	3 59.2
26 Th	12 20 33	3 14 11	18 01 54	24 46 46	11 04.0	19 36.6	18 31.0	24 09.0	25 41.6	14 53.0	13 59.8	25 53.0	25 33.0	4 00.2
27 F	12 24 30	4 13 04	1♌38 23	8♌36 48	11 03.3	21 08.3	19 36.3	24 47.5	26 07.7	14 48.6	13 56.7	25 51.7	25 35.3	4 01.2
28 Sa	12 28 26	5 12 00	15 41 58	22 53 36	11 02.6	22 39.0	20 41.8	25 26.1	26 33.7	14 44.1	13 53.6	25 50.5	25 37.5	4 02.1
29 Su	12 32 23	6 10 58	0♍11 20	7♍34 32	11 02.0	24 08.9	21 47.6	26 04.6	26 59.8	14 39.3	13 50.4	25 49.1	25 39.7	4 03.1
30 M	12 36 20	7 09 59	15 02 28	22 34 11	11 01.6	25 37.8	22 53.6	26 43.2	27 25.8	14 34.4	13 47.0	25 47.7	25 41.9	4 04.0

LONGITUDE — October 1940

Day	Sid.Time	☉	0 hr ☽	Noon ☽	True ☊	☿	♀	♂	⚳	♃	♄	♅	♆	♇
1 Tu	12 40 16	8♎09 01	0♎08 38	7♎44 40	11♎01.5	27♎05.9	23♌59.8	27♍21.8	27♎51.9	14♉29.3	13♉43.6	25♉46.3	25♍44.0	4♌04.9
2 W	12 44 13	9 08 05	15 21 04	22 56 36	11D 01.5	28 33.0	25 06.3	28 00.4	28 18.0	14R 24.1	13R 40.2	25R 44.9	25 46.2	4 05.7
3 Th	12 48 09	10 07 12	0♏30 07	8♏00 29	11R 01.6	29 59.2	26 13.0	28 39.0	28 44.2	14 18.7	13 36.6	25 43.4	25 48.4	4 06.6
4 F	12 52 06	11 06 20	15 26 44	22 48 01	11 01.6	1♏24.4	27 19.9	29 17.6	29 10.3	14 13.1	13 33.0	25 41.8	25 50.6	4 07.4
5 Sa	12 56 02	12 05 30	0♐03 41	7♐13 13	11 01.6	2 48.7	28 27.0	29 56.2	29 36.5	14 07.4	13 29.3	25 40.2	25 52.7	4 08.2
6 Su	12 59 59	13 04 42	14 16 18	21 12 46	11 01.4	4 11.9	29 34.3	0♎34.9	0♏02.7	14 01.5	13 25.5	25 38.6	25 54.9	4 09.0
7 M	13 03 55	14 03 56	28 02 37	4♑45 57	11D 01.3	5 34.2	0♍41.8	1 13.5	0 28.8	13 55.5	13 21.7	25 36.9	25 57.1	4 09.7
8 Tu	13 07 52	15 03 12	11♑23 01	17 54 08	11 01.3	6 55.3	1 49.5	1 52.2	0 55.0	13 49.3	13 17.8	25 35.3	25 59.2	4 10.4
9 W	13 11 49	16 02 29	24 19 39	0♒40 03	11 01.4	8 15.3	2 57.3	2 30.9	1 21.3	13 43.0	13 13.8	25 33.5	26 01.3	4 11.1
10 Th	13 15 45	17 01 48	6♒55 45	13 07 15	11 01.9	9 34.2	4 05.4	3 09.6	1 47.5	13 36.5	13 09.8	25 31.7	26 03.4	4 11.8
11 F	13 19 42	18 01 09	19 15 03	25 19 37	11 02.5	10 51.7	5 13.7	3 48.3	2 13.7	13 29.9	13 05.7	25 29.9	26 05.5	4 12.5
12 Sa	13 23 38	19 00 31	1♓21 25	7♓20 54	11 03.3	12 08.0	6 22.1	4 27.0	2 39.9	13 23.2	13 01.5	25 28.1	26 07.6	4 13.1
13 Su	13 27 35	19 59 56	13 18 30	19 14 38	11 04.1	13 22.9	7 30.7	5 05.8	3 06.2	13 16.4	12 57.3	25 26.2	26 09.7	4 13.7
14 M	13 31 31	20 59 22	25 09 39	1♈03 55	11R 04.7	14 36.2	8 39.5	5 44.5	3 32.4	13 09.4	12 53.1	25 24.3	26 11.8	4 14.3
15 Tu	13 35 28	21 58 50	6♈57 47	12 51 32	11 04.9	15 48.0	9 48.5	6 23.3	3 58.7	13 02.4	12 48.7	25 22.4	26 13.8	4 14.8
16 W	13 39 24	22 58 20	18 45 29	24 39 53	11 04.5	16 57.9	10 57.6	7 02.1	4 24.9	12 55.2	12 44.4	25 20.4	26 15.9	4 15.3
17 Th	13 43 21	23 57 53	0♉35 01	6♉31 08	11 03.5	18 06.0	12 06.9	7 40.9	4 51.2	12 47.9	12 40.0	25 18.4	26 17.9	4 15.8
18 F	13 47 17	24 57 27	12 28 29	18 27 21	11 01.8	19 12.0	13 16.4	8 19.7	5 17.5	12 40.6	12 35.5	25 16.3	26 19.9	4 16.3
19 Sa	13 51 14	25 57 04	24 27 58	0♊30 39	10 59.6	20 15.7	14 26.0	8 58.6	5 43.7	12 33.1	12 31.0	25 14.3	26 21.9	4 16.8
20 Su	13 55 11	26 56 43	6♊35 39	12 43 17	10 57.2	21 16.9	15 35.7	9 37.4	6 10.0	12 25.5	12 26.5	25 12.2	26 23.9	4 17.2
21 M	13 59 07	27 56 24	18 53 53	25 07 46	10 54.8	22 15.3	16 45.7	10 16.3	6 36.3	12 17.9	12 21.9	25 10.1	26 25.9	4 17.6
22 Tu	14 03 04	28 56 07	1♋25 18	7♋46 48	10 53.0	23 10.7	17 55.8	10 55.2	7 02.6	12 10.2	12 17.3	25 07.9	26 27.8	4 18.0
23 W	14 07 00	29 55 52	14 12 40	20 43 14	10D 51.8	24 02.7	19 06.0	11 34.1	7 28.9	12 02.4	12 12.6	25 05.7	26 29.8	4 18.3
24 Th	14 10 57	0♏55 40	27 18 49	3♌59 45	10 51.6	24 51.1	20 16.3	12 13.1	7 55.2	11 54.5	12 07.9	25 03.5	26 31.7	4 18.6
25 F	14 14 53	1 55 30	10♌46 17	17 38 35	10 52.2	25 35.3	21 26.8	12 52.0	8 21.5	11 46.6	12 03.2	25 01.3	26 33.6	4 18.9
26 Sa	14 18 50	2 55 22	24 36 48	1♍40 54	10 53.5	26 14.9	22 37.5	13 31.0	8 47.8	11 38.6	11 58.5	24 59.1	26 35.5	4 19.2
27 Su	14 22 46	3 55 17	8♍50 47	16 06 12	10 54.9	26 49.5	23 48.3	14 10.0	9 14.0	11 30.6	11 53.7	24 56.8	26 37.4	4 19.4
28 M	14 26 43	4 55 13	23 26 42	0♎51 44	10R 56.0	27 18.4	24 59.2	14 49.0	9 40.3	11 22.6	11 48.9	24 54.5	26 39.2	4 19.6
29 Tu	14 30 40	5 55 12	8♎20 34	15 52 17	10 56.2	27 41.2	26 10.2	15 28.1	10 06.6	11 14.5	11 44.1	24 52.2	26 41.0	4 19.8
30 W	14 34 36	6 55 13	23 25 51	1♏00 11	10 55.1	27 57.3	27 21.3	16 07.1	10 32.9	11 06.3	11 39.3	24 49.8	26 42.9	4 20.0
31 Th	14 38 33	7 55 15	8♏34 03	16 06 17	10 52.6	28R 05.9	28 32.6	16 46.2	10 59.2	10 58.2	11 34.5	24 47.5	26 44.6	4 20.1

Astro Data (Dy Hr Mn)

	Dy Hr Mn
♅ R	1 4:00
⚳0S	2 8:07
☽ 0S	3 8:10
♃ R	4 13:00
☿0S	15 14:38
☽ 0N	16 21:46
☉0S	23 4:45
☽ 0S	30 19:05
♅△♆	2 2:57
♂0S	9 0:50
☽ 0N	14 3:47
♃☌♄	20 4:37
♃□♆	26 19:40
☽ 0S	28 5:54
♄□♆	29 23:13

Planet Ingress

	Dy Hr Mn
♀ ♌	8 16:59
☿ ♎	14 11:34
☉ ♎	23 4:46
☿ ♏	3 12:14
♂ ♎	5 14:21
⚳ ♏	6 9:34
♀ ♍	6 21:10
☉ ♏	23 13:39

Last Aspect / ☽ Ingress (September)

Last Aspect Dy Hr Mn		☽ Ingress Dy Hr Mn
1 6:43	♅ □	♍ 1 12:57
3 6:45	♅ △	♎ 3 12:54
5 7:53	♀ □	♏ 5 13:16
7 13:40	♀ △	♐ 7 15:36
9 11:33	♆ □	♑ 9 20:45
11 21:24	♅ △	♒ 12 4:51
14 7:38	♅ □	♓ 14 15:25
16 19:42	♅ ⚹	♈ 17 3:43
17 22:50	♀ △	♉ 19 16:45
22 3:00	☉ △	♊ 22 5:05
24 6:26	♆ □	♋ 24 14:57
26 13:56	♅ ⚹	♌ 26 21:09
28 16:52	♅ □	♍ 28 23:41
30 18:52	♂ ☌	♎ 30 23:46

Last Aspect / ☽ Ingress (October)

Last Aspect Dy Hr Mn		☽ Ingress Dy Hr Mn
2 21:50	☿ ☌	♏ 2 23:12
4 23:13	♂ ⚹	♐ 4 23:54
6 20:16	♆ □	♑ 7 3:28
9 3:10	♆ △	♒ 9 10:44
11 12:20	♅ □	♓ 11 21:18
14 2:04	♆ ☍	♈ 14 9:50
16 8:15	☉ ☍	♉ 16 22:49
19 3:45	♆ △	♊ 19 10:59
21 17:50	☉ △	♋ 21 21:18
23 22:33	♆ ⚹	♌ 24 4:51
26 2:21	☿ □	♍ 26 9:10
28 6:05	☿ ⚹	♎ 28 10:37
29 11:20	♂ ☌	♏ 30 10:25

☽ Phases & Eclipses

Dy Hr Mn		
2 4:15	●	9♍32
8 19:32	☽	15♐58
16 14:41	○	23♓34
24 17:47	☾	1♋31
1 12:41	●	8♎11
1 12:43:41	●	T 05'36"
8 6:18	☽	14♑49
16 8:15	○	22♈49
16 8:01	●	A 0.715
24 6:04	☾	0♌41
30 22:03	●	7♏20

Astro Data

1 September 1940
Julian Day # 14854
SVP 6♓05'13"
GC 26♐00.6 ⚴ 26♍44.0
Eris 4♈47.7R ⚵ 27♋47.5
⚷ 27♋40.8 ⚶ 27♋59.4
☽ Mean ☊ 12♎36.4

1 October 1940
Julian Day # 14884
SVP 6♓05'11"
GC 26♐00.7 ⚴ 10♎22.8
Eris 4♈29.0R ⚵ 12♌25.1
⚷ 0♌05.3 ⚶ 9♌40.7
☽ Mean ☊ 11♎01.1

November 1940 LONGITUDE

Day	Sid.Time	☉	0 hr ☽	Noon ☽	True ☊	☿	♀	♂	⚳	♃	♄	♅	♆	♇
1 F	14 42 29	8♏55 20	23♏35 41	1♐01 10	10♎49.0	28♏06.4	29♍43.9	17♎25.3	11♏25.5	10♉50.0	11♉29.7	24♉45.1	26♍46.4	4♌20.2
2 Sa	14 46 26	9 55 26	8♐21 46	15 36 41	10R44.7	27R58.3	0♎55.4	18 04.4	11 51.7	10R41.9	11R24.8	24R42.7	26 48.2	4 20.3
3 Su	14 50 22	10 55 34	22 45 16	29 47 04	10 40.3	27 41.1	2 07.0	18 43.5	12 18.0	10 33.7	11 20.0	24 40.3	26 49.9	4 20.4
4 M	14 54 19	11 55 44	6♑41 49	13♑29 28	10 36.5	27 14.2	3 18.7	19 22.7	12 44.2	10 25.5	11 15.1	24 37.9	26 51.6	4R20.4
5 Tu	14 58 15	12 55 55	20 10 05	26 43 53	10 33.9	26 37.7	4 30.5	20 01.8	13 10.5	10 17.4	11 10.3	24 35.5	26 53.3	4 20.4
6 W	15 02 12	13 56 08	3♒11 14	9♒32 34	10D32.6	25 51.4	5 42.4	20 41.0	13 36.7	10 09.2	11 05.5	24 33.0	26 55.0	4 20.4
7 Th	15 06 09	14 56 22	15 48 25	21 59 19	10 32.8	24 55.9	6 54.4	21 20.2	14 02.9	10 01.1	11 00.6	24 30.6	26 56.6	4 20.3
8 F	15 10 05	15 56 38	28 05 55	4♓08 48	10 34.0	23 51.9	8 06.4	21 59.4	14 29.1	9 53.0	10 55.8	24 28.1	26 58.2	4 20.2
9 Sa	15 14 02	16 56 55	10♓08 37	16 05 59	10 35.8	22 40.9	9 18.6	22 38.6	14 55.3	9 45.0	10 51.0	24 25.7	26 59.8	4 20.1
10 Su	15 17 58	17 57 13	22 01 29	27 55 42	10 37.4	21 24.5	10 30.9	23 17.9	15 21.5	9 37.0	10 46.2	24 23.2	27 01.4	4 20.0
11 M	15 21 55	18 57 33	3♈49 12	9♈42 27	10R38.2	20 05.0	11 43.2	23 57.1	15 47.6	9 29.0	10 41.4	24 20.7	27 02.9	4 19.8
12 Tu	15 25 51	19 57 55	15 35 57	21 30 06	10 37.4	18 44.8	12 55.7	24 36.4	16 13.8	9 21.1	10 36.7	24 18.2	27 04.4	4 19.7
13 W	15 29 48	20 58 18	27 25 18	3♉21 53	10 34.9	17 26.5	14 08.2	25 15.7	16 39.9	9 13.3	10 32.0	24 15.7	27 05.9	4 19.4
14 Th	15 33 44	21 58 42	9♉20 08	15 20 18	10 30.2	16 12.8	15 20.8	25 55.0	17 06.0	9 05.5	10 27.3	24 13.2	27 07.4	4 19.2
15 F	15 37 41	22 59 09	21 22 36	27 27 12	10 23.7	15 06.0	16 33.6	26 34.3	17 32.1	8 57.8	10 22.6	24 10.7	27 08.8	4 18.9
16 Sa	15 41 38	23 59 37	3♊34 16	9♊43 53	10 15.9	14 07.9	17 46.3	27 13.7	17 58.2	8 50.2	10 17.9	24 08.2	27 10.2	4 18.7
17 Su	15 45 34	25 00 06	15 56 11	22 11 14	10 07.3	13 20.1	18 59.2	27 53.1	18 24.3	8 42.7	10 13.3	24 05.7	27 11.6	4 18.3
18 M	15 49 31	26 00 37	28 29 09	4♋49 59	9 59.0	12 43.5	20 12.2	28 32.5	18 50.3	8 35.2	10 08.8	24 03.2	27 13.0	4 18.0
19 Tu	15 53 27	27 01 10	11♋13 51	17 40 52	9 51.8	12 18.6	21 25.2	29 11.9	19 16.3	8 27.9	10 04.2	24 00.7	27 14.3	4 17.6
20 W	15 57 24	28 01 45	24 11 08	0♌44 49	9 46.4	12D05.3	22 38.3	29 51.3	19 42.3	8 20.6	9 59.7	23 58.2	27 15.6	4 17.2
21 Th	16 01 20	29 02 21	7♌22 03	14 03 00	9 43.1	12 03.4	23 51.5	0♏30.8	20 08.3	8 13.5	9 55.3	23 55.7	27 16.9	4 16.8
22 F	16 05 17	0♐02 59	20 47 50	27 36 44	9D41.9	12 12.3	25 04.7	1 10.3	20 34.3	8 06.4	9 50.9	23 53.2	27 18.1	4 16.4
23 Sa	16 09 13	1 03 39	4♍29 48	11♍27 10	9 42.2	12 31.1	26 18.0	1 49.8	21 00.2	7 59.5	9 46.5	23 50.7	27 19.3	4 15.9
24 Su	16 13 10	2 04 21	18 28 51	25 34 51	9R43.2	12 59.1	27 31.4	2 29.3	21 26.1	7 52.7	9 42.2	23 48.3	27 20.5	4 15.4
25 M	16 17 07	3 05 04	2♎45 00	9♎59 05	9 43.8	13 35.4	28 44.9	3 08.9	21 52.0	7 46.0	9 38.0	23 45.8	27 21.7	4 14.9
26 Tu	16 21 03	4 05 48	17 16 44	24 37 26	9 42.9	14 19.0	29 58.4	3 48.5	22 17.9	7 39.5	9 33.8	23 43.3	27 22.8	4 14.4
27 W	16 25 00	5 06 35	2♏00 31	9♏25 13	9 39.6	15 09.1	1♏11.9	4 28.0	22 43.7	7 33.1	9 29.7	23 40.9	27 23.9	4 13.8
28 Th	16 28 56	6 07 22	16 50 38	24 15 46	9 33.8	16 05.0	2 25.6	5 07.7	23 09.5	7 26.8	9 25.6	23 38.5	27 25.0	4 13.2
29 F	16 32 53	7 08 11	1♐39 35	9♐01 01	9 25.6	17 05.8	3 39.3	5 47.3	23 35.3	7 20.7	9 21.6	23 36.0	27 26.0	4 12.6
30 Sa	16 36 49	8 09 02	16 19 04	23 32 47	9 15.9	18 11.0	4 53.0	6 26.9	24 01.0	7 14.7	9 17.7	23 33.6	27 27.0	4 12.0

December 1940 LONGITUDE

Day	Sid.Time	☉	0 hr ☽	Noon ☽	True ☊	☿	♀	♂	⚳	♃	♄	♅	♆	♇
1 Su	16 40 46	9♐09 53	0♑41 22	7♑44 08	9♎05.8	19♏20.0	6♏06.8	7♏06.6	24♏26.8	7♉08.9	9♉13.8	23♉31.2	27♍28.0	4♌11.3
2 M	16 44 42	10 10 45	14 40 35	21 30 25	8R56.4	20 32.2	7 20.6	7 46.3	24 52.5	7R03.3	9R10.0	23R28.9	27 28.9	4R10.6
3 Tu	16 48 39	11 11 39	28 13 27	4♒49 44	8 48.7	21 47.2	8 34.5	8 26.0	25 18.1	6 57.8	9 06.3	23 26.5	27 29.9	4 09.9
4 W	16 52 36	12 12 33	11♒19 27	17 42 54	8 43.3	23 04.6	9 48.4	9 05.7	25 43.7	6 52.4	9 02.6	23 24.2	27 30.7	4 09.2
5 Th	16 56 32	13 13 28	24 00 31	0♓12 49	8 40.4	24 24.1	11 02.4	9 45.5	26 09.3	6 47.3	8 59.1	23 21.9	27 31.6	4 08.4
6 F	17 00 29	14 14 23	6♓20 23	12 23 52	8D39.4	25 45.3	12 16.4	10 25.2	26 34.8	6 42.3	8 55.6	23 19.6	27 32.4	4 07.6
7 Sa	17 04 25	15 15 19	18 23 57	24 21 19	8 39.7	27 08.1	13 30.4	11 05.0	27 00.3	6 37.5	8 52.1	23 17.3	27 33.2	4 06.9
8 Su	17 08 22	16 16 16	0♈16 40	6♈10 41	8R40.1	28 32.2	14 44.5	11 44.8	27 25.8	6 32.9	8 48.8	23 15.0	27 33.9	4 06.0
9 M	17 12 18	17 17 14	12 04 04	17 57 26	8 39.7	29 57.4	15 58.6	12 24.6	27 51.2	6 28.4	8 45.6	23 12.8	27 34.6	4 05.2
10 Tu	17 16 15	18 18 12	23 51 25	29 46 34	8 37.5	1♐23.5	17 12.8	13 04.4	28 16.6	6 24.2	8 42.4	23 10.6	27 35.3	4 04.3
11 W	17 20 11	19 19 11	5♉43 26	11♉42 26	8 32.7	2 50.5	18 27.0	13 44.3	28 42.0	6 20.1	8 39.3	23 08.4	27 36.0	4 03.5
12 Th	17 24 08	20 20 11	17 44 01	23 48 29	8 25.0	4 18.2	19 41.2	14 24.2	29 07.2	6 16.2	8 36.3	23 06.3	27 36.6	4 02.6
13 F	17 28 05	21 21 11	29 56 06	6♊07 05	8 14.7	5 46.5	20 55.5	15 04.1	29 32.5	6 12.5	8 33.4	23 04.1	27 37.2	4 01.6
14 Sa	17 32 01	22 22 12	12♊21 33	18 39 32	8 02.3	7 15.4	22 09.8	15 44.0	29 57.7	6 09.1	8 30.6	23 02.0	27 37.7	4 00.7
15 Su	17 35 58	23 23 14	25 01 03	1♋26 02	7 49.0	8 44.8	23 24.2	16 23.9	0♐22.9	6 05.8	8 27.9	23 00.0	27 38.2	3 59.7
16 M	17 39 54	24 24 17	7♋54 22	14 25 54	7 35.8	10 14.5	24 38.5	17 03.9	0 48.0	6 02.7	8 25.3	22 57.9	27 38.7	3 58.8
17 Tu	17 43 51	25 25 20	21 00 28	27 37 55	7 24.0	11 44.7	25 53.0	17 43.8	1 13.1	5 59.7	8 22.8	22 55.9	27 39.2	3 57.8
18 W	17 47 47	26 26 24	4♌18 03	11♌00 44	7 14.7	13 15.2	27 07.4	18 23.9	1 38.1	5 57.0	8 20.4	22 54.0	27 39.6	3 56.8
19 Th	17 51 44	27 27 28	17 45 49	24 33 12	7 08.3	14 46.1	28 21.9	19 03.9	2 03.1	5 54.5	8 18.0	22 52.0	27 40.0	3 55.7
20 F	17 55 40	28 28 34	1♍22 50	8♍14 41	7 04.8	16 17.2	29 36.4	19 43.9	2 28.0	5 52.2	8 15.8	22 50.1	27 40.3	3 54.7
21 Sa	17 59 37	29 29 40	15 08 44	22 05 00	7D03.6	17 48.6	0♐50.9	20 24.0	2 52.9	5 50.1	8 13.7	22 48.2	27 40.6	3 53.6
22 Su	18 03 34	0♑30 47	29 03 30	6♎04 15	7R03.5	19 20.3	2 05.5	21 04.1	3 17.7	5 48.2	8 11.7	22 46.4	27 40.9	3 52.5
23 M	18 07 30	1 31 55	13♎07 13	20 12 19	7 03.2	20 52.2	3 20.1	21 44.2	3 42.5	5 46.5	8 09.7	22 44.6	27 41.1	3 51.4
24 Tu	18 11 27	2 33 03	27 19 26	4♏28 21	7 01.2	22 24.4	4 34.7	22 24.3	4 07.3	5 45.1	8 07.9	22 42.8	27 41.3	3 50.3
25 W	18 15 23	3 34 12	11♏38 44	18 50 11	6 56.7	23 56.9	5 49.3	23 04.5	4 31.9	5 43.8	8 06.2	22 41.1	27 41.5	3 49.2
26 Th	18 19 20	4 35 22	26 02 11	3♐14 08	6 49.1	25 29.6	7 04.0	23 44.6	4 56.5	5 42.7	8 04.6	22 39.4	27 41.7	3 48.0
27 F	18 23 16	5 36 32	10♐25 19	17 35 02	6 38.6	27 02.6	8 18.7	24 24.8	5 21.1	5 41.9	8 03.1	22 37.7	27 41.8	3 46.9
28 Sa	18 27 13	6 37 42	24 42 29	1♑46 56	6 26.2	28 35.9	9 33.4	25 05.1	5 45.6	5 41.2	8 01.7	22 36.1	27 41.8	3 45.7
29 Su	18 31 09	7 38 53	8♑47 40	15 44 02	6 13.1	0♑09.4	10 48.1	25 45.3	6 10.0	5 40.8	8 00.4	22 34.6	27R41.9	3 44.5
30 M	18 35 06	8 40 04	22 35 30	29 21 38	6 00.6	1 43.3	12 02.8	26 25.5	6 34.4	5D40.6	7 59.3	22 33.0	27 41.9	3 43.3
31 Tu	18 39 03	9 41 15	6♒02 09	12♒36 55	5 49.9	3 17.4	13 17.6	27 05.8	6 58.7	5 40.6	7 58.2	22 31.5	27 41.8	3 42.1

Astro Data	Planet Ingress	Last Aspect	☽ Ingress	Last Aspect	☽ Ingress	☽ Phases & Eclipses	Astro Data
Dy Hr Mn	Dy Hr Mn	Dy Hr Mn	Dy Hr Mn	Dy Hr Mn	Dy Hr Mn	Dy Hr Mn	1 November 1940
☿R 1 1:39	♀ ♎ 1 17:24	1 9:44 ♀ ✶	♐ 1 10:21	2 22:41 ♆ △	♒ 3 3:12	6 21:08 ☽ 14♒19	Julian Day # 14915
♀0S 4 19:16	♂ ♏ 20 17:16	3 6:56 ♆ □	♑ 3 12:22	4 23:25 ☿ □	♓ 5 11:35	15 2:23 ○ 22♉35	SVP 6♓05'08"
♇R 5 1:30	☉ ♐ 22 10:49	5 12:17 ♆ △	♒ 5 18:03	7 18:29 ♆ ☍	♈ 7 23:26	22 16:36 ☾ 0♍15	GC 26♐00.8 ⚴ 24♎20.1
☽0N 10 10:31	♀ ♏ 26 12:32	7 17:19 ☿ □	♓ 8 3:46	9 10:30 ☉ △	♉ 10 12:27	29 8:42 ● 7♐00	Eris 4♈10.4R ⚵ 25♌12.9
☿D 21 4:03		10 10:09 ♆ ☍	♈ 10 16:13	12 19:28 ♆ △	♊ 13 0:08		⚷ 1♌23.6 ⚶ 20♌09.1
☽0S 24 15:11	☿ ♐ 9 12:45	12 18:40 ♂ ☍	♉ 13 5:13	15 4:54 ♆ □	♋ 15 9:20	6 16:01 ☽ 14♓25	☽ Mean ☊ 9♎22.6
	⚳ ♐ 14 14:10	15 11:24 ♆ △	♊ 15 17:00	17 12:02 ♆ ✶	♌ 17 16:16	14 19:38 ○ 22♊42	
☽0N 7 18:55	♀ ♐ 20 19:36	17 23:27 ♂ △	♋ 18 2:52	19 19:23 ♀ □	♍ 19 21:35	22 1:45 ☾ 0♎05	1 December 1940
☽0S 21 22:32	☉ ♑ 21 23:55	20 10:17 ♂ □	♌ 20 10:38	21 21:38 ♆ ☌	♎ 22 1:37	28 20:56 ● 7♑00	Julian Day # 14945
♆R 30 0:04	☿ ♑ 29 9:35	22 7:07 ♀ ✶	♍ 22 16:11	23 13:16 ☿ ✶	♏ 24 4:30		SVP 6♓05'04"
♃D 31 1:20		24 14:58 ♆ ☌	♎ 24 19:25	26 2:46 ♆ ✶	♐ 26 6:36		GC 26♐00.8 ⚴ 7♏25.6
		25 2:30 ♇ ✶	♏ 26 20:44	28 5:55 ☿ ☌	♑ 28 8:58		Eris 3♈58.5R ⚵ 4♍05.1
		28 17:07 ♆ ✶	♐ 28 21:18	30 9:02 ♆ △	♒ 30 13:09		⚷ 1♌13.1R ⚶ 27♌25.3
		30 18:33 ♆ □	♑ 30 22:50				☽ Mean ☊ 7♎47.3

LONGITUDE — January 1941

Day	Sid.Time	☉	0 hr ☽	Noon ☽	True ☊	☿	♀	♂	⚳	♃	♄	♅	♆	♇
1 W	18 42 59	10♑42 25	19♒05 55	25♒29 17	5♎41.8	4♑51.8	14♐32.4	27♏46.1	7♐22.9	5♉40.8	7♉57.2	22♉30.1	27♍41.8	3♌40.9
2 Th	18 46 56	11 43 36	1♓47 15	8♓00 12	5R36.6	6 26.6	15 47.1	28 26.4	7 47.1	5 41.2	7R56.4	22R28.7	27R41.6	3R39.7
3 F	18 50 52	12 44 46	14 08 35	20 12 55	5 34.0	8 01.7	17 01.9	29 06.7	8 11.2	5 41.8	7 55.7	22 27.3	27 41.5	3 38.4
4 Sa	18 54 49	13 45 56	26 13 48	2♈11 52	5D33.2	9 37.2	18 16.7	29 47.1	8 35.2	5 42.6	7 55.0	22 26.0	27 41.3	3 37.2
5 Su	18 58 45	14 47 05	8♈07 49	14 02 20	5R33.2	11 13.0	19 31.5	0♐27.4	8 59.2	5 43.7	7 54.5	22 24.8	27 41.1	3 35.9
6 M	19 02 42	15 48 15	19 56 08	25 49 54	5 32.9	12 49.2	20 46.4	1 07.8	9 23.1	5 44.9	7 54.1	22 23.5	27 40.9	3 34.6
7 Tu	19 06 38	16 49 23	1♉44 22	7♉40 10	5 31.0	14 25.8	22 01.2	1 48.2	9 46.9	5 46.3	7 53.9	22 22.4	27 40.6	3 33.3
8 W	19 10 35	17 50 32	13 37 58	19 38 22	5 26.9	16 02.8	23 16.0	2 28.6	10 10.6	5 48.0	7 53.7	22 21.2	27 40.3	3 32.0
9 Th	19 14 32	18 51 40	25 41 53	1♊49 00	5 20.1	17 40.3	24 30.9	3 09.0	10 34.3	5 49.9	7D53.6	22 20.2	27 40.0	3 30.7
10 F	19 18 28	19 52 47	8♊00 09	14 15 37	5 10.6	19 18.2	25 45.8	3 49.4	10 57.9	5 51.9	7 53.7	22 19.1	27 39.6	3 29.4
11 Sa	19 22 25	20 53 54	20 35 38	27 00 21	4 59.0	20 56.5	27 00.6	4 29.9	11 21.4	5 54.2	7 53.8	22 18.2	27 39.2	3 28.1
12 Su	19 26 21	21 55 01	3♋29 47	10♋03 52	4 46.3	22 35.3	28 15.5	5 10.4	11 44.8	5 56.6	7 54.1	22 17.2	27 38.7	3 26.8
13 M	19 30 18	22 56 07	16 42 25	23 25 11	4 33.6	24 14.6	29 30.4	5 50.9	12 08.2	5 59.3	7 54.5	22 16.3	27 38.3	3 25.5
14 Tu	19 34 14	23 57 13	0♌11 50	7♌01 57	4 22.3	25 54.4	0♑45.3	6 31.4	12 31.5	6 02.2	7 55.0	22 15.5	27 37.8	3 24.1
15 W	19 38 11	24 58 18	13 55 07	20 50 53	4 13.3	27 34.6	2 00.2	7 12.0	12 54.7	6 05.2	7 55.6	22 14.7	27 37.2	3 22.8
16 Th	19 42 08	25 59 23	27 48 46	4♍48 21	4 07.2	29 15.4	3 15.1	7 52.6	13 17.8	6 08.5	7 56.4	22 14.0	27 36.7	3 21.5
17 F	19 46 04	27 00 28	11♍49 14	18 51 03	4 04.0	0♒56.6	4 30.0	8 33.1	13 40.8	6 11.9	7 57.2	22 13.3	27 36.1	3 20.1
18 Sa	19 50 01	28 01 32	25 53 30	2♎56 20	4D03.0	2 38.2	5 45.0	9 13.8	14 03.7	6 15.6	7 58.1	22 12.6	27 35.4	3 18.8
19 Su	19 53 57	29 02 36	9♎59 21	17 02 25	4R03.4	4 20.4	6 59.9	9 54.4	14 26.5	6 19.4	7 59.2	22 12.1	27 34.8	3 17.4
20 M	19 57 54	0♒03 40	24 05 24	1♏08 12	4 03.7	6 02.9	8 14.9	10 35.0	14 49.3	6 23.4	8 00.4	22 11.5	27 34.1	3 16.0
21 Tu	20 01 50	1 04 43	8♏10 44	15 12 52	4 02.8	7 45.9	9 29.8	11 15.7	15 12.0	6 27.6	8 01.7	22 11.0	27 33.3	3 14.7
22 W	20 05 47	2 05 46	22 14 28	29 15 22	3 59.8	9 29.2	10 44.8	11 56.4	15 34.5	6 32.0	8 03.0	22 10.6	27 32.6	3 13.3
23 Th	20 09 43	3 06 49	6♐15 22	13♐14 10	3 54.1	11 12.8	11 59.7	12 37.1	15 57.0	6 36.6	8 04.6	22 10.2	27 31.8	3 12.0
24 F	20 13 40	4 07 51	20 11 30	27 06 59	3 46.1	12 56.6	13 14.7	13 17.9	16 19.4	6 41.4	8 06.2	22 09.9	27 31.0	3 10.6
25 Sa	20 17 37	5 08 52	4♑00 15	10♑50 54	3 36.2	14 40.6	14 29.7	13 58.6	16 41.6	6 46.3	8 07.9	22 09.6	27 30.1	3 09.3
26 Su	20 21 33	6 09 53	17 38 33	24 22 49	3 25.7	16 24.6	15 44.7	14 39.4	17 03.8	6 51.5	8 09.7	22 09.4	27 29.3	3 07.9
27 M	20 25 30	7 10 52	1♒03 21	7♒39 52	3 15.5	18 08.5	16 59.7	15 20.2	17 25.9	6 56.8	8 11.7	22 09.2	27 28.4	3 06.5
28 Tu	20 29 26	8 11 51	14 12 10	20 40 05	3 06.8	19 52.2	18 14.6	16 01.0	17 47.8	7 02.3	8 13.7	22 09.1	27 27.4	3 05.2
29 W	20 33 23	9 12 49	27 03 33	3♓22 38	3 00.3	21 35.4	19 29.6	16 41.8	18 09.7	7 07.9	8 15.9	22D09.1	27 26.5	3 03.8
30 Th	20 37 19	10 13 46	9♓37 25	15 48 07	2 56.2	23 17.9	20 44.6	17 22.6	18 31.4	7 13.8	8 18.1	22 09.1	27 25.5	3 02.5
31 F	20 41 16	11 14 41	21 55 03	27 58 33	2D54.5	24 59.6	21 59.6	18 03.4	18 53.1	7 19.8	8 20.5	22 09.1	27 24.5	3 01.1

LONGITUDE — February 1941

Day	Sid.Time	☉	0 hr ☽	Noon ☽	True ☊	☿	♀	♂	⚳	♃	♄	♅	♆	♇
1 Sa	20 45 12	12♒15 36	3♈59 04	9♈57 06	2♎54.6	26♒39.9	23♑14.5	18♐44.3	19♐14.6	7♉26.0	8♉23.0	22♉09.2	27♍23.4	2♌59.8
2 Su	20 49 09	13 16 28	15 53 11	21 47 56	2 55.7	28 18.7	24 29.5	19 25.2	19 36.0	7 32.3	8 25.6	22 09.3	27R22.4	2R58.4
3 M	20 53 05	14 17 20	27 41 57	3♉35 53	2R57.1	29 55.5	25 44.5	20 06.1	19 57.3	7 38.8	8 28.2	22 09.5	27 21.3	2 57.1
4 Tu	20 57 02	15 18 10	9♉30 25	15 26 13	2 57.7	1♓29.8	26 59.4	20 47.0	20 18.4	7 45.5	8 31.0	22 09.8	27 20.1	2 55.8
5 W	21 00 59	16 18 59	21 23 57	27 24 17	2 56.8	3 01.2	28 14.4	21 27.9	20 39.5	7 52.4	8 33.9	22 10.1	27 19.0	2 54.5
6 Th	21 04 55	17 19 47	3♊27 49	9♊35 10	2 54.1	4 29.0	29 29.4	22 08.8	21 00.4	7 59.4	8 36.9	22 10.5	27 17.8	2 53.1
7 F	21 08 52	18 20 32	15 46 52	22 03 24	2 49.5	5 52.6	0♒44.3	22 49.8	21 21.2	8 06.5	8 40.0	22 10.9	27 16.7	2 51.8
8 Sa	21 12 48	19 21 17	28 25 09	4♋52 26	2 43.3	7 11.4	1 59.3	23 30.7	21 41.9	8 13.8	8 43.2	22 11.4	27 15.4	2 50.5
9 Su	21 16 45	20 22 00	11♋25 26	18 04 14	2 36.1	8 24.6	3 14.2	24 11.7	22 02.4	8 21.3	8 46.5	22 11.9	27 14.2	2 49.3
10 M	21 20 41	21 22 41	24 48 47	1♌38 56	2 28.8	9 31.6	4 29.1	24 52.7	22 22.8	8 28.9	8 49.9	22 12.4	27 13.0	2 48.0
11 Tu	21 24 38	22 23 21	8♌34 20	15 34 35	2 22.2	10 31.5	5 44.1	25 33.7	22 43.1	8 36.7	8 53.4	22 13.1	27 11.7	2 46.7
12 W	21 28 34	23 24 00	22 39 09	29 47 24	2 17.1	11 23.7	6 59.0	26 14.8	23 03.3	8 44.6	8 56.9	22 13.7	27 10.4	2 45.4
13 Th	21 32 31	24 24 37	6♍58 37	14♍12 07	2 13.8	12 07.4	8 13.9	26 55.8	23 23.3	8 52.7	9 00.6	22 14.5	27 09.0	2 44.2
14 F	21 36 28	25 25 12	21 27 06	28 42 53	2D12.5	12 42.0	9 28.8	27 36.9	23 43.2	9 00.9	9 04.4	22 15.3	27 07.7	2 42.9
15 Sa	21 40 24	26 25 47	5♎58 45	13♎14 03	2 12.9	13 07.1	10 43.8	28 18.0	24 02.9	9 09.2	9 08.2	22 16.1	27 06.3	2 41.7
16 Su	21 44 21	27 26 20	20 28 15	27 40 51	2 14.2	13R22.1	11 58.7	28 59.1	24 22.5	9 17.7	9 12.2	22 17.0	27 05.0	2 40.5
17 M	21 48 17	28 26 52	4♏51 26	11♏59 41	2 15.7	13 26.8	13 13.6	29 40.2	24 42.0	9 26.3	9 16.2	22 17.9	27 03.6	2 39.3
18 Tu	21 52 14	29 27 23	19 05 21	26 08 15	2R16.5	13 21.2	14 28.5	0♑21.4	25 01.3	9 35.1	9 20.3	22 18.9	27 02.2	2 38.1
19 W	21 56 10	0♓27 52	3♐08 14	10♐05 12	2 16.2	13 05.4	15 43.4	1 02.5	25 20.5	9 44.0	9 24.6	22 19.9	27 00.7	2 36.9
20 Th	22 00 07	1 28 21	16 59 06	23 49 52	2 14.4	12 39.8	16 58.4	1 43.7	25 39.5	9 53.0	9 28.9	22 21.0	26 59.3	2 35.7
21 F	22 04 03	2 28 48	0♑37 29	7♑21 54	2 11.2	12 05.1	18 13.3	2 24.9	25 58.4	10 02.2	9 33.3	22 22.1	26 57.8	2 34.6
22 Sa	22 08 00	3 29 14	14 03 06	20 41 02	2 07.0	11 22.1	19 28.2	3 06.1	26 17.1	10 11.5	9 37.8	22 23.3	26 56.3	2 33.4
23 Su	22 11 57	4 29 38	27 15 42	3♒47 04	2 02.3	10 31.9	20 43.1	3 47.3	26 35.6	10 20.9	9 42.3	22 24.6	26 54.8	2 32.3
24 M	22 15 53	5 30 00	10♒15 06	16 39 47	1 57.8	9 36.0	21 58.0	4 28.6	26 54.0	10 30.4	9 47.0	22 25.9	26 53.3	2 31.2
25 Tu	22 19 50	6 30 21	23 01 08	29 19 10	1 53.9	8 35.7	23 12.8	5 09.8	27 12.2	10 40.1	9 51.7	22 27.2	26 51.8	2 30.1
26 W	22 23 46	7 30 41	5♓33 58	11♓45 35	1 51.2	7 32.7	24 27.7	5 51.0	27 30.2	10 49.9	9 56.5	22 28.6	26 50.2	2 29.0
27 Th	22 27 43	8 30 58	17 54 10	23 59 52	1D49.8	6 28.5	25 42.6	6 32.3	27 48.1	10 59.8	10 01.4	22 30.0	26 48.7	2 27.9
28 F	22 31 39	9 31 14	0♈02 54	6♈03 31	1 49.6	5 24.8	26 57.4	7 13.6	28 05.8	11 09.8	10 06.4	22 31.5	26 47.1	2 26.9

Astro Data

	Dy Hr Mn
☽0N	4 4:43
♄ D	9 12:20
☽0S	18 5:13
♅ D	30 5:02
☽0N	31 14:31
☽0S	14 13:09
♃☌♄	15 6:37
☿ R	17 10:57
☽0N	27 22:56

Planet Ingress

		Dy Hr Mn
♂	♐	4 19:42
♀	♑	13 21:29
☿	♒	16 22:36
☉	♒	20 10:34
☿	♓	3 13:08
♀	♒	6 21:49
♂	♑	17 23:32
☉	♓	19 0:56

Last Aspect / ☽ Ingress

Last Aspect Dy Hr Mn			☽ Ingress	Dy Hr Mn
1 16:34	♂	□	♓	1 20:35
4 6:51	♂	△	♈	4 7:34
6 0:29	♀	△	♉	6 20:28
9 3:53	♆	△	♊	9 8:27
11 13:12	♆	□	♋	11 17:33
13 19:29	♆	⚹	♌	13 23:39
15 14:25	♅	□	♍	16 3:45
18 2:59	☉	△	♎	18 7:00
20 10:01	☉	□	♏	20 10:04
22 9:04	♆	⚹	♐	22 13:16
24 12:42	♆	□	♑	24 17:01
26 17:34	♆	△	♒	26 22:06
28 14:46	♅	□	♓	29 5:34
31 10:52	♆	☍	♈	31 16:02

Last Aspect / ☽ Ingress

Last Aspect Dy Hr Mn			☽ Ingress	Dy Hr Mn
3 3:21	☿	⚹	♉	3 4:41
5 13:51	♀	△	♊	5 17:09
7 21:51	♆	□	♋	8 2:57
10 4:15	♆	⚹	♌	10 9:07
12 5:45	♂	△	♍	12 12:21
14 10:06	♂	□	♎	14 14:07
16 14:17	♂	⚹	♏	16 15:52
18 18:07	☉	□	♐	18 18:37
20 17:33	♆	□	♑	20 22:54
22 23:23	♆	△	♒	23 5:02
24 23:06	♀	☌	♓	25 13:18
27 17:34	♆	☍	♈	27 23:54

☽ Phases & Eclipses

Dy Hr Mn		
5 13:40	☽	14♈51
13 11:04	○	22♋54
20 10:01	☾	29♎59
27 11:03	●	7♒08
4 11:42	☽	15♉17
12 0:26	○	22♌55
18 18:07	☾	29♏43
26 3:02	●	7♓08

Astro Data

1 January 1941
Julian Day # 14976
SVP 6♓04'58"
GC 26♐00.9 ⚵ 20♏04.3
Eris 3♈56.4 ⚶ 7♍34.0R
⚷ 29♋39.6R ⚴ 29♌47.2R
☽ Mean ☊ 6♎08.8

1 February 1941
Julian Day # 15007
SVP 6♓04'54"
GC 26♐01.0 ⚵ 1♐02.8
Eris 4♈05.7 ⚶ 3♍41.7R
⚷ 27♋27.0R ⚴ 25♌11.0R
☽ Mean ☊ 4♎30.3

March 1941 LONGITUDE

Day	Sid.Time	☉	0 hr ☽	Noon ☽	True ☊	☿	♀	♂	⚳	♃	♄	♅	♆	♇
1 Sa	22 35 36	10♓31 27	12♈02 02	17♈58 47	1♎50.5	4♓22.8	28♒12.3	7♑54.9	28♐23.3	11♉19.9	10♉11.5	22♉33.0	26♍45.5	2♌25.8
2 Su	22 39 32	11 31 39	23 54 08	29 48 34	1 51.9	3R 24.0	29 27.1	8 36.1	28 40.7	11 30.2	10 16.6	22 34.6	26R 44.0	2R 24.8
3 M	22 43 29	12 31 49	5♉42 31	11♉36 29	1 53.6	2 29.5	0♓41.9	9 17.4	28 57.8	11 40.5	10 21.8	22 36.2	26 42.4	2 23.8
4 Tu	22 47 26	13 31 57	17 31 03	23 26 44	1 55.1	1 40.1	1 56.7	9 58.8	29 14.8	11 51.0	10 27.1	22 37.9	26 40.8	2 22.8
5 W	22 51 22	14 32 03	29 24 09	5♊23 54	1R 56.1	0 56.5	3 11.5	10 40.1	29 31.6	12 01.6	10 32.5	22 39.6	26 39.1	2 21.9
6 Th	22 55 19	15 32 06	11♊26 35	17 32 47	1 56.3	0 19.2	4 26.3	11 21.4	29 48.2	12 12.3	10 37.9	22 41.4	26 37.5	2 20.9
7 F	22 59 15	16 32 08	23 43 06	29 58 06	1 55.8	29♒48.5	5 41.1	12 02.7	0♑04.6	12 23.0	10 43.4	22 43.2	26 35.9	2 20.0
8 Sa	23 03 12	17 32 07	6♋18 17	12♋44 07	1 54.7	29 24.5	6 55.9	12 44.1	0 20.9	12 33.9	10 49.0	22 45.0	26 34.3	2 19.1
9 Su	23 07 08	18 32 04	19 15 58	25 54 09	1 53.1	29 07.2	8 10.6	13 25.5	0 36.9	12 44.9	10 54.7	22 46.9	26 32.6	2 18.2
10 M	23 11 05	19 32 00	2♌38 49	9♌30 02	1 51.4	28 56.6	9 25.4	14 06.8	0 52.7	12 56.0	11 00.4	22 48.9	26 31.0	2 17.4
11 Tu	23 15 01	20 31 52	16 27 42	23 31 36	1 49.8	28D 52.4	10 40.1	14 48.2	1 08.3	13 07.2	11 06.2	22 50.8	26 29.3	2 16.5
12 W	23 18 58	21 31 43	0♍41 18	7♍56 18	1 48.7	28 54.5	11 54.8	15 29.6	1 23.7	13 18.4	11 12.0	22 52.9	26 27.7	2 15.7
13 Th	23 22 55	22 31 32	15 15 52	22 39 11	1D 48.1	29 02.6	13 09.5	16 11.0	1 38.9	13 29.8	11 17.9	22 54.9	26 26.0	2 14.9
14 F	23 26 51	23 31 19	0♎05 21	7♎33 23	1 48.1	29 16.3	14 24.2	16 52.4	1 53.9	13 41.2	11 23.9	22 57.0	26 24.4	2 14.1
15 Sa	23 30 48	24 31 03	15 02 13	22 30 51	1 48.4	29 35.4	15 38.9	17 33.8	2 08.7	13 52.8	11 29.9	22 59.2	26 22.7	2 13.3
16 Su	23 34 44	25 30 47	29 58 18	7♏23 39	1 48.9	29 59.5	16 53.6	18 15.3	2 23.3	14 04.4	11 36.0	23 01.4	26 21.0	2 12.6
17 M	23 38 41	26 30 28	14♏46 04	22 04 52	1 49.5	0♓28.5	18 08.2	18 56.7	2 37.6	14 16.1	11 42.2	23 03.6	26 19.4	2 11.9
18 Tu	23 42 37	27 30 08	29 19 26	6♐29 22	1 49.9	1 01.9	19 22.9	19 38.2	2 51.7	14 27.9	11 48.4	23 05.9	26 17.7	2 11.2
19 W	23 46 34	28 29 46	13♐34 21	20 34 10	1R 50.1	1 39.5	20 37.5	20 19.6	3 05.6	14 39.8	11 54.7	23 08.2	26 16.0	2 10.5
20 Th	23 50 30	29 29 22	27 28 46	4♑18 09	1 50.1	2 21.1	21 52.2	21 01.1	3 19.3	14 51.8	12 01.0	23 10.5	26 14.4	2 09.9
21 F	23 54 27	0♈28 56	11♑02 25	17 41 44	1 50.1	3 06.4	23 06.8	21 42.6	3 32.7	15 03.8	12 07.4	23 12.9	26 12.7	2 09.3
22 Sa	23 58 23	1 28 29	24 16 19	0♒46 25	1D 50.0	3 55.2	24 21.4	22 24.1	3 45.9	15 15.9	12 13.9	23 15.3	26 11.1	2 08.7
23 Su	0 02 20	2 28 00	7♒12 17	13 34 12	1 50.0	4 47.3	25 36.0	23 05.5	3 58.9	15 28.1	12 20.4	23 17.8	26 09.4	2 08.1
24 M	0 06 17	3 27 29	19 52 27	26 07 19	1 50.2	5 42.5	26 50.6	23 47.0	4 11.6	15 40.4	12 26.9	23 20.3	26 07.8	2 07.5
25 Tu	0 10 13	4 26 57	2♓19 04	8♓27 59	1 50.4	6 40.5	28 05.2	24 28.5	4 24.0	15 52.7	12 33.5	23 22.8	26 06.1	2 07.0
26 W	0 14 10	5 26 22	14 34 18	20 38 17	1R 50.6	7 41.3	29 19.7	25 10.0	4 36.2	16 05.1	12 40.2	23 25.4	26 04.5	2 06.5
27 Th	0 18 06	6 25 45	26 40 10	2♈40 12	1 50.7	8 44.8	0♈34.3	25 51.5	4 48.1	16 17.6	12 46.9	23 28.0	26 02.8	2 06.0
28 F	0 22 03	7 25 07	8♈38 36	14 35 37	1 50.5	9 50.6	1 48.8	26 33.0	4 59.8	16 30.2	12 53.6	23 30.6	26 01.2	2 05.6
29 Sa	0 25 59	8 24 26	20 31 31	26 26 32	1 50.0	10 58.9	3 03.3	27 14.5	5 11.2	16 42.8	13 00.4	23 33.3	25 59.6	2 05.1
30 Su	0 29 56	9 23 43	2♉20 59	8♉15 09	1 49.2	12 09.4	4 17.9	27 56.0	5 22.3	16 55.5	13 07.3	23 36.0	25 58.0	2 04.7
31 M	0 33 52	10 22 58	14 09 21	20 03 57	1 48.0	13 22.0	5 32.4	28 37.5	5 33.2	17 08.2	13 14.2	23 38.7	25 56.4	2 04.3

April 1941 LONGITUDE

Day	Sid.Time	☉	0 hr ☽	Noon ☽	True ☊	☿	♀	♂	⚳	♃	♄	♅	♆	♇
1 Tu	0 37 49	11♈22 11	25♉59 18	1♊55 50	1♎46.7	14♓36.7	6♈46.8	29♑18.9	5♑43.8	17♉21.0	13♉21.1	23♉41.5	25♍54.8	2♌04.0
2 W	0 41 46	12 21 21	7♊53 57	13 54 09	1R 45.4	15 53.4	8 01.3	0♒00.4	5 54.1	17 33.9	13 28.1	23 44.2	25R 53.2	2R 03.6
3 Th	0 45 42	13 20 30	19 56 53	26 02 39	1 44.3	17 12.1	9 15.7	0 41.9	6 04.1	17 46.8	13 35.1	23 47.1	25 51.6	2 03.3
4 F	0 49 39	14 19 36	2♋11 59	8♋25 23	1D 43.7	18 32.5	10 30.2	1 23.4	6 13.9	17 59.8	13 42.1	23 49.9	25 50.0	2 03.1
5 Sa	0 53 35	15 18 39	14 43 23	21 06 27	1 43.7	19 54.8	11 44.6	2 04.8	6 23.3	18 12.8	13 49.2	23 52.8	25 48.5	2 02.8
6 Su	0 57 32	16 17 41	27 35 05	4♌09 42	1 44.3	21 18.9	12 59.0	2 46.3	6 32.5	18 25.9	13 56.3	23 55.7	25 46.9	2 02.6
7 M	1 01 28	17 16 40	10♌50 38	17 38 09	1 45.4	22 44.6	14 13.4	3 27.7	6 41.4	18 39.0	14 03.5	23 58.7	25 45.4	2 02.4
8 Tu	1 05 25	18 15 37	24 32 27	1♍33 31	1 46.6	24 12.1	15 27.7	4 09.2	6 49.9	18 52.2	14 10.7	24 01.6	25 43.9	2 02.2
9 W	1 09 21	19 14 31	8♍41 16	15 55 24	1 47.7	25 41.2	16 42.1	4 50.6	6 58.2	19 05.5	14 17.9	24 04.6	25 42.4	2 02.0
10 Th	1 13 18	20 13 23	23 15 27	0♎40 47	1R 48.1	27 12.0	17 56.4	5 32.1	7 06.2	19 18.8	14 25.2	24 07.6	25 40.9	2 01.9
11 F	1 17 14	21 12 13	8♎10 34	15 43 50	1 47.7	28 44.4	19 10.7	6 13.5	7 13.8	19 32.1	14 32.5	24 10.7	25 39.4	2 01.8
12 Sa	1 21 11	22 11 02	23 19 27	0♏56 14	1 46.3	0♈18.5	20 25.0	6 55.0	7 21.2	19 45.5	14 39.8	24 13.7	25 38.0	2 01.7
13 Su	1 25 08	23 09 48	8♏32 54	16 08 12	1 44.0	1 54.1	21 39.3	7 36.4	7 28.2	19 58.9	14 47.1	24 16.8	25 36.5	2 01.7
14 M	1 29 04	24 08 32	23 40 55	1♐09 59	1 41.1	3 31.4	22 53.5	8 17.8	7 34.9	20 12.3	14 54.5	24 19.9	25 35.1	2D 01.7
15 Tu	1 33 01	25 07 15	8♐34 23	15 53 21	1 38.1	5 10.2	24 07.8	8 59.2	7 41.3	20 25.9	15 01.9	24 23.1	25 33.7	2 01.7
16 W	1 36 57	26 05 56	23 06 16	0♑12 42	1 35.5	6 50.7	25 22.0	9 40.6	7 47.4	20 39.4	15 09.3	24 26.2	25 32.3	2 01.7
17 Th	1 40 54	27 04 35	7♑12 25	14 05 20	1 33.8	8 32.8	26 36.3	10 22.0	7 53.1	20 53.0	15 16.8	24 29.4	25 31.0	2 01.8
18 F	1 44 50	28 03 13	20 51 33	27 31 16	1D 33.2	10 16.5	27 50.5	11 03.4	7 58.5	21 06.6	15 24.3	24 32.6	25 29.6	2 01.9
19 Sa	1 48 47	29 01 49	4♒04 48	10♒32 31	1 33.6	12 01.8	29 04.7	11 44.8	8 03.6	21 20.3	15 31.8	24 35.8	25 28.3	2 02.0
20 Su	1 52 43	0♉00 23	16 54 53	23 12 24	1 34.9	13 48.8	0♉18.9	12 26.2	8 08.3	21 34.0	15 39.3	24 39.0	25 27.0	2 02.1
21 M	1 56 40	0 58 56	29 25 32	5♓34 48	1 36.7	15 37.4	1 33.1	13 07.5	8 12.7	21 47.7	15 46.9	24 42.3	25 25.7	2 02.3
22 Tu	2 00 37	1 57 27	11♓40 42	17 43 44	1 38.2	17 27.6	2 47.2	13 48.8	8 16.7	22 01.5	15 54.4	24 45.6	25 24.4	2 02.5
23 W	2 04 33	2 55 56	23 44 21	29 42 59	1R 39.0	19 19.5	4 01.4	14 30.1	8 20.4	22 15.2	16 02.0	24 48.9	25 23.1	2 02.7
24 Th	2 08 30	3 54 23	5♈40 02	11♈35 52	1 38.5	21 13.1	5 15.5	15 11.4	8 23.7	22 29.1	16 09.6	24 52.2	25 21.9	2 02.9
25 F	2 12 26	4 52 49	17 30 50	23 25 16	1 36.4	23 08.3	6 29.7	15 52.7	8 26.7	22 42.9	16 17.2	24 55.5	25 20.7	2 03.2
26 Sa	2 16 23	5 51 13	29 19 25	5♉13 34	1 32.6	25 05.1	7 43.8	16 33.9	8 29.3	22 56.8	16 24.8	24 58.8	25 19.5	2 03.5
27 Su	2 20 19	6 49 35	11♉07 59	17 02 52	1 27.4	27 03.6	8 57.9	17 15.1	8 31.5	23 10.7	16 32.5	25 02.2	25 18.3	2 03.8
28 M	2 24 16	7 47 56	22 58 29	28 55 03	1 21.0	29 03.7	10 11.9	17 56.3	8 33.4	23 24.6	16 40.1	25 05.5	25 17.2	2 04.1
29 Tu	2 28 12	8 46 14	4♊52 48	10♊52 00	1 14.1	1♉05.3	11 26.0	18 37.4	8 34.9	23 38.6	16 47.8	25 08.9	25 16.1	2 04.5
30 W	2 32 09	9 44 31	16 52 54	22 55 48	1 07.4	3 08.4	12 40.1	19 18.6	8 36.1	23 52.6	16 55.5	25 12.3	25 15.0	2 04.9

Astro Data	Dy Hr Mn
♃⚼♆	3 15:39
☿ D	11 15:53
☽ 0S	13 23:04
♄⚼♆	14 13:25
☉0N	21 0:20
☽ 0N	27 5:39
♀0N	29 16:08
☽ 0S	10 10:07
♇ D	14 18:26
☿0N	15 19:18
☽ 0N	23 11:41

Planet Ingress	Dy Hr Mn
♀ ♓	2 22:33
☿ ♒R	7 2:22
⚳ ♑	7 5:11
☿ ♓	16 12:26
☉ ♈	21 0:20
♀ ♈	27 0:58
♂ ♒	2 11:46
☿ ♈	12 7:19
♀ ♉	20 5:53
☉ ♉	20 11:50
☿ ♉	28 23:09

Last Aspect Dy Hr Mn		☽ Ingress Dy Hr Mn
2 11:11	♀ ⚹	♉ 2 12:23
4 18:30	♆ △	♊ 5 1:12
7 11:42	☿ △	♋ 7 12:04
9 13:09	♆ ⚹	♌ 9 19:19
11 20:59	☿ ☍	♍ 11 22:51
13 18:06	♆ ☌	♎ 13 23:51
15 23:41	☿ △	♏ 16 0:03
17 19:52	☉ △	♐ 18 1:08
20 2:51	☉ □	♑ 20 4:25
22 3:32	♆ △	♒ 22 10:34
24 6:37	♅ □	♓ 24 19:30
26 22:47	♆ ☍	♈ 27 6:39
29 13:43	♂ □	♉ 29 19:14

Last Aspect Dy Hr Mn		☽ Ingress Dy Hr Mn
1 6:24	♂ △	♊ 1 8:06
3 11:38	♆ □	♋ 3 19:44
5 20:43	♆ ⚹	♌ 6 4:26
7 23:04	♅ □	♍ 8 9:21
10 5:45	☿ ☍	♎ 10 10:54
11 21:15	☉ ☍	♏ 12 10:31
14 3:03	♆ ⚹	♐ 14 10:07
16 4:31	☉ △	♑ 16 11:38
18 13:03	☉ □	♒ 18 16:31
20 14:47	♅ □	♓ 21 1:07
23 3:19	♆ ☍	♈ 23 12:34
25 11:19	☿ ☌	♉ 26 1:23
28 4:41	♆ △	♊ 28 14:11

☽ Phases & Eclipses Dy Hr Mn	
6 7:42	☽ 15♊21
13 11:47	○ 22♍31
13 11:55	☍ P 0.323
20 2:51	☾ 29♐07
27 20:14	● 6♈46
27 20:07:43	● A 07'41"
5 0:12	☽ 14♋50
11 21:15	○ 21♎35
18 13:03	☾ 28♑06
26 13:23	● 5♉55

Astro Data

1 March 1941
Julian Day # 15035
SVP 6♓04'51"
GC 26♐01.1 ⚴ 8♐26.9
Eris 4♈21.7 ⚵ 26♌44.1R
⚷ 25♋49.8R ⚶ 18♌06.1R
☽ Mean ☊ 3♎01.3

1 April 1941
Julian Day # 15066
SVP 6♓04'49"
GC 26♐01.1 ⚴ 11♐57.5
Eris 4♈43.5 ⚵ 22♌26.6R
⚷ 25♋15.9 ⚶ 14♌40.5
☽ Mean ☊ 1♎22.8

LONGITUDE — May 1941

Day	Sid.Time	☉	0 hr ☽	Noon ☽	True ☊	☿	♀	♂	⚳	♃	♄	♅	♆	♇
1 Th	2 36 06	10♉42 45	29♊00 59	5♋08 49	1♎01.6	5♉12.9	13♉54.1	19♒59.6	8♑36.8	24♉06.5	17♉03.2	25♉15.7	25♍13.9	2♌05.3
2 F	2 40 02	11 40 58	11♋19 38	17 33 50	0R57.2	7 18.8	15 08.1	20 40.7	8R37.2	24 20.6	17 10.9	25 19.1	25R12.9	2 05.8
3 Sa	2 43 59	12 39 09	23 51 49	0♌14 00	0 54.7	9 25.8	16 22.1	21 21.7	8 37.3	24 34.6	17 18.6	25 22.6	25 11.9	2 06.2
4 Su	2 47 55	13 37 17	6♌40 48	13 12 39	0D53.9	11 33.9	17 36.1	22 02.7	8 36.9	24 48.6	17 26.3	25 26.0	25 10.9	2 06.7
5 M	2 51 52	14 35 24	19 49 56	26 33 01	0 54.4	13 42.9	18 50.1	22 43.7	8 36.2	25 02.7	17 34.0	25 29.4	25 09.9	2 07.2
6 Tu	2 55 48	15 33 28	3♍22 11	10♍17 40	0 55.6	15 52.6	20 04.0	23 24.6	8 35.2	25 16.8	17 41.7	25 32.9	25 09.0	2 07.8
7 W	2 59 45	16 31 31	17 19 34	24 27 51	0R56.6	18 02.8	21 18.0	24 05.5	8 33.7	25 30.9	17 49.4	25 36.3	25 08.1	2 08.4
8 Th	3 03 41	17 29 32	1♎42 22	9♎02 44	0 56.5	20 13.2	22 31.9	24 46.3	8 31.9	25 45.0	17 57.1	25 39.8	25 07.2	2 09.0
9 F	3 07 38	18 27 31	16 28 24	23 58 39	0 54.6	22 23.6	23 45.8	25 27.1	8 29.7	25 59.1	18 04.9	25 43.3	25 06.3	2 09.6
10 Sa	3 11 35	19 25 28	1♏32 31	9♏08 55	0 50.6	24 33.6	24 59.7	26 07.9	8 27.1	26 13.2	18 12.6	25 46.7	25 05.5	2 10.2
11 Su	3 15 31	20 23 24	16 46 37	24 24 16	0 44.6	26 43.1	26 13.5	26 48.6	8 24.2	26 27.3	18 20.3	25 50.2	25 04.7	2 10.9
12 M	3 19 28	21 21 18	2♐00 32	9♐34 06	0 37.3	28 51.7	27 27.4	27 29.3	8 20.9	26 41.4	18 28.0	25 53.7	25 03.9	2 11.6
13 Tu	3 23 24	22 19 11	17 03 44	24 28 20	0 29.6	0♊59.1	28 41.2	28 10.0	8 17.2	26 55.6	18 35.7	25 57.2	25 03.2	2 12.3
14 W	3 27 21	23 17 02	1♑47 01	8♑59 03	0 22.5	3 05.1	29 55.1	28 50.6	8 13.1	27 09.7	18 43.4	26 00.7	25 02.5	2 13.0
15 Th	3 31 17	24 14 53	16 03 58	23 01 31	0 16.8	5 09.3	1♊08.9	29 31.2	8 08.7	27 23.9	18 51.1	26 04.2	25 01.8	2 13.8
16 F	3 35 14	25 12 42	29 51 36	6♒34 22	0 13.1	7 11.7	2 22.7	0♓11.7	8 03.9	27 38.0	18 58.8	26 07.7	25 01.1	2 14.6
17 Sa	3 39 10	26 10 30	13♒10 03	19 39 03	0D11.4	9 11.9	3 36.5	0 52.1	7 58.8	27 52.2	19 06.5	26 11.2	25 00.5	2 15.4
18 Su	3 43 07	27 08 16	26 01 51	2♓19 01	0 11.3	11 09.7	4 50.3	1 32.6	7 53.3	28 06.4	19 14.2	26 14.7	24 59.9	2 16.2
19 M	3 47 04	28 06 02	8♓31 09	14 38 53	0 12.1	13 05.1	6 04.1	2 12.9	7 47.4	28 20.5	19 21.9	26 18.2	24 59.3	2 17.1
20 Tu	3 51 00	29 03 46	20 42 50	26 43 38	0R12.7	14 57.9	7 17.8	2 53.2	7 41.2	28 34.7	19 29.5	26 21.6	24 58.8	2 17.9
21 W	3 54 57	0♊01 29	2♈41 55	8♈38 15	0 12.4	16 47.9	8 31.6	3 33.4	7 34.6	28 48.8	19 37.2	26 25.1	24 58.3	2 18.8
22 Th	3 58 53	0 59 11	14 33 11	20 27 15	0 10.3	18 35.0	9 45.3	4 13.6	7 27.7	29 03.0	19 44.8	26 28.6	24 57.8	2 19.8
23 F	4 02 50	1 56 53	26 20 54	2♉14 33	0 05.7	20 19.3	10 59.1	4 53.7	7 20.4	29 17.1	19 52.4	26 32.1	24 57.4	2 20.7
24 Sa	4 06 46	2 54 32	8♉08 36	14 03 22	29♍58.6	22 00.6	12 12.8	5 33.7	7 12.8	29 31.3	20 00.0	26 35.6	24 57.0	2 21.7
25 Su	4 10 43	3 52 11	19 59 09	25 56 12	29 49.1	23 38.8	13 26.5	6 13.6	7 04.8	29 45.4	20 07.6	26 39.1	24 56.6	2 22.7
26 M	4 14 39	4 49 49	1♊54 42	7♊54 52	29 37.9	25 14.0	14 40.2	6 53.5	6 56.5	29 59.5	20 15.2	26 42.5	24 56.2	2 23.7
27 Tu	4 18 36	5 47 26	13 56 51	20 00 47	29 25.8	26 46.0	15 53.9	7 33.3	6 48.0	0♊13.6	20 22.7	26 46.0	24 55.9	2 24.7
28 W	4 22 33	6 45 01	26 06 49	2♋15 03	29 13.9	28 15.0	17 07.6	8 13.0	6 39.1	0 27.8	20 30.3	26 49.5	24 55.6	2 25.7
29 Th	4 26 29	7 42 35	8♋25 40	14 38 47	29 03.3	29 40.7	18 21.3	8 52.6	6 29.8	0 41.9	20 37.8	26 52.9	24 55.4	2 26.8
30 F	4 30 26	8 40 08	20 54 36	27 13 18	28 54.8	1♋03.2	19 34.9	9 32.2	6 20.3	0 55.9	20 45.3	26 56.4	24 55.2	2 27.9
31 Sa	4 34 22	9 37 39	3♌35 07	10♌00 17	28 48.9	2 22.4	20 48.5	10 11.6	6 10.6	1 10.0	20 52.8	26 59.8	24 55.0	2 29.0

LONGITUDE — June 1941

Day	Sid.Time	☉	0 hr ☽	Noon ☽	True ☊	☿	♀	♂	⚳	♃	♄	♅	♆	♇
1 Su	4 38 19	10♊35 09	16♌29 06	23♌01 50	28♍45.6	3♋38.3	22♊02.2	10♓51.0	6♑00.5	1♊24.0	21♉00.2	27♉03.2	24♍54.8	2♌30.1
2 M	4 42 15	11 32 38	29 38 49	6♍20 20	28D44.4	4 50.9	23 15.8	11 30.2	5R50.2	1 38.1	21 07.6	27 06.7	24R54.7	2 31.3
3 Tu	4 46 12	12 30 06	13♍06 41	19 58 07	28R44.5	6 00.0	24 29.4	12 09.4	5 39.6	1 52.1	21 15.0	27 10.1	24 54.6	2 32.4
4 W	4 50 08	13 27 32	26 54 47	3♎56 50	28 44.5	7 05.7	25 43.0	12 48.5	5 28.7	2 06.1	21 22.4	27 13.5	24 54.5	2 33.6
5 Th	4 54 05	14 24 57	11♎04 14	18 16 52	28 43.3	8 07.8	26 56.5	13 27.5	5 17.7	2 20.1	21 29.7	27 16.8	24D54.5	2 34.8
6 F	4 58 02	15 22 21	25 34 25	2♏56 25	28 40.1	9 06.3	28 10.1	14 06.3	5 06.4	2 34.0	21 37.0	27 20.2	24 54.5	2 36.1
7 Sa	5 01 58	16 19 44	10♏22 13	17 51 01	28 34.2	10 01.1	29 23.6	14 45.1	4 54.8	2 47.9	21 44.3	27 23.6	24 54.5	2 37.3
8 Su	5 05 55	17 17 06	25 21 48	2♐53 28	28 25.8	10 52.2	0♋37.1	15 23.8	4 43.1	3 01.8	21 51.6	27 26.9	24 54.6	2 38.5
9 M	5 09 51	18 14 27	10♐24 49	17 54 37	28 15.5	11 39.4	1 50.6	16 02.3	4 31.2	3 15.7	21 58.8	27 30.2	24 54.7	2 39.8
10 Tu	5 13 48	19 11 47	25 21 38	2♑44 45	28 04.7	12 22.6	3 04.1	16 40.8	4 19.1	3 29.6	22 06.0	27 33.5	24 54.8	2 41.1
11 W	5 17 44	20 09 06	10♑02 55	17 15 19	27 54.3	13 01.8	4 17.6	17 19.1	4 06.9	3 43.4	22 13.1	27 36.8	24 55.0	2 42.4
12 Th	5 21 41	21 06 25	24 21 16	1♒20 20	27 45.6	13 36.9	5 31.1	17 57.4	3 54.4	3 57.2	22 20.2	27 40.1	24 55.2	2 43.7
13 F	5 25 37	22 03 44	8♒12 16	14 57 00	27 39.3	14 07.7	6 44.6	18 35.5	3 41.9	4 11.0	22 27.3	27 43.4	24 55.4	2 45.1
14 Sa	5 29 34	23 01 02	21 34 39	28 05 29	27 35.5	14 34.2	7 58.0	19 13.4	3 29.2	4 24.7	22 34.4	27 46.6	24 55.7	2 46.4
15 Su	5 33 31	23 58 19	4♓29 56	10♓48 27	27 33.7	14 56.3	9 11.5	19 51.3	3 16.3	4 38.4	22 41.4	27 49.9	24 56.0	2 47.8
16 M	5 37 27	24 55 36	17 01 39	23 10 08	27 33.4	15 14.0	10 24.9	20 29.0	3 03.4	4 52.1	22 48.3	27 53.1	24 56.3	2 49.2
17 Tu	5 41 24	25 52 53	29 14 35	5♈15 40	27 33.3	15 27.2	11 38.3	21 06.6	2 50.4	5 05.8	22 55.3	27 56.3	24 56.6	2 50.6
18 W	5 45 20	26 50 10	11♈14 03	17 10 25	27 32.4	15 35.8	12 51.7	21 44.0	2 37.3	5 19.4	23 02.1	27 59.4	24 57.0	2 52.0
19 Th	5 49 17	27 47 26	23 05 25	28 59 39	27 29.7	15R39.8	14 05.1	22 21.3	2 24.1	5 33.0	23 09.0	28 02.6	24 57.5	2 53.4
20 F	5 53 13	28 44 42	4♉53 42	10♉48 06	27 24.6	15 39.3	15 18.5	22 58.4	2 10.9	5 46.5	23 15.8	28 05.7	24 57.9	2 54.9
21 Sa	5 57 10	29 41 58	16 43 20	22 39 51	27 16.7	15 34.3	16 31.9	23 35.3	1 57.6	6 00.0	23 22.6	28 08.8	24 58.4	2 56.3
22 Su	6 01 06	0♋39 14	28 38 00	4♊38 07	27 06.3	15 24.9	17 45.3	24 12.1	1 44.3	6 13.5	23 29.3	28 11.9	24 58.9	2 57.8
23 M	6 05 03	1 36 30	10♊40 27	16 45 14	26 54.0	15 11.2	18 58.7	24 48.7	1 31.1	6 26.9	23 35.9	28 15.0	24 59.5	2 59.3
24 Tu	6 09 00	2 33 45	22 52 36	29 02 39	26 40.7	14 53.5	20 12.0	25 25.2	1 17.8	6 40.3	23 42.6	28 18.0	25 00.0	3 00.8
25 W	6 12 56	3 31 00	5♋15 29	11♋31 07	26 27.6	14 32.0	21 25.4	26 01.4	1 04.5	6 53.6	23 49.1	28 21.0	25 00.7	3 02.3
26 Th	6 16 53	4 28 14	17 49 34	24 10 50	26 15.8	14 07.0	22 38.7	26 37.5	0 51.3	7 06.9	23 55.7	28 24.0	25 01.3	3 03.8
27 F	6 20 49	5 25 28	0♌34 55	7♌01 48	26 06.3	13 38.8	23 52.0	27 13.4	0 38.2	7 20.2	24 02.1	28 27.0	25 02.0	3 05.4
28 Sa	6 24 46	6 22 42	13 31 31	20 04 07	25 59.5	13 07.9	25 05.3	27 49.1	0 25.1	7 33.4	24 08.6	28 29.9	25 02.7	3 06.9
29 Su	6 28 42	7 19 55	26 39 38	3♍18 09	25 55.6	12 34.8	26 18.6	28 24.5	0 12.1	7 46.5	24 14.9	28 32.8	25 03.4	3 08.5
30 M	6 32 39	8 17 08	9♍59 48	16 44 42	25D54.0	12 00.0	27 31.8	28 59.8	29♐59.2	7 59.6	24 21.2	28 35.7	25 04.2	3 10.0

Astro Data

	Dy Hr Mn
♅△♆	1 2:22
⚳R	3 2:21
♃△♆	5 23:33
☽0S	7 20:46
♃☌♅	8 0:22
☽0N	20 18:27
☽0S	4 5:50
♆D	5 22:54
♃⚹♇	6 15:52
☽0N	17 2:45
☿R	19 21:18

Planet Ingress

	Dy Hr Mn
☿ ♊	13 0:50
♀ ♊	14 13:36
♂ ♓	16 5:05
☉ ♊	21 11:23
☊ ♍R	24 7:47
♃ ♊	26 12:48
☿ ♋	29 17:32
♀ ♋	7 23:53
☉ ♋	21 19:33
⚳ ♐R	30 10:26

Last Aspect / ☽ Ingress

Last Aspect Dy Hr Mn		☽ Ingress	Dy Hr Mn
30 16:35	♆ ☐	♋	1 1:56
3 2:49	♅ ⚹	♌	3 11:34
5 10:07	♅ ☐	♍	5 18:06
7 13:55	♅ △	♎	7 21:11
9 14:27	♂ △	♏	9 21:34
11 16:15	☿ ☍	♐	11 20:49
13 18:20	♂ ⚹	♑	13 21:03
15 19:47	♃ △	♒	16 0:15
18 3:47	♃ ☐	♓	18 7:33
20 17:06	☉ ⚹	♈	20 18:34
22 7:31	☿ ⚹	♉	23 7:26
25 19:50	♃ ☌	♊	25 20:10
28 3:07	☿ ☌	♋	28 7:36
30 11:28	♅ ⚹	♌	30 17:15

Last Aspect / ☽ Ingress

Last Aspect Dy Hr Mn		☽ Ingress	Dy Hr Mn
1 19:21	♅ ☐	♍	2 0:38
4 0:29	♅ △	♎	4 5:17
6 3:32	♀ △	♏	6 7:13
8 3:18	♅ ☍	♐	8 7:24
9 23:17	♆ ☐	♑	10 7:31
12 5:39	♅ △	♒	12 9:41
14 11:25	♅ ☐	♓	14 15:33
16 21:21	♅ ⚹	♈	17 1:30
19 9:20	☉ ⚹	♉	19 14:03
21 23:04	♅ ☌	♊	22 2:44
24 4:36	♂ ☐	♋	24 13:51
26 19:57	♅ ⚹	♌	26 22:55
29 3:23	♅ ☐	♍	29 6:03

☽ Phases & Eclipses

Dy Hr Mn	
4 12:48	☽ 13♌39
11 5:15	○ 20♏07
18 1:17	☾ 26♒42
26 5:18	● 4♊34
2 21:56	☽ 11♍56
9 12:34	○ 18♐16
16 15:45	☾ 25♓05
24 19:22	● 2♋51

Astro Data

1 May 1941
Julian Day # 15096
SVP 6♓04'46"
GC 26♐01.2 ⚴ 8♐39.0R
Eris 5♈03.6 ⚵ 24♌15.7
⚷ 26♋12.0 ⚶ 18♌09.4
☽ Mean ☊ 29♍47.5

1 June 1941
Julian Day # 15127
SVP 6♓04'41"
GC 26♐01.3 ⚴ 29♏56.5R
Eris 5♈18.4 ⚵ 0♍37.9
⚷ 28♋29.9 ⚶ 26♌51.1
☽ Mean ☊ 28♍09.0

July 1941 LONGITUDE

Day	Sid.Time	☉	0 hr ☽	Noon ☽	True ☊	☿	♀	♂	⚳	♃	♄	♅	♆	♇
1 Tu	6 36 35	9♋14 21	23♍32 59	0♎24 47	25♍53.8	11♋24.0	28♋45.1	29♓34.9	29♐46.4	8♊12.7	24♉27.5	28♉38.6	25♍05.0	3♌11.6
2 W	6 40 32	10 11 33	7♎20 12	14 19 19	25R53.9	10R47.4	29 58.3	0♈09.7	29R33.7	8 25.7	24 33.7	28 41.4	25 05.8	3 13.2
3 Th	6 44 29	11 08 45	21 22 08	28 28 35	25 52.9	10 11.0	1♌11.6	0 44.4	29 21.2	8 38.6	24 39.8	28 44.2	25 06.7	3 14.8
4 F	6 48 25	12 05 56	5♏38 30	12♏51 35	25 50.0	9 35.2	2 24.8	1 18.8	29 08.8	8 51.5	24 45.9	28 47.0	25 07.6	3 16.4
5 Sa	6 52 22	13 03 07	20 07 26	27 25 31	25 44.6	9 00.8	3 37.9	1 53.0	28 56.6	9 04.4	24 51.9	28 49.7	25 08.5	3 18.0
6 Su	6 56 18	14 00 19	4♐45 08	12♐05 32	25 36.8	8 28.4	4 51.1	2 27.0	28 44.5	9 17.1	24 57.9	28 52.4	25 09.4	3 19.6
7 M	7 00 15	14 57 30	19 25 48	26 45 02	25 27.2	7 58.4	6 04.2	3 00.7	28 32.7	9 29.8	25 03.8	28 55.1	25 10.4	3 21.2
8 Tu	7 04 11	15 54 41	4♑02 17	11♑16 36	25 16.9	7 31.5	7 17.4	3 34.2	28 21.0	9 42.5	25 09.7	28 57.7	25 11.4	3 22.9
9 W	7 08 08	16 51 52	18 27 07	25 33 04	25 07.1	7 08.1	8 30.5	4 07.4	28 09.5	9 55.1	25 15.5	29 00.3	25 12.5	3 24.5
10 Th	7 12 05	17 49 03	2♒33 49	9♒28 52	24 58.7	6 48.8	9 43.6	4 40.4	27 58.3	10 07.6	25 21.2	29 02.9	25 13.5	3 26.2
11 F	7 16 01	18 46 15	16 17 52	23 00 38	24 52.5	6 33.7	10 56.7	5 13.1	27 47.3	10 20.1	25 26.8	29 05.5	25 14.6	3 27.8
12 Sa	7 19 58	19 43 26	29 37 10	6♓07 33	24 48.7	6 23.3	12 09.7	5 45.6	27 36.5	10 32.5	25 32.4	29 08.0	25 15.7	3 29.5
13 Su	7 23 54	20 40 39	12♓32 03	18 51 02	24D47.2	6D17.9	13 22.8	6 17.8	27 26.0	10 44.9	25 37.9	29 10.5	25 16.9	3 31.1
14 M	7 27 51	21 37 52	25 04 57	1♈14 18	24 47.2	6 17.7	14 35.8	6 49.7	27 15.7	10 57.1	25 43.4	29 12.9	25 18.1	3 32.8
15 Tu	7 31 47	22 35 05	7♈19 41	13 21 43	24R47.8	6 22.7	15 48.8	7 21.2	27 05.7	11 09.4	25 48.8	29 15.3	25 19.3	3 34.5
16 W	7 35 44	23 32 19	19 21 03	25 18 20	24 48.1	6 33.2	17 01.8	7 52.5	26 56.0	11 21.5	25 54.1	29 17.7	25 20.5	3 36.2
17 Th	7 39 40	24 29 34	1♉14 14	7♉09 25	24 47.2	6 49.2	18 14.8	8 23.5	26 46.5	11 33.6	25 59.4	29 20.0	25 21.8	3 37.9
18 F	7 43 37	25 26 49	13 04 30	19 00 06	24 44.3	7 10.8	19 27.7	8 54.1	26 37.4	11 45.6	26 04.5	29 22.3	25 23.1	3 39.5
19 Sa	7 47 33	26 24 05	24 56 47	0♊55 06	24 39.3	7 38.1	20 40.7	9 24.5	26 28.5	11 57.5	26 09.6	29 24.6	25 24.4	3 41.2
20 Su	7 51 30	27 21 22	6♊55 29	12 58 25	24 32.2	8 10.9	21 53.6	9 54.4	26 20.0	12 09.3	26 14.7	29 26.8	25 25.7	3 42.9
21 M	7 55 27	28 18 40	19 04 13	25 13 13	24 23.3	8 49.3	23 06.5	10 24.0	26 11.7	12 21.1	26 19.6	29 29.0	25 27.1	3 44.6
22 Tu	7 59 23	29 15 58	1♋25 37	7♋41 37	24 13.6	9 33.2	24 19.4	10 53.3	26 03.8	12 32.8	26 24.5	29 31.1	25 28.5	3 46.3
23 W	8 03 20	0♌13 17	14 01 18	20 24 40	24 04.0	10 22.7	25 32.3	11 22.2	25 56.2	12 44.4	26 29.3	29 33.2	25 29.9	3 48.0
24 Th	8 07 16	1 10 37	26 51 44	3♌22 24	23 55.3	11 17.6	26 45.2	11 50.7	25 48.9	12 55.9	26 34.0	29 35.3	25 31.3	3 49.8
25 F	8 11 13	2 07 57	9♌56 32	16 34 00	23 48.5	12 17.8	27 58.0	12 18.8	25 42.0	13 07.4	26 38.7	29 37.3	25 32.8	3 51.5
26 Sa	8 15 09	3 05 18	23 14 35	29 58 08	23 43.9	13 23.3	29 10.8	12 46.5	25 35.4	13 18.7	26 43.3	29 39.3	25 34.3	3 53.2
27 Su	8 19 06	4 02 39	6♍44 27	13♍33 21	23D41.5	14 34.0	0♍23.6	13 13.8	25 29.2	13 30.0	26 47.7	29 41.3	25 35.8	3 54.9
28 M	8 23 02	5 00 01	20 24 40	27 18 15	23 41.1	15 49.8	1 36.4	13 40.7	25 23.3	13 41.2	26 52.1	29 43.2	25 37.4	3 56.6
29 Tu	8 26 59	5 57 23	4♎13 59	11♎11 44	23 41.9	17 10.4	2 49.2	14 07.1	25 17.7	13 52.2	26 56.5	29 45.0	25 38.9	3 58.3
30 W	8 30 56	6 54 46	18 11 25	25 12 53	23R43.0	18 35.8	4 01.9	14 33.2	25 12.5	14 03.2	27 00.7	29 46.8	25 40.5	4 00.0
31 Th	8 34 52	7 52 10	2♏16 03	9♏20 45	23 43.5	20 05.8	5 14.6	14 58.7	25 07.7	14 14.1	27 04.9	29 48.6	25 42.1	4 01.7

August 1941 LONGITUDE

Day	Sid.Time	☉	0 hr ☽	Noon ☽	True ☊	☿	♀	♂	⚳	♃	♄	♅	♆	♇
1 F	8 38 49	8♌49 34	16♏26 48	23♏33 58	23♍42.5	21♋40.2	6♍27.3	15♈23.9	25♐03.2	14♊24.9	27♉08.9	29♉50.3	25♍43.7	4♌03.4
2 Sa	8 42 45	9 46 58	0♐41 58	7♐50 27	23R39.8	23 18.7	7 39.9	15 48.5	24R59.1	14 35.7	27 12.9	29 52.0	25 45.4	4 05.1
3 Su	8 46 42	10 44 24	14 59 01	22 07 10	23 35.3	25 01.1	8 52.5	16 12.7	24 55.3	14 46.3	27 16.8	29 53.7	25 47.1	4 06.8
4 M	8 50 38	11 41 50	29 14 26	6♑20 13	23 29.5	26 47.1	10 05.1	16 36.5	24 51.9	14 56.8	27 20.6	29 55.3	25 48.8	4 08.5
5 Tu	8 54 35	12 39 17	13♑23 58	20 25 07	23 23.1	28 36.3	11 17.6	16 59.7	24 48.9	15 07.2	27 24.3	29 56.8	25 50.5	4 10.2
6 W	8 58 32	13 36 44	27 23 07	4♒17 28	23 16.9	0♌28.5	12 30.2	17 22.4	24 46.2	15 17.5	27 28.0	29 58.3	25 52.2	4 11.9
7 Th	9 02 28	14 34 13	11♒07 43	17 53 31	23 11.8	2 23.3	13 42.7	17 44.6	24 43.9	15 27.7	27 31.5	29 59.8	25 54.0	4 13.6
8 F	9 06 25	15 31 42	24 34 36	1♓10 47	23 08.1	4 20.3	14 55.1	18 06.3	24 42.0	15 37.8	27 34.9	0♊01.2	25 55.8	4 15.3
9 Sa	9 10 21	16 29 13	7♓42 00	14 08 17	23D06.2	6 19.1	16 07.6	18 27.4	24 40.4	15 47.8	27 38.3	0 02.6	25 57.6	4 16.9
10 Su	9 14 18	17 26 45	20 29 45	26 46 37	23 05.9	8 19.3	17 20.0	18 48.0	24 39.1	15 57.7	27 41.6	0 03.9	25 59.4	4 18.6
11 M	9 18 14	18 24 18	2♈59 11	9♈07 49	23 06.8	10 20.7	18 32.4	19 08.0	24 38.2	16 07.5	27 44.7	0 05.2	26 01.2	4 20.3
12 Tu	9 22 11	19 21 53	15 12 59	21 15 08	23 08.4	12 22.8	19 44.7	19 27.4	24D37.7	16 17.2	27 47.8	0 06.4	26 03.1	4 21.9
13 W	9 26 07	20 19 29	27 14 49	3♉12 37	23 10.0	14 25.4	20 57.0	19 46.3	24 37.5	16 26.7	27 50.8	0 07.6	26 04.9	4 23.6
14 Th	9 30 04	21 17 07	9♉09 06	15 04 53	23R11.1	16 28.1	22 09.3	20 04.5	24 37.7	16 36.2	27 53.7	0 08.7	26 06.8	4 25.3
15 F	9 34 00	22 14 46	21 00 36	26 56 50	23 11.2	18 30.7	23 21.6	20 22.0	24 38.3	16 45.5	27 56.5	0 09.8	26 08.7	4 26.9
16 Sa	9 37 57	23 12 26	2♊54 13	8♊53 20	23 10.0	20 32.9	24 33.8	20 39.0	24 39.2	16 54.7	27 59.2	0 10.9	26 10.7	4 28.5
17 Su	9 41 54	24 10 09	14 54 44	20 58 58	23 07.6	22 34.6	25 46.0	20 55.2	24 40.4	17 03.8	28 01.7	0 11.8	26 12.6	4 30.2
18 M	9 45 50	25 07 53	27 06 29	3♋17 45	23 04.1	24 35.6	26 58.2	21 10.8	24 42.0	17 12.8	28 04.2	0 12.8	26 14.5	4 31.8
19 Tu	9 49 47	26 05 38	9♋33 07	15 52 52	23 00.0	26 35.7	28 10.4	21 25.8	24 43.9	17 21.6	28 06.6	0 13.7	26 16.5	4 33.4
20 W	9 53 43	27 03 25	22 17 14	28 46 22	22 55.9	28 34.8	29 22.5	21 40.0	24 46.2	17 30.3	28 08.9	0 14.5	26 18.5	4 35.0
21 Th	9 57 40	28 01 13	5♌20 17	11♌58 58	22 52.1	0♍32.9	0♎34.6	21 53.4	24 48.9	17 38.9	28 11.1	0 15.3	26 20.5	4 36.6
22 F	10 01 36	28 59 03	18 42 17	25 30 02	22 49.3	2 29.8	1 46.6	22 06.2	24 51.8	17 47.4	28 13.2	0 16.1	26 22.5	4 38.2
23 Sa	10 05 33	29 56 55	2♍21 54	9♍17 34	22D47.6	4 25.5	2 58.7	22 18.2	24 55.1	17 55.7	28 15.2	0 16.8	26 24.6	4 39.8
24 Su	10 09 29	0♍54 47	16 16 35	23 18 32	22 47.1	6 19.9	4 10.6	22 29.5	24 58.8	18 03.9	28 17.1	0 17.4	26 26.6	4 41.3
25 M	10 13 26	1 52 41	0♎22 56	7♎29 17	22 47.5	8 13.1	5 22.6	22 40.0	25 02.8	18 12.0	28 18.9	0 18.0	26 28.7	4 42.9
26 Tu	10 17 23	2 50 37	14 37 06	21 45 55	22 48.7	10 05.0	6 34.5	22 49.7	25 07.1	18 19.9	28 20.5	0 18.5	26 30.7	4 44.4
27 W	10 21 19	3 48 34	28 55 16	6♏04 45	22 50.0	11 55.6	7 46.4	22 58.6	25 11.7	18 27.6	28 22.1	0 19.0	26 32.8	4 46.0
28 Th	10 25 16	4 46 32	13♏13 58	20 22 32	22 51.0	13 44.9	8 58.2	23 06.8	25 16.7	18 35.3	28 23.6	0 19.5	26 34.9	4 47.5
29 F	10 29 12	5 44 31	27 30 08	4♐36 29	22R51.4	15 32.9	10 10.0	23 14.1	25 21.9	18 42.8	28 24.9	0 19.9	26 37.0	4 49.0
30 Sa	10 33 09	6 42 32	11♐41 17	18 44 18	22 51.1	17 19.6	11 21.8	23 20.7	25 27.5	18 50.1	28 26.2	0 20.2	26 39.1	4 50.5
31 Su	10 37 05	7 40 34	25 45 16	2♑43 59	22 50.1	19 05.0	12 33.5	23 26.4	25 33.4	18 57.3	28 27.3	0 20.5	26 41.2	4 52.0

Astro Data Dy Hr Mn	Planet Ingress Dy Hr Mn	Last Aspect Dy Hr Mn	☽ Ingress Dy Hr Mn	Last Aspect Dy Hr Mn	☽ Ingress Dy Hr Mn	☽ Phases & Eclipses Dy Hr Mn
☽0S 1 13:06	♂ ♈ 2 5:17	1 10:29 ♂ ☍	♎ 1 11:17	1 22:34 ♅ ☍	♐ 1 22:49	2 4:24 ☽ 9♎53
♄△♆ 8 20:51	♀ ♌ 2 12:33	2 6:12 ☿ □	♏ 3 14:34	3 18:11 ♆ □	♑ 4 1:17	8 20:17 ○ 16♑14
☿ D 14 1:14	☉ ♌ 23 6:26	5 14:18 ♅ ☍	♐ 5 16:13	6 4:28 ♅ △	♒ 6 4:32	16 8:07 ☾ 23♈23
☽0N 14 12:13	♀ ♍ 27 4:12	7 9:25 ♆ □	♑ 7 17:21	8 5:25 ♄ □	♓ 8 9:51	24 7:39 ● 1♌00
♂0N 17 15:57		9 17:55 ♅ △	♒ 9 19:36	10 13:46 ♄ ⚹	♈ 10 18:13	31 9:19 ☽ 7♏46
☽0S 28 19:32	☿ ♌ 6 5:57	11 23:04 ♅ □	♓ 12 0:42	12 8:19 ♂ ☌	♉ 13 5:32	
	♅ ♊ 7 15:32	14 8:02 ♅ ⚹	♈ 14 9:35	15 14:01 ♄ ☌	♊ 15 18:09	7 5:38 ○ 14♒19
☽0N 10 21:45	♀ ♎ 21 0:29	16 8:07 ☉ □	♉ 16 21:30	17 22:24 ♀ □	♋ 18 5:37	15 1:40 ☾ 21♉50
⚳ D 13 11:21	☿ ♍ 21 5:18	19 8:58 ♅ ☌	♊ 19 10:10	20 13:13 ♀ ⚹	♌ 20 14:15	22 18:34 ● 29♌15
♀0S 22 12:54	☉ ♍ 23 13:17	21 12:27 ♆ □	♋ 21 21:15	22 18:34 ☉ ☌	♍ 22 19:53	29 14:04 ☽ 5♐49
☽0S 25 2:37		24 5:01 ♅ ⚹	♌ 24 5:48	24 20:28 ♄ △	♎ 24 23:21	
		26 11:26 ♅ □	♍ 26 12:03	26 13:48 ♂ ☍	♏ 27 1:49	
		28 16:12 ♅ △	♎ 28 16:41	29 1:31 ♄ ☍	♐ 29 4:13	
		29 23:24 ☿ □	♏ 30 20:09	31 1:34 ♆ □	♑ 31 7:18	

Astro Data

1 July 1941
Julian Day # 15157
SVP 6♓04'37"
GC 26♐01.3 ⚵ 23♏48.0R
Eris 5♈23.6R ⚴ 9♍18.3
⚷ 1♌36.7 ⚶ 8♍17.1
☽ Mean ☊ 26♍33.6

1 August 1941
Julian Day # 15188
SVP 6♓04'32"
GC 26♐01.4 ⚵ 24♏12.9
Eris 5♈18.5R ⚴ 19♍40.1
⚷ 5♌16.7 ⚶ 22♍01.1
☽ Mean ☊ 24♍55.2

LONGITUDE — September 1941

Day	Sid.Time	☉	0 hr ☽	Noon ☽	True ☊	☿	♀	♂	⚳	♃	♄	♅	♆	♇
1 M	10 41 02	8♍38 37	9♑40 13	16♑33 46	22♍48.5	20♍49.2	13♎45.2	23♈31.3	25♐39.6	19♊04.4	28♉28.4	0♊20.7	26♍43.4	4♌53.5
2 Tu	10 44 58	9 36 42	23 24 28	0♒12 05	22R46.8	22 32.1	14 56.8	23 35.4	25 46.2	19 11.3	28 29.3	0 20.9	26 45.5	4 54.9
3 W	10 48 55	10 34 48	6♒56 29	13 37 30	22 45.1	24 13.8	16 08.4	23 38.6	25 53.0	19 18.0	28 30.2	0 21.1	26 47.7	4 56.4
4 Th	10 52 52	11 32 56	20 15 01	26 48 55	22 43.8	25 54.2	17 19.9	23 41.0	26 00.1	19 24.7	28 30.9	0 21.2	26 49.8	4 57.8
5 F	10 56 48	12 31 05	3♓19 08	9♓45 37	22 43.0	27 33.5	18 31.4	23 42.5	26 07.5	19 31.1	28 31.5	0R21.2	26 52.0	4 59.2
6 Sa	11 00 45	13 29 16	16 08 24	22 27 31	22D42.8	29 11.6	19 42.8	23R43.2	26 15.2	19 37.4	28 32.0	0 21.2	26 54.2	5 00.6
7 Su	11 04 41	14 27 29	28 43 04	4♈55 11	22 43.0	0♎48.4	20 54.2	23 43.0	26 23.1	19 43.5	28 32.4	0 21.1	26 56.3	5 02.0
8 M	11 08 38	15 25 44	11♈04 06	17 10 01	22 43.5	2 24.2	22 05.5	23 41.9	26 31.4	19 49.5	28 32.7	0 21.0	26 58.5	5 03.4
9 Tu	11 12 34	16 24 01	23 13 14	29 14 07	22 44.2	3 58.8	23 16.8	23 40.0	26 39.9	19 55.3	28 32.9	0 20.8	27 00.7	5 04.7
10 W	11 16 31	17 22 19	5♉13 01	11♉10 23	22 44.8	5 32.2	24 28.1	23 37.2	26 48.7	20 01.0	28R33.0	0 20.6	27 02.9	5 06.1
11 Th	11 20 27	18 20 40	17 06 39	23 02 20	22 45.3	7 04.5	25 39.3	23 33.5	26 57.8	20 06.5	28 32.9	0 20.4	27 05.1	5 07.4
12 F	11 24 24	19 19 03	28 57 56	4♊54 01	22 45.6	8 35.7	26 50.4	23 28.9	27 07.1	20 11.8	28 32.8	0 20.1	27 07.3	5 08.7
13 Sa	11 28 20	20 17 28	10♊51 08	16 49 52	22R45.8	10 05.7	28 01.5	23 23.5	27 16.8	20 17.0	28 32.6	0 19.7	27 09.5	5 10.0
14 Su	11 32 17	21 15 55	22 50 47	28 54 29	22 45.8	11 34.6	29 12.6	23 17.2	27 26.6	20 21.9	28 32.2	0 19.3	27 11.8	5 11.3
15 M	11 36 14	22 14 24	5♋01 30	11♋12 23	22D45.7	13 02.4	0♏23.6	23 10.1	27 36.8	20 26.8	28 31.8	0 18.8	27 14.0	5 12.5
16 Tu	11 40 10	23 12 56	17 27 38	23 47 42	22 45.7	14 29.0	1 34.6	23 02.1	27 47.1	20 31.4	28 31.2	0 18.3	27 16.2	5 13.8
17 W	11 44 07	24 11 29	0♌13 00	6♌43 51	22 45.8	15 54.4	2 45.5	22 53.3	27 57.8	20 35.9	28 30.5	0 17.7	27 18.4	5 15.0
18 Th	11 48 03	25 10 05	13 20 29	20 03 02	22 46.0	17 18.7	3 56.3	22 43.6	28 08.7	20 40.1	28 29.7	0 17.1	27 20.7	5 16.2
19 F	11 52 00	26 08 43	26 51 30	3♍45 48	22 46.3	18 41.8	5 07.1	22 33.2	28 19.8	20 44.2	28 28.8	0 16.5	27 22.9	5 17.4
20 Sa	11 55 56	27 07 23	10♍45 42	17 50 49	22R46.4	20 03.6	6 17.9	22 22.0	28 31.2	20 48.2	28 27.8	0 15.7	27 25.1	5 18.5
21 Su	11 59 53	28 06 04	25 00 41	2♎14 39	22 46.4	21 24.1	7 28.6	22 10.0	28 42.8	20 51.9	28 26.7	0 15.0	27 27.3	5 19.7
22 M	12 03 49	29 04 48	9♎32 01	16 51 58	22 46.0	22 43.4	8 39.2	21 57.4	28 54.6	20 55.5	28 25.5	0 14.2	27 29.6	5 20.8
23 Tu	12 07 46	0♎03 34	24 13 40	1♏36 13	22 45.4	24 01.2	9 49.8	21 44.0	29 06.7	20 58.8	28 24.2	0 13.3	27 31.8	5 21.9
24 W	12 11 43	1 02 21	8♏58 44	16 20 23	22 44.5	25 17.7	11 00.3	21 30.0	29 19.0	21 02.0	28 22.8	0 12.4	27 34.0	5 23.0
25 Th	12 15 39	2 01 10	23 40 21	0♐57 58	22 43.5	26 32.6	12 10.8	21 15.3	29 31.5	21 05.0	28 21.2	0 11.5	27 36.3	5 24.1
26 F	12 19 36	3 00 01	8♐12 35	15 23 44	22 42.7	27 46.0	13 21.2	21 00.1	29 44.3	21 07.8	28 19.6	0 10.5	27 38.5	5 25.1
27 Sa	12 23 32	3 58 54	22 31 00	29 34 08	22D42.3	28 57.7	14 31.5	20 44.3	29 57.3	21 10.4	28 17.9	0 09.4	27 40.7	5 26.1
28 Su	12 27 29	4 57 48	6♑32 56	13♑27 20	22 42.4	0♏07.6	15 41.8	20 28.1	0♑10.5	21 12.9	28 16.0	0 08.3	27 42.9	5 27.1
29 M	12 31 25	5 56 45	20 17 19	27 02 57	22 43.0	1 15.7	16 52.0	20 11.4	0 23.9	21 15.1	28 14.1	0 07.2	27 45.1	5 28.1
30 Tu	12 35 22	6 55 42	3♒44 19	10♒21 35	22 44.1	2 21.7	18 02.1	19 54.2	0 37.5	21 17.1	28 12.0	0 06.0	27 47.4	5 29.1

LONGITUDE — October 1941

Day	Sid.Time	☉	0 hr ☽	Noon ☽	True ☊	☿	♀	♂	⚳	♃	♄	♅	♆	♇
1 W	12 39 18	7♎54 42	16♒54 54	23♒24 28	22♍45.3	3♏25.5	19♏12.1	19♈36.7	0♑51.3	21♊19.0	28♉09.9	0♊04.8	27♍49.6	5♌30.0
2 Th	12 43 15	8 53 43	29 50 28	6♓13 05	22 46.4	4 27.0	20 22.1	19R18.9	1 05.3	21 20.6	28R07.7	0R03.5	27 51.8	5 30.9
3 F	12 47 12	9 52 47	12♓32 31	18 48 55	22R47.1	5 26.0	21 32.0	19 00.7	1 19.5	21 22.1	28 05.3	0 02.2	27 53.9	5 31.8
4 Sa	12 51 08	10 51 52	25 02 30	1♈13 24	22 46.9	6 22.3	22 41.8	18 42.3	1 33.9	21 23.4	28 02.9	0 00.8	27 56.1	5 32.7
5 Su	12 55 05	11 50 59	7♈21 49	13 27 54	22 45.7	7 15.5	23 51.5	18 23.8	1 48.4	21 24.4	28 00.4	29♉59.4	27 58.3	5 33.5
6 M	12 59 01	12 50 08	19 31 50	25 33 49	22 43.6	8 05.6	25 01.1	18 05.0	2 03.2	21 25.3	27 57.8	29 58.0	28 00.5	5 34.3
7 Tu	13 02 58	13 49 19	1♉34 03	7♉32 45	22 40.5	8 52.0	26 10.7	17 46.2	2 18.2	21 26.0	27 55.0	29 56.5	28 02.7	5 35.1
8 W	13 06 54	14 48 33	13 30 10	19 26 36	22 36.9	9 34.6	27 20.1	17 27.4	2 33.3	21 26.4	27 52.2	29 55.0	28 04.8	5 35.9
9 Th	13 10 51	15 47 49	25 22 20	1♊17 43	22 33.0	10 13.0	28 29.5	17 08.5	2 48.6	21R26.7	27 49.3	29 53.4	28 07.0	5 36.6
10 F	13 14 47	16 47 07	7♊13 08	13 09 00	22 29.4	10 46.7	29 38.8	16 49.7	3 04.1	21 26.8	27 46.4	29 51.8	28 09.1	5 37.4
11 Sa	13 18 44	17 46 27	19 05 44	25 03 51	22 26.5	11 15.4	0♐48.0	16 30.9	3 19.8	21 26.6	27 43.3	29 50.2	28 11.2	5 38.1
12 Su	13 22 40	18 45 50	1♋03 51	7♋06 15	22 24.7	11 38.5	1 57.1	16 12.3	3 35.6	21 26.3	27 40.1	29 48.5	28 13.4	5 38.7
13 M	13 26 37	19 45 15	13 11 38	19 20 32	22D24.0	11 55.6	3 06.1	15 53.9	3 51.6	21 25.7	27 36.9	29 46.7	28 15.5	5 39.4
14 Tu	13 30 34	20 44 42	25 33 32	1♌51 11	22 24.5	12R06.2	4 15.0	15 35.8	4 07.8	21 25.0	27 33.6	29 45.0	28 17.6	5 40.0
15 W	13 34 30	21 44 11	8♌14 01	14 42 33	22 25.8	12 09.8	5 23.8	15 17.9	4 24.1	21 24.1	27 30.2	29 43.2	28 19.7	5 40.6
16 Th	13 38 27	22 43 43	21 17 12	27 58 20	22 27.5	12 05.7	6 32.5	15 00.3	4 40.6	21 22.9	27 26.7	29 41.4	28 21.7	5 41.2
17 F	13 42 23	23 43 17	4♍46 12	11♍40 56	22R28.8	11 53.7	7 41.1	14 43.2	4 57.3	21 21.6	27 23.1	29 39.5	28 23.8	5 41.7
18 Sa	13 46 20	24 42 53	18 42 32	25 50 48	22 29.1	11 33.3	8 49.6	14 26.4	5 14.1	21 20.0	27 19.4	29 37.6	28 25.9	5 42.3
19 Su	13 50 16	25 42 32	3♎05 22	10♎25 41	22 28.0	11 04.2	9 58.0	14 10.1	5 31.1	21 18.3	27 15.7	29 35.7	28 27.9	5 42.8
20 M	13 54 13	26 42 12	17 51 00	25 20 24	22 25.2	10 26.3	11 06.3	13 54.3	5 48.2	21 16.3	27 11.9	29 33.7	28 29.9	5 43.2
21 Tu	13 58 09	27 41 55	2♏52 48	10♏27 00	22 20.8	9 39.8	12 14.4	13 39.1	6 05.5	21 14.1	27 08.1	29 31.7	28 31.9	5 43.7
22 W	14 02 06	28 41 39	18 01 46	25 35 48	22 15.5	8 45.2	13 22.5	13 24.4	6 22.9	21 11.8	27 04.1	29 29.7	28 33.9	5 44.1
23 Th	14 06 03	29 41 26	3♐07 54	10♐36 55	22 09.9	7 43.1	14 30.4	13 10.4	6 40.5	21 09.2	27 00.1	29 27.6	28 35.9	5 44.5
24 F	14 09 59	0♏41 14	18 01 51	25 21 52	22 05.0	6 34.7	15 38.2	12 57.0	6 58.2	21 06.5	26 56.0	29 25.5	28 37.9	5 44.9
25 Sa	14 13 56	1 41 04	2♑36 21	9♑44 50	22 01.4	5 21.7	16 45.8	12 44.3	7 16.1	21 03.5	26 51.9	29 23.4	28 39.8	5 45.2
26 Su	14 17 52	2 40 56	16 47 03	23 42 56	21D59.4	4 05.8	17 53.3	12 32.2	7 34.1	21 00.4	26 47.7	29 21.2	28 41.7	5 45.5
27 M	14 21 49	3 40 49	0♒32 31	7♒16 01	21 59.1	2 49.3	19 00.7	12 20.9	7 52.2	20 57.1	26 43.5	29 19.1	28 43.7	5 45.8
28 Tu	14 25 45	4 40 44	13 53 42	20 25 55	22 00.0	1 34.6	20 07.8	12 10.4	8 10.4	20 53.5	26 39.2	29 16.9	28 45.6	5 46.1
29 W	14 29 42	5 40 40	26 53 07	3♓15 41	22 01.4	0 23.8	21 14.9	12 00.6	8 28.8	20 49.8	26 34.8	29 14.6	28 47.4	5 46.3
30 Th	14 33 38	6 40 38	9♓34 07	15 48 50	22R02.6	29♎19.4	22 21.7	11 51.5	8 47.3	20 45.9	26 30.4	29 12.4	28 49.3	5 46.5
31 F	14 37 35	7 40 38	22 00 17	28 08 52	22 02.6	28 23.1	23 28.4	11 43.3	9 06.0	20 41.8	26 26.0	29 10.1	28 51.1	5 46.7

Astro Data

	Dy Hr Mn
♅ R	5 17:36
♂ R	6 18:34
☽ 0N	7 6:16
☿ 0S	7 10:29
♄ R	10 17:39
♃∠♇	11 17:32
☽ 0S	21 11:31
☉ 0S	23 10:33
☽ 0N	4 13:23
♄△♆	5 22:24
♃ R	10 8:00
☿ R	15 11:30
☽ 0S	18 22:11
♃∠♇	30 8:31
☽ 0N	31 19:43

Planet Ingress

		Dy Hr Mn
☿	♎	6 23:58
♀	♏	15 4:01
☉	♎	23 10:33
⚳	♑	27 17:00
☿	♏	28 9:21
♅	♉R	5 2:08
♀	♐	10 19:21
☉	♏	23 19:27
☿	♎R	29 20:34

Last Aspect / ☽ Ingress (September)

Last Aspect Dy Hr Mn			☽ Ingress	Dy Hr Mn
2 8:58	♄	△	♒	2 11:39
4 15:08	♄	□	♓	4 17:52
6 23:39	♄	⚹	♈	7 2:28
9 0:55	♂	☌	♉	9 13:32
11 23:09	♄	☌	♊	12 2:06
14 12:40	♀	△	♋	14 14:09
16 20:50	♄	⚹	♌	16 23:36
19 2:51	♄	□	♍	19 5:29
21 5:43	♄	△	♎	21 8:17
22 22:29	☿	☌	♏	23 9:24
25 7:42	♄	☍	♐	25 10:24
27 10:52	☿	⚹	♑	27 12:44
29 14:07	♄	△	♒	29 17:17

Last Aspect / ☽ Ingress (October)

Last Aspect Dy Hr Mn			☽ Ingress	Dy Hr Mn
1 20:50	♄	□	♓	2 0:18
4 5:51	♄	⚹	♈	4 9:37
6 3:45	♃	⚹	♉	6 20:52
9 9:10	♅	☌	♊	9 9:23
11 18:16	♆	□	♋	11 21:53
14 8:01	♅	⚹	♌	14 8:29
16 15:03	♅	□	♍	16 15:36
18 18:16	♅	△	♎	18 18:54
20 14:20	☉	☌	♏	20 19:25
22 18:11	♅	☍	♐	22 19:00
24 17:24	♆	□	♑	24 19:40
26 21:52	♅	△	♒	26 23:02
29 4:27	♅	□	♓	29 5:51
31 14:00	♅	⚹	♈	31 15:38

☽ Phases & Eclipses

Dy Hr Mn		
5 17:36	○	12♓45
5 17:47	☍	P 0.051
13 19:31	☾	20♊36
21 4:38	●	27♍48
21 4:33:38	☌	T 03'22"
27 20:09	☽	4♑19
5 8:32	○	11♈42
13 12:52	☾	19♋47
20 14:20	●	26♎48
27 5:04	☽	3♒24

Astro Data

1 September 1941
Julian Day # 15219
SVP 6♓04'29"
GC 26♐01.5 ⚴ 0♐07.0
Eris 5♈04.2R ✱ 0♎44.7
⚷ 8♌54.8 ⚵ 7♎01.0
☽ Mean ☊ 23♍16.7

1 October 1941
Julian Day # 15249
SVP 6♓04'26"
GC 26♐01.5 ⚴ 8♐56.9
Eris 4♈45.6R ✱ 11♎41.7
⚷ 11♌55.2 ⚵ 22♎20.2
☽ Mean ☊ 21♍41.3

November 1941 LONGITUDE

Day	Sid.Time	☉	0 hr ☽	Noon ☽	True ☊	☿	♀	♂	⚳	♃	♄	♅	♆	♇
1 Sa	14 41 32	8♏40 39	4♈14 58	10♈18 55	22♍00.7	27♎36.5	24♐35.0	11♈35.8	9♑24.7	20♊37.6	26♉21.5	29♉07.8	28♍52.9	5♌46.9
2 Su	14 45 28	9 40 42	16 21 03	22 21 37	21R 56.6	27R 00.6	25 41.3	11R 29.1	9 43.6	20R 33.1	26R 16.9	29R 05.5	28 54.7	5 47.0
3 M	14 49 25	10 40 47	28 20 55	4♉19 08	21 50.1	26 36.2	26 47.4	11 23.2	10 02.6	20 28.5	26 12.3	29 03.2	28 56.5	5 47.1
4 Tu	14 53 21	11 40 54	10♉16 30	16 13 11	21 41.6	26D 23.5	27 53.4	11 18.1	10 21.7	20 23.7	26 07.7	29 00.8	28 58.3	5 47.2
5 W	14 57 18	12 41 02	22 09 23	28 05 17	21 31.7	26 22.2	28 59.1	11 13.9	10 40.9	20 18.8	26 03.0	28 58.5	29 00.0	5 47.2
6 Th	15 01 14	13 41 13	4♊01 05	9♊56 59	21 21.2	26 31.9	0♑04.7	11 10.4	11 00.2	20 13.6	25 58.3	28 56.1	29 01.7	5R 47.2
7 F	15 05 11	14 41 25	15 53 13	21 50 03	21 11.0	26 52.1	1 10.0	11 07.7	11 19.7	20 08.3	25 53.6	28 53.7	29 03.4	5 47.2
8 Sa	15 09 07	15 41 40	27 47 45	3♋46 41	21 02.2	27 21.9	2 15.1	11 05.8	11 39.2	20 02.9	25 48.9	28 51.3	29 05.1	5 47.2
9 Su	15 13 04	16 41 56	9♋47 11	15 49 41	20 55.3	28 00.5	3 20.0	11D 04.8	11 58.9	19 57.2	25 44.1	28 48.8	29 06.7	5 47.2
10 M	15 17 01	17 42 15	21 54 37	28 02 28	20 50.8	28 46.9	4 24.7	11 04.5	12 18.7	19 51.5	25 39.3	28 46.4	29 08.4	5 47.1
11 Tu	15 20 57	18 42 35	4♌13 46	10♌29 02	20D 48.6	29 40.4	5 29.1	11 05.0	12 38.6	19 45.5	25 34.5	28 43.9	29 10.0	5 47.0
12 W	15 24 54	19 42 57	16 48 49	23 13 42	20 48.3	0♏39.9	6 33.3	11 06.3	12 58.5	19 39.4	25 29.6	28 41.5	29 11.6	5 46.8
13 Th	15 28 50	20 43 21	29 44 12	6♍20 49	20 49.0	1 44.8	7 37.2	11 08.3	13 18.6	19 33.2	25 24.8	28 39.0	29 13.1	5 46.7
14 F	15 32 47	21 43 47	13♍03 59	19 54 04	20R 49.5	2 54.4	8 40.9	11 11.2	13 38.8	19 26.8	25 19.9	28 36.5	29 14.6	5 46.5
15 Sa	15 36 43	22 44 15	26 51 18	3♎55 46	20 48.8	4 07.9	9 44.3	11 14.8	13 59.1	19 20.3	25 15.0	28 34.0	29 16.1	5 46.2
16 Su	15 40 40	23 44 45	11♎07 22	18 25 47	20 45.9	5 24.9	10 47.4	11 19.2	14 19.4	19 13.7	25 10.1	28 31.5	29 17.6	5 46.0
17 M	15 44 36	24 45 16	25 50 31	3♏20 48	20 40.4	6 44.7	11 50.2	11 24.3	14 39.9	19 06.9	25 05.2	28 29.0	29 19.1	5 45.7
18 Tu	15 48 33	25 45 50	10♏55 37	18 33 48	20 32.4	8 07.0	12 52.7	11 30.2	15 00.5	19 00.0	25 00.3	28 26.5	29 20.5	5 45.4
19 W	15 52 30	26 46 24	26 13 59	3♐54 42	20 22.6	9 31.3	13 54.9	11 36.8	15 21.1	18 53.0	24 55.4	28 24.0	29 21.9	5 45.1
20 Th	15 56 26	27 47 01	11♐34 28	19 11 48	20 12.1	10 57.4	14 56.8	11 44.2	15 41.9	18 45.8	24 50.6	28 21.5	29 23.3	5 44.8
21 F	16 00 23	28 47 39	26 45 23	4♑13 59	20 02.4	12 24.9	15 58.3	11 52.2	16 02.7	18 38.6	24 45.7	28 19.0	29 24.6	5 44.4
22 Sa	16 04 19	29 48 18	11♑36 39	18 52 38	19 54.4	13 53.5	16 59.5	12 01.0	16 23.6	18 31.3	24 40.8	28 16.5	29 25.9	5 44.0
23 Su	16 08 16	0♐48 58	26 01 26	3♒02 47	19 48.9	15 23.2	18 00.3	12 10.5	16 44.6	18 23.8	24 36.0	28 14.0	29 27.2	5 43.6
24 M	16 12 12	1 49 39	9♒56 38	16 43 06	19 46.0	16 53.7	19 00.7	12 20.6	17 05.7	18 16.3	24 31.1	28 11.4	29 28.5	5 43.1
25 Tu	16 16 09	2 50 21	23 22 31	29 55 15	19D 45.0	18 24.8	20 00.7	12 31.4	17 26.8	18 08.7	24 26.3	28 08.9	29 29.7	5 42.6
26 W	16 20 05	3 51 05	6♓21 50	12♓42 49	19R 45.2	19 56.4	21 00.3	12 42.9	17 48.1	18 01.0	24 21.5	28 06.4	29 30.9	5 42.1
27 Th	16 24 02	4 51 49	18 58 48	25 10 24	19 45.1	21 28.5	21 59.5	12 55.0	18 09.4	17 53.3	24 16.7	28 03.9	29 32.1	5 41.6
28 F	16 27 59	5 52 34	1♈18 14	7♈22 51	19 43.8	23 00.9	22 58.2	13 07.7	18 30.7	17 45.4	24 12.0	28 01.5	29 33.2	5 41.0
29 Sa	16 31 55	6 53 21	13 24 51	19 24 45	19 40.2	24 33.6	23 56.4	13 21.0	18 52.2	17 37.5	24 07.3	27 59.0	29 34.3	5 40.5
30 Su	16 35 52	7 54 08	25 23 01	1♉20 06	19 33.8	26 06.4	24 54.2	13 34.9	19 13.7	17 29.6	24 02.6	27 56.5	29 35.4	5 39.9

December 1941 LONGITUDE

Day	Sid.Time	☉	0 hr ☽	Noon ☽	True ☊	☿	♀	♂	⚳	♃	♄	♅	♆	♇
1 M	16 39 48	8♐54 56	7♉16 22	13♉12 09	19♍24.3	27♏39.5	25♑51.4	13♈49.4	19♑35.3	17♊21.6	23♉57.9	27♉54.1	29♍36.4	5♌39.2
2 Tu	16 43 45	9 55 46	19 07 46	25 03 27	19R 12.1	29 12.7	26 48.1	14 04.5	19 57.0	17R 13.5	23R 53.3	27R 51.6	29 37.5	5R 38.6
3 W	16 47 41	10 56 37	0♊59 25	6♊55 51	18 57.9	0♐45.9	27 44.3	14 20.1	20 18.7	17 05.5	23 48.8	27 49.2	29 38.5	5 37.9
4 Th	16 51 38	11 57 28	12 52 55	18 50 45	18 43.0	2 19.3	28 39.9	14 36.3	20 40.5	16 57.3	23 44.3	27 46.8	29 39.4	5 37.2
5 F	16 55 34	12 58 21	24 49 29	0♋49 17	18 28.4	3 52.7	29 34.8	14 53.0	21 02.4	16 49.2	23 39.8	27 44.4	29 40.3	5 36.5
6 Sa	16 59 31	13 59 15	6♋50 16	12 52 39	18 15.3	5 26.2	0♒29.2	15 10.2	21 24.3	16 41.1	23 35.3	27 42.0	29 41.2	5 35.8
7 Su	17 03 28	15 00 10	18 56 38	25 02 26	18 04.7	6 59.7	1 23.0	15 27.9	21 46.3	16 32.9	23 31.0	27 39.6	29 42.1	5 35.0
8 M	17 07 24	16 01 06	1♌10 20	7♌20 39	17 57.2	8 33.3	2 16.0	15 46.1	22 08.3	16 24.7	23 26.6	27 37.3	29 42.9	5 34.2
9 Tu	17 11 21	17 02 04	13 33 45	19 50 03	17 52.7	10 06.9	3 08.4	16 04.7	22 30.5	16 16.5	23 22.4	27 34.9	29 43.7	5 33.4
10 W	17 15 17	18 03 02	26 09 57	2♍33 56	17 50.7	11 40.5	4 00.1	16 23.8	22 52.6	16 08.4	23 18.2	27 32.6	29 44.5	5 32.6
11 Th	17 19 14	19 04 01	9♍02 28	15 36 01	17 50.3	13 14.2	4 51.0	16 43.4	23 14.8	16 00.2	23 14.0	27 30.3	29 45.2	5 31.7
12 F	17 23 10	20 05 02	22 15 04	29 00 00	17 50.2	14 48.0	5 41.1	17 03.5	23 37.1	15 52.0	23 09.9	27 28.0	29 45.9	5 30.9
13 Sa	17 27 07	21 06 04	5♎51 10	12♎48 48	17 49.1	16 21.9	6 30.5	17 23.9	23 59.5	15 43.9	23 05.9	27 25.8	29 46.6	5 30.0
14 Su	17 31 03	22 07 07	19 53 03	27 03 49	17 45.8	17 55.8	7 19.0	17 44.8	24 21.9	15 35.8	23 01.9	27 23.6	29 47.2	5 29.1
15 M	17 35 00	23 08 10	4♏20 53	11♏43 48	17 39.8	19 29.9	8 06.6	18 06.1	24 44.3	15 27.8	22 58.0	27 21.4	29 47.8	5 28.1
16 Tu	17 38 57	24 09 15	19 11 52	26 44 11	17 30.9	21 04.0	8 53.4	18 27.9	25 06.8	15 19.7	22 54.2	27 19.2	29 48.4	5 27.2
17 W	17 42 53	25 10 21	4♐19 39	11♐56 59	17 20.0	22 38.3	9 39.2	18 50.0	25 29.4	15 11.8	22 50.4	27 17.0	29 48.9	5 26.2
18 Th	17 46 50	26 11 27	19 34 48	27 11 39	17 08.2	24 12.7	10 24.0	19 12.5	25 52.0	15 03.9	22 46.8	27 14.9	29 49.4	5 25.2
19 F	17 50 46	27 12 34	4♑46 07	12♑16 53	16 56.9	25 47.3	11 07.8	19 35.4	26 14.6	14 56.0	22 43.2	27 12.8	29 49.9	5 24.2
20 Sa	17 54 43	28 13 42	19 42 44	27 02 42	16 47.4	27 22.1	11 50.5	19 58.7	26 37.3	14 48.3	22 39.7	27 10.8	29 50.3	5 23.2
21 Su	17 58 39	29 14 49	4♒16 01	11♒22 08	16 40.5	28 57.0	12 32.1	20 22.4	27 00.0	14 40.6	22 36.2	27 08.8	29 50.7	5 22.2
22 M	18 02 36	0♑15 57	18 20 47	25 11 52	16 36.4	0♑32.1	13 12.6	20 46.4	27 22.8	14 32.9	22 32.9	27 06.8	29 51.1	5 21.1
23 Tu	18 06 32	1 17 05	1♓55 30	8♓31 57	16D 34.8	2 07.5	13 51.8	21 10.7	27 45.7	14 25.4	22 29.6	27 04.8	29 51.4	5 20.0
24 W	18 10 29	2 18 13	15 01 39	21 25 05	16R 34.6	3 43.1	14 29.7	21 35.4	28 08.5	14 18.0	22 26.5	27 02.9	29 51.7	5 18.9
25 Th	18 14 26	3 19 22	27 42 50	3♈55 33	16 34.8	5 18.9	15 06.4	22 00.4	28 31.4	14 10.6	22 23.4	27 01.0	29 51.9	5 17.8
26 F	18 18 22	4 20 30	10♈03 53	16 08 29	16 34.1	6 54.9	15 41.6	22 25.7	28 54.3	14 03.4	22 20.4	26 59.1	29 52.1	5 16.7
27 Sa	18 22 19	5 21 38	22 10 01	28 09 08	16 31.6	8 31.2	16 15.4	22 51.4	29 17.3	13 56.3	22 17.5	26 57.3	29 52.3	5 15.6
28 Su	18 26 15	6 22 46	4♉06 25	10♉02 28	16 26.5	10 07.8	16 47.7	23 17.3	29 40.3	13 49.2	22 14.7	26 55.5	29 52.5	5 14.4
29 M	18 30 12	7 23 55	15 57 47	21 52 51	16 18.6	11 44.7	17 18.5	23 43.5	0♒03.4	13 42.3	22 12.0	26 53.8	29 52.6	5 13.2
30 Tu	18 34 08	8 25 03	27 48 06	3♊43 54	16 08.2	13 21.8	17 47.7	24 10.0	0 26.4	13 35.6	22 09.3	26 52.0	29 52.7	5 12.0
31 W	18 38 05	9 26 11	9♊40 36	15 38 27	15 56.0	14 59.2	18 15.1	24 36.8	0 49.6	13 28.9	22 06.8	26 50.4	29R 52.7	5 10.9

Astro Data

	Dy Hr Mn
☿ D	5 2:39
♅△♆	5 2:58
♇ R	6 20:45
♂ D	10 8:33
☽ 0S	15 9:20
☽ 0N	28 2:33
☽ 0S	12 19:08
☽ 0N	25 10:57

Planet Ingress

	Dy Hr Mn
♀ ♑	6 10:17
☿ ♏	11 20:11
☉ ♐	22 16:38
☿ ♐	3 0:11
♀ ♒	5 23:04
☿ ♑	22 3:54
☉ ♑	22 5:44
⚳ ♒	29 8:29

Last Aspect / ☽ Ingress (November)

Last Aspect Dy Hr Mn		☽ Ingress Dy Hr Mn
2 20:58	☿ ☍	♉ 3 3:19
5 13:51	♆ △	♊ 5 15:52
8 2:34	♆ □	♋ 8 4:26
10 14:09	♆ ⚹	♌ 10 15:49
12 22:03	♅ □	♍ 13 0:29
15 4:06	♆ ☌	♎ 15 5:22
16 13:17	♃ △	♏ 17 6:40
19 4:53	♆ ⚹	♐ 19 5:53
21 4:14	♆ □	♑ 21 5:11
23 5:50	♆ △	♒ 23 6:46
25 8:45	♅ □	♓ 25 12:09
27 20:32	♆ ☍	♈ 27 21:26
29 21:54	♀ □	♉ 30 9:18

Last Aspect / ☽ Ingress (December)

Last Aspect Dy Hr Mn		☽ Ingress Dy Hr Mn
2 21:40	☿ ☍	♊ 2 22:00
5 9:42	♆ □	♋ 5 10:22
7 21:08	♆ ⚹	♌ 7 21:43
10 2:37	♅ □	♍ 10 7:12
12 13:21	♆ ☌	♎ 12 13:46
14 3:07	☉ ⚹	♏ 14 16:51
16 16:52	♆ ⚹	♐ 16 17:10
18 16:10	♆ □	♑ 18 16:26
20 16:37	♆ △	♒ 20 16:53
22 15:23	♅ □	♓ 22 20:33
25 4:08	♆ ☍	♈ 25 4:24
27 0:59	♂ ☌	♉ 27 15:43
30 4:12	♆ △	♊ 30 4:27

☽ Phases & Eclipses

Dy Hr Mn	
4 2:00	○ 11♉16
12 4:53	☾ 19♌25
19 0:04	● 26♏16
25 17:52	☽ 3♓05
3 20:51	○ 11♊19
11 18:48	☾ 19♍21
18 10:18	● 26♐07
25 10:43	☽ 3♈16

Astro Data

1 November 1941
Julian Day # 15280
SVP 6♓04'24"
GC 26♐01.6 ⚵ 19♐51.2
Eris 4♈26.9R ⚶ 22♎51.0
⚷ 13♌59.0 ⚴ 8♏41.8
☽ Mean ☊ 20♍02.8

1 December 1941
Julian Day # 15310
SVP 6♓04'20"
GC 26♐01.7 ⚵ 1♑16.5
Eris 4♈14.9R ⚶ 3♏02.8
⚷ 14♌33.1R ⚴ 24♏45.8
☽ Mean ☊ 18♍27.5

LONGITUDE — January 1942

Day	Sid.Time	☉	0 hr ☽	Noon ☽	True ☊	☿	♀	♂	⚳	♃	♄	♅	♆	♇
1 Th	18 42 01	10♑27 20	21♊37 40	27♊38 28	15♍42.9	16♑36.9	18♒40.8	25♈03.8	1♒12.7	13♊22.4	22♉04.4	26♉48.7	29♍52.7	5♌09.6
2 F	18 45 58	11 28 28	3♋40 58	9♋45 19	15R 30.1	18 14.9	19 04.8	25 31.1	1 35.9	13R 16.0	22R 02.1	26R 47.2	29R 52.7	5R 08.4
3 Sa	18 49 55	12 29 36	15 51 35	21 59 53	15 18.6	19 53.1	19 26.8	25 58.7	1 59.1	13 09.8	21 59.9	26 45.6	29 52.7	5 07.2
4 Su	18 53 51	13 30 44	28 10 17	4♌22 52	15 09.4	21 31.5	19 46.9	26 26.4	2 22.3	13 03.7	21 57.8	26 44.1	29 52.6	5 05.9
5 M	18 57 48	14 31 53	10♌37 44	16 55 02	15 02.9	23 10.2	20 05.0	26 54.5	2 45.5	12 57.8	21 55.7	26 42.6	29 52.5	5 04.7
6 Tu	19 01 44	15 33 01	23 14 54	29 37 31	14 59.3	24 49.0	20 21.1	27 22.7	3 08.8	12 52.0	21 53.8	26 41.2	29 52.3	5 03.4
7 W	19 05 41	16 34 09	6♍03 06	12♍31 54	14D 58.0	26 28.0	20 35.0	27 51.2	3 32.1	12 46.3	21 52.0	26 39.8	29 52.1	5 02.2
8 Th	19 09 37	17 35 18	19 04 10	25 40 11	14 58.4	28 07.0	20 46.8	28 19.9	3 55.5	12 40.9	21 50.3	26 38.5	29 51.9	5 00.9
9 F	19 13 34	18 36 26	2♎20 15	9♎04 39	14R 59.3	29 46.0	20 56.3	28 48.8	4 18.8	12 35.6	21 48.7	26 37.2	29 51.6	4 59.6
10 Sa	19 17 30	19 37 35	15 53 36	22 47 18	14 59.6	1♒24.9	21 03.5	29 18.0	4 42.2	12 30.4	21 47.2	26 36.0	29 51.3	4 58.3
11 Su	19 21 27	20 38 43	29 45 54	6♏49 24	14 58.3	3 03.7	21 08.4	29 47.3	5 05.6	12 25.4	21 45.9	26 34.8	29 51.0	4 57.0
12 M	19 25 24	21 39 52	13♏57 42	21 10 34	14 54.9	4 42.1	21R 10.9	0♉16.8	5 29.0	12 20.6	21 44.6	26 33.6	29 50.6	4 55.6
13 Tu	19 29 20	22 41 00	28 27 37	5♐48 16	14 49.2	6 20.0	21 11.0	0 46.6	5 52.5	12 16.0	21 43.4	26 32.5	29 50.3	4 54.3
14 W	19 33 17	23 42 09	13♐11 49	20 37 24	14 41.8	7 57.2	21 08.6	1 16.5	6 15.9	12 11.6	21 42.4	26 31.5	29 49.8	4 53.0
15 Th	19 37 13	24 43 17	28 04 00	5♑30 35	14 33.5	9 33.6	21 03.7	1 46.6	6 39.4	12 07.3	21 41.4	26 30.5	29 49.4	4 51.6
16 F	19 41 10	25 44 25	12♑56 00	20 19 10	14 25.5	11 08.7	20 56.3	2 16.9	7 02.9	12 03.2	21 40.6	26 29.5	29 48.9	4 50.3
17 Sa	19 45 06	26 45 32	27 39 02	4♒54 38	14 18.7	12 42.5	20 46.4	2 47.4	7 26.4	11 59.4	21 39.9	26 28.6	29 48.4	4 49.0
18 Su	19 49 03	27 46 38	12♒05 09	19 09 57	14 13.8	14 14.4	20 34.0	3 18.1	7 49.9	11 55.7	21 39.3	26 27.7	29 47.8	4 47.6
19 M	19 53 00	28 47 44	26 08 32	3♓00 38	14D 11.2	15 44.0	20 19.1	3 48.9	8 13.5	11 52.2	21 38.8	26 26.9	29 47.2	4 46.2
20 Tu	19 56 56	29 48 49	9♓46 06	16 24 58	14 10.6	17 11.0	20 01.8	4 20.0	8 37.0	11 48.8	21 38.5	26 26.2	29 46.6	4 44.9
21 W	20 00 53	0♒49 53	22 57 27	29 23 49	14 11.5	18 34.8	19 42.0	4 51.1	9 00.6	11 45.7	21 38.2	26 25.5	29 45.9	4 43.5
22 Th	20 04 49	1 50 57	5♈44 29	11♈59 58	14 13.0	19 54.7	19 19.9	5 22.4	9 24.2	11 42.8	21D 38.0	26 24.8	29 45.3	4 42.2
23 F	20 08 46	2 51 59	18 10 47	24 17 33	14R 14.3	21 10.1	18 55.6	5 53.9	9 47.7	11 40.1	21 38.0	26 24.2	29 44.5	4 40.8
24 Sa	20 12 42	3 53 00	0♉20 52	6♉21 24	14 14.7	22 20.4	18 29.2	6 25.5	10 11.3	11 37.6	21 38.1	26 23.6	29 43.8	4 39.4
25 Su	20 16 39	4 54 00	12 19 45	18 16 34	14 13.5	23 24.6	18 00.7	6 57.3	10 34.9	11 35.3	21 38.3	26 23.1	29 43.0	4 38.1
26 M	20 20 35	5 54 59	24 12 28	0♊08 01	14 10.6	24 22.1	17 30.4	7 29.2	10 58.5	11 33.1	21 38.6	26 22.7	29 42.2	4 36.7
27 Tu	20 24 32	6 55 57	6♊03 46	12 00 15	14 06.0	25 11.9	16 58.5	8 01.3	11 22.1	11 31.2	21 39.0	26 22.3	29 41.4	4 35.3
28 W	20 28 29	7 56 54	17 57 54	23 57 10	14 00.1	25 53.3	16 25.1	8 33.4	11 45.7	11 29.5	21 39.6	26 21.9	29 40.5	4 34.0
29 Th	20 32 25	8 57 50	29 58 24	6♋01 55	13 53.5	26 25.5	15 50.4	9 05.7	12 09.3	11 28.0	21 40.2	26 21.6	29 39.6	4 32.6
30 F	20 36 22	9 58 44	12♋08 01	18 16 52	13 47.0	26 47.6	15 14.7	9 38.1	12 32.9	11 26.7	21 41.0	26 21.4	29 38.7	4 31.2
31 Sa	20 40 18	10 59 38	24 28 38	0♌43 27	13 41.2	26R 59.2	14 38.3	10 10.7	12 56.5	11 25.6	21 41.8	26 21.2	29 37.8	4 29.9

LONGITUDE — February 1942

Day	Sid.Time	☉	0 hr ☽	Noon ☽	True ☊	☿	♀	♂	⚳	♃	♄	♅	♆	♇
1 Su	20 44 15	12♒00 30	7♌01 23	13♌22 27	13♍36.7	26♒59.8	14♒01.3	10♉43.3	13♒20.1	11♊24.7	21♉42.8	26♉21.1	29♍36.8	4♌28.5
2 M	20 48 11	13 01 22	19 46 41	26 14 02	13R 33.8	26R 49.1	13R 24.0	11 16.1	13 43.7	11R 24.0	21 43.9	26R 21.0	29R 35.8	4R 27.2
3 Tu	20 52 08	14 02 12	2♍44 28	9♍17 58	13D 32.5	26 27.4	12 46.7	11 49.0	14 07.3	11 23.5	21 45.1	26D 21.0	29 34.8	4 25.8
4 W	20 56 04	15 03 01	15 54 28	22 33 56	13 32.7	25 54.9	12 09.7	12 21.9	14 30.9	11D 23.2	21 46.4	26 21.0	29 33.7	4 24.5
5 Th	21 00 01	16 03 49	29 16 19	6♎01 35	13 33.9	25 12.5	11 33.2	12 55.0	14 54.5	11 23.2	21 47.9	26 21.1	29 32.6	4 23.1
6 F	21 03 57	17 04 36	12♎49 44	19 40 43	13 35.6	24 21.1	10 57.4	13 28.2	15 18.1	11 23.3	21 49.4	26 21.2	29 31.5	4 21.8
7 Sa	21 07 54	18 05 23	26 34 31	3♏31 04	13 36.9	23 22.2	10 22.7	14 01.5	15 41.7	11 23.6	21 51.0	26 21.4	29 30.4	4 20.5
8 Su	21 11 51	19 06 08	10♏30 19	17 32 10	13R 37.6	22 17.5	9 49.2	14 34.9	16 05.3	11 24.1	21 52.8	26 21.6	29 29.3	4 19.2
9 M	21 15 47	20 06 52	24 36 26	1♐42 57	13 37.2	21 08.8	9 17.2	15 08.3	16 28.9	11 24.8	21 54.7	26 21.9	29 28.1	4 17.8
10 Tu	21 19 44	21 07 36	8♐51 26	16 01 31	13 35.6	19 58.1	8 46.8	15 41.9	16 52.4	11 25.8	21 56.6	26 22.2	29 26.9	4 16.5
11 W	21 23 40	22 08 18	23 12 48	0♑24 47	13 33.2	18 47.3	8 18.2	16 15.6	17 16.0	11 26.9	21 58.7	26 22.6	29 25.7	4 15.2
12 Th	21 27 37	23 09 00	7♑36 56	14 48 37	13 30.4	17 38.3	7 51.6	16 49.3	17 39.6	11 28.2	22 00.9	26 23.1	29 24.4	4 14.0
13 F	21 31 33	24 09 40	21 59 13	29 08 04	13 27.5	16 32.7	7 27.1	17 23.2	18 03.1	11 29.8	22 03.2	26 23.6	29 23.1	4 12.7
14 Sa	21 35 30	25 10 19	6♒14 31	13♒17 57	13 25.1	15 31.9	7 04.7	17 57.1	18 26.6	11 31.5	22 05.6	26 24.1	29 21.9	4 11.4
15 Su	21 39 27	26 10 56	20 17 48	27 13 33	13 23.6	14 37.0	6 44.6	18 31.1	18 50.2	11 33.4	22 08.1	26 24.7	29 20.5	4 10.1
16 M	21 43 23	27 11 32	4♓04 47	10♓51 11	13D 23.0	13 48.9	6 26.9	19 05.2	19 13.7	11 35.6	22 10.8	26 25.4	29 19.2	4 08.9
17 Tu	21 47 20	28 12 06	17 32 33	24 08 44	13 23.2	13 08.0	6 11.6	19 39.4	19 37.2	11 37.9	22 13.5	26 26.1	29 17.9	4 07.7
18 W	21 51 16	29 12 39	0♈39 46	7♈05 42	13 24.1	12 34.7	5 58.7	20 13.7	20 00.6	11 40.4	22 16.3	26 26.8	29 16.5	4 06.4
19 Th	21 55 13	0♓13 09	13 26 46	19 43 13	13 25.3	12 09.1	5 48.3	20 48.0	20 24.1	11 43.1	22 19.2	26 27.7	29 15.1	4 05.2
20 F	21 59 09	1 13 39	25 55 23	2♉03 42	13 26.5	11 51.0	5 40.3	21 22.4	20 47.5	11 46.0	22 22.2	26 28.5	29 13.7	4 04.0
21 Sa	22 03 06	2 14 06	8♉08 39	14 10 42	13 27.5	11 40.4	5 34.9	21 56.9	21 10.9	11 49.1	22 25.4	26 29.4	29 12.3	4 02.8
22 Su	22 07 02	3 14 31	20 10 26	26 08 25	13R 28.1	11D 36.9	5D 31.8	22 31.4	21 34.3	11 52.4	22 28.6	26 30.4	29 10.8	4 01.7
23 M	22 10 59	4 14 55	2♊05 13	8♊01 28	13 28.2	11 40.2	5 31.2	23 06.1	21 57.7	11 55.9	22 31.9	26 31.4	29 09.4	4 00.5
24 Tu	22 14 55	5 15 16	13 57 43	19 54 35	13 27.8	11 49.9	5 33.0	23 40.7	22 21.1	11 59.6	22 35.3	26 32.5	29 07.9	3 59.4
25 W	22 18 52	6 15 36	25 52 38	1♋52 24	13 27.1	12 05.7	5 37.2	24 15.5	22 44.4	12 03.4	22 38.9	26 33.6	29 06.4	3 58.2
26 Th	22 22 49	7 15 54	7♋54 26	13 59 10	13 26.3	12 27.1	5 43.6	24 50.3	23 07.7	12 07.4	22 42.5	26 34.8	29 04.9	3 57.1
27 F	22 26 45	8 16 10	20 07 05	26 18 32	13 25.6	12 53.7	5 52.3	25 25.1	23 31.0	12 11.7	22 46.2	26 36.0	29 03.4	3 56.0
28 Sa	22 30 42	9 16 23	2♌33 51	8♌53 18	13 25.0	13 25.3	6 03.2	26 00.0	23 54.2	12 16.1	22 50.0	26 37.3	29 01.8	3 54.9

Astro Data Dy Hr Mn	Planet Ingress Dy Hr Mn	Last Aspect Dy Hr Mn	☽ Ingress Dy Hr Mn	Last Aspect Dy Hr Mn	☽ Ingress Dy Hr Mn	☽ Phases & Eclipses Dy Hr Mn
♆R 1 10:32	☿ ♒ 9 15:24	1 16:27 ♆ □	♋ 1 16:42	2 13:04 ☿ ☍	♍ 2 18:57	2 15:42 ○ 11♋38
☽0S 9 2:39	♂ ♉ 11 22:21	4 3:18 ♆ ✱	♌ 4 3:32	5 0:30 ♆ ☌	♎ 5 1:18	10 6:05 ☾ 19♎22
♀R 13 0:41	☉ ♒ 20 16:24	6 7:37 ♂ △	♍ 6 12:42	6 19:37 ☿ △	♏ 7 5:56	16 21:32 ● 26♑09
☽0N 21 20:49		8 19:34 ♆ ☌	♎ 8 19:48	9 8:13 ♆ ✱	♐ 9 9:07	24 6:36 ☽ 3♉39
♄D 23 7:01	☉ ♓ 19 6:47	10 23:36 ♂ ☍	♏ 11 0:24	11 10:22 ♆ □	♑ 11 11:19	
		13 2:16 ♆ ✱	♐ 13 2:31	13 12:25 ♆ △	♒ 13 13:27	1 9:12 ○ 11♌53
☿R 1 1:13		15 2:50 ♆ □	♑ 15 3:07	15 10:35 ♅ □	♓ 15 16:50	8 14:52 ☾ 19♏13
♅D 3 14:50		17 3:33 ♆ △	♒ 17 3:52	17 21:27 ♆ ☍	♈ 17 22:46	15 10:03 ● 26♒06
☽0S 5 8:55		19 0:33 ♅ □	♓ 19 6:43	18 21:59 ☿ ✱	♉ 20 7:57	23 3:40 ☽ 3♊54
♃D 5 10:02		21 12:42 ♆ ☍	♈ 21 13:08	22 18:07 ♆ △	♊ 22 19:47	
☽0N 18 6:54		23 5:10 ♆ ✱	♉ 23 23:18	25 6:29 ♆ □	♋ 25 8:15	
☿D 22 12:08		26 11:08 ♆ △	♊ 26 11:44	27 17:16 ♆ ✱	♌ 27 19:06	
♀D 23 6:01		28 23:24 ♆ □	♋ 29 0:03			
		31 9:54 ♆ ✱	♌ 31 10:37			

Astro Data

1 January 1942
Julian Day # 15341
SVP 6♓04'14"
GC 26♐01.8 ⚴ 13♑20.4
Eris 4♈12.7 ⚵ 12♏19.9
⚷ 13♌32.5R ⚶ 11♐17.4
☽ Mean ☊ 16♍49.0

1 February 1942
Julian Day # 15372
SVP 6♓04'09"
GC 26♐01.8 ⚴ 25♑08.4
Eris 4♈21.7 ⚵ 19♏23.5
⚷ 11♌24.5R ⚶ 27♐20.5
☽ Mean ☊ 15♍10.5

March 1942 LONGITUDE

Day	Sid.Time	☉	0 hr ☽	Noon ☽	True ☊	☿	♀	♂	⚳	♃	♄	♅	♆	♇
1 Su	22 34 38	10♓16 35	15♌17 04	21♌45 17	13♍24.6	14♒01.4	6♒16.3	26♉35.0	24♒17.4	12♊20.6	22♉53.9	26♉38.6	29♍00.3	3♌53.9
2 M	22 38 35	11 16 45	28 17 58	4♍55 06	13D 24.4	14 41.7	6 31.5	27 10.0	24 40.6	12 25.4	22 57.9	26 40.0	28R 58.7	3R 52.8
3 Tu	22 42 31	12 16 53	11♍36 34	18 22 12	13 24.4	15 25.9	6 48.7	27 45.1	25 03.8	12 30.3	23 02.0	26 41.4	28 57.2	3 51.8
4 W	22 46 28	13 17 00	25 11 44	2♎04 52	13R 24.4	16 13.8	7 07.8	28 20.2	25 26.9	12 35.4	23 06.1	26 42.8	28 55.6	3 50.8
5 Th	22 50 24	14 17 04	9♎01 15	16 00 30	13 24.4	17 05.1	7 28.9	28 55.3	25 50.1	12 40.6	23 10.4	26 44.4	28 54.0	3 49.8
6 F	22 54 21	15 17 07	23 02 11	0♏05 53	13 24.2	17 59.5	7 51.8	29 30.5	26 13.1	12 46.0	23 14.7	26 45.9	28 52.4	3 48.8
7 Sa	22 58 18	16 17 09	7♏11 09	14 17 33	13 24.0	18 56.9	8 16.5	0♊05.8	26 36.2	12 51.6	23 19.2	26 47.5	28 50.8	3 47.8
8 Su	23 02 14	17 17 08	21 24 40	28 32 08	13 23.7	19 57.1	8 42.8	0 41.1	26 59.2	12 57.4	23 23.7	26 49.2	28 49.2	3 46.9
9 M	23 06 11	18 17 06	5♐39 32	12♐46 33	13D 23.5	20 59.8	9 10.9	1 16.4	27 22.2	13 03.3	23 28.3	26 50.9	28 47.6	3 46.0
10 Tu	23 10 07	19 17 03	19 52 53	26 58 12	13 23.5	22 05.0	9 40.5	1 51.8	27 45.1	13 09.4	23 33.0	26 52.6	28 45.9	3 45.1
11 W	23 14 04	20 16 58	4♑02 16	11♑04 49	13 23.9	23 12.4	10 11.7	2 27.2	28 08.1	13 15.7	23 37.8	26 54.4	28 44.3	3 44.2
12 Th	23 18 00	21 16 52	18 05 37	25 04 27	13 24.5	24 22.1	10 44.3	3 02.7	28 30.9	13 22.1	23 42.6	26 56.2	28 42.7	3 43.3
13 F	23 21 57	22 16 43	2♒01 05	8♒55 19	13 25.3	25 33.7	11 18.3	3 38.2	28 53.8	13 28.6	23 47.5	26 58.1	28 41.0	3 42.5
14 Sa	23 25 53	23 16 33	15 46 55	22 35 42	13 26.1	26 47.4	11 53.6	4 13.8	29 16.6	13 35.3	23 52.6	27 00.0	28 39.4	3 41.7
15 Su	23 29 50	24 16 21	29 21 28	6♓04 03	13R 26.6	28 02.9	12 30.3	4 49.4	29 39.4	13 42.2	23 57.6	27 02.0	28 37.7	3 40.9
16 M	23 33 47	25 16 07	12♓43 15	19 18 58	13 26.6	29 20.2	13 08.1	5 25.0	0♓02.1	13 49.2	24 02.8	27 04.0	28 36.0	3 40.1
17 Tu	23 37 43	26 15 51	25 51 04	2♈19 28	13 26.0	0♓39.2	13 47.2	6 00.7	0 24.8	13 56.4	24 08.1	27 06.1	28 34.4	3 39.3
18 W	23 41 40	27 15 34	8♈44 09	15 05 07	13 24.6	1 59.8	14 27.4	6 36.4	0 47.4	14 03.7	24 13.4	27 08.2	28 32.7	3 38.6
19 Th	23 45 36	28 15 14	21 22 27	27 36 15	13 22.6	3 22.1	15 08.7	7 12.1	1 10.0	14 11.2	24 18.8	27 10.3	28 31.1	3 37.9
20 F	23 49 33	29 14 52	3♉46 42	9♉54 02	13 20.2	4 45.9	15 51.0	7 47.9	1 32.6	14 18.8	24 24.3	27 12.5	28 29.4	3 37.2
21 Sa	23 53 29	0♈14 27	15 58 31	22 00 31	13 17.7	6 11.2	16 34.4	8 23.8	1 55.0	14 26.5	24 29.8	27 14.7	28 27.7	3 36.5
22 Su	23 57 26	1 14 01	28 00 24	3♊58 36	13 15.4	7 38.0	17 18.7	8 59.6	2 17.5	14 34.4	24 35.4	27 16.9	28 26.1	3 35.9
23 M	0 01 22	2 13 32	9♊55 36	15 51 55	13 13.7	9 06.3	18 03.9	9 35.5	2 39.9	14 42.4	24 41.1	27 19.2	28 24.4	3 35.3
24 Tu	0 05 19	3 13 01	21 48 05	27 44 39	13D 12.7	10 36.0	18 50.0	10 11.4	3 02.3	14 50.6	24 46.8	27 21.6	28 22.8	3 34.7
25 W	0 09 15	4 12 28	3♋42 14	9♋41 25	13 12.8	12 07.2	19 37.0	10 47.4	3 24.6	14 58.9	24 52.7	27 24.0	28 21.1	3 34.1
26 Th	0 13 12	5 11 53	15 42 48	21 46 57	13 13.6	13 39.7	20 24.8	11 23.3	3 46.8	15 07.3	24 58.5	27 26.4	28 19.5	3 33.5
27 F	0 17 09	6 11 15	27 54 29	4♌05 54	13 15.1	15 13.6	21 13.4	11 59.3	4 09.0	15 15.9	25 04.5	27 28.8	28 17.8	3 33.0
28 Sa	0 21 05	7 10 35	10♌21 45	16 42 28	13 16.7	16 49.0	22 02.8	12 35.3	4 31.1	15 24.6	25 10.5	27 31.3	28 16.2	3 32.5
29 Su	0 25 02	8 09 52	23 08 26	29 39 59	13 18.1	18 25.7	22 52.9	13 11.4	4 53.2	15 33.4	25 16.6	27 33.8	28 14.5	3 32.1
30 M	0 28 58	9 09 08	6♍17 18	13♍00 30	13R 18.6	20 03.8	23 43.7	13 47.4	5 15.2	15 42.3	25 22.7	27 36.4	28 12.9	3 31.6
31 Tu	0 32 55	10 08 21	19 49 34	26 44 21	13 18.0	21 43.3	24 35.2	14 23.5	5 37.2	15 51.3	25 28.9	27 39.0	28 11.3	3 31.2

April 1942 LONGITUDE

Day	Sid.Time	☉	0 hr ☽	Noon ☽	True ☊	☿	♀	♂	⚳	♃	♄	♅	♆	♇
1 W	0 36 51	11♈07 32	3♎44 32	10♎49 43	13♍16.0	23♓24.1	25♒27.3	14♊59.6	5♓59.1	16♊00.5	25♉35.2	27♉41.6	28♍09.7	3♌30.8
2 Th	0 40 48	12 06 41	17 59 20	25 12 43	13R 12.8	25 06.4	26 20.1	15 35.8	6 21.0	16 09.8	25 41.5	27 44.2	28R 08.1	3R 30.4
3 F	0 44 44	13 05 48	2♏29 06	9♏47 37	13 08.6	26 50.1	27 13.5	16 11.9	6 42.8	16 19.2	25 47.8	27 46.9	28 06.5	3 30.1
4 Sa	0 48 41	14 04 53	17 07 24	24 27 35	13 04.2	28 35.3	28 07.5	16 48.1	7 04.5	16 28.7	25 54.2	27 49.6	28 04.9	3 29.7
5 Su	0 52 38	15 03 56	1♐47 17	9♐05 44	13 00.0	0♈21.9	29 02.0	17 24.3	7 26.2	16 38.3	26 00.7	27 52.4	28 03.3	3 29.4
6 M	0 56 34	16 02 58	16 22 11	23 36 03	12 56.9	2 09.9	29 57.1	18 00.5	7 47.8	16 48.0	26 07.3	27 55.2	28 01.7	3 29.2
7 Tu	1 00 31	17 01 58	0♑46 50	7♑54 08	12D 55.2	3 59.4	0♓52.8	18 36.7	8 09.3	16 57.9	26 13.8	27 58.0	28 00.2	3 28.9
8 W	1 04 27	18 00 56	14 57 43	21 57 25	12 54.9	5 50.3	1 48.9	19 13.0	8 30.8	17 07.8	26 20.5	28 00.8	27 58.6	3 28.7
9 Th	1 08 24	18 59 53	28 53 09	5♒44 56	12 55.8	7 42.7	2 45.5	19 49.2	8 52.2	17 17.9	26 27.2	28 03.7	27 57.1	3 28.5
10 F	1 12 20	19 58 48	12♒32 50	19 16 57	12 57.3	9 36.6	3 42.6	20 25.5	9 13.6	17 28.1	26 33.9	28 06.6	27 55.6	3 28.3
11 Sa	1 16 17	20 57 41	25 57 25	2♓34 23	12R 58.6	11 32.0	4 40.2	21 01.8	9 34.8	17 38.3	26 40.7	28 09.6	27 54.1	3 28.2
12 Su	1 20 13	21 56 32	9♓08 01	15 38 26	12 59.0	13 28.8	5 38.1	21 38.2	9 56.0	17 48.7	26 47.5	28 12.5	27 52.6	3 28.1
13 M	1 24 10	22 55 21	22 05 46	28 30 09	12 57.8	15 27.1	6 36.5	22 14.5	10 17.2	17 59.2	26 54.4	28 15.5	27 51.1	3 28.0
14 Tu	1 28 07	23 54 09	4♈51 41	11♈10 26	12 54.6	17 26.8	7 35.3	22 50.9	10 38.2	18 09.7	27 01.3	28 18.5	27 49.6	3 27.9
15 W	1 32 03	24 52 54	17 26 31	23 39 59	12 49.4	19 27.8	8 34.5	23 27.3	10 59.2	18 20.4	27 08.2	28 21.5	27 48.2	3D 27.9
16 Th	1 36 00	25 51 38	29 50 55	5♉59 25	12 42.5	21 30.2	9 34.0	24 03.7	11 20.1	18 31.1	27 15.2	28 24.6	27 46.7	3 27.9
17 F	1 39 56	26 50 20	12♉05 36	18 09 35	12 34.3	23 33.8	10 33.9	24 40.1	11 40.9	18 42.0	27 22.3	28 27.7	27 45.3	3 27.9
18 Sa	1 43 53	27 48 59	24 11 33	0♊11 42	12 25.8	25 38.5	11 34.1	25 16.6	12 01.7	18 52.9	27 29.4	28 30.8	27 43.9	3 27.9
19 Su	1 47 49	28 47 37	6♊10 16	12 07 33	12 17.6	27 44.3	12 34.7	25 53.1	12 22.3	19 03.9	27 36.5	28 33.9	27 42.6	3 28.0
20 M	1 51 46	29 46 12	18 03 53	23 59 39	12 10.7	29 51.0	13 35.6	26 29.5	12 42.9	19 15.0	27 43.6	28 37.1	27 41.2	3 28.1
21 Tu	1 55 42	0♉44 46	29 55 16	5♋51 13	12 05.5	1♉58.3	14 36.7	27 06.0	13 03.4	19 26.2	27 50.8	28 40.3	27 39.9	3 28.2
22 W	1 59 39	1 43 17	11♋48 01	17 46 13	12 02.3	4 06.2	15 38.2	27 42.5	13 23.8	19 37.5	27 58.1	28 43.5	27 38.5	3 28.3
23 Th	2 03 35	2 41 46	23 46 23	29 49 08	12D 01.1	6 14.4	16 40.0	28 19.1	13 44.1	19 48.9	28 05.3	28 46.7	27 37.2	3 28.5
24 F	2 07 32	3 40 13	5♌55 04	12♌04 51	12 01.4	8 22.6	17 42.1	28 55.6	14 04.3	20 00.3	28 12.6	28 49.9	27 36.0	3 28.7
25 Sa	2 11 29	4 38 38	18 19 05	24 38 21	12 02.4	10 30.7	18 44.4	29 32.1	14 24.4	20 11.8	28 20.0	28 53.2	27 34.7	3 28.9
26 Su	2 15 25	5 37 00	1♍03 13	7♍34 10	12R 03.3	12 38.2	19 47.0	0♋08.7	14 44.5	20 23.4	28 27.3	28 56.4	27 33.5	3 29.2
27 M	2 19 22	6 35 21	14 11 38	20 55 55	12 03.0	14 44.8	20 49.8	0 45.2	15 04.4	20 35.1	28 34.7	28 59.7	27 32.2	3 29.5
28 Tu	2 23 18	7 33 39	27 47 11	4♎45 27	12 00.8	16 50.4	21 52.9	1 21.8	15 24.3	20 46.8	28 42.1	29 03.0	27 31.1	3 29.8
29 W	2 27 15	8 31 56	11♎50 35	19 02 12	11 56.4	18 54.5	22 56.3	1 58.4	15 44.0	20 58.6	28 49.6	29 06.4	27 29.9	3 30.1
30 Th	2 31 11	9 30 11	26 19 45	3♏42 30	11 49.8	20 56.9	23 59.8	2 35.0	16 03.7	21 10.5	28 57.0	29 09.7	27 28.7	3 30.5

Astro Data (Dy Hr Mn)

☽0S 4 15:59
☽0N 17 15:47
☉0N 21 6:11

☽0S 1 1:01
☿0N 7 22:02
♅△♆ 7 23:53
☽0N 13 23:04
♃∠♇ 16 4:44
♇ D 16 11:02
♄△♆ 20 5:07
☽0S 28 11:35

Planet Ingress (Dy Hr Mn)

♂ ♊ 7 8:04
⚳ ♓ 16 9:47
☿ ♓ 17 0:10
☉ ♈ 21 6:11

☿ ♈ 5 7:06
♀ ♓ 6 13:14
☿ ♉ 20 13:42
☉ ♉ 20 17:39
♂ ♋ 26 6:18

Last Aspect / ☽ Ingress (Dy Hr Mn)

Last Aspect		☽ Ingress
1 21:17	♂ □	♍ 2 3:06
4 6:31	♆ ☌	♎ 4 8:23
5 13:58	☿ △	♏ 6 11:50
8 12:29	♆ ⚹	♐ 8 14:28
10 15:02	♆ □	♑ 10 17:08
12 18:16	♆ △	♒ 12 20:30
14 20:11	☿ ☌	♓ 15 1:09
17 5:03	♆ ☍	♈ 17 7:41
18 10:44	♀ ⚹	♉ 19 16:39
22 0:53	♆ △	♊ 22 4:00
24 13:17	♆ □	♋ 24 16:33
27 0:47	♆ ⚹	♌ 27 4:04
29 8:08	♅ □	♍ 29 12:37
31 14:29	♆ ☌	♎ 31 17:36

Last Aspect		☽ Ingress
2 13:59	♀ △	♏ 2 19:54
4 19:41	☿ △	♐ 4 21:04
6 19:23	♆ □	♑ 6 22:41
8 22:31	♅ △	♒ 9 1:56
11 3:57	♅ □	♓ 11 7:19
13 11:32	♅ ⚹	♈ 13 14:49
15 14:33	☉ ☌	♉ 16 0:18
18 8:37	♅ ☌	♊ 18 11:37
20 19:28	♆ □	♋ 21 0:10
23 9:56	♅ ⚹	♌ 23 12:21
25 21:38	♂ ⚹	♍ 25 22:03
28 2:09	♅ △	♎ 28 3:50
29 15:15	♃ △	♏ 30 5:59

☽ Phases & Eclipses (Dy Hr Mn)

3 0:20 ○ 11♍48
3 0:21 • T 1.561
9 22:00 ☾ 18♐42
16 23:50 ● 25♓46
16 23:36:41 • P 0.639
25 0:01 ☽ 3♋43

1 12:32 ○ 11♎09
8 4:43 ☾ 17♑43
15 14:33 ● 24♈59
23 18:10 ☽ 2♌57
30 21:59 ○ 9♏54

Astro Data

1 March 1942
Julian Day # 15400
SVP 6♓04'06"
GC 26♐01.9 ⚳ 5♒06.8
Eris 4♈37.5 ⚵ 22♏43.8
⚷ 9♌26.5R ⚶ 11♑00.1
☽ Mean ☊ 13♍41.5

1 April 1942
Julian Day # 15431
SVP 6♓04'04"
GC 26♐02.0 ⚳ 14♒48.2
Eris 4♈59.3 ⚵ 21♏44.4R
⚷ 8♌15.8R ⚶ 24♑30.9
☽ Mean ☊ 12♍03.0

LONGITUDE — May 1942

Day	Sid.Time	☉	0 hr ☽	Noon ☽	True ☊	☿	♀	♂	⚳	♃	♄	♅	♆	♇
1 F	2 35 08	10♉28 24	11♏09 30	18♏39 39	11♍41.5	22♉57.3	25♓03.6	3♋11.6	16♓23.2	21♊22.4	29♉04.5	29♉13.0	27♍27.6	3♌30.8
2 Sa	2 39 04	11 26 35	26 11 46	3♐44 35	11R32.5	24 55.3	26 07.7	3 48.2	16 42.7	21 34.4	29 12.0	29 16.4	27R26.5	3 31.2
3 Su	2 43 01	12 24 45	11♐16 50	18 47 18	11 24.0	26 50.9	27 11.9	4 24.8	17 02.1	21 46.5	29 19.6	29 19.8	27 25.4	3 31.7
4 M	2 46 58	13 22 53	26 14 55	3♑38 41	11 17.0	28 43.6	28 16.4	5 01.5	17 21.3	21 58.6	29 27.1	29 23.2	27 24.4	3 32.1
5 Tu	2 50 54	14 21 00	10♑57 52	18 11 51	11 12.1	0♊33.4	29 21.0	5 38.1	17 40.5	22 10.9	29 34.7	29 26.6	27 23.4	3 32.6
6 W	2 54 51	15 19 05	25 20 14	2♒22 50	11 09.5	2 20.1	0♈25.9	6 14.8	17 59.5	22 23.1	29 42.3	29 30.0	27 22.4	3 33.1
7 Th	2 58 47	16 17 09	9♒19 34	16 10 31	11D08.8	4 03.5	1 31.0	6 51.4	18 18.4	22 35.4	29 49.9	29 33.4	27 21.4	3 33.7
8 F	3 02 44	17 15 11	22 55 54	29 35 59	11R09.2	5 43.5	2 36.2	7 28.1	18 37.3	22 47.8	29 57.6	29 36.9	27 20.4	3 34.2
9 Sa	3 06 40	18 13 13	6♓11 06	12♓41 38	11 09.4	7 20.0	3 41.6	8 04.8	18 56.0	23 00.3	0♊05.2	29 40.3	27 19.5	3 34.8
10 Su	3 10 37	19 11 13	19 07 57	25 30 28	11 08.5	8 52.9	4 47.2	8 41.5	19 14.6	23 12.8	0 12.9	29 43.8	27 18.6	3 35.4
11 M	3 14 33	20 09 11	1♈49 32	8♈05 29	11 05.5	10 22.1	5 53.0	9 18.2	19 33.1	23 25.3	0 20.6	29 47.2	27 17.7	3 36.0
12 Tu	3 18 30	21 07 08	14 18 40	20 29 22	10 59.8	11 47.5	6 58.9	9 55.0	19 51.4	23 37.9	0 28.3	29 50.7	27 16.9	3 36.7
13 W	3 22 27	22 05 04	26 37 48	2♉44 13	10 51.3	13 09.2	8 04.9	10 31.7	20 09.7	23 50.6	0 36.0	29 54.2	27 16.1	3 37.4
14 Th	3 26 23	23 02 58	8♉48 47	14 51 42	10 40.4	14 27.0	9 11.2	11 08.5	20 27.8	24 03.3	0 43.7	29 57.7	27 15.3	3 38.1
15 F	3 30 20	24 00 51	20 53 05	26 53 05	10 27.7	15 40.8	10 17.5	11 45.2	20 45.8	24 16.1	0 51.4	0♊01.2	27 14.5	3 38.8
16 Sa	3 34 16	24 58 43	2♊51 52	8♊49 35	10 14.3	16 50.7	11 24.0	12 22.0	21 03.6	24 28.9	0 59.2	0 04.6	27 13.8	3 39.6
17 Su	3 38 13	25 56 33	14 46 23	20 42 29	10 01.4	17 56.5	12 30.7	12 58.8	21 21.3	24 41.8	1 06.9	0 08.1	27 13.1	3 40.3
18 M	3 42 09	26 54 21	26 38 05	2♋33 30	9 49.9	18 58.3	13 37.5	13 35.6	21 38.9	24 54.7	1 14.7	0 11.6	27 12.4	3 41.1
19 Tu	3 46 06	27 52 08	8♋28 59	14 24 56	9 40.7	19 55.8	14 44.4	14 12.4	21 56.4	25 07.6	1 22.4	0 15.2	27 11.8	3 42.0
20 W	3 50 02	28 49 54	20 21 43	26 19 48	9 34.2	20 49.1	15 51.4	14 49.2	22 13.7	25 20.6	1 30.2	0 18.7	27 11.2	3 42.8
21 Th	3 53 59	29 47 38	2♌19 40	8♌21 50	9 30.4	21 38.1	16 58.6	15 26.1	22 30.9	25 33.6	1 38.0	0 22.2	27 10.6	3 43.7
22 F	3 57 56	0♊45 20	14 26 54	20 35 27	9D28.8	22 22.8	18 05.8	16 02.9	22 47.9	25 46.7	1 45.7	0 25.7	27 10.1	3 44.6
23 Sa	4 01 52	1 43 00	26 48 06	3♍05 28	9R28.5	23 03.0	19 13.2	16 39.7	23 04.8	25 59.8	1 53.5	0 29.2	27 09.6	3 45.5
24 Su	4 05 49	2 40 40	9♍28 10	15 56 46	9 28.5	23 38.6	20 20.7	17 16.6	23 21.6	26 12.9	2 01.3	0 32.7	27 09.1	3 46.4
25 M	4 09 45	3 38 17	22 31 50	29 13 48	9 27.5	24 09.8	21 28.3	17 53.4	23 38.2	26 26.1	2 09.0	0 36.2	27 08.6	3 47.4
26 Tu	4 13 42	4 35 53	6♎03 00	12♎59 40	9 24.6	24 36.2	22 36.0	18 30.3	23 54.6	26 39.3	2 16.8	0 39.7	27 08.2	3 48.4
27 W	4 17 38	5 33 28	20 03 48	27 15 16	9 19.2	24 58.0	23 43.9	19 07.2	24 11.0	26 52.6	2 24.5	0 43.2	27 07.8	3 49.4
28 Th	4 21 35	6 31 01	4♏33 40	11♏58 22	9 11.2	25 15.2	24 51.8	19 44.1	24 27.1	27 05.8	2 32.3	0 46.7	27 07.4	3 50.4
29 F	4 25 31	7 28 33	19 28 32	27 03 04	9 01.3	25 27.6	25 59.8	20 20.9	24 43.1	27 19.1	2 40.1	0 50.2	27 07.1	3 51.4
30 Sa	4 29 28	8 26 04	4♐40 44	12♐20 06	8 50.5	25 35.3	27 08.0	20 57.8	24 58.9	27 32.5	2 47.8	0 53.6	27 06.8	3 52.5
31 Su	4 33 25	9 23 34	19 59 45	27 38 13	8 40.1	25R38.4	28 16.2	21 34.7	25 14.6	27 45.8	2 55.5	0 57.1	27 06.5	3 53.6

LONGITUDE — June 1942

Day	Sid.Time	☉	0 hr ☽	Noon ☽	True ☊	☿	♀	♂	⚳	♃	♄	♅	♆	♇
1 M	4 37 21	10♊21 03	5♑14 06	12♑46 09	8♍31.2	25♊36.9	29♈24.6	22♋11.7	25♓30.1	27♊59.2	3♊03.3	1♊00.6	27♍06.3	3♌54.7
2 Tu	4 41 18	11 18 31	20 13 18	27 34 43	8R24.8	25R30.9	0♉33.0	22 48.6	25 45.5	28 12.7	3 11.0	1 04.1	27R06.1	3 55.8
3 W	4 45 14	12 15 58	4♒49 45	11♒58 00	8 20.9	25 20.7	1 41.5	23 25.5	26 00.7	28 26.1	3 18.7	1 07.5	27 05.9	3 56.9
4 Th	4 49 11	13 13 25	18 59 19	25 53 41	8D19.2	25 06.3	2 50.2	24 02.4	26 15.7	28 39.6	3 26.4	1 11.0	27 05.8	3 58.1
5 F	4 53 07	14 10 51	2♓41 15	9♓22 20	8R19.0	24 48.2	3 58.9	24 39.4	26 30.5	28 53.0	3 34.1	1 14.4	27 05.6	3 59.3
6 Sa	4 57 04	15 08 16	15 57 18	22 26 37	8 18.9	24 26.5	5 07.7	25 16.4	26 45.2	29 06.6	3 41.8	1 17.9	27 05.6	4 00.5
7 Su	5 01 00	16 05 41	28 50 47	5♈10 18	8 17.8	24 01.7	6 16.6	25 53.3	26 59.7	29 20.1	3 49.4	1 21.3	27D05.5	4 01.7
8 M	5 04 57	17 03 05	11♈25 42	17 37 28	8 14.7	23 34.1	7 25.6	26 30.3	27 14.0	29 33.6	3 57.1	1 24.7	27 05.5	4 02.9
9 Tu	5 08 54	18 00 28	23 46 06	29 52 02	8 09.0	23 04.2	8 34.6	27 07.3	27 28.1	29 47.2	4 04.7	1 28.1	27 05.5	4 04.2
10 W	5 12 50	18 57 51	5♉55 42	11♉57 26	8 00.5	22 32.6	9 43.8	27 44.3	27 42.0	0♋00.8	4 12.3	1 31.5	27 05.6	4 05.5
11 Th	5 16 47	19 55 14	17 57 36	23 56 28	7 49.6	21 59.7	10 53.0	28 21.3	27 55.7	0 14.4	4 19.9	1 34.9	27 05.6	4 06.7
12 F	5 20 43	20 52 35	29 54 19	5♊51 22	7 36.9	21 26.1	12 02.3	28 58.4	28 09.2	0 28.0	4 27.5	1 38.2	27 05.8	4 08.1
13 Sa	5 24 40	21 49 56	11♊47 48	17 43 50	7 23.4	20 52.4	13 11.7	29 35.4	28 22.6	0 41.6	4 35.1	1 41.6	27 05.9	4 09.4
14 Su	5 28 36	22 47 17	23 39 38	29 35 23	7 10.4	20 19.1	14 21.1	0♌12.5	28 35.7	0 55.3	4 42.6	1 44.9	27 06.1	4 10.7
15 M	5 32 33	23 44 37	5♋31 15	11♋27 27	6 58.8	19 46.9	15 30.6	0 49.5	28 48.6	1 08.9	4 50.1	1 48.2	27 06.3	4 12.1
16 Tu	5 36 29	24 41 56	17 24 12	23 21 46	6 49.4	19 16.2	16 40.2	1 26.6	29 01.3	1 22.6	4 57.6	1 51.5	27 06.6	4 13.5
17 W	5 40 26	25 39 14	29 20 25	5♌20 28	6 42.7	18 47.7	17 49.9	2 03.7	29 13.8	1 36.3	5 05.1	1 54.8	27 06.8	4 14.8
18 Th	5 44 23	26 36 32	11♌22 18	17 26 20	6 38.8	18 21.7	18 59.6	2 40.8	29 26.1	1 50.0	5 12.5	1 58.1	27 07.1	4 16.2
19 F	5 48 19	27 33 49	23 32 59	29 42 44	6D37.2	17 58.8	20 09.3	3 17.9	29 38.1	2 03.7	5 19.9	2 01.3	27 07.5	4 17.7
20 Sa	5 52 16	28 31 05	5♍56 08	12♍13 40	6 37.1	17 39.2	21 19.2	3 55.0	29 50.0	2 17.3	5 27.3	2 04.6	27 07.9	4 19.1
21 Su	5 56 12	29 28 21	18 35 55	25 03 23	6R37.5	17 23.4	22 29.1	4 32.2	0♈01.6	2 31.0	5 34.7	2 07.8	27 08.3	4 20.5
22 M	6 00 09	0♋25 35	1♎36 37	8♎16 03	6 37.3	17 11.6	23 39.0	5 09.3	0 13.0	2 44.7	5 42.0	2 11.0	27 08.7	4 22.0
23 Tu	6 04 05	1 22 49	15 02 05	21 55 01	6 35.6	17 04.2	24 49.1	5 46.4	0 24.1	2 58.4	5 49.3	2 14.2	27 09.2	4 23.5
24 W	6 08 02	2 20 03	28 54 59	6♏02 00	6 31.7	17D01.1	25 59.2	6 23.6	0 35.1	3 12.1	5 56.5	2 17.3	27 09.7	4 25.0
25 Th	6 11 58	3 17 16	13♏15 51	20 36 08	6 25.7	17 02.7	27 09.3	7 00.8	0 45.7	3 25.8	6 03.7	2 20.4	27 10.2	4 26.5
26 F	6 15 55	4 14 28	28 02 13	5♐33 14	6 17.8	17 09.0	28 19.5	7 37.9	0 56.2	3 39.5	6 10.9	2 23.5	27 10.8	4 28.0
27 Sa	6 19 52	5 11 40	13♐08 09	20 45 42	6 09.0	17 20.1	29 29.8	8 15.1	1 06.4	3 53.2	6 18.1	2 26.6	27 11.4	4 29.5
28 Su	6 23 48	6 08 52	28 24 34	6♑03 19	6 00.4	17 36.0	0♊40.1	8 52.3	1 16.4	4 06.9	6 25.2	2 29.7	27 12.0	4 31.0
29 M	6 27 45	7 06 03	13♑40 32	21 14 54	5 53.1	17 56.7	1 50.5	9 29.5	1 26.1	4 20.6	6 32.3	2 32.7	27 12.7	4 32.6
30 Tu	6 31 41	8 03 15	28 45 11	6♒10 21	5 47.8	18 22.3	3 01.0	10 06.8	1 35.5	4 34.2	6 39.3	2 35.8	27 13.4	4 34.1

Astro Data

Aspect	Dy Hr Mn
♄☌♅	3 13:20
♀0N	9 2:05
☽0N	11 5:27
☽0S	25 22:13
♃□♆	28 14:47
☿R	31 16:03
☽0N	7 12:14
♆D	8 11:44
♄⚹♇	9 9:57
♃⚺♅	19 6:42
☽0S	22 7:25
☿D	24 15:54
♃⚺♇	30 11:47

Planet Ingress

		Dy Hr Mn
☿	♊	5 4:37
♀	♈	6 2:26
♄	♊	8 19:39
♅	♊	15 4:05
☉	♊	21 17:09
♀	♉	2 0:26
♃	♋	10 10:36
♂	♌	14 3:56
⚳	♈	21 8:40
☉	♋	22 1:16
♀	♊	27 22:18

Last Aspect / ☽ Ingress (May)

Last Aspect Dy Hr Mn		☽ Ingress	Dy Hr Mn
2 4:52	♅ ☍	♐	2 6:03
4 2:35	♀ □	♑	4 6:01
6 7:23	♄ △	♒	6 7:56
8 12:40	♄ □	♓	8 12:44
10 20:03	♅ ⚹	♈	10 20:31
12 18:14	♃ ⚹	♉	13 6:37
15 12:43	♆ △	♊	15 18:15
18 1:10	♆ □	♋	18 6:49
20 17:27	☉ ⚹	♌	20 19:21
22 22:13	♃ ⚹	♍	23 6:07
25 8:17	♆ ☌	♎	25 13:22
27 11:22	♃ △	♏	27 16:32
29 12:06	♆ ⚹	♐	29 16:39
31 13:05	♀ △	♑	31 15:43

Last Aspect / ☽ Ingress (June)

Last Aspect Dy Hr Mn		☽ Ingress	Dy Hr Mn
2 11:13	♆ △	♒	2 15:59
4 16:57	♃ △	♓	4 19:14
7 0:43	♃ □	♈	7 2:11
9 11:50	♃ ⚹	♉	9 12:16
11 21:22	♂ ⚹	♊	12 0:11
14 6:58	♆ □	♋	14 12:50
16 19:32	♆ ⚹	♌	17 1:19
19 7:29	☉ ⚹	♍	19 12:33
21 20:44	☉ □	♎	21 21:04
23 3:38	♆ ⚹	♏	24 1:50
25 23:29	♀ ☍	♐	26 3:09
27 22:06	♆ □	♑	28 2:30
29 21:32	♆ △	♒	30 2:00

☽ Phases & Eclipses

Dy Hr Mn		
7 12:13	☾	16♒18
15 5:45	●	23♉46
23 9:11	☽	1♍36
30 5:29	○	8♐10
5 21:26	☾	14♓33
13 21:02	●	22♊12
21 20:44	☽	29♍49
28 12:09	○	6♑09

Astro Data

1 May 1942
Julian Day # 15461
SVP 6♓04'02"
GC 26♐02.0 ⚴ 22♒01.5
Eris 5♈19.4 ⚵ 16♏16.9R
⚷ 8♌38.5 ⚶ 4♒55.7
☽ Mean ☊ 10♍27.7

1 June 1942
Julian Day # 15492
SVP 6♓03'57"
GC 26♐02.1 ⚴ 26♒00.8
Eris 5♈34.3 ⚵ 9♏51.0R
⚷ 10♌33.9 ⚶ 11♒07.1
☽ Mean ☊ 8♍49.2

July 1942 — **LONGITUDE**

Day	Sid.Time	☉	0 hr ☽	Noon ☽	True ☊	☿	♀	♂	⚳	♃	♄	♅	♆	♇
1 W	6 35 38	9♋00 26	13♒29 35	20♒42 16	5♍44.8	18♊52.7	4♊11.5	10♌44.0	1♈44.7	4♋47.9	6♊46.4	2♊38.7	27♍14.1	4♌35.7
2 Th	6 39 34	9 57 38	27 47 59	4♓46 34	5D43.9	19 27.8	5 22.1	11 21.2	1 53.7	5 01.6	6 53.3	2 41.7	27 14.8	4 37.3
3 F	6 43 31	10 54 49	11♓38 01	18 22 28	5 44.4	20 07.7	6 32.8	11 58.5	2 02.3	5 15.2	7 00.2	2 44.6	27 15.6	4 38.9
4 Sa	6 47 28	11 52 01	25 00 13	1♈31 39	5R45.3	20 52.3	7 43.5	12 35.8	2 10.7	5 28.9	7 07.1	2 47.6	27 16.4	4 40.5
5 Su	6 51 24	12 49 13	7♈57 15	14 17 31	5 45.7	21 41.6	8 54.2	13 13.1	2 18.9	5 42.5	7 14.0	2 50.4	27 17.3	4 42.1
6 M	6 55 21	13 46 25	20 33 01	26 44 17	5 44.7	22 35.4	10 05.1	13 50.4	2 26.7	5 56.1	7 20.8	2 53.3	27 18.1	4 43.7
7 Tu	6 59 17	14 43 38	2♉51 54	8♉56 24	5 41.9	23 33.7	11 16.0	14 27.7	2 34.3	6 09.7	7 27.5	2 56.1	27 19.1	4 45.3
8 W	7 03 14	15 40 51	14 58 20	20 58 09	5 36.9	24 36.5	12 26.9	15 05.0	2 41.6	6 23.3	7 34.2	2 58.9	27 20.0	4 47.0
9 Th	7 07 10	16 38 05	26 56 22	2♊53 22	5 30.1	25 43.7	13 37.9	15 42.3	2 48.5	6 36.9	7 40.9	3 01.7	27 21.0	4 48.6
10 F	7 11 07	17 35 19	8♊49 34	14 45 18	5 21.9	26 55.2	14 49.0	16 19.7	2 55.2	6 50.5	7 47.5	3 04.4	27 21.9	4 50.2
11 Sa	7 15 03	18 32 33	20 40 53	26 36 37	5 13.1	28 11.0	16 00.1	16 57.1	3 01.7	7 04.0	7 54.0	3 07.1	27 23.0	4 51.9
12 Su	7 19 00	19 29 47	2♋32 43	8♋29 27	5 04.5	29 31.0	17 11.3	17 34.5	3 07.8	7 17.5	8 00.5	3 09.8	27 24.0	4 53.6
13 M	7 22 57	20 27 02	14 27 01	20 25 36	4 56.9	0♋55.2	18 22.5	18 11.9	3 13.6	7 31.0	8 07.0	3 12.5	27 25.1	4 55.2
14 Tu	7 26 53	21 24 17	26 25 25	2♌26 39	4 50.9	2 23.4	19 33.7	18 49.3	3 19.0	7 44.5	8 13.4	3 15.1	27 26.2	4 56.9
15 W	7 30 50	22 21 32	8♌29 32	14 34 14	4 46.9	3 55.6	20 45.1	19 26.8	3 24.2	7 58.0	8 19.7	3 17.6	27 27.4	4 58.6
16 Th	7 34 46	23 18 48	20 41 02	26 50 11	4D45.0	5 31.6	21 56.4	20 04.2	3 29.1	8 11.4	8 26.0	3 20.2	27 28.5	5 00.3
17 F	7 38 43	24 16 04	3♍01 58	9♍16 41	4 44.7	7 11.4	23 07.9	20 41.7	3 33.6	8 24.8	8 32.3	3 22.7	27 29.7	5 02.0
18 Sa	7 42 39	25 13 19	15 34 41	21 56 18	4 45.7	8 54.7	24 19.3	21 19.2	3 37.9	8 38.2	8 38.4	3 25.2	27 30.9	5 03.7
19 Su	7 46 36	26 10 35	28 21 55	4♎51 53	4 47.2	10 41.5	25 30.9	21 56.7	3 41.7	8 51.5	8 44.6	3 27.6	27 32.2	5 05.4
20 M	7 50 32	27 07 52	11♎26 34	18 06 18	4R48.3	12 31.4	26 42.4	22 34.2	3 45.3	9 04.8	8 50.6	3 30.0	27 33.5	5 07.1
21 Tu	7 54 29	28 05 08	24 51 22	1♏42 00	4 48.6	14 24.3	27 54.0	23 11.7	3 48.6	9 18.1	8 56.6	3 32.4	27 34.8	5 08.8
22 W	7 58 26	29 02 25	8♏38 19	15 40 22	4 47.5	16 20.0	29 05.7	23 49.3	3 51.5	9 31.4	9 02.6	3 34.7	27 36.1	5 10.5
23 Th	8 02 22	29 59 42	22 48 03	0♐01 06	4 44.9	18 18.1	0♋17.4	24 26.8	3 54.1	9 44.6	9 08.4	3 37.0	27 37.4	5 12.2
24 F	8 06 19	0♌57 00	7♐19 07	14 41 30	4 41.1	20 18.3	1 29.2	25 04.4	3 56.3	9 57.8	9 14.2	3 39.2	27 38.8	5 13.9
25 Sa	8 10 15	1 54 18	22 07 31	29 36 15	4 36.6	22 20.3	2 41.0	25 42.0	3 58.2	10 11.0	9 20.0	3 41.5	27 40.2	5 15.7
26 Su	8 14 12	2 51 36	7♑06 43	14♑37 47	4 32.2	24 23.8	3 52.9	26 19.6	3 59.8	10 24.1	9 25.7	3 43.6	27 41.7	5 17.4
27 M	8 18 08	3 48 55	22 08 18	29 37 08	4 28.4	26 28.5	5 04.8	26 57.2	4 01.0	10 37.2	9 31.3	3 45.8	27 43.1	5 19.1
28 Tu	8 22 05	4 46 15	7♒03 11	14♒25 27	4 25.8	28 34.0	6 16.8	27 34.9	4 01.9	10 50.2	9 36.9	3 47.9	27 44.6	5 20.8
29 W	8 26 01	5 43 35	21 43 03	28 55 16	4D24.7	0♌40.0	7 28.8	28 12.5	4R02.4	11 03.2	9 42.3	3 49.9	27 46.1	5 22.5
30 Th	8 29 58	6 40 56	6♓01 33	13♓01 30	4 24.8	2 46.2	8 40.9	28 50.2	4 02.6	11 16.2	9 47.7	3 52.0	27 47.6	5 24.3
31 F	8 33 55	7 38 18	19 54 56	26 41 46	4 25.9	4 52.3	9 53.0	29 27.9	4 02.4	11 29.1	9 53.1	3 53.9	27 49.2	5 26.0

August 1942 — **LONGITUDE**

Day	Sid.Time	☉	0 hr ☽	Noon ☽	True ☊	☿	♀	♂	⚳	♃	♄	♅	♆	♇
1 Sa	8 37 51	8♌35 42	3♈22 06	9♈56 09	4♍27.4	6♌58.1	11♋05.2	0♍05.6	4♈01.9	11♋42.0	9♊58.4	3♊55.9	27♍50.8	5♌27.7
2 Su	8 41 48	9 33 06	16 24 13	22 46 43	4 28.8	9 03.4	12 17.5	0 43.3	4R01.0	11 54.8	10 03.6	3 57.8	27 52.3	5 29.4
3 M	8 45 44	10 30 31	29 04 05	5♉16 52	4R29.6	11 07.9	13 29.8	1 21.1	3 59.7	12 07.6	10 08.7	3 59.6	27 54.0	5 31.1
4 Tu	8 49 41	11 27 58	11♉25 34	17 30 47	4 29.6	13 11.5	14 42.1	1 58.8	3 58.1	12 20.3	10 13.7	4 01.4	27 55.6	5 32.9
5 W	8 53 37	12 25 26	23 33 03	29 32 57	4 28.6	15 14.1	15 54.5	2 36.6	3 56.1	12 33.0	10 18.7	4 03.2	27 57.3	5 34.6
6 Th	8 57 34	13 22 56	5♊31 01	11♊27 48	4 26.6	17 15.5	17 07.0	3 14.4	3 53.8	12 45.7	10 23.6	4 04.9	27 59.0	5 36.3
7 F	9 01 30	14 20 26	17 23 48	23 19 30	4 24.0	19 15.7	18 19.5	3 52.3	3 51.1	12 58.3	10 28.4	4 06.6	28 00.7	5 38.0
8 Sa	9 05 27	15 17 58	29 15 20	5♋11 44	4 21.0	21 14.5	19 32.0	4 30.1	3 48.0	13 10.8	10 33.2	4 08.2	28 02.4	5 39.7
9 Su	9 09 24	16 15 31	11♋09 03	17 07 40	4 18.0	23 12.0	20 44.6	5 08.0	3 44.6	13 23.3	10 37.8	4 09.8	28 04.1	5 41.4
10 M	9 13 20	17 13 05	23 07 51	29 09 53	4 15.5	25 08.0	21 57.3	5 45.9	3 40.8	13 35.8	10 42.4	4 11.4	28 05.9	5 43.1
11 Tu	9 17 17	18 10 41	5♌14 02	11♌20 28	4 13.6	27 02.6	23 10.0	6 23.8	3 36.6	13 48.1	10 46.9	4 12.9	28 07.7	5 44.8
12 W	9 21 13	19 08 17	17 29 24	23 41 00	4D12.6	28 55.7	24 22.7	7 01.7	3 32.1	14 00.5	10 51.3	4 14.3	28 09.5	5 46.5
13 Th	9 25 10	20 05 55	29 55 24	6♍12 44	4 12.3	0♍47.3	25 35.5	7 39.7	3 27.2	14 12.7	10 55.7	4 15.7	28 11.3	5 48.2
14 F	9 29 06	21 03 34	12♍33 07	18 56 42	4 12.7	2 37.5	26 48.4	8 17.7	3 22.0	14 24.9	10 59.9	4 17.1	28 13.2	5 49.8
15 Sa	9 33 03	22 01 14	25 23 33	1♎53 48	4 13.6	4 26.1	28 01.3	8 55.7	3 16.4	14 37.1	11 04.1	4 18.4	28 15.1	5 51.5
16 Su	9 36 59	22 58 55	8♎27 33	15 04 54	4 14.6	6 13.4	29 14.2	9 33.7	3 10.4	14 49.1	11 08.2	4 19.6	28 16.9	5 53.2
17 M	9 40 56	23 56 37	21 45 57	28 30 46	4 15.5	7 59.1	0♌27.2	10 11.8	3 04.1	15 01.1	11 12.2	4 20.9	28 18.8	5 54.8
18 Tu	9 44 52	24 54 20	5♏19 23	12♏11 51	4R16.1	9 43.4	1 40.2	10 49.8	2 57.5	15 13.1	11 16.1	4 22.0	28 20.7	5 56.5
19 W	9 48 49	25 52 04	19 08 09	26 08 11	4 16.3	11 26.3	2 53.2	11 27.9	2 50.5	15 25.0	11 19.9	4 23.1	28 22.7	5 58.1
20 Th	9 52 46	26 49 50	3♐11 50	10♐18 53	4 16.1	13 07.8	4 06.3	12 06.0	2 43.2	15 36.8	11 23.6	4 24.2	28 24.6	5 59.8
21 F	9 56 42	27 47 36	17 29 04	24 41 59	4 15.6	14 47.8	5 19.5	12 44.1	2 35.5	15 48.5	11 27.2	4 25.2	28 26.6	6 01.4
22 Sa	10 00 39	28 45 24	1♑57 10	9♑14 06	4 15.1	16 26.5	6 32.7	13 22.3	2 27.6	16 00.2	11 30.8	4 26.2	28 28.6	6 03.0
23 Su	10 04 35	29 43 12	16 32 08	23 50 34	4 14.5	18 03.8	7 45.9	14 00.5	2 19.3	16 11.7	11 34.2	4 27.1	28 30.6	6 04.6
24 M	10 08 32	0♍41 02	1♒08 42	8♒25 45	4 14.1	19 39.7	8 59.2	14 38.7	2 10.7	16 23.3	11 37.6	4 28.0	28 32.6	6 06.2
25 Tu	10 12 28	1 38 54	15 40 57	22 53 34	4D13.9	21 14.2	10 12.5	15 16.9	2 01.7	16 34.7	11 40.8	4 28.9	28 34.6	6 07.8
26 W	10 16 25	2 36 46	0♓02 54	7♓08 19	4 13.9	22 47.3	11 25.9	15 55.1	1 52.5	16 46.1	11 44.0	4 29.6	28 36.6	6 09.4
27 Th	10 20 21	3 34 40	14 09 17	21 05 21	4R13.9	24 19.1	12 39.3	16 33.4	1 43.0	16 57.3	11 47.1	4 30.4	28 38.7	6 10.9
28 F	10 24 18	4 32 36	27 56 12	4♈41 35	4 14.0	25 49.6	13 52.8	17 11.6	1 33.2	17 08.5	11 50.0	4 31.0	28 40.7	6 12.5
29 Sa	10 28 15	5 30 34	11♈21 26	17 55 43	4 13.9	27 18.7	15 06.3	17 50.0	1 23.1	17 19.6	11 52.9	4 31.7	28 42.8	6 14.0
30 Su	10 32 11	6 28 33	24 24 35	0♉48 13	4 13.7	28 46.4	16 19.9	18 28.3	1 12.7	17 30.7	11 55.7	4 32.2	28 44.9	6 15.6
31 M	10 36 08	7 26 34	7♉06 54	13 21 01	4 13.4	0♎12.7	17 33.5	19 06.6	1 02.1	17 41.6	11 58.4	4 32.8	28 47.0	6 17.1

Astro Data

	Dy Hr Mn
☽0N	4 20:17
♃⚺♄	18 12:55
☽0S	19 14:36
⚳R	30 11:48
☽0N	1 5:34
☽0S	15 20:30
☽0N	28 15:20
☿0S	30 17:11

Planet Ingress

		Dy Hr Mn
☿	♋	12 20:24
♀	♋	23 6:10
☉	♌	23 12:07
☿	♌	29 4:24
♂	♍	1 8:27
☿	♍	13 1:48
♀	♌	17 3:04
☉	♍	23 18:58
☿	♎	31 8:27

Last Aspect / ☽ Ingress

Last Aspect Dy Hr Mn			☽ Ingress	Dy Hr Mn
1 8:49	♆	△	♓	2 3:46
4 4:09	♆	☍	♈	4 9:10
6 3:18	♆	⚹	♉	6 18:23
9 0:49	♆	△	♊	9 6:10
11 15:34	☿	☌	♋	11 18:51
14 2:00	♆	⚹	♌	14 7:08
16 1:26	♀	⚹	♍	16 18:08
18 22:26	♆	☌	♎	19 3:02
21 5:13	☉	□	♏	21 9:02
23 11:57	☉	△	♐	23 11:58
25 8:54	♆	□	♑	25 12:38
27 8:56	♆	△	♒	27 12:37
29 10:45	♂	☍	♓	29 13:49
31 14:01	♆	☍	♈	31 17:55

Last Aspect / ☽ Ingress

Last Aspect Dy Hr Mn			☽ Ingress	Dy Hr Mn
1 15:19	♃	□	♉	3 1:47
5 8:48	♆	△	♊	5 12:54
7 21:30	♆	□	♋	8 1:30
10 9:53	♆	⚹	♌	10 13:39
12 23:52	♆	☌	♍	13 0:09
15 5:16	♆	☌	♎	15 8:31
17 3:16	☉	⚹	♏	17 14:38
19 15:50	♆	⚹	♐	19 18:35
21 18:13	♆	□	♑	21 20:46
23 19:41	♆	△	♒	23 22:07
24 17:18	♄	△	♓	25 23:55
28 1:17	♆	☍	♈	28 3:39
29 10:53	♃	□	♉	30 10:29

☽ Phases & Eclipses

Dy Hr Mn		
5 8:58	☾	12♈42
13 12:03	●	20♋27
21 5:13	☽	27♎49
27 19:14	○	4♒06
3 23:04	☾	10♉57
12 2:28	●	18♌45
12 2:44:47	●	P 0.056
19 11:30	☽	25♏51
26 3:46	○	2♓17
26 3:48	●	T 1.535

Astro Data

1 July 1942
Julian Day # 15522
SVP 6♓03'52"
GC 26♐02.2 ⚳ 25♒04.0R
Eris 5♈39.7 ⚵ 7♏16.0R
⚷ 13♌33.3 ⚶ 10♒32.5R
☽ Mean ☊ 7♍13.9

1 August 1942
Julian Day # 15553
SVP 6♓03'48"
GC 26♐02.2 ⚳ 18♒53.9R
Eris 5♈34.7R ⚵ 9♏25.7
⚷ 17♌20.5 ⚶ 3♒55.3R
☽ Mean ☊ 5♍35.4

LONGITUDE — September 1942

Day	Sid.Time	☉	0 hr ☽	Noon☽	True☊	☿	♀	♂	⚳	♃	♄	♅	♆	♇
1 Tu	10 40 04	8♍24 37	19♉31 00	25♉37 19	4♍13.1	1♎37.6	18♌47.1	19♍45.0	0♈51.2	17♋52.5	12♊00.9	4♊33.2	28♍49.1	6♌18.6
2 W	10 44 01	9 22 42	1♊40 29	7♊41 04	4D 13.0	3 01.1	20 00.8	20 23.4	0R 40.1	18 03.3	12 03.4	4 33.7	28 51.2	6 20.1
3 Th	10 47 57	10 20 49	13 39 36	19 36 42	4 13.1	4 23.1	21 14.5	21 01.9	0 28.7	18 14.0	12 05.8	4 34.1	28 53.4	6 21.6
4 F	10 51 54	11 18 58	25 32 56	1♋28 53	4 13.5	5 43.6	22 28.3	21 40.4	0 17.1	18 24.6	12 08.1	4 34.4	28 55.5	6 23.0
5 Sa	10 55 50	12 17 09	7♋25 06	13 22 08	4 14.1	7 02.6	23 42.2	22 18.9	0 05.3	18 35.1	12 10.3	4 34.7	28 57.6	6 24.5
6 Su	10 59 47	13 15 22	19 20 30	25 20 42	4 15.0	8 20.1	24 56.0	22 57.4	29♓53.2	18 45.5	12 12.3	4 34.9	28 59.8	6 25.9
7 M	11 03 44	14 13 37	1♌23 10	7♌28 19	4 16.0	9 35.9	26 09.9	23 35.9	29 41.0	18 55.8	12 14.3	4 35.0	29 02.0	6 27.4
8 Tu	11 07 40	15 11 54	13 36 31	19 48 05	4 16.7	10 50.0	27 23.9	24 14.5	29 28.6	19 06.0	12 16.2	4 35.2	29 04.1	6 28.8
9 W	11 11 37	16 10 12	26 03 15	2♍22 13	4R 17.1	12 02.4	28 37.9	24 53.1	29 16.0	19 16.1	12 17.9	4R 35.2	29 06.3	6 30.2
10 Th	11 15 33	17 08 33	8♍45 08	15 12 04	4 16.8	13 12.9	29 51.9	25 31.8	29 03.3	19 26.1	12 19.6	4 35.3	29 08.5	6 31.6
11 F	11 19 30	18 06 55	21 43 02	28 17 58	4 15.9	14 21.5	1♍05.9	26 10.4	28 50.4	19 36.0	12 21.1	4 35.2	29 10.7	6 32.9
12 Sa	11 23 26	19 05 19	4♎56 46	11♎39 19	4 14.4	15 28.0	2 20.0	26 49.1	28 37.4	19 45.8	12 22.5	4 35.1	29 12.9	6 34.3
13 Su	11 27 23	20 03 44	18 25 23	25 14 44	4 12.3	16 32.4	3 34.2	27 27.8	28 24.3	19 55.5	12 23.9	4 35.0	29 15.1	6 35.6
14 M	11 31 19	21 02 12	2♏07 08	9♏02 17	4 10.1	17 34.4	4 48.3	28 06.6	28 11.1	20 05.1	12 25.1	4 34.8	29 17.3	6 36.9
15 Tu	11 35 16	22 00 41	15 59 53	22 59 39	4 08.1	18 34.0	6 02.5	28 45.3	27 57.8	20 14.5	12 26.2	4 34.6	29 19.5	6 38.2
16 W	11 39 13	22 59 12	0♐01 16	7♐04 27	4 06.6	19 31.0	7 16.8	29 24.1	27 44.4	20 23.9	12 27.2	4 34.3	29 21.7	6 39.5
17 Th	11 43 09	23 57 44	14 08 54	21 14 21	4D 06.0	20 25.2	8 31.1	0♎03.0	27 31.0	20 33.1	12 28.1	4 33.9	29 24.0	6 40.8
18 F	11 47 06	24 56 18	28 20 30	5♑27 05	4 06.3	21 16.4	9 45.4	0 41.8	27 17.5	20 42.3	12 28.9	4 33.6	29 26.2	6 42.0
19 Sa	11 51 02	25 54 53	12♑33 50	19 40 27	4 07.3	22 04.3	10 59.7	1 20.7	27 04.0	20 51.3	12 29.6	4 33.1	29 28.4	6 43.2
20 Su	11 54 59	26 53 31	26 46 38	3♒52 06	4 08.7	22 48.7	12 14.0	1 59.6	26 50.5	21 00.2	12 30.2	4 32.6	29 30.6	6 44.4
21 M	11 58 55	27 52 10	10♒56 31	17 59 31	4 10.0	23 29.4	13 28.4	2 38.5	26 37.0	21 08.9	12 30.6	4 32.1	29 32.9	6 45.6
22 Tu	12 02 52	28 50 50	25 00 47	1♓59 55	4R 10.6	24 06.0	14 42.9	3 17.5	26 23.5	21 17.6	12 31.0	4 31.5	29 35.1	6 46.8
23 W	12 06 48	29 49 32	8♓56 33	15 50 20	4 10.2	24 38.2	15 57.3	3 56.5	26 10.0	21 26.1	12 31.2	4 30.9	29 37.3	6 47.9
24 Th	12 10 45	0♎48 17	22 40 54	29 27 56	4 08.4	25 05.6	17 11.8	4 35.5	25 56.6	21 34.5	12R 31.4	4 30.2	29 39.5	6 49.1
25 F	12 14 41	1 47 03	6♈11 09	12♈50 18	4 05.3	25 27.9	18 26.3	5 14.5	25 43.3	21 42.8	12 31.4	4 29.4	29 41.8	6 50.2
26 Sa	12 18 38	2 45 51	19 25 12	25 55 45	4 01.1	25 44.6	19 40.9	5 53.6	25 30.0	21 50.9	12 31.3	4 28.6	29 44.0	6 51.3
27 Su	12 22 35	3 44 41	2♉21 54	8♉43 42	3 56.2	25 55.5	20 55.4	6 32.7	25 16.8	21 58.9	12 31.1	4 27.8	29 46.2	6 52.3
28 M	12 26 31	4 43 34	15 01 16	21 14 46	3 51.2	25R 59.9	22 10.0	7 11.8	25 03.7	22 06.8	12 30.8	4 26.9	29 48.5	6 53.4
29 Tu	12 30 28	5 42 29	27 24 29	3♊30 45	3 46.8	25 57.7	23 24.7	7 51.0	24 50.7	22 14.5	12 30.4	4 26.0	29 50.7	6 54.4
30 W	12 34 24	6 41 26	9♊33 58	15 34 35	3 43.3	25 48.3	24 39.3	8 30.2	24 37.8	22 22.1	12 29.9	4 25.0	29 52.9	6 55.4

LONGITUDE — October 1942

Day	Sid.Time	☉	0 hr ☽	Noon☽	True☊	☿	♀	♂	⚳	♃	♄	♅	♆	♇
1 Th	12 38 21	7♎40 25	21♊33 06	27♊30 04	3♍41.3	25♎31.6	25♍54.0	9♎09.5	24♓25.1	22♋29.6	12♊29.3	4♊24.0	29♍55.1	6♌56.4
2 F	12 42 17	8 39 27	3♋26 04	9♋21 41	3D 40.6	25R 07.1	27 08.8	9 48.7	24R 12.6	22 36.9	12R 28.5	4R 22.9	29 57.3	6 57.3
3 Sa	12 46 14	9 38 31	15 17 33	21 14 17	3 41.3	24 34.9	28 23.5	10 28.0	24 00.2	22 44.1	12 27.7	4 21.8	29 59.5	6 58.3
4 Su	12 50 10	10 37 37	27 12 32	3♌12 54	3 42.8	23 55.0	29 38.3	11 07.4	23 48.0	22 51.1	12 26.7	4 20.7	0♎01.7	6 59.2
5 M	12 54 07	11 36 46	9♌16 00	15 22 23	3 44.5	23 07.7	0♎53.1	11 46.7	23 36.0	22 58.0	12 25.7	4 19.5	0 03.9	7 00.1
6 Tu	12 58 04	12 35 56	21 32 36	27 47 06	3R 45.6	22 13.3	2 08.0	12 26.1	23 24.1	23 04.8	12 24.5	4 18.2	0 06.1	7 01.0
7 W	13 02 00	13 35 09	4♍06 18	10♍30 33	3 45.5	21 12.8	3 22.8	13 05.6	23 12.6	23 11.4	12 23.2	4 16.9	0 08.3	7 01.8
8 Th	13 05 57	14 34 24	17 00 04	23 34 59	3 43.8	20 07.3	4 37.7	13 45.0	23 01.2	23 17.8	12 21.8	4 15.6	0 10.5	7 02.6
9 F	13 09 53	15 33 42	0♎15 20	7♎01 00	3 40.0	18 58.0	5 52.6	14 24.5	22 50.1	23 24.1	12 20.3	4 14.2	0 12.7	7 03.4
10 Sa	13 13 50	16 33 01	13 51 48	20 47 21	3 34.4	17 46.8	7 07.5	15 04.1	22 39.2	23 30.2	12 18.7	4 12.8	0 14.8	7 04.2
11 Su	13 17 46	17 32 22	27 47 14	4♏50 53	3 27.6	16 35.4	8 22.5	15 43.6	22 28.6	23 36.2	12 17.0	4 11.3	0 17.0	7 04.9
12 M	13 21 43	18 31 46	11♏57 39	19 06 53	3 20.2	15 25.8	9 37.5	16 23.2	22 18.3	23 42.0	12 15.2	4 09.8	0 19.1	7 05.7
13 Tu	13 25 39	19 31 11	26 17 50	3♐29 49	3 13.3	14 20.2	10 52.4	17 02.9	22 08.2	23 47.6	12 13.3	4 08.2	0 21.3	7 06.4
14 W	13 29 36	20 30 38	10♐42 09	17 54 10	3 07.7	13 20.3	12 07.5	17 42.5	21 58.5	23 53.1	12 11.3	4 06.6	0 23.4	7 07.0
15 Th	13 33 33	21 30 07	25 05 20	2♑15 09	3 04.1	12 28.0	13 22.5	18 22.2	21 49.0	23 58.4	12 09.1	4 05.0	0 25.5	7 07.7
16 F	13 37 29	22 29 38	9♑23 14	16 29 16	3D 02.4	11 44.6	14 37.5	19 02.0	21 39.9	24 03.6	12 06.9	4 03.3	0 27.6	7 08.3
17 Sa	13 41 26	23 29 10	23 33 03	0♒34 26	3 02.5	11 11.3	15 52.6	19 41.7	21 31.1	24 08.6	12 04.6	4 01.6	0 29.7	7 08.9
18 Su	13 45 22	24 28 44	7♒33 20	14 29 41	3 03.4	10 48.7	17 07.6	20 21.5	21 22.6	24 13.4	12 02.2	3 59.9	0 31.8	7 09.5
19 M	13 49 19	25 28 20	21 23 29	28 14 44	3R 04.3	10D 37.4	18 22.7	21 01.3	21 14.4	24 18.0	11 59.7	3 58.1	0 33.9	7 10.0
20 Tu	13 53 15	26 27 57	5♓03 26	11♓49 34	3 04.0	10 37.2	19 37.8	21 41.2	21 06.6	24 22.5	11 57.1	3 56.3	0 35.9	7 10.6
21 W	13 57 12	27 27 37	18 33 07	25 14 02	3 01.8	10 48.0	20 52.9	22 21.1	20 59.1	24 26.8	11 54.4	3 54.4	0 38.0	7 11.1
22 Th	14 01 08	28 27 18	1♈52 14	8♈27 40	2 57.0	11 09.2	22 08.0	23 01.0	20 52.0	24 30.9	11 51.6	3 52.5	0 40.0	7 11.5
23 F	14 05 05	29 27 01	15 00 11	21 29 43	2 49.7	11 40.4	23 23.2	23 41.0	20 45.2	24 34.8	11 48.7	3 50.6	0 42.0	7 12.0
24 Sa	14 09 01	0♏26 45	27 56 09	4♉19 24	2 40.2	12 20.6	24 38.3	24 21.0	20 38.8	24 38.6	11 45.7	3 48.6	0 44.0	7 12.4
25 Su	14 12 58	1 26 32	10♉39 25	16 56 08	2 29.4	13 09.1	25 53.5	25 01.0	20 32.7	24 42.2	11 42.6	3 46.6	0 46.0	7 12.8
26 M	14 16 55	2 26 21	23 09 37	29 19 54	2 18.1	14 05.1	27 08.7	25 41.0	20 27.0	24 45.6	11 39.5	3 44.6	0 48.0	7 13.2
27 Tu	14 20 51	3 26 12	5♊27 08	11♊31 30	2 07.4	15 07.7	28 23.9	26 21.1	20 21.6	24 48.8	11 36.2	3 42.6	0 49.9	7 13.5
28 W	14 24 48	4 26 06	17 33 16	23 32 43	1 58.3	16 16.0	29 39.1	27 01.3	20 16.6	24 51.8	11 32.9	3 40.5	0 51.9	7 13.8
29 Th	14 28 44	5 26 01	29 30 16	5♋26 21	1 51.5	17 29.4	0♏54.3	27 41.5	20 12.0	24 54.7	11 29.5	3 38.4	0 53.8	7 14.1
30 F	14 32 41	6 25 58	11♋21 27	17 16 06	1 47.1	18 47.0	2 09.5	28 21.7	20 07.8	24 57.3	11 26.0	3 36.2	0 55.7	7 14.4
31 Sa	14 36 37	7 25 58	23 10 54	29 06 29	1D 45.1	20 08.4	3 24.8	29 01.9	20 03.9	24 59.8	11 22.4	3 34.1	0 57.6	7 14.6

Astro Data	Dy Hr Mn
♅ R	10 7:42
♃∠♅	11 10:05
☽ 0S	12 2:48
♂ 0S	20 6:38
☉ 0S	23 16:16
☽ 0N	25 0:31
♄ R	25 5:39
☿ R	28 16:13
♀ 0S	7 11:23
☽ 0S	9 11:02
☿ D	20 0:19
☽ 0N	22 8:28

Planet Ingress		Dy Hr Mn
⚳	♓R	5 22:33
♀	♍	10 14:38
♂	♎	17 10:11
☉	♎	23 16:16
♆	♎	3 17:00
♀	♎	4 18:58
☉	♏	24 1:15
♀	♏	28 18:40

Last Aspect Dy Hr Mn		☽ Ingress	Dy Hr Mn
1 18:21	♆ △	♊	1 20:40
4 6:49	♆ □	♋	4 9:00
6 19:17	♆ ⚹	♌	6 21:15
9 4:09	♀ ☌	♍	9 7:31
11 13:36	♆ ☌	♎	11 15:05
13 2:32	♃ □	♏	13 20:19
15 22:51	♆ ⚹	♐	15 23:58
18 1:49	♆ □	♑	18 2:48
20 4:36	♆ △	♒	20 5:27
21 21:50	☿ △	♓	22 8:34
24 12:21	♆ ☍	♈	24 12:57
26 11:39	☿ ☍	♉	26 19:34
29 4:45	♆ △	♊	29 5:05

Last Aspect Dy Hr Mn		☽ Ingress	Dy Hr Mn
1 16:54	♆ □	♋	1 17:03
4 4:02	♀ ⚹	♌	4 5:35
6 2:04	☿ ⚹	♍	6 16:13
8 11:29	♃ ⚹	♎	8 23:33
10 16:42	♃ □	♏	11 3:46
12 19:43	♃ △	♐	13 6:10
14 16:40	☉ ⚹	♑	15 8:13
17 0:57	♃ ☍	♒	17 11:01
19 6:45	☉ △	♓	19 15:05
21 10:34	♃ △	♈	21 20:37
23 17:46	♃ □	♉	24 3:52
26 3:04	♃ ⚹	♊	26 13:18
28 19:25	♂ △	♋	29 1:00
31 11:50	♂ □	♌	31 13:48

☽ Phases & Eclipses Dy Hr Mn		
2 15:42	☾	9♊32
10 15:53	●	17♍18
10 15:39:06	●	P 0.523
17 16:57	☽	24♐10
24 14:34	○	0♈55
2 10:27	☾	8♋36
10 4:06	●	16♎13
16 22:58	☽	22♑57
24 4:05	○	0♉07

Astro Data

1 September 1942
Julian Day # 15584
SVP 6♓03'44"
GC 26♐02.3 ⚴ 11♒20.4R
Eris 5♈20.6R ⚵ 15♏20.4
⚷ 21♌20.3 ⚶ 28♑40.0R
☽ Mean ☊ 3♍56.9

1 October 1942
Julian Day # 15614
SVP 6♓03'42"
GC 26♐02.4 ⚴ 7♒49.5R
Eris 5♈02.0R ⚵ 23♏23.4
⚷ 24♌55.0 ⚶ 0♒08.4
☽ Mean ☊ 2♍21.5

November 1942 LONGITUDE

Day	Sid.Time	☉	0 hr ☽	Noon ☽	True ☊	☿	♀	♂	⚳	♃	♄	♅	♆	♇
1 Su	14 40 34	8♏26 00	5♌03 29	11♌02 35	1♍44.7	21♎32.8	4♏40.1	29♎42.2	20♓00.4	25♋02.1	11♊18.8	3♊31.9	0♎59.5	7♌14.8
2 M	14 44 30	9 26 04	17 04 27	23 09 47	1R 45.2	22 59.9	5 55.3	0♏22.5	19R 57.3	25 04.2	11R 15.0	3R 29.7	1 01.3	7 15.0
3 Tu	14 48 27	10 26 09	29 19 14	5♍33 27	1 45.3	24 29.1	7 10.6	1 02.9	19 54.6	25 06.1	11 11.2	3 27.4	1 03.1	7 15.1
4 W	14 52 24	11 26 17	11♍53 00	18 18 23	1 44.1	26 00.1	8 25.9	1 43.3	19 52.2	25 07.8	11 07.4	3 25.2	1 04.9	7 15.3
5 Th	14 56 20	12 26 27	24 50 04	1♎28 20	1 40.6	27 32.5	9 41.2	2 23.7	19 50.2	25 09.3	11 03.4	3 22.9	1 06.7	7 15.4
6 F	15 00 17	13 26 40	8♎13 21	15 05 10	1 34.5	29 06.0	10 56.5	3 04.2	19 48.6	25 10.6	10 59.4	3 20.6	1 08.5	7 15.4
7 Sa	15 04 13	14 26 54	22 03 36	29 08 20	1 25.7	0♏40.5	12 11.9	3 44.7	19 47.4	25 11.7	10 55.3	3 18.2	1 10.3	7 15.5
8 Su	15 08 10	15 27 09	6♏18 49	13♏34 20	1 15.0	2 15.6	13 27.2	4 25.2	19 46.6	25 12.6	10 51.2	3 15.9	1 12.0	7R 15.5
9 M	15 12 06	16 27 27	20 54 03	28 16 56	1 03.5	3 51.3	14 42.6	5 05.8	19D 46.1	25 13.3	10 47.0	3 13.5	1 13.7	7 15.5
10 Tu	15 16 03	17 27 47	5♐41 55	13♐07 52	0 52.4	5 27.3	15 57.9	5 46.4	19 46.0	25 13.9	10 42.7	3 11.1	1 15.4	7 15.4
11 W	15 19 59	18 28 08	20 33 40	27 58 18	0 43.0	7 03.6	17 13.3	6 27.1	19 46.3	25 14.2	10 38.4	3 08.7	1 17.0	7 15.4
12 Th	15 23 56	19 28 30	5♑20 48	12♑40 22	0 36.2	8 40.1	18 28.6	7 07.8	19 47.0	25R 14.3	10 34.0	3 06.3	1 18.7	7 15.3
13 F	15 27 53	20 28 54	19 56 20	27 08 15	0 32.2	10 16.6	19 44.0	7 48.5	19 48.1	25 14.2	10 29.5	3 03.9	1 20.3	7 15.2
14 Sa	15 31 49	21 29 19	4♒15 46	11♒18 44	0D 30.6	11 53.1	20 59.4	8 29.3	19 49.5	25 13.9	10 25.1	3 01.4	1 21.9	7 15.0
15 Su	15 35 46	22 29 46	18 17 04	25 10 52	0R 30.3	13 29.6	22 14.8	9 10.1	19 51.3	25 13.5	10 20.5	2 58.9	1 23.4	7 14.8
16 M	15 39 42	23 30 14	2♓00 15	8♓45 26	0 30.2	15 06.0	23 30.1	9 50.9	19 53.4	25 12.8	10 16.0	2 56.5	1 25.0	7 14.6
17 Tu	15 43 39	24 30 43	15 26 39	22 04 08	0 28.9	16 42.3	24 45.5	10 31.8	19 56.0	25 11.9	10 11.3	2 54.0	1 26.5	7 14.4
18 W	15 47 35	25 31 13	28 38 09	5♈08 56	0 25.3	18 18.4	26 00.9	11 12.7	19 58.8	25 10.8	10 06.7	2 51.5	1 28.0	7 14.2
19 Th	15 51 32	26 31 45	11♈36 41	18 01 34	0 18.7	19 54.4	27 16.3	11 53.6	20 02.1	25 09.5	10 02.0	2 49.0	1 29.4	7 13.9
20 F	15 55 28	27 32 18	24 23 45	0♉43 20	0 09.0	21 30.2	28 31.7	12 34.6	20 05.7	25 08.1	9 57.3	2 46.5	1 30.9	7 13.6
21 Sa	15 59 25	28 32 52	7♉00 24	13 15 01	29♌56.7	23 05.8	29 47.1	13 15.6	20 09.6	25 06.4	9 52.5	2 44.0	1 32.3	7 13.2
22 Su	16 03 22	29 33 28	19 27 14	25 37 05	29 42.6	24 41.3	1♐02.4	13 56.6	20 13.9	25 04.5	9 47.7	2 41.5	1 33.7	7 12.9
23 M	16 07 18	0♐34 05	1♊44 37	7♊49 54	29 27.9	26 16.6	2 17.8	14 37.7	20 18.5	25 02.5	9 42.9	2 39.0	1 35.0	7 12.5
24 Tu	16 11 15	1 34 44	13 53 01	19 54 05	29 13.8	27 51.7	3 33.2	15 18.8	20 23.5	25 00.2	9 38.1	2 36.4	1 36.3	7 12.1
25 W	16 15 11	2 35 24	25 53 16	1♋50 46	29 01.5	29 26.7	4 48.6	16 00.0	20 28.8	24 57.7	9 33.2	2 33.9	1 37.6	7 11.7
26 Th	16 19 08	3 36 06	7♋46 51	13 41 49	28 51.7	1♐01.5	6 04.0	16 41.2	20 34.4	24 55.1	9 28.3	2 31.4	1 38.9	7 11.2
27 F	16 23 04	4 36 49	19 36 02	25 29 56	28 44.9	2 36.2	7 19.5	17 22.4	20 40.4	24 52.2	9 23.5	2 28.9	1 40.2	7 10.7
28 Sa	16 27 01	5 37 33	1♌23 58	7♌18 42	28 41.0	4 10.8	8 34.9	18 03.7	20 46.7	24 49.2	9 18.6	2 26.4	1 41.4	7 10.2
29 Su	16 30 57	6 38 19	13 14 41	19 12 31	28D 39.4	5 45.3	9 50.3	18 45.1	20 53.3	24 46.0	9 13.6	2 23.9	1 42.6	7 09.7
30 M	16 34 54	7 39 07	25 12 53	1♍16 26	28R 39.2	7 19.6	11 05.7	19 26.4	21 00.2	24 42.6	9 08.7	2 21.3	1 43.7	7 09.1

December 1942 LONGITUDE

Day	Sid.Time	☉	0 hr ☽	Noon ☽	True ☊	☿	♀	♂	⚳	♃	♄	♅	♆	♇
1 Tu	16 38 51	8♐39 56	7♍23 52	13♍35 52	28♌39.1	8♐53.9	12♐21.1	20♏07.8	21♓07.4	24♋38.9	9♊03.8	2♊18.8	1♎44.8	7♌08.5
2 W	16 42 47	9 40 46	19 53 06	26 16 12	28R 38.1	10 28.2	13 36.6	20 49.3	21 15.0	24R 35.2	8R 58.9	2R 16.3	1 45.9	7R 07.9
3 Th	16 46 44	10 41 38	2♎45 45	9♎22 13	28 35.2	12 02.4	14 52.0	21 30.7	21 22.9	24 31.2	8 53.9	2 13.8	1 47.0	7 07.3
4 F	16 50 40	11 42 31	16 06 00	22 57 19	28 29.6	13 36.5	16 07.4	22 12.3	21 31.0	24 27.0	8 49.0	2 11.4	1 48.0	7 06.6
5 Sa	16 54 37	12 43 26	29 56 14	7♏02 35	28 21.4	15 10.6	17 22.9	22 53.8	21 39.5	24 22.7	8 44.1	2 08.9	1 49.0	7 05.9
6 Su	16 58 33	13 44 22	14♏16 02	21 35 58	28 11.2	16 44.8	18 38.3	23 35.4	21 48.3	24 18.2	8 39.2	2 06.4	1 50.0	7 05.2
7 M	17 02 30	14 45 19	29 01 33	6♐31 47	27 59.8	18 18.9	19 53.7	24 17.1	21 57.3	24 13.5	8 34.3	2 04.0	1 50.9	7 04.5
8 Tu	17 06 26	15 46 17	14♐05 27	21 41 14	27 48.8	19 53.1	21 09.2	24 58.7	22 06.7	24 08.6	8 29.4	2 01.5	1 51.8	7 03.8
9 W	17 10 23	16 47 16	29 17 45	6♑53 38	27 39.3	21 27.3	22 24.6	25 40.5	22 16.3	24 03.6	8 24.6	1 59.1	1 52.7	7 03.0
10 Th	17 14 20	17 48 16	14♑27 34	21 58 23	27 32.4	23 01.6	23 40.1	26 22.2	22 26.3	23 58.4	8 19.7	1 56.7	1 53.6	7 02.2
11 F	17 18 16	18 49 17	29 25 04	6♒46 49	27 28.3	24 35.9	24 55.5	27 04.0	22 36.5	23 53.0	8 14.9	1 54.3	1 54.4	7 01.4
12 Sa	17 22 13	19 50 18	14♒03 02	21 13 18	27D 26.6	26 10.3	26 11.0	27 45.8	22 47.0	23 47.5	8 10.2	1 52.0	1 55.2	7 00.5
13 Su	17 26 09	20 51 19	28 17 25	5♓15 21	27 26.7	27 44.7	27 26.4	28 27.7	22 57.7	23 41.8	8 05.4	1 49.6	1 55.9	6 59.7
14 M	17 30 06	21 52 21	12♓07 13	18 53 14	27R 27.1	29 19.2	28 41.8	29 09.6	23 08.7	23 36.0	8 00.7	1 47.3	1 56.6	6 58.8
15 Tu	17 34 02	22 53 24	25 33 41	2♈08 57	27 26.7	0♑53.8	29 57.2	29 51.5	23 20.0	23 30.0	7 56.0	1 45.0	1 57.3	6 57.9
16 W	17 37 59	23 54 26	8♈39 24	15 05 28	27 24.5	2 28.4	1♑12.7	0♐33.5	23 31.6	23 23.9	7 51.4	1 42.7	1 57.9	6 57.0
17 Th	17 41 55	24 55 30	21 27 32	27 46 00	27 19.7	4 03.1	2 28.1	1 15.5	23 43.4	23 17.6	7 46.8	1 40.4	1 58.5	6 56.0
18 F	17 45 52	25 56 33	4♉01 14	10♉13 34	27 12.3	5 37.9	3 43.5	1 57.5	23 55.4	23 11.2	7 42.2	1 38.2	1 59.1	6 55.1
19 Sa	17 49 49	26 57 37	16 23 19	22 30 43	27 02.6	7 12.7	4 58.9	2 39.6	24 07.7	23 04.7	7 37.7	1 36.0	1 59.7	6 54.1
20 Su	17 53 45	27 58 42	28 36 02	4♊39 28	26 51.3	8 47.5	6 14.3	3 21.7	24 20.2	22 58.0	7 33.2	1 33.8	2 00.2	6 53.1
21 M	17 57 42	28 59 47	10♊41 12	16 41 24	26 39.4	10 22.2	7 29.7	4 03.9	24 33.0	22 51.3	7 28.8	1 31.6	2 00.7	6 52.1
22 Tu	18 01 38	0♑00 52	22 40 14	28 37 51	26 28.0	11 56.9	8 45.1	4 46.1	24 46.0	22 44.4	7 24.5	1 29.5	2 01.1	6 51.0
23 W	18 05 35	1 01 58	4♋34 24	10♋30 05	26 18.0	13 31.5	10 00.5	5 28.3	24 59.2	22 37.4	7 20.2	1 27.4	2 01.5	6 50.0
24 Th	18 09 31	2 03 04	16 25 05	22 19 38	26 10.3	15 05.9	11 15.8	6 10.6	25 12.7	22 30.3	7 15.9	1 25.3	2 01.9	6 48.9
25 F	18 13 28	3 04 11	28 14 00	4♌08 28	26 05.0	16 40.0	12 31.2	6 52.9	25 26.3	22 23.1	7 11.7	1 23.2	2 02.2	6 47.8
26 Sa	18 17 25	4 05 18	10♌03 23	15 59 08	26D 02.3	18 13.8	13 46.6	7 35.3	25 40.2	22 15.8	7 07.6	1 21.2	2 02.5	6 46.7
27 Su	18 21 21	5 06 26	21 56 08	27 54 52	26 01.7	19 47.2	15 02.0	8 17.7	25 54.4	22 08.4	7 03.6	1 19.2	2 02.8	6 45.6
28 M	18 25 18	6 07 34	3♍55 51	9♍59 36	26 02.5	21 19.9	16 17.3	9 00.1	26 08.7	22 00.9	6 59.6	1 17.3	2 03.0	6 44.5
29 Tu	18 29 14	7 08 42	16 06 44	22 17 49	26 03.8	22 51.8	17 32.7	9 42.6	26 23.2	21 53.3	6 55.7	1 15.4	2 03.2	6 43.3
30 W	18 33 11	8 09 51	28 33 29	4♎54 18	26R 04.7	24 22.9	18 48.1	10 25.1	26 38.0	21 45.7	6 51.8	1 13.5	2 03.4	6 42.2
31 Th	18 37 07	9 11 00	11♎20 51	17 53 40	26 04.3	25 52.7	20 03.4	11 07.7	26 52.9	21 37.9	6 48.0	1 11.6	2 03.5	6 41.0

Astro Data

	Dy Hr Mn
☽ 0S	5 21:20
♇ R	8 14:41
⚳ D	10 4:55
♃ R	12 14:25
♃∠♄	17 8:21
☽ 0N	18 15:17
☽ 0S	3 8:17
♅△♆	11 11:38
☽ 0N	15 22:02
♃∠♄	28 20:40
☽ 0S	30 17:47

Planet Ingress

		Dy Hr Mn
♂	♏	1 22:36
☿	♏	7 1:44
☊	♌R	21 5:55
♀	♐	21 16:07
☉	♐	22 22:30
☿	♐	25 20:26
☿	♑	14 22:21
♀	♑	15 12:53
♂	♐	15 16:51
☉	♑	22 11:40

Last Aspect / ☽ Ingress (November)

Last Aspect Dy Hr Mn		☽ Ingress	Dy Hr Mn
2 11:38	☿ ⚹	♍	3 1:19
5 0:34	♃ ⚹	♎	5 9:21
7 5:20	♃ □	♏	7 13:27
9 7:02	♃ △	♐	9 14:47
10 8:07	♄ ☍	♑	11 15:18
13 8:49	♃ ☍	♒	13 16:48
15 6:57	☉ □	♓	15 20:28
17 17:42	♃ △	♈	18 2:30
20 1:25	♃ □	♉	20 10:38
22 20:24	☉ ☍	♊	22 20:35
23 15:42	♄ ☌	♋	25 8:17
27 10:44	♃ ☌	♌	27 21:09
29 11:02	♂ □	♍	30 9:29

Last Aspect / ☽ Ingress (December)

Last Aspect Dy Hr Mn		☽ Ingress	Dy Hr Mn
2 8:52	♃ ⚹	♎	2 18:55
4 14:34	♃ □	♏	5 0:06
6 16:22	♃ △	♐	7 1:34
8 11:05	♀ ☌	♑	9 1:07
10 19:25	♂ ⚹	♒	11 0:57
12 23:41	♂ □	♓	13 2:56
15 7:35	♂ △	♈	15 8:04
17 6:06	☉ △	♉	17 16:16
19 13:06	♃ ⚹	♊	20 2:46
20 17:43	♄ ☌	♋	22 14:46
24 12:21	♃ ☌	♌	25 3:35
25 18:10	♄ ⚹	♍	27 16:10
29 13:15	☿ △	♎	30 2:44

☽ Phases & Eclipses

Dy Hr Mn		
1 6:18	☾	8♌12
8 15:19	●	15♏35
15 6:57	☽	22♒17
22 20:24	○	29♉55
1 1:37	☾	8♍14
8 1:59	●	15♐21
14 17:47	☽	22♓07
22 15:03	○	0♋09
30 18:37	☾	8♎27

Astro Data

1 November 1942
Julian Day # 15645
SVP 6♓03'39"
GC 26♐02.5 ⚴ 9♒29.4
Eris 4♈43.3R ⚵ 3♐11.5
⚷ 27♌46.9 ⚶ 7♒30.5
☽ Mean ☊ 0♍43.0

1 December 1942
Julian Day # 15675
SVP 6♓03'35"
GC 26♐02.5 ⚴ 14♒58.3
Eris 4♈31.2R ⚵ 13♐29.1
⚷ 29♌14.4 ⚶ 18♒06.8
☽ Mean ☊ 29♌07.7

LONGITUDE

January 1943

Day	Sid.Time	☉	0 hr ☽	Noon ☽	True ☊	☿	♀	♂	⚳	♃	♄	♅	♆	♇
1 F	18 41 04	10♑12 10	24♎33 13	1♏19 52	26♌02.2	27♑21.1	21♑18.8	11♐50.2	27♓08.1	21♋30.2	6♊44.4	1♊09.8	2♎03.6	6♌39.8
2 Sa	18 45 00	11 13 20	8♏13 49	15 15 11	25R 58.1	28 47.8	22 34.1	12 32.9	27 23.4	21R 22.3	6R 40.7	1R 08.1	2 03.7	6R 38.6
3 Su	18 48 57	12 14 31	22 23 50	29 39 29	25 52.3	0♒12.4	23 49.5	13 15.6	27 38.9	21 14.4	6 37.2	1 06.3	2R 03.7	6 37.4
4 M	18 52 54	13 15 42	7♐01 35	14♐29 22	25 45.6	1 34.4	25 04.8	13 58.3	27 54.7	21 06.5	6 33.7	1 04.6	2 03.7	6 36.1
5 Tu	18 56 50	14 16 53	22 01 53	29 38 00	25 38.9	2 53.5	26 20.2	14 41.0	28 10.6	20 58.5	6 30.4	1 03.0	2 03.7	6 34.9
6 W	19 00 47	15 18 04	7♑16 24	14♑55 43	25 33.1	4 09.1	27 35.5	15 23.8	28 26.7	20 50.5	6 27.1	1 01.4	2 03.6	6 33.6
7 Th	19 04 43	16 19 15	22 34 34	0♒11 34	25 28.9	5 20.5	28 50.8	16 06.6	28 43.0	20 42.4	6 23.9	0 59.8	2 03.5	6 32.4
8 F	19 08 40	17 20 25	7♒45 28	15 15 10	25D 26.7	6 27.1	0♒06.1	16 49.5	28 59.5	20 34.3	6 20.8	0 58.3	2 03.4	6 31.1
9 Sa	19 12 36	18 21 35	22 39 42	29 58 22	25 26.4	7 28.1	1 21.4	17 32.4	29 16.1	20 26.3	6 17.8	0 56.8	2 03.2	6 29.8
10 Su	19 16 33	19 22 45	7♓10 37	14♓16 07	25 27.4	8 22.8	2 36.7	18 15.3	29 33.0	20 18.2	6 14.9	0 55.3	2 03.0	6 28.5
11 M	19 20 29	20 23 54	21 14 45	28 06 33	25 29.0	9 10.2	3 52.0	18 58.3	29 50.0	20 10.1	6 12.0	0 53.9	2 02.7	6 27.2
12 Tu	19 24 26	21 25 02	4♈51 39	11♈30 21	25R 30.3	9 49.4	5 07.3	19 41.3	0♈07.1	20 02.0	6 09.3	0 52.6	2 02.5	6 25.9
13 W	19 28 23	22 26 10	18 03 00	24 30 03	25 30.7	10 19.7	6 22.5	20 24.3	0 24.4	19 53.9	6 06.7	0 51.3	2 02.1	6 24.6
14 Th	19 32 19	23 27 17	0♉51 57	7♉09 11	25 29.7	10 40.0	7 37.7	21 07.4	0 41.9	19 45.8	6 04.1	0 50.0	2 01.8	6 23.2
15 F	19 36 16	24 28 24	13 22 15	19 31 40	25 27.2	10R 49.7	8 53.0	21 50.5	0 59.6	19 37.8	6 01.7	0 48.8	2 01.4	6 21.9
16 Sa	19 40 12	25 29 30	25 37 53	1♊41 23	25 23.3	10 48.2	10 08.2	22 33.6	1 17.4	19 29.7	5 59.4	0 47.6	2 01.0	6 20.6
17 Su	19 44 09	26 30 35	7♊42 36	13 41 55	25 18.5	10 35.0	11 23.4	23 16.8	1 35.3	19 21.7	5 57.1	0 46.5	2 00.6	6 19.2
18 M	19 48 05	27 31 39	19 39 42	25 36 20	25 13.3	10 10.0	12 38.5	24 00.0	1 53.4	19 13.8	5 55.0	0 45.4	2 00.1	6 17.9
19 Tu	19 52 02	28 32 43	1♋32 05	7♋27 16	25 08.2	9 33.7	13 53.7	24 43.2	2 11.6	19 05.9	5 53.0	0 44.4	1 59.6	6 16.5
20 W	19 55 58	29 33 46	13 22 09	19 16 58	25 03.9	8 46.5	15 08.9	25 26.5	2 30.0	18 58.1	5 51.1	0 43.4	1 59.0	6 15.1
21 Th	19 59 55	0♒34 48	25 11 59	1♌07 24	25 00.7	7 49.8	16 24.0	26 09.8	2 48.5	18 50.3	5 49.3	0 42.5	1 58.5	6 13.8
22 F	20 03 52	1 35 50	7♌03 27	13 00 23	24 58.8	6 45.0	17 39.1	26 53.2	3 07.2	18 42.5	5 47.6	0 41.6	1 57.9	6 12.4
23 Sa	20 07 48	2 36 51	18 58 27	24 57 53	24D 58.2	5 34.1	18 54.2	27 36.6	3 26.0	18 34.9	5 46.0	0 40.8	1 57.2	6 11.0
24 Su	20 11 45	3 37 51	0♍58 59	7♍02 03	24 58.7	4 19.3	20 09.3	28 20.0	3 44.9	18 27.3	5 44.5	0 40.0	1 56.5	6 09.7
25 M	20 15 41	4 38 50	13 07 23	19 15 22	25 00.0	3 02.8	21 24.3	29 03.5	4 04.0	18 19.8	5 43.1	0 39.3	1 55.8	6 08.3
26 Tu	20 19 38	5 39 49	25 26 21	1♎40 43	25 01.6	1 47.0	22 39.4	29 47.0	4 23.1	18 12.3	5 41.8	0 38.6	1 55.1	6 06.9
27 W	20 23 34	6 40 48	7♎58 53	14 21 16	25 03.1	0 34.0	23 54.4	0♑30.5	4 42.5	18 05.0	5 40.6	0 37.9	1 54.4	6 05.5
28 Th	20 27 31	7 41 45	20 48 16	27 20 17	25R 04.1	29♑25.6	25 09.4	1 14.1	5 01.9	17 57.8	5 39.6	0 37.4	1 53.6	6 04.2
29 F	20 31 27	8 42 42	3♏57 40	10♏40 44	25 04.3	28 23.4	26 24.4	1 57.7	5 21.5	17 50.6	5 38.6	0 36.8	1 52.8	6 02.8
30 Sa	20 35 24	9 43 39	17 29 44	24 24 48	25 03.8	27 28.5	27 39.4	2 41.4	5 41.1	17 43.6	5 37.8	0 36.4	1 51.9	6 01.4
31 Su	20 39 21	10 44 34	1♐26 00	8♐33 12	25 02.7	26 41.7	28 54.3	3 25.1	6 00.9	17 36.6	5 37.1	0 35.9	1 51.0	6 00.0

LONGITUDE

February 1943

Day	Sid.Time	☉	0 hr ☽	Noon ☽	True ☊	☿	♀	♂	⚳	♃	♄	♅	♆	♇
1 M	20 43 17	11♒45 30	15♐46 12	23♐04 34	25♌01.1	26♑03.4	0♓09.3	4♑08.8	6♈20.9	17♋29.8	5♊36.5	0♊35.6	1♎50.1	5♌58.7
2 Tu	20 47 14	12 46 24	0♑27 43	7♑54 56	24R 59.5	25R 33.8	1 24.2	4 52.6	6 40.9	17R 23.1	5R 36.0	0R 35.2	1R 49.2	5R 57.3
3 W	20 51 10	13 47 17	15 25 18	22 57 48	24 58.1	25 12.7	2 39.1	5 36.4	7 01.0	17 16.6	5 35.6	0 35.0	1 48.2	5 55.9
4 Th	20 55 07	14 48 10	0♒31 20	8♒04 42	24 57.2	25 00.0	3 54.0	6 20.2	7 21.3	17 10.1	5 35.4	0 34.8	1 47.2	5 54.6
5 F	20 59 03	15 49 01	15 36 45	23 06 20	24D 56.9	24D 55.3	5 08.9	7 04.1	7 41.7	17 03.8	5D 35.2	0 34.6	1 46.2	5 53.2
6 Sa	21 03 00	16 49 51	0♓32 23	7♓53 59	24 57.0	24 58.1	6 23.7	7 48.0	8 02.2	16 57.7	5 35.2	0 34.5	1 45.2	5 51.9
7 Su	21 06 56	17 50 39	15 10 19	22 20 46	24 57.5	25 07.9	7 38.5	8 31.9	8 22.7	16 51.6	5 35.3	0D 34.4	1 44.1	5 50.5
8 M	21 10 53	18 51 26	29 24 52	6♈22 20	24 58.2	25 24.4	8 53.3	9 15.8	8 43.4	16 45.8	5 35.4	0 34.4	1 43.0	5 49.2
9 Tu	21 14 50	19 52 12	13♈13 02	19 57 01	24 58.7	25 46.9	10 08.1	9 59.8	9 04.2	16 40.0	5 35.7	0 34.5	1 41.9	5 47.9
10 W	21 18 46	20 52 56	26 34 25	3♉05 32	24 59.1	26 15.0	11 22.8	10 43.8	9 25.1	16 34.5	5 36.2	0 34.6	1 40.8	5 46.5
11 Th	21 22 43	21 53 38	9♉30 43	15 50 24	24R 59.3	26 48.2	12 37.5	11 27.9	9 46.0	16 29.1	5 36.7	0 34.8	1 39.6	5 45.2
12 F	21 26 39	22 54 19	22 05 06	28 15 20	24 59.3	27 26.2	13 52.2	12 11.9	10 07.1	16 23.8	5 37.3	0 35.0	1 38.4	5 43.9
13 Sa	21 30 36	23 54 58	4♊21 39	10♊24 37	24D 59.3	28 08.5	15 06.8	12 56.0	10 28.3	16 18.7	5 38.1	0 35.2	1 37.2	5 42.6
14 Su	21 34 32	24 55 36	16 24 48	22 22 46	24 59.2	28 54.8	16 21.4	13 40.2	10 49.5	16 13.8	5 39.0	0 35.6	1 36.0	5 41.3
15 M	21 38 29	25 56 12	28 19 03	4♋14 10	24 59.3	29 44.8	17 36.0	14 24.3	11 10.9	16 09.0	5 40.0	0 35.9	1 34.7	5 40.0
16 Tu	21 42 25	26 56 46	10♋08 37	16 02 51	24 59.5	0♒38.1	18 50.5	15 08.5	11 32.3	16 04.5	5 41.1	0 36.4	1 33.4	5 38.8
17 W	21 46 22	27 57 19	21 57 18	27 52 22	24 59.8	1 34.5	20 05.0	15 52.8	11 53.8	16 00.1	5 42.3	0 36.8	1 32.1	5 37.5
18 Th	21 50 19	28 57 49	3♌48 24	9♌45 45	25 00.1	2 33.8	21 19.5	16 37.0	12 15.4	15 55.8	5 43.6	0 37.4	1 30.8	5 36.2
19 F	21 54 15	29 58 19	15 44 42	21 45 31	25R 00.2	3 35.8	22 33.9	17 21.3	12 37.0	15 51.8	5 45.0	0 37.9	1 29.5	5 35.0
20 Sa	21 58 12	0♓58 46	27 48 27	3♍53 41	25 00.2	4 40.2	23 48.3	18 05.6	12 58.8	15 47.9	5 46.6	0 38.6	1 28.1	5 33.8
21 Su	22 02 08	1 59 12	10♍01 26	16 11 52	24 59.7	5 46.8	25 02.7	18 50.0	13 20.6	15 44.2	5 48.2	0 39.3	1 26.7	5 32.6
22 M	22 06 05	2 59 36	22 25 08	28 41 23	24 58.9	6 55.6	26 17.0	19 34.4	13 42.5	15 40.7	5 50.0	0 40.0	1 25.3	5 31.4
23 Tu	22 10 01	3 59 59	5♎00 45	11♎23 23	24 57.8	8 06.5	27 31.3	20 18.8	14 04.5	15 37.4	5 51.8	0 40.8	1 23.9	5 30.2
24 W	22 13 58	5 00 20	17 49 23	24 18 55	24 56.4	9 19.2	28 45.6	21 03.2	14 26.5	15 34.2	5 53.8	0 41.6	1 22.5	5 29.0
25 Th	22 17 54	6 00 40	0♏52 05	7♏29 01	24 55.1	10 33.7	29 59.8	21 47.7	14 48.6	15 31.3	5 55.9	0 42.5	1 21.0	5 27.8
26 F	22 21 51	7 00 59	14 09 49	20 54 35	24 54.1	11 49.8	1♈14.0	22 32.2	15 10.8	15 28.5	5 58.1	0 43.5	1 19.6	5 26.7
27 Sa	22 25 47	8 01 16	27 43 23	4♐36 17	24D 53.7	13 07.6	2 28.1	23 16.7	15 33.1	15 25.9	6 00.4	0 44.5	1 18.1	5 25.5
28 Su	22 29 44	9 01 32	11♐33 15	18 34 16	24 53.8	14 26.9	3 42.2	24 01.3	15 55.4	15 23.6	6 02.8	0 45.5	1 16.6	5 24.4

Astro Data (Dy Hr Mn)

♄⚹♇ 3 10:24
♆ R 3 21:20
☽ 0N 12 6:01
☿ R 15 20:48
☽ 0S 27 0:48

☿ D 5 14:50
♄ D 6 7:52
♅ D 8 0:53
☽ 0N 8 15:39
♄⚹♇ 15 12:37
♃∠♅ 22 15:55
☽ 0S 23 6:27
♀0N 27 10:34
⚳0N 28 8:37

Planet Ingress (Dy Hr Mn)

☿ ♒ 3 8:27
♀ ♒ 8 10:03
⚳ ♈ 12 2:04
☉ ♒ 20 22:19
♂ ♑ 26 19:10
☿ ♑R 27 23:42

♀ ♓ 1 9:02
☿ ♒ 15 19:00
☉ ♓ 19 12:40
♀ ♈ 25 12:04

Last Aspect (Dy Hr Mn) — **☽ Ingress** (Dy Hr Mn)

1 4:08 ☿ □ ♏ 1 9:40
3 1:27 ♀ ⚹ ♐ 3 12:34
4 11:08 ♂ ☌ ♑ 5 12:35
7 9:41 ♀ ☌ ♒ 7 11:42
8 14:40 ♂ ⚹ ♓ 9 12:03
10 22:16 ♃ △ ♈ 11 15:20
13 7:49 ☉ □ ♉ 13 22:22
15 22:36 ☉ △ ♊ 16 8:39
18 8:33 ♂ ☍ ♋ 18 20:54
20 11:22 ♃ ☌ ♌ 21 9:44
23 17:37 ♂ △ ♍ 23 22:03
26 8:09 ♂ □ ♎ 26 8:47
28 15:31 ☿ □ ♏ 28 16:51
30 18:06 ♀ □ ♐ 30 21:34

Last Aspect (Dy Hr Mn) — **☽ Ingress** (Dy Hr Mn)

31 15:56 ☉ ⚹ ♑ 1 23:15
3 15:30 ☿ ☌ ♒ 3 23:10
4 23:29 ☉ ☌ ♓ 5 23:07
7 16:47 ☿ ⚹ ♈ 8 1:00
9 22:55 ☿ □ ♉ 10 6:17
12 10:19 ☿ △ ♊ 12 15:25
14 17:37 ☉ △ ♋ 15 3:24
16 18:21 ♀ △ ♌ 17 16:18
18 3:51 ♄ ⚹ ♍ 20 4:20
22 6:54 ♀ ☍ ♎ 22 14:30
24 5:37 ♂ □ ♏ 24 22:25
26 15:02 ♂ ⚹ ♐ 27 3:59

☽ Phases & Eclipses (Dy Hr Mn)

6 12:38 ● 15♑20
13 7:49 ☽ 22♈15
21 10:48 ○ 0♌32
29 8:13 ☾ 8♏33

4 23:29 ● 15♒17
4 23:37:45 ● T 02'35"
12 0:40 ☽ 22♉26
20 5:45 ○ 0♍43
20 5:38 ● P 0.761
27 18:22 ☾ 8♐17

Astro Data

1 January 1943
Julian Day # 15706
SVP 6♓03'30"
GC 26♐02.6 ⚵ 23♒07.6
Eris 4♈28.8 ⚶ 24♐24.7
⚷ 29♌03.1R ⚴ 1♓05.1
☽ Mean ☊ 27♌29.2

1 February 1943
Julian Day # 15737
SVP 6♓03'25"
GC 26♐02.7 ⚵ 2♓43.1
Eris 4♈37.6 ⚶ 5♑05.6
⚷ 27♌19.1R ⚴ 15♓07.6
☽ Mean ☊ 25♌50.7

March 1943 — LONGITUDE

Day	Sid.Time	☉	0 hr ☽	Noon ☽	True ☊	☿	♀	♂	⚳	♃	♄	♅	♆	♇
1 M	22 33 41	10♓01 46	25♐39 11	2♑47 49	24♌54.6	15♒47.7	4♈56.3	24♑45.9	16♈17.8	15♋21.4	6♊05.3	0♊46.6	1♎15.1	5♌23.3
2 Tu	22 37 37	11 01 59	9♑59 54	17 15 01	24 55.7	17 09.9	6 10.3	25 30.5	16 40.3	15R 19.4	6 07.9	0 47.8	1R 13.5	5R 22.2
3 W	22 41 34	12 02 10	24 32 43	1♒52 26	24 56.9	18 33.5	7 24.3	26 15.1	17 02.8	15 17.6	6 10.6	0 49.0	1 12.0	5 21.2
4 Th	22 45 30	13 02 20	9♒13 28	16 35 07	24R 57.8	19 58.3	8 38.3	26 59.8	17 25.4	15 16.0	6 13.4	0 50.2	1 10.5	5 20.1
5 F	22 49 27	14 02 28	23 56 32	1♓16 55	24 57.8	21 24.5	9 52.2	27 44.5	17 48.0	15 14.6	6 16.4	0 51.5	1 08.9	5 19.1
6 Sa	22 53 23	15 02 34	8♓35 22	15 51 05	24 56.8	22 52.0	11 06.1	28 29.2	18 10.8	15 13.4	6 19.4	0 52.9	1 07.3	5 18.1
7 Su	22 57 20	16 02 38	23 03 16	0♈11 11	24 54.8	24 20.6	12 19.9	29 13.9	18 33.5	15 12.4	6 22.5	0 54.3	1 05.7	5 17.1
8 M	23 01 16	17 02 40	7♈14 14	14 11 55	24 51.8	25 50.5	13 33.7	29 58.7	18 56.4	15 11.6	6 25.7	0 55.7	1 04.1	5 16.1
9 Tu	23 05 13	18 02 40	21 03 52	27 49 50	24 48.3	27 21.6	14 47.4	0♒43.5	19 19.2	15 11.0	6 29.1	0 57.2	1 02.5	5 15.1
10 W	23 09 10	19 02 38	4♉29 43	11♉03 34	24 44.8	28 53.9	16 01.1	1 28.3	19 42.2	15 10.6	6 32.5	0 58.8	1 00.9	5 14.2
11 Th	23 13 06	20 02 34	17 31 32	23 53 52	24 41.7	0♓27.4	17 14.8	2 13.1	20 05.2	15D 10.3	6 36.0	1 00.3	0 59.3	5 13.3
12 F	23 17 03	21 02 28	0♊10 56	6♊23 10	24 39.6	2 02.1	18 28.4	2 58.0	20 28.2	15 10.3	6 39.6	1 02.0	0 57.7	5 12.4
13 Sa	23 20 59	22 02 20	12 31 04	18 35 11	24D 38.6	3 37.9	19 41.9	3 42.8	20 51.3	15 10.5	6 43.3	1 03.7	0 56.1	5 11.5
14 Su	23 24 56	23 02 09	24 36 07	0♋34 28	24 38.8	5 15.0	20 55.4	4 27.7	21 14.4	15 10.9	6 47.1	1 05.4	0 54.4	5 10.6
15 M	23 28 52	24 01 57	6♋30 52	12 25 56	24 40.0	6 53.2	22 08.9	5 12.6	21 37.6	15 11.5	6 51.0	1 07.2	0 52.8	5 09.8
16 Tu	23 32 49	25 01 42	18 20 19	24 14 35	24 41.8	8 32.7	23 22.2	5 57.5	22 00.9	15 12.2	6 55.0	1 09.0	0 51.1	5 09.0
17 W	23 36 45	26 01 24	0♌09 21	6♌05 10	24 43.6	10 13.3	24 35.6	6 42.5	22 24.1	15 13.2	6 59.1	1 10.9	0 49.5	5 08.2
18 Th	23 40 42	27 01 05	12 02 33	18 02 00	24R 44.8	11 55.1	25 48.9	7 27.4	22 47.5	15 14.3	7 03.3	1 12.8	0 47.8	5 07.4
19 F	23 44 39	28 00 43	24 03 55	0♍08 42	24 44.8	13 38.2	27 02.1	8 12.4	23 10.8	15 15.7	7 07.5	1 14.7	0 46.2	5 06.7
20 Sa	23 48 35	29 00 19	6♍16 41	12 28 07	24 43.4	15 22.6	28 15.2	8 57.4	23 34.2	15 17.2	7 11.9	1 16.7	0 44.5	5 05.9
21 Su	23 52 32	29 59 53	18 43 12	25 02 05	24 40.2	17 08.1	29 28.3	9 42.4	23 57.7	15 18.9	7 16.3	1 18.7	0 42.9	5 05.2
22 M	23 56 28	0♈59 25	1♎24 51	7♎51 30	24 35.4	18 55.0	0♉41.4	10 27.5	24 21.1	15 20.8	7 20.8	1 20.8	0 41.2	5 04.5
23 Tu	0 00 25	1 58 55	14 21 59	20 56 12	24 29.4	20 43.1	1 54.4	11 12.5	24 44.7	15 22.9	7 25.4	1 22.9	0 39.5	5 03.9
24 W	0 04 21	2 58 24	27 34 01	4♏15 15	24 22.8	22 32.5	3 07.3	11 57.6	25 08.2	15 25.2	7 30.1	1 25.1	0 37.9	5 03.2
25 Th	0 08 18	3 57 50	10♏59 41	17 47 07	24 16.6	24 23.3	4 20.1	12 42.7	25 31.8	15 27.7	7 34.9	1 27.3	0 36.2	5 02.6
26 F	0 12 14	4 57 14	24 37 18	1♐30 01	24 11.3	26 15.3	5 33.0	13 27.8	25 55.5	15 30.3	7 39.7	1 29.5	0 34.6	5 02.0
27 Sa	0 16 11	5 56 37	8♐25 03	15 22 11	24 07.6	28 08.6	6 45.7	14 13.0	26 19.1	15 33.1	7 44.7	1 31.8	0 32.9	5 01.5
28 Su	0 20 08	6 55 58	22 21 14	29 22 02	24D 05.8	0♈03.2	7 58.4	14 58.1	26 42.8	15 36.2	7 49.7	1 34.2	0 31.3	5 00.9
29 M	0 24 04	7 55 17	6♑24 26	13♑28 15	24 05.7	1 59.2	9 11.0	15 43.3	27 06.6	15 39.4	7 54.8	1 36.5	0 29.6	5 00.4
30 Tu	0 28 01	8 54 35	20 33 19	27 39 29	24 06.6	3 56.4	10 23.6	16 28.5	27 30.4	15 42.7	7 59.9	1 38.9	0 28.0	4 59.9
31 W	0 31 57	9 53 51	4♒46 31	11♒54 11	24R 07.8	5 54.8	11 36.1	17 13.7	27 54.2	15 46.3	8 05.2	1 41.3	0 26.3	4 59.4

April 1943 — LONGITUDE

Day	Sid.Time	☉	0 hr ☽	Noon ☽	True ☊	☿	♀	♂	⚳	♃	♄	♅	♆	♇
1 Th	0 35 54	10♈53 05	19♒02 11	26♒10 12	24♌08.3	7♈54.4	12♉48.6	17♒58.9	28♈18.0	15♋50.0	8♊10.5	1♊43.8	0♎24.7	4♌59.0
2 F	0 39 50	11 52 17	3♓17 49	10♓24 36	24R 07.1	9 55.2	14 00.9	18 44.1	28 41.9	15 53.9	8 15.9	1 46.3	0R 23.1	4R 58.6
3 Sa	0 43 47	12 51 27	17 30 03	24 33 39	24 03.8	11 57.0	15 13.3	19 29.3	29 05.8	15 58.0	8 21.3	1 48.9	0 21.5	4 58.2
4 Su	0 47 43	13 50 35	1♈34 51	8♈33 08	23 58.1	13 59.8	16 25.5	20 14.5	29 29.7	16 02.2	8 26.9	1 51.4	0 19.9	4 57.8
5 M	0 51 40	14 49 41	15 27 57	22 18 51	23 50.4	16 03.4	17 37.7	20 59.8	29 53.6	16 06.6	8 32.5	1 54.1	0 18.3	4 57.5
6 Tu	0 55 36	15 48 46	29 05 24	5♉47 17	23 41.5	18 07.7	18 49.8	21 45.0	0♉17.6	16 11.2	8 38.2	1 56.7	0 16.7	4 57.2
7 W	0 59 33	16 47 48	12♉24 15	18 56 11	23 32.2	20 12.5	20 01.9	22 30.3	0 41.6	16 16.0	8 43.9	1 59.4	0 15.1	4 56.9
8 Th	1 03 30	17 46 48	25 23 02	1♊44 53	23 23.6	22 17.6	21 13.9	23 15.5	1 05.6	16 20.9	8 49.7	2 02.1	0 13.5	4 56.6
9 F	1 07 26	18 45 45	8♊01 56	14 14 26	23 16.4	24 22.8	22 25.8	24 00.8	1 29.7	16 26.0	8 55.6	2 04.9	0 12.0	4 56.4
10 Sa	1 11 23	19 44 41	20 22 46	26 27 22	23 11.4	26 27.9	23 37.6	24 46.1	1 53.8	16 31.3	9 01.6	2 07.6	0 10.4	4 56.1
11 Su	1 15 19	20 43 34	2♋28 45	8♋27 28	23 08.5	28 32.5	24 49.4	25 31.3	2 17.8	16 36.7	9 07.6	2 10.4	0 08.9	4 56.0
12 M	1 19 16	21 42 25	14 24 08	20 19 22	23D 07.6	0♉36.3	26 01.1	26 16.6	2 41.9	16 42.2	9 13.6	2 13.3	0 07.3	4 55.8
13 Tu	1 23 12	22 41 14	26 13 52	2♌08 16	23 08.0	2 39.1	27 12.7	27 01.9	3 06.1	16 48.0	9 19.8	2 16.1	0 05.8	4 55.7
14 W	1 27 09	23 40 00	8♌03 16	13 59 31	23R 08.8	4 40.3	28 24.2	27 47.1	3 30.2	16 53.8	9 26.0	2 19.0	0 04.3	4 55.6
15 Th	1 31 05	24 38 45	19 57 40	25 58 21	23 09.0	6 39.9	29 35.6	28 32.4	3 54.4	16 59.9	9 32.2	2 22.0	0 02.9	4 55.5
16 F	1 35 02	25 37 27	2♍02 08	8♍09 34	23 07.8	8 37.3	0♊47.0	29 17.7	4 18.6	17 06.1	9 38.5	2 24.9	0 01.4	4 55.4
17 Sa	1 38 59	26 36 06	14 21 05	20 37 07	23 04.5	10 32.2	1 58.2	0♓03.0	4 42.7	17 12.4	9 44.9	2 27.9	29♍59.9	4D 55.4
18 Su	1 42 55	27 34 44	26 57 57	3♎23 48	22 58.6	12 24.4	3 09.4	0 48.2	5 06.9	17 18.9	9 51.3	2 30.9	29 58.5	4 55.4
19 M	1 46 52	28 33 20	9♎54 47	16 30 53	22 50.4	14 13.5	4 20.5	1 33.5	5 31.2	17 25.5	9 57.8	2 33.9	29 57.1	4 55.4
20 Tu	1 50 48	29 31 53	23 12 00	29 57 55	22 40.3	15 59.2	5 31.5	2 18.8	5 55.4	17 32.3	10 04.3	2 37.0	29 55.7	4 55.5
21 W	1 54 45	0♉30 25	6♏48 16	13♏42 39	22 29.4	17 41.4	6 42.4	3 04.1	6 19.6	17 39.2	10 10.9	2 40.1	29 54.3	4 55.5
22 Th	1 58 41	1 28 55	20 40 34	27 41 27	22 18.7	19 19.7	7 53.2	3 49.4	6 43.9	17 46.2	10 17.5	2 43.2	29 52.9	4 55.6
23 F	2 02 38	2 27 23	4♐44 43	11♐49 46	22 09.4	20 54.0	9 04.0	4 34.6	7 08.2	17 53.4	10 24.2	2 46.3	29 51.6	4 55.8
24 Sa	2 06 34	3 25 50	18 56 02	26 03 00	22 02.4	22 24.2	10 14.6	5 19.9	7 32.4	18 00.7	10 30.9	2 49.4	29 50.3	4 55.9
25 Su	2 10 31	4 24 15	3♑10 09	10♑17 06	21 58.0	23 50.0	11 25.2	6 05.2	7 56.7	18 08.2	10 37.7	2 52.6	29 48.9	4 56.1
26 M	2 14 28	5 22 38	17 23 30	24 29 04	21D 56.0	25 11.4	12 35.6	6 50.5	8 21.0	18 15.8	10 44.6	2 55.8	29 47.7	4 56.3
27 Tu	2 18 24	6 21 00	1♒33 38	8♒37 02	21R 55.6	26 28.2	13 46.0	7 35.7	8 45.3	18 23.5	10 51.4	2 59.0	29 46.4	4 56.6
28 W	2 22 21	7 19 21	15 39 09	22 39 55	21 55.7	27 40.3	14 56.2	8 21.0	9 09.7	18 31.3	10 58.3	3 02.3	29 45.1	4 56.8
29 Th	2 26 17	8 17 39	29 39 16	6♓37 06	21 55.1	28 47.7	16 06.4	9 06.2	9 34.0	18 39.3	11 05.3	3 05.5	29 43.9	4 57.1
30 F	2 30 14	9 15 57	13♓33 21	20 27 53	21 52.5	29 50.2	17 16.5	9 51.5	9 58.3	18 47.4	11 12.3	3 08.8	29 42.7	4 57.4

Astro Data	Dy Hr Mn
☽0N	8 1:59
♅△♆	11 4:19
♃D	12 2:11
☉0N	21 12:02
☽0S	22 12:50
☿0N	30 9:22
☽0N	4 11:35
♇D	18 3:04
☽0S	18 21:10
♃∠♅	21 17:35

Planet Ingress	Dy Hr Mn
♂ ♒	8 12:42
☿ ♓	11 4:59
☉ ♈	21 12:03
♀ ♉	21 22:24
☿ ♈	28 11:19
⚳ ♉	5 18:23
☿ ♉	12 4:56
♀ ♊	15 20:12
♂ ♓	17 10:25
♆ ♍R	17 10:56
☉ ♉	20 23:32
☿ ♊	30 15:56

Last Aspect Dy Hr Mn		☽ Ingress	Dy Hr Mn
28 4:14	☿ ⚹	♑	1 7:19
3 2:18	♂ ☌	♒	3 8:56
4 18:07	☿ ☌	♓	5 9:54
7 10:18	♂ ⚹	♈	7 11:41
9 11:03	☿ ⚹	♉	9 15:53
11 4:06	☉ ⚹	♊	11 23:39
13 19:30	☉ □	♋	14 10:51
16 13:44	☉ △	♌	16 23:41
19 5:11	♀ △	♍	19 11:43
20 18:30	☿ ☍	♎	21 21:21
23 1:50	♃ □	♏	24 4:23
26 1:25	☿ △	♐	26 9:23
27 9:54	♂ ⚹	♑	28 13:05
29 15:43	♃ ☍	♒	30 15:57

Last Aspect Dy Hr Mn		☽ Ingress	Dy Hr Mn
31 21:27	♂ ☌	♓	1 18:27
2 21:20	♃ △	♈	3 21:17
5 9:33	♂ ⚹	♉	6 1:37
7 19:02	♂ □	♊	8 8:41
10 12:01	☿ ⚹	♋	10 19:03
13 0:52	♀ ⚹	♌	13 7:39
15 19:58	♀ □	♍	15 19:59
18 5:39	♆ ☌	♎	18 5:41
20 11:10	☉ ☍	♏	20 12:04
22 15:44	♆ ⚹	♐	22 15:56
24 18:22	♆ □	♑	24 18:39
26 20:59	♆ △	♒	26 21:21
28 21:22	☿ □	♓	29 0:36

☽ Phases & Eclipses Dy Hr Mn	
6 10:34	● 14♓59
13 19:30	☽ 22♊21
21 22:08	○ 0♎25
29 1:52	☾ 7♑30
4 21:53	● 14♈15
12 15:04	☽ 21♋50
20 11:10	○ 29♎30
27 7:51	☾ 6♒11

Astro Data

1 March 1943
Julian Day # 15765
SVP 6♓03'22"
GC 26♐02.7 ⚵ 11♓58.6
Eris 4♈53.3 ⚶ 14♑00.5
⚷ 25♌10.8R ⚴ 28♓12.5
☽ Mean ☊ 24♌21.7

1 April 1943
Julian Day # 15796
SVP 6♓03'19"
GC 26♐02.8 ⚵ 22♓21.7
Eris 5♈15.0 ⚶ 22♑17.9
⚷ 23♌22.1R ⚴ 12♈44.2
☽ Mean ☊ 22♌43.2

LONGITUDE — May 1943

Day	Sid.Time	☉	0 hr ☽	Noon ☽	True ☊	☿	♀	♂	⚳	♃	♄	♅	♆	♇
1 Sa	2 34 10	10♉14 12	27♓20 33	4♈11 09	21♌47.3	0♊47.8	18♊26.4	10♓36.7	10♉22.7	18♋55.6	11♊19.3	3♊12.1	29♍41.5	4♌57.8
2 Su	2 38 07	11 12 26	10♈59 28	17 45 15	21R 39.1	1 40.5	19 36.3	11 21.9	10 47.0	19 04.0	11 26.4	3 15.4	29R 40.4	4 58.1
3 M	2 42 03	12 10 39	24 28 14	1♉08 08	21 28.4	2 28.1	20 46.1	12 07.1	11 11.4	19 12.5	11 33.6	3 18.7	29 39.2	4 58.5
4 Tu	2 46 00	13 08 50	7♉44 43	14 17 43	21 16.0	3 10.5	21 55.7	12 52.3	11 35.7	19 21.1	11 40.7	3 22.0	29 38.1	4 58.9
5 W	2 49 57	14 06 59	20 46 58	27 12 19	21 03.0	3 47.8	23 05.3	13 37.4	12 00.1	19 29.8	11 47.9	3 25.4	29 37.0	4 59.4
6 Th	2 53 53	15 05 06	3♊33 41	9♊51 05	20 50.7	4 20.0	24 14.7	14 22.6	12 24.4	19 38.6	11 55.2	3 28.8	29 36.0	4 59.9
7 F	2 57 50	16 03 12	16 04 34	22 14 19	20 40.0	4 46.9	25 24.1	15 07.7	12 48.8	19 47.5	12 02.4	3 32.2	29 34.9	5 00.4
8 Sa	3 01 46	17 01 16	28 20 33	4♋23 36	20 31.8	5 08.5	26 33.3	15 52.8	13 13.2	19 56.6	12 09.7	3 35.6	29 33.9	5 00.9
9 Su	3 05 43	17 59 18	10♋23 50	16 21 42	20 26.2	5 24.9	27 42.4	16 37.9	13 37.5	20 05.8	12 17.1	3 39.0	29 32.9	5 01.4
10 M	3 09 39	18 57 19	22 17 44	28 12 29	20 23.2	5 36.2	28 51.3	17 22.9	14 01.9	20 15.0	12 24.4	3 42.4	29 32.0	5 02.0
11 Tu	3 13 36	19 55 17	4♌06 34	10♌00 37	20 22.1	5R 42.3	0♋00.2	18 08.0	14 26.2	20 24.4	12 31.8	3 45.8	29 31.0	5 02.6
12 W	3 17 32	20 53 14	15 55 18	21 51 19	20 22.0	5 43.4	1 08.9	18 53.0	14 50.6	20 33.9	12 39.3	3 49.3	29 30.1	5 03.2
13 Th	3 21 29	21 51 08	27 49 22	3♍50 06	20 21.7	5 39.6	2 17.5	19 37.9	15 14.9	20 43.5	12 46.7	3 52.7	29 29.3	5 03.9
14 F	3 25 26	22 49 01	9♍54 14	16 02 22	20 20.3	5 31.1	3 25.9	20 22.9	15 39.3	20 53.2	12 54.2	3 56.2	29 28.4	5 04.5
15 Sa	3 29 22	23 46 52	22 15 08	28 33 02	20 16.8	5 18.1	4 34.2	21 07.8	16 03.6	21 03.0	13 01.7	3 59.6	29 27.6	5 05.2
16 Su	3 33 19	24 44 42	4♎56 32	11♎25 58	20 10.8	5 00.9	5 42.4	21 52.7	16 27.9	21 12.8	13 09.2	4 03.1	29 26.8	5 05.9
17 M	3 37 15	25 42 30	18 01 36	24 43 31	20 02.3	4 39.9	6 50.4	22 37.6	16 52.2	21 22.8	13 16.8	4 06.6	29 26.0	5 06.7
18 Tu	3 41 12	26 40 16	1♏31 41	8♏25 52	19 51.9	4 15.5	7 58.2	23 22.5	17 16.5	21 32.9	13 24.3	4 10.1	29 25.3	5 07.4
19 W	3 45 08	27 38 01	15 25 44	22 30 46	19 40.4	3 48.0	9 05.9	24 07.3	17 40.8	21 43.1	13 31.9	4 13.6	29 24.6	5 08.2
20 Th	3 49 05	28 35 44	29 40 18	6♐53 33	19 29.1	3 18.0	10 13.5	24 52.1	18 05.1	21 53.3	13 39.5	4 17.1	29 23.9	5 09.0
21 F	3 53 01	29 33 27	14♐09 42	21 27 49	19 19.2	2 46.1	11 20.9	25 36.9	18 29.4	22 03.7	13 47.2	4 20.6	29 23.2	5 09.9
22 Sa	3 56 58	0♊31 08	28 46 59	6♑06 20	19 11.6	2 12.8	12 28.1	26 21.6	18 53.7	22 14.1	13 54.8	4 24.1	29 22.6	5 10.7
23 Su	4 00 55	1 28 48	13♑25 02	20 42 22	19 06.7	1 38.7	13 35.2	27 06.3	19 18.0	22 24.6	14 02.5	4 27.6	29 22.0	5 11.6
24 M	4 04 51	2 26 26	27 57 42	5♒10 33	19D 04.4	1 04.3	14 42.1	27 51.0	19 42.3	22 35.3	14 10.2	4 31.1	29 21.5	5 12.5
25 Tu	4 08 48	3 24 04	12♒20 31	19 27 22	19 03.9	0 30.4	15 48.9	28 35.6	20 06.5	22 45.9	14 17.9	4 34.6	29 20.9	5 13.5
26 W	4 12 44	4 21 41	26 30 54	3♓31 05	19R 04.0	29♉57.4	16 55.5	29 20.2	20 30.8	22 56.7	14 25.6	4 38.2	29 20.4	5 14.4
27 Th	4 16 41	5 19 17	10♓27 53	17 21 19	19 03.6	29 25.9	18 01.9	0♈04.8	20 55.0	23 07.6	14 33.3	4 41.7	29 19.9	5 15.4
28 F	4 20 37	6 16 52	24 11 29	0♈58 27	19 01.4	28 56.6	19 08.1	0 49.3	21 19.2	23 18.5	14 41.1	4 45.2	29 19.5	5 16.4
29 Sa	4 24 34	7 14 27	7♈42 17	14 23 04	18 56.8	28 29.7	20 14.2	1 33.8	21 43.4	23 29.5	14 48.8	4 48.7	29 19.1	5 17.4
30 Su	4 28 30	8 12 00	21 00 50	27 35 37	18 49.5	28 05.8	21 20.0	2 18.2	22 07.6	23 40.6	14 56.6	4 52.2	29 18.7	5 18.4
31 M	4 32 27	9 09 32	4♉07 25	10♉36 14	18 39.8	27 45.2	22 25.7	3 02.6	22 31.8	23 51.8	15 04.3	4 55.7	29 18.4	5 19.5

LONGITUDE — June 1943

Day	Sid.Time	☉	0 hr ☽	Noon ☽	True ☊	☿	♀	♂	⚳	♃	♄	♅	♆	♇
1 Tu	4 36 24	10♊07 04	17♉02 03	23♉24 48	18♌28.5	27♉28.3	23♋31.2	3♈47.0	22♉55.9	24♋03.0	15♊12.1	4♊59.2	29♍18.0	5♌20.6
2 W	4 40 20	11 04 35	29 44 31	6♊01 09	18R 16.7	27R 15.2	24 36.4	4 31.3	23 20.1	24 14.4	15 19.9	5 02.7	29R 17.8	5 21.7
3 Th	4 44 17	12 02 04	12♊14 43	18 25 16	18 05.4	27 06.3	25 41.5	5 15.5	23 44.2	24 25.7	15 27.7	5 06.2	29 17.5	5 22.8
4 F	4 48 13	12 59 33	24 32 54	0♋37 43	17 55.5	27D 01.6	26 46.4	5 59.7	24 08.3	24 37.2	15 35.5	5 09.7	29 17.3	5 23.9
5 Sa	4 52 10	13 57 01	6♋39 55	12 39 44	17 47.9	27 01.4	27 51.0	6 43.9	24 32.4	24 48.7	15 43.3	5 13.2	29 17.1	5 25.1
6 Su	4 56 06	14 54 27	18 37 27	24 33 26	17 42.8	27 05.6	28 55.4	7 28.0	24 56.4	25 00.3	15 51.1	5 16.7	29 16.9	5 26.2
7 M	5 00 03	15 51 53	0♌28 03	6♌21 47	17D 40.2	27 14.2	29 59.6	8 12.0	25 20.5	25 12.0	15 58.9	5 20.2	29 16.8	5 27.4
8 Tu	5 03 59	16 49 17	12 15 08	18 08 38	17 39.5	27 27.4	1♌03.6	8 56.0	25 44.5	25 23.7	16 06.7	5 23.7	29 16.7	5 28.7
9 W	5 07 56	17 46 41	24 02 52	29 58 29	17 40.0	27 45.1	2 07.3	9 39.9	26 08.5	25 35.5	16 14.5	5 27.1	29 16.7	5 29.9
10 Th	5 11 53	18 44 03	5♍56 06	11♍56 23	17R 40.8	28 07.2	3 10.7	10 23.7	26 32.5	25 47.3	16 22.3	5 30.6	29D 16.6	5 31.1
11 F	5 15 49	19 41 24	18 00 00	24 07 37	17 40.8	28 33.7	4 13.9	11 07.5	26 56.4	25 59.2	16 30.1	5 34.0	29 16.6	5 32.4
12 Sa	5 19 46	20 38 45	0♎19 53	6♎37 23	17 39.5	29 04.5	5 16.8	11 51.2	27 20.3	26 11.2	16 37.9	5 37.4	29 16.7	5 33.7
13 Su	5 23 42	21 36 04	13 00 40	19 30 14	17 36.1	29 39.6	6 19.4	12 34.9	27 44.2	26 23.2	16 45.6	5 40.9	29 16.7	5 35.0
14 M	5 27 39	22 33 22	26 06 26	2♏49 31	17 30.8	0♊18.9	7 21.8	13 18.5	28 08.1	26 35.3	16 53.4	5 44.3	29 16.8	5 36.3
15 Tu	5 31 35	23 30 40	9♏39 37	16 36 39	17 23.8	1 02.3	8 23.8	14 02.1	28 31.9	26 47.4	17 01.2	5 47.7	29 17.0	5 37.7
16 W	5 35 32	24 27 56	23 40 23	0♐50 26	17 15.8	1 49.7	9 25.6	14 45.5	28 55.7	26 59.6	17 08.9	5 51.0	29 17.1	5 39.0
17 Th	5 39 28	25 25 12	8♐06 09	15 26 47	17 07.8	2 41.1	10 27.0	15 28.9	29 19.5	27 11.8	17 16.7	5 54.4	29 17.3	5 40.4
18 F	5 43 25	26 22 28	22 51 25	0♑18 59	17 00.8	3 36.4	11 28.1	16 12.3	29 43.2	27 24.1	17 24.4	5 57.8	29 17.6	5 41.8
19 Sa	5 47 22	27 19 43	7♑48 24	15 18 31	16 55.6	4 35.5	12 28.9	16 55.6	0♊07.0	27 36.4	17 32.2	6 01.1	29 17.8	5 43.2
20 Su	5 51 18	28 16 58	22 48 15	0♒16 31	16 52.5	5 38.3	13 29.3	17 38.8	0 30.7	27 48.8	17 39.9	6 04.4	29 18.1	5 44.6
21 M	5 55 15	29 14 12	7♒42 24	15 05 05	16D 51.4	6 44.9	14 29.4	18 21.9	0 54.3	28 01.2	17 47.6	6 07.7	29 18.4	5 46.0
22 Tu	5 59 11	0♋11 26	22 23 55	29 38 23	16 51.9	7 55.1	15 29.1	19 05.0	1 17.9	28 13.6	17 55.3	6 11.0	29 18.8	5 47.5
23 W	6 03 08	1 08 40	6♓48 06	13♓52 53	16 53.0	9 08.9	16 28.5	19 48.0	1 41.5	28 26.1	18 03.0	6 14.3	29 19.2	5 48.9
24 Th	6 07 04	2 05 54	20 52 35	27 47 15	16R 53.8	10 26.2	17 27.5	20 30.9	2 05.1	28 38.7	18 10.6	6 17.6	29 19.6	5 50.4
25 F	6 11 01	3 03 07	4♈36 55	11♈21 46	16 53.6	11 47.1	18 26.1	21 13.7	2 28.6	28 51.3	18 18.3	6 20.8	29 20.1	5 51.9
26 Sa	6 14 57	4 00 21	18 01 58	24 37 46	16 51.7	13 11.4	19 24.3	21 56.5	2 52.1	29 03.9	18 25.9	6 24.0	29 20.6	5 53.4
27 Su	6 18 54	4 57 35	1♉09 22	7♉37 02	16 48.0	14 39.2	20 22.1	22 39.2	3 15.6	29 16.6	18 33.5	6 27.2	29 21.1	5 54.9
28 M	6 22 51	5 54 49	14 00 59	20 21 28	16 42.6	16 10.3	21 19.4	23 21.8	3 39.0	29 29.3	18 41.1	6 30.4	29 21.6	5 56.4
29 Tu	6 26 47	6 52 02	26 38 40	2♊52 49	16 36.1	17 44.8	22 16.3	24 04.3	4 02.4	29 42.0	18 48.6	6 33.6	29 22.2	5 58.0
30 W	6 30 44	7 49 16	9♊04 05	15 12 41	16 29.2	19 22.6	23 12.8	24 46.7	4 25.7	29 54.8	18 56.2	6 36.7	29 22.8	5 59.5

Astro Data

	Dy Hr Mn
☽0N	1 19:36
☿R	12 5:13
☽0S	16 7:04
☽0N	29 2:17
♂0N	1 23:10
☿D	5 1:28
♅✶♇	10 18:23
♆D	10 22:05
☽0S	12 17:05
☽0N	25 8:45
♃✶♆	27 20:54

Planet Ingress

		Dy Hr Mn
♀	♋	11 11:56
☉	♊	21 23:03
☿	♉R	26 10:04
♂	♈	27 9:25
♀	♌	7 12:09
☿	♊	14 0:46
⚳	♊	19 4:57
☉	♋	22 7:12
♃	♌	30 21:46

Last Aspect / ☽ Ingress

Last Aspect Dy Hr Mn			☽ Ingress	Dy Hr Mn
1 4:07	♆	☍	♈	1 4:39
2 15:37	♀	✶	♉	3 9:57
5 16:32	♆	△	♊	5 17:16
8 2:26	♆	□	♋	8 3:17
10 14:41	♆	✶	♌	10 15:39
12 9:52	☉	□	♍	13 4:21
15 13:43	♆	☌	♎	15 14:44
17 5:57	♃	□	♏	17 21:19
19 23:33	♆	✶	♐	20 0:33
22 0:59	♆	□	♑	22 2:00
24 2:19	♆	△	♒	24 3:23
25 3:13	♄	△	♓	26 5:58
28 9:05	♆	☍	♈	28 10:16
30 4:45	♃	□	♉	30 16:25

Last Aspect / ☽ Ingress

Last Aspect Dy Hr Mn			☽ Ingress	Dy Hr Mn
1 23:09	♆	△	♊	2 0:29
4 9:21	♆	□	♋	4 10:45
6 21:45	♀	☌	♌	6 23:03
9 7:23	☿	□	♍	9 12:03
11 21:58	♆	☌	♎	11 23:22
14 0:42	♃	□	♏	14 6:59
16 9:25	♆	✶	♐	16 10:36
18 10:21	♆	□	♑	18 11:30
20 10:26	♆	△	♒	20 11:33
21 17:39	♂	✶	♓	22 12:36
24 14:42	♆	☍	♈	24 15:52
26 20:17	♃	□	♉	26 21:52
29 5:46	♃	✶	♊	29 6:27

☽ Phases & Eclipses

Dy Hr Mn		
4 9:43	●	13♉03
12 9:52	☽	20♌48
19 21:13	○	28♏00
26 13:34	☾	4♓25
2 22:33	●	11♊30
11 2:35	☽	19♍19
18 5:14	○	26♐06
24 20:08	☾	2♈25

Astro Data

1 May 1943
Julian Day # 15826
SVP 6♓03'16"
GC 26♐02.9 ⚴ 2♈06.1
Eris 5♈35.1 ⚵ 27♑38.0
⚷ 23♌01.1 ⚶ 26♈33.0
☽ Mean ☊ 21♌07.9

1 June 1943
Julian Day # 15857
SVP 6♓03'12"
GC 26♐02.9 ⚴ 11♈19.2
Eris 5♈50.1 ⚵ 28♑47.1R
⚷ 24♌20.4 ⚶ 10♉17.4
☽ Mean ☊ 19♌29.4

July 1943

LONGITUDE

Day	Sid.Time	☉	0 hr ☽	Noon ☽	True ☊	☿	♀	♂	⚳	♃	♄	♅	♆	♇
1 Th	6 34 40	8♋46 30	21♊18 45	27♊22 29	16♌22.6	21♊03.7	24♌08.8	25♈29.0	4♊49.0	0♌07.6	19♊03.7	6♊39.8	29♍23.5	6♌01.1
2 F	6 38 37	9 43 44	3♋24 04	9♋23 42	16R 16.9	22 47.9	25 04.3	26 11.2	5 12.3	0 20.5	19 11.2	6 42.9	29 24.1	6 02.7
3 Sa	6 42 33	10 40 57	15 21 35	21 17 56	16 12.7	24 35.1	25 59.3	26 53.3	5 35.5	0 33.3	19 18.7	6 46.0	29 24.8	6 04.3
4 Su	6 46 30	11 38 11	27 13 02	3♌07 09	16 10.2	26 25.4	26 53.8	27 35.3	5 58.7	0 46.2	19 26.1	6 49.0	29 25.6	6 05.9
5 M	6 50 26	12 35 24	9♌00 36	14 53 45	16D 09.3	28 18.5	27 47.8	28 17.3	6 21.8	0 59.2	19 33.5	6 52.0	29 26.4	6 07.5
6 Tu	6 54 23	13 32 38	20 46 58	26 40 42	16 09.8	0♋14.2	28 41.2	28 59.1	6 44.8	1 12.1	19 40.9	6 55.0	29 27.2	6 09.1
7 W	6 58 20	14 29 51	2♍35 24	8♍31 34	16 11.2	2 12.4	29 34.0	29 40.8	7 07.9	1 25.1	19 48.3	6 58.0	29 28.0	6 10.7
8 Th	7 02 16	15 27 04	14 29 43	20 30 25	16 12.9	4 13.0	0♍26.2	0♉22.4	7 30.9	1 38.2	19 55.6	7 00.9	29 28.8	6 12.3
9 F	7 06 13	16 24 17	26 34 13	2♎41 42	16 14.3	6 15.6	1 17.7	1 03.9	7 53.8	1 51.2	20 02.9	7 03.8	29 29.7	6 14.0
10 Sa	7 10 09	17 21 29	8♎53 28	15 10 04	16R 15.0	8 19.9	2 08.7	1 45.3	8 16.7	2 04.3	20 10.1	7 06.7	29 30.7	6 15.6
11 Su	7 14 06	18 18 42	21 32 05	27 59 58	16 14.6	10 25.8	2 58.9	2 26.5	8 39.5	2 17.3	20 17.3	7 09.6	29 31.6	6 17.3
12 M	7 18 02	19 15 54	4♏34 12	11♏15 07	16 13.1	12 32.9	3 48.4	3 07.7	9 02.2	2 30.4	20 24.5	7 12.4	29 32.6	6 18.9
13 Tu	7 21 59	20 13 07	18 02 58	24 57 52	16 10.6	14 40.9	4 37.3	3 48.7	9 25.0	2 43.6	20 31.7	7 15.2	29 33.6	6 20.6
14 W	7 25 55	21 10 20	1♐59 47	9♐08 29	16 07.4	16 49.5	5 25.3	4 29.7	9 47.6	2 56.7	20 38.8	7 18.0	29 34.6	6 22.3
15 Th	7 29 52	22 07 32	16 23 36	23 44 33	16 04.1	18 58.4	6 12.6	5 10.5	10 10.2	3 09.9	20 45.8	7 20.7	29 35.7	6 24.0
16 F	7 33 49	23 04 46	1♑10 35	8♑40 45	16 01.3	21 07.4	6 59.0	5 51.2	10 32.8	3 23.0	20 52.9	7 23.4	29 36.8	6 25.7
17 Sa	7 37 45	24 01 59	16 14 01	23 49 13	15 59.2	23 16.1	7 44.6	6 31.8	10 55.3	3 36.2	20 59.9	7 26.1	29 37.9	6 27.4
18 Su	7 41 42	24 59 12	1♒25 09	9♒00 35	15D 58.2	25 24.3	8 29.3	7 12.2	11 17.7	3 49.4	21 06.8	7 28.7	29 39.1	6 29.1
19 M	7 45 38	25 56 27	16 34 21	24 05 21	15 58.2	27 31.8	9 13.2	7 52.6	11 40.1	4 02.6	21 13.7	7 31.3	29 40.3	6 30.8
20 Tu	7 49 35	26 53 41	1♓32 38	8♓55 23	15 59.0	29 38.3	9 56.0	8 32.8	12 02.4	4 15.9	21 20.6	7 33.9	29 41.5	6 32.5
21 W	7 53 31	27 50 57	16 12 54	23 24 43	16 00.2	1♌43.8	10 37.9	9 12.9	12 24.6	4 29.1	21 27.4	7 36.4	29 42.7	6 34.2
22 Th	7 57 28	28 48 13	0♈30 30	7♈30 04	16 01.4	3 48.1	11 18.8	9 52.8	12 46.8	4 42.3	21 34.2	7 38.9	29 44.0	6 35.9
23 F	8 01 24	29 45 30	14 23 23	21 10 31	16R 02.2	5 51.1	11 58.6	10 32.7	13 08.9	4 55.6	21 40.9	7 41.4	29 45.2	6 37.7
24 Sa	8 05 21	0♌42 48	27 51 39	4♉27 03	16 02.3	7 52.6	12 37.4	11 12.3	13 31.0	5 08.9	21 47.6	7 43.9	29 46.5	6 39.4
25 Su	8 09 18	1 40 06	10♉57 02	17 21 56	16 01.8	9 52.7	13 15.0	11 51.9	13 53.0	5 22.1	21 54.2	7 46.3	29 47.9	6 41.1
26 M	8 13 14	2 37 26	23 42 11	29 58 10	16 00.6	11 51.2	13 51.4	12 31.3	14 14.9	5 35.4	22 00.8	7 48.6	29 49.3	6 42.8
27 Tu	8 17 11	3 34 47	6♊10 17	12♊18 57	15 59.1	13 48.1	14 26.7	13 10.5	14 36.8	5 48.7	22 07.4	7 51.0	29 50.7	6 44.6
28 W	8 21 07	4 32 09	18 24 34	24 27 31	15 57.4	15 43.3	15 00.7	13 49.6	14 58.5	6 02.0	22 13.8	7 53.2	29 52.1	6 46.3
29 Th	8 25 04	5 29 31	0♋28 09	6♋26 50	15 55.9	17 36.9	15 33.3	14 28.6	15 20.2	6 15.3	22 20.3	7 55.5	29 53.5	6 48.1
30 F	8 29 00	6 26 55	12 23 53	18 19 37	15 54.7	19 28.9	16 04.6	15 07.4	15 41.9	6 28.6	22 26.6	7 57.7	29 55.0	6 49.8
31 Sa	8 32 57	7 24 19	24 14 21	0♌08 22	15 53.9	21 19.2	16 34.5	15 46.0	16 03.4	6 41.8	22 33.0	7 59.9	29 56.5	6 51.5

August 1943

LONGITUDE

Day	Sid.Time	☉	0 hr ☽	Noon ☽	True ☊	☿	♀	♂	⚳	♃	♄	♅	♆	♇
1 Su	8 36 53	8♌21 44	6♌01 58	11♌55 24	15♌53.5	23♌07.9	17♍02.9	16♉24.5	16♊24.9	6♌55.1	22♊39.2	8♊02.0	29♍58.0	6♌53.3
2 M	8 40 50	9 19 10	17 48 59	23 43 00	15D 53.6	24 54.9	17 29.8	17 02.8	16 46.3	7 08.4	22 45.4	8 04.1	29 59.5	6 55.0
3 Tu	8 44 47	10 16 37	29 37 44	5♍33 32	15 53.9	26 40.3	17 55.1	17 40.9	17 07.6	7 21.7	22 51.6	8 06.2	0♎01.1	6 56.7
4 W	8 48 43	11 14 05	11♍30 41	17 29 34	15 54.4	28 24.0	18 18.8	18 18.8	17 28.8	7 34.9	22 57.7	8 08.2	0 02.7	6 58.5
5 Th	8 52 40	12 11 33	23 30 32	29 33 59	15 54.8	0♍06.1	18 40.7	18 56.6	17 49.9	7 48.2	23 03.7	8 10.1	0 04.3	7 00.2
6 F	8 56 36	13 09 02	5♎40 18	11♎49 55	15 55.2	1 46.6	19 00.9	19 34.2	18 11.0	8 01.5	23 09.6	8 12.1	0 05.9	7 01.9
7 Sa	9 00 33	14 06 32	18 03 16	24 20 46	15 55.4	3 25.5	19 19.3	20 11.6	18 31.9	8 14.7	23 15.5	8 14.0	0 07.6	7 03.7
8 Su	9 04 29	15 04 03	0♏42 52	7♏09 59	15 55.4	5 02.8	19 35.8	20 48.8	18 52.8	8 27.9	23 21.4	8 15.8	0 09.3	7 05.4
9 M	9 08 26	16 01 35	13 42 29	20 20 44	15 55.5	6 38.5	19 50.3	21 25.9	19 13.6	8 41.2	23 27.1	8 17.6	0 11.0	7 07.1
10 Tu	9 12 22	16 59 07	27 05 01	3♐55 31	15 55.5	8 12.5	20 02.8	22 02.7	19 34.3	8 54.4	23 32.8	8 19.4	0 12.7	7 08.8
11 W	9 16 19	17 56 40	10♐52 22	17 55 33	15 55.6	9 45.0	20 13.2	22 39.4	19 54.8	9 07.6	23 38.5	8 21.1	0 14.4	7 10.5
12 Th	9 20 16	18 54 15	25 04 54	2♑20 08	15 55.9	11 15.9	20 21.5	23 15.8	20 15.3	9 20.7	23 44.0	8 22.7	0 16.2	7 12.3
13 F	9 24 12	19 51 50	9♑40 47	17 06 13	15 56.2	12 45.2	20 27.6	23 52.1	20 35.7	9 33.9	23 49.5	8 24.4	0 18.0	7 14.0
14 Sa	9 28 09	20 49 26	24 35 40	2♒08 11	15R 56.5	14 12.9	20 31.5	24 28.2	20 56.0	9 47.1	23 55.0	8 25.9	0 19.8	7 15.7
15 Su	9 32 05	21 47 03	9♒42 43	17 18 09	15 56.6	15 38.9	20R 33.1	25 04.0	21 16.2	10 00.2	24 00.3	8 27.5	0 21.6	7 17.4
16 M	9 36 02	22 44 42	24 53 18	2♓26 59	15 56.4	17 03.2	20 32.4	25 39.7	21 36.3	10 13.3	24 05.6	8 29.0	0 23.4	7 19.0
17 Tu	9 39 58	23 42 21	9♓58 03	17 25 28	15 55.8	18 25.9	20 29.3	26 15.1	21 56.2	10 26.4	24 10.8	8 30.4	0 25.3	7 20.7
18 W	9 43 55	24 40 02	24 48 17	2♈05 42	15 54.9	19 46.9	20 23.9	26 50.4	22 16.1	10 39.5	24 16.0	8 31.8	0 27.1	7 22.4
19 Th	9 47 51	25 37 45	9♈17 07	16 22 04	15 53.8	21 06.1	20 16.1	27 25.4	22 35.8	10 52.5	24 21.0	8 33.1	0 29.0	7 24.1
20 F	9 51 48	26 35 29	23 20 18	0♉11 40	15 52.8	22 23.5	20 05.9	28 00.1	22 55.5	11 05.5	24 26.0	8 34.4	0 30.9	7 25.7
21 Sa	9 55 45	27 33 15	6♉56 14	13 34 09	15 51.9	23 39.0	19 53.3	28 34.7	23 15.0	11 18.5	24 30.9	8 35.7	0 32.9	7 27.4
22 Su	9 59 41	28 31 03	20 05 43	26 31 18	15D 51.6	24 52.7	19 38.4	29 09.0	23 34.4	11 31.5	24 35.8	8 36.9	0 34.8	7 29.0
23 M	10 03 38	29 28 52	2♊51 19	9♊06 17	15 51.8	26 04.3	19 21.2	29 43.1	23 53.7	11 44.4	24 40.5	8 38.1	0 36.8	7 30.7
24 Tu	10 07 34	0♍26 43	15 16 44	21 23 12	15 52.5	27 14.0	19 01.7	0♊16.9	24 12.9	11 57.3	24 45.2	8 39.2	0 38.7	7 32.3
25 W	10 11 31	1 24 36	27 26 13	3♋26 22	15 53.7	28 21.4	18 40.1	0 50.5	24 31.9	12 10.2	24 49.8	8 40.2	0 40.7	7 33.9
26 Th	10 15 27	2 22 31	9♋24 11	15 20 09	15 55.2	29 26.7	18 16.2	1 23.8	24 50.8	12 23.1	24 54.3	8 41.2	0 42.7	7 35.5
27 F	10 19 24	3 20 27	21 14 48	27 08 35	15 56.5	0♎29.6	17 50.4	1 56.9	25 09.6	12 35.9	24 58.7	8 42.2	0 44.7	7 37.1
28 Sa	10 23 20	4 18 25	3♌01 56	8♌55 16	15R 57.3	1 30.0	17 22.6	2 29.7	25 28.3	12 48.7	25 03.1	8 43.1	0 46.8	7 38.7
29 Su	10 27 17	5 16 24	14 48 56	20 43 19	15 57.4	2 27.8	16 53.1	3 02.2	25 46.8	13 01.5	25 07.3	8 44.0	0 48.8	7 40.3
30 M	10 31 14	6 14 25	26 38 42	2♍35 23	15 56.5	3 22.8	16 21.9	3 34.4	26 05.2	13 14.2	25 11.5	8 44.8	0 50.9	7 41.9
31 Tu	10 35 10	7 12 28	8♍33 37	14 33 39	15 54.5	4 14.9	15 49.3	4 06.3	26 23.4	13 26.9	25 15.6	8 45.6	0 52.9	7 43.4

Astro Data	Dy Hr Mn
☽0S	10 1:45
☽0N	22 16:11
♄∠♇	22 20:20
♃☌♇	1 8:10
☽0S	6 8:23
♃⚹♅	7 10:25
♃∠♄	7 14:42
♀0S	9 11:29
♀R	15 16:37
☽0N	19 1:07
☿0S	24 0:32

Planet Ingress		Dy Hr Mn
☿	♋	6 9:05
♂	♉	7 23:05
♀	♍	7 23:56
☿	♌	20 16:08
☉	♌	23 18:05
♆	♎	2 19:10
☿	♍	5 10:33
♂	♊	23 23:58
☉	♍	24 0:55
☿	♎	27 0:36

Last Aspect Dy Hr Mn			☽ Ingress	Dy Hr Mn
1 16:01	♆	□	♋	1 17:13
4 4:29	♆	⚹	♌	4 5:39
6 16:59	♂	△	♍	6 18:45
9 5:44	♆	☌	♎	9 6:44
10 21:32	♄	△	♏	11 15:40
13 19:52	♆	⚹	♐	13 20:37
15 21:28	♆	□	♑	15 22:07
17 21:11	♆	△	♒	17 21:46
19 7:23	♄	△	♓	19 21:30
21 22:40	♆	☍	♈	21 23:08
23 12:55	♄	⚹	♉	24 3:53
26 11:43	♆	△	♊	26 12:04
28 22:49	♆	□	♋	28 23:04
31 11:36	♆	⚹	♌	31 11:43

Last Aspect Dy Hr Mn			☽ Ingress	Dy Hr Mn
2 14:52	☿	☌	♍	3 0:45
4 23:00	♄	□	♎	5 12:51
7 9:55	♄	△	♏	7 22:40
9 14:02	♂	☍	♐	10 5:08
11 21:40	♄	☍	♑	12 8:09
13 23:18	♂	△	♒	14 8:36
16 0:47	♂	□	♓	16 8:06
18 2:58	♂	⚹	♈	18 8:32
20 5:12	☉	△	♉	20 11:39
22 17:12	♂	☌	♊	22 18:34
25 0:48	☿	□	♋	25 5:07
26 17:45	♀	⚹	♌	27 17:49
29 20:58	♄	⚹	♍	30 6:47

☽ Phases & Eclipses Dy Hr Mn		
2 12:44	●	9♋45
10 16:29	☽	17♎32
17 12:22	○	24♑03
24 4:38	☾	0♉25
1 4:06	●	8♌03
1 4:15:48	●	A 06'58"
9 3:36	☽	15♏41
15 19:34	○	22♒05
15 19:28	●	P 0.870
22 16:04	☾	28♉41
30 19:59	●	6♍34

Astro Data

1 July 1943
Julian Day # 15887
SVP 6♓03'07"
GC 26♐03.0 ⚳ 18♈42.8
Eris 5♈55.6 ⚵ 24♑41.2R
⚷ 26♌59.9 ⚶ 22♉45.7
☽ Mean ☊ 17♌54.1

1 August 1943
Julian Day # 15918
SVP 6♓03'02"
GC 26♐03.1 ⚳ 23♈32.8
Eris 5♈50.9R ⚵ 17♑36.1R
⚷ 0♍43.1 ⚶ 4♊18.4
☽ Mean ☊ 16♌15.6

LONGITUDE

September 1943

Day	Sid.Time	☉	0 hr ☽	Noon ☽	True ☊	☿	♀	♂	⚳	♃	♄	♅	♆	♇
1 W	10 39 07	8♍10 33	20♍35 43	26♍40 02	15♌51.6	5♎03.9	15♍15.4	4♊38.0	26♊41.5	13♌39.5	25♊19.6	8♊46.3	0♎55.0	7♌45.0
2 Th	10 43 03	9 08 39	2♎46 48	8♎56 12	15R 48.0	5 49.5	14R 40.4	5 09.3	26 59.4	13 52.1	25 23.5	8 46.9	0 57.1	7 46.5
3 F	10 47 00	10 06 46	15 08 28	21 23 47	15 44.2	6 31.7	14 04.5	5 40.4	27 17.2	14 04.6	25 27.3	8 47.5	0 59.2	7 48.0
4 Sa	10 50 56	11 04 55	27 42 22	4♏04 26	15 40.5	7 10.0	13 28.0	6 11.1	27 34.9	14 17.2	25 31.0	8 48.1	1 01.3	7 49.5
5 Su	10 54 53	12 03 05	10♏30 12	16 59 54	15 37.6	7 44.4	12 51.0	6 41.5	27 52.4	14 29.6	25 34.6	8 48.6	1 03.5	7 51.0
6 M	10 58 49	13 01 17	23 33 45	0♐11 58	15 35.7	8 14.4	12 13.9	7 11.6	28 09.7	14 42.0	25 38.2	8 49.1	1 05.6	7 52.5
7 Tu	11 02 46	13 59 31	6♐54 45	13 42 16	15D 35.1	8 39.8	11 36.8	7 41.3	28 26.8	14 54.4	25 41.6	8 49.5	1 07.7	7 54.0
8 W	11 06 43	14 57 46	20 34 40	27 31 59	15 35.6	9 00.4	11 00.0	8 10.8	28 43.8	15 06.7	25 45.0	8 49.8	1 09.9	7 55.4
9 Th	11 10 39	15 56 02	4♑34 16	11♑41 24	15 36.8	9 15.7	10 23.8	8 39.8	29 00.7	15 19.0	25 48.2	8 50.1	1 12.0	7 56.8
10 F	11 14 36	16 54 20	18 53 12	26 09 22	15 38.3	9 25.4	9 48.3	9 08.6	29 17.3	15 31.2	25 51.4	8 50.4	1 14.2	7 58.3
11 Sa	11 18 32	17 52 40	3♒29 27	10♒52 52	15R 39.2	9R 29.3	9 13.8	9 37.0	29 33.8	15 43.4	25 54.4	8 50.6	1 16.4	7 59.7
12 Su	11 22 29	18 51 01	18 18 55	25 46 46	15 38.9	9 27.1	8 40.5	10 05.0	29 50.2	15 55.5	25 57.4	8 50.8	1 18.6	8 01.1
13 M	11 26 25	19 49 24	3♓15 29	10♓44 04	15 37.1	9 18.4	8 08.7	10 32.7	0♋06.3	16 07.6	26 00.2	8 50.9	1 20.8	8 02.4
14 Tu	11 30 22	20 47 48	18 11 27	25 36 35	15 33.6	9 03.0	7 38.4	11 00.0	0 22.3	16 19.6	26 03.0	8R 50.9	1 23.0	8 03.8
15 W	11 34 18	21 46 15	2♈58 26	10♈16 05	15 28.7	8 40.9	7 09.9	11 26.9	0 38.0	16 31.5	26 05.7	8 50.9	1 25.2	8 05.1
16 Th	11 38 15	22 44 43	17 28 43	24 35 37	15 23.0	8 11.9	6 43.3	11 53.4	0 53.6	16 43.4	26 08.2	8 50.9	1 27.4	8 06.4
17 F	11 42 11	23 43 13	1♉36 18	8♉30 24	15 17.2	7 36.1	6 18.7	12 19.6	1 09.0	16 55.2	26 10.7	8 50.7	1 29.6	8 07.7
18 Sa	11 46 08	24 41 46	15 17 45	21 58 18	15 12.2	6 53.8	5 56.3	12 45.3	1 24.2	17 07.0	26 13.1	8 50.6	1 31.8	8 09.0
19 Su	11 50 05	25 40 21	28 32 13	4♊59 45	15 08.5	6 05.3	5 36.2	13 10.6	1 39.2	17 18.7	26 15.3	8 50.4	1 34.0	8 10.3
20 M	11 54 01	26 38 58	11♊21 16	17 37 15	15D 06.4	5 11.2	5 18.3	13 35.5	1 54.0	17 30.3	26 17.5	8 50.1	1 36.2	8 11.6
21 Tu	11 57 58	27 37 37	23 48 13	29 54 45	15 06.0	4 12.4	5 02.9	13 59.9	2 08.6	17 41.9	26 19.5	8 49.8	1 38.5	8 12.8
22 W	12 01 54	28 36 19	5♋57 30	11♋57 05	15 06.8	3 10.0	4 49.8	14 23.9	2 23.0	17 53.4	26 21.5	8 49.5	1 40.7	8 14.0
23 Th	12 05 51	29 35 02	17 54 10	23 49 23	15 08.3	2 05.2	4 39.2	14 47.4	2 37.2	18 04.9	26 23.3	8 49.1	1 42.9	8 15.2
24 F	12 09 47	0♎33 48	29 43 23	5♌36 46	15R 09.6	0 59.5	4 31.0	15 10.5	2 51.1	18 16.2	26 25.0	8 48.6	1 45.2	8 16.4
25 Sa	12 13 44	1 32 36	11♌30 07	17 23 58	15 10.0	29♍54.5	4 25.3	15 33.1	3 04.8	18 27.5	26 26.7	8 48.1	1 47.4	8 17.5
26 Su	12 17 40	2 31 27	23 18 49	29 15 09	15 08.8	28 51.8	4D 22.0	15 55.2	3 18.3	18 38.7	26 28.2	8 47.5	1 49.6	8 18.7
27 M	12 21 37	3 30 19	5♍13 20	11♍13 45	15 05.5	27 53.2	4 21.1	16 16.8	3 31.6	18 49.9	26 29.6	8 46.9	1 51.8	8 19.8
28 Tu	12 25 34	4 29 13	17 16 42	23 22 25	15 00.0	27 00.2	4 22.5	16 37.8	3 44.6	19 00.9	26 30.9	8 46.3	1 54.1	8 20.9
29 W	12 29 30	5 28 10	29 31 05	5♎42 51	14 52.4	26 14.3	4 26.3	16 58.4	3 57.4	19 11.9	26 32.1	8 45.5	1 56.3	8 21.9
30 Th	12 33 27	6 27 08	11♎57 48	18 15 59	14 43.4	25 36.6	4 32.4	17 18.4	4 09.9	19 22.8	26 33.1	8 44.8	1 58.5	8 23.0

LONGITUDE

October 1943

Day	Sid.Time	☉	0 hr ☽	Noon ☽	True ☊	☿	♀	♂	⚳	♃	♄	♅	♆	♇
1 F	12 37 23	7♎26 09	24♎37 25	1♏02 05	14♌33.7	25♍08.2	4♍40.6	17♊37.8	4♋22.2	19♌33.6	26♊34.1	8♊44.0	2♎00.8	8♌24.0
2 Sa	12 41 20	8 25 11	7♏29 56	14 00 55	14R 24.4	24R 49.6	4 51.1	17 56.7	4 34.2	19 44.4	26 35.0	8R 43.1	2 03.0	8 25.0
3 Su	12 45 16	9 24 15	20 35 00	27 12 07	14 16.4	24D 41.5	5 03.7	18 15.0	4 46.0	19 55.0	26 35.7	8 42.2	2 05.2	8 26.0
4 M	12 49 13	10 23 22	3♐52 15	10♐35 21	14 10.4	24 43.8	5 18.4	18 32.8	4 57.5	20 05.6	26 36.4	8 41.3	2 07.4	8 27.0
5 Tu	12 53 09	11 22 30	17 21 26	24 10 31	14 06.8	24 56.6	5 35.0	18 49.9	5 08.8	20 16.0	26 36.9	8 40.3	2 09.6	8 27.9
6 W	12 57 06	12 21 39	1♑02 36	7♑57 43	14D 05.4	25 19.5	5 53.7	19 06.5	5 19.7	20 26.4	26 37.3	8 39.2	2 11.8	8 28.8
7 Th	13 01 03	13 20 51	14 55 53	21 57 04	14 05.6	25 52.1	6 14.2	19 22.4	5 30.4	20 36.7	26 37.6	8 38.1	2 14.0	8 29.7
8 F	13 04 59	14 20 04	29 01 14	6♒08 17	14R 06.3	26 33.8	6 36.5	19 37.8	5 40.9	20 46.9	26 37.8	8 37.0	2 16.2	8 30.6
9 Sa	13 08 56	15 19 19	13♒18 01	20 30 11	14 06.3	27 24.0	7 00.6	19 52.4	5 51.0	20 57.0	26R 37.9	8 35.8	2 18.4	8 31.5
10 Su	13 12 52	16 18 36	27 44 25	5♓00 15	14 04.6	28 21.9	7 26.5	20 06.5	6 00.9	21 07.0	26 37.9	8 34.6	2 20.6	8 32.3
11 M	13 16 49	17 17 54	12♓17 06	19 34 18	14 00.4	29 26.8	7 54.0	20 19.9	6 10.4	21 16.9	26 37.7	8 33.3	2 22.8	8 33.1
12 Tu	13 20 45	18 17 15	26 51 06	4♈06 41	13 53.6	0♎37.9	8 23.1	20 32.6	6 19.7	21 26.7	26 37.5	8 32.0	2 25.0	8 33.8
13 W	13 24 42	19 16 37	11♈20 13	18 30 51	13 44.4	1 54.3	8 53.8	20 44.6	6 28.6	21 36.4	26 37.1	8 30.6	2 27.1	8 34.6
14 Th	13 28 38	20 16 01	25 37 49	2♉40 24	13 33.7	3 15.6	9 26.0	20 55.9	6 37.3	21 46.0	26 36.7	8 29.2	2 29.3	8 35.3
15 F	13 32 35	21 15 28	9♉37 57	16 30 00	13 22.7	4 40.8	9 59.6	21 06.6	6 45.7	21 55.5	26 36.1	8 27.7	2 31.4	8 36.0
16 Sa	13 36 31	22 14 56	23 16 12	29 56 20	13 12.5	6 09.5	10 34.7	21 16.5	6 53.7	22 04.8	26 35.4	8 26.2	2 33.5	8 36.7
17 Su	13 40 28	23 14 27	6♊30 22	12♊58 23	13 04.2	7 41.0	11 11.1	21 25.6	7 01.4	22 14.1	26 34.6	8 24.7	2 35.7	8 37.4
18 M	13 44 25	24 14 00	19 20 36	25 37 21	12 58.2	9 14.9	11 48.7	21 34.0	7 08.8	22 23.3	26 33.7	8 23.1	2 37.8	8 38.0
19 Tu	13 48 21	25 13 36	1♋49 04	7♋56 16	12 54.7	10 50.8	12 27.7	21 41.7	7 15.9	22 32.3	26 32.7	8 21.5	2 39.9	8 38.6
20 W	13 52 18	26 13 13	13 59 33	19 59 32	12D 53.3	12 28.1	13 07.8	21 48.6	7 22.6	22 41.3	26 31.5	8 19.9	2 42.0	8 39.2
21 Th	13 56 14	27 12 53	25 56 53	1♌52 18	12R 53.1	14 06.7	13 49.1	21 54.6	7 29.0	22 50.1	26 30.3	8 18.2	2 44.0	8 39.7
22 F	14 00 11	28 12 36	7♌46 28	13 40 06	12 53.3	15 46.1	14 31.6	21 59.9	7 35.0	22 58.8	26 29.0	8 16.4	2 46.1	8 40.2
23 Sa	14 04 07	29 12 20	19 33 52	25 28 26	12 52.7	17 26.2	15 15.1	22 04.3	7 40.7	23 07.4	26 27.5	8 14.7	2 48.2	8 40.7
24 Su	14 08 04	0♏12 07	1♍24 26	7♍22 26	12 50.2	19 06.7	15 59.6	22 08.0	7 46.0	23 15.8	26 25.9	8 12.9	2 50.2	8 41.2
25 M	14 12 00	1 11 55	13 23 01	19 26 38	12 45.2	20 47.6	16 45.1	22 10.7	7 51.0	23 24.1	26 24.3	8 11.0	2 52.2	8 41.6
26 Tu	14 15 57	2 11 46	25 33 41	1♎44 31	12 37.4	22 28.5	17 31.6	22 12.7	7 55.6	23 32.4	26 22.5	8 09.1	2 54.2	8 42.1
27 W	14 19 54	3 11 39	7♎59 24	14 18 29	12 26.9	24 09.5	18 19.0	22R 13.7	7 59.9	23 40.4	26 20.6	8 07.2	2 56.2	8 42.5
28 Th	14 23 50	4 11 34	20 41 51	27 09 28	12 14.5	25 50.3	19 07.2	22 13.9	8 03.7	23 48.4	26 18.6	8 05.3	2 58.2	8 42.8
29 F	14 27 47	5 11 31	3♏41 17	10♏17 05	12 01.1	27 31.0	19 56.4	22 13.2	8 07.2	23 56.2	26 16.5	8 03.3	3 00.2	8 43.2
30 Sa	14 31 43	6 11 30	16 56 39	23 39 40	11 48.2	29 11.5	20 46.3	22 11.7	8 10.3	24 03.9	26 14.4	8 01.3	3 02.1	8 43.5
31 Su	14 35 40	7 11 31	0♐25 49	7♐14 46	11 36.8	0♏51.6	21 37.0	22 09.2	8 13.1	24 11.4	26 12.1	7 59.2	3 04.0	8 43.7

Astro Data

	Dy Hr Mn
☽0S	2 13:47
♀0N	10 19:29
☿ R	11 15:23
♃∠♆	14 20:18
♅ R	14 22:36
☽0N	15 11:13
☉0S	23 22:12
♀ D	27 9:15
☿0N	28 21:38
☽0S	29 19:41
☿ D	3 18:43
♄ R	9 18:17
♅✶♇	11 14:20
☽0N	12 21:20
☿0S	15 10:05

Planet Ingress

		Dy Hr Mn
⚳	♋	13 2:37
☉	♎	23 22:12
☿	♍R	25 9:56
☿	♎	11 23:27
☉	♏	24 7:08
☿	♏	30 23:37

☽0S27 3:28
♂ R28 5:15

Last Aspect Dy Hr Mn			☽ Ingress	Dy Hr Mn
1 9:21	♄	□	♎	1 18:33
3 19:46	♄	△	♏	4 4:20
5 7:19	♃	□	♐	6 11:38
8 8:55	♄	☍	♑	8 16:13
9 19:36	☉	△	♒	10 18:18
12 12:17	♄	△	♓	12 18:46
14 12:43	♄	□	♈	14 19:09
16 14:38	♄	✶	♉	16 21:14
18 17:21	☉	△	♊	19 2:42
21 7:06	☉	□	♋	21 12:10
21 22:00	♀	✶	♌	24 0:34
26 6:22	♄	✶	♍	26 13:30
28 18:40	☿	☌	♎	29 0:56

Last Aspect Dy Hr Mn			☽ Ingress	Dy Hr Mn
1 3:38	♄	△	♏	1 10:04
3 7:29	☿	✶	♐	3 17:03
5 16:16	♄	☍	♑	5 22:11
7 18:59	☿	△	♒	8 1:39
9 22:10	♄	△	♓	10 3:44
11 23:38	♄	□	♈	12 5:12
14 1:40	♄	✶	♉	14 7:26
15 21:43	♃	□	♊	16 12:07
18 13:48	♄	☌	♋	18 20:28
21 1:42	☉	□	♌	21 8:12
23 20:15	☉	✶	♍	23 21:10
26 1:37	♄	□	♎	26 8:38
28 10:26	♄	△	♏	28 17:14
30 12:43	♃	□	♐	30 23:14

☽ Phases & Eclipses

Dy Hr Mn	
7 12:33	☽ 14♐01
14 3:40	○ 20♓28
21 7:06	☾ 27♊26
29 11:29	● 5♎27
6 20:10	☽ 12♑42
13 13:23	○ 19♈20
21 1:42	☾ 26♋47
29 1:59	● 4♏47

Astro Data

1 September 1943
Julian Day # 15949
SVP 6♓02'59"
GC 26♐03.2 ⚴ 23♈36.2R
Eris 5♈36.9R ⚵ 13♑36.2R
⚷ 4♍55.5 ⚶ 13♊37.9
☽ Mean ☊ 14♌37.1

1 October 1943
Julian Day # 15979
SVP 6♓02'56"
GC 26♐03.2 ⚴ 17♈44.0R
Eris 5♈18.4R ⚵ 15♑25.8
⚷ 8♍57.9 ⚶ 19♊06.8
☽ Mean ☊ 13♌01.8

November 1943 LONGITUDE

Day	Sid.Time	☉	0 hr ☽	Noon ☽	True ☊	☿	♀	♂	⚳	♃	♄	♅	♆	♇
1 M	14 39 36	8♏11 34	14♐06 08	20♐59 35	11♌28.0	2♏31.5	22♍28.5	22♊05.9	8♋15.4	24♌18.8	26♊09.7	7♊57.1	3♎06.0	8♌44.0
2 Tu	14 43 33	9 11 38	27 54 50	4♑51 35	11R 22.2	4 11.0	23 20.8	22R 01.6	8 17.3	24 26.1	26R 07.2	7R 55.0	3 07.9	8 44.2
3 W	14 47 29	10 11 44	11♑49 38	18 48 48	11 19.2	5 50.1	24 13.7	21 56.5	8 18.9	24 33.2	26 04.6	7 52.9	3 09.7	8 44.4
4 Th	14 51 26	11 11 52	25 48 57	2♒49 58	11 18.3	7 28.9	25 07.3	21 50.5	8 20.1	24 40.2	26 01.9	7 50.7	3 11.6	8 44.6
5 F	14 55 23	12 12 00	9♒51 48	16 54 23	11 18.2	9 07.2	26 01.5	21 43.7	8 20.8	24 47.1	25 59.1	7 48.6	3 13.4	8 44.8
6 Sa	14 59 19	13 12 11	23 57 37	1♓01 25	11 17.6	10 45.2	26 56.4	21 35.9	8R 21.2	24 53.8	25 56.3	7 46.3	3 15.2	8 44.9
7 Su	15 03 16	14 12 23	8♓05 38	15 10 05	11 15.2	12 22.8	27 51.9	21 27.3	8 21.1	25 00.3	25 53.3	7 44.1	3 17.0	8 45.0
8 M	15 07 12	15 12 36	22 14 30	29 18 34	11 10.1	13 59.9	28 48.1	21 17.8	8 20.7	25 06.7	25 50.2	7 41.8	3 18.8	8 45.0
9 Tu	15 11 09	16 12 51	6♈21 52	13♈23 59	11 02.1	15 36.8	29 44.7	21 07.4	8 19.8	25 13.0	25 47.1	7 39.5	3 20.6	8R 45.1
10 W	15 15 05	17 13 07	20 24 23	27 22 34	10 51.4	17 13.2	0♎42.0	20 56.3	8 18.6	25 19.0	25 43.9	7 37.2	3 22.3	8 45.1
11 Th	15 19 02	18 13 25	4♉17 58	11♉10 05	10 39.0	18 49.3	1 39.8	20 44.2	8 16.9	25 25.0	25 40.5	7 34.9	3 24.0	8 45.1
12 F	15 22 58	19 13 45	17 58 24	24 42 31	10 26.1	20 25.1	2 38.1	20 31.4	8 14.8	25 30.8	25 37.1	7 32.6	3 25.7	8 45.0
13 Sa	15 26 55	20 14 06	1♊22 05	7♊56 50	10 13.9	22 00.5	3 36.9	20 17.7	8 12.3	25 36.4	25 33.6	7 30.2	3 27.4	8 45.0
14 Su	15 30 52	21 14 30	14 26 39	20 51 29	10 03.6	23 35.7	4 36.2	20 03.3	8 09.4	25 41.9	25 30.1	7 27.8	3 29.0	8 44.9
15 M	15 34 48	22 14 55	27 11 24	3♋26 36	9 55.8	25 10.5	5 36.0	19 48.0	8 06.1	25 47.2	25 26.4	7 25.4	3 30.7	8 44.7
16 Tu	15 38 45	23 15 22	9♋37 21	15 44 01	9 50.9	26 45.1	6 36.3	19 32.1	8 02.4	25 52.3	25 22.7	7 23.0	3 32.3	8 44.6
17 W	15 42 41	24 15 50	21 47 04	27 47 01	9 48.5	28 19.5	7 37.0	19 15.4	7 58.2	25 57.3	25 18.9	7 20.5	3 33.8	8 44.4
18 Th	15 46 38	25 16 21	3♌44 26	9♌39 58	9D 47.9	29 53.6	8 38.1	18 57.9	7 53.7	26 02.1	25 15.0	7 18.1	3 35.4	8 44.2
19 F	15 50 34	26 16 53	15 34 14	21 27 57	9R 48.1	1♐27.4	9 39.7	18 39.9	7 48.7	26 06.7	25 11.1	7 15.6	3 36.9	8 44.0
20 Sa	15 54 31	27 17 27	27 21 49	3♍16 31	9 48.0	3 01.1	10 41.6	18 21.1	7 43.3	26 11.2	25 07.1	7 13.2	3 38.4	8 43.7
21 Su	15 58 27	28 18 02	9♍12 45	15 11 12	9 46.6	4 34.5	11 44.0	18 01.8	7 37.5	26 15.5	25 03.0	7 10.7	3 39.9	8 43.4
22 M	16 02 24	29 18 40	21 12 30	27 17 17	9 43.0	6 07.8	12 46.7	17 41.9	7 31.3	26 19.6	24 58.8	7 08.2	3 41.3	8 43.1
23 Tu	16 06 21	0♐19 19	3♎26 04	9♎39 22	9 36.8	7 40.9	13 49.8	17 21.4	7 24.7	26 23.6	24 54.6	7 05.7	3 42.8	8 42.8
24 W	16 10 17	1 20 00	15 57 33	22 20 57	9 28.2	9 13.9	14 53.2	17 00.5	7 17.7	26 27.4	24 50.3	7 03.2	3 44.2	8 42.4
25 Th	16 14 14	2 20 42	28 49 45	5♏24 01	9 17.6	10 46.7	15 57.0	16 39.1	7 10.4	26 30.9	24 46.0	7 00.6	3 45.5	8 42.0
26 F	16 18 10	3 21 26	12♏03 44	18 48 42	9 06.0	12 19.4	17 01.1	16 17.3	7 02.6	26 34.4	24 41.6	6 58.1	3 46.9	8 41.6
27 Sa	16 22 07	4 22 11	25 38 39	2♐33 10	8 54.6	13 51.9	18 05.5	15 55.2	6 54.4	26 37.6	24 37.2	6 55.6	3 48.2	8 41.2
28 Su	16 26 03	5 22 58	9♐31 45	16 33 49	8 44.6	15 24.3	19 10.2	15 32.8	6 45.9	26 40.6	24 32.7	6 53.1	3 49.5	8 40.7
29 M	16 30 00	6 23 45	23 38 44	0♑45 50	8 36.9	16 56.6	20 15.2	15 10.1	6 37.0	26 43.5	24 28.1	6 50.5	3 50.7	8 40.2
30 Tu	16 33 56	7 24 34	7♑54 28	15 04 01	8 32.0	18 28.7	21 20.5	14 47.2	6 27.7	26 46.2	24 23.6	6 48.0	3 51.9	8 39.7

December 1943 LONGITUDE

Day	Sid.Time	☉	0 hr ☽	Noon ☽	True ☊	☿	♀	♂	⚳	♃	♄	♅	♆	♇
1 W	16 37 53	8♐25 24	22♑13 54	29♑23 35	8♌29.7	20♐00.6	22♎26.0	14♊24.2	6♋18.1	26♌48.7	24♊18.9	6♊45.5	3♎53.1	8♌39.1
2 Th	16 41 50	9 26 15	6♒32 40	13♒40 46	8D 29.5	21 32.4	23 31.9	14R 01.0	6R 08.1	26 51.0	24R 14.3	6R 42.9	3 54.3	8R 38.6
3 F	16 45 46	10 27 07	20 47 36	27 52 58	8R 30.2	23 04.1	24 37.9	13 37.9	5 57.8	26 53.1	24 09.5	6 40.4	3 55.5	8 38.0
4 Sa	16 49 43	11 27 59	4♓56 42	11♓58 42	8 30.6	24 35.5	25 44.3	13 14.7	5 47.2	26 55.0	24 04.8	6 37.9	3 56.6	8 37.3
5 Su	16 53 39	12 28 53	18 58 51	25 57 07	8 29.7	26 06.6	26 50.8	12 51.7	5 36.2	26 56.7	24 00.0	6 35.4	3 57.6	8 36.7
6 M	16 57 36	13 29 46	2♈53 25	9♈47 39	8 26.7	27 37.5	27 57.6	12 28.7	5 25.0	26 58.3	23 55.2	6 32.9	3 58.7	8 36.0
7 Tu	17 01 32	14 30 41	16 39 44	23 29 32	8 21.3	29 08.1	29 04.7	12 05.9	5 13.5	26 59.6	23 50.4	6 30.4	3 59.7	8 35.3
8 W	17 05 29	15 31 37	0♉16 54	7♉01 40	8 13.7	0♑38.3	0♏12.0	11 43.4	5 01.7	27 00.8	23 45.5	6 27.9	4 00.7	8 34.6
9 Th	17 09 25	16 32 33	13 43 39	20 22 38	8 04.7	2 08.1	1 19.4	11 21.0	4 49.6	27 01.8	23 40.6	6 25.4	4 01.6	8 33.9
10 F	17 13 22	17 33 30	26 58 26	3♊30 53	7 55.2	3 37.3	2 27.1	10 59.0	4 37.3	27 02.5	23 35.8	6 22.9	4 02.5	8 33.1
11 Sa	17 17 19	18 34 28	9♊59 48	16 25 05	7 46.2	5 05.9	3 35.0	10 37.4	4 24.8	27 03.1	23 30.8	6 20.4	4 03.4	8 32.3
12 Su	17 21 15	19 35 27	22 46 40	29 04 31	7 38.6	6 33.7	4 43.1	10 16.1	4 12.0	27 03.5	23 25.9	6 18.0	4 04.3	8 31.5
13 M	17 25 12	20 36 26	5♋18 42	11♋29 17	7 33.0	8 00.6	5 51.4	9 55.3	3 59.0	27R 03.7	23 21.0	6 15.6	4 05.1	8 30.7
14 Tu	17 29 08	21 37 27	17 36 29	23 40 31	7 29.7	9 26.5	6 59.9	9 34.9	3 45.8	27 03.7	23 16.0	6 13.1	4 05.9	8 29.9
15 W	17 33 05	22 38 28	29 41 42	5♌40 24	7D 28.6	10 51.1	8 08.6	9 15.1	3 32.4	27 03.5	23 11.1	6 10.7	4 06.7	8 29.0
16 Th	17 37 01	23 39 31	11♌37 03	17 32 06	7 29.0	12 14.2	9 17.5	8 55.8	3 18.9	27 03.1	23 06.2	6 08.4	4 07.4	8 28.1
17 F	17 40 58	24 40 34	23 26 07	29 19 40	7 30.5	13 35.6	10 26.5	8 37.0	3 05.2	27 02.5	23 01.2	6 06.0	4 08.1	8 27.2
18 Sa	17 44 55	25 41 38	5♍13 19	11♍07 44	7 32.1	14 54.8	11 35.7	8 18.9	2 51.4	27 01.7	22 56.3	6 03.6	4 08.8	8 26.3
19 Su	17 48 51	26 42 42	17 03 33	23 01 26	7R 33.1	16 11.7	12 45.1	8 01.4	2 37.4	27 00.7	22 51.3	6 01.3	4 09.4	8 25.3
20 M	17 52 48	27 43 48	29 02 03	5♎06 02	7 32.9	17 25.7	13 54.6	7 44.6	2 23.4	26 59.5	22 46.4	5 59.0	4 10.0	8 24.3
21 Tu	17 56 44	28 44 55	11♎14 01	17 26 36	7 31.0	18 36.3	15 04.3	7 28.4	2 09.3	26 58.1	22 41.5	5 56.7	4 10.5	8 23.3
22 W	18 00 41	29 46 02	23 44 19	0♏07 37	7 27.4	19 43.1	16 14.1	7 13.0	1 55.1	26 56.6	22 36.6	5 54.5	4 11.1	8 22.3
23 Th	18 04 37	0♑47 10	6♏36 55	13 12 28	7 22.4	20 45.4	17 24.0	6 58.3	1 40.9	26 54.8	22 31.7	5 52.2	4 11.6	8 21.3
24 F	18 08 34	1 48 18	19 54 25	26 42 48	7 16.6	21 42.5	18 34.2	6 44.3	1 26.6	26 52.8	22 26.8	5 50.0	4 12.0	8 20.3
25 Sa	18 12 30	2 49 28	3♐37 28	10♐38 09	7 10.7	22 33.7	19 44.4	6 31.2	1 12.3	26 50.7	22 22.0	5 47.8	4 12.4	8 19.2
26 Su	18 16 27	3 50 37	17 44 23	24 55 35	7 05.4	23 18.1	20 54.7	6 18.8	0 58.1	26 48.3	22 17.2	5 45.7	4 12.8	8 18.1
27 M	18 20 24	4 51 47	2♑11 03	9♑29 58	7 01.6	23 54.9	22 05.2	6 07.2	0 43.8	26 45.8	22 12.4	5 43.5	4 13.2	8 17.0
28 Tu	18 24 20	5 52 58	16 51 24	24 14 27	6D 59.3	24 23.1	23 15.8	5 56.4	0 29.6	26 43.0	22 07.7	5 41.4	4 13.5	8 15.9
29 W	18 28 17	6 54 08	1♒38 10	9♒01 39	6 58.8	24 41.9	24 26.5	5 46.5	0 15.5	26 40.1	22 03.0	5 39.4	4 13.8	8 14.8
30 Th	18 32 13	7 55 19	16 24 02	23 44 33	6 59.6	24R 50.4	25 37.3	5 37.4	0 01.5	26 37.0	21 58.3	5 37.3	4 14.0	8 13.6
31 F	18 36 10	8 56 29	1♓02 34	8♓17 32	7 01.0	24 47.8	26 48.3	5 29.1	29♊47.6	26 33.7	21 53.7	5 35.3	4 14.3	8 12.5

Astro Data

	Dy Hr Mn
♆0S	1 8:37
⚳ R	6 21:27
☽0N	9 6:10
♇ R	10 9:01
♀0S	11 20:31
♃✱♄	13 4:45
☽0S	23 13:07
☽0N	6 13:13
♄∠♇	11 3:15
♃ R	13 23:25
☽0S	20 23:08
☿ R	30 18:33

Planet Ingress

		Dy Hr Mn
♀	♎	9 18:25
☿	♐	18 13:39
☉	♐	23 4:22
☿	♑	8 1:47
♀	♏	8 7:45
☉	♑	22 17:29
⚳	♊R	30 14:34

Last Aspect / ☽ Ingress (November)

Last Aspect Dy Hr Mn			☽ Ingress	Dy Hr Mn
1 20:56	♄	☍	♑	2 3:37
3 21:55	♀	△	♒	4 7:10
6 3:23	♄	△	♓	6 10:16
8 11:04	♀	☍	♈	8 13:10
10 9:10	♄	✱	♉	10 16:32
12 13:27	♃	□	♊	12 21:31
14 21:13	♃	✱	♋	15 5:22
17 13:15	☿	△	♌	17 16:27
19 22:43	☉	□	♍	20 5:21
22 16:19	☉	✱	♎	22 17:19
24 19:40	♃	✱	♏	25 2:09
27 1:40	♃	□	♐	27 7:35
29 5:11	♃	△	♑	29 10:43

Last Aspect / ☽ Ingress (December)

Last Aspect Dy Hr Mn			☽ Ingress	Dy Hr Mn
30 23:23	♀	□	♒	1 13:01
3 10:18	♃	☍	♓	3 15:36
5 12:18	☿	□	♈	5 19:00
7 23:13	☿	△	♉	7 23:30
10 0:07	♃	□	♊	10 5:32
12 8:09	♃	✱	♋	12 13:46
13 4:20	☿	☍	♌	15 0:37
17 7:21	♃	☌	♍	17 13:22
19 20:03	☉	□	♎	20 1:55
22 11:16	☉	✱	♏	22 11:46
24 12:17	♃	□	♐	24 17:44
26 15:06	♃	△	♑	26 20:24
28 12:14	☿	☌	♒	28 21:21
30 16:42	♃	☍	♓	30 22:17

☽ Phases & Eclipses

Dy Hr Mn		
5 3:22	☽	11♒50
12 1:27	○	18♉47
19 22:43	☾	26♌44
27 15:23	●	4♐31
4 11:03	☽	11♓26
11 16:24	○	18♊46
19 20:03	☾	27♍03
27 3:50	●	4♑31

Astro Data

1 November 1943
Julian Day # 16010
SVP 6♓02'53"
GC 26♐03.3 ⚴ 8♈55.7R
Eris 4♈59.6R ⚵ 22♑17.5
⚷ 12♍34.3 ⚶ 19♊01.0R
☽ Mean ☊ 11♌23.2

1 December 1943
Julian Day # 16040
SVP 6♓02'49"
GC 26♐03.4 ⚴ 4♈55.2R
Eris 4♈47.4R ⚵ 2♒13.7
⚷ 14♍58.0 ⚶ 12♊53.2R
☽ Mean ☊ 9♌47.9

LONGITUDE — January 1944

Day	Sid.Time	☉	0 hr ☽	Noon ☽	True ☊	☿	♀	♂	⚳	♃	♄	♅	♆	♇
1 Sa	18 40 06	9♑57 39	15♓28 59	22♓36 37	7♌02.5	24♑33.6	27♏59.3	5♊21.6	29♊33.8	26♌30.2	21♊49.1	5♊33.4	4♎14.4	8♌11.3
2 Su	18 44 03	10 58 49	29 40 13	6♈39 39	7R 03.3	24R 07.5	29 10.4	5R 15.0	29R 20.1	26R 26.5	21R 44.5	5R 31.4	4 14.6	8R 10.1
3 M	18 47 59	11 59 59	13♈34 52	20 25 51	7 03.1	23 29.6	0♐21.6	5 09.2	29 06.6	26 22.7	21 40.0	5 29.5	4 14.7	8 08.9
4 Tu	18 51 56	13 01 08	27 12 42	3♉55 29	7 01.7	22 40.6	1 32.9	5 04.2	28 53.2	26 18.7	21 35.6	5 27.6	4 14.8	8 07.7
5 W	18 55 53	14 02 17	10♉34 20	17 09 21	6 59.2	21 41.3	2 44.3	5 00.1	28 40.1	26 14.5	21 31.2	5 25.8	4R 14.8	8 06.4
6 Th	18 59 49	15 03 26	23 40 42	0♊08 30	6 56.0	20 33.4	3 55.8	4 56.8	28 27.1	26 10.1	21 26.9	5 24.0	4 14.8	8 05.2
7 F	19 03 46	16 04 34	6♊32 53	12 53 59	6 52.5	19 18.9	5 07.4	4 54.2	28 14.4	26 05.5	21 22.6	5 22.3	4 14.8	8 03.9
8 Sa	19 07 42	17 05 42	19 11 57	25 26 53	6 49.2	18 00.1	6 19.0	4 52.5	28 01.9	26 00.8	21 18.4	5 20.6	4 14.7	8 02.7
9 Su	19 11 39	18 06 50	1♋38 55	7♋48 12	6 46.5	16 39.7	7 30.8	4D 51.6	27 49.7	25 56.0	21 14.3	5 18.9	4 14.6	8 01.4
10 M	19 15 35	19 07 58	13 54 53	19 59 07	6 44.7	15 20.2	8 42.6	4 51.5	27 37.7	25 50.9	21 10.2	5 17.3	4 14.5	8 00.1
11 Tu	19 19 32	20 09 05	26 01 05	2♌01 00	6D 43.9	14 04.1	9 54.5	4 52.1	27 26.0	25 45.7	21 06.2	5 15.7	4 14.4	7 58.8
12 W	19 23 28	21 10 12	7♌59 06	13 55 39	6 44.0	12 53.4	11 06.5	4 53.5	27 14.6	25 40.4	21 02.3	5 14.1	4 14.2	7 57.5
13 Th	19 27 25	22 11 19	19 50 56	25 45 18	6 44.8	11 49.8	12 18.5	4 55.6	27 03.4	25 34.9	20 58.4	5 12.6	4 13.9	7 56.2
14 F	19 31 22	23 12 25	1♍39 06	7♍32 46	6 46.0	10 54.6	13 30.6	4 58.4	26 52.6	25 29.2	20 54.6	5 11.1	4 13.7	7 54.9
15 Sa	19 35 18	24 13 31	13 26 44	19 21 28	6 47.4	10 08.6	14 42.8	5 02.0	26 42.1	25 23.4	20 50.9	5 09.7	4 13.4	7 53.5
16 Su	19 39 15	25 14 37	25 17 28	1♎15 17	6 48.5	9 32.2	15 55.1	5 06.3	26 32.0	25 17.5	20 47.2	5 08.3	4 13.0	7 52.2
17 M	19 43 11	26 15 43	7♎15 28	13 18 35	6 49.3	9 05.4	17 07.4	5 11.3	26 22.1	25 11.4	20 43.7	5 07.0	4 12.7	7 50.9
18 Tu	19 47 08	27 16 49	19 25 12	25 35 56	6R 49.7	8 48.0	18 19.8	5 17.0	26 12.7	25 05.2	20 40.2	5 05.7	4 12.3	7 49.5
19 W	19 51 04	28 17 54	1♏51 18	8♏11 53	6 49.5	8D 39.7	19 32.3	5 23.4	26 03.5	24 58.8	20 36.8	5 04.4	4 11.8	7 48.2
20 Th	19 55 01	29 18 59	14 38 08	21 10 31	6 49.0	8 39.9	20 44.8	5 30.5	25 54.8	24 52.4	20 33.5	5 03.2	4 11.4	7 46.8
21 F	19 58 57	0♒20 03	27 49 23	4♐34 58	6 48.3	8 48.0	21 57.4	5 38.2	25 46.4	24 45.8	20 30.3	5 02.1	4 10.9	7 45.4
22 Sa	20 02 54	1 21 08	11♐27 24	18 26 40	6 47.6	9 03.6	23 10.0	5 46.5	25 38.5	24 39.1	20 27.2	5 01.0	4 10.4	7 44.1
23 Su	20 06 51	2 22 11	25 32 38	2♑44 55	6 47.0	9 25.9	24 22.7	5 55.5	25 30.9	24 32.2	20 24.1	4 59.9	4 09.8	7 42.7
24 M	20 10 47	3 23 15	10♑03 01	17 26 16	6 46.6	9 54.3	25 35.4	6 05.2	25 23.7	24 25.3	20 21.2	4 58.9	4 09.2	7 41.3
25 Tu	20 14 44	4 24 17	24 53 48	2♒24 38	6D 46.5	10 28.4	26 48.2	6 15.4	25 16.9	24 18.3	20 18.3	4 58.0	4 08.6	7 39.9
26 W	20 18 40	5 25 19	9♒57 41	17 31 48	6 46.5	11 07.5	28 01.0	6 26.2	25 10.5	24 11.1	20 15.6	4 57.1	4 07.9	7 38.5
27 Th	20 22 37	6 26 19	25 05 48	2♓38 31	6R 46.6	11 51.3	29 13.9	6 37.6	25 04.6	24 03.9	20 12.9	4 56.2	4 07.3	7 37.2
28 F	20 26 33	7 27 19	10♓08 53	17 35 53	6 46.6	12 39.2	0♑26.8	6 49.6	24 59.0	23 56.6	20 10.3	4 55.4	4 06.5	7 35.8
29 Sa	20 30 30	8 28 17	24 58 40	2♈16 33	6 46.4	13 30.9	1 39.7	7 02.2	24 53.9	23 49.2	20 07.9	4 54.6	4 05.8	7 34.4
30 Su	20 34 26	9 29 15	9♈28 58	16 35 34	6 46.2	14 26.1	2 52.7	7 15.3	24 49.3	23 41.7	20 05.5	4 53.9	4 05.0	7 33.0
31 M	20 38 23	10 30 10	23 36 06	0♉30 30	6D 46.0	15 24.4	4 05.7	7 29.0	24 45.0	23 34.2	20 03.3	4 53.3	4 04.2	7 31.6

LONGITUDE — February 1944

Day	Sid.Time	☉	0 hr ☽	Noon ☽	True ☊	☿	♀	♂	⚳	♃	♄	♅	♆	♇
1 Tu	20 42 20	11♒31 05	7♉18 49	14♉01 12	6♌46.0	16♑25.5	5♑18.7	7♊43.1	24♊41.2	23♌26.6	20♊01.1	4♊52.7	4♎03.4	7♌30.2
2 W	20 46 16	12 31 58	20 37 54	27 09 14	6 46.2	17 29.3	6 31.8	7 57.8	24R 37.8	23R 18.9	19R 59.1	4R 52.1	4R 02.5	7R 28.9
3 Th	20 50 13	13 32 50	3♊35 31	9♊57 10	6 46.7	18 35.4	7 44.9	8 13.0	24 34.8	23 11.2	19 57.1	4 51.6	4 01.6	7 27.5
4 F	20 54 09	14 33 41	16 14 35	22 28 09	6 47.4	19 43.7	8 58.0	8 28.7	24 32.3	23 03.4	19 55.3	4 51.2	4 00.7	7 26.1
5 Sa	20 58 06	15 34 30	28 38 18	4♋45 23	6 48.3	20 54.0	10 11.2	8 44.8	24 30.2	22 55.6	19 53.6	4 50.8	3 59.7	7 24.7
6 Su	21 02 02	16 35 18	10♋49 49	16 51 55	6 49.2	22 06.2	11 24.4	9 01.4	24 28.6	22 47.7	19 51.9	4 50.5	3 58.7	7 23.4
7 M	21 05 59	17 36 05	22 52 03	28 50 31	6R 49.8	23 20.1	12 37.6	9 18.5	24 27.3	22 39.9	19 50.4	4 50.2	3 57.8	7 22.0
8 Tu	21 09 55	18 36 50	4♌47 36	10♌43 36	6 49.9	24 35.7	13 50.9	9 36.0	24 26.5	22 32.0	19 49.0	4 49.9	3 56.7	7 20.7
9 W	21 13 52	19 37 34	16 38 46	22 33 22	6 49.3	25 52.7	15 04.2	9 53.9	24D 26.1	22 24.0	19 47.7	4 49.7	3 55.7	7 19.3
10 Th	21 17 49	20 38 16	28 27 40	4♍21 53	6 48.0	27 11.2	16 17.5	10 12.2	24 26.2	22 16.1	19 46.6	4 49.6	3 54.6	7 18.0
11 F	21 21 45	21 38 58	10♍16 19	16 11 13	6 46.0	28 31.1	17 30.9	10 30.9	24 26.6	22 08.1	19 45.5	4 49.5	3 53.5	7 16.6
12 Sa	21 25 42	22 39 38	22 06 53	28 03 36	6 43.6	29 52.2	18 44.2	10 50.1	24 27.5	22 00.2	19 44.5	4D 49.5	3 52.4	7 15.3
13 Su	21 29 38	23 40 16	4♎01 42	10♎01 33	6 40.8	1♒14.5	19 57.6	11 09.6	24 28.8	21 52.2	19 43.7	4 49.5	3 51.2	7 14.0
14 M	21 33 35	24 40 54	16 03 29	22 07 57	6 38.2	2 38.1	21 11.1	11 29.5	24 30.5	21 44.3	19 42.9	4 49.6	3 50.0	7 12.6
15 Tu	21 37 31	25 41 30	28 15 19	4♏26 04	6 36.1	4 02.8	22 24.5	11 49.7	24 32.7	21 36.4	19 42.3	4 49.7	3 48.8	7 11.3
16 W	21 41 28	26 42 05	10♏40 39	16 59 31	6D 34.9	5 28.6	23 38.0	12 10.4	24 35.2	21 28.5	19 41.8	4 49.9	3 47.6	7 10.0
17 Th	21 45 24	27 42 39	23 22 03	29 51 56	6 34.5	6 55.4	24 51.5	12 31.3	24 38.1	21 20.6	19 41.4	4 50.2	3 46.4	7 08.8
18 F	21 49 21	28 43 12	6♐26 22	13♐06 47	6 35.2	8 23.3	26 05.0	12 52.7	24 41.5	21 12.8	19 41.1	4 50.5	3 45.1	7 07.5
19 Sa	21 53 18	29 43 44	19 53 30	26 46 44	6 36.5	9 52.3	27 18.5	13 14.3	24 45.2	21 05.0	19 40.9	4 50.8	3 43.8	7 06.2
20 Su	21 57 14	0♓44 14	3♑46 36	10♑53 03	6 38.0	11 22.2	28 32.1	13 36.3	24 49.4	20 57.2	19D 40.8	4 51.2	3 42.5	7 05.0
21 M	22 01 11	1 44 43	18 05 55	25 24 51	6R 39.2	12 53.2	29 45.7	13 58.6	24 53.9	20 49.5	19 40.9	4 51.7	3 41.2	7 03.7
22 Tu	22 05 07	2 45 11	2♒49 19	10♒18 33	6 39.4	14 25.1	0♒59.3	14 21.2	24 58.9	20 41.8	19 41.0	4 52.2	3 39.8	7 02.5
23 W	22 09 04	3 45 37	17 51 41	25 27 38	6 38.4	15 58.0	2 12.9	14 44.2	25 04.2	20 34.2	19 41.3	4 52.7	3 38.4	7 01.3
24 Th	22 13 00	4 46 01	3♓05 11	10♓43 05	6 36.0	17 32.0	3 26.5	15 07.4	25 09.9	20 26.7	19 41.7	4 53.4	3 37.1	7 00.1
25 F	22 16 57	5 46 23	18 20 00	25 54 38	6 32.3	19 06.9	4 40.2	15 31.0	25 16.0	20 19.2	19 42.2	4 54.0	3 35.6	6 58.9
26 Sa	22 20 53	6 46 44	3♈25 46	10♈52 20	6 27.9	20 42.8	5 53.8	15 54.8	25 22.4	20 11.8	19 42.8	4 54.7	3 34.2	6 57.7
27 Su	22 24 50	7 47 03	18 13 23	25 28 12	6 23.3	22 19.7	7 07.5	16 18.9	25 29.3	20 04.5	19 43.6	4 55.5	3 32.8	6 56.5
28 M	22 28 47	8 47 20	2♉36 14	9♉37 10	6 19.4	23 57.6	8 21.1	16 43.3	25 36.5	19 57.3	19 44.4	4 56.3	3 31.3	6 55.4
29 Tu	22 32 43	9 47 35	16 30 52	23 17 22	6 16.7	25 36.5	9 34.8	17 07.9	25 44.0	19 50.2	19 45.4	4 57.2	3 29.8	6 54.2

Astro Data (Dy Hr Mn)
☽ 0N 2 19:27
♆ R 6 6:23
♂ D 10 4:37
☽ 0S 17 7:38
☿ D 19 23:21
☽ 0N 30 2:45

⚳ D 9 21:38
♅ D 12 12:14
☽ 0S 13 14:02
♄ D 20 13:18
☽ 0N 26 12:09

Planet Ingress (Dy Hr Mn)
♀ ♐ 3 4:43
☉ ♒ 21 4:07
♀ ♑ 28 3:11

☿ ♒ 12 14:17
☉ ♓ 19 18:27
♀ ♒ 21 16:40

Last Aspect (Dy Hr Mn) — **☽ Ingress** (Dy Hr Mn)
1 21:58 ♀ △ ♈ 2 0:34
3 22:28 ♃ △ ♉ 4 4:58
6 4:39 ♃ □ ♊ 6 11:44
8 13:05 ♃ ⚹ ♋ 8 20:48
10 10:09 ☉ ☍ ♌ 11 7:58
13 11:39 ♃ ☌ ♍ 13 20:38
15 22:46 ☉ △ ♎ 16 9:29
18 15:32 ☉ □ ♏ 18 20:27
21 3:52 ☉ ⚹ ♐ 21 3:53
22 22:25 ♃ △ ♑ 23 7:27
23 23:20 ☿ ☌ ♒ 25 8:09
27 6:06 ♀ ⚹ ♓ 27 7:48
28 16:10 ♄ □ ♈ 29 8:15
31 0:03 ♃ △ ♉ 31 11:07

Last Aspect (Dy Hr Mn) — **☽ Ingress** (Dy Hr Mn)
2 4:59 ♃ □ ♊ 2 17:17
4 13:08 ♃ ⚹ ♋ 5 2:40
6 23:40 ☿ ☍ ♌ 7 14:20
9 11:41 ♃ ☌ ♍ 10 3:08
11 19:13 ♄ □ ♎ 12 15:54
14 17:28 ☉ △ ♏ 15 3:24
17 7:42 ☉ □ ♐ 17 12:15
19 17:29 ☉ ⚹ ♑ 19 17:33
19 23:54 ♆ □ ♒ 21 19:27
23 4:21 ♃ ☍ ♓ 23 19:09
25 2:10 ♄ □ ♈ 25 18:31
27 6:07 ☿ ⚹ ♉ 27 19:36

☽ Phases & Eclipses (Dy Hr Mn)
2 20:04 ☽ 11♈19
10 10:09 ○ 19♋03
18 15:32 ☾ 27♎26
25 15:24 ● 4♒33
25 15:26:16 ● T 04'09"

1 7:08 ☽ 11♉19
9 5:29 ○ 19♌21
9 5:14 ● A 0.579
17 7:42 ☾ 27♏32
24 1:59 ● 4♓21

Astro Data
1 January 1944
Julian Day # 16071
SVP 6♓02'43"
GC 26♐03.4 ⚴ 8♈02.9
Eris 4♈44.8 ⚵ 14♒44.4
⚷ 15♍48.7R ⚶ 5♊47.6R
☽ Mean ☊ 8♌09.5

1 February 1944
Julian Day # 16102
SVP 6♓02'39"
GC 26♐03.5 ⚴ 16♈50.5
Eris 4♈53.4 ⚵ 28♒46.6
⚷ 14♍51.0R ⚶ 4♊32.7
☽ Mean ☊ 6♌31.0

March 1944 LONGITUDE

Day	Sid.Time	☉	0 hr ☽	Noon ☽	True ☊	☿	♀	♂	⚳	♃	♄	♅	♆	♇
1 W	22 36 40	10♓47 48	29♉56 53	6♊29 43	6♌15.5	27♒16.4	10♒48.5	17♊32.8	25♊51.9	19♌43.2	19♊46.4	4♊58.1	3♎28.4	6♌53.1
2 Th	22 40 36	11 47 58	12♊56 17	19 17 05	6D 15.7	28 57.4	12 02.2	17 58.0	26 00.2	19R 36.3	19 47.6	4 59.1	3R 26.9	6R 52.0
3 F	22 44 33	12 48 07	25 32 40	1♋43 37	6 16.9	0♓39.4	13 15.9	18 23.4	26 08.8	19 29.5	19 48.9	5 00.1	3 25.3	6 50.9
4 Sa	22 48 29	13 48 14	7♋50 30	13 53 55	6 18.6	2 22.5	14 29.6	18 49.0	26 17.8	19 22.8	19 50.3	5 01.2	3 23.8	6 49.9
5 Su	22 52 26	14 48 18	19 54 27	25 52 38	6R 20.1	4 06.7	15 43.3	19 14.9	26 27.0	19 16.2	19 51.8	5 02.4	3 22.3	6 48.8
6 M	22 56 22	15 48 21	1♌49 00	7♌44 03	6 20.6	5 52.0	16 57.0	19 41.0	26 36.7	19 09.7	19 53.4	5 03.5	3 20.7	6 47.8
7 Tu	23 00 19	16 48 21	13 38 14	19 31 58	6 19.6	7 38.4	18 10.7	20 07.3	26 46.6	19 03.4	19 55.2	5 04.8	3 19.1	6 46.8
8 W	23 04 16	17 48 19	25 25 37	1♍19 32	6 16.6	9 25.9	19 24.5	20 33.8	26 56.9	18 57.2	19 57.0	5 06.0	3 17.6	6 45.8
9 Th	23 08 12	18 48 15	7♍14 01	13 09 19	6 11.5	11 14.5	20 38.2	21 00.5	27 07.4	18 51.1	19 59.0	5 07.4	3 16.0	6 44.8
10 F	23 12 09	19 48 10	19 05 40	25 03 19	6 04.6	13 04.2	21 51.9	21 27.5	27 18.3	18 45.2	20 01.0	5 08.7	3 14.4	6 43.8
11 Sa	23 16 05	20 48 02	1♎02 25	7♎03 11	5 56.3	14 55.1	23 05.7	21 54.6	27 29.5	18 39.3	20 03.2	5 10.2	3 12.8	6 42.9
12 Su	23 20 02	21 47 53	13 05 47	19 10 23	5 47.4	16 47.1	24 19.5	22 21.9	27 41.0	18 33.7	20 05.4	5 11.6	3 11.2	6 42.0
13 M	23 23 58	22 47 41	25 17 10	1♏26 21	5 38.8	18 40.3	25 33.2	22 49.5	27 52.7	18 28.2	20 07.8	5 13.2	3 09.6	6 41.1
14 Tu	23 27 55	23 47 28	7♏38 07	13 52 44	5 31.3	20 34.6	26 47.0	23 17.2	28 04.8	18 22.8	20 10.3	5 14.7	3 07.9	6 40.2
15 W	23 31 51	24 47 14	20 10 27	26 31 32	5 25.5	22 29.9	28 00.8	23 45.1	28 17.2	18 17.6	20 12.9	5 16.3	3 06.3	6 39.3
16 Th	23 35 48	25 46 57	2♐56 19	9♐25 06	5 22.0	24 26.3	29 14.6	24 13.1	28 29.8	18 12.5	20 15.5	5 18.0	3 04.7	6 38.5
17 F	23 39 44	26 46 39	15 58 14	22 36 01	5D 20.5	26 23.7	0♓28.4	24 41.4	28 42.7	18 07.6	20 18.3	5 19.7	3 03.0	6 37.7
18 Sa	23 43 41	27 46 19	29 18 47	6♑06 49	5 20.7	28 22.1	1 42.2	25 09.8	28 55.9	18 02.9	20 21.2	5 21.5	3 01.4	6 36.9
19 Su	23 47 38	28 45 58	13♑00 20	19 59 30	5 21.7	0♈21.3	2 56.0	25 38.3	29 09.4	17 58.3	20 24.2	5 23.3	2 59.7	6 36.1
20 M	23 51 34	29 45 34	27 04 20	4♒14 48	5R 22.3	2 21.3	4 09.8	26 07.1	29 23.1	17 53.9	20 27.3	5 25.1	2 58.1	6 35.4
21 Tu	23 55 31	0♈45 09	11♒30 39	18 51 30	5 21.6	4 21.9	5 23.6	26 36.0	29 37.1	17 49.6	20 30.5	5 27.0	2 56.4	6 34.6
22 W	23 59 27	1 44 42	26 16 46	3♓45 44	5 18.7	6 23.0	6 37.4	27 05.1	29 51.3	17 45.6	20 33.8	5 29.0	2 54.8	6 33.9
23 Th	0 03 24	2 44 14	11♓17 26	18 50 49	5 13.3	8 24.4	7 51.3	27 34.3	0♋05.9	17 41.7	20 37.2	5 30.9	2 53.1	6 33.2
24 F	0 07 20	3 43 43	26 24 41	3♈57 46	5 05.6	10 25.8	9 05.1	28 03.7	0 20.6	17 37.9	20 40.6	5 32.9	2 51.4	6 32.6
25 Sa	0 11 17	4 43 10	11♈28 48	18 56 33	4 56.4	12 27.1	10 18.9	28 33.2	0 35.6	17 34.4	20 44.2	5 35.0	2 49.8	6 31.9
26 Su	0 15 13	5 42 35	26 19 54	3♉37 52	4 46.8	14 27.9	11 32.7	29 02.9	0 50.9	17 31.0	20 47.9	5 37.1	2 48.1	6 31.3
27 M	0 19 10	6 41 58	10♉49 39	17 54 39	4 38.0	16 28.0	12 46.5	29 32.7	1 06.3	17 27.8	20 51.7	5 39.3	2 46.5	6 30.7
28 Tu	0 23 07	7 41 18	24 52 30	1♊42 59	4 30.8	18 26.9	14 00.3	0♋02.6	1 22.1	17 24.8	20 55.5	5 41.5	2 44.8	6 30.2
29 W	0 27 03	8 40 37	8♊26 09	15 02 11	4 26.0	20 24.5	15 14.1	0 32.7	1 38.0	17 22.0	20 59.5	5 43.7	2 43.2	6 29.6
30 Th	0 31 00	9 39 53	21 31 23	27 54 13	4 23.4	22 20.2	16 27.9	1 02.9	1 54.2	17 19.4	21 03.5	5 46.0	2 41.5	6 29.1
31 F	0 34 56	10 39 07	4♋11 12	10♋22 58	4D 22.7	24 13.6	17 41.7	1 33.3	2 10.6	17 16.9	21 07.7	5 48.3	2 39.9	6 28.6

April 1944 LONGITUDE

Day	Sid.Time	☉	0 hr ☽	Noon ☽	True ☊	☿	♀	♂	⚳	♃	♄	♅	♆	♇
1 Sa	0 38 53	11♈38 18	16♋30 08	22♋33 23	4♌23.1	26♈04.5	18♓55.5	2♋03.8	2♋27.2	17♌14.6	21♊11.9	5♊50.6	2♎38.2	6♌28.2
2 Su	0 42 49	12 37 27	28 33 23	4♌30 50	4R 23.4	27 52.3	20 09.3	2 34.3	2 44.0	17R 12.6	21 16.2	5 53.0	2R 36.6	6R 27.7
3 M	0 46 46	13 36 34	10♌26 22	16 20 37	4 22.7	29 36.7	21 23.1	3 05.1	3 01.0	17 10.7	21 20.6	5 55.4	2 35.0	6 27.3
4 Tu	0 50 42	14 35 39	22 14 11	28 07 37	4 20.1	1♉17.3	22 36.9	3 35.9	3 18.3	17 09.0	21 25.1	5 57.9	2 33.4	6 26.9
5 W	0 54 39	15 34 41	4♍01 26	9♍56 04	4 14.8	2 53.9	23 50.7	4 06.8	3 35.7	17 07.4	21 29.6	6 00.4	2 31.8	6 26.6
6 Th	0 58 36	16 33 41	15 51 57	21 49 25	4 06.9	4 26.0	25 04.4	4 37.9	3 53.3	17 06.1	21 34.3	6 02.9	2 30.2	6 26.2
7 F	1 02 32	17 32 39	27 48 46	3♎50 15	3 56.4	5 53.3	26 18.2	5 09.0	4 11.2	17 05.0	21 39.0	6 05.5	2 28.6	6 25.9
8 Sa	1 06 29	18 31 34	9♎54 03	16 00 19	3 44.0	7 15.7	27 32.0	5 40.3	4 29.2	17 04.0	21 43.8	6 08.1	2 27.0	6 25.6
9 Su	1 10 25	19 30 28	22 09 08	28 20 37	3 30.8	8 32.9	28 45.8	6 11.6	4 47.4	17 03.2	21 48.7	6 10.7	2 25.4	6 25.4
10 M	1 14 22	20 29 20	4♏34 46	10♏51 39	3 17.8	9 44.7	29 59.5	6 43.1	5 05.7	17 02.7	21 53.7	6 13.4	2 23.8	6 25.2
11 Tu	1 18 18	21 28 10	17 11 16	23 33 38	3 06.3	10 50.9	1♈13.3	7 14.7	5 24.3	17 02.3	21 58.8	6 16.1	2 22.3	6 25.0
12 W	1 22 15	22 26 58	29 58 50	6♐26 52	2 57.1	11 51.4	2 27.1	7 46.3	5 43.0	17D 02.1	22 03.9	6 18.8	2 20.7	6 24.8
13 Th	1 26 11	23 25 44	12♐57 51	19 31 52	2 50.7	12 46.0	3 40.8	8 18.1	6 02.0	17 02.0	22 09.1	6 21.6	2 19.2	6 24.6
14 F	1 30 08	24 24 29	26 09 03	2♑49 34	2 47.1	13 34.6	4 54.6	8 49.9	6 21.1	17 02.2	22 14.4	6 24.4	2 17.7	6 24.5
15 Sa	1 34 04	25 23 12	9♑33 35	16 21 16	2D 45.7	14 17.2	6 08.3	9 21.9	6 40.3	17 02.6	22 19.7	6 27.2	2 16.2	6 24.4
16 Su	1 38 01	26 21 53	23 12 47	0♒08 17	2R 45.6	14 53.7	7 22.1	9 53.9	6 59.7	17 03.1	22 25.2	6 30.1	2 14.7	6 24.3
17 M	1 41 58	27 20 33	7♒07 52	14 11 32	2 45.4	15 24.0	8 35.9	10 26.0	7 19.3	17 03.8	22 30.7	6 33.0	2 13.2	6 24.3
18 Tu	1 45 54	28 19 11	21 19 14	28 30 48	2 43.8	15 48.2	9 49.6	10 58.2	7 39.1	17 04.8	22 36.2	6 35.9	2 11.8	6D 24.3
19 W	1 49 51	29 17 47	5♓45 55	13♓04 08	2 39.9	16 06.2	11 03.4	11 30.5	7 59.0	17 05.9	22 41.9	6 38.8	2 10.3	6 24.3
20 Th	1 53 47	0♉16 21	20 24 52	27 47 22	2 33.2	16 18.1	12 17.1	12 02.9	8 19.1	17 07.1	22 47.6	6 41.8	2 08.9	6 24.3
21 F	1 57 44	1 14 54	5♈10 47	12♈34 09	2 23.8	16R 24.1	13 30.9	12 35.4	8 39.3	17 08.6	22 53.3	6 44.8	2 07.5	6 24.3
22 Sa	2 01 40	2 13 25	19 56 26	27 16 37	2 12.7	16 24.3	14 44.6	13 08.0	8 59.6	17 10.2	22 59.2	6 47.8	2 06.1	6 24.4
23 Su	2 05 37	3 11 54	4♉33 39	11♉46 38	2 00.8	16 18.8	15 58.4	13 40.6	9 20.2	17 12.1	23 05.1	6 50.9	2 04.7	6 24.5
24 M	2 09 33	4 10 21	18 54 42	25 57 12	1 49.7	16 07.9	17 12.1	14 13.3	9 40.8	17 14.1	23 11.1	6 53.9	2 03.4	6 24.7
25 Tu	2 13 30	5 08 47	2♊53 35	9♊43 32	1 40.3	15 52.0	18 25.8	14 46.1	10 01.6	17 16.3	23 17.1	6 57.0	2 02.0	6 24.9
26 W	2 17 27	6 07 10	16 26 52	23 03 36	1 33.4	15 31.3	19 39.6	15 19.0	10 22.6	17 18.7	23 23.2	7 00.2	2 00.7	6 25.0
27 Th	2 21 23	7 05 31	29 33 53	5♋58 01	1 29.1	15 06.4	20 53.3	15 52.0	10 43.7	17 21.2	23 29.4	7 03.3	1 59.4	6 25.3
28 F	2 25 20	8 03 51	12♋16 23	18 29 31	1 27.2	14 37.8	22 07.0	16 25.0	11 04.9	17 24.0	23 35.6	7 06.5	1 58.2	6 25.5
29 Sa	2 29 16	9 02 08	24 37 59	0♌42 24	1 26.8	14 05.9	23 20.7	16 58.1	11 26.3	17 26.9	23 41.9	7 09.7	1 56.9	6 25.8
30 Su	2 33 13	10 00 23	6♌43 26	12 41 46	1 26.8	13 31.5	24 34.4	17 31.3	11 47.7	17 29.9	23 48.2	7 12.9	1 55.7	6 26.1

Astro Data	Dy Hr Mn
♃✶♄	1 2:21
♆0N	7 15:02
☽0S	11 19:29
♃∠♆	19 0:13
☿0N	20 13:59
☉0N	20 17:49
☽0N	24 22:52
♄∠♇	4 21:07
☽0S	8 1:39
♃ D	13 2:10
♀0N	13 9:05
♅✶♇	14 12:55
♇ D	18 19:22
♃∠♆	21 3:04
☽0N	21 9:11

Planet Ingress		Dy Hr Mn
☿	♓	3 2:45
♀	♓	17 2:46
☿	♈	19 7:43
☉	♈	20 17:49
⚳	♋	23 2:22
♂	♋	28 9:54
☿	♉	3 17:29
♀	♈	10 12:09
☉	♉	20 5:18
☿ R		22 0:33

Last Aspect Dy Hr Mn			☽ Ingress	Dy Hr Mn
29 16:45	☿	□	♊	1 0:06
2 12:58	♄	☌	♋	3 8:38
4 11:48	☉	△	♌	5 20:19
7 13:15	♂	✶	♍	8 9:18
10 4:29	♂	□	♎	10 21:55
12 23:15	♀	△	♏	13 9:12
15 15:05	♀	□	♐	15 18:31
17 20:05	☉	□	♑	18 1:13
20 3:57	☉	✶	♒	20 4:55
22 0:56	♂	△	♓	22 5:59
24 2:18	♂	□	♈	24 5:42
26 4:11	♂	✶	♉	26 6:01
27 11:14	♃	□	♊	28 8:58
29 23:41	☿	✶	♋	30 15:59

Last Aspect Dy Hr Mn			☽ Ingress	Dy Hr Mn
1 20:17	☿	□	♌	2 2:54
3 22:15	♄	✶	♍	4 15:49
6 19:16	♀	☍	♎	7 4:22
8 23:15	♄	△	♏	9 15:12
10 23:43	♃	□	♐	12 0:02
13 19:39	☉	△	♑	14 6:56
16 4:59	☉	□	♒	16 11:46
18 11:39	☉	✶	♓	18 14:28
20 3:49	♄	□	♈	20 15:35
22 4:56	♄	✶	♉	22 16:28
23 21:08	♃	□	♊	24 18:59
26 12:36	♄	☌	♋	27 0:49
28 19:51	♀	□	♌	29 10:36

☽ Phases & Eclipses Dy Hr Mn	
1 20:40	☽ 11♊10
10 0:28	○ 19♍19
17 20:05	☾ 27♐07
24 11:36	● 3♈43
31 12:34	☽ 10♋41
8 17:22	○ 18♎45
16 4:59	☾ 26♑05
22 20:43	● 2♉35
30 6:06	☽ 9♌46

Astro Data

1 March 1944
Julian Day # 16131
SVP 6♓02'35"
GC 26♐03.6 ⚴ 28♈28.7
Eris 5♈09.6 ⚵ 12♓51.0
⚷ 12♍47.8R ⚶ 9♊04.4
☽ Mean ☊ 4♌58.8

1 April 1944
Julian Day # 16162
SVP 6♓02'33"
GC 26♐03.6 ⚴ 13♉23.5
Eris 5♈31.3 ⚵ 28♓35.0
⚷ 10♍31.6R ⚶ 17♊54.5
☽ Mean ☊ 3♌20.3

LONGITUDE — May 1944

Day	Sid.Time	☉	0 hr ☽	Noon ☽	True ☊	☿	♀	♂	⚳	♃	♄	♅	♆	♇
1 M	2 37 09	10♉58 36	18♌38 04	24♌33 04	1♌26.1	12♉55.1	25♈48.1	18♋04.6	12♋09.4	17♌33.2	23♊54.6	7♊16.1	1♎54.5	6♌26.4
2 Tu	2 41 06	11 56 47	0♍27 23	6♍21 42	1R 23.9	12R 17.5	27 01.8	18 37.9	12 31.1	17 36.6	24 01.0	7 19.4	1R 53.3	6 26.8
3 W	2 45 02	12 54 56	12 16 36	18 12 39	1 19.2	11 39.3	28 15.4	19 11.3	12 52.9	17 40.2	24 07.5	7 22.7	1 52.1	6 27.1
4 Th	2 48 59	13 53 03	24 10 23	0♎10 15	1 12.0	11 01.2	29 29.1	19 44.7	13 14.9	17 44.0	24 14.1	7 25.9	1 51.0	6 27.5
5 F	2 52 56	14 51 08	6♎12 39	12 17 56	1 02.3	10 23.9	0♉42.8	20 18.2	13 37.0	17 47.9	24 20.7	7 29.2	1 49.8	6 28.0
6 Sa	2 56 52	15 49 12	18 26 22	24 38 08	0 50.8	9 48.0	1 56.4	20 51.8	13 59.2	17 52.0	24 27.3	7 32.6	1 48.7	6 28.4
7 Su	3 00 49	16 47 13	0♏53 24	7♏12 12	0 38.3	9 14.1	3 10.1	21 25.4	14 21.5	17 56.2	24 34.0	7 35.9	1 47.7	6 28.9
8 M	3 04 45	17 45 13	13 34 32	20 00 22	0 26.1	8 42.8	4 23.7	21 59.1	14 44.0	18 00.6	24 40.8	7 39.3	1 46.6	6 29.4
9 Tu	3 08 42	18 43 12	26 29 35	3♐02 05	0 15.1	8 14.5	5 37.4	22 32.8	15 06.5	18 05.2	24 47.6	7 42.6	1 45.6	6 29.9
10 W	3 12 38	19 41 09	9♐37 41	16 16 13	0 06.4	7 49.6	6 51.0	23 06.6	15 29.2	18 10.0	24 54.4	7 46.0	1 44.6	6 30.5
11 Th	3 16 35	20 39 04	22 57 32	29 41 29	0 00.4	7 28.6	8 04.7	23 40.5	15 51.9	18 14.8	25 01.3	7 49.4	1 43.6	6 31.1
12 F	3 20 31	21 36 59	6♑27 56	13♑16 47	29♋57.2	7 11.6	9 18.3	24 14.4	16 14.8	18 19.9	25 08.2	7 52.8	1 42.7	6 31.7
13 Sa	3 24 28	22 34 52	20 07 56	27 01 21	29D 56.1	6 58.9	10 32.0	24 48.4	16 37.8	18 25.1	25 15.2	7 56.2	1 41.8	6 32.3
14 Su	3 28 25	23 32 43	3♒56 58	10♒54 48	29R 56.3	6 50.6	11 45.6	25 22.4	17 00.8	18 30.4	25 22.2	7 59.7	1 40.9	6 33.0
15 M	3 32 21	24 30 34	17 54 46	24 56 52	29 56.6	6D 46.9	12 59.3	25 56.5	17 24.0	18 36.0	25 29.3	8 03.1	1 40.0	6 33.7
16 Tu	3 36 18	25 28 23	2♓00 58	9♓06 58	29 55.9	6 47.7	14 12.9	26 30.7	17 47.2	18 41.6	25 36.4	8 06.6	1 39.2	6 34.4
17 W	3 40 14	26 26 11	16 14 40	23 23 47	29 53.2	6 53.1	15 26.6	27 04.9	18 10.6	18 47.4	25 43.5	8 10.0	1 38.4	6 35.1
18 Th	3 44 11	27 23 58	0♈33 57	7♈44 43	29 48.2	7 03.1	16 40.2	27 39.1	18 34.1	18 53.4	25 50.7	8 13.5	1 37.6	6 35.9
19 F	3 48 07	28 21 44	14 55 35	22 05 55	29 40.8	7 17.6	17 53.9	28 13.4	18 57.6	18 59.4	25 57.9	8 17.0	1 36.8	6 36.6
20 Sa	3 52 04	29 19 29	29 15 06	6♉22 26	29 31.9	7 36.6	19 07.5	28 47.8	19 21.3	19 05.7	26 05.2	8 20.5	1 36.1	6 37.4
21 Su	3 56 00	0♊17 12	13♉27 13	20 28 48	29 22.3	7 59.9	20 21.2	29 22.3	19 45.0	19 12.1	26 12.4	8 24.0	1 35.4	6 38.3
22 M	3 59 57	1 14 54	27 26 34	4♊19 59	29 13.2	8 27.5	21 34.8	29 56.7	20 08.8	19 18.6	26 19.7	8 27.5	1 34.7	6 39.1
23 Tu	4 03 54	2 12 35	11♊08 36	17 52 06	29 05.5	8 59.2	22 48.4	0♌31.3	20 32.7	19 25.2	26 27.1	8 31.0	1 34.1	6 40.0
24 W	4 07 50	3 10 15	24 30 17	1♋03 03	28 59.9	9 34.9	24 02.1	1 05.9	20 56.7	19 32.0	26 34.5	8 34.5	1 33.5	6 40.9
25 Th	4 11 47	4 07 54	7♋30 26	13 52 36	28 56.6	10 14.6	25 15.7	1 40.5	21 20.8	19 39.0	26 41.9	8 38.0	1 32.9	6 41.8
26 F	4 15 43	5 05 31	20 09 48	26 22 23	28D 55.4	10 58.1	26 29.4	2 15.2	21 45.0	19 46.0	26 49.3	8 41.6	1 32.4	6 42.8
27 Sa	4 19 40	6 03 06	2♌30 46	8♌35 28	28 55.7	11 45.2	27 43.0	2 49.9	22 09.3	19 53.2	26 56.8	8 45.1	1 31.9	6 43.7
28 Su	4 23 36	7 00 40	14 37 01	20 36 01	28 56.8	12 36.0	28 56.6	3 24.7	22 33.6	20 00.6	27 04.3	8 48.6	1 31.4	6 44.7
29 M	4 27 33	7 58 13	26 33 06	2♍28 53	28R 57.8	13 30.2	0♊10.3	3 59.6	22 58.0	20 08.0	27 11.8	8 52.2	1 30.9	6 45.7
30 Tu	4 31 29	8 55 44	8♍24 03	14 19 14	28 57.7	14 27.9	1 23.9	4 34.4	23 22.5	20 15.6	27 19.3	8 55.7	1 30.5	6 46.7
31 W	4 35 26	9 53 14	20 15 04	26 12 11	28 56.1	15 28.8	2 37.5	5 09.4	23 47.0	20 23.3	27 26.9	8 59.2	1 30.1	6 47.8

LONGITUDE — June 1944

Day	Sid.Time	☉	0 hr ☽	Noon ☽	True ☊	☿	♀	♂	⚳	♃	♄	♅	♆	♇
1 Th	4 39 23	10♊50 43	2♎11 10	8♎12 35	28♋52.7	16♉33.0	3♊51.1	5♌44.3	24♋11.6	20♌31.2	27♊34.5	9♊02.7	1♎29.7	6♌48.9
2 F	4 43 19	11 48 10	14 16 57	20 24 41	28R 47.3	17 40.4	5 04.8	6 19.3	24 36.3	20 39.1	27 42.1	9 06.2	1R 29.4	6 49.9
3 Sa	4 47 16	12 45 37	26 36 13	2♏51 51	28 40.6	18 50.9	6 18.4	6 54.4	25 01.1	20 47.2	27 49.7	9 09.8	1 29.1	6 51.1
4 Su	4 51 12	13 43 02	9♏11 50	15 36 18	28 33.0	20 04.4	7 32.0	7 29.5	25 25.9	20 55.4	27 57.3	9 13.3	1 28.8	6 52.2
5 M	4 55 09	14 40 26	22 05 20	28 38 56	28 25.5	21 20.9	8 45.6	8 04.6	25 50.8	21 03.7	28 05.0	9 16.8	1 28.6	6 53.3
6 Tu	4 59 05	15 37 49	5♐16 58	11♐59 17	28 18.8	22 40.3	9 59.2	8 39.8	26 15.8	21 12.1	28 12.7	9 20.3	1 28.4	6 54.5
7 W	5 03 02	16 35 12	18 45 36	25 35 38	28 13.6	24 02.7	11 12.9	9 15.0	26 40.8	21 20.6	28 20.4	9 23.8	1 28.2	6 55.7
8 Th	5 06 58	17 32 33	2♑29 02	9♑25 23	28 10.3	25 28.0	12 26.5	9 50.3	27 05.9	21 29.2	28 28.1	9 27.3	1 28.1	6 56.9
9 F	5 10 55	18 29 54	16 24 18	23 25 22	28D 08.9	26 56.1	13 40.1	10 25.6	27 31.1	21 38.0	28 35.8	9 30.8	1 28.0	6 58.2
10 Sa	5 14 52	19 27 14	0♒28 12	7♒32 25	28 09.1	28 27.1	14 53.8	11 01.0	27 56.3	21 46.9	28 43.5	9 34.3	1 27.9	6 59.4
11 Su	5 18 48	20 24 34	14 37 40	21 43 37	28 10.3	0♊00.9	16 07.4	11 36.3	28 21.6	21 55.8	28 51.3	9 37.8	1D 27.9	7 00.7
12 M	5 22 45	21 21 53	28 49 59	5♓56 29	28 11.6	1 37.5	17 21.1	12 11.8	28 47.0	22 04.9	28 59.0	9 41.3	1 27.8	7 02.0
13 Tu	5 26 41	22 19 12	13♓02 53	20 08 55	28R 12.4	3 16.9	18 34.7	12 47.3	29 12.4	22 14.1	29 06.8	9 44.8	1 27.9	7 03.3
14 W	5 30 38	23 16 31	27 14 23	4♈19 01	28 11.9	4 59.1	19 48.4	13 22.8	29 37.9	22 23.3	29 14.6	9 48.2	1 27.9	7 04.6
15 Th	5 34 34	24 13 49	11♈22 35	18 24 49	28 10.0	6 44.0	21 02.0	13 58.3	0♌03.4	22 32.7	29 22.4	9 51.7	1 28.0	7 05.9
16 F	5 38 31	25 11 07	25 25 26	2♉24 10	28 06.6	8 31.6	22 15.7	14 33.9	0 29.0	22 42.2	29 30.1	9 55.1	1 28.1	7 07.3
17 Sa	5 42 27	26 08 24	9♉20 41	16 14 41	28 02.3	10 21.8	23 29.4	15 09.6	0 54.6	22 51.8	29 37.9	9 58.5	1 28.3	7 08.6
18 Su	5 46 24	27 05 42	23 05 51	29 53 54	27 57.5	12 14.6	24 43.1	15 45.3	1 20.3	23 01.4	29 45.7	10 02.0	1 28.4	7 10.0
19 M	5 50 21	28 02 59	6♊38 33	13♊19 32	27 53.0	14 09.9	25 56.8	16 21.0	1 46.1	23 11.2	29 53.6	10 05.4	1 28.6	7 11.4
20 Tu	5 54 17	29 00 15	19 56 41	26 29 49	27 49.2	16 07.6	27 10.5	16 56.8	2 11.9	23 21.1	0♋01.4	10 08.8	1 28.9	7 12.8
21 W	5 58 14	29 57 31	2♋58 50	9♋23 44	27 46.6	18 07.6	28 24.2	17 32.6	2 37.8	23 31.0	0 09.2	10 12.1	1 29.2	7 14.3
22 Th	6 02 10	0♋54 47	15 44 31	22 01 18	27D 45.4	20 09.8	29 37.9	18 08.5	3 03.7	23 41.1	0 17.0	10 15.5	1 29.5	7 15.7
23 F	6 06 07	1 52 02	28 14 15	4♌23 36	27 45.4	22 13.8	0♋51.6	18 44.4	3 29.6	23 51.2	0 24.8	10 18.8	1 29.8	7 17.2
24 Sa	6 10 03	2 49 17	10♌29 39	16 32 45	27 46.4	24 19.6	2 05.3	19 20.4	3 55.6	24 01.4	0 32.6	10 22.2	1 30.2	7 18.7
25 Su	6 14 00	3 46 31	22 33 19	28 31 47	27 48.0	26 27.0	3 19.1	19 56.4	4 21.7	24 11.7	0 40.4	10 25.5	1 30.6	7 20.2
26 M	6 17 57	4 43 45	4♍28 39	10♍24 28	27 49.6	28 35.5	4 32.8	20 32.4	4 47.8	24 22.1	0 48.2	10 28.8	1 31.1	7 21.7
27 Tu	6 21 53	5 40 58	16 19 46	22 15 09	27 50.9	0♋45.1	5 46.5	21 08.4	5 14.0	24 32.6	0 56.0	10 32.1	1 31.5	7 23.2
28 W	6 25 50	6 38 11	28 11 11	4♎08 30	27R 51.6	2 55.4	7 00.2	21 44.5	5 40.2	24 43.1	1 03.8	10 35.3	1 32.0	7 24.7
29 Th	6 29 46	7 35 23	10♎07 40	16 09 17	27 51.3	5 06.2	8 14.0	22 20.7	6 06.4	24 53.7	1 11.6	10 38.6	1 32.6	7 26.2
30 F	6 33 43	8 32 35	22 13 55	28 22 07	27 50.2	7 17.1	9 27.7	22 56.9	6 32.7	25 04.4	1 19.3	10 41.8	1 33.1	7 27.8

Astro Data

	Dy Hr Mn
☽ 0S	5 9:24
☿ D	15 19:40
☽ 0N	18 17:44
☽ 0S	1 18:20
♆ D	12 10:25
☽ 0N	15 0:22
☽ 0S	29 3:16

Planet Ingress

		Dy Hr Mn
♀	♉	4 22:04
☊	♋R	11 14:29
☉	♊	21 4:51
♂	♌	22 14:16
♀	♊	29 8:39
☿	♊	11 11:46
⚳	♌	15 8:49
♄	♋	20 7:48
☉	♋	21 13:02
♀	♋	22 19:12
☿	♋	27 3:40

Last Aspect / ☽ Ingress (May)

Last Aspect Dy Hr Mn			☽ Ingress	Dy Hr Mn
1 14:50	♀	△	♍	1 23:04
4 0:01	♄	□	♎	4 11:40
6 11:39	♄	△	♏	6 22:18
8 15:50	♂	△	♐	9 6:27
11 3:37	♄	☍	♑	11 12:33
13 7:59	♂	☍	♒	13 17:10
15 12:56	♄	△	♓	15 20:35
17 18:26	♂	△	♈	17 23:03
19 22:42	♂	□	♉	20 1:15
22 4:01	♂	⚹	♊	22 4:26
24 3:42	♄	☌	♋	24 10:04
26 12:15	♀	⚹	♌	26 19:04
29 6:47	♀	□	♍	29 6:58
31 14:32	♄	□	♎	31 19:37

Last Aspect / ☽ Ingress (June)

Last Aspect Dy Hr Mn			☽ Ingress	Dy Hr Mn
3 2:15	♄	△	♏	3 6:32
4 21:57	♃	□	♐	5 14:27
7 16:50	♄	☍	♑	7 19:41
9 18:42	☿	△	♒	9 23:12
12 0:09	♄	△	♓	12 1:58
14 3:19	♄	□	♈	14 4:41
16 6:58	♄	⚹	♉	16 7:52
17 23:44	♃	□	♊	18 12:11
20 17:00	☉	☌	♋	20 18:28
20 21:13	♆	□	♌	23 3:25
25 6:54	☿	⚹	♍	25 14:58
26 12:09	♅	□	♎	28 3:40
30 5:29	♃	⚹	♏	30 15:10

☽ Phases & Eclipses

Dy Hr Mn		
8 7:28	○	17♏34
15 11:12	☾	24♒29
22 6:12	●	1♊01
30 0:06	☽	8♍27
6 18:58	○	15♐54
13 15:56	☾	22♓29
20 17:00	●	29♊12
28 17:27	☽	6♎51

Astro Data

1 May 1944
Julian Day # 16192
SVP 6♓02'29"
GC 26♐03.7 ⚵ 29♉32.8
Eris 5♈51.3 ✱ 14♈15.9
⚷ 9♍24.0R ⚶ 28♊46.0
☽ Mean ☊ 1♌45.0

1 June 1944
Julian Day # 16223
SVP 6♓02'25"
GC 26♐03.8 ⚵ 17♊26.6
Eris 6♈06.1 ✱ 0♉43.9
⚷ 9♍55.9 ⚶ 11♋21.8
☽ Mean ☊ 0♌06.5

July 1944

LONGITUDE

Day	Sid.Time	☉	0 hr ☽	Noon ☽	True ☊	☿	♀	♂	⚳	♃	♄	♅	♆	♇
1 Sa	6 37 39	9♋29 46	4♏34 22	10♏51 09	27♋48.4	9♋27.8	10♋41.5	23♌33.1	6♌59.0	25♌15.2	1♋27.1	10♊45.0	1♎33.7	7♌29.4
2 Su	6 41 36	10 26 57	17 12 49	23 39 42	27R 46.1	11 38.2	11 55.2	24 09.3	7 25.4	25 26.1	1 34.8	10 48.2	1 34.4	7 30.9
3 M	6 45 32	11 24 08	0♐12 01	6♐49 54	27 43.8	13 47.9	13 09.0	24 45.6	7 51.8	25 37.0	1 42.6	10 51.3	1 35.0	7 32.5
4 Tu	6 49 29	12 21 19	13 33 22	20 22 20	27 41.8	15 56.8	14 22.7	25 21.9	8 18.2	25 48.0	1 50.3	10 54.5	1 35.7	7 34.1
5 W	6 53 26	13 18 30	27 16 36	4♑15 51	27 40.3	18 04.6	15 36.5	25 58.3	8 44.7	25 59.1	1 58.0	10 57.6	1 36.4	7 35.8
6 Th	6 57 22	14 15 41	11♑19 40	18 27 31	27D 39.5	20 11.2	16 50.2	26 34.7	9 11.2	26 10.2	2 05.7	11 00.7	1 37.2	7 37.4
7 F	7 01 19	15 12 52	25 38 48	2♒52 52	27 39.4	22 16.3	18 04.0	27 11.1	9 37.8	26 21.4	2 13.4	11 03.8	1 38.0	7 39.0
8 Sa	7 05 15	16 10 03	10♒08 59	17 26 27	27 39.9	24 20.0	19 17.8	27 47.6	10 04.4	26 32.7	2 21.1	11 06.8	1 38.8	7 40.6
9 Su	7 09 12	17 07 14	24 44 30	2♓02 27	27 40.7	26 22.1	20 31.6	28 24.1	10 31.0	26 44.0	2 28.7	11 09.8	1 39.6	7 42.3
10 M	7 13 08	18 04 26	9♓19 38	16 35 26	27 41.5	28 22.5	21 45.4	29 00.7	10 57.7	26 55.4	2 36.4	11 12.8	1 40.5	7 43.9
11 Tu	7 17 05	19 01 38	23 49 19	1♈00 47	27 42.1	0♌21.2	22 59.2	29 37.3	11 24.4	27 06.9	2 44.0	11 15.8	1 41.4	7 45.6
12 W	7 21 01	19 58 50	8♈09 28	15 15 02	27R 42.4	2 18.1	24 13.0	0♍13.9	11 51.1	27 18.4	2 51.6	11 18.7	1 42.3	7 47.3
13 Th	7 24 58	20 56 04	22 17 14	29 15 54	27 42.4	4 13.2	25 26.8	0 50.5	12 17.9	27 30.0	2 59.1	11 21.7	1 43.3	7 49.0
14 F	7 28 55	21 53 18	6♉10 54	13♉02 09	27 42.0	6 06.4	26 40.7	1 27.3	12 44.7	27 41.7	3 06.7	11 24.5	1 44.3	7 50.7
15 Sa	7 32 51	22 50 32	19 49 38	26 33 20	27 41.6	7 57.8	27 54.5	2 04.0	13 11.5	27 53.4	3 14.2	11 27.4	1 45.3	7 52.3
16 Su	7 36 48	23 47 47	3♊13 17	9♊49 31	27 41.1	9 47.4	29 08.4	2 40.8	13 38.4	28 05.1	3 21.7	11 30.2	1 46.4	7 54.1
17 M	7 40 44	24 45 03	16 22 06	22 51 06	27 40.7	11 35.1	0♌22.2	3 17.6	14 05.3	28 16.9	3 29.2	11 33.0	1 47.5	7 55.8
18 Tu	7 44 41	25 42 20	29 16 36	5♋38 42	27 40.5	13 20.9	1 36.1	3 54.5	14 32.2	28 28.8	3 36.7	11 35.8	1 48.6	7 57.5
19 W	7 48 37	26 39 37	11♋57 31	18 13 08	27D 40.4	15 04.9	2 50.0	4 31.4	14 59.2	28 40.7	3 44.1	11 38.5	1 49.7	7 59.2
20 Th	7 52 34	27 36 54	24 25 43	0♌35 24	27R 40.4	16 47.1	4 03.9	5 08.4	15 26.2	28 52.7	3 51.5	11 41.3	1 50.9	8 00.9
21 F	7 56 30	28 34 12	6♌42 23	12 46 50	27 40.3	18 27.4	5 17.7	5 45.4	15 53.2	29 04.8	3 58.9	11 43.9	1 52.1	8 02.6
22 Sa	8 00 27	29 31 30	18 49 01	24 49 09	27 40.2	20 05.9	6 31.6	6 22.4	16 20.3	29 16.8	4 06.2	11 46.6	1 53.3	8 04.4
23 Su	8 04 24	0♌28 49	0♍47 33	6♍44 32	27 40.0	21 42.5	7 45.5	6 59.5	16 47.3	29 29.0	4 13.5	11 49.2	1 54.5	8 06.1
24 M	8 08 20	1 26 09	12 40 26	18 35 40	27 39.5	23 17.3	8 59.4	7 36.6	17 14.4	29 41.1	4 20.8	11 51.8	1 55.8	8 07.9
25 Tu	8 12 17	2 23 28	24 30 39	0♎25 49	27 39.0	24 50.3	10 13.4	8 13.7	17 41.6	29 53.3	4 28.0	11 54.3	1 57.1	8 09.6
26 W	8 16 13	3 20 49	6♎21 40	12 18 42	27 38.5	26 21.4	11 27.3	8 50.9	18 08.7	0♍05.6	4 35.2	11 56.8	1 58.4	8 11.3
27 Th	8 20 10	4 18 09	18 17 26	24 18 26	27D 38.1	27 50.6	12 41.2	9 28.1	18 35.9	0 17.9	4 42.3	11 59.3	1 59.8	8 13.1
28 F	8 24 06	5 15 30	0♏22 14	6♏29 24	27 38.0	29 18.0	13 55.1	10 05.4	19 03.1	0 30.2	4 49.5	12 01.7	2 01.2	8 14.8
29 Sa	8 28 03	6 12 52	12 40 29	18 56 01	27 38.2	0♍43.5	15 09.0	10 42.7	19 30.3	0 42.6	4 56.5	12 04.1	2 02.6	8 16.6
30 Su	8 31 59	7 10 14	25 16 29	1♐42 22	27 38.8	2 07.0	16 22.9	11 20.0	19 57.5	0 55.0	5 03.6	12 06.5	2 04.0	8 18.3
31 M	8 35 56	8 07 37	8♐14 03	14 51 51	27 39.6	3 28.6	17 36.9	11 57.4	20 24.8	1 07.5	5 10.6	12 08.8	2 05.5	8 20.1

August 1944

LONGITUDE

Day	Sid.Time	☉	0 hr ☽	Noon ☽	True ☊	☿	♀	♂	⚳	♃	♄	♅	♆	♇
1 Tu	8 39 53	9♌05 01	21♐36 00	28♐26 37	27♋40.6	4♍48.1	18♌50.8	12♍34.8	20♌52.1	1♍20.0	5♋17.6	12♊11.1	2♎07.0	8♌21.8
2 W	8 43 49	10 02 25	5♑23 40	12♑27 00	27 41.3	6 05.6	20 04.7	13 12.2	21 19.4	1 32.5	5 24.5	12 13.3	2 08.5	8 23.6
3 Th	8 47 46	10 59 50	19 36 19	26 51 07	27R 41.7	7 21.1	21 18.7	13 49.7	21 46.7	1 45.0	5 31.4	12 15.5	2 10.0	8 25.3
4 F	8 51 42	11 57 16	4♒10 48	11♒34 34	27 41.4	8 34.3	22 32.6	14 27.3	22 14.0	1 57.6	5 38.2	12 17.7	2 11.5	8 27.1
5 Sa	8 55 39	12 54 43	19 01 32	26 30 42	27 40.3	9 45.4	23 46.5	15 04.8	22 41.4	2 10.3	5 45.0	12 19.8	2 13.1	8 28.8
6 Su	8 59 35	13 52 11	4♓00 59	11♓31 19	27 38.7	10 54.1	25 00.5	15 42.4	23 08.7	2 22.9	5 51.7	12 21.9	2 14.7	8 30.6
7 M	9 03 32	14 49 40	19 00 37	26 27 50	27 36.6	12 00.5	26 14.4	16 20.0	23 36.1	2 35.6	5 58.4	12 24.0	2 16.3	8 32.3
8 Tu	9 07 28	15 47 10	3♈52 05	11♈12 32	27 34.5	13 04.4	27 28.3	16 57.7	24 03.5	2 48.3	6 05.0	12 26.0	2 18.0	8 34.1
9 W	9 11 25	16 44 42	18 28 32	25 39 33	27 32.8	14 05.7	28 42.3	17 35.4	24 30.9	3 01.0	6 11.6	12 27.9	2 19.6	8 35.8
10 Th	9 15 22	17 42 15	2♉45 14	9♉45 21	27D 31.8	15 04.4	29 56.3	18 13.2	24 58.3	3 13.8	6 18.2	12 29.9	2 21.3	8 37.5
11 F	9 19 18	18 39 49	16 39 50	23 28 42	27 31.7	16 00.2	1♍10.2	18 51.0	25 25.8	3 26.6	6 24.7	12 31.7	2 23.0	8 39.3
12 Sa	9 23 15	19 37 25	0♊12 07	6♊50 15	27 32.5	16 53.0	2 24.2	19 28.9	25 53.3	3 39.4	6 31.1	12 33.6	2 24.8	8 41.0
13 Su	9 27 11	20 35 03	13 23 24	19 51 53	27 33.8	17 42.8	3 38.2	20 06.7	26 20.7	3 52.2	6 37.5	12 35.4	2 26.5	8 42.7
14 M	9 31 08	21 32 42	26 16 00	2♋36 08	27 35.4	18 29.3	4 52.1	20 44.7	26 48.2	4 05.1	6 43.8	12 37.1	2 28.3	8 44.5
15 Tu	9 35 04	22 30 23	8♋52 37	15 05 47	27 36.7	19 12.3	6 06.1	21 22.6	27 15.7	4 17.9	6 50.1	12 38.8	2 30.1	8 46.2
16 W	9 39 01	23 28 04	21 15 59	27 23 31	27R 37.2	19 51.6	7 20.1	22 00.7	27 43.3	4 30.8	6 56.3	12 40.5	2 31.9	8 47.9
17 Th	9 42 57	24 25 48	3♌28 40	9♌31 44	27 36.6	20 27.1	8 34.1	22 38.7	28 10.8	4 43.7	7 02.4	12 42.1	2 33.7	8 49.6
18 F	9 46 54	25 23 33	15 32 57	21 32 34	27 34.6	20 58.6	9 48.1	23 16.8	28 38.3	4 56.7	7 08.5	12 43.7	2 35.6	8 51.3
19 Sa	9 50 51	26 21 19	27 30 49	3♍27 57	27 31.3	21 25.7	11 02.0	23 55.0	29 05.9	5 09.6	7 14.6	12 45.2	2 37.4	8 53.0
20 Su	9 54 47	27 19 06	9♍24 10	15 19 43	27 26.7	21 48.3	12 16.0	24 33.2	29 33.4	5 22.6	7 20.5	12 46.7	2 39.3	8 54.7
21 M	9 58 44	28 16 55	21 14 52	27 09 50	27 21.4	22 06.1	13 30.0	25 11.4	0♍01.0	5 35.5	7 26.4	12 48.1	2 41.2	8 56.3
22 Tu	10 02 40	29 14 45	3♎04 57	9♎00 29	27 15.8	22 18.8	14 44.0	25 49.6	0 28.6	5 48.5	7 32.3	12 49.5	2 43.1	8 58.0
23 W	10 06 37	0♍12 36	14 56 48	20 54 16	27 10.5	22R 26.3	15 58.0	26 28.0	0 56.1	6 01.5	7 38.0	12 50.8	2 45.1	8 59.6
24 Th	10 10 33	1 10 28	26 53 16	2♏54 14	27 06.2	22 28.3	17 11.9	27 06.3	1 23.7	6 14.5	7 43.7	12 52.1	2 47.0	9 01.3
25 F	10 14 30	2 08 22	8♏57 39	15 03 58	27 03.2	22 24.5	18 25.9	27 44.7	1 51.3	6 27.5	7 49.4	12 53.4	2 49.0	9 02.9
26 Sa	10 18 26	3 06 17	21 13 43	27 27 25	27D 01.8	22 14.9	19 39.9	28 23.1	2 18.9	6 40.5	7 55.0	12 54.6	2 51.0	9 04.6
27 Su	10 22 23	4 04 14	3♐45 36	10♐08 47	27 01.8	21 59.3	20 53.8	29 01.6	2 46.5	6 53.6	8 00.5	12 55.7	2 53.0	9 06.2
28 M	10 26 19	5 02 12	16 37 27	23 12 05	27 02.9	21 37.6	22 07.8	29 40.1	3 14.1	7 06.6	8 05.9	12 56.8	2 55.0	9 07.8
29 Tu	10 30 16	6 00 11	29 53 04	6♑40 44	27 04.3	21 09.9	23 21.8	0♎18.7	3 41.7	7 19.6	8 11.2	12 57.9	2 57.0	9 09.4
30 W	10 34 13	6 58 11	13♑35 17	20 36 48	27R 05.4	20 36.2	24 35.7	0 57.3	4 09.3	7 32.6	8 16.5	12 58.9	2 59.0	9 11.0
31 Th	10 38 09	7 56 13	27 45 13	5♒00 15	27 05.3	19 56.9	25 49.7	1 35.9	4 36.9	7 45.7	8 21.7	12 59.8	3 01.1	9 12.6

Astro Data

	Dy Hr Mn
♄□♆	2 10:21
☽0N	12 6:13
☽0S	26 11:03
♃⚻♆	5 18:13
☽0N	8 12:57
☿0S	20 16:00
☽0S	22 17:20
☿R	24 8:25
♂0S	31 9:01
☿0N	31 22:32

Planet Ingress

	Dy Hr Mn
☿ ♌	11 7:41
♂ ♍	12 2:54
♀ ♌	17 4:47
☉ ♌	22 23:56
♃ ♍	26 1:04
☿ ♍	28 23:44
♀ ♍	10 13:13
⚳ ♍	21 11:09
☉ ♍	23 6:46
♂ ♎	29 0:23

Last Aspect Dy Hr Mn		☽ Ingress	Dy Hr Mn
2 15:19	♃ □	♐	2 23:38
4 21:34	♃ △	♑	5 4:42
6 15:23	☿ ☍	♒	7 7:14
9 5:45	♂ ☍	♓	9 8:39
10 21:22	♀ △	♈	11 10:18
13 8:55	♃ △	♉	13 13:16
15 14:40	♀ ⚹	♊	15 18:11
17 22:18	♃ ⚹	♋	18 1:21
20 5:42	☉ ☌	♌	20 10:51
22 21:07	♃ ☌	♍	22 22:24
23 22:18	♅ □	♎	25 11:08
27 19:59	☿ ⚹	♏	27 23:16
29 3:58	♀ □	♐	30 8:50

Last Aspect Dy Hr Mn		☽ Ingress	Dy Hr Mn
31 17:25	♀ △	♑	1 14:42
2 13:20	♂ △	♒	3 17:10
5 7:14	♀ ☍	♓	5 17:35
6 19:00	♂ ☍	♈	7 17:43
9 17:37	♀ △	♉	9 19:19
11 3:26	♂ △	♊	11 23:38
13 13:27	☉ ⚹	♋	14 7:03
16 0:53	♂ ⚹	♌	16 17:08
18 20:25	☉ ☌	♍	19 5:01
21 7:46	♂ ☌	♎	21 17:45
22 19:44	♅ △	♏	24 6:13
26 13:52	♂ ⚹	♐	26 16:52
29 0:12	♂ □	♑	29 0:12
30 19:21	♀ △	♒	31 3:44

☽ Phases & Eclipses

Dy Hr Mn	
6 4:27	○ 13♑58
6 4:40	A 0.533
12 20:39	☾ 20♈19
20 5:42	● 27♋22
20 5:42:46	A 03'42"
28 9:23	☽ 5♏09
4 12:39	○ 11♒59
4 12:26	A 0.478
11 2:52	☾ 18♉18
18 20:25	● 25♌44
26 23:39	☽ 3♐34

Astro Data

1 July 1944
Julian Day # 16253
SVP 6♓02'20"
GC 26♐03.8 ⚴ 5♋23.8
Eris 6♈11.5 ⚵ 16♉40.4
⚷ 12♍02.0 ⚶ 24♋20.9
☽ Mean ☊ 28♋31.2

1 August 1944
Julian Day # 16284
SVP 6♓02'15"
GC 26♐03.9 ⚴ 24♋00.9
Eris 6♈06.6R ⚵ 2♊44.2
⚷ 15♍27.3 ⚶ 8♌14.8
☽ Mean ☊ 26♋52.7

LONGITUDE — September 1944

Day	Sid.Time	☉	0 hr ☽	Noon ☽	True ☊	☿	♀	♂	⚳	♃	♄	♅	♆	♇
1 F	10 42 06	8♍54 16	12♒21 28	19♒48 11	27♋03.5	19♍12.4	27♍03.6	2♎14.6	5♍04.5	7♍58.7	8♋26.9	13♊00.7	3♎03.1	9♌14.1
2 Sa	10 46 02	9 52 21	27 19 33	4♓54 31	26R 59.8	18R 23.2	28 17.5	2 53.3	5 32.1	8 11.7	8 31.9	13 01.6	3 05.2	9 15.7
3 Su	10 49 59	10 50 27	12♓31 54	20 10 21	26 54.3	17 30.0	29 31.4	3 32.0	5 59.6	8 24.7	8 36.9	13 02.4	3 07.3	9 17.2
4 M	10 53 55	11 48 35	27 48 31	5♈25 03	26 47.8	16 33.7	0♎45.4	4 10.8	6 27.2	8 37.7	8 41.8	13 03.1	3 09.4	9 18.8
5 Tu	10 57 52	12 46 45	12♈58 38	20 28 07	26 41.1	15 35.4	1 59.3	4 49.7	6 54.8	8 50.8	8 46.7	13 03.8	3 11.5	9 20.3
6 W	11 01 48	13 44 57	27 52 30	5♉10 57	26 35.2	14 36.2	3 13.2	5 28.6	7 22.4	9 03.8	8 51.4	13 04.4	3 13.6	9 21.8
7 Th	11 05 45	14 43 11	12♉22 54	19 27 58	26 30.7	13 37.5	4 27.1	6 07.5	7 50.0	9 16.8	8 56.1	13 05.0	3 15.8	9 23.3
8 F	11 09 42	15 41 27	26 25 57	3♊16 54	26 28.1	12 40.5	5 41.0	6 46.5	8 17.6	9 29.8	9 00.6	13 05.6	3 17.9	9 24.7
9 Sa	11 13 38	16 39 46	10♊00 56	16 38 23	26D 27.3	11 46.7	6 54.9	7 25.5	8 45.2	9 42.7	9 05.2	13 06.1	3 20.1	9 26.2
10 Su	11 17 35	17 38 06	23 09 38	29 35 09	26 27.9	10 57.2	8 08.8	8 04.6	9 12.8	9 55.7	9 09.6	13 06.5	3 22.2	9 27.7
11 M	11 21 31	18 36 28	5♋55 26	12♋11 02	26 29.0	10 13.4	9 22.7	8 43.7	9 40.4	10 08.7	9 13.9	13 06.9	3 24.4	9 29.1
12 Tu	11 25 28	19 34 53	18 22 31	24 30 24	26R 29.7	9 36.3	10 36.6	9 22.9	10 07.9	10 21.6	9 18.2	13 07.3	3 26.6	9 30.5
13 W	11 29 24	20 33 19	0♌35 13	6♌37 28	26 29.1	9 06.9	11 50.4	10 02.1	10 35.5	10 34.6	9 22.3	13 07.6	3 28.7	9 31.9
14 Th	11 33 21	21 31 48	12 37 37	18 36 04	26 26.6	8 45.9	13 04.3	10 41.3	11 03.1	10 47.5	9 26.4	13 07.8	3 30.9	9 33.3
15 F	11 37 17	22 30 18	24 33 15	0♍29 28	26 21.5	8D 33.9	14 18.2	11 20.6	11 30.6	11 00.4	9 30.4	13 08.0	3 33.1	9 34.6
16 Sa	11 41 14	23 28 51	6♍25 02	12 20 15	26 14.0	8 31.2	15 32.1	12 00.0	11 58.1	11 13.3	9 34.3	13 08.1	3 35.3	9 36.0
17 Su	11 45 11	24 27 25	18 15 21	24 10 32	26 04.3	8 38.0	16 45.9	12 39.4	12 25.7	11 26.2	9 38.0	13 08.2	3 37.5	9 37.3
18 M	11 49 07	25 26 02	0♎06 00	6♎01 58	25 53.1	8 54.5	17 59.8	13 18.8	12 53.2	11 39.0	9 41.8	13R 08.2	3 39.7	9 38.6
19 Tu	11 53 04	26 24 40	11 58 36	17 56 05	25 41.4	9 20.3	19 13.6	13 58.3	13 20.7	11 51.8	9 45.4	13 08.2	3 41.9	9 39.9
20 W	11 57 00	27 23 20	23 54 39	29 54 29	25 30.1	9 55.3	20 27.5	14 37.8	13 48.2	12 04.6	9 48.9	13 08.1	3 44.2	9 41.2
21 Th	12 00 57	28 22 02	5♏55 51	11♏59 01	25 20.3	10 39.0	21 41.3	15 17.4	14 15.7	12 17.4	9 52.3	13 08.0	3 46.4	9 42.5
22 F	12 04 53	29 20 46	18 04 17	24 12 02	25 12.6	11 31.0	22 55.1	15 57.0	14 43.1	12 30.2	9 55.6	13 07.8	3 48.6	9 43.7
23 Sa	12 08 50	0♎19 31	0♐22 37	6♐36 27	25 07.6	12 30.6	24 08.9	16 36.7	15 10.6	12 42.9	9 58.9	13 07.6	3 50.8	9 44.9
24 Su	12 12 46	1 18 19	12 54 00	19 15 42	25D 05.0	13 37.4	25 22.7	17 16.4	15 38.0	12 55.6	10 02.0	13 07.3	3 53.1	9 46.1
25 M	12 16 43	2 17 08	25 42 04	2♑13 33	25 04.3	14 50.6	26 36.5	17 56.2	16 05.4	13 08.2	10 05.0	13 07.0	3 55.3	9 47.3
26 Tu	12 20 40	3 15 59	8♑50 38	15 33 43	25R 04.6	16 09.5	27 50.3	18 36.0	16 32.8	13 20.9	10 08.0	13 06.6	3 57.5	9 48.5
27 W	12 24 36	4 14 51	22 23 09	29 19 13	25 04.7	17 33.5	29 04.1	19 15.8	17 00.2	13 33.5	10 10.8	13 06.2	3 59.8	9 49.6
28 Th	12 28 33	5 13 45	6♒22 02	13♒31 35	25 03.5	19 01.9	0♏17.8	19 55.7	17 27.6	13 46.0	10 13.5	13 05.7	4 02.0	9 50.7
29 F	12 32 29	6 12 41	20 47 41	28 09 55	25 00.1	20 34.2	1 31.6	20 35.7	17 54.9	13 58.5	10 16.2	13 05.2	4 04.2	9 51.8
30 Sa	12 36 26	7 11 39	5♓37 41	13♓10 06	24 53.9	22 09.6	2 45.3	21 15.6	18 22.2	14 11.0	10 18.7	13 04.6	4 06.5	9 52.9

LONGITUDE — October 1944

Day	Sid.Time	☉	0 hr ☽	Noon ☽	True ☊	☿	♀	♂	⚳	♃	♄	♅	♆	♇
1 Su	12 40 22	8♎10 38	20♓46 08	28♓24 32	24♋45.3	23♍47.8	3♏59.0	21♎55.7	18♍49.5	14♍23.5	10♋21.1	13♊04.0	4♎08.7	9♌54.0
2 M	12 44 19	9 09 40	6♈03 56	13♈42 54	24R 35.1	25 28.1	5 12.7	22 35.7	19 16.8	14 35.9	10 23.4	13R 03.3	4 10.9	9 55.0
3 Tu	12 48 15	10 08 43	21 19 59	28 53 47	24 24.3	27 10.2	6 26.4	23 15.9	19 44.0	14 48.3	10 25.6	13 02.5	4 13.1	9 56.0
4 W	12 52 12	11 07 49	6♉23 04	13♉46 44	24 14.3	28 53.6	7 40.0	23 56.0	20 11.3	15 00.6	10 27.8	13 01.8	4 15.4	9 57.0
5 Th	12 56 08	12 06 57	21 03 56	28 14 04	24 06.3	0♎38.0	8 53.7	24 36.2	20 38.5	15 12.9	10 29.8	13 00.9	4 17.6	9 58.0
6 F	13 00 05	13 06 07	5♊16 44	12♊11 45	24 00.7	2 23.2	10 07.4	25 16.5	21 05.6	15 25.1	10 31.7	13 00.1	4 19.8	9 58.9
7 Sa	13 04 02	14 05 20	18 59 13	25 39 18	23 57.6	4 08.8	11 21.0	25 56.8	21 32.8	15 37.3	10 33.5	12 59.1	4 22.0	9 59.8
8 Su	13 07 58	15 04 35	2♋12 23	8♋38 56	23D 56.5	5 54.6	12 34.6	26 37.2	21 59.9	15 49.5	10 35.2	12 58.2	4 24.2	10 00.7
9 M	13 11 55	16 03 52	14 59 32	21 14 46	23R 56.4	7 40.5	13 48.3	27 17.6	22 27.0	16 01.6	10 36.8	12 57.1	4 26.4	10 01.6
10 Tu	13 15 51	17 03 12	27 25 16	3♌31 44	23 56.2	9 26.3	15 01.9	27 58.0	22 54.1	16 13.7	10 38.2	12 56.1	4 28.6	10 02.5
11 W	13 19 48	18 02 33	9♌34 46	15 35 02	23 54.7	11 11.9	16 15.5	28 38.6	23 21.2	16 25.7	10 39.6	12 55.0	4 30.8	10 03.3
12 Th	13 23 44	19 01 58	21 33 07	27 29 36	23 50.9	12 57.2	17 29.1	29 19.1	23 48.2	16 37.6	10 40.8	12 53.8	4 33.0	10 04.1
13 F	13 27 41	20 01 24	3♍25 00	9♍19 47	23 44.4	14 42.1	18 42.7	29 59.7	24 15.2	16 49.5	10 42.0	12 52.6	4 35.1	10 04.9
14 Sa	13 31 37	21 00 52	15 14 23	21 09 10	23 34.8	16 26.6	19 56.2	0♏40.4	24 42.1	17 01.4	10 43.0	12 51.3	4 37.3	10 05.6
15 Su	13 35 34	22 00 23	27 04 29	3♎00 35	23 22.7	18 10.5	21 09.8	1 21.1	25 09.0	17 13.2	10 43.9	12 50.0	4 39.5	10 06.3
16 M	13 39 31	22 59 56	8♎57 43	14 56 05	23 08.7	19 53.9	22 23.3	2 01.9	25 35.9	17 24.9	10 44.8	12 48.7	4 41.6	10 07.0
17 Tu	13 43 27	23 59 31	20 55 49	26 57 04	22 54.0	21 36.7	23 36.9	2 42.7	26 02.7	17 36.6	10 45.4	12 47.3	4 43.8	10 07.7
18 W	13 47 24	24 59 07	2♏59 57	9♏04 34	22 39.7	23 18.9	24 50.4	3 23.5	26 29.5	17 48.2	10 46.0	12 45.9	4 45.9	10 08.4
19 Th	13 51 20	25 58 46	15 11 04	21 19 32	22 27.2	25 00.6	26 03.9	4 04.4	26 56.3	17 59.7	10 46.5	12 44.4	4 48.0	10 09.0
20 F	13 55 17	26 58 27	27 30 07	3♐42 59	22 17.2	26 41.6	27 17.4	4 45.4	27 23.0	18 11.2	10 46.9	12 42.9	4 50.1	10 09.6
21 Sa	13 59 13	27 58 10	9♐58 21	16 16 26	22 10.2	28 22.0	28 30.9	5 26.4	27 49.7	18 22.6	10 47.1	12 41.3	4 52.2	10 10.2
22 Su	14 03 10	28 57 54	22 37 30	29 01 52	22 06.2	0♏01.9	29 44.3	6 07.4	28 16.4	18 33.9	10R 47.3	12 39.7	4 54.3	10 10.7
23 M	14 07 06	29 57 40	5♑29 52	12♑01 50	22D 04.5	1 41.1	0♐57.8	6 48.5	28 43.0	18 45.2	10 47.3	12 38.1	4 56.4	10 11.3
24 Tu	14 11 03	0♏57 28	18 38 09	25 19 10	22R 04.3	3 19.8	2 11.2	7 29.7	29 09.5	18 56.4	10 47.2	12 36.4	4 58.4	10 11.8
25 W	14 15 00	1 57 18	2♒05 13	8♒56 35	22 04.3	4 57.9	3 24.6	8 10.9	29 36.0	19 07.5	10 47.0	12 34.7	5 00.5	10 12.2
26 Th	14 18 56	2 57 09	15 53 28	22 56 00	22 03.0	6 35.4	4 38.0	8 52.1	0♎02.5	19 18.6	10 46.7	12 32.9	5 02.5	10 12.7
27 F	14 22 53	3 57 02	0♓04 08	7♓17 42	21 59.7	8 12.4	5 51.4	9 33.4	0 28.9	19 29.5	10 46.3	12 31.1	5 04.5	10 13.1
28 Sa	14 26 49	4 56 56	14 36 21	21 59 32	21 53.6	9 48.9	7 04.7	10 14.8	0 55.2	19 40.4	10 45.7	12 29.3	5 06.5	10 13.5
29 Su	14 30 46	5 56 52	29 26 31	6♈56 22	21 45.0	11 24.9	8 18.0	10 56.1	1 21.5	19 51.2	10 45.1	12 27.4	5 08.5	10 13.8
30 M	14 34 42	6 56 50	14♈28 01	22 00 16	21 34.5	13 00.4	9 31.3	11 37.6	1 47.8	20 02.0	10 44.3	12 25.5	5 10.5	10 14.2
31 Tu	14 38 39	7 56 50	29 31 50	7♉01 27	21 23.4	14 35.4	10 44.6	12 19.0	2 14.0	20 12.6	10 43.5	12 23.6	5 12.4	10 14.5

Astro Data

	Dy Hr Mn
♆0S	4 14:28
☽0N	4 21:43
♃✶♄	4 23:59
♀0S	5 23:10
♃⚻♇	8 1:33
☿ D	16 6:46
♄⚻♇	17 4:54
♅ R	18 13:31
☽0S	18 22:50
☉0S	23 4:02
♃□♅	25 9:45
☽0N	2 8:20
☿0S	7 13:14
☽0S	16 4:50
♄ R	23 5:37

Planet Ingress

		Dy Hr Mn
♀	♎	3 21:16
☉	♎	23 4:02
♀	♏	28 6:12
☿	♎	5 3:17
♂	♏	13 12:09
☿	♏	22 11:33
♀	♐	22 17:07
☉	♏	23 12:56
⚳	♎	26 9:46

☽0N29 19:16

Last Aspect / ☽ Ingress (September)

Last Aspect Dy Hr Mn			☽ Ingress	Dy Hr Mn
1 1:03	♅	△	♓	2 4:14
3 8:02	☿	☍	♈	4 3:27
5 0:08	♅	✶	♉	6 3:28
7 3:21	☉	△	♊	8 6:13
9 12:03	☉	□	♋	10 12:47
12 1:31	☉	✶	♌	12 22:50
14 1:00	♅	✶	♍	15 11:00
17 12:37	☉	☌	♎	17 23:48
19 14:54	♀	☌	♏	20 12:11
22 22:52	☉	✶	♐	22 23:16
25 0:36	♀	✶	♑	25 7:55
27 11:31	♀	□	♒	27 13:10
28 23:05	♂	△	♓	29 14:58

Last Aspect / ☽ Ingress (October)

Last Aspect Dy Hr Mn			☽ Ingress	Dy Hr Mn
1 3:53	☿	☍	♈	1 14:30
3 2:39	♂	☍	♉	3 13:46
4 14:03	♃	△	♊	5 14:59
7 12:34	♂	△	♋	7 19:56
10 0:26	♂	□	♌	10 5:03
12 15:55	♂	✶	♍	12 17:04
14 9:15	♀	✶	♎	15 5:55
17 5:35	☉	☌	♏	17 18:03
19 22:14	♀	☌	♐	20 4:50
22 11:52	☉	✶	♑	22 13:48
24 0:23	♃	△	♒	24 20:19
25 18:17	♅	△	♓	26 23:53
28 8:12	♃	☍	♈	29 0:54
29 20:47	♅	✶	♉	31 0:45

☽ Phases & Eclipses

Dy Hr Mn		
2 20:21	○	10♓13
9 12:03	☾	16♊40
17 12:37	●	24♍29
25 12:07	☽	2♑17
2 4:22	○	8♈51
9 1:12	☾	15♋37
17 5:35	●	23♎44
24 22:48	☽	1♒24
31 13:35	○	8♉01

Astro Data

1 September 1944
Julian Day # 16315
SVP 6♓02'11"
GC 26♐04.0 ⚴ 12♌06.0
Eris 5♈52.5R ⚵ 17♊37.0
⚷ 19♍38.8 ⚶ 22♌23.1
☽ Mean ☊ 25♋14.2

1 October 1944
Julian Day # 16345
SVP 6♓02'09"
GC 26♐04.1 ⚴ 28♌33.5
Eris 5♈34.0R ⚵ 29♊32.8
⚷ 23♍56.6 ⚶ 6♍03.4
☽ Mean ☊ 23♋38.8

November 1944 — LONGITUDE

Day	Sid.Time	☉	0 hr ☽	Noon ☽	True ☊	☿	♀	♂	⚳	♃	♄	♅	♆	♇
1 W	14 42 35	8♏56 51	14♉27 54	21♉50 02	21♋13.0	16♏10.0	11♐57.8	13♏00.6	2♎40.2	20♍23.2	10♋42.5	12♊21.6	5♎14.4	10♌14.8
2 Th	14 46 32	9 56 55	29 06 54	6♊17 42	21R04.3	17 44.1	13 11.1	13 42.2	3 06.3	20 33.6	10R41.4	12R19.6	5 16.3	10 15.0
3 F	14 50 29	10 57 00	13♊21 51	20 19 00	20 58.2	19 17.8	14 24.3	14 23.8	3 32.3	20 44.0	10 40.2	12 17.6	5 18.2	10 15.2
4 Sa	14 54 25	11 57 08	27 08 58	3♋51 46	20 54.7	20 51.2	15 37.5	15 05.5	3 58.3	20 54.4	10 38.9	12 15.5	5 20.1	10 15.4
5 Su	14 58 22	12 57 17	10♋27 36	16 56 47	20D53.4	22 24.1	16 50.6	15 47.2	4 24.2	21 04.6	10 37.5	12 13.4	5 21.9	10 15.6
6 M	15 02 18	13 57 29	23 19 46	29 37 05	20 53.6	23 56.6	18 03.8	16 29.0	4 50.1	21 14.7	10 36.0	12 11.3	5 23.8	10 15.8
7 Tu	15 06 15	14 57 43	5♌49 18	11♌57 06	20R54.0	25 28.8	19 16.9	17 10.8	5 15.9	21 24.7	10 34.3	12 09.1	5 25.6	10 15.9
8 W	15 10 11	15 57 58	18 01 07	24 02 02	20 53.7	27 00.6	20 30.0	17 52.7	5 41.7	21 34.7	10 32.6	12 06.9	5 27.4	10 16.0
9 Th	15 14 08	16 58 16	0♍00 30	5♍57 11	20 51.7	28 32.1	21 43.1	18 34.7	6 07.4	21 44.5	10 30.8	12 04.7	5 29.2	10 16.0
10 F	15 18 04	17 58 36	11 52 43	17 47 39	20 47.3	0♐03.2	22 56.1	19 16.7	6 33.0	21 54.2	10 28.8	12 02.5	5 31.0	10R16.1
11 Sa	15 22 01	18 58 57	23 42 34	29 37 58	20 40.4	1 34.0	24 09.1	19 58.7	6 58.5	22 03.9	10 26.8	12 00.2	5 32.7	10 16.1
12 Su	15 25 58	19 59 20	5♎34 17	11♎31 55	20 31.2	3 04.4	25 22.1	20 40.8	7 24.0	22 13.4	10 24.6	11 57.9	5 34.5	10 16.1
13 M	15 29 54	20 59 46	17 31 13	23 32 28	20 20.3	4 34.5	26 35.1	21 22.9	7 49.4	22 22.8	10 22.3	11 55.6	5 36.2	10 16.0
14 Tu	15 33 51	22 00 13	29 35 54	5♏41 42	20 08.6	6 04.2	27 48.1	22 05.2	8 14.8	22 32.2	10 20.0	11 53.3	5 37.8	10 15.9
15 W	15 37 47	23 00 41	11♏49 59	18 00 52	19 57.3	7 33.5	29 01.0	22 47.4	8 40.1	22 41.4	10 17.5	11 51.0	5 39.5	10 15.8
16 Th	15 41 44	24 01 12	24 14 22	0♐30 33	19 47.3	9 02.4	0♑13.9	23 29.7	9 05.3	22 50.5	10 14.9	11 48.6	5 41.1	10 15.7
17 F	15 45 40	25 01 44	6♐49 26	13 10 59	19 39.5	10 31.0	1 26.7	24 12.0	9 30.4	22 59.5	10 12.3	11 46.2	5 42.7	10 15.5
18 Sa	15 49 37	26 02 17	19 35 15	26 02 14	19 34.3	11 59.0	2 39.6	24 54.4	9 55.4	23 08.3	10 09.5	11 43.8	5 44.3	10 15.4
19 Su	15 53 33	27 02 52	2♑31 59	9♑04 32	19D31.6	13 26.6	3 52.4	25 36.9	10 20.4	23 17.1	10 06.7	11 41.4	5 45.9	10 15.1
20 M	15 57 30	28 03 28	15 40 00	22 18 28	19 31.1	14 53.7	5 05.1	26 19.4	10 45.3	23 25.7	10 03.7	11 38.9	5 47.4	10 14.9
21 Tu	16 01 27	29 04 06	29 00 03	5♒44 54	19 31.9	16 20.1	6 17.9	27 01.9	11 10.1	23 34.2	10 00.7	11 36.5	5 48.9	10 14.6
22 W	16 05 23	0♐04 44	12♒33 09	19 24 55	19R33.1	17 45.9	7 30.5	27 44.5	11 34.8	23 42.6	9 57.6	11 34.0	5 50.4	10 14.3
23 Th	16 09 20	1 05 24	26 20 18	3♓19 20	19 33.5	19 11.0	8 43.2	28 27.1	11 59.4	23 50.9	9 54.3	11 31.5	5 51.9	10 14.0
24 F	16 13 16	2 06 04	10♓22 00	17 28 12	19 32.3	20 35.2	9 55.8	29 09.8	12 23.9	23 59.1	9 51.0	11 29.0	5 53.3	10 13.7
25 Sa	16 17 13	3 06 46	24 37 44	1♈50 15	19 29.2	21 58.5	11 08.3	29 52.5	12 48.3	24 07.1	9 47.7	11 26.5	5 54.7	10 13.3
26 Su	16 21 09	4 07 28	9♈05 19	16 22 23	19 24.1	23 20.7	12 20.8	0♐35.3	13 12.7	24 15.0	9 44.2	11 24.0	5 56.1	10 12.9
27 M	16 25 06	5 08 12	23 40 45	0♉59 39	19 17.5	24 41.7	13 33.2	1 18.1	13 36.9	24 22.7	9 40.6	11 21.5	5 57.5	10 12.5
28 Tu	16 29 02	6 08 57	8♉18 13	15 35 36	19 10.4	26 01.3	14 45.6	2 01.0	14 01.1	24 30.4	9 37.0	11 19.0	5 58.8	10 12.0
29 W	16 32 59	7 09 43	22 50 51	0♊03 09	19 03.6	27 19.2	15 58.0	2 43.9	14 25.1	24 37.9	9 33.3	11 16.5	6 00.1	10 11.5
30 Th	16 36 56	8 10 30	7♊11 40	14 15 43	18 58.0	28 35.4	17 10.3	3 26.9	14 49.1	24 45.2	9 29.5	11 13.9	6 01.3	10 11.0

December 1944 — LONGITUDE

Day	Sid.Time	☉	0 hr ☽	Noon ☽	True ☊	☿	♀	♂	⚳	♃	♄	♅	♆	♇
1 F	16 40 52	9♐11 19	21♊14 42	28♊08 12	18♋54.2	29♐49.4	18♑22.5	4♐09.9	15♎13.0	24♍52.5	9♋25.6	11♊11.4	6♎02.6	10♌10.5
2 Sa	16 44 49	10 12 08	4♋55 52	11♋37 36	18D52.3	1♑00.9	19 34.7	4 53.0	15 36.7	24 59.6	9R21.7	11R08.9	6 03.8	10R10.0
3 Su	16 48 45	11 13 00	18 13 20	24 43 13	18 52.2	2 09.6	20 46.8	5 36.1	16 00.4	25 06.5	9 17.7	11 06.3	6 05.0	10 09.4
4 M	16 52 42	12 13 52	1♌07 28	7♌26 26	18 53.4	3 15.1	21 58.8	6 19.3	16 23.9	25 13.3	9 13.6	11 03.8	6 06.1	10 08.8
5 Tu	16 56 38	13 14 45	13 40 31	19 50 12	18 55.1	4 16.9	23 10.8	7 02.5	16 47.4	25 20.0	9 09.5	11 01.2	6 07.3	10 08.2
6 W	17 00 35	14 15 40	25 56 03	1♍58 39	18 56.7	5 14.3	24 22.8	7 45.8	17 10.7	25 26.5	9 05.3	10 58.7	6 08.3	10 07.5
7 Th	17 04 31	15 16 36	7♍58 36	13 56 32	18R57.5	6 06.9	25 34.7	8 29.1	17 33.9	25 32.9	9 01.0	10 56.2	6 09.4	10 06.8
8 F	17 08 28	16 17 33	19 53 04	25 48 51	18 56.9	6 53.9	26 46.5	9 12.5	17 57.0	25 39.1	8 56.7	10 53.6	6 10.4	10 06.1
9 Sa	17 12 25	17 18 32	1♎44 29	7♎40 35	18 54.9	7 34.6	27 58.2	9 55.9	18 20.0	25 45.1	8 52.3	10 51.1	6 11.4	10 05.4
10 Su	17 16 21	18 19 31	13 37 41	19 36 19	18 51.5	8 08.2	29 09.9	10 39.4	18 42.8	25 51.0	8 47.8	10 48.6	6 12.4	10 04.7
11 M	17 20 18	19 20 32	25 37 00	1♏40 08	18 47.0	8 33.8	0♒21.5	11 22.9	19 05.6	25 56.8	8 43.4	10 46.1	6 13.3	10 03.9
12 Tu	17 24 14	20 21 33	7♏46 06	13 55 15	18 41.9	8 50.5	1 33.0	12 06.5	19 28.2	26 02.4	8 38.8	10 43.6	6 14.2	10 03.1
13 W	17 28 11	21 22 36	20 07 50	26 24 02	18 36.9	8R57.4	2 44.5	12 50.1	19 50.7	26 07.8	8 34.2	10 41.1	6 15.1	10 02.3
14 Th	17 32 07	22 23 40	2♐43 59	9♐07 46	18 32.6	8 53.9	3 55.9	13 33.8	20 13.0	26 13.1	8 29.6	10 38.6	6 15.9	10 01.4
15 F	17 36 04	23 24 44	15 35 23	22 06 46	18 29.3	8 39.2	5 07.2	14 17.5	20 35.3	26 18.2	8 24.9	10 36.2	6 16.8	10 00.6
16 Sa	17 40 00	24 25 49	28 41 51	5♑20 27	18D27.3	8 13.0	6 18.4	15 01.3	20 57.4	26 23.2	8 20.2	10 33.7	6 17.5	9 59.7
17 Su	17 43 57	25 26 55	12♑02 25	18 47 32	18 26.7	7 35.1	7 29.6	15 45.1	21 19.3	26 28.0	8 15.5	10 31.3	6 18.3	9 58.8
18 M	17 47 54	26 28 01	25 35 35	2♒26 22	18 27.3	6 46.0	8 40.6	16 29.0	21 41.1	26 32.6	8 10.7	10 28.8	6 19.0	9 57.9
19 Tu	17 51 50	27 29 08	9♒19 38	16 15 10	18 28.5	5 46.4	9 51.6	17 12.9	22 02.8	26 37.0	8 05.9	10 26.4	6 19.7	9 56.9
20 W	17 55 47	28 30 15	23 12 45	0♓12 10	18 30.0	4 37.7	11 02.4	17 56.8	22 24.3	26 41.3	8 01.0	10 24.1	6 20.3	9 56.0
21 Th	17 59 43	29 31 22	7♓13 14	14 15 45	18 31.2	3 22.0	12 13.2	18 40.8	22 45.6	26 45.4	7 56.2	10 21.7	6 20.9	9 55.0
22 F	18 03 40	0♑32 29	21 19 29	28 24 13	18R31.8	2 01.5	13 23.8	19 24.8	23 06.8	26 49.3	7 51.3	10 19.3	6 21.5	9 54.0
23 Sa	18 07 36	1 33 36	5♈29 45	12♈35 47	18 31.5	0 39.0	14 34.3	20 08.9	23 27.9	26 53.1	7 46.4	10 17.0	6 22.0	9 53.0
24 Su	18 11 33	2 34 43	19 42 04	26 48 15	18 30.4	29♐17.2	15 44.7	20 53.0	23 48.8	26 56.7	7 41.5	10 14.7	6 22.5	9 51.9
25 M	18 15 29	3 35 50	3♉54 01	10♉58 57	18 28.7	27 58.8	16 55.0	21 37.2	24 09.5	27 00.1	7 36.5	10 12.4	6 23.0	9 50.9
26 Tu	18 19 26	4 36 58	18 02 40	25 04 44	18 26.8	26 46.1	18 05.2	22 21.4	24 30.1	27 03.3	7 31.6	10 10.2	6 23.4	9 49.8
27 W	18 23 23	5 38 05	2♊04 42	9♊02 10	18 25.0	25 41.2	19 15.2	23 05.7	24 50.5	27 06.3	7 26.6	10 07.9	6 23.8	9 48.7
28 Th	18 27 19	6 39 13	15 56 42	22 47 54	18 23.6	24 45.3	20 25.1	23 50.0	25 10.7	27 09.2	7 21.7	10 05.7	6 24.2	9 47.6
29 F	18 31 16	7 40 21	29 35 26	6♋19 01	18D22.7	23 59.5	21 34.9	24 34.3	25 30.8	27 11.9	7 16.7	10 03.6	6 24.5	9 46.5
30 Sa	18 35 12	8 41 29	12♋58 24	19 33 25	18 22.5	23 24.1	22 44.5	25 18.7	25 50.7	27 14.4	7 11.8	10 01.4	6 24.8	9 45.3
31 Su	18 39 09	9 42 37	26 04 00	2♌30 08	18 22.8	22 59.2	23 54.0	26 03.2	26 10.5	27 16.7	7 06.8	9 59.3	6 25.1	9 44.2

Astro Data

	Dy Hr Mn
♇ R	11 5:11
☽ 0S	12 12:13
♄⊻♇	16 4:42
☽ 0N	26 4:34
♃∠♇	3 21:19
☽ 0S	9 20:48
☿ R	13 16:11
⚳ 0S	22 0:09
☽ 0N	23 11:18

Planet Ingress

	Dy Hr Mn
☿ ♐	10 11:09
♀ ♑	16 7:26
☉ ♐	22 10:08
♂ ♐	25 16:11
☿ ♑	1 15:31
♀ ♒	11 4:47
☉ ♑	21 23:15
☿ ♐R	23 23:21

Last Aspect / ☽ Ingress (November)

Dy Hr Mn	Aspect	☽ Ingress Dy Hr Mn
1 9:36	♃ △	♊ 2 1:28
3 12:44	♃ □	♋ 4 5:04
5 23:40	☿ △	♌ 6 12:44
8 18:51	☿ □	♍ 8 23:59
10 23:38	♀ □	♎ 11 12:45
13 18:43	♀ ⚹	♏ 14 0:48
15 22:29	☉ ☌	♐ 16 11:02
18 6:33	♃ □	♑ 18 19:20
20 23:09	☉ ⚹	♒ 21 1:47
23 3:12	♂ □	♓ 23 6:18
25 8:34	♂ △	♈ 25 8:57
27 0:37	☿ △	♉ 27 10:22
29 2:53	♃ △	♊ 29 11:55

Last Aspect / ☽ Ingress (December)

Dy Hr Mn	Aspect	☽ Ingress Dy Hr Mn
1 15:15	☿ ☍	♋ 1 15:16
3 12:44	♃ ⚹	♌ 3 21:53
4 22:02	☉ △	♍ 6 8:04
8 14:10	♀ △	♎ 8 20:28
10 9:12	☉ ⚹	♏ 11 8:42
13 11:29	♃ ⚹	♐ 13 18:50
15 19:42	♃ □	♑ 16 2:22
18 1:37	♃ △	♒ 18 7:44
20 8:52	☉ ⚹	♓ 20 11:39
22 9:19	♃ ☍	♈ 22 14:42
24 15:50	☿ △	♉ 24 17:24
26 15:24	♃ △	♊ 26 20:26
28 19:42	♃ □	♋ 29 0:44
31 2:13	♃ ⚹	♌ 31 7:19

☽ Phases & Eclipses

Dy Hr Mn	
7 18:29	☾ 15♌14
15 22:29	● 23♏27
23 7:53	☽ 0♓55
30 0:52	○ 7♊42
7 14:57	☾ 15♍24
15 14:35	● 23♐31
22 15:54	☽ 0♈42
29 14:38	○ 7♋47
29 14:49	A 1.022

Astro Data

1 November 1944
Julian Day # 16376
SVP 6♓02'06"
GC 26♐04.1 ⚴ 13♍54.3
Eris 5♈15.3R ⚵ 6♋52.2
⚷ 28♍05.7 ⚶ 19♍49.7
☽ Mean ☊ 22♋00.3

1 December 1944
Julian Day # 16406
SVP 6♓02'01"
GC 26♐04.2 ⚴ 26♍24.0
Eris 5♈03.2R ⚵ 6♋14.0R
⚷ 1♎17.0 ⚶ 2♎16.6
☽ Mean ☊ 20♋25.0

LONGITUDE — January 1945

Day	Sid.Time	☉	0 hr ☽	Noon ☽	True ☊	☿	♀	♂	⚳	♃	♄	♅	♆	♇
1 M	18 43 05	10♑43 46	8♌51 53	15♌09 24	18♋23.4	22♐44.5	25♒03.3	26♐47.6	26♎30.0	27♍18.8	7♋01.9	9♊57.2	6♎25.3	9♌43.0
2 Tu	18 47 02	11 44 54	21 22 54	27 32 39	18 24.2	22D 39.5	26 12.5	27 32.2	26 49.4	27 20.8	6R 57.0	9R 55.2	6 25.5	9R 41.8
3 W	18 50 59	12 46 03	3♍39 01	9♍42 24	18 24.9	22 43.7	27 21.6	28 16.7	27 08.5	27 22.5	6 52.0	9 53.1	6 25.7	9 40.6
4 Th	18 54 55	13 47 12	15 43 16	21 42 05	18 25.4	22 56.3	28 30.4	29 01.3	27 27.5	27 24.1	6 47.1	9 51.1	6 25.8	9 39.4
5 F	18 58 52	14 48 21	27 39 25	3♎35 47	18 25.7	23 16.6	29 39.1	29 46.0	27 46.3	27 25.5	6 42.2	9 49.2	6 25.9	9 38.2
6 Sa	19 02 48	15 49 30	9♎31 48	15 28 03	18R 25.8	23 44.0	0♓47.7	0♑30.7	28 04.9	27 26.7	6 37.4	9 47.2	6 26.0	9 36.9
7 Su	19 06 45	16 50 39	21 25 07	27 23 36	18 25.7	24 17.7	1 56.0	1 15.5	28 23.3	27 27.7	6 32.5	9 45.4	6R 26.0	9 35.7
8 M	19 10 41	17 51 48	3♏24 05	9♏27 09	18D 25.7	24 57.0	3 04.2	2 00.2	28 41.5	27 28.5	6 27.7	9 43.5	6 26.0	9 34.4
9 Tu	19 14 38	18 52 58	15 33 19	21 43 05	18 25.7	25 41.5	4 12.2	2 45.1	28 59.5	27 29.1	6 22.9	9 41.7	6 25.9	9 33.1
10 W	19 18 34	19 54 07	27 56 54	4♐15 10	18 25.8	26 30.6	5 20.1	3 30.0	29 17.3	27 29.5	6 18.1	9 39.9	6 25.9	9 31.8
11 Th	19 22 31	20 55 17	10♐38 13	17 06 16	18 26.0	27 23.8	6 27.7	4 14.9	29 34.8	27R 29.8	6 13.4	9 38.2	6 25.8	9 30.5
12 F	19 26 28	21 56 26	23 39 29	0♑17 56	18 26.3	28 20.6	7 35.1	4 59.9	29 52.2	27 29.8	6 08.7	9 36.5	6 25.6	9 29.2
13 Sa	19 30 24	22 57 35	7♑01 35	13 50 16	18R 26.5	29 20.7	8 42.3	5 44.9	0♏09.3	27 29.7	6 04.1	9 34.8	6 25.4	9 27.9
14 Su	19 34 21	23 58 44	20 43 45	27 41 40	18 26.4	0♑23.8	9 49.4	6 29.9	0 26.2	27 29.3	5 59.5	9 33.2	6 25.2	9 26.6
15 M	19 38 17	24 59 52	4♒43 35	11♒48 59	18 26.1	1 29.5	10 56.1	7 15.0	0 42.9	27 28.8	5 54.9	9 31.6	6 25.0	9 25.3
16 Tu	19 42 14	26 00 59	18 57 16	26 07 49	18 25.3	2 37.6	12 02.7	8 00.1	0 59.3	27 28.0	5 50.4	9 30.1	6 24.7	9 23.9
17 W	19 46 10	27 02 06	3♓19 57	10♓33 01	18 24.3	3 47.8	13 09.0	8 45.3	1 15.4	27 27.1	5 46.0	9 28.6	6 24.4	9 22.6
18 Th	19 50 07	28 03 12	17 46 23	24 59 25	18 23.2	5 00.0	14 15.1	9 30.5	1 31.4	27 26.0	5 41.6	9 27.1	6 24.0	9 21.2
19 F	19 54 03	29 04 17	2♈11 35	9♈22 22	18 22.3	6 13.9	15 20.9	10 15.7	1 47.1	27 24.6	5 37.2	9 25.7	6 23.6	9 19.9
20 Sa	19 58 00	0♒05 21	16 31 21	23 38 10	18D 21.7	7 29.5	16 26.5	11 01.0	2 02.5	27 23.1	5 32.9	9 24.3	6 23.2	9 18.5
21 Su	20 01 57	1 06 25	0♉42 31	7♉44 12	18 21.7	8 46.5	17 31.8	11 46.3	2 17.7	27 21.4	5 28.7	9 23.0	6 22.8	9 17.1
22 M	20 05 53	2 07 27	14 43 02	21 38 55	18 22.3	10 04.9	18 36.7	12 31.6	2 32.6	27 19.6	5 24.6	9 21.8	6 22.3	9 15.7
23 Tu	20 09 50	3 08 28	28 31 46	5♊21 32	18 23.4	11 24.6	19 41.4	13 17.0	2 47.3	27 17.5	5 20.5	9 20.5	6 21.8	9 14.4
24 W	20 13 46	4 09 28	12♊08 11	18 51 43	18 24.7	12 45.5	20 45.8	14 02.4	3 01.7	27 15.2	5 16.4	9 19.4	6 21.2	9 13.0
25 Th	20 17 43	5 10 28	25 32 06	2♋09 22	18 25.9	14 07.5	21 49.9	14 47.8	3 15.8	27 12.8	5 12.5	9 18.2	6 20.6	9 11.6
26 F	20 21 39	6 11 26	8♋43 29	15 14 27	18R 26.5	15 30.5	22 53.7	15 33.3	3 29.6	27 10.1	5 08.6	9 17.2	6 20.0	9 10.2
27 Sa	20 25 36	7 12 23	21 42 18	28 07 00	18 26.3	16 54.6	23 57.1	16 18.8	3 43.2	27 07.3	5 04.8	9 16.1	6 19.4	9 08.8
28 Su	20 29 32	8 13 20	4♌28 36	10♌47 07	18 24.9	18 19.6	25 00.1	17 04.4	3 56.5	27 04.3	5 01.1	9 15.2	6 18.7	9 07.4
29 M	20 33 29	9 14 15	17 02 36	23 15 08	18 22.5	19 45.5	26 02.9	17 50.0	4 09.5	27 01.1	4 57.4	9 14.2	6 18.0	9 06.0
30 Tu	20 37 26	10 15 09	29 24 49	5♍31 49	18 19.2	21 12.2	27 05.2	18 35.6	4 22.2	26 57.8	4 53.8	9 13.3	6 17.3	9 04.6
31 W	20 41 22	11 16 03	11♍36 19	17 38 33	18 15.3	22 39.9	28 07.2	19 21.3	4 34.7	26 54.2	4 50.3	9 12.5	6 16.5	9 03.2

LONGITUDE — February 1945

Day	Sid.Time	☉	0 hr ☽	Noon ☽	True ☊	☿	♀	♂	⚳	♃	♄	♅	♆	♇
1 Th	20 45 19	12♒16 55	23♍38 47	29♍37 19	18♋11.2	24♑08.3	29♓08.7	20♑07.0	4♏46.8	26♍50.5	4♋46.9	9♊11.7	6♎15.7	9♌01.9
2 F	20 49 15	13 17 47	5♎34 34	11♎30 54	18R 07.4	25 37.6	0♈09.9	20 52.7	4 58.6	26R 46.6	4R 43.6	9R 11.0	6R 14.9	9R 00.5
3 Sa	20 53 12	14 18 37	17 26 47	23 22 43	18 04.5	27 07.7	1 10.6	21 38.4	5 10.1	26 42.6	4 40.3	9 10.3	6 14.1	8 59.1
4 Su	20 57 08	15 19 27	29 19 14	5♏16 51	18D 02.7	28 38.5	2 11.0	22 24.2	5 21.3	26 38.3	4 37.2	9 09.7	6 13.2	8 57.7
5 M	21 01 05	16 20 16	11♏16 12	17 17 50	18 02.1	0♒10.2	3 10.8	23 10.1	5 32.2	26 33.9	4 34.1	9 09.1	6 12.3	8 56.3
6 Tu	21 05 01	17 21 04	23 22 23	29 30 27	18 02.8	1 42.7	4 10.3	23 55.9	5 42.7	26 29.4	4 31.2	9 08.6	6 11.3	8 54.9
7 W	21 08 58	18 21 52	5♐42 38	11♐59 28	18 04.3	3 15.9	5 09.2	24 41.8	5 52.9	26 24.6	4 28.3	9 08.1	6 10.4	8 53.6
8 Th	21 12 55	19 22 38	18 21 30	24 49 12	18 06.0	4 50.0	6 07.7	25 27.8	6 02.8	26 19.8	4 25.5	9 07.7	6 09.4	8 52.2
9 F	21 16 51	20 23 23	1♑22 56	8♑03 01	18R 07.4	6 24.8	7 05.6	26 13.7	6 12.4	26 14.7	4 22.8	9 07.3	6 08.4	8 50.8
10 Sa	21 20 48	21 24 07	14 49 37	21 42 46	18 07.7	8 00.5	8 03.1	26 59.7	6 21.6	26 09.5	4 20.2	9 07.0	6 07.3	8 49.5
11 Su	21 24 44	22 24 50	28 42 21	5♒48 06	18 06.5	9 37.0	9 00.0	27 45.7	6 30.4	26 04.2	4 17.7	9 06.7	6 06.3	8 48.1
12 M	21 28 41	23 25 31	12♒59 33	20 16 04	18 03.5	11 14.3	9 56.3	28 31.8	6 38.9	25 58.7	4 15.3	9 06.5	6 05.2	8 46.8
13 Tu	21 32 37	24 26 11	27 36 53	5♓01 05	17 58.9	12 52.4	10 52.1	29 17.8	6 47.1	25 53.0	4 13.1	9 06.3	6 04.1	8 45.4
14 W	21 36 34	25 26 50	12♓27 37	19 55 23	17 53.2	14 31.4	11 47.2	0♒03.9	6 54.9	25 47.2	4 10.9	9 06.2	6 02.9	8 44.1
15 Th	21 40 30	26 27 27	27 23 17	4♈50 14	17 47.2	16 11.2	12 41.8	0 50.0	7 02.3	25 41.3	4 08.8	9D 06.2	6 01.7	8 42.8
16 F	21 44 27	27 28 02	12♈15 12	19 37 16	17 41.8	17 51.9	13 35.6	1 36.2	7 09.3	25 35.3	4 06.8	9 06.2	6 00.6	8 41.5
17 Sa	21 48 24	28 28 36	26 55 41	4♉09 50	17 37.7	19 33.5	14 28.8	2 22.3	7 16.0	25 29.1	4 04.9	9 06.2	5 59.3	8 40.2
18 Su	21 52 20	29 29 07	11♉19 15	18 23 38	17D 35.4	21 16.0	15 21.3	3 08.5	7 22.3	25 22.8	4 03.2	9 06.4	5 58.1	8 38.9
19 M	21 56 17	0♓29 37	25 22 52	2♊16 54	17 34.8	22 59.5	16 13.1	3 54.7	7 28.2	25 16.4	4 01.5	9 06.5	5 56.8	8 37.6
20 Tu	22 00 13	1 30 05	9♊05 50	15 49 51	17 35.6	24 43.8	17 04.1	4 41.0	7 33.7	25 09.8	4 00.0	9 06.7	5 55.6	8 36.3
21 W	22 04 10	2 30 31	22 29 12	29 04 08	17 37.0	26 29.1	17 54.3	5 27.2	7 38.9	25 03.2	3 58.5	9 07.0	5 54.3	8 35.0
22 Th	22 08 06	3 30 56	5♋34 59	12♋02 03	17R 38.1	28 15.4	18 43.6	6 13.5	7 43.6	24 56.4	3 57.2	9 07.3	5 52.9	8 33.8
23 F	22 12 03	4 31 18	18 25 39	24 46 03	17 38.0	0♓02.6	19 32.1	6 59.8	7 48.0	24 49.6	3 56.0	9 07.7	5 51.6	8 32.6
24 Sa	22 15 59	5 31 38	1♌03 33	7♌18 23	17 35.9	1 50.8	20 19.8	7 46.1	7 52.0	24 42.6	3 54.9	9 08.1	5 50.2	8 31.3
25 Su	22 19 56	6 31 57	13 30 46	19 40 53	17 31.5	3 39.9	21 06.5	8 32.5	7 55.5	24 35.6	3 53.9	9 08.6	5 48.9	8 30.1
26 M	22 23 53	7 32 14	25 48 54	1♍54 59	17 24.8	5 30.0	21 52.2	9 18.8	7 58.7	24 28.5	3 53.0	9 09.2	5 47.5	8 28.9
27 Tu	22 27 49	8 32 29	7♍59 14	14 01 49	17 15.9	7 21.0	22 36.9	10 05.2	8 01.4	24 21.3	3 52.2	9 09.8	5 46.1	8 27.8
28 W	22 31 46	9 32 42	20 02 52	26 02 31	17 05.7	9 13.0	23 20.6	10 51.6	8 03.8	24 14.0	3 51.6	9 10.4	5 44.6	8 26.6

Astro Data	Dy Hr Mn
☿ D	2 12:45
☽ 0S	6 5:30
♆ R	7 16:34
♄□♆	8 20:36
♃ R	12 4:51
☽ 0N	19 16:46
♀ 0N	1 0:24
☽ 0S	2 13:12
♅ D	15 23:25
☽ 0N	15 23:32

Planet Ingress		Dy Hr Mn
♀	♓	5 19:18
♂	♑	5 19:31
⚳	♏	12 22:55
☿	♑	14 3:04
☉	♒	20 9:54
♀	♈	2 8:07
☿	♒	5 9:20
♂	♒	14 9:58
☉	♓	19 0:15
☿	♓	23 11:25

Last Aspect Dy Hr Mn		☽ Ingress	Dy Hr Mn
2 11:59	♂ △	♍	2 16:49
5 3:45	♂ □	♎	5 4:44
7 5:27	☿ ⚹	♏	7 17:13
9 23:07	♃ ⚹	♐	10 3:55
12 8:12	☿ ☌	♑	12 11:28
14 11:39	♃ △	♒	14 15:57
15 8:08	♅ △	♓	16 18:27
18 17:29	☉ ⚹	♈	18 20:21
19 13:34	♂ □	♉	20 22:48
22 21:52	♃ △	♊	23 2:35
25 3:04	♃ □	♋	25 8:05
27 10:08	♃ ⚹	♌	27 15:33
28 9:05	♅ ⚹	♍	30 1:09

Last Aspect Dy Hr Mn		☽ Ingress	Dy Hr Mn
1 10:57	♀ ☍	♎	1 12:46
3 20:41	☿ □	♏	4 1:22
6 6:09	♃ ⚹	♐	6 12:57
8 14:45	♃ □	♑	8 21:29
10 21:36	♂ ☌	♒	11 2:12
12 17:33	☉ ☌	♓	13 3:52
14 21:22	♃ ☍	♈	15 4:12
17 1:51	☉ ⚹	♉	17 5:05
18 23:54	♃ △	♊	19 8:01
21 6:33	☿ △	♋	21 13:42
23 12:07	♃ ⚹	♌	23 21:58
25 14:58	♀ △	♍	26 8:13
28 8:25	♃ ☌	♎	28 19:57

☽ Phases & Eclipses Dy Hr Mn		
6 12:47	☾	15♎52
14 5:07	●	23♑41
14 5:01:16	●	A 00'15"
20 23:48	☽	0♉35
28 6:41	○	8♌00
5 9:55	☾	16♏15
12 17:33	●	23♒40
19 8:38	☽	0♊21
27 0:07	○	8♍03

Astro Data

1 January 1945
Julian Day # 16437
SVP 6♓01'56"
GC 26♐04.3 ⚳ 5♎32.5
Eris 5♈00.8 ⚵ 29♊25.4R
⚷ 3♎09.0 ⚶ 13♎16.1
☽ Mean ☊ 18♋46.5

1 February 1945
Julian Day # 16468
SVP 6♓01'51"
GC 26♐04.3 ⚳ 8♎34.1R
Eris 5♈09.6 ⚵ 26♊06.5
⚷ 3♎10.6R ⚶ 20♎39.6
☽ Mean ☊ 17♋08.1

March 1945

LONGITUDE

Day	Sid.Time	☉	0 hr ☽	Noon ☽	True ☊	☿	♀	♂	⚷	♃	♄	♅	♆	♇
1 Th	22 35 42	10♓32 53	2♎00 57	7♎58 20	16♋55.1	11♓05.9	24♈03.2	11♒38.0	8♏05.7	24♍06.6	3♋51.0	9♊11.1	5♎43.2	8♌25.4
2 F	22 39 39	11 33 03	13 54 55	19 50 57	16R44.8	12 59.6	24 44.8	12 24.4	8 07.2	23R59.2	3R50.6	9 11.8	5R41.7	8R24.3
3 Sa	22 43 35	12 33 11	25 46 44	1♏42 37	16 36.0	14 54.1	25 25.1	13 10.9	8 08.4	23 51.7	3 50.2	9 12.6	5 40.2	8 23.2
4 Su	22 47 32	13 33 18	7♏39 00	13 36 18	16 29.2	16 49.3	26 04.3	13 57.4	8 09.0	23 44.1	3 50.0	9 13.5	5 38.7	8 22.1
5 M	22 51 28	14 33 23	19 35 01	25 35 41	16 24.9	18 45.2	26 42.2	14 43.9	8R09.3	23 36.6	3D49.9	9 14.4	5 37.2	8 21.0
6 Tu	22 55 25	15 33 27	1♐38 50	7♐45 04	16D22.8	20 41.6	27 18.8	15 30.4	8 09.2	23 28.9	3 49.9	9 15.3	5 35.7	8 19.9
7 W	22 59 22	16 33 28	13 55 00	20 09 14	16 22.5	22 38.3	27 54.1	16 16.9	8 08.6	23 21.2	3 50.0	9 16.3	5 34.2	8 18.9
8 Th	23 03 18	17 33 29	26 28 25	2♑53 06	16 23.1	24 35.3	28 28.0	17 03.5	8 07.6	23 13.5	3 50.3	9 17.4	5 32.6	8 17.8
9 F	23 07 15	18 33 28	9♑23 53	16 01 13	16R23.6	26 32.3	29 00.5	17 50.0	8 06.1	23 05.8	3 50.6	9 18.5	5 31.1	8 16.8
10 Sa	23 11 11	19 33 25	22 45 31	29 37 04	16 22.8	28 29.1	29 31.4	18 36.6	8 04.3	22 58.0	3 51.1	9 19.7	5 29.5	8 15.8
11 Su	23 15 08	20 33 20	6♒35 58	13♒42 12	16 20.0	0♈25.4	0♉00.9	19 23.2	8 02.0	22 50.2	3 51.6	9 20.9	5 27.9	8 14.8
12 M	23 19 04	21 33 14	20 55 29	28 15 21	16 14.5	2 20.9	0 28.7	20 09.8	7 59.3	22 42.4	3 52.3	9 22.1	5 26.3	8 13.9
13 Tu	23 23 01	22 33 05	5♓41 05	13♓11 46	16 06.6	4 15.2	0 54.8	20 56.4	7 56.1	22 34.6	3 53.1	9 23.4	5 24.7	8 12.9
14 W	23 26 57	23 32 55	20 46 15	28 23 16	15 56.8	6 08.1	1 19.2	21 43.0	7 52.6	22 26.8	3 54.0	9 24.8	5 23.1	8 12.0
15 Th	23 30 54	24 32 43	6♈01 24	13♈39 14	15 46.4	7 59.0	1 41.8	22 29.6	7 48.6	22 19.0	3 55.0	9 26.2	5 21.5	8 11.1
16 F	23 34 50	25 32 28	21 15 22	28 48 28	15 36.7	9 47.6	2 02.5	23 16.2	7 44.2	22 11.2	3 56.2	9 27.6	5 19.9	8 10.2
17 Sa	23 38 47	26 32 12	6♉17 24	13♉41 12	15 28.6	11 33.4	2 21.4	24 02.9	7 39.4	22 03.4	3 57.4	9 29.1	5 18.2	8 09.4
18 Su	23 42 44	27 31 53	20 59 06	28 10 37	15 23.1	13 16.0	2 38.2	24 49.5	7 34.1	21 55.6	3 58.7	9 30.7	5 16.6	8 08.5
19 M	23 46 40	28 31 32	5♊15 25	12♊13 25	15 20.1	14 54.7	2 52.9	25 36.2	7 28.5	21 47.9	4 00.2	9 32.3	5 15.0	8 07.7
20 Tu	23 50 37	29 31 09	19 04 41	25 49 27	15D19.1	16 29.3	3 05.6	26 22.8	7 22.5	21 40.2	4 01.8	9 33.9	5 13.3	8 06.9
21 W	23 54 33	0♈30 43	2♋28 02	9♋00 51	15R19.2	17 59.2	3 16.0	27 09.5	7 16.1	21 32.6	4 03.5	9 35.6	5 11.7	8 06.1
22 Th	23 58 30	1 30 16	15 28 22	21 51 06	15 19.1	19 24.0	3 24.2	27 56.1	7 09.2	21 24.9	4 05.2	9 37.4	5 10.0	8 05.4
23 F	0 02 26	2 29 45	28 09 32	4♌24 11	15 17.7	20 43.3	3 30.1	28 42.8	7 02.0	21 17.4	4 07.1	9 39.2	5 08.4	8 04.7
24 Sa	0 06 23	3 29 13	10♌35 32	16 44 01	15 14.0	21 56.8	3R33.7	29 29.4	6 54.5	21 09.9	4 09.1	9 41.0	5 06.7	8 04.0
25 Su	0 10 19	4 28 38	22 50 04	28 54 02	15 07.5	23 04.0	3 34.8	0♓16.1	6 46.5	21 02.4	4 11.2	9 42.9	5 05.1	8 03.3
26 M	0 14 16	5 28 01	4♍56 15	10♍57 02	14 58.1	24 04.7	3 33.6	1 02.8	6 38.2	20 55.1	4 13.5	9 44.8	5 03.4	8 02.6
27 Tu	0 18 13	6 27 22	16 56 36	22 55 12	14 46.0	24 58.6	3 29.8	1 49.4	6 29.5	20 47.7	4 15.8	9 46.7	5 01.8	8 02.0
28 W	0 22 09	7 26 41	28 53 00	4♎50 11	14 32.2	25 45.6	3 23.6	2 36.1	6 20.5	20 40.5	4 18.2	9 48.7	5 00.1	8 01.4
29 Th	0 26 06	8 25 58	10♎46 55	16 43 20	14 17.7	26 25.5	3 14.8	3 22.7	6 11.2	20 33.4	4 20.7	9 50.8	4 58.5	8 00.8
30 F	0 30 02	9 25 12	22 39 36	28 35 55	14 03.7	26 58.1	3 03.6	4 09.4	6 01.5	20 26.3	4 23.3	9 52.9	4 56.8	8 00.3
31 Sa	0 33 59	10 24 25	4♏32 27	10♏29 26	13 51.2	27 23.3	2 49.9	4 56.1	5 51.5	20 19.3	4 26.1	9 55.0	4 55.1	7 59.7

April 1945

LONGITUDE

Day	Sid.Time	☉	0 hr ☽	Noon ☽	True ☊	☿	♀	♂	⚷	♃	♄	♅	♆	♇
1 Su	0 37 55	11♈23 36	16♏27 08	22♏25 51	13♋41.3	27♈41.3	2♉33.8	5♓42.7	5♏41.1	20♍12.4	4♋28.9	9♊57.2	4♎53.5	7♌59.2
2 M	0 41 52	12 22 45	28 25 56	4♐27 45	13R34.2	27 52.0	2R15.2	6 29.4	5R30.5	20R05.6	4 31.8	9 59.4	4R51.9	7R58.7
3 Tu	0 45 48	13 21 52	10♐31 45	16 38 24	13 30.0	27R55.6	1 54.3	7 16.0	5 19.6	19 58.9	4 34.8	10 01.6	4 50.2	7 58.3
4 W	0 49 45	14 20 57	22 48 14	29 01 47	13 28.2	27 52.2	1 31.2	8 02.7	5 08.4	19 52.3	4 38.0	10 03.9	4 48.6	7 57.8
5 Th	0 53 42	15 20 01	5♑19 38	11♑42 19	13 27.8	27 42.2	1 05.8	8 49.3	4 57.0	19 45.9	4 41.2	10 06.3	4 47.0	7 57.4
6 F	0 57 38	16 19 03	18 10 27	24 44 32	13 27.7	27 25.8	0 38.5	9 36.0	4 45.3	19 39.5	4 44.5	10 08.6	4 45.4	7 57.1
7 Sa	1 01 35	17 18 03	1♒25 03	8♒12 26	13 26.6	27 03.6	0 09.2	10 22.6	4 33.3	19 33.3	4 47.9	10 11.0	4 43.7	7 56.7
8 Su	1 05 31	18 17 02	15 06 57	22 08 45	13 23.6	26 36.0	29♈38.2	11 09.3	4 21.1	19 27.1	4 51.5	10 13.5	4 42.1	7 56.4
9 M	1 09 28	19 15 58	29 17 47	6♓33 50	13 18.0	26 03.8	29 05.6	11 55.9	4 08.8	19 21.2	4 55.1	10 16.0	4 40.5	7 56.1
10 Tu	1 13 24	20 14 53	13♓56 25	21 24 50	13 09.8	25 27.5	28 31.5	12 42.5	3 56.2	19 15.3	4 58.8	10 18.5	4 39.0	7 55.8
11 W	1 17 21	21 13 46	28 58 08	6♈35 09	12 59.6	24 47.9	27 56.3	13 29.1	3 43.4	19 09.6	5 02.6	10 21.0	4 37.4	7 55.5
12 Th	1 21 17	22 12 37	14♈14 34	21 54 56	12 48.5	24 05.8	27 20.2	14 15.7	3 30.5	19 04.0	5 06.4	10 23.6	4 35.8	7 55.3
13 F	1 25 14	23 11 26	29 34 46	7♉12 34	12 37.9	23 22.2	26 43.2	15 02.3	3 17.4	18 58.5	5 10.4	10 26.2	4 34.2	7 55.1
14 Sa	1 29 10	24 10 13	14♉47 00	22 16 49	12 29.0	22 37.7	26 05.7	15 48.8	3 04.2	18 53.2	5 14.5	10 28.9	4 32.7	7 54.9
15 Su	1 33 07	25 08 58	29 41 00	6♊58 48	12 22.6	21 53.3	25 28.0	16 35.4	2 50.9	18 48.1	5 18.7	10 31.6	4 31.2	7 54.8
16 M	1 37 04	26 07 41	14♊09 38	21 13 12	12 18.9	21 09.8	24 50.2	17 21.9	2 37.4	18 43.0	5 22.9	10 34.3	4 29.7	7 54.7
17 Tu	1 41 00	27 06 21	28 09 24	4♋58 19	12D17.4	20 27.9	24 12.7	18 08.4	2 23.9	18 38.2	5 27.2	10 37.1	4 28.1	7 54.6
18 W	1 44 57	28 05 00	11♋40 12	18 15 24	12R17.3	19 48.4	23 35.5	18 54.9	2 10.4	18 33.5	5 31.7	10 39.9	4 26.7	7 54.5
19 Th	1 48 53	29 03 36	24 44 25	1♌07 44	12 17.5	19 11.8	22 59.1	19 41.4	1 56.8	18 29.0	5 36.2	10 42.7	4 25.2	7D54.5
20 F	1 52 50	0♉02 10	7♌25 57	13 39 38	12 16.6	18 38.7	22 23.7	20 27.9	1 43.2	18 24.6	5 40.8	10 45.6	4 23.7	7 54.5
21 Sa	1 56 46	1 00 41	19 49 23	25 55 46	12 13.9	18 09.5	21 49.3	21 14.3	1 29.5	18 20.4	5 45.4	10 48.4	4 22.3	7 54.5
22 Su	2 00 43	1 59 11	1♍59 20	8♍00 35	12 08.7	17 44.6	21 16.4	22 00.7	1 15.9	18 16.3	5 50.2	10 51.3	4 20.8	7 54.5
23 M	2 04 40	2 57 38	14 00 01	19 58 04	12 00.9	17 24.3	20 45.0	22 47.1	1 02.3	18 12.4	5 55.0	10 54.3	4 19.4	7 54.6
24 Tu	2 08 36	3 56 03	25 55 06	1♎51 30	11 50.7	17 08.7	20 15.3	23 33.5	0 48.7	18 08.7	5 59.9	10 57.2	4 18.0	7 54.7
25 W	2 12 33	4 54 26	7♎47 33	13 43 31	11 38.9	16 58.0	19 47.5	24 19.8	0 35.2	18 05.2	6 04.9	11 00.2	4 16.6	7 54.8
26 Th	2 16 29	5 52 48	19 39 40	25 36 10	11 26.4	16D52.3	19 21.7	25 06.2	0 21.7	18 01.8	6 10.0	11 03.2	4 15.3	7 54.9
27 F	2 20 26	6 51 07	1♏33 13	7♏31 01	11 14.3	16 51.5	18 58.1	25 52.5	0 08.4	17 58.6	6 15.1	11 06.3	4 13.9	7 55.1
28 Sa	2 24 22	7 49 25	13 29 41	19 29 26	11 03.6	16 55.6	18 36.7	26 38.8	29♎55.1	17 55.6	6 20.3	11 09.4	4 12.6	7 55.3
29 Su	2 28 19	8 47 41	25 30 25	1♐32 51	10 55.1	17 04.6	18 17.6	27 25.0	29 42.0	17 52.7	6 25.6	11 12.5	4 11.3	7 55.5
30 M	2 32 15	9 45 55	7♐36 56	13 42 55	10 49.1	17 18.4	18 00.9	28 11.3	29 29.0	17 50.1	6 31.0	11 15.6	4 10.0	7 55.8

Astro Data	Dy Hr Mn
☽0S	1 19:42
⚷R	5 15:14
♄D	5 22:43
♃∠♇	7 20:33
☿0N	11 19:07
☽0N	15 8:55
☉0N	20 23:38
♀R	25 11:24
☽0S	29 1:39
☿R	3 12:12
♄□♆	6 15:59
☽0N	11 19:57
⚷0N	16 6:18
♇D	20 10:22
☽0S	25 7:55

Planet Ingress	Dy Hr Mn
☿ ♈	11 6:45
♀ ♉	11 11:17
☉ ♈	20 23:37
♂ ♓	25 3:43
♀ ♈R	7 19:15
☉ ♉	20 11:07
⚷ ♎R	28 3:10
☿ D	27 3:46

Last Aspect Dy Hr Mn		☽ Ingress	Dy Hr Mn
2 22:31	♀ ☍	♏	3 8:32
5 8:05	♃ ⚹	♐	5 20:45
8 3:22	♀ △	♑	8 6:37
10 11:50	♀ □	♒	10 12:40
11 22:00	♂ ☌	♓	12 14:50
14 3:51	☉ ☌	♈	14 14:32
16 2:43	♂ ⚹	♉	16 13:54
18 10:50	☉ ⚹	♊	18 15:04
20 19:11	☉ □	♋	20 19:31
22 11:11	♃ ⚹	♌	23 3:32
24 23:19	☿ △	♍	25 14:11
27 7:46	♃ ☌	♎	28 2:15
30 8:34	☿ ☍	♏	30 14:50

Last Aspect Dy Hr Mn		☽ Ingress	Dy Hr Mn
1 7:35	♃ ⚹	♐	2 3:08
4 9:48	☿ △	♑	4 13:51
6 16:44	☿ □	♒	6 21:28
9 0:07	♀ ⚹	♓	9 1:10
10 8:34	♃ ☍	♈	11 1:38
12 20:09	♀ ☌	♉	13 0:40
14 6:35	♃ △	♊	15 0:31
16 21:07	☉ ⚹	♋	17 3:13
19 7:46	☉ □	♌	19 9:52
21 4:16	♀ △	♍	21 20:03
23 18:04	♂ ☍	♎	24 8:15
25 23:50	♀ ☍	♏	26 20:52
29 3:14	♂ △	♐	29 8:56

☽ Phases & Eclipses Dy Hr Mn	
7 4:30	☾ 16♐15
14 3:51	● 23♓13
20 19:11	☽ 29♊49
28 17:44	○ 7♎41
5 19:18	☾ 15♑38
12 12:30	● 22♈14
19 7:46	☽ 28♋53
27 10:33	○ 6♏48

Astro Data

1 March 1945
Julian Day # 16496
SVP 6♓01'48"
GC 26♐04.4 ⚳ 4♎11.9R
Eris 5♈25.2 ⚵ 29♊41.8
⚷ 1♎44.0R ⚶ 22♎07.7R
☽ Mean ☊ 15♋39.1

1 April 1945
Julian Day # 16527
SVP 6♓01'45"
GC 26♐04.5 ⚳ 24♍42.8R
Eris 5♈46.8 ⚵ 8♋39.1
⚷ 29♍20.8R ⚶ 16♎53.3R
☽ Mean ☊ 14♋00.6

LONGITUDE — May 1945

Day	Sid.Time	☉	0 hr ☽	Noon ☽	True ☊	☿	♀	♂	⚳	♃	♄	♅	♆	♇
1 Tu	2 36 12	10♉44 08	19♐51 06	26♐01 48	10♋45.8	17♈36.7	17♈46.6	28♓57.5	29♎16.2	17♍47.6	6♋36.4	11♊18.7	4♎08.8	7♌56.1
2 W	2 40 08	11 42 19	2♑15 21	8♑32 08	10D 44.7	17 59.5	17R 34.7	29 43.7	29R 03.5	17R 45.2	6 41.9	11 21.9	4R 07.5	7 56.4
3 Th	2 44 05	12 40 29	14 52 35	21 17 07	10 45.0	18 26.7	17 25.3	0♈29.8	28 51.0	17 43.1	6 47.5	11 25.1	4 06.3	7 56.7
4 F	2 48 02	13 38 37	27 46 09	4♒20 08	10R 45.8	18 58.1	17 18.4	1 16.0	28 38.7	17 41.1	6 53.1	11 28.3	4 05.1	7 57.1
5 Sa	2 51 58	14 36 44	10♒59 27	17 44 29	10 46.1	19 33.5	17 13.9	2 02.1	28 26.5	17 39.3	6 58.8	11 31.5	4 03.9	7 57.5
6 Su	2 55 55	15 34 49	24 35 28	1♓32 38	10 44.9	20 12.8	17D 11.8	2 48.2	28 14.7	17 37.7	7 04.6	11 34.8	4 02.8	7 57.9
7 M	2 59 51	16 32 53	8♓36 01	15 45 31	10 41.8	20 55.8	17 12.1	3 34.2	28 03.0	17 36.3	7 10.5	11 38.0	4 01.6	7 58.3
8 Tu	3 03 48	17 30 56	23 00 52	0♈21 36	10 36.5	21 42.4	17 14.7	4 20.3	27 51.6	17 35.1	7 16.4	11 41.3	4 00.5	7 58.8
9 W	3 07 44	18 28 57	7♈47 05	15 16 27	10 29.6	22 32.5	17 19.6	5 06.3	27 40.4	17 34.0	7 22.3	11 44.6	3 59.4	7 59.3
10 Th	3 11 41	19 26 57	22 48 40	0♉22 35	10 21.9	23 25.9	17 26.8	5 52.2	27 29.5	17 33.2	7 28.4	11 47.9	3 58.4	7 59.8
11 F	3 15 37	20 24 56	7♉56 56	15 30 26	10 14.5	24 22.5	17 36.1	6 38.1	27 18.9	17 32.5	7 34.5	11 51.3	3 57.3	8 00.3
12 Sa	3 19 34	21 22 53	23 01 50	0♊29 54	10 08.2	25 22.2	17 47.5	7 24.0	27 08.6	17 32.0	7 40.6	11 54.6	3 56.3	8 00.9
13 Su	3 23 31	22 20 48	7♊53 35	15 11 59	10 03.8	26 24.8	18 01.0	8 09.9	26 58.6	17 31.6	7 46.8	11 58.0	3 55.4	8 01.5
14 M	3 27 27	23 18 42	22 24 23	29 30 15	10D 01.5	27 30.4	18 16.5	8 55.7	26 48.9	17D 31.5	7 53.1	12 01.4	3 54.4	8 02.1
15 Tu	3 31 24	24 16 34	6♋29 17	13♋21 22	10 01.1	28 38.8	18 33.9	9 41.5	26 39.6	17 31.6	7 59.4	12 04.8	3 53.5	8 02.8
16 W	3 35 20	25 14 25	20 06 31	26 44 57	10 01.9	29 49.8	18 53.2	10 27.2	26 30.6	17 31.8	8 05.8	12 08.2	3 52.6	8 03.5
17 Th	3 39 17	26 12 14	3♌16 57	9♌42 56	10 03.3	1♉03.6	19 14.3	11 12.9	26 21.9	17 32.2	8 12.3	12 11.6	3 51.7	8 04.1
18 F	3 43 13	27 10 01	16 03 24	22 18 53	10R 04.2	2 19.9	19 37.1	11 58.5	26 13.5	17 32.8	8 18.8	12 15.1	3 50.8	8 04.9
19 Sa	3 47 10	28 07 46	28 29 56	4♍37 08	10 04.1	3 38.8	20 01.6	12 44.1	26 05.5	17 33.6	8 25.3	12 18.5	3 50.0	8 05.6
20 Su	3 51 06	29 05 30	10♍41 06	16 42 24	10 02.4	5 00.2	20 27.8	13 29.7	25 57.9	17 34.5	8 31.9	12 22.0	3 49.2	8 06.4
21 M	3 55 03	0♊03 12	22 41 36	28 39 14	9 59.0	6 24.1	20 55.5	14 15.2	25 50.6	17 35.7	8 38.6	12 25.5	3 48.5	8 07.2
22 Tu	3 59 00	1 00 52	4♎35 49	10♎31 49	9 54.0	7 50.4	21 24.7	15 00.7	25 43.7	17 37.0	8 45.2	12 28.9	3 47.7	8 08.0
23 W	4 02 56	1 58 31	16 27 40	22 23 46	9 47.8	9 19.1	21 55.4	15 46.1	25 37.2	17 38.5	8 52.0	12 32.4	3 47.0	8 08.8
24 Th	4 06 53	2 56 09	28 20 29	4♏18 07	9 41.2	10 50.2	22 27.5	16 31.5	25 31.1	17 40.1	8 58.8	12 35.9	3 46.3	8 09.7
25 F	4 10 49	3 53 45	10♏16 58	16 17 17	9 34.7	12 23.7	23 00.9	17 16.8	25 25.3	17 42.0	9 05.6	12 39.4	3 45.7	8 10.6
26 Sa	4 14 46	4 51 20	22 19 15	28 23 06	9 29.0	13 59.6	23 35.6	18 02.1	25 19.9	17 44.0	9 12.5	12 42.9	3 45.1	8 11.5
27 Su	4 18 42	5 48 54	4♐28 59	10♐37 04	9 24.6	15 37.8	24 11.6	18 47.4	25 14.9	17 46.2	9 19.4	12 46.5	3 44.5	8 12.4
28 M	4 22 39	6 46 27	16 47 29	23 00 24	9 21.8	17 18.3	24 48.8	19 32.6	25 10.3	17 48.6	9 26.4	12 50.0	3 43.9	8 13.4
29 Tu	4 26 35	7 43 59	29 15 57	5♑34 18	9D 20.7	19 01.3	25 27.2	20 17.7	25 06.1	17 51.1	9 33.4	12 53.5	3 43.4	8 14.3
30 W	4 30 32	8 41 29	11♑55 36	18 20 02	9 20.9	20 46.5	26 06.7	21 02.8	25 02.2	17 53.8	9 40.4	12 57.0	3 42.9	8 15.3
31 Th	4 34 29	9 38 59	24 47 48	1♒19 04	9 22.1	22 34.1	26 47.2	21 47.9	24 58.8	17 56.7	9 47.5	13 00.6	3 42.4	8 16.4

LONGITUDE — June 1945

Day	Sid.Time	☉	0 hr ☽	Noon ☽	True ☊	☿	♀	♂	⚳	♃	♄	♅	♆	♇
1 F	4 38 25	10♊36 28	7♒54 04	14♒32 58	9♋23.7	24♉24.0	27♈28.8	22♈32.9	24♎55.7	17♍59.7	9♋54.6	13♊04.1	3♎42.0	8♌17.4
2 Sa	4 42 22	11 33 56	21 15 57	28 03 11	9 25.0	26 16.2	28 11.4	23 17.9	24R 53.1	18 03.0	10 01.8	13 07.6	3R 41.6	8 18.5
3 Su	4 46 18	12 31 24	4♓54 46	11♓50 47	9R 25.5	28 10.7	28 54.9	24 02.8	24 50.8	18 06.3	10 09.0	13 11.2	3 41.2	8 19.6
4 M	4 50 15	13 28 51	18 51 12	25 55 56	9 25.0	0♊07.4	29 39.4	24 47.7	24 48.9	18 09.9	10 16.2	13 14.7	3 40.8	8 20.7
5 Tu	4 54 11	14 26 17	3♈04 46	10♈17 23	9 23.4	2 06.2	0♉24.7	25 32.5	24 47.4	18 13.6	10 23.5	13 18.3	3 40.5	8 21.8
6 W	4 58 08	15 23 43	17 33 21	24 52 06	9 20.9	4 07.1	1 10.9	26 17.3	24 46.3	18 17.5	10 30.8	13 21.8	3 40.2	8 22.9
7 Th	5 02 04	16 21 07	2♉12 58	9♉35 11	9 17.9	6 09.9	1 57.9	27 02.0	24 45.6	18 21.5	10 38.1	13 25.3	3 40.0	8 24.1
8 F	5 06 01	17 18 32	16 57 53	24 20 10	9 15.0	8 14.6	2 45.7	27 46.6	24D 45.3	18 25.7	10 45.5	13 28.9	3 39.8	8 25.3
9 Sa	5 09 58	18 15 56	1♊41 07	8♊59 49	9 12.5	10 21.0	3 34.2	28 31.2	24 45.3	18 30.1	10 52.9	13 32.4	3 39.6	8 26.5
10 Su	5 13 54	19 13 19	16 15 26	23 27 11	9 11.0	12 28.9	4 23.4	29 15.8	24 45.8	18 34.6	11 00.3	13 35.9	3 39.4	8 27.7
11 M	5 17 51	20 10 41	0♋34 22	7♋36 28	9D 10.4	14 38.0	5 13.3	0♉00.2	24 46.6	18 39.2	11 07.8	13 39.5	3 39.3	8 29.0
12 Tu	5 21 47	21 08 03	14 33 03	21 23 51	9 10.7	16 48.3	6 03.9	0 44.7	24 47.9	18 44.1	11 15.2	13 43.0	3 39.2	8 30.2
13 W	5 25 44	22 05 23	28 08 43	4♌47 38	9 11.7	18 59.4	6 55.1	1 29.0	24 49.5	18 49.1	11 22.7	13 46.5	3 39.1	8 31.5
14 Th	5 29 40	23 02 43	11♌20 43	17 48 11	9 13.0	21 11.0	7 46.9	2 13.3	24 51.5	18 54.2	11 30.3	13 50.0	3D 39.1	8 32.8
15 F	5 33 37	24 00 22	24 10 20	0♍27 33	9 14.2	23 22.9	8 39.3	2 57.5	24 53.8	18 59.5	11 37.8	13 53.5	3 39.1	8 34.1
16 Sa	5 37 34	24 57 20	6♍40 17	12 49 02	9 15.1	25 34.8	9 32.3	3 41.7	24 56.6	19 04.9	11 45.4	13 57.0	3 39.2	8 35.5
17 Su	5 41 30	25 54 37	18 54 19	24 56 42	9R 15.4	27 46.4	10 25.8	4 25.8	24 59.7	19 10.5	11 53.0	14 00.5	3 39.2	8 36.8
18 M	5 45 27	26 51 53	0♎56 45	6♎55 01	9 15.2	29 57.5	11 19.9	5 09.8	25 03.1	19 16.2	12 00.6	14 04.0	3 39.3	8 38.2
19 Tu	5 49 23	27 49 08	12 52 06	18 48 33	9 14.4	2♋07.9	12 14.5	5 53.8	25 07.0	19 22.1	12 08.2	14 07.5	3 39.5	8 39.6
20 W	5 53 20	28 46 23	24 44 53	0♏41 38	9 13.3	4 17.2	13 09.5	6 37.7	25 11.1	19 28.1	12 15.9	14 10.9	3 39.6	8 41.0
21 Th	5 57 16	29 43 37	6♏39 16	12 38 16	9 12.0	6 25.3	14 05.1	7 21.5	25 15.7	19 34.2	12 23.5	14 14.4	3 39.8	8 42.4
22 F	6 01 13	0♋40 51	18 39 01	24 41 55	9 10.7	8 32.0	15 01.1	8 05.3	25 20.5	19 40.5	12 31.2	14 17.8	3 40.0	8 43.8
23 Sa	6 05 09	1 38 04	0♐47 18	6♐55 26	9 09.7	10 37.1	15 57.6	8 49.0	25 25.8	19 46.9	12 38.9	14 21.2	3 40.3	8 45.3
24 Su	6 09 06	2 35 17	13 06 35	19 20 57	9 09.1	12 40.6	16 54.5	9 32.6	25 31.3	19 53.5	12 46.6	14 24.6	3 40.6	8 46.7
25 M	6 13 03	3 32 29	25 38 41	1♑59 54	9D 08.8	14 42.2	17 51.9	10 16.2	25 37.2	20 00.2	12 54.3	14 28.0	3 40.9	8 48.2
26 Tu	6 16 59	4 29 41	8♑24 40	14 53 01	9 08.7	16 42.0	18 49.6	10 59.7	25 43.5	20 07.0	13 02.1	14 31.4	3 41.3	8 49.7
27 W	6 20 56	5 26 53	21 24 57	28 00 26	9 08.9	18 39.9	19 47.8	11 43.1	25 50.0	20 14.0	13 09.8	14 34.8	3 41.7	8 51.2
28 Th	6 24 52	6 24 05	4♒39 25	11♒21 48	9 09.2	20 35.7	20 46.4	12 26.5	25 56.9	20 21.1	13 17.6	14 38.1	3 42.1	8 52.7
29 F	6 28 49	7 21 16	18 07 30	24 56 21	9 09.4	22 29.6	21 45.3	13 09.8	26 04.1	20 28.3	13 25.3	14 41.5	3 42.6	8 54.3
30 Sa	6 32 45	8 18 28	1♓48 16	8♓43 03	9R 09.5	24 21.3	22 44.6	13 53.0	26 11.6	20 35.6	13 33.1	14 44.8	3 43.1	8 55.8

Astro Data

	Dy Hr Mn
♂0N	6 16:35
♀D	6 21:04
☽0N	9 6:34
♃D	14 17:27
♄⚺♇	16 2:02
☽0S	22 15:00
⚳0S	23 18:50
☽0N	5 15:07
⚳D	8 19:42
♆D	14 20:49
☽0S	18 22:46

Planet Ingress

	Dy Hr Mn
♂ ♈	2 20:29
☿ ♉	16 15:21
☉ ♊	21 10:40
☿ ♊	4 10:30
♀ ♉	4 22:58
♂ ♉	11 11:52
☿ ♋	18 12:27
☉ ♋	21 18:52

Last Aspect / ☽ Ingress (May)

Last Aspect Dy Hr Mn		☽ Ingress Dy Hr Mn
1 18:02 ♂ □	♑	1 19:40
3 6:30 ☿ □	♒	4 4:06
5 15:21 ☿ ⚹	♓	6 9:21
7 15:04 ♃ ☍	♈	8 11:25
10 0:17 ☿ ☌	♉	10 11:24
11 20:21 ☉ ☌	♊	12 11:12
14 8:19 ☿ ⚹	♋	14 12:51
16 9:02 ☉ ⚹	♌	16 17:57
18 22:12 ☉ □	♍	19 2:56
20 13:44 ♃ ☌	♎	21 14:43
23 11:00 ♀ ☍	♏	24 3:21
25 14:49 ♃ ⚹	♐	26 15:11
28 15:40 ♀ △	♑	29 1:24
31 3:13 ♀ □	♒	31 9:35

Last Aspect / ☽ Ingress (June)

Last Aspect Dy Hr Mn		☽ Ingress Dy Hr Mn
2 12:15 ♀ ⚹	♓	2 15:25
3 22:46 ♃ ☍	♈	4 18:51
6 14:27 ♂ ☌	♉	6 20:23
8 2:20 ♃ △	♊	8 21:15
10 22:19 ♂ ⚹	♋	10 23:02
12 7:17 ♃ ⚹	♌	13 3:20
14 22:40 ☉ ⚹	♍	15 11:07
17 18:55 ☿ □	♎	17 22:06
20 7:47 ☉ △	♏	20 10:36
22 1:57 ♃ ⚹	♐	22 22:27
24 13:03 ♃ □	♑	25 8:14
26 21:43 ♃ △	♒	27 15:36
29 5:58 ♀ □	♓	29 20:51

☽ Phases & Eclipses

Dy Hr Mn	
5 6:02	☾ 14♒22
11 20:21	● 20♉45
18 22:12	☽ 27♌35
27 1:49	○ 5♐24
3 13:15	☾ 12♓34
10 4:26	● 18♊55
17 14:05	☽ 26♍00
25 15:08	○ 3♑40
25 15:14	☍ P 0.859

Astro Data

1 May 1945
Julian Day # 16557
SVP 6♓01'42"
GC 26♐04.5 ⚴ 19♍31.4R
Eris 6♈06.8 ⚵ 19♋54.0
⚷ 27♍28.7R ⚶ 10♎06.8R
☽ Mean ☊ 12♋25.2

1 June 1945
Julian Day # 16588
SVP 6♓01'37"
GC 26♐04.6 ⚴ 21♍29.5
Eris 6♈21.8 ⚵ 2♌43.4
⚷ 27♍00.3 ⚶ 9♎11.0
☽ Mean ☊ 10♋46.7

July 1945

LONGITUDE

Day	Sid.Time	☉	0 hr ☽	Noon ☽	True ☊	☿	♀	♂	⚳	♃	♄	♅	♆	♇
1 Su	6 36 42	9♋15 40	15♓40 32	22♓40 33	9♋09.6	26♋11.0	23♉44.2	14♉36.2	26♎19.4	20♍43.1	13♋40.9	14♊48.1	3♎43.6	8♌57.4
2 M	6 40 38	10 12 52	29 42 52	6♈47 14	9D 09.6	27 58.6	24 44.2	15 19.2	26 27.6	20 50.7	13 48.6	14 51.4	3 44.1	8 58.9
3 Tu	6 44 35	11 10 04	13♈53 26	21 01 07	9 09.6	29 44.2	25 44.5	16 02.2	26 36.0	20 58.4	13 56.4	14 54.7	3 44.7	9 00.5
4 W	6 48 32	12 07 16	28 10 00	5♉19 42	9 09.7	1♌27.6	26 45.1	16 45.2	26 44.7	21 06.2	14 04.2	14 57.9	3 45.3	9 02.1
5 Th	6 52 28	13 04 29	12♉29 49	19 39 56	9 10.0	3 08.9	27 46.1	17 28.0	26 53.7	21 14.2	14 12.0	15 01.2	3 46.0	9 03.7
6 F	6 56 25	14 01 42	26 49 35	3♊58 16	9 10.4	4 48.1	28 47.3	18 10.8	27 03.1	21 22.3	14 19.8	15 04.4	3 46.6	9 05.3
7 Sa	7 00 21	14 58 56	11♊05 31	18 10 48	9 10.9	6 25.3	29 48.9	18 53.5	27 12.7	21 30.5	14 27.6	15 07.6	3 47.3	9 07.0
8 Su	7 04 18	15 56 10	25 13 38	2♋13 33	9R 11.2	8 00.3	0♊50.7	19 36.2	27 22.6	21 38.8	14 35.4	15 10.7	3 48.1	9 08.6
9 M	7 08 14	16 53 24	9♋10 06	16 02 53	9 11.1	9 33.2	1 52.8	20 18.7	27 32.7	21 47.2	14 43.2	15 13.9	3 48.8	9 10.2
10 Tu	7 12 11	17 50 38	22 51 34	29 35 53	9 10.7	11 04.0	2 55.1	21 01.2	27 43.2	21 55.7	14 51.0	15 17.0	3 49.6	9 11.9
11 W	7 16 07	18 47 52	6♌15 37	12♌50 40	9 09.9	12 32.6	3 57.7	21 43.5	27 53.9	22 04.4	14 58.8	15 20.1	3 50.5	9 13.6
12 Th	7 20 04	19 45 07	19 21 00	25 46 39	9 08.6	13 59.0	5 00.5	22 25.8	28 04.9	22 13.1	15 06.6	15 23.2	3 51.3	9 15.2
13 F	7 24 01	20 42 21	2♍07 45	8♍24 32	9 07.1	15 23.3	6 03.6	23 08.0	28 16.2	22 22.0	15 14.3	15 26.2	3 52.2	9 16.9
14 Sa	7 27 57	21 39 35	14 37 14	20 46 14	9 05.6	16 45.3	7 06.9	23 50.1	28 27.7	22 30.9	15 22.1	15 29.3	3 53.2	9 18.6
15 Su	7 31 54	22 36 50	26 51 54	2♎54 43	9 04.3	18 05.1	8 10.5	24 32.2	28 39.4	22 40.0	15 29.9	15 32.3	3 54.1	9 20.3
16 M	7 35 50	23 34 05	8♎55 09	14 53 45	9D 03.5	19 22.5	9 14.2	25 14.1	28 51.5	22 49.2	15 37.6	15 35.2	3 55.1	9 22.0
17 Tu	7 39 47	24 31 19	20 51 03	26 47 38	9 03.3	20 37.6	10 18.2	25 56.0	29 03.7	22 58.4	15 45.4	15 38.2	3 56.1	9 23.7
18 W	7 43 43	25 28 34	2♏44 04	8♏40 57	9 03.8	21 50.2	11 22.4	26 37.7	29 16.2	23 07.8	15 53.1	15 41.1	3 57.1	9 25.4
19 Th	7 47 40	26 25 50	14 38 52	20 38 23	9 04.8	23 00.4	12 26.8	27 19.4	29 29.0	23 17.3	16 00.8	15 44.0	3 58.2	9 27.2
20 F	7 51 36	27 23 05	26 40 03	2♐44 22	9 06.2	24 08.0	13 31.5	28 01.0	29 42.0	23 26.8	16 08.5	15 46.8	3 59.3	9 28.9
21 Sa	7 55 33	28 20 21	8♐51 51	15 02 55	9 07.7	25 13.0	14 36.3	28 42.5	29 55.2	23 36.5	16 16.2	15 49.7	4 00.4	9 30.6
22 Su	7 59 30	29 17 37	21 17 58	27 37 19	9R 08.7	26 15.2	15 41.3	29 23.9	0♏08.6	23 46.2	16 23.9	15 52.5	4 01.6	9 32.4
23 M	8 03 26	0♌14 54	4♑01 14	10♑29 52	9 09.1	27 14.5	16 46.5	0♊05.2	0 22.3	23 56.1	16 31.5	15 55.2	4 02.7	9 34.1
24 Tu	8 07 23	1 12 11	17 03 20	23 41 37	9 08.5	28 10.9	17 51.9	0 46.4	0 36.1	24 06.0	16 39.2	15 58.0	4 04.0	9 35.9
25 W	8 11 19	2 09 29	0♒24 39	7♒12 13	9 06.8	29 04.3	18 57.5	1 27.5	0 50.2	24 16.0	16 46.8	16 00.7	4 05.2	9 37.6
26 Th	8 15 16	3 06 47	14 04 05	20 59 52	9 04.1	29 54.4	20 03.2	2 08.6	1 04.5	24 26.1	16 54.4	16 03.4	4 06.5	9 39.4
27 F	8 19 12	4 04 07	27 59 10	5♓01 29	9 00.7	0♍41.2	21 09.2	2 49.5	1 19.0	24 36.3	17 02.0	16 06.0	4 07.7	9 41.1
28 Sa	8 23 09	5 01 27	12♓06 18	19 13 05	8 57.2	1 24.4	22 15.3	3 30.4	1 33.7	24 46.6	17 09.5	16 08.6	4 09.1	9 42.9
29 Su	8 27 05	5 58 48	26 21 16	3♈30 19	8 54.0	2 04.0	23 21.6	4 11.1	1 48.6	24 56.9	17 17.1	16 11.2	4 10.4	9 44.6
30 M	8 31 02	6 56 10	10♈39 42	17 48 58	8 51.6	2 39.8	24 28.1	4 51.8	2 03.8	25 07.3	17 24.6	16 13.7	4 11.8	9 46.4
31 Tu	8 34 59	7 53 33	24 57 41	2♉05 28	8D 50.5	3 11.6	25 34.7	5 32.3	2 19.1	25 17.9	17 32.1	16 16.2	4 13.1	9 48.2

August 1945

LONGITUDE

Day	Sid.Time	☉	0 hr ☽	Noon ☽	True ☊	☿	♀	♂	⚳	♃	♄	♅	♆	♇
1 W	8 38 55	8♌50 57	9♉11 59	16♉17 00	8♋50.5	3♍39.2	26♊41.5	6♊12.8	2♏34.6	25♍28.4	17♋39.6	16♊18.7	4♎14.6	9♌49.9
2 Th	8 42 52	9 48 23	23 20 15	0♊21 34	8 51.5	4 02.5	27 48.5	6 53.2	2 50.2	25 39.1	17 47.0	16 21.1	4 16.0	9 51.7
3 F	8 46 48	10 45 50	7♊20 48	14 17 47	8 53.0	4 21.1	28 55.6	7 33.4	3 06.1	25 49.9	17 54.4	16 23.5	4 17.5	9 53.5
4 Sa	8 50 45	11 43 18	21 12 24	28 04 32	8R 54.3	4 35.1	0♋02.8	8 13.6	3 22.2	26 00.7	18 01.8	16 25.9	4 19.0	9 55.2
5 Su	8 54 41	12 40 47	4♋54 03	11♋40 49	8 54.6	4 44.1	1 10.3	8 53.6	3 38.4	26 11.6	18 09.2	16 28.2	4 20.5	9 57.0
6 M	8 58 38	13 38 18	18 24 41	25 05 33	8 53.5	4R 48.0	2 17.8	9 33.6	3 54.8	26 22.6	18 16.5	16 30.5	4 22.0	9 58.8
7 Tu	9 02 35	14 35 49	1♌43 15	8♌17 41	8 50.8	4 46.7	3 25.5	10 13.4	4 11.4	26 33.6	18 23.8	16 32.8	4 23.6	10 00.5
8 W	9 06 31	15 33 22	14 48 42	21 16 15	8 46.3	4 40.5	4 33.4	10 53.1	4 28.2	26 44.7	18 31.0	16 35.0	4 25.2	10 02.3
9 Th	9 10 28	16 30 55	27 40 16	4♍00 43	8 40.4	4 28.1	5 41.3	11 32.7	4 45.1	26 55.9	18 38.3	16 37.1	4 26.8	10 04.1
10 F	9 14 24	17 28 30	10♍17 40	16 31 10	8 33.6	4 10.7	6 49.4	12 12.2	5 02.2	27 07.2	18 45.4	16 39.3	4 28.4	10 05.8
11 Sa	9 18 21	18 26 06	22 41 22	28 48 29	8 26.7	3 47.9	7 57.7	12 51.6	5 19.5	27 18.5	18 52.6	16 41.4	4 30.1	10 07.6
12 Su	9 22 17	19 23 42	4♎52 45	10♎54 29	8 20.5	3 19.9	9 06.0	13 30.9	5 36.9	27 29.9	18 59.7	16 43.4	4 31.8	10 09.3
13 M	9 26 14	20 21 20	16 54 05	22 51 56	8 15.5	2 47.0	10 14.5	14 10.0	5 54.5	27 41.3	19 06.8	16 45.4	4 33.5	10 11.1
14 Tu	9 30 10	21 18 58	28 48 33	4♏44 25	8 12.1	2 09.3	11 23.1	14 49.0	6 12.3	27 52.8	19 13.8	16 47.4	4 35.2	10 12.8
15 W	9 34 07	22 16 38	10♏40 07	16 36 13	8D 10.5	1 27.5	12 31.9	15 27.9	6 30.2	28 04.4	19 20.8	16 49.3	4 36.9	10 14.5
16 Th	9 38 03	23 14 19	22 33 20	28 32 05	8 10.5	0 41.9	13 40.7	16 06.7	6 48.2	28 16.0	19 27.7	16 51.2	4 38.7	10 16.3
17 F	9 42 00	24 12 00	4♐33 07	10♐37 03	8 11.5	29♌53.5	14 49.7	16 45.3	7 06.4	28 27.7	19 34.7	16 53.0	4 40.5	10 18.0
18 Sa	9 45 57	25 09 43	16 44 30	22 56 04	8 12.8	29 02.8	15 58.8	17 23.9	7 24.7	28 39.4	19 41.5	16 54.8	4 42.3	10 19.7
19 Su	9 49 53	26 07 27	29 12 17	5♑33 40	8R 13.7	28 10.9	17 08.0	18 02.3	7 43.2	28 51.2	19 48.3	16 56.5	4 44.1	10 21.4
20 M	9 53 50	27 05 12	12♑00 36	18 33 26	8 13.2	27 18.7	18 17.3	18 40.6	8 01.8	29 03.0	19 55.1	16 58.2	4 45.9	10 23.2
21 Tu	9 57 46	28 02 58	25 12 23	1♒57 32	8 10.8	26 27.2	19 26.8	19 18.7	8 20.5	29 14.9	20 01.8	16 59.9	4 47.8	10 24.9
22 W	10 01 43	29 00 46	8♒48 52	15 46 08	8 06.3	25 37.5	20 36.3	19 56.8	8 39.4	29 26.9	20 08.5	17 01.5	4 49.7	10 26.6
23 Th	10 05 39	29 58 35	22 49 01	29 57 00	7 59.9	24 50.7	21 46.0	20 34.7	8 58.4	29 38.9	20 15.1	17 03.1	4 51.6	10 28.2
24 F	10 09 36	0♍56 25	7♓09 24	14♓25 27	7 52.0	24 07.7	22 55.8	21 12.5	9 17.6	29 50.9	20 21.7	17 04.6	4 53.5	10 29.9
25 Sa	10 13 32	1 54 17	21 44 16	29 04 54	7 43.7	23 29.6	24 05.7	21 50.1	9 36.8	0♎03.0	20 28.2	17 06.0	4 55.4	10 31.6
26 Su	10 17 29	2 52 10	6♈26 24	13♈47 48	7 36.0	22 57.3	25 15.7	22 27.6	9 56.2	0 15.1	20 34.7	17 07.5	4 57.3	10 33.3
27 M	10 21 26	3 50 06	21 08 12	28 26 49	7 29.8	22 31.4	26 25.8	23 05.0	10 15.7	0 27.3	20 41.1	17 08.8	4 59.3	10 34.9
28 Tu	10 25 22	4 48 03	5♉42 57	12♉56 02	7 25.6	22 12.6	27 36.0	23 42.3	10 35.3	0 39.5	20 47.5	17 10.2	5 01.3	10 36.6
29 W	10 29 19	5 46 02	20 05 39	27 11 30	7D 23.7	22D 01.5	28 46.4	24 19.4	10 55.1	0 51.8	20 53.8	17 11.5	5 03.2	10 38.2
30 Th	10 33 15	6 44 03	4♊13 23	11♊11 17	7 23.4	21 58.4	29 56.8	24 56.3	11 14.9	1 04.1	21 00.0	17 12.7	5 05.2	10 39.8
31 F	10 37 12	7 42 06	18 05 10	24 55 09	7R 24.1	22 03.6	1♌07.4	25 33.2	11 34.9	1 16.4	21 06.2	17 13.9	5 07.3	10 41.4

Astro Data

	Dy Hr Mn
☽ 0N	2 21:18
♄⚺♅	15 23:59
☽ 0S	16 6:41
♃∠♇	28 1:40
☽ 0N	30 2:28
☿ R	6 18:11
☽ 0S	12 14:08
☽ 0N	26 8:46
☿ D	30 9:01

Planet Ingress

		Dy Hr Mn
☿	♌	3 15:39
♀	♊	7 16:20
⚳	♏	21 20:41
☉	♌	23 5:45
♂	♊	23 8:59
☿	♍	26 14:48
♀	♋	4 10:59
☿	♌R	17 8:50
☉	♍	23 12:35
♃	♎	25 6:06
♀	♌	30 13:05

Last Aspect / ☽ Ingress (July)

Last Aspect Dy Hr Mn		☽ Ingress Dy Hr Mn
1 18:52	☿ △	♈ 2 0:29
3 1:41	♅ ✱	♉ 4 3:04
6 2:37	♀ ☌	♊ 6 5:20
7 17:43	♃ □	♋ 8 8:10
9 22:12	♃ ✱	♌ 10 12:43
12 5:22	☿ ☌	♍ 12 19:58
14 18:23	♂ △	♎ 15 6:13
17 7:01	☉ □	♏ 17 18:29
20 2:06	♂ ☍	♐ 20 6:36
22 9:11	☿ △	♑ 22 16:29
24 12:44	♃ △	♒ 24 23:16
26 10:14	♀ △	♓ 27 3:27
28 21:28	♃ ☍	♈ 29 6:07
31 0:07	♀ ✱	♉ 31 8:29

Last Aspect / ☽ Ingress (August)

Last Aspect Dy Hr Mn		☽ Ingress Dy Hr Mn
2 3:51	♃ △	♊ 2 11:23
4 8:20	♃ □	♋ 4 15:23
6 14:21	♃ ✱	♌ 6 20:53
8 3:15	♅ ✱	♍ 9 4:24
11 9:00	♃ ☌	♎ 11 14:21
13 6:30	☉ ✱	♏ 14 2:24
16 11:27	♃ ✱	♐ 16 14:56
18 23:08	♃ □	♑ 19 1:31
21 7:08	♃ △	♒ 21 8:32
23 12:03	☉ ☍	♓ 23 12:05
25 3:09	♀ △	♈ 25 13:30
27 8:24	♀ □	♉ 27 14:33
29 14:56	♀ ✱	♊ 29 16:47
31 13:10	♂ ☌	♋ 31 21:00

☽ Phases & Eclipses

Dy Hr Mn	
2 18:13	☾ 10♈28
9 13:35	● 16♋57
9 13:27:17	● T 01'16"
17 7:01	☽ 24♎19
25 2:25	○ 1♒47
31 22:30	☾ 8♉19
8 0:32	● 15♌06
16 0:27	☽ 22♏47
23 12:03	○ 29♒59
30 3:44	☾ 6♊24

Astro Data

1 July 1945
Julian Day # 16618
SVP 6♓01'32"
GC 26♐04.7 ⚳ 28♍24.8
Eris 6♈27.3 ⚵ 15♌34.5
⚷ 28♓14.2 ⚶ 14♎59.0
☽ Mean ☊ 9♋11.4

1 August 1945
Julian Day # 16649
SVP 6♓01'27"
GC 26♐04.8 ⚳ 8♎34.8
Eris 6♈22.5R ⚵ 28♌54.2
⚷ 1♈01.5 ⚶ 25♎32.7
☽ Mean ☊ 7♋33.0

LONGITUDE — September 1945

Day	Sid.Time	☉	0 hr ☽	Noon☽	True☊	☿	♀	♂	⚳	♃	♄	♅	♆	♇
1 Sa	10 41 08	8♍40 11	1♋41 22	8♋23 57	7♋24.5	22♌17.3	2♌18.0	26♊09.9	11♏55.0	1♎28.8	21♋12.4	17♊15.0	5♎09.3	10♌43.0
2 Su	10 45 05	9 38 17	15 03 06	21 38 58	7R 23.5	22 39.4	3 28.8	26 46.4	12 15.2	1 41.2	21 18.5	17 16.1	5 11.3	10 44.6
3 M	10 49 01	10 36 26	28 11 42	4♌41 27	7 20.4	23 09.9	4 39.6	27 22.8	12 35.5	1 53.7	21 24.5	17 17.1	5 13.4	10 46.2
4 Tu	10 52 58	11 34 37	11♌08 19	17 32 23	7 14.7	23 48.7	5 50.6	27 59.0	12 56.0	2 06.2	21 30.4	17 18.1	5 15.5	10 47.8
5 W	10 56 55	12 32 49	23 53 43	0♍12 22	7 06.2	24 35.5	7 01.6	28 35.1	13 16.5	2 18.7	21 36.3	17 19.1	5 17.6	10 49.3
6 Th	11 00 51	13 31 03	6♍28 22	12 41 46	6 55.5	25 29.9	8 12.8	29 11.0	13 37.1	2 31.3	21 42.1	17 20.0	5 19.7	10 50.9
7 F	11 04 48	14 29 19	18 52 35	25 00 54	6 43.4	26 31.7	9 24.0	29 46.7	13 57.9	2 43.9	21 47.9	17 20.8	5 21.8	10 52.4
8 Sa	11 08 44	15 27 36	1♎06 47	7♎10 21	6 30.8	27 40.3	10 35.3	0♋22.3	14 18.7	2 56.5	21 53.6	17 21.6	5 23.9	10 53.9
9 Su	11 12 41	16 25 55	13 11 46	19 11 15	6 19.0	28 55.3	11 46.7	0 57.7	14 39.7	3 09.2	21 59.2	17 22.3	5 26.0	10 55.4
10 M	11 16 37	17 24 16	25 09 01	1♏05 24	6 08.9	0♍16.1	12 58.2	1 33.0	15 00.7	3 21.8	22 04.7	17 23.0	5 28.1	10 56.9
11 Tu	11 20 34	18 22 39	7♏00 45	12 55 29	6 01.2	1 42.2	14 09.7	2 08.1	15 21.8	3 34.6	22 10.2	17 23.6	5 30.3	10 58.4
12 W	11 24 30	19 21 03	18 50 04	24 45 01	5 56.1	3 13.0	15 21.4	2 43.0	15 43.1	3 47.3	22 15.6	17 24.2	5 32.4	10 59.8
13 Th	11 28 27	20 19 29	0♐40 54	6♐38 19	5 53.4	4 48.0	16 33.1	3 17.7	16 04.4	4 00.0	22 20.9	17 24.7	5 34.6	11 01.2
14 F	11 32 24	21 17 56	12 37 52	18 40 15	5D 52.6	6 26.6	17 45.0	3 52.3	16 25.8	4 12.8	22 26.2	17 25.2	5 36.8	11 02.7
15 Sa	11 36 20	22 16 25	24 46 06	0♑56 07	5R 52.7	8 08.2	18 56.9	4 26.6	16 47.3	4 25.6	22 31.4	17 25.7	5 39.0	11 04.1
16 Su	11 40 17	23 14 56	7♑10 56	13 31 11	5 52.6	9 52.4	20 08.9	5 00.8	17 08.9	4 38.4	22 36.5	17 26.0	5 41.1	11 05.5
17 M	11 44 13	24 13 28	19 57 26	26 30 12	5 51.2	11 38.6	21 20.9	5 34.8	17 30.5	4 51.3	22 41.5	17 26.4	5 43.3	11 06.9
18 Tu	11 48 10	25 12 02	3♒09 52	9♒56 43	5 47.6	13 26.5	22 33.1	6 08.6	17 52.3	5 04.1	22 46.5	17 26.6	5 45.5	11 08.2
19 W	11 52 06	26 10 38	16 50 52	23 52 14	5 41.4	15 15.6	23 45.3	6 42.3	18 14.1	5 17.0	22 51.4	17 26.9	5 47.7	11 09.5
20 Th	11 56 03	27 09 15	1♓00 35	8♓15 25	5 32.6	17 05.6	24 57.6	7 15.7	18 36.0	5 29.9	22 56.2	17 27.0	5 49.9	11 10.9
21 F	11 59 59	28 07 55	15 36 03	23 01 36	5 22.1	18 56.2	26 10.0	7 48.9	18 58.0	5 42.8	23 00.9	17 27.1	5 52.2	11 12.2
22 Sa	12 03 56	29 06 36	0♈30 58	8♈02 59	5 10.8	20 47.1	27 22.4	8 22.0	19 20.1	5 55.7	23 05.5	17R 27.2	5 54.4	11 13.5
23 Su	12 07 52	0♎05 19	15 36 21	23 09 45	5 00.1	22 38.0	28 35.0	8 54.8	19 42.2	6 08.6	23 10.0	17 27.2	5 56.6	11 14.7
24 M	12 11 49	1 04 04	0♉41 55	8♉11 41	4 51.2	24 28.9	29 47.6	9 27.5	20 04.4	6 21.6	23 14.5	17 27.2	5 58.8	11 16.0
25 Tu	12 15 46	2 02 51	15 38 01	23 00 04	4 44.9	26 19.5	1♍00.3	9 59.9	20 26.7	6 34.5	23 18.9	17 27.1	6 01.0	11 17.2
26 W	12 19 42	3 01 41	0♊17 10	7♊28 52	4 41.3	28 09.7	2 13.0	10 32.2	20 49.0	6 47.5	23 23.2	17 27.0	6 03.3	11 18.4
27 Th	12 23 39	4 00 33	14 34 53	21 35 07	4 39.8	29 59.4	3 25.9	11 04.2	21 11.5	7 00.4	23 27.4	17 26.8	6 05.5	11 19.6
28 F	12 27 35	4 59 28	28 29 35	5♋18 29	4 39.6	1♎48.5	4 38.8	11 36.0	21 34.0	7 13.4	23 31.5	17 26.5	6 07.7	11 20.8
29 Sa	12 31 32	5 58 24	12♋02 04	18 40 37	4 39.4	3 36.9	5 51.8	12 07.5	21 56.5	7 26.4	23 35.5	17 26.2	6 10.0	11 21.9
30 Su	12 35 28	6 57 24	25 14 30	1♌44 05	4 37.9	5 24.7	7 04.8	12 38.9	22 19.2	7 39.4	23 39.5	17 25.9	6 12.2	11 23.0

LONGITUDE — October 1945

Day	Sid.Time	☉	0 hr ☽	Noon☽	True☊	☿	♀	♂	⚳	♃	♄	♅	♆	♇
1 M	12 39 25	7♎56 25	8♌09 45	14♌31 51	4♋34.0	7♎11.7	8♍18.0	13♋10.0	22♏41.9	7♎52.3	23♋43.3	17♊25.5	6♎14.4	11♌24.1
2 Tu	12 43 21	8 55 28	20 50 43	27 06 40	4R 27.2	8 57.9	9 31.2	13 40.8	23 04.6	8 05.3	23 47.1	17R 25.0	6 16.7	11 25.2
3 W	12 47 18	9 54 34	3♍19 56	9♍30 46	4 17.5	10 43.3	10 44.4	14 11.5	23 27.5	8 18.3	23 50.8	17 24.5	6 18.9	11 26.3
4 Th	12 51 15	10 53 42	15 39 22	21 45 54	4 05.3	12 27.9	11 57.7	14 41.8	23 50.3	8 31.3	23 54.3	17 24.0	6 21.1	11 27.3
5 F	12 55 11	11 52 52	27 50 32	3♎53 22	3 51.4	14 11.7	13 11.1	15 11.9	24 13.3	8 44.3	23 57.8	17 23.4	6 23.4	11 28.4
6 Sa	12 59 08	12 52 04	9♎54 33	15 54 12	3 37.1	15 54.7	14 24.6	15 41.8	24 36.3	8 57.3	24 01.2	17 22.7	6 25.6	11 29.3
7 Su	13 03 04	13 51 18	21 52 27	27 49 28	3 23.4	17 36.9	15 38.1	16 11.4	24 59.4	9 10.2	24 04.5	17 22.0	6 27.8	11 30.3
8 M	13 07 01	14 50 34	3♏45 26	9♏40 33	3 11.6	19 18.3	16 51.6	16 40.7	25 22.5	9 23.2	24 07.6	17 21.2	6 30.0	11 31.3
9 Tu	13 10 57	15 49 52	15 35 05	21 29 21	3 02.3	20 58.9	18 05.2	17 09.7	25 45.7	9 36.1	24 10.7	17 20.4	6 32.2	11 32.2
10 W	13 14 54	16 49 12	27 23 40	3♐18 27	2 56.0	22 38.8	19 18.9	17 38.5	26 08.9	9 49.1	24 13.7	17 19.6	6 34.4	11 33.1
11 Th	13 18 50	17 48 34	9♐14 08	15 11 14	2 52.4	24 17.9	20 32.6	18 07.0	26 32.2	10 02.0	24 16.6	17 18.7	6 36.6	11 34.0
12 F	13 22 47	18 47 57	21 10 17	27 11 51	2D 51.0	25 56.3	21 46.4	18 35.2	26 55.6	10 15.0	24 19.4	17 17.7	6 38.8	11 34.8
13 Sa	13 26 44	19 47 23	3♑16 33	9♑25 02	2R 51.0	27 33.9	23 00.2	19 03.1	27 19.0	10 27.9	24 22.0	17 16.7	6 41.0	11 35.7
14 Su	13 30 40	20 46 50	15 37 56	21 55 54	2 51.2	29 10.9	24 14.1	19 30.7	27 42.4	10 40.8	24 24.6	17 15.7	6 43.2	11 36.5
15 M	13 34 37	21 46 19	28 19 34	4♒49 31	2 50.5	0♏47.2	25 28.0	19 58.0	28 05.9	10 53.6	24 27.1	17 14.6	6 45.4	11 37.2
16 Tu	13 38 33	22 45 50	11♒26 15	18 10 12	2 47.9	2 22.8	26 42.0	20 25.0	28 29.5	11 06.5	24 29.5	17 13.5	6 47.6	11 38.0
17 W	13 42 30	23 45 22	25 01 40	2♓00 46	2 42.9	3 57.7	27 56.1	20 51.6	28 53.1	11 19.3	24 31.7	17 12.3	6 49.7	11 38.7
18 Th	13 46 26	24 44 56	9♓07 28	16 21 30	2 35.6	5 32.1	29 10.1	21 18.0	29 16.7	11 32.2	24 33.9	17 11.0	6 51.9	11 39.4
19 F	13 50 23	25 44 32	23 42 21	1♈09 17	2 26.3	7 05.8	0♎24.2	21 44.0	29 40.4	11 45.0	24 35.9	17 09.8	6 54.0	11 40.1
20 Sa	13 54 19	26 44 10	8♈41 20	16 17 20	2 16.3	8 38.9	1 38.4	22 09.7	0♐04.1	11 57.7	24 37.9	17 08.4	6 56.2	11 40.8
21 Su	13 58 16	27 43 49	23 55 57	1♉35 47	2 06.7	10 11.4	2 52.6	22 35.0	0 27.8	12 10.5	24 39.7	17 07.1	6 58.3	11 41.4
22 M	14 02 13	28 43 31	9♉15 21	16 53 15	1 58.6	11 43.3	4 06.9	23 00.0	0 51.6	12 23.2	24 41.4	17 05.7	7 00.4	11 42.0
23 Tu	14 06 09	29 43 15	24 28 09	1♊58 54	1 52.9	13 14.6	5 21.2	23 24.7	1 15.5	12 35.9	24 43.1	17 04.2	7 02.5	11 42.6
24 W	14 10 06	0♏43 01	9♊24 31	16 44 16	1 49.7	14 45.4	6 35.5	23 49.0	1 39.4	12 48.6	24 44.6	17 02.7	7 04.6	11 43.1
25 Th	14 14 02	1 42 50	23 57 37	1♋04 15	1D 48.8	16 15.6	7 49.9	24 12.9	2 03.3	13 01.3	24 46.0	17 01.2	7 06.7	11 43.6
26 F	14 17 59	2 42 40	8♋04 03	14 57 04	1 49.3	17 45.3	9 04.4	24 36.5	2 27.2	13 13.9	24 47.3	16 59.6	7 08.7	11 44.1
27 Sa	14 21 55	3 42 33	21 43 29	28 23 37	1R 50.0	19 14.3	10 18.9	24 59.6	2 51.2	13 26.5	24 48.5	16 58.0	7 10.8	11 44.6
28 Su	14 25 52	4 42 28	4♌57 51	11♌26 37	1 49.9	20 42.9	11 33.4	25 22.4	3 15.3	13 39.1	24 49.5	16 56.3	7 12.8	11 45.1
29 M	14 29 48	5 42 25	17 50 23	24 09 39	1 48.0	22 10.8	12 48.0	25 44.8	3 39.3	13 51.6	24 50.5	16 54.6	7 14.8	11 45.5
30 Tu	14 33 45	6 42 24	0♍24 54	6♍36 35	1 43.9	23 38.1	14 02.6	26 06.7	4 03.4	14 04.1	24 51.4	16 52.9	7 16.9	11 45.9
31 W	14 37 42	7 42 26	12 45 10	18 51 04	1 37.3	25 04.9	15 17.2	26 28.2	4 27.6	14 16.5	24 52.1	16 51.1	7 18.8	11 46.2

Astro Data

	Dy Hr Mn
♃0S	6 16:54
☽0S	8 20:55
♃☌♆	22 9:00
☽0N	22 17:36
♅R	23 5:56
☉0S	23 9:49
☿0S	29 10:10
☽0S	6 3:13
♃✶♇	19 2:23
☽0N	20 4:36
♀0S	22 1:54

Planet Ingress

	Dy Hr Mn
♂ ♋	7 20:56
☿ ♍	10 7:21
☉ ♎	23 9:50
♀ ♍	24 16:06
☿ ♎	27 12:08
☿ ♏	15 0:13
♀ ♎	19 4:09
⚳ ♐	20 7:52
☉ ♏	23 18:44

Last Aspect / ☽ Ingress (September)

Last Aspect Dy Hr Mn		☽ Ingress	Dy Hr Mn
2 11:22	♄ ☌	♌	3 3:20
5 8:45	♂ ✶	♍	5 11:36
7 5:39	♄ ✶	♎	7 21:48
9 17:40	♄ □	♏	10 9:48
12 6:55	♄ △	♐	12 22:37
14 17:38	☉ □	♑	15 10:11
17 7:31	☉ △	♒	17 18:20
19 11:47	♀ ☍	♓	19 22:19
21 20:46	☉ ☍	♈	21 23:11
23 21:23	♀ △	♉	23 22:53
25 18:15	☿ △	♊	25 23:32
27 4:53	♅ ☌	♋	28 2:38
29 21:01	♄ ☌	♌	30 8:47

Last Aspect / ☽ Ingress (October)

Last Aspect Dy Hr Mn		☽ Ingress	Dy Hr Mn
1 17:29	♅ ✶	♍	2 17:34
4 16:14	♄ ✶	♎	5 4:17
7 4:24	♄ □	♏	7 16:24
9 17:29	♄ △	♐	10 5:17
12 9:07	☿ ✶	♑	12 17:33
14 16:48	♀ △	♒	15 3:07
16 20:41	☉ △	♓	17 8:34
19 1:25	♄ △	♈	19 10:09
21 5:32	☉ ☍	♉	21 9:30
23 0:22	♄ ✶	♊	23 8:49
24 12:30	♅ ☌	♋	25 10:11
27 5:41	♂ ☌	♌	27 14:55
29 7:44	☿ □	♍	29 23:12

☽ Phases & Eclipses

Dy Hr Mn	
6 13:44	● 13♍35
14 17:38	☽ 21♐32
21 20:46	○ 28♓29
28 11:24	☾ 4♋58
6 5:22	● 12♎36
14 9:38	☽ 20♑41
21 5:32	○ 27♈28
27 22:30	☾ 4♌09

Astro Data

1 September 1945
Julian Day # 16680
SVP 6♓01'23"
GC 26♐04.8 ⚴ 20♎31.0
Eris 6♈08.6R ⚵ 12♍00.6
⚷ 4♎53.6 ⚶ 8♏51.5
☽ Mean ☊ 5♋54.5

1 October 1945
Julian Day # 16710
SVP 6♓01'20"
GC 26♐04.9 ⚴ 3♏02.9
Eris 5♈50.2R ⚵ 24♍14.7
⚷ 9♎10.5 ⚶ 23♏18.4
☽ Mean ☊ 4♋19.1

November 1945 — LONGITUDE

Day	Sid.Time	☉	0 hr ☽	Noon ☽	True ☊	☿	♀	♂	⚳	♃	♄	♅	♆	♇
1 Th	14 41 38	8♏42 29	24♍54 39	0♎56 16	1♋28.8	26♏30.9	16♎31.9	26♋49.3	4♐51.7	14♎28.9	24♋52.7	16♊49.3	7♎20.8	11♌46.6
2 F	14 45 35	9 42 34	6♎56 14	12 54 50	1R 18.8	27 56.3	17 46.6	27 09.9	5 15.9	14 41.3	24 53.2	16R 47.4	7 22.8	11 46.9
3 Sa	14 49 31	10 42 42	18 52 18	24 48 53	1 08.4	29 21.1	19 01.4	27 30.1	5 40.1	14 53.7	24 53.6	16 45.5	7 24.7	11 47.1
4 Su	14 53 28	11 42 51	0♏44 46	6♏40 09	0 58.5	0♐45.0	20 16.1	27 49.8	6 04.4	15 05.9	24 53.9	16 43.6	7 26.7	11 47.4
5 M	14 57 24	12 43 02	12 35 14	18 30 13	0 50.0	2 08.1	21 30.9	28 09.1	6 28.7	15 18.2	24 54.1	16 41.6	7 28.6	11 47.6
6 Tu	15 01 21	13 43 15	24 25 18	0♐20 43	0 43.5	3 30.4	22 45.8	28 27.8	6 53.0	15 30.4	24R 54.2	16 39.6	7 30.5	11 47.8
7 W	15 05 17	14 43 30	6♐16 42	12 13 33	0 39.3	4 51.7	24 00.7	28 46.1	7 17.3	15 42.6	24 54.1	16 37.6	7 32.3	11 48.0
8 Th	15 09 14	15 43 46	18 11 33	24 11 05	0D 37.3	6 12.0	25 15.5	29 03.8	7 41.7	15 54.7	24 53.9	16 35.6	7 34.2	11 48.1
9 F	15 13 11	16 44 04	0♑11 30	6♑16 14	0 37.2	7 31.1	26 30.5	29 21.1	8 06.1	16 06.7	24 53.7	16 33.5	7 36.0	11 48.2
10 Sa	15 17 07	17 44 24	12 22 45	18 32 31	0 38.4	8 49.0	27 45.4	29 37.8	8 30.5	16 18.7	24 53.3	16 31.3	7 37.9	11 48.3
11 Su	15 21 04	18 44 45	24 46 05	1♒03 56	0 39.9	10 05.4	29 00.4	29 54.0	8 54.9	16 30.7	24 52.8	16 29.2	7 39.7	11 48.4
12 M	15 25 00	19 45 07	7♒26 37	13 54 38	0R 41.0	11 20.3	0♏15.4	0♌09.7	9 19.4	16 42.6	24 52.2	16 27.0	7 41.4	11R 48.4
13 Tu	15 28 57	20 45 31	20 28 29	27 08 35	0 41.0	12 33.3	1 30.4	0 24.8	9 43.9	16 54.4	24 51.4	16 24.8	7 43.2	11 48.4
14 W	15 32 53	21 45 56	3♓55 17	10♓48 50	0 39.3	13 44.4	2 45.4	0 39.3	10 08.4	17 06.2	24 50.6	16 22.6	7 44.9	11 48.4
15 Th	15 36 50	22 46 22	17 49 19	24 56 42	0 36.0	14 53.2	4 00.5	0 53.3	10 32.9	17 17.9	24 49.6	16 20.3	7 46.6	11 48.3
16 F	15 40 46	23 46 50	2♈10 45	9♈31 01	0 31.3	15 59.5	5 15.5	1 06.6	10 57.4	17 29.6	24 48.6	16 18.0	7 48.3	11 48.3
17 Sa	15 44 43	24 47 19	16 56 50	24 27 23	0 25.9	17 02.9	6 30.6	1 19.4	11 21.9	17 41.2	24 47.4	16 15.7	7 50.0	11 48.2
18 Su	15 48 40	25 47 49	2♉01 37	9♉38 20	0 20.6	18 03.1	7 45.7	1 31.6	11 46.5	17 52.7	24 46.1	16 13.4	7 51.6	11 48.0
19 M	15 52 36	26 48 21	17 16 16	24 54 03	0 16.2	18 59.6	9 00.9	1 43.1	12 11.0	18 04.2	24 44.7	16 11.1	7 53.3	11 47.9
20 Tu	15 56 33	27 48 54	2♊30 22	10♊03 55	0 13.2	19 51.9	10 16.0	1 54.1	12 35.6	18 15.6	24 43.2	16 08.7	7 54.9	11 47.7
21 W	16 00 29	28 49 29	17 33 35	24 58 21	0D 11.9	20 39.5	11 31.2	2 04.4	13 00.2	18 26.9	24 41.6	16 06.3	7 56.4	11 47.5
22 Th	16 04 26	29 50 06	2♋17 25	9♋30 10	0 12.1	21 21.9	12 46.4	2 14.0	13 24.8	18 38.2	24 39.9	16 03.9	7 58.0	11 47.2
23 F	16 08 22	0♐50 44	16 36 11	23 35 14	0 13.3	21 58.2	14 01.6	2 23.0	13 49.5	18 49.4	24 38.1	16 01.5	7 59.5	11 46.9
24 Sa	16 12 19	1 51 24	0♌27 18	7♌12 28	0 14.9	22 27.8	15 16.8	2 31.3	14 14.1	19 00.5	24 36.2	15 59.1	8 01.0	11 46.6
25 Su	16 16 15	2 52 05	13 50 58	20 23 08	0 16.3	22 49.9	16 32.1	2 38.8	14 38.7	19 11.5	24 34.2	15 56.6	8 02.5	11 46.3
26 M	16 20 12	3 52 48	26 49 24	3♍10 15	0R 16.9	23 03.8	17 47.4	2 45.7	15 03.4	19 22.5	24 32.0	15 54.1	8 03.9	11 46.0
27 Tu	16 24 09	4 53 33	9♍26 11	15 37 44	0 16.4	23R 08.6	19 02.7	2 51.9	15 28.0	19 33.4	24 29.8	15 51.7	8 05.3	11 45.6
28 W	16 28 05	5 54 19	21 45 28	27 49 54	0 14.7	23 03.5	20 18.0	2 57.3	15 52.7	19 44.2	24 27.5	15 49.2	8 06.7	11 45.2
29 Th	16 32 02	6 55 06	3♎51 35	9♎51 00	0 11.9	22 48.1	21 33.3	3 02.0	16 17.4	19 54.9	24 25.0	15 46.7	8 08.1	11 44.7
30 F	16 35 58	7 55 55	15 48 40	21 45 00	0 08.3	22 21.7	22 48.6	3 05.9	16 42.1	20 05.6	24 22.5	15 44.1	8 09.4	11 44.3

December 1945 — LONGITUDE

Day	Sid.Time	☉	0 hr ☽	Noon ☽	True ☊	☿	♀	♂	⚳	♃	♄	♅	♆	♇
1 Sa	16 39 55	8♐56 45	27♎40 26	3♏35 22	0♋04.5	21♐44.2	24♏03.9	3♌09.0	17♐06.8	20♎16.2	24♋19.8	15♊41.6	8♎10.7	11♌43.8
2 Su	16 43 51	9 57 37	9♏30 08	15 25 04	0R 00.9	20R 55.8	25 19.3	3 11.4	17 31.4	20 26.6	24R 17.1	15R 39.1	8 12.0	11R 43.3
3 M	16 47 48	10 58 30	21 20 27	27 16 34	29♊57.9	19 57.2	26 34.7	3 12.9	17 56.1	20 37.0	24 14.3	15 36.5	8 13.3	11 42.7
4 Tu	16 51 44	11 59 24	3♐13 40	9♐11 57	29 55.7	18 49.5	27 50.0	3R 13.7	18 20.8	20 47.3	24 11.4	15 34.0	8 14.5	11 42.2
5 W	16 55 41	13 00 19	15 11 40	21 13 01	29D 54.5	17 34.4	29 05.4	3 13.7	18 45.5	20 57.5	24 08.3	15 31.5	8 15.7	11 41.6
6 Th	16 59 38	14 01 16	27 16 12	3♑21 27	29 54.4	16 14.2	0♐20.8	3 12.8	19 10.2	21 07.7	24 05.2	15 28.9	8 16.9	11 41.0
7 F	17 03 34	15 02 13	9♑28 59	15 39 01	29 54.9	14 51.4	1 36.2	3 11.1	19 34.9	21 17.7	24 02.0	15 26.4	8 18.0	11 40.4
8 Sa	17 07 31	16 03 11	21 51 49	28 07 38	29 56.0	13 28.9	2 51.6	3 08.6	19 59.6	21 27.6	23 58.7	15 23.8	8 19.1	11 39.7
9 Su	17 11 27	17 04 10	4♒26 45	10♒49 27	29 57.3	12 09.5	4 07.1	3 05.3	20 24.3	21 37.4	23 55.4	15 21.3	8 20.2	11 39.0
10 M	17 15 24	18 05 09	17 16 01	23 46 44	29 58.4	10 55.7	5 22.5	3 01.1	20 49.0	21 47.1	23 51.9	15 18.7	8 21.2	11 38.3
11 Tu	17 19 20	19 06 09	0♓21 55	7♓01 48	29R 59.1	9 49.6	6 37.9	2 56.1	21 13.7	21 56.8	23 48.4	15 16.2	8 22.2	11 37.6
12 W	17 23 17	20 07 09	13 46 36	20 36 31	29 59.4	8 52.9	7 53.3	2 50.2	21 38.4	22 06.3	23 44.7	15 13.6	8 23.2	11 36.8
13 Th	17 27 13	21 08 10	27 31 38	4♈31 58	29 59.1	8 06.7	9 08.8	2 43.5	22 03.0	22 15.7	23 41.0	15 11.1	8 24.2	11 36.0
14 F	17 31 10	22 09 11	11♈37 26	18 47 50	29 58.5	7 31.6	10 24.2	2 36.0	22 27.7	22 25.0	23 37.3	15 08.6	8 25.1	11 35.2
15 Sa	17 35 07	23 10 13	26 02 49	3♉21 54	29 57.7	7 07.6	11 39.6	2 27.6	22 52.3	22 34.2	23 33.4	15 06.0	8 26.0	11 34.4
16 Su	17 39 03	24 11 15	10♉44 29	18 09 49	29 57.0	6D 54.6	12 55.1	2 18.4	23 17.0	22 43.2	23 29.5	15 03.5	8 26.8	11 33.5
17 M	17 43 00	25 12 18	25 37 02	3♊05 12	29 56.5	6 52.0	14 10.5	2 08.4	23 41.6	22 52.2	23 25.5	15 01.0	8 27.6	11 32.7
18 Tu	17 46 56	26 13 21	10♊33 18	18 00 18	29D 56.2	6 59.1	15 26.0	1 57.6	24 06.2	23 01.1	23 21.4	14 58.5	8 28.4	11 31.8
19 W	17 50 53	27 14 25	25 25 10	2♋46 56	29 56.1	7 15.2	16 41.4	1 45.9	24 30.8	23 09.8	23 17.3	14 56.1	8 29.2	11 30.9
20 Th	17 54 49	28 15 29	10♋04 43	17 17 46	29 56.2	7 39.6	17 56.9	1 33.4	24 55.4	23 18.4	23 13.1	14 53.6	8 29.9	11 29.9
21 F	17 58 46	29 16 34	24 25 24	1♌27 10	29R 56.3	8 11.3	19 12.3	1 20.2	25 20.0	23 26.9	23 08.9	14 51.1	8 30.6	11 29.0
22 Sa	18 02 43	0♑17 40	8♌22 42	15 11 50	29 56.3	8 49.6	20 27.8	1 06.1	25 44.6	23 35.3	23 04.6	14 48.7	8 31.2	11 28.0
23 Su	18 06 39	1 18 46	21 54 30	28 30 50	29 56.2	9 33.8	21 43.3	0 51.3	26 09.1	23 43.6	23 00.2	14 46.3	8 31.9	11 27.0
24 M	18 10 36	2 19 53	5♍01 00	11♍25 21	29 56.0	10 23.2	22 58.7	0 35.7	26 33.7	23 51.7	22 55.8	14 43.9	8 32.5	11 26.0
25 Tu	18 14 32	3 21 00	17 44 16	23 58 13	29D 55.9	11 17.3	24 14.2	0 19.3	26 58.2	23 59.7	22 51.3	14 41.5	8 33.0	11 25.0
26 W	18 18 29	4 22 08	0♎07 43	6♎13 19	29 55.8	12 15.4	25 29.7	0 02.2	27 22.7	24 07.6	22 46.8	14 39.1	8 33.5	11 23.9
27 Th	18 22 25	5 23 17	12 15 36	18 15 10	29 56.0	13 17.2	26 45.2	29♋44.5	27 47.2	24 15.3	22 42.2	14 36.8	8 34.0	11 22.9
28 F	18 26 22	6 24 26	24 12 36	0♏08 30	29 56.4	14 22.1	28 00.7	29 26.0	28 11.6	24 23.0	22 37.6	14 34.5	8 34.5	11 21.8
29 Sa	18 30 18	7 25 35	6♏03 25	11 57 55	29 57.2	15 29.9	29 16.2	29 06.9	28 36.1	24 30.4	22 32.9	14 32.2	8 34.9	11 20.7
30 Su	18 34 15	8 26 45	17 52 32	23 47 44	29 58.1	16 40.1	0♑31.7	28 47.2	29 00.5	24 37.8	22 28.2	14 29.9	8 35.3	11 19.6
31 M	18 38 12	9 27 55	29 44 00	5♐41 44	29 59.0	17 52.6	1 47.1	28 26.9	29 24.9	24 45.0	22 23.5	14 27.6	8 35.6	11 18.4

Astro Data

	Dy Hr Mn
☽0S	2 9:30
♄ R	6 13:02
♃△♅	11 9:29
♇ R	13 1:53
☽0N	16 15:46
☿ R	27 12:00
☽0S	29 16:13
♂ R	4 22:49
☽0N	14 0:42
☿ D	17 6:10
♃□♄	20 2:04
☽0S	26 23:36

Planet Ingress

	Dy Hr Mn
☿ ♐	3 23:06
♂ ♌	11 21:05
♀ ♏	12 7:05
☉ ♐	22 15:55
☊ ♊R	2 18:35
♀ ♐	6 5:22
☉ ♑	22 5:04
♂ ♋R	26 15:04
♀ ♑	30 1:56

Last Aspect / ☽ Ingress

Last Aspect Dy Hr Mn		☽ Ingress Dy Hr Mn
1 3:33 ♂ ✶	♎	1 10:08
3 17:35 ♂ □	♏	3 22:29
6 8:05 ♂ △	♐	6 11:18
8 14:24 ♀ ✶	♑	8 23:35
11 9:45 ♂ ☍	♒	11 9:59
12 23:34 ☉ □	♓	13 17:05
15 11:48 ♄ △	♈	15 20:24
17 12:32 ♄ □	♉	17 20:48
19 15:13 ☉ ☍	♊	19 20:02
21 4:37 ☿ ☍	♋	21 20:14
23 13:49 ♄ ☌	♌	23 23:12
25 16:39 ☿ △	♍	26 5:59
28 5:21 ♄ ✶	♎	28 16:18

Last Aspect / ☽ Ingress

Last Aspect Dy Hr Mn		☽ Ingress Dy Hr Mn
30 17:18 ♄ □	♏	1 4:43
3 10:25 ♀ ☌	♐	3 17:30
5 11:29 ♃ ✶	♑	6 5:23
8 4:06 ♄ ☍	♒	8 15:34
10 8:18 ♃ △	♓	10 23:20
12 17:26 ♄ △	♈	13 4:15
14 19:58 ♄ □	♉	15 6:30
16 20:33 ♄ ✶	♊	17 7:03
19 2:17 ☉ ☍	♋	19 7:27
20 22:13 ♃ □	♌	21 9:30
23 3:12 ♃ ✶	♍	23 14:44
25 12:35 ♀ □	♎	25 23:45
28 10:36 ♂ □	♏	28 11:43
30 21:49 ♂ △	♐	31 0:32

☽ Phases & Eclipses

Dy Hr Mn	
4 23:11	● 12♏11
12 23:34	☽ 20♒14
19 15:13	○ 26♉56
26 13:28	☾ 3♍57
4 18:07	● 12♐15
12 11:05	☽ 20♓05
19 2:17	○ 26♊50
19 2:20	☊ T 1.343
26 8:00	☾ 4♎12

Astro Data

1 November 1945
Julian Day # 16741
SVP 6♓01'17"
GC 26♐05.0 ⚵ 16♏31.4
Eris 5♈31.5R ✴ 6♎06.0
⚷ 13♎37.5 ⚶ 9♐12.6
☽ Mean ☊ 2♋40.6

1 December 1945
Julian Day # 16771
SVP 6♓01'12"
GC 26♐05.0 ⚵ 29♏40.7
Eris 5♈19.3R ✴ 16♎19.3
⚷ 17♎24.7 ⚶ 25♐07.3
☽ Mean ☊ 1♋05.3

LONGITUDE — January 1946

Day	Sid.Time	☉	0 hr ☽	Noon ☽	True ☊	☿	♀	♂	⚳	♃	♄	♅	♆	♇
1 Tu	18 42 08	10♑29 06	11♐41 20	17♐43 07	29♊59.8	19♐07.0	3♑02.6	28♋06.1	29♐49.3	24♎52.1	22♋18.7	14♊25.4	8♎35.9	11♌17.3
2 W	18 46 05	11 30 17	23 47 22	29 54 22	0♋00.1	20 23.2	4 18.1	27R 44.7	0♑13.6	24 59.0	22R 13.9	14R 23.2	8 36.2	11R 16.1
3 Th	18 50 01	12 31 27	6♑04 17	12♑17 18	29♊59.7	21 40.9	5 33.6	27 22.9	0 38.0	25 05.8	22 09.1	14 21.0	8 36.5	11 14.9
4 F	18 53 58	13 32 38	18 33 32	24 53 03	29R 58.7	23 00.0	6 49.1	27 00.7	1 02.3	25 12.4	22 04.2	14 18.9	8 36.7	11 13.7
5 Sa	18 57 54	14 33 49	1♒15 57	7♒42 13	29 57.0	24 20.4	8 04.6	26 38.0	1 26.6	25 18.9	21 59.4	14 16.8	8 36.9	11 12.5
6 Su	19 01 51	15 34 59	14 11 52	20 44 52	29 54.7	25 41.9	9 20.1	26 15.0	1 50.8	25 25.2	21 54.5	14 14.7	8 37.0	11 11.3
7 M	19 05 47	16 36 09	27 21 14	4♓00 53	29 52.3	27 04.5	10 35.6	25 51.7	2 15.0	25 31.4	21 49.6	14 12.6	8 37.1	11 10.0
8 Tu	19 09 44	17 37 19	10♓43 47	17 29 53	29 50.0	28 28.0	11 51.1	25 28.2	2 39.2	25 37.5	21 44.6	14 10.6	8 37.2	11 08.8
9 W	19 13 41	18 38 28	24 19 08	1♈11 27	29 48.3	29 52.4	13 06.5	25 04.5	3 03.3	25 43.3	21 39.7	14 08.6	8R 37.2	11 07.5
10 Th	19 17 37	19 39 37	8♈06 46	15 05 00	29D 47.5	1♑17.6	14 22.0	24 40.6	3 27.5	25 49.1	21 34.7	14 06.7	8 37.2	11 06.2
11 F	19 21 34	20 40 44	22 06 01	29 09 41	29 47.7	2 43.6	15 37.5	24 16.6	3 51.5	25 54.6	21 29.8	14 04.8	8 37.2	11 05.0
12 Sa	19 25 30	21 41 52	6♉15 48	13♉24 09	29 48.6	4 10.3	16 52.9	23 52.6	4 15.6	26 00.0	21 24.8	14 02.9	8 37.1	11 03.7
13 Su	19 29 27	22 42 59	20 34 27	27 46 19	29 50.1	5 37.6	18 08.4	23 28.6	4 39.6	26 05.3	21 19.9	14 01.1	8 37.0	11 02.3
14 M	19 33 23	23 44 05	4♊59 21	12♊13 05	29 51.5	7 05.7	19 23.8	23 04.6	5 03.6	26 10.4	21 15.0	13 59.3	8 36.9	11 01.0
15 Tu	19 37 20	24 45 10	19 26 57	26 40 22	29R 52.2	8 34.3	20 39.2	22 40.7	5 27.5	26 15.3	21 10.0	13 57.5	8 36.7	10 59.7
16 W	19 41 16	25 46 15	3♋52 42	11♋03 17	29 51.9	10 03.6	21 54.7	22 16.9	5 51.4	26 20.1	21 05.1	13 55.8	8 36.5	10 58.4
17 Th	19 45 13	26 47 19	18 11 27	25 16 33	29 50.1	11 33.5	23 10.1	21 53.4	6 15.3	26 24.7	21 00.2	13 54.1	8 36.3	10 57.0
18 F	19 49 10	27 48 23	2♌18 00	9♌15 15	29 46.9	13 04.0	24 25.5	21 30.0	6 39.1	26 29.1	20 55.3	13 52.4	8 36.0	10 55.7
19 Sa	19 53 06	28 49 26	16 07 50	22 55 23	29 42.5	14 35.1	25 40.9	21 06.9	7 02.8	26 33.4	20 50.4	13 50.8	8 35.7	10 54.3
20 Su	19 57 03	29 50 29	29 37 38	6♍14 28	29 37.5	16 06.7	26 56.3	20 44.1	7 26.6	26 37.5	20 45.5	13 49.3	8 35.4	10 53.0
21 M	20 00 59	0♒51 31	12♍45 49	19 11 47	29 32.4	17 39.0	28 11.7	20 21.7	7 50.3	26 41.4	20 40.7	13 47.8	8 35.0	10 51.6
22 Tu	20 04 56	1 52 32	25 32 33	1♎48 24	29 27.9	19 11.8	29 27.1	19 59.7	8 13.9	26 45.1	20 35.9	13 46.3	8 34.6	10 50.2
23 W	20 08 52	2 53 33	7♎59 42	14 06 53	29 24.6	20 45.2	0♒42.5	19 38.0	8 37.5	26 48.7	20 31.1	13 44.8	8 34.2	10 48.8
24 Th	20 12 49	3 54 34	20 10 29	26 11 02	29D 22.8	22 19.3	1 57.9	19 16.9	9 01.1	26 52.1	20 26.4	13 43.5	8 33.7	10 47.4
25 F	20 16 45	4 55 34	2♏09 08	8♏05 25	29 22.5	23 53.9	3 13.3	18 56.2	9 24.6	26 55.3	20 21.6	13 42.1	8 33.2	10 46.0
26 Sa	20 20 42	5 56 33	14 00 31	19 55 05	29 23.4	25 29.2	4 28.7	18 36.1	9 48.0	26 58.4	20 16.9	13 40.8	8 32.7	10 44.7
27 Su	20 24 39	6 57 32	25 49 45	1♐45 10	29 25.1	27 05.1	5 44.1	18 16.6	10 11.4	27 01.3	20 12.3	13 39.6	8 32.1	10 43.3
28 M	20 28 35	7 58 30	7♐41 57	13 40 41	29 26.8	28 41.6	6 59.4	17 57.7	10 34.8	27 03.9	20 07.7	13 38.4	8 31.5	10 41.9
29 Tu	20 32 32	8 59 28	19 41 55	25 46 09	29R 27.9	0♒18.8	8 14.8	17 39.3	10 58.1	27 06.4	20 03.2	13 37.2	8 30.9	10 40.5
30 W	20 36 28	10 00 25	1♑53 50	8♑05 22	29 27.5	1 56.7	9 30.2	17 21.7	11 21.3	27 08.8	19 58.6	13 36.1	8 30.2	10 39.1
31 Th	20 40 25	11 01 21	14 21 03	20 41 06	29 25.3	3 35.2	10 45.5	17 04.7	11 44.5	27 10.9	19 54.2	13 35.0	8 29.6	10 37.7

LONGITUDE — February 1946

Day	Sid.Time	☉	0 hr ☽	Noon ☽	True ☊	☿	♀	♂	⚳	♃	♄	♅	♆	♇
1 F	20 44 21	12♒02 16	27♑05 42	3♒34 54	29♊21.0	5♒14.5	12♒00.9	16♋48.4	12♑07.7	27♎12.8	19♋49.8	13♊34.0	8♎28.8	10♌36.3
2 Sa	20 48 18	13 03 10	10♒08 39	16 46 50	29R 14.8	6 54.5	13 16.2	16R 32.9	12 30.8	27 14.6	19R 45.4	13R 33.1	8R 28.1	10R 34.9
3 Su	20 52 14	14 04 03	23 29 16	0♓15 38	29 07.3	8 35.2	14 31.5	16 18.1	12 53.8	27 16.2	19 41.1	13 32.2	8 27.3	10 33.5
4 M	20 56 11	15 04 54	7♓05 37	13 58 47	28 59.1	10 16.6	15 46.8	16 04.0	13 16.8	27 17.6	19 36.9	13 31.3	8 26.5	10 32.1
5 Tu	21 00 08	16 05 44	20 54 44	27 53 00	28 51.4	11 58.8	17 02.1	15 50.8	13 39.7	27 18.8	19 32.7	13 30.5	8 25.7	10 30.7
6 W	21 04 04	17 06 33	4♈53 08	11♈54 44	28 45.1	13 41.7	18 17.4	15 38.3	14 02.5	27 19.8	19 28.6	13 29.7	8 24.8	10 29.3
7 Th	21 08 01	18 07 21	18 57 23	26 00 45	28 40.7	15 25.5	19 32.7	15 26.6	14 25.3	27 20.6	19 24.6	13 29.0	8 23.9	10 27.9
8 F	21 11 57	19 08 06	3♉04 31	10♉08 26	28D 38.5	17 10.0	20 48.0	15 15.7	14 48.0	27 21.2	19 20.6	13 28.4	8 23.0	10 26.5
9 Sa	21 15 54	20 08 51	17 12 18	24 15 56	28 38.2	18 55.3	22 03.2	15 05.6	15 10.6	27 21.7	19 16.7	13 27.7	8 22.0	10 25.1
10 Su	21 19 50	21 09 33	1♊19 11	8♊21 56	28 39.0	20 41.3	23 18.4	14 56.3	15 33.2	27R 21.9	19 12.9	13 27.2	8 21.0	10 23.7
11 M	21 23 47	22 10 14	15 24 03	22 25 23	28R 40.0	22 28.2	24 33.7	14 47.8	15 55.7	27 22.0	19 09.2	13 26.7	8 20.0	10 22.4
12 Tu	21 27 43	23 10 54	29 25 47	6♋25 04	28 39.8	24 15.8	25 48.9	14 40.1	16 18.1	27 21.9	19 05.5	13 26.3	8 19.0	10 21.0
13 W	21 31 40	24 11 32	13♋23 00	20 19 18	28 37.7	26 04.2	27 04.0	14 33.2	16 40.5	27 21.6	19 01.9	13 25.9	8 18.0	10 19.6
14 Th	21 35 37	25 12 08	27 13 41	4♌05 48	28 33.1	27 53.2	28 19.2	14 27.2	17 02.8	27 21.1	18 58.4	13 25.5	8 16.9	10 18.3
15 F	21 39 33	26 12 42	10♌55 19	17 41 53	28 25.9	29 43.0	29 34.4	14 21.9	17 25.0	27 20.4	18 55.0	13 25.2	8 15.8	10 16.9
16 Sa	21 43 30	27 13 15	24 25 09	1♍04 48	28 16.4	1♓33.4	0♓49.5	14 17.4	17 47.1	27 19.5	18 51.7	13 25.0	8 14.6	10 15.6
17 Su	21 47 26	28 13 47	7♍40 34	14 12 13	28 05.5	3 24.3	2 04.6	14 13.7	18 09.2	27 18.4	18 48.4	13 24.8	8 13.5	10 14.3
18 M	21 51 23	29 14 17	20 39 37	27 02 42	27 54.3	5 15.7	3 19.8	14 10.7	18 31.1	27 17.2	18 45.3	13 24.7	8 12.3	10 13.0
19 Tu	21 55 19	0♓14 45	3♎21 30	9♎36 06	27 43.8	7 07.5	4 34.8	14 08.6	18 53.0	27 15.7	18 42.2	13 24.6	8 11.1	10 11.7
20 W	21 59 16	1 15 13	15 46 43	21 53 37	27 35.0	8 59.5	5 49.9	14 07.2	19 14.9	27 14.1	18 39.2	13D 24.6	8 09.9	10 10.3
21 Th	22 03 12	2 15 38	27 57 09	3♏57 47	27 28.6	10 51.6	7 05.0	14D 06.5	19 36.6	27 12.3	18 36.3	13 24.6	8 08.6	10 09.1
22 F	22 07 09	3 16 03	9♏55 58	15 52 17	27 24.6	12 43.6	8 20.1	14 06.6	19 58.3	27 10.3	18 33.5	13 24.7	8 07.4	10 07.8
23 Sa	22 11 06	4 16 26	21 47 20	27 41 43	27D 22.9	14 35.3	9 35.1	14 07.4	20 19.9	27 08.1	18 30.8	13 24.8	8 06.1	10 06.5
24 Su	22 15 02	5 16 48	3♐36 08	9♐31 16	27 22.7	16 26.4	10 50.1	14 09.0	20 41.4	27 05.7	18 28.2	13 25.0	8 04.8	10 05.3
25 M	22 18 59	6 17 08	15 27 46	21 26 22	27R 23.2	18 16.6	12 05.1	14 11.2	21 02.8	27 03.1	18 25.7	13 25.2	8 03.4	10 04.0
26 Tu	22 22 55	7 17 27	27 27 44	3♑32 29	27 23.1	20 05.6	13 20.1	14 14.2	21 24.1	27 00.4	18 23.3	13 25.5	8 02.1	10 02.8
27 W	22 26 52	8 17 45	9♑41 16	15 54 37	27 21.6	21 53.0	14 35.1	14 17.9	21 45.3	26 57.5	18 20.9	13 25.9	8 00.7	10 01.6
28 Th	22 30 48	9 18 00	22 13 02	28 36 54	27 17.6	23 38.3	15 50.1	14 22.2	22 06.5	26 54.4	18 18.7	13 26.3	7 59.3	10 00.4

Astro Data

	Dy Hr Mn
♆ R	10 1:15
☽ 0N	10 6:39
☽ 0S	23 7:32
☽ 0N	6 11:32
♃ R	11 8:26
☽ 0S	19 15:35
♅ D	20 12:13
♂ D	21 21:12

Planet Ingress

		Dy Hr Mn
⚳	♑	1 22:34
☊	♋	2 2:03
☊	♑R	2 22:11
☿	♑	9 14:09
☉	♒	20 15:45
♀	♒	22 22:28
☿	♒	29 7:22
☿	♓	15 15:43
♀	♓	15 20:11
☉	♓	19 6:09

Last Aspect / ☽ Ingress (January)

Last Aspect Dy Hr Mn			☽ Ingress	Dy Hr Mn
2 2:15	♃	⚹	♑	2 12:11
4 15:54	♂	☍	♒	4 21:38
6 22:03	☿	⚹	♓	7 4:47
9 9:27	☿	□	♈	9 9:56
11 6:27	♃	☍	♉	11 13:25
13 5:02	♂	⚹	♊	13 15:42
15 11:18	♃	△	♋	15 17:32
17 14:47	☉	☍	♌	17 20:03
19 18:31	♃	⚹	♍	20 0:40
22 6:58	♀	△	♎	22 8:31
24 13:23	♃	☌	♏	24 19:40
27 1:04	☿	⚹	♐	27 8:27
29 14:38	♃	⚹	♑	29 20:18

Last Aspect / ☽ Ingress (February)

Last Aspect Dy Hr Mn			☽ Ingress	Dy Hr Mn
1 0:12	♃	□	♒	1 5:23
3 6:42	♃	△	♓	3 11:32
4 21:43	♄	△	♈	5 15:38
7 14:16	♃	☍	♉	7 18:47
9 7:52	♀	□	♊	9 21:45
11 20:28	♃	△	♋	12 0:59
14 0:13	♃	□	♌	14 4:50
16 5:14	♃	⚹	♍	16 10:03
17 20:30	♄	⚹	♎	18 17:36
20 22:33	♃	☌	♏	21 4:05
22 17:25	♄	△	♐	23 16:41
25 23:09	♃	⚹	♑	26 5:01
28 8:49	♃	□	♒	28 14:34

☽ Phases & Eclipses

Dy Hr Mn		
3 12:30	●	12♑33
3 12:15:42	●	P 0.553
10 20:27	☽	20♈01
17 14:47	○	26♋54
25 5:00	☾	4♏38
2 4:43	●	12♒45
9 4:28	☽	19♉50
16 4:28	○	26♌54
24 2:36	☾	4♐53

Astro Data

1 January 1946
Julian Day # 16802
SVP 6♓01'07"
GC 26♐05.1 ⚴ 12♐56.5
Eris 5♈16.7 ⚵ 24♎46.3
⚷ 20♎12.1 ⚶ 11♑44.9
☽ Mean ☊ 29♊26.8

1 February 1946
Julian Day # 16833
SVP 6♓01'01"
GC 26♐05.2 ⚴ 25♐18.5
Eris 5♈25.3 ⚵ 29♎46.7
⚷ 21♎19.4 ⚶ 28♑14.1
☽ Mean ☊ 27♊48.4

March 1946 — LONGITUDE

Day	Sid.Time	☉	0 hr ☽	Noon ☽	True ☊	☿	♀	♂	⚳	♃	♄	♅	♆	♇
1 F	22 34 45	10♓18 15	5♒06 31	11♒42 03	27♊11.0	25♓21.2	17♓05.0	14♋27.2	22♑27.5	26♎51.1	18♋16.6	13♊26.7	7♎57.9	9♌59.2
2 Sa	22 38 41	11 18 27	18 23 33	25 10 55	27R01.8	27 01.1	18 20.0	14 32.9	22 48.5	26R47.7	18R14.6	13 27.2	7R56.5	9R58.0
3 Su	22 42 38	12 18 38	2♓03 53	9♓02 04	26 50.6	28 37.4	19 34.9	14 39.3	23 09.3	26 44.0	18 12.7	13 27.8	7 55.0	9 56.9
4 M	22 46 35	13 18 47	16 04 55	23 11 48	26 38.5	0♈09.7	20 49.8	14 46.3	23 30.0	26 40.2	18 10.9	13 28.4	7 53.6	9 55.7
5 Tu	22 50 31	14 18 55	0♈21 57	7♈34 33	26 26.9	1 37.3	22 04.7	14 53.9	23 50.7	26 36.3	18 09.2	13 29.1	7 52.1	9 54.6
6 W	22 54 28	15 19 00	14 48 47	22 03 48	26 17.0	2 59.7	23 19.5	15 02.2	24 11.2	26 32.1	18 07.6	13 29.8	7 50.6	9 53.5
7 Th	22 58 24	16 19 03	29 18 50	6♉33 09	26 09.6	4 16.3	24 34.4	15 11.1	24 31.7	26 27.8	18 06.2	13 30.6	7 49.1	9 52.4
8 F	23 02 21	17 19 04	13♉46 08	20 57 18	26 05.1	5 26.6	25 49.2	15 20.5	24 52.0	26 23.4	18 04.8	13 31.4	7 47.6	9 51.3
9 Sa	23 06 17	18 19 03	28 06 15	5♊12 40	26D03.1	6 30.0	27 04.0	15 30.6	25 12.2	26 18.7	18 03.5	13 32.3	7 46.1	9 50.3
10 Su	23 10 14	19 19 00	12♊16 25	19 17 23	26R02.7	7 26.3	28 18.7	15 41.2	25 32.3	26 14.0	18 02.4	13 33.2	7 44.5	9 49.2
11 M	23 14 10	20 18 54	26 15 32	3♋10 54	26 02.6	8 14.8	29 33.5	15 52.4	25 52.3	26 09.0	18 01.4	13 34.2	7 43.0	9 48.2
12 Tu	23 18 07	21 18 47	10♋03 31	16 53 29	26 01.5	8 55.3	0♈48.2	16 04.1	26 12.2	26 03.9	18 00.4	13 35.2	7 41.4	9 47.2
13 W	23 22 04	22 18 37	23 40 50	0♌25 37	25 58.3	9 27.5	2 02.9	16 16.3	26 32.0	25 58.7	17 59.6	13 36.3	7 39.9	9 46.2
14 Th	23 26 00	23 18 24	7♌07 51	13 47 32	25 52.2	9 51.3	3 17.5	16 29.1	26 51.6	25 53.4	17 58.9	13 37.5	7 38.3	9 45.3
15 F	23 29 57	24 18 10	20 24 36	26 59 00	25 43.1	10 06.5	4 32.2	16 42.4	27 11.2	25 47.8	17 58.3	13 38.6	7 36.7	9 44.3
16 Sa	23 33 53	25 17 54	3♍30 38	9♍59 24	25 31.4	10R13.1	5 46.8	16 56.2	27 30.6	25 42.2	17 57.8	13 39.9	7 35.1	9 43.4
17 Su	23 37 50	26 17 35	16 25 11	22 47 53	25 18.0	10 11.4	7 01.4	17 10.4	27 49.9	25 36.4	17 57.5	13 41.2	7 33.5	9 42.5
18 M	23 41 46	27 17 14	29 07 25	5♎23 46	25 04.1	10 01.4	8 15.9	17 25.2	28 09.1	25 30.5	17 57.2	13 42.5	7 31.8	9 41.6
19 Tu	23 45 43	28 16 52	11♎36 54	17 46 52	24 50.9	9 43.7	9 30.5	17 40.4	28 28.1	25 24.5	17D57.0	13 43.9	7 30.2	9 40.8
20 W	23 49 39	29 16 27	23 53 47	29 57 48	24 39.5	9 18.8	10 45.0	17 56.0	28 47.0	25 18.3	17 57.0	13 45.3	7 28.6	9 39.9
21 Th	23 53 36	0♈16 01	5♏59 11	11♏58 12	24 30.7	8 47.1	11 59.5	18 12.1	29 05.8	25 12.0	17 57.1	13 46.8	7 27.0	9 39.1
22 F	23 57 32	1 15 33	17 55 15	23 50 43	24 24.7	8 09.7	13 13.9	18 28.6	29 24.5	25 05.6	17 57.2	13 48.3	7 25.3	9 38.3
23 Sa	0 01 29	2 15 03	29 45 08	5♐38 59	24 21.4	7 27.2	14 28.4	18 45.5	29 43.0	24 59.1	17 57.5	13 49.9	7 23.7	9 37.6
24 Su	0 05 26	3 14 31	11♐32 54	17 27 29	24D20.2	6 40.7	15 42.8	19 02.9	0♒01.4	24 52.5	17 57.9	13 51.5	7 22.0	9 36.8
25 M	0 09 22	4 13 58	23 23 23	29 21 18	24R20.1	5 51.2	16 57.2	19 20.7	0 19.7	24 45.8	17 58.4	13 53.2	7 20.4	9 36.1
26 Tu	0 13 19	5 13 23	5♑21 54	11♑25 54	24 20.0	4 59.9	18 11.6	19 38.8	0 37.8	24 39.0	17 59.1	13 54.9	7 18.7	9 35.4
27 W	0 17 15	6 12 46	17 33 59	23 46 48	24 18.9	4 07.8	19 25.9	19 57.4	0 55.8	24 32.1	17 59.8	13 56.7	7 17.1	9 34.7
28 Th	0 21 12	7 12 07	0♒04 58	6♒29 01	24 15.7	3 16.0	20 40.2	20 16.3	1 13.6	24 25.1	18 00.6	13 58.5	7 15.4	9 34.1
29 F	0 25 08	8 11 27	12 59 24	19 36 29	24 10.1	2 25.4	21 54.5	20 35.6	1 31.3	24 18.0	18 01.6	14 00.3	7 13.8	9 33.4
30 Sa	0 29 05	9 10 44	26 20 28	3♓11 25	24 01.9	1 37.1	23 08.8	20 55.3	1 48.8	24 10.9	18 02.7	14 02.2	7 12.1	9 32.8
31 Su	0 33 01	10 10 00	10♓09 12	17 13 31	23 51.7	0 51.7	24 23.1	21 15.3	2 06.2	24 03.7	18 03.8	14 04.1	7 10.5	9 32.2

April 1946 — LONGITUDE

Day	Sid.Time	☉	0 hr ☽	Noon ☽	True ☊	☿	♀	♂	⚳	♃	♄	♅	♆	♇
1 M	0 36 58	11♈09 14	24♓23 52	1♈39 33	23♊40.6	0♈10.2	25♈37.3	21♋35.7	2♒23.4	23♎56.4	18♋05.1	14♊06.1	7♎08.8	9♌31.7
2 Tu	0 40 55	12 08 25	8♈59 45	16 23 27	23R29.7	29♓32.9	26 51.5	21 56.4	2 40.5	23R49.0	18 06.5	14 08.2	7R07.2	9R31.2
3 W	0 44 51	13 07 35	23 49 34	1♉17 00	23 20.3	29R00.4	28 05.7	22 17.5	2 57.4	23 41.6	18 08.0	14 10.2	7 05.5	9 30.6
4 Th	0 48 48	14 06 43	8♉44 35	16 11 17	23 13.3	28 33.0	29 19.8	22 38.8	3 14.1	23 34.1	18 09.6	14 12.3	7 03.9	9 30.2
5 F	0 52 44	15 05 48	23 36 07	0♊58 13	23 09.1	28 11.0	0♉33.9	23 00.6	3 30.7	23 26.6	18 11.3	14 14.5	7 02.2	9 29.7
6 Sa	0 56 41	16 04 51	8♊16 54	15 31 36	23D07.3	27 54.4	1 48.0	23 22.6	3 47.1	23 19.0	18 13.2	14 16.7	7 00.6	9 29.3
7 Su	1 00 37	17 03 52	22 41 58	29 47 44	23 07.3	27 43.3	3 02.1	23 44.9	4 03.4	23 11.4	18 15.1	14 18.9	6 59.0	9 28.9
8 M	1 04 34	18 02 51	6♋48 49	13♋45 13	23R07.7	27D37.8	4 16.1	24 07.5	4 19.4	23 03.8	18 17.1	14 21.2	6 57.4	9 28.5
9 Tu	1 08 30	19 01 47	20 37 00	27 24 19	23 07.5	27 37.6	5 30.1	24 30.5	4 35.3	22 56.2	18 19.3	14 23.5	6 55.7	9 28.2
10 W	1 12 27	20 00 41	4♌07 24	10♌46 25	23 05.5	27 42.8	6 44.0	24 53.7	4 51.1	22 48.5	18 21.5	14 25.9	6 54.1	9 27.8
11 Th	1 16 24	20 59 33	17 21 38	23 53 14	23 01.2	27 53.1	7 57.9	25 17.1	5 06.6	22 40.8	18 23.9	14 28.3	6 52.5	9 27.5
12 F	1 20 20	21 58 22	0♍21 27	6♍46 28	22 54.4	28 08.4	9 11.8	25 40.9	5 22.0	22 33.1	18 26.3	14 30.7	6 50.9	9 27.3
13 Sa	1 24 17	22 57 09	13 08 26	19 27 30	22 45.4	28 28.5	10 25.7	26 04.9	5 37.1	22 25.4	18 28.9	14 33.2	6 49.4	9 27.0
14 Su	1 28 13	23 55 54	25 43 47	1♎57 24	22 34.9	28 53.2	11 39.5	26 29.1	5 52.1	22 17.8	18 31.5	14 35.7	6 47.8	9 26.8
15 M	1 32 10	24 54 37	8♎08 27	14 17 00	22 24.0	29 22.4	12 53.3	26 53.6	6 06.9	22 10.1	18 34.3	14 38.2	6 46.2	9 26.6
16 Tu	1 36 06	25 53 18	20 23 12	26 27 07	22 13.6	29 55.7	14 07.1	27 18.4	6 21.5	22 02.4	18 37.1	14 40.8	6 44.7	9 26.4
17 W	1 40 03	26 51 57	2♏28 55	8♏28 45	22 04.7	0♈33.0	15 20.8	27 43.4	6 35.9	21 54.7	18 40.1	14 43.4	6 43.1	9 26.3
18 Th	1 43 59	27 50 34	14 26 48	20 23 19	21 57.8	1 14.2	16 34.5	28 08.6	6 50.1	21 47.1	18 43.1	14 46.0	6 41.6	9 26.2
19 F	1 47 56	28 49 09	26 18 35	2♐12 54	21 53.4	1 59.0	17 48.1	28 34.1	7 04.1	21 39.5	18 46.3	14 48.7	6 40.1	9 26.1
20 Sa	1 51 53	29 47 43	8♐06 40	14 00 15	21D51.2	2 47.4	19 01.8	28 59.8	7 17.9	21 31.9	18 49.5	14 51.4	6 38.6	9 26.0
21 Su	1 55 49	0♉46 15	19 54 09	25 48 51	21 50.9	3 39.0	20 15.4	29 25.7	7 31.5	21 24.4	18 52.9	14 54.2	6 37.1	9D26.0
22 M	1 59 46	1 44 45	1♑44 54	7♑42 53	21 51.8	4 33.8	21 28.9	29 51.8	7 44.9	21 16.9	18 56.3	14 57.0	6 35.7	9 26.0
23 Tu	2 03 42	2 43 13	13 43 23	19 47 03	21 53.1	5 31.7	22 42.5	0♌18.1	7 58.1	21 09.5	18 59.8	14 59.8	6 34.2	9 26.0
24 W	2 07 39	3 41 40	25 54 30	2♒06 24	21R53.8	6 32.4	23 56.0	0 44.6	8 11.1	21 02.1	19 03.5	15 02.6	6 32.8	9 26.1
25 Th	2 11 35	4 40 06	8♒23 19	14 45 53	21 53.3	7 35.9	25 09.5	1 11.4	8 23.8	20 54.8	19 07.2	15 05.5	6 31.4	9 26.1
26 F	2 15 32	5 38 29	21 14 36	27 49 56	21 51.0	8 42.2	26 22.9	1 38.3	8 36.3	20 47.5	19 11.0	15 08.4	6 30.0	9 26.2
27 Sa	2 19 28	6 36 51	4♓32 14	11♓21 42	21 46.9	9 50.9	27 36.3	2 05.5	8 48.6	20 40.3	19 14.9	15 11.3	6 28.6	9 26.4
28 Su	2 23 25	7 35 12	18 18 26	25 22 18	21 41.2	11 02.2	28 49.7	2 32.8	9 00.7	20 33.2	19 18.8	15 14.3	6 27.2	9 26.5
29 M	2 27 22	8 33 31	2♈33 01	9♈50 05	21 34.7	12 15.9	0♊03.1	3 00.3	9 12.5	20 26.1	19 22.9	15 17.3	6 25.8	9 26.7
30 Tu	2 31 18	9 31 48	17 12 48	24 40 16	21 28.2	13 32.0	1 16.4	3 28.1	9 24.1	20 19.2	19 27.1	15 20.3	6 24.5	9 26.9

Astro Data (Dy Hr Mn)

Astro Data	Dy Hr Mn
☿0N	3 13:47
☽0N	5 18:09
♀0N	14 4:37
☿R	16 18:56
☽0S	18 23:08
♄D	20 9:29
☉0N	21 5:32
☽0N	2 3:31
☿0S	5 8:44
☿D	9 0:37
☽0S	15 5:55
♇D	22 3:52
☿0N	24 0:16
☽0N	29 14:23

Planet Ingress (Dy Hr Mn)

Planet Ingress	Dy Hr Mn
☿ ♈	4 9:26
♀ ♈	11 20:32
☉ ♈	21 5:33
⚳ ♒	24 10:09
☿ ♓R	1 18:16
♀ ♉	5 1:01
☿ ♈	16 14:54
☉ ♉	20 17:02
♂ ♌	22 19:31
♀ ♊	29 10:59

Last Aspect Dy Hr Mn	☽ Ingress Dy Hr Mn	Last Aspect Dy Hr Mn	☽ Ingress Dy Hr Mn
2 14:49 ♃ △	♓ 2 20:25	31 18:55 ♂ △	♈ 1 9:16
4 7:38 ♀ ☌	♈ 4 23:23	3 6:24 ♀ ☌	♉ 3 9:56
6 19:22 ♃ ☍	♉ 7 1:08	5 7:33 ☿ ⚹	♊ 5 10:25
8 20:56 ♀ ⚹	♊ 9 3:12	7 8:31 ☿ □	♋ 7 12:21
11 5:05 ♀ □	♋ 11 6:29	9 12:24 ☿ △	♌ 9 16:37
13 4:08 ♃ □	♌ 13 11:14	11 9:48 ♃ ⚹	♍ 11 23:20
15 9:51 ♃ ⚹	♍ 15 17:32	14 5:51 ☿ ☍	♎ 14 8:13
17 19:11 ☉ ☍	♎ 18 1:40	16 13:45 ♂ △	♏ 16 19:03
20 2:51 ♃ ☌	♏ 20 12:04	19 4:19 ♂ △	♐ 19 7:30
22 0:52 ♂ △	♐ 23 0:30	21 3:09 ♃ ⚹	♑ 21 20:28
25 2:51 ♃ ⚹	♑ 25 13:18	23 18:23 ♀ △	♒ 24 7:56
27 13:26 ♃ □	♒ 27 23:51	26 9:06 ♀ □	♓ 26 15:54
29 20:19 ♃ △	♓ 30 6:26	28 18:20 ♀ ⚹	♈ 28 19:45
		30 5:04 ♃ ☍	♉ 30 20:31

☽ Phases & Eclipses (Dy Hr Mn)

Dy Hr Mn	Phase	Position
3 18:01	●	12♓34
10 12:03	☽	19♊19
17 19:11	○	26♍35
25 22:37	☾	4♑40
2 4:37	●	11♈50
8 20:04	☽	18♋23
16 10:47	○	25♎50
24 15:18	☾	3♒50

Astro Data

1 March 1946
Julian Day # 16861
SVP 6♓00'58"
GC 26♐05.2 ⚴ 5♑02.9
Eris 5♈40.8 ⚵ 0♏00.2R
⚷ 20♎43.9R ⚶ 12♒43.7
☽ Mean ☊ 26♊19.4

1 April 1946
Julian Day # 16892
SVP 6♓00'55"
GC 26♐05.3 ⚴ 13♑10.0
Eris 6♈02.3 ⚵ 25♎06.4R
⚷ 18♎43.0R ⚶ 27♒59.9
☽ Mean ☊ 24♊40.9

LONGITUDE — May 1946

Day	Sid.Time	☉	0 hr ☽	Noon ☽	True ☊	☿	♀	♂	⚳	♃	♄	♅	♆	♇
1 W	2 35 15	10♉30 04	2♉11 26	9♉45 09	21♊22.6	14♈50.3	2♊29.7	3♌56.0	9♒35.5	20♎12.3	19♋31.3	15♊23.3	6♎23.2	9♌27.2
2 Th	2 39 11	11 28 18	17 20 10	24 55 14	21R 18.6	16 10.8	3 43.0	4 24.1	9 46.6	20R 05.5	19 35.7	15 26.4	6R 21.9	9 27.4
3 F	2 43 08	12 26 30	2♊29 08	10♊00 42	21D 16.4	17 33.5	4 56.2	4 52.3	9 57.4	19 58.8	19 40.1	15 29.5	6 20.6	9 27.7
4 Sa	2 47 04	13 24 40	17 28 55	24 52 57	21 16.0	18 58.3	6 09.4	5 20.8	10 08.0	19 52.2	19 44.6	15 32.6	6 19.4	9 28.0
5 Su	2 51 01	14 22 49	2♋12 06	9♋25 50	21 16.9	20 25.2	7 22.6	5 49.4	10 18.4	19 45.8	19 49.2	15 35.7	6 18.1	9 28.4
6 M	2 54 57	15 20 55	16 33 48	23 35 51	21 18.3	21 54.2	8 35.7	6 18.2	10 28.4	19 39.4	19 53.8	15 38.9	6 16.9	9 28.8
7 Tu	2 58 54	16 19 00	0♌31 54	7♌22 02	21R 19.4	23 25.3	9 48.8	6 47.1	10 38.3	19 33.2	19 58.6	15 42.1	6 15.8	9 29.2
8 W	3 02 51	17 17 02	14 06 26	20 45 19	21 19.7	24 58.3	11 01.8	7 16.2	10 47.8	19 27.0	20 03.4	15 45.3	6 14.6	9 29.6
9 Th	3 06 47	18 15 03	27 19 01	3♍47 50	21 18.6	26 33.4	12 14.8	7 45.4	10 57.1	19 21.0	20 08.3	15 48.5	6 13.4	9 30.0
10 F	3 10 44	19 13 01	10♍12 08	16 32 17	21 16.0	28 10.5	13 27.8	8 14.8	11 06.2	19 15.1	20 13.3	15 51.7	6 12.3	9 30.5
11 Sa	3 14 40	20 10 58	22 48 39	29 01 35	21 12.2	29 49.6	14 40.7	8 44.4	11 14.9	19 09.4	20 18.4	15 55.0	6 11.2	9 31.0
12 Su	3 18 37	21 08 53	5♎11 24	11♎18 27	21 07.4	1♉30.8	15 53.6	9 14.1	11 23.4	19 03.7	20 23.5	15 58.3	6 10.2	9 31.5
13 M	3 22 33	22 06 47	17 23 01	23 25 23	21 02.4	3 13.9	17 06.4	9 43.9	11 31.6	18 58.2	20 28.7	16 01.6	6 09.1	9 32.1
14 Tu	3 26 30	23 04 38	29 25 49	5♏24 35	20 57.6	4 59.0	18 19.3	10 13.9	11 39.5	18 52.9	20 34.0	16 04.9	6 08.1	9 32.7
15 W	3 30 26	24 02 29	11♏21 56	17 18 06	20 53.5	6 46.2	19 32.0	10 44.0	11 47.1	18 47.7	20 39.3	16 08.3	6 07.1	9 33.3
16 Th	3 34 23	25 00 17	23 13 20	29 07 53	20 50.6	8 35.4	20 44.8	11 14.3	11 54.5	18 42.6	20 44.7	16 11.6	6 06.1	9 33.9
17 F	3 38 20	25 58 05	5♐01 59	10♐55 57	20D 49.0	10 26.6	21 57.4	11 44.6	12 01.5	18 37.7	20 50.2	16 15.0	6 05.2	9 34.6
18 Sa	3 42 16	26 55 51	16 50 03	22 44 37	20 48.6	12 19.8	23 10.1	12 15.1	12 08.3	18 32.9	20 55.8	16 18.4	6 04.3	9 35.2
19 Su	3 46 13	27 53 35	28 39 59	4♑36 31	20 49.2	14 15.0	24 22.7	12 45.8	12 14.7	18 28.3	21 01.4	16 21.8	6 03.4	9 35.9
20 M	3 50 09	28 51 19	10♑34 38	16 34 45	20 50.6	16 12.1	25 35.3	13 16.6	12 20.9	18 23.8	21 07.1	16 25.2	6 02.5	9 36.7
21 Tu	3 54 06	29 49 01	22 37 18	28 42 48	20 52.2	18 11.2	26 47.8	13 47.4	12 26.7	18 19.5	21 12.9	16 28.6	6 01.7	9 37.4
22 W	3 58 02	0♊46 43	4♒51 42	11♒04 32	20 53.6	20 12.2	28 00.3	14 18.5	12 32.3	18 15.4	21 18.7	16 32.1	6 00.9	9 38.2
23 Th	4 01 59	1 44 23	17 21 47	23 43 58	20R 54.5	22 14.9	29 12.8	14 49.6	12 37.5	18 11.4	21 24.6	16 35.5	6 00.1	9 39.0
24 F	4 05 55	2 42 02	0♓11 33	6♓44 57	20 54.6	24 19.4	0♋25.2	15 20.9	12 42.4	18 07.5	21 30.5	16 39.0	5 59.4	9 39.8
25 Sa	4 09 52	3 39 40	13 24 32	20 10 35	20 54.0	26 25.5	1 37.5	15 52.2	12 47.0	18 03.9	21 36.5	16 42.5	5 58.6	9 40.7
26 Su	4 13 49	4 37 18	27 03 18	4♈02 44	20 52.6	28 33.1	2 49.9	16 23.7	12 51.2	18 00.4	21 42.6	16 45.9	5 57.9	9 41.6
27 M	4 17 45	5 34 54	11♈08 48	18 21 13	20 50.9	0♊41.9	4 02.2	16 55.3	12 55.1	17 57.0	21 48.8	16 49.4	5 57.3	9 42.5
28 Tu	4 21 42	6 32 29	25 39 35	3♉03 17	20 49.1	2 51.9	5 14.4	17 27.1	12 58.7	17 53.9	21 54.9	16 52.9	5 56.6	9 43.4
29 W	4 25 38	7 30 04	10♉31 31	18 03 22	20 47.5	5 02.7	6 26.6	17 58.9	13 02.0	17 50.9	22 01.2	16 56.4	5 56.0	9 44.3
30 Th	4 29 35	8 27 37	25 37 46	3♊13 32	20 46.5	7 14.3	7 38.8	18 30.9	13 04.9	17 48.0	22 07.5	17 00.0	5 55.5	9 45.3
31 F	4 33 31	9 25 10	10♊49 28	18 24 22	20D 46.1	9 26.2	8 51.0	19 02.9	13 07.5	17 45.4	22 13.9	17 03.5	5 54.9	9 46.3

LONGITUDE — June 1946

Day	Sid.Time	☉	0 hr ☽	Noon ☽	True ☊	☿	♀	♂	⚳	♃	♄	♅	♆	♇
1 Sa	4 37 28	10♊22 42	25♊57 04	3♋26 27	20♊46.3	11♊38.3	10♋03.1	19♌35.1	13♒09.7	17♎42.9	22♋20.3	17♊07.0	5♎54.4	9♌47.3
2 Su	4 41 24	11 20 12	10♋51 36	18 11 42	20 46.9	13 50.3	11 15.1	20 07.4	13 11.6	17R 40.6	22 26.8	17 10.6	5R 53.9	9 48.3
3 M	4 45 21	12 17 41	25 26 06	2♌34 20	20 47.6	16 01.8	12 27.1	20 39.8	13 13.2	17 38.5	22 33.3	17 14.1	5 53.5	9 49.4
4 Tu	4 49 18	13 15 09	9♌36 06	16 31 15	20 48.3	18 12.7	13 39.1	21 12.3	13 14.4	17 36.6	22 39.8	17 17.7	5 53.0	9 50.5
5 W	4 53 14	14 12 36	23 19 48	0♍01 53	20 48.8	20 22.6	14 51.0	21 44.9	13 15.2	17 34.8	22 46.5	17 21.2	5 52.6	9 51.6
6 Th	4 57 11	15 10 01	6♍37 44	13 07 39	20R 49.0	22 31.4	16 02.8	22 17.6	13R 15.7	17 33.3	22 53.1	17 24.8	5 52.3	9 52.7
7 F	5 01 07	16 07 25	19 32 03	25 51 21	20 48.9	24 38.7	17 14.6	22 50.4	13 15.9	17 31.9	22 59.8	17 28.3	5 52.0	9 53.8
8 Sa	5 05 04	17 04 48	2♎06 02	8♎16 34	20 48.6	26 44.5	18 26.3	23 23.3	13 15.7	17 30.6	23 06.6	17 31.9	5 51.7	9 55.0
9 Su	5 09 00	18 02 10	14 23 27	20 27 11	20 48.3	28 48.5	19 38.0	23 56.2	13 15.1	17 29.6	23 13.4	17 35.4	5 51.4	9 56.2
10 M	5 12 57	18 59 31	26 28 14	2♏27 04	20 48.0	0♋50.6	20 49.7	24 29.3	13 14.2	17 28.7	23 20.3	17 39.0	5 51.1	9 57.4
11 Tu	5 16 53	19 56 51	8♏24 08	14 19 50	20D 47.9	2 50.7	22 01.3	25 02.5	13 12.9	17 28.1	23 27.2	17 42.5	5 50.9	9 58.6
12 W	5 20 50	20 54 11	20 14 35	26 08 44	20 47.8	4 48.7	23 12.8	25 35.7	13 11.3	17 27.6	23 34.1	17 46.1	5 50.8	9 59.8
13 Th	5 24 47	21 51 29	2♐02 40	7♐56 42	20 47.9	6 44.5	24 24.2	26 09.1	13 09.3	17 27.3	23 41.1	17 49.6	5 50.6	10 01.1
14 F	5 28 43	22 48 47	13 51 08	19 46 16	20R 47.9	8 38.0	25 35.7	26 42.5	13 07.0	17D 27.1	23 48.1	17 53.2	5 50.5	10 02.4
15 Sa	5 32 40	23 46 04	25 42 23	1♑39 45	20 47.9	10 29.2	26 47.0	27 16.0	13 04.3	17 27.2	23 55.1	17 56.7	5 50.4	10 03.7
16 Su	5 36 36	24 43 20	7♑38 38	13 39 19	20 47.6	12 18.1	27 58.3	27 49.6	13 01.3	17 27.4	24 02.2	18 00.2	5D 50.4	10 05.0
17 M	5 40 33	25 40 36	19 42 03	25 47 06	20 47.2	14 04.6	29 09.6	28 23.3	12 57.9	17 27.8	24 09.4	18 03.8	5 50.4	10 06.3
18 Tu	5 44 29	26 37 52	1♒54 45	8♒05 18	20 46.5	15 48.7	0♌20.7	28 57.1	12 54.1	17 28.4	24 16.5	18 07.3	5 50.4	10 07.7
19 W	5 48 26	27 35 07	14 19 01	20 36 13	20 45.7	17 30.4	1 31.9	29 31.0	12 50.0	17 29.1	24 23.7	18 10.8	5 50.5	10 09.0
20 Th	5 52 22	28 32 22	26 57 12	3♓22 16	20 45.0	19 09.7	2 42.9	0♍04.9	12 45.5	17 30.1	24 31.0	18 14.3	5 50.5	10 10.4
21 F	5 56 19	29 29 37	9♓51 43	16 25 50	20 44.4	20 46.6	3 53.9	0 39.0	12 40.7	17 31.2	24 38.2	18 17.8	5 50.7	10 11.8
22 Sa	6 00 16	0♋26 51	23 04 52	29 49 03	20D 44.1	22 21.0	5 04.9	1 13.1	12 35.5	17 32.5	24 45.5	18 21.3	5 50.8	10 13.2
23 Su	6 04 12	1 24 06	6♈38 33	13♈33 27	20 44.3	23 53.0	6 15.8	1 47.3	12 30.0	17 33.9	24 52.8	18 24.8	5 51.0	10 14.7
24 M	6 08 09	2 21 20	20 33 47	27 39 28	20 45.0	25 22.6	7 26.6	2 21.5	12 24.1	17 35.6	25 00.2	18 28.3	5 51.2	10 16.1
25 Tu	6 12 05	3 18 35	4♉50 17	12♉05 55	20 45.9	26 49.6	8 37.4	2 55.9	12 17.9	17 37.4	25 07.6	18 31.8	5 51.4	10 17.6
26 W	6 16 02	4 15 49	19 25 55	26 49 41	20 46.8	28 14.2	9 48.1	3 30.4	12 11.3	17 39.4	25 15.0	18 35.2	5 51.7	10 19.1
27 Th	6 19 58	5 13 04	4♊16 28	11♊45 27	20R 47.5	29 36.2	10 58.7	4 04.9	12 04.4	17 41.5	25 22.5	18 38.7	5 52.0	10 20.5
28 F	6 23 55	6 10 18	19 15 40	26 46 05	20 47.5	0♌55.6	12 09.3	4 39.5	11 57.2	17 43.9	25 29.9	18 42.1	5 52.4	10 22.1
29 Sa	6 27 52	7 07 32	4♋15 39	11♋43 19	20 46.8	2 12.3	13 19.8	5 14.2	11 49.7	17 46.4	25 37.4	18 45.5	5 52.8	10 23.6
30 Su	6 31 48	8 04 46	19 08 04	26 28 56	20 45.3	3 26.4	14 30.2	5 49.0	11 41.8	17 49.1	25 44.9	18 49.0	5 53.2	10 25.1

Astro Data
Dy Hr Mn
♃□♄ 5 4:36
☽0S 12 12:08
☽0N 27 0:34

⚳R 7 10:03
♃△♅ 8 5:46
☽0S 8 18:22
♃D 14 18:05
♆D 17 8:19
☽0N 23 8:27

Planet Ingress
Dy Hr Mn
☿ ♉ 11 14:29
☉ ♊ 21 16:34
♀ ♋ 24 3:39
☿ ♊ 27 4:13

☿ ♋ 10 2:00
♀ ♌ 18 5:00
♂ ♍ 20 8:31
☉ ♋ 22 0:44
☿ ♌ 27 19:07

Last Aspect / ☽ Ingress

Dy Hr Mn	Aspect	☽ Ingress Dy Hr Mn
2 3:32	♄ ✶	♊ 2 20:03
4 3:55	♃ △	♋ 4 20:23
6 8:45	☿ □	♌ 6 23:04
8 20:45	☿ △	♍ 9 4:57
10 19:05	♄ ✶	♎ 11 13:53
13 6:06	♄ □	♏ 14 1:08
16 2:52	☉ ☍	♐ 16 13:46
18 12:58	♀ ☍	♑ 19 2:42
21 14:21	☉ △	♒ 21 14:31
23 23:14	♀ △	♓ 23 23:39
26 0:53	☿ ✶	♈ 26 5:05
27 17:44	♄ □	♉ 28 7:04
29 18:20	♄ ✶	♊ 30 6:54

Last Aspect / ☽ Ingress

Dy Hr Mn	Aspect	☽ Ingress Dy Hr Mn
31 13:03	♂ ✶	♋ 1 6:28
2 19:05	♄ ☌	♌ 3 7:39
4 20:35	♂ ☌	♍ 5 11:57
7 9:14	☿ □	♎ 7 19:57
9 19:16	♂ ✶	♏ 10 7:04
12 10:50	♂ □	♐ 12 19:50
15 2:43	♂ △	♑ 15 8:39
17 19:20	♀ ☍	♒ 17 20:16
20 5:35	♂ ☍	♓ 20 5:43
22 2:55	♄ △	♈ 22 12:19
24 7:43	☿ □	♉ 24 15:56
26 14:30	☿ ✶	♊ 26 17:07
27 23:03	♅ ☌	♋ 28 17:10
30 10:47	♄ ☌	♌ 30 17:47

☽ Phases & Eclipses
Dy Hr Mn
1 13:16 ● 10♉33
8 5:13 ☽ 17♌01
16 2:52 ○ 24♏38
24 4:02 ☾ 2♓23
30 20:49 ● 8♊49
30 20:59:58 ● P 0.887

6 16:07 ☽ 15♍20
14 18:42 ○ 23♐05
14 18:39 • T 1.398
22 13:12 ☾ 0♈30
29 4:06 ● 6♋49
29 3:51:28 ● P 0.180

Astro Data
1 May 1946
Julian Day # 16922
SVP 6♓00'52"
GC 26♐05.4 ⚴ 16♑44.1
Eris 6♈22.3 ⚵ 18♎25.2R
⚷ 16♎27.1R ⚶ 11♓34.9
☽ Mean ☊ 23♊05.5

1 June 1946
Julian Day # 16953
SVP 6♓00'47"
GC 26♐05.5 ⚴ 14♑06.7R
Eris 6♈37.4 ⚵ 14♎46.3R
⚷ 15♎01.9R ⚶ 23♓43.3
☽ Mean ☊ 21♊27.1

July 1946 — LONGITUDE

Day	Sid.Time	☉	0 hr ☽	Noon ☽	True ☊	☿	♀	♂	⚳	♃	♄	♅	♆	♇
1 M	6 35 45	9♋02 00	3♌45 07	10♌55 52	20♊43.1	4♌37.8	15♌40.6	6♍23.8	11♒33.6	17♎51.9	25♋52.5	18♊52.3	5♎53.6	10♌26.7
2 Tu	6 39 41	9 59 14	18 00 40	24 59 08	20R 40.7	5 46.4	16 50.9	6 58.8	11R 25.1	17 55.0	26 00.0	18 55.7	5 54.1	10 28.2
3 W	6 43 38	10 56 27	1♍51 00	8♍36 14	20 38.2	6 52.0	18 01.1	7 33.8	11 16.3	17 58.2	26 07.6	18 59.1	5 54.6	10 29.8
4 Th	6 47 34	11 53 39	15 14 53	21 47 09	20 36.3	7 54.7	19 11.3	8 08.9	11 07.2	18 01.5	26 15.2	19 02.4	5 55.1	10 31.4
5 F	6 51 31	12 50 52	28 13 20	4♎33 51	20D 35.1	8 54.4	20 21.3	8 44.0	10 57.8	18 05.0	26 22.8	19 05.8	5 55.7	10 33.0
6 Sa	6 55 27	13 48 04	10♎49 09	16 59 45	20 34.9	9 50.9	21 31.3	9 19.2	10 48.1	18 08.7	26 30.5	19 09.1	5 56.3	10 34.6
7 Su	6 59 24	14 45 16	23 06 13	29 09 08	20 35.6	10 44.1	22 41.2	9 54.5	10 38.2	18 12.6	26 38.1	19 12.4	5 56.9	10 36.2
8 M	7 03 21	15 42 28	5♏09 06	11♏06 42	20 37.0	11 34.0	23 51.0	10 29.9	10 28.0	18 16.6	26 45.8	19 15.7	5 57.6	10 37.9
9 Tu	7 07 17	16 39 40	17 02 32	22 57 08	20 38.7	12 20.3	25 00.7	11 05.3	10 17.5	18 20.8	26 53.4	19 18.9	5 58.3	10 39.5
10 W	7 11 14	17 36 52	28 51 05	4♐44 52	20 40.2	13 03.0	26 10.4	11 40.9	10 06.8	18 25.1	27 01.1	19 22.2	5 59.0	10 41.2
11 Th	7 15 10	18 34 04	10♐38 59	16 33 53	20R 41.1	13 42.0	27 19.9	12 16.4	9 55.9	18 29.6	27 08.8	19 25.4	5 59.7	10 42.8
12 F	7 19 07	19 31 16	22 29 59	28 27 38	20 40.9	14 17.0	28 29.4	12 52.1	9 44.7	18 34.2	27 16.5	19 28.6	6 00.5	10 44.5
13 Sa	7 23 03	20 28 28	4♑27 11	10♑28 54	20 39.4	14 48.0	29 38.7	13 27.8	9 33.3	18 39.0	27 24.3	19 31.7	6 01.3	10 46.2
14 Su	7 27 00	21 25 40	16 33 03	22 39 51	20 36.4	15 14.8	0♍48.0	14 03.6	9 21.8	18 44.0	27 32.0	19 34.9	6 02.2	10 47.9
15 M	7 30 56	22 22 53	28 49 28	5♒02 03	20 32.1	15 37.3	1 57.2	14 39.5	9 10.0	18 49.1	27 39.7	19 38.0	6 03.1	10 49.6
16 Tu	7 34 53	23 20 06	11♒17 43	17 36 34	20 27.0	15 55.3	3 06.2	15 15.4	8 58.0	18 54.3	27 47.5	19 41.1	6 04.0	10 51.3
17 W	7 38 50	24 17 19	23 58 39	0♓24 04	20 21.5	16 08.7	4 15.2	15 51.4	8 45.9	18 59.7	27 55.2	19 44.2	6 04.9	10 53.0
18 Th	7 42 46	25 14 33	6♓52 50	13 25 01	20 16.3	16 17.3	5 24.1	16 27.4	8 33.6	19 05.3	28 03.0	19 47.3	6 05.9	10 54.7
19 F	7 46 43	26 11 48	20 00 39	26 39 48	20 12.1	16R 21.2	6 32.8	17 03.6	8 21.1	19 11.0	28 10.7	19 50.3	6 06.9	10 56.4
20 Sa	7 50 39	27 09 03	3♈22 29	10♈08 46	20 09.2	16 20.1	7 41.5	17 39.8	8 08.5	19 16.8	28 18.5	19 53.3	6 07.9	10 58.2
21 Su	7 54 36	28 06 20	16 58 40	23 52 12	20D 08.0	16 14.2	8 50.0	18 16.0	7 55.8	19 22.8	28 26.3	19 56.3	6 08.9	10 59.9
22 M	7 58 32	29 03 37	0♉49 22	7♉50 09	20 08.2	16 03.3	9 58.5	18 52.4	7 43.0	19 28.9	28 34.0	19 59.2	6 10.0	11 01.6
23 Tu	8 02 29	0♌00 55	14 54 26	22 02 05	20 09.3	15 47.6	11 06.8	19 28.8	7 30.1	19 35.2	28 41.8	20 02.2	6 11.1	11 03.4
24 W	8 06 25	0 58 14	29 12 53	6♊26 32	20R 10.6	15 27.1	12 15.1	20 05.2	7 17.0	19 41.6	28 49.5	20 05.0	6 12.3	11 05.1
25 Th	8 10 22	1 55 34	13♊42 37	21 00 40	20 11.1	15 02.1	13 23.2	20 41.8	7 04.0	19 48.1	28 57.3	20 07.9	6 13.4	11 06.9
26 F	8 14 19	2 52 55	28 20 04	5♋40 09	20 10.2	14 32.7	14 31.2	21 18.4	6 50.8	19 54.8	29 05.0	20 10.8	6 14.6	11 08.7
27 Sa	8 18 15	3 50 16	13♋00 08	20 19 13	20 07.3	13 59.4	15 39.1	21 55.1	6 37.6	20 01.6	29 12.8	20 13.6	6 15.8	11 10.4
28 Su	8 22 12	4 47 39	27 36 33	4♌51 17	20 02.5	13 22.6	16 46.9	22 31.9	6 24.4	20 08.6	29 20.5	20 16.3	6 17.1	11 12.2
29 M	8 26 08	5 45 02	12♌02 35	19 09 45	19 56.0	12 42.7	17 54.5	23 08.7	6 11.2	20 15.7	29 28.3	20 19.1	6 18.4	11 14.0
30 Tu	8 30 05	6 42 26	26 12 05	3♍09 04	19 48.6	12 00.4	19 02.1	23 45.6	5 57.9	20 22.9	29 36.0	20 21.8	6 19.7	11 15.8
31 W	8 34 01	7 39 50	10♍00 17	16 45 29	19 41.1	11 16.3	20 09.5	24 22.5	5 44.7	20 30.2	29 43.7	20 24.5	6 21.0	11 17.5

August 1946 — LONGITUDE

Day	Sid.Time	☉	0 hr ☽	Noon ☽	True ☊	☿	♀	♂	⚳	♃	♄	♅	♆	♇
1 Th	8 37 58	8♌37 15	23♍24 34	29♍57 31	19♊34.4	10♌31.2	21♍16.7	24♍59.5	5♒31.5	20♎37.7	29♋51.4	20♊27.1	6♎22.4	11♌19.3
2 F	8 41 54	9 34 41	6♎24 32	12♎45 51	19R 29.3	9R 45.8	22 23.8	25 36.6	5R 18.3	20 45.3	29 59.1	20 29.7	6 23.7	11 21.1
3 Sa	8 45 51	10 32 07	19 01 51	25 13 01	19 26.0	9 01.1	23 30.8	26 13.8	5 05.2	20 53.0	0♌06.8	20 32.3	6 25.1	11 22.9
4 Su	8 49 48	11 29 34	1♏19 51	7♏22 57	19D 24.7	8 17.8	24 37.6	26 51.0	4 52.2	21 00.9	0 14.5	20 34.9	6 26.6	11 24.7
5 M	8 53 44	12 27 02	13 22 56	19 20 27	19 24.8	7 36.7	25 44.3	27 28.3	4 39.3	21 08.8	0 22.1	20 37.4	6 28.0	11 26.4
6 Tu	8 57 41	13 24 31	25 16 08	1♐10 41	19 25.8	6 58.7	26 50.8	28 05.6	4 26.4	21 16.9	0 29.8	20 39.8	6 29.5	11 28.2
7 W	9 01 37	14 22 00	7♐04 44	12 58 54	19R 26.7	6 24.6	27 57.2	28 43.0	4 13.7	21 25.1	0 37.4	20 42.3	6 31.0	11 30.0
8 Th	9 05 34	15 19 30	18 53 50	24 50 04	19 26.8	5 54.9	29 03.4	29 20.5	4 01.1	21 33.4	0 45.0	20 44.7	6 32.5	11 31.8
9 F	9 09 30	16 17 01	0♑48 10	6♑48 37	19 25.1	5 30.5	0♎09.4	29 58.0	3 48.6	21 41.9	0 52.6	20 47.0	6 34.1	11 33.6
10 Sa	9 13 27	17 14 33	12 51 50	18 58 11	19 21.3	5 11.7	1 15.3	0♎35.6	3 36.3	21 50.4	1 00.2	20 49.3	6 35.7	11 35.3
11 Su	9 17 23	18 12 06	25 08 00	1♒21 29	19 15.1	4 59.2	2 21.0	1 13.2	3 24.1	21 59.1	1 07.7	20 51.6	6 37.3	11 37.1
12 M	9 21 20	19 09 40	7♒38 50	14 00 06	19 06.7	4D 53.2	3 26.5	1 50.9	3 12.1	22 07.8	1 15.3	20 53.9	6 38.9	11 38.9
13 Tu	9 25 17	20 07 16	20 25 20	26 54 27	18 56.9	4 54.1	4 31.8	2 28.7	3 00.3	22 16.7	1 22.8	20 56.1	6 40.5	11 40.7
14 W	9 29 13	21 04 52	3♓27 21	10♓03 53	18 46.4	5 02.0	5 36.9	3 06.6	2 48.7	22 25.7	1 30.2	20 58.2	6 42.2	11 42.4
15 Th	9 33 10	22 02 30	16 43 50	23 26 57	18 36.3	5 17.2	6 41.8	3 44.5	2 37.3	22 34.8	1 37.7	21 00.4	6 43.9	11 44.2
16 F	9 37 06	23 00 09	0♈13 00	7♈01 44	18 27.8	5 39.6	7 46.6	4 22.4	2 26.1	22 44.0	1 45.1	21 02.5	6 45.6	11 45.9
17 Sa	9 41 03	23 57 49	13 52 53	20 46 15	18 21.4	6 09.4	8 51.1	5 00.4	2 15.1	22 53.2	1 52.5	21 04.5	6 47.3	11 47.7
18 Su	9 44 59	24 55 32	27 41 37	4♉38 49	18 17.5	6 46.5	9 55.4	5 38.5	2 04.4	23 02.6	1 59.9	21 06.5	6 49.1	11 49.4
19 M	9 48 56	25 53 15	11♉37 43	18 38 11	18D 15.9	7 30.7	10 59.5	6 16.7	1 53.9	23 12.1	2 07.3	21 08.5	6 50.8	11 51.2
20 Tu	9 52 52	26 51 01	25 40 07	2♊43 25	18 15.8	8 22.0	12 03.4	6 54.9	1 43.6	23 21.7	2 14.6	21 10.4	6 52.6	11 52.9
21 W	9 56 49	27 48 48	9♊47 58	16 53 39	18R 16.1	9 20.0	13 07.1	7 33.2	1 33.7	23 31.4	2 21.9	21 12.3	6 54.5	11 54.6
22 Th	10 00 46	28 46 38	24 00 17	1♋07 38	18 15.6	10 24.7	14 10.6	8 11.5	1 24.0	23 41.2	2 29.1	21 14.1	6 56.3	11 56.4
23 F	10 04 42	29 44 28	8♋15 26	15 23 19	18 13.1	11 35.7	15 13.8	8 50.0	1 14.5	23 51.1	2 36.3	21 15.9	6 58.1	11 58.1
24 Sa	10 08 39	0♍42 21	22 30 53	29 37 37	18 08.1	12 52.7	16 16.8	9 28.4	1 05.4	24 01.1	2 43.5	21 17.6	7 00.0	11 59.8
25 Su	10 12 35	1 40 15	6♌42 59	13♌46 25	18 00.2	14 15.2	17 19.5	10 07.0	0 56.6	24 11.1	2 50.7	21 19.3	7 01.9	12 01.5
26 M	10 16 32	2 38 11	20 47 19	27 45 05	17 50.0	15 43.0	18 22.0	10 45.6	0 48.0	24 21.3	2 57.8	21 21.0	7 03.8	12 03.2
27 Tu	10 20 28	3 36 08	4♍39 11	11♍29 07	17 38.4	17 15.6	19 24.3	11 24.3	0 39.8	24 31.5	3 04.9	21 22.6	7 05.7	12 04.9
28 W	10 24 25	4 34 06	18 14 27	24 54 53	17 26.5	18 52.5	20 26.2	12 03.0	0 31.9	24 41.9	3 11.9	21 24.1	7 07.6	12 06.6
29 Th	10 28 21	5 32 06	1♎30 10	8♎00 14	17 15.5	20 33.3	21 27.9	12 41.8	0 24.3	24 52.3	3 18.9	21 25.6	7 09.6	12 08.2
30 F	10 32 18	6 30 08	14 25 05	20 44 51	17 06.3	22 17.5	22 29.3	13 20.7	0 17.0	25 02.8	3 25.9	21 27.1	7 11.6	12 09.9
31 Sa	10 36 15	7 28 11	26 59 47	3♏10 12	16 59.7	24 04.6	23 30.4	13 59.6	0 10.1	25 13.4	3 32.8	21 28.5	7 13.5	12 11.5

Astro Data	Dy Hr Mn
☽ 0S	6 1:12
☿ R	19 18:56
☽ 0N	20 13:58
♃△♅	30 6:14
☽ 0S	2 8:52
♀0S	9 10:25
♂0S	11 10:54
☿ D	12 21:04
☽ 0N	16 18:45
☽ 0S	29 17:04

Planet Ingress	Dy Hr Mn
♀ ♍	13 19:22
☉ ♌	23 11:37
♄ ♌	2 14:42
♀ ♎	9 8:34
♂ ♎	9 13:17
☉ ♍	23 18:26

Last Aspect Dy Hr Mn	☽ Ingress Dy Hr Mn
2 1:32 ♅ ⚹	♍ 2 20:45
4 20:24 ♄ ⚹	♎ 5 3:21
7 6:56 ♄ □	♏ 7 13:41
9 20:06 ♄ △	♐ 10 2:20
12 12:04 ♀ △	♑ 12 15:05
14 21:36 ♄ ☍	♒ 15 2:17
16 15:56 ♅ △	♓ 17 11:15
19 14:45 ♄ △	♈ 19 17:59
21 19:58 ♄ □	♉ 21 22:35
23 23:14 ♄ ⚹	♊ 24 1:18
25 11:28 ♂ □	♋ 26 2:44
28 2:47 ♄ ☌	♌ 28 3:57
29 13:58 ♅ ⚹	♍ 30 6:32

Last Aspect Dy Hr Mn	☽ Ingress Dy Hr Mn
1 11:49 ♄ ⚹	♎ 1 12:05
3 3:29 ♃ ☌	♏ 3 21:23
6 5:23 ♂ ⚹	♐ 6 9:36
8 21:34 ♂ □	♑ 8 22:23
10 17:40 ♃ □	♒ 11 9:24
13 3:21 ♃ △	♓ 13 17:41
15 7:38 ♅ □	♈ 15 23:37
17 17:57 ☉ △	♉ 18 3:59
20 1:17 ☉ □	♊ 20 7:22
22 7:45 ☉ ⚹	♋ 22 10:06
24 2:25 ♃ □	♌ 24 12:38
26 6:04 ♃ ⚹	♍ 26 15:54
28 5:39 ♅ □	♎ 28 21:15
30 20:21 ♃ ☌	♏ 31 5:49

☽ Phases & Eclipses Dy Hr Mn	
6 5:15	☽ 13♎32
14 9:23	○ 21♑19
21 19:52	☾ 28♈25
28 11:54	● 4♌47
4 20:55	☽ 11♏51
12 22:26	○ 19♒35
20 1:17	☾ 26♉25
26 21:07	● 3♍00

Astro Data

1 July 1946
Julian Day # 16983
SVP 6♓00'41"
GC 26♐05.5 ⚴ 6♑22.0R
Eris 6♈43.0 ⚵ 16♎06.0
⚷ 15♎13.8 ⚶ 2♈34.4
☽ Mean ☊ 19♊51.8

1 August 1946
Julian Day # 17014
SVP 6♓00'36"
GC 26♐05.6 ⚴ 29♐21.4R
Eris 6♈38.5R ⚵ 21♎24.6
⚷ 17♎06.8 ⚶ 6♈54.0
☽ Mean ☊ 18♊13.3

LONGITUDE

September 1946

Day	Sid.Time	☉	0 hr ☽	Noon ☽	True ☊	☿	♀	♂	⚳	♃	♄	♅	♆	♇
1 Su	10 40 11	8♍26 15	9♏16 33	15♏19 18	16♊55.6	25♌54.1	24♎31.1	14♎38.6	0♒03.5	25♎24.0	3♌39.6	21♊29.9	7♎15.5	12♌13.2
2 M	10 44 08	9 24 21	21 19 02	27 16 21	16R53.7	27 45.6	25 31.6	15 17.6	29♑57.3	25 34.8	3 46.5	21 31.2	7 17.5	12 14.8
3 Tu	10 48 04	10 22 28	3♐11 54	9♐06 21	16 53.3	29 38.7	26 31.7	15 56.7	29R51.4	25 45.6	3 53.3	21 32.5	7 19.6	12 16.4
4 W	10 52 01	11 20 37	15 00 23	20 54 43	16 53.3	1♍33.0	27 31.5	16 35.9	29 45.9	25 56.5	4 00.0	21 33.7	7 21.6	12 18.0
5 Th	10 55 57	12 18 47	26 50 01	2♑46 57	16 52.6	3 28.1	28 30.9	17 15.1	29 40.7	26 07.5	4 06.7	21 34.9	7 23.7	12 19.6
6 F	10 59 54	13 16 59	8♑46 11	14 48 18	16 50.3	5 23.7	29 30.0	17 54.4	29 35.8	26 18.6	4 13.3	21 36.0	7 25.7	12 21.2
7 Sa	11 03 50	14 15 12	20 53 53	27 03 24	16 45.6	7 19.6	0♏28.6	18 33.8	29 31.4	26 29.7	4 19.9	21 37.1	7 27.8	12 22.7
8 Su	11 07 47	15 13 27	3♒17 17	9♒35 52	16 38.2	9 15.4	1 26.9	19 13.2	29 27.2	26 40.9	4 26.4	21 38.1	7 29.9	12 24.3
9 M	11 11 44	16 11 44	15 59 24	22 28 01	16 28.3	11 11.0	2 24.8	19 52.7	29 23.5	26 52.1	4 32.9	21 39.1	7 32.0	12 25.8
10 Tu	11 15 40	17 10 02	29 01 44	5♓40 28	16 16.6	13 06.3	3 22.2	20 32.2	29 20.0	27 03.5	4 39.3	21 40.0	7 34.1	12 27.4
11 W	11 19 37	18 08 21	12♓24 02	19 12 06	16 04.1	15 00.9	4 19.2	21 11.8	29 17.0	27 14.9	4 45.7	21 40.9	7 36.2	12 28.9
12 Th	11 23 33	19 06 43	26 04 17	3♈00 07	15 52.1	16 54.9	5 15.8	21 51.5	29 14.3	27 26.3	4 52.0	21 41.7	7 38.4	12 30.4
13 F	11 27 30	20 05 06	9♈59 02	17 00 31	15 41.7	18 48.2	6 11.9	22 31.2	29 12.0	27 37.9	4 58.3	21 42.5	7 40.5	12 31.8
14 Sa	11 31 26	21 03 32	24 03 58	1♉08 50	15 33.9	20 40.6	7 07.4	23 11.0	29 10.0	27 49.5	5 04.5	21 43.2	7 42.7	12 33.3
15 Su	11 35 23	22 01 59	8♉14 37	15 20 51	15 28.9	22 32.1	8 02.5	23 50.8	29 08.4	28 01.1	5 10.6	21 43.9	7 44.8	12 34.8
16 M	11 39 19	23 00 29	22 27 08	29 33 08	15 26.5	24 22.7	8 57.1	24 30.7	29 07.1	28 12.8	5 16.7	21 44.5	7 47.0	12 36.2
17 Tu	11 43 16	23 59 01	6♊38 35	13♊43 18	15 25.9	26 12.3	9 51.2	25 10.7	29 06.2	28 24.6	5 22.7	21 45.1	7 49.2	12 37.6
18 W	11 47 12	24 57 35	20 47 08	27 49 59	15 25.9	28 00.9	10 44.7	25 50.7	29 05.7	28 36.5	5 28.7	21 45.6	7 51.3	12 39.0
19 Th	11 51 09	25 56 12	4♋51 44	11♋52 20	15 25.2	29 48.6	11 37.6	26 30.8	29D 05.5	28 48.3	5 34.6	21 46.1	7 53.5	12 40.4
20 F	11 55 06	26 54 51	18 51 39	25 49 37	15 22.6	1♎35.2	12 30.0	27 11.0	29 05.7	29 00.3	5 40.4	21 46.5	7 55.7	12 41.8
21 Sa	11 59 02	27 53 31	2♌46 03	9♌40 47	15 17.4	3 20.8	13 21.7	27 51.2	29 06.2	29 12.3	5 46.2	21 46.9	7 57.9	12 43.1
22 Su	12 02 59	28 52 15	16 33 36	23 24 15	15 09.4	5 05.4	14 12.8	28 31.5	29 07.1	29 24.4	5 51.9	21 47.2	8 00.1	12 44.5
23 M	12 06 55	29 51 00	0♍12 26	6♍57 52	14 59.0	6 49.1	15 03.3	29 11.9	29 08.3	29 36.5	5 57.6	21 47.4	8 02.4	12 45.8
24 Tu	12 10 52	0♎49 47	13 40 14	20 19 14	14 47.0	8 31.7	15 53.0	29 52.3	29 09.9	29 48.6	6 03.1	21 47.7	8 04.6	12 47.1
25 W	12 14 48	1 48 36	26 54 37	3♎26 10	14 34.6	10 13.4	16 42.1	0♏32.8	29 11.8	0♏00.9	6 08.6	21 47.8	8 06.8	12 48.3
26 Th	12 18 45	2 47 27	9♎53 42	16 17 07	14 23.1	11 54.2	17 30.4	1 13.3	29 14.1	0 13.1	6 14.0	21 47.9	8 09.0	12 49.6
27 F	12 22 41	3 46 20	22 36 25	28 51 38	14 13.4	13 34.0	18 17.9	1 53.9	29 16.7	0 25.4	6 19.4	21R48.0	8 11.2	12 50.8
28 Sa	12 26 38	4 45 15	5♏02 54	11♏10 27	14 06.2	15 12.9	19 04.6	2 34.6	29 19.7	0 37.8	6 24.7	21 47.9	8 13.5	12 52.0
29 Su	12 30 35	5 44 12	17 14 36	23 15 41	14 01.7	16 50.9	19 50.5	3 15.3	29 23.0	0 50.2	6 29.9	21 47.9	8 15.7	12 53.2
30 M	12 34 31	6 43 11	29 14 09	5♐10 31	13D 59.6	18 28.1	20 35.5	3 56.1	29 26.7	1 02.6	6 35.0	21 47.8	8 17.9	12 54.4

LONGITUDE

October 1946

Day	Sid.Time	☉	0 hr ☽	Noon ☽	True ☊	☿	♀	♂	⚳	♃	♄	♅	♆	♇
1 Tu	12 38 28	7♎42 12	11♐05 20	16♐59 11	13♊59.2	20♎04.3	21♏19.6	4♏37.0	29♑30.7	1♏15.1	6♌40.0	21♊47.6	8♎20.2	12♌55.6
2 W	12 42 24	8 41 14	22 52 43	28 46 34	13R 59.7	21 39.8	22 02.8	5 17.9	29 35.0	1 27.6	6 45.0	21R47.4	8 22.4	12 56.7
3 Th	12 46 21	9 40 19	4♑41 27	10♑38 02	14 00.0	23 14.4	22 44.9	5 58.9	29 39.6	1 40.2	6 49.9	21 47.2	8 24.6	12 57.8
4 F	12 50 17	10 39 25	16 37 00	22 39 02	13 59.2	24 48.1	23 26.0	6 39.9	29 44.6	1 52.8	6 54.7	21 46.8	8 26.9	12 58.9
5 Sa	12 54 14	11 38 32	28 44 46	4♒54 49	13 56.5	26 21.1	24 06.0	7 21.0	29 49.9	2 05.4	6 59.4	21 46.5	8 29.1	13 00.0
6 Su	12 58 10	12 37 42	11♒09 44	17 30 00	13 51.5	27 53.3	24 44.9	8 02.2	29 55.5	2 18.1	7 04.1	21 46.0	8 31.3	13 01.0
7 M	13 02 07	13 36 53	23 55 59	0♓27 59	13 44.3	29 24.6	25 22.7	8 43.4	0♒01.4	2 30.8	7 08.7	21 45.6	8 33.6	13 02.0
8 Tu	13 06 04	14 36 06	7♓06 09	13 50 31	13 35.4	0♏55.2	25 59.2	9 24.7	0 07.6	2 43.5	7 13.1	21 45.1	8 35.8	13 03.0
9 W	13 10 00	15 35 21	20 40 57	27 37 11	13 25.7	2 25.0	26 34.4	10 06.0	0 14.2	2 56.3	7 17.5	21 44.5	8 38.0	13 04.0
10 Th	13 13 57	16 34 38	4♈38 48	11♈45 13	13 16.2	3 54.0	27 08.4	10 47.4	0 21.0	3 09.1	7 21.8	21 43.9	8 40.2	13 05.0
11 F	13 17 53	17 33 57	18 55 46	26 09 41	13 08.1	5 22.2	27 40.9	11 28.9	0 28.1	3 21.9	7 26.1	21 43.2	8 42.4	13 05.9
12 Sa	13 21 50	18 33 18	3♉26 08	10♉44 14	13 02.0	6 49.6	28 12.1	12 10.4	0 35.5	3 34.7	7 30.2	21 42.5	8 44.7	13 06.8
13 Su	13 25 46	19 32 41	18 03 09	25 22 03	12 58.5	8 16.2	28 41.7	12 52.0	0 43.3	3 47.6	7 34.2	21 41.7	8 46.9	13 07.7
14 M	13 29 43	20 32 07	2♊40 12	9♊56 55	12D 57.2	9 42.0	29 09.8	13 33.6	0 51.3	4 00.5	7 38.2	21 40.9	8 49.1	13 08.5
15 Tu	13 33 39	21 31 35	17 11 39	24 23 57	12 57.5	11 07.0	29 36.4	14 15.3	0 59.5	4 13.4	7 42.1	21 40.0	8 51.3	13 09.4
16 W	13 37 36	22 31 05	1♋33 28	8♋39 57	12 58.6	12 31.1	0♐01.3	14 57.1	1 08.1	4 26.4	7 45.8	21 39.1	8 53.5	13 10.2
17 Th	13 41 33	23 30 38	15 43 13	22 43 11	12R 59.2	13 54.2	0 24.4	15 38.9	1 17.0	4 39.4	7 49.5	21 38.1	8 55.6	13 11.0
18 F	13 45 29	24 30 12	29 39 49	6♌33 06	12 58.5	15 16.5	0 45.9	16 20.8	1 26.1	4 52.4	7 53.1	21 37.1	8 57.8	13 11.7
19 Sa	13 49 26	25 29 49	13♌23 04	20 09 44	12 55.8	16 37.7	1 05.5	17 02.8	1 35.5	5 05.4	7 56.6	21 36.0	9 00.0	13 12.5
20 Su	13 53 22	26 29 29	26 53 10	3♍33 22	12 51.1	17 58.0	1 23.2	17 44.8	1 45.1	5 18.4	8 00.0	21 34.9	9 02.1	13 13.2
21 M	13 57 19	27 29 10	10♍10 22	16 44 11	12 44.5	19 17.1	1 39.0	18 26.9	1 55.1	5 31.4	8 03.3	21 33.8	9 04.3	13 13.9
22 Tu	14 01 15	28 28 54	23 14 49	29 42 15	12 36.7	20 35.0	1 52.7	19 09.0	2 05.2	5 44.5	8 06.5	21 32.5	9 06.4	13 14.5
23 W	14 05 12	29 28 40	6♎06 30	12♎27 32	12 28.6	21 51.6	2 04.4	19 51.3	2 15.7	5 57.6	8 09.6	21 31.3	9 08.5	13 15.2
24 Th	14 09 08	0♏28 28	18 45 24	25 00 06	12 21.1	23 06.9	2 13.9	20 33.5	2 26.4	6 10.7	8 12.6	21 30.0	9 10.7	13 15.8
25 F	14 13 05	1 28 18	1♏11 42	7♏20 17	12 14.8	24 20.7	2 21.3	21 15.9	2 37.4	6 23.8	8 15.5	21 28.6	9 12.8	13 16.3
26 Sa	14 17 01	2 28 09	13 26 00	19 29 01	12 10.3	25 32.9	2 26.4	21 58.3	2 48.6	6 36.9	8 18.3	21 27.2	9 14.9	13 16.9
27 Su	14 20 58	3 28 03	25 29 33	1♐27 52	12D 07.8	26 43.2	2R 29.2	22 40.7	3 00.0	6 50.0	8 21.0	21 25.8	9 17.0	13 17.4
28 M	14 24 55	4 27 59	7♐24 18	13 19 12	12 07.1	27 51.6	2 29.7	23 23.2	3 11.7	7 03.1	8 23.6	21 24.3	9 19.0	13 17.9
29 Tu	14 28 51	5 27 56	19 13 00	25 06 09	12 07.9	28 57.8	2 27.8	24 05.8	3 23.6	7 16.2	8 26.1	21 22.8	9 21.1	13 18.4
30 W	14 32 48	6 27 55	0♑59 10	6♑52 35	12 09.6	0♐01.6	2 23.5	24 48.5	3 35.8	7 29.4	8 28.4	21 21.2	9 23.1	13 18.8
31 Th	14 36 44	7 27 56	12 46 58	18 42 57	12 11.3	1 02.7	2 16.7	25 31.2	3 48.2	7 42.5	8 30.7	21 19.6	9 25.2	13 19.2

Astro Data

	Dy Hr Mn
☽0N	13 1:01
⚳D	19 12:19
☿0S	21 1:13
☉0S	23 15:41
☽0S	26 1:09
♅R	27 22:01
♄∠♅	2 23:10
☽0N	10 9:55
☽0S	23 8:24
♃□♅	25 20:05
♀R	28 4:52

Planet Ingress

		Dy Hr Mn
⚳	♑R	2 1:27
☿	♍	3 16:29
♀	♏	7 0:16
☿	♎	19 14:34
☉	♎	23 15:41
♂	♏	24 16:35
♃	♏	25 10:19
⚳	♒	7 6:26
☿	♏	7 21:21
♀	♐	16 10:45
☉	♏	24 0:35
☿	♐	30 11:23

Last Aspect / ☽ Ingress (September)

Last Aspect Dy Hr Mn			☽ Ingress	Dy Hr Mn
2 13:10	☿	□	♐	2 17:31
5 2:37	♀	⚹	♑	5 6:24
7 10:54	♃	□	♒	7 17:41
9 20:11	♃	△	♓	10 1:46
11 16:21	♅	□	♈	12 6:49
14 6:18	♃	☍	♉	14 10:03
16 1:57	☿	△	♊	16 12:45
18 13:20	♃	△	♋	18 15:42
20 17:34	♃	□	♌	20 19:13
22 22:45	♃	⚹	♍	22 23:38
24 14:40	♅	□	♎	25 5:40
26 22:28	♅	△	♏	27 14:12
29 4:43	♀	☌	♐	30 1:32

Last Aspect / ☽ Ingress (October)

Last Aspect Dy Hr Mn			☽ Ingress	Dy Hr Mn
1 21:47	♅	☍	♑	2 14:29
4 16:52	☿	□	♒	5 2:27
7 9:49	☿	△	♓	7 11:09
9 10:07	♀	△	♈	9 16:05
11 4:39	♅	⚹	♉	11 18:20
13 17:39	♀	☍	♊	13 19:37
15 7:27	♅	☌	♋	15 21:23
17 13:28	☉	□	♌	18 0:35
19 22:16	☉	⚹	♍	20 5:35
21 20:52	♅	□	♎	22 12:33
24 5:16	♅	△	♏	24 21:41
27 1:26	☿	☌	♐	27 9:03
29 4:26	♅	☍	♑	29 21:59

☽ Phases & Eclipses

Dy Hr Mn		
3 14:49	☽	10♐29
11 9:59	○	18♓03
18 6:44	☾	24♊45
25 8:45	●	1♎41
3 9:53	☽	9♑35
10 20:40	○	16♈56
17 13:28	☾	23♋34
24 23:32	●	0♏57

Astro Data

1 September 1946
Julian Day # 17045
SVP 6♓00'32"
GC 26♐05.7 ⚴ 28♐17.1
Eris 6♈24.7R ⚵ 29♎17.6
⚷ 20♎21.4 ⚶ 4♈21.7R
☽ Mean ☊ 16♊34.8

1 October 1946
Julian Day # 17075
SVP 6♓00'29"
GC 26♐05.7 ⚴ 2♑25.3
Eris 6♈06.3R ⚵ 8♏23.9
⚷ 24♎19.5 ⚶ 27♓09.3R
☽ Mean ☊ 14♊59.4

November 1946 — LONGITUDE

Day	Sid.Time	☉	0 hr ☽	Noon☽	True☊	☿	♀	♂	⚳	♃	♄	♅	♆	♇
1 F	14 40 41	8♏27 58	24♑41 08	0♒42 10	12♊12.6	2♐00.9	2♐07.5	26♏13.9	4♒00.8	7♏55.7	8♌32.9	21♊18.0	9♎27.2	13♌19.6
2 Sa	14 44 37	9 28 02	6♒46 41	12 55 18	12R 12.9	2 55.7	1R 55.9	26 56.7	4 13.6	8 08.8	8 35.0	21R 16.3	9 29.2	13 20.0
3 Su	14 48 34	10 28 08	19 08 39	25 27 17	12 11.7	3 46.7	1 41.8	27 39.6	4 26.7	8 21.9	8 36.9	21 14.6	9 31.2	13 20.3
4 M	14 52 31	11 28 15	1♓51 44	8♓22 25	12 09.2	4 33.7	1 25.3	28 22.5	4 40.0	8 35.1	8 38.8	21 12.8	9 33.1	13 20.6
5 Tu	14 56 27	12 28 23	14 59 40	21 43 44	12 05.6	5 16.0	1 06.5	29 05.5	4 53.5	8 48.2	8 40.5	21 11.0	9 35.1	13 20.9
6 W	15 00 24	13 28 34	28 34 41	5♈32 28	12 01.3	5 53.1	0 45.4	29 48.6	5 07.2	9 01.3	8 42.1	21 09.2	9 37.0	13 21.2
7 Th	15 04 20	14 28 45	12♈36 51	19 47 25	11 57.0	6 24.5	0 22.1	0♐31.7	5 21.1	9 14.4	8 43.7	21 07.3	9 38.9	13 21.4
8 F	15 08 17	15 28 59	27 03 36	4♉24 39	11 53.3	6 49.4	29♏56.6	1 14.8	5 35.2	9 27.6	8 45.1	21 05.4	9 40.8	13 21.6
9 Sa	15 12 13	16 29 14	11♉49 41	19 17 43	11 50.7	7 07.4	29 29.2	1 58.0	5 49.5	9 40.7	8 46.4	21 03.4	9 42.7	13 21.7
10 Su	15 16 10	17 29 31	26 47 41	4♊18 28	11D 49.4	7R 17.5	29 00.0	2 41.3	6 04.0	9 53.8	8 47.6	21 01.5	9 44.6	13 21.9
11 M	15 20 06	18 29 49	11♊49 00	19 18 13	11 49.4	7 19.2	28 29.2	3 24.6	6 18.7	10 06.8	8 48.7	20 59.5	9 46.4	13 22.0
12 Tu	15 24 03	19 30 10	26 45 09	4♋09 00	11 50.3	7 11.8	27 56.8	4 08.0	6 33.5	10 19.9	8 49.6	20 57.4	9 48.3	13 22.1
13 W	15 28 00	20 30 33	11♋29 01	18 44 38	11 51.7	6 54.8	27 23.2	4 51.5	6 48.6	10 33.0	8 50.5	20 55.3	9 50.1	13 22.1
14 Th	15 31 56	21 30 57	25 55 25	3♌01 06	11 53.0	6 27.6	26 48.6	5 35.0	7 03.9	10 46.0	8 51.3	20 53.2	9 51.9	13R 22.2
15 F	15 35 53	22 31 24	10♌01 29	16 56 33	11R 53.8	5 50.2	26 13.1	6 18.6	7 19.3	10 59.1	8 51.9	20 51.1	9 53.6	13 22.2
16 Sa	15 39 49	23 31 52	23 46 20	0♍30 56	11 53.7	5 02.6	25 37.1	7 02.2	7 34.9	11 12.1	8 52.4	20 48.9	9 55.4	13 22.1
17 Su	15 43 46	24 32 22	7♍10 34	13 45 25	11 52.8	4 05.3	25 00.7	7 45.9	7 50.7	11 25.1	8 52.8	20 46.7	9 57.1	13 22.1
18 M	15 47 42	25 32 54	20 15 47	26 41 54	11 51.1	2 59.3	24 24.3	8 29.7	8 06.6	11 38.0	8 53.1	20 44.5	9 58.8	13 22.0
19 Tu	15 51 39	26 33 27	3♎04 03	9♎22 33	11 48.9	1 46.2	23 48.0	9 13.5	8 22.8	11 51.0	8 53.3	20 42.3	10 00.5	13 21.9
20 W	15 55 35	27 34 02	15 37 38	21 49 34	11 46.6	0 27.8	23 12.2	9 57.3	8 39.1	12 03.9	8R 53.4	20 40.0	10 02.1	13 21.7
21 Th	15 59 32	28 34 39	27 58 38	4♏05 04	11 44.5	29♏06.5	22 37.0	10 41.2	8 55.5	12 16.8	8 53.4	20 37.7	10 03.8	13 21.6
22 F	16 03 29	29 35 18	10♏09 05	16 10 57	11 42.9	27 45.1	22 02.7	11 25.2	9 12.2	12 29.7	8 53.2	20 35.4	10 05.4	13 21.4
23 Sa	16 07 25	0♐35 58	22 10 51	28 09 02	11 41.9	26 26.2	21 29.5	12 09.3	9 29.0	12 42.6	8 52.9	20 33.0	10 07.0	13 21.2
24 Su	16 11 22	1 36 40	4♐05 45	10♐01 13	11D 41.5	25 12.4	20 57.7	12 53.4	9 45.9	12 55.4	8 52.6	20 30.6	10 08.5	13 20.9
25 M	16 15 18	2 37 23	15 55 42	21 49 29	11 41.7	24 06.1	20 27.3	13 37.5	10 03.0	13 08.2	8 52.1	20 28.3	10 10.1	13 20.6
26 Tu	16 19 15	3 38 07	27 42 51	3♑36 09	11 42.3	23 08.9	19 58.7	14 21.7	10 20.3	13 21.0	8 51.5	20 25.9	10 11.6	13 20.3
27 W	16 23 11	4 38 52	9♑29 42	15 23 55	11 43.1	22 22.4	19 31.9	15 06.0	10 37.7	13 33.7	8 50.7	20 23.4	10 13.1	13 20.0
28 Th	16 27 08	5 39 39	21 19 12	27 15 58	11 43.8	21 47.1	19 07.1	15 50.3	10 55.3	13 46.4	8 49.9	20 21.0	10 14.5	13 19.6
29 F	16 31 04	6 40 26	3♒14 44	9♒15 57	11 44.5	21 23.5	18 44.4	16 34.7	11 13.0	13 59.1	8 49.0	20 18.5	10 15.9	13 19.2
30 Sa	16 35 01	7 41 15	15 20 09	21 27 53	11 44.9	21D 11.3	18 23.9	17 19.1	11 30.8	14 11.7	8 47.9	20 16.1	10 17.4	13 18.8

December 1946 — LONGITUDE

Day	Sid.Time	☉	0 hr ☽	Noon☽	True☊	☿	♀	♂	⚳	♃	♄	♅	♆	♇
1 Su	16 38 58	8♐42 04	27♒39 39	3♓56 00	11♊45.0	21♏10.2	18♏05.8	18♐03.6	11♒48.8	14♏24.3	8♌46.8	20♊13.6	10♎18.7	13♌18.4
2 M	16 42 54	9 42 54	10♓17 28	16 44 31	11R 45.0	21 19.4	17R 50.0	18 48.1	12 07.0	14 36.8	8R 45.5	20R 11.1	10 20.1	13R 17.9
3 Tu	16 46 51	10 43 45	23 17 37	29 57 07	11D 44.9	21 38.2	17 36.6	19 32.7	12 25.2	14 49.3	8 44.1	20 08.6	10 21.4	13 17.4
4 W	16 50 47	11 44 37	6♈43 19	13♈36 23	11 44.9	22 05.7	17 25.7	20 17.3	12 43.6	15 01.7	8 42.6	20 06.1	10 22.7	13 16.9
5 Th	16 54 44	12 45 30	20 36 23	27 43 12	11 44.9	22 41.0	17 17.3	21 02.0	13 02.1	15 14.1	8 41.0	20 03.5	10 23.9	13 16.4
6 F	16 58 40	13 46 23	4♉56 35	12♉16 03	11 45.1	23 23.3	17 11.4	21 46.7	13 20.8	15 26.5	8 39.3	20 01.0	10 25.2	13 15.8
7 Sa	17 02 37	14 47 18	19 40 59	27 10 34	11R 45.3	24 11.9	17D 07.9	22 31.5	13 39.5	15 38.8	8 37.5	19 58.4	10 26.4	13 15.2
8 Su	17 06 33	15 48 13	4♊43 51	12♊19 42	11 45.4	25 05.9	17 06.9	23 16.3	13 58.4	15 51.1	8 35.6	19 55.9	10 27.6	13 14.6
9 M	17 10 30	16 49 10	19 56 56	27 34 17	11 45.2	26 04.6	17 08.4	24 01.2	14 17.4	16 03.3	8 33.6	19 53.4	10 28.7	13 13.9
10 Tu	17 14 27	17 50 07	5♋10 31	12♋44 25	11 44.8	27 07.6	17 12.3	24 46.1	14 36.6	16 15.5	8 31.5	19 50.8	10 29.8	13 13.3
11 W	17 18 23	18 51 05	20 14 51	27 40 51	11 44.1	28 14.2	17 18.6	25 31.1	14 55.8	16 27.6	8 29.2	19 48.3	10 30.9	13 12.6
12 Th	17 22 20	19 52 05	5♌01 35	12♌16 24	11 43.2	29 23.9	17 27.1	26 16.1	15 15.2	16 39.7	8 26.9	19 45.7	10 32.0	13 11.9
13 F	17 26 16	20 53 05	19 24 51	26 26 36	11 42.2	0♐36.4	17 38.0	27 01.2	15 34.6	16 51.7	8 24.5	19 43.1	10 33.0	13 11.1
14 Sa	17 30 13	21 54 06	3♍21 35	10♍09 49	11D 41.6	1 51.4	17 51.1	27 46.3	15 54.2	17 03.6	8 22.0	19 40.6	10 34.0	13 10.4
15 Su	17 34 09	22 55 09	16 51 27	23 26 46	11 41.3	3 08.3	18 06.3	28 31.5	16 13.9	17 15.5	8 19.3	19 38.0	10 35.0	13 09.6
16 M	17 38 06	23 56 12	29 56 08	6♎19 58	11 41.6	4 27.1	18 23.6	29 16.7	16 33.7	17 27.3	8 16.6	19 35.5	10 35.9	13 08.8
17 Tu	17 42 02	24 57 16	12♎38 43	18 52 53	11 42.5	5 47.5	18 42.9	0♑02.0	16 53.6	17 39.1	8 13.8	19 32.9	10 36.8	13 07.9
18 W	17 45 59	25 58 21	25 02 59	1♏09 30	11 43.8	7 09.3	19 04.2	0 47.4	17 13.6	17 50.8	8 10.9	19 30.4	10 37.7	13 07.1
19 Th	17 49 56	26 59 27	7♏12 56	13 13 45	11 45.2	8 32.2	19 27.4	1 32.7	17 33.8	18 02.4	8 07.9	19 27.8	10 38.5	13 06.2
20 F	17 53 52	28 00 34	19 12 24	25 09 19	11 46.4	9 56.3	19 52.4	2 18.2	17 54.0	18 14.0	8 04.8	19 25.3	10 39.3	13 05.3
21 Sa	17 57 49	29 01 42	1♐04 52	6♐59 27	11R 47.2	11 21.2	20 19.1	3 03.7	18 14.3	18 25.5	8 01.6	19 22.8	10 40.1	13 04.4
22 Su	18 01 45	0♑02 50	12 53 23	18 46 59	11 47.1	12 47.0	20 47.6	3 49.2	18 34.7	18 36.9	7 58.3	19 20.3	10 40.8	13 03.4
23 M	18 05 42	1 03 58	24 40 32	0♑34 19	11 45.9	14 13.5	21 17.6	4 34.8	18 55.2	18 48.3	7 55.0	19 17.8	10 41.5	13 02.5
24 Tu	18 09 38	2 05 07	6♑28 34	12 23 33	11 43.7	15 40.7	21 49.2	5 20.4	19 15.8	18 59.5	7 51.5	19 15.3	10 42.2	13 01.5
25 W	18 13 35	3 06 17	18 19 29	24 16 38	11 40.6	17 08.5	22 22.4	6 06.0	19 36.5	19 10.8	7 48.0	19 12.8	10 42.8	13 00.5
26 Th	18 17 32	4 07 26	0♒15 14	6♒15 32	11 36.7	18 36.8	22 56.9	6 51.7	19 57.3	19 21.9	7 44.4	19 10.4	10 43.4	12 59.4
27 F	18 21 28	5 08 36	12 17 49	18 22 22	11 32.6	20 05.6	23 32.9	7 37.5	20 18.1	19 32.9	7 40.7	19 07.9	10 44.0	12 58.4
28 Sa	18 25 25	6 09 46	24 29 30	0♓39 33	11 28.8	21 34.9	24 10.2	8 23.3	20 39.1	19 43.9	7 36.9	19 05.5	10 44.5	12 57.3
29 Su	18 29 21	7 10 55	6♓52 52	13 09 49	11 25.7	23 04.6	24 48.7	9 09.1	21 00.1	19 54.8	7 33.1	19 03.1	10 45.0	12 56.3
30 M	18 33 18	8 12 05	19 30 47	25 56 10	11 23.8	24 34.7	25 28.5	9 55.0	21 21.3	20 05.6	7 29.2	19 00.7	10 45.5	12 55.2
31 Tu	18 37 14	9 13 14	2♈26 21	9♈01 42	11D 23.1	26 05.2	26 09.5	10 40.9	21 42.4	20 16.3	7 25.2	18 58.4	10 45.9	12 54.0

Astro Data	Dy Hr Mn
♃□♄	4 19:48
☽0N	6 20:43
♃⚺♆	9 16:25
☿R	11 4:42
♇R	15 0:40
☽0S	19 14:36
♄R	20 15:21
♃□♇	26 10:49
☿D	1 2:31
☽0N	4 7:06
♀D	8 9:32
☽0S	16 20:24
♃⚻♅	25 15:40
☽0N	31 14:53

Planet Ingress	Dy Hr Mn
♂ ♐	6 18:22
♀ ♏R	8 8:56
☿ ♏R	20 20:16
☉ ♐	22 21:46
☿ ♐	13 0:03
♂ ♑	17 10:56
☉ ♑	22 10:53

Last Aspect Dy Hr Mn		☽ Ingress Dy Hr Mn
1 2:32	♂ ⚹	♒ 1 10:36
3 16:24	♂ □	♓ 3 20:32
6 1:36	♂ △	♈ 6 2:28
7 14:12	♅ ⚹	♉ 8 4:49
10 3:48	♀ ☍	♊ 10 5:07
11 14:42	♅ ☌	♋ 12 5:15
14 1:54	♀ △	♌ 14 6:53
16 3:39	♀ □	♍ 16 11:05
18 9:40	☉ ⚹	♎ 18 18:12
20 9:45	♅ △	♏ 21 3:58
23 8:53	☿ ☌	♐ 23 15:44
25 9:15	♅ ☍	♑ 26 4:40
28 1:25	☿ ⚹	♒ 28 17:30

Last Aspect Dy Hr Mn		☽ Ingress Dy Hr Mn
30 11:28	☿ □	♓ 1 4:30
2 20:35	☿ △	♈ 3 12:05
5 0:06	♂ △	♉ 5 15:48
7 6:57	☿ ☍	♊ 7 16:30
9 6:07	♂ ☍	♋ 9 15:50
11 12:59	☿ △	♌ 11 15:46
13 13:03	♂ △	♍ 13 18:09
15 21:57	♂ □	♎ 16 0:07
18 0:53	☉ ⚹	♏ 18 9:43
20 0:57	♀ ☌	♐ 20 21:48
22 13:08	♅ ☍	♑ 23 10:50
25 7:59	♀ ⚹	♒ 25 23:29
27 22:41	♀ □	♓ 28 10:43
30 11:06	♀ △	♈ 30 19:31

☽ Phases & Eclipses Dy Hr Mn	
2 4:40	☽ 9♒10
9 7:10	○ 16♉17
15 22:35	☾ 22♌58
23 17:24	● 0♐50
23 17:36:47	● P 0.776
1 21:48	☽ 9♓07
8 17:52	○ 16♊03
8 17:48	● T 1.164
15 10:57	☾ 22♍52
23 13:06	● 1♑07
31 12:23	☽ 9♈14

Astro Data

1 November 1946
Julian Day # 17106
SVP 6♓00'25"
GC 26♐05.8 ⚵ 10♑05.1
Eris 5♈47.7R ⚶ 18♏38.9
⚷ 28♎45.5 ⚴ 22♓22.9R
☽ Mean ☊ 13♊20.9

1 December 1946
Julian Day # 17136
SVP 6♓00'21"
GC 26♐05.9 ⚵ 19♑22.1
Eris 5♈35.3R ⚶ 28♏51.6
⚷ 2♏50.5 ⚴ 24♓17.7
☽ Mean ☊ 11♊45.6

LONGITUDE — January 1947

Day	Sid.Time	☉	0 hr ☽	Noon ☽	True ☊	☿	♀	♂	⚳	♃	♄	♅	♆	♇
1 W	18 41 11	10♑14 23	15♈42 33	22♈29 14	11♊23.6	27♐36.2	26♏51.7	11♑26.8	22♒03.7	20♏26.9	7♌21.1	18♊56.0	10♎46.3	12♌52.9
2 Th	18 45 07	11 15 32	29 21 56	6♉20 48	11 25.0	29 07.4	27 34.9	12 12.8	22 25.1	20 37.4	7R17.0	18R53.7	10 46.7	12R51.8
3 F	18 49 04	12 16 41	13♉25 52	20 37 01	11 26.6	0♑39.1	28 19.2	12 58.8	22 46.5	20 47.9	7 12.9	18 51.4	10 47.0	12 50.6
4 Sa	18 53 01	13 17 50	27 53 59	5♊16 20	11R27.7	2 11.2	29 04.4	13 44.9	23 08.0	20 58.2	7 08.6	18 49.1	10 47.3	12 49.4
5 Su	18 56 57	14 18 58	12♊43 26	20 14 30	11 27.5	3 43.6	29 50.7	14 31.0	23 29.6	21 08.5	7 04.3	18 46.9	10 47.5	12 48.2
6 M	19 00 54	15 20 06	27 48 34	5♋24 31	11 25.7	5 16.4	0♐37.9	15 17.1	23 51.2	21 18.7	7 00.0	18 44.7	10 47.8	12 47.0
7 Tu	19 04 50	16 21 14	13♋01 09	20 37 10	11 22.2	6 49.6	1 26.1	16 03.3	24 12.9	21 28.7	6 55.6	18 42.5	10 48.0	12 45.8
8 W	19 08 47	17 22 22	28 11 16	5♌42 15	11 17.2	8 23.2	2 15.1	16 49.5	24 34.7	21 38.7	6 51.1	18 40.3	10 48.1	12 44.6
9 Th	19 12 43	18 23 30	13♌08 56	20 30 20	11 11.3	9 57.2	3 04.9	17 35.8	24 56.5	21 48.6	6 46.6	18 38.2	10 48.3	12 43.3
10 F	19 16 40	19 24 37	27 45 37	4♍54 11	11 05.5	11 31.6	3 55.6	18 22.1	25 18.4	21 58.3	6 42.1	18 36.1	10 48.3	12 42.1
11 Sa	19 20 36	20 25 45	11♍55 36	18 49 39	11 00.4	13 06.4	4 47.0	19 08.4	25 40.4	22 08.0	6 37.5	18 34.0	10 48.4	12 40.8
12 Su	19 24 33	21 26 52	25 36 19	2♎15 45	10 56.8	14 41.7	5 39.2	19 54.8	26 02.4	22 17.5	6 32.8	18 32.0	10R48.4	12 39.5
13 M	19 28 30	22 28 00	8♎48 13	15 14 08	10D54.9	16 17.5	6 32.0	20 41.2	26 24.5	22 27.0	6 28.2	18 30.0	10 48.4	12 38.2
14 Tu	19 32 26	23 29 07	21 34 01	27 48 25	10 54.7	17 53.7	7 25.6	21 27.6	26 46.6	22 36.3	6 23.4	18 28.0	10 48.3	12 36.9
15 W	19 36 23	24 30 14	3♏57 56	10♏03 13	10 55.7	19 30.5	8 19.8	22 14.1	27 08.8	22 45.6	6 18.7	18 26.0	10 48.3	12 35.6
16 Th	19 40 19	25 31 21	16 04 56	22 03 42	10 57.3	21 07.7	9 14.7	23 00.6	27 31.1	22 54.7	6 13.9	18 24.1	10 48.1	12 34.2
17 F	19 44 16	26 32 27	28 00 09	3♐54 53	10R58.5	22 45.5	10 10.2	23 47.1	27 53.4	23 03.7	6 09.1	18 22.3	10 48.0	12 32.9
18 Sa	19 48 12	27 33 34	9♐48 29	15 41 29	10 58.7	24 23.7	11 06.2	24 33.7	28 15.8	23 12.6	6 04.3	18 20.4	10 47.8	12 31.5
19 Su	19 52 09	28 34 40	21 34 21	27 27 34	10 57.0	26 02.6	12 02.9	25 20.3	28 38.2	23 21.3	5 59.4	18 18.6	10 47.6	12 30.2
20 M	19 56 05	29 35 45	3♑21 30	9♑16 31	10 53.0	27 42.0	13 00.0	26 06.9	29 00.7	23 30.0	5 54.6	18 16.9	10 47.3	12 28.8
21 Tu	20 00 02	0♒36 50	15 12 55	21 10 58	10 46.6	29 22.0	13 57.7	26 53.6	29 23.2	23 38.5	5 49.7	18 15.2	10 47.0	12 27.5
22 W	20 03 59	1 37 55	27 10 52	3♒12 49	10 38.1	1♒02.5	14 55.9	27 40.3	29 45.8	23 46.9	5 44.8	18 13.5	10 46.7	12 26.1
23 Th	20 07 55	2 38 58	9♒16 58	15 23 26	10 28.0	2 43.6	15 54.5	28 27.0	0♓08.4	23 55.2	5 39.9	18 11.9	10 46.4	12 24.7
24 F	20 11 52	3 40 01	21 32 19	27 43 44	10 17.4	4 25.4	16 53.6	29 13.7	0 31.1	24 03.4	5 34.9	18 10.3	10 46.0	12 23.3
25 Sa	20 15 48	4 41 03	3♓57 45	10♓14 29	10 07.2	6 07.7	17 53.1	0♒00.5	0 53.8	24 11.4	5 30.0	18 08.7	10 45.6	12 21.9
26 Su	20 19 45	5 42 03	16 34 02	22 56 32	9 58.4	7 50.6	18 53.1	0 47.3	1 16.6	24 19.3	5 25.1	18 07.2	10 45.1	12 20.5
27 M	20 23 41	6 43 03	29 22 07	5♈51 00	9 51.7	9 34.1	19 53.5	1 34.1	1 39.4	24 27.0	5 20.1	18 05.8	10 44.6	12 19.1
28 Tu	20 27 38	7 44 01	12♈23 20	18 59 21	9 47.5	11 18.2	20 54.2	2 21.0	2 02.2	24 34.6	5 15.2	18 04.4	10 44.1	12 17.7
29 W	20 31 34	8 44 59	25 39 16	2♉23 20	9D45.7	13 02.8	21 55.4	3 07.8	2 25.1	24 42.1	5 10.3	18 03.0	10 43.5	12 16.3
30 Th	20 35 31	9 45 55	9♉11 45	16 04 42	9 45.7	14 48.0	22 56.9	3 54.7	2 48.0	24 49.5	5 05.4	18 01.7	10 43.0	12 14.9
31 F	20 39 28	10 46 50	23 02 21	0♊04 45	9R46.4	16 33.6	23 58.8	4 41.6	3 11.0	24 56.7	5 00.5	18 00.4	10 42.4	12 13.5

LONGITUDE — February 1947

Day	Sid.Time	☉	0 hr ☽	Noon ☽	True ☊	☿	♀	♂	⚳	♃	♄	♅	♆	♇
1 Sa	20 43 24	11♒47 43	7♊11 52	14♊23 36	9♊46.6	18♒19.7	25♐01.0	5♒28.6	3♓34.0	25♏03.7	4♌55.6	17♊59.2	10♎41.7	12♌12.1
2 Su	20 47 21	12 48 36	21 39 38	28 59 35	9R45.1	20 06.1	26 03.5	6 15.5	3 57.0	25 10.7	4R50.8	17R58.0	10R41.0	12R10.7
3 M	20 51 17	13 49 27	6♋22 52	13♋48 43	9 41.1	21 52.8	27 06.4	7 02.5	4 20.1	25 17.4	4 45.9	17 56.8	10 40.3	12 09.3
4 Tu	20 55 14	14 50 16	21 16 15	28 44 28	9 34.4	23 39.7	28 09.6	7 49.5	4 43.2	25 24.1	4 41.1	17 55.8	10 39.6	12 07.9
5 W	20 59 10	15 51 05	6♌12 16	13♌38 30	9 25.3	25 26.7	29 13.0	8 36.5	5 06.3	25 30.6	4 36.3	17 54.7	10 38.8	12 06.5
6 Th	21 03 07	16 51 52	21 02 03	28 21 50	9 14.6	27 13.5	0♑16.8	9 23.5	5 29.4	25 36.9	4 31.6	17 53.7	10 38.0	12 05.1
7 F	21 07 03	17 52 37	5♍36 52	12♍46 19	9 03.6	29 00.1	1 20.9	10 10.6	5 52.6	25 43.1	4 26.8	17 52.8	10 37.2	12 03.6
8 Sa	21 11 00	18 53 22	19 49 34	26 46 07	8 53.4	0♓46.2	2 25.2	10 57.6	6 15.8	25 49.1	4 22.1	17 51.9	10 36.4	12 02.2
9 Su	21 14 57	19 54 06	3♎35 42	10♎18 14	8 45.2	2 31.6	3 29.8	11 44.7	6 39.1	25 55.0	4 17.5	17 51.1	10 35.5	12 00.8
10 M	21 18 53	20 54 48	16 53 49	23 22 42	8 39.5	4 16.0	4 34.7	12 31.8	7 02.3	26 00.8	4 12.9	17 50.3	10 34.6	11 59.4
11 Tu	21 22 50	21 55 30	29 45 13	6♏01 54	8 36.3	5 59.0	5 39.8	13 18.9	7 25.6	26 06.3	4 08.3	17 49.5	10 33.6	11 58.1
12 W	21 26 46	22 56 10	12♏13 16	18 20 00	8D35.1	7 40.2	6 45.1	14 06.0	7 48.9	26 11.8	4 03.7	17 48.8	10 32.7	11 56.7
13 Th	21 30 43	23 56 50	24 22 43	0♐22 09	8R35.1	9 19.2	7 50.7	14 53.2	8 12.3	26 17.0	3 59.2	17 48.2	10 31.7	11 55.3
14 F	21 34 39	24 57 28	6♐18 59	12 13 56	8 35.2	10 55.6	8 56.5	15 40.3	8 35.6	26 22.1	3 54.8	17 47.6	10 30.7	11 53.9
15 Sa	21 38 36	25 58 05	18 07 40	24 00 53	8 34.2	12 28.8	10 02.5	16 27.5	8 59.0	26 27.0	3 50.4	17 47.1	10 29.6	11 52.6
16 Su	21 42 32	26 58 41	29 54 10	5♑48 07	8 31.2	13 58.1	11 08.7	17 14.7	9 22.4	26 31.8	3 46.1	17 46.6	10 28.5	11 51.2
17 M	21 46 29	27 59 15	11♑43 17	17 40 09	8 25.4	15 23.1	12 15.1	18 01.9	9 45.8	26 36.4	3 41.8	17 46.2	10 27.5	11 49.8
18 Tu	21 50 26	28 59 49	23 39 07	29 40 35	8 16.7	16 42.9	13 21.7	18 49.1	10 09.3	26 40.8	3 37.6	17 45.8	10 26.3	11 48.5
19 W	21 54 22	0♓00 20	5♒44 48	11♒52 02	8 05.4	17 57.0	14 28.5	19 36.3	10 32.7	26 45.1	3 33.4	17 45.5	10 25.2	11 47.2
20 Th	21 58 19	1 00 51	18 02 25	24 16 03	7 52.1	19 04.7	15 35.5	20 23.6	10 56.2	26 49.2	3 29.3	17 45.2	10 24.0	11 45.8
21 F	22 02 15	2 01 19	0♓32 59	6♓53 12	7 37.9	20 05.3	16 42.6	21 10.8	11 19.7	26 53.1	3 25.3	17 45.0	10 22.8	11 44.5
22 Sa	22 06 12	3 01 46	13 16 38	19 43 11	7 24.2	20 58.1	17 49.9	21 58.0	11 43.2	26 56.8	3 21.4	17 44.8	10 21.6	11 43.2
23 Su	22 10 08	4 02 11	26 12 45	2♈45 14	7 12.1	21 42.6	18 57.4	22 45.3	12 06.8	27 00.4	3 17.5	17 44.7	10 20.4	11 41.9
24 M	22 14 05	5 02 35	9♈20 29	15 58 24	7 02.6	22 18.3	20 05.0	23 32.5	12 30.3	27 03.8	3 13.6	17D44.7	10 19.1	11 40.6
25 Tu	22 18 01	6 02 56	22 38 56	29 22 01	6 56.2	22 44.7	21 12.8	24 19.8	12 53.8	27 07.0	3 09.9	17 44.7	10 17.8	11 39.4
26 W	22 21 58	7 03 16	6♉07 38	12♉55 48	6 52.7	23 01.5	22 20.7	25 07.1	13 17.4	27 10.0	3 06.2	17 44.7	10 16.5	11 38.1
27 Th	22 25 55	8 03 34	19 46 33	26 39 57	6 51.5	23R08.7	23 28.7	25 54.3	13 40.9	27 12.9	3 02.7	17 44.8	10 15.2	11 36.9
28 F	22 29 51	9 03 49	3♊36 03	10♊34 53	6 51.4	23 06.1	24 36.9	26 41.6	14 04.5	27 15.6	2 59.2	17 45.0	10 13.9	11 35.6

Astro Data

	Dy Hr Mn
♆R	12 12:25
☽0S	13 3:08
☽0N	27 20:02
♃∠♆	6 15:50
☽0S	9 11:31
☽0N	24 0:49
♅D	25 0:29
☿R	27 17:36
☿0N	28 10:07

Planet Ingress

		Dy Hr Mn
☿	♑	3 1:46
♀	♐	5 16:45
☉	♒	20 21:32
☿	♒	21 21:06
⚳	♓	23 3:04
♂	♒	25 11:44
♀	♑	6 5:41
☿	♓	8 1:31
☉	♓	19 11:52

Last Aspect / ☽ Ingress

Last Aspect Dy Hr Mn			☽ Ingress	Dy Hr Mn
1 22:03	☿	△	♉	2 1:06
4 1:22	♀	☍	♊	4 3:26
5 9:41	♅	☌	♋	6 3:28
7 13:22	♃	△	♌	8 2:53
9 14:10	♃	□	♍	10 3:45
11 17:54	♃	✶	♎	12 7:54
14 2:56	☉	□	♏	14 16:15
16 19:38	☉	✶	♐	17 4:03
18 17:24	♅	☍	♑	19 17:10
22 0:13	♂	☌	♒	22 5:37
24 4:49	♃	□	♓	24 16:23
26 14:37	♃	△	♈	27 1:10
28 15:45	♀	△	♉	29 7:45
31 3:11	♃	☍	♊	31 11:52

Last Aspect / ☽ Ingress

Last Aspect Dy Hr Mn			☽ Ingress	Dy Hr Mn
2 6:50	♀	☍	♋	2 13:38
4 6:36	♃	△	♌	4 14:01
6 9:52	☿	☍	♍	6 14:42
8 10:20	♃	✶	♎	8 17:39
10 7:01	☉	△	♏	11 0:28
13 3:45	♃	☌	♐	13 11:15
15 16:21	☉	✶	♑	16 0:12
18 6:00	♃	✶	♒	18 12:39
20 16:55	♃	□	♓	20 22:57
23 1:25	♃	△	♈	23 6:58
25 2:27	♂	✶	♉	25 13:08
27 12:57	♃	☍	♊	27 17:47

☽ Phases & Eclipses

Dy Hr Mn		
7 4:47	○	16♋03
14 2:56	☾	23♎06
22 8:34	●	1♒29
30 0:07	☽	9♉16
5 15:50	○	16♌01
12 21:58	☾	23♏21
21 2:00	●	1♓36
28 9:12	☽	8♊57

Astro Data

1 January 1947
Julian Day # 17167
SVP 6♓00'15"
GC 26♐05.9 ⚴ 29♑55.7
Eris 5♈32.5 ⚵ 9♐11.3
⚷ 6♏15.8 ⚶ 1♈38.3
☽ Mean ☊ 10♊07.2

1 February 1947
Julian Day # 17198
SVP 6♓00'10"
GC 26♐06.0 ⚴ 10♒47.0
Eris 5♈40.9 ⚵ 18♐39.4
⚷ 8♏18.2 ⚶ 12♈13.5
☽ Mean ☊ 8♊28.7

March 1947 LONGITUDE

Day	Sid.Time	☉	0 hr ☽	Noon ☽	True ☊	☿	♀	♂	⚳	♃	♄	♅	♆	♇
1 Sa	22 33 48	10♓04 03	17♊36 29	24♊40 49	6♊51.0	22♓53.9	25♑45.2	27♒28.8	14♓28.1	27♏18.1	2♌55.7	17♊45.2	10♎12.5	11♌34.4
2 Su	22 37 44	11 04 15	1♋47 46	8♋57 08	6R 49.0	22R 32.6	26 53.6	28 16.1	14 51.7	27 20.4	2R 52.4	17 45.5	10R 11.1	11R 33.2
3 M	22 41 41	12 04 24	16 08 38	23 21 52	6 44.6	22 02.7	28 02.2	29 03.4	15 15.3	27 22.5	2 49.1	17 45.8	10 09.7	11 32.0
4 Tu	22 45 37	13 04 32	0♌36 17	7♌51 18	6 37.2	21 25.0	29 10.9	29 50.6	15 38.9	27 24.5	2 46.0	17 46.2	10 08.3	11 30.8
5 W	22 49 34	14 04 37	15 06 09	22 20 05	6 27.3	20 40.3	0♒19.6	0♓37.9	16 02.4	27 26.2	2 42.9	17 46.6	10 06.9	11 29.7
6 Th	22 53 30	15 04 40	29 32 15	6♍41 50	6 15.5	19 50.0	1 28.6	1 25.1	16 26.0	27 27.8	2 39.9	17 47.1	10 05.4	11 28.5
7 F	22 57 27	16 04 42	13♍48 01	20 50 05	6 03.3	18 55.1	2 37.6	2 12.3	16 49.6	27 29.2	2 37.0	17 47.6	10 04.0	11 27.4
8 Sa	23 01 24	17 04 41	27 47 23	4♎39 24	5 51.8	17 57.2	3 46.7	2 59.6	17 13.2	27 30.4	2 34.2	17 48.2	10 02.5	11 26.3
9 Su	23 05 20	18 04 39	11♎25 46	18 06 14	5 42.2	16 57.6	4 56.0	3 46.8	17 36.8	27 31.5	2 31.5	17 48.9	10 01.0	11 25.2
10 M	23 09 17	19 04 35	24 40 45	1♏09 21	5 35.2	15 57.6	6 05.3	4 34.1	18 00.4	27 32.3	2 28.9	17 49.6	9 59.5	11 24.1
11 Tu	23 13 13	20 04 29	7♏32 13	13 49 42	5 30.9	14 58.7	7 14.8	5 21.3	18 24.0	27 32.9	2 26.4	17 50.3	9 58.0	11 23.1
12 W	23 17 10	21 04 21	20 02 10	26 10 09	5D 28.9	14 01.9	8 24.3	6 08.5	18 47.6	27 33.4	2 23.9	17 51.1	9 56.4	11 22.0
13 Th	23 21 06	22 04 12	2♐14 11	8♐14 54	5 28.6	13 08.5	9 34.0	6 55.7	19 11.2	27R 33.7	2 21.6	17 51.9	9 54.9	11 21.0
14 F	23 25 03	23 04 02	14 12 57	20 09 01	5R 28.9	12 19.3	10 43.7	7 42.9	19 34.8	27 33.8	2 19.4	17 52.8	9 53.3	11 20.0
15 Sa	23 28 59	24 03 49	26 03 48	1♑57 58	5 28.7	11 35.1	11 53.5	8 30.2	19 58.4	27 33.7	2 17.2	17 53.8	9 51.8	11 19.0
16 Su	23 32 56	25 03 35	7♑52 14	13 47 14	5 26.9	10 56.3	13 03.5	9 17.4	20 22.0	27 33.4	2 15.2	17 54.8	9 50.2	11 18.1
17 M	23 36 53	26 03 19	19 43 37	25 41 59	5 22.9	10 23.5	14 13.5	10 04.5	20 45.5	27 32.9	2 13.3	17 55.9	9 48.6	11 17.1
18 Tu	23 40 49	27 03 02	1♒42 53	7♒46 48	5 16.3	9 56.8	15 23.6	10 51.7	21 09.1	27 32.3	2 11.5	17 57.0	9 47.0	11 16.2
19 W	23 44 46	28 02 42	13 54 09	20 05 18	5 07.3	9 36.3	16 33.7	11 38.9	21 32.7	27 31.4	2 09.8	17 58.1	9 45.4	11 15.3
20 Th	23 48 42	29 02 21	26 20 30	2♓39 58	4 56.5	9 22.1	17 44.0	12 26.0	21 56.2	27 30.4	2 08.2	17 59.3	9 43.8	11 14.4
21 F	23 52 39	0♈01 57	9♓03 46	15 31 55	4 44.8	9D 14.1	18 54.3	13 13.2	22 19.7	27 29.1	2 06.6	18 00.6	9 42.2	11 13.6
22 Sa	23 56 35	1 01 32	22 04 21	28 40 54	4 33.4	9 12.1	20 04.6	14 00.3	22 43.3	27 27.7	2 05.2	18 01.9	9 40.5	11 12.7
23 Su	0 00 32	2 01 05	5♈21 20	12♈05 21	4 23.4	9 15.9	21 15.1	14 47.4	23 06.8	27 26.1	2 04.0	18 03.3	9 38.9	11 11.9
24 M	0 04 28	3 00 36	18 52 40	25 42 54	4 15.5	9 25.3	22 25.6	15 34.5	23 30.3	27 24.3	2 02.8	18 04.7	9 37.3	11 11.1
25 Tu	0 08 25	4 00 04	2♉35 41	9♉30 42	4 10.4	9 40.2	23 36.1	16 21.6	23 53.8	27 22.3	2 01.7	18 06.1	9 35.6	11 10.3
26 W	0 12 21	4 59 31	16 27 35	23 26 04	4D 07.9	10 00.1	24 46.7	17 08.7	24 17.3	27 20.2	2 00.7	18 07.6	9 34.0	11 09.6
27 Th	0 16 18	5 58 55	0♊25 51	7♊26 45	4 07.5	10 24.9	25 57.4	17 55.7	24 40.7	27 17.8	1 59.9	18 09.2	9 32.3	11 08.9
28 F	0 20 15	6 58 17	14 28 32	21 31 05	4 08.1	10 54.2	27 08.1	18 42.7	25 04.2	27 15.3	1 59.1	18 10.8	9 30.7	11 08.2
29 Sa	0 24 11	7 57 36	28 34 15	5♋37 54	4R 08.8	11 28.0	28 18.9	19 29.7	25 27.6	27 12.6	1 58.5	18 12.4	9 29.0	11 07.5
30 Su	0 28 08	8 56 53	12♋41 54	19 46 06	4 08.2	12 05.8	29 29.8	20 16.7	25 51.0	27 09.7	1 58.0	18 14.1	9 27.4	11 06.8
31 M	0 32 04	9 56 08	26 50 19	3♌54 20	4 05.8	12 47.4	0♓40.6	21 03.7	26 14.4	27 06.7	1 57.6	18 15.9	9 25.7	11 06.2

April 1947 LONGITUDE

Day	Sid.Time	☉	0 hr ☽	Noon ☽	True ☊	☿	♀	♂	⚳	♃	♄	♅	♆	♇
1 Tu	0 36 01	10♈55 21	10♌57 52	18♌00 37	4♊01.2	13♓32.8	1♓51.6	21♓50.6	26♓37.7	27♏03.5	1♌57.3	18♊17.7	9♎24.1	11♌05.6
2 W	0 39 57	11 54 31	25 02 11	2♍02 12	3R 54.5	14 21.6	3 02.6	22 37.5	27 01.1	27R 00.1	1R 57.1	18 19.5	9R 22.4	11R 05.0
3 Th	0 43 54	12 53 39	9♍00 13	15 55 46	3 46.3	15 13.6	4 13.6	23 24.4	27 24.4	26 56.5	1D 57.0	18 21.4	9 20.8	11 04.5
4 F	0 47 50	13 52 44	22 48 25	29 37 45	3 37.7	16 08.8	5 24.7	24 11.2	27 47.7	26 52.7	1 57.0	18 23.3	9 19.1	11 04.0
5 Sa	0 51 47	14 51 48	6♎23 22	13♎04 55	3 29.6	17 06.8	6 35.8	24 58.1	28 10.9	26 48.8	1 57.1	18 25.3	9 17.5	11 03.5
6 Su	0 55 44	15 50 49	19 42 10	26 14 55	3 22.9	18 07.7	7 47.0	25 44.9	28 34.2	26 44.8	1 57.4	18 27.3	9 15.8	11 03.0
7 M	0 59 40	16 49 48	2♏43 05	9♏06 39	3 18.1	19 11.3	8 58.2	26 31.6	28 57.4	26 40.5	1 57.7	18 29.3	9 14.2	11 02.5
8 Tu	1 03 37	17 48 46	15 25 42	21 40 26	3D 15.4	20 17.3	10 09.5	27 18.4	29 20.6	26 36.1	1 58.2	18 31.4	9 12.6	11 02.1
9 W	1 07 33	18 47 42	27 51 05	3♐58 00	3 14.6	21 25.8	11 20.8	28 05.1	29 43.8	26 31.6	1 58.7	18 33.5	9 10.9	11 01.7
10 Th	1 11 30	19 46 36	10♐01 35	16 02 19	3 15.3	22 36.7	12 32.1	28 51.8	0♈06.9	26 26.9	1 59.4	18 35.7	9 09.3	11 01.3
11 F	1 15 26	20 45 28	22 00 42	27 57 18	3 16.8	23 49.7	13 43.5	29 38.5	0 30.0	26 22.0	2 00.2	18 37.9	9 07.7	11 01.0
12 Sa	1 19 23	21 44 19	3♑52 43	9♑47 34	3 18.3	25 05.0	14 55.0	0♈25.2	0 53.1	26 17.0	2 01.1	18 40.2	9 06.1	11 00.7
13 Su	1 23 19	22 43 07	15 42 29	21 38 07	3R 19.0	26 22.3	16 06.5	1 11.8	1 16.2	26 11.9	2 02.1	18 42.5	9 04.5	11 00.4
14 M	1 27 16	23 41 54	27 35 06	3♒34 05	3 18.4	27 41.6	17 18.0	1 58.4	1 39.2	26 06.6	2 03.2	18 44.8	9 02.9	11 00.1
15 Tu	1 31 13	24 40 40	9♒35 39	15 40 24	3 16.3	29 02.9	18 29.6	2 45.0	2 02.2	26 01.1	2 04.4	18 47.2	9 01.3	10 59.9
16 W	1 35 09	25 39 23	21 48 52	28 01 31	3 12.5	0♈26.2	19 41.1	3 31.5	2 25.1	25 55.6	2 05.7	18 49.6	8 59.7	10 59.6
17 Th	1 39 06	26 38 05	4♓18 46	10♓40 58	3 07.4	1 51.3	20 52.8	4 18.0	2 48.1	25 49.8	2 07.2	18 52.1	8 58.2	10 59.4
18 F	1 43 02	27 36 45	17 08 22	23 41 05	3 01.6	3 18.2	22 04.4	5 04.5	3 11.0	25 44.0	2 08.7	18 54.6	8 56.6	10 59.3
19 Sa	1 46 59	28 35 23	0♈19 12	7♈02 37	2 55.8	4 47.0	23 16.1	5 50.9	3 33.8	25 38.0	2 10.4	18 57.1	8 55.1	10 59.1
20 Su	1 50 55	29 33 59	13 51 09	20 44 32	2 50.7	6 17.5	24 27.8	6 37.3	3 56.6	25 31.9	2 12.1	18 59.6	8 53.5	10 59.0
21 M	1 54 52	0♉32 34	27 42 22	4♉44 11	2 46.9	7 49.8	25 39.6	7 23.7	4 19.4	25 25.7	2 14.0	19 02.2	8 52.0	10 59.0
22 Tu	1 58 48	1 31 06	11♉49 25	18 57 29	2D 44.6	9 23.9	26 51.4	8 10.1	4 42.2	25 19.4	2 15.9	19 04.9	8 50.5	10 58.9
23 W	2 02 45	2 29 37	26 07 45	3♊19 35	2 44.0	10 59.7	28 03.1	8 56.4	5 04.9	25 12.9	2 18.0	19 07.5	8 49.0	10D 58.9
24 Th	2 06 42	3 28 06	10♊32 22	17 45 30	2 44.6	12 37.2	29 15.0	9 42.6	5 27.5	25 06.4	2 20.2	19 10.2	8 47.6	10 58.9
25 F	2 10 38	4 26 32	24 58 27	2♋10 42	2 45.9	14 16.5	0♈26.8	10 28.8	5 50.2	24 59.8	2 22.4	19 13.0	8 46.1	10 58.9
26 Sa	2 14 35	5 24 57	9♋21 49	16 31 25	2 47.4	15 57.5	1 38.7	11 15.0	6 12.7	24 53.0	2 24.8	19 15.7	8 44.7	10 59.0
27 Su	2 18 31	6 23 19	23 39 11	0♌44 51	2R 48.2	17 40.3	2 50.6	12 01.2	6 35.3	24 46.2	2 27.3	19 18.5	8 43.2	10 59.1
28 M	2 22 28	7 21 39	7♌48 10	14 48 59	2 48.1	19 24.8	4 02.5	12 47.3	6 57.7	24 39.3	2 29.9	19 21.4	8 41.8	10 59.2
29 Tu	2 26 24	8 19 57	21 47 07	28 42 26	2 46.9	21 11.0	5 14.4	13 33.3	7 20.2	24 32.3	2 32.5	19 24.2	8 40.4	10 59.3
30 W	2 30 21	9 18 13	5♍34 49	12♍24 10	2 44.7	22 59.0	6 26.4	14 19.3	7 42.6	24 25.2	2 35.3	19 27.1	8 39.1	10 59.5

Astro Data	Dy Hr Mn
☿0S	3 17:49
♄∠♅	4 10:34
☽0S	8 20:53
♃ R	14 11:36
☉0N	21 11:13
☿ D	22 8:05
☽0N	23 7:35
♄ D	3 19:38
☽0S	5 5:45
♂0N	14 22:30
☽0N	19 16:37
☿0N	20 9:15
♇ D	23 20:48
♀0N	28 4:46

Planet Ingress	Dy Hr Mn
♂ ♓	4 16:46
♀ ♒	5 5:09
☉ ♈	21 11:13
♀ ♓	30 22:14
⚳ ♈	10 4:51
♂ ♈	11 23:03
☿ ♈	16 4:31
☉ ♉	20 22:39
♀ ♈	25 3:03

Last Aspect Dy Hr Mn		☽ Ingress Dy Hr Mn
1 17:00	♂ △	♋ 1 20:59
3 20:25	♀ ☍	♌ 3 23:00
5 20:31	♃ □	♍ 6 0:46
7 23:30	♃ ⚹	♎ 8 3:51
9 11:29	♅ △	♏ 10 9:51
12 14:44	♃ ☌	♐ 12 19:34
14 18:28	☉ □	♑ 15 8:00
17 15:42	♃ ⚹	♒ 17 20:35
20 2:14	♃ □	♓ 20 6:57
22 9:48	♃ △	♈ 22 14:23
24 5:42	♀ ⚹	♉ 24 19:29
26 18:41	♃ ☍	♊ 26 23:16
28 22:26	♀ △	♋ 29 2:26
31 0:30	♃ △	♌ 31 5:22

Last Aspect Dy Hr Mn		☽ Ingress Dy Hr Mn
2 3:24	♃ □	♍ 2 8:30
4 7:10	♃ ⚹	♎ 4 12:39
5 21:41	♅ △	♏ 6 18:56
8 23:41	♂ △	♐ 9 4:12
11 15:39	♂ □	♑ 11 16:08
13 22:44	☿ ⚹	♒ 14 4:51
16 7:59	♃ □	♓ 16 15:47
18 15:42	♃ △	♈ 18 23:26
20 8:57	♅ ⚹	♉ 21 3:56
23 2:25	♀ ⚹	♊ 23 6:27
24 14:21	♅ ☌	♋ 25 8:22
27 1:58	♃ △	♌ 27 10:44
29 4:49	♃ □	♍ 29 14:15

☽ Phases & Eclipses Dy Hr Mn	
7 3:15	○ 15♍43
14 18:28	☾ 23♐20
22 16:34	● 1♈13
29 16:15	☽ 8♋08
5 15:28	○ 15♎00
13 14:23	☾ 22♑49
21 4:19	● 0♉14
27 22:18	☽ 6♌48

Astro Data

1 March 1947
Julian Day # 17226
SVP 6♓00'06"
GC 26♐06.1 ⚳ 20♒21.8
Eris 5♈56.3 ⚵ 25♐46.0
⚷ 8♏37.1R ⚶ 23♈19.3
☽Mean ☊ 6♊59.7

1 April 1947
Julian Day # 17257
SVP 6♓00'03"
GC 26♐06.2 ⚳ 0♓12.6
Eris 6♈17.7 ⚵ 0♑56.9
⚷ 7♏20.0R ⚶ 6♉28.6
☽Mean ☊ 5♊21.2

LONGITUDE — May 1947

Day	Sid.Time	☉	0 hr ☽	Noon ☽	True ☊	☿	♀	♂	⚳	♃	♄	♅	♆	♇
1 Th	2 34 17	10♉16 27	19♍10 22	25♍53 20	2♊41.7	24♈48.8	7♈38.3	15♈05.3	8♈04.9	24♏18.0	2♌38.2	19♊30.0	8♎37.7	10♌59.7
2 F	2 38 14	11 14 39	2♎33 00	9♎09 16	2R 38.4	26 40.3	8 50.3	15 51.2	8 27.2	24R 10.8	2 41.2	19 33.0	8R 36.4	10 59.9
3 Sa	2 42 11	12 12 49	15 42 06	22 11 27	2 35.4	28 33.6	10 02.3	16 37.1	8 49.4	24 03.5	2 44.2	19 36.0	8 35.0	11 00.1
4 Su	2 46 07	13 10 57	28 37 17	4♏59 38	2 33.0	0♉28.7	11 14.4	17 23.0	9 11.6	23 56.2	2 47.4	19 39.0	8 33.7	11 00.4
5 M	2 50 04	14 09 03	11♏18 31	17 34 01	2 31.4	2 25.5	12 26.4	18 08.8	9 33.8	23 48.8	2 50.6	19 42.0	8 32.4	11 00.7
6 Tu	2 54 00	15 07 08	23 46 14	29 55 21	2D 30.8	4 24.1	13 38.5	18 54.5	9 55.9	23 41.4	2 54.0	19 45.1	8 31.2	11 01.0
7 W	2 57 57	16 05 11	6♐01 32	12♐05 03	2 31.0	6 24.4	14 50.6	19 40.3	10 17.9	23 33.9	2 57.4	19 48.1	8 30.0	11 01.4
8 Th	3 01 53	17 03 13	18 06 10	24 05 13	2 31.9	8 26.3	16 02.7	20 26.0	10 39.9	23 26.4	3 01.0	19 51.2	8 28.7	11 01.8
9 F	3 05 50	18 01 14	0♑02 35	5♑58 41	2 33.1	10 29.8	17 14.9	21 11.6	11 01.8	23 18.8	3 04.6	19 54.4	8 27.5	11 02.2
10 Sa	3 09 46	18 59 12	11 53 57	17 48 53	2 34.4	12 34.8	18 27.1	21 57.2	11 23.7	23 11.2	3 08.3	19 57.5	8 26.4	11 02.6
11 Su	3 13 43	19 57 10	23 44 00	29 39 49	2 35.5	14 41.2	19 39.3	22 42.7	11 45.5	23 03.6	3 12.1	20 00.7	8 25.2	11 03.1
12 M	3 17 40	20 55 06	5♒36 55	11♒35 53	2R 36.2	16 48.9	20 51.5	23 28.2	12 07.2	22 56.0	3 16.0	20 03.9	8 24.1	11 03.6
13 Tu	3 21 36	21 53 01	17 37 16	23 41 39	2 36.4	18 57.7	22 03.7	24 13.7	12 28.9	22 48.4	3 20.0	20 07.1	8 23.0	11 04.1
14 W	3 25 33	22 50 55	29 49 38	6♓01 44	2 36.1	21 07.5	23 16.0	24 59.1	12 50.6	22 40.7	3 24.0	20 10.4	8 21.9	11 04.6
15 Th	3 29 29	23 48 47	12♓18 28	18 40 18	2 35.4	23 17.9	24 28.2	25 44.5	13 12.1	22 33.1	3 28.2	20 13.6	8 20.8	11 05.2
16 F	3 33 26	24 46 38	25 07 39	1♈40 50	2 34.5	25 29.0	25 40.5	26 29.8	13 33.6	22 25.4	3 32.4	20 16.9	8 19.8	11 05.8
17 Sa	3 37 22	25 44 28	8♈20 04	15 05 30	2 33.6	27 40.2	26 52.8	27 15.1	13 55.1	22 17.8	3 36.8	20 20.2	8 18.8	11 06.4
18 Su	3 41 19	26 42 16	21 57 07	28 54 48	2 32.9	29 51.5	28 05.2	28 00.3	14 16.4	22 10.2	3 41.2	20 23.5	8 17.8	11 07.0
19 M	3 45 15	27 40 04	5♉58 16	13♉07 08	2 32.4	2♊02.5	29 17.5	28 45.5	14 37.7	22 02.6	3 45.7	20 26.9	8 16.9	11 07.7
20 Tu	3 49 12	28 37 50	20 20 49	27 38 39	2D 32.2	4 12.9	0♉29.9	29 30.6	14 59.0	21 55.0	3 50.2	20 30.2	8 15.9	11 08.4
21 W	3 53 09	29 35 35	4♊59 53	12♊23 36	2 32.3	6 22.5	1 42.3	0♉15.7	15 20.2	21 47.5	3 54.9	20 33.6	8 15.0	11 09.1
22 Th	3 57 05	0♊33 18	19 48 55	27 14 52	2 32.4	8 30.9	2 54.6	1 00.7	15 41.2	21 40.0	3 59.6	20 37.0	8 14.2	11 09.8
23 F	4 01 02	1 31 01	4♋40 31	12♋04 57	2 32.5	10 38.0	4 07.1	1 45.6	16 02.3	21 32.5	4 04.4	20 40.4	8 13.3	11 10.6
24 Sa	4 04 58	2 28 41	19 27 21	26 46 57	2R 32.6	12 43.5	5 19.5	2 30.6	16 23.2	21 25.1	4 09.3	20 43.8	8 12.5	11 11.4
25 Su	4 08 55	3 26 20	4♌03 08	11♌15 22	2 32.6	14 47.2	6 31.9	3 15.4	16 44.1	21 17.7	4 14.3	20 47.3	8 11.7	11 12.2
26 M	4 12 51	4 23 58	18 23 15	25 26 30	2D 32.5	16 48.8	7 44.3	4 00.2	17 04.9	21 10.4	4 19.3	20 50.7	8 10.9	11 13.1
27 Tu	4 16 48	5 21 34	2♍24 56	9♍18 30	2 32.5	18 48.3	8 56.8	4 45.0	17 25.6	21 03.2	4 24.4	20 54.2	8 10.2	11 13.9
28 W	4 20 44	6 19 08	16 07 11	22 51 04	2 32.6	20 45.4	10 09.3	5 29.7	17 46.2	20 56.0	4 29.6	20 57.6	8 09.5	11 14.8
29 Th	4 24 41	7 16 41	29 30 18	6♎05 04	2 32.9	22 40.1	11 21.7	6 14.3	18 06.7	20 48.9	4 34.9	21 01.1	8 08.8	11 15.7
30 F	4 28 38	8 14 12	12♎35 34	19 02 02	2 33.4	24 32.3	12 34.2	6 58.9	18 27.2	20 41.9	4 40.2	21 04.6	8 08.2	11 16.7
31 Sa	4 32 34	9 11 43	25 24 43	1♏43 51	2 34.1	26 21.8	13 46.7	7 43.4	18 47.5	20 34.9	4 45.6	21 08.1	8 07.5	11 17.6

LONGITUDE — June 1947

Day	Sid.Time	☉	0 hr ☽	Noon ☽	True ☊	☿	♀	♂	⚳	♃	♄	♅	♆	♇
1 Su	4 36 31	10♊09 12	7♏59 42	14♏12 29	2♊34.6	28♊08.7	14♉59.3	8♉27.9	19♈07.8	20♏28.1	4♌51.1	21♊11.6	8♎07.0	11♌18.6
2 M	4 40 27	11 06 40	20 22 27	26 29 49	2R 35.0	29 52.9	16 11.8	9 12.3	19 28.0	20R 21.3	4 56.6	21 15.1	8R 06.4	11 19.6
3 Tu	4 44 24	12 04 07	2♐34 51	8♐37 45	2 35.0	1♋34.3	17 24.4	9 56.6	19 48.2	20 14.6	5 02.2	21 18.7	8 05.9	11 20.6
4 W	4 48 20	13 01 32	14 38 45	20 38 05	2 34.5	3 12.9	18 36.9	10 40.9	20 08.2	20 08.0	5 07.9	21 22.2	8 05.4	11 21.7
5 Th	4 52 17	13 58 58	26 36 00	2♑32 45	2 33.5	4 48.7	19 49.5	11 25.2	20 28.1	20 01.6	5 13.6	21 25.7	8 04.9	11 22.7
6 F	4 56 13	14 56 22	8♑28 37	14 23 54	2 31.9	6 21.7	21 02.1	12 09.4	20 48.0	19 55.2	5 19.4	21 29.3	8 04.5	11 23.8
7 Sa	5 00 10	15 53 45	20 18 54	26 13 58	2 30.0	7 51.7	22 14.8	12 53.5	21 07.7	19 48.9	5 25.3	21 32.8	8 04.1	11 24.9
8 Su	5 04 07	16 51 08	2♒09 28	8♒05 48	2 28.0	9 18.9	23 27.4	13 37.6	21 27.4	19 42.8	5 31.2	21 36.4	8 03.7	11 26.1
9 M	5 08 03	17 48 30	14 03 24	20 02 42	2 26.2	10 43.2	24 40.1	14 21.6	21 46.9	19 36.8	5 37.2	21 39.9	8 03.3	11 27.2
10 Tu	5 12 00	18 45 51	26 04 11	2♓08 21	2 24.7	12 04.5	25 52.8	15 05.6	22 06.4	19 30.9	5 43.2	21 43.5	8 03.0	11 28.4
11 W	5 15 56	19 43 12	8♓15 42	14 26 45	2D 24.0	13 22.8	27 05.5	15 49.5	22 25.7	19 25.1	5 49.3	21 47.1	8 02.7	11 29.6
12 Th	5 19 53	20 40 33	20 42 03	27 02 04	2 24.0	14 38.1	28 18.2	16 33.4	22 45.0	19 19.4	5 55.5	21 50.6	8 02.5	11 30.8
13 F	5 23 49	21 37 53	3♈27 19	9♈58 14	2 24.8	15 50.3	29 30.9	17 17.2	23 04.1	19 13.9	6 01.7	21 54.2	8 02.3	11 32.0
14 Sa	5 27 46	22 35 12	16 35 12	23 18 31	2 26.0	16 59.4	0♊43.7	18 00.9	23 23.1	19 08.5	6 07.9	21 57.7	8 02.1	11 33.3
15 Su	5 31 42	23 32 31	0♉08 26	7♉05 01	2 27.4	18 05.2	1 56.5	18 44.6	23 42.1	19 03.3	6 14.3	22 01.3	8 01.9	11 34.6
16 M	5 35 39	24 29 50	14 08 15	21 17 56	2R 28.4	19 07.8	3 09.3	19 28.2	24 00.9	18 58.2	6 20.6	22 04.9	8 01.8	11 35.9
17 Tu	5 39 36	25 27 09	28 33 41	5♊54 58	2 28.7	20 07.0	4 22.1	20 11.8	24 19.6	18 53.2	6 27.1	22 08.4	8 01.7	11 37.2
18 W	5 43 32	26 24 27	13♊21 04	20 51 05	2 27.8	21 02.7	5 35.0	20 55.3	24 38.2	18 48.4	6 33.5	22 12.0	8 01.6	11 38.5
19 Th	5 47 29	27 21 45	28 23 59	5♋58 38	2 25.8	21 55.0	6 47.8	21 38.7	24 56.7	18 43.7	6 40.1	22 15.6	8D 01.6	11 39.9
20 F	5 51 25	28 19 02	13♋33 48	21 08 17	2 22.9	22 43.6	8 00.7	22 22.1	25 15.0	18 39.2	6 46.7	22 19.1	8 01.6	11 41.2
21 Sa	5 55 22	29 16 18	28 40 51	6♌10 23	2 19.3	23 28.4	9 13.6	23 05.4	25 33.2	18 34.9	6 53.3	22 22.7	8 01.7	11 42.6
22 Su	5 59 18	0♋13 34	13♌35 54	20 56 31	2 15.8	24 09.4	10 26.5	23 48.7	25 51.3	18 30.7	7 00.0	22 26.2	8 01.7	11 44.0
23 M	6 03 15	1 10 49	28 11 34	5♍20 34	2 12.9	24 46.4	11 39.4	24 31.9	26 09.3	18 26.7	7 06.7	22 29.8	8 01.8	11 45.4
24 Tu	6 07 12	2 08 03	12♍23 12	19 19 19	2 11.0	25 19.4	12 52.3	25 15.0	26 27.1	18 22.8	7 13.5	22 33.3	8 02.0	11 46.9
25 W	6 11 08	3 05 17	26 08 58	2♎52 15	2D 10.3	25 48.2	14 05.3	25 58.0	26 44.9	18 19.1	7 20.3	22 36.8	8 02.1	11 48.3
26 Th	6 15 05	4 02 30	9♎29 27	16 00 55	2 10.9	26 12.6	15 18.3	26 41.0	27 02.4	18 15.6	7 27.1	22 40.3	8 02.3	11 49.8
27 F	6 19 01	4 59 43	22 27 01	28 48 13	2 12.2	26 32.7	16 31.3	27 23.9	27 19.9	18 12.2	7 34.0	22 43.9	8 02.6	11 51.2
28 Sa	6 22 58	5 56 55	5♏04 58	11♏17 45	2 13.8	26 48.3	17 44.3	28 06.8	27 37.2	18 09.0	7 41.0	22 47.3	8 02.8	11 52.7
29 Su	6 26 54	6 54 07	17 27 01	23 33 15	2R 15.1	26 59.4	18 57.3	28 49.6	27 54.4	18 06.0	7 47.9	22 50.8	8 03.1	11 54.2
30 M	6 30 51	7 51 18	29 36 52	5♐38 17	2 15.4	27R 05.8	20 10.3	29 32.3	28 11.4	18 03.1	7 54.9	22 54.3	8 03.4	11 55.8

Astro Data

	Dy Hr Mn
☽ 0S	2 13:01
♃∠♆	8 3:00
☽ 0N	17 2:34
♃⚻♅	28 8:16
☽ 0S	29 18:48
⚳ 0N	7 14:30
☽ 0N	13 11:33
♆ D	19 18:47
☽ 0S	26 0:16
♄∠♅	30 7:49

Planet Ingress

		Dy Hr Mn
☿	♉	4 6:03
☿	♊	18 13:33
♀	♉	20 2:06
♂	♉	21 3:40
☉	♊	21 22:09
☿	♋	2 13:40
♀	♊	13 21:35
☉	♋	22 6:19

Last Aspect / ☽ Ingress (May)

Last Aspect Dy Hr Mn			☽ Ingress	Dy Hr Mn
1 9:11	♃	⚹	♎	1 19:24
4 1:58	☿	☍	♏	4 2:35
5 23:58	♃	☌	♐	6 12:09
8 4:10	♂	△	♑	8 23:55
10 22:47	♃	⚹	♒	11 12:41
13 13:07	♂	⚹	♓	14 0:20
15 22:22	☿	⚹	♈	16 8:56
18 10:27	♀	☌	♉	18 13:51
20 13:44	☉	☌	♊	20 15:51
22 1:15	♅	☌	♋	22 16:27
24 3:17	♃	△	♌	24 17:18
26 4:47	♃	□	♍	26 19:50
28 8:36	♅	□	♎	29 0:54
31 0:06	☿	△	♏	31 8:42

Last Aspect / ☽ Ingress (June)

Last Aspect Dy Hr Mn			☽ Ingress	Dy Hr Mn
2 0:04	♃	☌	♐	2 18:54
4 13:29	♅	☍	♑	5 6:51
7 3:00	♀	△	♒	7 19:38
9 22:15	♀	□	♓	10 7:47
12 14:38	♀	⚹	♈	12 17:34
14 10:37	☉	⚹	♉	14 23:45
16 8:47	♂	☌	♊	17 2:22
18 21:26	☉	☌	♋	19 2:32
20 14:39	☿	☌	♌	21 2:06
22 16:59	♂	□	♍	23 3:01
24 22:59	♂	△	♎	25 6:51
27 7:37	☿	□	♏	27 14:17
29 23:05	♂	☍	♐	30 0:46

☽ Phases & Eclipses

Dy Hr Mn		
5 4:53	○	13♏52
13 8:08	☾	21♒44
20 13:44	●	28♉42
20 13:47:20	●	T 05'14"
27 4:36	☽	5♍04
3 19:27	○	12♐22
3 19:15	●	P 0.020
11 22:58	☾	20♓09
18 21:26	●	26♊47
25 12:25	☽	3♎06

Astro Data

1 May 1947
Julian Day # 17287
SVP 5♓59'59"
GC 26♐06.2 ⚴ 8♓22.5
Eris 6♈37.8 ⚵ 1♑53.7R
⚷ 5♏08.3R ⚶ 19♉34.7
☽ Mean ☊ 3♊45.9

1 June 1947
Julian Day # 17318
SVP 5♓59'55"
GC 26♐06.3 ⚴ 14♓30.4
Eris 6♈52.9 ⚵ 27♐49.4R
⚷ 3♏05.2R ⚶ 3♊08.8
☽ Mean ☊ 2♊07.4

July 1947

LONGITUDE

Day	Sid.Time	☉	0 hr ☽	Noon☽	True☊	☿	♀	♂	⚳	♃	♄	♅	♆	♇
1 Tu	6 34 47	8♋48 29	11♐37 53	17♐35 59	2♊14.2	27♋07.6	21♊23.4	0♊15.0	28♈28.3	18♏00.4	8♌02.0	22♊57.8	8♎03.8	11♌57.3
2 W	6 38 44	9 45 40	23 32 57	29 29 04	2R11.2	27R04.7	22 36.5	0 57.6	28 45.0	17R57.9	8 09.1	23 01.2	8 04.2	11 58.9
3 Th	6 42 41	10 42 51	5♑24 36	11♑19 48	2 06.5	26 57.3	23 49.6	1 40.1	29 01.6	17 55.6	8 16.2	23 04.7	8 04.6	12 00.4
4 F	6 46 37	11 40 02	17 14 55	23 10 10	2 00.3	26 45.3	25 02.7	2 22.6	29 18.1	17 53.4	8 23.4	23 08.1	8 05.1	12 02.0
5 Sa	6 50 34	12 37 12	29 05 48	5♒02 02	1 53.1	26 29.0	26 15.9	3 05.0	29 34.4	17 51.5	8 30.5	23 11.5	8 05.6	12 03.6
6 Su	6 54 30	13 34 23	10♒59 07	16 57 19	1 45.6	26 08.5	27 29.0	3 47.3	29 50.5	17 49.7	8 37.8	23 14.9	8 06.1	12 05.2
7 M	6 58 27	14 31 34	22 56 53	28 58 08	1 38.5	25 44.1	28 42.2	4 29.6	0♉06.5	17 48.0	8 45.0	23 18.3	8 06.6	12 06.8
8 Tu	7 02 23	15 28 45	5♓01 23	11♓07 00	1 32.5	25 16.0	29 55.4	5 11.8	0 22.3	17 46.6	8 52.3	23 21.7	8 07.2	12 08.4
9 W	7 06 20	16 25 57	17 15 22	23 26 54	1 28.1	24 44.8	1♋08.7	5 54.0	0 38.0	17 45.3	8 59.6	23 25.1	8 07.8	12 10.1
10 Th	7 10 16	17 23 09	29 42 00	6♈01 10	1D25.6	24 10.8	2 21.9	6 36.0	0 53.5	17 44.3	9 06.9	23 28.4	8 08.5	12 11.7
11 F	7 14 13	18 20 21	12♈24 49	18 53 25	1 24.9	23 34.6	3 35.2	7 18.1	1 08.8	17 43.3	9 14.3	23 31.7	8 09.1	12 13.4
12 Sa	7 18 10	19 17 34	25 27 26	2♉07 14	1 25.5	22 56.8	4 48.6	8 00.0	1 23.9	17 42.6	9 21.7	23 35.0	8 09.8	12 15.0
13 Su	7 22 06	20 14 48	8♉53 11	15 45 34	1 26.6	22 17.9	6 01.9	8 41.9	1 38.9	17 42.1	9 29.1	23 38.3	8 10.6	12 16.7
14 M	7 26 03	21 12 02	22 44 31	29 50 06	1R27.3	21 38.6	7 15.3	9 23.7	1 53.7	17 41.7	9 36.6	23 41.6	8 11.3	12 18.4
15 Tu	7 29 59	22 09 17	7♊02 10	14♊20 26	1 26.7	20 59.5	8 28.7	10 05.5	2 08.3	17D41.6	9 44.0	23 44.8	8 12.1	12 20.1
16 W	7 33 56	23 06 32	21 44 23	29 13 20	1 24.1	20 21.5	9 42.1	10 47.1	2 22.7	17 41.6	9 51.5	23 48.1	8 13.0	12 21.8
17 Th	7 37 52	24 03 48	6♋46 21	14♋22 21	1 19.2	19 45.1	10 55.5	11 28.8	2 37.0	17 41.8	9 59.0	23 51.3	8 13.8	12 23.5
18 F	7 41 49	25 01 04	22 00 07	29 38 18	1 12.5	19 11.0	12 09.0	12 10.3	2 51.0	17 42.1	10 06.6	23 54.5	8 14.7	12 25.3
19 Sa	7 45 46	25 58 21	7♌15 31	14♌50 26	1 04.5	18 39.8	13 22.5	12 51.8	3 04.9	17 42.7	10 14.1	23 57.6	8 15.7	12 27.0
20 Su	7 49 42	26 55 38	22 21 46	29 48 21	0 56.4	18 12.2	14 36.0	13 33.2	3 18.5	17 43.4	10 21.7	24 00.8	8 16.6	12 28.7
21 M	7 53 39	27 52 55	7♍09 16	14♍23 45	0 49.1	17 48.5	15 49.5	14 14.5	3 32.0	17 44.3	10 29.3	24 03.9	8 17.6	12 30.5
22 Tu	7 57 35	28 50 12	21 31 17	28 31 32	0 43.6	17 29.4	17 03.1	14 55.7	3 45.2	17 45.4	10 36.9	24 07.0	8 18.6	12 32.2
23 W	8 01 32	29 47 30	5♎24 26	12♎10 02	0 40.1	17 15.2	18 16.6	15 36.9	3 58.3	17 46.7	10 44.5	24 10.0	8 19.6	12 34.0
24 Th	8 05 28	0♌44 48	18 48 35	25 20 27	0D38.6	17 06.2	19 30.2	16 18.0	4 11.1	17 48.2	10 52.1	24 13.1	8 20.7	12 35.7
25 F	8 09 25	1 42 06	1♏46 06	8♏06 03	0 38.6	17D02.7	20 43.8	16 59.0	4 23.7	17 49.8	10 59.8	24 16.1	8 21.8	12 37.5
26 Sa	8 13 21	2 39 25	14 20 55	20 31 16	0R39.3	17 05.0	21 57.5	17 40.0	4 36.1	17 51.6	11 07.4	24 19.1	8 22.9	12 39.3
27 Su	8 17 18	3 36 44	26 37 44	2♐40 56	0 39.6	17 13.2	23 11.1	18 20.8	4 48.2	17 53.6	11 15.1	24 22.0	8 24.1	12 41.0
28 M	8 21 14	4 34 04	8♐41 26	14 39 48	0 38.6	17 27.4	24 24.8	19 01.6	5 00.2	17 55.8	11 22.7	24 24.9	8 25.2	12 42.8
29 Tu	8 25 11	5 31 25	20 36 33	26 32 12	0 35.5	17 47.8	25 38.5	19 42.4	5 11.9	17 58.1	11 30.4	24 27.8	8 26.5	12 44.6
30 W	8 29 08	6 28 46	2♑27 09	8♑21 50	0 29.8	18 14.4	26 52.2	20 23.0	5 23.4	18 00.6	11 38.1	24 30.7	8 27.7	12 46.4
31 Th	8 33 04	7 26 07	14 16 34	20 11 42	0 21.6	18 47.1	28 05.9	21 03.6	5 34.7	18 03.3	11 45.8	24 33.6	8 29.0	12 48.2

August 1947

LONGITUDE

Day	Sid.Time	☉	0 hr ☽	Noon☽	True☊	☿	♀	♂	⚳	♃	♄	♅	♆	♇
1 F	8 37 01	8♌23 30	26♑07 28	2♒04 07	0♊11.1	19♋26.0	29♋19.7	21♊44.1	5♉45.7	18♏06.2	11♌53.5	24♊36.4	8♎30.2	12♌50.0
2 Sa	8 40 57	9 20 53	8♒01 51	14 00 51	29♉59.2	20 11.1	0♌33.5	22 24.6	5 56.5	18 09.2	12 01.2	24 39.1	8 31.6	12 51.8
3 Su	8 44 54	10 18 17	20 01 16	26 03 16	29R46.6	21 02.1	1 47.3	23 04.9	6 07.0	18 12.4	12 08.9	24 41.9	8 32.9	12 53.6
4 M	8 48 50	11 15 42	2♓07 00	8♓12 37	29 34.6	21 59.2	3 01.2	23 45.2	6 17.3	18 15.8	12 16.6	24 44.6	8 34.3	12 55.4
5 Tu	8 52 47	12 13 08	14 20 18	20 30 13	29 24.1	23 02.1	4 15.0	24 25.4	6 27.3	18 19.4	12 24.3	24 47.3	8 35.7	12 57.2
6 W	8 56 44	13 10 35	26 42 36	2♈57 43	29 15.9	24 10.6	5 28.9	25 05.6	6 37.1	18 23.1	12 32.0	24 49.9	8 37.1	12 58.9
7 Th	9 00 40	14 08 04	9♈15 48	15 37 12	29 10.4	25 24.7	6 42.8	25 45.6	6 46.6	18 26.9	12 39.7	24 52.5	8 38.5	13 00.7
8 F	9 04 37	15 05 33	22 02 13	28 31 14	29 07.4	26 44.2	7 56.7	26 25.6	6 55.8	18 31.0	12 47.4	24 55.1	8 40.0	13 02.5
9 Sa	9 08 33	16 03 04	5♉04 37	11♉42 43	29D06.5	28 08.8	9 10.7	27 05.5	7 04.8	18 35.2	12 55.1	24 57.7	8 41.5	13 04.3
10 Su	9 12 30	17 00 37	18 25 53	25 14 27	29R06.5	29 38.2	10 24.7	27 45.4	7 13.5	18 39.5	13 02.8	25 00.2	8 43.0	13 06.1
11 M	9 16 26	17 58 11	2♊08 39	9♊08 38	29 06.3	1♌12.2	11 38.7	28 25.2	7 21.9	18 44.0	13 10.5	25 02.7	8 44.5	13 07.9
12 Tu	9 20 23	18 55 47	16 14 27	23 26 00	29 04.7	2 50.5	12 52.8	29 04.8	7 30.1	18 48.7	13 18.2	25 05.1	8 46.1	13 09.7
13 W	9 24 19	19 53 24	0♋43 02	8♋05 05	29 00.7	4 32.8	14 06.8	29 44.5	7 37.9	18 53.6	13 25.9	25 07.5	8 47.7	13 11.5
14 Th	9 28 16	20 51 02	15 31 31	23 01 28	28 54.1	6 18.5	15 20.9	0♋24.0	7 45.5	18 58.6	13 33.6	25 09.9	8 49.3	13 13.3
15 F	9 32 13	21 48 42	0♌33 57	8♌07 46	28 45.0	8 07.5	16 35.0	1 03.4	7 52.8	19 03.7	13 41.3	25 12.2	8 50.9	13 15.1
16 Sa	9 36 09	22 46 23	15 41 40	23 14 20	28 34.3	9 59.3	17 49.2	1 42.8	7 59.7	19 09.1	13 48.9	25 14.5	8 52.6	13 16.9
17 Su	9 40 06	23 44 05	0♍44 29	8♍10 54	28 23.2	11 53.4	19 03.3	2 22.1	8 06.4	19 14.5	13 56.6	25 16.7	8 54.3	13 18.7
18 M	9 44 02	24 41 49	15 32 29	22 48 18	28 12.9	13 49.4	20 17.5	3 01.3	8 12.8	19 20.2	14 04.2	25 18.9	8 56.0	13 20.4
19 Tu	9 47 59	25 39 33	29 57 40	7♎00 05	28 04.6	15 47.0	21 31.7	3 40.4	8 18.8	19 25.9	14 11.8	25 21.1	8 57.7	13 22.2
20 W	9 51 55	26 37 19	13♎55 15	20 43 06	27 58.9	17 45.9	22 45.9	4 19.4	8 24.5	19 31.8	14 19.4	25 23.2	8 59.4	13 24.0
21 Th	9 55 52	27 35 06	27 23 43	3♏57 24	27 55.6	19 45.5	24 00.1	4 58.4	8 29.9	19 37.9	14 27.0	25 25.3	9 01.2	13 25.7
22 F	9 59 48	28 32 54	10♏24 31	16 45 34	27D54.4	21 45.7	25 14.3	5 37.2	8 35.0	19 44.1	14 34.6	25 27.4	9 03.0	13 27.5
23 Sa	10 03 45	29 30 43	23 01 07	29 11 48	27R54.2	23 46.0	26 28.6	6 16.0	8 39.8	19 50.5	14 42.2	25 29.4	9 04.8	13 29.2
24 Su	10 07 41	0♍28 34	5♐18 15	11♐21 10	27 54.0	25 46.3	27 42.9	6 54.7	8 44.2	19 57.0	14 49.7	25 31.3	9 06.6	13 30.9
25 M	10 11 38	1 26 26	17 21 12	23 19 01	27 52.7	27 46.4	28 57.2	7 33.2	8 48.3	20 03.6	14 57.2	25 33.2	9 08.4	13 32.7
26 Tu	10 15 35	2 24 19	29 15 13	5♑10 25	27 49.2	29 45.9	0♍11.5	8 11.8	8 52.1	20 10.4	15 04.7	25 35.1	9 10.3	13 34.4
27 W	10 19 31	3 22 13	11♑05 10	16 59 59	27 43.2	1♍44.8	1 25.8	8 50.2	8 55.5	20 17.4	15 12.2	25 36.9	9 12.2	13 36.1
28 Th	10 23 28	4 20 09	22 55 18	28 51 33	27 34.4	3 43.0	2 40.2	9 28.5	8 58.6	20 24.4	15 19.6	25 38.7	9 14.1	13 37.8
29 F	10 27 24	5 18 06	4♒49 05	10♒48 11	27 23.2	5 40.2	3 54.5	10 06.7	9 01.4	20 31.6	15 27.0	25 40.4	9 16.0	13 39.5
30 Sa	10 31 21	6 16 04	16 49 07	22 52 05	27 10.4	7 36.5	5 08.9	10 44.9	9 03.8	20 39.0	15 34.4	25 42.1	9 17.9	13 41.2
31 Su	10 35 17	7 14 04	28 57 13	5♓04 39	26 56.9	9 31.7	6 23.3	11 23.0	9 05.8	20 46.4	15 41.8	25 43.8	9 19.8	13 42.9

Astro Data

	Dy Hr Mn
☿R	1 9:12
♄✶♆	1 18:29
☽0N	10 18:24
♃D	15 22:53
☽0S	23 6:49
☿D	25 14:38
☽0N	6 23:28
♄☌♇	11 1:21
☽0S	19 15:09

Planet Ingress

		Dy Hr Mn
♂	♊	1 3:34
⚳	♉	7 2:14
♀	♋	8 13:30
☉	♌	23 17:14
♀	♌	2 1:06
☊	♉R	2 10:22
☿	♌	10 17:40
♂	♋	13 21:26
☉	♍	24 0:09
♀	♍	26 8:17
☿	♍	26 14:50

Last Aspect / ☽ Ingress (July)

Last Aspect Dy Hr Mn			☽ Ingress	Dy Hr Mn
1 22:52	♅	☍	♑	2 13:03
4 19:07	☿	☍	♒	5 1:50
7 11:25	♀	△	♓	7 14:03
9 14:24	☿	△	♈	10 0:34
11 20:32	♅	✶	♉	12 8:12
13 22:44	☿	✶	♊	14 12:17
16 3:17	♅	☌	♋	16 13:14
18 4:15	☉	☌	♌	18 12:34
20 2:37	♅	✶	♍	20 12:19
22 12:35	☉	✶	♎	22 14:33
24 9:55	♅	△	♏	24 20:41
26 15:07	♀	△	♐	27 6:40
29 7:47	♅	☍	♑	29 19:01

Last Aspect / ☽ Ingress (August)

Last Aspect Dy Hr Mn			☽ Ingress	Dy Hr Mn
1 5:50	♀	☍	♒	1 7:50
3 9:18	♅	△	♓	3 19:49
5 20:19	♅	□	♈	6 6:20
8 8:20	☿	□	♉	8 14:43
10 0:20	♃	☍	♊	10 20:17
12 21:45	♂	☌	♋	12 22:49
14 5:30	♃	△	♌	14 23:06
16 15:12	♅	✶	♍	16 22:49
18 16:12	♅	□	♎	19 0:04
20 23:26	☉	✶	♏	21 4:44
23 12:40	☉	□	♐	23 13:34
26 0:43	♀	△	♑	26 1:31
27 18:44	♃	✶	♒	28 14:18
30 17:37	♅	△	♓	31 2:03

☽ Phases & Eclipses

Dy Hr Mn		
3 10:39	○	10♑40
11 10:54	☾	18♈18
18 4:15	●	24♋43
24 22:54	☽	1♏11
2 1:50	○	8♒57
9 20:22	☾	16♉23
16 11:12	●	22♌44
23 12:40	☽	29♏32
31 16:34	○	7♓25

Astro Data

1 July 1947
Julian Day # 17348
SVP 5♓59'49"
GC 26♐06.4 ⚴ 16♓58.4
Eris 6♈58.8 ✱ 21♐11.5R
⚷ 2♏18.2R ⚶ 16♊02.7
☽Mean ☊ 0♊32.1

1 August 1947
Julian Day # 17379
SVP 5♓59'43"
GC 26♐06.4 ⚴ 14♓33.0R
Eris 6♈54.4R ✱ 16♐45.5R
⚷ 3♏08.9 ⚶ 28♊50.6
☽Mean ☊ 28♉53.6

LONGITUDE — September 1947

Day	Sid.Time	⊙	0 hr ☽	Noon ☽	True ☊	☿	♀	♂	⚳	♃	♄	♅	♆	♇
1 M	10 39 14	8♍12 06	11♓14 27	17♓26 42	26♉43.9	11♍25.8	7♍37.7	12♋00.9	9♉07.5	20♏54.0	15♌49.2	25♊45.4	9♎21.8	13♌44.6
2 Tu	10 43 10	9 10 09	23 41 25	29 58 41	26R32.6	13 18.7	8 52.2	12 38.8	9 08.9	21 01.7	15 56.5	25 46.9	9 23.8	13 46.2
3 W	10 47 07	10 08 14	6♈18 31	12♈40 58	26 23.7	15 10.5	10 06.6	13 16.6	9 09.9	21 09.6	16 03.7	25 48.4	9 25.8	13 47.9
4 Th	10 51 04	11 06 21	19 06 09	25 34 09	26 17.6	17 01.1	11 21.1	13 54.3	9 10.5	21 17.5	16 11.0	25 49.9	9 27.8	13 49.5
5 F	10 55 00	12 04 30	2♉05 06	8♉39 10	26 14.3	18 50.5	12 35.6	14 32.0	9R 10.7	21 25.6	16 18.2	25 51.3	9 29.8	13 51.1
6 Sa	10 58 57	13 02 41	15 16 31	21 57 23	26D13.2	20 38.8	13 50.1	15 09.5	9 10.6	21 33.9	16 25.4	25 52.7	9 31.8	13 52.7
7 Su	11 02 53	14 00 54	28 41 57	5♊30 25	26R13.3	22 25.8	15 04.6	15 46.9	9 10.1	21 42.2	16 32.6	25 54.0	9 33.9	13 54.4
8 M	11 06 50	14 59 09	12♊22 58	19 19 43	26 13.4	24 11.7	16 19.1	16 24.3	9 09.3	21 50.7	16 39.7	25 55.3	9 35.9	13 55.9
9 Tu	11 10 46	15 57 26	26 20 45	3♋26 03	26 12.3	25 56.4	17 33.7	17 01.5	9 08.0	21 59.3	16 46.8	25 56.5	9 38.0	13 57.5
10 W	11 14 43	16 55 45	10♋35 27	17 48 43	26 09.1	27 39.9	18 48.2	17 38.6	9 06.4	22 08.0	16 53.8	25 57.7	9 40.1	13 59.1
11 Th	11 18 39	17 54 07	25 05 25	2♌25 00	26 03.3	29 22.3	20 02.8	18 15.7	9 04.4	22 16.8	17 00.9	25 58.8	9 42.2	14 00.6
12 F	11 22 36	18 52 30	9♌46 46	17 09 54	25 55.3	1♎03.6	21 17.4	18 52.6	9 02.1	22 25.7	17 07.8	25 59.9	9 44.3	14 02.2
13 Sa	11 26 33	19 50 55	24 33 27	1♍56 24	25 45.6	2 43.7	22 32.0	19 29.5	8 59.3	22 34.8	17 14.8	26 00.9	9 46.4	14 03.7
14 Su	11 30 29	20 49 23	9♍17 43	16 36 22	25 35.5	4 22.8	23 46.7	20 06.2	8 56.2	22 43.9	17 21.7	26 01.8	9 48.5	14 05.2
15 M	11 34 26	21 47 52	23 51 23	1♎01 55	25 26.0	6 00.8	25 01.3	20 42.9	8 52.7	22 53.2	17 28.5	26 02.8	9 50.7	14 06.7
16 Tu	11 38 22	22 46 23	8♎07 13	15 06 45	25 18.3	7 37.7	26 16.0	21 19.4	8 48.8	23 02.6	17 35.3	26 03.6	9 52.8	14 08.2
17 W	11 42 19	23 44 55	22 00 04	28 46 58	25 13.0	9 13.6	27 30.6	21 55.8	8 44.5	23 12.1	17 42.1	26 04.4	9 55.0	14 09.6
18 Th	11 46 15	24 43 30	5♏27 23	12♏01 24	25 10.1	10 48.5	28 45.3	22 32.1	8 39.9	23 21.7	17 48.8	26 05.2	9 57.1	14 11.1
19 F	11 50 12	25 42 06	18 29 16	24 51 18	25D09.2	12 22.3	29 60.0	23 08.3	8 34.9	23 31.3	17 55.4	26 05.9	9 59.3	14 12.5
20 Sa	11 54 08	26 40 44	1♐07 58	7♐19 48	25 09.7	13 55.1	1♎14.7	23 44.4	8 29.5	23 41.1	18 02.1	26 06.6	10 01.5	14 13.9
21 Su	11 58 05	27 39 24	13 27 20	19 31 14	25R10.5	15 26.9	2 29.4	24 20.4	8 23.7	23 51.1	18 08.6	26 07.2	10 03.7	14 15.3
22 M	12 02 02	28 38 05	25 32 08	1♑30 40	25 10.8	16 57.7	3 44.1	24 56.2	8 17.6	24 01.1	18 15.1	26 07.8	10 05.9	14 16.7
23 Tu	12 05 58	29 36 48	7♑27 31	13 23 20	25 09.6	18 27.5	4 58.8	25 32.0	8 11.1	24 11.1	18 21.6	26 08.3	10 08.1	14 18.1
24 W	12 09 55	0♎35 33	19 18 43	25 14 29	25 06.4	19 56.3	6 13.5	26 07.6	8 04.3	24 21.3	18 28.0	26 08.7	10 10.3	14 19.4
25 Th	12 13 51	1 34 20	1♒10 35	7♒08 08	25 01.0	21 24.1	7 28.2	26 43.1	7 57.1	24 31.6	18 34.4	26 09.1	10 12.5	14 20.7
26 F	12 17 48	2 33 08	13 07 25	19 08 50	24 53.6	22 50.8	8 42.9	27 18.5	7 49.5	24 42.0	18 40.6	26 09.5	10 14.7	14 22.0
27 Sa	12 21 44	3 31 58	25 12 45	1♓19 27	24 44.8	24 16.5	9 57.7	27 53.8	7 41.6	24 52.5	18 46.9	26 09.8	10 16.9	14 23.3
28 Su	12 25 41	4 30 50	7♓29 11	13 42 07	24 35.4	25 41.1	11 12.4	28 29.0	7 33.4	25 03.0	18 53.1	26 10.0	10 19.2	14 24.6
29 M	12 29 37	5 29 44	19 58 22	26 17 59	24 26.4	27 04.7	12 27.2	29 04.0	7 24.8	25 13.7	18 59.2	26 10.2	10 21.4	14 25.8
30 Tu	12 33 34	6 28 40	2♈40 58	9♈07 17	24 18.5	28 27.2	13 41.9	29 38.9	7 15.9	25 24.4	19 05.3	26 10.3	10 23.6	14 27.0

LONGITUDE — October 1947

Day	Sid.Time	⊙	0 hr ☽	Noon ☽	True ☊	☿	♀	♂	⚳	♃	♄	♅	♆	♇
1 W	12 37 31	7♎27 37	15♈36 52	22♈09 37	24♉12.5	29♎48.5	14♎56.7	0♌13.7	7♉06.7	25♏35.2	19♌11.3	26♊10.4	10♎25.8	14♌28.2
2 Th	12 41 27	8 26 37	28 45 24	5♉24 07	24R08.7	1♏08.6	16 11.4	0 48.4	6R57.2	25 46.1	19 17.2	26R10.5	10 28.1	14 29.4
3 F	12 45 24	9 25 40	12♉05 39	18 49 53	24D07.0	2 27.5	17 26.2	1 23.0	6 47.3	25 57.1	19 23.1	26 10.4	10 30.3	14 30.6
4 Sa	12 49 20	10 24 44	25 36 43	2♊26 05	24 07.2	3 45.1	18 41.0	1 57.4	6 37.2	26 08.2	19 28.9	26 10.4	10 32.5	14 31.7
5 Su	12 53 17	11 23 51	9♊17 55	16 12 09	24 08.3	5 01.4	19 55.8	2 31.7	6 26.7	26 19.3	19 34.6	26 10.3	10 34.8	14 32.9
6 M	12 57 13	12 23 00	23 08 44	0♋07 38	24R09.6	6 16.2	21 10.6	3 05.9	6 16.0	26 30.6	19 40.3	26 10.1	10 37.0	14 34.0
7 Tu	13 01 10	13 22 12	7♋08 44	14 11 57	24 10.1	7 29.5	22 25.4	3 39.9	6 05.0	26 41.9	19 45.9	26 09.9	10 39.2	14 35.0
8 W	13 05 06	14 21 25	21 17 08	28 24 03	24 09.3	8 41.2	23 40.2	4 13.8	5 53.7	26 53.3	19 51.5	26 09.6	10 41.5	14 36.1
9 Th	13 09 03	15 20 42	5♌32 26	12♌41 57	24 06.7	9 51.2	24 55.0	4 47.6	5 42.2	27 04.7	19 57.0	26 09.3	10 43.7	14 37.1
10 F	13 13 00	16 20 00	19 52 11	27 02 37	24 02.5	10 59.2	26 09.8	5 21.2	5 30.4	27 16.3	20 02.4	26 08.9	10 45.9	14 38.1
11 Sa	13 16 56	17 19 21	4♍12 42	11♍21 50	23 57.1	12 05.3	27 24.7	5 54.7	5 18.4	27 27.9	20 07.7	26 08.4	10 48.2	14 39.1
12 Su	13 20 53	18 18 44	18 29 24	25 34 45	23 51.4	13 09.1	28 39.5	6 28.0	5 06.2	27 39.5	20 13.0	26 07.9	10 50.4	14 40.1
13 M	13 24 49	19 18 09	2♎37 15	9♎36 20	23 46.0	14 10.5	29 54.4	7 01.2	4 53.7	27 51.3	20 18.2	26 07.4	10 52.6	14 41.0
14 Tu	13 28 46	20 17 36	16 31 27	23 22 10	23 41.7	15 09.4	1♏09.2	7 34.3	4 41.1	28 03.1	20 23.3	26 06.8	10 54.8	14 41.9
15 W	13 32 42	21 17 05	0♏08 09	6♏49 08	23 38.8	16 05.3	2 24.0	8 07.1	4 28.2	28 15.0	20 28.3	26 06.2	10 57.0	14 42.8
16 Th	13 36 39	22 16 36	13 24 59	19 55 40	23D37.7	16 58.1	3 38.9	8 39.9	4 15.3	28 26.9	20 33.2	26 05.5	10 59.2	14 43.7
17 F	13 40 35	23 16 10	26 21 16	2♐41 57	23 37.9	17 47.4	4 53.8	9 12.4	4 02.1	28 38.9	20 38.1	26 04.7	11 01.4	14 44.5
18 Sa	13 44 32	24 15 45	8♐57 59	15 09 44	23 39.2	18 32.9	6 08.6	9 44.8	3 48.8	28 51.0	20 42.9	26 03.9	11 03.6	14 45.3
19 Su	13 48 28	25 15 21	21 17 35	27 22 02	23 41.0	19 14.2	7 23.5	10 17.0	3 35.4	29 03.1	20 47.6	26 03.1	11 05.8	14 46.1
20 M	13 52 25	26 15 00	3♑23 35	9♑22 49	23 42.6	19 50.9	8 38.3	10 49.1	3 21.9	29 15.3	20 52.3	26 02.2	11 08.0	14 46.9
21 Tu	13 56 22	27 14 41	15 20 19	21 16 41	23R43.7	20 22.4	9 53.2	11 21.0	3 08.3	29 27.6	20 56.8	26 01.3	11 10.2	14 47.6
22 W	14 00 18	28 14 23	27 12 32	3♒08 30	23 43.7	20 48.3	11 08.0	11 52.7	2 54.6	29 39.9	21 01.3	26 00.3	11 12.3	14 48.3
23 Th	14 04 15	29 14 07	9♒05 09	15 03 07	23 42.6	21 08.0	12 22.9	12 24.3	2 40.9	29 52.3	21 05.6	25 59.2	11 14.5	14 49.0
24 F	14 08 11	0♏13 52	21 02 57	27 05 10	23 40.5	21 21.0	13 37.7	12 55.7	2 27.1	0♐04.7	21 09.9	25 58.1	11 16.6	14 49.7
25 Sa	14 12 08	1 13 39	3♓10 18	9♓18 46	23 37.5	21R26.7	14 52.6	13 26.9	2 13.3	0 17.1	21 14.1	25 57.0	11 18.8	14 50.3
26 Su	14 16 04	2 13 28	15 30 58	21 47 13	23 34.1	21 24.4	16 07.4	13 57.9	1 59.4	0 29.6	21 18.2	25 55.8	11 20.9	14 50.9
27 M	14 20 01	3 13 19	28 07 46	4♈32 48	23 30.8	21 13.7	17 22.3	14 28.7	1 45.6	0 42.2	21 22.3	25 54.6	11 23.0	14 51.5
28 Tu	14 23 57	4 13 11	11♈02 25	17 36 37	23 27.9	20 54.2	18 37.1	14 59.4	1 31.8	0 54.8	21 26.2	25 53.3	11 25.1	14 52.0
29 W	14 27 54	5 13 06	24 15 21	0♉58 27	23 25.9	20 25.4	19 52.0	15 29.8	1 18.0	1 07.5	21 30.0	25 52.0	11 27.2	14 52.6
30 Th	14 31 51	6 13 02	7♉45 42	14 36 50	23D24.8	19 47.2	21 06.8	16 00.1	1 04.3	1 20.2	21 33.8	25 50.6	11 29.3	14 53.1
31 F	14 35 47	7 13 01	21 31 29	28 29 16	23 24.7	18 59.8	22 21.6	16 30.2	0 50.6	1 32.9	21 37.4	25 49.2	11 31.3	14 53.5

Astro Data

	Dy Hr Mn
☽0N	3 4:23
⚳R	5 16:36
☿0S	12 17:46
☽0S	16 0:45
♀0S	21 22:05
⊙0S	23 21:28
♃∠♆	30 9:44
☽0N	30 10:52
♅R	2 16:05
♃⊼♅	4 16:40
☽0S	13 10:10
☿R	25 17:25
☽0N	27 19:29

Planet Ingress

	Dy Hr Mn
☿ ♎	11 20:54
♀ ♎	19 12:01
⊙ ♎	23 21:29
♂ ♌	1 2:31
☿ ♏	1 15:26
♀ ♏	13 13:49
♃ ♐	24 3:00
⊙ ♏	24 6:26

Last Aspect / ☽ Ingress (September)

Last Aspect Dy Hr Mn		☽ Ingress Dy Hr Mn
2 3:59	♅ □	♈ 2 12:03
4 12:29	♅ ⚹	♉ 4 20:10
6 11:17	♃ ☍	♊ 7 2:18
8 23:18	♅ ☌	♋ 9 6:12
11 6:22	☿ ⚹	♌ 11 8:03
13 2:21	♅ ⚹	♍ 13 8:51
15 3:38	♅ □	♎ 15 10:16
17 7:11	♅ △	♏ 17 14:10
19 13:45	⊙ ⚹	♐ 19 21:49
22 5:42	⊙ □	♑ 22 8:58
24 13:54	♂ ☍	♒ 24 21:38
27 1:52	♅ △	♓ 27 9:24
29 17:28	♂ △	♈ 29 18:58

Last Aspect / ☽ Ingress (October)

Last Aspect Dy Hr Mn		☽ Ingress Dy Hr Mn
1 19:19	♅ ⚹	♉ 2 2:15
4 0:46	♃ ☍	♊ 4 7:44
6 5:12	♅ ☌	♋ 6 11:47
8 9:25	♃ △	♌ 8 14:41
10 12:23	♃ □	♍ 10 16:57
12 15:35	♃ ⚹	♎ 12 19:31
14 16:51	♅ △	♏ 14 23:45
17 4:12	♃ ☌	♐ 17 6:53
19 9:24	♅ ☍	♑ 19 17:14
22 4:51	♃ ⚹	♒ 22 5:39
24 9:47	♅ △	♓ 24 17:46
26 19:51	♅ □	♈ 27 3:31
29 2:54	♅ ⚹	♉ 29 10:16
31 0:24	♀ ☍	♊ 31 14:36

☽ Phases & Eclipses

Dy Hr Mn		
8 3:57	☾	14♊40
14 19:28	●	21♍08
22 5:42	☽	28♐23
30 6:41	○	6♈16
7 10:29	☾	13♋18
14 6:10	●	20♎03
22 1:11	☽	27♑47
29 20:07	○	5♉33

Astro Data

1 September 1947
Julian Day # 17410
SVP 5♓59'39"
GC 26♐06.5 ⚳ 7♓33.5R
Eris 6♈40.8R ⚵ 17♐35.2
⚷ 5♏32.8 ⚶ 10♋40.3
☽ Mean ☊ 27♉15.1

1 October 1947
Julian Day # 17440
SVP 5♓59'37"
GC 26♐06.6 ⚳ 0♓48.4R
Eris 6♈22.5R ⚵ 22♐49.0
⚷ 8♏57.2 ⚶ 20♋29.9
☽ Mean ☊ 25♉39.8

November 1947 LONGITUDE

Day	Sid.Time	☉	0 hr ☽	Noon☽	True☊	☿	♀	♂	⚳	♃	♄	♅	♆	♇
1 Sa	14 39 44	8♏13 01	5♊29 47	12♊32 34	23♉25.3	18♏03.7	23♏36.5	17♌00.1	0♉37.0	1♐45.7	21♌41.0	25♊47.8	11♎33.4	14♌54.0
2 Su	14 43 40	9 13 03	19 37 13	26 43 15	23 26.3	16R59.7	24 51.3	17 29.8	0R23.5	1 58.5	21 44.5	25R46.3	11 35.4	14 54.4
3 M	14 47 37	10 13 08	3♋50 16	10♋57 51	23 27.5	15 49.1	26 06.2	17 59.2	0 10.1	2 11.4	21 47.9	25 44.7	11 37.4	14 54.8
4 Tu	14 51 33	11 13 15	18 05 37	25 13 14	23 28.3	14 33.6	27 21.0	18 28.5	29♈56.8	2 24.3	21 51.1	25 43.2	11 39.4	14 55.2
5 W	14 55 30	12 13 24	2♌20 21	9♌26 40	23R28.7	13 15.3	28 35.9	18 57.6	29 43.7	2 37.3	21 54.3	25 41.5	11 41.4	14 55.5
6 Th	14 59 27	13 13 35	16 31 56	23 35 51	23 28.6	11 56.6	29 50.7	19 26.4	29 30.7	2 50.3	21 57.4	25 39.9	11 43.4	14 55.8
7 F	15 03 23	14 13 48	0♍38 11	7♍38 43	23 28.0	10 40.0	1♐05.6	19 55.0	29 17.8	3 03.3	22 00.4	25 38.2	11 45.4	14 56.1
8 Sa	15 07 20	15 14 03	14 37 11	21 33 23	23 27.1	9 28.0	2 20.4	20 23.4	29 05.2	3 16.3	22 03.2	25 36.4	11 47.3	14 56.3
9 Su	15 11 16	16 14 20	28 27 05	5♎18 05	23 26.1	8 22.8	3 35.3	20 51.5	28 52.7	3 29.4	22 06.0	25 34.6	11 49.3	14 56.5
10 M	15 15 13	17 14 38	12♎06 09	18 51 06	23 25.3	7 26.4	4 50.1	21 19.4	28 40.5	3 42.6	22 08.7	25 32.8	11 51.2	14 56.7
11 Tu	15 19 09	18 14 59	25 32 46	2♏10 58	23 24.7	6 40.2	6 05.0	21 47.0	28 28.5	3 55.7	22 11.3	25 30.9	11 53.1	14 56.9
12 W	15 23 06	19 15 22	8♏45 35	15 16 30	23D24.4	6 05.1	7 19.8	22 14.4	28 16.7	4 08.9	22 13.7	25 29.1	11 54.9	14 57.0
13 Th	15 27 02	20 15 46	21 43 41	28 07 07	23 24.4	5 41.7	8 34.7	22 41.6	28 05.1	4 22.1	22 16.1	25 27.1	11 56.8	14 57.2
14 F	15 30 59	21 16 12	4♐26 49	10♐42 53	23 24.5	5D30.0	9 49.5	23 08.4	27 53.8	4 35.3	22 18.4	25 25.2	11 58.6	14 57.2
15 Sa	15 34 55	22 16 40	16 55 27	23 04 43	23 24.6	5 29.7	11 04.4	23 35.1	27 42.8	4 48.6	22 20.5	25 23.2	12 00.4	14 57.3
16 Su	15 38 52	23 17 09	29 10 55	5♑14 21	23R24.7	5 40.2	12 19.2	24 01.4	27 32.1	5 01.9	22 22.5	25 21.1	12 02.2	14R57.3
17 M	15 42 49	24 17 40	11♑15 22	17 14 22	23 24.7	6 00.8	13 34.1	24 27.5	27 21.7	5 15.2	22 24.5	25 19.0	12 04.0	14 57.3
18 Tu	15 46 45	25 18 12	23 11 47	29 08 06	23 24.5	6 30.6	14 48.9	24 53.2	27 11.5	5 28.5	22 26.3	25 17.0	12 05.8	14 57.3
19 W	15 50 42	26 18 45	5♒03 49	10♒59 30	23 24.3	7 08.8	16 03.7	25 18.7	27 01.7	5 41.9	22 28.0	25 14.8	12 07.5	14 57.2
20 Th	15 54 38	27 19 19	16 55 40	22 52 56	23D24.2	7 54.5	17 18.5	25 43.9	26 52.2	5 55.2	22 29.6	25 12.7	12 09.2	14 57.1
21 F	15 58 35	28 19 55	28 51 53	4♓53 07	23 24.2	8 46.8	18 33.4	26 08.8	26 43.1	6 08.6	22 31.1	25 10.5	12 10.9	14 57.0
22 Sa	16 02 31	29 20 31	10♓57 11	17 04 42	23 24.5	9 44.9	19 48.2	26 33.4	26 34.2	6 22.0	22 32.5	25 08.3	12 12.6	14 56.9
23 Su	16 06 28	0♐21 09	23 16 10	29 32 05	23 25.0	10 48.1	21 03.0	26 57.7	26 25.8	6 35.4	22 33.8	25 06.0	12 14.2	14 56.7
24 M	16 10 25	1 21 48	5♈52 56	12♈19 05	23 25.8	11 55.6	22 17.8	27 21.7	26 17.6	6 48.8	22 35.0	25 03.7	12 15.8	14 56.5
25 Tu	16 14 21	2 22 28	18 50 51	25 28 25	23 26.6	13 06.9	23 32.5	27 45.4	26 09.9	7 02.2	22 36.0	25 01.4	12 17.4	14 56.3
26 W	16 18 18	3 23 10	2♉11 55	9♉01 19	23 27.3	14 21.5	24 47.3	28 08.7	26 02.5	7 15.7	22 37.0	24 59.1	12 19.0	14 56.0
27 Th	16 22 14	4 23 53	15 56 30	22 57 10	23R27.6	15 38.8	26 02.1	28 31.7	25 55.4	7 29.1	22 37.8	24 56.8	12 20.5	14 55.7
28 F	16 26 11	5 24 37	0♊02 55	7♊13 13	23 27.3	16 58.5	27 16.9	28 54.4	25 48.7	7 42.6	22 38.6	24 54.4	12 22.1	14 55.4
29 Sa	16 30 07	6 25 22	14 27 24	21 44 44	23 26.4	18 20.2	28 31.6	29 16.7	25 42.5	7 56.0	22 39.2	24 52.1	12 23.6	14 55.1
30 Su	16 34 04	7 26 09	29 04 23	6♋25 27	23 24.8	19 43.7	29 46.4	29 38.6	25 36.5	8 09.5	22 39.7	24 49.7	12 25.0	14 54.7

December 1947 LONGITUDE

Day	Sid.Time	☉	0 hr ☽	Noon☽	True☊	☿	♀	♂	⚳	♃	♄	♅	♆	♇
1 M	16 38 00	8♐26 57	13♋47 05	21♋08 23	23♉22.9	21♏08.5	1♑01.1	0♍00.2	25♈31.0	8♐23.0	22♌40.1	24♊47.2	12♎26.5	14♌54.3
2 Tu	16 41 57	9 27 46	28 28 32	5♌46 46	23R20.9	22 34.7	2 15.9	0 21.5	25R25.9	8 36.4	22 40.4	24R44.8	12 27.9	14R53.9
3 W	16 45 54	10 28 37	13♌02 27	20 15 00	23 19.4	24 01.8	3 30.6	0 42.3	25 21.1	8 49.9	22R40.5	24 42.4	12 29.3	14 53.5
4 Th	16 49 50	11 29 29	27 24 01	4♍29 08	23D18.5	25 29.9	4 45.3	1 02.8	25 16.7	9 03.4	22 40.6	24 39.9	12 30.6	14 53.0
5 F	16 53 47	12 30 22	11♍30 10	18 26 59	23 18.4	26 58.7	6 00.0	1 22.8	25 12.7	9 16.8	22 40.5	24 37.4	12 32.0	14 52.5
6 Sa	16 57 43	13 31 17	25 19 33	2♎07 55	23 19.2	28 28.1	7 14.7	1 42.5	25 09.2	9 30.3	22 40.4	24 34.9	12 33.3	14 52.0
7 Su	17 01 40	14 32 13	8♎52 11	15 32 28	23 20.6	29 58.0	8 29.4	2 01.7	25 06.0	9 43.8	22 40.1	24 32.4	12 34.6	14 51.4
8 M	17 05 36	15 33 11	22 08 55	28 41 43	23 22.2	1♐28.4	9 44.1	2 20.5	25 03.2	9 57.2	22 39.7	24 29.9	12 35.8	14 50.8
9 Tu	17 09 33	16 34 09	5♏11 03	11♏37 04	23R23.5	2 59.2	10 58.8	2 38.9	25 00.8	10 10.7	22 39.2	24 27.3	12 37.0	14 50.2
10 W	17 13 29	17 35 09	17 59 56	24 19 50	23 23.9	4 30.3	12 13.5	2 56.8	24 58.8	10 24.1	22 38.5	24 24.8	12 38.2	14 49.6
11 Th	17 17 26	18 36 10	0♐36 52	6♐51 12	23 23.2	6 01.7	13 28.2	3 14.3	24 57.2	10 37.5	22 37.8	24 22.2	12 39.4	14 48.9
12 F	17 21 23	19 37 12	13 02 57	19 12 14	23 21.0	7 33.3	14 42.9	3 31.3	24 56.0	10 51.0	22 37.0	24 19.7	12 40.5	14 48.3
13 Sa	17 25 19	20 38 14	25 19 12	1♑23 59	23 17.4	9 05.2	15 57.5	3 47.8	24 55.2	11 04.4	22 36.0	24 17.1	12 41.6	14 47.6
14 Su	17 29 16	21 39 17	7♑26 43	13 27 37	23 12.7	10 37.2	17 12.1	4 03.9	24D54.8	11 17.8	22 34.9	24 14.6	12 42.7	14 46.8
15 M	17 33 12	22 40 21	19 26 51	25 24 41	23 07.2	12 09.5	18 26.8	4 19.4	24 54.8	11 31.1	22 33.8	24 12.0	12 43.7	14 46.1
16 Tu	17 37 09	23 41 26	1♒21 23	7♒17 14	23 01.5	13 41.9	19 41.4	4 34.4	24 55.2	11 44.5	22 32.5	24 09.4	12 44.7	14 45.3
17 W	17 41 05	24 42 31	13 12 38	19 07 56	22 56.4	15 14.5	20 56.0	4 49.0	24 56.0	11 57.8	22 31.1	24 06.9	12 45.7	14 44.5
18 Th	17 45 02	25 43 36	25 03 35	1♓00 04	22 52.2	16 47.2	22 10.6	5 03.0	24 57.2	12 11.1	22 29.6	24 04.3	12 46.6	14 43.7
19 F	17 48 58	26 44 42	6♓57 53	12 57 34	22 49.5	18 20.1	23 25.1	5 16.4	24 58.8	12 24.4	22 28.0	24 01.7	12 47.5	14 42.9
20 Sa	17 52 55	27 45 47	18 59 42	25 04 52	22D48.4	19 53.2	24 39.7	5 29.3	25 00.7	12 37.7	22 26.2	23 59.2	12 48.4	14 42.0
21 Su	17 56 52	28 46 54	1♈13 41	7♈26 43	22 48.8	21 26.4	25 54.2	5 41.7	25 03.1	12 51.0	22 24.4	23 56.6	12 49.3	14 41.1
22 M	18 00 48	29 48 00	13 44 34	20 07 49	22 50.1	22 59.9	27 08.7	5 53.5	25 05.8	13 04.2	22 22.5	23 54.0	12 50.1	14 40.2
23 Tu	18 04 45	0♑49 07	26 36 57	3♉12 26	22 51.8	24 33.5	28 23.2	6 04.7	25 08.9	13 17.4	22 20.5	23 51.5	12 50.9	14 39.2
24 W	18 08 41	1 50 13	9♉54 37	16 43 46	22R52.9	26 07.3	29 37.6	6 15.3	25 12.4	13 30.5	22 18.3	23 49.0	12 51.6	14 38.3
25 Th	18 12 38	2 51 20	23 39 57	0♊43 09	22 52.8	27 41.3	0♒52.1	6 25.3	25 16.2	13 43.7	22 16.1	23 46.4	12 52.3	14 37.3
26 F	18 16 34	3 52 28	7♊53 06	15 09 23	22 50.9	29 15.6	2 06.5	6 34.8	25 20.4	13 56.8	22 13.8	23 43.9	12 53.0	14 36.3
27 Sa	18 20 31	4 53 35	22 31 21	29 58 11	22 46.9	0♑50.1	3 20.9	6 43.6	25 25.0	14 09.9	22 11.3	23 41.4	12 53.7	14 35.3
28 Su	18 24 28	5 54 43	7♋28 51	15♋02 12	22 41.1	2 24.9	4 35.2	6 51.8	25 29.9	14 22.9	22 08.8	23 38.9	12 54.3	14 34.3
29 M	18 28 24	6 55 51	22 36 58	0♌11 52	22 34.2	3 59.9	5 49.6	6 59.3	25 35.2	14 35.9	22 06.2	23 36.4	12 54.9	14 33.2
30 Tu	18 32 21	7 56 59	7♌45 35	15 16 55	22 27.1	5 35.2	7 03.9	7 06.2	25 40.8	14 48.9	22 03.5	23 34.0	12 55.4	14 32.2
31 W	18 36 17	8 58 07	22 44 44	0♍08 06	22 20.8	7 10.9	8 18.2	7 12.4	25 46.8	15 01.8	22 00.6	23 31.5	12 55.9	14 31.1

Astro Data	Dy Hr Mn
☽ 0S	9 17:52
☿ D	15 0:38
♇ R	16 21:42
☽ 0N	24 5:09
♄ R	4 11:34
☽ 0S	6 23:30
⚳ D	14 23:44
♃⚹♆	21 8:43
☽ 0N	21 13:53
♃△♇	29 7:26

Planet Ingress		Dy Hr Mn
⚳	♈R	4 6:13
♀	♐	6 14:59
☉	♐	23 3:38
♀	♑	30 16:23
♂	♍	1 11:44
☿	♐	7 12:32
☉	♑	22 16:43
♀	♒	24 19:13
☿	♑	26 23:17

Last Aspect Dy Hr Mn			☽ Ingress	Dy Hr Mn
2 10:24	♅	☌	♋	2 17:32
4 15:56	♀	△	♌	4 20:03
6 15:31	♅	⚹	♍	6 22:55
8 19:02	♅	□	♎	9 2:42
10 23:58	♅	△	♏	11 8:02
13 1:26	♂	□	♐	13 15:33
15 16:31	♅	☍	♑	16 1:37
18 3:32	☉	⚹	♒	18 13:45
20 21:44	☉	□	♓	21 2:16
23 3:33	♅	□	♈	23 12:53
25 16:13	♂	△	♉	25 20:06
27 21:42	♂	□	♊	27 23:55
30 0:39	♂	⚹	♋	30 1:31

Last Aspect Dy Hr Mn			☽ Ingress	Dy Hr Mn
1 12:00	☿	△	♌	2 2:30
3 19:27	♅	⚹	♍	4 4:23
6 4:44	☿	⚹	♎	6 8:14
8 4:19	♅	△	♏	8 14:24
10 8:48	♄	□	♐	10 22:49
12 22:01	♅	☍	♑	13 9:14
14 20:22	♀	☌	♒	15 21:16
18 0:21	☉	⚹	♓	18 9:59
20 17:44	☉	□	♈	20 21:37
23 2:20	♀	□	♉	23 6:11
24 21:38	♄	□	♊	25 10:47
27 1:55	♅	☌	♋	27 12:03
28 8:37	♆	□	♌	29 11:41
31 1:17	♅	⚹	♍	31 11:47

☽ Phases & Eclipses Dy Hr Mn		
5 17:04	☾	12♌26
12 20:01	●	19♏36
12 20:05:09	●	A 03'59"
20 21:44	☽	27♒44
28 8:45	○	5♊16
28 8:34	○	A 0.868
5 0:55	☾	12♍02
12 12:53	●	19♐39
20 17:44	☽	28♓00
27 20:27	○	5♋15

Astro Data

1 November 1947
Julian Day # 17471
SVP 5♓59'33"
GC 26♐06.6 ⚴ 28♒29.1
Eris 6♈03.8R ⚵ 1♑23.2
⚷ 13♏05.6 ⚶ 27♋40.7
☽ Mean ☊ 24♉01.3

1 December 1947
Julian Day # 17501
SVP 5♓59'28"
GC 26♐06.7 ⚴ 1♓17.9
Eris 5♈51.4R ⚵ 11♑41.2
⚷ 17♏11.0 ⚶ 29♋46.1R
☽ Mean ☊ 22♉26.0

LONGITUDE — January 1948

Day	Sid.Time	☉	0 hr ☽	Noon ☽	True ☊	☿	♀	♂	⚳	♃	♄	♅	♆	♇
1 Th	18 40 14	9♑59 16	7♍26 16	14♍38 40	22♉16.1	8♑46.8	9♒32.4	7♍17.9	25♈53.1	15♐14.7	21♌57.7	23♊29.1	12♎56.4	14♌30.0
2 F	18 44 10	11 00 25	21 44 57	28 44 57	22D 13.3	10 23.1	10 46.6	7 22.8	25 59.7	15 27.5	21R 54.7	23R 26.6	12 56.9	14R 28.8
3 Sa	18 48 07	12 01 35	5♎38 38	12♎26 10	22 12.5	11 59.7	12 00.8	7 26.9	26 06.7	15 40.4	21 51.6	23 24.2	12 57.3	14 27.7
4 Su	18 52 03	13 02 45	19 07 46	25 43 48	22 13.2	13 36.7	13 15.0	7 30.3	26 14.0	15 53.1	21 48.4	23 21.8	12 57.6	14 26.5
5 M	18 56 00	14 03 55	2♏14 39	8♏40 45	22 14.3	15 14.1	14 29.2	7 33.0	26 21.7	16 05.8	21 45.2	23 19.5	12 58.0	14 25.4
6 Tu	18 59 57	15 05 05	15 02 31	21 20 27	22R 15.0	16 51.9	15 43.3	7 35.0	26 29.6	16 18.5	21 41.8	23 17.1	12 58.3	14 24.2
7 W	19 03 53	16 06 16	27 34 56	3♐46 23	22 14.3	18 30.0	16 57.4	7 36.2	26 37.9	16 31.1	21 38.4	23 14.8	12 58.6	14 23.0
8 Th	19 07 50	17 07 26	9♐55 12	16 01 43	22 11.3	20 08.5	18 11.4	7R 36.6	26 46.5	16 43.7	21 34.9	23 12.5	12 58.8	14 21.8
9 F	19 11 46	18 08 37	22 06 13	28 08 59	22 05.6	21 47.5	19 25.5	7 36.3	26 55.4	16 56.3	21 31.3	23 10.3	12 59.0	14 20.5
10 Sa	19 15 43	19 09 47	4♑10 15	10♑10 13	21 57.3	23 26.8	20 39.5	7 35.2	27 04.7	17 08.7	21 27.6	23 08.0	12 59.2	14 19.3
11 Su	19 19 39	20 10 57	16 09 04	22 06 58	21 46.7	25 06.6	21 53.4	7 33.3	27 14.2	17 21.1	21 23.8	23 05.8	12 59.3	14 18.0
12 M	19 23 36	21 12 07	28 04 05	4♒00 35	21 34.7	26 46.7	23 07.3	7 30.6	27 24.0	17 33.5	21 20.0	23 03.6	12 59.4	14 16.7
13 Tu	19 27 32	22 13 16	9♒56 36	15 52 21	21 22.1	28 27.2	24 21.2	7 27.1	27 34.1	17 45.8	21 16.1	23 01.5	12 59.5	14 15.5
14 W	19 31 29	23 14 25	21 48 01	27 43 52	21 10.2	0♒08.0	25 35.1	7 22.9	27 44.6	17 58.1	21 12.1	22 59.3	12R 59.5	14 14.2
15 Th	19 35 26	24 15 33	3♓40 10	9♓37 13	20 59.9	1 49.1	26 48.9	7 17.8	27 55.3	18 10.2	21 08.1	22 57.2	12 59.5	14 12.8
16 F	19 39 22	25 16 41	15 35 24	21 35 07	20 52.0	3 30.5	28 02.6	7 11.9	28 06.3	18 22.4	21 04.0	22 55.2	12 59.5	14 11.5
17 Sa	19 43 19	26 17 48	27 36 50	3♈41 01	20 46.8	5 12.2	29 16.3	7 05.2	28 17.5	18 34.4	20 59.8	22 53.1	12 59.4	14 10.2
18 Su	19 47 15	27 18 54	9♈48 12	15 58 59	20D 44.2	6 53.9	0♓30.0	6 57.8	28 29.1	18 46.4	20 55.6	22 51.1	12 59.3	14 08.9
19 M	19 51 12	28 19 59	22 13 55	28 33 36	20 43.5	8 35.8	1 43.6	6 49.5	28 40.9	18 58.3	20 51.3	22 49.2	12 59.2	14 07.5
20 Tu	19 55 08	29 21 03	4♉58 39	11♉29 37	20R 43.8	10 17.6	2 57.1	6 40.4	28 52.9	19 10.2	20 47.0	22 47.2	12 59.0	14 06.1
21 W	19 59 05	0♒22 07	18 07 01	24 51 19	20 44.0	11 59.3	4 10.7	6 30.5	29 05.3	19 21.9	20 42.6	22 45.3	12 58.8	14 04.8
22 Th	20 03 01	1 23 09	1♊42 50	8♊41 48	20 42.7	13 40.6	5 24.1	6 19.8	29 17.9	19 33.7	20 38.2	22 43.5	12 58.6	14 03.4
23 F	20 06 58	2 24 11	15 48 14	23 01 59	20 39.2	15 21.5	6 37.5	6 08.4	29 30.7	19 45.3	20 33.7	22 41.7	12 58.3	14 02.0
24 Sa	20 10 55	3 25 12	0♋22 40	7♋49 39	20 32.8	17 01.7	7 50.8	5 56.2	29 43.8	19 56.9	20 29.2	22 39.9	12 58.0	14 00.6
25 Su	20 14 51	4 26 12	15 22 04	22 58 48	20 23.9	18 40.9	9 04.1	5 43.2	29 57.1	20 08.4	20 24.6	22 38.2	12 57.6	13 59.3
26 M	20 18 48	5 27 10	0♌38 35	8♌19 58	20 13.2	20 18.9	10 17.3	5 29.4	0♉10.7	20 19.8	20 20.0	22 36.5	12 57.3	13 57.9
27 Tu	20 22 44	6 28 08	16 01 25	23 41 25	20 02.0	21 55.4	11 30.4	5 14.9	0 24.5	20 31.1	20 15.3	22 34.8	12 56.9	13 56.5
28 W	20 26 41	7 29 05	1♍18 30	8♍51 22	19 51.6	23 29.9	12 43.5	4 59.7	0 38.5	20 42.3	20 10.7	22 33.2	12 56.4	13 55.1
29 Th	20 30 37	8 30 02	16 18 52	23 40 08	19 43.1	25 01.9	13 56.5	4 43.8	0 52.8	20 53.5	20 05.9	22 31.6	12 56.0	13 53.6
30 F	20 34 34	9 30 57	0♎54 29	8♎01 32	19 37.3	26 31.1	15 09.5	4 27.1	1 07.3	21 04.6	20 01.2	22 30.1	12 55.5	13 52.2
31 Sa	20 38 30	10 31 52	15 01 06	21 53 14	19 34.2	27 56.9	16 22.4	4 09.8	1 22.0	21 15.6	19 56.4	22 28.6	12 54.9	13 50.8

LONGITUDE — February 1948

Day	Sid.Time	☉	0 hr ☽	Noon ☽	True ☊	☿	♀	♂	⚳	♃	♄	♅	♆	♇
1 Su	20 42 27	11♒32 46	28♎38 06	5♏16 04	19♉33.1	29♒18.5	17♓35.2	3♍51.8	1♉36.9	21♐26.5	19♌51.6	22♊27.1	12♎54.3	13♌49.4
2 M	20 46 24	12 33 40	11♏47 36	18 13 11	19R 33.0	0♓35.3	18 48.0	3R 33.1	1 52.1	21 37.3	19R 46.8	22R 25.7	12R 53.7	13R 48.0
3 Tu	20 50 20	13 34 32	24 33 25	0♐48 54	19 32.7	1 46.7	20 00.7	3 13.9	2 07.4	21 48.1	19 42.0	22 24.4	12 53.1	13 46.6
4 W	20 54 17	14 35 24	7♐00 13	13 07 57	19 31.0	2 51.8	21 13.3	2 54.0	2 23.0	21 58.7	19 37.1	22 23.1	12 52.5	13 45.1
5 Th	20 58 13	15 36 15	19 12 40	25 14 54	19 26.8	3 49.9	22 25.8	2 33.7	2 38.7	22 09.3	19 32.2	22 21.8	12 51.8	13 43.7
6 F	21 02 10	16 37 05	1♑15 07	7♑13 46	19 19.6	4 40.2	23 38.3	2 12.8	2 54.7	22 19.7	19 27.4	22 20.6	12 51.0	13 42.3
7 Sa	21 06 06	17 37 54	13 11 15	19 07 53	19 09.3	5 21.9	24 50.7	1 51.4	3 10.9	22 30.1	19 22.5	22 19.4	12 50.3	13 40.9
8 Su	21 10 03	18 38 42	25 03 59	0♒59 47	18 56.4	5 54.3	26 03.0	1 29.5	3 27.2	22 40.3	19 17.6	22 18.3	12 49.5	13 39.5
9 M	21 13 59	19 39 28	6♒55 32	12 51 24	18 41.6	6 16.8	27 15.2	1 07.3	3 43.8	22 50.5	19 12.7	22 17.3	12 48.7	13 38.1
10 Tu	21 17 56	20 40 14	18 47 33	24 44 08	18 26.3	6R 29.0	28 27.4	0 44.7	4 00.5	23 00.6	19 07.8	22 16.2	12 47.9	13 36.6
11 W	21 21 53	21 40 58	0♓41 18	6♓39 12	18 11.6	6 30.5	29 39.5	0 21.7	4 17.5	23 10.5	19 02.9	22 15.3	12 47.0	13 35.2
12 Th	21 25 49	22 41 40	12 38 00	18 37 53	17 58.7	6 21.3	0♈51.4	29♌58.5	4 34.6	23 20.3	18 58.0	22 14.3	12 46.1	13 33.8
13 F	21 29 46	23 42 21	24 39 03	0♈41 46	17 48.4	6 01.4	2 03.3	29 35.0	4 51.8	23 30.1	18 53.1	22 13.5	12 45.2	13 32.4
14 Sa	21 33 42	24 43 00	6♈46 18	12 53 01	17 41.2	5 31.5	3 15.1	29 11.4	5 09.3	23 39.7	18 48.3	22 12.6	12 44.2	13 31.0
15 Su	21 37 39	25 43 38	19 02 15	25 14 27	17 37.0	4 52.1	4 26.8	28 47.6	5 26.9	23 49.2	18 43.4	22 11.9	12 43.2	13 29.6
16 M	21 41 35	26 44 14	1♉30 03	7♉49 32	17D 35.4	4 04.3	5 38.4	28 23.7	5 44.7	23 58.6	18 38.6	22 11.2	12 42.2	13 28.3
17 Tu	21 45 32	27 44 48	14 13 25	20 42 13	17R 35.1	3 09.4	6 49.9	27 59.8	6 02.7	24 07.9	18 33.8	22 10.5	12 41.2	13 26.9
18 W	21 49 28	28 45 21	27 16 24	3♊56 28	17 35.1	2 08.8	8 01.3	27 35.9	6 20.8	24 17.1	18 29.0	22 09.9	12 40.1	13 25.5
19 Th	21 53 25	29 45 51	10♊42 49	17 35 45	17 34.0	1 04.3	9 12.6	27 12.0	6 39.1	24 26.1	18 24.3	22 09.3	12 39.0	13 24.2
20 F	21 57 22	0♓46 20	24 35 29	1♋42 04	17 30.9	29♒57.6	10 23.8	26 48.2	6 57.6	24 35.1	18 19.6	22 08.8	12 37.9	13 22.8
21 Sa	22 01 18	1 46 47	8♋55 23	16 15 03	17 25.2	28 50.3	11 34.8	26 24.5	7 16.2	24 43.9	18 14.9	22 08.4	12 36.8	13 21.5
22 Su	22 05 15	2 47 12	23 40 33	1♌11 04	17 16.9	27 44.3	12 45.8	26 01.0	7 34.9	24 52.6	18 10.2	22 08.0	12 35.6	13 20.1
23 M	22 09 11	3 47 36	8♌45 35	16 22 53	17 06.7	26 40.9	13 56.6	25 37.8	7 53.8	25 01.1	18 05.6	22 07.6	12 34.5	13 18.8
24 Tu	22 13 08	4 47 57	24 01 39	1♍40 25	16 55.8	25 41.6	15 07.3	25 14.7	8 12.9	25 09.6	18 01.0	22 07.3	12 33.3	13 17.5
25 W	22 17 04	5 48 17	9♍17 44	16 52 13	16 45.5	24 47.3	16 17.9	24 52.0	8 32.0	25 17.9	17 56.5	22 07.1	12 32.0	13 16.2
26 Th	22 21 01	6 48 35	24 22 33	1♎47 38	16 37.0	23 59.0	17 28.3	24 29.7	8 51.4	25 26.1	17 52.0	22 06.9	12 30.8	13 14.9
27 F	22 24 57	7 48 51	9♎06 34	16 18 41	16 31.1	23 17.3	18 38.7	24 07.7	9 10.8	25 34.1	17 47.5	22 06.7	12 29.5	13 13.6
28 Sa	22 28 54	8 49 06	23 23 31	0♏20 53	16 27.8	22 42.5	19 48.8	23 46.1	9 30.4	25 42.0	17 43.1	22 06.6	12 28.2	13 12.4
29 Su	22 32 51	9 49 20	7♏10 46	13 53 19	16D 26.7	22 14.7	20 58.9	23 24.9	9 50.1	25 49.8	17 38.8	22D 06.6	12 26.9	13 11.1

Astro Data

Dy Hr Mn	
☽0S	3 4:37
♂R	8 13:49
♆R	14 22:02
☽0N	17 20:26
♃△♄	26 12:20
☽0S	30 11:35
♃☍♅	6 13:50
☿R	11 3:21
♀0N	12 23:14
☽0N	14 1:27
☽0S	26 21:09
♅D	29 14:23

Planet Ingress

	Dy Hr Mn
☿ ♒	14 10:06
♀ ♓	18 2:14
☉ ♒	21 3:18
⚳ ♉	25 17:07
☿ ♓	2 0:46
♀ ♈	11 18:51
♂ ♌R	12 10:28
☉ ♓	19 17:37
☿ ♒R	20 11:08

Last Aspect / ☽ Ingress

Last Aspect Dy Hr Mn		☽ Ingress Dy Hr Mn
2 2:55	♅ □	♎ 2 14:10
4 7:42	♅ △	♏ 4 19:51
6 12:41	♄ □	♐ 7 4:41
9 2:09	♅ ☍	♑ 9 15:41
11 19:01	☿ ☌	♒ 12 3:54
14 7:09	♀ ☌	♓ 14 16:35
16 20:02	☉ ✶	♈ 17 4:44
19 11:32	☉ □	♉ 19 14:42
21 4:41	♄ □	♊ 21 21:01
23 11:26	♅ ☌	♋ 23 23:23
24 20:11	♆ □	♌ 25 23:00
27 10:16	♅ ✶	♍ 27 21:56
29 10:08	♅ □	♎ 29 22:29

Last Aspect / ☽ Ingress

Last Aspect Dy Hr Mn		☽ Ingress Dy Hr Mn
1 0:00	☿ △	♏ 1 2:27
2 14:55	♄ □	♐ 3 10:26
5 6:16	♅ ☍	♑ 5 21:30
8 0:52	♀ ✶	♒ 8 9:59
10 8:28	♃ ✶	♓ 10 22:37
12 21:31	♃ □	♈ 13 10:37
15 18:37	♂ △	♉ 15 21:08
18 1:55	☉ □	♊ 18 4:56
20 3:59	♂ ✶	♋ 20 9:09
21 6:04	♆ □	♌ 22 10:07
24 3:10	☿ ☍	♍ 24 9:22
26 1:37	♃ □	♎ 26 9:05
28 3:53	♃ ✶	♏ 28 11:24

☽ Phases & Eclipses

Dy Hr Mn	
3 11:13	☾ 12♎00
11 7:45	● 20♑00
19 11:32	☽ 28♈19
26 7:11	○ 5♌15
2 0:31	☾ 12♏05
10 3:02	● 20♒18
18 1:55	☽ 28♉20
24 17:16	○ 5♍01

Astro Data

1 January 1948
Julian Day # 17532
SVP 5♓59'22"
GC 26♐06.8 ⚴ 7♓59.7
Eris 5♈48.4 ⚵ 23♑38.7
⚷ 20♏55.7 ⚶ 25♋15.8R
☽ Mean ☊ 20♉47.5

1 February 1948
Julian Day # 17563
SVP 5♓59'16"
GC 26♐06.9 ⚴ 17♓08.0
Eris 5♈56.6 ⚵ 6♒23.6
⚷ 23♏36.0 ⚶ 17♋28.7R
☽ Mean ☊ 19♉09.0

March 1948 — LONGITUDE

Day	Sid.Time	☉	0 hr ☽	Noon ☽	True ☊	☿	♀	♂	⚳	♃	♄	♅	♆	♇
1 M	22 36 47	10♓49 32	20♏28 52	26♏57 50	16♉26.9	21♒54.1	22♈08.8	23♌04.3	10♉10.0	25♐57.5	17♌34.5	22♊06.6	12♎25.6	13♌09.9
2 Tu	22 40 44	11 49 42	3♐20 45	9♐38 12	16R 27.4	21R 40.6	23 18.6	22R 44.2	10 30.0	26 05.0	17R 30.2	22 06.7	12R 24.2	13R 08.7
3 W	22 44 40	12 49 51	15 50 46	21 59 08	16 27.0	21D 33.9	24 28.3	22 24.6	10 50.1	26 12.4	17 26.0	22 06.8	12 22.9	13 07.5
4 Th	22 48 37	13 49 59	28 03 53	4♑05 41	16 24.7	21 33.8	25 37.8	22 05.6	11 10.3	26 19.6	17 21.9	22 07.0	12 21.5	13 06.3
5 F	22 52 33	14 50 04	10♑05 06	16 02 44	16 20.1	21 40.0	26 47.2	21 47.2	11 30.7	26 26.7	17 17.8	22 07.3	12 20.1	13 05.1
6 Sa	22 56 30	15 50 09	21 59 04	27 54 37	16 12.9	21 52.2	27 56.4	21 29.4	11 51.2	26 33.6	17 13.8	22 07.6	12 18.6	13 03.9
7 Su	23 00 26	16 50 11	3♒49 50	9♒45 04	16 03.5	22 10.0	29 05.5	21 12.3	12 11.8	26 40.4	17 09.9	22 07.9	12 17.2	13 02.8
8 M	23 04 23	17 50 12	15 40 42	21 37 01	15 52.6	22 33.1	0♉14.4	20 55.8	12 32.5	26 47.1	17 06.0	22 08.3	12 15.7	13 01.6
9 Tu	23 08 20	18 50 11	27 34 16	3♓32 41	15 41.0	23 01.1	1 23.1	20 40.1	12 53.3	26 53.6	17 02.3	22 08.7	12 14.3	13 00.5
10 W	23 12 16	19 50 08	9♓32 26	15 33 42	15 29.9	23 33.8	2 31.7	20 25.0	13 14.3	27 00.0	16 58.5	22 09.2	12 12.8	12 59.4
11 Th	23 16 13	20 50 03	21 36 36	27 41 17	15 20.1	24 10.8	3 40.2	20 10.8	13 35.3	27 06.2	16 54.9	22 09.8	12 11.3	12 58.3
12 F	23 20 09	21 49 56	3♈47 52	9♈56 28	15 12.5	24 51.8	4 48.4	19 57.2	13 56.5	27 12.2	16 51.3	22 10.4	12 09.8	12 57.3
13 Sa	23 24 06	22 49 47	16 07 16	22 20 24	15 07.4	25 36.7	5 56.5	19 44.4	14 17.7	27 18.1	16 47.8	22 11.1	12 08.2	12 56.2
14 Su	23 28 02	23 49 36	28 36 04	4♉54 29	15D 04.8	26 25.1	7 04.4	19 32.4	14 39.1	27 23.8	16 44.4	22 11.8	12 06.7	12 55.2
15 M	23 31 59	24 49 22	11♉15 54	17 40 35	15 04.3	27 16.7	8 12.1	19 21.2	15 00.6	27 29.4	16 41.1	22 12.6	12 05.1	12 54.2
16 Tu	23 35 55	25 49 07	24 08 49	0♊40 55	15 05.1	28 11.5	9 19.6	19 10.7	15 22.2	27 34.8	16 37.9	22 13.4	12 03.6	12 53.2
17 W	23 39 52	26 48 50	7♊17 13	13 57 59	15 06.3	29 09.2	10 27.0	19 01.1	15 43.8	27 40.0	16 34.7	22 14.3	12 02.0	12 52.3
18 Th	23 43 49	27 48 30	20 43 31	27 34 02	15R 06.9	0♓09.7	11 34.1	18 52.2	16 05.6	27 45.1	16 31.7	22 15.2	12 00.4	12 51.3
19 F	23 47 45	28 48 08	4♋29 43	11♋30 36	15 06.1	1 12.7	12 41.0	18 44.1	16 27.5	27 50.0	16 28.7	22 16.2	11 58.8	12 50.4
20 Sa	23 51 42	29 47 43	18 36 40	25 47 42	15 03.5	2 18.2	13 47.7	18 36.9	16 49.4	27 54.8	16 25.8	22 17.2	11 57.2	12 49.5
21 Su	23 55 38	0♈47 17	3♌03 24	10♌23 15	14 59.0	3 26.0	14 54.2	18 30.4	17 11.4	27 59.4	16 23.0	22 18.3	11 55.6	12 48.6
22 M	23 59 35	1 46 47	17 46 35	25 12 35	14 53.1	4 36.0	16 00.4	18 24.7	17 33.6	28 03.8	16 20.3	22 19.4	11 54.0	12 47.8
23 Tu	0 03 31	2 46 16	2♍40 18	10♍08 41	14 46.5	5 48.1	17 06.4	18 19.7	17 55.8	28 08.1	16 17.7	22 20.6	11 52.4	12 46.9
24 W	0 07 28	3 45 42	17 36 37	25 02 59	14 40.2	7 02.3	18 12.2	18 15.6	18 18.1	28 12.1	16 15.2	22 21.8	11 50.8	12 46.1
25 Th	0 11 24	4 45 07	2♎26 40	9♎46 41	14 35.1	8 18.4	19 17.7	18 12.2	18 40.4	28 16.0	16 12.7	22 23.1	11 49.1	12 45.3
26 F	0 15 21	5 44 29	17 02 08	24 12 15	14 31.6	9 36.3	20 23.0	18 09.6	19 02.9	28 19.8	16 10.4	22 24.5	11 47.5	12 44.5
27 Sa	0 19 18	6 43 49	1♏16 29	8♏14 24	14D 30.0	10 56.1	21 28.0	18 07.7	19 25.4	28 23.3	16 08.2	22 25.8	11 45.8	12 43.8
28 Su	0 23 14	7 43 08	15 05 47	21 50 34	14 30.0	12 17.6	22 32.8	18 06.6	19 48.1	28 26.7	16 06.1	22 27.3	11 44.2	12 43.1
29 M	0 27 11	8 42 25	28 28 50	5♐00 49	14 31.2	13 40.8	23 37.3	18D 06.2	20 10.8	28 29.9	16 04.0	22 28.7	11 42.6	12 42.4
30 Tu	0 31 07	9 41 40	11♐26 49	17 47 16	14 32.9	15 05.6	24 41.5	18 06.6	20 33.5	28 33.0	16 02.1	22 30.3	11 40.9	12 41.7
31 W	0 35 04	10 40 53	24 02 39	0♑13 30	14R 34.3	16 32.1	25 45.4	18 07.6	20 56.4	28 35.8	16 00.3	22 31.8	11 39.3	12 41.0

April 1948 — LONGITUDE

Day	Sid.Time	☉	0 hr ☽	Noon ☽	True ☊	☿	♀	♂	⚳	♃	♄	♅	♆	♇
1 Th	0 39 00	11♈40 04	6♑20 25	12♑23 58	14♉34.8	18♓00.2	26♉49.1	18♌09.4	21♉19.3	28♐38.5	15♌58.6	22♊33.5	11♎37.6	12♌40.4
2 F	0 42 57	12 39 14	18 24 47	24 23 27	14R 34.0	19 29.9	27 52.5	18 11.9	21 42.3	28 41.0	15R 56.9	22 35.1	11R 36.0	12R 39.8
3 Sa	0 46 53	13 38 22	0♒20 35	6♒16 44	14 31.8	21 01.1	28 55.5	18 15.1	22 05.4	28 43.3	15 55.4	22 36.9	11 34.3	12 39.2
4 Su	0 50 50	14 37 28	12 12 27	18 08 16	14 28.4	22 33.8	29 58.3	18 19.0	22 28.5	28 45.4	15 54.0	22 38.6	11 32.7	12 38.7
5 M	0 54 47	15 36 32	24 04 38	0♓02 01	14 23.9	24 08.0	1♊00.7	18 23.5	22 51.7	28 47.4	15 52.7	22 40.4	11 31.0	12 38.2
6 Tu	0 58 43	16 35 34	6♓00 48	12 01 20	14 19.0	25 43.8	2 02.8	18 28.7	23 15.0	28 49.1	15 51.5	22 42.3	11 29.4	12 37.7
7 W	1 02 40	17 34 34	18 03 56	24 08 51	14 14.2	27 21.1	3 04.5	18 34.6	23 38.3	28 50.7	15 50.4	22 44.2	11 27.7	12 37.2
8 Th	1 06 36	18 33 33	0♈16 18	6♈26 28	14 10.1	28 59.9	4 06.0	18 41.1	24 01.7	28 52.1	15 49.4	22 46.1	11 26.1	12 36.7
9 F	1 10 33	19 32 29	12 39 30	18 55 29	14 07.0	0♈40.2	5 07.0	18 48.3	24 25.2	28 53.3	15 48.5	22 48.1	11 24.4	12 36.3
10 Sa	1 14 29	20 31 24	25 14 30	1♉36 37	14D 05.2	2 22.0	6 07.7	18 56.1	24 48.7	28 54.3	15 47.7	22 50.1	11 22.8	12 35.9
11 Su	1 18 26	21 30 16	8♉01 53	14 30 18	14 04.7	4 05.3	7 08.0	19 04.5	25 12.3	28 55.1	15 47.1	22 52.2	11 21.2	12 35.5
12 M	1 22 22	22 29 06	21 01 55	27 36 44	14 05.2	5 50.2	8 07.9	19 13.5	25 36.0	28 55.7	15 46.5	22 54.3	11 19.6	12 35.2
13 Tu	1 26 19	23 27 55	4♊14 46	10♊56 02	14 06.4	7 36.6	9 07.4	19 23.1	25 59.7	28 56.2	15 46.1	22 56.5	11 18.0	12 34.9
14 W	1 30 15	24 26 41	17 40 34	24 28 21	14 07.8	9 24.6	10 06.5	19 33.2	26 23.4	28R 56.4	15 45.7	22 58.7	11 16.3	12 34.6
15 Th	1 34 12	25 25 25	1♋19 24	8♋13 40	14 09.0	11 14.1	11 05.1	19 44.0	26 47.3	28 56.5	15 45.5	23 00.9	11 14.8	12 34.3
16 F	1 38 09	26 24 06	15 11 07	22 11 39	14R 09.7	13 05.1	12 03.3	19 55.3	27 11.1	28 56.4	15D 45.4	23 03.2	11 13.2	12 34.1
17 Sa	1 42 05	27 22 46	29 15 08	6♌21 21	14 09.5	14 57.8	13 01.0	20 07.2	27 35.1	28 56.1	15 45.4	23 05.5	11 11.6	12 33.9
18 Su	1 46 02	28 21 23	13♌30 03	20 40 52	14 08.6	16 52.0	13 58.2	20 19.6	27 59.0	28 55.6	15 45.4	23 07.9	11 10.0	12 33.7
19 M	1 49 58	29 19 57	27 53 24	5♍07 10	14 07.1	18 47.8	14 54.9	20 32.5	28 23.1	28 54.9	15 45.6	23 10.3	11 08.5	12 33.5
20 Tu	1 53 55	0♉18 30	12♍21 35	19 36 02	14 05.4	20 45.1	15 51.1	20 45.9	28 47.1	28 54.0	15 46.0	23 12.7	11 06.9	12 33.4
21 W	1 57 51	1 17 00	26 49 51	4♎02 23	14 03.8	22 44.0	16 46.7	20 59.8	29 11.3	28 52.9	15 46.4	23 15.2	11 05.4	12 33.3
22 Th	2 01 48	2 15 28	11♎12 55	18 20 48	14 02.5	24 44.3	17 41.8	21 14.2	29 35.4	28 51.7	15 46.9	23 17.7	11 03.9	12 33.2
23 F	2 05 44	3 13 55	25 25 25	2♏26 11	14D 01.7	26 46.2	18 36.3	21 29.1	29 59.6	28 50.3	15 47.5	23 20.2	11 02.4	12 33.2
24 Sa	2 09 41	4 12 19	9♏22 39	16 14 24	14 01.5	28 49.4	19 30.2	21 44.4	0♊23.9	28 48.6	15 48.3	23 22.8	11 00.9	12D 33.2
25 Su	2 13 38	5 10 42	23 01 10	29 42 45	14 01.8	0♉53.9	20 23.5	22 00.2	0 48.2	28 46.8	15 49.1	23 25.4	10 59.4	12 33.2
26 M	2 17 34	6 09 03	6♐19 05	12♐50 12	14 02.4	2 59.7	21 16.1	22 16.5	1 12.6	28 44.9	15 50.0	23 28.1	10 57.9	12 33.2
27 Tu	2 21 31	7 07 23	19 16 12	25 37 18	14 03.2	5 06.6	22 08.1	22 33.2	1 37.0	28 42.7	15 51.1	23 30.8	10 56.5	12 33.3
28 W	2 25 27	8 05 41	1♑53 48	8♑06 03	14 03.8	7 14.4	22 59.4	22 50.3	2 01.4	28 40.4	15 52.3	23 33.5	10 55.0	12 33.4
29 Th	2 29 24	9 03 57	14 14 30	20 19 35	14 04.3	9 23.0	23 50.1	23 07.8	2 25.9	28 37.8	15 53.5	23 36.2	10 53.6	12 33.5
30 F	2 33 20	10 02 12	26 21 50	2♒21 48	14R 04.6	11 32.2	24 39.9	23 25.8	2 50.4	28 35.1	15 54.9	23 39.0	10 52.2	12 33.6

Astro Data

	Dy Hr Mn
☿ D	4 0:18
☽ 0N	12 6:46
♃□♇	19 13:26
☉ 0N	20 16:56
☽ 0S	25 7:51
♂ D	29 12:33
☽ 0N	8 13:35
☿ 0N	12 4:47
♃ R	15 8:34
♄ D	17 3:20
☽ 0S	21 17:27
♇ D	24 16:58

Planet Ingress

		Dy Hr Mn
♀	♉	8 6:59
☿	♓	18 8:14
☉	♈	20 16:57
♀	♊	4 12:40
☿	♈	9 2:26
☉	♉	20 4:25
⚳	♊	23 12:21
☿	♉	25 1:38

Last Aspect / ☽ Ingress (March)

Last Aspect Dy Hr Mn		☽ Ingress	Dy Hr Mn
1 4:57	♂ □	♐	1 17:41
3 20:24	♃ ☌	♑	4 3:50
6 12:04	♀ □	♒	6 16:14
8 22:31	♃ ⚹	♓	9 4:53
11 10:50	♃ □	♈	11 16:33
13 21:35	♃ △	♉	14 2:40
16 7:06	☿ □	♊	16 10:45
18 12:27	☉ □	♋	18 16:14
19 14:10	♀ ⚹	♌	20 18:58
22 16:37	♃ △	♍	22 19:42
24 17:08	♃ □	♎	24 20:01
26 19:01	♃ ⚹	♏	26 21:49
28 13:23	♀ ☍	♐	29 2:46
31 8:49	♃ ☌	♑	31 11:34

Last Aspect / ☽ Ingress (April)

Last Aspect Dy Hr Mn		☽ Ingress	Dy Hr Mn
2 19:42	♀ △	♒	2 23:18
5 9:29	♃ ⚹	♓	5 11:56
7 21:14	♃ □	♈	7 23:28
10 6:54	♃ △	♉	10 8:58
11 20:30	♂ □	♊	12 16:20
14 19:50	♃ ☍	♋	14 21:41
16 19:42	☉ □	♌	17 1:16
19 1:43	♃ △	♍	19 3:30
21 3:25	♃ □	♎	21 5:16
23 5:50	♃ ⚹	♏	23 7:49
24 21:55	♂ □	♐	25 12:31
27 17:52	♃ ☌	♑	27 20:21
28 17:29	♆ □	♒	30 7:16

☽ Phases & Eclipses

Dy Hr Mn	
2 16:35	☾ 12♐01
10 21:15	● 20♓13
18 12:27	☽ 27♊50
25 3:10	○ 4♎23
1 10:25	☾ 11♑36
9 13:17	● 19♈36
16 19:42	☽ 26♋43
23 13:28	○ 3♏17
23 13:39	☍ P 0.023

Astro Data

1 March 1948
Julian Day # 17592
SVP 5♓59'13"
GC 26♐06.9 ⚳ 27♓01.8
Eris 6♈12.5 ⚵ 18♒38.9
⚷ 24♏41.7 ⚶ 14♋13.1R
☽ Mean ☊ 17♉36.9

1 April 1948
Julian Day # 17623
SVP 5♓59'09"
GC 26♐07.0 ⚳ 8♈27.7
Eris 6♈33.9 ⚵ 1♓44.7
⚷ 24♏11.0R ⚶ 17♋24.6
☽ Mean ☊ 15♉58.4

LONGITUDE — May 1948

Day	Sid.Time	☉	0 hr ☽	Noon ☽	True ☊	☿	♀	♂	⚳	♃	♄	♅	♆	♇
1 Sa	2 37 17	11♉00 25	8♒20 02	14♒17 06	14♉04.6	13♉41.7	25♊29.1	23♌44.1	3♊14.9	28♐32.3	15♌56.4	23♊41.8	10♎50.8	12♌33.8
2 Su	2 41 13	11 58 37	20 13 35	26 10 05	14R 04.5	15 51.3	26 17.4	24 02.9	3 39.5	28R 29.2	15 58.0	23 44.7	10R 49.5	12 34.0
3 M	2 45 10	12 56 47	2♓07 08	8♓05 18	14 04.4	18 00.7	27 05.0	24 22.0	4 04.2	28 26.0	15 59.6	23 47.6	10 48.1	12 34.2
4 Tu	2 49 07	13 54 56	14 05 07	20 07 03	14D 04.3	20 09.7	27 51.7	24 41.5	4 28.9	28 22.5	16 01.4	23 50.5	10 46.8	12 34.5
5 W	2 53 03	14 53 03	26 11 35	2♈19 08	14 04.4	22 17.9	28 37.5	25 01.4	4 53.6	28 18.9	16 03.3	23 53.4	10 45.5	12 34.8
6 Th	2 57 00	15 51 09	8♈30 02	14 44 38	14 04.5	24 25.0	29 22.4	25 21.7	5 18.3	28 15.2	16 05.3	23 56.4	10 44.2	12 35.1
7 F	3 00 56	16 49 13	21 03 10	27 25 49	14 04.7	26 30.8	0♋06.4	25 42.3	5 43.1	28 11.3	16 07.4	23 59.4	10 42.9	12 35.4
8 Sa	3 04 53	17 47 16	3♉52 42	10♉23 53	14R 04.8	28 35.0	0 49.5	26 03.3	6 07.9	28 07.2	16 09.6	24 02.4	10 41.7	12 35.8
9 Su	3 08 49	18 45 17	16 59 20	23 38 59	14 04.8	0♊37.3	1 31.5	26 24.6	6 32.8	28 02.9	16 11.9	24 05.4	10 40.4	12 36.1
10 M	3 12 46	19 43 16	0♊22 40	7♊10 12	14 04.4	2 37.5	2 12.4	26 46.3	6 57.7	27 58.5	16 14.3	24 08.5	10 39.2	12 36.6
11 Tu	3 16 42	20 41 15	14 01 18	20 55 40	14 03.8	4 35.3	2 52.3	27 08.3	7 22.6	27 53.9	16 16.8	24 11.6	10 38.0	12 37.0
12 W	3 20 39	21 39 11	27 52 57	4♋52 49	14 03.0	6 30.5	3 31.1	27 30.6	7 47.5	27 49.2	16 19.4	24 14.7	10 36.9	12 37.5
13 Th	3 24 36	22 37 06	11♋54 51	18 58 41	14 02.1	8 23.1	4 08.6	27 53.2	8 12.5	27 44.3	16 22.1	24 17.9	10 35.8	12 38.0
14 F	3 28 32	23 34 58	26 03 54	3♌10 09	14 01.3	10 12.7	4 44.9	28 16.2	8 37.5	27 39.3	16 24.9	24 21.1	10 34.6	12 38.5
15 Sa	3 32 29	24 32 49	10♌17 03	17 24 15	14D 00.8	11 59.4	5 20.0	28 39.5	9 02.5	27 34.1	16 27.8	24 24.3	10 33.5	12 39.1
16 Su	3 36 25	25 30 39	24 31 24	1♍38 12	14 00.8	13 43.0	5 53.7	29 03.0	9 27.6	27 28.8	16 30.8	24 27.5	10 32.5	12 39.6
17 M	3 40 22	26 28 26	8♍44 21	15 49 32	14 01.3	15 23.4	6 26.0	29 26.9	9 52.7	27 23.3	16 33.9	24 30.7	10 31.4	12 40.2
18 Tu	3 44 18	27 26 12	22 53 29	29 55 56	14 02.2	17 00.6	6 56.9	29 51.0	10 17.8	27 17.7	16 37.0	24 34.0	10 30.4	12 40.9
19 W	3 48 15	28 23 56	6♎56 36	13♎55 14	14 03.3	18 34.5	7 26.2	0♍15.4	10 42.9	27 12.0	16 40.3	24 37.3	10 29.4	12 41.5
20 Th	3 52 11	29 21 38	20 51 32	27 45 16	14 04.2	20 05.0	7 54.1	0 40.1	11 08.0	27 06.1	16 43.7	24 40.6	10 28.5	12 42.2
21 F	3 56 08	0♊19 19	4♏36 10	11♏24 00	14R 04.7	21 32.1	8 20.3	1 05.0	11 33.2	27 00.2	16 47.1	24 43.9	10 27.5	12 42.9
22 Sa	4 00 05	1 16 59	18 08 33	24 49 36	14 04.5	22 55.8	8 44.8	1 30.2	11 58.4	26 54.1	16 50.7	24 47.2	10 26.6	12 43.6
23 Su	4 04 01	2 14 37	1♐26 59	8♐00 34	14 03.3	24 16.0	9 07.7	1 55.7	12 23.6	26 47.8	16 54.3	24 50.6	10 25.7	12 44.4
24 M	4 07 58	3 12 14	14 30 17	20 56 05	14 01.3	25 32.7	9 28.7	2 21.4	12 48.9	26 41.5	16 58.0	24 53.9	10 24.9	12 45.2
25 Tu	4 11 54	4 09 50	27 17 59	3♑36 04	13 58.5	26 45.7	9 47.9	2 47.3	13 14.1	26 35.1	17 01.8	24 57.3	10 24.0	12 46.0
26 W	4 15 51	5 07 25	9♑50 27	16 01 21	13 55.3	27 55.2	10 05.2	3 13.5	13 39.4	26 28.5	17 05.7	25 00.7	10 23.2	12 46.8
27 Th	4 19 47	6 04 59	22 09 02	28 13 47	13 52.1	29 00.9	10 20.6	3 40.0	14 04.7	26 21.9	17 09.7	25 04.2	10 22.4	12 47.6
28 F	4 23 44	7 02 32	4♒15 58	10♒16 02	13 49.2	0♋02.9	10 33.9	4 06.6	14 30.0	26 15.1	17 13.8	25 07.6	10 21.7	12 48.5
29 Sa	4 27 41	8 00 04	16 14 24	22 11 36	13 47.2	1 01.1	10 45.2	4 33.5	14 55.4	26 08.3	17 17.9	25 11.0	10 21.0	12 49.4
30 Su	4 31 37	8 57 36	28 08 09	4♓04 38	13D 46.2	1 55.4	10 54.4	5 00.6	15 20.7	26 01.3	17 22.1	25 14.5	10 20.3	12 50.3
31 M	4 35 34	9 55 06	10♓01 35	15 59 38	13 46.2	2 45.7	11 01.4	5 28.0	15 46.1	25 54.3	17 26.5	25 18.0	10 19.6	12 51.3

LONGITUDE — June 1948

Day	Sid.Time	☉	0 hr ☽	Noon ☽	True ☊	☿	♀	♂	⚳	♃	♄	♅	♆	♇
1 Tu	4 39 30	10♊52 35	21♓59 22	28♓01 22	13♉47.2	3♋32.0	11♋06.1	5♍55.5	16♊11.5	25♐47.2	17♌30.9	25♊21.4	10♎19.0	12♌52.2
2 W	4 43 27	11 50 04	4♈06 13	10♈14 30	13 48.7	4 14.1	11R 08.6	6 23.3	16 36.9	25R 40.1	17 35.3	25 24.9	10R 18.4	12 53.2
3 Th	4 47 23	12 47 32	16 26 42	22 43 20	13 50.3	4 52.1	11 08.8	6 51.3	17 02.3	25 32.8	17 39.9	25 28.4	10 17.8	12 54.3
4 F	4 51 20	13 44 59	29 04 48	5♉31 26	13R 51.5	5 25.7	11 06.7	7 19.5	17 27.7	25 25.5	17 44.5	25 32.0	10 17.2	12 55.3
5 Sa	4 55 16	14 42 26	12♉03 31	18 41 11	13 51.7	5 55.0	11 02.2	7 47.9	17 53.2	25 18.1	17 49.2	25 35.5	10 16.7	12 56.3
6 Su	4 59 13	15 39 52	25 24 31	2♊13 25	13 50.4	6 19.9	10 55.3	8 16.5	18 18.7	25 10.7	17 54.0	25 39.0	10 16.2	12 57.4
7 M	5 03 10	16 37 17	9♊07 41	16 07 01	13 47.7	6 40.3	10 46.0	8 45.3	18 44.1	25 03.2	17 58.9	25 42.6	10 15.8	12 58.5
8 Tu	5 07 06	17 34 41	23 10 56	0♋18 53	13 43.6	6 56.1	10 34.3	9 14.3	19 09.6	24 55.7	18 03.9	25 46.1	10 15.4	12 59.7
9 W	5 11 03	18 32 05	7♋30 11	14 44 07	13 38.7	7 07.4	10 20.2	9 43.5	19 35.2	24 48.2	18 08.9	25 49.7	10 15.0	13 00.8
10 Th	5 14 59	19 29 28	21 59 53	29 16 40	13 33.5	7R 14.1	10 03.7	10 12.9	20 00.7	24 40.6	18 14.0	25 53.2	10 14.6	13 02.0
11 F	5 18 56	20 26 49	6♌33 40	13♌50 10	13 28.9	7 16.2	9 44.9	10 42.5	20 26.2	24 33.0	18 19.1	25 56.8	10 14.3	13 03.2
12 Sa	5 22 52	21 24 10	21 05 26	28 18 53	13 25.4	7 13.8	9 23.8	11 12.3	20 51.7	24 25.4	18 24.4	26 00.4	10 14.0	13 04.4
13 Su	5 26 49	22 21 29	5♍30 00	12♍38 24	13D 23.5	7 07.0	9 00.5	11 42.2	21 17.3	24 17.7	18 29.7	26 03.9	10 13.7	13 05.6
14 M	5 30 45	23 18 48	19 43 45	26 45 52	13 23.2	6 56.0	8 35.1	12 12.3	21 42.8	24 10.1	18 35.1	26 07.5	10 13.5	13 06.9
15 Tu	5 34 42	24 16 05	3♎44 36	10♎39 55	13 24.0	6 40.8	8 07.7	12 42.6	22 08.4	24 02.4	18 40.5	26 11.1	10 13.3	13 08.1
16 W	5 38 39	25 13 22	17 31 48	24 20 19	13 25.4	6 21.7	7 38.4	13 13.0	22 33.9	23 54.7	18 46.0	26 14.7	10 13.1	13 09.4
17 Th	5 42 35	26 10 38	1♏05 29	7♏47 25	13R 26.4	5 59.1	7 07.4	13 43.7	22 59.5	23 47.1	18 51.6	26 18.3	10 13.0	13 10.7
18 F	5 46 32	27 07 53	14 26 10	21 01 50	13 26.2	5 33.3	6 34.7	14 14.4	23 25.0	23 39.4	18 57.2	26 21.8	10 12.9	13 12.0
19 Sa	5 50 28	28 05 07	27 34 27	4♐04 06	13 24.3	5 04.6	6 00.8	14 45.4	23 50.6	23 31.8	19 02.9	26 25.4	10 12.8	13 13.4
20 Su	5 54 25	29 02 21	10♐30 47	16 54 34	13 20.4	4 33.6	5 25.6	15 16.5	24 16.2	23 24.2	19 08.7	26 29.0	10D 12.8	13 14.8
21 M	5 58 21	29 59 35	23 15 27	29 33 28	13 14.3	4 00.8	4 49.5	15 47.7	24 41.8	23 16.6	19 14.5	26 32.6	10 12.7	13 16.1
22 Tu	6 02 18	0♋56 48	5♑48 40	12♑01 05	13 06.6	3 26.6	4 12.6	16 19.1	25 07.3	23 09.1	19 20.4	26 36.1	10 12.8	13 17.5
23 W	6 06 14	1 54 01	18 10 49	24 17 59	12 57.9	2 51.7	3 35.2	16 50.7	25 32.9	23 01.6	19 26.3	26 39.7	10 12.8	13 18.9
24 Th	6 10 11	2 51 13	0♒22 42	6♒25 12	12 49.0	2 16.7	2 57.6	17 22.4	25 58.5	22 54.1	19 32.4	26 43.3	10 12.9	13 20.4
25 F	6 14 08	3 48 25	12 25 41	18 24 27	12 40.7	1 42.1	2 20.0	17 54.2	26 24.1	22 46.7	19 38.4	26 46.8	10 13.0	13 21.8
26 Sa	6 18 04	4 45 37	24 21 50	0♓18 14	12 33.9	1 08.6	1 42.6	18 26.2	26 49.7	22 39.3	19 44.5	26 50.4	10 13.2	13 23.3
27 Su	6 22 01	5 42 50	6♓14 05	12 09 52	12 28.9	0 36.7	1 05.6	18 58.4	27 15.3	22 32.0	19 50.7	26 53.9	10 13.3	13 24.8
28 M	6 25 57	6 40 02	18 06 05	24 03 18	12 26.1	0 07.0	0 29.4	19 30.7	27 40.9	22 24.7	19 56.9	26 57.5	10 13.6	13 26.3
29 Tu	6 29 54	7 37 14	0♈02 08	6♈03 11	12D 25.1	29♊40.0	29♊54.1	20 03.1	28 06.5	22 17.5	20 03.2	27 01.0	10 13.8	13 27.8
30 W	6 33 50	8 34 26	12 07 04	18 14 26	12 25.4	29 16.2	29 20.0	20 35.7	28 32.1	22 10.4	20 09.5	27 04.5	10 14.1	13 29.3

Astro Data

	Dy Hr Mn
☽0N	5 21:43
♃□♇	14 15:19
☽0S	19 0:37
☽0N	2 6:07
♀R	3 2:01
♃☍♅	3 21:42
☿R	11 11:15
☽0S	15 5:49
♆D	21 7:28
☽0N	29 13:39

Planet Ingress

	Dy Hr Mn
♀ ♋	7 8:27
☿ ♊	9 4:38
♂ ♍	18 20:54
☉ ♊	21 3:58
☿ ♋	28 10:50
☉ ♋	21 12:11
☿ ♊R	28 17:57
♀ ♊R	29 7:58

Last Aspect / ☽ Ingress (May)

Last Aspect Dy Hr Mn		☽ Ingress Dy Hr Mn
2 16:39	♃ ⚹	♓ 2 19:44
5 4:18	♀ □	♈ 5 7:28
7 13:25	♃ △	♉ 7 16:48
9 17:04	♂ □	♊ 9 23:20
11 23:58	♃ ☍	♋ 12 3:38
13 18:37	☉ ⚹	♌ 14 6:39
16 7:31	♂ ☌	♍ 16 9:14
18 7:32	♃ □	♎ 18 12:07
20 10:52	♃ ⚹	♏ 20 15:56
21 21:37	♄ □	♐ 22 21:22
24 22:45	♃ ☌	♑ 25 5:08
26 1:04	♆ □	♒ 27 15:31
29 19:53	♃ ⚹	♓ 30 3:46

Last Aspect / ☽ Ingress (June)

Last Aspect Dy Hr Mn		☽ Ingress Dy Hr Mn
1 7:36	♃ □	♈ 1 15:55
3 17:18	♃ △	♉ 4 1:43
5 10:26	♄ □	♊ 6 8:06
8 4:20	♅ ☌	♋ 8 11:28
9 4:50	♀ ☌	♌ 10 13:11
12 8:09	♅ ⚹	♍ 12 14:49
14 10:54	♅ □	♎ 14 17:33
16 15:24	♅ △	♏ 16 22:03
18 8:11	♄ □	♐ 19 4:28
21 6:13	♅ ☍	♑ 21 12:51
22 20:44	♂ △	♒ 23 23:15
26 4:58	♅ △	♓ 26 11:23
28 23:43	☿ □	♈ 28 23:56

☽ Phases & Eclipses

Dy Hr Mn	
1 4:48	☾ 10♒43
9 2:30	● 18♉22
9 2:25:35	● AT00'00"
16 0:55	☽ 25♌04
23 0:37	○ 1♐47
30 22:43	☾ 9♓23
7 12:55	● 16♊39
14 5:40	☽ 23♍04
21 12:54	○ 0♑02
29 15:23	☾ 7♈45

Astro Data

1 May 1948
Julian Day # 17653
SVP 5♓59'05"
GC 26♐07.1 ⚴ 19♈59.2
Eris 6♈53.9 ⚵ 14♓02.8
⚷ 22♏23.1R ⚶ 25♋17.0
☽ Mean ☊ 14♉23.1

1 June 1948
Julian Day # 17684
SVP 5♓59'00"
GC 26♐07.1 ⚴ 2♉05.1
Eris 7♈08.9 ⚵ 25♓51.2
⚷ 20♏08.0R ⚶ 6♌24.5
☽ Mean ☊ 12♉44.6

July 1948 — LONGITUDE

Day	Sid.Time	☉	0 hr ☽	Noon ☽	True ☊	☿	♀	♂	⚳	♃	♄	♅	♆	♇
1 Th	6 37 47	9♋31 38	24♈25 54	0♉42 05	12♉26.3	28♊55.9	28♊47.2	21♍08.4	28♊57.7	22♐03.4	20♌15.9	27♊08.1	10♎14.4	13♌30.8
2 F	6 41 43	10 28 51	7♉03 34	13 30 49	12R 26.7	28R 39.7	28R 16.0	21 41.2	29 23.2	21R 56.4	20 22.4	27 11.6	10 14.7	13 32.4
3 Sa	6 45 40	11 26 04	20 04 19	26 44 22	12 25.8	28 27.7	27 46.4	22 14.2	29 48.8	21 49.6	20 28.9	27 15.1	10 15.1	13 33.9
4 Su	6 49 37	12 23 17	3♊31 11	10♊24 49	12 22.8	28 20.3	27 18.7	22 47.3	0♋14.4	21 42.8	20 35.4	27 18.6	10 15.5	13 35.5
5 M	6 53 33	13 20 30	17 25 11	24 31 58	12 17.5	28D 17.7	26 52.9	23 20.6	0 40.0	21 36.1	20 42.0	27 22.1	10 16.0	13 37.1
6 Tu	6 57 30	14 17 44	1♋44 42	9♋02 43	12 10.0	28 19.9	26 29.3	23 54.0	1 05.6	21 29.5	20 48.6	27 25.5	10 16.4	13 38.7
7 W	7 01 26	15 14 58	16 25 09	23 51 02	12 01.0	28 27.2	26 07.7	24 27.5	1 31.2	21 23.0	20 55.3	27 29.0	10 16.9	13 40.4
8 Th	7 05 23	16 12 11	1♌19 14	8♌48 35	11 51.6	28 39.7	25 48.4	25 01.1	1 56.7	21 16.7	21 02.0	27 32.4	10 17.5	13 42.0
9 F	7 09 19	17 09 25	16 17 55	23 46 04	11 42.9	28 57.3	25 31.4	25 34.9	2 22.3	21 10.4	21 08.8	27 35.9	10 18.0	13 43.6
10 Sa	7 13 16	18 06 38	1♍11 59	8♍34 46	11 35.9	29 20.2	25 16.8	26 08.8	2 47.8	21 04.3	21 15.6	27 39.3	10 18.6	13 45.3
11 Su	7 17 13	19 03 52	15 53 37	23 07 58	11 31.2	29 48.2	25 04.4	26 42.9	3 13.4	20 58.3	21 22.4	27 42.7	10 19.3	13 46.9
12 M	7 21 09	20 01 05	0♎17 24	7♎21 39	11D 28.8	0♋21.5	24 54.5	27 17.0	3 38.9	20 52.4	21 29.3	27 46.1	10 19.9	13 48.6
13 Tu	7 25 06	20 58 18	14 20 37	21 14 21	11 28.2	1 00.0	24 46.9	27 51.3	4 04.4	20 46.6	21 36.3	27 49.4	10 20.6	13 50.3
14 W	7 29 02	21 55 32	28 02 58	4♏46 41	11R 28.5	1 43.6	24 41.7	28 25.7	4 29.9	20 41.0	21 43.2	27 52.8	10 21.3	13 52.0
15 Th	7 32 59	22 52 45	11♏25 46	18 00 32	11 28.4	2 32.3	24D 38.8	29 00.2	4 55.4	20 35.5	21 50.2	27 56.1	10 22.1	13 53.7
16 F	7 36 55	23 49 59	24 31 18	0♐58 22	11 27.0	3 26.1	24 38.3	29 34.8	5 20.9	20 30.2	21 57.3	27 59.4	10 22.9	13 55.4
17 Sa	7 40 52	24 47 13	7♐22 03	13 42 38	11 23.2	4 24.8	24 40.1	0♎09.5	5 46.3	20 24.9	22 04.3	28 02.7	10 23.7	13 57.1
18 Su	7 44 48	25 44 27	20 00 22	26 15 28	11 16.7	5 28.5	24 44.1	0 44.4	6 11.8	20 19.9	22 11.4	28 06.0	10 24.5	13 58.9
19 M	7 48 45	26 41 41	2♑28 07	8♑38 30	11 07.5	6 37.1	24 50.4	1 19.3	6 37.2	20 15.0	22 18.6	28 09.3	10 25.4	14 00.6
20 Tu	7 52 42	27 38 56	14 46 45	20 53 00	10 56.1	7 50.4	24 58.8	1 54.4	7 02.6	20 10.2	22 25.8	28 12.5	10 26.3	14 02.4
21 W	7 56 38	28 36 11	26 57 22	2♒59 57	10 43.1	9 08.4	25 09.4	2 29.6	7 28.1	20 05.6	22 33.0	28 15.7	10 27.2	14 04.1
22 Th	8 00 35	29 33 27	9♒00 54	15 00 22	10 29.9	10 31.0	25 22.0	3 04.9	7 53.4	20 01.2	22 40.2	28 18.9	10 28.2	14 05.9
23 F	8 04 31	0♌30 43	20 58 29	26 55 29	10 17.3	11 58.0	25 36.6	3 40.3	8 18.8	19 56.9	22 47.4	28 22.1	10 29.2	14 07.6
24 Sa	8 08 28	1 28 01	2♓51 35	8♓47 05	10 06.5	13 29.4	25 53.2	4 15.8	8 44.2	19 52.7	22 54.7	28 25.2	10 30.2	14 09.4
25 Su	8 12 24	2 25 18	14 42 17	20 37 34	9 58.1	15 04.9	26 11.7	4 51.4	9 09.5	19 48.8	23 02.0	28 28.3	10 31.3	14 11.2
26 M	8 16 21	3 22 37	26 33 22	2♈30 09	9 52.4	16 44.4	26 32.0	5 27.1	9 34.8	19 44.9	23 09.4	28 31.4	10 32.4	14 13.0
27 Tu	8 20 17	4 19 57	8♈28 26	14 28 46	9 49.3	18 27.6	26 54.1	6 02.9	10 00.2	19 41.3	23 16.7	28 34.5	10 33.5	14 14.7
28 W	8 24 14	5 17 18	20 31 45	26 37 59	9D 48.2	20 14.3	27 17.9	6 38.8	10 25.4	19 37.8	23 24.1	28 37.5	10 34.6	14 16.5
29 Th	8 28 11	6 14 39	2♉48 07	9♉02 49	9R 48.0	22 04.3	27 43.4	7 14.9	10 50.7	19 34.5	23 31.5	28 40.6	10 35.8	14 18.3
30 F	8 32 07	7 12 02	15 22 40	21 48 18	9 47.8	23 57.2	28 10.5	7 51.0	11 16.0	19 31.4	23 39.0	28 43.6	10 37.0	14 20.1
31 Sa	8 36 04	8 09 26	28 20 16	4♊59 02	9 46.3	25 52.8	28 39.1	8 27.2	11 41.2	19 28.5	23 46.4	28 46.5	10 38.2	14 21.9

August 1948 — LONGITUDE

Day	Sid.Time	☉	0 hr ☽	Noon ☽	True ☊	☿	♀	♂	⚳	♃	♄	♅	♆	♇
1 Su	8 40 00	9♌06 51	11♊44 58	18♊38 17	9♉42.8	27♋50.6	29♊09.1	9♎03.6	12♋06.4	19♐25.7	23♌53.9	28♊49.5	10♎39.4	14♌23.7
2 M	8 43 57	10 04 18	25 39 05	2♋47 12	9R 36.6	29 50.4	29 40.6	9 40.0	12 31.6	19R 23.1	24 01.4	28 52.4	10 40.7	14 25.6
3 Tu	8 47 53	11 01 45	10♋02 19	17 23 50	9 28.1	1♌51.8	0♋13.5	10 16.6	12 56.7	19 20.7	24 08.9	28 55.3	10 42.0	14 27.4
4 W	8 51 50	11 59 14	24 50 57	2♌22 40	9 17.7	3 54.4	0 47.7	10 53.3	13 21.9	19 18.4	24 16.4	28 58.1	10 43.3	14 29.2
5 Th	8 55 46	12 56 44	9♌57 46	17 34 55	9 06.7	5 57.9	1 23.2	11 30.0	13 47.0	19 16.4	24 24.0	29 00.9	10 44.7	14 31.0
6 F	8 59 43	13 54 14	25 12 43	2♍49 45	8 56.4	8 01.9	1 59.8	12 06.9	14 12.0	19 14.5	24 31.5	29 03.7	10 46.1	14 32.8
7 Sa	9 03 40	14 51 45	10♍24 40	17 56 15	8 48.0	10 06.2	2 37.7	12 43.9	14 37.1	19 12.8	24 39.1	29 06.5	10 47.5	14 34.6
8 Su	9 07 36	15 49 17	25 23 26	2♎45 22	8 42.1	12 10.4	3 16.6	13 20.9	15 02.1	19 11.3	24 46.7	29 09.2	10 48.9	14 36.4
9 M	9 11 33	16 46 50	10♎01 26	17 11 10	8 38.8	14 14.4	3 56.7	13 58.1	15 27.1	19 10.0	24 54.3	29 11.9	10 50.4	14 38.2
10 Tu	9 15 29	17 44 24	24 14 23	1♏11 03	8D 37.6	16 17.9	4 37.8	14 35.3	15 52.0	19 08.9	25 01.9	29 14.5	10 51.9	14 40.1
11 W	9 19 26	18 41 59	8♏01 16	14 45 18	8R 37.5	18 20.7	5 19.9	15 12.7	16 17.0	19 07.9	25 09.5	29 17.1	10 53.4	14 41.9
12 Th	9 23 22	19 39 35	21 23 27	27 56 09	8 37.3	20 22.6	6 02.9	15 50.1	16 41.8	19 07.2	25 17.1	29 19.7	10 54.9	14 43.7
13 F	9 27 19	20 37 12	4♐23 50	10♐46 58	8 35.9	22 23.6	6 47.0	16 27.7	17 06.7	19 06.6	25 24.7	29 22.3	10 56.4	14 45.5
14 Sa	9 31 15	21 34 49	17 06 00	23 21 23	8 32.3	24 23.4	7 31.9	17 05.3	17 31.5	19 06.2	25 32.4	29 24.8	10 58.0	14 47.3
15 Su	9 35 12	22 32 28	29 33 33	5♑42 54	8 26.1	26 22.1	8 17.7	17 43.0	17 56.3	19D 06.0	25 40.0	29 27.3	10 59.6	14 49.1
16 M	9 39 09	23 30 08	11♑49 47	17 54 32	8 17.1	28 19.6	9 04.3	18 20.8	18 21.0	19 06.0	25 47.7	29 29.7	11 01.2	14 50.9
17 Tu	9 43 05	24 27 49	23 57 26	29 58 45	8 05.9	0♍15.8	9 51.8	18 58.7	18 45.7	19 06.2	25 55.3	29 32.1	11 02.9	14 52.7
18 W	9 47 02	25 25 31	5♒58 42	11♒57 28	7 53.3	2 10.6	10 40.0	19 36.7	19 10.4	19 06.6	26 02.9	29 34.5	11 04.6	14 54.5
19 Th	9 50 58	26 23 14	17 55 16	23 52 16	7 40.3	4 04.0	11 29.0	20 14.8	19 35.0	19 07.1	26 10.6	29 36.8	11 06.3	14 56.3
20 F	9 54 55	27 20 59	29 48 37	5♓44 30	7 28.0	5 56.1	12 18.8	20 53.0	19 59.6	19 07.9	26 18.2	29 39.1	11 08.0	14 58.1
21 Sa	9 58 51	28 18 45	11♓40 08	17 35 41	7 17.4	7 46.9	13 09.2	21 31.2	20 24.1	19 08.8	26 25.9	29 41.3	11 09.7	14 59.8
22 Su	10 02 48	29 16 32	23 31 26	29 27 38	7 09.1	9 36.2	14 00.4	22 09.6	20 48.6	19 09.9	26 33.5	29 43.5	11 11.4	15 01.6
23 M	10 06 44	0♍14 21	5♈24 37	11♈22 42	7 03.5	11 24.2	14 52.2	22 48.0	21 13.1	19 11.2	26 41.1	29 45.7	11 13.2	15 03.4
24 Tu	10 10 41	1 12 12	17 22 18	23 23 52	7 00.5	13 10.8	15 44.7	23 26.6	21 37.5	19 12.7	26 48.8	29 47.8	11 15.0	15 05.1
25 W	10 14 38	2 10 05	29 27 51	5♉34 46	6D 59.6	14 56.1	16 37.7	24 05.2	22 01.9	19 14.3	26 56.4	29 49.9	11 16.8	15 06.9
26 Th	10 18 34	3 07 59	11♉45 11	17 59 39	6 59.9	16 40.0	17 31.4	24 43.9	22 26.2	19 16.2	27 04.0	29 52.0	11 18.6	15 08.6
27 F	10 22 31	4 05 55	24 18 44	0♊43 02	7R 00.4	18 22.7	18 25.7	25 22.7	22 50.5	19 18.2	27 11.6	29 54.0	11 20.5	15 10.4
28 Sa	10 26 27	5 03 53	7♊13 03	13 49 19	7 00.2	20 04.0	19 20.5	26 01.6	23 14.7	19 20.4	27 19.2	29 55.9	11 22.4	15 12.1
29 Su	10 30 24	6 01 53	20 32 15	27 22 11	6 58.2	21 44.0	20 15.9	26 40.5	23 38.9	19 22.8	27 26.8	29 57.8	11 24.2	15 13.8
30 M	10 34 20	6 59 55	4♋19 18	11♋23 39	6 54.0	23 22.8	21 11.8	27 19.6	24 03.0	19 25.4	27 34.4	29 59.7	11 26.1	15 15.5
31 Tu	10 38 17	7 57 59	18 35 04	25 53 12	6 47.8	25 00.3	22 08.2	27 58.8	24 27.1	19 28.1	27 42.0	0♋01.5	11 28.1	15 17.3

Astro Data

	Dy Hr Mn
☿ D	5 13:04
♃△♄	9 15:00
☽ 0S	12 10:52
♀ D	16 5:25
♂ 0S	18 17:07
☽ 0N	26 19:53
☽ 0S	8 17:45
♃ D	16 0:40
♄∠♆	18 18:32
☽ 0N	23 1:16

Planet Ingress

		Dy Hr Mn
⚳	♋	3 22:28
☿	♋	11 20:56
♂	♎	17 5:25
☉	♌	22 23:08
☿	♌	2 13:54
♀	♋	3 2:15
☿	♍	17 8:44
☉	♍	23 6:03
♅	♋	30 15:40

Last Aspect / ☽ Ingress

Last Aspect Dy Hr Mn		☽ Ingress Dy Hr Mn
1 8:43	☿ ⚹	♉ 1 10:40
3 3:34	♂ △	♊ 3 17:48
5 18:17	☿ ☌	♋ 5 21:07
7 13:01	♂ ⚹	♌ 7 21:53
9 20:34	☿ ⚹	♍ 9 22:03
11 19:41	♅ □	♎ 11 23:31
13 23:39	♅ △	♏ 14 3:28
16 9:17	♂ ⚹	♐ 16 10:11
18 15:34	♅ ☍	♑ 18 19:13
21 2:31	☉ ☍	♒ 21 6:02
23 14:56	♅ △	♓ 23 18:13
26 3:56	♅ □	♈ 26 6:57
28 15:54	♅ ⚹	♉ 28 18:34
30 16:39	☿ ⚹	♊ 31 3:01

Last Aspect / ☽ Ingress

Last Aspect Dy Hr Mn		☽ Ingress Dy Hr Mn
2 6:35	♀ ☌	♋ 2 7:20
3 1:04	♆ □	♌ 4 8:13
6 6:03	♅ ⚹	♍ 6 7:32
8 6:06	♅ □	♎ 8 7:30
10 8:37	♅ △	♏ 10 9:56
12 7:04	♄ □	♐ 12 15:49
14 23:45	♅ ☍	♑ 15 0:51
16 12:55	♂ □	♒ 17 12:03
19 23:38	♅ △	♓ 20 0:23
22 12:32	♅ □	♈ 22 13:05
25 0:42	♅ ⚹	♉ 25 1:03
27 5:21	♄ □	♊ 27 10:40
29 16:31	♅ ☌	♋ 29 16:34
31 15:34	♂ □	♌ 31 18:41

☽ Phases & Eclipses

Dy Hr Mn	
6 21:09	● 14♋40
13 11:30	☽ 20♎57
21 2:31	○ 28♑14
29 6:11	☾ 6♉01
5 4:13	● 12♌38
11 19:40	☽ 19♏00
19 17:32	○ 26♒37
27 18:46	☾ 4♊22

Astro Data

1 July 1948
Julian Day # 17714
SVP 5♓58'55"
GC 26♐07.2 ⚴ 13♉41.8
Eris 7♈14.5 ⚵ 5♈35.0
⚷ 18♏39.4R ⚶ 18♌56.4
☽ Mean ☊ 11♉09.3

1 August 1948
Julian Day # 17745
SVP 5♓58'50"
GC 26♐07.3 ⚴ 25♉09.5
Eris 7♈10.0R ⚵ 12♈21.0
⚷ 18♏34.4 ⚶ 3♍03.4
☽ Mean ☊ 9♉30.8

LONGITUDE — September 1948

Day	Sid.Time	☉	0 hr ☽	Noon ☽	True ☊	☿	♀	♂	⚳	♃	♄	♅	♆	♇
1 W	10 42 13	8♍56 05	3♌17 28	10♌47 02	6♉39.9	26♍36.5	23♋05.1	28♎38.0	24♋51.1	19♐31.0	27♌49.6	0♋03.3	11♎30.0	15♌18.9
2 Th	10 46 10	9 54 12	18 20 53	25 57 49	6R31.3	28 11.6	24 02.5	29 17.3	25 15.1	19 34.1	27 57.1	0 05.1	11 32.0	15 20.6
3 F	10 50 07	10 52 21	3♍36 30	11♍15 31	6 23.1	29 45.3	25 00.3	29 56.8	25 39.0	19 37.4	28 04.7	0 06.8	11 33.9	15 22.3
4 Sa	10 54 03	11 50 32	18 53 28	26 29 00	6 16.4	1♎17.9	25 58.6	0♏36.3	26 02.8	19 40.9	28 12.2	0 08.4	11 35.9	15 24.0
5 Su	10 58 00	12 48 44	4♎00 51	11♎27 58	6 11.8	2 49.2	26 57.3	1 15.9	26 26.6	19 44.5	28 19.7	0 10.0	11 37.9	15 25.6
6 M	11 01 56	13 46 58	18 49 28	26 04 41	6D09.5	4 19.3	27 56.4	1 55.5	26 50.3	19 48.3	28 27.2	0 11.5	11 39.9	15 27.3
7 Tu	11 05 53	14 45 14	3♏13 11	10♏14 43	6 09.2	5 48.1	28 55.9	2 35.3	27 14.0	19 52.3	28 34.6	0 13.0	11 41.9	15 28.9
8 W	11 09 49	15 43 31	17 09 15	23 56 52	6 10.0	7 15.7	29 55.8	3 15.2	27 37.6	19 56.5	28 42.1	0 14.5	11 44.0	15 30.5
9 Th	11 13 46	16 41 49	0♐37 50	7♐12 30	6R11.1	8 42.1	0♌56.1	3 55.1	28 01.1	20 00.8	28 49.5	0 15.9	11 46.0	15 32.1
10 F	11 17 42	17 40 10	13 41 16	20 04 39	6 11.4	10 07.1	1 56.8	4 35.1	28 24.5	20 05.3	28 56.9	0 17.3	11 48.1	15 33.7
11 Sa	11 21 39	18 38 32	26 23 08	2♑37 16	6 10.3	11 30.9	2 57.8	5 15.2	28 47.9	20 10.0	29 04.2	0 18.6	11 50.2	15 35.3
12 Su	11 25 36	19 36 55	8♑47 35	14 54 35	6 07.2	12 53.4	3 59.1	5 55.4	29 11.2	20 14.8	29 11.6	0 19.8	11 52.3	15 36.9
13 M	11 29 32	20 35 20	20 58 46	27 00 37	6 02.2	14 14.5	5 00.9	6 35.6	29 34.5	20 19.8	29 18.9	0 21.1	11 54.4	15 38.4
14 Tu	11 33 29	21 33 46	3♒00 34	8♒59 01	5 55.4	15 34.2	6 02.9	7 16.0	29 57.6	20 25.0	29 26.2	0 22.2	11 56.5	15 39.9
15 W	11 37 25	22 32 15	14 56 20	20 52 52	5 47.6	16 52.5	7 05.3	7 56.4	0♌20.7	20 30.3	29 33.5	0 23.3	11 58.6	15 41.5
16 Th	11 41 22	23 30 45	26 48 53	2♓44 41	5 39.4	18 09.3	8 08.0	8 36.9	0 43.7	20 35.8	29 40.7	0 24.4	12 00.8	15 43.0
17 F	11 45 18	24 29 16	8♓40 31	14 36 36	5 31.7	19 24.6	9 11.0	9 17.5	1 06.7	20 41.4	29 47.9	0 25.4	12 02.9	15 44.4
18 Sa	11 49 15	25 27 50	20 33 09	26 30 23	5 25.1	20 38.2	10 14.3	9 58.1	1 29.5	20 47.2	29 55.1	0 26.4	12 05.1	15 45.9
19 Su	11 53 11	26 26 26	2♈28 29	8♈27 41	5 20.2	21 50.1	11 17.9	10 38.9	1 52.3	20 53.2	0♍02.2	0 27.3	12 07.2	15 47.4
20 M	11 57 08	27 25 03	14 28 12	20 30 17	5 17.2	23 00.2	12 21.8	11 19.7	2 15.0	20 59.3	0 09.3	0 28.1	12 09.4	15 48.8
21 Tu	12 01 04	28 23 43	26 34 12	2♉40 12	5D16.1	24 08.5	13 26.0	12 00.6	2 37.6	21 05.5	0 16.4	0 29.0	12 11.6	15 50.2
22 W	12 05 01	29 22 25	8♉48 39	14 59 51	5 16.4	25 14.7	14 30.5	12 41.5	3 00.1	21 11.9	0 23.4	0 29.7	12 13.7	15 51.6
23 Th	12 08 58	0♎21 09	21 14 11	27 32 01	5 17.8	26 18.7	15 35.3	13 22.6	3 22.6	21 18.5	0 30.4	0 30.4	12 15.9	15 53.0
24 F	12 12 54	1 19 55	3♊53 47	10♊19 53	5 19.4	27 20.5	16 40.3	14 03.7	3 44.9	21 25.2	0 37.4	0 31.1	12 18.1	15 54.4
25 Sa	12 16 51	2 18 44	16 50 42	23 26 37	5R20.6	28 19.8	17 45.6	14 44.9	4 07.2	21 32.1	0 44.3	0 31.7	12 20.3	15 55.8
26 Su	12 20 47	3 17 34	0♋07 58	6♋55 03	5 20.9	29 16.5	18 51.1	15 26.2	4 29.3	21 39.1	0 51.2	0 32.2	12 22.5	15 57.1
27 M	12 24 44	4 16 28	13 48 03	20 47 04	5 19.8	0♏10.3	19 56.9	16 07.6	4 51.4	21 46.2	0 58.0	0 32.7	12 24.8	15 58.4
28 Tu	12 28 40	5 15 23	27 52 03	5♌02 51	5 17.5	1 00.9	21 02.9	16 49.1	5 13.4	21 53.5	1 04.8	0 33.2	12 27.0	15 59.7
29 W	12 32 37	6 14 21	12♌19 05	19 40 16	5 14.0	1 48.2	22 09.1	17 30.6	5 35.2	22 01.0	1 11.6	0 33.6	12 29.2	16 01.0
30 Th	12 36 34	7 13 21	27 05 40	4♍34 26	5 10.0	2 31.9	23 15.6	18 12.2	5 57.0	22 08.5	1 18.3	0 33.9	12 31.4	16 02.2

LONGITUDE — October 1948

Day	Sid.Time	☉	0 hr ☽	Noon ☽	True ☊	☿	♀	♂	⚳	♃	♄	♅	♆	♇
1 F	12 40 30	8♎12 23	12♍05 36	19♍38 01	5♉06.2	3♏11.5	24♌22.3	18♏53.9	6♌18.6	22♐16.2	1♍24.9	0♋34.2	12♎33.7	16♌03.5
2 Sa	12 44 27	9 11 27	27 10 33	4♎41 59	5R03.1	3 46.8	25 29.2	19 35.7	6 40.2	22 24.1	1 31.5	0 34.4	12 35.9	16 04.7
3 Su	12 48 23	10 10 34	12♎11 10	19 37 01	5 01.2	4 17.5	26 36.3	20 17.5	7 01.6	22 32.1	1 38.1	0 34.6	12 38.1	16 05.9
4 M	12 52 20	11 09 42	26 58 35	4♏15 01	5D00.5	4 42.9	27 43.6	20 59.4	7 22.9	22 40.2	1 44.6	0 34.7	12 40.4	16 07.0
5 Tu	12 56 16	12 08 52	11♏25 42	18 30 09	5 00.9	5 02.8	28 51.1	21 41.4	7 44.1	22 48.5	1 51.1	0R34.8	12 42.6	16 08.2
6 W	13 00 13	13 08 04	25 28 04	2♐19 18	5 02.2	5 16.7	29 58.8	22 23.5	8 05.2	22 56.8	1 57.5	0 34.8	12 44.8	16 09.3
7 Th	13 04 09	14 07 19	9♐03 53	15 41 59	5 03.7	5R24.1	1♍06.7	23 05.7	8 26.2	23 05.4	2 03.8	0 34.8	12 47.1	16 10.4
8 F	13 08 06	15 06 34	22 13 52	28 39 52	5 05.0	5 24.4	2 14.8	23 47.9	8 47.0	23 14.0	2 10.1	0 34.7	12 49.3	16 11.5
9 Sa	13 12 02	16 05 52	5♑00 27	11♑16 06	5R05.7	5 17.4	3 23.0	24 30.2	9 07.7	23 22.8	2 16.4	0 34.6	12 51.5	16 12.6
10 Su	13 15 59	17 05 12	17 27 20	23 34 43	5 05.6	5 02.6	4 31.5	25 12.6	9 28.3	23 31.7	2 22.6	0 34.4	12 53.8	16 13.6
11 M	13 19 56	18 04 33	29 38 48	5♒40 09	5 04.7	4 39.6	5 40.1	25 55.0	9 48.8	23 40.7	2 28.7	0 34.1	12 56.0	16 14.6
12 Tu	13 23 52	19 03 56	11♒39 18	17 36 48	5 03.1	4 08.3	6 48.8	26 37.6	10 09.1	23 49.8	2 34.8	0 33.8	12 58.2	16 15.6
13 W	13 27 49	20 03 20	23 33 09	29 28 50	5 01.0	3 28.7	7 57.8	27 20.2	10 29.3	23 59.1	2 40.8	0 33.5	13 00.4	16 16.6
14 Th	13 31 45	21 02 47	5♓24 19	11♓20 01	4 58.8	2 41.0	9 06.9	28 02.8	10 49.3	24 08.4	2 46.7	0 33.1	13 02.7	16 17.5
15 F	13 35 42	22 02 15	17 16 18	23 13 31	4 56.7	1 45.6	10 16.2	28 45.5	11 09.2	24 17.9	2 52.6	0 32.6	13 04.9	16 18.4
16 Sa	13 39 38	23 01 45	29 12 01	5♈12 03	4 55.0	0 43.4	11 25.6	29 28.4	11 29.0	24 27.5	2 58.5	0 32.1	13 07.1	16 19.3
17 Su	13 43 35	24 01 18	11♈13 53	17 17 44	4 53.9	29♎35.6	12 35.2	0♐11.2	11 48.6	24 37.2	3 04.2	0 31.6	13 09.3	16 20.2
18 M	13 47 31	25 00 52	23 23 49	29 32 18	4D53.4	28 23.6	13 44.9	0 54.2	12 08.0	24 47.0	3 09.9	0 31.0	13 11.5	16 21.0
19 Tu	13 51 28	26 00 28	5♉43 22	11♉57 09	4 53.4	27 09.4	14 54.8	1 37.2	12 27.3	24 56.9	3 15.5	0 30.3	13 13.7	16 21.9
20 W	13 55 25	27 00 07	18 13 48	24 33 28	4 53.8	25 54.9	16 04.9	2 20.3	12 46.5	25 07.0	3 21.1	0 29.6	13 15.9	16 22.7
21 Th	13 59 21	27 59 47	0♊56 17	7♊22 22	4 54.5	24 42.5	17 15.0	3 03.4	13 05.5	25 17.1	3 26.6	0 28.8	13 18.1	16 23.4
22 F	14 03 18	28 59 30	13 51 53	20 24 57	4 55.1	23 34.2	18 25.4	3 46.7	13 24.4	25 27.4	3 32.0	0 28.0	13 20.2	16 24.2
23 Sa	14 07 14	29 59 15	27 01 42	3♋42 15	4 55.7	22 32.3	19 35.8	4 30.0	13 43.0	25 37.7	3 37.4	0 27.2	13 22.4	16 24.9
24 Su	14 11 11	0♏59 02	10♋26 42	17 15 08	4 56.0	21 38.4	20 46.5	5 13.3	14 01.5	25 48.2	3 42.6	0 26.3	13 24.6	16 25.6
25 M	14 15 07	1 58 52	24 07 36	1♌04 05	4R56.1	20 54.0	21 57.2	5 56.8	14 19.9	25 58.7	3 47.8	0 25.3	13 26.7	16 26.2
26 Tu	14 19 04	2 58 44	8♌04 32	15 08 49	4 56.0	20 20.3	23 08.1	6 40.3	14 38.1	26 09.4	3 53.0	0 24.3	13 28.9	16 26.9
27 W	14 23 00	3 58 38	22 16 44	29 27 59	4D55.9	19 57.8	24 19.1	7 23.9	14 56.0	26 20.1	3 58.0	0 23.3	13 31.0	16 27.5
28 Th	14 26 57	4 58 34	6♍42 10	13♍58 48	4 55.9	19D46.8	25 30.2	8 07.5	15 13.8	26 30.9	4 03.0	0 22.1	13 33.1	16 28.1
29 F	14 30 54	5 58 32	21 17 17	28 36 59	4 56.0	19 47.2	26 41.4	8 51.2	15 31.4	26 41.9	4 07.9	0 21.0	13 35.2	16 28.6
30 Sa	14 34 50	6 58 33	5♎57 09	13♎17 00	4 56.1	19 58.7	27 52.8	9 35.0	15 48.9	26 52.9	4 12.7	0 19.8	13 37.3	16 29.2
31 Su	14 38 47	7 58 35	20 35 42	27 52 28	4R56.2	20 20.5	29 04.2	10 18.9	16 06.1	27 04.0	4 17.5	0 18.5	13 39.4	16 29.7

Astro Data

	Dy Hr Mn
☿0S	3 17:12
☽0S	5 3:07
☽0N	19 6:50
☉0S	23 3:22
♄⚹♅	23 12:04
☽0S	2 13:55
♅R	6 9:51
☿R	8 1:22
☽0N	16 13:26
☿D	28 23:08
☽0S	29 23:58

Planet Ingress

	Dy Hr Mn
♂ ♏	3 13:58
☿ ♎	3 15:47
♀ ♌	8 13:40
⚳ ♌	14 14:27
♄ ♍	19 4:36
☉ ♎	23 3:22
☿ ♏	27 7:19
♀ ♍	6 12:25
☿ ♎R	17 3:33
♂ ♐	17 5:43
☉ ♏	23 12:18

Last Aspect / ☽ Ingress (September)

Last Aspect Dy Hr Mn		☽ Ingress Dy Hr Mn
2 17:27	♂ ⚹	♍ 2 18:20
4 11:09	♀ ⚹	♎ 4 17:35
6 16:00	♄ ⚹	♏ 6 18:34
8 20:36	♄ □	♐ 8 22:52
11 5:05	♄ △	♑ 11 6:56
12 22:06	☉ △	♒ 13 17:58
16 5:44	♄ ☍	♓ 16 6:27
18 9:43	☉ ☍	♈ 18 19:02
20 17:28	☿ ☍	♉ 21 6:45
22 13:40	♇ □	♊ 23 16:40
25 21:27	☿ △	♋ 25 23:46
27 3:36	♂ △	♌ 28 3:35
29 16:21	♀ ☌	♍ 30 4:40

Last Aspect / ☽ Ingress (October)

Last Aspect Dy Hr Mn		☽ Ingress Dy Hr Mn
1 16:14	♃ □	♎ 2 4:30
4 0:20	♀ ⚹	♏ 4 4:58
6 7:31	♀ □	♐ 6 7:55
8 1:45	♃ ☌	♑ 8 14:31
10 15:25	♂ ⚹	♒ 11 0:42
13 7:23	♂ □	♓ 13 13:03
15 23:49	♂ △	♈ 16 1:36
18 9:58	☿ ☍	♉ 18 12:54
19 20:27	♇ □	♊ 20 22:15
23 4:48	☉ △	♋ 23 5:21
24 19:15	☿ □	♌ 25 10:10
27 6:43	♃ △	♍ 27 12:53
29 8:49	♃ □	♎ 29 14:16
31 10:39	♃ ⚹	♏ 31 15:31

☽ Phases & Eclipses

Dy Hr Mn	
3 11:21	● 10♍51
10 7:05	☽ 17♐28
18 9:43	○ 25♓22
26 5:07	☾ 3♋01
2 19:42	● 9♎30
9 22:10	☽ 16♑31
18 2:23	○ 24♈37
18 2:35	☍ A 1.014
25 13:41	☾ 2♌03

Astro Data

1 September 1948
Julian Day # 17776
SVP 5♓58'45"
GC 26♐07.3 ⚴ 5♊12.0
Eris 6♈56.3R ⚵ 13♈21.1R
⚷ 20♏05.6 ⚶ 17♍58.5
☽ Mean ☊ 7♉52.3

1 October 1948
Julian Day # 17806
SVP 5♓58'42"
GC 26♐07.4 ⚴ 11♊48.6
Eris 6♈38.0R ⚵ 7♈55.6R
⚷ 22♏49.6 ⚶ 2♎55.0
☽ Mean ☊ 6♉17.0

November 1948 — LONGITUDE

Day	Sid.Time	☉	0 hr ☽	Noon ☽	True ☊	☿	♀	♂	⚳	♃	♄	♅	♆	♇
1 M	14 42 43	8♏58 40	5♏06 29	12♏17 01	4♉56.2	20♎52.0	0♎15.8	11♐02.8	16♌23.1	27♐15.2	4♍22.1	0♋17.2	13♎41.5	16♌30.1
2 Tu	14 46 40	9 58 46	19 23 25	26 25 06	4R56.0	21 32.3	1 27.5	11 46.8	16 39.9	27 26.5	4 26.7	0R15.9	13 43.5	16 30.6
3 W	14 50 36	10 58 54	3♐21 37	10♐12 38	4 55.4	22 20.6	2 39.3	12 30.9	16 56.5	27 37.9	4 31.2	0 14.5	13 45.6	16 31.0
4 Th	14 54 33	11 59 04	16 57 56	23 37 26	4 54.6	23 16.0	3 51.2	13 15.0	17 13.0	27 49.4	4 35.6	0 13.1	13 47.6	16 31.4
5 F	14 58 29	12 59 16	0♑11 09	6♑39 15	4 53.6	24 17.6	5 03.2	13 59.2	17 29.1	28 01.0	4 39.9	0 11.6	13 49.6	16 31.8
6 Sa	15 02 26	13 59 29	13 01 58	19 19 37	4 52.6	25 24.6	6 15.2	14 43.4	17 45.1	28 12.6	4 44.1	0 10.1	13 51.6	16 32.1
7 Su	15 06 23	14 59 43	25 32 38	1♒41 27	4 51.8	26 36.4	7 27.4	15 27.8	18 00.9	28 24.3	4 48.3	0 08.5	13 53.6	16 32.4
8 M	15 10 19	16 00 00	7♒46 38	13 48 41	4D51.5	27 52.1	8 39.7	16 12.1	18 16.4	28 36.1	4 52.3	0 06.9	13 55.6	16 32.7
9 Tu	15 14 16	17 00 17	19 48 13	25 45 49	4 51.6	29 11.4	9 52.0	16 56.6	18 31.7	28 48.0	4 56.3	0 05.3	13 57.5	16 32.9
10 W	15 18 12	18 00 36	1♓42 04	7♓37 35	4 52.4	0♏33.5	11 04.4	17 41.1	18 46.7	28 59.9	5 00.2	0 03.6	13 59.5	16 33.1
11 Th	15 22 09	19 00 56	13 32 57	19 28 43	4 53.5	1 58.0	12 17.0	18 25.6	19 01.5	29 11.9	5 03.9	0 01.9	14 01.4	16 33.3
12 F	15 26 05	20 01 18	25 25 27	1♈23 40	4 55.0	3 24.6	13 29.6	19 10.3	19 16.1	29 24.0	5 07.6	0 00.1	14 03.3	16 33.5
13 Sa	15 30 02	21 01 41	7♈23 49	13 26 22	4 56.3	4 52.9	14 42.3	19 54.9	19 30.4	29 36.2	5 11.2	29♊58.3	14 05.2	16 33.6
14 Su	15 33 58	22 02 06	19 31 41	25 40 06	4R57.2	6 22.6	15 55.0	20 39.7	19 44.5	29 48.4	5 14.7	29 56.5	14 07.0	16 33.7
15 M	15 37 55	23 02 32	1♉51 54	8♉07 19	4 57.4	7 53.4	17 07.9	21 24.5	19 58.3	0♑00.7	5 18.1	29 54.6	14 08.9	16 33.8
16 Tu	15 41 52	24 03 00	14 26 31	20 49 35	4 56.7	9 25.1	18 20.8	22 09.3	20 11.9	0 13.1	5 21.4	29 52.7	14 10.7	16 33.9
17 W	15 45 48	25 03 30	27 16 34	3♊47 26	4 54.9	10 57.6	19 33.8	22 54.3	20 25.2	0 25.5	5 24.6	29 50.7	14 12.5	16R33.9
18 Th	15 49 45	26 04 01	10♊22 07	17 00 30	4 52.2	12 30.7	20 46.9	23 39.2	20 38.2	0 38.0	5 27.8	29 48.7	14 14.3	16 33.9
19 F	15 53 41	27 04 34	23 42 24	0♋27 38	4 48.9	14 04.2	22 00.0	24 24.3	20 50.9	0 50.5	5 30.8	29 46.7	14 16.1	16 33.9
20 Sa	15 57 38	28 05 08	7♋15 57	14 07 07	4 45.5	15 38.0	23 13.3	25 09.4	21 03.4	1 03.1	5 33.7	29 44.7	14 17.8	16 33.8
21 Su	16 01 34	29 05 44	21 00 53	27 56 58	4 42.4	17 12.1	24 26.5	25 54.5	21 15.6	1 15.8	5 36.5	29 42.6	14 19.5	16 33.7
22 M	16 05 31	0♐06 22	4♌55 07	11♌55 06	4 40.1	18 46.4	25 39.9	26 39.7	21 27.5	1 28.6	5 39.2	29 40.5	14 21.2	16 33.6
23 Tu	16 09 27	1 07 01	18 56 41	25 59 38	4D39.0	20 20.8	26 53.3	27 25.0	21 39.1	1 41.3	5 41.8	29 38.3	14 22.9	16 33.4
24 W	16 13 24	2 07 42	3♍03 44	10♍08 45	4 39.1	21 55.2	28 06.8	28 10.3	21 50.4	1 54.2	5 44.4	29 36.1	14 24.5	16 33.3
25 Th	16 17 21	3 08 25	17 14 29	24 20 42	4 40.2	23 29.7	29 20.4	28 55.7	22 01.4	2 07.1	5 46.8	29 33.9	14 26.2	16 33.1
26 F	16 21 17	4 09 10	1♎27 08	8♎33 31	4 41.7	25 04.2	0♏34.0	29 41.1	22 12.1	2 20.0	5 49.1	29 31.7	14 27.8	16 32.8
27 Sa	16 25 14	5 09 55	15 39 33	22 44 52	4R43.1	26 38.7	1 47.7	0♑26.6	22 22.4	2 33.0	5 51.3	29 29.4	14 29.4	16 32.6
28 Su	16 29 10	6 10 43	29 49 06	6♏51 52	4 43.5	28 13.2	3 01.4	1 12.1	22 32.5	2 46.1	5 53.4	29 27.2	14 30.9	16 32.3
29 M	16 33 07	7 11 32	13♏52 42	20 51 12	4 42.5	29 47.6	4 15.2	1 57.7	22 42.2	2 59.2	5 55.3	29 24.8	14 32.5	16 32.0
30 Tu	16 37 03	8 12 22	27 46 53	4♐39 20	4 39.7	1♐22.0	5 29.1	2 43.4	22 51.6	3 12.3	5 57.2	29 22.5	14 34.0	16 31.6

December 1948 — LONGITUDE

Day	Sid.Time	☉	0 hr ☽	Noon ☽	True ☊	☿	♀	♂	⚳	♃	♄	♅	♆	♇
1 W	16 41 00	9♐13 14	11♐28 10	18♐13 01	4♉35.2	2♐56.3	6♏42.9	3♑29.1	23♌00.6	3♑25.5	5♍59.0	29♊20.2	14♎35.4	16♌31.2
2 Th	16 44 57	10 14 06	24 53 35	1♑29 39	4R29.3	4 30.6	7 56.9	4 14.8	23 09.3	3 38.8	6 00.6	29R17.8	14 36.9	16R30.8
3 F	16 48 53	11 15 00	8♑01 05	14 27 49	4 22.7	6 04.9	9 10.9	5 00.6	23 17.7	3 52.1	6 02.2	29 15.4	14 38.3	16 30.4
4 Sa	16 52 50	12 15 55	20 49 54	27 07 28	4 16.1	7 39.1	10 24.9	5 46.5	23 25.7	4 05.4	6 03.6	29 13.0	14 39.7	16 30.0
5 Su	16 56 46	13 16 50	3♒20 44	9♒30 00	4 10.2	9 13.2	11 38.9	6 32.4	23 33.3	4 18.7	6 05.0	29 10.5	14 41.1	16 29.5
6 M	17 00 43	14 17 46	15 35 38	21 38 05	4 05.8	10 47.4	12 53.0	7 18.4	23 40.6	4 32.1	6 06.2	29 08.1	14 42.4	16 29.0
7 Tu	17 04 39	15 18 43	27 37 51	3♓35 30	4 03.1	12 21.6	14 07.2	8 04.4	23 47.5	4 45.6	6 07.3	29 05.6	14 43.8	16 28.5
8 W	17 08 36	16 19 41	9♓31 36	15 26 47	4D02.2	13 55.7	15 21.4	8 50.4	23 54.0	4 59.0	6 08.3	29 03.1	14 45.0	16 27.9
9 Th	17 12 32	17 20 39	21 21 42	27 16 59	4 02.7	15 29.9	16 35.6	9 36.5	24 00.2	5 12.5	6 09.2	29 00.6	14 46.3	16 27.3
10 F	17 16 29	18 21 38	3♈13 18	9♈11 19	4 04.1	17 04.1	17 49.8	10 22.6	24 06.0	5 26.1	6 10.0	28 58.1	14 47.5	16 26.7
11 Sa	17 20 26	19 22 37	15 11 38	21 14 53	4 05.6	18 38.4	19 04.1	11 08.8	24 11.4	5 39.6	6 10.6	28 55.6	14 48.7	16 26.1
12 Su	17 24 22	20 23 37	27 21 37	3♉32 21	4R06.4	20 12.7	20 18.4	11 55.0	24 16.4	5 53.2	6 11.2	28 53.0	14 49.9	16 25.4
13 M	17 28 19	21 24 38	9♉47 32	16 07 33	4 05.6	21 47.2	21 32.8	12 41.2	24 21.0	6 06.8	6 11.6	28 50.5	14 51.0	16 24.7
14 Tu	17 32 15	22 25 39	22 32 40	29 03 06	4 02.7	23 21.7	22 47.1	13 27.5	24 25.2	6 20.5	6 12.0	28 48.0	14 52.2	16 24.0
15 W	17 36 12	23 26 41	5♊38 54	12♊20 03	3 57.5	24 56.3	24 01.5	14 13.9	24 29.0	6 34.2	6 12.2	28 45.4	14 53.2	16 23.3
16 Th	17 40 08	24 27 44	19 06 21	25 57 33	3 50.3	26 31.1	25 16.0	15 00.3	24 32.5	6 47.9	6R12.3	28 42.8	14 54.3	16 22.5
17 F	17 44 05	25 28 47	2♋53 14	9♋52 54	3 41.6	28 06.0	26 30.5	15 46.7	24 35.5	7 01.6	6 12.3	28 40.3	14 55.3	16 21.7
18 Sa	17 48 01	26 29 51	16 55 58	24 01 47	3 32.5	29 41.1	27 45.0	16 33.1	24 38.1	7 15.3	6 12.2	28 37.7	14 56.3	16 20.9
19 Su	17 51 58	27 30 56	1♌09 41	8♌18 58	3 24.0	1♑16.3	28 59.5	17 19.6	24 40.3	7 29.1	6 12.0	28 35.1	14 57.3	16 20.1
20 M	17 55 55	28 32 01	15 28 58	22 39 05	3 17.2	2 51.7	0♐14.1	18 06.2	24 42.0	7 42.9	6 11.6	28 32.6	14 58.2	16 19.3
21 Tu	17 59 51	29 33 08	29 48 45	6♍57 30	3 12.6	4 27.3	1 28.7	18 52.8	24 43.4	7 56.7	6 11.2	28 30.0	14 59.1	16 18.4
22 W	18 03 48	0♑34 14	14♍04 57	21 10 48	3D10.3	6 03.1	2 43.3	19 39.4	24 44.3	8 10.5	6 10.6	28 27.4	14 59.9	16 17.5
23 Th	18 07 44	1 35 22	28 14 50	5♎16 54	3 09.9	7 39.1	3 57.9	20 26.0	24R44.7	8 24.3	6 10.0	28 24.8	15 00.8	16 16.6
24 F	18 11 41	2 36 30	12♎16 56	19 14 53	3 10.6	9 15.3	5 12.6	21 12.7	24 44.8	8 38.2	6 09.2	28 22.3	15 01.6	16 15.6
25 Sa	18 15 37	3 37 39	26 10 42	3♏04 25	3R11.1	10 51.6	6 27.3	21 59.4	24 44.4	8 52.0	6 08.3	28 19.7	15 02.3	16 14.7
26 Su	18 19 34	4 38 48	9♏56 00	16 45 25	3 10.2	12 28.2	7 42.0	22 46.2	24 43.5	9 05.9	6 07.3	28 17.1	15 03.1	16 13.7
27 M	18 23 30	5 39 58	23 32 37	0♐17 31	3 07.1	14 04.9	8 56.8	23 33.0	24 42.3	9 19.8	6 06.2	28 14.6	15 03.8	16 12.7
28 Tu	18 27 27	6 41 09	7♐00 00	13 39 54	3 01.1	15 41.8	10 11.5	24 19.8	24 40.6	9 33.7	6 05.0	28 12.0	15 04.4	16 11.6
29 W	18 31 24	7 42 20	20 17 05	26 51 21	2 52.2	17 18.8	11 26.3	25 06.7	24 38.4	9 47.6	6 03.6	28 09.5	15 05.0	16 10.6
30 Th	18 35 20	8 43 31	3♑22 32	9♑50 28	2 41.0	18 55.9	12 41.1	25 53.6	24 35.8	10 01.5	6 02.2	28 07.0	15 05.6	16 09.5
31 F	18 39 17	9 44 42	16 15 01	22 36 05	2 28.4	20 33.0	13 55.9	26 40.6	24 32.8	10 15.4	6 00.7	28 04.5	15 06.2	16 08.5

Astro Data

	Dy Hr Mn
♀0S	4 8:24
☽0N	12 21:03
♃☍♅	15 1:39
♇R	17 20:17
♃□♇	22 21:21
☽0S	26 7:25
☽0N	10 4:58
♃△♄	13 20:39
♄R	17 0:20
☽0S	23 12:21
⚳R	24 2:14

Planet Ingress

	Dy Hr Mn
♀ ♎	1 6:42
☿ ♏	10 2:19
♅ ♊R	12 13:27
♃ ♑	15 10:38
☉ ♐	22 9:29
♀ ♏	26 0:55
♂ ♑	26 21:59
☿ ♐	29 15:09
☿ ♑	18 16:46
♀ ♐	20 7:28
☉ ♑	21 22:33

Last Aspect / ☽ Ingress (November)

Last Aspect Dy Hr Mn		☽ Ingress Dy Hr Mn
1 19:07	♇ □	♐ 2 18:10
4 19:46	♃ ☌	♑ 4 23:39
7 0:59	♅ ☍	♒ 7 8:41
9 19:49	♅ △	♓ 9 20:34
12 7:56	♃ □	♈ 12 9:12
14 20:16	♅ ✶	♉ 14 20:24
16 18:31	☉ ☍	♊ 17 5:02
19 10:48	♅ ☌	♋ 19 11:11
21 14:08	☉ △	♌ 21 15:32
23 18:11	♅ ✶	♍ 23 18:48
25 20:47	♅ □	♎ 25 21:33
27 23:25	♅ △	♏ 28 0:19
29 4:34	♇ □	♐ 30 3:52

Last Aspect / ☽ Ingress (December)

Last Aspect Dy Hr Mn		☽ Ingress Dy Hr Mn
2 8:00	♅ ☍	♑ 2 9:16
3 12:20	♆ □	♒ 4 17:32
7 2:58	♅ △	♓ 7 4:46
9 15:29	♅ □	♈ 9 17:30
12 3:00	♅ ✶	♉ 12 5:09
13 23:13	♀ ☍	♊ 14 13:44
16 16:46	♅ ☌	♋ 16 19:01
18 18:52	♀ △	♌ 18 22:03
20 22:37	☉ △	♍ 21 0:19
23 0:19	♅ □	♎ 23 2:59
25 3:46	♅ △	♏ 25 6:39
26 23:17	♂ ✶	♐ 27 11:29
29 14:23	♅ ☍	♑ 29 17:47

☽ Phases & Eclipses

Dy Hr Mn	
1 6:03	● 8♏44
1 5:58:49	• T 01'56"
8 16:46	☽ 16♒12
16 18:31	○ 24♉19
23 21:22	☾ 1♍31
30 18:44	● 8♐29
8 13:57	☽ 16♓25
16 9:11	○ 24♊21
23 5:12	☾ 1♎18
30 9:45	● 8♑38

Astro Data

1 November 1948
Julian Day # 17837
SVP 5♓58'38"
GC 26♐07.5 ⚴ 12♊01.3R
Eris 6♈19.4R ⚵ 1♈56.4R
⚷ 26♏30.1 ⚶ 18♎38.1
☽ Mean ☊ 4♉38.5

1 December 1948
Julian Day # 17867
SVP 5♓58'33"
GC 26♐07.6 ⚴ 3♊53.5R
Eris 6♈07.1R ⚵ 3♈09.7
⚷ 0♐23.0 ⚶ 3♏50.1
☽ Mean ☊ 3♉03.2

LONGITUDE

January 1949

Day	Sid.Time	☉	0 hr ☽	Noon ☽	True ☊	☿	♀	♂	⚳	♃	♄	♅	♆	♇
1 Sa	18 43 13	10♑45 53	28♑53 36	5♒07 36	2♉15.5	22♑10.1	15♐10.7	27♑27.5	24♌29.3	10♑29.3	5♍59.0	28♊02.0	15♎06.7	16♌07.4
2 Su	18 47 10	11 47 04	11♒18 09	17 25 24	2R 03.6	23 47.2	16 25.6	28 14.5	24R 25.4	10 43.2	5R 57.3	27R 59.5	15 07.2	16R 06.2
3 M	18 51 06	12 48 15	23 29 33	29 30 55	1 53.6	25 24.0	17 40.4	29 01.5	24 21.0	10 57.1	5 55.4	27 57.0	15 07.7	16 05.1
4 Tu	18 55 03	13 49 26	5♓29 50	11♓26 45	1 46.1	27 00.6	18 55.3	29 48.6	24 16.2	11 11.0	5 53.4	27 54.5	15 08.1	16 04.0
5 W	18 59 00	14 50 36	17 22 09	23 16 34	1 41.4	28 36.8	20 10.1	0♒35.6	24 11.0	11 24.9	5 51.4	27 52.1	15 08.5	16 02.8
6 Th	19 02 56	15 51 46	29 10 35	5♈04 51	1D 39.1	0♒12.4	21 25.0	1 22.7	24 05.4	11 38.8	5 49.2	27 49.7	15 08.9	16 01.6
7 F	19 06 53	16 52 56	11♈00 01	16 56 47	1 38.6	1 47.3	22 39.9	2 09.8	23 59.3	11 52.7	5 46.9	27 47.3	15 09.2	16 00.4
8 Sa	19 10 49	17 54 05	22 55 50	28 57 53	1R 38.7	3 21.3	23 54.8	2 57.0	23 52.8	12 06.6	5 44.6	27 44.9	15 09.5	15 59.2
9 Su	19 14 46	18 55 13	5♉03 37	11♉13 42	1 38.4	4 54.0	25 09.7	3 44.1	23 45.9	12 20.5	5 42.1	27 42.5	15 09.7	15 57.9
10 M	19 18 42	19 56 21	17 28 45	23 49 20	1 36.6	6 25.3	26 24.6	4 31.3	23 38.6	12 34.3	5 39.5	27 40.2	15 09.9	15 56.7
11 Tu	19 22 39	20 57 29	0♊15 55	6♊48 53	1 32.3	7 54.8	27 39.5	5 18.5	23 30.9	12 48.2	5 36.9	27 37.9	15 10.1	15 55.4
12 W	19 26 35	21 58 36	13 28 30	20 14 52	1 25.2	9 22.0	28 54.4	6 05.7	23 22.8	13 02.0	5 34.1	27 35.6	15 10.3	15 54.2
13 Th	19 30 32	22 59 43	27 07 55	4♋07 24	1 15.5	10 46.6	0♑09.3	6 53.0	23 14.3	13 15.9	5 31.3	27 33.3	15 10.4	15 52.9
14 F	19 34 29	24 00 49	11♋12 55	18 23 52	1 03.9	12 08.0	1 24.3	7 40.2	23 05.4	13 29.7	5 28.4	27 31.1	15 10.5	15 51.6
15 Sa	19 38 25	25 01 55	25 39 27	2♌58 48	0 51.6	13 25.7	2 39.2	8 27.5	22 56.2	13 43.5	5 25.4	27 28.9	15R 10.5	15 50.3
16 Su	19 42 22	26 03 00	10♌20 52	17 44 37	0 39.9	14 38.9	3 54.2	9 14.8	22 46.6	13 57.2	5 22.2	27 26.7	15 10.5	15 49.0
17 M	19 46 18	27 04 04	25 08 56	2♍32 48	0 30.1	15 47.1	5 09.1	10 02.1	22 36.7	14 11.0	5 19.1	27 24.6	15 10.5	15 47.6
18 Tu	19 50 15	28 05 09	9♍55 14	17 15 25	0 23.0	16 49.3	6 24.1	10 49.4	22 26.3	14 24.7	5 15.8	27 22.4	15 10.5	15 46.3
19 W	19 54 11	29 06 13	24 32 38	1♎46 21	0 18.9	17 44.8	7 39.1	11 36.8	22 15.7	14 38.5	5 12.4	27 20.3	15 10.4	15 45.0
20 Th	19 58 08	0♒07 16	8♎56 09	16 01 49	0 17.1	18 32.7	8 54.0	12 24.1	22 04.8	14 52.2	5 09.0	27 18.3	15 10.3	15 43.6
21 F	20 02 04	1 08 19	23 03 13	0♏00 22	0 16.9	19 12.2	10 09.0	13 11.5	21 53.5	15 05.8	5 05.4	27 16.3	15 10.1	15 42.2
22 Sa	20 06 01	2 09 22	6♏53 20	13 42 16	0 16.7	19 42.4	11 24.0	13 58.9	21 41.9	15 19.5	5 01.8	27 14.3	15 09.9	15 40.8
23 Su	20 09 58	3 10 24	20 27 22	27 08 50	0 15.2	20 02.6	12 39.0	14 46.3	21 30.0	15 33.1	4 58.2	27 12.3	15 09.7	15 39.5
24 M	20 13 54	4 11 26	3♐46 53	10♐21 43	0 11.3	20R 12.0	13 54.0	15 33.7	21 17.9	15 46.7	4 54.4	27 10.4	15 09.4	15 38.1
25 Tu	20 17 51	5 12 28	16 53 30	23 22 23	0 04.4	20 10.3	15 09.0	16 21.1	21 05.5	16 00.3	4 50.6	27 08.5	15 09.1	15 36.7
26 W	20 21 47	6 13 29	29 48 30	6♑11 54	29♈54.5	19 57.0	16 24.0	17 08.5	20 52.9	16 13.8	4 46.7	27 06.7	15 08.8	15 35.3
27 Th	20 25 44	7 14 29	12♑32 39	18 50 48	29 42.0	19 32.4	17 39.1	17 56.0	20 40.1	16 27.3	4 42.7	27 04.9	15 08.4	15 33.9
28 F	20 29 40	8 15 28	25 06 21	1♒19 20	29 27.8	18 56.8	18 54.1	18 43.4	20 27.0	16 40.8	4 38.7	27 03.1	15 08.1	15 32.5
29 Sa	20 33 37	9 16 26	7♒29 45	13 37 39	29 13.3	18 11.0	20 09.1	19 30.9	20 13.7	16 54.2	4 34.6	27 01.4	15 07.6	15 31.0
30 Su	20 37 33	10 17 23	19 43 05	25 46 09	28 59.6	17 16.1	21 24.1	20 18.3	20 00.3	17 07.6	4 30.5	26 59.7	15 07.2	15 29.6
31 M	20 41 30	11 18 19	1♓46 59	7♓45 48	28 47.9	16 13.7	22 39.1	21 05.8	19 46.7	17 20.9	4 26.3	26 58.0	15 06.7	15 28.2

LONGITUDE

February 1949

Day	Sid.Time	☉	0 hr ☽	Noon ☽	True ☊	☿	♀	♂	⚳	♃	♄	♅	♆	♇
1 Tu	20 45 27	12♒19 14	13♓42 48	19♓38 18	28♈38.9	15♒05.5	23♑54.1	21♒53.3	19♌33.0	17♑34.2	4♍22.0	26♊56.4	15♎06.2	15♌26.8
2 W	20 49 23	13 20 08	25 32 39	1♈26 16	28R 32.8	13R 53.7	25 09.1	22 40.8	19R 19.2	17 47.5	4R 17.7	26R 54.9	15R 05.6	15R 25.3
3 Th	20 53 20	14 21 00	7♈19 37	13 13 12	28 29.6	12 40.3	26 24.1	23 28.2	19 05.2	18 00.7	4 13.3	26 53.3	15 05.0	15 23.9
4 F	20 57 16	15 21 51	19 07 37	25 03 26	28D 28.5	11 27.4	27 39.1	24 15.7	18 51.2	18 13.9	4 08.9	26 51.9	15 04.4	15 22.5
5 Sa	21 01 13	16 22 40	1♉01 20	7♉01 57	28R 28.6	10 16.9	28 54.1	25 03.2	18 37.1	18 27.1	4 04.4	26 50.4	15 03.7	15 21.0
6 Su	21 05 09	17 23 28	13 06 01	19 14 11	28 28.8	9 10.5	0♒09.1	25 50.6	18 23.0	18 40.1	3 59.9	26 49.1	15 03.1	15 19.6
7 M	21 09 06	18 24 15	25 27 10	1♊45 35	28 27.9	8 09.8	1 24.1	26 38.1	18 08.9	18 53.2	3 55.4	26 47.7	15 02.3	15 18.2
8 Tu	21 13 02	19 25 00	8♊10 04	14 41 09	28 25.1	7 15.6	2 39.1	27 25.6	17 54.7	19 06.2	3 50.8	26 46.4	15 01.6	15 16.8
9 W	21 16 59	20 25 44	21 19 16	28 04 43	28 19.9	6 28.9	3 54.0	28 13.0	17 40.6	19 19.1	3 46.2	26 45.2	15 00.8	15 15.3
10 Th	21 20 56	21 26 26	4♋57 39	11♋58 03	28 12.2	5 50.0	5 09.0	29 00.5	17 26.5	19 32.0	3 41.5	26 44.0	15 00.0	15 13.9
11 F	21 24 52	22 27 06	19 05 41	26 20 06	28 02.7	5 19.1	6 24.0	29 48.0	17 12.5	19 44.8	3 36.8	26 42.8	14 59.2	15 12.5
12 Sa	21 28 49	23 27 45	3♌40 39	11♌06 26	27 52.3	4 56.3	7 38.9	0♓35.4	16 58.5	19 57.6	3 32.1	26 41.7	14 58.4	15 11.1
13 Su	21 32 45	24 28 22	18 36 26	26 09 24	27 42.3	4 41.5	8 53.9	1 22.8	16 44.7	20 10.3	3 27.4	26 40.7	14 57.5	15 09.7
14 M	21 36 42	25 28 58	3♍44 05	11♍19 09	27 33.9	4D 34.3	10 08.8	2 10.3	16 30.9	20 23.0	3 22.6	26 39.7	14 56.6	15 08.3
15 Tu	21 40 38	26 29 33	18 53 18	26 25 20	27 27.9	4 34.3	11 23.8	2 57.7	16 17.3	20 35.6	3 17.9	26 38.7	14 55.6	15 06.9
16 W	21 44 35	27 30 06	3♎54 10	11♎18 54	27 24.5	4 41.3	12 38.7	3 45.1	16 03.8	20 48.1	3 13.1	26 37.8	14 54.7	15 05.5
17 Th	21 48 31	28 30 37	18 38 48	25 53 22	27D 23.4	4 54.6	13 53.6	4 32.5	15 50.4	21 00.6	3 08.2	26 37.0	14 53.7	15 04.1
18 F	21 52 28	29 31 08	3♏02 15	10♏05 17	27 23.9	5 14.0	15 08.6	5 19.9	15 37.3	21 13.0	3 03.4	26 36.2	14 52.6	15 02.7
19 Sa	21 56 25	0♓31 37	17 02 26	23 53 50	27R 24.6	5 39.0	16 23.5	6 07.3	15 24.3	21 25.4	2 58.6	26 35.4	14 51.6	15 01.3
20 Su	22 00 21	1 32 06	0♐39 39	7♐20 12	27 24.7	6 09.2	17 38.4	6 54.7	15 11.5	21 37.6	2 53.7	26 34.7	14 50.5	15 00.0
21 M	22 04 18	2 32 32	13 55 46	20 26 42	27 22.9	6 44.1	18 53.4	7 42.1	14 59.0	21 49.9	2 48.9	26 34.1	14 49.4	14 58.6
22 Tu	22 08 14	3 32 58	26 53 23	3♑16 09	27 19.0	7 23.5	20 08.3	8 29.4	14 46.7	22 02.0	2 44.1	26 33.5	14 48.3	14 57.3
23 W	22 12 11	4 33 22	9♑35 21	15 51 19	27 12.6	8 06.9	21 23.2	9 16.8	14 34.7	22 14.1	2 39.2	26 32.9	14 47.2	14 55.9
24 Th	22 16 07	5 33 45	22 04 18	28 14 37	27 04.3	8 54.2	22 38.1	10 04.1	14 22.9	22 26.1	2 34.4	26 32.5	14 46.0	14 54.6
25 F	22 20 04	6 34 06	4♒22 28	10♒28 04	26 54.6	9 44.9	23 53.0	10 51.4	14 11.5	22 38.0	2 29.5	26 32.0	14 44.8	14 53.3
26 Sa	22 24 00	7 34 25	16 31 38	22 33 19	26 44.6	10 38.8	25 07.9	11 38.7	14 00.3	22 49.8	2 24.7	26 31.6	14 43.6	14 52.0
27 Su	22 27 57	8 34 43	28 33 19	4♓31 46	26 35.1	11 35.7	26 22.8	12 26.0	13 49.4	23 01.6	2 19.9	26 31.3	14 42.3	14 50.7
28 M	22 31 54	9 34 59	10♓28 53	16 24 49	26 27.1	12 35.5	27 37.7	13 13.3	13 38.9	23 13.3	2 15.1	26 31.0	14 41.1	14 49.4

Astro Data	Dy Hr Mn
☽ 0N	6 12:16
♆ R	16 9:35
☽ 0S	19 17:22
♃□♆	21 19:24
♃⚻♇	23 22:12
☿ R	24 20:19
☽ 0N	2 18:41
♃⚼♄	7 14:59
☿ D	14 23:46
☽ 0S	16 1:05

Planet Ingress		Dy Hr Mn
♂	♒	4 17:50
☿	♒	6 8:53
♀	♑	13 9:01
☉	♒	20 9:09
☊	♈R	25 23:36
♀	♒	6 9:05
♂	♓	11 18:05
☉	♓	18 23:27

Last Aspect Dy Hr Mn			☽ Ingress	Dy Hr Mn
31 20:16	♂	☌	♒	1 2:07
3 8:53	♅	△	♓	3 12:58
6 0:33	☿	⚹	♈	6 1:40
8 9:36	♅	⚹	♉	8 14:03
10 4:02	☉	△	♊	10 23:31
13 4:33	♀	☍	♋	13 4:57
14 21:59	☉	☍	♌	15 7:08
17 3:41	♅	⚹	♍	17 7:52
19 7:13	☉	△	♎	19 9:03
21 7:17	♅	△	♏	21 11:59
22 22:59	☿	□	♐	23 17:09
25 19:00	♅	☍	♑	26 0:22
27 9:28	♀	☌	♒	28 9:26
30 14:26	♅	△	♓	30 20:26

Last Aspect Dy Hr Mn			☽ Ingress	Dy Hr Mn
2 2:49	♅	□	♈	2 9:04
4 17:51	♀	□	♉	4 21:57
7 1:37	♂	□	♊	7 8:40
9 12:15	♂	△	♋	9 15:22
11 0:55	♃	☍	♌	11 18:01
13 12:50	♅	⚹	♍	13 18:05
15 12:22	♅	□	♎	15 17:44
17 16:43	☉	△	♏	17 18:53
19 7:35	♃	⚹	♐	19 22:49
21 23:23	♅	☍	♑	22 5:50
24 0:31	♃	☌	♒	24 15:26
26 19:56	♅	△	♓	27 2:54

☽ Phases & Eclipses Dy Hr Mn		
7 11:52	☽	16♈53
14 21:59	○	24♋26
21 14:07	☾	1♏14
29 2:42	●	8♒53
6 8:05	☽	17♉14
13 9:08	○	24♌21
20 0:43	☾	1♐04
27 20:55	●	8♓57

Astro Data

1 January 1949
Julian Day # 17898
SVP 5♓58'27"
GC 26♐07.6 ⚴ 26♉11.0R
Eris 6♈04.3 ⚵ 11♈49.4
⚷ 4♐10.5 ⚶ 19♏07.3
☽ Mean ☊ 1♉24.7

1 February 1949
Julian Day # 17929
SVP 5♓58'21"
GC 26♐07.7 ⚴ 28♉54.2
Eris 6♈12.7 ⚵ 25♈13.7
⚷ 7♐10.4 ⚶ 3♐22.1
☽ Mean ☊ 29♈46.3

March 1949

LONGITUDE

Day	Sid.Time	☉	0 hr ☽	Noon ☽	True ☊	☿	♀	♂	⚳	♃	♄	♅	♆	♇
1 Tu	22 35 50	10♓35 13	22♓19 48	28♓14 03	26♈21.0	13♒37.8	28♒52.5	14♓00.6	13♌28.7	23♑24.9	2♍10.3	26♊30.8	14♎39.8	14♌48.1
2 W	22 39 47	11 35 25	4♈07 50	10♈01 28	26R 17.2	14 42.5	0♓07.4	14 47.8	13R 18.8	23 36.4	2R 05.6	26R 30.6	14R 38.5	14R 46.8
3 Th	22 43 43	12 35 35	15 55 16	21 49 38	26D 15.6	15 49.6	1 22.2	15 35.0	13 09.4	23 47.9	2 00.8	26 30.5	14 37.2	14 45.6
4 F	22 47 40	13 35 43	27 44 58	3♉41 45	26 15.8	16 58.7	2 37.1	16 22.2	13 00.3	23 59.2	1 56.1	26D 30.4	14 35.8	14 44.4
5 Sa	22 51 36	14 35 50	9♉40 29	15 41 41	26 17.1	18 09.9	3 51.9	17 09.4	12 51.5	24 10.5	1 51.5	26 30.4	14 34.4	14 43.2
6 Su	22 55 33	15 35 54	21 45 56	27 53 49	26 18.7	19 23.1	5 06.7	17 56.5	12 43.2	24 21.7	1 46.8	26 30.5	14 33.1	14 42.0
7 M	22 59 29	16 35 56	4♊05 55	10♊22 51	26R 19.8	20 38.0	6 21.5	18 43.6	12 35.2	24 32.7	1 42.2	26 30.6	14 31.7	14 40.8
8 Tu	23 03 26	17 35 56	16 45 10	23 13 26	26 19.9	21 54.7	7 36.3	19 30.7	12 27.7	24 43.7	1 37.6	26 30.7	14 30.3	14 39.6
9 W	23 07 23	18 35 54	29 48 08	6♋29 40	26 18.3	23 13.0	8 51.0	20 17.8	12 20.5	24 54.6	1 33.1	26 30.9	14 28.8	14 38.5
10 Th	23 11 19	19 35 49	13♋18 20	20 14 18	26 15.2	24 33.0	10 05.8	21 04.8	12 13.8	25 05.4	1 28.6	26 31.2	14 27.4	14 37.3
11 F	23 15 16	20 35 43	27 17 33	4♌27 54	26 10.8	25 54.4	11 20.5	21 51.9	12 07.5	25 16.1	1 24.2	26 31.5	14 25.9	14 36.2
12 Sa	23 19 12	21 35 34	11♌44 58	19 08 10	26 05.7	27 17.4	12 35.3	22 38.9	12 01.6	25 26.7	1 19.8	26 31.9	14 24.4	14 35.1
13 Su	23 23 09	22 35 23	26 36 41	4♍09 31	26 00.6	28 41.9	13 50.0	23 25.8	11 56.2	25 37.3	1 15.4	26 32.3	14 22.9	14 34.0
14 M	23 27 05	23 35 10	11♍45 31	19 23 27	25 56.3	0♓07.7	15 04.7	24 12.7	11 51.1	25 47.7	1 11.1	26 32.8	14 21.4	14 33.0
15 Tu	23 31 02	24 34 54	27 01 57	4♎39 42	25 53.3	1 35.0	16 19.4	24 59.6	11 46.5	25 58.0	1 06.9	26 33.3	14 19.9	14 31.9
16 W	23 34 58	25 34 37	12♎15 25	19 47 56	25D 52.0	3 03.6	17 34.1	25 46.5	11 42.3	26 08.2	1 02.7	26 33.9	14 18.4	14 30.9
17 Th	23 38 55	26 34 18	27 16 13	4♏39 23	25 52.1	4 33.5	18 48.7	26 33.4	11 38.6	26 18.3	0 58.6	26 34.5	14 16.8	14 29.9
18 F	23 42 52	27 33 58	11♏56 48	19 07 57	25 53.2	6 04.8	20 03.4	27 20.2	11 35.3	26 28.2	0 54.5	26 35.2	14 15.3	14 28.9
19 Sa	23 46 48	28 33 35	26 12 32	3♐10 27	25 54.7	7 37.4	21 18.1	28 07.0	11 32.4	26 38.1	0 50.5	26 35.9	14 13.7	14 27.9
20 Su	23 50 45	29 33 11	10♐01 44	16 46 30	25 56.1	9 11.3	22 32.7	28 53.7	11 29.9	26 47.9	0 46.5	26 36.7	14 12.1	14 27.0
21 M	23 54 41	0♈32 45	23 25 01	29 57 37	25R 56.6	10 46.6	23 47.3	29 40.5	11 27.9	26 57.5	0 42.6	26 37.6	14 10.6	14 26.0
22 Tu	23 58 38	1 32 18	6♑24 43	12♑46 44	25 56.1	12 23.1	25 02.0	0♈27.2	11 26.3	27 07.1	0 38.8	26 38.5	14 09.0	14 25.1
23 W	0 02 34	2 31 49	19 04 07	25 17 21	25 54.5	14 00.9	26 16.6	1 13.8	11 25.2	27 16.5	0 35.1	26 39.4	14 07.4	14 24.3
24 Th	0 06 31	3 31 18	1♒26 53	7♒33 10	25 51.8	15 40.1	27 31.2	2 00.5	11 24.5	27 25.8	0 31.4	26 40.4	14 05.7	14 23.4
25 F	0 10 27	4 30 45	13 36 40	19 37 45	25 48.6	17 20.6	28 45.7	2 47.1	11D 24.2	27 35.0	0 27.8	26 41.5	14 04.1	14 22.6
26 Sa	0 14 24	5 30 10	25 36 50	1♓34 18	25 45.1	19 02.3	0♈00.3	3 33.7	11 24.4	27 44.1	0 24.3	26 42.6	14 02.5	14 21.7
27 Su	0 18 21	6 29 33	7♓30 27	13 25 37	25 41.8	20 45.5	1 14.9	4 20.2	11 25.0	27 53.0	0 20.8	26 43.7	14 00.9	14 20.9
28 M	0 22 17	7 28 54	19 20 07	25 14 13	25 39.1	22 29.9	2 29.4	5 06.7	11 26.0	28 01.8	0 17.5	26 44.9	13 59.2	14 20.2
29 Tu	0 26 14	8 28 13	1♈08 11	7♈02 16	25 37.2	24 15.7	3 44.0	5 53.2	11 27.4	28 10.5	0 14.2	26 46.2	13 57.6	14 19.4
30 W	0 30 10	9 27 30	12 56 45	18 51 53	25D 36.3	26 02.9	4 58.5	6 39.6	11 29.3	28 19.1	0 11.0	26 47.5	13 55.9	14 18.7
31 Th	0 34 07	10 26 45	24 47 55	0♉45 09	25 36.2	27 51.5	6 13.0	7 26.0	11 31.6	28 27.5	0 07.9	26 48.8	13 54.3	14 18.0

April 1949

LONGITUDE

Day	Sid.Time	☉	0 hr ☽	Noon ☽	True ☊	☿	♀	♂	⚳	♃	♄	♅	♆	♇
1 F	0 38 03	11♈25 58	6♉43 53	12♉44 24	25♈36.8	29♓41.4	7♈27.5	8♈12.3	11♌34.3	28♑35.8	0♍04.8	26♊50.2	13♎52.6	14♌17.3
2 Sa	0 42 00	12 25 09	18 47 03	24 52 11	25 37.9	1♈32.7	8 41.9	8 58.6	11 37.4	28 44.0	0R 01.9	26 51.7	13R 51.0	14R 16.7
3 Su	0 45 56	13 24 18	1♊00 11	7♊11 25	25 39.1	3 25.4	9 56.4	9 44.9	11 41.0	28 52.0	29♌59.0	26 53.2	13 49.3	14 16.0
4 M	0 49 53	14 23 24	13 26 19	19 45 17	25 40.2	5 19.6	11 10.8	10 31.1	11 44.9	28 59.9	29 56.2	26 54.7	13 47.7	14 15.4
5 Tu	0 53 49	15 22 28	26 08 43	2♋37 02	25 40.9	7 15.1	12 25.3	11 17.3	11 49.3	29 07.7	29 53.6	26 56.3	13 46.0	14 14.9
6 W	0 57 46	16 21 30	9♋10 36	15 49 46	25R 41.1	9 12.0	13 39.7	12 03.5	11 54.0	29 15.3	29 51.0	26 58.0	13 44.4	14 14.3
7 Th	1 01 43	17 20 30	22 34 48	29 25 54	25 40.9	11 10.2	14 54.0	12 49.6	11 59.2	29 22.8	29 48.5	26 59.7	13 42.8	14 13.8
8 F	1 05 39	18 19 27	6♌23 10	13♌26 35	25 40.4	13 09.8	16 08.4	13 35.7	12 04.7	29 30.1	29 46.1	27 01.4	13 41.1	14 13.3
9 Sa	1 09 36	19 18 22	20 36 00	27 51 06	25 39.7	15 10.6	17 22.8	14 21.7	12 10.6	29 37.3	29 43.8	27 03.2	13 39.5	14 12.8
10 Su	1 13 32	20 17 14	5♍11 27	12♍36 23	25 39.1	17 12.7	18 37.1	15 07.6	12 16.9	29 44.3	29 41.6	27 05.0	13 37.8	14 12.4
11 M	1 17 29	21 16 04	20 05 07	27 36 45	25 38.6	19 15.9	19 51.4	15 53.6	12 23.6	29 51.2	29 39.5	27 06.9	13 36.2	14 12.0
12 Tu	1 21 25	22 14 52	5♎10 13	12♎44 25	25D 38.3	21 20.1	21 05.7	16 39.4	12 30.6	29 58.0	29 37.5	27 08.8	13 34.6	14 11.6
13 W	1 25 22	23 13 38	20 18 10	27 50 19	25 38.3	23 25.2	22 20.0	17 25.3	12 38.0	0♒04.6	29 35.6	27 10.8	13 32.9	14 11.2
14 Th	1 29 18	24 12 22	5♏19 46	12♏45 29	25 38.3	25 31.2	23 34.2	18 11.1	12 45.7	0 11.0	29 33.7	27 12.8	13 31.3	14 10.9
15 F	1 33 15	25 11 05	20 06 33	27 22 15	25R 38.4	27 37.7	24 48.5	18 56.8	12 53.8	0 17.3	29 32.0	27 14.8	13 29.7	14 10.5
16 Sa	1 37 12	26 09 45	4♐31 57	11♐35 15	25 38.4	29 44.5	26 02.7	19 42.6	13 02.3	0 23.5	29 30.4	27 16.9	13 28.1	14 10.3
17 Su	1 41 08	27 08 24	18 31 52	25 21 44	25 38.3	1♉51.6	27 17.0	20 28.2	13 11.1	0 29.5	29 28.9	27 19.1	13 26.5	14 10.0
18 M	1 45 05	28 07 01	2♑04 52	8♑41 28	25 38.1	3 58.5	28 31.2	21 13.8	13 20.2	0 35.3	29 27.5	27 21.2	13 24.9	14 09.8
19 Tu	1 49 01	29 05 37	15 11 48	21 36 15	25D 38.0	6 05.0	29 45.4	21 59.4	13 29.7	0 41.0	29 26.2	27 23.5	13 23.3	14 09.6
20 W	1 52 58	0♉04 11	27 55 14	4♒09 16	25 37.9	8 10.9	0♉59.6	22 45.0	13 39.5	0 46.5	29 25.0	27 25.7	13 21.8	14 09.4
21 Th	1 56 54	1 02 43	10♒18 52	16 24 35	25 38.1	10 15.7	2 13.7	23 30.5	13 49.6	0 51.8	29 23.9	27 28.0	13 20.2	14 09.2
22 F	2 00 51	2 01 13	22 26 59	28 26 37	25 38.6	12 19.3	3 27.9	24 15.9	14 00.1	0 57.0	29 22.9	27 30.4	13 18.7	14 09.1
23 Sa	2 04 47	2 59 42	4♓24 02	10♓19 45	25 39.3	14 21.1	4 42.1	25 01.3	14 10.8	1 02.0	29 22.0	27 32.7	13 17.1	14 09.0
24 Su	2 08 44	3 58 09	16 14 18	22 08 08	25 40.2	16 21.1	5 56.2	25 46.6	14 21.9	1 06.9	29 21.2	27 35.1	13 15.6	14 08.9
25 M	2 12 41	4 56 34	28 01 45	3♈55 32	25 41.0	18 18.7	7 10.3	26 32.0	14 33.3	1 11.5	29 20.5	27 37.6	13 14.1	14 08.9
26 Tu	2 16 37	5 54 58	9♈49 54	15 45 11	25R 41.6	20 13.8	8 24.4	27 17.2	14 45.0	1 16.0	29 20.0	27 40.1	13 12.6	14D 08.9
27 W	2 20 34	6 53 20	21 41 45	27 39 52	25 41.8	22 06.1	9 38.5	28 02.4	14 57.0	1 20.4	29 19.5	27 42.6	13 11.1	14 08.9
28 Th	2 24 30	7 51 40	3♉39 49	9♉41 50	25 41.3	23 55.3	10 52.6	28 47.6	15 09.2	1 24.5	29 19.1	27 45.2	13 09.6	14 08.9
29 F	2 28 27	8 49 58	15 46 10	21 53 01	25 40.3	25 41.3	12 06.6	29 32.7	15 21.8	1 28.5	29 18.9	27 47.8	13 08.2	14 09.0
30 Sa	2 32 23	9 48 15	28 02 33	4♊14 59	25 38.6	27 23.8	13 20.7	0♉17.7	15 34.7	1 32.3	29D 18.7	27 50.4	13 06.7	14 09.1

Astro Data

	Dy Hr Mn
☽ 0N	2 0:38
♅ D	5 4:08
☽ 0S	15 11:37
♃⚻♅	19 6:15
☉0N	20 22:48
♂0N	24 7:24
⚳ D	25 15:16
♀0N	29 2:53
☽ 0N	29 6:39
☿0N	3 23:38
♃⚻♄	10 4:50
☽ 0S	11 22:50
☽ 0N	25 13:02
♇ D	26 14:00

Planet Ingress

		Dy Hr Mn
♀	♓	2 9:38
☿	♓	14 9:52
☉	♈	20 22:48
♂	♈	21 22:02
♀	♈	26 11:54
☿	♈	1 16:02
♄	♌R	3 3:38
♃	♒	12 19:18
☿	♉	16 14:55
♀	♉	19 16:44
☉	♉	20 10:17
♂	♉	30 2:33

Last Aspect / ☽ Ingress (March)

Last Aspect Dy Hr Mn		☽ Ingress	Dy Hr Mn
1 8:30	♅ □	♈	1 15:36
3 21:29	♅ ⚹	♉	4 4:33
6 4:59	♃ △	♊	6 16:05
8 18:01	♅ ☌	♋	9 0:21
10 20:23	♃ ☍	♌	11 4:33
13 2:26	☿ ☍	♍	13 5:24
14 23:15	♅ □	♎	15 4:40
16 22:52	♅ △	♏	17 4:25
19 3:25	☉ △	♐	19 6:30
21 11:26	♂ □	♑	21 12:04
23 15:54	♃ ☌	♒	23 21:10
26 2:11	♅ △	♓	26 8:50
28 17:45	♃ ⚹	♈	28 21:41
31 7:20	♃ □	♉	31 10:29

Last Aspect / ☽ Ingress (April)

Last Aspect Dy Hr Mn		☽ Ingress	Dy Hr Mn
2 19:39	♃ △	♊	2 22:03
5 6:59	♄ ⚹	♋	5 7:10
7 11:54	♃ ☍	♌	7 12:59
9 15:04	♄ ☌	♍	9 15:32
11 15:35	♃ △	♎	11 15:48
13 14:48	♄ ⚹	♏	13 15:27
15 15:36	♄ □	♐	15 16:23
17 19:19	♄ △	♑	17 20:16
20 3:27	☉ □	♒	20 3:59
22 13:53	♄ ☍	♓	22 15:08
24 23:08	♅ □	♈	25 4:01
27 15:20	♄ △	♉	27 16:41
30 2:28	♄ □	♊	30 3:48

☽ Phases & Eclipses

Dy Hr Mn	
8 0:42	☽ 17♊08
14 19:03	○ 23♍53
21 13:10	☾ 0♑36
29 15:11	● 8♈36
6 13:01	☽ 16♋24
13 4:08	○ 22♎54
13 4:11	• T 1.425
20 3:27	☾ 29♑43
28 8:02	● 7♉42
28 7:48:23	• P 0.609

Astro Data

1 March 1949
Julian Day # 17957
SVP 5♓58'18"
GC 26♐07.8 ⚵ 8♊27.9
Eris 6♈28.0 ⚴ 9♉35.6
⚷ 8♐45.8 ⚶ 14♐32.1
☽ Mean ☊ 28♈17.3

1 April 1949
Julian Day # 17988
SVP 5♓58'15"
GC 26♐07.8 ⚵ 23♊00.2
Eris 6♈49.3 ⚴ 26♉43.4
⚷ 8♐59.2R ⚶ 23♐33.5
☽ Mean ☊ 26♈38.8

LONGITUDE

May 1949

Day	Sid.Time	☉	0 hr ☽	Noon ☽	True ☊	☿	♀	♂	⚳	♃	♄	♅	♆	♇
1 Su	2 36 20	10♉46 30	10♊30 27	16♊49 08	25♈36.5	29♉02.8	14♉34.7	1♉02.8	15♌47.8	1♒36.0	29♌18.7	27♊53.1	13♎05.3	14♌09.2
2 M	2 40 16	11 44 43	23 11 12	29 36 48	25R34.3	0♊37.9	15 48.7	1 47.7	16 01.2	1 39.4	29 18.8	27 55.8	13R03.9	14 09.4
3 Tu	2 44 13	12 42 53	6♋06 06	12♋39 14	25 32.2	2 09.3	17 02.7	2 32.6	16 14.9	1 42.7	29 18.9	27 58.5	13 02.5	14 09.6
4 W	2 48 10	13 41 02	19 16 23	25 57 39	25 30.7	3 36.7	18 16.7	3 17.5	16 28.8	1 45.8	29 19.2	28 01.3	13 01.1	14 09.8
5 Th	2 52 06	14 39 09	2♌43 10	9♌33 00	25D29.9	5 00.0	19 30.7	4 02.3	16 43.0	1 48.7	29 19.6	28 04.1	12 59.8	14 10.0
6 F	2 56 03	15 37 14	16 27 14	23 25 50	25 30.0	6 19.1	20 44.6	4 47.0	16 57.5	1 51.5	29 20.1	28 06.9	12 58.4	14 10.3
7 Sa	2 59 59	16 35 17	0♍28 44	7♍35 48	25 30.8	7 34.1	21 58.6	5 31.7	17 12.2	1 54.0	29 20.7	28 09.8	12 57.1	14 10.6
8 Su	3 03 56	17 33 18	14 46 49	22 01 27	25 32.1	8 44.8	23 12.5	6 16.4	17 27.2	1 56.4	29 21.4	28 12.7	12 55.8	14 10.9
9 M	3 07 52	18 31 17	29 19 15	6♎39 41	25 33.4	9 51.2	24 26.4	7 01.0	17 42.3	1 58.6	29 22.2	28 15.6	12 54.5	14 11.2
10 Tu	3 11 49	19 29 15	14♎02 08	21 25 50	25R34.1	10 53.1	25 40.2	7 45.5	17 57.8	2 00.6	29 23.1	28 18.6	12 53.3	14 11.6
11 W	3 15 45	20 27 10	28 49 58	6♏13 41	25 33.8	11 50.5	26 54.1	8 30.0	18 13.4	2 02.4	29 24.2	28 21.6	12 52.0	14 12.0
12 Th	3 19 42	21 25 04	13♏36 04	20 56 11	25 32.3	12 43.5	28 07.9	9 14.4	18 29.3	2 04.0	29 25.3	28 24.6	12 50.8	14 12.4
13 F	3 23 39	22 22 57	28 13 12	5♐26 17	25 29.6	13 31.8	29 21.8	9 58.8	18 45.4	2 05.5	29 26.5	28 27.6	12 49.6	14 12.9
14 Sa	3 27 35	23 20 48	12♐34 42	19 37 52	25 25.8	14 15.5	0♊35.6	10 43.1	19 01.8	2 06.7	29 27.8	28 30.7	12 48.4	14 13.3
15 Su	3 31 32	24 18 38	26 35 19	3♑26 41	25 21.6	14 54.4	1 49.4	11 27.4	19 18.3	2 07.8	29 29.3	28 33.8	12 47.3	14 13.8
16 M	3 35 28	25 16 26	10♑11 49	16 50 40	25 17.4	15 28.6	3 03.2	12 11.6	19 35.1	2 08.7	29 30.8	28 36.9	12 46.2	14 14.4
17 Tu	3 39 25	26 14 13	23 23 18	29 49 57	25 13.9	15 58.0	4 17.0	12 55.8	19 52.0	2 09.4	29 32.4	28 40.0	12 45.1	14 14.9
18 W	3 43 21	27 12 00	6♒10 56	12♒26 38	25 11.5	16 22.5	5 30.8	13 39.9	20 09.2	2 09.9	29 34.2	28 43.2	12 44.0	14 15.5
19 Th	3 47 18	28 09 44	18 37 33	24 44 13	25D10.4	16 42.2	6 44.5	14 24.0	20 26.6	2 10.2	29 36.0	28 46.4	12 42.9	14 16.1
20 F	3 51 15	29 07 28	0♓47 12	6♓47 07	25 10.6	16 57.0	7 58.3	15 08.0	20 44.2	2R10.3	29 38.0	28 49.6	12 41.9	14 16.8
21 Sa	3 55 11	0♊05 11	12 44 35	18 40 15	25 11.8	17 07.0	9 12.0	15 51.9	21 01.9	2 10.3	29 40.0	28 52.8	12 40.9	14 17.4
22 Su	3 59 08	1 02 52	24 34 44	0♈28 38	25 13.5	17R12.1	10 25.7	16 35.9	21 19.9	2 10.0	29 42.1	28 56.1	12 39.9	14 18.1
23 M	4 03 04	2 00 33	6♈22 34	12 17 04	25 15.1	17 12.6	11 39.5	17 19.7	21 38.1	2 09.6	29 44.4	28 59.4	12 39.0	14 18.8
24 Tu	4 07 01	2 58 12	18 12 42	24 09 56	25R15.8	17 08.4	12 53.2	18 03.5	21 56.4	2 08.9	29 46.7	29 02.7	12 38.0	14 19.6
25 W	4 10 57	3 55 51	0♉09 14	6♉10 59	25 15.2	16 59.9	14 06.9	18 47.3	22 14.9	2 08.1	29 49.2	29 06.0	12 37.1	14 20.3
26 Th	4 14 54	4 53 28	12 15 32	18 23 11	25 12.8	16 47.0	15 20.5	19 31.0	22 33.6	2 07.1	29 51.7	29 09.3	12 36.3	14 21.1
27 F	4 18 50	5 51 05	24 34 10	0♊48 39	25 08.6	16 30.2	16 34.2	20 14.6	22 52.5	2 05.9	29 54.3	29 12.7	12 35.4	14 21.9
28 Sa	4 22 47	6 48 40	7♊06 45	13 28 31	25 02.7	16 09.8	17 47.9	20 58.2	23 11.6	2 04.5	29 57.1	29 16.0	12 34.6	14 22.8
29 Su	4 26 44	7 46 14	19 53 59	26 23 05	24 55.7	15 46.0	19 01.5	21 41.7	23 30.8	2 02.9	29 59.9	29 19.4	12 33.8	14 23.6
30 M	4 30 40	8 43 47	2♋55 46	9♋31 54	24 48.3	15 19.4	20 15.2	22 25.2	23 50.2	2 01.1	0♍02.8	29 22.8	12 33.0	14 24.5
31 Tu	4 34 37	9 41 19	16 11 22	22 54 00	24 41.4	14 50.3	21 28.8	23 08.7	24 09.7	1 59.1	0 05.8	29 26.3	12 32.3	14 25.4

LONGITUDE

June 1949

Day	Sid.Time	☉	0 hr ☽	Noon ☽	True ☊	☿	♀	♂	⚳	♃	♄	♅	♆	♇
1 W	4 38 33	10♊38 49	29♋39 40	6♌28 13	24♈35.7	14♊19.2	22♊42.4	23♉52.0	24♌29.5	1♒57.0	0♍08.9	29♊29.7	12♎31.6	14♌26.4
2 Th	4 42 30	11 36 18	13♌19 29	20 13 20	24R31.8	13R46.8	23 56.0	24 35.3	24 49.3	1R54.7	0 12.1	29 33.1	12R30.9	14 27.3
3 F	4 46 26	12 33 46	27 09 39	4♍08 19	24D29.9	13 13.4	25 09.6	25 18.6	25 09.4	1 52.1	0 15.4	29 36.6	12 30.3	14 28.3
4 Sa	4 50 23	13 31 13	11♍09 12	18 12 12	24 29.7	12 39.9	26 23.1	26 01.8	25 29.6	1 49.4	0 18.8	29 40.1	12 29.7	14 29.3
5 Su	4 54 19	14 28 38	25 17 09	2♎23 55	24 30.5	12 06.6	27 36.7	26 44.9	25 49.9	1 46.6	0 22.3	29 43.6	12 29.1	14 30.3
6 M	4 58 16	15 26 02	9♎32 16	16 41 57	24R31.4	11 34.2	28 50.2	27 28.0	26 10.4	1 43.5	0 25.8	29 47.1	12 28.5	14 31.4
7 Tu	5 02 13	16 23 25	23 52 40	1♏04 02	24 31.5	11 03.2	0♋03.7	28 11.0	26 31.0	1 40.3	0 29.5	29 50.6	12 28.0	14 32.5
8 W	5 06 09	17 20 47	8♏15 35	15 26 49	24 29.7	10 34.2	1 17.2	28 54.0	26 51.7	1 36.9	0 33.2	29 54.1	12 27.5	14 33.6
9 Th	5 10 06	18 18 08	22 37 10	29 46 01	24 25.7	10 07.6	2 30.7	29 36.9	27 12.6	1 33.3	0 37.0	29 57.6	12 27.0	14 34.7
10 F	5 14 02	19 15 28	6♐52 43	13♐56 39	24 19.5	9 43.9	3 44.2	0♊19.7	27 33.6	1 29.5	0 40.9	0♋01.2	12 26.6	14 35.8
11 Sa	5 17 59	20 12 47	20 57 12	27 53 46	24 11.3	9 23.5	4 57.6	1 02.5	27 54.8	1 25.6	0 44.9	0 04.7	12 26.2	14 37.0
12 Su	5 21 55	21 10 06	4♑45 53	11♑33 08	24 02.1	9 06.7	6 11.1	1 45.3	28 16.1	1 21.5	0 49.0	0 08.3	12 25.8	14 38.2
13 M	5 25 52	22 07 24	18 15 12	24 51 54	23 52.7	8 53.8	7 24.5	2 28.0	28 37.5	1 17.3	0 53.2	0 11.8	12 25.5	14 39.4
14 Tu	5 29 48	23 04 42	1♒23 10	7♒49 03	23 44.3	8 45.0	8 38.0	3 10.6	28 59.0	1 12.8	0 57.4	0 15.4	12 25.1	14 40.6
15 W	5 33 45	24 01 59	14 09 42	20 25 24	23 37.5	8D40.5	9 51.4	3 53.2	29 20.7	1 08.3	1 01.7	0 19.0	12 24.9	14 41.8
16 Th	5 37 42	24 59 16	26 36 30	2♓43 26	23 32.9	8 40.5	11 04.8	4 35.7	29 42.5	1 03.5	1 06.1	0 22.5	12 24.6	14 43.1
17 F	5 41 38	25 56 32	8♓46 43	14 46 55	23 30.4	8 45.0	12 18.1	5 18.2	0♍04.4	0 58.6	1 10.6	0 26.1	12 24.4	14 44.4
18 Sa	5 45 35	26 53 48	20 44 39	26 40 33	23D29.7	8 54.2	13 31.5	6 00.6	0 26.4	0 53.6	1 15.1	0 29.7	12 24.2	14 45.7
19 Su	5 49 31	27 51 04	2♈35 17	8♈29 31	23 30.0	9 08.0	14 44.9	6 43.0	0 48.5	0 48.4	1 19.8	0 33.3	12 24.0	14 47.0
20 M	5 53 28	28 48 19	14 23 56	20 19 12	23R30.5	9 26.4	15 58.2	7 25.3	1 10.8	0 43.0	1 24.5	0 36.9	12 23.9	14 48.3
21 Tu	5 57 24	29 45 35	26 15 57	2♉14 48	23 30.2	9 49.4	17 11.6	8 07.5	1 33.1	0 37.5	1 29.3	0 40.5	12 23.8	14 49.7
22 W	6 01 21	0♋42 50	8♉16 19	14 21 02	23 28.2	10 17.1	18 24.9	8 49.8	1 55.6	0 31.9	1 34.1	0 44.1	12 23.8	14 51.1
23 Th	6 05 17	1 40 05	20 29 25	26 41 52	23 23.9	10 49.3	19 38.3	9 31.9	2 18.2	0 26.1	1 39.1	0 47.7	12D23.7	14 52.5
24 F	6 09 14	2 37 20	2♊58 41	9♊20 07	23 17.0	11 26.0	20 51.6	10 14.0	2 40.9	0 20.2	1 44.1	0 51.3	12 23.7	14 53.9
25 Sa	6 13 11	3 34 35	15 46 17	22 17 13	23 07.9	12 07.2	22 04.9	10 56.0	3 03.7	0 14.2	1 49.1	0 54.9	12 23.8	14 55.3
26 Su	6 17 07	4 31 49	28 52 51	5♋33 02	22 57.1	12 52.7	23 18.2	11 38.0	3 26.6	0 08.0	1 54.3	0 58.4	12 23.8	14 56.8
27 M	6 21 04	5 29 04	12♋17 31	19 05 56	22 45.7	13 42.5	24 31.4	12 20.0	3 49.6	0 01.7	1 59.5	1 02.0	12 23.9	14 58.2
28 Tu	6 25 00	6 26 18	25 57 55	2♌53 00	22 34.9	14 36.6	25 44.7	13 01.8	4 12.7	29♑55.3	2 04.8	1 05.6	12 24.1	14 59.7
29 W	6 28 57	7 23 31	9♌50 43	16 50 35	22 25.7	15 34.9	26 57.9	13 43.6	4 35.8	29 48.8	2 10.2	1 09.2	12 24.2	15 01.2
30 Th	6 32 53	8 20 45	23 52 09	0♍54 57	22 18.9	16 37.3	28 11.2	14 25.4	4 59.1	29 42.2	2 15.6	1 12.8	12 24.4	15 02.7

Astro Data

	Dy Hr Mn
♄ D	1 8:34
☽ 0S	9 8:18
♃ R	20 15:34
☽ 0N	22 19:48
☿ R	23 2:15
♅∠♇	31 4:10
☽ 0S	5 14:56
☿ D	16 0:07
♃⚻♄	16 5:15
☽ 0N	19 2:46
♃⚻♅	21 4:11
♆ D	23 20:46

Planet Ingress

	Dy Hr Mn
☿ ♊	2 2:19
♀ ♊	14 0:25
☉ ♊	21 9:51
♄ ♍	29 12:59
♀ ♋	7 10:47
♂ ♊	10 0:57
♅ ♋	10 4:08
⚳ ♍	17 7:13
☉ ♋	21 18:03
♃ ♑R	27 18:29

Last Aspect / ☽ Ingress (May)

Last Aspect Dy Hr Mn		☽ Ingress Dy Hr Mn
2 11:26	♄ ⚹	♋ 2 12:43
3 20:48	♀ ⚹	♌ 4 19:11
6 22:04	♄ ☌	♍ 6 23:11
8 22:13	♅ □	♎ 9 1:07
11 0:55	♄ ⚹	♏ 11 1:54
13 2:01	♄ □	♐ 13 2:57
15 5:02	♄ △	♑ 15 5:57
17 4:44	☉ △	♒ 17 12:19
19 21:40	♄ ☍	♓ 19 22:26
22 8:51	♅ □	♈ 22 11:02
24 23:17	♄ △	♉ 24 23:42
27 10:16	♄ □	♊ 27 10:27
29 17:26	♅ ☌	♋ 29 18:39

Last Aspect / ☽ Ingress (June)

Last Aspect Dy Hr Mn		☽ Ingress Dy Hr Mn
31 12:28	♂ ⚹	♌ 1 0:36
3 4:11	♅ ⚹	♍ 3 4:53
5 7:29	♅ □	♎ 5 7:58
7 10:10	♀ △	♏ 7 10:13
9 11:44	♂ ☍	♐ 9 12:24
10 21:45	☉ ☍	♑ 11 15:40
12 13:34	♆ □	♒ 13 21:26
15 19:34	☉ △	♓ 16 6:38
18 12:29	☉ □	♈ 18 18:45
21 6:35	☉ ⚹	♉ 21 7:30
22 20:50	♀ ⚹	♊ 23 18:20
24 22:24	♇ ⚹	♋ 26 2:01
28 6:55	♃ ☍	♌ 28 7:01
29 9:40	☿ ⚹	♍ 30 10:27

☽ Phases & Eclipses

Dy Hr Mn	
5 21:33	☽ 15♌02
12 12:51	○ 21♏27
19 19:22	☾ 28♒27
27 22:24	● 6♊16
4 3:27	☽ 13♍11
10 21:45	○ 19♐39
18 12:29	☾ 26♓55
26 10:02	● 4♋27

Astro Data

1 May 1949
Julian Day # 18018
SVP 5♓58'11"
GC 26♐07.9 ⚴ 8♋41.7
Eris 7♈09.4 ⚵ 13♊43.4
⚷ 7♐45.0R ⚶ 26♐46.9R
☽ Mean ☊ 25♈03.5

1 June 1949
Julian Day # 18049
SVP 5♓58'05"
GC 26♐08.0 ⚴ 25♋17.9
Eris 7♈24.4 ⚵ 1♋10.6
⚷ 5♐37.3R ⚶ 22♐49.7R
☽ Mean ☊ 23♈25.0

July 1949 — LONGITUDE

Day	Sid.Time	☉	0 hr ☽	Noon ☽	True ☊	☿	♀	♂	⚳	♃	♄	♅	♆	♇
1 F	6 36 50	9♋17 57	7♍58 37	15♍02 49	22♈14.8	17♊43.8	29♋24.4	15♊07.1	5♍22.5	29♑35.4	2♍21.1	1♋16.4	12♎24.7	15♌04.2
2 Sa	6 40 47	10 15 10	22 07 15	29 11 41	22D13.0	18 54.3	0♌37.6	15 48.7	5 46.0	29R28.6	2 26.6	1 19.9	12 24.9	15 05.8
3 Su	6 44 43	11 12 22	6♎15 58	13♎19 55	22R12.7	20 08.8	1 50.8	16 30.3	6 09.5	29 21.7	2 32.2	1 23.5	12 25.2	15 07.3
4 M	6 48 40	12 09 34	20 23 26	27 26 24	22 12.7	21 27.2	3 03.9	17 11.8	6 33.2	29 14.7	2 37.9	1 27.0	12 25.5	15 08.9
5 Tu	6 52 36	13 06 45	4♏28 41	11♏30 11	22 11.7	22 49.5	4 17.1	17 53.3	6 56.9	29 07.6	2 43.7	1 30.6	12 25.9	15 10.5
6 W	6 56 33	14 03 56	18 30 41	25 30 00	22 08.7	24 15.6	5 30.2	18 34.7	7 20.7	29 00.4	2 49.5	1 34.1	12 26.3	15 12.1
7 Th	7 00 29	15 01 08	2♐27 54	9♐24 03	22 03.0	25 45.4	6 43.3	19 16.1	7 44.6	28 53.2	2 55.3	1 37.6	12 26.7	15 13.7
8 F	7 04 26	15 58 19	16 18 09	23 09 50	21 54.6	27 19.0	7 56.4	19 57.4	8 08.6	28 45.9	3 01.3	1 41.1	12 27.2	15 15.3
9 Sa	7 08 22	16 55 30	29 58 45	6♑44 30	21 43.8	28 56.1	9 09.4	20 38.6	8 32.6	28 38.5	3 07.2	1 44.6	12 27.7	15 16.9
10 Su	7 12 19	17 52 41	13♑26 45	20 05 12	21 31.6	0♋36.8	10 22.5	21 19.8	8 56.7	28 31.0	3 13.3	1 48.1	12 28.2	15 18.6
11 M	7 16 16	18 49 53	26 39 35	3♒09 43	21 19.2	2 20.9	11 35.5	22 00.9	9 20.9	28 23.5	3 19.4	1 51.6	12 28.7	15 20.2
12 Tu	7 20 12	19 47 04	9♒35 28	15 56 50	21 07.7	4 08.2	12 48.5	22 42.0	9 45.2	28 16.0	3 25.5	1 55.1	12 29.3	15 21.9
13 W	7 24 09	20 44 17	22 13 53	28 26 45	20 58.1	5 58.6	14 01.5	23 23.0	10 09.5	28 08.4	3 31.7	1 58.5	12 29.9	15 23.6
14 Th	7 28 05	21 41 29	4♓35 40	10♓40 59	20 51.0	7 52.0	15 14.5	24 04.0	10 34.0	28 00.8	3 37.9	2 02.0	12 30.6	15 25.3
15 F	7 32 02	22 38 42	16 43 04	22 42 25	20 46.5	9 48.0	16 27.4	24 44.9	10 58.5	27 53.1	3 44.2	2 05.4	12 31.2	15 27.0
16 Sa	7 35 58	23 35 56	28 39 32	4♈35 01	20 44.3	11 46.5	17 40.4	25 25.8	11 23.0	27 45.4	3 50.6	2 08.8	12 32.0	15 28.7
17 Su	7 39 55	24 33 10	10♈29 28	16 23 32	20 43.7	13 47.2	18 53.3	26 06.6	11 47.6	27 37.7	3 57.0	2 12.2	12 32.7	15 30.4
18 M	7 43 51	25 30 25	22 17 54	28 13 15	20 43.6	15 49.9	20 06.2	26 47.3	12 12.3	27 29.9	4 03.4	2 15.6	12 33.5	15 32.1
19 Tu	7 47 48	26 27 40	4♉10 16	10♉09 38	20 43.1	17 54.1	21 19.1	27 28.0	12 37.1	27 22.2	4 09.9	2 19.0	12 34.3	15 33.9
20 W	7 51 45	27 24 57	16 12 00	22 18 01	20 41.2	19 59.6	22 31.9	28 08.7	13 01.9	27 14.4	4 16.5	2 22.3	12 35.1	15 35.6
21 Th	7 55 41	28 22 14	28 28 15	4♊43 13	20 37.0	22 06.0	23 44.8	28 49.3	13 26.8	27 06.7	4 23.1	2 25.6	12 35.9	15 37.4
22 F	7 59 38	29 19 32	11♊03 22	17 29 03	20 30.3	24 13.1	24 57.6	29 29.8	13 51.8	26 58.9	4 29.7	2 28.9	12 36.8	15 39.1
23 Sa	8 03 34	0♌16 51	24 00 29	0♋37 48	20 21.2	26 20.6	26 10.4	0♋10.3	14 16.8	26 51.2	4 36.4	2 32.2	12 37.8	15 40.9
24 Su	8 07 31	1 14 11	7♋20 59	14 09 53	20 10.4	28 28.1	27 23.2	0 50.7	14 41.9	26 43.5	4 43.1	2 35.5	12 38.7	15 42.7
25 M	8 11 27	2 11 31	21 04 11	28 03 26	19 58.8	0♌35.3	28 36.0	1 31.1	15 07.0	26 35.8	4 49.9	2 38.7	12 39.7	15 44.5
26 Tu	8 15 24	3 08 52	5♌07 07	12♌14 32	19 47.8	2 42.2	29 48.7	2 11.4	15 32.2	26 28.1	4 56.7	2 42.0	12 40.7	15 46.3
27 W	8 19 20	4 06 14	19 24 59	26 37 39	19 38.3	4 48.3	1♍01.4	2 51.7	15 57.5	26 20.4	5 03.5	2 45.2	12 41.7	15 48.1
28 Th	8 23 17	5 03 36	3♍51 47	11♍06 36	19 31.4	6 53.6	2 14.1	3 31.9	16 22.8	26 12.8	5 10.4	2 48.4	12 42.8	15 49.9
29 F	8 27 14	6 00 58	18 21 23	25 35 29	19 27.1	8 57.8	3 26.8	4 12.0	16 48.2	26 05.3	5 17.3	2 51.5	12 43.9	15 51.7
30 Sa	8 31 10	6 58 22	2♎48 22	9♎59 35	19D25.3	11 00.9	4 39.5	4 52.1	17 13.6	25 57.8	5 24.3	2 54.6	12 45.0	15 53.5
31 Su	8 35 07	7 55 45	17 08 46	24 15 39	19 25.1	13 02.8	5 52.1	5 32.1	17 39.1	25 50.3	5 31.3	2 57.7	12 46.2	15 55.3

August 1949 — LONGITUDE

Day	Sid.Time	☉	0 hr ☽	Noon ☽	True ☊	☿	♀	♂	⚳	♃	♄	♅	♆	♇
1 M	8 39 03	8♌53 10	1♏20 04	8♏21 54	19♈25.4	15♌03.2	7♍04.7	6♋12.1	18♍04.6	25♑42.9	5♍38.3	3♋00.8	12♎47.3	15♌57.1
2 Tu	8 43 00	9 50 35	15 21 05	22 17 35	19R24.8	17 02.3	8 17.2	6 52.0	18 30.2	25R35.6	5 45.4	3 03.9	12 48.6	15 58.9
3 W	8 46 56	10 48 00	29 11 25	6♐02 33	19 22.4	18 59.9	9 29.8	7 31.9	18 55.8	25 28.3	5 52.4	3 06.9	12 49.8	16 00.7
4 Th	8 50 53	11 45 27	12♐50 59	19 36 41	19 17.6	20 55.9	10 42.3	8 11.7	19 21.4	25 21.2	5 59.6	3 09.9	12 51.1	16 02.6
5 F	8 54 49	12 42 54	26 19 36	2♑59 41	19 10.3	22 50.5	11 54.8	8 51.4	19 47.2	25 14.1	6 06.7	3 12.9	12 52.3	16 04.4
6 Sa	8 58 46	13 40 22	9♑36 51	16 10 58	19 00.8	24 43.5	13 07.2	9 31.1	20 12.9	25 07.1	6 13.9	3 15.8	12 53.7	16 06.2
7 Su	9 02 43	14 37 51	22 41 58	29 09 44	18 50.1	26 34.9	14 19.6	10 10.7	20 38.7	25 00.2	6 21.1	3 18.7	12 55.0	16 08.1
8 M	9 06 39	15 35 20	5♒34 12	11♒55 17	18 39.0	28 24.8	15 32.0	10 50.3	21 04.6	24 53.3	6 28.3	3 21.6	12 56.4	16 09.9
9 Tu	9 10 36	16 32 51	18 12 58	24 27 16	18 28.8	0♍13.1	16 44.3	11 29.8	21 30.4	24 46.6	6 35.6	3 24.5	12 57.8	16 11.7
10 W	9 14 32	17 30 23	0♓38 15	6♓46 02	18 20.3	1 59.9	17 56.6	12 09.3	21 56.4	24 40.0	6 42.9	3 27.3	12 59.2	16 13.6
11 Th	9 18 29	18 27 56	12 50 47	18 52 46	18 14.0	3 45.2	19 08.9	12 48.7	22 22.3	24 33.5	6 50.2	3 30.1	13 00.6	16 15.4
12 F	9 22 25	19 25 30	24 52 15	0♈49 37	18 10.1	5 28.9	20 21.2	13 28.0	22 48.3	24 27.1	6 57.5	3 32.8	13 02.1	16 17.2
13 Sa	9 26 22	20 23 06	6♈45 15	12 39 39	18D08.4	7 11.2	21 33.4	14 07.3	23 14.4	24 20.8	7 04.9	3 35.6	13 03.6	16 19.0
14 Su	9 30 18	21 20 43	18 33 19	24 26 49	18 08.4	8 51.9	22 45.6	14 46.6	23 40.5	24 14.7	7 12.2	3 38.3	13 05.1	16 20.9
15 M	9 34 15	22 18 22	0♉20 43	6♉15 41	18 09.3	10 31.2	23 57.7	15 25.8	24 06.6	24 08.6	7 19.6	3 40.9	13 06.6	16 22.7
16 Tu	9 38 12	23 16 02	12 12 20	18 11 21	18R10.2	12 09.0	25 09.9	16 04.9	24 32.8	24 02.7	7 27.0	3 43.6	13 08.2	16 24.5
17 W	9 42 08	24 13 43	24 13 23	0♊19 06	18 10.1	13 45.3	26 22.0	16 44.0	24 59.0	23 57.0	7 34.5	3 46.1	13 09.8	16 26.3
18 Th	9 46 05	25 11 27	6♊29 08	12 44 05	18 08.4	15 20.2	27 34.0	17 23.0	25 25.2	23 51.3	7 41.9	3 48.7	13 11.4	16 28.1
19 F	9 50 01	26 09 12	19 04 30	25 30 50	18 04.8	16 53.6	28 46.1	18 02.0	25 51.5	23 45.8	7 49.4	3 51.2	13 13.0	16 30.0
20 Sa	9 53 58	27 06 59	2♋03 29	8♋42 42	17 59.2	18 25.5	29 58.1	18 40.9	26 17.8	23 40.5	7 56.9	3 53.7	13 14.7	16 31.8
21 Su	9 57 54	28 04 47	15 28 38	22 21 15	17 52.2	19 56.0	1♎10.0	19 19.8	26 44.1	23 35.3	8 04.4	3 56.2	13 16.4	16 33.6
22 M	10 01 51	29 02 37	29 20 22	6♌25 37	17 44.4	21 25.1	2 22.0	19 58.6	27 10.5	23 30.3	8 11.9	3 58.6	13 18.1	16 35.4
23 Tu	10 05 47	0♍00 28	13♌36 30	20 52 18	17 36.9	22 52.6	3 33.9	20 37.3	27 36.9	23 25.4	8 19.4	4 00.9	13 19.8	16 37.2
24 W	10 09 44	0 58 21	28 12 14	5♍35 20	17 30.5	24 18.7	4 45.7	21 16.0	28 03.3	23 20.6	8 26.9	4 03.3	13 21.6	16 39.0
25 Th	10 13 41	1 56 15	13♍00 37	20 27 02	17 26.0	25 43.2	5 57.6	21 54.6	28 29.8	23 16.1	8 34.5	4 05.6	13 23.3	16 40.7
26 F	10 17 37	2 54 11	27 53 34	5♎19 16	17D23.5	27 06.2	7 09.4	22 33.2	28 56.3	23 11.7	8 42.0	4 07.8	13 25.1	16 42.5
27 Sa	10 21 34	3 52 08	12♎43 13	20 04 39	17 23.0	28 27.7	8 21.1	23 11.7	29 22.8	23 07.4	8 49.6	4 10.0	13 26.9	16 44.3
28 Su	10 25 30	4 50 06	27 22 56	4♏37 31	17 23.8	29 47.5	9 32.8	23 50.1	29 49.4	23 03.4	8 57.1	4 12.2	13 28.7	16 46.0
29 M	10 29 27	5 48 06	11♏48 03	18 54 14	17 25.0	1♎05.7	10 44.5	24 28.5	0♎16.0	22 59.5	9 04.7	4 14.3	13 30.6	16 47.8
30 Tu	10 33 23	6 46 07	25 55 56	2♐53 05	17R25.9	2 22.2	11 56.1	25 06.9	0 42.6	22 55.8	9 12.3	4 16.4	13 32.4	16 49.5
31 W	10 37 20	7 44 10	9♐45 43	16 33 53	17 25.6	3 37.0	13 07.7	25 45.1	1 09.2	22 52.2	9 19.8	4 18.5	13 34.3	16 51.3

Astro Data

	Dy Hr Mn
☽0S	2 19:39
☽0N	16 9:44
☽0S	30 0:45
☽0N	12 16:33
♀0S	22 0:32
♃⚼♄	23 23:39
☽0S	26 8:12
☿0S	27 7:37

Planet Ingress

		Dy Hr Mn
♀	♌	1 23:40
☿	♋	10 3:19
☉	♌	23 4:57
♂	♋	23 5:54
☿	♌	25 5:20
♀	♍	26 15:43
☿	♍	9 9:04
♀	♎	20 12:39
☉	♍	23 11:48
☿	♎	28 15:48
⚳	♎	28 21:35

Last Aspect / ☽ Ingress

Last Aspect Dy Hr Mn			☽ Ingress	Dy Hr Mn
2 12:29	♃	△	♎	2 13:22
4 15:03	♃	□	♏	4 16:22
6 17:59	♃	✶	♐	6 19:45
8 20:16	☿	☍	♑	9 0:02
11 3:16	♃	☌	♒	11 6:09
13 1:39	♂	△	♓	13 15:01
15 22:19	♃	✶	♈	16 2:43
18 10:33	♃	□	♉	18 15:36
20 22:47	☉	✶	♊	21 2:57
23 3:08	♀	✶	♋	23 10:52
25 9:31	♃	☍	♌	25 15:19
26 17:55	♇	☌	♍	27 17:36
29 12:49	♃	△	♎	29 19:20
31 14:39	♃	□	♏	31 21:44

Last Aspect / ☽ Ingress

Last Aspect Dy Hr Mn			☽ Ingress	Dy Hr Mn
2 17:41	♃	✶	♐	3 1:25
4 14:45	☿	△	♑	5 6:36
7 4:20	♃	☌	♒	7 13:34
8 20:06	♇	☍	♓	9 22:45
11 23:16	♃	✶	♈	12 10:20
14 11:35	♃	□	♉	14 23:18
17 3:23	♀	△	♊	17 11:23
19 18:36	♀	□	♋	19 20:15
21 14:07	♃	☍	♌	22 1:08
23 4:59	♇	☌	♍	24 2:56
25 21:22	☿	☌	♎	26 3:24
27 17:21	♂	□	♏	28 4:19
29 21:57	♂	△	♐	30 7:00

☽ Phases & Eclipses

Dy Hr Mn		
3 8:08	☽	11♎03
10 7:41	○	17♑42
18 6:02	☾	25♈16
25 19:33	●	2♌30
1 12:57	☽	8♏55
8 19:33	○	15♒53
16 22:59	☾	23♉42
24 3:59	●	0♍39
30 19:16	☽	7♐04

Astro Data

1 July 1949
Julian Day # 18079
SVP 5♓58'00"
GC 26♐08.0 ⚴ 11♌10.5
Eris 7♈30.2 ⚵ 17♋37.2
⚷ 3♐43.9R ⚶ 16♐06.7R
☽ Mean ☊ 21♈49.7

1 August 1949
Julian Day # 18110
SVP 5♓57'54"
GC 26♐08.1 ⚴ 27♌09.2
Eris 7♈25.9R ⚵ 3♌55.1
⚷ 2♐52.0R ⚶ 14♐19.8
☽ Mean ☊ 20♈11.2

LONGITUDE — September 1949

Day	Sid.Time	☉	0 hr ☽	Noon ☽	True ☊	☿	♀	♂	⚳	♃	♄	♅	♆	♇
1 Th	10 41 16	8♍42 14	23♐17 44	29♐57 24	17♈23.7	4♎49.9	14♎19.2	26♋23.3	1♎35.8	22♑48.9	9♍27.4	4♋20.5	13♎36.2	16♌53.0
2 F	10 45 13	9 40 19	6♑33 03	13♑04 52	17R 20.1	6 00.9	15 30.7	27 01.5	2 02.5	22R 45.7	9 35.0	4 22.4	13 38.1	16 54.7
3 Sa	10 49 10	10 38 25	19 33 00	25 57 38	17 15.1	7 09.9	16 42.2	27 39.5	2 29.2	22 42.7	9 42.5	4 24.3	13 40.0	16 56.5
4 Su	10 53 06	11 36 33	2♒18 55	8♒37 01	17 09.1	8 16.8	17 53.6	28 17.6	2 55.9	22 39.9	9 50.1	4 26.2	13 42.0	16 58.2
5 M	10 57 03	12 34 43	14 52 04	21 04 13	17 03.0	9 21.6	19 04.9	28 55.5	3 22.7	22 37.2	9 57.7	4 28.0	13 43.9	16 59.8
6 Tu	11 00 59	13 32 54	27 13 36	3♓20 23	16 57.3	10 24.0	20 16.2	29 33.4	3 49.4	22 34.8	10 05.2	4 29.8	13 45.9	17 01.5
7 W	11 04 56	14 31 07	9♓24 42	15 26 45	16 52.7	11 24.0	21 27.4	0♌11.3	4 16.2	22 32.5	10 12.8	4 31.5	13 47.9	17 03.2
8 Th	11 08 52	15 29 22	21 26 43	27 24 49	16 49.5	12 21.3	22 38.6	0 49.0	4 43.0	22 30.4	10 20.4	4 33.2	13 49.9	17 04.8
9 F	11 12 49	16 27 38	3♈21 19	9♈16 30	16D 47.9	13 15.9	23 49.7	1 26.8	5 09.8	22 28.5	10 27.9	4 34.9	13 51.9	17 06.5
10 Sa	11 16 45	17 25 56	15 10 40	21 04 11	16 47.7	14 07.6	25 00.8	2 04.4	5 36.6	22 26.8	10 35.4	4 36.5	13 54.0	17 08.1
11 Su	11 20 42	18 24 17	26 57 26	2♉50 52	16 48.6	14 56.1	26 11.9	2 42.0	6 03.4	22 25.3	10 43.0	4 38.0	13 56.0	17 09.7
12 M	11 24 39	19 22 39	8♉44 55	14 40 06	16 50.2	15 41.2	27 22.8	3 19.6	6 30.3	22 24.0	10 50.5	4 39.5	13 58.1	17 11.3
13 Tu	11 28 35	20 21 03	20 36 58	26 36 02	16 52.0	16 22.6	28 33.8	3 57.0	6 57.2	22 22.9	10 58.0	4 41.0	14 00.1	17 12.9
14 W	11 32 32	21 19 30	2♊37 53	8♊43 08	16 53.4	17 00.2	29 44.6	4 34.5	7 24.1	22 22.0	11 05.5	4 42.4	14 02.2	17 14.5
15 Th	11 36 28	22 17 59	14 52 21	21 06 07	16R 54.0	17 33.6	0♏55.5	5 11.8	7 51.0	22 21.2	11 13.0	4 43.7	14 04.3	17 16.1
16 F	11 40 25	23 16 30	27 24 59	3♋49 30	16 53.6	18 02.4	2 06.2	5 49.1	8 17.9	22 20.7	11 20.5	4 45.1	14 06.4	17 17.6
17 Sa	11 44 21	24 15 03	10♋20 06	16 57 12	16 52.1	18 26.4	3 17.0	6 26.3	8 44.8	22 20.4	11 27.9	4 46.3	14 08.6	17 19.1
18 Su	11 48 18	25 13 39	23 41 04	0♌31 53	16 49.8	18 45.2	4 27.6	7 03.5	9 11.8	22D 20.2	11 35.4	4 47.5	14 10.7	17 20.7
19 M	11 52 14	26 12 16	7♌29 40	14 34 17	16 47.1	18 58.5	5 38.2	7 40.6	9 38.7	22 20.2	11 42.8	4 48.7	14 12.8	17 22.2
20 Tu	11 56 11	27 10 56	21 45 26	29 02 37	16 44.4	19R 05.8	6 48.8	8 17.7	10 05.7	22 20.5	11 50.2	4 49.8	14 15.0	17 23.7
21 W	12 00 08	28 09 37	6♍25 09	13♍52 14	16 42.1	19 06.8	7 59.3	8 54.6	10 32.7	22 20.9	11 57.6	4 50.9	14 17.1	17 25.1
22 Th	12 04 04	29 08 21	21 22 53	28 55 59	16 40.6	19 01.2	9 09.7	9 31.5	10 59.7	22 21.5	12 05.0	4 51.9	14 19.3	17 26.6
23 F	12 08 01	0♎07 06	6♎30 24	14♎04 56	16D 40.0	18 48.6	10 20.1	10 08.4	11 26.7	22 22.4	12 12.3	4 52.8	14 21.5	17 28.0
24 Sa	12 11 57	1 05 54	21 38 25	29 09 46	16 40.2	18 28.9	11 30.4	10 45.1	11 53.7	22 23.4	12 19.7	4 53.7	14 23.7	17 29.4
25 Su	12 15 54	2 04 43	6♏37 57	14♏02 07	16 41.0	18 01.8	12 40.7	11 21.8	12 20.7	22 24.6	12 26.9	4 54.6	14 25.9	17 30.8
26 M	12 19 50	3 03 35	21 21 33	28 35 40	16 42.1	17 27.3	13 50.8	11 58.4	12 47.7	22 26.0	12 34.2	4 55.4	14 28.0	17 32.2
27 Tu	12 23 47	4 02 28	5♐44 04	12♐46 32	16 43.1	16 45.6	15 01.0	12 35.0	13 14.8	22 27.6	12 41.5	4 56.1	14 30.3	17 33.6
28 W	12 27 43	5 01 23	19 42 55	26 33 16	16R 43.7	15 57.0	16 11.0	13 11.5	13 41.8	22 29.4	12 48.7	4 56.8	14 32.5	17 34.9
29 Th	12 31 40	6 00 19	3♑17 42	9♑56 26	16 43.8	15 02.1	17 21.0	13 47.9	14 08.8	22 31.4	12 55.9	4 57.5	14 34.7	17 36.2
30 F	12 35 37	6 59 17	16 29 43	22 57 53	16 43.4	14 01.8	18 30.8	14 24.2	14 35.9	22 33.6	13 03.0	4 58.1	14 36.9	17 37.6

LONGITUDE — October 1949

Day	Sid.Time	☉	0 hr ☽	Noon ☽	True ☊	☿	♀	♂	⚳	♃	♄	♅	♆	♇
1 Sa	12 39 33	7♎58 17	29♑21 19	5♒40 22	16♈42.6	12♎57.0	19♏40.6	15♌00.5	15♎02.9	22♑36.0	13♍10.2	4♋58.6	14♎39.1	17♌38.8
2 Su	12 43 30	8 57 19	11♒55 25	18 06 53	16R 41.6	11R 49.2	20 50.4	15 36.6	15 29.9	22 38.5	13 17.3	4 59.1	14 41.3	17 40.1
3 M	12 47 26	9 56 22	24 15 07	0♓20 29	16 40.6	10 40.1	22 00.0	16 12.8	15 57.0	22 41.3	13 24.3	4 59.5	14 43.6	17 41.3
4 Tu	12 51 23	10 55 28	6♓23 21	12 24 02	16 39.8	9 31.3	23 09.5	16 48.8	16 24.0	22 44.2	13 31.4	4 59.9	14 45.8	17 42.6
5 W	12 55 19	11 54 35	18 22 53	24 20 10	16 39.2	8 24.7	24 19.0	17 24.8	16 51.0	22 47.3	13 38.4	5 00.2	14 48.0	17 43.8
6 Th	12 59 16	12 53 44	0♈16 11	6♈11 14	16D 38.9	7 22.3	25 28.4	18 00.6	17 18.1	22 50.6	13 45.3	5 00.5	14 50.3	17 45.0
7 F	13 03 12	13 52 55	12 05 34	17 59 28	16 38.8	6 25.8	26 37.6	18 36.5	17 45.1	22 54.1	13 52.2	5 00.7	14 52.5	17 46.1
8 Sa	13 07 09	14 52 08	23 53 12	29 47 04	16 38.9	5 36.8	27 46.8	19 12.2	18 12.1	22 57.8	13 59.1	5 00.9	14 54.7	17 47.2
9 Su	13 11 05	15 51 24	5♉41 20	11♉36 19	16R 39.0	4 56.5	28 55.9	19 47.9	18 39.1	23 01.6	14 06.0	5 01.0	14 57.0	17 48.4
10 M	13 15 02	16 50 41	17 32 21	23 29 45	16 39.0	4 26.1	0♐04.9	20 23.5	19 06.2	23 05.7	14 12.8	5R 01.1	14 59.2	17 49.4
11 Tu	13 18 59	17 50 01	29 28 53	5♊30 08	16 38.9	4 06.2	1 13.8	20 59.0	19 33.2	23 09.9	14 19.5	5 01.1	15 01.4	17 50.5
12 W	13 22 55	18 49 23	11♊33 56	17 40 40	16 38.7	3D 57.2	2 22.6	21 34.4	20 00.2	23 14.3	14 26.2	5 01.1	15 03.7	17 51.6
13 Th	13 26 52	19 48 48	23 50 49	0♋04 48	16 38.4	3 59.1	3 31.2	22 09.8	20 27.2	23 18.8	14 32.9	5 01.0	15 05.9	17 52.6
14 F	13 30 48	20 48 14	6♋23 05	12 46 08	16D 38.2	4 11.8	4 39.8	22 45.0	20 54.2	23 23.6	14 39.5	5 00.8	15 08.1	17 53.6
15 Sa	13 34 45	21 47 43	19 14 22	25 48 10	16 38.2	4 34.8	5 48.3	23 20.2	21 21.2	23 28.5	14 46.1	5 00.6	15 10.4	17 54.6
16 Su	13 38 41	22 47 15	2♌27 55	9♌13 53	16 38.4	5 07.7	6 56.7	23 55.4	21 48.2	23 33.6	14 52.7	5 00.4	15 12.6	17 55.5
17 M	13 42 38	23 46 48	16 06 16	23 05 08	16 38.9	5 49.6	8 04.9	24 30.4	22 15.2	23 38.8	14 59.1	5 00.1	15 14.8	17 56.4
18 Tu	13 46 34	24 46 24	0♍10 29	7♍22 06	16 39.6	6 39.8	9 13.0	25 05.3	22 42.2	23 44.3	15 05.6	4 59.7	15 17.0	17 57.3
19 W	13 50 31	25 46 02	14 39 38	22 02 33	16 40.3	7 37.5	10 21.0	25 40.2	23 09.1	23 49.9	15 12.0	4 59.3	15 19.2	17 58.2
20 Th	13 54 28	26 45 42	29 30 10	7♎01 38	16R 40.8	8 41.9	11 28.9	26 14.9	23 36.1	23 55.6	15 18.3	4 58.8	15 21.4	17 59.1
21 F	13 58 24	27 45 25	14♎35 55	22 11 55	16 40.9	9 52.1	12 36.7	26 49.6	24 03.0	24 01.6	15 24.6	4 58.3	15 23.6	17 59.9
22 Sa	14 02 21	28 45 09	29 48 25	7♏24 11	16 40.4	11 07.5	13 44.3	27 24.2	24 30.0	24 07.7	15 30.8	4 57.7	15 25.8	18 00.7
23 Su	14 06 17	29 44 56	14♏58 00	22 28 43	16 39.2	12 27.2	14 51.8	27 58.7	24 56.9	24 13.9	15 37.0	4 57.1	15 28.0	18 01.5
24 M	14 10 14	0♏44 44	29 55 16	7♐16 45	16 37.5	13 50.7	15 59.2	28 33.1	25 23.8	24 20.4	15 43.1	4 56.4	15 30.2	18 02.2
25 Tu	14 14 10	1 44 34	14♐32 25	21 41 43	16 35.6	15 17.4	17 06.4	29 07.4	25 50.7	24 27.0	15 49.1	4 55.7	15 32.4	18 02.9
26 W	14 18 07	2 44 26	28 44 16	5♑39 52	16 33.8	16 46.7	18 13.5	29 41.6	26 17.6	24 33.7	15 55.1	4 54.9	15 34.5	18 03.6
27 Th	14 22 03	3 44 20	12♑28 30	19 10 17	16 32.5	18 18.2	19 20.4	0♍15.7	26 44.4	24 40.6	16 01.0	4 54.1	15 36.7	18 04.3
28 F	14 26 00	4 44 15	25 45 27	2♒14 21	16D 31.9	19 51.4	20 27.1	0 49.7	27 11.2	24 47.7	16 06.9	4 53.2	15 38.8	18 04.9
29 Sa	14 29 57	5 44 12	8♒37 25	14 55 09	16 32.2	21 26.1	21 33.7	1 23.5	27 38.1	24 54.9	16 12.7	4 52.3	15 41.0	18 05.6
30 Su	14 33 53	6 44 10	21 08 03	27 16 42	16 33.2	23 01.9	22 40.1	1 57.3	28 04.9	25 02.3	16 18.4	4 51.3	15 43.1	18 06.1
31 M	14 37 50	7 44 10	3♓21 38	9♓23 26	16 34.7	24 38.5	23 46.3	2 31.0	28 31.6	25 09.8	16 24.1	4 50.3	15 45.2	18 06.7

Astro Data

	Dy Hr Mn
☽0N	8 23:05
♃ D	18 18:47
☿ R	21 3:49
☽0S	22 18:17
☉0S	23 9:06
⚳0S	3 15:05
☽0N	6 5:21
♅ R	11 5:14
☿ D	12 19:47
☽0S	20 5:27
♄⊻♆	21 6:30

Planet Ingress

	Dy Hr Mn
♂ ♌	7 4:51
♀ ♏	14 17:12
☉ ♎	23 9:06
♀ ♐	10 10:18
☉ ♏	23 18:03
♂ ♍	27 0:58

Last Aspect / ☽ Ingress (September)

Last Aspect Dy Hr Mn		☽ Ingress	Dy Hr Mn
31 12:31	♇ △	♑	1 12:05
3 15:22	♂ ☍	♒	3 19:37
5 7:44	♀ △	♓	6 5:26
8 2:10	♃ ⚹	♈	8 17:13
10 20:56	♀ ☍	♉	11 6:12
13 3:34	♃ △	♊	13 18:47
15 14:29	☉ □	♋	16 4:52
18 2:00	☉ ⚹	♌	18 11:05
19 19:27	☿ ⚹	♍	20 13:34
22 12:21	☉ ☌	♎	22 13:42
24 1:11	♃ □	♏	24 13:20
26 1:45	♃ ⚹	♐	26 14:21
27 20:16	♇ △	♑	28 18:07

Last Aspect / ☽ Ingress (October)

Last Aspect Dy Hr Mn		☽ Ingress	Dy Hr Mn
30 11:15	♃ ☌	♒	1 1:13
2 17:52	♀ □	♓	3 11:19
5 11:57	♀ △	♈	5 23:27
7 22:03	♃ □	♉	8 12:26
10 11:11	♃ △	♊	11 1:02
12 19:58	♂ ⚹	♋	13 11:51
15 7:44	♃ ☍	♌	15 19:35
17 14:31	♂ ☌	♍	17 23:42
19 14:54	♃ △	♎	20 0:48
21 21:23	☉ ☌	♏	22 0:18
23 21:13	♂ □	♐	24 0:08
26 1:12	♂ △	♑	26 2:10
27 22:07	♃ ☌	♒	28 7:50
30 2:27	☿ △	♓	30 17:21

☽ Phases & Eclipses

Dy Hr Mn	
7 9:59	○ 14♓26
15 14:29	☾ 22♊24
22 12:21	● 29♍09
29 4:18	☽ 5♑41
7 2:53	○ 13♈30
7 2:56	T 1.224
15 4:06	☾ 21♋28
21 21:23	● 28♎09
21 21:12:31	P 0.964
28 17:04	☽ 4♒57

Astro Data

1 September 1949
Julian Day # 18141
SVP 5♓57'50"
GC 26♐08.2 ⚳ 12♍37.5
Eris 7♈12.4R ⚵ 19♌18.7
⚷ 3♐30.9 ⚶ 19♐35.5
☽ Mean ☊ 18♈32.7

1 October 1949
Julian Day # 18171
SVP 5♓57'46"
GC 26♐08.2 ⚳ 27♍04.2
Eris 6♈54.1R ⚵ 3♍06.3
⚷ 5♐30.3 ⚶ 29♐15.4
☽ Mean ☊ 16♈57.4

November 1949 LONGITUDE

Day	Sid.Time	☉	0 hr ☽	Noon ☽	True ☊	☿	♀	♂	⚳	♃	♄	♅	♆	♇
1 Tu	14 41 46	8♏44 11	15♓22 37	21♓19 44	16♈36.4	26♎15.8	24♐52.3	3♍04.6	28♎58.4	25♑17.4	16♍29.7	4♋49.2	15♎47.3	18♌07.2
2 W	14 45 43	9 44 15	27 15 17	3♈09 43	16 37.8	27 53.5	25 58.1	3 38.1	29 25.1	25 25.2	16 35.3	4R48.1	15 49.4	18 07.7
3 Th	14 49 39	10 44 20	9♈03 29	14 57 00	16R38.5	29 31.5	27 03.7	4 11.5	29 51.8	25 33.2	16 40.7	4 46.9	15 51.5	18 08.2
4 F	14 53 36	11 44 26	20 50 37	26 44 41	16 38.1	1♏09.7	28 09.1	4 44.7	0♏18.5	25 41.3	16 46.1	4 45.7	15 53.5	18 08.7
5 Sa	14 57 32	12 44 35	2♉39 30	8♉35 20	16 36.3	2 48.0	29 14.3	5 17.9	0 45.1	25 49.5	16 51.4	4 44.4	15 55.6	18 09.1
6 Su	15 01 29	13 44 45	14 32 27	20 31 05	16 33.2	4 26.3	0♑19.2	5 50.9	1 11.8	25 57.9	16 56.7	4 43.1	15 57.6	18 09.5
7 M	15 05 26	14 44 57	26 31 26	2♊33 42	16 28.8	6 04.5	1 24.0	6 23.9	1 38.4	26 06.4	17 01.9	4 41.8	15 59.6	18 09.8
8 Tu	15 09 22	15 45 11	8♊38 06	14 44 48	16 23.7	7 42.6	2 28.4	6 56.7	2 05.0	26 15.0	17 07.0	4 40.4	16 01.6	18 10.2
9 W	15 13 19	16 45 27	20 54 02	27 05 58	16 18.4	9 20.5	3 32.7	7 29.4	2 31.5	26 23.8	17 12.0	4 38.9	16 03.6	18 10.5
10 Th	15 17 15	17 45 45	3♋20 51	9♋38 54	16 13.4	10 58.2	4 36.7	8 02.0	2 58.1	26 32.7	17 17.0	4 37.4	16 05.6	18 10.8
11 F	15 21 12	18 46 05	16 00 21	22 25 30	16 09.4	12 35.7	5 40.4	8 34.5	3 24.6	26 41.8	17 21.9	4 35.9	16 07.6	18 11.0
12 Sa	15 25 08	19 46 26	28 54 34	5♌27 52	16 06.9	14 12.9	6 43.9	9 06.9	3 51.0	26 50.9	17 26.7	4 34.3	16 09.5	18 11.2
13 Su	15 29 05	20 46 50	12♌05 38	18 48 09	16D05.9	15 49.9	7 47.0	9 39.1	4 17.5	27 00.2	17 31.4	4 32.7	16 11.5	18 11.4
14 M	15 33 01	21 47 16	25 35 38	2♍28 15	16 06.3	17 26.6	8 49.9	10 11.2	4 43.9	27 09.6	17 36.1	4 31.0	16 13.4	18 11.6
15 Tu	15 36 58	22 47 43	9♍26 07	16 29 17	16 07.6	19 03.0	9 52.5	10 43.2	5 10.3	27 19.2	17 40.6	4 29.3	16 15.3	18 11.7
16 W	15 40 55	23 48 12	23 37 40	0♎51 04	16 09.0	20 39.2	10 54.8	11 15.0	5 36.6	27 28.9	17 45.1	4 27.6	16 17.1	18 11.8
17 Th	15 44 51	24 48 43	8♎09 10	15 31 28	16R09.7	22 15.2	11 56.7	11 46.7	6 02.9	27 38.6	17 49.5	4 25.8	16 19.0	18 11.9
18 F	15 48 48	25 49 16	22 57 19	0♏25 57	16 09.0	23 50.9	12 58.4	12 18.3	6 29.2	27 48.6	17 53.8	4 24.0	16 20.8	18 12.0
19 Sa	15 52 44	26 49 51	7♏56 24	15 27 38	16 06.2	25 26.3	13 59.7	12 49.7	6 55.4	27 58.6	17 58.0	4 22.1	16 22.6	18R12.0
20 Su	15 56 41	27 50 27	22 58 31	0♐27 53	16 01.4	27 01.6	15 00.6	13 21.0	7 21.6	28 08.7	18 02.2	4 20.2	16 24.4	18 12.0
21 M	16 00 37	28 51 05	7♐54 36	15 17 33	15 55.0	28 36.6	16 01.2	13 52.2	7 47.8	28 19.0	18 06.2	4 18.3	16 26.2	18 11.9
22 Tu	16 04 34	29 51 44	22 35 47	29 48 27	15 47.8	0♐11.4	17 01.4	14 23.2	8 13.9	28 29.4	18 10.2	4 16.3	16 28.0	18 11.9
23 W	16 08 31	0♐52 25	6♑54 53	13♑54 36	15 40.6	1 46.1	18 01.2	14 54.0	8 40.0	28 39.9	18 14.0	4 14.3	16 29.7	18 11.8
24 Th	16 12 27	1 53 06	20 47 20	27 32 58	15 34.5	3 20.5	19 00.5	15 24.7	9 06.1	28 50.4	18 17.8	4 12.3	16 31.4	18 11.7
25 F	16 16 24	2 53 49	4♒11 34	10♒43 21	15 30.0	4 54.8	19 59.4	15 55.2	9 32.1	29 01.1	18 21.5	4 10.2	16 33.1	18 11.5
26 Sa	16 20 20	3 54 33	17 08 41	23 28 01	15D27.4	6 29.0	20 57.9	16 25.6	9 58.0	29 12.0	18 25.1	4 08.1	16 34.7	18 11.3
27 Su	16 24 17	4 55 18	29 41 52	5♓50 52	15 26.8	8 03.1	21 55.9	16 55.8	10 23.9	29 22.9	18 28.6	4 06.0	16 36.4	18 11.1
28 M	16 28 13	5 56 03	11♓55 37	17 56 48	15 27.5	9 37.0	22 53.4	17 25.8	10 49.8	29 33.9	18 32.0	4 03.8	16 38.0	18 10.9
29 Tu	16 32 10	6 56 50	23 55 05	29 51 08	15 28.7	11 10.9	23 50.4	17 55.7	11 15.6	29 45.0	18 35.3	4 01.6	16 39.6	18 10.6
30 W	16 36 06	7 57 38	5♈45 37	11♈39 08	15R29.7	12 44.6	24 46.8	18 25.4	11 41.3	29 56.2	18 38.5	3 59.4	16 41.1	18 10.3

December 1949 LONGITUDE

Day	Sid.Time	☉	0 hr ☽	Noon ☽	True ☊	☿	♀	♂	⚳	♃	♄	♅	♆	♇
1 Th	16 40 03	8♐58 26	17♈32 18	23♈25 39	15♈29.4	14♐18.3	25♑42.7	18♍54.9	12♏07.0	0♒07.5	18♍41.6	3♋57.1	16♎42.7	18♌10.0
2 F	16 44 00	9 59 16	29 19 44	5♉14 58	15R27.1	15 52.0	26 38.0	19 24.3	12 32.7	0 18.9	18 44.6	3R54.9	16 44.2	18R09.7
3 Sa	16 47 56	11 00 07	11♉11 48	17 10 35	15 22.3	17 25.6	27 32.7	19 53.5	12 58.3	0 30.4	18 47.5	3 52.6	16 45.7	18 09.3
4 Su	16 51 53	12 00 58	23 11 37	29 15 08	15 15.0	18 59.2	28 26.8	20 22.5	13 23.8	0 41.9	18 50.3	3 50.2	16 47.2	18 08.9
5 M	16 55 49	13 01 51	5♊21 21	11♊30 22	15 05.6	20 32.8	29 20.2	20 51.3	13 49.3	0 53.6	18 53.1	3 47.9	16 48.6	18 08.5
6 Tu	16 59 46	14 02 45	17 42 19	23 57 14	14 54.6	22 06.3	0♒12.9	21 20.0	14 14.8	1 05.4	18 55.7	3 45.5	16 50.0	18 08.0
7 W	17 03 42	15 03 40	0♋15 09	6♋36 02	14 43.0	23 39.8	1 04.9	21 48.4	14 40.2	1 17.2	18 58.2	3 43.1	16 51.4	18 07.5
8 Th	17 07 39	16 04 36	12 59 53	19 26 39	14 32.1	25 13.3	1 56.2	22 16.7	15 05.5	1 29.2	19 00.6	3 40.7	16 52.8	18 07.0
9 F	17 11 35	17 05 33	25 56 20	2♌28 55	14 22.7	26 46.8	2 46.8	22 44.7	15 30.8	1 41.2	19 02.9	3 38.3	16 54.1	18 06.5
10 Sa	17 15 32	18 06 31	9♌04 24	15 42 48	14 15.8	28 20.3	3 36.5	23 12.6	15 56.0	1 53.3	19 05.1	3 35.8	16 55.4	18 05.9
11 Su	17 19 29	19 07 30	22 24 11	29 08 37	14 11.5	29 53.7	4 25.5	23 40.2	16 21.1	2 05.4	19 07.2	3 33.4	16 56.7	18 05.3
12 M	17 23 25	20 08 30	5♍56 12	12♍47 01	14D09.7	1♑27.1	5 13.5	24 07.7	16 46.2	2 17.7	19 09.2	3 30.9	16 57.9	18 04.7
13 Tu	17 27 22	21 09 31	19 41 10	26 38 44	14 09.5	3 00.3	6 00.7	24 34.9	17 11.3	2 30.0	19 11.1	3 28.4	16 59.1	18 04.1
14 W	17 31 18	22 10 34	3♎39 46	10♎44 14	14R09.9	4 33.5	6 47.0	25 01.9	17 36.2	2 42.4	19 12.9	3 25.9	17 00.3	18 03.4
15 Th	17 35 15	23 11 37	17 52 03	25 03 01	14 09.5	6 06.5	7 32.3	25 28.7	18 01.1	2 54.9	19 14.5	3 23.4	17 01.4	18 02.7
16 F	17 39 11	24 12 42	2♏16 51	9♏33 08	14 07.2	7 39.3	8 16.6	25 55.2	18 26.0	3 07.5	19 16.1	3 20.8	17 02.6	18 02.0
17 Sa	17 43 08	25 13 47	16 51 17	24 10 40	14 02.1	9 11.9	8 59.8	26 21.5	18 50.7	3 20.1	19 17.5	3 18.3	17 03.7	18 01.2
18 Su	17 47 04	26 14 53	1♐30 29	8♐49 52	13 54.1	10 44.1	9 42.0	26 47.6	19 15.4	3 32.8	19 18.9	3 15.7	17 04.7	18 00.5
19 M	17 51 01	27 16 00	16 07 52	23 23 34	13 43.6	12 15.9	10 23.1	27 13.4	19 40.1	3 45.6	19 20.1	3 13.2	17 05.8	17 59.7
20 Tu	17 54 58	28 17 08	0♑36 03	7♑44 26	13 31.7	13 47.1	11 03.0	27 38.9	20 04.6	3 58.4	19 21.3	3 10.6	17 06.8	17 58.9
21 W	17 58 54	29 18 16	14 47 58	21 46 02	13 19.5	15 17.7	11 41.6	28 04.2	20 29.1	4 11.3	19 22.3	3 08.0	17 07.7	17 58.0
22 Th	18 02 51	0♑19 24	28 38 09	5♒24 01	13 08.4	16 47.4	12 19.0	28 29.2	20 53.5	4 24.3	19 23.2	3 05.5	17 08.7	17 57.2
23 F	18 06 47	1 20 33	12♒03 29	18 36 33	12 59.5	18 16.1	12 55.0	28 54.0	21 17.8	4 37.3	19 24.0	3 02.9	17 09.6	17 56.3
24 Sa	18 10 44	2 21 42	25 03 24	1♓24 18	12 53.2	19 43.6	13 29.6	29 18.5	21 42.1	4 50.4	19 24.7	3 00.3	17 10.5	17 55.4
25 Su	18 14 40	3 22 50	7♓39 42	13 50 04	12 49.6	21 09.6	14 02.8	29 42.7	22 06.2	5 03.6	19 25.2	2 57.7	17 11.3	17 54.5
26 M	18 18 37	4 23 59	19 55 59	25 58 09	12D48.2	22 33.8	14 34.5	0♎06.6	22 30.3	5 16.8	19 25.7	2 55.1	17 12.1	17 53.5
27 Tu	18 22 34	5 25 08	1♈57 05	7♈53 37	12R48.0	23 55.8	15 04.6	0 30.2	22 54.3	5 30.0	19 26.0	2 52.5	17 12.9	17 52.5
28 W	18 26 30	6 26 17	13 48 26	19 42 14	12 47.9	25 15.4	15 33.0	0 53.5	23 18.2	5 43.3	19 26.3	2 50.0	17 13.6	17 51.5
29 Th	18 30 27	7 27 26	25 35 43	1♉29 33	12 46.7	26 32.0	15 59.8	1 16.5	23 42.0	5 56.7	19R26.4	2 47.4	17 14.3	17 50.5
30 F	18 34 23	8 28 34	7♉24 22	13 20 48	12 43.5	27 45.1	16 24.8	1 39.2	24 05.7	6 10.1	19 26.4	2 44.8	17 15.0	17 49.5
31 Sa	18 38 20	9 29 43	19 19 23	25 20 37	12 37.6	28 54.1	16 47.9	2 01.6	24 29.4	6 23.6	19 26.3	2 42.2	17 15.6	17 48.4

Astro Data Dy Hr Mn	Planet Ingress Dy Hr Mn
☽0N 2 11:27	☿ ♏ 3 18:58
☽0S 16 15:11	⚳ ♏ 3 19:22
♇R 19 18:22	♀ ♑ 6 4:53
♄⚺♇ 22 22:18	☿ ♐ 22 9:06
☽0N 29 17:40	☉ ♐ 22 15:16
	♃ ♒ 30 20:08
☽0S 13 21:50	
♃⚻♅ 17 9:07	♀ ♒ 6 6:06
♃⚼♄ 22 9:46	☿ ♑ 11 13:37
☽0N 27 0:25	☉ ♑ 22 4:23
♅∠♇ 27 11:56	♂ ♎ 26 5:23
♄R 30 4:04	

Last Aspect Dy Hr Mn	☽ Ingress Dy Hr Mn	Last Aspect Dy Hr Mn	☽ Ingress Dy Hr Mn
1 20:06 ♃ ⚹	♈ 2 5:34	1 17:03 ♀ □	♉ 2 1:22
4 15:09 ♀ △	♉ 4 18:37	4 10:17 ♀ △	♊ 4 13:28
6 23:01 ♃ △	♊ 7 6:55	6 7:57 ☿ ☍	♋ 6 23:31
8 18:41 ♇ ⚹	♋ 9 17:35	8 17:27 ♂ ⚹	♌ 9 7:28
11 20:01 ♃ ☍	♌ 12 2:00	11 13:30 ☿ △	♍ 11 13:31
13 15:48 ☉ □	♍ 14 7:42	13 8:20 ♂ ☌	♎ 13 17:45
16 6:21 ♃ △	♎ 16 10:36	15 8:40 ☉ ⚹	♏ 15 20:13
18 7:45 ♃ □	♏ 18 11:18	17 15:41 ♂ ⚹	♐ 17 21:32
20 8:14 ♃ ⚹	♐ 20 11:15	19 18:56 ☉ ☌	♑ 19 23:00
21 16:46 ♇ △	♑ 22 12:19	21 23:21 ♂ △	♒ 22 2:24
24 14:21 ♃ ☌	♒ 24 16:24	23 10:46 ♇ ☍	♓ 24 9:20
26 1:58 ♇ ☍	♓ 27 0:35	26 4:20 ☿ ⚹	♈ 26 20:05
29 11:47 ♃ ⚹	♈ 29 12:18	29 0:42 ☿ □	♉ 29 8:58
		31 19:45 ☿ △	♊ 31 21:13

☽ Phases & Eclipses Dy Hr Mn	
5 21:09	○ 13♉08
13 15:48	☾ 20♌56
20 7:29	● 27♏39
27 10:01	☽ 4♓50
5 15:13	○ 13♊10
13 1:48	☾ 20♍44
19 18:56	● 27♐34
27 6:31	☽ 5♈11

Astro Data

1 November 1949
Julian Day # 18202
SVP 5♓57'43"
GC 26♐08.3 ⚴ 11♎19.9
Eris 6♈35.5R ⚵ 15♍48.0
⚷ 8♐36.2 ⚶ 12♑00.0
☽ Mean ☊ 15♈18.9

1 December 1949
Julian Day # 18232
SVP 5♓57'38"
GC 26♐08.4 ⚴ 24♎13.6
Eris 6♈23.1R ⚵ 25♍52.0
⚷ 12♐08.8 ⚶ 25♑51.1
☽ Mean ☊ 13♈43.6

LONGITUDE — January 1950

Day	Sid.Time	☉	0 hr ☽	Noon ☽	True ☊	☿	♀	♂	⚳	♃	♄	♅	♆	♇
1 Su	18 42 16	10♑30 52	1♊24 56	7♊32 40	12♈28.8	29♑58.3	17♒09.1	2♎23.7	24♏52.9	6♒37.1	19♍26.1	2♋39.7	17♎16.3	17♌47.4
2 M	18 46 13	11 32 00	13 44 08	19 59 30	12R 17.4	0♒57.1	17 28.4	2 45.4	25 16.4	6 50.6	19R 25.8	2R 37.1	17 16.8	17R 46.3
3 Tu	18 50 09	12 33 09	26 18 54	2♋42 20	12 04.1	1 49.5	17 45.7	3 06.8	25 39.7	7 04.2	19 25.4	2 34.6	17 17.4	17 45.2
4 W	18 54 06	13 34 17	9♋09 47	15 41 06	11 50.1	2 34.9	18 00.8	3 27.9	26 03.0	7 17.9	19 24.9	2 32.1	17 17.9	17 44.1
5 Th	18 58 03	14 35 26	22 16 05	28 54 32	11 36.7	3 12.2	18 13.8	3 48.6	26 26.2	7 31.6	19 24.2	2 29.6	17 18.4	17 42.9
6 F	19 01 59	15 36 34	5♌36 08	12♌20 36	11 25.1	3 40.5	18 24.6	4 09.0	26 49.2	7 45.3	19 23.5	2 27.1	17 18.8	17 41.7
7 Sa	19 05 56	16 37 42	19 07 38	25 56 58	11 16.3	3 59.0	18 33.1	4 29.0	27 12.2	7 59.1	19 22.6	2 24.6	17 19.2	17 40.6
8 Su	19 09 52	17 38 50	2♍48 18	9♍41 27	11 10.5	4R 06.8	18 39.2	4 48.6	27 35.1	8 12.9	19 21.7	2 22.1	17 19.6	17 39.4
9 M	19 13 49	18 39 59	16 36 13	23 32 27	11 07.6	4 03.4	18 43.0	5 07.8	27 57.8	8 26.7	19 20.6	2 19.6	17 19.9	17 38.2
10 Tu	19 17 45	19 41 07	0♎30 04	7♎29 00	11 06.8	3 48.3	18R 44.4	5 26.6	28 20.5	8 40.6	19 19.4	2 17.2	17 20.2	17 36.9
11 W	19 21 42	20 42 15	14 29 11	21 30 36	11 06.8	3 21.4	18 43.3	5 45.1	28 43.0	8 54.5	19 18.1	2 14.8	17 20.5	17 35.7
12 Th	19 25 38	21 43 24	28 33 11	5♏36 51	11 06.2	2 42.8	18 39.8	6 03.1	29 05.5	9 08.5	19 16.7	2 12.4	17 20.7	17 34.4
13 F	19 29 35	22 44 32	12♏41 31	19 46 57	11 03.9	1 53.4	18 33.8	6 20.7	29 27.8	9 22.4	19 15.2	2 10.0	17 20.9	17 33.2
14 Sa	19 33 32	23 45 40	26 52 56	3♐59 08	10 58.8	0 54.3	18 25.2	6 37.9	29 50.0	9 36.5	19 13.6	2 07.6	17 21.1	17 31.9
15 Su	19 37 28	24 46 48	11♐05 08	18 10 27	10 50.9	29♑47.1	18 14.2	6 54.6	0♐12.1	9 50.5	19 11.9	2 05.3	17 21.2	17 30.6
16 M	19 41 25	25 47 56	25 14 33	2♑16 51	10 40.4	28 33.9	18 00.7	7 10.9	0 34.1	10 04.6	19 10.1	2 03.0	17 21.3	17 29.3
17 Tu	19 45 21	26 49 04	9♑16 45	16 13 38	10 28.3	27 16.9	17 44.7	7 26.7	0 56.0	10 18.7	19 08.2	2 00.7	17 21.4	17 28.0
18 W	19 49 18	27 50 11	23 06 57	29 56 11	10 15.8	25 58.6	17 26.3	7 42.1	1 17.7	10 32.8	19 06.2	1 58.5	17R 21.4	17 26.6
19 Th	19 53 14	28 51 17	6♒40 54	13♒20 47	10 04.3	24 41.4	17 05.5	7 56.9	1 39.4	10 46.9	19 04.0	1 56.2	17 21.4	17 25.3
20 F	19 57 11	29 52 23	19 55 35	26 25 12	9 54.8	23 27.4	16 42.5	8 11.3	2 00.8	11 01.1	19 01.8	1 54.0	17 21.4	17 24.0
21 Sa	20 01 07	0♒53 28	2♓49 40	9♓09 05	9 47.9	22 18.8	16 17.3	8 25.1	2 22.2	11 15.3	18 59.5	1 51.8	17 21.3	17 22.6
22 Su	20 05 04	1 54 31	15 23 42	21 33 50	9 43.8	21 16.9	15 50.0	8 38.5	2 43.4	11 29.5	18 57.1	1 49.7	17 21.2	17 21.2
23 M	20 09 01	2 55 34	27 39 54	3♈42 25	9D 42.1	20 22.8	15 20.9	8 51.3	3 04.5	11 43.7	18 54.6	1 47.6	17 21.0	17 19.8
24 Tu	20 12 57	3 56 36	9♈41 56	15 39 02	9 42.0	19 37.4	14 49.9	9 03.6	3 25.5	11 57.9	18 52.0	1 45.5	17 20.8	17 18.5
25 W	20 16 54	4 57 37	21 34 24	27 28 40	9R 42.6	19 01.0	14 17.4	9 15.3	3 46.3	12 12.2	18 49.3	1 43.4	17 20.6	17 17.1
26 Th	20 20 50	5 58 37	3♉22 33	9♉16 44	9 42.8	18 33.7	13 43.5	9 26.5	4 06.9	12 26.4	18 46.5	1 41.4	17 20.4	17 15.7
27 F	20 24 47	6 59 35	15 11 55	21 08 46	9 41.5	18 15.3	13 08.5	9 37.2	4 27.5	12 40.7	18 43.6	1 39.4	17 20.1	17 14.2
28 Sa	20 28 43	8 00 33	27 07 56	3♊10 01	9 38.2	18D 05.4	12 32.5	9 47.3	4 47.9	12 55.0	18 40.6	1 37.5	17 19.8	17 12.8
29 Su	20 32 40	9 01 29	9♊15 37	15 25 12	9 32.4	18 03.8	11 55.9	9 56.8	5 08.1	13 09.3	18 37.6	1 35.6	17 19.4	17 11.4
30 M	20 36 36	10 02 25	21 39 14	27 58 02	9 24.4	18 09.7	11 18.8	10 05.7	5 28.2	13 23.6	18 34.4	1 33.7	17 19.1	17 10.0
31 Tu	20 40 33	11 03 19	4♋21 52	10♋50 53	9 14.7	18 22.8	10 41.5	10 13.9	5 48.1	13 37.9	18 31.2	1 31.9	17 18.7	17 08.6

LONGITUDE — February 1950

Day	Sid.Time	☉	0 hr ☽	Noon ☽	True ☊	☿	♀	♂	⚳	♃	♄	♅	♆	♇
1 W	20 44 30	12♒04 12	17♋25 06	24♋04 28	9♈04.3	18♑42.5	10♒04.4	10♎21.6	6♐07.9	13♒52.2	18♍27.9	1♋30.1	17♎18.2	17♌07.1
2 Th	20 48 26	13 05 03	0♌48 47	7♌37 44	8R 54.2	19 08.3	9R 27.6	10 28.7	6 27.5	14 06.5	18R 24.5	1R 28.3	17R 17.7	17R 05.7
3 F	20 52 23	14 05 54	14 30 58	21 27 58	8 45.5	19 39.6	8 51.4	10 35.1	6 47.0	14 20.8	18 21.1	1 26.6	17 17.2	17 04.3
4 Sa	20 56 19	15 06 43	28 28 15	5♍31 12	8 38.9	20 15.9	8 16.1	10 40.9	7 06.3	14 35.1	18 17.5	1 24.9	17 16.7	17 02.8
5 Su	21 00 16	16 07 32	12♍36 16	19 42 51	8 34.9	20 56.9	7 41.9	10 46.0	7 25.5	14 49.4	18 13.9	1 23.3	17 16.1	17 01.4
6 M	21 04 12	17 08 19	26 50 27	3♎58 31	8D 33.3	21 42.1	7 09.0	10 50.5	7 44.5	15 03.7	18 10.2	1 21.7	17 15.5	17 00.0
7 Tu	21 08 09	18 09 05	11♎06 39	18 14 27	8 33.5	22 31.2	6 37.6	10 54.2	8 03.3	15 18.1	18 06.5	1 20.2	17 14.9	16 58.5
8 W	21 12 05	19 09 50	25 21 37	2♏27 52	8 34.6	23 23.9	6 08.0	10 57.3	8 21.9	15 32.4	18 02.6	1 18.7	17 14.2	16 57.1
9 Th	21 16 02	20 10 35	9♏33 00	16 36 52	8R 35.4	24 19.7	5 40.3	10 59.6	8 40.4	15 46.7	17 58.7	1 17.2	17 13.5	16 55.6
10 F	21 19 59	21 11 18	23 39 19	0♐40 13	8 35.1	25 18.5	5 14.5	11 01.3	8 58.7	16 01.0	17 54.8	1 15.8	17 12.8	16 54.2
11 Sa	21 23 55	22 12 01	7♐39 27	14 36 54	8 32.8	26 20.1	4 51.0	11R 02.2	9 16.8	16 15.3	17 50.8	1 14.4	17 12.0	16 52.8
12 Su	21 27 52	23 12 42	21 32 25	28 25 49	8 28.5	27 24.1	4 29.7	11 02.4	9 34.7	16 29.5	17 46.7	1 13.1	17 11.3	16 51.3
13 M	21 31 48	24 13 22	5♑16 57	12♑05 35	8 22.3	28 30.5	4 10.7	11 01.8	9 52.5	16 43.8	17 42.5	1 11.8	17 10.4	16 49.9
14 Tu	21 35 45	25 14 02	18 51 31	25 34 32	8 14.9	29 39.0	3 54.1	11 00.5	10 10.1	16 58.1	17 38.3	1 10.6	17 09.6	16 48.5
15 W	21 39 41	26 14 39	2♒14 23	8♒50 52	8 07.2	0♒49.6	3 40.0	10 58.4	10 27.4	17 12.3	17 34.1	1 09.4	17 08.7	16 47.1
16 Th	21 43 38	27 15 15	15 23 48	21 53 03	8 00.1	2 02.0	3 28.3	10 55.6	10 44.6	17 26.6	17 29.8	1 08.3	17 07.8	16 45.7
17 F	21 47 35	28 15 50	28 18 30	4♓40 06	7 54.2	3 16.1	3 19.1	10 51.9	11 01.5	17 40.8	17 25.4	1 07.2	17 06.9	16 44.3
18 Sa	21 51 31	29 16 23	10♓57 52	17 11 53	7 50.2	4 31.9	3 12.4	10 47.5	11 18.3	17 55.0	17 21.0	1 06.1	17 05.9	16 42.8
19 Su	21 55 28	0♓16 55	23 22 16	29 29 15	7D 48.1	5 49.3	3 08.1	10 42.3	11 34.9	18 09.2	17 16.6	1 05.2	17 04.9	16 41.4
20 M	21 59 24	1 17 24	5♈33 06	11♈34 09	7 47.7	7 08.1	3D 06.3	10 36.3	11 51.2	18 23.3	17 12.1	1 04.2	17 03.9	16 40.1
21 Tu	22 03 21	2 17 52	17 32 48	23 29 29	7 48.8	8 28.4	3 06.9	10 29.6	12 07.3	18 37.5	17 07.6	1 03.3	17 02.9	16 38.7
22 W	22 07 17	3 18 19	29 24 44	5♉19 03	7 50.5	9 50.0	3 09.9	10 22.1	12 23.2	18 51.6	17 03.0	1 02.5	17 01.8	16 37.3
23 Th	22 11 14	4 18 43	11♉13 01	17 07 16	7 52.3	11 12.9	3 15.2	10 13.7	12 38.9	19 05.7	16 58.4	1 01.7	17 00.7	16 35.9
24 F	22 15 10	5 19 05	23 02 23	28 59 01	7R 53.5	12 37.1	3 22.7	10 04.7	12 54.4	19 19.7	16 53.8	1 01.0	16 59.6	16 34.6
25 Sa	22 19 07	6 19 26	4♊57 50	10♊59 26	7 53.6	14 02.4	3 32.6	9 54.8	13 09.7	19 33.8	16 49.1	1 00.3	16 58.5	16 33.2
26 Su	22 23 03	7 19 45	17 04 27	23 13 29	7 52.3	15 29.0	3 44.5	9 44.2	13 24.7	19 47.8	16 44.5	0 59.7	16 57.3	16 31.9
27 M	22 27 00	8 20 01	29 27 04	5♋45 42	7 49.7	16 56.8	3 58.6	9 32.8	13 39.5	20 01.8	16 39.8	0 59.1	16 56.1	16 30.6
28 Tu	22 30 57	9 20 16	12♋09 49	18 39 44	7 46.0	18 25.7	4 14.8	9 20.6	13 54.0	20 15.7	16 35.0	0 58.6	16 54.9	16 29.3

Astro Data Dy Hr Mn	Planet Ingress Dy Hr Mn	Last Aspect Dy Hr Mn	☽ Ingress Dy Hr Mn	Last Aspect Dy Hr Mn	☽ Ingress Dy Hr Mn	☽ Phases & Eclipses Dy Hr Mn	Astro Data
☿ R 8 16:55	☿ ♒ 1 12:39	2 10:56 ♄ □	♋ 3 6:56	1 2:04 ☿ ☍	♌ 1 22:34	4 7:48 ○ 13♋24	1 January 1950
☽ 0S 10 2:22	⚳ ♐ 14 22:48	4 18:48 ♄ ⚹	♌ 5 13:58	3 4:48 ♆ ⚹	♍ 4 2:37	11 10:31 ☾ 20♎38	Julian Day # 18263
♀ R 10 13:35	☿ ♑R 15 7:35	6 22:51 ♀ ☍	♍ 7 19:06	5 14:12 ☿ △	♎ 6 5:19	18 8:00 ● 27♑40	SVP 5♓57'32"
♂ 0S 13 12:16	☉ ♒ 20 15:00	9 4:45 ♄ ☌	♎ 9 23:08	7 19:40 ☿ □	♏ 8 7:50	26 4:39 ☽ 5♉40	GC 26♐08.5 ⚵ 6♏03.5
♆ R 18 19:19		11 10:31 ☉ □	♏ 12 2:28	10 2:08 ☿ ⚹	♐ 10 10:51		Eris 6♈20.2 ⚶ 2♎42.5
♆⚹♇ 22 12:53	☿ ♒ 14 19:12	13 17:23 ☉ ⚹	♐ 14 5:16	12 2:11 ☉ ⚹	♑ 12 14:45	2 22:16 ○ 13♌31	⚷ 15♐50.1 ⚴ 10♒59.8
☽ 0N 23 7:54	☉ ♓ 19 5:18	15 13:44 ♄ □	♑ 16 8:06	13 21:54 ♄ △	♒ 14 19:57	9 18:32 ☾ 20♏27	☽ Mean ☊ 12♈05.1
☿ D 29 5:02		18 8:00 ☉ ☌	♒ 18 12:07	16 22:53 ☉ ☌	♓ 17 3:11	16 22:53 ● 27♒43	
☽ 0S 6 7:47		19 19:24 ♇ ☍	♓ 20 18:41	18 12:18 ♄ ☍	♈ 19 13:01	25 1:52 ☽ 5♊54	1 February 1950
♃⚼♅ 11 10:43		22 11:29 ☿ ⚹	♈ 23 4:37	21 1:58 ♃ ⚹	♉ 22 1:12		Julian Day # 18294
♂ R 12 5:48		24 19:37 ☿ □	♉ 25 17:08	23 16:05 ♃ □	♊ 24 14:03		SVP 5♓57'26"
♃☍♇ 13 21:20		27 7:09 ♄ △	♊ 28 5:43	26 5:12 ♃ △	♋ 27 1:03		GC 26♐08.5 ⚵ 15♏19.7
♃△♆ 15 6:16		29 18:10 ♄ □	♋ 30 15:50				Eris 6♈28.4 ⚶ 4♎06.8R
♃⚻♄ 16 16:09	♀ D20 18:04						⚷ 18♐59.4 ⚴ 26♒29.0
☽ 0N 19 15:40	♄⊻⊻22 20:01						☽ Mean ☊ 10♈26.7

March 1950 — LONGITUDE

Day	Sid.Time	☉	0 hr ☽	Noon ☽	True ☊	☿	♀	♂	⚳	♃	♄	♅	♆	♇
1 W	22 34 53	10♓20 29	25♋15 42	1♌57 48	7♈41.8	19♒55.7	4♒32.9	9♎07.7	14♐08.4	20♒29.6	16♍30.3	0♋58.1	16♎53.7	16♌28.0
2 Th	22 38 50	11 20 39	8♌46 04	15 40 19	7R37.5	21 26.8	4 53.0	8R54.1	14 22.4	20 43.5	16R25.5	0R57.7	16R52.5	16R26.7
3 F	22 42 46	12 20 48	22 40 16	29 45 30	7 33.9	22 59.1	5 14.9	8 39.8	14 36.3	20 57.4	16 20.8	0 57.3	16 51.2	16 25.4
4 Sa	22 46 43	13 20 54	6♍55 27	14♍09 27	7 31.2	24 32.4	5 38.6	8 24.7	14 49.9	21 11.2	16 16.0	0 57.0	16 49.9	16 24.1
5 Su	22 50 39	14 20 59	21 26 45	28 46 30	7D29.9	26 06.9	6 04.1	8 09.0	15 03.2	21 25.0	16 11.2	0 56.8	16 48.6	16 22.9
6 M	22 54 36	15 21 02	6♎07 50	13♎29 55	7 29.8	27 42.4	6 31.2	7 52.6	15 16.3	21 38.7	16 06.4	0 56.6	16 47.2	16 21.6
7 Tu	22 58 32	16 21 03	20 51 52	28 12 55	7 30.6	29 19.1	7 00.0	7 35.5	15 29.1	21 52.4	16 01.6	0 56.4	16 45.9	16 20.4
8 W	23 02 29	17 21 03	5♏32 20	12♏49 29	7 31.9	0♓56.9	7 30.4	7 17.8	15 41.7	22 06.1	15 56.9	0 56.3	16 44.5	16 19.2
9 Th	23 06 26	18 21 01	20 03 49	27 14 55	7 33.2	2 35.8	8 02.2	6 59.4	15 54.0	22 19.7	15 52.1	0D56.3	16 43.1	16 18.0
10 F	23 10 22	19 20 58	4♐22 26	11♐26 07	7R34.0	4 15.8	8 35.5	6 40.5	16 06.0	22 33.3	15 47.3	0 56.3	16 41.7	16 16.8
11 Sa	23 14 19	20 20 53	18 25 48	25 21 25	7 34.1	5 57.0	9 10.2	6 21.0	16 17.8	22 46.8	15 42.5	0 56.3	16 40.3	16 15.7
12 Su	23 18 15	21 20 46	2♑12 55	9♑00 20	7 33.4	7 39.4	9 46.2	6 01.0	16 29.3	23 00.3	15 37.8	0 56.5	16 38.9	16 14.5
13 M	23 22 12	22 20 38	15 43 43	22 23 09	7 32.0	9 22.9	10 23.5	5 40.5	16 40.5	23 13.7	15 33.0	0 56.6	16 37.4	16 13.4
14 Tu	23 26 08	23 20 28	28 58 44	5♒30 35	7 30.1	11 07.5	11 02.0	5 19.5	16 51.4	23 27.1	15 28.3	0 56.8	16 35.9	16 12.3
15 W	23 30 05	24 20 16	11♒58 50	18 23 36	7 28.1	12 53.4	11 41.6	4 58.0	17 02.0	23 40.5	15 23.6	0 57.1	16 34.5	16 11.2
16 Th	23 34 01	25 20 03	24 45 00	1♓03 11	7 26.3	14 40.5	12 22.4	4 36.2	17 12.3	23 53.8	15 18.9	0 57.5	16 33.0	16 10.2
17 F	23 37 58	26 19 47	7♓18 15	13 30 23	7 25.0	16 28.8	13 04.3	4 14.0	17 22.3	24 07.0	15 14.2	0 57.8	16 31.4	16 09.1
18 Sa	23 41 55	27 19 29	19 39 42	25 46 22	7D24.1	18 18.3	13 47.2	3 51.5	17 32.0	24 20.2	15 09.6	0 58.3	16 29.9	16 08.1
19 Su	23 45 51	28 19 10	1♈50 34	7♈52 31	7 23.9	20 09.0	14 31.1	3 28.8	17 41.4	24 33.3	15 05.0	0 58.8	16 28.4	16 07.1
20 M	23 49 48	29 18 48	13 52 25	19 50 32	7 24.1	22 01.0	15 15.9	3 05.8	17 50.5	24 46.4	15 00.4	0 59.3	16 26.8	16 06.1
21 Tu	23 53 44	0♈18 25	25 47 09	1♉42 34	7 24.7	23 54.2	16 01.6	2 42.6	17 59.3	24 59.4	14 55.8	0 59.9	16 25.3	16 05.1
22 W	23 57 41	1 17 59	7♉37 09	13 31 16	7 25.4	25 48.6	16 48.2	2 19.3	18 07.8	25 12.3	14 51.3	1 00.6	16 23.7	16 04.1
23 Th	0 01 37	2 17 31	19 25 21	25 19 50	7 26.0	27 44.3	17 35.7	1 55.9	18 15.9	25 25.2	14 46.9	1 01.3	16 22.1	16 03.2
24 F	0 05 34	3 17 01	1♊15 12	7♊11 57	7 26.5	29 41.1	18 23.9	1 32.4	18 23.7	25 38.1	14 42.4	1 02.0	16 20.5	16 02.3
25 Sa	0 09 30	4 16 28	13 10 37	19 11 45	7 26.8	1♈39.1	19 13.0	1 09.0	18 31.2	25 50.8	14 38.1	1 02.9	16 18.9	16 01.4
26 Su	0 13 27	5 15 53	25 15 56	1♋23 42	7R27.0	3 38.1	20 02.8	0 45.6	18 38.4	26 03.5	14 33.7	1 03.7	16 17.3	16 00.6
27 M	0 17 24	6 15 16	7♋35 37	13 52 14	7 27.0	5 38.2	20 53.3	0 22.3	18 45.2	26 16.1	14 29.4	1 04.6	16 15.7	15 59.7
28 Tu	0 21 20	7 14 37	20 14 03	26 41 32	7D26.9	7 39.2	21 44.4	29♍59.1	18 51.7	26 28.7	14 25.2	1 05.6	16 14.1	15 58.9
29 W	0 25 17	8 13 55	3♌15 06	9♌55 03	7 26.9	9 41.1	22 36.3	29 36.1	18 57.9	26 41.2	14 21.0	1 06.6	16 12.4	15 58.1
30 Th	0 29 13	9 13 11	16 41 36	23 34 53	7 27.1	11 43.7	23 28.8	29 13.4	19 03.7	26 53.6	14 16.9	1 07.7	16 10.8	15 57.4
31 F	0 33 10	10 12 25	0♍34 49	7♍41 13	7 27.3	13 46.8	24 21.9	28 50.9	19 09.1	27 05.9	14 12.8	1 08.8	16 09.2	15 56.6

April 1950 — LONGITUDE

Day	Sid.Time	☉	0 hr ☽	Noon ☽	True ☊	☿	♀	♂	⚳	♃	♄	♅	♆	♇
1 Sa	0 37 06	11♈11 36	14♍53 45	22♍11 53	7♈27.5	15♈50.3	25♒15.6	28♍28.7	19♐14.2	27♒18.2	14♍08.8	1♋10.0	16♎07.5	15♌55.9
2 Su	0 41 03	12 10 45	29 34 56	7♎02 03	7R27.6	17 54.0	26 09.9	28R06.8	19 19.0	27 30.4	14R04.9	1 11.2	16R05.9	15R55.2
3 M	0 44 59	13 09 52	14♎32 17	22 04 33	7 27.5	19 57.6	27 04.7	27 45.4	19 23.3	27 42.5	14 01.0	1 12.5	16 04.2	15 54.5
4 Tu	0 48 56	14 08 58	29 37 44	7♏10 42	7 27.0	22 00.8	28 00.1	27 24.3	19 27.4	27 54.5	13 57.2	1 13.8	16 02.6	15 53.9
5 W	0 52 53	15 08 01	14♏42 17	22 11 28	7 26.3	24 03.4	28 56.0	27 03.7	19 31.0	28 06.5	13 53.4	1 15.2	16 00.9	15 53.2
6 Th	0 56 49	16 07 03	29 37 17	6♐58 53	7 25.3	26 05.0	29 52.4	26 43.6	19 34.4	28 18.4	13 49.8	1 16.6	15 59.3	15 52.6
7 F	1 00 46	17 06 02	14♐15 36	21 26 55	7 24.4	28 05.3	0♓49.3	26 24.0	19 37.3	28 30.2	13 46.2	1 18.1	15 57.7	15 52.1
8 Sa	1 04 42	18 05 00	28 32 29	5♑32 04	7D23.7	0♉03.9	1 46.6	26 04.9	19 39.8	28 41.9	13 42.6	1 19.6	15 56.0	15 51.5
9 Su	1 08 39	19 03 57	12♑25 37	19 13 11	7 23.5	2 00.4	2 44.4	25 46.5	19 42.0	28 53.5	13 39.2	1 21.2	15 54.4	15 51.0
10 M	1 12 35	20 02 51	25 54 55	2♒31 04	7 23.8	3 54.6	3 42.6	25 28.6	19 43.8	29 05.1	13 35.8	1 22.8	15 52.7	15 50.5
11 Tu	1 16 32	21 01 44	9♒01 57	15 27 55	7 24.6	5 45.9	4 41.2	25 11.3	19 45.3	29 16.5	13 32.5	1 24.5	15 51.1	15 50.0
12 W	1 20 28	22 00 35	21 49 19	28 06 34	7 25.8	7 34.2	5 40.3	24 54.7	19 46.3	29 27.9	13 29.2	1 26.2	15 49.4	15 49.6
13 Th	1 24 25	22 59 25	4♓20 03	10♓30 10	7 27.1	9 19.1	6 39.7	24 38.8	19 47.0	29 39.1	13 26.1	1 27.9	15 47.8	15 49.2
14 F	1 28 22	23 58 12	16 37 18	22 41 48	7 28.2	11 00.2	7 39.4	24 23.5	19R47.2	29 50.3	13 23.0	1 29.7	15 46.2	15 48.8
15 Sa	1 32 18	24 56 57	28 44 01	4♈44 16	7R28.7	12 37.4	8 39.6	24 09.0	19 47.1	0♓01.4	13 20.0	1 31.6	15 44.5	15 48.4
16 Su	1 36 15	25 55 41	10♈42 52	16 40 05	7 28.5	14 10.3	9 40.0	23 55.2	19 46.6	0 12.4	13 17.1	1 33.5	15 42.9	15 48.0
17 M	1 40 11	26 54 23	22 36 13	28 31 30	7 27.2	15 38.8	10 40.8	23 42.2	19 45.7	0 23.3	13 14.3	1 35.4	15 41.3	15 47.7
18 Tu	1 44 08	27 53 03	4♉26 13	10♉20 36	7 25.0	17 02.6	11 41.9	23 29.9	19 44.4	0 34.0	13 11.6	1 37.4	15 39.7	15 47.4
19 W	1 48 04	28 51 40	16 14 55	22 09 26	7 21.9	18 21.7	12 43.3	23 18.4	19 42.7	0 44.7	13 09.0	1 39.4	15 38.1	15 47.2
20 Th	1 52 01	29 50 16	28 04 25	4♊00 12	7 18.2	19 35.8	13 45.0	23 07.7	19 40.6	0 55.3	13 06.4	1 41.5	15 36.5	15 47.0
21 F	1 55 57	0♉48 50	9♊57 04	15 55 22	7 14.3	20 44.9	14 47.0	22 57.7	19 38.2	1 05.8	13 04.0	1 43.6	15 34.9	15 46.8
22 Sa	1 59 54	1 47 22	21 55 28	27 57 46	7 10.7	21 48.8	15 49.3	22 48.6	19 35.3	1 16.2	13 01.6	1 45.7	15 33.3	15 46.6
23 Su	2 03 51	2 45 52	4♋02 42	10♋10 41	7 07.9	22 47.4	16 51.8	22 40.2	19 32.1	1 26.4	12 59.4	1 47.9	15 31.8	15 46.4
24 M	2 07 47	3 44 19	16 22 11	22 37 40	7D06.2	23 40.7	17 54.6	22 32.7	19 28.5	1 36.6	12 57.2	1 50.2	15 30.2	15 46.3
25 Tu	2 11 44	4 42 44	28 57 38	5♌22 32	7 05.7	24 28.5	18 57.6	22 26.0	19 24.5	1 46.6	12 55.1	1 52.4	15 28.7	15 46.2
26 W	2 15 40	5 41 08	11♌52 50	18 28 56	7 06.3	25 10.8	20 00.9	22 20.0	19 20.1	1 56.5	12 53.2	1 54.8	15 27.1	15 46.2
27 Th	2 19 37	6 39 29	25 11 12	1♍59 56	7 07.6	25 47.6	21 04.4	22 14.9	19 15.3	2 06.3	12 51.3	1 57.1	15 25.6	15D46.1
28 F	2 23 33	7 37 48	8♍55 19	15 57 24	7 09.1	26 18.7	22 08.1	22 10.5	19 10.2	2 16.0	12 49.5	1 59.5	15 24.1	15 46.1
29 Sa	2 27 30	8 36 04	23 06 08	0♎21 15	7R10.1	26 44.3	23 12.0	22 06.9	19 04.7	2 25.6	12 47.8	2 01.9	15 22.6	15 46.1
30 Su	2 31 26	9 34 19	7♎42 20	15 08 47	7 10.0	27 04.3	24 16.2	22 04.1	18 58.8	2 35.1	12 46.3	2 04.4	15 21.1	15 46.2

Astro Data	Dy Hr Mn
♄⊻♇	2 4:17
♂0N	4 22:13
☽0S	5 16:08
♅ D	9 19:25
☽0N	18 22:55
☉0N	21 4:35
♅∠♇	24 15:53
☿0N	26 7:21
☽0S	2 2:47
♆⚹♇	12 9:11
⚳ R	14 16:22
☽0N	15 5:08
♃⚼♆	18 22:59
♃△♅	26 6:23
♇ D	28 8:40

Planet Ingress		Dy Hr Mn
☿	♓	7 22:04
☉	♈	21 4:35
☿	♈	24 15:52
♂	♍R	28 11:05
♀	♓	6 15:13
☿	♉	8 11:13
♃	♓	15 8:58
☉	♉	20 15:59
☽0S29 13:27		

Last Aspect Dy Hr Mn			☽ Ingress	Dy Hr Mn
28 8:48	♆	□	♌	1 8:30
2 23:07	☿	☍	♍	3 12:24
4 15:28	♄	☌	♎	5 14:00
7 14:02	☿	△	♏	7 14:55
9 3:38	♃	□	♐	9 16:37
11 7:27	♃	⚹	♑	11 20:07
13 11:55	☉	⚹	♒	14 1:52
15 22:08	♃	☌	♓	16 9:59
18 15:20	☉	☌	♈	18 20:21
20 22:08	♃	⚹	♉	21 8:32
23 17:50	☿	⚹	♊	23 21:28
26 1:23	♃	△	♋	26 9:17
28 17:53	♂	⚹	♌	28 18:05
30 17:47	♃	☍	♍	30 23:01

Last Aspect Dy Hr Mn			☽ Ingress	Dy Hr Mn
1 21:58	♂	☌	♎	2 0:41
3 21:04	♃	△	♏	4 0:35
5 23:37	♀	□	♐	6 0:37
8 1:04	☿	△	♑	8 2:29
9 23:29	♂	△	♒	10 7:24
12 14:39	♃	☌	♓	12 15:38
14 15:18	♂	☍	♈	15 2:32
17 8:25	☉	☌	♉	17 15:00
19 14:18	♂	△	♊	20 3:54
22 1:53	♂	□	♋	22 16:02
24 14:09	☿	⚹	♌	25 1:57
27 0:35	☿	□	♍	27 8:30
29 5:52	☿	△	♎	29 11:25

☽ Phases & Eclipses Dy Hr Mn	
4 10:34	○ 13♍17
11 2:38	☾ 19♐58
18 15:20	● 27♓28
18 15:31:31	● A non-C
26 20:10	☽ 5♋36
2 20:49	○ 12♎32
2 20:44	● T 1.033
9 11:42	☾ 19♑03
17 8:25	● 26♈46
25 10:40	☽ 4♌39

Astro Data

1 March 1950
Julian Day # 18322
SVP 5♓57'22"
GC 26♐08.6 ⚴ 19♏59.4
Eris 6♈43.6 ⚵ 29♍56.0R
⚷ 20♐56.4 ⚶ 10♓26.6
☽ Mean ☊ 8♈57.7

1 April 1950
Julian Day # 18353
SVP 5♓57'19"
GC 26♐08.7 ⚴ 18♏46.9R
Eris 7♈04.8 ⚵ 22♍35.9R
⚷ 21♐44.3 ⚶ 25♓34.3
☽ Mean ☊ 7♈19.2

LONGITUDE

May 1950

Day	Sid.Time	☉	0 hr ☽	Noon ☽	True ☊	☿	♀	♂	⚳	♃	♄	♅	♆	♇
1 M	2 35 23	10♉32 32	22♎39 47	0♏14 20	7♈08.5	27♉18.7	25♓20.6	22♍02.1	18♐52.6	2♓44.4	12♍44.8	2♋06.9	15♎19.7	15♌46.3
2 Tu	2 39 19	11 30 43	7♏51 18	15 29 28	7R 05.3	27 27.7	26 25.1	22R 00.9	18R 46.0	2 53.6	12R 43.4	2 09.5	15R 18.2	15 46.4
3 W	2 43 16	12 28 53	23 07 28	0♐44 00	7 00.8	27R 31.2	27 29.9	22D 00.4	18 39.0	3 02.7	12 42.1	2 12.1	15 16.8	15 46.5
4 Th	2 47 13	13 27 01	8♐17 48	15 47 39	6 55.6	27 29.5	28 34.9	22 00.6	18 31.7	3 11.7	12 40.9	2 14.7	15 15.4	15 46.7
5 F	2 51 09	14 25 07	23 12 33	0♑31 37	6 50.4	27 22.8	29 40.1	22 01.6	18 24.1	3 20.6	12 39.9	2 17.3	15 14.0	15 46.8
6 Sa	2 55 06	15 23 12	7♑44 14	14 49 55	6 46.0	27 11.2	0♈45.4	22 03.3	18 16.1	3 29.3	12 38.9	2 20.0	15 12.6	15 47.1
7 Su	2 59 02	16 21 16	21 48 28	28 39 49	6 43.0	26 55.1	1 51.0	22 05.8	18 07.8	3 37.9	12 38.0	2 22.7	15 11.2	15 47.3
8 M	3 02 59	17 19 18	5♒24 04	12♒01 28	6D 41.5	26 34.8	2 56.7	22 08.9	17 59.1	3 46.3	12 37.3	2 25.5	15 09.9	15 47.6
9 Tu	3 06 55	18 17 19	18 32 25	24 57 19	6 41.6	26 10.7	4 02.6	22 12.8	17 50.1	3 54.7	12 36.6	2 28.3	15 08.6	15 47.9
10 W	3 10 52	19 15 18	1♓16 44	7♓31 11	6 42.7	25 43.3	5 08.6	22 17.4	17 40.8	4 02.9	12 36.0	2 31.1	15 07.3	15 48.2
11 Th	3 14 49	20 13 16	13 41 14	19 47 30	6 44.1	25 13.2	6 14.8	22 22.7	17 31.2	4 10.9	12 35.6	2 33.9	15 06.0	15 48.5
12 F	3 18 45	21 11 13	25 50 30	1♈50 50	6R 45.2	24 40.7	7 21.1	22 28.6	17 21.3	4 18.8	12 35.2	2 36.8	15 04.7	15 48.9
13 Sa	3 22 42	22 09 08	7♈48 59	13 45 27	6 45.0	24 06.6	8 27.6	22 35.2	17 11.1	4 26.6	12 35.0	2 39.7	15 03.5	15 49.3
14 Su	3 26 38	23 07 02	19 40 42	25 35 07	6 43.1	23 31.5	9 34.2	22 42.5	17 00.7	4 34.3	12D 34.8	2 42.7	15 02.2	15 49.7
15 M	3 30 35	24 04 55	1♉29 07	7♉23 01	6 39.0	22 56.0	10 41.0	22 50.4	16 49.9	4 41.7	12 34.8	2 45.7	15 01.0	15 50.2
16 Tu	3 34 31	25 02 46	13 17 07	19 11 42	6 32.7	22 20.6	11 47.9	22 59.0	16 39.0	4 49.1	12 34.8	2 48.7	14 59.8	15 50.7
17 W	3 38 28	26 00 36	25 07 01	1♊03 15	6 24.6	21 46.1	12 54.9	23 08.2	16 27.7	4 56.3	12 35.0	2 51.7	14 58.7	15 51.2
18 Th	3 42 24	26 58 25	7♊00 39	12 59 24	6 15.3	21 12.9	14 02.0	23 18.0	16 16.3	5 03.3	12 35.3	2 54.7	14 57.5	15 51.7
19 F	3 46 21	27 56 12	18 59 40	25 01 40	6 05.6	20 41.7	15 09.3	23 28.5	16 04.6	5 10.2	12 35.7	2 57.8	14 56.4	15 52.3
20 Sa	3 50 18	28 53 58	1♋05 37	7♋11 43	5 56.4	20 13.0	16 16.7	23 39.5	15 52.7	5 17.0	12 36.1	3 00.9	14 55.3	15 52.9
21 Su	3 54 14	29 51 42	13 20 14	19 31 25	5 48.5	19 47.1	17 24.2	23 51.2	15 40.6	5 23.6	12 36.7	3 04.1	14 54.3	15 53.5
22 M	3 58 11	0♊49 24	25 45 33	2♌02 59	5 42.7	19 24.5	18 31.8	24 03.4	15 28.3	5 30.0	12 37.4	3 07.2	14 53.2	15 54.2
23 Tu	4 02 07	1 47 05	8♌24 03	14 49 07	5 39.1	19 05.6	19 39.5	24 16.2	15 15.9	5 36.3	12 38.2	3 10.4	14 52.2	15 54.9
24 W	4 06 04	2 44 45	21 18 33	27 52 44	5D 37.7	18 50.5	20 47.3	24 29.5	15 03.3	5 42.4	12 39.1	3 13.6	14 51.2	15 55.6
25 Th	4 10 00	3 42 22	4♍32 02	11♍16 47	5 37.7	18 39.6	21 55.2	24 43.4	14 50.5	5 48.4	12 40.1	3 16.8	14 50.3	15 56.3
26 F	4 13 57	4 39 59	18 07 16	25 03 42	5R 38.5	18 32.9	23 03.2	24 57.8	14 37.7	5 54.2	12 41.2	3 20.1	14 49.3	15 57.0
27 Sa	4 17 53	5 37 34	2♎06 11	9♎14 42	5 38.7	18D 30.5	24 11.4	25 12.7	14 24.7	5 59.8	12 42.4	3 23.4	14 48.4	15 57.8
28 Su	4 21 50	6 35 07	16 29 05	23 49 01	5 37.4	18 32.7	25 19.6	25 28.2	14 11.6	6 05.3	12 43.8	3 26.7	14 47.5	15 58.6
29 M	4 25 47	7 32 39	1♏13 56	8♏43 09	5 34.0	18 39.3	26 27.9	25 44.1	13 58.5	6 10.6	12 45.2	3 30.0	14 46.7	15 59.4
30 Tu	4 29 43	8 30 10	16 15 43	23 50 34	5 28.0	18 50.5	27 36.3	26 00.5	13 45.3	6 15.8	12 46.7	3 33.3	14 45.8	16 00.3
31 W	4 33 40	9 27 39	1♐26 30	9♐02 12	5 20.0	19 06.1	28 44.8	26 17.4	13 32.0	6 20.8	12 48.3	3 36.6	14 45.0	16 01.2

LONGITUDE

June 1950

Day	Sid.Time	☉	0 hr ☽	Noon ☽	True ☊	☿	♀	♂	⚳	♃	♄	♅	♆	♇
1 Th	4 37 36	10♊25 08	16♐36 20	24♐07 37	5♈10.6	19♉26.1	29♈53.4	26♍34.8	13♐18.7	6♓25.6	12♍50.0	3♋40.0	14♎44.3	16♌02.1
2 F	4 41 33	11 22 36	1♑34 49	8♑56 54	5R 01.1	19 50.5	1♉02.1	26 52.6	13R 05.3	6 30.2	12 51.8	3 43.4	14R 43.5	16 03.0
3 Sa	4 45 29	12 20 03	16 12 57	23 22 19	4 52.5	20 19.2	2 10.8	27 10.9	12 52.0	6 34.7	12 53.7	3 46.8	14 42.8	16 03.9
4 Su	4 49 26	13 17 29	0♒24 31	7♒19 20	4 45.8	20 52.1	3 19.7	27 29.6	12 38.6	6 39.0	12 55.7	3 50.2	14 42.1	16 04.9
5 M	4 53 22	14 14 54	14 06 42	20 46 46	4 41.4	21 29.1	4 28.6	27 48.8	12 25.3	6 43.1	12 57.9	3 53.7	14 41.4	16 05.9
6 Tu	4 57 19	15 12 19	27 19 50	3♓46 17	4D 39.1	22 10.1	5 37.7	28 08.3	12 12.0	6 47.1	13 00.1	3 57.1	14 40.8	16 06.9
7 W	5 01 16	16 09 43	10♓06 39	16 21 31	4 38.6	22 55.0	6 46.8	28 28.3	11 58.7	6 50.8	13 02.4	4 00.6	14 40.2	16 07.9
8 Th	5 05 12	17 07 06	22 31 30	28 37 16	4R 38.8	23 43.8	7 56.0	28 48.7	11 45.5	6 54.4	13 04.8	4 04.0	14 39.6	16 09.0
9 F	5 09 09	18 04 29	4♈39 28	10♈38 46	4 38.8	24 36.3	9 05.3	29 09.5	11 32.4	6 57.8	13 07.2	4 07.5	14 39.1	16 10.1
10 Sa	5 13 05	19 01 51	16 35 48	22 31 12	4 37.4	25 32.5	10 14.6	29 30.7	11 19.3	7 01.0	13 09.8	4 11.0	14 38.6	16 11.2
11 Su	5 17 02	19 59 13	28 25 33	4♉19 21	4 33.9	26 32.3	11 24.0	29 52.3	11 06.4	7 04.1	13 12.5	4 14.6	14 38.1	16 12.3
12 M	5 20 58	20 56 35	10♉13 09	16 07 21	4 27.8	27 35.5	12 33.5	0♎14.3	10 53.6	7 06.9	13 15.3	4 18.1	14 37.6	16 13.5
13 Tu	5 24 55	21 53 55	22 02 21	27 58 32	4 18.9	28 42.3	13 43.1	0 36.6	10 40.9	7 09.6	13 18.2	4 21.6	14 37.2	16 14.6
14 W	5 28 51	22 51 15	3♊56 09	9♊55 28	4 07.7	29 52.4	14 52.7	0 59.3	10 28.4	7 12.1	13 21.1	4 25.2	14 36.8	16 15.8
15 Th	5 32 48	23 48 35	15 56 40	21 59 57	3 54.9	1♊05.8	16 02.5	1 22.4	10 16.0	7 14.4	13 24.2	4 28.7	14 36.4	16 17.1
16 F	5 36 45	24 45 54	28 05 24	4♋13 10	3 41.5	2 22.6	17 12.2	1 45.9	10 03.8	7 16.5	13 27.4	4 32.3	14 36.1	16 18.3
17 Sa	5 40 41	25 43 13	10♋23 18	16 35 54	3 28.7	3 42.6	18 22.1	2 09.7	9 51.8	7 18.4	13 30.6	4 35.9	14 35.8	16 19.6
18 Su	5 44 38	26 40 30	22 51 02	29 08 47	3 17.6	5 05.8	19 32.0	2 33.8	9 40.0	7 20.2	13 33.9	4 39.4	14 35.6	16 20.8
19 M	5 48 34	27 37 48	5♌29 16	11♌52 37	3 09.0	6 32.2	20 41.9	2 58.2	9 28.4	7 21.7	13 37.3	4 43.0	14 35.3	16 22.1
20 Tu	5 52 31	28 35 04	18 18 58	24 48 30	3 03.2	8 01.7	21 51.9	3 23.0	9 17.0	7 23.1	13 40.9	4 46.6	14 35.1	16 23.5
21 W	5 56 27	29 32 20	1♍21 26	7♍57 59	3 00.1	9 34.4	23 02.0	3 48.2	9 05.9	7 24.2	13 44.4	4 50.2	14 34.9	16 24.8
22 Th	6 00 24	0♋29 34	14 38 23	21 22 54	2 59.0	11 10.2	24 12.1	4 13.6	8 55.0	7 25.2	13 48.1	4 53.8	14 34.8	16 26.1
23 F	6 04 21	1 26 49	28 11 44	5♎05 05	2 58.9	12 49.0	25 22.3	4 39.3	8 44.3	7 25.9	13 51.9	4 57.4	14 34.7	16 27.5
24 Sa	6 08 17	2 24 02	12♎03 06	19 05 51	2 58.5	14 30.9	26 32.6	5 05.4	8 34.0	7 26.5	13 55.7	5 01.0	14 34.6	16 28.9
25 Su	6 12 14	3 21 15	26 13 17	3♏25 15	2 56.6	16 15.7	27 42.9	5 31.7	8 23.9	7 26.9	13 59.7	5 04.6	14D 34.6	16 30.3
26 M	6 16 10	4 18 28	10♏41 27	18 01 24	2 52.5	18 03.4	28 53.2	5 58.3	8 14.1	7R 27.1	14 03.7	5 08.2	14 34.6	16 31.7
27 Tu	6 20 07	5 15 40	25 24 29	2♐49 55	2 45.6	19 54.0	0♊03.7	6 25.2	8 04.6	7 27.1	14 07.8	5 11.8	14 34.6	16 33.2
28 W	6 24 03	6 12 51	10♐16 47	17 44 03	2 36.4	21 47.2	1 14.2	6 52.4	7 55.4	7 26.9	14 12.0	5 15.4	14 34.6	16 34.6
29 Th	6 28 00	7 10 03	25 10 35	2♑35 17	2 25.6	23 43.1	2 24.7	7 19.9	7 46.4	7 26.5	14 16.2	5 19.0	14 34.7	16 36.1
30 F	6 31 56	8 07 14	9♑57 02	17 14 49	2 14.6	25 41.5	3 35.3	7 47.6	7 37.8	7 25.9	14 20.6	5 22.6	14 34.8	16 37.6

Astro Data (Dy Hr Mn)

♂ D 3 15:51
☿ R 3 16:07
♀0N 8 19:22
☽ 0N 12 10:38
♄ D 15 9:22
☽ 0S 26 22:04
☿ D 27 12:29

☽ 0N 8 16:18
♂0S 14 8:14
☽ 0S 23 4:02
♆ D 26 8:03
♃ R 27 0:14

Planet Ingress (Dy Hr Mn)

♀ ♈ 5 19:19
☉ ♊ 21 15:27

♀ ♉ 1 14:19
♂ ♎ 11 20:27
☿ ♊ 14 14:33
☉ ♋ 21 23:36
♀ ♊ 27 10:45

Last Aspect (Dy Hr Mn) — **☽ Ingress** (Dy Hr Mn)

30 13:00 ♇ ⚹ — ♏ 1 11:37
3 6:55 ☿ ☍ — ♐ 3 10:50
5 10:28 ♀ □ — ♑ 5 11:08
7 9:00 ☿ △ — ♒ 7 14:22
9 14:14 ☿ □ — ♓ 9 21:34
11 22:18 ☿ ⚹ — ♈ 12 8:18
13 16:11 ♇ △ — ♉ 14 20:59
17 0:54 ☉ ☌ — ♊ 17 9:52
19 8:52 ♂ □ — ♋ 19 21:50
21 20:29 ♂ ⚹ — ♌ 22 8:06
23 21:49 ♀ △ — ♍ 24 15:51
26 11:50 ♂ ☌ — ♎ 26 20:26
28 14:39 ♀ ☍ — ♏ 28 22:01
30 15:29 ♂ ⚹ — ♐ 30 21:43

Last Aspect (Dy Hr Mn) — **☽ Ingress** (Dy Hr Mn)

1 16:01 ♂ □ — ♑ 1 21:27
3 18:37 ♂ △ — ♒ 3 23:18
5 13:21 ☿ □ — ♓ 6 4:57
8 12:23 ♂ ☍ — ♈ 8 14:44
10 4:18 ☉ ⚹ — ♉ 11 3:12
13 13:38 ☿ ☌ — ♊ 13 16:05
15 15:53 ☉ ☌ — ♋ 16 3:45
17 15:45 ♀ ⚹ — ♌ 18 13:37
20 19:29 ☉ ⚹ — ♍ 20 21:31
22 17:27 ♀ △ — ♎ 23 3:09
24 7:33 ♇ ⚹ — ♏ 25 6:19
27 7:09 ♀ ☍ — ♐ 27 7:26
28 19:30 ☿ ☍ — ♑ 29 7:48

☽ Phases & Eclipses (Dy Hr Mn)

2 5:19 ○ 11♏15
8 22:32 ☾ 17♒45
17 0:54 ● 25♉34
24 21:28 ☽ 3♍07
31 12:43 ○ 9♐29

7 11:35 ☾ 16♓09
15 15:53 ● 23♊58
23 5:13 ☽ 1♎11
29 19:58 ○ 7♑29

Astro Data

1 May 1950
Julian Day # 18383
SVP 5♓57'15"
GC 26♐08.7 ⚵ 11♏07.0R
Eris 7♈24.8 ⚶ 18♍42.2R
⚷ 21♐03.7R ⚴ 9♈36.8
☽ Mean ☊ 5♈43.9

1 June 1950
Julian Day # 18414
SVP 5♓57'10"
GC 26♐08.8 ⚵ 3♏11.0R
Eris 7♈40.0 ⚶ 20♍10.8
⚷ 19♐15.1R ⚴ 23♈10.1
☽ Mean ☊ 4♈05.4

July 1950

LONGITUDE

Day	Sid.Time	☉	0 hr ☽	Noon ☽	True ☊	☿	♀	♂	⚳	♃	♄	♅	♆	♇
1 Sa	6 35 53	9♋04 25	24♑27 41	1♒34 56	2♈04.4	27♊42.1	4♊46.0	8♎15.6	7♐29.6	7♓25.2	14♍25.0	5♋26.2	14♎35.0	16♌39.1
2 Su	6 39 50	10 01 36	8♒35 57	15 30 21	1R 56.1	29 44.8	5 56.7	8 43.9	7R 21.6	7R 24.2	14 29.5	5 29.8	14 35.2	16 40.7
3 M	6 43 46	10 58 47	22 17 56	28 58 41	1 50.3	1♋49.3	7 07.5	9 12.4	7 14.0	7 23.1	14 34.1	5 33.4	14 35.4	16 42.2
4 Tu	6 47 43	11 55 58	5♓32 44	12♓00 21	1 47.1	3 55.5	8 18.3	9 41.1	7 06.7	7 21.7	14 38.7	5 37.0	14 35.6	16 43.7
5 W	6 51 39	12 53 09	18 21 57	24 38 01	1D 45.8	6 02.9	9 29.2	10 10.1	6 59.7	7 20.2	14 43.4	5 40.6	14 35.9	16 45.3
6 Th	6 55 36	13 50 21	0♈49 06	6♈55 51	1R 45.7	8 11.5	10 40.1	10 39.4	6 53.1	7 18.4	14 48.2	5 44.2	14 36.2	16 46.9
7 F	6 59 32	14 47 33	12 58 54	18 58 55	1 45.7	10 20.8	11 51.1	11 08.8	6 46.8	7 16.5	14 53.1	5 47.8	14 36.6	16 48.5
8 Sa	7 03 29	15 44 46	24 56 36	0♉52 35	1 44.8	12 30.5	13 02.2	11 38.6	6 40.8	7 14.4	14 58.0	5 51.3	14 36.9	16 50.1
9 Su	7 07 25	16 41 58	6♉47 33	12 42 06	1 42.0	14 40.4	14 13.3	12 08.5	6 35.3	7 12.1	15 03.0	5 54.9	14 37.3	16 51.7
10 M	7 11 22	17 39 12	18 36 50	24 32 18	1 36.8	16 50.2	15 24.5	12 38.7	6 30.1	7 09.6	15 08.1	5 58.5	14 37.8	16 53.4
11 Tu	7 15 19	18 36 25	0♊28 59	6♊27 21	1 29.1	18 59.6	16 35.7	13 09.1	6 25.2	7 06.9	15 13.2	6 02.0	14 38.2	16 55.0
12 W	7 19 15	19 33 39	12 27 46	18 30 35	1 19.1	21 08.4	17 47.0	13 39.8	6 20.7	7 04.0	15 18.5	6 05.6	14 38.7	16 56.7
13 Th	7 23 12	20 30 54	24 36 03	0♋44 23	1 07.6	23 16.4	18 58.3	14 10.7	6 16.6	7 01.0	15 23.8	6 09.1	14 39.3	16 58.4
14 F	7 27 08	21 28 09	6♋55 44	13 10 11	0 55.4	25 23.3	20 09.7	14 41.7	6 12.8	6 57.7	15 29.1	6 12.6	14 39.9	17 00.1
15 Sa	7 31 05	22 25 24	19 27 47	25 48 31	0 43.8	27 29.1	21 21.2	15 13.1	6 09.4	6 54.3	15 34.5	6 16.1	14 40.4	17 01.7
16 Su	7 35 01	23 22 40	2♌12 22	8♌39 17	0 33.7	29 33.5	22 32.7	15 44.6	6 06.4	6 50.7	15 40.0	6 19.6	14 41.1	17 03.5
17 M	7 38 58	24 19 55	15 09 11	21 42 00	0 25.9	1♌36.6	23 44.2	16 16.3	6 03.8	6 46.9	15 45.6	6 23.1	14 41.7	17 05.2
18 Tu	7 42 54	25 17 11	28 17 40	4♍56 07	0 20.8	3 38.1	24 55.8	16 48.2	6 01.5	6 43.0	15 51.2	6 26.6	14 42.4	17 06.9
19 W	7 46 51	26 14 28	11♍37 21	18 21 20	0D 18.3	5 38.0	26 07.4	17 20.4	5 59.6	6 38.8	15 56.8	6 30.0	14 43.2	17 08.6
20 Th	7 50 48	27 11 44	25 08 05	1♎57 37	0 17.7	7 36.2	27 19.1	17 52.7	5 58.0	6 34.5	16 02.6	6 33.4	14 43.9	17 10.4
21 F	7 54 44	28 09 01	8♎50 00	15 45 14	0R 18.2	9 32.8	28 30.8	18 25.3	5 56.8	6 30.1	16 08.4	6 36.9	14 44.7	17 12.1
22 Sa	7 58 41	29 06 18	22 43 22	29 44 21	0 18.5	11 27.6	29 42.6	18 58.0	5 56.0	6 25.4	16 14.2	6 40.3	14 45.5	17 13.9
23 Su	8 02 37	0♌03 35	6♏48 10	13♏54 40	0 17.7	13 20.8	0♋54.4	19 30.9	5D 55.6	6 20.6	16 20.1	6 43.7	14 46.3	17 15.7
24 M	8 06 34	1 00 53	21 03 38	28 14 47	0 15.0	15 12.1	2 06.3	20 04.0	5 55.5	6 15.7	16 26.1	6 47.0	14 47.2	17 17.5
25 Tu	8 10 30	1 58 11	5♐27 42	12♐41 53	0 10.0	17 01.8	3 18.2	20 37.3	5 55.8	6 10.5	16 32.1	6 50.4	14 48.1	17 19.2
26 W	8 14 27	2 55 29	19 56 44	27 11 34	0 03.0	18 49.7	4 30.1	21 10.8	5 56.4	6 05.3	16 38.2	6 53.7	14 49.1	17 21.0
27 Th	8 18 24	3 52 48	4♑25 38	11♑38 09	29♓54.7	20 35.9	5 42.2	21 44.4	5 57.5	5 59.9	16 44.3	6 57.1	14 50.0	17 22.8
28 F	8 22 20	4 50 08	18 48 19	25 55 24	29 46.0	22 20.3	6 54.2	22 18.2	5 58.8	5 54.3	16 50.5	7 00.4	14 51.0	17 24.6
29 Sa	8 26 17	5 47 28	2♒58 40	9♒57 31	29 38.0	24 03.0	8 06.3	22 52.2	6 00.5	5 48.6	16 56.7	7 03.6	14 52.1	17 26.5
30 Su	8 30 13	6 44 49	16 51 26	23 40 01	29 31.5	25 44.0	9 18.5	23 26.4	6 02.6	5 42.7	17 03.0	7 06.9	14 53.1	17 28.3
31 M	8 34 10	7 42 11	0♓23 02	7♓00 22	29 27.1	27 23.3	10 30.7	24 00.7	6 05.0	5 36.7	17 09.3	7 10.1	14 54.2	17 30.1

August 1950

LONGITUDE

Day	Sid.Time	☉	0 hr ☽	Noon ☽	True ☊	☿	♀	♂	⚳	♃	♄	♅	♆	♇
1 Tu	8 38 06	8♌39 34	13♓32 00	19♓58 05	29♓24.9	29♌00.9	11♋43.0	24♎35.2	6♐07.7	5♓30.6	17♍15.7	7♋13.3	14♎55.3	17♌31.9
2 W	8 42 03	9 36 57	26 18 52	2♈34 40	29D 24.5	0♍36.9	12 55.3	25 09.8	6 10.8	5R 24.4	17 22.1	7 16.5	14 56.4	17 33.7
3 Th	8 45 59	10 34 22	8♈45 57	14 53 10	29 25.3	2 11.1	14 07.7	25 44.6	6 14.2	5 18.0	17 28.6	7 19.7	14 57.6	17 35.6
4 F	8 49 56	11 31 48	20 56 54	26 57 42	29 26.6	3 43.6	15 20.1	26 19.6	6 18.0	5 11.5	17 35.1	7 22.8	14 58.8	17 37.4
5 Sa	8 53 52	12 29 16	2♉56 13	8♉53 05	29R 27.4	5 14.4	16 32.6	26 54.7	6 22.0	5 04.9	17 41.7	7 25.9	15 00.0	17 39.3
6 Su	8 57 49	13 26 44	14 48 55	20 44 22	29 27.2	6 43.5	17 45.1	27 30.0	6 26.5	4 58.1	17 48.3	7 29.0	15 01.2	17 41.1
7 M	9 01 46	14 24 14	26 40 05	2♊36 38	29 25.3	8 10.9	18 57.7	28 05.5	6 31.2	4 51.3	17 54.9	7 32.1	15 02.5	17 42.9
8 Tu	9 05 42	15 21 46	8♊34 37	14 34 35	29 21.6	9 36.5	20 10.3	28 41.1	6 36.3	4 44.3	18 01.6	7 35.1	15 03.8	17 44.8
9 W	9 09 39	16 19 18	20 37 00	26 42 20	29 16.3	11 00.4	21 23.0	29 16.9	6 41.7	4 37.3	18 08.3	7 38.2	15 05.2	17 46.6
10 Th	9 13 35	17 16 52	2♋50 58	9♋03 13	29 09.7	12 22.5	22 35.7	29 52.8	6 47.4	4 30.2	18 15.1	7 41.1	15 06.5	17 48.5
11 F	9 17 32	18 14 28	15 19 19	21 39 28	29 02.6	13 42.7	23 48.5	0♏28.9	6 53.4	4 22.9	18 21.9	7 44.1	15 07.9	17 50.3
12 Sa	9 21 28	19 12 04	28 03 46	4♌32 13	28 55.7	15 01.1	25 01.3	1 05.1	6 59.7	4 15.6	18 28.8	7 47.0	15 09.3	17 52.2
13 Su	9 25 25	20 09 42	11♌04 47	17 41 22	28 49.8	16 17.6	26 14.2	1 41.5	7 06.4	4 08.2	18 35.6	7 49.9	15 10.7	17 54.0
14 M	9 29 22	21 07 21	24 21 47	1♍05 50	28 45.4	17 32.0	27 27.1	2 18.0	7 13.3	4 00.7	18 42.6	7 52.8	15 12.2	17 55.9
15 Tu	9 33 18	22 05 01	7♍53 13	14 43 42	28 42.8	18 44.4	28 40.0	2 54.7	7 20.5	3 53.2	18 49.5	7 55.6	15 13.7	17 57.7
16 W	9 37 15	23 02 42	21 36 57	28 32 42	28D 42.0	19 54.7	29 53.0	3 31.5	7 28.1	3 45.6	18 56.5	7 58.4	15 15.2	17 59.6
17 Th	9 41 11	24 00 24	5♎30 36	12♎30 25	28 42.6	21 02.9	1♌06.1	4 08.5	7 35.9	3 37.9	19 03.5	8 01.2	15 16.7	18 01.4
18 F	9 45 08	24 58 08	19 31 51	26 34 39	28 44.0	22 08.7	2 19.2	4 45.6	7 44.0	3 30.2	19 10.5	8 03.9	15 18.3	18 03.2
19 Sa	9 49 04	25 55 52	3♏38 35	10♏43 24	28 45.3	23 12.1	3 32.3	5 22.8	7 52.4	3 22.5	19 17.6	8 06.6	15 19.8	18 05.1
20 Su	9 53 01	26 53 38	17 48 54	24 54 50	28R 46.0	24 13.0	4 45.5	6 00.2	8 01.1	3 14.7	19 24.7	8 09.3	15 21.4	18 06.9
21 M	9 56 57	27 51 24	2♐00 57	9♐07 00	28 45.6	25 11.2	5 58.7	6 37.7	8 10.1	3 06.9	19 31.9	8 11.9	15 23.1	18 08.7
22 Tu	10 00 54	28 49 12	16 12 43	23 17 46	28 43.8	26 06.7	7 11.9	7 15.4	8 19.3	2 59.0	19 39.0	8 14.5	15 24.7	18 10.6
23 W	10 04 51	29 47 01	0♑21 49	7♑24 30	28 40.8	26 59.3	8 25.2	7 53.1	8 28.8	2 51.2	19 46.2	8 17.1	15 26.4	18 12.4
24 Th	10 08 47	0♍44 51	14 25 27	21 24 15	28 37.0	27 48.7	9 38.6	8 31.0	8 38.6	2 43.3	19 53.4	8 19.6	15 28.1	18 14.2
25 F	10 12 44	1 42 43	28 20 32	5♒13 53	28 32.9	28 34.9	10 52.0	9 09.1	8 48.7	2 35.4	20 00.7	8 22.1	15 29.8	18 16.0
26 Sa	10 16 40	2 40 36	12♒03 57	18 50 24	28 29.2	29 17.5	12 05.4	9 47.2	8 58.9	2 27.5	20 07.9	8 24.5	15 31.5	18 17.8
27 Su	10 20 37	3 38 30	25 32 58	2♓11 25	28 26.3	29 56.5	13 18.9	10 25.5	9 09.5	2 19.6	20 15.2	8 27.0	15 33.3	18 19.6
28 M	10 24 33	4 36 25	8♓45 36	15 15 25	28 24.5	0♎31.5	14 32.4	11 03.9	9 20.3	2 11.7	20 22.5	8 29.3	15 35.1	18 21.4
29 Tu	10 28 30	5 34 23	21 40 53	28 02 01	28D 23.9	1 02.4	15 45.9	11 42.4	9 31.3	2 03.8	20 29.8	8 31.7	15 36.8	18 23.2
30 W	10 32 26	6 32 22	4♈19 00	10♈32 02	28 24.3	1 28.8	16 59.5	12 21.1	9 42.6	1 55.9	20 37.1	8 34.0	15 38.7	18 25.0
31 Th	10 36 23	7 30 22	16 41 22	22 47 22	28 25.5	1 50.5	18 13.2	12 59.8	9 54.1	1 48.1	20 44.5	8 36.2	15 40.5	18 26.7

Astro Data

	Dy Hr Mn
♄⚺♆	3 19:20
☽0N	5 22:59
☽0S	20 8:39
♃△♅	20 15:19
⚳ D	24 4:57
☽0N	2 6:51
♄⚺♇	4 23:48
☽0S	16 14:07
☿0S	21 12:24
☽0N	29 15:13

Planet Ingress

		Dy Hr Mn
☿	♋	2 14:57
☿	♌	16 17:08
♀	♋	22 17:50
☉	♌	23 10:30
☊	♓R	26 20:56
☿	♍	2 2:44
♂	♏	10 16:48
♀	♌	16 14:18
☉	♍	23 17:23
☿	♎	27 14:17

Last Aspect / ☽ Ingress

Last Aspect Dy Hr Mn		☽ Ingress	Dy Hr Mn
30 7:36	♆ □	♒	1 9:19
2 14:04	♇ ☍	♓	3 13:51
4 16:59	♄ ☍	♈	5 22:24
7 7:38	♇ △	♉	8 10:13
9 20:50	☉ ⚹	♊	10 23:02
12 10:24	♀ ☌	♋	13 10:34
15 15:46	☿ ☌	♌	15 19:52
17 16:05	♀ ⚹	♍	18 3:05
20 3:04	♀ □	♎	20 8:34
22 11:57	♀ △	♏	22 12:27
23 17:39	♇ □	♐	24 14:55
26 1:39	♂ ⚹	♑	26 16:39
28 5:38	♂ □	♒	28 18:55
30 16:12	☿ ☍	♓	30 23:19

Last Aspect / ☽ Ingress

Last Aspect Dy Hr Mn		☽ Ingress	Dy Hr Mn
1 6:53	♄ ☍	♈	2 7:03
4 10:40	♂ ☍	♉	4 18:06
6 6:00	♄ △	♊	7 6:44
9 17:18	♂ △	♋	9 18:27
11 16:28	♀ ☌	♌	12 3:36
13 16:48	☉ ☌	♍	14 10:03
15 19:39	☿ ☌	♎	16 14:31
18 9:04	☉ ⚹	♏	18 17:49
20 15:35	☉ □	♐	20 20:36
22 22:04	☉ △	♑	22 23:23
24 23:45	☿ △	♒	25 2:53
26 11:02	♇ ☍	♓	27 8:02
28 21:38	♄ ☍	♈	29 15:44

☽ Phases & Eclipses

Dy Hr Mn	
7 2:53	☾ 14♈26
15 5:05	● 22♋09
22 10:50	☽ 29♎04
29 4:18	○ 5♒29
5 19:56	☾ 12♉48
13 16:48	● 20♌21
20 15:35	☽ 27♏02
27 14:51	○ 3♓45

Astro Data

1 July 1950
Julian Day # 18444
SVP 5♓57'04"
GC 26♐08.9 ⚴ 1♏47.4
Eris 7♈46.0 ⚵ 25♍38.8
⚷ 17♐14.2R ⚶ 4♉54.2
☽ Mean ☊ 2♈30.1

1 August 1950
Julian Day # 18475
SVP 5♓56'58"
GC 26♐08.9 ⚴ 6♏34.8
Eris 7♈41.8R ⚵ 3♎50.6
⚷ 15♐50.3R ⚶ 14♉47.4
☽ Mean ☊ 0♈51.6

LONGITUDE — September 1950

Day	Sid.Time	☉	0 hr ☽	Noon☽	True☊	☿	♀	♂	⚳	♃	♄	♅	♆	♇
1 F	10 40 19	8♍28 25	28♈50 25	4♉50 57	28♓27.1	2♎07.2	19♌26.9	13♏38.7	10♐05.8	1♓40.3	20♍51.9	8♋38.4	15♎42.3	18♌28.5
2 Sa	10 44 16	9 26 30	10♉49 29	16 46 31	28 28.6	2 18.6	20 40.6	14 17.7	10 17.8	1R 32.5	20 59.2	8 40.6	15 44.2	18 30.3
3 Su	10 48 13	10 24 36	22 42 37	28 38 20	28 29.7	2R 24.5	21 54.4	14 56.9	10 30.0	1 24.8	21 06.6	8 42.7	15 46.1	18 32.0
4 M	10 52 09	11 22 44	4♊34 17	10♊31 02	28R 30.1	2 24.5	23 08.2	15 36.1	10 42.5	1 17.1	21 14.1	8 44.8	15 48.0	18 33.7
5 Tu	10 56 06	12 20 55	16 29 13	22 29 23	28 29.8	2 18.5	24 22.1	16 15.5	10 55.1	1 09.5	21 21.5	8 46.9	15 49.9	18 35.5
6 W	11 00 02	13 19 07	28 32 07	4♋37 57	28 28.8	2 06.2	25 36.0	16 55.0	11 08.0	1 01.9	21 28.9	8 48.9	15 51.9	18 37.2
7 Th	11 03 59	14 17 22	10♋47 25	17 00 57	28 27.3	1 47.5	26 50.0	17 34.6	11 21.1	0 54.4	21 36.4	8 50.9	15 53.8	18 38.9
8 F	11 07 55	15 15 38	23 18 58	29 41 48	28 25.5	1 22.3	28 03.9	18 14.3	11 34.4	0 47.0	21 43.9	8 52.8	15 55.8	18 40.6
9 Sa	11 11 52	16 13 56	6♌09 42	12♌42 50	28 23.7	0 50.6	29 18.0	18 54.2	11 47.9	0 39.6	21 51.3	8 54.6	15 57.8	18 42.3
10 Su	11 15 48	17 12 17	19 21 17	26 05 02	28 22.3	0 12.7	0♍32.0	19 34.1	12 01.7	0 32.3	21 58.8	8 56.5	15 59.8	18 43.9
11 M	11 19 45	18 10 39	2♍53 56	9♍47 45	28 21.3	29♍28.7	1 46.1	20 14.2	12 15.6	0 25.1	22 06.3	8 58.3	16 01.8	18 45.6
12 Tu	11 23 42	19 09 03	16 46 08	23 48 41	28D 20.9	28 39.3	3 00.3	20 54.4	12 29.7	0 18.0	22 13.8	9 00.0	16 03.8	18 47.2
13 W	11 27 38	20 07 29	0♎54 52	8♎04 07	28 21.0	27 45.0	4 14.5	21 34.7	12 44.1	0 11.0	22 21.3	9 01.7	16 05.9	18 48.9
14 Th	11 31 35	21 05 56	15 15 48	22 29 16	28 21.4	26 46.8	5 28.7	22 15.1	12 58.6	0 04.1	22 28.7	9 03.3	16 07.9	18 50.5
15 F	11 35 31	22 04 25	29 43 51	6♏58 54	28 21.9	25 45.8	6 42.9	22 55.6	13 13.3	29♒57.3	22 36.2	9 04.9	16 10.0	18 52.1
16 Sa	11 39 28	23 02 56	14♏13 46	21 27 55	28 22.5	24 43.1	7 57.2	23 36.2	13 28.3	29 50.6	22 43.7	9 06.5	16 12.1	18 53.7
17 Su	11 43 24	24 01 29	28 40 46	5♐51 52	28 22.8	23 40.2	9 11.5	24 16.9	13 43.4	29 44.0	22 51.2	9 08.0	16 14.2	18 55.3
18 M	11 47 21	25 00 04	13♐00 49	20 07 17	28R 23.0	22 38.6	10 25.8	24 57.8	13 58.6	29 37.6	22 58.7	9 09.4	16 16.3	18 56.8
19 Tu	11 51 17	25 58 40	27 10 58	4♑11 40	28 23.0	21 39.9	11 40.2	25 38.7	14 14.1	29 31.3	23 06.2	9 10.8	16 18.4	18 58.4
20 W	11 55 14	26 57 17	11♑09 12	18 03 28	28 22.9	20 45.4	12 54.6	26 19.8	14 29.7	29 25.1	23 13.7	9 12.2	16 20.5	18 59.9
21 Th	11 59 11	27 55 56	24 54 22	1♒41 50	28D 22.8	19 56.7	14 09.0	27 00.9	14 45.5	29 19.1	23 21.2	9 13.5	16 22.6	19 01.4
22 F	12 03 07	28 54 37	8♒25 52	15 06 25	28 22.8	19 15.1	15 23.5	27 42.2	15 01.5	29 13.2	23 28.7	9 14.7	16 24.8	19 02.9
23 Sa	12 07 04	29 53 20	21 43 31	28 17 09	28 22.9	18 41.5	16 38.0	28 23.5	15 17.7	29 07.4	23 36.1	9 16.0	16 26.9	19 04.4
24 Su	12 11 00	0♎52 04	4♓47 21	11♓14 10	28 23.1	18 16.9	17 52.5	29 04.9	15 34.0	29 01.8	23 43.6	9 17.1	16 29.1	19 05.9
25 M	12 14 57	1 50 50	17 37 38	23 57 49	28R 23.2	18D 01.8	19 07.0	29 46.5	15 50.4	28 56.3	23 51.0	9 18.2	16 31.3	19 07.3
26 Tu	12 18 53	2 49 38	0♈14 48	6♈28 41	28 23.2	17 56.8	20 21.6	0♐28.1	16 07.1	28 51.0	23 58.5	9 19.3	16 33.5	19 08.8
27 W	12 22 50	3 48 29	12 39 37	18 47 44	28 22.9	18 01.9	21 36.2	1 09.8	16 23.8	28 45.8	24 05.9	9 20.3	16 35.6	19 10.2
28 Th	12 26 46	4 47 21	24 53 13	0♉56 19	28 22.3	18 17.0	22 50.8	1 51.6	16 40.8	28 40.8	24 13.3	9 21.2	16 37.8	19 11.6
29 F	12 30 43	5 46 15	6♉57 17	12 56 24	28 21.3	18 42.1	24 05.5	2 33.6	16 57.9	28 36.0	24 20.7	9 22.1	16 40.0	19 12.9
30 Sa	12 34 40	6 45 12	18 54 00	24 50 28	28 20.2	19 16.6	25 20.2	3 15.6	17 15.1	28 31.3	24 28.1	9 23.0	16 42.2	19 14.3

LONGITUDE — October 1950

Day	Sid.Time	☉	0 hr ☽	Noon☽	True☊	☿	♀	♂	⚳	♃	♄	♅	♆	♇
1 Su	12 38 36	7♎44 11	0♊46 12	6♊41 39	28♓19.0	20♍00.1	26♍34.9	3♐57.7	17♐32.5	28♒26.8	24♍35.5	9♋23.8	16♎44.4	19♌15.6
2 M	12 42 33	8 43 12	12 37 17	18 33 37	28R 18.0	20 51.9	27 49.6	4 39.9	17 50.0	28R 22.5	24 42.9	9 24.5	16 46.7	19 16.9
3 Tu	12 46 29	9 42 15	24 31 10	0♋30 30	28D 17.3	21 51.4	29 04.4	5 22.2	18 07.7	28 18.4	24 50.2	9 25.2	16 48.9	19 18.2
4 W	12 50 26	10 41 21	6♋32 11	12 36 46	28 17.1	22 57.9	0♎19.2	6 04.5	18 25.5	28 14.4	24 57.5	9 25.8	16 51.1	19 19.5
5 Th	12 54 22	11 40 29	18 44 50	24 56 58	28 17.5	24 10.6	1 34.0	6 47.0	18 43.5	28 10.6	25 04.8	9 26.4	16 53.3	19 20.8
6 F	12 58 19	12 39 39	1♌13 40	7♌35 26	28 18.4	25 28.8	2 48.9	7 29.6	19 01.6	28 07.0	25 12.1	9 27.0	16 55.6	19 22.0
7 Sa	13 02 15	13 38 52	14 02 44	20 35 55	28 19.6	26 51.9	4 03.7	8 12.3	19 19.8	28 03.6	25 19.4	9 27.5	16 57.8	19 23.2
8 Su	13 06 12	14 38 07	27 15 18	4♍01 03	28 20.8	28 19.0	5 18.6	8 55.0	19 38.1	28 00.3	25 26.6	9 27.9	17 00.0	19 24.4
9 M	13 10 09	15 37 24	10♍53 13	17 51 45	28R 21.7	29 49.7	6 33.6	9 37.9	19 56.6	27 57.3	25 33.8	9 28.3	17 02.3	19 25.6
10 Tu	13 14 05	16 36 43	24 56 24	2♎06 48	28 21.9	1♎23.3	7 48.5	10 20.8	20 15.2	27 54.4	25 41.0	9 28.6	17 04.5	19 26.7
11 W	13 18 02	17 36 04	9♎22 23	16 42 27	28 21.2	2 59.4	9 03.5	11 03.8	20 34.0	27 51.8	25 48.2	9 28.8	17 06.7	19 27.9
12 Th	13 21 58	18 35 28	24 06 10	1♏32 36	28 19.4	4 37.4	10 18.5	11 46.9	20 52.8	27 49.3	25 55.3	9 29.1	17 09.0	19 29.0
13 F	13 25 55	19 34 53	9♏00 41	16 29 23	28 16.9	6 17.0	11 33.5	12 30.1	21 11.8	27 47.0	26 02.4	9 29.2	17 11.2	19 30.0
14 Sa	13 29 51	20 34 21	23 57 36	1♐24 18	28 13.9	7 57.8	12 48.5	13 13.4	21 30.9	27 45.0	26 09.5	9 29.3	17 13.4	19 31.1
15 Su	13 33 48	21 33 50	8♐48 33	16 09 30	28 11.0	9 39.5	14 03.5	13 56.8	21 50.2	27 43.1	26 16.5	9R 29.4	17 15.7	19 32.1
16 M	13 37 44	22 33 21	23 26 27	0♑38 51	28 08.6	11 21.8	15 18.6	14 40.2	22 09.5	27 41.4	26 23.5	9 29.4	17 17.9	19 33.1
17 Tu	13 41 41	23 32 54	7♑46 17	14 48 30	28D 07.3	13 04.5	16 33.6	15 23.8	22 29.0	27 39.9	26 30.5	9 29.3	17 20.1	19 34.1
18 W	13 45 38	24 32 28	21 45 22	28 36 54	28 07.1	14 47.5	17 48.7	16 07.4	22 48.5	27 38.7	26 37.4	9 29.2	17 22.4	19 35.1
19 Th	13 49 34	25 32 04	5♒23 11	12♒04 24	28 07.9	16 30.5	19 03.8	16 51.1	23 08.2	27 37.6	26 44.3	9 29.0	17 24.6	19 36.0
20 F	13 53 31	26 31 42	18 40 49	25 12 40	28 09.4	18 13.4	20 18.9	17 34.8	23 28.0	27 36.7	26 51.2	9 28.8	17 26.8	19 36.9
21 Sa	13 57 27	27 31 22	1♓40 18	8♓04 01	28 11.1	19 56.2	21 34.0	18 18.7	23 47.9	27 36.1	26 58.0	9 28.6	17 29.0	19 37.8
22 Su	14 01 24	28 31 03	14 24 09	20 40 59	28R 12.3	21 38.7	22 49.2	19 02.6	24 07.8	27 35.6	27 04.8	9 28.2	17 31.2	19 38.7
23 M	14 05 20	29 30 46	26 54 49	3♈05 57	28 12.4	23 21.0	24 04.3	19 46.6	24 27.9	27D 35.4	27 11.5	9 27.9	17 33.4	19 39.5
24 Tu	14 09 17	0♏30 31	9♈14 37	15 21 03	28 11.0	25 02.8	25 19.5	20 30.7	24 48.1	27 35.3	27 18.2	9 27.4	17 35.6	19 40.3
25 W	14 13 13	1 30 17	21 25 28	27 28 04	28 07.9	26 44.3	26 34.6	21 14.8	25 08.4	27 35.5	27 24.9	9 27.0	17 37.8	19 41.1
26 Th	14 17 10	2 30 06	3♉29 04	9♉28 38	28 03.2	28 25.3	27 49.8	21 59.0	25 28.8	27 35.8	27 31.5	9 26.4	17 40.0	19 41.8
27 F	14 21 07	3 29 57	15 26 57	21 24 14	27 57.1	0♏05.8	29 05.0	22 43.3	25 49.2	27 36.4	27 38.1	9 25.8	17 42.2	19 42.5
28 Sa	14 25 03	4 29 50	27 20 42	3♊16 34	27 50.1	1 45.9	0♏20.2	23 27.6	26 09.8	27 37.1	27 44.6	9 25.2	17 44.3	19 43.2
29 Su	14 29 00	5 29 45	9♊12 07	15 07 37	27 43.1	3 25.5	1 35.4	24 12.1	26 30.4	27 38.1	27 51.1	9 24.5	17 46.5	19 43.9
30 M	14 32 56	6 29 42	21 03 25	26 59 51	27 36.6	5 04.7	2 50.7	24 56.6	26 51.2	27 39.2	27 57.5	9 23.8	17 48.6	19 44.6
31 Tu	14 36 53	7 29 41	2♋57 19	8♋56 16	27 31.3	6 43.3	4 05.9	25 41.1	27 12.0	27 40.6	28 03.9	9 23.0	17 50.8	19 45.2

Astro Data

	Dy Hr Mn
☿R	4 0:13
♃⚼♆	7 13:29
☽0S	12 21:58
☿0N	18 0:58
☉0S	23 14:44
☽0N	25 22:59
☿D	26 11:59
♀0S	6 22:05
☽0S	10 8:00
☿0S	12 10:43
♅R	16 0:17
☽0N	23 5:22
♃D	24 6:34
♃⚻♄	27 5:05

Planet Ingress

	Dy Hr Mn
♀ ♍	10 1:37
☿ ♍R	10 19:16
♃ ♒R	15 2:23
☉ ♎	23 14:44
♂ ♐	25 19:48
♀ ♎	4 5:51
☿ ♎	9 14:40
☉ ♏	23 23:45
☿ ♏	27 10:36
♀ ♏	28 5:33

Last Aspect / ☽ Ingress (September)

Last Aspect Dy Hr Mn		☽ Ingress Dy Hr Mn
31 3:25	♇ △	♉ 1 2:19
2 20:48	♀ □	♊ 3 14:45
5 16:10	♀ ⚹	♋ 6 2:54
7 20:51	♄ ⚹	♌ 8 12:34
9 23:46	♂ □	♍ 10 18:55
12 19:43	☿ ☌	♎ 12 22:28
14 5:56	♇ ⚹	♏ 15 0:27
17 1:50	♃ □	♐ 17 2:12
19 4:03	♃ ⚹	♑ 19 4:49
21 4:49	☉ △	♒ 21 8:59
23 13:32	♃ ☌	♓ 23 15:09
25 11:47	♄ ☍	♈ 25 23:32
28 7:33	♃ ⚹	♉ 28 10:08
30 19:24	♃ □	♊ 30 22:26

Last Aspect / ☽ Ingress (October)

Last Aspect Dy Hr Mn		☽ Ingress Dy Hr Mn
3 8:48	♀ □	♋ 3 10:59
5 12:15	♄ ⚹	♌ 5 21:40
8 1:23	♃ ☍	♍ 8 4:54
10 1:10	♄ ☌	♎ 10 8:29
12 6:01	♃ △	♏ 12 9:31
14 6:07	♃ □	♐ 14 9:44
16 7:04	♃ ⚹	♑ 16 10:55
18 8:28	♄ △	♒ 18 14:27
20 16:26	♃ ☌	♓ 20 20:53
23 0:26	♄ ☍	♈ 23 5:59
25 12:15	♃ ⚹	♉ 25 17:03
28 0:42	♄ △	♊ 28 5:22
30 13:57	♄ □	♋ 30 18:03

☽ Phases & Eclipses

Dy Hr Mn	
4 13:53	☾ 11♊27
12 3:29	● 18♍48
12 3:38:16	◐ T 01'14"
18 20:54	☽ 25♐22
26 4:21	○ 2♈31
26 4:17	◑ T 1.079
4 7:53	☾ 10♋31
11 13:34	● 17♎40
18 4:18	☽ 24♑13
25 20:46	○ 1♉52

Astro Data

1 September 1950
Julian Day # 18506
SVP 5♓56'54"
GC 26♐09.0 ⚴ 15♏20.0
Eris 7♈28.4R ⚵ 13♎31.7
⚷ 15♐45.3 ⚶ 20♉57.4
☽ Mean ☊ 29♓13.1

1 October 1950
Julian Day # 18536
SVP 5♓56'51"
GC 26♐09.1 ⚴ 25♏56.8
Eris 7♈10.3R ⚵ 23♎39.2
⚷ 17♐02.7 ⚶ 21♉23.4R
☽ Mean ☊ 27♓37.8

November 1950 LONGITUDE

Day	Sid.Time	☉	0 hr ☽	Noon ☽	True ☊	☿	♀	♂	⚳	♃	♄	♅	♆	♇
1 W	14 40 49	8♏29 42	14♋57 11	21♋00 32	27♓27.7	8♏21.5	5♏21.2	26♐25.8	27♐32.9	27♒42.2	28♍10.2	9♋22.2	17♎52.9	19♌45.8
2 Th	14 44 46	9 29 45	27 06 53	3♌16 46	27D 26.0	9 59.2	6 36.5	27 10.5	27 53.9	27 43.9	28 16.5	9R 21.3	17 55.0	19 46.4
3 F	14 48 42	10 29 51	9♌30 45	15 49 26	27 25.9	11 36.5	7 51.7	27 55.3	28 15.0	27 45.9	28 22.7	9 20.3	17 57.1	19 46.9
4 Sa	14 52 39	11 29 58	22 13 20	28 43 01	27 26.9	13 13.4	9 07.0	28 40.1	28 36.2	27 48.0	28 28.9	9 19.3	17 59.2	19 47.4
5 Su	14 56 36	12 30 08	5♍18 56	12♍01 30	27 28.3	14 49.8	10 22.3	29 25.0	28 57.4	27 50.4	28 35.0	9 18.3	18 01.3	19 47.9
6 M	15 00 32	13 30 20	18 51 02	25 47 42	27R 29.0	16 25.8	11 37.7	0♑10.0	29 18.8	27 52.9	28 41.0	9 17.2	18 03.4	19 48.3
7 Tu	15 04 29	14 30 33	2♎51 31	10♎02 21	27 28.4	18 01.4	12 53.0	0 55.0	29 40.2	27 55.7	28 47.0	9 16.1	18 05.4	19 48.8
8 W	15 08 25	15 30 49	17 19 50	24 43 25	27 25.6	19 36.7	14 08.3	1 40.2	0♑01.6	27 58.6	28 53.0	9 14.9	18 07.5	19 49.1
9 Th	15 12 22	16 31 06	2♏12 18	9♏45 28	27 20.6	21 11.6	15 23.7	2 25.3	0 23.2	28 01.8	28 58.9	9 13.6	18 09.5	19 49.5
10 F	15 16 18	17 31 26	17 21 47	24 59 56	27 13.7	22 46.1	16 39.0	3 10.6	0 44.8	28 05.1	29 04.7	9 12.4	18 11.5	19 49.9
11 Sa	15 20 15	18 31 47	2♐38 30	10♐16 06	27 05.7	24 20.3	17 54.4	3 55.9	1 06.6	28 08.7	29 10.4	9 11.0	18 13.5	19 50.2
12 Su	15 24 11	19 32 10	17 51 21	25 23 00	26 57.6	25 54.2	19 09.7	4 41.3	1 28.3	28 12.4	29 16.1	9 09.7	18 15.5	19 50.4
13 M	15 28 08	20 32 34	2♑49 59	10♑11 22	26 50.5	27 27.8	20 25.1	5 26.7	1 50.2	28 16.3	29 21.8	9 08.2	18 17.5	19 50.7
14 Tu	15 32 05	21 33 00	17 26 30	24 34 54	26 45.2	29 01.2	21 40.5	6 12.2	2 12.1	28 20.4	29 27.3	9 06.8	18 19.4	19 50.9
15 W	15 36 01	22 33 26	1♒36 21	8♒30 47	26 42.2	0♐34.2	22 55.8	6 57.7	2 34.1	28 24.7	29 32.8	9 05.3	18 21.4	19 51.1
16 Th	15 39 58	23 33 55	15 18 20	21 59 16	26D 41.2	2 07.0	24 11.2	7 43.3	2 56.1	28 29.2	29 38.2	9 03.7	18 23.3	19 51.3
17 F	15 43 54	24 34 24	28 33 57	5♓02 49	26 41.6	3 39.5	25 26.6	8 29.0	3 18.2	28 33.9	29 43.6	9 02.1	18 25.2	19 51.4
18 Sa	15 47 51	25 34 55	11♓26 23	17 45 11	26R 42.4	5 11.8	26 42.0	9 14.7	3 40.4	28 38.7	29 48.8	9 00.5	18 27.1	19 51.5
19 Su	15 51 47	26 35 26	23 59 44	0♈10 35	26 42.6	6 43.8	27 57.4	10 00.4	4 02.6	28 43.7	29 54.1	8 58.8	18 28.9	19 51.6
20 M	15 55 44	27 36 00	6♈18 15	12 23 13	26 41.3	8 15.7	29 12.7	10 46.2	4 24.9	28 49.0	29 59.2	8 57.1	18 30.8	19 51.7
21 Tu	15 59 40	28 36 34	18 25 54	24 26 45	26 37.5	9 47.3	0♐28.1	11 32.1	4 47.2	28 54.3	0♎04.2	8 55.3	18 32.6	19R 51.7
22 W	16 03 37	29 37 10	0♉26 07	6♉24 19	26 30.9	11 18.6	1 43.5	12 18.0	5 09.6	28 59.9	0 09.2	8 53.5	18 34.4	19 51.7
23 Th	16 07 34	0♐37 47	12 21 38	18 18 19	26 21.6	12 49.7	2 58.9	13 04.0	5 32.1	29 05.6	0 14.1	8 51.7	18 36.2	19 51.6
24 F	16 11 30	1 38 26	24 14 36	0♊10 39	26 10.1	14 20.6	4 14.3	13 50.0	5 54.6	29 11.6	0 19.0	8 49.8	18 37.9	19 51.6
25 Sa	16 15 27	2 39 06	6♊06 39	12 02 46	25 57.1	15 51.2	5 29.7	14 36.0	6 17.1	29 17.6	0 23.7	8 47.9	18 39.7	19 51.5
26 Su	16 19 23	3 39 47	17 59 10	23 56 01	25 43.7	17 21.6	6 45.1	15 22.1	6 39.8	29 23.9	0 28.4	8 45.9	18 41.4	19 51.3
27 M	16 23 20	4 40 30	29 53 30	5♋51 51	25 31.0	18 51.7	8 00.5	16 08.2	7 02.4	29 30.3	0 33.0	8 44.0	18 43.1	19 51.2
28 Tu	16 27 16	5 41 14	11♋51 16	17 52 03	25 20.1	20 21.4	9 15.9	16 54.4	7 25.1	29 36.9	0 37.5	8 41.9	18 44.8	19 51.0
29 W	16 31 13	6 42 00	23 54 31	29 59 01	25 11.8	21 50.7	10 31.3	17 40.7	7 47.9	29 43.6	0 41.9	8 39.9	18 46.4	19 50.8
30 Th	16 35 09	7 42 47	6♌05 58	12♌15 46	25 06.3	23 19.7	11 46.7	18 26.9	8 10.7	29 50.6	0 46.3	8 37.8	18 48.0	19 50.6

December 1950 LONGITUDE

Day	Sid.Time	☉	0 hr ☽	Noon ☽	True ☊	☿	♀	♂	⚳	♃	♄	♅	♆	♇
1 F	16 39 06	8♐43 35	18♌28 56	24♌45 57	25♓03.4	24♐48.2	13♐02.1	19♑13.3	8♑33.5	29♒57.6	0♎50.6	8♋35.7	18♎49.7	19♌50.3
2 Sa	16 43 03	9 44 25	1♍07 22	7♍33 42	25D 02.6	26 16.1	14 17.5	19 59.6	8 56.4	0♓04.9	0 54.7	8R 33.5	18 51.2	19R 50.0
3 Su	16 46 59	10 45 16	14 05 29	20 43 13	25R 02.7	27 43.4	15 32.9	20 46.0	9 19.4	0 12.2	0 58.8	8 31.4	18 52.8	19 49.7
4 M	16 50 56	11 46 09	27 27 20	4♎18 13	25 02.5	29 10.0	16 48.3	21 32.5	9 42.3	0 19.8	1 02.8	8 29.2	18 54.3	19 49.3
5 Tu	16 54 52	12 47 03	11♎16 06	18 21 05	25 00.7	0♑35.8	18 03.7	22 19.0	10 05.4	0 27.5	1 06.7	8 26.9	18 55.8	19 48.9
6 W	16 58 49	13 47 59	25 33 05	2♏51 51	24 56.5	2 00.6	19 19.2	23 05.5	10 28.4	0 35.3	1 10.6	8 24.7	18 57.3	19 48.5
7 Th	17 02 45	14 48 55	10♏16 50	17 47 17	24 49.4	3 24.2	20 34.6	23 52.1	10 51.5	0 43.3	1 14.3	8 22.4	18 58.7	19 48.1
8 F	17 06 42	15 49 53	25 22 15	3♐00 30	24 39.7	4 46.5	21 50.0	24 38.7	11 14.7	0 51.5	1 18.0	8 20.0	19 00.2	19 47.6
9 Sa	17 10 38	16 50 52	10♐40 41	18 21 20	24 28.3	6 07.2	23 05.5	25 25.3	11 37.9	0 59.8	1 21.5	8 17.7	19 01.6	19 47.2
10 Su	17 14 35	17 51 52	26 00 55	3♑37 57	24 16.5	7 26.1	24 20.9	26 12.0	12 01.1	1 08.3	1 25.0	8 15.3	19 02.9	19 46.6
11 M	17 18 32	18 52 53	11♑11 06	18 39 07	24 05.9	8 42.9	25 36.3	26 58.7	12 24.4	1 16.9	1 28.3	8 13.0	19 04.3	19 46.1
12 Tu	17 22 28	19 53 54	26 01 02	3♒16 05	23 57.4	9 57.3	26 51.8	27 45.5	12 47.6	1 25.6	1 31.6	8 10.6	19 05.6	19 45.5
13 W	17 26 25	20 54 56	10♒23 47	17 23 51	23 51.6	11 08.7	28 07.2	28 32.3	13 11.0	1 34.5	1 34.8	8 08.1	19 06.9	19 44.9
14 Th	17 30 21	21 55 59	24 16 15	1♓01 08	23 48.6	12 16.8	29 22.6	29 19.1	13 34.3	1 43.5	1 37.8	8 05.7	19 08.1	19 44.3
15 F	17 34 18	22 57 01	7♓38 48	14 09 42	23 47.5	13 21.0	0♑38.0	0♒05.9	13 57.7	1 52.6	1 40.8	8 03.2	19 09.3	19 43.7
16 Sa	17 38 14	23 58 05	20 34 21	26 53 21	23 47.4	14 20.8	1 53.4	0 52.8	14 21.1	2 01.9	1 43.7	8 00.7	19 10.5	19 43.0
17 Su	17 42 11	24 59 08	3♈07 19	9♈16 54	23 47.0	15 15.5	3 08.8	1 39.7	14 44.5	2 11.3	1 46.5	7 58.3	19 11.7	19 42.3
18 M	17 46 08	26 00 12	15 22 46	21 25 30	23 45.1	16 04.2	4 24.2	2 26.6	15 08.0	2 20.9	1 49.1	7 55.7	19 12.8	19 41.6
19 Tu	17 50 04	27 01 16	27 25 45	3♉24 03	23 40.7	16 46.3	5 39.6	3 13.5	15 31.5	2 30.6	1 51.7	7 53.2	19 13.9	19 40.8
20 W	17 54 01	28 02 21	9♉20 56	15 16 53	23 33.3	17 20.9	6 55.0	4 00.5	15 55.0	2 40.4	1 54.2	7 50.7	19 15.0	19 40.0
21 Th	17 57 57	29 03 26	21 12 18	27 07 35	23 23.0	17 47.1	8 10.4	4 47.5	16 18.5	2 50.3	1 56.5	7 48.1	19 16.1	19 39.2
22 F	18 01 54	0♑04 31	3♊03 02	8♊58 56	23 10.2	18 03.9	9 25.8	5 34.5	16 42.1	3 00.3	1 58.8	7 45.6	19 17.1	19 38.4
23 Sa	18 05 50	1 05 37	14 55 32	20 53 00	22 55.7	18R 10.5	10 41.2	6 21.5	17 05.6	3 10.5	2 01.0	7 43.0	19 18.1	19 37.6
24 Su	18 09 47	2 06 44	26 51 30	2♋51 11	22 40.8	18 06.2	11 56.5	7 08.5	17 29.2	3 20.8	2 03.0	7 40.5	19 19.0	19 36.7
25 M	18 13 43	3 07 50	8♋52 10	14 54 34	22 26.6	17 50.4	13 11.9	7 55.6	17 52.8	3 31.2	2 05.0	7 37.9	19 19.9	19 35.8
26 Tu	18 17 40	4 08 57	20 58 30	27 04 07	22 14.3	17 22.8	14 27.3	8 42.7	18 16.5	3 41.7	2 06.9	7 35.3	19 20.8	19 34.9
27 W	18 21 37	5 10 04	3♌11 33	9♌20 59	22 04.7	16 43.4	15 42.6	9 29.8	18 40.1	3 52.3	2 08.6	7 32.7	19 21.7	19 34.0
28 Th	18 25 33	6 11 12	15 32 39	21 46 47	21 58.1	15 52.9	16 58.0	10 16.9	19 03.8	4 03.1	2 10.2	7 30.1	19 22.5	19 33.0
29 F	18 29 30	7 12 20	28 03 40	4♍23 40	21 54.5	14 52.1	18 13.3	11 04.0	19 27.5	4 13.9	2 11.8	7 27.5	19 23.3	19 32.0
30 Sa	18 33 26	8 13 29	10♍47 07	17 14 24	21D 53.3	13 42.7	19 28.7	11 51.2	19 51.2	4 24.9	2 13.2	7 25.0	19 24.0	19 31.0
31 Su	18 37 23	9 14 38	23 45 57	0♎22 09	21R 53.3	12 26.7	20 44.0	12 38.3	20 14.9	4 35.9	2 14.5	7 22.4	19 24.8	19 30.0

Astro Data	Planet Ingress	Last Aspect	☽ Ingress	Last Aspect	☽ Ingress	☽ Phases & Eclipses	Astro Data
Dy Hr Mn	Dy Hr Mn	Dy Hr Mn	Dy Hr Mn	Dy Hr Mn	Dy Hr Mn	Dy Hr Mn	1 November 1950
☽0S 6 18:26	♂ ♑ 6 6:40	2 2:11 ♄ ⚹	♌ 2 5:38	1 12:05 ☿ △	♍ 1 21:53	3 1:00 ☾ 10♌02	Julian Day # 18567
☽0N 19 10:34	⚳ ♑ 8 10:10	4 11:54 ♂ △	♍ 4 14:21	4 1:57 ☿ □	♎ 4 4:29	9 23:25 ● 17♏00	SVP 5♓56'47"
♇R 21 15:56	☿ ♐ 15 3:10	6 16:58 ♄ ☌	♎ 6 19:10	5 19:00 ♂ □	♏ 6 7:19	16 15:06 ☽ 23♒42	GC 26♐09.2 ⚴ 8♐07.0
	♄ ♎ 20 15:50	8 17:15 ♃ △	♏ 8 20:29	7 22:09 ♂ ⚹	♐ 8 7:17	24 15:14 ○ 1♊47	Eris 6♈51.7R ⚵ 4♏23.2
☽0S 4 3:00	♀ ♐ 21 3:03	10 18:27 ♄ ⚹	♐ 10 19:51	9 20:05 ♀ ☌	♑ 10 6:16		⚷ 19♐32.8 ⚶ 15♉26.2R
♃⊼♄ 13 13:10	☉ ♐ 22 21:03	12 18:17 ♄ □	♑ 12 19:25	12 2:21 ♂ ☌	♒ 12 6:34	2 16:22 ☾ 9♍55	☽ Mean ☊ 25♓59.3
☽0N 16 15:58		14 20:30 ☿ ⚹	♒ 14 21:14	14 8:45 ♀ ⚹	♓ 14 10:10	9 9:29 ● 16♐44	
☿R 23 14:49	♃ ♓ 1 19:57	16 23:56 ♃ ☌	♓ 17 2:38	16 5:56 ☉ □	♈ 16 17:58	16 5:56 ☽ 23♓43	1 December 1950
♃⚼♆ 30 10:04	☿ ♑ 5 1:57	19 11:28 ♄ ☍	♈ 19 11:39	18 22:00 ☉ △	♉ 19 5:10	24 10:23 ○ 2♋03	Julian Day # 18597
☽0S 31 8:51	♀ ♑ 14 23:54	21 21:00 ♃ ⚹	♉ 21 23:08	20 20:52 ♇ □	♊ 21 17:49		SVP 5♓56'42"
	♂ ♒ 15 8:59	24 9:59 ♃ □	♊ 24 11:38	23 9:28 ♇ ⚹	♋ 24 6:18		GC 26♐09.2 ⚴ 20♐25.0
	☉ ♑ 22 10:13	26 23:06 ♃ △	♋ 27 0:13	25 20:46 ♆ □	♌ 26 17:45		Eris 6♈39.2R ⚵ 14♏34.7
		28 13:45 ♆ □	♌ 29 12:02	28 7:44 ♇ ☌	♍ 29 3:41		⚷ 22♐41.2 ⚶ 8♉25.1R
				30 16:34 ♀ △	♎ 31 11:20		☽ Mean ☊ 24♓24.0

LONGITUDE

January 1951

Day	Sid.Time	☉	0 hr ☽	Noon ☽	True ☊	☿	♀	♂	⚳	♃	♄	♅	♆	♇
1 M	18 41 19	10♑15 47	7♎03 23	13♎50 01	21♓53.5	11♑06.7	21♑59.3	13♒25.5	20♑38.6	4♓47.1	2♎15.7	7♋19.8	19♎25.4	19♌29.0
2 Tu	18 45 16	11 16 57	20 42 21	27 40 33	21R52.4	9R45.1	23 14.7	14 12.7	21 02.3	4 58.4	2 16.8	7R17.2	19 26.1	19R27.9
3 W	18 49 12	12 18 07	4♏44 42	11♏54 45	21 49.1	8 24.8	24 30.0	14 59.9	21 26.1	5 09.7	2 17.8	7 14.6	19 26.7	19 26.8
4 Th	18 53 09	13 19 17	19 10 25	26 31 17	21 43.3	7 08.1	25 45.3	15 47.1	21 49.9	5 21.2	2 18.7	7 12.0	19 27.3	19 25.7
5 F	18 57 06	14 20 28	3♐56 43	11♐25 50	21 34.9	5 57.4	27 00.6	16 34.4	22 13.6	5 32.8	2 19.5	7 09.5	19 27.9	19 24.6
6 Sa	19 01 02	15 21 39	18 57 39	26 30 59	21 24.9	4 54.3	28 15.9	17 21.6	22 37.4	5 44.5	2 20.2	7 06.9	19 28.4	19 23.5
7 Su	19 04 59	16 22 50	4♑04 33	11♑37 02	21 14.4	4 00.0	29 31.2	18 08.9	23 01.2	5 56.2	2 20.7	7 04.4	19 28.9	19 22.3
8 M	19 08 55	17 24 01	19 07 09	26 33 39	21 04.6	3 15.3	0♒46.5	18 56.1	23 25.0	6 08.1	2 21.2	7 01.8	19 29.4	19 21.2
9 Tu	19 12 52	18 25 11	3♒55 26	11♒11 37	20 56.7	2 40.6	2 01.8	19 43.4	23 48.8	6 20.0	2 21.5	6 59.3	19 29.8	19 20.0
10 W	19 16 48	19 26 21	18 21 28	25 24 28	20 51.3	2 15.9	3 17.1	20 30.7	24 12.6	6 32.1	2 21.8	6 56.8	19 30.2	19 18.8
11 Th	19 20 45	20 27 31	2♓20 20	9♓08 59	20D48.6	2 00.9	4 32.4	21 17.9	24 36.4	6 44.2	2R21.9	6 54.3	19 30.5	19 17.6
12 F	19 24 42	21 28 40	15 50 29	22 25 06	20 47.9	1D55.2	5 47.6	22 05.2	25 00.2	6 56.4	2 21.9	6 51.8	19 30.8	19 16.3
13 Sa	19 28 38	22 29 48	28 53 12	5♈15 16	20 48.5	1 58.1	7 02.8	22 52.5	25 24.0	7 08.7	2 21.8	6 49.3	19 31.1	19 15.1
14 Su	19 32 35	23 30 55	11♈31 49	17 43 30	20R49.4	2 09.2	8 18.1	23 39.8	25 47.8	7 21.1	2 21.6	6 46.8	19 31.3	19 13.8
15 M	19 36 31	24 32 02	23 50 56	29 54 46	20 49.4	2 27.6	9 33.3	24 27.1	26 11.6	7 33.5	2 21.2	6 44.4	19 31.6	19 12.5
16 Tu	19 40 28	25 33 09	5♉55 40	11♉54 16	20 47.6	2 52.9	10 48.5	25 14.3	26 35.4	7 46.0	2 20.8	6 42.0	19 31.7	19 11.2
17 W	19 44 24	26 34 14	17 51 11	23 47 01	20 43.7	3 24.2	12 03.6	26 01.6	26 59.2	7 58.7	2 20.3	6 39.6	19 31.9	19 09.9
18 Th	19 48 21	27 35 19	29 42 19	5♊37 35	20 37.4	4 01.2	13 18.8	26 48.9	27 23.0	8 11.3	2 19.6	6 37.2	19 32.0	19 08.6
19 F	19 52 17	28 36 23	11♊33 18	17 29 52	20 29.2	4 43.2	14 33.9	27 36.1	27 46.8	8 24.1	2 18.9	6 34.8	19 32.1	19 07.3
20 Sa	19 56 14	29 37 27	23 27 40	29 26 58	20 19.5	5 29.7	15 49.1	28 23.4	28 10.6	8 36.9	2 18.0	6 32.5	19R32.1	19 05.9
21 Su	20 00 11	0♒38 29	5♋28 05	11♋31 11	20 09.4	6 20.3	17 04.2	29 10.6	28 34.4	8 49.8	2 17.1	6 30.2	19 32.1	19 04.6
22 M	20 04 07	1 39 31	17 36 28	23 44 03	19 59.7	7 14.6	18 19.3	29 57.9	28 58.2	9 02.8	2 16.0	6 27.9	19 32.1	19 03.2
23 Tu	20 08 04	2 40 32	29 54 02	6♌06 30	19 51.4	8 12.2	19 34.3	0♓45.1	29 21.9	9 15.8	2 14.8	6 25.7	19 32.0	19 01.9
24 W	20 12 00	3 41 32	12♌21 30	18 39 05	19 45.1	9 12.9	20 49.4	1 32.3	29 45.7	9 28.9	2 13.5	6 23.5	19 31.9	19 00.5
25 Th	20 15 57	4 42 32	24 59 18	1♍22 13	19 41.1	10 16.2	22 04.4	2 19.5	0♒09.4	9 42.1	2 12.1	6 21.3	19 31.8	18 59.1
26 F	20 19 53	5 43 30	7♍47 53	14 16 24	19D39.3	11 22.1	23 19.5	3 06.7	0 33.1	9 55.3	2 10.6	6 19.1	19 31.6	18 57.7
27 Sa	20 23 50	6 44 28	20 47 53	27 22 27	19 39.4	12 30.2	24 34.5	3 53.9	0 56.8	10 08.6	2 09.1	6 16.9	19 31.4	18 56.3
28 Su	20 27 46	7 45 26	4♎00 15	10♎41 26	19 40.6	13 40.4	25 49.4	4 41.1	1 20.6	10 21.9	2 07.4	6 14.8	19 31.2	18 54.9
29 M	20 31 43	8 46 23	17 26 10	24 14 36	19 42.1	14 52.5	27 04.4	5 28.3	1 44.2	10 35.3	2 05.6	6 12.8	19 30.9	18 53.5
30 Tu	20 35 40	9 47 19	1♏06 50	8♏02 58	19R42.9	16 06.3	28 19.3	6 15.4	2 07.9	10 48.8	2 03.7	6 10.7	19 30.6	18 52.0
31 W	20 39 36	10 48 14	15 03 00	22 06 54	19 42.3	17 21.7	29 34.3	7 02.6	2 31.6	11 02.3	2 01.7	6 08.7	19 30.3	18 50.6

LONGITUDE

February 1951

Day	Sid.Time	☉	0 hr ☽	Noon ☽	True ☊	☿	♀	♂	⚳	♃	♄	♅	♆	♇
1 Th	20 43 33	11♒49 09	29♏14 29	6♐25 31	19♓40.0	18♑38.7	0♓49.2	7♓49.7	2♒55.2	11♓15.8	1♎59.6	6♋06.7	19♎29.9	18♌49.2
2 F	20 47 29	12 50 03	13♐39 35	20 56 12	19R36.1	19 57.1	2 04.1	8 36.8	3 18.9	11 29.5	1R57.4	6R04.8	19R29.5	18R47.7
3 Sa	20 51 26	13 50 57	28 14 45	5♑34 28	19 31.0	21 16.7	3 19.0	9 24.0	3 42.5	11 43.1	1 55.1	6 02.9	19 29.1	18 46.3
4 Su	20 55 22	14 51 49	12♑54 32	20 14 06	19 25.4	22 37.6	4 33.8	10 11.0	4 06.1	11 56.9	1 52.7	6 01.0	19 28.7	18 44.9
5 M	20 59 19	15 52 41	27 32 13	4♒48 00	19 20.2	23 59.7	5 48.6	10 58.1	4 29.7	12 10.6	1 50.2	5 59.2	19 28.2	18 43.4
6 Tu	21 03 15	16 53 31	12♒00 36	19 09 15	19 16.0	25 22.9	7 03.4	11 45.2	4 53.2	12 24.4	1 47.6	5 57.4	19 27.6	18 42.0
7 W	21 07 12	17 54 20	26 13 15	3♓12 04	19 13.4	26 47.2	8 18.2	12 32.2	5 16.7	12 38.3	1 45.0	5 55.7	19 27.1	18 40.5
8 Th	21 11 09	18 55 07	10♓05 18	16 52 40	19D12.3	28 12.5	9 33.0	13 19.3	5 40.2	12 52.2	1 42.2	5 54.0	19 26.5	18 39.1
9 F	21 15 05	19 55 54	23 34 04	0♈09 31	19 12.7	29 38.8	10 47.7	14 06.3	6 03.7	13 06.1	1 39.4	5 52.3	19 25.9	18 37.6
10 Sa	21 19 02	20 56 38	6♈39 08	13 03 12	19 14.1	1♒06.1	12 02.4	14 53.2	6 27.2	13 20.1	1 36.4	5 50.7	19 25.2	18 36.2
11 Su	21 22 58	21 57 21	19 22 02	25 36 05	19 15.9	2 34.4	13 17.1	15 40.2	6 50.6	13 34.1	1 33.4	5 49.1	19 24.5	18 34.7
12 M	21 26 55	22 58 03	1♉45 50	7♉51 48	19 17.5	4 03.5	14 31.7	16 27.1	7 14.0	13 48.2	1 30.3	5 47.6	19 23.8	18 33.3
13 Tu	21 30 51	23 58 43	13 54 36	19 54 48	19R18.3	5 33.6	15 46.3	17 14.0	7 37.4	14 02.3	1 27.1	5 46.1	19 23.1	18 31.8
14 W	21 34 48	24 59 21	25 53 02	1♊49 53	19 18.2	7 04.6	17 00.9	18 00.9	8 00.7	14 16.4	1 23.8	5 44.6	19 22.3	18 30.4
15 Th	21 38 44	25 59 58	7♊45 59	13 41 54	19 16.9	8 36.5	18 15.4	18 47.8	8 24.0	14 30.6	1 20.5	5 43.2	19 21.5	18 29.0
16 F	21 42 41	27 00 32	19 38 14	25 35 29	19 14.6	10 09.3	19 29.9	19 34.6	8 47.3	14 44.8	1 17.1	5 41.9	19 20.6	18 27.5
17 Sa	21 46 38	28 01 06	1♋34 12	7♋34 48	19 11.6	11 43.0	20 44.4	20 21.4	9 10.5	14 59.0	1 13.6	5 40.6	19 19.8	18 26.1
18 Su	21 50 34	29 01 37	13 37 44	19 43 22	19 08.2	13 17.6	21 58.8	21 08.2	9 33.7	15 13.2	1 10.0	5 39.3	19 18.9	18 24.7
19 M	21 54 31	0♓02 07	25 52 00	2♌03 54	19 05.0	14 53.1	23 13.2	21 54.9	9 56.9	15 27.5	1 06.4	5 38.1	19 18.0	18 23.3
20 Tu	21 58 27	1 02 35	8♌19 16	14 38 15	19 02.2	16 29.5	24 27.6	22 41.6	10 20.0	15 41.8	1 02.6	5 36.9	19 17.0	18 21.9
21 W	22 02 24	2 03 01	21 00 56	27 27 20	19 00.3	18 06.9	25 41.9	23 28.3	10 43.1	15 56.1	0 58.9	5 35.8	19 16.1	18 20.4
22 Th	22 06 20	3 03 26	3♍57 27	10♍31 13	18D59.3	19 45.2	26 56.2	24 14.9	11 06.2	16 10.5	0 55.0	5 34.7	19 15.1	18 19.0
23 F	22 10 17	4 03 49	17 08 31	23 49 15	18 59.2	21 24.4	28 10.4	25 01.5	11 29.2	16 24.8	0 51.0	5 33.7	19 14.0	18 17.7
24 Sa	22 14 13	5 04 10	0♎33 13	7♎20 16	18 59.7	23 04.6	29 24.6	25 48.1	11 52.2	16 39.2	0 47.1	5 32.7	19 13.0	18 16.3
25 Su	22 18 10	6 04 30	14 10 13	21 02 50	19 00.7	24 45.8	0♈38.8	26 34.7	12 15.1	16 53.6	0 43.1	5 31.8	19 11.9	18 14.9
26 M	22 22 07	7 04 48	27 57 56	4♏55 18	19 01.8	26 28.0	1 52.9	27 21.2	12 38.0	17 08.1	0 39.0	5 30.9	19 10.8	18 13.5
27 Tu	22 26 03	8 05 05	11♏54 45	18 56 02	19 02.7	28 11.1	3 07.0	28 07.7	13 00.9	17 22.5	0 34.9	5 30.1	19 09.7	18 12.2
28 W	22 30 00	9 05 21	25 58 58	3♐03 17	19R03.2	29 55.3	4 21.1	28 54.1	13 23.7	17 37.0	0 30.7	5 29.3	19 08.5	18 10.8

Astro Data

	Dy Hr Mn
♆✶♇	3 13:30
♄ R	12 1:17
♃△♅	12 4:27
☿ D	12 15:34
☽0N	12 23:09
♆R	21 5:28
☽0S	27 13:32
☽0N	9 8:17
☽0S	23 19:36
♀0N	26 21:37

Planet Ingress

	Dy Hr Mn
♀ ♒	7 21:10
☉ ♒	20 20:52
♂ ♓	22 13:05
⚳ ♒	25 2:29
♀ ♓	31 20:14
☿ ♒	9 17:50
☉ ♓	19 11:10
♀ ♈	24 23:26
☿ ♓	28 13:04

Last Aspect Dy Hr Mn			☽ Ingress	Dy Hr Mn
2 3:38	♀	□	♏	2 15:58
4 10:38	♀	✶	♐	4 17:38
6 0:49	♆	✶	♑	6 17:32
8 0:35	♆	□	♒	8 17:35
10 3:09	♂	☌	♓	10 19:56
12 10:08	☉	✶	♈	13 2:05
15 0:26	♂	✶	♉	15 12:10
17 18:11	☉	△	♊	18 0:36
20 9:44	♂	△	♋	20 13:06
22 3:47	♆	□	♌	23 0:12
24 16:34	♀	☍	♍	25 9:26
26 6:07	☿	△	♎	27 16:46
29 17:27	♀	△	♏	29 22:04

Last Aspect Dy Hr Mn			☽ Ingress	Dy Hr Mn
31 6:28	♇	□	♐	1 1:16
2 9:37	♆	✶	♑	3 2:52
4 16:20	☿	☌	♒	5 4:04
6 12:31	♆	△	♓	7 6:29
9 10:57	☿	✶	♈	9 11:43
11 4:21	☉	✶	♉	11 20:33
13 20:55	☉	□	♊	14 8:18
16 15:07	☉	△	♋	16 20:51
18 16:55	♀	△	♌	19 8:01
20 20:45	♆	✶	♍	21 16:43
23 20:33	♀	☍	♎	23 23:01
25 19:21	☿	△	♏	26 3:31
28 5:57	☿	□	♐	28 6:49

☽ Phases & Eclipses

Dy Hr Mn		
1 5:11	☾	9♎58
7 20:10	●	16♑44
15 0:23	☽	24♈02
23 4:47	○	2♌22
30 15:14	☾	9♏56
6 7:54	●	16♒43
13 20:55	☽	24♉21
21 21:12	○	2♍26
28 22:59	☾	9♐33

Astro Data

1 January 1951
Julian Day # 18628
SVP 5♓56'36"
GC 26♐09.3 ⚴ 3♑08.3
Eris 6♈36.1 ⚵ 24♏20.9
⚷ 26♐09.8 ⚶ 6♉41.5
☽ Mean ☊ 22♓45.5

1 February 1951
Julian Day # 18659
SVP 5♓56'30"
GC 26♐09.4 ⚴ 15♑21.7
Eris 6♈44.0 ⚵ 2♐33.8
⚷ 29♐20.1 ⚶ 11♉20.3
☽ Mean ☊ 21♓07.1

March 1951 LONGITUDE

Day	Sid.Time	☉	0 hr ☽	Noon ☽	True ☊	☿	♀	♂	⚳	♃	♄	♅	♆	♇
1 Th	22 33 56	10♓05 35	10♐08 46	17♐15 08	19♓03.1	1♓40.6	5♈35.1	29♓40.6	13♒46.4	17♓51.4	0♎26.4	5♋28.6	19♎07.4	18♌09.5
2 F	22 37 53	11 05 48	24 22 07	1♑29 21	19R 02.7	3 26.8	6 49.1	0♈27.0	14 09.2	18 05.9	0R 22.2	5R 28.0	19R 06.2	18R 08.2
3 Sa	22 41 49	12 06 00	8♑36 32	15 43 16	19 02.0	5 14.2	8 03.0	1 13.3	14 31.9	18 20.4	0 17.8	5 27.4	19 05.0	18 06.9
4 Su	22 45 46	13 06 09	22 49 09	29 53 46	19 01.3	7 02.6	9 16.9	1 59.7	14 54.5	18 34.9	0 13.4	5 26.8	19 03.7	18 05.6
5 M	22 49 42	14 06 17	6♒56 40	13♒57 24	19 00.6	8 52.0	10 30.8	2 45.9	15 17.1	18 49.4	0 09.0	5 26.3	19 02.5	18 04.3
6 Tu	22 53 39	15 06 24	20 55 34	27 50 43	19 00.2	10 42.6	11 44.6	3 32.2	15 39.6	19 04.0	0 04.5	5 25.8	19 01.2	18 03.0
7 W	22 57 36	16 06 28	4♓42 28	11♓30 30	19D 00.0	12 34.2	12 58.4	4 18.4	16 02.1	19 18.5	0 00.0	5 25.4	18 59.9	18 01.8
8 Th	23 01 32	17 06 31	18 14 31	24 54 18	19 00.0	14 26.8	14 12.1	5 04.6	16 24.5	19 33.0	29♍55.5	5 25.1	18 58.5	18 00.5
9 F	23 05 29	18 06 32	1♈29 41	8♈00 36	19R 00.1	16 20.5	15 25.8	5 50.8	16 46.9	19 47.6	29 50.9	5 24.8	18 57.2	17 59.3
10 Sa	23 09 25	19 06 30	14 27 03	20 49 06	19 00.1	18 15.1	16 39.4	6 36.9	17 09.2	20 02.1	29 46.3	5 24.5	18 55.8	17 58.1
11 Su	23 13 22	20 06 27	27 06 53	3♉20 39	19 00.0	20 10.7	17 53.0	7 22.9	17 31.5	20 16.7	29 41.7	5 24.4	18 54.4	17 56.9
12 M	23 17 18	21 06 22	9♉30 41	15 37 20	18 59.8	22 07.3	19 06.5	8 09.0	17 53.7	20 31.2	29 37.1	5 24.2	18 53.0	17 55.7
13 Tu	23 21 15	22 06 14	21 41 00	27 42 08	18 59.5	24 04.6	20 20.0	8 54.9	18 15.8	20 45.7	29 32.4	5D 24.1	18 51.6	17 54.5
14 W	23 25 11	23 06 04	3♊41 15	9♊38 51	18 59.2	26 02.7	21 33.4	9 40.9	18 37.9	21 00.3	29 27.7	5 24.1	18 50.2	17 53.4
15 Th	23 29 08	24 05 52	15 35 31	21 31 48	18D 59.1	28 01.4	22 46.8	10 26.8	18 59.9	21 14.8	29 23.0	5 24.1	18 48.7	17 52.3
16 F	23 33 05	25 05 38	27 28 18	3♋25 37	18 59.2	0♈00.6	24 00.1	11 12.6	19 21.9	21 29.4	29 18.3	5 24.2	18 47.3	17 51.2
17 Sa	23 37 01	26 05 22	9♋24 18	15 24 58	18 59.5	2 00.1	25 13.4	11 58.5	19 43.8	21 43.9	29 13.6	5 24.4	18 45.8	17 50.1
18 Su	23 40 58	27 05 03	21 28 09	27 34 22	19 00.2	3 59.7	26 26.6	12 44.2	20 05.6	21 58.4	29 08.9	5 24.6	18 44.3	17 49.0
19 M	23 44 54	28 04 42	3♌44 07	9♌57 51	19 01.1	5 59.2	27 39.7	13 30.0	20 27.4	22 12.9	29 04.2	5 24.8	18 42.8	17 47.9
20 Tu	23 48 51	29 04 19	16 15 56	22 38 41	19 02.0	7 58.3	28 52.8	14 15.6	20 49.1	22 27.4	28 59.4	5 25.1	18 41.3	17 46.9
21 W	23 52 47	0♈03 54	29 06 21	5♍39 06	19 02.7	9 56.8	0♉05.8	15 01.3	21 10.7	22 41.9	28 54.7	5 25.5	18 39.8	17 45.9
22 Th	23 56 44	1 03 26	12♍16 58	18 59 56	19R 03.0	11 54.3	1 18.8	15 46.9	21 32.2	22 56.3	28 50.0	5 25.9	18 38.2	17 44.9
23 F	0 00 40	2 02 57	25 47 51	2♎40 29	19 02.7	13 50.4	2 31.7	16 32.4	21 53.7	23 10.8	28 45.2	5 26.3	18 36.6	17 43.9
24 Sa	0 04 37	3 02 25	9♎37 31	16 38 29	19 01.7	15 44.8	3 44.5	17 17.9	22 15.1	23 25.2	28 40.5	5 26.8	18 35.1	17 43.0
25 Su	0 08 33	4 01 51	23 42 55	0♏50 14	19 00.0	17 37.0	4 57.3	18 03.3	22 36.5	23 39.6	28 35.8	5 27.4	18 33.5	17 42.0
26 M	0 12 30	5 01 16	7♏59 49	15 11 02	18 58.0	19 26.7	6 10.0	18 48.8	22 57.8	23 54.0	28 31.1	5 28.0	18 31.9	17 41.1
27 Tu	0 16 27	6 00 39	22 23 14	29 35 47	18 55.8	21 13.3	7 22.6	19 34.1	23 19.0	24 08.4	28 26.5	5 28.7	18 30.3	17 40.2
28 W	0 20 23	7 00 00	6♐48 07	13♐59 40	18 54.1	22 56.6	8 35.2	20 19.4	23 40.1	24 22.8	28 21.8	5 29.4	18 28.7	17 39.4
29 Th	0 24 20	7 59 19	21 09 58	28 18 35	18D 53.0	24 36.0	9 47.8	21 04.7	24 01.1	24 37.1	28 17.2	5 30.2	18 27.1	17 38.5
30 F	0 28 16	8 58 37	5♑25 10	12♑29 27	18 52.8	26 11.3	11 00.2	21 50.0	24 22.1	24 51.5	28 12.5	5 31.0	18 25.5	17 37.7
31 Sa	0 32 13	9 57 53	19 31 13	26 30 18	18 53.4	27 41.9	12 12.6	22 35.1	24 43.0	25 05.8	28 08.0	5 31.9	18 23.9	17 36.9

April 1951 LONGITUDE

Day	Sid.Time	☉	0 hr ☽	Noon ☽	True ☊	☿	♀	♂	⚳	♃	♄	♅	♆	♇
1 Su	0 36 09	10♈57 07	3♒26 35	10♒19 58	18♓54.7	29♈07.6	13♉25.0	23♈20.3	25♒03.8	25♓20.0	28♍03.4	5♋32.8	18♎22.3	17♌36.2
2 M	0 40 06	11 56 19	17 10 24	23 57 51	18 56.2	0♉28.0	14 37.2	24 05.4	25 24.5	25 34.3	27R 58.9	5 33.8	18R 20.6	17R 35.4
3 Tu	0 44 02	12 55 29	0♓42 16	7♓23 38	18R 57.4	1 42.9	15 49.4	24 50.4	25 45.1	25 48.5	27 54.4	5 34.9	18 19.0	17 34.7
4 W	0 47 59	13 54 38	14 01 55	20 37 06	18 57.8	2 52.1	17 01.6	25 35.4	26 05.7	26 02.7	27 49.9	5 35.9	18 17.3	17 34.0
5 Th	0 51 56	14 53 44	27 09 08	3♈38 00	18 57.0	3 55.2	18 13.6	26 20.4	26 26.1	26 16.9	27 45.5	5 37.1	18 15.7	17 33.3
6 F	0 55 52	15 52 49	10♈03 41	16 26 12	18 54.8	4 52.1	19 25.6	27 05.3	26 46.5	26 31.0	27 41.1	5 38.3	18 14.0	17 32.6
7 Sa	0 59 49	16 51 51	22 45 31	29 01 43	18 51.2	5 42.7	20 37.6	27 50.2	27 06.7	26 45.1	27 36.7	5 39.5	18 12.4	17 32.0
8 Su	1 03 45	17 50 51	5♉14 52	11♉25 03	18 46.6	6 26.9	21 49.4	28 35.0	27 26.9	26 59.2	27 32.4	5 40.8	18 10.7	17 31.4
9 M	1 07 42	18 49 50	17 32 26	23 37 14	18 41.3	7 04.4	23 01.2	29 19.7	27 47.0	27 13.2	27 28.2	5 42.1	18 09.1	17 30.8
10 Tu	1 11 38	19 48 46	29 39 39	5♊40 00	18 36.0	7 35.4	24 12.9	0♉04.4	28 07.0	27 27.2	27 24.0	5 43.5	18 07.4	17 30.3
11 W	1 15 35	20 47 40	11♊38 38	17 35 55	18 31.3	7 59.7	25 24.5	0 49.1	28 26.9	27 41.2	27 19.8	5 45.0	18 05.8	17 29.8
12 Th	1 19 31	21 46 32	23 32 19	29 28 16	18 27.6	8 17.4	26 36.1	1 33.7	28 46.6	27 55.1	27 15.7	5 46.5	18 04.2	17 29.3
13 F	1 23 28	22 45 22	5♋24 19	11♋21 00	18 25.4	8 28.5	27 47.6	2 18.3	29 06.3	28 08.9	27 11.7	5 48.0	18 02.5	17 28.8
14 Sa	1 27 25	23 44 09	17 18 53	23 18 35	18D 24.6	8R 33.2	28 58.9	3 02.8	29 25.9	28 22.8	27 07.7	5 49.6	18 00.9	17 28.4
15 Su	1 31 21	24 42 54	29 20 41	5♌25 49	18 25.2	8 31.6	0♊10.2	3 47.3	29 45.4	28 36.6	27 03.8	5 51.2	17 59.2	17 27.9
16 M	1 35 18	25 41 37	11♌34 35	17 47 34	18 26.6	8 24.0	1 21.4	4 31.7	0♓04.7	28 50.3	26 59.9	5 52.9	17 57.6	17 27.6
17 Tu	1 39 14	26 40 17	24 05 20	0♍28 21	18 28.2	8 10.6	2 32.6	5 16.0	0 24.0	29 04.0	26 56.1	5 54.6	17 56.0	17 27.2
18 W	1 43 11	27 38 55	6♍57 06	13 31 54	18R 29.2	7 51.9	3 43.6	6 00.3	0 43.1	29 17.7	26 52.4	5 56.4	17 54.3	17 26.9
19 Th	1 47 07	28 37 32	20 13 02	27 00 36	18 29.0	7 28.2	4 54.5	6 44.6	1 02.1	29 31.3	26 48.7	5 58.2	17 52.7	17 26.5
20 F	1 51 04	29 36 05	3♎54 37	10♎54 53	18 27.0	7 00.1	6 05.4	7 28.8	1 21.1	29 44.8	26 45.1	6 00.1	17 51.1	17 26.3
21 Sa	1 55 00	0♉34 37	18 01 05	25 12 43	18 23.2	6 28.2	7 16.1	8 12.9	1 39.9	29 58.3	26 41.6	6 02.0	17 49.5	17 26.0
22 Su	1 58 57	1 33 08	2♏29 05	9♏49 25	18 17.7	5 53.1	8 26.7	8 57.0	1 58.5	0♈11.8	26 38.1	6 04.0	17 47.9	17 25.8
23 M	2 02 54	2 31 36	17 12 44	24 38 02	18 11.1	5 15.4	9 37.3	9 41.0	2 17.1	0 25.2	26 34.8	6 06.0	17 46.3	17 25.6
24 Tu	2 06 50	3 30 03	2♐04 15	9♐30 19	18 04.3	4 36.0	10 47.8	10 25.0	2 35.6	0 38.6	26 31.5	6 08.0	17 44.8	17 25.4
25 W	2 10 47	4 28 28	16 55 12	24 17 57	17 58.2	3 55.6	11 58.1	11 09.0	2 53.9	0 51.9	26 28.2	6 10.1	17 43.2	17 25.3
26 Th	2 14 43	5 26 51	1♑37 46	8♑53 57	17 53.7	3 14.9	13 08.4	11 52.9	3 12.1	1 05.1	26 25.1	6 12.2	17 41.6	17 25.2
27 F	2 18 40	6 25 13	16 05 59	23 13 29	17 51.0	2 34.6	14 18.5	12 36.7	3 30.2	1 18.3	26 22.0	6 14.4	17 40.1	17 25.1
28 Sa	2 22 36	7 23 33	0♒16 14	7♒14 06	17D 50.2	1 55.6	15 28.6	13 20.5	3 48.1	1 31.4	26 19.0	6 16.6	17 38.6	17 25.0
29 Su	2 26 33	8 21 52	14 07 08	20 55 26	17 50.7	1 18.3	16 38.6	14 04.3	4 05.9	1 44.5	26 16.1	6 18.8	17 37.0	17D 25.0
30 M	2 30 29	9 20 09	27 39 10	4♓18 34	17 51.8	0 43.5	17 48.4	14 48.0	4 23.6	1 57.5	26 13.3	6 21.1	17 35.5	17 25.0

Astro Data	Dy Hr Mn
♃⊼♇	2 15:27
♂0N	3 19:47
♃⊼♆	6 7:45
☽0N	8 17:45
♅ D	14 10:41
☿0N	17 11:16
☉0N	21 10:26
☽0S	23 4:00
☽0N	5 1:43
♃☍♄	10 7:44
☿ R	14 17:51
☽0S	19 13:46
♇ D	30 5:20

Planet Ingress		Dy Hr Mn
♂	♈	1 22:03
♄	♍R	7 12:12
☿	♈	16 11:53
♀	♉	21 10:05
☉	♈	21 10:26
☿	♉	2 3:27
♂	♉	10 9:37
♀	♊	15 8:33
⚳	♓	16 6:08
☉	♉	20 21:48
♃	♈	21 14:57

Last Aspect Dy Hr Mn			☽ Ingress	Dy Hr Mn
1 15:09	♆	⚹	♑	2 9:29
3 17:40	♆	□	♒	4 12:11
5 20:44	♆	△	♓	6 15:45
8 21:05	♄	☍	♈	8 21:16
10 8:26	♆	☍	♉	11 5:33
13 15:39	♄	△	♊	13 16:36
16 3:45	♄	□	♋	16 5:06
18 15:04	♄	⚹	♌	18 16:44
21 0:47	♀	△	♍	21 1:39
23 5:13	♄	☌	♎	23 7:21
24 15:18	♆	☌	♏	25 10:36
27 10:05	♄	⚹	♐	27 12:40
29 11:58	♄	□	♑	29 14:51
31 14:48	♄	△	♒	31 18:02

Last Aspect Dy Hr Mn			☽ Ingress	Dy Hr Mn
2 12:14	♂	⚹	♓	2 22:44
5 1:11	♄	☍	♈	5 5:16
7 9:34	♂	☌	♉	7 13:52
9 19:36	♄	△	♊	10 0:41
12 8:48	♃	□	♋	12 13:04
15 0:31	♀	⚹	♌	15 1:18
17 4:17	☉	△	♍	17 11:07
19 16:28	♃	☍	♎	19 17:13
20 23:42	♆	☌	♏	21 19:55
23 15:08	♄	⚹	♐	23 20:40
25 15:32	♄	□	♑	25 21:19
27 17:19	♄	△	♒	27 23:32
29 6:10	♆	△	♓	30 4:13

☽ Phases & Eclipses Dy Hr Mn		
7 20:51	●	16♓29
7 20:53:10	●	A 00'59"
15 17:40	☽	24♊20
23 10:50	○	2♎00
23 10:37	◑	A 0.642
30 5:35	☾	8♑43
6 10:52	●	15♈50
14 12:56	☽	23♋46
21 21:30	○	0♏58
28 12:18	☾	7♒24

Astro Data

1 March 1951
Julian Day # 18687
SVP 5♓56'26"
GC 26♐09.4 ⚴ 25♑29.0
Eris 6♈59.1 ⚵ 7♐43.2
⚷ 1♑29.7 ⚶ 19♉11.1
☽ Mean ☊ 19♓38.1

1 April 1951
Julian Day # 18718
SVP 5♓56'22"
GC 26♐09.5 ⚴ 4♒58.7
Eris 7♈20.3 ⚵ 9♐35.0R
⚷ 2♑42.6 ⚶ 0♊12.4
☽ Mean ☊ 17♓59.6

LONGITUDE

May 1951

Day	Sid.Time	☉	0 hr ☽	Noon ☽	True ☊	☿	♀	♂	⚴	♃	♄	♅	♆	♇
1 Tu	2 34 26	10♉18 24	10♓53 54	17♓25 25	17♓52.4	0♉11.6	18♊58.2	15♉31.6	4♓41.2	2♈10.4	26♍10.6	6♋23.5	17♎34.0	17♌25.0
2 W	2 38 23	11 16 38	23 53 23	0♈18 04	17R51.6	29♈43.1	20 07.8	16 15.2	4 58.6	2 23.3	26R07.9	6 25.8	17R32.5	17 25.0
3 Th	2 42 19	12 14 51	6♈39 42	12 58 29	17 48.7	29R18.5	21 17.4	16 58.7	5 15.9	2 36.1	26 05.3	6 28.2	17 31.1	17 25.1
4 F	2 46 16	13 13 02	19 14 38	25 28 16	17 43.3	28 58.0	22 26.8	17 42.2	5 33.0	2 48.9	26 02.9	6 30.7	17 29.6	17 25.2
5 Sa	2 50 12	14 11 11	1♉39 33	7♉48 37	17 35.5	28 41.8	23 36.1	18 25.7	5 50.0	3 01.5	26 00.5	6 33.2	17 28.2	17 25.4
6 Su	2 54 09	15 09 19	13 55 34	20 00 31	17 25.7	28 30.1	24 45.3	19 09.1	6 06.8	3 14.1	25 58.2	6 35.7	17 26.7	17 25.5
7 M	2 58 05	16 07 25	26 03 35	2♊04 55	17 14.7	28D23.1	25 54.4	19 52.4	6 23.5	3 26.7	25 56.0	6 38.3	17 25.3	17 25.7
8 Tu	3 02 02	17 05 29	8♊04 40	14 03 02	17 03.5	28 20.8	27 03.3	20 35.7	6 40.0	3 39.1	25 53.9	6 40.9	17 23.9	17 25.9
9 W	3 05 58	18 03 32	20 00 12	25 56 28	16 53.0	28 23.2	28 12.2	21 19.0	6 56.4	3 51.5	25 51.9	6 43.5	17 22.6	17 26.2
10 Th	3 09 55	19 01 32	1♋52 07	7♋47 31	16 44.1	28 30.3	29 20.9	22 02.1	7 12.6	4 03.8	25 50.0	6 46.2	17 21.2	17 26.5
11 F	3 13 52	19 59 31	13 43 04	19 39 11	16 37.5	28 41.9	0♋29.4	22 45.3	7 28.7	4 16.1	25 48.1	6 48.9	17 19.9	17 26.8
12 Sa	3 17 48	20 57 29	25 36 24	1♌35 13	16 33.3	28 58.2	1 37.9	23 28.4	7 44.6	4 28.2	25 46.4	6 51.6	17 18.6	17 27.1
13 Su	3 21 45	21 55 24	7♌36 13	13 40 00	16D31.4	29 18.9	2 46.2	24 11.4	8 00.3	4 40.3	25 44.8	6 54.4	17 17.3	17 27.5
14 M	3 25 41	22 53 18	19 47 11	25 58 24	16 31.1	29 43.9	3 54.3	24 54.4	8 15.8	4 52.3	25 43.3	6 57.2	17 16.0	17 27.8
15 Tu	3 29 38	23 51 09	2♍14 17	8♍35 26	16R31.5	0♉13.1	5 02.3	25 37.3	8 31.2	5 04.2	25 41.8	7 00.0	17 14.7	17 28.3
16 W	3 33 34	24 48 59	15 02 26	21 35 49	16 31.6	0 46.4	6 10.2	26 20.2	8 46.5	5 16.0	25 40.5	7 02.9	17 13.5	17 28.7
17 Th	3 37 31	25 46 48	28 16 00	5♎03 18	16 30.2	1 23.6	7 17.9	27 03.0	9 01.5	5 27.7	25 39.3	7 05.8	17 12.3	17 29.2
18 F	3 41 27	26 44 34	11♎57 55	18 59 50	16 26.7	2 04.7	8 25.4	27 45.7	9 16.4	5 39.4	25 38.1	7 08.7	17 11.1	17 29.7
19 Sa	3 45 24	27 42 19	26 08 55	3♏24 43	16 20.7	2 49.5	9 32.8	28 28.5	9 31.1	5 50.9	25 37.1	7 11.7	17 09.9	17 30.2
20 Su	3 49 21	28 40 03	10♏46 40	18 13 55	16 12.4	3 37.9	10 40.0	29 11.1	9 45.6	6 02.4	25 36.2	7 14.7	17 08.8	17 30.7
21 M	3 53 17	29 37 45	25 45 25	3♐19 58	16 02.5	4 29.8	11 47.1	29 53.7	9 59.9	6 13.8	25 35.4	7 17.7	17 07.7	17 31.3
22 Tu	3 57 14	0♊35 26	10♐56 16	18 32 56	15 52.2	5 25.0	12 54.0	0♊36.3	10 14.1	6 25.1	25 34.6	7 20.7	17 06.6	17 31.9
23 W	4 01 10	1 33 06	26 08 35	3♑41 55	15 42.7	6 23.5	14 00.7	1 18.8	10 28.0	6 36.3	25 34.0	7 23.8	17 05.5	17 32.5
24 Th	4 05 07	2 30 44	11♑11 46	18 37 08	15 35.1	7 25.1	15 07.2	2 01.3	10 41.8	6 47.4	25 33.5	7 26.9	17 04.4	17 33.2
25 F	4 09 03	3 28 22	25 57 13	3♒11 26	15 29.9	8 29.8	16 13.6	2 43.7	10 55.3	6 58.4	25 33.1	7 30.0	17 03.4	17 33.9
26 Sa	4 13 00	4 25 59	10♒19 24	17 20 56	15 27.2	9 37.6	17 19.8	3 26.0	11 08.7	7 09.3	25 32.8	7 33.2	17 02.4	17 34.6
27 Su	4 16 57	5 23 34	24 16 03	1♓04 53	15D26.3	10 48.2	18 25.8	4 08.4	11 21.9	7 20.1	25 32.5	7 36.3	17 01.4	17 35.3
28 M	4 20 53	6 21 09	7♓47 41	14 24 48	15R26.3	12 01.8	19 31.6	4 50.6	11 34.8	7 30.8	25D32.4	7 39.5	17 00.5	17 36.1
29 Tu	4 24 50	7 18 43	20 56 39	27 23 40	15 26.0	13 18.1	20 37.2	5 32.8	11 47.6	7 41.4	25 32.4	7 42.8	16 59.5	17 36.9
30 W	4 28 46	8 16 16	3♈46 18	10♈05 00	15 24.1	14 37.3	21 42.6	6 15.0	12 00.1	7 51.9	25 32.5	7 46.0	16 58.6	17 37.7
31 Th	4 32 43	9 13 48	16 20 13	22 32 20	15 19.9	15 59.1	22 47.8	6 57.1	12 12.4	8 02.3	25 32.7	7 49.3	16 57.8	17 38.5

LONGITUDE

June 1951

Day	Sid.Time	☉	0 hr ☽	Noon ☽	True ☊	☿	♀	♂	⚴	♃	♄	♅	♆	♇
1 F	4 36 39	10♊11 19	28♈41 45	4♉48 48	15♓12.8	17♉23.7	23♋52.8	7♊39.2	12♓24.6	8♈12.6	25♍33.0	7♋52.5	16♎56.9	17♌39.4
2 Sa	4 40 36	11 08 49	10♉53 46	16 56 56	15R02.9	18 50.9	24 57.6	8 21.2	12 36.4	8 22.7	25 33.4	7 55.9	16R56.1	17 40.2
3 Su	4 44 32	12 06 19	22 58 32	28 58 46	14 50.7	20 20.8	26 02.1	9 03.2	12 48.1	8 32.8	25 33.9	7 59.2	16 55.3	17 41.2
4 M	4 48 29	13 03 47	4♊57 49	10♊55 50	14 37.0	21 53.2	27 06.5	9 45.1	12 59.5	8 42.8	25 34.5	8 02.5	16 54.6	17 42.1
5 Tu	4 52 26	14 01 15	16 52 59	22 49 26	14 22.9	23 28.3	28 10.6	10 27.0	13 10.7	8 52.6	25 35.2	8 05.9	16 53.8	17 43.1
6 W	4 56 22	14 58 42	28 45 22	4♋40 58	14 09.7	25 06.0	29 14.5	11 08.9	13 21.7	9 02.3	25 36.0	8 09.3	16 53.1	17 44.0
7 Th	5 00 19	15 56 08	10♋36 26	16 32 03	13 58.2	26 46.3	0♌18.1	11 50.6	13 32.4	9 11.9	25 36.9	8 12.7	16 52.4	17 45.0
8 F	5 04 15	16 53 33	22 28 04	28 24 51	13 49.3	28 29.1	1 21.5	12 32.4	13 42.8	9 21.4	25 37.9	8 16.1	16 51.8	17 46.1
9 Sa	5 08 12	17 50 56	4♌22 45	10♌22 12	13 43.3	0♊14.5	2 24.6	13 14.1	13 53.1	9 30.7	25 39.0	8 19.5	16 51.2	17 47.1
10 Su	5 12 08	18 48 19	16 23 39	22 27 36	13 39.9	2 02.5	3 27.4	13 55.7	14 03.0	9 39.9	25 40.3	8 23.0	16 50.6	17 48.2
11 M	5 16 05	19 45 41	28 34 38	4♍45 17	13D38.6	3 52.9	4 30.0	14 37.3	14 12.8	9 49.0	25 41.6	8 26.5	16 50.0	17 49.3
12 Tu	5 20 01	20 43 01	11♍00 09	17 19 50	13R38.5	5 45.7	5 32.3	15 18.8	14 22.2	9 58.0	25 43.0	8 29.9	16 49.5	17 50.4
13 W	5 23 58	21 40 21	23 44 56	0♎16 00	13 38.3	7 41.0	6 34.2	16 00.3	14 31.4	10 06.9	25 44.5	8 33.4	16 49.0	17 51.6
14 Th	5 27 55	22 37 39	6♎53 33	13 38 00	13 37.0	9 38.5	7 35.9	16 41.7	14 40.4	10 15.6	25 46.1	8 36.9	16 48.5	17 52.7
15 F	5 31 51	23 34 57	20 29 40	27 28 45	13 33.7	11 38.3	8 37.2	17 23.1	14 49.0	10 24.2	25 47.8	8 40.4	16 48.1	17 53.9
16 Sa	5 35 48	24 32 14	4♏35 13	11♏48 54	13 28.0	13 40.2	9 38.3	18 04.5	14 57.4	10 32.6	25 49.6	8 44.0	16 47.7	17 55.1
17 Su	5 39 44	25 29 30	19 09 21	26 35 56	13 19.9	15 44.0	10 39.0	18 45.7	15 05.6	10 40.9	25 51.5	8 47.5	16 47.3	17 56.3
18 M	5 43 41	26 26 45	4♐07 43	11♐43 37	13 10.1	17 49.6	11 39.3	19 27.0	15 13.4	10 49.1	25 53.6	8 51.1	16 47.0	17 57.6
19 Tu	5 47 37	27 24 00	19 22 21	27 02 29	12 59.8	19 56.8	12 39.3	20 08.2	15 21.0	10 57.2	25 55.7	8 54.6	16 46.7	17 58.9
20 W	5 51 34	28 21 15	4♑42 34	12♑21 08	12 50.2	22 05.4	13 38.9	20 49.3	15 28.3	11 05.1	25 57.9	8 58.2	16 46.4	18 00.2
21 Th	5 55 30	29 18 29	19 56 49	27 28 22	12 42.4	24 15.1	14 38.1	21 30.4	15 35.4	11 12.9	26 00.2	9 01.8	16 46.1	18 01.5
22 F	5 59 27	0♋15 42	4♒54 44	12♒15 07	12 37.1	26 25.6	15 37.0	22 11.5	15 42.1	11 20.5	26 02.5	9 05.4	16 45.9	18 02.8
23 Sa	6 03 24	1 12 56	19 28 53	26 35 42	12 34.2	28 36.7	16 35.4	22 52.5	15 48.5	11 28.0	26 05.0	9 08.9	16 45.7	18 04.2
24 Su	6 07 20	2 10 09	3♓35 22	10♓27 56	12D33.3	0♋48.1	17 33.5	23 33.5	15 54.7	11 35.3	26 07.6	9 12.5	16 45.6	18 05.5
25 M	6 11 17	3 07 22	17 13 34	23 52 36	12R33.5	2 59.5	18 31.1	24 14.4	16 00.5	11 42.5	26 10.3	9 16.1	16 45.4	18 06.9
26 Tu	6 15 13	4 04 35	0♈25 24	6♈52 29	12 33.7	5 10.7	19 28.3	24 55.3	16 06.0	11 49.5	26 13.0	9 19.7	16 45.3	18 08.3
27 W	6 19 10	5 01 48	13 14 21	19 31 31	12 32.7	7 21.3	20 25.0	25 36.1	16 11.2	11 56.4	26 15.9	9 23.4	16 45.3	18 09.7
28 Th	6 23 06	5 59 01	25 44 33	1♉53 59	12 29.8	9 31.2	21 21.3	26 16.9	16 16.2	12 03.2	26 18.8	9 27.0	16D45.3	18 11.2
29 F	6 27 03	6 56 14	8♉00 18	14 04 01	12 24.4	11 40.1	22 17.1	26 57.7	16 20.8	12 09.7	26 21.9	9 30.6	16 45.3	18 12.6
30 Sa	6 30 59	7 53 28	20 05 33	26 05 20	12 16.5	13 47.8	23 12.4	27 38.4	16 25.0	12 16.2	26 25.0	9 34.2	16 45.3	18 14.1

Astro Data	Dy Hr Mn
☽0N	2 7:33
♃⚼♇	2 15:16
♃0N	3 4:38
♆⚹♇	7 6:22
☿ D	8 11:50
☽0S	16 23:02
♄ D	29 3:37
☽0N	29 12:18
♃□♅	29 16:25
☽0S	13 6:29
☽0N	25 17:50
♆ D	28 21:51

Planet Ingress		Dy Hr Mn
☿	♈R	1 21:25
♀	♋	11 1:41
☿	♉	15 1:40
♂	♊	21 15:32
☉	♊	21 21:15
♀	♌	7 5:10
☿	♊	9 8:43
☉	♋	22 5:25
☿	♋	24 3:13

Last Aspect Dy Hr Mn			☽ Ingress	Dy Hr Mn
2 4:13	♄	☍	♈	2 11:26
4 18:37	☿	☌	♉	4 20:47
6 23:47	♄	△	♊	7 7:51
9 17:04	♀	☌	♋	9 20:13
12 6:37	☿	□	♌	12 8:49
14 19:30	☿	△	♍	14 19:44
16 21:02	♂	△	♎	17 3:05
18 9:27	♇	⚹	♏	19 6:23
21 6:18	♂	☍	♐	21 6:44
22 23:06	♄	□	♑	23 6:07
24 23:21	♄	△	♒	25 6:41
26 12:24	♇	☍	♓	27 10:05
29 8:32	♄	☍	♈	29 16:53

Last Aspect Dy Hr Mn			☽ Ingress	Dy Hr Mn
31 12:33	♀	□	♉	1 2:33
3 5:32	♀	⚹	♊	3 14:03
5 17:36	♄	□	♋	6 2:31
8 12:10	☿	⚹	♌	8 15:12
10 4:10	☉	⚹	♍	11 2:47
13 3:40	♄	☌	♎	13 11:31
15 4:50	☉	△	♏	15 16:17
17 10:49	♄	⚹	♐	17 17:26
19 12:36	☉	☍	♑	19 16:38
21 9:39	♄	△	♒	21 16:04
23 16:05	☿	△	♓	23 17:49
25 16:12	♄	☍	♈	25 23:13
28 0:25	♂	⚹	♉	28 8:17
30 12:40	♄	△	♊	30 19:51

☽ Phases & Eclipses Dy Hr Mn	
6 1:36	● 14♉44
14 5:32	☽ 22♌38
21 5:45	○ 29♏23
27 20:17	☾ 5♓43
4 16:40	● 13♊15
12 18:52	☽ 20♍59
19 12:36	○ 27♐25
26 6:21	☾ 3♈51

Astro Data

1 May 1951
Julian Day # 18748
SVP 5♓56'19"
GC 26♐09.6 ⚳ 11♒27.2
Eris 7♈40.3 ⚵ 6♐33.4R
⚷ 2♑31.1R ⚶ 12♊11.1
☽ Mean ☊ 16♓24.3

1 June 1951
Julian Day # 18779
SVP 5♓56'14"
GC 26♐09.6 ⚳ 13♒49.6R
Eris 7♈55.6 ⚵ 29♏58.6R
⚷ 1♑05.6R ⚶ 25♊17.1
☽ Mean ☊ 14♓45.8

July 1951

LONGITUDE

Day	Sid.Time	☉	0 hr ☽	Noon ☽	True ☊	☿	♀	♂	⚳	♃	♄	♅	♆	♇
1 Su	6 34 56	8♋50 41	2♊03 42	8♊01 01	12♓07.6	15♋54.2	24♌07.2	28♊19.0	16♓29.0	12♈22.4	26♍28.2	9♋37.8	16♎45.4	18♌15.6
2 M	6 38 53	9 47 54	13 57 34	19 53 36	11R55.4	17 59.1	25 01.5	28 59.7	16 32.6	12 28.5	26 31.5	9 41.4	16 45.5	18 17.1
3 Tu	6 42 49	10 45 08	25 49 22	1♋45 04	11 43.8	20 02.5	25 55.2	29 40.2	16 35.9	12 34.5	26 34.9	9 45.1	16 45.6	18 18.6
4 W	6 46 46	11 42 21	7♋40 54	13 37 03	11 32.8	22 04.1	26 48.4	0♋20.8	16 38.9	12 40.3	26 38.4	9 48.7	16 45.8	18 20.2
5 Th	6 50 42	12 39 35	19 33 44	25 31 08	11 23.4	24 03.9	27 41.0	1 01.3	16 41.5	12 45.9	26 41.9	9 52.3	16 46.0	18 21.7
6 F	6 54 39	13 36 48	1♌29 28	7♌28 58	11 16.2	26 01.9	28 32.9	1 41.7	16 43.8	12 51.3	26 45.6	9 55.9	16 46.2	18 23.3
7 Sa	6 58 35	14 34 01	13 29 54	19 32 33	11 11.5	27 58.0	29 24.3	2 22.1	16 45.7	12 56.6	26 49.3	9 59.6	16 46.5	18 24.9
8 Su	7 02 32	15 31 14	25 37 16	1♍44 23	11D09.2	29 52.2	0♍14.9	3 02.5	16 47.4	13 01.7	26 53.1	10 03.2	16 46.8	18 26.5
9 M	7 06 29	16 28 27	7♍54 20	14 07 31	11 08.7	1♌44.5	1 04.9	3 42.8	16 48.6	13 06.6	26 57.0	10 06.8	16 47.1	18 28.1
10 Tu	7 10 25	17 25 40	20 24 25	26 45 28	11 09.5	3 34.8	1 54.2	4 23.0	16 49.5	13 11.4	27 01.0	10 10.4	16 47.4	18 29.7
11 W	7 14 22	18 22 53	3♎11 11	9♎42 01	11R10.4	5 23.2	2 42.8	5 03.3	16 50.1	13 16.0	27 05.1	10 14.0	16 47.8	18 31.4
12 Th	7 18 18	19 20 05	16 18 24	23 00 44	11 10.6	7 09.7	3 30.5	5 43.4	16R50.3	13 20.4	27 09.2	10 17.6	16 48.2	18 33.0
13 F	7 22 15	20 17 18	29 49 20	6♏44 25	11 09.4	8 54.1	4 17.5	6 23.6	16 50.2	13 24.6	27 13.5	10 21.1	16 48.7	18 34.7
14 Sa	7 26 11	21 14 31	13♏46 04	20 54 15	11 06.2	10 36.7	5 03.7	7 03.7	16 49.7	13 28.7	27 17.8	10 24.7	16 49.2	18 36.4
15 Su	7 30 08	22 11 44	28 08 41	5♐28 58	11 01.2	12 17.2	5 49.0	7 43.7	16 48.9	13 32.6	27 22.1	10 28.3	16 49.7	18 38.1
16 M	7 34 04	23 08 57	12♐54 25	20 24 14	10 54.9	13 55.9	6 33.4	8 23.7	16 47.7	13 36.3	27 26.6	10 31.9	16 50.3	18 39.8
17 Tu	7 38 01	24 06 10	27 57 23	5♑32 41	10 48.0	15 32.5	7 16.9	9 03.7	16 46.2	13 39.8	27 31.1	10 35.4	16 50.8	18 41.5
18 W	7 41 58	25 03 23	13♑08 53	20 44 40	10 41.6	17 07.2	7 59.4	9 43.6	16 44.3	13 43.1	27 35.7	10 39.0	16 51.5	18 43.2
19 Th	7 45 54	26 00 37	28 18 43	5♒49 48	10 36.4	18 40.0	8 40.9	10 23.5	16 42.1	13 46.3	27 40.4	10 42.5	16 52.1	18 45.0
20 F	7 49 51	26 57 51	13♒16 47	20 38 44	10 32.9	20 10.8	9 21.4	11 03.3	16 39.5	13 49.3	27 45.2	10 46.0	16 52.8	18 46.7
21 Sa	7 53 47	27 55 06	27 54 52	5♓04 37	10D31.4	21 39.6	10 00.8	11 43.1	16 36.5	13 52.0	27 50.0	10 49.5	16 53.5	18 48.5
22 Su	7 57 44	28 52 22	12♓07 35	19 03 37	10 31.6	23 06.4	10 39.1	12 22.9	16 33.2	13 54.6	27 54.9	10 53.0	16 54.2	18 50.2
23 M	8 01 40	29 49 38	25 52 42	2♈34 58	10 32.7	24 31.1	11 16.3	13 02.6	16 29.5	13 57.0	27 59.9	10 56.5	16 55.0	18 52.0
24 Tu	8 05 37	0♌46 55	9♈10 41	15 40 14	10 34.1	25 53.9	11 52.2	13 42.3	16 25.5	13 59.3	28 04.9	10 59.9	16 55.8	18 53.8
25 W	8 09 33	1 44 13	22 04 02	28 22 37	10R35.0	27 14.5	12 27.0	14 21.9	16 21.1	14 01.3	28 10.0	11 03.4	16 56.6	18 55.5
26 Th	8 13 30	2 41 32	4♉36 31	10♉46 16	10 34.7	28 33.0	13 00.4	15 01.5	16 16.3	14 03.1	28 15.2	11 06.8	16 57.5	18 57.3
27 F	8 17 27	3 38 52	16 52 27	22 55 37	10 32.9	29 49.4	13 32.5	15 41.1	16 11.2	14 04.7	28 20.4	11 10.3	16 58.4	18 59.1
28 Sa	8 21 23	4 36 13	28 56 20	4♊55 05	10 29.5	1♍03.5	14 03.2	16 20.6	16 05.8	14 06.2	28 25.7	11 13.7	16 59.3	19 01.0
29 Su	8 25 20	5 33 35	10♊52 23	16 48 40	10 24.8	2 15.3	14 32.5	17 00.1	16 00.0	14 07.4	28 31.1	11 17.0	17 00.2	19 02.8
30 M	8 29 16	6 30 58	22 44 24	28 39 57	10 19.1	3 24.8	15 00.3	17 39.6	15 53.9	14 08.5	28 36.5	11 20.4	17 01.2	19 04.6
31 Tu	8 33 13	7 28 22	4♋35 40	10♋31 52	10 13.2	4 31.8	15 26.5	18 19.0	15 47.4	14 09.3	28 42.0	11 23.8	17 02.2	19 06.4

August 1951

LONGITUDE

Day	Sid.Time	☉	0 hr ☽	Noon ☽	True ☊	☿	♀	♂	⚳	♃	♄	♅	♆	♇
1 W	8 37 09	8♌25 47	16♋28 51	22♋26 53	10♓07.6	5♍36.3	15♍51.2	18♋58.4	15♓40.5	14♈10.0	28♍47.6	11♋27.1	17♎03.3	19♌08.3
2 Th	8 41 06	9 23 13	28 26 11	4♌26 59	10R02.9	6 38.1	16 14.2	19 37.7	15R33.4	14 10.4	28 53.2	11 30.4	17 04.3	19 10.1
3 F	8 45 02	10 20 39	10♌29 29	16 33 51	9 59.4	7 37.2	16 35.4	20 17.0	15 25.9	14R10.7	28 58.9	11 33.7	17 05.4	19 12.0
4 Sa	8 48 59	11 18 07	22 40 18	28 49 01	9D57.5	8 33.5	16 54.9	20 56.3	15 18.0	14 10.8	29 04.6	11 37.0	17 06.5	19 13.8
5 Su	8 52 56	12 15 35	5♍00 11	11♍14 01	9 57.0	9 26.7	17 12.5	21 35.5	15 09.9	14 10.6	29 10.4	11 40.2	17 07.7	19 15.7
6 M	8 56 52	13 13 05	17 30 45	23 50 36	9 57.6	10 16.9	17 28.3	22 14.6	15 01.4	14 10.3	29 16.3	11 43.4	17 08.9	19 17.5
7 Tu	9 00 49	14 10 35	0♎13 48	6♎40 37	9 59.0	11 03.7	17 42.0	22 53.8	14 52.7	14 09.7	29 22.2	11 46.6	17 10.1	19 19.4
8 W	9 04 45	15 08 05	13 11 19	19 46 09	10 00.5	11 47.0	17 53.8	23 32.9	14 43.6	14 09.0	29 28.1	11 49.8	17 11.3	19 21.2
9 Th	9 08 42	16 05 37	26 25 21	3♏09 08	10 01.7	12 26.8	18 03.4	24 11.9	14 34.2	14 08.1	29 34.2	11 53.0	17 12.6	19 23.1
10 F	9 12 38	17 03 10	9♏57 41	16 51 06	10R02.2	13 02.7	18 10.9	24 51.0	14 24.6	14 06.9	29 40.2	11 56.1	17 13.9	19 24.9
11 Sa	9 16 35	18 00 43	23 49 26	0♐52 37	10 01.7	13 34.5	18 16.2	25 29.9	14 14.6	14 05.6	29 46.4	11 59.2	17 15.2	19 26.8
12 Su	9 20 31	18 58 17	8♐00 31	15 12 49	10 00.3	14 02.1	18R19.3	26 08.9	14 04.4	14 04.1	29 52.5	12 02.3	17 16.5	19 28.7
13 M	9 24 28	19 55 53	22 29 07	29 48 52	9 58.2	14 25.3	18 20.1	26 47.8	13 54.0	14 02.4	29 58.8	12 05.3	17 17.9	19 30.5
14 Tu	9 28 25	20 53 29	7♑11 23	14♑35 53	9 55.7	14 43.8	18 18.5	27 26.7	13 43.3	14 00.4	0♎05.0	12 08.3	17 19.3	19 32.4
15 W	9 32 21	21 51 06	22 01 29	29 27 14	9 53.4	14 57.4	18 14.5	28 05.5	13 32.3	13 58.3	0 11.4	12 11.3	17 20.7	19 34.3
16 Th	9 36 18	22 48 44	6♒52 08	14♒15 13	9 51.7	15 05.9	18 08.2	28 44.3	13 21.2	13 56.0	0 17.7	12 14.3	17 22.2	19 36.1
17 F	9 40 14	23 46 24	21 35 33	28 52 15	9D50.6	15R09.1	17 59.5	29 23.0	13 09.7	13 53.5	0 24.1	12 17.2	17 23.6	19 38.0
18 Sa	9 44 11	24 44 04	6♓04 34	13♓11 51	9 50.4	15 06.8	17 48.4	0♌01.7	12 58.1	13 50.8	0 30.6	12 20.1	17 25.1	19 39.9
19 Su	9 48 07	25 41 46	20 13 37	27 09 30	9 50.9	14 58.9	17 34.9	0 40.4	12 46.3	13 48.0	0 37.1	12 23.0	17 26.7	19 41.7
20 M	9 52 04	26 39 30	3♈59 17	10♈42 54	9 51.9	14 45.2	17 19.0	1 19.1	12 34.3	13 44.9	0 43.6	12 25.9	17 28.2	19 43.6
21 Tu	9 56 00	27 37 15	17 20 24	23 51 58	9 52.9	14 25.8	17 00.9	1 57.7	12 22.1	13 41.6	0 50.2	12 28.7	17 29.8	19 45.4
22 W	9 59 57	28 35 02	0♉17 52	6♉38 28	9 53.9	14 00.7	16 40.4	2 36.3	12 09.7	13 38.2	0 56.8	12 31.4	17 31.4	19 47.3
23 Th	10 03 54	29 32 51	12 54 10	19 05 28	9R54.5	13 30.0	16 17.9	3 14.8	11 57.2	13 34.5	1 03.5	12 34.2	17 33.0	19 49.1
24 F	10 07 50	0♍30 41	25 12 54	1♊16 58	9 54.7	12 53.9	15 53.2	3 53.3	11 44.5	13 30.7	1 10.2	12 36.9	17 34.6	19 51.0
25 Sa	10 11 47	1 28 33	7♊18 17	13 17 23	9 54.5	12 12.8	15 26.5	4 31.8	11 31.7	13 26.7	1 17.0	12 39.6	17 36.3	19 52.8
26 Su	10 15 43	2 26 27	19 14 51	25 11 15	9 53.9	11 27.2	14 58.0	5 10.2	11 18.8	13 22.6	1 23.8	12 42.2	17 37.9	19 54.6
27 M	10 19 40	3 24 23	1♋07 05	7♋02 55	9 53.2	10 37.7	14 27.7	5 48.6	11 05.7	13 18.2	1 30.6	12 44.8	17 39.6	19 56.5
28 Tu	10 23 36	4 22 20	12 59 13	18 56 26	9 52.4	9 45.0	13 55.9	6 27.0	10 52.6	13 13.7	1 37.4	12 47.4	17 41.4	19 58.3
29 W	10 27 33	5 20 20	24 55 01	0♌55 20	9 51.7	8 50.2	13 22.8	7 05.3	10 39.4	13 09.0	1 44.3	12 49.9	17 43.1	20 00.1
30 Th	10 31 29	6 18 21	6♌57 44	13 02 32	9 51.3	7 54.2	12 48.4	7 43.6	10 26.1	13 04.1	1 51.2	12 52.4	17 44.9	20 01.9
31 F	10 35 26	7 16 23	19 10 00	25 20 21	9 51.0	6 58.1	12 13.0	8 21.9	10 12.8	12 59.1	1 58.2	12 54.9	17 46.7	20 03.7

Astro Data

	Dy Hr Mn
☽0S	10 12:05
⚳R	12 15:18
☽0N	23 1:25
♃R	4 6:53
☽0S	6 17:05
♀0S	11 7:24
♀R	13 7:51
☿R	17 14:04
☽0N	19 10:52

Planet Ingress

	Dy Hr Mn
♂ ♋	3 23:42
♀ ♍	8 4:54
☿ ♌	8 13:39
☉ ♌	23 16:21
☿ ♍	27 15:24
♄ ♎	13 16:44
♂ ♌	18 10:55
☉ ♍	23 23:16

Last Aspect / ☽ Ingress (July)

Last Aspect Dy Hr Mn		☽ Ingress Dy Hr Mn
3 7:32 ♂ ☌	♋	3 8:27
5 14:23 ♄ ✶	♌	5 21:00
7 9:46 ♇ ☌	♍	8 8:36
10 12:29 ♄ ☌	♎	10 18:04
12 4:56 ☉ □	♏	13 0:19
14 22:39 ♄ ✶	♐	15 3:03
16 23:15 ♄ □	♑	17 3:14
18 22:55 ♄ △	♒	19 2:41
20 11:09 ♇ ☍	♓	21 3:29
23 6:40 ☉ △	♈	23 7:21
25 9:34 ☿ △	♉	25 15:07
27 22:53 ♄ △	♊	28 2:08
30 11:53 ♄ □	♋	30 14:42

Last Aspect / ☽ Ingress (August)

Last Aspect Dy Hr Mn		☽ Ingress Dy Hr Mn
2 0:49 ♄ ✶	♌	2 3:08
3 17:12 ♇ ☌	♍	4 14:18
6 22:17 ♄ ☌	♎	6 23:34
8 19:11 ♂ □	♏	9 6:24
11 10:07 ♄ ✶	♐	11 10:31
13 12:16 ♄ □	♑	13 12:18
15 9:42 ♂ ☍	♒	15 12:53
17 2:59 ☉ ☍	♓	17 13:52
18 19:44 ♀ ☍	♈	19 16:58
21 19:33 ☉ △	♉	21 23:26
23 13:25 ♇ □	♊	24 9:27
26 1:19 ♇ ✶	♋	26 21:44
28 9:29 ♆ □	♌	29 10:10
31 1:43 ♇ ☌	♍	31 21:00

☽ Phases & Eclipses

Dy Hr Mn		
4 7:48	●	11♋32
12 4:56	☽	19♎03
18 19:17	○	25♑21
25 18:59	☾	2♉01
2 22:39	●	9♌49
10 12:22	☽	17♏04
17 2:59	○	23♒25
17 3:14	•	A 0.119
24 10:20	☾	0♊27

Astro Data

1 July 1951
Julian Day # 18809
SVP 5♓56'08"
GC 26♐09.7 ⚴ 10♒35.7R
Eris 8♈01.7 ⚵ 24♏52.3R
⚷ 29♐08.7R ⚶ 8♋18.1
☽ Mean ☊ 13♓10.5

1 August 1951
Julian Day # 18840
SVP 5♓56'03"
GC 26♐09.8 ⚴ 2♒53.9R
Eris 7♈57.7R ⚵ 24♏16.9
⚷ 27♐26.4R ⚶ 21♋50.0
☽ Mean ☊ 11♓32.0

LONGITUDE

September 1951

Day	Sid.Time	☉	0 hr ☽	Noon ☽	True ☊	☿	♀	♂	⚳	♃	♄	♅	♆	♇
1 Sa	10 39 23	8♍14 27	1♍33 46	7♍50 24	9♓50.9	6♍03.2	11♍36.8	9♌00.1	9♓59.4	12♈53.8	2♎05.2	12♋57.3	17♎48.5	20♌05.5
2 Su	10 43 19	9 12 33	14 10 22	20 33 44	9R 50.9	5R 10.7	11R 00.1	9 38.3	9R 46.0	12R 48.5	2 12.2	12 59.7	17 50.3	20 07.3
3 M	10 47 16	10 10 41	27 00 33	3♎30 50	9 51.0	4 21.7	10 23.1	10 16.5	9 32.6	12 43.0	2 19.2	13 02.0	17 52.1	20 09.1
4 Tu	10 51 12	11 08 50	10♎04 35	16 41 47	9 50.9	3 37.4	9 46.0	10 54.6	9 19.3	12 37.3	2 26.3	13 04.3	17 54.0	20 10.9
5 W	10 55 09	12 07 00	23 22 24	0♏06 22	9 50.7	2 58.9	9 09.1	11 32.6	9 05.9	12 31.4	2 33.4	13 06.6	17 55.9	20 12.6
6 Th	10 59 05	13 05 12	6♏53 36	13 44 03	9 50.4	2 27.1	8 32.5	12 10.7	8 52.6	12 25.5	2 40.5	13 08.8	17 57.8	20 14.4
7 F	11 03 02	14 03 26	20 37 35	27 34 06	9 50.1	2 02.8	7 56.6	12 48.7	8 39.3	12 19.4	2 47.7	13 11.0	17 59.7	20 16.1
8 Sa	11 06 58	15 01 41	4♐33 27	11♐35 27	9D 49.9	1 46.7	7 21.5	13 26.6	8 26.2	12 13.1	2 54.8	13 13.1	18 01.6	20 17.8
9 Su	11 10 55	15 59 58	18 39 55	25 46 36	9 50.0	1D 39.1	6 47.4	14 04.6	8 13.0	12 06.7	3 02.0	13 15.2	18 03.6	20 19.6
10 M	11 14 52	16 58 16	2♑55 12	10♑05 22	9 50.4	1 40.5	6 14.7	14 42.5	8 00.0	12 00.2	3 09.2	13 17.3	18 05.5	20 21.3
11 Tu	11 18 48	17 56 36	17 16 45	24 28 53	9 51.0	1 50.9	5 43.4	15 20.3	7 47.1	11 53.6	3 16.5	13 19.3	18 07.5	20 23.0
12 W	11 22 45	18 54 57	1♒41 18	8♒53 28	9 51.7	2 10.5	5 13.7	15 58.1	7 34.4	11 46.8	3 23.7	13 21.3	18 09.5	20 24.7
13 Th	11 26 41	19 53 20	16 04 50	23 14 49	9 52.4	2 39.1	4 45.9	16 35.9	7 21.7	11 39.9	3 31.0	13 23.2	18 11.5	20 26.3
14 F	11 30 38	20 51 45	0♓22 50	7♓28 19	9R 52.7	3 16.4	4 20.0	17 13.6	7 09.2	11 32.9	3 38.3	13 25.1	18 13.5	20 28.0
15 Sa	11 34 34	21 50 11	14 30 44	21 29 32	9 52.5	4 02.1	3 56.2	17 51.3	6 56.9	11 25.9	3 45.6	13 26.9	18 15.6	20 29.6
16 Su	11 38 31	22 48 39	28 24 19	5♈14 41	9 51.6	4 55.9	3 34.5	18 29.0	6 44.7	11 18.7	3 52.9	13 28.7	18 17.6	20 31.3
17 M	11 42 27	23 47 09	12♈00 20	18 41 03	9 50.1	5 57.2	3 15.1	19 06.6	6 32.8	11 11.4	4 00.2	13 30.4	18 19.7	20 32.9
18 Tu	11 46 24	24 45 41	25 16 45	1♉47 24	9 48.2	7 05.5	2 58.1	19 44.2	6 21.0	11 04.0	4 07.6	13 32.1	18 21.7	20 34.5
19 W	11 50 21	25 44 16	8♉13 04	14 33 56	9 45.9	8 20.1	2 43.4	20 21.8	6 09.4	10 56.5	4 14.9	13 33.7	18 23.8	20 36.1
20 Th	11 54 17	26 42 52	20 50 13	27 02 16	9 43.8	9 40.5	2 31.1	20 59.3	5 58.1	10 49.0	4 22.3	13 35.3	18 25.9	20 37.7
21 F	11 58 14	27 41 31	3♊10 28	9♊15 17	9 42.1	11 06.0	2 21.3	21 36.8	5 46.9	10 41.4	4 29.7	13 36.9	18 28.0	20 39.2
22 Sa	12 02 10	28 40 12	15 17 10	21 16 42	9D 41.1	12 36.0	2 14.0	22 14.3	5 36.0	10 33.7	4 37.0	13 38.4	18 30.2	20 40.8
23 Su	12 06 07	29 38 55	27 14 25	3♋10 56	9 40.9	14 10.0	2 09.1	22 51.7	5 25.4	10 25.9	4 44.4	13 39.8	18 32.3	20 42.3
24 M	12 10 03	0♎37 40	9♋06 49	15 02 42	9 41.6	15 47.2	2D 06.6	23 29.1	5 15.0	10 18.1	4 51.8	13 41.3	18 34.4	20 43.8
25 Tu	12 14 00	1 36 28	20 59 09	26 56 47	9 42.9	17 27.3	2 06.5	24 06.5	5 04.9	10 10.2	4 59.2	13 42.6	18 36.6	20 45.3
26 W	12 17 56	2 35 18	2♌56 09	8♌57 48	9 44.6	19 09.6	2 08.7	24 43.8	4 55.1	10 02.3	5 06.7	13 43.9	18 38.8	20 46.8
27 Th	12 21 53	3 34 10	15 02 14	21 09 55	9 46.2	20 53.7	2 13.3	25 21.1	4 45.5	9 54.3	5 14.1	13 45.2	18 40.9	20 48.3
28 F	12 25 50	4 33 04	27 21 16	3♍36 36	9R 47.1	22 39.3	2 20.2	25 58.3	4 36.3	9 46.3	5 21.5	13 46.4	18 43.1	20 49.7
29 Sa	12 29 46	5 32 00	9♍56 13	16 20 20	9 47.1	24 25.9	2 29.3	26 35.6	4 27.3	9 38.3	5 28.9	13 47.5	18 45.3	20 51.1
30 Su	12 33 43	6 30 59	22 49 03	29 22 24	9 45.8	26 13.3	2 40.5	27 12.7	4 18.7	9 30.3	5 36.3	13 48.6	18 47.5	20 52.5

LONGITUDE

October 1951

Day	Sid.Time	☉	0 hr ☽	Noon ☽	True ☊	☿	♀	♂	⚳	♃	♄	♅	♆	♇
1 M	12 37 39	7♎29 59	6♎00 21	12♎42 46	9♓43.2	28♍01.1	2♍53.8	27♌49.8	4♓10.4	9♈22.2	5♎43.7	13♋49.7	18♎49.7	20♌53.9
2 Tu	12 41 36	8 29 01	19 29 25	26 20 00	9R 39.3	29 49.1	3 09.2	28 26.9	4R 02.4	9R 14.1	5 51.1	13 50.7	18 51.9	20 55.3
3 W	12 45 32	9 28 06	3♏14 10	10♏11 29	9 34.8	1♎37.2	3 26.6	29 04.0	3 54.7	9 06.1	5 58.6	13 51.6	18 54.1	20 56.6
4 Th	12 49 29	10 27 12	17 11 31	24 13 46	9 30.2	3 25.1	3 45.9	29 41.0	3 47.4	8 58.0	6 06.0	13 52.5	18 56.3	20 58.0
5 F	12 53 25	11 26 21	1♐17 47	8♐23 04	9 26.1	5 12.8	4 07.1	0♍18.0	3 40.4	8 49.9	6 13.4	13 53.4	18 58.5	20 59.3
6 Sa	12 57 22	12 25 31	15 29 10	22 35 42	9 23.2	7 00.1	4 30.1	0 54.9	3 33.8	8 41.9	6 20.8	13 54.2	19 00.7	21 00.6
7 Su	13 01 18	13 24 43	29 42 16	6♑48 33	9D 21.8	8 46.9	4 54.8	1 31.8	3 27.6	8 33.9	6 28.2	13 54.9	19 03.0	21 01.8
8 M	13 05 15	14 23 56	13♑54 17	20 59 11	9 21.8	10 33.3	5 21.2	2 08.6	3 21.6	8 25.9	6 35.5	13 55.6	19 05.2	21 03.1
9 Tu	13 09 12	15 23 12	28 03 05	5♒05 46	9 22.8	12 19.0	5 49.3	2 45.4	3 16.1	8 17.9	6 42.9	13 56.2	19 07.4	21 04.3
10 W	13 13 08	16 22 29	12♒07 05	19 06 51	9 24.3	14 04.1	6 18.9	3 22.2	3 10.9	8 10.0	6 50.3	13 56.8	19 09.7	21 05.5
11 Th	13 17 05	17 21 47	26 04 54	3♓01 05	9R 25.4	15 48.5	6 50.1	3 58.9	3 06.1	8 02.1	6 57.6	13 57.3	19 11.9	21 06.7
12 F	13 21 01	18 21 08	9♓55 10	16 46 59	9 25.3	17 32.3	7 22.7	4 35.6	3 01.6	7 54.3	7 04.9	13 57.8	19 14.1	21 07.9
13 Sa	13 24 58	19 20 30	23 36 17	0♈22 51	9 23.5	19 15.3	7 56.7	5 12.2	2 57.5	7 46.6	7 12.2	13 58.2	19 16.4	21 09.0
14 Su	13 28 54	20 19 54	7♈06 27	13 46 50	9 19.6	20 57.7	8 32.2	5 48.8	2 53.7	7 38.9	7 19.5	13 58.6	19 18.6	21 10.1
15 M	13 32 51	21 19 21	20 23 48	26 57 11	9 13.8	22 39.4	9 08.9	6 25.4	2 50.4	7 31.3	7 26.8	13 58.9	19 20.8	21 11.2
16 Tu	13 36 47	22 18 49	3♉26 48	9♉52 34	9 06.5	24 20.4	9 47.0	7 01.9	2 47.4	7 23.7	7 34.1	13 59.2	19 23.1	21 12.3
17 W	13 40 44	23 18 20	16 14 27	22 32 27	8 58.4	26 00.8	10 26.3	7 38.4	2 44.8	7 16.3	7 41.3	13 59.4	19 25.3	21 13.3
18 Th	13 44 41	24 17 53	28 46 40	4♊57 16	8 50.4	27 40.4	11 06.7	8 14.8	2 42.5	7 08.9	7 48.5	13 59.5	19 27.6	21 14.3
19 F	13 48 37	25 17 28	11♊04 28	17 08 35	8 43.2	29 19.4	11 48.3	8 51.2	2 40.6	7 01.6	7 55.7	13 59.6	19 29.8	21 15.3
20 Sa	13 52 34	26 17 05	23 09 58	29 09 03	8 37.6	0♏57.8	12 31.0	9 27.6	2 39.1	6 54.4	8 02.9	13R 59.7	19 32.0	21 16.3
21 Su	13 56 30	27 16 45	5♋06 19	11♋02 18	8 33.9	2 35.6	13 14.8	10 03.9	2 38.0	6 47.3	8 10.1	13 59.7	19 34.2	21 17.2
22 M	14 00 27	28 16 26	16 57 33	22 52 43	8D 32.2	4 12.7	13 59.6	10 40.1	2 37.2	6 40.4	8 17.2	13 59.6	19 36.5	21 18.1
23 Tu	14 04 23	29 16 10	28 48 24	4♌45 15	8 32.2	5 49.3	14 45.4	11 16.4	2D 36.8	6 33.5	8 24.3	13 59.5	19 38.7	21 19.0
24 W	14 08 20	0♏15 56	10♌43 57	16 45 08	8 33.2	7 25.3	15 32.2	11 52.6	2 36.7	6 26.7	8 31.4	13 59.3	19 40.9	21 19.9
25 Th	14 12 16	1 15 45	22 49 27	28 57 32	8R 34.3	9 00.7	16 19.8	12 28.7	2 37.1	6 20.1	8 38.5	13 59.1	19 43.1	21 20.7
26 F	14 16 13	2 15 35	5♍09 57	11♍27 13	8 34.7	10 35.6	17 08.3	13 04.8	2 37.7	6 13.6	8 45.5	13 58.8	19 45.3	21 21.5
27 Sa	14 20 10	3 15 28	17 49 49	24 18 05	8 33.3	12 10.0	17 57.7	13 40.8	2 38.8	6 07.3	8 52.5	13 58.5	19 47.5	21 22.3
28 Su	14 24 06	4 15 23	0♎52 18	7♎32 35	8 29.8	13 43.9	18 47.9	14 16.8	2 40.2	6 01.0	8 59.5	13 58.1	19 49.7	21 23.1
29 M	14 28 03	5 15 20	14 18 58	21 11 16	8 23.8	15 17.3	19 38.8	14 52.8	2 42.0	5 55.0	9 06.4	13 57.7	19 51.8	21 23.8
30 Tu	14 31 59	6 15 19	28 09 13	5♏12 21	8 15.7	16 50.2	20 30.5	15 28.7	2 44.1	5 49.0	9 13.3	13 57.2	19 54.0	21 24.5
31 W	14 35 56	7 15 20	12♏20 03	19 31 38	8 06.1	18 22.6	21 23.0	16 04.5	2 46.6	5 43.2	9 20.2	13 56.6	19 56.2	21 25.2

Astro Data

	Dy Hr Mn
♃□♅	1 1:09
☽0S	2 23:03
♀0N	5 0:05
☿D	9 20:23
☽0N	15 20:42
☉0S	23 20:38
♀D	25 0:58
♄0S	25 4:58
☽0S	30 6:47
♄∠♇	3 4:27
☿0S	4 19:01
☽0N	13 5:06
♃☍♄	15 19:12
♅R	20 20:55
⚳D	24 2:40
♃⚼⚼	25 10:01
☽0S	27 15:49

Planet Ingress

	Dy Hr Mn
☉ ♎	23 20:37
☿ ♎	2 14:25
♂ ♍	5 0:20
☿ ♏	19 21:52
☉ ♏	24 5:36

Last Aspect / ☽ Ingress (September)

Last Aspect Dy Hr Mn		☽ Ingress	Dy Hr Mn
1 21:44	♅ ⚹	♎	3 5:32
4 18:17	♇ ⚹	♏	5 11:49
6 23:21	♇ □	♐	7 16:11
9 2:47	♇ △	♑	9 19:06
11 1:23	♆ □	♒	11 21:11
13 7:17	♇ ☍	♓	13 23:21
15 12:38	☉ ☍	♈	16 2:47
17 15:23	♇ △	♉	18 8:41
20 11:19	☉ △	♊	20 17:47
23 4:13	☉ □	♋	23 5:34
24 19:09	♆ □	♌	25 18:08
27 20:34	♂ ☌	♍	28 5:05
30 5:20	☿ ☌	♎	30 13:08

Last Aspect / ☽ Ingress (October)

Last Aspect Dy Hr Mn		☽ Ingress	Dy Hr Mn
2 15:52	♂ ⚹	♏	2 18:23
4 21:41	♂ □	♐	4 21:48
6 9:19	♇ △	♑	7 0:30
8 8:46	♆ □	♒	9 3:19
10 15:24	♇ ☍	♓	11 6:46
12 7:04	♅ △	♈	13 11:19
15 2:58	☿ ☍	♉	15 17:37
17 9:28	♇ □	♊	18 2:22
20 5:43	☉ △	♋	20 13:42
22 23:55	☉ □	♌	23 2:25
24 21:04	♇ ☌	♍	25 14:01
26 23:26	♀ ☌	♎	27 22:25
29 12:22	♇ ⚹	♏	30 3:09

☽ Phases & Eclipses

Dy Hr Mn		
1 12:50	●	8♍16
1 12:51:21	●	A 02'36"
8 18:16	☽	15♐17
15 12:38	○	21♓52
15 12:27	●	A 0.804
23 4:13	☾	29♊20
1 1:57	●	7♎05
8 0:00	☽	13♑54
15 0:51	○	20♈52
22 23:55	☾	28♋46
30 13:54	●	6♏20

Astro Data

1 September 1951
Julian Day # 18871
SVP 5♓55'58"
GC 26♐09.9 ⚴ 26♑29.0R
Eris 7♈44.5R ⚵ 28♏19.4
⚷ 26♐47.8 ⚶ 5♌11.0
☽ Mean ☊ 9♓53.5

1 October 1951
Julian Day # 18901
SVP 5♓55'55"
GC 26♐09.9 ⚴ 25♑23.6
Eris 7♈26.4R ⚵ 5♐21.7
⚷ 27♐28.5 ⚶ 17♌35.3
☽ Mean ☊ 8♓18.2

November 1951 LONGITUDE

Day	Sid.Time	☉	0 hr ☽	Noon ☽	True ☊	☿	♀	♂	⚳	♃	♄	♅	♆	♇
1 Th	14 39 52	8♏15 22	26♏46 16	4♐03 03	7♓56.3	19♏54.6	22♍16.1	16♍40.3	2♓49.5	5♈37.6	9♎27.0	13♋56.0	19♎58.3	21♌25.9
2 F	14 43 49	9 15 27	11♐21 05	18 39 29	7R47.3	21 26.1	23 09.9	17 16.1	2 52.7	5R32.2	9 33.8	13R55.4	20 00.5	21 26.5
3 Sa	14 47 45	10 15 33	25 57 23	3♑14 01	7 40.2	22 57.2	24 04.4	17 51.8	2 56.3	5 26.9	9 40.6	13 54.7	20 02.6	21 27.1
4 Su	14 51 42	11 15 41	10♑28 43	17 40 57	7 35.5	24 27.9	24 59.4	18 27.4	3 00.2	5 21.7	9 47.3	13 53.9	20 04.7	21 27.7
5 M	14 55 39	12 15 51	24 50 17	1♒56 25	7D33.2	25 58.1	25 55.1	19 03.0	3 04.4	5 16.8	9 53.9	13 53.1	20 06.9	21 28.2
6 Tu	14 59 35	13 16 01	8♒59 12	15 58 32	7 32.8	27 27.8	26 51.4	19 38.5	3 09.0	5 12.0	10 00.6	13 52.3	20 09.0	21 28.7
7 W	15 03 32	14 16 14	22 54 25	29 46 54	7R33.3	28 57.1	27 48.2	20 14.0	3 13.9	5 07.4	10 07.2	13 51.4	20 11.1	21 29.2
8 Th	15 07 28	15 16 27	6♓36 06	13♓22 08	7 33.3	0♐25.9	28 45.6	20 49.4	3 19.2	5 02.9	10 13.7	13 50.4	20 13.1	21 29.7
9 F	15 11 25	16 16 42	20 05 07	26 45 10	7 31.7	1 54.3	29 43.5	21 24.8	3 24.8	4 58.7	10 20.2	13 49.4	20 15.2	21 30.1
10 Sa	15 15 21	17 16 59	3♈22 24	9♈56 52	7 27.7	3 22.1	0♎41.9	22 00.1	3 30.7	4 54.6	10 26.6	13 48.3	20 17.2	21 30.5
11 Su	15 19 18	18 17 17	16 28 37	22 57 39	7 20.7	4 49.5	1 40.9	22 35.3	3 36.9	4 50.7	10 33.0	13 47.2	20 19.3	21 30.9
12 M	15 23 14	19 17 37	29 24 00	5♉47 36	7 10.8	6 16.3	2 40.3	23 10.5	3 43.5	4 47.1	10 39.4	13 46.1	20 21.3	21 31.2
13 Tu	15 27 11	20 17 58	12♉08 26	18 26 28	6 58.7	7 42.5	3 40.1	23 45.7	3 50.3	4 43.6	10 45.7	13 44.9	20 23.3	21 31.5
14 W	15 31 08	21 18 21	24 41 39	0♊54 01	6 45.2	9 08.1	4 40.5	24 20.8	3 57.5	4 40.3	10 51.9	13 43.6	20 25.3	21 31.8
15 Th	15 35 04	22 18 46	7♊03 35	13 10 25	6 31.6	10 32.9	5 41.3	24 55.8	4 04.9	4 37.1	10 58.1	13 42.3	20 27.3	21 32.0
16 F	15 39 01	23 19 13	19 14 38	25 16 26	6 19.0	11 57.1	6 42.5	25 30.8	4 12.7	4 34.2	11 04.3	13 41.0	20 29.2	21 32.3
17 Sa	15 42 57	24 19 41	1♋16 00	7♋13 40	6 08.5	13 20.3	7 44.1	26 05.7	4 20.8	4 31.5	11 10.4	13 39.6	20 31.2	21 32.5
18 Su	15 46 54	25 20 11	13 09 47	19 04 44	6 00.6	14 42.7	8 46.1	26 40.5	4 29.2	4 29.0	11 16.4	13 38.2	20 33.1	21 32.6
19 M	15 50 50	26 20 43	24 59 01	0♌53 09	5 55.5	16 04.0	9 48.5	27 15.3	4 37.8	4 26.7	11 22.4	13 36.7	20 35.0	21 32.8
20 Tu	15 54 47	27 21 16	6♌47 41	12 43 15	5 52.9	17 24.2	10 51.3	27 50.1	4 46.8	4 24.6	11 28.3	13 35.2	20 36.9	21 32.9
21 W	15 58 43	28 21 52	18 40 30	24 40 06	5 52.1	18 43.0	11 54.5	28 24.7	4 56.0	4 22.7	11 34.2	13 33.6	20 38.8	21 33.0
22 Th	16 02 40	29 22 29	0♍42 45	6♍49 08	5 52.1	20 00.4	12 58.0	28 59.3	5 05.5	4 21.0	11 40.0	13 32.0	20 40.6	21 33.0
23 F	16 06 37	0♐23 07	12 59 56	19 15 50	5 51.7	21 16.0	14 01.8	29 33.9	5 15.3	4 19.5	11 45.7	13 30.4	20 42.4	21R33.0
24 Sa	16 10 33	1 23 47	25 37 26	2♎05 17	5 49.6	22 29.7	15 06.0	0♎08.3	5 25.3	4 18.2	11 51.4	13 28.7	20 44.3	21 33.0
25 Su	16 14 30	2 24 29	8♎39 51	15 21 27	5 45.2	23 41.3	16 10.4	0 42.7	5 35.7	4 17.1	11 57.0	13 26.9	20 46.0	21 33.0
26 M	16 18 26	3 25 13	22 10 16	29 06 21	5 37.9	24 50.3	17 15.2	1 17.1	5 46.3	4 16.2	12 02.6	13 25.2	20 47.8	21 32.9
27 Tu	16 22 23	4 25 58	6♏09 31	13♏19 23	5 28.0	25 56.4	18 20.3	1 51.3	5 57.1	4 15.5	12 08.0	13 23.3	20 49.6	21 32.8
28 W	16 26 19	5 26 44	20 35 21	27 56 37	5 16.4	26 59.3	19 25.7	2 25.5	6 08.2	4 15.1	12 13.5	13 21.5	20 51.3	21 32.7
29 Th	16 30 16	6 27 32	5♐22 13	12♐51 01	5 04.2	27 58.4	20 31.3	2 59.6	6 19.6	4D14.8	12 18.8	13 19.6	20 53.0	21 32.6
30 F	16 34 13	7 28 22	20 21 47	27 53 16	4 52.8	28 53.3	21 37.2	3 33.7	6 31.3	4 14.8	12 24.1	13 17.7	20 54.7	21 32.4

December 1951 LONGITUDE

Day	Sid.Time	☉	0 hr ☽	Noon ☽	True ☊	☿	♀	♂	⚳	♃	♄	♅	♆	♇
1 Sa	16 38 09	8♐29 12	5♑24 12	12♑53 25	4♓43.6	29♐43.3	22♎43.4	4♎07.7	6♓43.1	4♈15.0	12♎29.3	13♋15.7	20♎56.4	21♌32.2
2 Su	16 42 06	9 30 03	20 19 52	27 42 41	4R37.1	0♑27.7	23 49.8	4 41.5	6 55.3	4 15.3	12 34.4	13R13.7	20 58.0	21R31.9
3 M	16 46 02	10 30 55	5♒01 07	12♒14 41	4 33.5	1 05.9	24 56.4	5 15.3	7 07.6	4 15.9	12 39.5	13 11.7	20 59.6	21 31.7
4 Tu	16 49 59	11 31 48	19 23 01	26 25 59	4D32.3	1 37.1	26 03.3	5 49.0	7 20.2	4 16.7	12 44.5	13 09.6	21 01.2	21 31.4
5 W	16 53 55	12 32 42	3♓23 34	10♓15 50	4R32.2	2 00.3	27 10.4	6 22.7	7 33.1	4 17.7	12 49.4	13 07.5	21 02.8	21 31.0
6 Th	16 57 52	13 33 36	17 03 01	23 45 22	4 31.9	2R14.9	28 17.7	6 56.2	7 46.2	4 19.0	12 54.2	13 05.4	21 04.3	21 30.7
7 F	17 01 48	14 34 31	0♈23 12	6♈56 49	4 30.2	2 19.9	29 25.3	7 29.7	7 59.4	4 20.4	12 59.0	13 03.2	21 05.8	21 30.3
8 Sa	17 05 45	15 35 27	13 26 34	19 52 47	4 26.0	2 14.6	0♏33.0	8 03.1	8 13.0	4 22.0	13 03.6	13 01.0	21 07.3	21 29.9
9 Su	17 09 42	16 36 23	26 15 43	2♉35 40	4 18.9	1 58.4	1 41.0	8 36.4	8 26.7	4 23.8	13 08.2	12 58.8	21 08.7	21 29.4
10 M	17 13 38	17 37 20	8♉52 51	15 07 28	4 08.8	1 30.8	2 49.1	9 09.6	8 40.6	4 25.9	13 12.8	12 56.5	21 10.2	21 29.0
11 Tu	17 17 35	18 38 18	21 19 41	27 29 39	3 56.4	0 51.7	3 57.5	9 42.7	8 54.8	4 28.1	13 17.2	12 54.3	21 11.6	21 28.5
12 W	17 21 31	19 39 17	3♊37 27	9♊43 12	3 42.6	0 01.5	5 06.0	10 15.7	9 09.1	4 30.6	13 21.5	12 52.0	21 13.0	21 28.0
13 Th	17 25 28	20 40 17	15 47 01	21 48 59	3 28.6	29♐01.0	6 14.7	10 48.7	9 23.7	4 33.2	13 25.8	12 49.6	21 14.3	21 27.4
14 F	17 29 24	21 41 17	27 49 13	3♋47 51	3 15.6	27 51.6	7 23.6	11 21.5	9 38.5	4 36.1	13 30.0	12 47.3	21 15.6	21 26.9
15 Sa	17 33 21	22 42 18	9♋45 02	15 41 00	3 04.5	26 35.2	8 32.7	11 54.3	9 53.5	4 39.1	13 34.1	12 44.9	21 16.9	21 26.3
16 Su	17 37 17	23 43 20	21 35 59	27 30 15	2 56.1	25 14.2	9 41.9	12 27.0	10 08.6	4 42.3	13 38.1	12 42.5	21 18.2	21 25.6
17 M	17 41 14	24 44 23	3♌24 10	9♌18 07	2 50.5	23 51.2	10 51.3	12 59.5	10 24.0	4 45.8	13 42.0	12 40.1	21 19.4	21 25.0
18 Tu	17 45 11	25 45 27	15 12 32	21 07 55	2D47.7	22 29.1	12 00.8	13 32.0	10 39.5	4 49.4	13 45.9	12 37.7	21 20.6	21 24.3
19 W	17 49 07	26 46 31	27 04 48	3♍03 45	2 47.0	21 10.6	13 10.6	14 04.4	10 55.2	4 53.2	13 49.6	12 35.2	21 21.8	21 23.6
20 Th	17 53 04	27 47 36	9♍05 24	15 10 23	2 47.4	19 58.2	14 20.4	14 36.6	11 11.1	4 57.2	13 53.3	12 32.7	21 23.0	21 22.9
21 F	17 57 00	28 48 42	21 19 22	27 33 01	2R47.9	18 53.7	15 30.4	15 08.8	11 27.2	5 01.4	13 56.9	12 30.2	21 24.1	21 22.1
22 Sa	18 00 57	29 49 49	3♎51 58	10♎16 50	2 47.3	17 58.7	16 40.6	15 40.9	11 43.5	5 05.8	14 00.3	12 27.7	21 25.2	21 21.3
23 Su	18 04 53	0♑50 56	16 48 12	23 26 32	2 44.9	17 14.0	17 50.8	16 12.8	11 59.9	5 10.4	14 03.7	12 25.2	21 26.2	21 20.5
24 M	18 08 50	1 52 04	0♏12 13	7♏05 29	2 40.1	16 40.1	19 01.2	16 44.6	12 16.5	5 15.2	14 07.0	12 22.7	21 27.3	21 19.7
25 Tu	18 12 46	2 53 13	14 06 23	21 14 46	2 33.0	16 16.9	20 11.8	17 16.4	12 33.3	5 20.2	14 10.2	12 20.1	21 28.3	21 18.8
26 W	18 16 43	3 54 23	28 30 17	5♐52 21	2 24.2	16D04.3	21 22.4	17 48.0	12 50.3	5 25.3	14 13.3	12 17.6	21 29.2	21 18.0
27 Th	18 20 40	4 55 33	13♐20 08	20 52 37	2 14.7	16 01.6	22 33.2	18 19.4	13 07.4	5 30.6	14 16.3	12 15.0	21 30.2	21 17.1
28 F	18 24 36	5 56 43	28 28 33	6♑06 38	2 05.8	16 08.3	23 44.1	18 50.8	13 24.7	5 36.1	14 19.2	12 12.5	21 31.1	21 16.2
29 Sa	18 28 33	6 57 54	13♑45 26	21 23 32	1 58.4	16 23.5	24 55.1	19 22.0	13 42.1	5 41.8	14 22.0	12 09.9	21 31.9	21 15.2
30 Su	18 32 29	7 59 05	28 59 36	6♒32 24	1 53.4	16 46.5	26 06.1	19 53.1	13 59.7	5 47.7	14 24.7	12 07.3	21 32.8	21 14.3
31 M	18 36 26	9 00 15	14♒00 53	21 24 10	1D50.9	17 16.6	27 17.3	20 24.1	14 17.4	5 53.7	14 27.3	12 04.7	21 33.6	21 13.3

Astro Data	Dy Hr Mn
☽0N	9 11:05
♀0S	12 0:32
♇ R	23 16:29
☽0S	24 0:41
♃ D	30 4:08
♂0S	30 20:59
☽0N	6 15:39
☿ R	7 11:57
♄□♅	8 2:48
♆⚹♇	20 10:37
☽0S	21 7:59
☿ D	27 6:37

Planet Ingress		Dy Hr Mn
☿	♐	8 4:59
♀	♎	9 18:48
☉	♐	23 2:51
♂	♎	24 6:11
☿	♑	1 20:41
♀	♏	8 0:19
☿	♐R	12 12:39
☉	♑	22 16:00

Last Aspect Dy Hr Mn			☽ Ingress	Dy Hr Mn
31 15:17	♀	⚹	♐	1 5:20
2 19:54	♀	□	♑	3 6:40
5 1:07	♀	△	♒	5 8:43
7 10:22	☿	□	♓	7 12:23
9 17:48	♀	☍	♈	9 17:53
11 9:19	♇	△	♉	12 1:07
13 22:42	♂	△	♊	14 10:15
16 12:30	♂	□	♋	16 21:27
19 4:14	♂	⚹	♌	19 10:12
21 20:01	☉	□	♍	21 22:35
23 16:13	☿	□	♎	24 8:09
26 3:59	☿	⚹	♏	26 13:32
28 1:34	♇	□	♐	28 15:20
30 13:42	☿	☌	♑	30 15:22

Last Aspect Dy Hr Mn			☽ Ingress	Dy Hr Mn
2 5:10	♀	□	♒	2 15:45
4 11:18	♀	△	♓	4 18:08
5 17:02	♅	△	♈	6 23:18
8 15:02	♇	△	♉	9 7:04
11 0:18	♇	□	♊	11 16:54
14 1:10	☿	☍	♋	14 4:22
15 23:23	♆	□	♌	16 17:05
18 22:13	☉	△	♍	19 5:52
21 14:37	☉	□	♎	21 16:41
23 8:24	♆	☌	♏	23 23:38
25 12:07	♇	□	♐	26 2:27
27 12:59	♆	⚹	♑	28 2:24
29 18:02	♀	⚹	♒	30 1:36

☽ Phases & Eclipses Dy Hr Mn	
6 6:59	☽ 13♒03
13 15:52	○ 20♉28
21 20:01	☾ 28♌42
29 1:00	● 6♐00
5 16:20	☽ 12♓44
13 9:30	○ 20♊34
21 14:37	☾ 28♍55
28 11:43	● 5♑56

Astro Data

1 November 1951
Julian Day # 18932
SVP 5♓55'52"
GC 26♐10.0 ⚴ 29♑12.0
Eris 7♈07.8R ⚵ 14♐43.3
⚷ 29♐24.5 ⚶ 29♌17.5
☽ Mean ☊ 6♓39.7

1 December 1951
Julian Day # 18962
SVP 5♓55'46"
GC 26♐10.1 ⚴ 6♒02.8
Eris 6♈55.2R ⚵ 25♐01.8
⚷ 2♑07.8 ⚶ 8♍32.6
☽ Mean ☊ 5♓04.4

LONGITUDE — January 1952

Day	Sid.Time	☉	0 hr ☽	Noon ☽	True ☊	☿	♀	♂	⚳	♃	♄	♅	♆	♇
1 Tu	18 40 22	10♑01 26	28♒41 37	5♓52 46	1♓50.5	17♐53.0	28♏28.6	20♎54.9	14♓35.3	5♈59.9	14♎29.9	12♋02.1	21♎34.3	21♌12.3
2 W	18 44 19	11 02 36	12♓57 24	19 55 27	1 51.4	18 35.1	29 40.0	21 25.6	14 53.4	6 06.3	14 32.3	11R59.5	21 35.1	21R11.2
3 Th	18 48 16	12 03 46	26 46 58	3♈32 12	1R52.4	19 22.3	0♐51.4	21 56.2	15 11.5	6 12.9	14 34.6	11 56.9	21 35.8	21 10.2
4 F	18 52 12	13 04 55	10♈11 27	16 45 04	1 52.7	20 14.0	2 03.0	22 26.6	15 29.9	6 19.6	14 36.8	11 54.3	21 36.4	21 09.1
5 Sa	18 56 09	14 06 05	23 13 29	29 37 09	1 51.3	21 09.7	3 14.6	22 56.8	15 48.3	6 26.5	14 38.9	11 51.7	21 37.1	21 08.0
6 Su	19 00 05	15 07 14	5♉56 30	12♉12 00	1 47.7	22 09.0	4 26.3	23 27.0	16 06.9	6 33.5	14 40.9	11 49.1	21 37.7	21 06.9
7 M	19 04 02	16 08 22	18 24 04	24 33 06	1 42.1	23 11.5	5 38.1	23 57.0	16 25.6	6 40.7	14 42.7	11 46.5	21 38.2	21 05.8
8 Tu	19 07 58	17 09 31	0♊39 29	6♊43 34	1 34.7	24 16.8	6 49.9	24 26.8	16 44.5	6 48.1	14 44.5	11 44.0	21 38.8	21 04.6
9 W	19 11 55	18 10 39	12 45 39	18 46 02	1 26.3	25 24.7	8 01.9	24 56.5	17 03.5	6 55.6	14 46.2	11 41.4	21 39.3	21 03.5
10 Th	19 15 51	19 11 47	24 44 57	0♋42 39	1 17.6	26 34.8	9 13.9	25 26.0	17 22.6	7 03.3	14 47.8	11 38.8	21 39.8	21 02.3
11 F	19 19 48	20 12 54	6♋39 21	12 35 14	1 09.6	27 47.0	10 26.0	25 55.4	17 41.9	7 11.2	14 49.3	11 36.3	21 40.2	21 01.1
12 Sa	19 23 45	21 14 01	18 30 32	24 25 27	1 02.8	29 01.0	11 38.2	26 24.6	18 01.2	7 19.1	14 50.6	11 33.7	21 40.6	20 59.9
13 Su	19 27 41	22 15 07	0♌20 10	6♌14 56	0 57.9	0♑16.7	12 50.4	26 53.6	18 20.7	7 27.3	14 51.9	11 31.2	21 41.0	20 58.7
14 M	19 31 38	23 16 14	12 10 00	18 05 38	0 55.0	1 33.9	14 02.7	27 22.5	18 40.3	7 35.6	14 53.1	11 28.6	21 41.3	20 57.4
15 Tu	19 35 34	24 17 20	24 02 09	29 59 52	0D54.0	2 52.5	15 15.1	27 51.2	19 00.0	7 44.0	14 54.1	11 26.1	21 41.6	20 56.2
16 W	19 39 31	25 18 25	5♍59 11	12♍00 30	0 54.6	4 12.3	16 27.5	28 19.8	19 19.8	7 52.5	14 55.1	11 23.6	21 41.8	20 54.9
17 Th	19 43 27	26 19 31	18 04 16	24 10 57	0 56.1	5 33.4	17 40.0	28 48.1	19 39.7	8 01.3	14 55.9	11 21.1	21 42.1	20 53.6
18 F	19 47 24	27 20 36	0♎21 04	6♎35 07	0 57.9	6 55.4	18 52.6	29 16.3	19 59.8	8 10.1	14 56.6	11 18.6	21 42.3	20 52.3
19 Sa	19 51 20	28 21 40	12 53 38	19 17 09	0R59.3	8 18.5	20 05.2	29 44.3	20 19.9	8 19.1	14 57.2	11 16.2	21 42.4	20 51.0
20 Su	19 55 17	29 22 45	25 46 09	2♏21 07	0 59.6	9 42.6	21 17.8	0♏12.1	20 40.2	8 28.2	14 57.7	11 13.7	21 42.5	20 49.6
21 M	19 59 14	0♒23 49	9♏02 26	15 50 24	0 58.6	11 07.5	22 30.6	0 39.7	21 00.6	8 37.5	14 58.1	11 11.3	21 42.6	20 48.3
22 Tu	20 03 10	1 24 53	22 45 15	29 47 00	0 56.2	12 33.3	23 43.4	1 07.1	21 21.0	8 46.9	14 58.4	11 08.9	21 42.7	20 47.0
23 W	20 07 07	2 25 56	6♐55 34	14♐10 40	0 52.7	13 59.9	24 56.2	1 34.3	21 41.6	8 56.4	14 58.6	11 06.5	21R42.7	20 45.6
24 Th	20 11 03	3 26 59	21 31 49	28 58 18	0 48.6	15 27.3	26 09.1	2 01.3	22 02.3	9 06.1	14R58.7	11 04.2	21 42.7	20 44.2
25 F	20 15 00	4 28 02	6♑29 15	14♑03 38	0 44.7	16 55.5	27 22.0	2 28.0	22 23.0	9 15.8	14 58.7	11 01.9	21 42.7	20 42.9
26 Sa	20 18 56	5 29 03	21 40 15	29 17 49	0 41.5	18 24.4	28 34.9	2 54.6	22 43.9	9 25.7	14 58.5	10 59.6	21 42.6	20 41.5
27 Su	20 22 53	6 30 04	6♒55 02	14♒30 35	0 39.5	19 54.0	29 47.9	3 20.9	23 04.8	9 35.8	14 58.3	10 57.3	21 42.5	20 40.1
28 M	20 26 49	7 31 04	22 03 16	29 31 59	0D38.8	21 24.3	1♑01.0	3 47.0	23 25.9	9 45.9	14 57.9	10 55.0	21 42.3	20 38.7
29 Tu	20 30 46	8 32 03	6♓55 46	14♓13 51	0 39.2	22 55.3	2 14.1	4 12.8	23 47.0	9 56.2	14 57.5	10 52.8	21 42.1	20 37.3
30 W	20 34 43	9 33 00	21 25 40	28 30 50	0 40.4	24 27.1	3 27.2	4 38.4	24 08.2	10 06.6	14 56.9	10 50.6	21 41.9	20 35.8
31 Th	20 38 39	10 33 57	5♈29 08	12♈20 32	0 41.9	25 59.5	4 40.3	5 03.8	24 29.5	10 17.1	14 56.2	10 48.4	21 41.6	20 34.4

LONGITUDE — February 1952

Day	Sid.Time	☉	0 hr ☽	Noon ☽	True ☊	☿	♀	♂	⚳	♃	♄	♅	♆	♇
1 F	20 42 36	11♒34 52	19♈05 09	25♈43 13	0♓43.2	27♑32.6	5♑53.5	5♏28.9	24♓50.9	10♈27.7	14♎55.4	10♋46.3	21♎41.4	20♌33.0
2 Sa	20 46 32	12 35 46	2♉15 03	8♉41 03	0R43.8	29 06.4	7 06.7	5 53.8	25 12.4	10 38.4	14R54.6	10R44.2	21R41.0	20R31.5
3 Su	20 50 29	13 36 38	15 01 42	21 17 30	0 43.7	0♒41.0	8 19.9	6 18.3	25 33.9	10 49.3	14 53.6	10 42.1	21 40.7	20 30.1
4 M	20 54 25	14 37 29	27 28 57	3♊36 36	0 42.7	2 16.2	9 33.1	6 42.7	25 55.6	11 00.2	14 52.5	10 40.1	21 40.3	20 28.6
5 Tu	20 58 22	15 38 19	9♊40 58	15 42 33	0 41.1	3 52.2	10 46.4	7 06.7	26 17.3	11 11.2	14 51.3	10 38.1	21 39.9	20 27.2
6 W	21 02 18	16 39 07	21 41 53	27 39 24	0 39.0	5 28.9	11 59.7	7 30.5	26 39.0	11 22.4	14 50.0	10 36.1	21 39.4	20 25.7
7 Th	21 06 15	17 39 54	3♋35 34	9♋30 46	0 36.9	7 06.4	13 13.1	7 54.0	27 00.9	11 33.6	14 48.6	10 34.2	21 39.0	20 24.3
8 F	21 10 12	18 40 40	15 25 26	21 19 52	0 34.9	8 44.7	14 26.4	8 17.2	27 22.8	11 45.0	14 47.0	10 32.3	21 38.4	20 22.8
9 Sa	21 14 08	19 41 24	27 14 26	3♌09 26	0 33.4	10 23.7	15 39.8	8 40.2	27 44.8	11 56.4	14 45.4	10 30.5	21 37.9	20 21.4
10 Su	21 18 05	20 42 06	9♌05 07	15 01 46	0 32.4	12 03.5	16 53.2	9 02.8	28 06.8	12 08.0	14 43.7	10 28.7	21 37.3	20 19.9
11 M	21 22 01	21 42 48	20 59 37	26 58 54	0D32.0	13 44.2	18 06.7	9 25.1	28 28.9	12 19.6	14 41.9	10 26.9	21 36.7	20 18.5
12 Tu	21 25 58	22 43 28	2♍59 52	9♍02 43	0 32.1	15 25.6	19 20.2	9 47.1	28 51.1	12 31.3	14 40.0	10 25.1	21 36.1	20 17.0
13 W	21 29 54	23 44 06	15 07 42	21 15 03	0 32.5	17 07.9	20 33.6	10 08.8	29 13.4	12 43.1	14 38.0	10 23.4	21 35.4	20 15.5
14 Th	21 33 51	24 44 43	27 25 00	3♎37 49	0 33.1	18 51.1	21 47.2	10 30.2	29 35.7	12 55.1	14 35.9	10 21.8	21 34.7	20 14.1
15 F	21 37 47	25 45 20	9♎53 47	16 13 09	0 33.7	20 35.1	23 00.7	10 51.2	29 58.0	13 07.0	14 33.7	10 20.2	21 34.0	20 12.6
16 Sa	21 41 44	26 45 54	22 36 13	29 03 17	0 34.2	22 20.0	24 14.3	11 11.9	0♈20.5	13 19.1	14 31.4	10 18.6	21 33.2	20 11.2
17 Su	21 45 41	27 46 28	5♏34 37	12♏10 29	0 34.4	24 05.8	25 27.8	11 32.2	0 43.0	13 31.3	14 29.0	10 17.1	21 32.4	20 09.7
18 M	21 49 37	28 47 01	18 51 09	25 36 48	0R34.5	25 52.5	26 41.4	11 52.2	1 05.5	13 43.5	14 26.5	10 15.6	21 31.6	20 08.3
19 Tu	21 53 34	29 47 32	2♐27 35	9♐23 37	0D34.5	27 40.1	27 55.1	12 11.7	1 28.1	13 55.9	14 24.0	10 14.2	21 30.7	20 06.9
20 W	21 57 30	0♓48 02	16 24 52	23 31 13	0 34.5	29 28.6	29 08.7	12 31.0	1 50.8	14 08.3	14 21.3	10 12.8	21 29.9	20 05.4
21 Th	22 01 27	1 48 31	0♑42 28	7♑58 15	0 34.6	1♓18.0	0♒22.4	12 49.8	2 13.5	14 20.7	14 18.6	10 11.4	21 29.0	20 04.0
22 F	22 05 23	2 48 58	15 18 06	22 41 21	0 34.8	3 08.2	1 36.1	13 08.2	2 36.3	14 33.3	14 15.7	10 10.1	21 28.0	20 02.6
23 Sa	22 09 20	3 49 24	0♒07 17	7♒35 02	0 35.0	4 59.2	2 49.8	13 26.2	2 59.1	14 45.9	14 12.8	10 08.9	21 27.1	20 01.2
24 Su	22 13 16	4 49 49	15 03 39	22 32 07	0R35.2	6 51.1	4 03.5	13 43.8	3 22.0	14 58.7	14 09.8	10 07.7	21 26.1	19 59.8
25 M	22 17 13	5 50 11	29 59 24	7♓24 29	0 35.2	8 43.7	5 17.2	14 01.0	3 44.9	15 11.4	14 06.7	10 06.5	21 25.1	19 58.4
26 Tu	22 21 10	6 50 33	14♓46 24	22 04 16	0 34.9	10 37.0	6 30.9	14 17.7	4 07.9	15 24.3	14 03.6	10 05.4	21 24.0	19 57.0
27 W	22 25 06	7 50 52	29 17 18	6♈24 53	0 34.2	12 30.8	7 44.6	14 34.0	4 30.9	15 37.2	14 00.3	10 04.4	21 23.0	19 55.6
28 Th	22 29 03	8 51 09	13♈26 30	20 21 50	0 33.3	14 25.2	8 58.4	14 49.8	4 54.0	15 50.2	13 57.0	10 03.3	21 21.9	19 54.2
29 F	22 32 59	9 51 24	27 10 42	3♉53 03	0 32.1	16 19.9	10 12.1	15 05.2	5 17.1	16 03.2	13 53.6	10 02.4	21 20.8	19 52.9

Astro Data

	Dy Hr Mn
☽0N	2 21:21
♃□♇	3 3:32
☽0S	17 13:43
♆R	23 16:28
♄R	24 17:55
☽0N	30 6:00
♃□♅	2 22:47
☽0S	13 19:11
♃☍♄	21 8:36
☽0N	26 16:46

Planet Ingress

	Dy Hr Mn
♀ ♐	2 18:44
☿ ♑	13 6:44
♂ ♏	20 1:33
☉ ♒	21 2:38
♀ ♑	27 15:58
☿ ♒	3 1:38
⚳ ♈	15 14:06
☉ ♓	19 16:57
☿ ♓	20 18:55
♀ ♒	21 4:42

Last Aspect / ☽ Ingress

Last Aspect Dy Hr Mn	☽ Ingress Dy Hr Mn
31 22:32 ♀ □	♓ 1 2:10
2 9:33 ☿ □	♈ 3 5:42
4 22:58 ♂ ☍	♉ 5 12:43
7 5:15 ♇ □	♊ 7 22:42
10 2:46 ☿ ☍	♋ 10 10:34
12 16:12 ♂ □	♌ 12 23:19
15 7:31 ♂ ⚹	♍ 15 12:00
17 16:34 ☉ △	♎ 17 23:19
20 6:09 ☉ □	♏ 20 7:44
21 20:37 ♇ □	♐ 22 12:22
24 7:04 ♀ ☌	♑ 24 13:39
26 0:04 ♆ □	♒ 26 13:06
27 23:27 ♆ △	♓ 28 12:45
30 4:16 ☿ ⚹	♈ 30 14:32

Last Aspect Dy Hr Mn	☽ Ingress Dy Hr Mn
1 15:47 ☿ □	♉ 1 19:51
3 10:29 ♇ □	♊ 4 4:55
5 23:56 ♆ △	♋ 6 16:44
8 12:38 ♆ □	♌ 9 5:36
11 1:15 ♆ ⚹	♍ 11 18:02
13 10:30 ♀ △	♎ 14 5:00
16 7:24 ☉ △	♏ 16 13:45
18 18:01 ☉ □	♐ 18 19:42
20 8:36 ♆ ⚹	♑ 20 22:49
22 10:01 ♆ □	♒ 22 23:48
24 10:14 ♆ △	♓ 25 0:01
25 22:58 ♂ △	♈ 27 1:11
28 13:45 ♆ ☍	♉ 29 5:02

☽ Phases & Eclipses

Dy Hr Mn	
4 4:42	☽ 12♈46
12 4:55	○ 20♋56
20 6:09	☾ 29♎08
26 22:26	● 5♒56
2 20:01	☽ 12♉56
11 0:28	○ 21♌14
11 0:39	☍ P 0.083
18 18:01	☾ 29♏02
25 9:16	● 5♓43
25 9:11:05	● T 03'09"

Astro Data

1 January 1952
Julian Day # 18993
SVP 5♓55'40"
GC 26♐10.1 ⚴ 15♒01.9
Eris 6♈51.9 ⚵ 6♑22.5
⚷ 5♑20.7 ⚶ 14♍09.4
☽ Mean ☊ 3♓25.9

1 February 1952
Julian Day # 19024
SVP 5♓55'35"
GC 26♐10.2 ⚴ 25♒00.8
Eris 6♈59.7 ⚵ 17♑54.8
⚷ 8♑26.6 ⚶ 13♍18.8R
☽ Mean ☊ 1♓47.5

March 1952 — LONGITUDE

Day	Sid.Time	☉	0 hr ☽	Noon☽	True☊	☿	♀	♂	⚳	♃	♄	♅	♆	♇
1 Sa	22 36 56	10♓51 38	10♉29 00	16♉58 47	0♓31.0	18♓14.9	11♒25.9	15♏20.0	5♈40.2	16♈16.3	13♎50.1	10♋01.5	21♎19.6	19♌51.5
2 Su	22 40 52	11 51 49	23 22 42	29 41 09	0R30.2	20 09.9	12 39.7	15 34.4	6 03.4	16 29.5	13R46.6	10R00.6	21R18.5	19R50.2
3 M	22 44 49	12 51 59	5♊54 38	12♊03 40	0D29.9	22 04.7	13 53.4	15 48.3	6 26.6	16 42.7	13 43.0	9 59.8	21 17.3	19 48.8
4 Tu	22 48 45	13 52 06	18 08 48	24 10 38	0 30.2	23 59.0	15 07.2	16 01.8	6 49.9	16 56.0	13 39.3	9 59.1	21 16.1	19 47.5
5 W	22 52 42	14 52 11	0♋09 46	6♋06 47	0 31.0	25 52.6	16 21.0	16 14.7	7 13.2	17 09.3	13 35.5	9 58.4	21 14.8	19 46.2
6 Th	22 56 39	15 52 14	12 02 16	17 56 48	0 32.3	27 45.2	17 34.8	16 27.0	7 36.6	17 22.7	13 31.7	9 57.7	21 13.6	19 44.9
7 F	23 00 35	16 52 15	23 50 56	29 45 11	0 33.8	29 36.3	18 48.6	16 38.9	7 59.9	17 36.2	13 27.8	9 57.1	21 12.3	19 43.7
8 Sa	23 04 32	17 52 14	5♌40 03	11♌35 58	0 35.2	1♈25.6	20 02.4	16 50.2	8 23.3	17 49.7	13 23.9	9 56.6	21 11.0	19 42.4
9 Su	23 08 28	18 52 11	17 33 23	23 32 39	0R36.0	3 12.7	21 16.2	17 00.9	8 46.8	18 03.2	13 19.9	9 56.1	21 09.7	19 41.1
10 M	23 12 25	19 52 05	29 34 07	5♍38 04	0 36.1	4 57.0	22 30.0	17 11.1	9 10.2	18 16.8	13 15.9	9 55.7	21 08.4	19 39.9
11 Tu	23 16 21	20 51 58	11♍44 44	17 54 21	0 35.1	6 38.0	23 43.8	17 20.8	9 33.7	18 30.5	13 11.8	9 55.3	21 07.0	19 38.7
12 W	23 20 18	21 51 49	24 07 03	0♎22 58	0 33.1	8 15.4	24 57.6	17 29.8	9 57.3	18 44.1	13 07.6	9 54.9	21 05.6	19 37.5
13 Th	23 24 14	22 51 37	6♎42 11	13 04 46	0 30.2	9 48.5	26 11.4	17 38.2	10 20.8	18 57.9	13 03.4	9 54.7	21 04.2	19 36.3
14 F	23 28 11	23 51 24	19 30 45	26 00 08	0 26.6	11 16.8	27 25.2	17 46.1	10 44.4	19 11.6	12 59.2	9 54.4	21 02.8	19 35.1
15 Sa	23 32 08	24 51 09	2♏32 55	9♏09 04	0 22.8	12 40.0	28 39.1	17 53.3	11 08.0	19 25.5	12 54.9	9 54.3	21 01.4	19 34.0
16 Su	23 36 04	25 50 53	15 48 33	22 31 22	0 19.4	13 57.4	29 52.9	17 59.8	11 31.7	19 39.3	12 50.6	9 54.1	21 00.0	19 32.8
17 M	23 40 01	26 50 35	29 17 27	6♐06 45	0 16.8	15 08.7	1♓06.8	18 05.8	11 55.4	19 53.2	12 46.2	9D54.1	20 58.5	19 31.7
18 Tu	23 43 57	27 50 15	12♐59 14	19 54 50	0D15.4	16 13.4	2 20.6	18 11.0	12 19.1	20 07.2	12 41.8	9 54.1	20 57.0	19 30.6
19 W	23 47 54	28 49 53	26 53 28	3♑55 02	0 15.2	17 11.3	3 34.5	18 15.6	12 42.8	20 21.1	12 37.3	9 54.1	20 55.6	19 29.6
20 Th	23 51 50	29 49 30	10♑59 24	18 06 23	0 16.1	18 01.9	4 48.4	18 19.6	13 06.5	20 35.1	12 32.9	9 54.2	20 54.1	19 28.5
21 F	23 55 47	0♈49 05	25 15 45	2♒27 12	0 17.6	18 45.1	6 02.2	18 22.8	13 30.3	20 49.2	12 28.4	9 54.4	20 52.6	19 27.5
22 Sa	23 59 43	1 48 38	9♒40 22	16 54 49	0R18.9	19 20.7	7 16.1	18 25.3	13 54.1	21 03.3	12 23.8	9 54.6	20 51.0	19 26.4
23 Su	0 03 40	2 48 09	24 10 02	1♓25 25	0 19.5	19 48.5	8 30.0	18 27.1	14 17.9	21 17.4	12 19.3	9 54.8	20 49.5	19 25.4
24 M	0 07 37	3 47 39	8♓40 22	15 54 10	0 18.6	20 08.4	9 43.8	18R28.2	14 41.7	21 31.5	12 14.7	9 55.1	20 47.9	19 24.5
25 Tu	0 11 33	4 47 06	23 06 07	0♈15 30	0 15.9	20 20.6	10 57.7	18 28.5	15 05.6	21 45.6	12 10.1	9 55.5	20 46.4	19 23.5
26 W	0 15 30	5 46 31	7♈21 39	14 23 55	0 11.6	20R25.0	12 11.6	18 28.1	15 29.4	21 59.8	12 05.4	9 55.9	20 44.8	19 22.6
27 Th	0 19 26	6 45 55	21 21 44	28 14 38	0 06.0	20 21.9	13 25.4	18 27.0	15 53.3	22 14.1	12 00.8	9 56.4	20 43.2	19 21.7
28 F	0 23 23	7 45 16	5♉02 15	11♉44 20	29♒59.7	20 11.5	14 39.3	18 25.1	16 17.2	22 28.3	11 56.1	9 56.9	20 41.6	19 20.8
29 Sa	0 27 19	8 44 35	18 20 47	24 51 34	29 53.5	19 54.2	15 53.1	18 22.4	16 41.1	22 42.6	11 51.5	9 57.5	20 40.0	19 19.9
30 Su	0 31 16	9 43 52	1♊16 50	7♊36 47	29 48.1	19 30.4	17 07.0	18 19.0	17 05.0	22 56.8	11 46.8	9 58.1	20 38.4	19 19.1
31 M	0 35 12	10 43 06	13 51 46	20 02 10	29 44.2	19 00.9	18 20.9	18 14.9	17 29.0	23 11.1	11 42.1	9 58.8	20 36.8	19 18.2

April 1952 — LONGITUDE

Day	Sid.Time	☉	0 hr ☽	Noon☽	True☊	☿	♀	♂	⚳	♃	♄	♅	♆	♇
1 Tu	0 39 09	11♈42 19	26♊08 29	2♋11 16	29♒42.0	18♈26.2	19♓34.7	18♏09.9	17♈52.9	23♈25.5	11♎37.5	9♋59.6	20♎35.2	19♌17.4
2 W	0 43 06	12 41 29	8♋11 04	14 08 32	29D41.4	17R47.1	20 48.5	18R04.2	18 16.9	23 39.8	11R32.8	10 00.4	20R33.6	19R16.7
3 Th	0 47 02	13 40 36	20 04 18	25 59 00	29 42.2	17 04.5	22 02.4	17 57.8	18 40.9	23 54.2	11 28.1	10 01.2	20 31.9	19 15.9
4 F	0 50 59	14 39 42	1♌53 19	7♌47 52	29 43.6	16 19.2	23 16.2	17 50.6	19 04.8	24 08.5	11 23.5	10 02.1	20 30.3	19 15.2
5 Sa	0 54 55	15 38 45	13 43 17	19 40 11	29R45.0	15 32.3	24 30.0	17 42.6	19 28.8	24 22.9	11 18.8	10 03.1	20 28.7	19 14.5
6 Su	0 58 52	16 37 45	25 39 08	1♍40 39	29 45.4	14 44.6	25 43.8	17 33.8	19 52.8	24 37.3	11 14.2	10 04.1	20 27.0	19 13.8
7 M	1 02 48	17 36 44	7♍45 12	13 53 14	29 44.3	13 57.1	26 57.7	17 24.3	20 16.8	24 51.7	11 09.5	10 05.1	20 25.4	19 13.2
8 Tu	1 06 45	18 35 40	20 05 04	26 21 00	29 41.1	13 10.6	28 11.5	17 14.1	20 40.8	25 06.1	11 04.9	10 06.2	20 23.7	19 12.5
9 W	1 10 41	19 34 34	2♎41 13	9♎05 50	29 35.7	12 26.1	29 25.3	17 03.1	21 04.8	25 20.5	11 00.3	10 07.4	20 22.1	19 11.9
10 Th	1 14 38	20 33 26	15 34 53	22 08 19	29 28.3	11 44.2	0♈39.1	16 51.3	21 28.8	25 35.0	10 55.7	10 08.6	20 20.4	19 11.4
11 F	1 18 34	21 32 16	28 46 00	5♏27 42	29 19.7	11 05.5	1 52.9	16 38.9	21 52.8	25 49.4	10 51.2	10 09.8	20 18.8	19 10.8
12 Sa	1 22 31	22 31 04	12♏13 09	19 02 02	29 10.7	10 30.8	3 06.7	16 25.7	22 16.8	26 03.8	10 46.6	10 11.1	20 17.1	19 10.3
13 Su	1 26 28	23 29 51	25 53 58	2♐48 34	29 02.2	10 00.3	4 20.5	16 11.8	22 40.8	26 18.3	10 42.1	10 12.5	20 15.5	19 09.8
14 M	1 30 24	24 28 36	9♐45 27	16 44 13	28 55.3	9 34.5	5 34.3	15 57.3	23 04.8	26 32.7	10 37.6	10 13.9	20 13.9	19 09.3
15 Tu	1 34 21	25 27 19	23 44 32	0♑46 04	28 50.5	9 13.6	6 48.1	15 42.0	23 28.9	26 47.2	10 33.2	10 15.4	20 12.2	19 08.9
16 W	1 38 17	26 26 00	7♑48 32	14 51 41	28D48.0	8 57.8	8 01.9	15 26.1	23 52.9	27 01.6	10 28.8	10 16.9	20 10.6	19 08.5
17 Th	1 42 14	27 24 40	21 55 19	28 59 16	28 47.4	8 47.1	9 15.7	15 09.6	24 16.9	27 16.1	10 24.4	10 18.4	20 09.0	19 08.1
18 F	1 46 10	28 23 17	6♒03 22	13♒07 30	28 47.9	8D41.6	10 29.5	14 52.4	24 40.9	27 30.5	10 20.1	10 20.0	20 07.3	19 07.7
19 Sa	1 50 07	29 21 54	20 11 30	27 15 13	28R48.4	8 41.3	11 43.3	14 34.6	25 05.0	27 45.0	10 15.8	10 21.7	20 05.7	19 07.4
20 Su	1 54 03	0♉20 28	4♓18 28	11♓21 01	28 47.8	8 46.1	12 57.0	14 16.3	25 29.0	27 59.4	10 11.5	10 23.4	20 04.1	19 07.1
21 M	1 58 00	1 19 01	18 22 36	25 22 54	28 45.1	8 55.8	14 10.8	13 57.5	25 53.0	28 13.9	10 07.3	10 25.1	20 02.5	19 06.8
22 Tu	2 01 57	2 17 32	2♈21 33	9♈18 11	28 39.7	9 10.3	15 24.6	13 38.1	26 17.0	28 28.3	10 03.2	10 26.9	20 00.9	19 06.5
23 W	2 05 53	3 16 02	16 12 22	23 03 42	28 31.8	9 29.6	16 38.4	13 18.3	26 41.0	28 42.7	9 59.0	10 28.7	19 59.3	19 06.3
24 Th	2 09 50	4 14 29	29 51 44	6♉36 07	28 21.7	9 53.4	17 52.1	12 58.0	27 05.0	28 57.2	9 55.0	10 30.6	19 57.7	19 06.1
25 F	2 13 46	5 12 55	13♉16 31	19 52 37	28 10.3	10 21.5	19 05.9	12 37.4	27 29.0	29 11.6	9 51.0	10 32.5	19 56.1	19 05.9
26 Sa	2 17 43	6 11 19	26 24 16	2♊51 19	27 58.9	10 53.8	20 19.7	12 16.4	27 53.0	29 26.0	9 47.0	10 34.5	19 54.5	19 05.8
27 Su	2 21 39	7 09 41	9♊13 47	15 31 43	27 48.5	11 30.1	21 33.4	11 55.1	28 16.9	29 40.3	9 43.1	10 36.5	19 53.0	19 05.7
28 M	2 25 36	8 08 01	21 45 19	27 54 49	27 40.0	12 10.3	22 47.2	11 33.5	28 40.9	29 54.7	9 39.3	10 38.6	19 51.4	19 05.6
29 Tu	2 29 32	9 06 19	4♋00 35	10♋03 02	27 33.9	12 54.1	24 00.9	11 11.8	29 04.8	0♉09.1	9 35.6	10 40.7	19 49.9	19 05.5
30 W	2 33 29	10 04 35	16 02 40	22 00 01	27 30.2	13 41.5	25 14.6	10 49.8	29 28.8	0 23.4	9 31.9	10 42.8	19 48.3	19D05.5

Astro Data	Planet Ingress	Last Aspect	☽ Ingress	Last Aspect	☽ Ingress	☽ Phases & Eclipses
Dy Hr Mn	Dy Hr Mn	Dy Hr Mn	Dy Hr Mn	Dy Hr Mn	Dy Hr Mn	Dy Hr Mn
☿0N 7 19:38	☿ ♈ 7 17:10	1 17:22 ♇ □	♊ 2 12:36	31 18:18 ♃ ⚹	♋ 1 7:39	3 13:43 ☽ 12♊56
☽0S 12 1:39	♀ ♓ 16 14:18	4 11:32 ☿ □	♋ 4 23:40	3 7:41 ♃ □	♌ 3 20:10	11 18:14 ○ 21♍08
♃△♇ 16 1:38	⊙ ♈ 20 16:14	7 11:39 ☿ △	♌ 7 12:30	5 21:39 ♃ △	♍ 6 8:40	19 2:40 ☾ 28♐27
♅D 18 4:11	☊ ♒R 28 10:45	9 7:14 ♆ ⚹	♍ 10 0:51	8 15:53 ♀ ☍	♎ 8 18:56	25 20:13 ● 5♈07
⊙0N 20 16:14		11 18:14 ⊙ ☍	♎ 12 11:16	10 18:22 ♃ ☍	♏ 11 2:13	
♃☍♆ 21 17:12	♀ ♈ 9 23:17	14 14:53 ♀ △	♏ 14 19:20	12 12:14 ♇ □	♐ 13 7:08	2 8:48 ☽ 12♋34
☽0N 25 3:08	⊙ ♉ 20 3:37	16 18:23 ⊙ △	♐ 17 1:15	15 5:05 ♃ △	♑ 15 10:41	10 8:53 ○ 20♎26
♂R 25 11:07	♃ ♉ 28 20:50	19 2:40 ⊙ □	♑ 19 5:19	17 9:07 ⊙ □	♒ 17 13:43	17 9:07 ☾ 27♑18
☿R 26 13:55		20 16:41 ♆ □	♒ 21 7:55	19 15:51 ⊙ ⚹	♓ 19 16:40	24 7:27 ● 4♉03
⚳0N 28 16:13		22 18:58 ♃ ⚹	♓ 23 9:39	20 16:53 ♂ △	♈ 21 19:56	
☽0S 8 9:18		24 16:16 ♂ △	♈ 25 11:34	23 22:09 ♃ ☌	♉ 24 0:15	
♀0N 12 20:02		27 1:20 ♃ ☌	♉ 27 15:05	25 10:35 ♇ □	♊ 26 6:40	
♄□♅ 18 12:13		29 1:49 ♇ □	♊ 29 21:36	28 16:00 ♃ ⚹	♋ 28 16:06	
☿D 19 1:32						
☽0N 21 11:04	♇ D30 23:20					

Astro Data

1 March 1952
Julian Day # 19053
SVP 5♓55'31"
GC 26♐10.3 ⚴ 4♓38.9
Eris 7♈15.2 ⚵ 28♑25.6
⚷ 10♑46.5 ⚶ 6♍47.2R
☽ Mean ☊ 0♓15.3

1 April 1952
Julian Day # 19084
SVP 5♓55'27"
GC 26♐10.3 ⚴ 14♓44.7
Eris 7♈36.4 ⚵ 8♒47.6
⚷ 12♑14.3 ⚶ 0♍31.5R
☽ Mean ☊ 28♒36.8

LONGITUDE — May 1952

Day	Sid.Time	☉	0 hr ☽	Noon ☽	True ☊	☿	♀	♂	⚳	♃	♄	♅	♆	♇
1 Th	2 37 26	11♉02 49	27♋55 42	3♌50 20	27♒28.7	14♈32.2	26♈28.4	10♏27.7	29♈52.7	0♉37.7	9♎28.2	10♋45.0	19♎46.8	19♌05.5
2 F	2 41 22	12 01 00	9♌44 34	15 39 07	27R 28.6	15 26.2	27 42.1	10R 05.6	0♉16.6	0 52.0	9R 24.6	10 47.2	19R 45.3	19 05.5
3 Sa	2 45 19	12 59 10	21 34 38	27 31 49	27 28.7	16 23.4	28 55.8	9 43.4	0 40.5	1 06.3	9 21.1	10 49.5	19 43.8	19 05.6
4 Su	2 49 15	13 57 18	3♍31 21	9♍33 51	27 28.2	17 23.5	0♉09.5	9 21.2	1 04.4	1 20.6	9 17.7	10 51.8	19 42.4	19 05.7
5 M	2 53 12	14 55 24	15 39 57	21 50 11	27 26.0	18 26.5	1 23.2	8 59.0	1 28.3	1 34.8	9 14.4	10 54.2	19 40.9	19 05.8
6 Tu	2 57 08	15 53 28	28 05 05	4♎25 01	27 21.4	19 32.3	2 36.9	8 37.0	1 52.1	1 49.0	9 11.1	10 56.6	19 39.4	19 05.9
7 W	3 01 05	16 51 30	10♎50 19	17 21 13	27 14.2	20 40.8	3 50.6	8 15.1	2 15.9	2 03.2	9 07.9	10 59.0	19 38.0	19 06.1
8 Th	3 05 01	17 49 30	23 57 47	0♏39 58	27 04.6	21 51.9	5 04.2	7 53.4	2 39.7	2 17.4	9 04.7	11 01.4	19 36.6	19 06.3
9 F	3 08 58	18 47 29	7♏27 37	14 20 26	26 53.3	23 05.6	6 17.9	7 31.9	3 03.5	2 31.5	9 01.7	11 03.9	19 35.2	19 06.5
10 Sa	3 12 55	19 45 26	21 17 57	28 19 38	26 41.5	24 21.7	7 31.6	7 10.7	3 27.3	2 45.6	8 58.7	11 06.5	19 33.8	19 06.8
11 Su	3 16 51	20 43 22	5♐24 52	12♐32 56	26 30.3	25 40.3	8 45.3	6 49.8	3 51.1	2 59.7	8 55.8	11 09.1	19 32.5	19 07.1
12 M	3 20 48	21 41 16	19 43 06	26 54 38	26 20.9	27 01.3	9 58.9	6 29.2	4 14.8	3 13.7	8 53.0	11 11.7	19 31.1	19 07.4
13 Tu	3 24 44	22 39 09	4♑06 49	11♑19 01	26 14.0	28 24.5	11 12.6	6 09.0	4 38.5	3 27.8	8 50.3	11 14.3	19 29.8	19 07.7
14 W	3 28 41	23 37 01	18 30 37	25 41 08	26 09.9	29 50.1	12 26.3	5 49.2	5 02.2	3 41.7	8 47.6	11 17.0	19 28.5	19 08.1
15 Th	3 32 37	24 34 51	2♒50 11	9♒57 28	26 08.2	1♉18.0	13 39.9	5 29.9	5 25.9	3 55.7	8 45.1	11 19.7	19 27.2	19 08.5
16 F	3 36 34	25 32 41	17 02 45	24 05 53	26 07.9	2 48.1	14 53.6	5 11.1	5 49.6	4 09.6	8 42.6	11 22.5	19 26.0	19 08.9
17 Sa	3 40 31	26 30 29	1♓06 48	8♓05 27	26 07.7	4 20.5	16 07.3	4 52.8	6 13.2	4 23.5	8 40.2	11 25.3	19 24.7	19 09.3
18 Su	3 44 27	27 28 15	15 01 49	21 55 54	26 06.4	5 55.0	17 20.9	4 35.1	6 36.8	4 37.4	8 37.9	11 28.1	19 23.5	19 09.8
19 M	3 48 24	28 26 01	28 47 40	5♈37 05	26 03.0	7 31.8	18 34.6	4 17.9	7 00.4	4 51.2	8 35.7	11 30.9	19 22.3	19 10.3
20 Tu	3 52 20	29 23 46	12♈24 07	19 08 39	25 56.8	9 10.8	19 48.3	4 01.4	7 24.0	5 04.9	8 33.6	11 33.8	19 21.1	19 10.8
21 W	3 56 17	0♊21 29	25 50 35	2♉29 47	25 47.7	10 52.0	21 01.9	3 45.5	7 47.5	5 18.7	8 31.6	11 36.7	19 19.9	19 11.4
22 Th	4 00 13	1 19 12	9♉06 06	15 39 21	25 36.4	12 35.3	22 15.6	3 30.3	8 11.0	5 32.4	8 29.7	11 39.7	19 18.8	19 12.0
23 F	4 04 10	2 16 53	22 09 23	28 36 04	25 23.6	14 20.9	23 29.3	3 15.9	8 34.5	5 46.0	8 27.8	11 42.6	19 17.7	19 12.6
24 Sa	4 08 06	3 14 33	4♊59 18	11♊18 59	25 10.7	16 08.6	24 42.9	3 02.1	8 57.9	5 59.6	8 26.1	11 45.6	19 16.6	19 13.2
25 Su	4 12 03	4 12 12	17 35 07	23 47 45	24 58.7	17 58.6	25 56.6	2 49.1	9 21.3	6 13.2	8 24.4	11 48.7	19 15.5	19 13.9
26 M	4 16 00	5 09 49	29 56 58	6♋02 57	24 48.7	19 50.7	27 10.2	2 36.8	9 44.7	6 26.7	8 22.9	11 51.7	19 14.5	19 14.6
27 Tu	4 19 56	6 07 25	12♋05 56	18 06 15	24 41.2	21 44.9	28 23.9	2 25.3	10 08.1	6 40.1	8 21.5	11 54.8	19 13.5	19 15.3
28 W	4 23 53	7 05 00	24 04 14	0♌00 22	24 36.5	23 41.2	29 37.6	2 14.7	10 31.4	6 53.6	8 20.1	11 57.9	19 12.5	19 16.1
29 Th	4 27 49	8 02 34	5♌55 07	11 49 02	24 34.1	25 39.6	0♊51.2	2 04.8	10 54.6	7 06.9	8 18.8	12 01.1	19 11.5	19 16.8
30 F	4 31 46	9 00 06	17 42 42	23 36 45	24D 33.5	27 40.0	2 04.9	1 55.7	11 17.9	7 20.2	8 17.7	12 04.2	19 10.6	19 17.6
31 Sa	4 35 42	9 57 36	29 31 51	5♍28 40	24R 33.7	29 42.4	3 18.5	1 47.4	11 41.1	7 33.5	8 16.6	12 07.4	19 09.7	19 18.4

LONGITUDE — June 1952

Day	Sid.Time	☉	0 hr ☽	Noon ☽	True ☊	☿	♀	♂	⚳	♃	♄	♅	♆	♇
1 Su	4 39 39	10♊55 06	11♍27 53	17♍30 11	24♒33.5	1♊46.5	4♊32.1	1♏40.0	12♉04.3	7♉46.7	8♎15.7	12♋10.6	19♎08.8	19♌19.3
2 M	4 43 35	11 52 34	23 36 14	29 46 41	24R 32.2	3 52.3	5 45.8	1R 33.4	12 27.4	7 59.8	8R 14.8	12 13.9	19R 07.9	19 20.2
3 Tu	4 47 32	12 50 00	6♎02 08	12♎23 07	24 28.8	5 59.7	6 59.4	1 27.6	12 50.5	8 12.9	8 14.0	12 17.1	19 07.1	19 21.0
4 W	4 51 29	13 47 26	18 50 05	25 23 23	24 23.0	8 08.4	8 13.1	1 22.6	13 13.5	8 25.9	8 13.4	12 20.4	19 06.3	19 22.0
5 Th	4 55 25	14 44 50	2♏03 16	8♏49 47	24 15.1	10 18.3	9 26.7	1 18.5	13 36.5	8 38.9	8 12.8	12 23.7	19 05.5	19 22.9
6 F	4 59 22	15 42 14	15 42 54	22 42 21	24 05.5	12 29.2	10 40.3	1 15.2	13 59.5	8 51.8	8 12.4	12 27.0	19 04.8	19 23.9
7 Sa	5 03 18	16 39 36	29 47 44	6♐58 27	23 55.2	14 40.7	11 54.0	1 12.6	14 22.4	9 04.6	8 12.0	12 30.3	19 04.1	19 24.9
8 Su	5 07 15	17 36 58	14♐13 47	21 32 52	23 45.5	16 52.6	13 07.6	1 11.0	14 45.3	9 17.4	8 11.8	12 33.7	19 03.4	19 25.9
9 M	5 11 11	18 34 19	28 54 44	6♑18 23	23 37.3	19 04.7	14 21.3	1D 10.1	15 08.1	9 30.1	8 11.6	12 37.1	19 02.7	19 26.9
10 Tu	5 15 08	19 31 39	13♑42 48	21 07 00	23 31.4	21 16.7	15 34.9	1 10.0	15 30.9	9 42.8	8D 11.5	12 40.5	19 02.1	19 28.0
11 W	5 19 04	20 28 59	28 30 04	5♒51 11	23 28.0	23 28.3	16 48.6	1 10.7	15 53.7	9 55.4	8 11.6	12 43.9	19 01.5	19 29.1
12 Th	5 23 01	21 26 18	13♒09 41	20 24 59	23D 26.9	25 39.2	18 02.2	1 12.2	16 16.4	10 07.9	8 11.7	12 47.3	19 00.9	19 30.2
13 F	5 26 58	22 23 36	27 36 41	4♓44 29	23 27.1	27 49.2	19 15.9	1 14.4	16 39.0	10 20.4	8 12.0	12 50.8	19 00.4	19 31.3
14 Sa	5 30 54	23 20 54	11♓48 12	18 47 46	23R 27.7	29 58.1	20 29.6	1 17.4	17 01.6	10 32.7	8 12.3	12 54.2	18 59.9	19 32.5
15 Su	5 34 51	24 18 12	25 43 11	2♈34 31	23 27.5	2♋05.6	21 43.2	1 21.2	17 24.2	10 45.0	8 12.8	12 57.7	18 59.4	19 33.7
16 M	5 38 47	25 15 30	9♈21 52	16 05 21	23 25.6	4 11.6	22 56.9	1 25.8	17 46.7	10 57.3	8 13.3	13 01.2	18 58.9	19 34.9
17 Tu	5 42 44	26 12 47	22 45 08	29 21 21	23 21.4	6 16.0	24 10.6	1 31.1	18 09.2	11 09.4	8 13.9	13 04.7	18 58.5	19 36.1
18 W	5 46 40	27 10 04	5♉54 07	12♉23 34	23 15.0	8 18.6	25 24.3	1 37.2	18 31.6	11 21.5	8 14.7	13 08.2	18 58.1	19 37.3
19 Th	5 50 37	28 07 21	18 49 49	25 12 56	23 06.7	10 19.2	26 38.0	1 43.9	18 53.9	11 33.5	8 15.5	13 11.8	18 57.7	19 38.6
20 F	5 54 33	29 04 37	1♊33 00	7♊50 05	22 57.2	12 17.9	27 51.7	1 51.5	19 16.2	11 45.4	8 16.5	13 15.3	18 57.4	19 39.9
21 Sa	5 58 30	0♋01 53	14 04 16	20 15 38	22 47.6	14 14.5	29 05.4	1 59.7	19 38.5	11 57.3	8 17.5	13 18.9	18 57.1	19 41.2
22 Su	6 02 27	0 59 09	26 24 15	2♋30 15	22 38.6	16 09.0	0♋19.1	2 08.6	20 00.6	12 09.0	8 18.7	13 22.4	18 56.9	19 42.5
23 M	6 06 23	1 56 24	8♋33 45	14 34 56	22 31.2	18 01.4	1 32.9	2 18.3	20 22.8	12 20.7	8 19.9	13 26.0	18 56.6	19 43.8
24 Tu	6 10 20	2 53 39	20 34 00	26 31 13	22 25.8	19 51.5	2 46.6	2 28.6	20 44.8	12 32.3	8 21.3	13 29.6	18 56.4	19 45.2
25 W	6 14 16	3 50 54	2♌26 51	8♌21 15	22 22.7	21 39.5	4 00.3	2 39.6	21 06.8	12 43.8	8 22.7	13 33.2	18 56.2	19 46.6
26 Th	6 18 13	4 48 08	14 14 50	20 07 59	22D 21.5	23 25.3	5 14.1	2 51.2	21 28.7	12 55.2	8 24.3	13 36.8	18 56.1	19 48.0
27 F	6 22 09	5 45 21	26 01 12	1♍55 01	22 21.9	25 08.9	6 27.8	3 03.6	21 50.6	13 06.5	8 25.9	13 40.4	18 56.0	19 49.4
28 Sa	6 26 06	6 42 34	7♍49 57	13 46 37	22 23.1	26 50.2	7 41.5	3 16.5	22 12.4	13 17.7	8 27.7	13 44.0	18 55.9	19 50.8
29 Su	6 30 02	7 39 47	19 45 37	25 47 34	22 24.5	28 29.3	8 55.3	3 30.1	22 34.1	13 28.9	8 29.5	13 47.6	18D 55.9	19 52.3
30 M	6 33 59	8 36 59	1♎53 07	8♎02 54	22R 25.1	0♌06.2	10 09.0	3 44.3	22 55.8	13 39.9	8 31.4	13 51.2	18 55.9	19 53.8

Astro Data

	Dy Hr Mn
☽0S	5 17:26
☽0N	18 16:25
♆⚹♇	26 10:46
☽0S	2 1:09
♃⚻♄	3 14:00
♂ D	10 2:45
♄ D	10 13:19
☽0N	14 21:00
☽0S	29 7:58
♆ D	30 9:23

Planet Ingress

		Dy Hr Mn
⚳	♉	1 19:19
♀	♉	4 8:55
☿	♉	14 14:43
☉	♊	21 3:04
♀	♊	28 19:19
☿	♊	31 15:26
☿	♋	14 12:22
☉	♋	21 11:13
♀	♋	22 5:46
☿	♌	30 10:27

Last Aspect / ☽ Ingress (May)

Last Aspect Dy Hr Mn			☽ Ingress	Dy Hr Mn
30 19:19	♀	□	♌	1 4:12
3 15:08	♀	△	♍	3 16:57
4 21:23	☉	△	♎	6 3:39
7 18:39	☿	☍	♏	8 10:49
9 20:16	☉	☍	♐	10 14:50
12 12:12	☿	△	♑	12 17:09
14 8:17	☉	△	♒	14 19:14
16 14:39	☉	□	♓	16 22:05
18 22:25	☉	⚹	♈	19 2:07
20 12:22	♆	☍	♉	21 7:29
23 1:28	♀	☌	♊	23 14:37
25 3:14	♆	△	♋	26 0:06
28 11:09	♀	⚹	♌	28 11:59
30 21:56	☿	□	♍	31 0:57

Last Aspect / ☽ Ingress (June)

Last Aspect Dy Hr Mn			☽ Ingress	Dy Hr Mn
1 1:22	♅	⚹	♎	2 12:26
4 0:58	♇	⚹	♏	4 20:19
6 6:20	♇	□	♐	7 0:21
8 8:32	♇	△	♑	9 1:46
10 8:38	♆	□	♒	11 2:26
12 22:17	☿	△	♓	13 4:00
14 20:28	☉	□	♈	15 7:29
17 5:50	☉	⚹	♉	17 13:11
19 1:30	♇	□	♊	19 21:03
21 10:53	♇	⚹	♋	22 7:04
23 20:44	♆	□	♌	24 19:02
26 11:19	♇	☌	♍	27 8:06
29 18:09	☿	⚹	♎	29 20:18

☽ Phases & Eclipses

Dy Hr Mn		
2 3:58	☽	11♌42
9 20:16	○	19♏07
16 14:39	☾	25♒39
23 19:28	●	2♊35
31 21:46	☽	10♍21
8 5:07	○	17♐21
14 20:28	☾	23♓41
22 8:45	●	0♋51
30 13:11	☽	8♎40

Astro Data

1 May 1952
Julian Day # 19114
SVP 5♓55'23"
GC 26♐10.4 ⚴ 23♓48.9
Eris 7♈56.3 ⚵ 17♒11.9
⚷ 12♑23.9R ⚶ 1♍02.8
☽ Mean ☊ 27♒01.5

1 June 1952
Julian Day # 19145
SVP 5♓55'18"
GC 26♐10.5 ⚴ 1♈48.6
Eris 8♈11.4 ⚵ 22♒57.0
⚷ 11♑19.0R ⚶ 7♍52.9
☽ Mean ☊ 25♒23.0

July 1952 — LONGITUDE

Day	Sid.Time	☉	0 hr ☽	Noon ☽	True ☊	☿	♀	♂	⚳	♃	♄	♅	♆	♇
1 Tu	6 37 56	9♋34 11	14♎17 32	20♎37 34	22♒24.4	1♌40.8	11♋22.8	3♏59.1	23♉17.4	13♉50.8	8♎33.5	13♋54.9	18♎55.9	19♌55.3
2 W	6 41 52	10 31 22	27 03 34	3♏35 58	22R 22.1	3 13.2	12 36.5	4 14.5	23 38.9	14 01.7	8 35.6	13 58.5	18 55.9	19 56.8
3 Th	6 45 49	11 28 34	10♏15 08	17 01 18	22 18.2	4 43.3	13 50.3	4 30.5	24 00.4	14 12.4	8 37.8	14 02.1	18 56.0	19 58.3
4 F	6 49 45	12 25 45	23 54 33	0♐54 51	22 13.1	6 11.1	15 04.0	4 47.0	24 21.7	14 23.1	8 40.1	14 05.8	18 56.1	19 59.8
5 Sa	6 53 42	13 22 56	8♐01 55	15 15 20	22 07.4	7 36.5	16 17.8	5 04.1	24 43.0	14 33.6	8 42.5	14 09.4	18 56.3	20 01.4
6 Su	6 57 38	14 20 06	22 34 29	29 58 34	22 01.8	8 59.7	17 31.6	5 21.8	25 04.3	14 44.0	8 45.0	14 13.0	18 56.5	20 03.0
7 M	7 01 35	15 17 17	7♑26 38	14♑57 36	21 57.2	10 20.4	18 45.3	5 40.0	25 25.4	14 54.4	8 47.6	14 16.7	18 56.7	20 04.6
8 Tu	7 05 32	16 14 28	22 30 21	0♒03 40	21 54.1	11 38.8	19 59.1	5 58.7	25 46.5	15 04.6	8 50.3	14 20.3	18 56.9	20 06.2
9 W	7 09 28	17 11 39	7♒36 24	15 07 27	21D 52.6	12 54.6	21 12.9	6 17.9	26 07.5	15 14.7	8 53.1	14 23.9	18 57.2	20 07.8
10 Th	7 13 25	18 08 50	22 35 48	0♓00 36	21 52.6	14 08.0	22 26.7	6 37.6	26 28.4	15 24.7	8 56.0	14 27.6	18 57.5	20 09.4
11 F	7 17 21	19 06 02	7♓21 07	14 36 48	21 53.7	15 18.7	23 40.5	6 57.8	26 49.2	15 34.6	8 58.9	14 31.2	18 57.9	20 11.0
12 Sa	7 21 18	20 03 14	21 47 13	28 52 07	21 55.1	16 26.8	24 54.3	7 18.5	27 10.0	15 44.4	9 02.0	14 34.8	18 58.2	20 12.7
13 Su	7 25 14	21 00 26	5♈51 23	12♈45 00	21R 56.2	17 32.2	26 08.1	7 39.6	27 30.6	15 54.1	9 05.1	14 38.4	18 58.7	20 14.4
14 M	7 29 11	21 57 40	19 33 04	26 15 45	21 56.4	18 34.8	27 21.9	8 01.3	27 51.2	16 03.6	9 08.3	14 42.0	18 59.1	20 16.0
15 Tu	7 33 07	22 54 54	2♉53 16	9♉25 54	21 55.3	19 34.4	28 35.8	8 23.4	28 11.7	16 13.1	9 11.6	14 45.7	18 59.6	20 17.7
16 W	7 37 04	23 52 08	15 53 56	22 17 40	21 53.0	20 31.0	29 49.6	8 45.9	28 32.1	16 22.4	9 15.0	14 49.3	19 00.1	20 19.5
17 Th	7 41 01	24 49 24	28 37 27	4♊53 34	21 49.6	21 24.5	1♌03.4	9 08.9	28 52.4	16 31.6	9 18.5	14 52.9	19 00.6	20 21.2
18 F	7 44 57	25 46 40	11♊06 20	17 16 03	21 45.6	22 14.8	2 17.3	9 32.3	29 12.6	16 40.6	9 22.0	14 56.5	19 01.2	20 22.9
19 Sa	7 48 54	26 43 56	23 22 58	29 27 22	21 41.4	23 01.6	3 31.2	9 56.2	29 32.7	16 49.6	9 25.7	15 00.0	19 01.8	20 24.6
20 Su	7 52 50	27 41 13	5♋29 32	11♋29 40	21 37.5	23 44.9	4 45.0	10 20.5	29 52.7	16 58.4	9 29.4	15 03.6	19 02.4	20 26.4
21 M	7 56 47	28 38 31	17 28 03	23 24 55	21 34.5	24 24.6	5 58.9	10 45.2	0♊12.6	17 07.1	9 33.2	15 07.2	19 03.1	20 28.2
22 Tu	8 00 43	29 35 49	29 20 31	5♌15 06	21 32.4	25 00.4	7 12.8	11 10.3	0 32.5	17 15.6	9 37.1	15 10.7	19 03.7	20 29.9
23 W	8 04 40	0♌33 08	11♌08 57	17 02 20	21D 31.5	25 32.2	8 26.7	11 35.8	0 52.2	17 24.1	9 41.1	15 14.3	19 04.5	20 31.7
24 Th	8 08 36	1 30 27	22 55 35	28 49 01	21 31.6	25 59.8	9 40.6	12 01.7	1 11.8	17 32.4	9 45.2	15 17.8	19 05.2	20 33.5
25 F	8 12 33	2 27 47	4♍43 00	10♍37 55	21 32.5	26 23.1	10 54.5	12 28.0	1 31.2	17 40.5	9 49.3	15 21.3	19 06.0	20 35.3
26 Sa	8 16 30	3 25 08	16 34 11	22 32 15	21 33.9	26 41.9	12 08.4	12 54.7	1 50.6	17 48.5	9 53.5	15 24.9	19 06.8	20 37.1
27 Su	8 20 26	4 22 28	28 32 35	4♎35 41	21 35.3	26 56.0	13 22.3	13 21.7	2 09.9	17 56.4	9 57.8	15 28.3	19 07.7	20 38.9
28 M	8 24 23	5 19 50	10♎42 03	16 52 12	21 36.5	27 05.3	14 36.2	13 49.1	2 29.0	18 04.1	10 02.2	15 31.8	19 08.5	20 40.7
29 Tu	8 28 19	6 17 12	23 06 40	29 25 57	21R 37.2	27R 09.6	15 50.1	14 16.9	2 48.0	18 11.7	10 06.6	15 35.3	19 09.4	20 42.6
30 W	8 32 16	7 14 34	5♏50 34	12♏20 58	21 37.2	27 08.8	17 04.0	14 45.0	3 07.0	18 19.1	10 11.2	15 38.7	19 10.4	20 44.4
31 Th	8 36 12	8 11 57	18 57 32	25 40 35	21 36.7	27 02.9	18 17.9	15 13.4	3 25.7	18 26.4	10 15.8	15 42.2	19 11.3	20 46.2

August 1952 — LONGITUDE

Day	Sid.Time	☉	0 hr ☽	Noon ☽	True ☊	☿	♀	♂	⚳	♃	♄	♅	♆	♇
1 F	8 40 09	9♌09 21	2♐30 22	9♐26 58	21♒35.6	26♌51.8	19♌31.8	15♏42.2	3♊44.4	18♉33.6	10♎20.4	15♋45.6	19♎12.3	20♌48.1
2 Sa	8 44 05	10 06 45	16 30 21	23 40 18	21R 34.3	26R 35.6	20 45.7	16 11.3	4 02.9	18 40.6	10 25.2	15 49.0	19 13.4	20 49.9
3 Su	8 48 02	11 04 10	0♑56 29	8♑18 20	21 33.0	26 14.2	21 59.7	16 40.7	4 21.4	18 47.4	10 30.0	15 52.4	19 14.4	20 51.8
4 M	8 51 59	12 01 36	15 45 08	23 16 00	21 32.0	25 47.9	23 13.6	17 10.5	4 39.7	18 54.1	10 34.9	15 55.7	19 15.5	20 53.7
5 Tu	8 55 55	12 59 02	0♒49 55	8♒25 44	21D 31.4	25 16.8	24 27.5	17 40.5	4 57.8	19 00.6	10 39.8	15 59.1	19 16.6	20 55.5
6 W	8 59 52	13 56 30	16 02 16	23 38 18	21 31.3	24 41.4	25 41.4	18 10.9	5 15.8	19 07.0	10 44.8	16 02.4	19 17.8	20 57.4
7 Th	9 03 48	14 53 58	1♓12 38	8♓44 09	21 31.5	24 02.0	26 55.3	18 41.5	5 33.7	19 13.2	10 49.9	16 05.7	19 18.9	20 59.3
8 F	9 07 45	15 51 28	16 11 51	23 34 51	21 31.9	23 19.1	28 09.2	19 12.4	5 51.5	19 19.3	10 55.1	16 09.0	19 20.1	21 01.1
9 Sa	9 11 41	16 48 59	0♈52 26	8♈04 02	21 32.4	22 33.5	29 23.2	19 43.6	6 09.1	19 25.2	11 00.3	16 12.2	19 21.3	21 03.0
10 Su	9 15 38	17 46 31	15 09 19	22 08 02	21 32.7	21 45.8	0♍37.1	20 15.1	6 26.5	19 31.0	11 05.6	16 15.5	19 22.6	21 04.9
11 M	9 19 34	18 44 05	29 00 09	5♉45 43	21 33.0	20 56.9	1 51.0	20 46.9	6 43.9	19 36.5	11 10.9	16 18.7	19 23.9	21 06.8
12 Tu	9 23 31	19 41 40	12♉24 56	18 58 05	21R 33.0	20 07.7	3 04.9	21 18.9	7 01.0	19 41.9	11 16.3	16 21.9	19 25.2	21 08.7
13 W	9 27 28	20 39 17	25 25 30	1♊47 37	21D 33.0	19 19.0	4 18.9	21 51.2	7 18.0	19 47.2	11 21.8	16 25.0	19 26.5	21 10.5
14 Th	9 31 24	21 36 55	8♊04 52	14 17 44	21 33.0	18 31.8	5 32.8	22 23.8	7 34.9	19 52.3	11 27.3	16 28.2	19 27.8	21 12.4
15 F	9 35 21	22 34 35	20 26 40	26 32 11	21 33.1	17 47.1	6 46.8	22 56.6	7 51.6	19 57.2	11 32.9	16 31.3	19 29.2	21 14.3
16 Sa	9 39 17	23 32 17	2♋34 44	8♋34 46	21 33.2	17 05.9	8 00.7	23 29.7	8 08.2	20 01.9	11 38.6	16 34.4	19 30.6	21 16.2
17 Su	9 43 14	24 29 59	14 32 44	20 29 03	21 33.5	16 29.0	9 14.7	24 03.1	8 24.6	20 06.4	11 44.3	16 37.5	19 32.1	21 18.1
18 M	9 47 10	25 27 44	26 24 06	2♌18 16	21 33.8	15 57.1	10 28.6	24 36.7	8 40.8	20 10.8	11 50.1	16 40.5	19 33.5	21 20.0
19 Tu	9 51 07	26 25 29	8♌11 54	14 05 19	21R 34.1	15 31.0	11 42.6	25 10.5	8 56.8	20 15.0	11 55.9	16 43.5	19 35.0	21 21.9
20 W	9 55 03	27 23 16	19 58 50	25 52 44	21 34.1	15 11.4	12 56.5	25 44.6	9 12.7	20 19.0	12 01.8	16 46.5	19 36.5	21 23.7
21 Th	9 59 00	28 21 05	1♍47 19	7♍42 51	21 33.8	14 58.7	14 10.5	26 18.9	9 28.4	20 22.8	12 07.7	16 49.4	19 38.1	21 25.6
22 F	10 02 57	29 18 55	13 39 37	19 37 53	21 33.2	14D 53.4	15 24.4	26 53.5	9 43.9	20 26.5	12 13.7	16 52.3	19 39.6	21 27.5
23 Sa	10 06 53	0♍16 46	25 37 56	1♎40 02	21 32.1	14 55.7	16 38.4	27 28.3	9 59.2	20 29.9	12 19.7	16 55.2	19 41.2	21 29.3
24 Su	10 10 50	1 14 38	7♎44 30	13 51 39	21 30.9	15 05.8	17 52.3	28 03.3	10 14.3	20 33.2	12 25.8	16 58.1	19 42.8	21 31.2
25 M	10 14 46	2 12 32	20 01 46	26 15 13	21 29.5	15 23.9	19 06.2	28 38.6	10 29.3	20 36.3	12 32.0	17 00.9	19 44.4	21 33.1
26 Tu	10 18 43	3 10 27	2♏32 19	8♏53 26	21 28.2	15 50.0	20 20.2	29 14.0	10 44.0	20 39.2	12 38.1	17 03.7	19 46.1	21 34.9
27 W	10 22 39	4 08 24	15 18 54	21 49 04	21D 27.4	16 23.9	21 34.1	29 49.7	10 58.6	20 41.9	12 44.4	17 06.4	19 47.7	21 36.8
28 Th	10 26 36	5 06 22	28 24 14	5♐04 41	21 27.1	17 05.7	22 48.0	0♐25.6	11 12.9	20 44.4	12 50.7	17 09.1	19 49.4	21 38.6
29 F	10 30 32	6 04 21	11♐50 41	18 42 22	21 27.4	17 55.0	24 01.9	1 01.7	11 27.1	20 46.7	12 57.0	17 11.8	19 51.1	21 40.5
30 Sa	10 34 29	7 02 21	25 39 52	2♑43 09	21 28.3	18 51.6	25 15.9	1 38.0	11 41.0	20 48.9	13 03.4	17 14.5	19 52.9	21 42.3
31 Su	10 38 26	8 00 23	9♑52 06	17 06 28	21 29.4	19 55.2	26 29.8	2 14.5	11 54.8	20 50.8	13 09.8	17 17.1	19 54.6	21 44.1

Astro Data Dy Hr Mn	Planet Ingress Dy Hr Mn	Last Aspect Dy Hr Mn	☽ Ingress Dy Hr Mn	Last Aspect Dy Hr Mn	☽ Ingress Dy Hr Mn	☽ Phases & Eclipses Dy Hr Mn	Astro Data
♃✶♅ 2 1:20	♀ ♌ 16 15:23	1 10:40 ♇ ✶	♏ 2 5:25	2 16:44 ☿ △	♑ 2 22:27	7 12:33 ○ 15♑19	1 July 1952
☽0N 12 3:07	⚳ ♊ 20 20:44	3 17:10 ♇ □	♐ 4 10:27	4 5:36 ♆ □	♒ 4 22:41	14 3:42 ☾ 21♈38	Julian Day # 19175
☽0S 26 13:59	☉ ♌ 22 22:07	5 19:51 ♇ △	♑ 6 12:02	6 15:32 ♀ ☍	♓ 6 22:05	21 23:31 ● 29♋06	SVP 5♓55'13"
☿R 29 20:31		7 18:35 ♀ ☍	♒ 8 11:54	8 5:01 ♃ ✶	♈ 8 22:33	30 1:51 ☽ 6♏50	GC 26♐10.6 ⚴ 7♈17.1
	♀ ♍ 9 23:58	9 20:03 ♇ ☍	♓ 10 11:59	10 11:24 ☿ △	♉ 11 1:46		Eris 8♈17.4 ⚵ 23♒57.3R
☽0N 8 11:53	☉ ♍ 23 5:03	12 4:37 ♀ △	♈ 12 13:56	12 16:32 ♂ ☍	♊ 13 8:36	5 19:40 ○ 13♒17	⚷ 9♑31.6R ⚶ 18♍23.1
♃⚻♆ 8 16:02	♂ ♐ 27 18:53	14 14:11 ♀ □	♉ 14 18:45	15 3:31 ☉ ✶	♋ 15 18:52	5 19:47 ☍ P 0.532	☽ Mean ☊ 23♒47.7
☿D 22 16:55		16 15:13 ☉ ✶	♊ 17 2:37	17 19:35 ♂ △	♌ 18 7:19	12 13:27 ☾ 19♉45	
☽0S 22 19:46		18 22:27 ☿ ✶	♋ 19 13:05	20 15:20 ☉ ☌	♍ 20 20:22	20 15:20 ● 27♌31	1 August 1952
		21 23:31 ☉ ☌	♌ 22 1:20	23 3:15 ♂ ✶	♎ 23 8:42	20 15:13:05 ● A 06'40"	Julian Day # 19206
		24 6:02 ☿ ☌	♍ 24 14:24	25 2:55 ♇ ✶	♏ 25 19:10	28 12:03 ☽ 5♐06	SVP 5♓55'08"
		26 2:23 ♃ △	♎ 27 2:54	27 11:37 ♇ □	♐ 28 2:53		GC 26♐10.6 ⚴ 9♈07.7R
		29 7:41 ☿ ✶	♏ 29 13:04	29 22:05 ♀ □	♑ 30 7:24		Eris 8♈13.2R ⚵ 19♒10.8R
		31 14:24 ☿ □	♐ 31 19:37				⚷ 7♑42.3R ⚶ 1♎39.8
							☽ Mean ☊ 22♒09.2

LONGITUDE — September 1952

Day	Sid.Time	☉	0 hr ☽	Noon ☽	True ☊	☿	♀	♂	⚳	♃	♄	♅	♆	♇
1 M	10 42 22	8♍58 26	24♑25 51	1♒49 41	21♒30.5	21♌05.5	27♍43.7	2♐51.2	12♊08.3	20♉52.5	13♎16.3	17♋19.7	19♎56.4	21♌45.9
2 Tu	10 46 19	9 56 31	9♒17 16	16 47 46	21R 31.1	22 21.9	28 57.6	3 28.1	12 21.6	20 54.1	13 22.8	17 22.2	19 58.2	21 47.8
3 W	10 50 15	10 54 37	24 20 12	1♓53 30	21 30.9	23 44.0	0♎11.4	4 05.2	12 34.7	20 55.5	13 29.3	17 24.7	20 00.0	21 49.6
4 Th	10 54 12	11 52 45	9♓26 33	16 58 12	21 29.7	25 11.4	1 25.3	4 42.4	12 47.5	20 56.6	13 35.9	17 27.2	20 01.9	21 51.4
5 F	10 58 08	12 50 54	24 27 18	1♈52 50	21 27.6	26 43.5	2 39.2	5 19.9	13 00.2	20 57.6	13 42.5	17 29.6	20 03.7	21 53.1
6 Sa	11 02 05	13 49 05	9♈13 50	16 29 28	21 24.7	28 19.9	3 53.0	5 57.5	13 12.6	20 58.3	13 49.2	17 32.0	20 05.6	21 54.9
7 Su	11 06 01	14 47 19	23 39 06	0♉42 14	21 21.5	29 59.9	5 06.9	6 35.3	13 24.7	20 58.9	13 55.9	17 34.3	20 07.5	21 56.7
8 M	11 09 58	15 45 34	7♉38 35	14 28 01	21 18.6	1♍43.0	6 20.7	7 13.2	13 36.7	20 59.3	14 02.6	17 36.7	20 09.4	21 58.4
9 Tu	11 13 55	16 43 51	21 10 32	27 46 19	21 16.3	3 28.8	7 34.6	7 51.4	13 48.4	20R 59.4	14 09.4	17 38.9	20 11.3	22 00.2
10 W	11 17 51	17 42 11	4♊15 39	10♊38 56	21D 15.0	5 16.8	8 48.4	8 29.7	13 59.8	20 59.4	14 16.2	17 41.2	20 13.2	22 01.9
11 Th	11 21 48	18 40 33	16 56 38	23 09 16	21 14.9	7 06.5	10 02.3	9 08.2	14 11.0	20 59.1	14 23.1	17 43.3	20 15.2	22 03.7
12 F	11 25 44	19 38 56	29 17 25	5♋21 39	21 15.8	8 57.6	11 16.1	9 46.8	14 21.9	20 58.7	14 29.9	17 45.5	20 17.2	22 05.4
13 Sa	11 29 41	20 37 22	11♋22 36	17 20 52	21 17.4	10 49.6	12 29.9	10 25.6	14 32.6	20 58.1	14 36.8	17 47.6	20 19.1	22 07.1
14 Su	11 33 37	21 35 50	23 17 03	29 11 42	21 19.1	12 42.3	13 43.8	11 04.6	14 43.0	20 57.2	14 43.8	17 49.7	20 21.2	22 08.8
15 M	11 37 34	22 34 20	5♌05 23	10♌58 37	21R 20.5	14 35.3	14 57.6	11 43.7	14 53.1	20 56.2	14 50.7	17 51.7	20 23.2	22 10.5
16 Tu	11 41 30	23 32 52	16 51 53	22 45 39	21 21.0	16 28.4	16 11.4	12 23.0	15 03.0	20 54.9	14 57.7	17 53.6	20 25.2	22 12.1
17 W	11 45 27	24 31 26	28 40 17	4♍36 11	21 20.1	18 21.4	17 25.2	13 02.5	15 12.5	20 53.5	15 04.7	17 55.6	20 27.2	22 13.8
18 Th	11 49 24	25 30 02	10♍33 39	16 33 00	21 17.5	20 14.1	18 39.0	13 42.1	15 21.8	20 51.8	15 11.8	17 57.5	20 29.3	22 15.4
19 F	11 53 20	26 28 40	22 34 26	28 38 13	21 13.3	22 06.4	19 52.8	14 21.9	15 30.8	20 49.9	15 18.9	17 59.3	20 31.4	22 17.0
20 Sa	11 57 17	27 27 20	4♎44 29	10♎53 25	21 07.6	23 58.2	21 06.6	15 01.8	15 39.5	20 47.9	15 26.0	18 01.1	20 33.5	22 18.6
21 Su	12 01 13	28 26 02	17 05 07	23 19 43	21 01.1	25 49.3	22 20.4	15 41.8	15 47.9	20 45.6	15 33.1	18 02.8	20 35.5	22 20.2
22 M	12 05 10	29 24 46	29 37 20	5♏58 02	20 54.4	27 39.7	23 34.1	16 22.1	15 56.0	20 43.2	15 40.2	18 04.5	20 37.7	22 21.8
23 Tu	12 09 06	0♎23 31	12♏21 56	18 49 07	20 48.2	29 29.3	24 47.9	17 02.4	16 03.8	20 40.5	15 47.4	18 06.2	20 39.8	22 23.4
24 W	12 13 03	1 22 19	25 19 43	1♐53 50	20 43.2	1♎18.1	26 01.6	17 42.9	16 11.3	20 37.7	15 54.5	18 07.8	20 41.9	22 24.9
25 Th	12 16 59	2 21 08	8♐31 35	15 13 06	20 40.0	3 06.0	27 15.4	18 23.5	16 18.5	20 34.6	16 01.7	18 09.3	20 44.0	22 26.4
26 F	12 20 56	3 19 59	21 58 31	28 47 57	20D 38.6	4 53.1	28 29.1	19 04.3	16 25.3	20 31.4	16 08.9	18 10.8	20 46.2	22 28.0
27 Sa	12 24 53	4 18 51	5♑41 28	12♑39 08	20 38.8	6 39.2	29 42.8	19 45.2	16 31.8	20 28.0	16 16.2	18 12.3	20 48.4	22 29.4
28 Su	12 28 49	5 17 46	19 40 59	26 46 54	20 39.9	8 24.5	0♏56.5	20 26.2	16 38.0	20 24.4	16 23.4	18 13.7	20 50.5	22 30.9
29 M	12 32 46	6 16 42	3♒56 47	11♒10 21	20R 41.0	10 08.9	2 10.2	21 07.4	16 43.9	20 20.6	16 30.7	18 15.0	20 52.7	22 32.4
30 Tu	12 36 42	7 15 40	18 27 16	25 47 02	20 41.2	11 52.3	3 23.9	21 48.7	16 49.4	20 16.6	16 37.9	18 16.3	20 54.9	22 33.8

LONGITUDE — October 1952

Day	Sid.Time	☉	0 hr ☽	Noon ☽	True ☊	☿	♀	♂	⚳	♃	♄	♅	♆	♇
1 W	12 40 39	8♎14 39	3♓09 03	10♓32 34	20♒39.7	13♎34.9	4♏37.5	22♐30.1	16♊54.6	20♉12.4	16♎45.2	18♋17.6	20♎57.1	22♌35.2
2 Th	12 44 35	9 13 40	17 56 46	25 20 44	20R 35.9	15 16.6	5 51.1	23 11.6	16 59.5	20R 08.1	16 52.5	18 18.8	20 59.3	22 36.6
3 F	12 48 32	10 12 44	2♈43 30	10♈04 05	20 30.0	16 57.5	7 04.8	23 53.2	17 04.0	20 03.6	16 59.8	18 19.9	21 01.5	22 38.0
4 Sa	12 52 28	11 11 49	17 21 31	24 34 55	20 22.3	18 37.5	8 18.4	24 34.9	17 08.1	19 58.9	17 07.1	18 21.0	21 03.7	22 39.4
5 Su	12 56 25	12 10 56	1♉43 29	8♉46 33	20 13.8	20 16.7	9 32.0	25 16.8	17 12.0	19 54.0	17 14.4	18 22.1	21 05.9	22 40.7
6 M	13 00 21	13 10 06	15 43 36	22 34 17	20 05.5	21 55.1	10 45.6	25 58.8	17 15.4	19 49.0	17 21.8	18 23.1	21 08.1	22 42.1
7 Tu	13 04 18	14 09 18	29 18 25	5♊55 58	19 58.3	23 32.8	11 59.1	26 40.8	17 18.5	19 43.8	17 29.1	18 24.0	21 10.3	22 43.4
8 W	13 08 15	15 08 32	12♊27 04	18 51 58	19 52.8	25 09.6	13 12.7	27 23.0	17 21.2	19 38.4	17 36.4	18 24.9	21 12.5	22 44.6
9 Th	13 12 11	16 07 49	25 11 03	1♋24 46	19 49.5	26 45.7	14 26.2	28 05.3	17 23.5	19 32.9	17 43.8	18 25.8	21 14.8	22 45.9
10 F	13 16 08	17 07 08	7♋33 41	13 38 23	19D 48.2	28 21.1	15 39.8	28 47.8	17 25.5	19 27.2	17 51.1	18 26.6	21 17.0	22 47.1
11 Sa	13 20 04	18 06 29	19 39 31	25 37 45	19 48.4	29 55.7	16 53.3	29 30.3	17 27.1	19 21.3	17 58.4	18 27.3	21 19.2	22 48.4
12 Su	13 24 01	19 05 53	1♌33 46	7♌28 14	19 49.3	1♏29.7	18 06.8	0♑12.9	17 28.3	19 15.3	18 05.8	18 28.0	21 21.5	22 49.5
13 M	13 27 57	20 05 19	13 21 51	19 15 14	19R 49.8	3 02.9	19 20.3	0 55.6	17 29.1	19 09.2	18 13.1	18 28.6	21 23.7	22 50.7
14 Tu	13 31 54	21 04 47	25 09 01	1♍03 47	19 49.1	4 35.5	20 33.8	1 38.4	17R 29.6	19 02.9	18 20.5	18 29.2	21 26.0	22 51.9
15 W	13 35 50	22 04 17	7♍00 05	12 58 23	19 46.3	6 07.4	21 47.3	2 21.4	17 29.6	18 56.4	18 27.8	18 29.7	21 28.2	22 53.0
16 Th	13 39 47	23 03 49	18 59 08	25 02 41	19 41.0	7 38.7	23 00.8	3 04.4	17 29.3	18 49.9	18 35.1	18 30.2	21 30.4	22 54.1
17 F	13 43 44	24 03 24	1♎09 22	7♎19 24	19 33.0	9 09.2	24 14.2	3 47.5	17 28.5	18 43.2	18 42.4	18 30.6	21 32.7	22 55.2
18 Sa	13 47 40	25 03 01	13 32 56	19 50 06	19 22.8	10 39.2	25 27.7	4 30.8	17 27.4	18 36.3	18 49.8	18 31.0	21 34.9	22 56.2
19 Su	13 51 37	26 02 39	26 10 54	2♏35 19	19 11.1	12 08.4	26 41.1	5 14.1	17 25.8	18 29.4	18 57.1	18 31.3	21 37.1	22 57.2
20 M	13 55 33	27 02 20	9♏03 16	15 34 37	18 59.0	13 37.0	27 54.5	5 57.5	17 23.9	18 22.3	19 04.4	18 31.5	21 39.4	22 58.2
21 Tu	13 59 30	28 02 03	22 09 12	28 46 52	18 47.6	15 05.0	29 07.9	6 41.0	17 21.5	18 15.2	19 11.7	18 31.7	21 41.6	22 59.2
22 W	14 03 26	29 01 48	5♐27 25	12♐10 39	18 38.1	16 32.3	0♐21.3	7 24.6	17 18.8	18 07.9	19 18.9	18 31.9	21 43.8	23 00.2
23 Th	14 07 23	0♏01 34	18 56 27	25 44 38	18 31.1	17 58.8	1 34.7	8 08.3	17 15.6	18 00.5	19 26.2	18 32.0	21 46.1	23 01.1
24 F	14 11 19	1 01 22	2♑35 08	9♑27 49	18 27.0	19 24.7	2 48.0	8 52.1	17 12.1	17 53.0	19 33.5	18R 32.0	21 48.3	23 02.0
25 Sa	14 15 16	2 01 12	16 22 41	23 19 40	18D 25.3	20 49.8	4 01.3	9 36.0	17 08.2	17 45.5	19 40.7	18 32.0	21 50.5	23 02.9
26 Su	14 19 13	3 01 04	0♒18 45	7♒19 55	18R 25.1	22 14.1	5 14.7	10 19.9	17 03.8	17 37.9	19 47.9	18 31.9	21 52.7	23 03.7
27 M	14 23 09	4 00 57	14 23 06	21 28 14	18 25.2	23 37.6	6 27.9	11 03.9	16 59.1	17 30.1	19 55.1	18 31.8	21 54.9	23 04.6
28 Tu	14 27 06	5 00 51	28 35 11	5♓43 44	18 24.2	25 00.3	7 41.2	11 48.0	16 53.9	17 22.4	20 02.3	18 31.6	21 57.1	23 05.3
29 W	14 31 02	6 00 48	12♓53 36	20 04 24	18 21.2	26 22.0	8 54.4	12 32.2	16 48.4	17 14.5	20 09.5	18 31.4	21 59.3	23 06.1
30 Th	14 34 59	7 00 46	27 15 40	4♈26 51	18 15.3	27 42.7	10 07.6	13 16.4	16 42.5	17 06.6	20 16.6	18 31.1	22 01.5	23 06.9
31 F	14 38 55	8 00 45	11♈37 18	18 46 22	18 06.4	29 02.4	11 20.8	14 00.7	16 36.2	16 58.6	20 23.8	18 30.8	22 03.6	23 07.6

Astro Data

	Dy Hr Mn
☽0N	4 22:31
♀0S	5 9:55
♃R	9 19:40
☽0S	19 1:58
☉0S	23 2:23
♃⚻♆	23 15:41
☿0S	25 12:10
☽0N	2 9:04
⚳R	15 2:30
♄□♅	15 18:51
☽0S	16 8:53
♃⚻♄	17 13:14
♃⚹♅	19 5:44
♅R	24 16:47
☽0N	29 17:25

Planet Ingress

		Dy Hr Mn
♀	♎	3 8:17
☿	♍	7 12:02
☉	♎	23 2:24
☿	♎	23 18:45
♀	♏	27 17:36
☿	♏	11 13:05
♂	♑	12 4:45
♀	♐	22 5:02
☉	♏	23 11:22

Last Aspect / ☽ Ingress (September)

Last Aspect Dy Hr Mn			☽ Ingress	Dy Hr Mn
1 4:45	♀	△	♒	1 9:03
2 21:44	☿	☍	♓	3 9:00
4 18:22	♃	⚹	♈	5 8:57
7 10:38	☿	△	♉	7 10:48
9 1:28	♇	□	♊	9 16:06
11 9:52	♇	⚹	♋	12 1:24
13 19:18	♃	⚹	♌	14 13:38
16 10:52	♇	☌	♍	17 2:42
19 7:22	☉	☌	♎	19 14:41
21 10:06	♇	⚹	♏	22 0:43
23 18:37	♇	□	♐	24 8:33
26 11:24	♀	⚹	♑	26 14:06
28 1:56	♆	□	♒	28 17:24
30 6:44	♇	☍	♓	30 18:52

Last Aspect / ☽ Ingress (October)

Last Aspect Dy Hr Mn			☽ Ingress	Dy Hr Mn
2 8:20	♂	□	♈	2 19:34
4 12:00	♂	△	♉	4 21:05
6 12:14	♇	□	♊	7 1:15
9 5:11	♂	☍	♋	9 9:16
11 3:18	♆	□	♌	11 20:50
13 19:19	♇	☌	♍	14 9:51
16 7:32	♀	⚹	♎	16 21:44
18 22:42	☉	☌	♏	19 7:10
21 12:42	♀	☌	♐	21 14:12
23 7:12	♇	△	♑	23 19:28
25 9:26	♆	□	♒	25 23:28
27 16:02	☿	□	♓	28 2:23
29 23:36	☿	△	♈	30 4:34

☽ Phases & Eclipses

Dy Hr Mn		
4 3:19	○	11♓32
11 2:36	☾	18♊18
19 7:22	●	26♍17
26 20:31	☽	3♑41
3 12:15	○	10♈13
10 19:33	☾	17♋26
18 22:42	●	25♎30
26 4:04	☽	2♒41

Astro Data

1 September 1952
Julian Day # 19237
SVP 5♓55'03"
GC 26♐10.7 ⚴ 5♈31.2R
Eris 7♈59.9R ⚵ 11♒59.2R
⚷ 6♑41.8R ⚶ 16♎29.3
☽ Mean ☊ 20♒30.7

1 October 1952
Julian Day # 19267
SVP 5♓55'00"
GC 26♐10.8 ⚴ 27♓49.5R
Eris 7♈41.8R ⚵ 9♒15.7
⚷ 6♑54.6 ⚶ 1♏47.3
☽ Mean ☊ 18♒55.4

November 1952 — LONGITUDE

Day	Sid.Time	☉	0 hr ☽	Noon ☽	True ☊	☿	♀	♂	⚳	♃	♄	♅	♆	♇
1 Sa	14 42 52	9♏00 47	25♈53 18	2♉57 23	17♒55.3	0♐20.9	12♐34.0	14♑45.1	16♊29.5	16♉50.6	20♎30.9	18♋30.4	22♎05.8	23♌08.3
2 Su	14 46 48	10 00 50	9♉57 57	16 54 21	17R 42.8	1 38.2	13 47.1	15 29.5	16R 22.5	16R 42.6	20 37.9	18R 29.9	22 08.0	23 08.9
3 M	14 50 45	11 00 55	23 46 04	0♊32 38	17 30.3	2 54.1	15 00.2	16 14.0	16 15.0	16 34.5	20 45.0	18 29.4	22 10.1	23 09.5
4 Tu	14 54 42	12 01 03	7♊13 46	13 49 17	17 19.0	4 08.4	16 13.3	16 58.6	16 07.2	16 26.4	20 52.0	18 28.9	22 12.3	23 10.2
5 W	14 58 38	13 01 12	20 19 09	26 43 26	17 09.9	5 21.1	17 26.4	17 43.2	15 59.1	16 18.2	20 59.0	18 28.3	22 14.4	23 10.7
6 Th	15 02 35	14 01 23	3♋02 21	9♋16 13	17 03.5	6 31.9	18 39.4	18 27.9	15 50.5	16 10.1	21 06.0	18 27.6	22 16.5	23 11.3
7 F	15 06 31	15 01 36	15 25 28	21 30 35	16 59.7	7 40.6	19 52.4	19 12.7	15 41.7	16 01.9	21 12.9	18 26.9	22 18.6	23 11.8
8 Sa	15 10 28	16 01 52	27 32 09	3♌30 46	16 58.1	8 47.0	21 05.4	19 57.5	15 32.4	15 53.7	21 19.9	18 26.1	22 20.7	23 12.3
9 Su	15 14 24	17 02 09	9♌27 07	15 21 52	16 57.8	9 50.7	22 18.4	20 42.4	15 22.8	15 45.6	21 26.7	18 25.3	22 22.8	23 12.8
10 M	15 18 21	18 02 28	21 15 44	27 09 25	16 57.7	10 51.5	23 31.3	21 27.4	15 12.9	15 37.4	21 33.6	18 24.5	22 24.9	23 13.2
11 Tu	15 22 17	19 02 49	3♍03 37	8♍59 01	16 56.6	11 49.0	24 44.2	22 12.4	15 02.7	15 29.2	21 40.4	18 23.5	22 26.9	23 13.6
12 W	15 26 14	20 03 12	14 56 17	20 56 01	16 53.6	12 42.8	25 57.1	22 57.4	14 52.1	15 21.1	21 47.2	18 22.6	22 29.0	23 14.0
13 Th	15 30 11	21 03 37	26 58 47	3♎05 07	16 47.9	13 32.3	27 10.0	23 42.6	14 41.2	15 13.0	21 53.9	18 21.6	22 31.0	23 14.3
14 F	15 34 07	22 04 04	9♎15 25	15 30 04	16 39.3	14 17.2	28 22.8	24 27.7	14 30.1	15 04.9	22 00.6	18 20.5	22 33.0	23 14.6
15 Sa	15 38 04	23 04 32	21 49 18	28 13 18	16 28.3	14 56.7	29 35.6	25 13.0	14 18.6	14 56.9	22 07.3	18 19.4	22 35.0	23 14.9
16 Su	15 42 00	24 05 02	4♏42 08	11♏15 44	16 15.5	15 30.3	0♑48.4	25 58.3	14 06.9	14 48.9	22 13.9	18 18.2	22 37.0	23 15.2
17 M	15 45 57	25 05 34	17 53 58	24 36 35	16 02.2	15 57.3	2 01.1	26 43.6	13 54.9	14 41.0	22 20.5	18 17.0	22 39.0	23 15.4
18 Tu	15 49 53	26 06 08	1♐23 15	8♐13 33	15 49.6	16 16.9	3 13.8	27 29.0	13 42.7	14 33.1	22 27.0	18 15.7	22 40.9	23 15.6
19 W	15 53 50	27 06 43	15 07 02	22 03 14	15 39.0	16R 28.3	4 26.5	28 14.4	13 30.2	14 25.3	22 33.6	18 14.4	22 42.8	23 15.8
20 Th	15 57 46	28 07 20	29 01 40	6♑01 49	15 31.1	16 30.9	5 39.1	28 59.9	13 17.6	14 17.6	22 40.0	18 13.1	22 44.8	23 15.9
21 F	16 01 43	29 07 57	13♑03 17	20 05 39	15 26.3	16 23.9	6 51.7	29 45.5	13 04.7	14 09.9	22 46.4	18 11.7	22 46.7	23 16.0
22 Sa	16 05 40	0♐08 36	27 08 35	4♒11 48	15D 24.2	16 06.7	8 04.3	0♒31.0	12 51.6	14 02.4	22 52.8	18 10.2	22 48.5	23 16.1
23 Su	16 09 36	1 09 16	11♒15 06	18 18 18	15R 23.8	15 38.9	9 16.8	1 16.7	12 38.3	13 54.9	22 59.1	18 08.7	22 50.4	23 16.2
24 M	16 13 33	2 09 57	25 21 17	2♓23 58	15 24.0	15 00.3	10 29.2	2 02.3	12 24.9	13 47.5	23 05.4	18 07.2	22 52.2	23R 16.2
25 Tu	16 17 29	3 10 39	9♓26 14	16 28 02	15 23.3	14 11.1	11 41.6	2 48.0	12 11.3	13 40.2	23 11.6	18 05.6	22 54.1	23 16.2
26 W	16 21 26	4 11 22	23 29 13	0♈29 41	15 20.7	13 11.9	12 54.0	3 33.7	11 57.7	13 33.1	23 17.7	18 04.0	22 55.9	23 16.1
27 Th	16 25 22	5 12 07	7♈29 14	14 27 39	15 15.5	12 03.9	14 06.3	4 19.5	11 43.9	13 26.0	23 23.8	18 02.3	22 57.6	23 16.1
28 F	16 29 19	6 12 52	21 24 39	28 19 55	15 07.5	10 48.7	15 18.5	5 05.3	11 30.0	13 19.1	23 29.9	18 00.6	22 59.4	23 16.0
29 Sa	16 33 15	7 13 38	5♉13 05	12♉03 47	14 57.2	9 28.6	16 30.7	5 51.1	11 16.0	13 12.2	23 35.9	17 58.9	23 01.1	23 15.9
30 Su	16 37 12	8 14 25	18 51 36	25 36 12	14 45.6	8 06.1	17 42.8	6 36.9	11 01.9	13 05.5	23 41.8	17 57.1	23 02.8	23 15.7

December 1952 — LONGITUDE

Day	Sid.Time	☉	0 hr ☽	Noon ☽	True ☊	☿	♀	♂	⚳	♃	♄	♅	♆	♇
1 M	16 41 09	9♐15 14	2♊17 12	8♊54 17	14♒33.8	6♐44.0	18♑54.9	7♒22.8	10♊47.9	12♉59.0	23♎47.7	17♋55.2	23♎04.5	23♌15.5
2 Tu	16 45 05	10 16 03	15 27 15	21 55 53	14R 23.1	5R 25.0	20 06.9	8 08.7	10R 33.7	12R 52.5	23 53.5	17R 53.4	23 06.2	23R 15.3
3 W	16 49 02	11 16 54	28 20 07	4♋39 57	14 14.4	4 11.7	21 18.9	8 54.7	10 19.6	12 46.3	23 59.3	17 51.5	23 07.9	23 15.1
4 Th	16 52 58	12 17 46	10♋55 29	17 06 52	14 08.2	3 06.3	22 30.7	9 40.6	10 05.5	12 40.1	24 05.0	17 49.5	23 09.5	23 14.8
5 F	16 56 55	13 18 40	23 14 24	29 18 24	14 04.6	2 10.5	23 42.6	10 26.6	9 51.4	12 34.1	24 10.6	17 47.6	23 11.1	23 14.5
6 Sa	17 00 51	14 19 34	5♌19 18	11♌17 35	14D 03.4	1 25.4	24 54.3	11 12.6	9 37.3	12 28.3	24 16.2	17 45.6	23 12.6	23 14.2
7 Su	17 04 48	15 20 30	17 13 48	23 08 31	14 03.7	0 51.5	26 06.0	11 58.6	9 23.3	12 22.6	24 21.7	17 43.5	23 14.2	23 13.8
8 M	17 08 45	16 21 27	29 02 22	4♍56 01	14 04.6	0 29.1	27 17.6	12 44.7	9 09.4	12 17.1	24 27.2	17 41.4	23 15.7	23 13.4
9 Tu	17 12 41	17 22 25	10♍50 08	16 45 24	14R 05.2	0D 17.8	28 29.2	13 30.8	8 55.5	12 11.7	24 32.6	17 39.3	23 17.2	23 13.0
10 W	17 16 38	18 23 24	22 42 30	28 42 08	14 04.5	0 17.1	29 40.6	14 16.9	8 41.7	12 06.5	24 37.9	17 37.2	23 18.7	23 12.6
11 Th	17 20 34	19 24 24	4♎44 56	10♎51 31	14 01.9	0 26.4	0♒52.0	15 03.0	8 28.1	12 01.5	24 43.1	17 35.0	23 20.1	23 12.1
12 F	17 24 31	20 25 25	17 02 27	23 18 16	13 57.1	0 44.8	2 03.3	15 49.1	8 14.6	11 56.6	24 48.3	17 32.8	23 21.5	23 11.6
13 Sa	17 28 27	21 26 28	29 39 22	6♏06 05	13 50.1	1 11.6	3 14.6	16 35.3	8 01.2	11 51.9	24 53.4	17 30.5	23 22.9	23 11.1
14 Su	17 32 24	22 27 31	12♏38 39	19 17 09	13 41.7	1 45.8	4 25.7	17 21.4	7 48.1	11 47.4	24 58.5	17 28.3	23 24.3	23 10.6
15 M	17 36 20	23 28 35	26 01 34	2♐51 42	13 32.6	2 26.7	5 36.8	18 07.6	7 35.1	11 43.1	25 03.4	17 26.0	23 25.6	23 10.0
16 Tu	17 40 17	24 29 41	9♐47 16	16 47 49	13 23.9	3 13.5	6 47.8	18 53.8	7 22.3	11 39.0	25 08.3	17 23.7	23 26.9	23 09.4
17 W	17 44 14	25 30 47	23 52 47	1♑01 29	13 16.6	4 05.5	7 58.7	19 40.1	7 09.7	11 35.1	25 13.1	17 21.3	23 28.2	23 08.7
18 Th	17 48 10	26 31 53	8♑13 13	15 27 12	13 11.4	5 02.1	9 09.5	20 26.3	6 57.4	11 31.3	25 17.9	17 19.0	23 29.5	23 08.1
19 F	17 52 07	27 33 00	22 42 39	29 58 47	13D 08.5	6 02.8	10 20.2	21 12.6	6 45.3	11 27.8	25 22.5	17 16.6	23 30.7	23 07.4
20 Sa	17 56 03	28 34 07	7♒14 53	14♒30 18	13 07.7	7 07.0	11 30.8	21 58.8	6 33.5	11 24.4	25 27.1	17 14.2	23 31.9	23 06.7
21 Su	18 00 00	29 35 15	21 44 27	28 56 51	13 08.5	8 14.4	12 41.3	22 45.1	6 21.9	11 21.3	25 31.6	17 11.8	23 33.1	23 06.0
22 M	18 03 56	0♑36 22	6♓07 08	13♓14 58	13 09.9	9 24.4	13 51.6	23 31.3	6 10.7	11 18.3	25 36.0	17 09.3	23 34.2	23 05.2
23 Tu	18 07 53	1 37 30	20 20 08	27 22 30	13R 10.8	10 36.9	15 01.9	24 17.6	5 59.7	11 15.6	25 40.4	17 06.8	23 35.3	23 04.4
24 W	18 11 49	2 38 38	4♈21 56	11♈18 24	13 10.5	11 51.5	16 12.0	25 03.9	5 49.0	11 13.0	25 44.6	17 04.4	23 36.4	23 03.6
25 Th	18 15 46	3 39 45	18 11 51	25 02 16	13 08.5	13 07.9	17 22.0	25 50.2	5 38.7	11 10.7	25 48.8	17 01.9	23 37.4	23 02.8
26 F	18 19 43	4 40 53	1♉49 39	8♉33 58	13 04.6	14 26.0	18 31.9	26 36.4	5 28.7	11 08.6	25 52.9	16 59.3	23 38.4	23 01.9
27 Sa	18 23 39	5 42 01	15 15 13	21 53 22	12 59.2	15 45.5	19 41.6	27 22.7	5 19.0	11 06.6	25 56.9	16 56.8	23 39.4	23 01.0
28 Su	18 27 36	6 43 09	28 28 22	5♊00 11	12 52.9	17 06.3	20 51.2	28 09.0	5 09.7	11 04.9	26 00.8	16 54.3	23 40.3	23 00.1
29 M	18 31 32	7 44 17	11♊28 47	17 54 08	12 46.4	18 28.3	22 00.7	28 55.3	5 00.7	11 03.4	26 04.6	16 51.7	23 41.2	22 59.2
30 Tu	18 35 29	8 45 25	24 16 12	0♋35 00	12 40.5	19 51.3	23 10.0	29 41.5	4 52.1	11 02.1	26 08.3	16 49.2	23 42.1	22 58.3
31 W	18 39 25	9 46 34	6♋50 32	13 02 54	12 35.8	21 15.3	24 19.1	0♓27.8	4 43.9	11 01.0	26 12.0	16 46.6	23 43.0	22 57.3

Astro Data

	Dy Hr Mn
☽0S	12 16:19
☿R	20 6:43
♄☌♆	21 13:17
♇R	24 17:04
☽0N	25 22:56
♄✶♇	26 5:53
♆✶♇	7 7:24
☽0S	9 23:47
☿D	10 1:27
☽0N	23 3:31

Planet Ingress

		Dy Hr Mn
☿	♐	1 5:34
♀	♑	15 20:03
♂	♒	21 19:40
☉	♐	22 8:36
♀	♒	10 18:30
☉	♑	21 21:43
♂	♓	30 21:35

Last Aspect / ☽ Ingress (November)

Last Aspect Dy Hr Mn		☽ Ingress	Dy Hr Mn
31 19:20	♇ △	♉	1 6:58
2 22:55	♇ □	♊	3 11:02
5 5:20	♇ ✶	♋	5 18:12
7 13:36	♆ □	♌	8 4:56
10 3:59	♇ ☌	♍	10 17:47
12 23:05	♀ □	♎	13 5:57
15 14:49	♀ ✶	♏	15 15:18
17 15:59	♂ ✶	♐	17 21:33
19 14:05	♇ △	♑	20 1:40
22 4:34	☉ ✶	♒	22 4:52
23 20:27	♇ ☍	♓	24 7:55
25 14:46	♅ △	♈	26 11:09
28 3:33	♄ ☍	♉	28 14:54
30 7:49	♇ □	♊	30 19:53

Last Aspect / ☽ Ingress (December)

Last Aspect Dy Hr Mn		☽ Ingress	Dy Hr Mn
2 15:41	♄ △	♋	3 3:09
5 1:46	♄ □	♌	5 13:23
7 14:30	♄ ✶	♍	8 1:57
10 14:09	♀ △	♎	10 14:35
12 14:52	♄ ☌	♏	13 0:39
14 18:56	♇ □	♐	15 7:00
17 2:12	♄ ✶	♑	17 10:17
19 4:22	♄ □	♒	19 12:02
21 13:09	☉ ✶	♓	21 13:45
22 18:35	♅ △	♈	23 16:30
25 13:29	♂ ✶	♉	25 20:46
27 22:37	♂ □	♊	28 2:48
30 10:11	♂ △	♋	30 10:53

☽ Phases & Eclipses

Dy Hr Mn		
1 23:10	○	9♉29
9 15:43	☾	17♌11
17 12:56	●	25♏08
24 11:34	☽	2♓09
1 12:41	○	9♊17
9 13:22	☾	17♍26
17 2:02	●	25♐05
23 19:52	☽	1♈58
31 5:06	○	9♋29

Astro Data

1 November 1952
Julian Day # 19298
SVP 5♓54'56"
GC 26♐10.8 ⚵ 21♓16.2R
Eris 7♈23.3R ⚴ 13♒08.0
⚷ 8♑22.1 ⚶ 18♏13.2
☽ Mean ☊ 17♒16.9

1 December 1952
Julian Day # 19328
SVP 5♓54'51"
GC 26♐10.9 ⚵ 20♓38.3
Eris 7♈10.8R ⚴ 21♒55.3
⚷ 10♑42.6 ⚶ 4♐25.4
☽ Mean ☊ 15♒41.6

LONGITUDE

January 1953

Day	Sid.Time	☉	0 hr ☽	Noon ☽	True ☊	☿	♀	♂	⚳	♃	♄	♅	♆	♇
1 Th	18 43 22	10♑47 42	19♋12 10	25♋18 28	12♒32.7	22♐40.1	25♒28.1	1♓14.0	4♊36.0	11♉00.1	26♎15.6	16♋44.0	23♎43.8	22♌56.3
2 F	18 47 19	11 48 50	1♌22 02	7♌23 03	12D31.2	24 05.7	26 36.9	2 00.3	4R28.6	10R59.4	26 19.0	16R41.4	23 44.6	22R55.3
3 Sa	18 51 15	12 49 59	13 21 51	19 18 45	12 31.3	25 32.0	27 45.6	2 46.5	4 21.5	10 58.9	26 22.4	16 38.8	23 45.3	22 54.2
4 Su	18 55 12	13 51 07	25 14 08	1♍08 25	12 32.5	26 59.0	28 54.0	3 32.8	4 14.7	10D58.6	26 25.7	16 36.3	23 46.0	22 53.2
5 M	18 59 08	14 52 16	7♍02 06	12 55 42	12 34.4	28 26.6	0♓02.4	4 19.0	4 08.4	10 58.6	26 28.9	16 33.7	23 46.7	22 52.1
6 Tu	19 03 05	15 53 25	18 49 44	24 44 48	12 36.2	29 54.8	1 10.5	5 05.2	4 02.5	10 58.7	26 32.0	16 31.0	23 47.4	22 51.0
7 W	19 07 01	16 54 34	0♎41 30	6♎40 27	12R37.6	1♑23.6	2 18.4	5 51.4	3 57.0	10 59.1	26 35.0	16 28.4	23 48.0	22 49.9
8 Th	19 10 58	17 55 43	12 42 17	18 47 36	12 38.0	2 52.9	3 26.2	6 37.6	3 51.9	10 59.6	26 37.9	16 25.8	23 48.6	22 48.8
9 F	19 14 54	18 56 52	24 57 02	1♏11 10	12 37.4	4 22.8	4 33.7	7 23.8	3 47.2	11 00.4	26 40.7	16 23.2	23 49.1	22 47.6
10 Sa	19 18 51	19 58 01	7♏30 32	13 55 37	12 35.7	5 53.1	5 41.1	8 10.0	3 42.9	11 01.3	26 43.4	16 20.6	23 49.6	22 46.4
11 Su	19 22 48	20 59 10	20 26 50	27 04 28	12 33.1	7 24.0	6 48.2	8 56.2	3 39.1	11 02.5	26 46.0	16 18.0	23 50.1	22 45.3
12 M	19 26 44	22 00 19	3♐48 44	10♐39 42	12 30.1	8 55.4	7 55.2	9 42.3	3 35.6	11 03.9	26 48.5	16 15.5	23 50.6	22 44.1
13 Tu	19 30 41	23 01 28	17 37 15	24 41 10	12 27.1	10 27.2	9 01.9	10 28.5	3 32.6	11 05.5	26 50.9	16 12.9	23 51.0	22 42.8
14 W	19 34 37	24 02 37	1♑51 02	9♑06 16	12 24.6	11 59.6	10 08.4	11 14.6	3 30.0	11 07.3	26 53.3	16 10.3	23 51.4	22 41.6
15 Th	19 38 34	25 03 45	16 26 08	23 49 49	12 22.9	13 32.4	11 14.6	12 00.7	3 27.8	11 09.3	26 55.5	16 07.7	23 51.7	22 40.3
16 F	19 42 30	26 04 53	1♒16 21	8♒44 41	12D22.3	15 05.8	12 20.6	12 46.8	3 26.1	11 11.5	26 57.6	16 05.2	23 52.0	22 39.1
17 Sa	19 46 27	27 06 00	16 13 48	23 42 38	12 22.5	16 39.7	13 26.4	13 32.9	3 24.7	11 13.9	26 59.6	16 02.6	23 52.3	22 37.8
18 Su	19 50 23	28 07 06	1♓10 12	8♓35 34	12 23.3	18 14.1	14 31.9	14 19.0	3 23.8	11 16.5	27 01.5	16 00.1	23 52.5	22 36.5
19 M	19 54 20	29 08 12	15 57 57	23 16 38	12 24.4	19 49.0	15 37.1	15 05.1	3D23.3	11 19.3	27 03.3	15 57.6	23 52.7	22 35.2
20 Tu	19 58 17	0♒09 16	0♈31 04	7♈40 50	12 25.4	21 24.5	16 42.0	15 51.1	3 23.2	11 22.3	27 05.0	15 55.1	23 52.9	22 33.9
21 W	20 02 13	1 10 20	14 45 40	21 45 22	12R26.0	23 00.5	17 46.6	16 37.1	3 23.5	11 25.5	27 06.6	15 52.6	23 53.0	22 32.5
22 Th	20 06 10	2 11 23	28 39 53	5♉29 16	12 26.2	24 37.1	18 51.0	17 23.1	3 24.3	11 28.9	27 08.1	15 50.1	23 53.1	22 31.2
23 F	20 10 06	3 12 24	12♉13 37	18 53 06	12 25.8	26 14.3	19 55.0	18 09.0	3 25.4	11 32.5	27 09.5	15 47.6	23 53.2	22 29.8
24 Sa	20 14 03	4 13 25	25 27 55	1♊58 19	12 25.0	27 52.1	20 58.7	18 55.0	3 27.0	11 36.3	27 10.8	15 45.2	23R53.3	22 28.4
25 Su	20 17 59	5 14 25	8♊24 35	14 46 57	12 24.1	29 30.5	22 02.0	19 40.9	3 29.0	11 40.2	27 11.9	15 42.8	23 53.3	22 27.1
26 M	20 21 56	6 15 23	21 05 42	27 21 07	12 23.2	1♒09.5	23 05.0	20 26.8	3 31.3	11 44.4	27 13.0	15 40.4	23 53.2	22 25.7
27 Tu	20 25 52	7 16 21	3♋33 26	9♋42 54	12 22.4	2 49.2	24 07.7	21 12.6	3 34.1	11 48.7	27 14.0	15 38.0	23 53.2	22 24.3
28 W	20 29 49	8 17 17	15 49 47	21 54 17	12 21.9	4 29.5	25 10.0	21 58.5	3 37.3	11 53.3	27 14.8	15 35.7	23 53.1	22 22.9
29 Th	20 33 46	9 18 13	27 56 39	3♌57 06	12D21.7	6 10.5	26 11.8	22 44.3	3 40.8	11 58.0	27 15.6	15 33.4	23 52.9	22 21.5
30 F	20 37 42	10 19 07	9♌55 52	15 53 11	12 21.7	7 52.2	27 13.3	23 30.0	3 44.7	12 02.9	27 16.2	15 31.1	23 52.7	22 20.0
31 Sa	20 41 39	11 20 00	21 49 17	27 44 25	12 21.7	9 34.6	28 14.4	24 15.8	3 49.0	12 08.0	27 16.8	15 28.8	23 52.5	22 18.6

LONGITUDE

February 1953

Day	Sid.Time	☉	0 hr ☽	Noon ☽	True ☊	☿	♀	♂	⚳	♃	♄	♅	♆	♇
1 Su	20 45 35	12♒20 53	3♍38 53	9♍32 58	12♒21.8	11♒17.7	29♓15.0	25♓01.5	3♊53.7	12♉13.2	27♎17.2	15♋26.5	23♎52.3	22♌17.2
2 M	20 49 32	13 21 44	15 27 00	21 21 19	12R21.7	13 01.5	0♈15.3	25 47.2	3 58.8	12 18.6	27 17.5	15R24.3	23R52.0	22R15.7
3 Tu	20 53 28	14 22 35	27 16 18	3♎12 21	12 21.5	14 46.0	1 15.0	26 32.8	4 04.2	12 24.2	27 17.8	15 22.1	23 51.7	22 14.3
4 W	20 57 25	15 23 24	9♎09 54	15 09 26	12 21.2	16 31.2	2 14.3	27 18.4	4 10.0	12 30.0	27R17.9	15 20.0	23 51.4	22 12.8
5 Th	21 01 21	16 24 13	21 11 26	27 16 23	12 20.8	18 17.1	3 13.1	28 04.0	4 16.2	12 35.9	27 17.9	15 17.8	23 51.0	22 11.4
6 F	21 05 18	17 25 00	3♏24 50	9♏37 18	12D20.6	20 03.7	4 11.4	28 49.6	4 22.7	12 42.0	27 17.8	15 15.7	23 50.6	22 09.9
7 Sa	21 09 15	18 25 47	15 54 18	22 16 20	12 20.5	21 50.9	5 09.3	29 35.1	4 29.6	12 48.3	27 17.6	15 13.7	23 50.2	22 08.5
8 Su	21 13 11	19 26 33	28 43 55	5♐17 28	12 20.8	23 38.8	6 06.5	0♈20.6	4 36.8	12 54.8	27 17.3	15 11.6	23 49.7	22 07.0
9 M	21 17 08	20 27 18	11♐57 20	18 43 49	12 21.4	25 27.2	7 03.3	1 06.1	4 44.4	13 01.4	27 16.9	15 09.6	23 49.2	22 05.5
10 Tu	21 21 04	21 28 02	25 37 05	2♑37 12	12 22.2	27 16.1	7 59.4	1 51.5	4 52.3	13 08.2	27 16.4	15 07.7	23 48.7	22 04.1
11 W	21 25 01	22 28 44	9♑44 02	16 57 21	12 23.0	29 05.4	8 55.0	2 37.0	5 00.6	13 15.1	27 15.8	15 05.8	23 48.1	22 02.6
12 Th	21 28 57	23 29 26	24 16 39	1♒41 21	12R23.6	0♓55.1	9 50.0	3 22.3	5 09.2	13 22.2	27 15.0	15 03.9	23 47.5	22 01.1
13 F	21 32 54	24 30 06	9♒10 37	16 43 30	12 23.7	2 45.0	10 44.3	4 07.7	5 18.1	13 29.4	27 14.2	15 02.0	23 46.9	21 59.7
14 Sa	21 36 50	25 30 45	24 18 52	1♓55 32	12 23.2	4 35.0	11 38.0	4 53.0	5 27.4	13 36.8	27 13.3	15 00.2	23 46.2	21 58.2
15 Su	21 40 47	26 31 22	9♓32 15	17 07 46	12 22.0	6 24.8	12 31.0	5 38.3	5 36.9	13 44.4	27 12.2	14 58.4	23 45.6	21 56.7
16 M	21 44 44	27 31 58	24 40 52	2♈10 26	12 20.1	8 14.3	13 23.3	6 23.5	5 46.8	13 52.1	27 11.1	14 56.7	23 44.8	21 55.3
17 Tu	21 48 40	28 32 31	9♈35 30	16 55 14	12 18.1	10 03.3	14 14.8	7 08.7	5 57.0	13 59.9	27 09.8	14 55.0	23 44.1	21 53.8
18 W	21 52 37	29 33 03	24 09 01	1♉16 24	12 16.1	11 51.5	15 05.6	7 53.9	6 07.5	14 07.9	27 08.5	14 53.4	23 43.3	21 52.3
19 Th	21 56 33	0♓33 34	8♉17 07	15 11 03	12 14.6	13 38.4	15 55.6	8 39.0	6 18.3	14 16.1	27 07.0	14 51.8	23 42.5	21 50.9
20 F	22 00 30	1 34 02	21 58 18	28 39 01	12D14.0	15 23.8	16 44.8	9 24.1	6 29.5	14 24.4	27 05.5	14 50.2	23 41.7	21 49.5
21 Sa	22 04 26	2 34 29	5♊13 31	11♊42 09	12 14.2	17 07.3	17 33.1	10 09.1	6 40.9	14 32.8	27 03.8	14 48.7	23 40.8	21 48.0
22 Su	22 08 23	3 34 54	18 05 22	24 23 38	12 15.3	18 48.3	18 20.4	10 54.1	6 52.6	14 41.4	27 02.1	14 47.2	23 39.9	21 46.6
23 M	22 12 19	4 35 17	0♋37 27	6♋47 19	12 16.9	20 26.5	19 06.9	11 39.1	7 04.5	14 50.1	27 00.2	14 45.8	23 39.0	21 45.2
24 Tu	22 16 16	5 35 37	12 53 44	18 57 11	12 18.6	22 01.1	19 52.4	12 24.0	7 16.8	14 58.9	26 58.3	14 44.4	23 38.0	21 43.7
25 W	22 20 13	6 35 56	24 58 09	0♌57 03	12R19.9	23 31.7	20 36.9	13 08.9	7 29.3	15 07.8	26 56.3	14 43.1	23 37.1	21 42.3
26 Th	22 24 09	7 36 13	6♌54 18	12 50 17	12 20.4	24 57.7	21 20.3	13 53.7	7 42.1	15 16.9	26 54.1	14 41.8	23 36.1	21 40.9
27 F	22 28 06	8 36 29	18 45 21	24 39 49	12 19.7	26 18.3	22 02.6	14 38.5	7 55.2	15 26.2	26 51.9	14 40.6	23 35.0	21 39.5
28 Sa	22 32 02	9 36 42	0♍34 00	6♍28 10	12 17.6	27 33.1	22 43.8	15 23.3	8 08.5	15 35.5	26 49.6	14 39.4	23 34.0	21 38.1

Astro Data

	Dy Hr Mn
♃ D	5 7:52
☽ 0S	6 6:54
☽ 0N	19 10:10
⚳ D	20 4:56
♆ R	25 0:57
♀ 0N	31 17:35
☽ 0S	2 13:36
♄ R	5 2:31
♂ 0N	9 11:53
☽ 0N	15 20:00
♃ ⚹ ♅	23 1:57
☿ 0N	28 6:51

Planet Ingress

	Dy Hr Mn
♀ ♓	5 11:10
☿ ♑	6 13:24
☉ ♒	20 8:21
☿ ♒	25 19:10
♀ ♈	2 5:54
♂ ♈	8 1:07
☿ ♓	11 23:57
☉ ♓	18 22:41

Last Aspect / ☽ Ingress

Last Aspect Dy Hr Mn		☽ Ingress Dy Hr Mn
1 13:53	♄ □	♌ 1 21:17
4 6:58	♀ ☍	♍ 4 9:41
5 19:22	♅ ⚹	♎ 6 22:36
9 3:18	♄ ☌	♏ 9 9:44
11 4:13	♇ □	♐ 11 17:14
13 15:39	♄ ⚹	♑ 13 20:55
15 17:01	♄ □	♒ 15 21:57
17 17:17	♄ △	♓ 17 22:07
19 22:26	☉ ⚹	♈ 19 23:08
21 21:18	♄ ☍	♉ 22 2:20
24 3:20	☿ △	♊ 24 8:21
26 11:44	♄ △	♋ 26 17:07
28 22:37	♄ □	♌ 29 4:06
31 11:04	♄ ⚹	♍ 31 16:35

Last Aspect / ☽ Ingress

Last Aspect Dy Hr Mn		☽ Ingress Dy Hr Mn
2 21:36	♂ ☍	♎ 3 5:31
5 12:03	♄ ☌	♏ 5 17:21
7 11:45	♇ □	♐ 8 2:20
10 2:52	♄ ⚹	♑ 10 7:32
12 4:50	♄ □	♒ 12 9:17
14 4:36	♄ △	♓ 14 8:58
15 8:36	♅ △	♈ 16 8:30
18 8:52	☉ ⚹	♉ 18 9:50
19 23:46	♇ □	♊ 20 14:27
22 17:03	♄ △	♋ 22 22:48
25 3:58	♄ □	♌ 25 10:05
27 16:28	♄ ⚹	♍ 27 22:51

☽ Phases & Eclipses

Dy Hr Mn	
8 10:09	☾ 17♎51
15 14:08	● 25♑09
22 5:43	☽ 1♉55
29 23:44	○ 9♌48
29 23:47	● T 1.331
7 4:09	☾ 18♏06
14 1:10	● 25♒03
14 0:59:00	● P 0.760
20 17:44	☽ 1♊49
28 18:59	○ 9♍54

Astro Data

1 January 1953
Julian Day # 19359
SVP 5♓54'45"
GC 26♐11.0 ⚴ 25♓41.0
Eris 7♈07.7 ⚵ 4♓26.9
⚷ 13♑39.1 ⚶ 21♐10.0
☽ Mean ☊ 14♒03.1

1 February 1953
Julian Day # 19390
SVP 5♓54'39"
GC 26♐11.0 ⚴ 4♈45.5
Eris 7♈15.6 ⚵ 19♓16.7
⚷ 16♑37.2 ⚶ 7♑33.2
☽ Mean ☊ 12♒24.7

March 1953

LONGITUDE

Day	Sid.Time	☉	0 hr ☽	Noon ☽	True ☊	☿	♀	♂	⚳	♃	♄	♅	♆	♇
1 Su	22 35 59	10♓36 54	12♍22 33	18♍17 25	12♒14.0	28♓41.5	23♈23.8	16♈08.0	8♊22.0	15♉45.0	26♎47.2	14♋38.2	23♎32.9	21♌36.7
2 M	22 39 55	11 37 03	24 13 00	0♎09 31	12R 09.3	29 42.7	24 02.6	16 52.6	8 35.9	15 54.5	26R 44.7	14R 37.1	23R 31.8	21R 35.4
3 Tu	22 43 52	12 37 11	6♎07 13	12 06 19	12 03.8	0♈36.4	24 40.1	17 37.3	8 49.9	16 04.3	26 42.1	14 36.1	23 30.7	21 34.0
4 W	22 47 48	13 37 18	18 07 07	24 09 50	11 58.1	1 22.1	25 16.3	18 21.8	9 04.2	16 14.1	26 39.5	14 35.1	23 29.5	21 32.7
5 Th	22 51 45	14 37 22	0♏14 49	6♏22 21	11 52.8	1 59.3	25 51.2	19 06.4	9 18.8	16 24.0	26 36.7	14 34.1	23 28.3	21 31.3
6 F	22 55 42	15 37 26	12 32 47	18 46 28	11 48.6	2 27.8	26 24.6	19 50.9	9 33.6	16 34.1	26 33.9	14 33.3	23 27.1	21 30.0
7 Sa	22 59 38	16 37 27	25 03 49	1♐25 12	11 45.8	2 47.3	26 56.6	20 35.3	9 48.6	16 44.2	26 30.9	14 32.4	23 25.9	21 28.7
8 Su	23 03 35	17 37 27	7♐51 03	14 21 45	11D 44.6	2R 57.7	27 27.0	21 19.7	10 03.8	16 54.5	26 27.9	14 31.6	23 24.7	21 27.4
9 M	23 07 31	18 37 26	20 57 41	27 39 13	11 44.9	2 59.1	27 55.9	22 04.1	10 19.3	17 04.9	26 24.9	14 30.9	23 23.4	21 26.1
10 Tu	23 11 28	19 37 22	4♑26 40	11♑20 14	11 46.1	2 51.7	28 23.1	22 48.4	10 35.0	17 15.4	26 21.7	14 30.2	23 22.1	21 24.8
11 W	23 15 24	20 37 18	18 20 05	25 26 14	11 47.6	2 35.7	28 48.7	23 32.7	10 50.9	17 26.0	26 18.5	14 29.6	23 20.8	21 23.6
12 Th	23 19 21	21 37 11	2♒38 31	9♒56 41	11R 48.4	2 11.6	29 12.5	24 17.0	11 07.1	17 36.7	26 15.1	14 29.0	23 19.5	21 22.4
13 F	23 23 17	22 37 03	17 20 14	24 48 30	11 47.7	1 40.1	29 34.4	25 01.2	11 23.4	17 47.5	26 11.8	14 28.4	23 18.2	21 21.1
14 Sa	23 27 14	23 36 52	2♓20 38	9♓55 37	11 45.2	1 02.0	29 54.5	25 45.3	11 40.0	17 58.4	26 08.3	14 28.0	23 16.8	21 19.9
15 Su	23 31 11	24 36 40	17 32 15	25 09 18	11 40.6	0 18.2	0♉12.7	26 29.4	11 56.7	18 09.4	26 04.8	14 27.5	23 15.4	21 18.7
16 M	23 35 07	25 36 26	2♈45 26	10♈19 19	11 34.4	29♓29.8	0 28.8	27 13.5	12 13.7	18 20.5	26 01.2	14 27.1	23 14.0	21 17.5
17 Tu	23 39 04	26 36 10	17 49 43	25 15 29	11 27.3	28 37.8	0 42.9	27 57.5	12 30.8	18 31.7	25 57.5	14 26.8	23 12.6	21 16.4
18 W	23 43 00	27 35 52	2♉35 41	9♉49 31	11 20.3	27 43.5	0 54.9	28 41.5	12 48.2	18 43.0	25 53.8	14 26.6	23 11.2	21 15.2
19 Th	23 46 57	28 35 31	16 56 26	23 56 05	11 14.3	26 48.1	1 04.6	29 25.4	13 05.7	18 54.4	25 50.0	14 26.3	23 09.7	21 14.1
20 F	23 50 53	29 35 09	0♊48 19	7♊33 10	11 10.0	25 52.9	1 12.1	0♉09.3	13 23.4	19 05.9	25 46.1	14 26.2	23 08.3	21 13.0
21 Sa	23 54 50	0♈34 44	14 10 52	20 41 44	11D 07.7	24 58.8	1 17.3	0 53.2	13 41.4	19 17.4	25 42.2	14 26.1	23 06.8	21 11.9
22 Su	23 58 46	1 34 17	27 06 13	3♋24 52	11 07.2	24 07.0	1R 20.1	1 37.0	13 59.4	19 29.1	25 38.3	14D 26.0	23 05.3	21 10.9
23 M	0 02 43	2 33 47	9♋38 15	15 47 00	11 07.9	23 18.4	1 20.5	2 20.7	14 17.7	19 40.8	25 34.2	14 26.0	23 03.8	21 09.8
24 Tu	0 06 40	3 33 15	21 51 45	27 53 08	11 09.1	22 33.7	1 18.4	3 04.4	14 36.2	19 52.6	25 30.2	14 26.1	23 02.3	21 08.8
25 W	0 10 36	4 32 41	3♌51 48	9♌48 21	11R 09.8	21 53.6	1 13.9	3 48.1	14 54.8	20 04.5	25 26.1	14 26.2	23 00.7	21 07.8
26 Th	0 14 33	5 32 05	15 43 22	21 37 22	11 09.1	21 18.5	1 06.8	4 31.7	15 13.5	20 16.5	25 21.9	14 26.4	22 59.2	21 06.8
27 F	0 18 29	6 31 26	27 30 53	3♍24 21	11 06.4	20 48.9	0 57.3	5 15.2	15 32.5	20 28.5	25 17.7	14 26.6	22 57.6	21 05.9
28 Sa	0 22 26	7 30 45	9♍18 11	15 12 44	11 01.3	20 25.0	0 45.2	5 58.7	15 51.6	20 40.6	25 13.4	14 26.9	22 56.1	21 04.9
29 Su	0 26 22	8 30 02	21 08 21	27 05 17	10 53.7	20 06.9	0 30.7	6 42.2	16 10.8	20 52.8	25 09.1	14 27.2	22 54.5	21 04.0
30 M	0 30 19	9 29 17	3♎03 46	9♎04 01	10 44.0	19 54.6	0 13.7	7 25.6	16 30.2	21 05.1	25 04.8	14 27.6	22 52.9	21 03.1
31 Tu	0 34 15	10 28 29	15 06 10	21 10 23	10 32.9	19D 48.1	29♈54.3	8 08.9	16 49.8	21 17.4	25 00.4	14 28.0	22 51.3	21 02.2

April 1953

LONGITUDE

Day	Sid.Time	☉	0 hr ☽	Noon ☽	True ☊	☿	♀	♂	⚳	♃	♄	♅	♆	♇
1 W	0 38 12	11♈27 40	27♎16 47	3♏25 29	10♒21.3	19♓47.2	29♈32.6	8♉52.2	17♊09.5	21♉29.8	24♎56.0	14♋28.5	22♎49.7	21♌01.4
2 Th	0 42 08	12 26 49	9♏36 35	15 50 13	10R 10.4	19 51.9	29R 08.7	9 35.5	17 29.3	21 42.3	24R 51.6	14 29.0	22R 48.1	21R 00.6
3 F	0 46 05	13 25 56	22 06 31	28 25 38	10 01.1	20 01.9	28 42.6	10 18.7	17 49.3	21 54.8	24 47.2	14 29.6	22 46.5	20 59.8
4 Sa	0 50 02	14 25 02	4♐47 44	11♐13 01	9 54.1	20 17.1	28 14.5	11 01.9	18 09.5	22 07.4	24 42.7	14 30.3	22 44.9	20 59.0
5 Su	0 53 58	15 24 05	17 41 42	24 14 04	9 49.7	20 37.2	27 44.5	11 45.0	18 29.7	22 20.1	24 38.2	14 31.0	22 43.3	20 58.2
6 M	0 57 55	16 23 07	0♑50 20	7♑30 47	9D 47.7	21 02.1	27 12.8	12 28.1	18 50.2	22 32.8	24 33.6	14 31.7	22 41.6	20 57.5
7 Tu	1 01 51	17 22 07	14 15 41	21 05 17	9 47.4	21 31.4	26 39.6	13 11.2	19 10.7	22 45.6	24 29.1	14 32.6	22 40.0	20 56.8
8 W	1 05 48	18 21 05	27 59 46	4♒59 16	9R 47.8	22 05.0	26 05.1	13 54.2	19 31.4	22 58.4	24 24.5	14 33.4	22 38.4	20 56.1
9 Th	1 09 44	19 20 02	12♒03 50	19 13 24	9 47.6	22 42.6	25 29.5	14 37.1	19 52.2	23 11.3	24 19.9	14 34.3	22 36.7	20 55.5
10 F	1 13 41	20 18 56	26 27 46	3♓46 34	9 45.6	23 24.1	24 52.9	15 20.0	20 13.2	23 24.3	24 15.3	14 35.3	22 35.1	20 54.9
11 Sa	1 17 37	21 17 49	11♓09 16	18 35 11	9 41.1	24 09.2	24 15.8	16 02.9	20 34.3	23 37.3	24 10.7	14 36.3	22 33.4	20 54.2
12 Su	1 21 34	22 16 40	26 03 27	3♈33 04	9 33.9	24 57.8	23 38.2	16 45.7	20 55.5	23 50.4	24 06.1	14 37.4	22 31.8	20 53.7
13 M	1 25 31	23 15 30	11♈02 55	18 31 49	9 24.4	25 49.6	23 00.4	17 28.4	21 16.8	24 03.5	24 01.5	14 38.5	22 30.1	20 53.1
14 Tu	1 29 27	24 14 17	25 58 35	3♉22 04	9 13.4	26 44.6	22 22.7	18 11.2	21 38.2	24 16.6	23 56.9	14 39.7	22 28.5	20 52.6
15 W	1 33 24	25 13 02	10♉41 12	17 55 04	9 02.4	27 42.6	21 45.3	18 53.8	21 59.8	24 29.9	23 52.3	14 40.9	22 26.8	20 52.1
16 Th	1 37 20	26 11 46	25 02 54	2♊04 09	8 52.4	28 43.4	21 08.5	19 36.5	22 21.5	24 43.1	23 47.6	14 42.1	22 25.2	20 51.6
17 F	1 41 17	27 10 27	8♊58 28	15 45 41	8 44.5	29 47.0	20 32.5	20 19.1	22 43.3	24 56.4	23 43.0	14 43.5	22 23.6	20 51.2
18 Sa	1 45 13	28 09 06	22 25 48	28 59 02	8 39.2	0♈53.1	19 57.5	21 01.6	23 05.2	25 09.8	23 38.4	14 44.8	22 21.9	20 50.8
19 Su	1 49 10	29 07 43	5♋25 42	11♋46 14	8 36.3	2 01.8	19 23.7	21 44.1	23 27.2	25 23.2	23 33.8	14 46.3	22 20.3	20 50.4
20 M	1 53 06	0♉06 17	18 01 11	24 11 08	8D 35.3	3 12.8	18 51.3	22 26.5	23 49.3	25 36.6	23 29.3	14 47.7	22 18.7	20 50.0
21 Tu	1 57 03	1 04 50	0♌16 45	6♌18 43	8R 35.2	4 26.2	18 20.6	23 08.9	24 11.6	25 50.1	23 24.7	14 49.3	22 17.0	20 49.7
22 W	2 01 00	2 03 20	12 17 42	18 14 24	8 35.0	5 41.9	17 51.6	23 51.3	24 33.9	26 03.6	23 20.2	14 50.8	22 15.4	20 49.4
23 Th	2 04 56	3 01 48	24 09 30	0♍03 38	8 33.5	6 59.7	17 24.6	24 33.6	24 56.3	26 17.2	23 15.6	14 52.4	22 13.8	20 49.1
24 F	2 08 53	4 00 14	5♍57 25	11 51 26	8 29.9	8 19.6	16 59.6	25 15.8	25 18.9	26 30.7	23 11.1	14 54.1	22 12.2	20 48.9
25 Sa	2 12 49	4 58 38	17 46 13	23 42 15	8 23.7	9 41.6	16 36.7	25 58.0	25 41.5	26 44.4	23 06.7	14 55.8	22 10.6	20 48.6
26 Su	2 16 46	5 56 59	29 39 57	5♎39 41	8 14.6	11 05.7	16 16.2	26 40.2	26 04.2	26 58.0	23 02.2	14 57.6	22 09.0	20 48.4
27 M	2 20 42	6 55 19	11♎41 46	17 46 26	8 03.2	12 31.8	15 57.9	27 22.3	26 27.0	27 11.7	22 57.8	14 59.4	22 07.4	20 48.3
28 Tu	2 24 39	7 53 37	23 53 52	0♏04 13	7 50.2	13 59.8	15 42.0	28 04.3	26 49.9	27 25.4	22 53.4	15 01.2	22 05.8	20 48.1
29 W	2 28 35	8 51 53	6♏17 32	12 33 52	7 36.6	15 29.7	15 28.6	28 46.4	27 12.9	27 39.1	22 49.1	15 03.1	22 04.3	20 48.0
30 Th	2 32 32	9 50 08	18 53 12	25 15 32	7 23.7	17 01.6	15 17.6	29 28.3	27 36.0	27 52.9	22 44.7	15 05.0	22 02.7	20 47.9

Astro Data

	Dy Hr Mn
☽0S	1 19:58
☿R	9 3:43
☽0N	15 7:23
☉0N	20 22:00
☿0S	22 19:23
♅D	22 21:22
♀R	23 3:52
☽0S	29 2:11
♃□♇	30 8:26
☿D	1 3:35
♃⚻♆	7 2:43
☽0N	11 17:40
♃⚻♄	13 9:20
☿0N	23 0:09
☽0S	25 8:30

Planet Ingress

	Dy Hr Mn
☿ ♈	2 19:21
♀ ♉	14 18:58
☿ ♓R	15 21:16
♂ ♉	20 6:54
☉ ♈	20 22:01
♀ ♈R	31 5:17
☿ ♈	17 16:48
☉ ♉	20 9:25

Last Aspect / ☽ Ingress

Last Aspect Dy Hr Mn		☽ Ingress	Dy Hr Mn
2 11:01	☿ ☍	♎	2 11:41
4 16:55	♄ ☌	♏	4 23:31
6 17:12	♇ □	♐	7 9:20
9 12:31	♀ △	♑	9 16:10
11 17:48	♀ □	♒	11 19:37
13 19:47	♀ ⚹	♓	13 20:17
15 11:05	☉ ☌	♈	15 19:39
17 16:38	♂ ☌	♉	17 19:44
19 20:45	☉ ⚹	♊	19 22:35
21 21:19	♄ △	♋	22 5:29
24 7:16	♄ □	♌	24 16:14
26 19:35	♄ ⚹	♍	27 5:04
28 23:16	♃ △	♎	29 17:51

Last Aspect / ☽ Ingress

Last Aspect Dy Hr Mn		☽ Ingress	Dy Hr Mn
1 4:39	♀ ☍	♏	1 5:19
2 23:25	♃ ☍	♐	3 14:58
5 18:09	♀ △	♑	5 22:29
7 21:19	♀ □	♒	8 3:27
9 21:59	♀ ⚹	♓	10 5:49
11 21:27	♀ ☌	♈	12 6:19
13 20:48	♄ ☍	♉	14 6:31
16 5:48	☿ ⚹	♊	16 8:27
18 10:20	☉ ⚹	♋	18 13:53
20 14:51	♃ ⚹	♌	20 23:27
23 4:10	♃ □	♍	23 11:53
25 18:14	♃ △	♎	26 0:40
27 22:07	♄ ☌	♏	28 11:52
30 20:20	♂ ☍	♐	30 20:52

☽ Phases & Eclipses

Dy Hr Mn		
8 18:26	☾	17♐54
15 11:05	●	24♓34
22 8:11	☽	1♋25
30 12:55	○	9♎32
7 4:58	☾	17♑05
13 20:09	●	23♈35
21 0:41	☽	0♌37
29 4:20	○	8♏33

Astro Data

1 March 1953
Julian Day # 19418
SVP 5♓54'36"
GC 26♐11.1 ⚴ 15♈16.3
Eris 7♈30.6 ⚵ 4♈00.8
⚷ 18♑54.0 ⚶ 21♑41.4
☽ Mean ☊ 10♒55.7

1 April 1953
Julian Day # 19449
SVP 5♓54'33"
GC 26♐11.2 ⚴ 28♈42.8
Eris 7♈51.7 ⚵ 21♈20.1
⚷ 20♑33.9 ⚶ 6♒05.2
☽ Mean ☊ 9♒17.2

LONGITUDE — May 1953

Day	Sid.Time	☉	0 hr ☽	Noon ☽	True ☊	☿	♀	♂	⚳	♃	♄	♅	♆	♇
1 F	2 36 29	10♉48 21	1♐40 47	8♐08 55	7♒12.6	18♈35.5	15♈09.1	0♊10.3	27♊59.2	28♉06.7	22♎40.5	15♋07.0	22♎01.2	20♌47.9
2 Sa	2 40 25	11 46 32	14 39 53	21 13 39	7R 04.0	20 11.2	15R 03.0	0 52.1	28 22.5	28 20.5	22R 36.2	15 09.0	21R 59.6	20D 47.9
3 Su	2 44 22	12 44 42	27 50 12	4♑29 32	6 58.3	21 48.8	14 59.3	1 34.0	28 45.8	28 34.4	22 32.0	15 11.1	21 58.1	20 47.9
4 M	2 48 18	13 42 50	11♑11 43	17 56 48	6 55.4	23 28.3	14D 58.1	2 15.8	29 09.2	28 48.3	22 27.9	15 13.2	21 56.6	20 47.9
5 Tu	2 52 15	14 40 57	24 44 51	1♒35 59	6D 54.5	25 09.6	14 59.2	2 57.5	29 32.8	29 02.1	22 23.8	15 15.4	21 55.1	20 48.0
6 W	2 56 11	15 39 02	8♒30 16	15 27 48	6R 54.5	26 52.9	15 02.6	3 39.2	29 56.4	29 16.1	22 19.7	15 17.6	21 53.6	20 48.0
7 Th	3 00 08	16 37 06	22 28 35	29 32 37	6 54.1	28 38.1	15 08.4	4 20.9	0♋20.0	29 30.0	22 15.7	15 19.8	21 52.2	20 48.2
8 F	3 04 04	17 35 08	6♓39 48	13♓49 55	6 52.1	0♉25.2	15 16.3	5 02.5	0 43.8	29 44.0	22 11.8	15 22.1	21 50.7	20 48.3
9 Sa	3 08 01	18 33 10	21 02 41	28 17 41	6 47.7	2 14.2	15 26.5	5 44.1	1 07.6	29 57.9	22 07.9	15 24.4	21 49.3	20 48.5
10 Su	3 11 58	19 31 10	5♈34 20	12♈52 01	6 40.6	4 05.1	15 38.7	6 25.6	1 31.5	0♊11.9	22 04.0	15 26.8	21 47.9	20 48.7
11 M	3 15 54	20 29 08	20 09 56	27 27 16	6 31.2	5 57.9	15 53.0	7 07.1	1 55.5	0 25.9	22 00.2	15 29.2	21 46.5	20 48.9
12 Tu	3 19 51	21 27 05	4♉43 08	11♉56 37	6 20.4	7 52.5	16 09.3	7 48.6	2 19.6	0 39.9	21 56.5	15 31.6	21 45.1	20 49.2
13 W	3 23 47	22 25 01	19 06 52	26 13 06	6 09.3	9 49.1	16 27.5	8 30.0	2 43.7	0 54.0	21 52.9	15 34.1	21 43.7	20 49.4
14 Th	3 27 44	23 22 55	3♊14 36	10♊10 48	5 59.1	11 47.5	16 47.5	9 11.4	3 07.9	1 08.0	21 49.3	15 36.6	21 42.4	20 49.8
15 F	3 31 40	24 20 48	17 01 16	23 45 46	5 50.9	13 47.7	17 09.3	9 52.7	3 32.2	1 22.1	21 45.7	15 39.2	21 41.0	20 50.1
16 Sa	3 35 37	25 18 39	0♋24 08	6♋56 26	5 45.2	15 49.7	17 32.9	10 34.0	3 56.5	1 36.2	21 42.3	15 41.8	21 39.7	20 50.5
17 Su	3 39 33	26 16 29	13 22 48	19 43 33	5 41.9	17 53.4	17 58.1	11 15.3	4 20.9	1 50.2	21 38.9	15 44.4	21 38.4	20 50.9
18 M	3 43 30	27 14 17	25 59 04	2♌09 49	5D 40.8	19 58.6	18 24.9	11 56.5	4 45.4	2 04.3	21 35.6	15 47.1	21 37.1	20 51.3
19 Tu	3 47 27	28 12 03	8♌16 22	14 19 18	5 41.0	22 05.4	18 53.2	12 37.6	5 09.9	2 18.4	21 32.3	15 49.8	21 35.9	20 51.8
20 W	3 51 23	29 09 47	20 19 16	26 16 56	5R 41.4	24 13.4	19 23.0	13 18.7	5 34.5	2 32.5	21 29.2	15 52.5	21 34.7	20 52.2
21 Th	3 55 20	0♊07 30	2♍12 57	8♍08 01	5 41.1	26 22.7	19 54.3	13 59.8	5 59.2	2 46.6	21 26.1	15 55.2	21 33.4	20 52.8
22 F	3 59 16	1 05 11	14 02 46	19 57 52	5 39.2	28 32.9	20 26.9	14 40.8	6 23.9	3 00.7	21 23.0	15 58.0	21 32.3	20 53.3
23 Sa	4 03 13	2 02 51	25 53 54	1♎51 29	5 35.2	0♊43.9	21 00.8	15 21.8	6 48.7	3 14.7	21 20.1	16 00.9	21 31.1	20 53.9
24 Su	4 07 09	3 00 29	7♎51 07	13 53 16	5 28.8	2 55.4	21 36.1	16 02.8	7 13.5	3 28.8	21 17.2	16 03.7	21 29.9	20 54.4
25 M	4 11 06	3 58 06	19 58 23	26 06 48	5 20.4	5 07.2	22 12.5	16 43.7	7 38.4	3 42.9	21 14.4	16 06.6	21 28.8	20 55.1
26 Tu	4 15 02	4 55 41	2♏18 48	8♏34 34	5 10.5	7 19.0	22 50.2	17 24.5	8 03.4	3 57.0	21 11.7	16 09.6	21 27.7	20 55.7
27 W	4 18 59	5 53 16	14 54 16	21 17 57	5 00.0	9 30.6	23 29.0	18 05.3	8 28.4	4 11.1	21 09.1	16 12.5	21 26.6	20 56.4
28 Th	4 22 56	6 50 49	27 45 34	4♐17 04	4 50.1	11 41.6	24 08.9	18 46.1	8 53.4	4 25.2	21 06.6	16 15.5	21 25.6	20 57.1
29 F	4 26 52	7 48 20	10♐52 18	17 31 04	4 41.5	13 51.8	24 49.8	19 26.9	9 18.5	4 39.2	21 04.2	16 18.5	21 24.6	20 57.8
30 Sa	4 30 49	8 45 51	24 13 09	0♑58 19	4 35.1	16 00.9	25 31.8	20 07.6	9 43.7	4 53.3	21 01.8	16 21.5	21 23.6	20 58.6
31 Su	4 34 45	9 43 21	7♑46 17	14 36 49	4 31.1	18 08.7	26 14.7	20 48.2	10 08.9	5 07.3	20 59.5	16 24.6	21 22.6	20 59.3

LONGITUDE — June 1953

Day	Sid.Time	☉	0 hr ☽	Noon ☽	True ☊	☿	♀	♂	⚳	♃	♄	♅	♆	♇
1 M	4 38 42	10♊40 50	21♑29 40	28♑24 37	4♒29.4	20♊14.9	26♈58.6	21♊28.9	10♋34.1	5♊21.4	20♎57.3	16♋27.7	21♎21.7	21♌00.1
2 Tu	4 42 38	11 38 18	5♒21 28	12♒20 02	4D 29.5	22 19.5	27 43.4	22 09.4	10 59.5	5 35.4	20R 55.2	16 30.8	21R 20.7	21 01.0
3 W	4 46 35	12 35 46	19 20 10	26 21 45	4 30.4	24 22.1	28 29.1	22 50.0	11 24.8	5 49.5	20 53.2	16 34.0	21 19.8	21 01.8
4 Th	4 50 32	13 33 13	3♓24 37	10♓28 39	4R 31.1	26 22.7	29 15.6	23 30.5	11 50.2	6 03.5	20 51.3	16 37.2	21 19.0	21 02.7
5 F	4 54 28	14 30 39	17 33 41	24 39 32	4 30.7	28 21.2	0♉02.9	24 11.0	12 15.7	6 17.5	20 49.5	16 40.4	21 18.1	21 03.6
6 Sa	4 58 25	15 28 04	1♈45 58	8♈52 42	4 28.5	0♋17.3	0 50.9	24 51.4	12 41.2	6 31.5	20 47.8	16 43.6	21 17.3	21 04.5
7 Su	5 02 21	16 25 29	15 59 25	23 05 43	4 24.4	2 11.2	1 39.7	25 31.8	13 06.7	6 45.4	20 46.1	16 46.8	21 16.5	21 05.5
8 M	5 06 18	17 22 53	0♉11 11	7♉15 19	4 18.4	4 02.6	2 29.3	26 12.2	13 32.3	6 59.4	20 44.6	16 50.1	21 15.7	21 06.5
9 Tu	5 10 14	18 20 17	14 17 38	21 17 36	4 11.4	5 51.6	3 19.5	26 52.5	13 58.0	7 13.3	20 43.1	16 53.4	21 15.0	21 07.5
10 W	5 14 11	19 17 40	28 14 42	5♊08 27	4 04.1	7 38.1	4 10.3	27 32.8	14 23.7	7 27.2	20 41.8	16 56.7	21 14.3	21 08.5
11 Th	5 18 07	20 15 03	11♊58 24	18 44 12	3 57.4	9 22.1	5 01.8	28 13.1	14 49.4	7 41.1	20 40.5	17 00.0	21 13.6	21 09.6
12 F	5 22 04	21 12 25	25 25 32	2♋02 10	3 52.1	11 03.5	5 53.9	28 53.3	15 15.2	7 55.0	20 39.4	17 03.4	21 13.0	21 10.6
13 Sa	5 26 01	22 09 46	8♋34 01	15 01 02	3 48.5	12 42.3	6 46.6	29 33.5	15 41.0	8 08.9	20 38.3	17 06.8	21 12.4	21 11.7
14 Su	5 29 57	23 07 06	21 23 19	27 41 00	3D 46.9	14 18.6	7 39.9	0♋13.7	16 06.8	8 22.7	20 37.3	17 10.2	21 11.8	21 12.9
15 M	5 33 54	24 04 25	3♌54 22	10♌03 44	3 46.9	15 52.3	8 33.7	0 53.8	16 32.7	8 36.5	20 36.5	17 13.6	21 11.2	21 14.0
16 Tu	5 37 50	25 01 44	16 09 31	22 12 09	3 48.0	17 23.4	9 28.0	1 33.9	16 58.6	8 50.3	20 35.7	17 17.0	21 10.7	21 15.2
17 W	5 41 47	25 59 01	28 12 10	4♍10 07	3 49.6	18 51.8	10 22.8	2 14.0	17 24.6	9 04.0	20 35.0	17 20.5	21 10.2	21 16.4
18 Th	5 45 43	26 56 18	10♍06 34	16 02 09	3R 51.0	20 17.5	11 18.1	2 54.0	17 50.6	9 17.8	20 34.5	17 23.9	21 09.7	21 17.6
19 F	5 49 40	27 53 35	21 57 29	27 53 11	3 51.6	21 40.6	12 13.9	3 33.9	18 16.6	9 31.4	20 34.0	17 27.4	21 09.3	21 18.8
20 Sa	5 53 36	28 50 50	3♎49 52	9♎48 10	3 50.9	23 00.9	13 10.1	4 13.9	18 42.7	9 45.1	20 33.6	17 30.9	21 08.9	21 20.1
21 Su	5 57 33	29 48 05	15 48 39	21 51 53	3 48.8	24 18.4	14 06.7	4 53.8	19 08.8	9 58.7	20 33.3	17 34.4	21 08.5	21 21.3
22 M	6 01 30	0♋45 19	27 58 24	4♏08 39	3 45.3	25 33.1	15 03.8	5 33.7	19 34.9	10 12.3	20 33.2	17 37.9	21 08.2	21 22.6
23 Tu	6 05 26	1 42 32	10♏23 03	16 41 56	3 40.9	26 45.0	16 01.4	6 13.5	20 01.1	10 25.9	20D 33.1	17 41.4	21 07.9	21 23.9
24 W	6 09 23	2 39 45	23 05 34	29 34 08	3 36.0	27 53.8	16 59.3	6 53.3	20 27.3	10 39.4	20 33.1	17 45.0	21 07.6	21 25.3
25 Th	6 13 19	3 36 58	6♐07 42	12♐46 16	3 31.3	28 59.7	17 57.6	7 33.1	20 53.5	10 52.9	20 33.2	17 48.5	21 07.3	21 26.6
26 F	6 17 16	4 34 10	19 29 44	26 17 52	3 27.2	0♌02.5	18 56.3	8 12.8	21 19.8	11 06.3	20 33.5	17 52.1	21 07.1	21 28.0
27 Sa	6 21 12	5 31 22	3♑10 24	10♑06 58	3 24.4	1 02.2	19 55.3	8 52.5	21 46.0	11 19.7	20 33.8	17 55.7	21 06.9	21 29.4
28 Su	6 25 09	6 28 34	17 07 08	24 10 24	3D 22.9	1 58.5	20 54.7	9 32.2	22 12.3	11 33.1	20 34.2	17 59.3	21 06.8	21 30.8
29 M	6 29 05	7 25 45	1♒16 16	8♒24 11	3 22.7	2 51.5	21 54.5	10 11.8	22 38.7	11 46.4	20 34.8	18 02.9	21 06.7	21 32.3
30 Tu	6 33 02	8 22 57	15 33 37	22 44 03	3 23.5	3 41.0	22 54.6	10 51.4	23 05.1	11 59.7	20 35.4	18 06.5	21 06.6	21 33.7

Astro Data

	Dy Hr Mn
♇ D	2 20:21
♀ D	4 12:33
☽0N	9 1:11
♃∠♅	11 18:44
♄☌♆	17 17:28
☽0S	22 15:11
♄✶♇	31 13:29
♃⚼♄	3 17:41
☽0N	5 6:21
♃⚼♆	5 13:03
♆✶♇	13 21:03
☽0S	18 22:19
♄ D	23 17:26

Planet Ingress

	Dy Hr Mn
♂ ♊	1 6:08
⚳ ♋	6 15:42
☿ ♉	8 6:24
♃ ♊	9 15:33
☉ ♊	21 8:53
☿ ♊	23 3:58
♀ ♉	5 10:34
☿ ♋	6 8:23
♂ ♋	14 3:49
☉ ♋	21 17:00
☿ ♌	26 11:01

Last Aspect / ☽ Ingress (May)

Last Aspect Dy Hr Mn		☽ Ingress Dy Hr Mn
2 14:30	♄ ✶	♑ 3 3:55
5 7:27	♃ △	♒ 5 9:12
7 11:55	♃ □	♓ 7 12:46
9 14:48	♃ ✶	♈ 9 14:49
11 3:04	♄ ☍	♉ 11 16:12
13 5:06	☉ ☌	♊ 13 18:27
15 8:26	♄ △	♋ 15 23:16
18 1:37	☉ ✶	♌ 18 7:47
20 18:20	☉ □	♍ 20 19:31
22 3:52	♅ ✶	♎ 23 8:16
25 3:59	♀ ☍	♏ 25 19:32
27 11:20	♇ □	♐ 28 4:08
30 1:48	♀ △	♑ 30 10:17

Last Aspect / ☽ Ingress (June)

Last Aspect Dy Hr Mn		☽ Ingress Dy Hr Mn
1 9:23	♀ □	♒ 1 14:45
3 15:50	♀ ✶	♓ 3 18:12
5 19:14	☿ □	♈ 5 21:01
7 16:19	♂ ✶	♉ 7 23:41
9 11:43	♇ □	♊ 10 3:03
12 5:58	♂ ☌	♋ 12 8:17
13 23:39	♆ □	♌ 14 16:27
16 18:08	☉ ✶	♍ 17 3:37
19 12:01	☉ □	♎ 19 16:16
21 17:22	♅ □	♏ 22 3:57
24 8:37	☿ △	♐ 24 12:48
26 3:29	♇ △	♑ 26 18:29
28 6:48	♆ □	♒ 28 21:51

☽ Phases & Eclipses

Dy Hr Mn	
6 12:21	☾ 15♒40
13 5:06	● 22♉08
20 18:20	☽ 29♌25
28 17:03	○ 7♐03
4 17:35	☾ 13♓47
11 14:55	● 20♊22
19 12:01	☽ 27♍54
27 3:29	○ 5♑11

Astro Data

1 May 1953
Julian Day # 19479
SVP 5♓54'29"
GC 26♐11.2 ⚴ 13♉06.4
Eris 8♈11.7 ⚵ 8♉45.0
⚷ 21♑02.1R ⚶ 18♒00.3
☽ Mean ☊ 7♒41.9

1 June 1953
Julian Day # 19510
SVP 5♓54'24"
GC 26♐11.3 ⚴ 29♉09.2
Eris 8♈26.9 ⚵ 27♉04.5
⚷ 20♑17.8R ⚶ 26♒55.1
☽ Mean ☊ 6♒03.4

July 1953 LONGITUDE

Day	Sid.Time	☉	0 hr ☽	Noon ☽	True ☊	☿	♀	♂	⚳	♃	♄	♅	♆	♇
1 W	6 36 59	9♋20 08	29♒54 58	7♓05 55	3♒24.9	4♌27.0	23♉55.0	11♋31.0	23♋31.5	12♊12.9	20♎36.1	18♋10.1	21♎06.5	21♌35.2
2 Th	6 40 55	10 17 20	14♓16 27	21 26 11	3 26.1	5 09.2	24 55.8	12 10.6	23 57.9	12 26.1	20 36.9	18 13.7	21D 06.5	21 36.7
3 F	6 44 52	11 14 32	28 34 46	5♈41 53	3R 26.9	5 47.6	25 56.8	12 50.1	24 24.3	12 39.3	20 37.8	18 17.3	21 06.5	21 38.2
4 Sa	6 48 48	12 11 44	12♈47 16	19 50 39	3 26.8	6 22.1	26 58.2	13 29.6	24 50.8	12 52.4	20 38.8	18 21.0	21 06.5	21 39.7
5 Su	6 52 45	13 08 57	26 51 49	3♉50 34	3 25.8	6 52.5	27 59.8	14 09.1	25 17.3	13 05.4	20 40.0	18 24.6	21 06.6	21 41.2
6 M	6 56 41	14 06 09	10♉46 42	17 40 02	3 24.0	7 18.7	29 01.7	14 48.5	25 43.8	13 18.4	20 41.2	18 28.2	21 06.7	21 42.8
7 Tu	7 00 38	15 03 23	24 30 25	1♊17 40	3 21.7	7 40.5	0♊03.9	15 27.9	26 10.4	13 31.4	20 42.5	18 31.9	21 06.8	21 44.4
8 W	7 04 34	16 00 36	8♊01 40	14 42 15	3 19.2	7 57.9	1 06.4	16 07.3	26 37.0	13 44.3	20 43.9	18 35.5	21 07.0	21 45.9
9 Th	7 08 31	16 57 50	21 19 21	27 52 51	3 17.0	8 10.8	2 09.1	16 46.7	27 03.6	13 57.1	20 45.4	18 39.2	21 07.2	21 47.6
10 F	7 12 28	17 55 04	4♋22 42	10♋48 51	3 15.4	8 18.9	3 12.0	17 26.0	27 30.2	14 09.9	20 47.0	18 42.8	21 07.4	21 49.2
11 Sa	7 16 24	18 52 19	17 11 21	23 30 13	3D 14.4	8R 22.4	4 15.2	18 05.3	27 56.8	14 22.7	20 48.7	18 46.5	21 07.7	21 50.8
12 Su	7 20 21	19 49 33	29 45 33	5♌57 30	3 14.2	8 21.1	5 18.6	18 44.6	28 23.5	14 35.3	20 50.5	18 50.1	21 08.0	21 52.5
13 M	7 24 17	20 46 48	12♌06 15	18 12 01	3 14.7	8 15.0	6 22.3	19 23.8	28 50.2	14 48.0	20 52.4	18 53.8	21 08.3	21 54.1
14 Tu	7 28 14	21 44 03	24 15 06	0♍15 49	3 15.5	8 04.2	7 26.2	20 03.0	29 16.9	15 00.5	20 54.4	18 57.4	21 08.7	21 55.8
15 W	7 32 10	22 41 18	6♍14 32	12 11 41	3 16.6	7 48.7	8 30.2	20 42.2	29 43.6	15 13.0	20 56.5	19 01.1	21 09.1	21 57.5
16 Th	7 36 07	23 38 33	18 07 41	24 03 02	3 17.6	7 28.7	9 34.5	21 21.4	0♌10.4	15 25.4	20 58.6	19 04.7	21 09.5	21 59.2
17 F	7 40 03	24 35 48	29 58 14	5♎53 51	3 18.3	7 04.3	10 39.0	22 00.5	0 37.1	15 37.8	21 00.9	19 08.4	21 09.9	22 00.9
18 Sa	7 44 00	25 33 03	11♎50 25	17 48 30	3R 18.7	6 36.0	11 43.7	22 39.6	1 03.9	15 50.1	21 03.3	19 12.0	21 10.4	22 02.6
19 Su	7 47 57	26 30 19	23 48 41	29 51 34	3 18.8	6 03.9	12 48.6	23 18.7	1 30.7	16 02.3	21 05.7	19 15.6	21 10.9	22 04.3
20 M	7 51 53	27 27 35	5♏57 41	12♏07 35	3 18.6	5 28.6	13 53.7	23 57.7	1 57.5	16 14.5	21 08.3	19 19.2	21 11.5	22 06.1
21 Tu	7 55 50	28 24 51	18 21 47	24 40 46	3 18.2	4 50.6	14 58.9	24 36.8	2 24.3	16 26.6	21 10.9	19 22.9	21 12.1	22 07.8
22 W	7 59 46	29 22 07	1♐04 57	7♐34 39	3 17.7	4 10.3	16 04.4	25 15.7	2 51.1	16 38.6	21 13.6	19 26.5	21 12.7	22 09.6
23 Th	8 03 43	0♌19 24	14 10 10	20 51 38	3 17.3	3 28.6	17 10.0	25 54.7	3 18.0	16 50.5	21 16.5	19 30.1	21 13.3	22 11.4
24 F	8 07 39	1 16 42	27 39 06	4♑32 31	3 17.1	2 46.0	18 15.8	26 33.7	3 44.8	17 02.4	21 19.4	19 33.7	21 14.0	22 13.2
25 Sa	8 11 36	2 13 59	11♑31 40	18 36 15	3 17.0	2 03.4	19 21.8	27 12.6	4 11.7	17 14.2	21 22.4	19 37.3	21 14.7	22 15.0
26 Su	8 15 33	3 11 18	25 45 46	2♒59 39	3 17.0	1 21.4	20 27.9	27 51.5	4 38.5	17 25.9	21 25.5	19 40.9	21 15.5	22 16.8
27 M	8 19 29	4 08 37	10♒17 13	17 37 40	3 16.9	0 40.9	21 34.2	28 30.3	5 05.4	17 37.6	21 28.6	19 44.4	21 16.2	22 18.6
28 Tu	8 23 26	5 05 57	25 00 09	2♓23 48	3 16.8	0 02.6	22 40.7	29 09.2	5 32.3	17 49.1	21 31.9	19 48.0	21 17.0	22 20.4
29 W	8 27 22	6 03 17	9♓47 41	17 10 57	3 16.6	29♋27.2	23 47.4	29 48.0	5 59.2	18 00.6	21 35.2	19 51.5	21 17.9	22 22.3
30 Th	8 31 19	7 00 39	24 32 47	1♈52 24	3 16.3	28 55.4	24 54.2	0♌26.8	6 26.1	18 12.0	21 38.6	19 55.1	21 18.7	22 24.1
31 F	8 35 15	7 58 01	9♈09 09	16 22 29	3 15.9	28 27.9	26 01.2	1 05.6	6 53.1	18 23.3	21 42.2	19 58.6	21 19.6	22 25.9

August 1953 LONGITUDE

Day	Sid.Time	☉	0 hr ☽	Noon ☽	True ☊	☿	♀	♂	⚳	♃	♄	♅	♆	♇
1 Sa	8 39 12	8♌55 25	23♈31 58	0♉37 14	3♒15.7	28♋05.2	27♊08.3	1♌44.3	7♌20.0	18♊34.5	21♎45.7	20♋02.1	21♎20.5	22♌27.8
2 Su	8 43 08	9 52 50	7♉38 05	14 34 22	3D 15.6	27R 47.8	28 15.6	2 23.1	7 47.0	18 45.7	21 49.4	20 05.6	21 21.5	22 29.7
3 M	8 47 05	10 50 17	21 26 03	28 13 09	3 15.9	27 36.1	29 23.0	3 01.8	8 13.9	18 56.7	21 53.2	20 09.1	21 22.5	22 31.5
4 Tu	8 51 02	11 47 44	4♊55 46	11♊34 01	3 16.5	27D 30.5	0♋30.6	3 40.5	8 40.9	19 07.7	21 57.0	20 12.5	21 23.5	22 33.4
5 W	8 54 58	12 45 13	18 08 05	24 38 09	3 17.3	27 31.2	1 38.3	4 19.2	9 07.8	19 18.6	22 00.9	20 16.0	21 24.5	22 35.3
6 Th	8 58 55	13 42 43	1♋04 24	7♋27 03	3 18.2	27 38.5	2 46.2	4 57.8	9 34.8	19 29.3	22 05.0	20 19.4	21 25.6	22 37.1
7 F	9 02 51	14 40 14	13 46 20	20 02 25	3 18.9	27 52.4	3 54.2	5 36.5	10 01.8	19 40.0	22 09.0	20 22.8	21 26.7	22 39.0
8 Sa	9 06 48	15 37 47	26 15 32	2♌25 52	3R 19.3	28 13.2	5 02.3	6 15.1	10 28.8	19 50.6	22 13.2	20 26.2	21 27.8	22 40.9
9 Su	9 10 44	16 35 20	8♌33 38	14 39 01	3 19.0	28 40.7	6 10.5	6 53.7	10 55.8	20 01.1	22 17.4	20 29.6	21 29.0	22 42.8
10 M	9 14 41	17 32 54	20 42 13	26 43 29	3 18.0	29 15.0	7 18.9	7 32.3	11 22.8	20 11.5	22 21.7	20 33.0	21 30.1	22 44.7
11 Tu	9 18 37	18 30 30	2♍43 00	8♍41 03	3 16.3	29 56.1	8 27.4	8 10.8	11 49.8	20 21.8	22 26.1	20 36.3	21 31.4	22 46.6
12 W	9 22 34	19 28 07	14 37 51	20 33 43	3 14.0	0♌43.9	9 36.1	8 49.3	12 16.8	20 31.9	22 30.6	20 39.6	21 32.6	22 48.5
13 Th	9 26 31	20 25 44	26 28 58	2♎23 55	3 11.4	1 38.2	10 44.8	9 27.8	12 43.8	20 42.0	22 35.1	20 42.9	21 33.9	22 50.4
14 F	9 30 27	21 23 23	8♎18 57	14 14 28	3 08.7	2 38.9	11 53.7	10 06.3	13 10.8	20 52.0	22 39.7	20 46.2	21 35.1	22 52.3
15 Sa	9 34 24	22 21 03	20 10 55	26 08 45	3 06.4	3 45.8	13 02.7	10 44.8	13 37.8	21 01.8	22 44.4	20 49.4	21 36.5	22 54.2
16 Su	9 38 20	23 18 43	2♏08 27	8♏10 32	3 04.7	4 58.7	14 11.8	11 23.2	14 04.8	21 11.5	22 49.2	20 52.7	21 37.8	22 56.1
17 M	9 42 17	24 16 25	14 15 32	20 24 00	3D 04.0	6 17.3	15 21.0	12 01.7	14 31.7	21 21.2	22 54.0	20 55.9	21 39.2	22 58.0
18 Tu	9 46 13	25 14 08	26 36 29	2♐53 29	3 04.1	7 41.2	16 30.3	12 40.1	14 58.7	21 30.7	22 58.9	20 59.0	21 40.6	22 59.9
19 W	9 50 10	26 11 52	9♐15 33	15 43 10	3 05.1	9 10.2	17 39.7	13 18.5	15 25.7	21 40.1	23 03.9	21 02.2	21 42.0	23 01.8
20 Th	9 54 06	27 09 38	22 16 45	28 56 39	3 06.5	10 43.9	18 49.3	13 56.8	15 52.7	21 49.4	23 08.9	21 05.3	21 43.4	23 03.7
21 F	9 58 03	28 07 24	5♑43 10	12♑36 25	3 07.9	12 21.9	19 58.9	14 35.2	16 19.7	21 58.5	23 14.0	21 08.4	21 44.9	23 05.6
22 Sa	10 02 00	29 05 11	19 36 26	26 43 05	3R 08.8	14 03.7	21 08.7	15 13.5	16 46.6	22 07.6	23 19.2	21 11.5	21 46.4	23 07.5
23 Su	10 05 56	0♍03 00	3♒56 04	11♒14 53	3 08.8	15 49.0	22 18.6	15 51.8	17 13.6	22 16.5	23 24.4	21 14.5	21 47.9	23 09.4
24 M	10 09 53	1 00 50	18 38 52	26 07 10	3 07.4	17 37.3	23 28.6	16 30.1	17 40.6	22 25.3	23 29.7	21 17.5	21 49.5	23 11.3
25 Tu	10 13 49	1 58 42	3♓38 48	11♓12 38	3 04.7	19 28.2	24 38.6	17 08.4	18 07.5	22 34.0	23 35.0	21 20.5	21 51.1	23 13.2
26 W	10 17 46	2 56 35	18 47 28	26 22 04	3 01.0	21 21.1	25 48.8	17 46.6	18 34.4	22 42.5	23 40.4	21 23.5	21 52.6	23 15.1
27 Th	10 21 42	3 54 29	3♈55 11	11♈25 41	2 56.7	23 15.8	26 59.1	18 24.8	19 01.4	22 50.9	23 45.9	21 26.4	21 54.3	23 16.9
28 F	10 25 39	4 52 26	18 52 31	26 14 47	2 52.6	25 11.7	28 09.5	19 03.1	19 28.3	22 59.2	23 51.4	21 29.3	21 55.9	23 18.8
29 Sa	10 29 35	5 50 24	3♉31 46	10♉42 55	2 49.3	27 08.6	29 20.1	19 41.3	19 55.2	23 07.4	23 57.0	21 32.2	21 57.6	23 20.7
30 Su	10 33 32	6 48 24	17 47 54	24 46 30	2D 47.3	29 06.1	0♌30.7	20 19.5	20 22.1	23 15.4	24 02.7	21 35.0	21 59.2	23 22.5
31 M	10 37 28	7 46 26	1♊38 44	8♊24 43	2 46.6	1♍03.9	1 41.4	20 57.6	20 49.0	23 23.3	24 08.4	21 37.8	22 00.9	23 24.4

Astro Data	Planet Ingress	Last Aspect	☽ Ingress	Last Aspect	☽ Ingress	☽ Phases & Eclipses	Astro Data
Dy Hr Mn	Dy Hr Mn	Dy Hr Mn	Dy Hr Mn	Dy Hr Mn	Dy Hr Mn	Dy Hr Mn	
☽0N 2 11:17	♀ ♊ 7 10:30	30 12:19 ♀ □	♓ 1 0:08	1 7:48 ☿ □	♉ 1 10:57	3 22:03 ☾ 11♈38	1 July 1953
♆D 2 22:13	⚳ ♌ 16 2:42	2 18:19 ♀ ✶	♈ 3 2:23	3 10:55 ☿ ✶	♊ 3 15:10	11 2:28 ● 18♋30	Julian Day # 19540
☿R 11 17:26	☉ ♌ 23 3:52	4 15:06 ♇ △	♉ 5 5:23	5 8:12 ♇ ✶	♋ 5 21:59	11 2:43:38 ● P 0.202	SVP 5♓54'18"
☽0S 16 5:41	☿ ♋R 28 13:40	7 9:38 ♀ ☌	♊ 7 9:42	8 3:32 ☿ ☌	♌ 8 7:16	19 4:47 ☽ 26♎13	GC 26♐11.4 ⚴ 15♊37.2
♄☌♆ 22 1:22	♂ ♌ 29 19:25	9 0:50 ♇ ✶	♋ 9 15:54	10 4:02 ♇ ☌	♍ 10 18:33	26 12:21 ○ 3♒12	Eris 8♈33.0 ⚵ 14♊47.1
☽0N 29 18:06		11 7:28 ♆ □	♌ 12 0:28	12 12:12 ♅ ✶	♎ 13 7:08	26 12:21 ● T 1.863	⚷ 18♑43.0R ⚶ 0♓16.7
	♀ ♋ 4 1:08	13 19:21 ♇ ☌	♍ 14 11:28	15 5:28 ♇ ✶	♏ 15 19:43		☽ Mean ☊ 4♒28.1
☿D 4 21:22	☿ ♌ 11 14:04	16 11:06 ☉ ✶	♎ 17 0:04	17 20:08 ☉ □	♐ 18 6:30	2 3:16 ☾ 9♉32	
☽0S 12 12:50	☉ ♍ 23 10:45	19 4:47 ☉ □	♏ 19 12:17	20 8:34 ☉ △	♑ 20 13:53	9 16:10 ● 16♌45	1 August 1953
♃⚺♅ 13 15:15	♀ ♌ 30 1:35	21 19:35 ☉ △	♐ 21 21:59	22 6:15 ♄ □	♒ 22 17:29	9 15:54:32 ● P 0.373	Julian Day # 19571
♄✶♇ 18 19:52	☿ ♍ 30 22:59	23 14:22 ♇ △	♑ 24 4:07	24 7:46 ♄ △	♓ 24 18:12	17 20:08 ☽ 24♏36	SVP 5♓54'13"
♃△♆ 19 17:47		26 3:05 ♂ ☍	♒ 26 7:03	26 11:03 ♀ △	♈ 26 17:46	24 20:21 ○ 1♓21	GC 26♐11.5 ⚴ 3♋18.4
☽0N 26 3:31		27 19:38 ♇ ☍	♓ 28 8:07	28 15:25 ♀ □	♉ 28 18:10	31 10:46 ☾ 7♊43	Eris 8♈29.0R ⚵ 2♋39.1
♃✶♇ 31 16:25		30 7:19 ☿ △	♈ 30 8:56	30 20:48 ☿ □	♊ 30 21:07		⚷ 16♑52.2R ⚶ 26♒38.9R
							☽ Mean ☊ 2♒49.6

LONGITUDE — September 1953

Day	Sid.Time	☉	0 hr ☽	Noon ☽	True ☊	☿	♀	♂	⚳	♃	♄	♅	♆	♇
1 Tu	10 41 25	8♍44 30	15♊04 38	21♊38 51	2♒47.3	3♍01.8	2♌52.2	21♌35.8	21♌15.9	23♊31.1	24♎14.2	21♋40.6	22♎02.7	23♌26.3
2 W	10 45 22	9 42 36	28 07 42	4♋31 39	2 48.7	4 59.4	4 03.1	22 14.0	21 42.8	23 38.7	24 20.0	21 43.3	22 04.4	23 28.1
3 Th	10 49 18	10 40 44	10♋51 06	17 06 32	2 50.2	6 56.7	5 14.1	22 52.1	22 09.7	23 46.1	24 25.9	21 46.0	22 06.2	23 29.9
4 F	10 53 15	11 38 54	23 18 23	29 27 05	2R51.2	8 53.5	6 25.3	23 30.2	22 36.5	23 53.5	24 31.8	21 48.7	22 08.0	23 31.8
5 Sa	10 57 11	12 37 06	5♌33 02	11♌36 38	2 50.8	10 49.5	7 36.5	24 08.3	23 03.4	24 00.6	24 37.8	21 51.3	22 09.8	23 33.6
6 Su	11 01 08	13 35 20	17 38 13	23 38 07	2 48.7	12 44.8	8 47.7	24 46.4	23 30.2	24 07.7	24 43.8	21 53.9	22 11.6	23 35.4
7 M	11 05 04	14 33 35	29 36 37	5♍34 00	2 44.5	14 39.2	9 59.1	25 24.5	23 57.0	24 14.5	24 49.9	21 56.4	22 13.4	23 37.2
8 Tu	11 09 01	15 31 52	11♍30 30	17 26 21	2 38.4	16 32.6	11 10.6	26 02.5	24 23.8	24 21.3	24 56.0	21 58.9	22 15.3	23 39.0
9 W	11 12 57	16 30 11	23 21 47	29 16 58	2 30.8	18 25.1	12 22.1	26 40.6	24 50.5	24 27.8	25 02.2	22 01.4	22 17.2	23 40.8
10 Th	11 16 54	17 28 32	5♎12 10	11♎07 35	2 22.2	20 16.5	13 33.8	27 18.6	25 17.3	24 34.2	25 08.4	22 03.8	22 19.1	23 42.6
11 F	11 20 51	18 26 54	17 03 27	23 00 03	2 13.5	22 06.8	14 45.5	27 56.6	25 44.0	24 40.5	25 14.7	22 06.2	22 21.0	23 44.3
12 Sa	11 24 47	19 25 18	28 57 38	4♏56 33	2 05.5	23 56.0	15 57.3	28 34.6	26 10.7	24 46.6	25 21.0	22 08.6	22 22.9	23 46.1
13 Su	11 28 44	20 23 44	10♏57 08	16 59 46	1 58.9	25 44.2	17 09.1	29 12.6	26 37.4	24 52.5	25 27.4	22 10.9	22 24.9	23 47.8
14 M	11 32 40	21 22 11	23 04 52	29 12 54	1 54.3	27 31.3	18 21.1	29 50.5	27 04.1	24 58.3	25 33.8	22 13.2	22 26.8	23 49.6
15 Tu	11 36 37	22 20 40	5♐24 19	11♐39 39	1D51.8	29 17.3	19 33.1	0♍28.5	27 30.7	25 03.9	25 40.2	22 15.4	22 28.8	23 51.3
16 W	11 40 33	23 19 11	17 59 23	24 24 03	1 51.2	1♎02.2	20 45.3	1 06.4	27 57.3	25 09.4	25 46.7	22 17.6	22 30.8	23 53.0
17 Th	11 44 30	24 17 44	0♑54 09	7♑30 10	1 51.8	2 46.0	21 57.4	1 44.3	28 23.9	25 14.7	25 53.3	22 19.8	22 32.8	23 54.7
18 F	11 48 26	25 16 18	14 12 31	21 01 31	1R52.8	4 28.8	23 09.7	2 22.2	28 50.5	25 19.8	25 59.8	22 21.9	22 34.9	23 56.4
19 Sa	11 52 23	26 14 53	27 57 27	5♒00 23	1 53.1	6 10.6	24 22.1	3 00.1	29 17.0	25 24.7	26 06.4	22 23.9	22 36.9	23 58.0
20 Su	11 56 20	27 13 31	12♒10 17	19 26 54	1 51.8	7 51.3	25 34.5	3 38.0	29 43.5	25 29.5	26 13.1	22 26.0	22 39.0	23 59.7
21 M	12 00 16	28 12 09	26 49 47	4♓18 15	1 48.4	9 31.1	26 47.0	4 15.8	0♍10.0	25 34.1	26 19.8	22 27.9	22 41.0	24 01.3
22 Tu	12 04 13	29 10 50	11♓51 25	19 28 12	1 42.5	11 09.8	27 59.5	4 53.7	0 36.4	25 38.5	26 26.5	22 29.9	22 43.1	24 03.0
23 W	12 08 09	0♎09 33	27 07 19	4♈47 23	1 34.7	12 47.6	29 12.2	5 31.5	1 02.9	25 42.7	26 33.2	22 31.8	22 45.2	24 04.6
24 Th	12 12 06	1 08 17	12♈26 59	20 04 39	1 25.8	14 24.4	0♍24.9	6 09.3	1 29.2	25 46.8	26 40.0	22 33.6	22 47.3	24 06.2
25 F	12 16 02	2 07 04	27 39 03	5♉08 56	1 16.9	16 00.3	1 37.7	6 47.1	1 55.6	25 50.7	26 46.8	22 35.4	22 49.4	24 07.7
26 Sa	12 19 59	3 05 53	12♉33 16	19 51 14	1 09.2	17 35.3	2 50.5	7 24.9	2 21.9	25 54.4	26 53.6	22 37.1	22 51.5	24 09.3
27 Su	12 23 55	4 04 45	27 02 15	4♊05 56	1 03.4	19 09.3	4 03.5	8 02.6	2 48.2	25 57.9	27 00.5	22 38.8	22 53.7	24 10.8
28 M	12 27 52	5 03 38	11♊02 09	17 50 57	0 59.9	20 42.5	5 16.5	8 40.4	3 14.5	26 01.3	27 07.4	22 40.5	22 55.8	24 12.4
29 Tu	12 31 49	6 02 34	24 32 34	1♋07 20	0D58.6	22 14.8	6 29.5	9 18.2	3 40.7	26 04.5	27 14.4	22 42.1	22 58.0	24 13.9
30 W	12 35 45	7 01 32	7♋35 43	13 58 15	0 58.6	23 46.2	7 42.7	9 55.9	4 06.9	26 07.4	27 21.3	22 43.7	23 00.1	24 15.4

LONGITUDE — October 1953

Day	Sid.Time	☉	0 hr ☽	Noon ☽	True ☊	☿	♀	♂	⚳	♃	♄	♅	♆	♇
1 Th	12 39 42	8♎00 33	20♋15 30	26♋28 04	0♒59.1	25♎16.7	8♍55.9	10♍33.6	4♍33.0	26♊10.2	27♎28.3	22♋45.2	23♎02.3	24♌16.9
2 F	12 43 38	8 59 36	2♌36 35	8♌41 37	0R58.9	26 46.3	10 09.2	11 11.4	4 59.1	26 12.8	27 35.3	22 46.6	23 04.5	24 18.3
3 Sa	12 47 35	9 58 40	14 43 47	20 43 36	0 57.0	28 15.1	11 22.5	11 49.1	5 25.2	26 15.2	27 42.3	22 48.0	23 06.7	24 19.8
4 Su	12 51 31	10 57 48	26 41 36	2♍38 15	0 52.7	29 43.0	12 35.9	12 26.7	5 51.2	26 17.4	27 49.4	22 49.4	23 08.9	24 21.2
5 M	12 55 28	11 56 57	8♍33 57	14 29 06	0 45.5	1♏10.0	13 49.4	13 04.4	6 17.2	26 19.4	27 56.5	22 50.7	23 11.1	24 22.6
6 Tu	12 59 24	12 56 08	20 24 01	26 18 59	0 35.5	2 36.1	15 02.9	13 42.1	6 43.2	26 21.2	28 03.5	22 52.0	23 13.3	24 23.9
7 W	13 03 21	13 55 22	2♎14 16	8♎10 04	0 23.3	4 01.3	16 16.5	14 19.7	7 09.1	26 22.9	28 10.7	22 53.2	23 15.5	24 25.3
8 Th	13 07 18	14 54 38	14 06 35	20 03 58	0 09.6	5 25.5	17 30.1	14 57.4	7 34.9	26 24.3	28 17.8	22 54.3	23 17.7	24 26.6
9 F	13 11 14	15 53 56	26 02 24	2♏02 00	29♑55.7	6 48.8	18 43.8	15 35.0	8 00.7	26 25.5	28 24.9	22 55.4	23 19.9	24 27.9
10 Sa	13 15 11	16 53 15	8♏02 56	14 05 24	29 42.6	8 11.1	19 57.6	16 12.6	8 26.5	26 26.5	28 32.1	22 56.5	23 22.1	24 29.2
11 Su	13 19 07	17 52 37	20 09 33	26 15 38	29 31.5	9 32.3	21 11.4	16 50.2	8 52.1	26 27.3	28 39.3	22 57.5	23 24.4	24 30.5
12 M	13 23 04	18 52 01	2♐23 53	8♐34 36	29 23.0	10 52.4	22 25.2	17 27.8	9 17.8	26 28.0	28 46.5	22 58.4	23 26.6	24 31.8
13 Tu	13 27 00	19 51 26	14 48 07	21 04 47	29 17.5	12 11.3	23 39.1	18 05.3	9 43.4	26 28.4	28 53.7	22 59.3	23 28.8	24 33.0
14 W	13 30 57	20 50 54	27 25 01	3♑49 13	29 14.6	13 29.1	24 53.1	18 42.9	10 08.9	26R28.6	29 00.9	23 00.1	23 31.1	24 34.2
15 Th	13 34 53	21 50 23	10♑17 50	16 51 19	29 13.8	14 45.5	26 07.1	19 20.4	10 34.4	26 28.6	29 08.1	23 00.9	23 33.3	24 35.4
16 F	13 38 50	22 49 53	23 30 06	0♒14 34	29 13.7	16 00.6	27 21.1	19 58.0	10 59.8	26 28.5	29 15.4	23 01.7	23 35.6	24 36.5
17 Sa	13 42 47	23 49 26	7♒05 04	14 01 50	29 13.3	17 14.1	28 35.2	20 35.5	11 25.2	26 28.1	29 22.6	23 02.4	23 37.8	24 37.7
18 Su	13 46 43	24 49 00	21 05 01	28 14 34	29 11.2	18 26.0	29 49.3	21 12.9	11 50.5	26 27.5	29 29.9	23 03.0	23 40.0	24 38.8
19 M	13 50 40	25 48 36	5♓30 19	12♓51 52	29 06.5	19 36.2	1♎03.5	21 50.4	12 15.7	26 26.7	29 37.1	23 03.6	23 42.3	24 39.9
20 Tu	13 54 36	26 48 13	20 18 36	27 49 41	28 59.1	20 44.4	2 17.7	22 27.9	12 40.9	26 25.7	29 44.4	23 04.1	23 44.5	24 40.9
21 W	13 58 33	27 47 53	5♈24 06	13♈00 37	28 49.3	21 50.6	3 32.0	23 05.3	13 06.0	26 24.6	29 51.6	23 04.5	23 46.7	24 42.0
22 Th	14 02 29	28 47 34	20 37 56	28 14 37	28 38.0	22 54.5	4 46.3	23 42.7	13 31.0	26 23.2	29 58.9	23 04.9	23 49.0	24 43.0
23 F	14 06 26	29 47 18	5♉49 16	13♉20 33	28 26.5	23 55.8	6 00.7	24 20.2	13 56.0	26 21.6	0♏06.2	23 05.3	23 51.2	24 44.0
24 Sa	14 10 22	0♏47 03	20 47 14	28 08 18	28 16.2	24 54.3	7 15.1	24 57.6	14 20.9	26 19.8	0 13.4	23 05.6	23 53.4	24 44.9
25 Su	14 14 19	1 46 51	5♊22 55	12♊30 28	28 08.1	25 49.8	8 29.5	25 35.0	14 45.8	26 17.8	0 20.7	23 05.9	23 55.7	24 45.9
26 M	14 18 16	2 46 41	19 30 37	26 23 13	28 02.7	26 41.8	9 44.0	26 12.4	15 10.5	26 15.7	0 28.0	23 06.1	23 57.9	24 46.8
27 Tu	14 22 12	3 46 33	3♋08 18	9♋46 07	27 59.9	27 30.1	10 58.5	26 49.7	15 35.3	26 13.3	0 35.3	23 06.2	24 00.1	24 47.7
28 W	14 26 09	4 46 27	16 17 02	22 41 32	27D58.9	28 14.1	12 13.1	27 27.1	15 59.9	26 10.7	0 42.5	23 06.3	24 02.3	24 48.5
29 Th	14 30 05	5 46 23	29 00 09	5♌13 33	27R58.9	28 53.5	13 27.7	28 04.4	16 24.4	26 08.0	0 49.8	23R06.3	24 04.5	24 49.4
30 F	14 34 02	6 46 22	11♌22 22	17 27 17	27 58.6	29 27.6	14 42.4	28 41.8	16 48.9	26 05.0	0 57.0	23 06.3	24 06.7	24 50.2
31 Sa	14 37 58	7 46 23	23 28 57	29 28 01	27 56.8	29 56.0	15 57.0	29 19.1	17 13.3	26 01.8	1 04.3	23 06.2	24 08.9	24 51.0

Astro Data

	Dy Hr Mn
☽0S	8 19:22
☿0S	17 3:07
☽0N	22 14:29
☉0S	23 8:06
☽0S	6 1:15
♃R	15 2:56
☽0N	20 0:52
♀0S	21 13:01
♅R	29 14:19

Planet Ingress

		Dy Hr Mn
♂	♍	14 17:59
☿	♎	15 21:45
⚳	♍	21 2:56
☉	♎	23 8:06
♀	♍	24 3:48
☿	♏	4 16:40
☊	♑R	9 4:29
♀	♎	18 15:27
♄	♏	22 15:36
☉	♏	23 17:06
☿	♐	31 15:49

Last Aspect / ☽ Ingress (September)

Last Aspect Dy Hr Mn			☽ Ingress	Dy Hr Mn
1 16:49	♄	△	♋	2 3:30
4 2:18	♄	□	♌	4 13:05
6 14:25	♂	☌	♍	7 0:47
9 2:08	♃	□	♎	9 13:27
11 22:31	♂	⚹	♏	12 2:05
14 13:17	♂	□	♐	14 13:32
16 14:35	♄	⚹	♑	16 22:21
18 20:42	♄	□	♒	19 3:30
20 23:06	♄	△	♓	21 5:06
23 4:16	☉	☍	♈	23 4:30
24 22:31	♄	☍	♉	25 3:45
26 19:11	♇	□	♊	27 5:01
29 4:50	♄	△	♋	29 9:56

Last Aspect / ☽ Ingress (October)

Last Aspect Dy Hr Mn			☽ Ingress	Dy Hr Mn
1 13:58	♄	□	♌	1 18:53
4 5:16	☿	⚹	♍	4 6:40
6 12:05	♃	□	♎	6 19:28
9 4:41	♄	☌	♏	9 7:56
11 8:33	♇	□	♐	11 19:19
14 2:55	♄	⚹	♑	14 4:51
16 10:14	♄	□	♒	16 11:34
18 14:06	♄	△	♓	18 14:55
20 9:47	♃	□	♈	20 15:27
22 14:46	♄	☍	♉	22 14:47
24 6:34	♂	△	♊	24 15:04
26 11:47	♃	☌	♋	26 18:24
28 23:08	☿	△	♌	29 1:55
31 12:58	☿	□	♍	31 13:04

☽ Phases & Eclipses

Dy Hr Mn		
8 7:48	●	15♍22
16 9:49	☽	23♐14
23 4:16	○	29♓51
29 21:51	☾	6♋27
8 0:40	●	14♎27
15 21:44	☽	22♑15
22 12:56	○	28♈50
29 13:09	☾	5♌49

Astro Data

1 September 1953
Julian Day # 19602
SVP 5♓54'09"
GC 26♐11.5 ⚵ 21♋10.1
Eris 8♈15.8R ⚶ 19♋33.9
⚷ 15♑35.2R ⚴ 19♒20.9R
☽ Mean ☊ 1♒11.1

1 October 1953
Julian Day # 19632
SVP 5♓54'06"
GC 26♐11.6 ⚵ 7♌50.4
Eris 7♈57.8R ⚶ 4♌22.6
⚷ 15♑23.6 ⚴ 16♒28.3
☽ Mean ☊ 29♑35.8

November 1953 — LONGITUDE

Day	Sid.Time	☉	0 hr ☽	Noon ☽	True ☊	☿	♀	♂	⚳	♃	♄	♅	♆	♇
1 Su	14 41 55	8♏46 25	5♍25 09	11♍20 55	27♑52.7	0♐18.1	17♎11.8	29♍56.4	17♍37.6	25♊58.5	1♏11.5	23♋06.1	24♎11.1	24♌51.7
2 M	14 45 51	9 46 30	17 15 52	23 10 30	27R 45.7	0 33.2	18 26.5	0♎33.7	18 01.8	25R 54.9	1 18.7	23R 05.9	24 13.3	24 52.4
3 Tu	14 49 48	10 46 37	29 05 18	5♎00 39	27 35.9	0R 40.7	19 41.3	1 11.0	18 26.0	25 51.2	1 25.9	23 05.7	24 15.5	24 53.1
4 W	14 53 44	11 46 46	10♎56 54	16 54 21	27 23.8	0 39.9	20 56.1	1 48.2	18 50.0	25 47.3	1 33.1	23 05.4	24 17.6	24 53.8
5 Th	14 57 41	12 46 57	22 53 15	28 53 48	27 10.2	0 30.2	22 11.0	2 25.5	19 14.0	25 43.1	1 40.3	23 05.0	24 19.8	24 54.4
6 F	15 01 38	13 47 10	4♏56 08	11♏00 24	26 56.2	0 11.2	23 25.8	3 02.7	19 37.9	25 38.9	1 47.5	23 04.6	24 21.9	24 55.1
7 Sa	15 05 34	14 47 24	17 06 42	23 15 06	26 43.1	29♏42.4	24 40.7	3 39.9	20 01.7	25 34.4	1 54.7	23 04.2	24 24.1	24 55.6
8 Su	15 09 31	15 47 41	29 25 40	5♐38 29	26 31.8	29 03.7	25 55.7	4 17.1	20 25.4	25 29.7	2 01.8	23 03.6	24 26.2	24 56.2
9 M	15 13 27	16 47 59	11♐53 38	18 11 13	26 23.3	28 15.2	27 10.6	4 54.3	20 48.9	25 24.9	2 09.0	23 03.1	24 28.3	24 56.7
10 Tu	15 17 24	17 48 18	24 31 21	0♑54 12	26 17.7	27 17.5	28 25.6	5 31.5	21 12.4	25 19.9	2 16.1	23 02.5	24 30.4	24 57.2
11 W	15 21 20	18 48 40	7♑19 57	13 48 49	26D 14.9	26 11.6	29 40.6	6 08.6	21 35.8	25 14.7	2 23.2	23 01.8	24 32.5	24 57.7
12 Th	15 25 17	19 49 02	20 21 03	26 56 55	26 14.3	24 58.8	0♏55.6	6 45.7	21 59.1	25 09.4	2 30.2	23 01.1	24 34.6	24 58.1
13 F	15 29 14	20 49 26	3♒36 42	10♒20 41	26R 14.7	23 41.1	2 10.7	7 22.8	22 22.2	25 03.9	2 37.3	23 00.3	24 36.6	24 58.5
14 Sa	15 33 10	21 49 51	17 09 05	24 02 09	26 14.9	22 20.7	3 25.8	7 59.9	22 45.3	24 58.3	2 44.3	22 59.5	24 38.7	24 58.9
15 Su	15 37 07	22 50 18	1♓00 00	8♓02 43	26 13.9	21 00.4	4 40.8	8 37.0	23 08.2	24 52.5	2 51.3	22 58.6	24 40.7	24 59.3
16 M	15 41 03	23 50 46	15 10 12	22 22 16	26 10.7	19 42.6	5 55.9	9 14.0	23 31.1	24 46.5	2 58.2	22 57.7	24 42.7	24 59.6
17 Tu	15 45 00	24 51 15	29 38 35	6♈58 38	26 05.1	18 30.0	7 11.1	9 51.0	23 53.8	24 40.4	3 05.2	22 56.7	24 44.7	24 59.9
18 W	15 48 56	25 51 45	14♈21 42	21 47 00	25 57.3	17 24.8	8 26.2	10 28.1	24 16.4	24 34.1	3 12.1	22 55.7	24 46.7	25 00.1
19 Th	15 52 53	26 52 17	29 13 32	6♉40 14	25 48.0	16 28.9	9 41.4	11 05.0	24 38.9	24 27.8	3 19.0	22 54.6	24 48.7	25 00.4
20 F	15 56 49	27 52 50	14♉06 01	21 29 44	25 38.5	15 43.5	10 56.5	11 42.0	25 01.2	24 21.2	3 25.8	22 53.5	24 50.7	25 00.6
21 Sa	16 00 46	28 53 25	28 50 18	6♊06 44	25 29.9	15 09.5	12 11.7	12 19.0	25 23.5	24 14.6	3 32.7	22 52.3	24 52.6	25 00.8
22 Su	16 04 43	29 54 01	13♊18 11	20 23 57	25 23.1	14 47.2	13 26.9	12 55.9	25 45.6	24 07.8	3 39.5	22 51.1	24 54.5	25 00.9
23 M	16 08 39	0♐54 39	27 23 31	4♋16 32	25 18.7	14D 36.5	14 42.2	13 32.8	26 07.6	24 00.9	3 46.2	22 49.8	24 56.4	25 01.0
24 Tu	16 12 36	1 55 18	11♋02 51	17 42 29	25D 16.6	14 37.0	15 57.4	14 09.7	26 29.4	23 53.9	3 52.9	22 48.5	24 58.3	25 01.1
25 W	16 16 32	2 55 59	24 15 35	0♌42 28	25 16.4	14 47.9	17 12.7	14 46.6	26 51.2	23 46.8	3 59.6	22 47.1	25 00.2	25 01.2
26 Th	16 20 29	3 56 42	7♌03 31	13 19 14	25 17.4	15 08.7	18 28.0	15 23.5	27 12.7	23 39.5	4 06.3	22 45.7	25 02.0	25R 01.2
27 F	16 24 25	4 57 26	19 30 11	25 36 57	25R 18.6	15 38.2	19 43.3	16 00.3	27 34.2	23 32.2	4 12.9	22 44.2	25 03.9	25 01.2
28 Sa	16 28 22	5 58 11	1♍40 11	7♍40 31	25 19.0	16 15.8	20 58.6	16 37.1	27 55.5	23 24.8	4 19.5	22 42.7	25 05.7	25 01.2
29 Su	16 32 18	6 58 58	13 38 38	19 35 10	25 17.9	17 00.4	22 13.9	17 14.0	28 16.7	23 17.2	4 26.0	22 41.2	25 07.5	25 01.1
30 M	16 36 15	7 59 46	25 30 45	1♎25 59	25 14.9	17 51.4	23 29.3	17 50.7	28 37.7	23 09.6	4 32.5	22 39.6	25 09.2	25 01.0

December 1953 — LONGITUDE

Day	Sid.Time	☉	0 hr ☽	Noon ☽	True ☊	☿	♀	♂	⚳	♃	♄	♅	♆	♇
1 Tu	16 40 12	9♐00 36	7♎21 26	13♎17 38	25♑09.8	18♏47.8	24♏44.6	18♎27.5	28♍58.5	23♊01.9	4♏38.9	22♋38.0	25♎11.0	25♌00.9
2 W	16 44 08	10 01 28	19 15 03	25 14 09	25R 02.8	19 49.0	26 00.0	19 04.2	29 19.2	22R 54.2	4 45.3	22R 36.3	25 12.7	25R 00.7
3 Th	16 48 05	11 02 20	1♏15 17	7♏18 47	24 54.7	20 54.4	27 15.4	19 41.0	29 39.8	22 46.3	4 51.7	22 34.6	25 14.4	25 00.5
4 F	16 52 01	12 03 14	13 24 54	19 33 52	24 46.1	22 03.5	28 30.8	20 17.6	0♎00.2	22 38.4	4 58.0	22 32.8	25 16.1	25 00.3
5 Sa	16 55 58	13 04 10	25 45 49	2♐00 51	24 38.1	23 15.6	29 46.2	20 54.3	0 20.4	22 30.5	5 04.3	22 31.0	25 17.7	25 00.1
6 Su	16 59 54	14 05 06	8♐19 02	14 40 21	24 31.3	24 30.5	1♐01.6	21 31.0	0 40.4	22 22.5	5 10.5	22 29.2	25 19.4	24 59.8
7 M	17 03 51	15 06 03	21 04 48	27 32 21	24 26.3	25 47.7	2 17.0	22 07.6	1 00.3	22 14.4	5 16.6	22 27.3	25 21.0	24 59.5
8 Tu	17 07 47	16 07 01	4♑02 54	10♑36 26	24 23.4	27 06.9	3 32.4	22 44.2	1 20.0	22 06.3	5 22.7	22 25.4	25 22.6	24 59.2
9 W	17 11 44	17 08 00	17 12 50	23 52 06	24D 22.4	28 27.9	4 47.9	23 20.7	1 39.5	21 58.2	5 28.8	22 23.4	25 24.1	24 58.8
10 Th	17 15 41	18 09 00	0♒34 08	7♒18 56	24 23.0	29 50.3	6 03.3	23 57.3	1 58.9	21 50.1	5 34.8	22 21.4	25 25.7	24 58.5
11 F	17 19 37	19 10 00	14 06 29	20 56 46	24 24.5	1♐14.0	7 18.8	24 33.8	2 18.0	21 41.9	5 40.8	22 19.4	25 27.2	24 58.0
12 Sa	17 23 34	20 11 01	27 49 46	4♓45 28	24 26.0	2 38.8	8 34.2	25 10.2	2 37.0	21 33.7	5 46.7	22 17.3	25 28.7	24 57.6
13 Su	17 27 30	21 12 03	11♓43 51	18 44 50	24R 26.8	4 04.6	9 49.7	25 46.7	2 55.8	21 25.6	5 52.5	22 15.2	25 30.1	24 57.1
14 M	17 31 27	22 13 04	25 48 19	2♈54 07	24 26.4	5 31.2	11 05.1	26 23.1	3 14.3	21 17.4	5 58.3	22 13.1	25 31.5	24 56.6
15 Tu	17 35 23	23 14 06	10♈02 00	17 11 40	24 24.4	6 58.5	12 20.6	26 59.5	3 32.7	21 09.2	6 04.0	22 10.9	25 32.9	24 56.1
16 W	17 39 20	24 15 09	24 22 42	1♉34 38	24 21.2	8 26.4	13 36.0	27 35.8	3 50.9	21 01.1	6 09.6	22 08.8	25 34.3	24 55.5
17 Th	17 43 16	25 16 12	8♉46 55	15 58 56	24 17.0	9 55.0	14 51.5	28 12.1	4 08.9	20 52.9	6 15.2	22 06.5	25 35.7	24 55.0
18 F	17 47 13	26 17 16	23 10 02	0♊19 30	24 12.5	11 24.0	16 06.9	28 48.4	4 26.7	20 44.8	6 20.8	22 04.3	25 37.0	24 54.4
19 Sa	17 51 10	27 18 20	7♊26 42	14 30 57	24 08.5	12 53.4	17 22.4	29 24.7	4 44.2	20 36.8	6 26.2	22 02.0	25 38.3	24 53.7
20 Su	17 55 06	28 19 24	21 31 38	28 28 13	24 05.4	14 23.3	18 37.9	0♏00.9	5 01.6	20 28.7	6 31.6	21 59.7	25 39.5	24 53.1
21 M	17 59 03	29 20 29	5♋20 15	12♋07 24	24D 03.6	15 53.5	19 53.3	0 37.2	5 18.7	20 20.8	6 37.0	21 57.4	25 40.8	24 52.4
22 Tu	18 02 59	0♑21 35	18 49 24	25 26 09	24 03.1	17 24.1	21 08.8	1 13.3	5 35.6	20 12.8	6 42.2	21 55.1	25 42.0	24 51.7
23 W	18 06 56	1 22 41	1♌57 36	8♌23 53	24 03.7	18 55.0	22 24.3	1 49.5	5 52.3	20 04.9	6 47.5	21 52.7	25 43.1	24 50.9
24 Th	18 10 52	2 23 47	14 45 09	21 01 42	24 05.2	20 26.2	23 39.8	2 25.6	6 08.7	19 57.1	6 52.6	21 50.3	25 44.3	24 50.2
25 F	18 14 49	3 24 54	27 13 53	3♍22 08	24 06.8	21 57.7	24 55.2	3 01.7	6 24.9	19 49.4	6 57.6	21 47.9	25 45.4	24 49.4
26 Sa	18 18 46	4 26 02	9♍26 55	15 28 46	24 08.4	23 29.6	26 10.7	3 37.7	6 40.9	19 41.7	7 02.6	21 45.4	25 46.5	24 48.6
27 Su	18 22 42	5 27 10	21 28 16	27 25 58	24R 09.4	25 01.7	27 26.2	4 13.7	6 56.6	19 34.1	7 07.6	21 43.0	25 47.5	24 47.7
28 M	18 26 39	6 28 18	3♎22 30	9♎18 28	24 09.6	26 34.0	28 41.7	4 49.7	7 12.1	19 26.6	7 12.4	21 40.5	25 48.6	24 46.9
29 Tu	18 30 35	7 29 28	15 14 28	21 11 07	24 08.9	28 06.7	29 57.2	5 25.7	7 27.3	19 19.1	7 17.2	21 38.0	25 49.5	24 46.0
30 W	18 34 32	8 30 37	27 08 58	3♏08 37	24 07.6	29 39.7	1♑12.7	6 01.6	7 42.3	19 11.8	7 21.9	21 35.5	25 50.5	24 45.1
31 Th	18 38 28	9 31 47	9♏10 34	15 15 17	24 05.7	1♑13.0	2 28.2	6 37.4	7 57.0	19 04.6	7 26.5	21 33.0	25 51.4	24 44.1

Astro Data

	Dy Hr Mn
☽0S	2 6:58
☿R	3 21:50
♂0S	6 6:32
♃⚹♇	14 9:25
☽0N	16 8:47
♃△♆	16 23:10
☿D	23 22:57
♆⚹♇	26 0:50
♇R	26 20:44
☽0S	29 13:18
♃⚺♅	5 9:58
☽0N	13 14:10
♃⚼♄	15 21:06
☽0S	26 20:50

Planet Ingress

		Dy Hr Mn
♂	♎	1 14:19
☿	♏R	6 22:19
♀	♏	11 18:12
☉	♐	22 14:22
⚳	♎	4 11:49
♀	♐	5 16:24
☿	♐	10 14:48
♂	♏	20 11:22
☉	♑	22 3:31
♀	♑	29 12:53
☿	♑	30 17:14

Last Aspect / ☽ Ingress (November)

Last Aspect Dy Hr Mn			☽ Ingress	Dy Hr Mn
2 17:32	♃	□	♎	3 1:51
5 5:42	♃	△	♏	5 14:12
7 23:57	☿	☌	♐	8 1:06
10 6:51	♀	⚹	♑	10 10:18
12 8:44	☿	⚹	♒	12 17:31
14 13:38	♇	☍	♓	14 22:17
16 15:57	♃	□	♈	17 0:35
18 17:12	♇	△	♉	19 1:15
20 23:12	☉	☍	♊	21 1:55
22 19:54	♇	⚹	♋	23 4:31
25 1:21	♆	□	♌	25 10:40
27 10:55	♆	⚹	♍	27 20:41
29 19:25	♃	□	♎	30 9:06

Last Aspect / ☽ Ingress (December)

Last Aspect Dy Hr Mn			☽ Ingress	Dy Hr Mn
2 11:57	♆	☌	♏	2 21:30
5 7:13	♀	☌	♐	5 8:09
7 7:56	♆	⚹	♑	7 16:33
9 21:10	☿	⚹	♒	9 22:59
11 19:53	♆	△	♓	12 3:46
13 17:57	♅	△	♈	14 7:06
16 5:05	♂	☍	♉	16 9:22
18 2:55	♇	□	♊	18 11:27
20 11:44	☉	☍	♋	20 14:40
22 12:29	♆	□	♌	22 20:23
24 21:07	♆	⚹	♍	25 5:24
27 12:01	♀	□	♎	27 17:11
30 4:00	☿	⚹	♏	30 5:43

☽ Phases & Eclipses

Dy Hr Mn		
6 17:58	●	14♏02
14 7:52	☽	21♒39
20 23:12	○	28♉21
28 8:16	☾	5♍49
6 10:48	●	14♐02
13 16:30	☽	21♓23
20 11:44	○	28♊19
28 5:43	☾	6♎12

Astro Data

1 November 1953
Julian Day # 19663
SVP 5♓54'02"
GC 26♐11.7 ⚴ 23♌14.0
Eris 7♈39.2R ⚵ 17♌03.1
⚷ 16♑24.4 ⚶ 20♒20.1
☽ Mean ☊ 27♑57.3

1 December 1953
Julian Day # 19693
SVP 5♓53'58"
GC 26♐11.7 ⚴ 4♍36.8
Eris 7♈26.6R ⚵ 25♌10.3
⚷ 18♑22.4 ⚶ 28♒48.7
☽ Mean ☊ 26♑22.0

LONGITUDE

January 1954

Day	Sid.Time	☉	0 hr ☽	Noon ☽	True ☊	☿	♀	♂	⚳	♃	♄	♅	♆	♇
1 F	18 42 25	10♑32 57	21♏23 14	27♏34 46	24♑03.5	2♑46.6	3♑43.7	7♏13.3	8♎11.4	18♊57.5	7♏31.0	21♋30.4	25♎52.3	24♌43.2
2 Sa	18 46 21	11 34 08	3♐50 14	10♐09 50	24R 01.6	4 20.5	4 59.2	7 49.1	8 25.5	18R 50.5	7 35.5	21R 27.9	25 53.2	24R 42.2
3 Su	18 50 18	12 35 19	16 33 48	23 02 11	23 59.9	5 54.8	6 14.7	8 24.8	8 39.4	18 43.6	7 39.9	21 25.3	25 54.0	24 41.2
4 M	18 54 15	13 36 30	29 35 02	6♑12 17	23 58.9	7 29.4	7 30.2	9 00.5	8 53.0	18 36.8	7 44.2	21 22.8	25 54.8	24 40.2
5 Tu	18 58 11	14 37 41	12♑53 48	19 39 23	23D 58.4	9 04.4	8 45.7	9 36.2	9 06.3	18 30.2	7 48.4	21 20.2	25 55.6	24 39.1
6 W	19 02 08	15 38 52	26 28 48	3♒21 41	23 58.5	10 39.7	10 01.2	10 11.8	9 19.3	18 23.7	7 52.5	21 17.6	25 56.3	24 38.1
7 Th	19 06 04	16 40 02	10♒17 44	17 16 31	23 59.0	12 15.4	11 16.7	10 47.4	9 32.0	18 17.3	7 56.6	21 15.0	25 57.0	24 37.0
8 F	19 10 01	17 41 12	24 17 39	1♓20 42	23 59.6	13 51.6	12 32.2	11 22.9	9 44.4	18 11.1	8 00.6	21 12.4	25 57.7	24 35.9
9 Sa	19 13 57	18 42 22	8♓25 16	15 30 57	24 00.2	15 28.1	13 47.7	11 58.3	9 56.5	18 05.0	8 04.4	21 09.8	25 58.3	24 34.8
10 Su	19 17 54	19 43 31	22 37 21	29 44 06	24 00.6	17 05.1	15 03.1	12 33.8	10 08.3	17 59.1	8 08.2	21 07.2	25 58.9	24 33.6
11 M	19 21 50	20 44 39	6♈50 53	13♈57 21	24R 00.8	18 42.5	16 18.6	13 09.1	10 19.8	17 53.3	8 11.9	21 04.6	25 59.5	24 32.5
12 Tu	19 25 47	21 45 47	21 03 13	28 08 13	24 00.8	20 20.4	17 34.1	13 44.5	10 31.0	17 47.7	8 15.6	21 02.0	26 00.0	24 31.3
13 W	19 29 44	22 46 54	5♉12 05	12♉14 35	24 00.7	21 58.8	18 49.5	14 19.7	10 41.8	17 42.2	8 19.1	20 59.4	26 00.5	24 30.1
14 Th	19 33 40	23 48 01	19 15 26	26 14 26	24D 00.6	23 37.6	20 05.0	14 54.9	10 52.3	17 37.0	8 22.5	20 56.8	26 00.9	24 28.9
15 F	19 37 37	24 49 07	3♊11 20	10♊05 53	24 00.7	25 17.0	21 20.4	15 30.1	11 02.5	17 31.8	8 25.9	20 54.2	26 01.4	24 27.6
16 Sa	19 41 33	25 50 12	16 57 54	23 47 07	24 00.8	26 56.8	22 35.9	16 05.2	11 12.3	17 26.9	8 29.1	20 51.6	26 01.8	24 26.4
17 Su	19 45 30	26 51 17	0♋33 20	7♋16 21	24 01.0	28 37.2	23 51.3	16 40.3	11 21.8	17 22.1	8 32.3	20 49.0	26 02.1	24 25.1
18 M	19 49 26	27 52 21	13 56 00	20 32 07	24R 01.2	0♒18.0	25 06.7	17 15.3	11 31.0	17 17.5	8 35.4	20 46.4	26 02.5	24 23.9
19 Tu	19 53 23	28 53 24	27 04 34	3♌33 17	24 01.1	1 59.4	26 22.1	17 50.3	11 39.8	17 13.1	8 38.3	20 43.8	26 02.7	24 22.6
20 W	19 57 19	29 54 27	9♌58 15	16 19 27	24 00.7	3 41.3	27 37.5	18 25.2	11 48.2	17 08.9	8 41.2	20 41.3	26 03.0	24 21.3
21 Th	20 01 16	0♒55 29	22 36 57	28 50 54	24 00.0	5 23.6	28 53.0	19 00.1	11 56.3	17 04.8	8 44.0	20 38.7	26 03.2	24 20.0
22 F	20 05 13	1 56 30	5♍01 26	11♍08 50	23 59.0	7 06.5	0♒08.4	19 34.9	12 04.0	17 01.0	8 46.7	20 36.1	26 03.4	24 18.6
23 Sa	20 09 09	2 57 31	17 13 21	23 15 20	23 57.7	8 49.8	1 23.8	20 09.6	12 11.3	16 57.3	8 49.3	20 33.6	26 03.6	24 17.3
24 Su	20 13 06	3 58 31	29 15 11	5♎13 19	23 56.4	10 33.5	2 39.1	20 44.3	12 18.3	16 53.8	8 51.8	20 31.1	26 03.7	24 15.9
25 M	20 17 02	4 59 31	11♎10 14	17 06 26	23 55.4	12 17.6	3 54.5	21 18.9	12 24.9	16 50.5	8 54.2	20 28.6	26 03.8	24 14.6
26 Tu	20 20 59	6 00 30	23 02 27	28 58 52	23D 54.7	14 01.9	5 09.9	21 53.5	12 31.1	16 47.4	8 56.5	20 26.1	26R 03.8	24 13.2
27 W	20 24 55	7 01 29	4♏56 16	10♏55 13	23 54.6	15 46.5	6 25.3	22 28.0	12 36.9	16 44.5	8 58.7	20 23.6	26 03.8	24 11.8
28 Th	20 28 52	8 02 27	16 56 21	23 00 15	23 55.1	17 31.3	7 40.7	23 02.4	12 42.3	16 41.7	9 00.8	20 21.2	26 03.8	24 10.4
29 F	20 32 48	9 03 24	29 07 28	5♐18 34	23 56.2	19 16.0	8 56.0	23 36.8	12 47.3	16 39.2	9 02.8	20 18.7	26 03.8	24 09.0
30 Sa	20 36 45	10 04 21	11♐34 04	17 54 24	23 57.6	21 00.6	10 11.4	24 11.1	12 51.9	16 36.9	9 04.7	20 16.3	26 03.7	24 07.6
31 Su	20 40 42	11 05 16	24 19 58	0♑51 05	23 59.0	22 45.0	11 26.7	24 45.3	12 56.1	16 34.8	9 06.5	20 13.9	26 03.6	24 06.1

LONGITUDE

February 1954

Day	Sid.Time	☉	0 hr ☽	Noon ☽	True ☊	☿	♀	♂	⚳	♃	♄	♅	♆	♇
1 M	20 44 38	12♒06 12	7♑27 57	14♑10 41	23♑59.9	24♒28.8	12♒42.1	25♏19.5	12♎59.9	16♊32.9	9♏08.2	20♋11.5	26♎03.4	24♌04.7
2 Tu	20 48 35	13 07 06	20 59 17	27 53 35	24R 00.1	26 12.0	13 57.4	25 53.5	13 03.3	16R 31.2	9 09.8	20R 09.2	26R 03.2	24R 03.3
3 W	20 52 31	14 07 59	4♒53 19	11♒58 04	23 59.3	27 54.1	15 12.7	26 27.5	13 06.3	16 29.6	9 11.3	20 06.9	26 03.0	24 01.8
4 Th	20 56 28	15 08 51	19 07 18	26 20 21	23 57.4	29 34.9	16 28.0	27 01.5	13 08.8	16 28.3	9 12.7	20 04.6	26 02.7	24 00.4
5 F	21 00 24	16 09 41	3♓36 27	10♓54 48	23 54.6	1♓13.9	17 43.4	27 35.3	13 10.9	16 27.2	9 13.9	20 02.3	26 02.4	23 58.9
6 Sa	21 04 21	17 10 30	18 14 30	25 34 41	23 51.3	2 50.9	18 58.6	28 09.1	13 12.6	16 26.3	9 15.1	20 00.0	26 02.1	23 57.5
7 Su	21 08 17	18 11 18	2♈54 30	10♈13 09	23 48.0	4 25.2	20 13.9	28 42.7	13 13.8	16 25.6	9 16.2	19 57.8	26 01.8	23 56.0
8 M	21 12 14	19 12 05	17 29 54	24 44 08	23 45.3	5 56.4	21 29.2	29 16.3	13 14.6	16 25.1	9 17.2	19 55.6	26 01.4	23 54.5
9 Tu	21 16 11	20 12 49	1♉55 19	9♉03 05	23D 43.6	7 23.8	22 44.4	29 49.8	13R 15.0	16D 24.9	9 18.0	19 53.5	26 00.9	23 53.0
10 W	21 20 07	21 13 33	16 07 07	23 07 15	23 43.2	8 46.9	23 59.7	0♐23.3	13 15.0	16 24.8	9 18.8	19 51.3	26 00.5	23 51.6
11 Th	21 24 04	22 14 14	0♊03 23	6♊55 31	23 43.9	10 05.0	25 14.9	0 56.6	13 14.5	16 24.9	9 19.4	19 49.3	26 00.0	23 50.1
12 F	21 28 00	23 14 54	13 43 43	20 28 03	23 45.4	11 17.3	26 30.1	1 29.8	13 13.6	16 25.2	9 20.0	19 47.2	25 59.5	23 48.6
13 Sa	21 31 57	24 15 33	27 08 40	3♋45 43	23 47.0	12 23.1	27 45.3	2 03.0	13 12.3	16 25.8	9 20.4	19 45.2	25 58.9	23 47.2
14 Su	21 35 53	25 16 09	10♋19 21	16 49 44	23R 48.2	13 21.7	29 00.4	2 36.0	13 10.5	16 26.5	9 20.8	19 43.2	25 58.4	23 45.7
15 M	21 39 50	26 16 44	23 16 59	29 41 15	23 48.2	14 12.4	0♓15.6	3 09.0	13 08.3	16 27.4	9 21.0	19 41.2	25 57.7	23 44.2
16 Tu	21 43 46	27 17 17	6♌02 39	12♌21 17	23 46.7	14 54.5	1 30.7	3 41.9	13 05.6	16 28.5	9R 21.1	19 39.3	25 57.1	23 42.7
17 W	21 47 43	28 17 49	18 37 15	24 50 38	23 43.3	15 27.5	2 45.9	4 14.7	13 02.6	16 29.9	9 21.2	19 37.4	25 56.4	23 41.3
18 Th	21 51 40	29 18 19	1♍01 32	7♍10 04	23 38.2	15 50.9	4 01.0	4 47.3	12 59.1	16 31.4	9 21.1	19 35.6	25 55.7	23 39.8
19 F	21 55 36	0♓18 48	13 16 19	19 20 25	23 31.8	16R 04.2	5 16.1	5 19.9	12 55.1	16 33.1	9 20.9	19 33.8	25 55.0	23 38.3
20 Sa	21 59 33	1 19 15	25 22 34	1♎22 55	23 24.5	16 07.5	6 31.1	5 52.4	12 50.8	16 35.0	9 20.6	19 32.0	25 54.2	23 36.9
21 Su	22 03 29	2 19 41	7♎21 44	13 19 15	23 17.2	16 00.5	7 46.2	6 24.8	12 46.0	16 37.1	9 20.2	19 30.3	25 53.4	23 35.4
22 M	22 07 26	3 20 05	19 15 49	25 11 47	23 10.6	15 43.6	9 01.2	6 57.0	12 40.8	16 39.4	9 19.7	19 28.6	25 52.6	23 33.9
23 Tu	22 11 22	4 20 28	1♏07 33	7♏03 34	23 05.3	15 17.1	10 16.3	7 29.2	12 35.1	16 41.9	9 19.1	19 27.0	25 51.8	23 32.5
24 W	22 15 19	5 20 49	13 00 20	18 58 22	23 01.8	14 41.8	11 31.3	8 01.3	12 29.1	16 44.6	9 18.5	19 25.4	25 50.9	23 31.0
25 Th	22 19 15	6 21 09	24 58 15	1♐00 32	23D 00.1	13 58.6	12 46.3	8 33.2	12 22.6	16 47.5	9 17.7	19 23.8	25 50.0	23 29.6
26 F	22 23 12	7 21 28	7♐05 52	13 14 50	23 00.1	13 08.5	14 01.3	9 05.0	12 15.7	16 50.6	9 16.8	19 22.3	25 49.0	23 28.2
27 Sa	22 27 09	8 21 45	19 28 04	25 46 10	23 01.2	12 12.9	15 16.2	9 36.7	12 08.5	16 53.8	9 15.7	19 20.9	25 48.1	23 26.7
28 Su	22 31 05	9 22 01	2♑09 41	8♑39 10	23 02.6	11 13.3	16 31.2	10 08.3	12 00.8	16 57.3	9 14.6	19 19.4	25 47.1	23 25.3

Astro Data

	Dy Hr Mn
☽0N	9 19:18
☽0S	23 5:13
♆R	27 10:50
☽0N	6 2:44
⚳R	9 21:40
♃D	10 9:26
♄R	17 6:16
☽0S	19 13:18
☿R	20 7:32

Planet Ingress

		Dy Hr Mn
☿	♒	18 7:43
☉	♒	20 14:11
♀	♒	22 9:20
☿	♓	4 18:03
♂	♐	9 19:18
♀	♓	15 7:01
☉	♓	19 4:32

Last Aspect / ☽ Ingress

Last Aspect Dy Hr Mn			☽ Ingress	Dy Hr Mn
1 6:29	♇	□	♐	1 16:39
3 17:16	♆	⚹	♑	4 0:45
5 23:02	♆	□	♒	6 6:09
8 2:50	♆	△	♓	8 9:43
9 21:31	♅	△	♈	10 12:27
12 8:22	♆	☍	♉	12 15:10
14 8:59	♇	□	♊	14 18:29
16 15:58	♆	△	♋	16 23:01
19 2:37	☉	☍	♌	19 5:24
21 6:36	♆	⚹	♍	21 14:14
23 6:39	♅	⚹	♎	24 1:30
26 6:07	♆	☌	♏	26 14:03
28 14:18	♇	□	♐	29 1:42
31 3:12	♆	⚹	♑	31 10:27

Last Aspect / ☽ Ingress

Last Aspect Dy Hr Mn			☽ Ingress	Dy Hr Mn
2 8:49	♆	□	♒	2 15:38
4 13:11	♂	□	♓	4 18:03
6 16:23	♂	△	♈	6 19:14
8 14:09	♆	☍	♉	8 20:47
10 13:39	♀	□	♊	10 23:54
12 23:58	♀	△	♋	13 5:10
15 5:01	♆	□	♌	15 12:35
17 19:17	☉	☍	♍	17 22:00
19 12:26	♅	⚹	♎	20 9:14
22 13:23	♆	☌	♏	22 21:43
24 21:05	♇	□	♐	25 10:00
27 12:04	♆	⚹	♑	27 19:58

☽ Phases & Eclipses

Dy Hr Mn		
5 2:21	●	14♑13
5 2:31:27	●	A 01'42"
12 0:22	☽	21♈16
19 2:37	○	28♋30
19 2:32	●	T 1.032
27 3:28	☾	6♏40
3 15:55	●	14♒18
10 8:29	☽	21♉05
17 19:17	○	28♌36
25 23:29	☾	6♐50

Astro Data

1 January 1954
Julian Day # 19724
SVP 5♓53'52"
GC 26♐11.8 ⚴ 9♍53.1
Eris 7♈23.3 ⚵ 26♌54.0R
⚷ 21♑02.2 ⚶ 10♓24.8
☽ Mean ☊ 24♑43.5

1 February 1954
Julian Day # 19755
SVP 5♓53'46"
GC 26♐11.9 ⚴ 5♍33.6R
Eris 7♈31.1 ⚵ 21♌09.3R
⚷ 23♑51.7 ⚶ 23♓34.9
☽ Mean ☊ 23♑05.0

March 1954 — LONGITUDE

Day	Sid.Time	☉	0 hr ☽	Noon ☽	True ☊	☿	♀	♂	⚳	♃	♄	♅	♆	♇
1 M	22 35 02	10♓22 15	15♑15 01	21♑57 35	23♑03.3	10♓11.2	17♓46.1	10♐39.7	11♎52.7	17♊00.9	9♏13.4	19♋18.1	25♎46.1	23♌23.9
2 Tu	22 38 58	11 22 27	28 47 07	5♒43 40	23R 02.6	9R 08.1	19 01.1	11 11.0	11R 44.3	17 04.7	9R 12.1	19R 16.8	25R 45.0	23R 22.5
3 W	22 42 55	12 22 38	12♒47 09	19 57 16	22 59.8	8 05.5	20 16.0	11 42.2	11 35.5	17 08.7	9 10.7	19 15.5	25 44.0	23 21.1
4 Th	22 46 51	13 22 48	27 13 33	4♓35 18	22 54.7	7 04.8	21 30.9	12 13.2	11 26.3	17 12.9	9 09.2	19 14.2	25 42.9	23 19.8
5 F	22 50 48	14 22 55	12♓01 39	19 31 31	22 47.6	6 07.2	22 45.7	12 44.1	11 16.8	17 17.2	9 07.6	19 13.1	25 41.8	23 18.4
6 Sa	22 54 44	15 23 00	27 03 46	4♈37 06	22 39.4	5 13.9	24 00.6	13 14.8	11 06.9	17 21.8	9 05.9	19 11.9	25 40.6	23 17.0
7 Su	22 58 41	16 23 04	12♈10 16	19 41 58	22 31.0	4 25.6	25 15.4	13 45.4	10 56.7	17 26.5	9 04.1	19 10.8	25 39.4	23 15.7
8 M	23 02 38	17 23 05	27 11 05	4♉36 34	22 23.6	3 43.0	26 30.2	14 15.9	10 46.2	17 31.4	9 02.2	19 09.8	25 38.3	23 14.4
9 Tu	23 06 34	18 23 05	11♉57 33	19 13 23	22 18.0	3 06.6	27 45.0	14 46.2	10 35.3	17 36.4	9 00.2	19 08.8	25 37.0	23 13.0
10 W	23 10 31	19 23 02	26 23 34	3♊27 51	22 14.7	2 36.6	28 59.7	15 16.3	10 24.2	17 41.7	8 58.2	19 07.9	25 35.8	23 11.7
11 Th	23 14 27	20 22 57	10♊26 06	17 18 22	22D 13.5	2 13.3	0♈14.4	15 46.3	10 12.8	17 47.1	8 56.0	19 07.0	25 34.6	23 10.4
12 F	23 18 24	21 22 50	24 04 50	0♋45 45	22 13.8	1 56.5	1 29.1	16 16.1	10 01.1	17 52.6	8 53.7	19 06.2	25 33.3	23 09.2
13 Sa	23 22 20	22 22 41	7♋21 28	13 52 21	22R 14.5	1 46.2	2 43.8	16 45.7	9 49.2	17 58.4	8 51.4	19 05.4	25 32.0	23 07.9
14 Su	23 26 17	23 22 29	20 18 50	26 41 18	22 14.7	1D 42.3	3 58.5	17 15.2	9 37.0	18 04.2	8 48.9	19 04.7	25 30.7	23 06.7
15 M	23 30 13	24 22 15	3♌00 11	9♌15 52	22 13.2	1 44.6	5 13.1	17 44.5	9 24.6	18 10.3	8 46.4	19 04.0	25 29.4	23 05.4
16 Tu	23 34 10	25 21 59	15 28 41	21 38 59	22 09.3	1 52.7	6 27.7	18 13.6	9 12.1	18 16.5	8 43.8	19 03.4	25 28.0	23 04.2
17 W	23 38 07	26 21 41	27 47 02	3♍53 07	22 02.6	2 06.4	7 42.3	18 42.6	8 59.3	18 22.9	8 41.1	19 02.8	25 26.6	23 03.0
18 Th	23 42 03	27 21 21	9♍57 25	16 00 09	21 53.3	2 25.4	8 56.8	19 11.3	8 46.3	18 29.4	8 38.3	19 02.3	25 25.2	23 01.8
19 F	23 46 00	28 20 58	22 01 29	28 01 33	21 41.7	2 49.5	10 11.3	19 39.9	8 33.2	18 36.1	8 35.5	19 01.8	25 23.8	23 00.7
20 Sa	23 49 56	29 20 34	4♎00 31	9♎58 32	21 28.9	3 18.3	11 25.8	20 08.3	8 19.9	18 42.9	8 32.5	19 01.4	25 22.4	22 59.5
21 Su	23 53 53	0♈20 07	15 55 45	21 52 20	21 15.8	3 51.6	12 40.3	20 36.5	8 06.5	18 49.8	8 29.5	19 01.0	25 21.0	22 58.4
22 M	23 57 49	1 19 39	27 48 29	3♏44 27	21 03.5	4 29.0	13 54.7	21 04.5	7 53.0	18 57.0	8 26.4	19 00.7	25 19.5	22 57.3
23 Tu	0 01 46	2 19 09	9♏40 28	15 36 53	20 53.0	5 10.4	15 09.2	21 32.3	7 39.4	19 04.2	8 23.2	19 00.4	25 18.0	22 56.2
24 W	0 05 42	3 18 37	21 34 01	27 32 18	20 45.1	5 55.5	16 23.6	21 59.9	7 25.7	19 11.6	8 20.0	19 00.2	25 16.6	22 55.1
25 Th	0 09 39	4 18 03	3♐32 09	9♐34 05	20 39.9	6 44.1	17 37.9	22 27.3	7 12.0	19 19.2	8 16.7	19 00.1	25 15.1	22 54.1
26 F	0 13 35	5 17 28	15 38 37	21 46 20	20 37.3	7 36.0	18 52.3	22 54.4	6 58.2	19 26.9	8 13.3	19 00.0	25 13.5	22 53.1
27 Sa	0 17 32	6 16 50	27 57 49	4♑13 40	20D 36.5	8 31.0	20 06.6	23 21.4	6 44.4	19 34.7	8 09.8	19D 00.0	25 12.0	22 52.0
28 Su	0 21 29	7 16 11	10♑34 31	17 00 56	20R 36.6	9 29.0	21 20.9	23 48.0	6 30.6	19 42.7	8 06.3	19 00.0	25 10.5	22 51.1
29 M	0 25 25	8 15 31	23 33 29	0♒12 41	20 36.4	10 29.6	22 35.2	24 14.5	6 16.8	19 50.8	8 02.7	19 00.0	25 08.9	22 50.1
30 Tu	0 29 22	9 14 48	6♒58 54	13 52 28	20 34.7	11 33.0	23 49.4	24 40.7	6 03.1	19 59.0	7 59.0	19 00.2	25 07.4	22 49.1
31 W	0 33 18	10 14 04	20 53 28	28 01 53	20 30.6	12 38.8	25 03.6	25 06.7	5 49.3	20 07.4	7 55.3	19 00.3	25 05.8	22 48.2

April 1954 — LONGITUDE

Day	Sid.Time	☉	0 hr ☽	Noon ☽	True ☊	☿	♀	♂	⚳	♃	♄	♅	♆	♇
1 Th	0 37 15	11♈13 17	5♓17 25	12♓39 37	20♑23.8	13♓47.0	26♈17.8	25♐32.3	5♎35.7	20♊15.8	7♏51.5	19♋00.6	25♎04.2	22♌47.3
2 F	0 41 11	12 12 29	20 07 43	27 40 45	20R 14.5	14 57.5	27 32.0	25 57.8	5R 22.1	20 24.5	7R 47.7	19 00.8	25R 02.6	22R 46.4
3 Sa	0 45 08	13 11 39	5♈17 32	12♈56 44	20 03.7	16 10.1	28 46.1	26 22.9	5 08.7	20 33.2	7 43.8	19 01.2	25 01.0	22 45.6
4 Su	0 49 04	14 10 47	20 36 53	28 16 29	19 52.4	17 24.8	0♉00.3	26 47.8	4 55.3	20 42.1	7 39.8	19 01.6	24 59.4	22 44.8
5 M	0 53 01	15 09 53	5♉54 06	13♉28 21	19 42.2	18 41.6	1 14.3	27 12.3	4 42.1	20 51.1	7 35.8	19 02.0	24 57.8	22 44.0
6 Tu	0 56 58	16 08 56	20 58 04	28 22 16	19 34.0	20 00.3	2 28.4	27 36.6	4 29.1	21 00.2	7 31.8	19 02.5	24 56.2	22 43.2
7 W	1 00 54	17 07 58	5♊40 10	12♊51 17	19 28.6	21 20.9	3 42.4	28 00.6	4 16.2	21 09.4	7 27.7	19 03.1	24 54.6	22 42.4
8 Th	1 04 51	18 06 57	19 55 18	26 52 09	19 25.7	22 43.3	4 56.4	28 24.3	4 03.6	21 18.8	7 23.6	19 03.7	24 53.0	22 41.7
9 F	1 08 47	19 05 54	3♋41 57	10♋24 57	19 24.8	24 07.5	6 10.4	28 47.7	3 51.1	21 28.2	7 19.4	19 04.4	24 51.3	22 41.0
10 Sa	1 12 44	20 04 49	17 01 30	23 32 04	19 24.7	25 33.5	7 24.3	29 10.7	3 38.9	21 37.8	7 15.1	19 05.1	24 49.7	22 40.3
11 Su	1 16 40	21 03 41	29 57 09	6♌17 18	19 24.2	27 01.2	8 38.2	29 33.5	3 26.9	21 47.5	7 10.9	19 05.8	24 48.1	22 39.7
12 M	1 20 37	22 02 31	12♌33 04	18 44 59	19 22.2	28 30.6	9 52.1	29 55.9	3 15.1	21 57.3	7 06.6	19 06.7	24 46.4	22 39.0
13 Tu	1 24 33	23 01 18	24 53 36	0♍59 24	19 17.8	0♈01.6	11 05.9	0♑17.9	3 03.6	22 07.1	7 02.3	19 07.5	24 44.8	22 38.4
14 W	1 28 30	24 00 04	7♍02 51	13 04 21	19 10.5	1 34.4	12 19.7	0 39.7	2 52.4	22 17.1	6 57.9	19 08.4	24 43.1	22 37.8
15 Th	1 32 27	24 58 47	19 04 18	25 03 01	19 00.4	3 08.7	13 33.4	1 01.0	2 41.4	22 27.2	6 53.5	19 09.4	24 41.5	22 37.3
16 F	1 36 23	25 57 28	1♎00 48	6♎57 54	18 48.0	4 44.8	14 47.1	1 22.0	2 30.8	22 37.4	6 49.1	19 10.4	24 39.8	22 36.8
17 Sa	1 40 20	26 56 07	12 54 32	18 50 54	18 34.2	6 22.4	16 00.8	1 42.7	2 20.4	22 47.7	6 44.6	19 11.5	24 38.2	22 36.3
18 Su	1 44 16	27 54 44	24 47 11	0♏43 32	18 20.1	8 01.7	17 14.5	2 03.0	2 10.4	22 58.1	6 40.2	19 12.7	24 36.6	22 35.8
19 M	1 48 13	28 53 20	6♏40 07	12 37 07	18 06.8	9 42.7	18 28.1	2 22.8	2 00.7	23 08.6	6 35.7	19 13.8	24 34.9	22 35.3
20 Tu	1 52 09	29 51 53	18 34 43	24 33 06	17 55.4	11 25.2	19 41.7	2 42.3	1 51.4	23 19.2	6 31.2	19 15.1	24 33.3	22 34.9
21 W	1 56 06	0♉50 25	0♐32 32	6♐33 16	17 46.5	13 09.5	20 55.3	3 01.4	1 42.3	23 29.9	6 26.6	19 16.3	24 31.7	22 34.5
22 Th	2 00 02	1 48 55	12 35 37	18 39 56	17 40.5	14 55.4	22 08.8	3 20.1	1 33.7	23 40.6	6 22.1	19 17.7	24 30.0	22 34.2
23 F	2 03 59	2 47 23	24 46 36	0♑56 04	17 37.3	16 42.9	23 22.3	3 38.3	1 25.4	23 51.5	6 17.6	19 19.1	24 28.4	22 33.8
24 Sa	2 07 56	3 45 50	7♑08 47	13 25 16	17D 36.2	18 32.2	24 35.8	3 56.1	1 17.4	24 02.4	6 13.0	19 20.5	24 26.8	22 33.5
25 Su	2 11 52	4 44 15	19 46 01	26 11 34	17R 36.3	20 23.1	25 49.2	4 13.5	1 09.8	24 13.5	6 08.5	19 22.0	24 25.2	22 33.3
26 M	2 15 49	5 42 38	2♒42 25	9♒19 05	17 36.4	22 15.7	27 02.6	4 30.4	1 02.6	24 24.6	6 03.9	19 23.5	24 23.6	22 33.0
27 Tu	2 19 45	6 41 00	16 01 58	22 51 27	17 35.4	24 10.0	28 16.0	4 46.8	0 55.8	24 35.8	5 59.3	19 25.1	24 22.0	22 32.8
28 W	2 23 42	7 39 21	29 47 44	6♓50 58	17 32.4	26 05.9	29 29.3	5 02.7	0 49.4	24 47.1	5 54.8	19 26.7	24 20.4	22 32.6
29 Th	2 27 38	8 37 39	14♓01 02	21 17 40	17 27.0	28 03.6	0♊42.6	5 18.1	0 43.4	24 58.4	5 50.2	19 28.4	24 18.8	22 32.4
30 F	2 31 35	9 35 57	28 40 24	6♈08 31	17 19.3	0♉02.8	1 55.9	5 33.1	0 37.7	25 09.9	5 45.7	19 30.1	24 17.2	22 32.3

Astro Data

	Dy Hr Mn
☽0N	5 12:48
♀0N	13 15:15
☿D	14 15:07
☽0S	18 20:04
☉0N	21 3:54
♃⊻♅	22 23:57
♅D	27 17:31
☽0N	1 23:43
♃Q♄	13 3:46
☽0S	15 1:34
♃✶♇	16 10:30
☿0N	17 3:43
♃△♆	26 10:03
☽0N	29 9:15

Planet Ingress

		Dy Hr Mn
♀	♈	11 7:22
☉	♈	21 3:53
♀	♉	4 11:55
♂	♑	12 16:28
☿	♈	13 11:34
☉	♉	20 15:20
♀	♊	28 22:03
☿	♉	30 11:26

Last Aspect / ☽ Ingress (March)

Last Aspect Dy Hr Mn			☽ Ingress	Dy Hr Mn
1 18:43	♆	□	♒	2 2:07
3 21:32	♆	△	♓	4 4:32
5 17:37	♀	☌	♈	6 4:40
7 21:32	♆	☍	♉	8 4:32
10 3:40	♀	✶	♊	10 6:06
12 2:39	♆	△	♋	12 10:37
14 9:47	♆	□	♌	14 18:17
16 19:27	♆	✶	♍	17 4:21
19 12:42	☉	☍	♎	19 15:57
21 19:01	♆	☌	♏	22 4:26
24 2:44	♇	□	♐	24 16:56
26 18:42	♆	✶	♑	27 3:55
29 2:54	♆	□	♒	29 11:37
31 7:06	♆	△	♓	31 15:16

Last Aspect / ☽ Ingress (April)

Last Aspect Dy Hr Mn			☽ Ingress	Dy Hr Mn
2 9:12	♂	□	♈	2 15:40
4 9:37	♂	△	♉	4 14:43
6 2:50	♇	□	♊	6 14:40
8 14:46	♂	☍	♋	8 17:29
10 16:15	☿	△	♌	11 0:05
12 23:44	♆	✶	♍	13 10:03
15 6:43	♃	□	♎	15 21:58
18 5:48	☉	☍	♏	18 10:32
20 8:03	♇	□	♐	20 22:55
22 23:26	♆	✶	♑	23 10:11
25 11:14	♀	△	♒	25 19:02
27 22:16	♀	□	♓	28 0:21
29 18:05	♃	□	♈	30 2:08

☽ Phases & Eclipses

Dy Hr Mn		
5 3:11	●	14♓01
11 17:52	☽	20♊38
19 12:42	○	28♍23
27 16:14	☾	6♑27
3 12:25	●	13♈13
10 5:05	☽	19♋48
18 5:48	○	27♎40
26 4:57	☾	5♒26

Astro Data

1 March 1954
Julian Day # 19783
SVP 5♓53'42"
GC 26♐11.9 ⚴ 26♌31.8R
Eris 7♈45.9 ⚵ 14♌35.0R
⚷ 26♑08.3 ⚶ 6♈08.5
☽ Mean ☊ 21♑36.1

1 April 1954
Julian Day # 19814
SVP 5♓53'39"
GC 26♐12.0 ⚴ 21♌20.5R
Eris 8♈06.9 ⚵ 12♌40.3
⚷ 27♑56.2 ⚶ 20♈18.0
☽ Mean ☊ 19♑57.6

LONGITUDE — May 1954

Day	Sid.Time	☉	0 hr ☽	Noon ☽	True ☊	☿	♀	♂	⚳	♃	♄	♅	♆	♇
1 Sa	2 35 31	10♉34 12	13♈41 03	21♈16 55	17♑10.0	2♉03.7	3♊09.1	5♑47.5	0♎32.5	25♊21.4	5♏41.1	19♋31.9	24♎15.6	22♌32.2
2 Su	2 39 28	11 32 26	28 54 47	6♉33 18	17R 00.2	4 06.1	4 22.3	6 01.3	0R 27.7	25 33.0	5R 36.6	19 33.7	24R 14.1	22R 32.1
3 M	2 43 25	12 30 39	14♉11 00	21 46 32	16 51.2	6 10.1	5 35.5	6 14.6	0 23.3	25 44.6	5 32.1	19 35.5	24 12.5	22 32.0
4 Tu	2 47 21	13 28 49	29 18 33	6♊45 56	16 44.0	8 15.4	6 48.6	6 27.4	0 19.3	25 56.4	5 27.5	19 37.4	24 11.0	22D 32.0
5 W	2 51 18	14 26 58	14♊07 42	21 23 07	16 39.2	10 22.0	8 01.7	6 39.6	0 15.7	26 08.2	5 23.1	19 39.4	24 09.5	22 32.0
6 Th	2 55 14	15 25 06	28 31 40	5♋33 03	16D 36.8	12 29.7	9 14.8	6 51.2	0 12.5	26 20.1	5 18.6	19 41.4	24 07.9	22 32.1
7 F	2 59 11	16 23 11	12♋27 10	19 14 07	16 36.3	14 38.5	10 27.8	7 02.3	0 09.7	26 32.0	5 14.2	19 43.4	24 06.5	22 32.1
8 Sa	3 03 07	17 21 14	25 54 07	2♌27 32	16 36.9	16 48.1	11 40.8	7 12.8	0 07.4	26 44.0	5 09.7	19 45.5	24 05.0	22 32.2
9 Su	3 07 04	18 19 15	8♌54 49	15 16 30	16R 37.5	18 58.3	12 53.8	7 22.6	0 05.5	26 56.1	5 05.4	19 47.6	24 03.5	22 32.3
10 M	3 11 00	19 17 14	21 33 08	27 45 17	16 37.2	21 08.8	14 06.7	7 31.9	0 03.9	27 08.2	5 01.0	19 49.8	24 02.0	22 32.5
11 Tu	3 14 57	20 15 12	3♍53 34	9♍58 33	16 35.0	23 19.5	15 19.6	7 40.5	0 02.8	27 20.4	4 56.7	19 52.0	24 00.6	22 32.7
12 W	3 18 54	21 13 08	16 00 48	22 00 51	16 30.8	25 30.0	16 32.4	7 48.5	0 02.1	27 32.7	4 52.4	19 54.3	23 59.2	22 32.9
13 Th	3 22 50	22 11 01	27 59 13	3♎56 21	16 24.3	27 40.1	17 45.2	7 55.8	0D 01.8	27 45.0	4 48.1	19 56.5	23 57.8	22 33.1
14 F	3 26 47	23 08 54	9♎52 41	15 48 36	16 15.9	29 49.5	18 57.9	8 02.5	0 02.0	27 57.4	4 43.9	19 58.9	23 56.4	22 33.4
15 Sa	3 30 43	24 06 44	21 44 26	27 40 30	16 06.4	1♊57.9	20 10.6	8 08.6	0 02.5	28 09.8	4 39.7	20 01.2	23 55.0	22 33.7
16 Su	3 34 40	25 04 33	3♏37 04	9♏34 22	15 56.6	4 05.0	21 23.3	8 13.9	0 03.4	28 22.3	4 35.6	20 03.7	23 53.6	22 34.0
17 M	3 38 36	26 02 21	15 32 37	21 31 59	15 47.4	6 10.6	22 35.9	8 18.6	0 04.7	28 34.8	4 31.5	20 06.1	23 52.3	22 34.3
18 Tu	3 42 33	27 00 07	27 32 40	3♐34 50	15 39.6	8 14.3	23 48.5	8 22.6	0 06.4	28 47.4	4 27.5	20 08.6	23 51.0	22 34.7
19 W	3 46 29	27 57 52	9♐38 39	15 44 18	15 33.7	10 16.1	25 01.0	8 25.9	0 08.5	29 00.0	4 23.5	20 11.1	23 49.7	22 35.1
20 Th	3 50 26	28 55 35	21 51 59	28 01 54	15 30.0	12 15.7	26 13.5	8 28.5	0 11.0	29 12.7	4 19.5	20 13.7	23 48.4	22 35.5
21 F	3 54 23	29 53 18	4♑14 17	10♑29 24	15D 28.4	14 12.9	27 26.0	8 30.4	0 13.9	29 25.4	4 15.6	20 16.3	23 47.1	22 36.0
22 Sa	3 58 19	0♊50 59	16 47 32	23 09 00	15 28.6	16 07.6	28 38.4	8 31.5	0 17.1	29 38.2	4 11.8	20 18.9	23 45.9	22 36.5
23 Su	4 02 16	1 48 39	29 34 06	6♒03 12	15 29.7	17 59.7	29 50.8	8R 31.9	0 20.8	29 51.0	4 08.0	20 21.6	23 44.7	22 37.0
24 M	4 06 12	2 46 18	12♒36 38	19 14 43	15 31.0	19 49.0	1♋03.1	8 31.6	0 24.8	0♋03.9	4 04.3	20 24.3	23 43.5	22 37.5
25 Tu	4 10 09	3 43 56	25 57 45	2♓45 59	15R 31.7	21 35.6	2 15.4	8 30.5	0 29.2	0 16.8	4 00.6	20 27.0	23 42.3	22 38.1
26 W	4 14 05	4 41 33	9♓39 36	16 38 41	15 31.1	23 19.2	3 27.6	8 28.6	0 33.9	0 29.8	3 57.0	20 29.8	23 41.1	22 38.7
27 Th	4 18 02	5 39 09	23 43 13	0♈53 02	15 28.8	25 00.0	4 39.8	8 26.0	0 39.0	0 42.8	3 53.5	20 32.6	23 40.0	22 39.3
28 F	4 21 58	6 36 44	8♈07 51	15 27 09	15 25.0	26 37.7	5 52.0	8 22.6	0 44.5	0 55.8	3 50.0	20 35.5	23 38.9	22 40.0
29 Sa	4 25 55	7 34 19	22 50 19	0♉16 33	15 20.0	28 12.5	7 04.1	8 18.4	0 50.3	1 08.8	3 46.6	20 38.3	23 37.8	22 40.7
30 Su	4 29 52	8 31 53	7♉44 55	15 14 23	15 14.6	29 44.2	8 16.2	8 13.5	0 56.5	1 21.9	3 43.2	20 41.2	23 36.7	22 41.4
31 M	4 33 48	9 29 25	22 43 50	0♊12 07	15 09.6	1♋12.9	9 28.3	8 07.8	1 03.0	1 35.1	3 40.0	20 44.2	23 35.7	22 42.1

LONGITUDE — June 1954

Day	Sid.Time	☉	0 hr ☽	Noon ☽	True ☊	☿	♀	♂	⚳	♃	♄	♅	♆	♇
1 Tu	4 37 45	10♊26 57	7♊38 09	15♊00 52	15♑05.7	2♋38.4	10♋40.2	8♑01.3	1♎09.9	1♋48.3	3♏36.8	20♋47.2	23♎34.7	22♌42.9
2 W	4 41 41	11 24 28	22 19 21	29 32 47	15R 03.2	4 00.8	11 52.2	7R 54.1	1 17.1	2 01.5	3R 33.6	20 50.2	23R 33.7	22 43.7
3 Th	4 45 38	12 21 57	6♋40 34	13♋42 13	15D 02.3	5 20.0	13 04.1	7 46.2	1 24.6	2 14.7	3 30.6	20 53.2	23 32.8	22 44.5
4 F	4 49 34	13 19 26	20 37 27	27 26 09	15 02.8	6 35.9	14 15.9	7 37.5	1 32.5	2 28.0	3 27.6	20 56.2	23 31.8	22 45.3
5 Sa	4 53 31	14 16 53	4♌08 20	10♌44 10	15 04.2	7 48.6	15 27.7	7 28.1	1 40.7	2 41.3	3 24.7	20 59.3	23 30.9	22 46.2
6 Su	4 57 27	15 14 19	17 13 56	23 37 59	15 05.7	8 58.0	16 39.5	7 18.1	1 49.3	2 54.6	3 21.9	21 02.4	23 30.0	22 47.1
7 M	5 01 24	16 11 44	29 56 47	6♍10 50	15R 07.0	10 03.9	17 51.2	7 07.3	1 58.1	3 07.9	3 19.2	21 05.6	23 29.2	22 48.0
8 Tu	5 05 21	17 09 08	12♍20 39	18 26 49	15 07.4	11 06.4	19 02.8	6 55.9	2 07.3	3 21.3	3 16.5	21 08.7	23 28.3	22 48.9
9 W	5 09 17	18 06 31	24 29 55	0♎30 30	15 06.7	12 05.3	20 14.4	6 43.8	2 16.7	3 34.7	3 13.9	21 11.9	23 27.5	22 49.9
10 Th	5 13 14	19 03 52	6♎29 09	12 26 25	15 04.8	13 00.6	21 25.9	6 31.1	2 26.5	3 48.1	3 11.4	21 15.1	23 26.8	22 50.9
11 F	5 17 10	20 01 13	18 22 50	24 18 54	15 01.9	13 52.3	22 37.4	6 17.8	2 36.6	4 01.6	3 09.0	21 18.4	23 26.0	22 51.9
12 Sa	5 21 07	20 58 33	0♏15 04	6♏11 48	14 58.3	14 40.1	23 48.8	6 03.9	2 46.9	4 15.0	3 06.7	21 21.6	23 25.3	22 52.9
13 Su	5 25 03	21 55 51	12 09 28	18 08 26	14 54.5	15 24.0	25 00.2	5 49.4	2 57.6	4 28.5	3 04.5	21 24.9	23 24.6	22 54.0
14 M	5 29 00	22 53 09	24 09 02	0♐11 31	14 50.9	16 04.0	26 11.5	5 34.4	3 08.5	4 42.0	3 02.3	21 28.2	23 24.0	22 55.1
15 Tu	5 32 56	23 50 27	6♐16 10	12 23 11	14 48.0	16 39.8	27 22.7	5 19.0	3 19.7	4 55.5	3 00.3	21 31.5	23 23.3	22 56.2
16 W	5 36 53	24 47 44	18 32 45	24 45 00	14 45.9	17 11.5	28 33.9	5 03.0	3 31.2	5 09.0	2 58.3	21 34.9	23 22.7	22 57.3
17 Th	5 40 50	25 45 00	1♑00 06	7♑18 09	14D 44.9	17 38.9	29 45.0	4 46.6	3 42.9	5 22.6	2 56.4	21 38.2	23 22.2	22 58.5
18 F	5 44 46	26 42 15	13 39 15	20 03 29	14 44.8	18 02.0	0♌56.0	4 29.8	3 54.9	5 36.1	2 54.6	21 41.6	23 21.6	22 59.7
19 Sa	5 48 43	27 39 31	26 30 57	3♒01 43	14 45.5	18 20.6	2 07.0	4 12.7	4 07.2	5 49.7	2 52.9	21 45.0	23 21.1	23 00.9
20 Su	5 52 39	28 36 45	9♒35 52	16 13 29	14 46.6	18 34.7	3 17.9	3 55.2	4 19.7	6 03.2	2 51.3	21 48.5	23 20.6	23 02.1
21 M	5 56 36	29 34 00	22 54 36	29 39 17	14 47.8	18 44.2	4 28.8	3 37.4	4 32.5	6 16.8	2 49.8	21 51.9	23 20.2	23 03.3
22 Tu	6 00 32	0♋31 14	6♓27 35	13♓19 30	14 48.8	18R 49.2	5 39.6	3 19.3	4 45.5	6 30.4	2 48.4	21 55.3	23 19.8	23 04.6
23 W	6 04 29	1 28 29	20 15 00	27 14 03	14R 49.3	18 49.6	6 50.3	3 01.0	4 58.8	6 44.0	2 47.1	21 58.8	23 19.4	23 05.9
24 Th	6 08 26	2 25 43	4♈16 30	11♈22 10	14 49.2	18 45.5	8 01.0	2 42.6	5 12.3	6 57.6	2 45.8	22 02.3	23 19.0	23 07.2
25 F	6 12 22	3 22 57	18 30 48	25 42 04	14 48.5	18 36.9	9 11.6	2 24.0	5 26.1	7 11.3	2 44.7	22 05.8	23 18.7	23 08.5
26 Sa	6 16 19	4 20 11	2♉55 32	10♉10 42	14 47.5	18 24.1	10 22.1	2 05.4	5 40.1	7 24.9	2 43.6	22 09.3	23 18.4	23 09.9
27 Su	6 20 15	5 17 26	17 27 00	24 43 47	14 46.4	18 07.0	11 32.6	1 46.7	5 54.3	7 38.5	2 42.7	22 12.9	23 18.1	23 11.2
28 M	6 24 12	6 14 40	2♊00 22	9♊16 01	14 45.4	17 46.1	12 43.0	1 28.0	6 08.7	7 52.1	2 41.8	22 16.4	23 17.9	23 12.6
29 Tu	6 28 08	7 11 54	16 30 01	23 41 38	14 44.7	17 21.5	13 53.3	1 09.4	6 23.4	8 05.8	2 41.1	22 20.0	23 17.7	23 14.0
30 W	6 32 05	8 09 09	0♋50 12	7♋55 05	14D 44.4	16 53.6	15 03.6	0 50.9	6 38.3	8 19.4	2 40.4	22 23.5	23 17.5	23 15.5

Astro Data

	Dy Hr Mn
♇ D	4 17:45
☽ 0S	12 6:52
⚳ D	13 17:10
♂ R	23 12:47
☽ 0N	26 16:23
♃△♄	8 4:48
☽ 0S	8 13:15
☽ 0N	22 21:47
☿ R	23 2:08
♃∠♇	30 4:14

Planet Ingress

		Dy Hr Mn
☿	♊	14 13:57
☉	♊	21 14:47
♀	♋	23 15:04
♃	♋	24 4:43
☿	♋	30 16:13
♀	♌	17 17:04
☉	♋	21 22:54

Last Aspect / ☽ Ingress (May)

Last Aspect Dy Hr Mn			☽ Ingress	Dy Hr Mn
1 18:30	♃	✶	♉	2 1:42
3 13:12	♇	□	♊	4 1:06
5 20:04	♃	☌	♋	6 2:30
7 20:44	♆	□	♌	8 7:29
10 10:47	♃	✶	♍	10 16:23
12 23:18	♃	□	♎	13 4:03
15 13:00	♃	△	♏	15 16:42
17 21:47	☉	☍	♐	18 4:53
20 14:20	♃	☍	♑	20 15:49
22 13:09	♆	□	♒	23 0:48
24 20:00	♆	△	♓	25 7:08
27 0:51	☿	□	♈	27 10:32
29 8:17	☿	✶	♉	29 11:33
30 23:57	♇	□	♊	31 11:40

Last Aspect / ☽ Ingress (June)

Last Aspect Dy Hr Mn			☽ Ingress	Dy Hr Mn
2 2:04	♆	△	♋	2 12:46
4 5:06	♆	□	♌	4 16:34
6 11:45	♆	✶	♍	7 0:06
8 17:22	♅	✶	♎	9 10:59
11 10:13	♆	☌	♏	11 23:30
14 3:12	♀	△	♐	14 11:37
16 12:06	☉	☍	♑	16 22:05
18 18:09	♆	□	♒	19 6:26
21 11:50	☉	△	♓	21 12:37
23 2:57	♅	△	♈	23 16:44
25 8:01	♆	☍	♉	25 19:09
27 9:27	♇	□	♊	27 20:41
29 11:20	♆	△	♋	29 22:35

☽ Phases & Eclipses

Dy Hr Mn		
2 20:22	●	11♉53
9 18:17	☽	18♌34
17 21:47	○	26♏26
25 13:49	☾	3♓48
1 4:03	●	10♊08
8 9:14	☽	17♍03
16 12:06	○	24♐48
23 19:46	☾	1♈47
30 12:26	●	8♋10
30 12:32:05	●	T 02'35"

Astro Data

1 May 1954
Julian Day # 19844
SVP 5♓53'36"
GC 26♐12.1 ⚴ 24♌00.3
Eris 8♈26.9 ⚵ 16♌40.5
⚷ 28♑39.0 ⚶ 3♉55.4
☽ Mean ☊ 18♑22.2

1 June 1954
Julian Day # 19875
SVP 5♓53'31"
GC 26♐12.2 ⚴ 1♍52.6
Eris 8♈42.2 ⚵ 24♌36.3
⚷ 28♑12.7R ⚶ 17♉38.3
☽ Mean ☊ 16♑43.7

July 1954 — LONGITUDE

Day	Sid.Time	☉	0 hr ☽	Noon ☽	True ☊	☿	♀	♂	⚳	♃	♄	♅	♆	♇
1 Th	6 36 01	9♋06 23	14♋55 46	21♋51 46	14♑44.4	16♋22.9	16♌13.8	0♑32.6	6♎53.4	8♋33.0	2♏39.9	22♋27.1	23♎17.4	23♌16.9
2 F	6 39 58	10 03 37	28 42 45	5♌28 30	14 44.6	15R 49.8	17 23.9	0R 14.4	7 08.7	8 46.6	2R 39.4	22 30.7	23R 17.3	23 18.4
3 Sa	6 43 55	11 00 50	12♌08 51	18 43 48	14 45.0	15 14.8	18 33.9	29♐56.6	7 24.3	9 00.3	2 39.1	22 34.3	23 17.2	23 19.9
4 Su	6 47 51	11 58 03	25 13 26	1♍37 55	14 45.3	14 38.4	19 43.9	29 39.0	7 40.0	9 13.9	2 38.8	22 37.9	23D 17.2	23 21.4
5 M	6 51 48	12 55 17	7♍57 32	14 12 37	14 45.6	14 01.3	20 53.7	29 21.8	7 55.9	9 27.5	2 38.6	22 41.6	23 17.1	23 22.9
6 Tu	6 55 44	13 52 29	20 23 33	26 30 48	14R 45.7	13 24.2	22 03.5	29 05.1	8 12.1	9 41.1	2D 38.6	22 45.2	23 17.2	23 24.4
7 W	6 59 41	14 49 42	2♎34 53	8♎36 18	14D 45.7	12 47.6	23 13.2	28 48.7	8 28.4	9 54.7	2 38.6	22 48.8	23 17.2	23 26.0
8 Th	7 03 37	15 46 55	14 35 37	20 33 25	14 45.7	12 12.2	24 22.8	28 32.8	8 44.9	10 08.3	2 38.7	22 52.4	23 17.3	23 27.5
9 F	7 07 34	16 44 07	26 30 15	2♏26 41	14 45.8	11 38.6	25 32.4	28 17.4	9 01.6	10 21.8	2 39.0	22 56.1	23 17.4	23 29.1
10 Sa	7 11 30	17 41 19	8♏23 17	14 20 37	14 46.0	11 07.4	26 41.8	28 02.6	9 18.5	10 35.4	2 39.3	22 59.7	23 17.6	23 30.7
11 Su	7 15 27	18 38 32	20 19 11	26 19 29	14 46.4	10 39.2	27 51.1	27 48.4	9 35.6	10 49.0	2 39.7	23 03.4	23 17.8	23 32.3
12 M	7 19 24	19 35 44	2♐21 59	8♐27 06	14 46.8	10 14.4	29 00.3	27 34.7	9 52.8	11 02.5	2 40.3	23 07.0	23 18.0	23 34.0
13 Tu	7 23 20	20 32 56	14 35 13	20 46 39	14 47.3	9 53.6	0♍09.5	27 21.7	10 10.2	11 16.0	2 40.9	23 10.7	23 18.2	23 35.6
14 W	7 27 17	21 30 09	27 01 41	3♑20 33	14R 47.7	9 37.2	1 18.5	27 09.4	10 27.8	11 29.5	2 41.6	23 14.4	23 18.5	23 37.3
15 Th	7 31 13	22 27 22	9♑43 22	16 10 17	14 47.9	9 25.5	2 27.4	26 57.8	10 45.6	11 43.0	2 42.4	23 18.0	23 18.8	23 39.0
16 F	7 35 10	23 24 35	22 41 17	29 16 22	14 47.6	9D 18.7	3 36.2	26 46.8	11 03.5	11 56.5	2 43.4	23 21.7	23 19.2	23 40.7
17 Sa	7 39 06	24 21 49	5♒55 27	12♒38 23	14 46.9	9 17.2	4 45.0	26 36.6	11 21.5	12 09.9	2 44.4	23 25.3	23 19.5	23 42.4
18 Su	7 43 03	25 19 02	19 24 59	26 15 01	14 45.8	9 21.1	5 53.6	26 27.1	11 39.8	12 23.3	2 45.5	23 29.0	23 19.9	23 44.1
19 M	7 46 59	26 16 17	3♓08 12	10♓04 14	14 44.5	9 30.5	7 02.1	26 18.4	11 58.2	12 36.7	2 46.7	23 32.7	23 20.4	23 45.8
20 Tu	7 50 56	27 13 32	17 02 50	24 03 38	14 43.1	9 45.6	8 10.4	26 10.4	12 16.7	12 50.1	2 48.0	23 36.3	23 20.8	23 47.5
21 W	7 54 53	28 10 48	1♈06 18	8♈10 30	14 42.0	10 06.5	9 18.7	26 03.2	12 35.4	13 03.5	2 49.4	23 40.0	23 21.4	23 49.3
22 Th	7 58 49	29 08 05	15 15 55	22 22 12	14D 41.3	10 33.0	10 26.9	25 56.9	12 54.2	13 16.8	2 50.9	23 43.6	23 21.9	23 51.0
23 F	8 02 46	0♌05 22	29 29 02	6♉36 08	14 41.3	11 05.4	11 34.9	25 51.3	13 13.2	13 30.1	2 52.5	23 47.3	23 22.4	23 52.8
24 Sa	8 06 42	1 02 41	13♉43 09	20 49 49	14 41.9	11 43.4	12 42.8	25 46.5	13 32.3	13 43.4	2 54.2	23 50.9	23 23.0	23 54.6
25 Su	8 10 39	2 00 01	27 55 49	5♊00 51	14 43.0	12 27.2	13 50.7	25 42.6	13 51.6	13 56.7	2 56.0	23 54.6	23 23.7	23 56.4
26 M	8 14 35	2 57 21	12♊04 35	19 06 43	14 44.3	13 16.6	14 58.4	25 39.5	14 11.0	14 09.9	2 57.9	23 58.2	23 24.3	23 58.2
27 Tu	8 18 32	3 54 43	26 06 56	3♋04 53	14R 45.2	14 11.6	16 05.9	25 37.3	14 30.5	14 23.1	2 59.8	24 01.8	23 25.0	24 00.0
28 W	8 22 28	4 52 05	10♋00 16	16 52 45	14 45.5	15 12.0	17 13.4	25 35.9	14 50.2	14 36.2	3 01.9	24 05.5	23 25.8	24 01.9
29 Th	8 26 25	5 49 28	23 42 02	0♌27 51	14 44.8	16 17.9	18 20.7	25D 35.4	15 10.0	14 49.4	3 04.1	24 09.1	23 26.5	24 03.7
30 F	8 30 22	6 46 52	7♌09 57	13 48 08	14 43.1	17 29.1	19 27.8	25 35.7	15 30.0	15 02.5	3 06.3	24 12.7	23 27.3	24 05.5
31 Sa	8 34 18	7 44 17	20 22 16	26 52 13	14 40.3	18 45.4	20 34.9	25 36.8	15 50.0	15 15.5	3 08.7	24 16.3	23 28.1	24 07.4

August 1954 — LONGITUDE

Day	Sid.Time	☉	0 hr ☽	Noon ☽	True ☊	☿	♀	♂	⚳	♃	♄	♅	♆	♇
1 Su	8 38 15	8♌41 42	3♍18 00	9♍39 37	14♑36.7	20♋06.7	21♍41.8	25♐38.8	16♎10.2	15♋28.5	3♏11.1	24♋19.9	23♎29.0	24♌09.2
2 M	8 42 11	9 39 08	15 57 11	22 10 53	14R 32.8	21 32.8	22 48.5	25 41.7	16 30.6	15 41.5	3 13.6	24 23.4	23 29.8	24 11.1
3 Tu	8 46 08	10 36 35	28 20 57	4♎27 41	14 29.1	23 03.6	23 55.1	25 45.4	16 51.0	15 54.5	3 16.3	24 27.0	23 30.7	24 13.0
4 W	8 50 04	11 34 02	10♎31 28	16 32 43	14 25.9	24 38.7	25 01.5	25 49.9	17 11.6	16 07.4	3 19.0	24 30.5	23 31.7	24 14.8
5 Th	8 54 01	12 31 31	22 31 53	28 29 30	14 23.8	26 17.9	26 07.8	25 55.3	17 32.2	16 20.2	3 21.8	24 34.1	23 32.6	24 16.7
6 F	8 57 57	13 29 00	4♏26 06	10♏22 15	14D 22.9	28 01.0	27 13.9	26 01.4	17 53.0	16 33.0	3 24.7	24 37.6	23 33.6	24 18.6
7 Sa	9 01 54	14 26 29	16 18 32	22 15 35	14 23.1	29 47.7	28 19.9	26 08.4	18 13.9	16 45.8	3 27.7	24 41.1	23 34.7	24 20.5
8 Su	9 05 51	15 24 00	28 13 59	4♐14 21	14 24.3	1♌37.5	29 25.6	26 16.2	18 34.9	16 58.5	3 30.7	24 44.6	23 35.7	24 22.4
9 M	9 09 47	16 21 31	10♐17 15	16 23 17	14 25.9	3 30.1	0♎31.2	26 24.8	18 56.0	17 11.2	3 33.9	24 48.1	23 36.8	24 24.3
10 Tu	9 13 44	17 19 04	22 32 57	28 46 46	14 27.5	5 25.2	1 36.6	26 34.1	19 17.2	17 23.8	3 37.1	24 51.5	23 37.9	24 26.2
11 W	9 17 40	18 16 37	5♑05 08	11♑28 26	14R 28.3	7 22.4	2 41.9	26 44.2	19 38.6	17 36.4	3 40.4	24 55.0	23 39.1	24 28.1
12 Th	9 21 37	19 14 11	17 56 57	24 30 50	14 27.9	9 21.2	3 46.9	26 55.0	20 00.0	17 48.9	3 43.9	24 58.4	23 40.2	24 30.0
13 F	9 25 33	20 11 46	1♒10 12	7♒55 00	14 26.0	11 21.4	4 51.7	27 06.6	20 21.5	18 01.4	3 47.4	25 01.8	23 41.4	24 32.0
14 Sa	9 29 30	21 09 23	14 45 03	21 40 07	14 22.4	13 22.5	5 56.3	27 18.9	20 43.1	18 13.8	3 50.9	25 05.2	23 42.7	24 33.9
15 Su	9 33 26	22 07 00	28 39 47	5♓43 32	14 17.4	15 24.2	7 00.7	27 31.9	21 04.8	18 26.1	3 54.6	25 08.6	23 43.9	24 35.8
16 M	9 37 23	23 04 39	12♓50 47	20 00 51	14 11.6	17 26.3	8 04.9	27 45.6	21 26.6	18 38.5	3 58.3	25 11.9	23 45.2	24 37.7
17 Tu	9 41 20	24 02 19	27 13 02	4♈26 35	14 05.7	19 28.4	9 08.9	28 00.0	21 48.5	18 50.7	4 02.1	25 15.3	23 46.5	24 39.6
18 W	9 45 16	25 00 01	11♈40 45	18 54 52	14 00.6	21 30.3	10 12.7	28 15.1	22 10.5	19 02.9	4 06.0	25 18.6	23 47.8	24 41.5
19 Th	9 49 13	25 57 44	26 08 16	3♉20 24	13 56.9	23 31.7	11 16.2	28 30.8	22 32.6	19 15.0	4 10.0	25 21.9	23 49.2	24 43.5
20 F	9 53 09	26 55 29	10♉30 46	17 38 59	13D 55.0	25 32.6	12 19.5	28 47.1	22 54.7	19 27.1	4 14.1	25 25.1	23 50.6	24 45.4
21 Sa	9 57 06	27 53 16	24 44 45	1♊47 52	13 54.7	27 32.7	13 22.5	29 04.1	23 17.0	19 39.1	4 18.2	25 28.4	23 52.0	24 47.3
22 Su	10 01 02	28 51 05	8♊48 10	15 45 35	13 55.5	29 31.9	14 25.3	29 21.8	23 39.3	19 51.0	4 22.4	25 31.6	23 53.4	24 49.2
23 M	10 04 59	29 48 55	22 40 05	29 31 39	13 56.7	1♍30.1	15 27.9	29 40.0	24 01.8	20 02.9	4 26.7	25 34.8	23 54.9	24 51.1
24 Tu	10 08 55	0♍46 47	6♋20 18	13♋06 03	13R 57.4	3 27.2	16 30.2	29 58.9	24 24.3	20 14.7	4 31.1	25 37.9	23 56.4	24 53.1
25 W	10 12 52	1 44 41	19 48 55	26 28 55	13 56.6	5 23.1	17 32.2	0♑18.4	24 46.9	20 26.5	4 35.5	25 41.1	23 57.9	24 55.0
26 Th	10 16 49	2 42 36	3♌06 00	9♌40 12	13 53.9	7 17.9	18 34.0	0 38.4	25 09.5	20 38.1	4 40.0	25 44.2	23 59.4	24 56.9
27 F	10 20 45	3 40 33	16 11 25	22 39 40	13 48.8	9 11.4	19 35.5	0 59.1	25 32.3	20 49.7	4 44.6	25 47.3	24 01.0	24 58.8
28 Sa	10 24 42	4 38 31	29 04 51	5♍26 58	13 41.5	11 03.7	20 36.7	1 20.3	25 55.1	21 01.3	4 49.2	25 50.3	24 02.5	25 00.7
29 Su	10 28 38	5 36 31	11♍45 59	18 01 53	13 32.6	12 54.7	21 37.6	1 42.0	26 18.0	21 12.7	4 54.0	25 53.4	24 04.1	25 02.6
30 M	10 32 35	6 34 33	24 14 44	0♎24 36	13 22.8	14 44.4	22 38.1	2 04.3	26 41.0	21 24.1	4 58.8	25 56.4	24 05.8	25 04.5
31 Tu	10 36 31	7 32 36	6♎31 37	12 35 56	13 13.1	16 32.9	23 38.4	2 27.2	27 04.0	21 35.4	5 03.6	25 59.3	24 07.4	25 06.4

Astro Data

	Dy Hr Mn
♆✶♇	1 19:09
♆ D	5 8:33
☽ 0S	5 21:10
♄ D	6 15:53
♅□♆	15 17:36
☿ D	17 6:50
☽ 0N	20 3:18
♅⊻♇	26 11:58
♂ D	29 15:20
⚳ 0S	1 2:54
☽ 0S	2 5:56
♀ 0S	9 0:31
☽ 0N	16 10:31
☽ 0S	29 14:16

Planet Ingress

	Dy Hr Mn
♂ ♐R	3 7:23
♀ ♍	13 8:43
☉ ♌	23 9:45
☿ ♌	7 14:44
♀ ♎	9 0:34
☿ ♍	22 17:42
☉ ♍	23 16:36
♂ ♑	24 13:22

Last Aspect / ☽ Ingress

Last Aspect Dy Hr Mn		☽ Ingress Dy Hr Mn
1 14:29 ♆ □	♌	2 2:16
4 8:21 ♂ △	♍	4 8:56
6 16:58 ♂ □	♎	6 18:53
9 3:47 ♂ ✶	♏	9 7:04
11 15:22 ♀ □	♐	11 19:19
14 0:26 ♂ ☌	♑	14 5:40
16 1:11 ♅ ☍	♒	16 13:19
18 12:21 ♂ ✶	♓	18 18:33
20 17:47 ☉ △	♈	20 22:07
23 0:14 ☉ □	♉	23 0:52
24 17:13 ♇ □	♊	25 3:30
26 23:11 ♂ ☍	♋	27 6:41
29 0:45 ♅ ☌	♌	29 11:10
31 9:40 ♂ △	♍	31 17:49

Last Aspect Dy Hr Mn		☽ Ingress Dy Hr Mn
2 18:51 ♂ □	♎	3 3:14
5 6:51 ☿ □	♏	5 15:03
8 1:26 ♀ ✶	♐	8 3:32
10 7:42 ♂ ☌	♑	10 14:20
12 12:50 ♅ ☍	♒	12 21:54
14 21:51 ♂ ✶	♓	15 2:17
17 1:07 ♂ □	♈	17 4:37
19 3:48 ♂ △	♉	19 6:26
21 4:51 ☉ □	♊	21 8:56
23 12:33 ☉ ✶	♋	23 12:50
25 10:33 ♅ ☌	♌	25 18:22
27 16:20 ♇ ☌	♍	28 1:44
30 3:15 ♅ ✶	♎	30 11:12

☽ Phases & Eclipses

Dy Hr Mn	
8 1:33	☽ 15♎22
16 0:29	○ 22♑57
16 0:20	• P 0.405
23 0:14	☾ 29♈37
29 22:20	● 6♌14
6 18:51	☽ 13♏45
14 11:03	○ 21♒07
21 4:51	☾ 27♉36
28 10:21	● 4♍35

Astro Data

1 July 1954
Julian Day # 19905
SVP 5♓53'25"
GC 26♐12.2 ⚴ 12♍10.8
Eris 8♈48.4 ✱ 4♍16.6
⚷ 26♑51.3R ⚶ 0♊16.8
☽ Mean ☊ 15♑08.4

1 August 1954
Julian Day # 19936
SVP 5♓53'20"
GC 26♐12.3 ⚴ 24♍20.8
Eris 8♈44.6R ✱ 15♍19.8
⚷ 25♑03.3R ⚶ 12♊17.2
☽ Mean ☊ 13♑30.0

LONGITUDE — September 1954

Day	Sid.Time	☉	0 hr ☽	Noon ☽	True ☊	☿	♀	♂	⚳	♃	♄	♅	♆	♇
1 W	10 40 28	8♍30 40	18♎37 49	24♎37 33	13♑04.3	18♍20.1	24♎38.3	2♑50.5	27♎27.2	21♋46.6	5♏08.6	26♋02.3	24♎09.1	25♌08.3
2 Th	10 44 24	9 28 46	0♏35 28	6♏31 59	12R57.3	20 06.0	25 37.9	3 14.4	27 50.3	21 57.7	5 13.6	26 05.2	24 10.8	25 10.1
3 F	10 48 21	10 26 54	12 27 33	18 22 40	12 52.5	21 50.7	26 37.1	3 38.8	28 13.6	22 08.7	5 18.6	26 08.0	24 12.5	25 12.0
4 Sa	10 52 18	11 25 03	24 17 53	0♐13 47	12 49.8	23 34.2	27 35.9	4 03.7	28 36.9	22 19.7	5 23.8	26 10.9	24 14.2	25 13.9
5 Su	10 56 14	12 23 13	6♐10 59	12 10 08	12D49.1	25 16.4	28 34.3	4 29.0	29 00.3	22 30.6	5 29.0	26 13.7	24 16.0	25 15.7
6 M	11 00 11	13 21 25	18 11 53	24 16 53	12 49.5	26 57.5	29 32.4	4 54.8	29 23.8	22 41.4	5 34.2	26 16.5	24 17.8	25 17.6
7 Tu	11 04 07	14 19 38	0♑25 47	6♑39 13	12R50.2	28 37.3	0♏30.0	5 21.1	29 47.3	22 52.1	5 39.6	26 19.2	24 19.6	25 19.4
8 W	11 08 04	15 17 53	12 57 46	19 21 58	12 50.2	0♎16.0	1 27.2	5 47.8	0♏10.9	23 02.7	5 45.0	26 21.9	24 21.4	25 21.3
9 Th	11 12 00	16 16 10	25 52 17	2♒29 02	12 48.5	1 53.6	2 24.0	6 14.9	0 34.5	23 13.2	5 50.4	26 24.6	24 23.2	25 23.1
10 F	11 15 57	17 14 27	9♒12 29	16 02 43	12 44.5	3 30.0	3 20.3	6 42.5	0 58.2	23 23.6	5 55.9	26 27.2	24 25.1	25 24.9
11 Sa	11 19 53	18 12 47	22 59 38	0♓02 59	12 38.0	5 05.2	4 16.1	7 10.5	1 21.9	23 33.9	6 01.5	26 29.8	24 27.0	25 26.7
12 Su	11 23 50	19 11 08	7♓12 21	14 27 05	12 29.4	6 39.4	5 11.4	7 38.8	1 45.7	23 44.1	6 07.1	26 32.4	24 28.9	25 28.5
13 M	11 27 47	20 09 31	21 46 24	29 09 20	12 19.4	8 12.4	6 06.2	8 07.6	2 09.6	23 54.3	6 12.8	26 34.9	24 30.8	25 30.3
14 Tu	11 31 43	21 07 56	6♈34 51	14♈01 49	12 09.2	9 44.3	7 00.5	8 36.7	2 33.5	24 04.3	6 18.5	26 37.4	24 32.7	25 32.0
15 W	11 35 40	22 06 23	21 29 06	28 55 36	12 00.0	11 15.2	7 54.2	9 06.2	2 57.5	24 14.2	6 24.3	26 39.8	24 34.6	25 33.8
16 Th	11 39 36	23 04 52	6♉20 18	13♉42 17	11 52.9	12 44.9	8 47.3	9 36.1	3 21.5	24 24.0	6 30.1	26 42.2	24 36.6	25 35.6
17 F	11 43 33	24 03 23	21 00 49	28 15 19	11 48.2	14 13.5	9 39.9	10 06.3	3 45.6	24 33.8	6 36.0	26 44.6	24 38.6	25 37.3
18 Sa	11 47 29	25 01 57	5♊25 20	12♊30 38	11D45.9	15 41.1	10 31.9	10 36.9	4 09.7	24 43.4	6 42.0	26 46.9	24 40.6	25 39.0
19 Su	11 51 26	26 00 33	19 31 05	26 26 42	11 45.4	17 07.5	11 23.2	11 07.8	4 33.9	24 52.9	6 48.0	26 49.2	24 42.6	25 40.7
20 M	11 55 22	26 59 11	3♋17 35	10♋03 54	11R45.5	18 32.7	12 13.9	11 39.0	4 58.1	25 02.3	6 54.0	26 51.5	24 44.6	25 42.4
21 Tu	11 59 19	27 57 51	16 45 54	23 23 50	11 45.1	19 56.9	13 03.9	12 10.6	5 22.3	25 11.6	7 00.1	26 53.7	24 46.6	25 44.1
22 W	12 03 16	28 56 33	29 57 59	6♌28 36	11 43.0	21 19.8	13 53.2	12 42.5	5 46.7	25 20.7	7 06.2	26 55.8	24 48.7	25 45.8
23 Th	12 07 12	29 55 18	12♌55 56	19 20 13	11 38.3	22 41.5	14 41.8	13 14.7	6 11.0	25 29.8	7 12.4	26 58.0	24 50.7	25 47.5
24 F	12 11 09	0♎54 04	25 41 39	2♍00 23	11 30.6	24 02.0	15 29.6	13 47.3	6 35.4	25 38.7	7 18.7	27 00.0	24 52.8	25 49.1
25 Sa	12 15 05	1 52 53	8♍16 34	14 30 17	11 20.0	25 21.2	16 16.7	14 20.1	6 59.9	25 47.5	7 25.0	27 02.1	24 54.9	25 50.7
26 Su	12 19 02	2 51 44	20 41 40	26 50 45	11 07.3	26 39.1	17 02.9	14 53.2	7 24.4	25 56.2	7 31.3	27 04.0	24 57.0	25 52.3
27 M	12 22 58	3 50 37	2♎57 39	9♎02 25	10 53.3	27 55.6	17 48.3	15 26.7	7 48.9	26 04.8	7 37.7	27 06.0	24 59.1	25 53.9
28 Tu	12 26 55	4 49 31	15 05 09	21 05 59	10 39.2	29 10.5	18 32.7	16 00.4	8 13.5	26 13.2	7 44.1	27 07.9	25 01.2	25 55.5
29 W	12 30 51	5 48 28	27 05 04	3♏02 36	10 26.3	0♏24.0	19 16.3	16 34.4	8 38.1	26 21.5	7 50.5	27 09.7	25 03.3	25 57.1
30 Th	12 34 48	6 47 27	8♏58 48	14 53 59	10 15.4	1 35.8	19 58.9	17 08.6	9 02.8	26 29.7	7 57.0	27 11.5	25 05.5	25 58.6

LONGITUDE — October 1954

Day	Sid.Time	☉	0 hr ☽	Noon ☽	True ☊	☿	♀	♂	⚳	♃	♄	♅	♆	♇
1 F	12 38 44	7♎46 27	20♏48 28	26♏42 39	10♑07.3	2♏45.8	20♏40.5	17♑43.2	9♏27.5	26♋37.8	8♏03.5	27♋13.3	25♎07.6	26♌00.1
2 Sa	12 42 41	8 45 30	2♐36 59	8♐31 57	10R02.1	3 54.0	21 21.0	18 18.0	9 52.2	26 45.7	8 10.1	27 15.0	25 09.8	26 01.6
3 Su	12 46 38	9 44 34	14 28 05	20 26 00	9 59.4	5 00.1	22 00.4	18 53.0	10 17.0	26 53.5	8 16.7	27 16.6	25 12.0	26 03.1
4 M	12 50 34	10 43 40	26 26 19	2♑29 40	9 58.5	6 04.1	22 38.7	19 28.3	10 41.8	27 01.1	8 23.4	27 18.2	25 14.1	26 04.6
5 Tu	12 54 31	11 42 48	8♑36 43	14 48 10	9 58.5	7 05.8	23 15.9	20 03.9	11 06.6	27 08.6	8 30.0	27 19.8	25 16.3	26 06.1
6 W	12 58 27	12 41 58	21 04 39	27 26 50	9 58.0	8 04.9	23 51.7	20 39.6	11 31.5	27 16.0	8 36.8	27 21.3	25 18.5	26 07.5
7 Th	13 02 24	13 41 09	3♒55 17	10♒30 31	9 56.1	9 01.2	24 26.3	21 15.6	11 56.4	27 23.2	8 43.5	27 22.8	25 20.7	26 08.9
8 F	13 06 20	14 40 22	17 12 57	24 02 51	9 51.8	9 54.6	24 59.6	21 51.8	12 21.3	27 30.3	8 50.3	27 24.2	25 22.9	26 10.3
9 Sa	13 10 17	15 39 37	1♓00 20	8♓05 19	9 44.9	10 44.7	25 31.4	22 28.2	12 46.3	27 37.2	8 57.1	27 25.5	25 25.1	26 11.7
10 Su	13 14 13	16 38 53	15 17 31	22 36 24	9 35.5	11 31.1	26 01.8	23 04.9	13 11.3	27 44.0	9 03.9	27 26.8	25 27.3	26 13.0
11 M	13 18 10	17 38 12	0♈01 13	7♈31 01	9 24.6	12 13.7	26 30.7	23 41.7	13 36.3	27 50.7	9 10.8	27 28.1	25 29.6	26 14.4
12 Tu	13 22 07	18 37 32	15 04 38	22 40 45	9 13.3	12 51.9	26 58.0	24 18.7	14 01.3	27 57.2	9 17.6	27 29.3	25 31.8	26 15.7
13 W	13 26 03	19 36 55	0♉17 59	7♉54 57	9 03.0	13 25.5	27 23.6	24 55.9	14 26.4	28 03.5	9 24.5	27 30.5	25 34.0	26 16.9
14 Th	13 30 00	20 36 20	15 30 17	23 02 44	8 54.8	13 53.8	27 47.6	25 33.3	14 51.5	28 09.7	9 31.5	27 31.6	25 36.2	26 18.2
15 F	13 33 56	21 35 47	0♊31 13	7♊54 51	8 49.3	14 16.5	28 09.9	26 10.9	15 16.6	28 15.7	9 38.4	27 32.6	25 38.5	26 19.5
16 Sa	13 37 53	22 35 16	15 12 56	22 25 02	8 46.4	14 33.1	28 30.3	26 48.6	15 41.7	28 21.6	9 45.4	27 33.6	25 40.7	26 20.7
17 Su	13 41 49	23 34 48	29 30 50	6♋30 18	8D45.6	14R42.9	28 48.9	27 26.5	16 06.9	28 27.3	9 52.4	27 34.6	25 43.0	26 21.9
18 M	13 45 46	24 34 22	13♋23 29	20 10 35	8R45.7	14 45.5	29 05.6	28 04.6	16 32.1	28 32.9	9 59.5	27 35.5	25 45.2	26 23.1
19 Tu	13 49 42	25 33 58	26 51 53	3♌27 47	8 45.6	14 40.4	29 20.3	28 42.9	16 57.3	28 38.3	10 06.5	27 36.3	25 47.4	26 24.2
20 W	13 53 39	26 33 36	9♌58 39	16 24 55	8 43.9	14 27.1	29 32.9	29 21.3	17 22.5	28 43.5	10 13.6	27 37.1	25 49.7	26 25.3
21 Th	13 57 36	27 33 17	22 47 02	29 05 25	8 39.9	14 05.2	29 43.5	29 59.9	17 47.8	28 48.6	10 20.7	27 37.8	25 51.9	26 26.4
22 F	14 01 32	28 33 00	5♍20 27	11♍32 30	8 33.1	13 34.5	29 51.9	0♒38.7	18 13.0	28 53.5	10 27.8	27 38.5	25 54.2	26 27.5
23 Sa	14 05 29	29 32 45	17 41 55	23 48 59	8 23.5	12 54.9	29 58.1	1 17.6	18 38.3	28 58.2	10 34.9	27 39.1	25 56.4	26 28.6
24 Su	14 09 25	0♏32 32	29 53 57	5♎57 05	8 11.9	12 06.5	0♐02.0	1 56.6	19 03.6	29 02.7	10 42.0	27 39.7	25 58.6	26 29.6
25 M	14 13 22	1 32 22	11♎58 33	17 58 32	7 59.0	11 09.9	0R03.6	2 35.8	19 29.0	29 07.1	10 49.1	27 40.2	26 00.9	26 30.6
26 Tu	14 17 18	2 32 13	23 57 13	29 54 44	7 46.1	10 06.0	0 02.9	3 15.2	19 54.3	29 11.3	10 56.3	27 40.7	26 03.1	26 31.6
27 W	14 21 15	3 32 06	5♏51 16	11♏46 58	7 34.1	8 56.0	29♏59.8	3 54.7	20 19.7	29 15.3	11 03.5	27 41.1	26 05.3	26 32.5
28 Th	14 25 11	4 32 02	17 42 02	23 36 41	7 24.1	7 41.6	29 54.3	4 34.3	20 45.1	29 19.2	11 10.6	27 41.5	26 07.6	26 33.4
29 F	14 29 08	5 31 59	29 31 08	5♐25 42	7 16.6	6 24.8	29 46.3	5 14.1	21 10.4	29 22.8	11 17.8	27 41.8	26 09.8	26 34.3
30 Sa	14 33 05	6 31 58	11♐20 40	17 16 26	7 11.9	5 07.9	29 35.9	5 54.0	21 35.8	29 26.3	11 25.0	27 42.0	26 12.0	26 35.2
31 Su	14 37 01	7 31 59	23 13 23	29 12 00	7D09.7	3 53.3	29 23.1	6 34.0	22 01.3	29 29.6	11 32.2	27 42.2	26 14.2	26 36.0

Astro Data

	Dy Hr Mn
☿0S	8 21:51
☽0N	12 19:50
♃□♆	18 3:03
☉0S	23 13:55
☽0S	25 21:08
♃⚺♇	25 22:47
♃☌♅	7 10:02
☽0N	10 6:14
☿R	18 8:25
☽0S	23 2:28
♀R	25 16:36

Planet Ingress

	Dy Hr Mn
♀ ♏	6 23:29
⚳ ♏	8 0:57
☿ ♎	8 8:05
☉ ♎	23 13:55
☿ ♏	29 4:06
♂ ♒	21 12:03
♀ ♐	23 22:07
☉ ♏	23 22:56
♀ ♏R	27 10:42

Last Aspect / ☽ Ingress

Last Aspect Dy Hr Mn		☽ Ingress Dy Hr Mn
1 14:51 ♅ □	♏	1 22:49
4 3:47 ♅ △	♐	4 11:32
6 23:08 ♀ ⚹	♑	6 23:10
9 0:57 ♅ ☍	♒	9 7:31
11 4:10 ♇ ☍	♓	11 11:55
13 7:49 ♅ △	♈	13 13:22
15 8:20 ♅ □	♉	15 13:44
17 9:29 ♅ ⚹	♊	17 14:55
19 11:11 ☉ □	♋	19 18:13
21 21:00 ☉ ⚹	♌	22 0:04
24 0:13 ♇ ☌	♍	24 8:11
26 12:26 ♅ ⚹	♎	26 18:11
29 0:07 ♅ □	♏	29 5:52

Last Aspect / ☽ Ingress

Last Aspect Dy Hr Mn		☽ Ingress Dy Hr Mn
1 13:02 ♅ △	♐	1 18:41
3 23:15 ♇ △	♑	4 7:04
6 11:50 ♅ ☍	♒	6 16:45
8 15:41 ♇ ☍	♓	8 22:17
10 20:23 ♃ △	♈	10 23:58
12 20:22 ♃ □	♉	12 23:32
14 20:15 ♃ ⚹	♊	14 23:10
16 18:38 ♇ ⚹	♋	17 0:50
19 4:21 ♀ △	♌	19 5:41
21 13:14 ♀ □	♍	21 13:44
23 22:14 ♃ ⚹	♎	24 0:12
26 10:32 ♃ □	♏	26 12:11
29 0:39 ♀ ☌	♐	29 0:59
31 6:47 ♇ △	♑	31 13:36

☽ Phases & Eclipses

Dy Hr Mn	
5 12:28	☽ 12♐24
12 20:19	○ 19♓31
19 11:11	☾ 25♊59
27 0:50	● 3♎23
5 5:31	☽ 11♑27
12 5:10	○ 18♈21
18 20:30	☾ 24♋55
26 17:47	● 2♏47

Astro Data

1 September 1954
Julian Day # 19967
SVP 5♓53'17"
GC 26♐12.4 ⚴ 7♎24.1
Eris 8♈31.5R ⚵ 26♍52.2
⚷ 23♑36.0R ⚶ 22♊31.8
☽ Mean ☊ 11♑51.5

1 October 1954
Julian Day # 19997
SVP 5♓53'14"
GC 26♐12.4 ⚴ 20♎30.8
Eris 8♈13.6R ⚵ 8♎06.7
⚷ 23♑05.3 ⚶ 29♊35.8
☽ Mean ☊ 10♑16.1

November 1954 LONGITUDE

Day	Sid.Time	☉	0 hr ☽	Noon ☽	True ☊	☿	♀	♂	⚳	♃	♄	♅	♆	♇
1 M	14 40 58	8♏32 01	5♑12 45	11♑16 12	7♑09.4	2♏43.3	29♏07.9	7♒14.2	22♏26.7	29♋32.7	11♏39.4	27♋42.3	26♎16.4	26♌36.9
2 Tu	14 44 54	9 32 05	17 22 54	23 33 27	7 10.2	1R 40.1	28R 50.4	7 54.5	22 52.1	29 35.6	11 46.6	27R 42.4	26 18.6	26 37.6
3 W	14 48 51	10 32 11	29 48 28	6♒08 33	7R 11.0	0 45.5	28 30.5	8 34.8	23 17.6	29 38.4	11 53.8	27 42.4	26 20.8	26 38.4
4 Th	14 52 47	11 32 18	12♒34 17	19 06 13	7 10.7	0 01.0	28 08.3	9 15.3	23 43.0	29 40.9	12 01.0	27 42.4	26 23.0	26 39.1
5 F	14 56 44	12 32 26	25 44 51	2♓30 33	7 08.8	29♎27.5	27 44.0	9 55.9	24 08.5	29 43.3	12 08.2	27 42.3	26 25.2	26 39.8
6 Sa	15 00 40	13 32 36	9♓23 37	16 24 09	7 04.7	29 05.6	27 17.7	10 36.6	24 33.9	29 45.5	12 15.4	27 42.2	26 27.3	26 40.5
7 Su	15 04 37	14 32 48	23 32 06	0♈47 10	6 58.5	28D 55.3	26 49.4	11 17.4	24 59.4	29 47.4	12 22.7	27 42.0	26 29.5	26 41.2
8 M	15 08 34	15 33 01	8♈08 53	15 36 31	6 51.0	28 56.5	26 19.4	11 58.3	25 24.8	29 49.2	12 29.9	27 41.7	26 31.6	26 41.8
9 Tu	15 12 30	16 33 16	23 09 07	0♉45 32	6 42.9	29 08.5	25 47.8	12 39.3	25 50.3	29 50.8	12 37.1	27 41.4	26 33.8	26 42.4
10 W	15 16 27	17 33 32	8♉24 28	16 04 31	6 35.5	29 30.8	25 14.8	13 20.4	26 15.8	29 52.2	12 44.2	27 41.1	26 35.9	26 42.9
11 Th	15 20 23	18 33 50	23 44 15	1♊22 16	6 29.6	0♏02.4	24 40.7	14 01.6	26 41.3	29 53.4	12 51.4	27 40.7	26 38.0	26 43.5
12 F	15 24 20	19 34 10	8♊57 15	16 28 02	6 25.8	0 42.4	24 05.6	14 42.8	27 06.7	29 54.4	12 58.6	27 40.2	26 40.1	26 44.0
13 Sa	15 28 16	20 34 32	23 53 38	1♋13 17	6D 24.2	1 30.1	23 29.7	15 24.1	27 32.2	29 55.3	13 05.8	27 39.7	26 42.2	26 44.5
14 Su	15 32 13	21 34 56	8♋26 26	15 32 44	6 24.4	2 24.5	22 53.4	16 05.5	27 57.7	29 55.9	13 13.0	27 39.1	26 44.3	26 44.9
15 M	15 36 09	22 35 22	22 32 02	29 24 21	6 25.6	3 24.8	22 16.9	16 47.0	28 23.2	29 56.3	13 20.1	27 38.5	26 46.4	26 45.3
16 Tu	15 40 06	23 35 49	6♌09 53	12♌48 53	6R 26.9	4 30.2	21 40.4	17 28.6	28 48.7	29R 56.5	13 27.3	27 37.8	26 48.4	26 45.7
17 W	15 44 03	24 36 18	19 21 45	25 48 55	6 27.4	5 40.1	21 04.2	18 10.2	29 14.2	29 56.6	13 34.4	27 37.1	26 50.5	26 46.1
18 Th	15 47 59	25 36 49	2♍10 53	8♍28 09	6 26.5	6 53.8	20 28.6	18 51.9	29 39.6	29 56.4	13 41.5	27 36.3	26 52.5	26 46.4
19 F	15 51 56	26 37 22	14 41 13	20 50 38	6 23.7	8 10.7	19 53.7	19 33.7	0♐05.1	29 56.0	13 48.6	27 35.5	26 54.5	26 46.7
20 Sa	15 55 52	27 37 57	26 56 51	3♎00 22	6 19.0	9 30.4	19 19.9	20 15.5	0 30.6	29 55.4	13 55.7	27 34.6	26 56.5	26 47.0
21 Su	15 59 49	28 38 33	9♎01 36	15 00 58	6 13.0	10 52.4	18 47.2	20 57.4	0 56.0	29 54.7	14 02.8	27 33.7	26 58.5	26 47.2
22 M	16 03 45	29 39 11	20 58 52	26 55 36	6 06.0	12 16.5	18 16.1	21 39.4	1 21.5	29 53.7	14 09.8	27 32.7	27 00.5	26 47.4
23 Tu	16 07 42	0♐39 51	2♏51 30	8♏46 50	5 58.9	13 42.1	17 46.5	22 21.5	1 47.0	29 52.5	14 16.8	27 31.6	27 02.4	26 47.6
24 W	16 11 38	1 40 32	14 41 53	20 36 52	5 52.3	15 09.2	17 18.7	23 03.6	2 12.4	29 51.1	14 23.9	27 30.5	27 04.3	26 47.8
25 Th	16 15 35	2 41 14	26 32 00	2♐27 31	5 47.0	16 37.4	16 52.8	23 45.8	2 37.9	29 49.6	14 30.8	27 29.4	27 06.3	26 47.9
26 F	16 19 32	3 41 58	8♐23 37	14 20 32	5 43.2	18 06.6	16 29.1	24 28.0	3 03.3	29 47.8	14 37.8	27 28.2	27 08.2	26 48.0
27 Sa	16 23 28	4 42 44	20 18 30	26 17 45	5D 41.1	19 36.6	16 07.5	25 10.3	3 28.7	29 45.8	14 44.8	27 27.0	27 10.0	26 48.0
28 Su	16 27 25	5 43 30	2♑18 34	8♑21 15	5 40.7	21 07.2	15 48.1	25 52.6	3 54.1	29 43.6	14 51.7	27 25.7	27 11.9	26R 48.1
29 M	16 31 21	6 44 18	14 26 06	20 33 29	5 41.6	22 38.3	15 31.1	26 35.0	4 19.5	29 41.3	14 58.6	27 24.4	27 13.7	26 48.1
30 Tu	16 35 18	7 45 06	26 43 46	2♒57 22	5 43.2	24 09.9	15 16.5	27 17.5	4 44.9	29 38.7	15 05.4	27 23.0	27 15.6	26 48.0

December 1954 LONGITUDE

Day	Sid.Time	☉	0 hr ☽	Noon ☽	True ☊	☿	♀	♂	⚳	♃	♄	♅	♆	♇
1 W	16 39 14	8♐45 56	9♒14 42	15♒36 11	5♑45.0	25♏41.9	15♏04.3	27♒59.9	5♐10.3	29♋36.0	15♏12.2	27♋21.6	27♎17.4	26♌48.0
2 Th	16 43 11	9 46 46	22 02 16	28 33 22	5R 46.3	27 14.1	14R 54.6	28 42.5	5 35.6	29R 33.0	15 19.0	27R 20.1	27 19.1	26R 47.9
3 F	16 47 07	10 47 38	5♓09 52	11♓52 07	5 46.7	28 46.5	14 47.3	29 25.0	6 01.0	29 29.9	15 25.8	27 18.6	27 20.9	26 47.7
4 Sa	16 51 04	11 48 30	18 40 22	25 34 50	5 46.1	0♐19.2	14 42.6	0♓07.7	6 26.3	29 26.6	15 32.5	27 17.0	27 22.6	26 47.6
5 Su	16 55 01	12 49 23	2♈35 34	9♈42 30	5 44.3	1 51.9	14D 40.3	0 50.3	6 51.6	29 23.0	15 39.2	27 15.4	27 24.3	26 47.4
6 M	16 58 57	13 50 16	16 55 23	24 13 50	5 41.7	3 24.8	14 40.4	1 33.0	7 16.9	29 19.3	15 45.9	27 13.8	27 26.0	26 47.2
7 Tu	17 02 54	14 51 11	1♉37 16	9♉04 55	5 38.8	4 57.8	14 43.0	2 15.7	7 42.1	29 15.5	15 52.5	27 12.1	27 27.7	26 47.0
8 W	17 06 50	15 52 06	16 35 53	24 09 05	5 36.1	6 30.9	14 47.9	2 58.4	8 07.4	29 11.4	15 59.1	27 10.3	27 29.3	26 46.7
9 Th	17 10 47	16 53 02	1♊43 23	9♊17 34	5 33.9	8 04.1	14 55.2	3 41.2	8 32.6	29 07.2	16 05.7	27 08.6	27 30.9	26 46.4
10 F	17 14 43	17 53 59	16 50 25	24 20 46	5D 32.7	9 37.4	15 04.7	4 24.0	8 57.8	29 02.8	16 12.2	27 06.8	27 32.5	26 46.1
11 Sa	17 18 40	18 54 57	1♋47 33	9♋09 46	5 32.5	11 10.7	15 16.6	5 06.8	9 22.9	28 58.2	16 18.6	27 04.9	27 34.1	26 45.7
12 Su	17 22 37	19 55 56	16 26 39	23 37 32	5 33.1	12 44.1	15 30.6	5 49.7	9 48.1	28 53.4	16 25.1	27 03.0	27 35.7	26 45.3
13 M	17 26 33	20 56 56	0♌42 00	7♌39 44	5 34.2	14 17.6	15 46.7	6 32.6	10 13.2	28 48.5	16 31.5	27 01.1	27 37.2	26 44.9
14 Tu	17 30 30	21 57 57	14 30 40	21 14 49	5 35.4	15 51.2	16 04.9	7 15.4	10 38.3	28 43.4	16 37.8	26 59.1	27 38.7	26 44.5
15 W	17 34 26	22 58 59	27 52 21	4♍23 35	5 36.4	17 24.9	16 25.1	7 58.3	11 03.4	28 38.1	16 44.1	26 57.1	27 40.1	26 44.0
16 Th	17 38 23	24 00 01	10♍48 52	17 08 40	5R 37.0	18 58.7	16 47.2	8 41.3	11 28.4	28 32.7	16 50.4	26 55.1	27 41.6	26 43.5
17 F	17 42 19	25 01 05	23 23 29	29 33 51	5 37.1	20 32.6	17 11.2	9 24.2	11 53.5	28 27.1	16 56.6	26 53.0	27 43.0	26 43.0
18 Sa	17 46 16	26 02 10	5♎40 20	11♎43 30	5 36.7	22 06.6	17 36.9	10 07.2	12 18.5	28 21.4	17 02.7	26 50.9	27 44.4	26 42.4
19 Su	17 50 12	27 03 15	17 43 54	23 42 06	5 35.8	23 40.8	18 04.4	10 50.2	12 43.4	28 15.5	17 08.8	26 48.8	27 45.7	26 41.8
20 M	17 54 09	28 04 22	29 38 38	5♏34 01	5 34.8	25 15.2	18 33.6	11 33.2	13 08.4	28 09.5	17 14.9	26 46.6	27 47.1	26 41.2
21 Tu	17 58 06	29 05 29	11♏28 43	17 23 12	5 33.7	26 49.7	19 04.4	12 16.2	13 33.3	28 03.3	17 20.9	26 44.4	27 48.4	26 40.6
22 W	18 02 02	0♑06 36	23 17 53	29 13 09	5 32.9	28 24.4	19 36.8	12 59.2	13 58.1	27 57.0	17 26.8	26 42.2	27 49.6	26 39.9
23 Th	18 05 59	1 07 45	5♐09 20	11♐06 47	5 32.3	29 59.4	20 10.6	13 42.3	14 23.0	27 50.6	17 32.7	26 39.9	27 50.9	26 39.2
24 F	18 09 55	2 08 54	17 05 45	23 06 31	5 32.0	1♑34.5	20 45.8	14 25.4	14 47.8	27 44.0	17 38.6	26 37.7	27 52.1	26 38.5
25 Sa	18 13 52	3 10 03	29 09 17	5♑14 16	5D 31.9	3 09.9	21 22.4	15 08.4	15 12.5	27 37.3	17 44.3	26 35.3	27 53.3	26 37.8
26 Su	18 17 48	4 11 13	11♑21 39	17 31 37	5 31.9	4 45.5	22 00.4	15 51.5	15 37.3	27 30.5	17 50.1	26 33.0	27 54.5	26 37.0
27 M	18 21 45	5 12 23	23 44 18	29 59 52	5R 32.0	6 21.4	22 39.6	16 34.6	16 02.0	27 23.5	17 55.7	26 30.7	27 55.6	26 36.2
28 Tu	18 25 41	6 13 33	6♒18 28	12♒40 15	5 32.0	7 57.6	23 20.0	17 17.8	16 26.6	27 16.5	18 01.3	26 28.3	27 56.7	26 35.4
29 W	18 29 38	7 14 43	19 05 21	25 33 56	5 31.8	9 34.0	24 01.5	18 00.9	16 51.2	27 09.3	18 06.9	26 25.9	27 57.7	26 34.6
30 Th	18 33 35	8 15 53	2♓06 08	8♓42 06	5 31.6	11 10.8	24 44.2	18 44.0	17 15.8	27 02.1	18 12.4	26 23.4	27 58.8	26 33.7
31 F	18 37 31	9 17 03	15 21 58	22 05 51	5 31.3	12 47.8	25 27.9	19 27.1	17 40.3	26 54.7	18 17.8	26 21.0	27 59.8	26 32.8

Astro Data Dy Hr Mn	Planet Ingress Dy Hr Mn	Last Aspect Dy Hr Mn	☽ Ingress Dy Hr Mn	Last Aspect Dy Hr Mn	☽ Ingress Dy Hr Mn	☽ Phases & Eclipses Dy Hr Mn	Astro Data
♅R 3 10:58	☿ ♎R 4 12:37	2 23:38 ♃ ☍	♒ 3 0:22	2 12:18 ♂ ☌	♓ 2 14:38	3 20:55 ☽ 10♒55	1 November 1954
☽0N 6 15:53	☿ ♏ 11 10:25	5 6:48 ☿ △	♓ 5 7:34	4 18:36 ♃ △	♈ 4 19:35	10 14:29 ○ 17♉40	Julian Day # 20028
☿D 7 21:33	⚳ ♐ 19 7:11	7 10:21 ♃ △	♈ 7 10:42	6 20:15 ♃ □	♉ 6 21:23	17 9:33 ☾ 24♌30	SVP 5♓53'10"
♆⚹♇ 14 20:48	☉ ♐ 22 20:14	9 10:34 ♃ □	♉ 9 10:48	8 19:57 ♃ ⚹	♊ 8 21:16	25 12:30 ● 2♐43	GC 26♐12.5 ⚴ 4♏15.2
♃R 17 3:02		11 9:40 ♃ ⚹	♊ 11 9:50	10 17:09 ♆ △	♋ 10 21:06		Eris 7♈55.0R ⚵ 19♎25.8
☽0S 19 7:30	☿ ♐ 4 7:02	13 4:38 ♇ ⚹	♋ 13 9:59	12 20:52 ♃ ☌	♌ 12 22:48	3 9:56 ☽ 10♓42	⚷ 23♑43.1 ⚶ 2♋00.3R
♇R 28 23:44	♂ ♓ 4 7:41	15 12:56 ♃ ☌	♌ 15 13:03	14 23:36 ♆ ⚹	♍ 15 3:54	10 0:57 ○ 17♊26	☽ Mean ☊ 8♑37.6
	☉ ♑ 22 9:24	17 13:56 ♆ ⚹	♍ 17 19:52	17 9:51 ♃ ⚹	♎ 17 12:51	17 2:21 ☾ 24♍37	
♅□♆ 2 19:06	☿ ♑ 23 12:10	20 5:53 ♃ ⚹	♎ 20 6:02	19 21:07 ♃ □	♏ 20 0:43	25 7:33 ● 2♑59	1 December 1954
☽0N 3 23:25		22 18:00 ♃ □	♏ 22 18:13	22 9:27 ♃ △	♐ 22 13:35	25 7:36:11 ☀ A 07'39"	Julian Day # 20058
♀D 5 22:39		25 6:41 ♃ △	♐ 25 7:01	24 21:28 ♆ ⚹	♑ 25 1:40		SVP 5♓53'05"
☽0S 16 14:08		27 13:45 ♆ ⚹	♑ 27 19:24	27 8:02 ♆ □	♒ 27 12:00		GC 26♐12.6 ⚴ 17♏25.4
♃□♆ 23 10:57		30 5:39 ♃ ☍	♒ 30 6:19	29 16:25 ♆ △	♓ 29 20:09		Eris 7♈42.3R ⚵ 29♎39.3
♅⚺♇ 23 22:40							⚷ 25♑20.8 ⚶ 27♊59.3R
☽0N 31 5:07							☽ Mean ☊ 7♑02.3

LONGITUDE — January 1955

Day	Sid.Time	☉	0 hr ☽	Noon ☽	True ☊	☿	♀	♂	⚳	♃	♄	♅	♆	♇
1 Sa	18 41 28	10♑18 12	28♓53 52	5♈46 04	5♑31.1	14♑25.1	26♏12.7	20♓10.2	18♐04.8	26♋47.3	18♏23.1	26♋18.5	28♎00.7	26♌31.9
2 Su	18 45 24	11 19 22	12♈42 28	19 43 01	5D31.1	16 02.8	26 58.5	20 53.4	18 29.2	26R39.8	18 28.4	26R16.0	28 01.7	26R31.0
3 M	18 49 21	12 20 31	26 47 37	3♉56 03	5 31.5	17 40.7	27 45.2	21 36.5	18 53.6	26 32.2	18 33.6	26 13.5	28 02.6	26 30.0
4 Tu	18 53 17	13 21 40	11♉08 03	18 23 12	5 32.1	19 19.0	28 32.9	22 19.6	19 17.9	26 24.5	18 38.8	26 11.0	28 03.5	26 29.0
5 W	18 57 14	14 22 49	25 41 02	3♊00 56	5 32.9	20 57.6	29 21.4	23 02.7	19 42.2	26 16.8	18 43.8	26 08.5	28 04.3	26 28.0
6 Th	19 01 10	15 23 57	10♊22 15	17 44 11	5 33.6	22 36.4	0♐10.8	23 45.8	20 06.5	26 09.0	18 48.8	26 05.9	28 05.1	26 27.0
7 F	19 05 07	16 25 05	25 05 56	2♋26 38	5R34.0	24 15.5	1 01.0	24 28.9	20 30.7	26 01.2	18 53.8	26 03.4	28 05.9	26 25.9
8 Sa	19 09 04	17 26 13	9♋45 26	17 01 30	5 33.8	25 54.8	1 52.0	25 12.0	20 54.8	25 53.3	18 58.6	26 00.8	28 06.6	26 24.9
9 Su	19 13 00	18 27 21	24 14 01	1♌22 18	5 32.9	27 34.3	2 43.7	25 55.1	21 18.9	25 45.4	19 03.4	25 58.2	28 07.4	26 23.8
10 M	19 16 57	19 28 28	8♌25 43	15 23 48	5 31.4	29 14.0	3 36.2	26 38.2	21 42.9	25 37.4	19 08.2	25 55.7	28 08.0	26 22.7
11 Tu	19 20 53	20 29 36	22 16 09	29 02 33	5 29.3	0♒53.7	4 29.4	27 21.2	22 06.9	25 29.4	19 12.8	25 53.1	28 08.7	26 21.5
12 W	19 24 50	21 30 43	5♍42 55	12♍17 15	5 27.0	2 33.4	5 23.3	28 04.3	22 30.8	25 21.3	19 17.4	25 50.5	28 09.3	26 20.4
13 Th	19 28 46	22 31 50	18 45 44	25 08 35	5 24.9	4 13.1	6 17.8	28 47.3	22 54.7	25 13.3	19 21.9	25 47.9	28 09.9	26 19.2
14 F	19 32 43	23 32 57	1♎26 11	7♎38 57	5 23.3	5 52.5	7 13.0	29 30.3	23 18.5	25 05.2	19 26.3	25 45.3	28 10.4	26 18.0
15 Sa	19 36 39	24 34 03	13 47 21	19 51 58	5D22.4	7 31.5	8 08.8	0♈13.3	23 42.3	24 57.1	19 30.6	25 42.6	28 10.9	26 16.8
16 Su	19 40 36	25 35 10	25 53 21	1♏52 07	5 22.5	9 10.1	9 05.1	0 56.3	24 06.0	24 49.1	19 34.9	25 40.0	28 11.4	26 15.6
17 M	19 44 33	26 36 16	7♏48 52	13 44 15	5 23.4	10 47.9	10 02.0	1 39.3	24 29.6	24 41.0	19 39.0	25 37.4	28 11.8	26 14.4
18 Tu	19 48 29	27 37 22	19 38 51	25 33 17	5 25.0	12 24.8	10 59.4	2 22.3	24 53.2	24 32.9	19 43.1	25 34.8	28 12.2	26 13.1
19 W	19 52 26	28 38 28	1♐28 09	7♐23 58	5 26.8	14 00.5	11 57.4	3 05.3	25 16.7	24 24.9	19 47.1	25 32.2	28 12.6	26 11.9
20 Th	19 56 22	29 39 33	13 21 18	19 20 35	5 28.4	15 34.6	12 55.8	3 48.3	25 40.1	24 16.9	19 51.0	25 29.6	28 13.0	26 10.6
21 F	20 00 19	0♒40 38	25 22 17	1♑26 47	5R29.3	17 06.8	13 54.7	4 31.2	26 03.5	24 08.9	19 54.9	25 27.0	28 13.3	26 09.3
22 Sa	20 04 15	1 41 43	7♑34 23	13 45 24	5 29.1	18 36.6	14 54.1	5 14.2	26 26.8	24 00.9	19 58.6	25 24.4	28 13.5	26 08.0
23 Su	20 08 12	2 42 47	20 00 01	26 18 22	5 27.5	20 03.6	15 53.9	5 57.1	26 50.1	23 53.0	20 02.3	25 21.8	28 13.8	26 06.6
24 M	20 12 08	3 43 50	2♒40 35	9♒06 38	5 24.4	21 27.1	16 54.1	6 40.0	27 13.2	23 45.1	20 05.9	25 19.2	28 14.0	26 05.3
25 Tu	20 16 05	4 44 52	15 36 32	22 10 09	5 20.1	22 46.7	17 54.7	7 22.9	27 36.3	23 37.3	20 09.4	25 16.6	28 14.1	26 03.9
26 W	20 20 02	5 45 53	28 47 24	5♓28 04	5 15.1	24 01.6	18 55.8	8 05.8	27 59.4	23 29.5	20 12.8	25 14.1	28 14.3	26 02.6
27 Th	20 23 58	6 46 53	12♓11 59	18 58 56	5 09.9	25 11.0	19 57.1	8 48.6	28 22.3	23 21.8	20 16.1	25 11.5	28 14.4	26 01.2
28 F	20 27 55	7 47 52	25 48 40	2♈40 59	5 05.2	26 14.3	20 58.9	9 31.5	28 45.2	23 14.2	20 19.3	25 09.0	28 14.4	25 59.8
29 Sa	20 31 51	8 48 50	9♈35 38	16 32 25	5 01.8	27 10.5	22 01.0	10 14.3	29 08.0	23 06.7	20 22.4	25 06.5	28R14.5	25 58.4
30 Su	20 35 48	9 49 47	23 31 08	0♉31 37	4D59.9	27 58.8	23 03.4	10 57.1	29 30.7	22 59.2	20 25.4	25 03.9	28 14.5	25 57.0
31 M	20 39 44	10 50 42	7♉33 40	14 37 07	4 59.6	28 38.5	24 06.1	11 39.9	29 53.3	22 51.8	20 28.4	25 01.5	28 14.4	25 55.6

LONGITUDE — February 1955

Day	Sid.Time	☉	0 hr ☽	Noon ☽	True ☊	☿	♀	♂	⚳	♃	♄	♅	♆	♇
1 Tu	20 43 41	11♒51 37	21♉41 48	28♉47 31	5♑00.5	29♒08.8	25♐09.2	12♈22.6	0♑15.9	22♋44.6	20♏31.2	24♋59.0	28♎14.3	25♌54.2
2 W	20 47 37	12 52 29	5♊54 04	13♊01 13	5 02.0	29 29.0	26 12.6	13 05.3	0 38.3	22R37.4	20 34.0	24R56.5	28R14.2	25R52.7
3 Th	20 51 34	13 53 21	20 08 41	27 16 08	5R03.2	29R38.5	27 16.2	13 48.0	1 00.7	22 30.3	20 36.6	24 54.1	28 14.1	25 51.3
4 F	20 55 31	14 54 11	4♋23 12	11♋29 27	5 03.2	29 37.1	28 20.2	14 30.7	1 23.0	22 23.4	20 39.2	24 51.7	28 13.9	25 49.8
5 Sa	20 59 27	15 55 00	18 34 26	25 37 40	5 01.5	29 24.6	29 24.4	15 13.4	1 45.2	22 16.5	20 41.6	24 49.3	28 13.7	25 48.4
6 Su	21 03 24	16 55 47	2♌38 37	9♌36 46	4 57.6	29 01.1	0♑28.9	15 56.0	2 07.3	22 09.8	20 44.0	24 46.9	28 13.5	25 46.9
7 M	21 07 20	17 56 34	16 31 37	23 22 43	4 51.7	28 27.2	1 33.7	16 38.6	2 29.4	22 03.1	20 46.3	24 44.6	28 13.2	25 45.5
8 Tu	21 11 17	18 57 18	0♍09 39	6♍52 05	4 44.3	27 43.5	2 38.7	17 21.2	2 51.3	21 56.7	20 48.4	24 42.2	28 12.9	25 44.0
9 W	21 15 13	19 58 02	13 29 45	20 02 30	4 36.0	26 51.4	3 43.9	18 03.7	3 13.1	21 50.3	20 50.5	24 39.9	28 12.5	25 42.5
10 Th	21 19 10	20 58 44	26 30 17	2♎53 09	4 28.0	25 52.1	4 49.4	18 46.2	3 34.9	21 44.1	20 52.5	24 37.7	28 12.2	25 41.0
11 F	21 23 06	21 59 26	9♎11 14	15 24 46	4 20.9	24 47.5	5 55.1	19 28.7	3 56.5	21 38.0	20 54.4	24 35.4	28 11.8	25 39.6
12 Sa	21 27 03	23 00 06	21 34 06	27 39 38	4 15.5	23 39.2	7 01.1	20 11.2	4 18.1	21 32.0	20 56.1	24 33.2	28 11.3	25 38.1
13 Su	21 31 00	24 00 45	3♏41 51	9♏41 17	4 12.1	22 29.2	8 07.2	20 53.6	4 39.5	21 26.2	20 57.8	24 31.0	28 10.8	25 36.6
14 M	21 34 56	25 01 23	15 38 30	21 34 09	4D10.7	21 19.5	9 13.6	21 36.0	5 00.9	21 20.6	20 59.4	24 28.9	28 10.3	25 35.1
15 Tu	21 38 53	26 02 00	27 28 52	3♐23 19	4 10.9	20 11.7	10 20.1	22 18.4	5 22.2	21 15.0	21 00.8	24 26.7	28 09.8	25 33.6
16 W	21 42 49	27 02 36	9♐18 11	15 14 07	4 12.0	19 07.5	11 26.9	23 00.8	5 43.3	21 09.7	21 02.2	24 24.7	28 09.2	25 32.1
17 Th	21 46 46	28 03 10	21 11 47	27 11 50	4R13.0	18 08.2	12 33.8	23 43.1	6 04.4	21 04.5	21 03.5	24 22.6	28 08.6	25 30.6
18 F	21 50 42	29 03 43	3♑14 50	9♑21 22	4 13.1	17 14.7	13 40.9	24 25.4	6 25.3	20 59.5	21 04.7	24 20.6	28 08.0	25 29.2
19 Sa	21 54 39	0♓04 15	15 31 54	21 46 54	4 11.4	16 27.9	14 48.2	25 07.7	6 46.1	20 54.6	21 05.7	24 18.6	28 07.4	25 27.7
20 Su	21 58 35	1 04 46	28 06 41	4♒31 31	4 07.3	15 48.3	15 55.7	25 49.9	7 06.8	20 49.9	21 06.7	24 16.6	28 06.7	25 26.2
21 M	22 02 32	2 05 15	11♒01 33	17 36 49	4 00.7	15 16.1	17 03.3	26 32.2	7 27.4	20 45.4	21 07.5	24 14.7	28 05.9	25 24.7
22 Tu	22 06 29	3 05 42	24 17 14	1♓02 37	3 52.0	14 51.4	18 11.0	27 14.4	7 47.9	20 41.1	21 08.3	24 12.9	28 05.2	25 23.2
23 W	22 10 25	4 06 07	7♓52 38	14 46 53	3 41.8	14 34.3	19 19.0	27 56.5	8 08.3	20 36.9	21 08.9	24 11.0	28 04.4	25 21.8
24 Th	22 14 22	5 06 31	21 44 52	28 46 01	3 31.2	14D24.3	20 27.0	28 38.7	8 28.5	20 32.9	21 09.5	24 09.2	28 03.6	25 20.3
25 F	22 18 18	6 06 53	5♈49 44	12♈55 21	3 21.5	14 21.4	21 35.2	29 20.8	8 48.6	20 29.1	21 09.9	24 07.5	28 02.8	25 18.8
26 Sa	22 22 15	7 07 14	20 02 17	27 09 55	3 13.7	14 25.2	22 43.5	0♉02.9	9 08.6	20 25.5	21 10.2	24 05.7	28 01.9	25 17.4
27 Su	22 26 11	8 07 32	4♉17 45	11♉25 17	3 08.3	14 35.3	23 51.9	0 44.9	9 28.5	20 22.0	21 10.5	24 04.1	28 01.0	25 15.9
28 M	22 30 08	9 07 48	18 32 09	25 38 02	3 05.5	14 51.3	25 00.5	1 26.9	9 48.2	20 18.8	21R10.6	24 02.4	28 00.1	25 14.5

Astro Data

	Dy Hr Mn
♃×♇	3 19:56
♃☌♅	7 2:00
☽0S	12 23:06
♂0N	16 4:42
☽0N	27 10:59
♆R	29 19:18
☿R	3 20:57
☽0S	9 9:11
♃△♄	17 15:55
☽0N	23 18:37
☿D	25 10:17

Planet Ingress

	Dy Hr Mn
♀ ♐	6 6:48
☿ ♒	10 23:05
♂ ♈	15 4:33
☉ ♒	20 20:02
⚳ ♑	31 19:07
♀ ♑	6 1:15
☉ ♓	19 10:19
♂ ♉	26 10:22

Last Aspect / ☽ Ingress

Last Aspect Dy Hr Mn		☽ Ingress Dy Hr Mn
31 20:26 ♃ △	♈	1 1:56
3 2:06 ♆ ☍	♉	3 5:24
5 5:40 ♀ ☍	♊	5 7:04
7 4:53 ♆ △	♋	7 8:00
9 6:31 ♆ □	♌	9 9:41
11 10:24 ♆ ⚹	♍	11 13:43
13 19:21 ♂ ☍	♎	13 21:15
16 4:36 ♆ ☌	♏	16 8:15
18 16:36 ☉ ⚹	♐	18 21:01
21 5:38 ♆ ⚹	♑	21 9:09
23 15:38 ♆ □	♒	23 18:58
25 23:00 ♆ △	♓	26 2:11
27 22:53 ♅ △	♈	28 7:19
30 8:05 ♆ ☍	♉	30 11:06

Last Aspect / ☽ Ingress

Last Aspect Dy Hr Mn		☽ Ingress Dy Hr Mn
1 12:37 ☿ □	♊	1 14:02
3 16:01 ☿ △	♋	3 16:36
5 16:26 ♆ △	♌	5 19:28
7 20:33 ♆ ⚹	♍	7 23:43
9 20:33 ♅ ⚹	♎	10 6:33
12 13:03 ♆ ☌	♏	12 16:38
14 20:08 ♇ □	♐	15 5:07
17 13:53 ♆ ⚹	♑	17 17:34
20 0:01 ♆ □	♒	20 3:33
22 6:46 ♆ △	♓	22 10:09
24 4:08 ♅ △	♈	24 14:06
26 13:27 ♆ ☍	♉	26 16:46
28 11:20 ♇ □	♊	28 19:24

☽ Phases & Eclipses

Dy Hr Mn	
1 20:29	☽ 10♈40
8 12:44	○ 17♋28
8 12:33	• A 0.856
15 22:14	☾ 25♎00
24 1:07	● 3♒16
31 5:05	☽ 10♉33
7 1:43	○ 17♌31
14 19:40	☾ 25♏21
22 15:54	● 3♓16

Astro Data

1 January 1955
Julian Day # 20089
SVP 5♓53'00"
GC 26♐12.6 ⚴ 0♐27.8
Eris 7♈38.8 ⚵ 8♏48.6
⚷ 27♑44.6 ⚶ 20♊11.9R
☽ Mean ☊ 5♑23.8

1 February 1955
Julian Day # 20120
SVP 5♓52'55"
GC 26♐12.7 ⚴ 12♐16.8
Eris 7♈46.4 ⚵ 15♏31.3
⚷ 0♒24.8 ⚶ 16♊18.9R
☽ Mean ☊ 3♑45.4

March 1955

LONGITUDE

Day	Sid.Time	☉	0 hr ☽	Noon ☽	True ☊	☿	♀	♂	⚳	♃	♄	♅	♆	♇
1 Tu	22 34 04	10♓08 03	2♊42 43	9♊46 00	3♑04.8	15♒12.8	26♑09.2	2♉08.9	10♑07.8	20♋15.7	21♏10.6	24♋00.8	27♎59.1	25♌13.1
2 W	22 38 01	11 08 15	16 47 48	23 48 02	3R 05.1	15 39.6	27 18.0	2 50.9	10 27.3	20R 12.9	21R 10.6	23R 59.3	27R 58.2	25R 11.6
3 Th	22 41 58	12 08 25	0♋46 39	7♋43 37	3 05.2	16 11.2	28 26.9	3 32.8	10 46.6	20 10.2	21 10.4	23 57.8	27 57.2	25 10.2
4 F	22 45 54	13 08 33	14 38 53	21 32 22	3 03.9	16 47.3	29 35.9	4 14.7	11 05.8	20 07.7	21 10.1	23 56.3	27 56.1	25 08.8
5 Sa	22 49 51	14 08 39	28 23 58	5♌13 34	3 00.1	17 27.5	0♒45.1	4 56.5	11 24.9	20 05.4	21 09.7	23 54.9	27 55.1	25 07.4
6 Su	22 53 47	15 08 43	12♌00 59	18 46 02	2 53.5	18 11.7	1 54.3	5 38.4	11 43.8	20 03.3	21 09.2	23 53.6	27 54.0	25 06.0
7 M	22 57 44	16 08 45	25 28 29	2♍08 05	2 44.0	18 59.5	3 03.7	6 20.1	12 02.6	20 01.4	21 08.6	23 52.3	27 52.9	25 04.7
8 Tu	23 01 40	17 08 44	8♍44 37	15 17 50	2 32.3	19 50.7	4 13.1	7 01.9	12 21.2	19 59.6	21 07.9	23 51.0	27 51.8	25 03.3
9 W	23 05 37	18 08 42	21 47 33	28 13 35	2 19.3	20 45.1	5 22.6	7 43.6	12 39.7	19 58.1	21 07.2	23 49.8	27 50.6	25 01.9
10 Th	23 09 33	19 08 38	4♎35 52	10♎54 19	2 06.3	21 42.3	6 32.3	8 25.3	12 58.1	19 56.8	21 06.3	23 48.6	27 49.4	25 00.6
11 F	23 13 30	20 08 33	17 08 59	23 19 58	1 54.3	22 42.4	7 42.0	9 06.9	13 16.2	19 55.6	21 05.3	23 47.5	27 48.2	24 59.3
12 Sa	23 17 27	21 08 25	29 27 27	5♏31 42	1 44.5	23 45.0	8 51.9	9 48.5	13 34.3	19 54.7	21 04.2	23 46.4	27 47.0	24 58.0
13 Su	23 21 23	22 08 16	11♏33 02	17 31 53	1 37.3	24 50.1	10 01.8	10 30.1	13 52.2	19 53.9	21 03.0	23 45.4	27 45.8	24 56.7
14 M	23 25 20	23 08 05	23 28 42	29 24 00	1 32.8	25 57.6	11 11.8	11 11.7	14 09.9	19 53.4	21 01.7	23 44.4	27 44.5	24 55.4
15 Tu	23 29 16	24 07 52	5♐18 24	11♐12 29	1 30.7	27 07.1	12 21.9	11 53.2	14 27.5	19 53.0	21 00.3	23 43.4	27 43.2	24 54.1
16 W	23 33 13	25 07 38	17 06 56	23 02 24	1 30.2	28 18.8	13 32.1	12 34.7	14 44.9	19D 52.8	20 58.9	23 42.6	27 41.9	24 52.9
17 Th	23 37 09	26 07 22	28 59 37	4♑59 15	1 30.2	29 32.5	14 42.3	13 16.1	15 02.1	19 52.9	20 57.3	23 41.7	27 40.6	24 51.6
18 F	23 41 06	27 07 04	11♑02 00	17 08 32	1 29.5	0♓48.0	15 52.6	13 57.5	15 19.2	19 53.1	20 55.6	23 41.0	27 39.3	24 50.4
19 Sa	23 45 02	28 06 44	23 19 30	29 35 29	1 27.2	2 05.4	17 03.0	14 38.9	15 36.1	19 53.5	20 53.9	23 40.2	27 37.9	24 49.2
20 Su	23 48 59	29 06 23	5♒56 58	12♒24 24	1 22.5	3 24.5	18 13.5	15 20.3	15 52.8	19 54.1	20 52.0	23 39.6	27 36.5	24 48.0
21 M	23 52 56	0♈06 00	18 58 05	25 38 12	1 14.9	4 45.2	19 24.0	16 01.6	16 09.3	19 54.9	20 50.0	23 39.0	27 35.1	24 46.8
22 Tu	23 56 52	1 05 35	2♓24 46	9♓17 40	1 04.9	6 07.6	20 34.7	16 42.9	16 25.7	19 55.9	20 48.0	23 38.4	27 33.7	24 45.7
23 W	0 00 49	2 05 08	16 16 36	23 21 06	0 53.2	7 31.6	21 45.3	17 24.2	16 41.9	19 57.1	20 45.9	23 37.9	27 32.3	24 44.5
24 Th	0 04 45	3 04 39	0♈30 32	7♈44 08	0 41.0	8 57.2	22 56.0	18 05.4	16 57.9	19 58.5	20 43.6	23 37.4	27 30.8	24 43.4
25 F	0 08 42	4 04 08	15 01 01	22 20 15	0 29.5	10 24.2	24 06.8	18 46.6	17 13.7	20 00.0	20 41.3	23 37.0	27 29.3	24 42.3
26 Sa	0 12 38	5 03 34	29 40 51	7♉01 51	0 20.1	11 52.8	25 17.6	19 27.8	17 29.3	20 01.8	20 38.9	23 36.6	27 27.9	24 41.2
27 Su	0 16 35	6 02 59	14♉22 19	21 41 26	0 13.4	13 22.8	26 28.5	20 08.9	17 44.7	20 03.7	20 36.4	23 36.3	27 26.4	24 40.2
28 M	0 20 31	7 02 22	28 58 29	6♊12 53	0 09.5	14 54.3	27 39.5	20 50.0	17 59.9	20 05.9	20 33.8	23 36.1	27 24.9	24 39.1
29 Tu	0 24 28	8 01 42	13♊24 12	20 32 07	0D 08.1	16 27.1	28 50.4	21 31.1	18 14.9	20 08.2	20 31.2	23 35.9	27 23.4	24 38.1
30 W	0 28 25	9 01 00	27 36 26	4♋37 04	0R 07.9	18 01.5	0♓01.5	22 12.1	18 29.8	20 10.7	20 28.4	23 35.8	27 21.8	24 37.1
31 Th	0 32 21	10 00 15	11♋34 01	18 27 20	0 07.8	19 37.2	1 12.6	22 53.1	18 44.4	20 13.4	20 25.6	23 35.7	27 20.3	24 36.2

April 1955

LONGITUDE

Day	Sid.Time	☉	0 hr ☽	Noon ☽	True ☊	☿	♀	♂	⚳	♃	♄	♅	♆	♇
1 F	0 36 18	10♈59 28	25♋17 09	2♌03 33	0♑06.3	21♓14.3	2♓23.7	23♉34.1	18♑58.8	20♋16.3	20♏22.7	23♋35.7	27♎18.7	24♌35.2
2 Sa	0 40 14	11 58 39	8♌46 42	15 26 44	0R 02.7	22 52.9	3 34.8	24 15.0	19 12.9	20 19.3	20R 19.8	23D 35.7	27R 17.2	24R 34.3
3 Su	0 44 11	12 57 47	22 03 44	28 37 48	29♐56.2	24 32.9	4 46.0	24 55.9	19 26.9	20 22.6	20 16.7	23 35.8	27 15.6	24 33.4
4 M	0 48 07	13 56 53	5♍09 00	11♍37 22	29 46.9	26 14.3	5 57.3	25 36.7	19 40.7	20 26.0	20 13.6	23 35.9	27 14.0	24 32.5
5 Tu	0 52 04	14 55 57	18 02 54	24 25 37	29 35.4	27 57.1	7 08.6	26 17.6	19 54.2	20 29.5	20 10.4	23 36.1	27 12.4	24 31.7
6 W	0 56 00	15 54 59	0♎45 29	7♎02 30	29 22.7	29 41.4	8 19.9	26 58.3	20 07.5	20 33.3	20 07.1	23 36.3	27 10.8	24 30.8
7 Th	0 59 57	16 53 58	13 16 40	19 28 01	29 09.8	1♈27.2	9 31.3	27 39.1	20 20.6	20 37.2	20 03.8	23 36.6	27 09.2	24 30.0
8 F	1 03 53	17 52 56	25 36 35	1♏42 27	28 57.9	3 14.4	10 42.7	28 19.8	20 33.5	20 41.3	20 00.4	23 37.0	27 07.6	24 29.2
9 Sa	1 07 50	18 51 52	7♏45 46	13 46 43	28 48.0	5 03.1	11 54.2	29 00.5	20 46.1	20 45.6	19 56.9	23 37.4	27 06.0	24 28.5
10 Su	1 11 47	19 50 46	19 45 32	25 42 30	28 40.6	6 53.3	13 05.7	29 41.1	20 58.5	20 50.0	19 53.3	23 37.8	27 04.4	24 27.7
11 M	1 15 43	20 49 38	1♐37 59	7♐32 22	28 36.0	8 44.9	14 17.2	0♊21.8	21 10.6	20 54.6	19 49.7	23 38.3	27 02.7	24 27.0
12 Tu	1 19 40	21 48 28	13 26 08	19 19 47	28D 33.8	10 38.1	15 28.8	1 02.3	21 22.6	20 59.4	19 46.1	23 38.9	27 01.1	24 26.3
13 W	1 23 36	22 47 16	25 13 52	1♑08 59	28 33.4	12 32.8	16 40.4	1 42.9	21 34.2	21 04.3	19 42.4	23 39.5	26 59.5	24 25.7
14 Th	1 27 33	23 46 03	7♑05 46	13 04 51	28R 33.9	14 29.0	17 52.1	2 23.4	21 45.6	21 09.4	19 38.6	23 40.2	26 57.9	24 25.0
15 F	1 31 29	24 44 48	19 06 56	25 12 41	28 34.3	16 26.6	19 03.8	3 03.9	21 56.8	21 14.7	19 34.7	23 40.9	26 56.2	24 24.4
16 Sa	1 35 26	25 43 31	1♒22 45	7♒37 48	28 33.5	18 25.7	20 15.5	3 44.4	22 07.7	21 20.1	19 30.9	23 41.7	26 54.6	24 23.9
17 Su	1 39 22	26 42 13	13 58 25	20 25 09	28 30.9	20 26.2	21 27.3	4 24.8	22 18.3	21 25.6	19 26.9	23 42.5	26 52.9	24 23.3
18 M	1 43 19	27 40 53	26 58 27	3♓38 39	28 26.1	22 28.1	22 39.1	5 05.2	22 28.7	21 31.4	19 22.9	23 43.4	26 51.3	24 22.8
19 Tu	1 47 16	28 39 31	10♓25 58	17 20 26	28 19.1	24 31.3	23 50.9	5 45.6	22 38.8	21 37.2	19 18.9	23 44.3	26 49.6	24 22.3
20 W	1 51 12	29 38 07	24 21 56	1♈30 08	28 10.5	26 35.7	25 02.7	6 25.9	22 48.7	21 43.3	19 14.8	23 45.3	26 48.0	24 21.8
21 Th	1 55 09	0♉36 42	8♈44 31	16 04 20	28 01.4	28 41.3	26 14.6	7 06.2	22 58.2	21 49.4	19 10.7	23 46.3	26 46.4	24 21.3
22 F	1 59 05	1 35 14	23 28 44	0♉56 38	27 52.7	0♉47.8	27 26.5	7 46.5	23 07.5	21 55.8	19 06.5	23 47.4	26 44.7	24 20.9
23 Sa	2 03 02	2 33 45	8♉26 55	15 58 24	27 45.6	2 55.1	28 38.4	8 26.7	23 16.5	22 02.3	19 02.3	23 48.5	26 43.1	24 20.5
24 Su	2 06 58	3 32 14	23 29 51	1♊00 09	27 40.7	5 03.1	29 50.4	9 06.9	23 25.2	22 08.9	18 58.0	23 49.7	26 41.4	24 20.2
25 M	2 10 55	4 30 42	8♊28 15	15 53 14	27D 38.1	7 11.5	1♈02.3	9 47.1	23 33.6	22 15.6	18 53.8	23 51.0	26 39.8	24 19.8
26 Tu	2 14 51	5 29 07	23 14 20	0♋30 57	27 37.6	9 20.2	2 14.3	10 27.3	23 41.7	22 22.6	18 49.4	23 52.3	26 38.2	24 19.5
27 W	2 18 48	6 27 29	7♋42 40	14 49 12	27 38.4	11 28.7	3 26.3	11 07.4	23 49.5	22 29.6	18 45.1	23 53.6	26 36.6	24 19.3
28 Th	2 22 45	7 25 50	21 50 26	28 46 21	27R 39.3	13 37.0	4 38.3	11 47.5	23 57.1	22 36.8	18 40.7	23 55.0	26 35.0	24 19.0
29 F	2 26 41	8 24 09	5♌37 02	12♌22 39	27 39.5	15 44.6	5 50.4	12 27.6	24 04.3	22 44.1	18 36.3	23 56.5	26 33.4	24 18.8
30 Sa	2 30 38	9 22 25	19 03 25	25 39 37	27 38.2	17 51.2	7 02.4	13 07.6	24 11.2	22 51.6	18 31.9	23 58.0	26 31.8	24 18.6

Astro Data	Dy Hr Mn
♄ R	1 6:19
☽ 0S	8 18:13
♃ D	16 20:38
☉ 0N	21 9:34
☽ 0N	23 3:59
♅ D	1 12:50
♃ △ ♄	2 13:41
☽ 0S	5 0:55
☿ 0N	9 10:17
☽ 0N	19 13:43
♀ 0N	27 16:45

Planet Ingress		Dy Hr Mn
♀	♒	4 20:22
☿	♓	17 20:49
☉	♈	21 9:35
♀	♓	30 11:30
☊	♐R	2 23:08
☿	♈	6 16:14
♂	♊	10 23:09
☉	♉	20 20:58
☿	♉	22 2:57
♀	♈	24 15:13

Last Aspect Dy Hr Mn			☽ Ingress	Dy Hr Mn
2 19:09	♆	△	♋	2 22:40
4 23:10	♆	□	♌	5 2:48
7 4:20	♆	⚹	♍	7 8:09
9 3:48	♅	⚹	♎	9 15:20
11 20:44	♆	☌	♏	12 1:04
14 4:17	☿	□	♐	14 13:13
16 23:51	☿	⚹	♑	17 2:01
19 8:56	☉	⚹	♒	19 12:47
21 15:28	♆	△	♓	21 19:45
23 12:28	♅	△	♈	23 23:09
25 20:24	♆	☍	♉	26 0:31
27 20:34	♀	□	♊	28 1:42
30 3:24	♀	△	♋	30 4:05

Last Aspect Dy Hr Mn			☽ Ingress	Dy Hr Mn
1 3:36	♆	□	♌	1 8:20
3 9:30	♆	⚹	♍	3 14:31
5 19:44	☿	☍	♎	5 22:34
8 3:00	♆	☌	♏	8 8:38
10 20:32	♂	☍	♐	10 20:41
13 3:36	♆	⚹	♑	13 9:40
15 15:22	♆	□	♒	15 21:20
18 0:26	☉	⚹	♓	18 5:28
20 0:09	♀	☌	♈	20 9:29
22 5:16	♆	☍	♉	22 10:29
24 9:59	♀	⚹	♊	24 10:24
26 5:36	♆	△	♋	26 11:09
28 8:12	♆	□	♌	28 14:08
30 13:35	♆	⚹	♍	30 19:58

☽ Phases & Eclipses Dy Hr Mn		
1 12:40	☽	10♊10
8 15:41	○	17♍18
16 16:36	☾	25♐19
24 3:42	●	2♈44
30 20:10	☽	9♋21
7 6:35	○	16♎41
15 11:01	☾	24♑42
22 13:06	●	1♉38
29 4:23	☽	8♌06

Astro Data

1 March 1955
Julian Day # 20148
SVP 5♓52'51"
GC 26♐12.8 ⚴ 21♐03.8
Eris 8♈01.1 ⚵ 18♏18.1
⚷ 2♒39.4 ⚶ 18♊38.8
☽ Mean ☊ 2♑16.4

1 April 1955
Julian Day # 20179
SVP 5♓52'48"
GC 26♐12.9 ⚴ 27♐13.2
Eris 8♈22.0 ⚵ 16♏29.8R
⚷ 4♒32.5 ⚶ 26♊04.0
☽ Mean ☊ 0♑37.9

LONGITUDE

May 1955

Day	Sid.Time	☉	0 hr ☽	Noon ☽	True ☊	☿	♀	♂	⚳	♃	♄	♅	♆	♇
1 Su	2 34 34	10♉20 40	2♍11 30	8♍39 21	27♐34.8	19♉56.6	8♈14.5	13♊47.6	24♑17.8	22♋59.1	18♏27.5	23♋59.5	26♎30.2	24♌18.4
2 M	2 38 31	11 18 52	15 03 27	21 24 05	27R29.5	22 00.5	9 26.6	14 27.6	24 24.1	23 06.9	18R23.0	24 01.1	26R28.6	24R18.3
3 Tu	2 42 27	12 17 02	27 41 28	3♎55 51	27 22.6	24 02.5	10 38.7	15 07.5	24 30.0	23 14.7	18 18.6	24 02.7	26 27.0	24 18.2
4 W	2 46 24	13 15 11	10♎07 26	16 16 26	27 14.7	26 02.4	11 50.8	15 47.4	24 35.7	23 22.7	18 14.1	24 04.4	26 25.5	24 18.1
5 Th	2 50 20	14 13 17	22 23 02	28 27 23	27 06.6	27 59.9	13 03.0	16 27.3	24 41.0	23 30.8	18 09.6	24 06.1	26 23.9	24 18.0
6 F	2 54 17	15 11 22	4♏29 41	10♏30 07	26 59.3	29 54.9	14 15.2	17 07.1	24 46.0	23 39.0	18 05.1	24 07.9	26 22.4	24D18.0
7 Sa	2 58 14	16 09 26	16 28 50	22 26 04	26 53.2	1♊47.0	15 27.4	17 46.9	24 50.7	23 47.3	18 00.6	24 09.7	26 20.9	24 18.0
8 Su	3 02 10	17 07 27	28 22 02	4♐16 59	26 48.9	3 36.2	16 39.6	18 26.7	24 55.1	23 55.8	17 56.1	24 11.6	26 19.3	24 18.1
9 M	3 06 07	18 05 28	10♐11 11	16 04 58	26D46.5	5 22.3	17 51.8	19 06.5	24 59.1	24 04.3	17 51.6	24 13.5	26 17.8	24 18.1
10 Tu	3 10 03	19 03 26	21 58 41	27 52 42	26 45.9	7 05.1	19 04.1	19 46.2	25 02.8	24 13.0	17 47.0	24 15.5	26 16.4	24 18.2
11 W	3 14 00	20 01 24	3♑47 28	9♑43 26	26 46.6	8 44.5	20 16.3	20 25.9	25 06.1	24 21.8	17 42.5	24 17.5	26 14.9	24 18.3
12 Th	3 17 56	20 59 19	15 41 06	21 41 00	26 48.1	10 20.5	21 28.6	21 05.6	25 09.1	24 30.7	17 38.0	24 19.5	26 13.4	24 18.5
13 F	3 21 53	21 57 14	27 43 40	3♒49 42	26 49.8	11 52.9	22 40.9	21 45.2	25 11.8	24 39.8	17 33.5	24 21.6	26 12.0	24 18.7
14 Sa	3 25 49	22 55 07	9♒59 41	16 14 11	26R50.9	13 21.8	23 53.3	22 24.8	25 14.1	24 48.9	17 29.0	24 23.7	26 10.5	24 18.9
15 Su	3 29 46	23 52 59	22 33 46	28 58 59	26 51.0	14 46.9	25 05.6	23 04.4	25 16.0	24 58.1	17 24.6	24 25.9	26 09.1	24 19.1
16 M	3 33 43	24 50 50	5♓30 18	12♓08 08	26 49.8	16 08.4	26 18.0	23 44.0	25 17.6	25 07.5	17 20.1	24 28.1	26 07.7	24 19.4
17 Tu	3 37 39	25 48 40	18 52 49	25 44 32	26 47.2	17 26.1	27 30.4	24 23.5	25 18.9	25 16.9	17 15.6	24 30.4	26 06.3	24 19.7
18 W	3 41 36	26 46 28	2♈43 20	9♈49 06	26 43.6	18 39.9	28 42.8	25 03.0	25 19.7	25 26.5	17 11.2	24 32.7	26 05.0	24 20.0
19 Th	3 45 32	27 44 15	17 01 33	24 20 10	26 39.6	19 49.9	29 55.2	25 42.5	25R20.3	25 36.1	17 06.8	24 35.0	26 03.6	24 20.3
20 F	3 49 29	28 42 02	1♉44 18	9♉13 03	26 35.6	20 55.9	1♉07.6	26 22.0	25 20.4	25 45.9	17 02.4	24 37.4	26 02.3	24 20.7
21 Sa	3 53 25	29 39 47	16 45 26	24 20 17	26 32.4	21 57.9	2 20.1	27 01.4	25 20.2	25 55.8	16 58.1	24 39.8	26 01.0	24 21.1
22 Su	3 57 22	0♊37 30	1♊56 23	9♊32 29	26 30.4	22 55.9	3 32.6	27 40.9	25 19.6	26 05.7	16 53.7	24 42.3	25 59.7	24 21.6
23 M	4 01 18	1 35 13	17 07 22	24 39 51	26D29.6	23 49.7	4 45.1	28 20.3	25 18.7	26 15.8	16 49.4	24 44.8	25 58.4	24 22.0
24 Tu	4 05 15	2 32 54	2♋08 55	9♋33 39	26 30.0	24 39.4	5 57.5	28 59.6	25 17.4	26 25.9	16 45.2	24 47.3	25 57.2	24 22.5
25 W	4 09 12	3 30 33	16 53 19	24 07 21	26 31.2	25 24.7	7 10.0	29 39.0	25 15.7	26 36.1	16 40.9	24 49.9	25 55.9	24 23.1
26 Th	4 13 08	4 28 11	1♌15 22	8♌17 07	26 32.6	26 05.7	8 22.6	0♋18.3	25 13.7	26 46.5	16 36.7	24 52.5	25 54.7	24 23.6
27 F	4 17 05	5 25 48	15 12 33	22 01 41	26 33.7	26 42.3	9 35.1	0 57.6	25 11.3	26 56.9	16 32.6	24 55.2	25 53.6	24 24.2
28 Sa	4 21 01	6 23 23	28 44 43	5♍21 51	26R34.2	27 14.4	10 47.6	1 36.9	25 08.5	27 07.4	16 28.5	24 57.8	25 52.4	24 24.8
29 Su	4 24 58	7 20 56	11♍53 26	18 19 50	26 33.8	27 41.9	12 00.2	2 16.1	25 05.4	27 18.0	16 24.4	25 00.5	25 51.2	24 25.4
30 M	4 28 54	8 18 28	24 41 25	0♎58 37	26 32.6	28 04.9	13 12.7	2 55.3	25 01.9	27 28.6	16 20.3	25 03.3	25 50.1	24 26.1
31 Tu	4 32 51	9 15 59	7♎11 51	13 21 32	26 30.7	28 23.2	14 25.3	3 34.5	24 58.0	27 39.4	16 16.4	25 06.1	25 49.0	24 26.8

LONGITUDE

June 1955

Day	Sid.Time	☉	0 hr ☽	Noon ☽	True ☊	☿	♀	♂	⚳	♃	♄	♅	♆	♇
1 W	4 36 47	10♊13 29	19♎28 05	25♎31 53	26♐28.3	28♊36.8	15♉37.9	4♋13.7	24♑53.8	27♋50.2	16♏12.4	25♋08.9	25♎48.0	24♌27.5
2 Th	4 40 44	11 10 57	1♏33 20	7♏32 46	26R26.0	28 45.8	16 50.5	4 52.8	24R49.2	28 01.1	16R08.6	25 11.8	25R46.9	24 28.2
3 F	4 44 41	12 08 24	13 30 33	19 26 59	26 23.8	28R50.1	18 03.1	5 31.9	24 44.3	28 12.1	16 04.7	25 14.6	25 45.9	24 29.0
4 Sa	4 48 37	13 05 50	25 22 23	1♐17 02	26 22.2	28 49.9	19 15.7	6 11.0	24 39.0	28 23.1	16 01.0	25 17.6	25 44.9	24 29.8
5 Su	4 52 34	14 03 15	7♐11 14	13 05 15	26 21.2	28 45.2	20 28.4	6 50.1	24 33.4	28 34.3	15 57.2	25 20.5	25 43.9	24 30.6
6 M	4 56 30	15 00 40	18 59 21	24 53 51	26D20.8	28 36.2	21 41.1	7 29.1	24 27.4	28 45.5	15 53.6	25 23.5	25 43.0	24 31.5
7 Tu	5 00 27	15 58 03	0♑49 00	6♑45 07	26 21.0	28 23.0	22 53.7	8 08.1	24 21.1	28 56.7	15 50.0	25 26.5	25 42.1	24 32.3
8 W	5 04 23	16 55 26	12 42 30	18 41 29	26 21.6	28 05.8	24 06.5	8 47.1	24 14.4	29 08.1	15 46.4	25 29.5	25 41.2	24 33.2
9 Th	5 08 20	17 52 47	24 42 26	0♒45 41	26 22.4	27 45.1	25 19.2	9 26.1	24 07.4	29 19.5	15 43.0	25 32.6	25 40.3	24 34.2
10 F	5 12 16	18 50 09	6♒51 37	13 00 40	26 23.2	27 21.1	26 31.9	10 05.1	24 00.1	29 31.0	15 39.6	25 35.7	25 39.5	24 35.1
11 Sa	5 16 13	19 47 29	19 13 13	25 29 42	26 23.9	26 54.1	27 44.7	10 44.0	23 52.4	29 42.5	15 36.2	25 38.8	25 38.6	24 36.1
12 Su	5 20 10	20 44 49	1♓50 31	8♓16 07	26 24.3	26 24.7	28 57.4	11 23.0	23 44.4	29 54.1	15 32.9	25 41.9	25 37.9	24 37.1
13 M	5 24 06	21 42 09	14 46 51	21 23 06	26R24.4	25 53.4	0♊10.2	12 01.9	23 36.1	0♌05.8	15 29.7	25 45.1	25 37.1	24 38.1
14 Tu	5 28 03	22 39 28	28 05 09	4♈53 14	26 24.3	25 20.6	1 23.0	12 40.7	23 27.5	0 17.5	15 26.6	25 48.3	25 36.4	24 39.1
15 W	5 31 59	23 36 47	11♈47 30	18 47 57	26 24.1	24 46.9	2 35.9	13 19.6	23 18.6	0 29.3	15 23.5	25 51.5	25 35.7	24 40.2
16 Th	5 35 56	24 34 06	25 54 32	3♉06 59	26 23.9	24 12.9	3 48.7	13 58.5	23 09.3	0 41.2	15 20.5	25 54.8	25 35.0	24 41.3
17 F	5 39 52	25 31 24	10♉24 54	17 47 44	26D23.8	23 39.2	5 01.6	14 37.3	22 59.8	0 53.1	15 17.6	25 58.0	25 34.3	24 42.4
18 Sa	5 43 49	26 28 42	25 14 46	2♊45 09	26 23.8	23 06.4	6 14.5	15 16.1	22 50.0	1 05.1	15 14.8	26 01.3	25 33.7	24 43.6
19 Su	5 47 45	27 26 00	10♊17 53	17 51 54	26R23.8	22 35.0	7 27.4	15 54.9	22 39.9	1 17.1	15 12.0	26 04.6	25 33.1	24 44.7
20 M	5 51 42	28 23 17	25 26 03	2♋59 11	26 23.8	22 05.5	8 40.3	16 33.7	22 29.6	1 29.2	15 09.3	26 08.0	25 32.6	24 45.9
21 Tu	5 55 39	29 20 34	10♋30 10	17 57 56	26 23.7	21 38.4	9 53.3	17 12.5	22 19.0	1 41.3	15 06.7	26 11.3	25 32.1	24 47.1
22 W	5 59 35	0♋17 50	25 21 32	2♌40 08	26 23.4	21 14.3	11 06.2	17 51.2	22 08.2	1 53.5	15 04.2	26 14.7	25 31.6	24 48.4
23 Th	6 03 32	1 15 06	9♌53 04	16 59 50	26 22.9	20 53.4	12 19.2	18 29.9	21 57.1	2 05.7	15 01.7	26 18.1	25 31.1	24 49.6
24 F	6 07 28	2 12 21	24 00 05	0♍53 40	26 22.4	20 36.3	13 32.2	19 08.7	21 45.8	2 18.0	14 59.4	26 21.5	25 30.7	24 50.9
25 Sa	6 11 25	3 09 35	7♍40 32	14 20 48	26 21.8	20 23.1	14 45.2	19 47.3	21 34.3	2 30.4	14 57.1	26 25.0	25 30.3	24 52.2
26 Su	6 15 21	4 06 49	20 54 43	27 22 35	26D21.5	20 14.2	15 58.2	20 26.0	21 22.6	2 42.7	14 54.9	26 28.4	25 29.9	24 53.5
27 M	6 19 18	5 04 02	3♎44 50	10♎01 53	26 21.5	20D09.7	17 11.2	21 04.7	21 10.6	2 55.1	14 52.8	26 31.9	25 29.6	24 54.9
28 Tu	6 23 15	6 01 15	16 14 16	22 22 30	26 21.8	20 09.9	18 24.3	21 43.3	20 58.6	3 07.6	14 50.8	26 35.4	25 29.2	24 56.2
29 W	6 27 11	6 58 27	28 27 07	4♏28 41	26 22.6	20 14.8	19 37.4	22 21.9	20 46.3	3 20.1	14 48.9	26 38.9	25 29.0	24 57.6
30 Th	6 31 08	7 55 39	10♏27 43	16 24 45	26 23.6	20 24.6	20 50.4	23 00.5	20 33.9	3 32.7	14 47.1	26 42.4	25 28.7	24 59.0

Astro Data	Dy Hr Mn
☽0S	2 5:55
♇D	6 18:29
♃☌♅	10 20:38
♃⚺♇	11 2:26
♅⚺♇	11 23:19
☽0N	16 22:25
⚳R	20 10:11
♃□♆	21 23:11
☽0S	29 11:09
☿R	3 22:47
♅□♆	11 11:08
☽0N	13 5:30
☽0S	25 18:18
☿D	27 23:12

Planet Ingress		Dy Hr Mn
☿	♊	6 13:05
♀	♉	19 13:35
☉	♊	21 20:24
♂	♋	26 0:50
♃	♌	13 0:07
♀	♊	13 8:38
☉	♋	22 4:31

Last Aspect Dy Hr Mn			☽ Ingress	Dy Hr Mn
2 16:59	♅	⚹	♎	3 4:26
5 7:56	♆	☌	♏	5 15:04
7 15:46	♇	□	♐	8 3:19
10 8:45	♆	⚹	♑	10 16:19
12 21:00	♆	□	♒	13 4:29
15 6:44	♆	△	♓	15 13:53
17 12:08	☉	⚹	♈	17 19:21
19 14:48	♆	☍	♉	19 21:12
21 14:32	♃	⚹	♊	21 20:56
23 18:09	♂	☌	♋	23 20:33
25 16:12	♃	☌	♌	25 21:52
27 20:42	☿	⚹	♍	28 2:16
30 6:18	☿	□	♎	30 10:08

Last Aspect Dy Hr Mn			☽ Ingress	Dy Hr Mn
1 18:13	☿	△	♏	1 20:54
4 6:01	♃	△	♐	4 9:24
6 19:24	☿	☍	♑	6 22:21
9 9:07	♃	☍	♒	9 10:30
11 16:43	♀	□	♓	11 20:32
13 19:52	♅	△	♈	14 3:24
15 23:58	♅	□	♉	16 6:50
18 1:12	♅	⚹	♊	18 7:37
20 4:12	☉	☌	♋	20 7:15
22 1:24	♅	☌	♌	22 7:36
24 2:37	♆	⚹	♍	24 10:26
26 10:18	♅	⚹	♎	26 16:55
28 20:21	♅	□	♏	29 3:04

☽ Phases & Eclipses Dy Hr Mn	
6 22:14	○ 15♏36
15 1:42	☾ 23♒28
21 20:59	● 0♊01
28 14:01	☽ 6♍28
5 14:08	○ 14♐08
5 14:23	A 0.622
13 12:37	☾ 21♓44
20 4:12	● 28♊05
20 4:10:11	T 07'08"
27 1:44	☽ 4♎40

Astro Data

1 May 1955
Julian Day # 20209
SVP 5♓52'45"
GC 26♐12.9 ⚴ 27♐34.1R
Eris 8♈41.9 ⚵ 10♏32.9R
⚷ 5♒26.7 ⚶ 6♋12.1
☽ Mean ☊ 29♐02.6

1 June 1955
Julian Day # 20240
SVP 5♓52'40"
GC 26♐13.0 ⚴ 21♐08.6R
Eris 8♈57.3 ⚵ 4♏27.3R
⚷ 5♒15.7R ⚶ 18♋27.5
☽ Mean ☊ 27♐24.1

July 1955

LONGITUDE

Day	Sid.Time	☉	0 hr ☽	Noon ☽	True ☊	☿	♀	♂	⚳	♃	♄	♅	♆	♇
1 F	6 35 04	8♋52 50	22♏20 16	28♏14 46	26♐24.8	20♊39.2	22♊03.5	23♋39.1	20♑21.4	3♌45.2	14♏45.3	26♋45.9	25♎28.5	25♌00.4
2 Sa	6 39 01	9 50 01	4♐08 42	10♐02 29	26 25.7	20 58.8	23 16.7	24 17.7	20R 08.7	3 57.9	14R 43.7	26 49.5	25R 28.3	25 01.9
3 Su	6 42 57	10 47 13	15 56 31	21 51 09	26R 26.3	21 23.3	24 29.8	24 56.3	19 56.0	4 10.5	14 42.1	26 53.0	25 28.2	25 03.3
4 M	6 46 54	11 44 24	27 46 43	3♑43 33	26 26.2	21 52.7	25 43.0	25 34.8	19 43.1	4 23.2	14 40.7	26 56.6	25 28.0	25 04.8
5 Tu	6 50 50	12 41 34	9♑41 55	15 42 05	26 25.3	22 27.0	26 56.2	26 13.3	19 30.1	4 35.9	14 39.3	27 00.2	25 28.0	25 06.3
6 W	6 54 47	13 38 45	21 44 16	27 48 43	26 23.7	23 06.1	28 09.4	26 51.8	19 17.1	4 48.7	14 38.0	27 03.8	25 27.9	25 07.8
7 Th	6 58 44	14 35 56	3♒55 39	10♒05 15	26 21.3	23 50.0	29 22.6	27 30.3	19 04.0	5 01.5	14 36.8	27 07.4	25D 27.9	25 09.4
8 F	7 02 40	15 33 07	16 17 42	22 33 14	26 18.6	24 38.7	0♋35.9	28 08.8	18 50.8	5 14.3	14 35.7	27 11.0	25 27.9	25 10.9
9 Sa	7 06 37	16 30 19	28 52 02	5♓14 16	26 15.7	25 32.1	1 49.1	28 47.3	18 37.6	5 27.2	14 34.7	27 14.6	25 27.9	25 12.5
10 Su	7 10 33	17 27 30	11♓40 09	18 09 53	26 13.2	26 30.2	3 02.4	29 25.8	18 24.4	5 40.0	14 33.8	27 18.2	25 28.0	25 14.1
11 M	7 14 30	18 24 43	24 43 39	1♈21 37	26 11.3	27 32.8	4 15.8	0♌04.2	18 11.2	5 53.0	14 33.0	27 21.9	25 28.1	25 15.7
12 Tu	7 18 26	19 21 55	8♈03 58	14 50 50	26D 10.5	28 39.9	5 29.1	0 42.6	17 58.0	6 05.9	14 32.3	27 25.5	25 28.2	25 17.3
13 W	7 22 23	20 19 08	21 42 20	28 38 29	26 10.6	29 51.5	6 42.5	1 21.1	17 44.8	6 18.9	14 31.7	27 29.2	25 28.4	25 18.9
14 Th	7 26 19	21 16 22	5♉39 19	12♉44 43	26 11.6	1♋07.6	7 55.9	1 59.5	17 31.6	6 31.8	14 31.2	27 32.8	25 28.6	25 20.6
15 F	7 30 16	22 13 37	19 54 31	27 08 27	26 12.9	2 27.9	9 09.3	2 37.9	17 18.5	6 44.9	14 30.8	27 36.5	25 28.8	25 22.2
16 Sa	7 34 13	23 10 52	4♊26 06	11♊46 58	26R 14.2	3 52.5	10 22.8	3 16.3	17 05.5	6 57.9	14 30.4	27 40.2	25 29.1	25 23.9
17 Su	7 38 09	24 08 08	19 10 25	26 35 41	26 14.7	5 21.2	11 36.2	3 54.7	16 52.5	7 11.0	14 30.2	27 43.8	25 29.4	25 25.6
18 M	7 42 06	25 05 24	4♋01 57	11♋28 18	26 14.0	6 53.9	12 49.7	4 33.1	16 39.6	7 24.0	14D 30.1	27 47.5	25 29.7	25 27.3
19 Tu	7 46 02	26 02 41	18 53 45	26 17 19	26 11.9	8 30.6	14 03.2	5 11.5	16 26.9	7 37.1	14 30.0	27 51.2	25 30.1	25 29.0
20 W	7 49 59	26 59 58	3♌38 03	10♌55 04	26 08.4	10 11.0	15 16.8	5 49.8	16 14.2	7 50.3	14 30.1	27 54.9	25 30.5	25 30.8
21 Th	7 53 55	27 57 15	18 07 32	25 14 46	26 04.0	11 55.0	16 30.4	6 28.2	16 01.7	8 03.4	14 30.3	27 58.5	25 30.9	25 32.5
22 F	7 57 52	28 54 33	2♍16 13	9♍11 29	25 59.1	13 42.4	17 43.9	7 06.6	15 49.3	8 16.5	14 30.5	28 02.2	25 31.3	25 34.3
23 Sa	8 01 48	29 51 52	16 00 21	22 42 42	25 54.5	15 33.0	18 57.5	7 44.9	15 37.1	8 29.7	14 30.9	28 05.9	25 31.8	25 36.0
24 Su	8 05 45	0♌49 10	29 18 36	5♎48 15	25 50.8	17 26.5	20 11.2	8 23.2	15 25.0	8 42.9	14 31.4	28 09.6	25 32.4	25 37.8
25 M	8 09 42	1 46 29	12♎11 56	18 30 04	25 48.4	19 22.7	21 24.8	9 01.5	15 13.2	8 56.0	14 31.9	28 13.2	25 32.9	25 39.6
26 Tu	8 13 38	2 43 48	24 43 07	0♏51 39	25D 47.5	21 21.2	22 38.5	9 39.8	15 01.5	9 09.2	14 32.6	28 16.9	25 33.5	25 41.4
27 W	8 17 35	3 41 08	6♏56 12	12 57 25	25 47.9	23 21.7	23 52.2	10 18.1	14 50.1	9 22.4	14 33.3	28 20.6	25 34.1	25 43.2
28 Th	8 21 31	4 38 28	18 55 55	24 52 20	25 49.2	25 23.9	25 05.9	10 56.4	14 38.8	9 35.6	14 34.2	28 24.2	25 34.8	25 45.0
29 F	8 25 28	5 35 49	0♐47 17	6♐41 23	25 50.8	27 27.4	26 19.6	11 34.7	14 27.8	9 48.8	14 35.1	28 27.9	25 35.4	25 46.9
30 Sa	8 29 24	6 33 11	12 35 14	18 29 22	25R 52.1	29 32.0	27 33.3	12 13.0	14 17.1	10 02.1	14 36.2	28 31.5	25 36.1	25 48.7
31 Su	8 33 21	7 30 33	24 24 19	0♑20 35	25 52.2	1♌37.3	28 47.1	12 51.2	14 06.5	10 15.3	14 37.3	28 35.2	25 36.9	25 50.6

August 1955

LONGITUDE

Day	Sid.Time	☉	0 hr ☽	Noon ☽	True ☊	☿	♀	♂	⚳	♃	♄	♅	♆	♇
1 M	8 37 17	8♌27 55	6♑18 35	12♑18 44	25♐50.8	3♌42.9	0♌00.9	13♌29.5	13♑56.3	10♌28.5	14♏38.5	28♋38.8	25♎37.7	25♌52.4
2 Tu	8 41 14	9 25 19	18 21 21	24 26 44	25R 47.4	5 48.6	1 14.7	14 07.7	13R 46.3	10 41.7	14 39.9	28 42.5	25 38.5	25 54.3
3 W	8 45 11	10 22 43	0♒35 07	6♒46 41	25 42.1	7 54.2	2 28.5	14 46.0	13 36.5	10 55.0	14 41.3	28 46.1	25 39.3	25 56.2
4 Th	8 49 07	11 20 08	13 01 34	19 19 49	25 35.2	9 59.3	3 42.4	15 24.2	13 27.1	11 08.2	14 42.8	28 49.7	25 40.2	25 58.0
5 F	8 53 04	12 17 34	25 41 30	2♓06 36	25 27.3	12 03.8	4 56.3	16 02.4	13 17.9	11 21.4	14 44.5	28 53.3	25 41.0	25 59.9
6 Sa	8 57 00	13 15 01	8♓35 06	15 06 55	25 19.2	14 07.5	6 10.2	16 40.7	13 09.0	11 34.6	14 46.2	28 56.9	25 42.0	26 01.8
7 Su	9 00 57	14 12 29	21 41 59	28 20 13	25 11.8	16 10.3	7 24.1	17 18.9	13 00.5	11 47.8	14 48.0	29 00.5	25 42.9	26 03.7
8 M	9 04 53	15 09 59	5♈01 33	11♈45 53	25 05.9	18 11.9	8 38.1	17 57.1	12 52.2	12 01.1	14 49.9	29 04.1	25 43.9	26 05.6
9 Tu	9 08 50	16 07 30	18 33 10	25 23 20	25 01.9	20 12.4	9 52.0	18 35.3	12 44.2	12 14.3	14 51.9	29 07.6	25 44.9	26 07.5
10 W	9 12 46	17 05 02	2♉16 21	9♉12 09	25D 00.0	22 11.6	11 06.0	19 13.5	12 36.6	12 27.5	14 53.9	29 11.2	25 45.9	26 09.4
11 Th	9 16 43	18 02 35	16 10 41	23 11 54	24 59.8	24 09.4	12 20.1	19 51.7	12 29.3	12 40.7	14 56.1	29 14.7	25 47.0	26 11.4
12 F	9 20 40	19 00 11	0♊15 44	7♊22 02	25 00.6	26 05.9	13 34.1	20 29.9	12 22.3	12 53.9	14 58.4	29 18.2	25 48.1	26 13.3
13 Sa	9 24 36	19 57 47	14 30 37	21 41 16	25R 01.3	28 01.0	14 48.2	21 08.1	12 15.7	13 07.1	15 00.8	29 21.8	25 49.2	26 15.2
14 Su	9 28 33	20 55 25	28 53 39	6♋07 21	25 00.8	29 54.7	16 02.3	21 46.4	12 09.3	13 20.2	15 03.2	29 25.3	25 50.4	26 17.2
15 M	9 32 29	21 53 05	13♋21 53	20 36 41	24 58.4	1♍46.9	17 16.4	22 24.6	12 03.4	13 33.4	15 05.8	29 28.7	25 51.6	26 19.1
16 Tu	9 36 26	22 50 46	27 51 05	5♌04 23	24 53.6	3 37.6	18 30.6	23 02.8	11 57.8	13 46.5	15 08.4	29 32.2	25 52.8	26 21.0
17 W	9 40 22	23 48 28	12♌15 51	19 24 43	24 46.3	5 27.0	19 44.7	23 41.0	11 52.5	13 59.7	15 11.1	29 35.6	25 54.0	26 23.0
18 Th	9 44 19	24 46 12	26 30 15	3♍31 48	24 37.2	7 14.8	20 58.9	24 19.2	11 47.6	14 12.8	15 13.9	29 39.1	25 55.3	26 24.9
19 F	9 48 15	25 43 57	10♍28 45	17 20 37	24 27.3	9 01.3	22 13.1	24 57.4	11 43.0	14 25.9	15 16.8	29 42.5	25 56.6	26 26.8
20 Sa	9 52 12	26 41 43	24 07 02	0♎47 46	24 17.5	10 46.3	23 27.4	25 35.5	11 38.8	14 39.0	15 19.8	29 45.8	25 57.9	26 28.8
21 Su	9 56 09	27 39 30	7♎22 41	13 51 50	24 08.9	12 29.9	24 41.6	26 13.7	11 35.0	14 52.0	15 22.9	29 49.2	25 59.3	26 30.7
22 M	10 00 05	28 37 19	20 15 22	26 33 33	24 02.3	14 12.1	25 55.8	26 51.9	11 31.5	15 05.1	15 26.1	29 52.5	26 00.6	26 32.7
23 Tu	10 04 02	29 35 08	2♏46 46	8♏55 27	23 58.1	15 52.9	27 10.1	27 30.1	11 28.4	15 18.1	15 29.3	29 55.9	26 02.0	26 34.6
24 W	10 07 58	0♍32 59	15 00 09	21 01 26	23D 56.0	17 32.4	28 24.4	28 08.3	11 25.6	15 31.1	15 32.7	29 59.2	26 03.4	26 36.5
25 Th	10 11 55	1 30 51	26 59 57	2♐56 21	23 55.5	19 10.5	29 38.7	28 46.5	11 23.2	15 44.0	15 36.1	0♌02.4	26 04.9	26 38.5
26 F	10 15 51	2 28 45	8♐51 18	14 45 29	23R 55.9	20 47.2	0♍53.1	29 24.7	11 21.2	15 57.0	15 39.6	0 05.7	26 06.4	26 40.4
27 Sa	10 19 48	3 26 40	20 39 35	26 34 16	23 56.1	22 22.6	2 07.4	0♍02.8	11 19.5	16 09.9	15 43.2	0 08.9	26 07.9	26 42.3
28 Su	10 23 44	4 24 36	2♑30 10	8♑27 53	23 55.1	23 56.7	3 21.7	0 41.0	11 18.2	16 22.8	15 46.8	0 12.1	26 09.4	26 44.3
29 M	10 27 41	5 22 33	14 28 00	20 31 01	23 52.1	25 29.4	4 36.1	1 19.2	11 17.3	16 35.6	15 50.6	0 15.3	26 11.0	26 46.2
30 Tu	10 31 38	6 20 32	26 37 24	2♒47 30	23 46.6	27 00.8	5 50.5	1 57.4	11 16.7	16 48.4	15 54.4	0 18.5	26 12.5	26 48.1
31 W	10 35 34	7 18 32	9♒01 40	15 20 05	23 38.5	28 30.9	7 04.9	2 35.5	11D 16.5	17 01.2	15 58.3	0 21.6	26 14.1	26 50.0

Astro Data	Dy Hr Mn
♆ D	7 19:39
☽ 0N	10 11:30
♄ D	19 7:30
♆ ⚹ ♇	20 6:43
☽ 0S	23 3:32
☽ 0N	6 17:33
☽ 0S	19 13:37
♃ □ ♄	24 16:02
⚳ D	31 15:38

Planet Ingress	Dy Hr Mn
♀ ♋	8 0:15
♂ ♌	11 9:22
☿ ♋	13 14:44
☉ ♌	23 15:25
☿ ♌	30 17:22
♀ ♌	1 11:43
☿ ♍	14 13:08
☉ ♍	23 22:19
♅ ♌	24 18:04
♀ ♍	25 18:52
♂ ♍	27 10:13

Last Aspect Dy Hr Mn		☽ Ingress	Dy Hr Mn
1 8:58	♅ △	♐	1 15:34
3 19:20	♆ ⚹	♑	4 4:29
6 10:31	♅ ☍	♒	6 16:18
8 17:33	♆ △	♓	9 2:09
11 4:45	♅ △	♈	11 9:33
13 14:18	☿ ⚹	♉	13 14:20
15 12:46	♅ ⚹	♊	15 16:43
17 10:13	♆ △	♋	17 17:30
19 14:34	♅ ☌	♌	19 18:03
21 12:30	♇ ☌	♍	21 20:06
23 21:50	♅ ⚹	♎	24 1:16
26 6:55	♅ □	♏	26 10:19
28 19:12	♅ △	♐	28 22:24
31 2:53	♇ △	♑	31 11:18

Last Aspect Dy Hr Mn		☽ Ingress	Dy Hr Mn
2 20:23	♅ ☍	♒	2 22:52
5 0:33	♇ ☍	♓	5 8:04
7 13:13	♅ △	♈	7 15:00
9 18:33	♅ □	♉	9 20:03
11 22:19	♅ ⚹	♊	11 23:33
14 0:08	☿ ⚹	♋	14 1:50
16 2:46	♅ ☌	♌	16 3:34
17 23:49	♇ ☌	♍	18 5:57
20 10:08	♅ ⚹	♎	20 10:34
22 18:25	♅ □	♏	22 18:37
25 4:34	♀ □	♐	25 6:03
27 12:16	♇ △	♑	27 18:57
29 23:11	☿ △	♒	30 6:35

☽ Phases & Eclipses Dy Hr Mn	
5 5:29	○ 12♑26
12 20:31	☾ 19♈42
19 11:35	● 26♋02
26 16:00	☽ 2♏53
3 19:30	○ 10♒41
11 2:33	☾ 17♉40
17 19:58	● 24♌08
25 8:52	☽ 1♐23

Astro Data

1 July 1955
Julian Day # 20270
SVP 5♓52'35"
GC 26♐13.1 ⚴ 12♐54.2R
Eris 9♈03.7 ⚵ 2♏38.4
⚷ 4♒07.4R ⚶ 1♌22.0
☽ Mean ☊ 25♐48.8

1 August 1955
Julian Day # 20301
SVP 5♓52'30"
GC 26♐13.1 ⚴ 9♐26.0R
Eris 9♈00.0R ⚵ 5♏28.8
⚷ 2♒25.0R ⚶ 15♌23.0
☽ Mean ☊ 24♐10.3

LONGITUDE September 1955

Day	Sid.Time	☉	0 hr ☽	Noon ☽	True ☊	☿	♀	♂	⚳	♃	♄	♅	♆	♇
1 Th	10 39 31	8♍16 34	21♒42 54	28♒10 10	23♐28.2	29♍59.6	8♍19.3	3♍13.7	11♑16.6	17♌14.0	16♏02.3	0♌24.7	26♎15.7	26♌51.9
2 F	10 43 27	9 14 37	4♓41 50	11♓17 45	23R16.4	1♎27.0	9 33.8	3 51.9	11 17.1	17 26.7	16 06.4	0 27.7	26 17.4	26 53.9
3 Sa	10 47 24	10 12 42	17 57 43	24 41 27	23 04.3	2 53.1	10 48.2	4 30.1	11 17.9	17 39.4	16 10.5	0 30.8	26 19.0	26 55.8
4 Su	10 51 20	11 10 48	1♈28 37	8♈18 51	22 53.1	4 17.7	12 02.7	5 08.2	11 19.1	17 52.0	16 14.7	0 33.8	26 20.7	26 57.6
5 M	10 55 17	12 08 57	15 11 45	22 06 56	22 43.8	5 41.0	13 17.1	5 46.4	11 20.6	18 04.6	16 19.0	0 36.8	26 22.4	26 59.5
6 Tu	10 59 13	13 07 07	29 04 02	6♉02 41	22 37.2	7 02.8	14 31.6	6 24.6	11 22.5	18 17.2	16 23.4	0 39.7	26 24.1	27 01.4
7 W	11 03 10	14 05 20	13♉02 36	20 03 31	22 33.2	8 23.2	15 46.1	7 02.8	11 24.7	18 29.7	16 27.8	0 42.6	26 25.9	27 03.3
8 Th	11 07 06	15 03 34	27 05 14	4♊07 34	22D31.7	9 42.1	17 00.7	7 41.0	11 27.2	18 42.2	16 32.3	0 45.5	26 27.7	27 05.2
9 F	11 11 03	16 01 51	11♊10 24	18 13 37	22R31.4	10 59.4	18 15.2	8 19.2	11 30.1	18 54.7	16 36.9	0 48.4	26 29.5	27 07.0
10 Sa	11 15 00	17 00 10	25 17 07	2♋20 47	22 31.3	12 15.2	19 29.8	8 57.4	11 33.3	19 07.1	16 41.6	0 51.2	26 31.3	27 08.9
11 Su	11 18 56	17 58 30	9♋24 30	16 28 07	22 29.9	13 29.2	20 44.4	9 35.6	11 36.9	19 19.4	16 46.3	0 54.0	26 33.1	27 10.7
12 M	11 22 53	18 56 53	23 31 24	0♌34 06	22 26.3	14 41.6	21 59.0	10 13.8	11 40.8	19 31.8	16 51.1	0 56.8	26 34.9	27 12.6
13 Tu	11 26 49	19 55 18	7♌35 53	14 36 23	22 19.8	15 52.1	23 13.6	10 52.1	11 45.0	19 44.0	16 56.0	0 59.5	26 36.8	27 14.4
14 W	11 30 46	20 53 45	21 35 10	28 31 47	22 10.5	17 00.7	24 28.2	11 30.3	11 49.6	19 56.2	17 00.9	1 02.2	26 38.7	27 16.2
15 Th	11 34 42	21 52 14	5♍25 46	12♍16 38	21 59.0	18 07.2	25 42.8	12 08.5	11 54.4	20 08.4	17 05.9	1 04.8	26 40.6	27 18.0
16 F	11 38 39	22 50 45	19 03 57	25 47 18	21 46.3	19 11.7	26 57.5	12 46.8	11 59.6	20 20.5	17 11.0	1 07.4	26 42.5	27 19.8
17 Sa	11 42 35	23 49 18	2♎26 22	9♎00 52	21 33.7	20 13.8	28 12.1	13 25.0	12 05.2	20 32.6	17 16.1	1 10.0	26 44.4	27 21.6
18 Su	11 46 32	24 47 52	15 30 41	21 55 42	21 22.3	21 13.5	29 26.8	14 03.2	12 11.0	20 44.5	17 21.3	1 12.5	26 46.4	27 23.3
19 M	11 50 29	25 46 29	28 16 00	4♏31 42	21 13.1	22 10.6	0♎41.4	14 41.5	12 17.1	20 56.5	17 26.6	1 15.0	26 48.4	27 25.1
20 Tu	11 54 25	26 45 07	10♏43 03	16 50 21	21 06.7	23 04.8	1 56.1	15 19.7	12 23.6	21 08.4	17 31.9	1 17.5	26 50.4	27 26.8
21 W	11 58 22	27 43 47	22 54 03	28 54 37	21 02.9	23 56.1	3 10.8	15 58.0	12 30.3	21 20.2	17 37.3	1 19.9	26 52.4	27 28.6
22 Th	12 02 18	28 42 29	4♐52 36	10♐48 34	21D01.2	24 44.1	4 25.5	16 36.2	12 37.4	21 31.9	17 42.7	1 22.3	26 54.4	27 30.3
23 F	12 06 15	29 41 12	16 43 12	22 37 07	21R00.9	25 28.6	5 40.2	17 14.5	12 44.7	21 43.6	17 48.2	1 24.6	26 56.4	27 32.0
24 Sa	12 10 11	0♎39 57	28 31 02	4♑25 39	21 01.0	26 09.3	6 54.9	17 52.8	12 52.4	21 55.3	17 53.8	1 26.9	26 58.4	27 33.7
25 Su	12 14 08	1 38 44	10♑21 38	16 19 42	21 00.2	26 45.8	8 09.6	18 31.0	13 00.3	22 06.8	17 59.4	1 29.1	27 00.5	27 35.4
26 M	12 18 04	2 37 32	22 20 28	28 24 36	20 57.6	27 17.9	9 24.4	19 09.3	13 08.5	22 18.3	18 05.1	1 31.4	27 02.6	27 37.0
27 Tu	12 22 01	3 36 23	4♒32 40	10♒45 10	20 52.6	27 45.2	10 39.1	19 47.6	13 17.0	22 29.7	18 10.8	1 33.5	27 04.7	27 38.7
28 W	12 25 58	4 35 15	17 02 34	23 25 10	20 45.1	28 07.3	11 53.8	20 25.9	13 25.8	22 41.1	18 16.6	1 35.6	27 06.7	27 40.3
29 Th	12 29 54	5 34 08	29 53 16	6♓26 57	20 35.3	28 23.8	13 08.5	21 04.2	13 34.9	22 52.4	18 22.4	1 37.7	27 08.9	27 41.9
30 F	12 33 51	6 33 04	13♓06 14	19 51 00	20 24.0	28 34.2	14 23.3	21 42.5	13 44.2	23 03.6	18 28.3	1 39.7	27 11.0	27 43.5

LONGITUDE October 1955

Day	Sid.Time	☉	0 hr ☽	Noon ☽	True ☊	☿	♀	♂	⚳	♃	♄	♅	♆	♇
1 Sa	12 37 47	7♎32 02	26♓40 59	3♈35 47	20♐12.2	28♎38.1	15♎38.0	22♍20.8	13♑53.8	23♌14.7	18♏34.3	1♌41.7	27♎13.1	27♌45.1
2 Su	12 41 44	8 31 01	10♈34 57	17 37 51	20R01.3	28R35.2	16 52.8	22 59.1	14 03.6	23 25.7	18 40.2	1 43.7	27 15.2	27 46.6
3 M	12 45 40	9 30 03	24 43 52	1♉52 18	19 52.2	28 25.0	18 07.5	23 37.4	14 13.7	23 36.7	18 46.3	1 45.6	27 17.4	27 48.2
4 Tu	12 49 37	10 29 07	9♉02 26	16 13 35	19 45.7	28 07.2	19 22.3	24 15.7	14 24.1	23 47.6	18 52.4	1 47.4	27 19.5	27 49.7
5 W	12 53 33	11 28 13	23 25 08	0♊36 29	19 42.0	27 41.6	20 37.0	24 54.1	14 34.7	23 58.4	18 58.5	1 49.2	27 21.7	27 51.2
6 Th	12 57 30	12 27 21	7♊47 08	14 56 41	19D40.6	27 08.1	21 51.8	25 32.4	14 45.5	24 09.2	19 04.7	1 51.0	27 23.9	27 52.7
7 F	13 01 27	13 26 32	22 04 48	29 11 14	19 40.8	26 26.7	23 06.6	26 10.8	14 56.6	24 19.8	19 10.9	1 52.7	27 26.1	27 54.2
8 Sa	13 05 23	14 25 46	6♋15 48	13♋18 22	19R41.2	25 37.8	24 21.4	26 49.1	15 08.0	24 30.4	19 17.2	1 54.4	27 28.2	27 55.6
9 Su	13 09 20	15 25 01	20 18 52	27 17 15	19 40.6	24 41.9	25 36.2	27 27.5	15 19.6	24 40.9	19 23.5	1 56.0	27 30.4	27 57.1
10 M	13 13 16	16 24 19	4♌13 26	11♌07 24	19 38.1	23 39.9	26 51.0	28 05.9	15 31.4	24 51.2	19 29.8	1 57.6	27 32.6	27 58.5
11 Tu	13 17 13	17 23 39	17 59 04	24 48 21	19 33.0	22 32.8	28 05.8	28 44.3	15 43.4	25 01.5	19 36.2	1 59.1	27 34.9	27 59.9
12 W	13 21 09	18 23 01	1♍35 08	8♍19 18	19 25.5	21 22.3	29 20.6	29 22.7	15 55.7	25 11.7	19 42.7	2 00.5	27 37.1	28 01.2
13 Th	13 25 06	19 22 26	15 00 40	21 39 05	19 16.0	20 10.1	0♏35.4	0♎01.1	16 08.2	25 21.8	19 49.2	2 01.9	27 39.3	28 02.6
14 F	13 29 02	20 21 53	28 14 24	4♎46 24	19 05.4	18 58.1	1 50.2	0 39.5	16 21.0	25 31.8	19 55.7	2 03.3	27 41.5	28 03.9
15 Sa	13 32 59	21 21 21	11♎14 59	17 40 01	18 54.8	17 48.4	3 05.0	1 17.9	16 33.9	25 41.8	20 02.2	2 04.6	27 43.7	28 05.2
16 Su	13 36 55	22 20 52	24 01 25	0♏19 10	18 45.2	16 43.0	4 19.9	1 56.4	16 47.1	25 51.6	20 08.8	2 05.9	27 46.0	28 06.5
17 M	13 40 52	23 20 25	6♏33 17	12 43 52	18 37.6	15 43.9	5 34.7	2 34.8	17 00.5	26 01.3	20 15.4	2 07.1	27 48.2	28 07.7
18 Tu	13 44 49	24 20 00	18 51 04	24 55 07	18 32.2	14 52.8	6 49.5	3 13.3	17 14.1	26 10.9	20 22.1	2 08.3	27 50.4	28 09.0
19 W	13 48 45	25 19 37	0♐56 18	6♐54 58	18D29.3	14 11.1	8 04.3	3 51.7	17 27.9	26 20.4	20 28.8	2 09.4	27 52.7	28 10.2
20 Th	13 52 42	26 19 16	12 51 32	18 46 29	18 28.5	13 39.7	9 19.2	4 30.2	17 41.9	26 29.8	20 35.5	2 10.4	27 54.9	28 11.4
21 F	13 56 38	27 18 56	24 40 19	0♑33 36	18 29.1	13 19.3	10 34.0	5 08.7	17 56.1	26 39.0	20 42.3	2 11.4	27 57.2	28 12.5
22 Sa	14 00 35	28 18 39	6♑26 56	12 20 57	18 30.4	13D10.2	11 48.8	5 47.2	18 10.5	26 48.2	20 49.0	2 12.4	27 59.4	28 13.7
23 Su	14 04 31	29 18 23	18 16 19	24 13 42	18R31.4	13 12.3	13 03.7	6 25.6	18 25.2	26 57.3	20 55.9	2 13.3	28 01.7	28 14.8
24 M	14 08 28	0♏18 08	0♒13 45	6♒17 08	18 31.3	13 25.4	14 18.5	7 04.1	18 39.9	27 06.2	21 02.7	2 14.1	28 03.9	28 15.9
25 Tu	14 12 24	1 17 56	12 24 31	18 36 30	18 29.5	13 48.8	15 33.3	7 42.6	18 54.9	27 15.0	21 09.6	2 14.9	28 06.1	28 17.0
26 W	14 16 21	2 17 44	24 53 38	1♓16 26	18 25.9	14 21.9	16 48.1	8 21.2	19 10.1	27 23.7	21 16.4	2 15.6	28 08.4	28 18.0
27 Th	14 20 18	3 17 35	7♓45 16	14 20 27	18 20.4	15 03.8	18 03.0	8 59.7	19 25.4	27 32.3	21 23.3	2 16.3	28 10.6	28 19.0
28 F	14 24 14	4 17 28	21 02 11	27 50 28	18 13.7	15 53.8	19 17.8	9 38.2	19 41.0	27 40.8	21 30.3	2 16.9	28 12.8	28 20.0
29 Sa	14 28 11	5 17 22	4♈45 12	11♈46 06	18 06.5	16 51.0	20 32.6	10 16.7	19 56.7	27 49.1	21 37.2	2 17.5	28 15.1	28 20.9
30 Su	14 32 07	6 17 18	18 52 43	26 04 28	17 59.6	17 54.5	21 47.4	10 55.3	20 12.5	27 57.3	21 44.2	2 18.0	28 17.3	28 21.9
31 M	14 36 04	7 17 15	3♉20 38	10♉40 20	17 54.0	19 03.5	23 02.2	11 33.9	20 28.6	28 05.4	21 51.2	2 18.5	28 19.5	28 22.8

Astro Data

	Dy Hr Mn
☿0S	1 2:14
☽0N	3 0:42
☽0S	15 22:46
♀0S	21 8:34
⊙0S	23 19:41
☽0N	30 9:15
☿R	1 13:58
☽0S	13 5:44
♂0S	17 4:26
☿D	22 19:24
☽0N	27 18:34

Planet Ingress

	Dy Hr Mn
☿ ♎	1 12:06
♀ ♎	18 22:41
⊙ ♎	23 19:41
♀ ♏	13 0:39
♂ ♎	13 11:20
⊙ ♏	24 4:43

Last Aspect Dy Hr Mn		☽ Ingress Dy Hr Mn	
1 9:35	♇ ☍	♓	1 15:23
2 20:43	♄ △	♈	3 21:24
5 20:27	♇ △	♉	6 1:36
7 23:58	♇ □	♊	8 4:58
10 3:09	♇ ⚹	♋	10 8:01
12 5:12	♆ □	♌	12 11:02
14 9:49	♇ ☌	♍	14 14:33
16 14:19	♀ ☌	♎	16 19:35
18 22:21	♇ ⚹	♏	19 3:18
21 9:26	⊙ ⚹	♐	21 14:11
23 22:01	♇ △	♑	24 3:01
26 9:43	☿ □	♒	26 15:07
28 20:57	☿ △	♓	29 0:12

Last Aspect Dy Hr Mn		☽ Ingress Dy Hr Mn	
30 15:26	♂ ☍	♈	1 5:46
3 6:17	☿ ☍	♉	3 8:52
5 7:24	♇ □	♊	5 10:59
7 9:49	♇ ⚹	♋	7 13:23
9 12:23	♆ □	♌	9 16:41
11 18:24	♀ ⚹	♍	11 21:11
13 8:39	♄ ⚹	♎	14 3:13
16 7:46	♇ ⚹	♏	16 11:23
18 18:26	♇ □	♐	18 22:07
21 7:12	♇ △	♑	21 10:52
23 23:05	⊙ □	♒	23 23:33
26 6:25	♇ ☍	♓	26 9:37
28 0:44	♄ △	♈	28 15:46
30 15:48	♇ △	♉	30 18:30

☽ Phases & Eclipses

Dy Hr Mn		
2 7:59	○	9♓05
9 7:59	☾	15♊52
16 6:19	●	22♍37
24 3:41	☽	0♑20
1 19:17	○	7♈50
8 14:04	☾	14♋31
15 19:32	●	21♎40
23 23:05	☽	29♑46
31 6:04	○	7♉02

Astro Data

1 September 1955
Julian Day # 20332
SVP 5♓52'26"
GC 26♐13.2 ⚵ 12♐19.6
Eris 8♈47.1R ⚶ 11♏48.8
⚷ 0♒51.8R ⚴ 29♌49.1
☽ Mean ☊ 22♐31.8

1 October 1955
Julian Day # 20362
SVP 5♓52'23"
GC 26♐13.3 ⚵ 19♐13.8
Eris 8♈29.3R ⚶ 20♏04.6
⚷ 0♒06.4R ⚴ 13♍57.7
☽ Mean ☊ 20♐56.4

November 1955 LONGITUDE

Day	Sid.Time	☉	0 hr ☽	Noon ☽	True ☊	☿	♀	♂	⚳	♃	♄	♅	♆	♇
1 Tu	14 40 00	8♏17 15	18♉02 40	25♉26 40	17♐50.3	20♎17.4	24♏17.0	12♎12.4	20♑44.8	28♌13.4	21♏58.2	2♌18.9	28♎21.7	28♌23.7
2 W	14 43 57	9 17 17	2♊51 21	10♊15 46	17D48.5	21 35.3	25 31.8	12 51.0	21 01.2	28 21.2	22 05.2	2 19.2	28 24.0	28 24.5
3 Th	14 47 53	10 17 21	17 39 03	25 00 24	17 48.4	22 56.8	26 46.6	13 29.6	21 17.7	28 28.9	22 12.3	2 19.5	28 26.2	28 25.4
4 F	14 51 50	11 17 27	2♋19 10	9♋34 46	17 49.6	24 21.2	28 01.4	14 08.2	21 34.4	28 36.5	22 19.4	2 19.8	28 28.4	28 26.2
5 Sa	14 55 47	12 17 35	16 46 46	23 54 51	17 51.0	25 48.0	29 16.3	14 46.9	21 51.2	28 44.0	22 26.4	2 20.0	28 30.6	28 26.9
6 Su	14 59 43	13 17 45	0♌58 49	7♌58 32	17R52.0	27 16.9	0♐31.1	15 25.5	22 08.2	28 51.3	22 33.5	2 20.1	28 32.8	28 27.7
7 M	15 03 40	14 17 57	14 53 58	21 45 08	17 51.9	28 47.5	1 45.9	16 04.1	22 25.4	28 58.4	22 40.6	2R20.2	28 34.9	28 28.4
8 Tu	15 07 36	15 18 11	28 32 08	5♍15 02	17 50.3	0♏19.5	3 00.7	16 42.8	22 42.7	29 05.4	22 47.7	2 20.2	28 37.1	28 29.1
9 W	15 11 33	16 18 28	11♍54 00	18 29 08	17 47.2	1 52.5	4 15.5	17 21.5	23 00.2	29 12.3	22 54.9	2 20.2	28 39.3	28 29.7
10 Th	15 15 29	17 18 46	25 00 35	1♎28 31	17 42.8	3 26.4	5 30.3	18 00.1	23 17.8	29 19.0	23 02.0	2 20.1	28 41.4	28 30.4
11 F	15 19 26	18 19 06	7♎53 01	14 14 15	17 37.8	5 00.9	6 45.1	18 38.8	23 35.5	29 25.6	23 09.1	2 19.9	28 43.6	28 31.0
12 Sa	15 23 22	19 19 28	20 32 19	26 47 21	17 32.7	6 36.0	7 59.9	19 17.5	23 53.4	29 32.0	23 16.3	2 19.7	28 45.7	28 31.5
13 Su	15 27 19	20 19 52	2♏59 28	9♏08 47	17 28.1	8 11.4	9 14.8	19 56.2	24 11.4	29 38.3	23 23.4	2 19.5	28 47.8	28 32.1
14 M	15 31 16	21 20 17	15 15 26	21 19 36	17 24.6	9 47.1	10 29.6	20 35.0	24 29.6	29 44.4	23 30.6	2 19.2	28 49.9	28 32.6
15 Tu	15 35 12	22 20 45	27 21 26	3♐21 09	17 22.4	11 23.0	11 44.4	21 13.7	24 47.9	29 50.4	23 37.8	2 18.8	28 52.0	28 33.1
16 W	15 39 09	23 21 14	9♐18 58	15 15 09	17D21.5	12 58.9	12 59.2	21 52.4	25 06.3	29 56.2	23 44.9	2 18.4	28 54.1	28 33.5
17 Th	15 43 05	24 21 44	21 10 00	27 03 51	17 21.9	14 34.9	14 14.0	22 31.2	25 24.9	0♍01.9	23 52.1	2 17.9	28 56.2	28 34.0
18 F	15 47 02	25 22 16	2♑57 06	8♑50 08	17 23.1	16 10.8	15 28.8	23 10.0	25 43.6	0 07.4	23 59.2	2 17.4	28 58.3	28 34.4
19 Sa	15 50 58	26 22 49	14 43 25	20 37 26	17 24.8	17 46.7	16 43.6	23 48.7	26 02.4	0 12.7	24 06.4	2 16.8	29 00.3	28 34.7
20 Su	15 54 55	27 23 23	26 32 43	2♒29 48	17 26.5	19 22.5	17 58.4	24 27.5	26 21.3	0 17.9	24 13.6	2 16.2	29 02.4	28 35.1
21 M	15 58 51	28 23 59	8♒29 15	14 31 41	17 27.8	20 58.2	19 13.2	25 06.3	26 40.4	0 22.9	24 20.7	2 15.5	29 04.4	28 35.4
22 Tu	16 02 48	29 24 36	20 37 40	26 47 49	17R28.4	22 33.7	20 27.9	25 45.1	26 59.6	0 27.7	24 27.9	2 14.8	29 06.4	28 35.7
23 W	16 06 45	0♐25 14	3♓02 43	9♓22 54	17 28.2	24 09.1	21 42.7	26 23.9	27 18.9	0 32.4	24 35.0	2 14.0	29 08.4	28 35.9
24 Th	16 10 41	1 25 53	15 48 53	22 21 07	17 27.1	25 44.4	22 57.5	27 02.7	27 38.3	0 36.9	24 42.1	2 13.1	29 10.3	28 36.1
25 F	16 14 38	2 26 33	28 59 56	5♈45 37	17 25.5	27 19.5	24 12.2	27 41.5	27 57.8	0 41.2	24 49.2	2 12.2	29 12.3	28 36.3
26 Sa	16 18 34	3 27 14	12♈38 17	19 37 55	17 23.7	28 54.5	25 26.9	28 20.4	28 17.4	0 45.3	24 56.4	2 11.3	29 14.2	28 36.4
27 Su	16 22 31	4 27 57	26 44 19	3♉57 08	17 21.9	0♐29.3	26 41.7	28 59.2	28 37.1	0 49.3	25 03.5	2 10.3	29 16.2	28 36.6
28 M	16 26 27	5 28 40	11♉15 50	18 39 41	17 20.5	2 04.1	27 56.4	29 38.1	28 57.0	0 53.1	25 10.6	2 09.2	29 18.1	28 36.7
29 Tu	16 30 24	6 29 25	26 07 50	3♊39 16	17D19.6	3 38.7	29 11.1	0♏16.9	29 16.9	0 56.8	25 17.6	2 08.2	29 19.9	28 36.7
30 W	16 34 20	7 30 11	11♊12 52	18 47 28	17 19.4	5 13.2	0♑25.8	0 55.8	29 36.9	1 00.2	25 24.7	2 07.0	29 21.8	28R36.8

December 1955 LONGITUDE

Day	Sid.Time	☉	0 hr ☽	Noon ☽	True ☊	☿	♀	♂	⚳	♃	♄	♅	♆	♇
1 Th	16 38 17	8♐30 59	26♊21 54	3♋54 59	17♐19.7	6♐47.6	1♑40.5	1♏34.7	29♑57.1	1♍03.5	25♏31.7	2♌05.8	29♎23.7	28♌36.8
2 F	16 42 14	9 31 47	11♋25 39	18 52 55	17 20.3	8 22.0	2 55.2	2 13.6	0♒17.3	1 06.6	25 38.8	2R04.6	29 25.5	28R36.7
3 Sa	16 46 10	10 32 37	26 15 56	3♌34 03	17 21.0	9 56.2	4 09.9	2 52.5	0 37.7	1 09.5	25 45.8	2 03.3	29 27.3	28 36.7
4 Su	16 50 07	11 33 29	10♌46 42	17 53 32	17 21.5	11 30.5	5 24.6	3 31.4	0 58.1	1 12.2	25 52.8	2 01.9	29 29.1	28 36.6
5 M	16 54 03	12 34 22	24 54 20	1♍49 03	17R21.9	13 04.7	6 39.3	4 10.4	1 18.6	1 14.7	25 59.8	2 00.6	29 30.9	28 36.5
6 Tu	16 58 00	13 35 16	8♍37 42	15 20 28	17 22.0	14 38.9	7 53.9	4 49.3	1 39.2	1 17.1	26 06.7	1 59.1	29 32.6	28 36.3
7 W	17 01 56	14 36 11	21 57 34	28 29 18	17 21.9	16 13.1	9 08.6	5 28.3	1 59.9	1 19.3	26 13.6	1 57.6	29 34.3	28 36.2
8 Th	17 05 53	15 37 08	4♎56 01	11♎18 05	17 21.7	17 47.3	10 23.2	6 07.3	2 20.7	1 21.2	26 20.6	1 56.1	29 36.0	28 35.9
9 F	17 09 50	16 38 05	17 35 54	23 49 51	17D21.6	19 21.6	11 37.9	6 46.2	2 41.6	1 23.0	26 27.4	1 54.5	29 37.7	28 35.7
10 Sa	17 13 46	17 39 04	0♏00 19	6♏07 41	17 21.5	20 55.9	12 52.5	7 25.2	3 02.6	1 24.6	26 34.3	1 52.9	29 39.3	28 35.4
11 Su	17 17 43	18 40 05	12 12 19	18 14 33	17 21.6	22 30.2	14 07.1	8 04.3	3 23.6	1 26.0	26 41.1	1 51.3	29 41.0	28 35.1
12 M	17 21 39	19 41 06	24 14 43	0♐13 08	17 21.8	24 04.7	15 21.7	8 43.3	3 44.7	1 27.2	26 47.9	1 49.6	29 42.6	28 34.8
13 Tu	17 25 36	20 42 08	6♐10 04	12 05 49	17R21.9	25 39.2	16 36.3	9 22.3	4 06.0	1 28.2	26 54.7	1 47.8	29 44.2	28 34.5
14 W	17 29 32	21 43 11	18 00 38	23 54 48	17 21.9	27 13.8	17 50.9	10 01.3	4 27.3	1 29.1	27 01.5	1 46.1	29 45.7	28 34.1
15 Th	17 33 29	22 44 15	29 48 33	5♑42 09	17 21.6	28 48.5	19 05.5	10 40.4	4 48.6	1 29.7	27 08.2	1 44.2	29 47.3	28 33.7
16 F	17 37 25	23 45 19	11♑35 54	17 30 02	17 21.0	0♑23.3	20 20.1	11 19.4	5 10.1	1 30.1	27 14.9	1 42.4	29 48.8	28 33.2
17 Sa	17 41 22	24 46 24	23 24 53	29 20 46	17 20.1	1 58.2	21 34.6	11 58.5	5 31.6	1R30.4	27 21.5	1 40.5	29 50.2	28 32.8
18 Su	17 45 19	25 47 29	5♒18 01	11♒16 59	17 18.9	3 33.2	22 49.1	12 37.6	5 53.2	1 30.4	27 28.1	1 38.5	29 51.7	28 32.3
19 M	17 49 15	26 48 35	17 18 05	23 21 43	17 17.6	5 08.3	24 03.6	13 16.6	6 14.9	1 30.2	27 34.7	1 36.6	29 53.1	28 31.7
20 Tu	17 53 12	27 49 41	29 28 20	5♓38 22	17 16.4	6 43.5	25 18.1	13 55.7	6 36.6	1 29.9	27 41.2	1 34.5	29 54.5	28 31.2
21 W	17 57 08	28 50 47	11♓52 19	18 10 37	17D15.7	8 18.8	26 32.6	14 34.8	6 58.4	1 29.3	27 47.7	1 32.5	29 55.9	28 30.6
22 Th	18 01 05	29 51 54	24 33 46	1♈02 13	17 15.4	9 54.1	27 47.1	15 13.9	7 20.3	1 28.6	27 54.2	1 30.4	29 57.2	28 30.0
23 F	18 05 01	0♑53 01	7♈36 22	14 16 37	17 15.8	11 29.4	29 01.5	15 53.0	7 42.2	1 27.6	28 00.6	1 28.3	29 58.5	28 29.3
24 Sa	18 08 58	1 54 07	21 03 14	27 56 27	17 16.7	13 04.8	0♒15.9	16 32.1	8 04.2	1 26.5	28 06.9	1 26.1	29 59.8	28 28.7
25 Su	18 12 54	2 55 14	4♉56 21	12♉02 54	17 17.9	14 40.1	1 30.3	17 11.2	8 26.3	1 25.2	28 13.3	1 24.0	0♏01.1	28 28.0
26 M	18 16 51	3 56 22	19 15 54	26 34 59	17 19.1	16 15.3	2 44.6	17 50.4	8 48.4	1 23.6	28 19.6	1 21.8	0 02.3	28 27.3
27 Tu	18 20 48	4 57 29	3♊59 36	11♊29 00	17R19.8	17 50.3	3 58.9	18 29.5	9 10.6	1 21.9	28 25.8	1 19.5	0 03.5	28 26.5
28 W	18 24 44	5 58 37	19 02 18	26 38 25	17 19.7	19 25.1	5 13.2	19 08.7	9 32.8	1 20.0	28 32.0	1 17.3	0 04.7	28 25.7
29 Th	18 28 41	6 59 44	4♋16 11	11♋54 18	17 18.5	20 59.5	6 27.5	19 47.8	9 55.1	1 17.9	28 38.1	1 15.0	0 05.8	28 25.0
30 F	18 32 37	8 00 52	19 31 30	27 06 28	17 16.4	22 33.4	7 41.8	20 27.0	10 17.4	1 15.6	28 44.2	1 12.7	0 06.9	28 24.1
31 Sa	18 36 34	9 02 00	4♌38 03	12♌05 07	17 13.5	24 06.8	8 56.0	21 06.2	10 39.8	1 13.1	28 50.3	1 10.3	0 08.0	28 23.3

Astro Data	Dy Hr Mn
♆✶♇	2 22:02
♃☌♇	2 23:26
♃✶♆	2 23:47
♅ R	8 9:29
☽0S	9 10:51
☽0N	24 3:28
♇ R	1 4:47
☽0S	6 16:10
♃ R	18 4:30
☽0N	21 11:03
♃⚺♅	24 3:19
♄□♇	27 14:29

Planet Ingress		Dy Hr Mn
♀	♐	6 2:02
☿	♏	8 6:57
♃	♍	17 3:59
☉	♐	23 2:01
☿	♐	27 4:34
♂	♏	29 1:33
♀	♑	30 3:42
⚳	♒	1 15:28
☿	♑	16 6:06
☉	♑	22 15:11
♀	♒	24 6:52
♆	♏	24 15:22

Last Aspect Dy Hr Mn			☽ Ingress	Dy Hr Mn
1 16:47	♇	□	♊	1 19:23
3 17:45	♃	✶	♋	3 20:11
5 21:58	♀	△	♌	5 22:20
8 2:03	☿	✶	♍	8 2:36
9 20:13	♄	✶	♎	10 9:15
12 17:21	♃	✶	♏	12 18:12
15 4:54	♃	□	♐	15 5:17
17 15:50	♆	✶	♑	17 17:59
20 5:01	♆	□	♒	20 6:58
22 17:29	☉	□	♓	22 18:10
24 18:58	☿	△	♈	25 1:47
27 4:13	♆	☍	♉	27 5:27
29 3:58	♇	□	♊	29 6:11

Last Aspect Dy Hr Mn			☽ Ingress	Dy Hr Mn
1 4:48	♆	△	♋	1 5:46
3 5:13	♆	□	♌	3 6:07
5 7:58	♆	✶	♍	5 8:50
7 7:47	♄	✶	♎	7 14:48
9 23:17	♆	☌	♏	9 23:59
12 8:42	♇	□	♐	12 11:34
14 23:56	♆	✶	♑	15 0:23
17 13:00	♆	□	♒	17 13:19
20 0:50	♆	△	♓	20 1:02
22 9:39	☉	□	♈	22 10:05
24 15:33	♆	☍	♉	24 15:33
26 15:02	♇	□	♊	26 17:33
28 14:49	♇	✶	♋	28 17:17
30 14:36	♄	△	♌	30 16:36

☽ Phases & Eclipses Dy Hr Mn		
6 21:56	☾	13♌43
14 12:02	●	21♏20
22 17:29	☽	29♒38
29 16:50	○	6♊42
29 16:59	•	P 0.119
6 8:35	☾	13♍27
14 7:07	●	21♐31
14 7:01:54	•	A 12'09"
22 9:39	☽	29♓46
29 3:44	○	6♋39

Astro Data

1 November 1955
Julian Day # 20393
SVP 5♓52'20"
GC 26♐13.3 ⚳ 28♐48.2
Eris 8♈10.6R ⚵ 29♏57.0
⚷ 0♒24.8 ⚶ 28♍28.4
☽ Mean ☊ 19♐17.9

1 December 1955
Julian Day # 20423
SVP 5♓52'15"
GC 26♐13.4 ⚳ 9♑19.9
Eris 7♈57.8R ⚵ 10♐11.8
⚷ 1♒44.2 ⚶ 12♎00.5
☽ Mean ☊ 17♐42.6

LONGITUDE January 1956

Day	Sid.Time	☉	0 hr ☽	Noon ☽	True ☊	☿	♀	♂	⚳	♃	♄	♅	♆	♇
1 Su	18 40 30	10♑03 08	19♌26 46	26♌42 16	17♐10.3	25♑39.3	10♒10.2	21♏45.3	11♒02.3	1♍10.5	28♏56.3	1♌07.9	0♏09.1	28♌22.4
2 M	18 44 27	11 04 17	3♍51 04	10♍52 50	17R 07.3	27 10.9	11 24.3	22 24.5	11 24.8	1R 07.6	29 02.2	1R 05.6	0 10.1	28R 21.5
3 Tu	18 48 23	12 05 26	17 47 23	24 34 46	17 05.1	28 41.2	12 38.5	23 03.8	11 47.3	1 04.6	29 08.1	1 03.1	0 11.1	28 20.6
4 W	18 52 20	13 06 35	1♎15 08	7♎48 48	17D 03.9	0♒10.0	13 52.6	23 43.0	12 09.9	1 01.3	29 13.9	1 00.7	0 12.0	28 19.7
5 Th	18 56 17	14 07 45	14 16 08	20 37 39	17 04.0	1 37.0	15 06.6	24 22.2	12 32.5	0 57.9	29 19.7	0 58.2	0 12.9	28 18.7
6 F	19 00 13	15 08 54	26 53 51	3♏05 18	17 05.1	3 01.8	16 20.7	25 01.4	12 55.2	0 54.3	29 25.4	0 55.8	0 13.8	28 17.7
7 Sa	19 04 10	16 10 04	9♏12 36	15 16 18	17 06.8	4 24.0	17 34.7	25 40.7	13 18.0	0 50.5	29 31.1	0 53.3	0 14.7	28 16.7
8 Su	19 08 06	17 11 14	21 17 00	27 15 15	17 08.7	5 43.0	18 48.7	26 19.9	13 40.8	0 46.6	29 36.7	0 50.8	0 15.5	28 15.7
9 M	19 12 03	18 12 24	3♐11 34	9♐06 27	17R 10.0	6 58.4	20 02.6	26 59.2	14 03.6	0 42.4	29 42.2	0 48.2	0 16.3	28 14.6
10 Tu	19 15 59	19 13 34	15 00 21	20 53 43	17 10.3	8 09.4	21 16.5	27 38.5	14 26.5	0 38.1	29 47.7	0 45.7	0 17.1	28 13.5
11 W	19 19 56	20 14 44	26 46 55	2♑40 18	17 08.9	9 15.3	22 30.4	28 17.8	14 49.4	0 33.6	29 53.1	0 43.2	0 17.8	28 12.4
12 Th	19 23 52	21 15 54	8♑34 11	14 28 51	17 05.9	10 15.5	23 44.2	28 57.0	15 12.3	0 29.0	29 58.5	0 40.6	0 18.5	28 11.3
13 F	19 27 49	22 17 03	20 24 33	26 21 30	17 01.0	11 09.0	24 58.0	29 36.3	15 35.3	0 24.2	0♐03.8	0 38.0	0 19.1	28 10.2
14 Sa	19 31 46	23 18 12	2♒19 54	8♒19 58	16 54.7	11 55.1	26 11.8	0♐15.6	15 58.4	0 19.2	0 09.0	0 35.4	0 19.8	28 09.0
15 Su	19 35 42	24 19 21	14 21 51	20 25 46	16 47.5	12 32.7	27 25.5	0 54.9	16 21.4	0 14.0	0 14.2	0 32.8	0 20.3	28 07.9
16 M	19 39 39	25 20 28	26 31 54	2♓40 26	16 40.1	13 01.0	28 39.1	1 34.2	16 44.5	0 08.7	0 19.3	0 30.2	0 20.9	28 06.7
17 Tu	19 43 35	26 21 36	8♓51 36	15 05 37	16 33.3	13 19.3	29 52.7	2 13.5	17 07.6	0 03.3	0 24.3	0 27.6	0 21.4	28 05.5
18 W	19 47 32	27 22 42	21 22 46	27 43 17	16 27.9	13R 26.7	1♓06.3	2 52.8	17 30.8	29♌57.7	0 29.2	0 25.0	0 21.9	28 04.2
19 Th	19 51 28	28 23 48	4♈07 30	10♈35 43	16 24.3	13 22.8	2 19.8	3 32.1	17 54.0	29 51.9	0 34.1	0 22.4	0 22.4	28 03.0
20 F	19 55 25	29 24 52	17 08 14	23 45 24	16D 22.6	13 07.3	3 33.3	4 11.4	18 17.2	29 46.0	0 38.9	0 19.8	0 22.8	28 01.7
21 Sa	19 59 21	0♒25 56	0♉27 30	7♉14 48	16 22.7	12 40.1	4 46.7	4 50.7	18 40.5	29 40.0	0 43.6	0 17.2	0 23.2	28 00.4
22 Su	20 03 18	1 26 59	14 07 33	21 05 52	16 23.8	12 01.6	6 00.0	5 30.1	19 03.7	29 33.8	0 48.3	0 14.5	0 23.5	27 59.1
23 M	20 07 15	2 28 01	28 09 50	5♊19 22	16R 25.0	11 12.8	7 13.3	6 09.4	19 27.0	29 27.5	0 52.9	0 11.9	0 23.8	27 57.8
24 Tu	20 11 11	3 29 02	12♊34 18	19 54 15	16 25.3	10 14.8	8 26.6	6 48.7	19 50.4	29 21.1	0 57.4	0 09.3	0 24.1	27 56.5
25 W	20 15 08	4 30 02	27 18 42	4♋46 55	16 23.9	9 09.1	9 39.7	7 28.1	20 13.7	29 14.6	1 01.8	0 06.7	0 24.4	27 55.2
26 Th	20 19 04	5 31 01	12♋18 04	19 51 05	16 20.3	7 57.9	10 52.8	8 07.4	20 37.1	29 07.9	1 06.2	0 04.1	0 24.6	27 53.8
27 F	20 23 01	6 31 59	27 24 49	4♌58 04	16 14.3	6 43.3	12 05.8	8 46.7	21 00.5	29 01.2	1 10.5	0 01.5	0 24.8	27 52.5
28 Sa	20 26 57	7 32 56	12♌29 33	19 58 04	16 06.6	5 27.5	13 18.8	9 26.1	21 23.9	28 54.3	1 14.7	29♋58.9	0 24.9	27 51.1
29 Su	20 30 54	8 33 52	27 22 27	4♍41 42	15 57.9	4 12.7	14 31.7	10 05.5	21 47.3	28 47.3	1 18.8	29 56.3	0 25.0	27 49.7
30 M	20 34 51	9 34 48	11♍54 58	19 01 36	15 49.4	3 01.1	15 44.5	10 44.8	22 10.8	28 40.2	1 22.8	29 53.8	0 25.1	27 48.3
31 Tu	20 38 47	10 35 42	26 01 10	2♎53 25	15 42.1	1 54.3	16 57.3	11 24.2	22 34.3	28 33.1	1 26.8	29 51.2	0R 25.2	27 46.9

LONGITUDE February 1956

Day	Sid.Time	☉	0 hr ☽	Noon ☽	True ☊	☿	♀	♂	⚳	♃	♄	♅	♆	♇
1 W	20 42 44	11♒36 36	9♎38 18	16♎15 57	15♐36.8	0♒53.8	18♓10.0	12♐03.6	22♒57.7	28♌25.8	1♐30.6	29♋48.6	0♏25.2	27♌45.5
2 Th	20 46 40	12 37 29	22 46 40	29 10 51	15R 33.7	0R 00.6	19 22.6	12 42.9	23 21.2	28R 18.5	1 34.4	29R 46.1	0R 25.2	27R 44.1
3 F	20 50 37	13 38 21	5♏28 59	11♏41 42	15D 32.6	29♑15.4	20 35.1	13 22.3	23 44.8	28 11.0	1 38.1	29 43.6	0 25.1	27 42.6
4 Sa	20 54 33	14 39 13	17 49 35	23 53 20	15 32.9	28 38.7	21 47.6	14 01.7	24 08.3	28 03.5	1 41.7	29 41.1	0 25.0	27 41.2
5 Su	20 58 30	15 40 03	29 53 38	5♐51 09	15R 33.8	28 10.4	23 00.0	14 41.1	24 31.9	27 56.0	1 45.2	29 38.6	0 24.9	27 39.8
6 M	21 02 26	16 40 53	11♐46 34	17 40 32	15 34.1	27 50.6	24 12.3	15 20.5	24 55.4	27 48.3	1 48.7	29 36.1	0 24.7	27 38.3
7 Tu	21 06 23	17 41 42	23 33 40	29 26 33	15 32.9	27 39.0	25 24.5	15 59.9	25 19.0	27 40.7	1 52.0	29 33.6	0 24.5	27 36.8
8 W	21 10 20	18 42 29	5♑19 43	11♑13 38	15 29.5	27D 35.2	26 36.7	16 39.3	25 42.6	27 32.9	1 55.3	29 31.2	0 24.3	27 35.4
9 Th	21 14 16	19 43 16	17 08 46	23 05 28	15 23.3	27 38.7	27 48.8	17 18.7	26 06.2	27 25.1	1 58.5	29 28.8	0 24.0	27 33.9
10 F	21 18 13	20 44 01	29 04 05	5♒04 52	15 14.5	27 49.2	29 00.8	17 58.1	26 29.8	27 17.3	2 01.5	29 26.4	0 23.7	27 32.4
11 Sa	21 22 09	21 44 45	11♒08 02	17 13 45	15 03.3	28 06.1	0♈12.7	18 37.5	26 53.4	27 09.4	2 04.5	29 24.0	0 23.4	27 30.9
12 Su	21 26 06	22 45 28	23 22 08	29 33 15	14 50.6	28 29.0	1 24.5	19 16.9	27 17.0	27 01.6	2 07.4	29 21.7	0 23.1	27 29.4
13 M	21 30 02	23 46 09	5♓47 08	12♓03 50	14 37.5	28 57.4	2 36.2	19 56.3	27 40.7	26 53.7	2 10.2	29 19.3	0 22.7	27 27.9
14 Tu	21 33 59	24 46 49	18 23 20	24 45 39	14 25.3	29 30.9	3 47.8	20 35.7	28 04.3	26 45.7	2 12.9	29 17.0	0 22.2	27 26.4
15 W	21 37 55	25 47 27	1♈10 46	7♈38 44	14 15.0	0♒09.0	4 59.3	21 15.0	28 27.9	26 37.8	2 15.5	29 14.8	0 21.8	27 24.9
16 Th	21 41 52	26 48 04	14 09 34	20 43 52	14 07.3	0 51.4	6 10.7	21 54.4	28 51.6	26 29.9	2 18.0	29 12.5	0 21.3	27 23.4
17 F	21 45 48	27 48 39	27 20 11	4♉00 11	14 02.5	1 37.8	7 22.0	22 33.8	29 15.2	26 21.9	2 20.5	29 10.3	0 20.8	27 21.9
18 Sa	21 49 45	28 49 12	10♉43 29	17 30 15	14D 00.4	2 27.7	8 33.2	23 13.2	29 38.8	26 14.0	2 22.8	29 08.1	0 20.2	27 20.5
19 Su	21 53 42	29 49 43	24 20 38	1♊14 47	13R 59.9	3 21.0	9 44.3	23 52.5	0♓02.5	26 06.1	2 25.0	29 06.0	0 19.6	27 19.0
20 M	21 57 38	0♓50 13	8♊12 48	15 14 45	14 00.1	4 17.4	10 55.3	24 31.9	0 26.1	25 58.2	2 27.2	29 03.8	0 19.0	27 17.5
21 Tu	22 01 35	1 50 40	22 20 36	29 30 15	13 59.4	5 16.6	12 06.1	25 11.3	0 49.7	25 50.3	2 29.2	29 01.8	0 18.4	27 16.0
22 W	22 05 31	2 51 06	6♋43 26	13♋59 49	13 56.7	6 18.5	13 16.9	25 50.6	1 13.4	25 42.5	2 31.1	28 59.7	0 17.7	27 14.5
23 Th	22 09 28	3 51 30	21 18 53	28 39 57	13 51.2	7 22.8	14 27.5	26 30.0	1 37.0	25 34.7	2 33.0	28 57.7	0 17.0	27 13.0
24 F	22 13 24	4 51 52	6♌02 17	13♌24 57	13 42.9	8 29.5	15 37.9	27 09.4	2 00.6	25 27.0	2 34.7	28 55.7	0 16.2	27 11.5
25 Sa	22 17 21	5 52 12	20 47 00	28 07 23	13 32.2	9 38.2	16 48.3	27 48.7	2 24.2	25 19.3	2 36.3	28 53.8	0 15.5	27 10.0
26 Su	22 21 17	6 52 30	5♍25 07	12♍39 12	13 20.1	10 49.0	17 58.5	28 28.1	2 47.8	25 11.6	2 37.9	28 51.9	0 14.7	27 08.6
27 M	22 25 14	7 52 46	19 48 47	26 53 06	13 08.0	12 01.7	19 08.6	29 07.4	3 11.4	25 04.0	2 39.3	28 50.0	0 13.9	27 07.1
28 Tu	22 29 11	8 53 01	3♎51 32	10♎43 41	12 57.2	13 16.1	20 18.5	29 46.8	3 35.0	24 56.5	2 40.6	28 48.1	0 13.0	27 05.6
29 W	22 33 07	9 53 15	17 29 18	24 08 16	12 48.5	14 32.3	21 28.3	0♑26.1	3 58.6	24 49.0	2 41.9	28 46.4	0 12.1	27 04.2

Astro Data

	Dy Hr Mn
☽0S	2 23:57
♃⚻♅	5 3:58
♃⚹♆	14 9:31
♃□♄	15 11:39
♄⚻♆	16 20:43
☽0N	17 17:30
♄△♅	17 22:34
☿R	18 15:53
♅□♆	19 12:12
☽0S	30 10:27
♆R	1 6:32
♃☌♇	8 2:39
☿D	8 12:10
♀0N	12 11:25
☽0N	13 23:51

Planet Ingress

	Dy Hr Mn
☿ ♒	4 9:16
♄ ♐	12 18:46
♂ ♐	14 2:28
♀ ♓	17 14:22
♃ ♌R	18 2:04
☉ ♒	21 1:48
♅ ♋R	28 1:57
☿ ♑R	2 12:18
♀ ♈	11 7:46
☿ ♒	15 6:34
⚳ ♓	19 9:29
☉ ♓	19 16:05
♂ ♑	28 20:05
☽0S	26 21:36

Last Aspect / ☽ Ingress (January)

Last Aspect Dy Hr Mn		☽ Ingress Dy Hr Mn
1 15:45	♄ □	♍ 1 17:31
3 20:17	☿ △	♎ 3 21:44
6 2:43	♇ ⚹	♏ 6 6:00
8 16:48	♄ ☌	♐ 8 17:32
11 2:55	♇ △	♑ 11 6:33
13 18:54	♂ ⚹	♒ 13 19:19
16 3:17	♀ ☌	♓ 16 6:47
18 11:18	☉ ⚹	♈ 18 16:17
20 22:58	☉ □	♉ 20 23:11
23 2:15	♃ □	♊ 23 3:06
25 3:11	♃ ⚹	♋ 25 4:20
25 20:29	♀ △	♌ 27 4:06
29 2:23	♃ ☌	♍ 29 4:17
31 6:41	♅ ⚹	♎ 31 6:56

Last Aspect / ☽ Ingress (February)

Last Aspect Dy Hr Mn		☽ Ingress Dy Hr Mn
2 13:28	☿ □	♏ 2 13:33
4 23:32	♅ △	♐ 5 0:13
7 8:26	♃ △	♑ 7 13:08
10 0:47	♅ ☍	♒ 10 1:52
12 8:01	♇ ☍	♓ 12 12:52
14 21:20	☿ ⚹	♈ 14 21:48
17 3:20	♅ □	♉ 17 4:48
19 9:21	☉ □	♊ 19 9:50
21 8:16	♇ ⚹	♋ 21 12:50
23 12:29	♅ ☌	♌ 23 14:10
25 11:28	♂ △	♍ 25 15:05
27 16:01	♂ □	♎ 27 17:20
29 20:28	♅ □	♏ 29 22:45

☽ Phases & Eclipses

Dy Hr Mn	
4 22:41	☾ 13♎34
13 3:01	● 21♑54
20 22:58	☽ 29♈53
27 14:40	○ 6♌39
3 16:08	☾ 13♏49
11 21:38	● 22♒09
19 9:21	☽ 29♉43
26 1:42	○ 6♍27

Astro Data

1 January 1956
Julian Day # 20454
SVP 5♓52'10"
GC 26♐13.5 ⚴ 20♑45.6
Eris 7♈54.2 ⚵ 20♐57.8
⚷ 3♒52.8 ⚶ 24♎46.3
☽ Mean ☊ 16♐04.2

1 February 1956
Julian Day # 20485
SVP 5♓52'05"
GC 26♐13.6 ⚴ 2♒09.5
Eris 8♈01.5 ⚵ 1♑21.3
⚷ 6♒23.6 ⚶ 5♏04.4
☽ Mean ☊ 14♐25.7

March 1956 LONGITUDE

Day	Sid.Time	☉	0 hr ☽	Noon ☽	True ☊	☿	♀	♂	⚳	♃	♄	♅	♆	♇
1 Th	22 37 04	10♓53 26	0♏40 42	7♏06 48	12♐42.6	15♒50.1	22♈37.9	1♑05.4	4♓22.1	24♌41.7	2♐43.0	28♋44.6	0♏11.2	27♌02.7
2 F	22 41 00	11 53 37	13 26 57	19 41 36	12R 39.3	17 09.5	23 47.5	1 44.8	4 45.7	24R 34.4	2 44.1	28R 42.9	0R 10.3	27R 01.3
3 Sa	22 44 57	12 53 45	25 51 18	1♐56 39	12D 38.1	18 30.3	24 56.8	2 24.1	5 09.2	24 27.1	2 45.0	28 41.2	0 09.3	26 59.8
4 Su	22 48 53	13 53 53	7♐58 19	13 56 59	12R 37.9	19 52.6	26 06.0	3 03.4	5 32.8	24 20.0	2 45.8	28 39.6	0 08.3	26 58.4
5 M	22 52 50	14 53 58	19 53 20	25 48 07	12 37.7	21 16.3	27 15.1	3 42.8	5 56.3	24 13.0	2 46.6	28 38.0	0 07.3	26 57.0
6 Tu	22 56 46	15 54 02	1♑41 59	7♑35 38	12 36.3	22 41.4	28 24.0	4 22.1	6 19.8	24 06.0	2 47.2	28 36.5	0 06.3	26 55.6
7 W	23 00 43	16 54 05	13 29 43	19 24 50	12 32.7	24 07.7	29 32.8	5 01.4	6 43.3	23 59.2	2 47.7	28 35.0	0 05.2	26 54.2
8 Th	23 04 40	17 54 05	25 21 32	1♒20 21	12 26.5	25 35.4	0♉41.3	5 40.7	7 06.8	23 52.5	2 48.2	28 33.5	0 04.1	26 52.8
9 F	23 08 36	18 54 04	7♒21 44	13 26 03	12 17.4	27 04.3	1 49.8	6 20.0	7 30.2	23 45.8	2 48.5	28 32.1	0 03.0	26 51.4
10 Sa	23 12 33	19 54 02	19 33 37	25 44 40	12 05.9	28 34.5	2 58.0	6 59.2	7 53.7	23 39.3	2 48.7	28 30.7	0 01.9	26 50.1
11 Su	23 16 29	20 53 57	1♓59 22	8♓17 47	11 52.7	0♓05.9	4 06.1	7 38.5	8 17.1	23 33.0	2R 48.8	28 29.4	0 00.7	26 48.7
12 M	23 20 26	21 53 50	14 39 58	21 05 49	11 39.1	1 38.5	5 14.0	8 17.7	8 40.5	23 26.7	2 48.8	28 28.2	29♎59.5	26 47.4
13 Tu	23 24 22	22 53 42	27 35 15	4♈08 06	11 26.2	3 12.4	6 21.7	8 57.0	9 03.9	23 20.6	2 48.7	28 26.9	29 58.3	26 46.1
14 W	23 28 19	23 53 31	10♈44 11	17 23 16	11 15.3	4 47.5	7 29.2	9 36.2	9 27.2	23 14.6	2 48.6	28 25.8	29 57.1	26 44.7
15 Th	23 32 15	24 53 19	24 05 08	0♉49 35	11 07.1	6 23.8	8 36.5	10 15.4	9 50.6	23 08.7	2 48.3	28 24.6	29 55.8	26 43.5
16 F	23 36 12	25 53 04	7♉36 26	14 25 29	11 01.9	8 01.3	9 43.6	10 54.5	10 13.9	23 03.0	2 47.9	28 23.6	29 54.5	26 42.2
17 Sa	23 40 09	26 52 47	21 16 39	28 09 47	10D 59.4	9 40.0	10 50.6	11 33.7	10 37.2	22 57.5	2 47.4	28 22.6	29 53.2	26 40.9
18 Su	23 44 05	27 52 28	5♊04 52	12♊01 50	10 58.9	11 19.9	11 57.3	12 12.9	11 00.4	22 52.1	2 46.8	28 21.6	29 51.9	26 39.7
19 M	23 48 02	28 52 06	19 00 39	26 01 18	10R 59.1	13 01.1	13 03.7	12 52.0	11 23.6	22 46.8	2 46.1	28 20.7	29 50.6	26 38.4
20 Tu	23 51 58	29 51 43	3♋03 44	10♋07 51	10 58.8	14 43.6	14 10.0	13 31.1	11 46.8	22 41.7	2 45.3	28 19.8	29 49.2	26 37.2
21 W	23 55 55	0♈51 17	17 13 33	24 20 38	10 56.8	16 27.3	15 16.0	14 10.2	12 10.0	22 36.8	2 44.4	28 19.0	29 47.9	26 36.0
22 Th	23 59 51	1 50 48	1♌28 49	8♌37 45	10 52.3	18 12.2	16 21.8	14 49.2	12 33.1	22 32.0	2 43.4	28 18.2	29 46.5	26 34.8
23 F	0 03 48	2 50 17	15 46 59	22 56 00	10 45.2	19 58.5	17 27.3	15 28.3	12 56.2	22 27.3	2 42.4	28 17.5	29 45.1	26 33.7
24 Sa	0 07 44	3 49 44	0♍04 14	7♍11 02	10 35.8	21 46.0	18 32.6	16 07.3	13 19.3	22 22.9	2 41.2	28 16.8	29 43.6	26 32.5
25 Su	0 11 41	4 49 09	14 15 43	21 17 39	10 25.2	23 34.9	19 37.6	16 46.4	13 42.4	22 18.6	2 39.9	28 16.2	29 42.2	26 31.4
26 M	0 15 37	5 48 31	28 16 11	5♎10 45	10 14.5	25 25.0	20 42.3	17 25.3	14 05.4	22 14.5	2 38.5	28 15.7	29 40.7	26 30.3
27 Tu	0 19 34	6 47 52	12♎00 50	18 46 04	10 04.8	27 16.5	21 46.8	18 04.3	14 28.3	22 10.5	2 37.0	28 15.2	29 39.3	26 29.2
28 W	0 23 31	7 47 11	25 26 08	2♏00 54	9 56.9	29 09.3	22 51.0	18 43.3	14 51.3	22 06.7	2 35.5	28 14.7	29 37.8	26 28.2
29 Th	0 27 27	8 46 27	8♏30 18	14 54 26	9 51.6	1♈03.5	23 54.9	19 22.2	15 14.2	22 03.1	2 33.8	28 14.3	29 36.3	26 27.1
30 F	0 31 24	9 45 42	21 13 28	27 27 42	9 48.7	2 59.0	24 58.5	20 01.2	15 37.0	21 59.7	2 32.1	28 14.0	29 34.8	26 26.1
31 Sa	0 35 20	10 44 55	3♐37 31	9♐43 23	9D 47.9	4 55.7	26 01.8	20 40.1	15 59.9	21 56.4	2 30.2	28 13.7	29 33.3	26 25.1

April 1956 LONGITUDE

Day	Sid.Time	☉	0 hr ☽	Noon ☽	True ☊	☿	♀	♂	⚳	♃	♄	♅	♆	♇
1 Su	0 39 17	11♈44 06	15♐45 50	21♐45 25	9♐48.4	6♈53.8	27♉04.8	21♑18.9	16♓22.7	21♌53.3	2♐28.3	28♋13.4	29♎31.7	26♌24.1
2 M	0 43 13	12 43 16	27 42 46	3♑38 33	9R 49.3	8 53.1	28 07.5	21 57.8	16 45.4	21R 50.4	2R 26.3	28R 13.2	29R 30.2	26R 23.2
3 Tu	0 47 10	13 42 24	9♑33 24	15 27 59	9 49.7	10 53.6	29 09.9	22 36.6	17 08.1	21 47.7	2 24.2	28 13.1	29 28.6	26 22.2
4 W	0 51 06	14 41 29	21 23 00	27 19 05	9 48.6	12 55.2	0♊11.9	23 15.4	17 30.8	21 45.2	2 22.0	28D 13.0	29 27.1	26 21.3
5 Th	0 55 03	15 40 33	3♒16 52	9♒16 58	9 45.7	14 57.9	1 13.6	23 54.2	17 53.4	21 42.8	2 19.7	28 13.0	29 25.5	26 20.4
6 F	0 59 00	16 39 36	15 19 56	21 26 16	9 40.6	17 01.4	2 14.9	24 32.9	18 16.0	21 40.6	2 17.3	28 13.0	29 23.9	26 19.6
7 Sa	1 02 56	17 38 36	27 36 25	3♓50 46	9 33.5	19 05.8	3 15.9	25 11.6	18 38.6	21 38.7	2 14.8	28 13.1	29 22.3	26 18.7
8 Su	1 06 53	18 37 34	10♓09 35	16 33 05	9 25.1	21 10.8	4 16.5	25 50.3	19 01.1	21 36.9	2 12.3	28 13.2	29 20.7	26 17.9
9 M	1 10 49	19 36 31	23 01 22	29 34 27	9 16.1	23 16.3	5 16.7	26 28.9	19 23.5	21 35.2	2 09.7	28 13.4	29 19.1	26 17.1
10 Tu	1 14 46	20 35 26	6♈12 14	12♈54 34	9 07.6	25 22.0	6 16.5	27 07.5	19 45.9	21 33.8	2 07.0	28 13.7	29 17.5	26 16.4
11 W	1 18 42	21 34 19	19 41 09	26 31 40	9 00.4	27 27.7	7 15.9	27 46.0	20 08.3	21 32.6	2 04.2	28 14.0	29 15.9	26 15.6
12 Th	1 22 39	22 33 09	3♉25 42	10♉22 49	8 55.2	29 33.1	8 14.9	28 24.5	20 30.6	21 31.5	2 01.3	28 14.3	29 14.2	26 14.9
13 F	1 26 35	23 31 58	17 22 34	24 24 29	8 52.2	1♉37.9	9 13.5	29 02.9	20 52.8	21 30.7	1 58.4	28 14.7	29 12.6	26 14.2
14 Sa	1 30 32	24 30 45	1♊28 05	8♊32 57	8D 51.3	3 41.9	10 11.5	29 41.4	21 15.0	21 30.0	1 55.3	28 15.2	29 11.0	26 13.6
15 Su	1 34 29	25 29 29	15 38 41	22 44 55	8 51.9	5 44.6	11 09.2	0♒19.7	21 37.1	21 29.5	1 52.2	28 15.7	29 09.4	26 12.9
16 M	1 38 25	26 28 11	29 51 20	6♋57 40	8 53.2	7 45.8	12 06.3	0 58.0	21 59.2	21 29.2	1 49.1	28 16.3	29 07.7	26 12.3
17 Tu	1 42 22	27 26 51	14♋03 39	21 09 06	8R 54.2	9 45.1	13 02.9	1 36.3	22 21.3	21D 29.1	1 45.8	28 16.9	29 06.1	26 11.7
18 W	1 46 18	28 25 29	28 13 47	5♌17 32	8 54.1	11 42.1	13 59.0	2 14.5	22 43.2	21 29.2	1 42.5	28 17.6	29 04.4	26 11.2
19 Th	1 50 15	29 24 04	12♌20 08	19 21 24	8 52.5	13 36.6	14 54.5	2 52.7	23 05.1	21 29.5	1 39.2	28 18.3	29 02.8	26 10.6
20 F	1 54 11	0♉22 37	26 21 07	3♍19 01	8 49.1	15 28.2	15 49.5	3 30.8	23 27.0	21 30.0	1 35.7	28 19.1	29 01.2	26 10.1
21 Sa	1 58 08	1 21 08	10♍14 52	17 08 23	8 44.3	17 16.7	16 43.9	4 08.9	23 48.8	21 30.6	1 32.2	28 19.9	28 59.5	26 09.7
22 Su	2 02 04	2 19 37	23 59 18	0♎47 20	8 38.6	19 01.9	17 37.7	4 46.9	24 10.5	21 31.4	1 28.7	28 20.8	28 57.9	26 09.2
23 M	2 06 01	3 18 04	7♎32 13	14 13 40	8 32.7	20 43.4	18 30.9	5 24.9	24 32.1	21 32.4	1 25.0	28 21.8	28 56.2	26 08.8
24 Tu	2 09 58	4 16 29	20 51 30	27 25 31	8 27.5	22 21.1	19 23.4	6 02.8	24 53.7	21 33.6	1 21.4	28 22.8	28 54.6	26 08.4
25 W	2 13 54	5 14 52	3♏55 36	10♏21 39	8 23.3	23 54.9	20 15.2	6 40.6	25 15.3	21 35.0	1 17.6	28 23.8	28 53.0	26 08.0
26 Th	2 17 51	6 13 13	16 43 41	23 01 44	8 20.7	25 24.5	21 06.4	7 18.4	25 36.7	21 36.6	1 13.8	28 24.9	28 51.4	26 07.7
27 F	2 21 47	7 11 32	29 15 56	5♐26 28	8D 19.7	26 49.9	21 56.8	7 56.2	25 58.1	21 38.3	1 10.0	28 26.0	28 49.7	26 07.4
28 Sa	2 25 44	8 09 50	11♐33 37	17 37 40	8 20.0	28 10.9	22 46.5	8 33.9	26 19.5	21 40.2	1 06.1	28 27.2	28 48.1	26 07.1
29 Su	2 29 40	9 08 06	23 39 00	29 38 03	8 21.3	29 27.4	23 35.4	9 11.5	26 40.7	21 42.3	1 02.1	28 28.5	28 46.5	26 06.8
30 M	2 33 37	10 06 21	5♑35 17	11♑31 13	8 23.0	0♊39.3	24 23.6	9 49.0	27 01.9	21 44.6	0 58.2	28 29.8	28 44.9	26 06.6

Astro Data (Dy Hr Mn)

	Dy Hr Mn
♄ R	12 3:29
☽ 0N	12 7:02
☉ 0N	20 15:20
☽ 0S	25 7:00
☿ 0N	30 23:26
♅ D	5 11:22
☽ 0N	8 15:09
♃ D	17 12:59
☽ 0S	21 13:42

Planet Ingress (Dy Hr Mn)

		Dy Hr Mn
♀	♉	7 21:31
☿	♓	11 10:27
♆	♎R	12 1:53
☉	♈	20 15:20
☿	♈	28 22:41
♀	♊	4 7:23
☿	♉	12 17:10
♂	♒	14 23:40
☉	♉	20 2:43
☿	♊	29 22:41

Last Aspect / ☽ Ingress (March)

Last Aspect Dy Hr Mn			☽ Ingress	Dy Hr Mn
3 5:35	♅	△	♐	3 8:09
5 15:16	♀	△	♑	5 20:32
8 6:26	♅	☍	♒	8 9:19
10 18:12	☿	☌	♓	10 20:11
13 1:36	♅	△	♈	13 4:26
15 10:25	♆	☍	♉	15 10:32
17 12:22	♅	⚹	♊	17 15:11
19 18:31	♆	△	♋	19 18:47
21 21:09	♆	□	♌	21 21:31
23 23:27	♆	⚹	♍	23 23:53
25 24:00	♅	⚹	♎	26 3:00
28 7:38	♆	☌	♏	28 8:18
30 13:30	♅	△	♐	30 16:56

Last Aspect / ☽ Ingress (April)

Last Aspect Dy Hr Mn			☽ Ingress	Dy Hr Mn
2 3:38	♆	⚹	♑	2 4:37
4 16:17	♆	□	♒	4 17:24
7 3:26	♆	△	♓	7 4:37
9 9:32	♅	△	♈	9 12:47
11 16:46	♆	☍	♉	11 18:03
13 20:16	♂	△	♊	13 21:30
15 22:48	♆	△	♋	16 0:15
18 1:27	♆	□	♌	18 3:00
20 4:36	♆	⚹	♍	20 6:17
22 7:41	♅	⚹	♎	22 10:36
24 14:43	♆	☌	♏	24 16:44
26 22:22	♅	△	♐	27 1:25
29 10:17	♆	⚹	♑	29 12:44

☽ Phases & Eclipses (Dy Hr Mn)

Dy Hr Mn		
4 11:53	☾	13♐54
12 13:37	●	21♓58
19 17:14	☽	29♊05
26 13:11	○	5♎51
3 8:06	☾	13♑33
11 2:39	●	21♈11
17 23:28	☽	27♋55
25 1:41	○	4♏50

Astro Data

1 March 1956
Julian Day # 20514
SVP 5♓52'01"
GC 26♐13.6 ⚵ 12♒18.7
Eris 8♈16.7 ✱ 10♑08.4
⚷ 8♒39.6 ⚶ 10♏40.6
☽ Mean ☊ 12♐53.5

1 April 1956
Julian Day # 20545
SVP 5♓51'58"
GC 26♐13.7 ⚵ 22♒03.4
Eris 8♈37.6 ✱ 17♑39.5
⚷ 10♒34.5 ⚶ 9♏57.0R
☽ Mean ☊ 11♐15.0

LONGITUDE — May 1956

Day	Sid.Time	☉	0 hr ☽	Noon ☽	True ☊	☿	♀	♂	⚳	♃	♄	♅	♆	♇
1 Tu	2 37 33	11♉04 34	17♑26 24	23♑21 24	8♐24.7	1♊46.6	25♊10.9	10♒26.5	27♓23.1	21♌47.0	0♐54.1	28♋31.1	28♎43.3	26♌06.4
2 W	2 41 30	12 02 45	29 16 49	5♒13 15	8R 25.7	2 49.2	25 57.3	11 04.0	27 44.1	21 49.7	0R 50.0	28 32.5	28R 41.7	26R 06.3
3 Th	2 45 27	13 00 55	11♒11 20	17 11 39	8 25.9	3 47.0	26 42.9	11 41.3	28 05.1	21 52.5	0 45.9	28 34.0	28 40.1	26 06.1
4 F	2 49 23	13 59 03	23 14 50	29 21 24	8 24.9	4 40.0	27 27.6	12 18.6	28 26.0	21 55.4	0 41.8	28 35.5	28 38.6	26 06.0
5 Sa	2 53 20	14 57 11	5♓31 57	11♓46 56	8 22.9	5 28.0	28 11.3	12 55.8	28 46.8	21 58.6	0 37.6	28 37.0	28 37.0	26 05.9
6 Su	2 57 16	15 55 16	18 06 47	24 31 53	8 20.2	6 11.0	28 54.0	13 32.9	29 07.6	22 01.9	0 33.3	28 38.6	28 35.4	26 05.9
7 M	3 01 13	16 53 20	1♈02 30	7♈38 48	8 17.1	6 49.0	29 35.7	14 09.9	29 28.2	22 05.4	0 29.1	28 40.2	28 33.9	26D 05.8
8 Tu	3 05 09	17 51 23	14 20 52	21 08 38	8 14.0	7 22.0	0♋16.3	14 46.8	29 48.8	22 09.0	0 24.8	28 41.9	28 32.4	26 05.8
9 W	3 09 06	18 49 24	28 01 56	5♉00 29	8 11.5	7 49.8	0 55.9	15 23.6	0♈09.3	22 12.8	0 20.4	28 43.7	28 30.8	26 05.9
10 Th	3 13 02	19 47 24	12♉03 52	19 11 34	8 09.8	8 12.5	1 34.3	16 00.3	0 29.7	22 16.8	0 16.1	28 45.4	28 29.3	26 05.9
11 F	3 16 59	20 45 22	26 22 58	3♊37 23	8D 09.1	8 30.1	2 11.5	16 37.0	0 50.1	22 21.0	0 11.7	28 47.3	28 27.8	26 06.0
12 Sa	3 20 56	21 43 19	10♊54 05	18 12 18	8 09.2	8 42.6	2 47.4	17 13.5	1 10.3	22 25.3	0 07.3	28 49.2	28 26.4	26 06.2
13 Su	3 24 52	22 41 14	25 31 15	2♋50 12	8 10.0	8 50.1	3 22.1	17 49.9	1 30.4	22 29.8	0 02.9	28 51.1	28 24.9	26 06.3
14 M	3 28 49	23 39 08	10♋08 27	17 25 21	8 11.1	8R 52.6	3 55.4	18 26.2	1 50.5	22 34.4	29♏58.5	28 53.0	28 23.4	26 06.5
15 Tu	3 32 45	24 36 59	24 40 19	1♌52 51	8 12.1	8 50.2	4 27.3	19 02.4	2 10.5	22 39.2	29 54.0	28 55.1	28 22.0	26 06.7
16 W	3 36 42	25 34 49	9♌02 34	16 09 06	8R 12.8	8 43.2	4 57.8	19 38.5	2 30.3	22 44.2	29 49.6	28 57.1	28 20.6	26 07.0
17 Th	3 40 38	26 32 37	23 12 14	0♍11 44	8 12.9	8 31.6	5 26.8	20 14.5	2 50.1	22 49.3	29 45.1	28 59.2	28 19.2	26 07.2
18 F	3 44 35	27 30 23	7♍07 31	13 59 29	8 12.5	8 15.9	5 54.2	20 50.4	3 09.7	22 54.5	29 40.6	29 01.4	28 17.8	26 07.5
19 Sa	3 48 31	28 28 08	20 47 38	27 31 57	8 11.6	7 56.3	6 20.0	21 26.1	3 29.3	23 00.0	29 36.2	29 03.5	28 16.4	26 07.9
20 Su	3 52 28	29 25 50	4♎12 29	10♎49 16	8 10.6	7 33.1	6 44.1	22 01.7	3 48.8	23 05.5	29 31.7	29 05.8	28 15.1	26 08.2
21 M	3 56 25	0♊23 32	17 22 22	23 51 54	8 09.6	7 06.8	7 06.4	22 37.2	4 08.1	23 11.2	29 27.2	29 08.0	28 13.7	26 08.6
22 Tu	4 00 21	1 21 12	0♏17 55	6♏40 32	8 08.7	6 37.9	7 26.9	23 12.6	4 27.4	23 17.1	29 22.7	29 10.3	28 12.4	26 09.0
23 W	4 04 18	2 18 50	12 59 52	19 16 01	8 08.1	6 06.8	7 45.6	23 47.9	4 46.6	23 23.1	29 18.3	29 12.7	28 11.1	26 09.4
24 Th	4 08 14	3 16 27	25 29 08	1♐39 22	8D 07.8	5 34.2	8 02.4	24 23.0	5 05.6	23 29.2	29 13.8	29 15.1	28 09.8	26 09.9
25 F	4 12 11	4 14 04	7♐46 52	13 51 51	8 07.8	5 00.6	8 17.1	24 57.9	5 24.5	23 35.5	29 09.4	29 17.5	28 08.6	26 10.4
26 Sa	4 16 07	5 11 38	19 54 31	25 55 08	8 08.0	4 26.5	8 29.8	25 32.8	5 43.4	23 41.9	29 04.9	29 20.0	28 07.3	26 10.9
27 Su	4 20 04	6 09 12	1♑53 57	7♑51 16	8 08.2	3 52.7	8 40.5	26 07.5	6 02.1	23 48.5	29 00.5	29 22.5	28 06.1	26 11.5
28 M	4 24 00	7 06 45	13 47 27	19 42 51	8 08.4	3 19.5	8 49.0	26 42.0	6 20.7	23 55.2	28 56.1	29 25.0	28 04.9	26 12.1
29 Tu	4 27 57	8 04 17	25 37 52	1♒32 56	8R 08.4	2 47.8	8 55.2	27 16.4	6 39.2	24 02.0	28 51.7	29 27.6	28 03.7	26 12.7
30 W	4 31 54	9 01 48	7♒28 32	13 25 08	8 08.4	2 17.9	8 59.3	27 50.6	6 57.6	24 09.0	28 47.3	29 30.2	28 02.6	26 13.3
31 Th	4 35 50	9 59 18	19 23 16	25 23 27	8 08.3	1 50.3	9R 01.0	28 24.7	7 15.8	24 16.1	28 43.0	29 32.9	28 01.5	26 14.0

LONGITUDE — June 1956

Day	Sid.Time	☉	0 hr ☽	Noon ☽	True ☊	☿	♀	♂	⚳	♃	♄	♅	♆	♇
1 F	4 39 47	10♊56 47	1♓26 14	7♓32 11	8♐08.2	1♊25.5	9♋00.4	28♒58.6	7♈33.9	24♌23.3	28♏38.6	29♋35.6	28♎00.4	26♌14.7
2 Sa	4 43 43	11 54 15	13 41 49	19 55 42	8D 08.3	1R 04.0	8R 57.5	29 32.3	7 51.9	24 30.7	28R 34.3	29 38.3	27R 59.3	26 15.4
3 Su	4 47 40	12 51 43	26 14 20	2♈38 12	8 08.5	0 45.9	8 52.2	0♓05.8	8 09.8	24 38.1	28 30.0	29 41.0	27 58.2	26 16.1
4 M	4 51 36	13 49 10	9♈07 43	15 43 13	8 08.9	0 31.7	8 44.5	0 39.1	8 27.6	24 45.8	28 25.8	29 43.8	27 57.2	26 16.9
5 Tu	4 55 33	14 46 36	22 24 59	29 13 11	8 09.5	0 21.6	8 34.4	1 12.2	8 45.2	24 53.5	28 21.6	29 46.6	27 56.2	26 17.7
6 W	4 59 29	15 44 02	6♉07 51	13♉08 52	8 10.1	0D 15.6	8 21.9	1 45.2	9 02.7	25 01.3	28 17.4	29 49.5	27 55.2	26 18.5
7 Th	5 03 26	16 41 27	20 16 00	27 28 51	8R 10.5	0 14.1	8 07.0	2 17.9	9 20.0	25 09.3	28 13.3	29 52.4	27 54.2	26 19.4
8 F	5 07 23	17 38 52	4♊46 50	12♊09 15	8 10.6	0 16.9	7 49.8	2 50.4	9 37.2	25 17.4	28 09.2	29 55.3	27 53.3	26 20.3
9 Sa	5 11 19	18 36 15	19 35 15	27 03 53	8 10.3	0 24.3	7 30.3	3 22.6	9 54.3	25 25.6	28 05.1	29 58.3	27 52.4	26 21.2
10 Su	5 15 16	19 33 38	4♋34 05	12♋04 47	8 09.4	0 36.2	7 08.5	3 54.7	10 11.2	25 34.0	28 01.1	0♌01.3	27 51.5	26 22.1
11 M	5 19 12	20 31 00	19 34 54	27 03 23	8 08.1	0 52.6	6 44.6	4 26.5	10 28.0	25 42.4	27 57.1	0 04.3	27 50.7	26 23.1
12 Tu	5 23 09	21 28 21	4♌29 15	11♌51 40	8 06.6	1 13.5	6 18.6	4 58.1	10 44.6	25 51.0	27 53.2	0 07.3	27 49.8	26 24.1
13 W	5 27 05	22 25 41	19 09 52	26 23 17	8 05.2	1 38.9	5 50.6	5 29.4	11 01.1	25 59.7	27 49.3	0 10.4	27 49.0	26 25.1
14 Th	5 31 02	23 23 00	3♍31 28	10♍34 08	8D 04.2	2 08.6	5 20.8	6 00.5	11 17.4	26 08.4	27 45.5	0 13.5	27 48.3	26 26.1
15 F	5 34 58	24 20 18	17 31 07	24 22 25	8 03.8	2 42.7	4 49.3	6 31.3	11 33.6	26 17.3	27 41.7	0 16.6	27 47.5	26 27.1
16 Sa	5 38 55	25 17 35	1♎08 07	7♎48 22	8 04.2	3 21.0	4 16.3	7 01.8	11 49.6	26 26.3	27 38.0	0 19.8	27 46.8	26 28.2
17 Su	5 42 52	26 14 51	14 23 26	20 53 36	8 05.2	4 03.5	3 41.9	7 32.1	12 05.4	26 35.4	27 34.4	0 23.0	27 46.1	26 29.3
18 M	5 46 48	27 12 07	27 19 11	3♏40 33	8 06.6	4 50.2	3 06.4	8 02.2	12 21.1	26 44.6	27 30.8	0 26.2	27 45.5	26 30.5
19 Tu	5 50 45	28 09 22	9♏58 02	16 12 02	8 08.0	5 40.9	2 30.1	8 31.9	12 36.6	26 53.9	27 27.2	0 29.4	27 44.8	26 31.6
20 W	5 54 41	29 06 36	22 22 51	28 30 51	8R 09.0	6 35.5	1 53.0	9 01.4	12 52.0	27 03.3	27 23.8	0 32.7	27 44.2	26 32.8
21 Th	5 58 38	0♋03 49	4♐36 21	10♐39 38	8 09.2	7 34.1	1 15.6	9 30.5	13 07.2	27 12.8	27 20.4	0 35.9	27 43.7	26 34.0
22 F	6 02 34	1 01 03	16 41 00	22 40 44	8 08.5	8 36.5	0 37.9	9 59.4	13 22.2	27 22.4	27 17.0	0 39.3	27 43.1	26 35.2
23 Sa	6 06 31	1 58 15	28 39 04	4♑36 16	8 06.6	9 42.8	0 00.3	10 28.0	13 37.0	27 32.1	27 13.8	0 42.6	27 42.6	26 36.5
24 Su	6 10 27	2 55 28	10♑32 34	16 28 14	8 03.5	10 52.7	29♊22.9	10 56.2	13 51.7	27 41.9	27 10.5	0 45.9	27 42.1	26 37.7
25 M	6 14 24	3 52 40	22 23 29	28 18 37	7 59.6	12 06.4	28 46.2	11 24.1	14 06.1	27 51.7	27 07.4	0 49.3	27 41.7	26 39.0
26 Tu	6 18 21	4 49 52	4♒13 54	10♒09 38	7 55.1	13 23.7	28 10.2	11 51.7	14 20.4	28 01.7	27 04.3	0 52.7	27 41.3	26 40.3
27 W	6 22 17	5 47 04	16 06 07	22 03 42	7 50.6	14 44.6	27 35.1	12 18.9	14 34.5	28 11.7	27 01.3	0 56.1	27 40.9	26 41.7
28 Th	6 26 14	6 44 16	28 02 46	4♓03 43	7 46.6	16 09.1	27 01.3	12 45.8	14 48.5	28 21.9	26 58.4	0 59.5	27 40.5	26 43.0
29 F	6 30 10	7 41 27	10♓06 58	16 12 58	7 43.6	17 37.1	26 29.0	13 12.3	15 02.2	28 32.1	26 55.6	1 02.9	27 40.2	26 44.4
30 Sa	6 34 07	8 38 39	22 22 12	28 35 09	7D 41.8	19 08.6	25 58.2	13 38.4	15 15.7	28 42.4	26 52.8	1 06.4	27 39.9	26 45.8

Astro Data	Dy Hr Mn
♅□♆	5 11:52
☽0N	5 23:42
♇ D	7 19:59
☿ R	14 12:12
☽0S	18 18:50
♄△♅	24 7:37
♀ R	31 18:04
☽0N	2 8:01
☿ D	7 8:33
♄⚺♆	13 14:23
☽0S	15 0:39
♃☌♇	16 17:45
♃□♄	22 2:03
♃⚹♆	24 12:39
☽0N	29 15:35

Planet Ingress		Dy Hr Mn
♀	♋	8 2:17
⚳	♈	9 1:05
♄	♏R	14 3:45
☉	♊	21 2:13
♂	♓	3 7:51
♅	♌	10 1:48
☉	♋	21 10:24
♀	♊R	23 12:10

Last Aspect Dy Hr Mn		☽ Ingress Dy Hr Mn
1 22:51	♆ □	♒ 2 1:27
4 10:36	♆ △	♓ 4 13:15
6 20:32	♀ □	♈ 6 22:05
9 1:11	♅ □	♉ 9 3:24
11 3:59	♅ ⚹	♊ 11 6:00
13 4:45	♆ △	♋ 13 7:21
15 8:43	♄ △	♌ 15 8:52
17 11:14	♄ □	♍ 17 11:40
19 15:41	♄ ⚹	♎ 19 16:25
21 21:51	♅ □	♏ 21 23:26
24 7:18	♄ ☌	♐ 24 8:46
26 16:24	♆ ⚹	♑ 26 20:11
29 7:45	♅ ☍	♒ 29 8:52
31 18:34	♄ □	♓ 31 21:09

Last Aspect Dy Hr Mn		☽ Ingress Dy Hr Mn
3 6:28	♅ △	♈ 3 7:05
5 12:59	♅ □	♉ 5 13:22
7 15:58	♅ ⚹	♊ 7 16:09
9 13:18	♆ △	♋ 9 16:42
11 13:26	♄ △	♌ 11 16:45
13 14:23	♆ ⚹	♍ 13 18:03
15 17:51	♄ ⚹	♎ 15 21:58
18 0:50	♆ ☌	♏ 18 5:03
20 9:49	♄ ☌	♐ 20 14:55
22 22:07	♆ ⚹	♑ 23 2:43
25 10:45	♆ □	♒ 25 15:26
28 0:28	♃ ☍	♓ 28 3:54
30 8:44	♄ △	♈ 30 14:43

☽ Phases & Eclipses Dy Hr Mn	
3 2:55	☾ 12♒39
10 13:04	● 19♉50
17 5:15	☽ 26♌16
24 15:26	○ 3♐25
24 15:31	P 0.965
1 19:13	☾ 11♓14
8 21:29	● 18♊02
8 21:20:09	T 04'44"
15 11:56	☽ 24♍20
23 6:14	○ 1♑44

Astro Data

1 May 1956
Julian Day # 20575
SVP 5♓51'55"
GC 26♐13.8 ⚴ 29♒41.3
Eris 8♈57.5 ⚵ 21♑52.5
⚷ 11♒35.8 ⚶ 3♏21.7R
☽ Mean ☊ 9♐39.7

1 June 1956
Julian Day # 20606
SVP 5♓51'51"
GC 26♐13.8 ⚴ 4♓38.0
Eris 9♈12.7 ⚵ 21♑30.4R
⚷ 11♒35.8R ⚶ 28♎15.6R
☽ Mean ☊ 8♐01.2

July 1956 — LONGITUDE

Day	Sid.Time	☉	0 hr ☽	Noon ☽	True ☊	☿	♀	♂	⚷	♃	♄	♅	♆	♇
1 Su	6 38 03	9♋35 51	4♈52 18	11♈14 10	7♐41.3	20♊43.5	25♊29.1	14♓04.1	15♈29.0	28♌52.8	26♏50.1	1♌09.9	27♎39.6	26♌47.2
2 M	6 42 00	10 33 04	17 41 14	24 13 55	7 42.0	22 21.8	25R 01.9	14 29.4	15 42.2	29 03.3	26R 47.5	1 13.4	27R 39.4	26 48.6
3 Tu	6 45 56	11 30 16	0♉52 39	7♉37 44	7 43.3	24 03.4	24 36.8	14 54.4	15 55.1	29 13.8	26 44.9	1 16.9	27 39.2	26 50.1
4 W	6 49 53	12 27 29	14 29 27	21 27 54	7 44.7	25 48.2	24 13.8	15 18.8	16 07.8	29 24.4	26 42.5	1 20.4	27 39.0	26 51.5
5 Th	6 53 50	13 24 42	28 33 04	5♊44 48	7R 45.5	27 36.1	23 53.0	15 42.9	16 20.3	29 35.2	26 40.1	1 24.0	27 38.9	26 53.0
6 F	6 57 46	14 21 56	13♊02 44	20 26 19	7 44.9	29 27.0	23 34.4	16 06.5	16 32.6	29 45.9	26 37.8	1 27.5	27 38.8	26 54.5
7 Sa	7 01 43	15 19 09	27 54 49	5♋27 19	7 42.7	1♋20.7	23 18.2	16 29.6	16 44.6	29 56.8	26 35.6	1 31.1	27 38.7	26 56.1
8 Su	7 05 39	16 16 23	13♋02 42	20 39 46	7 38.8	3 17.0	23 04.3	16 52.3	16 56.4	0♍07.7	26 33.5	1 34.7	27D 38.7	26 57.6
9 M	7 09 36	17 13 37	28 17 12	5♌53 42	7 33.6	5 15.9	22 52.8	17 14.4	17 08.0	0 18.8	26 31.4	1 38.3	27 38.7	26 59.2
10 Tu	7 13 32	18 10 51	13♌27 57	20 58 45	7 27.8	7 16.9	22 43.7	17 36.1	17 19.4	0 29.8	26 29.5	1 41.9	27 38.7	27 00.8
11 W	7 17 29	19 08 05	28 25 02	5♍45 53	7 22.2	9 19.9	22 36.9	17 57.3	17 30.5	0 41.0	26 27.6	1 45.5	27 38.7	27 02.4
12 Th	7 21 26	20 05 18	13♍00 37	20 08 44	7 17.6	11 24.6	22 32.5	18 17.9	17 41.4	0 52.2	26 25.9	1 49.1	27 38.8	27 04.0
13 F	7 25 22	21 02 32	27 09 56	4♎04 07	7 14.5	13 30.7	22D 30.4	18 38.0	17 52.1	1 03.5	26 24.2	1 52.8	27 39.0	27 05.6
14 Sa	7 29 19	21 59 46	10♎51 22	17 31 52	7D 13.2	15 37.8	22 30.7	18 57.6	18 02.5	1 14.8	26 22.6	1 56.4	27 39.1	27 07.3
15 Su	7 33 15	22 57 00	24 05 58	0♏34 04	7 13.4	17 45.8	22 33.2	19 16.7	18 12.6	1 26.2	26 21.1	2 00.0	27 39.3	27 08.9
16 M	7 37 12	23 54 14	6♏56 39	13 14 15	7 14.5	19 54.2	22 38.0	19 35.1	18 22.5	1 37.7	26 19.7	2 03.7	27 39.5	27 10.6
17 Tu	7 41 08	24 51 28	19 27 24	25 36 38	7R 15.7	22 02.8	22 45.0	19 53.1	18 32.2	1 49.2	26 18.4	2 07.4	27 39.8	27 12.3
18 W	7 45 05	25 48 43	1♐42 31	7♐45 33	7 16.2	24 11.3	22 54.1	20 10.4	18 41.6	2 00.8	26 17.2	2 11.0	27 40.0	27 14.0
19 Th	7 49 01	26 45 57	13 46 14	19 45 02	7 15.4	26 19.5	23 05.3	20 27.2	18 50.7	2 12.5	26 16.1	2 14.7	27 40.4	27 15.7
20 F	7 52 58	27 43 12	25 42 22	1♑38 38	7 12.5	28 27.0	23 18.6	20 43.3	18 59.5	2 24.2	26 15.0	2 18.4	27 40.7	27 17.5
21 Sa	7 56 55	28 40 28	7♑34 10	13 29 18	7 07.3	0♌33.8	23 33.8	20 58.8	19 08.1	2 35.9	26 14.1	2 22.1	27 41.1	27 19.2
22 Su	8 00 51	29 37 44	19 24 19	25 19 28	7 00.0	2 39.6	23 51.0	21 13.7	19 16.5	2 47.8	26 13.2	2 25.8	27 41.5	27 21.0
23 M	8 04 48	0♌35 00	1♒14 58	7♒11 03	6 50.9	4 44.3	24 10.0	21 28.0	19 24.5	2 59.6	26 12.5	2 29.4	27 41.9	27 22.7
24 Tu	8 08 44	1 32 17	13 07 54	19 05 44	6 40.8	6 47.7	24 30.8	21 41.6	19 32.3	3 11.5	26 11.9	2 33.1	27 42.4	27 24.5
25 W	8 12 41	2 29 35	25 04 44	1♓05 07	6 30.6	8 49.7	24 53.4	21 54.5	19 39.7	3 23.5	26 11.3	2 36.8	27 42.9	27 26.3
26 Th	8 16 37	3 26 54	7♓07 06	13 10 56	6 21.1	10 50.3	25 17.7	22 06.7	19 46.9	3 35.5	26 10.8	2 40.5	27 43.4	27 28.1
27 F	8 20 34	4 24 13	19 16 53	25 25 15	6 13.3	12 49.4	25 43.7	22 18.3	19 53.8	3 47.6	26 10.5	2 44.2	27 44.0	27 29.9
28 Sa	8 24 30	5 21 33	1♈36 23	7♈50 37	6 07.6	14 47.0	26 11.2	22 29.1	20 00.4	3 59.7	26 10.2	2 47.9	27 44.6	27 31.8
29 Su	8 28 27	6 18 55	14 08 22	20 30 02	6 04.3	16 42.9	26 40.2	22 39.2	20 06.7	4 11.9	26 10.0	2 51.6	27 45.2	27 33.6
30 M	8 32 23	7 16 17	26 56 02	3♉26 48	6D 03.0	18 37.3	27 10.7	22 48.5	20 12.7	4 24.1	26D 09.9	2 55.2	27 45.9	27 35.5
31 Tu	8 36 20	8 13 41	10♉02 47	16 44 20	6 03.2	20 30.0	27 42.6	22 57.1	20 18.4	4 36.3	26 10.0	2 58.9	27 46.6	27 37.3

August 1956 — LONGITUDE

Day	Sid.Time	☉	0 hr ☽	Noon ☽	True ☊	☿	♀	♂	⚷	♃	♄	♅	♆	♇
1 W	8 40 17	9♌11 06	23♉31 49	0♊25 29	6♐03.7	22♌21.1	28♊15.9	23♓05.0	20♈23.8	4♍48.6	26♏10.1	3♌02.6	27♎47.3	27♌39.2
2 Th	8 44 13	10 08 32	7♊25 32	14 31 58	6R 03.5	24 10.6	28 50.5	23 12.0	20 28.9	5 00.9	26 10.3	3 06.3	27 48.1	27 41.1
3 F	8 48 10	11 05 59	21 44 41	29 03 24	6 01.7	25 58.5	29 26.4	23 18.3	20 33.6	5 13.3	26 10.6	3 10.0	27 48.9	27 42.9
4 Sa	8 52 06	12 03 28	6♋27 34	13♋56 32	5 57.4	27 44.7	0♋03.4	23 23.7	20 38.0	5 25.7	26 11.0	3 13.6	27 49.7	27 44.8
5 Su	8 56 03	13 00 57	21 29 21	29 04 56	5 50.6	29 29.3	0 41.6	23 28.4	20 42.1	5 38.2	26 11.5	3 17.3	27 50.5	27 46.7
6 M	8 59 59	13 58 28	6♌42 03	14♌19 20	5 41.8	1♍12.4	1 21.0	23 32.2	20 45.8	5 50.7	26 12.2	3 20.9	27 51.4	27 48.7
7 Tu	9 03 56	14 56 00	21 55 25	29 28 56	5 31.9	2 53.8	2 01.4	23 35.2	20 49.2	6 03.2	26 12.9	3 24.6	27 52.3	27 50.6
8 W	9 07 53	15 53 32	6♍58 37	14♍23 21	5 22.1	4 33.7	2 42.8	23 37.4	20 52.3	6 15.7	26 13.7	3 28.2	27 53.2	27 52.5
9 Th	9 11 49	16 51 06	21 42 10	28 54 22	5 13.5	6 12.0	3 25.3	23 38.8	20 55.1	6 28.3	26 14.6	3 31.8	27 54.2	27 54.4
10 F	9 15 46	17 48 40	5♎59 27	12♎57 08	5 07.1	7 48.8	4 08.6	23R 39.4	20 57.4	6 40.9	26 15.6	3 35.4	27 55.2	27 56.3
11 Sa	9 19 42	18 46 15	19 47 20	26 30 12	5 03.0	9 23.9	4 52.9	23 39.1	20 59.5	6 53.6	26 16.7	3 39.0	27 56.2	27 58.3
12 Su	9 23 39	19 43 51	3♏05 59	9♏35 06	5D 01.2	10 57.5	5 38.1	23 38.0	21 01.2	7 06.2	26 17.8	3 42.6	27 57.3	28 00.2
13 M	9 27 35	20 41 29	15 58 02	22 15 23	5 00.8	12 29.6	6 24.2	23 36.1	21 02.5	7 19.0	26 19.1	3 46.2	27 58.4	28 02.2
14 Tu	9 31 32	21 39 07	28 27 44	4♐35 45	5R 01.0	14 00.1	7 11.1	23 33.5	21 03.5	7 31.7	26 20.5	3 49.8	27 59.5	28 04.1
15 W	9 35 28	22 36 46	10♐40 04	16 41 20	5 00.5	15 29.0	7 58.8	23 30.0	21 04.2	7 44.4	26 22.0	3 53.3	28 00.6	28 06.0
16 Th	9 39 25	23 34 26	22 40 11	28 37 11	4 58.4	16 56.3	8 47.2	23 25.7	21R 04.4	7 57.2	26 23.6	3 56.8	28 01.8	28 08.0
17 F	9 43 22	24 32 07	4♑32 54	10♑27 50	4 53.9	18 22.1	9 36.4	23 20.6	21 04.4	8 10.0	26 25.2	4 00.4	28 03.0	28 10.0
18 Sa	9 47 18	25 29 50	16 22 29	22 17 15	4 46.7	19 46.1	10 26.4	23 14.7	21 03.9	8 22.8	26 27.0	4 03.9	28 04.2	28 11.9
19 Su	9 51 15	26 27 33	28 12 29	4♒08 32	4 36.8	21 08.6	11 17.0	23 08.1	21 03.1	8 35.7	26 28.9	4 07.4	28 05.5	28 13.9
20 M	9 55 11	27 25 18	10♒05 39	16 04 04	4 24.6	22 29.3	12 08.3	23 00.8	21 02.0	8 48.5	26 30.8	4 10.8	28 06.8	28 15.8
21 Tu	9 59 08	28 23 04	22 04 44	28 05 34	4 11.2	23 48.4	13 00.2	22 52.6	21 00.5	9 01.4	26 32.8	4 14.3	28 08.1	28 17.8
22 W	10 03 04	29 20 52	4♓08 56	10♓14 13	3 57.5	25 05.6	13 52.8	22 43.8	20 58.6	9 14.3	26 35.0	4 17.7	28 09.4	28 19.7
23 Th	10 07 01	0♍18 41	16 21 29	22 30 53	3 44.7	26 21.0	14 46.0	22 34.3	20 56.3	9 27.2	26 37.2	4 21.1	28 10.8	28 21.7
24 F	10 10 57	1 16 31	28 42 31	4♈56 31	3 33.9	27 34.6	15 39.9	22 24.0	20 53.7	9 40.1	26 39.5	4 24.5	28 12.2	28 23.7
25 Sa	10 14 54	2 14 24	11♈13 02	17 32 16	3 25.7	28 46.2	16 34.2	22 13.1	20 50.7	9 53.0	26 41.9	4 27.9	28 13.6	28 25.6
26 Su	10 18 50	3 12 18	23 54 24	0♉19 42	3 20.4	29 55.7	17 29.2	22 01.6	20 47.3	10 06.0	26 44.4	4 31.3	28 15.0	28 27.6
27 M	10 22 47	4 10 13	6♉48 26	13 20 54	3 17.8	1♎03.2	18 24.6	21 49.5	20 43.6	10 18.9	26 47.0	4 34.6	28 16.5	28 29.5
28 Tu	10 26 44	5 08 11	19 57 24	26 38 16	3 17.0	2 08.4	19 20.7	21 36.7	20 39.5	10 31.9	26 49.7	4 37.9	28 18.0	28 31.5
29 W	10 30 40	6 06 11	3♊23 47	10♊14 13	3 16.9	3 11.3	20 17.2	21 23.5	20 35.0	10 44.9	26 52.5	4 41.2	28 19.5	28 33.4
30 Th	10 34 37	7 04 12	17 09 46	24 10 33	3 16.4	4 11.7	21 14.2	21 09.6	20 30.2	10 57.9	26 55.3	4 44.5	28 21.0	28 35.4
31 F	10 38 33	8 02 16	1♋16 36	8♋27 47	3 14.1	5 09.6	22 11.6	20 55.4	20 25.0	11 10.9	26 58.3	4 47.7	28 22.6	28 37.3

Astro Data

	Dy Hr Mn
♄□♇	2 5:08
♆ D	9 6:10
☽0S	12 8:42
♀ D	13 21:20
♃⚺♅	19 18:41
☽0N	26 22:20
♄ D	30 18:36
☽0S	8 18:51
♆✶♇	9 7:11
♂ R	10 16:18
⚷ R	16 19:01
☽0N	23 4:41
☿0S	24 3:52

Planet Ingress

	Dy Hr Mn
☿ ♋	6 19:02
♃ ♍	7 19:01
☿ ♌	21 5:35
☉ ♌	22 21:20
♀ ♋	4 9:49
☿ ♍	5 19:06
☉ ♍	23 4:15
☿ ♎	26 13:30

Last Aspect / ☽ Ingress

Last Aspect Dy Hr Mn		☽ Ingress Dy Hr Mn
2 20:51	♃ △	♉ 2 22:26
5 1:36	♃ □	♊ 5 2:26
7 3:08	♃ ✶	♋ 7 3:20
8 22:59	♆ □	♌ 9 2:42
10 22:45	♆ ✶	♍ 11 2:34
12 22:43	♄ ✶	♎ 13 4:54
15 6:34	♆ ☌	♏ 15 10:56
17 15:08	♇ □	♐ 17 20:38
20 3:59	♆ ✶	♑ 20 8:40
22 16:48	♆ □	♒ 22 21:28
25 5:16	♆ △	♓ 25 9:50
27 13:28	♄ △	♈ 27 20:54
30 1:32	♆ ☍	♉ 30 5:40

Last Aspect / ☽ Ingress

Last Aspect Dy Hr Mn		☽ Ingress Dy Hr Mn
1 7:11	♇ □	♊ 1 11:16
3 12:39	♀ ☌	♋ 3 13:32
5 10:02	♆ □	♌ 5 13:27
7 9:26	♆ ✶	♍ 7 12:50
9 7:32	♄ ✶	♎ 9 13:50
11 14:40	♇ ✶	♏ 11 18:20
13 23:12	♇ □	♐ 14 3:00
16 11:01	♇ △	♑ 16 14:47
18 23:45	♆ □	♒ 19 3:38
21 12:38	☉ ☍	♓ 21 15:47
23 20:16	☿ ☍	♈ 24 2:30
26 8:31	♇ △	♉ 26 11:23
28 15:22	♇ □	♊ 28 17:59
30 19:30	♇ ✶	♋ 30 21:51

☽ Phases & Eclipses

Dy Hr Mn		
1 8:41	☾	9♈28
8 4:38	●	15♋59
14 20:47	☽	22♎21
22 21:29	○	0♒00
30 19:31	☾	7♉34
6 11:25	●	13♌57
13 8:45	☽	20♏34
21 12:38	○	28♒25
29 4:13	☾	5♊47

Astro Data

1 July 1956
Julian Day # 20636
SVP 5♓51'46"
GC 26♐13.9 ⚳ 5♓11.2R
Eris 9♈18.9 ⚵ 16♑14.3R
⚷ 10♒38.3R ⚶ 0♏15.7
☽ Mean ☊ 6♐25.9

1 August 1956
Julian Day # 20667
SVP 5♓51'41"
GC 26♐14.0 ⚳ 0♓29.0R
Eris 9♈15.1R ⚵ 9♑26.1R
⚷ 9♒02.1R ⚶ 8♏22.4
☽ Mean ☊ 4♐47.4

LONGITUDE — September 1956

Day	Sid.Time	☉	0 hr ☽	Noon ☽	True ☊	☿	♀	♂	⚳	♃	♄	♅	♆	♇
1 Sa	10 42 30	9♍00 21	15♋43 50	23♋04 17	3♐09.3	6♎04.7	23♋09.6	20♓40.6	20♈19.4	11♍23.9	27♏01.3	4♌50.9	28♎24.2	28♌39.2
2 Su	10 46 26	9 58 29	0♌28 30	7♌55 41	3R 01.9	6 56.9	24 07.9	20R 25.5	20R 13.5	11 36.9	27 04.4	4 54.1	28 25.8	28 41.2
3 M	10 50 23	10 56 38	15 24 53	22 54 58	2 52.2	7 45.9	25 06.7	20 10.0	20 07.2	11 49.9	27 07.6	4 57.3	28 27.4	28 43.1
4 Tu	10 54 19	11 54 48	0♍24 46	7♍53 05	2 41.1	8 31.7	26 05.9	19 54.2	20 00.6	12 02.9	27 10.9	5 00.4	28 29.0	28 45.0
5 W	10 58 16	12 53 01	15 18 41	22 40 28	2 30.0	9 13.9	27 05.5	19 38.1	19 53.6	12 15.9	27 14.3	5 03.5	28 30.7	28 46.9
6 Th	11 02 13	13 51 15	29 57 26	7♎08 45	2 20.2	9 52.4	28 05.5	19 21.8	19 46.2	12 28.9	27 17.7	5 06.6	28 32.4	28 48.9
7 F	11 06 09	14 49 31	14♎13 46	21 12 03	2 12.5	10 26.7	29 05.9	19 05.4	19 38.5	12 41.9	27 21.3	5 09.7	28 34.1	28 50.8
8 Sa	11 10 06	15 47 49	28 03 21	4♏47 37	2 07.4	10 56.8	0♌06.6	18 48.8	19 30.5	12 54.9	27 24.9	5 12.7	28 35.9	28 52.7
9 Su	11 14 02	16 46 08	11♏24 58	17 55 39	2 04.9	11 22.2	1 07.7	18 32.2	19 22.1	13 07.9	27 28.6	5 15.7	28 37.6	28 54.5
10 M	11 17 59	17 44 28	24 20 06	0♐38 46	2D 04.1	11 42.7	2 09.1	18 15.6	19 13.5	13 20.9	27 32.4	5 18.7	28 39.4	28 56.4
11 Tu	11 21 55	18 42 51	6♐52 14	13 01 07	2R 04.3	11 57.9	3 10.9	17 59.0	19 04.5	13 33.9	27 36.2	5 21.6	28 41.2	28 58.3
12 W	11 25 52	19 41 15	19 06 04	25 07 45	2 04.3	12 07.4	4 13.0	17 42.6	18 55.1	13 46.9	27 40.2	5 24.5	28 43.0	29 00.2
13 Th	11 29 48	20 39 40	1♑06 50	7♑03 59	2 03.0	12R 11.1	5 15.4	17 26.2	18 45.5	13 59.9	27 44.2	5 27.4	28 44.9	29 02.0
14 F	11 33 45	21 38 07	12 59 50	18 55 00	1 59.6	12 08.5	6 18.2	17 10.1	18 35.6	14 12.8	27 48.3	5 30.2	28 46.7	29 03.9
15 Sa	11 37 42	22 36 36	24 50 03	0♒45 30	1 53.8	11 59.3	7 21.2	16 54.1	18 25.4	14 25.8	27 52.5	5 33.0	28 48.6	29 05.7
16 Su	11 41 38	23 35 06	6♒41 50	12 39 30	1 45.4	11 43.4	8 24.6	16 38.5	18 15.0	14 38.7	27 56.7	5 35.8	28 50.5	29 07.5
17 M	11 45 35	24 33 38	18 38 50	24 40 11	1 34.9	11 20.5	9 28.2	16 23.2	18 04.2	14 51.6	28 01.1	5 38.5	28 52.4	29 09.3
18 Tu	11 49 31	25 32 12	0♓43 48	6♓49 52	1 23.2	10 50.6	10 32.1	16 08.2	17 53.2	15 04.5	28 05.5	5 41.2	28 54.3	29 11.1
19 W	11 53 28	26 30 47	12 58 33	19 09 56	1 11.2	10 13.8	11 36.3	15 53.6	17 42.0	15 17.4	28 09.9	5 43.8	28 56.3	29 12.9
20 Th	11 57 24	27 29 25	25 24 07	1♈41 05	0 59.9	9 30.4	12 40.8	15 39.5	17 30.5	15 30.3	28 14.5	5 46.4	28 58.3	29 14.7
21 F	12 01 21	28 28 04	8♈00 53	14 23 28	0 50.5	8 40.6	13 45.5	15 25.8	17 18.8	15 43.1	28 19.1	5 49.0	29 00.2	29 16.4
22 Sa	12 05 17	29 26 46	20 48 49	27 16 57	0 43.5	7 45.3	14 50.5	15 12.6	17 06.8	15 55.9	28 23.8	5 51.6	29 02.2	29 18.2
23 Su	12 09 14	0♎25 29	3♉47 51	10♉21 32	0 39.2	6 45.2	15 55.8	15 00.0	16 54.7	16 08.7	28 28.5	5 54.1	29 04.2	29 19.9
24 M	12 13 10	1 24 15	16 58 02	23 37 26	0D 37.3	5 41.5	17 01.3	14 47.9	16 42.3	16 21.5	28 33.4	5 56.5	29 06.3	29 21.7
25 Tu	12 17 07	2 23 04	0♊19 48	7♊05 14	0 37.2	4 35.5	18 07.1	14 36.4	16 29.8	16 34.3	28 38.3	5 59.0	29 08.3	29 23.4
26 W	12 21 04	3 21 54	13 53 50	20 45 44	0R 38.0	3 28.9	19 13.1	14 25.5	16 17.1	16 47.0	28 43.2	6 01.4	29 10.3	29 25.1
27 Th	12 25 00	4 20 59	27 40 59	4♋39 38	0 38.5	2 23.2	20 19.3	14 15.2	16 04.2	16 59.7	28 48.3	6 03.7	29 12.4	29 26.7
28 F	12 28 57	5 19 42	11♋41 41	18 47 03	0 37.6	1 20.1	21 25.8	14 05.6	15 51.2	17 12.4	28 53.3	6 06.0	29 14.5	29 28.4
29 Sa	12 32 53	6 18 39	25 55 32	3♌06 53	0 34.8	0 21.5	22 32.5	13 56.8	15 38.1	17 25.1	28 58.5	6 08.3	29 16.6	29 30.1
30 Su	12 36 50	7 17 39	10♌20 41	17 36 26	0 29.8	29♍28.8	23 39.4	13 48.6	15 24.8	17 37.7	29 03.7	6 10.5	29 18.7	29 31.7

LONGITUDE — October 1956

Day	Sid.Time	☉	0 hr ☽	Noon ☽	True ☊	☿	♀	♂	⚳	♃	♄	♅	♆	♇
1 M	12 40 46	8♎16 41	24♌53 30	2♍11 10	0♐22.9	28♍43.6	24♌46.5	13♓41.1	15♈11.4	17♍50.3	29♏09.0	6♌12.7	29♎20.8	29♌33.3
2 Tu	12 44 43	9 15 45	9♍28 36	16 44 58	0R 14.9	28R 06.9	25 53.8	13R 34.4	14R 58.0	18 02.9	29 14.4	6 14.8	29 22.9	29 34.9
3 W	12 48 39	10 14 51	23 59 24	1♎11 02	0 06.7	27 39.8	27 01.3	13 28.4	14 44.4	18 15.4	29 19.8	6 16.9	29 25.0	29 36.5
4 Th	12 52 36	11 13 59	8♎19 04	15 22 48	29♏59.3	27 22.9	28 09.0	13 23.3	14 30.8	18 27.9	29 25.2	6 18.9	29 27.2	29 38.0
5 F	12 56 33	12 13 10	22 21 37	29 15 03	29 53.7	27D 16.6	29 16.9	13 18.9	14 17.2	18 40.4	29 30.7	6 20.9	29 29.3	29 39.6
6 Sa	13 00 29	13 12 22	6♏02 48	12♏44 39	29 50.1	27 20.8	0♍25.0	13 15.3	14 03.5	18 52.8	29 36.3	6 22.9	29 31.5	29 41.1
7 Su	13 04 26	14 11 36	19 20 34	25 50 39	29D 48.7	27 35.6	1 33.2	13 12.5	13 49.9	19 05.1	29 42.0	6 24.8	29 33.7	29 42.6
8 M	13 08 22	15 10 52	2♐15 08	8♐34 18	29 49.0	28 00.5	2 41.7	13 10.6	13 36.2	19 17.5	29 47.7	6 26.6	29 35.9	29 44.1
9 Tu	13 12 19	16 10 10	14 48 34	20 58 26	29 50.2	28 35.0	3 50.3	13D 09.4	13 22.6	19 29.8	29 53.4	6 28.4	29 38.1	29 45.6
10 W	13 16 15	17 09 30	27 04 26	3♑07 09	29 51.7	29 18.5	4 59.0	13 09.1	13 08.9	19 42.0	29 59.2	6 30.2	29 40.2	29 47.0
11 Th	13 20 12	18 08 52	9♑07 11	15 05 11	29R 52.6	0♎10.3	6 08.0	13 09.6	12 55.4	19 54.2	0♐05.1	6 31.9	29 42.5	29 48.4
12 F	13 24 08	19 08 15	21 01 47	26 57 36	29 52.3	1 09.6	7 17.1	13 10.8	12 41.9	20 06.4	0 11.0	6 33.6	29 44.7	29 49.9
13 Sa	13 28 05	20 07 40	2♒53 18	8♒49 27	29 50.3	2 15.6	8 26.3	13 12.9	12 28.5	20 18.5	0 16.9	6 35.2	29 46.9	29 51.2
14 Su	13 32 02	21 07 07	14 46 39	20 45 25	29 46.6	3 27.6	9 35.7	13 15.8	12 15.2	20 30.5	0 23.0	6 36.8	29 49.1	29 52.6
15 M	13 35 58	22 06 35	26 46 15	2♓49 36	29 41.5	4 44.8	10 45.3	13 19.4	12 02.0	20 42.5	0 29.0	6 38.3	29 51.3	29 53.9
16 Tu	13 39 55	23 06 06	8♓55 51	15 05 20	29 35.3	6 06.5	11 55.0	13 23.8	11 48.9	20 54.5	0 35.1	6 39.8	29 53.5	29 55.3
17 W	13 43 51	24 05 38	21 18 19	27 35 00	29 28.9	7 32.0	13 04.9	13 29.0	11 35.9	21 06.3	0 41.3	6 41.2	29 55.8	29 56.5
18 Th	13 47 48	25 05 12	3♈55 30	10♈19 53	29 22.8	9 00.8	14 14.9	13 35.0	11 23.2	21 18.2	0 47.4	6 42.5	29 58.0	29 57.8
19 F	13 51 44	26 04 48	16 48 10	23 20 15	29 17.8	10 32.3	15 25.0	13 41.7	11 10.5	21 30.0	0 53.7	6 43.9	0♏00.2	29 59.1
20 Sa	13 55 41	27 04 26	29 56 02	6♉35 23	29 14.3	12 06.0	16 35.3	13 49.1	10 58.1	21 41.7	1 00.0	6 45.1	0 02.5	0♍00.3
21 Su	13 59 37	28 04 06	13♉18 04	20 03 54	29D 12.5	13 41.5	17 45.7	13 57.3	10 45.8	21 53.3	1 06.3	6 46.3	0 04.7	0 01.5
22 M	14 03 34	29 03 49	26 52 37	3♊44 00	29 12.2	15 18.3	18 56.3	14 06.1	10 33.8	22 04.9	1 12.6	6 47.5	0 07.0	0 02.7
23 Tu	14 07 31	0♏03 33	10♊37 49	17 33 49	29 13.1	16 56.4	20 07.0	14 15.7	10 22.0	22 16.5	1 19.0	6 48.6	0 09.2	0 03.8
24 W	14 11 27	1 03 20	24 31 47	1♋31 31	29 14.7	18 35.2	21 17.8	14 26.0	10 10.3	22 28.0	1 25.5	6 49.7	0 11.4	0 05.0
25 Th	14 15 24	2 03 09	8♋32 49	15 35 29	29 16.1	20 14.7	22 28.8	14 36.9	9 59.0	22 39.4	1 32.0	6 50.7	0 13.7	0 06.1
26 F	14 19 20	3 03 00	22 39 19	29 44 06	29R 16.9	21 54.5	23 39.9	14 48.5	9 47.9	22 50.7	1 38.5	6 51.6	0 15.9	0 07.2
27 Sa	14 23 17	4 02 54	6♌49 37	13♌55 38	29 16.6	23 34.7	24 51.1	15 00.7	9 37.0	23 02.0	1 45.0	6 52.5	0 18.2	0 08.2
28 Su	14 27 13	5 02 49	21 01 51	28 07 59	29 15.1	25 14.9	26 02.4	15 13.6	9 26.4	23 13.2	1 51.6	6 53.4	0 20.4	0 09.2
29 M	14 31 10	6 02 47	5♍13 40	12♍18 31	29 12.7	26 55.2	27 13.9	15 27.2	9 16.1	23 24.3	1 58.3	6 54.2	0 22.6	0 10.2
30 Tu	14 35 06	7 02 47	19 22 09	26 24 07	29 09.6	28 35.3	28 25.4	15 41.3	9 06.1	23 35.4	2 04.9	6 54.9	0 24.9	0 11.2
31 W	14 39 03	8 02 49	3♎23 58	10♎21 17	29 06.3	0♏15.3	29 37.1	15 56.1	8 56.4	23 46.4	2 11.6	6 55.6	0 27.1	0 12.2

Astro Data

	Dy Hr Mn
☽0S	5 5:41
♃∠♆	12 3:42
☿R	13 14:08
☽0N	19 11:19
☉0S	23 1:35
☿0N	2 6:27
☽0S	2 15:17
♄⊻♆	5 2:03
☿D	5 14:21
♄□♇	7 15:42
♂D	10 10:06
☿0S	15 6:34
☽0N	16 18:49
♆✱♇	18 7:31
♃∠♅	20 19:55

Planet Ingress

		Dy Hr Mn
♀	♌	8 9:23
☉	♎	23 1:35
☿	♍R	29 21:25
☊	♏R	4 9:37
♀	♍	6 3:12
♄	♐	10 15:11
☿	♎	11 7:30
♆	♏	19 9:28
♇	♍	20 6:12
☉	♏	23 10:34
☿	♏	31 8:19
♀	♎	31 19:40

☽0S29 22:30

Last Aspect / ☽ Ingress (September)

Last Aspect Dy Hr Mn			☽ Ingress	Dy Hr Mn
1 20:40	♆	□	♌	1 23:14
3 21:18	♇	☌	♍	3 23:20
5 19:48	♀	✱	♎	6 0:04
8 2:58	♀	□	♏	8 3:26
10 8:44	♇	□	♐	10 10:46
12 19:47	♇	△	♑	12 21:46
15 8:03	♆	□	♒	15 10:28
17 20:55	♇	☍	♓	17 22:34
20 5:24	♄	△	♈	20 8:47
22 15:44	♇	△	♉	22 17:01
24 22:18	♇	□	♊	24 23:25
27 3:01	♇	✱	♋	27 4:00
29 5:35	♆	□	♌	29 6:49

Last Aspect / ☽ Ingress (October)

Last Aspect Dy Hr Mn			☽ Ingress	Dy Hr Mn
1 7:40	♇	☌	♍	1 8:24
3 8:53	♄	✱	♎	3 10:01
5 12:43	♇	✱	♏	5 13:19
7 19:15	♄	☌	♐	7 19:46
10 5:21	♇	△	♑	10 5:48
12 17:39	♆	□	♒	12 18:09
15 6:12	♇	☍	♓	15 6:25
16 23:25	♃	☍	♈	17 16:35
20 0:07	♇	△	♉	20 0:07
21 15:16	♃	△	♊	22 5:29
23 20:14	♃	□	♋	24 9:23
26 0:46	♀	✱	♌	26 12:27
28 6:29	☿	✱	♍	28 15:09
30 15:47	♀	☌	♎	30 18:10

☽ Phases & Eclipses

Dy Hr Mn		
4 18:57	●	12♍12
12 0:13	☽	19♐13
20 3:19	○	27♓08
27 11:25	☾	4♋19
4 4:25	●	10♎55
11 18:44	☽	18♑26
19 17:25	○	26♈18
26 18:02	☾	3♌18

Astro Data

1 September 1956
Julian Day # 20698
SVP 5♓51'37"
GC 26♐14.0 ⚴ 22♒47.4R
Eris 9♈02.1R ⚵ 6♑48.2
⚷ 7♒27.0R ⚶ 20♏14.7
☽ Mean ☊ 3♐08.9

1 October 1956
Julian Day # 20728
SVP 5♓51'34"
GC 26♐14.1 ⚴ 17♒44.1R
Eris 8♈44.2R ⚵ 9♑45.4
⚷ 6♒32.1R ⚶ 3♐49.7
☽ Mean ☊ 1♐33.6

November 1956 LONGITUDE

Day	Sid.Time	☉	0 hr ☽	Noon☽	True☊	☿	♀	♂	⚳	♃	♄	♅	♆	♇
1 Th	14 43 00	9♏02 53	17♎15 38	24♎06 37	29♏03.5	1♏55.1	0♎48.9	16♓11.5	8♈46.9	23♍57.3	2♐18.3	6♌56.2	0♏29.3	0♍13.1
2 F	14 46 56	10 02 59	0♏53 53	7♏37 08	29R01.5	3 34.6	2 00.7	16 27.5	8R37.9	24 08.1	2 25.1	6 56.8	0 31.6	0 14.0
3 Sa	14 50 53	11 03 07	14 16 08	20 50 43	29D00.4	5 13.8	3 12.7	16 44.0	8 29.1	24 18.8	2 31.9	6 57.3	0 33.8	0 14.8
4 Su	14 54 49	12 03 17	27 20 49	3♐46 25	29 00.2	6 52.7	4 24.8	17 01.2	8 20.7	24 29.5	2 38.7	6 57.7	0 36.0	0 15.7
5 M	14 58 46	13 03 28	10♐07 37	16 24 33	29 00.9	8 31.3	5 36.9	17 18.9	8 12.6	24 40.1	2 45.5	6 58.2	0 38.2	0 16.5
6 Tu	15 02 42	14 03 41	22 37 27	28 46 37	29 02.1	10 09.5	6 49.2	17 37.1	8 04.9	24 50.6	2 52.3	6 58.5	0 40.4	0 17.3
7 W	15 06 39	15 03 56	4♑52 25	10♑55 17	29 03.5	11 47.4	8 01.5	17 55.9	7 57.5	25 01.0	2 59.2	6 58.8	0 42.6	0 18.0
8 Th	15 10 35	16 04 12	16 55 39	22 54 03	29 04.7	13 24.8	9 14.0	18 15.2	7 50.5	25 11.3	3 06.1	6 59.0	0 44.8	0 18.8
9 F	15 14 32	17 04 30	28 51 01	4♒47 07	29 05.6	15 02.0	10 26.5	18 35.0	7 43.8	25 21.5	3 13.1	6 59.2	0 47.0	0 19.5
10 Sa	15 18 29	18 04 49	10♒42 57	16 39 05	29R05.9	16 38.8	11 39.1	18 55.3	7 37.5	25 31.6	3 20.0	6 59.3	0 49.1	0 20.1
11 Su	15 22 25	19 05 10	22 36 08	28 34 43	29 05.8	18 15.2	12 51.7	19 16.1	7 31.6	25 41.7	3 27.0	6R59.4	0 51.3	0 20.8
12 M	15 26 22	20 05 32	4♓35 22	10♓38 41	29 05.1	19 51.3	14 04.5	19 37.4	7 26.1	25 51.6	3 33.9	6 59.4	0 53.4	0 21.4
13 Tu	15 30 18	21 05 55	16 45 12	22 55 22	29 04.2	21 27.1	15 17.3	19 59.1	7 20.9	26 01.4	3 40.9	6 59.4	0 55.6	0 22.0
14 W	15 34 15	22 06 20	29 09 39	5♈28 26	29 03.2	23 02.6	16 30.2	20 21.3	7 16.2	26 11.2	3 48.0	6 59.3	0 57.7	0 22.5
15 Th	15 38 11	23 06 46	11♈52 01	18 20 37	29 02.4	24 37.8	17 43.2	20 43.9	7 11.8	26 20.8	3 55.0	6 59.2	0 59.8	0 23.0
16 F	15 42 08	24 07 14	24 54 23	1♉33 21	29 01.8	26 12.8	18 56.3	21 06.9	7 07.7	26 30.3	4 02.0	6 58.9	1 01.9	0 23.5
17 Sa	15 46 04	25 07 43	8♉17 29	15 06 36	29 01.4	27 47.4	20 09.4	21 30.3	7 04.1	26 39.8	4 09.1	6 58.7	1 04.0	0 24.0
18 Su	15 50 01	26 08 13	22 00 28	28 58 42	29D01.3	29 21.9	21 22.6	21 54.1	7 00.9	26 49.1	4 16.1	6 58.4	1 06.1	0 24.4
19 M	15 53 58	27 08 45	6♊00 52	13♊06 27	29 01.4	0♐56.1	22 35.9	22 18.3	6 58.0	26 58.3	4 23.2	6 58.0	1 08.2	0 24.8
20 Tu	15 57 54	28 09 19	20 14 54	27 25 33	29R01.5	2 30.1	23 49.2	22 42.9	6 55.5	27 07.4	4 30.3	6 57.6	1 10.2	0 25.2
21 W	16 01 51	29 09 55	4♋37 48	11♋51 00	29 01.5	4 03.9	25 02.6	23 07.8	6 53.5	27 16.4	4 37.4	6 57.1	1 12.3	0 25.6
22 Th	16 05 47	0♐10 32	19 04 30	26 17 44	29 01.5	5 37.6	26 16.1	23 33.1	6 51.8	27 25.3	4 44.5	6 56.6	1 14.3	0 25.9
23 F	16 09 44	1 11 11	3♌30 08	10♌41 13	29 01.3	7 11.1	27 29.6	23 58.8	6 50.5	27 34.1	4 51.6	6 56.0	1 16.3	0 26.2
24 Sa	16 13 40	2 11 51	17 50 33	24 57 46	29D01.2	8 44.4	28 43.2	24 24.8	6 49.5	27 42.7	4 58.7	6 55.4	1 18.3	0 26.4
25 Su	16 17 37	3 12 33	2♍02 35	9♍04 45	29 01.2	10 17.6	29 56.9	24 51.1	6D49.0	27 51.3	5 05.9	6 54.7	1 20.3	0 26.6
26 M	16 21 33	4 13 17	16 04 05	23 00 27	29 01.4	11 50.7	1♏10.6	25 17.8	6 48.8	27 59.7	5 13.0	6 53.9	1 22.3	0 26.8
27 Tu	16 25 30	5 14 02	29 53 45	6♎43 54	29 01.9	13 23.7	2 24.4	25 44.7	6 49.0	28 08.0	5 20.1	6 53.1	1 24.2	0 27.0
28 W	16 29 27	6 14 49	13♎30 52	20 14 37	29 02.6	14 56.5	3 38.2	26 12.0	6 49.6	28 16.2	5 27.2	6 52.3	1 26.1	0 27.1
29 Th	16 33 23	7 15 37	26 55 08	3♏32 23	29 03.3	16 29.3	4 52.1	26 39.6	6 50.6	28 24.2	5 34.3	6 51.4	1 28.0	0 27.2
30 F	16 37 20	8 16 26	10♏06 22	16 37 05	29R03.9	18 01.9	6 06.0	27 07.5	6 52.0	28 32.1	5 41.5	6 50.4	1 29.9	0 27.3

December 1956 LONGITUDE

Day	Sid.Time	☉	0 hr ☽	Noon☽	True☊	☿	♀	♂	⚳	♃	♄	♅	♆	♇
1 Sa	16 41 16	9♐17 18	23♏04 33	29♏28 45	29♏04.2	19♐34.5	7♏20.0	27♓35.7	6♈53.7	28♍39.9	5♐48.6	6♌49.4	1♏31.8	0♍27.3
2 Su	16 45 13	10 18 10	5♐49 45	12♐07 35	29R03.8	21 06.9	8 34.0	28 04.1	6 55.8	28 47.5	5 55.7	6R48.4	1 33.7	0R27.3
3 M	16 49 09	11 19 03	18 22 19	24 34 03	29 02.9	22 39.2	9 48.1	28 32.9	6 58.3	28 55.1	6 02.8	6 47.3	1 35.5	0 27.3
4 Tu	16 53 06	12 19 58	0♑42 55	6♑49 05	29 01.2	24 11.4	11 02.2	29 01.9	7 01.2	29 02.4	6 09.9	6 46.1	1 37.3	0 27.3
5 W	16 57 02	13 20 53	12 52 46	18 54 13	28 59.0	25 43.4	12 16.3	29 31.2	7 04.4	29 09.7	6 17.0	6 44.9	1 39.1	0 27.2
6 Th	17 00 59	14 21 49	24 53 42	0♒51 34	28 56.6	27 15.3	13 30.5	0♈00.7	7 08.0	29 16.8	6 24.1	6 43.7	1 40.9	0 27.1
7 F	17 04 56	15 22 46	6♒48 13	12 44 02	28 54.2	28 46.9	14 44.7	0 30.5	7 12.0	29 23.8	6 31.2	6 42.4	1 42.7	0 26.9
8 Sa	17 08 52	16 23 44	18 39 30	24 35 07	28 52.2	0♑18.3	15 59.0	1 00.6	7 16.3	29 30.6	6 38.2	6 41.0	1 44.4	0 26.7
9 Su	17 12 49	17 24 42	0♓31 23	6♓28 53	28D50.9	1 49.4	17 13.3	1 30.8	7 20.9	29 37.2	6 45.3	6 39.6	1 46.1	0 26.5
10 M	17 16 45	18 25 41	12 28 10	18 29 51	28 50.4	3 20.1	18 27.6	2 01.3	7 26.0	29 43.8	6 52.3	6 38.2	1 47.8	0 26.3
11 Tu	17 20 42	19 26 40	24 34 30	0♈42 44	28 50.9	4 50.4	19 42.0	2 32.1	7 31.3	29 50.1	6 59.3	6 36.7	1 49.4	0 26.0
12 W	17 24 38	20 27 40	6♈55 07	13 12 12	28 52.1	6 20.2	20 56.4	3 03.0	7 37.0	29 56.4	7 06.3	6 35.1	1 51.1	0 25.7
13 Th	17 28 35	21 28 41	19 34 29	26 02 26	28 53.7	7 49.3	22 10.8	3 34.1	7 43.1	0♎02.4	7 13.3	6 33.6	1 52.7	0 25.4
14 F	17 32 31	22 29 42	2♉36 25	9♉16 43	28 55.2	9 17.7	23 25.2	4 05.5	7 49.4	0 08.4	7 20.3	6 31.9	1 54.3	0 25.1
15 Sa	17 36 28	23 30 44	16 03 29	22 56 46	28R56.2	10 45.1	24 39.7	4 37.0	7 56.1	0 14.1	7 27.2	6 30.3	1 55.8	0 24.7
16 Su	17 40 25	24 31 46	29 56 27	7♊02 16	28 56.1	12 11.5	25 54.2	5 08.7	8 03.2	0 19.7	7 34.2	6 28.6	1 57.4	0 24.3
17 M	17 44 21	25 32 49	14♊13 45	21 30 19	28 54.6	13 36.5	27 08.7	5 40.6	8 10.5	0 25.2	7 41.1	6 26.8	1 58.9	0 23.8
18 Tu	17 48 18	26 33 52	28 51 11	6♋15 29	28 51.8	15 00.0	28 23.3	6 12.7	8 18.2	0 30.5	7 48.0	6 25.0	2 00.4	0 23.4
19 W	17 52 14	27 34 57	13♋42 11	21 10 14	28 47.9	16 21.7	29 37.9	6 44.9	8 26.1	0 35.6	7 54.8	6 23.2	2 01.9	0 22.9
20 Th	17 56 11	28 36 01	28 38 31	6♌05 57	28 43.5	17 41.3	0♐52.5	7 17.4	8 34.4	0 40.6	8 01.7	6 21.3	2 03.3	0 22.3
21 F	18 00 07	29 37 07	13♌31 32	20 54 19	28 39.2	18 58.3	2 07.2	7 49.9	8 43.0	0 45.4	8 08.5	6 19.4	2 04.7	0 21.8
22 Sa	18 04 04	0♑38 13	28 13 33	5♍28 33	28 35.8	20 12.3	3 21.8	8 22.7	8 51.9	0 50.1	8 15.2	6 17.5	2 06.1	0 21.2
23 Su	18 08 00	1 39 19	12♍38 51	19 44 08	28D33.6	21 22.9	4 36.5	8 55.6	9 01.1	0 54.5	8 22.0	6 15.5	2 07.4	0 20.6
24 M	18 11 57	2 40 27	26 44 11	3♎38 59	28 33.0	22 29.4	5 51.2	9 28.6	9 10.6	0 58.8	8 28.7	6 13.5	2 08.8	0 19.9
25 Tu	18 15 54	3 41 35	10♎28 35	17 13 08	28 33.7	23 31.2	7 06.0	10 01.8	9 20.3	1 03.0	8 35.4	6 11.4	2 10.1	0 19.3
26 W	18 19 50	4 42 44	23 52 52	0♏28 02	28 35.2	24 27.6	8 20.7	10 35.2	9 30.4	1 06.9	8 42.1	6 09.3	2 11.3	0 18.6
27 Th	18 23 47	5 43 53	6♏58 58	13 25 57	28 36.9	25 17.9	9 35.5	11 08.6	9 40.7	1 10.7	8 48.7	6 07.2	2 12.6	0 17.9
28 F	18 27 43	6 45 03	19 49 19	26 09 22	28R37.8	26 01.1	10 50.3	11 42.3	9 51.3	1 14.3	8 55.3	6 05.0	2 13.8	0 17.1
29 Sa	18 31 40	7 46 13	2♐26 22	8♐40 36	28 37.2	26 36.4	12 05.1	12 16.0	10 02.2	1 17.8	9 01.9	6 02.9	2 15.0	0 16.3
30 Su	18 35 36	8 47 23	14 52 18	21 01 40	28 34.8	27 02.8	13 20.0	12 49.9	10 13.4	1 21.0	9 08.4	6 00.6	2 16.1	0 15.5
31 M	18 39 33	9 48 34	27 08 53	3♑14 09	28 30.2	27 19.6	14 34.8	13 24.0	10 24.8	1 24.1	9 14.9	5 58.4	2 17.3	0 14.7

Astro Data	Dy Hr Mn
♀0S	3 21:14
♅ R	12 6:51
☽0N	13 3:12
☽0S	26 4:00
⚳ D	26 10:11
♇ R	2 7:16
♂0N	8 8:45
♄△♅	8 19:56
☽0N	10 11:57
♃⚺♇	17 6:21
☽0S	23 10:06

Planet Ingress		Dy Hr Mn
☿	♐	18 21:42
☉	♐	22 7:50
♀	♏	25 13:01
♂	♈	6 11:24
☿	♑	8 7:11
♃	♎	13 2:17
♀	♐	19 19:07
☉	♑	21 20:59

Last Aspect Dy Hr Mn			☽ Ingress	Dy Hr Mn
31 6:04	♅	⚹	♏	1 22:24
3 18:28	♃	⚹	♐	4 4:56
6 4:12	♃	□	♑	6 14:24
8 16:41	♃	△	♒	9 2:19
10 15:09	☉	□	♓	11 14:51
13 18:04	♃	☍	♈	14 1:36
15 10:44	♀	☍	♉	16 9:12
18 12:45	☿	☍	♊	18 13:45
20 11:29	♃	□	♋	20 16:18
22 13:54	♃	⚹	♌	22 18:10
24 18:58	♀	⚹	♍	24 20:32
26 20:46	♃	☌	♎	27 0:11
28 1:19	☿	⚹	♏	29 5:34

Last Aspect Dy Hr Mn			☽ Ingress	Dy Hr Mn
1 10:27	♃	⚹	♐	1 12:59
3 20:34	♃	□	♑	3 22:36
6 10:13	♂	⚹	♒	6 10:16
7 17:52	☉	⚹	♓	8 22:57
11 10:17	♃	☍	♈	11 10:37
13 2:50	☉	△	♉	13 19:15
15 15:15	♀	☍	♊	16 0:06
17 19:06	☉	☍	♋	18 1:52
19 3:30	☿	☍	♌	20 2:11
20 15:08	♄	△	♍	22 2:56
23 15:03	☿	△	♎	24 5:39
26 0:14	☿	□	♏	26 11:09
28 11:43	☿	⚹	♐	28 19:20
29 19:20	♀	☌	♑	31 5:37

☽ Phases & Eclipses Dy Hr Mn		
2 16:44	●	10♏15
10 15:09	☽	18♒13
18 6:45	○	25♉55
18 6:48	☍	T 1.317
25 1:13	☾	2♍45
2 8:13	●	10♐09
2 8:00:04	☌	P 0.805
10 11:51	☽	18♓25
17 19:06	○	25♊51
24 10:10	☾	2♎36

Astro Data

1 November 1956
Julian Day # 20759
SVP 5♓51'32"
GC 26♐14.2 ⚴ 17♒47.1
Eris 8♈25.6R ⚵ 17♑14.5
⚷ 6♒36.2 ⚶ 19♐08.1
☽ Mean ☊ 29♏55.0

1 December 1956
Julian Day # 20789
SVP 5♓51'27"
GC 26♐14.3 ⚴ 22♒13.5
Eris 8♈13.0R ⚵ 27♑22.7
⚷ 7♒41.1 ⚶ 4♑38.4
☽ Mean ☊ 28♏19.7

LONGITUDE — January 1957

Day	Sid.Time	☉	0 hr ☽	Noon ☽	True ☊	☿	♀	♂	⚳	♃	♄	♅	♆	♇
1 Tu	18 43 29	10♑49 45	9♑17 36	15♑19 24	28♏23.5	27♑25.7	15♐49.7	13♈58.1	10♈36.5	1♎27.0	9♐21.3	5♌56.1	2♏18.3	0♍13.9
2 W	18 47 26	11 50 56	21 19 41	27 18 37	28R 15.3	27R 20.7	17 04.6	14 32.4	10 48.5	1 29.7	9 27.7	5R 53.8	2 19.4	0R 13.0
3 Th	18 51 23	12 52 07	3♒16 23	9♒13 11	28 06.1	27 03.9	18 19.5	15 06.8	11 00.7	1 32.2	9 34.1	5 51.5	2 20.4	0 12.1
4 F	18 55 19	13 53 17	15 09 14	21 04 47	27 57.0	26 35.2	19 34.4	15 41.3	11 13.2	1 34.6	9 40.4	5 49.1	2 21.4	0 11.2
5 Sa	18 59 16	14 54 27	27 00 09	2♓55 41	27 48.7	25 54.9	20 49.3	16 16.0	11 25.9	1 36.7	9 46.7	5 46.8	2 22.4	0 10.2
6 Su	19 03 12	15 55 37	8♓51 44	14 48 45	27 42.0	25 03.6	22 04.2	16 50.7	11 38.8	1 38.7	9 52.9	5 44.4	2 23.3	0 09.3
7 M	19 07 09	16 56 47	20 47 11	26 47 34	27 37.4	24 02.4	23 19.1	17 25.6	11 52.0	1 40.5	9 59.1	5 41.9	2 24.2	0 08.3
8 Tu	19 11 05	17 57 56	2♈50 25	8♈56 20	27D 35.1	22 53.2	24 34.0	18 00.5	12 05.4	1 42.1	10 05.2	5 39.5	2 25.1	0 07.2
9 W	19 15 02	18 59 05	15 05 55	21 19 45	27 34.6	21 37.9	25 49.0	18 35.6	12 19.1	1 43.5	10 11.3	5 37.0	2 25.9	0 06.2
10 Th	19 18 58	20 00 13	27 38 27	4♉02 37	27 35.4	20 19.1	27 03.9	19 10.7	12 33.0	1 44.7	10 17.3	5 34.5	2 26.7	0 05.1
11 F	19 22 55	21 01 21	10♉32 47	17 09 28	27R 36.4	18 59.1	28 18.9	19 46.0	12 47.1	1 45.7	10 23.3	5 32.0	2 27.5	0 04.1
12 Sa	19 26 52	22 02 28	23 53 04	0♊43 53	27 36.8	17 40.7	29 33.8	20 21.3	13 01.4	1 46.5	10 29.3	5 29.5	2 28.2	0 03.0
13 Su	19 30 48	23 03 35	7♊42 04	14 47 36	27 35.4	16 26.0	0♑48.8	20 56.7	13 16.0	1 47.2	10 35.1	5 27.0	2 29.0	0 01.8
14 M	19 34 45	24 04 41	22 00 16	29 19 39	27 31.7	15 17.1	2 03.8	21 32.2	13 30.7	1 47.6	10 41.0	5 24.4	2 29.6	0 00.7
15 Tu	19 38 41	25 05 46	6♋45 06	14♋15 42	27 25.6	14 15.5	3 18.7	22 07.8	13 45.7	1R 47.9	10 46.7	5 21.9	2 30.3	29♌59.6
16 W	19 42 38	26 06 51	21 50 24	29 27 54	27 17.3	13 22.3	4 33.7	22 43.4	14 00.9	1 48.0	10 52.5	5 19.3	2 30.9	29 58.4
17 Th	19 46 34	27 07 55	7♌06 50	14♌45 46	27 07.9	12 38.3	5 48.7	23 19.2	14 16.2	1 47.9	10 58.1	5 16.7	2 31.5	29 57.2
18 F	19 50 31	28 08 59	22 23 16	29 57 57	26 58.5	12 03.8	7 03.7	23 54.9	14 31.8	1 47.6	11 03.7	5 14.2	2 32.0	29 56.0
19 Sa	19 54 28	29 10 02	7♍28 37	14♍54 14	26 50.2	11 38.8	8 18.7	24 30.8	14 47.5	1 47.0	11 09.3	5 11.6	2 32.5	29 54.7
20 Su	19 58 24	0♒11 05	22 13 59	29 27 16	26 44.1	11 22.9	9 33.7	25 06.7	15 03.5	1 46.4	11 14.8	5 09.0	2 33.0	29 53.5
21 M	20 02 21	1 12 07	6♎33 44	13♎33 13	26 40.4	11D 15.9	10 48.7	25 42.7	15 19.6	1 45.5	11 20.2	5 06.3	2 33.4	29 52.2
22 Tu	20 06 17	2 13 09	20 25 45	27 11 32	26D 39.0	11 17.3	12 03.7	26 18.8	15 36.0	1 44.4	11 25.5	5 03.7	2 33.8	29 50.9
23 W	20 10 14	3 14 11	3♏50 53	10♏24 12	26 39.0	11 26.4	13 18.7	26 54.9	15 52.5	1 43.1	11 30.8	5 01.1	2 34.2	29 49.6
24 Th	20 14 10	4 15 12	16 51 57	23 14 41	26R 39.5	11 42.7	14 33.8	27 31.1	16 09.1	1 41.7	11 36.1	4 58.5	2 34.5	29 48.3
25 F	20 18 07	5 16 13	29 32 53	5♐47 07	26 39.1	12 05.6	15 48.8	28 07.4	16 26.0	1 40.0	11 41.2	4 55.9	2 34.8	29 47.0
26 Sa	20 22 03	6 17 13	11♐57 53	18 05 40	26 36.9	12 34.6	17 03.8	28 43.7	16 43.1	1 38.2	11 46.3	4 53.2	2 35.1	29 45.6
27 Su	20 26 00	7 18 13	24 10 55	0♑14 02	26 32.1	13 09.0	18 18.9	29 20.1	17 00.3	1 36.1	11 51.4	4 50.6	2 35.3	29 44.3
28 M	20 29 57	8 19 12	6♑15 23	12 15 18	26 24.2	13 48.4	19 33.9	29 56.5	17 17.6	1 33.9	11 56.3	4 48.0	2 35.5	29 42.9
29 Tu	20 33 53	9 20 10	18 14 04	24 11 54	26 13.4	14 32.3	20 48.9	0♉33.0	17 35.2	1 31.5	12 01.2	4 45.4	2 35.7	29 41.5
30 W	20 37 50	10 21 07	0♒09 02	6♒05 37	26 00.3	15 20.3	22 04.0	1 09.5	17 52.9	1 28.9	12 06.1	4 42.8	2 35.8	29 40.1
31 Th	20 41 46	11 22 03	12 01 51	17 57 52	25 45.8	16 12.1	23 19.0	1 46.1	18 10.8	1 26.1	12 10.8	4 40.2	2 35.9	29 38.7

LONGITUDE — February 1957

Day	Sid.Time	☉	0 hr ☽	Noon ☽	True ☊	☿	♀	♂	⚳	♃	♄	♅	♆	♇
1 F	20 45 43	12♒22 57	23♒53 50	29♒49 54	25♏31.2	17♑07.3	24♑34.1	2♉22.8	18♈28.8	1♎23.2	12♐15.5	4♌37.6	2♏35.9	29♌37.3
2 Sa	20 49 39	13 23 51	5♓46 15	11♓43 05	25R 17.6	18 05.6	25 49.1	2 59.5	18 47.0	1R 20.0	12 20.1	4R 35.0	2R 36.0	29R 35.9
3 Su	20 53 36	14 24 44	17 40 38	23 39 11	25 06.0	19 06.6	27 04.1	3 36.2	19 05.3	1 16.7	12 24.6	4 32.4	2 36.0	29 34.4
4 M	20 57 32	15 25 35	29 39 01	5♈40 32	24 57.3	20 10.3	28 19.1	4 13.0	19 23.8	1 13.2	12 29.1	4 29.8	2 35.9	29 33.0
5 Tu	21 01 29	16 26 24	11♈44 06	17 50 12	24 51.6	21 16.4	29 34.1	4 49.9	19 42.4	1 09.5	12 33.4	4 27.3	2 35.8	29 31.5
6 W	21 05 25	17 27 13	23 59 18	0♉11 56	24 48.6	22 24.6	0♒49.2	5 26.8	20 01.2	1 05.6	12 37.7	4 24.7	2 35.7	29 30.1
7 Th	21 09 22	18 28 00	6♉28 40	12 50 04	24 47.7	23 34.8	2 04.2	6 03.7	20 20.1	1 01.6	12 41.9	4 22.2	2 35.6	29 28.6
8 F	21 13 19	19 28 45	19 16 42	25 49 07	24 47.6	24 46.9	3 19.2	6 40.6	20 39.2	0 57.4	12 46.1	4 19.7	2 35.4	29 27.1
9 Sa	21 17 15	20 29 29	2♊27 49	9♊13 16	24 47.2	26 00.8	4 34.2	7 17.6	20 58.3	0 53.1	12 50.1	4 17.2	2 35.2	29 25.7
10 Su	21 21 12	21 30 11	16 05 48	23 05 37	24 45.1	27 16.3	5 49.2	7 54.7	21 17.6	0 48.5	12 54.1	4 14.7	2 34.9	29 24.2
11 M	21 25 08	22 30 52	0♋12 47	7♋27 08	24 40.6	28 33.3	7 04.1	8 31.7	21 37.1	0 43.8	12 58.0	4 12.3	2 34.7	29 22.7
12 Tu	21 29 05	23 31 31	14 48 17	22 15 37	24 33.2	29 51.8	8 19.1	9 08.8	21 56.7	0 39.0	13 01.8	4 09.8	2 34.3	29 21.2
13 W	21 33 01	24 32 08	29 48 17	7♌25 11	24 23.4	1♒11.6	9 34.1	9 46.0	22 16.3	0 34.0	13 05.5	4 07.4	2 34.0	29 19.7
14 Th	21 36 58	25 32 44	15♌05 01	22 46 21	24 12.0	2 32.7	10 49.1	10 23.1	22 36.2	0 28.8	13 09.2	4 05.0	2 33.6	29 18.2
15 F	21 40 55	26 33 18	0♍27 39	8♍07 25	24 00.4	3 55.1	12 04.0	11 00.3	22 56.1	0 23.5	13 12.7	4 02.6	2 33.2	29 16.7
16 Sa	21 44 51	27 33 51	15 44 09	23 16 33	23 50.0	5 18.7	13 19.0	11 37.5	23 16.1	0 18.1	13 16.2	4 00.3	2 32.8	29 15.2
17 Su	21 48 48	28 34 23	0♎43 29	8♎04 03	23 41.9	6 43.5	14 33.9	12 14.7	23 36.3	0 12.5	13 19.6	3 58.0	2 32.3	29 13.7
18 M	21 52 44	29 34 53	15 17 35	22 23 42	23 36.5	8 09.4	15 48.9	12 51.9	23 56.6	0 06.8	13 22.9	3 55.7	2 31.8	29 12.2
19 Tu	21 56 41	0♓35 22	29 22 12	6♏13 08	23 33.7	9 36.4	17 03.8	13 29.2	24 17.0	0 00.9	13 26.1	3 53.4	2 31.2	29 10.7
20 W	22 00 37	1 35 49	12♏56 42	19 33 14	23D 32.9	11 04.4	18 18.8	14 06.5	24 37.5	29♍54.9	13 29.2	3 51.2	2 30.7	29 09.2
21 Th	22 04 34	2 36 16	26 03 13	2♐27 11	23R 32.9	12 33.5	19 33.7	14 43.8	24 58.1	29 48.8	13 32.3	3 49.0	2 30.1	29 07.7
22 F	22 08 30	3 36 41	8♐45 44	14 59 27	23 32.5	14 03.7	20 48.6	15 21.2	25 18.8	29 42.5	13 35.2	3 46.8	2 29.4	29 06.2
23 Sa	22 12 27	4 37 05	21 09 00	27 14 58	23 30.5	15 34.9	22 03.6	15 58.6	25 39.6	29 36.1	13 38.0	3 44.6	2 28.8	29 04.7
24 Su	22 16 23	5 37 27	3♑17 58	9♑18 32	23 26.1	17 07.1	23 18.5	16 36.0	26 00.5	29 29.6	13 40.8	3 42.5	2 28.1	29 03.2
25 M	22 20 20	6 37 48	15 17 13	21 14 30	23 18.7	18 40.4	24 33.4	17 13.4	26 21.6	29 23.0	13 43.5	3 40.4	2 27.4	29 01.7
26 Tu	22 24 17	7 38 07	27 10 47	3♒06 28	23 08.6	20 14.6	25 48.3	17 50.8	26 42.7	29 16.3	13 46.0	3 38.4	2 26.6	29 00.2
27 W	22 28 13	8 38 24	9♒01 53	14 57 20	22 56.1	21 49.9	27 03.2	18 28.3	27 03.9	29 09.5	13 48.5	3 36.3	2 25.8	28 58.7
28 Th	22 32 10	9 38 40	20 53 04	26 49 17	22 42.3	23 26.2	28 18.1	19 05.7	27 25.2	29 02.6	13 50.9	3 34.4	2 25.0	28 57.2

Astro Data	Planet Ingress	Last Aspect	☽ Ingress	Last Aspect	☽ Ingress	☽ Phases & Eclipses	Astro Data
Dy Hr Mn	Dy Hr Mn	Dy Hr Mn	Dy Hr Mn	Dy Hr Mn	Dy Hr Mn	Dy Hr Mn	1 January 1957
☿ R 1 13:23	♀ ♑ 12 20:23	2 12:04 ☿ ☌	♒ 2 17:25	1 11:35 ♇ ☍	♓ 1 12:20	1 2:14 ● 10♑25	Julian Day # 20820
☽ 0N 6 20:11	♇ ♌R 15 2:45	4 8:35 ♀ ⚹	♓ 5 6:04	3 19:38 ♀ ⚹	♈ 4 0:42	9 7:06 ☽ 18♈47	SVP 5♓51'21"
♃ R 16 9:22	☉ ♒ 20 7:39	7 6:58 ☿ ⚹	♈ 7 18:23	6 10:40 ♇ △	♉ 6 11:37	16 6:21 ○ 25♋52	GC 26♐14.3 ⚴ 29♒48.1
☽ 0S 19 18:50	♂ ♉ 28 14:19	9 21:29 ♀ △	♉ 10 4:27	8 18:34 ♇ □	♊ 8 19:34	22 21:48 ☾ 2♏38	Eris 8♈09.5 ⚵ 9♒49.4
☿ D 21 19:56		11 19:29 ☉ △	♊ 12 10:44	10 22:38 ♇ ⚹	♋ 10 23:39	30 21:25 ● 10♒45	⚷ 9♒36.9 ⚶ 20♑58.3
⚳ 0N 26 7:36	♀ ♒ 5 20:16	13 22:41 ♂ ⚹	♋ 14 13:06	11 13:51 ♂ ⚹	♌ 13 0:19		☽ Mean ☊ 26♏41.2
	☿ ♒ 12 14:30	16 6:21 ☉ ☍	♌ 16 12:50	14 22:11 ♇ ☌	♍ 14 23:17	7 23:23 ☽ 18♉57	
♆ R 2 15:51	☉ ♓ 18 21:58	18 11:57 ♇ ☌	♍ 18 12:03	15 20:03 ♄ □	♎ 16 22:50	14 16:38 ○ 25♌44	1 February 1957
☽ 0N 3 3:26	♃ ♍R 19 15:37	19 6:51 ☿ △	♎ 20 12:55	18 23:41 ♇ ⚹	♏ 19 1:06	21 12:19 ☾ 2♐37	Julian Day # 20851
☽ 0S 16 5:59		22 16:46 ♇ ⚹	♏ 22 17:02	21 7:04 ♃ ⚹	♐ 21 7:23		SVP 5♓51'17"
		25 0:28 ♇ □	♐ 25 0:52	23 16:37 ♃ □	♑ 23 17:27		GC 26♐14.4 ⚴ 9♓11.6
		27 11:01 ♇ △	♑ 27 11:32	26 4:18 ♃ △	♒ 26 5:42		Eris 8♈17.0 ⚵ 23♒35.8
		29 4:24 ♀ ☌	♒ 29 23:42	28 16:18 ♇ ☍	♓ 28 18:25		⚷ 11♒58.7 ⚶ 7♒16.1
							☽ Mean ☊ 25♏02.8

March 1957 — LONGITUDE

Day	Sid.Time	☉	0 hr ☽	Noon ☽	True ☊	☿	♀	♂	⚸	♃	♄	♅	♆	♇
1 F	22 36 06	10♓38 55	2♓46 10	8♓43 53	22♏28.2	25♒03.6	29♒33.0	19♉43.2	27♈46.7	28♍55.6	13♐53.2	3♌32.4	2♏24.2	28♌55.7
2 Sa	22 40 03	11 39 07	14 42 35	20 42 24	22R 15.1	26 41.9	0♓47.9	20 20.8	28 08.2	28R 48.5	13 55.3	3R 30.5	2R 23.3	28R 54.3
3 Su	22 43 59	12 39 17	26 43 30	2♈46 01	22 03.9	28 21.4	2 02.7	20 58.3	28 29.8	28 41.3	13 57.4	3 28.6	2 22.4	28 52.8
4 M	22 47 56	13 39 26	8♈50 09	14 56 06	21 55.4	0♓01.8	3 17.6	21 35.8	28 51.4	28 34.0	13 59.4	3 26.8	2 21.5	28 51.3
5 Tu	22 51 52	14 39 33	21 04 06	27 14 26	21 49.9	1 43.4	4 32.4	22 13.4	29 13.2	28 26.7	14 01.3	3 25.0	2 20.5	28 49.9
6 W	22 55 49	15 39 37	3♉27 24	9♉43 22	21D 47.1	3 26.0	5 47.3	22 51.0	29 35.1	28 19.3	14 03.1	3 23.3	2 19.5	28 48.5
7 Th	22 59 46	16 39 40	16 02 42	22 25 50	21 46.4	5 09.7	7 02.1	23 28.6	29 57.0	28 11.8	14 04.8	3 21.5	2 18.5	28 47.0
8 F	23 03 42	17 39 41	28 53 11	5♊25 14	21R 46.9	6 54.6	8 16.9	24 06.2	0♉19.0	28 04.3	14 06.4	3 19.9	2 17.5	28 45.6
9 Sa	23 07 39	18 39 39	12♊02 16	18 44 49	21 47.3	8 40.5	9 31.7	24 43.8	0 41.1	27 56.7	14 07.9	3 18.3	2 16.5	28 44.2
10 Su	23 11 35	19 39 35	25 33 10	2♋27 35	21 46.5	10 27.6	10 46.4	25 21.4	1 03.3	27 49.1	14 09.3	3 16.7	2 15.4	28 42.8
11 M	23 15 32	20 39 29	9♋28 11	16 34 59	21 43.8	12 15.9	12 01.2	25 59.1	1 25.5	27 41.5	14 10.6	3 15.1	2 14.3	28 41.4
12 Tu	23 19 28	21 39 21	23 47 49	1♌06 20	21 38.7	14 05.3	13 16.0	26 36.7	1 47.9	27 33.8	14 11.8	3 13.7	2 13.1	28 40.1
13 W	23 23 25	22 39 10	8♌29 59	15 58 00	21 31.5	15 55.8	14 30.7	27 14.4	2 10.2	27 26.1	14 12.9	3 12.2	2 12.0	28 38.7
14 Th	23 27 21	23 38 57	23 29 26	1♍03 10	21 22.9	17 47.5	15 45.4	27 52.0	2 32.7	27 18.3	14 13.9	3 10.8	2 10.8	28 37.4
15 F	23 31 18	24 38 42	8♍37 59	16 12 32	21 13.9	19 40.4	17 00.1	28 29.7	2 55.2	27 10.6	14 14.8	3 09.5	2 09.6	28 36.0
16 Sa	23 35 15	25 38 25	23 45 32	1♎15 41	21 05.7	21 34.4	18 14.8	29 07.3	3 17.8	27 02.8	14 15.6	3 08.1	2 08.4	28 34.7
17 Su	23 39 11	26 38 06	8♎41 49	16 02 55	20 59.3	23 29.5	19 29.5	29 45.0	3 40.5	26 55.0	14 16.4	3 06.9	2 07.2	28 33.4
18 M	23 43 08	27 37 46	23 18 09	0♏26 53	20 55.2	25 25.8	20 44.2	0♊22.7	4 03.2	26 47.2	14 17.0	3 05.7	2 05.9	28 32.1
19 Tu	23 47 04	28 37 23	7♏28 43	14 23 26	20D 53.4	27 23.1	21 58.8	1 00.3	4 26.0	26 39.4	14 17.5	3 04.5	2 04.6	28 30.8
20 W	23 51 01	29 36 59	21 11 00	27 51 34	20 53.4	29 21.4	23 13.5	1 38.0	4 48.9	26 31.7	14 17.9	3 03.4	2 03.3	28 29.6
21 Th	23 54 57	0♈36 33	4♐25 24	10♐52 54	20 54.4	1♈20.6	24 28.1	2 15.7	5 11.8	26 23.9	14 18.2	3 02.3	2 02.0	28 28.4
22 F	23 58 54	1 36 05	17 14 34	23 30 55	20R 55.5	3 20.7	25 42.7	2 53.4	5 34.8	26 16.2	14 18.4	3 01.3	2 00.6	28 27.1
23 Sa	0 02 50	2 35 35	29 42 33	5♑50 05	20 55.8	5 21.4	26 57.3	3 31.1	5 57.8	26 08.4	14R 18.5	3 00.3	1 59.3	28 25.9
24 Su	0 06 47	3 35 04	11♑54 08	17 55 19	20 54.5	7 22.8	28 12.0	4 08.8	6 20.9	26 00.8	14 18.5	2 59.4	1 57.9	28 24.7
25 M	0 10 44	4 34 31	23 54 15	29 51 31	20 51.3	9 24.6	29 26.5	4 46.5	6 44.0	25 53.1	14 18.4	2 58.5	1 56.5	28 23.6
26 Tu	0 14 40	5 33 56	5♒47 38	11♒43 58	20 46.0	11 26.6	0♈41.1	5 24.2	7 07.3	25 45.5	14 18.2	2 57.7	1 55.1	28 22.4
27 W	0 18 37	6 33 19	17 38 30	23 34 08	20 39.1	13 28.6	1 55.7	6 01.9	7 30.5	25 37.9	14 17.9	2 57.0	1 53.7	28 21.3
28 Th	0 22 33	7 32 40	29 30 26	5♓27 44	20 31.1	15 30.4	3 10.2	6 39.6	7 53.9	25 30.4	14 17.5	2 56.2	1 52.2	28 20.2
29 F	0 26 30	8 32 00	11♓26 21	17 26 30	20 22.9	17 31.6	4 24.8	7 17.3	8 17.2	25 23.0	14 17.0	2 55.6	1 50.8	28 19.1
30 Sa	0 30 26	9 31 17	23 28 25	29 32 18	20 15.2	19 31.9	5 39.3	7 55.1	8 40.7	25 15.6	14 16.4	2 55.0	1 49.3	28 18.0
31 Su	0 34 23	10 30 32	5♈38 16	11♈46 29	20 08.7	21 31.0	6 53.8	8 32.8	9 04.1	25 08.3	14 15.7	2 54.4	1 47.8	28 16.9

April 1957 — LONGITUDE

Day	Sid.Time	☉	0 hr ☽	Noon ☽	True ☊	☿	♀	♂	⚸	♃	♄	♅	♆	♇
1 M	0 38 19	11♈29 46	17♈57 03	24♈10 05	20♏04.0	23♈28.5	8♈08.3	9♊10.5	9♉27.7	25♍01.0	14♐14.9	2♌53.9	1♏46.3	28♌15.9
2 Tu	0 42 16	12 28 57	0♉25 42	6♉43 59	20R 01.2	25 24.0	9 22.8	9 48.2	9 51.2	24R 53.8	14R 14.0	2R 53.5	1R 44.8	28R 14.9
3 W	0 46 12	13 28 06	13 05 06	19 29 09	20D 00.3	27 17.2	10 37.3	10 26.0	10 14.8	24 46.8	14 13.0	2 53.1	1 43.2	28 13.9
4 Th	0 50 09	14 27 13	25 56 19	2♊26 45	20 00.9	29 07.6	11 51.7	11 03.7	10 38.5	24 39.8	14 11.9	2 52.7	1 41.7	28 13.0
5 F	0 54 06	15 26 18	9♊00 39	15 38 11	20 02.3	0♉54.9	13 06.2	11 41.5	11 02.2	24 32.9	14 10.7	2 52.4	1 40.1	28 12.0
6 Sa	0 58 02	16 25 21	22 19 33	29 04 55	20 03.9	2 38.8	14 20.6	12 19.2	11 26.0	24 26.0	14 09.5	2 52.2	1 38.6	28 11.1
7 Su	1 01 59	17 24 21	5♋54 25	12♋48 11	20R 04.8	4 18.8	15 35.0	12 56.9	11 49.8	24 19.3	14 08.1	2 52.0	1 37.0	28 10.2
8 M	1 05 55	18 23 19	19 46 14	26 48 32	20 04.6	5 54.6	16 49.3	13 34.7	12 13.6	24 12.7	14 06.6	2 51.9	1 35.4	28 09.3
9 Tu	1 09 52	19 22 14	3♌54 58	11♌05 18	20 03.0	7 26.0	18 03.7	14 12.4	12 37.5	24 06.3	14 05.0	2D 51.8	1 33.9	28 08.5
10 W	1 13 48	20 21 07	18 19 10	25 36 05	20 00.2	8 52.7	19 18.0	14 50.1	13 01.4	23 59.9	14 03.4	2 51.8	1 32.3	28 07.7
11 Th	1 17 45	21 19 58	2♍55 28	10♍16 34	19 56.5	10 14.5	20 32.4	15 27.9	13 25.3	23 53.6	14 01.6	2 51.8	1 30.7	28 06.9
12 F	1 21 41	22 18 46	17 38 36	25 00 40	19 52.4	11 31.1	21 46.7	16 05.6	13 49.3	23 47.5	13 59.8	2 51.9	1 29.0	28 06.1
13 Sa	1 25 38	23 17 33	2♎21 52	9♎41 15	19 48.8	12 42.4	23 01.0	16 43.3	14 13.3	23 41.5	13 57.9	2 52.1	1 27.4	28 05.4
14 Su	1 29 35	24 16 17	16 57 56	24 11 05	19 46.0	13 48.2	24 15.2	17 21.0	14 37.4	23 35.6	13 55.9	2 52.3	1 25.8	28 04.6
15 M	1 33 31	25 15 00	1♏19 57	8♏23 57	19D 44.4	14 48.4	25 29.5	17 58.7	15 01.4	23 29.9	13 53.8	2 52.5	1 24.2	28 03.9
16 Tu	1 37 28	26 13 40	15 22 34	22 15 27	19 44.0	15 42.9	26 43.7	18 36.4	15 25.6	23 24.3	13 51.6	2 52.8	1 22.6	28 03.3
17 W	1 41 24	27 12 19	29 02 24	5♐43 22	19 44.7	16 31.5	27 57.9	19 14.1	15 49.7	23 18.8	13 49.3	2 53.2	1 20.9	28 02.6
18 Th	1 45 21	28 10 56	12♐18 23	18 47 38	19 46.0	17 14.3	29 12.2	19 51.8	16 13.9	23 13.5	13 46.9	2 53.6	1 19.3	28 02.0
19 F	1 49 17	29 09 31	25 11 24	1♑30 02	19 47.6	17 51.0	0♉26.4	20 29.5	16 38.1	23 08.3	13 44.5	2 54.1	1 17.7	28 01.4
20 Sa	1 53 14	0♉08 05	7♑43 59	13 53 43	19 48.9	18 21.8	1 40.5	21 07.2	17 02.3	23 03.2	13 42.0	2 54.6	1 16.0	28 00.9
21 Su	1 57 10	1 06 37	19 59 47	26 02 44	19R 49.6	18 46.6	2 54.7	21 44.9	17 26.6	22 58.3	13 39.4	2 55.2	1 14.4	28 00.3
22 M	2 01 07	2 05 07	2♒03 09	8♒01 37	19 49.6	19 05.4	4 08.9	22 22.6	17 50.9	22 53.6	13 36.7	2 55.8	1 12.8	27 59.8
23 Tu	2 05 04	3 03 36	13 58 44	19 55 03	19 48.8	19 18.2	5 23.0	23 00.3	18 15.2	22 49.0	13 33.9	2 56.5	1 11.1	27 59.3
24 W	2 09 00	4 02 03	25 51 09	1♓47 34	19 47.3	19R 25.2	6 37.1	23 37.9	18 39.6	22 44.6	13 31.1	2 57.2	1 09.5	27 58.9
25 Th	2 12 57	5 00 28	7♓44 48	13 43 20	19 45.3	19 26.5	7 51.3	24 15.6	19 04.0	22 40.3	13 28.2	2 58.0	1 07.8	27 58.5
26 F	2 16 53	5 58 52	19 43 36	25 46 00	19 43.2	19 22.3	9 05.4	24 53.3	19 28.4	22 36.2	13 25.2	2 58.8	1 06.2	27 58.1
27 Sa	2 20 50	6 57 14	1♈50 54	7♈58 35	19 41.2	19 12.8	10 19.4	25 31.0	19 52.8	22 32.3	13 22.1	2 59.7	1 04.6	27 57.7
28 Su	2 24 46	7 55 34	14 09 19	20 23 18	19 39.7	18 58.2	11 33.5	26 08.7	20 17.3	22 28.5	13 19.0	3 00.7	1 02.9	27 57.3
29 M	2 28 43	8 53 53	26 40 42	3♉01 37	19 38.7	18 39.0	12 47.6	26 46.3	20 41.7	22 24.9	13 15.7	3 01.6	1 01.3	27 57.0
30 Tu	2 32 39	9 52 10	9♉26 07	15 54 14	19D 38.2	18 15.6	14 01.6	27 24.0	21 06.3	22 21.5	13 12.5	3 02.7	0 59.7	27 56.7

Astro Data (Dy Hr Mn)

Astro Data	Dy Hr Mn
♃⚺♇	1 11:16
☽0N	2 9:52
☽0S	15 17:24
☉0N	20 21:16
☿0N	22 4:46
♄ R	24 0:45
♀0N	28 13:34
☽0N	29 16:14
♅ D	10 8:21
☽0S	12 2:57
☿ R	25 5:31
☽0N	25 23:17

Planet Ingress

		Dy Hr Mn
♀	♓	1 20:39
☿	♓	4 11:34
⚸	♉	7 15:17
♂	♊	17 21:34
☿	♈	20 19:48
☉	♈	20 21:16
♀	♈	25 22:46
☿	♉	4 23:37
♀	♉	19 3:28
☉	♉	20 8:41

Last Aspect / ☽ Ingress (March)

Last Aspect Dy Hr Mn		☽ Ingress	Dy Hr Mn
3 3:59	♃ ☍	♈	3 6:31
5 15:04	♇ △	♉	5 17:20
7 23:47	♇ □	♊	8 2:03
10 5:31	♇ ⚹	♋	10 7:45
12 6:15	♃ ⚹	♌	12 10:12
14 8:09	♇ ☌	♍	14 10:20
16 8:25	♂ △	♎	16 9:59
18 8:47	♇ ⚹	♏	18 11:15
20 15:27	☉ △	♐	20 15:53
22 21:32	♇ △	♑	23 0:34
25 11:04	♀ ⚹	♒	25 12:17
27 21:39	♇ ☍	♓	28 1:00
30 3:38	♃ ☍	♈	30 12:55

Last Aspect / ☽ Ingress (April)

Last Aspect Dy Hr Mn		☽ Ingress	Dy Hr Mn
1 19:51	♇ △	♉	1 23:11
4 4:13	♇ □	♊	4 7:30
6 10:25	♇ ⚹	♋	6 13:37
8 7:37	♃ ⚹	♌	8 17:24
10 16:09	♇ ☌	♍	10 19:13
12 10:02	♃ ☌	♎	12 20:08
14 18:31	♇ ⚹	♏	14 21:45
16 22:14	♇ □	♐	17 1:43
19 7:09	☉ △	♑	19 9:08
21 5:56	♃ △	♒	21 19:53
24 4:18	♇ ☍	♓	24 8:23
26 10:10	♂ □	♈	26 20:22
29 2:25	♇ △	♉	29 6:18

☽ Phases & Eclipses

Dy Hr Mn	Phase	Position
1 16:12	●	10♓49
9 11:50	☽	18♊39
16 2:22	○	25♍14
23 5:04	☾	2♑18
31 9:19	●	10♈24
7 20:33	☽	17♋45
14 12:09	○	24♎17
21 23:01	☾	1♒33
29 23:54	●	9♉23
30 0:04:54	●	A non-C

Astro Data

1 March 1957
Julian Day # 20879
SVP 5♓51'13"
GC 26♐14.5 ⚳ 18♓32.3
Eris 8♈31.6 ⚵ 6♓47.9
⚷ 14♒06.5 ⚶ 21♒41.4
☽ Mean ☊ 23♏33.8

1 April 1957
Julian Day # 20910
SVP 5♓51'11"
GC 26♐14.5 ⚳ 29♓18.1
Eris 8♈52.5 ⚵ 21♓58.0
⚷ 16♒03.4 ⚶ 7♓01.4
☽ Mean ☊ 21♏55.3

LONGITUDE — May 1957

Day	Sid.Time	☉	0 hr ☽	Noon ☽	True ☊	☿	♀	♂	⚳	♃	♄	♅	♆	♇
1 W	2 36 36	10♉50 25	22♉25 56	29♉01 11	19♏38.3	17♉48.4	15♉15.7	28♊01.7	21♉30.8	22♍18.2	13♐09.1	3♌03.8	0♏58.1	27♌56.5
2 Th	2 40 32	11 48 38	5♊39 54	12♊22 00	19 38.8	17R 17.9	16 29.7	28 39.4	21 55.3	22R 15.2	13R 05.7	3 05.0	0R 56.5	27R 56.3
3 F	2 44 29	12 46 50	19 07 20	25 55 47	19 39.4	16 44.8	17 43.7	29 17.1	22 19.9	22 12.3	13 02.2	3 06.2	0 54.9	27 56.1
4 Sa	2 48 26	13 44 59	2♋47 11	9♋41 24	19 40.0	16 09.6	18 57.6	29 54.7	22 44.5	22 09.5	12 58.7	3 07.4	0 53.3	27 55.9
5 Su	2 52 22	14 43 07	16 38 14	23 37 30	19 40.5	15 33.0	20 11.6	0♋32.4	23 09.1	22 07.0	12 55.1	3 08.7	0 51.7	27 55.8
6 M	2 56 19	15 41 13	0♌39 00	7♌42 31	19R 40.7	14 55.7	21 25.6	1 10.1	23 33.7	22 04.6	12 51.4	3 10.1	0 50.1	27 55.6
7 Tu	3 00 15	16 39 16	14 47 47	21 54 33	19 40.7	14 18.3	22 39.5	1 47.7	23 58.3	22 02.4	12 47.7	3 11.5	0 48.6	27 55.6
8 W	3 04 12	17 37 18	29 02 30	6♍11 17	19 40.6	13 41.5	23 53.4	2 25.4	24 22.9	22 00.4	12 44.0	3 12.9	0 47.0	27 55.5
9 Th	3 08 08	18 35 17	13♍20 33	20 29 53	19 40.5	13 05.9	25 07.3	3 03.0	24 47.6	21 58.6	12 40.1	3 14.4	0 45.5	27D 55.5
10 F	3 12 05	19 33 15	27 38 51	4♎47 00	19D 40.5	12 32.1	26 21.2	3 40.6	25 12.2	21 56.9	12 36.3	3 16.0	0 43.9	27 55.5
11 Sa	3 16 01	20 31 11	11♎53 49	18 58 51	19 40.5	12 00.7	27 35.0	4 18.3	25 36.9	21 55.5	12 32.4	3 17.6	0 42.4	27 55.5
12 Su	3 19 58	21 29 06	26 01 37	3♏01 37	19 40.6	11 32.1	28 48.8	4 55.9	26 01.6	21 54.2	12 28.4	3 19.2	0 40.9	27 55.6
13 M	3 23 55	22 26 58	9♏58 27	16 51 41	19R 40.7	11 06.9	0♊02.7	5 33.5	26 26.3	21 53.1	12 24.4	3 20.9	0 39.4	27 55.7
14 Tu	3 27 51	23 24 50	23 40 59	0♐26 05	19 40.6	10 45.2	1 16.5	6 11.1	26 51.0	21 52.1	12 20.4	3 22.7	0 37.9	27 55.8
15 W	3 31 48	24 22 40	7♐06 45	13 42 50	19 40.3	10 27.5	2 30.3	6 48.8	27 15.7	21 51.4	12 16.3	3 24.4	0 36.4	27 56.0
16 Th	3 35 44	25 20 28	20 14 18	26 41 09	19 39.8	10 14.0	3 44.1	7 26.4	27 40.5	21 50.8	12 12.1	3 26.3	0 35.0	27 56.2
17 F	3 39 41	26 18 15	3♑03 29	9♑21 30	19 39.0	10 04.8	4 57.8	8 04.0	28 05.2	21 50.5	12 08.0	3 28.2	0 33.5	27 56.4
18 Sa	3 43 37	27 16 01	15 35 25	21 45 33	19 38.1	10D 00.0	6 11.6	8 41.6	28 30.0	21D 50.3	12 03.8	3 30.1	0 32.1	27 56.6
19 Su	3 47 34	28 13 46	27 52 18	3♒56 03	19 37.2	9 59.8	7 25.3	9 19.2	28 54.7	21 50.2	11 59.6	3 32.1	0 30.7	27 56.9
20 M	3 51 31	29 11 29	9♒57 18	15 56 33	19 36.5	10 04.2	8 39.1	9 56.8	29 19.5	21 50.4	11 55.3	3 34.1	0 29.3	27 57.2
21 Tu	3 55 27	0♊09 12	21 54 20	27 51 12	19D 36.2	10 13.1	9 52.8	10 34.4	29 44.3	21 50.8	11 51.0	3 36.1	0 27.9	27 57.5
22 W	3 59 24	1 06 53	3♓47 44	9♓44 31	19 36.4	10 26.5	11 06.5	11 12.0	0♊09.0	21 51.3	11 46.7	3 38.2	0 26.5	27 57.9
23 Th	4 03 20	2 04 34	15 42 08	21 41 09	19 37.0	10 44.4	12 20.2	11 49.6	0 33.8	21 52.0	11 42.4	3 40.4	0 25.2	27 58.2
24 F	4 07 17	3 02 13	27 42 07	3♈45 35	19 38.0	11 06.7	13 33.9	12 27.2	0 58.6	21 52.9	11 38.0	3 42.6	0 23.9	27 58.6
25 Sa	4 11 13	3 59 51	9♈52 03	16 01 58	19 39.3	11 33.2	14 47.6	13 04.8	1 23.4	21 53.9	11 33.6	3 44.8	0 22.6	27 59.1
26 Su	4 15 10	4 57 29	22 15 46	28 33 48	19 40.4	12 04.0	16 01.2	13 42.4	1 48.2	21 55.2	11 29.2	3 47.1	0 21.3	27 59.6
27 M	4 19 06	5 55 05	4♉56 21	11♉23 38	19R 41.2	12 38.8	17 14.9	14 20.0	2 13.0	21 56.6	11 24.8	3 49.4	0 20.0	28 00.1
28 Tu	4 23 03	6 52 40	17 55 46	24 32 49	19 41.3	13 17.6	18 28.5	14 57.6	2 37.8	21 58.2	11 20.4	3 51.7	0 18.8	28 00.6
29 W	4 26 59	7 50 15	1♊14 43	8♊01 20	19 40.5	14 00.3	19 42.1	15 35.2	3 02.6	22 00.0	11 16.0	3 54.1	0 17.5	28 01.1
30 Th	4 30 56	8 47 48	14 52 25	21 47 39	19 38.9	14 46.7	20 55.8	16 12.8	3 27.5	22 01.9	11 11.5	3 56.6	0 16.3	28 01.7
31 F	4 34 53	9 45 20	28 46 37	5♋48 53	19 36.5	15 36.7	22 09.4	16 50.4	3 52.3	22 04.1	11 07.1	3 59.0	0 15.1	28 02.4

LONGITUDE — June 1957

Day	Sid.Time	☉	0 hr ☽	Noon ☽	True ☊	☿	♀	♂	⚳	♃	♄	♅	♆	♇
1 Sa	4 38 49	10♊42 51	12♋53 53	20♋01 05	19♏33.7	16♉30.3	23♊23.0	17♋27.9	4♊17.1	22♍06.4	11♐02.6	4♌01.5	0♏14.0	28♌03.0
2 Su	4 42 46	11 40 21	27 09 54	4♌19 45	19R 31.0	17 27.4	24 36.5	18 05.5	4 41.9	22 08.8	10R 58.2	4 04.1	0R 12.8	28 03.7
3 M	4 46 42	12 37 49	11♌30 07	18 40 26	19 28.7	18 27.9	25 50.1	18 43.1	5 06.7	22 11.5	10 53.7	4 06.7	0 11.7	28 04.4
4 Tu	4 50 39	13 35 16	25 50 14	2♍59 07	19D 27.4	19 31.6	27 03.6	19 20.7	5 31.5	22 14.3	10 49.3	4 09.3	0 10.6	28 05.1
5 W	4 54 35	14 32 42	10♍06 41	17 12 38	19 27.0	20 38.6	28 17.2	19 58.3	5 56.3	22 17.3	10 44.8	4 12.0	0 09.6	28 05.8
6 Th	4 58 32	15 30 06	24 16 42	1♎18 41	19 27.7	21 48.8	29 30.7	20 35.9	6 21.1	22 20.5	10 40.4	4 14.7	0 08.5	28 06.6
7 F	5 02 29	16 27 30	8♎18 24	15 15 42	19 29.0	23 02.1	0♋44.2	21 13.5	6 45.8	22 23.8	10 36.0	4 17.4	0 07.5	28 07.4
8 Sa	5 06 25	17 24 52	22 10 28	29 02 35	19 30.5	24 18.4	1 57.6	21 51.0	7 10.6	22 27.3	10 31.6	4 20.2	0 06.5	28 08.3
9 Su	5 10 22	18 22 13	5♏51 58	12♏38 31	19R 31.5	25 37.8	3 11.1	22 28.6	7 35.4	22 30.9	10 27.2	4 23.0	0 05.5	28 09.1
10 M	5 14 18	19 19 34	19 22 07	26 02 41	19 31.5	27 00.2	4 24.6	23 06.2	8 00.1	22 34.7	10 22.8	4 25.8	0 04.6	28 10.0
11 Tu	5 18 15	20 16 53	2♐40 07	9♐14 21	19 30.1	28 25.5	5 38.0	23 43.8	8 24.9	22 38.7	10 18.5	4 28.7	0 03.7	28 10.9
12 W	5 22 11	21 14 12	15 45 17	22 12 51	19 27.2	29 53.8	6 51.4	24 21.3	8 49.6	22 42.9	10 14.2	4 31.6	0 02.8	28 11.9
13 Th	5 26 08	22 11 30	28 37 02	4♑57 49	19 22.8	1♊25.0	8 04.8	24 58.9	9 14.4	22 47.2	10 09.8	4 34.5	0 01.9	28 12.8
14 F	5 30 04	23 08 48	11♑15 14	17 29 21	19 17.4	2 59.1	9 18.2	25 36.5	9 39.1	22 51.6	10 05.6	4 37.5	0 01.1	28 13.8
15 Sa	5 34 01	24 06 05	23 40 18	29 48 15	19 11.5	4 36.0	10 31.6	26 14.1	10 03.8	22 56.2	10 01.3	4 40.4	0 00.3	28 14.8
16 Su	5 37 58	25 03 21	5♒53 25	11♒56 06	19 05.7	6 15.8	11 45.0	26 51.6	10 28.5	23 01.0	9 57.1	4 43.5	29♎59.5	28 15.9
17 M	5 41 54	26 00 37	17 56 36	23 55 20	19 00.7	7 58.5	12 58.3	27 29.2	10 53.2	23 05.9	9 52.9	4 46.5	29 58.7	28 16.9
18 Tu	5 45 51	26 57 53	29 52 43	5♓49 13	18 57.0	9 43.9	14 11.6	28 06.8	11 17.9	23 10.9	9 48.7	4 49.6	29 58.0	28 18.0
19 W	5 49 47	27 55 08	11♓45 21	17 41 41	18D 54.8	11 32.0	15 25.0	28 44.4	11 42.6	23 16.2	9 44.6	4 52.7	29 57.3	28 19.1
20 Th	5 53 44	28 52 24	23 38 47	29 37 15	18 54.2	13 22.9	16 38.3	29 21.9	12 07.2	23 21.5	9 40.5	4 55.8	29 56.6	28 20.3
21 F	5 57 40	29 49 39	5♈37 42	11♈40 45	18 54.8	15 16.3	17 51.6	29 59.5	12 31.9	23 27.0	9 36.5	4 59.0	29 56.0	28 21.4
22 Sa	6 01 37	0♋46 53	17 47 00	23 57 03	18 56.2	17 12.3	19 04.9	0♌37.1	12 56.5	23 32.7	9 32.5	5 02.2	29 55.4	28 22.6
23 Su	6 05 33	1 44 08	0♉11 28	6♉30 46	18R 57.5	19 10.7	20 18.2	1 14.7	13 21.1	23 38.5	9 28.5	5 05.4	29 54.8	28 23.8
24 M	6 09 30	2 41 23	12 55 25	19 25 47	18 58.1	21 11.3	21 31.4	1 52.3	13 45.8	23 44.4	9 24.6	5 08.6	29 54.2	28 25.0
25 Tu	6 13 27	3 38 38	26 02 10	2♊44 44	18 57.2	23 14.0	22 44.7	2 29.9	14 10.3	23 50.5	9 20.8	5 11.9	29 53.7	28 26.3
26 W	6 17 23	4 35 52	9♊33 31	16 28 25	18 54.5	25 18.6	23 57.9	3 07.5	14 34.9	23 56.8	9 16.9	5 15.2	29 53.2	28 27.6
27 Th	6 21 20	5 33 06	23 29 10	0♋35 22	18 49.7	27 24.8	25 11.2	3 45.1	14 59.5	24 03.1	9 13.2	5 18.5	29 52.7	28 28.9
28 F	6 25 16	6 30 21	7♋46 25	15 01 38	18 43.3	29 32.5	26 24.4	4 22.8	15 24.0	24 09.6	9 09.5	5 21.8	29 52.3	28 30.2
29 Sa	6 29 13	7 27 35	22 20 08	29 41 03	18 36.0	1♋41.4	27 37.6	5 00.4	15 48.5	24 16.3	9 05.8	5 25.2	29 51.9	28 31.5
30 Su	6 33 09	8 24 48	7♌03 22	14♌26 06	18 28.7	3 51.1	28 50.8	5 38.0	16 13.0	24 23.1	9 02.2	5 28.6	29 51.5	28 32.9

Astro Data
Dy Hr Mn
☽0S 9 10:01
♇D 9 19:51
☿D 19 1:03
♃D 19 2:20
☽0N 23 7:19

☽0S 5 15:48
☽0N 19 15:57

Planet Ingress
Dy Hr Mn
♂ ♋ 4 15:22
♀ ♊ 13 11:08
☉ ♊ 21 8:10
⚳ ♊ 22 3:15

♀ ♋ 6 21:35
☿ ♊ 12 13:40
♆ ♎R 15 20:07
♂ ♌ 21 12:18
☉ ♋ 21 16:21
☿ ♋ 28 17:08

Last Aspect Dy Hr Mn		☽ Ingress Dy Hr Mn
1 10:03	♇ □	♊ 1 13:47
3 18:10	♂ ☌	♋ 3 19:08
5 9:25	♃ ⚹	♌ 5 22:54
7 22:07	♇ ☌	♍ 8 1:37
9 20:29	☿ △	♎ 10 3:57
12 3:15	♇ ⚹	♏ 12 6:48
14 7:32	♇ □	♐ 14 11:13
16 14:21	♇ △	♑ 16 18:13
18 23:44	☉ △	♒ 19 4:12
21 12:13	♇ ☍	♓ 21 16:20
23 12:22	♃ ☍	♈ 24 4:34
26 10:55	♇ △	♉ 26 14:43
28 18:14	♇ □	♊ 28 21:47
30 22:44	♇ ⚹	♋ 31 2:05

Last Aspect Dy Hr Mn		☽ Ingress Dy Hr Mn
1 15:31	♃ ⚹	♌ 2 4:45
4 3:46	♇ ☌	♍ 4 6:59
6 8:38	♀ □	♎ 6 9:45
8 10:25	♇ ⚹	♏ 8 13:41
10 15:50	♇ □	♐ 10 19:09
12 23:13	♇ △	♑ 13 2:36
15 4:38	♂ ☍	♒ 15 12:23
18 0:11	♆ △	♓ 18 0:15
20 11:28	♂ △	♈ 20 12:46
22 23:29	♆ ☍	♉ 22 23:38
25 4:18	♇ □	♊ 25 7:07
27 10:48	♆ △	♋ 27 11:01
29 12:18	♆ □	♌ 29 12:31

☽ Phases & Eclipses
Dy Hr Mn
7 2:29 ☽ 16♌16
13 22:34 ○ 22♏52
13 22:31 T 1.299
21 17:03 ☾ 0♓21
29 11:39 ● 7♊49

5 7:10 ☽ 14♍21
12 10:02 ○ 21♐10
20 10:22 ☾ 28♓49
27 20:53 ● 5♋54

Astro Data
1 May 1957
Julian Day # 20940
SVP 5♓51'08"
GC 26♐14.6 ⚴ 9♈43.6
Eris 9♈12.3 ⚵ 6♈58.6
⚷ 17♒11.9 ⚶ 20♓52.9
☽ Mean ☊ 20♏19.9

1 June 1957
Julian Day # 20971
SVP 5♓51'03"
GC 26♐14.7 ⚴ 20♈05.3
Eris 9♈27.7 ⚵ 22♈36.9
⚷ 17♒23.3R ⚶ 3♈40.4
☽ Mean ☊ 18♏41.4

July 1957 — LONGITUDE

Day	Sid.Time	☉	0 hr ☽	Noon ☽	True ☊	☿	♀	♂	⚳	♃	♄	♅	♆	♇
1 M	6 37 06	9♋22 01	21♌48 19	29♌09 06	18♏22.4	6♋01.4	0♌04.0	6♌15.6	16♊37.5	24♍30.0	8♐58.7	5♌32.0	29♎51.2	28♌34.3
2 Tu	6 41 02	10 19 14	6♍27 41	13♍43 23	18R17.7	8 12.1	1 17.1	6 53.3	17 01.9	24 37.0	8R55.2	5 35.4	29R50.9	28 35.7
3 W	6 44 59	11 16 27	20 55 39	28 04 07	18D15.1	10 22.7	2 30.2	7 30.9	17 26.4	24 44.2	8 51.8	5 38.8	29 50.6	28 37.1
4 Th	6 48 56	12 13 39	5♎08 29	12♎08 39	18 14.3	12 33.1	3 43.4	8 08.5	17 50.8	24 51.5	8 48.5	5 42.3	29 50.4	28 38.6
5 F	6 52 52	13 10 51	19 04 32	25 56 13	18 14.8	14 43.0	4 56.4	8 46.2	18 15.1	24 58.9	8 45.2	5 45.8	29 50.1	28 40.0
6 Sa	6 56 49	14 08 03	2♏43 47	9♏27 24	18R15.7	16 52.1	6 09.5	9 23.8	18 39.5	25 06.5	8 42.0	5 49.2	29 50.0	28 41.5
7 Su	7 00 45	15 05 14	16 07 15	22 43 32	18 15.8	19 00.3	7 22.6	10 01.5	19 03.8	25 14.1	8 38.9	5 52.7	29 49.8	28 43.0
8 M	7 04 42	16 02 25	29 16 27	5♐46 10	18 14.4	21 07.4	8 35.6	10 39.1	19 28.1	25 21.9	8 35.8	5 56.3	29 49.7	28 44.6
9 Tu	7 08 38	16 59 37	12♐12 51	18 36 38	18 10.7	23 13.2	9 48.6	11 16.8	19 52.4	25 29.8	8 32.8	5 59.8	29 49.6	28 46.1
10 W	7 12 35	17 56 48	24 57 40	1♑16 02	18 04.5	25 17.5	11 01.6	11 54.4	20 16.6	25 37.9	8 29.9	6 03.4	29 49.5	28 47.7
11 Th	7 16 31	18 54 00	7♑31 48	13 45 05	17 55.9	27 20.3	12 14.6	12 32.1	20 40.8	25 46.0	8 27.0	6 06.9	29D49.5	28 49.2
12 F	7 20 28	19 51 11	19 55 55	26 04 23	17 45.5	29 21.5	13 27.5	13 09.8	21 05.0	25 54.3	8 24.2	6 10.5	29 49.5	28 50.8
13 Sa	7 24 25	20 48 23	2♒10 35	8♒14 39	17 34.1	1♌21.1	14 40.5	13 47.5	21 29.2	26 02.6	8 21.5	6 14.1	29 49.6	28 52.4
14 Su	7 28 21	21 45 36	14 16 42	20 16 55	17 22.8	3 18.8	15 53.4	14 25.1	21 53.3	26 11.1	8 18.9	6 17.7	29 49.6	28 54.1
15 M	7 32 18	22 42 49	26 15 32	2♓12 48	17 12.5	5 14.8	17 06.3	15 02.8	22 17.4	26 19.7	8 16.4	6 21.3	29 49.7	28 55.7
16 Tu	7 36 14	23 40 02	8♓09 03	14 04 38	17 04.1	7 09.1	18 19.1	15 40.5	22 41.4	26 28.4	8 13.9	6 24.9	29 49.9	28 57.4
17 W	7 40 11	24 37 16	19 59 59	25 55 32	16 58.0	9 01.5	19 32.0	16 18.2	23 05.4	26 37.2	8 11.5	6 28.6	29 50.0	28 59.0
18 Th	7 44 07	25 34 30	1♈51 50	7♈49 24	16 54.4	10 52.0	20 44.8	16 55.9	23 29.4	26 46.1	8 09.2	6 32.2	29 50.2	29 00.7
19 F	7 48 04	26 31 45	13 48 50	19 50 45	16D52.8	12 40.8	21 57.6	17 33.7	23 53.4	26 55.1	8 07.0	6 35.9	29 50.5	29 02.4
20 Sa	7 52 00	27 29 01	25 55 47	2♉04 35	16 52.7	14 27.7	23 10.4	18 11.4	24 17.3	27 04.2	8 04.9	6 39.5	29 50.7	29 04.2
21 Su	7 55 57	28 26 18	8♉17 47	14 36 02	16R53.0	16 12.9	24 23.2	18 49.1	24 41.2	27 13.5	8 02.8	6 43.2	29 51.0	29 05.9
22 M	7 59 54	29 23 36	20 59 55	27 29 57	16 52.6	17 56.2	25 35.9	19 26.9	25 05.0	27 22.8	8 00.9	6 46.9	29 51.4	29 07.6
23 Tu	8 03 50	0♌20 54	4♊06 35	10♊50 11	16 50.6	19 37.7	26 48.7	20 04.7	25 28.8	27 32.2	7 59.0	6 50.6	29 51.7	29 09.4
24 W	8 07 47	1 18 13	17 40 56	24 38 54	16 46.2	21 17.4	28 01.4	20 42.4	25 52.6	27 41.7	7 57.2	6 54.2	29 52.1	29 11.2
25 Th	8 11 43	2 15 34	1♋43 56	8♋55 41	16 39.3	22 55.3	29 14.1	21 20.2	26 16.3	27 51.3	7 55.5	6 57.9	29 52.5	29 13.0
26 F	8 15 40	3 12 55	16 13 36	23 36 55	16 30.2	24 31.4	0♍26.7	21 58.0	26 40.0	28 01.1	7 53.9	7 01.6	29 53.0	29 14.8
27 Sa	8 19 36	4 10 16	1♌04 39	8♌35 43	16 19.7	26 05.7	1 39.4	22 35.8	27 03.7	28 10.9	7 52.4	7 05.3	29 53.5	29 16.6
28 Su	8 23 33	5 07 39	16 08 49	23 42 42	16 09.2	27 38.2	2 52.0	23 13.7	27 27.2	28 20.8	7 51.0	7 09.0	29 54.0	29 18.4
29 M	8 27 29	6 05 02	1♍16 02	8♍47 34	15 59.7	29 08.9	4 04.6	23 51.5	27 50.8	28 30.7	7 49.6	7 12.7	29 54.6	29 20.3
30 Tu	8 31 26	7 02 25	16 16 11	23 40 54	15 52.3	0♍37.8	5 17.2	24 29.3	28 14.3	28 40.8	7 48.4	7 16.4	29 55.2	29 22.1
31 W	8 35 23	7 59 49	1♎00 55	8♎15 40	15 47.6	2 04.8	6 29.7	25 07.2	28 37.7	28 51.0	7 47.2	7 20.1	29 55.8	29 24.0

August 1957 — LONGITUDE

Day	Sid.Time	☉	0 hr ☽	Noon ☽	True ☊	☿	♀	♂	⚳	♃	♄	♅	♆	♇
1 Th	8 39 19	8♌57 14	15♎24 45	22♎27 56	15♏45.2	3♍30.0	7♍42.2	25♌45.0	29♊01.1	29♍01.2	7♐46.2	7♌23.8	29♎56.4	29♌25.8
2 F	8 43 16	9 54 40	29 25 12	6♏16 38	15R44.6	4 53.3	8 54.7	26 22.9	29 24.5	29 11.5	7R45.2	7 27.5	29 57.1	29 27.7
3 Sa	8 47 12	10 52 06	13♏02 27	19 42 55	15 44.6	6 14.6	10 07.2	27 00.8	29 47.8	29 22.0	7 44.4	7 31.2	29 57.8	29 29.6
4 Su	8 51 09	11 49 32	26 18 24	2♐49 16	15 43.9	7 34.0	11 19.6	27 38.7	0♋11.0	29 32.5	7 43.6	7 34.9	29 58.5	29 31.5
5 M	8 55 05	12 47 00	9♐15 55	15 38 44	15 41.5	8 51.3	12 32.0	28 16.6	0 34.2	29 43.0	7 42.9	7 38.6	29 59.3	29 33.4
6 Tu	8 59 02	13 44 28	21 58 05	28 14 20	15 36.6	10 06.6	13 44.3	28 54.5	0 57.3	29 53.7	7 42.4	7 42.3	0♏00.1	29 35.3
7 W	9 02 58	14 41 57	4♑27 46	10♑38 41	15 28.8	11 19.8	14 56.7	29 32.4	1 20.4	0♎04.4	7 41.9	7 46.0	0 01.0	29 37.2
8 Th	9 06 55	15 39 27	16 47 20	22 53 55	15 18.3	12 30.8	16 09.0	0♍10.4	1 43.4	0 15.2	7 41.5	7 49.7	0 01.8	29 39.1
9 F	9 10 52	16 36 58	28 58 39	5♒01 39	15 05.7	13 39.5	17 21.2	0 48.3	2 06.4	0 26.1	7 41.2	7 53.4	0 02.7	29 41.1
10 Sa	9 14 48	17 34 30	11♒03 07	17 03 10	14 52.0	14 45.9	18 33.4	1 26.3	2 29.3	0 37.0	7 41.0	7 57.0	0 03.6	29 43.0
11 Su	9 18 45	18 32 03	23 01 56	28 59 35	14 38.3	15 49.8	19 45.6	2 04.2	2 52.1	0 48.0	7D40.9	8 00.7	0 04.6	29 44.9
12 M	9 22 41	19 29 37	4♓56 18	10♓52 15	14 25.7	16 51.2	20 57.8	2 42.2	3 14.9	0 59.1	7 40.9	8 04.3	0 05.6	29 46.9
13 Tu	9 26 38	20 27 12	16 47 41	22 42 52	14 15.1	17 49.9	22 09.9	3 20.2	3 37.6	1 10.3	7 41.0	8 08.0	0 06.6	29 48.8
14 W	9 30 34	21 24 49	28 38 05	4♈33 43	14 07.2	18 45.7	23 22.0	3 58.2	4 00.2	1 21.5	7 41.2	8 11.6	0 07.6	29 50.8
15 Th	9 34 31	22 22 27	10♈30 10	16 27 51	14 02.0	19 38.7	24 34.0	4 36.2	4 22.8	1 32.8	7 41.5	8 15.2	0 08.7	29 52.8
16 F	9 38 27	23 20 07	22 27 17	28 29 00	13 59.4	20 28.5	25 46.0	5 14.3	4 45.3	1 44.1	7 41.9	8 18.9	0 09.8	29 54.7
17 Sa	9 42 24	24 17 48	4♉33 34	10♉41 36	13D58.7	21 15.1	26 58.0	5 52.3	5 07.8	1 55.5	7 42.4	8 22.5	0 10.9	29 56.7
18 Su	9 46 21	25 15 31	16 53 41	23 10 29	13R58.7	21 58.3	28 10.0	6 30.4	5 30.2	2 07.0	7 43.0	8 26.0	0 12.1	29 58.7
19 M	9 50 17	26 13 16	29 32 35	6♊00 35	13 58.4	22 37.8	29 21.9	7 08.5	5 52.5	2 18.5	7 43.6	8 29.6	0 13.3	0♍00.6
20 Tu	9 54 14	27 11 02	12♊35 01	19 16 21	13 56.8	23 13.4	0♎33.7	7 46.6	6 14.7	2 30.1	7 44.4	8 33.2	0 14.5	0 02.6
21 W	9 58 10	28 08 50	26 04 55	3♋00 56	13 53.0	23 45.0	1 45.6	8 24.7	6 36.9	2 41.8	7 45.3	8 36.7	0 15.7	0 04.6
22 Th	10 02 07	29 06 40	10♋04 26	17 15 15	13 46.6	24 12.2	2 57.4	9 02.9	6 59.0	2 53.5	7 46.3	8 40.3	0 17.0	0 06.6
23 F	10 06 03	0♍04 31	24 33 02	1♌57 07	13 38.1	24 34.9	4 09.2	9 41.1	7 21.0	3 05.3	7 47.3	8 43.8	0 18.3	0 08.5
24 Sa	10 10 00	1 02 24	9♌26 41	17 00 39	13 28.1	24 52.8	5 20.9	10 19.2	7 42.9	3 17.1	7 48.5	8 47.3	0 19.6	0 10.5
25 Su	10 13 56	2 00 18	24 37 48	2♍16 43	13 17.9	25 05.6	6 32.6	10 57.4	8 04.7	3 29.0	7 49.8	8 50.8	0 21.0	0 12.5
26 M	10 17 53	2 58 14	9♍56 00	17 34 11	13 08.6	25R13.1	7 44.3	11 35.7	8 26.5	3 40.9	7 51.1	8 54.3	0 22.3	0 14.5
27 Tu	10 21 50	3 56 11	25 09 55	2♎41 58	13 01.4	25 15.0	8 55.9	12 13.9	8 48.1	3 52.9	7 52.6	8 57.7	0 23.7	0 16.5
28 W	10 25 46	4 54 10	10♎09 15	17 30 57	12 56.7	25 11.1	10 07.5	12 52.1	9 09.7	4 05.0	7 54.1	9 01.1	0 25.2	0 18.4
29 Th	10 29 43	5 52 10	24 46 25	1♏55 16	12D54.4	25 01.3	11 19.0	13 30.4	9 31.2	4 17.0	7 55.8	9 04.6	0 26.6	0 20.4
30 F	10 33 39	6 50 12	8♏57 17	15 52 26	12 54.0	24 45.3	12 30.5	14 08.7	9 52.6	4 29.2	7 57.5	9 07.9	0 28.1	0 22.4
31 Sa	10 37 36	7 48 15	22 40 54	29 22 55	12R54.5	24 23.2	13 42.0	14 47.0	10 13.9	4 41.3	7 59.3	9 11.3	0 29.6	0 24.3

Astro Data	Dy Hr Mn	Planet Ingress	Dy Hr Mn
☽0S	2 22:14	♀ ♌	1 10:42
♆D	11 17:50	☿ ♌	12 19:41
☽0N	17 0:20	☉ ♌	23 3:15
☽0S	30 6:39	♀ ♍	26 3:10
		☿ ♍	30 1:44
♃⊻♇	4 9:18		
♄△♅	6 12:14	⚳ ♋	4 0:38
♃⊻♆	7 3:40	♆ ♏	6 8:25
♄D	11 23:57	♃ ♎	7 2:11
☽0N	13 7:46	♂ ♍	8 5:27
☿0S	20 5:31	♇ ♍	19 4:23
♃0S	21 3:35	♀ ♎	20 0:44
♀0S	21 12:06	☉ ♍	23 10:08
☽0S	26 16:58		
☿R	27 8:04		

Last Aspect Dy Hr Mn	☽ Ingress Dy Hr Mn	Last Aspect Dy Hr Mn	☽ Ingress Dy Hr Mn
1 13:09 ♆ ⚹	♍ 1 13:23	2 0:55 ♆ ☌	♏ 2 1:01
3 6:20 ♃ ☌	♎ 3 15:16	4 5:54 ♇ □	♐ 4 6:47
5 18:52 ♆ ☌	♏ 5 19:10	6 15:14 ♃ □	♑ 6 15:23
7 23:00 ♇ □	♐ 8 1:20	7 21:18 ♀ △	♒ 9 2:01
10 9:15 ♆ ⚹	♑ 10 9:35	11 13:32 ♇ ☍	♓ 11 14:02
12 19:22 ♆ □	♒ 12 19:43	13 10:46 ♀ ☍	♈ 14 2:46
15 7:11 ♆ △	♓ 15 7:32	16 14:50 ♇ △	♉ 16 15:00
17 13:25 ♃ ☍	♈ 17 20:14	19 0:51 ♇ □	♊ 19 0:51
20 7:40 ♆ ☍	♉ 20 7:58	21 2:58 ☉ ⚹	♋ 21 6:48
22 15:44 ☉ ⚹	♊ 22 16:34	22 23:45 ☿ ⚹	♌ 23 8:51
24 20:52 ♆ △	♋ 24 21:05	23 22:54 ♅ ☌	♍ 25 8:26
26 22:05 ♆ □	♌ 26 22:16	27 0:08 ☿ ☌	♎ 27 7:41
28 21:50 ♆ ⚹	♍ 28 21:59	27 22:54 ♀ ☌	♏ 29 8:45
30 20:16 ♃ ☌	♎ 30 22:20	31 3:18 ☿ ⚹	♐ 31 13:07

☽ Phases & Eclipses Dy Hr Mn	
4 12:09	☽ 12♎14
11 22:50	○ 19♑20
20 2:17	☾ 27♈06
27 4:28	● 3♌52
2 18:55	☽ 10♏11
10 13:08	○ 17♒37
18 16:16	☾ 25♉26
25 11:33	● 1♍59

Astro Data

1 July 1957
Julian Day # 21001
SVP 5♓50'58"
GC 26♐14.7 ⚵ 29♈11.5
Eris 9♈34.0 ⚴ 7♉35.6
⚷ 16♒37.1R ⚶ 13♈46.0
☽ Mean ☊ 17♏06.1

1 August 1957
Julian Day # 21032
SVP 5♓50'54"
GC 26♐14.8 ⚵ 6♉43.9
Eris 9♈30.4R ⚴ 22♉25.0
⚷ 15♒08.3R ⚶ 20♈23.2
☽ Mean ☊ 15♏27.6

LONGITUDE — September 1957

Day	Sid.Time	☉	0 hr ☽	Noon ☽	True ☊	☿	♀	♂	⚳	♃	♄	♅	♆	♇
1 Su	10 41 32	8♍46 19	5♐58 52	12♐29 09	12♏54.6	23♍54.9	14♎53.4	15♍25.3	10♋35.1	4♎53.6	8♐01.3	9♌14.7	0♏31.1	0♍26.3
2 M	10 45 29	9 44 24	18 54 16	25 14 42	12R53.4	23R20.7	16 04.7	16 03.7	10 56.2	5 05.8	8 03.3	9 18.0	0 32.7	0 28.3
3 Tu	10 49 25	10 42 31	1♑30 56	7♑43 29	12 50.1	22 40.6	17 16.0	16 42.0	11 17.2	5 18.1	8 05.4	9 21.3	0 34.2	0 30.2
4 W	10 53 22	11 40 40	13 52 48	19 59 20	12 44.3	21 55.2	18 27.2	17 20.4	11 38.1	5 30.5	8 07.6	9 24.6	0 35.8	0 32.2
5 Th	10 57 19	12 38 50	26 03 30	2♒05 39	12 36.2	21 05.0	19 38.4	17 58.8	11 59.0	5 42.8	8 09.9	9 27.8	0 37.5	0 34.1
6 F	11 01 15	13 37 01	8♒06 08	14 05 14	12 26.3	20 10.8	20 49.6	18 37.2	12 19.7	5 55.3	8 12.3	9 31.1	0 39.1	0 36.1
7 Sa	11 05 12	14 35 14	20 03 15	26 00 23	12 15.3	19 13.4	22 00.7	19 15.6	12 40.3	6 07.7	8 14.8	9 34.3	0 40.8	0 38.0
8 Su	11 09 08	15 33 29	1♓56 54	7♓52 57	12 04.3	18 14.1	23 11.7	19 54.0	13 00.7	6 20.2	8 17.3	9 37.4	0 42.4	0 39.9
9 M	11 13 05	16 31 46	13 48 46	19 44 31	11 54.3	17 13.9	24 22.7	20 32.5	13 21.1	6 32.7	8 20.0	9 40.6	0 44.2	0 41.9
10 Tu	11 17 01	17 30 04	25 40 25	1♈36 40	11 45.9	16 14.2	25 33.6	21 11.0	13 41.4	6 45.3	8 22.7	9 43.7	0 45.9	0 43.8
11 W	11 20 58	18 28 24	7♈33 29	13 31 09	11 39.8	15 16.4	26 44.4	21 49.5	14 01.5	6 57.9	8 25.6	9 46.8	0 47.6	0 45.7
12 Th	11 24 54	19 26 46	19 29 56	25 30 10	11 36.1	14 22.0	27 55.3	22 28.0	14 21.6	7 10.5	8 28.5	9 49.9	0 49.4	0 47.6
13 F	11 28 51	20 25 10	1♉32 11	7♉36 23	11D34.7	13 32.1	29 06.0	23 06.5	14 41.5	7 23.1	8 31.5	9 52.9	0 51.2	0 49.5
14 Sa	11 32 47	21 23 36	13 43 13	19 53 08	11 34.9	12 48.2	0♏16.7	23 45.1	15 01.3	7 35.8	8 34.6	9 55.9	0 53.0	0 51.3
15 Su	11 36 44	22 22 05	26 06 37	2♊24 10	11 36.0	12 11.3	1 27.3	24 23.7	15 21.0	7 48.5	8 37.8	9 58.9	0 54.8	0 53.2
16 M	11 40 41	23 20 35	8♊46 18	15 13 33	11R37.1	11 42.4	2 37.9	25 02.3	15 40.5	8 01.2	8 41.0	10 01.8	0 56.7	0 55.1
17 Tu	11 44 37	24 19 08	21 46 21	28 25 11	11 37.3	11 22.1	3 48.4	25 41.0	15 59.9	8 14.0	8 44.4	10 04.7	0 58.6	0 56.9
18 W	11 48 34	25 17 43	5♋10 23	12♋02 14	11 35.9	11D11.1	4 58.9	26 19.6	16 19.2	8 26.8	8 47.8	10 07.6	1 00.4	0 58.8
19 Th	11 52 30	26 16 21	19 00 53	26 06 09	11 32.8	11 09.6	6 09.3	26 58.3	16 38.4	8 39.6	8 51.3	10 10.5	1 02.4	1 00.6
20 F	11 56 27	27 15 00	3♌18 22	10♌36 39	11 27.8	11 17.9	7 19.7	27 37.0	16 57.4	8 52.4	8 54.9	10 13.3	1 04.3	1 02.4
21 Sa	12 00 23	28 13 41	18 00 35	25 29 22	11 21.7	11 35.8	8 29.9	28 15.8	17 16.2	9 05.2	8 58.6	10 16.1	1 06.2	1 04.3
22 Su	12 04 20	29 12 25	3♍02 02	10♍37 25	11 15.3	12 03.3	9 40.2	28 54.5	17 35.0	9 18.1	9 02.4	10 18.8	1 08.2	1 06.0
23 M	12 08 16	0♎11 11	18 14 17	25 51 17	11 09.4	12 39.9	10 50.3	29 33.3	17 53.5	9 31.0	9 06.2	10 21.5	1 10.1	1 07.8
24 Tu	12 12 13	1 09 58	3♎27 05	11♎00 24	11 04.9	13 25.2	12 00.4	0♎12.1	18 12.0	9 43.9	9 10.2	10 24.2	1 12.1	1 09.6
25 W	12 16 10	2 08 48	18 30 05	25 55 04	11 02.2	14 18.8	13 10.4	0 50.9	18 30.2	9 56.8	9 14.2	10 26.8	1 14.1	1 11.4
26 Th	12 20 06	3 07 40	3♏14 32	10♏27 49	11D01.3	15 19.9	14 20.4	1 29.8	18 48.4	10 09.7	9 18.2	10 29.4	1 16.1	1 13.1
27 F	12 24 03	4 06 33	17 34 29	24 34 17	11 01.9	16 27.9	15 30.3	2 08.7	19 06.3	10 22.6	9 22.4	10 32.0	1 18.2	1 14.8
28 Sa	12 27 59	5 05 28	1♐27 08	8♐13 07	11 03.3	17 42.1	16 40.1	2 47.6	19 24.1	10 35.6	9 26.6	10 34.5	1 20.2	1 16.5
29 Su	12 31 56	6 04 25	14 52 28	21 25 31	11 04.7	19 02.0	17 49.8	3 26.5	19 41.7	10 48.6	9 31.0	10 37.0	1 22.3	1 18.2
30 M	12 35 52	7 03 24	27 52 39	4♑14 22	11R05.6	20 26.7	18 59.4	4 05.4	19 59.2	11 01.5	9 35.4	10 39.4	1 24.4	1 19.9

LONGITUDE — October 1957

Day	Sid.Time	☉	0 hr ☽	Noon ☽	True ☊	☿	♀	♂	⚳	♃	♄	♅	♆	♇
1 Tu	12 39 49	8♎02 24	10♑31 10	16♑43 34	11♏05.2	21♍55.6	20♏09.0	4♎44.4	20♋16.5	11♎14.5	9♐39.8	10♌41.8	1♏26.4	1♍21.6
2 W	12 43 45	9 01 27	22 52 09	28 57 26	11R03.4	23 28.2	21 18.4	5 23.4	20 33.6	11 27.5	9 44.3	10 44.1	1 28.5	1 23.2
3 Th	12 47 42	10 00 31	4♒59 58	11♒00 14	11 00.2	25 03.7	22 27.8	6 02.4	20 50.5	11 40.5	9 49.0	10 46.4	1 30.7	1 24.9
4 F	12 51 39	10 59 36	16 58 43	22 55 53	10 55.8	26 41.8	23 37.1	6 41.4	21 07.3	11 53.4	9 53.6	10 48.7	1 32.8	1 26.5
5 Sa	12 55 35	11 58 44	28 52 09	4♓47 53	10 50.8	28 21.9	24 46.3	7 20.5	21 23.8	12 06.4	9 58.4	10 50.9	1 34.9	1 28.1
6 Su	12 59 32	12 57 53	10♓43 27	16 39 10	10 45.7	0♎03.7	25 55.4	7 59.6	21 40.2	12 19.4	10 03.2	10 53.1	1 37.0	1 29.7
7 M	13 03 28	13 57 05	22 35 20	28 32 11	10 41.0	1 46.6	27 04.4	8 38.7	21 56.4	12 32.4	10 08.1	10 55.3	1 39.2	1 31.2
8 Tu	13 07 25	14 56 18	4♈30 00	10♈28 58	10 37.3	3 30.5	28 13.3	9 17.8	22 12.4	12 45.4	10 13.0	10 57.4	1 41.4	1 32.8
9 W	13 11 21	15 55 33	16 29 19	22 31 16	10 34.8	5 15.0	29 22.0	9 57.0	22 28.2	12 58.4	10 18.0	10 59.4	1 43.5	1 34.3
10 Th	13 15 18	16 54 51	28 35 00	4♉40 44	10D33.6	6 59.9	0♐30.7	10 36.2	22 43.8	13 11.4	10 23.1	11 01.4	1 45.7	1 35.8
11 F	13 19 14	17 54 10	10♉48 41	16 59 04	10 33.6	8 45.0	1 39.3	11 15.4	22 59.2	13 24.3	10 28.2	11 03.4	1 47.9	1 37.3
12 Sa	13 23 11	18 53 32	23 12 09	29 28 11	10 34.5	10 30.2	2 47.8	11 54.6	23 14.3	13 37.3	10 33.4	11 05.3	1 50.1	1 38.7
13 Su	13 27 07	19 52 56	5♊47 26	12♊10 10	10 36.0	12 15.2	3 56.1	12 33.9	23 29.3	13 50.3	10 38.7	11 07.1	1 52.3	1 40.2
14 M	13 31 04	20 52 22	18 36 43	25 07 21	10 37.5	14 00.0	5 04.3	13 13.2	23 44.1	14 03.2	10 44.0	11 09.0	1 54.5	1 41.6
15 Tu	13 35 01	21 51 51	1♋42 22	8♋22 01	10 38.6	15 44.5	6 12.4	13 52.5	23 58.6	14 16.2	10 49.4	11 10.7	1 56.7	1 43.0
16 W	13 38 57	22 51 22	15 06 31	21 56 05	10R39.1	17 28.6	7 20.4	14 31.9	24 12.9	14 29.1	10 54.9	11 12.5	1 58.9	1 44.4
17 Th	13 42 54	23 50 55	28 50 47	5♌50 41	10 38.7	19 12.3	8 28.3	15 11.3	24 27.0	14 42.0	11 00.4	11 14.1	2 01.1	1 45.8
18 F	13 46 50	24 50 31	12♌55 40	20 05 32	10 37.7	20 55.4	9 36.1	15 50.7	24 40.8	14 55.0	11 06.0	11 15.8	2 03.4	1 47.1
19 Sa	13 50 47	25 50 09	27 19 58	4♍38 29	10 36.0	22 38.1	10 43.7	16 30.1	24 54.4	15 07.9	11 11.6	11 17.3	2 05.6	1 48.4
20 Su	13 54 43	26 49 49	12♍00 27	19 25 09	10 34.3	24 20.2	11 51.2	17 09.6	25 07.7	15 20.7	11 17.3	11 18.9	2 07.8	1 49.7
21 M	13 58 40	27 49 31	26 51 43	4♎19 12	10 32.6	26 01.7	12 58.5	17 49.1	25 20.8	15 33.6	11 23.0	11 20.3	2 10.1	1 51.0
22 Tu	14 02 36	28 49 15	11♎46 34	19 12 49	10 31.5	27 42.7	14 05.7	18 28.6	25 33.7	15 46.4	11 28.8	11 21.8	2 12.3	1 52.2
23 W	14 06 33	29 49 02	26 36 56	3♏57 56	10D30.9	29 23.2	15 12.8	19 08.2	25 46.3	15 59.3	11 34.6	11 23.1	2 14.5	1 53.4
24 Th	14 10 30	0♏48 50	11♏14 59	18 27 18	10 30.9	1♏03.0	16 19.7	19 47.8	25 58.6	16 12.1	11 40.5	11 24.4	2 16.8	1 54.6
25 F	14 14 26	1 48 41	25 34 16	2♐35 26	10 31.4	2 42.3	17 26.5	20 27.4	26 10.6	16 24.9	11 46.5	11 25.7	2 19.0	1 55.8
26 Sa	14 18 23	2 48 33	9♐30 27	16 19 10	10 32.1	4 21.0	18 33.1	21 07.0	26 22.4	16 37.6	11 52.5	11 26.9	2 21.3	1 56.9
27 Su	14 22 19	3 48 27	23 01 33	29 37 42	10 32.9	5 59.2	19 39.5	21 46.7	26 33.9	16 50.3	11 58.5	11 28.1	2 23.5	1 58.1
28 M	14 26 16	4 48 22	6♑07 50	12♑32 17	10 33.4	7 36.9	20 45.7	22 26.4	26 45.1	17 03.0	12 04.6	11 29.2	2 25.8	1 59.2
29 Tu	14 30 12	5 48 20	18 51 25	25 05 43	10R33.8	9 14.0	21 51.8	23 06.1	26 56.1	17 15.7	12 10.8	11 30.3	2 28.0	2 00.2
30 W	14 34 09	6 48 18	1♒15 40	7♒21 51	10 33.9	10 50.7	22 57.7	23 45.9	27 06.7	17 28.4	12 17.0	11 31.3	2 30.3	2 01.3
31 Th	14 38 05	7 48 19	13 24 47	19 25 05	10 33.8	12 26.8	24 03.3	24 25.6	27 17.0	17 41.0	12 23.2	11 32.2	2 32.5	2 02.3

Astro Data

	Dy Hr Mn
☿0N	6 9:01
☽0N	9 14:10
☿ D	19 3:35
♃⚹♄	20 18:41
☽0S	23 3:59
☉0S	23 7:26
♂0S	27 6:08
♃⚹♅	28 9:25
☽0N	6 20:13
☿0S	8 23:27
☽0S	20 13:57
♄△♅	20 20:59
♃∠♇	28 3:58

Planet Ingress

		Dy Hr Mn
♀	♏	14 6:20
☉	♎	23 7:26
♂	♎	24 4:31
☿	♎	6 11:09
♀	♐	10 1:16
☉	♏	23 16:24
☿	♏	23 20:50

Last Aspect / ☽ Ingress

Last Aspect Dy Hr Mn			☽ Ingress	Dy Hr Mn
2 8:33	☿	□	♑	2 21:05
4 15:34	☿	△	♒	5 7:50
7 3:03	♀	△	♓	7 20:04
9 13:43	♂	☍	♈	10 8:45
12 17:20	♀	☍	♉	12 20:57
14 19:52	♂	△	♊	15 7:26
17 6:50	♂	□	♋	17 14:50
19 13:31	♂	⚹	♌	19 18:31
20 11:22	♅	☌	♍	21 19:11
23 18:06	♂	☌	♎	23 18:33
24 11:02	♅	⚹	♏	25 18:40
26 20:53	☿	⚹	♐	27 21:27
29 7:05	☿	□	♑	30 3:59

Last Aspect / ☽ Ingress

Last Aspect Dy Hr Mn			☽ Ingress	Dy Hr Mn
1 23:36	☿	△	♒	2 14:04
4 13:32	♀	□	♓	5 2:17
7 8:44	♀	△	♈	7 14:57
8 21:42	☉	☍	♉	10 2:48
11 0:27	♅	□	♊	12 13:01
14 3:32	☉	△	♋	14 20:54
16 13:44	☉	□	♌	17 1:59
18 20:28	☉	⚹	♍	19 4:23
19 22:45	♄	□	♎	21 5:03
23 4:43	☉	☌	♏	23 5:31
24 0:15	♅	□	♐	25 7:33
26 21:01	♂	⚹	♑	27 12:41
29 7:56	♂	□	♒	29 21:32

☽ Phases & Eclipses

Dy Hr Mn		
1 4:35	☽	8♐28
9 4:55	○	16♓15
17 4:02	☾	24♊00
23 19:18	●	0♎29
30 17:49	☽	7♑18
8 21:42	○	15♈20
16 13:44	☾	22♋56
23 4:43	●	29♎31
23 4:53:28	●	T non-C
30 10:48	☽	6♒45

Astro Data

1 September 1957
Julian Day # 21063
SVP 5♓50'50"
GC 26♐14.9 ⚵ 10♉41.5
Eris 9♈17.5R ⚶ 5♊36.4
⚷ 13♒32.5R ⚴ 21♈00.9R
☽ Mean ☊ 13♏49.1

1 October 1957
Julian Day # 21093
SVP 5♓50'48"
GC 26♐15.0 ⚵ 8♉41.3R
Eris 8♈59.7R ⚶ 15♊03.1
⚷ 12♒29.0R ⚴ 15♈17.5R
☽ Mean ☊ 12♏13.8

November 1957 LONGITUDE

Day	Sid.Time	☉	0 hr ☽	Noon ☽	True ☊	☿	♀	♂	⚳	♃	♄	♅	♆	♇
1 F	14 42 02	8♏48 21	25♒23 19	1♓20 02	10♏33.6	14♏02.5	25♐08.8	25♎05.4	27♋27.1	17♎53.5	12♐29.5	11♌33.1	2♏34.7	2♍03.3
2 Sa	14 45 59	9 48 24	7♓15 48	13 11 10	10D 33.5	15 37.7	26 14.1	25 45.3	27 36.8	18 06.1	12 35.8	11 34.0	2 37.0	2 04.2
3 Su	14 49 55	10 48 30	19 06 37	25 02 38	10 33.5	17 12.5	27 19.1	26 25.1	27 46.3	18 18.6	12 42.1	11 34.8	2 39.2	2 05.2
4 M	14 53 52	11 48 37	0♈59 40	6♈58 07	10 33.6	18 46.9	28 23.9	27 05.0	27 55.4	18 31.1	12 48.5	11 35.5	2 41.4	2 06.1
5 Tu	14 57 48	12 48 45	12 58 21	19 00 42	10 33.8	20 20.9	29 28.4	27 44.9	28 04.2	18 43.5	12 54.9	11 36.2	2 43.6	2 07.0
6 W	15 01 45	13 48 55	25 05 27	1♉12 50	10R 33.9	21 54.5	0♑32.8	28 24.9	28 12.7	18 55.9	13 01.4	11 36.8	2 45.8	2 07.8
7 Th	15 05 41	14 49 07	7♉23 03	13 36 18	10 34.0	23 27.7	1 36.8	29 04.9	28 20.8	19 08.2	13 07.9	11 37.4	2 48.0	2 08.6
8 F	15 09 38	15 49 21	19 52 41	26 12 19	10 33.8	25 00.5	2 40.6	29 44.9	28 28.6	19 20.5	13 14.4	11 37.9	2 50.3	2 09.4
9 Sa	15 13 34	16 49 37	2♊35 14	9♊01 31	10 33.3	26 33.1	3 44.2	0♏24.9	28 36.1	19 32.8	13 21.0	11 38.3	2 52.4	2 10.2
10 Su	15 17 31	17 49 54	15 31 10	22 04 12	10 32.5	28 05.2	4 47.4	1 05.0	28 43.3	19 45.0	13 27.6	11 38.7	2 54.6	2 10.9
11 M	15 21 28	18 50 14	28 40 34	5♋20 17	10 31.4	29 37.1	5 50.4	1 45.1	28 50.1	19 57.2	13 34.3	11 39.1	2 56.8	2 11.7
12 Tu	15 25 24	19 50 35	12♋03 18	18 49 34	10 30.4	1♐08.6	6 53.1	2 25.2	28 56.5	20 09.3	13 41.0	11 39.4	2 59.0	2 12.3
13 W	15 29 21	20 50 58	25 39 02	2♌31 38	10 29.5	2 39.8	7 55.5	3 05.4	29 02.6	20 21.4	13 47.7	11 39.6	3 01.2	2 13.0
14 Th	15 33 17	21 51 23	9♌27 17	16 25 53	10D 29.0	4 10.7	8 57.5	3 45.6	29 08.3	20 33.4	13 54.4	11 39.8	3 03.3	2 13.6
15 F	15 37 14	22 51 50	23 27 17	0♍31 20	10 29.0	5 41.3	9 59.2	4 25.8	29 13.7	20 45.4	14 01.2	11 39.9	3 05.5	2 14.2
16 Sa	15 41 10	23 52 19	7♍37 48	14 46 25	10 29.6	7 11.5	11 00.6	5 06.1	29 18.7	20 57.3	14 07.9	11R 40.0	3 07.6	2 14.8
17 Su	15 45 07	24 52 50	21 56 54	29 08 50	10 30.7	8 41.5	12 01.7	5 46.4	29 23.3	21 09.2	14 14.8	11 40.0	3 09.7	2 15.3
18 M	15 49 03	25 53 23	6♎21 48	13♎35 18	10 31.8	10 11.0	13 02.4	6 26.7	29 27.5	21 21.0	14 21.6	11 40.0	3 11.8	2 15.8
19 Tu	15 53 00	26 53 57	20 48 47	28 01 38	10R 32.8	11 40.3	14 02.7	7 07.1	29 31.3	21 32.8	14 28.5	11 39.9	3 13.9	2 16.3
20 W	15 56 57	27 54 33	5♏13 15	12♏22 59	10 33.1	13 09.1	15 02.6	7 47.5	29 34.8	21 44.4	14 35.3	11 39.7	3 16.0	2 16.7
21 Th	16 00 53	28 55 10	19 30 11	26 34 16	10 32.5	14 37.5	16 02.1	8 27.9	29 37.8	21 56.1	14 42.3	11 39.5	3 18.1	2 17.1
22 F	16 04 50	29 55 50	3♐34 39	10♐30 49	10 30.8	16 05.4	17 01.2	9 08.4	29 40.5	22 07.6	14 49.2	11 39.3	3 20.2	2 17.5
23 Sa	16 08 46	0♐56 30	17 22 22	24 08 58	10 28.2	17 32.9	17 59.9	9 48.9	29 42.7	22 19.1	14 56.1	11 39.0	3 22.2	2 17.9
24 Su	16 12 43	1 57 12	0♑50 22	7♑26 27	10 24.9	18 59.7	18 58.1	10 29.4	29 44.5	22 30.6	15 03.1	11 38.6	3 24.3	2 18.2
25 M	16 16 39	2 57 55	13 57 13	20 22 45	10 21.4	20 25.9	19 55.8	11 10.0	29 46.0	22 41.9	15 10.1	11 38.2	3 26.3	2 18.5
26 Tu	16 20 36	3 58 39	26 43 15	2♒58 58	10 18.1	21 51.4	20 53.0	11 50.5	29 47.0	22 53.2	15 17.1	11 37.7	3 28.3	2 18.8
27 W	16 24 32	4 59 24	9♒10 18	15 17 39	10 15.6	23 16.1	21 49.7	12 31.1	29R 47.6	23 04.4	15 24.1	11 37.1	3 30.3	2 19.0
28 Th	16 28 29	6 00 10	21 21 32	27 22 28	10D 14.0	24 39.8	22 45.9	13 11.8	29 47.8	23 15.6	15 31.1	11 36.5	3 32.2	2 19.2
29 F	16 32 26	7 00 57	3♓21 02	9♓17 51	10 13.7	26 02.5	23 41.5	13 52.4	29 47.6	23 26.7	15 38.2	11 35.9	3 34.2	2 19.4
30 Sa	16 36 22	8 01 45	15 13 31	21 08 40	10 14.5	27 23.9	24 36.5	14 33.1	29 46.9	23 37.6	15 45.2	11 35.2	3 36.1	2 19.5

December 1957 LONGITUDE

Day	Sid.Time	☉	0 hr ☽	Noon ☽	True ☊	☿	♀	♂	⚳	♃	♄	♅	♆	♇
1 Su	16 40 19	9♐02 34	27♓03 56	2♈59 56	10♏16.0	28♐43.9	25♑30.9	15♏13.9	29♋45.8	23♎48.6	15♐52.3	11♌34.5	3♏38.0	2♍19.6
2 M	16 44 15	10 03 24	8♈57 15	14 56 28	10 17.9	0♑02.2	26 24.6	15 54.6	29R 44.4	23 59.4	15 59.3	11R 33.6	3 39.9	2 19.7
3 Tu	16 48 12	11 04 15	20 58 08	27 02 44	10 19.5	1 18.7	27 17.7	16 35.4	29 42.4	24 10.1	16 06.4	11 32.8	3 41.8	2R 19.7
4 W	16 52 08	12 05 06	3♉10 42	9♉22 26	10R 20.2	2 32.9	28 10.2	17 16.2	29 40.1	24 20.8	16 13.5	11 31.9	3 43.7	2 19.7
5 Th	16 56 05	13 05 59	15 38 15	21 58 23	10 19.6	3 44.6	29 01.8	17 57.1	29 37.4	24 31.4	16 20.6	11 30.9	3 45.5	2 19.7
6 F	17 00 01	14 06 52	28 23 00	4♊52 10	10 17.3	4 53.5	29 52.8	18 38.0	29 34.2	24 41.9	16 27.7	11 29.9	3 47.4	2 19.7
7 Sa	17 03 58	15 07 47	11♊25 54	18 04 04	10 13.3	5 58.9	0♒42.9	19 18.9	29 30.6	24 52.3	16 34.8	11 28.9	3 49.2	2 19.6
8 Su	17 07 55	16 08 43	24 46 31	1♋32 57	10 07.9	7 00.5	1 32.3	19 59.8	29 26.6	25 02.6	16 41.9	11 27.7	3 51.0	2 19.5
9 M	17 11 51	17 09 39	8♋23 05	15 16 30	10 01.7	7 57.7	2 20.8	20 40.8	29 22.1	25 12.9	16 48.9	11 26.6	3 52.7	2 19.3
10 Tu	17 15 48	18 10 37	22 12 48	29 11 31	9 55.4	8 49.7	3 08.4	21 21.8	29 17.3	25 23.0	16 56.0	11 25.4	3 54.5	2 19.2
11 W	17 19 44	19 11 35	6♌12 13	13♌14 27	9 50.0	9 36.0	3 55.2	22 02.9	29 12.0	25 33.1	17 03.1	11 24.1	3 56.2	2 19.0
12 Th	17 23 41	20 12 35	20 17 48	27 21 53	9 46.0	10 15.7	4 41.0	22 44.0	29 06.3	25 43.0	17 10.2	11 22.8	3 57.9	2 18.7
13 F	17 27 37	21 13 36	4♍26 23	11♍30 59	9D 43.8	10 48.0	5 25.8	23 25.1	29 00.1	25 52.9	17 17.3	11 21.5	3 59.6	2 18.5
14 Sa	17 31 34	22 14 38	18 35 27	25 39 33	9 43.4	11 12.0	6 09.5	24 06.3	28 53.6	26 02.6	17 24.4	11 20.1	4 01.2	2 18.2
15 Su	17 35 30	23 15 41	2♎43 09	9♎46 03	9 44.3	11R 26.9	6 52.3	24 47.4	28 46.7	26 12.3	17 31.5	11 18.6	4 02.8	2 17.9
16 M	17 39 27	24 16 44	16 48 09	23 49 16	9 45.6	11 31.8	7 33.9	25 28.7	28 39.3	26 21.8	17 38.6	11 17.1	4 04.4	2 17.5
17 Tu	17 43 24	25 17 49	0♏49 15	7♏47 56	9R 46.4	11 25.9	8 14.3	26 09.9	28 31.6	26 31.3	17 45.6	11 15.6	4 06.0	2 17.1
18 W	17 47 20	26 18 55	14 45 06	21 40 30	9 45.8	11 08.6	8 53.6	26 51.2	28 23.5	26 40.6	17 52.7	11 14.0	4 07.6	2 16.7
19 Th	17 51 17	27 20 01	28 33 53	5♐24 57	9 43.0	10 39.7	9 31.6	27 32.5	28 14.9	26 49.8	17 59.7	11 12.3	4 09.1	2 16.3
20 F	17 55 13	28 21 09	12♐13 24	18 58 53	9 37.7	9 59.1	10 08.4	28 13.9	28 06.0	26 58.9	18 06.8	11 10.7	4 10.6	2 15.8
21 Sa	17 59 10	29 22 16	25 41 08	2♑19 51	9 30.2	9 07.4	10 43.8	28 55.3	27 56.8	27 07.9	18 13.8	11 09.0	4 12.1	2 15.3
22 Su	18 03 06	0♑23 25	8♑54 46	15 25 43	9 21.0	8 05.6	11 17.7	29 36.7	27 47.1	27 16.8	18 20.8	11 07.2	4 13.5	2 14.8
23 M	18 07 03	1 24 33	21 52 33	28 15 12	9 11.0	6 55.1	11 50.2	0♐18.2	27 37.2	27 25.6	18 27.8	11 05.4	4 14.9	2 14.2
24 Tu	18 11 00	2 25 42	4♒33 42	10♒48 08	9 01.2	5 38.2	12 21.2	0 59.6	27 26.8	27 34.3	18 34.7	11 03.6	4 16.3	2 13.7
25 W	18 14 56	3 26 51	16 58 41	23 05 37	8 52.6	4 17.2	12 50.6	1 41.2	27 16.2	27 42.8	18 41.7	11 01.7	4 17.7	2 13.0
26 Th	18 18 53	4 28 00	29 09 16	5♓10 02	8 46.0	2 54.8	13 18.3	2 22.7	27 05.2	27 51.2	18 48.6	10 59.8	4 19.0	2 12.4
27 F	18 22 49	5 29 09	11♓08 26	17 04 57	8 41.6	1 33.8	13 44.3	3 04.3	26 53.9	27 59.5	18 55.5	10 57.8	4 20.3	2 11.7
28 Sa	18 26 46	6 30 18	23 00 11	28 54 45	8D 39.5	0 16.8	14 08.5	3 45.9	26 42.4	28 07.6	19 02.4	10 55.8	4 21.6	2 11.0
29 Su	18 30 42	7 31 27	4♈49 17	10♈44 29	8 39.2	29♐06.1	14 30.8	4 27.5	26 30.5	28 15.7	19 09.3	10 53.8	4 22.9	2 10.3
30 M	18 34 39	8 32 36	16 41 00	22 39 33	8 39.9	28 03.3	14 51.3	5 09.2	26 18.4	28 23.6	19 16.2	10 51.7	4 24.1	2 09.6
31 Tu	18 38 35	9 33 44	28 40 47	4♉45 21	8R 40.6	27 09.8	15 09.7	5 50.9	26 06.0	28 31.3	19 23.0	10 49.6	4 25.3	2 08.8

Astro Data Dy Hr Mn	Planet Ingress Dy Hr Mn	Last Aspect Dy Hr Mn	☽ Ingress Dy Hr Mn	Last Aspect Dy Hr Mn	☽ Ingress Dy Hr Mn	☽ Phases & Eclipses Dy Hr Mn
☽0N 3 2:59	♀ ♑ 5 23:46	31 22:39 ♂ △	♓ 1 9:18	1 2:17 ☿ □	♈ 1 5:56	7 14:32 ○ 14♉55
☽0S 16 21:47	♂ ♏ 8 21:04	3 17:03 ♀ □	♈ 3 22:00	3 12:32 ♀ □	♉ 3 17:48	7 14:27 ☍ T 1.030
♅R 17 6:27	☿ ♐ 11 18:00	6 6:13 ♂ ☍	♉ 6 9:38	6 2:08 ♀ △	♊ 6 3:00	14 21:59 ☾ 22♌17
⚳R 28 10:53	☉ ♐ 22 13:39	8 9:26 ☿ ☍	♊ 8 19:09	8 0:20 ♃ △	♋ 8 9:16	21 16:19 ● 29♏06
☽0N 30 11:11		10 7:42 ♃ △	♋ 11 2:24	10 5:23 ♃ □	♌ 10 13:23	29 6:58 ☽ 6♓48
	☿ ♑ 2 11:19	12 14:23 ♃ □	♌ 13 7:36	12 9:10 ♃ ⚹	♍ 12 16:28	
♇R 4 10:31	♀ ♒ 6 15:26	14 21:59 ☉ □	♍ 15 11:07	14 9:13 ♂ ⚹	♎ 14 19:23	7 6:16 ○ 14♊53
☽0S 14 4:02	☉ ♑ 22 2:49	17 4:21 ☉ ⚹	♎ 17 13:25	16 16:24 ♃ ☌	♏ 16 22:35	14 5:45 ☾ 21♍59
☿R 16 11:05	♂ ♐ 23 1:29	19 1:04 ♃ ☌	♏ 19 15:17	18 21:29 ♂ ☌	♐ 19 2:30	21 6:12 ● 29♐07
☽0N 27 20:29	☿ ♐R 28 17:30	21 16:19 ☉ ☌	♐ 21 17:52	21 6:12 ☉ ☌	♑ 21 7:47	29 4:52 ☽ 7♈13
♄∠♆ 31 21:52		23 8:42 ♃ ⚹	♑ 23 22:29	23 10:25 ♃ □	♒ 23 15:19	
		25 16:26 ♃ □	♒ 26 6:16	25 21:15 ♃ △	♓ 26 1:41	
		28 5:52 ☿ ⚹	♓ 28 17:16	27 15:46 ♄ □	♈ 28 14:13	
				30 23:33 ♃ ☍	♉ 31 2:37	

Astro Data

1 November 1957
Julian Day # 21124
SVP 5♓50'45"
GC 26♐15.0 ⚴ 0♉06.2R
Eris 8♈41.1R ⚵ 18♊22.8R
⚷ 12♒19.2 ⚶ 8♈13.6R
☽ Mean ☊ 10♏35.3

1 December 1957
Julian Day # 21154
SVP 5♓50'41"
GC 26♐15.1 ⚴ 22♈30.7R
Eris 8♈28.3R ⚵ 13♊52.9R
⚷ 13♒09.6 ⚶ 6♈52.3
☽ Mean ☊ 9♏00.0

LONGITUDE — January 1958

Day	Sid.Time	☉	0 hr ☽	Noon ☽	True ☊	☿	♀	♂	⚳	♃	♄	♅	♆	♇
1 W	18 42 32	10♑34 53	10♉53 53	17♉06 56	8♏40.3	26♐26.3	15♒26.1	6♐32.6	25♋53.4	28♎39.0	19♐29.8	10♌47.5	4♏26.5	2♍08.0
2 Th	18 46 28	11 36 02	23 25 01	29 48 33	8R38.1	25R53.2	15 40.3	7 14.3	25R40.6	28 46.5	19 36.5	10R45.3	4 27.6	2R07.2
3 F	18 50 25	12 37 10	6♊17 51	12♊53 07	8 33.3	25 30.4	15 52.3	7 56.1	25 27.5	28 53.9	19 43.3	10 43.1	4 28.7	2 06.3
4 Sa	18 54 22	13 38 18	19 34 27	26 21 45	8 26.0	25D17.5	16 02.2	8 37.9	25 14.3	29 01.1	19 50.0	10 40.9	4 29.8	2 05.4
5 Su	18 58 18	14 39 26	3♋14 49	10♋13 17	8 16.3	25 14.2	16 09.6	9 19.8	25 00.9	29 08.2	19 56.7	10 38.6	4 30.8	2 04.5
6 M	19 02 15	15 40 34	17 16 36	24 24 10	8 05.3	25 19.8	16 14.8	10 01.7	24 47.3	29 15.2	20 03.3	10 36.4	4 31.8	2 03.6
7 Tu	19 06 11	16 41 42	1♌35 12	8♌48 52	7 54.1	25 33.6	16R17.5	10 43.6	24 33.6	29 22.0	20 09.9	10 34.1	4 32.8	2 02.7
8 W	19 10 08	17 42 50	16 04 19	23 20 40	7 43.9	25 54.9	16 17.8	11 25.6	24 19.7	29 28.7	20 16.5	10 31.7	4 33.7	2 01.7
9 Th	19 14 04	18 43 57	0♍37 04	7♍52 45	7 35.9	26 23.0	16 15.6	12 07.6	24 05.8	29 35.2	20 23.1	10 29.4	4 34.7	2 00.7
10 F	19 18 01	19 45 05	15 07 04	22 19 24	7 30.5	26 57.3	16 10.9	12 49.6	23 51.7	29 41.6	20 29.6	10 27.0	4 35.5	1 59.7
11 Sa	19 21 58	20 46 12	29 29 20	6♎36 33	7 27.8	27 37.1	16 03.7	13 31.6	23 37.6	29 47.8	20 36.1	10 24.6	4 36.4	1 58.6
12 Su	19 25 54	21 47 20	13♎40 49	20 42 02	7D27.1	28 21.9	15 54.0	14 13.7	23 23.4	29 53.9	20 42.5	10 22.1	4 37.2	1 57.6
13 M	19 29 51	22 48 28	27 40 09	4♏35 13	7R27.2	29 11.2	15 41.8	14 55.9	23 09.2	29 59.8	20 48.9	10 19.7	4 38.0	1 56.5
14 Tu	19 33 47	23 49 35	11♏27 18	18 16 30	7 26.9	0♑04.5	15 27.1	15 38.0	22 54.9	0♏05.6	20 55.3	10 17.2	4 38.8	1 55.4
15 W	19 37 44	24 50 43	25 02 54	1♐46 36	7 24.8	1 01.3	15 10.0	16 20.2	22 40.7	0 11.2	21 01.6	10 14.7	4 39.5	1 54.3
16 Th	19 41 40	25 51 50	8♐27 39	15 06 07	7 20.0	2 01.4	14 50.5	17 02.4	22 26.4	0 16.6	21 07.8	10 12.2	4 40.2	1 53.1
17 F	19 45 37	26 52 57	21 42 00	28 15 15	7 12.1	3 04.4	14 28.8	17 44.7	22 12.2	0 21.9	21 14.1	10 09.7	4 40.8	1 51.9
18 Sa	19 49 33	27 54 03	4♑45 50	11♑13 40	7 01.2	4 10.0	14 04.7	18 27.0	21 58.1	0 27.1	21 20.3	10 07.2	4 41.4	1 50.8
19 Su	19 53 30	28 55 09	17 38 40	24 00 45	6 48.0	5 18.0	13 38.6	19 09.3	21 44.0	0 32.0	21 26.4	10 04.6	4 42.0	1 49.6
20 M	19 57 27	29 56 15	0♒19 49	6♒35 51	6 33.6	6 28.1	13 10.5	19 51.7	21 30.0	0 36.8	21 32.5	10 02.1	4 42.6	1 48.3
21 Tu	20 01 23	0♒57 19	12 48 49	18 58 44	6 19.3	7 40.1	12 40.6	20 34.0	21 16.2	0 41.5	21 38.5	9 59.5	4 43.1	1 47.1
22 W	20 05 20	1 58 23	25 05 42	1♓09 50	6 06.3	8 53.9	12 09.0	21 16.4	21 02.4	0 46.0	21 44.5	9 56.9	4 43.6	1 45.8
23 Th	20 09 16	2 59 26	7♓11 21	13 10 31	5 55.6	10 09.3	11 36.0	21 58.9	20 48.9	0 50.3	21 50.5	9 54.3	4 44.0	1 44.6
24 F	20 13 13	4 00 28	19 07 40	25 03 12	5 47.7	11 26.3	11 01.6	22 41.4	20 35.4	0 54.4	21 56.3	9 51.7	4 44.5	1 43.3
25 Sa	20 17 09	5 01 29	0♈57 34	6♈51 17	5 42.8	12 44.6	10 26.3	23 23.8	20 22.2	0 58.3	22 02.2	9 49.1	4 44.8	1 42.0
26 Su	20 21 06	6 02 29	12 44 55	18 39 05	5 40.4	14 04.1	9 50.1	24 06.4	20 09.2	1 02.1	22 08.0	9 46.4	4 45.2	1 40.6
27 M	20 25 02	7 03 28	24 34 25	0♉31 38	5 39.7	15 24.9	9 13.3	24 48.9	19 56.4	1 05.7	22 13.7	9 43.8	4 45.5	1 39.3
28 Tu	20 28 59	8 04 26	6♉31 23	12 34 25	5 39.7	16 46.8	8 36.2	25 31.5	19 43.8	1 09.2	22 19.3	9 41.2	4 45.8	1 37.9
29 W	20 32 56	9 05 22	18 41 24	24 53 02	5 39.0	18 09.8	7 59.1	26 14.1	19 31.4	1 12.4	22 25.0	9 38.6	4 46.0	1 36.6
30 Th	20 36 52	10 06 17	1♊09 58	7♊32 46	5 36.7	19 33.8	7 22.1	26 56.8	19 19.4	1 15.5	22 30.5	9 36.0	4 46.2	1 35.2
31 F	20 40 49	11 07 12	14 01 58	20 37 57	5 32.0	20 58.8	6 45.7	27 39.4	19 07.6	1 18.4	22 36.0	9 33.3	4 46.4	1 33.8

LONGITUDE — February 1958

Day	Sid.Time	☉	0 hr ☽	Noon ☽	True ☊	☿	♀	♂	⚳	♃	♄	♅	♆	♇
1 Sa	20 44 45	12♒08 04	27♊21 00	4♋11 13	5♏24.4	22♑24.7	6♒09.9	28♐22.1	18♋56.1	1♏21.1	22♐41.4	9♌30.7	4♏46.5	1♍32.4
2 Su	20 48 42	13 08 56	11♋08 33	18 12 45	5R14.5	23 51.5	5R35.1	29 04.9	18R44.9	1 23.7	22 46.8	9R28.1	4 46.7	1R31.0
3 M	20 52 38	14 09 46	25 23 21	2♌39 41	5 02.9	25 19.2	5 01.5	29 47.6	18 34.0	1 26.0	22 52.1	9 25.5	4 46.7	1 29.6
4 Tu	20 56 35	15 10 35	10♌00 55	17 26 02	4 50.9	26 47.7	4 29.3	0♑30.4	18 23.4	1 28.2	22 57.3	9 22.9	4R46.8	1 28.1
5 W	21 00 31	16 11 23	24 53 54	2♍23 21	4 40.0	28 17.1	3 58.6	1 13.2	18 13.2	1 30.2	23 02.5	9 20.3	4 46.8	1 26.7
6 Th	21 04 28	17 12 10	9♍53 08	17 22 07	4 31.1	29 47.4	3 29.8	1 56.1	18 03.3	1 32.0	23 07.6	9 17.7	4 46.7	1 25.2
7 F	21 08 25	18 12 56	24 49 12	2♎13 28	4 25.0	1♒18.4	3 02.9	2 39.0	17 53.8	1 33.6	23 12.7	9 15.1	4 46.7	1 23.8
8 Sa	21 12 21	19 13 40	9♎34 06	16 50 31	4 21.8	2 50.3	2 38.1	3 21.9	17 44.6	1 35.1	23 17.7	9 12.5	4 46.6	1 22.3
9 Su	21 16 18	20 14 24	24 02 15	1♏09 04	4D20.8	4 23.0	2 15.6	4 04.9	17 35.8	1 36.3	23 22.6	9 09.9	4 46.4	1 20.8
10 M	21 20 14	21 15 07	8♏10 49	15 07 31	4R21.0	5 56.5	1 55.3	4 47.8	17 27.3	1 37.4	23 27.4	9 07.4	4 46.3	1 19.3
11 Tu	21 24 11	22 15 49	21 59 17	28 46 18	4 20.9	7 30.8	1 37.4	5 30.9	17 19.3	1 38.3	23 32.2	9 04.8	4 46.1	1 17.9
12 W	21 28 07	23 16 29	5♐28 48	12♐07 03	4 19.4	9 06.0	1 21.9	6 13.9	17 11.7	1 39.0	23 36.9	9 02.3	4 45.9	1 16.4
13 Th	21 32 04	24 17 09	18 41 20	25 11 56	4 15.5	10 42.0	1 08.9	6 57.0	17 04.4	1 39.5	23 41.5	8 59.8	4 45.6	1 14.9
14 F	21 36 00	25 17 47	1♑39 05	8♑03 04	4 08.8	12 18.9	0 58.4	7 40.1	16 57.6	1 39.8	23 46.1	8 57.3	4 45.3	1 13.4
15 Sa	21 39 57	26 18 25	14 24 03	20 42 14	3 59.4	13 56.6	0 50.4	8 23.2	16 51.1	1R39.9	23 50.5	8 54.8	4 45.0	1 11.9
16 Su	21 43 54	27 19 01	26 57 45	3♒10 45	3 47.9	15 35.2	0 44.8	9 06.4	16 45.1	1 39.8	23 54.9	8 52.3	4 44.6	1 10.3
17 M	21 47 50	28 19 35	9♒21 20	15 29 34	3 35.2	17 14.6	0D41.7	9 49.6	16 39.5	1 39.6	23 59.3	8 49.9	4 44.2	1 08.8
18 Tu	21 51 47	29 20 08	21 35 35	27 39 27	3 22.5	18 55.0	0 41.1	10 32.8	16 34.4	1 39.1	24 03.5	8 47.5	4 43.8	1 07.3
19 W	21 55 43	0♓20 39	3♓41 17	9♓41 14	3 10.9	20 36.3	0 42.9	11 16.0	16 29.7	1 38.5	24 07.7	8 45.1	4 43.3	1 05.8
20 Th	21 59 40	1 21 09	15 39 25	21 36 05	3 01.3	22 18.5	0 47.0	11 59.3	16 25.4	1 37.6	24 11.8	8 42.7	4 42.8	1 04.3
21 F	22 03 36	2 21 37	27 31 26	3♈25 45	2 54.3	24 01.6	0 53.4	12 42.6	16 21.5	1 36.6	24 15.8	8 40.3	4 42.3	1 02.8
22 Sa	22 07 33	3 22 03	9♈19 24	15 12 44	2 50.0	25 45.7	1 02.1	13 25.9	16 18.1	1 35.4	24 19.7	8 38.0	4 41.7	1 01.2
23 Su	22 11 29	4 22 28	21 06 12	27 00 16	2D48.2	27 30.7	1 13.0	14 09.2	16 15.1	1 34.0	24 23.5	8 35.7	4 41.1	0 59.7
24 M	22 15 26	5 22 51	2♉55 28	8♉52 23	2 48.2	29 16.7	1 26.1	14 52.6	16 12.5	1 32.4	24 27.3	8 33.5	4 40.5	0 58.2
25 Tu	22 19 22	6 23 11	14 51 36	20 53 45	2 49.1	1♓03.7	1 41.2	15 36.0	16 10.4	1 30.6	24 31.0	8 31.2	4 39.9	0 56.7
26 W	22 23 19	7 23 30	26 59 30	3♊09 30	2R49.9	2 51.7	1 58.3	16 19.4	16 08.7	1 28.7	24 34.5	8 29.0	4 39.2	0 55.2
27 Th	22 27 16	8 23 47	9♊24 24	15 44 50	2 49.6	4 40.7	2 17.4	17 02.8	16 07.5	1 26.5	24 38.1	8 26.8	4 38.5	0 53.7
28 F	22 31 12	9 24 02	22 11 22	28 44 32	2 47.7	6 30.7	2 38.4	17 46.3	16 06.7	1 24.2	24 41.5	8 24.7	4 37.7	0 52.2

Astro Data

	Dy Hr Mn
☿ D	5 8:38
♀ R	8 2:46
☽ 0S	10 10:46
☽ 0N	24 5:39
♃ ⚹ ♇	4 11:32
♆ R	5 3:14
☽ 0S	6 19:41
♃ R	15 14:58
♄ ⚼ ♅	16 2:53
♀ D	18 6:17
☽ 0N	20 13:29

Planet Ingress

	Dy Hr Mn
♃ ♏	13 12:52
☿ ♑	14 10:03
☉ ♒	20 13:28
♂ ♑	3 18:57
☿ ♒	6 15:21
☉ ♓	19 3:48
☿ ♓	24 21:44

Last Aspect / ☽ Ingress (January)

Last Aspect Dy Hr Mn		☽ Ingress	Dy Hr Mn
1 8:42	♀ □	♊	2 12:21
4 16:41	♃ △	♋	4 18:22
6 20:11	♃ □	♌	6 21:21
8 22:12	♃ ⚹	♍	8 22:59
10 20:06	☿ □	♎	11 0:52
13 3:58	♃ ☌	♏	13 4:02
14 22:38	☉ ⚹	♐	15 8:49
16 23:03	♄ ☌	♑	17 15:13
19 22:08	☉ ☌	♒	19 23:22
21 17:15	♄ ⚹	♓	22 9:41
24 6:54	♂ □	♈	24 22:03
26 23:45	♂ △	♉	27 10:56
28 21:19	☿ △	♊	29 21:47

Last Aspect / ☽ Ingress (February)

Last Aspect Dy Hr Mn		☽ Ingress	Dy Hr Mn
1 1:14	♂ ☍	♋	1 4:41
2 22:31	☿ ☍	♌	3 7:38
4 20:56	♄ △	♍	5 8:11
6 21:19	♄ □	♎	7 8:23
8 22:49	♄ ⚹	♏	9 10:03
10 23:34	☉ □	♐	11 14:11
13 10:10	☉ ⚹	♑	13 20:55
14 11:14	♂ ☌	♒	16 5:51
18 15:38	☉ ☌	♓	18 16:39
20 17:17	♄ □	♈	21 5:02
23 13:13	☿ ⚹	♉	23 18:05
25 0:48	♂ △	♊	26 5:52
28 4:34	♄ ☍	♋	28 14:17

☽ Phases & Eclipses

Dy Hr Mn		
5 20:09	○	15♋00
12 14:01	☾	21♎52
19 22:08	●	29♑21
28 2:16	☽	7♉40
4 8:05	○	15♌01
10 23:34	☾	21♏44
18 15:38	●	29♒29
26 20:52	☽	7♊46

Astro Data

1 January 1958
Julian Day # 21185
SVP 5♓50'36"
GC 26♐15.2 ⚳ 22♈50.0
Eris 8♈24.6 ⚵ 8♊14.8R
⚷ 14♒52.5 ⚶ 11♈47.7
☽ Mean ☊ 7♏21.5

1 February 1958
Julian Day # 21216
SVP 5♓50'31"
GC 26♐15.2 ⚳ 0♉55.7
Eris 8♈32.0 ⚵ 9♊58.9
⚷ 17♒05.4 ⚶ 20♈55.0
☽ Mean ☊ 5♏43.0

March 1958 LONGITUDE

Day	Sid.Time	☉	0 hr ☽	Noon ☽	True ☊	☿	♀	♂	⚳	♃	♄	♅	♆	♇
1 Sa	22 35 09	10♓24 15	5♋24 46	12♋12 20	2♏43.6	8♓21.6	3♒01.2	18♑29.7	16♋06.3	1♏21.7	24♐44.8	8♌22.6	4♏37.0	0♍50.7
2 Su	22 39 05	11 24 26	19 07 25	26 09 58	2R37.6	10 13.5	3 25.7	19 13.2	16D06.4	1R19.0	24 48.1	8R20.5	4R36.2	0R49.2
3 M	22 43 02	12 24 34	3♌19 47	10♌36 24	2 30.1	12 06.4	3 52.0	19 56.8	16 06.9	1 16.1	24 51.2	8 18.4	4 35.4	0 47.7
4 Tu	22 46 58	13 24 41	17 59 11	25 27 14	2 22.2	14 00.1	4 19.9	20 40.3	16 07.8	1 13.1	24 54.3	8 16.4	4 34.5	0 46.2
5 W	22 50 55	14 24 46	2♍59 31	10♍34 50	2 14.8	15 54.7	4 49.4	21 23.9	16 09.2	1 09.8	24 57.3	8 14.4	4 33.6	0 44.8
6 Th	22 54 51	15 24 49	18 11 52	25 49 16	2 08.9	17 50.1	5 20.5	22 07.5	16 10.9	1 06.4	25 00.2	8 12.5	4 32.7	0 43.3
7 F	22 58 48	16 24 50	3♎25 44	10♎59 59	2 05.0	19 46.2	5 53.0	22 51.1	16 13.1	1 02.9	25 03.0	8 10.6	4 31.8	0 41.8
8 Sa	23 02 45	17 24 49	18 30 55	25 57 33	2D03.3	21 42.9	6 26.9	23 34.8	16 15.7	0 59.1	25 05.7	8 08.7	4 30.8	0 40.4
9 Su	23 06 41	18 24 47	3♏19 08	10♏35 03	2 03.4	23 40.1	7 02.2	24 18.5	16 18.7	0 55.2	25 08.3	8 06.9	4 29.8	0 39.0
10 M	23 10 38	19 24 43	17 44 57	24 48 34	2 04.6	25 37.6	7 38.8	25 02.2	16 22.1	0 51.1	25 10.8	8 05.1	4 28.8	0 37.5
11 Tu	23 14 34	20 24 37	1♐45 54	8♐36 59	2R05.9	27 35.3	8 16.7	25 45.9	16 25.9	0 46.9	25 13.2	8 03.3	4 27.7	0 36.1
12 W	23 18 31	21 24 30	15 22 02	22 01 19	2 06.4	29 33.0	8 55.8	26 29.7	16 30.1	0 42.5	25 15.6	8 01.6	4 26.7	0 34.7
13 Th	23 22 27	22 24 21	28 35 10	5♑03 58	2 05.6	1♈30.3	9 36.0	27 13.5	16 34.7	0 37.9	25 17.8	8 00.0	4 25.6	0 33.3
14 F	23 26 24	23 24 11	11♑28 06	17 47 58	2 03.0	3 27.0	10 17.3	27 57.3	16 39.7	0 33.2	25 20.0	7 58.4	4 24.5	0 31.9
15 Sa	23 30 20	24 23 59	24 03 59	0♒16 32	1 58.6	5 22.9	10 59.7	28 41.1	16 45.1	0 28.3	25 22.0	7 56.8	4 23.3	0 30.6
16 Su	23 34 17	25 23 45	6♒25 59	12 32 41	1 52.8	7 17.4	11 43.2	29 25.0	16 50.8	0 23.3	25 24.0	7 55.2	4 22.2	0 29.2
17 M	23 38 14	26 23 29	18 36 57	24 39 05	1 46.3	9 10.4	12 27.6	0♒08.8	16 57.0	0 18.1	25 25.8	7 53.7	4 21.0	0 27.9
18 Tu	23 42 10	27 23 11	0♓39 21	6♓38 00	1 39.7	11 01.2	13 12.9	0 52.7	17 03.5	0 12.8	25 27.6	7 52.3	4 19.8	0 26.5
19 W	23 46 07	28 22 52	12 35 17	18 31 26	1 33.6	12 49.6	13 59.1	1 36.6	17 10.4	0 07.3	25 29.3	7 50.9	4 18.5	0 25.2
20 Th	23 50 03	29 22 30	24 26 40	0♈21 12	1 28.8	14 35.1	14 46.2	2 20.5	17 17.6	0 01.7	25 30.8	7 49.5	4 17.3	0 23.9
21 F	23 54 00	0♈22 06	6♈15 17	12 09 10	1 25.4	16 17.1	15 34.1	3 04.4	17 25.3	29♎56.0	25 32.3	7 48.2	4 16.0	0 22.6
22 Sa	23 57 56	1 21 41	18 03 06	23 57 22	1D23.7	17 55.3	16 22.8	3 48.4	17 33.3	29 50.1	25 33.7	7 47.0	4 14.7	0 21.4
23 Su	0 01 53	2 21 13	29 52 18	5♉48 15	1 23.5	19 29.1	17 12.3	4 32.4	17 41.6	29 44.1	25 34.9	7 45.8	4 13.4	0 20.1
24 M	0 05 49	3 20 43	11♉45 34	17 44 41	1 24.5	20 58.3	18 02.5	5 16.3	17 50.3	29 38.0	25 36.1	7 44.6	4 12.1	0 18.9
25 Tu	0 09 46	4 20 11	23 46 01	29 50 03	1 26.2	22 22.2	18 53.4	6 00.3	17 59.3	29 31.7	25 37.2	7 43.5	4 10.7	0 17.7
26 W	0 13 42	5 19 37	5♊57 17	12♊08 14	1 27.9	23 40.7	19 45.0	6 44.3	18 08.7	29 25.4	25 38.2	7 42.4	4 09.3	0 16.5
27 Th	0 17 39	6 19 00	18 23 23	24 43 18	1R29.2	24 53.3	20 37.2	7 28.3	18 18.4	29 18.9	25 39.0	7 41.4	4 07.9	0 15.3
28 F	0 21 36	7 18 21	1♋08 27	7♋39 20	1 29.7	25 59.8	21 30.0	8 12.4	18 28.4	29 12.3	25 39.8	7 40.4	4 06.5	0 14.1
29 Sa	0 25 32	8 17 40	14 16 21	20 59 51	1 29.1	26 59.8	22 23.5	8 56.4	18 38.8	29 05.6	25 40.5	7 39.5	4 05.1	0 13.0
30 Su	0 29 29	9 16 57	27 50 06	4♌47 12	1 27.5	27 53.1	23 17.5	9 40.5	18 49.5	28 58.9	25 41.1	7 38.7	4 03.7	0 11.9
31 M	0 33 25	10 16 11	11♌51 10	19 01 48	1 25.2	28 39.6	24 12.1	10 24.5	19 00.5	28 52.0	25 41.6	7 37.8	4 02.2	0 10.8

April 1958 LONGITUDE

Day	Sid.Time	☉	0 hr ☽	Noon ☽	True ☊	☿	♀	♂	⚳	♃	♄	♅	♆	♇
1 Tu	0 37 22	11♈15 22	26♌18 44	3♍41 26	1♏22.5	29♈19.1	25♒07.2	11♒08.6	19♋11.7	28♎45.0	25♐41.9	7♌37.1	4♏00.8	0♍09.7
2 W	0 41 18	12 14 32	11♍09 08	18 40 56	1R19.9	29 51.6	26 02.9	11 52.7	19 23.3	28R38.0	25 42.2	7R36.4	3R59.3	0R08.6
3 Th	0 45 15	13 13 39	26 15 46	3♎52 27	1 17.9	0♉16.8	26 59.0	12 36.8	19 35.2	28 30.9	25 42.4	7 35.7	3 57.8	0 07.6
4 F	0 49 11	14 12 44	11♎29 45	19 06 22	1D16.7	0 35.0	27 55.7	13 20.9	19 47.4	28 23.7	25R42.5	7 35.1	3 56.3	0 06.6
5 Sa	0 53 08	15 11 48	26 41 06	4♏12 46	1 16.5	0 46.0	28 52.8	14 05.1	19 59.9	28 16.4	25 42.5	7 34.6	3 54.8	0 05.6
6 Su	0 57 05	16 10 49	11♏40 21	19 02 57	1 17.0	0R50.1	29 50.4	14 49.2	20 12.6	28 09.1	25 42.3	7 34.1	3 53.2	0 04.6
7 M	1 01 01	17 09 48	26 19 52	3♐30 34	1 18.0	0 47.5	0♓48.4	15 33.4	20 25.7	28 01.7	25 42.1	7 33.6	3 51.7	0 03.7
8 Tu	1 04 58	18 08 46	10♐34 42	17 32 05	1 19.1	0 38.3	1 46.8	16 17.6	20 39.0	27 54.3	25 41.8	7 33.2	3 50.1	0 02.7
9 W	1 08 54	19 07 42	24 22 40	1♑06 36	1 20.0	0 23.0	2 45.7	17 01.7	20 52.5	27 46.8	25 41.4	7 32.9	3 48.6	0 01.8
10 Th	1 12 51	20 06 37	7♑44 05	14 15 27	1R20.5	0 01.9	3 44.9	17 45.9	21 06.4	27 39.3	25 40.9	7 32.6	3 47.0	0 01.0
11 F	1 16 47	21 05 29	20 41 04	27 01 24	1 20.5	29♈35.5	4 44.6	18 30.1	21 20.5	27 31.7	25 40.3	7 32.4	3 45.4	0 00.1
12 Sa	1 20 44	22 04 20	3♒16 55	9♒28 08	1 20.0	29 04.5	5 44.6	19 14.3	21 34.8	27 24.1	25 39.6	7 32.2	3 43.8	29♌59.3
13 Su	1 24 40	23 03 09	15 35 32	21 39 38	1 19.2	28 29.5	6 44.9	19 58.6	21 49.4	27 16.5	25 38.8	7 32.1	3 42.2	29 58.5
14 M	1 28 37	24 01 56	27 40 56	3♓39 55	1 18.3	27 51.3	7 45.6	20 42.8	22 04.3	27 08.8	25 37.9	7D32.0	3 40.6	29 57.7
15 Tu	1 32 34	25 00 42	9♓37 02	15 32 43	1 17.3	27 10.5	8 46.6	21 27.0	22 19.4	27 01.2	25 36.9	7 32.0	3 39.0	29 56.9
16 W	1 36 30	25 59 25	21 27 23	27 21 25	1 16.5	26 28.0	9 47.9	22 11.2	22 34.8	26 53.5	25 35.8	7 32.0	3 37.4	29 56.2
17 Th	1 40 27	26 58 07	3♈15 10	9♈08 57	1 16.0	25 44.7	10 49.5	22 55.4	22 50.3	26 45.8	25 34.6	7 32.1	3 35.8	29 55.5
18 F	1 44 23	27 56 47	15 03 07	20 57 55	1D15.7	25 01.3	11 51.4	23 39.7	23 06.2	26 38.1	25 33.3	7 32.2	3 34.1	29 54.8
19 Sa	1 48 20	28 55 25	26 53 40	2♉50 36	1 15.7	24 18.6	12 53.6	24 23.9	23 22.2	26 30.4	25 31.9	7 32.4	3 32.5	29 54.2
20 Su	1 52 16	29 54 01	8♉48 59	14 49 05	1 15.7	23 37.4	13 56.1	25 08.1	23 38.5	26 22.7	25 30.5	7 32.7	3 30.9	29 53.5
21 M	1 56 13	0♉52 35	20 51 09	26 55 27	1R15.8	22 58.4	14 58.8	25 52.3	23 55.0	26 15.1	25 28.9	7 33.0	3 29.2	29 52.9
22 Tu	2 00 09	1 51 08	3♊02 14	9♊11 47	1 15.8	22 22.2	16 01.7	26 36.5	24 11.7	26 07.4	25 27.2	7 33.4	3 27.6	29 52.4
23 W	2 04 06	2 49 38	15 24 23	21 40 19	1 15.6	21 49.3	17 05.0	27 20.7	24 28.6	25 59.8	25 25.5	7 33.8	3 26.0	29 51.8
24 Th	2 08 03	3 48 06	27 59 55	4♋23 27	1 15.4	21 20.2	18 08.4	28 04.9	24 45.8	25 52.3	25 23.7	7 34.3	3 24.3	29 51.3
25 F	2 11 59	4 46 32	10♋51 15	17 23 34	1 15.2	20 55.2	19 12.1	28 49.1	25 03.1	25 44.7	25 21.7	7 34.8	3 22.7	29 50.8
26 Sa	2 15 56	5 44 56	24 00 42	0♌42 53	1D15.0	20 34.6	20 16.0	29 33.3	25 20.7	25 37.2	25 19.7	7 35.4	3 21.1	29 50.4
27 Su	2 19 52	6 43 17	7♌30 18	14 23 05	1 15.0	20 18.7	21 20.1	0♓17.5	25 38.4	25 29.8	25 17.6	7 36.0	3 19.4	29 50.0
28 M	2 23 49	7 41 37	21 21 17	28 24 51	1 15.3	20 07.5	22 24.4	1 01.6	25 56.4	25 22.4	25 15.4	7 36.7	3 17.8	29 49.6
29 Tu	2 27 45	8 39 54	5♍33 39	12♍47 22	1 15.9	20D01.2	23 28.9	1 45.8	26 14.5	25 15.0	25 13.2	7 37.4	3 16.2	29 49.2
30 W	2 31 42	9 38 10	20 05 37	27 27 51	1 16.5	19 59.8	24 33.6	2 29.9	26 32.8	25 07.8	25 10.8	7 38.2	3 14.5	29 48.8

Astro Data	Dy Hr Mn
⚳ D	1 20:21
☽ 0S	6 6:34
☿ 0N	13 9:18
♃ ⚹ ♇	14 20:53
☽ 0N	19 19:50
☉ 0N	21 3:06
☽ 0S	2 17:45
♄ R	4 19:38
☿ R	6 14:25
♅ D	15 8:27
☽ 0N	16 1:40
♃ ⚹ ♄	29 21:05
☽ 0S	30 3:33
☿ D	30 6:57

Planet Ingress	Dy Hr Mn
☿ ♈	12 17:31
♂ ♒	17 7:11
♃ ♎R	20 19:13
☉ ♈	21 3:06
☿ ♉	2 19:17
♀ ♓	6 16:00
☿ ♈R	10 13:51
♇ ♌R	11 14:59
☉ ♉	20 14:27
♂ ♓	27 2:31

Last Aspect Dy Hr Mn		☽ Ingress Dy Hr Mn
1 23:31	♂ ☍	♌ 2 18:27
4 11:07	♄ △	♍ 4 19:15
6 10:42	♄ □	♎ 6 18:35
8 10:36	♄ ⚹	♏ 8 18:34
10 13:38	☿ △	♐ 10 20:56
12 17:55	♄ ☌	♑ 13 2:36
15 8:43	♂ ☌	♒ 15 11:28
17 13:33	♄ ⚹	♓ 17 22:41
20 9:50	☉ ☌	♈ 20 11:17
22 23:50	♃ ☍	♉ 23 0:16
24 12:38	♀ □	♊ 25 12:20
27 20:32	♃ △	♋ 27 21:53
30 2:04	♃ □	♌ 30 3:46

Last Aspect Dy Hr Mn		☽ Ingress Dy Hr Mn
1 4:36	☿ △	♍ 1 6:01
2 23:07	♄ □	♎ 3 5:54
5 2:55	♀ △	♏ 5 5:16
6 4:45	♂ □	♐ 7 6:07
9 6:06	♃ ⚹	♑ 9 10:00
11 16:43	☿ □	♒ 11 17:41
14 4:34	♇ ☍	♓ 14 4:38
16 8:25	♄ □	♈ 16 17:23
19 6:05	♇ △	♉ 19 6:16
21 17:49	♇ □	♊ 21 18:03
24 3:30	♇ ⚹	♋ 24 3:46
26 2:59	♃ □	♌ 26 10:44
28 14:23	♇ ☌	♍ 28 14:41
30 8:18	♄ □	♎ 30 16:06

☽ Phases & Eclipses Dy Hr Mn	
5 18:28	○ 14♍41
12 10:48	☾ 21♐21
20 9:50	● 29♓17
28 11:18	☽ 7♋17
4 3:45	○ 13♎52
4 4:00	A 0.013
10 23:50	☾ 20♑36
19 3:23	● 28♈34
19 3:26:44	A 07'07"
26 21:36	☽ 6♌08

Astro Data

1 March 1958
Julian Day # 21244
SVP 5♓50'27"
GC 26♐15.3 ⚴ 12♉35.3
Eris 8♈46.5 ⚵ 17♊23.9
⚷ 19♒09.5 ⚶ 1♉12.5
☽ Mean ☊ 4♏14.0

1 April 1958
Julian Day # 21275
SVP 5♓50'25"
GC 26♐15.4 ⚴ 28♉25.4
Eris 9♈07.2 ⚵ 29♊09.6
⚷ 21♒07.4 ⚶ 13♉49.6
☽ Mean ☊ 2♏35.5

LONGITUDE

May 1958

Day	Sid.Time	☉	0 hr ☽	Noon ☽	True ☊	☿	♀	♂	⚳	♃	♄	♅	♆	♇
1 Th	2 35 38	10♉36 23	4♎53 23	12♎21 24	1♏17.2	20♈03.3	25♓38.6	3♓14.1	26♋51.3	25♎00.6	25♐08.4	7♌39.0	3♏12.9	29♌48.5
2 F	2 39 35	11 34 34	19 51 01	27 21 13	1R17.5	20 11.5	26 43.7	3 58.2	27 10.0	24R53.4	25R05.9	7 39.9	3R11.3	29R48.2
3 Sa	2 43 31	12 32 44	4♏50 59	12♏19 14	1 17.4	20 24.5	27 48.9	4 42.3	27 28.9	24 46.4	25 03.3	7 40.9	3 09.7	29 48.0
4 Su	2 47 28	13 30 52	19 44 57	27 07 11	1 16.7	20 42.1	28 54.4	5 26.4	27 47.9	24 39.4	25 00.6	7 41.9	3 08.1	29 47.7
5 M	2 51 25	14 28 58	4♐25 03	11♐37 47	1 15.3	21 04.1	0♈00.0	6 10.5	28 07.1	24 32.5	24 57.8	7 42.9	3 06.5	29 47.5
6 Tu	2 55 21	15 27 03	18 44 49	25 45 40	1 13.6	21 30.5	1 05.9	6 54.6	28 26.4	24 25.7	24 55.0	7 44.0	3 04.9	29 47.4
7 W	2 59 18	16 25 07	2♑40 02	9♑27 49	1 11.7	22 01.2	2 11.8	7 38.7	28 46.0	24 19.0	24 52.1	7 45.2	3 03.3	29 47.2
8 Th	3 03 14	17 23 09	16 09 00	22 43 43	1 10.0	22 35.8	3 18.0	8 22.8	29 05.7	24 12.4	24 49.1	7 46.4	3 01.7	29 47.1
9 F	3 07 11	18 21 09	29 12 15	5♒34 56	1 08.8	23 14.4	4 24.3	9 06.8	29 25.5	24 05.9	24 46.1	7 47.7	3 00.1	29 47.0
10 Sa	3 11 07	19 19 08	11♒52 12	18 04 33	1D08.4	23 56.8	5 30.7	9 50.9	29 45.5	23 59.5	24 43.0	7 49.0	2 58.6	29 47.0
11 Su	3 15 04	20 17 06	24 12 32	0♓16 42	1 08.7	24 42.7	6 37.3	10 34.9	0♌05.7	23 53.3	24 39.8	7 50.3	2 57.0	29D46.9
12 M	3 19 01	21 15 03	6♓17 39	12 16 00	1 09.7	25 32.2	7 44.1	11 18.9	0 26.0	23 47.1	24 36.5	7 51.7	2 55.5	29 46.9
13 Tu	3 22 57	22 12 58	18 12 18	24 07 09	1 11.2	26 25.0	8 50.9	12 02.8	0 46.5	23 41.0	24 33.2	7 53.2	2 54.0	29 47.0
14 W	3 26 54	23 10 52	0♈01 08	5♈54 45	1 12.8	27 21.1	9 57.9	12 46.8	1 07.1	23 35.1	24 29.8	7 54.7	2 52.4	29 47.0
15 Th	3 30 50	24 08 45	11 48 31	17 42 55	1 14.2	28 20.4	11 05.1	13 30.7	1 27.9	23 29.3	24 26.3	7 56.2	2 50.9	29 47.1
16 F	3 34 47	25 06 36	23 38 23	29 35 18	1R14.8	29 22.6	12 12.3	14 14.6	1 48.8	23 23.6	24 22.8	7 57.8	2 49.4	29 47.3
17 Sa	3 38 43	26 04 26	5♉34 03	11♉34 56	1 14.4	0♉27.8	13 19.7	14 58.4	2 09.8	23 18.1	24 19.2	7 59.5	2 48.0	29 47.4
18 Su	3 42 40	27 02 15	17 38 14	23 44 10	1 12.7	1 35.9	14 27.2	15 42.2	2 31.0	23 12.7	24 15.6	8 01.2	2 46.5	29 47.6
19 M	3 46 36	28 00 02	29 52 58	6♊04 46	1 09.8	2 46.8	15 34.8	16 26.0	2 52.3	23 07.4	24 11.9	8 02.9	2 45.0	29 47.8
20 Tu	3 50 33	28 57 48	12♊19 43	18 37 54	1 05.9	4 00.3	16 42.5	17 09.8	3 13.8	23 02.3	24 08.2	8 04.7	2 43.6	29 48.0
21 W	3 54 29	29 55 33	24 59 24	1♋24 16	1 01.3	5 16.5	17 50.3	17 53.5	3 35.3	22 57.4	24 04.4	8 06.5	2 42.2	29 48.3
22 Th	3 58 26	0♊53 16	7♋52 34	14 24 18	0 56.7	6 35.4	18 58.3	18 37.2	3 57.0	22 52.5	24 00.5	8 08.4	2 40.8	29 48.6
23 F	4 02 23	1 50 58	20 59 31	27 38 14	0 52.6	7 56.7	20 06.3	19 20.8	4 18.9	22 47.9	23 56.6	8 10.4	2 39.4	29 48.9
24 Sa	4 06 19	2 48 38	4♌20 27	11♌06 11	0 49.5	9 20.6	21 14.4	20 04.4	4 40.8	22 43.4	23 52.7	8 12.3	2 38.0	29 49.3
25 Su	4 10 16	3 46 16	17 55 27	24 48 15	0D47.9	10 47.0	22 22.6	20 48.0	5 02.9	22 39.0	23 48.7	8 14.4	2 36.7	29 49.7
26 M	4 14 12	4 43 53	1♍44 31	8♍44 14	0 47.6	12 15.8	23 30.9	21 31.5	5 25.1	22 34.8	23 44.7	8 16.4	2 35.3	29 50.1
27 Tu	4 18 09	5 41 28	15 47 18	22 53 34	0 48.5	13 47.1	24 39.3	22 15.0	5 47.4	22 30.8	23 40.6	8 18.5	2 34.0	29 50.5
28 W	4 22 05	6 39 02	0♎02 51	7♎14 51	0 49.8	15 20.9	25 47.8	22 58.4	6 09.8	22 26.9	23 36.5	8 20.7	2 32.7	29 51.0
29 Th	4 26 02	7 36 35	14 29 14	21 45 33	0R51.0	16 57.0	26 56.4	23 41.8	6 32.4	22 23.2	23 32.3	8 22.9	2 31.5	29 51.5
30 F	4 29 58	8 34 06	29 03 17	6♏21 49	0 51.1	18 35.6	28 05.0	24 25.1	6 55.0	22 19.7	23 28.2	8 25.1	2 30.2	29 52.1
31 Sa	4 33 55	9 31 36	13♏40 28	20 58 29	0 49.7	20 16.6	29 13.8	25 08.4	7 17.7	22 16.3	23 23.9	8 27.4	2 29.0	29 52.6

LONGITUDE

June 1958

Day	Sid.Time	☉	0 hr ☽	Noon ☽	True ☊	☿	♀	♂	⚳	♃	♄	♅	♆	♇
1 Su	4 37 52	10♊29 05	28♏15 05	5♐29 29	0♏46.4	21♉59.9	0♉22.6	25♓51.7	7♌40.6	22♎13.1	23♐19.7	8♌29.7	2♏27.8	29♌53.2
2 M	4 41 48	11 26 33	12♐40 54	19 48 36	0R41.4	23 45.7	1 31.5	26 34.9	8 03.5	22R10.0	23R15.5	8 32.1	2R26.6	29 53.8
3 Tu	4 45 45	12 24 00	26 51 54	3♑50 16	0 35.1	25 33.8	2 40.5	27 18.0	8 26.6	22 07.2	23 11.2	8 34.5	2 25.4	29 54.5
4 W	4 49 41	13 21 26	10♑43 13	17 30 28	0 28.4	27 24.4	3 49.6	28 01.1	8 49.7	22 04.5	23 06.9	8 36.9	2 24.2	29 55.1
5 Th	4 53 38	14 18 51	24 11 48	0♒47 10	0 21.9	29 17.2	4 58.8	28 44.2	9 13.0	22 02.0	23 02.5	8 39.4	2 23.1	29 55.8
6 F	4 57 34	15 16 15	7♒16 38	13 40 26	0 16.4	1♊12.3	6 08.0	29 27.2	9 36.3	21 59.6	22 58.2	8 41.9	2 22.0	29 56.6
7 Sa	5 01 31	16 13 39	19 58 49	26 12 13	0 12.5	3 09.7	7 17.4	0♈10.1	9 59.8	21 57.4	22 53.8	8 44.4	2 20.9	29 57.3
8 Su	5 05 28	17 11 02	2♓21 05	8♓25 58	0D10.4	5 09.2	8 26.8	0 53.0	10 23.3	21 55.5	22 49.4	8 47.0	2 19.9	29 58.1
9 M	5 09 24	18 08 25	14 27 27	20 26 09	0 10.0	7 10.7	9 36.2	1 35.8	10 46.9	21 53.6	22 45.0	8 49.7	2 18.8	29 58.9
10 Tu	5 13 21	19 05 47	26 22 42	2♈17 46	0 10.7	9 14.2	10 45.8	2 18.6	11 10.6	21 52.0	22 40.6	8 52.3	2 17.8	29 59.8
11 W	5 17 17	20 03 08	8♈11 59	14 06 02	0 12.0	11 19.5	11 55.4	3 01.2	11 34.4	21 50.5	22 36.2	8 55.0	2 16.8	0♍00.6
12 Th	5 21 14	21 00 29	20 00 30	25 56 01	0R12.9	13 26.5	13 05.1	3 43.9	11 58.3	21 49.2	22 31.7	8 57.8	2 15.9	0 01.5
13 F	5 25 10	21 57 50	1♉53 08	7♉52 23	0 12.6	15 34.8	14 14.9	4 26.4	12 22.3	21 48.1	22 27.3	9 00.5	2 15.0	0 02.4
14 Sa	5 29 07	22 55 10	13 54 16	19 59 11	0 10.6	17 44.4	15 24.7	5 08.9	12 46.4	21 47.2	22 22.9	9 03.3	2 14.1	0 03.4
15 Su	5 33 03	23 52 30	26 07 29	2♊19 30	0 06.4	19 54.9	16 34.6	5 51.3	13 10.5	21 46.5	22 18.5	9 06.2	2 13.2	0 04.3
16 M	5 37 00	24 49 49	8♊35 24	14 55 23	29♎59.9	22 06.2	17 44.5	6 33.6	13 34.8	21 45.9	22 14.0	9 09.0	2 12.3	0 05.3
17 Tu	5 40 57	25 47 07	21 19 29	27 47 42	29 51.6	24 17.9	18 54.6	7 15.8	13 59.1	21 45.6	22 09.6	9 11.9	2 11.5	0 06.4
18 W	5 44 53	26 44 25	4♋19 57	10♋56 06	29 42.2	26 29.8	20 04.6	7 58.0	14 23.5	21D45.4	22 05.2	9 14.9	2 10.7	0 07.4
19 Th	5 48 50	27 41 43	17 35 57	24 19 16	29 32.5	28 41.5	21 14.8	8 40.0	14 48.0	21 45.3	22 00.8	9 17.9	2 09.9	0 08.5
20 F	5 52 46	28 39 00	1♌05 45	7♌55 08	29 23.8	0♋52.8	22 25.0	9 22.0	15 12.5	21 45.5	21 56.4	9 20.9	2 09.2	0 09.6
21 Sa	5 56 43	29 36 16	14 47 06	21 41 23	29 16.7	3 03.5	23 35.2	10 03.9	15 37.1	21 45.9	21 52.0	9 23.9	2 08.5	0 10.7
22 Su	6 00 39	0♋33 31	28 37 42	5♍35 49	29 12.0	5 13.4	24 45.5	10 45.7	16 01.8	21 46.4	21 47.7	9 26.9	2 07.8	0 11.8
23 M	6 04 36	1 30 46	12♍35 30	19 36 36	29D09.5	7 22.1	25 55.9	11 27.4	16 26.6	21 47.1	21 43.3	9 30.0	2 07.1	0 13.0
24 Tu	6 08 32	2 28 00	26 38 56	3♎42 21	29 09.0	9 29.5	27 06.3	12 09.0	16 51.4	21 48.0	21 39.0	9 33.1	2 06.5	0 14.2
25 W	6 12 29	3 25 13	10♎46 44	17 51 56	29R09.4	11 35.5	28 16.7	12 50.5	17 16.3	21 49.0	21 34.7	9 36.3	2 05.9	0 15.4
26 Th	6 16 26	4 22 26	24 57 48	2♏04 08	29 09.6	13 39.9	29 27.3	13 31.9	17 41.3	21 50.3	21 30.4	9 39.5	2 05.3	0 16.7
27 F	6 20 22	5 19 39	9♏10 42	16 17 12	29 08.5	15 42.5	0♊37.8	14 13.2	18 06.3	21 51.7	21 26.2	9 42.7	2 04.8	0 17.9
28 Sa	6 24 19	6 16 50	23 23 18	0♐28 36	29 05.3	17 43.4	1 48.5	14 54.4	18 31.4	21 53.3	21 22.0	9 45.9	2 04.3	0 19.2
29 Su	6 28 15	7 14 02	7♐32 39	14 34 58	28 59.4	19 42.3	2 59.1	15 35.5	18 56.6	21 55.1	21 17.8	9 49.1	2 03.8	0 20.5
30 M	6 32 12	8 11 13	21 35 00	28 32 14	28 51.0	21 39.3	4 09.9	16 16.5	19 21.8	21 57.0	21 13.7	9 52.4	2 03.4	0 21.9

Astro Data

	Dy Hr Mn
♀0N	8 12:22
♇ D	11 22:01
☽0N	13 8:22
☽0S	27 11:21
♄□♅	30 23:21
☽0N	9 16:37
♂0N	14 7:12
♃ D	19 1:44
♃✶♄	22 18:10
☽0S	23 17:51

Planet Ingress

		Dy Hr Mn
♀	♈	5 11:59
⚳	♌	11 5:14
☿	♉	17 1:53
☉	♊	21 13:51
♀	♉	1 4:07
☿	♊	5 20:59
♂	♈	7 6:21
♇	♍	10 18:50
☊	♎R	16 11:42
☿	♋	20 2:20
☉	♋	21 21:57
♀	♊	26 23:08

Last Aspect / ☽ Ingress

Last Aspect Dy Hr Mn			☽ Ingress	Dy Hr Mn
2 15:55	♇	✶	♏	2 16:14
4 16:23	♇	□	♐	4 16:43
6 18:59	♇	△	♑	6 19:21
8 14:42	♃	□	♒	9 1:29
11 11:01	♇	☍	♓	11 11:27
13 12:53	♄	□	♈	13 23:58
16 12:24	♇	△	♉	16 12:50
18 23:50	♇	□	♊	19 0:14
21 9:01	♇	✶	♋	21 9:23
23 3:19	♃	□	♌	23 16:15
25 20:42	♇	☌	♍	25 21:00
27 13:19	♄	□	♎	27 23:55
30 1:20	♇	✶	♏	30 1:33

Last Aspect / ☽ Ingress

Last Aspect Dy Hr Mn			☽ Ingress	Dy Hr Mn
1 2:42	♇	□	♐	1 2:54
3 5:13	♇	△	♑	3 5:23
5 8:47	☿	△	♒	5 10:34
7 19:19	♇	☍	♓	7 19:24
9 16:38	♄	□	♈	10 7:20
12 5:09	♄	△	♉	12 20:12
14 2:02	♀	☌	♊	15 7:31
17 7:59	☉	☌	♋	17 16:04
19 7:26	♃	□	♌	19 22:04
21 15:35	♀	□	♍	22 2:22
23 23:45	♀	△	♎	24 5:42
25 18:42	♃	☌	♏	26 8:30
27 10:52	☿	△	♐	28 11:12
30 0:36	♃	✶	♑	30 14:32

☽ Phases & Eclipses

Dy Hr Mn	
3 12:23	○ 12♏34
3 12:13	☍ P 0.009
10 14:38	☾ 19♒25
18 19:00	● 27♉19
26 4:38	☽ 4♍26
1 20:55	○ 10♐50
9 6:59	☾ 17♓56
17 7:59	● 25♊38
24 9:45	☽ 2♎23

Astro Data

1 May 1958
Julian Day # 21305
SVP 5♓50'22"
GC 26♐15.4 ⚴ 15♊25.5
Eris 9♈27.1 ⚵ 12♋12.0
⚷ 22♒21.7 ⚶ 26♉38.6
☽ Mean ☊ 1♏00.2

1 June 1958
Julian Day # 21336
SVP 5♓50'18"
GC 26♐15.5 ⚴ 3♋45.1
Eris 9♈42.5 ⚵ 26♋18.9
⚷ 22♒42.8R ⚶ 10♊06.3
☽ Mean ☊ 29♎21.7

July 1958 — LONGITUDE

Day	Sid.Time	☉	0 hr ☽	Noon ☽	True ☊	☿	♀	♂	⚳	♃	♄	♅	♆	♇
1 Tu	6 36 08	9♋08 24	5♑26 10	12♑16 18	28♎40.6	23♋34.4	5♊20.7	16♈57.4	19♌47.1	21♎59.2	21♐09.6	9♌55.7	2♏03.0	0♍23.2
2 W	6 40 05	10 05 35	19 02 14	25 43 38	28R 29.4	25 27.4	6 31.5	17 38.1	20 12.4	22 01.4	21R 05.5	9 59.0	2R 02.6	0 24.6
3 Th	6 44 01	11 02 46	2♒20 13	8♒51 50	28 18.3	27 18.4	7 42.4	18 18.8	20 37.8	22 03.9	21 01.5	10 02.4	2 02.2	0 26.0
4 F	6 47 58	11 59 57	15 18 28	21 40 08	28 08.5	29 07.3	8 53.4	18 59.4	21 03.3	22 06.5	20 57.5	10 05.7	2 01.9	0 27.4
5 Sa	6 51 55	12 57 08	27 57 02	4♓09 25	28 00.7	0♌54.2	10 04.4	19 39.8	21 28.8	22 09.3	20 53.5	10 09.1	2 01.6	0 28.8
6 Su	6 55 51	13 54 20	10♓17 37	16 22 06	27 55.4	2 39.1	11 15.5	20 20.1	21 54.4	22 12.3	20 49.6	10 12.5	2 01.3	0 30.3
7 M	6 59 48	14 51 31	22 23 21	28 21 56	27 52.4	4 21.9	12 26.6	21 00.3	22 20.0	22 15.4	20 45.8	10 15.9	2 01.1	0 31.8
8 Tu	7 03 44	15 48 43	4♈18 27	10♈13 33	27D 51.3	6 02.6	13 37.8	21 40.4	22 45.7	22 18.7	20 42.0	10 19.4	2 00.9	0 33.3
9 W	7 07 41	16 45 56	16 07 53	22 02 09	27R 51.3	7 41.3	14 49.0	22 20.3	23 11.4	22 22.2	20 38.2	10 22.8	2 00.7	0 34.8
10 Th	7 11 37	17 43 08	27 57 01	3♉53 10	27 51.2	9 17.9	16 00.3	23 00.1	23 37.2	22 25.8	20 34.5	10 26.3	2 00.6	0 36.3
11 F	7 15 34	18 40 22	9♉51 17	15 51 59	27 50.2	10 52.4	17 11.6	23 39.8	24 03.0	22 29.6	20 30.9	10 29.8	2 00.5	0 37.9
12 Sa	7 19 30	19 37 35	21 55 53	28 03 30	27 47.1	12 24.9	18 23.0	24 19.3	24 28.9	22 33.6	20 27.3	10 33.3	2 00.4	0 39.4
13 Su	7 23 27	20 34 49	4♊15 20	10♊31 48	27 41.6	13 55.2	19 34.5	24 58.7	24 54.9	22 37.7	20 23.8	10 36.9	2D 00.4	0 41.0
14 M	7 27 24	21 32 04	16 53 11	23 19 44	27 33.5	15 23.5	20 46.0	25 37.9	25 20.9	22 42.0	20 20.3	10 40.4	2 00.4	0 42.6
15 Tu	7 31 20	22 29 19	29 51 33	6♋28 37	27 23.2	16 49.7	21 57.5	26 16.9	25 46.9	22 46.5	20 16.9	10 44.0	2 00.4	0 44.3
16 W	7 35 17	23 26 35	13♋10 49	19 57 53	27 11.4	18 13.7	23 09.1	26 55.8	26 13.0	22 51.1	20 13.5	10 47.5	2 00.4	0 45.9
17 Th	7 39 13	24 23 51	26 49 29	3♌45 10	26 59.4	19 35.5	24 20.8	27 34.6	26 39.2	22 55.8	20 10.3	10 51.1	2 00.5	0 47.6
18 F	7 43 10	25 21 07	10♌44 24	17 46 36	26 48.3	20 55.0	25 32.5	28 13.2	27 05.3	23 00.7	20 07.0	10 54.7	2 00.7	0 49.2
19 Sa	7 47 06	26 18 24	24 51 09	1♍57 26	26 39.3	22 12.4	26 44.2	28 51.6	27 31.6	23 05.8	20 03.9	10 58.4	2 00.8	0 50.9
20 Su	7 51 03	27 15 40	9♍04 51	16 12 53	26 32.9	23 27.3	27 56.0	29 29.8	27 57.8	23 11.0	20 00.8	11 02.0	2 01.0	0 52.6
21 M	7 54 59	28 12 58	23 21 01	0♎28 49	26 29.2	24 39.9	29 07.8	0♉07.8	28 24.1	23 16.4	19 57.8	11 05.6	2 01.2	0 54.4
22 Tu	7 58 56	29 10 15	7♎35 59	14 42 13	26D 28.7	25 50.1	0♋19.7	0 45.7	28 50.5	23 21.9	19 54.9	11 09.3	2 01.5	0 56.1
23 W	8 02 53	0♌07 32	21 47 19	28 51 08	26R 27.6	26 57.7	1 31.6	1 23.4	29 16.9	23 27.6	19 52.0	11 12.9	2 01.7	0 57.9
24 Th	8 06 49	1 04 50	5♏53 34	12♏54 31	26 27.4	28 02.7	2 43.6	2 00.9	29 43.3	23 33.4	19 49.3	11 16.6	2 02.0	0 59.6
25 F	8 10 46	2 02 09	19 53 56	26 51 43	26 25.9	29 05.0	3 55.6	2 38.2	0♍09.8	23 39.3	19 46.6	11 20.3	2 02.4	1 01.4
26 Sa	8 14 42	2 59 27	3♐47 47	10♐42 00	26 22.1	0♍04.5	5 07.6	3 15.3	0 36.3	23 45.4	19 43.9	11 23.9	2 02.8	1 03.2
27 Su	8 18 39	3 56 47	17 34 13	24 24 14	26 15.5	1 01.1	6 19.7	3 52.3	1 02.8	23 51.7	19 41.4	11 27.6	2 03.2	1 05.0
28 M	8 22 35	4 54 06	1♑11 51	7♑56 48	26 06.4	1 54.6	7 31.9	4 29.0	1 29.4	23 58.0	19 38.9	11 31.3	2 03.6	1 06.8
29 Tu	8 26 32	5 51 27	14 38 51	21 17 45	25 55.1	2 44.9	8 44.1	5 05.6	1 56.0	24 04.6	19 36.5	11 35.0	2 04.1	1 08.6
30 W	8 30 28	6 48 47	27 53 14	4♒25 08	25 42.9	3 32.0	9 56.3	5 41.9	2 22.6	24 11.2	19 34.2	11 38.7	2 04.6	1 10.5
31 Th	8 34 25	7 46 09	10♒53 14	17 17 27	25 30.8	4 15.5	11 08.6	6 18.0	2 49.3	24 18.0	19 32.0	11 42.4	2 05.1	1 12.3

August 1958 — LONGITUDE

Day	Sid.Time	☉	0 hr ☽	Noon ☽	True ☊	☿	♀	♂	⚳	♃	♄	♅	♆	♇
1 F	8 38 22	8♌43 32	23♒37 43	29♒54 04	25♎19.9	4♍55.4	12♋21.0	6♉53.9	3♍16.0	24♎24.9	19♐29.9	11♌46.1	2♏05.7	1♍14.2
2 Sa	8 42 18	9 40 55	6♓06 34	12♓15 25	25R 11.1	5 31.4	13 33.4	7 29.6	3 42.7	24 32.0	19R 27.8	11 49.8	2 06.3	1 16.1
3 Su	8 46 15	10 38 20	18 20 51	24 23 11	25 04.8	6 03.5	14 45.8	8 05.1	4 09.5	24 39.1	19 25.9	11 53.5	2 06.9	1 17.9
4 M	8 50 11	11 35 45	0♈22 48	6♈20 10	25 01.1	6 31.4	15 58.3	8 40.3	4 36.3	24 46.5	19 24.0	11 57.3	2 07.6	1 19.8
5 Tu	8 54 08	12 33 12	12 15 48	18 10 14	24D 59.6	6 54.9	17 10.8	9 15.3	5 03.1	24 53.9	19 22.2	12 01.0	2 08.3	1 21.7
6 W	8 58 04	13 30 40	24 04 05	29 58 00	24 59.5	7 13.9	18 23.4	9 50.1	5 30.0	25 01.5	19 20.5	12 04.7	2 09.0	1 23.6
7 Th	9 02 01	14 28 10	5♉52 36	11♉48 36	24R 59.8	7 28.0	19 36.1	10 24.6	5 56.9	25 09.1	19 18.9	12 08.4	2 09.8	1 25.6
8 F	9 05 57	15 25 40	17 46 41	23 47 30	24 59.5	7 37.2	20 48.8	10 58.9	6 23.8	25 17.0	19 17.4	12 12.1	2 10.6	1 27.5
9 Sa	9 09 54	16 23 13	29 51 44	6♊00 01	24 57.7	7R 41.4	22 01.5	11 32.9	6 50.7	25 24.9	19 15.9	12 15.8	2 11.4	1 29.4
10 Su	9 13 51	17 20 46	12♊12 56	18 31 01	24 53.8	7 40.2	23 14.3	12 06.6	7 17.7	25 32.9	19 14.6	12 19.5	2 12.2	1 31.4
11 M	9 17 47	18 18 21	24 54 42	1♋24 20	24 47.6	7 33.6	24 27.2	12 40.1	7 44.7	25 41.1	19 13.3	12 23.2	2 13.1	1 33.3
12 Tu	9 21 44	19 15 57	8♋00 10	14 42 18	24 39.2	7 21.6	25 40.1	13 13.3	8 11.7	25 49.4	19 12.2	12 26.9	2 14.0	1 35.3
13 W	9 25 40	20 13 35	21 30 41	28 25 07	24 29.5	7 04.1	26 53.0	13 46.2	8 38.8	25 57.8	19 11.1	12 30.6	2 15.0	1 37.2
14 Th	9 29 37	21 11 13	5♌25 16	12♌30 36	24 19.3	6 41.2	28 06.0	14 18.8	9 05.9	26 06.4	19 10.2	12 34.3	2 15.9	1 39.2
15 F	9 33 33	22 08 54	19 40 30	26 54 13	24 10.0	6 12.9	29 19.0	14 51.1	9 33.0	26 15.0	19 09.3	12 38.0	2 16.9	1 41.2
16 Sa	9 37 30	23 06 35	4♍10 53	11♍29 37	24 02.4	5 39.5	0♌32.1	15 23.1	10 00.1	26 23.8	19 08.5	12 41.7	2 18.0	1 43.1
17 Su	9 41 26	24 04 17	18 49 32	26 09 45	23 57.2	5 01.4	1 45.2	15 54.7	10 27.3	26 32.6	19 07.8	12 45.3	2 19.0	1 45.1
18 M	9 45 23	25 02 01	3♎29 25	10♎47 50	23D 54.4	4 18.9	2 58.3	16 26.1	10 54.4	26 41.6	19 07.2	12 49.0	2 20.1	1 47.1
19 Tu	9 49 20	25 59 46	18 04 21	25 18 26	23 53.8	3 32.6	4 11.5	16 57.1	11 21.6	26 50.7	19 06.7	12 52.6	2 21.2	1 49.1
20 W	9 53 16	26 57 31	2♏29 41	9♏37 48	23 54.3	2 43.3	5 24.8	17 27.8	11 48.8	26 59.8	19 06.4	12 56.3	2 22.4	1 51.1
21 Th	9 57 13	27 55 18	16 42 34	23 43 53	23R 55.0	1 51.7	6 38.0	17 58.2	12 16.0	27 09.1	19 06.1	12 59.9	2 23.5	1 53.1
22 F	10 01 09	28 53 06	0♐41 42	7♐36 00	23 54.7	0 58.8	7 51.3	18 28.2	12 43.3	27 18.5	19 05.9	13 03.5	2 24.7	1 55.1
23 Sa	10 05 06	29 50 56	14 26 49	21 14 13	23 52.7	0 05.6	9 04.7	18 57.8	13 10.5	27 28.0	19D 05.8	13 07.1	2 26.0	1 57.1
24 Su	10 09 02	0♍48 46	27 58 15	4♑38 58	23 48.5	29♌13.1	10 18.1	19 27.1	13 37.8	27 37.6	19 05.8	13 10.7	2 27.2	1 59.1
25 M	10 12 59	1 46 38	11♑16 26	17 50 41	23 42.1	28 22.4	11 31.6	19 56.1	14 05.1	27 47.3	19 05.9	13 14.3	2 28.5	2 01.1
26 Tu	10 16 55	2 44 31	24 21 44	0♒49 36	23 34.2	27 34.7	12 45.0	20 24.6	14 32.4	27 57.1	19 06.1	13 17.9	2 29.8	2 03.1
27 W	10 20 52	3 42 25	7♒14 19	13 35 52	23 25.3	26 51.0	13 58.6	20 52.8	14 59.7	28 07.0	19 06.3	13 21.4	2 31.2	2 05.1
28 Th	10 24 49	4 40 21	19 54 18	26 09 37	23 16.5	26 12.2	15 12.1	21 20.6	15 27.0	28 16.9	19 06.7	13 24.9	2 32.5	2 07.1
29 F	10 28 45	5 38 18	2♓21 54	8♓31 13	23 08.7	25 39.4	16 25.7	21 48.0	15 54.3	28 27.0	19 07.2	13 28.5	2 33.9	2 09.1
30 Sa	10 32 42	6 36 16	14 37 41	20 41 28	23 02.5	25 13.3	17 39.4	22 15.0	16 21.7	28 37.1	19 07.8	13 32.0	2 35.3	2 11.1
31 Su	10 36 38	7 34 17	26 42 45	2♈41 48	22 58.3	24 54.5	18 53.1	22 41.6	16 49.0	28 47.4	19 08.5	13 35.4	2 36.8	2 13.0

Astro Data

	Dy Hr Mn
☽0N	7 1:56
♆D	14 5:52
☽0S	21 0:33
☽0N	3 11:08
☿R	9 18:47
☽0S	17 8:41
♄D	24 0:31
☽0N	30 19:07

Planet Ingress

		Dy Hr Mn
☿	♌	4 23:46
♂	♉	21 7:03
♀	♋	22 5:26
☉	♌	23 8:50
⚳	♍	25 3:08
☿	♍	26 10:08
♀	♌	16 1:28
☿	♌R	23 14:31
☉	♍	23 15:46

Last Aspect / ☽ Ingress

Dy Hr Mn			☽ Ingress	Dy Hr Mn
2 11:26	☿	☍	♒	2 19:44
4 12:50	♃	△	♓	5 3:57
6 20:50	♄	□	♈	7 15:18
9 12:41	♃	☍	♉	10 4:09
11 18:02	☉	⚹	♊	12 15:46
14 16:28	♂	⚹	♋	15 0:15
17 0:47	♂	□	♌	17 5:31
19 6:32	♂	△	♍	19 8:42
21 9:31	♀	□	♎	21 11:11
23 8:31	☿	⚹	♏	23 13:57
25 16:08	☿	□	♐	25 17:25
27 11:02	♃	⚹	♑	27 21:53
29 17:05	♃	□	♒	30 3:52

Last Aspect / ☽ Ingress

Dy Hr Mn			☽ Ingress	Dy Hr Mn
1 1:24	♃	△	♓	1 12:11
3 2:10	♄	□	♈	3 23:14
6 1:50	♃	☍	♉	6 12:04
8 5:24	♀	⚹	♊	9 0:16
11 1:20	♃	△	♋	11 9:25
13 9:05	♀	☌	♌	13 14:43
15 10:54	♃	⚹	♍	15 17:07
17 0:30	♄	□	♎	17 18:17
19 14:35	♃	☌	♏	19 19:50
21 19:45	☉	□	♐	21 22:48
24 2:50	☿	△	♑	24 3:38
26 6:35	♃	□	♒	26 10:28
28 16:09	♃	△	♓	28 19:25
30 15:13	♂	⚹	♈	31 6:35

☽ Phases & Eclipses

Dy Hr Mn		
1 6:05	○	8♑54
9 0:21	☾	16♈18
16 18:33	●	23♋42
23 14:20	☽	0♏13
30 16:47	○	7♒00
7 17:49	☾	14♉42
15 3:33	●	21♌49
21 19:45	☽	28♏14
29 5:53	○	5♓24

Astro Data

1 July 1958
Julian Day # 21366
SVP 5♓50'13"
GC 26♐15.6 ⚴ 21♋31.1
Eris 9♈49.0 ⚵ 10♌04.4
⚷ 22♒07.0R ⚶ 23♊04.1
☽ Mean ☊ 27♎46.4

1 August 1958
Julian Day # 21397
SVP 5♓50'08"
GC 26♐15.6 ⚴ 9♌23.6
Eris 9♈45.5R ⚵ 24♌05.7
⚷ 20♒45.9R ⚶ 6♋07.7
☽ Mean ☊ 26♎07.9

LONGITUDE — September 1958

Day	Sid.Time	☉	0 hr ☽	Noon ☽	True ☊	☿	♀	♂	⚳	♃	♄	♅	♆	♇
1 M	10 40 35	8♍32 19	8♈38 55	14♈34 25	22♎56.1	24♌43.5	20♌06.8	23♉07.8	17♍16.4	28♎57.7	19♐09.2	13♌38.9	2♏38.2	2♍15.0
2 Tu	10 44 31	9 30 23	20 28 44	26 22 17	22D55.8	24D40.8	21 20.6	23 33.5	17 43.8	29 08.1	19 10.1	13 42.3	2 39.7	2 17.0
3 W	10 48 28	10 28 29	2♉15 32	8♉09 03	22 56.7	24 46.6	22 34.4	23 58.8	18 11.2	29 18.6	19 11.1	13 45.8	2 41.2	2 19.0
4 Th	10 52 24	11 26 37	14 03 21	19 59 04	22 58.2	25 01.1	23 48.3	24 23.6	18 38.6	29 29.2	19 12.1	13 49.2	2 42.8	2 21.0
5 F	10 56 21	12 24 47	25 56 47	1♊57 08	22R59.6	25 24.1	25 02.2	24 48.0	19 06.0	29 39.8	19 13.3	13 52.5	2 44.3	2 23.0
6 Sa	11 00 17	13 22 58	8♊00 46	14 08 19	23 00.1	25 55.8	26 16.1	25 11.9	19 33.4	29 50.6	19 14.5	13 55.9	2 45.9	2 24.9
7 Su	11 04 14	14 21 12	20 20 24	26 37 35	22 59.3	26 35.7	27 30.1	25 35.2	20 00.9	0♏01.4	19 15.9	13 59.3	2 47.5	2 26.9
8 M	11 08 11	15 19 28	3♋00 26	9♋29 24	22 56.9	27 23.8	28 44.1	25 58.1	20 28.3	0 12.3	19 17.3	14 02.6	2 49.1	2 28.9
9 Tu	11 12 07	16 17 46	16 04 51	22 47 04	22 53.1	28 19.5	29 58.2	26 20.5	20 55.8	0 23.3	19 18.9	14 05.9	2 50.8	2 30.8
10 W	11 16 04	17 16 06	29 36 10	6♌32 09	22 48.2	29 22.5	1♍12.3	26 42.3	21 23.2	0 34.4	19 20.5	14 09.1	2 52.5	2 32.8
11 Th	11 20 00	18 14 28	13♌34 50	20 43 51	22 42.8	0♍32.4	2 26.4	27 03.6	21 50.7	0 45.5	19 22.2	14 12.4	2 54.2	2 34.7
12 F	11 23 57	19 12 52	27 58 39	5♍18 33	22 37.8	1 48.5	3 40.6	27 24.4	22 18.1	0 56.7	19 24.1	14 15.6	2 55.9	2 36.7
13 Sa	11 27 53	20 11 18	12♍42 41	20 10 05	22 33.8	3 10.3	4 54.8	27 44.5	22 45.6	1 08.0	19 26.0	14 18.8	2 57.6	2 38.6
14 Su	11 31 50	21 09 45	27 39 40	5♎10 20	22 31.3	4 37.2	6 09.1	28 04.1	23 13.1	1 19.3	19 28.0	14 22.0	2 59.4	2 40.5
15 M	11 35 46	22 08 15	12♎40 59	20 10 33	22D30.3	6 08.7	7 23.3	28 23.1	23 40.6	1 30.7	19 30.1	14 25.1	3 01.2	2 42.4
16 Tu	11 39 43	23 06 46	27 38 04	5♏02 38	22 30.7	7 44.2	8 37.6	28 41.5	24 08.0	1 42.2	19 32.3	14 28.2	3 03.0	2 44.3
17 W	11 43 40	24 05 19	12♏23 32	19 40 09	22 32.0	9 23.1	9 52.0	28 59.3	24 35.5	1 53.8	19 34.6	14 31.3	3 04.8	2 46.2
18 Th	11 47 36	25 03 54	26 52 03	3♐58 55	22 33.4	11 04.9	11 06.4	29 16.5	25 03.0	2 05.4	19 37.0	14 34.3	3 06.7	2 48.1
19 F	11 51 33	26 02 30	11♐00 33	17 56 54	22R34.5	12 49.1	12 20.8	29 33.0	25 30.5	2 17.1	19 39.5	14 37.3	3 08.5	2 50.0
20 Sa	11 55 29	27 01 08	24 48 00	1♑33 56	22 34.6	14 35.1	13 35.2	29 48.9	25 57.9	2 28.8	19 42.0	14 40.3	3 10.4	2 51.8
21 Su	11 59 26	27 59 47	8♑14 53	14 51 04	22 33.6	16 22.7	14 49.6	0♊04.1	26 25.4	2 40.6	19 44.7	14 43.3	3 12.3	2 53.7
22 M	12 03 22	28 58 29	21 22 43	27 50 05	22 31.5	18 11.4	16 04.1	0 18.7	26 52.9	2 52.5	19 47.5	14 46.2	3 14.2	2 55.5
23 Tu	12 07 19	29 57 12	4♒13 28	10♒33 08	22 28.6	20 00.8	17 18.6	0 32.6	27 20.3	3 04.4	19 50.3	14 49.1	3 16.2	2 57.4
24 W	12 11 15	0♎55 56	16 49 20	23 02 19	22 25.2	21 50.7	18 33.2	0 45.7	27 47.8	3 16.3	19 53.2	14 52.0	3 18.1	2 59.2
25 Th	12 15 12	1 54 43	29 12 22	5♓19 42	22 21.8	23 40.9	19 47.7	0 58.2	28 15.2	3 28.4	19 56.2	14 54.8	3 20.1	3 01.0
26 F	12 19 09	2 53 31	11♓24 33	17 27 09	22 18.8	25 31.1	21 02.3	1 10.0	28 42.6	3 40.4	19 59.3	14 57.6	3 22.0	3 02.8
27 Sa	12 23 05	3 52 21	23 27 43	29 26 30	22 16.6	27 21.2	22 16.9	1 21.1	29 10.1	3 52.6	20 02.5	15 00.3	3 24.0	3 04.5
28 Su	12 27 02	4 51 13	5♈23 43	11♈19 37	22D15.3	29 10.9	23 31.6	1 31.4	29 37.5	4 04.7	20 05.8	15 03.0	3 26.0	3 06.3
29 M	12 30 58	5 50 07	17 14 27	23 08 31	22 15.0	1♎00.3	24 46.3	1 40.9	0♎04.9	4 17.0	20 09.1	15 05.7	3 28.1	3 08.1
30 Tu	12 34 55	6 49 04	29 02 06	4♉55 33	22 15.4	2 49.1	26 01.0	1 49.7	0 32.3	4 29.2	20 12.6	15 08.3	3 30.1	3 09.8

LONGITUDE — October 1958

Day	Sid.Time	☉	0 hr ☽	Noon ☽	True ☊	☿	♀	♂	⚳	♃	♄	♅	♆	♇
1 W	12 38 51	7♎48 02	10♉49 12	16♉43 26	22♎16.4	4♎37.3	27♍15.7	1♊57.7	0♎59.7	4♏41.6	20♐16.1	15♌10.9	3♏32.2	3♍11.5
2 Th	12 42 48	8 47 03	22 38 40	28 35 21	22 17.7	6 24.9	28 30.5	2 04.8	1 27.1	4 53.9	20 19.7	15 13.5	3 34.2	3 13.2
3 F	12 46 44	9 46 06	4♊33 57	10♊34 58	22 18.9	8 11.8	29 45.3	2 11.2	1 54.5	5 06.3	20 23.4	15 16.0	3 36.3	3 14.9
4 Sa	12 50 41	10 45 11	16 38 54	22 46 17	22 19.9	9 57.9	1♎00.1	2 16.8	2 21.9	5 18.8	20 27.2	15 18.5	3 38.4	3 16.6
5 Su	12 54 37	11 44 19	28 57 39	5♋13 33	22R20.4	11 43.3	2 14.9	2 21.5	2 49.2	5 31.3	20 31.0	15 21.0	3 40.5	3 18.2
6 M	12 58 34	12 43 29	11♋34 30	18 00 58	22 20.4	13 28.0	3 29.8	2 25.4	3 16.6	5 43.9	20 34.9	15 23.4	3 42.6	3 19.9
7 Tu	13 02 31	13 42 41	24 33 24	1♌12 10	22 20.0	15 11.8	4 44.6	2 28.4	3 43.9	5 56.4	20 38.9	15 25.7	3 44.8	3 21.5
8 W	13 06 27	14 41 55	7♌57 34	14 49 47	22 19.4	16 54.9	5 59.6	2 30.5	4 11.2	6 09.1	20 43.0	15 28.1	3 46.9	3 23.1
9 Th	13 10 24	15 41 12	21 48 51	28 54 40	22 18.6	18 37.2	7 14.5	2R31.8	4 38.6	6 21.7	20 47.2	15 30.3	3 49.0	3 24.7
10 F	13 14 20	16 40 31	6♍06 59	13♍25 20	22 17.9	20 18.8	8 29.4	2 32.1	5 05.8	6 34.4	20 51.4	15 32.6	3 51.2	3 26.2
11 Sa	13 18 17	17 39 53	20 49 07	28 17 32	22 17.4	21 59.6	9 44.4	2 31.6	5 33.1	6 47.1	20 55.8	15 34.8	3 53.4	3 27.8
12 Su	13 22 13	18 39 16	5♎49 37	13♎24 19	22D17.1	23 39.6	10 59.4	2 30.2	6 00.4	6 59.9	21 00.1	15 36.9	3 55.5	3 29.3
13 M	13 26 10	19 38 41	21 00 26	28 36 46	22 17.1	25 18.9	12 14.4	2 27.8	6 27.6	7 12.7	21 04.6	15 39.0	3 57.7	3 30.8
14 Tu	13 30 06	20 38 09	6♏12 06	13♏45 16	22 17.2	26 57.5	13 29.5	2 24.6	6 54.8	7 25.5	21 09.2	15 41.1	3 59.9	3 32.3
15 W	13 34 03	21 37 39	21 15 09	28 40 49	22R17.3	28 35.4	14 44.5	2 20.4	7 22.0	7 38.4	21 13.8	15 43.1	4 02.1	3 33.7
16 Th	13 38 00	22 37 10	6♐01 27	13♐16 24	22 17.3	0♏12.7	15 59.6	2 15.4	7 49.2	7 51.3	21 18.4	15 45.1	4 04.3	3 35.2
17 F	13 41 56	23 36 43	20 25 12	27 27 34	22 17.2	1 49.2	17 14.7	2 09.5	8 16.4	8 04.2	21 23.2	15 47.0	4 06.5	3 36.6
18 Sa	13 45 53	24 36 18	4♑23 21	11♑12 33	22 17.1	3 25.2	18 29.7	2 02.6	8 43.5	8 17.1	21 28.0	15 48.9	4 08.7	3 38.0
19 Su	13 49 49	25 35 55	17 55 20	24 31 55	22D17.1	5 00.4	19 44.9	1 54.9	9 10.6	8 30.1	21 32.9	15 50.7	4 11.0	3 39.4
20 M	13 53 46	26 35 33	1♒02 38	7♒27 52	22 17.1	6 35.1	21 00.0	1 46.4	9 37.7	8 43.1	21 37.9	15 52.5	4 13.2	3 40.7
21 Tu	13 57 42	27 35 13	13 48 03	20 03 38	22 17.5	8 09.2	22 15.1	1 36.9	10 04.7	8 56.1	21 42.9	15 54.2	4 15.4	3 42.1
22 W	14 01 39	28 34 55	26 15 05	2♓22 54	22 18.0	9 42.7	23 30.2	1 26.6	10 31.8	9 09.1	21 48.0	15 55.9	4 17.7	3 43.4
23 Th	14 05 35	29 34 38	8♓27 33	14 29 28	22 18.8	11 15.6	24 45.4	1 15.5	10 58.8	9 22.2	21 53.2	15 57.5	4 19.9	3 44.7
24 F	14 09 32	0♏34 23	20 29 06	26 26 52	22 19.6	12 47.9	26 00.5	1 03.5	11 25.7	9 35.2	21 58.4	15 59.1	4 22.1	3 45.9
25 Sa	14 13 29	1 34 10	2♈23 09	8♈18 19	22 20.2	14 19.7	27 15.7	0 50.8	11 52.7	9 48.3	22 03.6	16 00.6	4 24.4	3 47.1
26 Su	14 17 25	2 33 59	14 12 43	20 06 39	22R20.6	15 51.0	28 30.9	0 37.2	12 19.6	10 01.4	22 09.0	16 02.1	4 26.6	3 48.4
27 M	14 21 22	3 33 50	26 00 26	1♉54 20	22 20.4	17 21.7	29 46.1	0 22.9	12 46.5	10 14.5	22 14.4	16 03.5	4 28.9	3 49.5
28 Tu	14 25 18	4 33 43	7♉48 38	13 43 36	22 19.6	18 51.9	1♏01.3	0 07.8	13 13.3	10 27.6	22 19.8	16 04.9	4 31.1	3 50.7
29 W	14 29 15	5 33 38	19 39 29	25 36 32	22 18.1	20 21.6	2 16.5	29♉52.0	13 40.1	10 40.7	22 25.4	16 06.2	4 33.3	3 51.8
30 Th	14 33 11	6 33 34	1♊35 02	7♊35 15	22 16.1	21 50.7	3 31.8	29 35.5	14 06.9	10 53.9	22 30.9	16 07.5	4 35.6	3 53.0
31 F	14 37 08	7 33 33	13 37 29	19 42 00	22 13.8	23 19.3	4 47.0	29 18.4	14 33.6	11 07.0	22 36.6	16 08.7	4 37.8	3 54.0

Astro Data

	Dy Hr Mn
☿D	2 7:41
☽0S	13 18:35
♃✶♇	22 19:20
☉0S	23 13:10
♃☌♆	24 16:12
☽0N	27 1:37
☿0S	30 22:37
♃∠♄	5 11:10
♀0S	6 8:49
♂R	10 9:46
☽0S	11 5:29
☽0N	24 7:30

Planet Ingress

		Dy Hr Mn
♃	♏	7 8:52
♀	♍	9 12:35
☿	♍	11 1:10
♂	♊	21 5:26
☉	♎	23 13:09
☿	♎	28 22:45
⚳	♎	29 7:42
♀	♎	3 16:44
☿	♏	16 8:52
☉	♏	23 22:11
♀	♏	27 16:26
♂	♉R	29 0:01

Last Aspect / ☽ Ingress (September)

Last Aspect Dy Hr Mn			☽ Ingress	Dy Hr Mn
2 17:43	♃	☍	♉	2 19:24
4 22:26	☿	□	♊	5 8:07
7 13:50	♀	✶	♋	7 18:22
9 18:27	♂	✶	♌	10 0:42
11 22:45	♂	□	♍	12 3:19
14 0:24	♂	△	♎	14 3:44
15 10:55	♄	✶	♏	16 3:49
18 3:53	♂	☍	♐	18 5:16
20 3:18	☉	□	♑	20 9:13
22 14:18	☉	△	♒	22 16:03
24 5:53	♄	✶	♓	25 1:33
27 7:03	☿	☍	♈	27 13:07
29 5:53	♄	△	♉	30 1:58

Last Aspect / ☽ Ingress (October)

Last Aspect Dy Hr Mn			☽ Ingress	Dy Hr Mn
2 11:49	♀	△	♊	2 14:50
4 7:27	♄	☍	♋	5 2:00
6 2:13	☿	□	♌	7 9:51
8 22:11	♄	△	♍	9 13:49
11 0:07	♄	□	♎	11 14:44
13 6:10	☿	☌	♏	13 14:11
14 15:05	♅	□	♐	15 14:09
17 4:55	☉	✶	♑	17 16:23
19 14:07	☉	□	♒	19 22:04
22 3:53	☉	△	♓	22 7:19
24 2:55	♄	□	♈	24 19:10
27 7:08	♀	☍	♉	27 8:07
29 20:22	♂	☌	♊	29 20:49

☽ Phases & Eclipses

Dy Hr Mn	
6 10:24	☾ 13♊19
13 12:02	● 20♍11
20 3:18	☽ 26♐40
27 21:44	○ 4♈16
6 1:20	☾ 12♋17
12 20:52	● 19♎01
12 20:54:55	• T 05'11"
19 14:07	☽ 25♑41
27 15:41	○ 3♉43
27 15:27	• A 0.782

Astro Data

1 September 1958
Julian Day # 21428
SVP 5♓50'05"
GC 26♐15.7 ⚴ 26♌27.0
Eris 9♈32.8R ⚵ 7♍42.5
⚷ 19♒11.0R ⚶ 18♋29.2
☽ Mean ☊ 24♎29.4

1 October 1958
Julian Day # 21458
SVP 5♓50'03"
GC 26♐15.8 ⚴ 11♍58.1
Eris 9♈15.0R ⚵ 20♍17.2
⚷ 18♒01.2R ⚶ 29♋13.3
☽ Mean ☊ 22♎54.0

November 1958 — LONGITUDE

Day	Sid.Time	☉	0 hr ☽	Noon ☽	True ☊	☿	♀	♂	⚳	♃	♄	♅	♆	♇
1 Sa	14 41 04	8♏33 34	25♊49 10	1♋59 17	22♎11.4	24♏47.3	6♏02.3	29♉00.6	15♎00.4	11♏20.2	22♐42.3	16♌09.9	4♏40.1	3♍55.1
2 Su	14 45 01	9 33 37	8♋12 43	14 29 50	22R09.4	26 14.7	7 17.5	28R42.2	15 27.0	11 33.3	22 48.0	16 11.0	4 42.3	3 56.1
3 M	14 48 58	10 33 42	20 51 00	27 16 36	22 07.9	27 41.6	8 32.8	28 23.3	15 53.7	11 46.5	22 53.8	16 12.0	4 44.6	3 57.1
4 Tu	14 52 54	11 33 50	3♌47 00	10♌22 33	22D07.4	29 07.9	9 48.1	28 03.8	16 20.3	11 59.7	22 59.7	16 13.0	4 46.8	3 58.1
5 W	14 56 51	12 33 59	17 03 34	23 50 20	22 07.8	0♐33.5	11 03.4	27 43.9	16 46.8	12 12.9	23 05.6	16 14.0	4 49.0	3 59.1
6 Th	15 00 47	13 34 10	0♍43 01	7♍41 44	22 08.8	1 58.4	12 18.7	27 23.5	17 13.4	12 26.0	23 11.5	16 14.9	4 51.3	4 00.0
7 F	15 04 44	14 34 24	14 46 30	21 57 09	22 10.3	3 22.6	13 34.0	27 02.7	17 39.9	12 39.2	23 17.5	16 15.7	4 53.5	4 00.9
8 Sa	15 08 40	15 34 39	29 13 27	6♎34 55	22 11.5	4 46.0	14 49.4	26 41.6	18 06.3	12 52.4	23 23.6	16 16.5	4 55.7	4 01.8
9 Su	15 12 37	16 34 57	14♎00 58	21 30 48	22R12.1	6 08.6	16 04.7	26 20.2	18 32.7	13 05.6	23 29.7	16 17.3	4 57.9	4 02.6
10 M	15 16 33	17 35 16	29 03 31	6♏38 02	22 11.5	7 30.2	17 20.1	25 58.5	18 59.1	13 18.8	23 35.8	16 18.0	5 00.1	4 03.4
11 Tu	15 20 30	18 35 37	14♏13 12	21 47 47	22 09.6	8 50.8	18 35.4	25 36.7	19 25.4	13 31.9	23 42.0	16 18.6	5 02.3	4 04.2
12 W	15 24 26	19 36 00	29 20 34	6♐50 22	22 06.4	10 10.2	19 50.8	25 14.7	19 51.6	13 45.1	23 48.2	16 19.2	5 04.5	4 04.9
13 Th	15 28 23	20 36 25	14♐16 05	21 36 45	22 02.2	11 28.4	21 06.1	24 52.6	20 17.8	13 58.2	23 54.5	16 19.7	5 06.7	4 05.7
14 F	15 32 20	21 36 51	28 51 35	5♑59 58	21 57.8	12 45.2	22 21.5	24 30.5	20 44.0	14 11.4	24 00.9	16 20.1	5 08.9	4 06.4
15 Sa	15 36 16	22 37 18	13♑01 27	19 55 49	21 53.8	14 00.4	23 36.9	24 08.5	21 10.1	14 24.5	24 07.2	16 20.5	5 11.0	4 07.0
16 Su	15 40 13	23 37 47	26 43 02	3♒23 11	21 50.7	15 13.7	24 52.3	23 46.5	21 36.1	14 37.6	24 13.6	16 20.9	5 13.2	4 07.7
17 M	15 44 09	24 38 17	9♒56 31	16 23 25	21D49.0	16 25.1	26 07.6	23 24.7	22 02.1	14 50.8	24 20.1	16 21.2	5 15.4	4 08.3
18 Tu	15 48 06	25 38 48	22 44 20	28 59 48	21 48.7	17 34.1	27 23.0	23 03.0	22 28.1	15 03.8	24 26.5	16 21.4	5 17.5	4 08.8
19 W	15 52 02	26 39 21	5♓10 24	11♓16 44	21 49.7	18 40.6	28 38.4	22 41.6	22 54.0	15 16.9	24 33.1	16 21.6	5 19.6	4 09.4
20 Th	15 55 59	27 39 54	17 19 25	23 19 05	21 51.3	19 44.1	29 53.8	22 20.5	23 19.8	15 30.0	24 39.6	16 21.7	5 21.7	4 09.9
21 F	15 59 55	28 40 29	29 16 20	5♈11 47	21 53.1	20 44.3	1♐09.1	21 59.7	23 45.6	15 43.0	24 46.2	16R21.8	5 23.8	4 10.4
22 Sa	16 03 52	29 41 06	11♈05 58	16 59 26	21R54.2	21 40.7	2 24.5	21 39.3	24 11.3	15 56.0	24 52.8	16 21.8	5 25.9	4 10.8
23 Su	16 07 49	0♐41 43	22 52 39	28 46 07	21 54.1	22 32.8	3 39.9	21 19.3	24 36.9	16 09.0	24 59.4	16 21.7	5 28.0	4 11.3
24 M	16 11 45	1 42 22	4♉40 12	10♉35 17	21 52.1	23 20.0	4 55.3	20 59.8	25 02.5	16 22.0	25 06.1	16 21.6	5 30.1	4 11.7
25 Tu	16 15 42	2 43 02	16 31 41	22 29 42	21 48.2	24 01.7	6 10.7	20 40.7	25 28.0	16 34.9	25 12.8	16 21.5	5 32.1	4 12.0
26 W	16 19 38	3 43 43	28 29 32	4♊31 26	21 42.3	24 37.3	7 26.1	20 22.2	25 53.5	16 47.9	25 19.6	16 21.3	5 34.2	4 12.4
27 Th	16 23 35	4 44 26	10♊35 32	16 41 59	21 34.8	25 05.8	8 41.5	20 04.3	26 18.8	17 00.7	25 26.3	16 21.0	5 36.2	4 12.7
28 F	16 27 31	5 45 10	22 50 56	29 02 28	21 26.3	25 26.7	9 56.8	19 46.9	26 44.2	17 13.6	25 33.1	16 20.7	5 38.2	4 12.9
29 Sa	16 31 28	6 45 56	5♋16 41	11♋33 43	21 17.8	25R39.0	11 12.2	19 30.2	27 09.4	17 26.5	25 39.9	16 20.3	5 40.2	4 13.2
30 Su	16 35 25	7 46 42	17 53 39	24 16 36	21 10.0	25 42.0	12 27.6	19 14.1	27 34.6	17 39.3	25 46.8	16 19.9	5 42.2	4 13.4

December 1958 — LONGITUDE

Day	Sid.Time	☉	0 hr ☽	Noon ☽	True ☊	☿	♀	♂	⚳	♃	♄	♅	♆	♇
1 M	16 39 21	8♐47 31	0♌42 43	7♌12 08	21♎03.8	25♐34.8	13♐43.0	18♉58.7	27♎59.7	17♏52.0	25♐53.6	16♌19.4	5♏44.2	4♍13.6
2 Tu	16 43 18	9 48 20	13 45 02	20 21 36	20R59.7	25R17.0	14 58.4	18R44.0	28 24.8	18 04.8	26 00.5	16R18.9	5 46.1	4 13.7
3 W	16 47 14	10 49 11	27 02 01	3♍46 29	20D57.8	24 48.1	16 13.8	18 30.1	28 49.7	18 17.5	26 07.4	16 18.3	5 48.0	4 13.8
4 Th	16 51 11	11 50 04	10♍35 10	17 28 15	20 57.6	24 08.0	17 29.2	18 16.8	29 14.6	18 30.2	26 14.4	16 17.6	5 50.0	4 13.9
5 F	16 55 07	12 50 58	24 25 49	1♎27 57	20 58.6	23 17.0	18 44.7	18 04.3	29 39.4	18 42.8	26 21.3	16 16.9	5 51.8	4 13.9
6 Sa	16 59 04	13 51 53	8♎34 35	15 45 35	20R59.4	22 15.9	20 00.1	17 52.6	0♏04.2	18 55.4	26 28.3	16 16.2	5 53.7	4R14.0
7 Su	17 03 00	14 52 49	23 00 43	0♏19 33	20 59.2	21 06.1	21 15.5	17 41.7	0 28.8	19 07.9	26 35.2	16 15.4	5 55.6	4 14.0
8 M	17 06 57	15 53 47	7♏41 33	15 06 02	20 56.8	19 49.5	22 30.9	17 31.6	0 53.4	19 20.4	26 42.2	16 14.5	5 57.4	4 13.9
9 Tu	17 10 54	16 54 46	22 32 09	29 58 58	20 52.0	18 28.3	23 46.3	17 22.3	1 17.9	19 32.9	26 49.2	16 13.6	5 59.2	4 13.8
10 W	17 14 50	17 55 46	7♐25 26	14♐50 29	20 44.6	17 05.3	25 01.7	17 13.8	1 42.3	19 45.3	26 56.3	16 12.6	6 01.0	4 13.7
11 Th	17 18 47	18 56 47	22 13 01	29 32 00	20 35.4	15 43.3	26 17.2	17 06.2	2 06.6	19 57.7	27 03.3	16 11.6	6 02.8	4 13.6
12 F	17 22 43	19 57 48	6♑46 28	13♑55 36	20 25.3	14 25.0	27 32.6	16 59.4	2 30.8	20 10.0	27 10.4	16 10.6	6 04.5	4 13.4
13 Sa	17 26 40	20 58 51	20 58 45	27 55 26	20 15.5	13 12.9	28 48.0	16 53.4	2 55.0	20 22.3	27 17.4	16 09.4	6 06.3	4 13.3
14 Su	17 30 36	21 59 53	4♒45 19	11♒28 19	20 07.2	12 09.0	0♑03.4	16 48.2	3 19.0	20 34.5	27 24.5	16 08.3	6 08.0	4 13.0
15 M	17 34 33	23 00 57	18 04 27	24 33 57	20 01.0	11 14.8	1 18.8	16 43.9	3 42.9	20 46.7	27 31.5	16 07.0	6 09.7	4 12.8
16 Tu	17 38 29	24 02 00	0♓57 09	7♓14 30	19 57.2	10 31.2	2 34.2	16 40.4	4 06.8	20 58.8	27 38.6	16 05.8	6 11.3	4 12.5
17 W	17 42 26	25 03 04	13 26 31	19 33 50	19D55.7	9 58.6	3 49.6	16 37.8	4 30.5	21 10.9	27 45.7	16 04.5	6 13.0	4 12.2
18 Th	17 46 23	26 04 09	25 37 05	1♈36 58	19 55.6	9 37.1	5 05.0	16 35.9	4 54.1	21 22.9	27 52.8	16 03.1	6 14.6	4 11.8
19 F	17 50 19	27 05 14	7♈34 10	13 29 23	19R56.2	9D26.3	6 20.4	16D34.9	5 17.7	21 34.8	27 59.9	16 01.7	6 16.2	4 11.4
20 Sa	17 54 16	28 06 19	19 23 19	25 16 37	19 56.2	9 25.7	7 35.8	16 34.7	5 41.1	21 46.7	28 07.0	16 00.2	6 17.7	4 11.0
21 Su	17 58 12	29 07 24	1♉09 56	7♉03 51	19 54.6	9 34.5	8 51.2	16 35.3	6 04.4	21 58.5	28 14.0	15 58.7	6 19.3	4 10.6
22 M	18 02 09	0♑08 30	12 58 57	18 55 42	19 50.7	9 52.1	10 06.5	16 36.6	6 27.6	22 10.2	28 21.1	15 57.2	6 20.8	4 10.1
23 Tu	18 06 05	1 09 36	24 54 34	0♊55 56	19 44.0	10 17.6	11 21.9	16 38.7	6 50.7	22 21.9	28 28.2	15 55.6	6 22.2	4 09.6
24 W	18 10 02	2 10 42	7♊00 07	13 07 21	19 34.5	10 50.3	12 37.2	16 41.6	7 13.7	22 33.5	28 35.3	15 53.9	6 23.7	4 09.1
25 Th	18 13 58	3 11 49	19 17 50	25 31 41	19 22.6	11 29.3	13 52.6	16 45.2	7 36.6	22 45.1	28 42.4	15 52.3	6 25.1	4 08.5
26 F	18 17 55	4 12 56	1♋48 56	8♋09 35	19 09.4	12 14.1	15 07.9	16 49.6	7 59.4	22 56.5	28 49.4	15 50.5	6 26.5	4 08.0
27 Sa	18 21 52	5 14 03	14 33 34	21 00 48	18 55.9	13 03.9	16 23.3	16 54.7	8 22.0	23 07.9	28 56.5	15 48.8	6 27.9	4 07.3
28 Su	18 25 48	6 15 10	27 31 09	4♌04 28	18 43.4	13 58.2	17 38.6	17 00.5	8 44.6	23 19.3	29 03.5	15 47.0	6 29.3	4 06.7
29 M	18 29 45	7 16 18	10♌40 36	17 19 26	18 33.1	14 56.4	18 54.0	17 06.9	9 07.0	23 30.5	29 10.6	15 45.1	6 30.6	4 06.0
30 Tu	18 33 41	8 17 26	24 00 49	0♍44 41	18 25.5	15 58.2	20 09.3	17 14.1	9 29.3	23 41.7	29 17.6	15 43.2	6 31.9	4 05.4
31 W	18 37 38	9 18 35	7♍30 58	14 19 38	18 21.0	17 03.1	21 24.6	17 21.9	9 51.4	23 52.8	29 24.6	15 41.3	6 33.2	4 04.6

Astro Data

	Dy Hr Mn
☽0S	7 15:53
⚳0S	8 11:31
☽0N	20 14:14
♅R	22 4:49
♃□♅	24 11:23
☿R	30 7:15
☽0S	5 0:32
♇R	6 15:43
☽0N	17 22:50
☿D	20 1:26
♂D	20 6:45

Planet Ingress

	Dy Hr Mn
☿ ♐	5 2:36
♀ ♐	20 13:59
☉ ♐	22 19:29
⚳ ♏	6 7:57
♀ ♑	14 10:55
☉ ♑	22 8:40

Last Aspect / ☽ Ingress

Last Aspect Dy Hr Mn	☽ Ingress Dy Hr Mn
31 17:46 ♄ ☍	♋ 1 8:09
3 14:01 ♂ ✶	♌ 3 17:02
5 18:39 ♂ □	♍ 5 22:45
7 20:13 ♂ △	♎ 8 1:16
9 15:11 ♄ ✶	♏ 10 1:30
11 17:55 ♂ ☍	♐ 12 1:03
13 15:49 ♄ ☌	♑ 14 1:54
15 19:14 ♂ △	♒ 16 5:53
18 8:33 ♀ □	♓ 18 13:56
20 21:34 ☉ △	♈ 21 1:28
23 4:14 ♄ △	♉ 23 14:30
25 8:27 ♂ ☌	♊ 26 3:00
28 5:11 ♄ ☍	♋ 28 13:51
30 2:43 ♂ ✶	♌ 30 22:41

Last Aspect / ☽ Ingress

Last Aspect Dy Hr Mn	☽ Ingress Dy Hr Mn
2 22:15 ♄ △	♍ 3 5:18
5 3:13 ♄ □	♎ 5 9:31
7 5:50 ♄ ✶	♏ 7 11:28
8 18:57 ♃ ☌	♐ 9 12:02
11 7:53 ♄ ☌	♑ 11 12:46
12 22:46 ♃ ✶	♒ 13 15:38
15 17:35 ♄ ✶	♓ 15 22:12
18 4:26 ♄ □	♈ 18 8:45
20 18:19 ☉ △	♉ 20 21:38
22 18:37 ♃ ☍	♊ 23 10:09
25 18:08 ♄ ☍	♋ 25 20:33
27 15:59 ♃ △	♌ 28 4:33
30 9:24 ♄ △	♍ 30 10:41

☽ Phases & Eclipses

Dy Hr Mn	
4 14:19	☾ 11♌40
11 6:34	● 18♏22
18 4:59	☽ 25♒21
26 10:17	○ 3♊39
4 1:24	☾ 11♍23
10 17:23	● 18♐09
17 23:52	☽ 25♓33
26 3:54	○ 3♋52

Astro Data

1 November 1958
Julian Day # 21489
SVP 5♓50'00"
GC 26♐15.9 ⚴ 26♍44.6
Eris 8♈56.4R ⚵ 2♎20.8
⚷ 17♒39.6 ⚶ 8♌00.8
☽ Mean ☊ 21♎15.5

1 December 1958
Julian Day # 21519
SVP 5♓49'55"
GC 26♐15.9 ⚴ 9♎25.1
Eris 8♈43.6R ⚵ 12♎36.3
⚷ 18♒17.0 ⚶ 12♌35.1
☽ Mean ☊ 19♎40.2

LONGITUDE — January 1959

Day	Sid.Time	☉	0 hr ☽	Noon ☽	True ☊	☿	♀	♂	⚳	♃	♄	♅	♆	♇
1 Th	18 41 34	10♑19 44	21♍10 41	28♍04 08	18♎19.0	18♐10.7	22♑39.9	17♉30.4	10♏13.5	24♏03.8	29♐31.7	15♌39.4	6♏34.4	4♍03.9
2 F	18 45 31	11 20 53	5♎00 03	11♎58 26	18R 18.6	19 20.8	23 55.2	17 39.6	10 35.4	24 14.8	29 38.6	15R 37.4	6 35.6	4R 03.1
3 Sa	18 49 27	12 22 03	18 59 19	26 02 40	18 18.5	20 33.1	25 10.5	17 49.3	10 57.1	24 25.6	29 45.6	15 35.3	6 36.8	4 02.3
4 Su	18 53 24	13 23 13	3♏08 26	10♏16 26	18 17.4	21 47.3	26 25.8	17 59.7	11 18.8	24 36.4	29 52.6	15 33.2	6 37.9	4 01.5
5 M	18 57 21	14 24 23	17 26 27	24 38 07	18 13.9	23 03.2	27 41.1	18 10.7	11 40.3	24 47.1	29 59.6	15 31.1	6 39.0	4 00.6
6 Tu	19 01 17	15 25 34	1♐50 59	9♐04 30	18 07.5	24 20.7	28 56.4	18 22.3	12 01.6	24 57.7	0♑06.5	15 29.0	6 40.1	3 59.7
7 W	19 05 14	16 26 44	16 18 00	23 30 45	17 58.1	25 39.6	0♒11.7	18 34.6	12 22.8	25 08.2	0 13.4	15 26.8	6 41.2	3 58.8
8 Th	19 09 10	17 27 55	0♑41 58	7♑50 51	17 46.3	26 59.8	1 27.0	18 47.3	12 43.9	25 18.6	0 20.3	15 24.6	6 42.2	3 57.9
9 F	19 13 07	18 29 05	14 56 35	21 58 28	17 33.3	28 21.1	2 42.2	19 00.7	13 04.8	25 29.0	0 27.2	15 22.4	6 43.2	3 57.0
10 Sa	19 17 03	19 30 15	28 55 49	5♒48 05	17 20.5	29 43.4	3 57.5	19 14.6	13 25.6	25 39.2	0 34.0	15 20.1	6 44.2	3 56.0
11 Su	19 21 00	20 31 25	12♒34 52	19 15 52	17 09.1	1♑06.8	5 12.7	19 29.0	13 46.2	25 49.3	0 40.8	15 17.9	6 45.1	3 55.0
12 M	19 24 56	21 32 34	25 50 58	2♓20 12	17 00.1	2 31.0	6 28.0	19 44.0	14 06.6	25 59.4	0 47.6	15 15.5	6 46.0	3 54.0
13 Tu	19 28 53	22 33 43	8♓43 41	15 01 42	16 54.0	3 56.1	7 43.2	19 59.5	14 26.9	26 09.3	0 54.4	15 13.2	6 46.9	3 52.9
14 W	19 32 50	23 34 51	21 14 38	27 22 58	16 50.6	5 21.9	8 58.4	20 15.5	14 47.0	26 19.1	1 01.2	15 10.8	6 47.7	3 51.8
15 Th	19 36 46	24 35 58	3♈27 15	9♈28 04	16D 49.3	6 48.5	10 13.6	20 32.0	15 07.0	26 28.8	1 07.9	15 08.4	6 48.5	3 50.8
16 F	19 40 43	25 37 05	15 26 06	21 22 01	16R 49.2	8 15.8	11 28.7	20 48.9	15 26.8	26 38.4	1 14.5	15 06.0	6 49.2	3 49.6
17 Sa	19 44 39	26 38 11	27 16 31	3♉10 20	16 49.1	9 43.8	12 43.9	21 06.4	15 46.4	26 47.9	1 21.2	15 03.6	6 50.0	3 48.5
18 Su	19 48 36	27 39 16	9♉04 08	14 58 39	16 47.8	11 12.5	13 59.0	21 24.3	16 05.8	26 57.3	1 27.8	15 01.1	6 50.7	3 47.4
19 M	19 52 32	28 40 20	20 54 30	26 52 20	16 44.5	12 41.8	15 14.2	21 42.6	16 25.1	27 06.6	1 34.4	14 58.6	6 51.3	3 46.2
20 Tu	19 56 29	29 41 24	2♊52 45	8♊56 14	16 38.6	14 11.7	16 29.3	22 01.4	16 44.2	27 15.8	1 41.0	14 56.1	6 52.0	3 45.0
21 W	20 00 25	0♒42 26	15 03 16	21 14 13	16 29.9	15 42.2	17 44.3	22 20.6	17 03.1	27 24.9	1 47.5	14 53.6	6 52.6	3 43.8
22 Th	20 04 22	1 43 28	27 29 24	3♋49 01	16 18.9	17 13.4	18 59.4	22 40.2	17 21.8	27 33.8	1 53.9	14 51.1	6 53.1	3 42.6
23 F	20 08 19	2 44 29	10♋13 12	16 41 56	16 06.4	18 45.2	20 14.5	23 00.2	17 40.3	27 42.6	2 00.4	14 48.6	6 53.7	3 41.3
24 Sa	20 12 15	3 45 29	23 15 10	29 52 42	15 53.6	20 17.6	21 29.5	23 20.5	17 58.7	27 51.4	2 06.8	14 46.0	6 54.2	3 40.1
25 Su	20 16 12	4 46 28	6♌34 18	13♌19 39	15 41.6	21 50.6	22 44.5	23 41.3	18 16.8	27 59.9	2 13.2	14 43.4	6 54.6	3 38.8
26 M	20 20 08	5 47 27	20 08 23	27 00 03	15 31.7	23 24.2	23 59.5	24 02.4	18 34.8	28 08.4	2 19.5	14 40.9	6 55.1	3 37.5
27 Tu	20 24 05	6 48 25	3♍54 17	10♍50 38	15 24.4	24 58.5	25 14.5	24 23.9	18 52.5	28 16.8	2 25.7	14 38.3	6 55.5	3 36.2
28 W	20 28 01	7 49 22	17 48 43	24 48 11	15 20.2	26 33.4	26 29.4	24 45.7	19 10.1	28 25.0	2 32.0	14 35.7	6 55.8	3 34.8
29 Th	20 31 58	8 50 18	1♎48 42	8♎50 02	15D 18.4	28 08.9	27 44.3	25 07.9	19 27.4	28 33.1	2 38.2	14 33.1	6 56.2	3 33.5
30 F	20 35 54	9 51 13	15 51 56	22 54 16	15 18.4	29 45.2	28 59.2	25 30.4	19 44.6	28 41.0	2 44.3	14 30.5	6 56.5	3 32.1
31 Sa	20 39 51	10 52 08	29 56 54	6♏59 42	15R 18.9	1♒22.1	0♓14.1	25 53.2	20 01.5	28 48.9	2 50.4	14 27.8	6 56.7	3 30.8

LONGITUDE — February 1959

Day	Sid.Time	☉	0 hr ☽	Noon ☽	True ☊	☿	♀	♂	⚳	♃	♄	♅	♆	♇
1 Su	20 43 48	11♒53 02	14♏02 35	21♏05 27	15♎18.6	2♒59.7	1♓29.0	26♉16.4	20♏18.2	28♏56.6	2♑56.5	14♌25.2	6♏56.9	3♍29.4
2 M	20 47 44	12 53 56	28 08 10	5♐10 36	15R 16.5	4 38.0	2 43.9	26 39.8	20 34.7	29 04.1	3 02.5	14R 22.6	6 57.1	3R 28.0
3 Tu	20 51 41	13 54 49	12♐12 31	19 13 41	15 11.9	6 17.0	3 58.7	27 03.6	20 50.9	29 11.5	3 08.4	14 20.0	6 57.3	3 26.6
4 W	20 55 37	14 55 41	26 13 48	3♑12 30	15 04.7	7 56.7	5 13.5	27 27.6	21 07.0	29 18.8	3 14.3	14 17.3	6 57.4	3 25.1
5 Th	20 59 34	15 56 32	10♑09 25	17 04 07	14 55.5	9 37.2	6 28.3	27 52.0	21 22.7	29 26.0	3 20.2	14 14.7	6 57.5	3 23.7
6 F	21 03 30	16 57 22	23 56 10	0♒45 08	14 45.1	11 18.5	7 43.1	28 16.6	21 38.3	29 33.0	3 26.0	14 12.1	6 57.6	3 22.3
7 Sa	21 07 27	17 58 10	7♒30 37	14 12 16	14 34.8	13 00.5	8 57.8	28 41.5	21 53.6	29 39.8	3 31.7	14 09.4	6R 57.6	3 20.8
8 Su	21 11 23	18 58 58	20 49 47	27 22 55	14 25.6	14 43.4	10 12.5	29 06.7	22 08.7	29 46.6	3 37.4	14 06.8	6 57.6	3 19.3
9 M	21 15 20	19 59 44	3♓51 33	10♓15 37	14 18.3	16 27.0	11 27.2	29 32.2	22 23.5	29 53.1	3 43.0	14 04.2	6 57.5	3 17.9
10 Tu	21 19 17	21 00 29	16 35 10	22 50 20	14 13.4	18 11.4	12 41.9	29 57.9	22 38.1	29 59.5	3 48.6	14 01.6	6 57.4	3 16.4
11 W	21 23 13	22 01 12	29 01 20	5♈08 29	14D 10.9	19 56.6	13 56.5	0♊23.9	22 52.4	0♐05.8	3 54.1	13 59.0	6 57.3	3 14.9
12 Th	21 27 10	23 01 54	11♈12 10	17 12 49	14 10.5	21 42.7	15 11.1	0 50.1	23 06.4	0 11.9	3 59.6	13 56.4	6 57.2	3 13.4
13 F	21 31 06	24 02 34	23 10 58	29 07 11	14 11.4	23 29.5	16 25.6	1 16.5	23 20.2	0 17.9	4 04.9	13 53.8	6 57.0	3 11.9
14 Sa	21 35 03	25 03 12	5♉02 02	10♉56 11	14 12.7	25 17.2	17 40.2	1 43.2	23 33.7	0 23.7	4 10.3	13 51.2	6 56.8	3 10.4
15 Su	21 38 59	26 03 49	16 50 17	22 44 59	14R 13.6	27 05.6	18 54.7	2 10.1	23 46.9	0 29.3	4 15.5	13 48.7	6 56.5	3 08.9
16 M	21 42 56	27 04 24	28 40 58	4♊38 54	14 13.3	28 54.8	20 09.1	2 37.2	23 59.9	0 34.8	4 20.7	13 46.1	6 56.2	3 07.4
17 Tu	21 46 52	28 04 57	10♊39 26	16 43 10	14 11.2	0♓44.8	21 23.6	3 04.6	24 12.6	0 40.1	4 25.9	13 43.6	6 55.9	3 05.9
18 W	21 50 49	29 05 29	22 50 41	29 02 31	14 07.2	2 35.4	22 38.0	3 32.1	24 25.0	0 45.3	4 30.9	13 41.1	6 55.6	3 04.3
19 Th	21 54 46	0♓05 59	5♋19 07	11♋40 51	14 01.5	4 26.6	23 52.3	3 59.9	24 37.1	0 50.3	4 35.9	13 38.6	6 55.2	3 02.8
20 F	21 58 42	1 06 27	18 08 00	24 40 46	13 54.5	6 18.4	25 06.6	4 27.8	24 48.9	0 55.1	4 40.9	13 36.1	6 54.8	3 01.3
21 Sa	22 02 39	2 06 53	1♌19 11	8♌03 12	13 47.1	8 10.7	26 20.9	4 56.0	25 00.4	0 59.8	4 45.7	13 33.6	6 54.3	2 59.8
22 Su	22 06 35	3 07 18	14 52 37	21 47 09	13 40.1	10 03.3	27 35.1	5 24.3	25 11.7	1 04.3	4 50.5	13 31.2	6 53.8	2 58.2
23 M	22 10 32	4 07 40	28 46 21	5♍49 43	13 34.4	11 56.1	28 49.3	5 52.8	25 22.6	1 08.7	4 55.3	13 28.8	6 53.3	2 56.7
24 Tu	22 14 28	5 08 01	12♍56 37	20 06 25	13 30.4	13 48.9	0♈03.5	6 21.4	25 33.2	1 12.8	4 59.9	13 26.4	6 52.8	2 55.2
25 W	22 18 25	6 08 21	27 18 25	4♎31 54	13D 28.4	15 41.6	1 17.6	6 50.3	25 43.5	1 16.8	5 04.5	13 24.0	6 52.2	2 53.7
26 Th	22 22 21	7 08 39	11♎46 11	19 00 37	13 28.2	17 33.9	2 31.6	7 19.3	25 53.5	1 20.7	5 09.0	13 21.7	6 51.6	2 52.1
27 F	22 26 18	8 08 55	26 14 37	3♏27 39	13 29.3	19 25.5	3 45.7	7 48.5	26 03.2	1 24.3	5 13.4	13 19.3	6 51.0	2 50.6
28 Sa	22 30 15	9 09 10	10♏39 16	17 49 05	13 30.7	21 16.1	4 59.7	8 17.8	26 12.6	1 27.8	5 17.8	13 17.0	6 50.3	2 49.1

Astro Data

	Dy Hr Mn
☽0S	1 7:28
♄□♅	8 23:26
☽0N	14 8:55
☽0S	28 14:18
♄△♇	5 23:41
♆R	7 13:35
☽0N	10 18:50
☽0S	24 22:38
♀0N	26 8:44

Planet Ingress

		Dy Hr Mn
♄	♑	5 13:33
♀	♒	7 8:16
☿	♑	10 16:48
☉	♒	20 19:19
☿	♒	30 15:41
♀	♓	31 7:28
♃	♐	10 13:46
♂	♊	10 13:57
☿	♓	17 2:15
☉	♓	19 9:38
♀	♈	24 10:53

Last Aspect / ☽ Ingress (January)

Last Aspect Dy Hr Mn		☽ Ingress Dy Hr Mn
1 14:33 ♄ □	♎	1 15:21
3 18:21 ♄ ⚹	♏	3 18:42
5 17:34 ♀ ⚹	♐	5 20:56
7 15:57 ☿ ☌	♑	7 22:50
9 18:07 ♃ ⚹	♒	10 1:52
12 0:06 ♃ □	♓	12 7:39
14 9:53 ♃ △	♈	14 17:09
16 21:27 ☉ □	♉	17 5:33
19 15:56 ☉ △	♊	19 18:16
21 4:28 ♀ △	♋	22 4:47
24 8:19 ♃ △	♌	24 12:13
26 14:00 ♃ □	♍	26 17:13
28 18:15 ♃ ⚹	♎	28 20:54
30 23:22 ♀ △	♏	31 0:05

Last Aspect / ☽ Ingress (February)

Last Aspect Dy Hr Mn		☽ Ingress Dy Hr Mn
2 1:30 ♃ ☌	♐	2 3:11
3 3:39 ♅ △	♑	4 6:29
6 9:51 ♃ ⚹	♒	6 10:40
8 16:27 ♃ □	♓	8 16:50
9 14:30 ♀ ☌	♈	11 1:55
13 0:47 ☉ ⚹	♉	13 13:47
15 22:23 ☿ □	♊	16 2:39
18 12:06 ☉ △	♋	18 13:51
20 12:52 ♀ △	♌	20 21:38
21 21:40 ♅ ☍	♍	23 2:06
23 23:52 ☿ ☍	♎	25 4:29
26 2:40 ♅ ⚹	♏	27 6:14

☽ Phases & Eclipses

Dy Hr Mn		
2 10:50	☾	11♎18
9 5:34	●	18♑13
16 21:27	☽	26♈01
24 19:32	○	4♌05
31 19:06	☾	11♏10
7 19:22	●	18♒17
15 19:20	☽	26♉22
23 8:54	○	4♍00

Astro Data

1 January 1959
Julian Day # 21550
SVP 5♓49'50"
GC 26♐16.0 ⚴ 20♎00.6
Eris 8♈39.8 ⚵ 20♎52.0
⚷ 19♒48.0 ⚶ 10♌59.7R
☽Mean ☊ 18♎01.7

1 February 1959
Julian Day # 21581
SVP 5♓49'46"
GC 26♐16.1 ⚴ 26♎28.9
Eris 8♈46.9 ⚵ 25♎22.1
⚷ 21♒52.4 ⚶ 3♌39.4R
☽Mean ☊ 16♎23.2

March 1959

LONGITUDE

Day	Sid.Time	☉	0 hr ☽	Noon ☽	True ☊	☿	♀	♂	⚳	♃	♄	♅	♆	♇
1 Su	22 34 11	10♓09 24	24♏56 47	2♐02 08	13♎31.9	23♓05.4	6♈13.6	8♊47.3	26♏21.6	1♐31.1	5♑22.1	13♌14.8	6♏49.6	2♍47.6
2 M	22 38 08	11 09 36	9♐04 57	16 05 04	13R32.1	24 52.9	7 27.5	9 16.9	26 30.3	1 34.2	5 26.3	13R12.5	6R48.9	2R46.1
3 Tu	22 42 04	12 09 47	23 02 24	29 56 51	13 30.8	26 38.3	8 41.4	9 46.7	26 38.7	1 37.2	5 30.4	13 10.3	6 48.1	2 44.6
4 W	22 46 01	13 09 56	6♑48 20	13♑36 48	13 28.1	28 21.0	9 55.2	10 16.7	26 46.7	1 40.0	5 34.4	13 08.1	6 47.3	2 43.1
5 Th	22 49 57	14 10 03	20 22 11	27 04 26	13 24.2	0♈00.5	11 09.0	10 46.8	26 54.3	1 42.6	5 38.4	13 06.0	6 46.5	2 41.6
6 F	22 53 54	15 10 09	3♒43 29	10♒19 15	13 19.6	1 36.4	12 22.8	11 17.0	27 01.7	1 45.0	5 42.3	13 03.9	6 45.7	2 40.1
7 Sa	22 57 50	16 10 13	16 51 42	23 20 48	13 15.0	3 08.0	13 36.5	11 47.4	27 08.6	1 47.2	5 46.1	13 01.8	6 44.8	2 38.6
8 Su	23 01 47	17 10 16	29 46 29	6♓08 46	13 10.9	4 34.8	14 50.1	12 17.9	27 15.2	1 49.2	5 49.8	12 59.7	6 43.9	2 37.1
9 M	23 05 44	18 10 16	12♓27 40	18 43 13	13 07.8	5 56.3	16 03.7	12 48.5	27 21.4	1 51.1	5 53.5	12 57.7	6 43.0	2 35.6
10 Tu	23 09 40	19 10 15	24 55 30	1♈04 39	13D05.9	7 11.9	17 17.3	13 19.3	27 27.3	1 52.8	5 57.0	12 55.7	6 42.0	2 34.2
11 W	23 13 37	20 10 12	7♈10 50	13 14 16	13 05.3	8 21.2	18 30.8	13 50.2	27 32.8	1 54.2	6 00.5	12 53.8	6 41.0	2 32.7
12 Th	23 17 33	21 10 06	19 15 13	25 14 00	13 05.8	9 23.6	19 44.2	14 21.2	27 37.9	1 55.5	6 03.9	12 51.9	6 40.0	2 31.3
13 F	23 21 30	22 09 59	1♉10 59	7♉06 32	13 07.1	10 18.7	20 57.6	14 52.4	27 42.7	1 56.6	6 07.2	12 50.0	6 39.0	2 29.9
14 Sa	23 25 26	23 09 49	13 01 08	18 55 15	13 08.8	11 06.2	22 11.0	15 23.7	27 47.0	1 57.6	6 10.4	12 48.2	6 37.9	2 28.4
15 Su	23 29 23	24 09 37	24 49 24	0♊44 09	13 10.4	11 45.8	23 24.3	15 55.0	27 51.0	1 58.3	6 13.5	12 46.4	6 36.9	2 27.0
16 M	23 33 19	25 09 24	6♊40 03	12 37 42	13 11.6	12 17.2	24 37.5	16 26.5	27 54.6	1 58.9	6 16.5	12 44.7	6 35.8	2 25.7
17 Tu	23 37 16	26 09 07	18 37 42	24 40 39	13R12.0	12 40.2	25 50.7	16 58.1	27 57.8	1 59.2	6 19.5	12 43.0	6 34.6	2 24.3
18 W	23 41 12	27 08 49	0♋47 10	6♋57 49	13 11.8	12 55.0	27 03.8	17 29.9	28 00.7	1R59.4	6 22.3	12 41.3	6 33.5	2 22.9
19 Th	23 45 09	28 08 28	13 13 08	19 33 39	13 10.8	13R01.3	28 16.8	18 01.7	28 03.1	1 59.4	6 25.1	12 39.7	6 32.3	2 21.6
20 F	23 49 06	29 08 05	25 59 47	2♌31 54	13 09.2	12 59.5	29 29.8	18 33.6	28 05.1	1 59.2	6 27.8	12 38.1	6 31.1	2 20.2
21 Sa	23 53 02	0♈07 40	9♌10 16	15 55 03	13 07.5	12 49.7	0♉42.8	19 05.6	28 06.8	1 58.8	6 30.3	12 36.6	6 29.9	2 18.9
22 Su	23 56 59	1 07 13	22 46 16	29 43 50	13 05.8	12 32.4	1 55.6	19 37.7	28 08.0	1 58.2	6 32.8	12 35.1	6 28.6	2 17.6
23 M	0 00 55	2 06 43	6♍47 27	13♍56 45	13 04.5	12 07.9	3 08.4	20 09.9	28 08.9	1 57.4	6 35.2	12 33.6	6 27.4	2 16.3
24 Tu	0 04 52	3 06 11	21 11 10	28 30 00	13D03.7	11 37.1	4 21.2	20 42.2	28R09.3	1 56.5	6 37.5	12 32.2	6 26.1	2 15.0
25 W	0 08 48	4 05 37	5♎52 27	13♎17 36	13 03.5	11 00.5	5 33.9	21 14.5	28 09.4	1 55.4	6 39.7	12 30.9	6 24.8	2 13.7
26 Th	0 12 45	5 05 01	20 44 30	28 12 08	13 03.7	10 19.0	6 46.5	21 47.0	28 09.0	1 54.0	6 41.8	12 29.6	6 23.5	2 12.5
27 F	0 16 41	6 04 24	5♏39 32	13♏05 45	13 04.2	9 33.6	7 59.0	22 19.5	28 08.2	1 52.5	6 43.9	12 28.3	6 22.1	2 11.3
28 Sa	0 20 38	7 03 44	20 29 53	27 51 10	13 04.8	8 45.4	9 11.5	22 52.1	28 07.1	1 50.8	6 45.8	12 27.1	6 20.8	2 10.1
29 Su	0 24 35	8 03 03	5♐08 56	12♐22 37	13 05.3	7 55.2	10 23.9	23 24.8	28 05.5	1 49.0	6 47.6	12 25.9	6 19.4	2 08.9
30 M	0 28 31	9 02 20	19 31 49	26 36 13	13 05.6	7 04.2	11 36.3	23 57.6	28 03.5	1 46.9	6 49.4	12 24.8	6 18.0	2 07.7
31 Tu	0 32 28	10 01 35	3♑35 39	10♑30 02	13R05.6	6 13.5	12 48.5	24 30.4	28 01.1	1 44.7	6 51.0	12 23.8	6 16.6	2 06.6

April 1959

LONGITUDE

Day	Sid.Time	☉	0 hr ☽	Noon ☽	True ☊	☿	♀	♂	⚳	♃	♄	♅	♆	♇
1 W	0 36 24	11♈00 49	17♑19 23	24♑03 46	13♎05.6	5♈23.9	14♉00.8	25♊03.4	27♏58.3	1♐42.2	6♑52.5	12♌22.8	6♏15.2	2♍05.4
2 Th	0 40 21	12 00 01	0♒43 22	7♒18 21	13R05.5	4R36.5	15 12.9	25 36.4	27R55.1	1R39.6	6 54.0	12R21.8	6R13.7	2R04.3
3 F	0 44 17	12 59 10	13 48 57	20 15 25	13D05.4	3 51.9	16 25.0	26 09.5	27 51.5	1 36.8	6 55.3	12 20.9	6 12.2	2 03.2
4 Sa	0 48 14	13 58 18	26 38 00	2♓56 58	13 05.5	3 11.0	17 37.0	26 42.6	27 47.5	1 33.9	6 56.6	12 20.0	6 10.8	2 02.2
5 Su	0 52 10	14 57 25	9♓12 34	15 25 03	13 05.6	2 34.2	18 48.9	27 15.9	27 43.0	1 30.7	6 57.7	12 19.2	6 09.3	2 01.1
6 M	0 56 07	15 56 29	21 34 41	27 41 41	13 05.8	2 02.1	20 00.8	27 49.2	27 38.2	1 27.4	6 58.8	12 18.4	6 07.8	2 00.1
7 Tu	1 00 03	16 55 31	3♈46 17	9♈48 45	13R05.9	1 34.9	21 12.6	28 22.6	27 33.0	1 23.9	6 59.7	12 17.7	6 06.3	1 59.1
8 W	1 04 00	17 54 32	15 49 16	21 48 06	13 05.9	1 12.9	22 24.3	28 56.0	27 27.4	1 20.3	7 00.6	12 17.1	6 04.7	1 58.1
9 Th	1 07 57	18 53 30	27 45 29	3♉41 40	13 05.5	0 56.3	23 35.9	29 29.5	27 21.4	1 16.4	7 01.3	12 16.5	6 03.2	1 57.1
10 F	1 11 53	19 52 26	9♉36 56	15 31 32	13 04.9	0 45.1	24 47.5	0♋03.1	27 15.0	1 12.4	7 02.0	12 15.9	6 01.6	1 56.2
11 Sa	1 15 50	20 51 20	21 25 49	27 20 06	13 03.9	0D39.3	25 59.0	0 36.8	27 08.2	1 08.3	7 02.6	12 15.4	6 00.1	1 55.3
12 Su	1 19 46	21 50 12	3♊14 45	9♊10 08	13 02.7	0 38.9	27 10.4	1 10.5	27 01.1	1 04.0	7 03.0	12 15.0	5 58.5	1 54.4
13 M	1 23 43	22 49 02	15 06 42	21 04 53	13 01.4	0 43.7	28 21.7	1 44.3	26 53.6	0 59.5	7 03.4	12 14.6	5 56.9	1 53.5
14 Tu	1 27 39	23 47 50	27 05 09	3♋08 00	13 00.3	0 53.7	29 32.9	2 18.1	26 45.7	0 54.8	7 03.6	12 14.2	5 55.4	1 52.7
15 W	1 31 36	24 46 35	9♋13 56	15 23 29	12D59.6	1 08.6	0♊44.1	2 52.0	26 37.5	0 50.0	7 03.8	12 14.0	5 53.8	1 51.9
16 Th	1 35 32	25 45 19	21 37 10	27 55 31	12 59.5	1 28.2	1 55.1	3 25.9	26 29.0	0 45.1	7R03.9	12 13.7	5 52.2	1 51.1
17 F	1 39 29	26 44 00	4♌19 00	10♌48 06	12 59.9	1 52.5	3 06.1	3 59.9	26 20.1	0 40.0	7 03.8	12 13.6	5 50.6	1 50.3
18 Sa	1 43 26	27 42 38	17 23 13	24 04 42	13 00.8	2 21.2	4 16.9	4 34.0	26 10.8	0 34.8	7 03.7	12 13.4	5 49.0	1 49.6
19 Su	1 47 22	28 41 15	0♍52 49	7♍47 40	13 01.9	2 54.0	5 27.7	5 08.1	26 01.3	0 29.4	7 03.5	12D13.4	5 47.3	1 48.9
20 M	1 51 19	29 39 49	14 49 18	21 57 32	13 03.1	3 30.9	6 38.4	5 42.2	25 51.5	0 23.9	7 03.1	12 13.3	5 45.7	1 48.2
21 Tu	1 55 15	0♉38 21	29 12 05	6♎32 27	13R03.8	4 11.6	7 49.0	6 16.4	25 41.3	0 18.3	7 02.7	12 13.4	5 44.1	1 47.6
22 W	1 59 12	1 36 51	13♎57 57	21 27 46	13 03.7	4 56.0	8 59.4	6 50.7	25 30.9	0 12.5	7 02.2	12 13.5	5 42.5	1 46.9
23 Th	2 03 08	2 35 19	29 00 53	6♏36 11	13 02.7	5 43.9	10 09.8	7 25.0	25 20.2	0 06.6	7 01.6	12 13.6	5 40.8	1 46.3
24 F	2 07 05	3 33 45	14♏12 28	21 48 38	13 00.7	6 35.1	11 20.1	7 59.3	25 09.2	0 00.5	7 00.9	12 13.8	5 39.2	1 45.7
25 Sa	2 11 01	4 32 10	29 22 59	6♐54 49	12 58.1	7 29.5	12 30.2	8 33.7	24 58.0	29♏54.4	7 00.0	12 14.1	5 37.6	1 45.2
26 Su	2 14 58	5 30 33	14♐22 53	21 46 17	12 55.2	8 27.0	13 40.3	9 08.1	24 46.5	29 48.1	6 59.1	12 14.4	5 35.9	1 44.7
27 M	2 18 55	6 28 55	29 04 14	6♑16 10	12 52.5	9 27.5	14 50.2	9 42.6	24 34.8	29 41.8	6 58.1	12 14.8	5 34.3	1 44.2
28 Tu	2 22 51	7 27 14	13♑21 41	20 20 35	12 50.5	10 30.7	16 00.1	10 17.1	24 22.9	29 35.3	6 57.0	12 15.2	5 32.7	1 43.7
29 W	2 26 48	8 25 33	27 12 48	3♒58 27	12D49.6	11 36.7	17 09.8	10 51.7	24 10.7	29 28.7	6 55.9	12 15.6	5 31.0	1 43.3
30 Th	2 30 44	9 23 49	10♒37 44	17 10 57	12 49.7	12 45.3	18 19.5	11 26.3	23 58.4	29 22.0	6 54.6	12 16.2	5 29.4	1 42.9

Astro Data	Planet Ingress	Last Aspect	☽ Ingress	Last Aspect	☽ Ingress	☽ Phases & Eclipses	Astro Data
Dy Hr Mn	Dy Hr Mn	Dy Hr Mn	Dy Hr Mn	Dy Hr Mn	Dy Hr Mn	Dy Hr Mn	1 March 1959
☿0N 5 0:12	☿ ♈ 5 11:52	28 18:39 ☿ △	♐ 1 8:33	31 16:26 ♀ △	♒ 1 22:41	2 2:54 ☾ 10♐47	Julian Day # 21609
☽0N 10 3:09	♀ ♉ 20 21:55	3 5:25 ☿ □	♑ 3 12:05	3 23:36 ♂ △	♓ 4 6:23	9 10:51 ● 18♓07	SVP 5♓49'43"
♃R 18 22:09	⊙ ♈ 21 8:55	4 11:09 ⊙ ✶	♒ 5 17:16	6 12:15 ♂ □	♈ 6 16:33	17 15:10 ☽ 26♊17	GC 26♐16.1 ⚴ 26♎46.2R
☿R 19 18:35		6 17:00 ♅ ☍	♓ 8 0:25	9 3:05 ♂ ✶	♉ 9 4:32	24 20:02 ○ 3♎26	Eris 9♈01.3 ⚵ 24♎51.3R
⊙0N 21 8:55	♂ ♋ 10 9:46	9 10:51 ⊙ ☌	♈ 10 9:53	11 8:57 ♀ ☌	♊ 11 17:25	24 20:11 • P 0.264	⚷ 23♒52.5 ⚶ 28♋07.3R
♄✶♆ 21 9:10	♀ ♊ 14 21:08	11 23:43 ♀ ☌	♉ 12 21:37	13 15:47 ⊙ ✶	♋ 14 5:48	31 11:06 ☾ 9♑59	☽ Mean ☊ 14♎54.3
☽0S 24 8:45	⊙ ♉ 20 20:17	14 21:25 ⊙ ✶	♊ 15 10:31	16 7:33 ⊙ □	♌ 16 15:55		
⚳R 25 2:31	♃ ♏R 24 14:10	17 15:10 ⊙ □	♋ 17 22:28	18 18:56 ⊙ △	♍ 18 22:27	8 3:29 ● 17♈34	1 April 1959
☽0N 6 9:39		20 5:53 ♀ □	♌ 20 7:22	19 10:44 ♄ △	♎ 21 1:19	8 3:23:36 • A 07'25"	Julian Day # 21640
☿0S 11 18:47		21 17:49 ♂ ✶	♍ 22 12:28	21 21:12 ♅ ✶	♏ 23 1:34	16 7:33 ☽ 25♋34	SVP 5♓49'40"
☿D 12 1:52		23 22:43 ♂ □	♎ 24 14:27	25 0:54 ♃ ☌	♐ 25 0:59	23 5:13 ○ 2♏19	GC 26♐16.2 ⚴ 19♎55.0R
♄R 16 15:32		26 1:17 ♂ △	♏ 26 14:53	25 21:44 ♀ ☍	♑ 27 1:32	29 20:38 ☾ 8♒47	Eris 9♈21.9 ⚵ 19♎15.0R
♅D 20 6:57		27 11:00 ♅ □	♐ 28 15:31	29 4:04 ♃ ✶	♒ 29 4:55		⚷ 25♒50.8 ⚶ 28♋28.5
☽0S 20 19:35		30 7:19 ♂ ☍	♑ 30 17:49				☽ Mean ☊ 13♎15.7
☿0N 23 2:59							

LONGITUDE — May 1959

Day	Sid.Time	☉	0 hr ☽	Noon ☽	True ☊	☿	♀	♂	⚳	♃	♄	♅	♆	♇
1 F	2 34 41	10♉22 05	23♒38 31	0♓00 52	12♎50.8	13♈56.4	19♊29.0	12♋01.0	23♏45.8	29♏15.2	6♑53.2	12♌16.7	5♏27.8	1♍42.5
2 Sa	2 38 37	11 20 18	6♓18 27	12 31 46	12 52.4	15 10.0	20 38.4	12 35.7	23R 33.1	29R 08.4	6R 51.7	12 17.4	5R 26.1	1R 42.1
3 Su	2 42 34	12 18 31	18 41 18	24 47 33	12 54.0	16 25.9	21 47.7	13 10.4	23 20.3	29 01.4	6 50.2	12 18.1	5 24.5	1 41.8
4 M	2 46 30	13 16 41	0♈50 58	6♈51 59	12R 55.1	17 44.2	22 56.9	13 45.2	23 07.3	28 54.4	6 48.5	12 18.8	5 22.9	1 41.5
5 Tu	2 50 27	14 14 50	12 51 02	18 48 29	12 55.1	19 04.7	24 05.9	14 20.1	22 54.2	28 47.2	6 46.8	12 19.6	5 21.3	1 41.3
6 W	2 54 24	15 12 58	24 44 42	0♉40 01	12 53.6	20 27.4	25 14.9	14 54.9	22 41.0	28 40.0	6 44.9	12 20.4	5 19.6	1 41.0
7 Th	2 58 20	16 11 04	6♉34 42	12 29 04	12 50.5	21 52.3	26 23.7	15 29.9	22 27.7	28 32.8	6 43.0	12 21.3	5 18.0	1 40.8
8 F	3 02 17	17 09 08	18 23 22	24 17 50	12 45.8	23 19.4	27 32.4	16 04.8	22 14.3	28 25.5	6 41.0	12 22.3	5 16.4	1 40.6
9 Sa	3 06 13	18 07 11	0♊12 42	6♊08 14	12 39.9	24 48.6	28 40.9	16 39.8	22 00.9	28 18.1	6 38.9	12 23.3	5 14.9	1 40.5
10 Su	3 10 10	19 05 12	12 04 38	18 02 11	12 33.3	26 19.8	29 49.3	17 14.9	21 47.4	28 10.7	6 36.7	12 24.3	5 13.3	1 40.4
11 M	3 14 06	20 03 11	24 01 07	0♋01 44	12 26.6	27 53.2	0♋57.6	17 49.9	21 33.9	28 03.2	6 34.4	12 25.4	5 11.7	1 40.3
12 Tu	3 18 03	21 01 09	6♋04 20	12 09 15	12 20.6	29 28.6	2 05.8	18 25.1	21 20.4	27 55.7	6 32.1	12 26.6	5 10.1	1 40.2
13 W	3 21 59	21 59 05	18 16 50	24 27 28	12 15.9	1♉06.0	3 13.8	19 00.2	21 06.9	27 48.1	6 29.7	12 27.8	5 08.6	1D 40.2
14 Th	3 25 56	22 56 59	0♌41 34	6♌59 31	12 12.9	2 45.5	4 21.6	19 35.4	20 53.4	27 40.6	6 27.1	12 29.0	5 07.0	1 40.2
15 F	3 29 53	23 54 51	13 21 48	19 48 49	12D 11.5	4 27.1	5 29.3	20 10.6	20 40.0	27 33.0	6 24.5	12 30.4	5 05.5	1 40.2
16 Sa	3 33 49	24 52 42	26 21 01	2♍58 48	12 11.7	6 10.7	6 36.9	20 45.9	20 26.6	27 25.3	6 21.9	12 31.7	5 04.0	1 40.3
17 Su	3 37 46	25 50 31	9♍42 30	16 32 26	12 12.8	7 56.4	7 44.2	21 21.2	20 13.3	27 17.7	6 19.1	12 33.1	5 02.5	1 40.4
18 M	3 41 42	26 48 18	23 28 48	0♎31 41	12R 14.0	9 44.1	8 51.4	21 56.5	20 00.1	27 10.1	6 16.3	12 34.6	5 01.0	1 40.5
19 Tu	3 45 39	27 46 03	7♎41 02	14 56 38	12 14.4	11 33.9	9 58.5	22 31.9	19 47.0	27 02.4	6 13.4	12 36.1	4 59.5	1 40.7
20 W	3 49 35	28 43 47	22 18 06	29 44 50	12 13.3	13 25.8	11 05.4	23 07.2	19 34.0	26 54.8	6 10.4	12 37.6	4 58.0	1 40.8
21 Th	3 53 32	29 41 29	7♏16 01	14♏50 43	12 10.1	15 19.6	12 12.1	23 42.7	19 21.2	26 47.2	6 07.4	12 39.2	4 56.6	1 41.1
22 F	3 57 28	0♊39 10	22 27 45	0♐05 53	12 04.8	17 15.5	13 18.6	24 18.1	19 08.4	26 39.6	6 04.3	12 40.9	4 55.1	1 41.3
23 Sa	4 01 25	1 36 50	7♐43 45	15 20 00	11 58.1	19 13.4	14 24.9	24 53.6	18 55.9	26 32.0	6 01.1	12 42.6	4 53.7	1 41.6
24 Su	4 05 22	2 34 28	22 53 19	0♑22 30	11 50.5	21 13.2	15 31.0	25 29.1	18 43.5	26 24.4	5 57.8	12 44.3	4 52.3	1 41.9
25 M	4 09 18	3 32 06	7♑46 29	15 04 24	11 43.3	23 14.9	16 37.0	26 04.6	18 31.3	26 16.8	5 54.5	12 46.1	4 50.9	1 42.2
26 Tu	4 13 15	4 29 42	22 15 35	29 19 36	11 37.2	25 18.4	17 42.7	26 40.2	18 19.3	26 09.3	5 51.2	12 48.0	4 49.5	1 42.6
27 W	4 17 11	5 27 17	6♒16 14	13♒05 26	11 33.0	27 23.5	18 48.3	27 15.8	18 07.6	26 01.8	5 47.7	12 49.9	4 48.2	1 42.9
28 Th	4 21 08	6 24 52	19 47 22	26 22 18	11D 30.7	29 30.3	19 53.6	27 51.4	17 56.0	25 54.4	5 44.2	12 51.8	4 46.8	1 43.4
29 F	4 25 04	7 22 25	2♓50 40	9♓12 57	11 30.2	1♊38.4	20 58.8	28 27.1	17 44.7	25 47.0	5 40.6	12 53.8	4 45.5	1 43.8
30 Sa	4 29 01	8 19 58	15 29 42	21 41 33	11 30.8	3 47.8	22 03.7	29 02.8	17 33.6	25 39.7	5 37.0	12 55.8	4 44.2	1 44.3
31 Su	4 32 57	9 17 30	27 49 05	3♈52 58	11R 31.7	5 58.3	23 08.4	29 38.5	17 22.7	25 32.4	5 33.3	12 57.8	4 42.9	1 44.8

LONGITUDE — June 1959

Day	Sid.Time	☉	0 hr ☽	Noon ☽	True ☊	☿	♀	♂	⚳	♃	♄	♅	♆	♇
1 M	4 36 54	10♊15 01	9♈53 47	15♈52 08	11♎31.8	8♊09.5	24♋12.9	0♌14.3	17♏12.2	25♏25.2	5♑29.6	12♌59.9	4♏41.6	1♍45.3
2 Tu	4 40 51	11 12 31	21 48 36	27 43 43	11R 30.3	10 21.3	25 17.2	0 50.1	17R 01.9	25R 18.0	5R 25.8	13 02.1	4R 40.4	1 45.9
3 W	4 44 47	12 10 00	3♉37 57	9♉31 47	11 26.6	12 33.3	26 21.2	1 25.9	16 51.9	25 11.0	5 22.0	13 04.3	4 39.2	1 46.5
4 Th	4 48 44	13 07 29	15 25 35	21 19 43	11 20.4	14 45.4	27 25.0	2 01.7	16 42.2	25 04.0	5 18.1	13 06.5	4 37.9	1 47.1
5 F	4 52 40	14 04 56	27 14 31	3♊10 15	11 11.8	16 57.3	28 28.6	2 37.6	16 32.8	24 57.1	5 14.2	13 08.8	4 36.8	1 47.7
6 Sa	4 56 37	15 02 23	9♊07 09	15 05 26	11 01.1	19 08.6	29 31.8	3 13.5	16 23.7	24 50.3	5 10.2	13 11.1	4 35.6	1 48.4
7 Su	5 00 33	15 59 49	21 05 16	27 06 48	10 49.4	21 19.1	0♌34.9	3 49.5	16 15.0	24 43.5	5 06.2	13 13.5	4 34.5	1 49.1
8 M	5 04 30	16 57 14	3♋10 13	9♋15 37	10 37.5	23 28.6	1 37.6	4 25.5	16 06.5	24 36.9	5 02.1	13 15.9	4 33.4	1 49.8
9 Tu	5 08 26	17 54 39	15 23 12	21 33 06	10 26.4	25 36.9	2 40.1	5 01.5	15 58.5	24 30.4	4 58.0	13 18.3	4 32.3	1 50.6
10 W	5 12 23	18 52 02	27 45 29	4♌00 34	10 17.3	27 43.6	3 42.3	5 37.5	15 50.7	24 23.9	4 53.9	13 20.8	4 31.2	1 51.4
11 Th	5 16 20	19 49 24	10♌18 35	16 39 47	10 10.5	29 48.7	4 44.2	6 13.6	15 43.3	24 17.6	4 49.7	13 23.3	4 30.2	1 52.2
12 F	5 20 16	20 46 45	23 04 27	29 32 53	10 06.4	1♋52.1	5 45.8	6 49.7	15 36.3	24 11.4	4 45.5	13 25.9	4 29.1	1 53.0
13 Sa	5 24 13	21 44 05	6♍05 24	12♍42 21	10D 04.7	3 53.4	6 47.1	7 25.8	15 29.6	24 05.3	4 41.3	13 28.5	4 28.1	1 53.9
14 Su	5 28 09	22 41 24	19 24 02	26 10 45	10 04.4	5 52.8	7 48.0	8 01.9	15 23.3	23 59.4	4 37.0	13 31.1	4 27.2	1 54.8
15 M	5 32 06	23 38 42	3♎02 46	10♎00 16	10R 04.6	7 50.0	8 48.6	8 38.1	15 17.3	23 53.5	4 32.8	13 33.8	4 26.2	1 55.7
16 Tu	5 36 02	24 36 00	17 03 20	24 11 57	10 04.0	9 45.0	9 48.9	9 14.3	15 11.8	23 47.8	4 28.5	13 36.5	4 25.3	1 56.7
17 W	5 39 59	25 33 16	1♏25 56	8♏44 58	10 01.6	11 37.8	10 48.8	9 50.5	15 06.6	23 42.2	4 24.1	13 39.2	4 24.4	1 57.7
18 Th	5 43 55	26 30 32	16 08 30	23 35 51	9 56.7	13 28.3	11 48.3	10 26.8	15 01.7	23 36.8	4 19.8	13 42.0	4 23.5	1 58.7
19 F	5 47 52	27 27 47	1♐06 09	8♐38 19	9 49.2	15 16.5	12 47.4	11 03.1	14 57.3	23 31.5	4 15.4	13 44.8	4 22.7	1 59.7
20 Sa	5 51 49	28 25 01	16 11 13	23 43 35	9 39.6	17 02.4	13 46.2	11 39.4	14 53.2	23 26.3	4 11.1	13 47.7	4 21.9	2 00.7
21 Su	5 55 45	29 22 15	1♑14 10	8♑41 43	9 28.9	18 45.9	14 44.5	12 15.7	14 49.5	23 21.3	4 06.7	13 50.5	4 21.1	2 01.8
22 M	5 59 42	0♋19 29	16 05 07	23 23 20	9 18.3	20 27.0	15 42.4	12 52.0	14 46.2	23 16.5	4 02.3	13 53.4	4 20.4	2 02.9
23 Tu	6 03 38	1 16 42	0♒35 33	7♒41 09	9 09.1	22 05.8	16 39.9	13 28.4	14 43.2	23 11.7	3 57.9	13 56.4	4 19.6	2 04.1
24 W	6 07 35	2 13 55	14 39 43	21 31 42	9 02.0	23 42.3	17 36.9	14 04.8	14 40.6	23 07.2	3 53.5	13 59.4	4 18.9	2 05.2
25 Th	6 11 31	3 11 08	28 15 06	4♓52 04	8 57.5	25 16.3	18 33.5	14 41.3	14 38.4	23 02.7	3 49.0	14 02.4	4 18.3	2 06.4
26 F	6 15 28	4 08 21	11♓22 14	17 46 02	8 55.2	26 47.9	19 29.6	15 17.7	14 36.6	22 58.5	3 44.6	14 05.4	4 17.6	2 07.6
27 Sa	6 19 24	5 05 33	24 04 00	0♈16 42	8 54.5	28 17.2	20 25.2	15 54.2	14 35.2	22 54.4	3 40.2	14 08.5	4 17.0	2 08.8
28 Su	6 23 21	6 02 46	6♈24 46	12 28 54	8 54.5	29 43.9	21 20.3	16 30.7	14 34.1	22 50.4	3 35.8	14 11.5	4 16.4	2 10.1
29 M	6 27 18	6 59 59	18 29 45	24 27 59	8 53.9	1♌08.2	22 14.9	17 07.3	14 33.4	22 46.6	3 31.4	14 14.7	4 15.9	2 11.3
30 Tu	6 31 14	7 57 12	0♉24 16	6♉19 15	8 51.9	2 30.1	23 09.0	17 43.9	14D 33.1	22 43.0	3 27.0	14 17.8	4 15.4	2 12.6

Astro Data

	Dy Hr Mn
☽0N	3 15:34
♇D	13 21:51
☽0S	18 5:42
☽0N	30 22:28
☽0S	14 14:12
♄✶♆	17 10:02
☽0N	27 7:04
⚳D	30 20:26

Planet Ingress

		Dy Hr Mn
♀	♋	10 15:45
☿	♉	12 19:48
☉	♊	21 19:42
☿	♊	28 17:35
♂	♌	1 2:26
♀	♌	6 22:43
☿	♋	11 14:11
☉	♋	22 3:50
☿	♌	28 16:31

Last Aspect / ☽ Ingress (May)

Last Aspect Dy Hr Mn		☽ Ingress Dy Hr Mn
1 10:34	♃ □	♓ 1 11:58
3 20:18	♃ △	♈ 3 22:19
5 23:50	♀ ✶	♉ 6 10:39
8 20:17	♃ ☍	♊ 8 23:34
11 7:05	☿ ✶	♋ 11 11:57
13 18:23	♃ △	♌ 13 22:40
16 2:03	♃ □	♍ 16 6:38
18 6:21	♃ ✶	♎ 18 11:06
20 0:53	♂ □	♏ 20 12:24
22 6:38	♃ ☌	♐ 22 11:51
23 7:51	♅ △	♑ 24 11:24
26 7:16	♂ ☍	♒ 26 13:09
28 11:09	♃ □	♓ 28 18:42
31 3:10	♂ △	♈ 31 4:18

Last Aspect / ☽ Ingress (June)

Last Aspect Dy Hr Mn		☽ Ingress Dy Hr Mn
2 6:33	♀ □	♉ 2 16:37
5 1:34	♀ ✶	♊ 5 5:35
6 21:55	☿ ☌	♋ 7 17:44
9 17:40	♃ △	♌ 10 4:19
12 2:09	♃ □	♍ 12 12:50
14 8:10	♃ ✶	♎ 14 18:42
16 12:43	☉ △	♏ 16 21:38
18 12:01	♃ ☌	♐ 18 22:14
20 20:00	☉ ☍	♑ 20 22:01
22 11:49	♃ ✶	♒ 22 23:00
24 14:49	♃ □	♓ 25 3:09
27 7:37	☿ △	♈ 27 11:28
29 7:10	♀ △	♉ 29 23:11

☽ Phases & Eclipses

Dy Hr Mn		
7 20:11	●	16♉31
15 20:09	☽	24♌14
22 12:56	○	0♐41
29 8:14	☾	7♓13
6 11:53	●	15♊02
14 5:22	☽	22♍26
20 20:00	○	28♐44
27 22:12	☾	5♈30

Astro Data

1 May 1959
Julian Day # 21670
SVP 5♓49'37"
GC 26♐16.3 ⚴ 11♎20.1R
Eris 9♈41.8 ⚵ 12♎42.6R
⚷ 27♒09.8 ⚶ 4♌39.7
☽ Mean ☊ 11♎40.4

1 June 1959
Julian Day # 21701
SVP 5♓49'33"
GC 26♐16.3 ⚴ 8♎19.2
Eris 9♈57.3 ⚵ 9♎53.5R
⚷ 27♒39.5 ⚶ 14♌53.1
☽ Mean ☊ 10♎01.9

July 1959 — LONGITUDE

Day	Sid.Time	☉	0 hr ☽	Noon ☽	True ☊	☿	♀	♂	⚳	♃	♄	♅	♆	♇
1 W	6 35 11	8♋54 25	12♉13 30	18♉07 36	8♎47.6	3♌49.3	24♌02.5	18♌20.5	14♏33.1	22♏39.6	3♑22.6	14♌21.0	4♏14.9	2♍13.9
2 Th	6 39 07	9 51 38	24 02 04	29 57 20	8R 40.5	5 06.1	24 55.4	18 57.1	14 33.6	22R 36.3	3R 18.2	14 24.2	4R 14.4	2 15.3
3 F	6 43 04	10 48 51	5♊53 50	11♊51 55	8 30.8	6 20.1	25 47.7	19 33.8	14 34.4	22 33.2	3 13.8	14 27.4	4 14.0	2 16.6
4 Sa	6 47 00	11 46 05	17 51 52	23 53 57	8 18.9	7 31.5	26 39.5	20 10.5	14 35.5	22 30.2	3 09.5	14 30.7	4 13.6	2 18.0
5 Su	6 50 57	12 43 18	29 58 22	6♋05 14	8 05.8	8 40.1	27 30.5	20 47.2	14 37.1	22 27.5	3 05.1	14 34.0	4 13.2	2 19.4
6 M	6 54 53	13 40 32	12♋14 40	18 26 45	7 52.4	9 45.9	28 21.0	21 24.0	14 39.0	22 24.9	3 00.8	14 37.3	4 12.8	2 20.9
7 Tu	6 58 50	14 37 45	24 41 30	0♌58 58	7 40.0	10 48.8	29 10.7	22 00.8	14 41.2	22 22.5	2 56.5	14 40.6	4 12.5	2 22.3
8 W	7 02 47	15 34 58	7♌19 10	13 42 07	7 29.5	11 48.7	29 59.7	22 37.6	14 43.9	22 20.2	2 52.3	14 43.9	4 12.3	2 23.8
9 Th	7 06 43	16 32 12	20 07 50	26 36 24	7 21.8	12 45.5	0♍48.0	23 14.4	14 46.8	22 18.2	2 48.0	14 47.3	4 12.0	2 25.3
10 F	7 10 40	17 29 25	3♍07 52	9♍42 21	7 16.9	13 39.0	1 35.5	23 51.3	14 50.2	22 16.3	2 43.8	14 50.7	4 11.8	2 26.8
11 Sa	7 14 36	18 26 38	16 19 57	23 00 50	7 14.5	14 29.2	2 22.2	24 28.2	14 53.9	22 14.6	2 39.6	14 54.1	4 11.6	2 28.3
12 Su	7 18 33	19 23 51	29 45 09	6♎33 05	7 14.0	15 16.0	3 08.1	25 05.1	14 57.9	22 13.1	2 35.5	14 57.5	4 11.5	2 29.8
13 M	7 22 29	20 21 05	13♎24 46	20 20 20	7 14.1	15 59.1	3 53.1	25 42.1	15 02.3	22 11.7	2 31.4	15 01.0	4 11.3	2 31.4
14 Tu	7 26 26	21 18 18	27 19 52	4♏23 22	7 13.6	16 38.5	4 37.2	26 19.0	15 07.0	22 10.6	2 27.3	15 04.5	4 11.2	2 33.0
15 W	7 30 22	22 15 31	11♏30 45	18 41 49	7 11.4	17 14.1	5 20.4	26 56.0	15 12.0	22 09.6	2 23.3	15 08.0	4 11.2	2 34.6
16 Th	7 34 19	23 12 44	25 56 17	3♐13 39	7 06.8	17 45.6	6 02.6	27 33.1	15 17.4	22 08.8	2 19.3	15 11.5	4D 11.2	2 36.2
17 F	7 38 16	24 09 57	10♐33 21	17 54 38	6 59.8	18 12.9	6 43.8	28 10.1	15 23.1	22 08.2	2 15.3	15 15.0	4 11.2	2 37.9
18 Sa	7 42 12	25 07 11	25 16 41	2♑38 33	6 50.7	18 35.9	7 23.9	28 47.2	15 29.1	22 07.8	2 11.5	15 18.5	4 11.2	2 39.5
19 Su	7 46 09	26 04 25	9♑59 16	17 17 50	6 40.5	18 54.4	8 02.9	29 24.3	15 35.5	22D 07.5	2 07.6	15 22.1	4 11.3	2 41.2
20 M	7 50 05	27 01 39	24 33 16	1♒44 42	6 30.3	19 08.3	8 40.8	0♍01.5	15 42.1	22 07.5	2 03.8	15 25.6	4 11.4	2 42.9
21 Tu	7 54 02	27 58 54	8♒51 22	15 52 36	6 21.2	19 17.5	9 17.5	0 38.6	15 49.1	22 07.6	2 00.1	15 29.2	4 11.5	2 44.6
22 W	7 57 58	28 56 09	22 47 55	29 37 02	6 14.2	19R 21.8	9 53.0	1 15.8	15 56.4	22 07.9	1 56.4	15 32.8	4 11.7	2 46.3
23 Th	8 01 55	29 53 25	6♓19 46	12♓56 07	6 09.7	19 21.2	10 27.2	1 53.1	16 03.9	22 08.4	1 52.7	15 36.4	4 11.9	2 48.0
24 F	8 05 51	0♌50 42	19 26 16	25 50 28	6D 07.4	19 15.6	11 00.1	2 30.3	16 11.8	22 09.1	1 49.1	15 40.1	4 12.1	2 49.8
25 Sa	8 09 48	1 47 59	2♈09 08	8♈22 42	6 07.0	19 05.0	11 31.7	3 07.6	16 20.0	22 09.9	1 45.6	15 43.7	4 12.4	2 51.5
26 Su	8 13 45	2 45 18	14 31 45	20 36 51	6 07.5	18 49.5	12 01.8	3 44.9	16 28.4	22 10.9	1 42.1	15 47.3	4 12.7	2 53.3
27 M	8 17 41	3 42 37	26 38 39	2♉37 48	6R 08.0	18 29.1	12 30.5	4 22.2	16 37.2	22 12.1	1 38.7	15 51.0	4 13.0	2 55.1
28 Tu	8 21 38	4 39 58	8♉34 58	14 30 49	6 07.4	18 04.1	12 57.7	4 59.6	16 46.2	22 13.5	1 35.4	15 54.7	4 13.4	2 56.9
29 W	8 25 34	5 37 19	20 25 58	26 21 04	6 05.1	17 34.6	13 23.3	5 37.0	16 55.5	22 15.1	1 32.1	15 58.3	4 13.8	2 58.7
30 Th	8 29 31	6 34 42	2♊16 43	8♊13 27	6 00.7	17 01.1	13 47.3	6 14.5	17 05.1	22 16.8	1 28.9	16 02.0	4 14.2	3 00.6
31 F	8 33 27	7 32 06	14 11 47	20 12 12	5 54.0	16 23.8	14 09.6	6 52.0	17 15.0	22 18.7	1 25.7	16 05.7	4 14.7	3 02.4

August 1959 — LONGITUDE

Day	Sid.Time	☉	0 hr ☽	Noon ☽	True ☊	☿	♀	♂	⚳	♃	♄	♅	♆	♇
1 Sa	8 37 24	8♌29 30	26♊15 04	2♋20 45	5♎45.4	15♌43.4	14♍30.1	7♍29.5	17♏25.1	22♏20.8	1♑22.6	16♌09.4	4♏15.1	3♍04.3
2 Su	8 41 20	9 26 56	8♋29 32	14 41 37	5R 35.7	15R 00.5	14 48.9	8 07.0	17 35.5	22 23.1	1R 19.6	16 13.1	4 15.7	3 06.1
3 M	8 45 17	10 24 22	20 57 09	27 16 13	5 25.7	14 15.6	15 05.8	8 44.6	17 46.1	22 25.5	1 16.7	16 16.8	4 16.2	3 08.0
4 Tu	8 49 14	11 21 50	3♌38 51	10♌05 00	5 16.4	13 29.6	15 20.8	9 22.2	17 57.0	22 28.2	1 13.8	16 20.5	4 16.8	3 09.9
5 W	8 53 10	12 19 18	16 34 37	23 07 34	5 08.7	12 43.3	15 33.8	9 59.8	18 08.2	22 31.0	1 11.1	16 24.2	4 17.4	3 11.8
6 Th	8 57 07	13 16 48	29 43 44	6♍22 57	5 03.1	11 57.5	15 44.7	10 37.5	18 19.6	22 33.9	1 08.3	16 28.0	4 18.1	3 13.7
7 F	9 01 03	14 14 18	13♍05 04	19 49 56	5 00.0	11 13.0	15 53.6	11 15.2	18 31.3	22 37.1	1 05.7	16 31.7	4 18.8	3 15.6
8 Sa	9 05 00	15 11 49	26 37 25	3♎27 23	4D 58.9	10 30.9	16 00.3	11 52.9	18 43.2	22 40.4	1 03.2	16 35.4	4 19.5	3 17.6
9 Su	9 08 56	16 09 21	10♎19 45	17 14 24	4 59.4	9 51.8	16 04.8	12 30.7	18 55.4	22 43.9	1 00.7	16 39.1	4 20.2	3 19.5
10 M	9 12 53	17 06 54	24 11 15	1♏10 15	5 00.4	9 16.5	16R 07.0	13 08.5	19 07.8	22 47.6	0 58.3	16 42.9	4 21.0	3 21.5
11 Tu	9 16 49	18 04 28	8♏11 18	15 14 18	5R 01.2	8 45.9	16 06.9	13 46.3	19 20.4	22 51.4	0 56.0	16 46.6	4 21.8	3 23.4
12 W	9 20 46	19 02 02	22 19 06	29 25 31	5 00.7	8 20.6	16 04.5	14 24.1	19 33.2	22 55.4	0 53.8	16 50.3	4 22.6	3 25.4
13 Th	9 24 43	19 59 37	6♐33 19	13♐42 11	4 58.6	8 01.1	15 59.7	15 02.0	19 46.3	22 59.5	0 51.6	16 54.0	4 23.5	3 27.3
14 F	9 28 39	20 57 14	20 51 45	28 01 33	4 54.6	7 47.9	15 52.5	15 39.9	19 59.6	23 03.9	0 49.6	16 57.8	4 24.4	3 29.3
15 Sa	9 32 36	21 54 51	5♑11 05	12♑19 47	4 49.0	7D 41.4	15 43.0	16 17.9	20 13.1	23 08.4	0 47.6	17 01.5	4 25.3	3 31.3
16 Su	9 36 32	22 52 30	19 27 04	26 32 18	4 42.6	7 42.0	15 31.0	16 55.9	20 26.8	23 13.0	0 45.7	17 05.2	4 26.3	3 33.3
17 M	9 40 29	23 50 09	3♒34 53	10♒34 13	4 36.2	7 49.8	15 16.6	17 33.9	20 40.7	23 17.8	0 44.0	17 08.9	4 27.2	3 35.3
18 Tu	9 44 25	24 47 50	17 29 48	24 21 09	4 30.5	8 05.1	14 59.9	18 11.9	20 54.9	23 22.8	0 42.3	17 12.6	4 28.3	3 37.3
19 W	9 48 22	25 45 32	1♓07 53	7♓49 45	4 26.2	8 27.8	14 40.9	18 50.0	21 09.2	23 27.9	0 40.6	17 16.3	4 29.3	3 39.3
20 Th	9 52 18	26 43 15	14 26 35	20 58 17	4 23.6	8 58.0	14 19.6	19 28.1	21 23.7	23 33.2	0 39.1	17 20.0	4 30.4	3 41.3
21 F	9 56 15	27 41 00	27 24 56	3♈46 39	4D 22.8	9 35.6	13 56.1	20 06.2	21 38.5	23 38.6	0 37.7	17 23.7	4 31.5	3 43.3
22 Sa	10 00 12	28 38 46	10♈03 40	16 16 19	4 23.3	10 20.6	13 30.6	20 44.4	21 53.4	23 44.2	0 36.3	17 27.4	4 32.6	3 45.3
23 Su	10 04 08	29 36 34	22 25 00	28 30 09	4 24.8	11 12.6	13 03.2	21 22.6	22 08.5	23 49.9	0 35.1	17 31.0	4 33.8	3 47.3
24 M	10 08 05	0♍34 24	4♉32 17	10♉31 57	4 26.5	12 11.6	12 33.9	22 00.9	22 23.8	23 55.8	0 33.9	17 34.7	4 34.9	3 49.3
25 Tu	10 12 01	1 32 15	16 29 43	22 26 12	4R 27.8	13 17.2	12 03.0	22 39.1	22 39.3	24 01.8	0 32.9	17 38.3	4 36.2	3 51.3
26 W	10 15 58	2 30 09	28 22 01	4♊17 46	4 28.2	14 29.2	11 30.6	23 17.4	22 54.9	24 08.0	0 31.9	17 42.0	4 37.4	3 53.3
27 Th	10 19 54	3 28 04	10♊14 05	16 11 34	4 27.3	15 47.1	10 56.8	23 55.8	23 10.8	24 14.3	0 31.0	17 45.6	4 38.7	3 55.3
28 F	10 23 51	4 26 01	22 10 48	28 12 19	4 25.2	17 10.7	10 22.0	24 34.2	23 26.8	24 20.8	0 30.3	17 49.2	4 40.0	3 57.4
29 Sa	10 27 47	5 23 59	4♋16 39	10♋24 15	4 21.8	18 39.3	9 46.2	25 12.6	23 43.0	24 27.4	0 29.6	17 52.8	4 41.3	3 59.4
30 Su	10 31 44	6 22 00	16 35 33	22 50 52	4 17.7	20 12.7	9 09.8	25 51.1	23 59.3	24 34.1	0 29.0	17 56.4	4 42.6	4 01.4
31 M	10 35 41	7 20 02	29 10 30	5♌34 39	4 13.3	21 50.3	8 32.9	26 29.6	24 15.9	24 41.0	0 28.5	18 00.0	4 44.0	4 03.4

Astro Data

	Dy Hr Mn
☽ 0S	11 21:10
♄△♇	13 11:49
♆ D	16 16:51
♃ D	20 8:00
☿ R	22 21:03
☽ 0N	24 16:54
♄□♅	3 11:36
☽ 0S	8 3:39
♀ R	10 23:16
♀ 0S	14 15:47
☿ D	15 22:06
☽ 0N	21 2:41
♀ 0N	28 18:02

Planet Ingress

		Dy Hr Mn
♀	♍	8 12:08
♂	♍	20 11:03
☉	♌	23 14:45
☉	♍	23 21:44

Last Aspect / ☽ Ingress (July)

Last Aspect Dy Hr Mn			☽ Ingress	Dy Hr Mn
2 0:59	♀	□	♊	2 12:05
4 17:52	♀	✶	♋	5 0:03
6 19:37	♃	△	♌	7 10:08
9 5:28	♂	☌	♍	9 18:15
11 10:37	♃	✶	♎	12 0:26
13 21:38	♂	✶	♏	14 4:33
16 2:15	♂	□	♐	16 6:42
18 5:26	♂	△	♑	18 7:42
20 3:33	☉	☍	♒	20 9:05
21 22:50	♃	□	♓	22 12:41
24 5:03	♃	△	♈	24 19:53
26 8:33	☿	△	♉	27 6:43
29 3:40	♃	☍	♊	29 19:23

Last Aspect / ☽ Ingress (August)

Last Aspect Dy Hr Mn			☽ Ingress	Dy Hr Mn
31 4:47	☿	✶	♋	1 7:24
3 2:47	♃	△	♌	3 17:09
5 10:53	♃	□	♍	6 0:29
7 16:57	♃	✶	♎	8 5:56
9 10:59	♅	✶	♏	10 10:00
12 0:58	♃	☌	♐	12 12:58
13 23:18	☉	△	♑	14 15:18
16 6:20	♃	✶	♒	16 17:53
18 12:51	☉	☍	♓	18 21:59
20 16:49	♃	△	♈	21 4:51
23 14:23	☉	△	♉	23 14:58
25 15:15	♃	☍	♊	26 3:18
28 4:22	♂	□	♋	28 15:33
30 18:01	♂	✶	♌	31 1:33

☽ Phases & Eclipses

Dy Hr Mn		
6 2:00	●	13♋17
13 12:01	☽	20♎21
20 3:33	○	26♑42
27 14:22	☾	3♉48
4 14:34	●	11♌28
11 17:10	☽	18♏17
18 12:51	○	24♒50
26 8:03	☾	2♊21

Astro Data

1 July 1959
Julian Day # 21731
SVP 5♓49'28"
GC 26♐16.4 ⚳ 11♎55.9
Eris 10♈04.0 ⚵ 12♎00.8
⚷ 27♒13.2R ⚶ 27♌01.7
☽ Mean ☊ 8♎26.6

1 August 1959
Julian Day # 21762
SVP 5♓49'24"
GC 26♐16.5 ⚳ 20♎05.1
Eris 10♈00.6R ⚵ 17♎54.0
⚷ 25♒59.8R ⚶ 11♍02.4
☽ Mean ☊ 6♎48.1

LONGITUDE — September 1959

Day	Sid.Time	☉	0 hr ☽	Noon ☽	True ☊	☿	♀	♂	⚳	♃	♄	♅	♆	♇
1 Tu	10 39 37	8♍18 06	12♌03 25	18♌36 52	4♎09.2	23♌31.6	7♍55.8	27♍08.1	24♏32.6	24♏48.1	0♑28.1	18♌03.6	4♏45.4	4♍05.4
2 W	10 43 34	9 16 12	25 14 55	1♍57 27	4R 05.9	25 16.2	7R 18.7	27 46.7	24 49.4	24 55.2	0R 27.8	18 07.1	4 46.8	4 07.4
3 Th	10 47 30	10 14 19	8♍44 14	15 35 01	4 03.7	27 03.5	6 41.9	28 25.3	25 06.5	25 02.5	0 27.6	18 10.6	4 48.3	4 09.5
4 F	10 51 27	11 12 28	22 29 27	29 27 08	4D 02.7	28 53.0	6 05.6	29 03.9	25 23.6	25 10.0	0D 27.5	18 14.1	4 49.8	4 11.5
5 Sa	10 55 23	12 10 39	6♎27 40	13♎30 35	4 02.8	0♍44.5	5 29.9	29 42.6	25 41.0	25 17.6	0 27.5	18 17.6	4 51.3	4 13.5
6 Su	10 59 20	13 08 51	20 35 28	27 41 50	4 03.8	2 37.3	4 55.3	0♎21.3	25 58.5	25 25.3	0 27.6	18 21.1	4 52.8	4 15.5
7 M	11 03 16	14 07 05	4♏49 17	11♏57 23	4 05.1	4 31.2	4 21.7	1 00.1	26 16.1	25 33.1	0 27.8	18 24.6	4 54.4	4 17.5
8 Tu	11 07 13	15 05 21	19 05 45	26 14 01	4 06.3	6 25.8	3 49.5	1 38.9	26 33.9	25 41.1	0 28.1	18 28.0	4 55.9	4 19.5
9 W	11 11 09	16 03 38	3♐21 52	10♐28 58	4R 07.0	8 20.9	3 18.8	2 17.7	26 51.8	25 49.2	0 28.5	18 31.4	4 57.5	4 21.4
10 Th	11 15 06	17 01 56	17 35 02	24 39 48	4 07.0	10 16.0	2 49.9	2 56.6	27 09.9	25 57.4	0 29.0	18 34.8	4 59.2	4 23.4
11 F	11 19 03	18 00 16	1♑43 01	8♑44 24	4 06.1	12 11.1	2 22.7	3 35.5	27 28.1	26 05.7	0 29.6	18 38.2	5 00.8	4 25.4
12 Sa	11 22 59	18 58 37	15 43 44	22 40 46	4 04.7	14 05.9	1 57.6	4 14.4	27 46.5	26 14.2	0 30.2	18 41.6	5 02.5	4 27.4
13 Su	11 26 56	19 57 00	29 35 17	6♒27 01	4 02.9	16 00.3	1 34.5	4 53.4	28 05.0	26 22.8	0 31.0	18 44.9	5 04.2	4 29.3
14 M	11 30 52	20 55 25	13♒15 47	20 01 21	4 01.0	17 54.1	1 13.6	5 32.4	28 23.6	26 31.5	0 31.9	18 48.2	5 05.9	4 31.3
15 Tu	11 34 49	21 53 51	26 43 34	3♓22 15	3 59.5	19 47.2	0 55.0	6 11.4	28 42.3	26 40.3	0 32.9	18 51.5	5 07.6	4 33.3
16 W	11 38 45	22 52 19	9♓57 17	16 28 34	3 58.5	21 39.5	0 38.7	6 50.5	29 01.2	26 49.2	0 33.9	18 54.7	5 09.4	4 35.2
17 Th	11 42 42	23 50 49	22 56 03	29 19 43	3D 58.0	23 31.0	0 24.9	7 29.6	29 20.2	26 58.2	0 35.1	18 58.0	5 11.1	4 37.1
18 F	11 46 38	24 49 21	5♈39 37	11♈55 51	3 58.1	25 21.6	0 13.4	8 08.8	29 39.3	27 07.4	0 36.4	19 01.2	5 12.9	4 39.0
19 Sa	11 50 35	25 47 55	18 08 33	24 17 55	3 58.5	27 11.3	0 04.4	8 48.0	29 58.5	27 16.7	0 37.7	19 04.3	5 14.7	4 41.0
20 Su	11 54 32	26 46 31	0♉24 14	6♉27 45	3 59.2	29 00.0	29♌57.8	9 27.2	0♐17.9	27 26.0	0 39.2	19 07.5	5 16.6	4 42.9
21 M	11 58 28	27 45 09	12 28 52	18 27 57	3 59.9	0♎47.8	29 53.7	10 06.5	0 37.3	27 35.5	0 40.7	19 10.6	5 18.4	4 44.8
22 Tu	12 02 25	28 43 49	24 25 26	0♊21 48	4 00.6	2 34.6	29D 52.0	10 45.8	0 56.9	27 45.1	0 42.4	19 13.7	5 20.3	4 46.6
23 W	12 06 21	29 42 31	6♊17 34	12 13 14	4 01.0	4 20.4	29 52.6	11 25.2	1 16.6	27 54.8	0 44.1	19 16.7	5 22.2	4 48.5
24 Th	12 10 18	0♎41 16	18 09 24	24 06 36	4R 01.2	6 05.3	29 55.7	12 04.6	1 36.4	28 04.6	0 46.0	19 19.8	5 24.1	4 50.4
25 F	12 14 14	1 40 03	0♋05 26	6♋06 29	4 01.2	7 49.1	0♍01.0	12 44.0	1 56.4	28 14.5	0 47.9	19 22.8	5 26.0	4 52.2
26 Sa	12 18 11	2 38 53	12 10 19	18 17 30	4 01.1	9 32.1	0 08.6	13 23.5	2 16.4	28 24.5	0 49.9	19 25.7	5 28.0	4 54.1
27 Su	12 22 07	3 37 44	24 28 33	0♌43 58	4D 01.1	11 14.1	0 18.4	14 03.0	2 36.5	28 34.6	0 52.1	19 28.7	5 29.9	4 55.9
28 M	12 26 04	4 36 38	7♌04 13	13 29 39	4 01.1	12 55.1	0 30.3	14 42.6	2 56.8	28 44.8	0 54.3	19 31.6	5 31.9	4 57.7
29 Tu	12 30 01	5 35 34	20 00 36	26 37 15	4 01.2	14 35.3	0 44.4	15 22.2	3 17.1	28 55.1	0 56.6	19 34.5	5 33.9	4 59.5
30 W	12 33 57	6 34 32	3♍19 45	10♍08 05	4 01.4	16 14.5	1 00.5	16 01.8	3 37.6	29 05.5	0 59.0	19 37.3	5 35.9	5 01.3

LONGITUDE — October 1959

Day	Sid.Time	☉	0 hr ☽	Noon ☽	True ☊	☿	♀	♂	⚳	♃	♄	♅	♆	♇
1 Th	12 37 54	7♎33 32	17♍02 07	24♍01 37	4♎01.6	17♎52.9	1♍18.5	16♎41.5	3♐58.1	29♏16.0	1♑01.5	19♌40.1	5♏37.9	5♍03.1
2 F	12 41 50	8 32 34	1♎06 12	8♎15 21	4R 01.6	19 30.5	1 38.5	17 21.2	4 18.8	29 26.5	1 04.1	19 42.8	5 40.0	5 04.8
3 Sa	12 45 47	9 31 39	15 28 29	22 44 52	4 01.4	21 07.2	2 00.3	18 01.0	4 39.5	29 37.2	1 06.7	19 45.6	5 42.0	5 06.6
4 Su	12 49 43	10 30 45	0♏03 43	7♏24 12	4 00.9	22 43.0	2 23.9	18 40.8	5 00.4	29 47.9	1 09.5	19 48.3	5 44.1	5 08.3
5 M	12 53 40	11 29 54	14 45 29	22 06 41	4 00.1	24 18.1	2 49.2	19 20.7	5 21.3	29 58.8	1 12.4	19 50.9	5 46.1	5 10.0
6 Tu	12 57 36	12 29 04	29 27 01	6♐45 44	3 59.2	25 52.3	3 16.2	20 00.6	5 42.3	0♐09.7	1 15.3	19 53.5	5 48.2	5 11.7
7 W	13 01 33	13 28 16	14♐02 08	21 15 41	3 58.3	27 25.8	3 44.8	20 40.5	6 03.4	0 20.7	1 18.3	19 56.1	5 50.3	5 13.3
8 Th	13 05 29	14 27 30	28 25 53	5♑32 24	3D 57.8	28 58.5	4 15.0	21 20.5	6 24.7	0 31.8	1 21.5	19 58.6	5 52.4	5 15.0
9 F	13 09 26	15 26 46	12♑34 56	19 33 21	3 57.7	0♏30.4	4 46.6	22 00.5	6 45.9	0 43.0	1 24.7	20 01.1	5 54.6	5 16.6
10 Sa	13 13 23	16 26 03	26 27 33	3♒17 32	3 58.2	2 01.6	5 19.7	22 40.6	7 07.3	0 54.3	1 28.0	20 03.6	5 56.7	5 18.3
11 Su	13 17 19	17 25 22	10♒03 21	16 45 05	3 59.1	3 32.0	5 54.2	23 20.7	7 28.8	1 05.6	1 31.3	20 06.0	5 58.8	5 19.9
12 M	13 21 16	18 24 43	23 22 51	29 56 49	4 00.3	5 01.7	6 30.0	24 00.8	7 50.3	1 17.0	1 34.8	20 08.4	6 01.0	5 21.4
13 Tu	13 25 12	19 24 05	6♓27 07	12♓53 57	4 01.5	6 30.6	7 07.1	24 41.0	8 11.9	1 28.5	1 38.4	20 10.7	6 03.2	5 23.0
14 W	13 29 09	20 23 30	19 17 26	25 37 48	4R 02.3	7 58.7	7 45.5	25 21.2	8 33.6	1 40.1	1 42.0	20 13.0	6 05.3	5 24.6
15 Th	13 33 05	21 22 56	1♈55 05	8♈09 32	4 02.4	9 26.1	8 25.1	26 01.5	8 55.4	1 51.7	1 45.7	20 15.2	6 07.5	5 26.1
16 F	13 37 02	22 22 24	14 21 17	20 30 29	4 01.6	10 52.7	9 05.9	26 41.8	9 17.2	2 03.4	1 49.5	20 17.4	6 09.7	5 27.6
17 Sa	13 40 58	23 21 55	26 37 17	2♉41 51	3 59.8	12 18.5	9 47.8	27 22.1	9 39.1	2 15.1	1 53.4	20 19.6	6 11.9	5 29.1
18 Su	13 44 55	24 21 27	8♉44 22	14 45 03	3 57.1	13 43.5	10 30.8	28 02.5	10 01.1	2 27.0	1 57.3	20 21.7	6 14.1	5 30.5
19 M	13 48 52	25 21 02	20 44 07	26 41 48	3 53.7	15 07.7	11 14.8	28 42.9	10 23.1	2 38.9	2 01.3	20 23.8	6 16.3	5 32.0
20 Tu	13 52 48	26 20 39	2♊38 25	8♊34 16	3 49.9	16 31.0	11 59.9	29 23.4	10 45.3	2 50.9	2 05.5	20 25.8	6 18.5	5 33.4
21 W	13 56 45	27 20 18	14 29 43	20 25 09	3 46.2	17 53.3	12 45.9	0♏03.9	11 07.5	3 02.9	2 09.6	20 27.8	6 20.7	5 34.8
22 Th	14 00 41	28 19 59	26 21 00	2♋17 43	3 43.0	19 14.7	13 32.9	0 44.5	11 29.7	3 15.0	2 13.9	20 29.7	6 23.0	5 36.1
23 F	14 04 38	29 19 42	8♋15 47	14 15 45	3 40.9	20 35.1	14 20.7	1 25.1	11 52.0	3 27.2	2 18.2	20 31.6	6 25.2	5 37.5
24 Sa	14 08 34	0♏19 28	20 18 09	26 23 33	3D 39.8	21 54.4	15 09.5	2 05.8	12 14.4	3 39.4	2 22.7	20 33.4	6 27.4	5 38.8
25 Su	14 12 31	1 19 16	2♌32 32	8♌45 39	3 40.0	23 12.5	15 59.0	2 46.5	12 36.9	3 51.7	2 27.2	20 35.2	6 29.7	5 40.1
26 M	14 16 27	2 19 06	15 03 29	21 26 33	3 41.1	24 29.4	16 49.4	3 27.2	12 59.4	4 04.0	2 31.7	20 36.9	6 31.9	5 41.4
27 Tu	14 20 24	3 18 59	27 55 21	4♍30 19	3 42.7	25 44.8	17 40.6	4 08.0	13 22.0	4 16.4	2 36.4	20 38.6	6 34.1	5 42.7
28 W	14 24 21	4 18 53	11♍11 47	18 00 01	3 44.2	26 58.9	18 32.5	4 48.9	13 44.6	4 28.8	2 41.1	20 40.2	6 36.4	5 43.9
29 Th	14 28 17	5 18 50	24 55 06	1♎57 00	3R 45.0	28 11.2	19 25.1	5 29.8	14 07.3	4 41.3	2 45.8	20 41.8	6 38.6	5 45.1
30 F	14 32 14	6 18 49	9♎05 31	16 20 14	3 44.4	29 21.8	20 18.4	6 10.7	14 30.1	4 53.9	2 50.7	20 43.4	6 40.9	5 46.3
31 Sa	14 36 10	7 18 49	23 40 36	1♏05 50	3 42.2	0♐30.4	21 12.4	6 51.7	14 52.9	5 06.5	2 55.6	20 44.8	6 43.1	5 47.4

Astro Data (Dy Hr Mn)

☽0S 4 11:04
♄ D 5 1:01
♂0S 8 11:59
☽0N 17 11:15
☿0S 22 14:00
♀ D 22 17:15
☉0S 23 19:08

☽0S 1 20:17
♃⊻♄ 14 17:51
☽0N 14 18:15
☽0S 29 6:59

Planet Ingress (Dy Hr Mn)

☿ ♍ 5 2:28
♂ ♎ 5 22:46
⚳ ♐ 19 13:51
♀ ♌R 20 3:01
☿ ♎ 21 1:20
☉ ♎ 23 19:08
♀ ♍ 25 8:15

♃ ♐ 5 14:40
☿ ♏ 9 4:02
♂ ♏ 21 9:40
☉ ♏ 24 4:11
☿ ♐ 31 1:16

Last Aspect / ☽ Ingress (September)

Last Aspect Dy Hr Mn			☽ Ingress	Dy Hr Mn
1 23:18	♃	□	♍	2 8:31
4 11:18	♂	☌	♎	4 12:56
5 20:09	♅	⚹	♏	6 15:53
8 11:04	♃	☌	♐	8 18:20
10 1:39	♅	△	♑	10 21:04
12 18:14	♃	⚹	♒	13 0:43
14 23:46	♃	□	♓	15 5:54
17 7:31	♃	△	♈	17 13:16
19 1:46	♅	△	♉	19 23:12
22 11:00	♀	□	♊	22 11:16
24 23:45	♀	⚹	♋	24 23:49
27 7:49	♃	△	♌	27 10:36
29 16:11	♃	□	♍	29 18:04

Last Aspect / ☽ Ingress (October)

Last Aspect Dy Hr Mn			☽ Ingress	Dy Hr Mn
1 21:00	♃	⚹	♎	1 22:08
3 8:59	☿	☌	♏	3 23:54
5 8:18	♅	□	♐	6 0:54
7 23:34	☿	⚹	♑	8 2:38
9 16:28	♂	□	♒	10 6:12
12 0:34	♂	△	♓	12 12:06
13 0:41	♀	☍	♈	14 20:20
17 0:51	♂	☍	♉	17 6:40
18 23:17	♅	□	♊	19 18:40
22 3:17	☉	△	♋	22 7:22
24 2:06	☿	△	♌	24 19:03
26 18:17	☿	□	♍	27 3:48
29 5:00	☿	⚹	♎	29 8:41
30 19:12	♅	⚹	♏	31 10:14

☽ Phases & Eclipses (Dy Hr Mn)

3 1:56 ● 9♍50
9 22:07 ☽ 16♐28
17 0:52 ○ 23♓24
17 1:03 • A 0.987
25 2:22 ☾ 1♋16

2 12:31 ● 8♎34
2 12:26:27 • T 03'02"
9 4:22 ☽ 15♑08
16 15:59 ○ 22♈32
24 20:22 ☾ 0♌40
31 22:41 ● 7♏46

Astro Data

1 September 1959
Julian Day # 21793
SVP 5♓49'20"
GC 26♐16.6 ⚵ 0♏51.0
Eris 9♈48.1R ⚴ 26♎08.5
⚷ 24♒26.9R ⚶ 26♍02.7
☽ Mean ☊ 5♎09.6

1 October 1959
Julian Day # 21823
SVP 5♓49'18"
GC 26♐16.6 ⚵ 12♏41.7
Eris 9♈30.4R ⚴ 5♏26.7
⚷ 23♒12.4R ⚶ 11♎12.5
☽ Mean ☊ 3♎34.2

November 1959 LONGITUDE

Day	Sid.Time	☉	0 hr ☽	Noon ☽	True ☊	☿	♀	♂	⚳	♃	♄	♅	♆	♇
1 Su	14 40 07	8♏18 52	8♏34 59	16♏06 58	3♎38.4	1♐36.8	22♍07.1	7♏32.7	15♐15.8	5♐19.2	3♑00.6	20♌46.3	6♏45.4	5♍48.6
2 M	14 44 03	9 18 57	23 40 36	1♐14 37	3R 33.3	2 40.8	23 02.3	8 13.8	15 38.7	5 31.9	3 05.6	20 47.7	6 47.6	5 49.7
3 Tu	14 48 00	10 19 03	8♐47 48	16 18 55	3 27.8	3 42.0	23 58.2	8 54.9	16 01.7	5 44.6	3 10.8	20 49.0	6 49.9	5 50.7
4 W	14 51 56	11 19 12	23 46 52	1♑10 43	3 22.5	4 40.2	24 54.6	9 36.0	16 24.7	5 57.4	3 16.0	20 50.3	6 52.1	5 51.8
5 Th	14 55 53	12 19 21	8♑29 40	15 43 06	3 18.4	5 35.1	25 51.6	10 17.2	16 47.8	6 10.3	3 21.2	20 51.5	6 54.3	5 52.8
6 F	14 59 50	13 19 33	22 50 38	29 52 00	3 15.8	6 26.1	26 49.1	10 58.5	17 10.9	6 23.1	3 26.5	20 52.7	6 56.6	5 53.8
7 Sa	15 03 46	14 19 45	6♒47 09	13♒36 10	3D 14.9	7 12.8	27 47.1	11 39.8	17 34.1	6 36.1	3 31.9	20 53.8	6 58.8	5 54.8
8 Su	15 07 43	15 20 00	20 19 15	26 56 40	3 15.5	7 54.8	28 45.7	12 21.1	17 57.3	6 49.0	3 37.3	20 54.8	7 01.1	5 55.7
9 M	15 11 39	16 20 15	3♓28 48	9♓56 02	3 16.8	8 31.5	29 44.7	13 02.5	18 20.6	7 02.0	3 42.8	20 55.9	7 03.3	5 56.6
10 Tu	15 15 36	17 20 32	16 18 49	22 37 33	3R 18.2	9 02.3	0♎44.2	13 43.9	18 43.9	7 15.1	3 48.4	20 56.8	7 05.5	5 57.5
11 W	15 19 32	18 20 51	28 52 41	5♈04 38	3 18.7	9 26.4	1 44.2	14 25.3	19 07.2	7 28.1	3 54.0	20 57.7	7 07.7	5 58.4
12 Th	15 23 29	19 21 11	11♈13 46	17 20 28	3 17.5	9 43.3	2 44.6	15 06.8	19 30.6	7 41.2	3 59.6	20 58.6	7 09.9	5 59.2
13 F	15 27 25	20 21 32	23 25 02	29 27 46	3 14.2	9R 52.2	3 45.5	15 48.4	19 54.1	7 54.4	4 05.3	20 59.3	7 12.1	6 00.0
14 Sa	15 31 22	21 21 56	5♉28 55	11♉28 44	3 08.5	9 52.4	4 46.8	16 30.0	20 17.5	8 07.5	4 11.1	21 00.1	7 14.3	6 00.7
15 Su	15 35 19	22 22 20	17 27 25	23 25 10	3 00.6	9 43.3	5 48.4	17 11.6	20 41.0	8 20.7	4 16.9	21 00.8	7 16.5	6 01.5
16 M	15 39 15	23 22 47	29 22 10	5♊18 34	2 51.1	9 24.2	6 50.5	17 53.3	21 04.6	8 34.0	4 22.8	21 01.4	7 18.7	6 02.2
17 Tu	15 43 12	24 23 15	11♊14 36	17 10 25	2 40.6	8 54.9	7 53.0	18 35.0	21 28.2	8 47.2	4 28.7	21 02.0	7 20.9	6 02.9
18 W	15 47 08	25 23 45	23 06 15	29 02 21	2 30.2	8 15.1	8 55.8	19 16.8	21 51.8	9 00.5	4 34.7	21 02.5	7 23.0	6 03.5
19 Th	15 51 05	26 24 17	4♋58 59	10♋56 26	2 20.8	7 25.1	9 59.0	19 58.6	22 15.4	9 13.8	4 40.8	21 02.9	7 25.2	6 04.1
20 F	15 55 01	27 24 50	16 55 04	22 55 17	2 13.2	6 25.5	11 02.6	20 40.5	22 39.1	9 27.1	4 46.8	21 03.3	7 27.3	6 04.7
21 Sa	15 58 58	28 25 25	28 57 28	5♌02 08	2 07.9	5 17.4	12 06.5	21 22.4	23 02.9	9 40.5	4 53.0	21 03.7	7 29.5	6 05.3
22 Su	16 02 54	29 26 01	11♌09 45	17 20 53	2 04.9	4 02.5	13 10.7	22 04.4	23 26.6	9 53.9	4 59.1	21 04.0	7 31.6	6 05.8
23 M	16 06 51	0♐26 40	23 36 03	29 55 51	2D 04.0	2 42.8	14 15.2	22 46.4	23 50.4	10 07.3	5 05.3	21 04.2	7 33.7	6 06.3
24 Tu	16 10 48	1 27 20	6♍20 50	12♍51 33	2 04.5	1 21.0	15 20.1	23 28.5	24 14.2	10 20.7	5 11.6	21 04.4	7 35.8	6 06.8
25 W	16 14 44	2 28 01	19 28 29	26 12 06	2R 05.2	29♏59.6	16 25.2	24 10.6	24 38.1	10 34.1	5 17.9	21 04.5	7 37.9	6 07.2
26 Th	16 18 41	3 28 45	3♎02 44	10♎00 35	2 05.1	28 41.4	17 30.6	24 52.7	25 01.9	10 47.6	5 24.2	21R 04.6	7 40.0	6 07.6
27 F	16 22 37	4 29 30	17 05 45	24 18 04	2 03.0	27 29.1	18 36.3	25 34.9	25 25.8	11 01.0	5 30.6	21 04.6	7 42.0	6 08.0
28 Sa	16 26 34	5 30 16	1♏37 14	9♏02 40	1 58.5	26 24.7	19 42.3	26 17.2	25 49.8	11 14.5	5 37.1	21 04.6	7 44.1	6 08.3
29 Su	16 30 30	6 31 04	16 33 34	24 08 55	1 51.3	25 29.9	20 48.5	26 59.5	26 13.7	11 28.0	5 43.5	21 04.5	7 46.1	6 08.6
30 M	16 34 27	7 31 53	1♐47 28	9♐27 51	1 42.0	24 45.9	21 55.0	27 41.8	26 37.7	11 41.5	5 50.0	21 04.3	7 48.1	6 08.9

December 1959 LONGITUDE

Day	Sid.Time	☉	0 hr ☽	Noon ☽	True ☊	☿	♀	♂	⚳	♃	♄	♅	♆	♇
1 Tu	16 38 23	8♐32 44	17♐08 35	24♐48 11	1♎31.6	24♏13.3	23♎01.8	28♏24.2	27♐01.7	11♐55.0	5♑56.6	21♌04.1	7♏50.1	6♍09.2
2 W	16 42 20	9 33 36	2♑25 10	9♑58 14	1R 21.4	23R 52.3	24 08.7	29 06.6	27 25.7	12 08.5	6 03.1	21R 03.8	7 52.1	6 09.4
3 Th	16 46 17	10 34 28	17 26 13	24 48 10	1 12.7	23D 42.6	25 15.9	29 49.1	27 49.8	12 22.0	6 09.8	21 03.5	7 54.1	6 09.6
4 F	16 50 13	11 35 22	2♒03 22	9♒11 23	1 06.2	23 43.7	26 23.3	0♐31.6	28 13.8	12 35.6	6 16.4	21 03.1	7 56.1	6 09.7
5 Sa	16 54 10	12 36 16	16 11 58	23 05 06	1 02.4	23 54.9	27 30.9	1 14.2	28 37.9	12 49.1	6 23.1	21 02.7	7 58.0	6 09.9
6 Su	16 58 06	13 37 11	29 50 57	6♓29 49	1D 00.8	24 15.4	28 38.7	1 56.8	29 02.0	13 02.6	6 29.8	21 02.2	7 59.9	6 10.0
7 M	17 02 03	14 38 07	13♓02 08	19 28 25	1R 00.7	24 44.3	29 46.7	2 39.5	29 26.1	13 16.2	6 36.5	21 01.7	8 01.8	6 10.0
8 Tu	17 05 59	15 39 03	25 49 12	2♈05 07	1 00.9	25 20.8	0♏54.9	3 22.1	29 50.3	13 29.7	6 43.3	21 01.1	8 03.7	6R 10.0
9 W	17 09 56	16 40 00	8♈16 44	14 24 41	1 00.2	26 04.1	2 03.3	4 04.9	0♑14.4	13 43.2	6 50.0	21 00.4	8 05.6	6 10.0
10 Th	17 13 52	17 40 58	20 29 30	26 31 46	0 57.4	26 53.3	3 11.8	4 47.7	0 38.6	13 56.8	6 56.8	20 59.7	8 07.4	6 10.0
11 F	17 17 49	18 41 56	2♉31 57	8♉30 32	0 52.0	27 47.8	4 20.6	5 30.5	1 02.7	14 10.3	7 03.7	20 58.9	8 09.2	6 09.9
12 Sa	17 21 46	19 42 55	14 27 56	20 24 29	0 43.5	28 46.9	5 29.5	6 13.4	1 26.9	14 23.8	7 10.5	20 58.1	8 11.0	6 09.8
13 Su	17 25 42	20 43 55	26 20 33	2♊16 22	0 32.1	29 50.0	6 38.6	6 56.3	1 51.1	14 37.3	7 17.4	20 57.3	8 12.8	6 09.7
14 M	17 29 39	21 44 56	8♊12 11	14 08 12	0 18.4	0♐56.6	7 47.9	7 39.2	2 15.3	14 50.8	7 24.3	20 56.3	8 14.6	6 09.5
15 Tu	17 33 35	22 45 57	20 04 35	26 01 30	0 03.5	2 06.3	8 57.3	8 22.2	2 39.5	15 04.3	7 31.2	20 55.4	8 16.3	6 09.4
16 W	17 37 32	23 46 59	1♋59 05	7♋57 29	29♍48.6	3 18.6	10 06.9	9 05.3	3 03.7	15 17.8	7 38.2	20 54.4	8 18.0	6 09.1
17 Th	17 41 28	24 48 02	13 56 51	19 57 20	29 34.8	4 33.3	11 16.6	9 48.4	3 27.9	15 31.2	7 45.1	20 53.3	8 19.7	6 08.9
18 F	17 45 25	25 49 05	25 59 09	2♌02 30	29 23.2	5 50.1	12 26.5	10 31.5	3 52.2	15 44.7	7 52.1	20 52.2	8 21.4	6 08.6
19 Sa	17 49 21	26 50 10	8♌07 40	14 14 55	29 14.5	7 08.6	13 36.6	11 14.7	4 16.4	15 58.1	7 59.1	20 51.0	8 23.0	6 08.3
20 Su	17 53 18	27 51 15	20 24 38	26 37 10	29 09.0	8 28.6	14 46.7	11 57.9	4 40.7	16 11.5	8 06.1	20 49.8	8 24.6	6 08.0
21 M	17 57 15	28 52 20	2♍52 57	9♍12 27	29 06.1	9 50.0	15 57.0	12 41.2	5 04.9	16 25.0	8 13.1	20 48.5	8 26.2	6 07.6
22 Tu	18 01 11	29 53 27	15 36 09	22 04 31	29 05.3	11 12.7	17 07.5	13 24.5	5 29.1	16 38.3	8 20.2	20 47.2	8 27.8	6 07.2
23 W	18 05 08	0♑54 34	28 38 05	5♎17 17	29 05.2	12 36.3	18 18.1	14 07.9	5 53.4	16 51.7	8 27.2	20 45.8	8 29.4	6 06.7
24 Th	18 09 04	1 55 42	12♎02 33	18 54 13	29 04.6	14 01.0	19 28.7	14 51.3	6 17.7	17 05.0	8 34.3	20 44.4	8 30.9	6 06.3
25 F	18 13 01	2 56 51	25 52 31	2♏57 33	29 02.3	15 26.4	20 39.6	15 34.8	6 41.9	17 18.4	8 41.3	20 42.9	8 32.4	6 05.8
26 Sa	18 16 57	3 58 00	10♏09 16	17 27 21	28 57.3	16 52.6	21 50.5	16 18.3	7 06.2	17 31.7	8 48.4	20 41.4	8 33.9	6 05.3
27 Su	18 20 54	4 59 10	24 51 20	2♐20 29	28 49.4	18 19.5	23 01.5	17 01.9	7 30.4	17 44.9	8 55.5	20 39.9	8 35.3	6 04.7
28 M	18 24 50	6 00 21	9♐53 52	17 30 18	28 39.2	19 47.0	24 12.7	17 45.5	7 54.7	17 58.2	9 02.6	20 38.3	8 36.7	6 04.1
29 Tu	18 28 47	7 01 32	25 08 30	2♑47 02	28 27.5	21 15.1	25 23.9	18 29.1	8 18.9	18 11.4	9 09.7	20 36.6	8 38.1	6 03.5
30 W	18 32 44	8 02 43	10♑24 25	17 59 15	28 15.9	22 43.7	26 35.3	19 12.8	8 43.2	18 24.6	9 16.7	20 34.9	8 39.5	6 02.9
31 Th	18 36 40	9 03 54	25 30 11	2♒56 04	28 05.6	24 12.8	27 46.7	19 56.5	9 07.4	18 37.7	9 23.8	20 33.2	8 40.8	6 02.2

Astro Data Dy Hr Mn	Planet Ingress Dy Hr Mn	Last Aspect Dy Hr Mn	☽ Ingress Dy Hr Mn	Last Aspect Dy Hr Mn	☽ Ingress Dy Hr Mn	☽ Phases & Eclipses Dy Hr Mn	Astro Data
♃□♇ 4 0:30	♀ ♎ 9 18:11	1 22:09 ♀ ⚹	♐ 2 10:02	1 9:00 ♀ ⚹	♑ 1 20:11	7 13:24 ☽ 14♒23	1 November 1959
♃⚺♆ 9 14:47	☉ ♐ 23 1:27	4 1:08 ♀ □	♑ 4 10:05	3 12:49 ♀ □	♒ 3 20:35	15 9:42 ○ 22♉17	Julian Day # 21854
☽0N 11 0:29	☿ ♏R 25 11:53	6 6:23 ♀ △	♒ 6 12:14	5 20:33 ♀ △	♓ 6 0:16	23 13:03 ☾ 0♍29	SVP 5♓49'15"
♀0S 12 2:51		8 1:03 ♅ ☍	♓ 8 17:35	7 22:25 ☿ △	♈ 8 7:59	30 8:46 ● 7♐24	GC 26♐16.7 ⚴ 25♏43.6
☿R 14 0:35	♂ ♐ 3 18:09	10 1:05 ☉ △	♈ 11 2:10	10 1:00 ♅ △	♉ 10 18:56		Eris 9♈11.8R ⚵ 15♏47.0
☽0S 25 17:44	♀ ♏ 7 16:41	12 19:11 ♅ △	♉ 13 13:04	13 6:34 ☿ ☍	♊ 13 7:24	7 2:12 ☽ 14♓13	⚷ 22♒40.9R ⚶ 27♎16.8
♅R 27 4:47	⚳ ♑ 8 21:41	15 9:42 ☉ ☍	♊ 16 1:16	15 4:49 ☉ ☍	♋ 15 20:00	15 4:49 ○ 22♊28	☽ Mean ☊ 1♎55.7
	☿ ♐ 13 15:42	17 19:49 ♅ ⚹	♋ 18 13:56	16 16:47 ♀ △	♌ 18 7:58	23 3:28 ☾ 0♎33	
♄⚼♅ 2 14:24	☊ ♍R 15 17:36	20 21:45 ☉ △	♌ 21 2:04	20 14:35 ☉ △	♍ 20 18:29	29 19:09 ● 7♑20	1 December 1959
♄△♇ 3 11:22	☉ ♑ 22 14:34	22 21:37 ♂ □	♍ 23 12:08	22 1:55 ♀ ⚹	♎ 23 2:29		Julian Day # 21884
☿D 3 21:27		25 18:05 ♀ ⚹	♎ 25 18:41	24 15:10 ♅ ⚹	♏ 25 7:01		SVP 5♓49'11"
☽0N 8 7:30		27 6:39 ♅ ⚹	♏ 27 21:21	26 19:45 ♀ ☌	♐ 27 8:16		GC 26♐16.8 ⚴ 8♐37.2
♇R 8 20:26		29 16:41 ♂ ☌	♐ 29 21:12	28 16:55 ♅ △	♑ 29 7:38		Eris 8♈58.8R ⚵ 25♏59.2
☽0S 23 2:54				31 2:56 ♀ ⚹	♒ 31 7:15		⚷ 23♒06.7 ⚶ 12♏57.4
♄⚹♆ 23 21:22							☽ Mean ☊ 0♎20.4

LONGITUDE — January 1960

Day	Sid.Time	☉	0 hr ☽	Noon☽	True☊	☿	♀	♂	⚳	♃	♄	♅	♆	♇
1 F	18 40 37	10♑05 05	10♒15 54	17♒28 57	27♍57.7	25♐42.4	28♏58.2	20♐40.3	9♑31.7	18♐50.9	9♑30.9	20♌31.4	8♏42.1	6♍01.5
2 Sa	18 44 33	11 06 16	24 34 45	1♓33 00	27R 52.7	27 12.4	0♐09.8	21 24.1	9 55.9	19 03.9	9 38.0	20R 29.6	8 43.4	6R 00.8
3 Su	18 48 30	12 07 26	8♓23 41	15 06 54	27D 50.2	28 42.8	1 21.5	22 07.9	10 20.1	19 17.0	9 45.1	20 27.8	8 44.6	6 00.1
4 M	18 52 26	13 08 37	21 42 59	28 12 21	27 49.7	0♑13.6	2 33.3	22 51.8	10 44.3	19 30.0	9 52.2	20 25.9	8 45.9	5 59.3
5 Tu	18 56 23	14 09 47	4♈35 30	10♈53 03	27R 49.9	1 44.9	3 45.1	23 35.8	11 08.5	19 43.0	9 59.3	20 23.9	8 47.0	5 58.5
6 W	19 00 19	15 10 56	17 05 38	23 13 53	27 49.6	3 16.6	4 57.0	24 19.7	11 32.7	19 55.9	10 06.3	20 22.0	8 48.2	5 57.6
7 Th	19 04 16	16 12 05	29 18 28	5♉20 02	27 47.8	4 48.6	6 09.0	25 03.7	11 56.9	20 08.8	10 13.4	20 20.0	8 49.3	5 56.8
8 F	19 08 13	17 13 14	11♉19 13	17 16 37	27 43.6	6 21.1	7 21.1	25 47.8	12 21.0	20 21.6	10 20.5	20 17.9	8 50.4	5 55.9
9 Sa	19 12 09	18 14 23	23 12 46	29 08 11	27 36.6	7 54.0	8 33.2	26 31.9	12 45.2	20 34.4	10 27.5	20 15.8	8 51.5	5 55.0
10 Su	19 16 06	19 15 31	5♊03 20	10♊58 37	27 27.0	9 27.3	9 45.4	27 16.0	13 09.3	20 47.1	10 34.6	20 13.7	8 52.5	5 54.1
11 M	19 20 02	20 16 39	16 54 24	22 51 00	27 15.3	11 01.0	10 57.7	28 00.2	13 33.4	20 59.8	10 41.6	20 11.6	8 53.5	5 53.1
12 Tu	19 23 59	21 17 46	28 48 40	4♋47 37	27 02.3	12 35.2	12 10.1	28 44.4	13 57.5	21 12.5	10 48.6	20 09.4	8 54.5	5 52.1
13 W	19 27 55	22 18 53	10♋48 02	16 50 03	26 49.3	14 09.8	13 22.5	29 28.6	14 21.6	21 25.1	10 55.6	20 07.2	8 55.4	5 51.1
14 Th	19 31 52	23 19 59	22 53 48	28 59 22	26 37.2	15 44.9	14 35.0	0♑12.9	14 45.6	21 37.6	11 02.6	20 05.0	8 56.4	5 50.1
15 F	19 35 48	24 21 05	5♌06 53	11♌16 24	26 27.1	17 20.4	15 47.5	0 57.3	15 09.7	21 50.1	11 09.6	20 02.7	8 57.2	5 49.1
16 Sa	19 39 45	25 22 11	17 28 03	23 41 58	26 19.6	18 56.5	17 00.1	1 41.7	15 33.7	22 02.6	11 16.6	20 00.4	8 58.1	5 48.0
17 Su	19 43 42	26 23 16	29 58 17	6♍17 11	26 14.9	20 33.1	18 12.7	2 26.1	15 57.7	22 15.0	11 23.5	19 58.1	8 58.9	5 46.9
18 M	19 47 38	27 24 21	12♍38 52	19 03 36	26D 12.9	22 10.1	19 25.4	3 10.5	16 21.7	22 27.3	11 30.4	19 55.7	8 59.7	5 45.8
19 Tu	19 51 35	28 25 26	25 31 38	2♎03 16	26 12.8	23 47.8	20 38.2	3 55.0	16 45.6	22 39.5	11 37.3	19 53.4	9 00.4	5 44.7
20 W	19 55 31	29 26 30	8♎38 48	15 18 33	26 13.6	25 25.9	21 51.0	4 39.6	17 09.5	22 51.7	11 44.2	19 51.0	9 01.1	5 43.5
21 Th	19 59 28	0♒27 34	22 02 49	28 51 50	26R 14.2	27 04.7	23 03.9	5 24.1	17 33.4	23 03.9	11 51.0	19 48.6	9 01.8	5 42.3
22 F	20 03 24	1 28 37	5♏45 50	12♏44 54	26 13.6	28 44.0	24 16.8	6 08.8	17 57.3	23 16.0	11 57.9	19 46.1	9 02.5	5 41.1
23 Sa	20 07 21	2 29 40	19 49 05	26 58 15	26 11.1	0♒23.9	25 29.8	6 53.4	18 21.2	23 28.0	12 04.7	19 43.7	9 03.1	5 39.9
24 Su	20 11 17	3 30 43	4♐12 08	11♐30 19	26 06.2	2 04.4	26 42.8	7 38.1	18 45.0	23 39.9	12 11.5	19 41.2	9 03.7	5 38.7
25 M	20 15 14	4 31 45	18 52 13	26 17 02	25 59.4	3 45.6	27 55.8	8 22.9	19 08.8	23 51.8	12 18.2	19 38.7	9 04.2	5 37.4
26 Tu	20 19 11	5 32 47	3♑43 54	11♑11 46	25 51.4	5 27.4	29 08.9	9 07.7	19 32.6	24 03.6	12 25.0	19 36.2	9 04.7	5 36.2
27 W	20 23 07	6 33 48	18 39 31	26 06 01	25 43.2	7 09.7	0♑22.1	9 52.5	19 56.3	24 15.3	12 31.7	19 33.6	9 05.2	5 34.9
28 Th	20 27 04	7 34 48	3♒30 07	10♒50 46	25 35.8	8 52.8	1 35.2	10 37.3	20 20.0	24 27.0	12 38.4	19 31.1	9 05.7	5 33.6
29 F	20 31 00	8 35 47	18 07 00	25 18 01	25 30.2	10 36.4	2 48.4	11 22.2	20 43.7	24 38.6	12 45.0	19 28.5	9 06.1	5 32.2
30 Sa	20 34 57	9 36 45	2♓23 10	9♓22 00	25 26.8	12 20.6	4 01.7	12 07.1	21 07.3	24 50.1	12 51.6	19 25.9	9 06.4	5 30.9
31 Su	20 38 53	10 37 42	16 14 13	22 59 43	25D 25.6	14 05.5	5 14.9	12 52.1	21 30.9	25 01.5	12 58.2	19 23.4	9 06.8	5 29.6

LONGITUDE — February 1960

Day	Sid.Time	☉	0 hr ☽	Noon☽	True☊	☿	♀	♂	⚳	♃	♄	♅	♆	♇
1 M	20 42 50	11♒38 38	29♓38 35	6♈11 01	25♍26.0	15♒50.9	6♑28.2	13♑37.1	21♑54.5	25♐12.9	13♑04.7	19♌20.8	9♏07.1	5♍28.2
2 Tu	20 46 46	12 39 32	12♈37 19	18 57 55	25 27.4	17 36.8	7 41.5	14 22.1	22 18.0	25 24.1	13 11.2	19R 18.2	9 07.4	5R 26.8
3 W	20 50 43	13 40 25	25 13 19	1♉24 05	25 28.9	19 23.3	8 54.9	15 07.1	22 41.5	25 35.3	13 17.7	19 15.5	9 07.6	5 25.4
4 Th	20 54 40	14 41 16	7♉30 49	13 34 07	25R 29.6	21 10.2	10 08.3	15 52.2	23 04.9	25 46.4	13 24.1	19 12.9	9 07.8	5 24.0
5 F	20 58 36	15 42 07	19 34 39	25 33 02	25 29.0	22 57.4	11 21.6	16 37.3	23 28.3	25 57.4	13 30.5	19 10.3	9 08.0	5 22.6
6 Sa	21 02 33	16 42 55	1♊29 53	7♊25 48	25 26.6	24 45.0	12 35.1	17 22.5	23 51.7	26 08.3	13 36.8	19 07.7	9 08.1	5 21.2
7 Su	21 06 29	17 43 43	13 21 22	19 17 06	25 22.6	26 32.7	13 48.5	18 07.7	24 15.0	26 19.1	13 43.1	19 05.0	9 08.2	5 19.7
8 M	21 10 26	18 44 29	25 13 32	1♋11 04	25 17.0	28 20.4	15 02.0	18 52.9	24 38.3	26 29.9	13 49.4	19 02.4	9 08.3	5 18.3
9 Tu	21 14 22	19 45 13	7♋10 10	13 11 08	25 10.6	0♓08.0	16 15.5	19 38.1	25 01.5	26 40.5	13 55.6	18 59.8	9R 08.3	5 16.8
10 W	21 18 19	20 45 56	19 14 18	25 19 56	25 04.0	1 55.3	17 29.0	20 23.4	25 24.7	26 51.1	14 01.7	18 57.1	9 08.3	5 15.3
11 Th	21 22 15	21 46 38	1♌28 12	7♌39 18	24 57.8	3 42.0	18 42.5	21 08.7	25 47.8	27 01.5	14 07.9	18 54.5	9 08.3	5 13.9
12 F	21 26 12	22 47 18	13 53 19	20 10 19	24 52.8	5 27.9	19 56.1	21 54.1	26 10.9	27 11.9	14 13.9	18 51.9	9 08.2	5 12.4
13 Sa	21 30 09	23 47 56	26 30 23	2♍53 30	24 49.3	7 12.7	21 09.7	22 39.4	26 33.9	27 22.1	14 19.9	18 49.3	9 08.1	5 10.9
14 Su	21 34 05	24 48 33	9♍19 41	15 48 55	24D 47.4	8 56.0	22 23.3	23 24.8	26 56.9	27 32.3	14 25.9	18 46.7	9 08.0	5 09.4
15 M	21 38 02	25 49 09	22 21 10	28 56 27	24 47.2	10 37.5	23 36.9	24 10.3	27 19.8	27 42.3	14 31.8	18 44.0	9 07.8	5 07.9
16 Tu	21 41 58	26 49 44	5♎34 43	12♎16 00	24 48.1	12 16.6	24 50.5	24 55.7	27 42.7	27 52.3	14 37.7	18 41.4	9 07.6	5 06.3
17 W	21 45 55	27 50 17	19 00 16	25 47 33	24 49.6	13 52.8	26 04.2	25 41.2	28 05.5	28 02.1	14 43.5	18 38.8	9 07.4	5 04.8
18 Th	21 49 51	28 50 49	2♏37 49	9♏31 06	24 51.2	15 25.6	27 17.9	26 26.8	28 28.3	28 11.8	14 49.3	18 36.3	9 07.1	5 03.3
19 F	21 53 48	29 51 20	16 27 20	23 26 29	24R 52.1	16 54.5	28 31.6	27 12.3	28 51.0	28 21.5	14 55.0	18 33.7	9 06.8	5 01.8
20 Sa	21 57 44	0♓51 50	0♐28 26	7♐33 04	24 52.1	18 18.8	29 45.3	27 57.9	29 13.7	28 31.0	15 00.7	18 31.1	9 06.5	5 00.2
21 Su	22 01 41	1 52 18	14 40 08	21 49 22	24 51.0	19 37.7	0♒59.0	28 43.5	29 36.3	28 40.4	15 06.3	18 28.6	9 06.1	4 58.7
22 M	22 05 38	2 52 45	29 00 24	6♑12 46	24 48.9	20 50.8	2 12.8	29 29.2	29 58.9	28 49.7	15 11.8	18 26.0	9 05.7	4 57.2
23 Tu	22 09 34	3 53 11	13♑25 58	20 39 25	24 46.1	21 57.3	3 26.6	0♒14.9	0♒21.3	28 58.8	15 17.3	18 23.5	9 05.3	4 55.6
24 W	22 13 31	4 53 35	27 52 27	5♒04 24	24 43.2	22 56.6	4 40.3	1 00.6	0 43.8	29 07.9	15 22.7	18 21.0	9 04.8	4 54.1
25 Th	22 17 27	5 53 58	12♒14 35	19 22 19	24 40.6	23 48.0	5 54.1	1 46.3	1 06.1	29 16.8	15 28.1	18 18.5	9 04.3	4 52.6
26 F	22 21 24	6 54 19	26 26 57	3♓27 53	24 38.8	24 31.1	7 07.9	2 32.1	1 28.4	29 25.6	15 33.4	18 16.1	9 03.8	4 51.0
27 Sa	22 25 20	7 54 38	10♓24 36	17 16 42	24D 37.8	25 05.4	8 21.7	3 17.8	1 50.7	29 34.3	15 38.7	18 13.6	9 03.2	4 49.5
28 Su	22 29 17	8 54 56	24 03 51	0♈45 49	24 37.8	25 30.4	9 35.6	4 03.6	2 12.8	29 42.9	15 43.8	18 11.2	9 02.6	4 47.9
29 M	22 33 13	9 55 11	7♈22 31	13 53 56	24 38.5	25 46.0	10 49.4	4 49.4	2 34.9	29 51.3	15 48.9	18 08.8	9 02.0	4 46.4

Astro Data Dy Hr Mn	Planet Ingress Dy Hr Mn	Last Aspect Dy Hr Mn	☽ Ingress Dy Hr Mn	Last Aspect Dy Hr Mn	☽ Ingress Dy Hr Mn	☽ Phases & Eclipses Dy Hr Mn
☽0N 4 16:24	♀ ♐ 2 8:43	2 3:36 ☿ ⚹	♓ 2 9:19	31 15:42 ♃ □	♈ 1 0:39	5 18:53 ☽ 14♈27
♃△♅ 8 6:03	☿ ♑ 4 8:24	4 1:31 ♂ □	♈ 4 15:21	3 0:32 ♃ △	♉ 3 9:16	13 23:51 ○ 22♋49
☽0S 19 10:02	♂ ♑ 14 4:59	6 14:18 ♂ △	♉ 7 1:22	5 5:52 ☿ □	♊ 5 20:58	21 15:01 ☾ 0♏35
♃∠♆ 26 14:22	☉ ♒ 21 1:10	8 18:05 ♅ □	♊ 9 13:45	8 5:16 ☿ △	♋ 8 9:37	28 6:15 ● 7♒20
	☿ ♒ 23 6:16	11 23:03 ♂ ☍	♋ 12 2:23	10 1:38 ♂ ☍	♌ 10 21:08	
☽0N 1 2:51	♀ ♑ 27 4:46	13 23:51 ☉ ☍	♌ 14 13:59	13 1:29 ♃ △	♍ 13 6:35	4 14:26 ☽ 14♉47
♆R 10 0:07		16 8:46 ♃ △	♍ 17 0:03	15 9:44 ♃ □	♎ 15 13:55	12 17:24 ○ 23♌01
☽0S 15 16:26	☿ ♓ 9 10:13	19 4:47 ☉ △	♎ 19 8:14	17 16:00 ♃ ⚹	♏ 17 19:24	19 23:47 ☾ 0♐21
☿0N 27 6:41	☉ ♓ 19 15:26	21 8:26 ☿ □	♏ 21 13:59	19 21:31 ♀ ⚹	♐ 19 23:12	26 18:24 ● 7♓10
☽0N 28 13:14	♀ ♒ 20 16:47	22 23:53 ♅ □	♐ 23 17:03	21 23:34 ♃ ☌	♑ 22 1:39	
	⚳ ♒ 22 13:13	25 14:54 ♀ ☌	♑ 25 18:00	23 14:19 ☿ ⚹	♒ 24 3:32	
	♂ ♒ 23 4:11	26 13:59 ♄ ☌	♒ 27 18:19	26 5:00 ♃ ⚹	♓ 26 6:04	
		29 10:53 ♃ ⚹	♓ 29 19:56	28 10:05 ♃ □	♈ 28 10:37	

Astro Data

1 January 1960
Julian Day # 21915
SVP 5♓49'06"
GC 26♐16.8 ⚴ 21♐46.0
Eris 8♈54.8 ⚵ 6♐12.3
⚷ 24♒26.6 ⚶ 28♏56.1
☽ Mean ☊ 28♍41.9

1 February 1960
Julian Day # 21946
SVP 5♓49'01"
GC 26♐16.9 ⚴ 4♑12.2
Eris 9♈01.8 ⚵ 15♐26.3
⚷ 26♒22.9 ⚶ 14♐12.2
☽ Mean ☊ 27♍03.4

March 1960 LONGITUDE

Day	Sid.Time	☉	0 hr ☽	Noon ☽	True ☊	☿	♀	♂	⚳	♃	♄	♅	♆	♇
1 Tu	22 37 10	10♓55 25	20♈20 12	26♈41 30	24♍39.6	25♓52.0	12♒03.2	5♒35.3	2♒57.0	29♐59.6	15♑54.0	18♌06.4	9♏01.3	4♍44.9
2 W	22 41 07	11 55 36	2♉58 07	9♉10 26	24 40.9	25R48.6	13 17.0	6 21.1	3 18.9	0♑07.8	15 58.9	18R04.1	9R00.6	4R43.3
3 Th	22 45 03	12 55 46	15 18 52	21 23 53	24 41.9	25 35.8	14 30.9	7 07.0	3 40.8	0 15.8	16 03.9	18 01.8	8 59.9	4 41.8
4 F	22 49 00	13 55 54	27 26 00	3♊25 48	24R42.7	25 14.0	15 44.7	7 52.9	4 02.6	0 23.7	16 08.7	17 59.5	8 59.2	4 40.3
5 Sa	22 52 56	14 55 59	9♊23 49	15 20 41	24 42.9	24 44.0	16 58.6	8 38.9	4 24.3	0 31.5	16 13.5	17 57.2	8 58.4	4 38.8
6 Su	22 56 53	15 56 03	21 16 58	27 13 15	24 42.6	24 06.4	18 12.4	9 24.8	4 46.0	0 39.1	16 18.2	17 55.0	8 57.6	4 37.3
7 M	23 00 49	16 56 04	3♋10 08	9♋08 11	24 42.0	23 22.2	19 26.3	10 10.7	5 07.5	0 46.6	16 22.8	17 52.8	8 56.8	4 35.8
8 Tu	23 04 46	17 56 03	15 07 55	21 09 51	24 41.2	22 32.4	20 40.1	10 56.7	5 29.0	0 54.0	16 27.3	17 50.6	8 55.9	4 34.3
9 W	23 08 42	18 56 00	27 14 27	3♌22 08	24 40.4	21 38.4	21 54.0	11 42.7	5 50.5	1 01.2	16 31.8	17 48.4	8 55.0	4 32.8
10 Th	23 12 39	19 55 55	9♌33 17	15 48 13	24 39.7	20 41.5	23 07.9	12 28.7	6 11.8	1 08.2	16 36.2	17 46.3	8 54.1	4 31.3
11 F	23 16 36	20 55 48	22 07 09	28 30 18	24 39.2	19 43.0	24 21.7	13 14.7	6 33.0	1 15.2	16 40.5	17 44.2	8 53.2	4 29.9
12 Sa	23 20 32	21 55 38	4♍57 46	11♍29 35	24D39.0	18 44.2	25 35.6	14 00.8	6 54.2	1 21.9	16 44.8	17 42.2	8 52.2	4 28.4
13 Su	23 24 29	22 55 27	18 05 44	24 46 06	24 38.9	17 46.4	26 49.5	14 46.9	7 15.3	1 28.6	16 49.0	17 40.2	8 51.2	4 27.0
14 M	23 28 25	23 55 14	1♎30 31	8♎18 47	24R38.9	16 50.8	28 03.4	15 32.9	7 36.3	1 35.0	16 53.1	17 38.2	8 50.2	4 25.5
15 Tu	23 32 22	24 54 58	15 10 35	22 05 37	24 38.9	15 58.4	29 17.2	16 19.0	7 57.2	1 41.4	16 57.1	17 36.2	8 49.2	4 24.1
16 W	23 36 18	25 54 41	29 03 30	6♏03 52	24 38.9	15 10.1	0♓31.1	17 05.1	8 18.0	1 47.6	17 01.0	17 34.3	8 48.1	4 22.7
17 Th	23 40 15	26 54 23	13♏06 20	20 10 28	24 38.7	14 26.7	1 45.0	17 51.3	8 38.7	1 53.6	17 04.9	17 32.5	8 47.0	4 21.3
18 F	23 44 11	27 54 02	27 15 52	4♐22 11	24 38.4	13 48.7	2 58.9	18 37.4	8 59.3	1 59.5	17 08.6	17 30.6	8 45.9	4 19.9
19 Sa	23 48 08	28 53 40	11♐29 01	18 36 01	24D38.2	13 16.4	4 12.8	19 23.6	9 19.9	2 05.2	17 12.3	17 28.9	8 44.7	4 18.5
20 Su	23 52 04	29 53 16	25 42 52	2♑49 14	24 38.1	12 50.1	5 26.7	20 09.7	9 40.3	2 10.7	17 16.0	17 27.1	8 43.6	4 17.1
21 M	23 56 01	0♈52 51	9♑54 51	16 59 24	24 38.3	12 29.9	6 40.6	20 55.9	10 00.7	2 16.1	17 19.5	17 25.4	8 42.4	4 15.8
22 Tu	23 59 58	1 52 23	24 02 40	1♒04 21	24 38.8	12 15.9	7 54.6	21 42.1	10 20.9	2 21.4	17 22.9	17 23.7	8 41.2	4 14.4
23 W	0 03 54	2 51 54	8♒04 12	15 01 59	24 39.5	12D 08.0	9 08.5	22 28.3	10 41.1	2 26.4	17 26.3	17 22.1	8 39.9	4 13.1
24 Th	0 07 51	3 51 23	21 57 28	28 50 22	24 40.3	12 06.0	10 22.4	23 14.6	11 01.1	2 31.3	17 29.6	17 20.5	8 38.7	4 11.8
25 F	0 11 47	4 50 50	5♓40 29	12♓27 34	24R40.9	12 09.8	11 36.3	24 00.8	11 21.0	2 36.1	17 32.8	17 19.0	8 37.4	4 10.5
26 Sa	0 15 44	5 50 15	19 11 25	25 51 50	24 41.1	12 19.2	12 50.2	24 47.0	11 40.9	2 40.6	17 35.9	17 17.5	8 36.1	4 09.2
27 Su	0 19 40	6 49 39	2♈28 41	9♈01 49	24 40.8	12 33.9	14 04.1	25 33.3	12 00.6	2 45.0	17 38.9	17 16.1	8 34.8	4 08.0
28 M	0 23 37	7 49 00	15 31 09	21 56 39	24 39.7	12 53.6	15 18.0	26 19.5	12 20.2	2 49.2	17 41.8	17 14.7	8 33.5	4 06.8
29 Tu	0 27 33	8 48 19	28 18 19	4♉36 14	24 38.0	13 18.2	16 31.9	27 05.8	12 39.7	2 53.3	17 44.6	17 13.3	8 32.1	4 05.5
30 W	0 31 30	9 47 36	10♉50 31	17 01 21	24 35.8	13 47.3	17 45.8	27 52.0	12 59.1	2 57.2	17 47.4	17 12.0	8 30.7	4 04.3
31 Th	0 35 27	10 46 50	23 08 59	29 13 43	24 33.4	14 20.8	18 59.7	28 38.3	13 18.3	3 00.9	17 50.0	17 10.7	8 29.4	4 03.1

April 1960 LONGITUDE

Day	Sid.Time	☉	0 hr ☽	Noon ☽	True ☊	☿	♀	♂	⚳	♃	♄	♅	♆	♇
1 F	0 39 23	11♈46 03	5♊15 53	11♊15 54	24♍31.1	14♓58.3	20♓13.6	29♒24.5	13♒37.5	3♑04.4	17♑52.6	17♌09.5	8♏27.9	4♍02.0
2 Sa	0 43 20	12 45 13	17 14 13	23 11 18	24R29.2	15 39.8	21 27.5	0♓10.8	13 56.5	3 07.8	17 55.0	17R08.4	8R26.5	4R00.8
3 Su	0 47 16	13 44 21	29 07 41	5♋03 56	24D28.1	16 24.9	22 41.4	0 57.0	14 15.4	3 10.9	17 57.4	17 07.3	8 25.1	3 59.7
4 M	0 51 13	14 43 27	11♋00 36	16 58 16	24 27.8	17 13.4	23 55.2	1 43.3	14 34.2	3 13.9	17 59.7	17 06.2	8 23.6	3 58.6
5 Tu	0 55 09	15 42 30	22 57 33	28 59 02	24 28.4	18 05.2	25 09.1	2 29.6	14 52.8	3 16.7	18 01.9	17 05.2	8 22.2	3 57.5
6 W	0 59 06	16 41 31	5♌03 19	11♌10 56	24 29.7	19 00.2	26 23.0	3 15.8	15 11.4	3 19.4	18 04.0	17 04.2	8 20.7	3 56.5
7 Th	1 03 02	17 40 30	17 22 27	23 38 20	24 31.3	19 58.1	27 36.8	4 02.1	15 29.8	3 21.8	18 06.0	17 03.3	8 19.2	3 55.5
8 F	1 06 59	18 39 26	29 59 04	6♍24 58	24 32.8	20 58.8	28 50.7	4 48.3	15 48.0	3 24.1	18 07.9	17 02.5	8 17.7	3 54.4
9 Sa	1 10 56	19 38 20	12♍56 22	19 33 33	24R33.7	22 02.1	0♈04.5	5 34.6	16 06.1	3 26.2	18 09.7	17 01.6	8 16.2	3 53.4
10 Su	1 14 52	20 37 12	26 16 16	3♎04 50	24 33.5	23 08.1	1 18.3	6 20.8	16 24.1	3 28.1	18 11.4	17 00.9	8 14.6	3 52.5
11 M	1 18 49	21 36 02	9♎58 57	16 58 20	24 32.1	24 16.5	2 32.2	7 07.1	16 42.0	3 29.8	18 13.0	17 00.2	8 13.1	3 51.5
12 Tu	1 22 45	22 34 50	24 02 34	1♏11 05	24 29.3	25 27.2	3 46.0	7 53.3	16 59.7	3 31.3	18 14.5	16 59.5	8 11.5	3 50.6
13 W	1 26 42	23 33 36	8♏23 14	15 38 17	24 25.5	26 40.2	4 59.8	8 39.5	17 17.3	3 32.7	18 16.0	16 58.9	8 10.0	3 49.7
14 Th	1 30 38	24 32 20	22 55 24	0♐13 45	24 21.2	27 55.4	6 13.6	9 25.8	17 34.7	3 33.9	18 17.3	16 58.4	8 08.4	3 48.8
15 F	1 34 35	25 31 03	7♐32 30	14 50 50	24 16.9	29 12.7	7 27.5	10 12.0	17 52.0	3 34.8	18 18.5	16 57.9	8 06.8	3 48.0
16 Sa	1 38 31	26 29 43	22 07 59	29 23 18	24 13.5	0♈32.1	8 41.3	10 58.2	18 09.2	3 35.6	18 19.7	16 57.4	8 05.2	3 47.2
17 Su	1 42 28	27 28 22	6♑36 11	13♑46 12	24 11.3	1 53.5	9 55.1	11 44.5	18 26.2	3 36.2	18 20.7	16 57.0	8 03.7	3 46.4
18 M	1 46 24	28 27 00	20 52 57	27 56 12	24D10.5	3 16.8	11 08.9	12 30.7	18 43.0	3 36.7	18 21.7	16 56.7	8 02.1	3 45.6
19 Tu	1 50 21	29 25 36	4♒55 48	11♒51 41	24 11.1	4 42.0	12 22.7	13 16.9	18 59.7	3R36.9	18 22.5	16 56.4	8 00.4	3 44.9
20 W	1 54 18	0♉24 10	18 43 49	25 32 16	24 12.4	6 09.2	13 36.6	14 03.1	19 16.3	3 36.9	18 23.3	16 56.2	7 58.8	3 44.2
21 Th	1 58 14	1 22 42	2♓17 07	8♓58 28	24 13.9	7 38.1	14 50.4	14 49.3	19 32.6	3 36.8	18 23.9	16 56.0	7 57.2	3 43.5
22 F	2 02 11	2 21 13	15 36 27	22 11 10	24R14.7	9 08.9	16 04.2	15 35.4	19 48.8	3 36.4	18 24.5	16 55.9	7 55.6	3 42.8
23 Sa	2 06 07	3 19 42	28 42 43	5♈11 14	24 14.1	10 41.5	17 18.0	16 21.6	20 04.9	3 35.9	18 24.9	16D55.8	7 54.0	3 42.2
24 Su	2 10 04	4 18 09	11♈36 46	17 59 25	24 11.7	12 15.9	18 31.8	17 07.7	20 20.7	3 35.2	18 25.3	16 55.8	7 52.3	3 41.5
25 M	2 14 00	5 16 34	24 19 14	0♉36 18	24 07.3	13 52.0	19 45.5	17 53.9	20 36.4	3 34.3	18 25.5	16 55.8	7 50.7	3 41.0
26 Tu	2 17 57	6 14 58	6♉50 39	13 02 22	24 01.1	15 29.9	20 59.3	18 40.0	20 52.0	3 33.2	18 25.7	16 55.9	7 49.1	3 40.4
27 W	2 21 53	7 13 20	19 11 32	25 18 16	23 53.5	17 09.7	22 13.1	19 26.1	21 07.3	3 31.9	18R25.7	16 56.1	7 47.4	3 39.9
28 Th	2 25 50	8 11 40	1♊22 42	7♊25 00	23 45.2	18 51.1	23 26.9	20 12.1	21 22.5	3 30.4	18 25.7	16 56.3	7 45.8	3 39.4
29 F	2 29 47	9 09 58	13 25 24	19 24 09	23 37.0	20 34.4	24 40.7	20 58.2	21 37.5	3 28.8	18 25.6	16 56.5	7 44.1	3 38.9
30 Sa	2 33 43	10 08 14	25 21 32	1♋17 56	23 29.8	22 19.4	25 54.4	21 44.2	21 52.3	3 26.9	18 25.3	16 56.8	7 42.5	3 38.5

Astro Data

	Dy Hr Mn
☿ R	1 15:11
☿0S	9 14:10
☽0S	13 23:53
☉0N	20 14:42
♄⚻♅	22 15:49
♃⚼♅	22 20:27
☿ D	24 8:04
☽0N	26 22:06
☽0S	10 9:08
♀0N	12 7:07
♃ R	20 4:55
☿0N	20 12:58
☽0N	23 5:11
♅ D	24 7:46
♄ R	27 14:06

Planet Ingress

		Dy Hr Mn
♃	♑	1 13:10
♀	♓	16 1:53
☉	♈	20 14:43
♂	♓	2 6:24
♀	♈	9 10:32
☿	♈	16 2:22
☉	♉	20 2:06

Last Aspect / ☽ Ingress

Last Aspect Dy Hr Mn			☽ Ingress	Dy Hr Mn
29 19:53	♅	△	♉	1 18:18
3 20:08	☿	⚹	♊	4 5:08
6 6:03	☿	□	♋	6 17:37
8 14:33	☿	△	♌	9 5:25
11 3:24	♀	☍	♍	11 14:47
13 8:26	☉	☍	♎	13 21:19
16 1:35	♀	△	♏	16 1:37
18 0:15	☉	△	♐	18 4:37
20 6:40	☉	□	♑	20 7:14
21 12:34	♄	☌	♒	22 10:10
24 1:39	♂	☌	♓	24 14:02
25 21:06	♄	⚹	♈	26 19:29
28 20:47	♂	⚹	♉	29 3:13
31 10:45	♂	□	♊	31 13:32

Last Aspect / ☽ Ingress

Last Aspect Dy Hr Mn			☽ Ingress	Dy Hr Mn
2 8:06	♀	□	♋	3 1:46
5 3:30	♀	△	♌	5 14:01
6 23:36	☉	△	♍	8 0:02
9 16:50	☿	☍	♎	10 6:36
11 20:27	☉	☍	♏	12 10:01
14 7:51	☿	△	♐	14 11:37
16 6:52	☉	△	♑	16 13:01
18 12:57	☉	□	♒	18 15:32
19 20:52	♅	☍	♓	20 19:55
22 5:06	♄	⚹	♈	23 2:23
24 13:08	♀	☌	♉	25 10:50
26 23:42	♂	⚹	♊	27 21:16
29 23:51	♀	⚹	♋	30 9:22

☽ Phases & Eclipses

Dy Hr Mn		
5 11:06	☽	14♊54
13 8:26	○	22♍47
13 8:28	☍	T 1.514
20 6:40	☾	29♐40
27 7:37	●	6♈39
27 7:24:34	●	P 0.706
4 7:05	☽	14♋31
11 20:27	○	21♎57
18 12:57	☾	28♑29
25 21:44	●	5♉40

Astro Data

1 March 1960
Julian Day # 21975
SVP 5♓48'58"
GC 26♐17.0 ⚴ 14♑35.5
Eris 9♈16.6 ⚵ 22♐23.4
⚷ 28♒23.2 ⚶ 27♐12.9
☽ Mean ☊ 25♍31.3

1 April 1960
Julian Day # 22006
SVP 5♓48'56"
GC 26♐17.0 ⚴ 23♑27.4
Eris 9♈37.3 ⚵ 26♐49.7
⚷ 0♓20.5 ⚶ 8♑42.9
☽ Mean ☊ 23♍52.8

LONGITUDE — May 1960

Day	Sid.Time	☉	0 hr ☽	Noon ☽	True ☊	☿	♀	♂	⚴	♃	♄	♅	♆	♇
1 Su	2 37 40	11♉06 28	7♋13 45	13♋09 24	23♍24.2	24♈06.3	27♈08.2	22♓30.2	22♒06.9	3♑24.9	18♑25.0	16♌57.2	7♏40.9	3♍38.0
2 M	2 41 36	12 04 41	19 05 24	25 02 16	23R 20.5	25 54.9	28 21.9	23 16.2	22 21.3	3R 22.7	18R 24.6	16 57.6	7R 39.2	3R 37.7
3 Tu	2 45 33	13 02 51	1♌00 33	7♌00 52	23D 18.8	27 45.3	29 35.6	24 02.2	22 35.5	3 20.3	18 24.0	16 58.1	7 37.6	3 37.3
4 W	2 49 29	14 00 59	13 03 49	19 10 01	23 18.7	29 37.6	0♉49.4	24 48.1	22 49.6	3 17.7	18 23.4	16 58.6	7 36.0	3 37.0
5 Th	2 53 26	14 59 05	25 20 07	1♍34 42	23 19.6	1♉31.6	2 03.1	25 34.0	23 03.4	3 15.0	18 22.7	16 59.2	7 34.4	3 36.7
6 F	2 57 22	15 57 10	7♍54 23	14 19 41	23R 20.6	3 27.4	3 16.8	26 19.9	23 17.0	3 12.1	18 21.9	16 59.8	7 32.8	3 36.4
7 Sa	3 01 19	16 55 12	20 51 06	27 29 01	23 20.9	5 25.0	4 30.5	27 05.8	23 30.4	3 08.9	18 21.0	17 00.5	7 31.1	3 36.2
8 Su	3 05 16	17 53 12	4♎13 41	11♎05 17	23 19.4	7 24.3	5 44.2	27 51.6	23 43.7	3 05.7	18 20.0	17 01.2	7 29.5	3 36.0
9 M	3 09 12	18 51 11	18 03 47	25 09 00	23 15.9	9 25.3	6 57.9	28 37.4	23 56.7	3 02.2	18 18.9	17 02.0	7 27.9	3 35.8
10 Tu	3 13 09	19 49 08	2♏20 33	9♏37 51	23 10.0	11 28.0	8 11.6	29 23.2	24 09.5	2 58.6	18 17.7	17 02.9	7 26.3	3 35.6
11 W	3 17 05	20 47 03	17 00 07	24 26 25	23 02.4	13 32.3	9 25.3	0♈08.9	24 22.1	2 54.8	18 16.4	17 03.8	7 24.8	3 35.5
12 Th	3 21 02	21 44 57	1♐55 40	9♐26 41	22 53.6	15 38.0	10 39.0	0 54.7	24 34.4	2 50.9	18 15.0	17 04.7	7 23.2	3 35.4
13 F	3 24 58	22 42 50	16 58 14	24 29 06	22 45.0	17 45.2	11 52.7	1 40.4	24 46.6	2 46.7	18 13.5	17 05.7	7 21.6	3 35.3
14 Sa	3 28 55	23 40 41	1♑58 07	9♑24 15	22 37.4	19 53.5	13 06.4	2 26.0	24 58.5	2 42.5	18 12.0	17 06.8	7 20.1	3D 35.3
15 Su	3 32 51	24 38 31	16 46 35	24 04 24	22 31.9	22 02.9	14 20.0	3 11.7	25 10.2	2 38.0	18 10.3	17 07.9	7 18.5	3 35.3
16 M	3 36 48	25 36 20	1♒17 09	8♒24 29	22 28.6	24 13.2	15 33.7	3 57.3	25 21.7	2 33.4	18 08.6	17 09.0	7 17.0	3 35.3
17 Tu	3 40 45	26 34 07	15 26 12	22 22 17	22D 27.3	26 24.1	16 47.4	4 42.9	25 32.9	2 28.7	18 06.8	17 10.2	7 15.5	3 35.4
18 W	3 44 41	27 31 54	29 12 48	5♓57 59	22 27.4	28 35.4	18 01.1	5 28.4	25 43.9	2 23.8	18 04.8	17 11.5	7 13.9	3 35.5
19 Th	3 48 38	28 29 39	12♓38 04	19 13 23	22R 27.9	0♊46.9	19 14.8	6 13.9	25 54.6	2 18.7	18 02.8	17 12.8	7 12.4	3 35.6
20 F	3 52 34	29 27 23	25 44 18	2♈11 09	22 27.5	2 58.2	20 28.4	6 59.4	26 05.1	2 13.5	18 00.7	17 14.1	7 10.9	3 35.7
21 Sa	3 56 31	0♊25 06	8♈34 19	14 54 09	22 25.4	5 09.1	21 42.1	7 44.8	26 15.4	2 08.1	17 58.6	17 15.6	7 09.5	3 35.9
22 Su	4 00 27	1 22 48	21 10 56	27 24 58	22 20.7	7 19.4	22 55.8	8 30.2	26 25.4	2 02.7	17 56.3	17 17.0	7 08.0	3 36.1
23 M	4 04 24	2 20 29	3♉36 31	9♉45 48	22 13.2	9 28.7	24 09.5	9 15.6	26 35.1	1 57.0	17 54.0	17 18.5	7 06.5	3 36.4
24 Tu	4 08 20	3 18 09	15 53 00	21 58 18	22 03.2	11 36.8	25 23.2	10 00.9	26 44.6	1 51.3	17 51.5	17 20.1	7 05.1	3 36.6
25 W	4 12 17	4 15 48	28 01 50	4♊03 45	21 51.1	13 43.4	26 36.8	10 46.2	26 53.8	1 45.4	17 49.0	17 21.7	7 03.7	3 36.9
26 Th	4 16 14	5 13 25	10♊04 12	16 03 18	21 38.1	15 48.3	27 50.5	11 31.4	27 02.7	1 39.3	17 46.4	17 23.3	7 02.3	3 37.3
27 F	4 20 10	6 11 01	22 01 13	27 58 08	21 25.0	17 51.3	29 04.2	12 16.6	27 11.4	1 33.2	17 43.8	17 25.0	7 00.9	3 37.6
28 Sa	4 24 07	7 08 36	3♋54 16	9♋49 50	21 13.1	19 52.3	0♊17.9	13 01.7	27 19.8	1 26.9	17 41.0	17 26.8	6 59.5	3 38.0
29 Su	4 28 03	8 06 10	15 45 09	21 40 31	21 03.3	21 51.1	1 31.5	13 46.8	27 27.9	1 20.6	17 38.2	17 28.6	6 58.2	3 38.4
30 M	4 32 00	9 03 43	27 36 19	3♌32 58	20 56.0	23 47.6	2 45.2	14 31.8	27 35.7	1 14.1	17 35.3	17 30.4	6 56.9	3 38.9
31 Tu	4 35 56	10 01 14	9♌30 57	15 30 46	20 51.4	25 41.6	3 58.9	15 16.8	27 43.3	1 07.5	17 32.3	17 32.3	6 55.5	3 39.3

LONGITUDE — June 1960

Day	Sid.Time	☉	0 hr ☽	Noon ☽	True ☊	☿	♀	♂	⚴	♃	♄	♅	♆	♇
1 W	4 39 53	10♊58 43	21♌32 58	27♌38 09	20♍49.3	27♊33.1	5♊12.5	16♈01.8	27♒50.5	1♑00.8	17♑29.3	17♌34.2	6♏54.2	3♍39.9
2 Th	4 43 49	11 56 12	3♍46 55	9♍59 54	20R 48.7	29 22.0	6 26.2	16 46.7	27 57.5	0R 54.0	17R 26.2	17 36.2	6R 53.0	3 40.4
3 F	4 47 46	12 53 39	16 17 43	22 40 59	20 48.7	1♋08.3	7 39.8	17 31.5	28 04.2	0 47.1	17 23.0	17 38.2	6 51.7	3 40.9
4 Sa	4 51 43	13 51 05	29 10 16	5♎46 07	20 48.2	2 51.9	8 53.5	18 16.3	28 10.5	0 40.2	17 19.8	17 40.3	6 50.5	3 41.5
5 Su	4 55 39	14 48 30	12♎28 56	19 19 04	20 46.0	4 32.8	10 07.2	19 01.0	28 16.6	0 33.1	17 16.4	17 42.4	6 49.3	3 42.2
6 M	4 59 36	15 45 53	26 16 39	3♏21 42	20 41.5	6 10.9	11 20.8	19 45.7	28 22.4	0 26.0	17 13.1	17 44.5	6 48.1	3 42.8
7 Tu	5 03 32	16 43 16	10♏34 01	17 53 08	20 34.4	7 46.3	12 34.5	20 30.3	28 27.9	0 18.8	17 09.6	17 46.7	6 46.9	3 43.5
8 W	5 07 29	17 40 38	25 18 24	2♐48 56	20 25.1	9 18.9	13 48.1	21 14.9	28 33.0	0 11.6	17 06.1	17 49.0	6 45.8	3 44.2
9 Th	5 11 25	18 37 58	10♐23 35	18 01 06	20 14.5	10 48.7	15 01.8	21 59.4	28 37.9	0 04.3	17 02.6	17 51.3	6 44.6	3 44.9
10 F	5 15 22	19 35 18	25 40 05	3♑19 04	20 03.8	12 15.7	16 15.4	22 43.9	28 42.4	29♐56.9	16 59.0	17 53.6	6 43.5	3 45.7
11 Sa	5 19 18	20 32 38	10♑56 39	18 31 27	19 54.3	13 39.8	17 29.1	23 28.3	28 46.6	29 49.5	16 55.3	17 55.9	6 42.5	3 46.5
12 Su	5 23 15	21 29 56	26 02 17	3♒28 09	19 47.0	15 01.0	18 42.8	24 12.6	28 50.5	29 42.0	16 51.6	17 58.4	6 41.4	3 47.3
13 M	5 27 12	22 27 15	10♒48 13	18 01 57	19 42.3	16 19.3	19 56.4	24 56.9	28 54.1	29 34.5	16 47.8	18 00.8	6 40.4	3 48.1
14 Tu	5 31 08	23 24 32	25 09 00	2♓09 12	19 40.0	17 34.6	21 10.1	25 41.2	28 57.3	29 26.9	16 44.0	18 03.3	6 39.4	3 49.0
15 W	5 35 05	24 21 50	9♓02 35	15 49 22	19 39.3	18 46.9	22 23.8	26 25.4	29 00.2	29 19.3	16 40.1	18 05.8	6 38.4	3 49.9
16 Th	5 39 01	25 19 07	22 29 49	29 04 21	19 39.3	19 56.1	23 37.5	27 09.5	29 02.8	29 11.7	16 36.2	18 08.3	6 37.4	3 50.8
17 F	5 42 58	26 16 24	5♈33 25	11♈57 29	19 38.7	21 02.2	24 51.2	27 53.5	29 05.0	29 04.0	16 32.2	18 10.9	6 36.5	3 51.8
18 Sa	5 46 54	27 13 40	18 17 03	24 32 38	19 36.3	22 05.0	26 04.9	28 37.5	29 06.9	28 56.4	16 28.2	18 13.6	6 35.6	3 52.8
19 Su	5 50 51	28 10 57	0♉44 42	6♉53 43	19 31.5	23 04.5	27 18.6	29 21.5	29 08.4	28 48.7	16 24.1	18 16.2	6 34.7	3 53.8
20 M	5 54 47	29 08 13	13 00 06	19 04 13	19 23.9	24 00.7	28 32.3	0♉05.3	29 09.6	28 41.0	16 20.0	18 19.0	6 33.9	3 54.8
21 Tu	5 58 44	0♋05 29	25 06 26	1♊07 03	19 13.7	24 53.3	29 46.0	0 49.1	29 10.5	28 33.4	16 15.9	18 21.7	6 33.0	3 55.9
22 W	6 02 41	1 02 44	7♊06 21	13 04 32	19 01.4	25 42.4	0♋59.7	1 32.9	29R 11.0	28 25.7	16 11.7	18 24.5	6 32.2	3 57.0
23 Th	6 06 37	1 59 59	19 01 51	24 58 28	18 48.1	26 27.8	2 13.4	2 16.5	29 11.1	28 18.0	16 07.5	18 27.3	6 31.5	3 58.1
24 F	6 10 34	2 57 14	0♋54 35	6♋50 22	18 34.7	27 09.4	3 27.2	3 00.1	29 10.9	28 10.4	16 03.3	18 30.1	6 30.7	3 59.2
25 Sa	6 14 30	3 54 29	12 46 00	18 41 40	18 22.5	27 47.1	4 40.9	3 43.6	29 10.4	28 02.8	15 59.1	18 33.0	6 30.0	4 00.4
26 Su	6 18 27	4 51 43	24 37 35	0♌33 59	18 12.3	28 20.8	5 54.6	4 27.0	29 09.4	27 55.2	15 54.8	18 35.9	6 29.3	4 01.5
27 M	6 22 23	5 48 57	6♌31 09	12 29 22	18 04.7	28 50.3	7 08.4	5 10.4	29 08.2	27 47.6	15 50.5	18 38.9	6 28.7	4 02.8
28 Tu	6 26 20	6 46 11	18 29 01	24 30 27	17 59.9	29 15.6	8 22.1	5 53.7	29 06.5	27 40.1	15 46.2	18 41.9	6 28.0	4 04.0
29 W	6 30 16	7 43 24	0♍34 07	6♍40 30	17D 57.6	29 36.5	9 35.9	6 36.9	29 04.5	27 32.6	15 41.8	18 44.9	6 27.4	4 05.2
30 Th	6 34 13	8 40 36	12 50 05	19 03 25	17 57.0	29 52.9	10 49.6	7 20.0	29 02.2	27 25.2	15 37.4	18 47.9	6 26.9	4 06.5

Astro Data

	Dy Hr Mn
☽0S	7 19:34
♇ D	15 0:50
♂0N	15 15:29
♃□♅	20 9:39
☽0N	20 11:31
♄⚻♅	31 12:13
☽0S	4 5:46
☽0N	16 18:32
⚴ R	23 9:52

Planet Ingress

		Dy Hr Mn
♀	♉	3 19:56
☿	♉	4 16:45
♂	♈	11 7:19
☿	♊	19 3:27
☉	♊	21 1:34
♀	♊	28 6:11
☿	♋	2 20:31
♃	♐R	10 1:52
♂	♉	20 9:05
☉	♋	21 9:42
♀	♋	21 16:34

Last Aspect / ☽ Ingress

Last Aspect Dy Hr Mn			☽ Ingress	Dy Hr Mn
2 19:28	♀	□	♌	2 21:59
4 7:42	♅	☌	♍	5 8:59
7 11:16	♂	☍	♎	7 16:30
9 0:27	♄	□	♏	9 20:07
11 5:42	☉	☍	♐	11 20:55
13 0:11	♅	△	♑	13 20:50
15 13:01	☉	△	♒	15 21:51
17 20:24	☿	□	♓	18 1:23
20 6:30	☉	⚹	♈	20 7:55
21 17:51	♄	□	♉	22 17:00
24 19:31	♀	☌	♊	25 3:55
26 14:41	♅	⚹	♋	27 16:06
29 3:51	♄	☍	♌	30 4:50

Last Aspect / ☽ Ingress

Last Aspect Dy Hr Mn			☽ Ingress	Dy Hr Mn
1 11:48	☿	⚹	♍	1 16:38
3 2:06	♄	△	♎	4 1:31
5 11:27	♂	☍	♏	6 6:20
7 11:49	♅	□	♐	8 7:31
10 6:45	♃	☌	♑	10 6:48
11 20:18	♂	□	♒	12 6:23
14 7:23	♃	⚹	♓	14 8:17
16 12:13	♃	□	♈	16 13:42
18 20:25	♃	△	♉	18 22:33
20 22:36	☿	⚹	♊	21 9:46
23 18:39	♃	☍	♋	23 22:10
26 7:18	☿	☌	♌	26 10:51
28 18:12	♃	△	♍	28 22:53

☽ Phases & Eclipses

Dy Hr Mn		
4 1:00	☽	13♌34
11 5:42	○	20♏32
17 19:54	☾	26♒53
25 12:26	●	4♊17
2 16:01	☽	12♍06
9 13:02	○	18♐40
16 4:35	☾	25♓01
24 3:27	●	2♋37

Astro Data

1 May 1960
Julian Day # 22036
SVP 5♓48'53"
GC 26♐17.1 ⚳ 28♑30.4
Eris 9♈57.1 ⚵ 26♐48.1R
⚷ 1♓42.1 ⚶ 15♑49.3
☽ Mean ☊ 22♍17.4

1 June 1960
Julian Day # 22067
SVP 5♓48'49"
GC 26♐17.2 ⚳ 28♑15.7R
Eris 10♈12.5 ⚵ 21♐53.1R
⚷ 2♓17.4 ⚶ 16♑39.1R
☽ Mean ☊ 20♍38.9

July 1960 LONGITUDE

Day	Sid.Time	☉	0 hr ☽	Noon ☽	True ☊	☿	♀	♂	⚷	♃	♄	♅	♆	♇
1 F	6 38 10	9♋37 49	25♍21 03	1♎43 32	17♍57.4	0♌04.8	12♋03.4	8♉03.0	28♒59.5	27♐17.8	15♑33.1	18♌51.0	6♏26.3	4♍07.8
2 Sa	6 42 06	10 35 01	8♎11 25	14 45 13	17R 57.5	0 12.0	13 17.1	8 46.0	28R 56.4	27R 10.5	15R 28.7	18 54.1	6R 25.8	4 09.2
3 Su	6 46 03	11 32 12	21 25 23	28 12 20	17 56.3	0R 14.6	14 30.9	9 28.9	28 53.0	27 03.3	15 24.3	18 57.2	6 25.3	4 10.5
4 M	6 49 59	12 29 23	5♏06 18	12♏07 26	17 53.1	0 12.5	15 44.7	10 11.7	28 49.2	26 56.1	15 19.9	19 00.3	6 24.9	4 11.9
5 Tu	6 53 56	13 26 35	19 15 41	26 30 48	17 47.7	0 05.8	16 58.4	10 54.4	28 45.1	26 49.0	15 15.4	19 03.5	6 24.5	4 13.3
6 W	6 57 52	14 23 45	3♐52 20	11♐19 37	17 40.3	29♋54.4	18 12.2	11 37.0	28 40.6	26 42.0	15 11.0	19 06.7	6 24.1	4 14.7
7 Th	7 01 49	15 20 56	18 51 42	26 27 31	17 31.6	29 38.6	19 26.0	12 19.6	28 35.8	26 35.0	15 06.6	19 10.0	6 23.7	4 16.1
8 F	7 05 45	16 18 07	4♑05 46	11♑45 04	17 22.7	29 18.6	20 39.8	13 02.0	28 30.6	26 28.2	15 02.2	19 13.2	6 23.4	4 17.6
9 Sa	7 09 42	17 15 18	19 24 01	27 01 11	17 14.8	28 54.5	21 53.5	13 44.4	28 25.1	26 21.4	14 57.8	19 16.5	6 23.1	4 19.1
10 Su	7 13 39	18 12 29	4♒35 15	12♒05 02	17 08.7	28 26.6	23 07.3	14 26.7	28 19.2	26 14.8	14 53.4	19 19.8	6 22.9	4 20.6
11 M	7 17 35	19 09 41	19 29 32	26 47 58	17 04.9	27 55.4	24 21.1	15 08.9	28 13.0	26 08.2	14 49.0	19 23.1	6 22.6	4 22.1
12 Tu	7 21 32	20 06 52	3♓59 45	11♓04 34	17D 03.3	27 21.3	25 34.9	15 51.0	28 06.5	26 01.8	14 44.6	19 26.5	6 22.4	4 23.6
13 W	7 25 28	21 04 05	18 02 14	24 52 47	17 03.3	26 44.7	26 48.7	16 33.1	27 59.6	25 55.4	14 40.2	19 29.9	6 22.3	4 25.2
14 Th	7 29 25	22 01 18	1♈36 26	8♈13 28	17 04.2	26 06.4	28 02.5	17 15.0	27 52.4	25 49.2	14 35.8	19 33.3	6 22.1	4 26.7
15 F	7 33 21	22 58 31	14 44 18	21 09 24	17R 04.8	25 26.8	29 16.4	17 56.9	27 44.9	25 43.1	14 31.4	19 36.7	6 22.0	4 28.3
16 Sa	7 37 18	23 55 45	27 29 17	3♉44 30	17 04.3	24 46.7	0♌30.2	18 38.6	27 37.0	25 37.1	14 27.1	19 40.1	6 21.9	4 30.0
17 Su	7 41 14	24 53 00	9♉55 37	16 03 09	17 02.0	24 06.7	1 44.0	19 20.3	27 28.8	25 31.2	14 22.8	19 43.6	6D 21.9	4 31.6
18 M	7 45 11	25 50 15	22 07 40	28 09 39	16 57.6	23 27.6	2 57.9	20 01.8	27 20.4	25 25.5	14 18.5	19 47.0	6 21.9	4 33.2
19 Tu	7 49 08	26 47 32	4♊09 35	10♊07 55	16 51.2	22 50.0	4 11.7	20 43.3	27 11.6	25 19.9	14 14.2	19 50.5	6 21.9	4 34.9
20 W	7 53 04	27 44 49	16 05 02	22 01 20	16 43.1	22 14.7	5 25.6	21 24.7	27 02.5	25 14.4	14 10.0	19 54.1	6 22.0	4 36.6
21 Th	7 57 01	28 42 06	27 57 07	3♋52 43	16 34.3	21 42.2	6 39.5	22 05.9	26 53.1	25 09.1	14 05.8	19 57.6	6 22.1	4 38.3
22 F	8 00 57	29 39 24	9♋48 22	15 44 19	16 25.3	21 13.2	7 53.3	22 47.1	26 43.4	25 03.9	14 01.6	20 01.1	6 22.2	4 40.0
23 Sa	8 04 54	0♌36 43	21 40 49	27 38 02	16 17.1	20 48.3	9 07.2	23 28.1	26 33.4	24 58.9	13 57.4	20 04.7	6 22.3	4 41.7
24 Su	8 08 50	1 34 03	3♌36 12	9♌35 30	16 10.4	20 27.9	10 21.1	24 09.1	26 23.2	24 54.0	13 53.3	20 08.3	6 22.5	4 43.5
25 M	8 12 47	2 31 23	15 36 08	21 38 21	16 05.6	20 12.4	11 35.0	24 49.9	26 12.7	24 49.3	13 49.2	20 11.9	6 22.7	4 45.3
26 Tu	8 16 43	3 28 43	27 42 21	3♍48 25	16D 02.9	20 02.3	12 48.9	25 30.6	26 02.0	24 44.7	13 45.2	20 15.5	6 23.0	4 47.0
27 W	8 20 40	4 26 04	9♍56 49	16 07 52	16 02.1	19D 57.9	14 02.8	26 11.2	25 51.0	24 40.3	13 41.2	20 19.1	6 23.3	4 48.8
28 Th	8 24 37	5 23 26	22 21 55	28 39 19	16 02.8	19 59.3	15 16.6	26 51.7	25 39.8	24 36.0	13 37.2	20 22.7	6 23.6	4 50.6
29 F	8 28 33	6 20 48	5♎00 26	11♎25 40	16 04.1	20 06.7	16 30.5	27 32.1	25 28.4	24 31.9	13 33.3	20 26.4	6 23.9	4 52.5
30 Sa	8 32 30	7 18 11	17 55 25	24 30 03	16 05.5	20 20.4	17 44.4	28 12.4	25 16.8	24 28.0	13 29.4	20 30.0	6 24.3	4 54.3
31 Su	8 36 26	8 15 34	1♏09 56	7♏55 20	16R 06.1	20 40.3	18 58.3	28 52.5	25 05.0	24 24.3	13 25.6	20 33.7	6 24.7	4 56.1

August 1960 LONGITUDE

Day	Sid.Time	☉	0 hr ☽	Noon ☽	True ☊	☿	♀	♂	⚷	♃	♄	♅	♆	♇
1 M	8 40 23	9♌12 58	14♏46 30	21♏43 33	16♍05.4	21♋06.5	20♌12.2	29♉32.5	24♒53.0	24♐20.7	13♑21.9	20♌37.4	6♏25.2	4♍58.0
2 Tu	8 44 19	10 10 23	28 46 31	5♐55 17	16R 03.2	21 39.1	21 26.1	0♊12.4	24R 40.8	24R 17.3	13R 18.2	20 41.0	6 25.6	4 59.9
3 W	8 48 16	11 07 48	13♐09 33	20 28 53	15 59.7	22 18.1	22 40.0	0 52.2	24 28.4	24 14.0	13 14.5	20 44.7	6 26.1	5 01.8
4 Th	8 52 12	12 05 14	27 52 38	5♑20 02	15 55.3	23 03.2	23 53.9	1 31.8	24 16.0	24 11.0	13 10.9	20 48.4	6 26.7	5 03.7
5 F	8 56 09	13 02 41	12♑50 08	20 21 51	15 50.6	23 54.6	25 07.8	2 11.4	24 03.3	24 08.1	13 07.4	20 52.1	6 27.2	5 05.6
6 Sa	9 00 06	14 00 08	27 54 03	5♒25 34	15 46.4	24 52.1	26 21.7	2 50.8	23 50.6	24 05.4	13 03.9	20 55.9	6 27.9	5 07.5
7 Su	9 04 02	14 57 37	12♒55 11	20 21 50	15 43.3	25 55.5	27 35.6	3 30.1	23 37.7	24 02.8	13 00.5	20 59.6	6 28.5	5 09.4
8 M	9 07 59	15 55 06	27 44 30	5♓02 18	15D 41.5	27 04.7	28 49.5	4 09.2	23 24.8	24 00.5	12 57.2	21 03.3	6 29.1	5 11.3
9 Tu	9 11 55	16 52 37	12♓14 33	19 20 43	15 41.2	28 19.5	0♍03.4	4 48.3	23 11.7	23 58.3	12 53.9	21 07.0	6 29.8	5 13.3
10 W	9 15 52	17 50 09	26 20 26	3♈13 30	15 42.0	29 39.8	1 17.3	5 27.2	22 58.6	23 56.3	12 50.6	21 10.7	6 30.6	5 15.2
11 Th	9 19 48	18 47 42	9♈59 56	16 39 49	15 43.5	1♌05.1	2 31.2	6 06.0	22 45.4	23 54.5	12 47.5	21 14.5	6 31.3	5 17.2
12 F	9 23 45	19 45 17	23 13 24	29 41 01	15 45.0	2 35.4	3 45.1	6 44.6	22 32.2	23 52.9	12 44.4	21 18.2	6 32.1	5 19.2
13 Sa	9 27 41	20 42 53	6♉03 04	12♉20 03	15R 46.0	4 10.2	4 59.0	7 23.1	22 19.0	23 51.4	12 41.4	21 21.9	6 32.9	5 21.1
14 Su	9 31 38	21 40 31	18 32 29	24 40 53	15 46.3	5 49.2	6 12.9	8 01.5	22 05.7	23 50.2	12 38.5	21 25.7	6 33.8	5 23.1
15 M	9 35 35	22 38 10	0♊45 50	6♊47 54	15 45.5	7 32.1	7 26.8	8 39.7	21 52.4	23 49.1	12 35.6	21 29.4	6 34.7	5 25.1
16 Tu	9 39 31	23 35 51	12 47 39	18 45 35	15 43.7	9 18.4	8 40.7	9 17.8	21 39.1	23 48.2	12 32.8	21 33.2	6 35.6	5 27.1
17 W	9 43 28	24 33 33	24 42 16	0♋38 10	15 41.1	11 07.8	9 54.7	9 55.7	21 25.9	23 47.5	12 30.1	21 36.9	6 36.5	5 29.1
18 Th	9 47 24	25 31 17	6♋33 46	12 29 29	15 38.0	12 59.9	11 08.6	10 33.5	21 12.7	23 47.0	12 27.4	21 40.6	6 37.5	5 31.1
19 F	9 51 21	26 29 03	18 25 43	24 22 51	15 34.8	14 54.1	12 22.5	11 11.1	20 59.5	23 46.7	12 24.9	21 44.4	6 38.5	5 33.1
20 Sa	9 55 17	27 26 49	0♌21 11	6♌21 02	15 32.0	16 50.2	13 36.4	11 48.6	20 46.4	23D 46.6	12 22.4	21 48.1	6 39.5	5 35.2
21 Su	9 59 14	28 24 38	12 22 39	18 26 16	15 29.7	18 47.7	14 50.3	12 25.9	20 33.4	23 46.6	12 20.0	21 51.8	6 40.6	5 37.2
22 M	10 03 10	29 22 28	24 32 06	0♍40 20	15 28.3	20 46.2	16 04.2	13 03.1	20 20.5	23 46.9	12 17.7	21 55.5	6 41.6	5 39.2
23 Tu	10 07 07	0♍20 19	6♍51 07	13 04 39	15D 27.8	22 45.5	17 18.1	13 40.1	20 07.7	23 47.3	12 15.5	21 59.2	6 42.8	5 41.2
24 W	10 11 04	1 18 12	19 21 02	25 40 25	15 28.0	24 45.1	18 32.0	14 16.9	19 55.0	23 47.9	12 13.3	22 02.9	6 43.9	5 43.3
25 Th	10 15 00	2 16 06	2♎02 58	8♎28 47	15 28.7	26 44.9	19 45.9	14 53.6	19 42.4	23 48.7	12 11.2	22 06.6	6 45.1	5 45.3
26 F	10 18 57	3 14 01	14 58 01	21 30 48	15 29.8	28 44.5	20 59.8	15 30.0	19 30.0	23 49.7	12 09.3	22 10.3	6 46.3	5 47.3
27 Sa	10 22 53	4 11 58	28 07 15	4♏47 31	15 30.8	0♍43.7	22 13.7	16 06.4	19 17.8	23 50.9	12 07.4	22 14.0	6 47.5	5 49.4
28 Su	10 26 50	5 09 56	11♏31 40	18 19 49	15 31.6	2 42.5	23 27.6	16 42.5	19 05.7	23 52.3	12 05.6	22 17.7	6 48.8	5 51.4
29 M	10 30 46	6 07 55	25 11 58	2♐08 10	15R 31.9	4 40.5	24 41.5	17 18.5	18 53.9	23 53.9	12 03.9	22 21.3	6 50.1	5 53.4
30 Tu	10 34 43	7 05 56	9♐08 19	16 12 18	15 31.8	6 37.7	25 55.4	17 54.2	18 42.2	23 55.6	12 02.3	22 25.0	6 51.4	5 55.5
31 W	10 38 39	8 03 58	23 19 55	0♑30 51	15 31.4	8 34.1	27 09.3	18 29.8	18 30.7	23 57.6	12 00.8	22 28.6	6 52.7	5 57.5

Astro Data	Planet Ingress	Last Aspect	☽ Ingress	Last Aspect	☽ Ingress	☽ Phases & Eclipses	Astro Data
Dy Hr Mn	Dy Hr Mn	Dy Hr Mn	Dy Hr Mn	Dy Hr Mn	Dy Hr Mn	Dy Hr Mn	1 July 1960
☽0S 1 14:29	☿ ♌ 1 1:13	1 3:46 ♃ □	♎ 1 8:46	2 1:57 ♂ ☍	♐ 2 2:04	2 3:48 ☽ 10♎15	Julian Day # 22097
☿R 3 13:15	☿ ♋R 6 1:23	3 10:00 ♃ ✶	♏ 3 15:08	3 18:05 ♃ ☌	♑ 4 3:25	8 19:37 ○ 16♑36	SVP 5♓48'44"
☽0N 14 3:05	♀ ♌ 16 2:11	4 23:37 ♅ □	♐ 5 17:42	5 18:01 ☿ ☍	♒ 6 3:21	15 15:43 ☾ 23♈07	GC 26♐17.3 ⚳ 22♑11.7R
♆D 18 6:55	☉ ♌ 22 20:37	7 12:12 ♃ ☌	♑ 7 17:34	8 0:50 ♀ ☍	♓ 8 3:42	23 18:31 ● 0♌52	Eris 10♈19.0 ⚴ 15♐21.1R
☿D 27 18:25		9 14:54 ☿ ☍	♒ 9 16:43	10 5:05 ☿ △	♈ 10 6:21	31 12:38 ☽ 8♏17	⚵ 1♓58.1R ⚶ 10♑57.7R
☽0S 28 21:24	♂ ♊ 2 4:32	11 10:55 ♃ ✶	♓ 11 17:19	12 1:14 ♃ △	♉ 12 12:36		☽ Mean ☊ 19♍03.6
	♀ ♍ 9 10:54	13 15:46 ♀ △	♈ 13 21:07	14 5:37 ☉ □	♊ 14 22:29	7 2:41 ○ 14♒35	
☽0N 10 12:56	☿ ♌ 10 17:49	15 20:34 ♃ △	♉ 16 4:48	16 22:37 ☉ ✶	♋ 17 10:43	14 5:37 ☾ 21♉25	1 August 1960
♃D 20 16:40	☉ ♍ 23 3:34	18 6:58 ☉ ✶	♊ 18 15:40	18 11:56 ♄ ☍	♌ 19 23:18	22 9:15 ● 29♌16	Julian Day # 22128
☽0S 25 3:22	☿ ♍ 27 3:11	20 18:28 ♃ ☍	♋ 21 4:09	22 9:15 ☉ ☌	♍ 22 10:41	29 19:22 ☽ 6♐26	SVP 5♓48'40"
		23 3:06 ♂ ✶	♌ 23 16:46	24 8:27 ♃ □	♎ 24 20:09		GC 26♐17.3 ⚳ 14♑07.5R
		25 18:42 ♂ □	♍ 26 4:31	26 16:13 ♃ ✶	♏ 27 3:24		Eris 10♈15.5R ⚴ 11♐49.6R
		28 8:24 ♂ △	♎ 28 14:33	28 21:51 ♀ ✶	♐ 29 8:19		⚵ 0♓51.1R ⚶ 4♑59.2R
		30 11:56 ♃ ✶	♏ 30 21:55	31 5:52 ♀ □	♑ 31 11:09		☽ Mean ☊ 17♍25.1

LONGITUDE — September 1960

Day	Sid.Time	☉	0 hr ☽	Noon ☽	True ☊	☿	♀	♂	⚳	♃	♄	♅	♆	♇
1 Th	10 42 36	9♍02 01	7♑44 44	15♑01 03	15♍30.8	10♍29.4	28♍23.1	19♊05.3	18♒19.5	23♐59.7	11♑59.3	22♌32.3	6♏54.1	5♍59.6
2 F	10 46 33	10 00 06	22 19 14	29 38 38	15R 30.1	12 23.7	29 37.0	19 40.5	18R 08.5	24 02.0	11R 58.0	22 35.9	6 55.5	6 01.6
3 Sa	10 50 29	10 58 12	6♒58 30	14♒18 03	15 29.6	14 16.8	0♎50.8	20 15.5	17 57.7	24 04.5	11 56.8	22 39.5	6 56.9	6 03.6
4 Su	10 54 26	11 56 20	21 36 31	28 53 04	15 29.3	16 08.9	2 04.6	20 50.4	17 47.2	24 07.1	11 55.6	22 43.1	6 58.3	6 05.7
5 M	10 58 22	12 54 29	6♓06 56	13♓17 23	15D 29.2	17 59.7	3 18.5	21 25.0	17 36.9	24 10.0	11 54.5	22 46.6	6 59.8	6 07.7
6 Tu	11 02 19	13 52 40	20 23 48	27 25 35	15 29.2	19 49.5	4 32.3	21 59.5	17 26.9	24 13.0	11 53.6	22 50.2	7 01.3	6 09.7
7 W	11 06 15	14 50 53	4♈22 19	11♈13 40	15R 29.3	21 38.0	5 46.1	22 33.8	17 17.2	24 16.2	11 52.7	22 53.7	7 02.8	6 11.7
8 Th	11 10 12	15 49 08	17 59 25	24 39 29	15 29.3	23 25.4	6 59.9	23 07.8	17 07.8	24 19.5	11 51.9	22 57.3	7 04.3	6 13.7
9 F	11 14 08	16 47 25	1♉13 52	7♉42 44	15 29.2	25 11.6	8 13.7	23 41.7	16 58.6	24 23.1	11 51.3	23 00.8	7 05.9	6 15.8
10 Sa	11 18 05	17 45 43	14 06 16	20 24 49	15 29.0	26 56.7	9 27.5	24 15.3	16 49.8	24 26.8	11 50.7	23 04.3	7 07.5	6 17.8
11 Su	11 22 01	18 44 04	26 38 45	2♊48 31	15 28.8	28 40.7	10 41.2	24 48.8	16 41.2	24 30.7	11 50.2	23 07.7	7 09.1	6 19.8
12 M	11 25 58	19 42 27	8♊54 36	14 57 32	15D 28.6	0♎23.5	11 55.0	25 22.0	16 33.0	24 34.8	11 49.8	23 11.2	7 10.7	6 21.8
13 Tu	11 29 55	20 40 53	20 57 54	26 56 15	15 28.7	2 05.2	13 08.8	25 55.0	16 25.1	24 39.0	11 49.5	23 14.6	7 12.4	6 23.8
14 W	11 33 51	21 39 20	2♋53 10	8♋49 14	15 29.0	3 45.9	14 22.6	26 27.7	16 17.5	24 43.4	11 49.3	23 18.0	7 14.1	6 25.8
15 Th	11 37 48	22 37 49	14 45 01	20 41 06	15 29.5	5 25.5	15 36.3	27 00.2	16 10.2	24 48.0	11D 49.2	23 21.4	7 15.8	6 27.7
16 F	11 41 44	23 36 21	26 37 59	2♌36 12	15 30.3	7 04.0	16 50.1	27 32.5	16 03.3	24 52.8	11 49.2	23 24.8	7 17.5	6 29.7
17 Sa	11 45 41	24 34 55	8♌36 13	14 38 29	15 31.2	8 41.4	18 03.8	28 04.6	15 56.7	24 57.7	11 49.3	23 28.1	7 19.2	6 31.7
18 Su	11 49 37	25 33 30	20 43 23	26 51 16	15 32.0	10 17.9	19 17.6	28 36.4	15 50.4	25 02.8	11 49.5	23 31.4	7 21.0	6 33.6
19 M	11 53 34	26 32 08	3♍02 25	9♍17 06	15R 32.5	11 53.3	20 31.3	29 07.9	15 44.5	25 08.0	11 49.8	23 34.7	7 22.8	6 35.6
20 Tu	11 57 30	27 30 48	15 35 29	21 57 42	15 32.5	13 27.8	21 45.0	29 39.2	15 39.0	25 13.4	11 50.2	23 38.0	7 24.6	6 37.5
21 W	12 01 27	28 29 30	28 23 48	4♎53 50	15 31.8	15 01.2	22 58.7	0♋10.2	15 33.8	25 19.0	11 50.7	23 41.2	7 26.4	6 39.4
22 Th	12 05 24	29 28 13	11♎27 44	18 05 25	15 30.5	16 33.7	24 12.4	0 40.9	15 28.9	25 24.7	11 51.3	23 44.5	7 28.3	6 41.3
23 F	12 09 20	0♎26 59	24 46 44	1♏31 32	15 28.7	18 05.2	25 26.1	1 11.4	15 24.5	25 30.6	11 52.0	23 47.6	7 30.1	6 43.3
24 Sa	12 13 17	1 25 46	8♏19 35	15 10 41	15 26.6	19 35.8	26 39.8	1 41.6	15 20.3	25 36.7	11 52.8	23 50.8	7 32.0	6 45.1
25 Su	12 17 13	2 24 36	22 04 34	29 00 59	15 24.5	21 05.3	27 53.5	2 11.5	15 16.6	25 42.9	11 53.7	23 53.9	7 33.9	6 47.0
26 M	12 21 10	3 23 27	5♐59 39	13♐00 20	15 22.8	22 33.9	29 07.2	2 41.1	15 13.2	25 49.3	11 54.7	23 57.0	7 35.8	6 48.9
27 Tu	12 25 06	4 22 19	20 02 44	27 06 37	15D 21.9	24 01.5	0♏20.8	3 10.4	15 10.2	25 55.8	11 55.8	24 00.1	7 37.8	6 50.8
28 W	12 29 03	5 21 14	4♑11 43	11♑17 46	15 21.9	25 28.1	1 34.5	3 39.4	15 07.6	26 02.5	11 57.0	24 03.2	7 39.7	6 52.6
29 Th	12 32 59	6 20 10	18 24 30	25 31 38	15 22.7	26 53.7	2 48.1	4 08.1	15 05.3	26 09.3	11 58.3	24 06.2	7 41.7	6 54.4
30 F	12 36 56	7 19 08	2♒38 52	9♒45 55	15 24.0	28 18.3	4 01.7	4 36.6	15 03.4	26 16.2	11 59.7	24 09.1	7 43.7	6 56.3

LONGITUDE — October 1960

Day	Sid.Time	☉	0 hr ☽	Noon ☽	True ☊	☿	♀	♂	⚳	♃	♄	♅	♆	♇
1 Sa	12 40 53	8♎18 08	16♒52 25	23♒58 02	15♍25.3	29♎41.8	5♏15.3	5♋04.7	15♒01.9	26♐23.3	12♑01.2	24♌12.1	7♏45.7	6♍58.1
2 Su	12 44 49	9 17 09	1♓02 23	8♓05 03	15R 26.3	1♏04.2	6 28.8	5 32.4	15R 00.7	26 30.6	12 02.7	24 15.0	7 47.7	6 59.9
3 M	12 48 46	10 16 12	15 05 40	22 03 47	15 26.3	2 25.5	7 42.4	5 59.9	14 59.9	26 38.0	12 04.4	24 17.9	7 49.7	7 01.6
4 Tu	12 52 42	11 15 17	28 59 01	5♈50 58	15 25.0	3 45.7	8 55.9	6 27.0	14D 59.4	26 45.5	12 06.2	24 20.7	7 51.8	7 03.4
5 W	12 56 39	12 14 25	12♈39 16	19 23 39	15 22.4	5 04.7	10 09.5	6 53.8	14 59.3	26 53.2	12 08.0	24 23.5	7 53.8	7 05.1
6 Th	13 00 35	13 13 34	26 03 49	2♉39 35	15 18.6	6 22.3	11 23.0	7 20.2	14 59.6	27 01.0	12 10.0	24 26.3	7 55.9	7 06.9
7 F	13 04 32	14 12 45	9♉10 52	15 37 35	15 14.0	7 38.7	12 36.5	7 46.3	15 00.2	27 09.0	12 12.1	24 29.0	7 58.0	7 08.6
8 Sa	13 08 28	15 11 59	21 59 49	28 17 40	15 09.0	8 53.6	13 50.0	8 12.1	15 01.2	27 17.0	12 14.2	24 31.7	8 00.1	7 10.3
9 Su	13 12 25	16 11 15	4♊31 21	10♊41 09	15 04.4	10 07.1	15 03.4	8 37.4	15 02.5	27 25.3	12 16.5	24 34.4	8 02.2	7 11.9
10 M	13 16 21	17 10 33	16 47 26	22 50 36	15 00.6	11 18.9	16 16.9	9 02.4	15 04.2	27 33.6	12 18.8	24 37.0	8 04.3	7 13.6
11 Tu	13 20 18	18 09 54	28 51 07	4♋49 31	14 58.2	12 29.0	17 30.4	9 27.0	15 06.3	27 42.1	12 21.2	24 39.6	8 06.4	7 15.3
12 W	13 24 15	19 09 17	10♋46 21	16 42 12	14D 57.1	13 37.2	18 43.8	9 51.2	15 08.7	27 50.7	12 23.7	24 42.2	8 08.6	7 16.9
13 Th	13 28 11	20 08 42	22 37 43	28 33 29	14 57.5	14 43.3	19 57.2	10 15.0	15 11.4	27 59.4	12 26.4	24 44.7	8 10.7	7 18.5
14 F	13 32 08	21 08 09	4♌30 08	10♌28 20	14 58.8	15 47.3	21 10.6	10 38.4	15 14.5	28 08.3	12 29.1	24 47.1	8 12.9	7 20.1
15 Sa	13 36 04	22 07 39	16 28 40	22 31 44	15 00.5	16 48.9	22 24.0	11 01.4	15 17.9	28 17.3	12 31.9	24 49.6	8 15.0	7 21.6
16 Su	13 40 01	23 07 11	28 38 05	4♍48 15	15R 01.9	17 47.8	23 37.4	11 24.0	15 21.7	28 26.4	12 34.7	24 51.9	8 17.2	7 23.2
17 M	13 43 57	24 06 45	11♍02 41	17 21 46	15 02.3	18 43.8	24 50.8	11 46.0	15 25.8	28 35.6	12 37.7	24 54.3	8 19.4	7 24.7
18 Tu	13 47 54	25 06 21	23 45 50	0♎15 04	15 01.2	19 36.7	26 04.1	12 07.7	15 30.2	28 44.9	12 40.8	24 56.6	8 21.6	7 26.2
19 W	13 51 50	26 06 00	6♎49 36	13 29 27	14 58.1	20 26.0	27 17.5	12 28.9	15 35.0	28 54.4	12 43.9	24 58.8	8 23.8	7 27.7
20 Th	13 55 47	27 05 41	20 14 29	27 04 28	14 53.1	21 11.4	28 30.8	12 49.6	15 40.0	29 04.0	12 47.2	25 01.0	8 26.0	7 29.1
21 F	13 59 44	28 05 23	3♏59 05	10♏57 52	14 46.6	21 52.5	29 44.1	13 09.8	15 45.5	29 13.7	12 50.5	25 03.2	8 28.2	7 30.6
22 Sa	14 03 40	29 05 08	18 00 16	25 05 42	14 39.3	22 29.0	0♐57.4	13 29.5	15 51.2	29 23.5	12 53.9	25 05.3	8 30.4	7 32.0
23 Su	14 07 37	0♏04 54	2♐13 30	9♐22 58	14 32.1	23 00.1	2 10.7	13 48.8	15 57.3	29 33.4	12 57.4	25 07.4	8 32.7	7 33.4
24 M	14 11 33	1 04 43	16 33 28	23 44 20	14 25.9	23 25.5	3 24.0	14 07.5	16 03.7	29 43.5	13 01.0	25 09.4	8 34.9	7 34.8
25 Tu	14 15 30	2 04 33	0♑54 59	8♑04 54	14 21.5	23 44.6	4 37.2	14 25.7	16 10.3	29 53.6	13 04.7	25 11.4	8 37.1	7 36.1
26 W	14 19 26	3 04 24	15 13 39	22 20 51	14D 19.1	23 56.8	5 50.4	14 43.3	16 17.3	0♑03.8	13 08.4	25 13.3	8 39.4	7 37.4
27 Th	14 23 23	4 04 18	29 26 15	6♒29 37	14 18.6	24R 01.5	7 03.6	15 00.5	16 24.6	0 14.2	13 12.3	25 15.2	8 41.6	7 38.7
28 F	14 27 19	5 04 13	13♒30 51	20 29 51	14 19.3	23 58.0	8 16.8	15 17.0	16 32.2	0 24.7	13 16.2	25 17.1	8 43.8	7 40.0
29 Sa	14 31 16	6 04 09	27 26 34	4♓20 57	14R 20.4	23 45.9	9 29.9	15 33.1	16 40.1	0 35.2	13 20.2	25 18.8	8 46.1	7 41.2
30 Su	14 35 13	7 04 07	11♓13 00	18 02 41	14 20.7	23 24.7	10 43.0	15 48.5	16 48.3	0 45.9	13 24.2	25 20.6	8 48.3	7 42.5
31 M	14 39 09	8 04 07	24 49 57	1♈34 44	14 19.2	22 54.1	11 56.1	16 03.4	16 56.8	0 56.6	13 28.4	25 22.3	8 50.6	7 43.7

Astro Data

	Dy Hr Mn
♀0S	4 20:52
☽0N	6 23:06
☿0S	13 5:57
♄D	15 22:48
☽0S	21 10:02
⊙0S	23 0:59
☽0N	4 8:27
⚳D	5 6:04
☽0S	18 18:37
☿R	27 14:02
☽0N	31 16:17

Planet Ingress

	Dy Hr Mn
♀ ♎	2 19:29
☿ ♎	12 6:29
♂ ♋	21 4:06
⊙ ♎	23 0:59
♀ ♏	27 5:13
☿ ♏	1 17:17
♀ ♐	21 17:12
⊙ ♏	23 10:02
♃ ♑	26 3:01

Last Aspect / ☽ Ingress (September)

Last Aspect Dy Hr Mn		☽ Ingress Dy Hr Mn
2 11:57 ♀ △	♒	2 12:35
4 4:07 ♃ ✶	♓	4 13:51
6 6:29 ♃ □	♈	6 16:26
8 11:24 ♃ △	♉	8 21:44
11 2:38 ☿ △	♊	11 6:31
13 9:51 ♂ ☌	♋	13 18:10
15 16:17 ⊙ ✶	♌	16 6:46
18 15:34 ♂ ✶	♍	18 18:07
21 2:55 ♂ □	♎	21 2:58
23 1:14 ♃ ✶	♏	23 9:18
25 3:08 ♅ □	♐	25 13:42
27 9:59 ♃ ☌	♑	27 16:54
29 14:34 ☿ □	♒	29 19:32

Last Aspect / ☽ Ingress (October)

Last Aspect Dy Hr Mn		☽ Ingress Dy Hr Mn
1 16:08 ♃ ✶	♓	1 22:14
3 19:59 ♃ □	♈	4 1:46
6 1:37 ♃ △	♉	6 7:09
8 4:47 ♅ □	♊	8 15:16
10 21:32 ♃ ☍	♋	11 2:18
12 17:25 ⊙ □	♌	13 14:55
15 23:28 ♃ △	♍	16 2:40
18 9:12 ♃ □	♎	18 11:32
20 15:31 ♃ ✶	♏	20 17:06
22 11:59 ♅ □	♐	22 20:16
24 22:07 ♃ ☌	♑	24 22:28
26 14:44 ♅ ☍	♒	27 0:57
28 20:17 ♅ ☍	♓	29 4:26
30 21:10 ☿ △	♈	31 9:11

☽ Phases & Eclipses

Dy Hr Mn	
5 11:19	○ 12♓53
5 11:21	• T 1.424
12 22:19	☾ 20♊08
20 23:12	● 27♍58
20 22:59:22	• P 0.614
28 1:13	☽ 4♑55
4 22:16	○ 11♈41
12 17:25	☾ 19♋23
20 12:02	● 27♎06
27 7:34	☽ 3♒53

Astro Data

1 September 1960
Julian Day # 22159
SVP 5♓48'36"
GC 26♐17.4 ⚴ 10♑27.1R
Eris 10♈02.8R ⚵ 13♐32.3
⚷ 29♒20.7R ⚶ 5♑35.9
☽ Mean ☊ 15♍46.6

1 October 1960
Julian Day # 22189
SVP 5♓48'33"
GC 26♐17.5 ⚴ 12♑25.3
Eris 9♈45.1R ⚵ 19♐17.7
⚷ 28♒03.9R ⚶ 12♑15.1
☽ Mean ☊ 14♍11.3

November 1960 — LONGITUDE

Day	Sid.Time	☉	0 hr ☽	Noon ☽	True ☊	☿	♀	♂	⚳	♃	♄	♅	♆	♇
1 Tu	14 43 06	9♏04 08	8♈16 58	14♈56 32	14♍15.4	22♏13.9	13♐09.2	16♋17.6	17♒05.6	1♑07.5	13♑32.6	25♌23.9	8♏52.8	7♍44.8
2 W	14 47 02	10 04 12	21 33 18	28 07 08	14R 09.0	21R 24.5	14 22.2	16 31.3	17 14.6	1 18.4	13 36.9	25 25.5	8 55.1	7 46.0
3 Th	14 50 59	11 04 17	4♉37 55	11♉05 29	14 00.2	20 26.3	15 35.3	16 44.3	17 23.9	1 29.4	13 41.3	25 27.0	8 57.3	7 47.1
4 F	14 54 55	12 04 24	17 29 46	23 50 40	13 49.7	19 20.4	16 48.2	16 56.8	17 33.5	1 40.6	13 45.8	25 28.5	8 59.6	7 48.2
5 Sa	14 58 52	13 04 32	0♊08 10	6♊22 16	13 38.5	18 08.0	18 01.2	17 08.6	17 43.4	1 51.8	13 50.3	25 30.0	9 01.8	7 49.3
6 Su	15 02 48	14 04 43	12 33 03	18 40 38	13 27.5	16 51.2	19 14.1	17 19.7	17 53.5	2 03.1	13 54.9	25 31.4	9 04.0	7 50.3
7 M	15 06 45	15 04 56	24 45 15	0♋47 10	13 17.8	15 32.1	20 27.0	17 30.1	18 03.9	2 14.5	13 59.6	25 32.7	9 06.3	7 51.3
8 Tu	15 10 42	16 05 11	6♋46 42	12 44 15	13 10.2	14 13.1	21 39.9	17 39.9	18 14.5	2 25.9	14 04.3	25 34.0	9 08.5	7 52.3
9 W	15 14 38	17 05 27	18 40 17	24 35 19	13 05.0	12 56.8	22 52.8	17 49.0	18 25.4	2 37.5	14 09.2	25 35.2	9 10.8	7 53.3
10 Th	15 18 35	18 05 46	0♌29 54	6♌24 38	13 02.3	11 45.8	24 05.6	17 57.4	18 36.6	2 49.1	14 14.0	25 36.4	9 13.0	7 54.2
11 F	15 22 31	19 06 06	12 20 10	18 17 09	13D 01.5	10 42.2	25 18.4	18 05.0	18 47.9	3 00.9	14 19.0	25 37.5	9 15.2	7 55.1
12 Sa	15 26 28	20 06 29	24 16 17	0♍18 13	13 01.8	9 47.7	26 31.1	18 11.9	18 59.6	3 12.7	14 24.0	25 38.6	9 17.4	7 56.0
13 Su	15 30 24	21 06 53	6♍23 40	12 33 16	13R 02.2	9 03.8	27 43.9	18 18.1	19 11.5	3 24.6	14 29.1	25 39.6	9 19.6	7 56.8
14 M	15 34 21	22 07 20	18 47 39	25 07 23	13 01.5	8 31.3	28 56.6	18 23.5	19 23.6	3 36.5	14 34.3	25 40.5	9 21.9	7 57.6
15 Tu	15 38 17	23 07 48	1♎32 59	8♎04 49	12 58.8	8 10.5	0♑09.2	18 28.1	19 35.9	3 48.6	14 39.5	25 41.4	9 24.1	7 58.4
16 W	15 42 14	24 08 18	14 43 12	21 28 17	12 53.6	8D 01.3	1 21.9	18 31.9	19 48.5	4 00.7	14 44.8	25 42.3	9 26.2	7 59.1
17 Th	15 46 11	25 08 49	28 20 02	5♏18 17	12 45.6	8 03.3	2 34.5	18 35.0	20 01.3	4 12.9	14 50.1	25 43.1	9 28.4	7 59.9
18 F	15 50 07	26 09 23	12♏22 40	19 32 38	12 35.4	8 16.1	3 47.0	18 37.2	20 14.4	4 25.1	14 55.6	25 43.8	9 30.6	8 00.6
19 Sa	15 54 04	27 09 58	26 47 28	4♐06 18	12 23.9	8 38.6	4 59.6	18 38.6	20 27.7	4 37.4	15 01.0	25 44.5	9 32.8	8 01.2
20 Su	15 58 00	28 10 35	11♐28 07	18 51 53	12 12.4	9 10.1	6 12.0	18R 39.2	20 41.1	4 49.8	15 06.6	25 45.1	9 34.9	8 01.9
21 M	16 01 57	29 11 13	26 16 30	3♑40 54	12 02.2	9 49.8	7 24.5	18 39.0	20 54.9	5 02.3	15 12.2	25 45.7	9 37.1	8 02.5
22 Tu	16 05 53	0♐11 52	11♑04 05	18 25 08	11 54.3	10 36.6	8 36.9	18 37.9	21 08.8	5 14.8	15 17.8	25 46.2	9 39.2	8 03.0
23 W	16 09 50	1 12 32	25 43 20	2♒58 03	11 49.2	11 29.7	9 49.3	18 36.0	21 22.9	5 27.4	15 23.5	25 46.7	9 41.4	8 03.6
24 Th	16 13 46	2 13 14	10♒08 51	17 15 27	11 46.8	12 28.5	11 01.6	18 33.2	21 37.2	5 40.1	15 29.3	25 47.1	9 43.5	8 04.1
25 F	16 17 43	3 13 56	24 17 41	1♓15 32	11 46.2	13 32.0	12 13.8	18 29.6	21 51.8	5 52.8	15 35.1	25 47.4	9 45.6	8 04.6
26 Sa	16 21 40	4 14 40	8♓09 04	14 58 25	11 46.2	14 39.8	13 26.0	18 25.1	22 06.5	6 05.5	15 41.0	25 47.7	9 47.7	8 05.0
27 Su	16 25 36	5 15 24	21 43 47	28 25 22	11 45.4	15 51.2	14 38.2	18 19.8	22 21.4	6 18.4	15 46.9	25 48.0	9 49.8	8 05.4
28 M	16 29 33	6 16 09	5♈03 26	11♈38 10	11 42.7	17 05.7	15 50.3	18 13.6	22 36.5	6 31.3	15 52.9	25 48.1	9 51.8	8 05.8
29 Tu	16 33 29	7 16 56	18 09 47	24 38 28	11 37.2	18 22.9	17 02.3	18 06.5	22 51.8	6 44.2	15 58.9	25 48.3	9 53.9	8 06.2
30 W	16 37 26	8 17 43	1♉04 21	7♉27 34	11 28.6	19 42.4	18 14.3	17 58.7	23 07.3	6 57.2	16 05.0	25R 48.3	9 55.9	8 06.5

December 1960 — LONGITUDE

Day	Sid.Time	☉	0 hr ☽	Noon ☽	True ☊	☿	♀	♂	⚳	♃	♄	♅	♆	♇
1 Th	16 41 22	9♐18 32	13♉48 10	20♉06 14	11♍17.1	21♏03.8	19♑26.2	17♋49.9	23♒22.9	7♑10.2	16♑11.1	25♌48.3	9♏57.9	8♍06.8
2 F	16 45 19	10 19 22	26 21 47	2♊34 52	11R 03.5	22 26.9	20 38.0	17R 40.3	23 38.8	7 23.3	16 17.3	25R 48.3	10 00.0	8 07.0
3 Sa	16 49 15	11 20 13	8♊45 29	14 53 41	10 48.8	23 51.3	21 49.8	17 29.9	23 54.8	7 36.4	16 23.5	25 48.2	10 02.0	8 07.3
4 Su	16 53 12	12 21 05	20 59 30	27 03 04	10 34.4	25 17.0	23 01.5	17 18.6	24 11.0	7 49.6	16 29.7	25 48.0	10 03.9	8 07.5
5 M	16 57 09	13 21 58	3♋04 27	9♋03 51	10 21.3	26 43.8	24 13.1	17 06.5	24 27.4	8 02.8	16 36.0	25 47.8	10 05.9	8 07.6
6 Tu	17 01 05	14 22 52	15 01 29	20 57 36	10 10.6	28 11.3	25 24.7	16 53.6	24 43.9	8 16.1	16 42.4	25 47.6	10 07.8	8 07.8
7 W	17 05 02	15 23 47	26 52 33	2♌46 42	10 02.8	29 39.7	26 36.2	16 39.9	25 00.6	8 29.4	16 48.8	25 47.2	10 09.8	8 07.9
8 Th	17 08 58	16 24 44	8♌40 30	14 34 27	9 57.9	1♐08.6	27 47.6	16 25.3	25 17.4	8 42.8	16 55.2	25 46.9	10 11.7	8 07.9
9 F	17 12 55	17 25 41	20 29 04	26 24 59	9 55.6	2 38.1	28 58.9	16 10.0	25 34.4	8 56.2	17 01.6	25 46.4	10 13.6	8R 08.0
10 Sa	17 16 51	18 26 40	2♍22 47	8♍23 10	9 55.0	4 08.1	0♒10.2	15 54.0	25 51.6	9 09.6	17 08.1	25 45.9	10 15.4	8 08.0
11 Su	17 20 48	19 27 40	14 26 48	20 34 22	9 55.1	5 38.5	1 21.3	15 37.2	26 08.9	9 23.1	17 14.7	25 45.4	10 17.3	8 08.0
12 M	17 24 44	20 28 41	26 46 35	3♎04 05	9 54.5	7 09.2	2 32.4	15 19.7	26 26.4	9 36.6	17 21.3	25 44.8	10 19.1	8 07.9
13 Tu	17 28 41	21 29 43	9♎27 31	15 57 27	9 52.3	8 40.3	3 43.4	15 01.4	26 44.0	9 50.2	17 27.9	25 44.1	10 20.9	8 07.8
14 W	17 32 38	22 30 46	22 34 21	29 18 33	9 47.7	10 11.6	4 54.4	14 42.6	27 01.8	10 03.7	17 34.5	25 43.4	10 22.7	8 07.7
15 Th	17 36 34	23 31 50	6♏10 17	13♏09 33	9 40.3	11 43.1	6 05.2	14 23.1	27 19.7	10 17.4	17 41.2	25 42.7	10 24.5	8 07.5
16 F	17 40 31	24 32 56	20 16 12	27 29 48	9 30.6	13 14.9	7 15.9	14 03.0	27 37.8	10 31.0	17 47.9	25 41.8	10 26.2	8 07.4
17 Sa	17 44 27	25 34 02	4♐49 46	12♐15 13	9 19.4	14 46.9	8 26.6	13 42.3	27 56.0	10 44.7	17 54.6	25 41.0	10 28.0	8 07.1
18 Su	17 48 24	26 35 08	19 45 08	27 18 19	9 08.1	16 19.1	9 37.1	13 21.1	28 14.3	10 58.4	18 01.4	25 40.1	10 29.7	8 06.9
19 M	17 52 20	27 36 15	4♑53 25	12♑29 06	8 57.8	17 51.6	10 47.5	12 59.5	28 32.8	11 12.1	18 08.2	25 39.1	10 31.4	8 06.6
20 Tu	17 56 17	28 37 23	20 04 01	27 36 53	8 49.8	19 24.2	11 57.8	12 37.4	28 51.4	11 25.9	18 15.0	25 38.1	10 33.0	8 06.3
21 W	18 00 13	29 38 31	5♒06 35	12♒32 09	8 44.6	20 57.0	13 08.1	12 14.9	29 10.2	11 39.7	18 21.9	25 37.0	10 34.6	8 06.0
22 Th	18 04 10	0♑39 39	19 52 49	27 08 01	8D 42.1	22 30.0	14 18.1	11 52.1	29 29.0	11 53.5	18 28.7	25 35.9	10 36.3	8 05.6
23 F	18 08 07	1 40 48	4♓17 24	11♓20 46	8 41.7	24 03.2	15 28.1	11 29.0	29 48.0	12 07.3	18 35.6	25 34.7	10 37.8	8 05.2
24 Sa	18 12 03	2 41 56	18 18 06	25 09 32	8R 42.1	25 36.6	16 37.9	11 05.6	0♓07.1	12 21.1	18 42.5	25 33.4	10 39.4	8 04.8
25 Su	18 16 00	3 43 04	1♈55 17	8♈35 38	8 42.2	27 10.3	17 47.6	10 42.0	0 26.4	12 35.0	18 49.5	25 32.2	10 40.9	8 04.3
26 M	18 19 56	4 44 13	15 10 57	21 41 36	8 40.7	28 44.1	18 57.2	10 18.3	0 45.7	12 48.9	18 56.4	25 30.8	10 42.4	8 03.8
27 Tu	18 23 53	5 45 21	28 07 59	4♉30 29	8 36.9	0♑18.3	20 06.6	9 54.5	1 05.2	13 02.8	19 03.4	25 29.5	10 43.9	8 03.3
28 W	18 27 49	6 46 30	10♉49 28	17 05 17	8 30.4	1 52.7	21 15.9	9 30.6	1 24.8	13 16.7	19 10.4	25 28.0	10 45.4	8 02.8
29 Th	18 31 46	7 47 38	23 18 13	29 28 35	8 21.4	3 27.3	22 25.0	9 06.8	1 44.5	13 30.6	19 17.4	25 26.6	10 46.8	8 02.2
30 F	18 35 42	8 48 47	5♊36 36	11♊42 29	8 10.6	5 02.3	23 33.9	8 42.9	2 04.3	13 44.5	19 24.4	25 25.1	10 48.2	8 01.6
31 Sa	18 39 39	9 49 55	17 46 27	23 48 39	7 58.8	6 37.5	24 42.7	8 19.2	2 24.2	13 58.5	19 31.4	25 23.5	10 49.6	8 00.9

Astro Data

	Dy Hr Mn
☽ 0S	15 4:58
☿ D	16 19:28
♂ R	20 17:04
☽ 0N	27 23:00
♅ R	1 4:21
♃△♇	5 20:46
♇ R	10 4:38
☽ 0S	12 15:33
♃⚹♆	16 2:23
♃⚼♅	17 5:52
☽ 0N	25 5:59

Planet Ingress

	Dy Hr Mn
♀ ♑	15 8:57
☉ ♐	22 7:18
☿ ♐	7 17:30
♀ ♒	10 8:34
☉ ♑	21 20:26
⚳ ♓	24 3:03
☿ ♑	27 7:21

Last Aspect / ☽ Ingress (November)

Last Aspect Dy Hr Mn		☽ Ingress Dy Hr Mn
2 7:03	♅ △	♉ 2 15:27
4 15:06	♅ □	♊ 4 23:44
7 1:33	♅ ⚹	♋ 7 10:26
8 22:06	♂ ☌	♌ 9 22:59
12 3:39	♀ △	♍ 12 11:24
14 19:54	♀ □	♎ 14 21:07
16 19:26	♅ ⚹	♏ 17 2:53
18 23:46	☉ ☌	♐ 19 5:17
20 23:10	♅ △	♑ 21 6:02
22 12:21	♂ ☍	♒ 23 7:04
25 2:34	♅ ☍	♓ 25 9:49
26 18:04	♂ △	♈ 27 14:51
29 14:10	♅ △	♉ 29 22:00

Last Aspect / ☽ Ingress (December)

Last Aspect Dy Hr Mn		☽ Ingress Dy Hr Mn
1 22:56	♅ □	♊ 2 7:01
4 9:31	♅ ⚹	♋ 4 17:52
7 4:45	☿ △	♌ 7 6:21
9 10:42	♅ ☌	♍ 9 19:13
11 9:38	☉ □	♎ 12 6:10
14 5:39	♅ ⚹	♏ 14 13:13
16 9:02	♅ □	♐ 16 16:07
18 10:47	☉ ☌	♑ 18 16:16
19 21:01	♄ ☌	♒ 20 15:49
22 9:27	♅ ☍	♓ 22 16:47
24 12:54	☿ □	♈ 24 20:34
27 2:58	☿ △	♉ 27 3:30
29 4:10	♅ □	♊ 29 13:01

☽ Phases & Eclipses

Dy Hr Mn	
3 11:58	○ 11♉04
11 13:47	☾ 19♌11
18 23:46	● 26♏39
25 15:42	☽ 3♓23
3 4:24	○ 11♊01
11 9:38	☾ 19♍22
18 10:47	● 26♐32
25 2:30	☽ 3♈19

Astro Data

1 November 1960
Julian Day # 22220
SVP 5♓48'31"
GC 26♐17.5 ⚴ 18♑32.6
Eris 9♈26.6R ⚵ 28♐06.8
⚷ 27♒25.6R ⚶ 23♑04.1
☽ Mean ☊ 12♍32.8

1 December 1960
Julian Day # 22250
SVP 5♓48'27"
GC 26♐17.6 ⚴ 26♑50.5
Eris 9♈13.8R ⚵ 8♑26.9
⚷ 27♒42.8 ⚶ 5♒43.7
☽ Mean ☊ 10♍57.4

LONGITUDE — January 1961

Day	Sid.Time	☉	0 hr ☽	Noon ☽	True ☊	☿	♀	♂	⚷	♃	♄	♅	♆	♇
1 Su	18 43 36	10♑51 04	29♊49 14	5♋48 21	7♍47.1	8♑13.1	25♒51.3	7♋55.6	2♓44.2	14♑12.4	19♑38.5	25♌21.9	10♏50.9	8♍00.3
2 M	18 47 32	11 52 13	11♋46 11	17 42 52	7R36.5	9 49.0	26 59.8	7R32.2	3 04.3	14 26.4	19 45.5	25R20.3	10 52.2	7R59.6
3 Tu	18 51 29	12 53 21	23 38 35	29 33 32	7 27.9	11 25.3	28 08.0	7 09.1	3 24.5	14 40.3	19 52.6	25 18.6	10 53.5	7 58.9
4 W	18 55 25	13 54 30	5♌27 58	11♌22 10	7 21.8	13 01.9	29 16.1	6 46.2	3 44.9	14 54.3	19 59.7	25 16.8	10 54.8	7 58.1
5 Th	18 59 22	14 55 39	17 16 25	23 11 05	7 18.2	14 38.9	0♓24.0	6 23.6	4 05.3	15 08.3	20 06.8	25 15.1	10 56.0	7 57.4
6 F	19 03 18	15 56 47	29 06 35	5♍03 20	7D17.0	16 16.3	1 31.7	6 01.4	4 25.8	15 22.2	20 13.9	25 13.2	10 57.2	7 56.6
7 Sa	19 07 15	16 57 56	11♍01 51	17 02 38	7 17.4	17 54.1	2 39.2	5 39.6	4 46.4	15 36.2	20 21.0	25 11.4	10 58.4	7 55.7
8 Su	19 11 11	17 59 05	23 06 16	29 13 20	7 18.6	19 32.4	3 46.4	5 18.2	5 07.1	15 50.2	20 28.1	25 09.5	10 59.5	7 54.9
9 M	19 15 08	19 00 14	5♎24 26	11♎40 12	7R19.8	21 11.0	4 53.5	4 57.3	5 27.9	16 04.1	20 35.2	25 07.5	11 00.6	7 54.0
10 Tu	19 19 05	20 01 22	18 01 13	24 28 04	7 19.9	22 50.1	6 00.4	4 37.0	5 48.8	16 18.1	20 42.3	25 05.6	11 01.7	7 53.1
11 W	19 23 01	21 02 31	1♏01 17	7♏41 18	7 18.5	24 29.6	7 07.0	4 17.1	6 09.7	16 32.1	20 49.3	25 03.6	11 02.8	7 52.2
12 Th	19 26 58	22 03 40	14 28 28	21 23 01	7 15.0	26 09.5	8 13.4	3 57.9	6 30.8	16 46.0	20 56.5	25 01.5	11 03.8	7 51.2
13 F	19 30 54	23 04 49	28 25 00	5♐34 17	7 09.8	27 49.9	9 19.6	3 39.3	6 51.9	17 00.0	21 03.6	24 59.4	11 04.8	7 50.2
14 Sa	19 34 51	24 05 58	12♐50 30	20 13 08	7 03.3	29 30.6	10 25.5	3 21.3	7 13.2	17 13.9	21 10.7	24 57.3	11 05.7	7 49.2
15 Su	19 38 47	25 07 06	27 41 21	5♑14 12	6 56.4	1♒11.8	11 31.2	3 04.0	7 34.5	17 27.8	21 17.8	24 55.2	11 06.6	7 48.2
16 M	19 42 44	26 08 15	12♑50 29	20 28 56	6 50.2	2 53.3	12 36.6	2 47.4	7 55.9	17 41.8	21 24.9	24 53.0	11 07.5	7 47.1
17 Tu	19 46 41	27 09 22	28 08 09	5♒46 44	6 45.4	4 35.2	13 41.7	2 31.5	8 17.3	17 55.7	21 32.0	24 50.8	11 08.4	7 46.1
18 W	19 50 37	28 10 29	13♒23 22	20 56 47	6 42.4	6 17.4	14 46.6	2 16.3	8 38.9	18 09.6	21 39.1	24 48.5	11 09.2	7 45.0
19 Th	19 54 34	29 11 35	28 25 56	5♓49 52	6D41.5	7 59.7	15 51.2	2 02.0	9 00.5	18 23.5	21 46.2	24 46.3	11 10.0	7 43.9
20 F	19 58 30	0♒12 41	13♓07 55	20 19 34	6 42.1	9 42.3	16 55.4	1 48.3	9 22.2	18 37.3	21 53.2	24 44.0	11 10.8	7 42.7
21 Sa	20 02 27	1 13 45	27 24 31	4♈22 39	6 43.5	11 24.9	17 59.4	1 35.5	9 44.0	18 51.2	22 00.3	24 41.6	11 11.5	7 41.6
22 Su	20 06 23	2 14 48	11♈14 01	17 58 48	6 45.0	13 07.4	19 03.0	1 23.5	10 05.8	19 05.0	22 07.3	24 39.3	11 12.2	7 40.4
23 M	20 10 20	3 15 51	24 37 15	1♉09 45	6R45.8	14 49.8	20 06.3	1 12.2	10 27.7	19 18.8	22 14.4	24 36.9	11 12.9	7 39.2
24 Tu	20 14 16	4 16 52	7♉36 44	13 58 39	6 45.3	16 31.9	21 09.3	1 01.8	10 49.6	19 32.6	22 21.4	24 34.5	11 13.5	7 37.9
25 W	20 18 13	5 17 52	20 15 58	26 29 12	6 43.4	18 13.4	22 11.8	0 52.2	11 11.7	19 46.3	22 28.4	24 32.1	11 14.1	7 36.7
26 Th	20 22 10	6 18 52	2♊38 48	8♊45 15	6 39.9	19 54.2	23 14.0	0 43.4	11 33.8	20 00.0	22 35.4	24 29.6	11 14.6	7 35.5
27 F	20 26 06	7 19 50	14 49 00	20 50 26	6 35.4	21 34.0	24 15.8	0 35.4	11 55.9	20 13.7	22 42.3	24 27.2	11 15.2	7 34.2
28 Sa	20 30 03	8 20 47	26 49 58	2♋47 57	6 30.2	23 12.4	25 17.3	0 28.3	12 18.1	20 27.4	22 49.3	24 24.7	11 15.7	7 32.9
29 Su	20 33 59	9 21 43	8♋44 43	14 40 35	6 25.1	24 49.2	26 18.3	0 21.9	12 40.4	20 41.0	22 56.2	24 22.2	11 16.1	7 31.6
30 M	20 37 56	10 22 38	20 35 47	26 30 38	6 20.4	26 23.9	27 18.8	0 16.4	13 02.7	20 54.7	23 03.1	24 19.7	11 16.5	7 30.3
31 Tu	20 41 52	11 23 31	2♌25 20	8♌20 09	6 16.8	27 56.1	28 18.9	0 11.6	13 25.1	21 08.2	23 10.0	24 17.1	11 16.9	7 28.9

LONGITUDE — February 1961

Day	Sid.Time	☉	0 hr ☽	Noon ☽	True ☊	☿	♀	♂	⚷	♃	♄	♅	♆	♇
1 W	20 45 49	12♒24 24	14♌15 19	20♌11 03	6♍14.4	29♒25.2	29♓18.6	0♋07.7	13♓47.5	21♑21.8	23♑16.9	24♌14.6	11♏17.3	7♍27.6
2 Th	20 49 45	13 25 16	26 07 36	2♍05 13	6D13.4	0♓50.6	0♈17.8	0R04.5	14 10.0	21 35.3	23 23.7	24R12.0	11 17.6	7R26.2
3 F	20 53 42	14 26 06	8♍04 11	14 04 48	6 13.6	2 11.7	1 16.5	0 02.1	14 32.6	21 48.8	23 30.5	24 09.5	11 17.9	7 24.8
4 Sa	20 57 39	15 26 56	20 07 21	26 12 12	6 14.6	3 27.9	2 14.7	0 00.5	14 55.2	22 02.2	23 37.3	24 06.9	11 18.2	7 23.4
5 Su	21 01 35	16 27 44	2♎19 43	8♎30 17	6 16.1	4 38.3	3 12.3	29♊59.7	15 17.8	22 15.6	23 44.0	24 04.3	11 18.4	7 22.0
6 M	21 05 32	17 28 32	14 44 18	21 02 12	6 17.7	5 42.3	4 09.5	29D59.6	15 40.5	22 29.0	23 50.8	24 01.7	11 18.6	7 20.6
7 Tu	21 09 28	18 29 18	27 24 24	3♏51 19	6 18.9	6 39.0	5 06.0	0♋00.3	16 03.2	22 42.3	23 57.5	23 59.1	11 18.7	7 19.1
8 W	21 13 25	19 30 04	10♏23 23	17 00 56	6R19.5	7 27.7	6 02.0	0 01.6	16 26.0	22 55.6	24 04.1	23 56.4	11 18.8	7 17.7
9 Th	21 17 21	20 30 49	23 44 18	0♐33 43	6 19.3	8 07.7	6 57.4	0 03.8	16 48.8	23 08.8	24 10.8	23 53.8	11 18.9	7 16.2
10 F	21 21 18	21 31 32	7♐29 19	14 31 10	6 18.3	8 38.3	7 52.2	0 06.6	17 11.7	23 22.0	24 17.4	23 51.2	11R19.0	7 14.7
11 Sa	21 25 14	22 32 15	21 39 07	28 52 56	6 16.8	8 59.0	8 46.3	0 10.2	17 34.6	23 35.1	24 24.0	23 48.5	11 19.0	7 13.3
12 Su	21 29 11	23 32 56	6♑12 09	13♑36 11	6 15.2	9R09.4	9 39.8	0 14.4	17 57.6	23 48.2	24 30.5	23 45.9	11 19.0	7 11.8
13 M	21 33 08	24 33 37	21 04 16	28 35 28	6 13.7	9 09.2	10 32.6	0 19.4	18 20.6	24 01.3	24 37.0	23 43.3	11 18.9	7 10.3
14 Tu	21 37 04	25 34 16	6♒08 43	13♒42 55	6 12.6	8 58.4	11 24.7	0 25.0	18 43.7	24 14.3	24 43.5	23 40.6	11 18.8	7 08.8
15 W	21 41 01	26 34 53	21 16 51	28 49 20	6D12.0	8 37.2	12 16.0	0 31.3	19 06.8	24 27.2	24 49.9	23 38.0	11 18.7	7 07.3
16 Th	21 44 57	27 35 30	6♓19 14	13♓45 29	6 12.0	8 06.2	13 06.6	0 38.2	19 29.9	24 40.1	24 56.3	23 35.4	11 18.5	7 05.7
17 F	21 48 54	28 36 04	21 07 09	28 23 28	6 12.4	7 26.1	13 56.3	0 45.8	19 53.0	24 52.9	25 02.6	23 32.8	11 18.3	7 04.2
18 Sa	21 52 50	29 36 37	5♈33 49	12♈37 45	6 13.1	6 37.9	14 45.2	0 54.0	20 16.2	25 05.7	25 08.9	23 30.1	11 18.1	7 02.7
19 Su	21 56 47	0♓37 08	19 35 00	26 25 28	6 13.7	5 43.0	15 33.3	1 02.9	20 39.5	25 18.4	25 15.2	23 27.5	11 17.9	7 01.2
20 M	22 00 43	1 37 37	3♉09 12	9♉46 22	6 14.1	4 42.7	16 20.5	1 12.3	21 02.7	25 31.0	25 21.4	23 24.9	11 17.6	6 59.6
21 Tu	22 04 40	2 38 04	16 17 15	22 42 14	6R14.4	3 38.8	17 06.7	1 22.4	21 26.0	25 43.6	25 27.5	23 22.3	11 17.2	6 58.1
22 W	22 08 36	3 38 29	29 01 45	5♊16 18	6 14.5	2 33.0	17 51.9	1 33.0	21 49.3	25 56.1	25 33.6	23 19.7	11 16.9	6 56.5
23 Th	22 12 33	4 38 53	11♊26 26	17 32 40	6 14.4	1 26.8	18 36.1	1 44.2	22 12.7	26 08.6	25 39.7	23 17.2	11 16.5	6 55.0
24 F	22 16 30	5 39 14	23 35 36	29 35 45	6D14.3	0 22.0	19 19.2	1 55.9	22 36.0	26 21.0	25 45.7	23 14.6	11 16.1	6 53.4
25 Sa	22 20 26	6 39 34	5♋33 42	11♋29 57	6 14.3	29♒20.0	20 01.3	2 08.2	22 59.4	26 33.3	25 51.7	23 12.1	11 15.6	6 51.9
26 Su	22 24 23	7 39 52	17 25 02	23 19 26	6 14.4	28 22.0	20 42.1	2 21.0	23 22.8	26 45.5	25 57.6	23 09.5	11 15.2	6 50.3
27 M	22 28 19	8 40 07	29 13 34	5♌07 53	6 14.7	27 29.0	21 21.8	2 34.3	23 46.3	26 57.7	26 03.5	23 07.0	11 14.6	6 48.8
28 Tu	22 32 16	9 40 21	11♌02 46	16 58 33	6 15.0	26 41.9	22 00.3	2 48.2	24 09.7	27 09.8	26 09.3	23 04.5	11 14.1	6 47.2

Astro Data

	Dy Hr Mn
☽0S	9 0:31
☽0N	21 14:37
♄□♇	26 12:16
♀0N	31 11:18
☽0S	5 7:17
♃□♇	5 22:21
♂ D	6 2:51
♄⚻♅	7 16:04
♆ R	11 11:32
♃⚻♅	12 8:29
☿ R	12 23:35
☽0N	18 0:56
♃☌♄	19 0:02

Planet Ingress

		Dy Hr Mn
♀	♓	5 3:31
☿	♒	14 18:58
☉	♒	20 7:01
☿	♓	1 21:39
♀	♈	2 4:46
♂	♊R	5 0:22
♂	♋	7 5:26
☉	♓	18 21:16
☿	♒R	24 20:22

Last Aspect / ☽ Ingress (January)

Last Aspect Dy Hr Mn			☽ Ingress	Dy Hr Mn
31 15:09	♅	⚹	♋	1 0:22
2 16:11	♄	☍	♌	3 12:54
5 16:11	♅	☌	♍	6 1:48
7 18:37	♄	△	♎	8 13:31
10 13:09	♅	⚹	♏	10 22:09
12 21:16	☿	⚹	♐	13 2:40
14 19:36	♅	△	♑	15 3:41
16 21:30	☉	☌	♒	17 2:55
18 18:10	♅	☍	♓	19 2:32
20 14:39	♄	⚹	♈	21 4:26
23 0:02	♅	△	♉	23 9:51
25 8:14	♅	□	♊	25 18:50
27 19:29	♀	□	♋	28 6:22
30 13:47	♀	△	♌	30 19:05

Last Aspect / ☽ Ingress (February)

Last Aspect Dy Hr Mn			☽ Ingress	Dy Hr Mn
1 20:10	♅	☌	♍	2 7:48
4 6:52	♄	△	♎	4 19:27
7 4:51	♂	△	♏	7 4:51
9 0:41	♄	⚹	♐	9 11:01
11 3:37	♅	△	♑	11 13:50
13 5:37	♄	☌	♒	13 14:14
15 8:10	☉	☌	♓	15 13:53
17 6:25	♄	⚹	♈	17 14:41
19 10:00	♃	□	♉	19 18:21
21 17:49	♃	△	♊	22 1:51
23 23:21	♅	⚹	♋	24 12:49
26 19:06	♃	☍	♌	27 1:34

☽ Phases & Eclipses

Dy Hr Mn	
1 23:06	○ 11♋19
10 3:02	☾ 19♎39
16 21:30	● 26♑32
23 16:13	☽ 3♉27
31 18:47	○ 11♌41
8 16:49	☾ 19♏42
15 8:10	● 26♒25
15 8:19:15	● T 02'45"
22 8:34	☽ 3♊30

Astro Data

1 January 1961
Julian Day # 22281
SVP 5♓48'21"
GC 26♐17.7 ⚳ 6♒44.6
Eris 9♈10.0 ⚵ 20♑17.0
⚴ 28♒54.0 ⚶ 20♒03.0
☽ Mean ☊ 9♍19.0

1 February 1961
Julian Day # 22312
SVP 5♓48'16"
GC 26♐17.7 ⚳ 17♒12.4
Eris 9♈17.1 ⚵ 2♒45.6
⚴ 0♓43.4 ⚶ 4♓58.3
☽ Mean ☊ 7♍40.5

March 1961 — LONGITUDE

Day	Sid.Time	☉	0 hr ☽	Noon ☽	True ☊	☿	♀	♂	⚳	♃	♄	♅	♆	♇
1 W	22 36 12	10♓40 33	22♌55 35	28♌54 09	6♍15.2	26♒01.2	22♈37.5	3♋02.5	24♓33.2	27♑21.9	26♑15.1	23♌02.0	11♏13.5	6♍45.7
2 Th	22 40 09	11 40 43	4♍54 30	10♍56 52	6R 15.2	25R 27.3	23 13.3	3 17.3	24 56.7	27 33.8	26 20.8	22R 59.6	11R 12.9	6R 44.2
3 F	22 44 05	12 40 51	17 01 30	23 08 34	6 14.9	25 00.3	23 47.7	3 32.5	25 20.3	27 45.7	26 26.4	22 57.1	11 12.3	6 42.6
4 Sa	22 48 02	13 40 58	29 18 16	5♎30 45	6 14.3	24 40.4	24 20.7	3 48.3	25 43.8	27 57.5	26 32.0	22 54.7	11 11.6	6 41.1
5 Su	22 51 59	14 41 02	11♎46 11	18 04 44	6 13.3	24 27.3	24 52.2	4 04.4	26 07.4	28 09.2	26 37.5	22 52.3	11 10.9	6 39.5
6 M	22 55 55	15 41 05	24 26 33	0♏51 48	6 12.0	24D 21.0	25 22.1	4 21.0	26 31.0	28 20.9	26 43.0	22 49.9	11 10.2	6 38.0
7 Tu	22 59 52	16 41 06	7♏20 36	13 53 08	6 10.7	24 21.2	25 50.5	4 38.1	26 54.6	28 32.4	26 48.4	22 47.6	11 09.4	6 36.5
8 W	23 03 48	17 41 06	20 29 32	27 09 55	6 09.6	24 27.6	26 17.1	4 55.5	27 18.2	28 43.9	26 53.8	22 45.3	11 08.6	6 35.0
9 Th	23 07 45	18 41 04	3♐54 25	10♐43 07	6D 08.9	24 39.9	26 42.1	5 13.4	27 41.8	28 55.3	26 59.1	22 43.0	11 07.8	6 33.5
10 F	23 11 41	19 41 01	17 36 05	24 33 19	6 08.9	24 57.7	27 05.2	5 31.6	28 05.5	29 06.6	27 04.3	22 40.7	11 07.0	6 32.0
11 Sa	23 15 38	20 40 56	1♑34 46	8♑40 18	6 09.4	25 20.8	27 26.6	5 50.3	28 29.2	29 17.8	27 09.5	22 38.4	11 06.1	6 30.5
12 Su	23 19 34	21 40 49	15 49 43	23 02 44	6 10.4	25 48.8	27 46.0	6 09.3	28 52.8	29 29.0	27 14.6	22 36.2	11 05.2	6 29.0
13 M	23 23 31	22 40 41	0♒18 56	7♒37 49	6 11.6	26 21.4	28 03.5	6 28.7	29 16.5	29 40.0	27 19.6	22 34.1	11 04.3	6 27.5
14 Tu	23 27 28	23 40 30	14 58 46	22 21 05	6R 12.6	26 58.3	28 18.9	6 48.5	29 40.2	29 50.9	27 24.6	22 31.9	11 03.3	6 26.0
15 W	23 31 24	24 40 18	29 44 00	7♓06 39	6 13.0	27 39.3	28 32.3	7 08.6	0♈04.0	0♒01.8	27 29.5	22 29.8	11 02.3	6 24.5
16 Th	23 35 21	25 40 04	14♓28 11	21 47 42	6 12.4	28 24.0	28 43.5	7 29.1	0 27.7	0 12.5	27 34.3	22 27.7	11 01.3	6 23.1
17 F	23 39 17	26 39 49	29 04 21	6♈17 18	6 10.8	29 12.3	28 52.5	7 49.9	0 51.4	0 23.2	27 39.1	22 25.6	11 00.3	6 21.7
18 Sa	23 43 14	27 39 31	13♈25 52	20 29 24	6 08.2	0♓03.8	28 59.2	8 11.1	1 15.1	0 33.7	27 43.8	22 23.6	10 59.2	6 20.2
19 Su	23 47 10	28 39 10	27 27 25	4♉19 34	6 04.9	0 58.5	29 03.6	8 32.6	1 38.9	0 44.2	27 48.4	22 21.7	10 58.1	6 18.8
20 M	23 51 07	29 38 48	11♉05 37	17 45 30	6 01.5	1 56.1	29R 05.6	8 54.4	2 02.6	0 54.5	27 52.9	22 19.7	10 57.0	6 17.4
21 Tu	23 55 03	0♈38 24	24 19 15	0♊47 04	5 58.3	2 56.5	29 05.2	9 16.5	2 26.4	1 04.8	27 57.4	22 17.8	10 55.9	6 16.0
22 W	23 59 00	1 37 57	7♊09 13	13 26 05	5 55.9	3 59.5	29 02.4	9 39.0	2 50.1	1 14.9	28 01.8	22 15.9	10 54.7	6 14.6
23 Th	0 02 56	2 37 28	19 38 06	25 45 48	5D 54.6	5 04.9	28 57.1	10 01.7	3 13.9	1 24.9	28 06.1	22 14.1	10 53.6	6 13.3
24 F	0 06 53	3 36 57	1♋49 44	7♋50 29	5 54.4	6 12.7	28 49.2	10 24.7	3 37.7	1 34.8	28 10.4	22 12.3	10 52.4	6 11.9
25 Sa	0 10 50	4 36 23	13 48 42	19 44 58	5 55.4	7 22.7	28 38.9	10 48.0	4 01.4	1 44.6	28 14.5	22 10.6	10 51.1	6 10.6
26 Su	0 14 46	5 35 47	25 39 56	1♌34 13	5 57.0	8 34.8	28 26.1	11 11.6	4 25.2	1 54.3	28 18.6	22 08.9	10 49.9	6 09.3
27 M	0 18 43	6 35 09	7♌28 24	13 23 04	5 58.8	9 48.9	28 10.8	11 35.4	4 48.9	2 03.9	28 22.6	22 07.2	10 48.6	6 08.0
28 Tu	0 22 39	7 34 28	19 18 46	25 15 59	6R 00.3	11 05.1	27 53.0	11 59.6	5 12.7	2 13.3	28 26.6	22 05.6	10 47.3	6 06.7
29 W	0 26 36	8 33 46	1♍15 14	7♍16 53	6 00.8	12 23.1	27 32.8	12 23.9	5 36.4	2 22.7	28 30.4	22 04.0	10 46.0	6 05.4
30 Th	0 30 32	9 33 01	13 21 20	19 28 53	5 59.9	13 42.9	27 10.4	12 48.5	6 00.2	2 31.9	28 34.2	22 02.5	10 44.7	6 04.2
31 F	0 34 29	10 32 13	25 39 48	1♎54 16	5 57.3	15 04.5	26 45.7	13 13.4	6 23.9	2 41.0	28 37.9	22 01.0	10 43.4	6 02.9

April 1961 — LONGITUDE

Day	Sid.Time	☉	0 hr ☽	Noon ☽	True ☊	☿	♀	♂	⚳	♃	♄	♅	♆	♇
1 Sa	0 38 25	11♈31 24	8♎12 25	14♎34 20	5♍53.1	16♓27.9	26♈18.9	13♋38.5	6♈47.6	2♒50.0	28♑41.5	21♌59.5	10♏42.0	6♍01.7
2 Su	0 42 22	12 30 33	21 00 02	27 29 29	5R 47.5	17 52.9	25R 50.1	14 03.8	7 11.4	2 58.8	28 45.0	21R 58.2	10R 40.6	6R 00.5
3 M	0 46 19	13 29 40	4♏02 35	10♏39 14	5 41.2	19 19.6	25 19.4	14 29.3	7 35.1	3 07.5	28 48.4	21 56.8	10 39.2	5 59.4
4 Tu	0 50 15	14 28 45	17 19 16	24 02 30	5 34.8	20 47.9	24 47.2	14 55.1	7 58.8	3 16.1	28 51.8	21 55.5	10 37.8	5 58.2
5 W	0 54 12	15 27 48	0♐48 46	7♐37 51	5 29.2	22 17.8	24 13.4	15 21.1	8 22.5	3 24.6	28 55.0	21 54.2	10 36.4	5 57.1
6 Th	0 58 08	16 26 49	14 29 35	21 23 46	5 25.0	23 49.3	23 38.4	15 47.3	8 46.2	3 33.0	28 58.2	21 53.0	10 35.0	5 56.0
7 F	1 02 05	17 25 49	28 20 14	5♑18 50	5D 22.5	25 22.3	23 02.4	16 13.7	9 09.9	3 41.2	29 01.3	21 51.9	10 33.5	5 54.9
8 Sa	1 06 01	18 24 46	12♑19 24	19 21 47	5 21.9	26 56.9	22 25.5	16 40.3	9 33.6	3 49.2	29 04.3	21 50.8	10 32.0	5 53.8
9 Su	1 09 58	19 23 43	26 25 51	3♒31 25	5 22.5	28 33.1	21 48.1	17 07.1	9 57.2	3 57.2	29 07.3	21 49.7	10 30.5	5 52.8
10 M	1 13 54	20 22 37	10♒38 19	17 46 19	5 23.8	0♈10.8	21 10.3	17 34.1	10 20.9	4 05.0	29 10.1	21 48.7	10 29.0	5 51.7
11 Tu	1 17 51	21 21 30	24 55 08	2♓04 27	5R 24.6	1 50.0	20 32.5	18 01.3	10 44.5	4 12.6	29 12.8	21 47.7	10 27.5	5 50.7
12 W	1 21 48	22 20 21	9♓13 55	16 23 03	5 24.1	3 30.8	19 54.9	18 28.7	11 08.2	4 20.2	29 15.5	21 46.8	10 26.0	5 49.8
13 Th	1 25 44	23 19 10	23 31 24	0♈38 24	5 21.7	5 13.2	19 17.7	18 56.3	11 31.8	4 27.5	29 18.0	21 45.9	10 24.5	5 48.8
14 F	1 29 41	24 17 57	7♈43 30	14 46 07	5 16.9	6 57.0	18 41.1	19 24.0	11 55.4	4 34.8	29 20.5	21 45.1	10 22.9	5 47.9
15 Sa	1 33 37	25 16 42	21 45 41	28 41 38	5 10.1	8 42.5	18 05.5	19 52.0	12 19.0	4 41.9	29 22.9	21 44.4	10 21.3	5 47.0
16 Su	1 37 34	26 15 25	5♉33 29	12♉20 50	5 01.7	10 29.5	17 30.9	20 20.1	12 42.5	4 48.8	29 25.2	21 43.6	10 19.8	5 46.1
17 M	1 41 30	27 14 06	19 03 20	25 40 45	4 52.6	12 18.1	16 57.7	20 48.4	13 06.1	4 55.6	29 27.4	21 43.0	10 18.2	5 45.2
18 Tu	1 45 27	28 12 46	2♊12 59	8♊40 00	4 43.9	14 08.4	16 25.9	21 16.8	13 29.6	5 02.2	29 29.5	21 42.4	10 16.6	5 44.4
19 W	1 49 23	29 11 23	15 01 54	21 18 55	4 36.4	16 00.2	15 55.9	21 45.5	13 53.1	5 08.7	29 31.5	21 41.8	10 15.0	5 43.6
20 Th	1 53 20	0♉09 58	27 31 20	3♋39 32	4 30.8	17 53.5	15 27.7	22 14.2	14 16.6	5 15.0	29 33.4	21 41.3	10 13.4	5 42.8
21 F	1 57 17	1 08 30	9♋43 58	15 45 12	4 27.3	19 48.5	15 01.4	22 43.2	14 40.1	5 21.2	29 35.2	21 40.9	10 11.8	5 42.0
22 Sa	2 01 13	2 07 01	21 43 46	27 40 19	4D 25.9	21 45.1	14 37.3	23 12.3	15 03.5	5 27.2	29 36.9	21 40.5	10 10.2	5 41.3
23 Su	2 05 10	3 05 30	3♌35 29	9♌29 55	4 26.0	23 43.3	14 15.3	23 41.5	15 26.9	5 33.1	29 38.5	21 40.2	10 08.6	5 40.6
24 M	2 09 06	4 03 56	15 24 19	21 19 20	4 26.8	25 43.0	13 55.6	24 10.9	15 50.3	5 38.8	29 40.0	21 39.9	10 07.0	5 39.9
25 Tu	2 13 03	5 02 20	27 15 38	3♍13 51	4R 27.4	27 44.2	13 38.2	24 40.5	16 13.7	5 44.3	29 41.5	21 39.6	10 05.4	5 39.3
26 W	2 16 59	6 00 42	9♍14 35	15 18 24	4 26.8	29 46.8	13 23.2	25 10.1	16 37.0	5 49.7	29 42.8	21 39.5	10 03.7	5 38.7
27 Th	2 20 56	6 59 02	21 25 50	27 37 18	4 24.2	1♉50.9	13 10.7	25 39.9	17 00.3	5 54.9	29 44.0	21 39.3	10 02.1	5 38.1
28 F	2 24 52	7 57 20	3♎53 11	10♎13 45	4 19.2	3 56.2	13 00.5	26 09.9	17 23.6	6 00.0	29 45.2	21D 39.3	10 00.5	5 37.5
29 Sa	2 28 49	8 55 36	16 39 14	23 09 42	4 11.8	6 02.7	12 52.9	26 40.0	17 46.9	6 04.8	29 46.2	21 39.3	9 58.8	5 37.0
30 Su	2 32 45	9 53 50	29 45 07	6♏25 24	4 02.4	8 10.3	12 47.6	27 10.1	18 10.1	6 09.5	29 47.2	21 39.3	9 57.2	5 36.5

Astro Data (Dy Hr Mn)	Planet Ingress (Dy Hr Mn)	Last Aspect (Dy Hr Mn)	☽ Ingress (Dy Hr Mn)	Last Aspect (Dy Hr Mn)	☽ Ingress (Dy Hr Mn)	☽ Phases & Eclipses (Dy Hr Mn)	Astro Data
☽0S 4 13:08	⚳ ♈ 15 8:00	1 6:31 ☿ ☍	♍ 1 14:12	2 14:19 ♄ □	♏ 2 16:36	2 13:35 ○ 11♍45	1 March 1961
☿D 6 23:16	♃ ♒ 15 8:01	3 21:09 ♃ △	♎ 4 1:21	4 20:35 ♄ ⚹	♐ 4 22:34	2 13:28 ☍ P 0.800	Julian Day # 22340
☽0N 17 11:39	☿ ♓ 18 10:16	6 7:14 ♃ □	♏ 6 10:24	6 16:43 ☿ □	♑ 7 2:52	10 2:57 ☾ 19♐18	SVP 5♓48'13"
♀R 20 20:13	☉ ♈ 20 20:32	8 14:50 ♃ ⚹	♐ 8 17:04	9 4:32 ♄ ☌	♒ 9 6:03	16 18:51 ● 25♓57	GC 26♐17.8 ⚴ 26♒38.2
☉0N 20 20:33		10 16:27 ♀ △	♑ 10 21:19	10 18:47 ♅ ☍	♓ 11 8:31	24 2:48 ☽ 3♋14	Eris 9♈31.4 ⚵ 14♒12.8
☽0S 31 19:53	☿ ♈ 10 9:22	12 22:46 ♃ ☌	♒ 12 23:29	13 9:44 ♄ ⚹	♈ 13 10:55		⚷ 2♓35.8 ⚶ 18♓34.9
	☉ ♉ 20 7:55	14 21:51 ♀ ⚹	♓ 15 0:26	15 13:12 ♄ □	♉ 15 14:16	1 5:47 ○ 11♎16	☽ Mean ☊ 6♍11.5
☿0N 13 15:18	☿ ♉ 26 14:34	16 21:34 ♄ ⚹	♈ 17 1:32	17 18:56 ♄ △	♊ 17 19:55	8 10:16 ☾ 18♑21	
☽0N 13 21:13		19 2:45 ♀ ☌	♉ 19 4:25	20 4:34 ☉ ⚹	♋ 20 4:50	15 5:37 ● 25♈01	1 April 1961
♃⊼♇ 24 16:25		21 6:42 ♄ △	♊ 21 10:32	22 15:57 ♄ ☍	♌ 22 16:43	22 21:49 ☽ 2♌31	Julian Day # 22371
☽0S 28 4:24		23 18:14 ♀ ⚹	♋ 23 20:22	24 22:42 ☿ △	♍ 25 5:31	30 18:40 ○ 10♏10	SVP 5♓48'11"
♅D 29 7:50		26 5:45 ♀ □	♌ 26 8:48	27 16:04 ♄ △	♎ 27 16:34		GC 26♐17.9 ⚴ 6♓32.6
⚳0N 29 22:57		28 17:07 ♀ △	♍ 28 21:30	30 0:03 ♄ □	♏ 30 0:27		Eris 9♈52.0 ⚵ 26♒42.7
		31 5:41 ♄ △	♎ 31 8:21				⚷ 4♓32.6 ⚶ 3♈28.4
							☽ Mean ☊ 4♍33.0

LONGITUDE — May 1961

Day	Sid.Time	☉	0 hr ☽	Noon ☽	True ☊	☿	♀	♂	⚳	♃	♄	♅	♆	♇
1 M	2 36 42	10♉52 03	13♏10 17	19♏59 28	3♍51.7	10♉18.7	12♈44.8	27♋40.5	18♈33.3	6♒14.1	29♑48.0	21♌39.4	9♏55.6	5♍36.0
2 Tu	2 40 39	11 50 14	26 52 32	3♐49 01	3R40.9	12 27.9	12D44.4	28 10.9	18 56.4	6 18.5	29 48.8	21 39.5	9R53.9	5R35.5
3 W	2 44 35	12 48 23	10♐48 23	17 50 05	3 31.1	14 37.5	12 46.3	28 41.5	19 19.6	6 22.7	29 49.4	21 39.7	9 52.3	5 35.1
4 Th	2 48 32	13 46 31	24 53 36	1♑58 22	3 23.3	16 47.4	12 50.6	29 12.2	19 42.7	6 26.7	29 50.0	21 40.0	9 50.7	5 34.7
5 F	2 52 28	14 44 37	9♑03 56	16 09 52	3 18.0	18 57.3	12 57.1	29 43.0	20 05.8	6 30.6	29 50.4	21 40.3	9 49.0	5 34.4
6 Sa	2 56 25	15 42 42	23 15 46	0♒21 21	3 15.2	21 06.8	13 05.8	0♌13.9	20 28.8	6 34.2	29 50.8	21 40.7	9 47.4	5 34.0
7 Su	3 00 21	16 40 45	7♒26 23	14 30 40	3D14.4	23 15.8	13 16.8	0 44.9	20 51.8	6 37.7	29 51.1	21 41.1	9 45.8	5 33.7
8 M	3 04 18	17 38 48	21 34 05	28 36 30	3R14.5	25 23.9	13 29.8	1 16.1	21 14.8	6 41.1	29 51.2	21 41.5	9 44.2	5 33.4
9 Tu	3 08 14	18 36 48	5♓37 50	12♓37 59	3 14.3	27 30.8	13 44.8	1 47.4	21 37.7	6 44.2	29R51.3	21 42.1	9 42.6	5 33.2
10 W	3 12 11	19 34 48	19 36 52	26 34 20	3 12.6	29 36.3	14 01.8	2 18.7	22 00.6	6 47.2	29 51.3	21 42.6	9 40.9	5 33.0
11 Th	3 16 08	20 32 46	3♈30 14	10♈24 22	3 08.4	1♊40.1	14 20.7	2 50.2	22 23.5	6 49.9	29 51.1	21 43.2	9 39.3	5 32.8
12 F	3 20 04	21 30 43	17 16 29	24 06 20	3 01.4	3 41.9	14 41.4	3 21.8	22 46.3	6 52.5	29 50.9	21 43.9	9 37.7	5 32.6
13 Sa	3 24 01	22 28 38	0♉53 36	7♉37 59	2 51.6	5 41.5	15 03.9	3 53.5	23 09.1	6 55.0	29 50.6	21 44.7	9 36.2	5 32.5
14 Su	3 27 57	23 26 32	14 19 12	20 56 56	2 39.9	7 38.6	15 28.1	4 25.3	23 31.8	6 57.2	29 50.2	21 45.5	9 34.6	5 32.4
15 M	3 31 54	24 24 25	27 30 57	4♊01 03	2 27.2	9 33.3	15 54.0	4 57.2	23 54.5	6 59.2	29 49.7	21 46.3	9 33.0	5 32.3
16 Tu	3 35 50	25 22 16	10♊27 05	16 48 59	2 14.7	11 25.2	16 21.4	5 29.2	24 17.1	7 01.1	29 49.0	21 47.2	9 31.4	5D32.3
17 W	3 39 47	26 20 05	23 06 46	29 20 31	2 03.5	13 14.2	16 50.4	6 01.4	24 39.7	7 02.7	29 48.3	21 48.1	9 29.9	5 32.3
18 Th	3 43 43	27 17 53	5♋30 24	11♋36 43	1 54.6	15 00.3	17 20.8	6 33.6	25 02.3	7 04.2	29 47.5	21 49.1	9 28.3	5 32.3
19 F	3 47 40	28 15 40	17 39 46	23 39 58	1 48.3	16 43.3	17 52.6	7 05.9	25 24.8	7 05.5	29 46.6	21 50.2	9 26.8	5 32.4
20 Sa	3 51 37	29 13 25	29 37 47	5♌33 47	1 44.6	18 23.2	18 25.8	7 38.3	25 47.3	7 06.6	29 45.6	21 51.3	9 25.3	5 32.5
21 Su	3 55 33	0♊11 08	11♌28 31	17 22 37	1 43.0	20 00.0	19 00.3	8 10.8	26 09.7	7 07.5	29 44.5	21 52.4	9 23.8	5 32.6
22 M	3 59 30	1 08 49	23 16 44	29 11 33	1 42.7	21 33.5	19 36.0	8 43.3	26 32.0	7 08.2	29 43.3	21 53.6	9 22.3	5 32.7
23 Tu	4 03 26	2 06 29	5♍07 45	11♍06 01	1 42.6	23 03.7	20 13.0	9 16.0	26 54.3	7 08.7	29 42.1	21 54.9	9 20.8	5 32.9
24 W	4 07 23	3 04 08	17 07 03	23 11 30	1 41.7	24 30.6	20 51.1	9 48.8	27 16.6	7 09.1	29 40.7	21 56.2	9 19.3	5 33.1
25 Th	4 11 19	4 01 45	29 20 00	5♎33 06	1 38.9	25 54.1	21 30.3	10 21.6	27 38.8	7R09.2	29 39.2	21 57.6	9 17.9	5 33.3
26 F	4 15 16	4 59 20	11♎51 20	18 15 07	1 33.7	27 14.2	22 10.6	10 54.5	28 00.9	7 09.2	29 37.7	21 59.0	9 16.4	5 33.6
27 Sa	4 19 12	5 56 55	24 44 46	1♏20 29	1 26.0	28 30.9	22 51.9	11 27.5	28 23.0	7 08.9	29 36.0	22 00.4	9 15.0	5 33.9
28 Su	4 23 09	6 54 27	8♏02 21	14 50 16	1 16.0	29 44.1	23 34.3	12 00.6	28 45.1	7 08.5	29 34.3	22 01.9	9 13.6	5 34.2
29 M	4 27 06	7 51 59	21 44 02	28 43 16	1 04.7	0♋53.7	24 17.6	12 33.8	29 07.0	7 07.9	29 32.5	22 03.5	9 12.2	5 34.6
30 Tu	4 31 02	8 49 30	5♐47 26	12♐55 53	0 53.2	1 59.7	25 01.8	13 07.0	29 29.0	7 07.1	29 30.6	22 05.1	9 10.8	5 35.0
31 W	4 34 59	9 46 59	20 07 52	27 22 34	0 42.7	3 02.0	25 46.9	13 40.3	29 50.8	7 06.1	29 28.6	22 06.7	9 09.5	5 35.4

LONGITUDE — June 1961

Day	Sid.Time	☉	0 hr ☽	Noon ☽	True ☊	☿	♀	♂	⚳	♃	♄	♅	♆	♇
1 Th	4 38 55	10♊44 28	4♑39 05	11♑56 35	0♍34.2	4♋00.6	26♈32.9	14♌13.7	0♉12.6	7♒05.0	29♑26.5	22♌08.4	9♏08.1	5♍35.8
2 F	4 42 52	11 41 56	19 14 14	26 31 16	0R28.3	4 55.4	27 19.7	14 47.2	0 34.4	7R03.6	29R24.3	22 10.2	9R06.8	5 36.3
3 Sa	4 46 48	12 39 23	3♒47 01	11♒00 54	0 25.2	5 46.3	28 07.2	15 20.8	0 56.1	7 02.0	29 22.1	22 12.0	9 05.5	5 36.8
4 Su	4 50 45	13 36 49	18 12 29	25 21 25	0D24.1	6 33.3	28 55.6	15 54.4	1 17.7	7 00.3	29 19.7	22 13.8	9 04.2	5 37.3
5 M	4 54 41	14 34 14	2♓27 29	9♓30 30	0R24.1	7 16.1	29 44.7	16 28.1	1 39.2	6 58.4	29 17.3	22 15.7	9 03.0	5 37.9
6 Tu	4 58 38	15 31 39	16 30 26	23 27 14	0 24.0	7 54.9	0♉34.5	17 01.9	2 00.7	6 56.3	29 14.8	22 17.6	9 01.7	5 38.5
7 W	5 02 35	16 29 04	0♈20 58	7♈11 38	0 22.5	8 29.4	1 25.0	17 35.7	2 22.2	6 54.0	29 12.2	22 19.6	9 00.5	5 39.1
8 Th	5 06 31	17 26 27	13 59 19	20 44 02	0 18.8	8 59.7	2 16.1	18 09.6	2 43.5	6 51.5	29 09.6	22 21.6	8 59.3	5 39.8
9 F	5 10 28	18 23 51	27 25 50	4♉04 43	0 12.4	9 25.5	3 07.9	18 43.6	3 04.8	6 48.8	29 06.8	22 23.7	8 58.1	5 40.4
10 Sa	5 14 24	19 21 13	10♉40 40	17 13 40	0 03.5	9 46.9	4 00.2	19 17.7	3 26.0	6 45.9	29 04.0	22 25.8	8 56.9	5 41.1
11 Su	5 18 21	20 18 35	23 43 39	0♊10 35	29♌52.7	10 03.8	4 53.1	19 51.9	3 47.2	6 42.9	29 01.1	22 27.9	8 55.8	5 41.9
12 M	5 22 17	21 15 57	6♊34 23	12 55 01	29 40.9	10 16.2	5 46.6	20 26.1	4 08.2	6 39.7	28 58.2	22 30.1	8 54.7	5 42.6
13 Tu	5 26 14	22 13 18	19 12 29	25 26 45	29 29.3	10 24.0	6 40.7	21 00.4	4 29.2	6 36.3	28 55.1	22 32.4	8 53.6	5 43.4
14 W	5 30 10	23 10 38	1♋37 52	7♋45 57	29 18.9	10R27.2	7 35.2	21 34.7	4 50.1	6 32.7	28 52.0	22 34.6	8 52.5	5 44.3
15 Th	5 34 07	24 07 58	13 51 06	19 53 33	29 10.5	10 25.9	8 30.3	22 09.2	5 11.0	6 29.0	28 48.9	22 37.0	8 51.5	5 45.1
16 F	5 38 04	25 05 16	25 53 30	1♌51 19	29 04.6	10 20.2	9 25.8	22 43.7	5 31.7	6 25.1	28 45.6	22 39.3	8 50.5	5 46.0
17 Sa	5 42 00	26 02 34	7♌47 19	13 41 58	29 01.2	10 10.1	10 21.8	23 18.2	5 52.4	6 21.0	28 42.3	22 41.7	8 49.5	5 46.9
18 Su	5 45 57	26 59 52	19 35 42	25 29 05	28D59.9	9 55.8	11 18.2	23 52.9	6 13.0	6 16.7	28 38.9	22 44.2	8 48.5	5 47.8
19 M	5 49 53	27 57 08	1♍22 38	7♍16 59	29 00.1	9 37.6	12 15.1	24 27.6	6 33.5	6 12.3	28 35.5	22 46.7	8 47.6	5 48.8
20 Tu	5 53 50	28 54 24	13 12 46	19 10 37	29R00.8	9 15.8	13 12.3	25 02.3	6 53.9	6 07.7	28 32.0	22 49.2	8 46.6	5 49.8
21 W	5 57 46	29 51 39	25 11 14	1♎15 15	29 01.2	8 50.5	14 10.0	25 37.2	7 14.2	6 03.0	28 28.4	22 51.7	8 45.8	5 50.8
22 Th	6 01 43	0♋48 53	7♎23 21	13 36 09	29 00.3	8 22.3	15 08.1	26 12.1	7 34.4	5 58.1	28 24.8	22 54.3	8 44.9	5 51.8
23 F	6 05 39	1 46 07	19 54 15	26 18 11	28 57.5	7 51.6	16 06.6	26 47.0	7 54.6	5 53.0	28 21.1	22 57.0	8 44.1	5 52.9
24 Sa	6 09 36	2 43 20	2♏48 23	9♏25 12	28 52.7	7 18.8	17 05.4	27 22.0	8 14.6	5 47.8	28 17.4	22 59.6	8 43.2	5 54.0
25 Su	6 13 33	3 40 33	16 08 52	22 59 26	28 46.0	6 44.5	18 04.6	27 57.1	8 34.6	5 42.5	28 13.6	23 02.3	8 42.5	5 55.1
26 M	6 17 29	4 37 45	29 56 49	7♐00 46	28 38.1	6 09.3	19 04.1	28 32.2	8 54.4	5 37.0	28 09.8	23 05.1	8 41.7	5 56.2
27 Tu	6 21 26	5 34 57	14♐10 48	21 26 18	28 29.8	5 33.8	20 04.0	29 07.4	9 14.2	5 31.4	28 05.9	23 07.9	8 41.0	5 57.4
28 W	6 25 22	6 32 08	28 46 29	6♑10 25	28 22.3	4 58.5	21 04.2	29 42.7	9 33.9	5 25.6	28 02.0	23 10.7	8 40.3	5 58.6
29 Th	6 29 19	7 29 19	13♑37 04	21 05 22	28 16.2	4 24.1	22 04.7	0♍18.0	9 53.4	5 19.7	27 58.0	23 13.5	8 39.6	5 59.8
30 F	6 33 15	8 26 31	28 34 12	6♒02 30	28 12.3	3 51.2	23 05.6	0 53.3	10 12.9	5 13.7	27 54.0	23 16.4	8 39.0	6 01.0

Astro Data (Dy Hr Mn)

♀ D 2 4:15
♄ R 9 16:21
☽ 0N 11 5:02
♇ D 17 4:24
☽ 0S 25 14:13
♃ R 25 18:35

☽ 0N 7 11:38
☿ R 14 17:07
☽ 0S 21 23:57
♃⚻♇ 23 12:41

Planet Ingress (Dy Hr Mn)

♂ ♌ 6 1:13
☿ ♊ 10 16:34
☉ ♊ 21 7:22
☿ ♋ 28 17:23
⚳ ♉ 31 22:05

♀ ♉ 5 19:25
☊ ♌R 10 20:06
☉ ♋ 21 15:30
♂ ♍ 28 23:47

Last Aspect / ☽ Ingress (May)

Dy Hr Mn	Aspect	☽ Ingress	Dy Hr Mn
2 5:05	♄ ✶	♐	2 5:25
3 18:31	♅ △	♑	4 8:40
6 11:08	♄ ☌	♒	6 11:24
8 5:33	☿ □	♓	8 14:23
10 17:41	♄ ✶	♈	10 17:56
12 22:09	♄ □	♉	12 22:25
15 4:16	♄ △	♊	15 4:34
16 21:28	♅ ✶	♋	17 13:17
20 0:17	♄ ☍	♌	20 0:45
21 21:10	♅ ☌	♍	22 13:38
25 0:39	♄ △	♎	25 1:18
27 8:51	♄ □	♏	27 9:34
29 13:24	♄ ✶	♐	29 14:11
31 9:13	♀ △	♑	31 16:20

Last Aspect / ☽ Ingress (June)

Dy Hr Mn	Aspect	☽ Ingress	Dy Hr Mn
2 16:45	♄ ☌	♒	2 17:45
4 18:23	♀ ✶	♓	4 19:50
6 22:03	♄ ✶	♈	6 23:23
9 3:04	♄ □	♉	9 4:38
11 9:51	♄ △	♊	11 11:40
13 6:23	♅ ✶	♋	13 20:50
16 5:48	♄ ☍	♌	16 8:16
18 15:21	☉ ✶	♍	18 21:12
21 9:01	☉ □	♎	21 9:32
23 15:47	♄ □	♏	23 18:51
25 21:01	♄ ✶	♐	26 0:05
28 1:05	♂ △	♑	28 2:00
29 22:59	♄ ☌	♒	30 2:18

☽ Phases & Eclipses (Dy Hr Mn)

7 15:57 ☾ 16♒50
14 16:54 ● 23♉38
22 16:18 ☽ 1♍19
30 4:37 ○ 8♐32

5 21:19 ☾ 14♓57
13 5:16 ● 21♊57
21 9:01 ☽ 29♍45
28 12:37 ○ 6♑34

Astro Data

1 May 1961
Julian Day # 22401
SVP 5♓48'08"
GC 26♐18.0 ⚴ 15♓02.9
Eris 10♈11.9 ⚵ 8♓11.5
⚷ 5♓57.6 ⚶ 17♈26.1
☽ Mean ☊ 2♍57.6

1 June 1961
Julian Day # 22432
SVP 5♓48'04"
GC 26♐18.0 ⚴ 21♓55.6
Eris 10♈27.3 ⚵ 18♓45.5
⚷ 6♓39.6 ⚶ 1♉06.2
☽ Mean ☊ 1♍19.1

July 1961 — LONGITUDE

Day	Sid.Time	☉	0 hr ☽	Noon ☽	True ☊	☿	♀	♂	⚳	♃	♄	♅	♆	♇
1 Sa	6 37 12	9♋23 42	13♒29 17	20♒53 40	28♌10.5	3♋20.3	24♉06.7	1♍28.8	10♉32.3	5♒07.6	27♑50.0	23♌19.3	8♏38.4	6♍02.3
2 Su	6 41 09	10 20 53	28 14 52	5♓32 19	28D 10.5	2R 52.0	25 08.2	2 04.3	10 51.5	5R 01.3	27R 45.9	23 22.3	8R 37.8	6 03.6
3 M	6 45 05	11 18 05	12♓45 30	19 54 08	28 11.5	2 26.9	26 09.9	2 39.8	11 10.7	4 54.9	27 41.8	23 25.3	8 37.2	6 04.9
4 Tu	6 49 02	12 15 16	26 57 59	3♈56 59	28R 12.5	2 05.2	27 11.9	3 15.4	11 29.7	4 48.4	27 37.6	23 28.3	8 36.7	6 06.2
5 W	6 52 58	13 12 28	10♈51 08	17 40 32	28 12.7	1 47.5	28 14.2	3 51.1	11 48.6	4 41.8	27 33.4	23 31.3	8 36.2	6 07.6
6 Th	6 56 55	14 09 41	24 25 17	1♉05 36	28 11.3	1 34.1	29 16.8	4 26.8	12 07.5	4 35.1	27 29.2	23 34.4	8 35.7	6 08.9
7 F	7 00 51	15 06 53	7♉41 39	14 13 40	28 08.1	1 25.3	0♊19.6	5 02.6	12 26.2	4 28.2	27 24.9	23 37.5	8 35.3	6 10.3
8 Sa	7 04 48	16 04 06	20 41 52	27 06 26	28 03.2	1D 21.2	1 22.6	5 38.4	12 44.7	4 21.3	27 20.6	23 40.6	8 34.9	6 11.8
9 Su	7 08 44	17 01 20	3♊27 35	9♊45 29	27 56.8	1 22.1	2 25.9	6 14.3	13 03.2	4 14.3	27 16.3	23 43.7	8 34.5	6 13.2
10 M	7 12 41	17 58 34	16 00 20	22 12 18	27 49.8	1 28.2	3 29.4	6 50.3	13 21.6	4 07.2	27 12.0	23 46.9	8 34.2	6 14.7
11 Tu	7 16 38	18 55 48	28 21 32	4♋28 11	27 42.9	1 39.5	4 33.1	7 26.3	13 39.8	4 00.0	27 07.6	23 50.1	8 33.9	6 16.2
12 W	7 20 34	19 53 02	10♋32 26	16 34 27	27 36.7	1 56.1	5 37.1	8 02.4	13 57.9	3 52.7	27 03.2	23 53.4	8 33.6	6 17.7
13 Th	7 24 31	20 50 17	22 34 25	28 32 33	27 31.9	2 18.0	6 41.3	8 38.5	14 15.8	3 45.4	26 58.8	23 56.6	8 33.4	6 19.2
14 F	7 28 27	21 47 32	4♌29 05	10♌24 17	27 28.7	2 45.3	7 45.6	9 14.7	14 33.6	3 38.0	26 54.4	23 59.9	8 33.1	6 20.8
15 Sa	7 32 24	22 44 47	16 18 26	22 11 53	27D 27.3	3 17.9	8 50.2	9 51.0	14 51.3	3 30.5	26 50.0	24 03.2	8 33.0	6 22.3
16 Su	7 36 20	23 42 02	28 04 58	3♍58 08	27 27.3	3 55.8	9 55.0	10 27.3	15 08.9	3 23.0	26 45.6	24 06.6	8 32.8	6 23.9
17 M	7 40 17	24 39 18	9♍51 48	15 46 27	27 28.5	4 39.0	10 59.9	11 03.7	15 26.3	3 15.4	26 41.2	24 09.9	8 32.7	6 25.5
18 Tu	7 44 13	25 36 34	21 42 36	27 40 47	27 30.1	5 27.5	12 05.1	11 40.1	15 43.6	3 07.8	26 36.7	24 13.3	8 32.6	6 27.2
19 W	7 48 10	26 33 49	3♎41 34	9♎45 33	27 31.7	6 21.1	13 10.4	12 16.6	16 00.7	3 00.2	26 32.3	24 16.7	8 32.5	6 28.8
20 Th	7 52 07	27 31 06	15 53 18	22 05 26	27R 32.7	7 19.9	14 15.9	12 53.1	16 17.7	2 52.5	26 27.9	24 20.1	8D 32.5	6 30.5
21 F	7 56 03	28 28 22	28 22 30	4♏45 04	27 32.6	8 23.7	15 21.6	13 29.7	16 34.5	2 44.8	26 23.4	24 23.6	8 32.5	6 32.1
22 Sa	8 00 00	29 25 39	11♏13 37	17 48 34	27 31.4	9 32.5	16 27.5	14 06.3	16 51.2	2 37.0	26 19.0	24 27.1	8 32.6	6 33.8
23 Su	8 03 56	0♌22 56	24 30 16	1♐18 56	27 29.0	10 46.2	17 33.5	14 43.0	17 07.7	2 29.3	26 14.6	24 30.5	8 32.6	6 35.6
24 M	8 07 53	1 20 13	8♐14 40	15 17 22	27 25.9	12 04.7	18 39.7	15 19.8	17 24.1	2 21.5	26 10.2	24 34.0	8 32.7	6 37.3
25 Tu	8 11 49	2 17 31	22 26 49	29 42 35	27 22.4	13 27.8	19 46.0	15 56.6	17 40.3	2 13.7	26 05.8	24 37.6	8 32.9	6 39.0
26 W	8 15 46	3 14 50	7♑06 40	14♑30 25	27 19.2	14 55.4	20 52.5	16 33.4	17 56.4	2 06.0	26 01.4	24 41.1	8 33.0	6 40.8
27 Th	8 19 42	4 12 08	22 00 44	29 33 57	27 16.8	16 27.5	21 59.2	17 10.3	18 12.3	1 58.2	25 57.0	24 44.7	8 33.2	6 42.6
28 F	8 23 39	5 09 28	7♒08 54	14♒44 22	27D 15.3	18 03.7	23 06.0	17 47.3	18 28.0	1 50.5	25 52.7	24 48.2	8 33.5	6 44.4
29 Sa	8 27 36	6 06 49	22 19 09	29 52 06	27 15.0	19 43.8	24 13.0	18 24.3	18 43.5	1 42.7	25 48.3	24 51.8	8 33.7	6 46.2
30 Su	8 31 32	7 04 10	7♓22 11	14♓48 26	27 15.6	21 27.7	25 20.2	19 01.4	18 58.9	1 35.0	25 44.0	24 55.4	8 34.0	6 48.0
31 M	8 35 29	8 01 32	22 10 06	29 26 33	27 16.7	23 15.1	26 27.4	19 38.5	19 14.1	1 27.3	25 39.7	24 59.0	8 34.4	6 49.8

August 1961 — LONGITUDE

Day	Sid.Time	☉	0 hr ☽	Noon ☽	True ☊	☿	♀	♂	⚳	♃	♄	♅	♆	♇
1 Tu	8 39 25	8♌58 55	6♈37 19	13♈42 06	27♌17.9	25♋05.7	27♊34.9	20♍15.6	19♉29.2	1♒19.7	25♑35.5	25♌02.6	8♏34.7	6♍51.7
2 W	8 43 22	9 56 20	20 40 46	27 33 17	27 18.9	26 59.1	28 42.5	20 52.9	19 44.0	1R 12.0	25R 31.2	25 06.3	8 35.1	6 53.5
3 Th	8 47 18	10 53 46	4♉19 45	11♉00 21	27R 19.2	28 55.0	29 50.2	21 30.2	19 58.7	1 04.5	25 27.0	25 09.9	8 35.5	6 55.4
4 F	8 51 15	11 51 13	17 35 21	24 05 03	27 18.9	0♌53.1	0♋58.1	22 07.5	20 13.2	0 56.9	25 22.8	25 13.6	8 36.0	6 57.3
5 Sa	8 55 11	12 48 41	0♊29 49	6♊50 01	27 17.8	2 53.0	2 06.1	22 44.9	20 27.5	0 49.5	25 18.7	25 17.3	8 36.5	6 59.2
6 Su	8 59 08	13 46 10	13 06 03	19 18 19	27 16.3	4 54.4	3 14.2	23 22.3	20 41.5	0 42.0	25 14.6	25 20.9	8 37.0	7 01.1
7 M	9 03 05	14 43 41	25 27 11	1♋33 02	27 14.5	6 56.8	4 22.5	23 59.8	20 55.4	0 34.7	25 10.6	25 24.6	8 37.6	7 03.0
8 Tu	9 07 01	15 41 13	7♋36 15	13 37 10	27 12.8	9 00.0	5 30.9	24 37.4	21 09.1	0 27.4	25 06.5	25 28.3	8 38.2	7 05.0
9 W	9 10 58	16 38 46	19 36 06	25 33 24	27 11.3	11 03.7	6 39.4	25 15.0	21 22.6	0 20.2	25 02.6	25 32.0	8 38.8	7 06.9
10 Th	9 14 54	17 36 21	1♌29 20	7♌24 13	27 10.3	13 07.4	7 48.0	25 52.7	21 35.9	0 13.1	24 58.6	25 35.8	8 39.4	7 08.9
11 F	9 18 51	18 33 56	13 18 19	19 11 56	27D 09.7	15 11.1	8 56.8	26 30.4	21 48.9	0 06.1	24 54.7	25 39.5	8 40.1	7 10.8
12 Sa	9 22 47	19 31 33	25 05 20	0♍58 49	27 09.7	17 14.3	10 05.7	27 08.2	22 01.8	29♑59.1	24 50.9	25 43.2	8 40.8	7 12.8
13 Su	9 26 44	20 29 11	6♍52 40	12 47 11	27 09.9	19 17.1	11 14.7	27 46.0	22 14.4	29 52.3	24 47.1	25 46.9	8 41.6	7 14.8
14 M	9 30 40	21 26 50	18 42 43	24 39 35	27 10.4	21 19.0	12 23.8	28 23.9	22 26.8	29 45.5	24 43.4	25 50.7	8 42.3	7 16.8
15 Tu	9 34 37	22 24 30	0♎38 10	6♎38 50	27 11.0	23 20.1	13 33.0	29 01.9	22 39.0	29 38.9	24 39.7	25 54.4	8 43.1	7 18.8
16 W	9 38 33	23 22 11	12 41 59	18 48 03	27 11.5	25 20.1	14 42.4	29 39.9	22 50.9	29 32.3	24 36.1	25 58.2	8 44.0	7 20.8
17 Th	9 42 30	24 19 53	24 57 28	1♏10 42	27 11.8	27 19.1	15 51.8	0♎17.9	23 02.6	29 25.9	24 32.5	26 01.9	8 44.8	7 22.8
18 F	9 46 27	25 17 36	7♏28 10	13 50 20	27 11.9	29 16.8	17 01.3	0 56.0	23 14.1	29 19.6	24 29.0	26 05.6	8 45.7	7 24.8
19 Sa	9 50 23	26 15 20	20 17 38	26 50 27	27 12.0	1♍13.3	18 11.0	1 34.2	23 25.3	29 13.5	24 25.6	26 09.4	8 46.6	7 26.8
20 Su	9 54 20	27 13 06	3♐29 08	10♐13 59	27 12.0	3 08.6	19 20.8	2 12.4	23 36.2	29 07.4	24 22.2	26 13.1	8 47.6	7 28.8
21 M	9 58 16	28 10 52	17 05 11	24 02 51	27 12.0	5 02.5	20 30.6	2 50.7	23 47.0	29 01.5	24 18.9	26 16.9	8 48.6	7 30.9
22 Tu	10 02 13	29 08 40	1♑06 55	8♑17 15	27 12.2	6 55.0	21 40.6	3 29.0	23 57.4	28 55.7	24 15.7	26 20.6	8 49.6	7 32.9
23 W	10 06 09	0♍06 29	15 33 30	22 55 10	27 12.4	8 46.2	22 50.7	4 07.4	24 07.6	28 50.1	24 12.5	26 24.4	8 50.7	7 34.9
24 Th	10 10 06	1 04 19	0♒21 36	7♒51 59	27 12.7	10 36.1	24 00.8	4 45.8	24 17.6	28 44.6	24 09.4	26 28.1	8 51.7	7 37.0
25 F	10 14 03	2 02 11	15 25 19	23 00 48	27R 12.8	12 24.6	25 11.1	5 24.3	24 27.3	28 39.3	24 06.4	26 31.9	8 52.8	7 39.0
26 Sa	10 17 59	3 00 03	0♓36 31	8♓12 02	27 12.7	14 11.8	26 21.5	6 02.8	24 36.7	28 34.1	24 03.5	26 35.6	8 54.0	7 41.1
27 Su	10 21 56	3 57 58	15 45 52	23 16 56	27 12.4	15 57.6	27 32.0	6 41.4	24 45.9	28 29.0	24 00.6	26 39.3	8 55.1	7 43.1
28 M	10 25 52	4 55 54	0♈44 08	8♈06 35	27 11.7	17 42.2	28 42.5	7 20.0	24 54.7	28 24.1	23 57.8	26 43.0	8 56.3	7 45.2
29 Tu	10 29 49	5 53 52	15 23 31	22 34 20	27 10.7	19 25.4	29 53.2	7 58.7	25 03.3	28 19.4	23 55.1	26 46.7	8 57.5	7 47.2
30 W	10 33 45	6 51 51	29 38 37	6♉36 07	27 09.7	21 07.3	1♌04.0	8 37.4	25 11.6	28 14.8	23 52.4	26 50.4	8 58.8	7 49.3
31 Th	10 37 42	7 49 53	13♉26 46	20 10 37	27 08.8	22 48.0	2 14.9	9 16.2	25 19.6	28 10.4	23 49.8	26 54.1	9 00.0	7 51.4

Astro Data

	Dy Hr Mn
☽0N	4 18:20
☿D	8 19:37
☽0S	19 8:16
♆D	20 18:48
☽0N	1 2:17
♄⚻♅	5 16:29
☽0S	15 14:47
♂0S	19 2:44
☽0N	28 11:53

Planet Ingress

		Dy Hr Mn
♀	♊	7 4:32
☉	♌	23 2:24
♀	♋	3 15:28
☿	♌	4 1:15
♃	♑R	12 8:54
♂	♎	17 0:41
☿	♍	18 20:52
☉	♍	23 9:19
♀	♌	29 14:18

Last Aspect / ☽ Ingress

Last Aspect Dy Hr Mn			☽ Ingress	Dy Hr Mn
1 17:38	♀	□	♓	2 2:52
4 1:11	♄	⚹	♈	4 5:12
6 5:32	♄	□	♉	6 10:01
8 12:27	♄	△	♊	8 17:27
10 15:05	♅	⚹	♋	11 3:13
13 8:52	♄	☍	♌	13 14:56
15 15:48	♅	☌	♍	16 3:55
18 9:52	♄	△	♎	18 16:39
20 23:13	☉	□	♏	21 3:05
23 3:08	♄	⚹	♐	23 9:42
25 3:35	♅	△	♑	25 12:29
27 6:17	♄	☌	♒	27 12:41
29 4:00	♅	☍	♓	29 12:13
31 6:39	♀	□	♈	31 12:56

Last Aspect / ☽ Ingress

Last Aspect Dy Hr Mn			☽ Ingress	Dy Hr Mn
2 14:13	♀	⚹	♉	2 16:19
4 14:24	♄	△	♊	4 23:04
6 23:51	♅	⚹	♋	7 8:56
9 11:21	♂	⚹	♌	9 20:59
12 1:14	♅	☌	♍	12 10:00
14 22:09	♃	△	♎	14 22:44
17 8:40	♃	□	♏	17 9:44
19 16:17	♃	⚹	♐	19 17:44
21 19:33	☉	△	♑	21 22:07
23 21:29	♃	☌	♒	23 23:25
25 17:35	♅	☍	♓	25 23:02
27 20:19	♃	⚹	♈	27 22:49
29 21:42	♃	□	♉	30 0:37

☽ Phases & Eclipses

Dy Hr Mn		
5 3:32	☾	12♈52
12 19:11	●	20♋10
20 23:13	☽	27♎58
27 19:50	○	4♒31
3 11:47	☾	10♉53
11 10:36	●	18♌31
11 10:46:14	●	A 06'35"
19 10:51	☽	26♏13
26 3:13	○	2♓39
26 3:08	●	P 0.986

Astro Data

1 July 1961
Julian Day # 22462
SVP 5♓47'59"
GC 26♐18.1 ⚵ 25♓37.2
Eris 10♈33.9 ⚶ 26♓40.3
⚷ 6♓28.4R ⚴ 13♉12.8
☽ Mean ☊ 29♌43.8

1 August 1961
Julian Day # 22493
SVP 5♓47'54"
GC 26♐18.2 ⚵ 24♓51.5R
Eris 10♈30.6R ⚶ 0♈35.4
⚷ 5♓28.6R ⚴ 23♉55.6
☽ Mean ☊ 28♌05.4

LONGITUDE — September 1961

Day	Sid.Time	☉	0 hr ☽	Noon ☽	True ☊	☿	♀	♂	⚳	♃	♄	♅	♆	♇
1 F	10 41 38	8♍47 56	26♉47 51	3♊18 48	27♌08.3	24♍27.4	3♌25.9	9♎55.0	25♉27.4	28♑06.2	23♑47.3	26♌57.8	9♏01.3	7♍53.4
2 Sa	10 45 35	9 46 02	9♊43 49	16 03 21	27D08.4	26 05.6	4 36.9	10 34.0	25 34.8	28R02.1	23R44.9	27 01.5	9 02.7	7 55.5
3 Su	10 49 31	10 44 09	22 17 56	28 28 04	27 08.9	27 42.6	5 48.1	11 12.9	25 41.9	27 58.2	23 42.6	27 05.2	9 04.0	7 57.5
4 M	10 53 28	11 42 18	4♋34 17	10♋37 09	27 10.0	29 18.3	6 59.4	11 51.9	25 48.7	27 54.5	23 40.4	27 08.9	9 05.4	7 59.6
5 Tu	10 57 25	12 40 30	16 37 11	22 34 56	27 11.4	0♎52.9	8 10.7	12 31.0	25 55.2	27 50.9	23 38.2	27 12.5	9 06.8	8 01.6
6 W	11 01 21	13 38 43	28 30 54	4♌25 32	27 12.7	2 26.2	9 22.1	13 10.2	26 01.4	27 47.5	23 36.1	27 16.2	9 08.2	8 03.7
7 Th	11 05 18	14 36 58	10♌19 20	16 12 40	27R13.7	3 58.3	10 33.7	13 49.3	26 07.3	27 44.3	23 34.2	27 19.8	9 09.7	8 05.8
8 F	11 09 14	15 35 15	22 05 58	27 59 35	27 14.1	5 29.3	11 45.3	14 28.6	26 12.8	27 41.3	23 32.3	27 23.4	9 11.2	8 07.8
9 Sa	11 13 11	16 33 34	3♍53 50	9♍49 03	27 13.5	6 59.0	12 57.0	15 07.9	26 18.0	27 38.5	23 30.5	27 27.0	9 12.7	8 09.8
10 Su	11 17 07	17 31 54	15 45 28	21 43 23	27 12.0	8 27.6	14 08.7	15 47.3	26 22.9	27 35.9	23 28.8	27 30.6	9 14.2	8 11.9
11 M	11 21 04	18 30 16	27 43 01	3♎44 37	27 09.4	9 54.9	15 20.6	16 26.7	26 27.4	27 33.4	23 27.1	27 34.2	9 15.8	8 13.9
12 Tu	11 25 00	19 28 41	9♎48 22	15 54 31	27 06.1	11 21.1	16 32.5	17 06.1	26 31.6	27 31.2	23 25.6	27 37.7	9 17.3	8 15.9
13 W	11 28 57	20 27 06	22 03 16	28 14 51	27 02.3	12 45.9	17 44.5	17 45.7	26 35.4	27 29.1	23 24.2	27 41.3	9 18.9	8 18.0
14 Th	11 32 54	21 25 34	4♏29 27	10♏47 21	26 58.6	14 09.6	18 56.6	18 25.2	26 38.9	27 27.2	23 22.8	27 44.8	9 20.6	8 20.0
15 F	11 36 50	22 24 03	17 08 45	23 33 55	26 55.4	15 31.9	20 08.8	19 04.9	26 42.1	27 25.5	23 21.6	27 48.3	9 22.2	8 22.0
16 Sa	11 40 47	23 22 34	0♐03 06	6♐36 33	26 53.2	16 52.9	21 21.0	19 44.6	26 44.9	27 24.0	23 20.4	27 51.8	9 23.9	8 24.0
17 Su	11 44 43	24 21 07	13 14 30	19 57 10	26D52.2	18 12.6	22 33.3	20 24.3	26 47.3	27 22.7	23 19.4	27 55.2	9 25.6	8 26.0
18 M	11 48 40	25 19 41	26 44 45	3♑37 23	26 52.4	19 30.8	23 45.7	21 04.1	26 49.4	27 21.6	23 18.4	27 58.7	9 27.3	8 28.0
19 Tu	11 52 36	26 18 17	10♑35 09	17 38 04	26 53.5	20 47.6	24 58.2	21 44.0	26 51.1	27 20.7	23 17.6	28 02.1	9 29.0	8 30.0
20 W	11 56 33	27 16 54	24 46 02	1♒58 50	26 54.9	22 02.9	26 10.7	22 23.9	26 52.4	27 20.0	23 16.8	28 05.5	9 30.8	8 32.0
21 Th	12 00 29	28 15 34	9♒16 09	16 37 29	26R56.1	23 16.5	27 23.3	23 03.8	26 53.4	27 19.5	23 16.1	28 08.9	9 32.6	8 33.9
22 F	12 04 26	29 14 14	24 02 15	1♓29 41	26 56.3	24 28.5	28 36.0	23 43.8	26 54.0	27 19.2	23 15.6	28 12.2	9 34.4	8 35.9
23 Sa	12 08 23	0♎12 57	8♓58 55	16 28 56	26 55.1	25 38.7	29 48.7	24 23.9	26R54.2	27D19.1	23 15.1	28 15.5	9 36.2	8 37.8
24 Su	12 12 19	1 11 41	23 58 43	1♈27 10	26 52.2	26 47.0	1♍01.6	25 04.0	26 54.1	27 19.1	23 14.7	28 18.8	9 38.0	8 39.8
25 M	12 16 16	2 10 28	8♈53 11	16 15 44	26 47.8	27 53.3	2 14.4	25 44.2	26 53.6	27 19.4	23 14.4	28 22.1	9 39.9	8 41.7
26 Tu	12 20 12	3 09 16	23 33 53	0♉46 47	26 42.4	28 57.5	3 27.4	26 24.4	26 52.7	27 19.9	23 14.2	28 25.4	9 41.7	8 43.6
27 W	12 24 09	4 08 07	7♉53 48	14 54 24	26 36.7	29 59.3	4 40.4	27 04.7	26 51.4	27 20.5	23D14.2	28 28.6	9 43.6	8 45.5
28 Th	12 28 05	5 07 00	21 48 17	28 35 17	26 31.4	0♏58.7	5 53.5	27 45.0	26 49.7	27 21.4	23 14.2	28 31.8	9 45.5	8 47.4
29 F	12 32 02	6 05 55	5♊15 26	11♊48 52	26 27.3	1 55.5	7 06.7	28 25.4	26 47.7	27 22.4	23 14.3	28 35.0	9 47.5	8 49.3
30 Sa	12 35 58	7 04 53	18 15 53	24 36 53	26 24.7	2 49.3	8 19.9	29 05.9	26 45.3	27 23.6	23 14.5	28 38.1	9 49.4	8 51.2

LONGITUDE — October 1961

Day	Sid.Time	☉	0 hr ☽	Noon ☽	True ☊	☿	♀	♂	⚳	♃	♄	♅	♆	♇
1 Su	12 39 55	8♎03 52	0♋52 22	7♋02 52	26♌23.8	3♏40.0	9♍33.2	29♎46.4	26♉42.4	27♑25.1	23♑14.8	28♌41.2	9♏51.4	8♍53.0
2 M	12 43 51	9 02 55	13 09 00	19 11 23	26D24.3	4 27.4	10 46.6	0♏27.0	26R39.2	27 26.7	23 15.3	28 44.3	9 53.4	8 54.9
3 Tu	12 47 48	10 01 59	25 10 40	1♌07 30	26 25.7	5 11.0	12 00.0	1 07.6	26 35.6	27 28.5	23 15.8	28 47.4	9 55.3	8 56.7
4 W	12 51 45	11 01 06	7♌02 32	12 56 23	26 27.2	5 50.6	13 13.5	1 48.3	26 31.7	27 30.5	23 16.4	28 50.4	9 57.4	8 58.5
5 Th	12 55 41	12 00 14	18 49 39	24 42 54	26R28.0	6 25.8	14 27.0	2 29.1	26 27.3	27 32.7	23 17.1	28 53.4	9 59.4	9 00.3
6 F	12 59 38	12 59 26	0♍36 40	6♍31 25	26 27.4	6 56.1	15 40.6	3 09.9	26 22.5	27 35.1	23 17.9	28 56.3	10 01.4	9 02.1
7 Sa	13 03 34	13 58 39	12 27 37	18 25 39	26 24.8	7 21.3	16 54.3	3 50.7	26 17.4	27 37.7	23 18.8	28 59.3	10 03.5	9 03.9
8 Su	13 07 31	14 57 54	24 25 50	0♎28 28	26 20.0	7 40.8	18 08.0	4 31.7	26 11.8	27 40.5	23 19.8	29 02.1	10 05.5	9 05.6
9 M	13 11 27	15 57 12	6♎33 46	12 41 56	26 13.0	7 54.2	19 21.8	5 12.6	26 05.9	27 43.5	23 20.9	29 05.0	10 07.6	9 07.4
10 Tu	13 15 24	16 56 31	18 53 05	25 07 19	26 04.4	8R00.9	20 35.6	5 53.7	25 59.6	27 46.6	23 22.2	29 07.8	10 09.7	9 09.1
11 W	13 19 20	17 55 53	1♏24 39	7♏45 09	25 54.8	8 00.4	21 49.5	6 34.8	25 52.9	27 50.0	23 23.5	29 10.6	10 11.8	9 10.8
12 Th	13 23 17	18 55 16	14 08 46	20 35 31	25 45.2	7 52.4	23 03.4	7 15.9	25 45.9	27 53.5	23 24.9	29 13.3	10 13.9	9 12.4
13 F	13 27 14	19 54 42	27 05 22	3♐38 16	25 36.6	7 36.5	24 17.4	7 57.1	25 38.5	27 57.2	23 26.4	29 16.1	10 16.0	9 14.1
14 Sa	13 31 10	20 54 09	10♐14 15	16 53 16	25 29.8	7 12.2	25 31.4	8 38.4	25 30.7	28 01.1	23 28.0	29 18.7	10 18.2	9 15.8
15 Su	13 35 07	21 53 39	23 35 22	0♑20 34	25 25.3	6 39.4	26 45.5	9 19.7	25 22.6	28 05.2	23 29.7	29 21.4	10 20.3	9 17.4
16 M	13 39 03	22 53 10	7♑08 56	14 00 29	25D23.2	5 58.2	27 59.6	10 01.1	25 14.2	28 09.5	23 31.5	29 24.0	10 22.5	9 19.0
17 Tu	13 43 00	23 52 42	20 55 17	27 53 22	25 22.9	5 08.8	29 13.7	10 42.5	25 05.4	28 13.9	23 33.4	29 26.5	10 24.7	9 20.6
18 W	13 46 56	24 52 17	4♒54 44	11♒59 21	25R23.6	4 11.7	0♎27.9	11 24.0	24 56.2	28 18.5	23 35.4	29 29.0	10 26.8	9 22.1
19 Th	13 50 53	25 51 53	19 07 05	26 17 45	25 24.0	3 07.8	1 42.2	12 05.5	24 46.7	28 23.3	23 37.5	29 31.5	10 29.0	9 23.7
20 F	13 54 49	26 51 30	3♓31 04	10♓46 38	25 23.0	1 58.5	2 56.5	12 47.1	24 37.0	28 28.3	23 39.7	29 33.9	10 31.2	9 25.2
21 Sa	13 58 46	27 51 10	18 03 56	25 22 22	25 19.8	0 45.3	4 10.8	13 28.8	24 26.9	28 33.5	23 42.0	29 36.3	10 33.4	9 26.7
22 Su	14 02 43	28 50 51	2♈41 11	9♈59 35	25 13.9	29♎30.1	5 25.1	14 10.5	24 16.5	28 38.8	23 44.3	29 38.7	10 35.6	9 28.2
23 M	14 06 39	29 50 34	17 16 43	24 31 42	25 05.5	28 15.2	6 39.5	14 52.2	24 05.8	28 44.3	23 46.8	29 41.0	10 37.8	9 29.6
24 Tu	14 10 36	0♏50 19	1♉43 39	8♉51 44	24 55.3	27 02.7	7 54.0	15 34.0	23 54.8	28 49.9	23 49.4	29 43.2	10 40.0	9 31.1
25 W	14 14 32	1 50 06	15 55 14	22 53 32	24 44.2	25 55.0	9 08.5	16 15.9	23 43.5	28 55.7	23 52.0	29 45.4	10 42.3	9 32.5
26 Th	14 18 29	2 49 56	29 46 07	6♊32 40	24 33.7	24 54.1	10 23.0	16 57.8	23 32.0	29 01.7	23 54.8	29 47.6	10 44.5	9 33.9
27 F	14 22 25	3 49 47	13♊12 59	19 47 04	24 24.6	24 01.7	11 37.6	17 39.8	23 20.2	29 07.9	23 57.6	29 49.7	10 46.7	9 35.3
28 Sa	14 26 22	4 49 41	26 15 00	2♋37 03	24 17.8	23 19.3	12 52.2	18 21.9	23 08.2	29 14.2	24 00.5	29 51.8	10 48.9	9 36.6
29 Su	14 30 18	5 49 36	8♋53 35	15 05 03	24 13.5	22 47.7	14 06.8	19 04.0	22 55.9	29 20.7	24 03.6	29 53.9	10 51.2	9 37.9
30 M	14 34 15	6 49 34	21 11 59	27 14 59	24D11.5	22 27.6	15 21.5	19 46.1	22 43.5	29 27.3	24 06.7	29 55.9	10 53.4	9 39.2
31 Tu	14 38 12	7 49 34	3♌14 43	9♌11 51	24 11.1	22D19.0	16 36.2	20 28.3	22 30.8	29 34.1	24 09.9	29 57.8	10 55.7	9 40.5

Astro Data
Dy Hr Mn
☿0S 5 3:51
♃⊼♅ 11 8:59
☽0S 11 20:21
♄⊡♇ 15 8:48
☉0S 23 6:42
⚳R 23 15:02
♃D 23 15:27
☽0N 24 22:27
♄D 27 19:32

☽0S 9 2:37
☿R 10 22:42
♀0S 21 0:21
☽0N 22 8:42
☿D 31 18:02

Planet Ingress
Dy Hr Mn
☿ ♎ 4 22:32
☉ ♎ 23 6:42
♀ ♍ 23 15:43
☿ ♏ 27 12:16

♂ ♏ 1 20:02
♀ ♎ 18 2:58
☿ ♎R 22 2:29
☉ ♏ 23 15:47

Last Aspect / ☽ Ingress

Last Aspect Dy Hr Mn			☽ Ingress	Dy Hr Mn
1 2:26	♃	△	♊	1 5:52
3 10:18	☿	□	♋	3 15:00
5 22:36	♃	☍	♌	6 3:01
8 10:46	♅	☌	♍	8 16:05
10 23:43	♃	△	♎	11 4:33
13 10:55	♅	⚹	♏	13 15:23
15 19:54	♅	□	♐	15 23:54
18 2:07	♅	△	♑	18 5:42
20 4:17	♃	☌	♒	20 8:43
22 6:56	♀	☍	♓	22 9:36
24 5:21	♃	⚹	♈	24 9:40
26 8:43	☿	☍	♉	26 10:42
28 11:54	♅	□	♊	28 14:31
30 21:04	♂	△	♋	30 22:19

Last Aspect Dy Hr Mn			☽ Ingress	Dy Hr Mn
3 4:36	♃	☍	♌	3 9:43
5 20:32	♅	☌	♍	5 22:45
8 6:26	♃	△	♎	8 11:04
10 19:41	♅	⚹	♏	10 21:19
13 3:58	♅	□	♐	13 5:21
15 10:15	♅	△	♑	15 11:24
17 14:31	♀	△	♒	17 15:37
19 17:23	♅	☍	♓	19 18:10
21 17:15	♃	⚹	♈	21 19:36
23 20:36	♅	△	♉	23 21:07
26 0:01	♅	□	♊	26 0:24
28 6:47	♅	⚹	♋	28 7:03
30 16:27	♃	☍	♌	30 17:30

☽ Phases & Eclipses
Dy Hr Mn
1 23:05 ☾ 9♊15
10 2:50 ● 17♍10
17 20:23 ☽ 24♐42
24 11:33 ○ 1♈11

1 14:10 ☾ 8♋09
9 18:52 ● 16♎14
17 4:34 ☽ 23♑34
23 21:30 ○ 0♉14
31 8:58 ☾ 7♌42

Astro Data
1 September 1961
Julian Day # 22524
SVP 5♓47'51"
GC 26♐18.2 ⚵ 18♓54.0R
Eris 10♈18.1R ⚶ 28♓02.3R
⚷ 4♓01.5R ⚴ 1♊39.2
☽ Mean ☊ 26♌26.8

1 October 1961
Julian Day # 22554
SVP 5♓47'49"
GC 26♐18.3 ⚵ 11♓24.0R
Eris 10♈00.5R ⚶ 21♓06.3R
⚷ 2♓42.2R ⚴ 4♊28.9R
☽ Mean ☊ 24♌51.5

November 1961 — LONGITUDE

Day	Sid.Time	☉	0 hr ☽	Noon ☽	True ☊	☿	♀	♂	⚳	♃	♄	♅	♆	♇
1 W	14 42 08	8♏49 36	15♌07 05	21♌01 07	24♌11.3	22♎21.8	17♎51.0	21♏10.6	22♉17.9	29♑41.1	24♑13.1	29♌59.7	10♏57.9	9♍41.7
2 Th	14 46 05	9 49 40	26 54 38	2♍48 19	24R 11.1	22 35.5	19 05.8	21 52.9	22R 04.9	29 48.2	24 16.5	0♍01.5	11 00.2	9 42.9
3 F	14 50 01	10 49 47	8♍42 50	14 38 48	24 09.3	22 59.4	20 20.6	22 35.3	21 51.6	29 55.4	24 20.0	0 03.3	11 02.4	9 44.1
4 Sa	14 53 58	11 49 55	20 36 47	26 37 18	24 05.1	23 32.7	21 35.5	23 17.8	21 38.3	0♒02.9	24 23.5	0 05.1	11 04.7	9 45.3
5 Su	14 57 54	12 50 05	2♎40 48	8♎47 42	23 58.1	24 14.6	22 50.3	24 00.3	21 24.7	0 10.4	24 27.1	0 06.8	11 06.9	9 46.4
6 M	15 01 51	13 50 18	14 58 18	21 12 50	23 48.4	25 04.3	24 05.2	24 42.8	21 11.1	0 18.1	24 30.9	0 08.4	11 09.2	9 47.5
7 Tu	15 05 47	14 50 32	27 31 27	3♏54 13	23 36.4	26 00.7	25 20.2	25 25.5	20 57.4	0 26.0	24 34.7	0 10.0	11 11.4	9 48.6
8 W	15 09 44	15 50 48	10♏21 06	16 52 00	23 23.0	27 03.1	26 35.1	26 08.1	20 43.6	0 34.0	24 38.5	0 11.6	11 13.6	9 49.7
9 Th	15 13 40	16 51 06	23 26 46	0♐05 08	23 09.6	28 10.7	27 50.1	26 50.9	20 29.7	0 42.2	24 42.5	0 13.1	11 15.9	9 50.7
10 F	15 17 37	17 51 26	6♐46 52	13 31 37	22 57.4	29 22.8	29 05.2	27 33.7	20 15.7	0 50.5	24 46.5	0 14.5	11 18.1	9 51.7
11 Sa	15 21 34	18 51 47	20 19 05	27 08 57	22 47.5	0♏38.8	0♏20.2	28 16.5	20 01.7	0 58.9	24 50.7	0 15.9	11 20.4	9 52.7
12 Su	15 25 30	19 52 10	4♑00 56	10♑54 45	22 40.5	1 58.0	1 35.3	28 59.4	19 47.7	1 07.5	24 54.9	0 17.2	11 22.6	9 53.6
13 M	15 29 27	20 52 34	17 50 11	24 47 04	22 36.5	3 20.0	2 50.3	29 42.4	19 33.7	1 16.2	24 59.2	0 18.5	11 24.8	9 54.6
14 Tu	15 33 23	21 52 59	1♒45 14	8♒44 36	22D 34.9	4 44.4	4 05.4	0♐25.4	19 19.7	1 25.0	25 03.5	0 19.7	11 27.1	9 55.4
15 W	15 37 20	22 53 26	15 45 06	22 46 40	22R 34.6	6 10.7	5 20.5	1 08.4	19 05.8	1 34.0	25 08.0	0 20.9	11 29.3	9 56.3
16 Th	15 41 16	23 53 54	29 49 14	6♓52 45	22 34.4	7 38.6	6 35.7	1 51.6	18 51.8	1 43.1	25 12.5	0 22.0	11 31.5	9 57.1
17 F	15 45 13	24 54 23	13♓57 06	21 02 08	22 32.8	9 07.8	7 50.8	2 34.7	18 38.0	1 52.4	25 17.1	0 23.1	11 33.7	9 57.9
18 Sa	15 49 09	25 54 54	28 07 36	5♈13 14	22 28.8	10 38.1	9 06.0	3 17.9	18 24.2	2 01.7	25 21.7	0 24.1	11 35.9	9 58.7
19 Su	15 53 06	26 55 25	12♈18 40	19 23 28	22 21.8	12 09.3	10 21.2	4 01.2	18 10.5	2 11.2	25 26.5	0 25.1	11 38.1	9 59.4
20 M	15 57 03	27 55 59	26 27 07	3♉29 05	22 12.0	13 41.2	11 36.4	4 44.5	17 57.0	2 20.8	25 31.3	0 26.0	11 40.2	10 00.1
21 Tu	16 00 59	28 56 33	10♉28 47	17 25 38	22 00.0	15 13.7	12 51.6	5 27.9	17 43.5	2 30.6	25 36.1	0 26.8	11 42.4	10 00.8
22 W	16 04 56	29 57 09	24 19 05	1♊08 38	21 47.1	16 46.6	14 06.8	6 11.4	17 30.2	2 40.4	25 41.1	0 27.6	11 44.6	10 01.5
23 Th	16 08 52	0♐57 46	7♊53 48	14 34 16	21 34.5	18 19.9	15 22.1	6 54.8	17 17.1	2 50.4	25 46.1	0 28.4	11 46.7	10 02.1
24 F	16 12 49	1 58 25	21 09 46	27 40 10	21 23.4	19 53.5	16 37.3	7 38.4	17 04.1	3 00.5	25 51.2	0 29.1	11 48.9	10 02.7
25 Sa	16 16 45	2 59 06	4♋05 26	10♋25 40	21 14.8	21 27.2	17 52.6	8 22.0	16 51.3	3 10.7	25 56.3	0 29.7	11 51.0	10 03.2
26 Su	16 20 42	3 59 48	16 41 04	22 51 55	21 08.9	23 01.1	19 07.9	9 05.6	16 38.8	3 21.0	26 01.6	0 30.3	11 53.1	10 03.8
27 M	16 24 39	5 00 31	28 58 39	5♌01 42	21 05.7	24 35.1	20 23.2	9 49.3	16 26.4	3 31.4	26 06.8	0 30.8	11 55.3	10 04.3
28 Tu	16 28 35	6 01 16	11♌01 38	16 59 01	21D 04.5	26 09.1	21 38.5	10 33.1	16 14.2	3 42.0	26 12.2	0 31.3	11 57.4	10 04.7
29 W	16 32 32	7 02 02	22 54 30	28 48 46	21R 04.6	27 43.2	22 53.9	11 16.9	16 02.3	3 52.6	26 17.6	0 31.7	11 59.4	10 05.2
30 Th	16 36 28	8 02 50	4♍42 29	10♍36 22	21 04.7	29 17.2	24 09.2	12 00.8	15 50.6	4 03.4	26 23.1	0 32.0	12 01.5	10 05.6

December 1961 — LONGITUDE

Day	Sid.Time	☉	0 hr ☽	Noon ☽	True ☊	☿	♀	♂	⚳	♃	♄	♅	♆	♇
1 F	16 40 25	9♐03 40	16♍31 07	22♍27 26	21♌03.8	0♐51.3	25♏24.6	12♐44.7	15♉39.2	4♒14.3	26♑28.6	0♍32.3	12♏03.6	10♍05.9
2 Sa	16 44 21	10 04 30	28 25 58	4♎27 22	21R 01.0	2 25.4	26 40.0	13 28.7	15R 28.1	4 25.2	26 34.2	0 32.5	12 05.6	10 06.3
3 Su	16 48 18	11 05 22	10♎32 13	16 41 04	20 55.6	3 59.5	27 55.4	14 12.7	15 17.2	4 36.3	26 39.8	0 32.7	12 07.7	10 06.6
4 M	16 52 14	12 06 16	22 54 21	29 12 29	20 47.7	5 33.5	29 10.8	14 56.8	15 06.7	4 47.5	26 45.5	0 32.8	12 09.7	10 06.8
5 Tu	16 56 11	13 07 11	5♏35 43	12♏04 14	20 37.5	7 07.5	0♐26.2	15 41.0	14 56.5	4 58.7	26 51.3	0R 32.9	12 11.7	10 07.1
6 W	17 00 07	14 08 07	18 38 05	25 17 14	20 26.0	8 41.6	1 41.6	16 25.2	14 46.5	5 10.1	26 57.1	0 32.9	12 13.7	10 07.3
7 Th	17 04 04	15 09 04	2♐01 29	8♐50 32	20 14.3	10 15.6	2 57.0	17 09.4	14 36.9	5 21.6	27 03.0	0 32.9	12 15.6	10 07.5
8 F	17 08 01	16 10 02	15 44 00	22 41 22	20 03.5	11 49.6	4 12.5	17 53.7	14 27.7	5 33.1	27 08.9	0 32.8	12 17.6	10 07.6
9 Sa	17 11 57	17 11 01	29 42 05	6♑45 32	19 54.8	13 23.7	5 27.9	18 38.1	14 18.8	5 44.8	27 14.9	0 32.6	12 19.5	10 07.7
10 Su	17 15 54	18 12 01	13♑51 07	20 58 12	19 48.8	14 57.8	6 43.4	19 22.5	14 10.2	5 56.5	27 20.9	0 32.4	12 21.4	10 07.8
11 M	17 19 50	19 13 02	28 06 12	5♒14 37	19 45.5	16 31.9	7 58.8	20 06.9	14 02.1	6 08.4	27 27.0	0 32.1	12 23.3	10R 07.9
12 Tu	17 23 47	20 14 03	12♒22 56	19 30 48	19D 44.6	18 06.1	9 14.3	20 51.4	13 54.2	6 20.3	27 33.1	0 31.8	12 25.2	10 07.9
13 W	17 27 43	21 15 04	26 37 51	3♓43 52	19 45.1	19 40.4	10 29.8	21 36.0	13 46.8	6 32.3	27 39.3	0 31.4	12 27.1	10 07.9
14 Th	17 31 40	22 16 07	10♓48 39	17 52 03	19R 45.8	21 14.7	11 45.2	22 20.5	13 39.7	6 44.4	27 45.5	0 31.0	12 28.9	10 07.8
15 F	17 35 37	23 17 09	24 53 57	1♈54 16	19 45.5	22 49.1	13 00.7	23 05.2	13 33.0	6 56.5	27 51.8	0 30.5	12 30.7	10 07.7
16 Sa	17 39 33	24 18 12	8♈52 56	15 49 50	19 43.4	24 23.7	14 16.2	23 49.9	13 26.8	7 08.8	27 58.1	0 29.9	12 32.5	10 07.6
17 Su	17 43 30	25 19 15	22 44 52	29 37 54	19 38.8	25 58.4	15 31.6	24 34.6	13 20.9	7 21.1	28 04.5	0 29.3	12 34.3	10 07.5
18 M	17 47 26	26 20 19	6♉28 47	13♉17 20	19 32.0	27 33.2	16 47.1	25 19.4	13 15.3	7 33.5	28 10.9	0 28.7	12 36.1	10 07.3
19 Tu	17 51 23	27 21 23	20 03 20	26 46 34	19 23.4	29 08.2	18 02.6	26 04.2	13 10.2	7 46.0	28 17.3	0 28.0	12 37.8	10 07.1
20 W	17 55 19	28 22 27	3♊26 47	10♊03 43	19 14.0	0♑43.4	19 18.0	26 49.1	13 05.5	7 58.5	28 23.8	0 27.2	12 39.5	10 06.8
21 Th	17 59 16	29 23 32	16 37 21	23 07 19	19 04.7	2 18.7	20 33.5	27 34.0	13 01.2	8 11.1	28 30.3	0 26.4	12 41.2	10 06.6
22 F	18 03 12	0♑24 38	29 33 33	5♋55 57	18 56.5	3 54.3	21 49.0	28 19.0	12 57.3	8 23.8	28 36.8	0 25.5	12 42.9	10 06.3
23 Sa	18 07 09	1 25 44	12♋14 32	18 29 18	18 50.2	5 30.1	23 04.5	29 04.0	12 53.8	8 36.6	28 43.4	0 24.6	12 44.5	10 06.0
24 Su	18 11 06	2 26 50	24 40 24	0♌48 00	18 46.1	7 06.0	24 20.0	29 49.0	12 50.8	8 49.4	28 50.1	0 23.6	12 46.1	10 05.6
25 M	18 15 02	3 27 57	6♌52 22	12 53 48	18D 44.3	8 42.2	25 35.4	0♑34.1	12 48.1	9 02.3	28 56.7	0 22.6	12 47.7	10 05.2
26 Tu	18 18 59	4 29 04	18 52 42	24 49 29	18 44.3	10 18.7	26 50.9	1 19.3	12 45.8	9 15.3	29 03.4	0 21.5	12 49.3	10 04.8
27 W	18 22 55	5 30 12	0♍44 41	6♍38 49	18 45.5	11 55.3	28 06.4	2 04.5	12 43.9	9 28.3	29 10.1	0 20.4	12 50.8	10 04.3
28 Th	18 26 52	6 31 20	12 32 28	18 26 14	18 47.2	13 32.2	29 21.9	2 49.8	12 42.4	9 41.3	29 16.9	0 19.2	12 52.4	10 03.8
29 F	18 30 48	7 32 29	24 20 47	0♎16 45	18R 48.5	15 09.3	0♑37.4	3 35.0	12 41.4	9 54.5	29 23.7	0 18.0	12 53.8	10 03.3
30 Sa	18 34 45	8 33 38	6♎14 48	12 15 35	18 48.7	16 46.6	1 52.9	4 20.4	12 40.7	10 07.7	29 30.5	0 16.7	12 55.3	10 02.8
31 Su	18 38 41	9 34 47	18 19 46	24 27 57	18 47.4	18 24.0	3 08.4	5 05.8	12D 40.4	10 20.9	29 37.3	0 15.4	12 56.7	10 02.2

Astro Data	Dy Hr Mn	Planet Ingress	Dy Hr Mn	Last Aspect Dy Hr Mn		☽ Ingress	Dy Hr Mn	Last Aspect Dy Hr Mn		☽ Ingress	Dy Hr Mn	☽ Phases & Eclipses Dy Hr Mn	
♃⚻♅	4 21:11	♅ ♍	1 16:01	1 14:46	☿ ⚹	♍	2 6:17	1 20:09	♄ △	♎	2 3:08	8 9:58	● 15♏46
☽0S	5 10:42	♃ ♒	4 2:49	4 7:32	♄ △	♎	4 18:42	4 7:19	♄ □	♏	4 13:30	15 12:12	☽ 22♒54
♄⚼♇	12 2:58	☿ ♏	10 23:53	6 19:55	☿ ☌	♏	7 4:40	6 15:00	♄ ⚹	♐	6 20:25	22 9:44	○ 29♉51
☽0N	18 17:20	♀ ♏	11 5:33	9 5:50	♂ ☌	♐	9 11:51	8 3:17	♂ ☌	♑	9 0:31	30 6:18	☾ 7♍48
		♂ ♐	13 21:50	10 5:29	♇ □	♑	11 16:59	10 22:48	♄ ☌	♒	11 3:11		
☽0S	2 20:22	☉ ♐	22 13:08	13 20:56	♂ ⚹	♒	13 20:59	12 14:23	♂ ⚹	♓	13 5:41	7 23:52	● 15♐39
♅R	6 4:28	☿ ♐	30 22:54	15 12:12	☉ □	♓	16 0:18	15 5:01	♄ ⚹	♈	15 8:44	14 20:05	☽ 22♓37
♇R	12 11:54			17 19:14	♄ ⚹	♈	18 3:10	17 9:16	♄ □	♉	17 12:39	22 0:42	○ 29♊56
☽0N	16 0:11	♀ ♐	5 3:40	19 22:20	♄ □	♉	20 6:03	19 14:44	♄ △	♊	19 17:47	30 3:57	☾ 8♎13
♃⚻♇	30 3:27	☿ ♑	20 1:04	22 9:44	☉ ☍	♊	22 9:59	22 0:42	☉ ☍	♋	22 0:50		
☽0S	30 6:07	☉ ♑	22 2:19	23 3:49	♇ □	♋	24 16:20	24 8:06	♄ ☍	♌	24 10:26		
⚳D	31 15:28	♂ ♑	24 17:50	26 18:14	♄ ☍	♌	27 2:01	26 16:35	♀ △	♍	26 22:29		
		♀ ♑	29 0:07	29 9:26	☿ □	♍	29 14:25	29 10:12	♄ △	♎	29 11:26		
								31 22:04	♄ □	♏	31 22:42		

Astro Data

1 November 1961
Julian Day # 22585
SVP 5♓47'46"
GC 26♐18.4 ⚴ 7♓23.8R
Eris 9♈42.0R ⚵ 17♓23.7
⚷ 1♓56.6R ⚶ 0♊51.2R
☽ Mean ☊ 23♌13.0

1 December 1961
Julian Day # 22615
SVP 5♓47'41"
GC 26♐18.4 ⚴ 8♓58.9
Eris 9♈29.0R ⚵ 21♓20.5
⚷ 2♓04.3 ⚶ 23♉21.1R
☽ Mean ☊ 21♌37.7

LONGITUDE — January 1962

Day	Sid.Time	☉	0 hr ☽	Noon ☽	True ☊	☿	♀	♂	⚳	♃	♄	♅	♆	♇
1 M	18 42 38	10♑35 57	0♏40 44	6♏58 37	18♌44.3	20♑01.6	4♑23.9	5♑51.2	12♉40.6	10♒34.3	29♑44.2	0♍14.0	12♏58.2	10♍01.6
2 Tu	18 46 35	11 37 08	13 22 04	19 51 26	18R39.7	21 39.3	5 39.4	6 36.7	12 41.1	10 47.6	29 51.1	0R12.6	12 59.5	10R01.0
3 W	18 50 31	12 38 18	26 26 59	3♐08 50	18 34.0	23 17.1	6 54.9	7 22.2	12 42.1	11 01.1	29 58.0	0 11.1	13 00.9	10 00.3
4 Th	18 54 28	13 39 29	9♐57 00	16 51 19	18 28.0	24 54.9	8 10.4	8 07.8	12 43.4	11 14.5	0♒04.9	0 09.6	13 02.2	9 59.6
5 F	18 58 24	14 40 40	23 51 30	0♑57 04	18 22.4	26 32.6	9 25.9	8 53.4	12 45.2	11 28.1	0 11.9	0 08.0	13 03.5	9 58.9
6 Sa	19 02 21	15 41 51	8♑07 28	15 21 59	18 17.9	28 10.1	10 41.4	9 39.0	12 47.3	11 41.6	0 18.9	0 06.4	13 04.8	9 58.2
7 Su	19 06 17	16 43 02	22 39 48	0♒00 03	18 15.1	29 47.4	11 56.9	10 24.7	12 49.8	11 55.2	0 25.9	0 04.8	13 06.1	9 57.4
8 M	19 10 14	17 44 12	7♒21 50	14 44 14	18D13.9	1♒24.2	13 12.4	11 10.4	12 52.7	12 08.9	0 32.9	0 03.1	13 07.3	9 56.6
9 Tu	19 14 10	18 45 23	22 06 24	29 27 31	18 14.2	3 00.5	14 27.9	11 56.2	12 56.0	12 22.6	0 39.9	0 01.3	13 08.4	9 55.8
10 W	19 18 07	19 46 32	6♓46 52	14♓03 48	18 15.5	4 36.0	15 43.4	12 42.0	12 59.7	12 36.4	0 47.0	29♌59.5	13 09.6	9 54.9
11 Th	19 22 04	20 47 41	21 17 50	28 28 31	18 17.1	6 10.5	16 58.9	13 27.9	13 03.8	12 50.2	0 54.0	29 57.7	13 10.7	9 54.0
12 F	19 26 00	21 48 50	5♈35 34	12♈38 47	18R18.2	7 43.7	18 14.3	14 13.7	13 08.2	13 04.0	1 01.1	29 55.9	13 11.8	9 53.1
13 Sa	19 29 57	22 49 57	19 38 00	26 33 12	18 18.5	9 15.4	19 29.8	14 59.6	13 13.0	13 17.9	1 08.2	29 54.0	13 12.9	9 52.2
14 Su	19 33 53	23 51 05	3♉24 22	10♉11 33	18 17.5	10 45.2	20 45.3	15 45.6	13 18.2	13 31.8	1 15.3	29 52.0	13 13.9	9 51.2
15 M	19 37 50	24 52 11	16 54 48	23 34 15	18 15.4	12 12.6	22 00.7	16 31.6	13 23.7	13 45.7	1 22.4	29 50.0	13 14.9	9 50.3
16 Tu	19 41 46	25 53 17	0♊09 58	6♊42 05	18 12.4	13 37.2	23 16.1	17 17.6	13 29.6	13 59.7	1 29.5	29 48.0	13 15.9	9 49.3
17 W	19 45 43	26 54 22	13 10 42	19 35 57	18 08.9	14 58.5	24 31.6	18 03.6	13 35.8	14 13.7	1 36.6	29 46.0	13 16.8	9 48.2
18 Th	19 49 39	27 55 26	25 57 55	2♋16 43	18 05.5	16 15.9	25 47.0	18 49.7	13 42.4	14 27.7	1 43.8	29 43.9	13 17.7	9 47.2
19 F	19 53 36	28 56 30	8♋32 27	14 45 15	18 02.6	17 28.6	27 02.4	19 35.9	13 49.4	14 41.8	1 50.9	29 41.8	13 18.6	9 46.1
20 Sa	19 57 33	29 57 33	20 55 14	27 02 32	18 00.5	18 36.0	28 17.9	20 22.0	13 56.6	14 55.8	1 58.0	29 39.6	13 19.4	9 45.0
21 Su	20 01 29	0♒58 35	3♌07 20	9♌09 47	17D59.3	19 37.2	29 33.3	21 08.2	14 04.2	15 10.0	2 05.2	29 37.5	13 20.2	9 43.9
22 M	20 05 26	1 59 36	15 10 06	21 08 32	17 59.1	20 31.4	0♒48.7	21 54.4	14 12.2	15 24.1	2 12.3	29 35.2	13 21.0	9 42.8
23 Tu	20 09 22	3 00 37	27 05 21	3♍00 51	17 59.7	21 17.9	2 04.1	22 40.7	14 20.4	15 38.3	2 19.4	29 33.0	13 21.7	9 41.6
24 W	20 13 19	4 01 38	8♍55 23	14 49 20	18 00.8	21 55.6	3 19.5	23 27.0	14 29.0	15 52.4	2 26.6	29 30.7	13 22.4	9 40.4
25 Th	20 17 15	5 02 37	20 43 06	26 37 09	18 02.1	22 23.9	4 34.8	24 13.3	14 37.9	16 06.7	2 33.7	29 28.4	13 23.1	9 39.2
26 F	20 21 12	6 03 36	2♎31 58	8♎28 03	18 03.4	22 41.9	5 50.2	24 59.7	14 47.1	16 20.9	2 40.9	29 26.1	13 23.8	9 38.0
27 Sa	20 25 08	7 04 35	14 25 58	20 26 16	18 04.3	22R49.1	7 05.6	25 46.0	14 56.6	16 35.1	2 48.0	29 23.7	13 24.4	9 36.7
28 Su	20 29 05	8 05 32	26 29 32	2♏36 20	18R04.8	22 45.1	8 21.0	26 32.5	15 06.5	16 49.4	2 55.1	29 21.4	13 24.9	9 35.5
29 M	20 33 02	9 06 29	8♏47 16	15 02 52	18 04.8	22 29.7	9 36.3	27 18.9	15 16.6	17 03.7	3 02.2	29 19.0	13 25.5	9 34.2
30 Tu	20 36 58	10 07 26	21 23 42	27 50 14	18 04.4	22 03.1	10 51.7	28 05.4	15 27.0	17 18.0	3 09.3	29 16.5	13 26.0	9 32.9
31 W	20 40 55	11 08 22	4♐22 54	11♐02 02	18 03.7	21 25.7	12 07.0	28 51.9	15 37.7	17 32.3	3 16.5	29 14.1	13 26.5	9 31.6

LONGITUDE — February 1962

Day	Sid.Time	☉	0 hr ☽	Noon ☽	True ☊	☿	♀	♂	⚳	♃	♄	♅	♆	♇
1 Th	20 44 51	12♒09 17	17♐47 51	24♐40 30	18♌03.0	20♒38.5	13♒22.4	29♑38.5	15♉48.7	17♒46.6	3♒23.6	29♌11.6	13♏26.9	9♍30.3
2 F	20 48 48	13 10 11	1♑39 55	8♑45 56	18R02.3	19R42.6	14 37.7	0♒25.0	16 00.0	18 00.9	3 30.6	29R09.1	13 27.3	9R28.9
3 Sa	20 52 44	14 11 04	15 58 11	23 16 09	18 01.9	18 39.7	15 53.0	1 11.6	16 11.6	18 15.3	3 37.7	29 06.6	13 27.7	9 27.5
4 Su	20 56 41	15 11 57	0♒39 08	8♒06 16	18D01.7	17 31.5	17 08.3	1 58.3	16 23.5	18 29.6	3 44.8	29 04.1	13 28.0	9 26.2
5 M	21 00 37	16 12 48	15 36 35	23 09 01	18 01.7	16 20.1	18 23.6	2 44.9	16 35.6	18 44.0	3 51.8	29 01.6	13 28.3	9 24.8
6 Tu	21 04 34	17 13 38	0♓42 23	8♓15 34	18R01.7	15 07.4	19 38.9	3 31.6	16 48.0	18 58.3	3 58.9	28 59.0	13 28.6	9 23.4
7 W	21 08 31	18 14 26	15 47 25	23 16 53	18 01.7	13 55.7	20 54.2	4 18.3	17 00.6	19 12.7	4 05.9	28 56.5	13 28.8	9 21.9
8 Th	21 12 27	19 15 13	0♈42 59	8♈04 55	18 01.7	12 46.6	22 09.5	5 05.0	17 13.6	19 27.1	4 12.9	28 53.9	13 29.0	9 20.5
9 F	21 16 24	20 15 59	15 21 59	22 33 41	18 01.5	11 41.7	23 24.7	5 51.7	17 26.7	19 41.4	4 19.8	28 51.3	13 29.2	9 19.1
10 Sa	21 20 20	21 16 43	29 39 39	6♉39 41	18 01.3	10 42.5	24 40.0	6 38.5	17 40.2	19 55.8	4 26.8	28 48.7	13 29.3	9 17.6
11 Su	21 24 17	22 17 25	13♉33 43	20 21 47	18D01.2	9 50.0	25 55.2	7 25.2	17 53.8	20 10.2	4 33.7	28 46.1	13 29.4	9 16.1
12 M	21 28 13	23 18 06	27 04 03	3♊40 45	18 01.2	9 04.7	27 10.4	8 12.0	18 07.7	20 24.5	4 40.6	28 43.5	13 29.5	9 14.7
13 Tu	21 32 10	24 18 45	10♊12 11	16 38 42	18 01.6	8 27.2	28 25.6	8 58.9	18 21.9	20 38.9	4 47.5	28 40.8	13R29.5	9 13.2
14 W	21 36 06	25 19 22	23 00 39	29 18 26	18 02.3	7 57.6	29 40.8	9 45.7	18 36.3	20 53.2	4 54.4	28 38.2	13 29.5	9 11.7
15 Th	21 40 03	26 19 58	5♋32 27	11♋43 04	18 03.1	7 35.9	0♓55.9	10 32.5	18 50.9	21 07.6	5 01.2	28 35.6	13 29.5	9 10.2
16 F	21 44 00	27 20 32	17 50 39	23 55 35	18 04.0	7 22.0	2 11.1	11 19.4	19 05.7	21 21.9	5 08.0	28 33.0	13 29.4	9 08.7
17 Sa	21 47 56	28 21 04	29 58 11	5♌58 47	18 04.7	7D15.5	3 26.2	12 06.3	19 20.8	21 36.2	5 14.8	28 30.3	13 29.3	9 07.2
18 Su	21 51 53	29 21 35	11♌57 41	17 55 10	18R05.0	7 16.2	4 41.3	12 53.2	19 36.1	21 50.5	5 21.5	28 27.7	13 29.1	9 05.6
19 M	21 55 49	0♓22 04	23 51 29	29 46 56	18 04.7	7 23.6	5 56.4	13 40.1	19 51.6	22 04.8	5 28.3	28 25.1	13 29.0	9 04.1
20 Tu	21 59 46	1 22 31	5♍41 44	11♍36 10	18 03.7	7 37.4	7 11.4	14 27.0	20 07.3	22 19.1	5 34.9	28 22.4	13 28.7	9 02.6
21 W	22 03 42	2 22 57	17 30 28	23 24 55	18 01.9	7 57.1	8 26.5	15 14.0	20 23.2	22 33.4	5 41.6	28 19.8	13 28.5	9 01.0
22 Th	22 07 39	3 23 22	29 19 47	5♎15 22	17 59.6	8 22.2	9 41.5	16 00.9	20 39.3	22 47.6	5 48.2	28 17.2	13 28.2	8 59.5
23 F	22 11 35	4 23 44	11♎11 58	17 09 56	17 57.0	8 52.5	10 56.6	16 47.9	20 55.6	23 01.9	5 54.8	28 14.6	13 27.9	8 57.9
24 Sa	22 15 32	5 24 06	23 09 38	29 11 26	17 54.4	9 27.5	12 11.6	17 34.9	21 12.1	23 16.1	6 01.4	28 11.9	13 27.6	8 56.4
25 Su	22 19 29	6 24 26	5♏15 46	11♏23 04	17 52.1	10 06.9	13 26.6	18 21.9	21 28.8	23 30.3	6 07.9	28 09.3	13 27.2	8 54.8
26 M	22 23 25	7 24 44	17 33 46	23 48 21	17 50.6	10 50.3	14 41.5	19 08.9	21 45.7	23 44.5	6 14.3	28 06.7	13 26.8	8 53.2
27 Tu	22 27 22	8 25 01	0♐07 18	6♐31 05	17D49.9	11 37.5	15 56.5	19 55.9	22 02.8	23 58.6	6 20.8	28 04.2	13 26.4	8 51.7
28 W	22 31 18	9 25 17	13 00 08	19 34 53	17 50.2	12 28.1	17 11.4	20 42.9	22 20.1	24 12.7	6 27.2	28 01.6	13 25.9	8 50.1

Astro Data

	Dy Hr Mn
♄⚻♅	5 1:09
☽0N	12 6:38
♃□♆	13 2:40
☽0S	26 14:22
☿R	27 15:32
☽0N	8 14:35
♆R	13 20:07
☿D	17 21:36
☽0S	22 20:46

Planet Ingress

	Dy Hr Mn
♄ ♒	3 19:01
☿ ♒	7 15:08
♅ ♌R	10 5:53
☉ ♒	20 12:58
♀ ♒	21 20:31
♂ ♒	1 23:06
♀ ♓	14 18:09
☉ ♓	19 3:15

Last Aspect / ☽ Ingress (January)

Last Aspect Dy Hr Mn		☽ Ingress Dy Hr Mn
3 6:16	♄ ⚹	♐ 3 6:23
4 2:06	♃ ⚹	♑ 5 10:24
7 11:37	☿ ☌	♒ 7 12:00
8 9:22	♆ □	♓ 9 12:53
10 22:11	☉ ⚹	♈ 11 14:34
13 17:50	♅ △	♉ 13 18:01
15 23:22	♅ □	♊ 15 23:42
18 7:10	♅ ⚹	♋ 18 7:39
20 14:45	♀ ☍	♌ 20 17:50
23 5:00	♅ ☌	♍ 23 5:53
25 6:47	♂ △	♎ 25 18:52
28 5:39	♅ ⚹	♏ 28 6:54
30 14:39	♅ □	♐ 30 15:59

Last Aspect / ☽ Ingress (February)

Last Aspect Dy Hr Mn		☽ Ingress Dy Hr Mn
1 19:45	♅ △	♑ 1 21:10
2 19:50	♆ ⚹	♒ 3 22:57
5 21:18	♅ ☍	♓ 5 22:53
6 20:19	♆ △	♈ 7 22:50
9 22:36	♅ △	♉ 10 0:35
12 3:01	♅ □	♊ 12 5:18
14 12:48	♀ △	♋ 14 13:20
15 15:28	♆ △	♌ 17 0:04
19 9:15	♅ ☌	♍ 19 12:27
20 15:49	♆ ⚹	♎ 22 1:22
24 10:02	♅ ⚹	♏ 24 13:36
26 20:10	♅ □	♐ 26 23:46

☽ Phases & Eclipses

Dy Hr Mn	
6 12:35	● 15♑43
13 5:01	☽ 22♈32
20 18:16	○ 0♌13
28 23:36	☾ 8♏35
5 0:10	● 15♒43
5 0:12:04	● T 04'08"
11 15:43	☽ 22♉27
19 13:18	○ 0♍25
19 13:03	● A 0.612
27 15:50	☾ 8♐35

Astro Data

1 January 1962
Julian Day # 22646
SVP 5♓47'36"
GC 26♐18.5 ⚵ 15♓05.1
Eris 9♈25.1 ⚶ 1♈38.1
⚷ 3♓06.0 ⚴ 18♉54.8R
☽ Mean ☊ 19♌59.2

1 February 1962
Julian Day # 22677
SVP 5♓47'31"
GC 26♐18.6 ⚵ 24♓10.5
Eris 9♈32.0 ⚶ 15♈49.8
⚷ 4♓48.1 ⚴ 21♉12.2
☽ Mean ☊ 18♌20.7

March 1962 — LONGITUDE

Day	Sid.Time	☉	0 hr ☽	Noon ☽	True ☊	☿	♀	♂	⚳	♃	♄	♅	♆	♇
1 Th	22 35 15	10♓25 31	26♐15 42	3♑02 54	17♌51.3	13♒22.0	18♓26.4	21♒30.0	22♉37.5	24♒26.9	6♒33.5	27♌59.0	13♏25.4	8♍48.6
2 F	22 39 11	11 25 44	9♑56 40	16 57 07	17 52.8	14 18.9	19 41.3	22 17.1	22 55.2	24 40.9	6 39.9	27R 56.5	13R 24.9	8R 47.0
3 Sa	22 43 08	12 25 55	24 04 11	1♒17 41	17 54.2	15 18.5	20 56.2	23 04.1	23 13.0	24 55.0	6 46.1	27 53.9	13 24.3	8 45.5
4 Su	22 47 04	13 26 05	8♒37 13	16 02 13	17R 54.8	16 20.8	22 11.0	23 51.2	23 31.0	25 09.0	6 52.4	27 51.4	13 23.7	8 43.9
5 M	22 51 01	14 26 13	23 31 57	1♓05 27	17 54.3	17 25.5	23 25.9	24 38.3	23 49.1	25 23.0	6 58.5	27 48.9	13 23.1	8 42.3
6 Tu	22 54 58	15 26 19	8♓41 38	16 19 18	17 52.5	18 32.5	24 40.7	25 25.4	24 07.4	25 37.0	7 04.7	27 46.4	13 22.4	8 40.8
7 W	22 58 54	16 26 23	23 57 09	1♈33 52	17 49.2	19 41.7	25 55.5	26 12.4	24 25.9	25 50.9	7 10.8	27 44.0	13 21.7	8 39.2
8 Th	23 02 51	17 26 25	9♈08 10	16 38 51	17 45.1	20 52.9	27 10.3	26 59.5	24 44.6	26 04.8	7 16.8	27 41.5	13 21.0	8 37.7
9 F	23 06 47	18 26 25	24 04 51	1♉25 17	17 40.6	22 06.0	28 25.1	27 46.6	25 03.4	26 18.7	7 22.8	27 39.1	13 20.3	8 36.2
10 Sa	23 10 44	19 26 23	8♉39 25	15 46 47	17 36.5	23 21.0	29 39.8	28 33.7	25 22.3	26 32.5	7 28.7	27 36.7	13 19.5	8 34.6
11 Su	23 14 40	20 26 19	22 47 03	29 40 08	17 33.4	24 37.8	0♈54.6	29 20.8	25 41.4	26 46.3	7 34.6	27 34.3	13 18.7	8 33.1
12 M	23 18 37	21 26 12	6♊26 05	13♊05 08	17D 31.6	25 56.2	2 09.3	0♓07.9	26 00.7	27 00.0	7 40.4	27 32.0	13 17.8	8 31.6
13 Tu	23 22 33	22 26 04	19 37 35	26 03 52	17 31.4	27 16.3	3 23.9	0 55.0	26 20.1	27 13.8	7 46.2	27 29.7	13 17.0	8 30.1
14 W	23 26 30	23 25 53	2♋24 29	8♋39 59	17 32.3	28 37.9	4 38.6	1 42.1	26 39.7	27 27.4	7 51.9	27 27.4	13 16.1	8 28.6
15 Th	23 30 26	24 25 40	14 50 55	20 57 53	17 34.0	0♓01.0	5 53.2	2 29.2	26 59.4	27 41.0	7 57.6	27 25.1	13 15.2	8 27.1
16 F	23 34 23	25 25 25	27 01 26	3♌02 09	17 35.6	1 25.6	7 07.8	3 16.2	27 19.2	27 54.6	8 03.2	27 22.9	13 14.2	8 25.6
17 Sa	23 38 20	26 25 07	9♌00 34	14 57 11	17R 36.5	2 51.7	8 22.3	4 03.3	27 39.2	28 08.1	8 08.8	27 20.7	13 13.3	8 24.1
18 Su	23 42 16	27 24 47	20 52 29	26 46 53	17 36.1	4 19.2	9 36.9	4 50.4	27 59.3	28 21.6	8 14.2	27 18.5	13 12.3	8 22.7
19 M	23 46 13	28 24 26	2♍40 49	8♍34 38	17 33.8	5 48.0	10 51.4	5 37.4	28 19.5	28 35.0	8 19.7	27 16.3	13 11.3	8 21.2
20 Tu	23 50 09	29 24 02	14 28 38	20 23 08	17 29.4	7 18.3	12 05.9	6 24.5	28 39.8	28 48.4	8 25.0	27 14.2	13 10.2	8 19.8
21 W	23 54 06	0♈23 36	26 18 23	2♎14 37	17 23.2	8 49.9	13 20.3	7 11.5	29 00.3	29 01.7	8 30.3	27 12.1	13 09.1	8 18.4
22 Th	23 58 02	1 23 07	8♎12 03	14 10 52	17 15.4	10 22.8	14 34.7	7 58.6	29 20.9	29 15.0	8 35.6	27 10.1	13 08.0	8 16.9
23 F	0 01 59	2 22 37	20 11 16	26 13 25	17 06.7	11 57.1	15 49.1	8 45.6	29 41.7	29 28.2	8 40.8	27 08.1	13 06.9	8 15.5
24 Sa	0 05 55	3 22 05	2♏17 32	8♏23 48	16 58.0	13 32.7	17 03.5	9 32.7	0♊02.5	29 41.4	8 45.9	27 06.1	13 05.8	8 14.1
25 Su	0 09 52	4 21 32	14 32 26	20 43 41	16 50.2	15 09.7	18 17.8	10 19.7	0 23.5	29 54.5	8 50.9	27 04.1	13 04.6	8 12.8
26 M	0 13 49	5 20 56	26 57 47	3♐15 03	16 43.9	16 48.0	19 32.2	11 06.7	0 44.5	0♓07.5	8 55.9	27 02.2	13 03.4	8 11.4
27 Tu	0 17 45	6 20 19	9♐35 46	16 00 15	16 39.7	18 27.6	20 46.5	11 53.7	1 05.7	0 20.5	9 00.8	27 00.4	13 02.2	8 10.1
28 W	0 21 42	7 19 40	22 28 53	29 01 59	16D 37.6	20 08.6	22 00.7	12 40.7	1 27.0	0 33.5	9 05.7	26 58.5	13 01.0	8 08.7
29 Th	0 25 38	8 18 59	5♑39 54	12♑22 58	16 37.3	21 50.9	23 15.0	13 27.7	1 48.5	0 46.3	9 10.5	26 56.8	12 59.7	8 07.4
30 F	0 29 35	9 18 16	19 11 27	26 05 36	16 38.1	23 34.6	24 29.2	14 14.7	2 10.0	0 59.1	9 15.2	26 55.0	12 58.4	8 06.1
31 Sa	0 33 31	10 17 32	3♒05 33	10♒11 20	16R 38.9	25 19.7	25 43.4	15 01.7	2 31.6	1 11.9	9 19.8	26 53.3	12 57.2	8 04.8

April 1962 — LONGITUDE

Day	Sid.Time	☉	0 hr ☽	Noon ☽	True ☊	☿	♀	♂	⚳	♃	♄	♅	♆	♇
1 Su	0 37 28	11♈16 46	17♒22 51	24♒39 50	16♌38.8	27♓06.2	26♈57.6	15♓48.6	2♊53.4	1♓24.6	9♒24.4	26♌51.6	12♏55.8	8♍03.6
2 M	0 41 24	12 15 58	2♓01 53	9♓28 23	16R 36.8	28 54.0	28 11.7	16 35.6	3 15.2	1 37.2	9 28.9	26R 50.0	12R 54.5	8R 02.3
3 Tu	0 45 21	13 15 08	16 58 30	24 31 18	16 32.4	0♈43.3	29 25.8	17 22.5	3 37.2	1 49.7	9 33.3	26 48.4	12 53.1	8 01.1
4 W	0 49 18	14 14 16	2♈05 39	9♈40 18	16 25.6	2 34.0	0♉39.9	18 09.4	3 59.2	2 02.2	9 37.6	26 46.9	12 51.8	7 59.9
5 Th	0 53 14	15 13 22	17 14 00	24 45 26	16 17.0	4 26.1	1 53.9	18 56.3	4 21.3	2 14.6	9 41.9	26 45.4	12 50.4	7 58.7
6 F	0 57 11	16 12 26	2♉13 24	9♉36 44	16 07.6	6 19.6	3 08.0	19 43.2	4 43.6	2 26.9	9 46.1	26 44.0	12 49.0	7 57.6
7 Sa	1 01 07	17 11 28	16 54 31	24 05 58	15 58.6	8 14.5	4 22.0	20 30.0	5 05.9	2 39.1	9 50.2	26 42.6	12 47.6	7 56.4
8 Su	1 05 04	18 10 28	1♊10 31	8♊07 49	15 50.9	10 10.9	5 35.9	21 16.8	5 28.4	2 51.3	9 54.2	26 41.2	12 46.1	7 55.3
9 M	1 09 00	19 09 25	14 57 45	21 40 19	15 45.4	12 08.7	6 49.9	22 03.7	5 50.9	3 03.4	9 58.2	26 39.9	12 44.7	7 54.2
10 Tu	1 12 57	20 08 21	28 15 46	4♋44 26	15 42.2	14 07.8	8 03.8	22 50.4	6 13.5	3 15.4	10 02.0	26 38.6	12 43.2	7 53.1
11 W	1 16 53	21 07 13	11♋06 48	17 23 23	15D 41.0	16 08.2	9 17.6	23 37.2	6 36.2	3 27.3	10 05.8	26 37.4	12 41.7	7 52.0
12 Th	1 20 50	22 06 04	23 34 50	29 41 46	15 41.1	18 09.9	10 31.4	24 23.9	6 58.9	3 39.1	10 09.5	26 36.3	12 40.2	7 51.0
13 F	1 24 47	23 04 53	5♌44 51	11♌44 47	15R 41.6	20 12.9	11 45.2	25 10.6	7 21.8	3 50.9	10 13.1	26 35.2	12 38.7	7 50.0
14 Sa	1 28 43	24 03 39	17 42 13	23 37 47	15 41.4	22 16.9	12 59.0	25 57.3	7 44.7	4 02.6	10 16.7	26 34.1	12 37.2	7 49.0
15 Su	1 32 40	25 02 22	29 32 07	5♍25 47	15 39.4	24 21.9	14 12.7	26 44.0	8 07.8	4 14.2	10 20.1	26 33.1	12 35.7	7 48.0
16 M	1 36 36	26 01 04	11♍19 18	17 13 12	15 35.2	26 27.8	15 26.4	27 30.6	8 30.9	4 25.6	10 23.5	26 32.1	12 34.1	7 47.1
17 Tu	1 40 33	26 59 44	23 07 52	29 03 44	15 28.2	28 34.4	16 40.1	28 17.2	8 54.0	4 37.1	10 26.8	26 31.2	12 32.6	7 46.2
18 W	1 44 29	27 58 21	5♎01 06	11♎00 16	15 18.5	0♉41.6	17 53.7	29 03.8	9 17.3	4 48.4	10 30.0	26 30.3	12 31.0	7 45.3
19 Th	1 48 26	28 56 56	17 01 28	23 04 52	15 06.8	2 49.0	19 07.3	29 50.4	9 40.6	4 59.6	10 33.1	26 29.5	12 29.4	7 44.4
20 F	1 52 22	29 55 30	29 10 37	5♏18 49	14 53.9	4 56.4	20 20.8	0♈36.9	10 04.0	5 10.7	10 36.1	26 28.8	12 27.9	7 43.6
21 Sa	1 56 19	0♉54 02	11♏29 33	17 42 53	14 40.8	7 03.7	21 34.3	1 23.4	10 27.5	5 21.7	10 39.1	26 28.1	12 26.3	7 42.8
22 Su	2 00 15	1 52 31	23 58 51	0♐17 30	14 28.7	9 10.4	22 47.8	2 09.9	10 51.0	5 32.7	10 41.9	26 27.4	12 24.7	7 42.0
23 M	2 04 12	2 51 00	6♐38 53	13 03 04	14 18.7	11 16.3	24 01.3	2 56.3	11 14.6	5 43.5	10 44.7	26 26.8	12 23.1	7 41.2
24 Tu	2 08 09	3 49 26	19 30 09	26 00 14	14 11.4	13 21.1	25 14.7	3 42.7	11 38.3	5 54.2	10 47.4	26 26.2	12 21.5	7 40.5
25 W	2 12 05	4 47 51	2♑33 28	9♑10 00	14 06.9	15 24.4	26 28.1	4 29.1	12 02.0	6 04.9	10 50.0	26 25.7	12 19.9	7 39.8
26 Th	2 16 02	5 46 14	15 50 02	22 33 46	14 04.9	17 26.0	27 41.4	5 15.5	12 25.8	6 15.4	10 52.5	26 25.3	12 18.2	7 39.1
27 F	2 19 58	6 44 36	29 21 23	6♒13 04	14 04.4	19 25.5	28 54.7	6 01.8	12 49.7	6 25.8	10 54.9	26 24.9	12 16.6	7 38.4
28 Sa	2 23 55	7 42 56	13♒08 59	20 09 13	14 04.4	21 22.7	0♊08.0	6 48.1	13 13.6	6 36.2	10 57.2	26 24.6	12 15.0	7 37.8
29 Su	2 27 51	8 41 14	27 13 47	4♓22 35	14 03.5	23 17.2	1 21.2	7 34.3	13 37.6	6 46.4	10 59.4	26 24.3	12 13.4	7 37.2
30 M	2 31 48	9 39 32	11♓35 27	18 52 00	14 00.5	25 08.9	2 34.5	8 20.6	14 01.7	6 56.5	11 01.5	26 24.0	12 11.7	7 36.6

Astro Data (Dy Hr Mn)
☽0N 8 0:38
♀0N 13 2:09
♃☍♅ 14 11:57
♄⊼♇ 19 17:27
☉0N 21 2:29
☽0S 22 2:28

☽0N 4 11:38
☿0N 5 13:00
☽0S 18 8:56
♂0N 22 23:20

Planet Ingress (Dy Hr Mn)
♀ ♈ 10 18:28
♂ ♓ 12 7:58
☿ ♓ 15 11:43
☉ ♈ 21 2:30
⚳ ♊ 24 9:08
♃ ♓ 25 22:07

☿ ♈ 3 2:32
♀ ♉ 3 23:05
☿ ♉ 18 4:10
♂ ♈ 19 16:58
☉ ♉ 20 13:51
♀ ♊ 28 9:23

Last Aspect Dy Hr Mn		☽ Ingress Dy Hr Mn
1 3:05	♅ △	♑ 1 6:38
2 17:05	♀ ⚹	♒ 3 9:52
5 6:49	♅ ☍	♓ 5 10:16
7 2:19	♀ ☌	♈ 7 9:32
9 5:50	♅ △	♉ 9 9:40
11 11:24	♂ □	♊ 11 12:35
13 14:41	♅ ⚹	♋ 13 19:25
15 19:28	☉ △	♌ 16 5:56
18 15:16	♃ ☍	♍ 18 18:33
19 21:22	♆ ⚹	♎ 21 7:28
23 18:33	♃ △	♏ 23 19:29
26 0:10	♅ □	♐ 26 5:49
28 8:15	♅ △	♑ 28 13:46
30 8:57	♀ □	♒ 30 18:43

Last Aspect Dy Hr Mn		☽ Ingress Dy Hr Mn
1 16:06	♀ ⚹	♓ 1 20:42
3 0:01	♂ ☌	♈ 3 20:41
5 15:12	♅ △	♉ 5 20:25
7 16:24	♅ □	♊ 7 22:00
9 21:03	♅ ⚹	♋ 10 3:12
12 0:54	♂ △	♌ 12 12:36
14 17:57	♅ ☌	♍ 15 0:57
17 10:19	♂ ☍	♎ 17 13:54
20 0:33	☉ ☍	♏ 20 1:37
22 4:43	♅ □	♐ 22 11:27
24 12:48	♅ △	♑ 24 19:20
26 21:58	♀ △	♒ 27 1:08
28 22:37	♅ ☍	♓ 29 4:40

☽ Phases & Eclipses (Dy Hr Mn)
6 10:31 ● 15♓23
13 4:39 ☽ 22♊08
21 7:55 ○ 0♎13
29 4:11 ☾ 8♑00

4 19:45 ● 14♈33
11 19:50 ☽ 21♋26
20 0:33 ○ 29♎28
27 12:59 ☾ 6♒47

Astro Data
1 March 1962
Julian Day # 22705
SVP 5♓47'28"
GC 26♐18.6 ⚴ 4♈02.3
Eris 9♈46.2 ⚵ 0♉36.1
⚷ 6♓36.6 ⚶ 27♉43.1
☽ Mean ☊ 16♌51.7

1 April 1962
Julian Day # 22736
SVP 5♓47'25"
GC 26♐18.7 ⚴ 16♈10.1
Eris 10♈06.8 ⚵ 18♉06.6
⚷ 8♓32.8 ⚶ 7♊53.4
☽ Mean ☊ 15♌13.2

LONGITUDE

May 1962

Day	Sid.Time	☉	0 hr ☽	Noon ☽	True ☊	☿	♀	♂	⚳	♃	♄	♅	♆	♇
1 Tu	2 35 44	10♉37 47	26♓11 46	3♈34 05	13♌54.9	26♉57.5	3♊47.6	9♈06.8	14♊25.8	7♓06.5	11♒03.5	26♌23.8	12♏10.1	7♍36.1
2 W	2 39 41	11 36 01	10♈58 10	18 23 06	13R46.5	28 42.9	5 00.8	9 52.9	14 50.0	7 16.3	11 05.5	26R23.7	12R08.5	7R35.5
3 Th	2 43 38	12 34 13	25 47 52	3♉11 25	13 36.0	0♊24.8	6 13.9	10 39.0	15 14.2	7 26.1	11 07.3	26D23.6	12 06.8	7 35.1
4 F	2 47 34	13 32 24	10♉32 39	17 50 32	13 24.4	2 03.2	7 27.0	11 25.1	15 38.6	7 35.8	11 09.0	26 23.6	12 05.2	7 34.6
5 Sa	2 51 31	14 30 33	25 04 08	2♊12 37	13 13.0	3 37.9	8 40.0	12 11.1	16 02.9	7 45.3	11 10.7	26 23.7	12 03.6	7 34.2
6 Su	2 55 27	15 28 40	9♊15 18	16 11 43	13 03.1	5 08.8	9 53.0	12 57.2	16 27.3	7 54.7	11 12.2	26 23.7	12 01.9	7 33.8
7 M	2 59 24	16 26 46	23 01 32	29 44 37	12 55.4	6 35.8	11 06.0	13 43.1	16 51.8	8 04.0	11 13.7	26 23.9	12 00.3	7 33.4
8 Tu	3 03 20	17 24 50	6♋21 02	12♋50 56	12 50.4	7 58.8	12 18.9	14 29.0	17 16.3	8 13.1	11 15.1	26 24.1	11 58.7	7 33.0
9 W	3 07 17	18 22 51	19 14 40	25 32 40	12 47.8	9 17.8	13 31.8	15 14.9	17 40.9	8 22.2	11 16.3	26 24.3	11 57.1	7 32.7
10 Th	3 11 13	19 20 51	1♌45 27	7♌53 36	12D47.0	10 32.7	14 44.7	16 00.7	18 05.5	8 31.1	11 17.5	26 24.6	11 55.4	7 32.5
11 F	3 15 10	20 18 49	13 57 46	19 58 37	12R46.9	11 43.4	15 57.5	16 46.5	18 30.2	8 39.8	11 18.6	26 25.0	11 53.8	7 32.2
12 Sa	3 19 07	21 16 45	25 56 49	1♍53 04	12 46.6	12 49.9	17 10.3	17 32.3	18 54.9	8 48.5	11 19.5	26 25.4	11 52.2	7 32.0
13 Su	3 23 03	22 14 40	7♍48 03	13 42 25	12 44.9	13 52.1	18 23.0	18 18.0	19 19.7	8 57.0	11 20.4	26 25.9	11 50.6	7 31.8
14 M	3 27 00	23 12 32	19 36 48	25 31 46	12 41.1	14 50.0	19 35.7	19 03.6	19 44.5	9 05.4	11 21.2	26 26.4	11 49.0	7 31.6
15 Tu	3 30 56	24 10 23	1♎27 54	7♎25 40	12 34.6	15 43.4	20 48.3	19 49.2	20 09.3	9 13.6	11 21.8	26 27.0	11 47.4	7 31.5
16 W	3 34 53	25 08 12	13 25 32	19 27 51	12 25.7	16 32.3	22 00.9	20 34.8	20 34.2	9 21.7	11 22.4	26 27.6	11 45.8	7 31.4
17 Th	3 38 49	26 06 00	25 32 58	1♏41 06	12 14.6	17 16.7	23 13.4	21 20.3	20 59.1	9 29.7	11 22.9	26 28.3	11 44.2	7 31.3
18 F	3 42 46	27 03 46	7♏52 28	14 07 09	12 02.3	17 56.4	24 25.9	22 05.8	21 24.1	9 37.6	11 23.3	26 29.0	11 42.7	7D31.3
19 Sa	3 46 42	28 01 31	20 25 15	26 46 43	11 49.8	18 31.5	25 38.4	22 51.2	21 49.1	9 45.3	11 23.6	26 29.8	11 41.1	7 31.2
20 Su	3 50 39	28 59 14	3♐11 33	9♐39 39	11 38.2	19 01.9	26 50.8	23 36.6	22 14.2	9 52.8	11 23.8	26 30.6	11 39.6	7 31.3
21 M	3 54 36	29 56 56	16 10 54	22 45 11	11 28.7	19 27.5	28 03.2	24 21.9	22 39.3	10 00.2	11R23.9	26 31.5	11 38.0	7 31.3
22 Tu	3 58 32	0♊54 37	29 22 21	6♑02 17	11 21.7	19 48.3	29 15.5	25 07.2	23 04.4	10 07.5	11 23.9	26 32.5	11 36.5	7 31.4
23 W	4 02 29	1 52 17	12♑44 54	19 30 04	11 17.5	20 04.3	0♋27.8	25 52.4	23 29.6	10 14.6	11 23.8	26 33.5	11 35.0	7 31.5
24 Th	4 06 25	2 49 55	26 17 45	3♒07 54	11D15.7	20 15.6	1 40.0	26 37.6	23 54.8	10 21.6	11 23.6	26 34.5	11 33.5	7 31.6
25 F	4 10 22	3 47 33	10♒00 31	16 55 34	11 15.5	20R22.0	2 52.2	27 22.8	24 20.1	10 28.4	11 23.3	26 35.6	11 32.0	7 31.8
26 Sa	4 14 18	4 45 10	23 53 04	0♓52 59	11R15.9	20 23.8	4 04.4	28 07.9	24 45.4	10 35.1	11 22.9	26 36.8	11 30.5	7 32.0
27 Su	4 18 15	5 42 45	7♓55 18	14 59 55	11 15.7	20 21.0	5 16.5	28 52.9	25 10.7	10 41.6	11 22.4	26 37.9	11 29.1	7 32.2
28 M	4 22 11	6 40 20	22 06 41	29 15 23	11 13.7	20 13.7	6 28.6	29 37.9	25 36.1	10 48.0	11 21.8	26 39.2	11 27.6	7 32.5
29 Tu	4 26 08	7 37 54	6♈25 42	13♈37 16	11 09.5	20 02.2	7 40.6	0♉22.9	26 01.5	10 54.2	11 21.1	26 40.5	11 26.2	7 32.8
30 W	4 30 05	8 35 27	20 49 33	28 02 00	11 02.9	19 46.6	8 52.6	1 07.8	26 26.9	11 00.2	11 20.3	26 41.8	11 24.8	7 33.1
31 Th	4 34 01	9 33 00	5♉13 57	12♉24 42	10 54.4	19 27.3	10 04.5	1 52.6	26 52.4	11 06.1	11 19.5	26 43.2	11 23.4	7 33.5

LONGITUDE

June 1962

Day	Sid.Time	☉	0 hr ☽	Noon ☽	True ☊	☿	♀	♂	⚳	♃	♄	♅	♆	♇
1 F	4 37 58	10♊30 31	19♉33 32	26♉39 42	10♌44.9	19♊04.6	11♋16.4	2♉37.4	27♊17.9	11♓11.8	11♒18.5	26♌44.7	11♏22.0	7♍33.8
2 Sa	4 41 54	11 28 02	3♊42 31	10♊41 21	10R35.5	18R38.8	12 28.2	3 22.1	27 43.4	11 17.4	11R17.4	26 46.2	11R20.6	7 34.3
3 Su	4 45 51	12 25 31	17 35 38	24 24 58	10 27.3	18 10.5	13 40.0	4 06.8	28 09.0	11 22.8	11 16.3	26 47.8	11 19.3	7 34.7
4 M	4 49 47	13 23 00	1♋08 59	7♋47 32	10 20.9	17 40.1	14 51.7	4 51.4	28 34.6	11 28.0	11 15.0	26 49.4	11 17.9	7 35.2
5 Tu	4 53 44	14 20 27	14 20 31	20 48 00	10 16.8	17 08.1	16 03.4	5 36.0	29 00.2	11 33.0	11 13.7	26 51.0	11 16.6	7 35.7
6 W	4 57 40	15 17 54	27 10 11	3♌27 20	10D15.0	16 35.0	17 15.1	6 20.5	29 25.9	11 37.9	11 12.2	26 52.7	11 15.3	7 36.2
7 Th	5 01 37	16 15 19	9♌39 49	15 48 06	10 14.9	16 01.5	18 26.6	7 05.0	29 51.6	11 42.6	11 10.7	26 54.4	11 14.1	7 36.8
8 F	5 05 34	17 12 43	21 52 41	27 54 08	10 15.8	15 28.1	19 38.2	7 49.3	0♋17.3	11 47.2	11 09.1	26 56.2	11 12.8	7 37.4
9 Sa	5 09 30	18 10 06	3♍53 05	9♍50 08	10R16.8	14 55.4	20 49.6	8 33.7	0 43.0	11 51.5	11 07.3	26 58.1	11 11.6	7 38.0
10 Su	5 13 27	19 07 28	15 45 57	21 41 11	10 17.1	14 23.9	22 01.0	9 17.9	1 08.8	11 55.7	11 05.5	26 59.9	11 10.4	7 38.6
11 M	5 17 23	20 04 49	27 36 28	3♎32 27	10 16.0	13 54.1	23 12.4	10 02.1	1 34.5	11 59.7	11 03.6	27 01.9	11 09.2	7 39.3
12 Tu	5 21 20	21 02 09	9♎29 43	15 28 53	10 13.0	13 26.7	24 23.7	10 46.3	2 00.3	12 03.6	11 01.7	27 03.8	11 08.0	7 40.0
13 W	5 25 16	21 59 28	21 30 28	27 34 57	10 08.1	13 01.9	25 34.9	11 30.4	2 26.2	12 07.2	10 59.6	27 05.9	11 06.8	7 40.8
14 Th	5 29 13	22 56 46	3♏42 46	9♏54 18	10 01.6	12 40.4	26 46.1	12 14.4	2 52.0	12 10.7	10 57.4	27 07.9	11 05.7	7 41.5
15 F	5 33 09	23 54 03	16 09 50	22 29 35	9 54.0	12 22.3	27 57.2	12 58.3	3 17.9	12 14.0	10 55.2	27 10.0	11 04.6	7 42.3
16 Sa	5 37 06	24 51 20	28 53 42	5♐22 13	9 46.2	12 08.0	29 08.2	13 42.2	3 43.8	12 17.1	10 52.9	27 12.2	11 03.5	7 43.1
17 Su	5 41 03	25 48 36	11♐55 07	18 32 19	9 39.0	11 57.9	0♌19.2	14 26.1	4 09.7	12 20.0	10 50.5	27 14.4	11 02.5	7 44.0
18 M	5 44 59	26 45 51	25 13 36	1♑58 44	9 33.1	11D52.0	1 30.1	15 09.9	4 35.6	12 22.8	10 48.0	27 16.6	11 01.5	7 44.9
19 Tu	5 48 56	27 43 06	8♑47 27	15 39 25	9 29.1	11 50.5	2 40.9	15 53.6	5 01.6	12 25.4	10 45.4	27 18.9	11 00.5	7 45.8
20 W	5 52 52	28 40 21	22 34 15	29 31 37	9D27.0	11 53.6	3 51.7	16 37.3	5 27.5	12 27.7	10 42.8	27 21.2	10 59.5	7 46.7
21 Th	5 56 49	29 37 35	6♒31 09	13♒32 30	9 26.6	12 01.3	5 02.4	17 20.9	5 53.5	12 29.9	10 40.1	27 23.6	10 58.5	7 47.7
22 F	6 00 45	0♋34 49	20 35 19	27 39 19	9 27.5	12 13.8	6 13.0	18 04.4	6 19.5	12 31.9	10 37.3	27 26.0	10 57.6	7 48.7
23 Sa	6 04 42	1 32 02	4♓44 12	11♓49 42	9 28.9	12 30.9	7 23.6	18 47.9	6 45.5	12 33.7	10 34.4	27 28.4	10 56.7	7 49.7
24 Su	6 08 38	2 29 16	18 55 35	26 01 37	9R29.9	12 52.8	8 34.1	19 31.3	7 11.6	12 35.4	10 31.4	27 30.9	10 55.8	7 50.7
25 M	6 12 35	3 26 30	3♈07 34	10♈13 11	9 29.8	13 19.3	9 44.5	20 14.6	7 37.6	12 36.8	10 28.4	27 33.4	10 54.9	7 51.8
26 Tu	6 16 32	4 23 43	17 18 14	24 22 27	9 28.4	13 50.4	10 54.9	20 57.9	8 03.7	12 38.0	10 25.3	27 36.0	10 54.1	7 52.9
27 W	6 20 28	5 20 57	1♉25 33	8♉27 12	9 25.4	14 26.2	12 05.2	21 41.1	8 29.8	12 39.1	10 22.2	27 38.6	10 53.3	7 54.0
28 Th	6 24 25	6 18 11	15 27 05	22 24 52	9 21.3	15 06.5	13 15.4	22 24.3	8 55.9	12 39.9	10 18.9	27 41.2	10 52.6	7 55.1
29 F	6 28 21	7 15 24	29 20 11	6♊12 42	9 16.5	15 51.3	14 25.5	23 07.4	9 22.0	12 40.6	10 15.6	27 43.9	10 51.8	7 56.3
30 Sa	6 32 18	8 12 38	13♊02 04	19 47 58	9 11.7	16 40.6	15 35.6	23 50.4	9 48.2	12 41.1	10 12.2	27 46.6	10 51.1	7 57.5

Astro Data	Dy Hr Mn
☽0N	1 21:51
♅D	4 8:56
♃☍♇	4 9:13
☽0S	15 16:49
♇D	19 9:38
♄R	21 23:22
☿R	26 9:09
☽0N	29 6:07
♃⚺♄	2 12:10
♃△♆	2 23:30
☽0S	12 1:43
☿D	19 7:45
☽0N	25 12:36

Planet Ingress		Dy Hr Mn
☿	♊	3 6:05
☉	♊	21 13:17
♀	♋	23 2:46
♂	♉	28 23:47
⚳	♋	7 19:52
♀	♌	17 5:31
☉	♋	21 21:24

Last Aspect Dy Hr Mn			☽ Ingress	Dy Hr Mn
30 23:45	☿	⚹	♈	1 6:12
3 0:58	♅	△	♉	3 6:49
5 2:13	♅	□	♊	5 8:16
7 6:00	♅	⚹	♋	7 12:28
8 21:15	☉	⚹	♌	9 20:35
12 0:57	♅	☌	♍	12 8:11
14 6:53	☉	△	♎	14 21:03
17 1:48	♅	⚹	♏	17 8:43
19 14:32	☉	☍	♐	19 18:02
21 22:35	♀	☍	♑	22 1:08
23 23:55	♂	□	♒	24 6:31
26 7:01	♂	⚹	♓	26 10:29
27 20:58	☿	□	♈	28 13:15
30 9:46	♅	△	♉	30 15:17

Last Aspect Dy Hr Mn			☽ Ingress	Dy Hr Mn
1 12:09	♅	□	♊	1 17:40
3 16:14	♅	⚹	♋	3 21:56
5 2:17	♀	☌	♌	6 5:23
8 10:04	♅	☌	♍	8 16:12
10 12:45	♀	⚹	♎	11 4:51
13 11:03	♅	⚹	♏	13 16:45
15 23:17	♀	△	♐	16 2:03
18 3:38	♅	△	♑	18 8:30
19 12:26	♂	△	♒	20 12:49
22 11:37	♅	☍	♓	22 15:59
24 0:25	♂	⚹	♈	24 18:43
26 17:30	♅	△	♉	26 21:34
28 21:10	♅	□	♊	29 1:09

☽ Phases & Eclipses Dy Hr Mn	
4 4:25	● 13♉14
11 12:44	☽ 20♌21
19 14:32	○ 28♏08
26 19:05	☾ 5♓02
2 13:27	● 11♊31
10 6:21	☽ 18♍54
18 2:02	○ 26♐22
24 23:42	☾ 2♈57

Astro Data

1 May 1962
Julian Day # 22766
SVP 5♓47'23"
GC 26♐18.8 ⚴ 28♈45.8
Eris 10♈26.6 ✱ 5♊31.2
⚷ 10♓00.7 ⚵ 19♊26.3
☽ Mean ☊ 13♌37.9

1 June 1962
Julian Day # 22797
SVP 5♓47'18"
GC 26♐18.9 ⚴ 12♉26.3
Eris 10♈42.1 ✱ 23♊28.0
⚷ 10♓48.7 ⚵ 2♋21.4
☽ Mean ☊ 11♌59.4

July 1962 — LONGITUDE

Day	Sid.Time	☉	0 hr ☽	Noon ☽	True ☊	☿	♀	♂	⚳	♃	♄	♅	♆	♇
1 Su	6 36 14	9♋09 52	26♊30 08	3♋08 21	9♌07.5	17♊34.1	16♌45.6	24♉33.4	10♋14.3	12♓41.3	10♒08.8	27♌49.3	10♏50.4	7♍58.7
2 M	6 40 11	10 07 06	9♋42 26	16 12 18	9R 04.4	18 32.0	17 55.5	25 16.2	10 40.5	12R 41.4	10R 05.3	27 52.1	10R 49.8	8 00.0
3 Tu	6 44 08	11 04 19	22 37 53	28 59 15	9D 02.7	19 34.2	19 05.3	25 59.1	11 06.7	12 41.3	10 01.8	27 54.9	10 49.1	8 01.2
4 W	6 48 04	12 01 33	5♌16 30	11♌29 49	9 02.3	20 40.5	20 15.1	26 41.8	11 32.9	12 41.0	9 58.1	27 57.8	10 48.5	8 02.5
5 Th	6 52 01	12 58 46	17 39 27	23 45 43	9 03.0	21 51.0	21 24.7	27 24.5	11 59.1	12 40.4	9 54.5	28 00.7	10 48.0	8 03.9
6 F	6 55 57	13 55 59	29 48 58	5♍49 39	9 04.5	23 05.5	22 34.3	28 07.1	12 25.3	12 39.7	9 50.7	28 03.6	10 47.4	8 05.2
7 Sa	6 59 54	14 53 12	11♍48 13	17 45 11	9 06.1	24 24.1	23 43.8	28 49.6	12 51.5	12 38.8	9 47.0	28 06.5	10 46.9	8 06.6
8 Su	7 03 50	15 50 25	23 41 06	29 36 31	9 07.6	25 46.7	24 53.2	29 32.0	13 17.7	12 37.7	9 43.1	28 09.5	10 46.4	8 07.9
9 M	7 07 47	16 47 37	5♎32 02	11♎28 15	9R 08.4	27 13.1	26 02.5	0♊14.4	13 43.9	12 36.4	9 39.2	28 12.5	10 46.0	8 09.4
10 Tu	7 11 43	17 44 50	17 25 46	23 25 11	9 08.4	28 43.4	27 11.7	0 56.7	14 10.1	12 34.9	9 35.3	28 15.5	10 45.6	8 10.8
11 W	7 15 40	18 42 02	29 27 04	5♏31 59	9 07.5	0♋17.5	28 20.8	1 38.9	14 36.4	12 33.3	9 31.3	28 18.6	10 45.2	8 12.2
12 Th	7 19 37	19 39 15	11♏40 28	17 53 01	9 05.7	1 55.2	29 29.8	2 21.1	15 02.6	12 31.4	9 27.3	28 21.7	10 44.8	8 13.7
13 F	7 23 33	20 36 27	24 10 02	0♐31 54	9 03.4	3 36.5	0♍38.7	3 03.2	15 28.9	12 29.3	9 23.2	28 24.8	10 44.5	8 15.2
14 Sa	7 27 30	21 33 40	6♐58 55	13 31 15	9 01.0	5 21.2	1 47.4	3 45.2	15 55.1	12 27.1	9 19.1	28 28.0	10 44.2	8 16.7
15 Su	7 31 26	22 30 53	20 09 03	26 52 18	8 58.7	7 09.2	2 56.1	4 27.1	16 21.4	12 24.7	9 15.0	28 31.2	10 44.0	8 18.3
16 M	7 35 23	23 28 06	3♑40 53	10♑34 36	8 56.9	9 00.3	4 04.7	5 09.0	16 47.6	12 22.0	9 10.8	28 34.4	10 43.7	8 19.8
17 Tu	7 39 19	24 25 19	17 33 07	24 36 02	8 55.8	10 54.2	5 13.1	5 50.8	17 13.9	12 19.2	9 06.6	28 37.6	10 43.5	8 21.4
18 W	7 43 16	25 22 33	1♒42 49	8♒52 54	8D 55.4	12 50.8	6 21.4	6 32.5	17 40.2	12 16.2	9 02.4	28 40.9	10 43.4	8 23.0
19 Th	7 47 12	26 19 47	16 05 37	23 20 20	8 55.7	14 49.8	7 29.7	7 14.1	18 06.4	12 13.1	8 58.1	28 44.2	10 43.2	8 24.6
20 F	7 51 09	27 17 01	0♓36 19	7♓52 54	8 56.4	16 50.9	8 37.8	7 55.7	18 32.7	12 09.7	8 53.8	28 47.5	10 43.1	8 26.3
21 Sa	7 55 06	28 14 17	15 09 24	22 25 13	8 57.3	18 53.7	9 45.7	8 37.2	18 59.0	12 06.2	8 49.5	28 50.8	10 43.0	8 27.9
22 Su	7 59 02	29 11 33	29 39 47	6♈52 33	8 58.1	20 58.1	10 53.6	9 18.6	19 25.2	12 02.4	8 45.1	28 54.2	10D 43.0	8 29.6
23 M	8 02 59	0♌08 50	14♈03 07	21 11 05	8R 58.5	23 03.6	12 01.3	9 59.9	19 51.5	11 58.6	8 40.7	28 57.6	10 43.0	8 31.3
24 Tu	8 06 55	1 06 08	28 16 09	5♉18 05	8 58.6	25 09.9	13 08.9	10 41.2	20 17.8	11 54.5	8 36.4	29 01.0	10 43.0	8 33.0
25 W	8 10 52	2 03 27	12♉16 42	19 11 52	8 58.3	27 16.8	14 16.4	11 22.4	20 44.0	11 50.2	8 31.9	29 04.4	10 43.1	8 34.7
26 Th	8 14 48	3 00 47	26 03 29	2♊51 29	8 57.8	29 23.8	15 23.7	12 03.5	21 10.3	11 45.8	8 27.5	29 07.9	10 43.1	8 36.5
27 F	8 18 45	3 58 08	9♊35 52	16 16 37	8 57.2	1♌30.8	16 30.9	12 44.5	21 36.6	11 41.2	8 23.1	29 11.3	10 43.3	8 38.2
28 Sa	8 22 41	4 55 30	22 53 44	29 27 16	8 56.7	3 37.5	17 38.0	13 25.4	22 02.8	11 36.5	8 18.6	29 14.8	10 43.4	8 40.0
29 Su	8 26 38	5 52 52	5♋57 15	12♋23 45	8 56.3	5 43.7	18 45.0	14 06.3	22 29.1	11 31.6	8 14.2	29 18.3	10 43.6	8 41.8
30 M	8 30 35	6 50 16	18 46 49	25 06 33	8 56.1	7 49.1	19 51.8	14 47.1	22 55.4	11 26.5	8 09.7	29 21.9	10 43.8	8 43.6
31 Tu	8 34 31	7 47 41	1♌23 02	7♌36 24	8D 56.1	9 53.5	20 58.4	15 27.8	23 21.6	11 21.2	8 05.3	29 25.4	10 44.1	8 45.4

August 1962 — LONGITUDE

Day	Sid.Time	☉	0 hr ☽	Noon ☽	True ☊	☿	♀	♂	⚳	♃	♄	♅	♆	♇
1 W	8 38 28	8♌45 06	13♌46 48	19♌54 23	8♌56.1	11♌56.9	22♍04.9	16♊08.4	23♋47.9	11♓15.9	8♒00.8	29♌29.0	10♏44.4	8♍47.2
2 Th	8 42 24	9 42 32	25 59 22	2♍01 59	8R 56.1	13 59.1	23 11.3	16 48.9	24 14.1	11R 10.3	7R 56.3	29 32.5	10 44.7	8 49.1
3 F	8 46 21	10 39 59	8♍02 28	14 01 09	8 55.9	16 00.0	24 17.4	17 29.3	24 40.3	11 04.6	7 51.9	29 36.1	10 45.0	8 51.0
4 Sa	8 50 17	11 37 26	19 58 21	25 54 26	8 55.7	17 59.6	25 23.5	18 09.7	25 06.4	10 58.8	7 47.4	29 39.7	10 45.4	8 52.8
5 Su	8 54 14	12 34 55	1♎49 47	7♎44 52	8 55.3	19 57.7	26 29.3	18 50.0	25 32.8	10 52.8	7 43.0	29 43.4	10 45.8	8 54.7
6 M	8 58 10	13 32 24	13 40 09	19 36 06	8 54.8	21 54.3	27 35.0	19 30.1	25 59.0	10 46.7	7 38.6	29 47.0	10 46.2	8 56.6
7 Tu	9 02 07	14 29 54	25 33 15	1♏32 08	8 54.4	23 49.5	28 40.5	20 10.2	26 25.2	10 40.5	7 34.1	29 50.6	10 46.7	8 58.5
8 W	9 06 04	15 27 25	7♏33 19	13 37 21	8D 54.3	25 43.1	29 45.8	20 50.2	26 51.3	10 34.1	7 29.7	29 54.3	10 47.2	9 00.5
9 Th	9 10 00	16 24 56	19 44 47	25 56 12	8 54.4	27 35.2	0♎50.9	21 30.1	27 17.5	10 27.6	7 25.3	29 58.0	10 47.8	9 02.4
10 F	9 13 57	17 22 29	2♐12 05	8♐32 58	8 54.8	29 25.8	1 55.9	22 09.9	27 43.7	10 21.0	7 21.0	0♍01.6	10 48.3	9 04.4
11 Sa	9 17 53	18 20 02	14 59 16	21 31 23	8 55.6	1♍14.9	3 00.6	22 49.6	28 09.8	10 14.3	7 16.6	0 05.3	10 48.9	9 06.3
12 Su	9 21 50	19 17 36	28 09 37	4♑54 09	8 56.5	3 02.4	4 05.1	23 29.3	28 35.9	10 07.5	7 12.3	0 09.0	10 49.6	9 08.3
13 M	9 25 46	20 15 12	11♑45 06	18 42 24	8 57.3	4 48.5	5 09.4	24 08.8	29 02.0	10 00.5	7 08.0	0 12.7	10 50.2	9 10.3
14 Tu	9 29 43	21 12 48	25 45 53	2♒55 12	8R 57.8	6 33.0	6 13.5	24 48.3	29 28.1	9 53.5	7 03.8	0 16.5	10 50.9	9 12.3
15 W	9 33 39	22 10 25	10♒09 51	17 29 13	8 57.7	8 16.0	7 17.3	25 27.6	29 54.2	9 46.4	6 59.5	0 20.2	10 51.7	9 14.2
16 Th	9 37 36	23 08 04	24 52 29	2♓16 46	8 57.0	9 57.6	8 21.0	26 06.9	0♌20.3	9 39.2	6 55.3	0 23.9	10 52.4	9 16.3
17 F	9 41 33	24 05 44	9♓47 04	17 16 21	8 55.6	11 37.7	9 24.3	26 46.1	0 46.3	9 31.9	6 51.2	0 27.6	10 53.2	9 18.3
18 Sa	9 45 29	25 03 25	24 45 32	2♈13 35	8 53.7	13 16.4	10 27.5	27 25.2	1 12.4	9 24.5	6 47.0	0 31.4	10 54.0	9 20.3
19 Su	9 49 26	26 01 08	9♈39 31	17 02 27	8 51.7	14 53.6	11 30.4	28 04.2	1 38.4	9 17.0	6 43.0	0 35.1	10 54.9	9 22.3
20 M	9 53 22	26 58 52	24 21 37	1♉36 24	8 49.9	16 29.4	12 33.0	28 43.1	2 04.4	9 09.5	6 38.9	0 38.9	10 55.8	9 24.3
21 Tu	9 57 19	27 56 38	8♉46 19	15 51 01	8D 48.7	18 03.7	13 35.4	29 21.9	2 30.3	9 01.9	6 34.9	0 42.6	10 56.7	9 26.4
22 W	10 01 15	28 54 26	22 50 20	29 44 10	8 48.3	19 36.7	14 37.5	0♋00.6	2 56.3	8 54.3	6 30.9	0 46.4	10 57.6	9 28.4
23 Th	10 05 12	29 52 16	6♊32 36	13♊15 44	8 48.8	21 08.2	15 39.4	0 39.2	3 22.2	8 46.5	6 27.0	0 50.1	10 58.6	9 30.5
24 F	10 09 08	0♍50 08	19 53 47	26 27 01	8 50.0	22 38.3	16 40.9	1 17.7	3 48.1	8 38.8	6 23.2	0 53.9	10 59.6	9 32.5
25 Sa	10 13 05	1 48 01	2♋55 43	9♋20 12	8 51.5	24 07.0	17 42.2	1 56.2	4 14.0	8 31.0	6 19.4	0 57.6	11 00.6	9 34.6
26 Su	10 17 02	2 45 56	15 40 48	21 57 51	8 52.9	25 34.2	18 43.2	2 34.5	4 39.9	8 23.2	6 15.6	1 01.4	11 01.7	9 36.7
27 M	10 20 58	3 43 52	28 11 39	4♌22 31	8R 53.8	27 00.0	19 43.9	3 12.7	5 05.8	8 15.3	6 11.9	1 05.1	11 02.8	9 38.7
28 Tu	10 24 55	4 41 50	10♌30 43	16 36 33	8 53.6	28 24.3	20 44.2	3 50.8	5 31.6	8 07.4	6 08.2	1 08.9	11 03.9	9 40.8
29 W	10 28 51	5 39 50	22 40 15	28 42 04	8 52.1	29 47.0	21 44.3	4 28.8	5 57.4	7 59.5	6 04.6	1 12.6	11 05.0	9 42.9
30 Th	10 32 48	6 37 52	4♍42 13	10♍40 56	8 49.3	1♎08.3	22 44.0	5 06.7	6 23.1	7 51.6	6 01.1	1 16.4	11 06.2	9 44.9
31 F	10 36 44	7 35 55	16 38 27	22 34 58	8 45.2	2 28.0	23 43.3	5 44.5	6 48.8	7 43.6	5 57.6	1 20.1	11 07.4	9 47.0

Astro Data

	Dy Hr Mn
♃ R	2 8:58
☽ 0S	9 10:33
☽ 0N	22 18:37
♆ D	23 8:11
♄ ⚻ ♇	25 1:13
☽ 0S	5 18:17
♃ △ ♆	6 13:41
♀ 0S	8 15:08
♃ ☍ ♇	18 22:41
☽ 0N	19 1:51
☿ 0S	28 15:00

Planet Ingress

		Dy Hr Mn
♂	♊	9 3:50
☿	♋	11 7:36
♀	♍	12 22:32
☉	♌	23 8:18
☿	♌	26 18:50
♀	♎	8 17:13
♅	♍	10 1:19
☿	♍	10 19:29
⚳	♌	15 17:19
♂	♋	22 11:37
☉	♍	23 15:12
☿	♎	29 15:48

Last Aspect / ☽ Ingress (July)

Last Aspect Dy Hr Mn				☽ Ingress Dy Hr Mn
1 2:21	♅	⚹	♋	1 6:19
3 5:59	♂	⚹	♌	3 13:55
5 20:27	♅	☌	♍	6 0:22
8 11:50	♂	△	♎	8 12:48
11 0:07	☿	△	♏	11 1:05
13 8:00	♅	□	♐	13 11:00
15 14:56	♅	△	♑	15 17:32
17 11:40	☉	☍	♒	17 21:07
19 20:57	♅	☍	♓	19 23:00
21 22:19	☉	△	♈	22 0:34
24 1:14	♅	△	♉	24 2:57
26 5:23	♅	□	♊	26 6:57
28 11:37	♅	⚹	♋	28 13:00
30 1:05	♀	⚹	♌	30 21:21

Last Aspect / ☽ Ingress (August)

Last Aspect Dy Hr Mn				☽ Ingress Dy Hr Mn
2 7:01	♅	☌	♍	2 7:57
4 10:51	♀	☌	♎	4 20:17
7 8:36	♅	⚹	♏	7 8:56
9 19:46	♅	□	♐	9 19:48
11 14:30	♂	☍	♑	12 3:18
12 22:24	♆	⚹	♒	14 7:07
16 1:33	♂	△	♓	16 8:17
18 3:55	♂	□	♈	18 8:25
20 6:59	♂	⚹	♉	20 9:20
22 10:26	☉	□	♊	22 12:28
24 4:06	☿	□	♋	24 18:34
26 19:50	☿	⚹	♌	27 3:30
28 20:54	♀	⚹	♍	29 14:36

☽ Phases & Eclipses

Dy Hr Mn		
1 23:52	●	9♋38
9 23:39	☽	17♎15
17 11:40	○	24♑25
17 11:54	☍	A 0.392
24 4:18	☾	0♉48
31 12:24	●	7♌49
31 12:24:58	☌	A 03'33"
8 15:55	☽	15♏37
15 20:09	○	22♒30
15 19:57	☍	A 0.596
22 10:26	☾	28♉51
30 3:09	●	6♍16

Astro Data

1 July 1962
Julian Day # 22827
SVP 5♓47'13"
GC 26♐18.9 ⚴ 26♉10.2
Eris 10♈48.9 ⚵ 10♋26.0
⚷ 10♓45.0R ⚶ 15♋23.2
☽ Mean ☊ 10♌24.1

1 August 1962
Julian Day # 22858
SVP 5♓47'08"
GC 26♐19.0 ⚴ 10♊41.0
Eris 10♈45.8R ⚵ 27♋16.0
⚷ 9♓52.3R ⚶ 29♋06.4
☽ Mean ☊ 8♌45.6

LONGITUDE — September 1962

Day	Sid.Time	☉	0 hr ☽	Noon ☽	True ☊	☿	♀	♂	⚳	♃	♄	♅	♆	♇
1 Sa	10 40 41	8♍33 59	28♍30 44	4♎26 01	8♌40.1	3♎46.0	24♎42.3	6♋22.2	7♌14.5	7♓35.7	5♒54.2	1♍23.9	11♏08.6	9♍49.1
2 Su	10 44 37	9 32 05	10♎21 03	16 16 09	8R34.6	5 02.4	25 40.9	6 59.7	7 40.2	7R27.8	5R50.9	1 27.6	11 09.9	9 51.2
3 M	10 48 34	10 30 13	22 11 38	28 07 52	8 29.3	6 17.1	26 39.1	7 37.2	8 05.8	7 19.8	5 47.6	1 31.3	11 11.2	9 53.3
4 Tu	10 52 30	11 28 22	4♏05 12	10♏04 06	8 24.7	7 29.9	27 36.9	8 14.5	8 31.4	7 11.9	5 44.4	1 35.1	11 12.5	9 55.3
5 W	10 56 27	12 26 33	16 04 58	22 08 18	8 21.4	8 40.9	28 34.3	8 51.7	8 57.0	7 04.1	5 41.3	1 38.8	11 13.8	9 57.4
6 Th	11 00 24	13 24 45	28 14 37	4♐24 25	8D19.5	9 50.0	29 31.3	9 28.8	9 22.5	6 56.2	5 38.3	1 42.5	11 15.2	9 59.5
7 F	11 04 20	14 22 58	10♐38 14	16 56 38	8 19.1	10 56.9	0♏27.8	10 05.8	9 48.0	6 48.4	5 35.3	1 46.2	11 16.6	10 01.6
8 Sa	11 08 17	15 21 14	23 20 07	29 49 13	8 19.9	12 01.7	1 23.8	10 42.7	10 13.5	6 40.7	5 32.4	1 49.8	11 18.0	10 03.6
9 Su	11 12 13	16 19 30	6♑24 21	13♑05 56	8 21.4	13 04.2	2 19.4	11 19.5	10 38.9	6 32.9	5 29.5	1 53.5	11 19.5	10 05.7
10 M	11 16 10	17 17 48	19 54 16	26 49 34	8R22.7	14 04.3	3 14.4	11 56.1	11 04.3	6 25.3	5 26.8	1 57.2	11 20.9	10 07.8
11 Tu	11 20 06	18 16 08	3♒51 50	11♒01 01	8 23.1	15 01.7	4 08.9	12 32.6	11 29.6	6 17.7	5 24.1	2 00.8	11 22.4	10 09.8
12 W	11 24 03	19 14 29	18 16 46	25 38 38	8 21.9	15 56.4	5 02.9	13 09.0	11 54.9	6 10.1	5 21.5	2 04.5	11 23.9	10 11.9
13 Th	11 27 59	20 12 52	3♓05 53	10♓37 39	8 18.9	16 48.2	5 56.3	13 45.3	12 20.2	6 02.7	5 19.0	2 08.1	11 25.5	10 14.0
14 F	11 31 56	21 11 17	18 12 49	25 50 11	8 14.1	17 36.7	6 49.1	14 21.4	12 45.4	5 55.3	5 16.6	2 11.7	11 27.1	10 16.0
15 Sa	11 35 53	22 09 44	3♈28 26	11♈06 10	8 07.9	18 21.9	7 41.4	14 57.5	13 10.5	5 48.0	5 14.3	2 15.3	11 28.6	10 18.1
16 Su	11 39 49	23 08 12	18 42 04	26 14 51	8 01.2	19 03.4	8 33.0	15 33.4	13 35.6	5 40.7	5 12.0	2 18.9	11 30.3	10 20.1
17 M	11 43 46	24 06 43	3♉43 23	11♉06 43	7 54.9	19 41.0	9 23.9	16 09.2	14 00.7	5 33.6	5 09.8	2 22.4	11 31.9	10 22.1
18 Tu	11 47 42	25 05 16	18 24 04	25 34 55	7 49.9	20 14.3	10 14.2	16 44.8	14 25.8	5 26.5	5 07.7	2 26.0	11 33.6	10 24.2
19 W	11 51 39	26 03 51	2♊38 54	9♊35 53	7 46.7	20 43.1	11 03.8	17 20.3	14 50.7	5 19.6	5 05.7	2 29.5	11 35.2	10 26.2
20 Th	11 55 35	27 02 28	16 25 55	23 09 11	7D45.4	21 06.9	11 52.7	17 55.7	15 15.7	5 12.8	5 03.8	2 33.0	11 36.9	10 28.2
21 F	11 59 32	28 01 08	29 46 00	6♋16 45	7 45.6	21 25.5	12 40.8	18 31.0	15 40.6	5 06.0	5 02.0	2 36.5	11 38.7	10 30.2
22 Sa	12 03 28	28 59 50	12♋41 55	19 02 00	7 46.6	21 38.5	13 28.2	19 06.1	16 05.4	4 59.4	5 00.3	2 40.0	11 40.4	10 32.2
23 Su	12 07 25	29 58 34	25 17 33	1♌29 05	7R47.6	21R45.4	14 14.7	19 41.1	16 30.2	4 52.9	4 58.7	2 43.5	11 42.2	10 34.2
24 M	12 11 22	0♎57 20	7♌37 08	13 42 13	7 47.6	21 45.9	15 00.4	20 15.9	16 54.9	4 46.6	4 57.1	2 46.9	11 44.0	10 36.2
25 Tu	12 15 18	1 56 08	19 44 47	25 45 17	7 45.8	21 39.6	15 45.3	20 50.6	17 19.5	4 40.3	4 55.7	2 50.3	11 45.8	10 38.2
26 W	12 19 15	2 54 59	1♍44 08	7♍41 42	7 41.6	21 26.3	16 29.2	21 25.2	17 44.2	4 34.2	4 54.3	2 53.7	11 47.6	10 40.1
27 Th	12 23 11	3 53 51	13 38 17	19 34 10	7 34.9	21 05.6	17 12.2	21 59.6	18 08.7	4 28.2	4 53.1	2 57.1	11 49.5	10 42.1
28 F	12 27 08	4 52 46	25 29 39	1♎24 55	7 25.9	20 37.5	17 54.2	22 33.8	18 33.2	4 22.4	4 51.9	3 00.4	11 51.3	10 44.0
29 Sa	12 31 04	5 51 43	7♎20 12	13 15 42	7 15.1	20 01.8	18 35.3	23 07.9	18 57.6	4 16.7	4 50.8	3 03.7	11 53.2	10 45.9
30 Su	12 35 01	6 50 41	19 11 34	25 08 01	7 03.4	19 18.8	19 15.2	23 41.9	19 21.9	4 11.2	4 49.9	3 07.0	11 55.1	10 47.9

LONGITUDE — October 1962

Day	Sid.Time	☉	0 hr ☽	Noon ☽	True ☊	☿	♀	♂	⚳	♃	♄	♅	♆	♇
1 M	12 38 57	7♎49 42	1♏05 15	7♏03 27	6♌51.8	18♎28.8	19♏54.0	24♋15.6	19♌46.2	4♓05.8	4♒49.0	3♍10.3	11♏57.0	10♍49.8
2 Tu	12 42 54	8 48 44	13 02 53	19 03 47	6R41.3	17R32.5	20 31.7	24 49.3	20 10.4	4R00.6	4R48.2	3 13.5	11 59.0	10 51.7
3 W	12 46 50	9 47 49	25 06 28	1♐11 16	6 32.9	16 30.8	21 08.2	25 22.7	20 34.6	3 55.6	4 47.6	3 16.7	12 00.9	10 53.5
4 Th	12 50 47	10 46 55	7♐18 32	13 28 42	6 26.9	15 24.7	21 43.4	25 56.0	20 58.7	3 50.7	4 47.0	3 19.9	12 02.9	10 55.4
5 F	12 54 44	11 46 03	19 42 11	25 59 27	6 23.5	14 15.8	22 17.3	26 29.1	21 22.7	3 46.0	4 46.5	3 23.0	12 04.9	10 57.3
6 Sa	12 58 40	12 45 13	2♑21 01	8♑47 22	6D22.3	13 05.7	22 49.9	27 02.1	21 46.6	3 41.5	4 46.2	3 26.2	12 06.9	10 59.1
7 Su	13 02 37	13 44 24	15 18 59	21 56 22	6 22.4	11 56.4	23 21.0	27 34.8	22 10.4	3 37.1	4 45.9	3 29.3	12 08.9	11 00.9
8 M	13 06 33	14 43 38	28 39 54	5♒29 58	6R22.8	10 49.6	23 50.7	28 07.4	22 34.2	3 32.9	4 45.7	3 32.3	12 10.9	11 02.7
9 Tu	13 10 30	15 42 53	12♒26 49	19 30 34	6 22.2	9 47.4	24 18.8	28 39.9	22 57.9	3 28.9	4D45.7	3 35.4	12 13.0	11 04.5
10 W	13 14 26	16 42 10	26 41 10	3♓58 23	6 19.6	8 51.5	24 45.3	29 12.1	23 21.5	3 25.1	4 45.7	3 38.4	12 15.1	11 06.3
11 Th	13 18 23	17 41 28	11♓21 47	18 50 41	6 14.4	8 03.5	25 10.1	29 44.2	23 45.0	3 21.4	4 45.8	3 41.3	12 17.1	11 08.0
12 F	13 22 19	18 40 48	26 24 12	4♈01 13	6 06.6	7 24.6	25 33.3	0♌16.0	24 08.5	3 18.0	4 46.1	3 44.3	12 19.2	11 09.8
13 Sa	13 26 16	19 40 11	11♈40 27	19 20 30	5 56.7	6 55.9	25 54.6	0 47.7	24 31.8	3 14.7	4 46.4	3 47.2	12 21.3	11 11.5
14 Su	13 30 13	20 39 35	26 59 53	4♉37 09	5 46.0	6 37.9	26 14.2	1 19.2	24 55.1	3 11.6	4 46.8	3 50.0	12 23.4	11 13.2
15 M	13 34 09	21 39 02	12♉10 55	19 39 57	5 35.5	6D31.0	26 31.8	1 50.6	25 18.3	3 08.7	4 47.4	3 52.8	12 25.5	11 14.9
16 Tu	13 38 06	22 38 30	27 03 12	4♊19 50	5 26.7	6 35.1	26 47.4	2 21.7	25 41.4	3 06.0	4 48.0	3 55.6	12 27.7	11 16.5
17 W	13 42 02	23 38 02	11♊29 17	18 31 12	5 20.2	6 49.9	27 01.1	2 52.6	26 04.4	3 03.5	4 48.7	3 58.4	12 29.8	11 18.2
18 Th	13 45 59	24 37 35	25 25 28	2♋12 10	5 16.3	7 15.0	27 12.6	3 23.3	26 27.3	3 01.2	4 49.6	4 01.1	12 32.0	11 19.8
19 F	13 49 55	25 37 11	8♋51 32	15 23 59	5D14.6	7 49.7	27 22.1	3 53.9	26 50.1	2 59.1	4 50.5	4 03.8	12 34.1	11 21.4
20 Sa	13 53 52	26 36 48	21 49 59	28 10 06	5R14.3	8 33.3	27 29.3	4 24.2	27 12.8	2 57.2	4 51.5	4 06.4	12 36.3	11 23.0
21 Su	13 57 48	27 36 29	4♌24 58	10♌35 13	5 14.3	9 25.0	27 34.3	4 54.2	27 35.4	2 55.5	4 52.7	4 09.0	12 38.5	11 24.6
22 M	14 01 45	28 36 11	16 41 31	22 44 29	5 13.3	10 24.0	27R37.1	5 24.1	27 57.9	2 53.9	4 53.9	4 11.6	12 40.7	11 26.1
23 Tu	14 05 42	29 35 56	28 44 45	4♍42 54	5 10.4	11 29.4	27 37.5	5 53.7	28 20.3	2 52.6	4 55.2	4 14.1	12 42.9	11 27.7
24 W	14 09 38	0♏35 42	10♍39 29	16 35 00	5 04.7	12 40.4	27 35.5	6 23.2	28 42.6	2 51.5	4 56.7	4 16.6	12 45.1	11 29.2
25 Th	14 13 35	1 35 31	22 29 56	28 24 39	4 56.0	13 56.3	27 31.2	6 52.3	29 04.8	2 50.6	4 58.2	4 19.1	12 47.3	11 30.6
26 F	14 17 31	2 35 22	4♎19 32	10♎14 52	4 44.6	15 16.4	27 24.5	7 21.3	29 26.8	2 49.9	4 59.9	4 21.5	12 49.5	11 32.1
27 Sa	14 21 28	3 35 15	16 10 56	22 07 56	4 30.9	16 40.0	27 15.3	7 49.9	29 48.8	2 49.4	5 01.6	4 23.8	12 51.7	11 33.5
28 Su	14 25 24	4 35 10	28 06 04	4♏05 28	4 16.2	18 06.7	27 03.7	8 18.4	0♍10.6	2D49.1	5 03.4	4 26.1	12 53.9	11 35.0
29 M	14 29 21	5 35 07	10♏06 17	16 08 37	4 01.5	19 35.8	26 49.8	8 46.5	0 32.3	2 49.0	5 05.3	4 28.4	12 56.2	11 36.3
30 Tu	14 33 17	6 35 06	22 12 36	28 18 21	3 48.1	21 07.0	26 33.4	9 14.5	0 53.8	2 49.1	5 07.4	4 30.6	12 58.4	11 37.7
31 W	14 37 14	7 35 07	4♐26 01	10♐35 45	3 37.0	22 39.9	26 14.8	9 42.1	1 15.3	2 49.5	5 09.5	4 32.8	13 00.6	11 39.0

Astro Data

	Dy Hr Mn
☽0S	2 0:41
☽0N	15 11:13
♃⚹♄	22 7:39
⊙0S	23 12:35
☿R	24 1:52
☽0S	29 6:26
♃☍♅	8 13:55
♄D	9 16:25
☽0N	12 22:14
☿D	15 15:05
♀R	23 4:14
☽0S	26 12:43
♃D	29 10:31

Planet Ingress

	Dy Hr Mn
♀ ♏	7 0:11
⊙ ♎	23 12:35
♂ ♌	11 23:54
⊙ ♏	23 21:40
⚳ ♍	28 0:21

Last Aspect / ☽ Ingress

Last Aspect Dy Hr Mn		☽ Ingress Dy Hr Mn
30 12:51 ♆ ⚹	♎	1 3:01
3 8:45 ♀ ☌	♏	3 15:46
4 15:03 ⊙ ⚹	♐	6 3:26
7 6:44 ⊙ □	♑	8 12:20
9 18:09 ⊙ △	♒	10 17:26
11 19:06 ☿ △	♓	12 19:02
14 4:11 ⊙ ☍	♈	14 18:33
16 0:02 ☿ ☍	♉	16 18:00
18 11:07 ⊙ △	♊	18 19:29
20 19:36 ⊙ □	♋	21 0:26
23 8:49 ⊙ ⚹	♌	23 9:07
25 3:55 ☿ ⚹	♍	25 20:31
27 17:09 ♂ ⚹	♎	28 9:08
30 8:57 ♂ □	♏	30 21:49

Last Aspect / ☽ Ingress

Last Aspect Dy Hr Mn		☽ Ingress Dy Hr Mn
2 23:59 ♂ △	♐	3 9:40
4 15:26 ☿ ⚹	♑	5 19:35
7 22:30 ♂ ☍	♒	8 2:22
9 20:19 ♀ □	♓	10 5:29
11 22:19 ♀ △	♈	12 5:41
13 12:33 ⊙ ☍	♉	14 4:43
15 23:21 ♀ ☍	♊	16 4:50
17 21:33 ⊙ △	♋	18 8:05
20 10:42 ♀ △	♌	20 15:30
23 0:47 ⊙ ⚹	♍	23 2:31
25 10:12 ♀ ⚹	♎	25 15:14
26 23:30 ☿ ☌	♏	28 3:49
30 8:39 ♀ ☌	♐	30 15:19

☽ Phases & Eclipses

Dy Hr Mn	
7 6:44	☽ 14♐10
14 4:11	○ 20♓52
20 19:36	☾ 27♊21
28 19:39	● 5♎12
6 19:54	☽ 13♑05
13 12:33	○ 19♈42
20 8:47	☾ 26♋29
28 13:05	● 4♏38

Astro Data

1 September 1962
Julian Day # 22889
SVP 5♓47'05"
GC 26♐19.1 ⚴ 25♊07.3
Eris 10♈33.4R ⚵ 13♌08.2
⚷ 8♓28.7R ⚶ 12♌50.3
☽ Mean ☊ 7♌07.1

1 October 1962
Julian Day # 22919
SVP 5♓47'03"
GC 26♐19.1 ⚴ 8♋08.9
Eris 10♈15.9R ⚵ 27♌16.6
⚷ 7♓07.9R ⚶ 25♌51.4
☽ Mean ☊ 5♌31.7

November 1962 LONGITUDE

Day	Sid.Time	☉	0 hr ☽	Noon ☽	True ☊	☿	♀	♂	⚳	♃	♄	♅	♆	♇
1 Th	14 41 11	8♏35 09	16♐47 44	23♐02 12	3♌28.8	24♎14.1	25♏53.8	10♌09.5	1♍36.6	2♓50.0	5♒11.7	4♍34.9	13♏02.9	11♍40.4
2 F	14 45 07	9 35 13	29 19 26	5♑39 42	3R 23.7	25 49.3	25R 30.7	10 36.6	1 57.8	2 50.7	5 14.1	4 37.0	13 05.1	11 41.6
3 Sa	14 49 04	10 35 19	12♑03 20	18 30 43	3 21.3	27 25.4	25 05.5	11 03.5	2 18.8	2 51.7	5 16.5	4 39.1	13 07.4	11 42.9
4 Su	14 53 00	11 35 27	25 02 14	1♒38 15	3 20.7	29 02.0	24 38.3	11 30.0	2 39.7	2 52.8	5 19.0	4 41.1	13 09.6	11 44.2
5 M	14 56 57	12 35 35	8♒19 10	15 05 19	3 20.8	0♏39.1	24 09.3	11 56.3	3 00.5	2 54.1	5 21.6	4 43.0	13 11.9	11 45.4
6 Tu	15 00 53	13 35 46	21 57 00	28 54 25	3 20.1	2 16.5	23 38.6	12 22.2	3 21.1	2 55.7	5 24.3	4 44.9	13 14.1	11 46.6
7 W	15 04 50	14 35 58	5♓57 41	13♓06 45	3 17.5	3 54.1	23 06.3	12 47.9	3 41.6	2 57.4	5 27.1	4 46.7	13 16.4	11 47.7
8 Th	15 08 46	15 36 11	20 21 25	27 41 18	3 12.4	5 31.7	22 32.8	13 13.2	4 01.9	2 59.4	5 30.0	4 48.5	13 18.6	11 48.8
9 F	15 12 43	16 36 25	5♈05 49	12♈34 11	3 04.6	7 09.4	21 58.2	13 38.3	4 22.1	3 01.5	5 32.9	4 50.3	13 20.9	11 49.9
10 Sa	15 16 40	17 36 42	20 05 25	27 38 23	2 54.7	8 46.9	21 22.7	14 03.0	4 42.1	3 03.9	5 36.0	4 52.0	13 23.1	11 51.0
11 Su	15 20 36	18 37 00	5♉11 51	12♉44 30	2 43.6	10 24.4	20 46.6	14 27.4	5 02.0	3 06.4	5 39.2	4 53.6	13 25.4	11 52.1
12 M	15 24 33	19 37 19	20 15 02	27 42 11	2 32.7	12 01.7	20 10.1	14 51.5	5 21.7	3 09.2	5 42.4	4 55.2	13 27.6	11 53.1
13 Tu	15 28 29	20 37 41	5♊04 51	12♊22 02	2 23.2	13 38.8	19 33.5	15 15.2	5 41.2	3 12.1	5 45.7	4 56.8	13 29.8	11 54.1
14 W	15 32 26	21 38 04	19 33 00	26 37 10	2 16.1	15 15.8	18 57.0	15 38.7	6 00.6	3 15.2	5 49.2	4 58.3	13 32.1	11 55.0
15 Th	15 36 22	22 38 29	3♋34 11	10♋23 56	2 11.7	16 52.5	18 21.0	16 01.7	6 19.8	3 18.6	5 52.7	4 59.7	13 34.3	11 56.0
16 F	15 40 19	23 38 56	17 06 28	23 41 58	2D 09.7	18 29.0	17 45.6	16 24.4	6 38.8	3 22.1	5 56.3	5 01.1	13 36.5	11 56.9
17 Sa	15 44 15	24 39 24	0♌10 50	6♌33 30	2 09.5	20 05.2	17 11.0	16 46.7	6 57.7	3 25.8	6 00.0	5 02.5	13 38.7	11 57.8
18 Su	15 48 12	25 39 55	12 50 30	19 02 29	2R 10.0	21 41.3	16 37.6	17 08.7	7 16.4	3 29.7	6 03.7	5 03.8	13 41.0	11 58.6
19 M	15 52 09	26 40 27	25 10 04	1♍13 55	2 10.0	23 17.1	16 05.6	17 30.3	7 34.8	3 33.8	6 07.6	5 05.0	13 43.2	11 59.4
20 Tu	15 56 05	27 41 01	7♍14 43	13 13 07	2 08.6	24 52.7	15 35.1	17 51.4	7 53.1	3 38.1	6 11.5	5 06.2	13 45.4	12 00.2
21 W	16 00 02	28 41 37	19 09 46	25 05 16	2 05.0	26 28.0	15 06.2	18 12.2	8 11.2	3 42.5	6 15.5	5 07.3	13 47.6	12 01.0
22 Th	16 03 58	29 42 14	1♎00 13	6♎55 07	1 58.9	28 03.2	14 39.3	18 32.6	8 29.2	3 47.2	6 19.6	5 08.4	13 49.7	12 01.7
23 F	16 07 55	0♐42 53	12 50 29	18 46 44	1 50.2	29 38.2	14 14.3	18 52.5	8 46.9	3 52.0	6 23.8	5 09.4	13 51.9	12 02.4
24 Sa	16 11 51	1 43 34	24 44 15	0♏43 21	1 39.7	1♐13.0	13 51.5	19 12.0	9 04.4	3 57.0	6 28.1	5 10.4	13 54.1	12 03.1
25 Su	16 15 48	2 44 16	6♏44 20	12 47 23	1 28.0	2 47.6	13 30.9	19 31.1	9 21.7	4 02.2	6 32.4	5 11.3	13 56.3	12 03.7
26 M	16 19 44	3 45 00	18 52 41	25 00 22	1 16.3	4 22.2	13 12.7	19 49.7	9 38.7	4 07.6	6 36.8	5 12.1	13 58.4	12 04.3
27 Tu	16 23 41	4 45 45	1♐10 31	7♐23 12	1 05.6	5 56.5	12 56.8	20 07.8	9 55.6	4 13.1	6 41.3	5 12.9	14 00.5	12 04.9
28 W	16 27 38	5 46 31	13 38 26	19 56 16	0 56.9	7 30.8	12 43.3	20 25.5	10 12.3	4 18.9	6 45.9	5 13.7	14 02.7	12 05.4
29 Th	16 31 34	6 47 19	26 16 42	2♑39 48	0 50.7	9 04.9	12 32.3	20 42.7	10 28.7	4 24.8	6 50.5	5 14.4	14 04.8	12 05.9
30 F	16 35 31	7 48 07	9♑05 35	15 34 08	0 47.1	10 39.0	12 23.8	20 59.4	10 44.9	4 30.9	6 55.3	5 15.0	14 06.9	12 06.4

December 1962 LONGITUDE

Day	Sid.Time	☉	0 hr ☽	Noon ☽	True ☊	☿	♀	♂	⚳	♃	♄	♅	♆	♇
1 Sa	16 39 27	8♐48 57	22♑05 31	28♑39 53	0♌45.8	12♐13.0	12♏17.7	21♌15.6	11♍00.8	4♓37.1	7♒00.1	5♍15.6	14♏09.0	12♍06.9
2 Su	16 43 24	9 49 48	5♒17 20	11♒58 03	0D 46.3	13 46.9	12D 14.1	21 31.3	11 16.5	4 43.5	7 04.9	5 16.1	14 11.1	12 07.3
3 M	16 47 20	10 50 39	18 42 11	25 29 53	0 47.4	15 20.8	12 12.9	21 46.5	11 32.0	4 50.1	7 09.9	5 16.6	14 13.1	12 07.7
4 Tu	16 51 17	11 51 32	2♓21 20	9♓16 36	0R 48.2	16 54.7	12 14.2	22 01.2	11 47.2	4 56.9	7 14.9	5 17.0	14 15.2	12 08.0
5 W	16 55 13	12 52 25	16 15 45	23 18 46	0 47.7	18 28.5	12 17.8	22 15.3	12 02.2	5 03.8	7 20.0	5 17.3	14 17.2	12 08.3
6 Th	16 59 10	13 53 19	0♈25 33	7♈35 52	0 45.3	20 02.3	12 23.8	22 28.9	12 16.9	5 10.9	7 25.1	5 17.6	14 19.3	12 08.6
7 F	17 03 07	14 54 13	14 49 22	22 05 34	0 40.9	21 36.1	12 32.1	22 41.9	12 31.4	5 18.1	7 30.3	5 17.8	14 21.3	12 08.9
8 Sa	17 07 03	15 55 08	29 23 54	6♉43 37	0 34.7	23 10.0	12 42.7	22 54.3	12 45.5	5 25.5	7 35.6	5 18.0	14 23.3	12 09.1
9 Su	17 11 00	16 56 04	14♉03 55	21 23 54	0 27.7	24 43.8	12 55.5	23 06.2	12 59.5	5 33.1	7 40.9	5 18.1	14 25.2	12 09.3
10 M	17 14 56	17 57 01	28 42 37	5♊59 10	0 20.6	26 17.7	13 10.4	23 17.5	13 13.1	5 40.8	7 46.3	5R 18.2	14 27.2	12 09.4
11 Tu	17 18 53	18 57 59	13♊12 39	20 22 14	0 14.5	27 51.5	13 27.4	23 28.2	13 26.5	5 48.7	7 51.8	5 18.2	14 29.1	12 09.6
12 W	17 22 49	19 58 58	27 27 12	4♋26 58	0 10.0	29 25.4	13 46.4	23 38.2	13 39.6	5 56.7	7 57.3	5 18.2	14 31.1	12 09.7
13 Th	17 26 46	20 59 57	11♋21 05	18 09 16	0D 07.5	0♑59.3	14 07.4	23 47.7	13 52.4	6 04.8	8 02.9	5 18.1	14 33.0	12 09.7
14 F	17 30 42	22 00 58	24 51 23	1♌27 24	0 06.8	2 33.2	14 30.3	23 56.5	14 05.0	6 13.1	8 08.6	5 17.9	14 34.9	12R 09.7
15 Sa	17 34 39	23 01 59	7♌57 29	14 21 52	0 07.6	4 07.0	14 55.0	24 04.7	14 17.2	6 21.6	8 14.3	5 17.7	14 36.7	12 09.7
16 Su	17 38 36	24 03 01	20 40 53	26 55 00	0 09.2	5 40.8	15 21.6	24 12.1	14 29.1	6 30.2	8 20.1	5 17.4	14 38.6	12 09.7
17 M	17 42 32	25 04 04	3♍04 43	9♍10 34	0 10.9	7 14.4	15 49.8	24 19.0	14 40.7	6 38.9	8 25.9	5 17.1	14 40.4	12 09.6
18 Tu	17 46 29	26 05 08	15 13 09	21 13 05	0R 12.0	8 48.0	16 19.7	24 25.1	14 52.0	6 47.8	8 31.8	5 16.7	14 42.2	12 09.5
19 W	17 50 25	27 06 13	27 11 01	3♎07 33	0 11.9	10 21.4	16 51.1	24 30.5	15 03.0	6 56.8	8 37.7	5 16.3	14 44.0	12 09.4
20 Th	17 54 22	28 07 19	9♎03 20	14 58 57	0 10.4	11 54.5	17 24.1	24 35.2	15 13.7	7 05.9	8 43.7	5 15.8	14 45.8	12 09.2
21 F	17 58 18	29 08 25	20 55 01	26 52 04	0 07.4	13 27.2	17 58.6	24 39.2	15 24.0	7 15.2	8 49.7	5 15.3	14 47.5	12 09.0
22 Sa	18 02 15	0♑09 32	2♏50 37	8♏51 09	0 03.2	14 59.6	18 34.5	24 42.5	15 34.0	7 24.6	8 55.8	5 14.6	14 49.2	12 08.8
23 Su	18 06 11	1 10 40	14 54 05	20 59 47	29♋58.2	16 31.4	19 11.7	24 45.0	15 43.7	7 34.2	9 02.0	5 14.0	14 50.9	12 08.5
24 M	18 10 08	2 11 49	27 08 33	3♐20 39	29 53.0	18 02.5	19 50.2	24 46.7	15 53.0	7 43.9	9 08.2	5 13.3	14 52.6	12 08.3
25 Tu	18 14 05	3 12 58	9♐36 16	15 55 31	29 48.3	19 32.8	20 30.0	24R 47.7	16 01.9	7 53.7	9 14.4	5 12.5	14 54.2	12 07.9
26 W	18 18 01	4 14 07	22 18 28	28 45 08	29 44.6	21 02.0	21 11.0	24 47.9	16 10.5	8 03.6	9 20.7	5 11.7	14 55.9	12 07.6
27 Th	18 21 58	5 15 17	5♑15 28	11♑49 23	29 42.1	22 29.9	21 53.1	24 47.3	16 18.8	8 13.7	9 27.0	5 10.8	14 57.5	12 07.2
28 F	18 25 54	6 16 28	18 26 45	25 07 24	29D 41.1	23 56.3	22 36.3	24 45.9	16 26.7	8 23.8	9 33.4	5 09.9	14 59.1	12 06.8
29 Sa	18 29 51	7 17 38	1♒51 11	8♒37 53	29 41.2	25 20.9	23 20.5	24 43.8	16 34.2	8 34.1	9 39.8	5 08.9	15 00.6	12 06.3
30 Su	18 33 47	8 18 48	15 27 20	22 19 20	29 42.3	26 43.2	24 05.8	24 40.8	16 41.3	8 44.6	9 46.3	5 07.9	15 02.1	12 05.9
31 M	18 37 44	9 19 58	29 13 41	6♓10 13	29 43.8	28 02.9	24 52.1	24 37.0	16 48.1	8 55.1	9 52.8	5 06.8	15 03.7	12 05.4

Astro Data
Dy Hr Mn
☽0N 9 9:11
☽0S 22 20:17

♀D 3 11:26
☽0N 6 18:07
♃☍♅ 7 11:01
♅R 11 5:12
♇R 14 21:46
☽0S 20 4:55
♂R 26 6:11

Planet Ingress
Dy Hr Mn
☿ ♏ 5 2:20
☉ ♐ 22 19:02
☿ ♐ 23 17:31

☿ ♑ 12 20:51
☉ ♑ 22 8:15
☊ ♋R 23 3:32

Last Aspect / ☽ Ingress

Dy Hr Mn		☽ Ingress Dy Hr Mn
1 14:37	☿ ⚹	♑ 2 1:17
4 6:38	☿ □	♒ 4 9:02
6 3:16	♀ □	♓ 6 13:52
8 3:55	♀ △	♈ 8 15:45
9 13:45	♂ △	♉ 10 15:45
12 0:21	♀ ☍	♊ 12 15:43
13 16:56	♂ ⚹	♋ 14 17:49
16 11:54	☉ △	♌ 16 23:40
19 2:09	☉ □	♍ 19 9:33
21 20:00	☉ ⚹	♎ 21 21:58
23 12:12	♂ ⚹	♏ 24 10:33
26 1:36	♂ □	♐ 26 21:43
28 12:57	♂ △	♑ 29 7:00

Last Aspect / ☽ Ingress

Dy Hr Mn		☽ Ingress Dy Hr Mn
30 9:18	♆ ⚹	♒ 1 14:26
3 5:19	♂ ☍	♓ 3 19:53
5 2:45	☿ □	♈ 5 23:17
7 13:01	♂ △	♉ 8 0:59
9 14:50	♂ □	♊ 10 2:07
12 2:17	☿ ☍	♋ 12 4:21
13 5:36	♆ △	♌ 14 9:20
16 6:42	♂ ☌	♍ 16 17:59
18 22:42	☉ □	♎ 19 5:41
21 17:00	☉ ⚹	♏ 21 18:18
23 19:22	♂ □	♐ 24 5:33
26 4:39	♂ △	♑ 26 14:19
28 9:37	☿ ☌	♒ 28 20:42
30 16:05	♂ ☍	♓ 31 1:20

☽ Phases & Eclipses
Dy Hr Mn
5 7:15 ☽ 12♒24
11 22:03 ○ 19♉02
19 2:09 ☾ 26♌16
27 6:29 ● 4♐32

4 16:48 ☽ 12♓04
11 9:27 ○ 18♊52
18 22:42 ☾ 26♍32
26 22:59 ● 4♑42

Astro Data
1 November 1962
Julian Day # 22950
SVP 5♓47'00"
GC 26♐19.2 ⚴ 18♋35.4
Eris 9♈57.3R ⚵ 10♍08.3
⚷ 6♓15.9R ⚶ 8♍34.2
☽ Mean ☊ 3♌53.2

1 December 1962
Julian Day # 22980
SVP 5♓46'55"
GC 26♐19.3 ⚴ 21♋58.7R
Eris 9♈44.3R ⚵ 20♍04.3
⚷ 6♓15.1 ⚶ 19♍24.3
☽ Mean ☊ 2♌17.9

LONGITUDE — January 1963

Day	Sid.Time	☉	0 hr ☽	Noon ☽	True ☊	☿	♀	♂	⚳	♃	♄	♅	♆	♇
1 Tu	18 41 40	10♑21 08	13♓08 44	20♓09 04	29♋45.1	29♑19.5	25♏39.2	24♌32.4	16♍54.4	9♓05.7	9♒59.3	5♍05.7	15♏05.1	12♍04.8
2 W	18 45 37	11 22 18	27 11 03	4♈14 28	29R46.0	0♒32.4	26 27.3	24R27.0	17 00.4	9 16.5	10 05.9	5R04.5	15 06.6	12R04.2
3 Th	18 49 34	12 23 27	11♈19 07	18 24 47	29 46.0	1 41.1	27 16.2	24 20.8	17 06.0	9 27.3	10 12.5	5 03.3	15 08.0	12 03.6
4 F	18 53 30	13 24 36	25 31 11	2♉38 01	29 45.2	2 44.7	28 06.0	24 13.7	17 11.2	9 38.3	10 19.2	5 02.0	15 09.4	12 03.0
5 Sa	18 57 27	14 25 45	9♉44 58	16 51 40	29 43.7	3 42.7	28 56.6	24 05.9	17 16.0	9 49.4	10 25.8	5 00.6	15 10.8	12 02.4
6 Su	19 01 23	15 26 54	23 57 40	1♊02 34	29 41.8	4 34.1	29 47.9	23 57.2	17 20.4	10 00.6	10 32.6	4 59.3	15 12.1	12 01.7
7 M	19 05 20	16 28 02	8♊05 54	15 07 11	29 39.9	5 18.1	0♐40.0	23 47.7	17 24.3	10 11.9	10 39.3	4 57.8	15 13.4	12 01.0
8 Tu	19 09 16	17 29 10	22 05 58	29 01 48	29 38.3	5 53.7	1 32.8	23 37.5	17 27.9	10 23.2	10 46.1	4 56.4	15 14.7	12 00.2
9 W	19 13 13	18 30 18	5♋54 16	12♋43 00	29 37.3	6 20.2	2 26.3	23 26.4	17 31.1	10 34.7	10 52.9	4 54.9	15 15.9	11 59.5
10 Th	19 17 10	19 31 25	19 27 41	26 08 05	29D36.9	6R36.5	3 20.5	23 14.5	17 33.8	10 46.3	10 59.8	4 53.3	15 17.2	11 58.7
11 F	19 21 06	20 32 33	2♌44 01	9♌15 24	29 37.0	6 42.1	4 15.3	23 01.9	17 36.2	10 58.0	11 06.6	4 51.7	15 18.4	11 57.8
12 Sa	19 25 03	21 33 39	15 42 13	22 04 33	29 37.5	6 36.2	5 10.8	22 48.5	17 38.1	11 09.7	11 13.5	4 50.0	15 19.5	11 57.0
13 Su	19 28 59	22 34 46	28 22 33	4♍36 27	29 38.2	6 18.5	6 06.8	22 34.3	17 39.5	11 21.6	11 20.4	4 48.3	15 20.7	11 56.1
14 M	19 32 56	23 35 53	10♍46 32	16 53 10	29 39.0	5 49.1	7 03.4	22 19.3	17 40.6	11 33.5	11 27.4	4 46.6	15 21.8	11 55.2
15 Tu	19 36 52	24 36 59	22 56 46	28 57 47	29 39.6	5 08.3	8 00.5	22 03.6	17R41.2	11 45.6	11 34.4	4 44.8	15 22.8	11 54.3
16 W	19 40 49	25 38 05	4♎56 44	10♎54 10	29 40.0	4 16.9	8 58.2	21 47.2	17 41.3	11 57.7	11 41.3	4 43.0	15 23.9	11 53.3
17 Th	19 44 45	26 39 11	16 50 37	22 46 42	29R40.1	3 16.2	9 56.4	21 30.1	17 41.0	12 09.9	11 48.4	4 41.1	15 24.9	11 52.3
18 F	19 48 42	27 40 16	28 42 59	4♏40 05	29 40.1	2 08.0	10 55.1	21 12.3	17 40.3	12 22.2	11 55.4	4 39.2	15 25.9	11 51.3
19 Sa	19 52 38	28 41 22	10♏38 35	16 39 04	29D40.0	0 54.3	11 54.2	20 53.8	17 39.2	12 34.6	12 02.4	4 37.3	15 26.8	11 50.3
20 Su	19 56 35	29 42 27	22 42 05	28 48 10	29 40.0	29♑37.4	12 53.8	20 34.7	17 37.6	12 47.0	12 09.5	4 35.3	15 27.7	11 49.3
21 M	20 00 32	0♒43 31	4♐57 49	11♐11 27	29 40.1	28 19.7	13 53.9	20 15.0	17 35.5	12 59.6	12 16.6	4 33.3	15 28.6	11 48.2
22 Tu	20 04 28	1 44 36	17 29 28	23 52 10	29 40.3	27 03.6	14 54.3	19 54.7	17 33.0	13 12.2	12 23.7	4 31.3	15 29.5	11 47.1
23 W	20 08 25	2 45 39	0♑19 46	6♑52 27	29 40.5	25 51.1	15 55.2	19 33.9	17 30.1	13 24.9	12 30.8	4 29.2	15 30.3	11 46.0
24 Th	20 12 21	3 46 42	13 30 14	20 13 06	29R40.8	24 44.2	16 56.4	19 12.6	17 26.7	13 37.6	12 38.0	4 27.1	15 31.1	11 44.8
25 F	20 16 18	4 47 45	27 00 53	3♒53 20	29 40.8	23 44.2	17 58.1	18 50.9	17 22.9	13 50.5	12 45.1	4 24.9	15 31.8	11 43.7
26 Sa	20 20 14	5 48 46	10♒50 08	17 50 50	29 40.6	22 52.0	19 00.0	18 28.6	17 18.6	14 03.4	12 52.2	4 22.7	15 32.6	11 42.5
27 Su	20 24 11	6 49 47	24 54 56	2♓01 53	29 40.0	22 08.5	20 02.3	18 06.1	17 13.9	14 16.4	12 59.4	4 20.5	15 33.3	11 41.3
28 M	20 28 08	7 50 46	9♓11 05	16 21 53	29 39.0	21 33.8	21 05.0	17 43.1	17 08.8	14 29.4	13 06.6	4 18.3	15 33.9	11 40.1
29 Tu	20 32 04	8 51 45	23 33 41	0♈45 52	29 38.0	21 08.1	22 07.9	17 19.9	17 03.2	14 42.5	13 13.8	4 16.0	15 34.5	11 38.8
30 W	20 36 01	9 52 42	7♈57 51	15 09 06	29 36.9	20 51.0	23 11.2	16 56.4	16 57.2	14 55.7	13 20.9	4 13.7	15 35.1	11 37.5
31 Th	20 39 57	10 53 38	22 19 09	29 27 35	29D36.2	20D42.4	24 14.8	16 32.8	16 50.8	15 08.9	13 28.1	4 11.3	15 35.7	11 36.3

LONGITUDE — February 1963

Day	Sid.Time	☉	0 hr ☽	Noon ☽	True ☊	☿	♀	♂	⚳	♃	♄	♅	♆	♇
1 F	20 43 54	11♒54 32	6♉34 04	13♉38 18	29♋36.0	20♑41.8	25♐18.6	16♌08.9	16♍44.0	15♓22.2	13♒35.3	4♍09.0	15♏36.2	11♍35.0
2 Sa	20 47 50	12 55 26	20 40 05	27 39 14	29 36.4	20 48.6	26 22.7	15R45.0	16R36.7	15 35.6	13 42.5	4R06.6	15 36.7	11R33.6
3 Su	20 51 47	13 56 18	4♊35 37	11♊29 08	29 37.3	21 02.4	27 27.1	15 21.0	16 29.1	15 49.0	13 49.7	4 04.2	15 37.1	11 32.3
4 M	20 55 43	14 57 08	18 19 43	25 07 20	29 38.6	21 22.6	28 31.8	14 57.0	16 21.1	16 02.4	13 56.9	4 01.8	15 37.5	11 31.0
5 Tu	20 59 40	15 57 57	1♋51 55	8♋33 27	29 39.8	21 48.8	29 36.7	14 33.0	16 12.7	16 15.9	14 04.1	3 59.3	15 37.9	11 29.6
6 W	21 03 37	16 58 45	15 11 53	21 47 12	29R40.6	22 20.4	0♑41.9	14 09.1	16 03.9	16 29.5	14 11.3	3 56.9	15 38.3	11 28.2
7 Th	21 07 33	17 59 32	28 19 22	4♌48 21	29 40.7	22 56.9	1 47.3	13 45.3	15 54.7	16 43.1	14 18.4	3 54.4	15 38.6	11 26.8
8 F	21 11 30	19 00 17	11♌14 10	17 36 47	29 39.8	23 38.0	2 52.9	13 21.6	15 45.2	16 56.8	14 25.6	3 51.9	15 38.9	11 25.4
9 Sa	21 15 26	20 01 01	23 56 14	0♍12 33	29 37.8	24 23.3	3 58.7	12 58.2	15 35.4	17 10.5	14 32.8	3 49.4	15 39.1	11 24.0
10 Su	21 19 23	21 01 43	6♍25 50	12 36 10	29 34.8	25 12.4	5 04.8	12 35.0	15 25.1	17 24.3	14 39.9	3 46.8	15 39.3	11 22.5
11 M	21 23 19	22 02 25	18 43 43	24 48 40	29 31.1	26 05.0	6 11.1	12 12.1	15 14.6	17 38.1	14 47.1	3 44.3	15 39.5	11 21.1
12 Tu	21 27 16	23 03 05	0♎51 15	6♎51 46	29 27.0	27 00.9	7 17.6	11 49.6	15 03.7	17 52.0	14 54.3	3 41.7	15 39.7	11 19.6
13 W	21 31 12	24 03 44	12 50 32	18 47 56	29 23.2	27 59.6	8 24.3	11 27.4	14 52.6	18 05.8	15 01.4	3 39.1	15 39.8	11 18.1
14 Th	21 35 09	25 04 21	24 44 24	0♏40 23	29 20.0	29 01.1	9 31.1	11 05.6	14 41.1	18 19.8	15 08.5	3 36.6	15 39.8	11 16.7
15 F	21 39 05	26 04 58	6♏36 23	12 32 58	29 17.8	0♒05.0	10 38.2	10 44.2	14 29.4	18 33.8	15 15.6	3 34.0	15R39.9	11 15.2
16 Sa	21 43 02	27 05 33	18 30 40	24 30 04	29D16.9	1 11.3	11 45.4	10 23.4	14 17.3	18 47.8	15 22.7	3 31.3	15 39.9	11 13.7
17 Su	21 46 59	28 06 07	0♐31 48	6♐36 26	29 17.2	2 19.8	12 52.9	10 03.0	14 05.1	19 01.8	15 29.8	3 28.7	15 39.9	11 12.2
18 M	21 50 55	29 06 40	12 44 37	18 56 53	29 18.4	3 30.3	14 00.4	9 43.2	13 52.6	19 15.9	15 36.9	3 26.1	15 39.8	11 10.6
19 Tu	21 54 52	0♓07 12	25 13 50	1♑35 58	29 20.1	4 42.6	15 08.2	9 24.0	13 39.8	19 30.1	15 44.0	3 23.5	15 39.7	11 09.1
20 W	21 58 48	1 07 43	8♑03 43	14 37 29	29 21.7	5 56.7	16 16.1	9 05.4	13 26.9	19 44.2	15 51.0	3 20.9	15 39.6	11 07.6
21 Th	22 02 45	2 08 12	21 17 31	28 04 00	29R22.5	7 12.5	17 24.1	8 47.4	13 13.8	19 58.4	15 58.0	3 18.2	15 39.4	11 06.0
22 F	22 06 41	3 08 39	4♒56 56	11♒56 11	29 21.8	8 29.9	18 32.3	8 30.0	13 00.5	20 12.6	16 05.0	3 15.6	15 39.2	11 04.5
23 Sa	22 10 38	4 09 05	19 01 28	26 12 18	29 19.5	9 48.8	19 40.6	8 13.4	12 47.0	20 26.9	16 12.0	3 13.0	15 39.0	11 02.9
24 Su	22 14 34	5 09 30	3♓28 04	10♓47 59	29 15.5	11 09.1	20 49.1	7 57.4	12 33.4	20 41.2	16 18.9	3 10.3	15 38.8	11 01.4
25 M	22 18 31	6 09 52	18 11 09	25 36 32	29 10.2	12 30.8	21 57.7	7 42.2	12 19.7	20 55.5	16 25.9	3 07.7	15 38.5	10 59.8
26 Tu	22 22 28	7 10 13	3♈03 04	10♈29 41	29 04.2	13 53.9	23 06.4	7 27.7	12 05.9	21 09.8	16 32.8	3 05.1	15 38.1	10 58.3
27 W	22 26 24	8 10 32	17 55 20	25 19 02	28 58.6	15 18.2	24 15.2	7 14.0	11 52.1	21 24.2	16 39.6	3 02.4	15 37.8	10 56.7
28 Th	22 30 21	9 10 49	2♉39 55	9♉57 15	28 54.0	16 43.7	25 24.1	7 01.0	11 38.1	21 38.5	16 46.5	2 59.8	15 37.4	10 55.1

Astro Data

	Dy Hr Mn
☽0N	3 0:33
☿R	11 11:47
♃⚺♄	13 6:25
♃☍♇	16 4:00
⚳R	16 8:57
☽0S	16 13:38
♄⚻♇	17 23:56
☽0N	30 6:13
☿D	1 1:57
♃△♆	2 14:04
☽0S	12 21:29
♆R	16 6:05
♄□♆	18 21:48
☽0N	26 13:34

Planet Ingress

	Dy Hr Mn
☿ ♒	2 1:10
♀ ♐	6 17:35
☿ ♑R	20 4:59
☉ ♒	20 18:54
♀ ♑	5 20:36
☿ ♒	15 10:08
☉ ♓	19 9:09

Last Aspect / ☽ Ingress (January)

Last Aspect Dy Hr Mn		☽ Ingress Dy Hr Mn
1 21:57	♀ △	♈ 2 4:48
3 21:56	♂ △	♉ 4 7:34
6 9:45	♀ ☍	♊ 6 10:14
8 2:45	♂ ⚹	♋ 8 13:41
9 23:08	☉ ☍	♌ 10 19:01
12 13:22	♂ ☌	♍ 13 3:07
15 2:31	☉ △	♎ 15 14:05
17 20:34	☉ □	♏ 18 2:35
20 13:56	☉ ⚹	♐ 20 14:20
22 4:46	♂ △	♑ 22 23:23
24 19:25	☿ ☌	♒ 25 5:14
26 14:07	♀ ⚹	♓ 27 8:35
28 20:29	♀ □	♈ 29 10:44
31 2:32	♀ △	♉ 31 12:55

Last Aspect / ☽ Ingress (February)

Last Aspect Dy Hr Mn		☽ Ingress Dy Hr Mn
2 0:07	☿ △	♊ 2 16:03
4 18:35	♀ ☍	♋ 4 20:40
6 13:03	☿ ☍	♌ 7 3:06
8 14:52	☉ ☍	♍ 9 11:36
11 14:44	☿ △	♎ 11 22:18
14 8:20	☿ □	♏ 14 10:38
16 17:38	☉ □	♐ 16 22:57
19 8:59	☉ ⚹	♑ 19 9:00
20 21:23	♃ ⚹	♒ 21 15:23
22 19:06	♄ ☌	♓ 23 18:17
25 5:37	♀ ⚹	♈ 25 19:05
27 10:07	♀ □	♉ 27 19:38

☽ Phases & Eclipses

Dy Hr Mn	
3 1:02	☽ 11♈55
9 23:08	○ 18♋59
9 23:19	A 1.018
17 20:34	☾ 27♎01
25 13:42	● 4♒52
25 13:36:36	A 00'25"
1 8:50	☽ 11♉46
8 14:52	○ 19♌08
16 17:38	☾ 27♏20
24 2:06	● 4♓45

Astro Data

1 January 1963
Julian Day # 23011
SVP 5♓46'50"
GC 26♐19.4 ⚴ 15♋11.1R
Eris 9♈40.2 ⚵ 26♍17.3
⚷ 7♓07.9 ⚶ 27♍41.5
☽ Mean ☊ 0♌39.4

1 February 1963
Julian Day # 23042
SVP 5♓46'45"
GC 26♐19.4 ⚴ 6♋55.2R
Eris 9♈47.0 ⚵ 26♍28.0R
⚷ 8♓42.9 ⚶ 0♎43.6R
☽ Mean ☊ 29♋01.0

March 1963 — LONGITUDE

Day	Sid.Time	☉	0 hr ☽	Noon ☽	True ☊	☿	♀	♂	⚳	♃	♄	♅	♆	♇
1 F	22 34 17	10♓11 04	17♉10 27	24♉19 05	28♋51.0	18♒10.5	26♑33.1	6♌48.8	11♍24.2	21♓52.9	16♒53.3	2♍57.2	15♏36.9	10♍53.5
2 Sa	22 38 14	11 11 17	1♊22 54	8♊21 44	28D 49.9	19 38.4	27 42.3	6R 37.4	11R 10.2	22 07.3	17 00.1	2R 54.6	15R 36.5	10R 52.0
3 Su	22 42 10	12 11 28	15 15 35	22 04 33	28 50.2	21 07.6	28 51.5	6 26.8	10 56.2	22 21.8	17 06.9	2 52.0	15 36.0	10 50.4
4 M	22 46 07	13 11 37	28 48 47	5♋28 31	28 51.5	22 37.9	0♒00.9	6 17.0	10 42.2	22 36.2	17 13.6	2 49.4	15 35.5	10 48.8
5 Tu	22 50 03	14 11 43	12♋04 00	18 35 33	28R 52.8	24 09.3	1 10.4	6 07.9	10 28.3	22 50.7	17 20.3	2 46.9	15 34.9	10 47.3
6 W	22 54 00	15 11 48	25 03 25	1♌27 54	28 53.2	25 41.9	2 19.9	5 59.7	10 14.4	23 05.1	17 27.0	2 44.3	15 34.3	10 45.7
7 Th	22 57 57	16 11 50	7♌49 15	14 07 43	28 51.9	27 15.6	3 29.5	5 52.3	10 00.6	23 19.6	17 33.6	2 41.7	15 33.7	10 44.2
8 F	23 01 53	17 11 51	20 23 32	26 36 51	28 48.4	28 50.4	4 39.3	5 45.6	9 46.9	23 34.1	17 40.2	2 39.2	15 33.1	10 42.6
9 Sa	23 05 50	18 11 49	2♍47 53	8♍56 45	28 42.5	0♓26.4	5 49.1	5 39.7	9 33.3	23 48.6	17 46.7	2 36.7	15 32.4	10 41.0
10 Su	23 09 46	19 11 45	15 03 35	21 08 32	28 34.5	2 03.5	6 59.0	5 34.6	9 19.8	24 03.1	17 53.2	2 34.2	15 31.7	10 39.5
11 M	23 13 43	20 11 40	27 11 41	3♎13 13	28 24.8	3 41.7	8 09.0	5 30.3	9 06.5	24 17.6	17 59.7	2 31.7	15 31.0	10 37.9
12 Tu	23 17 39	21 11 32	9♎13 14	15 11 56	28 14.3	5 21.1	9 19.1	5 26.8	8 53.3	24 32.2	18 06.1	2 29.3	15 30.2	10 36.4
13 W	23 21 36	22 11 23	21 09 31	27 06 13	28 04.0	7 01.7	10 29.3	5 24.0	8 40.4	24 46.7	18 12.5	2 26.8	15 29.4	10 34.9
14 Th	23 25 32	23 11 12	3♏02 18	8♏58 05	27 54.8	8 43.4	11 39.6	5 22.0	8 27.6	25 01.2	18 18.9	2 24.4	15 28.6	10 33.3
15 F	23 29 29	24 10 59	14 53 56	20 50 16	27 47.4	10 26.3	12 49.9	5 20.7	8 15.0	25 15.8	18 25.2	2 22.0	15 27.8	10 31.8
16 Sa	23 33 26	25 10 45	26 47 32	2♐46 14	27 42.3	12 10.4	14 00.3	5D 20.2	8 02.6	25 30.3	18 31.5	2 19.6	15 26.9	10 30.3
17 Su	23 37 22	26 10 29	8♐46 54	14 50 07	27 39.5	13 55.8	15 10.8	5 20.4	7 50.5	25 44.8	18 37.7	2 17.3	15 26.0	10 28.8
18 M	23 41 19	27 10 11	20 56 28	27 06 35	27D 38.8	15 42.3	16 21.4	5 21.3	7 38.6	25 59.4	18 43.9	2 15.0	15 25.0	10 27.3
19 Tu	23 45 15	28 09 51	3♑21 05	9♑40 35	27 39.2	17 30.1	17 32.0	5 22.9	7 27.0	26 13.9	18 50.0	2 12.7	15 24.1	10 25.8
20 W	23 49 12	29 09 30	16 05 41	22 36 54	27R 39.9	19 19.1	18 42.7	5 25.3	7 15.7	26 28.5	18 56.1	2 10.4	15 23.1	10 24.3
21 Th	23 53 08	0♈09 07	29 14 44	5♒59 33	27 39.7	21 09.4	19 53.4	5 28.3	7 04.7	26 43.0	19 02.1	2 08.2	15 22.1	10 22.9
22 F	23 57 05	1 08 42	12♒51 36	19 50 59	27 37.6	23 00.9	21 04.2	5 32.1	6 54.0	26 57.5	19 08.1	2 06.0	15 21.1	10 21.4
23 Sa	0 01 01	2 08 16	26 57 37	4♓11 12	27 33.2	24 53.7	22 15.1	5 36.5	6 43.6	27 12.0	19 14.0	2 03.8	15 20.0	10 20.0
24 Su	0 04 58	3 07 47	11♓31 14	18 56 59	27 26.1	26 47.8	23 26.1	5 41.6	6 33.5	27 26.5	19 19.9	2 01.6	15 18.9	10 18.5
25 M	0 08 55	4 07 16	26 27 28	4♈01 34	27 17.0	28 43.1	24 37.0	5 47.3	6 23.8	27 41.0	19 25.7	1 59.5	15 17.8	10 17.1
26 Tu	0 12 51	5 06 44	11♈38 00	19 15 21	27 06.8	0♈39.6	25 48.1	5 53.7	6 14.4	27 55.5	19 31.5	1 57.4	15 16.7	10 15.7
27 W	0 16 48	6 06 09	26 52 14	4♉27 17	26 56.8	2 37.3	26 59.1	6 00.8	6 05.4	28 10.0	19 37.2	1 55.4	15 15.5	10 14.3
28 Th	0 20 44	7 05 32	11♉59 13	19 26 56	26 48.1	4 36.2	28 10.3	6 08.4	5 56.8	28 24.5	19 42.8	1 53.3	15 14.3	10 13.0
29 F	0 24 41	8 04 53	26 49 31	4♊06 17	26 41.7	6 36.1	29 21.4	6 16.7	5 48.6	28 38.9	19 48.4	1 51.4	15 13.1	10 11.6
30 Sa	0 28 37	9 04 12	11♊16 44	18 20 36	26 37.9	8 37.1	0♓32.7	6 25.6	5 40.7	28 53.3	19 53.9	1 49.4	15 11.9	10 10.3
31 Su	0 32 34	10 03 28	25 17 50	2♋08 30	26D 36.3	10 39.0	1 43.9	6 35.1	5 33.3	29 07.7	19 59.4	1 47.5	15 10.7	10 08.9

April 1963 — LONGITUDE

Day	Sid.Time	☉	0 hr ☽	Noon ☽	True ☊	☿	♀	♂	⚳	♃	♄	♅	♆	♇
1 M	0 36 30	11♈02 42	8♋52 51	15♋31 12	26♋36.2	12♈41.7	2♓55.2	6♌45.2	5♍26.2	29♓22.1	20♒04.8	1♍45.7	15♏09.4	10♍07.6
2 Tu	0 40 27	12 01 53	22 03 58	28 31 37	26R 36.3	14 45.1	4 06.6	6 55.8	5R 19.6	29 36.5	20 10.2	1R 43.8	15R 08.1	10R 06.3
3 W	0 44 23	13 01 03	4♌54 36	11♌13 26	26 35.5	16 48.9	5 17.9	7 07.0	5 13.3	29 50.9	20 15.5	1 42.1	15 06.8	10 05.1
4 Th	0 48 20	14 00 09	17 28 34	23 40 29	26 32.8	18 53.1	6 29.4	7 18.7	5 07.5	0♈05.2	20 20.7	1 40.3	15 05.5	10 03.8
5 F	0 52 17	14 59 14	29 49 36	5♍56 18	26 27.3	20 57.3	7 40.8	7 30.9	5 02.1	0 19.5	20 25.8	1 38.6	15 04.1	10 02.6
6 Sa	0 56 13	15 58 16	12♍00 56	18 03 47	26 18.9	23 01.4	8 52.3	7 43.7	4 57.1	0 33.7	20 30.9	1 36.9	15 02.8	10 01.4
7 Su	1 00 10	16 57 16	24 05 09	0♎05 16	26 07.8	25 05.0	10 03.8	7 57.0	4 52.5	0 48.0	20 35.9	1 35.3	15 01.4	10 00.2
8 M	1 04 06	17 56 15	6♎04 18	12 02 28	25 54.6	27 07.8	11 15.4	8 10.7	4 48.4	1 02.2	20 40.9	1 33.7	15 00.0	9 59.0
9 Tu	1 08 03	18 55 11	17 59 55	23 56 48	25 40.4	29 09.4	12 27.0	8 25.0	4 44.7	1 16.4	20 45.8	1 32.2	14 58.6	9 57.8
10 W	1 11 59	19 54 05	29 53 17	5♏49 31	25 26.2	1♉09.7	13 38.7	8 39.7	4 41.4	1 30.6	20 50.6	1 30.7	14 57.1	9 56.7
11 Th	1 15 56	20 52 57	11♏45 42	17 42 02	25 13.3	3 08.1	14 50.3	8 54.9	4 38.5	1 44.7	20 55.3	1 29.3	14 55.7	9 55.6
12 F	1 19 52	21 51 47	23 38 47	29 36 11	25 02.6	5 04.3	16 02.1	9 10.5	4 36.1	1 58.8	21 00.0	1 27.9	14 54.2	9 54.5
13 Sa	1 23 49	22 50 35	5♐34 36	11♐34 23	24 54.6	6 58.1	17 13.8	9 26.6	4 34.0	2 12.9	21 04.6	1 26.5	14 52.8	9 53.4
14 Su	1 27 46	23 49 22	17 35 56	23 39 43	24 49.5	8 48.9	18 25.6	9 43.1	4 32.5	2 26.9	21 09.2	1 25.2	14 51.3	9 52.4
15 M	1 31 42	24 48 07	29 46 14	5♑56 02	24 47.0	10 36.6	19 37.4	10 00.1	4 31.3	2 40.9	21 13.6	1 23.9	14 49.8	9 51.3
16 Tu	1 35 39	25 46 50	12♑09 39	18 27 40	24 46.3	12 20.9	20 49.3	10 17.4	4 30.5	2 54.9	21 18.0	1 22.7	14 48.3	9 50.3
17 W	1 39 35	26 45 32	24 50 41	1♒19 16	24 46.2	14 01.3	22 01.1	10 35.2	4D 30.2	3 08.8	21 22.3	1 21.6	14 46.8	9 49.4
18 Th	1 43 32	27 44 12	7♒53 57	14 35 13	24 45.6	15 37.8	23 13.0	10 53.3	4 30.3	3 22.7	21 26.6	1 20.5	14 45.2	9 48.4
19 F	1 47 28	28 42 50	21 23 26	28 18 53	24 43.4	17 10.1	24 25.0	11 11.9	4 30.9	3 36.5	21 30.7	1 19.4	14 43.7	9 47.5
20 Sa	1 51 25	29 41 26	5♓21 40	12♓31 43	24 38.7	18 38.0	25 37.0	11 30.9	4 31.8	3 50.3	21 34.8	1 18.4	14 42.1	9 46.6
21 Su	1 55 21	0♉40 01	19 48 45	27 12 16	24 31.4	20 01.3	26 48.9	11 50.2	4 33.2	4 04.1	21 38.8	1 17.4	14 40.5	9 45.7
22 M	1 59 18	1 38 34	4♈41 29	12♈15 25	24 21.8	21 20.0	28 01.0	12 09.9	4 34.9	4 17.8	21 42.7	1 16.5	14 39.0	9 44.8
23 Tu	2 03 15	2 37 05	19 52 53	27 32 31	24 11.0	22 33.8	29 13.0	12 29.9	4 37.1	4 31.5	21 46.6	1 15.6	14 37.4	9 44.0
24 W	2 07 11	3 35 35	5♉12 52	12♉52 26	24 00.1	23 42.6	0♈25.1	12 50.3	4 39.7	4 45.1	21 50.3	1 14.8	14 35.8	9 43.2
25 Th	2 11 08	4 34 02	20 29 46	28 03 31	23 50.6	24 46.4	1 37.1	13 11.1	4 42.7	4 58.7	21 54.0	1 14.0	14 34.2	9 42.4
26 F	2 15 04	5 32 28	5♊32 31	12♊55 48	23 43.3	25 45.0	2 49.2	13 32.2	4 46.1	5 12.2	21 57.6	1 13.3	14 32.6	9 41.7
27 Sa	2 19 01	6 30 51	20 12 37	27 22 29	23 38.7	26 38.5	4 01.3	13 53.7	4 49.9	5 25.7	22 01.1	1 12.7	14 31.0	9 41.0
28 Su	2 22 57	7 29 13	4♋25 06	11♋20 26	23D 36.6	27 26.6	5 13.5	14 15.4	4 54.2	5 39.1	22 04.5	1 12.1	14 29.4	9 40.3
29 M	2 26 54	8 27 32	18 08 34	24 49 48	23 36.1	28 09.4	6 25.6	14 37.5	4 58.8	5 52.5	22 07.8	1 11.5	14 27.7	9 39.6
30 Tu	2 30 50	9 25 50	1♌24 30	7♌53 07	23R 36.3	28 46.8	7 37.8	14 59.9	5 03.7	6 05.8	22 11.1	1 11.0	14 26.1	9 39.0

Astro Data	Dy Hr Mn
☽0S	12 4:13
♂D	16 17:21
☉0N	21 8:20
☽0N	25 23:26
☿0N	27 22:00
♃⚼♆	4 12:28
☽0S	8 10:23
♃⚻♅	10 12:14
♃0N	14 16:03
⚳D	17 18:03
☽0N	22 10:34
♀0N	27 5:01

Planet Ingress		Dy Hr Mn
♀	♒	4 11:41
☿	♓	9 5:26
☉	♈	21 8:20
☿	♈	26 3:52
♀	♓	30 1:00
♃	♈	4 3:19
☿	♉	9 22:03
☉	♉	20 19:36
♀	♈	24 3:39

Last Aspect Dy Hr Mn			☽ Ingress	Dy Hr Mn
1 16:07	♀	△	♊	1 21:39
3 12:31	♃	□	♋	4 2:08
5 20:02	♃	△	♌	6 9:15
8 16:57	☿	☍	♍	8 18:34
10 17:53	♃	☍	♎	11 5:35
12 17:54	♄	△	♏	13 17:51
15 21:06	♃	△	♐	16 6:27
18 12:08	☉	□	♑	18 17:35
21 0:48	☉	⚹	♒	21 1:21
22 14:16	♀	☌	♓	23 5:04
25 2:22	☿	☌	♈	25 5:38
26 23:11	♀	⚹	♉	27 4:57
29 3:28	♀	□	♊	29 5:13
31 6:36	♃	□	♋	31 8:13

Last Aspect Dy Hr Mn			☽ Ingress	Dy Hr Mn
2 14:04	♃	△	♌	2 14:45
4 5:30	♄	☍	♍	5 0:20
6 6:01	♆	⚹	♎	7 11:49
9 5:32	♄	△	♏	10 0:14
11 18:33	♄	□	♐	12 12:48
14 12:21	☉	△	♑	15 0:27
17 2:52	☉	□	♒	17 9:34
19 12:44	☉	⚹	♓	19 14:53
21 11:19	♀	☌	♈	21 16:30
23 2:56	♄	⚹	♉	23 15:51
25 6:24	☿	☌	♊	25 15:06
27 2:58	♄	△	♋	27 16:27
29 18:22	☿	⚹	♌	29 21:25

☽ Phases & Eclipses Dy Hr Mn	
2 17:17	☽ 11♊25
10 7:49	○ 19♍01
18 12:08	☾ 27♐10
25 12:10	● 4♈08
1 3:15	☽ 10♋41
9 0:57	○ 18♎28
17 2:52	☾ 26♑23
23 20:29	● 2♉58
30 15:08	☽ 9♌33

Astro Data

1 March 1963
Julian Day # 23070
SVP 5♓46'42"
GC 26♐19.5 ⚴ 7♋43.5
Eris 10♈01.0 ⚵ 21♍12.7R
⚷ 10♓27.7 ⚶ 27♍15.1R
☽ Mean ☊ 27♋32.0

1 April 1963
Julian Day # 23101
SVP 5♓46'39"
GC 26♐19.6 ⚴ 15♋58.6
Eris 10♈21.5 ⚵ 14♍04.9R
⚷ 12♓23.0 ⚶ 19♍37.6R
☽ Mean ☊ 25♋53.5

LONGITUDE May 1963

Day	Sid.Time	☉	0 hr ☽	Noon ☽	True ☊	☿	♀	♂	⚳	♃	♄	♅	♆	♇
1 W	2 34 47	10♉24 05	14♌16 13	20♌34 19	23♋35.9	29♉18.7	8♈50.0	15♌22.6	5♍09.1	6♈19.0	22♒14.3	1♍10.6	14♏24.5	9♍38.3
2 Th	2 38 44	11 22 18	26 48 00	2♍57 52	23R 33.9	29 45.2	10 02.2	15 45.6	5 14.8	6 32.2	22 17.3	1R 10.2	14R 22.9	9R 37.8
3 F	2 42 40	12 20 29	9♍04 26	15 08 15	23 29.5	0♊06.2	11 14.4	16 08.9	5 20.9	6 45.3	22 20.3	1 09.8	14 21.2	9 37.2
4 Sa	2 46 37	13 18 38	21 09 48	27 09 33	23 22.5	0 21.7	12 26.6	16 32.5	5 27.4	6 58.4	22 23.2	1 09.5	14 19.6	9 36.7
5 Su	2 50 33	14 16 45	3♎07 54	9♎05 14	23 13.1	0 31.9	13 38.9	16 56.3	5 34.3	7 11.4	22 26.0	1 09.3	14 18.0	9 36.2
6 M	2 54 30	15 14 51	15 01 52	20 58 06	23 01.7	0R 36.8	14 51.1	17 20.4	5 41.4	7 24.4	22 28.7	1 09.1	14 16.3	9 35.7
7 Tu	2 58 26	16 12 54	26 54 10	2♏50 19	22 49.3	0 36.4	16 03.4	17 44.8	5 49.0	7 37.3	22 31.4	1 09.0	14 14.7	9 35.3
8 W	3 02 23	17 10 56	8♏46 43	14 43 35	22 37.0	0 31.1	17 15.7	18 09.4	5 56.9	7 50.1	22 33.9	1D 08.9	14 13.1	9 34.9
9 Th	3 06 19	18 08 56	20 41 05	26 39 22	22 25.7	0 21.0	18 28.0	18 34.3	6 05.1	8 02.8	22 36.4	1 08.9	14 11.4	9 34.5
10 F	3 10 16	19 06 55	2♐38 38	8♐39 04	22 16.4	0 06.3	19 40.3	18 59.4	6 13.7	8 15.5	22 38.7	1 08.9	14 09.8	9 34.1
11 Sa	3 14 13	20 04 52	14 40 54	20 44 21	22 09.6	29♉47.5	20 52.7	19 24.8	6 22.6	8 28.1	22 41.0	1 09.0	14 08.2	9 33.8
12 Su	3 18 09	21 02 48	26 49 42	2♑57 16	22 05.4	29 24.8	22 05.1	19 50.4	6 31.8	8 40.7	22 43.2	1 09.1	14 06.6	9 33.5
13 M	3 22 06	22 00 43	9♑07 24	15 20 27	22D 03.5	28 58.7	23 17.5	20 16.3	6 41.4	8 53.2	22 45.2	1 09.3	14 04.9	9 33.3
14 Tu	3 26 02	22 58 36	21 36 51	27 57 01	22 03.4	28 29.7	24 29.9	20 42.4	6 51.2	9 05.6	22 47.2	1 09.6	14 03.3	9 33.0
15 W	3 29 59	23 56 28	4♒21 25	10♒50 30	22 04.2	27 58.3	25 42.3	21 08.7	7 01.4	9 17.9	22 49.1	1 09.9	14 01.7	9 32.8
16 Th	3 33 55	24 54 18	17 24 42	24 04 26	22R 04.7	27 25.2	26 54.7	21 35.2	7 11.9	9 30.2	22 50.9	1 10.2	14 00.1	9 32.6
17 F	3 37 52	25 52 08	0♓50 03	7♓41 49	22 04.1	26 50.8	28 07.2	22 01.9	7 22.7	9 42.3	22 52.6	1 10.6	13 58.5	9 32.5
18 Sa	3 41 48	26 49 56	14 39 56	21 44 25	22 01.6	26 15.8	29 19.7	22 28.9	7 33.8	9 54.4	22 54.2	1 11.1	13 56.9	9 32.4
19 Su	3 45 45	27 47 43	28 55 08	6♈11 47	21 57.0	25 40.8	0♉32.2	22 56.1	7 45.1	10 06.5	22 55.7	1 11.6	13 55.4	9 32.3
20 M	3 49 42	28 45 29	13♈33 51	21 00 38	21 50.6	25 06.4	1 44.7	23 23.5	7 56.8	10 18.4	22 57.2	1 12.2	13 53.8	9 32.3
21 Tu	3 53 38	29 43 14	28 31 14	6♉04 35	21 43.0	24 33.3	2 57.2	23 51.1	8 08.8	10 30.3	22 58.5	1 12.8	13 52.2	9D 32.2
22 W	3 57 35	0♊40 58	13♉39 28	21 14 36	21 35.3	24 01.9	4 09.7	24 18.8	8 21.0	10 42.0	22 59.7	1 13.4	13 50.7	9 32.3
23 Th	4 01 31	1 38 40	28 48 40	6♊20 24	21 28.5	23 32.8	5 22.3	24 46.8	8 33.5	10 53.7	23 00.8	1 14.2	13 49.1	9 32.3
24 F	4 05 28	2 36 22	13♊48 36	21 12 13	21 23.4	23 06.4	6 34.9	25 15.0	8 46.4	11 05.3	23 01.8	1 15.0	13 47.6	9 32.4
25 Sa	4 09 24	3 34 02	28 30 22	5♋42 23	21 20.3	22 43.1	7 47.4	25 43.4	8 59.4	11 16.8	23 02.8	1 15.8	13 46.1	9 32.5
26 Su	4 13 21	4 31 40	12♋47 46	19 46 15	21D 19.3	22 23.3	9 00.0	26 12.0	9 12.8	11 28.2	23 03.6	1 16.7	13 44.6	9 32.6
27 M	4 17 17	5 29 17	26 37 44	3♌22 18	21 19.8	22 07.3	10 12.6	26 40.8	9 26.4	11 39.5	23 04.3	1 17.6	13 43.1	9 32.8
28 Tu	4 21 14	6 26 53	10♌00 10	16 31 39	21 21.0	21 55.3	11 25.2	27 09.7	9 40.2	11 50.8	23 04.9	1 18.6	13 41.6	9 33.0
29 W	4 25 11	7 24 27	22 57 12	29 17 17	21R 22.1	21 47.5	12 37.8	27 38.8	9 54.3	12 01.9	23 05.5	1 19.7	13 40.1	9 33.2
30 Th	4 29 07	8 21 59	5♍32 28	11♍43 18	21 22.4	21D 44.0	13 50.5	28 08.1	10 08.7	12 12.9	23 05.9	1 20.8	13 38.7	9 33.5
31 F	4 33 04	9 19 31	17 50 22	23 54 15	21 21.1	21 45.0	15 03.1	28 37.5	10 23.3	12 23.8	23 06.2	1 21.9	13 37.2	9 33.7

LONGITUDE June 1963

Day	Sid.Time	☉	0 hr ☽	Noon ☽	True ☊	☿	♀	♂	⚳	♃	♄	♅	♆	♇
1 Sa	4 37 00	10♊17 01	29♍55 32	5♎54 45	21♋18.2	21♉50.4	16♉15.8	29♌07.2	10♍38.1	12♈34.7	23♒06.5	1♍23.1	13♏35.8	9♍34.1
2 Su	4 40 57	11 14 29	11♎52 26	17 49 04	21R 13.5	22 00.3	17 28.4	29 36.9	10 53.1	12 45.4	23R 06.6	1 24.3	13R 34.4	9 34.4
3 M	4 44 53	12 11 57	23 45 06	29 40 58	21 07.6	22 14.7	18 41.1	0♍06.9	11 08.4	12 56.0	23 06.6	1 25.6	13 33.0	9 34.8
4 Tu	4 48 50	13 09 23	5♏37 02	11♏33 39	21 00.8	22 33.6	19 53.8	0 37.0	11 23.9	13 06.6	23 06.6	1 27.0	13 31.6	9 35.2
5 W	4 52 46	14 06 48	17 31 07	23 29 43	20 54.1	22 56.8	21 06.5	1 07.2	11 39.7	13 17.0	23 06.4	1 28.4	13 30.3	9 35.6
6 Th	4 56 43	15 04 12	29 29 40	5♐31 11	20 47.9	23 24.4	22 19.2	1 37.6	11 55.6	13 27.3	23 06.2	1 29.8	13 28.9	9 36.1
7 F	5 00 40	16 01 36	11♐34 28	17 39 41	20 43.0	23 56.2	23 32.0	2 08.2	12 11.8	13 37.5	23 05.8	1 31.3	13 27.6	9 36.6
8 Sa	5 04 36	16 58 58	23 47 01	29 56 36	20 39.6	24 32.2	24 44.7	2 38.9	12 28.1	13 47.6	23 05.4	1 32.9	13 26.3	9 37.1
9 Su	5 08 33	17 56 20	6♑08 37	12♑23 14	20D 37.8	25 12.2	25 57.5	3 09.7	12 44.7	13 57.6	23 04.8	1 34.5	13 25.0	9 37.7
10 M	5 12 29	18 53 41	18 40 38	25 01 00	20 37.6	25 56.3	27 10.3	3 40.7	13 01.5	14 07.4	23 04.2	1 36.1	13 23.8	9 38.3
11 Tu	5 16 26	19 51 01	1♒24 32	7♒51 27	20 38.5	26 44.2	28 23.1	4 11.8	13 18.4	14 17.2	23 03.5	1 37.8	13 22.5	9 38.9
12 W	5 20 22	20 48 21	14 21 59	20 56 21	20 40.0	27 36.0	29 35.9	4 43.1	13 35.6	14 26.8	23 02.6	1 39.5	13 21.3	9 39.6
13 Th	5 24 19	21 45 41	27 34 47	4♓17 30	20 41.5	28 31.6	0♊48.7	5 14.5	13 52.9	14 36.3	23 01.7	1 41.3	13 20.1	9 40.2
14 F	5 28 15	22 42 59	11♓04 38	17 56 21	20R 42.3	29 30.8	2 01.6	5 46.0	14 10.5	14 45.7	23 00.7	1 43.2	13 18.9	9 40.9
15 Sa	5 32 12	23 40 18	24 52 43	1♈53 41	20 42.2	0♊33.6	3 14.5	6 17.7	14 28.2	14 55.0	22 59.6	1 45.0	13 17.8	9 41.7
16 Su	5 36 09	24 37 36	8♈59 11	16 08 59	20 40.9	1 39.9	4 27.4	6 49.5	14 46.1	15 04.2	22 58.4	1 46.9	13 16.6	9 42.4
17 M	5 40 05	25 34 54	23 22 44	0♉39 58	20 38.6	2 49.7	5 40.3	7 21.5	15 04.2	15 13.2	22 57.0	1 48.9	13 15.5	9 43.2
18 Tu	5 44 02	26 32 11	8♉00 05	15 22 22	20 35.6	4 03.0	6 53.2	7 53.5	15 22.4	15 22.1	22 55.6	1 50.9	13 14.4	9 44.1
19 W	5 47 58	27 29 29	22 46 00	0♊10 05	20 32.5	5 19.6	8 06.2	8 25.8	15 40.9	15 30.9	22 54.2	1 53.0	13 13.3	9 44.9
20 Th	5 51 55	28 26 46	7♊33 41	14 55 50	20 29.7	6 39.6	9 19.1	8 58.1	15 59.5	15 39.5	22 52.6	1 55.1	13 12.3	9 45.8
21 F	5 55 51	29 24 03	22 15 35	29 32 06	20 27.7	8 02.9	10 32.1	9 30.6	16 18.2	15 48.0	22 50.9	1 57.2	13 11.3	9 46.7
22 Sa	5 59 48	0♋21 19	6♋44 33	13♋52 17	20D 26.8	9 29.5	11 45.1	10 03.2	16 37.2	15 56.4	22 49.1	1 59.4	13 10.3	9 47.6
23 Su	6 03 44	1 18 35	20 54 46	27 51 34	20 26.8	10 59.3	12 58.1	10 35.9	16 56.3	16 04.6	22 47.3	2 01.7	13 09.3	9 48.6
24 M	6 07 41	2 15 50	4♌42 27	11♌27 17	20 27.6	12 32.3	14 11.2	11 08.7	17 15.5	16 12.7	22 45.3	2 03.9	13 08.4	9 49.6
25 Tu	6 11 38	3 13 04	18 06 05	24 38 59	20 28.8	14 08.5	15 24.2	11 41.7	17 35.0	16 20.7	22 43.3	2 06.3	13 07.5	9 50.6
26 W	6 15 34	4 10 19	1♍06 13	7♍28 07	20 30.2	15 47.8	16 37.3	12 14.7	17 54.5	16 28.5	22 41.2	2 08.6	13 06.6	9 51.6
27 Th	6 19 31	5 07 32	13 45 05	19 57 34	20 31.2	17 30.2	17 50.4	12 47.9	18 14.2	16 36.1	22 38.9	2 11.0	13 05.7	9 52.7
28 F	6 23 27	6 04 45	26 06 06	2♎11 11	20R 31.7	19 15.6	19 03.5	13 21.2	18 34.1	16 43.7	22 36.6	2 13.5	13 04.9	9 53.8
29 Sa	6 27 24	7 01 57	8♎13 24	14 13 19	20 31.6	21 04.0	20 16.6	13 54.7	18 54.1	16 51.1	22 34.3	2 15.9	13 04.1	9 54.9
30 Su	6 31 20	7 59 09	20 11 29	26 08 30	20 30.9	22 55.2	21 29.7	14 28.2	19 14.2	16 58.3	22 31.8	2 18.5	13 03.3	9 56.1

Astro Data	Dy Hr Mn
☽ 0S	5 16:48
♃∠♄	6 22:15
☿ R	6 22:30
♅ D	9 10:16
♃⊼♇	16 16:49
☽ 0N	19 20:57
♇ D	21 15:41
☿ D	30 18:52
☽ 0S	1 23:57
♄ R	3 9:39
♃⊼♆	6 15:26
☽ 0N	16 5:08
☽ 0S	29 7:50

Planet Ingress		Dy Hr Mn
☿	♊	3 4:17
☿	♉R	10 20:39
♀	♉	19 1:21
☉	♊	21 18:58
♂	♍	3 6:30
♀	♊	12 19:57
☿	♊	14 23:21
☉	♋	22 3:04

Last Aspect Dy Hr Mn			☽ Ingress	Dy Hr Mn
2 5:31	☿	□	♍	2 6:13
3 10:27	♆	⚹	♎	4 17:42
6 15:04	♄	△	♏	7 6:16
9 3:50	♄	□	♐	9 18:42
11 15:51	♄	⚹	♑	12 6:13
14 12:59	☿	△	♒	14 15:51
16 17:43	☿	□	♓	16 22:32
18 21:08	☉	⚹	♈	19 1:48
20 15:56	♂	△	♉	21 2:21
22 17:01	♂	□	♊	23 1:53
24 18:51	♂	⚹	♋	25 2:29
26 16:28	☿	⚹	♌	27 5:58
29 8:45	♂	☌	♍	29 13:22

Last Aspect Dy Hr Mn			☽ Ingress	Dy Hr Mn
31 7:43	☿	△	♎	1 0:09
2 22:42	♄	△	♏	3 12:39
5 11:13	♄	□	♐	6 1:01
7 22:39	♄	⚹	♑	8 12:07
10 16:29	♀	△	♒	10 21:22
13 0:55	☿	□	♓	13 4:21
14 20:53	☉	□	♈	15 8:46
17 3:03	☉	⚹	♉	17 10:54
19 0:14	♄	□	♊	19 11:44
21 11:46	☉	☌	♋	21 12:46
22 15:33	♃	□	♌	23 15:44
25 8:27	♄	☍	♍	25 21:56
27 7:26	♀	□	♎	28 7:41
30 4:44	♄	△	♏	30 19:48

☽ Phases & Eclipses Dy Hr Mn	
8 17:23	○ 17♏24
16 13:36	☾ 24♒58
23 4:00	● 1♊19
30 4:55	☽ 8♍05
7 8:31	○ 15♐53
14 20:53	☾ 23♓04
21 11:46	● 29♊23
28 20:24	☽ 6♎25

Astro Data

1 May 1963
Julian Day # 23131
SVP 5♓46'35"
GC 26♐19.6 ⚴ 27♋32.9
Eris 10♈41.4 ⚵ 11♍34.1
⚷ 13♓53.3 ⚶ 16♍22.3
☽ Mean ☊ 24♋18.1

1 June 1963
Julian Day # 23162
SVP 5♓46'31"
GC 26♐19.7 ⚴ 11♌03.2
Eris 10♈57.0 ⚵ 14♍27.0
⚷ 14♓46.9 ⚶ 20♍15.5
☽ Mean ☊ 22♋39.6

July 1963 — LONGITUDE

Day	Sid.Time	☉	0 hr ☽	Noon ☽	True ☊	☿	♀	♂	⚳	♃	♄	♅	♆	♇
1 M	6 35 17	8♋56 21	2♏04 52	8♏01 09	20♋29.8	24♊49.1	22♊42.9	15♍01.8	19♍34.5	17♈05.4	22♒29.3	2♍21.0	13♏02.5	9♍57.3
2 Tu	6 39 13	9 53 32	13 57 49	19 55 23	20R 28.4	26 45.6	23 56.0	15 35.6	19 54.9	17 12.3	22R 26.6	2 23.6	13R 01.8	9 58.5
3 W	6 43 10	10 50 44	25 54 15	1♐54 49	20 27.0	28 44.6	25 09.2	16 09.4	20 15.5	17 19.1	22 23.9	2 26.2	13 01.1	9 59.7
4 Th	6 47 07	11 47 54	7♐57 29	14 02 32	20 25.8	0♋45.7	26 22.4	16 43.4	20 36.2	17 25.7	22 21.1	2 28.9	13 00.4	10 00.9
5 F	6 51 03	12 45 05	20 10 15	26 20 53	20 24.9	2 48.9	27 35.6	17 17.4	20 57.0	17 32.2	22 18.3	2 31.6	12 59.8	10 02.2
6 Sa	6 55 00	13 42 16	2♑34 37	8♑51 37	20D 24.4	4 53.8	28 48.9	17 51.6	21 17.9	17 38.5	22 15.4	2 34.4	12 59.2	10 03.5
7 Su	6 58 56	14 39 27	15 11 59	21 35 47	20 24.3	7 00.3	0♋02.1	18 25.8	21 38.9	17 44.7	22 12.4	2 37.1	12 58.6	10 04.8
8 M	7 02 53	15 36 38	28 03 06	4♒33 54	20 24.4	9 07.9	1 15.4	19 00.2	22 00.1	17 50.7	22 09.3	2 40.0	12 58.0	10 06.2
9 Tu	7 06 49	16 33 49	11♒08 13	17 45 59	20 24.7	11 16.5	2 28.7	19 34.7	22 21.4	17 56.5	22 06.1	2 42.8	12 57.5	10 07.6
10 W	7 10 46	17 31 00	24 27 09	1♓11 39	20 25.1	13 25.7	3 42.1	20 09.2	22 42.8	18 02.2	22 02.9	2 45.7	12 57.0	10 08.9
11 Th	7 14 43	18 28 11	7♓59 24	14 50 17	20 25.3	15 35.2	4 55.4	20 43.9	23 04.3	18 07.7	21 59.6	2 48.6	12 56.6	10 10.4
12 F	7 18 39	19 25 23	21 44 10	28 40 56	20 25.4	17 44.8	6 08.8	21 18.7	23 25.9	18 13.0	21 56.3	2 51.5	12 56.1	10 11.8
13 Sa	7 22 36	20 22 36	5♈40 25	12♈42 24	20 25.5	19 54.1	7 22.2	21 53.5	23 47.7	18 18.2	21 52.8	2 54.5	12 55.7	10 13.3
14 Su	7 26 32	21 19 49	19 46 41	26 53 01	20 25.5	22 03.0	8 35.6	22 28.5	24 09.5	18 23.2	21 49.3	2 57.5	12 55.4	10 14.7
15 M	7 30 29	22 17 03	4♉01 05	11♉10 34	20 25.5	24 11.1	9 49.1	23 03.5	24 31.5	18 28.0	21 45.8	3 00.6	12 55.0	10 16.2
16 Tu	7 34 25	23 14 17	18 21 06	25 32 14	20 25.7	26 18.4	11 02.5	23 38.7	24 53.5	18 32.7	21 42.2	3 03.6	12 54.7	10 17.8
17 W	7 38 22	24 11 32	2♊43 31	9♊54 28	20 26.0	28 24.5	12 16.0	24 13.9	25 15.7	18 37.2	21 38.5	3 06.7	12 54.4	10 19.3
18 Th	7 42 18	25 08 48	17 04 33	24 13 14	20 26.4	0♌29.5	13 29.6	24 49.3	25 38.0	18 41.5	21 34.8	3 09.9	12 54.2	10 20.9
19 F	7 46 15	26 06 05	1♋19 58	8♋24 13	20R 26.7	2 33.0	14 43.1	25 24.8	26 00.4	18 45.6	21 31.0	3 13.0	12 54.0	10 22.5
20 Sa	7 50 12	27 03 22	15 25 28	22 23 16	20 26.8	4 35.2	15 56.7	26 00.3	26 22.8	18 49.6	21 27.2	3 16.2	12 53.8	10 24.1
21 Su	7 54 08	28 00 39	29 17 10	6♌06 50	20 26.6	6 35.7	17 10.3	26 35.9	26 45.4	18 53.3	21 23.3	3 19.4	12 53.6	10 25.7
22 M	7 58 05	28 57 57	12♌51 59	19 32 25	20 26.0	8 34.7	18 23.9	27 11.7	27 08.1	18 56.9	21 19.3	3 22.7	12 53.5	10 27.4
23 Tu	8 02 01	29 55 15	26 08 00	2♍38 44	20 24.9	10 32.1	19 37.5	27 47.5	27 30.8	19 00.3	21 15.3	3 26.0	12 53.4	10 29.0
24 W	8 05 58	0♌52 34	9♍04 40	15 25 56	20 23.6	12 27.7	20 51.2	28 23.4	27 53.7	19 03.5	21 11.3	3 29.2	12 53.4	10 30.7
25 Th	8 09 54	1 49 53	21 42 47	27 55 30	20 22.2	14 21.7	22 04.8	28 59.4	28 16.6	19 06.5	21 07.2	3 32.6	12D 53.3	10 32.4
26 F	8 13 51	2 47 13	4♎04 27	10♎10 02	20 20.9	16 14.0	23 18.5	29 35.5	28 39.6	19 09.4	21 03.1	3 35.9	12 53.3	10 34.1
27 Sa	8 17 47	3 44 32	16 12 45	22 13 04	20 20.0	18 04.5	24 32.2	0♎11.7	29 02.8	19 12.0	20 59.0	3 39.3	12 53.4	10 35.9
28 Su	8 21 44	4 41 53	28 11 34	4♏08 46	20D 19.7	19 53.4	25 46.0	0 48.0	29 26.0	19 14.5	20 54.8	3 42.6	12 53.5	10 37.6
29 M	8 25 41	5 39 14	10♏05 17	16 01 40	20 20.0	21 40.5	26 59.7	1 24.3	29 49.2	19 16.8	20 50.5	3 46.1	12 53.6	10 39.4
30 Tu	8 29 37	6 36 35	21 58 32	27 56 26	20 20.9	23 26.0	28 13.5	2 00.8	0♎12.6	19 18.8	20 46.3	3 49.5	12 53.7	10 41.2
31 W	8 33 34	7 33 57	3♐55 57	9♐57 36	20 22.2	25 09.7	29 27.3	2 37.3	0 36.0	19 20.7	20 42.0	3 52.9	12 53.9	10 43.0

August 1963 — LONGITUDE

Day	Sid.Time	☉	0 hr ☽	Noon ☽	True ☊	☿	♀	♂	⚳	♃	♄	♅	♆	♇
1 Th	8 37 30	8♌31 20	16♐01 55	22♐09 21	20♋23.6	26♌51.8	0♌41.1	3♎13.9	0♎59.5	19♈22.4	20♒37.7	3♍56.4	12♏54.1	10♍44.8
2 F	8 41 27	9 28 43	28 20 19	4♑35 13	20 24.8	28 32.2	1 54.9	3 50.6	1 23.1	19 23.9	20R 33.3	3 59.9	12 54.3	10 46.6
3 Sa	8 45 23	10 26 07	10♑54 20	17 17 54	20R 25.4	0♍10.9	3 08.8	4 27.4	1 46.8	19 25.2	20 28.9	4 03.4	12 54.6	10 48.5
4 Su	8 49 20	11 23 32	23 46 05	0♒18 58	20 25.2	1 47.9	4 22.7	5 04.3	2 10.5	19 26.3	20 24.5	4 06.9	12 54.9	10 50.4
5 M	8 53 16	12 20 58	6♒56 33	13 38 42	20 23.9	3 23.3	5 36.6	5 41.2	2 34.3	19 27.3	20 20.1	4 10.5	12 55.2	10 52.2
6 Tu	8 57 13	13 18 25	20 25 17	27 16 00	20 21.6	4 57.0	6 50.5	6 18.3	2 58.2	19 28.0	20 15.7	4 14.1	12 55.6	10 54.1
7 W	9 01 10	14 15 53	4♓10 32	11♓08 28	20 18.5	6 29.1	8 04.4	6 55.4	3 22.1	19 28.5	20 11.3	4 17.6	12 56.0	10 56.0
8 Th	9 05 06	15 13 21	18 09 22	25 12 45	20 15.0	7 59.5	9 18.4	7 32.6	3 46.1	19 28.8	20 06.8	4 21.2	12 56.4	10 57.9
9 F	9 09 03	16 10 52	2♈18 05	9♈24 52	20 11.7	9 28.2	10 32.4	8 09.8	4 10.2	19R 28.9	20 02.3	4 24.8	12 56.8	10 59.9
10 Sa	9 12 59	17 08 23	16 32 37	23 40 51	20 09.1	10 55.2	11 46.4	8 47.2	4 34.4	19 28.9	19 57.8	4 28.5	12 57.3	11 01.8
11 Su	9 16 56	18 05 56	0♉49 07	7♉57 02	20D 07.6	12 20.5	13 00.4	9 24.6	4 58.6	19 28.6	19 53.3	4 32.1	12 57.8	11 03.8
12 M	9 20 52	19 03 30	15 04 16	22 10 29	20 07.3	13 44.1	14 14.5	10 02.1	5 22.8	19 28.1	19 48.8	4 35.7	12 58.4	11 05.7
13 Tu	9 24 49	20 01 06	29 15 27	6♊18 55	20 08.0	15 05.9	15 28.5	10 39.8	5 47.2	19 27.5	19 44.4	4 39.4	12 59.0	11 07.7
14 W	9 28 45	20 58 44	13♊20 41	20 20 36	20 09.4	16 25.9	16 42.7	11 17.4	6 11.6	19 26.6	19 39.9	4 43.1	12 59.6	11 09.7
15 Th	9 32 42	21 56 23	27 18 28	4♋14 09	20 10.8	17 44.1	17 56.8	11 55.2	6 36.0	19 25.5	19 35.4	4 46.8	13 00.3	11 11.7
16 F	9 36 39	22 54 03	11♋07 29	17 58 18	20R 11.6	19 00.3	19 10.9	12 33.1	7 00.6	19 24.3	19 30.9	4 50.5	13 00.9	11 13.7
17 Sa	9 40 35	23 51 45	24 46 26	1♌31 42	20 11.1	20 14.7	20 25.1	13 11.0	7 25.1	19 22.8	19 26.4	4 54.2	13 01.7	11 15.7
18 Su	9 44 32	24 49 28	8♌13 55	14 52 57	20 08.9	21 27.0	21 39.3	13 49.0	7 49.8	19 21.2	19 21.9	4 57.9	13 02.4	11 17.7
19 M	9 48 28	25 47 13	21 28 36	28 00 46	20 05.1	22 37.2	22 53.5	14 27.1	8 14.5	19 19.3	19 17.5	5 01.6	13 03.2	11 19.8
20 Tu	9 52 25	26 44 59	4♍29 19	10♍54 13	19 59.7	23 45.3	24 07.8	15 05.3	8 39.2	19 17.2	19 13.0	5 05.3	13 04.0	11 21.8
21 W	9 56 21	27 42 46	17 15 24	23 32 56	19 53.3	24 51.1	25 22.0	15 43.6	9 04.0	19 15.0	19 08.6	5 09.1	13 04.8	11 23.8
22 Th	10 00 18	28 40 35	29 46 54	5♎57 26	19 46.6	25 54.5	26 36.3	16 21.9	9 28.9	19 12.5	19 04.2	5 12.8	13 05.7	11 25.9
23 F	10 04 14	29 38 24	12♎04 46	18 09 11	19 40.2	26 55.5	27 50.6	17 00.4	9 53.8	19 09.9	18 59.8	5 16.6	13 06.6	11 27.9
24 Sa	10 08 11	0♍36 15	24 10 59	0♏10 34	19 34.8	27 53.8	29 04.9	17 38.9	10 18.7	19 07.0	18 55.4	5 20.3	13 07.5	11 30.0
25 Su	10 12 07	1 34 08	6♏08 24	12 04 58	19 31.0	28 49.3	0♍19.2	18 17.4	10 43.7	19 04.0	18 51.1	5 24.1	13 08.5	11 32.1
26 M	10 16 04	2 32 01	18 00 48	23 56 28	19D 29.0	29 42.0	1 33.5	18 56.1	11 08.8	19 00.8	18 46.8	5 27.8	13 09.4	11 34.2
27 Tu	10 20 01	3 29 56	29 52 34	5♐49 43	19 28.6	0♎31.5	2 47.9	19 34.8	11 33.9	18 57.4	18 42.5	5 31.6	13 10.5	11 36.2
28 W	10 23 57	4 27 52	11♐48 32	17 49 41	19 29.4	1 17.8	4 02.2	20 13.6	11 59.0	18 53.8	18 38.2	5 35.4	13 11.5	11 38.3
29 Th	10 27 54	5 25 50	23 53 47	0♑01 26	19 30.7	2 00.6	5 16.6	20 52.5	12 24.2	18 50.0	18 34.0	5 39.1	13 12.6	11 40.4
30 F	10 31 50	6 23 49	6♑13 12	12 29 39	19R 31.9	2 39.7	6 31.0	21 31.5	12 49.4	18 46.1	18 29.9	5 42.9	13 13.7	11 42.5
31 Sa	10 35 47	7 21 49	18 51 14	25 18 21	19 31.9	3 14.8	7 45.4	22 10.5	13 14.7	18 41.9	18 25.7	5 46.6	13 14.8	11 44.6

Astro Data	Dy Hr Mn
♃□♅	5 8:19
☽0N	13 11:06
♆ D	25 19:14
☽0S	26 15:55
♂0S	28 19:43
♃ R	9 15:26
☽0N	9 16:25
♃□♅	10 14:41
♃✶♄	18 18:56
☿0S	22 10:11
☽0S	22 23:39

Planet Ingress		Dy Hr Mn
☿	♋	4 3:00
♀	♋	7 11:18
☿	♌	18 6:19
☉	♌	23 13:59
♂	♎	27 4:14
⚳	♎	29 23:05
♀	♌	31 22:38
☿	♍	3 9:20
☉	♍	23 20:58
♀	♍	25 5:49
☿	♎	26 20:33

Last Aspect Dy Hr Mn		☽ Ingress Dy Hr Mn
2 17:03	♄ □	♐ 3 8:11
5 14:40	♀ ☍	♑ 5 19:03
7 5:48	♂ △	♒ 8 3:36
9 19:46	♄ ☌	♓ 10 9:53
11 22:42	♂ ☍	♈ 12 14:16
14 3:30	♄ ✶	♉ 14 17:15
16 13:30	☿ ✶	♊ 16 19:27
18 13:03	♂ □	♋ 18 21:45
20 20:43	☉ ☌	♌ 21 1:15
22 15:13	♄ ☍	♍ 23 7:06
25 14:11	♂ ☌	♎ 25 16:02
27 17:11	♀ □	♏ 28 3:38
30 12:38	♀ △	♐ 30 16:08

Last Aspect Dy Hr Mn		☽ Ingress Dy Hr Mn
1 22:35	☿ △	♑ 2 3:12
3 15:57	♃ □	♒ 4 11:25
5 23:47	♄ ☌	♓ 6 16:46
7 15:04	♆ △	♈ 8 20:07
10 5:47	♄ ✶	♉ 10 22:37
12 8:02	♄ □	♊ 13 1:16
14 13:10	☉ ✶	♋ 15 4:39
16 14:31	♃ □	♌ 17 9:17
19 7:35	☉ ☌	♍ 19 15:40
21 14:44	☿ ☌	♎ 22 0:25
24 9:33	♀ ✶	♏ 24 11:39
26 1:37	♄ □	♐ 27 0:15
28 17:01	♂ ✶	♑ 29 11:57
31 5:53	♂ □	♒ 31 20:37

☽ Phases & Eclipses Dy Hr Mn	
6 21:55	○ 14♑06
6 22:02	☍ P 0.706
14 1:57	☾ 20♈56
20 20:43	● 27♋24
20 20:35:37	● T 01'40"
28 13:13	☽ 4♏45
5 9:31	○ 12♒15
12 6:21	☾ 18♉50
19 7:35	● 25♌37
27 6:54	☽ 3♐18

Astro Data

1 July 1963
Julian Day # 23192
SVP 5♓46'26"
GC 26♐19.8 ⚴ 24♌43.1
Eris 11♈03.9 ⚵ 20♍53.1
⚷ 14♓50.1R ⚶ 29♍08.0
☽ Mean ☊ 21♋04.3

1 August 1963
Julian Day # 23223
SVP 5♓46'21"
GC 26♐19.8 ⚴ 9♍03.1
Eris 11♈01.0R ⚵ 29♍44.9
⚷ 14♓04.2R ⚶ 11♎29.9
☽ Mean ☊ 19♋25.9

LONGITUDE — September 1963

Day	Sid.Time	☉	0 hr ☽	Noon ☽	True ☊	☿	♀	♂	⚳	♃	♄	♅	♆	♇
1 Su	10 39 43	8♍19 51	1♒51 18	8♒30 18	19♋30.2	3♎45.8	8♍59.8	22♎49.6	13♎40.0	18♈37.6	18♒21.6	5♍50.4	13♏16.0	11♍46.7
2 M	10 43 40	9 17 54	15 15 23	22 06 29	19R 26.5	4 12.2	10 14.2	23 28.8	14 05.3	18R 33.1	18R 17.6	5 54.2	13 17.2	11 48.8
3 Tu	10 47 36	10 15 58	29 03 23	6♓05 43	19 20.6	4 33.9	11 28.7	24 08.0	14 30.7	18 28.5	18 13.6	5 57.9	13 18.4	11 50.9
4 W	10 51 33	11 14 05	13♓12 56	20 24 23	19 13.2	4 50.6	12 43.1	24 47.4	14 56.1	18 23.6	18 09.6	6 01.7	13 19.6	11 53.0
5 Th	10 55 30	12 12 13	27 39 18	4♈56 49	19 04.9	5 01.9	13 57.6	25 26.8	15 21.6	18 18.6	18 05.7	6 05.4	13 20.9	11 55.1
6 F	10 59 26	13 10 22	12♈16 01	19 35 59	18 56.9	5R 07.6	15 12.1	26 06.2	15 47.1	18 13.5	18 01.9	6 09.2	13 22.2	11 57.2
7 Sa	11 03 23	14 08 34	26 55 48	4♉14 37	18 50.1	5 07.4	16 26.6	26 45.8	16 12.6	18 08.2	17 58.0	6 12.9	13 23.5	11 59.3
8 Su	11 07 19	15 06 48	11♉31 43	18 46 26	18 45.2	5 01.0	17 41.1	27 25.4	16 38.2	18 02.7	17 54.3	6 16.6	13 24.9	12 01.4
9 M	11 11 16	16 05 04	25 58 15	3♊06 47	18D 42.5	4 48.2	18 55.7	28 05.1	17 03.8	17 57.1	17 50.6	6 20.4	13 26.3	12 03.5
10 Tu	11 15 12	17 03 22	10♊11 46	17 13 03	18 41.8	4 28.9	20 10.2	28 44.9	17 29.4	17 51.3	17 47.0	6 24.1	13 27.7	12 05.6
11 W	11 19 09	18 01 42	24 10 34	1♋04 21	18 42.2	4 03.0	21 24.8	29 24.8	17 55.1	17 45.3	17 43.4	6 27.8	13 29.1	12 07.7
12 Th	11 23 05	19 00 05	7♋54 29	14 41 03	18R 42.9	3 30.5	22 39.4	0♏04.7	18 20.8	17 39.3	17 39.9	6 31.5	13 30.6	12 09.7
13 F	11 27 02	19 58 29	21 24 13	28 04 08	18 42.5	2 51.6	23 54.0	0 44.7	18 46.6	17 33.0	17 36.4	6 35.2	13 32.1	12 11.8
14 Sa	11 30 59	20 56 56	4♌40 54	11♌14 40	18 40.3	2 06.6	25 08.6	1 24.8	19 12.4	17 26.7	17 33.1	6 38.9	13 33.6	12 13.9
15 Su	11 34 55	21 55 24	17 45 31	24 13 31	18 35.5	1 16.0	26 23.2	2 04.9	19 38.2	17 20.2	17 29.7	6 42.6	13 35.1	12 16.0
16 M	11 38 52	22 53 55	0♍38 44	7♍01 12	18 28.0	0 20.6	27 37.8	2 45.2	20 04.0	17 13.6	17 26.5	6 46.2	13 36.7	12 18.1
17 Tu	11 42 48	23 52 27	13 20 55	19 37 54	18 18.0	29♍21.2	28 52.5	3 25.5	20 29.8	17 06.8	17 23.3	6 49.9	13 38.2	12 20.1
18 W	11 46 45	24 51 02	25 52 10	2♎03 46	18 06.2	28 19.0	0♎07.1	4 05.9	20 55.7	16 59.9	17 20.2	6 53.5	13 39.8	12 22.2
19 Th	11 50 41	25 49 38	8♎12 43	14 19 07	17 53.7	27 15.3	1 21.8	4 46.3	21 21.7	16 53.0	17 17.2	6 57.1	13 41.5	12 24.3
20 F	11 54 38	26 48 16	20 23 05	26 24 47	17 41.6	26 11.6	2 36.5	5 26.9	21 47.6	16 45.9	17 14.3	7 00.7	13 43.1	12 26.3
21 Sa	11 58 34	27 46 56	2♏24 26	8♏22 17	17 30.9	25 09.3	3 51.1	6 07.5	22 13.6	16 38.7	17 11.4	7 04.3	13 44.8	12 28.4
22 Su	12 02 31	28 45 38	14 18 41	20 14 00	17 22.4	24 10.1	5 05.8	6 48.2	22 39.5	16 31.4	17 08.6	7 07.9	13 46.5	12 30.4
23 M	12 06 28	29 44 21	26 08 40	2♐03 11	17 16.4	23 15.6	6 20.5	7 28.9	23 05.6	16 24.0	17 05.9	7 11.5	13 48.2	12 32.4
24 Tu	12 10 24	0♎43 07	7♐58 04	13 53 55	17 13.1	22 27.1	7 35.2	8 09.7	23 31.6	16 16.5	17 03.3	7 15.0	13 49.9	12 34.5
25 W	12 14 21	1 41 54	19 51 19	25 50 57	17D 11.8	21 46.0	8 49.9	8 50.6	23 57.7	16 09.0	17 00.7	7 18.5	13 51.7	12 36.5
26 Th	12 18 17	2 40 43	1♑53 27	7♑59 31	17R 11.7	21 13.3	10 04.6	9 31.6	24 23.7	16 01.4	16 58.2	7 22.0	13 53.5	12 38.5
27 F	12 22 14	3 39 33	14 09 49	20 24 59	17 11.8	20 49.8	11 19.3	10 12.7	24 49.8	15 53.7	16 55.9	7 25.5	13 55.3	12 40.5
28 Sa	12 26 10	4 38 25	26 45 40	3♒12 24	17 10.9	20D 36.2	12 34.1	10 53.8	25 15.9	15 45.9	16 53.6	7 29.0	13 57.1	12 42.5
29 Su	12 30 07	5 37 19	9♒45 41	16 25 53	17 08.1	20 32.7	13 48.8	11 34.9	25 42.1	15 38.1	16 51.4	7 32.4	13 59.0	12 44.4
30 M	12 34 03	6 36 15	23 13 14	0♓07 50	17 02.7	20 39.6	15 03.5	12 16.2	26 08.2	15 30.2	16 49.3	7 35.8	14 00.8	12 46.4

LONGITUDE — October 1963

Day	Sid.Time	☉	0 hr ☽	Noon ☽	True ☊	☿	♀	♂	⚳	♃	♄	♅	♆	♇
1 Tu	12 38 00	7♎35 13	7♓09 34	14♓18 08	16♋54.7	20♍56.5	16♎18.2	12♏57.5	26♎34.4	15♈22.3	16♒47.3	7♍39.2	14♏02.7	12♍48.4
2 W	12 41 56	8 34 12	21 33 03	28 53 33	16R 44.6	21 23.4	17 33.0	13 38.9	27 00.5	15R 14.3	16R 45.3	7 42.6	14 04.6	12 50.3
3 Th	12 45 53	9 33 13	6♈18 45	13♈47 34	16 33.3	21 59.7	18 47.7	14 20.3	27 26.7	15 06.3	16 43.5	7 46.0	14 06.5	12 52.2
4 F	12 49 50	10 32 17	21 18 47	28 51 08	16 22.1	22 44.9	20 02.4	15 01.8	27 52.9	14 58.3	16 41.7	7 49.3	14 08.4	12 54.1
5 Sa	12 53 46	11 31 23	6♉23 22	13♉54 13	16 12.4	23 38.2	21 17.2	15 43.4	28 19.1	14 50.3	16 40.1	7 52.6	14 10.4	12 56.0
6 Su	12 57 43	12 30 30	21 22 35	28 47 28	16 05.0	24 39.1	22 31.9	16 25.1	28 45.4	14 42.2	16 38.5	7 55.8	14 12.3	12 57.9
7 M	13 01 39	13 29 41	6♊08 06	13♊23 51	16 00.4	25 46.8	23 46.7	17 06.8	29 11.6	14 34.1	16 37.1	7 59.1	14 14.3	12 59.8
8 Tu	13 05 36	14 28 53	20 34 19	27 39 15	15 58.3	27 00.5	25 01.4	17 48.6	29 37.9	14 26.1	16 35.7	8 02.3	14 16.3	13 01.7
9 W	13 09 32	15 28 08	4♋38 35	11♋32 22	15 57.8	28 19.5	26 16.2	18 30.5	0♏04.1	14 18.0	16 34.4	8 05.5	14 18.3	13 03.5
10 Th	13 13 29	16 27 26	18 20 46	25 04 03	15 57.7	29 43.0	27 31.0	19 12.5	0 30.4	14 09.9	16 33.2	8 08.7	14 20.4	13 05.3
11 F	13 17 25	17 26 45	1♌42 32	8♌16 32	15 56.7	1♎10.6	28 45.8	19 54.5	0 56.7	14 01.8	16 32.2	8 11.8	14 22.4	13 07.1
12 Sa	13 21 22	18 26 07	14 46 25	21 12 31	15 53.8	2 41.4	0♏00.5	20 36.6	1 23.0	13 53.8	16 31.2	8 14.9	14 24.5	13 08.9
13 Su	13 25 19	19 25 31	27 35 11	3♍54 43	15 48.0	4 15.0	1 15.3	21 18.7	1 49.3	13 45.8	16 30.3	8 18.0	14 26.5	13 10.7
14 M	13 29 15	20 24 58	10♍11 22	16 25 24	15 39.2	5 50.9	2 30.1	22 01.0	2 15.6	13 37.8	16 29.5	8 21.0	14 28.6	13 12.5
15 Tu	13 33 12	21 24 26	22 37 00	28 46 21	15 27.6	7 28.6	3 44.9	22 43.3	2 42.0	13 29.8	16 28.8	8 24.0	14 30.7	13 14.2
16 W	13 37 08	22 23 57	4♎53 35	10♎58 51	15 14.1	9 07.8	4 59.7	23 25.7	3 08.3	13 21.9	16 28.3	8 27.0	14 32.8	13 16.0
17 Th	13 41 05	23 23 29	17 02 14	23 03 53	14 59.7	10 48.0	6 14.5	24 08.1	3 34.6	13 14.1	16 27.8	8 30.0	14 34.9	13 17.7
18 F	13 45 01	24 23 04	29 03 53	5♏02 24	14 45.6	12 29.1	7 29.3	24 50.6	4 01.0	13 06.3	16 27.4	8 32.9	14 37.0	13 19.4
19 Sa	13 48 58	25 22 41	10♏59 33	16 55 34	14 32.9	14 10.8	8 44.1	25 33.2	4 27.3	12 58.5	16 27.1	8 35.7	14 39.2	13 21.0
20 Su	13 52 54	26 22 20	22 50 39	28 45 05	14 22.7	15 52.9	9 58.9	26 15.8	4 53.7	12 50.9	16 26.9	8 38.6	14 41.3	13 22.7
21 M	13 56 51	27 22 00	4♐39 10	10♐33 17	14 15.3	17 35.1	11 13.7	26 58.6	5 20.0	12 43.3	16D 26.9	8 41.4	14 43.5	13 24.3
22 Tu	14 00 48	28 21 43	16 27 51	22 23 19	14 10.7	19 17.4	12 28.5	27 41.3	5 46.4	12 35.8	16 26.9	8 44.1	14 45.7	13 25.9
23 W	14 04 44	29 21 27	28 20 13	4♑19 06	14D 08.7	20 59.6	13 43.4	28 24.2	6 12.7	12 28.3	16 27.0	8 46.9	14 47.9	13 27.5
24 Th	14 08 41	0♏21 13	10♑20 34	16 25 15	14 08.4	22 41.7	14 58.2	29 07.1	6 39.1	12 21.0	16 27.3	8 49.6	14 50.0	13 29.1
25 F	14 12 37	1 21 01	22 33 47	28 46 51	14R 08.6	24 23.5	16 13.0	29 50.1	7 05.4	12 13.8	16 27.6	8 52.2	14 52.2	13 30.6
26 Sa	14 16 34	2 20 50	5♒05 06	11♒29 08	14 08.3	26 05.0	17 27.8	0♐33.1	7 31.8	12 06.7	16 28.1	8 54.8	14 54.4	13 32.2
27 Su	14 20 30	3 20 41	17 59 34	24 36 53	14 06.4	27 46.2	18 42.6	1 16.3	7 58.1	11 59.7	16 28.6	8 57.4	14 56.6	13 33.7
28 M	14 24 27	4 20 34	1♓21 30	8♓13 41	14 02.2	29 26.9	19 57.3	1 59.4	8 24.4	11 52.8	16 29.3	8 59.9	14 58.9	13 35.1
29 Tu	14 28 23	5 20 28	15 13 32	22 20 58	13 55.5	1♏07.3	21 12.1	2 42.7	8 50.8	11 46.0	16 30.0	9 02.4	15 01.1	13 36.6
30 W	14 32 20	6 20 24	29 35 41	6♈57 09	13 46.7	2 47.2	22 26.9	3 26.0	9 17.1	11 39.3	16 30.9	9 04.9	15 03.3	13 38.0
31 Th	14 36 17	7 20 22	14♈24 34	21 56 57	13 36.7	4 26.7	23 41.7	4 09.3	9 43.4	11 32.8	16 31.8	9 07.3	15 05.5	13 39.4

Astro Data	Dy Hr Mn
⚳0S	5 13:12
☽0N	5 23:11
☿R	6 23:10
♃⚹♄	12 6:14
☽0S	19 6:43
♀0S	20 19:25
☿0N	22 6:27
☉0S	23 18:24
☿D	29 8:03
☽0N	3 8:30
♃⚻♆	9 11:09
☿0S	13 16:55
☽0S	16 13:14
♃⚻♇	17 2:54
♄D	21 16:22

Planet Ingress	Dy Hr Mn
♂ ♏	12 9:11
☿ ♍R	16 20:29
♀ ♎	18 9:43
☉ ♎	23 18:24
⚳ ♏	9 8:13
☿ ♎	10 16:44
♀ ♏	12 11:50
☉ ♏	24 3:29
♂ ♐	25 17:31
☿ ♏	28 19:54
☽0N	30 19:43

Last Aspect Dy Hr Mn		☽ Ingress	Dy Hr Mn
2 14:30	♂ △	♓	3 1:37
4 0:10	♆ △	♈	5 3:52
6 23:09	♂ ☍	♉	7 5:02
8 10:34	♄ □	♊	9 6:45
11 8:57	♂ △	♋	11 10:08
13 3:43	♀ ⚹	♌	13 15:30
14 23:34	♄ ☍	♍	15 22:47
18 7:48	♀ ☌	♎	18 8:00
19 17:50	♄ △	♏	20 19:10
23 6:53	☉ ⚹	♐	23 7:50
25 4:15	☿ □	♑	25 20:15
27 12:46	☿ △	♒	28 6:03
29 12:45	♄ ☌	♓	30 11:47

Last Aspect Dy Hr Mn		☽ Ingress	Dy Hr Mn
1 23:19	☿ ☍	♈	2 13:48
3 20:42	♀ ☍	♉	4 13:50
6 4:47	☿ △	♊	6 13:58
8 10:47	☿ □	♋	8 16:01
10 16:52	♀ □	♌	10 20:54
12 10:49	♂ □	♍	13 4:34
14 23:29	♂ ⚹	♎	15 14:24
17 12:43	☉ ☌	♏	18 1:53
20 6:37	♂ ☌	♐	20 14:32
23 1:09	☉ ⚹	♑	23 3:21
25 14:08	♂ ⚹	♒	25 14:20
27 18:27	☿ △	♓	27 21:36
29 9:54	♀ △	♈	30 0:40

☽ Phases & Eclipses Dy Hr Mn	
3 19:33	○ 10♓34
10 11:42	☾ 17♊03
17 20:51	● 24♍14
26 0:38	☽ 2♑13
3 4:44	○ 9♈15
9 19:27	☾ 15♋47
17 12:43	● 23♎25
25 17:20	☽ 1♒34

Astro Data

1 September 1963
Julian Day # 23254
SVP 5♓46'17"
GC 26♐19.9 ⚴ 23♍25.1
Eris 10♈48.7R ⚵ 9♎52.0
⚷ 12♓44.5R ⚶ 25♎49.8
☽ Mean ☊ 17♋47.4

1 October 1963
Julian Day # 23284
SVP 5♓46'15"
GC 26♐20.0 ⚴ 7♎14.0
Eris 10♈31.3R ⚵ 20♎15.4
⚷ 11♓22.8R ⚶ 10♏52.0
☽ Mean ☊ 16♋12.0

November 1963 — LONGITUDE

Day	Sid.Time	☉	0 hr ☽	Noon ☽	True ☊	☿	♀	♂	⚳	♃	♄	♅	♆	♇
1 F	14 40 13	8♏20 21	29♈33 06	7♉11 41	13♋26.6	6♏05.7	24♏56.5	4♐52.7	10♏09.7	11♈26.4	16♒32.9	9♍09.6	15♏07.8	13♍40.8
2 Sa	14 44 10	9 20 23	14♉51 15	22 30 22	13R 17.8	7 44.3	26 11.3	5 36.2	10 36.0	11R 20.1	16 34.0	9 11.9	15 10.0	13 42.2
3 Su	14 48 06	10 20 26	0♊07 37	7♊41 45	13 11.1	9 22.4	27 26.0	6 19.8	11 02.3	11 14.0	16 35.3	9 14.2	15 12.2	13 43.5
4 M	14 52 03	11 20 32	15 11 37	22 36 17	13 07.0	11 00.1	28 40.8	7 03.4	11 28.6	11 08.1	16 36.6	9 16.5	15 14.5	13 44.8
5 Tu	14 55 59	12 20 39	29 55 04	7♋07 28	13D 05.3	12 37.4	29 55.6	7 47.1	11 54.8	11 02.2	16 38.1	9 18.6	15 16.7	13 46.1
6 W	14 59 56	13 20 49	14♋13 12	21 12 11	13 05.4	14 14.3	1♐10.4	8 30.8	12 21.1	10 56.6	16 39.7	9 20.8	15 19.0	13 47.4
7 Th	15 03 52	14 21 00	28 04 30	4♌50 21	13R 06.1	15 50.8	2 25.1	9 14.6	12 47.4	10 51.1	16 41.3	9 22.9	15 21.2	13 48.6
8 F	15 07 49	15 21 14	11♌30 02	18 03 58	13 06.4	17 26.8	3 39.9	9 58.5	13 13.6	10 45.7	16 43.1	9 24.9	15 23.5	13 49.8
9 Sa	15 11 46	16 21 30	24 32 33	0♍56 16	13 05.2	19 02.6	4 54.7	10 42.5	13 39.9	10 40.5	16 44.9	9 26.9	15 25.7	13 51.0
10 Su	15 15 42	17 21 48	7♍15 35	13 30 59	13 01.8	20 37.9	6 09.5	11 26.5	14 06.1	10 35.5	16 46.9	9 28.9	15 28.0	13 52.2
11 M	15 19 39	18 22 07	19 42 55	25 51 47	12 56.0	22 12.9	7 24.2	12 10.5	14 32.3	10 30.7	16 49.0	9 30.8	15 30.2	13 53.3
12 Tu	15 23 35	19 22 29	1♎58 00	8♎01 56	12 48.0	23 47.6	8 39.0	12 54.6	14 58.5	10 26.0	16 51.1	9 32.7	15 32.5	13 54.4
13 W	15 27 32	20 22 52	14 03 54	20 04 12	12 38.3	25 22.0	9 53.8	13 38.8	15 24.7	10 21.5	16 53.4	9 34.5	15 34.7	13 55.5
14 Th	15 31 28	21 23 17	26 03 05	2♏00 47	12 27.8	26 56.1	11 08.6	14 23.1	15 50.8	10 17.2	16 55.7	9 36.2	15 37.0	13 56.5
15 F	15 35 25	22 23 44	7♏57 31	13 53 29	12 17.6	28 29.9	12 23.3	15 07.4	16 17.0	10 13.0	16 58.2	9 37.9	15 39.2	13 57.5
16 Sa	15 39 21	23 24 13	19 48 53	25 43 53	12 08.4	0♐03.4	13 38.1	15 51.8	16 43.1	10 09.1	17 00.7	9 39.6	15 41.4	13 58.5
17 Su	15 43 18	24 24 43	1♐38 42	7♐33 33	12 01.0	1 36.7	14 52.9	16 36.2	17 09.2	10 05.4	17 03.4	9 41.2	15 43.7	13 59.5
18 M	15 47 15	25 25 15	13 28 39	19 24 15	11 56.0	3 09.8	16 07.6	17 20.7	17 35.3	10 01.8	17 06.1	9 42.7	15 45.9	14 00.4
19 Tu	15 51 11	26 25 48	25 20 41	1♑18 14	11D 53.2	4 42.6	17 22.4	18 05.3	18 01.4	9 58.4	17 08.9	9 44.2	15 48.1	14 01.3
20 W	15 55 08	27 26 23	7♑17 18	13 18 15	11 52.6	6 15.3	18 37.1	18 49.9	18 27.4	9 55.3	17 11.9	9 45.7	15 50.3	14 02.2
21 Th	15 59 04	28 26 59	19 21 34	25 27 41	11 53.4	7 47.7	19 51.9	19 34.5	18 53.4	9 52.3	17 14.9	9 47.1	15 52.6	14 03.0
22 F	16 03 01	29 27 36	1♒37 09	7♒50 27	11 54.9	9 19.9	21 06.6	20 19.3	19 19.4	9 49.6	17 18.0	9 48.4	15 54.8	14 03.8
23 Sa	16 06 57	0♐28 15	14 08 10	20 30 49	11R 56.2	10 51.9	22 21.4	21 04.1	19 45.4	9 47.0	17 21.2	9 49.7	15 57.0	14 04.6
24 Su	16 10 54	1 28 54	26 58 56	3♓33 00	11 56.7	12 23.7	23 36.1	21 48.9	20 11.3	9 44.6	17 24.5	9 51.0	15 59.2	14 05.3
25 M	16 14 50	2 29 34	10♓13 27	17 00 38	11 55.6	13 55.3	24 50.8	22 33.8	20 37.2	9 42.5	17 27.9	9 52.2	16 01.3	14 06.0
26 Tu	16 18 47	3 30 16	23 54 46	0♈55 58	11 52.8	15 26.7	26 05.5	23 18.7	21 03.1	9 40.5	17 31.3	9 53.3	16 03.5	14 06.7
27 W	16 22 44	4 30 58	8♈04 08	15 19 01	11 48.5	16 57.9	27 20.2	24 03.7	21 29.0	9 38.8	17 34.9	9 54.4	16 05.7	14 07.4
28 Th	16 26 40	5 31 42	22 40 09	0♉06 50	11 43.2	18 28.9	28 34.9	24 48.8	21 54.8	9 37.2	17 38.6	9 55.4	16 07.8	14 08.0
29 F	16 30 37	6 32 27	7♉38 12	15 13 11	11 37.7	19 59.6	29 49.6	25 33.9	22 20.6	9 35.9	17 42.3	9 56.3	16 10.0	14 08.6
30 Sa	16 34 33	7 33 13	22 50 33	0♊28 59	11 32.8	21 30.0	1♑04.2	26 19.0	22 46.4	9 34.8	17 46.1	9 57.3	16 12.1	14 09.1

December 1963 — LONGITUDE

Day	Sid.Time	☉	0 hr ☽	Noon ☽	True ☊	☿	♀	♂	⚳	♃	♄	♅	♆	♇
1 Su	16 38 30	8♐34 00	8♊07 09	15♊43 41	11♋29.3	23♐00.2	2♑18.9	27♐04.2	23♏12.1	9♈33.9	17♒50.0	9♍58.1	16♏14.2	14♍09.7
2 M	16 42 26	9 34 48	23 17 20	0♋46 57	11D 27.3	24 30.0	3 33.5	27 49.5	23 37.8	9R 33.1	17 54.0	9 58.9	16 16.3	14 10.2
3 Tu	16 46 23	10 35 38	8♋11 34	15 30 22	11 27.0	25 59.4	4 48.2	28 34.8	24 03.5	9 32.6	17 58.1	9 59.7	16 18.4	14 10.6
4 W	16 50 19	11 36 29	22 42 48	29 48 26	11 27.9	27 28.3	6 02.8	29 20.2	24 29.1	9D 32.3	18 02.2	10 00.4	16 20.5	14 11.1
5 Th	16 54 16	12 37 21	6♌47 06	13♌38 46	11 29.5	28 56.7	7 17.4	0♑05.6	24 54.7	9 32.3	18 06.5	10 01.0	16 22.6	14 11.5
6 F	16 58 13	13 38 15	20 23 34	27 01 43	11 31.0	0♑24.5	8 32.1	0 51.1	25 20.3	9 32.4	18 10.8	10 01.6	16 24.7	14 11.8
7 Sa	17 02 09	14 39 09	3♍33 36	9♍59 38	11R 31.9	1 51.6	9 46.7	1 36.6	25 45.8	9 32.7	18 15.2	10 02.1	16 26.7	14 12.2
8 Su	17 06 06	15 40 05	16 20 17	22 36 04	11 31.8	3 17.8	11 01.2	2 22.1	26 11.3	9 33.2	18 19.7	10 02.6	16 28.7	14 12.5
9 M	17 10 02	16 41 03	28 47 32	4♎55 12	11 30.5	4 43.0	12 15.8	3 07.8	26 36.7	9 34.0	18 24.2	10 03.0	16 30.7	14 12.7
10 Tu	17 13 59	17 42 01	10♎59 38	17 01 19	11 28.0	6 07.1	13 30.4	3 53.4	27 02.2	9 34.9	18 28.8	10 03.3	16 32.7	14 13.0
11 W	17 17 55	18 43 01	23 00 46	28 58 27	11 24.6	7 29.8	14 45.0	4 39.2	27 27.5	9 36.1	18 33.5	10 03.6	16 34.7	14 13.2
12 Th	17 21 52	19 44 01	4♏54 48	10♏50 14	11 20.8	8 50.9	15 59.5	5 24.9	27 52.9	9 37.5	18 38.3	10 03.9	16 36.7	14 13.3
13 F	17 25 48	20 45 03	16 45 07	22 39 48	11 17.0	10 10.2	17 14.1	6 10.8	28 18.1	9 39.0	18 43.2	10 04.0	16 38.6	14 13.5
14 Sa	17 29 45	21 46 06	28 34 34	4♐29 45	11 13.7	11 27.2	18 28.6	6 56.6	28 43.4	9 40.8	18 48.1	10 04.2	16 40.6	14 13.6
15 Su	17 33 42	22 47 09	10♐25 35	16 22 18	11 11.2	12 41.7	19 43.1	7 42.6	29 08.6	9 42.8	18 53.1	10R 04.2	16 42.5	14 13.7
16 M	17 37 38	23 48 13	22 20 09	28 19 22	11 09.7	13 53.2	20 57.6	8 28.5	29 33.7	9 45.0	18 58.2	10 04.2	16 44.4	14R 13.7
17 Tu	17 41 35	24 49 18	4♑20 08	10♑22 41	11D 09.2	15 01.2	22 12.1	9 14.5	29 58.8	9 47.4	19 03.3	10 04.2	16 46.3	14 13.7
18 W	17 45 31	25 50 24	16 27 15	22 34 03	11 09.5	16 05.2	23 26.6	10 00.6	0♐23.9	9 50.0	19 08.5	10 04.1	16 48.1	14 13.7
19 Th	17 49 28	26 51 30	28 43 21	4♒55 25	11 10.5	17 04.6	24 41.1	10 46.7	0 48.9	9 52.8	19 13.8	10 03.9	16 50.0	14 13.6
20 F	17 53 24	27 52 36	11♒10 30	17 28 56	11 11.7	17 58.6	25 55.5	11 32.8	1 13.8	9 55.8	19 19.2	10 03.7	16 51.8	14 13.5
21 Sa	17 57 21	28 53 43	23 51 00	0♓17 01	11 12.9	18 46.5	27 09.9	12 19.0	1 38.7	9 59.0	19 24.6	10 03.5	16 53.6	14 13.4
22 Su	18 01 17	29 54 50	6♓47 17	13 22 08	11 13.9	19 27.5	28 24.3	13 05.3	2 03.6	10 02.4	19 30.0	10 03.1	16 55.3	14 13.3
23 M	18 05 14	0♑55 57	20 01 48	26 46 33	11R 14.3	20 00.7	29 38.7	13 51.5	2 28.3	10 06.0	19 35.6	10 02.7	16 57.1	14 13.1
24 Tu	18 09 11	1 57 04	3♈36 33	10♈31 56	11 14.2	20 25.2	0♒53.0	14 37.8	2 53.1	10 09.8	19 41.2	10 02.3	16 58.8	14 12.9
25 W	18 13 07	2 58 11	17 32 41	24 38 43	11 13.7	20R 40.0	2 07.3	15 24.2	3 17.7	10 13.7	19 46.8	10 01.8	17 00.5	14 12.6
26 Th	18 17 04	3 59 18	1♉49 49	9♉05 38	11 12.9	20 44.4	3 21.6	16 10.5	3 42.3	10 17.9	19 52.5	10 01.3	17 02.2	14 12.3
27 F	18 21 00	5 00 25	16 25 41	23 49 17	11 12.2	20 37.6	4 35.9	16 56.9	4 06.9	10 22.3	19 58.3	10 00.7	17 03.9	14 12.0
28 Sa	18 24 57	6 01 33	1♊15 42	8♊44 01	11 11.5	20 19.2	5 50.1	17 43.4	4 31.4	10 26.8	20 04.2	10 00.0	17 05.5	14 11.7
29 Su	18 28 53	7 02 40	16 13 16	23 42 24	11 11.1	19 48.9	7 04.3	18 29.9	4 55.8	10 31.6	20 10.1	9 59.3	17 07.1	14 11.3
30 M	18 32 50	8 03 48	1♋10 21	8♋36 05	11D 11.0	19 06.9	8 18.5	19 16.4	5 20.1	10 36.5	20 16.0	9 58.5	17 08.7	14 10.9
31 Tu	18 36 47	9 04 56	15 58 37	23 17 03	11 11.1	18 14.0	9 32.7	20 03.0	5 44.4	10 41.6	20 22.0	9 57.7	17 10.3	14 10.5

Astro Data	Planet Ingress	Last Aspect	☽ Ingress	Last Aspect	☽ Ingress	☽ Phases & Eclipses	Astro Data
Dy Hr Mn	Dy Hr Mn	Dy Hr Mn	Dy Hr Mn	Dy Hr Mn	Dy Hr Mn	Dy Hr Mn	
☽0S 12 19:36	♀ ♐ 5 13:25	31 3:23 ♄ ⚹	♉ 1 0:42	2 7:00 ♂ ☍	♋ 2 10:44	1 13:55 ○ 8♉25	1 November 1963
♃⚻♅ 22 18:44	☿ ♐ 16 11:07	2 18:18 ♀ ☍	♊ 2 23:48	3 13:20 ♆ △	♌ 4 12:20	8 6:37 ☾ 15♌08	Julian Day # 23315
☽0N 27 6:39	☉ ♐ 23 0:49	4 2:16 ♄ △	♋ 5 0:08	5 19:57 ♄ ☍	♍ 6 17:26	16 6:50 ● 23♏11	SVP 5♓46'12"
	♀ ♑ 29 15:21	6 1:51 ♆ △	♌ 7 3:24	8 0:14 ♆ ⚹	♎ 9 2:21	24 7:56 ☽ 1♓19	GC 26♐20.0 ⚴ 21♎15.4
♃ D 5 10:11		8 10:42 ☿ □	♍ 9 10:14	10 14:56 ♄ △	♏ 11 14:04	30 23:54 ○ 8♊03	Eris 10♈12.7R ⚵ 1♏08.5
☽0S 10 2:24	♂ ♑ 5 9:03	11 3:49 ☿ ⚹	♎ 11 20:07	13 3:56 ♄ □	♐ 14 2:53		⚷ 10♓25.4R ⚶ 27♏09.0
♅ R 16 5:12	☿ ♑ 6 5:17	13 5:37 ♄ △	♏ 14 7:57	16 2:06 ☉ ☌	♑ 16 15:21	7 21:34 ☾ 15♍03	☽ Mean ☊ 14♋33.5
♇ R 17 7:07	⚳ ♐ 17 13:07	16 6:50 ☉ ☌	♐ 16 20:40	18 13:54 ♀ ☌	♒ 19 2:29	16 2:06 ● 23♐23	
♃⚻♅ 22 16:37	☉ ♑ 22 14:02	18 7:33 ♂ ☌	♑ 19 9:23	21 9:12 ☉ ⚹	♓ 21 11:28	23 19:54 ☽ 1♈16	1 December 1963
☽0N 24 15:05	♀ ♒ 23 18:53	21 18:22 ☉ ⚹	♒ 21 20:51	23 17:34 ♀ ⚹	♈ 23 17:41	30 11:04 ○ 8♋01	Julian Day # 23345
☿ R 26 9:39		23 15:48 ♀ ⚹	♓ 24 5:32	25 5:12 ☿ □	♉ 25 20:57	30 11:07 • T 1.335	SVP 5♓46'07"
		26 2:56 ♀ □	♈ 26 10:25	27 6:53 ☿ △	♊ 27 21:58		GC 26♐20.1 ⚴ 4♏19.5
		28 9:19 ♀ △	♉ 28 11:49	29 6:17 ♄ △	♋ 29 22:07		Eris 9♈59.6R ⚵ 11♏22.2
		29 15:56 ♄ □	♊ 30 11:14	31 6:22 ♂ ☍	♌ 31 23:09		⚷ 10♓16.7 ⚶ 13♐17.7
							☽ Mean ☊ 12♋58.2

LONGITUDE — January 1964

Day	Sid.Time	☉	0 hr ☽	Noon ☽	True ☊	☿	♀	♂	⚳	♃	♄	♅	♆	♇
1 W	18 40 43	10♑06 04	0♌30 36	7♌38 39	11♋11.2	17♑11.2	10♒46.8	20♑49.6	6♐08.7	10♈46.9	20♒28.1	9♍56.8	17♏11.8	14♍10.0
2 Th	18 44 40	11 07 12	14 40 41	21 36 23	11R 11.2	16R 00.3	12 00.9	21 36.2	6 32.8	10 52.3	20 34.2	9R 55.9	17 13.3	14R 09.5
3 F	18 48 36	12 08 21	28 25 36	5♍08 17	11 11.2	14 43.4	13 14.9	22 22.9	6 56.9	10 58.0	20 40.3	9 54.9	17 14.8	14 09.0
4 Sa	18 52 33	13 09 30	11♍44 34	18 14 39	11 11.0	13 23.1	14 28.9	23 09.6	7 21.0	11 03.8	20 46.5	9 53.9	17 16.3	14 08.4
5 Su	18 56 29	14 10 38	24 38 52	0♎57 38	11 10.8	12 01.9	15 42.9	23 56.3	7 44.9	11 09.8	20 52.8	9 52.8	17 17.7	14 07.8
6 M	19 00 26	15 11 47	7♎11 26	13 20 47	11D 10.7	10 42.5	16 56.9	24 43.0	8 08.8	11 15.9	20 59.1	9 51.7	17 19.1	14 07.2
7 Tu	19 04 22	16 12 57	19 26 14	25 28 23	11 10.8	9 27.4	18 10.8	25 29.8	8 32.6	11 22.3	21 05.4	9 50.5	17 20.5	14 06.5
8 W	19 08 19	17 14 06	1♏27 49	7♏25 07	11 11.2	8 18.5	19 24.7	26 16.7	8 56.4	11 28.8	21 11.8	9 49.3	17 21.9	14 05.9
9 Th	19 12 16	18 15 15	13 20 53	19 15 40	11 11.8	7 17.4	20 38.5	27 03.5	9 20.0	11 35.4	21 18.3	9 48.0	17 23.2	14 05.2
10 F	19 16 12	19 16 25	25 10 01	1♐04 28	11 12.7	6 25.3	21 52.3	27 50.4	9 43.6	11 42.3	21 24.7	9 46.7	17 24.5	14 04.4
11 Sa	19 20 09	20 17 34	6♐59 28	12 55 29	11 13.6	5 42.8	23 06.1	28 37.4	10 07.2	11 49.3	21 31.3	9 45.3	17 25.7	14 03.7
12 Su	19 24 05	21 18 44	18 52 55	24 52 09	11 14.5	5 10.2	24 19.9	29 24.3	10 30.6	11 56.4	21 37.8	9 43.9	17 27.0	14 02.9
13 M	19 28 02	22 19 53	0♑53 31	6♑57 16	11R 14.9	4 47.4	25 33.6	0♒11.3	10 53.9	12 03.8	21 44.5	9 42.4	17 28.2	14 02.0
14 Tu	19 31 58	23 21 02	13 03 40	19 12 55	11 14.8	4D 34.1	26 47.2	0 58.3	11 17.2	12 11.2	21 51.1	9 40.9	17 29.4	14 01.2
15 W	19 35 55	24 22 10	25 25 10	1♒40 34	11 14.0	4 29.9	28 00.8	1 45.4	11 40.4	12 18.9	21 57.8	9 39.3	17 30.5	14 00.3
16 Th	19 39 51	25 23 18	7♒59 11	14 21 06	11 12.5	4 34.1	29 14.4	2 32.4	12 03.5	12 26.7	22 04.5	9 37.7	17 31.6	13 59.4
17 F	19 43 48	26 24 26	20 46 21	27 14 58	11 10.5	4 46.2	0♓27.9	3 19.5	12 26.5	12 34.6	22 11.3	9 36.1	17 32.7	13 58.5
18 Sa	19 47 45	27 25 32	3♓46 55	10♓22 15	11 08.0	5 05.6	1 41.4	4 06.6	12 49.4	12 42.7	22 18.0	9 34.4	17 33.8	13 57.6
19 Su	19 51 41	28 26 38	17 00 54	23 42 53	11 05.7	5 31.5	2 54.8	4 53.7	13 12.2	12 51.0	22 24.9	9 32.6	17 34.8	13 56.6
20 M	19 55 38	29 27 43	0♈28 10	7♈16 43	11 03.7	6 03.4	4 08.1	5 40.9	13 34.9	12 59.3	22 31.7	9 30.8	17 35.8	13 55.6
21 Tu	19 59 34	0♒28 47	14 08 29	21 03 26	11D 02.6	6 40.8	5 21.4	6 28.1	13 57.5	13 07.9	22 38.6	9 29.0	17 36.7	13 54.5
22 W	20 03 31	1 29 51	28 01 28	5♉02 30	11 02.4	7 23.1	6 34.7	7 15.2	14 20.1	13 16.6	22 45.5	9 27.1	17 37.7	13 53.5
23 Th	20 07 27	2 30 53	12♉06 24	19 12 58	11 03.1	8 09.8	7 47.8	8 02.4	14 42.5	13 25.4	22 52.4	9 25.2	17 38.6	13 52.4
24 F	20 11 24	3 31 54	26 21 57	3♊33 05	11 04.4	9 00.5	9 00.9	8 49.7	15 04.8	13 34.3	22 59.4	9 23.3	17 39.4	13 51.3
25 Sa	20 15 20	4 32 54	10♊45 58	18 00 10	11 05.8	9 54.8	10 14.0	9 36.9	15 27.0	13 43.4	23 06.4	9 21.3	17 40.3	13 50.2
26 Su	20 19 17	5 33 53	25 15 10	2♋30 23	11R 06.9	10 52.4	11 27.0	10 24.1	15 49.2	13 52.6	23 13.4	9 19.3	17 41.1	13 49.1
27 M	20 23 14	6 34 51	9♋45 12	16 58 56	11 07.0	11 53.0	12 39.9	11 11.4	16 11.2	14 02.0	23 20.4	9 17.3	17 41.8	13 47.9
28 Tu	20 27 10	7 35 49	24 10 53	1♌20 21	11 05.8	12 56.3	13 52.7	11 58.7	16 33.1	14 11.5	23 27.5	9 15.2	17 42.6	13 46.7
29 W	20 31 07	8 36 45	8♌26 41	15 29 14	11 03.1	14 02.0	15 05.5	12 46.0	16 54.9	14 21.1	23 34.6	9 13.1	17 43.3	13 45.5
30 Th	20 35 03	9 37 40	22 27 26	29 20 50	10 59.1	15 10.0	16 18.2	13 33.3	17 16.6	14 30.8	23 41.7	9 10.9	17 43.9	13 44.3
31 F	20 39 00	10 38 34	6♍09 03	12♍51 50	10 54.3	16 20.1	17 30.8	14 20.6	17 38.2	14 40.7	23 48.8	9 08.7	17 44.6	13 43.0

LONGITUDE — February 1964

Day	Sid.Time	☉	0 hr ☽	Noon ☽	True ☊	☿	♀	♂	⚳	♃	♄	♅	♆	♇
1 Sa	20 42 56	11♒39 28	19♍29 03	26♍00 40	10♋49.2	17♑32.0	18♓43.3	15♒07.9	17♐59.7	14♈50.7	23♒55.9	9♍06.5	17♏45.2	13♍41.8
2 Su	20 46 53	12 40 20	2♎26 48	8♎47 39	10R 44.6	18 45.7	19 55.8	15 55.3	18 21.0	15 00.7	24 03.0	9R 04.3	17 45.7	13R 40.5
3 M	20 50 49	13 41 12	15 03 30	21 14 45	10 40.9	20 01.1	21 08.2	16 42.7	18 42.3	15 11.0	24 10.2	9 02.0	17 46.3	13 39.2
4 Tu	20 54 46	14 42 03	27 21 51	3♏25 21	10 38.6	21 17.9	22 20.5	17 30.0	19 03.4	15 21.3	24 17.4	8 59.7	17 46.8	13 37.9
5 W	20 58 43	15 42 53	9♏25 46	15 23 45	10D 37.8	22 36.2	23 32.7	18 17.4	19 24.4	15 31.7	24 24.6	8 57.4	17 47.2	13 36.5
6 Th	21 02 39	16 43 42	21 19 55	27 14 54	10 38.4	23 55.8	24 44.9	19 04.8	19 45.3	15 42.3	24 31.8	8 55.0	17 47.7	13 35.2
7 F	21 06 36	17 44 30	3♐09 21	9♐03 55	10 39.9	25 16.7	25 56.9	19 52.2	20 06.1	15 53.0	24 39.0	8 52.7	17 48.1	13 33.8
8 Sa	21 10 32	18 45 17	14 59 13	20 55 53	10 41.7	26 38.8	27 08.9	20 39.6	20 26.7	16 03.8	24 46.2	8 50.3	17 48.4	13 32.4
9 Su	21 14 29	19 46 04	26 54 28	2♑55 31	10R 43.0	28 02.0	28 20.8	21 27.0	20 47.2	16 14.7	24 53.4	8 47.8	17 48.8	13 31.0
10 M	21 18 25	20 46 49	8♑59 32	15 06 56	10 43.2	29 26.3	29 32.6	22 14.5	21 07.6	16 25.7	25 00.7	8 45.4	17 49.1	13 29.6
11 Tu	21 22 22	21 47 33	21 18 05	27 33 19	10 41.7	0♒51.7	0♈44.3	23 01.9	21 27.8	16 36.8	25 07.9	8 42.9	17 49.3	13 28.2
12 W	21 26 18	22 48 16	3♒52 49	10♒16 44	10 38.1	2 18.1	1 56.0	23 49.3	21 47.9	16 48.0	25 15.2	8 40.4	17 49.6	13 26.7
13 Th	21 30 15	23 48 57	16 45 08	23 17 58	10 32.6	3 45.5	3 07.5	24 36.8	22 07.9	16 59.3	25 22.4	8 37.9	17 49.8	13 25.3
14 F	21 34 12	24 49 37	29 55 07	6♓36 24	10 25.4	5 13.9	4 18.9	25 24.2	22 27.7	17 10.7	25 29.7	8 35.4	17 49.9	13 23.8
15 Sa	21 38 08	25 50 16	13♓21 31	20 10 11	10 17.4	6 43.2	5 30.2	26 11.6	22 47.3	17 22.2	25 36.9	8 32.9	17 50.0	13 22.3
16 Su	21 42 05	26 50 53	27 01 59	3♈56 33	10 09.5	8 13.5	6 41.4	26 59.1	23 06.9	17 33.8	25 44.2	8 30.3	17 50.1	13 20.8
17 M	21 46 01	27 51 28	10♈53 28	17 52 20	10 02.6	9 44.8	7 52.5	27 46.5	23 26.2	17 45.4	25 51.4	8 27.8	17 50.2	13 19.3
18 Tu	21 49 58	28 52 01	24 52 44	1♉54 21	9 57.4	11 16.9	9 03.5	28 33.9	23 45.5	17 57.2	25 58.7	8 25.2	17R 50.2	13 17.8
19 W	21 53 54	29 52 33	8♉56 51	15 59 57	9 54.5	12 50.0	10 14.4	29 21.4	24 04.5	18 09.1	26 05.9	8 22.6	17 50.2	13 16.3
20 Th	21 57 51	0♓53 03	23 03 27	0♊07 08	9D 53.5	14 24.0	11 25.1	0♓08.8	24 23.5	18 21.0	26 13.2	8 20.0	17 50.1	13 14.8
21 F	22 01 47	1 53 31	7♊10 50	14 14 25	9 54.0	15 59.0	12 35.8	0 56.2	24 42.2	18 33.1	26 20.4	8 17.4	17 50.1	13 13.2
22 Sa	22 05 44	2 53 57	21 17 45	28 20 40	9R 55.0	17 34.9	13 46.3	1 43.6	25 00.8	18 45.2	26 27.6	8 14.8	17 50.0	13 11.7
23 Su	22 09 41	3 54 21	5♋23 02	12♋24 38	9 55.4	19 11.7	14 56.6	2 31.0	25 19.3	18 57.4	26 34.8	8 12.2	17 49.8	13 10.2
24 M	22 13 37	4 54 44	19 25 15	26 24 37	9 54.2	20 49.5	16 06.9	3 18.4	25 37.5	19 09.7	26 42.0	8 09.5	17 49.6	13 08.6
25 Tu	22 17 34	5 55 04	3♌22 26	10♌18 20	9 50.6	22 28.3	17 17.0	4 05.8	25 55.6	19 22.0	26 49.2	8 06.9	17 49.4	13 07.0
26 W	22 21 30	6 55 23	17 11 58	24 02 57	9 44.3	24 08.1	18 26.9	4 53.2	26 13.6	19 34.5	26 56.4	8 04.3	17 49.2	13 05.5
27 Th	22 25 27	7 55 39	0♍50 52	7♍35 23	9 35.7	25 48.8	19 36.7	5 40.6	26 31.3	19 47.0	27 03.6	8 01.7	17 48.9	13 03.9
28 F	22 29 23	8 55 54	14 16 08	20 52 51	9 25.4	27 30.5	20 46.4	6 27.9	26 48.9	19 59.6	27 10.8	7 59.0	17 48.6	13 02.3
29 Sa	22 33 20	9 56 08	27 25 18	3♎53 21	9 14.3	29 13.3	21 55.9	7 15.3	27 06.3	20 12.2	27 17.9	7 56.4	17 48.2	13 00.8

Astro Data

	Dy Hr Mn
☽ 0S	6 10:02
☿ D	15 11:42
☽ 0N	20 20:43
♃⚻♇	26 3:45
☽ 0S	2 18:23
♀0N	11 23:59
☽ 0N	17 1:48
♃⚻♆	17 21:42
♆ R	18 14:29

Planet Ingress

		Dy Hr Mn
♂	♒	13 6:13
♀	♓	17 2:54
☉	♒	21 0:41
♀	♈	10 21:09
☿	♒	10 21:30
☉	♓	19 14:57
♂	♓	20 7:33
☿	♓	29 22:50

Last Aspect / ☽ Ingress

Last Aspect Dy Hr Mn			☽ Ingress	Dy Hr Mn
2 10:11	♄	☍	♍	3 2:48
4 21:48	♂	△	♎	5 10:10
7 12:03	♂	□	♏	7 21:04
10 4:58	♂	⚹	♐	10 9:49
12 10:48	♀	⚹	♑	12 22:14
14 20:43	☉	☌	♒	15 8:48
17 2:33	♄	☌	♓	17 17:04
19 21:06	☉	⚹	♈	19 23:10
21 14:46	♄	⚹	♉	22 3:23
23 18:12	♄	□	♊	24 6:05
25 20:31	♄	△	♋	26 7:51
27 13:11	♆	△	♌	28 9:45
30 2:04	♄	☍	♍	30 13:09

Last Aspect / ☽ Ingress

Last Aspect Dy Hr Mn			☽ Ingress	Dy Hr Mn
31 21:16	♀	☍	♎	1 19:25
3 17:47	♄	△	♏	4 5:12
6 6:26	♄	□	♐	6 17:35
9 1:52	♀	□	♑	9 6:11
10 17:16	♆	⚹	♒	11 16:39
13 15:48	♄	☌	♓	14 0:09
15 7:54	♆	△	♈	16 5:10
18 6:25	☉	⚹	♉	18 8:45
20 5:19	♄	□	♊	20 11:48
22 8:46	♄	△	♋	22 14:49
23 23:22	♃	□	♌	24 18:11
26 17:08	♄	☍	♍	26 22:30
28 6:25	♆	⚹	♎	29 4:46

☽ Phases & Eclipses

Dy Hr Mn		
6 15:58	☾	15♎22
14 20:43	●	23♑43
14 20:29:31	◐	P 0.559
22 5:29	☽	1♉13
28 23:23	○	8♌05
5 12:42	☾	15♏45
13 13:01	●	23♒52
20 13:24	☽	0♊57
27 12:39	○	7♍57

Astro Data

1 January 1964
Julian Day # 23376
SVP 5♓46'01"
GC 26♐20.2 ⚴ 16♏50.7
Eris 9♈55.3 ⚵ 21♏03.1
⚷ 11♓01.1 ⚶ 0♑03.5
☽ Mean ☊ 11♋19.7

1 February 1964
Julian Day # 23407
SVP 5♓45'56"
GC 26♐20.3 ⚴ 27♏33.2
Eris 10♈01.9 ⚵ 29♏00.7
⚷ 12♓29.4 ⚶ 16♑34.2
☽ Mean ☊ 9♋41.2

March 1964

LONGITUDE

Day	Sid.Time	☉	0 hr ☽	Noon ☽	True ☊	☿	♀	♂	⚳	♃	♄	♅	♆	♇
1 Su	22 37 16	10♓56 19	10♎16 56	16♎36 06	9♋03.6	0♓57.1	23♈05.3	8♓02.6	27♐23.6	20♈24.9	27♒25.0	7♍53.8	17♏47.8	12♍59.2
2 M	22 41 13	11 56 29	22 50 58	29 01 44	8R 54.4	2 41.9	24 14.5	8 50.0	27 40.6	20 37.7	27 32.1	7R 51.1	17R 47.4	12R 57.6
3 Tu	22 45 10	12 56 38	5♏08 43	11♏12 17	8 47.2	4 27.8	25 23.6	9 37.3	27 57.5	20 50.6	27 39.2	7 48.5	17 47.0	12 56.0
4 W	22 49 06	13 56 44	17 12 53	23 11 03	8 42.5	6 14.8	26 32.5	10 24.6	28 14.2	21 03.5	27 46.3	7 45.9	17 46.5	12 54.5
5 Th	22 53 03	14 56 50	29 07 19	5♐02 20	8D 40.2	8 02.9	27 41.2	11 11.9	28 30.7	21 16.5	27 53.4	7 43.3	17 46.0	12 52.9
6 F	22 56 59	15 56 53	10♐56 43	16 51 08	8 39.6	9 52.1	28 49.8	11 59.2	28 47.0	21 29.5	28 00.4	7 40.7	17 45.5	12 51.3
7 Sa	23 00 56	16 56 56	22 46 18	28 42 52	8R 40.0	11 42.3	29 58.2	12 46.5	29 03.1	21 42.7	28 07.4	7 38.1	17 44.9	12 49.7
8 Su	23 04 52	17 56 56	4♑41 33	10♑43 00	8 40.2	13 33.7	1♉06.4	13 33.7	29 19.0	21 55.8	28 14.4	7 35.5	17 44.3	12 48.2
9 M	23 08 49	18 56 55	16 47 51	22 56 43	8 39.3	15 26.1	2 14.5	14 21.0	29 34.7	22 09.1	28 21.4	7 33.0	17 43.7	12 46.6
10 Tu	23 12 45	19 56 52	29 10 06	5♒28 30	8 36.2	17 19.6	3 22.4	15 08.2	29 50.2	22 22.4	28 28.3	7 30.4	17 43.0	12 45.0
11 W	23 16 42	20 56 48	11♒52 16	18 21 41	8 30.6	19 14.1	4 30.1	15 55.4	0♑05.5	22 35.7	28 35.2	7 27.9	17 42.3	12 43.5
12 Th	23 20 39	21 56 41	24 56 54	1♓37 56	8 22.2	21 09.7	5 37.6	16 42.6	0 20.6	22 49.1	28 42.1	7 25.3	17 41.6	12 41.9
13 F	23 24 35	22 56 33	8♓24 39	15 16 49	8 11.7	23 06.2	6 44.9	17 29.8	0 35.4	23 02.6	28 48.9	7 22.8	17 40.9	12 40.3
14 Sa	23 28 32	23 56 23	22 14 00	29 15 42	7 59.8	25 03.6	7 52.0	18 16.9	0 50.0	23 16.1	28 55.8	7 20.3	17 40.1	12 38.8
15 Su	23 32 28	24 56 11	6♈21 15	13♈29 57	7 47.9	27 01.8	8 58.9	19 04.1	1 04.4	23 29.6	29 02.6	7 17.8	17 39.3	12 37.2
16 M	23 36 25	25 55 56	20 41 01	27 53 39	7 37.3	29 00.8	10 05.6	19 51.2	1 18.6	23 43.2	29 09.3	7 15.4	17 38.4	12 35.7
17 Tu	23 40 21	26 55 40	5♉07 05	12♉20 34	7 29.0	1♈00.3	11 12.0	20 38.3	1 32.6	23 56.8	29 16.0	7 12.9	17 37.6	12 34.2
18 W	23 44 18	27 55 21	19 33 26	26 45 09	7 23.5	3 00.3	12 18.3	21 25.3	1 46.3	24 10.5	29 22.7	7 10.5	17 36.7	12 32.7
19 Th	23 48 14	28 55 01	3♊55 12	11♊03 16	7 20.6	5 00.5	13 24.3	22 12.4	1 59.7	24 24.3	29 29.4	7 08.1	17 35.8	12 31.2
20 F	23 52 11	29 54 37	18 09 05	25 12 28	7 19.8	7 00.7	14 30.1	22 59.4	2 13.0	24 38.0	29 36.0	7 05.7	17 34.8	12 29.7
21 Sa	23 56 07	0♈54 12	2♋13 20	9♋11 40	7 19.8	9 00.8	15 35.6	23 46.4	2 26.0	24 51.8	29 42.6	7 03.4	17 33.8	12 28.2
22 Su	0 00 04	1 53 44	16 07 28	23 00 46	7 19.2	11 00.4	16 40.9	24 33.3	2 38.7	25 05.7	29 49.1	7 01.1	17 32.8	12 26.7
23 M	0 04 01	2 53 14	29 51 37	6♌40 01	7 16.9	12 59.2	17 45.9	25 20.2	2 51.2	25 19.6	29 55.6	6 58.8	17 31.8	12 25.2
24 Tu	0 07 57	3 52 42	13♌26 00	20 09 31	7 12.0	14 56.9	18 50.6	26 07.1	3 03.5	25 33.5	0♓02.1	6 56.5	17 30.8	12 23.8
25 W	0 11 54	4 52 07	26 50 33	3♍28 59	7 04.0	16 53.1	19 55.1	26 54.0	3 15.4	25 47.5	0 08.5	6 54.3	17 29.7	12 22.4
26 Th	0 15 50	5 51 30	10♍04 44	16 37 40	6 53.3	18 47.4	20 59.3	27 40.8	3 27.2	26 01.4	0 14.9	6 52.1	17 28.6	12 20.9
27 F	0 19 47	6 50 51	23 07 38	29 34 32	6 40.5	20 39.4	22 03.2	28 27.6	3 38.6	26 15.5	0 21.2	6 49.9	17 27.5	12 19.5
28 Sa	0 23 43	7 50 10	5♎58 13	12♎18 36	6 26.9	22 28.7	23 06.8	29 14.4	3 49.8	26 29.5	0 27.5	6 47.8	17 26.3	12 18.1
29 Su	0 27 40	8 49 27	18 35 39	24 49 22	6 13.5	24 14.9	24 10.0	0♈01.2	4 00.8	26 43.6	0 33.7	6 45.6	17 25.2	12 16.7
30 M	0 31 36	9 48 42	0♏59 47	7♏07 01	6 01.6	25 57.6	25 13.0	0 47.9	4 11.4	26 57.7	0 39.9	6 43.6	17 24.0	12 15.4
31 Tu	0 35 33	10 47 55	13 11 17	19 12 48	5 52.0	27 36.4	26 15.6	1 34.6	4 21.8	27 11.8	0 46.0	6 41.5	17 22.8	12 14.0

April 1964

LONGITUDE

Day	Sid.Time	☉	0 hr ☽	Noon ☽	True ☊	☿	♀	♂	⚳	♃	♄	♅	♆	♇
1 W	0 39 30	11♈47 06	25♏11 54	1♐08 59	5♋45.1	29♈10.9	27♉18.0	2♈21.2	4♑31.9	27♈26.0	0♓52.1	6♍39.5	17♏21.5	12♍12.7
2 Th	0 43 26	12 46 15	7♐04 29	12 58 54	5R 41.1	0♉40.8	28 19.9	3 07.8	4 41.7	27 40.2	0 58.1	6R 37.5	17R 20.3	12R 11.3
3 F	0 47 23	13 45 23	18 52 48	24 46 46	5D 39.3	2 05.7	29 21.5	3 54.4	4 51.3	27 54.4	1 04.1	6 35.6	17 19.0	12 10.0
4 Sa	0 51 19	14 44 29	0♑41 27	6♑37 31	5R 38.9	3 25.4	0♊22.8	4 41.0	5 00.5	28 08.6	1 10.1	6 33.7	17 17.7	12 08.8
5 Su	0 55 16	15 43 33	12 35 38	18 36 31	5 39.0	4 39.6	1 23.7	5 27.5	5 09.4	28 22.8	1 16.0	6 31.8	17 16.4	12 07.5
6 M	0 59 12	16 42 35	24 40 50	0♒49 17	5 38.3	5 48.1	2 24.2	6 14.0	5 18.1	28 37.1	1 21.8	6 30.0	17 15.1	12 06.2
7 Tu	1 03 09	17 41 35	7♒02 30	13 21 04	5 35.8	6 50.7	3 24.3	7 00.5	5 26.4	28 51.4	1 27.6	6 28.2	17 13.7	12 05.0
8 W	1 07 05	18 40 34	19 45 31	26 16 17	5 31.0	7 47.2	4 24.1	7 46.9	5 34.5	29 05.7	1 33.3	6 26.4	17 12.3	12 03.8
9 Th	1 11 02	19 39 31	2♓53 40	9♓37 52	5 23.6	8 37.5	5 23.4	8 33.3	5 42.2	29 20.0	1 38.9	6 24.7	17 10.9	12 02.6
10 F	1 14 59	20 38 26	16 28 53	23 26 36	5 14.1	9 21.6	6 22.3	9 19.6	5 49.6	29 34.4	1 44.5	6 23.1	17 09.5	12 01.4
11 Sa	1 18 55	21 37 19	0♈30 38	7♈40 30	5 03.1	9 59.2	7 20.7	10 06.0	5 56.6	29 48.7	1 50.1	6 21.4	17 08.1	12 00.3
12 Su	1 22 52	22 36 10	14 55 30	22 14 47	4 52.0	10 30.3	8 18.7	10 52.2	6 03.4	0♉03.1	1 55.6	6 19.9	17 06.7	11 59.1
13 M	1 26 48	23 34 59	29 37 22	7♉02 12	4 42.0	10 55.1	9 16.2	11 38.5	6 09.8	0 17.4	2 01.0	6 18.3	17 05.2	11 58.0
14 Tu	1 30 45	24 33 46	14♉28 11	21 54 15	4 34.1	11 13.3	10 13.2	12 24.7	6 15.9	0 31.8	2 06.3	6 16.8	17 03.7	11 57.0
15 W	1 34 41	25 32 31	29 19 23	6♊42 40	4 28.8	11 25.2	11 09.7	13 10.8	6 21.7	0 46.2	2 11.6	6 15.4	17 02.3	11 55.9
16 Th	1 38 38	26 31 14	14♊03 18	21 20 37	4D 26.2	11R 30.8	12 05.7	13 56.9	6 27.1	1 00.6	2 16.9	6 14.0	17 00.8	11 54.9
17 F	1 42 34	27 29 55	28 34 08	5♋43 31	4 25.7	11 30.3	13 01.2	14 43.0	6 32.2	1 15.0	2 22.0	6 12.6	16 59.3	11 53.9
18 Sa	1 46 31	28 28 34	12♋48 31	19 49 04	4R 26.0	11 23.8	13 56.0	15 29.0	6 36.9	1 29.4	2 27.1	6 11.3	16 57.8	11 52.9
19 Su	1 50 28	29 27 10	26 45 10	3♌36 54	4 26.1	11 11.7	14 50.3	16 15.0	6 41.4	1 43.8	2 32.2	6 10.1	16 56.2	11 51.9
20 M	1 54 24	0♉25 44	10♌24 24	17 07 50	4 24.9	10 54.3	15 44.0	17 01.0	6 45.4	1 58.2	2 37.1	6 08.9	16 54.7	11 51.0
21 Tu	1 58 21	1 24 16	23 47 25	0♍23 20	4 21.4	10 32.1	16 37.1	17 46.9	6 49.1	2 12.6	2 42.0	6 07.7	16 53.1	11 50.0
22 W	2 02 17	2 22 45	6♍55 45	13 24 53	4 15.5	10 05.4	17 29.4	18 32.7	6 52.5	2 27.0	2 46.8	6 06.6	16 51.6	11 49.2
23 Th	2 06 14	3 21 13	19 50 50	26 13 47	4 07.2	9 34.9	18 21.2	19 18.5	6 55.5	2 41.4	2 51.6	6 05.5	16 50.0	11 48.3
24 F	2 10 10	4 19 38	2♎33 49	8♎51 02	3 57.2	9 01.2	19 12.2	20 04.3	6 58.1	2 55.8	2 56.3	6 04.5	16 48.4	11 47.4
25 Sa	2 14 07	5 18 01	15 05 30	21 17 20	3 46.3	8 24.8	20 02.4	20 50.0	7 00.4	3 10.2	3 00.9	6 03.5	16 46.8	11 46.6
26 Su	2 18 03	6 16 23	27 26 35	3♏33 21	3 35.7	7 46.6	20 52.0	21 35.6	7 02.3	3 24.6	3 05.4	6 02.6	16 45.2	11 45.8
27 M	2 22 00	7 14 43	9♏37 45	15 39 55	3 26.2	7 07.2	21 40.7	22 21.3	7 03.9	3 39.0	3 09.9	6 01.7	16 43.6	11 45.1
28 Tu	2 25 56	8 13 00	21 40 01	27 38 15	3 18.7	6 27.4	22 28.6	23 06.8	7 05.1	3 53.4	3 14.2	6 00.9	16 42.0	11 44.3
29 W	2 29 53	9 11 17	3♐34 53	9♐30 11	3 13.4	5 47.9	23 15.7	23 52.4	7 05.9	4 07.7	3 18.5	6 00.1	16 40.4	11 43.6
30 Th	2 33 50	10 09 31	15 24 30	21 18 14	3 10.5	5 09.3	24 02.0	24 37.8	7R 06.4	4 22.1	3 22.8	5 59.4	16 38.8	11 43.0

Astro Data

	Dy Hr Mn
☽0S	1 2:50
♃□♅	11 0:09
☽0N	15 8:54
☿0N	18 2:08
⊙0N	20 14:10
☽0S	28 10:38
♃□♇	31 15:23
♂0N	1 1:53
☽0N	11 18:34
☿R	16 21:51
♃✶♄	24 13:05
☽0S	24 17:27

Planet Ingress

	Dy Hr Mn
♀ ♉	7 12:38
⚳ ♑	11 3:20
☿ ♈	16 23:54
⊙ ♈	20 14:10
♄ ♓	24 4:18
♂ ♈	29 11:24
☿ ♉	2 0:57
♀ ♊	4 3:03
♃ ♉	12 6:52
⊙ ♉	20 1:27

Last Aspect / ☽ Ingress

Last Aspect Dy Hr Mn		☽ Ingress Dy Hr Mn
2 9:04 ♄ △	♏	2 13:54
4 21:22 ♄ □	♐	5 1:47
7 10:48 ♄ ✶	♑	7 14:35
9 10:26 ♃ □	♒	10 1:35
12 6:43 ♄ ☌	♓	12 9:05
14 3:41 ☿ ☌	♈	14 13:15
16 14:07 ♄ ✶	♉	16 15:30
18 16:26 ♄ □	♊	18 17:26
20 19:34 ♄ △	♋	20 20:11
22 15:42 ♃ □	♌	23 0:15
24 21:52 ♃ △	♍	25 5:42
27 9:47 ♂ ☍	♎	27 12:48
29 15:46 ♃ ☍	♏	29 22:03

Last Aspect / ☽ Ingress

Last Aspect Dy Hr Mn		☽ Ingress Dy Hr Mn
1 3:29 ♀ ☍	♐	1 9:41
3 18:29 ♃ △	♑	3 22:36
6 7:38 ♃ □	♒	6 10:24
8 17:14 ♃ ✶	♓	8 18:47
10 1:12 ♆ △	♈	10 23:08
12 12:37 ⊙ ☌	♉	13 0:37
14 4:12 ♆ ☍	♊	15 1:06
16 21:13 ⊙ ✶	♋	17 2:23
19 4:09 ⊙ □	♌	19 5:40
20 11:47 ♂ △	♍	21 11:17
22 20:08 ♀ □	♎	23 19:08
25 11:03 ♂ ☍	♏	26 5:01
27 14:07 ♆ ☌	♐	28 16:46

☽ Phases & Eclipses

Dy Hr Mn	
6 10:00	☾ 15♐52
14 2:14	● 23♓32
20 20:39	☽ 0♋16
28 2:48	○ 7♎27
5 5:45	☾ 15♑28
12 12:37	● 22♈38
19 4:09	☽ 29♋08
26 17:50	○ 6♏31

Astro Data

1 March 1964
Julian Day # 23436
SVP 5♓45'53"
GC 26♐20.3 ⚴ 4♐42.2
Eris 10♈16.5 ⚵ 3♐51.4
⚷ 14♓14.3 ⚶ 1♒27.5
☽ Mean ☊ 8♋09.1

1 April 1964
Julian Day # 23467
SVP 5♓45'50"
GC 26♐20.4 ⚴ 7♐12.6R
Eris 10♈36.9 ⚵ 4♐50.9R
⚷ 16♓08.3 ⚶ 16♒21.0
☽ Mean ☊ 6♋30.6

LONGITUDE — May 1964

Day	Sid.Time	☉	0 hr ☽	Noon ☽	True ☊	☿	♀	♂	⚳	♃	♄	♅	♆	♇
1 F	2 37 46	11♉07 44	27♐11 48	3♑05 40	3♋09.7	4♉32.4	24♊47.3	25♈23.3	7♑06.5	4♉36.4	3♓26.9	5♍58.8	16♏37.2	11♍42.3
2 Sa	2 41 43	12 05 56	9♑00 23	14 56 30	3D 10.3	3R 57.8	25 31.7	26 08.7	7R 06.2	4 50.8	3 31.0	5R 58.2	16R 35.6	11R 41.7
3 Su	2 45 39	13 04 06	20 54 36	26 55 18	3 11.5	3 25.9	26 15.1	26 54.0	7 05.5	5 05.1	3 35.0	5 57.6	16 33.9	11 41.1
4 M	2 49 36	14 02 15	2♒59 14	9♒07 03	3R 12.4	2 57.2	26 57.5	27 39.3	7 04.5	5 19.4	3 38.9	5 57.1	16 32.3	11 40.5
5 Tu	2 53 32	15 00 22	15 19 23	21 36 51	3 12.3	2 32.3	27 38.9	28 24.6	7 03.1	5 33.7	3 42.8	5 56.6	16 30.7	11 40.0
6 W	2 57 29	15 58 27	28 00 01	4♓29 24	3 10.6	2 11.3	28 19.2	29 09.8	7 01.3	5 48.0	3 46.5	5 56.2	16 29.0	11 39.5
7 Th	3 01 25	16 56 31	11♓05 25	17 48 25	3 07.0	1 54.5	28 58.4	29 55.0	6 59.1	6 02.2	3 50.2	5 55.9	16 27.4	11 39.0
8 F	3 05 22	17 54 34	24 38 35	1♈35 56	3 01.7	1 42.2	29 36.4	0♉40.1	6 56.6	6 16.5	3 53.8	5 55.6	16 25.8	11 38.5
9 Sa	3 09 19	18 52 36	8♈40 21	15 51 29	2 55.3	1 34.4	0♋13.3	1 25.1	6 53.6	6 30.7	3 57.3	5 55.3	16 24.1	11 38.1
10 Su	3 13 15	19 50 36	23 08 47	0♉31 33	2 48.7	1D 31.3	0 48.8	2 10.2	6 50.3	6 44.9	4 00.7	5 55.1	16 22.5	11 37.7
11 M	3 17 12	20 48 34	7♉58 52	15 29 40	2 42.6	1 32.8	1 23.1	2 55.1	6 46.7	6 59.1	4 04.0	5 55.0	16 20.9	11 37.4
12 Tu	3 21 08	21 46 32	23 02 47	0♊37 01	2 37.9	1 39.0	1 56.0	3 40.0	6 42.6	7 13.2	4 07.3	5D 54.9	16 19.2	11 37.0
13 W	3 25 05	22 44 27	8♊11 07	15 43 55	2 35.0	1 49.8	2 27.6	4 24.9	6 38.2	7 27.3	4 10.4	5 54.9	16 17.6	11 36.7
14 Th	3 29 01	23 42 21	23 14 17	0♋41 17	2D 33.9	2 05.1	2 57.6	5 09.7	6 33.4	7 41.4	4 13.5	5 54.9	16 16.0	11 36.5
15 F	3 32 58	24 40 14	8♋04 05	15 22 03	2 34.4	2 24.9	3 26.2	5 54.5	6 28.2	7 55.5	4 16.5	5 55.0	16 14.4	11 36.2
16 Sa	3 36 55	25 38 04	22 34 41	29 41 41	2 35.7	2 49.0	3 53.1	6 39.2	6 22.7	8 09.6	4 19.4	5 55.1	16 12.8	11 36.0
17 Su	3 40 51	26 35 53	6♌42 54	13♌38 17	2 37.0	3 17.3	4 18.4	7 23.8	6 16.8	8 23.6	4 22.2	5 55.3	16 11.2	11 35.8
18 M	3 44 48	27 33 40	20 27 55	27 11 59	2R 37.6	3 49.7	4 42.1	8 08.4	6 10.6	8 37.6	4 24.9	5 55.6	16 09.6	11 35.7
19 Tu	3 48 44	28 31 25	3♍50 42	10♍24 23	2 36.9	4 26.2	5 03.9	8 52.9	6 04.0	8 51.5	4 27.5	5 55.9	16 08.0	11 35.6
20 W	3 52 41	29 29 09	16 53 20	23 17 53	2 34.8	5 06.5	5 23.9	9 37.4	5 57.1	9 05.4	4 30.0	5 56.2	16 06.4	11 35.5
21 Th	3 56 37	0♊26 51	29 38 22	5♎55 09	2 31.3	5 50.5	5 42.1	10 21.8	5 49.8	9 19.3	4 32.5	5 56.6	16 04.8	11 35.4
22 F	4 00 34	1 24 32	12♎08 33	18 18 52	2 26.7	6 38.2	5 58.3	11 06.2	5 42.2	9 33.1	4 34.8	5 57.1	16 03.3	11D 35.4
23 Sa	4 04 30	2 22 11	24 26 24	0♏31 27	2 21.6	7 29.4	6 12.5	11 50.5	5 34.3	9 47.0	4 37.1	5 57.6	16 01.7	11 35.4
24 Su	4 08 27	3 19 48	6♏34 16	12 35 06	2 16.5	8 24.0	6 24.6	12 34.8	5 26.0	10 00.7	4 39.2	5 58.2	16 00.2	11 35.4
25 M	4 12 23	4 17 25	18 34 12	24 31 49	2 12.1	9 21.9	6 34.6	13 19.0	5 17.5	10 14.5	4 41.3	5 58.8	15 58.6	11 35.5
26 Tu	4 16 20	5 15 00	0♐28 11	6♐23 31	2 08.7	10 23.1	6 42.5	14 03.1	5 08.6	10 28.1	4 43.3	5 59.4	15 57.1	11 35.6
27 W	4 20 17	6 12 34	12 18 06	18 12 11	2 06.6	11 27.4	6 48.1	14 47.2	4 59.4	10 41.8	4 45.2	6 00.2	15 55.6	11 35.7
28 Th	4 24 13	7 10 07	24 06 02	29 59 60	2D 05.8	12 34.7	6R 51.4	15 31.3	4 49.9	10 55.4	4 46.9	6 00.9	15 54.1	11 35.9
29 F	4 28 10	8 07 39	5♑54 23	11♑49 32	2 06.1	13 45.1	6 52.4	16 15.2	4 40.2	11 09.0	4 48.6	6 01.8	15 52.6	11 36.1
30 Sa	4 32 06	9 05 09	17 45 52	23 43 47	2 07.3	14 58.3	6 51.1	16 59.2	4 30.1	11 22.5	4 50.2	6 02.6	15 51.1	11 36.3
31 Su	4 36 03	10 02 39	29 43 44	5♒46 11	2 08.8	16 14.5	6 47.4	17 43.1	4 19.8	11 36.0	4 51.7	6 03.6	15 49.7	11 36.5

LONGITUDE — June 1964

Day	Sid.Time	☉	0 hr ☽	Noon ☽	True ☊	☿	♀	♂	⚳	♃	♄	♅	♆	♇
1 M	4 39 59	11♊00 09	11♒51 37	18♒00 34	2♋10.4	17♉33.5	6♋41.3	18♉26.9	4♑09.2	11♉49.4	4♓53.1	6♍04.6	15♏48.2	11♍36.8
2 Tu	4 43 56	11 57 37	24 13 31	0♓31 01	2R 11.5	18 55.3	6R 32.8	19 10.7	3R 58.4	12 02.8	4 54.4	6 05.6	15R 46.8	11 37.1
3 W	4 47 53	12 55 04	6♓53 33	13 21 36	2 11.9	20 19.9	6 21.9	19 54.4	3 47.3	12 16.1	4 55.6	6 06.7	15 45.4	11 37.5
4 Th	4 51 49	13 52 31	19 55 34	26 35 51	2 11.4	21 47.2	6 08.6	20 38.1	3 36.0	12 29.4	4 56.7	6 07.8	15 44.0	11 37.9
5 F	4 55 46	14 49 58	3♈22 41	10♈16 16	2 10.2	23 17.2	5 52.9	21 21.7	3 24.5	12 42.6	4 57.7	6 09.0	15 42.6	11 38.3
6 Sa	4 59 42	15 47 23	17 16 37	24 23 36	2 08.5	24 49.9	5 34.9	22 05.2	3 12.8	12 55.8	4 58.6	6 10.2	15 41.2	11 38.7
7 Su	5 03 39	16 44 48	1♉36 57	8♉56 11	2 06.5	26 25.3	5 14.6	22 48.7	3 00.8	13 08.9	4 59.4	6 11.5	15 39.9	11 39.2
8 M	5 07 35	17 42 13	16 20 40	23 49 34	2 04.8	28 03.3	4 52.1	23 32.2	2 48.7	13 22.0	5 00.1	6 12.9	15 38.6	11 39.7
9 Tu	5 11 32	18 39 36	1♊21 57	8♊56 41	2 03.5	29 44.0	4 27.5	24 15.5	2 36.4	13 35.0	5 00.8	6 14.3	15 37.2	11 40.2
10 W	5 15 28	19 36 59	16 32 37	24 08 31	2D 02.8	1♊27.4	4 00.8	24 58.9	2 23.9	13 47.9	5 01.3	6 15.7	15 35.9	11 40.7
11 Th	5 19 25	20 34 22	1♋43 12	9♋15 29	2 02.8	3 13.3	3 32.3	25 42.2	2 11.3	14 00.8	5 01.7	6 17.2	15 34.7	11 41.3
12 F	5 23 22	21 31 43	16 44 21	24 08 50	2 03.3	5 01.8	3 02.0	26 25.4	1 58.6	14 13.6	5 02.0	6 18.8	15 33.4	11 41.9
13 Sa	5 27 18	22 29 04	1♌28 11	8♌41 46	2 04.1	6 52.8	2 30.0	27 08.5	1 45.8	14 26.4	5 02.2	6 20.3	15 32.2	11 42.6
14 Su	5 31 15	23 26 24	15 49 11	22 50 08	2 04.8	8 46.4	1 56.6	27 51.6	1 32.8	14 39.1	5R 02.3	6 22.0	15 31.0	11 43.3
15 M	5 35 11	24 23 42	29 44 32	6♍32 22	2 05.4	10 42.3	1 22.0	28 34.6	1 19.8	14 51.7	5 02.3	6 23.7	15 29.8	11 44.0
16 Tu	5 39 08	25 21 00	13♍13 49	19 49 08	2R 05.7	12 40.5	0 46.2	29 17.6	1 06.6	15 04.3	5 02.3	6 25.4	15 28.6	11 44.7
17 W	5 43 04	26 18 17	26 18 37	2♎42 41	2 05.7	14 41.0	0 09.7	0♊00.5	0 53.5	15 16.8	5 02.1	6 27.2	15 27.5	11 45.5
18 Th	5 47 01	27 15 33	9♎01 44	15 16 16	2 05.5	16 43.5	29♊32.5	0 43.4	0 40.2	15 29.2	5 01.8	6 29.0	15 26.3	11 46.3
19 F	5 50 57	28 12 48	21 26 44	27 33 37	2 05.1	18 47.9	28 55.0	1 26.2	0 27.0	15 41.5	5 01.4	6 30.9	15 25.2	11 47.1
20 Sa	5 54 54	29 10 03	3♏37 24	9♏38 33	2 04.7	20 54.0	28 17.3	2 08.9	0 13.7	15 53.8	5 00.9	6 32.8	15 24.2	11 47.9
21 Su	5 58 51	0♋07 17	15 37 29	21 34 40	2 04.5	23 01.7	27 39.8	2 51.6	0 00.5	16 06.0	5 00.4	6 34.8	15 23.1	11 48.8
22 M	6 02 47	1 04 30	27 30 29	3♐25 19	2 04.2	25 10.6	27 02.6	3 34.2	29♐47.2	16 18.1	4 59.7	6 36.8	15 22.1	11 49.7
23 Tu	6 06 44	2 01 43	9♐19 32	15 13 28	2D 04.2	27 20.5	26 26.0	4 16.7	29 34.0	16 30.2	4 58.9	6 38.8	15 21.1	11 50.7
24 W	6 10 40	2 58 56	21 07 26	27 01 44	2R 04.2	29 31.1	25 50.3	4 59.2	29 20.8	16 42.2	4 58.1	6 40.9	15 20.1	11 51.6
25 Th	6 14 37	3 56 08	2♑56 41	8♑52 32	2 04.2	1♋42.2	25 15.6	5 41.7	29 07.6	16 54.0	4 57.1	6 43.1	15 19.1	11 52.6
26 F	6 18 33	4 53 20	14 49 34	20 48 04	2 04.1	3 53.5	24 42.2	6 24.0	28 54.6	17 05.9	4 56.0	6 45.3	15 18.2	11 53.6
27 Sa	6 22 30	5 50 32	26 48 18	2♒50 33	2 03.8	6 04.6	24 10.2	7 06.4	28 41.6	17 17.6	4 54.9	6 47.5	15 17.3	11 54.7
28 Su	6 26 26	6 47 43	8♒55 06	15 02 14	2 03.3	8 15.4	23 39.9	7 48.6	28 28.7	17 29.3	4 53.6	6 49.8	15 16.4	11 55.8
29 M	6 30 23	7 44 55	21 12 17	27 25 31	2 02.6	10 25.6	23 11.4	8 30.8	28 15.9	17 40.8	4 52.3	6 52.1	15 15.6	11 56.9
30 Tu	6 34 20	8 42 07	3♓42 18	10♓02 56	2 01.9	12 34.9	22 44.8	9 13.0	28 03.2	17 52.3	4 50.9	6 54.4	15 14.8	11 58.0

Astro Data Dy Hr Mn	Planet Ingress Dy Hr Mn	Last Aspect Dy Hr Mn	☽ Ingress Dy Hr Mn	Last Aspect Dy Hr Mn	☽ Ingress Dy Hr Mn	☽ Phases & Eclipses Dy Hr Mn
⚳R 1 5:47	♂ ♉ 7 14:41	30 19:14 ♂ △	♑ 1 5:42	1 12:54 ♂ □	♓ 2 11:01	4 22:20 ☾ 14♒27
♃△♅ 7 1:34	♀ ♋ 9 3:16	3 11:57 ♂ □	♒ 3 18:06	4 2:17 ☿ ✶	♈ 4 18:03	11 21:02 ● 21♉10
☽0N 9 5:20	☉ ♊ 21 0:50	6 1:33 ♂ ✶	♓ 6 3:43	5 20:24 ☉ ✶	♉ 6 21:20	18 12:42 ☽ 27♌35
☿D 10 16:09		8 8:25 ♀ □	♈ 8 9:16	8 19:34 ☿ ☌	♊ 8 21:50	26 9:29 ○ 5♐09
♅D 13 11:26	☿ ♊ 9 15:45	8 8:25 ♀ □	♉ 10 11:09	10 4:22 ☉ ☌	♋ 10 21:16	
☽0S 21 23:39	♂ ♊ 17 11:43	11 21:02 ☉ ☌	♊ 12 11:01	12 15:54 ♂ ✶	♌ 12 21:35	3 11:07 ☾ 12♓53
♇D 22 21:29	♀ ♊R 17 18:17	13 5:27 ♇ □	♋ 14 10:53	14 21:11 ♂ □	♍ 15 0:27	10 4:22 ● 19♊19
♀R 29 10:29	☉ ♋ 21 8:57	16 4:38 ☉ ✶	♌ 16 12:31	17 6:37 ♂ △	♎ 17 6:54	10 4:33:33 ☌ P 0.755
♃△♇ 31 13:04	⚳ ♐R 21 12:49	18 12:42 ☉ □	♍ 18 17:02	19 14:33 ♀ △	♏ 19 16:49	16 23:02 ☽ 25♍47
	☿ ♋ 24 17:17	21 0:40 ☉ △	♎ 21 0:41	21 0:46 ♃ ☍	♐ 22 5:03	25 1:08 ○ 3♑30
☽0N 5 15:08		21 11:34 ♀ □	♏ 23 10:58	24 9:42 ♀ ☍	♑ 24 18:02	25 1:06 ☍ T 1.556
♄R 15 3:25		24 18:50 ♆ ☌	♐ 25 23:03	26 4:27 ♃ △	♒ 27 6:22	
☽0S 18 5:58		26 22:34 ♇ □	♑ 28 12:00	29 4:08 ♀ △	♓ 29 16:56	
♃☍♆ 18 6:58		29 21:32 ♂ △	♒ 31 0:32			

Astro Data

1 May 1964
Julian Day # 23497
SVP 5♓45'47"
GC 26♐20.5 ⚳ 2♐43.9R
Eris 10♈56.7 ✵ 0♐57.9R
⚷ 17♓39.8 ⚶ 29♒10.5
☽ Mean ☊ 4♋55.2

1 June 1964
Julian Day # 23528
SVP 5♓45'42"
GC 26♐20.5 ⚳ 23♏46.9R
Eris 11♈12.2 ✵ 24♏14.1R
⚷ 18♓36.9 ⚶ 9♓49.2
☽ Mean ☊ 3♋16.8

July 1964

LONGITUDE

Day	Sid.Time	☉	0 hr ☽	Noon☽	True☊	☿	♀	♂	⚳	♃	♄	♅	♆	♇
1 W	6 38 16	9♋39 18	16♓27 45	22♓57 05	2♋01.3	14♋43.1	22♊20.2	9♊55.1	27♐50.7	18♉03.7	4♓49.3	6♍56.8	15♏14.0	11♍59.1
2 Th	6 42 13	10 36 30	29 31 12	6♈10 24	2D 01.0	16 50.1	21R 57.8	10 37.1	27R 38.3	18 15.0	4R 47.7	6 59.2	15R 13.2	12 00.3
3 F	6 46 09	11 33 42	12♈54 53	19 44 52	2 01.1	18 55.7	21 37.7	11 19.1	27 26.0	18 26.2	4 46.0	7 01.7	15 12.4	12 01.5
4 Sa	6 50 06	12 30 55	26 40 25	3♉41 33	2 01.5	20 59.8	21 19.9	12 01.0	27 14.0	18 37.3	4 44.2	7 04.2	15 11.7	12 02.7
5 Su	6 54 02	13 28 07	10♉48 10	18 00 03	2 02.3	23 02.2	21 04.4	12 42.8	27 02.1	18 48.4	4 42.3	7 06.8	15 11.0	12 04.0
6 M	6 57 59	14 25 20	25 16 50	2♊38 03	2 03.3	25 03.0	20 51.2	13 24.6	26 50.4	18 59.3	4 40.3	7 09.4	15 10.4	12 05.3
7 Tu	7 01 55	15 22 34	10♊03 03	17 31 04	2R 04.0	27 01.9	20 40.5	14 06.4	26 38.9	19 10.1	4 38.2	7 12.0	15 09.8	12 06.6
8 W	7 05 52	16 19 48	25 01 11	2♋32 27	2 04.3	28 59.1	20 32.2	14 48.1	26 27.7	19 20.9	4 36.1	7 14.7	15 09.2	12 07.9
9 Th	7 09 49	17 17 02	10♋03 47	17 34 07	2 03.9	0♌54.3	20 26.2	15 29.7	26 16.6	19 31.5	4 33.8	7 17.4	15 08.6	12 09.3
10 F	7 13 45	18 14 16	25 02 20	2♌27 27	2 02.8	2 47.7	20 22.6	16 11.2	26 05.9	19 42.0	4 31.5	7 20.1	15 08.1	12 10.6
11 Sa	7 17 42	19 11 30	9♌48 30	17 04 39	2 00.9	4 39.2	20D 21.4	16 52.7	25 55.3	19 52.5	4 29.1	7 22.9	15 07.6	12 12.0
12 Su	7 21 38	20 08 44	24 15 15	1♍19 44	1 58.6	6 28.8	20 22.4	17 34.2	25 45.1	20 02.8	4 26.6	7 25.7	15 07.1	12 13.5
13 M	7 25 35	21 05 58	8♍17 45	15 09 07	1 56.2	8 16.4	20 25.7	18 15.5	25 35.1	20 13.0	4 24.0	7 28.6	15 06.6	12 14.9
14 Tu	7 29 31	22 03 12	21 53 46	28 31 50	1 54.2	10 02.1	20 31.3	18 56.8	25 25.3	20 23.1	4 21.3	7 31.5	15 06.2	12 16.4
15 W	7 33 28	23 00 27	5♎03 30	11♎29 08	1D 52.9	11 46.0	20 39.0	19 38.1	25 15.9	20 33.1	4 18.6	7 34.4	15 05.8	12 17.9
16 Th	7 37 24	23 57 41	17 49 06	24 03 56	1 52.4	13 27.9	20 48.8	20 19.3	25 06.8	20 43.0	4 15.7	7 37.3	15 05.5	12 19.4
17 F	7 41 21	24 54 55	0♏14 07	6♏20 15	1 52.9	15 07.8	21 00.7	21 00.4	24 57.9	20 52.7	4 12.8	7 40.3	15 05.1	12 20.9
18 Sa	7 45 18	25 52 10	12 22 54	18 22 39	1 54.1	16 45.9	21 14.6	21 41.4	24 49.4	21 02.4	4 09.8	7 43.3	15 04.8	12 22.5
19 Su	7 49 14	26 49 25	24 20 05	0♐15 48	1 55.7	18 22.1	21 30.4	22 22.4	24 41.2	21 11.9	4 06.8	7 46.3	15 04.6	12 24.0
20 M	7 53 11	27 46 40	6♐10 20	12 04 12	1 57.4	19 56.3	21 48.2	23 03.4	24 33.3	21 21.4	4 03.6	7 49.4	15 04.4	12 25.6
21 Tu	7 57 07	28 43 56	17 57 56	23 52 00	1R 58.5	21 28.7	22 07.8	23 44.2	24 25.8	21 30.7	4 00.4	7 52.5	15 04.2	12 27.3
22 W	8 01 04	29 41 12	29 46 48	5♑42 45	1 58.7	22 59.0	22 29.2	24 25.0	24 18.5	21 39.8	3 57.2	7 55.6	15 04.0	12 28.9
23 Th	8 05 00	0♌38 28	11♑40 12	17 39 28	1 57.7	24 27.5	22 52.3	25 05.8	24 11.6	21 48.9	3 53.8	7 58.8	15 03.9	12 30.6
24 F	8 08 57	1 35 45	23 40 51	29 44 33	1 55.2	25 54.0	23 17.1	25 46.5	24 05.1	21 57.8	3 50.4	8 02.0	15 03.8	12 32.2
25 Sa	8 12 54	2 33 03	5♒50 49	11♒59 48	1 51.4	27 18.5	23 43.5	26 27.1	23 58.9	22 06.6	3 47.0	8 05.2	15 03.7	12 33.9
26 Su	8 16 50	3 30 21	18 11 39	24 26 31	1 46.6	28 40.9	24 11.4	27 07.7	23 53.0	22 15.3	3 43.4	8 08.4	15D 03.6	12 35.6
27 M	8 20 47	4 27 40	0♓44 29	7♓05 39	1 41.3	0♍01.4	24 40.9	27 48.2	23 47.5	22 23.9	3 39.8	8 11.7	15 03.6	12 37.4
28 Tu	8 24 43	5 25 00	13 30 06	19 57 56	1 36.0	1 19.7	25 11.8	28 28.6	23 42.3	22 32.3	3 36.2	8 15.0	15 03.7	12 39.1
29 W	8 28 40	6 22 21	26 29 11	3♈03 58	1 31.5	2 35.9	25 44.1	29 09.0	23 37.4	22 40.5	3 32.4	8 18.3	15 03.7	12 40.9
30 Th	8 32 36	7 19 43	9♈42 21	16 24 24	1 28.2	3 49.8	26 17.8	29 49.3	23 33.0	22 48.7	3 28.7	8 21.7	15 03.8	12 42.7
31 F	8 36 33	8 17 06	23 10 11	29 59 47	1D 26.5	5 01.6	26 52.8	0♋29.6	23 28.9	22 56.7	3 24.8	8 25.0	15 03.9	12 44.5

August 1964

LONGITUDE

Day	Sid.Time	☉	0 hr ☽	Noon☽	True☊	☿	♀	♂	⚳	♃	♄	♅	♆	♇
1 Sa	8 40 29	9♌14 30	6♉53 14	13♉50 32	1♋26.3	6♍11.0	27♊29.0	1♋09.8	23♐25.1	23♉04.6	3♓20.9	8♍28.4	15♏04.1	12♍46.3
2 Su	8 44 26	10 11 56	20 51 40	27 56 33	1 27.2	7 18.0	28 06.4	1 49.9	23R 21.7	23 12.3	3R 17.0	8 31.8	15 04.3	12 48.1
3 M	8 48 22	11 09 22	5♊05 02	12♊16 52	1 28.5	8 22.5	28 44.9	2 30.0	23 18.7	23 19.9	3 13.0	8 35.2	15 04.5	12 50.0
4 Tu	8 52 19	12 06 50	19 31 45	26 49 13	1R 29.4	9 24.3	29 24.6	3 10.0	23 16.0	23 27.4	3 09.0	8 38.7	15 04.7	12 51.8
5 W	8 56 16	13 04 19	4♋08 46	11♋29 43	1 29.1	10 23.5	0♋05.4	3 50.0	23 13.7	23 34.7	3 04.9	8 42.2	15 05.0	12 53.7
6 Th	9 00 12	14 01 50	18 51 22	26 12 53	1 27.1	11 19.9	0 47.1	4 29.9	23 11.7	23 41.8	3 00.8	8 45.7	15 05.3	12 55.6
7 F	9 04 09	14 59 21	3♌33 25	10♌52 03	1 23.0	12 13.3	1 29.9	5 09.7	23 10.2	23 48.8	2 56.6	8 49.2	15 05.7	12 57.5
8 Sa	9 08 05	15 56 54	18 07 55	25 20 11	1 17.1	13 03.5	2 13.6	5 49.4	23 08.9	23 55.7	2 52.4	8 52.7	15 06.0	12 59.4
9 Su	9 12 02	16 54 27	2♍28 05	9♍30 57	1 10.0	13 50.5	2 58.2	6 29.1	23 08.1	24 02.4	2 48.1	8 56.3	15 06.5	13 01.3
10 M	9 15 58	17 52 01	16 28 15	23 19 37	1 02.6	14 34.1	3 43.6	7 08.8	23D 07.6	24 08.9	2 43.8	8 59.8	15 06.9	13 03.3
11 Tu	9 19 55	18 49 37	0♎04 48	6♎43 43	0 55.7	15 14.0	4 30.0	7 48.3	23 07.5	24 15.3	2 39.5	9 03.4	15 07.4	13 05.2
12 W	9 23 51	19 47 13	13 16 24	19 43 03	0 50.2	15 50.1	5 17.1	8 27.8	23 07.7	24 21.5	2 35.2	9 07.0	15 07.9	13 07.2
13 Th	9 27 48	20 44 50	26 03 59	2♏19 34	0 46.4	16 22.2	6 05.0	9 07.2	23 08.3	24 27.5	2 30.8	9 10.6	15 08.4	13 09.2
14 F	9 31 45	21 42 29	8♏30 19	14 36 45	0D 44.6	16 50.0	6 53.7	9 46.6	23 09.2	24 33.4	2 26.4	9 14.3	15 09.0	13 11.2
15 Sa	9 35 41	22 40 08	20 39 30	26 39 10	0 44.4	17 13.4	7 43.1	10 25.9	23 10.5	24 39.2	2 22.0	9 17.9	15 09.6	13 13.2
16 Su	9 39 38	23 37 48	2♐36 25	8♐31 55	0 45.2	17 32.1	8 33.2	11 05.1	23 12.1	24 44.7	2 17.5	9 21.6	15 10.2	13 15.2
17 M	9 43 34	24 35 29	14 26 19	20 20 15	0R 46.3	17 45.9	9 24.0	11 44.3	23 14.1	24 50.2	2 13.0	9 25.2	15 10.9	13 17.2
18 Tu	9 47 31	25 33 12	26 14 22	2♑09 15	0 46.8	17 54.5	10 15.5	12 23.4	23 16.5	24 55.4	2 08.6	9 28.9	15 11.6	13 19.2
19 W	9 51 27	26 30 56	8♑05 27	14 03 31	0 45.7	17R 57.7	11 07.6	13 02.4	23 19.1	25 00.5	2 04.1	9 32.6	15 12.3	13 21.3
20 Th	9 55 24	27 28 40	20 03 53	26 06 58	0 42.7	17 55.4	12 00.4	13 41.4	23 22.1	25 05.3	1 59.6	9 36.3	15 13.1	13 23.3
21 F	9 59 21	28 26 26	2♒13 08	8♒22 39	0 37.2	17 47.5	12 53.7	14 20.3	23 25.5	25 10.1	1 55.0	9 40.0	15 13.9	13 25.4
22 Sa	10 03 17	29 24 14	14 35 44	20 52 33	0 29.5	17 33.7	13 47.6	14 59.1	23 29.2	25 14.6	1 50.5	9 43.7	15 14.7	13 27.5
23 Su	10 07 14	0♍22 02	27 13 10	3♓37 35	0 20.1	17 14.0	14 42.1	15 37.9	23 33.2	25 19.0	1 46.0	9 47.5	15 15.6	13 29.5
24 M	10 11 10	1 19 53	10♓05 45	16 37 35	0 09.7	16 48.5	15 37.1	16 16.6	23 37.5	25 23.2	1 41.4	9 51.2	15 16.4	13 31.6
25 Tu	10 15 07	2 17 44	23 12 54	29 51 33	29♊59.3	16 17.2	16 32.7	16 55.2	23 42.2	25 27.2	1 36.9	9 54.9	15 17.3	13 33.7
26 W	10 19 03	3 15 38	6♈33 18	13♈17 57	29 50.1	15 40.5	17 28.8	17 33.7	23 47.1	25 31.0	1 32.4	9 58.7	15 18.3	13 35.8
27 Th	10 23 00	4 13 33	20 05 17	26 55 06	29 42.9	14 58.7	18 25.4	18 12.2	23 52.4	25 34.7	1 27.8	10 02.4	15 19.3	13 37.8
28 F	10 26 56	5 11 30	3♉47 13	10♉41 28	29 38.2	14 12.2	19 22.5	18 50.7	23 58.0	25 38.2	1 23.3	10 06.2	15 20.3	13 39.9
29 Sa	10 30 53	6 09 28	17 37 44	24 35 54	29D 35.8	13 21.7	20 20.0	19 29.0	24 04.0	25 41.4	1 18.8	10 09.9	15 21.3	13 42.0
30 Su	10 34 49	7 07 29	1♊35 54	8♊37 37	29 35.3	12 28.0	21 18.0	20 07.3	24 10.2	25 44.5	1 14.3	10 13.7	15 22.4	13 44.2
31 M	10 38 46	8 05 32	15 40 59	22 45 54	29R 35.6	11 32.1	22 16.5	20 45.6	24 16.7	25 47.4	1 09.8	10 17.5	15 23.4	13 46.3

Astro Data	Planet Ingress	Last Aspect	☽ Ingress	Last Aspect	☽ Ingress	☽ Phases & Eclipses	Astro Data
Dy Hr Mn	Dy Hr Mn	Dy Hr Mn	Dy Hr Mn	Dy Hr Mn	Dy Hr Mn	Dy Hr Mn	
☽0N 2 22:37	☿ ♌ 9 0:38	1 10:54 ♀ □	♈ 2 0:52	2 3:55 ♃ ☌	♊ 2 15:28	2 20:31 ☾ 10♈57	1 July 1964
♀D 11 13:00	☉ ♌ 22 19:53	3 15:12 ♀ ⚹	♉ 4 5:42	4 16:27 ♀ ☌	♋ 4 17:13	9 11:31 ● 17♋16	Julian Day # 23558
☽0S 15 13:06	☿ ♍ 27 11:35	5 21:39 ☿ ⚹	♊ 6 7:43	6 7:52 ♃ ⚹	♌ 6 18:11	9 11:17:16 ● P 0.322	SVP 5♓45'37"
♆D 27 7:02	♂ ♋ 30 18:23	7 17:00 ♀ ☌	♋ 8 7:57	8 9:38 ♃ □	♍ 8 19:50	16 11:47 ☽ 23♎57	GC 26♐20.6 ⚳ 18♏39.5R
☽0N 30 3:56		9 15:10 ♃ ⚹	♌ 10 8:01	10 13:28 ♃ △	♎ 10 23:51	24 15:58 ○ 1♒45	Eris 11♈19.0 ⚵ 19♏51.5R
	♀ ♋ 5 8:53	11 17:28 ♀ ⚹	♍ 12 9:44	12 12:09 ☉ ⚹	♏ 13 7:31		⚷ 18♓45.1R ⚶ 16♓03.0
⚳D 11 9:03	☉ ♍ 23 2:51	13 23:23 ☉ ⚹	♎ 14 14:41	15 7:57 ♃ ☍	♐ 15 18:44	1 3:29 ☾ 8♉54	☽ Mean ☊ 1♋41.5
☽0S 11 21:12	☊ ♊R 25 10:22	16 11:47 ☉ □	♏ 16 23:32	17 21:25 ☉ △	♑ 18 7:38	7 19:17 ● 15♌17	
☿R 19 14:14		19 4:25 ☉ △	♐ 19 11:28	20 9:57 ♃ △	♒ 20 19:39	15 3:19 ☽ 22♏19	1 August 1964
☽0N 26 8:53		21 11:43 ♂ ☍	♑ 22 0:27	22 20:19 ♃ □	♓ 23 5:13	23 5:25 ○ 0♓06	Julian Day # 23589
		23 20:24 ♃ △	♒ 24 12:30	25 4:01 ♃ ⚹	♈ 25 12:15	30 9:15 ☾ 7♊01	SVP 5♓45'32"
		26 21:03 ☿ ☍	♓ 26 22:36	26 19:57 ♀ □	♉ 27 17:24		GC 26♐20.7 ⚳ 20♏12.9
		29 4:29 ♂ □	♈ 29 6:25	29 13:53 ♃ ☌	♊ 29 21:16		Eris 11♈15.9R ⚵ 20♏11.2
		31 6:17 ♀ ⚹	♉ 31 12:00				⚷ 18♓04.3R ⚶ 16♓06.8R
							☽ Mean ☊ 0♋03.0

LONGITUDE — September 1964

Day	Sid.Time	☉	0 hr ☽	Noon☽	True☊	☿	♀	♂	⚳	♃	♄	♅	♆	♇
1 Tu	10 42 43	9♍03 37	29♊52 13	6♋59 45	29♊35.6	10♍35.0	23♋15.3	21♋23.7	24♐23.5	25♉50.2	1♓05.3	10♍21.3	15♏24.6	13♍48.4
2 W	10 46 39	10 01 43	14♋08 15	21 17 23	29R 33.9	9R 38.0	24 14.6	22 01.8	24 30.7	25 52.7	1R 00.8	10 25.0	15 25.7	13 50.5
3 Th	10 50 36	10 59 52	28 26 46	5♌35 55	29 29.9	8 42.1	25 14.3	22 39.9	24 38.1	25 55.0	0 56.4	10 28.8	15 26.9	13 52.6
4 F	10 54 32	11 58 02	12♌44 18	19 51 20	29 23.0	7 48.8	26 14.4	23 17.8	24 45.8	25 57.2	0 52.0	10 32.6	15 28.1	13 54.7
5 Sa	10 58 29	12 56 15	26 56 22	3♍58 47	29 13.6	6 59.2	27 14.8	23 55.7	24 53.8	25 59.1	0 47.6	10 36.3	15 29.3	13 56.9
6 Su	11 02 25	13 54 29	10♍57 56	17 53 14	29 02.4	6 14.5	28 15.6	24 33.5	25 02.1	26 00.9	0 43.2	10 40.1	15 30.6	13 59.0
7 M	11 06 22	14 52 44	24 44 12	1♎30 22	28 50.5	5 35.8	29 16.8	25 11.2	25 10.6	26 02.4	0 38.8	10 43.9	15 31.9	14 01.1
8 Tu	11 10 18	15 51 02	8♎11 26	14 47 11	28 39.1	5 04.1	0♌18.3	25 48.9	25 19.5	26 03.8	0 34.5	10 47.6	15 33.2	14 03.2
9 W	11 14 15	16 49 20	21 17 32	27 42 32	28 29.3	4 40.1	1 20.1	26 26.4	25 28.6	26 04.9	0 30.3	10 51.4	15 34.5	14 05.3
10 Th	11 18 12	17 47 41	4♏02 20	10♏17 11	28 21.8	4 24.5	2 22.2	27 03.9	25 38.0	26 05.9	0 26.0	10 55.2	15 35.9	14 07.5
11 F	11 22 08	18 46 03	16 27 29	22 33 39	28 17.0	4D 17.7	3 24.7	27 41.3	25 47.6	26 06.6	0 21.8	10 58.9	15 37.3	14 09.6
12 Sa	11 26 05	19 44 27	28 36 13	4♐35 45	28 14.5	4 20.1	4 27.5	28 18.7	25 57.5	26 07.2	0 17.7	11 02.6	15 38.7	14 11.7
13 Su	11 30 01	20 42 53	10♐32 54	16 28 19	28 13.7	4 31.8	5 30.6	28 55.9	26 07.7	26 07.6	0 13.5	11 06.4	15 40.2	14 13.8
14 M	11 33 58	21 41 20	22 22 40	28 16 40	28 13.7	4 52.7	6 33.9	29 33.1	26 18.1	26R 07.7	0 09.5	11 10.1	15 41.7	14 15.9
15 Tu	11 37 54	22 39 49	4♑11 00	10♑06 20	28 13.3	5 22.7	7 37.6	0♌10.2	26 28.8	26 07.7	0 05.5	11 13.8	15 43.2	14 18.0
16 W	11 41 51	23 38 19	16 03 22	22 02 42	28 11.6	6 01.5	8 41.5	0 47.3	26 39.8	26 07.4	0 01.5	11 17.5	15 44.7	14 20.1
17 Th	11 45 47	24 36 51	28 04 56	4♒10 36	28 07.6	6 48.7	9 45.7	1 24.2	26 50.9	26 07.0	29♒57.6	11 21.3	15 46.2	14 22.2
18 F	11 49 44	25 35 25	10♒20 11	16 34 05	28 01.0	7 43.9	10 50.2	2 01.1	27 02.3	26 06.3	29 53.7	11 24.9	15 47.8	14 24.3
19 Sa	11 53 41	26 34 01	22 52 35	29 15 56	27 51.8	8 46.5	11 55.0	2 37.9	27 14.0	26 05.5	29 49.9	11 28.6	15 49.4	14 26.4
20 Su	11 57 37	27 32 38	5♓44 14	12♓17 28	27 40.4	9 56.0	13 00.0	3 14.6	27 25.9	26 04.5	29 46.1	11 32.3	15 51.0	14 28.5
21 M	12 01 34	28 31 17	18 55 34	25 38 17	27 27.9	11 11.7	14 05.2	3 51.2	27 38.0	26 03.2	29 42.4	11 35.9	15 52.7	14 30.6
22 Tu	12 05 30	29 29 58	2♈25 21	9♈16 20	27 15.4	12 33.0	15 10.7	4 27.8	27 50.3	26 01.8	29 38.8	11 39.6	15 54.3	14 32.6
23 W	12 09 27	0♎28 41	16 10 48	23 08 15	27 04.2	13 59.3	16 16.4	5 04.3	28 02.8	26 00.1	29 35.2	11 43.2	15 56.0	14 34.7
24 Th	12 13 23	1 27 26	0♉08 09	7♉09 57	26 55.2	15 29.9	17 22.4	5 40.6	28 15.6	25 58.3	29 31.7	11 46.8	15 57.7	14 36.7
25 F	12 17 20	2 26 14	14 13 11	21 17 22	26 49.1	17 04.2	18 28.6	6 17.0	28 28.6	25 56.2	29 28.3	11 50.4	15 59.4	14 38.8
26 Sa	12 21 16	3 25 03	28 22 05	5♊26 59	26 45.8	18 41.6	19 35.1	6 53.2	28 41.8	25 54.0	29 24.9	11 54.0	16 01.2	14 40.8
27 Su	12 25 13	4 23 55	12♊31 48	19 36 18	26D 44.6	20 21.6	20 41.8	7 29.3	28 55.2	25 51.5	29 21.6	11 57.6	16 03.0	14 42.8
28 M	12 29 10	5 22 50	26 40 19	3♋43 43	26R 44.6	22 03.8	21 48.6	8 05.4	29 08.8	25 48.9	29 18.4	12 01.1	16 04.8	14 44.9
29 Tu	12 33 06	6 21 46	10♋46 24	17 48 17	26 44.3	23 47.6	22 55.7	8 41.4	29 22.6	25 46.1	29 15.2	12 04.7	16 06.6	14 46.9
30 W	12 37 03	7 20 46	24 49 17	1♌49 16	26 42.5	25 32.8	24 03.0	9 17.3	29 36.6	25 43.1	29 12.2	12 08.2	16 08.4	14 48.9

LONGITUDE — October 1964

Day	Sid.Time	☉	0 hr ☽	Noon☽	True☊	☿	♀	♂	⚳	♃	♄	♅	♆	♇
1 Th	12 40 59	8♎19 47	8♌48 07	15♌45 38	26♊38.2	27♍18.8	25♌10.5	9♌53.1	29♐50.9	25♉39.8	29♒09.1	12♍11.7	16♏10.3	14♍50.9
2 F	12 44 56	9 18 50	22 41 37	29 35 48	26R 31.1	29 05.6	26 18.2	10 28.8	0♑05.3	25R 36.4	29R 06.2	12 15.2	16 12.1	14 52.8
3 Sa	12 48 52	10 17 56	6♍27 51	13♍17 29	26 21.4	0♎52.7	27 26.1	11 04.4	0 19.9	25 32.8	29 03.4	12 18.6	16 14.0	14 54.8
4 Su	12 52 49	11 17 04	20 04 20	26 48 03	26 09.7	2 40.0	28 34.2	11 39.9	0 34.7	25 29.0	29 00.6	12 22.0	16 15.9	14 56.8
5 M	12 56 45	12 16 14	3♎28 20	10♎04 52	25 57.3	4 27.3	29 42.4	12 15.3	0 49.7	25 25.0	28 57.9	12 25.4	16 17.8	14 58.7
6 Tu	13 00 42	13 15 26	16 37 26	23 05 50	25 45.3	6 14.5	0♍50.9	12 50.7	1 04.8	25 20.9	28 55.3	12 28.8	16 19.8	15 00.6
7 W	13 04 38	14 14 40	29 29 59	5♏49 51	25 34.8	8 01.3	1 59.5	13 25.9	1 20.2	25 16.5	28 52.8	12 32.2	16 21.7	15 02.5
8 Th	13 08 35	15 13 56	12♏05 31	18 17 07	25 26.7	9 47.8	3 08.2	14 01.0	1 35.7	25 12.0	28 50.4	12 35.5	16 23.7	15 04.4
9 F	13 12 32	16 13 14	24 24 54	0♐29 10	25 21.2	11 33.9	4 17.1	14 36.1	1 51.4	25 07.3	28 48.0	12 38.8	16 25.7	15 06.3
10 Sa	13 16 28	17 12 34	6♐30 20	12 28 50	25 18.3	13 19.4	5 26.2	15 11.0	2 07.3	25 02.4	28 45.8	12 42.1	16 27.7	15 08.2
11 Su	13 20 25	18 11 56	18 25 13	24 20 02	25D 17.5	15 04.3	6 35.5	15 45.8	2 23.3	24 57.3	28 43.6	12 45.4	16 29.7	15 10.0
12 M	13 24 21	19 11 19	0♑13 53	6♑07 27	25 17.8	16 48.6	7 44.9	16 20.6	2 39.6	24 52.1	28 41.6	12 48.6	16 31.8	15 11.9
13 Tu	13 28 18	20 10 44	12 01 23	17 56 22	25R 18.3	18 32.3	8 54.4	16 55.2	2 55.9	24 46.7	28 39.6	12 51.8	16 33.8	15 13.7
14 W	13 32 14	21 10 11	23 53 06	29 52 15	25 17.9	20 15.4	10 04.1	17 29.7	3 12.5	24 41.2	28 37.7	12 55.0	16 35.9	15 15.5
15 Th	13 36 11	22 09 40	5♒54 30	12♒00 30	25 15.8	21 57.8	11 14.0	18 04.1	3 29.2	24 35.5	28 35.9	12 58.1	16 38.0	15 17.3
16 F	13 40 07	23 09 11	18 10 48	24 25 59	25 11.4	23 39.5	12 23.9	18 38.4	3 46.0	24 29.6	28 34.2	13 01.2	16 40.1	15 19.1
17 Sa	13 44 04	24 08 43	0♓46 28	7♓12 38	25 04.8	25 20.5	13 34.1	19 12.6	4 03.0	24 23.6	28 32.6	13 04.3	16 42.2	15 20.8
18 Su	13 48 01	25 08 17	13 44 44	20 22 54	24 56.2	27 01.0	14 44.3	19 46.7	4 20.2	24 17.5	28 31.1	13 07.4	16 44.3	15 22.6
19 M	13 51 57	26 07 53	27 07 07	3♈57 16	24 46.4	28 40.7	15 54.7	20 20.6	4 37.5	24 11.2	28 29.7	13 10.4	16 46.4	15 24.3
20 Tu	13 55 54	27 07 31	10♈53 01	17 53 58	24 36.6	0♏19.8	17 05.2	20 54.5	4 54.9	24 04.8	28 28.4	13 13.4	16 48.5	15 26.0
21 W	13 59 50	28 07 11	24 59 33	2♉09 04	24 27.7	1 58.4	18 15.9	21 28.3	5 12.5	23 58.2	28 27.2	13 16.3	16 50.7	15 27.6
22 Th	14 03 47	29 06 53	9♉21 47	16 36 53	24 20.7	3 36.3	19 26.7	22 01.9	5 30.2	23 51.5	28 26.1	13 19.2	16 52.8	15 29.3
23 F	14 07 43	0♏06 37	23 53 32	1♊10 55	24 16.1	5 13.6	20 37.6	22 35.4	5 48.1	23 44.7	28 25.1	13 22.1	16 55.0	15 30.9
24 Sa	14 11 40	1 06 23	8♊28 17	15 44 55	24D 14.0	6 50.3	21 48.7	23 08.8	6 06.1	23 37.8	28 24.2	13 24.9	16 57.2	15 32.5
25 Su	14 15 36	2 06 11	23 00 11	0♋13 36	24 13.8	8 26.5	22 59.8	23 42.1	6 24.2	23 30.7	28 23.4	13 27.8	16 59.4	15 34.1
26 M	14 19 33	3 06 02	7♋24 45	14 33 17	24 14.7	10 02.2	24 11.1	24 15.3	6 42.5	23 23.6	28 22.7	13 30.5	17 01.6	15 35.7
27 Tu	14 23 30	4 05 55	21 39 00	28 41 44	24R 15.6	11 37.4	25 22.5	24 48.3	7 00.9	23 16.3	28 22.1	13 33.3	17 03.8	15 37.3
28 W	14 27 26	5 05 50	5♌41 24	12♌37 58	24 15.5	13 12.0	26 34.1	25 21.3	7 19.4	23 08.9	28 21.6	13 36.0	17 06.0	15 38.8
29 Th	14 31 23	6 05 47	19 31 24	26 21 43	24 13.5	14 46.2	27 45.7	25 54.0	7 38.0	23 01.5	28 21.2	13 38.6	17 08.2	15 40.3
30 F	14 35 19	7 05 47	3♍08 56	9♍53 03	24 09.5	16 19.8	28 57.4	26 26.7	7 56.8	22 53.9	28 20.9	13 41.3	17 10.4	15 41.8
31 Sa	14 39 16	8 05 48	16 34 05	23 12 01	24 03.4	17 53.1	0♎09.3	26 59.2	8 15.7	22 46.3	28 20.7	13 43.8	17 12.6	15 43.2

Astro Data

	Dy Hr Mn
☽0S	8 5:50
☿D	11 17:50
♃R	14 19:01
☽0N	22 15:32
☉0S	23 0:16
☿0S	5 6:46
☽0S	5 14:11
☽0N	20 0:46

Planet Ingress

	Dy Hr Mn
♀ ♌	8 4:53
♂ ♌	15 5:22
♄ ♒R	16 21:04
☉ ♎	23 0:17
⚳ ♑	2 3:15
☿ ♎	3 0:12
♀ ♍	5 18:10
☿ ♏	20 7:11
☉ ♏	23 9:21
♀ ♎	31 8:54

Last Aspect / ☽ Ingress (September)

Last Aspect Dy Hr Mn		☽ Ingress Dy Hr Mn
30 20:43	♇ □	♋ 1 0:13
2 19:43	♃ ⚹	♌ 3 2:36
4 22:21	♃ □	♍ 5 5:12
7 7:43	♀ ⚹	♎ 7 9:19
9 9:30	♂ □	♏ 9 16:19
11 22:44	♂ △	♐ 12 2:47
13 21:24	☉ □	♑ 14 15:30
16 20:07	♃ △	♒ 17 3:47
19 13:03	♄ ☌	♓ 19 13:22
21 17:31	☉ ☍	♈ 21 19:44
23 23:01	♄ ⚹	♉ 23 23:46
26 1:49	♄ □	♊ 26 2:46
28 4:30	♄ △	♋ 28 5:39
30 1:34	♃ ⚹	♌ 30 8:52

Last Aspect / ☽ Ingress (October)

Last Aspect Dy Hr Mn		☽ Ingress Dy Hr Mn
2 11:09	♄ ☍	♍ 2 12:42
4 9:39	♃ △	♎ 4 17:44
6 22:53	♄ △	♏ 7 0:57
9 8:40	♄ □	♐ 9 11:02
11 20:55	♄ ⚹	♑ 11 23:32
14 1:42	♃ △	♒ 14 12:15
16 19:50	♄ ☌	♓ 16 22:33
18 18:56	♃ ⚹	♈ 19 5:05
21 5:49	♄ ⚹	♉ 21 8:24
23 7:27	♄ □	♊ 23 10:03
25 8:57	♄ △	♋ 25 11:37
27 5:49	♀ ⚹	♌ 27 14:14
29 15:31	♄ ☍	♍ 29 18:25

☽ Phases & Eclipses

Dy Hr Mn	
6 4:34	● 13♍36
13 21:24	☽ 21♐06
21 17:31	○ 28♓45
28 15:01	☾ 5♋30
5 16:20	● 12♎27
13 16:56	☽ 20♑23
21 4:45	○ 27♈49
27 21:59	☾ 4♌31

Astro Data

1 September 1964
Julian Day # 23620
SVP 5♓45'28"
GC 26♐20.7 ⚴ 26♏53.5
Eris 11♈03.5R ⚵ 24♏52.7
⚷ 16♓47.9R ⚶ 9♓43.3R
☽ Mean ☊ 28♊24.5

1 October 1964
Julian Day # 23650
SVP 5♓45'25"
GC 26♐20.8 ⚴ 6♐12.3
Eris 10♈46.1R ⚵ 2♐16.5
⚷ 15♓26.2R ⚶ 3♓38.1R
☽ Mean ☊ 26♊49.1

November 1964 — LONGITUDE

Day	Sid.Time	☉	0 hr ☽	Noon ☽	True ☊	☿	♀	♂	⚳	♃	♄	♅	♆	♇
1 Su	14 43 12	9♏05 52	29♍46 49	6♎18 28	23♊55.9	19♏25.9	1♎21.2	27♌31.6	8♑34.7	22♉38.5	28♒20.6	13♍46.4	17♏14.8	15♍44.7
2 M	14 47 09	10 05 57	12♎46 56	19 12 10	23R47.7	20 58.2	2 33.3	28 03.9	8 53.9	22R30.7	28D20.6	13 48.9	17 17.1	15 46.1
3 Tu	14 51 05	11 06 05	25 34 10	1♏52 54	23 39.8	22 30.2	3 45.4	28 36.0	9 13.1	22 22.9	28 20.7	13 51.3	17 19.3	15 47.5
4 W	14 55 02	12 06 15	8♏08 24	14 20 43	23 32.9	24 01.7	4 57.7	29 07.9	9 32.5	22 15.0	28 21.0	13 53.7	17 21.6	15 48.8
5 Th	14 58 59	13 06 26	20 29 55	26 36 09	23 27.7	25 32.8	6 10.0	29 39.8	9 52.0	22 07.0	28 21.3	13 56.1	17 23.8	15 50.2
6 F	15 02 55	14 06 39	2♐39 35	8♐40 27	23 24.5	27 03.5	7 22.4	0♍11.4	10 11.6	21 59.0	28 21.7	13 58.4	17 26.1	15 51.5
7 Sa	15 06 52	15 06 54	14 39 02	20 35 39	23D23.3	28 33.8	8 34.9	0 42.9	10 31.3	21 50.9	28 22.3	14 00.7	17 28.3	15 52.8
8 Su	15 10 48	16 07 10	26 30 41	2♑24 35	23 23.6	0♐03.6	9 47.5	1 14.3	10 51.1	21 42.8	28 22.9	14 03.0	17 30.6	15 54.0
9 M	15 14 45	17 07 28	8♑17 48	14 10 52	23 25.1	1 33.1	11 00.2	1 45.5	11 11.0	21 34.7	28 23.7	14 05.1	17 32.8	15 55.2
10 Tu	15 18 41	18 07 48	20 04 20	25 58 48	23 26.9	3 02.1	12 12.9	2 16.6	11 31.0	21 26.5	28 24.5	14 07.3	17 35.1	15 56.5
11 W	15 22 38	19 08 09	1♒54 53	7♒53 11	23 28.4	4 30.7	13 25.7	2 47.4	11 51.1	21 18.3	28 25.5	14 09.4	17 37.3	15 57.6
12 Th	15 26 34	20 08 31	13 54 23	19 59 06	23R29.0	5 58.8	14 38.6	3 18.2	12 11.3	21 10.2	28 26.5	14 11.4	17 39.6	15 58.8
13 F	15 30 31	21 08 55	26 07 58	2♓21 36	23 28.3	7 26.4	15 51.6	3 48.7	12 31.6	21 02.0	28 27.7	14 13.5	17 41.8	15 59.9
14 Sa	15 34 28	22 09 20	8♓40 32	15 05 18	23 26.2	8 53.5	17 04.6	4 19.1	12 52.0	20 53.8	28 29.0	14 15.4	17 44.1	16 01.0
15 Su	15 38 24	23 09 46	21 36 17	28 13 51	23 22.8	10 20.0	18 17.8	4 49.3	13 12.5	20 45.6	28 30.3	14 17.3	17 46.3	16 02.0
16 M	15 42 21	24 10 14	4♈58 10	11♈49 19	23 18.6	11 45.9	19 30.9	5 19.4	13 33.1	20 37.5	28 31.8	14 19.2	17 48.5	16 03.1
17 Tu	15 46 17	25 10 43	18 47 12	25 51 35	23 14.2	13 11.2	20 44.2	5 49.2	13 53.7	20 29.4	28 33.4	14 21.0	17 50.8	16 04.1
18 W	15 50 14	26 11 14	3♉02 01	10♉17 56	23 10.1	14 35.6	21 57.5	6 18.9	14 14.5	20 21.3	28 35.1	14 22.7	17 53.0	16 05.1
19 Th	15 54 10	27 11 46	17 38 33	25 03 01	23 07.0	15 59.3	23 10.9	6 48.4	14 35.3	20 13.2	28 36.8	14 24.5	17 55.2	16 06.0
20 F	15 58 07	28 12 19	2♊30 19	9♊59 25	23D05.2	17 22.1	24 24.3	7 17.7	14 56.3	20 05.2	28 38.7	14 26.1	17 57.5	16 06.9
21 Sa	16 02 03	29 12 54	17 29 15	24 58 43	23 04.7	18 43.8	25 37.8	7 46.9	15 17.3	19 57.2	28 40.7	14 27.7	17 59.7	16 07.8
22 Su	16 06 00	0♐13 31	2♋26 51	9♋52 41	23 05.4	20 04.3	26 51.4	8 15.8	15 38.4	19 49.3	28 42.8	14 29.3	18 01.9	16 08.7
23 M	16 09 57	1 14 09	17 15 27	24 34 26	23 06.7	21 23.5	28 05.1	8 44.6	15 59.5	19 41.4	28 45.0	14 30.8	18 04.1	16 09.5
24 Tu	16 13 53	2 14 49	1♌49 07	8♌59 05	23 08.1	22 41.2	29 18.8	9 13.1	16 20.8	19 33.6	28 47.2	14 32.3	18 06.3	16 10.3
25 W	16 17 50	3 15 31	16 04 04	23 03 55	23R09.1	23 57.2	0♏32.5	9 41.5	16 42.1	19 25.9	28 49.6	14 33.7	18 08.5	16 11.1
26 Th	16 21 46	4 16 14	29 58 35	6♍48 07	23 09.4	25 11.2	1 46.3	10 09.6	17 03.5	19 18.2	28 52.1	14 35.0	18 10.7	16 11.8
27 F	16 25 43	5 16 59	13♍32 38	20 12 19	23 08.7	26 22.9	3 00.2	10 37.5	17 25.0	19 10.7	28 54.7	14 36.3	18 12.9	16 12.5
28 Sa	16 29 39	6 17 45	26 47 21	3♎18 00	23 07.3	27 32.1	4 14.1	11 05.2	17 46.5	19 03.2	28 57.3	14 37.6	18 15.0	16 13.2
29 Su	16 33 36	7 18 33	9♎44 31	16 07 09	23 05.2	28 38.3	5 28.1	11 32.7	18 08.1	18 55.8	29 00.1	14 38.8	18 17.2	16 13.8
30 M	16 37 32	8 19 22	22 26 10	28 41 50	23 02.9	29 41.1	6 42.1	11 59.9	18 29.8	18 48.5	29 02.9	14 39.9	18 19.4	16 14.4

December 1964 — LONGITUDE

Day	Sid.Time	☉	0 hr ☽	Noon ☽	True ☊	☿	♀	♂	⚳	♃	♄	♅	♆	♇
1 Tu	16 41 29	9♐20 13	4♏54 22	11♏04 01	23♊00.6	0♑40.1	7♏56.2	12♍26.9	18♑51.6	18♉41.3	29♒05.9	14♍41.0	18♏21.5	16♍15.0
2 W	16 45 26	10 21 05	17 11 01	23 15 36	22R58.8	1 34.6	9 10.3	12 53.7	19 13.4	18R34.2	29 08.9	14 42.0	18 23.6	16 15.6
3 Th	16 49 22	11 21 58	29 17 57	5♐18 18	22 57.6	2 24.1	10 24.5	13 20.2	19 35.3	18 27.2	29 12.1	14 43.0	18 25.7	16 16.1
4 F	16 53 19	12 22 52	11♐16 53	17 13 55	22D57.0	3 07.9	11 38.7	13 46.5	19 57.3	18 20.4	29 15.3	14 43.9	18 27.8	16 16.6
5 Sa	16 57 15	13 23 48	23 09 38	29 04 18	22 57.0	3 45.2	12 52.9	14 12.5	20 19.3	18 13.7	29 18.7	14 44.7	18 29.9	16 17.0
6 Su	17 01 12	14 24 44	4♑58 13	10♑51 39	22 57.4	4 15.1	14 07.2	14 38.3	20 41.4	18 07.1	29 22.1	14 45.5	18 32.0	16 17.4
7 M	17 05 08	15 25 41	16 44 58	22 38 30	22 58.2	4 37.0	15 21.5	15 03.8	21 03.5	18 00.7	29 25.6	14 46.3	18 34.1	16 17.8
8 Tu	17 09 05	16 26 40	28 32 40	4♒27 52	22 59.0	4R49.8	16 35.8	15 29.0	21 25.7	17 54.4	29 29.2	14 47.0	18 36.1	16 18.2
9 W	17 13 01	17 27 38	10♒24 34	16 23 15	22 59.7	4 52.9	17 50.2	15 53.9	21 48.0	17 48.2	29 32.9	14 47.6	18 38.2	16 18.5
10 Th	17 16 58	18 28 38	22 24 25	28 28 35	23 00.2	4 45.3	19 04.6	16 18.6	22 10.3	17 42.2	29 36.7	14 48.2	18 40.2	16 18.8
11 F	17 20 55	19 29 38	4♓36 19	10♓48 08	23R00.4	4 26.6	20 19.0	16 43.0	22 32.7	17 36.4	29 40.5	14 48.7	18 42.2	16 19.0
12 Sa	17 24 51	20 30 38	17 04 36	23 26 13	23 00.5	3 56.4	21 33.5	17 07.1	22 55.1	17 30.7	29 44.5	14 49.2	18 44.2	16 19.2
13 Su	17 28 48	21 31 39	29 53 28	6♈26 50	23 00.4	3 14.7	22 48.0	17 30.8	23 17.6	17 25.1	29 48.5	14 49.6	18 46.2	16 19.4
14 M	17 32 44	22 32 40	13♈06 39	19 53 12	23D00.3	2 21.9	24 02.5	17 54.3	23 40.1	17 19.8	29 52.7	14 49.9	18 48.1	16 19.6
15 Tu	17 36 41	23 33 42	26 46 39	3♉47 03	23 00.3	1 19.2	25 17.0	18 17.5	24 02.7	17 14.6	29 56.9	14 50.2	18 50.1	16 19.7
16 W	17 40 37	24 34 45	10♉54 16	18 08 01	23 00.5	0 07.9	26 31.6	18 40.4	24 25.3	17 09.5	0♓01.1	14 50.5	18 52.0	16 19.8
17 Th	17 44 34	25 35 48	25 27 48	2♊53 00	23 00.7	28♐50.1	27 46.2	19 02.9	24 48.0	17 04.7	0 05.5	14 50.7	18 53.9	16 19.8
18 F	17 48 31	26 36 51	10♊22 47	17 56 08	23R00.8	27 28.4	29 00.8	19 25.1	25 10.7	17 00.0	0 10.0	14 50.8	18 55.8	16R19.9
19 Sa	17 52 27	27 37 55	25 31 57	3♋09 02	23 00.7	26 05.5	0♐15.4	19 47.0	25 33.4	16 55.5	0 14.5	14R50.9	18 57.6	16 19.8
20 Su	17 56 24	28 39 00	10♋46 08	18 22 00	23 00.4	24 44.2	1 30.1	20 08.6	25 56.2	16 51.2	0 19.1	14 50.9	18 59.5	16 19.8
21 M	18 00 20	29 40 05	25 55 26	3♌25 21	22 59.8	23 27.0	2 44.8	20 29.7	26 19.1	16 47.1	0 23.8	14 50.8	19 01.3	16 19.7
22 Tu	18 04 17	0♑41 11	10♌50 45	18 10 52	22 58.9	22 16.4	3 59.5	20 50.6	26 42.0	16 43.1	0 28.5	14 50.7	19 03.1	16 19.6
23 W	18 08 13	1 42 17	25 25 04	2♍32 54	22 58.0	21 14.1	5 14.3	21 11.1	27 04.9	16 39.4	0 33.4	14 50.6	19 04.9	16 19.5
24 Th	18 12 10	2 43 24	9♍34 05	16 28 33	22 57.2	20 21.5	6 29.0	21 31.2	27 27.8	16 35.8	0 38.3	14 50.4	19 06.7	16 19.3
25 F	18 16 06	3 44 31	23 16 21	29 57 37	22D56.8	19 39.2	7 43.8	21 50.9	27 50.8	16 32.5	0 43.3	14 50.1	19 08.4	16 19.1
26 Sa	18 20 03	4 45 40	6♎32 40	13♎01 51	22 56.9	19 07.7	8 58.6	22 10.2	28 13.9	16 29.3	0 48.3	14 49.8	19 10.1	16 18.9
27 Su	18 24 00	5 46 48	19 25 35	25 44 20	22 57.6	18 46.8	10 13.5	22 29.1	28 36.9	16 26.3	0 53.4	14 49.4	19 11.8	16 18.6
28 M	18 27 56	6 47 58	1♏58 34	8♏08 47	22 58.7	18D36.1	11 28.3	22 47.6	29 00.0	16 23.5	0 58.6	14 49.0	19 13.5	16 18.3
29 Tu	18 31 53	7 49 07	14 15 29	20 19 08	23 00.1	18 35.2	12 43.2	23 05.7	29 23.2	16 21.0	1 03.9	14 48.5	19 15.1	16 18.0
30 W	18 35 49	8 50 18	26 20 12	2♐19 07	23 01.5	18 43.4	13 58.1	23 23.3	29 46.4	16 18.6	1 09.2	14 47.9	19 16.8	16 17.6
31 Th	18 39 46	9 51 28	8♐16 18	14 12 06	23R02.4	18 59.9	15 13.0	23 40.6	0♒09.6	16 16.4	1 14.6	14 47.3	19 18.4	16 17.2

Astro Data

	Dy Hr Mn
♄ D	1 20:44
☽ 0S	1 21:27
♀ 0S	3 10:20
☽ 0N	16 11:32
☽ 0S	29 3:33
♃ ☍ ♆	3 16:01
☿ R	9 7:04
☽ 0N	13 21:28
♇ R	18 18:38
♅ R	20 6:45
☽ 0S	26 9:29
☿ D	29 2:14
♃ △ ♇	31 1:16

Planet Ingress

		Dy Hr Mn
♂	♍	6 3:20
☿	♐	8 11:02
☉	♐	22 6:39
♀	♏	25 1:25
☿	♑	30 19:30
♄	♓	16 5:39
☿	♐R	16 14:31
♀	♐	19 7:02
☉	♑	21 19:50
⚳	♒	31 2:07

Last Aspect / ☽ Ingress (November)

Last Aspect Dy Hr Mn			☽ Ingress	Dy Hr Mn
31 11:14	♃	△	♎	1 0:24
3 5:28	♂	✶	♏	3 8:25
5 18:20	♂	□	♐	5 18:43
8 3:48	♄	✶	♑	8 7:06
10 2:53	♃	△	♒	10 20:08
13 4:30	♄	☌	♓	13 7:28
15 2:05	☉	△	♈	15 15:10
17 16:32	♄	✶	♉	17 18:57
19 17:45	♄	□	♊	19 19:58
21 17:57	♄	△	♋	21 20:04
23 18:20	♀	□	♌	23 20:59
25 22:01	♄	☍	♍	26 0:02
28 0:21	☿	□	♎	28 5:54
30 14:04	☿	✶	♏	30 14:31

Last Aspect / ☽ Ingress (December)

Last Aspect Dy Hr Mn			☽ Ingress	Dy Hr Mn
2 23:45	♄	□	♐	3 1:24
5 12:29	♄	✶	♑	5 13:53
7 3:41	♆	✶	♒	8 2:57
10 14:15	♄	☌	♓	10 15:00
12 8:06	♀	△	♈	13 0:12
15 5:25	♄	✶	♉	15 5:33
17 2:59	♀	☍	♊	17 7:21
19 2:41	☉	☍	♋	19 7:02
20 14:53	♂	✶	♌	21 6:31
22 18:17	☿	△	♍	23 7:41
24 21:07	♂	☌	♎	25 12:04
26 23:06	☿	✶	♏	27 20:11
29 17:40	♂	✶	♐	30 7:20

☽ Phases & Eclipses

Dy Hr Mn	
4 7:16	● 11♏54
12 12:20	☽ 20♒09
19 15:43	○ 27♉21
26 7:10	☾ 4♍04
4 1:18	● 11♐56
4 1:31:21	● P 0.752
12 6:01	☽ 20♓15
19 2:41	○ 27♊14
19 2:37	● T 1.175
25 19:27	☾ 4♎03

Astro Data

1 November 1964
Julian Day # 23681
SVP 5♓45'21"
GC 26♐20.9 ⚵ 17♐26.6
Eris 10♈27.6R ✵ 11♐47.9
⚷ 14♓25.2R ⚶ 3♓40.9
☽ Mean ☊ 25♊10.6

1 December 1964
Julian Day # 23711
SVP 5♓45'17"
GC 26♐21.0 ⚵ 29♐05.3
Eris 10♈14.6R ✵ 22♐06.7
⚷ 14♓10.9 ⚶ 9♓38.8
☽ Mean ☊ 23♊35.3

LONGITUDE

January 1965

Day	Sid.Time	☉	0 hr ☽	Noon ☽	True ☊	☿	♀	♂	⚳	♃	♄	♅	♆	♇
1 F	18 43 42	10♑52 39	20♐06 54	26♐01 01	23♊02.6	19♐23.9	16♐27.9	23♍57.3	0♒32.8	16♉14.5	1♓20.1	14♍46.7	19♏19.9	16♍16.8
2 Sa	18 47 39	11 53 50	1♑54 45	7♑48 23	23R 01.9	19 54.9	17 42.8	24 13.6	0 56.1	16R 12.7	1 25.6	14R 46.0	19 21.5	16R 16.3
3 Su	18 51 35	12 55 01	13 42 10	19 36 22	23 00.1	20 31.9	18 57.7	24 29.4	1 19.4	16 11.2	1 31.2	14 45.2	19 23.0	16 15.8
4 M	18 55 32	13 56 11	25 31 14	1♒26 59	22 57.2	21 14.5	20 12.7	24 44.8	1 42.7	16 09.9	1 36.9	14 44.4	19 24.5	16 15.3
5 Tu	18 59 29	14 57 22	7♒23 53	13 22 11	22 53.5	22 02.1	21 27.6	24 59.6	2 06.0	16 08.7	1 42.6	14 43.5	19 26.0	16 14.8
6 W	19 03 25	15 58 32	19 22 08	25 24 02	22 49.5	22 54.0	22 42.6	25 14.0	2 29.4	16 07.8	1 48.4	14 42.6	19 27.4	16 14.2
7 Th	19 07 22	16 59 42	1♓28 12	7♓34 56	22 45.5	23 49.8	23 57.6	25 27.8	2 52.8	16 07.1	1 54.3	14 41.6	19 28.8	16 13.6
8 F	19 11 18	18 00 52	13 44 36	19 57 34	22 42.1	24 49.2	25 12.5	25 41.2	3 16.2	16 06.6	2 00.2	14 40.6	19 30.2	16 12.9
9 Sa	19 15 15	19 02 01	26 14 13	2♈34 57	22 39.7	25 51.6	26 27.5	25 54.0	3 39.7	16D 06.3	2 06.1	14 39.5	19 31.6	16 12.2
10 Su	19 19 11	20 03 10	9♈00 11	15 30 18	22D 38.6	26 56.9	27 42.5	26 06.2	4 03.1	16 06.2	2 12.1	14 38.3	19 32.9	16 11.5
11 M	19 23 08	21 04 18	22 05 42	28 46 44	22 38.7	28 04.6	28 57.5	26 17.9	4 26.6	16 06.3	2 18.2	14 37.2	19 34.2	16 10.8
12 Tu	19 27 04	22 05 25	5♉33 41	12♉26 47	22 39.9	29 14.6	0♑12.5	26 29.1	4 50.1	16 06.7	2 24.3	14 35.9	19 35.5	16 10.1
13 W	19 31 01	23 06 32	19 26 11	26 31 53	22 41.5	0♑26.6	1 27.5	26 39.7	5 13.6	16 07.2	2 30.5	14 34.6	19 36.7	16 09.3
14 Th	19 34 58	24 07 38	3♊43 45	11♊01 31	22R 42.8	1 40.5	2 42.5	26 49.7	5 37.1	16 08.0	2 36.7	14 33.3	19 38.0	16 08.5
15 F	19 38 54	25 08 43	18 24 41	25 52 39	22 43.2	2 56.0	3 57.5	26 59.1	6 00.6	16 08.9	2 43.0	14 31.9	19 39.2	16 07.6
16 Sa	19 42 51	26 09 48	3♋24 33	10♋59 23	22 42.0	4 13.0	5 12.5	27 07.9	6 24.2	16 10.1	2 49.3	14 30.5	19 40.3	16 06.8
17 Su	19 46 47	27 10 53	18 36 02	26 13 15	22 39.1	5 31.4	6 27.5	27 16.1	6 47.7	16 11.5	2 55.7	14 29.1	19 41.5	16 05.9
18 M	19 50 44	28 11 56	3♌49 43	11♌24 08	22 34.6	6 51.0	7 42.5	27 23.7	7 11.3	16 13.0	3 02.1	14 27.5	19 42.6	16 04.9
19 Tu	19 54 40	29 13 00	18 55 16	26 21 58	22 29.0	8 11.9	8 57.6	27 30.7	7 34.9	16 14.8	3 08.6	14 26.0	19 43.6	16 04.0
20 W	19 58 37	0♒14 02	3♍43 14	10♍58 18	22 23.1	9 33.8	10 12.6	27 37.0	7 58.5	16 16.8	3 15.1	14 24.4	19 44.7	16 03.0
21 Th	20 02 34	1 15 04	18 06 33	25 07 35	22 17.7	10 56.8	11 27.6	27 42.6	8 22.1	16 18.9	3 21.6	14 22.7	19 45.7	16 02.0
22 F	20 06 30	2 16 06	2♎01 12	8♎47 27	22 13.6	12 20.7	12 42.7	27 47.6	8 45.7	16 21.3	3 28.2	14 21.0	19 46.6	16 01.0
23 Sa	20 10 27	3 17 07	15 26 27	21 58 31	22D 11.1	13 45.6	13 57.7	27 51.9	9 09.3	16 23.9	3 34.8	14 19.3	19 47.6	16 00.0
24 Su	20 14 23	4 18 08	28 24 06	4♏43 41	22 10.4	15 11.3	15 12.8	27 55.5	9 33.0	16 26.6	3 41.5	14 17.5	19 48.5	15 58.9
25 M	20 18 20	5 19 08	10♏57 50	17 07 12	22 11.0	16 37.9	16 27.8	27 58.4	9 56.6	16 29.6	3 48.2	14 15.7	19 49.4	15 57.8
26 Tu	20 22 16	6 20 08	23 12 22	29 14 01	22 12.5	18 05.3	17 42.9	28 00.6	10 20.2	16 32.8	3 54.9	14 13.8	19 50.2	15 56.7
27 W	20 26 13	7 21 07	5♐12 47	11♐09 16	22R 14.0	19 33.4	18 58.0	28 02.0	10 43.9	16 36.1	4 01.7	14 11.9	19 51.0	15 55.5
28 Th	20 30 09	8 22 05	17 04 03	22 57 44	22 14.6	21 02.4	20 13.0	28R 02.7	11 07.5	16 39.7	4 08.5	14 10.0	19 51.8	15 54.4
29 F	20 34 06	9 23 03	28 50 47	4♑43 43	22 13.6	22 32.1	21 28.1	28 02.7	11 31.2	16 43.4	4 15.4	14 08.0	19 52.6	15 53.2
30 Sa	20 38 03	10 24 00	10♑36 56	16 30 51	22 10.4	24 02.5	22 43.1	28 01.9	11 54.8	16 47.3	4 22.3	14 06.0	19 53.3	15 52.0
31 Su	20 41 59	11 24 56	22 25 46	28 22 00	22 04.8	25 33.7	23 58.2	28 00.3	12 18.5	16 51.4	4 29.2	14 04.0	19 54.0	15 50.8

LONGITUDE

February 1965

Day	Sid.Time	☉	0 hr ☽	Noon ☽	True ☊	☿	♀	♂	⚳	♃	♄	♅	♆	♇
1 M	20 45 56	12♒25 51	4♒19 49	10♒19 23	21♊57.0	27♑05.6	25♑13.3	27♍58.0	12♒42.1	16♉55.8	4♓36.2	14♍01.9	19♏54.6	15♍49.5
2 Tu	20 49 52	13 26 44	16 20 55	22 24 33	21R 47.4	28 38.2	26 28.3	27R 54.9	13 05.8	17 00.2	4 43.1	13R 59.8	19 55.2	15R 48.2
3 W	20 53 49	14 27 37	28 30 25	4♓38 37	21 36.9	0♒11.6	27 43.4	27 51.0	13 29.4	17 04.9	4 50.1	13 57.6	19 55.8	15 47.0
4 Th	20 57 45	15 28 29	10♓49 17	17 02 31	21 26.4	1 45.7	28 58.4	27 46.3	13 53.1	17 09.8	4 57.2	13 55.4	19 56.3	15 45.7
5 F	21 01 42	16 29 19	23 18 25	29 37 09	21 17.1	3 20.5	0♒13.5	27 40.8	14 16.7	17 14.8	5 04.2	13 53.2	19 56.9	15 44.3
6 Sa	21 05 38	17 30 07	5♈58 51	12♈23 41	21 09.6	4 56.1	1 28.5	27 34.6	14 40.3	17 20.0	5 11.3	13 51.0	19 57.3	15 43.0
7 Su	21 09 35	18 30 54	18 51 53	25 23 38	21 04.5	6 32.5	2 43.5	27 27.5	15 03.9	17 25.4	5 18.4	13 48.7	19 57.8	15 41.6
8 M	21 13 31	19 31 40	1♉59 13	8♉38 51	21D 01.9	8 09.6	3 58.6	27 19.7	15 27.5	17 31.0	5 25.5	13 46.4	19 58.2	15 40.3
9 Tu	21 17 28	20 32 24	15 22 47	22 11 16	21 01.3	9 47.5	5 13.6	27 11.1	15 51.1	17 36.7	5 32.7	13 44.1	19 58.6	15 38.9
10 W	21 21 25	21 33 07	29 04 30	6♊02 37	21 01.9	11 26.2	6 28.6	27 01.7	16 14.7	17 42.6	5 39.8	13 41.7	19 58.9	15 37.5
11 Th	21 25 21	22 33 48	13♊05 41	20 13 40	21R 02.4	13 05.8	7 43.6	26 51.5	16 38.3	17 48.7	5 47.0	13 39.4	19 59.2	15 36.0
12 F	21 29 18	23 34 27	27 26 25	4♋43 38	21 01.7	14 46.1	8 58.6	26 40.6	17 01.9	17 54.9	5 54.2	13 37.0	19 59.5	15 34.6
13 Sa	21 33 14	24 35 05	12♋04 52	19 29 29	20 58.7	16 27.3	10 13.6	26 28.9	17 25.4	18 01.3	6 01.4	13 34.5	19 59.7	15 33.2
14 Su	21 37 11	25 35 41	26 56 41	4♌25 33	20 53.1	18 09.3	11 28.6	26 16.4	17 48.9	18 07.9	6 08.7	13 32.1	20 00.0	15 31.7
15 M	21 41 07	26 36 16	11♌55 01	19 23 58	20 44.9	19 52.3	12 43.6	26 03.2	18 12.5	18 14.6	6 15.9	13 29.6	20 00.1	15 30.2
16 Tu	21 45 04	27 36 49	26 51 11	4♍15 33	20 34.7	21 36.1	13 58.6	25 49.3	18 36.0	18 21.5	6 23.2	13 27.2	20 00.3	15 28.8
17 W	21 49 01	28 37 20	11♍35 57	18 51 26	20 23.8	23 20.8	15 13.5	25 34.6	18 59.5	18 28.6	6 30.4	13 24.7	20 00.4	15 27.3
18 Th	21 52 57	29 37 50	26 01 09	3♎04 29	20 13.4	25 06.4	16 28.5	25 19.2	19 22.9	18 35.8	6 37.7	13 22.1	20 00.4	15 25.8
19 F	21 56 54	0♓38 18	10♎01 00	16 50 26	20 04.5	26 52.9	17 43.4	25 03.1	19 46.4	18 43.1	6 45.0	13 19.6	20R 00.5	15 24.2
20 Sa	22 00 50	1 38 45	23 32 44	0♏08 02	19 58.0	28 40.4	18 58.4	24 46.3	20 09.8	18 50.6	6 52.3	13 17.1	20 00.5	15 22.7
21 Su	22 04 47	2 39 11	6♏36 36	12 58 49	19 54.0	0♓28.7	20 13.3	24 28.9	20 33.2	18 58.2	6 59.6	13 14.5	20 00.4	15 21.2
22 M	22 08 43	3 39 36	19 15 11	25 26 18	19D 52.3	2 18.0	21 28.3	24 10.8	20 56.6	19 06.0	7 06.9	13 11.9	20 00.4	15 19.6
23 Tu	22 12 40	4 39 59	1♐32 48	7♐35 21	19 52.0	4 08.2	22 43.2	23 52.1	21 20.0	19 14.0	7 14.2	13 09.4	20 00.3	15 18.1
24 W	22 16 36	5 40 21	13 34 39	19 31 24	19R 52.2	5 59.2	23 58.2	23 32.9	21 43.3	19 22.1	7 21.5	13 06.8	20 00.2	15 16.5
25 Th	22 20 33	6 40 41	25 26 19	1♑20 03	19 51.7	7 51.1	25 13.1	23 13.0	22 06.7	19 30.3	7 28.9	13 04.2	20 00.0	15 15.0
26 F	22 24 29	7 41 00	7♑13 16	13 06 34	19 49.4	9 43.8	26 28.0	22 52.7	22 30.0	19 38.7	7 36.2	13 01.6	19 59.8	15 13.4
27 Sa	22 28 26	8 41 18	19 00 32	24 55 41	19 44.6	11 37.3	27 42.9	22 31.8	22 53.2	19 47.2	7 43.5	12 58.9	19 59.6	15 11.8
28 Su	22 32 23	9 41 34	0♒52 28	6♒51 18	19 36.9	13 31.4	28 57.8	22 10.5	23 16.5	19 55.8	7 50.8	12 56.3	19 59.3	15 10.3

Astro Data	Dy Hr Mn
☽ 0N	10 4:42
♃ D	10 9:33
♃△♇	14 18:44
☽ 0S	22 16:41
♂ R	28 22:38
☽ 0N	6 9:39
☽ 0S	19 1:40
♆ R	20 1:23
♃☍♆	28 21:19

Planet Ingress		Dy Hr Mn
♀	♑	12 8:00
☿	♑	13 3:12
☉	♒	20 6:29
☿	♒	3 9:02
♀	♒	5 7:41
☉	♓	18 20:48
☿	♓	21 5:40

Last Aspect Dy Hr Mn		☽ Ingress	Dy Hr Mn
1 7:42	♂ □	♑	1 20:06
3 22:08	♂ △	♒	4 9:04
6 6:38	☿ ⚹	♓	6 21:06
8 23:09	♀ □	♈	9 7:08
11 12:21	♀ △	♉	11 14:10
13 12:13	♂ △	♊	13 17:48
15 13:47	♂ □	♋	15 18:35
17 13:40	♂ ⚹	♌	17 17:57
19 1:17	♆ □	♍	19 17:55
21 16:30	♂ ☌	♎	21 20:28
22 19:47	♀ □	♏	24 3:01
26 9:33	♂ ⚹	♐	26 13:32
28 22:22	♂ □	♑	29 2:21
31 11:16	♂ △	♒	31 15:18

Last Aspect Dy Hr Mn		☽ Ingress	Dy Hr Mn
2 7:05	♆ □	♓	3 2:56
5 8:21	♂ ☍	♈	5 12:43
6 22:17	☉ ⚹	♉	7 20:24
9 20:38	♂ △	♊	10 1:36
11 22:54	♂ □	♋	12 4:14
13 23:06	♂ ⚹	♌	14 4:54
16 0:27	☉ ☍	♍	16 5:05
17 23:03	♂ ☌	♎	18 6:45
20 8:54	☿ △	♏	20 11:45
22 9:36	♂ ⚹	♐	22 20:57
24 22:05	♀ ⚹	♑	25 9:17
27 7:17	♂ △	♒	27 22:14

☽ Phases & Eclipses Dy Hr Mn	
2 21:07	● 12♑17
10 20:59	☽ 20♈26
17 13:37	○ 27♋15
24 11:07	☾ 4♏16
1 16:36	● 12♒37
9 8:53	☽ 20♉25
16 0:27	○ 27♌08
23 5:39	☾ 4♐24

Astro Data

1 January 1965
Julian Day # 23742
SVP 5♓45'11"
GC 26♐21.0 ⚵ 11♑18.9
Eris 10♈10.5 ⚶ 3♑19.6
⚷ 14♓49.1 ⚴ 19♓39.4
☽ Mean ☊ 21♊56.9

1 February 1965
Julian Day # 23773
SVP 5♓45'06"
GC 26♐21.1 ⚵ 23♑12.6
Eris 10♈17.3 ⚶ 14♑35.7
⚷ 16♓12.2 ⚴ 1♈51.0
☽ Mean ☊ 20♊18.4

March 1965 LONGITUDE

Day	Sid.Time	☉	0 hr ☽	Noon☽	True☊	☿	♀	♂	⚳	♃	♄	♅	♆	♇
1 M	22 36 19	10♓41 48	12♒52 32	18♒56 26	19♊26.5	15♓26.2	0♓12.7	21♍48.7	23♒39.7	20♉04.6	7♓58.2	12♍53.7	19♏59.0	15♍08.7
2 Tu	22 40 16	11 42 00	25 03 14	1♓13 03	19R 13.8	17 21.3	1 27.6	21R 26.5	24 02.9	20 13.5	8 05.5	12R 51.1	19R 58.7	15R 07.1
3 W	22 44 12	12 42 11	7♓26 00	13 42 07	18 59.8	19 16.9	2 42.5	21 04.0	24 26.1	20 22.5	8 12.8	12 48.4	19 58.3	15 05.5
4 Th	22 48 09	13 42 20	20 01 24	26 23 47	18 45.8	21 12.6	3 57.4	20 41.2	24 49.2	20 31.7	8 20.1	12 45.8	19 57.9	15 03.9
5 F	22 52 05	14 42 27	2♈49 12	9♈17 34	18 33.1	23 08.2	5 12.2	20 18.2	25 12.3	20 40.9	8 27.4	12 43.2	19 57.5	15 02.3
6 Sa	22 56 02	15 42 32	15 48 47	22 22 47	18 22.6	25 03.6	6 27.1	19 54.9	25 35.4	20 50.4	8 34.7	12 40.5	19 57.0	15 00.8
7 Su	22 59 58	16 42 35	28 59 29	5♉38 52	18 15.1	26 58.5	7 41.9	19 31.4	25 58.4	20 59.9	8 42.0	12 37.9	19 56.5	14 59.2
8 M	23 03 55	17 42 35	12♉20 54	19 05 37	18 10.7	28 52.5	8 56.7	19 07.9	26 21.4	21 09.5	8 49.2	12 35.3	19 56.0	14 57.6
9 Tu	23 07 52	18 42 34	25 53 04	2♊43 18	18 08.7	0♈45.4	10 11.5	18 44.2	26 44.4	21 19.3	8 56.5	12 32.7	19 55.4	14 56.0
10 W	23 11 48	19 42 31	9♊36 25	16 32 29	18 08.4	2 36.7	11 26.3	18 20.5	27 07.3	21 29.2	9 03.7	12 30.1	19 54.9	14 54.4
11 Th	23 15 45	20 42 25	23 31 33	0♋33 39	18 08.2	4 26.0	12 41.1	17 56.9	27 30.2	21 39.2	9 11.0	12 27.5	19 54.2	14 52.8
12 F	23 19 41	21 42 18	7♋38 43	14 46 39	18 07.0	6 12.9	13 55.9	17 33.3	27 53.0	21 49.3	9 18.2	12 24.9	19 53.6	14 51.3
13 Sa	23 23 38	22 42 07	21 57 12	29 10 04	18 03.6	7 56.9	15 10.6	17 09.8	28 15.8	21 59.5	9 25.4	12 22.3	19 52.9	14 49.7
14 Su	23 27 34	23 41 55	6♌24 46	13♌40 46	17 57.3	9 37.6	16 25.3	16 46.4	28 38.6	22 09.9	9 32.6	12 19.8	19 52.2	14 48.1
15 M	23 31 31	24 41 41	20 57 23	28 13 50	17 48.3	11 14.3	17 40.1	16 23.3	29 01.3	22 20.3	9 39.8	12 17.2	19 51.5	14 46.6
16 Tu	23 35 27	25 41 24	5♍29 16	12♍42 51	17 37.3	12 46.7	18 54.8	16 00.3	29 24.0	22 30.9	9 46.9	12 14.7	19 50.7	14 45.0
17 W	23 39 24	26 41 05	19 53 42	27 00 58	17 25.2	14 14.3	20 09.4	15 37.7	29 46.6	22 41.5	9 54.0	12 12.2	19 49.9	14 43.4
18 Th	23 43 21	27 40 44	4♎03 56	11♎01 57	17 13.5	15 36.5	21 24.1	15 15.3	0♓09.2	22 52.2	10 01.1	12 09.6	19 49.1	14 41.9
19 F	23 47 17	28 40 21	17 54 31	24 41 15	17 03.2	16 53.0	22 38.8	14 53.3	0 31.7	23 03.1	10 08.2	12 07.2	19 48.2	14 40.4
20 Sa	23 51 14	29 39 57	1♏21 56	7♏56 33	16 55.4	18 03.3	23 53.4	14 31.7	0 54.2	23 14.0	10 15.3	12 04.7	19 47.4	14 38.8
21 Su	23 55 10	0♈39 30	14 25 09	20 47 58	16 50.2	19 07.1	25 08.1	14 10.5	1 16.6	23 25.0	10 22.3	12 02.2	19 46.5	14 37.3
22 M	23 59 07	1 39 02	27 05 20	3♐17 41	16 47.6	20 04.1	26 22.7	13 49.7	1 39.0	23 36.1	10 29.3	11 59.8	19 45.5	14 35.8
23 Tu	0 03 03	2 38 32	9♐25 31	15 29 26	16D 46.9	20 53.9	27 37.3	13 29.5	2 01.4	23 47.4	10 36.3	11 57.4	19 44.6	14 34.3
24 W	0 07 00	3 38 01	21 30 04	27 28 04	16R 47.1	21 36.4	28 51.9	13 09.7	2 23.7	23 58.7	10 43.3	11 55.0	19 43.6	14 32.8
25 Th	0 10 56	4 37 27	3♑24 06	9♑18 54	16 47.1	22 11.4	0♈06.5	12 50.5	2 45.9	24 10.1	10 50.2	11 52.6	19 42.6	14 31.4
26 F	0 14 53	5 36 52	15 13 07	21 07 28	16 45.9	22 38.8	1 21.1	12 31.9	3 08.1	24 21.6	10 57.1	11 50.3	19 41.5	14 29.9
27 Sa	0 18 50	6 36 15	27 02 33	2♒59 02	16 42.6	22 58.6	2 35.7	12 13.9	3 30.3	24 33.1	11 04.0	11 48.0	19 40.5	14 28.4
28 Su	0 22 46	7 35 36	8♒57 28	14 58 24	16 36.9	23 10.7	3 50.2	11 56.6	3 52.4	24 44.8	11 10.8	11 45.7	19 39.4	14 27.0
29 M	0 26 43	8 34 56	21 02 17	27 09 32	16 28.7	23R 15.3	5 04.8	11 39.9	4 14.4	24 56.5	11 17.6	11 43.4	19 38.3	14 25.6
30 Tu	0 30 39	9 34 13	3♓20 28	9♓35 21	16 18.4	23 12.5	6 19.3	11 23.8	4 36.4	25 08.3	11 24.4	11 41.2	19 37.1	14 24.2
31 W	0 34 36	10 33 29	15 54 20	22 17 31	16 06.8	23 02.7	7 33.8	11 08.5	4 58.3	25 20.2	11 31.1	11 38.9	19 36.0	14 22.8

April 1965 LONGITUDE

Day	Sid.Time	☉	0 hr ☽	Noon☽	True☊	☿	♀	♂	⚳	♃	♄	♅	♆	♇
1 Th	0 38 32	11♈32 42	28♓44 54	5♈16 23	15♊55.2	22♈46.2	8♈48.3	10♍53.9	5♓20.1	25♉32.2	11♓37.8	11♍36.8	19♏34.8	14♍21.4
2 F	0 42 29	12 31 54	11♈51 49	18 31 00	15R 44.5	22R 23.4	10 02.8	10R 40.0	5 41.9	25 44.2	11 44.5	11R 34.6	19R 33.6	14R 20.0
3 Sa	0 46 25	13 31 03	25 13 40	1♉59 30	15 35.8	21 54.9	11 17.3	10 26.9	6 03.6	25 56.4	11 51.1	11 32.5	19 32.4	14 18.6
4 Su	0 50 22	14 30 11	8♉48 13	15 39 29	15 29.7	21 21.4	12 31.7	10 14.6	6 25.3	26 08.6	11 57.7	11 30.4	19 31.1	14 17.3
5 M	0 54 18	15 29 16	22 32 59	29 28 26	15 26.3	20 43.5	13 46.2	10 03.0	6 46.9	26 20.8	12 04.2	11 28.4	19 29.9	14 16.0
6 Tu	0 58 15	16 28 19	6♊25 35	13♊24 14	15D 25.1	20 02.2	15 00.6	9 52.2	7 08.4	26 33.2	12 10.7	11 26.4	19 28.6	14 14.7
7 W	1 02 12	17 27 20	20 24 10	27 25 14	15 25.5	19 18.3	16 15.0	9 42.2	7 29.9	26 45.6	12 17.2	11 24.4	19 27.3	14 13.4
8 Th	1 06 08	18 26 18	4♋27 19	11♋30 17	15R 26.3	18 32.6	17 29.4	9 32.9	7 51.3	26 58.0	12 23.6	11 22.4	19 25.9	14 12.2
9 F	1 10 05	19 25 14	18 34 01	25 38 22	15 26.2	17 46.0	18 43.8	9 24.5	8 12.6	27 10.6	12 30.0	11 20.5	19 24.6	14 10.9
10 Sa	1 14 01	20 24 08	2♌43 11	9♌48 15	15 24.6	16 59.6	19 58.1	9 16.9	8 33.8	27 23.2	12 36.3	11 18.7	19 23.2	14 09.7
11 Su	1 17 58	21 23 00	16 53 20	23 58 06	15 20.7	16 14.1	21 12.4	9 10.0	8 55.0	27 35.8	12 42.6	11 16.9	19 21.9	14 08.5
12 M	1 21 54	22 21 49	1♍02 13	8♍05 16	15 14.7	15 30.3	22 26.8	9 04.0	9 16.1	27 48.5	12 48.8	11 15.1	19 20.5	14 07.3
13 Tu	1 25 51	23 20 36	15 06 47	22 06 17	15 07.0	14 49.0	23 41.0	8 58.7	9 37.1	28 01.3	12 55.0	11 13.3	19 19.0	14 06.1
14 W	1 29 47	24 19 20	29 03 18	5♎57 20	14 58.5	14 10.9	24 55.3	8 54.2	9 58.0	28 14.1	13 01.1	11 11.6	19 17.6	14 05.0
15 Th	1 33 44	25 18 03	12♎47 56	19 34 41	14 50.2	13 36.4	26 09.6	8 50.5	10 18.9	28 27.0	13 07.2	11 10.0	19 16.2	14 03.9
16 F	1 37 41	26 16 44	26 17 15	2♏55 21	14 42.9	13 06.1	27 23.8	8 47.6	10 39.7	28 39.9	13 13.2	11 08.3	19 14.7	14 02.8
17 Sa	1 41 37	27 15 22	9♏28 48	15 57 31	14 37.4	12 40.3	28 38.0	8 45.4	11 00.4	28 52.9	13 19.2	11 06.7	19 13.2	14 01.7
18 Su	1 45 34	28 13 59	22 21 31	28 40 54	14 34.0	12 19.2	29 52.2	8 43.9	11 21.0	29 06.0	13 25.1	11 05.2	19 11.8	14 00.7
19 M	1 49 30	29 12 35	4♐55 51	11♐06 40	14D 32.7	12 03.1	1♉06.4	8D 43.3	11 41.5	29 19.1	13 31.0	11 03.7	19 10.3	13 59.6
20 Tu	1 53 27	0♉11 08	17 13 41	23 17 21	14 33.0	11 52.1	2 20.6	8 43.3	12 02.0	29 32.2	13 36.8	11 02.3	19 08.7	13 58.6
21 W	1 57 23	1 09 40	29 18 08	5♑16 35	14 34.3	11D 46.1	3 34.8	8 44.1	12 22.4	29 45.4	13 42.5	11 00.9	19 07.2	13 57.7
22 Th	2 01 20	2 08 10	11♑13 15	17 08 46	14 35.8	11 45.3	4 48.9	8 45.6	12 42.6	29 58.6	13 48.2	10 59.5	19 05.7	13 56.7
23 F	2 05 16	3 06 39	23 03 44	28 58 48	14R 36.8	11 49.5	6 03.1	8 47.9	13 02.8	0♊11.9	13 53.9	10 58.2	19 04.1	13 55.8
24 Sa	2 09 13	4 05 06	4♒54 37	10♒51 49	14 36.6	11 58.6	7 17.2	8 50.8	13 22.9	0 25.2	13 59.5	10 56.9	19 02.6	13 54.9
25 Su	2 13 10	5 03 31	16 51 01	22 52 49	14 34.9	12 12.5	8 31.3	8 54.5	13 42.9	0 38.5	14 05.0	10 55.7	19 01.0	13 54.0
26 M	2 17 06	6 01 55	28 57 47	5♓06 26	14 31.5	12 31.1	9 45.4	8 58.8	14 02.9	0 51.9	14 10.4	10 54.6	18 59.5	13 53.1
27 Tu	2 21 03	7 00 17	11♓19 14	17 36 34	14 26.7	12 54.3	10 59.5	9 03.8	14 22.7	1 05.4	14 15.8	10 53.4	18 57.9	13 52.3
28 W	2 24 59	7 58 37	23 58 45	0♈26 00	14 21.0	13 21.8	12 13.6	9 09.5	14 42.4	1 18.9	14 21.2	10 52.4	18 56.3	13 51.5
29 Th	2 28 56	8 56 56	6♈58 26	13 36 07	14 15.0	13 53.5	13 27.6	9 15.9	15 02.0	1 32.4	14 26.4	10 51.3	18 54.7	13 50.7
30 F	2 32 52	9 55 13	20 18 55	27 06 41	14 09.5	14 29.2	14 41.6	9 22.9	15 21.6	1 45.9	14 31.6	10 50.4	18 53.1	13 50.0

Astro Data	Planet Ingress	Last Aspect	☽ Ingress	Last Aspect	☽ Ingress	☽ Phases & Eclipses	Astro Data
Dy Hr Mn	Dy Hr Mn	Dy Hr Mn	Dy Hr Mn	Dy Hr Mn	Dy Hr Mn	Dy Hr Mn	1 March 1965
☽0N 5 14:44	♀ ♓ 1 7:55	1 14:16 ♃ □	♓ 2 9:38	31 17:46 ♃ ⚹	♈ 1 2:19	3 9:56 ● 12♓37	Julian Day # 23801
☿0N 9 9:03	☿ ♈ 9 2:19	4 1:34 ♂ ☍	♈ 4 18:45	2 18:43 ☿ ☌	♉ 3 8:29	10 17:52 ☽ 19♊57	SVP 5♓45'02"
☽0S 18 11:25	⚳ ♓ 18 2:15	4 1:34 ♂ ☍	♉ 7 1:49	5 6:30 ♃ ☌	♊ 5 12:55	17 11:24 ○ 26♍40	GC 26♐21.2 ⚴ 3♒12.6
☉0N 20 20:04	☉ ♈ 20 20:05	8 15:42 ♃ ☌	♊ 9 7:14	6 22:49 ☿ ⚹	♋ 7 16:24	25 1:37 ☾ 4♑12	Eris 10♈31.3 ⚵ 24♑21.6
♀0N 28 0:32	♀ ♈ 25 9:54	10 17:52 ☉ □	♋ 11 11:03	9 14:39 ♃ ⚹	♌ 9 19:24		⚷ 17♓50.1 ⚶ 13♈50.9
☿ R 29 14:53		13 0:27 ☉ △	♌ 13 13:23	11 18:15 ♃ □	♍ 11 22:14	2 0:21 ● 12♈03	☽ Mean ☊ 18♊49.4
	♀ ♉ 18 14:31	15 2:10 ♃ □	♍ 15 14:55	13 22:22 ♃ △	♎ 14 1:38	9 0:40 ☽ 18♋57	
♄☍♅ 1 9:07	☉ ♉ 20 7:26	17 11:24 ☉ ☍	♎ 17 17:04	16 0:58 ♀ ☍	♏ 16 6:42	15 23:02 ○ 25♎45	1 April 1965
☽0N 1 21:49	♃ ♊ 22 14:32	18 20:48 ☿ ☍	♏ 19 21:32	18 12:49 ♃ ☍	♐ 18 14:31	23 21:07 ☾ 3♒29	Julian Day # 23832
☽0S 14 20:18		21 21:10 ♀ △	♐ 22 5:37	19 17:38 ♇ □	♑ 21 1:24		SVP 5♓44'59"
♂ D 19 21:56		24 15:09 ♀ □	♑ 24 17:07	22 15:57 ♆ ⚹	♒ 23 14:04		GC 26♐21.2 ⚴ 12♒50.5
☿ D 22 4:00		26 18:40 ♃ △	♒ 27 5:59	25 4:20 ♆ □	♓ 26 2:02		Eris 10♈51.7 ⚵ 4♒06.1
♄☍♇ 23 18:58		29 7:36 ♃ □	♓ 29 17:32	27 14:34 ♆ △	♈ 28 11:12		⚷ 19♓43.1 ⚶ 27♈37.3
☽0N 29 6:55				29 12:33 ☿ ☌	♉ 30 17:04		☽ Mean ☊ 17♊10.9

LONGITUDE — May 1965

Day	Sid.Time	☉	0 hr ☽	Noon ☽	True ☊	☿	♀	♂	⚴	♃	♄	♅	♆	♇
1 Sa	2 36 49	10♉53 28	3♉59 07	10♉55 49	14♊05.1	15♈08.8	15♉55.7	9♍30.5	15♓41.0	1♊59.5	14♓36.7	10♍49.4	18♏51.5	13♍49.3
2 Su	2 40 45	11 51 42	17 56 21	25 00 10	14R 02.2	15 52.1	17 09.7	9 38.8	16 00.3	2 13.1	14 41.8	10R 48.6	18R 49.8	13R 48.6
3 M	2 44 42	12 49 54	2♊06 45	9♊15 28	14D 01.0	16 39.0	18 23.7	9 47.7	16 19.5	2 26.8	14 46.8	10 47.7	18 48.2	13 47.9
4 Tu	2 48 39	13 48 05	16 25 45	23 37 01	14 01.2	17 29.3	19 37.7	9 57.2	16 38.6	2 40.4	14 51.7	10 47.0	18 46.6	13 47.3
5 W	2 52 35	14 46 13	0♋48 43	8♋00 22	14 02.3	18 22.8	20 51.6	10 07.3	16 57.6	2 54.1	14 56.6	10 46.3	18 45.0	13 46.7
6 Th	2 56 32	15 44 19	15 11 29	22 21 40	14 03.8	19 19.5	22 05.6	10 18.1	17 16.4	3 07.9	15 01.4	10 45.6	18 43.4	13 46.1
7 F	3 00 28	16 42 24	29 30 33	6♌37 51	14R 04.9	20 19.3	23 19.5	10 29.3	17 35.2	3 21.6	15 06.1	10 45.0	18 41.7	13 45.5
8 Sa	3 04 25	17 40 26	13♌43 18	20 46 39	14 05.2	21 21.9	24 33.4	10 41.2	17 53.8	3 35.4	15 10.7	10 44.4	18 40.1	13 45.0
9 Su	3 08 21	18 38 27	27 47 43	4♍46 20	14 04.3	22 27.4	25 47.3	10 53.6	18 12.4	3 49.2	15 15.3	10 43.9	18 38.5	13 44.5
10 M	3 12 18	19 36 25	11♍42 20	18 35 33	14 02.4	23 35.7	27 01.2	11 06.5	18 30.8	4 03.0	15 19.8	10 43.4	18 36.8	13 44.1
11 Tu	3 16 14	20 34 22	25 25 52	2♎13 09	13 59.5	24 46.6	28 15.0	11 20.0	18 49.0	4 16.9	15 24.2	10 43.0	18 35.2	13 43.6
12 W	3 20 11	21 32 17	8♎57 16	15 38 06	13 56.2	26 00.1	29 28.8	11 34.0	19 07.2	4 30.7	15 28.5	10 42.7	18 33.6	13 43.2
13 Th	3 24 08	22 30 10	22 15 32	28 49 31	13 53.0	27 16.1	0♊42.7	11 48.5	19 25.2	4 44.6	15 32.8	10 42.4	18 31.9	13 42.9
14 F	3 28 04	23 28 02	5♏19 57	11♏46 48	13 50.3	28 34.6	1 56.5	12 03.5	19 43.1	4 58.5	15 37.0	10 42.1	18 30.3	13 42.5
15 Sa	3 32 01	24 25 52	18 10 04	24 29 46	13 48.3	29 55.5	3 10.2	12 19.0	20 00.9	5 12.4	15 41.1	10 41.9	18 28.7	13 42.2
16 Su	3 35 57	25 23 40	0♐45 59	6♐58 50	13D 47.4	1♉18.8	4 24.0	12 34.9	20 18.6	5 26.3	15 45.1	10 41.8	18 27.1	13 41.9
17 M	3 39 54	26 21 28	13 08 27	19 15 04	13 47.3	2 44.4	5 37.8	12 51.3	20 36.1	5 40.3	15 49.0	10 41.7	18 25.5	13 41.7
18 Tu	3 43 50	27 19 14	25 18 55	1♑20 19	13 48.0	4 12.4	6 51.5	13 08.2	20 53.5	5 54.2	15 52.9	10D 41.7	18 23.9	13 41.5
19 W	3 47 47	28 16 59	7♑19 36	13 17 09	13 49.2	5 42.6	8 05.3	13 25.5	21 10.7	6 08.2	15 56.7	10 41.7	18 22.3	13 41.3
20 Th	3 51 43	29 14 42	19 13 24	25 08 49	13 50.5	7 15.2	9 19.0	13 43.3	21 27.8	6 22.2	16 00.4	10 41.8	18 20.7	13 41.1
21 F	3 55 40	0♊12 25	1♒03 53	6♒59 09	13 51.8	8 50.0	10 32.7	14 01.5	21 44.8	6 36.2	16 04.0	10 41.9	18 19.1	13 41.0
22 Sa	3 59 37	1 10 06	12 55 09	18 52 28	13 52.6	10 27.1	11 46.4	14 20.1	22 01.6	6 50.2	16 07.5	10 42.1	18 17.5	13 40.9
23 Su	4 03 33	2 07 46	24 51 40	0♓53 19	13R 52.9	12 06.4	13 00.0	14 39.1	22 18.3	7 04.2	16 11.0	10 42.3	18 15.9	13 40.8
24 M	4 07 30	3 05 26	6♓58 02	13 06 21	13 52.7	13 48.0	14 13.7	14 58.5	22 34.9	7 18.2	16 14.4	10 42.6	18 14.3	13D 40.8
25 Tu	4 11 26	4 03 04	19 18 49	25 35 55	13 52.1	15 31.8	15 27.4	15 18.4	22 51.2	7 32.2	16 17.6	10 42.9	18 12.8	13 40.8
26 W	4 15 23	5 00 41	1♈58 08	8♈25 49	13 51.2	17 17.9	16 41.0	15 38.6	23 07.5	7 46.2	16 20.8	10 43.3	18 11.2	13 40.8
27 Th	4 19 19	5 58 18	14 59 17	21 38 44	13 50.2	19 06.2	17 54.6	15 59.2	23 23.5	8 00.2	16 23.9	10 43.8	18 09.7	13 40.8
28 F	4 23 16	6 55 53	28 24 17	5♉15 55	13 49.3	20 56.8	19 08.3	16 20.2	23 39.4	8 14.3	16 26.9	10 44.3	18 08.1	13 40.9
29 Sa	4 27 12	7 53 27	12♉13 27	19 16 38	13 48.7	22 49.5	20 21.9	16 41.5	23 55.2	8 28.3	16 29.8	10 44.8	18 06.6	13 41.1
30 Su	4 31 09	8 51 01	26 25 01	3♊38 03	13D 48.4	24 44.4	21 35.5	17 03.3	24 10.8	8 42.3	16 32.7	10 45.5	18 05.1	13 41.2
31 M	4 35 06	9 48 34	10♊55 04	18 15 18	13 48.3	26 41.4	22 49.1	17 25.4	24 26.2	8 56.3	16 35.4	10 46.1	18 03.6	13 41.4

LONGITUDE — June 1965

Day	Sid.Time	☉	0 hr ☽	Noon ☽	True ☊	☿	♀	♂	⚴	♃	♄	♅	♆	♇
1 Tu	4 39 02	10♊46 05	25♊37 55	3♋01 59	13♊48.4	28♉40.6	24♊02.6	17♍47.8	24♓41.4	9♊10.3	16♓38.1	10♍46.8	18♏02.1	13♍41.6
2 W	4 42 59	11 43 36	10♋26 37	17 50 54	13 48.6	0♊41.7	25 16.2	18 10.6	24 56.5	9 24.4	16 40.6	10 47.6	18R 00.7	13 41.9
3 Th	4 46 55	12 41 05	25 13 58	2♌35 03	13 48.8	2 44.7	26 29.7	18 33.7	25 11.4	9 38.4	16 43.1	10 48.4	17 59.2	13 42.1
4 F	4 50 52	13 38 33	9♌53 25	17 08 29	13R 48.9	4 49.6	27 43.3	18 57.2	25 26.1	9 52.4	16 45.4	10 49.3	17 57.8	13 42.4
5 Sa	4 54 48	14 35 59	24 19 45	1♍26 51	13D 48.8	6 56.0	28 56.8	19 20.9	25 40.6	10 06.4	16 47.7	10 50.2	17 56.4	13 42.8
6 Su	4 58 45	15 33 25	8♍29 30	15 27 32	13 48.8	9 04.0	0♋10.3	19 45.0	25 55.0	10 20.3	16 49.9	10 51.2	17 55.0	13 43.1
7 M	5 02 42	16 30 49	22 20 54	29 09 34	13 48.9	11 13.2	1 23.7	20 09.4	26 09.2	10 34.3	16 52.0	10 52.2	17 53.6	13 43.5
8 Tu	5 06 38	17 28 12	5♎53 37	12♎33 11	13 49.1	13 23.5	2 37.2	20 34.1	26 23.1	10 48.3	16 54.0	10 53.3	17 52.2	13 44.0
9 W	5 10 35	18 25 34	19 08 25	25 39 30	13 49.5	15 34.6	3 50.6	20 59.1	26 36.9	11 02.2	16 55.9	10 54.5	17 50.8	13 44.4
10 Th	5 14 31	19 22 54	2♏06 39	8♏30 04	13 50.0	17 46.3	5 04.1	21 24.4	26 50.5	11 16.1	16 57.6	10 55.6	17 49.5	13 44.9
11 F	5 18 28	20 20 14	14 50 00	21 06 38	13 50.5	19 58.3	6 17.5	21 50.0	27 03.9	11 30.0	16 59.3	10 56.9	17 48.2	13 45.4
12 Sa	5 22 24	21 17 34	27 20 13	3♐30 57	13R 51.0	22 10.4	7 30.9	22 15.8	27 17.1	11 43.9	17 01.0	10 58.2	17 46.9	13 46.0
13 Su	5 26 21	22 14 52	9♐39 03	15 44 44	13 51.1	24 22.2	8 44.3	22 42.0	27 30.1	11 57.8	17 02.5	10 59.5	17 45.6	13 46.6
14 M	5 30 17	23 12 10	21 48 14	27 49 45	13 50.8	26 33.4	9 57.6	23 08.4	27 42.8	12 11.7	17 03.9	11 00.9	17 44.3	13 47.2
15 Tu	5 34 14	24 09 27	3♑49 32	9♑47 48	13 50.0	28 44.0	11 11.0	23 35.0	27 55.4	12 25.5	17 05.2	11 02.3	17 43.1	13 47.8
16 W	5 38 11	25 06 44	15 44 51	21 40 55	13 48.7	0♋53.5	12 24.3	24 01.9	28 07.8	12 39.4	17 06.4	11 03.8	17 41.9	13 48.5
17 Th	5 42 07	26 04 00	27 36 21	3♒31 27	13 47.1	3 01.7	13 37.6	24 29.1	28 19.9	12 53.2	17 07.5	11 05.3	17 40.7	13 49.2
18 F	5 46 04	27 01 16	9♒26 34	15 22 07	13 45.2	5 08.6	14 50.9	24 56.5	28 31.9	13 06.9	17 08.5	11 06.9	17 39.5	13 50.0
19 Sa	5 50 00	27 58 31	21 18 28	27 16 06	13 43.4	7 13.9	16 04.2	25 24.1	28 43.6	13 20.7	17 09.5	11 08.5	17 38.3	13 50.7
20 Su	5 53 57	28 55 46	3♓15 27	9♓17 02	13 41.9	9 17.5	17 17.5	25 52.0	28 55.1	13 34.4	17 10.3	11 10.2	17 37.2	13 51.5
21 M	5 57 53	29 53 01	15 21 20	21 28 53	13D 41.0	11 19.3	18 30.8	26 20.2	29 06.3	13 48.1	17 11.0	11 11.9	17 36.1	13 52.3
22 Tu	6 01 50	0♋50 16	27 40 13	3♈55 50	13 40.8	13 19.1	19 44.0	26 48.6	29 17.3	14 01.8	17 11.6	11 13.7	17 35.0	13 53.2
23 W	6 05 46	1 47 30	10♈16 16	16 42 00	13 41.4	15 17.0	20 57.3	27 17.2	29 28.1	14 15.5	17 12.1	11 15.5	17 33.9	13 54.0
24 Th	6 09 43	2 44 45	23 13 27	29 51 00	13 42.5	17 12.8	22 10.5	27 46.0	29 38.6	14 29.1	17 12.6	11 17.4	17 32.9	13 54.9
25 F	6 13 40	3 41 59	6♉34 57	13♉25 30	13 43.8	19 06.5	23 23.7	28 15.1	29 48.9	14 42.7	17 12.9	11 19.3	17 31.9	13 55.9
26 Sa	6 17 36	4 39 14	20 22 42	27 26 30	13 45.0	20 58.1	24 36.9	28 44.3	29 59.0	14 56.3	17 13.1	11 21.3	17 30.9	13 56.8
27 Su	6 21 33	5 36 28	4♊36 41	11♊52 49	13R 45.6	22 47.6	25 50.1	29 13.8	0♈08.8	15 09.8	17R 13.2	11 23.3	17 29.9	13 57.8
28 M	6 25 29	6 33 43	19 14 21	26 40 32	13 45.2	24 34.9	27 03.3	29 43.6	0 18.3	15 23.3	17 13.3	11 25.3	17 29.0	13 58.9
29 Tu	6 29 26	7 30 57	4♋10 26	11♋43 02	13 43.7	26 20.0	28 16.4	0♎13.5	0 27.6	15 36.8	17 13.2	11 27.4	17 28.0	13 59.9
30 W	6 33 22	8 28 11	19 17 11	26 51 40	13 41.1	28 03.0	29 29.6	0 43.7	0 36.6	15 50.2	17 13.0	11 29.6	17 27.2	14 01.0

Astro Data

	Dy Hr Mn
☽0S	12 3:25
♅D	18 14:32
♇D	25 5:21
☽0N	26 16:36
☽0S	8 9:06
♃□♅	8 21:29
♃□♇	21 19:49
☽0N	23 1:10
♄R	28 5:32
♂0S	30 13:14

Planet Ingress

	Dy Hr Mn
♀ ♊	12 22:08
☿ ♉	15 13:19
☉ ♊	21 6:50
☿ ♊	2 3:47
♀ ♋	6 8:39
☿ ♋	16 2:04
☉ ♋	21 14:56
⚴ ♈	26 14:28
♂ ♎	29 1:12
♀ ♌	30 21:59

Last Aspect / ☽ Ingress (May)

Last Aspect Dy Hr Mn		☽ Ingress Dy Hr Mn
2 1:32	♆ ☍	♊ 2 20:26
4 1:07	☿ ⚹	♋ 4 22:39
6 11:31	♀ ⚹	♌ 7 0:50
8 19:04	♀ □	♍ 9 3:47
11 4:16	♀ △	♎ 11 8:04
13 8:50	☿ ☍	♏ 13 14:10
15 11:52	☉ ☍	♐ 15 22:32
17 5:13	♄ □	♑ 18 9:20
20 21:03	☉ △	♒ 20 21:50
22 10:50	♆ □	♓ 23 10:14
24 21:55	♆ △	♈ 25 20:19
27 4:36	♀ ⚹	♉ 28 2:48
29 18:54	☿ ☌	♊ 30 5:58

Last Aspect / ☽ Ingress (June)

Last Aspect Dy Hr Mn		☽ Ingress Dy Hr Mn
31 20:06	♀ ☌	♋ 1 7:05
2 12:33	♂ ⚹	♌ 3 7:46
5 7:22	♀ ⚹	♍ 5 9:33
6 19:41	♂ ☌	♎ 7 13:29
8 21:39	☉ △	♏ 9 20:04
11 13:26	♂ ⚹	♐ 12 5:10
14 8:54	☿ ☍	♑ 14 16:20
16 16:57	♂ △	♒ 17 4:51
19 13:33	☉ △	♓ 19 17:29
21 21:48	♂ ☍	♈ 22 4:29
23 20:39	♀ □	♉ 24 12:16
26 14:16	♂ △	♊ 26 16:18
28 17:04	♂ □	♋ 28 17:20
30 16:32	♀ ☌	♌ 30 16:59

☽ Phases & Eclipses

Dy Hr Mn	
1 11:56	● 10♉53
8 6:20	☽ 17♌27
15 11:52	○ 24♏26
23 14:40	☾ 2♓14
30 21:12	● 9♊13
30 21:16:55	● T 05'15"
6 12:11	☽ 15♍34
14 1:59	○ 22♐48
14 1:49	● P 0.177
22 5:36	☾ 0♈35
29 4:52	● 7♋14

Astro Data

1 May 1965
Julian Day # 23862
SVP 5♓44'56"
GC 26♐21.3 ⚳ 19♒52.6
Eris 11♈11.5 ⚵ 11♒35.7
⚷ 21♓16.6 ⚶ 11♉03.1
☽ Mean ☊ 15♊35.6

1 June 1965
Julian Day # 23893
SVP 5♓44'51"
GC 26♐21.4 ⚳ 23♒28.6
Eris 11♈27.1 ⚵ 15♒56.7
⚷ 22♓18.4 ⚶ 24♉44.0
☽ Mean ☊ 13♊57.1

July 1965 — LONGITUDE

Day	Sid.Time	☉	0 hr ☽	Noon ☽	True ☊	☿	♀	♂	⚷	♃	♄	♅	♆	♇
1 Th	6 37 19	9♋25 25	4♌25 16	11♌56 50	13♊37.8	29♋43.8	0♌42.7	1♎14.0	0♈45.4	16♊03.6	17♓12.7	11♍31.7	17♏26.3	14♍02.1
2 F	6 41 15	10 22 38	19 25 16	26 49 35	13R 34.3	1♌22.4	1 55.8	1 44.6	0 53.8	16 16.9	17R 12.3	11 34.0	17R 25.5	14 03.2
3 Sa	6 45 12	11 19 52	4♍09 01	11♍22 54	13 31.3	2 58.8	3 08.9	2 15.3	1 02.0	16 30.2	17 11.9	11 36.2	17 24.7	14 04.4
4 Su	6 49 09	12 17 04	18 30 47	25 32 25	13 29.1	4 33.0	4 22.0	2 46.3	1 09.9	16 43.5	17 11.3	11 38.5	17 23.9	14 05.5
5 M	6 53 05	13 14 17	2♎27 39	9♎16 33	13D 28.1	6 05.0	5 35.0	3 17.4	1 17.6	16 56.7	17 10.6	11 40.9	17 23.1	14 06.8
6 Tu	6 57 02	14 11 29	15 59 16	22 36 03	13 28.3	7 34.7	6 48.0	3 48.8	1 24.9	17 09.9	17 09.8	11 43.3	17 22.4	14 08.0
7 W	7 00 58	15 08 41	29 07 15	5♏33 15	13 29.4	9 02.2	8 01.0	4 20.3	1 32.0	17 23.0	17 09.0	11 45.7	17 21.7	14 09.2
8 Th	7 04 55	16 05 53	11♏54 29	18 11 23	13 31.0	10 27.5	9 14.0	4 52.0	1 38.8	17 36.1	17 08.0	11 48.2	17 21.0	14 10.5
9 F	7 08 51	17 03 05	24 24 27	0♐34 05	13 32.5	11 50.4	10 27.0	5 23.8	1 45.3	17 49.1	17 06.9	11 50.7	17 20.4	14 11.8
10 Sa	7 12 48	18 00 16	6♐40 44	12 44 49	13R 33.2	13 11.0	11 39.9	5 55.9	1 51.5	18 02.1	17 05.8	11 53.2	17 19.8	14 13.2
11 Su	7 16 44	18 57 28	18 46 43	24 46 47	13 32.5	14 29.2	12 52.8	6 28.1	1 57.4	18 15.0	17 04.5	11 55.8	17 19.2	14 14.5
12 M	7 20 41	19 54 40	0♑45 22	6♑42 45	13 30.2	15 45.0	14 05.7	7 00.5	2 02.9	18 27.9	17 03.1	11 58.5	17 18.6	14 15.9
13 Tu	7 24 38	20 51 53	12 39 13	18 35 03	13 26.2	16 58.4	15 18.6	7 33.1	2 08.2	18 40.8	17 01.7	12 01.1	17 18.1	14 17.3
14 W	7 28 34	21 49 05	24 30 28	0♒25 42	13 20.6	18 09.1	16 31.5	8 05.8	2 13.2	18 53.5	17 00.2	12 03.8	17 17.6	14 18.7
15 Th	7 32 31	22 46 18	6♒21 01	12 16 36	13 13.8	19 17.3	17 44.3	8 38.7	2 17.9	19 06.3	16 58.5	12 06.6	17 17.2	14 20.2
16 F	7 36 27	23 43 31	18 12 44	24 09 38	13 06.4	20 22.7	18 57.1	9 11.8	2 22.2	19 18.9	16 56.8	12 09.3	17 16.7	14 21.7
17 Sa	7 40 24	24 40 45	0♓07 36	6♓06 54	12 59.3	21 25.4	20 09.9	9 45.0	2 26.2	19 31.6	16 55.0	12 12.1	17 16.3	14 23.2
18 Su	7 44 20	25 37 59	12 07 52	18 10 50	12 53.0	22 25.2	21 22.6	10 18.4	2 29.9	19 44.1	16 53.1	12 15.0	17 16.0	14 24.7
19 M	7 48 17	26 35 14	24 16 11	0♈24 20	12 48.1	23 22.0	22 35.4	10 51.9	2 33.3	19 56.6	16 51.0	12 17.9	17 15.6	14 26.2
20 Tu	7 52 13	27 32 29	6♈35 43	12 50 46	12 45.1	24 15.7	23 48.1	11 25.6	2 36.3	20 09.0	16 48.9	12 20.8	17 15.3	14 27.8
21 W	7 56 10	28 29 46	19 09 58	25 33 47	12D 44.0	25 06.2	25 00.8	11 59.4	2 39.0	20 21.4	16 46.8	12 23.7	17 15.0	14 29.4
22 Th	8 00 07	29 27 03	2♉02 42	8♉37 09	12 44.3	25 53.3	26 13.5	12 33.4	2 41.4	20 33.7	16 44.5	12 26.7	17 14.8	14 31.0
23 F	8 04 03	0♌24 21	15 17 33	22 04 14	12 45.3	26 36.9	27 26.1	13 07.6	2 43.4	20 45.9	16 42.1	12 29.7	17 14.6	14 32.6
24 Sa	8 08 00	1 21 40	28 57 28	5♊57 24	12R 46.3	27 16.9	28 38.7	13 41.9	2 45.1	20 58.1	16 39.7	12 32.7	17 14.4	14 34.2
25 Su	8 11 56	2 19 00	13♊04 01	20 17 11	12 46.2	27 53.0	29 51.4	14 16.3	2 46.4	21 10.2	16 37.2	12 35.8	17 14.2	14 35.9
26 M	8 15 53	3 16 21	27 36 32	5♋01 33	12 44.4	28 25.2	1♍03.9	14 50.9	2 47.4	21 22.3	16 34.5	12 38.9	17 14.1	14 37.6
27 Tu	8 19 49	4 13 43	12♋31 27	20 05 17	12 40.4	28 53.2	2 16.5	15 25.7	2 48.0	21 34.2	16 31.8	12 42.0	17 14.0	14 39.3
28 W	8 23 46	5 11 05	27 41 56	5♌20 08	12 34.3	29 16.9	3 29.1	16 00.6	2R 48.3	21 46.1	16 29.1	12 45.2	17 14.0	14 41.0
29 Th	8 27 43	6 08 28	12♌58 30	20 35 41	12 26.8	29 36.0	4 41.6	16 35.6	2 48.2	21 57.9	16 26.2	12 48.4	17D 13.9	14 42.8
30 F	8 31 39	7 05 52	28 10 18	5♍41 06	12 18.7	29 50.5	5 54.1	17 10.8	2 47.7	22 09.7	16 23.3	12 51.6	17 13.9	14 44.5
31 Sa	8 35 36	8 03 17	13♍07 00	20 27 04	12 11.1	0♍00.2	7 06.5	17 46.2	2 46.9	22 21.4	16 20.2	12 54.8	17 14.0	14 46.3

August 1965 — LONGITUDE

Day	Sid.Time	☉	0 hr ☽	Noon ☽	True ☊	☿	♀	♂	⚷	♃	♄	♅	♆	♇
1 Su	8 39 32	9♌00 42	27♍40 37	4♎47 08	12♊05.0	0♍04.8	8♍18.9	18♎21.6	2♈45.8	22♊32.9	16♓17.1	12♍58.1	17♏14.1	14♍48.1
2 M	8 43 29	9 58 08	11♎46 23	18 38 18	12R 00.9	0R 04.4	9 31.3	18 57.2	2R 44.3	22 44.4	16R 14.0	13 01.4	17 14.2	14 49.9
3 Tu	8 47 25	10 55 34	25 22 59	2♏00 42	11D 58.9	29♌58.7	10 43.7	19 33.0	2 42.4	22 55.9	16 10.7	13 04.7	17 14.3	14 51.7
4 W	8 51 22	11 53 01	8♏31 52	14 56 56	11 58.6	29 47.8	11 56.0	20 08.8	2 40.1	23 07.2	16 07.4	13 08.1	17 14.5	14 53.6
5 Th	8 55 18	12 50 29	21 16 26	27 30 58	11 59.2	29 31.6	13 08.3	20 44.8	2 37.5	23 18.4	16 04.0	13 11.4	17 14.7	14 55.4
6 F	8 59 15	13 47 57	3♐41 07	9♐47 30	11R 59.7	29 10.3	14 20.6	21 21.0	2 34.6	23 29.6	16 00.6	13 14.8	17 14.9	14 57.3
7 Sa	9 03 12	14 45 26	15 50 42	21 51 18	11 59.3	28 43.8	15 32.8	21 57.2	2 31.2	23 40.7	15 57.1	13 18.2	17 15.2	14 59.2
8 Su	9 07 08	15 42 57	27 49 50	3♑46 48	11 56.9	28 12.5	16 45.0	22 33.6	2 27.5	23 51.7	15 53.5	13 21.7	17 15.5	15 01.1
9 M	9 11 05	16 40 28	9♑42 39	15 37 50	11 52.1	27 36.7	17 57.2	23 10.1	2 23.5	24 02.6	15 49.8	13 25.1	17 15.8	15 03.0
10 Tu	9 15 01	17 38 00	21 32 42	27 27 36	11 44.8	26 56.8	19 09.3	23 46.7	2 19.1	24 13.4	15 46.1	13 28.6	17 16.2	15 05.0
11 W	9 18 58	18 35 33	3♒22 48	9♒18 35	11 35.0	26 13.4	20 21.4	24 23.5	2 14.3	24 24.1	15 42.4	13 32.1	17 16.6	15 06.9
12 Th	9 22 54	19 33 07	15 15 09	21 12 42	11 23.4	25 27.0	21 33.4	25 00.4	2 09.2	24 34.7	15 38.5	13 35.6	17 17.0	15 08.9
13 F	9 26 51	20 30 42	27 11 25	3♓11 27	11 10.9	24 38.4	22 45.4	25 37.3	2 03.8	24 45.2	15 34.7	13 39.1	17 17.5	15 10.8
14 Sa	9 30 47	21 28 19	9♓12 58	15 16 08	10 58.6	23 48.5	23 57.4	26 14.5	1 58.0	24 55.6	15 30.7	13 42.7	17 18.0	15 12.8
15 Su	9 34 44	22 25 56	21 21 07	27 28 06	10 47.5	22 58.2	25 09.3	26 51.7	1 51.8	25 06.0	15 26.7	13 46.3	17 18.5	15 14.8
16 M	9 38 40	23 23 36	3♈37 18	9♈48 58	10 38.5	22 08.4	26 21.2	27 29.0	1 45.3	25 16.2	15 22.7	13 49.8	17 19.0	15 16.8
17 Tu	9 42 37	24 21 16	16 03 23	22 20 50	10 32.0	21 20.1	27 33.1	28 06.5	1 38.4	25 26.3	15 18.6	13 53.4	17 19.6	15 18.8
18 W	9 46 34	25 18 59	28 41 40	5♉06 16	10 28.3	20 34.4	28 44.9	28 44.1	1 31.2	25 36.3	15 14.5	13 57.0	17 20.2	15 20.8
19 Th	9 50 30	26 16 42	11♉34 59	18 08 15	10D 26.8	19 52.2	29 56.7	29 21.8	1 23.7	25 46.2	15 10.3	14 00.7	17 20.9	15 22.9
20 F	9 54 27	27 14 28	24 46 25	1♊29 52	10R 26.6	19 14.3	1♎08.4	29 59.6	1 15.8	25 56.0	15 06.1	14 04.3	17 21.6	15 24.9
21 Sa	9 58 23	28 12 16	8♊18 55	15 13 49	10 26.6	18 41.7	2 20.2	0♏37.5	1 07.6	26 05.7	15 01.8	14 08.0	17 22.3	15 27.0
22 Su	10 02 20	29 10 05	22 14 42	29 21 38	10 25.6	18 15.1	3 31.8	1 15.6	0 59.1	26 15.3	14 57.5	14 11.7	17 23.0	15 29.0
23 M	10 06 16	0♍07 56	6♋34 27	13♋52 51	10 22.6	17 55.1	4 43.5	1 53.7	0 50.3	26 24.7	14 53.2	14 15.3	17 23.8	15 31.1
24 Tu	10 10 13	1 05 48	21 16 22	28 44 16	10 16.9	17 42.2	5 55.1	2 32.0	0 41.2	26 34.1	14 48.8	14 19.0	17 24.6	15 33.2
25 W	10 14 10	2 03 42	6♌15 40	13♌49 29	10 08.6	17D 36.9	7 06.6	3 10.4	0 31.7	26 43.3	14 44.4	14 22.7	17 25.5	15 35.3
26 Th	10 18 06	3 01 38	21 24 30	28 59 24	9 58.3	17 39.4	8 18.2	3 48.9	0 22.0	26 52.4	14 40.0	14 26.5	17 26.3	15 37.4
27 F	10 22 03	3 59 35	6♍32 51	14♍03 33	9 47.1	17 50.0	9 29.6	4 27.5	0 12.0	27 01.4	14 35.5	14 30.2	17 27.2	15 39.5
28 Sa	10 25 59	4 57 34	21 30 14	28 51 52	9 36.4	18 08.6	10 41.1	5 06.3	0 01.7	27 10.3	14 31.0	14 33.9	17 28.2	15 41.6
29 Su	10 29 56	5 55 34	6♎07 32	13♎16 33	9 27.4	18 35.5	11 52.5	5 45.1	29♓51.1	27 19.0	14 26.5	14 37.7	17 29.1	15 43.7
30 M	10 33 52	6 53 35	20 18 29	27 13 03	9 20.8	19 10.4	13 03.8	6 24.0	29 40.2	27 27.6	14 22.0	14 41.4	17 30.1	15 45.8
31 Tu	10 37 49	7 51 38	4♏00 15	10♏40 13	9 16.7	19 53.1	14 15.1	7 03.1	29 29.2	27 36.1	14 17.5	14 45.2	17 31.1	15 47.9

Astro Data

	Dy Hr Mn
☽0S	5 14:43
♃□♄	6 11:55
♃⊼♆	7 9:42
☽0N	20 7:41
⚷R	28 18:13
♆D	29 17:40
☽0S	1 21:41
☿R	1 21:56
☽0N	16 12:42
♄☍♇	17 11:11
♀0S	20 23:56
☿D	25 16:25
♄☍♅	28 3:36
☽0S	29 6:33

Planet Ingress

	Dy Hr Mn
☿ ♌	1 15:55
☉ ♌	23 1:48
♀ ♍	25 14:51
☿ ♍	31 11:24
☿ ♌R	3 8:09
♀ ♎	19 13:06
♂ ♏	20 12:16
☉ ♍	23 8:43
⚷ ♓R	28 15:47

Last Aspect / ☽ Ingress (July)

Last Aspect Dy Hr Mn		☽ Ingress Dy Hr Mn
1 20:48 ♆ □	♍	2 17:11
3 22:07 ♆ ⚹	♎	4 19:43
6 1:57 ♃ △	♏	7 1:38
8 10:23 ♆ ☌	♐	9 10:53
10 22:43 ♃ ☍	♑	11 22:29
13 17:01 ☉ ☍	♒	14 11:08
16 3:37 ☿ ☍	♓	16 23:45
19 3:55 ☉ △	♈	19 11:13
21 17:53 ☉ □	♉	21 20:14
23 22:16 ♀ □	♊	24 1:48
26 0:56 ☿ ⚹	♋	26 3:53
27 7:29 ♆ △	♌	28 3:37
30 2:31 ☿ ☌	♍	30 2:55

Last Aspect / ☽ Ingress (August)

Last Aspect Dy Hr Mn		☽ Ingress Dy Hr Mn
31 15:11 ♃ □	♎	1 3:54
3 8:20 ☿ ⚹	♏	3 8:20
5 15:48 ☿ □	♐	5 16:49
8 1:15 ☿ △	♑	8 4:22
10 4:08 ♂ □	♒	10 17:09
12 20:02 ♂ △	♓	13 5:37
15 7:18 ♃ □	♈	15 16:57
17 23:28 ♂ ☍	♉	18 2:27
20 3:50 ☉ □	♊	20 9:20
22 11:39 ☉ ⚹	♋	22 13:04
23 17:44 ♆ △	♌	24 14:01
26 8:37 ♃ ⚹	♍	26 13:36
28 9:12 ♃ □	♎	28 13:52
30 12:26 ♃ △	♏	30 16:54

☽ Phases & Eclipses

Dy Hr Mn	
5 19:36	☽ 13♎32
13 17:01	○ 21♑04
21 17:53	☾ 28♈44
28 11:45	● 5♌10
4 5:47	☽ 11♏38
12 8:22	○ 19♒24
20 3:50	☾ 26♉55
26 18:50	● 3♍18

Astro Data

1 July 1965
Julian Day # 23923
SVP 5♓44'45"
GC 26♐21.4 ⚳ 21♒57.9R
Eris 11♈33.9 ⚵ 15♒11.9R
⚷ 22♓32.7R ⚶ 7♊31.1
☽ Mean ☊ 12♊21.8

1 August 1965
Julian Day # 23954
SVP 5♓44'40"
GC 26♐21.5 ⚳ 15♒20.5R
Eris 11♈31.0R ⚵ 9♒09.0R
⚷ 21♓58.4R ⚶ 19♊55.1
☽ Mean ☊ 10♊43.3

LONGITUDE — September 1965

Day	Sid.Time	☉	0 hr ☽	Noon ☽	True ☊	☿	♀	♂	⚳	♃	♄	♅	♆	♇
1 W	10 41 45	8♍49 43	17♏13 14	23♏39 43	9♊14.9	20♌43.6	15♎26.3	7♏42.3	29♓17.9	27♊44.5	14♓12.9	14♍48.9	17♏32.2	15♍50.1
2 Th	10 45 42	9 47 49	0♐00 12	6♐15 16	9R 14.5	21 41.3	16 37.5	8 21.5	29R 06.3	27 52.7	14R 08.3	14 52.7	17 33.2	15 52.2
3 F	10 49 38	10 45 56	12 25 32	18 31 41	9 14.5	22 46.1	17 48.7	9 00.9	28 54.6	28 00.8	14 03.8	14 56.4	17 34.4	15 54.3
4 Sa	10 53 35	11 44 04	24 34 23	0♑34 16	9 13.5	23 57.5	18 59.8	9 40.4	28 42.6	28 08.7	13 59.2	15 00.2	17 35.5	15 56.5
5 Su	10 57 32	12 42 14	6♑31 59	12 28 11	9 10.8	25 15.0	20 10.8	10 19.9	28 30.5	28 16.6	13 54.6	15 04.0	17 36.7	15 58.6
6 M	11 01 28	13 40 26	18 23 24	24 18 12	9 05.6	26 38.1	21 21.8	10 59.6	28 18.1	28 24.2	13 50.0	15 07.8	17 37.9	16 00.7
7 Tu	11 05 25	14 38 39	0♒13 03	6♒08 24	8 57.5	28 06.4	22 32.7	11 39.4	28 05.6	28 31.8	13 45.4	15 11.6	17 39.1	16 02.9
8 W	11 09 21	15 36 54	12 04 39	18 02 06	8 46.9	29 39.2	23 43.6	12 19.2	27 53.0	28 39.2	13 40.8	15 15.3	17 40.3	16 05.0
9 Th	11 13 18	16 35 10	24 01 04	0♓01 45	8 34.3	1♍16.1	24 54.4	12 59.2	27 40.2	28 46.4	13 36.2	15 19.1	17 41.6	16 07.2
10 F	11 17 14	17 33 28	6♓04 22	12 09 01	8 20.7	2 56.5	26 05.1	13 39.3	27 27.2	28 53.5	13 31.7	15 22.9	17 42.9	16 09.3
11 Sa	11 21 11	18 31 48	18 15 51	24 24 57	8 07.3	4 39.9	27 15.8	14 19.4	27 14.2	29 00.5	13 27.1	15 26.6	17 44.2	16 11.4
12 Su	11 25 07	19 30 09	0♈36 21	6♈50 08	7 55.1	6 25.7	28 26.4	14 59.7	27 01.0	29 07.3	13 22.5	15 30.4	17 45.6	16 13.6
13 M	11 29 04	20 28 33	13 06 22	19 25 06	7 45.2	8 13.6	29 37.0	15 40.0	26 47.8	29 14.0	13 18.0	15 34.2	17 47.0	16 15.7
14 Tu	11 33 01	21 26 58	25 46 26	2♉10 29	7 38.0	10 03.0	0♏47.5	16 20.5	26 34.4	29 20.5	13 13.5	15 37.9	17 48.4	16 17.9
15 W	11 36 57	22 25 26	8♉37 22	15 07 16	7 33.7	11 53.7	1 57.9	17 01.0	26 21.0	29 26.8	13 08.9	15 41.7	17 49.8	16 20.0
16 Th	11 40 54	23 23 56	21 40 23	28 16 56	7D 31.9	13 45.2	3 08.3	17 41.7	26 07.6	29 33.0	13 04.5	15 45.5	17 51.3	16 22.1
17 F	11 44 50	24 22 28	4♊57 08	11♊41 15	7 31.7	15 37.3	4 18.6	18 22.4	25 54.1	29 39.1	13 00.0	15 49.2	17 52.8	16 24.2
18 Sa	11 48 47	25 21 02	18 29 29	25 22 03	7R 31.9	17 29.6	5 28.9	19 03.2	25 40.6	29 45.0	12 55.6	15 53.0	17 54.3	16 26.4
19 Su	11 52 43	26 19 39	2♋19 04	9♋20 37	7 31.3	19 22.0	6 39.0	19 44.2	25 27.1	29 50.7	12 51.1	15 56.7	17 55.8	16 28.5
20 M	11 56 40	27 18 17	16 26 40	23 37 04	7 28.8	21 14.2	7 49.2	20 25.2	25 13.6	29 56.2	12 46.8	16 00.4	17 57.4	16 30.6
21 Tu	12 00 36	28 16 58	0♌51 32	8♌09 36	7 24.0	23 06.1	8 59.2	21 06.3	25 00.1	0♋01.6	12 42.4	16 04.2	17 59.0	16 32.7
22 W	12 04 33	29 15 42	15 30 40	22 54 00	7 16.6	24 57.5	10 09.2	21 47.5	24 46.7	0 06.9	12 38.1	16 07.9	18 00.6	16 34.8
23 Th	12 08 30	0♎14 27	0♍18 43	7♍43 48	7 07.3	26 48.4	11 19.1	22 28.8	24 33.3	0 11.9	12 33.8	16 11.6	18 02.2	16 36.9
24 F	12 12 26	1 13 14	15 08 12	22 30 49	6 57.1	28 38.6	12 29.0	23 10.3	24 20.0	0 16.8	12 29.6	16 15.3	18 03.9	16 39.0
25 Sa	12 16 23	2 12 03	29 50 38	7♎06 37	6 47.1	0♎28.1	13 38.7	23 51.7	24 06.7	0 21.5	12 25.4	16 18.9	18 05.5	16 41.1
26 Su	12 20 19	3 10 55	14♎17 55	21 23 48	6 38.7	2 16.9	14 48.4	24 33.3	23 53.6	0 26.0	12 21.2	16 22.6	18 07.2	16 43.2
27 M	12 24 16	4 09 48	28 23 42	5♏17 14	6 32.4	4 04.8	15 58.1	25 15.0	23 40.6	0 30.4	12 17.1	16 26.3	18 09.0	16 45.3
28 Tu	12 28 12	5 08 43	12♏04 11	18 44 33	6 28.6	5 51.9	17 07.6	25 56.8	23 27.7	0 34.6	12 13.1	16 29.9	18 10.7	16 47.3
29 W	12 32 09	6 07 40	25 18 26	1♐46 05	6D 27.1	7 38.2	18 17.1	26 38.6	23 14.9	0 38.5	12 09.1	16 33.5	18 12.5	16 49.4
30 Th	12 36 05	7 06 39	8♐07 53	14 24 18	6 27.3	9 23.6	19 26.4	27 20.6	23 02.3	0 42.4	12 05.1	16 37.1	18 14.3	16 51.4

LONGITUDE — October 1965

Day	Sid.Time	☉	0 hr ☽	Noon ☽	True ☊	☿	♀	♂	⚳	♃	♄	♅	♆	♇
1 F	12 40 02	8♎05 39	20♐35 52	26♐43 11	6♊28.1	11♎08.1	20♏35.7	28♏02.6	22♓49.9	0♋46.0	12♓01.2	16♍40.7	18♏16.1	16♍53.5
2 Sa	12 43 59	9 04 41	2♑46 53	8♑47 37	6R 28.6	12 51.7	21 44.9	28 44.7	22R 37.6	0 49.5	11R 57.4	16 44.3	18 17.9	16 55.5
3 Su	12 47 55	10 03 45	14 46 03	20 42 49	6 27.9	14 34.5	22 54.0	29 26.9	22 25.6	0 52.7	11 53.6	16 47.9	18 19.7	16 57.5
4 M	12 51 52	11 02 51	26 38 35	2♒33 57	6 25.2	16 16.5	24 03.0	0♐09.2	22 13.7	0 55.8	11 49.9	16 51.4	18 21.6	16 59.5
5 Tu	12 55 48	12 01 59	8♒29 30	14 25 48	6 20.4	17 57.6	25 11.9	0 51.6	22 02.1	0 58.7	11 46.3	16 54.9	18 23.5	17 01.5
6 W	12 59 45	13 01 08	20 23 20	26 22 33	6 13.5	19 37.9	26 20.7	1 34.0	21 50.7	1 01.4	11 42.7	16 58.4	18 25.4	17 03.5
7 Th	13 03 41	14 00 19	2♓23 51	8♓27 35	6 04.9	21 17.3	27 29.4	2 16.6	21 39.6	1 03.9	11 39.2	17 01.9	18 27.3	17 05.4
8 F	13 07 38	14 59 32	14 34 00	20 43 22	5 55.4	22 56.0	28 38.0	2 59.2	21 28.6	1 06.2	11 35.7	17 05.3	18 29.2	17 07.4
9 Sa	13 11 34	15 58 47	26 55 47	3♈11 24	5 45.8	24 34.0	29 46.4	3 41.9	21 18.0	1 08.4	11 32.3	17 08.8	18 31.2	17 09.3
10 Su	13 15 31	16 58 04	9♈30 15	15 52 20	5 37.3	26 11.1	0♐54.8	4 24.6	21 07.6	1 10.3	11 29.0	17 12.2	18 33.1	17 11.2
11 M	13 19 27	17 57 23	22 17 37	28 46 03	5 30.4	27 47.6	2 03.0	5 07.5	20 57.5	1 12.1	11 25.8	17 15.6	18 35.1	17 13.1
12 Tu	13 23 24	18 56 44	5♉17 33	11♉52 01	5 25.7	29 23.3	3 11.1	5 50.4	20 47.7	1 13.6	11 22.6	17 19.0	18 37.1	17 15.0
13 W	13 27 21	19 56 08	18 29 21	25 09 29	5D 23.3	0♏58.3	4 19.1	6 33.4	20 38.1	1 15.0	11 19.6	17 22.3	18 39.1	17 16.9
14 Th	13 31 17	20 55 33	1♊52 21	8♊37 52	5 22.8	2 32.7	5 26.9	7 16.5	20 28.9	1 16.1	11 16.6	17 25.6	18 41.2	17 18.8
15 F	13 35 14	21 55 01	15 26 00	22 16 44	5 23.7	4 06.3	6 34.7	7 59.7	20 20.0	1 17.1	11 13.6	17 28.9	18 43.2	17 20.6
16 Sa	13 39 10	22 54 32	29 10 03	6♋05 54	5 25.1	5 39.3	7 42.3	8 42.9	20 11.4	1 17.9	11 10.8	17 32.2	18 45.3	17 22.4
17 Su	13 43 07	23 54 04	13♋04 17	20 05 07	5R 26.0	7 11.7	8 49.8	9 26.3	20 03.2	1 18.4	11 08.1	17 35.4	18 47.4	17 24.3
18 M	13 47 03	24 53 39	27 08 18	4♌13 42	5 25.6	8 43.4	9 57.1	10 09.7	19 55.2	1 18.8	11 05.4	17 38.6	18 49.4	17 26.1
19 Tu	13 51 00	25 53 16	11♌21 06	18 30 12	5 23.6	10 14.5	11 04.3	10 53.2	19 47.6	1R 19.0	11 02.8	17 41.8	18 51.5	17 27.8
20 W	13 54 56	26 52 56	25 40 38	2♍51 58	5 19.9	11 45.0	12 11.3	11 36.7	19 40.3	1 18.9	11 00.3	17 45.0	18 53.7	17 29.6
21 Th	13 58 53	27 52 37	10♍03 39	17 15 06	5 14.8	13 14.9	13 18.2	12 20.4	19 33.4	1 18.7	10 57.9	17 48.1	18 55.8	17 31.3
22 F	14 02 50	28 52 21	24 25 40	1♎34 40	5 09.0	14 44.1	14 25.0	13 04.1	19 26.9	1 18.2	10 55.6	17 51.2	18 57.9	17 33.1
23 Sa	14 06 46	29 52 07	8♎41 27	15 45 19	5 03.3	16 12.7	15 31.6	13 47.9	19 20.7	1 17.6	10 53.3	17 54.2	19 00.0	17 34.8
24 Su	14 10 43	0♏51 55	22 45 41	29 41 59	4 58.5	17 40.7	16 38.0	14 31.8	19 14.8	1 16.8	10 51.2	17 57.3	19 02.2	17 36.4
25 M	14 14 39	1 51 45	6♏33 46	13♏20 39	4 55.1	19 08.0	17 44.2	15 15.7	19 09.3	1 15.7	10 49.1	18 00.2	19 04.4	17 38.1
26 Tu	14 18 36	2 51 37	20 02 25	26 38 54	4D 53.3	20 34.6	18 50.3	15 59.7	19 04.2	1 14.4	10 47.2	18 03.2	19 06.5	17 39.7
27 W	14 22 32	3 51 31	3♐10 06	9♐36 06	4 53.1	22 00.6	19 56.2	16 43.8	18 59.5	1 13.0	10 45.4	18 06.1	19 08.7	17 41.4
28 Th	14 26 29	4 51 26	15 57 05	22 13 20	4 54.1	23 25.9	21 01.9	17 28.0	18 55.2	1 11.3	10 43.6	18 09.0	19 10.9	17 43.0
29 F	14 30 25	5 51 24	28 25 14	4♑33 11	4 55.8	24 50.4	22 07.5	18 12.2	18 51.2	1 09.5	10 41.9	18 11.9	19 13.1	17 44.5
30 Sa	14 34 22	6 51 23	10♑37 41	16 39 17	4 57.6	26 14.1	23 12.8	18 56.5	18 47.6	1 07.4	10 40.4	18 14.7	19 15.3	17 46.1
31 Su	14 38 19	7 51 23	22 38 33	28 36 04	4R 58.9	27 37.0	24 17.9	19 40.9	18 44.4	1 05.2	10 38.9	18 17.5	19 17.5	17 47.6

Astro Data

	Dy Hr Mn
☽0N	12 17:49
☉0S	23 6:06
☽0S	25 16:32
☿0S	27 1:04
♅☌♇	9 20:17
☽0N	10 0:36
♃R	19 19:32
☽0S	23 2:01

Planet Ingress

	Dy Hr Mn
☿ ♍	8 17:14
♀ ♏	13 19:50
♃ ♋	21 4:40
☉ ♎	23 6:06
☿ ♎	25 5:49
♂ ♐	4 6:46
♀ ♐	9 16:46
☿ ♏	12 21:15
☉ ♏	23 15:10

Last Aspect / ☽ Ingress (September)

Last Aspect Dy Hr Mn		☽ Ingress	Dy Hr Mn
1 6:06	☿ □	♐	1 24:00
4 7:05	♃ ☍	♑	4 10:51
6 5:22	♀ □	♒	6 23:34
9 9:28	♃ △	♓	9 11:57
11 21:00	♃ □	♈	11 22:50
14 6:39	♃ ⚹	♉	14 7:56
16 2:26	☉ △	♊	16 15:06
18 19:38	♃ ☌	♋	18 20:01
20 18:34	☉ ⚹	♌	20 22:35
22 10:07	♂ □	♍	22 23:30
24 23:28	☿ ☌	♎	25 0:15
25 3:18	☉ ☌	♏	27 2:47
29 1:56	♂ ☌	♐	29 8:42

Last Aspect / ☽ Ingress (October)

Last Aspect Dy Hr Mn		☽ Ingress	Dy Hr Mn
30 16:45	♇ □	♑	1 18:29
3 16:54	♀ ⚹	♒	4 6:48
6 11:56	♀ □	♓	6 19:14
9 4:48	♀ △	♈	9 5:54
11 9:57	☿ ☍	♉	11 14:16
13 0:16	♆ ☍	♊	13 20:40
15 11:19	☉ △	♋	16 1:27
17 19:00	☉ □	♌	18 4:51
20 1:16	☉ ⚹	♍	20 7:13
21 14:49	♆ ⚹	♎	22 9:21
23 11:35	♀ ⚹	♏	24 12:31
25 23:38	☿ ☌	♐	26 18:09
28 9:30	♀ ☌	♑	29 3:05
31 9:45	☿ ⚹	♒	31 14:49

☽ Phases & Eclipses

Dy Hr Mn	
2 19:27	☽ 10♐06
10 23:32	○ 18♓01
18 11:58	☾ 25♊21
25 3:18	● 1♎51
2 12:37	☽ 9♑06
10 14:14	○ 17♈04
17 19:00	☾ 24♋11
24 14:11	● 0♏57

Astro Data

1 September 1965
Julian Day # 23985
SVP 5♓44'36"
GC 26♐21.6 ⚴ 7♒58.3R
Eris 11♈18.8R ⚵ 2♒36.0R
⚷ 20♓46.0R ⚶ 0♋55.8
☽ Mean ☊ 9♊04.8

1 October 1965
Julian Day # 24015
SVP 5♓44'33"
GC 26♐21.7 ⚴ 5♒02.4R
Eris 11♈01.4R ⚵ 1♒24.8
⚷ 19♓24.4R ⚶ 9♋19.6
☽ Mean ☊ 7♊29.5

November 1965 LONGITUDE

Day	Sid.Time	☉	0 hr ☽	Noon☽	True☊	☿	♀	♂	⚳	♃	♄	♅	♆	♇
1 M	14 42 15	8♏51 25	4♒32 27	10♒28 19	4♊59.2	28♏58.9	25♐22.7	20♐25.3	18♓41.6	1♋02.7	10♓37.6	18♍20.2	19♏19.8	17♍49.1
2 Tu	14 46 12	9 51 29	16 24 18	22 20 59	4R 58.5	0♐19.9	26 27.4	21 09.9	18R 39.1	1R 00.1	10R 36.3	18 22.9	19 22.0	17 50.6
3 W	14 50 08	10 51 35	28 18 58	4♓18 48	4 56.6	1 39.9	27 31.8	21 54.4	18 37.0	0 57.2	10 35.2	18 25.6	19 24.2	17 52.1
4 Th	14 54 05	11 51 42	10♓21 00	16 26 04	4 53.7	2 58.7	28 35.9	22 39.1	18 35.3	0 54.2	10 34.1	18 28.2	19 26.4	17 53.5
5 F	14 58 01	12 51 50	22 34 26	28 46 27	4 50.3	4 16.3	29 39.8	23 23.8	18 34.0	0 51.0	10 33.1	18 30.8	19 28.7	17 54.9
6 Sa	15 01 58	13 52 00	5♈02 26	11♈22 38	4 46.8	5 32.4	0♑43.5	24 08.5	18 33.1	0 47.6	10 32.3	18 33.3	19 30.9	17 56.3
7 Su	15 05 54	14 52 12	17 47 13	24 16 14	4 43.7	6 47.1	1 46.8	24 53.3	18D 32.5	0 44.0	10 31.5	18 35.8	19 33.2	17 57.6
8 M	15 09 51	15 52 25	0♉49 44	7♉27 37	4 41.3	8 00.0	2 49.9	25 38.2	18 32.3	0 40.2	10 30.9	18 38.3	19 35.4	17 59.0
9 Tu	15 13 48	16 52 41	14 09 44	20 55 54	4 39.8	9 11.1	3 52.7	26 23.2	18 32.5	0 36.2	10 30.4	18 40.7	19 37.6	18 00.3
10 W	15 17 44	17 52 58	27 45 48	4♊39 09	4D 39.3	10 20.0	4 55.1	27 08.2	18 33.1	0 32.0	10 29.9	18 43.1	19 39.9	18 01.6
11 Th	15 21 41	18 53 16	11♊35 34	18 34 41	4 39.7	11 26.6	5 57.3	27 53.3	18 34.0	0 27.7	10 29.6	18 45.4	19 42.1	18 02.8
12 F	15 25 37	19 53 37	25 36 04	2♋39 19	4 40.7	12 30.5	6 59.1	28 38.4	18 35.3	0 23.2	10 29.4	18 47.7	19 44.4	18 04.1
13 Sa	15 29 34	20 54 00	9♋44 02	16 49 50	4 41.9	13 31.3	8 00.6	29 23.6	18 37.0	0 18.5	10D 29.3	18 50.0	19 46.7	18 05.3
14 Su	15 33 30	21 54 24	23 56 20	1♌03 11	4 42.9	14 28.8	9 01.8	0♑08.8	18 39.0	0 13.6	10 29.2	18 52.2	19 48.9	18 06.4
15 M	15 37 27	22 54 51	8♌10 04	15 16 39	4R 43.5	15 22.4	10 02.6	0 54.2	18 41.4	0 08.6	10 29.3	18 54.3	19 51.2	18 07.6
16 Tu	15 41 23	23 55 19	22 22 41	29 27 52	4 43.5	16 11.8	11 03.0	1 39.5	18 44.1	0 03.4	10 29.5	18 56.4	19 53.4	18 08.7
17 W	15 45 20	24 55 49	6♍31 56	13♍34 38	4 43.0	16 56.2	12 03.0	2 25.0	18 47.2	29♊58.0	10 29.8	18 58.5	19 55.7	18 09.8
18 Th	15 49 17	25 56 21	20 35 43	27 34 57	4 42.2	17 35.2	13 02.7	3 10.4	18 50.7	29 52.5	10 30.2	19 00.5	19 57.9	18 10.8
19 F	15 53 13	26 56 55	4♎32 03	11♎26 47	4 41.2	18 08.0	14 01.9	3 56.0	18 54.5	29 46.8	10 30.7	19 02.5	20 00.1	18 11.9
20 Sa	15 57 10	27 57 30	18 18 54	25 08 10	4 40.3	18 34.0	15 00.7	4 41.6	18 58.6	29 40.9	10 31.4	19 04.4	20 02.4	18 12.9
21 Su	16 01 06	28 58 07	1♏54 22	8♏37 15	4 39.6	18 52.4	15 59.1	5 27.3	19 03.2	29 34.9	10 32.1	19 06.2	20 04.6	18 13.8
22 M	16 05 03	29 58 46	15 16 40	21 52 27	4D 39.2	19R 02.4	16 57.0	6 13.0	19 08.0	29 28.8	10 32.9	19 08.1	20 06.8	18 14.8
23 Tu	16 08 59	0♐59 26	28 24 29	4♐52 41	4 39.1	19 03.3	17 54.4	6 58.8	19 13.2	29 22.5	10 33.9	19 09.8	20 09.1	18 15.7
24 W	16 12 56	2 00 08	11♐17 03	17 37 34	4 39.2	18 54.3	18 51.3	7 44.6	19 18.7	29 16.0	10 34.9	19 11.5	20 11.3	18 16.6
25 Th	16 16 52	3 00 51	23 54 22	0♑07 33	4 39.3	18 34.9	19 47.7	8 30.5	19 24.6	29 09.5	10 36.1	19 13.2	20 13.5	18 17.4
26 F	16 20 49	4 01 35	6♑17 20	12 23 58	4R 39.4	18 04.7	20 43.6	9 16.4	19 30.8	29 02.8	10 37.3	19 14.8	20 15.7	18 18.2
27 Sa	16 24 46	5 02 21	18 27 45	24 29 02	4 39.5	17 23.7	21 38.9	10 02.4	19 37.3	28 56.0	10 38.7	19 16.4	20 17.9	18 19.0
28 Su	16 28 42	6 03 07	0♒28 15	6♒25 50	4 39.4	16 32.0	22 33.6	10 48.4	19 44.1	28 49.0	10 40.1	19 17.9	20 20.1	18 19.8
29 M	16 32 39	7 03 55	12 22 16	18 18 05	4 39.2	15 30.5	23 27.7	11 34.5	19 51.3	28 42.0	10 41.7	19 19.4	20 22.3	18 20.5
30 Tu	16 36 35	8 04 43	24 13 50	0♓10 04	4D 39.0	14 20.4	24 21.1	12 20.6	19 58.8	28 34.8	10 43.4	19 20.8	20 24.5	18 21.2

December 1965 LONGITUDE

Day	Sid.Time	☉	0 hr ☽	Noon☽	True☊	☿	♀	♂	⚳	♃	♄	♅	♆	♇
1 W	16 40 32	9♐05 32	6♓07 23	12♓06 23	4♊39.0	13♐03.7	25♑13.9	13♑06.8	20♓06.6	28♊27.5	10♓45.2	19♍22.1	20♏26.6	18♍21.9
2 Th	16 44 28	10 06 22	18 07 38	24 11 45	4 39.2	11R 42.6	26 05.9	13 53.0	20 14.6	28R 20.2	10 47.0	19 23.4	20 28.8	18 22.5
3 F	16 48 25	11 07 13	0♈19 17	6♈30 46	4 39.6	10 19.8	26 57.3	14 39.3	20 23.0	28 12.7	10 49.0	19 24.7	20 30.9	18 23.1
4 Sa	16 52 22	12 08 05	12 46 41	19 07 29	4 40.3	8 58.0	27 47.9	15 25.6	20 31.7	28 05.2	10 51.1	19 25.8	20 33.1	18 23.6
5 Su	16 56 18	13 08 58	25 33 32	2♉05 08	4 41.2	7 40.1	28 37.7	16 11.9	20 40.7	27 57.5	10 53.3	19 27.0	20 35.2	18 24.2
6 M	17 00 15	14 09 51	8♉42 29	15 25 40	4 41.9	6 28.5	29 26.6	16 58.3	20 50.0	27 49.8	10 55.6	19 28.1	20 37.3	18 24.7
7 Tu	17 04 11	15 10 46	22 14 39	29 09 17	4R 42.4	5 25.3	0♒14.7	17 44.7	20 59.5	27 42.1	10 58.0	19 29.1	20 39.4	18 25.1
8 W	17 08 08	16 11 41	6♊09 18	13♊14 17	4 42.3	4 31.9	1 01.9	18 31.2	21 09.4	27 34.2	11 00.4	19 30.1	20 41.5	18 25.6
9 Th	17 12 04	17 12 38	20 23 40	27 36 51	4 41.6	3 49.3	1 48.2	19 17.7	21 19.5	27 26.3	11 03.0	19 31.0	20 43.5	18 26.0
10 F	17 16 01	18 13 35	4♋53 04	12♋11 31	4 40.3	3 18.0	2 33.5	20 04.2	21 29.9	27 18.4	11 05.7	19 31.9	20 45.6	18 26.4
11 Sa	17 19 57	19 14 33	19 31 21	26 51 43	4 38.4	2 58.0	3 17.8	20 50.8	21 40.5	27 10.4	11 08.5	19 32.7	20 47.6	18 26.7
12 Su	17 23 54	20 15 33	4♌11 46	11♌30 43	4 36.5	2D 49.0	4 01.1	21 37.4	21 51.4	27 02.3	11 11.4	19 33.4	20 49.7	18 27.0
13 M	17 27 51	21 16 33	18 47 51	26 02 31	4 34.7	2 50.4	4 43.3	22 24.1	22 02.6	26 54.3	11 14.3	19 34.1	20 51.7	18 27.3
14 Tu	17 31 47	22 17 34	3♍14 13	10♍22 31	4D 33.5	3 01.4	5 24.3	23 10.8	22 14.0	26 46.2	11 17.4	19 34.8	20 53.7	18 27.5
15 W	17 35 44	23 18 37	17 27 08	24 27 51	4 33.1	3 21.3	6 04.2	23 57.5	22 25.7	26 38.0	11 20.6	19 35.3	20 55.7	18 27.7
16 Th	17 39 40	24 19 40	1♎24 32	8♎17 11	4 33.6	3 49.3	6 42.8	24 44.2	22 37.7	26 29.9	11 23.8	19 35.9	20 57.6	18 27.9
17 F	17 43 37	25 20 44	15 05 48	21 50 29	4 34.9	4 24.5	7 20.2	25 31.0	22 49.9	26 21.7	11 27.2	19 36.3	20 59.6	18 28.0
18 Sa	17 47 33	26 21 50	28 31 21	5♏08 31	4 36.4	5 06.2	7 56.3	26 17.9	23 02.3	26 13.5	11 30.6	19 36.7	21 01.5	18 28.1
19 Su	17 51 30	27 22 56	11♏42 08	18 12 22	4 37.9	5 53.5	8 30.9	27 04.7	23 15.0	26 05.4	11 34.2	19 37.1	21 03.4	18 28.2
20 M	17 55 26	28 24 03	24 39 21	1♐03 14	4R 38.7	6 46.0	9 04.2	27 51.6	23 27.9	25 57.2	11 37.8	19 37.4	21 05.3	18R 28.2
21 Tu	17 59 23	29 25 10	7♐24 08	13 42 10	4 38.4	7 42.8	9 36.0	28 38.6	23 41.0	25 49.1	11 41.5	19 37.6	21 07.2	18 28.3
22 W	18 03 20	0♑26 18	19 57 27	26 10 06	4 36.8	8 43.7	10 06.2	29 25.5	23 54.4	25 40.9	11 45.3	19 37.8	21 09.0	18 28.2
23 Th	18 07 16	1 27 27	2♑20 13	8♑27 56	4 33.7	9 47.9	10 34.8	0♒12.5	24 08.0	25 32.9	11 49.2	19 38.0	21 10.9	18 28.2
24 F	18 11 13	2 28 36	14 33 22	20 36 41	4 29.3	10 55.2	11 01.7	0 59.5	24 21.9	25 24.8	11 53.2	19R 38.0	21 12.7	18 28.1
25 Sa	18 15 09	3 29 45	26 38 03	2♒37 40	4 24.0	12 05.1	11 26.9	1 46.6	24 35.9	25 16.8	11 57.3	19 38.0	21 14.5	18 28.0
26 Su	18 19 06	4 30 54	8♒35 47	14 32 42	4 18.3	13 17.4	11 50.3	2 33.7	24 50.2	25 08.8	12 01.4	19 38.0	21 16.3	18 27.8
27 M	18 23 02	5 32 04	20 28 42	26 24 21	4 13.0	14 31.8	12 11.8	3 20.8	25 04.7	25 00.9	12 05.7	19 37.9	21 18.0	18 27.6
28 Tu	18 26 59	6 33 13	2♓19 32	8♓15 12	4 08.4	15 48.0	12 31.4	4 07.9	25 19.4	24 53.0	12 10.0	19 37.7	21 19.7	18 27.4
29 W	18 30 55	7 34 23	14 11 40	20 09 28	4 05.2	17 05.8	12 48.9	4 55.0	25 34.2	24 45.2	12 14.4	19 37.5	21 21.4	18 27.1
30 Th	18 34 52	8 35 32	26 09 09	2♈11 17	4D 03.6	18 25.1	13 04.4	5 42.2	25 49.3	24 37.5	12 18.9	19 37.3	21 23.1	18 26.8
31 F	18 38 49	9 36 41	8♈16 29	14 25 21	4 03.5	19 45.6	13 17.7	6 29.3	26 04.6	24 29.8	12 23.4	19 36.9	21 24.8	18 26.5

Astro Data	Dy Hr Mn
☽0N	6 9:19
⚳D	8 11:56
♄D	14 3:17
☽0S	19 9:30
☿R	23 2:14
☽0N	3 18:44
☿D	12 20:41
☽0S	16 14:57
♇R	21 5:06
♅R	25 6:06
☽0N	31 2:59

Planet Ingress		Dy Hr Mn
☿	♐	2 6:04
♀	♑	5 19:36
♂	♑	14 7:19
♃	♊R	17 3:08
☉	♐	22 12:29
♀	♒	7 4:37
☉	♑	22 1:40
♂	♒	23 5:36

Last Aspect Dy Hr Mn		☽ Ingress Dy Hr Mn
2 21:05	♀ ⚹	♓ 3 3:23
5 13:52	♀ □	♈ 5 14:21
7 13:12	♂ △	♉ 7 22:29
9 9:41	♆ ☍	♊ 10 3:54
12 4:47	♂ ☍	♋ 12 7:29
13 19:24	☉ △	♌ 14 10:13
16 1:54	☉ □	♍ 16 12:54
18 15:55	♃ □	♎ 18 16:10
20 19:59	♃ △	♏ 20 20:37
22 8:47	♆ ☌	♐ 23 2:56
25 10:09	♃ ☍	♑ 25 11:45
27 5:52	♀ ☌	♒ 27 23:03
30 8:50	♃ △	♓ 30 11:40

Last Aspect Dy Hr Mn		☽ Ingress Dy Hr Mn
2 20:03	♃ □	♈ 2 23:22
5 5:14	♀ □	♉ 5 8:11
6 21:11	♆ ☍	♊ 7 13:27
9 11:43	♃ ☌	♋ 9 15:57
11 2:03	♆ △	♌ 11 17:08
13 13:25	♃ ⚹	♍ 13 18:35
15 15:42	♃ □	♎ 15 21:33
17 20:02	♃ △	♏ 18 2:40
20 5:37	♂ ⚹	♐ 20 10:01
22 11:04	♃ ☍	♑ 22 19:27
24 13:12	♆ ⚹	♒ 25 6:44
27 9:13	♃ △	♓ 27 19:17
29 21:07	♃ □	♈ 30 7:40

☽ Phases & Eclipses Dy Hr Mn		
1 8:26	☽	8♒42
9 4:15	○	16♉33
16 1:54	☾	23♌30
23 4:10	●	0♐40
23 4:14:15	•	A 04'02"
1 5:24	☽	8♓49
8 17:21	○	16♊25
8 17:10	•	A 0.882
15 9:52	☾	23♍13
22 21:03	●	0♑49
31 1:46	☽	9♈11

Astro Data

1 November 1965
Julian Day # 24046
SVP 5♓44'29"
GC 26♐21.7 ⚴ 7♒15.2
Eris 10♈42.9R ⚵ 6♒22.7
⚷ 18♓19.2R ⚶ 13♋58.7
☽Mean ☊ 5♊51.0

1 December 1965
Julian Day # 24076
SVP 5♓44'25"
GC 26♐21.8 ⚴ 13♒05.0
Eris 10♈29.8R ⚵ 15♒35.0
⚷ 17♓58.2 ⚶ 12♋31.9R
☽Mean ☊ 4♊15.7

LONGITUDE — January 1966

Day	Sid.Time	☉	0 hr ☽	Noon ☽	True ☊	☿	♀	♂	⚳	♃	♄	♅	♆	♇
1 Sa	18 42 45	10♑37 50	20♈38 29	26♈56 28	4♊04.6	21♐07.3	13♒28.8	7♒16.5	26♓20.1	24♊22.3	12♓28.1	19♍36.6	21♏26.4	18♍26.1
2 Su	18 46 42	11 38 59	3♉19 51	9♉49 10	4 06.2	22 30.1	13 37.6	8 03.8	26 35.8	24R 14.8	12 32.8	19R 36.1	21 28.0	18R 25.8
3 M	18 50 38	12 40 08	16 24 50	23 07 13	4R 07.6	23 53.8	13 44.1	8 51.0	26 51.7	24 07.4	12 37.6	19 35.6	21 29.6	18 25.3
4 Tu	18 54 35	13 41 16	29 56 31	6♊52 50	4 08.0	25 18.4	13 48.2	9 38.2	27 07.7	24 00.1	12 42.5	19 35.1	21 31.2	18 24.9
5 W	18 58 31	14 42 24	13♊56 05	21 06 01	4 06.8	26 43.7	13R 49.9	10 25.5	27 24.0	23 53.0	12 47.4	19 34.5	21 32.7	18 24.4
6 Th	19 02 28	15 43 32	28 22 10	5♋43 52	4 03.6	28 09.8	13 49.1	11 12.8	27 40.4	23 45.9	12 52.5	19 33.8	21 34.2	18 23.9
7 F	19 06 25	16 44 40	13♋10 18	20 40 26	3 58.4	29 36.6	13 45.8	12 00.1	27 56.9	23 39.0	12 57.6	19 33.1	21 35.7	18 23.4
8 Sa	19 10 21	17 45 48	28 13 06	5♌47 04	3 51.8	1♑04.1	13 40.0	12 47.4	28 13.7	23 32.1	13 02.7	19 32.4	21 37.1	18 22.8
9 Su	19 14 18	18 46 56	13♌21 02	20 53 44	3 44.7	2 32.2	13 31.7	13 34.7	28 30.6	23 25.4	13 08.0	19 31.5	21 38.6	18 22.2
10 M	19 18 14	19 48 03	28 24 00	5♍50 44	3 37.9	4 00.8	13 20.8	14 22.0	28 47.7	23 18.8	13 13.3	19 30.7	21 40.0	18 21.6
11 Tu	19 22 11	20 49 10	13♍13 03	20 30 14	3 32.6	5 30.0	13 07.4	15 09.3	29 05.0	23 12.4	13 18.7	19 29.8	21 41.4	18 20.9
12 W	19 26 07	21 50 17	27 41 44	4♎47 15	3 29.1	6 59.8	12 51.6	15 56.7	29 22.4	23 06.0	13 24.1	19 28.8	21 42.7	18 20.2
13 Th	19 30 04	22 51 25	11♎46 36	18 39 50	3D 27.6	8 30.2	12 33.4	16 44.0	29 39.9	22 59.9	13 29.6	19 27.7	21 44.0	18 19.5
14 F	19 34 00	23 52 32	25 27 03	2♏08 32	3 27.8	10 01.0	12 12.8	17 31.4	29 57.7	22 53.8	13 35.2	19 26.7	21 45.3	18 18.7
15 Sa	19 37 57	24 53 39	8♏44 35	15 15 37	3 28.9	11 32.4	11 49.9	18 18.8	0♈15.5	22 48.0	13 40.9	19 25.5	21 46.6	18 18.0
16 Su	19 41 54	25 54 46	21 42 02	28 04 16	3R 29.9	13 04.3	11 24.9	19 06.1	0 33.6	22 42.2	13 46.6	19 24.4	21 47.8	18 17.2
17 M	19 45 50	26 55 52	4♐22 44	10♐37 50	3 29.7	14 36.8	10 57.9	19 53.5	0 51.8	22 36.6	13 52.3	19 23.1	21 49.0	18 16.3
18 Tu	19 49 47	27 56 59	16 49 59	23 00 31	3 27.6	16 09.8	10 28.9	20 40.9	1 10.1	22 31.2	13 58.2	19 21.9	21 50.2	18 15.5
19 W	19 53 43	28 58 04	29 06 45	5♑11 58	3 22.9	17 43.3	9 58.2	21 28.4	1 28.6	22 26.0	14 04.1	19 20.5	21 51.3	18 14.6
20 Th	19 57 40	29 59 10	11♑15 25	17 17 19	3 15.5	19 17.4	9 26.0	22 15.8	1 47.2	22 20.9	14 10.0	19 19.2	21 52.4	18 13.7
21 F	20 01 36	1♒00 15	23 17 51	29 17 11	3 05.7	20 52.0	8 52.4	23 03.2	2 05.9	22 16.0	14 16.0	19 17.7	21 53.5	18 12.7
22 Sa	20 05 33	2 01 19	5♒15 29	11♒12 55	2 54.1	22 27.2	8 17.6	23 50.6	2 24.8	22 11.3	14 22.1	19 16.3	21 54.6	18 11.8
23 Su	20 09 29	3 02 22	17 09 36	23 05 44	2 41.7	24 03.0	7 41.9	24 38.0	2 43.8	22 06.7	14 28.2	19 14.8	21 55.6	18 10.8
24 M	20 13 26	4 03 24	29 01 31	4♓57 08	2 29.5	25 39.4	7 05.5	25 25.4	3 03.0	22 02.3	14 34.4	19 13.2	21 56.6	18 09.7
25 Tu	20 17 23	5 04 26	10♓52 52	16 49 00	2 18.6	27 16.4	6 28.7	26 12.8	3 22.3	21 58.1	14 40.6	19 11.6	21 57.5	18 08.7
26 W	20 21 19	6 05 26	22 45 51	28 43 50	2 09.8	28 53.9	5 51.6	27 00.2	3 41.7	21 54.1	14 46.9	19 09.9	21 58.4	18 07.6
27 Th	20 25 16	7 06 25	4♈43 20	10♈44 51	2 03.7	0♒32.2	5 14.7	27 47.6	4 01.2	21 50.3	14 53.3	19 08.2	21 59.3	18 06.5
28 F	20 29 12	8 07 24	16 48 53	22 55 59	2 00.2	2 11.0	4 38.0	28 35.0	4 20.9	21 46.7	14 59.6	19 06.5	22 00.2	18 05.4
29 Sa	20 33 09	9 08 21	29 06 44	5♉21 44	1D 59.0	3 50.6	4 02.0	29 22.4	4 40.6	21 43.2	15 06.1	19 04.7	22 01.0	18 04.3
30 Su	20 37 05	10 09 16	11♉41 34	18 06 51	1 59.1	5 30.8	3 26.7	0♓09.8	5 00.5	21 40.0	15 12.5	19 02.9	22 01.8	18 03.1
31 M	20 41 02	11 10 11	24 38 10	1♊16 00	1R 59.5	7 11.7	2 52.5	0 57.2	5 20.5	21 36.9	15 19.1	19 01.0	22 02.6	18 01.9

LONGITUDE — February 1966

Day	Sid.Time	☉	0 hr ☽	Noon ☽	True ☊	☿	♀	♂	⚳	♃	♄	♅	♆	♇
1 Tu	20 44 58	12♒11 04	8♊00 48	14♊52 54	1♊58.8	8♒53.3	2♒19.6	1♓44.6	5♈40.6	21♊34.1	15♓25.6	18♍59.1	22♏03.3	18♍00.7
2 W	20 48 55	13 11 56	21 52 28	28 59 32	1R 56.2	10 35.6	1R 48.2	2 31.9	6 00.9	21R 31.4	15 32.3	18R 57.2	22 04.0	17R 59.5
3 Th	20 52 52	14 12 47	6♋13 55	13♋35 09	1 50.9	12 18.6	1 18.4	3 19.3	6 21.2	21 28.9	15 38.9	18 55.2	22 04.7	17 58.3
4 F	20 56 48	15 13 36	21 02 37	28 35 23	1 42.9	14 02.4	0 50.5	4 06.6	6 41.6	21 26.7	15 45.6	18 53.2	22 05.3	17 57.0
5 Sa	21 00 45	16 14 24	6♌12 20	13♌52 09	1 32.7	15 46.9	0 24.5	4 53.9	7 02.1	21 24.6	15 52.3	18 51.2	22 05.9	17 55.7
6 Su	21 04 41	17 15 11	21 33 22	29 14 29	1 21.6	17 32.1	0 00.7	5 41.2	7 22.8	21 22.7	15 59.1	18 49.1	22 06.4	17 54.4
7 M	21 08 38	18 15 57	6♍53 58	14♍30 23	1 10.8	19 18.1	29♑39.2	6 28.5	7 43.5	21 21.1	16 05.9	18 47.0	22 07.0	17 53.1
8 Tu	21 12 34	19 16 41	22 02 29	29 29 09	1 01.6	21 04.8	29 19.9	7 15.8	8 04.3	21 19.6	16 12.8	18 44.9	22 07.5	17 51.8
9 W	21 16 31	20 17 25	6♎49 32	14♎03 02	0 54.8	22 52.1	29 03.1	8 03.1	8 25.3	21 18.3	16 19.6	18 42.7	22 07.9	17 50.4
10 Th	21 20 27	21 18 07	21 09 16	28 08 06	0 50.8	24 40.2	28 48.8	8 50.3	8 46.3	21 17.3	16 26.5	18 40.5	22 08.4	17 49.0
11 F	21 24 24	22 18 48	4♏59 35	11♏43 57	0D 49.1	26 28.8	28 36.9	9 37.6	9 07.4	21 16.4	16 33.5	18 38.2	22 08.7	17 47.6
12 Sa	21 28 21	23 19 29	18 21 32	24 52 49	0R 48.8	28 18.1	28 27.5	10 24.8	9 28.6	21 15.7	16 40.5	18 36.0	22 09.1	17 46.2
13 Su	21 32 17	24 20 08	1♐18 17	7♐38 32	0 48.7	0♓07.8	28 20.6	11 12.0	9 49.9	21 15.3	16 47.5	18 33.7	22 09.4	17 44.8
14 M	21 36 14	25 20 46	13 54 08	20 05 40	0 47.6	1 58.0	28 16.3	11 59.2	10 11.3	21D 15.0	16 54.5	18 31.4	22 09.7	17 43.4
15 Tu	21 40 10	26 21 23	26 13 42	2♑18 48	0 44.4	3 48.5	28D 14.4	12 46.4	10 32.8	21 14.9	17 01.6	18 29.0	22 10.0	17 41.9
16 W	21 44 07	27 21 59	8♑21 26	14 22 04	0 38.3	5 39.2	28 14.9	13 33.6	10 54.3	21 15.1	17 08.7	18 26.7	22 10.2	17 40.5
17 Th	21 48 03	28 22 33	20 21 09	26 19 01	0 29.1	7 29.9	28 17.8	14 20.7	11 16.0	21 15.4	17 15.8	18 24.3	22 10.4	17 39.0
18 F	21 52 00	29 23 06	2♒16 00	8♒12 24	0 17.0	9 20.4	28 23.1	15 07.9	11 37.7	21 16.0	17 23.0	18 21.8	22 10.5	17 37.5
19 Sa	21 55 56	0♓23 38	14 08 25	20 04 18	0 02.9	11 10.6	28 30.7	15 55.0	11 59.5	21 16.7	17 30.1	18 19.4	22 10.7	17 36.0
20 Su	21 59 53	1 24 07	26 00 11	1♓56 16	29♉47.7	13 00.1	28 40.5	16 42.0	12 21.4	21 17.7	17 37.3	18 16.9	22 10.8	17 34.5
21 M	22 03 50	2 24 36	7♓52 42	13 49 36	29 32.7	14 48.7	28 52.5	17 29.1	12 43.3	21 18.8	17 44.5	18 14.5	22R 10.8	17 33.0
22 Tu	22 07 46	3 25 02	19 47 09	25 45 32	29 19.2	16 36.0	29 06.6	18 16.1	13 05.3	21 20.2	17 51.8	18 12.0	22 10.8	17 31.4
23 W	22 11 43	4 25 27	1♈44 56	7♈45 35	29 08.0	18 21.7	29 22.7	19 03.1	13 27.5	21 21.7	17 59.0	18 09.4	22 10.8	17 29.9
24 Th	22 15 39	5 25 50	13 47 46	19 51 47	28 59.7	20 05.2	29 40.9	19 50.1	13 49.6	21 23.4	18 06.3	18 06.9	22 10.7	17 28.4
25 F	22 19 36	6 26 11	25 57 59	2♉06 47	28 54.6	21 46.2	0♒01.0	20 37.1	14 11.9	21 25.4	18 13.6	18 04.4	22 10.7	17 26.8
26 Sa	22 23 32	7 26 31	8♉18 37	14 33 57	28 52.1	23 24.1	0 22.9	21 24.0	14 34.2	21 27.5	18 20.9	18 01.8	22 10.5	17 25.2
27 Su	22 27 29	8 26 48	20 53 17	27 17 10	28 51.5	24 58.3	0 46.6	22 10.9	14 56.6	21 29.8	18 28.2	17 59.3	22 10.4	17 23.7
28 M	22 31 25	9 27 03	3♊46 06	10♊20 35	28 51.6	26 28.3	1 12.0	22 57.8	15 19.0	21 32.4	18 35.6	17 56.7	22 10.2	17 22.1

Astro Data

	Dy Hr Mn
♀ R	5 16:21
☽ 0S	12 20:18
♃⚻♆	25 14:57
☽ 0N	27 9:13
☽ 0S	9 3:52
♃ D	15 6:57
♀ D	15 18:41
♄☍♇	20 4:11
♆ R	22 10:42
☽ 0N	23 14:19
♄☍♅	24 13:30

Planet Ingress

	Dy Hr Mn
☿ ♑	7 18:26
⚳ ♈	14 15:09
☉ ♒	20 12:20
☿ ♒	27 4:10
♂ ♓	30 7:01
♀ ♑R	6 12:46
☿ ♓	13 10:17
☉ ♓	19 2:38
☊ ♉R	19 16:40
♀ ♒	25 10:55

Last Aspect / ☽ Ingress (January)

Last Aspect Dy Hr Mn		☽ Ingress Dy Hr Mn
1 7:10 ♃ ⚹	♉	1 17:46
3 9:06 ♆ ☍	♊	4 0:06
5 22:19 ☿ ☍	♋	6 2:40
7 13:28 ♆ △	♌	8 2:50
9 16:00 ♃ ⚹	♍	10 2:34
11 16:28 ♃ □	♎	12 3:53
13 20:00 ☉ □	♏	14 8:08
16 7:34 ☉ ⚹	♐	16 15:39
18 11:05 ♃ ☍	♑	19 1:45
20 21:10 ♆ ⚹	♒	21 13:26
23 15:20 ♂ ☌	♓	24 1:58
26 12:24 ☿ ⚹	♈	26 14:33
28 23:44 ♂ ⚹	♉	29 1:43
30 19:14 ♆ ☍	♊	31 9:43

Last Aspect / ☽ Ingress (February)

Last Aspect Dy Hr Mn		☽ Ingress Dy Hr Mn
1 23:26 ♃ ☌	♋	2 13:41
4 1:40 ♆ △	♌	4 14:14
6 0:51 ♆ □	♍	6 13:11
8 11:45 ♀ △	♎	8 12:50
10 13:10 ♀ □	♏	10 15:15
12 19:26 ☿ □	♐	12 21:33
14 23:12 ☉ ⚹	♑	15 7:26
17 16:01 ♀ ☌	♒	17 19:26
19 16:16 ♆ □	♓	20 8:05
22 18:52 ♀ ⚹	♈	22 20:30
25 7:48 ♀ □	♉	25 7:53
27 7:05 ☿ ⚹	♊	27 17:03

☽ Phases & Eclipses

Dy Hr Mn	
7 5:16	○ 16♋28
13 20:00	☾ 23♎12
21 15:46	● 1♒10
29 19:48	☽ 9♉28
5 15:58	○ 16♌24
12 8:53	☾ 23♏12
20 10:49	● 1♓21
28 10:15	☽ 9♊23

Astro Data

1 January 1966
Julian Day # 24107
SVP 5♓44'19"
GC 26♐21.9 ⚵ 21♒26.7
Eris 10♈25.6 ⚶ 28♒05.6
⚷ 18♓28.8 ⚴ 5♋21.6R
☽ Mean ☊ 2♊37.2

1 February 1966
Julian Day # 24138
SVP 5♓44'14"
GC 26♐21.9 ⚵ 1♓07.5
Eris 10♈32.1 ⚶ 12♓37.9
⚷ 19♓45.7 ⚴ 29♊12.4R
☽ Mean ☊ 0♊58.7

March 1966

LONGITUDE

Day	Sid.Time	☉	0 hr ☽	Noon☽	True☊	☿	♀	♂	⚳	♃	♄	♅	♆	♇
1 Tu	22 35 22	10♓27 17	17♊01 07	23♊48 04	28♉51.0	27♓53.5	1♒39.1	23♓44.6	15♈41.5	21♊35.1	18♓42.9	17♍54.1	22♏10.0	17♍20.5
2 W	22 39 19	11 27 28	0♋41 46	7♋42 24	28R 48.7	29 13.3	2 07.9	24 31.5	16 04.1	21 38.0	18 50.3	17R 51.5	22R 09.7	17R 18.9
3 Th	22 43 15	12 27 37	14 49 59	22 04 21	28 44.0	0♈27.1	2 38.1	25 18.2	16 26.7	21 41.1	18 57.6	17 48.9	22 09.5	17 17.4
4 F	22 47 12	13 27 45	29 25 08	6♌51 42	28 36.6	1 34.3	3 09.9	26 05.0	16 49.4	21 44.3	19 05.0	17 46.3	22 09.1	17 15.8
5 Sa	22 51 08	14 27 50	14♌23 14	21 58 40	28 27.0	2 34.3	3 43.1	26 51.7	17 12.1	21 47.8	19 12.4	17 43.7	22 08.8	17 14.2
6 Su	22 55 05	15 27 53	29 36 45	7♍16 06	28 16.3	3 26.8	4 17.7	27 38.4	17 34.9	21 51.4	19 19.7	17 41.1	22 08.4	17 12.6
7 M	22 59 01	16 27 54	14♍55 16	22 32 47	28 05.8	4 11.3	4 53.6	28 25.0	17 57.8	21 55.3	19 27.1	17 38.4	22 08.0	17 11.0
8 Tu	23 02 58	17 27 53	0♎07 15	7♎37 24	27 56.6	4 47.3	5 30.8	29 11.6	18 20.7	21 59.2	19 34.5	17 35.8	22 07.5	17 09.4
9 W	23 06 54	18 27 50	15 02 10	22 20 39	27 49.7	5 14.7	6 09.3	29 58.2	18 43.6	22 03.4	19 41.9	17 33.2	22 07.1	17 07.8
10 Th	23 10 51	19 27 46	29 32 14	6♏36 30	27 45.5	5 33.3	6 48.9	0♈44.8	19 06.6	22 07.8	19 49.3	17 30.6	22 06.6	17 06.2
11 F	23 14 48	20 27 40	13♏33 17	20 22 36	27D 43.8	5R 43.0	7 29.7	1 31.3	19 29.7	22 12.3	19 56.7	17 27.9	22 06.0	17 04.6
12 Sa	23 18 44	21 27 33	27 04 39	3♐39 45	27 43.7	5 43.8	8 11.6	2 17.8	19 52.8	22 17.0	20 04.1	17 25.3	22 05.4	17 03.0
13 Su	23 22 41	22 27 23	10♐08 22	16 31 00	27R 44.2	5 36.0	8 54.5	3 04.2	20 16.0	22 21.9	20 11.5	17 22.7	22 04.8	17 01.4
14 M	23 26 37	23 27 13	22 48 15	29 00 44	27 44.1	5 19.9	9 38.4	3 50.6	20 39.2	22 26.9	20 18.9	17 20.1	22 04.2	16 59.8
15 Tu	23 30 34	24 27 00	5♑09 04	11♑13 52	27 42.6	4 56.0	10 23.3	4 37.0	21 02.5	22 32.1	20 26.3	17 17.5	22 03.6	16 58.2
16 W	23 34 30	25 26 46	17 15 46	23 15 19	27 38.8	4 24.9	11 09.1	5 23.3	21 25.8	22 37.5	20 33.7	17 14.9	22 02.9	16 56.7
17 Th	23 38 27	26 26 30	29 13 06	5♒09 36	27 32.5	3 47.4	11 55.8	6 09.7	21 49.1	22 43.1	20 41.1	17 12.3	22 02.1	16 55.1
18 F	23 42 23	27 26 12	11♒05 18	17 00 36	27 23.7	3 04.4	12 43.4	6 55.9	22 12.5	22 48.8	20 48.4	17 09.8	22 01.4	16 53.5
19 Sa	23 46 20	28 25 53	22 55 54	28 51 31	27 13.2	2 16.9	13 31.7	7 42.2	22 35.9	22 54.7	20 55.8	17 07.2	22 00.6	16 52.0
20 Su	23 50 17	29 25 31	4♓47 43	10♓44 47	27 01.8	1 26.0	14 20.9	8 28.3	22 59.4	23 00.7	21 03.2	17 04.6	21 59.8	16 50.4
21 M	23 54 13	0♈25 08	16 42 54	22 42 15	26 50.4	0 32.8	15 10.8	9 14.5	23 22.9	23 06.9	21 10.5	17 02.1	21 59.0	16 48.9
22 Tu	23 58 10	1 24 42	28 43 00	4♈45 17	26 40.1	29♓38.6	16 01.4	10 00.6	23 46.5	23 13.2	21 17.8	16 59.6	21 58.1	16 47.3
23 W	0 02 06	2 24 14	10♈49 16	16 55 04	26 31.7	28 44.5	16 52.7	10 46.7	24 10.1	23 19.7	21 25.2	16 57.1	21 57.2	16 45.8
24 Th	0 06 03	3 23 45	23 02 51	29 12 46	26 25.7	27 51.6	17 44.7	11 32.7	24 33.7	23 26.4	21 32.5	16 54.6	21 56.3	16 44.3
25 F	0 09 59	4 23 13	5♉25 01	11♉39 49	26 22.2	27 00.8	18 37.3	12 18.7	24 57.4	23 33.2	21 39.8	16 52.1	21 55.3	16 42.7
26 Sa	0 13 56	5 22 39	17 57 25	24 18 05	26D 21.0	26 13.1	19 30.5	13 04.7	25 21.0	23 40.1	21 47.0	16 49.6	21 54.4	16 41.2
27 Su	0 17 52	6 22 03	0♊42 07	7♊09 50	26 21.4	25 29.2	20 24.3	13 50.6	25 44.8	23 47.2	21 54.3	16 47.2	21 53.4	16 39.8
28 M	0 21 49	7 21 25	13 41 34	20 17 40	26 22.6	24 49.8	21 18.7	14 36.4	26 08.5	23 54.5	22 01.5	16 44.8	21 52.3	16 38.3
29 Tu	0 25 45	8 20 44	26 58 27	3♋44 11	26R 23.5	24 15.3	22 13.6	15 22.2	26 32.3	24 01.9	22 08.7	16 42.4	21 51.3	16 36.8
30 W	0 29 42	9 20 01	10♋35 07	17 31 24	26 23.3	23 46.1	23 09.0	16 08.0	26 56.2	24 09.4	22 16.0	16 40.1	21 50.2	16 35.4
31 Th	0 33 39	10 19 16	24 33 06	1♌40 09	26 21.3	23 22.4	24 05.0	16 53.7	27 20.0	24 17.1	22 23.1	16 37.7	21 49.1	16 33.9

April 1966

LONGITUDE

Day	Sid.Time	☉	0 hr ☽	Noon☽	True☊	☿	♀	♂	⚳	♃	♄	♅	♆	♇
1 F	0 37 35	11♈18 28	8♌52 21	16♌09 18	26♉17.5	23♓04.4	25♒01.4	17♈39.4	27♈43.9	24♊24.9	22♓30.3	16♍35.4	21♏48.0	16♍32.5
2 Sa	0 41 32	12 17 38	23 30 29	0♍55 11	26R 12.0	22R 52.1	25 58.4	18 25.1	28 07.8	24 32.8	22 37.4	16R 33.1	21R 46.8	16R 31.1
3 Su	0 45 28	13 16 46	8♍22 33	15 51 34	26 05.6	22D 45.5	26 55.7	19 10.6	28 31.7	24 40.9	22 44.5	16 30.9	21 45.7	16 29.7
4 M	0 49 25	14 15 51	23 21 08	0♎50 08	25 59.1	22 44.5	27 53.5	19 56.2	28 55.7	24 49.1	22 51.6	16 28.6	21 44.5	16 28.3
5 Tu	0 53 21	15 14 54	8♎17 24	15 41 49	25 53.5	22 48.9	28 51.8	20 41.7	29 19.6	24 57.5	22 58.6	16 26.4	21 43.3	16 27.0
6 W	0 57 18	16 13 55	23 02 22	0♏18 11	25 49.4	22 58.7	29 50.5	21 27.1	29 43.6	25 05.9	23 05.7	16 24.2	21 42.0	16 25.6
7 Th	1 01 14	17 12 55	7♏28 30	14 32 47	25D 47.1	23 13.5	0♓49.5	22 12.5	0♉07.6	25 14.5	23 12.7	16 22.1	21 40.8	16 24.3
8 F	1 05 11	18 11 52	21 30 39	28 21 54	25 46.6	23 33.3	1 49.0	22 57.9	0 31.7	25 23.2	23 19.6	16 20.0	21 39.5	16 23.0
9 Sa	1 09 08	19 10 48	5♐06 28	11♐44 30	25 47.4	23 57.7	2 48.8	23 43.2	0 55.7	25 32.0	23 26.6	16 17.9	21 38.2	16 21.7
10 Su	1 13 04	20 09 42	18 16 13	24 41 57	25 49.0	24 26.7	3 49.0	24 28.4	1 19.8	25 41.0	23 33.5	16 15.9	21 36.9	16 20.4
11 M	1 17 01	21 08 34	1♑02 10	7♑17 20	25 50.5	24 59.9	4 49.5	25 13.6	1 43.9	25 50.0	23 40.3	16 13.8	21 35.6	16 19.1
12 Tu	1 20 57	22 07 25	13 28 01	19 34 48	25R 51.3	25 37.1	5 50.4	25 58.8	2 08.1	25 59.2	23 47.2	16 11.9	21 34.2	16 17.9
13 W	1 24 54	23 06 14	25 38 15	1♒39 01	25 51.0	26 18.2	6 51.6	26 43.9	2 32.2	26 08.5	23 54.0	16 09.9	21 32.8	16 16.7
14 Th	1 28 50	24 05 01	7♒37 39	13 34 46	25 49.2	27 02.9	7 53.1	27 29.0	2 56.4	26 17.9	24 00.7	16 08.0	21 31.5	16 15.5
15 F	1 32 47	25 03 46	19 30 55	25 26 38	25 46.0	27 51.2	8 55.0	28 14.0	3 20.6	26 27.5	24 07.5	16 06.2	21 30.0	16 14.3
16 Sa	1 36 43	26 02 30	1♓22 25	7♓18 43	25 41.8	28 42.7	9 57.1	28 59.0	3 44.8	26 37.1	24 14.2	16 04.3	21 28.6	16 13.2
17 Su	1 40 40	27 01 11	13 15 59	19 14 34	25 36.9	29 37.5	10 59.4	29 44.0	4 09.0	26 46.8	24 20.8	16 02.5	21 27.2	16 12.0
18 M	1 44 37	27 59 51	25 14 50	1♈17 04	25 31.9	0♈35.2	12 02.1	0♉28.8	4 33.2	26 56.7	24 27.4	16 00.8	21 25.7	16 10.9
19 Tu	1 48 33	28 58 29	7♈21 31	13 28 23	25 27.5	1 35.8	13 05.0	1 13.7	4 57.4	27 06.6	24 34.0	15 59.1	21 24.3	16 09.8
20 W	1 52 30	29 57 05	19 37 52	25 50 05	25 23.9	2 39.1	14 08.2	1 58.5	5 21.7	27 16.7	24 40.5	15 57.4	21 22.8	16 08.7
21 Th	1 56 26	0♉55 40	2♉05 10	8♉23 11	25 21.6	3 45.1	15 11.6	2 43.2	5 45.9	27 26.8	24 47.0	15 55.8	21 21.3	16 07.7
22 F	2 00 23	1 54 12	14 44 14	21 08 22	25D 20.6	4 53.6	16 15.2	3 27.9	6 10.2	27 37.1	24 53.4	15 54.2	21 19.8	16 06.7
23 Sa	2 04 19	2 52 43	27 35 38	4♊06 05	25 20.8	6 04.6	17 19.1	4 12.5	6 34.5	27 47.5	24 59.8	15 52.7	21 18.3	16 05.7
24 Su	2 08 16	3 51 11	10♊39 47	17 16 45	25 21.8	7 17.9	18 23.1	4 57.1	6 58.8	27 57.9	25 06.2	15 51.2	21 16.7	16 04.7
25 M	2 12 12	4 49 38	23 57 03	0♋40 44	25 23.2	8 33.5	19 27.4	5 41.6	7 23.1	28 08.4	25 12.4	15 49.7	21 15.2	16 03.8
26 Tu	2 16 09	5 48 02	7♋27 50	14 18 22	25 24.6	9 51.3	20 31.9	6 26.1	7 47.4	28 19.1	25 18.7	15 48.3	21 13.7	16 02.9
27 W	2 20 06	6 46 25	21 12 20	28 09 42	25R 25.4	11 11.3	21 36.6	7 10.6	8 11.7	28 29.8	25 24.9	15 47.0	21 12.1	16 02.0
28 Th	2 24 02	7 44 45	5♌10 23	12♌14 15	25 25.6	12 33.4	22 41.5	7 54.9	8 36.0	28 40.6	25 31.0	15 45.7	21 10.5	16 01.1
29 F	2 27 59	8 43 03	19 21 04	26 30 35	25 24.9	13 57.5	23 46.5	8 39.2	9 00.4	28 51.5	25 37.1	15 44.4	21 09.0	16 00.3
30 Sa	2 31 55	9 41 19	3♍42 25	10♍56 08	25 23.6	15 23.7	24 51.7	9 23.5	9 24.7	29 02.5	25 43.2	15 43.2	21 07.4	15 59.5

Astro Data	Dy Hr Mn
☿0N	1 12:30
⚳0N	2 0:22
☽0S	8 13:57
♃⚻♆	10 6:04
♂0N	11 15:08
☿R	12 2:17
☉0N	21 1:53
☽0N	22 19:54
♄△♆	27 9:17
☿0S	27 19:26
☿D	4 4:24
♅☌♇	4 20:31
☽0S	5 0:46
☽0N	19 2:50
☿0N	23 16:40

Planet Ingress		Dy Hr Mn
☿	♈	3 2:57
♂	♈	9 12:55
☉	♈	21 1:53
☿	♓R	22 2:34
♀	♓	6 15:53
⚳	♉	7 4:22
♂	♉	17 20:35
☿	♈	17 21:31
☉	♉	20 13:12

Last Aspect Dy Hr Mn			☽ Ingress	Dy Hr Mn
1 19:55	☿	□	♋	1 22:48
3 17:36	♂	△	♌	4 0:57
5 12:16	♆	□	♍	6 0:36
7 21:48	♂	☍	♎	7 23:48
9 11:32	♃	△	♏	10 0:47
11 15:04	♆	☌	♐	12 5:18
14 0:19	☉	□	♑	14 13:55
16 16:48	☉	⚹	♒	17 1:35
18 23:51	♃	△	♓	19 14:19
21 12:50	♃	□	♈	22 2:33
24 0:40	♃	⚹	♉	24 13:32
26 15:24	☿	⚹	♊	26 22:41
28 19:49	☿	□	♋	29 5:23
30 22:22	☿	△	♌	31 9:12

Last Aspect Dy Hr Mn			☽ Ingress	Dy Hr Mn
2 3:27	♀	☍	♍	2 10:31
4 2:16	♃	□	♎	4 10:40
6 11:11	♀	△	♏	6 11:30
8 3:20	☿	△	♐	8 14:54
10 13:52	♃	☍	♑	10 22:02
13 1:32	♂	□	♒	13 8:42
15 18:02	♂	⚹	♓	15 21:13
18 3:16	♃	□	♈	18 9:27
20 14:49	♃	⚹	♉	20 20:00
22 19:03	♄	⚹	♊	23 4:27
25 7:25	♃	☌	♋	25 10:48
27 7:14	♄	△	♌	27 15:09
29 15:58	♃	⚹	♍	29 17:50

☽ Phases & Eclipses Dy Hr Mn		
7 1:45	○	16♍02
14 0:19	☾	22♐58
22 4:46	●	1♈07
29 20:43	☽	8♋42
5 11:13	○	15♎13
12 17:28	☾	22♑21
20 20:35	●	0♉18
28 3:49	☽	7♌25

Astro Data

1 March 1966
Julian Day # 24166
SVP 5♓44'10"
GC 26♐22.0 ⚴ 10♓23.1
Eris 10♈46.0 ⚵ 26♓57.9
⚷ 21♓20.2 ⚶ 29♊16.6
☽ Mean ☊ 29♉29.8

1 April 1966
Julian Day # 24197
SVP 5♓44'06"
GC 26♐22.1 ⚴ 20♓41.3
Eris 11♈06.4 ⚵ 13♈45.9
⚷ 23♓12.1 ⚶ 5♋04.4
☽ Mean ☊ 27♉51.2

LONGITUDE — May 1966

Day	Sid.Time	☉	0 hr ☽	Noon ☽	True ☊	☿	♀	♂	⚳	♃	♄	♅	♆	♇
1 Su	2 35 52	10♉39 33	18♍11 11	25♍27 00	25♉21.8	16♈51.9	25♓57.2	10♉07.7	9♉49.0	29♊13.6	25♓49.1	15♍42.0	21♏05.8	15♍58.7
2 M	2 39 48	11 37 44	2♎42 53	9♎58 10	25R 20.0	18 22.1	27 02.7	10 51.9	10 13.3	29 24.7	25 55.1	15R 40.9	21R 04.2	15R 57.9
3 Tu	2 43 45	12 35 54	17 12 06	24 23 59	25 18.5	19 54.2	28 08.5	11 36.0	10 37.7	29 35.9	26 00.9	15 39.8	21 02.6	15 57.2
4 W	2 47 41	13 34 02	1♏33 07	8♏38 52	25 17.5	21 28.3	29 14.4	12 20.0	11 02.0	29 47.3	26 06.8	15 38.8	21 01.0	15 56.5
5 Th	2 51 38	14 32 09	15 40 37	22 37 55	25D 17.2	23 04.3	0♈20.5	13 04.1	11 26.3	29 58.6	26 12.5	15 37.8	20 59.3	15 55.8
6 F	2 55 35	15 30 14	29 30 22	6♐17 40	25 17.3	24 42.3	1 26.8	13 48.0	11 50.7	0♋10.1	26 18.2	15 36.9	20 57.7	15 55.1
7 Sa	2 59 31	16 28 17	12♐59 40	19 36 17	25 17.9	26 22.1	2 33.2	14 31.9	12 15.0	0 21.6	26 23.9	15 36.0	20 56.1	15 54.5
8 Su	3 03 28	17 26 19	26 07 34	2♑33 39	25 18.6	28 04.0	3 39.7	15 15.8	12 39.3	0 33.2	26 29.4	15 35.2	20 54.5	15 53.9
9 M	3 07 24	18 24 19	8♑54 46	15 11 14	25 19.3	29 47.7	4 46.4	15 59.6	13 03.7	0 44.9	26 35.0	15 34.4	20 52.9	15 53.4
10 Tu	3 11 21	19 22 19	21 23 26	27 31 47	25 19.9	1♉33.4	5 53.2	16 43.3	13 28.0	0 56.7	26 40.4	15 33.7	20 51.2	15 52.8
11 W	3 15 17	20 20 16	3♒36 47	9♒38 58	25R 20.3	3 21.1	7 00.2	17 27.0	13 52.3	1 08.5	26 45.8	15 33.0	20 49.6	15 52.3
12 Th	3 19 14	21 18 13	15 38 51	21 37 00	25 20.4	5 10.7	8 07.3	18 10.7	14 16.6	1 20.4	26 51.1	15 32.4	20 48.0	15 51.9
13 F	3 23 10	22 16 08	27 34 02	3♓30 29	25 20.3	7 02.2	9 14.6	18 54.3	14 41.0	1 32.3	26 56.4	15 31.8	20 46.3	15 51.4
14 Sa	3 27 07	23 14 02	9♓26 57	15 23 58	25 20.1	8 55.7	10 21.9	19 37.8	15 05.3	1 44.3	27 01.6	15 31.3	20 44.7	15 51.0
15 Su	3 31 04	24 11 54	21 22 06	27 21 51	25 20.0	10 51.0	11 29.4	20 21.3	15 29.6	1 56.4	27 06.7	15 30.8	20 43.1	15 50.6
16 M	3 35 00	25 09 45	3♈23 41	9♈28 05	25D 19.9	12 48.3	12 37.0	21 04.7	15 53.9	2 08.5	27 11.8	15 30.4	20 41.5	15 50.3
17 Tu	3 38 57	26 07 35	15 35 24	21 46 01	25 19.9	14 47.5	13 44.7	21 48.1	16 18.2	2 20.7	27 16.8	15 30.0	20 39.8	15 49.9
18 W	3 42 53	27 05 24	28 00 13	4♉18 15	25 20.1	16 48.5	14 52.5	22 31.5	16 42.5	2 33.0	27 21.7	15 29.7	20 38.2	15 49.6
19 Th	3 46 50	28 03 12	10♉40 17	17 06 27	25R 20.2	18 51.2	16 00.4	23 14.8	17 06.8	2 45.3	27 26.6	15 29.5	20 36.6	15 49.4
20 F	3 50 46	29 00 58	23 36 46	0♊11 14	25 20.2	20 55.6	17 08.5	23 58.0	17 31.0	2 57.7	27 31.3	15 29.3	20 35.0	15 49.1
21 Sa	3 54 43	29 58 43	6♊49 47	13 32 17	25 20.0	23 01.6	18 16.6	24 41.2	17 55.3	3 10.1	27 36.0	15 29.1	20 33.4	15 48.9
22 Su	3 58 39	0♊56 27	20 18 32	27 08 18	25 19.6	25 09.0	19 24.8	25 24.3	18 19.6	3 22.6	27 40.7	15 29.0	20 31.8	15 48.8
23 M	4 02 36	1 54 09	4♋01 19	10♋57 17	25 18.9	27 17.7	20 33.1	26 07.4	18 43.8	3 35.1	27 45.2	15D 29.0	20 30.2	15 48.6
24 Tu	4 06 33	2 51 49	17 55 51	24 56 42	25 18.1	29 27.5	21 41.5	26 50.4	19 08.0	3 47.7	27 49.7	15 29.0	20 28.6	15 48.5
25 W	4 10 29	3 49 29	1♌59 27	9♌03 46	25 17.3	1♊38.2	22 50.0	27 33.4	19 32.2	4 00.3	27 54.1	15 29.1	20 27.0	15 48.5
26 Th	4 14 26	4 47 06	16 09 17	23 15 40	25D 16.7	3 49.6	23 58.6	28 16.3	19 56.4	4 13.0	27 58.4	15 29.2	20 25.4	15D 48.4
27 F	4 18 22	5 44 42	0♍22 35	7♍29 43	25 16.6	6 01.3	25 07.3	28 59.2	20 20.6	4 25.7	28 02.7	15 29.4	20 23.9	15 48.4
28 Sa	4 22 19	6 42 17	14 36 44	21 43 19	25 16.9	8 13.3	26 16.0	29 42.0	20 44.8	4 38.5	28 06.8	15 29.6	20 22.3	15 48.4
29 Su	4 26 15	7 39 50	28 49 11	5♎54 02	25 17.6	10 25.1	27 24.8	0♊24.7	21 08.9	4 51.3	28 10.9	15 29.9	20 20.8	15 48.5
30 M	4 30 12	8 37 22	12♎57 32	19 59 25	25 18.6	12 36.6	28 33.7	1 07.4	21 33.0	5 04.1	28 14.9	15 30.2	20 19.2	15 48.5
31 Tu	4 34 08	9 34 52	26 59 20	3♏57 02	25 19.6	14 47.3	29 42.7	1 50.0	21 57.1	5 17.0	28 18.8	15 30.6	20 17.7	15 48.7

LONGITUDE — June 1966

Day	Sid.Time	☉	0 hr ☽	Noon ☽	True ☊	☿	♀	♂	⚳	♃	♄	♅	♆	♇
1 W	4 38 05	10♊32 21	10♏52 10	17♏44 29	25♉20.3	16♊57.2	0♉51.8	2♊32.6	22♉21.2	5♋29.9	28♓22.7	15♍31.1	20♏16.2	15♍48.8
2 Th	4 42 02	11 29 50	24 33 41	1♐19 32	25R 20.3	19 05.9	2 00.9	3 15.2	22 45.3	5 42.9	28 26.4	15 31.6	20R 14.7	15 49.0
3 F	4 45 58	12 27 17	8♐01 47	14 40 15	25 19.5	21 13.2	3 10.2	3 57.7	23 09.3	5 55.9	28 30.1	15 32.1	20 13.2	15 49.2
4 Sa	4 49 55	13 24 43	21 14 48	27 45 20	25 17.9	23 18.8	4 19.5	4 40.1	23 33.4	6 08.9	28 33.7	15 32.7	20 11.8	15 49.4
5 Su	4 53 51	14 22 08	4♑11 49	10♑34 16	25 15.4	25 22.7	5 28.8	5 22.5	23 57.4	6 22.0	28 37.2	15 33.4	20 10.3	15 49.7
6 M	4 57 48	15 19 33	16 52 46	23 07 29	25 12.5	27 24.7	6 38.3	6 04.8	24 21.4	6 35.1	28 40.6	15 34.1	20 08.9	15 50.0
7 Tu	5 01 44	16 16 57	29 18 36	5♒26 23	25 09.4	29 24.5	7 47.8	6 47.1	24 45.4	6 48.2	28 44.0	15 34.8	20 07.4	15 50.3
8 W	5 05 41	17 14 20	11♒31 12	17 33 25	25 06.6	1♋22.2	8 57.4	7 29.3	25 09.3	7 01.4	28 47.2	15 35.7	20 06.0	15 50.7
9 Th	5 09 38	18 11 42	23 33 28	29 31 49	25 04.4	3 17.7	10 07.1	8 11.5	25 33.2	7 14.6	28 50.4	15 36.5	20 04.6	15 51.1
10 F	5 13 34	19 09 04	5♓28 59	11♓25 31	25D 03.1	5 10.8	11 16.8	8 53.6	25 57.1	7 27.8	28 53.5	15 37.4	20 03.2	15 51.5
11 Sa	5 17 31	20 06 25	17 21 59	23 18 58	25 02.9	7 01.5	12 26.6	9 35.7	26 21.0	7 41.1	28 56.4	15 38.4	20 01.9	15 51.9
12 Su	5 21 27	21 03 46	29 17 04	5♈16 52	25 03.6	8 49.8	13 36.5	10 17.8	26 44.8	7 54.4	28 59.3	15 39.4	20 00.5	15 52.4
13 M	5 25 24	22 01 07	11♈18 58	17 23 56	25 05.1	10 35.7	14 46.5	10 59.7	27 08.7	8 07.7	29 02.1	15 40.5	19 59.2	15 52.9
14 Tu	5 29 20	22 58 27	23 32 19	29 44 38	25 06.7	12 19.1	15 56.5	11 41.7	27 32.5	8 21.0	29 04.8	15 41.6	19 57.9	15 53.5
15 W	5 33 17	23 55 46	6♉01 20	12♉22 48	25R 08.1	14 00.0	17 06.5	12 23.6	27 56.2	8 34.4	29 07.4	15 42.8	19 56.6	15 54.1
16 Th	5 37 13	24 53 05	18 49 24	25 21 19	25 08.6	15 38.3	18 16.7	13 05.4	28 20.0	8 47.7	29 09.9	15 44.0	19 55.3	15 54.7
17 F	5 41 10	25 50 24	1♊58 44	8♊41 40	25 07.9	17 14.2	19 26.8	13 47.2	28 43.7	9 01.1	29 12.4	15 45.3	19 54.1	15 55.3
18 Sa	5 45 07	26 47 43	15 30 01	22 23 36	25 05.8	18 47.5	20 37.1	14 28.9	29 07.3	9 14.6	29 14.7	15 46.6	19 52.8	15 56.0
19 Su	5 49 03	27 45 01	29 22 03	6♋24 55	25 02.2	20 18.2	21 47.4	15 10.6	29 31.0	9 28.0	29 16.9	15 48.0	19 51.6	15 56.7
20 M	5 53 00	28 42 18	13♋31 41	20 41 40	24 57.6	21 46.4	22 57.8	15 52.2	29 54.6	9 41.4	29 19.1	15 49.4	19 50.4	15 57.4
21 Tu	5 56 56	29 39 35	27 54 10	5♌08 27	24 52.6	23 12.0	24 08.2	16 33.8	0♊18.2	9 54.9	29 21.1	15 50.9	19 49.3	15 58.2
22 W	6 00 53	0♋36 51	12♌23 43	19 39 15	24 47.8	24 34.9	25 18.6	17 15.3	0 41.7	10 08.4	29 23.1	15 52.4	19 48.1	15 59.0
23 Th	6 04 49	1 34 06	26 54 20	4♍08 18	24 44.0	25 55.1	26 29.1	17 56.8	1 05.2	10 21.9	29 24.9	15 54.0	19 47.0	15 59.8
24 F	6 08 46	2 31 21	11♍20 38	18 30 49	24 41.6	27 12.6	27 39.7	18 38.2	1 28.7	10 35.4	29 26.7	15 55.6	19 45.9	16 00.6
25 Sa	6 12 42	3 28 35	25 38 30	2♎43 24	24D 40.8	28 27.4	28 50.3	19 19.6	1 52.1	10 48.9	29 28.3	15 57.3	19 44.8	16 01.5
26 Su	6 16 39	4 25 49	9♎45 18	16 44 05	24 41.3	29 39.3	0♊01.0	20 00.9	2 15.5	11 02.4	29 29.9	15 59.0	19 43.8	16 02.4
27 M	6 20 36	5 23 02	23 39 41	0♏32 06	24 42.6	0♌48.3	1 11.7	20 42.2	2 38.8	11 16.0	29 31.3	16 00.8	19 42.7	16 03.3
28 Tu	6 24 32	6 20 14	7♏21 19	14 07 23	24R 43.8	1 54.4	2 22.5	21 23.4	3 02.1	11 29.5	29 32.7	16 02.6	19 41.7	16 04.3
29 W	6 28 29	7 17 26	20 50 21	27 30 15	24 44.2	2 57.5	3 33.3	22 04.6	3 25.4	11 43.0	29 34.0	16 04.5	19 40.8	16 05.3
30 Th	6 32 25	8 14 38	4♐07 07	10♐40 59	24 43.0	3 57.4	4 44.2	22 45.7	3 48.6	11 56.6	29 35.1	16 06.4	19 39.8	16 06.3

Astro Data	Dy Hr Mn
☽0S	2 10:09
♀0N	8 5:15
☽0N	16 10:51
♅D	23 16:37
♇D	27 11:12
☽0S	29 17:02
♃⚻♆	31 13:11
☽0N	12 18:58
☽0S	25 22:07
♅☌♇	30 9:58

Planet Ingress	Dy Hr Mn
♀ ♈	5 4:33
♃ ♋	5 14:52
☿ ♉	9 14:48
☉ ♊	21 12:32
☿ ♊	24 17:59
♂ ♊	28 22:07
♀ ♉	31 18:00
☿ ♋	7 19:11
⚳ ♊	20 17:30
☉ ♋	21 20:33
♀ ♊	26 11:40
☿ ♌	26 19:05

Last Aspect Dy Hr Mn		☽ Ingress Dy Hr Mn
1 18:19	♃ □	♎ 1 19:31
3 20:50	♃ △	♏ 3 21:23
5 18:16	♄ △	♐ 6 0:52
8 2:19	☿ △	♑ 8 7:12
10 10:18	♄ ✶	♒ 10 16:52
12 11:19	☉ □	♓ 13 4:55
15 11:30	♄ ☌	♈ 15 17:15
16 18:49	♀ ☌	♉ 18 3:49
20 9:42	☉ ☌	♊ 20 11:40
22 12:57	♄ □	♋ 22 17:00
24 16:57	♄ △	♌ 24 20:37
26 20:54	♂ □	♍ 26 23:22
28 22:51	♀ ☍	♎ 29 2:00
31 4:02	♀ ☍	♏ 31 5:11

Last Aspect Dy Hr Mn		☽ Ingress Dy Hr Mn
2 6:51	♄ △	♐ 2 9:38
4 13:30	♄ □	♑ 4 16:10
6 22:49	♄ ✶	♒ 7 1:21
8 17:04	♆ □	♓ 9 12:57
11 23:21	♄ ☌	♈ 12 1:26
13 21:48	☉ ✶	♉ 14 12:30
16 18:57	♄ ✶	♊ 16 20:26
18 23:49	♄ □	♋ 19 1:05
21 2:23	♄ △	♌ 21 3:29
22 22:11	♀ □	♍ 23 5:08
25 6:28	♄ ☍	♎ 25 7:23
26 17:58	♂ △	♏ 27 11:04
29 15:44	♄ △	♐ 29 16:31

☽ Phases & Eclipses Dy Hr Mn	
4 21:00	○ 13♏56
4 21:11	• A 0.916
12 11:19	☾ 21♒17
20 9:42	● 28♉55
20 9:38:24	• A 00'04"
27 8:50	☽ 5♍37
3 7:40	○ 12♐17
11 4:58	☾ 19♓50
18 20:09	● 27♊07
25 13:22	☽ 3♎32

Astro Data

1 May 1966
Julian Day # 24227
SVP 5♓44'03"
GC 26♐22.1 ⚴ 0♈15.3
Eris 11♈26.2 ⚵ 0♉39.9
⚷ 24♓47.3 ⚶ 14♋21.6
☽ Mean ☊ 26♉15.9

1 June 1966
Julian Day # 24258
SVP 5♓43'58"
GC 26♐22.2 ⚴ 9♈10.0
Eris 11♈41.8 ⚵ 18♉31.0
⚷ 25♓53.5 ⚶ 26♋11.7
☽ Mean ☊ 24♉37.4

July 1966

LONGITUDE

Day	Sid.Time	☉	0 hr ☽	Noon ☽	True ☊	☿	♀	♂	⚳	♃	♄	♅	♆	♇
1 F	6 36 22	9♋11 49	17♐11 52	23♐39 46	24♉39.8	4♌54.1	5♊55.1	23♊26.8	4♊11.8	12♋10.1	29♓36.2	16♍08.3	19♏38.9	16♍07.4
2 Sa	6 40 18	10 09 01	0♑04 41	6♑26 37	24R 34.6	5 47.4	7 06.1	24 07.8	4 34.9	12 23.7	29 37.1	16 10.3	19R 38.0	16 08.4
3 Su	6 44 15	11 06 12	12 45 35	19 01 36	24 27.6	6 37.4	8 17.1	24 48.8	4 58.0	12 37.3	29 38.0	16 12.4	19 37.1	16 09.5
4 M	6 48 11	12 03 23	25 14 44	1♒25 02	24 19.3	7 23.8	9 28.2	25 29.7	5 21.0	12 50.8	29 38.8	16 14.5	19 36.3	16 10.7
5 Tu	6 52 08	13 00 34	7♒32 38	13 37 41	24 10.5	8 06.6	10 39.3	26 10.5	5 44.0	13 04.4	29 39.4	16 16.6	19 35.4	16 11.8
6 W	6 56 05	13 57 46	19 40 24	25 41 01	24 02.2	8 45.5	11 50.5	26 51.4	6 07.0	13 17.9	29 40.0	16 18.8	19 34.6	16 13.0
7 Th	7 00 01	14 54 57	1♓39 51	7♓37 15	23 55.0	9 20.5	13 01.7	27 32.2	6 29.9	13 31.5	29 40.4	16 21.0	19 33.9	16 14.2
8 F	7 03 58	15 52 09	13 33 38	19 29 27	23 49.5	9 51.5	14 13.0	28 12.9	6 52.7	13 45.0	29 40.8	16 23.2	19 33.1	16 15.4
9 Sa	7 07 54	16 49 21	25 25 11	1♈21 24	23 46.1	10 18.3	15 24.4	28 53.6	7 15.5	13 58.6	29 41.1	16 25.5	19 32.4	16 16.7
10 Su	7 11 51	17 46 34	7♈18 40	13 17 35	23D 44.7	10 40.7	16 35.8	29 34.2	7 38.2	14 12.1	29 41.2	16 27.9	19 31.7	16 18.0
11 M	7 15 47	18 43 47	19 18 46	25 22 52	23 44.8	10 58.7	17 47.2	0♋14.8	8 00.9	14 25.7	29R 41.3	16 30.3	19 31.1	16 19.3
12 Tu	7 19 44	19 41 00	1♉30 31	7♉42 20	23 45.6	11 12.2	18 58.7	0 55.3	8 23.6	14 39.2	29 41.2	16 32.7	19 30.4	16 20.6
13 W	7 23 40	20 38 14	13 58 55	20 20 49	23R 46.3	11 21.0	20 10.3	1 35.9	8 46.2	14 52.7	29 41.1	16 35.2	19 29.8	16 22.0
14 Th	7 27 37	21 35 29	26 48 33	3♊22 29	23 46.0	11R 25.0	21 21.9	2 16.3	9 08.7	15 06.2	29 40.8	16 37.7	19 29.3	16 23.4
15 F	7 31 34	22 32 44	10♊02 58	16 50 08	23 43.8	11 24.3	22 33.5	2 56.7	9 31.2	15 19.7	29 40.5	16 40.2	19 28.7	16 24.8
16 Sa	7 35 30	23 30 00	23 44 02	0♋44 31	23 39.3	11 18.7	23 45.2	3 37.1	9 53.6	15 33.2	29 40.0	16 42.8	19 28.2	16 26.2
17 Su	7 39 27	24 27 16	7♋51 16	15 03 47	23 32.5	11 08.3	24 57.0	4 17.4	10 15.9	15 46.7	29 39.5	16 45.4	19 27.8	16 27.7
18 M	7 43 23	25 24 33	22 21 20	29 43 06	23 23.9	10 53.2	26 08.8	4 57.7	10 38.2	16 00.1	29 38.8	16 48.1	19 27.3	16 29.1
19 Tu	7 47 20	26 21 50	7♌08 05	14♌35 10	23 14.6	10 33.5	27 20.6	5 37.9	11 00.4	16 13.6	29 38.1	16 50.8	19 26.9	16 30.7
20 W	7 51 16	27 19 07	22 03 14	29 31 08	23 05.6	10 09.3	28 32.5	6 18.1	11 22.6	16 27.0	29 37.2	16 53.5	19 26.5	16 32.2
21 Th	7 55 13	28 16 25	6♍57 45	14♍22 07	22 57.9	9 41.0	29 44.4	6 58.2	11 44.7	16 40.4	29 36.3	16 56.3	19 26.2	16 33.7
22 F	7 59 09	29 13 43	21 43 22	29 00 46	22 52.5	9 08.9	0♋56.4	7 38.3	12 06.7	16 53.8	29 35.2	16 59.1	19 25.8	16 35.3
23 Sa	8 03 06	0♌11 01	6♎13 47	13♎22 02	22 49.3	8 33.4	2 08.4	8 18.3	12 28.7	17 07.2	29 34.1	17 01.9	19 25.5	16 36.9
24 Su	8 07 03	1 08 19	20 25 19	27 23 32	22D 48.3	7 55.0	3 20.5	8 58.3	12 50.5	17 20.5	29 32.8	17 04.8	19 25.3	16 38.5
25 M	8 10 59	2 05 38	4♏16 45	11♏05 05	22R 48.4	7 14.2	4 32.6	9 38.2	13 12.3	17 33.8	29 31.5	17 07.7	19 25.1	16 40.1
26 Tu	8 14 56	3 02 57	17 48 45	24 28 01	22 48.6	6 31.8	5 44.7	10 18.1	13 34.1	17 47.1	29 30.0	17 10.6	19 24.9	16 41.8
27 W	8 18 52	4 00 17	1♐03 09	7♐34 27	22 47.8	5 48.4	6 56.9	10 57.9	13 55.7	18 00.4	29 28.5	17 13.6	19 24.7	16 43.5
28 Th	8 22 49	4 57 37	14 02 12	20 26 40	22 44.9	5 04.8	8 09.2	11 37.7	14 17.3	18 13.6	29 26.9	17 16.6	19 24.6	16 45.1
29 F	8 26 45	5 54 58	26 48 07	3♑06 45	22 39.4	4 21.8	9 21.5	12 17.5	14 38.8	18 26.8	29 25.2	17 19.7	19 24.5	16 46.9
30 Sa	8 30 42	6 52 19	9♑22 46	15 36 20	22 31.1	3 40.1	10 33.8	12 57.2	15 00.2	18 40.0	29 23.3	17 22.7	19 24.4	16 48.6
31 Su	8 34 39	7 49 41	21 47 34	27 56 37	22 20.4	3 00.6	11 46.2	13 36.8	15 21.6	18 53.2	29 21.4	17 25.8	19D 24.4	16 50.3

August 1966

LONGITUDE

Day	Sid.Time	☉	0 hr ☽	Noon ☽	True ☊	☿	♀	♂	⚳	♃	♄	♅	♆	♇
1 M	8 38 35	8♌47 04	4♒03 33	10♒08 30	22♉07.9	2♌24.0	12♋58.6	14♋16.4	15♊42.8	19♋06.3	29♓19.4	17♍28.9	19♏24.3	16♍52.1
2 Tu	8 42 32	9 44 28	16 11 35	22 12 54	21R 54.6	1R 51.0	14 11.1	14 56.0	16 04.0	19 19.4	29R 17.3	17 32.1	19 24.4	16 53.9
3 W	8 46 28	10 41 52	28 12 36	4♓10 52	21 41.8	1 22.2	15 23.6	15 35.5	16 25.1	19 32.4	29 15.1	17 35.3	19 24.4	16 55.7
4 Th	8 50 25	11 39 18	10♓07 55	16 03 59	21 30.4	0 58.4	16 36.2	16 15.0	16 46.1	19 45.4	29 12.9	17 38.5	19 24.5	16 57.5
5 F	8 54 21	12 36 45	21 59 23	27 54 27	21 21.2	0 40.0	17 48.8	16 54.4	17 07.1	19 58.4	29 10.5	17 41.7	19 24.6	16 59.4
6 Sa	8 58 18	13 34 12	3♈49 35	9♈45 14	21 14.7	0 27.4	19 01.4	17 33.8	17 27.9	20 11.4	29 08.1	17 45.0	19 24.8	17 01.2
7 Su	9 02 14	14 31 41	15 41 53	21 40 04	21 10.8	0D 21.0	20 14.2	18 13.1	17 48.6	20 24.3	29 05.5	17 48.3	19 25.0	17 03.1
8 M	9 06 11	15 29 12	27 40 23	3♉43 24	21 09.1	0 21.1	21 26.9	18 52.4	18 09.3	20 37.2	29 02.9	17 51.6	19 25.2	17 05.0
9 Tu	9 10 07	16 26 43	9♉49 48	16 00 12	21 08.8	0 27.9	22 39.7	19 31.7	18 29.8	20 50.0	29 00.2	17 54.9	19 25.4	17 06.9
10 W	9 14 04	17 24 16	22 15 15	28 35 36	21 08.7	0 41.5	23 52.6	20 10.9	18 50.3	21 02.8	28 57.4	17 58.3	19 25.7	17 08.8
11 Th	9 18 01	18 21 51	5♊01 50	11♊34 29	21 07.8	1 02.2	25 05.5	20 50.1	19 10.7	21 15.5	28 54.5	18 01.7	19 26.0	17 10.7
12 F	9 21 57	19 19 27	18 14 01	25 00 46	21 04.9	1 29.8	26 18.5	21 29.2	19 30.9	21 28.2	28 51.6	18 05.1	19 26.4	17 12.7
13 Sa	9 25 54	20 17 04	1♋54 56	8♋56 33	20 59.6	2 04.4	27 31.5	22 08.3	19 51.1	21 40.9	28 48.5	18 08.5	19 26.8	17 14.6
14 Su	9 29 50	21 14 43	16 05 26	23 21 12	20 51.8	2 45.9	28 44.5	22 47.3	20 11.1	21 53.5	28 45.4	18 12.0	19 27.2	17 16.6
15 M	9 33 47	22 12 24	0♌43 13	8♌10 39	20 41.8	3 34.2	29 57.6	23 26.3	20 31.1	22 06.1	28 42.2	18 15.5	19 27.6	17 18.6
16 Tu	9 37 43	23 10 05	15 42 26	23 17 22	20 30.8	4 29.2	1♌10.7	24 05.3	20 50.9	22 18.6	28 39.0	18 19.0	19 28.1	17 20.6
17 W	9 41 40	24 07 48	0♍54 06	8♍31 13	20 20.1	5 30.7	2 23.9	24 44.2	21 10.6	22 31.0	28 35.6	18 22.5	19 28.6	17 22.6
18 Th	9 45 37	25 05 32	16 07 22	23 41 13	20 10.8	6 38.4	3 37.1	25 23.1	21 30.2	22 43.4	28 32.2	18 26.0	19 29.2	17 24.6
19 F	9 49 33	26 03 17	1♎11 35	8♎37 28	20 03.9	7 52.2	4 50.4	26 01.9	21 49.7	22 55.8	28 28.7	18 29.6	19 29.7	17 26.6
20 Sa	9 53 30	27 01 03	15 58 05	23 12 50	19 59.7	9 11.7	6 03.7	26 40.6	22 09.1	23 08.1	28 25.2	18 33.1	19 30.3	17 28.7
21 Su	9 57 26	27 58 50	0♏21 21	7♏23 27	19D 57.8	10 36.5	7 17.0	27 19.4	22 28.3	23 20.3	28 21.5	18 36.7	19 31.0	17 30.7
22 M	10 01 23	28 56 38	14 19 09	21 08 34	19R 57.5	12 06.4	8 30.4	27 58.0	22 47.4	23 32.5	28 17.9	18 40.3	19 31.6	17 32.8
23 Tu	10 05 19	29 54 28	27 51 57	4♐29 41	19 57.5	13 40.9	9 43.8	28 36.7	23 06.4	23 44.6	28 14.1	18 44.0	19 32.3	17 34.9
24 W	10 09 16	0♍52 19	11♐02 07	17 29 43	19 56.6	15 19.6	10 57.3	29 15.3	23 25.3	23 56.6	28 10.3	18 47.6	19 33.1	17 36.9
25 Th	10 13 12	1 50 11	23 52 54	0♑12 08	19 53.7	17 02.0	12 10.8	29 53.8	23 44.0	24 08.6	28 06.5	18 51.2	19 33.8	17 39.0
26 F	10 17 09	2 48 04	6♑27 50	12 40 24	19 48.3	18 47.8	13 24.3	0♌32.3	24 02.6	24 20.6	28 02.5	18 54.9	19 34.6	17 41.1
27 Sa	10 21 06	3 45 59	18 50 13	24 57 37	19 40.2	20 36.4	14 37.9	1 10.7	24 21.1	24 32.4	27 58.6	18 58.6	19 35.5	17 43.2
28 Su	10 25 02	4 43 55	1♒02 52	7♒06 16	19 29.5	22 27.3	15 51.5	1 49.1	24 39.4	24 44.2	27 54.5	19 02.3	19 36.3	17 45.3
29 M	10 28 59	5 41 52	13 08 02	19 08 23	19 17.1	24 20.3	17 05.2	2 27.5	24 57.6	24 55.9	27 50.4	19 06.0	19 37.2	17 47.5
30 Tu	10 32 55	6 39 51	25 07 29	1♓05 31	19 04.0	26 14.8	18 18.9	3 05.8	25 15.7	25 07.6	27 46.3	19 09.7	19 38.1	17 49.6
31 W	10 36 52	7 37 51	7♓02 39	12 59 02	18 51.2	28 10.4	19 32.6	3 44.1	25 33.6	25 19.2	27 42.1	19 13.4	19 39.1	17 51.7

Astro Data

	Dy Hr Mn
☽0N	10 2:16
♄R	11 13:03
☿R	14 20:15
♃✶♇	20 22:27
♃✶♅	23 0:02
☽0S	23 3:23
♆D	1 4:30
♃△♆	2 21:13
☽0N	6 8:26
☿D	7 23:43
☽0S	19 10:43

Planet Ingress

	Dy Hr Mn
♂ ♋	11 3:15
♀ ♋	21 17:11
☉ ♌	23 7:23
♀ ♌	15 12:47
☉ ♍	23 14:18
♂ ♌	25 15:52

Last Aspect Dy Hr Mn		☽ Ingress Dy Hr Mn
1 23:07	♄ □	♑ 1 23:51
4 8:33	♄ ✶	♒ 4 9:14
6 14:29	♂ △	♓ 6 20:39
9 8:37	♄ ☌	♈ 9 9:16
10 21:43	☉ □	♉ 11 21:03
14 5:16	♄ ✶	♊ 14 5:51
16 10:10	♄ □	♋ 16 10:44
18 11:53	♄ △	♌ 18 12:27
20 10:18	♀ ✶	♍ 20 12:46
22 12:57	♄ ☍	♎ 22 13:38
23 18:28	♃ □	♏ 24 16:32
26 21:09	♄ △	♐ 26 22:04
29 4:59	♄ □	♑ 29 6:04
31 14:46	♄ ✶	♒ 31 16:02

Last Aspect Dy Hr Mn		☽ Ingress Dy Hr Mn
2 6:24	♆ □	♓ 3 3:36
5 14:34	♄ ☌	♈ 5 16:15
7 9:25	♃ □	♉ 8 4:38
10 12:41	♄ ✶	♊ 10 14:38
12 18:41	♄ □	♋ 12 20:41
14 21:35	♀ ☌	♌ 14 22:50
16 11:48	☉ ☌	♍ 16 22:35
18 19:43	♄ ☍	♎ 18 22:05
20 18:50	☉ ✶	♏ 20 23:24
23 3:02	☉ □	♐ 23 3:51
25 8:02	♄ □	♑ 25 11:37
27 17:54	♄ ✶	♒ 27 21:56
30 0:24	☿ ☍	♓ 30 9:48

☽ Phases & Eclipses

Dy Hr Mn		
2 19:36	○	10♑27
10 21:43	☾	18♈10
18 4:30	●	25♋07
24 19:00	☽	1♏25
1 9:05	○	8♒40
9 12:55	☾	16♉29
16 11:48	●	23♌10
23 3:02	☽	29♏33
31 0:14	○	7♓09

Astro Data

1 July 1966
Julian Day # 24288
SVP 5♓43'53"
GC 26♐22.3 ⚴ 16♈05.0
Eris 11♈48.9 ⚵ 5♊52.5
⚷ 26♓13.8R ⚶ 8♌58.5
☽ Mean ☊ 23♉02.1

1 August 1966
Julian Day # 24319
SVP 5♓43'47"
GC 26♐22.4 ⚴ 20♈09.8
Eris 11♈46.1R ⚵ 23♊30.0
⚷ 25♓45.8R ⚶ 23♌03.2
☽ Mean ☊ 21♉23.7

LONGITUDE — September 1966

Day	Sid.Time	☉	0 hr ☽	Noon ☽	True ☊	☿	♀	♂	⚳	♃	♄	♅	♆	♇
1 Th	10 40 48	8♍35 53	18♓54 52	24♓50 20	18♉39.7	0♍06.9	20♌46.4	4♌22.3	25♊51.3	25♋30.7	27♓37.9	19♍17.1	19♏40.0	17♍53.8
2 F	10 44 45	9 33 57	0♈45 40	6♈41 07	18R 30.5	2 03.8	22 00.2	5 00.5	26 08.9	25 42.1	27R 33.6	19 20.8	19 41.1	17 56.0
3 Sa	10 48 41	10 32 02	12 36 58	18 33 32	18 24.0	4 01.0	23 14.1	5 38.6	26 26.4	25 53.5	27 29.3	19 24.6	19 42.1	17 58.1
4 Su	10 52 38	11 30 10	24 31 14	0♉30 26	18 20.1	5 58.1	24 28.0	6 16.7	26 43.7	26 04.8	27 25.0	19 28.3	19 43.1	18 00.3
5 M	10 56 34	12 28 19	6♉31 38	12 35 19	18D 18.5	7 55.0	25 41.9	6 54.8	27 00.8	26 16.0	27 20.6	19 32.1	19 44.2	18 02.4
6 Tu	11 00 31	13 26 30	18 42 01	24 52 19	18 18.5	9 51.4	26 55.9	7 32.8	27 17.8	26 27.1	27 16.2	19 35.8	19 45.4	18 04.6
7 W	11 04 28	14 24 43	1♊06 46	7♊26 00	18R 19.1	11 47.2	28 09.9	8 10.8	27 34.6	26 38.2	27 11.7	19 39.6	19 46.5	18 06.7
8 Th	11 08 24	15 22 59	13 50 33	20 21 00	18 19.2	13 42.4	29 24.0	8 48.7	27 51.3	26 49.2	27 07.2	19 43.4	19 47.7	18 08.9
9 F	11 12 21	16 21 16	26 57 50	3♋41 29	18 17.8	15 36.7	0♍38.1	9 26.6	28 07.7	27 00.0	27 02.7	19 47.2	19 48.9	18 11.1
10 Sa	11 16 17	17 19 36	10♋32 16	17 30 20	18 14.3	17 30.2	1 52.2	10 04.4	28 24.0	27 10.8	26 58.2	19 50.9	19 50.1	18 13.2
11 Su	11 20 14	18 17 57	24 35 43	1♌48 12	18 08.6	19 22.7	3 06.4	10 42.2	28 40.2	27 21.6	26 53.6	19 54.7	19 51.4	18 15.4
12 M	11 24 10	19 16 21	9♌07 25	16 32 41	18 01.0	21 14.2	4 20.6	11 20.0	28 56.1	27 32.2	26 49.1	19 58.5	19 52.7	18 17.6
13 Tu	11 28 07	20 14 47	24 03 11	1♍37 49	17 52.4	23 04.7	5 34.8	11 57.7	29 11.8	27 42.7	26 44.5	20 02.3	19 54.0	18 19.7
14 W	11 32 03	21 13 14	9♍15 21	16 54 26	17 43.8	24 54.2	6 49.1	12 35.3	29 27.4	27 53.1	26 39.9	20 06.1	19 55.4	18 21.9
15 Th	11 36 00	22 11 44	24 33 39	2♎11 34	17 36.3	26 42.6	8 03.4	13 13.0	29 42.8	28 03.5	26 35.2	20 09.9	19 56.7	18 24.0
16 F	11 39 57	23 10 15	9♎46 50	17 18 15	17 30.9	28 29.9	9 17.8	13 50.5	29 57.9	28 13.7	26 30.6	20 13.6	19 58.1	18 26.2
17 Sa	11 43 53	24 08 48	24 44 47	2♏05 34	17 27.7	0♎16.2	10 32.1	14 28.0	0♋12.9	28 23.9	26 25.9	20 17.4	19 59.6	18 28.4
18 Su	11 47 50	25 07 22	9♏20 01	16 27 42	17D 26.8	2 01.5	11 46.5	15 05.5	0 27.6	28 33.9	26 21.3	20 21.2	20 01.0	18 30.5
19 M	11 51 46	26 05 59	23 28 25	0♐22 10	17 27.3	3 45.6	13 01.0	15 42.9	0 42.2	28 43.8	26 16.6	20 25.0	20 02.5	18 32.7
20 Tu	11 55 43	27 04 37	7♐09 04	13 49 24	17 28.3	5 28.8	14 15.4	16 20.3	0 56.5	28 53.7	26 12.0	20 28.7	20 04.0	18 34.8
21 W	11 59 39	28 03 17	20 23 31	26 51 51	17R 29.0	7 10.9	15 29.9	16 57.6	1 10.6	29 03.4	26 07.3	20 32.5	20 05.5	18 37.0
22 Th	12 03 36	29 01 58	3♑14 54	9♑33 09	17 28.3	8 52.1	16 44.4	17 34.9	1 24.5	29 13.0	26 02.7	20 36.3	20 07.1	18 39.1
23 F	12 07 32	0♎00 41	15 47 09	21 57 25	17 25.9	10 32.2	17 59.0	18 12.1	1 38.2	29 22.6	25 58.1	20 40.0	20 08.7	18 41.2
24 Sa	12 11 29	0 59 26	28 04 26	4♒08 47	17 21.3	12 11.4	19 13.5	18 49.3	1 51.7	29 32.0	25 53.4	20 43.7	20 10.3	18 43.4
25 Su	12 15 26	1 58 13	10♒10 40	16 10 45	17 15.0	13 49.6	20 28.1	19 26.4	2 04.9	29 41.3	25 48.8	20 47.5	20 11.9	18 45.5
26 M	12 19 22	2 57 01	22 09 20	28 06 46	17 07.2	15 26.9	21 42.7	20 03.5	2 17.9	29 50.4	25 44.2	20 51.2	20 13.5	18 47.6
27 Tu	12 23 19	3 55 51	4♓03 22	9♓59 26	16 58.9	17 03.3	22 57.4	20 40.5	2 30.6	29 59.5	25 39.6	20 54.9	20 15.2	18 49.7
28 W	12 27 15	4 54 45	15 55 12	21 50 55	16 50.8	18 38.8	24 12.0	21 17.5	2 43.1	0♌08.5	25 35.1	20 58.6	20 16.9	18 51.8
29 Th	12 31 12	5 53 37	27 46 48	3♈43 04	16 43.6	20 13.4	25 26.7	21 54.4	2 55.4	0 17.3	25 30.5	21 02.3	20 18.6	18 53.9
30 F	12 35 08	6 52 33	9♈39 55	15 37 35	16 37.9	21 47.1	26 41.5	22 31.3	3 07.4	0 26.0	25 26.0	21 06.0	20 20.3	18 56.0

LONGITUDE — October 1966

Day	Sid.Time	☉	0 hr ☽	Noon ☽	True ☊	☿	♀	♂	⚳	♃	♄	♅	♆	♇
1 Sa	12 39 05	7♎51 31	21♈36 15	27♈36 11	16♉34.2	23♎19.9	27♍56.2	23♌08.1	3♋19.2	0♌34.6	25♓21.5	21♍09.7	20♏22.1	18♍58.0
2 Su	12 43 01	8 50 31	3♉37 37	9♉40 51	16D 32.4	24 51.9	29 11.0	23 44.9	3 30.7	0 43.0	25R 17.0	21 13.3	20 23.9	19 00.1
3 M	12 46 58	9 49 33	15 46 10	21 53 55	16 32.3	26 23.1	0♎25.8	24 21.6	3 41.9	0 51.4	25 12.6	21 17.0	20 25.7	19 02.2
4 Tu	12 50 55	10 48 38	28 04 28	4♊18 11	16 33.4	27 53.4	1 40.6	24 58.3	3 52.9	0 59.6	25 08.2	21 20.6	20 27.5	19 04.2
5 W	12 54 51	11 47 44	10♊35 30	16 56 50	16 35.0	29 22.8	2 55.4	25 35.0	4 03.6	1 07.7	25 03.9	21 24.2	20 29.3	19 06.3
6 Th	12 58 48	12 46 54	23 22 36	29 53 14	16 36.4	0♏51.4	4 10.3	26 11.5	4 14.0	1 15.7	24 59.5	21 27.8	20 31.2	19 08.3
7 F	13 02 44	13 46 05	6♋29 08	13♋10 38	16R 37.1	2 19.2	5 25.2	26 48.1	4 24.1	1 23.5	24 55.2	21 31.4	20 33.0	19 10.3
8 Sa	13 06 41	14 45 19	19 58 02	26 51 31	16 36.5	3 46.1	6 40.1	27 24.6	4 34.0	1 31.2	24 51.0	21 35.0	20 34.9	19 12.3
9 Su	13 10 37	15 44 35	3♌51 11	10♌57 00	16 34.5	5 12.1	7 55.1	28 01.0	4 43.5	1 38.7	24 46.8	21 38.5	20 36.8	19 14.3
10 M	13 14 34	16 43 54	18 08 44	25 26 02	16 31.3	6 37.3	9 10.0	28 37.4	4 52.8	1 46.1	24 42.7	21 42.0	20 38.8	19 16.3
11 Tu	13 18 30	17 43 14	2♍48 20	10♍14 55	16 27.3	8 01.5	10 25.0	29 13.7	5 01.7	1 53.4	24 38.6	21 45.6	20 40.7	19 18.2
12 W	13 22 27	18 42 37	17 44 52	25 17 09	16 23.2	9 24.8	11 40.0	29 50.0	5 10.4	2 00.5	24 34.5	21 49.0	20 42.7	19 20.2
13 Th	13 26 24	19 42 02	2♎50 37	10♎24 05	16 19.7	10 47.1	12 55.0	0♍26.2	5 18.7	2 07.5	24 30.5	21 52.5	20 44.7	19 22.1
14 F	13 30 20	20 41 30	17 56 19	25 26 09	16 17.3	12 08.4	14 10.0	1 02.4	5 26.7	2 14.3	24 26.6	21 56.0	20 46.7	19 24.0
15 Sa	13 34 17	21 40 59	2♏52 29	10♏14 22	16D 16.1	13 28.7	15 25.1	1 38.5	5 34.4	2 21.0	24 22.7	21 59.4	20 48.7	19 25.9
16 Su	13 38 13	22 40 30	17 30 59	24 41 42	16 16.2	14 47.7	16 40.2	2 14.5	5 41.8	2 27.6	24 18.9	22 02.8	20 50.7	19 27.8
17 M	13 42 10	23 40 03	1♐46 04	8♐43 48	16 17.2	16 05.6	17 55.3	2 50.5	5 48.8	2 33.9	24 15.2	22 06.1	20 52.7	19 29.7
18 Tu	13 46 06	24 39 38	15 34 48	22 19 05	16 18.7	17 22.3	19 10.4	3 26.5	5 55.5	2 40.2	24 11.5	22 09.5	20 54.8	19 31.6
19 W	13 50 03	25 39 15	28 56 52	5♑28 25	16 20.2	18 37.5	20 25.5	4 02.3	6 01.9	2 46.2	24 07.9	22 12.8	20 56.9	19 33.4
20 Th	13 53 59	26 38 53	11♑54 06	18 14 23	16R 21.1	19 51.2	21 40.6	4 38.1	6 07.9	2 52.2	24 04.3	22 16.1	20 58.9	19 35.2
21 F	13 57 56	27 38 33	24 29 45	0♒40 44	16 21.3	21 03.4	22 55.7	5 13.9	6 13.6	2 57.9	24 00.8	22 19.4	21 01.0	19 37.0
22 Sa	14 01 53	28 38 15	6♒47 55	12 51 49	16 20.6	22 13.7	24 10.9	5 49.6	6 18.9	3 03.5	23 57.4	22 22.6	21 03.2	19 38.8
23 Su	14 05 49	29 37 59	18 53 01	24 52 02	16 19.2	23 22.2	25 26.0	6 25.2	6 23.8	3 08.9	23 54.1	22 25.9	21 05.3	19 40.6
24 M	14 09 46	0♏37 44	0♓49 26	6♓45 40	16 17.1	24 28.6	26 41.2	7 00.7	6 28.4	3 14.2	23 50.9	22 29.0	21 07.4	19 42.3
25 Tu	14 13 42	1 37 31	12 41 15	18 36 36	16 14.8	25 32.6	27 56.4	7 36.2	6 32.7	3 19.3	23 47.7	22 32.2	21 09.5	19 44.0
26 W	14 17 39	2 37 20	24 32 07	0♈28 12	16 12.6	26 34.1	29 11.6	8 11.7	6 36.5	3 24.2	23 44.6	22 35.3	21 11.7	19 45.8
27 Th	14 21 35	3 37 10	6♈25 09	12 23 19	16 10.6	27 32.7	0♏26.7	8 47.0	6 40.0	3 29.0	23 41.6	22 38.4	21 13.8	19 47.4
28 F	14 25 32	4 37 02	18 22 56	24 24 17	16 09.3	28 28.3	1 42.0	9 22.4	6 43.2	3 33.6	23 38.6	22 41.5	21 16.0	19 49.1
29 Sa	14 29 28	5 36 57	0♉27 34	6♉33 00	16D 08.5	29 20.3	2 57.2	9 57.6	6 45.9	3 38.0	23 35.8	22 44.5	21 18.2	19 50.7
30 Su	14 33 25	6 36 53	12 40 45	18 51 00	16 08.3	0♐08.4	4 12.4	10 32.8	6 48.3	3 42.3	23 33.0	22 47.5	21 20.4	19 52.4
31 M	14 37 21	7 36 51	25 03 55	1♊19 39	16 08.7	0 52.3	5 27.6	11 07.9	6 50.2	3 46.4	23 30.3	22 50.5	21 22.6	19 54.0

Astro Data Dy Hr Mn	Planet Ingress Dy Hr Mn	Last Aspect Dy Hr Mn	☽ Ingress Dy Hr Mn	Last Aspect Dy Hr Mn	☽ Ingress Dy Hr Mn	☽ Phases & Eclipses Dy Hr Mn	Astro Data
☽0N 2 13:57	☿ ♍ 1 10:35	1 17:38 ♄ ☌	♈ 1 22:27	1 2:35 ♂ △	♉ 1 16:47	8 2:07 ☾ 14♊59	1 September 1966
♃△♄ 9 16:13	♀ ♍ 8 23:40	4 2:59 ♃ □	♉ 4 10:59	3 18:25 ♄ ⚹	♊ 4 3:43	14 19:13 ● 21♍31	Julian Day # 24350
♅⚹♆ 10 4:28	⚳ ♋ 16 15:19	6 16:36 ♄ ⚹	♊ 6 21:52	6 4:52 ♂ ⚹	♋ 6 12:12	21 14:25 ☽ 28♐09	SVP 5♓43'43"
☽0S 15 20:32	☿ ♎ 17 8:19	9 0:13 ♄ □	♋ 9 5:26	8 8:32 ♄ △	♌ 8 17:25	29 16:47 ○ 6♈05	GC 26♐22.4 ⚴ 19♈12.5R
☿0S 18 15:53	☉ ♎ 23 11:43	11 4:32 ♃ ☌	♌ 11 9:01	10 17:26 ♂ ☌	♍ 10 19:27		Eris 11♈34.0R ⚵ 10♋14.2
☉0S 23 11:43	♃ ♌ 27 13:19	12 17:21 ♆ □	♍ 13 9:26	12 10:53 ♄ ☍	♎ 12 19:29	7 13:08 ☾ 13♋49	⚷ 24♓37.7R ⚶ 7♍42.7
☽0N 29 19:44		15 5:25 ♃ ⚹	♎ 15 8:33	14 3:52 ☉ ☌	♏ 14 19:21	14 3:52 ● 20♎21	☽ Mean ☊ 19♉45.2
	♀ ♎ 3 3:44	17 5:52 ♃ □	♏ 17 8:34	16 11:22 ♄ △	♐ 16 20:59	21 5:34 ☽ 27♑23	
♀0S 5 19:39	☿ ♏ 5 22:03	19 9:06 ♃ △	♐ 19 11:21	18 16:34 ☉ ⚹	♑ 19 1:55	29 10:00 ○ 5♉32	1 October 1966
☽0S 13 7:32	♂ ♍ 12 18:37	21 14:25 ☉ □	♑ 21 17:52	21 5:34 ☉ □	♒ 21 10:41	29 10:12 ☍ A 0.952	Julian Day # 24380
☽0N 27 2:25	☉ ♏ 23 20:51	24 2:45 ♃ ☍	♒ 24 3:48	23 13:16 ♀ △	♓ 23 22:20		SVP 5♓43'40"
	♀ ♏ 27 3:28	25 20:05 ♆ □	♓ 26 15:48	26 3:23 ☿ △	♈ 26 11:03		GC 26♐22.5 ⚴ 12♈37.4R
	☿ ♐ 30 7:38	28 19:31 ♄ ☌	♈ 29 4:29	26 17:58 ♃ △	♉ 28 23:05		Eris 11♈16.7R ⚵ 24♋46.8
				30 21:03 ♄ ⚹	♊ 31 9:28		⚷ 23♓16.5R ⚶ 22♍13.5
							☽ Mean ☊ 18♉09.8

November 1966 LONGITUDE

Day	Sid.Time	☉	0 hr ☽	Noon ☽	True ☊	☿	♀	♂	⚳	♃	♄	♅	♆	♇
1 Tu	14 41 18	8♏36 51	7♊38 21	14♊00 10	16♉09.3	1♐31.3	6♏42.9	11♍43.0	6♋51.8	3♌50.3	23♓27.8	22♍53.4	21♏24.8	19♍55.5
2 W	14 45 15	9 36 54	20 25 18	26 53 51	16 10.0	2 05.0	7 58.1	12 17.9	6 53.0	3 54.0	23R 25.3	22 56.3	21 27.0	19 57.1
3 Th	14 49 11	10 36 58	3♋26 02	10♋01 58	16 10.6	2 32.9	9 13.4	12 52.9	6 53.8	3 57.5	23 22.9	22 59.2	21 29.2	19 58.6
4 F	14 53 08	11 37 05	16 41 48	23 25 40	16 11.1	2 54.1	10 28.7	13 27.7	6R 54.2	4 00.9	23 20.5	23 02.0	21 31.4	20 00.1
5 Sa	14 57 04	12 37 13	0♌13 41	7♌05 53	16R 11.2	3 08.2	11 44.0	14 02.5	6 54.2	4 04.1	23 18.3	23 04.8	21 33.7	20 01.6
6 Su	15 01 01	13 37 24	14 02 18	21 02 53	16 11.2	3R 14.5	12 59.3	14 37.2	6 53.8	4 07.1	23 16.2	23 07.5	21 35.9	20 03.1
7 M	15 04 57	14 37 37	28 07 30	5♍15 57	16 11.1	3 12.3	14 14.6	15 11.9	6 53.0	4 09.9	23 14.1	23 10.2	21 38.1	20 04.5
8 Tu	15 08 54	15 37 51	12♍27 55	19 43 00	16D 11.0	3 00.9	15 29.9	15 46.4	6 51.7	4 12.5	23 12.2	23 12.9	21 40.4	20 05.9
9 W	15 12 50	16 38 08	27 00 41	4♎20 22	16 11.0	2 40.0	16 45.2	16 20.9	6 50.1	4 14.9	23 10.4	23 15.5	21 42.6	20 07.3
10 Th	15 16 47	17 38 27	11♎41 20	19 02 49	16 11.1	2 09.1	18 00.6	16 55.3	6 48.0	4 17.2	23 08.6	23 18.1	21 44.9	20 08.7
11 F	15 20 44	18 38 47	26 24 01	3♏44 02	16R 11.3	1 28.2	19 15.9	17 29.7	6 45.5	4 19.2	23 07.0	23 20.7	21 47.1	20 10.0
12 Sa	15 24 40	19 39 10	11♏02 04	18 17 16	16 11.3	0 37.5	20 31.3	18 03.9	6 42.6	4 21.1	23 05.4	23 23.2	21 49.4	20 11.3
13 Su	15 28 37	20 39 34	25 28 53	2♐36 13	16 11.2	29♏37.6	21 46.6	18 38.1	6 39.3	4 22.7	23 04.0	23 25.7	21 51.6	20 12.6
14 M	15 32 33	21 40 00	9♐38 43	16 35 54	16 10.7	28 29.7	23 02.0	19 12.2	6 35.6	4 24.2	23 02.7	23 28.1	21 53.9	20 13.9
15 Tu	15 36 30	22 40 27	23 27 26	0♑13 07	16 10.0	27 15.2	24 17.4	19 46.2	6 31.4	4 25.5	23 01.4	23 30.5	21 56.1	20 15.1
16 W	15 40 26	23 40 56	6♑52 52	13 26 45	16 09.1	25 56.3	25 32.7	20 20.1	6 26.9	4 26.5	23 00.3	23 32.8	21 58.4	20 16.3
17 Th	15 44 23	24 41 26	19 54 54	26 17 36	16 08.1	24 35.3	26 48.1	20 54.0	6 21.9	4 27.4	22 59.3	23 35.1	22 00.6	20 17.4
18 F	15 48 20	25 41 57	2♒35 10	8♒48 04	16 07.3	23 15.0	28 03.5	21 27.7	6 16.5	4 28.1	22 58.4	23 37.3	22 02.9	20 18.6
19 Sa	15 52 16	26 42 30	14 56 45	21 01 45	16D 06.8	21 57.9	29 18.8	22 01.4	6 10.8	4 28.6	22 57.5	23 39.5	22 05.1	20 19.7
20 Su	15 56 13	27 43 04	27 03 38	3♓02 59	16 06.8	20 46.7	0♐34.2	22 34.9	6 04.6	4R 28.9	22 56.8	23 41.7	22 07.4	20 20.8
21 M	16 00 09	28 43 39	9♓00 24	14 56 29	16 07.3	19 43.3	1 49.6	23 08.4	5 58.0	4 28.9	22 56.2	23 43.8	22 09.6	20 21.8
22 Tu	16 04 06	29 44 15	20 51 49	26 47 00	16 08.4	18 49.6	3 05.0	23 41.8	5 51.1	4 28.8	22 55.7	23 45.9	22 11.9	20 22.9
23 W	16 08 02	0♐44 53	2♈42 36	8♈39 08	16 09.8	18 06.8	4 20.3	24 15.1	5 43.7	4 28.5	22 55.3	23 47.9	22 14.1	20 23.8
24 Th	16 11 59	1 45 31	14 37 08	20 37 01	16 11.2	17 35.4	5 35.7	24 48.3	5 36.0	4 28.0	22 55.1	23 49.8	22 16.3	20 24.8
25 F	16 15 55	2 46 11	26 39 15	2♉44 12	16 12.3	17 15.7	6 51.1	25 21.4	5 27.9	4 27.3	22 54.9	23 51.8	22 18.6	20 25.7
26 Sa	16 19 52	3 46 52	8♉52 11	15 03 29	16R 12.8	17D 07.5	8 06.5	25 54.4	5 19.4	4 26.4	22D 54.8	23 53.6	22 20.8	20 26.6
27 Su	16 23 49	4 47 34	21 18 17	27 36 47	16 12.4	17 10.2	9 21.8	26 27.3	5 10.5	4 25.3	22 54.8	23 55.5	22 23.0	20 27.5
28 M	16 27 45	5 48 18	3♊59 02	10♊25 07	16 11.0	17 23.2	10 37.2	27 00.1	5 01.3	4 24.0	22 55.0	23 57.2	22 25.2	20 28.4
29 Tu	16 31 42	6 49 03	16 54 59	23 28 35	16 08.6	17 45.7	11 52.6	27 32.8	4 51.8	4 22.5	22 55.2	23 58.9	22 27.4	20 29.2
30 W	16 35 38	7 49 49	0♋05 48	6♋46 29	16 05.4	18 16.7	13 08.0	28 05.4	4 41.9	4 20.8	22 55.6	24 00.6	22 29.6	20 30.0

December 1966 LONGITUDE

Day	Sid.Time	☉	0 hr ☽	Noon ☽	True ☊	☿	♀	♂	⚳	♃	♄	♅	♆	♇
1 Th	16 39 35	8♐50 37	13♋30 28	20♋17 32	16♉01.9	18♏55.5	14♐23.4	28♍38.0	4♋31.6	4♌18.9	22♓56.1	24♍02.2	22♏31.8	20♍30.7
2 F	16 43 31	9 51 26	27 07 29	4♌00 04	15R 58.6	19 41.1	15 38.7	29 10.4	4R 21.1	4R 16.8	22 56.6	24 03.8	22 34.0	20 31.4
3 Sa	16 47 28	10 52 17	10♌55 04	17 52 17	15 56.0	20 32.7	16 54.1	29 42.7	4 10.2	4 14.6	22 57.3	24 05.3	22 36.1	20 32.1
4 Su	16 51 24	11 53 08	24 51 28	1♍52 26	15D 54.4	21 29.6	18 09.5	0♎14.9	3 59.0	4 12.1	22 58.1	24 06.8	22 38.3	20 32.8
5 M	16 55 21	12 54 01	8♍54 58	15 58 53	15 54.1	22 31.1	19 24.9	0 46.9	3 47.5	4 09.4	22 59.0	24 08.2	22 40.5	20 33.4
6 Tu	16 59 18	13 54 56	23 03 58	0♎09 59	15 54.9	23 36.7	20 40.3	1 18.9	3 35.8	4 06.6	23 00.0	24 09.6	22 42.6	20 34.0
7 W	17 03 14	14 55 52	7♎16 44	14 23 55	15 56.3	24 45.8	21 55.7	1 50.7	3 23.7	4 03.5	23 01.1	24 10.9	22 44.7	20 34.5
8 Th	17 07 11	15 56 49	21 31 15	28 38 23	15 57.8	25 57.9	23 11.1	2 22.5	3 11.4	4 00.3	23 02.3	24 12.1	22 46.8	20 35.0
9 F	17 11 07	16 57 47	5♏44 59	12♏50 36	15R 58.7	27 12.6	24 26.5	2 54.1	2 58.9	3 56.8	23 03.7	24 13.3	22 48.9	20 35.5
10 Sa	17 15 04	17 58 46	19 54 49	26 57 09	15 58.2	28 29.6	25 41.9	3 25.5	2 46.1	3 53.2	23 05.1	24 14.4	22 51.0	20 36.0
11 Su	17 19 00	18 59 47	3♐57 06	10♐54 13	15 56.1	29 48.5	26 57.3	3 56.9	2 33.1	3 49.4	23 06.6	24 15.5	22 53.1	20 36.4
12 M	17 22 57	20 00 48	17 48 02	24 38 06	15 52.2	1♐09.1	28 12.7	4 28.1	2 19.9	3 45.4	23 08.3	24 16.6	22 55.2	20 36.8
13 Tu	17 26 53	21 01 51	1♑24 04	8♑05 37	15 46.8	2 31.2	29 28.1	4 59.2	2 06.6	3 41.2	23 10.0	24 17.5	22 57.2	20 37.2
14 W	17 30 50	22 02 54	14 42 31	21 14 38	15 40.4	3 54.6	0♑43.5	5 30.1	1 53.1	3 36.9	23 11.9	24 18.5	22 59.3	20 37.5
15 Th	17 34 47	23 03 57	27 41 55	4♒04 25	15 33.7	5 19.0	1 58.9	6 00.9	1 39.4	3 32.4	23 13.8	24 19.3	23 01.3	20 37.8
16 F	17 38 43	24 05 01	10♒22 16	16 35 43	15 27.6	6 44.4	3 14.3	6 31.6	1 25.6	3 27.7	23 15.9	24 20.1	23 03.3	20 38.0
17 Sa	17 42 40	25 06 05	22 45 04	28 50 44	15 22.6	8 10.6	4 29.7	7 02.1	1 11.6	3 22.8	23 18.1	24 20.9	23 05.3	20 38.2
18 Su	17 46 36	26 07 10	4♓53 09	10♓52 51	15 19.4	9 37.6	5 45.1	7 32.5	0 57.6	3 17.8	23 20.3	24 21.6	23 07.3	20 38.4
19 M	17 50 33	27 08 15	16 50 25	22 46 25	15D 17.9	11 05.2	7 00.5	8 02.7	0 43.5	3 12.6	23 22.7	24 22.2	23 09.2	20 38.6
20 Tu	17 54 29	28 09 21	28 41 30	4♈36 18	15 18.0	12 33.4	8 15.8	8 32.8	0 29.3	3 07.2	23 25.2	24 22.8	23 11.1	20 38.7
21 W	17 58 26	29 10 26	10♈31 30	16 27 44	15 19.2	14 02.1	9 31.2	9 02.7	0 15.1	3 01.7	23 27.8	24 23.3	23 13.1	20 38.8
22 Th	18 02 22	0♑11 32	22 25 40	28 25 54	15 20.8	15 31.2	10 46.6	9 32.5	0 00.9	2 56.0	23 30.4	24 23.8	23 15.0	20 38.9
23 F	18 06 19	1 12 38	4♉29 03	10♉35 39	15R 21.9	17 00.8	12 01.9	10 02.1	29♊46.7	2 50.2	23 33.2	24 24.2	23 16.8	20R 38.9
24 Sa	18 10 16	2 13 44	16 46 14	23 01 12	15 21.7	18 30.8	13 17.3	10 31.6	29 32.4	2 44.2	23 36.1	24 24.6	23 18.7	20 38.9
25 Su	18 14 12	3 14 51	29 20 56	5♊45 42	15 19.5	20 01.2	14 32.6	11 00.8	29 18.2	2 38.1	23 39.0	24 24.9	23 20.5	20 38.8
26 M	18 18 09	4 15 58	12♊15 39	18 50 52	15 15.1	21 31.9	15 47.9	11 30.0	29 04.1	2 31.9	23 42.1	24 25.1	23 22.4	20 38.7
27 Tu	18 22 05	5 17 05	25 31 17	2♋16 45	15 08.5	23 02.9	17 03.3	11 58.9	28 50.0	2 25.5	23 45.3	24 25.3	23 24.2	20 38.6
28 W	18 26 02	6 18 12	9♋06 56	16 01 30	15 00.3	24 34.3	18 18.6	12 27.7	28 36.0	2 19.0	23 48.5	24 25.4	23 26.0	20 38.5
29 Th	18 29 58	7 19 20	22 59 54	0♌01 37	14 51.1	26 06.0	19 33.9	12 56.3	28 22.1	2 12.4	23 51.9	24R 25.5	23 27.7	20 38.3
30 F	18 33 55	8 20 28	7♌06 01	14 12 27	14 42.3	27 38.0	20 49.2	13 24.7	28 08.3	2 05.7	23 55.3	24 25.5	23 29.5	20 38.1
31 Sa	18 37 52	9 21 36	21 20 17	28 28 53	14 34.7	29 10.4	22 04.5	13 53.0	27 54.6	1 58.8	23 58.9	24 25.5	23 31.2	20 37.9

Astro Data Dy Hr Mn	Planet Ingress Dy Hr Mn	Last Aspect Dy Hr Mn	☽ Ingress Dy Hr Mn	Last Aspect Dy Hr Mn	☽ Ingress Dy Hr Mn	☽ Phases & Eclipses Dy Hr Mn
⚳ R 4 23:32	☿ ♏R 13 3:26	2 5:36 ♄ □	♋ 2 17:43	2 3:14 ♂ ⚹	♌ 2 5:02	5 22:18 ☾ 13♌03
☿ R 6 17:56	♀ ♐ 20 1:06	4 11:51 ♄ △	♌ 4 23:36	3 20:09 ♆ □	♍ 4 8:48	12 14:26 ● 19♏45
♄☍♅ 8 8:21	☉ ♐ 22 18:14	6 12:56 ♆ □	♍ 7 3:10	6 1:50 ♅ ☌	♎ 6 11:43	12 14:22:50 ☛ T 01'58"
☽0S 9 17:24		8 17:47 ♅ ☌	♎ 9 4:54	8 1:55 ♀ ⚹	♏ 8 14:18	20 0:20 ☽ 27♒14
♃ R 21 10:22	♂ ♎ 4 0:55	9 11:51 ♃ ⚹	♏ 11 5:53	10 14:54 ☿ ☌	♐ 10 17:13	28 2:40 ○ 5♊25
☽0N 23 9:56	☿ ♐ 11 15:27	13 7:19 ☿ ☌	♐ 13 7:36	12 18:59 ♀ ☌	♑ 12 21:30	
♄ D 26 15:33	♀ ♑ 13 22:09	15 0:03 ♅ □	♑ 15 11:37	14 17:41 ♅ △	♒ 15 4:19	5 6:22 ☾ 12♍40
☿ D 26 17:50	☉ ♑ 22 7:28	17 13:04 ♀ ⚹	♒ 17 19:03	17 3:57 ☉ ⚹	♓ 17 14:17	12 3:13 ● 19♐38
	⚳ ♊R 22 13:31	20 0:20 ☉ □	♓ 20 5:53	19 21:41 ☉ □	♈ 20 2:39	19 21:41 ☽ 27♓33
☽0S 7 0:26		22 5:52 ♅ ☍	♈ 22 18:31	21 6:24 ☿ △	♉ 22 15:07	27 17:43 ○ 5♋32
♂0S 12 6:03		23 3:34 ♃ △	♉ 25 6:37	24 14:39 ♅ △	♊ 25 1:14	
☽0N 20 17:37		27 9:42 ♂ △	♊ 27 16:31	26 22:02 ♅ □	♋ 27 7:58	
♇ R 23 15:37		29 19:42 ♂ □	♋ 29 23:50	29 2:27 ♅ ⚹	♌ 29 11:57	
♅ R 30 7:30				31 13:18 ☿ △	♍ 31 14:33	

Astro Data

1 November 1966
Julian Day # 24411
SVP 5♓43'36"
GC 26♐22.6 ⚵ 4♈13.8R
Eris 10♈58.2R ⚶ 6♌45.8
⚷ 22♓07.6R ⚴ 7♎18.2
☽ Mean ☊ 16♉31.3

1 December 1966
Julian Day # 24441
SVP 5♓43'31"
GC 26♐22.6 ⚵ 1♈10.4
Eris 10♈45.0R ⚶ 13♌20.4
⚷ 21♓40.3R ⚴ 21♎38.6
☽ Mean ☊ 14♉56.0

LONGITUDE — January 1967

Day	Sid.Time	☉	0 hr ☽	Noon ☽	True ☊	☿	♀	♂	⚳	♃	♄	♅	♆	♇
1 Su	18 41 48	10♑22 45	5♍37 41	12♍46 09	14♉29.1	0♑43.0	23♑19.8	14♎21.1	27♊41.1	1♌51.8	24♓02.5	24♍25.4	23♏32.9	20♍37.6
2 M	18 45 45	11 23 53	19 53 53	27 00 31	14R 26.0	2 16.0	24 35.1	14 48.9	27R 27.7	1R 44.7	24 06.2	24R 25.2	23 34.5	20R 37.3
3 Tu	18 49 41	12 25 02	4♎05 46	11♎09 27	14D 25.0	3 49.4	25 50.4	15 16.6	27 14.6	1 37.5	24 10.0	24 25.0	23 36.2	20 36.9
4 W	18 53 38	13 26 12	18 11 25	25 11 36	14 25.4	5 23.1	27 05.6	15 44.1	27 01.6	1 30.3	24 13.9	24 24.8	23 37.8	20 36.6
5 Th	18 57 34	14 27 22	2♏09 56	9♏06 24	14R 26.1	6 57.1	28 20.9	16 11.3	26 48.8	1 22.9	24 17.9	24 24.4	23 39.4	20 36.2
6 F	19 01 31	15 28 32	16 00 58	22 53 34	14 25.9	8 31.5	29 36.2	16 38.4	26 36.3	1 15.4	24 22.0	24 24.1	23 41.0	20 35.7
7 Sa	19 05 27	16 29 42	29 44 10	6♐32 39	14 23.7	10 06.3	0♒51.4	17 05.2	26 24.0	1 07.9	24 26.2	24 23.6	23 42.5	20 35.3
8 Su	19 09 24	17 30 52	13♐18 55	20 02 48	14 18.8	11 41.5	2 06.7	17 31.8	26 11.9	1 00.3	24 30.4	24 23.1	23 44.0	20 34.8
9 M	19 13 21	18 32 03	26 44 07	3♑22 40	14 11.0	13 17.1	3 21.9	17 58.2	26 00.2	0 52.6	24 34.7	24 22.6	23 45.5	20 34.2
10 Tu	19 17 17	19 33 13	9♑58 14	16 30 38	14 00.6	14 53.1	4 37.2	18 24.4	25 48.7	0 44.8	24 39.2	24 22.0	23 47.0	20 33.7
11 W	19 21 14	20 34 23	22 59 40	29 25 10	13 48.4	16 29.6	5 52.4	18 50.3	25 37.5	0 37.0	24 43.7	24 21.3	23 48.4	20 33.1
12 Th	19 25 10	21 35 32	5♒47 04	12♒05 17	13 35.6	18 06.5	7 07.6	19 16.0	25 26.6	0 29.1	24 48.3	24 20.6	23 49.8	20 32.5
13 F	19 29 07	22 36 41	18 19 51	24 30 49	13 23.3	19 43.9	8 22.8	19 41.4	25 16.1	0 21.2	24 52.9	24 19.9	23 51.2	20 31.8
14 Sa	19 33 03	23 37 50	0♓38 23	6♓42 45	13 12.6	21 21.7	9 38.0	20 06.6	25 05.8	0 13.3	24 57.7	24 19.1	23 52.6	20 31.1
15 Su	19 37 00	24 38 57	12 44 15	18 43 15	13 04.3	23 00.1	10 53.2	20 31.5	24 56.0	0 05.3	25 02.5	24 18.2	23 53.9	20 30.4
16 M	19 40 56	25 40 04	24 40 12	0♈35 35	12 58.7	24 38.9	12 08.3	20 56.2	24 46.4	29♋57.3	25 07.4	24 17.3	23 55.2	20 29.7
17 Tu	19 44 53	26 41 11	6♈30 00	12 24 00	12 55.7	26 18.3	13 23.5	21 20.5	24 37.3	29 49.2	25 12.4	24 16.3	23 56.5	20 28.9
18 W	19 48 50	27 42 16	18 18 17	24 13 29	12D 54.7	27 58.2	14 38.6	21 44.7	24 28.5	29 41.2	25 17.4	24 15.3	23 57.7	20 28.1
19 Th	19 52 46	28 43 21	0♉10 18	6♉09 26	12R 54.7	29 38.6	15 53.7	22 08.5	24 20.1	29 33.1	25 22.6	24 14.2	23 58.9	20 27.3
20 F	19 56 43	29 44 25	12 11 36	18 17 28	12 54.7	1♒19.6	17 08.8	22 32.1	24 12.1	29 25.1	25 27.8	24 13.1	24 00.1	20 26.4
21 Sa	20 00 39	0♒45 28	24 27 42	0♊42 53	12 53.5	3 01.1	18 23.8	22 55.3	24 04.5	29 17.0	25 33.0	24 11.9	24 01.3	20 25.6
22 Su	20 04 36	1 46 30	7♊03 36	13 30 17	12 50.1	4 43.2	19 38.9	23 18.3	23 57.2	29 09.0	25 38.4	24 10.6	24 02.4	20 24.6
23 M	20 08 32	2 47 32	20 03 17	26 42 50	12 44.0	6 25.8	20 53.9	23 41.0	23 50.4	29 01.0	25 43.8	24 09.4	24 03.5	20 23.7
24 Tu	20 12 29	3 48 32	3♋29 01	10♋21 46	12 35.2	8 08.8	22 08.9	24 03.4	23 44.0	28 52.9	25 49.3	24 08.1	24 04.6	20 22.8
25 W	20 16 25	4 49 31	17 20 47	24 25 40	12 24.1	9 52.4	23 23.9	24 25.4	23 38.0	28 45.0	25 54.8	24 06.7	24 05.6	20 21.8
26 Th	20 20 22	5 50 30	1♌35 47	8♌50 22	12 11.9	11 36.5	24 38.9	24 47.2	23 32.4	28 37.0	26 00.5	24 05.3	24 06.6	20 20.8
27 F	20 24 19	6 51 28	16 08 33	23 29 19	11 59.8	13 21.0	25 53.8	25 08.6	23 27.2	28 29.1	26 06.1	24 03.8	24 07.6	20 19.7
28 Sa	20 28 15	7 52 25	0♍51 39	8♍14 29	11 49.1	15 05.8	27 08.7	25 29.7	23 22.5	28 21.3	26 11.9	24 02.3	24 08.5	20 18.7
29 Su	20 32 12	8 53 21	15 36 51	22 57 50	11 41.0	16 51.0	28 23.6	25 50.4	23 18.2	28 13.4	26 17.7	24 00.7	24 09.4	20 17.6
30 M	20 36 08	9 54 16	0♎16 38	7♎32 36	11 35.7	18 36.3	29 38.5	26 10.8	23 14.2	28 05.7	26 23.6	23 59.1	24 10.3	20 16.5
31 Tu	20 40 05	10 55 10	14 45 14	21 54 09	11 33.2	20 21.8	0♓53.4	26 30.8	23 10.8	27 58.0	26 29.5	23 57.5	24 11.1	20 15.3

LONGITUDE — February 1967

Day	Sid.Time	☉	0 hr ☽	Noon ☽	True ☊	☿	♀	♂	⚳	♃	♄	♅	♆	♇
1 W	20 44 01	11♒56 04	28♎59 09	6♏00 08	11♉32.5	22♒07.3	2♓08.2	26♎50.5	23♊07.7	27♋50.4	26♓35.5	23♍55.8	24♏11.9	20♍14.2
2 Th	20 47 58	12 56 58	12♏57 05	19 50 06	11R 32.5	23 52.7	3 23.0	27 09.8	23R 05.1	27R 42.8	26 41.5	23R 54.1	24 12.7	20R 13.0
3 F	20 51 54	13 57 50	26 39 19	3♐24 54	11 31.6	25 37.7	4 37.8	27 28.7	23 02.9	27 35.3	26 47.6	23 52.3	24 13.4	20 11.8
4 Sa	20 55 51	14 58 42	10♐07 02	16 45 55	11 28.8	27 22.2	5 52.6	27 47.2	23 01.1	27 27.9	26 53.8	23 50.5	24 14.2	20 10.6
5 Su	20 59 48	15 59 33	23 21 42	29 54 31	11 23.1	29 05.9	7 07.3	28 05.3	22 59.8	27 20.6	27 00.0	23 48.6	24 14.8	20 09.3
6 M	21 03 44	17 00 22	6♑24 30	12♑51 44	11 14.3	0♓48.5	8 22.1	28 23.0	22 58.8	27 13.4	27 06.3	23 46.7	24 15.5	20 08.1
7 Tu	21 07 41	18 01 11	19 16 15	25 38 05	11 02.7	2 29.6	9 36.8	28 40.2	22D 58.4	27 06.3	27 12.6	23 44.8	24 16.1	20 06.8
8 W	21 11 37	19 01 59	1♒57 15	8♒13 44	10 49.1	4 08.9	10 51.4	28 57.0	22 58.3	26 59.3	27 19.0	23 42.8	24 16.7	20 05.5
9 Th	21 15 34	20 02 45	14 27 33	20 38 41	10 34.6	5 46.0	12 06.1	29 13.4	22 58.7	26 52.4	27 25.4	23 40.8	24 17.2	20 04.2
10 F	21 19 30	21 03 30	26 47 11	2♓53 07	10 20.7	7 20.2	13 20.7	29 29.4	22 59.4	26 45.6	27 31.9	23 38.8	24 17.7	20 02.8
11 Sa	21 23 27	22 04 14	8♓56 34	14 57 41	10 08.3	8 51.2	14 35.3	29 44.8	23 00.7	26 38.9	27 38.4	23 36.7	24 18.2	20 01.5
12 Su	21 27 23	23 04 56	20 56 40	26 53 47	9 58.3	10 18.2	15 49.8	29 59.8	23 02.3	26 32.4	27 45.0	23 34.6	24 18.6	20 00.1
13 M	21 31 20	24 05 37	2♈49 21	8♈43 43	9 51.4	11 40.7	17 04.4	0♏14.3	23 04.3	26 25.9	27 51.6	23 32.5	24 19.0	19 58.7
14 Tu	21 35 17	25 06 16	14 37 19	20 30 39	9 47.2	12 57.9	18 18.9	0 28.3	23 06.8	26 19.7	27 58.3	23 30.3	24 19.4	19 57.3
15 W	21 39 13	26 06 53	26 24 14	2♉18 40	9D 45.5	14 09.2	19 33.3	0 41.8	23 09.7	26 13.5	28 05.0	23 28.1	24 19.7	19 55.9
16 Th	21 43 10	27 07 29	8♉14 34	14 12 34	9 45.4	15 13.8	20 47.7	0 54.8	23 12.9	26 07.5	28 11.7	23 25.8	24 20.0	19 54.4
17 F	21 47 06	28 08 03	20 13 22	26 17 40	9R 45.6	16 11.1	22 02.1	1 07.3	23 16.6	26 01.7	28 18.5	23 23.6	24 20.3	19 53.0
18 Sa	21 51 03	29 08 35	2♊26 08	8♊39 28	9 45.2	17 00.3	23 16.5	1 19.3	23 20.7	25 56.0	28 25.3	23 21.3	24 20.5	19 51.5
19 Su	21 54 59	0♓09 05	14 58 18	21 23 13	9 43.2	17 40.9	24 30.8	1 30.7	23 25.2	25 50.4	28 32.2	23 19.0	24 20.8	19 50.0
20 M	21 58 56	1 09 34	27 54 46	4♋33 19	9 38.8	18 12.3	25 45.0	1 41.6	23 30.0	25 45.0	28 39.1	23 16.6	24 20.9	19 48.5
21 Tu	22 02 52	2 10 01	11♋19 10	18 12 27	9 31.9	18 34.2	26 59.3	1 51.9	23 35.3	25 39.8	28 46.0	23 14.3	24 21.1	19 47.0
22 W	22 06 49	3 10 26	25 13 05	2♌20 50	9 23.0	18R 46.1	28 13.5	2 01.6	23 40.9	25 34.7	28 53.0	23 11.9	24 21.2	19 45.5
23 Th	22 10 46	4 10 49	9♌35 12	16 55 31	9 12.8	18 47.9	29 27.6	2 10.8	23 46.9	25 29.8	29 00.0	23 09.5	24 21.2	19 44.0
24 F	22 14 42	5 11 10	24 20 53	1♍50 14	9 02.5	18 39.8	0♈41.7	2 19.3	23 53.3	25 25.0	29 07.1	23 07.0	24R 21.3	19 42.5
25 Sa	22 18 39	6 11 29	9♍22 24	16 56 06	8 53.4	18 21.9	1 55.8	2 27.3	24 00.0	25 20.4	29 14.1	23 04.6	24 21.3	19 40.9
26 Su	22 22 35	7 11 47	24 30 02	2♎02 58	8 46.5	17 54.8	3 09.8	2 34.7	24 07.1	25 16.0	29 21.2	23 02.1	24 21.2	19 39.4
27 M	22 26 32	8 12 04	9♎33 44	17 01 17	8 42.1	17 19.1	4 23.7	2 41.4	24 14.6	25 11.8	29 28.3	22 59.6	24 21.1	19 37.8
28 Tu	22 30 28	9 12 18	24 24 48	1♏43 35	8D 40.3	16 35.7	5 37.7	2 47.5	24 22.4	25 07.7	29 35.5	22 57.1	24 21.0	19 36.2

Astro Data	Dy Hr Mn
☽0S	3 5:12
♄☍♅	6 22:53
☽0N	17 0:48
♅⚹♆	25 22:52
☽0S	30 10:33
♃△♄	7 0:41
⚳D	8 3:20
☽0N	13 7:20
☿R	23 4:24
♆R	24 22:07
♀0N	25 20:00
☽0S	26 18:48

Planet Ingress		Dy Hr Mn
☿	♑	1 0:52
♀	♒	6 19:36
♃	♋R	16 3:50
☿	♒	19 17:05
☉	♒	20 18:08
♀	♓	30 18:53
☿	♓	6 0:38
♂	♏	12 12:20
☉	♓	19 8:24
♀	♈	23 22:30

Last Aspect Dy Hr Mn			☽ Ingress	Dy Hr Mn
2 7:38	♅	☌	♎	2 17:04
4 15:35	♀	□	♏	4 20:16
6 14:38	♅	⚹	♐	7 0:28
8 20:02	♄	□	♑	9 5:53
11 3:11	♄	⚹	♒	11 13:05
13 10:43	♆	□	♓	13 22:45
16 10:43	♃	△	♈	16 10:48
18 22:54	♃	□	♉	18 23:39
21 9:18	♃	⚹	♊	21 10:38
23 10:14	♄	□	♋	23 17:51
25 19:11	♃	☌	♌	25 21:20
27 16:17	♀	☍	♍	27 22:36
29 20:33	♃	⚹	♎	29 23:33

Last Aspect Dy Hr Mn			☽ Ingress	Dy Hr Mn
31 22:10	♃	□	♏	1 1:44
3 1:45	♃	△	♐	3 5:55
5 10:17	☿	⚹	♑	5 12:10
7 17:53	♂	□	♒	7 20:17
10 5:10	♂	△	♓	10 6:19
12 13:45	♄	☌	♈	12 18:17
14 23:45	♃	□	♉	15 7:19
17 15:59	♄	⚹	♊	17 19:16
20 1:15	♄	□	♋	20 3:48
22 6:09	♄	△	♌	22 8:04
24 0:01	♆	□	♍	24 9:04
26 7:41	♄	☍	♎	26 8:44
28 1:13	♃	□	♏	28 9:09

☽ Phases & Eclipses Dy Hr Mn	
3 14:19	☾ 12♎31
10 18:06	● 19♑49
18 19:41	☽ 28♈02
26 6:40	○ 5♌37
1 23:03	☾ 12♏24
9 10:44	● 20♒00
17 15:56	☽ 28♉18
24 17:43	○ 5♍26

Astro Data

1 January 1967
Julian Day # 24472
SVP 5♓43'25"
GC 26♐22.7 ⚴ 4♈54.2
Eris 10♈40.6 ⚵ 12♌24.3R
⚷ 22♓03.8 ⚶ 5♏39.8
☽ Mean ☊ 13♉17.6

1 February 1967
Julian Day # 24503
SVP 5♓43'20"
GC 26♐22.8 ⚴ 13♈50.2
Eris 10♈47.0 ⚵ 5♌08.5R
⚷ 23♓14.7 ⚶ 17♏59.3
☽ Mean ☊ 11♉39.1

March 1967 — LONGITUDE

Day	Sid.Time	☉	0 hr ☽	Noon ☽	True ☊	☿	♀	♂	⚳	♃	♄	♅	♆	♇
1 W	22 34 25	10♓12 32	8♏57 08	16♏05 10	8♉40.2	15♓45.9	6♈51.5	2♏52.9	24♊30.5	25♋03.8	29♓42.7	22♍54.6	24♏20.9	19♍34.7
2 Th	22 38 21	11 12 44	23 07 31	0♐04 11	8R 41.0	14R 50.8	8 05.4	2 57.7	24 39.0	25R 00.1	29 49.9	22R 52.1	24R 20.7	19R 33.1
3 F	22 42 18	12 12 54	6♐55 17	13 41 00	8 41.4	13 51.9	9 19.2	3 01.8	24 47.9	24 56.6	29 57.1	22 49.5	24 20.5	19 31.5
4 Sa	22 46 15	13 13 03	20 21 37	26 57 24	8 40.4	12 50.7	10 33.0	3 05.2	24 57.0	24 53.2	0♈04.4	22 47.0	24 20.3	19 29.9
5 Su	22 50 11	14 13 11	3♑28 43	9♑55 53	8 37.3	11 48.6	11 46.7	3 07.9	25 06.5	24 50.1	0 11.7	22 44.4	24 20.0	19 28.3
6 M	22 54 08	15 13 16	16 19 15	22 39 06	8 31.8	10 47.2	13 00.3	3 09.9	25 16.4	24 47.1	0 19.0	22 41.8	24 19.7	19 26.7
7 Tu	22 58 04	16 13 21	28 55 44	5♒09 26	8 24.1	9 47.7	14 14.0	3 11.1	25 26.5	24 44.3	0 26.3	22 39.2	24 19.4	19 25.1
8 W	23 02 01	17 13 23	11♒20 26	17 28 57	8 14.8	8 51.3	15 27.5	3R 11.7	25 37.0	24 41.7	0 33.6	22 36.6	24 19.0	19 23.5
9 Th	23 05 57	18 13 24	23 35 11	29 39 17	8 04.9	7 59.1	16 41.1	3 11.5	25 47.8	24 39.3	0 41.0	22 34.0	24 18.6	19 21.9
10 F	23 09 54	19 13 22	5♓41 27	11♓41 49	7 55.2	7 11.9	17 54.5	3 10.6	25 58.9	24 37.1	0 48.4	22 31.4	24 18.2	19 20.3
11 Sa	23 13 50	20 13 19	17 40 35	23 37 53	7 46.6	6 30.2	19 08.0	3 08.9	26 10.3	24 35.0	0 55.7	22 28.8	24 17.7	19 18.7
12 Su	23 17 47	21 13 14	29 33 56	5♈28 57	7 39.9	5 54.6	20 21.3	3 06.4	26 22.0	24 33.2	1 03.1	22 26.2	24 17.2	19 17.1
13 M	23 21 44	22 13 07	11♈23 10	17 16 53	7 35.3	5 25.4	21 34.6	3 03.2	26 33.9	24 31.6	1 10.6	22 23.5	24 16.7	19 15.5
14 Tu	23 25 40	23 12 58	23 10 23	29 04 02	7D 33.0	5 02.6	22 47.9	2 59.2	26 46.2	24 30.1	1 18.0	22 20.9	24 16.2	19 13.9
15 W	23 29 37	24 12 47	4♉58 15	10♉53 27	7 32.6	4 46.2	24 01.1	2 54.5	26 58.8	24 28.9	1 25.4	22 18.3	24 15.6	19 12.3
16 Th	23 33 33	25 12 33	16 50 07	22 48 47	7 33.6	4 36.3	25 14.3	2 49.0	27 11.6	24 27.8	1 32.9	22 15.7	24 14.9	19 10.7
17 F	23 37 30	26 12 18	28 49 59	4♊54 18	7 35.2	4D 32.6	26 27.4	2 42.7	27 24.8	24 27.0	1 40.3	22 13.1	24 14.3	19 09.1
18 Sa	23 41 26	27 12 00	11♊02 21	17 14 42	7R 36.6	4 35.0	27 40.4	2 35.6	27 38.2	24 26.3	1 47.8	22 10.5	24 13.6	19 07.5
19 Su	23 45 23	28 11 40	23 31 58	29 54 44	7 37.0	4 43.2	28 53.4	2 27.8	27 51.8	24 25.9	1 55.3	22 07.9	24 12.9	19 05.9
20 M	23 49 19	29 11 18	6♋23 33	12♋58 51	7 36.0	4 56.9	0♉06.3	2 19.2	28 05.7	24D 25.6	2 02.7	22 05.3	24 12.2	19 04.3
21 Tu	23 53 16	0♈10 53	19 41 04	26 30 27	7 33.4	5 15.8	1 19.1	2 09.8	28 19.9	24 25.5	2 10.2	22 02.7	24 11.4	19 02.8
22 W	23 57 13	1 10 26	3♌27 09	10♌31 08	7 29.3	5 39.8	2 31.9	1 59.7	28 34.4	24 25.6	2 17.7	22 00.1	24 10.6	19 01.2
23 Th	0 01 09	2 09 57	17 42 10	24 59 50	7 24.3	6 08.4	3 44.6	1 48.9	28 49.0	24 25.9	2 25.2	21 57.5	24 09.8	18 59.7
24 F	0 05 06	3 09 26	2♍23 30	9♍52 21	7 19.1	6 41.5	4 57.3	1 37.2	29 04.0	24 26.4	2 32.7	21 55.0	24 08.9	18 58.1
25 Sa	0 09 02	4 08 52	17 25 22	25 01 22	7 14.4	7 18.8	6 09.8	1 24.9	29 19.1	24 27.1	2 40.1	21 52.4	24 08.1	18 56.6
26 Su	0 12 59	5 08 16	2♎39 06	10♎17 14	7 10.9	8 00.0	7 22.3	1 11.8	29 34.5	24 28.0	2 47.6	21 49.9	24 07.1	18 55.0
27 M	0 16 55	6 07 38	17 54 27	25 29 31	7D 09.0	8 44.9	8 34.8	0 58.0	29 50.1	24 29.1	2 55.1	21 47.4	24 06.2	18 53.5
28 Tu	0 20 52	7 06 59	3♏01 16	10♏28 43	7 08.6	9 33.3	9 47.1	0 43.5	0♋06.0	24 30.3	3 02.5	21 44.9	24 05.3	18 52.0
29 W	0 24 48	8 06 17	17 51 03	25 07 36	7 09.4	10 25.0	10 59.4	0 28.3	0 22.0	24 31.8	3 10.0	21 42.4	24 04.3	18 50.5
30 Th	0 28 45	9 05 34	2♐17 57	9♐21 48	7 10.8	11 19.8	12 11.7	0 12.4	0 38.3	24 33.4	3 17.5	21 39.9	24 03.3	18 49.0
31 F	0 32 42	10 04 49	16 19 05	23 09 48	7 12.3	12 17.5	13 23.8	29♎55.9	0 54.9	24 35.3	3 24.9	21 37.5	24 02.2	18 47.5

April 1967 — LONGITUDE

Day	Sid.Time	☉	0 hr ☽	Noon ☽	True ☊	☿	♀	♂	⚳	♃	♄	♅	♆	♇
1 Sa	0 36 38	11♈04 02	29♐54 08	6♑32 21	7♉13.1	13♓18.1	14♉35.9	29♎38.8	1♋11.6	24♋37.3	3♈32.4	21♍35.0	24♏01.2	18♍46.1
2 Su	0 40 35	12 03 14	13♑04 45	19 31 46	7R 13.0	14 21.3	15 47.9	29R 21.0	1 28.5	24 39.5	3 39.8	21R 32.6	24R 00.1	18R 44.6
3 M	0 44 31	13 02 24	25 53 47	2♒11 16	7 11.7	15 27.0	16 59.9	29 02.6	1 45.6	24 41.8	3 47.2	21 30.3	23 59.0	18 43.2
4 Tu	0 48 28	14 01 32	8♒24 40	14 34 25	7 09.4	16 35.1	18 11.7	28 43.7	2 03.0	24 44.4	3 54.6	21 27.9	23 57.8	18 41.7
5 W	0 52 24	15 00 38	20 40 58	26 44 43	7 06.2	17 45.6	19 23.5	28 24.2	2 20.5	24 47.1	4 02.1	21 25.6	23 56.7	18 40.3
6 Th	0 56 21	15 59 42	2♓46 05	8♓45 26	7 02.7	18 58.2	20 35.3	28 04.2	2 38.3	24 50.1	4 09.4	21 23.2	23 55.5	18 38.9
7 F	1 00 17	16 58 44	14 43 07	20 39 27	6 59.2	20 13.0	21 46.9	27 43.8	2 56.2	24 53.2	4 16.8	21 20.9	23 54.3	18 37.6
8 Sa	1 04 14	17 57 44	26 34 45	2♈29 18	6 56.2	21 29.8	22 58.5	27 22.9	3 14.3	24 56.4	4 24.2	21 18.7	23 53.1	18 36.2
9 Su	1 08 11	18 56 43	8♈23 24	14 17 17	6 54.0	22 48.5	24 10.0	27 01.6	3 32.6	24 59.9	4 31.5	21 16.4	23 51.8	18 34.8
10 M	1 12 07	19 55 39	20 11 13	26 05 29	6D 52.8	24 09.2	25 21.4	26 40.0	3 51.1	25 03.5	4 38.8	21 14.2	23 50.6	18 33.5
11 Tu	1 16 04	20 54 34	2♉00 20	7♉56 03	6 52.4	25 31.8	26 32.7	26 18.1	4 09.8	25 07.3	4 46.1	21 12.1	23 49.3	18 32.2
12 W	1 20 00	21 53 26	13 52 55	19 51 15	6 52.8	26 56.2	27 44.0	25 55.9	4 28.6	25 11.3	4 53.4	21 09.9	23 48.0	18 30.9
13 Th	1 23 57	22 52 16	25 51 22	1♊53 38	6 53.8	28 22.3	28 55.1	25 33.5	4 47.7	25 15.5	5 00.7	21 07.8	23 46.6	18 29.6
14 F	1 27 53	23 51 05	7♊58 24	14 06 05	6 55.0	29 50.3	0♊06.2	25 10.9	5 06.9	25 19.8	5 07.9	21 05.7	23 45.3	18 28.4
15 Sa	1 31 50	24 49 51	20 17 04	26 31 48	6 56.2	1♈19.9	1 17.2	24 48.2	5 26.2	25 24.3	5 15.1	21 03.7	23 43.9	18 27.2
16 Su	1 35 46	25 48 34	2♋50 42	9♋14 11	6 57.0	2 51.3	2 28.1	24 25.4	5 45.8	25 28.9	5 22.3	21 01.7	23 42.6	18 25.9
17 M	1 39 43	26 47 16	15 42 40	22 16 33	6R 57.5	4 24.3	3 38.9	24 02.5	6 05.4	25 33.7	5 29.5	20 59.7	23 41.2	18 24.8
18 Tu	1 43 40	27 45 55	28 56 09	5♌41 45	6 57.4	5 59.1	4 49.6	23 39.7	6 25.3	25 38.7	5 36.6	20 57.8	23 39.7	18 23.6
19 W	1 47 36	28 44 32	12♌33 33	19 31 38	6 56.9	7 35.5	6 00.1	23 16.9	6 45.3	25 43.9	5 43.7	20 55.9	23 38.3	18 22.4
20 Th	1 51 33	29 43 07	26 35 58	3♍46 22	6 56.2	9 13.5	7 10.6	22 54.2	7 05.4	25 49.1	5 50.8	20 54.0	23 36.9	18 21.3
21 F	1 55 29	0♉41 40	11♍02 30	18 23 52	6 55.5	10 53.3	8 21.0	22 31.6	7 25.7	25 54.6	5 57.8	20 52.2	23 35.4	18 20.2
22 Sa	1 59 26	1 40 10	25 49 48	3♎19 29	6 54.9	12 34.7	9 31.3	22 09.2	7 46.2	26 00.2	6 04.9	20 50.4	23 33.9	18 19.1
23 Su	2 03 22	2 38 38	10♎51 58	18 26 09	6 54.5	14 17.8	10 41.5	21 47.1	8 06.8	26 06.0	6 11.8	20 48.6	23 32.5	18 18.1
24 M	2 07 19	3 37 05	26 00 55	3♏35 04	6D 54.4	16 02.6	11 51.5	21 25.2	8 27.5	26 11.9	6 18.8	20 46.9	23 31.0	18 17.0
25 Tu	2 11 15	4 35 29	11♏07 28	18 36 59	6 54.4	17 49.0	13 01.5	21 03.6	8 48.3	26 17.9	6 25.7	20 45.3	23 29.5	18 16.0
26 W	2 15 12	5 33 52	26 02 37	3♐23 29	6 54.5	19 37.2	14 11.4	20 42.4	9 09.3	26 24.1	6 32.6	20 43.6	23 27.9	18 15.1
27 Th	2 19 08	6 32 13	10♐38 50	17 48 06	6R 54.6	21 27.1	15 21.1	20 21.5	9 30.5	26 30.5	6 39.4	20 42.1	23 26.4	18 14.1
28 F	2 23 05	7 30 33	24 50 54	1♑47 00	6 54.6	23 18.7	16 30.7	20 01.1	9 51.7	26 37.0	6 46.3	20 40.5	23 24.9	18 13.2
29 Sa	2 27 02	8 28 51	8♑36 19	15 18 56	6 54.5	25 12.0	17 40.2	19 41.1	10 13.1	26 43.6	6 53.0	20 39.0	23 23.3	18 12.3
30 Su	2 30 58	9 27 08	21 55 02	28 24 54	6D 54.4	27 07.1	18 49.6	19 21.6	10 34.7	26 50.4	6 59.8	20 37.6	23 21.8	18 11.4

Astro Data

	Dy Hr Mn
♂R	8 17:44
☽0N	12 13:28
☿D	17 14:27
⊙0N	21 7:36
♃D	21 9:16
☽0S	26 5:36
☽0N	8 19:35
♄0N	12 13:49
☿0N	18 11:13
☽0S	22 16:40

Planet Ingress

	Dy Hr Mn
♄ ♈	3 21:32
♀ ♉	20 9:56
☉ ♈	21 7:37
⚳ ♋	28 3:00
♂ ♎R	31 6:10
♀ ♊	14 9:54
☿ ♈	14 14:38
☉ ♉	20 18:55

Last Aspect / ☽ Ingress

Last Aspect Dy Hr Mn		☽ Ingress Dy Hr Mn
2 11:35	♄ △	♐ 2 11:53
4 4:25	♅ □	♑ 4 17:35
6 16:03	♃ ☍	♒ 7 2:03
9 1:26	♆ □	♓ 9 12:41
11 13:55	♃ △	♈ 12 0:53
14 2:44	♃ □	♉ 14 13:54
16 17:13	☉ ⚹	♊ 17 2:19
19 9:53	♀ ⚹	♋ 19 12:10
21 8:22	♃ ☌	♌ 21 18:04
23 10:38	♆ □	♍ 23 20:08
25 11:06	♃ ⚹	♎ 25 19:50
27 10:24	♃ □	♏ 27 19:10
29 11:01	♃ △	♐ 29 20:08

Last Aspect Dy Hr Mn		☽ Ingress Dy Hr Mn
31 23:48	♂ ⚹	♑ 1 0:11
3 6:08	♂ □	♒ 3 7:49
5 15:12	♂ △	♓ 5 18:29
7 20:36	♃ △	♈ 8 6:57
10 13:08	♂ ☍	♉ 10 19:56
13 5:27	♀ ☌	♊ 13 8:15
15 8:47	♂ △	♋ 15 18:37
17 20:48	☉ □	♌ 18 1:54
20 4:45	☉ △	♍ 20 5:43
22 0:12	♃ ⚹	♎ 22 6:41
24 0:13	♃ □	♏ 24 6:19
26 0:30	♃ △	♐ 26 6:27
27 19:08	☿ △	♑ 28 8:54
30 9:10	☿ □	♒ 30 14:57

☽ Phases & Eclipses

Dy Hr Mn		
3 9:10	☾	12♐06
11 4:30	●	19♓55
19 8:31	☽	28♊03
26 3:21	○	4♎47
1 20:58	☾	11♑26
9 22:20	●	19♈22
17 20:48	☽	27♋09
24 12:03	○	3♏37
24 12:06	•	T 1.336

Astro Data

1 March 1967
Julian Day # 24531
SVP 5♓43'16"
GC 26♐22.8 ⚴ 24♈54.0
Eris 11♈00.7 ⚵ 0♌24.3R
⚷ 24♓45.7 ⚶ 26♏25.3
☽ Mean ☊ 10♉10.1

1 April 1967
Julian Day # 24562
SVP 5♓43'12"
GC 26♐22.9 ⚴ 9♉27.0
Eris 11♈21.0 ⚵ 1♌46.2
⚷ 26♓36.4 ⚶ 0♐37.2
☽ Mean ☊ 8♉31.6

LONGITUDE

May 1967

Day	Sid.Time	☉	0 hr ☽	Noon ☽	True ☊	☿	♀	♂	⚳	♃	♄	♅	♆	♇
1 M	2 34 55	10♉25 23	4♒48 57	11♒07 36	6♉54.3	29♈03.8	19♊58.9	19♎02.6	10♋56.3	26♋57.3	7♈06.5	20♍36.2	23♏20.2	18♍10.5
2 Tu	2 38 51	11 23 36	17 21 21	23 30 44	6 54.4	1♉02.2	21 08.1	18R 44.2	11 18.1	27 04.4	7 13.1	20R 34.8	23R 18.6	18R 09.7
3 W	2 42 48	12 21 48	29 36 18	5♓38 35	6 54.8	3 02.3	22 17.1	18 26.3	11 40.0	27 11.6	7 19.7	20 33.5	23 17.0	18 08.9
4 Th	2 46 44	13 19 58	11♓38 09	17 35 31	6 55.3	5 03.9	23 26.0	18 09.1	12 02.0	27 18.9	7 26.3	20 32.2	23 15.4	18 08.1
5 F	2 50 41	14 18 07	23 31 13	29 25 45	6 56.1	7 07.1	24 34.8	17 52.5	12 24.1	27 26.4	7 32.8	20 31.0	23 13.8	18 07.4
6 Sa	2 54 37	15 16 15	5♈19 34	11♈13 07	6 56.9	9 11.8	25 43.5	17 36.5	12 46.4	27 34.0	7 39.3	20 29.8	23 12.2	18 06.6
7 Su	2 58 34	16 14 21	17 06 48	23 01 01	6 57.5	11 17.9	26 52.0	17 21.3	13 08.7	27 41.7	7 45.7	20 28.7	23 10.6	18 06.0
8 M	3 02 31	17 12 25	28 56 07	4♉52 24	6R 57.8	13 25.2	28 00.4	17 06.7	13 31.2	27 49.5	7 52.1	20 27.6	23 09.0	18 05.3
9 Tu	3 06 27	18 10 28	10♉50 10	16 49 42	6 57.7	15 33.7	29 08.7	16 52.9	13 53.8	27 57.5	7 58.4	20 26.6	23 07.4	18 04.7
10 W	3 10 24	19 08 29	22 51 14	28 55 00	6 56.9	17 43.0	0♋16.8	16 39.9	14 16.5	28 05.6	8 04.7	20 25.6	23 05.7	18 04.0
11 Th	3 14 20	20 06 29	5♊01 12	11♊10 04	6 55.5	19 53.1	1 24.8	16 27.6	14 39.3	28 13.9	8 10.9	20 24.7	23 04.1	18 03.5
12 F	3 18 17	21 04 27	17 21 46	23 36 30	6 53.6	22 03.8	2 32.6	16 16.0	15 02.2	28 22.2	8 17.1	20 23.8	23 02.5	18 02.9
13 Sa	3 22 13	22 02 23	29 54 26	6♋15 47	6 51.5	24 14.7	3 40.3	16 05.3	15 25.2	28 30.7	8 23.3	20 22.9	23 00.9	18 02.4
14 Su	3 26 10	23 00 18	12♋40 44	19 09 26	6 49.5	26 25.6	4 47.8	15 55.4	15 48.3	28 39.3	8 29.3	20 22.2	22 59.2	18 01.9
15 M	3 30 07	23 58 11	25 42 06	2♌18 52	6 47.8	28 36.2	5 55.2	15 46.2	16 11.5	28 48.0	8 35.4	20 21.4	22 57.6	18 01.5
16 Tu	3 34 03	24 56 02	8♌59 56	15 45 24	6D 46.8	0♊46.3	7 02.4	15 37.9	16 34.8	28 56.8	8 41.3	20 20.8	22 56.0	18 01.0
17 W	3 38 00	25 53 51	22 35 23	29 29 56	6 46.6	2 55.5	8 09.4	15 30.4	16 58.2	29 05.7	8 47.2	20 20.1	22 54.3	18 00.6
18 Th	3 41 56	26 51 39	6♍29 04	13♍32 41	6 47.2	5 03.6	9 16.3	15 23.7	17 21.7	29 14.7	8 53.1	20 19.6	22 52.7	18 00.3
19 F	3 45 53	27 49 25	20 40 40	27 52 45	6 48.4	7 10.3	10 23.0	15 17.8	17 45.3	29 23.9	8 58.9	20 19.0	22 51.1	17 59.9
20 Sa	3 49 49	28 47 09	5♎08 35	12♎27 42	6 49.7	9 15.4	11 29.4	15 12.7	18 08.9	29 33.1	9 04.6	20 18.6	22 49.5	17 59.6
21 Su	3 53 46	29 44 52	19 49 31	27 13 22	6R 50.6	11 18.6	12 35.8	15 08.5	18 32.7	29 42.5	9 10.3	20 18.1	22 47.9	17 59.4
22 M	3 57 42	0♊42 33	4♏38 28	12♏03 56	6 50.8	13 19.8	13 41.9	15 05.0	18 56.5	29 51.9	9 15.9	20 17.8	22 46.2	17 59.1
23 Tu	4 01 39	1 40 12	19 28 53	26 52 21	6 49.8	15 18.8	14 47.8	15 02.3	19 20.4	0♌01.5	9 21.4	20 17.5	22 44.6	17 58.9
24 W	4 05 36	2 37 51	4♐13 24	11♐31 09	6 47.5	17 15.3	15 53.5	15 00.5	19 44.4	0 11.1	9 26.9	20 17.2	22 43.0	17 58.7
25 Th	4 09 32	3 35 28	18 44 46	25 53 33	6 44.2	19 09.3	16 59.0	14D 59.4	20 08.5	0 20.9	9 32.3	20 17.0	22 41.4	17 58.6
26 F	4 13 29	4 33 05	2♑56 54	9♑54 21	6 40.3	21 00.7	18 04.3	14 59.1	20 32.7	0 30.7	9 37.7	20 16.9	22 39.9	17 58.5
27 Sa	4 17 25	5 30 40	16 45 36	23 30 29	6 36.2	22 49.5	19 09.4	14 59.5	20 56.9	0 40.7	9 43.0	20 16.8	22 38.3	17 58.4
28 Su	4 21 22	6 28 14	0♒08 59	6♒41 13	6 32.6	24 35.4	20 14.3	15 00.8	21 21.3	0 50.7	9 48.2	20D 16.7	22 36.7	17 58.3
29 M	4 25 18	7 25 47	13 07 26	19 27 58	6 29.9	26 18.5	21 18.9	15 02.8	21 45.6	1 00.8	9 53.3	20 16.7	22 35.1	17D 58.3
30 Tu	4 29 15	8 23 20	25 43 14	1♓53 44	6D 28.5	27 58.7	22 23.4	15 05.5	22 10.1	1 11.0	9 58.4	20 16.8	22 33.6	17 58.3
31 W	4 33 11	9 20 51	8♓00 02	14 02 41	6 28.4	29 36.0	23 27.6	15 09.0	22 34.7	1 21.3	10 03.4	20 16.9	22 32.0	17 58.3

LONGITUDE

June 1967

Day	Sid.Time	☉	0 hr ☽	Noon ☽	True ☊	☿	♀	♂	⚳	♃	♄	♅	♆	♇
1 Th	4 37 08	10♊18 22	20♓02 20	25♓59 35	6♉29.3	1♋10.4	24♋31.5	15♎13.2	22♋59.3	1♌31.7	10♈08.4	20♍17.0	22♏30.5	17♍58.4
2 F	4 41 05	11 15 52	1♈55 04	7♈49 25	6 30.9	2 41.7	25 35.2	15 18.2	23 24.0	1 42.2	10 13.3	20 17.3	22R 29.0	17 58.5
3 Sa	4 45 01	12 13 21	13 43 12	19 37 02	6 32.6	4 10.1	26 38.7	15 23.8	23 48.7	1 52.8	10 18.1	20 17.5	22 27.4	17 58.6
4 Su	4 48 58	13 10 49	25 31 28	1♉27 00	6R 33.7	5 35.4	27 41.9	15 30.2	24 13.6	2 03.4	10 22.8	20 17.9	22 25.9	17 58.8
5 M	4 52 54	14 08 17	7♉24 06	13 23 13	6 33.5	6 57.7	28 44.8	15 37.3	24 38.5	2 14.2	10 27.4	20 18.2	22 24.4	17 59.0
6 Tu	4 56 51	15 05 44	19 24 44	25 28 58	6 31.8	8 16.8	29 47.5	15 45.0	25 03.4	2 25.0	10 32.0	20 18.7	22 23.0	17 59.2
7 W	5 00 47	16 03 10	1♊36 13	7♊46 41	6 28.3	9 32.8	0♌49.9	15 53.5	25 28.5	2 35.9	10 36.5	20 19.2	22 21.5	17 59.5
8 Th	5 04 44	17 00 35	14 00 32	20 17 53	6 23.0	10 45.6	1 52.0	16 02.6	25 53.6	2 46.8	10 40.9	20 19.7	22 20.1	17 59.7
9 F	5 08 40	17 58 00	26 38 49	3♋03 19	6 16.5	11 55.2	2 53.8	16 12.4	26 18.8	2 57.9	10 45.3	20 20.3	22 18.6	18 00.1
10 Sa	5 12 37	18 55 23	9♋31 23	16 02 57	6 09.3	13 01.4	3 55.3	16 22.9	26 44.0	3 09.0	10 49.5	20 20.9	22 17.2	18 00.4
11 Su	5 16 34	19 52 46	22 37 55	29 16 13	6 02.2	14 04.2	4 56.5	16 33.9	27 09.3	3 20.2	10 53.7	20 21.6	22 15.8	18 00.8
12 M	5 20 30	20 50 08	5♌57 42	12♌42 17	5 56.2	15 03.5	5 57.3	16 45.7	27 34.6	3 31.4	10 57.8	20 22.4	22 14.4	18 01.2
13 Tu	5 24 27	21 47 29	19 29 49	26 20 13	5 51.7	15 59.3	6 57.9	16 58.0	28 00.0	3 42.8	11 01.8	20 23.2	22 13.0	18 01.7
14 W	5 28 23	22 44 48	3♍13 23	10♍09 13	5D 49.2	16 51.5	7 58.0	17 10.9	28 25.5	3 54.2	11 05.8	20 24.1	22 11.7	18 02.2
15 Th	5 32 20	23 42 07	17 07 37	24 08 30	5 48.5	17 39.9	8 57.8	17 24.5	28 51.0	4 05.6	11 09.6	20 25.0	22 10.3	18 02.7
16 F	5 36 16	24 39 25	1♎11 44	8♎17 12	5 49.0	18 24.5	9 57.3	17 38.6	29 16.6	4 17.2	11 13.4	20 25.9	22 09.0	18 03.2
17 Sa	5 40 13	25 36 42	15 24 43	22 34 04	5R 50.1	19 05.2	10 56.3	17 53.3	29 42.2	4 28.8	11 17.1	20 26.9	22 07.7	18 03.8
18 Su	5 44 09	26 33 58	29 44 58	6♏57 05	5 50.6	19 41.9	11 54.9	18 08.5	0♌07.9	4 40.4	11 20.7	20 28.0	22 06.4	18 04.4
19 M	5 48 06	27 31 13	14♏09 58	21 23 08	5 49.6	20 14.4	12 53.2	18 24.3	0 33.6	4 52.1	11 24.2	20 29.1	22 05.2	18 05.0
20 Tu	5 52 03	28 28 28	28 36 01	5♐48 00	5 46.5	20 42.7	13 50.9	18 40.6	0 59.4	5 03.9	11 27.6	20 30.3	22 03.9	18 05.7
21 W	5 55 59	29 25 42	12♐58 26	20 06 36	5 41.1	21 06.6	14 48.3	18 57.5	1 25.3	5 15.7	11 31.0	20 31.5	22 02.7	18 06.4
22 Th	5 59 56	0♋22 56	27 11 51	4♑13 32	5 33.7	21 26.1	15 45.2	19 14.8	1 51.1	5 27.6	11 34.2	20 32.8	22 01.5	18 07.1
23 F	6 03 52	1 20 10	11♑11 03	18 03 54	5 24.9	21 41.2	16 41.6	19 32.7	2 17.1	5 39.6	11 37.4	20 34.1	22 00.4	18 07.8
24 Sa	6 07 49	2 17 23	24 51 41	1♒34 06	5 15.7	21 51.7	17 37.6	19 51.1	2 43.0	5 51.6	11 40.4	20 35.5	21 59.2	18 08.6
25 Su	6 11 45	3 14 35	8♒10 59	14 42 17	5 07.1	21R 57.6	18 33.0	20 09.9	3 09.1	6 03.6	11 43.4	20 36.9	21 58.1	18 09.4
26 M	6 15 42	4 11 48	21 08 04	27 28 32	4 59.9	21 58.9	19 28.0	20 29.2	3 35.1	6 15.7	11 46.3	20 38.4	21 57.0	18 10.3
27 Tu	6 19 39	5 09 01	3♓43 58	9♓54 46	4 54.7	21 55.6	20 22.4	20 49.0	4 01.2	6 27.9	11 49.1	20 39.9	21 55.9	18 11.2
28 W	6 23 35	6 06 13	16 01 24	22 04 23	4 51.6	21 47.8	21 16.2	21 09.2	4 27.4	6 40.1	11 51.8	20 41.4	21 54.8	18 12.1
29 Th	6 27 32	7 03 26	28 04 19	4♈01 48	4D 50.5	21 35.7	22 09.5	21 29.9	4 53.6	6 52.3	11 54.4	20 43.1	21 53.8	18 13.0
30 F	6 31 28	8 00 38	9♈57 31	15 52 07	4 50.7	21 19.3	23 02.2	21 51.0	5 19.8	7 04.6	11 56.9	20 44.7	21 52.7	18 13.9

Astro Data

	Dy Hr Mn
☽0N	6 1:54
♄□♆	10 15:06
☽0S	20 1:45
♂ D	26 9:29
♅ D	28 21:36
♇ D	29 20:30
☽0N	2 8:32
♃∠♇	9 16:55
☽0S	16 8:02
♃∠♅	22 23:40
☿ R	26 6:50
☽0N	29 15:28

Planet Ingress

		Dy Hr Mn
☿	♉	1 23:26
♀	♋	10 6:05
☿	♊	16 3:27
☉	♊	21 18:18
♃	♌	23 8:21
☿	♋	31 18:02
♀	♌	6 16:48
⚳	♌	18 4:37
☉	♋	22 2:23

Last Aspect / ☽ Ingress (May)

Last Aspect Dy Hr Mn			☽ Ingress	Dy Hr Mn
2 11:36	♆	□	♓	3 0:47
5 7:55	♃	△	♈	5 13:10
7 21:36	♃	□	♉	8 2:09
10 10:21	♃	✶	♊	10 14:08
12 5:51	♅	□	♋	13 0:11
15 5:34	♃	☌	♌	15 7:49
17 5:18	☉	□	♍	17 12:52
19 14:33	♃	✶	♎	19 15:31
21 16:04	♃	□	♏	21 16:30
23 5:18	♆	☌	♐	23 17:06
25 2:34	♅	□	♑	25 18:58
27 10:27	♆	✶	♒	27 23:44
30 3:12	☿	△	♓	30 8:18

Last Aspect / ☽ Ingress (June)

Last Aspect Dy Hr Mn			☽ Ingress	Dy Hr Mn
1 8:45	♀	△	♈	1 20:07
4 3:40	♀	□	♉	4 9:04
6 5:54	♆	☍	♊	6 20:52
8 12:03	♅	□	♋	9 6:18
10 23:21	♆	△	♌	11 13:19
13 4:48	♆	□	♍	13 18:24
15 11:12	☉	□	♎	15 21:58
17 17:27	☉	△	♏	18 0:25
19 13:10	♆	☌	♐	20 2:20
21 12:42	♅	□	♑	22 4:46
23 18:56	♆	✶	♒	24 9:11
26 1:33	♆	□	♓	26 16:49
28 11:41	♆	△	♈	29 3:53

☽ Phases & Eclipses

Dy Hr Mn		
1 10:33	☾	10♒22
9 14:55	●	18♉18
9 14:42:09	●	P 0.720
17 5:18	☽	25♌38
23 20:22	○	2♐00
31 1:52	☾	8♓57
8 5:13	●	16♊44
15 11:12	☽	23♍40
22 4:57	○	0♑06
29 18:39	☾	7♈19

Astro Data

1 May 1967
Julian Day # 24592
SVP 5♓43'08"
GC 26♐23.0 ⚴ 25♉13.2
Eris 11♈40.8 ⚵ 8♌12.6
⚷ 28♓13.3 ⚶ 27♏38.8R
☽ Mean ☊ 6♉56.3

1 June 1967
Julian Day # 24623
SVP 5♓43'04"
GC 26♐23.1 ⚴ 12♊47.3
Eris 11♈56.5 ⚵ 17♌48.3
⚷ 29♓23.7 ⚶ 20♏31.2R
☽ Mean ☊ 5♉17.8

July 1967 — LONGITUDE

Day	Sid.Time	☉	0 hr ☽	Noon ☽	True ☊	☿	♀	♂	⚳	♃	♄	♅	♆	♇
1 Sa	6 35 25	8♋57 51	21♈46 16	27♈40 40	4♉51.3	20♋58.8	23♌54.3	22♎12.6	5♌46.1	7♌17.0	11♈59.3	20♍46.4	21♏51.8	18♍14.9
2 Su	6 39 21	9 55 04	3♉35 56	9♉32 43	4R 51.4	20R 34.7	24 45.8	22 34.6	6 12.5	7 29.4	12 01.7	20 48.2	21R 50.8	18 15.9
3 M	6 43 18	10 52 17	15 31 37	21 33 11	4 50.0	20 07.1	25 36.6	22 57.0	6 38.8	7 41.8	12 03.9	20 50.0	21 49.8	18 17.0
4 Tu	6 47 14	11 49 30	27 37 55	3♊46 17	4 46.5	19 36.5	26 26.8	23 19.8	7 05.3	7 54.3	12 06.0	20 51.8	21 48.9	18 18.0
5 W	6 51 11	12 46 44	9♊58 37	16 15 15	4 40.4	19 03.3	27 16.2	23 43.1	7 31.7	8 06.8	12 08.1	20 53.7	21 48.0	18 19.1
6 Th	6 55 08	13 43 57	22 36 21	29 02 04	4 32.0	18 28.0	28 05.0	24 06.7	7 58.2	8 19.3	12 10.0	20 55.7	21 47.2	18 20.3
7 F	6 59 04	14 41 11	5♋32 23	12♋07 15	4 21.7	17 51.3	28 53.0	24 30.7	8 24.7	8 31.9	12 11.9	20 57.7	21 46.3	18 21.4
8 Sa	7 03 01	15 38 25	18 46 29	25 29 51	4 10.4	17 13.7	29 40.2	24 55.1	8 51.3	8 44.6	12 13.6	20 59.7	21 45.5	18 22.6
9 Su	7 06 57	16 35 39	2♌17 00	9♌07 36	3 59.2	16 35.8	0♍26.6	25 19.9	9 17.9	8 57.3	12 15.2	21 01.8	21 44.8	18 23.8
10 M	7 10 54	17 32 53	16 01 12	22 57 22	3 49.4	15 58.4	1 12.2	25 45.1	9 44.6	9 10.0	12 16.8	21 03.9	21 44.0	18 25.1
11 Tu	7 14 50	18 30 07	29 55 42	6♍55 45	3 41.7	15 21.9	1 56.9	26 10.6	10 11.2	9 22.7	12 18.2	21 06.1	21 43.3	18 26.3
12 W	7 18 47	19 27 20	13♍57 08	20 59 31	3 36.7	14 47.2	2 40.7	26 36.5	10 37.9	9 35.5	12 19.6	21 08.3	21 42.6	18 27.6
13 Th	7 22 43	20 24 34	28 02 37	5♎06 11	3 34.2	14 14.8	3 23.5	27 02.7	11 04.7	9 48.3	12 20.8	21 10.5	21 41.9	18 28.9
14 F	7 26 40	21 21 48	12♎10 01	19 13 57	3D 33.5	13 45.3	4 05.4	27 29.3	11 31.4	10 01.1	12 21.9	21 12.8	21 41.3	18 30.3
15 Sa	7 30 37	22 19 01	26 17 51	3♏21 37	3R 33.6	13 19.2	4 46.2	27 56.2	11 58.2	10 13.9	12 23.0	21 15.2	21 40.7	18 31.6
16 Su	7 34 33	23 16 15	10♏25 07	17 28 12	3 33.1	12 57.0	5 26.0	28 23.4	12 25.1	10 26.8	12 23.9	21 17.5	21 40.1	18 33.0
17 M	7 38 30	24 13 29	24 30 43	1♐32 28	3 30.9	12 39.2	6 04.6	28 51.0	12 51.9	10 39.7	12 24.7	21 20.0	21 39.5	18 34.4
18 Tu	7 42 26	25 10 43	8♐33 11	15 32 35	3 26.2	12 26.1	6 42.1	29 18.9	13 18.8	10 52.7	12 25.5	21 22.4	21 39.0	18 35.9
19 W	7 46 23	26 07 58	22 30 18	29 25 59	3 18.8	12 18.1	7 18.4	29 47.1	13 45.7	11 05.6	12 26.1	21 24.9	21 38.5	18 37.3
20 Th	7 50 19	27 05 12	6♑19 12	13♑09 34	3 08.8	12D 15.3	7 53.5	0♏15.5	14 12.7	11 18.6	12 26.6	21 27.5	21 38.1	18 38.8
21 F	7 54 16	28 02 27	19 56 40	26 40 08	2 57.0	12 18.1	8 27.2	0 44.3	14 39.6	11 31.6	12 27.1	21 30.0	21 37.6	18 40.3
22 Sa	7 58 12	28 59 43	3♒19 37	9♒54 51	2 44.6	12 26.6	8 59.7	1 13.4	15 06.6	11 44.6	12 27.4	21 32.7	21 37.2	18 41.8
23 Su	8 02 09	29 56 59	16 25 40	22 51 57	2 32.8	12 40.8	9 30.7	1 42.7	15 33.6	11 57.6	12 27.6	21 35.3	21 36.9	18 43.4
24 M	8 06 06	0♌54 16	29 13 40	5♓30 56	2 22.6	13 00.9	10 00.3	2 12.4	16 00.7	12 10.7	12R 27.7	21 38.0	21 36.5	18 45.0
25 Tu	8 10 02	1 51 33	11♓43 53	17 52 49	2 14.7	13 26.8	10 28.4	2 42.3	16 27.7	12 23.8	12 27.7	21 40.7	21 36.2	18 46.6
26 W	8 13 59	2 48 51	23 58 05	0♈00 04	2 09.4	13 58.7	10 55.0	3 12.5	16 54.8	12 36.9	12 27.6	21 43.5	21 35.9	18 48.2
27 Th	8 17 55	3 46 11	5♈59 18	11 56 18	2 06.5	14 36.5	11 20.0	3 42.9	17 21.9	12 50.0	12 27.5	21 46.3	21 35.7	18 49.8
28 F	8 21 52	4 43 31	17 51 41	23 46 04	2D 05.5	15 20.1	11 43.3	4 13.6	17 49.1	13 03.1	12 27.2	21 49.1	21 35.5	18 51.5
29 Sa	8 25 48	5 40 52	29 40 08	5♉34 33	2R 05.4	16 09.5	12 04.9	4 44.6	18 16.2	13 16.2	12 26.8	21 52.0	21 35.3	18 53.1
30 Su	8 29 45	6 38 14	11♉30 00	17 27 10	2 05.1	17 04.6	12 24.7	5 15.8	18 43.4	13 29.3	12 26.3	21 54.9	21 35.1	18 54.8
31 M	8 33 41	7 35 38	23 26 45	29 29 23	2 03.7	18 05.4	12 42.8	5 47.3	19 10.6	13 42.5	12 25.7	21 57.8	21 35.0	18 56.6

August 1967 — LONGITUDE

Day	Sid.Time	☉	0 hr ☽	Noon ☽	True ☊	☿	♀	♂	⚳	♃	♄	♅	♆	♇
1 Tu	8 37 38	8♌33 02	5♊35 41	11♊46 12	2♉00.2	19♋11.7	12♍58.9	6♏19.0	19♌37.8	13♌55.7	12♈25.0	22♍00.8	21♏34.9	18♍58.3
2 W	8 41 35	9 30 28	18 01 27	24 21 49	1R 54.2	20 23.3	13 13.1	6 51.0	20 05.1	14 08.8	12R 24.2	22 03.8	21R 34.9	19 00.1
3 Th	8 45 31	10 27 54	0♋47 39	7♋19 09	1 45.7	21 40.3	13 25.3	7 23.3	20 32.3	14 22.0	12 23.3	22 06.8	21D 34.9	19 01.8
4 F	8 49 28	11 25 22	13 56 23	20 39 19	1 35.2	23 02.3	13 35.4	7 55.7	20 59.6	14 35.2	12 22.3	22 09.9	21 34.9	19 03.6
5 Sa	8 53 24	12 22 51	27 27 47	4♌21 27	1 23.6	24 29.1	13 43.5	8 28.4	21 26.9	14 48.4	12 21.2	22 13.0	21 34.9	19 05.4
6 Su	8 57 21	13 20 21	11♌19 52	18 22 29	1 12.1	26 00.6	13 49.3	9 01.4	21 54.3	15 01.6	12 20.0	22 16.1	21 35.0	19 07.3
7 M	9 01 17	14 17 52	25 28 39	2♍37 41	1 01.8	27 36.5	13 53.0	9 34.6	22 21.6	15 14.8	12 18.7	22 19.3	21 35.1	19 09.1
8 Tu	9 05 14	15 15 23	9♍48 48	17 01 17	0 53.8	29 16.5	13R 54.4	10 08.0	22 48.9	15 28.0	12 17.3	22 22.4	21 35.2	19 11.0
9 W	9 09 10	16 12 56	24 14 26	1♎27 33	0 48.6	1♌00.3	13 53.5	10 41.6	23 16.3	15 41.2	12 15.8	22 25.6	21 35.4	19 12.9
10 Th	9 13 07	17 10 29	8♎40 05	15 51 30	0 45.9	2 47.5	13 50.2	11 15.5	23 43.7	15 54.4	12 14.2	22 28.9	21 35.6	19 14.8
11 F	9 17 04	18 08 03	23 01 26	0♏09 32	0D 45.3	4 37.9	13 44.6	11 49.5	24 11.1	16 07.5	12 12.5	22 32.1	21 35.9	19 16.7
12 Sa	9 21 00	19 05 38	7♏15 36	14 19 27	0R 45.5	6 30.9	13 36.5	12 23.8	24 38.5	16 20.7	12 10.7	22 35.4	21 36.1	19 18.6
13 Su	9 24 57	20 03 14	21 20 59	28 20 08	0 45.3	8 26.2	13 26.1	12 58.3	25 05.9	16 33.9	12 08.8	22 38.7	21 36.4	19 20.5
14 M	9 28 53	21 00 51	5♐16 53	12♐11 11	0 43.6	10 23.5	13 13.3	13 33.0	25 33.3	16 47.1	12 06.9	22 42.1	21 36.8	19 22.5
15 Tu	9 32 50	21 58 29	19 03 00	25 52 19	0 39.6	12 22.3	12 58.1	14 07.8	26 00.7	17 00.2	12 04.8	22 45.5	21 37.1	19 24.5
16 W	9 36 46	22 56 08	2♑39 03	9♑23 06	0 33.1	14 22.3	12 40.5	14 42.9	26 28.2	17 13.4	12 02.6	22 48.8	21 37.5	19 26.5
17 Th	9 40 43	23 53 48	16 04 23	22 42 46	0 24.2	16 23.1	12 20.7	15 18.2	26 55.6	17 26.5	12 00.4	22 52.3	21 38.0	19 28.5
18 F	9 44 39	24 51 29	29 18 06	5♒50 16	0 13.6	18 24.4	11 58.6	15 53.7	27 23.1	17 39.7	11 58.0	22 55.7	21 38.4	19 30.5
19 Sa	9 48 36	25 49 11	12♒19 08	18 44 35	0 02.5	20 25.9	11 34.4	16 29.3	27 50.6	17 52.8	11 55.6	22 59.1	21 38.9	19 32.5
20 Su	9 52 33	26 46 55	25 06 33	1♓24 59	29♈51.8	22 27.3	11 08.1	17 05.1	28 18.0	18 05.9	11 53.1	23 02.6	21 39.5	19 34.5
21 M	9 56 29	27 44 40	7♓39 55	13 51 23	29 42.5	24 28.5	10 40.0	17 41.2	28 45.5	18 19.0	11 50.4	23 06.1	21 40.0	19 36.6
22 Tu	10 00 26	28 42 26	19 59 33	26 04 35	29 35.3	26 29.1	10 10.0	18 17.4	29 13.0	18 32.1	11 47.7	23 09.6	21 40.6	19 38.6
23 W	10 04 22	29 40 14	2♈06 44	8♈06 19	29 30.6	28 29.1	9 38.4	18 53.7	29 40.5	18 45.1	11 45.0	23 13.1	21 41.2	19 40.7
24 Th	10 08 19	0♍38 03	14 03 44	19 59 23	29D 28.3	0♍28.3	9 05.4	19 30.3	0♍08.0	18 58.2	11 42.1	23 16.7	21 41.9	19 42.8
25 F	10 12 15	1 35 54	25 53 47	1♉47 27	29 27.8	2 26.5	8 31.2	20 07.0	0 35.5	19 11.2	11 39.1	23 20.3	21 42.6	19 44.8
26 Sa	10 16 12	2 33 47	7♉40 57	13 34 55	29 28.5	4 23.8	7 55.9	20 43.9	1 03.0	19 24.2	11 36.1	23 23.8	21 43.3	19 46.9
27 Su	10 20 08	3 31 42	19 29 59	25 26 48	29R 29.4	6 19.9	7 19.8	21 20.9	1 30.5	19 37.2	11 33.0	23 27.5	21 44.0	19 49.0
28 M	10 24 05	4 29 39	1♊26 02	7♊28 21	29 29.6	8 14.9	6 43.0	21 58.2	1 58.1	19 50.2	11 29.8	23 31.1	21 44.8	19 51.2
29 Tu	10 28 02	5 27 37	13 34 25	19 44 52	29 28.5	10 08.7	6 06.0	22 35.6	2 25.6	20 03.1	11 26.5	23 34.7	21 45.6	19 53.3
30 W	10 31 58	6 25 37	26 00 16	2♋21 09	29 25.4	12 01.3	5 28.8	23 13.1	2 53.1	20 16.0	11 23.2	23 38.4	21 46.4	19 55.4
31 Th	10 35 55	7 23 40	8♋47 58	15 21 05	29 20.2	13 52.7	4 51.7	23 50.9	3 20.7	20 28.9	11 19.8	23 42.0	21 47.3	19 57.5

Astro Data	Dy Hr Mn
☽ 0S	13 12:41
☿ D	20 12:01
♅ ⚹ ♆	24 0:24
♄ R	25 4:08
♃ △ ♄	25 19:16
☽ 0N	26 22:34
♆ D	3 15:20
♀ R	8 14:29
☽ 0S	9 18:01
☽ 0N	23 5:36
♃ ⚺ ♇	28 14:11

Planet Ingress		Dy Hr Mn
♀	♍	8 22:11
♂	♏	19 22:56
☉	♌	23 13:16
☿	♌	8 22:09
☊	♈R	19 17:23
☉	♍	23 20:12
⚳	♍	24 5:01
☿	♍	24 6:17

Last Aspect Dy Hr Mn			☽ Ingress	Dy Hr Mn
1 3:44	♀	△	♉	1 16:43
3 20:37	♀	□	♊	4 4:39
6 10:07	♀	⚹	♋	6 13:47
8 10:56	♂	□	♌	8 19:58
10 16:58	♂	⚹	♍	11 0:07
12 13:13	♆	⚹	♎	13 3:20
15 2:29	♂	☌	♏	15 6:17
16 22:36	☉	△	♐	17 9:22
19 12:38	♂	⚹	♑	19 12:59
21 14:39	☉	☍	♒	21 17:59
23 9:40	♆	□	♓	24 1:28
25 19:30	♅	☍	♈	26 12:00
27 17:44	☿	□	♉	29 0:40
30 20:59	♅	△	♊	31 13:00

Last Aspect Dy Hr Mn			☽ Ingress	Dy Hr Mn
2 7:39	♅	□	♋	2 22:32
4 16:42	☿	☌	♌	5 4:26
6 17:26	♆	□	♍	7 7:36
8 20:56	♅	☌	♎	9 9:34
10 14:22	☉	⚹	♏	11 11:44
13 2:11	♅	⚹	♐	13 14:52
15 6:29	♅	□	♑	15 19:18
17 12:17	♅	△	♒	18 1:17
20 2:27	☉	☍	♓	20 9:18
22 6:13	♅	☍	♈	22 19:47
24 9:54	♃	△	♉	25 8:21
27 7:58	♅	△	♊	27 21:08
29 19:24	♅	□	♋	30 7:34

☽ Phases & Eclipses Dy Hr Mn		
7 17:00	●	14♋53
14 15:53	☽	21♎31
21 14:39	○	28♑09
29 12:14	☾	5♉41
6 2:48	●	12♌58
12 20:44	☽	19♏27
20 2:27	○	26♒24
28 5:35	☾	4♊14

Astro Data

1 July 1967
Julian Day # 24653
SVP 5♓42'58"
GC 26♐23.1 ⚵ 0♋34.2
Eris 12♈03.7 ⚶ 28♌32.8
⚷ 29♓49.7 ⚴ 17♏48.1
☽ Mean ☊ 3♉42.5

1 August 1967
Julian Day # 24684
SVP 5♓42'53"
GC 26♐23.2 ⚵ 19♋12.4
Eris 12♈01.1R ⚶ 10♍21.4
⚷ 29♓27.8R ⚴ 22♏11.3
☽ Mean ☊ 2♉04.0

LONGITUDE — September 1967

Day	Sid.Time	☉	0 hr ☽	Noon ☽	True ☊	☿	♀	♂	⚳	♃	♄	♅	♆	♇
1 F	10 39 51	8♍21 44	22♋00 43	28♋46 59	29♈13.4	15♍42.8	4♍15.0	24♏28.8	3♍48.2	20♌41.8	11♈16.3	23♍45.7	21♏48.2	19♍59.7
2 Sa	10 43 48	9 19 49	5♌39 49	12♌39 01	29R 05.6	17 31.7	3R 38.9	25 06.8	4 15.7	20 54.6	11R 12.7	23 49.4	21 49.2	20 01.8
3 Su	10 47 44	10 17 57	19 44 10	26 54 46	28 57.6	19 19.3	3 03.6	25 45.0	4 43.3	21 07.5	11 09.1	23 53.1	21 50.1	20 04.0
4 M	10 51 41	11 16 06	4♍10 04	11♍29 17	28 50.6	21 05.7	2 29.3	26 23.4	5 10.8	21 20.2	11 05.4	23 56.8	21 51.1	20 06.2
5 Tu	10 55 37	12 14 17	18 51 29	26 15 40	28 45.2	22 50.9	1 56.3	27 01.9	5 38.3	21 33.0	11 01.6	24 00.5	21 52.1	20 08.3
6 W	10 59 34	13 12 30	3♎40 51	11♎06 02	28 41.9	24 34.9	1 24.7	27 40.6	6 05.8	21 45.7	10 57.8	24 04.2	21 53.2	20 10.5
7 Th	11 03 31	14 10 44	18 30 18	25 52 49	28D 40.7	26 17.7	0 54.6	28 19.4	6 33.4	21 58.3	10 53.9	24 08.0	21 54.3	20 12.6
8 F	11 07 27	15 09 00	3♏12 51	10♏29 47	28 41.1	27 59.3	0 26.4	28 58.4	7 00.9	22 11.0	10 49.9	24 11.7	21 55.4	20 14.8
9 Sa	11 11 24	16 07 17	17 43 10	24 52 37	28 42.3	29 39.7	29♌60.0	29 37.5	7 28.4	22 23.6	10 45.9	24 15.5	21 56.5	20 17.0
10 Su	11 15 20	17 05 36	1♐57 55	8♐58 56	28R 43.4	1♎19.0	29 35.6	0♐16.8	7 55.9	22 36.1	10 41.9	24 19.2	21 57.7	20 19.2
11 M	11 19 17	18 03 56	15 55 36	22 47 56	28 43.5	2 57.1	29 13.3	0 56.2	8 23.4	22 48.7	10 37.7	24 23.0	21 58.9	20 21.4
12 Tu	11 23 13	19 02 18	29 36 02	6♑19 59	28 42.1	4 34.2	28 53.3	1 35.8	8 50.9	23 01.1	10 33.6	24 26.8	22 00.1	20 23.5
13 W	11 27 10	20 00 42	12♑59 55	19 36 00	28 39.0	6 10.1	28 35.5	2 15.5	9 18.3	23 13.6	10 29.4	24 30.6	22 01.4	20 25.7
14 Th	11 31 06	20 59 07	26 08 21	2♒37 07	28 34.3	7 44.9	28 20.1	2 55.3	9 45.8	23 26.0	10 25.1	24 34.3	22 02.7	20 27.9
15 F	11 35 03	21 57 33	9♒02 27	15 24 29	28 28.5	9 18.7	28 07.1	3 35.2	10 13.3	23 38.3	10 20.8	24 38.1	22 04.0	20 30.1
16 Sa	11 39 00	22 56 02	21 43 20	27 59 07	28 22.2	10 51.3	27 56.4	4 15.3	10 40.7	23 50.6	10 16.4	24 41.9	22 05.3	20 32.3
17 Su	11 42 56	23 54 32	4♓11 59	10♓22 01	28 16.1	12 22.9	27 48.2	4 55.5	11 08.1	24 02.8	10 12.0	24 45.7	22 06.7	20 34.5
18 M	11 46 53	24 53 04	16 29 23	22 34 13	28 11.0	13 53.5	27 42.5	5 35.8	11 35.5	24 15.0	10 07.6	24 49.5	22 08.0	20 36.6
19 Tu	11 50 49	25 51 37	28 36 41	4♈37 00	28 07.2	15 22.9	27D 39.1	6 16.3	12 03.0	24 27.2	10 03.1	24 53.2	22 09.5	20 38.8
20 W	11 54 46	26 50 13	10♈35 22	16 32 03	28D 05.0	16 51.3	27 38.2	6 56.9	12 30.3	24 39.3	9 58.6	24 57.0	22 10.9	20 41.0
21 Th	11 58 42	27 48 51	22 27 20	28 21 33	28 04.3	18 18.6	27 39.6	7 37.6	12 57.7	24 51.3	9 54.1	25 00.8	22 12.4	20 43.2
22 F	12 02 39	28 47 31	4♉15 04	10♉08 18	28 04.9	19 44.8	27 43.3	8 18.4	13 25.1	25 03.3	9 49.6	25 04.6	22 13.9	20 45.3
23 Sa	12 06 35	29 46 13	16 01 40	21 55 41	28 06.4	21 09.9	27 49.4	8 59.4	13 52.5	25 15.2	9 45.0	25 08.4	22 15.4	20 47.5
24 Su	12 10 32	0♎44 57	27 50 50	3♊47 41	28 08.2	22 33.9	27 57.7	9 40.4	14 19.8	25 27.1	9 40.4	25 12.1	22 16.9	20 49.7
25 M	12 14 29	1 43 44	9♊46 47	15 48 43	28 09.7	23 56.8	28 08.2	10 21.6	14 47.1	25 38.9	9 35.7	25 15.9	22 18.5	20 51.8
26 Tu	12 18 25	2 42 32	21 54 06	28 03 32	28R 10.6	25 18.5	28 20.8	11 02.9	15 14.4	25 50.6	9 31.1	25 19.7	22 20.1	20 54.0
27 W	12 22 22	3 41 24	4♋17 35	10♋36 49	28 10.5	26 38.9	28 35.6	11 44.3	15 41.7	26 02.3	9 26.4	25 23.5	22 21.7	20 56.1
28 Th	12 26 18	4 40 17	17 01 45	23 32 51	28 09.4	27 58.1	28 52.3	12 25.9	16 09.0	26 14.0	9 21.7	25 27.2	22 23.3	20 58.3
29 F	12 30 15	5 39 13	0♌10 29	6♌54 55	28 07.2	29 16.0	29 11.0	13 07.5	16 36.2	26 25.5	9 17.0	25 31.0	22 25.0	21 00.4
30 Sa	12 34 11	6 38 10	13 46 18	20 44 38	28 04.5	0♏32.4	29 31.6	13 49.3	17 03.5	26 37.0	9 12.3	25 34.7	22 26.7	21 02.5

LONGITUDE — October 1967

Day	Sid.Time	☉	0 hr ☽	Noon ☽	True ☊	☿	♀	♂	⚳	♃	♄	♅	♆	♇
1 Su	12 38 08	7♎37 11	27♌49 46	5♍01 21	28♈01.6	1♏47.5	29♌54.0	14♐31.2	17♍30.7	26♌48.4	9♈07.6	25♍38.4	22♏28.4	21♍04.6
2 M	12 42 04	8 36 13	12♍18 52	19 41 37	27R 59.0	3 01.0	0♍18.2	15 13.1	17 57.9	26 59.8	9R 02.9	25 42.2	22 30.1	21 06.7
3 Tu	12 46 01	9 35 17	27 08 46	4♎39 18	27 57.1	4 12.9	0 44.1	15 55.2	18 25.0	27 11.1	8 58.2	25 45.9	22 31.8	21 08.8
4 W	12 49 58	10 34 23	12♎12 09	19 46 07	27D 56.1	5 23.0	1 11.6	16 37.5	18 52.2	27 22.3	8 53.5	25 49.6	22 33.6	21 10.9
5 Th	12 53 54	11 33 32	27 20 04	4♏52 50	27 56.1	6 31.3	1 40.8	17 19.8	19 19.3	27 33.4	8 48.8	25 53.3	22 35.4	21 13.0
6 F	12 57 51	12 32 42	12♏23 21	19 50 38	27 56.7	7 37.6	2 11.4	18 02.2	19 46.4	27 44.5	8 44.1	25 56.9	22 37.2	21 15.1
7 Sa	13 01 47	13 31 55	27 13 52	4♐32 20	27 57.8	8 41.7	2 43.6	18 44.7	20 13.4	27 55.5	8 39.4	26 00.6	22 39.0	21 17.1
8 Su	13 05 44	14 31 09	11♐45 32	18 53 04	27 58.9	9 43.5	3 17.1	19 27.4	20 40.5	28 06.4	8 34.7	26 04.3	22 40.9	21 19.2
9 M	13 09 40	15 30 25	25 54 44	2♑50 26	27 59.7	10 42.8	3 52.1	20 10.1	21 07.5	28 17.2	8 30.0	26 07.9	22 42.8	21 21.2
10 Tu	13 13 37	16 29 42	9♑40 12	16 24 11	27R 59.9	11 39.3	4 28.3	20 52.9	21 34.4	28 27.9	8 25.4	26 11.5	22 44.6	21 23.3
11 W	13 17 33	17 29 02	23 02 34	29 35 38	27 59.7	12 32.7	5 05.8	21 35.9	22 01.4	28 38.6	8 20.7	26 15.1	22 46.5	21 25.3
12 Th	13 21 30	18 28 23	6♒03 43	12♒27 09	27 58.9	13 22.8	5 44.6	22 18.9	22 28.3	28 49.1	8 16.1	26 18.7	22 48.5	21 27.3
13 F	13 25 27	19 27 46	18 46 18	25 01 33	27 57.9	14 09.3	6 24.5	23 02.0	22 55.1	28 59.6	8 11.6	26 22.3	22 50.4	21 29.3
14 Sa	13 29 23	20 27 10	1♓13 15	7♓21 46	27 56.9	14 51.8	7 05.6	23 45.2	23 22.0	29 10.0	8 07.0	26 25.8	22 52.4	21 31.2
15 Su	13 33 20	21 26 37	13 27 28	19 30 40	27 55.9	15 29.9	7 47.8	24 28.5	23 48.8	29 20.3	8 02.5	26 29.4	22 54.3	21 33.2
16 M	13 37 16	22 26 05	25 31 42	1♈30 50	27 55.1	16 03.2	8 31.1	25 11.9	24 15.5	29 30.4	7 58.0	26 32.9	22 56.3	21 35.1
17 Tu	13 41 13	23 25 35	7♈28 24	13 24 40	27 54.7	16 31.3	9 15.4	25 55.3	24 42.2	29 40.6	7 53.5	26 36.4	22 58.3	21 37.1
18 W	13 45 09	24 25 07	19 19 53	25 14 20	27D 54.5	16 53.5	10 00.7	26 38.9	25 08.9	29 50.6	7 49.1	26 39.8	23 00.4	21 39.0
19 Th	13 49 06	25 24 41	1♉08 18	7♉02 02	27 54.6	17 09.4	10 46.9	27 22.5	25 35.6	0♍00.5	7 44.7	26 43.3	23 02.4	21 40.9
20 F	13 53 02	26 24 18	12 55 49	18 49 57	27 54.7	17R 18.5	11 34.1	28 06.2	26 02.2	0 10.3	7 40.4	26 46.7	23 04.4	21 42.8
21 Sa	13 56 59	27 23 56	24 44 45	0♊40 33	27R 54.8	17 20.2	12 22.2	28 50.0	26 28.7	0 20.0	7 36.1	26 50.1	23 06.5	21 44.6
22 Su	14 00 55	28 23 37	6♊37 41	12 36 33	27 54.8	17 13.9	13 11.1	29 33.9	26 55.3	0 29.6	7 31.8	26 53.5	23 08.6	21 46.5
23 M	14 04 52	29 23 20	18 37 31	24 41 02	27 54.7	16 59.2	14 00.9	0♑17.9	27 21.7	0 39.1	7 27.6	26 56.8	23 10.7	21 48.3
24 Tu	14 08 49	0♏23 05	0♋47 32	6♋57 28	27 54.5	16 35.8	14 51.4	1 01.9	27 48.2	0 48.5	7 23.5	27 00.2	23 12.8	21 50.1
25 W	14 12 45	1 22 52	13 11 18	19 29 30	27D 54.3	16 03.3	15 42.8	1 46.1	28 14.6	0 57.8	7 19.4	27 03.5	23 14.9	21 51.9
26 Th	14 16 42	2 22 42	25 52 33	2♌20 52	27 54.2	15 21.8	16 34.9	2 30.3	28 40.9	1 07.0	7 15.3	27 06.8	23 17.0	21 53.7
27 F	14 20 38	3 22 34	8♌54 53	15 34 56	27 54.3	14 31.5	17 27.7	3 14.6	29 07.2	1 16.1	7 11.3	27 10.0	23 19.2	21 55.4
28 Sa	14 24 35	4 22 28	22 21 18	29 14 12	27 54.7	13 33.0	18 21.1	3 58.9	29 33.5	1 25.0	7 07.4	27 13.2	23 21.3	21 57.2
29 Su	14 28 31	5 22 24	6♍13 41	13♍19 42	27 55.3	12 27.2	19 15.3	4 43.4	29 59.7	1 33.9	7 03.5	27 16.4	23 23.5	21 58.9
30 M	14 32 28	6 22 22	20 32 03	27 50 20	27 56.0	11 15.6	20 10.1	5 27.9	0♎25.8	1 42.6	6 59.7	27 19.6	23 25.6	22 00.6
31 Tu	14 36 24	7 22 22	5♎14 02	12♎42 24	27 56.6	9 59.9	21 05.5	6 12.5	0 51.9	1 51.2	6 56.0	27 22.7	23 27.8	22 02.3

Astro Data

	Dy Hr Mn
☽0S	6 1:51
♃□♆	7 3:32
☿0S	10 9:39
☽0N	19 12:20
♀D	20 9:34
♃⚼♄	21 16:06
♃⚺♅	22 15:52
☉0S	23 17:39
☽0S	3 12:13
♄⚼♆	16 18:07
☽0N	16 18:38
☿R	21 5:15
☽0S	30 23:19

Planet Ingress

		Dy Hr Mn
♀	♌R	9 11:58
☿	♎	9 16:53
♂	♐	10 1:44
☉	♎	23 17:38
☿	♏	30 1:46
♀	♍	1 18:07
♃	♍	19 10:51
♂	♑	23 2:14
☉	♏	24 2:44
⚳	♎	29 12:18

Last Aspect / ☽ Ingress (September)

Last Aspect Dy Hr Mn			☽ Ingress	Dy Hr Mn
1 4:01	♂	△	♌	1 14:08
3 9:58	♂	□	♍	3 17:07
5 13:18	♂	⚹	♎	5 18:03
7 5:33	♃	⚹	♏	7 18:44
9 20:25	♂	☌	♐	9 20:40
11 23:03	♀	△	♑	12 0:43
13 21:03	♅	△	♒	14 7:08
16 11:55	♀	☍	♓	16 15:53
18 16:59	☉	☍	♈	19 2:46
21 10:34	♀	△	♉	21 15:20
24 0:05	♀	□	♊	24 4:21
26 12:34	♀	⚹	♋	26 15:45
28 20:54	☿	□	♌	28 23:41

Last Aspect / ☽ Ingress (October)

Last Aspect Dy Hr Mn			☽ Ingress	Dy Hr Mn
1 3:14	♀	☌	♍	1 3:38
2 21:43	♅	☌	♎	3 4:34
5 0:13	♃	⚹	♏	5 4:14
7 1:00	♃	□	♐	7 4:32
9 3:59	♃	△	♑	9 7:04
11 5:50	♅	△	♒	11 12:45
13 19:47	♃	☍	♓	13 21:38
16 1:59	♅	☍	♈	16 8:58
18 21:30	♃	△	♉	18 21:41
21 4:12	♅	△	♊	21 10:38
23 22:04	☉	△	♋	23 22:27
26 2:16	♅	⚹	♌	26 7:40
28 1:44	♆	□	♍	28 13:19
30 11:09	♅	☌	♎	30 15:31

☽ Phases & Eclipses

Dy Hr Mn		
4 11:37	●	11♍15
11 3:06	☽	17♐42
18 16:59	○	25♓05
26 21:44	☾	3♋06
3 20:24	●	9♎56
10 12:11	☽	16♑30
18 10:11	○	24♈21
18 10:15	☍	T 1.143
26 12:04	☾	2♌23

Astro Data

1 September 1967
Julian Day # 24715
SVP 5♓42'48"
GC 26♐23.3 ⚴ 7♌28.8
Eris 11♈49.2R ⚵ 22♍25.2
⚷ 28♓24.1R ⚶ 1♐48.2
☽ Mean ☊ 0♉25.6

1 October 1967
Julian Day # 24745
SVP 5♓42'45"
GC 26♐23.3 ⚴ 24♌11.3
Eris 11♈31.9R ⚵ 4♎00.1
⚷ 27♓03.7R ⚶ 14♐03.2
☽ Mean ☊ 28♈50.2

November 1967 LONGITUDE

Day	Sid.Time	☉	0 hr ☽	Noon ☽	True ☊	☿	♀	♂	⚳	♃	♄	♅	♆	♇
1 W	14 40 21	8♏22 25	20♎14 33	27♎49 27	27♈56.9	8♏42.3	22♍01.5	6♑57.1	1♎18.0	1♍59.7	6♈52.3	27♍25.8	23♏30.0	22♍03.9
2 Th	14 44 18	9 22 29	5♏25 56	13♏02 48	27R 56.6	7R 25.1	22 58.1	7 41.9	1 43.9	2 08.0	6R 48.7	27 28.9	23 32.2	22 05.5
3 F	14 48 14	10 22 36	20 38 47	28 12 40	27 55.7	6 10.8	23 55.2	8 26.7	2 09.9	2 16.3	6 45.2	27 31.9	23 34.4	22 07.1
4 Sa	14 52 11	11 22 44	5♐43 18	13♐09 38	27 54.2	5 01.6	24 52.9	9 11.6	2 35.7	2 24.4	6 41.8	27 34.9	23 36.6	22 08.7
5 Su	14 56 07	12 22 54	20 30 46	27 46 01	27 52.3	3 59.9	25 51.1	9 56.5	3 01.5	2 32.4	6 38.4	27 37.9	23 38.8	22 10.3
6 M	15 00 04	13 23 05	4♑54 48	11♑56 48	27 50.5	3 07.2	26 49.7	10 41.5	3 27.3	2 40.2	6 35.1	27 40.8	23 41.0	22 11.8
7 Tu	15 04 00	14 23 18	18 51 50	25 39 55	27 49.0	2 24.9	27 48.9	11 26.6	3 53.0	2 47.9	6 31.9	27 43.7	23 43.3	22 13.3
8 W	15 07 57	15 23 32	2♒21 09	8♒55 49	27D 48.2	1 53.9	28 48.5	12 11.7	4 18.6	2 55.5	6 28.8	27 46.6	23 45.5	22 14.8
9 Th	15 11 54	16 23 48	15 24 17	21 46 59	27 48.1	1 34.6	29 48.6	12 56.9	4 44.1	3 02.9	6 25.7	27 49.4	23 47.7	22 16.3
10 F	15 15 50	17 24 05	28 04 25	4♓17 05	27 48.9	1D 26.9	0♎49.1	13 42.2	5 09.6	3 10.2	6 22.7	27 52.2	23 50.0	22 17.7
11 Sa	15 19 47	18 24 24	10♓25 34	16 30 25	27 50.3	1 30.4	1 50.0	14 27.5	5 35.0	3 17.4	6 19.9	27 55.0	23 52.2	22 19.1
12 Su	15 23 43	19 24 44	22 32 10	28 31 22	27 52.0	1 44.7	2 51.4	15 12.9	6 00.3	3 24.4	6 17.1	27 57.7	23 54.5	22 20.5
13 M	15 27 40	20 25 05	4♈28 31	10♈24 07	27 53.6	2 08.9	3 53.1	15 58.3	6 25.6	3 31.3	6 14.4	28 00.4	23 56.7	22 21.9
14 Tu	15 31 36	21 25 28	16 18 37	22 12 27	27R 54.6	2 42.2	4 55.3	16 43.8	6 50.8	3 38.1	6 11.7	28 03.0	23 59.0	22 23.2
15 W	15 35 33	22 25 53	28 06 00	3♉59 37	27 54.5	3 23.7	5 57.8	17 29.3	7 15.9	3 44.6	6 09.2	28 05.6	24 01.2	22 24.5
16 Th	15 39 29	23 26 19	9♉53 37	15 48 20	27 53.2	4 12.6	7 00.7	18 14.9	7 40.9	3 51.1	6 06.8	28 08.1	24 03.5	22 25.8
17 F	15 43 26	24 26 47	21 44 00	27 40 52	27 50.5	5 07.9	8 03.9	19 00.5	8 05.9	3 57.4	6 04.5	28 10.6	24 05.7	22 27.0
18 Sa	15 47 22	25 27 16	3♊39 10	9♊39 07	27 46.6	6 08.8	9 07.5	19 46.2	8 30.8	4 03.5	6 02.2	28 13.1	24 08.0	22 28.2
19 Su	15 51 19	26 27 47	15 40 55	21 44 47	27 41.7	7 14.7	10 11.5	20 31.9	8 55.6	4 09.5	6 00.1	28 15.5	24 10.2	22 29.4
20 M	15 55 16	27 28 20	27 50 53	3♋59 28	27 36.3	8 24.8	11 15.7	21 17.7	9 20.3	4 15.4	5 58.0	28 17.9	24 12.5	22 30.6
21 Tu	15 59 12	28 28 54	10♋10 44	16 24 57	27 31.1	9 38.6	12 20.3	22 03.5	9 45.0	4 21.0	5 56.1	28 20.3	24 14.7	22 31.7
22 W	16 03 09	29 29 30	22 42 20	29 03 10	27 26.8	10 55.4	13 25.2	22 49.4	10 09.5	4 26.6	5 54.2	28 22.6	24 17.0	22 32.9
23 Th	16 07 05	0♐30 08	5♌27 43	11♌56 19	27 23.6	12 15.0	14 30.4	23 35.3	10 34.0	4 31.9	5 52.5	28 24.8	24 19.2	22 33.9
24 F	16 11 02	1 30 47	18 29 13	25 06 44	27D 22.1	13 36.7	15 35.8	24 21.3	10 58.4	4 37.1	5 50.8	28 27.0	24 21.5	22 35.0
25 Sa	16 14 58	2 31 28	1♍49 08	8♍36 40	27 22.0	15 00.4	16 41.6	25 07.3	11 22.7	4 42.1	5 49.3	28 29.2	24 23.7	22 36.0
26 Su	16 18 55	3 32 10	15 29 30	22 27 46	27 23.1	16 25.7	17 47.6	25 53.3	11 46.9	4 47.0	5 47.8	28 31.3	24 26.0	22 37.0
27 M	16 22 52	4 32 54	29 31 30	6♎40 37	27 24.6	17 52.4	18 53.9	26 39.4	12 11.0	4 51.7	5 46.5	28 33.4	24 28.2	22 37.9
28 Tu	16 26 48	5 33 40	13♎54 55	21 14 03	27R 25.7	19 20.1	20 00.4	27 25.6	12 35.0	4 56.2	5 45.3	28 35.4	24 30.4	22 38.9
29 W	16 30 45	6 34 28	28 37 28	6♏04 31	27 25.5	20 48.8	21 07.2	28 11.7	12 58.9	5 00.6	5 44.1	28 37.4	24 32.6	22 39.8
30 Th	16 34 41	7 35 16	13♏34 22	21 06 00	27 23.5	22 18.3	22 14.2	28 57.9	13 22.7	5 04.8	5 43.1	28 39.3	24 34.8	22 40.6

December 1967 LONGITUDE

Day	Sid.Time	☉	0 hr ☽	Noon ☽	True ☊	☿	♀	♂	⚳	♃	♄	♅	♆	♇
1 F	16 38 38	8♐36 06	28♏38 22	6♐10 17	27♈19.5	23♏48.5	23♎21.4	29♑44.2	13♎46.4	5♍08.8	5♈42.2	28♍41.2	24♏37.1	22♍41.5
2 Sa	16 42 34	9 36 58	13♐40 33	21 07 59	27R 13.6	25 19.2	24 28.9	0♒30.5	14 10.0	5 12.6	5R 41.4	28 43.0	24 39.3	22 42.3
3 Su	16 46 31	10 37 50	28 31 31	5♑50 08	27 06.6	26 50.3	25 36.5	1 16.8	14 33.4	5 16.3	5 40.7	28 44.8	24 41.4	22 43.1
4 M	16 50 27	11 38 44	13♑03 00	20 09 30	26 59.3	28 21.8	26 44.4	2 03.2	14 56.8	5 19.8	5 40.1	28 46.5	24 43.6	22 43.8
5 Tu	16 54 24	12 39 38	27 09 09	4♒01 41	26 52.7	29 53.5	27 52.5	2 49.6	15 20.1	5 23.0	5 39.6	28 48.2	24 45.8	22 44.5
6 W	16 58 21	13 40 33	10♒47 03	17 25 19	26 47.6	1♐25.6	29 00.7	3 36.0	15 43.2	5 26.2	5 39.2	28 49.8	24 48.0	22 45.2
7 Th	17 02 17	14 41 29	23 56 44	0♓21 42	26 44.4	2 57.8	0♏09.1	4 22.4	16 06.2	5 29.1	5 39.0	28 51.3	24 50.1	22 45.8
8 F	17 06 14	15 42 26	6♓40 40	12 54 11	26D 43.2	4 30.2	1 17.8	5 08.9	16 29.1	5 31.8	5D 38.8	28 52.9	24 52.3	22 46.4
9 Sa	17 10 10	16 43 23	19 02 52	25 07 22	26 43.5	6 02.8	2 26.6	5 55.4	16 51.9	5 34.4	5 38.8	28 54.3	24 54.4	22 47.0
10 Su	17 14 07	17 44 21	1♈08 20	7♈06 28	26 44.7	7 35.5	3 35.5	6 41.9	17 14.6	5 36.8	5 38.8	28 55.7	24 56.5	22 47.5
11 M	17 18 03	18 45 19	13 02 23	18 56 46	26R 45.9	9 08.3	4 44.7	7 28.5	17 37.1	5 38.9	5 39.0	28 57.1	24 58.6	22 48.0
12 Tu	17 22 00	19 46 18	24 50 13	0♉43 20	26 46.1	10 41.2	5 54.0	8 15.1	17 59.5	5 40.9	5 39.3	28 58.4	25 00.7	22 48.5
13 W	17 25 56	20 47 18	6♉36 38	12 30 38	26 44.5	12 14.3	7 03.4	9 01.7	18 21.8	5 42.8	5 39.7	28 59.6	25 02.8	22 49.0
14 Th	17 29 53	21 48 18	18 25 47	24 22 28	26 40.6	13 47.4	8 13.0	9 48.3	18 43.9	5 44.4	5 40.2	29 00.8	25 04.9	22 49.4
15 F	17 33 50	22 49 19	0♊21 02	6♊21 47	26 34.1	15 20.7	9 22.8	10 34.9	19 05.9	5 45.8	5 40.8	29 02.0	25 06.9	22 49.8
16 Sa	17 37 46	23 50 21	12 24 55	18 30 39	26 25.3	16 54.0	10 32.7	11 21.5	19 27.8	5 47.1	5 41.5	29 03.1	25 09.0	22 50.1
17 Su	17 41 43	24 51 23	24 39 06	0♋50 21	26 14.6	18 27.5	11 42.8	12 08.2	19 49.5	5 48.1	5 42.3	29 04.1	25 11.0	22 50.4
18 M	17 45 39	25 52 26	7♋04 29	13 21 30	26 03.1	20 01.1	12 53.0	12 54.9	20 11.1	5 49.0	5 43.3	29 05.1	25 13.0	22 50.7
19 Tu	17 49 36	26 53 30	19 41 25	26 04 13	25 51.7	21 34.9	14 03.3	13 41.6	20 32.5	5 49.6	5 44.3	29 06.0	25 15.0	22 50.9
20 W	17 53 32	27 54 35	2♌29 54	8♌58 29	25 41.6	23 08.8	15 13.7	14 28.3	20 53.8	5 50.1	5 45.5	29 06.9	25 17.0	22 51.1
21 Th	17 57 29	28 55 40	15 29 58	22 04 24	25 33.7	24 42.9	16 24.3	15 15.0	21 15.0	5R 50.4	5 46.7	29 07.7	25 19.0	22 51.3
22 F	18 01 25	29 56 46	28 41 50	5♍22 21	25 28.4	26 17.1	17 35.1	16 01.7	21 36.0	5 50.5	5 48.1	29 08.4	25 20.9	22 51.5
23 Sa	18 05 22	0♑57 52	12♍06 04	18 53 05	25D 25.7	27 51.6	18 45.9	16 48.5	21 56.8	5 50.4	5 49.6	29 09.1	25 22.8	22 51.6
24 Su	18 09 19	1 58 59	25 43 33	2♎37 34	25 25.0	29 26.2	19 56.8	17 35.2	22 17.5	5 50.0	5 51.2	29 09.8	25 24.7	22 51.6
25 M	18 13 15	3 00 07	9♎35 14	16 36 35	25R 25.4	1♑01.1	21 07.9	18 22.0	22 38.0	5 49.5	5 52.9	29 10.4	25 26.6	22R 51.7
26 Tu	18 17 12	4 01 16	23 41 37	0♏50 14	25 25.5	2 36.2	22 19.1	19 08.8	22 58.4	5 48.8	5 54.7	29 10.9	25 28.5	22 51.7
27 W	18 21 08	5 02 25	8♏02 13	15 17 14	25 24.0	4 11.6	23 30.4	19 55.6	23 18.5	5 47.9	5 56.6	29 11.4	25 30.4	22 51.7
28 Th	18 25 05	6 03 35	22 34 51	29 54 28	25 20.0	5 47.3	24 41.8	20 42.4	23 38.6	5 46.8	5 58.6	29 11.8	25 32.2	22 51.6
29 F	18 29 01	7 04 46	7♐15 21	14♐36 40	25 13.1	7 23.2	25 53.2	21 29.2	23 58.4	5 45.6	6 00.7	29 12.1	25 34.0	22 51.5
30 Sa	18 32 58	8 05 56	21 57 31	29 16 55	25 03.4	8 59.4	27 04.8	22 16.0	24 18.1	5 44.1	6 02.9	29 12.4	25 35.8	22 51.4
31 Su	18 36 55	9 07 07	6♑33 53	13♑47 28	24 51.9	10 36.0	28 16.5	23 02.8	24 37.5	5 42.4	6 05.2	29 12.7	25 37.6	22 51.2

Astro Data	Dy Hr Mn
☿ D	10 16:17
♀ 0S	12 3:36
☽ 0N	13 0:37
♄ 0S	18 9:03
☽ 0S	27 8:37
♄ D	9 10:27
☽ 0N	10 6:46
♃⚻♄	11 12:46
♄ 0N	20 0:59
♃ R	22 10:02
♃⚻♄	23 22:13
☽ 0S	24 14:48
♇ R	26 4:48
⚳ 0S	29 11:11

Planet Ingress		Dy Hr Mn
♀	♎	9 16:32
☉	♐	23 0:04
♂	♒	1 20:12
☿	♐	5 13:41
♀	♏	7 8:48
☉	♑	22 13:16
☿	♑	24 20:33

Last Aspect Dy Hr Mn		☽ Ingress	Dy Hr Mn
31 2:47	♄ ☍	♏	1 15:26
3 10:55	♅ ⚹	♐	3 14:51
5 11:47	♅ □	♑	5 15:44
7 16:09	♀ △	♒	7 19:45
9 15:50	♆ □	♓	10 3:42
12 10:52	♅ ☍	♈	12 14:58
14 0:05	♂ □	♉	15 3:52
17 13:00	♅ △	♊	17 16:40
20 0:51	♅ □	♋	20 4:13
22 12:54	☉ △	♌	22 13:47
24 10:38	♆ □	♍	24 20:46
26 22:20	♅ ☌	♎	27 0:48
28 22:37	♂ □	♏	29 2:13

Last Aspect Dy Hr Mn		☽ Ingress	Dy Hr Mn
1 1:12	♂ ⚹	♐	1 2:10
3 0:20	♅ □	♑	3 2:25
5 3:51	☿ ⚹	♒	5 4:57
7 1:37	♆ □	♓	7 11:19
9 19:33	♅ ☍	♈	9 21:43
11 11:34	☉ △	♉	12 10:32
14 21:20	♅ △	♊	14 23:18
17 8:34	♅ □	♋	17 10:23
19 17:40	♅ ⚹	♌	19 19:21
22 1:27	☉ △	♍	22 2:21
24 5:59	♅ ☌	♎	24 7:27
25 15:10	♂ △	♏	26 10:36
28 10:50	♅ ⚹	♐	28 12:09
30 11:53	♅ □	♑	30 13:11

☽ Phases & Eclipses Dy Hr Mn		
2 5:48	●	9♏07
2 5:38:17	●	T non-C
9 1:00	☽	15♒56
17 4:53	○	24♉09
25 0:23	☾	2♍02
1 16:10	●	8♐47
8 17:57	☽	15♓58
16 23:21	○	24♊19
24 10:48	☾	1♎56
31 3:38	●	8♑46

Astro Data

1 November 1967
Julian Day # 24776
SVP 5♓42'42"
GC 26♐23.4 ⚴ 9♍44.3
Eris 11♈13.4R ⚵ 15♎31.8
⚷ 25♓51.7R ⚶ 28♐28.4
☽ Mean ☊ 27♈11.7

1 December 1967
Julian Day # 24806
SVP 5♓42'37"
GC 26♐23.5 ⚴ 22♍13.6
Eris 11♈00.1R ⚵ 25♎48.8
⚷ 25♓18.5R ⚶ 13♑23.9
☽ Mean ☊ 25♈36.4

LONGITUDE January 1968

Day	Sid.Time	☉	0 hr ☽	Noon ☽	True ☊	☿	♀	♂	⚳	♃	♄	♅	♆	♇
1 M	18 40 51	10♑08 18	20♑56 48	28♑01 06	24♈39.7	12♑12.8	29♏28.2	23♒49.7	24♎56.8	5♍40.5	6♈07.7	29♍12.9	25♏39.3	22♍51.0
2 Tu	18 44 48	11 09 29	4♒59 45	11♒52 17	24R 28.2	13 50.0	0♐40.0	24 36.5	25 15.9	5R 38.5	6 10.2	29 13.0	25 41.0	22R 50.8
3 W	18 48 44	12 10 40	18 38 24	25 17 59	24 18.5	15 27.5	1 51.9	25 23.3	25 34.8	5 36.2	6 12.8	29R 13.1	25 42.7	22 50.6
4 Th	18 52 41	13 11 51	1♓51 04	8♓17 51	24 11.3	17 05.4	3 03.9	26 10.2	25 53.5	5 33.7	6 15.6	29 13.1	25 44.4	22 50.3
5 F	18 56 37	14 13 01	14 38 39	20 53 53	24 06.8	18 43.5	4 16.0	26 57.0	26 12.0	5 31.1	6 18.4	29 13.1	25 46.1	22 49.9
6 Sa	19 00 34	15 14 11	27 04 05	3♈09 50	24 04.7	20 22.1	5 28.1	27 43.8	26 30.3	5 28.3	6 21.3	29 13.0	25 47.7	22 49.6
7 Su	19 04 30	16 15 20	9♈11 48	15 10 38	24 04.3	22 00.9	6 40.3	28 30.6	26 48.4	5 25.3	6 24.4	29 12.8	25 49.3	22 49.2
8 M	19 08 27	17 16 29	21 07 05	27 01 49	24 04.3	23 40.1	7 52.5	29 17.4	27 06.3	5 22.1	6 27.5	29 12.6	25 50.9	22 48.8
9 Tu	19 12 24	18 17 38	2♉55 34	8♉49 01	24 03.6	25 19.6	9 04.8	0♓04.2	27 24.0	5 18.7	6 30.7	29 12.3	25 52.4	22 48.3
10 W	19 16 20	19 18 46	14 42 50	20 37 39	24 01.2	26 59.3	10 17.2	0 51.0	27 41.4	5 15.1	6 34.0	29 12.0	25 54.0	22 47.8
11 Th	19 20 17	20 19 54	26 34 03	2♊32 34	23 56.2	28 39.4	11 29.7	1 37.8	27 58.7	5 11.4	6 37.5	29 11.6	25 55.5	22 47.3
12 F	19 24 13	21 21 01	8♊33 41	14 37 49	23 48.3	0♒19.6	12 42.2	2 24.6	28 15.7	5 07.5	6 41.0	29 11.2	25 57.0	22 46.8
13 Sa	19 28 10	22 22 08	20 45 17	26 56 23	23 37.7	1 59.9	13 54.8	3 11.4	28 32.5	5 03.4	6 44.6	29 10.7	25 58.4	22 46.2
14 Su	19 32 06	23 23 15	3♋11 15	9♋30 01	23 24.9	3 40.4	15 07.4	3 58.2	28 49.1	4 59.1	6 48.3	29 10.2	25 59.8	22 45.6
15 M	19 36 03	24 24 21	15 52 42	22 19 14	23 10.9	5 20.8	16 20.1	4 44.9	29 05.4	4 54.7	6 52.1	29 09.6	26 01.2	22 44.9
16 Tu	19 39 59	25 25 26	28 49 30	5♌23 19	22 57.1	7 01.2	17 32.8	5 31.6	29 21.5	4 50.1	6 56.0	29 08.9	26 02.6	22 44.3
17 W	19 43 56	26 26 31	12♌00 28	18 40 43	22 44.7	8 41.3	18 45.6	6 18.4	29 37.3	4 45.3	6 59.9	29 08.2	26 03.9	22 43.6
18 Th	19 47 53	27 27 36	25 23 45	2♍09 22	22 34.7	10 21.0	19 58.5	7 05.1	29 52.9	4 40.4	7 04.0	29 07.5	26 05.3	22 42.8
19 F	19 51 49	28 28 40	8♍57 16	15 47 15	22 27.8	12 00.2	21 11.4	7 51.8	0♏08.3	4 35.3	7 08.1	29 06.6	26 06.5	22 42.1
20 Sa	19 55 46	29 29 43	22 39 09	29 32 48	22 23.8	13 38.6	22 24.3	8 38.4	0 23.4	4 30.0	7 12.4	29 05.8	26 07.8	22 41.3
21 Su	19 59 42	0♒30 47	6♎28 07	13♎25 01	22D 22.4	15 16.0	23 37.3	9 25.1	0 38.2	4 24.6	7 16.7	29 04.9	26 09.0	22 40.5
22 M	20 03 39	1 31 49	20 23 27	27 23 25	22R 22.2	16 52.1	24 50.4	10 11.7	0 52.8	4 19.1	7 21.1	29 03.9	26 10.2	22 39.6
23 Tu	20 07 35	2 32 52	4♏24 52	11♏27 45	22 22.1	18 26.6	26 03.4	10 58.4	1 07.1	4 13.4	7 25.6	29 02.9	26 11.4	22 38.7
24 W	20 11 32	3 33 54	18 32 00	25 37 27	22 20.5	19 59.0	27 16.6	11 45.0	1 21.2	4 07.5	7 30.2	29 01.8	26 12.5	22 37.8
25 Th	20 15 28	4 34 56	2♐43 55	9♐51 07	22 16.6	21 28.9	28 29.8	12 31.6	1 35.0	4 01.6	7 34.8	29 00.7	26 13.6	22 36.9
26 F	20 19 25	5 35 58	16 58 40	24 06 07	22 09.7	22 55.8	29 43.0	13 18.2	1 48.4	3 55.4	7 39.6	28 59.5	26 14.7	22 36.0
27 Sa	20 23 22	6 36 58	1♑12 57	8♑18 36	22 00.2	24 19.1	0♑56.2	14 04.8	2 01.6	3 49.2	7 44.4	28 58.3	26 15.8	22 35.0
28 Su	20 27 18	7 37 58	15 22 24	22 23 43	21 48.6	25 38.3	2 09.5	14 51.3	2 14.5	3 42.8	7 49.3	28 57.0	26 16.8	22 34.0
29 M	20 31 15	8 38 57	29 21 56	6♒16 27	21 36.2	26 52.5	3 22.8	15 37.8	2 27.2	3 36.3	7 54.3	28 55.7	26 17.8	22 33.0
30 Tu	20 35 11	9 39 56	13♒06 44	19 52 21	21 24.3	28 01.0	4 36.2	16 24.3	2 39.5	3 29.7	7 59.3	28 54.3	26 18.7	22 31.9
31 W	20 39 08	10 40 53	26 32 58	3♓08 22	21 14.1	29 03.1	5 49.6	17 10.8	2 51.5	3 22.9	8 04.5	28 52.9	26 19.6	22 30.8

LONGITUDE February 1968

Day	Sid.Time	☉	0 hr ☽	Noon ☽	True ☊	☿	♀	♂	⚳	♃	♄	♅	♆	♇
1 Th	20 43 04	11♒41 48	9♓38 27	16♓03 15	21♈06.3	29♒58.0	7♑03.0	17♓57.3	3♏03.1	3♍16.1	8♈09.7	28♍51.4	26♏20.5	22♍29.7
2 F	20 47 01	12 42 43	22 22 54	28 37 40	21R 01.3	0♓44.8	8 16.4	18 43.7	3 14.5	3R 09.1	8 14.9	28R 49.9	26 21.4	22R 28.6
3 Sa	20 50 57	13 43 36	4♈47 54	10♈54 03	20D 58.9	1 22.8	9 29.9	19 30.1	3 25.6	3 02.1	8 20.3	28 48.4	26 22.2	22 27.4
4 Su	20 54 54	14 44 28	16 56 36	22 56 08	20 58.4	1 51.2	10 43.3	20 16.5	3 36.3	2 55.0	8 25.7	28 46.8	26 23.0	22 26.2
5 M	20 58 51	15 45 19	28 53 17	4♉48 42	20 58.9	2 09.4	11 56.8	21 02.9	3 46.7	2 47.7	8 31.2	28 45.1	26 23.7	22 25.1
6 Tu	21 02 47	16 46 08	10♉43 02	16 37 01	20R 59.3	2R 16.9	13 10.4	21 49.2	3 56.8	2 40.4	8 36.8	28 43.4	26 24.4	22 23.8
7 W	21 06 44	17 46 56	22 31 18	28 26 36	20 58.6	2 13.6	14 23.9	22 35.5	4 06.5	2 33.0	8 42.4	28 41.7	26 25.1	22 22.6
8 Th	21 10 40	18 47 42	4♊23 35	10♊22 52	20 56.0	1 59.3	15 37.5	23 21.8	4 16.0	2 25.6	8 48.1	28 39.9	26 25.8	22 21.3
9 F	21 14 37	19 48 27	16 25 03	22 30 42	20 51.0	1 34.2	16 51.1	24 08.0	4 25.0	2 18.0	8 53.8	28 38.1	26 26.4	22 20.0
10 Sa	21 18 33	20 49 11	28 40 18	4♋54 14	20 43.7	0 59.0	18 04.7	24 54.2	4 33.7	2 10.4	8 59.7	28 36.3	26 27.0	22 18.8
11 Su	21 22 30	21 49 52	11♋12 51	17 36 23	20 34.5	0 14.4	19 18.3	25 40.4	4 42.1	2 02.8	9 05.6	28 34.4	26 27.6	22 17.4
12 M	21 26 27	22 50 33	24 04 57	0♌38 35	20 24.2	29♒21.6	20 31.9	26 26.5	4 50.1	1 55.1	9 11.5	28 32.5	26 28.1	22 16.1
13 Tu	21 30 23	23 51 12	7♌17 10	14 00 33	20 13.8	28 22.2	21 45.6	27 12.6	4 57.8	1 47.3	9 17.5	28 30.5	26 28.6	22 14.7
14 W	21 34 20	24 51 49	20 48 25	27 40 24	20 04.4	27 17.7	22 59.3	27 58.7	5 05.1	1 39.6	9 23.6	28 28.5	26 29.0	22 13.4
15 Th	21 38 16	25 52 25	4♍36 02	11♍34 50	19 57.0	26 10.0	24 13.0	28 44.7	5 12.0	1 31.7	9 29.7	28 26.5	26 29.5	22 12.0
16 F	21 42 13	26 52 59	18 36 15	25 39 45	19 52.1	25 00.9	25 26.7	29 30.7	5 18.5	1 23.9	9 35.9	28 24.4	26 29.8	22 10.6
17 Sa	21 46 09	27 53 32	2♎44 48	9♎50 54	19D 49.6	23 52.2	26 40.4	0♈16.7	5 24.7	1 16.0	9 42.1	28 22.3	26 30.2	22 09.1
18 Su	21 50 06	28 54 04	16 57 37	24 04 32	19 49.3	22 45.7	27 54.2	1 02.6	5 30.5	1 08.1	9 48.4	28 20.2	26 30.5	22 07.7
19 M	21 54 02	29 54 34	1♏11 18	8♏17 39	19 50.1	21 42.9	29 08.0	1 48.5	5 35.9	1 00.2	9 54.8	28 18.0	26 30.8	22 06.3
20 Tu	21 57 59	0♓55 04	15 23 20	22 28 09	19R 51.2	20 44.9	0♒21.8	2 34.4	5 40.9	0 52.3	10 01.2	28 15.8	26 31.0	22 04.8
21 W	22 01 55	1 55 32	29 31 57	6♐34 35	19 51.3	19 52.7	1 35.6	3 20.2	5 45.6	0 44.4	10 07.6	28 13.6	26 31.3	22 03.3
22 Th	22 05 52	2 55 59	13♐35 55	20 35 49	19 49.8	19 07.2	2 49.4	4 06.0	5 49.8	0 36.5	10 14.1	28 11.3	26 31.5	22 01.8
23 F	22 09 49	3 56 24	27 34 06	4♑30 38	19 46.3	18 28.8	4 03.3	4 51.7	5 53.6	0 28.6	10 20.7	28 09.0	26 31.6	22 00.3
24 Sa	22 13 45	4 56 48	11♑25 11	18 17 32	19 40.8	17 57.6	5 17.1	5 37.5	5 57.0	0 20.7	10 27.3	28 06.7	26 31.7	21 58.8
25 Su	22 17 42	5 57 11	25 07 28	1♒54 42	19 33.8	17 33.9	6 31.0	6 23.2	6 00.0	0 12.9	10 33.9	28 04.4	26 31.8	21 57.3
26 M	22 21 38	6 57 32	8♒39 00	15 20 05	19 26.2	17 17.5	7 44.8	7 08.8	6 02.6	0 05.1	10 40.6	28 02.0	26R 31.9	21 55.7
27 Tu	22 25 35	7 57 51	21 57 45	28 31 46	19 18.8	17D 08.2	8 58.7	7 54.4	6 04.8	29♌57.3	10 47.4	27 59.6	26 31.9	21 54.2
28 W	22 29 31	8 58 09	5♓01 59	11♓28 18	19 12.4	17 05.8	10 12.6	8 40.0	6 06.6	29 49.5	10 54.2	27 57.2	26 31.8	21 52.6
29 Th	22 33 28	9 58 25	17 50 39	24 09 03	19 07.7	17 10.0	11 26.5	9 25.5	6 07.9	29 41.8	11 01.0	27 54.8	26 31.8	21 51.1

Astro Data (Dy Hr Mn)

	Dy Hr Mn
♅R	4 6:14
☽0N	6 13:41
☽0S	20 19:15
☽0N	2 21:30
☿R	6 16:41
☽0S	17 1:02
♂0N	18 18:25
♆R	27 8:55
☿D	28 8:36

Planet Ingress (Dy Hr Mn)

	Dy Hr Mn
♀ ♐	1 22:37
♂ ♓	9 9:49
☿ ♒	12 7:19
⚳ ♏	18 22:59
☉ ♒	20 23:54
♀ ♑	26 17:35
☿ ♓	1 12:57
☿ ♒R	11 18:54
♂ ♈	17 3:18
☉ ♓	19 14:09
♀ ♒	20 4:55
♃ ♌R	27 3:33

Last Aspect Dy Hr Mn	☽ Ingress Dy Hr Mn
1 14:43 ♀ ⚹	♒ 1 15:23
3 12:45 ♆ □	♓ 3 20:35
6 4:13 ♅ ☍	♈ 6 5:45
8 16:55 ♂ ⚹	♉ 8 18:02
11 5:17 ♅ △	♊ 11 6:54
13 16:19 ♅ □	♋ 13 17:54
16 0:36 ♅ ⚹	♌ 16 2:09
18 1:13 ♆ □	♍ 18 8:11
20 11:54 ☉ △	♎ 20 12:47
22 7:13 ♀ ⚹	♏ 22 16:28
24 17:45 ♅ ⚹	♐ 24 19:23
26 20:14 ♅ □	♑ 26 21:57
28 23:16 ♅ △	♒ 29 1:06
31 3:56 ☿ ☌	♓ 31 6:16

Last Aspect Dy Hr Mn	☽ Ingress Dy Hr Mn
2 12:24 ♅ ☍	♈ 2 14:39
3 18:07 ☉ ⚹	♉ 5 2:15
7 12:30 ♅ △	♊ 7 15:09
9 23:54 ♅ □	♋ 10 2:34
12 8:11 ♅ ⚹	♌ 12 10:50
14 11:23 ☿ ☍	♍ 14 16:02
16 18:54 ♂ ☍	♎ 16 19:21
18 20:46 ☉ △	♏ 18 22:00
20 21:49 ♅ ⚹	♐ 21 0:48
23 1:02 ♅ □	♑ 23 4:12
25 5:13 ♅ △	♒ 25 8:37
27 14:36 ♃ ☍	♓ 27 14:42
29 19:12 ♅ ☍	♈ 29 23:14

☽ Phases & Eclipses (Dy Hr Mn)

Dy Hr Mn	
7 14:23	☽ 16♈21
15 16:11	○ 24♋35
22 19:38	☾ 1♏51
29 16:29	● 8♒50
6 12:20	☽ 16♉47
14 6:43	○ 24♌38
21 3:28	☾ 1♐34
28 6:56	● 8♓45

Astro Data

1 January 1968
Julian Day # 24837
SVP 5♓42'30"
GC 26♐23.5 ⚳ 0♎57.0
Eris 10♈55.5 ✱ 4♏50.8
⚷ 25♓35.0 ⚵ 29♑19.0
☽ Mean ☊ 23♈58.0

1 February 1968
Julian Day # 24868
SVP 5♓42'24"
GC 26♐23.6 ⚳ 2♎55.0R
Eris 11♈01.7 ✱ 11♏10.9
⚷ 26♓40.1 ⚵ 15♒20.7
☽ Mean ☊ 22♈19.5

March 1968 — LONGITUDE

Day	Sid.Time	☉	0 hr ☽	Noon ☽	True ☊	☿	♀	♂	⚳	♃	♄	♅	♆	♇
1 F	22 37 24	10♓58 39	0♈23 35	6♈34 25	19♈05.0	17♒20.3	12♒40.4	10♈11.0	6♏08.9	29♌34.1	11♈07.8	27♍52.3	26♏31.7	21♍49.5
2 Sa	22 41 21	11 58 51	12 41 45	18 45 52	19D 04.1	17 36.5	13 54.3	10 56.5	6R 09.4	29R 26.5	11 14.7	27R 49.9	26R 31.6	21R 47.9
3 Su	22 45 18	12 59 01	24 47 09	0♉46 00	19 04.8	17 58.3	15 08.2	11 41.9	6 09.4	29 19.0	11 21.7	27 47.4	26 31.4	21 46.3
4 M	22 49 14	13 59 09	6♉42 52	12 38 16	19 06.3	18 25.1	16 22.1	12 27.3	6 09.1	29 11.5	11 28.7	27 44.9	26 31.2	21 44.7
5 Tu	22 53 11	14 59 15	18 32 44	24 26 53	19 08.2	18 56.7	17 36.0	13 12.6	6 08.3	29 04.2	11 35.7	27 42.4	26 31.0	21 43.1
6 W	22 57 07	15 59 20	0♊21 19	6♊16 39	19R 09.6	19 32.8	18 50.0	13 57.9	6 07.1	28 56.8	11 42.7	27 39.8	26 30.7	21 41.5
7 Th	23 01 04	16 59 21	12 13 32	18 12 35	19 10.0	20 13.0	20 03.9	14 43.1	6 05.5	28 49.6	11 49.8	27 37.3	26 30.5	21 39.9
8 F	23 05 00	17 59 21	24 14 27	0♋19 45	19 09.2	20 57.2	21 17.8	15 28.3	6 03.5	28 42.5	11 56.9	27 34.7	26 30.1	21 38.3
9 Sa	23 08 57	18 59 19	6♋29 03	12 42 52	19 07.0	21 44.9	22 31.7	16 13.5	6 01.0	28 35.4	12 04.1	27 32.2	26 29.8	21 36.7
10 Su	23 12 53	19 59 14	19 01 43	25 25 58	19 03.6	22 36.0	23 45.6	16 58.6	5 58.1	28 28.5	12 11.3	27 29.6	26 29.4	21 35.1
11 M	23 16 50	20 59 08	1♌55 56	8♌31 51	18 59.4	23 30.2	24 59.6	17 43.6	5 54.8	28 21.7	12 18.5	27 27.0	26 29.0	21 33.5
12 Tu	23 20 47	21 58 59	15 13 48	22 01 44	18 55.1	24 27.4	26 13.5	18 28.7	5 51.1	28 14.9	12 25.7	27 24.4	26 28.5	21 31.9
13 W	23 24 43	22 58 48	28 55 31	5♍54 50	18 51.1	25 27.4	27 27.4	19 13.6	5 47.0	28 08.3	12 33.0	27 21.8	26 28.1	21 30.3
14 Th	23 28 40	23 58 35	12♍59 15	20 08 14	18 48.1	26 30.0	28 41.4	19 58.5	5 42.4	28 01.8	12 40.3	27 19.2	26 27.5	21 28.6
15 F	23 32 36	24 58 19	27 21 07	4♎37 10	18D 46.2	27 35.0	29 55.3	20 43.4	5 37.5	27 55.4	12 47.6	27 16.6	26 27.0	21 27.0
16 Sa	23 36 33	25 58 02	11♎55 34	19 15 31	18 45.7	28 42.3	1♓09.2	21 28.2	5 32.1	27 49.1	12 54.9	27 14.0	26 26.4	21 25.4
17 Su	23 40 29	26 57 43	26 36 11	3♏56 45	18 46.2	29 51.9	2 23.2	22 13.0	5 26.3	27 43.0	13 02.2	27 11.4	26 25.8	21 23.8
18 M	23 44 26	27 57 23	11♏16 28	18 34 40	18 47.4	1♓03.5	3 37.1	22 57.8	5 20.1	27 37.0	13 09.6	27 08.8	26 25.2	21 22.2
19 Tu	23 48 22	28 57 00	25 50 44	3♐04 10	18 48.7	2 17.2	4 51.1	23 42.4	5 13.6	27 31.1	13 17.0	27 06.2	26 24.5	21 20.6
20 W	23 52 19	29 56 36	10♐14 32	17 21 32	18R 49.8	3 32.8	6 05.0	24 27.1	5 06.6	27 25.4	13 24.4	27 03.6	26 23.8	21 19.0
21 Th	23 56 16	0♈56 11	24 24 55	1♑24 31	18 50.2	4 50.2	7 19.0	25 11.7	4 59.3	27 19.8	13 31.9	27 00.9	26 23.1	21 17.4
22 F	0 00 12	1 55 43	8♑20 14	15 12 02	18 49.7	6 09.4	8 32.9	25 56.3	4 51.5	27 14.4	13 39.3	26 58.3	26 22.4	21 15.9
23 Sa	0 04 09	2 55 14	21 59 54	28 43 54	18 48.5	7 30.3	9 46.9	26 40.8	4 43.4	27 09.1	13 46.8	26 55.8	26 21.6	21 14.3
24 Su	0 08 05	3 54 43	5♒24 03	12♒00 28	18 46.7	8 52.8	11 00.9	27 25.2	4 35.0	27 03.9	13 54.3	26 53.2	26 20.8	21 12.7
25 M	0 12 02	4 54 10	18 33 12	25 02 23	18 44.7	10 17.0	12 14.8	28 09.7	4 26.1	26 58.9	14 01.8	26 50.6	26 19.9	21 11.1
26 Tu	0 15 58	5 53 35	1♓28 05	7♓50 25	18 42.8	11 42.7	13 28.8	28 54.0	4 16.9	26 54.1	14 09.3	26 48.0	26 19.1	21 09.6
27 W	0 19 55	6 52 59	14 09 29	20 25 24	18 41.2	13 10.0	14 42.7	29 38.4	4 07.4	26 49.4	14 16.8	26 45.4	26 18.2	21 08.0
28 Th	0 23 51	7 52 20	26 38 19	2♈48 21	18 40.2	14 38.8	15 56.7	0♉22.7	3 57.6	26 44.9	14 24.3	26 42.9	26 17.2	21 06.5
29 F	0 27 48	8 51 39	8♈55 39	15 00 25	18D 39.7	16 09.1	17 10.6	1 06.9	3 47.4	26 40.5	14 31.9	26 40.3	26 16.3	21 05.0
30 Sa	0 31 45	9 50 56	21 02 50	27 03 08	18 39.8	17 40.9	18 24.6	1 51.1	3 36.9	26 36.3	14 39.4	26 37.8	26 15.3	21 03.4
31 Su	0 35 41	10 50 11	3♉01 35	8♉58 27	18 40.3	19 14.1	19 38.5	2 35.2	3 26.1	26 32.3	14 46.9	26 35.3	26 14.3	21 01.9

April 1968 — LONGITUDE

Day	Sid.Time	☉	0 hr ☽	Noon ☽	True ☊	☿	♀	♂	⚳	♃	♄	♅	♆	♇
1 M	0 39 38	11♈49 24	14♉54 06	20♉48 51	18♈41.0	20♓48.8	20♓52.4	3♉19.3	3♏15.1	26♌28.5	14♈54.5	26♍32.8	26♏13.3	21♍00.5
2 Tu	0 43 34	12 48 35	26 43 07	2♊37 20	18 41.7	22 25.0	22 06.4	4 03.4	3R 03.7	26R 24.8	15 02.1	26R 30.3	26R 12.2	20R 59.0
3 W	0 47 31	13 47 44	8♊31 57	14 27 27	18 42.3	24 02.6	23 20.3	4 47.3	2 52.1	26 21.4	15 09.6	26 27.8	26 11.2	20 57.5
4 Th	0 51 27	14 46 50	20 24 22	26 23 14	18 42.7	25 41.6	24 34.2	5 31.3	2 40.3	26 18.0	15 17.2	26 25.4	26 10.1	20 56.1
5 F	0 55 24	15 45 54	2♋24 36	8♋29 03	18R 42.9	27 22.1	25 48.1	6 15.2	2 28.2	26 14.9	15 24.7	26 23.0	26 09.0	20 54.6
6 Sa	0 59 20	16 44 56	14 37 07	20 49 23	18 42.9	29 04.1	27 02.0	6 59.0	2 16.0	26 12.0	15 32.3	26 20.6	26 07.8	20 53.2
7 Su	1 03 17	17 43 55	27 06 23	3♌28 37	18 42.9	0♈47.5	28 15.9	7 42.8	2 03.5	26 09.2	15 39.9	26 18.2	26 06.6	20 51.8
8 M	1 07 14	18 42 52	9♌56 32	16 30 31	18D 42.8	2 32.4	29 29.8	8 26.6	1 50.8	26 06.6	15 47.4	26 15.8	26 05.4	20 50.4
9 Tu	1 11 10	19 41 47	23 10 52	29 57 47	18 42.9	4 18.8	0♈43.7	9 10.3	1 38.0	26 04.2	15 55.0	26 13.5	26 04.2	20 49.0
10 W	1 15 07	20 40 39	6♍51 21	13♍51 29	18 43.0	6 06.6	1 57.6	9 53.9	1 25.0	26 02.0	16 02.5	26 11.2	26 03.0	20 47.7
11 Th	1 19 03	21 39 30	20 58 00	28 10 30	18 43.2	7 56.0	3 11.4	10 37.5	1 11.9	26 00.0	16 10.1	26 08.9	26 01.7	20 46.3
12 F	1 23 00	22 38 18	5♎28 27	12♎51 09	18R 43.4	9 46.9	4 25.3	11 21.0	0 58.6	25 58.1	16 17.6	26 06.6	26 00.5	20 45.0
13 Sa	1 26 56	23 37 04	20 17 46	27 47 20	18 43.4	11 39.3	5 39.1	12 04.5	0 45.3	25 56.4	16 25.1	26 04.4	25 59.2	20 43.7
14 Su	1 30 53	24 35 48	5♏18 48	12♏51 03	18 43.1	13 33.3	6 53.0	12 47.9	0 31.8	25 55.0	16 32.6	26 02.2	25 57.9	20 42.4
15 M	1 34 49	25 34 30	20 22 58	27 53 27	18 42.4	15 28.7	8 06.9	13 31.3	0 18.3	25 53.7	16 40.2	26 00.0	25 56.5	20 41.1
16 Tu	1 38 46	26 33 11	5♐21 30	12♐46 11	18 41.6	17 25.7	9 20.7	14 14.7	0 04.7	25 52.6	16 47.7	25 57.9	25 55.2	20 39.9
17 W	1 42 43	27 31 50	20 06 42	27 22 24	18 40.7	19 24.2	10 34.6	14 58.0	29♎51.1	25 51.6	16 55.1	25 55.8	25 53.8	20 38.7
18 Th	1 46 39	28 30 27	4♑32 49	11♑37 36	18 40.0	21 24.1	11 48.4	15 41.2	29 37.5	25 50.9	17 02.6	25 53.7	25 52.4	20 37.5
19 F	1 50 36	29 29 02	18 36 34	25 29 38	18D 39.6	23 25.5	13 02.2	16 24.4	29 23.8	25 50.3	17 10.1	25 51.7	25 51.0	20 36.3
20 Sa	1 54 32	0♉27 36	2♒16 53	8♒58 28	18 39.7	25 28.2	14 16.1	17 07.6	29 10.2	25 50.0	17 17.5	25 49.7	25 49.6	20 35.1
21 Su	1 58 29	1 26 09	15 34 37	22 05 38	18 40.3	27 32.2	15 29.9	17 50.7	28 56.6	25D 49.8	17 25.0	25 47.7	25 48.2	20 34.0
22 M	2 02 25	2 24 39	28 31 51	4♓53 37	18 41.4	29 37.4	16 43.8	18 33.7	28 43.0	25 49.8	17 32.4	25 45.7	25 46.7	20 32.9
23 Tu	2 06 22	3 23 08	11♓11 18	17 25 18	18 42.6	1♉43.7	17 57.6	19 16.7	28 29.4	25 50.0	17 39.8	25 43.8	25 45.3	20 31.8
24 W	2 10 18	4 21 35	23 35 59	29 43 41	18 43.8	3 50.9	19 11.4	19 59.7	28 16.0	25 50.4	17 47.1	25 42.0	25 43.8	20 30.7
25 Th	2 14 15	5 20 01	5♈48 46	11♈51 33	18R 44.5	5 58.9	20 25.2	20 42.6	28 02.6	25 50.9	17 54.5	25 40.1	25 42.3	20 29.6
26 F	2 18 12	6 18 24	17 52 21	23 51 26	18 44.6	8 07.5	21 39.0	21 25.5	27 49.4	25 51.7	18 01.8	25 38.3	25 40.8	20 28.6
27 Sa	2 22 08	7 16 46	29 49 06	5♉45 35	18 43.7	10 16.4	22 52.8	22 08.3	27 36.3	25 52.6	18 09.1	25 36.6	25 39.3	20 27.6
28 Su	2 26 05	8 15 06	11♉41 11	17 36 07	18 41.9	12 25.4	24 06.6	22 51.1	27 23.3	25 53.7	18 16.4	25 34.9	25 37.7	20 26.6
29 M	2 30 01	9 13 25	23 30 39	29 25 04	18 39.1	14 34.2	25 20.4	23 33.8	27 10.5	25 55.0	18 23.6	25 33.2	25 36.2	20 25.7
30 Tu	2 33 58	10 11 41	5♊19 36	11♊14 35	18 35.7	16 42.5	26 34.2	24 16.4	26 57.9	25 56.5	18 30.9	25 31.6	25 34.7	20 24.8

Astro Data

	Dy Hr Mn
☽0N	1 5:34
⚳R	3 4:24
♄⚼♆	4 20:31
☽0S	15 9:44
♃⚼♄	16 1:49
☉0N	20 13:23
⚳0N	27 5:41
☽0N	28 12:52
♃⚺♅	29 14:46
♃□♆	9 11:32
☿0N	9 22:13
♀0N	11 18:11
☽0S	11 20:23
♃□♆	20 4:22
♃⚺♅	20 7:35

Planet Ingress

		Dy Hr Mn
♀	♓	15 13:32
☿	♓	17 14:45
☉	♈	20 13:22
♂	♉	27 23:43
☿	♈	7 1:01
♀	♈	8 21:48
⚳	♎R	16 20:21
☉	♉	20 0:41
☿	♉	22 16:18
♅⚹⚹		20 13:49
♃ D		21 23:26
☽0N		24 18:57

Last Aspect / ☽ Ingress (March)

Last Aspect Dy Hr Mn			☽ Ingress	Dy Hr Mn
3 9:07	♃	△	♉	3 10:27
5 21:18	♃	□	♊	5 23:17
8 8:51	♃	⚹	♋	8 11:21
10 15:49	♅	⚹	♌	10 20:27
12 22:45	♃	☌	♍	13 1:51
14 23:55	♅	☌	♎	15 4:23
17 4:45	☿	△	♏	17 5:33
19 4:39	☉	△	♐	19 6:53
21 5:02	♃	△	♑	21 9:34
23 8:47	♅	△	♒	23 14:16
25 18:10	♂	⚹	♓	25 21:15
28 0:11	♅	☍	♈	28 6:32
30 11:07	♃	△	♉	30 17:55

Last Aspect / ☽ Ingress (April)

Last Aspect Dy Hr Mn			☽ Ingress	Dy Hr Mn
1 23:37	♅	△	♊	2 6:40
4 12:04	♅	□	♋	4 19:13
7 1:08	♀	△	♌	7 5:28
9 5:09	♃	☌	♍	9 12:04
11 8:39	♅	☌	♎	11 15:01
13 9:03	♃	⚹	♏	13 15:32
15 8:59	♅	⚹	♐	15 15:23
17 12:17	☉	△	♑	17 16:23
19 19:35	☉	□	♒	19 19:57
22 0:06	☿	⚹	♓	22 2:46
24 4:11	♆	△	♈	24 12:32
26 16:02	♃	△	♉	27 0:22
29 4:52	♃	□	♊	29 13:11

☽ Phases & Eclipses

Dy Hr Mn	
7 9:20	☽ 16♊53
14 18:52	○ 24♍16
21 11:07	☾ 0♑54
28 22:48	● 8♈19
28 22:59:51	● P 0.899
6 3:27	☽ 16♋24
13 4:52	○ 23♎20
13 4:47	● T 1.111
19 19:35	☾ 29♑48
27 15:21	● 7♉25

Astro Data

1 March 1968
Julian Day # 24897
SVP 5♓42'21"
GC 26♐23.7 ⚴ 27♍02.8R
Eris 11♈15.9 ⚵ 13♏20.6R
⚷ 28♓11.1 ⚶ 0♓08.6
☽ Mean ☊ 20♈47.3

1 April 1968
Julian Day # 24928
SVP 5♓42'17"
GC 26♐23.8 ⚴ 17♍36.4R
Eris 11♈36.2 ⚵ 10♏30.2R
⚷ 0♈00.7 ⚶ 15♓27.2
☽ Mean ☊ 19♈08.8

LONGITUDE — May 1968

Day	Sid.Time	☉	0 hr ☽	Noon ☽	True ☊	☿	♀	♂	⚳	♃	♄	♅	♆	♇
1 W	2 37 54	11♉09 56	17♊10 17	23♊07 04	18♈32.0	18♉50.2	27♈48.0	24♉59.1	26♎45.4	25♌58.2	18♈38.1	25♍30.0	25♏33.1	20♍23.9
2 Th	2 41 51	12 08 09	29 05 17	5♋05 19	18R 28.5	20 56.7	29 01.8	25 41.7	26R 33.2	26 00.0	18 45.3	25R 28.5	25R 31.5	20R 23.0
3 F	2 45 47	13 06 20	11♋07 33	17 12 28	18 25.5	23 01.9	0♉15.5	26 24.2	26 21.2	26 02.0	18 52.4	25 27.0	25 30.0	20 22.1
4 Sa	2 49 44	14 04 28	23 20 29	29 32 06	18 23.5	25 05.4	1 29.3	27 06.7	26 09.4	26 04.2	18 59.5	25 25.5	25 28.4	20 21.3
5 Su	2 53 41	15 02 35	5♌47 46	12♌08 01	18D 22.6	27 07.0	2 43.1	27 49.1	25 57.9	26 06.6	19 06.6	25 24.1	25 26.8	20 20.5
6 M	2 57 37	16 00 40	18 33 18	25 04 04	18 22.9	29 06.4	3 56.8	28 31.5	25 46.6	26 09.2	19 13.7	25 22.7	25 25.2	20 19.8
7 Tu	3 01 34	16 58 43	1♍40 44	8♍23 40	18 24.0	1♊03.4	5 10.5	29 13.8	25 35.6	26 11.9	19 20.7	25 21.4	25 23.6	20 19.0
8 W	3 05 30	17 56 44	15 13 08	22 09 18	18 25.5	2 57.7	6 24.3	29 56.1	25 24.8	26 14.8	19 27.6	25 20.1	25 22.0	20 18.3
9 Th	3 09 27	18 54 43	29 12 12	6♎21 45	18R 26.8	4 49.3	7 38.0	0♊38.3	25 14.4	26 17.9	19 34.6	25 18.9	25 20.4	20 17.7
10 F	3 13 23	19 52 40	13♎37 39	20 59 27	18 27.1	6 37.8	8 51.7	1 20.5	25 04.2	26 21.1	19 41.5	25 17.7	25 18.8	20 17.0
11 Sa	3 17 20	20 50 36	28 26 30	5♏57 58	18 26.2	8 23.2	10 05.4	2 02.6	24 54.4	26 24.5	19 48.4	25 16.6	25 17.1	20 16.4
12 Su	3 21 16	21 48 30	13♏32 49	21 09 55	18 23.6	10 05.5	11 19.1	2 44.7	24 44.9	26 28.1	19 55.2	25 15.5	25 15.5	20 15.8
13 M	3 25 13	22 46 22	28 47 58	6♐25 41	18 19.7	11 44.3	12 32.8	3 26.7	24 35.7	26 31.9	20 02.0	25 14.5	25 13.9	20 15.2
14 Tu	3 29 10	23 44 13	14♐01 43	21 34 50	18 14.8	13 19.8	13 46.5	4 08.7	24 26.8	26 35.8	20 08.7	25 13.5	25 12.3	20 14.7
15 W	3 33 06	24 42 03	29 03 53	6♑27 51	18 09.7	14 51.9	15 00.2	4 50.6	24 18.3	26 39.9	20 15.5	25 12.6	25 10.7	20 14.2
16 Th	3 37 03	25 39 52	13♑45 57	20 57 33	18 05.1	16 20.3	16 13.9	5 32.5	24 10.1	26 44.1	20 22.1	25 11.7	25 09.0	20 13.7
17 F	3 40 59	26 37 39	28 02 16	4♒59 52	18 01.7	17 45.3	17 27.6	6 14.4	24 02.3	26 48.5	20 28.8	25 10.9	25 07.4	20 13.3
18 Sa	3 44 56	27 35 25	11♒50 21	18 33 51	17D 59.8	19 06.5	18 41.3	6 56.2	23 54.8	26 53.1	20 35.3	25 10.1	25 05.8	20 12.9
19 Su	3 48 52	28 33 10	25 10 38	1♓41 05	17 59.4	20 24.1	19 55.0	7 38.0	23 47.7	26 57.8	20 41.9	25 09.3	25 04.1	20 12.5
20 M	3 52 49	29 30 54	8♓05 37	14 24 48	18 00.3	21 38.0	21 08.7	8 19.7	23 40.9	27 02.6	20 48.4	25 08.6	25 02.5	20 12.1
21 Tu	3 56 45	0♊28 37	20 39 08	26 49 11	18 01.7	22 48.0	22 22.4	9 01.3	23 34.6	27 07.7	20 54.8	25 08.0	25 00.9	20 11.8
22 W	4 00 42	1 26 19	2♈55 33	8♈58 44	18R 03.0	23 54.3	23 36.1	9 43.0	23 28.6	27 12.8	21 01.2	25 07.4	24 59.3	20 11.5
23 Th	4 04 39	2 23 59	14 59 17	20 57 43	18 03.3	24 56.6	24 49.8	10 24.6	23 23.0	27 18.2	21 07.5	25 06.9	24 57.7	20 11.3
24 F	4 08 35	3 21 39	26 54 29	2♉50 02	18 02.0	25 54.9	26 03.5	11 06.1	23 17.7	27 23.6	21 13.8	25 06.4	24 56.1	20 11.0
25 Sa	4 12 32	4 19 18	8♉44 44	14 38 59	17 58.7	26 49.2	27 17.2	11 47.6	23 12.9	27 29.3	21 20.1	25 06.0	24 54.5	20 10.8
26 Su	4 16 28	5 16 55	20 33 04	26 27 17	17 53.3	27 39.4	28 30.8	12 29.1	23 08.5	27 35.0	21 26.3	25 05.6	24 52.9	20 10.7
27 M	4 20 25	6 14 31	2♊21 55	8♊17 11	17 45.9	28 25.5	29 44.5	13 10.5	23 04.4	27 41.0	21 32.4	25 05.3	24 51.3	20 10.5
28 Tu	4 24 21	7 12 07	14 13 18	20 10 29	17 37.0	29 07.2	0♊58.2	13 51.8	23 00.8	27 47.0	21 38.5	25 05.0	24 49.7	20 10.4
29 W	4 28 18	8 09 41	26 08 56	2♋08 50	17 27.5	29 44.7	2 11.9	14 33.2	22 57.5	27 53.3	21 44.5	25 04.8	24 48.1	20 10.4
30 Th	4 32 14	9 07 13	8♋10 25	14 13 54	17 18.2	0♋17.7	3 25.6	15 14.4	22 54.6	27 59.6	21 50.5	25 04.6	24 46.5	20D 10.3
31 F	4 36 11	10 04 45	20 19 32	26 27 33	17 10.0	0 46.3	4 39.3	15 55.7	22 52.2	28 06.1	21 56.4	25 04.5	24 45.0	20 10.3

LONGITUDE — June 1968

Day	Sid.Time	☉	0 hr ☽	Noon ☽	True ☊	☿	♀	♂	⚳	♃	♄	♅	♆	♇
1 Sa	4 40 08	11♊02 15	2♌38 17	8♌52 02	17♈03.6	1♋10.3	5♊53.0	16♊36.9	22♎50.1	28♌12.7	22♈02.2	25♍04.5	24♏43.4	20♍10.4
2 Su	4 44 04	11 59 44	15 09 09	21 30 00	16R 59.4	1 29.8	7 06.6	17 18.0	22R 48.4	28 19.5	22 08.0	25D 04.5	24R 41.9	20 10.4
3 M	4 48 01	12 57 12	27 54 59	4♍24 29	16D 57.3	1 44.6	8 20.3	17 59.1	22 47.2	28 26.4	22 13.7	25 04.5	24 40.4	20 10.5
4 Tu	4 51 57	13 54 39	10♍58 53	17 38 36	16 57.0	1 54.8	9 34.0	18 40.2	22 46.3	28 33.4	22 19.4	25 04.6	24 38.8	20 10.6
5 W	4 55 54	14 52 04	24 23 56	1♎15 10	16 57.7	2R 00.4	10 47.7	19 21.2	22D 45.8	28 40.6	22 25.0	25 04.8	24 37.3	20 10.8
6 Th	4 59 50	15 49 28	8♎12 32	15 16 06	16R 58.2	2 01.4	12 01.3	20 02.1	22 45.7	28 47.9	22 30.5	25 05.0	24 35.8	20 10.9
7 F	5 03 47	16 46 51	22 25 50	29 41 32	16 57.7	1 57.9	13 15.0	20 43.1	22 46.0	28 55.3	22 36.0	25 05.3	24 34.3	20 11.2
8 Sa	5 07 43	17 44 12	7♏02 48	14♏29 04	16 55.1	1 50.0	14 28.7	21 23.9	22 46.7	29 02.9	22 41.4	25 05.6	24 32.9	20 11.4
9 Su	5 11 40	18 41 33	21 59 34	29 33 19	16 50.1	1 37.9	15 42.3	22 04.8	22 47.7	29 10.5	22 46.7	25 06.0	24 31.4	20 11.7
10 M	5 15 37	19 38 54	7♐09 11	14♐45 56	16 42.8	1 21.8	16 56.0	22 45.6	22 49.2	29 18.3	22 52.0	25 06.4	24 30.0	20 12.0
11 Tu	5 19 33	20 36 13	22 22 13	29 56 41	16 33.9	1 02.0	18 09.7	23 26.3	22 51.0	29 26.2	22 57.2	25 06.9	24 28.6	20 12.4
12 W	5 23 30	21 33 32	7♑28 03	14♑55 05	16 24.5	0 38.7	19 23.3	24 07.0	22 53.2	29 34.3	23 02.3	25 07.4	24 27.1	20 12.7
13 Th	5 27 26	22 30 50	22 16 47	29 32 17	16 15.7	0 12.4	20 37.0	24 47.7	22 55.8	29 42.4	23 07.4	25 08.0	24 25.8	20 13.1
14 F	5 31 23	23 28 07	6♒40 57	13♒42 22	16 08.4	29♊43.5	21 50.7	25 28.3	22 58.7	29 50.7	23 12.4	25 08.6	24 24.4	20 13.6
15 Sa	5 35 19	24 25 24	20 36 20	27 22 51	16 03.3	29 12.4	23 04.4	26 08.9	23 02.0	29 59.0	23 17.3	25 09.3	24 23.0	20 14.0
16 Su	5 39 16	25 22 41	4♓02 06	10♓34 23	16 00.4	28 39.8	24 18.1	26 49.5	23 05.6	0♍07.5	23 22.2	25 10.1	24 21.7	20 14.5
17 M	5 43 13	26 19 58	17 00 09	23 19 56	15D 59.5	28 06.0	25 31.8	27 30.0	23 09.6	0 16.1	23 26.9	25 10.8	24 20.3	20 15.1
18 Tu	5 47 09	27 17 14	29 34 18	5♈43 54	15R 59.6	27 31.7	26 45.5	28 10.5	23 14.0	0 24.8	23 31.6	25 11.7	24 19.0	20 15.6
19 W	5 51 06	28 14 30	11♈49 24	17 51 25	15 59.8	26 57.6	27 59.2	28 50.9	23 18.7	0 33.6	23 36.3	25 12.6	24 17.7	20 16.2
20 Th	5 55 02	29 11 45	23 50 38	29 47 40	15 59.0	26 24.1	29 12.9	29 31.3	23 23.7	0 42.6	23 40.8	25 13.5	24 16.5	20 16.8
21 F	5 58 59	0♋09 01	5♉43 07	11♉37 33	15 56.2	25 51.8	0♋26.6	0♋11.7	23 29.1	0 51.6	23 45.3	25 14.5	24 15.2	20 17.5
22 Sa	6 02 55	1 06 16	17 31 28	23 25 21	15 51.0	25 21.3	1 40.3	0 52.0	23 34.9	1 00.7	23 49.7	25 15.6	24 14.0	20 18.2
23 Su	6 06 52	2 03 31	29 19 38	5♊14 40	15 43.0	24 53.2	2 54.1	1 32.3	23 40.9	1 10.0	23 54.0	25 16.7	24 12.8	20 18.9
24 M	6 10 48	3 00 46	11♊10 48	17 08 18	15 32.5	24 27.8	4 07.8	2 12.6	23 47.4	1 19.3	23 58.2	25 17.9	24 11.6	20 19.6
25 Tu	6 14 45	3 58 01	23 07 24	29 08 17	15 20.2	24 05.7	5 21.5	2 52.8	23 54.1	1 28.7	24 02.3	25 19.1	24 10.4	20 20.4
26 W	6 18 42	4 55 16	5♋11 07	11♋16 02	15 06.9	23 47.2	6 35.3	3 33.0	24 01.2	1 38.3	24 06.4	25 20.3	24 09.3	20 21.2
27 Th	6 22 38	5 52 30	17 23 07	23 32 30	14 53.8	23 32.6	7 49.0	4 13.1	24 08.5	1 47.9	24 10.4	25 21.6	24 08.2	20 22.1
28 F	6 26 35	6 49 44	29 44 15	5♌58 29	14 42.1	23 22.3	9 02.8	4 53.2	24 16.2	1 57.6	24 14.3	25 23.0	24 07.1	20 22.9
29 Sa	6 30 31	7 46 57	12♌15 19	18 34 52	14 32.6	23D 16.4	10 16.5	5 33.3	24 24.3	2 07.5	24 18.1	25 24.4	24 06.0	20 23.8
30 Su	6 34 28	8 44 10	24 57 18	1♍22 48	14 25.8	23 15.2	11 30.3	6 13.3	24 32.6	2 17.4	24 21.8	25 25.9	24 04.9	20 24.8

Astro Data

	Dy Hr Mn
☽0S	9 6:41
♅⚹♆	12 11:52
♄⚻♇	15 7:48
☽0N	22 0:20
♇D	31 4:01
♅D	2 0:37
☽0S	5 14:49
⚳0S	6 0:14
☿R	6 5:16
⚳D	6 5:53
☽0N	18 6:04
♄⚻♆	27 1:26
☿D	30 6:09

Planet Ingress

	Dy Hr Mn
♀ ♉	3 6:56
☿ ♊	6 22:56
♂ ♊	8 14:14
☉ ♊	21 0:06
♀ ♊	27 17:02
☿ ♋	29 22:44
☿ ♊R	13 22:32
♃ ♍	15 14:44
♀ ♋	21 3:20
♂ ♋	21 5:03
☉ ♋	21 8:13

Last Aspect / ☽ Ingress (May)

Last Aspect Dy Hr Mn		☽ Ingress Dy Hr Mn
1 22:30 ♀ ⚹	♋	2 1:50
4 7:02 ♂ ⚹	♌	4 12:54
6 20:38 ☿ □	♍	6 20:58
8 17:29 ♆ ⚹	♎	9 1:21
10 20:41 ♃ ⚹	♏	11 2:30
12 20:22 ♃ □	♐	13 1:53
14 20:04 ♃ △	♑	15 1:31
16 20:32 ☉ △	♒	17 3:22
19 5:44 ☉ □	♓	19 8:53
21 8:43 ♅ ☍	♈	21 18:14
24 0:54 ♃ △	♉	24 6:15
26 16:40 ♀ ☌	♊	26 19:12
29 6:57 ☿ ☌	♋	29 7:43
31 9:18 ♅ ⚹	♌	31 18:53

Last Aspect / ☽ Ingress (June)

Last Aspect Dy Hr Mn		☽ Ingress Dy Hr Mn
3 0:52 ♃ ☌	♍	3 3:52
5 1:12 ♅ ☌	♎	5 9:49
7 10:43 ♃ ⚹	♏	7 12:30
9 11:24 ♃ □	♐	9 12:42
11 11:11 ♃ △	♑	11 12:05
13 4:42 ♅ △	♒	13 12:46
15 15:09 ☿ △	♓	15 16:42
17 20:45 ☿ □	♈	18 0:50
20 11:25 ♂ ⚹	♉	20 12:25
22 15:44 ♅ △	♊	23 1:22
25 4:22 ♅ □	♋	25 13:43
27 15:32 ♅ ⚹	♌	28 0:30
29 22:50 ♄ △	♍	30 9:26

☽ Phases & Eclipses

Dy Hr Mn	
5 17:54	☽ 15♌17
12 13:05	○ 21♏51
19 5:44	☾ 28♒18
27 7:30	● 6♊04
4 4:47	☽ 13♍37
10 20:13	○ 19♐59
17 18:14	☾ 26♓35
25 22:24	● 4♋23

Astro Data

1 May 1968
Julian Day # 24958
SVP 5♓42'14"
GC 26♐23.8 ⚴ 13♍57.6
Eris 11♈55.9 ⚵ 4♏05.5R
⚷ 1♈38.5 ⚶ 29♓27.9
☽ Mean ☊ 17♈33.5

1 June 1968
Julian Day # 24989
SVP 5♓42'08"
GC 26♐23.9 ⚴ 17♍19.7
Eris 12♈11.6 ⚵ 28♎37.3R
⚷ 2♈51.7 ⚶ 12♈41.6
☽ Mean ☊ 15♈55.0

July 1968 — LONGITUDE

Day	Sid.Time	☉	0 hr ☽	Noon ☽	True ☊	☿	♀	♂	⚳	♃	♄	♅	♆	♇
1 M	6 38 24	9♋41 23	7♍51 36	14♍23 55	14♈21.8	23♊18.8	12♋44.0	6♋53.3	24♎41.2	2♍27.4	24♈25.5	25♍27.4	24♏03.9	20♍25.7
2 Tu	6 42 21	10 38 36	21 00 01	27 40 10	14R 20.2	23 27.3	13 57.8	7 33.2	24 50.1	2 37.5	24 29.0	25 28.9	24R 02.9	20 26.7
3 W	6 46 17	11 35 48	4♎24 38	11♎13 40	14 19.9	23 40.7	15 11.6	8 13.1	24 59.4	2 47.6	24 32.5	25 30.5	24 01.9	20 27.7
4 Th	6 50 14	12 32 59	18 07 29	25 06 12	14 19.7	23 59.1	16 25.3	8 53.0	25 08.9	2 57.9	24 35.8	25 32.2	24 01.0	20 28.7
5 F	6 54 11	13 30 11	2♏09 53	9♏18 28	14 18.5	24 22.6	17 39.1	9 32.9	25 18.7	3 08.2	24 39.1	25 33.9	24 00.0	20 29.8
6 Sa	6 58 07	14 27 22	16 31 47	23 49 28	14 15.2	24 51.0	18 52.9	10 12.7	25 28.7	3 18.6	24 42.3	25 35.6	23 59.1	20 30.9
7 Su	7 02 04	15 24 33	1♐11 01	8♐35 46	14 09.3	25 24.5	20 06.6	10 52.4	25 39.1	3 29.2	24 45.4	25 37.4	23 58.3	20 32.0
8 M	7 06 00	16 21 45	16 02 50	23 31 16	14 00.8	26 02.9	21 20.4	11 32.2	25 49.7	3 39.7	24 48.4	25 39.3	23 57.4	20 33.2
9 Tu	7 09 57	17 18 56	0♑59 59	8♑27 47	13 50.5	26 46.3	22 34.2	12 11.9	26 00.6	3 50.4	24 51.3	25 41.2	23 56.6	20 34.4
10 W	7 13 53	18 16 07	15 53 32	23 16 06	13 39.4	27 34.5	23 48.0	12 51.5	26 11.8	4 01.1	24 54.2	25 43.1	23 55.8	20 35.6
11 Th	7 17 50	19 13 18	0♒34 27	7♒47 40	13 28.8	28 27.6	25 01.8	13 31.1	26 23.2	4 11.9	24 56.9	25 45.1	23 55.1	20 36.8
12 F	7 21 46	20 10 30	14 55 00	21 55 56	13 19.9	29 25.4	26 15.6	14 10.7	26 34.8	4 22.8	24 59.5	25 47.1	23 54.3	20 38.1
13 Sa	7 25 43	21 07 42	28 50 05	5♓37 17	13 13.3	0♋28.0	27 29.4	14 50.3	26 46.8	4 33.8	25 02.1	25 49.2	23 53.6	20 39.4
14 Su	7 29 40	22 04 55	12♓17 34	18 51 06	13 09.2	1 35.1	28 43.2	15 29.8	26 58.9	4 44.8	25 04.5	25 51.3	23 52.9	20 40.7
15 M	7 33 36	23 02 08	25 18 11	1♈39 15	13D 07.4	2 46.9	29 57.0	16 09.3	27 11.3	4 55.9	25 06.9	25 53.4	23 52.3	20 42.0
16 Tu	7 37 33	23 59 22	7♈54 49	14 05 29	13R 07.0	4 03.2	1♌10.8	16 48.8	27 24.0	5 07.1	25 09.1	25 55.6	23 51.6	20 43.4
17 W	7 41 29	24 56 36	20 11 51	26 14 36	13 07.1	5 23.9	2 24.6	17 28.2	27 36.8	5 18.3	25 11.3	25 57.9	23 51.0	20 44.7
18 Th	7 45 26	25 53 51	2♉14 23	8♉11 54	13 06.5	6 48.9	3 38.4	18 07.6	27 49.9	5 29.6	25 13.3	26 00.2	23 50.5	20 46.2
19 F	7 49 22	26 51 07	14 07 48	20 02 44	13 04.4	8 18.1	4 52.3	18 47.0	28 03.3	5 41.0	25 15.3	26 02.5	23 49.9	20 47.6
20 Sa	7 53 19	27 48 24	25 57 18	1♊52 03	12 59.9	9 51.5	6 06.1	19 26.4	28 16.9	5 52.4	25 17.2	26 04.9	23 49.4	20 49.0
21 Su	7 57 15	28 45 41	7♊47 33	13 44 15	12 52.8	11 28.8	7 20.0	20 05.7	28 30.7	6 03.9	25 18.9	26 07.3	23 49.0	20 50.5
22 M	8 01 12	29 42 59	19 42 36	25 42 56	12 43.4	13 09.9	8 33.8	20 45.0	28 44.7	6 15.4	25 20.6	26 09.7	23 48.5	20 52.0
23 Tu	8 05 09	0♌40 18	1♋45 34	7♋50 46	12 32.0	14 54.6	9 47.7	21 24.2	28 58.9	6 27.0	25 22.1	26 12.2	23 48.1	20 53.6
24 W	8 09 05	1 37 38	13 58 43	20 09 32	12 19.8	16 42.7	11 01.6	22 03.4	29 13.3	6 38.7	25 23.6	26 14.8	23 47.7	20 55.1
25 Th	8 13 02	2 34 58	26 23 19	2♌40 07	12 07.7	18 33.9	12 15.5	22 42.6	29 28.0	6 50.4	25 24.9	26 17.3	23 47.4	20 56.7
26 F	8 16 58	3 32 19	8♌59 55	15 22 43	11 56.8	20 28.0	13 29.3	23 21.8	29 42.8	7 02.2	25 26.2	26 19.9	23 47.0	20 58.3
27 Sa	8 20 55	4 29 41	21 48 28	28 17 07	11 48.0	22 24.6	14 43.2	24 00.9	29 57.9	7 14.1	25 27.3	26 22.6	23 46.8	20 59.9
28 Su	8 24 51	5 27 03	4♍48 38	11♍22 58	11 41.9	24 23.4	15 57.1	24 40.0	0♏13.2	7 25.9	25 28.4	26 25.3	23 46.5	21 01.6
29 M	8 28 48	6 24 26	18 00 08	24 40 08	11 38.4	26 24.2	17 11.0	25 19.1	0 28.6	7 37.9	25 29.3	26 28.0	23 46.3	21 03.2
30 Tu	8 32 44	7 21 49	1♎22 59	8♎08 45	11D 37.2	28 26.5	18 24.9	25 58.1	0 44.3	7 49.9	25 30.2	26 30.7	23 46.1	21 04.9
31 W	8 36 41	8 19 13	14 57 29	21 49 16	11 37.4	0♌30.1	19 38.7	26 37.1	1 00.1	8 01.9	25 30.9	26 33.5	23 45.9	21 06.6

August 1968 — LONGITUDE

Day	Sid.Time	☉	0 hr ☽	Noon ☽	True ☊	☿	♀	♂	⚳	♃	♄	♅	♆	♇
1 Th	8 40 38	9♌16 37	28♎44 10	5♏42 12	11♈37.9	2♌34.5	20♌52.6	27♋16.1	1♏16.1	8♍14.0	25♈31.5	26♍36.4	23♏45.8	21♍08.4
2 F	8 44 34	10 14 02	12♏43 23	19 47 39	11R 37.6	4 39.5	22 06.5	27 55.1	1 32.3	8 26.1	25 32.0	26 39.2	23R 45.7	21 10.1
3 Sa	8 48 31	11 11 28	26 54 52	4♐04 48	11 35.6	6 44.7	23 20.4	28 34.0	1 48.7	8 38.3	25 32.5	26 42.1	23 45.6	21 11.9
4 Su	8 52 27	12 08 54	11♐17 08	18 31 25	11 31.3	8 49.9	24 34.3	29 12.9	2 05.3	8 50.5	25 32.8	26 45.0	23D 45.6	21 13.7
5 M	8 56 24	13 06 22	25 47 06	3♑03 32	11 24.8	10 54.8	25 48.2	29 51.7	2 22.0	9 02.8	25 33.0	26 48.0	23 45.6	21 15.5
6 Tu	9 00 20	14 03 50	10♑19 59	17 35 38	11 16.8	12 59.2	27 02.0	0♌30.5	2 38.9	9 15.1	25R 33.1	26 51.0	23 45.6	21 17.3
7 W	9 04 17	15 01 19	24 49 41	2♒01 16	11 08.0	15 02.9	28 15.9	1 09.3	2 55.9	9 27.4	25 33.1	26 54.0	23 45.7	21 19.1
8 Th	9 08 14	15 58 48	9♒09 36	16 13 58	10 59.5	17 05.8	29 29.8	1 48.1	3 13.1	9 39.8	25 33.0	26 57.1	23 45.7	21 21.0
9 F	9 12 10	16 56 19	23 13 43	0♓08 20	10 52.4	19 07.6	0♍43.7	2 26.9	3 30.5	9 52.2	25 32.8	27 00.2	23 45.9	21 22.9
10 Sa	9 16 07	17 53 51	6♓57 28	13 40 51	10 47.2	21 08.3	1 57.5	3 05.6	3 48.1	10 04.7	25 32.5	27 03.3	23 46.0	21 24.7
11 Su	9 20 03	18 51 24	20 18 23	26 50 06	10 44.2	23 07.8	3 11.4	3 44.3	4 05.7	10 17.1	25 32.1	27 06.4	23 46.2	21 26.6
12 M	9 24 00	19 48 59	3♈16 11	9♈36 52	10D 43.2	25 06.1	4 25.3	4 22.9	4 23.6	10 29.7	25 31.6	27 09.6	23 46.4	21 28.6
13 Tu	9 27 56	20 46 35	15 52 32	22 03 39	10 43.7	27 03.0	5 39.2	5 01.6	4 41.6	10 42.2	25 31.0	27 12.8	23 46.7	21 30.5
14 W	9 31 53	21 44 12	28 10 42	4♉14 15	10 44.9	28 58.5	6 53.0	5 40.2	4 59.7	10 54.8	25 30.3	27 16.0	23 47.0	21 32.4
15 Th	9 35 49	22 41 51	10♉14 55	16 13 20	10R 45.9	0♍52.7	8 06.9	6 18.8	5 18.0	11 07.4	25 29.5	27 19.3	23 47.3	21 34.4
16 F	9 39 46	23 39 31	22 10 07	28 05 55	10 46.0	2 45.4	9 20.8	6 57.3	5 36.4	11 20.1	25 28.5	27 22.6	23 47.6	21 36.4
17 Sa	9 43 43	24 37 14	4♊01 23	9♊57 08	10 44.6	4 36.7	10 34.7	7 35.9	5 55.0	11 32.7	25 27.5	27 25.9	23 48.0	21 38.4
18 Su	9 47 39	25 34 57	15 53 45	21 51 48	10 41.4	6 26.6	11 48.6	8 14.4	6 13.7	11 45.4	25 26.4	27 29.2	23 48.4	21 40.4
19 M	9 51 36	26 32 43	27 51 49	3♋54 17	10 36.3	8 15.1	13 02.4	8 52.9	6 32.5	11 58.2	25 25.2	27 32.6	23 48.9	21 42.4
20 Tu	9 55 32	27 30 30	9♋59 37	16 08 10	10 29.9	10 02.1	14 16.3	9 31.4	6 51.5	12 10.9	25 23.8	27 36.0	23 49.4	21 44.5
21 W	9 59 29	28 28 18	22 20 15	28 36 05	10 22.6	11 47.8	15 30.2	10 09.8	7 10.6	12 23.7	25 22.4	27 39.4	23 49.9	21 46.5
22 Th	10 03 25	29 26 08	4♌55 51	11♌19 36	10 15.3	13 32.1	16 44.1	10 48.2	7 29.9	12 36.5	25 20.9	27 42.8	23 50.4	21 48.6
23 F	10 07 22	0♍24 00	17 47 22	24 19 07	10 08.8	15 15.0	17 58.0	11 26.6	7 49.2	12 49.4	25 19.2	27 46.3	23 51.0	21 50.6
24 Sa	10 11 18	1 21 53	0♍54 42	7♍34 00	10 03.7	16 56.5	19 11.8	12 05.0	8 08.7	13 02.2	25 17.5	27 49.8	23 51.6	21 52.7
25 Su	10 15 15	2 19 47	14 16 46	21 02 49	10 00.4	18 36.7	20 25.7	12 43.4	8 28.3	13 15.1	25 15.7	27 53.2	23 52.2	21 54.8
26 M	10 19 11	3 17 43	27 51 51	4♎43 38	9D 58.9	20 15.6	21 39.6	13 21.7	8 48.1	13 27.9	25 13.8	27 56.8	23 52.9	21 56.9
27 Tu	10 23 08	4 15 40	11♎37 53	18 34 21	9 59.1	21 53.1	22 53.4	14 00.0	9 07.9	13 40.8	25 11.7	28 00.3	23 53.6	21 59.0
28 W	10 27 05	5 13 39	25 32 48	2♏33 00	10 00.2	23 29.4	24 07.3	14 38.2	9 27.9	13 53.7	25 09.6	28 03.8	23 54.3	22 01.1
29 Th	10 31 01	6 11 38	9♏34 43	16 37 46	10 01.7	25 04.3	25 21.1	15 16.5	9 48.0	14 06.7	25 07.4	28 07.4	23 55.1	22 03.3
30 F	10 34 58	7 09 40	23 41 56	0♐47 00	10R 02.7	26 37.9	26 35.0	15 54.7	10 08.2	14 19.6	25 05.1	28 11.0	23 55.9	22 05.4
31 Sa	10 38 54	8 07 42	7♐52 46	14 58 59	10 02.6	28 10.2	27 48.8	16 32.9	10 28.5	14 32.6	25 02.7	28 14.6	23 56.7	22 07.5

Astro Data

	Dy Hr Mn
☽0S	2 20:27
☽0N	15 13:04
☽0S	30 1:03
♆D	5 1:17
♄R	7 2:22
☽0N	11 21:18
♃⚼♄	12 15:35
☽0S	26 6:45

Planet Ingress

	Dy Hr Mn
☿ ♋	13 1:30
♀ ♌	15 12:59
☉ ♌	22 19:07
⚳ ♏	27 15:19
☿ ♌	31 6:11
♂ ♌	5 17:07
♀ ♍	8 21:49
☿ ♍	15 0:53
☉ ♍	23 2:03

Last Aspect / ☽ Ingress (July)

Last Aspect Dy Hr Mn		☽ Ingress Dy Hr Mn
2 8:04	♅ ☌	♎ 2 16:10
4 11:08	♄ ☍	♏ 4 20:20
6 14:54	♅ ⚹	♐ 6 22:05
8 16:15	☿ ☍	♑ 8 22:24
10 16:01	♅ △	♒ 10 23:03
12 17:19	♄ ⚹	♓ 13 2:03
15 8:25	♀ △	♈ 15 8:51
17 9:53	♄ ☌	♉ 17 19:30
20 3:02	☉ ⚹	♊ 20 8:13
22 12:54	♅ □	♋ 22 20:31
24 23:46	♅ ⚹	♌ 25 6:55
27 6:46	♄ △	♍ 27 15:10
29 15:40	☿ ⚹	♎ 29 21:32

Last Aspect / ☽ Ingress (August)

Last Aspect Dy Hr Mn		☽ Ingress Dy Hr Mn
31 20:45	♂ □	♏ 1 2:11
3 2:20	♂ △	♐ 3 5:11
5 1:38	♅ □	♑ 5 6:57
7 3:25	♅ △	♒ 7 8:37
9 4:01	♄ ⚹	♓ 9 11:45
11 12:30	♅ ☍	♈ 11 17:53
13 23:37	☿ △	♉ 14 3:36
16 10:32	♅ △	♊ 16 15:51
18 23:18	♅ □	♋ 19 4:15
21 10:11	♅ ⚹	♌ 21 14:40
23 13:50	♄ △	♍ 23 22:21
26 0:06	♅ ☌	♎ 26 3:45
27 23:22	♄ ☍	♏ 28 7:38
30 7:35	♅ ⚹	♐ 30 10:40

☽ Phases & Eclipses

Dy Hr Mn	
3 12:42	☽ 11♎37
10 3:18	○ 17♑55
17 9:11	☾ 24♈50
25 11:49	● 2♌35
1 18:34	☽ 9♏32
8 11:32	○ 15♒58
16 2:13	☾ 23♉16
23 23:57	● 0♍53
30 23:34	☽ 7♐38

Astro Data

1 July 1968
Julian Day # 25019
SVP 5♓42'02"
GC 26♐24.0 ⚴ 25♍04.7
Eris 12♈18.6 ⚵ 27♎49.9
⚷ 3♈21.8 ⚶ 23♈39.5
☽ Mean ☊ 14♈19.7

1 August 1968
Julian Day # 25050
SVP 5♓41'57"
GC 26♐24.0 ⚴ 5♎44.0
Eris 12♈15.8R ⚵ 1♏31.8
⚷ 3♈04.4R ⚶ 1♉57.6
☽ Mean ☊ 12♈41.3

LONGITUDE — September 1968

Day	Sid.Time	☉	0 hr ☽	Noon ☽	True ☊	☿	♀	♂	⚳	♃	♄	♅	♆	♇
1 Su	10 42 51	9♍05 47	22♐05 23	29♐11 40	10♈01.2	29♍41.3	29♍02.6	17♌11.0	10♏48.9	14♍45.5	25♈00.2	28♍18.2	23♏57.6	22♍09.7
2 M	10 46 47	10 03 52	6♑17 31	13♑22 33	9R 58.5	1♎11.0	0♎16.4	17 49.2	11 09.5	14 58.5	24R 57.6	28 21.9	23 58.5	22 11.9
3 Tu	10 50 44	11 01 59	20 26 22	27 28 34	9 54.8	2 39.5	1 30.2	18 27.3	11 30.1	15 11.5	24 55.0	28 25.5	23 59.4	22 14.0
4 W	10 54 41	12 00 07	4♒28 41	11♒26 19	9 50.7	4 06.6	2 44.0	19 05.4	11 50.8	15 24.4	24 52.2	28 29.2	24 00.4	22 16.2
5 Th	10 58 37	12 58 17	18 21 01	25 12 24	9 46.6	5 32.4	3 57.8	19 43.5	12 11.6	15 37.4	24 49.4	28 32.8	24 01.3	22 18.4
6 F	11 02 34	13 56 28	2♓00 06	8♓43 49	9 43.3	6 56.8	5 11.6	20 21.5	12 32.6	15 50.4	24 46.4	28 36.5	24 02.4	22 20.6
7 Sa	11 06 30	14 54 41	15 23 18	21 58 24	9 41.1	8 19.9	6 25.4	20 59.5	12 53.6	16 03.4	24 43.4	28 40.2	24 03.4	22 22.7
8 Su	11 10 27	15 52 56	28 29 01	4♈55 08	9D 40.0	9 41.6	7 39.1	21 37.5	13 14.7	16 16.4	24 40.3	28 43.9	24 04.5	22 24.9
9 M	11 14 23	16 51 13	11♈16 49	17 34 14	9 40.1	11 01.8	8 52.9	22 15.5	13 35.9	16 29.4	24 37.2	28 47.7	24 05.6	22 27.1
10 Tu	11 18 20	17 49 31	23 47 35	29 57 10	9 41.2	12 20.6	10 06.6	22 53.4	13 57.2	16 42.4	24 33.9	28 51.4	24 06.7	22 29.3
11 W	11 22 16	18 47 52	6♉03 21	12♉06 31	9 42.7	13 37.8	11 20.3	23 31.4	14 18.6	16 55.4	24 30.6	28 55.1	24 07.8	22 31.5
12 Th	11 26 13	19 46 15	18 07 09	24 05 44	9 44.3	14 53.5	12 34.1	24 09.3	14 40.0	17 08.4	24 27.2	28 58.9	24 09.0	22 33.7
13 F	11 30 09	20 44 40	0♊02 49	5♊58 57	9 45.5	16 07.5	13 47.8	24 47.2	15 01.6	17 21.4	24 23.7	29 02.6	24 10.2	22 35.9
14 Sa	11 34 06	21 43 07	11 54 44	17 50 45	9R 46.2	17 19.9	15 01.5	25 25.0	15 23.3	17 34.4	24 20.1	29 06.4	24 11.5	22 38.1
15 Su	11 38 03	22 41 36	23 47 36	29 45 53	9 46.1	18 30.4	16 15.2	26 02.9	15 45.0	17 47.3	24 16.5	29 10.1	24 12.7	22 40.3
16 M	11 41 59	23 40 07	5♋46 10	11♋49 02	9 45.2	19 39.0	17 28.9	26 40.7	16 06.8	18 00.3	24 12.8	29 13.9	24 14.0	22 42.5
17 Tu	11 45 56	24 38 41	17 55 00	24 04 34	9 43.7	20 45.6	18 42.6	27 18.5	16 28.7	18 13.3	24 09.0	29 17.7	24 15.4	22 44.7
18 W	11 49 52	25 37 17	0♌18 12	6♌36 15	9 41.9	21 50.1	19 56.3	27 56.3	16 50.7	18 26.2	24 05.2	29 21.5	24 16.7	22 46.9
19 Th	11 53 49	26 35 54	12 59 04	19 26 52	9 39.9	22 52.3	21 09.9	28 34.1	17 12.8	18 39.2	24 01.3	29 25.3	24 18.1	22 49.1
20 F	11 57 45	27 34 34	25 59 49	2♍37 57	9 38.3	23 52.0	22 23.6	29 11.8	17 34.9	18 52.1	23 57.3	29 29.1	24 19.5	22 51.3
21 Sa	12 01 42	28 33 16	9♍21 14	16 09 33	9 37.0	24 49.2	23 37.3	29 49.6	17 57.1	19 05.0	23 53.3	29 32.8	24 20.9	22 53.5
22 Su	12 05 38	29 32 00	23 02 37	0♎00 07	9D 36.4	25 43.6	24 50.9	0♍27.3	18 19.4	19 18.0	23 49.2	29 36.6	24 22.4	22 55.7
23 M	12 09 35	0♎30 46	7♎01 38	14 06 39	9 36.3	26 34.9	26 04.6	1 04.9	18 41.8	19 30.8	23 45.1	29 40.4	24 23.9	22 57.9
24 Tu	12 13 32	1 29 34	21 14 38	28 24 58	9 36.6	27 23.0	27 18.2	1 42.6	19 04.2	19 43.7	23 40.9	29 44.2	24 25.4	23 00.1
25 W	12 17 28	2 28 23	5♏37 02	12♏50 12	9 37.2	28 07.5	28 31.8	2 20.2	19 26.8	19 56.6	23 36.7	29 48.0	24 26.9	23 02.3
26 Th	12 21 25	3 27 15	20 03 52	27 17 25	9 37.8	28 48.2	29 45.4	2 57.8	19 49.3	20 09.4	23 32.4	29 51.8	24 28.4	23 04.5
27 F	12 25 21	4 26 08	4♐30 21	11♐42 07	9 38.3	29 24.7	0♏59.0	3 35.4	20 12.0	20 22.2	23 28.0	29 55.6	24 30.0	23 06.6
28 Sa	12 29 18	5 25 03	18 52 19	26 00 33	9R 38.5	29 56.7	2 12.6	4 12.9	20 34.7	20 35.0	23 23.6	29 59.3	24 31.6	23 08.8
29 Su	12 33 14	6 24 00	3♑06 30	10♑09 54	9 38.6	0♏23.9	3 26.1	4 50.5	20 57.5	20 47.8	23 19.2	0♎03.1	24 33.3	23 11.0
30 M	12 37 11	7 22 59	17 10 31	24 08 12	9 38.5	0 45.7	4 39.7	5 28.0	21 20.3	21 00.5	23 14.8	0 06.9	24 34.9	23 13.1

LONGITUDE — October 1968

Day	Sid.Time	☉	0 hr ☽	Noon ☽	True ☊	☿	♀	♂	⚳	♃	♄	♅	♆	♇
1 Tu	12 41 07	8♎21 59	1♒02 48	7♒54 13	9♈38.3	1♏01.8	5♏53.2	6♍05.5	21♏43.2	21♍13.2	23♈10.2	0♎10.7	24♏36.6	23♍15.3
2 W	12 45 04	9 21 01	14 42 22	21 27 13	9D 38.3	1R 11.8	7 06.7	6 42.9	22 06.2	21 25.9	23R 05.7	0 14.4	24 38.3	23 17.4
3 Th	12 49 01	10 20 05	28 08 41	4♓46 47	9 38.3	1 15.1	8 20.2	7 20.4	22 29.2	21 38.6	23 01.1	0 18.2	24 40.0	23 19.6
4 F	12 52 57	11 19 10	11♓21 28	17 52 44	9 38.4	1 11.4	9 33.7	7 57.8	22 52.3	21 51.2	22 56.5	0 21.9	24 41.7	23 21.7
5 Sa	12 56 54	12 18 17	24 20 36	0♈45 06	9R 38.5	1 00.3	10 47.2	8 35.2	23 15.4	22 03.8	22 51.9	0 25.6	24 43.5	23 23.8
6 Su	13 00 50	13 17 27	7♈06 15	13 24 09	9 38.5	0 41.5	12 00.6	9 12.5	23 38.6	22 16.3	22 47.2	0 29.4	24 45.3	23 25.9
7 M	13 04 47	14 16 38	19 38 52	25 50 31	9 38.4	0 14.7	13 14.0	9 49.9	24 01.8	22 28.9	22 42.6	0 33.1	24 47.1	23 28.0
8 Tu	13 08 43	15 15 52	1♉59 16	8♉05 18	9 37.9	29♎39.8	14 27.5	10 27.2	24 25.1	22 41.4	22 37.9	0 36.8	24 48.9	23 30.1
9 W	13 12 40	16 15 07	14 08 51	20 10 10	9 37.1	28 56.9	15 40.9	11 04.5	24 48.5	22 53.8	22 33.1	0 40.5	24 50.7	23 32.1
10 Th	13 16 36	17 14 25	26 09 33	2♊07 22	9 36.1	28 06.4	16 54.2	11 41.8	25 11.9	23 06.2	22 28.4	0 44.2	24 52.6	23 34.2
11 F	13 20 33	18 13 46	8♊03 58	13 59 49	9 35.0	27 08.8	18 07.6	12 19.0	25 35.3	23 18.6	22 23.7	0 47.8	24 54.5	23 36.3
12 Sa	13 24 30	19 13 08	19 55 20	25 51 01	9 33.9	26 05.2	19 21.0	12 56.3	25 58.8	23 30.9	22 18.9	0 51.5	24 56.4	23 38.3
13 Su	13 28 26	20 12 33	1♋47 23	7♋44 59	9 33.1	24 56.7	20 34.3	13 33.5	26 22.4	23 43.2	22 14.1	0 55.1	24 58.3	23 40.3
14 M	13 32 23	21 12 00	13 44 22	19 46 07	9D 32.8	23 44.9	21 47.6	14 10.7	26 46.0	23 55.5	22 09.4	0 58.7	25 00.2	23 42.3
15 Tu	13 36 19	22 11 30	25 50 48	1♌59 01	9 33.0	22 31.8	23 01.0	14 47.9	27 09.6	24 07.7	22 04.6	1 02.4	25 02.2	23 44.3
16 W	13 40 16	23 11 01	8♌11 17	14 28 10	9 33.7	21 19.3	24 14.3	15 25.0	27 33.3	24 19.9	21 59.8	1 05.9	25 04.2	23 46.3
17 Th	13 44 12	24 10 35	20 50 08	27 17 38	9 34.9	20 09.5	25 27.5	16 02.2	27 57.1	24 32.0	21 55.0	1 09.5	25 06.1	23 48.3
18 F	13 48 09	25 10 11	3♍51 02	10♍30 35	9 36.2	19 04.6	26 40.8	16 39.3	28 20.9	24 44.0	21 50.3	1 13.1	25 08.1	23 50.3
19 Sa	13 52 05	26 09 50	17 16 28	24 08 42	9 37.2	18 06.4	27 54.1	17 16.4	28 44.7	24 56.1	21 45.5	1 16.6	25 10.1	23 52.2
20 Su	13 56 02	27 09 30	1♎07 13	8♎11 45	9R 37.7	17 16.7	29 07.3	17 53.4	29 08.5	25 08.0	21 40.8	1 20.1	25 12.2	23 54.1
21 M	13 59 59	28 09 13	15 21 54	22 37 06	9 37.3	16 36.8	0♐20.5	18 30.4	29 32.5	25 19.9	21 36.0	1 23.6	25 14.2	23 56.0
22 Tu	14 03 55	29 08 57	29 56 38	7♏19 41	9 35.9	16 07.5	1 33.7	19 07.5	29 56.4	25 31.8	21 31.3	1 27.1	25 16.3	23 57.9
23 W	14 07 52	0♏08 44	14♏45 16	22 12 24	9 33.7	15 49.3	2 46.9	19 44.4	0♐20.4	25 43.6	21 26.6	1 30.6	25 18.4	23 59.8
24 Th	14 11 48	1 08 33	29 40 01	7♐07 05	9 30.8	15D 42.6	4 00.1	20 21.4	0 44.4	25 55.3	21 21.9	1 34.0	25 20.4	24 01.7
25 F	14 15 45	2 08 23	14♐32 35	21 55 38	9 27.8	15 47.1	5 13.2	20 58.3	1 08.5	26 07.0	21 17.3	1 37.4	25 22.5	24 03.5
26 Sa	14 19 41	3 08 15	29 15 24	6♑31 15	9 25.2	16 02.4	6 26.4	21 35.2	1 32.6	26 18.6	21 12.6	1 40.8	25 24.7	24 05.3
27 Su	14 23 38	4 08 09	13♑42 38	20 49 11	9 23.5	16 27.9	7 39.5	22 12.1	1 56.7	26 30.2	21 08.0	1 44.2	25 26.8	24 07.1
28 M	14 27 34	5 08 05	27 50 40	4♒46 59	9D 22.9	17 02.9	8 52.6	22 48.9	2 20.9	26 41.6	21 03.5	1 47.5	25 28.9	24 08.9
29 Tu	14 31 31	6 08 02	11♒38 08	18 24 13	9 23.4	17 46.5	10 05.6	23 25.7	2 45.1	26 53.1	20 58.9	1 50.8	25 31.1	24 10.7
30 W	14 35 28	7 08 00	25 05 26	1♓41 59	9 24.7	18 37.9	11 18.6	24 02.5	3 09.3	27 04.4	20 54.5	1 54.1	25 33.2	24 12.4
31 Th	14 39 24	8 08 00	8♓14 08	14 42 13	9 26.4	19 36.2	12 31.6	24 39.3	3 33.6	27 15.7	20 50.0	1 57.3	25 35.4	24 14.1

Astro Data

	Dy Hr Mn
☿0S	1 11:56
♀0S	4 7:44
☽0N	8 5:57
♄⊼♆	16 6:08
☽0S	22 14:53
☉0S	22 23:27
♄⊼♇	30 17:52
☿R	3 11:40
☽0N	5 13:46
♃⊼♄	8 7:07
♃☌♇	13 5:12
☽0S	20 0:57
♃⚹♆	20 22:06
☿D	24 14:18
♅0S	25 17:13

Planet Ingress

		Dy Hr Mn
☿	♎	1 16:59
♀	♎	2 6:39
♂	♍	21 18:39
☉	♎	22 23:26
♀	♏	26 16:45
☿	♏	28 14:40
♅	♎	28 16:09
☿	♎R	7 22:46
♀	♐	21 5:16
⚳	♐	22 15:36
☉	♏	23 8:30

Last Aspect / ☽ Ingress (September)

Last Aspect Dy Hr Mn			☽ Ingress	Dy Hr Mn
1 12:56	☿	□	♑	1 13:22
3 13:38	♅	△	♒	3 16:19
5 11:20	♄	⚹	♓	5 20:27
8 0:24	♅	☍	♈	8 2:49
10 1:33	♄	☌	♉	10 12:06
12 21:54	♅	△	♊	12 23:54
15 10:48	♅	□	♋	15 12:28
17 22:07	♅	⚹	♌	17 23:25
20 5:30	♂	☌	♍	20 7:15
22 11:19	♅	☌	♎	22 12:00
24 10:11	☿	☌	♏	24 14:39
26 16:18	♅	⚹	♐	26 16:30
28 7:37	♄	△	♑	28 18:44
30 12:46	♆	⚹	♒	30 22:11

Last Aspect / ☽ Ingress (October)

Last Aspect Dy Hr Mn			☽ Ingress	Dy Hr Mn
2 17:43	♆	□	♓	3 3:21
5 0:41	♆	△	♈	5 10:35
7 5:57	♄	☌	♉	7 20:07
9 21:23	♆	☍	♊	10 7:43
12 12:26	☿	△	♋	12 20:23
14 22:22	♆	△	♌	15 8:08
17 8:15	♀	□	♍	17 16:58
19 19:06	♀	⚹	♎	19 22:05
21 21:44	☉	☌	♏	22 0:05
23 17:44	♃	⚹	♐	24 0:32
25 18:56	♃	□	♑	26 1:13
27 21:50	♃	△	♒	28 3:43
30 0:48	♆	□	♓	30 8:54

☽ Phases & Eclipses

Dy Hr Mn	
6 22:07	○ 14♓21
14 20:31	☾ 22♊04
22 11:08	● 29♍30
22 11:18:06	● T 00'40"
29 5:07	☽ 6♑07
6 11:46	○ 13♈17
6 11:42	● T 1.169
14 15:05	☾ 21♋20
21 21:44	● 28♎33
28 12:40	☽ 5♒10

Astro Data

1 September 1968
Julian Day # 25081
SVP 5♓41'53"
GC 26♐24.1 ⚵ 17♎56.9
Eris 12♈03.7R ✱ 8♏25.0
⚷ 2♈04.2R ⚶ 5♉17.9
☽ Mean ☊ 11♈02.8

1 October 1968
Julian Day # 25111
SVP 5♓41'49"
GC 26♐24.2 ⚵ 0♏38.0
Eris 11♈46.5R ✱ 16♏59.1
⚷ 0♈44.7R ⚶ 2♉04.0R
☽ Mean ☊ 9♈27.4

November 1968 LONGITUDE

Day	Sid.Time	☉	0 hr ☽	Noon ☽	True ☊	☿	♀	♂	⚳	♃	♄	♅	♆	♇
1 F	14 43 21	9♏08 02	21♓06 29	27♓27 15	9♈27.9	20♎40.6	13♐44.6	25♍16.0	3♐57.8	27♍26.9	20♈45.6	2♎00.5	25♏37.6	24♍15.8
2 Sa	14 47 17	10 08 05	3♈44 48	9♈59 24	9R 28.4	21 50.3	14 57.5	25 52.7	4 22.1	27 38.0	20R 41.2	2 03.7	25 39.7	24 17.5
3 Su	14 51 14	11 08 10	16 11 19	22 20 45	9 27.6	23 04.5	16 10.4	26 29.4	4 46.5	27 49.1	20 36.9	2 06.9	25 41.9	24 19.1
4 M	14 55 10	12 08 17	28 27 56	4♉33 04	9 25.1	24 22.7	17 23.3	27 06.0	5 10.8	28 00.1	20 32.6	2 10.0	25 44.1	24 20.8
5 Tu	14 59 07	13 08 26	10♉36 20	16 37 54	9 20.9	25 44.2	18 36.2	27 42.7	5 35.2	28 11.0	20 28.4	2 13.1	25 46.3	24 22.4
6 W	15 03 03	14 08 36	22 37 57	28 36 41	9 15.2	27 08.5	19 49.0	28 19.3	5 59.6	28 21.8	20 24.2	2 16.2	25 48.5	24 24.0
7 Th	15 07 00	15 08 49	4♊34 16	10♊30 57	9 08.5	28 35.1	21 01.8	28 55.8	6 24.1	28 32.6	20 20.1	2 19.2	25 50.8	24 25.5
8 F	15 10 57	16 09 03	16 26 58	22 22 34	9 01.4	0♏03.7	22 14.5	29 32.4	6 48.5	28 43.2	20 16.1	2 22.3	25 53.0	24 27.1
9 Sa	15 14 53	17 09 19	28 18 03	4♋13 46	8 54.7	1 33.9	23 27.3	0♎08.9	7 13.0	28 53.8	20 12.1	2 25.2	25 55.2	24 28.6
10 Su	15 18 50	18 09 37	10♋10 05	16 07 26	8 48.9	3 05.4	24 40.0	0 45.4	7 37.5	29 04.3	20 08.2	2 28.2	25 57.5	24 30.1
11 M	15 22 46	19 09 57	22 06 14	28 07 00	8 44.8	4 37.9	25 52.6	1 21.8	8 02.0	29 14.8	20 04.3	2 31.1	25 59.7	24 31.5
12 Tu	15 26 43	20 10 19	4♌10 15	10♌16 31	8D 42.4	6 11.2	27 05.2	1 58.3	8 26.6	29 25.1	20 00.5	2 33.9	26 02.0	24 33.0
13 W	15 30 39	21 10 43	16 26 22	22 40 24	8 41.8	7 45.2	28 17.8	2 34.7	8 51.1	29 35.3	19 56.8	2 36.8	26 04.2	24 34.4
14 Th	15 34 36	22 11 09	28 59 11	5♍23 17	8 42.5	9 19.7	29 30.4	3 11.0	9 15.7	29 45.5	19 53.1	2 39.6	26 06.4	24 35.8
15 F	15 38 32	23 11 37	11♍53 14	18 29 29	8 43.9	10 54.5	0♑42.9	3 47.4	9 40.3	29 55.5	19 49.5	2 42.3	26 08.7	24 37.1
16 Sa	15 42 29	24 12 06	25 12 28	2♎02 26	8R 45.0	12 29.6	1 55.4	4 23.7	10 04.9	0♎05.5	19 46.0	2 45.0	26 11.0	24 38.5
17 Su	15 46 26	25 12 37	8♎59 35	16 03 55	8 45.0	14 04.9	3 07.9	4 59.9	10 29.6	0 15.4	19 42.6	2 47.7	26 13.2	24 39.8
18 M	15 50 22	26 13 10	23 15 14	0♏33 09	8 43.0	15 40.2	4 20.3	5 36.2	10 54.2	0 25.1	19 39.2	2 50.4	26 15.5	24 41.0
19 Tu	15 54 19	27 13 45	7♏57 04	15 26 10	8 38.8	17 15.7	5 32.7	6 12.4	11 18.9	0 34.8	19 35.9	2 53.0	26 17.7	24 42.3
20 W	15 58 15	28 14 22	22 59 26	0♐35 41	8 32.5	18 51.1	6 45.0	6 48.6	11 43.5	0 44.3	19 32.7	2 55.5	26 20.0	24 43.5
21 Th	16 02 12	29 15 00	8♐13 34	15 51 43	8 24.7	20 26.5	7 57.3	7 24.7	12 08.2	0 53.8	19 29.6	2 58.0	26 22.2	24 44.7
22 F	16 06 08	0♐15 39	23 28 44	1♑03 16	8 16.5	22 01.8	9 09.6	8 00.8	12 32.9	1 03.1	19 26.6	3 00.5	26 24.5	24 45.9
23 Sa	16 10 05	1 16 20	8♑34 05	16 00 09	8 08.9	23 37.0	10 21.8	8 36.9	12 57.6	1 12.4	19 23.7	3 02.9	26 26.7	24 47.0
24 Su	16 14 01	2 17 01	23 20 35	0♒34 46	8 02.9	25 12.2	11 33.9	9 12.9	13 22.4	1 21.5	19 20.8	3 05.3	26 29.0	24 48.1
25 M	16 17 58	3 17 44	7♒42 16	14 42 53	7 59.0	26 47.2	12 46.0	9 48.9	13 47.1	1 30.5	19 18.1	3 07.7	26 31.2	24 49.2
26 Tu	16 21 55	4 18 28	21 36 35	28 23 32	7D 57.3	28 22.1	13 58.1	10 24.8	14 11.8	1 39.4	19 15.4	3 10.0	26 33.5	24 50.2
27 W	16 25 51	5 19 12	5♓03 59	11♓38 19	7 57.3	29 56.9	15 10.0	11 00.7	14 36.5	1 48.2	19 12.8	3 12.2	26 35.7	24 51.2
28 Th	16 29 48	6 19 58	18 07 00	24 30 30	7 58.2	1♐31.6	16 22.0	11 36.5	15 01.3	1 56.9	19 10.4	3 14.4	26 38.0	24 52.2
29 F	16 33 44	7 20 45	0♈49 22	7♈04 06	7R 58.7	3 06.2	17 33.8	12 12.4	15 26.0	2 05.4	19 08.0	3 16.6	26 40.2	24 53.2
30 Sa	16 37 41	8 21 32	13 15 15	19 23 16	7 58.0	4 40.7	18 45.6	12 48.1	15 50.7	2 13.8	19 05.7	3 18.7	26 42.4	24 54.1

December 1968 LONGITUDE

Day	Sid.Time	☉	0 hr ☽	Noon ☽	True ☊	☿	♀	♂	⚳	♃	♄	♅	♆	♇
1 Su	16 41 37	9♐22 21	25♈28 39	1♉31 49	7♈55.1	6♐15.1	19♑57.3	13♎23.9	16♐15.5	2♎22.1	19♈03.5	3♎20.8	26♏44.6	24♍55.0
2 M	16 45 34	10 23 10	7♉33 09	13 32 59	7R 49.5	7 49.5	21 09.0	13 59.6	16 40.2	2 30.3	19R 01.4	3 22.8	26 46.8	24 55.8
3 Tu	16 49 30	11 24 01	19 31 38	25 29 21	7 41.1	9 23.8	22 20.6	14 35.2	17 05.0	2 38.4	18 59.4	3 24.8	26 49.0	24 56.7
4 W	16 53 27	12 24 53	1♊26 23	7♊22 56	7 30.2	10 58.1	23 32.1	15 10.9	17 29.7	2 46.3	18 57.6	3 26.7	26 51.2	24 57.5
5 Th	16 57 24	13 25 45	13 19 10	19 15 16	7 17.6	12 32.3	24 43.5	15 46.4	17 54.4	2 54.1	18 55.8	3 28.5	26 53.4	24 58.2
6 F	17 01 20	14 26 39	25 11 23	1♋07 41	7 04.1	14 06.5	25 54.9	16 22.0	18 19.2	3 01.8	18 54.1	3 30.4	26 55.6	24 59.0
7 Sa	17 05 17	15 27 34	7♋04 21	13 01 34	6 51.0	15 40.7	27 06.1	16 57.5	18 43.9	3 09.3	18 52.5	3 32.2	26 57.8	24 59.7
8 Su	17 09 13	16 28 30	18 59 34	24 58 36	6 39.4	17 15.0	28 17.3	17 32.9	19 08.7	3 16.7	18 51.1	3 33.9	26 59.9	25 00.3
9 M	17 13 10	17 29 27	0♌58 57	7♌00 59	6 30.0	18 49.2	29 28.4	18 08.3	19 33.4	3 24.0	18 49.7	3 35.6	27 02.1	25 01.0
10 Tu	17 17 06	18 30 26	13 05 02	19 11 33	6 23.5	20 23.6	0♒39.5	18 43.7	19 58.1	3 31.1	18 48.4	3 37.2	27 04.2	25 01.6
11 W	17 21 03	19 31 25	25 21 00	1♍33 52	6 19.8	21 58.0	1 50.4	19 19.0	20 22.8	3 38.1	18 47.3	3 38.7	27 06.4	25 02.1
12 Th	17 25 00	20 32 25	7♍50 40	14 11 59	6D 18.3	23 32.4	3 01.2	19 54.3	20 47.5	3 44.9	18 46.2	3 40.3	27 08.5	25 02.7
13 F	17 28 56	21 33 26	20 38 19	27 10 15	6R 18.2	25 07.0	4 12.0	20 29.5	21 12.2	3 51.6	18 45.3	3 41.7	27 10.6	25 03.2
14 Sa	17 32 53	22 34 29	3♎48 16	10♎32 49	6 18.3	26 41.7	5 22.6	21 04.7	21 36.9	3 58.2	18 44.5	3 43.1	27 12.7	25 03.6
15 Su	17 36 49	23 35 32	17 24 14	24 22 48	6 17.2	28 16.5	6 33.2	21 39.8	22 01.6	4 04.6	18 43.7	3 44.5	27 14.7	25 04.1
16 M	17 40 46	24 36 36	1♏28 33	8♏41 25	6 13.9	29 51.4	7 43.7	22 14.9	22 26.3	4 10.8	18 43.1	3 45.8	27 16.8	25 04.5
17 Tu	17 44 42	25 37 42	16 01 03	23 26 56	6 07.9	1♑26.4	8 54.0	22 49.9	22 51.0	4 16.9	18 42.6	3 47.1	27 18.8	25 04.8
18 W	17 48 39	26 38 48	0♐58 15	8♐33 58	5 59.0	3 01.6	10 04.3	23 24.9	23 15.6	4 22.9	18 42.2	3 48.3	27 20.9	25 05.2
19 Th	17 52 35	27 39 55	16 12 52	23 53 33	5 48.1	4 36.9	11 14.4	23 59.8	23 40.3	4 28.7	18 42.0	3 49.4	27 22.9	25 05.5
20 F	17 56 32	28 41 03	1♑34 31	9♑14 14	5 36.3	6 12.4	12 24.4	24 34.6	24 04.9	4 34.3	18D 41.8	3 50.5	27 24.9	25 05.7
21 Sa	18 00 29	29 42 11	16 51 14	24 24 09	5 25.1	7 48.0	13 34.3	25 09.4	24 29.5	4 39.8	18 41.7	3 51.5	27 26.9	25 06.0
22 Su	18 04 25	0♑43 19	1♒51 48	9♒13 14	5 15.7	9 23.7	14 44.1	25 44.2	24 54.1	4 45.1	18 41.8	3 52.5	27 28.9	25 06.2
23 M	18 08 22	1 44 27	16 27 43	23 34 49	5 08.9	10 59.5	15 53.7	26 18.9	25 18.7	4 50.3	18 42.0	3 53.4	27 30.8	25 06.3
24 Tu	18 12 18	2 45 36	0♓34 16	7♓26 05	5 04.9	12 35.4	17 03.2	26 53.5	25 43.3	4 55.3	18 42.2	3 54.3	27 32.8	25 06.4
25 W	18 16 15	3 46 44	14 10 26	20 47 38	5 03.3	14 11.3	18 12.6	27 28.0	26 07.8	5 00.1	18 42.6	3 55.1	27 34.7	25 06.5
26 Th	18 20 11	4 47 53	27 18 09	3♈42 30	5 03.0	15 47.2	19 21.8	28 02.5	26 32.3	5 04.8	18 43.1	3 55.9	27 36.6	25 06.6
27 F	18 24 08	5 49 01	10♈01 18	16 15 09	5 02.8	17 23.2	20 30.9	28 36.9	26 56.8	5 09.2	18 43.7	3 56.6	27 38.5	25R 06.6
28 Sa	18 28 04	6 50 10	22 24 44	28 30 38	5 01.5	18 59.0	21 39.8	29 11.3	27 21.3	5 13.6	18 44.5	3 57.2	27 40.3	25 06.6
29 Su	18 32 01	7 51 18	4♉33 30	10♉33 55	4 58.1	20 34.6	22 48.5	29 45.6	27 45.7	5 17.7	18 45.3	3 57.8	27 42.2	25 06.6
30 M	18 35 58	8 52 27	16 32 25	22 29 32	4 51.8	22 10.1	23 57.1	0♏19.8	28 10.2	5 21.7	18 46.2	3 58.3	27 44.0	25 06.5
31 Tu	18 39 54	9 53 35	28 25 41	4♊21 17	4 42.4	23 45.1	25 05.5	0 53.9	28 34.6	5 25.5	18 47.3	3 58.8	27 45.8	25 06.4

Astro Data

	Dy Hr Mn
☽0N	1 19:59
♂0S	14 11:43
☽0S	16 11:03
☽0N	29 1:02
♃0S	4 6:56
♃☌♅	11 14:59
☽0S	13 19:04
♄ D	21 11:38
☽0N	26 6:38
♇ R	27 17:05

Planet Ingress

		Dy Hr Mn
☿	♏	8 11:00
♂	♎	9 6:10
♀	♑	14 21:48
♃	♎	15 22:44
☉	♐	22 5:49
☿	♐	27 12:47
♀	♒	9 22:40
☿	♑	16 14:11
☉	♑	21 19:00
♂	♏	29 22:07

Last Aspect / ☽ Ingress (November)

Last Aspect Dy Hr Mn			☽ Ingress	Dy Hr Mn
1 11:59	♃	☍	♈	1 16:51
3 13:36	☿	☍	♉	4 3:01
6 11:30	♃	△	♊	6 14:48
9 3:18	♂	□	♋	9 3:26
11 14:17	♃	⚹	♌	11 15:45
13 23:49	♀	△	♍	14 1:55
16 1:42	♆	⚹	♎	16 8:26
17 18:05	♄	☍	♏	18 11:06
20 8:01	☉	☌	♐	20 11:04
22 2:01	♇	□	♑	22 10:19
24 5:10	♆	⚹	♒	24 11:02
26 11:57	☿	□	♓	26 14:52
28 16:02	♆	△	♈	28 22:26

Last Aspect / ☽ Ingress (December)

Last Aspect Dy Hr Mn			☽ Ingress	Dy Hr Mn
30 11:26	♄	☌	♉	1 8:58
3 14:41	♆	☍	♊	3 21:06
5 23:34	♇	□	♋	6 9:43
8 19:21	♀	☍	♌	8 22:02
11 3:23	♆	□	♍	11 8:59
13 12:01	♆	⚹	♎	13 17:08
15 19:26	☿	⚹	♏	15 21:31
17 18:12	♆	☌	♐	17 22:28
19 18:19	☉	☌	♑	19 21:32
21 16:54	♆	⚹	♒	21 20:59
23 18:45	♆	□	♓	23 23:01
26 0:33	♆	△	♈	26 5:02
28 13:24	♂	☍	♉	28 14:57
30 22:37	♆	☍	♊	31 3:11

☽ Phases & Eclipses

Dy Hr Mn		
5 4:25	○	12♉49
13 8:53	☾	21♌03
20 8:01	●	28♏04
26 23:30	☽	4♓48
4 23:07	○	12♊53
13 0:49	☾	21♍05
19 18:19	●	27♐56
26 14:14	☽	4♈54

Astro Data

1 November 1968
Julian Day # 25142
SVP 5♓41'45"
GC 26♐24.2 ⚴ 14♏11.5
Eris 11♈28.0R ⚵ 27♏00.3
⚷ 29♓30.6R ⚶ 24♈25.8R
☽ Mean ☊ 7♈48.9

1 December 1968
Julian Day # 25172
SVP 5♓41'41"
GC 26♐24.3 ⚴ 27♏22.5
Eris 11♈14.8R ⚵ 7♐15.4
⚷ 28♓53.3R ⚶ 20♈06.9R
☽ Mean ☊ 6♈13.6

LONGITUDE — January 1969

Day	Sid.Time	☉	0 hr ☽	Noon ☽	True ☊	☿	♀	♂	⚳	♃	♄	♅	♆	♇
1 W	18 43 51	10♑54 44	10♊16 42	16♊12 15	4♈30.3	25♑19.7	26♒13.7	1♏28.0	28♐58.9	5♎29.1	18♈48.5	3♎59.2	27♏47.6	25♍06.2
2 Th	18 47 47	11 55 52	22 08 10	28 04 40	4R 16.3	26 53.6	27 21.7	2 02.1	29 23.3	5 32.6	18 49.7	3 59.6	27 49.3	25R 06.1
3 F	18 51 44	12 57 01	4♋01 58	10♋00 12	4 01.3	28 26.8	28 29.5	2 36.0	29 47.6	5 35.9	18 51.1	3 59.9	27 51.0	25 05.9
4 Sa	18 55 40	13 58 09	15 59 30	22 00 01	3 46.7	29 58.8	29 37.2	3 09.9	0♑11.9	5 39.0	18 52.6	4 00.1	27 52.8	25 05.6
5 Su	18 59 37	14 59 17	28 01 50	4♌05 08	3 33.5	1♒29.6	0♓44.6	3 43.7	0 36.2	5 41.9	18 54.2	4 00.3	27 54.4	25 05.3
6 M	19 03 33	16 00 25	10♌10 01	16 16 42	3 22.9	2 58.9	1 51.8	4 17.5	1 00.4	5 44.6	18 55.9	4 00.4	27 56.1	25 05.0
7 Tu	19 07 30	17 01 33	22 25 21	28 36 13	3 15.2	4 26.2	2 58.8	4 51.1	1 24.6	5 47.2	18 57.7	4R 00.5	27 57.7	25 04.7
8 W	19 11 27	18 02 42	4♍49 35	11♍05 46	3 10.6	5 51.2	4 05.6	5 24.7	1 48.8	5 49.6	18 59.7	4 00.5	27 59.4	25 04.3
9 Th	19 15 23	19 03 50	17 25 07	23 48 01	3D 08.6	7 13.4	5 12.2	5 58.2	2 12.9	5 51.8	19 01.7	4 00.5	28 01.0	25 03.9
10 F	19 19 20	20 04 58	0♎14 54	6♎46 11	3 08.3	8 32.3	6 18.5	6 31.7	2 37.0	5 53.8	19 03.8	4 00.4	28 02.5	25 03.5
11 Sa	19 23 16	21 06 06	13 22 16	20 03 35	3R 08.6	9 47.3	7 24.5	7 05.0	3 01.1	5 55.6	19 06.0	4 00.2	28 04.1	25 03.0
12 Su	19 27 13	22 07 14	26 50 29	3♏43 15	3 08.1	10 57.8	8 30.4	7 38.3	3 25.1	5 57.2	19 08.4	4 00.0	28 05.6	25 02.5
13 M	19 31 09	23 08 22	10♏42 05	17 47 02	3 05.7	12 03.1	9 35.9	8 11.5	3 49.1	5 58.7	19 10.8	3 59.8	28 07.1	25 02.0
14 Tu	19 35 06	24 09 30	24 58 01	2♐14 45	3 00.8	13 02.3	10 41.3	8 44.6	4 13.1	5 59.9	19 13.4	3 59.4	28 08.5	25 01.4
15 W	19 39 03	25 10 38	9♐36 46	17 03 23	2 53.4	13 54.6	11 46.3	9 17.6	4 37.0	6 01.0	19 16.0	3 59.1	28 10.0	25 00.8
16 Th	19 42 59	26 11 46	24 33 42	2♑06 39	2 43.9	14 39.1	12 51.1	9 50.5	5 00.9	6 01.9	19 18.8	3 58.6	28 11.4	25 00.2
17 F	19 46 56	27 12 53	9♑41 02	17 15 32	2 33.4	15 15.0	13 55.5	10 23.4	5 24.7	6 02.5	19 21.7	3 58.2	28 12.8	24 59.5
18 Sa	19 50 52	28 14 00	24 48 48	2♒19 31	2 23.2	15 41.4	14 59.7	10 56.1	5 48.5	6 03.0	19 24.6	3 57.6	28 14.1	24 58.8
19 Su	19 54 49	29 15 06	9♒46 27	17 08 32	2 14.6	15R 57.5	16 03.6	11 28.7	6 12.3	6 03.3	19 27.7	3 57.0	28 15.4	24 58.1
20 M	19 58 45	0♒16 12	24 24 51	1♓34 42	2 08.3	16 02.6	17 07.1	12 01.2	6 36.0	6R 03.4	19 30.9	3 56.4	28 16.7	24 57.4
21 Tu	20 02 42	1 17 16	8♓37 36	15 33 18	2 04.6	15 56.4	18 10.3	12 33.7	6 59.6	6 03.3	19 34.1	3 55.7	28 18.0	24 56.6
22 W	20 06 38	2 18 20	22 21 44	29 03 00	2D 03.3	15 38.5	19 13.2	13 06.0	7 23.3	6 03.0	19 37.5	3 54.9	28 19.2	24 55.8
23 Th	20 10 35	3 19 22	5♈37 22	12♈05 15	2 03.6	15 09.1	20 15.7	13 38.2	7 46.8	6 02.6	19 40.9	3 54.1	28 20.5	24 55.0
24 F	20 14 32	4 20 24	18 27 06	24 43 31	2R 04.5	14 28.8	21 17.8	14 10.3	8 10.3	6 01.9	19 44.5	3 53.2	28 21.6	24 54.1
25 Sa	20 18 28	5 21 24	0♉55 05	7♉02 27	2 04.9	13 38.3	22 19.5	14 42.3	8 33.8	6 01.0	19 48.1	3 52.3	28 22.8	24 53.2
26 Su	20 22 25	6 22 24	13 06 16	19 07 11	2 03.8	12 39.1	23 20.8	15 14.2	8 57.2	6 00.0	19 51.9	3 51.3	28 23.9	24 52.3
27 M	20 26 21	7 23 22	25 05 49	1♊02 48	2 00.6	11 32.9	24 21.7	15 45.9	9 20.5	5 58.7	19 55.7	3 50.3	28 25.0	24 51.3
28 Tu	20 30 18	8 24 19	6♊58 42	12 54 02	1 55.1	10 21.5	25 22.2	16 17.6	9 43.8	5 57.3	19 59.6	3 49.2	28 26.0	24 50.4
29 W	20 34 14	9 25 15	18 49 20	24 45 02	1 47.5	9 07.2	26 22.2	16 49.1	10 07.1	5 55.7	20 03.6	3 48.1	28 27.1	24 49.4
30 Th	20 38 11	10 26 10	0♋41 31	6♋39 08	1 38.2	7 52.2	27 21.8	17 20.5	10 30.3	5 53.9	20 07.7	3 46.9	28 28.1	24 48.3
31 F	20 42 07	11 27 04	12 38 12	18 38 58	1 28.1	6 38.7	28 20.9	17 51.8	10 53.4	5 51.9	20 11.9	3 45.7	28 29.0	24 47.3

LONGITUDE — February 1969

Day	Sid.Time	☉	0 hr ☽	Noon ☽	True ☊	☿	♀	♂	⚳	♃	♄	♅	♆	♇
1 Sa	20 46 04	12♒27 56	24♋41 37	0♌46 20	1♈18.2	5♒28.5	29♓19.4	18♏23.0	11♑16.5	5♎49.7	20♈16.2	3♎44.5	28♏30.0	24♍46.2
2 Su	20 50 01	13 28 48	6♌53 15	13 02 27	1R 09.3	4R 23.3	0♈17.5	18 54.1	11 39.5	5R 47.3	20 20.6	3R 43.1	28 30.9	24R 45.1
3 M	20 53 57	14 29 38	19 14 02	25 28 04	1 02.2	3 24.4	1 15.0	19 25.0	12 02.4	5 44.8	20 25.0	3 41.8	28 31.7	24 44.0
4 Tu	20 57 54	15 30 27	1♍44 37	8♍03 45	0 57.3	2 32.9	2 12.0	19 55.8	12 25.3	5 42.1	20 29.5	3 40.4	28 32.6	24 42.9
5 W	21 01 50	16 31 15	14 25 34	20 50 08	0D 54.8	1 49.3	3 08.4	20 26.5	12 48.1	5 39.1	20 34.2	3 38.9	28 33.4	24 41.7
6 Th	21 05 47	17 32 02	27 17 36	3♎48 05	0 54.3	1 14.1	4 04.2	20 57.0	13 10.9	5 36.0	20 38.9	3 37.4	28 34.1	24 40.5
7 F	21 09 43	18 32 48	10♎21 45	16 58 46	0 55.2	0 47.1	4 59.4	21 27.4	13 33.6	5 32.8	20 43.6	3 35.8	28 34.9	24 39.3
8 Sa	21 13 40	19 33 33	23 39 20	0♏23 37	0 56.7	0 28.5	5 54.0	21 57.6	13 56.2	5 29.3	20 48.5	3 34.2	28 35.6	24 38.0
9 Su	21 17 36	20 34 17	7♏11 46	14 03 57	0R 57.8	0D 17.8	6 47.9	22 27.8	14 18.8	5 25.7	20 53.4	3 32.6	28 36.2	24 36.8
10 M	21 21 33	21 35 00	21 00 14	28 00 39	0 57.8	0 14.9	7 41.2	22 57.7	14 41.3	5 21.8	20 58.5	3 30.9	28 36.9	24 35.5
11 Tu	21 25 30	22 35 43	5♐05 08	12♐13 30	0 56.2	0 19.1	8 33.7	23 27.5	15 03.7	5 17.9	21 03.6	3 29.2	28 37.5	24 34.2
12 W	21 29 26	23 36 24	19 25 29	26 40 40	0 52.9	0 30.2	9 25.6	23 57.2	15 26.1	5 13.7	21 08.7	3 27.4	28 38.1	24 32.9
13 Th	21 33 23	24 37 04	3♑58 30	11♑18 20	0 48.1	0 47.6	10 16.7	24 26.7	15 48.4	5 09.4	21 14.0	3 25.6	28 38.6	24 31.6
14 F	21 37 19	25 37 43	18 39 23	26 00 48	0 42.7	1 10.8	11 07.0	24 56.0	16 10.6	5 04.9	21 19.3	3 23.8	28 39.1	24 30.2
15 Sa	21 41 16	26 38 20	3♒21 38	10♒40 59	0 37.2	1 39.4	11 56.5	25 25.1	16 32.7	5 00.3	21 24.7	3 21.9	28 39.6	24 28.8
16 Su	21 45 12	27 38 56	17 57 53	25 11 28	0 32.6	2 13.1	12 45.1	25 54.1	16 54.7	4 55.5	21 30.2	3 20.0	28 40.0	24 27.4
17 M	21 49 09	28 39 30	2♓20 58	9♓25 41	0 29.4	2 51.3	13 32.9	26 22.9	17 16.7	4 50.5	21 35.7	3 18.0	28 40.4	24 26.0
18 Tu	21 53 05	29 40 03	16 25 05	23 18 46	0D 27.8	3 33.8	14 19.8	26 51.5	17 38.6	4 45.4	21 41.3	3 16.0	28 40.8	24 24.6
19 W	21 57 02	0♓40 34	0♈06 29	6♈48 07	0 27.8	4 20.1	15 05.7	27 19.9	18 00.4	4 40.1	21 47.0	3 14.0	28 41.1	24 23.2
20 Th	22 00 59	1 41 04	13 23 44	19 53 27	0 28.9	5 10.1	15 50.6	27 48.2	18 22.1	4 34.7	21 52.8	3 11.9	28 41.4	24 21.7
21 F	22 04 55	2 41 31	26 17 34	2♉36 26	0 30.6	6 03.4	16 34.5	28 16.2	18 43.8	4 29.1	21 58.6	3 09.8	28 41.7	24 20.2
22 Sa	22 08 52	3 41 57	8♉50 30	15 00 15	0 32.3	6 59.7	17 17.3	28 44.1	19 05.3	4 23.4	22 04.4	3 07.7	28 41.9	24 18.8
23 Su	22 12 48	4 42 21	21 06 14	27 09 02	0R 33.4	7 58.9	17 59.0	29 11.7	19 26.8	4 17.6	22 10.4	3 05.5	28 42.1	24 17.3
24 M	22 16 45	5 42 43	3♊09 16	9♊07 31	0 33.6	9 00.7	18 39.6	29 39.2	19 48.1	4 11.6	22 16.4	3 03.3	28 42.3	24 15.8
25 Tu	22 20 41	6 43 03	15 04 24	21 00 31	0 32.6	10 05.0	19 18.9	0♐06.4	20 09.4	4 05.5	22 22.4	3 01.1	28 42.4	24 14.2
26 W	22 24 38	7 43 21	26 56 27	2♋52 46	0 30.6	11 11.6	19 57.0	0 33.4	20 30.6	3 59.3	22 28.6	2 58.9	28 42.5	24 12.7
27 Th	22 28 34	8 43 37	8♋49 59	14 48 35	0 27.8	12 20.3	20 33.8	1 00.2	20 51.7	3 52.9	22 34.7	2 56.6	28 42.6	24 11.2
28 F	22 32 31	9 43 51	20 49 03	26 51 45	0 24.5	13 31.0	21 09.2	1 26.8	21 12.7	3 46.5	22 41.0	2 54.3	28R 42.6	24 09.6

Astro Data

	Dy Hr Mn
♅ R	8 7:28
☽ 0S	10 0:31
☿ R	20 10:56
♃ R	20 12:29
☽ 0N	22 14:22
♀ 0N	31 5:32
☽ 0S	6 5:17
☿ D	10 9:38
☽ 0N	18 23:57
♆ R	28 20:20

Planet Ingress

	Dy Hr Mn
⚳ ♑	4 0:14
☿ ♒	4 12:18
♀ ♓	4 20:07
☉ ♒	20 5:38
♀ ♈	2 4:45
☉ ♓	18 19:55
♂ ♐	25 6:21

Last Aspect / ☽ Ingress (January)

Last Aspect Dy Hr Mn		☽ Ingress	Dy Hr Mn
2 10:24	♀ △	♋	2 15:53
4 23:44	♆ △	♌	5 3:55
7 10:45	♆ □	♍	7 14:42
9 19:53	♆ ⚹	♎	9 23:32
11 14:00	☉ □	♏	12 5:32
14 5:14	♆ ☌	♐	14 8:19
16 0:43	♇ □	♑	16 8:39
18 5:27	♆ ⚹	♒	18 8:17
20 6:27	♆ □	♓	20 9:20
22 10:41	♆ △	♈	22 13:43
24 2:24	♄ ☌	♉	24 22:13
27 6:41	♆ ☍	♊	27 9:53
29 15:34	♀ □	♋	29 22:36

Last Aspect / ☽ Ingress (February)

Last Aspect Dy Hr Mn		☽ Ingress	Dy Hr Mn
1 8:54	♀ △	♌	1 10:29
3 17:52	♆ □	♍	3 20:40
6 2:21	♆ ⚹	♎	6 5:00
7 18:47	♄ ☍	♏	8 11:18
10 13:02	♆ ☌	♐	10 15:23
12 8:29	♇ □	♑	12 17:28
14 16:19	♆ ⚹	♒	14 18:30
16 17:49	♆ □	♓	16 20:03
18 21:28	♆ △	♈	18 23:48
20 15:44	♄ ☌	♉	21 7:02
23 16:14	♂ ☍	♊	23 17:41
25 18:31	♇ □	♋	26 6:11
28 15:39	♆ △	♌	28 18:12

☽ Phases & Eclipses

Dy Hr Mn	
3 18:28	○ 13♋13
11 14:00	☾ 21♎11
18 4:59	● 27♑56
25 8:23	☽ 5♉12
2 12:56	○ 13♌31
10 0:08	☾ 21♏05
16 16:25	● 27♒50
24 4:30	☽ 5♊24

Astro Data

1 January 1969
Julian Day # 25203
SVP 5♓41'34"
GC 26♐24.4 ⚴ 10♐37.3
Eris 11♈10.4 ⚵ 17♐53.9
⚷ 29♓04.9 ⚶ 22♈20.9
☽ Mean ☊ 4♈35.2

1 February 1969
Julian Day # 25234
SVP 5♓41'28"
GC 26♐24.5 ⚴ 22♐54.2
Eris 11♈16.8 ⚵ 28♐00.6
⚷ 0♈05.6 ⚶ 29♈46.9
☽ Mean ☊ 2♈56.7

March 1969 LONGITUDE

Day	Sid.Time	☉	0 hr ☽	Noon ☽	True ☊	☿	♀	♂	⚳	♃	♄	♅	♆	♇
1 Sa	22 36 28	10♓44 03	2♌57 03	9♌05 16	0♈21.1	14♒43.7	21♈43.2	1♐53.2	21♑33.6	3♎39.9	22♈47.3	2♎52.0	28♏42.6	24♍08.1
2 Su	22 40 24	11 44 14	15 16 39	21 31 22	0R 18.1	15 58.2	22 15.8	2 19.3	21 54.3	3R 33.2	22 53.6	2R 49.6	28R 42.6	24R 06.5
3 M	22 44 21	12 44 22	27 49 35	4♍11 23	0 15.8	17 14.4	22 46.8	2 45.3	22 15.0	3 26.4	23 00.0	2 47.2	28 42.5	24 04.9
4 Tu	22 48 17	13 44 28	10♍36 48	17 05 49	0D 14.5	18 32.2	23 16.2	3 10.9	22 35.6	3 19.6	23 06.5	2 44.8	28 42.4	24 03.3
5 W	22 52 14	14 44 33	23 38 24	0♎14 27	0 14.1	19 51.6	23 44.0	3 36.3	22 56.1	3 12.6	23 13.0	2 42.4	28 42.2	24 01.7
6 Th	22 56 10	15 44 35	6♎53 53	13 36 34	0 14.4	21 12.6	24 10.1	4 01.5	23 16.5	3 05.5	23 19.5	2 40.0	28 42.1	24 00.1
7 F	23 00 07	16 44 36	20 22 20	27 11 02	0 15.3	22 35.0	24 34.5	4 26.4	23 36.8	2 58.4	23 26.1	2 37.5	28 41.9	23 58.5
8 Sa	23 04 03	17 44 36	4♏02 30	10♏56 34	0 16.4	23 58.8	24 57.0	4 51.1	23 56.9	2 51.2	23 32.8	2 35.0	28 41.6	23 56.9
9 Su	23 08 00	18 44 33	17 53 03	24 51 46	0 17.4	25 24.0	25 17.7	5 15.5	24 17.0	2 43.9	23 39.5	2 32.5	28 41.3	23 55.3
10 M	23 11 57	19 44 30	1♐52 32	8♐55 09	0R 18.0	26 50.5	25 36.4	5 39.6	24 37.0	2 36.5	23 46.2	2 30.0	28 41.0	23 53.7
11 Tu	23 15 53	20 44 24	15 59 24	23 05 02	0 18.2	28 18.4	25 53.2	6 03.4	24 56.8	2 29.1	23 53.0	2 27.5	28 40.7	23 52.1
12 W	23 19 50	21 44 17	0♑11 47	7♑19 20	0 17.9	29 47.6	26 07.9	6 27.0	25 16.5	2 21.6	23 59.9	2 25.0	28 40.3	23 50.5
13 Th	23 23 46	22 44 09	14 27 23	21 35 31	0 17.3	1♓18.0	26 20.5	6 50.2	25 36.1	2 14.1	24 06.8	2 22.4	28 39.9	23 48.9
14 F	23 27 43	23 43 58	28 43 22	5♒50 29	0 16.5	2 49.8	26 30.9	7 13.2	25 55.6	2 06.5	24 13.7	2 19.9	28 39.5	23 47.2
15 Sa	23 31 39	24 43 46	12♒56 24	20 00 39	0 15.8	4 22.7	26 39.0	7 35.8	26 15.0	1 58.8	24 20.6	2 17.3	28 39.0	23 45.6
16 Su	23 35 36	25 43 32	27 02 45	4♓02 15	0 15.2	5 57.0	26 44.9	7 58.1	26 34.2	1 51.2	24 27.6	2 14.7	28 38.5	23 44.0
17 M	23 39 32	26 43 16	10♓58 41	17 51 39	0D 14.9	7 32.4	26R 48.5	8 20.0	26 53.3	1 43.5	24 34.7	2 12.1	28 38.0	23 42.4
18 Tu	23 43 29	27 42 59	24 40 48	1♈25 50	0 14.9	9 09.1	26 49.7	8 41.6	27 12.3	1 35.7	24 41.8	2 09.5	28 37.5	23 40.7
19 W	23 47 26	28 42 39	8♈06 30	14 42 40	0 14.9	10 47.1	26 48.5	9 02.9	27 31.1	1 28.0	24 48.9	2 06.9	28 36.9	23 39.1
20 Th	23 51 22	29 42 17	21 14 14	27 41 13	0R 15.0	12 26.3	26 44.8	9 23.8	27 49.9	1 20.2	24 56.0	2 04.3	28 36.2	23 37.5
21 F	23 55 19	0♈41 53	4♉03 42	10♉21 50	0 15.0	14 06.8	26 38.6	9 44.4	28 08.4	1 12.4	25 03.2	2 01.7	28 35.6	23 35.9
22 Sa	23 59 15	1 41 26	16 35 52	22 46 07	0 14.9	15 48.6	26 29.9	10 04.6	28 26.9	1 04.6	25 10.4	1 59.1	28 34.9	23 34.3
23 Su	0 03 12	2 40 58	28 52 55	4♊56 41	0 14.6	17 31.6	26 18.8	10 24.4	28 45.2	0 56.9	25 17.6	1 56.5	28 34.2	23 32.7
24 M	0 07 08	3 40 27	10♊57 55	16 57 06	0 14.4	19 15.9	26 05.1	10 43.8	29 03.3	0 49.1	25 24.9	1 53.9	28 33.5	23 31.1
25 Tu	0 11 05	4 39 54	22 54 46	28 51 29	0D 14.2	21 01.5	25 49.0	11 02.8	29 21.4	0 41.4	25 32.2	1 51.3	28 32.7	23 29.5
26 W	0 15 01	5 39 19	4♋47 50	10♋44 24	0 14.2	22 48.4	25 30.5	11 21.5	29 39.2	0 33.6	25 39.5	1 48.7	28 31.9	23 27.9
27 Th	0 18 58	6 38 41	16 41 45	22 40 30	0 14.5	24 36.7	25 09.5	11 39.7	29 56.9	0 25.9	25 46.9	1 46.1	28 31.1	23 26.4
28 F	0 22 54	7 38 01	28 41 11	4♌44 22	0 15.0	26 26.3	24 46.3	11 57.5	0♒14.5	0 18.3	25 54.3	1 43.5	28 30.2	23 24.8
29 Sa	0 26 51	8 37 19	10♌50 34	17 00 14	0 15.8	28 17.2	24 20.9	12 14.9	0 31.9	0 10.6	26 01.7	1 40.9	28 29.3	23 23.2
30 Su	0 30 48	9 36 35	23 13 49	29 31 40	0 16.7	0♈09.5	23 53.4	12 31.9	0 49.2	0 03.0	26 09.1	1 38.3	28 28.4	23 21.7
31 M	0 34 44	10 35 48	5♍54 06	12♍21 21	0 17.5	2 03.1	23 24.0	12 48.4	1 06.3	29♍55.5	26 16.5	1 35.8	28 27.5	23 20.1

April 1969 LONGITUDE

Day	Sid.Time	☉	0 hr ☽	Noon ☽	True ☊	☿	♀	♂	⚳	♃	♄	♅	♆	♇
1 Tu	0 38 41	11♈34 59	18♍53 32	25♍30 44	0♈18.0	3♈58.1	22♈52.8	13♐04.4	1♒23.3	29♍48.0	26♈24.0	1♎33.2	28♏26.5	23♍18.6
2 W	0 42 37	12 34 08	2♎12 53	8♎59 52	0R 17.9	5 54.4	22R 19.9	13 20.0	1 40.0	29R 40.5	26 31.5	1R 30.7	28R 25.5	23R 17.1
3 Th	0 46 34	13 33 14	15 51 26	22 47 16	0 17.1	7 52.1	21 45.7	13 35.1	1 56.7	29 33.2	26 39.0	1 28.1	28 24.5	23 15.6
4 F	0 50 30	14 32 19	29 46 58	6♏50 02	0 15.7	9 51.0	21 10.2	13 49.8	2 13.1	29 25.8	26 46.5	1 25.6	28 23.5	23 14.1
5 Sa	0 54 27	15 31 22	13♏55 57	21 04 08	0 13.8	11 51.2	20 33.8	14 03.9	2 29.4	29 18.6	26 54.0	1 23.1	28 22.4	23 12.6
6 Su	0 58 23	16 30 24	28 13 58	5♐24 52	0 11.8	13 52.5	19 56.6	14 17.6	2 45.6	29 11.4	27 01.5	1 20.6	28 21.3	23 11.1
7 M	1 02 20	17 29 23	12♐36 14	19 47 31	0 09.9	15 55.0	19 19.0	14 30.7	3 01.5	29 04.3	27 09.1	1 18.1	28 20.2	23 09.7
8 Tu	1 06 17	18 28 21	26 58 11	4♑07 49	0 08.6	17 58.4	18 41.1	14 43.3	3 17.3	28 57.3	27 16.7	1 15.7	28 19.1	23 08.3
9 W	1 10 13	19 27 17	11♑15 59	18 22 22	0D 08.1	20 02.8	18 03.3	14 55.3	3 32.9	28 50.4	27 24.3	1 13.2	28 17.9	23 06.8
10 Th	1 14 10	20 26 11	25 26 40	2♒28 41	0 08.4	22 07.9	17 25.7	15 06.8	3 48.3	28 43.6	27 31.9	1 10.8	28 16.8	23 05.4
11 F	1 18 06	21 25 04	9♒28 14	16 25 11	0 09.5	24 13.6	16 48.7	15 17.7	4 03.5	28 36.9	27 39.5	1 08.4	28 15.6	23 04.0
12 Sa	1 22 03	22 23 54	23 19 26	0♓10 52	0 10.9	26 19.7	16 12.4	15 28.0	4 18.6	28 30.3	27 47.1	1 06.0	28 14.3	23 02.7
13 Su	1 25 59	23 22 43	6♓59 26	13 45 04	0 12.3	28 25.9	15 37.1	15 37.8	4 33.4	28 23.8	27 54.7	1 03.7	28 13.1	23 01.3
14 M	1 29 56	24 21 30	20 27 42	27 07 16	0R 13.0	0♉32.0	15 03.0	15 46.9	4 48.1	28 17.4	28 02.3	1 01.3	28 11.8	23 00.0
15 Tu	1 33 52	25 20 16	3♈43 42	10♈16 58	0 12.7	2 37.7	14 30.4	15 55.4	5 02.6	28 11.1	28 10.0	0 59.0	28 10.6	22 58.6
16 W	1 37 49	26 18 59	16 47 00	23 13 47	0 11.0	4 42.7	13 59.3	16 03.2	5 16.8	28 04.9	28 17.6	0 56.7	28 09.2	22 57.3
17 Th	1 41 46	27 17 40	29 37 15	5♉57 27	0 08.0	6 46.7	13 29.9	16 10.5	5 30.9	27 58.9	28 25.3	0 54.5	28 07.9	22 56.0
18 F	1 45 42	28 16 20	12♉14 24	18 28 11	0 03.9	8 49.3	13 02.5	16 17.1	5 44.7	27 53.0	28 32.9	0 52.2	28 06.6	22 54.8
19 Sa	1 49 39	29 14 58	24 38 54	0♊46 42	29♓58.9	10 50.3	12 37.0	16 23.0	5 58.3	27 47.2	28 40.5	0 50.0	28 05.2	22 53.5
20 Su	1 53 35	0♉13 33	6♊51 48	12 54 28	29 53.7	12 49.2	12 13.8	16 28.2	6 11.8	27 41.6	28 48.2	0 47.9	28 03.8	22 52.3
21 M	1 57 32	1 12 06	18 55 00	24 53 45	29 48.9	14 45.9	11 52.7	16 32.8	6 25.0	27 36.1	28 55.8	0 45.7	28 02.5	22 51.1
22 Tu	2 01 28	2 10 38	0♋51 08	6♋47 36	29 45.0	16 39.9	11 33.9	16 36.7	6 38.0	27 30.7	29 03.5	0 43.6	28 01.0	22 49.9
23 W	2 05 25	3 09 07	12 43 37	18 39 44	29 42.4	18 30.9	11 17.5	16 39.9	6 50.7	27 25.5	29 11.1	0 41.5	27 59.6	22 48.8
24 Th	2 09 21	4 07 34	24 36 30	0♌34 31	29D 41.3	20 18.8	11 03.5	16 42.4	7 03.3	27 20.4	29 18.7	0 39.5	27 58.2	22 47.6
25 F	2 13 18	5 05 59	6♌34 21	12 36 38	29 41.5	22 03.4	10 51.9	16 44.2	7 15.6	27 15.5	29 26.3	0 37.5	27 56.7	22 46.5
26 Sa	2 17 15	6 04 22	18 41 59	24 50 59	29 42.7	23 44.3	10 42.7	16R 45.2	7 27.7	27 10.7	29 33.9	0 35.5	27 55.3	22 45.4
27 Su	2 21 11	7 02 42	1♍04 12	7♍22 12	29 44.3	25 21.4	10 36.0	16 45.6	7 39.5	27 06.1	29 41.5	0 33.6	27 53.8	22 44.4
28 M	2 25 08	8 01 01	13 45 28	20 14 24	29R 45.6	26 54.6	10 31.7	16 45.2	7 51.2	27 01.7	29 49.1	0 31.7	27 52.3	22 43.3
29 Tu	2 29 04	8 59 17	26 49 21	3♎30 33	29 45.9	28 23.7	10D 29.8	16 44.1	8 02.5	26 57.4	29 56.7	0 29.8	27 50.8	22 42.3
30 W	2 33 01	9 57 32	10♎18 04	17 11 54	29 44.6	29 48.7	10 30.2	16 42.2	8 13.7	26 53.3	0♉04.3	0 28.0	27 49.2	22 41.3

Astro Data Dy Hr Mn	Planet Ingress Dy Hr Mn	Last Aspect Dy Hr Mn	☽ Ingress Dy Hr Mn	Last Aspect Dy Hr Mn	☽ Ingress Dy Hr Mn	☽ Phases & Eclipses Dy Hr Mn
♃0N 2 7:26	☿ ♓ 12 15:19	3 1:40 ♆ □	♍ 3 4:07	1 19:37 ♃ ☌	♎ 1 20:03	4 5:17 ○ 13♍28
☽0S 5 11:38	☉ ♈ 20 19:08	5 9:13 ♆ ✶	♎ 5 11:34	3 18:42 ♄ ☍	♏ 4 0:22	11 7:44 ☾ 20♐34
♄⚻♇ 11 9:19	⚳ ♒ 27 16:09	7 7:17 ♀ ☍	♏ 7 16:56	6 1:41 ♃ ✶	♐ 6 2:57	18 4:51 ● 27♓25
♃☌♅ 11 19:40	☿ ♈ 30 9:59	9 18:33 ♆ ☌	♐ 9 20:48	8 3:24 ♃ □	♑ 8 5:04	18 4:54:18 ● A 00'26"
☽0N 18 9:32	♃ ♍R 30 21:36	11 21:50 ☿ ✶	♑ 11 23:40	10 5:39 ♃ △	♒ 10 7:46	26 0:48 ☽ 5♋12
♀R 18 11:49		13 23:54 ♆ ✶	♒ 14 2:09	12 8:36 ♆ □	♓ 12 11:41	
☉0N 20 19:08	☿ ♉ 14 5:55	16 2:44 ♆ □	♓ 16 5:04	14 14:06 ♃ ☍	♈ 14 17:13	2 18:45 ○ 12♎51
♅0N 26 23:21	☊ ♓R 19 6:53	18 7:00 ♆ △	♈ 18 9:27	16 21:36 ♄ ☌	♉ 17 0:43	2 18:32 ● A 0.703
☿0N 1 13:27	☉ ♉ 20 6:27	20 10:15 ♀ ☌	♉ 20 16:20	19 6:44 ♆ ☍	♊ 19 10:28	9 13:58 ☾ 19♑32
☽0S 1 20:09	♄ ♉ 29 22:23	22 23:24 ♆ ☍	♊ 23 2:12	21 20:13 ♄ ✶	♋ 21 22:17	16 18:16 ● 26♈34
☽0N 14 17:17	☿ ♊ 30 15:18	25 6:00 ♀ ✶	♋ 25 14:18	24 9:26 ♄ □	♌ 24 10:51	24 19:45 ☽ 4♌26
♄⚻♆ 15 13:33		27 23:39 ♆ △	♌ 28 2:37	26 21:12 ♄ △	♍ 26 21:57	
♃⚻♄ 15 13:55		30 10:00 ♆ □	♍ 30 12:54	29 1:52 ♆ ✶	♎ 29 5:44	
♃✶♆ 15 14:34	☽0S29 5:39					
♂R 27 11:24	♀ D29 19:20					

Astro Data

1 March 1969
Julian Day # 25262
SVP 5♓41'25"
GC 26♐24.5 ⚴ 2♑28.8
Eris 11♈30.5 ⚵ 6♑05.2
⚷ 1♈30.5 ⚶ 9♉09.5
☽ Mean ☊ 1♈27.7

1 April 1969
Julian Day # 25293
SVP 5♓41'21"
GC 26♐24.6 ⚴ 10♑14.2
Eris 11♈50.7 ⚵ 12♑56.3
⚷ 3♈19.0 ⚶ 21♉10.5
☽ Mean ☊ 29♓49.2

LONGITUDE — May 1969

Day	Sid.Time	☉	0 hr ☽	Noon ☽	True ☊	☿	♀	♂	⚳	♃	♄	♅	♆	♇
1 Th	2 36 57	10♉55 44	24♎11 50	1♏17 32	29♓41.5	1♊09.3	10♈33.0	16♐39.6	8♒24.5	26♍49.3	0♉11.8	0♎26.2	27♏47.7	22♍40.4
2 F	2 40 54	11 53 55	8♏28 29	15 43 59	29R36.6	2 25.6	10 38.1	16R36.3	8 35.2	26R45.5	0 19.4	0R24.4	27R46.2	22R39.4
3 Sa	2 44 50	12 52 05	23 03 16	0♐25 23	29 30.4	3 37.4	10 45.4	16 32.2	8 45.6	26 41.9	0 26.9	0 22.7	27 44.6	22 38.5
4 Su	2 48 47	13 50 12	7♐49 21	15 14 07	29 23.7	4 44.7	10 55.0	16 27.3	8 55.7	26 38.4	0 34.4	0 21.1	27 43.1	22 37.6
5 M	2 52 44	14 48 19	22 38 42	0♑02 06	29 17.4	5 47.4	11 06.7	16 21.7	9 05.6	26 35.1	0 41.9	0 19.4	27 41.5	22 36.8
6 Tu	2 56 40	15 46 23	7♑23 25	14 41 53	29 12.4	6 45.4	11 20.4	16 15.3	9 15.2	26 32.0	0 49.4	0 17.8	27 39.9	22 35.9
7 W	3 00 37	16 44 27	21 56 52	29 07 53	29 09.1	7 38.6	11 36.2	16 08.2	9 24.6	26 29.1	0 56.9	0 16.3	27 38.3	22 35.1
8 Th	3 04 33	17 42 29	6♒14 33	13♒16 42	29D07.8	8 27.1	11 53.9	16 00.2	9 33.6	26 26.3	1 04.3	0 14.8	27 36.8	22 34.3
9 F	3 08 30	18 40 29	20 14 13	27 07 07	29 07.9	9 10.7	12 13.5	15 51.6	9 42.4	26 23.7	1 11.8	0 13.3	27 35.2	22 33.6
10 Sa	3 12 26	19 38 29	3♓55 31	10♓39 34	29 08.9	9 49.4	12 35.0	15 42.1	9 51.0	26 21.3	1 19.2	0 11.9	27 33.6	22 32.9
11 Su	3 16 23	20 36 26	17 19 28	23 55 28	29R09.8	10 23.2	12 58.2	15 32.0	9 59.2	26 19.0	1 26.5	0 10.6	27 31.9	22 32.2
12 M	3 20 19	21 34 23	0♈27 48	6♈56 42	29 09.6	10 51.9	13 23.0	15 21.0	10 07.2	26 16.9	1 33.9	0 09.2	27 30.3	22 31.5
13 Tu	3 24 16	22 32 18	13 22 22	19 45 03	29 07.6	11 15.7	13 49.5	15 09.4	10 14.8	26 15.0	1 41.2	0 07.9	27 28.7	22 30.9
14 W	3 28 13	23 30 12	26 04 53	2♉22 03	29 03.2	11 34.4	14 17.6	14 57.1	10 22.2	26 13.3	1 48.5	0 06.7	27 27.1	22 30.3
15 Th	3 32 09	24 28 05	8♉36 40	14 48 53	28 56.3	11 48.1	14 47.2	14 44.0	10 29.3	26 11.8	1 55.8	0 05.5	27 25.5	22 29.7
16 F	3 36 06	25 25 56	20 58 46	27 06 27	28 47.3	11 56.9	15 18.2	14 30.3	10 36.0	26 10.5	2 03.1	0 04.4	27 23.8	22 29.1
17 Sa	3 40 02	26 23 46	3♊12 01	9♊15 36	28 36.8	12R00.7	15 50.7	14 16.0	10 42.5	26 09.3	2 10.3	0 03.3	27 22.2	22 28.6
18 Su	3 43 59	27 21 34	15 17 19	21 17 22	28 25.7	11 59.7	16 24.4	14 01.0	10 48.7	26 08.3	2 17.5	0 02.3	27 20.6	22 28.1
19 M	3 47 55	28 19 21	27 15 54	3♋13 12	28 15.1	11 54.1	16 59.5	13 45.4	10 54.5	26 07.5	2 24.6	0 01.3	27 19.0	22 27.7
20 Tu	3 51 52	29 17 07	9♋09 30	15 05 10	28 05.9	11 44.0	17 35.7	13 29.2	11 00.1	26 06.9	2 31.8	0 00.3	27 17.3	22 27.2
21 W	3 55 48	0♊14 50	21 00 32	26 56 02	27 58.6	11 29.7	18 13.2	13 12.5	11 05.3	26 06.5	2 38.9	29♍59.4	27 15.7	22 26.8
22 Th	3 59 45	1 12 33	2♌52 09	8♌49 22	27 53.8	11 11.4	18 51.8	12 55.3	11 10.2	26D06.3	2 45.9	29 58.6	27 14.1	22 26.5
23 F	4 03 42	2 10 13	14 48 15	20 49 23	27 51.3	10 49.5	19 31.5	12 37.6	11 14.8	26 06.2	2 52.9	29 57.8	27 12.5	22 26.1
24 Sa	4 07 38	3 07 52	26 53 22	3♍00 50	27D50.6	10 24.4	20 12.2	12 19.4	11 19.0	26 06.3	2 59.9	29 57.1	27 10.8	22 25.8
25 Su	4 11 35	4 05 30	9♍12 25	15 28 45	27R51.0	9 56.5	20 54.0	12 00.9	11 23.0	26 06.6	3 06.9	29 56.4	27 09.2	22 25.5
26 M	4 15 31	5 03 06	21 50 27	28 18 04	27 51.3	9 26.3	21 36.7	11 42.0	11 26.6	26 07.1	3 13.8	29 55.7	27 07.6	22 25.3
27 Tu	4 19 28	6 00 41	4♎52 07	11♎32 59	27 50.6	8 54.4	22 20.4	11 22.7	11 29.8	26 07.8	3 20.6	29 55.1	27 06.0	22 25.1
28 W	4 23 24	6 58 14	18 20 59	25 16 14	27 47.9	8 21.2	23 05.0	11 03.2	11 32.8	26 08.6	3 27.4	29 54.6	27 04.4	22 24.9
29 Th	4 27 21	7 55 46	2♏18 45	9♏28 16	27 42.7	7 47.5	23 50.4	10 43.4	11 35.4	26 09.6	3 34.2	29 54.1	27 02.8	22 24.8
30 F	4 31 17	8 53 16	16 44 23	24 06 27	27 35.2	7 13.7	24 36.7	10 23.4	11 37.7	26 10.8	3 41.0	29 53.7	27 01.2	22 24.6
31 Sa	4 35 14	9 50 46	1♐33 34	9♐04 43	27 25.8	6 40.5	25 23.8	10 03.2	11 39.6	26 12.2	3 47.7	29 53.3	26 59.7	22 24.6

LONGITUDE — June 1969

Day	Sid.Time	☉	0 hr ☽	Noon ☽	True ☊	☿	♀	♂	⚳	♃	♄	♅	♆	♇
1 Su	4 39 11	10♊48 15	16♐38 40	24♐14 07	27♓15.6	6♊08.4	26♈11.7	9♐42.9	11♒41.2	26♍13.7	3♉54.3	29♍53.0	26♏58.1	22♍24.5
2 M	4 43 07	11 45 42	1♑49 43	9♑24 07	27R05.8	5R38.0	27 00.3	9R22.5	11 42.4	26 15.5	4 00.9	29R52.7	26R56.5	22D24.5
3 Tu	4 47 04	12 43 09	16 56 05	24 24 30	26 57.5	5 09.8	27 49.7	9 02.1	11 43.3	26 17.4	4 07.5	29 52.5	26 55.0	22 24.5
4 W	4 51 00	13 40 35	1♒48 24	9♒07 04	26 51.5	4 44.2	28 39.8	8 41.7	11 43.8	26 19.5	4 14.0	29 52.3	26 53.4	22 24.6
5 Th	4 54 57	14 38 01	16 19 56	23 26 42	26 48.1	4 21.6	29 30.5	8 21.3	11R44.0	26 21.7	4 20.5	29 52.2	26 51.9	22 24.6
6 F	4 58 53	15 35 25	0♓27 13	7♓21 29	26D46.7	4 02.5	0♉21.9	8 01.0	11 43.8	26 24.1	4 26.9	29D52.1	26 50.4	22 24.7
7 Sa	5 02 50	16 32 49	14 09 41	20 52 04	26R46.6	3 47.1	1 13.9	7 40.8	11 43.3	26 26.7	4 33.3	29 52.1	26 48.9	22 24.9
8 Su	5 06 47	17 30 13	27 28 58	4♈00 47	26 46.5	3 35.7	2 06.5	7 20.8	11 42.4	26 29.5	4 39.6	29 52.2	26 47.4	22 25.0
9 M	5 10 43	18 27 36	10♈27 58	16 50 54	26 45.3	3 28.4	2 59.7	7 01.0	11 41.2	26 32.4	4 45.8	29 52.3	26 45.9	22 25.2
10 Tu	5 14 40	19 24 58	23 10 04	29 25 49	26 41.9	3D25.5	3 53.4	6 41.5	11 39.6	26 35.5	4 52.0	29 52.4	26 44.4	22 25.5
11 W	5 18 36	20 22 20	5♉38 34	11♉48 39	26 35.9	3 27.0	4 47.7	6 22.4	11 37.6	26 38.8	4 58.2	29 52.6	26 42.9	22 25.7
12 Th	5 22 33	21 19 41	17 56 23	24 02 03	26 26.9	3 33.1	5 42.5	6 03.6	11 35.3	26 42.2	5 04.3	29 52.9	26 41.5	22 26.0
13 F	5 26 29	22 17 02	0♊05 51	6♊08 02	26 15.5	3 43.7	6 37.8	5 45.2	11 32.6	26 45.8	5 10.3	29 53.2	26 40.0	22 26.4
14 Sa	5 30 26	23 14 22	12 08 46	18 08 14	26 02.2	3 58.8	7 33.5	5 27.2	11 29.5	26 49.5	5 16.3	29 53.5	26 38.6	22 26.7
15 Su	5 34 22	24 11 42	24 06 34	0♋03 56	25 48.2	4 18.5	8 29.7	5 09.7	11 26.1	26 53.5	5 22.2	29 53.9	26 37.2	22 27.1
16 M	5 38 19	25 09 01	6♋00 29	11 56 26	25 34.7	4 42.7	9 26.4	4 52.8	11 22.3	26 57.6	5 28.1	29 54.4	26 35.8	22 27.6
17 Tu	5 42 16	26 06 19	17 51 56	23 47 16	25 22.6	5 11.4	10 23.4	4 36.4	11 18.2	27 01.8	5 33.9	29 54.9	26 34.5	22 28.0
18 W	5 46 12	27 03 37	29 42 40	5♌38 26	25 12.9	5 44.5	11 20.9	4 20.7	11 13.7	27 06.2	5 39.7	29 55.5	26 33.1	22 28.5
19 Th	5 50 09	28 00 54	11♌34 57	17 32 36	25 05.9	6 21.9	12 18.8	4 05.5	11 08.9	27 10.8	5 45.3	29 56.1	26 31.8	22 29.0
20 F	5 54 05	28 58 10	23 31 50	29 33 07	25 01.7	7 03.6	13 17.1	3 51.0	11 03.7	27 15.5	5 50.9	29 56.8	26 30.5	22 29.6
21 Sa	5 58 02	29 55 26	5♍37 00	11♍44 03	24 59.9	7 49.5	14 15.7	3 37.2	10 58.2	27 20.4	5 56.5	29 57.5	26 29.2	22 30.2
22 Su	6 01 58	0♋52 40	17 54 50	24 09 58	24 59.5	8 39.5	15 14.7	3 24.1	10 52.3	27 25.4	6 02.0	29 58.3	26 27.9	22 30.8
23 M	6 05 55	1 49 54	0♎30 04	6♎55 43	24 59.4	9 33.6	16 14.1	3 11.7	10 46.1	27 30.6	6 07.4	29 59.2	26 26.6	22 31.4
24 Tu	6 09 51	2 47 08	13 27 29	20 05 51	24 58.6	10 31.7	17 13.7	3 00.1	10 39.5	27 35.9	6 12.7	0♎00.1	26 25.4	22 32.1
25 W	6 13 48	3 44 21	26 51 16	3♏43 59	24 56.0	11 33.8	18 13.8	2 49.3	10 32.6	27 41.4	6 18.0	0 01.0	26 24.2	22 32.8
26 Th	6 17 45	4 41 33	10♏44 09	17 51 45	24 51.1	12 39.7	19 14.1	2 39.2	10 25.4	27 47.0	6 23.2	0 02.0	26 23.0	22 33.5
27 F	6 21 41	5 38 45	25 06 32	2♐28 00	24 43.7	13 49.5	20 14.8	2 29.9	10 17.8	27 52.8	6 28.3	0 03.0	26 21.8	22 34.3
28 Sa	6 25 38	6 35 57	9♐55 27	17 27 57	24 34.3	15 03.1	21 15.7	2 21.5	10 10.0	27 58.7	6 33.4	0 04.1	26 20.6	22 35.1
29 Su	6 29 34	7 33 08	25 04 19	2♑43 17	24 24.0	16 20.5	22 17.0	2 13.8	10 01.8	28 04.7	6 38.4	0 05.3	26 19.5	22 35.9
30 M	6 33 31	8 30 20	10♑23 23	18 03 09	24 14.0	17 41.5	23 18.5	2 07.0	9 53.4	28 10.9	6 43.3	0 06.5	26 18.4	22 36.8

Astro Data

	Dy Hr Mn
♄⚻♅	3 1:05
☽0N	11 22:53
☿R	17 19:07
♃D	23 8:20
☽0S	26 14:27
♇D	2 14:00
⚳R	5 12:26
♅D	7 6:34
☽0N	8 3:37
☿D	10 15:48
♃⚹♆	12 8:35
☽0S	22 21:28

Planet Ingress

		Dy Hr Mn
♅	♍R	20 20:51
☉	♊	21 5:50
♀	♉	6 1:48
☉	♋	21 13:55
♅	♎	24 10:36

Last Aspect / ☽ Ingress

Last Aspect Dy Hr Mn			☽ Ingress	Dy Hr Mn
30 11:09	♂	⚹	♏	1 9:50
3 7:39	♆	☌	♐	3 11:19
5 6:25	♃	□	♑	5 11:57
7 9:30	♆	⚹	♒	7 13:28
9 12:49	♆	□	♓	9 17:04
11 18:36	♆	△	♈	11 23:09
13 3:29	♂	△	♉	14 7:28
16 12:34	♆	☍	♊	16 17:41
18 21:43	♃	□	♋	19 5:30
21 18:11	♅	⚹	♌	21 18:12
24 0:36	♆	□	♍	24 6:07
26 14:59	♅	☌	♎	26 15:07
28 8:01	♀	☍	♏	28 20:05
30 21:20	♅	⚹	♐	30 21:30

Last Aspect / ☽ Ingress

Last Aspect Dy Hr Mn			☽ Ingress	Dy Hr Mn
1 20:55	♅	□	♑	1 21:07
3 20:51	♅	△	♒	3 21:03
5 23:03	♀	⚹	♓	5 23:13
8 4:22	♅	☍	♈	8 4:36
9 15:18	☉	⚹	♉	10 13:06
12 23:34	♅	△	♊	12 23:48
15 11:40	♅	□	♋	15 11:52
18 0:25	♅	⚹	♌	18 0:35
20 10:45	☉	⚹	♍	20 12:53
22 23:01	♅	☌	♎	22 23:03
23 17:14	☿	△	♏	25 5:31
27 4:29	♃	⚹	♐	27 8:00
29 4:40	♃	□	♑	29 7:44

☽ Phases & Eclipses

Dy Hr Mn		
2 5:13	○	11♏37
8 20:12	☾	18♒02
16 8:26	●	25♉17
24 12:15	☽	3♍08
31 13:18	○	9♐54
7 3:39	☾	16♓13
14 23:09	●	23♊41
23 1:44	☽	1♎25
29 20:04	○	7♑52

Astro Data

1 May 1969
Julian Day # 25323
SVP 5♓41'18"
GC 26♐24.7 ⚴ 13♑10.6
Eris 12♈10.4 ⚵ 16♑11.7
⚷ 4♈58.2 ⚶ 3♊40.6
☽ Mean ☊ 28♓13.9

1 June 1969
Julian Day # 25354
SVP 5♓41'12"
GC 26♐24.7 ⚴ 9♑41.1R
Eris 12♈26.1 ⚵ 14♑37.1R
⚷ 6♈15.4 ⚶ 17♊00.6
☽ Mean ☊ 26♓35.4

July 1969 LONGITUDE

Day	Sid.Time	☉	0 hr ☽	Noon ☽	True ☊	☿	♀	♂	⚳	♃	♄	♅	♆	♇
1 Tu	6 37 27	9♋27 31	25♑41 10	3♒16 04	24♓05.5	19♊06.2	24♉20.3	2♐00.9	9♒44.6	28♍17.2	6♉48.1	0♎07.7	26♏17.3	22♍37.7
2 W	6 41 24	10 24 42	10♒46 39	18 11 57	23R59.2	20 34.5	25 22.5	1R55.7	9R35.5	28 23.7	6 52.9	0 09.0	26R16.3	22 38.6
3 Th	6 45 21	11 21 53	25 31 11	2♓43 47	23 55.5	22 06.4	26 24.8	1 51.4	9 26.1	28 30.3	6 57.6	0 10.4	26 15.2	22 39.6
4 F	6 49 17	12 19 04	9♓49 26	16 48 02	23D54.0	23 41.8	27 27.5	1 47.8	9 16.5	28 37.0	7 02.2	0 11.8	26 14.2	22 40.5
5 Sa	6 53 14	13 16 16	23 39 37	0♈24 24	23 53.9	25 20.6	28 30.3	1 45.1	9 06.6	28 43.9	7 06.8	0 13.2	26 13.2	22 41.5
6 Su	6 57 10	14 13 28	7♈02 43	13 34 59	23R54.2	27 02.7	29 33.5	1 43.2	8 56.4	28 50.9	7 11.2	0 14.7	26 12.3	22 42.6
7 M	7 01 07	15 10 40	20 01 40	26 23 16	23 53.7	28 48.1	0♊36.8	1D42.2	8 45.9	28 58.0	7 15.6	0 16.3	26 11.3	22 43.6
8 Tu	7 05 03	16 07 53	2♉40 20	8♉53 22	23 51.4	0♋36.7	1 40.4	1 41.9	8 35.2	29 05.2	7 19.9	0 17.9	26 10.4	22 44.7
9 W	7 09 00	17 05 06	15 02 55	21 09 26	23 46.7	2 28.2	2 44.3	1 42.6	8 24.3	29 12.6	7 24.1	0 19.5	26 09.5	22 45.8
10 Th	7 12 56	18 02 19	27 13 23	3♊15 13	23 39.6	4 22.6	3 48.3	1 44.0	8 13.1	29 20.1	7 28.2	0 21.2	26 08.7	22 47.0
11 F	7 16 53	18 59 33	9♊15 17	15 13 57	23 30.1	6 19.5	4 52.6	1 46.3	8 01.7	29 27.8	7 32.3	0 22.9	26 07.8	22 48.2
12 Sa	7 20 50	19 56 47	21 11 31	27 08 16	23 19.1	8 18.9	5 57.0	1 49.4	7 50.1	29 35.5	7 36.2	0 24.7	26 07.0	22 49.4
13 Su	7 24 46	20 54 02	3♋04 26	9♋00 15	23 07.3	10 20.4	7 01.7	1 53.3	7 38.3	29 43.4	7 40.1	0 26.5	26 06.2	22 50.6
14 M	7 28 43	21 51 17	14 55 54	20 51 36	22 55.9	12 23.7	8 06.5	1 58.0	7 26.3	29 51.4	7 43.9	0 28.4	26 05.5	22 51.9
15 Tu	7 32 39	22 48 32	26 47 32	2♌43 53	22 45.8	14 28.7	9 11.6	2 03.6	7 14.1	29 59.5	7 47.6	0 30.3	26 04.8	22 53.1
16 W	7 36 36	23 45 48	8♌40 53	14 38 44	22 37.7	16 34.9	10 16.8	2 09.9	7 01.8	0♎07.7	7 51.2	0 32.3	26 04.1	22 54.5
17 Th	7 40 32	24 43 04	20 37 43	26 38 05	22 32.1	18 42.1	11 22.2	2 17.0	6 49.4	0 16.1	7 54.8	0 34.3	26 03.4	22 55.8
18 F	7 44 29	25 40 20	2♍40 10	8♍44 20	22 28.9	20 49.9	12 27.8	2 24.9	6 36.7	0 24.5	7 58.2	0 36.4	26 02.8	22 57.1
19 Sa	7 48 25	26 37 36	14 50 57	21 00 27	22D27.9	22 58.1	13 33.5	2 33.6	6 24.0	0 33.1	8 01.5	0 38.5	26 02.1	22 58.5
20 Su	7 52 22	27 34 52	27 13 17	3♎29 56	22 28.3	25 06.3	14 39.5	2 43.0	6 11.2	0 41.8	8 04.8	0 40.6	26 01.6	22 59.9
21 M	7 56 19	28 32 09	9♎50 55	16 16 41	22R29.3	27 14.4	15 45.5	2 53.1	5 58.2	0 50.5	8 07.9	0 42.8	26 01.0	23 01.4
22 Tu	8 00 15	29 29 26	22 47 45	29 24 33	22 29.8	29 21.9	16 51.8	3 04.0	5 45.2	0 59.4	8 11.0	0 45.1	26 00.5	23 02.8
23 W	8 04 12	0♌26 44	6♏07 30	12♏56 53	22 29.0	1♌28.8	17 58.2	3 15.6	5 32.2	1 08.4	8 14.0	0 47.3	26 00.0	23 04.3
24 Th	8 08 08	1 24 02	19 52 55	26 55 41	22 26.5	3 34.8	19 04.7	3 28.0	5 19.0	1 17.5	8 16.9	0 49.7	25 59.5	23 05.8
25 F	8 12 05	2 21 20	4♐05 05	11♐20 50	22 22.0	5 39.8	20 11.4	3 41.0	5 05.9	1 26.7	8 19.6	0 52.0	25 59.1	23 07.4
26 Sa	8 16 01	3 18 38	18 42 26	26 09 13	22 15.9	7 43.6	21 18.3	3 54.7	4 52.7	1 36.0	8 22.3	0 54.4	25 58.7	23 08.9
27 Su	8 19 58	4 15 58	3♑40 17	11♑14 34	22 09.0	9 46.1	22 25.3	4 09.0	4 39.4	1 45.4	8 24.9	0 56.9	25 58.4	23 10.5
28 M	8 23 54	5 13 17	18 50 51	26 27 50	22 02.1	11 47.3	23 32.5	4 24.0	4 26.2	1 54.9	8 27.4	0 59.4	25 58.0	23 12.1
29 Tu	8 27 51	6 10 38	4♒04 11	11♒38 34	21 56.3	13 46.9	24 39.8	4 39.7	4 13.0	2 04.5	8 29.8	1 01.9	25 57.7	23 13.7
30 W	8 31 48	7 07 59	19 09 45	26 36 39	21 52.1	15 45.1	25 47.2	4 55.9	3 59.9	2 14.2	8 32.1	1 04.5	25 57.4	23 15.4
31 Th	8 35 44	8 05 21	3♓58 18	11♓13 59	21D49.9	17 41.7	26 54.8	5 12.8	3 46.7	2 24.0	8 34.3	1 07.0	25 57.2	23 17.1

August 1969 LONGITUDE

Day	Sid.Time	☉	0 hr ☽	Noon ☽	True ☊	☿	♀	♂	⚳	♃	♄	♅	♆	♇
1 F	8 39 41	9♌02 44	18♓23 10	25♓25 30	21♓49.5	19♌36.7	28♊02.6	5♐30.3	3♒33.7	2♎33.8	8♉36.4	1♎09.7	25♏57.0	23♍18.7
2 Sa	8 43 37	10 00 08	2♈20 51	9♈09 14	21 50.4	21 30.2	29 10.4	5 48.4	3R20.7	2 43.8	8 38.4	1 12.4	25R56.8	23 20.4
3 Su	8 47 34	10 57 33	15 50 50	22 25 55	21 51.8	23 22.0	0♋18.4	6 07.0	3 07.7	2 53.8	8 40.3	1 15.1	25 56.7	23 22.2
4 M	8 51 30	11 55 00	28 54 53	5♉18 12	21R52.8	25 12.3	1 26.6	6 26.3	2 54.9	3 04.0	8 42.1	1 17.8	25 56.5	23 23.9
5 Tu	8 55 27	12 52 28	11♉36 21	17 49 54	21 52.9	27 00.9	2 34.9	6 46.0	2 42.2	3 14.2	8 43.8	1 20.6	25 56.4	23 25.7
6 W	8 59 23	13 49 57	23 59 24	0♊05 25	21 51.5	28 48.0	3 43.3	7 06.4	2 29.5	3 24.5	8 45.4	1 23.4	25 56.4	23 27.5
7 Th	9 03 20	14 47 27	6♊08 28	12 09 06	21 48.5	0♍33.5	4 51.8	7 27.3	2 17.1	3 34.9	8 46.9	1 26.3	25D56.4	23 29.3
8 F	9 07 17	15 44 59	18 07 50	24 05 07	21 44.0	2 17.4	6 00.4	7 48.7	2 04.7	3 45.4	8 48.3	1 29.2	25 56.4	23 31.1
9 Sa	9 11 13	16 42 32	0♋01 25	5♋57 07	21 38.4	3 59.7	7 09.2	8 10.7	1 52.6	3 55.9	8 49.6	1 32.1	25 56.4	23 33.0
10 Su	9 15 10	17 40 06	11 52 37	17 48 14	21 32.3	5 40.5	8 18.1	8 33.1	1 40.6	4 06.5	8 50.8	1 35.0	25 56.5	23 34.8
11 M	9 19 06	18 37 42	23 44 17	29 41 02	21 26.3	7 19.8	9 27.1	8 56.1	1 28.7	4 17.3	8 51.9	1 38.0	25 56.6	23 36.7
12 Tu	9 23 03	19 35 18	5♌38 45	11♌37 39	21 21.1	8 57.5	10 36.3	9 19.6	1 17.1	4 28.0	8 52.9	1 41.1	25 56.8	23 38.6
13 W	9 26 59	20 32 56	17 37 57	23 39 51	21 17.0	10 33.7	11 45.5	9 43.5	1 05.7	4 38.9	8 53.7	1 44.1	25 56.9	23 40.5
14 Th	9 30 56	21 30 35	29 43 33	5♍49 15	21 14.5	12 08.4	12 54.8	10 08.0	0 54.5	4 49.8	8 54.5	1 47.2	25 57.1	23 42.5
15 F	9 34 52	22 28 16	11♍57 09	18 07 28	21D13.5	13 41.5	14 04.3	10 32.9	0 43.5	5 00.9	8 55.2	1 50.3	25 57.4	23 44.4
16 Sa	9 38 49	23 25 57	24 20 26	0♎36 17	21 13.8	15 13.2	15 13.8	10 58.3	0 32.8	5 11.9	8 55.7	1 53.4	25 57.6	23 46.4
17 Su	9 42 46	24 23 39	6♎55 17	13 17 42	21 14.9	16 43.3	16 23.5	11 24.1	0 22.3	5 23.1	8 56.2	1 56.6	25 57.9	23 48.3
18 M	9 46 42	25 21 23	19 43 48	26 13 54	21 16.5	18 11.8	17 33.3	11 50.4	0 12.1	5 34.3	8 56.5	1 59.8	25 58.3	23 50.3
19 Tu	9 50 39	26 19 08	2♏48 15	9♏27 08	21 17.9	19 38.8	18 43.1	12 17.0	0 02.1	5 45.6	8 56.7	2 03.0	25 58.6	23 52.3
20 W	9 54 35	27 16 54	16 10 47	22 59 24	21R18.7	21 04.3	19 53.1	12 44.2	29♑52.5	5 56.9	8R56.9	2 06.3	25 59.0	23 54.4
21 Th	9 58 32	28 14 41	29 53 05	6♐51 53	21 18.5	22 28.1	21 03.1	13 11.7	29 43.1	6 08.4	8 56.9	2 09.6	25 59.5	23 56.4
22 F	10 02 28	29 12 29	13♐55 45	21 04 31	21 17.3	23 50.3	22 13.3	13 39.6	29 34.0	6 19.8	8 56.8	2 12.9	26 00.0	23 58.4
23 Sa	10 06 25	0♍10 18	28 17 51	5♑35 21	21 15.3	25 10.9	23 23.6	14 08.0	29 25.2	6 31.4	8 56.6	2 16.2	26 00.5	24 00.5
24 Su	10 10 21	1 08 09	12♑56 24	20 20 17	21 12.8	26 29.7	24 33.9	14 36.7	29 16.7	6 43.0	8 56.3	2 19.6	26 01.0	24 02.6
25 M	10 14 18	2 06 01	27 46 11	5♒13 10	21 10.3	27 46.9	25 44.4	15 05.8	29 08.5	6 54.6	8 55.9	2 23.0	26 01.5	24 04.7
26 Tu	10 18 15	3 03 54	12♒40 14	20 06 21	21 08.2	29 02.2	26 54.9	15 35.2	29 00.7	7 06.3	8 55.4	2 26.4	26 02.1	24 06.8
27 W	10 22 11	4 01 48	27 30 32	4♓51 47	21 06.8	0♎15.6	28 05.6	16 05.0	28 53.1	7 18.1	8 54.8	2 29.8	26 02.8	24 08.9
28 Th	10 26 08	4 59 44	12♓09 16	19 22 10	21D06.3	1 27.2	29 16.3	16 35.1	28 45.9	7 29.9	8 54.1	2 33.2	26 03.4	24 11.0
29 F	10 30 04	5 57 42	26 29 53	3♈31 54	21 06.6	2 36.7	0♌27.2	17 05.6	28 39.0	7 41.8	8 53.3	2 36.7	26 04.1	24 13.1
30 Sa	10 34 01	6 55 41	10♈27 53	17 17 40	21 07.4	3 44.1	1 38.1	17 36.5	28 32.4	7 53.7	8 52.4	2 40.2	26 04.8	24 15.2
31 Su	10 37 57	7 53 42	24 01 09	0♉38 28	21 08.5	4 49.3	2 49.2	18 07.6	28 26.2	8 05.7	8 51.3	2 43.7	26 05.6	24 17.4

Astro Data	Dy Hr Mn	Planet Ingress	Dy Hr Mn
☽ 0N	5 9:26	♀ ♊	6 22:04
♂ D	8 6:07	☿ ♋	8 3:58
♄□♇	17 23:49	♃ ♎	15 13:30
☽ 0S	20 2:52	☿ ♌	22 19:11
♃☌♅	20 7:57	☉ ♌	23 0:48
☽ 0N	1 17:28	♀ ♋	3 5:30
♃0S	2 12:39	☿ ♍	7 4:21
♆ D	7 14:55	⚳ ♑R	19 17:16
♅0S	11 1:31	☉ ♍	23 7:43
☽ 0S	16 7:56	☿ ♎	27 6:50
♄ R	21 5:44	♀ ♌	29 2:48
♄□♇	21 17:43		
☿0S	25 8:41		
☽ 0N	29 3:18		

Last Aspect Dy Hr Mn		☽ Ingress Dy Hr Mn	
1 4:03	♃ △	♒	1 6:49
3 1:14	♆ □	♓	3 7:26
5 8:59	♃ ☍	♈	5 11:16
7 17:21	☿ ⚹	♉	7 18:53
10 4:07	♃ △	♊	10 5:31
12 17:01	♃ □	♋	12 17:47
15 6:24	♃ ⚹	♌	15 6:29
17 10:51	♆ □	♍	17 18:42
19 23:45	☉ ⚹	♎	20 5:20
22 12:09	☉ □	♏	22 13:04
24 10:25	♆ ☌	♐	24 17:10
26 7:10	♇ □	♑	26 18:09
28 11:13	♆ ⚹	♒	28 17:34
30 10:57	♆ □	♓	30 17:30

Last Aspect Dy Hr Mn		☽ Ingress Dy Hr Mn	
1 16:55	♀ □	♈	1 19:54
3 14:00	☿ △	♉	4 2:02
6 9:01	☿ □	♊	6 11:49
8 10:51	♇ □	♋	8 23:57
11 4:27	♆ △	♌	11 12:38
13 16:32	♆ □	♍	14 0:32
16 3:07	♆ ⚹	♎	16 10:51
18 10:16	☉ ⚹	♏	18 18:54
20 20:03	☉ □	♐	21 0:12
23 2:28	☉ △	♑	23 2:49
24 22:54	☿ △	♒	25 3:36
26 21:37	♆ □	♓	27 4:03
28 23:16	♆ △	♈	29 5:57
30 12:35	♂ △	♉	31 10:50

☽ Phases & Eclipses Dy Hr Mn	
6 13:17	☾ 14♈17
14 14:11	● 21♋57
22 12:09	☽ 29♎30
29 2:45	○ 5♒49
5 1:38	☾ 12♉28
13 5:16	● 20♌17
20 20:03	☽ 27♏36
27 10:32	○ 3♓58
27 10:48	☍ A 0.013

Astro Data

1 July 1969
Julian Day # 25384
SVP 5♓41'06"
GC 26♐24.8 ⚴ 1♑34.6R
Eris 12♈33.3 ⚵ 8♑39.4R
⚷ 6♈50.9 ⚶ 0♋00.9
☽ Mean ☊ 25♓00.2

1 August 1969
Julian Day # 25415
SVP 5♓41'01"
GC 26♐24.9 ⚴ 25♐11.4R
Eris 12♈30.7R ⚵ 2♑23.0R
⚷ 6♈39.7R ⚶ 13♋17.9
☽ Mean ☊ 23♓21.7

LONGITUDE — September 1969

Day	Sid.Time	☉	0 hr ☽	Noon ☽	True ☊	☿	♀	♂	⚳	♃	♄	♅	♆	♇
1 M	10 41 54	8♍51 45	7♉09 46	13♉35 22	21♓09.6	5♎52.3	4♌00.3	18♐39.1	28♑20.4	8♎17.7	8♉50.2	2♎47.2	26♏06.4	24♍19.5
2 Tu	10 45 50	9 49 51	19 55 39	26 11 02	21 10.4	6 52.7	5 11.5	19 10.9	28R 14.8	8 29.8	8R 49.0	2 50.8	26 07.2	24 21.7
3 W	10 49 47	10 47 58	2♊22 02	8♊29 10	21R 10.7	7 50.6	6 22.8	19 43.0	28 09.6	8 41.9	8 47.7	2 54.4	26 08.0	24 23.8
4 Th	10 53 44	11 46 07	14 32 59	20 34 04	21 10.6	8 45.8	7 34.2	20 15.4	28 04.8	8 54.1	8 46.2	2 57.9	26 08.9	24 26.0
5 F	10 57 40	12 44 18	26 32 58	2♋30 15	21 10.1	9 38.0	8 45.7	20 48.1	28 00.3	9 06.3	8 44.7	3 01.5	26 09.8	24 28.2
6 Sa	11 01 37	13 42 31	8♋26 29	14 22 11	21 09.3	10 27.2	9 57.3	21 21.1	27 56.2	9 18.6	8 43.0	3 05.2	26 10.7	24 30.4
7 Su	11 05 33	14 40 46	20 17 52	26 14 00	21 08.4	11 13.0	11 09.0	21 54.4	27 52.4	9 30.9	8 41.3	3 08.8	26 11.7	24 32.6
8 M	11 09 30	15 39 03	2♌11 03	8♌09 24	21 07.6	11 55.3	12 20.7	22 28.0	27 49.0	9 43.2	8 39.5	3 12.4	26 12.7	24 34.8
9 Tu	11 13 26	16 37 21	14 09 27	20 11 31	21 06.9	12 33.7	13 32.5	23 01.8	27 46.0	9 55.6	8 37.5	3 16.1	26 13.7	24 37.0
10 W	11 17 23	17 35 42	26 15 55	2♍22 53	21 06.5	13 08.1	14 44.4	23 36.0	27 43.3	10 08.0	8 35.5	3 19.8	26 14.8	24 39.2
11 Th	11 21 19	18 34 05	8♍32 38	14 45 22	21D 06.4	13 38.2	15 56.4	24 10.4	27 41.0	10 20.5	8 33.3	3 23.5	26 15.9	24 41.4
12 F	11 25 16	19 32 29	21 01 13	27 20 17	21 06.4	14 03.5	17 08.5	24 45.1	27 39.0	10 33.0	8 31.1	3 27.2	26 17.0	24 43.6
13 Sa	11 29 13	20 30 55	3♎42 41	10♎08 27	21R 06.4	14 23.9	18 20.6	25 20.0	27 37.4	10 45.5	8 28.8	3 30.9	26 18.1	24 45.8
14 Su	11 33 09	21 29 23	16 37 37	23 10 14	21 06.4	14 38.9	19 32.9	25 55.2	27 36.2	10 58.1	8 26.3	3 34.6	26 19.3	24 48.0
15 M	11 37 06	22 27 53	29 46 16	6♏25 44	21 06.3	14 48.3	20 45.2	26 30.7	27 35.3	11 10.7	8 23.8	3 38.3	26 20.5	24 50.3
16 Tu	11 41 02	23 26 24	13♏08 36	19 54 49	21 06.1	14R 51.6	21 57.5	27 06.4	27D 34.8	11 23.4	8 21.2	3 42.1	26 21.7	24 52.5
17 W	11 44 59	24 24 57	26 44 21	3♐37 06	21 05.9	14 48.5	23 10.0	27 42.3	27 34.7	11 36.0	8 18.5	3 45.8	26 23.0	24 54.7
18 Th	11 48 55	25 23 32	10♐33 01	17 31 57	21D 05.7	14 38.8	24 22.5	28 18.5	27 34.9	11 48.7	8 15.7	3 49.6	26 24.3	24 56.9
19 F	11 52 52	26 22 09	24 33 46	1♑38 15	21 05.7	14 22.2	25 35.0	28 54.9	27 35.5	12 01.4	8 12.8	3 53.3	26 25.6	24 59.2
20 Sa	11 56 48	27 20 47	8♑45 11	15 54 16	21 05.9	13 58.6	26 47.7	29 31.5	27 36.4	12 14.2	8 09.9	3 57.1	26 26.9	25 01.4
21 Su	12 00 45	28 19 26	23 05 10	0♒17 27	21 06.4	13 27.8	28 00.4	0♑08.3	27 37.7	12 26.9	8 06.8	4 00.9	26 28.3	25 03.6
22 M	12 04 42	29 18 08	7♒30 41	14 44 21	21 07.1	12 49.9	29 13.2	0 45.4	27 39.3	12 39.7	8 03.7	4 04.6	26 29.7	25 05.8
23 Tu	12 08 38	0♎16 51	21 57 52	29 10 40	21 07.8	12 05.2	0♍26.0	1 22.6	27 41.3	12 52.5	8 00.5	4 08.4	26 31.1	25 08.0
24 W	12 12 35	1 15 36	6♓22 07	13♓31 36	21R 08.2	11 14.2	1 38.9	2 00.1	27 43.6	13 05.4	7 57.2	4 12.2	26 32.5	25 10.3
25 Th	12 16 31	2 14 22	20 38 29	27 42 13	21 08.2	10 17.6	2 51.9	2 37.7	27 46.3	13 18.2	7 53.8	4 16.0	26 34.0	25 12.5
26 F	12 20 28	3 13 11	4♈42 15	11♈38 07	21 07.7	9 16.2	4 05.0	3 15.5	27 49.3	13 31.1	7 50.3	4 19.8	26 35.5	25 14.7
27 Sa	12 24 24	4 12 01	18 29 25	25 15 52	21 06.4	8 11.2	5 18.1	3 53.6	27 52.6	13 44.0	7 46.8	4 23.6	26 37.0	25 16.9
28 Su	12 28 21	5 10 54	1♉57 13	8♉33 24	21 04.6	7 04.2	6 31.3	4 31.8	27 56.3	13 56.9	7 43.2	4 27.3	26 38.6	25 19.1
29 M	12 32 17	6 09 49	15 04 23	21 30 16	21 02.5	5 56.6	7 44.5	5 10.1	28 00.3	14 09.8	7 39.5	4 31.1	26 40.1	25 21.3
30 Tu	12 36 14	7 08 47	27 51 14	4♊07 32	21 00.4	4 50.3	8 57.8	5 48.7	28 04.6	14 22.8	7 35.8	4 34.9	26 41.7	25 23.5

LONGITUDE — October 1969

Day	Sid.Time	☉	0 hr ☽	Noon ☽	True ☊	☿	♀	♂	⚳	♃	♄	♅	♆	♇
1 W	12 40 10	8♎07 46	10♊19 32	16♊27 37	20♓58.6	3♎46.9	10♍11.2	6♑27.4	28♑09.3	14♎35.7	7♉32.0	4♎38.7	26♏43.3	25♍25.7
2 Th	12 44 07	9 06 48	22 32 17	28 34 00	20D 57.4	2R 48.3	11 24.6	7 06.4	28 14.2	14 48.7	7R 28.1	4 42.5	26 45.0	25 27.8
3 F	12 48 04	10 05 52	4♋33 21	10♋30 54	20 57.0	1 56.1	12 38.2	7 45.4	28 19.5	15 01.7	7 24.1	4 46.3	26 46.6	25 30.0
4 Sa	12 52 00	11 04 59	16 27 14	22 22 58	20 57.5	1 11.7	13 51.7	8 24.7	28 25.1	15 14.6	7 20.1	4 50.1	26 48.3	25 32.2
5 Su	12 55 57	12 04 07	28 18 42	4♌15 02	20 58.6	0 36.3	15 05.3	9 04.1	28 31.1	15 27.6	7 16.0	4 53.8	26 50.0	25 34.3
6 M	12 59 53	13 03 18	10♌12 33	16 11 48	21 00.2	0 10.7	16 19.0	9 43.7	28 37.3	15 40.6	7 11.9	4 57.6	26 51.8	25 36.5
7 Tu	13 03 50	14 02 32	22 17 37	28 17 37	21 01.9	29♍55.5	17 32.8	10 23.4	28 43.8	15 53.6	7 07.7	5 01.4	26 53.5	25 38.6
8 W	13 07 46	15 01 47	4♍25 07	10♍36 13	21R 03.1	29D 51.1	18 46.6	11 03.3	28 50.7	16 06.6	7 03.4	5 05.1	26 55.3	25 40.8
9 Th	13 11 43	16 01 05	16 51 15	23 10 29	21 03.5	29 57.4	20 00.4	11 43.3	28 57.8	16 19.7	6 59.1	5 08.9	26 57.1	25 42.9
10 F	13 15 39	17 00 24	29 34 07	6♎02 14	21 02.6	0♎14.2	21 14.3	12 23.5	29 05.3	16 32.7	6 54.8	5 12.6	26 58.9	25 45.0
11 Sa	13 19 36	17 59 46	12♎34 53	19 11 59	21 00.4	0 41.1	22 28.2	13 03.9	29 13.0	16 45.7	6 50.4	5 16.3	27 00.7	25 47.1
12 Su	13 23 33	18 59 10	25 53 25	2♏38 59	20 57.0	1 17.5	23 42.2	13 44.3	29 21.0	16 58.7	6 45.9	5 20.0	27 02.6	25 49.2
13 M	13 27 29	19 58 36	9♏28 21	16 21 13	20 52.7	2 02.8	24 56.3	14 25.0	29 29.4	17 11.7	6 41.4	5 23.7	27 04.5	25 51.2
14 Tu	13 31 26	20 58 04	23 17 11	0♐15 48	20 48.0	2 56.1	26 10.4	15 05.7	29 38.0	17 24.7	6 36.9	5 27.4	27 06.4	25 53.3
15 W	13 35 22	21 57 34	7♐16 40	14 19 19	20 43.7	3 56.7	27 24.5	15 46.6	29 46.8	17 37.7	6 32.3	5 31.1	27 08.3	25 55.4
16 Th	13 39 19	22 57 05	21 23 19	28 28 16	20 40.3	5 03.9	28 38.7	16 27.7	29 56.0	17 50.7	6 27.7	5 34.8	27 10.2	25 57.4
17 F	13 43 15	23 56 39	5♑33 47	12♑39 32	20D 38.3	6 16.7	29 52.9	17 08.8	0♒05.4	18 03.7	6 23.1	5 38.5	27 12.1	25 59.4
18 Sa	13 47 12	24 56 14	19 45 14	26 50 36	20 37.9	7 34.5	1♎07.2	17 50.1	0 15.1	18 16.7	6 18.4	5 42.1	27 14.1	26 01.5
19 Su	13 51 08	25 55 50	3♒55 24	10♒59 26	20 38.6	8 56.6	2 21.5	18 31.5	0 25.1	18 29.7	6 13.7	5 45.7	27 16.1	26 03.4
20 M	13 55 05	26 55 29	18 02 31	25 04 28	20 40.0	10 22.4	3 35.8	19 13.0	0 35.3	18 42.7	6 09.0	5 49.3	27 18.1	26 05.4
21 Tu	13 59 02	27 55 09	2♓05 06	9♓04 12	20R 41.4	11 51.2	4 50.2	19 54.7	0 45.8	18 55.6	6 04.3	5 52.9	27 20.1	26 07.4
22 W	14 02 58	28 54 50	16 01 34	22 57 00	20 41.8	13 22.5	6 04.6	20 36.4	0 56.5	19 08.5	5 59.5	5 56.5	27 22.1	26 09.3
23 Th	14 06 55	29 54 34	29 50 13	6♈40 58	20 40.7	14 55.9	7 19.1	21 18.2	1 07.5	19 21.5	5 54.7	6 00.1	27 24.2	26 11.3
24 F	14 10 51	0♏54 19	13♈28 59	20 13 59	20 37.6	16 31.0	8 33.6	22 00.2	1 18.7	19 34.4	5 49.9	6 03.6	27 26.2	26 13.2
25 Sa	14 14 48	1 54 06	26 55 43	3♉33 56	20 32.4	18 07.5	9 48.1	22 42.2	1 30.2	19 47.2	5 45.1	6 07.1	27 28.3	26 15.1
26 Su	14 18 44	2 53 56	10♉08 25	16 39 02	20 25.6	19 44.9	11 02.7	23 24.4	1 41.9	20 00.1	5 40.3	6 10.6	27 30.4	26 17.0
27 M	14 22 41	3 53 47	23 05 39	29 28 13	20 17.8	21 23.2	12 17.3	24 06.6	1 53.9	20 13.0	5 35.5	6 14.1	27 32.5	26 18.8
28 Tu	14 26 37	4 53 41	5♊46 46	12♊01 24	20 09.7	23 02.0	13 32.0	24 48.9	2 06.0	20 25.8	5 30.6	6 17.6	27 34.6	26 20.7
29 W	14 30 34	5 53 36	18 12 17	24 19 40	20 02.2	24 41.2	14 46.7	25 31.4	2 18.4	20 38.6	5 25.8	6 21.0	27 36.7	26 22.5
30 Th	14 34 31	6 53 34	0♋23 52	6♋25 16	19 56.0	26 20.6	16 01.4	26 13.9	2 31.1	20 51.4	5 21.0	6 24.4	27 38.8	26 24.3
31 F	14 38 27	7 53 34	12 24 19	18 21 31	19 51.7	28 00.2	17 16.1	26 56.5	2 43.9	21 04.1	5 16.1	6 27.8	27 41.0	26 26.1

Astro Data	Planet Ingress	Last Aspect	☽ Ingress	Last Aspect	☽ Ingress	☽ Phases & Eclipses	Astro Data
Dy Hr Mn	Dy Hr Mn	Dy Hr Mn	Dy Hr Mn	Dy Hr Mn	Dy Hr Mn	Dy Hr Mn	1 September 1969
♃⊼♄ 3 22:08	♂ ♑ 21 6:35	2 11:53 ♆ ☍	♊ 2 19:23	2 5:48 ♇ □	♋ 2 14:52	3 16:58 ☾ 11♊00	Julian Day # 25446
☽0S 12 14:05	♀ ♍ 23 3:26	4 19:46 ♇ □	♋ 5 6:57	4 20:58 ♆ △	♌ 5 3:25	11 19:56 ● 18♍53	SVP 5♓40'57"
♃∠♆ 16 8:33	☉ ♎ 23 5:07	7 11:55 ♆ △	♌ 7 19:36	7 9:14 ♆ □	♍ 7 15:21	11 19:58:19 ● A 03'11"	GC 26♐24.9 ⚴ 25♐01.1
☿R 16 12:41		9 23:57 ♆ □	♍ 10 7:20	9 19:07 ♆ ✶	♎ 10 0:48	19 2:24 ☽ 25♐59	Eris 12♈18.8R ⚵ 0♑51.1
⚳D 17 9:29	☿ ♍R 7 2:57	12 10:00 ♆ ✶	♎ 12 17:01	11 9:39 ☉ ☌	♏ 12 7:19	25 20:21 ○ 2♈35	⚷ 5♈44.0R ⚶ 26♋07.0
☉0S 23 5:07	☿ ♎ 9 16:56	14 17:15 ♂ ✶	♏ 15 0:25	14 6:34 ♆ ☌	♐ 14 11:33	25 20:10 ☍ A 0.901	☽ Mean ☊ 21♓43.2
☽0N 25 13:16	⚳ ♒ 16 22:15	16 23:21 ♆ ☌	♐ 17 5:42	16 12:19 ♀ □	♑ 16 14:35		
	♀ ♎ 17 14:17	19 7:11 ♂ ☌	♑ 19 9:14	18 12:40 ♆ ✶	♒ 18 17:21	3 11:05 ☾ 10♋04	1 October 1969
☿0N 7 0:26	☉ ♏ 23 14:11	21 8:29 ☉ △	♒ 21 11:31	20 15:49 ♆ □	♓ 20 20:26	11 9:39 ● 17♎54	Julian Day # 25476
☿D 8 9:53		23 7:34 ♆ □	♓ 23 13:22	22 19:43 ♆ △	♈ 23 0:17	18 8:32 ☽ 24♑48	SVP 5♓40'54"
☽0S 9 21:54		25 10:04 ♆ △	♈ 25 15:55	24 15:20 ♂ □	♉ 25 5:32	25 8:44 ○ 1♉46	GC 26♐25.0 ⚴ 29♐48.8
☿0S 15 16:14		26 15:20 ♃ ☍	♉ 27 20:29	27 8:21 ♆ ☍	♊ 27 13:00		Eris 12♈01.6R ⚵ 4♑34.6
♀0S 20 11:28		29 21:46 ♆ ☍	♊ 30 4:05	29 16:03 ♇ □	♋ 29 23:13		⚷ 4♈25.9R ⚶ 7♌37.6
♄⊼♅ 22 20:35							☽ Mean ☊ 20♓07.8
☽0N 22 21:29							

November 1969 LONGITUDE

Day	Sid.Time	☉	0 hr ☽	Noon ☽	True ☊	☿	♀	♂	⚳	♃	♄	♅	♆	♇
1 Sa	14 42 24	8♏53 36	24♋17 24	0♌12 34	19♓49.4	29♎39.7	18♎30.9	27♑39.2	2♒57.0	21♎16.9	5♉11.3	6♎31.1	27♏43.1	26♍27.9
2 Su	14 46 20	9 53 39	6♌07 38	12 03 15	19D 48.9	1♏19.2	19 45.8	28 21.9	3 10.3	21 29.6	5R 06.5	6 34.5	27 45.3	26 29.6
3 M	14 50 17	10 53 46	18 00 03	23 58 44	19 49.7	2 58.5	21 00.6	29 04.8	3 23.8	21 42.2	5 01.7	6 37.8	27 47.4	26 31.4
4 Tu	14 54 13	11 53 54	29 59 56	6♍04 17	19 50.9	4 37.6	22 15.5	29 47.7	3 37.5	21 54.9	4 56.9	6 41.1	27 49.6	26 33.1
5 W	14 58 10	12 54 04	12♍12 25	18 24 53	19R 51.6	6 16.5	23 30.4	0♒30.8	3 51.4	22 07.5	4 52.2	6 44.3	27 51.8	26 34.7
6 Th	15 02 06	13 54 16	24 42 11	1♎04 47	19 51.0	7 55.1	24 45.4	1 13.9	4 05.5	22 20.1	4 47.4	6 47.6	27 54.0	26 36.4
7 F	15 06 03	14 54 30	7♎33 01	14 07 07	19 48.2	9 33.4	26 00.3	1 57.1	4 19.8	22 32.6	4 42.7	6 50.8	27 56.2	26 38.0
8 Sa	15 10 00	15 54 46	20 47 11	27 33 14	19 43.0	11 11.4	27 15.3	2 40.3	4 34.3	22 45.1	4 38.0	6 53.9	27 58.4	26 39.6
9 Su	15 13 56	16 55 04	4♏25 03	11♏22 22	19 35.5	12 49.1	28 30.4	3 23.6	4 49.0	22 57.6	4 33.3	6 57.1	28 00.6	26 41.2
10 M	15 17 53	17 55 24	18 24 41	25 31 26	19 26.3	14 26.5	29 45.4	4 07.1	5 03.9	23 10.0	4 28.6	7 00.2	28 02.9	26 42.8
11 Tu	15 21 49	18 55 46	2♐41 53	9♐55 14	19 16.3	16 03.5	1♏00.5	4 50.5	5 19.0	23 22.4	4 24.0	7 03.2	28 05.1	26 44.3
12 W	15 25 46	19 56 09	17 10 39	24 27 13	19 06.8	17 40.2	2 15.6	5 34.1	5 34.3	23 34.7	4 19.5	7 06.3	28 07.3	26 45.9
13 Th	15 29 42	20 56 34	1♑44 07	9♑00 32	18 58.8	19 16.6	3 30.7	6 17.7	5 49.8	23 47.0	4 14.9	7 09.3	28 09.6	26 47.4
14 F	15 33 39	21 57 00	16 15 44	23 29 07	18 53.2	20 52.7	4 45.8	7 01.4	6 05.4	23 59.3	4 10.4	7 12.3	28 11.8	26 48.8
15 Sa	15 37 35	22 57 27	0♒40 10	7♒48 31	18 50.0	22 28.5	6 01.0	7 45.1	6 21.3	24 11.5	4 06.0	7 15.2	28 14.1	26 50.3
16 Su	15 41 32	23 57 56	14 53 53	21 56 08	18D 49.0	24 04.1	7 16.1	8 28.9	6 37.3	24 23.7	4 01.6	7 18.1	28 16.3	26 51.7
17 M	15 45 29	24 58 25	28 55 10	5♓51 00	18R 49.3	25 39.3	8 31.3	9 12.7	6 53.4	24 35.8	3 57.2	7 21.0	28 18.6	26 53.1
18 Tu	15 49 25	25 58 56	12♓43 41	19 33 18	18 49.6	27 14.3	9 46.5	9 56.6	7 09.7	24 47.8	3 52.9	7 23.8	28 20.8	26 54.4
19 W	15 53 22	26 59 29	26 19 58	3♈03 46	18 48.8	28 49.1	11 01.7	10 40.6	7 26.2	24 59.8	3 48.7	7 26.6	28 23.1	26 55.7
20 Th	15 57 18	28 00 02	9♈44 47	16 23 05	18 45.7	0♐23.6	12 16.9	11 24.6	7 42.9	25 11.8	3 44.5	7 29.4	28 25.3	26 57.0
21 F	16 01 15	29 00 37	22 58 44	29 31 41	18 39.8	1 57.9	13 32.2	12 08.6	7 59.7	25 23.7	3 40.4	7 32.1	28 27.6	26 58.3
22 Sa	16 05 11	0♐01 13	6♉01 58	12♉29 31	18 30.9	3 32.1	14 47.4	12 52.7	8 16.7	25 35.5	3 36.3	7 34.8	28 29.9	26 59.6
23 Su	16 09 08	1 01 51	18 54 16	25 16 11	18 19.5	5 06.0	16 02.7	13 36.8	8 33.8	25 47.3	3 32.3	7 37.4	28 32.1	27 00.8
24 M	16 13 04	2 02 29	1♊35 11	7♊51 15	18 06.3	6 39.8	17 18.0	14 21.0	8 51.1	25 59.0	3 28.4	7 40.0	28 34.4	27 02.0
25 Tu	16 17 01	3 03 10	14 04 21	20 14 32	17 52.6	8 13.5	18 33.3	15 05.2	9 08.5	26 10.6	3 24.5	7 42.5	28 36.6	27 03.1
26 W	16 20 58	4 03 52	26 21 51	2♋26 26	17 39.6	9 47.0	19 48.6	15 49.4	9 26.1	26 22.2	3 20.7	7 45.1	28 38.9	27 04.3
27 Th	16 24 54	5 04 35	8♋28 28	14 28 12	17 28.2	11 20.5	21 03.9	16 33.7	9 43.8	26 33.8	3 16.9	7 47.5	28 41.1	27 05.4
28 F	16 28 51	6 05 19	20 25 57	26 22 04	17 19.4	12 53.8	22 19.3	17 18.0	10 01.6	26 45.2	3 13.3	7 50.0	28 43.4	27 06.4
29 Sa	16 32 47	7 06 06	2♌17 00	8♌11 13	17 13.3	14 27.0	23 34.6	18 02.3	10 19.6	26 56.6	3 09.7	7 52.4	28 45.6	27 07.5
30 Su	16 36 44	8 06 53	14 05 17	19 59 46	17 10.0	16 00.2	24 50.0	18 46.7	10 37.8	27 08.0	3 06.2	7 54.7	28 47.8	27 08.5

December 1969 LONGITUDE

Day	Sid.Time	☉	0 hr ☽	Noon ☽	True ☊	☿	♀	♂	⚳	♃	♄	♅	♆	♇
1 M	16 40 40	9♐07 42	25♌55 18	1♍52 33	17♓08.7	17♐33.2	26♏05.4	19♒31.1	10♒56.0	27♎19.2	3♉02.7	7♎57.0	28♏50.1	27♍09.5
2 Tu	16 44 37	10 08 32	7♍52 11	13 54 55	17R 08.6	19 06.2	27 20.8	20 15.5	11 14.4	27 30.4	2R 59.4	7 59.3	28 52.3	27 10.4
3 W	16 48 34	11 09 24	20 01 27	26 12 27	17 08.4	20 39.1	28 36.2	21 00.0	11 33.0	27 41.5	2 56.1	8 01.5	28 54.5	27 11.3
4 Th	16 52 30	12 10 17	2♎28 35	8♎50 27	17 07.0	22 12.0	29 51.6	21 44.5	11 51.6	27 52.5	2 52.9	8 03.6	28 56.7	27 12.2
5 F	16 56 27	13 11 11	15 18 36	21 53 26	17 03.4	23 44.8	1♐07.0	22 29.0	12 10.4	28 03.5	2 49.8	8 05.7	28 58.9	27 13.1
6 Sa	17 00 23	14 12 07	28 35 17	5♏24 19	16 57.1	25 17.5	2 22.4	23 13.6	12 29.3	28 14.4	2 46.8	8 07.8	29 01.1	27 13.9
7 Su	17 04 20	15 13 04	12♏20 31	19 23 41	16 48.0	26 50.0	3 37.9	23 58.2	12 48.4	28 25.2	2 43.9	8 09.8	29 03.3	27 14.7
8 M	17 08 16	16 14 02	26 33 24	3♐49 03	16 36.8	28 22.5	4 53.3	24 42.8	13 07.5	28 35.9	2 41.1	8 11.8	29 05.5	27 15.4
9 Tu	17 12 13	17 15 01	11♐09 50	18 34 45	16 24.5	29 54.8	6 08.8	25 27.4	13 26.8	28 46.5	2 38.3	8 13.7	29 07.7	27 16.2
10 W	17 16 09	18 16 02	26 02 41	3♑32 26	16 12.6	1♑26.9	7 24.3	26 12.0	13 46.2	28 57.1	2 35.7	8 15.6	29 09.9	27 16.9
11 Th	17 20 06	19 17 02	11♑02 45	18 32 25	16 02.4	2 58.8	8 39.7	26 56.7	14 05.7	29 07.5	2 33.1	8 17.4	29 12.0	27 17.5
12 F	17 24 03	20 18 04	26 00 19	3♒25 27	15 54.8	4 30.5	9 55.2	27 41.4	14 25.3	29 17.9	2 30.7	8 19.2	29 14.2	27 18.1
13 Sa	17 27 59	21 19 06	10♒46 59	18 04 13	15 50.1	6 01.7	11 10.7	28 26.1	14 45.0	29 28.1	2 28.3	8 20.9	29 16.3	27 18.7
14 Su	17 31 56	22 20 09	25 16 43	2♓24 09	15D 48.1	7 32.6	12 26.2	29 10.8	15 04.9	29 38.3	2 26.1	8 22.6	29 18.4	27 19.3
15 M	17 35 52	23 21 11	9♓26 24	16 23 26	15R 47.7	9 02.9	13 41.6	29 55.6	15 24.8	29 48.4	2 23.9	8 24.2	29 20.5	27 19.8
16 Tu	17 39 49	24 22 15	23 15 23	0♈02 27	15 47.7	10 32.5	14 57.1	0♓40.3	15 44.9	29 58.4	2 21.9	8 25.8	29 22.6	27 20.3
17 W	17 43 45	25 23 18	6♈44 52	13 22 57	15 46.6	12 01.4	16 12.6	1 25.1	16 05.0	0♏08.3	2 19.9	8 27.3	29 24.7	27 20.7
18 Th	17 47 42	26 24 22	19 57 00	26 27 18	15 43.4	13 29.4	17 28.1	2 09.8	16 25.2	0 18.0	2 18.1	8 28.8	29 26.8	27 21.2
19 F	17 51 38	27 25 26	2♉54 11	9♉17 53	15 37.4	14 56.3	18 43.6	2 54.6	16 45.6	0 27.7	2 16.4	8 30.2	29 28.8	27 21.6
20 Sa	17 55 35	28 26 31	15 38 39	21 56 41	15 28.3	16 21.8	19 59.0	3 39.4	17 06.0	0 37.3	2 14.7	8 31.5	29 30.9	27 21.9
21 Su	17 59 32	29 27 36	28 12 09	4♊25 11	15 16.7	17 45.7	21 14.5	4 24.1	17 26.5	0 46.8	2 13.2	8 32.8	29 32.9	27 22.2
22 M	18 03 28	0♑28 41	10♊35 55	16 44 26	15 03.2	19 07.7	22 30.0	5 08.9	17 47.1	0 56.1	2 11.8	8 34.1	29 34.9	27 22.5
23 Tu	18 07 25	1 29 47	22 50 50	28 55 11	14 49.1	20 27.5	23 45.5	5 53.7	18 07.9	1 05.4	2 10.5	8 35.3	29 36.9	27 22.8
24 W	18 11 21	2 30 54	4♋57 35	10♋58 09	14 35.6	21 44.7	25 01.0	6 38.5	18 28.6	1 14.6	2 09.3	8 36.4	29 38.9	27 23.0
25 Th	18 15 18	3 32 00	16 57 01	22 54 22	14 23.8	22 58.7	26 16.5	7 23.2	18 49.5	1 23.6	2 08.2	8 37.5	29 40.9	27 23.2
26 F	18 19 14	4 33 07	28 50 23	4♌45 20	14 14.4	24 09.1	27 32.0	8 08.0	19 10.5	1 32.5	2 07.2	8 38.5	29 42.8	27 23.3
27 Sa	18 23 11	5 34 15	10♌39 33	16 33 21	14 07.9	25 15.3	28 47.5	8 52.8	19 31.5	1 41.3	2 06.3	8 39.5	29 44.7	27 23.4
28 Su	18 27 08	6 35 22	22 27 09	28 21 25	14 04.2	26 16.6	0♑03.0	9 37.5	19 52.7	1 50.0	2 05.6	8 40.4	29 46.6	27 23.5
29 M	18 31 04	7 36 30	4♍16 40	10♍13 26	14D 02.8	27 12.2	1 18.5	10 22.3	20 13.9	1 58.6	2 04.9	8 41.3	29 48.5	27R 23.6
30 Tu	18 35 01	8 37 39	16 12 19	22 13 57	14 03.0	28 01.5	2 33.9	11 07.0	20 35.1	2 07.1	2 04.4	8 42.1	29 50.4	27 23.6
31 W	18 38 57	9 38 48	28 19 00	4♎28 06	14R 03.6	28 43.4	3 49.4	11 51.8	20 56.5	2 15.4	2 03.9	8 42.9	29 52.2	27 23.6

Astro Data

	Dy Hr Mn
☽0S	6 6:44
☽0N	19 3:10
♃⚺♇	30 13:14
☽0S	3 15:08
♃⚺♆	12 1:11
☽0N	16 7:42
♃☍♄	30 4:44
♇R	30 8:07
☽0S	30 22:00

Planet Ingress

	Dy Hr Mn
☿ ♏	1 16:53
♂ ♒	4 18:51
♀ ♏	10 16:40
☿ ♐	20 6:00
☉ ♐	22 11:31
♀ ♐	4 14:41
☿ ♑	9 13:21
♂ ♓	15 14:22
♃ ♏	16 15:55
☉ ♑	22 0:44
♀ ♑	28 11:04

Last Aspect / ☽ Ingress

Last Aspect Dy Hr Mn		☽ Ingress Dy Hr Mn
1 10:43	♆ □	♌ 1 11:35
3 19:38	♆ □	♍ 4 0:00
6 6:01	♆ ⚹	♎ 6 9:59
8 11:25	♀ ☌	♏ 8 16:18
10 16:15	♆ ☌	♐ 10 19:30
12 15:49	♇ □	♑ 12 21:08
14 19:53	♆ ⚹	♒ 14 22:53
16 22:55	♆ □	♓ 17 1:52
19 3:38	♆ △	♈ 19 6:32
21 4:18	♃ ☍	♉ 21 12:52
23 18:13	♆ ☍	♊ 23 20:59
26 1:23	♇ □	♋ 26 7:10
28 16:47	♆ △	♌ 28 19:22

Last Aspect / ☽ Ingress

Last Aspect Dy Hr Mn		☽ Ingress Dy Hr Mn
1 5:52	♆ □	♍ 1 8:14
3 17:12	♆ ⚹	♎ 3 19:17
5 23:13	♃ ☌	♏ 6 2:30
8 4:11	♆ ☌	♐ 8 5:43
10 4:34	♃ ⚹	♑ 10 6:20
12 5:14	♃ □	♒ 12 6:27
14 7:16	♃ △	♓ 14 7:56
16 10:49	♆ △	♈ 16 11:56
18 11:54	☉ △	♉ 18 18:35
21 2:34	♆ ☍	♊ 21 3:28
23 8:57	♇ □	♋ 23 14:08
26 1:45	♆ △	♌ 26 2:21
28 14:53	♆ □	♍ 28 15:20
31 3:01	♆ ⚹	♎ 31 3:18

☽ Phases & Eclipses

Dy Hr Mn		
2 7:14	☾	9♌42
9 22:11	●	17♏21
16 15:45	☽	24♒07
23 23:54	○	1♊32
2 3:50	☾	9♍48
9 9:42	●	17♐09
16 1:09	☽	23♓55
23 17:35	○	1♋44
31 22:52	☾	10♎06

Astro Data

1 November 1969
Julian Day # 25507
SVP 5♓40'49"
GC 26♐25.1 ⚴ 7♑55.7
Eris 11♈43.1R ⚵ 12♑25.7
⚷ 3♈09.3R ⚶ 17♌46.8
☽ Mean ☊ 18♓29.3

1 December 1969
Julian Day # 25537
SVP 5♓40'44"
GC 26♐25.1 ⚴ 17♑29.8
Eris 11♈29.8R ⚵ 22♑36.8
⚷ 2♈26.6R ⚶ 24♌32.1
☽ Mean ☊ 16♓54.0

LONGITUDE — January 1970

Day	Sid.Time	☉	0 hr ☽	Noon ☽	True ☊	☿	♀	♂	⚳	♃	♄	♅	♆	♇
1 Th	18 42 54	10♑39 57	10♎41 56	17♎01 10	14♓03.5	29♑17.0	5♑04.9	12♓36.5	21♒18.0	2♏23.6	2♉03.6	8♎43.6	29♏54.1	27♍23.5
2 F	18 46 50	11 41 07	23 26 24	29 58 11	14R 01.7	29 41.6	6 20.4	13 21.3	21 39.5	2 31.7	2R 03.4	8 44.2	29 55.9	27R 23.4
3 Sa	18 50 47	12 42 17	6♏36 59	13♏23 10	13 57.8	29R 56.2	7 35.9	14 06.0	22 01.1	2 39.6	2D 03.3	8 44.8	29 57.7	27 23.3
4 Su	18 54 43	13 43 27	20 16 56	27 18 19	13 51.4	29 60.0	8 51.5	14 50.8	22 22.7	2 47.4	2 03.3	8 45.3	29 59.4	27 23.1
5 M	18 58 40	14 44 38	4♐27 09	11♐43 01	13 43.1	29 52.4	10 07.0	15 35.5	22 44.5	2 55.1	2 03.4	8 45.8	0♐01.2	27 22.9
6 Tu	19 02 37	15 45 49	19 05 20	26 33 13	13 33.7	29 33.0	11 22.5	16 20.2	23 06.3	3 02.7	2 03.7	8 46.2	0 02.9	27 22.7
7 W	19 06 33	16 46 59	4♑05 37	11♑41 20	13 24.4	29 01.8	12 38.0	17 04.9	23 28.1	3 10.1	2 04.0	8 46.6	0 04.6	27 22.5
8 Th	19 10 30	17 48 10	19 19 01	26 57 16	13 16.3	28 19.0	13 53.5	17 49.6	23 50.1	3 17.4	2 04.5	8 46.9	0 06.3	27 22.2
9 F	19 14 26	18 49 20	4♒34 41	12♒09 57	13 10.4	27 25.6	15 09.0	18 34.3	24 12.1	3 24.5	2 05.1	8 47.1	0 07.9	27 21.9
10 Sa	19 18 23	19 50 30	19 41 53	27 09 27	13 07.0	26 22.8	16 24.4	19 19.0	24 34.1	3 31.5	2 05.7	8 47.3	0 09.5	27 21.5
11 Su	19 22 19	20 51 39	4♓31 51	11♓48 27	13D 05.9	25 12.4	17 39.9	20 03.6	24 56.3	3 38.4	2 06.6	8 47.5	0 11.2	27 21.1
12 M	19 26 16	21 52 48	18 58 50	26 02 47	13 06.4	23 56.6	18 55.4	20 48.3	25 18.4	3 45.1	2 07.5	8R 47.5	0 12.7	27 20.7
13 Tu	19 30 12	22 53 56	3♈00 15	9♈51 22	13 07.5	22 37.8	20 10.9	21 32.9	25 40.7	3 51.7	2 08.5	8 47.5	0 14.3	27 20.2
14 W	19 34 09	23 55 03	16 36 18	23 15 23	13R 08.1	21 18.5	21 26.3	22 17.5	26 03.0	3 58.1	2 09.6	8 47.5	0 15.8	27 19.7
15 Th	19 38 06	24 56 10	29 48 58	6♉17 29	13 07.4	20 01.2	22 41.8	23 02.1	26 25.3	4 04.3	2 10.9	8 47.4	0 17.3	27 19.2
16 F	19 42 02	25 57 16	12♉41 20	19 00 58	13 04.6	18 48.1	23 57.2	23 46.7	26 47.7	4 10.5	2 12.2	8 47.2	0 18.8	27 18.7
17 Sa	19 45 59	26 58 21	25 16 49	1♊29 17	12 59.7	17 41.0	25 12.7	24 31.3	27 10.2	4 16.4	2 13.7	8 47.0	0 20.2	27 18.1
18 Su	19 49 55	27 59 25	7♊38 45	13 45 35	12 52.9	16 41.4	26 28.1	25 15.8	27 32.7	4 22.2	2 15.3	8 46.8	0 21.6	27 17.5
19 M	19 53 52	29 00 29	19 50 06	25 52 35	12 44.8	15 50.3	27 43.5	26 00.3	27 55.2	4 27.9	2 17.0	8 46.5	0 23.0	27 16.8
20 Tu	19 57 48	0♒01 32	1♋53 20	7♋52 33	12 36.1	15 08.3	28 58.9	26 44.8	28 17.8	4 33.4	2 18.8	8 46.1	0 24.4	27 16.2
21 W	20 01 45	1 02 34	13 50 30	19 47 22	12 27.8	14 35.6	0♒14.4	27 29.2	28 40.5	4 38.7	2 20.7	8 45.7	0 25.7	27 15.4
22 Th	20 05 41	2 03 36	25 43 21	1♌38 39	12 20.5	14 12.2	1 29.8	28 13.7	29 03.2	4 43.9	2 22.7	8 45.2	0 27.0	27 14.7
23 F	20 09 38	3 04 36	7♌33 29	13 28 04	12 14.9	13 57.8	2 45.1	28 58.1	29 25.9	4 48.9	2 24.8	8 44.6	0 28.3	27 14.0
24 Sa	20 13 35	4 05 36	19 22 37	25 17 25	12 11.3	13D 52.1	4 00.5	29 42.5	29 48.7	4 53.8	2 27.0	8 44.0	0 29.6	27 13.2
25 Su	20 17 31	5 06 35	1♍12 45	7♍08 55	12D 09.7	13 54.5	5 15.9	0♈26.8	0♓11.5	4 58.5	2 29.4	8 43.4	0 30.8	27 12.3
26 M	20 21 28	6 07 34	13 06 18	19 05 17	12 09.8	14 04.5	6 31.3	1 11.1	0 34.4	5 03.0	2 31.8	8 42.7	0 32.0	27 11.5
27 Tu	20 25 24	7 08 31	25 06 16	1♎09 46	12 11.1	14 21.5	7 46.7	1 55.4	0 57.3	5 07.3	2 34.3	8 41.9	0 33.1	27 10.6
28 W	20 29 21	8 09 28	7♎16 13	13 26 11	12 12.9	14 45.0	9 02.0	2 39.7	1 20.2	5 11.5	2 37.0	8 41.1	0 34.3	27 09.7
29 Th	20 33 17	9 10 25	19 40 10	25 58 42	12 14.5	15 14.3	10 17.4	3 24.0	1 43.2	5 15.5	2 39.7	8 40.3	0 35.4	27 08.8
30 F	20 37 14	10 11 21	2♏22 21	8♏51 35	12R 15.2	15 49.1	11 32.7	4 08.2	2 06.2	5 19.4	2 42.6	8 39.3	0 36.4	27 07.8
31 Sa	20 41 10	11 12 16	15 26 53	22 08 38	12 14.7	16 28.7	12 48.0	4 52.4	2 29.2	5 23.0	2 45.5	8 38.4	0 37.5	27 06.8

LONGITUDE — February 1970

Day	Sid.Time	☉	0 hr ☽	Noon ☽	True ☊	☿	♀	♂	⚳	♃	♄	♅	♆	♇
1 Su	20 45 07	12♒13 10	28♏57 09	5♐52 36	12♓12.7	17♑12.8	14♒03.4	5♈36.6	2♓52.3	5♏26.5	2♉48.6	8♎37.4	0♐38.5	27♍05.8
2 M	20 49 04	13 14 04	12♐55 02	20 04 20	12R 09.6	18 00.9	15 18.7	6 20.7	3 15.5	5 29.9	2 51.7	8R 36.3	0 39.5	27R 04.8
3 Tu	20 53 00	14 14 57	27 20 09	4♑41 59	12 05.7	18 52.7	16 34.0	7 04.8	3 38.6	5 33.0	2 55.0	8 35.2	0 40.4	27 03.7
4 W	20 56 57	15 15 49	12♑09 08	19 40 41	12 01.6	19 47.9	17 49.3	7 48.9	4 01.8	5 36.0	2 58.3	8 34.0	0 41.3	27 02.6
5 Th	21 00 53	16 16 40	27 15 32	4♒52 30	11 58.1	20 46.1	19 04.6	8 33.0	4 25.0	5 38.7	3 01.8	8 32.8	0 42.2	27 01.5
6 F	21 04 50	17 17 30	12♒30 18	20 07 37	11 55.6	21 47.2	20 19.9	9 17.0	4 48.3	5 41.3	3 05.3	8 31.5	0 43.1	27 00.3
7 Sa	21 08 46	18 18 18	27 43 08	5♓15 40	11D 54.4	22 50.8	21 35.2	10 01.0	5 11.6	5 43.7	3 09.0	8 30.2	0 43.9	26 59.2
8 Su	21 12 43	19 19 05	12♓44 08	20 07 35	11 54.4	23 56.7	22 50.5	10 45.0	5 34.9	5 46.0	3 12.7	8 28.8	0 44.7	26 58.0
9 M	21 16 39	20 19 51	27 25 17	4♈36 42	11 55.4	25 04.9	24 05.7	11 29.0	5 58.2	5 48.0	3 16.5	8 27.4	0 45.4	26 56.8
10 Tu	21 20 36	21 20 35	11♈41 27	18 39 21	11 56.9	26 15.1	25 20.9	12 12.9	6 21.5	5 49.9	3 20.5	8 26.0	0 46.1	26 55.5
11 W	21 24 33	22 21 17	25 30 23	2♉14 40	11 58.2	27 27.1	26 36.2	12 56.8	6 44.9	5 51.5	3 24.5	8 24.5	0 46.8	26 54.3
12 Th	21 28 29	23 21 58	8♉52 27	15 24 05	11R 59.1	28 40.9	27 51.4	13 40.6	7 08.3	5 53.0	3 28.6	8 22.9	0 47.5	26 53.0
13 F	21 32 26	24 22 38	21 49 56	28 10 30	11 59.3	29 56.4	29 06.5	14 24.4	7 31.7	5 54.3	3 32.8	8 21.3	0 48.1	26 51.7
14 Sa	21 36 22	25 23 15	4♊26 16	10♊37 44	11 58.6	1♒13.4	0♓21.7	15 08.2	7 55.2	5 55.4	3 37.1	8 19.7	0 48.7	26 50.4
15 Su	21 40 19	26 23 51	16 45 27	22 49 54	11 57.1	2 31.8	1 36.9	15 51.9	8 18.6	5 56.4	3 41.4	8 18.0	0 49.2	26 49.1
16 M	21 44 15	27 24 25	28 51 35	4♋51 01	11 55.2	3 51.7	2 52.0	16 35.6	8 42.1	5 57.1	3 45.9	8 16.3	0 49.8	26 47.7
17 Tu	21 48 12	28 24 58	10♋48 38	16 44 52	11 53.0	5 12.9	4 07.1	17 19.3	9 05.6	5 57.7	3 50.4	8 14.5	0 50.2	26 46.4
18 W	21 52 09	29 25 29	22 40 07	28 34 46	11 50.9	6 35.3	5 22.2	18 02.9	9 29.1	5 58.0	3 55.1	8 12.7	0 50.7	26 45.0
19 Th	21 56 05	0♓25 58	4♌29 09	10♌23 36	11 49.2	7 59.0	6 37.3	18 46.5	9 52.6	5R 58.2	3 59.8	8 10.9	0 51.1	26 43.6
20 F	22 00 02	1 26 25	16 18 23	22 13 49	11 48.0	9 23.8	7 52.4	19 30.1	10 16.1	5 58.2	4 04.6	8 09.0	0 51.5	26 42.1
21 Sa	22 03 58	2 26 51	28 10 07	4♍07 34	11D 47.4	10 49.8	9 07.4	20 13.6	10 39.7	5 58.0	4 09.4	8 07.1	0 51.8	26 40.7
22 Su	22 07 55	3 27 15	10♍06 23	16 06 49	11 47.3	12 17.0	10 22.4	20 57.1	11 03.2	5 57.6	4 14.4	8 05.1	0 52.2	26 39.3
23 M	22 11 51	4 27 37	22 09 06	28 13 29	11 47.7	13 45.2	11 37.5	21 40.5	11 26.8	5 57.0	4 19.4	8 03.2	0 52.4	26 37.8
24 Tu	22 15 48	5 27 58	4♎20 12	10♎29 31	11 48.2	15 14.5	12 52.4	22 23.9	11 50.4	5 56.2	4 24.5	8 01.1	0 52.7	26 36.3
25 W	22 19 44	6 28 18	16 41 44	22 57 07	11 48.9	16 44.9	14 07.4	23 07.3	12 14.0	5 55.3	4 29.7	7 59.1	0 52.9	26 34.8
26 Th	22 23 41	7 28 36	29 15 58	5♏38 36	11 49.4	18 16.4	15 22.4	23 50.6	12 37.5	5 54.1	4 35.0	7 57.0	0 53.1	26 33.3
27 F	22 27 37	8 28 52	12♏05 18	18 36 24	11 49.8	19 48.9	16 37.3	24 33.9	13 01.2	5 52.8	4 40.3	7 54.8	0 53.2	26 31.8
28 Sa	22 31 34	9 29 07	25 12 09	1♐52 50	11R 49.9	21 22.4	17 52.3	25 17.1	13 24.8	5 51.3	4 45.7	7 52.7	0 53.3	26 30.2

Astro Data

	Dy Hr Mn
♄ D	3 21:06
☿ R	4 8:09
☽ 0N	12 13:51
♅ R	13 6:09
☿ D	24 16:38
♂ 0N	26 1:42
☽ 0S	27 3:37
☽ 0N	8 23:05
♃ R	19 21:58
☽ 0S	23 9:14

Planet Ingress

		Dy Hr Mn
☿	♒	4 4:24
☿	♊R	4 11:54
♆	♐	4 19:55
☉	♒	20 11:24
♀	♒	21 7:26
♂	♈	24 21:29
⚳	♓	24 23:55
☿	♒	13 13:08
♀	♓	14 5:04
☉	♓	19 1:42

Last Aspect / ☽ Ingress (January)

Last Aspect Dy Hr Mn		☽ Ingress Dy Hr Mn
2 11:29	☿ □	♏ 2 12:03
4 16:32	♀ ☌	♐ 4 16:33
6 13:19	♇ □	♑ 6 17:30
8 14:02	♀ ☌	♒ 8 16:47
9 6:39	♅ △	♓ 10 16:37
12 14:14	♇ ☍	♈ 12 18:48
14 13:18	☉ □	♉ 15 0:20
17 3:54	♇ △	♊ 17 9:07
19 14:48	♇ □	♋ 19 20:13
22 4:37	♂ ☍	♌ 22 8:40
23 2:25	♅ ✱	♍ 24 21:33
27 4:07	♇ ☌	♎ 27 9:42
28 14:38	☿ □	♏ 29 19:34

Last Aspect / ☽ Ingress (February)

Last Aspect Dy Hr Mn		☽ Ingress Dy Hr Mn
31 20:46	♇ ✱	♐ 1 1:50
2 23:34	♇ □	♑ 3 4:22
4 23:39	♇ △	♒ 5 4:19
6 12:21	♀ ☌	♓ 7 3:37
8 23:14	♇ ☍	♈ 9 4:17
11 2:36	♅ □	♉ 11 7:59
13 13:59	☿ □	♊ 13 15:29
15 19:55	♇ □	♋ 16 2:17
18 8:17	♇ ✱	♌ 18 14:53
20 6:07	♂ △	♍ 21 3:42
23 8:52	♇ ☌	♎ 23 15:30
25 12:21	♂ ☍	♏ 26 1:23
28 2:22	♇ ✱	♐ 28 8:38

☽ Phases & Eclipses

Dy Hr Mn	
7 20:35	● 17♑09
14 13:18	☽ 23♈58
22 12:55	○ 2♌06
30 14:38	☾ 10♏18
6 7:13	● 17♒05
13 4:10	☽ 24♉03
21 8:19	○ 2♍18
21 8:30	☍ P 0.046

Astro Data

1 January 1970
Julian Day # 25568
SVP 5♓40'39"
GC 26♐25.2 ⚴ 28♑14.9
Eris 11♈25.2 ⚵ 4♒53.0
⚷ 2♈31.7 ⚶ 26♌05.6R
☽ Mean ☊ 15♓15.6

1 February 1970
Julian Day # 25599
SVP 5♓40'33"
GC 26♐25.3 ⚴ 9♒12.8
Eris 11♈31.4 ⚵ 18♒18.5
⚷ 3♈26.7 ⚶ 20♌45.5R
☽ Mean ☊ 13♓37.1

March 1970

LONGITUDE

Day	Sid.Time	☉	0 hr ☽	Noon ☽	True ☊	☿	♀	♂	?	♃	♄	♅	♆	♇
1 Su	22 35 31	10♓29 21	8♐38 39	15♐29 46	11♓49.9	22♒57.1	19♓07.2	26♈00.3	13♓48.4	5♏49.6	4♉51.2	7♎50.5	0♐53.4	26♍28.7
2 M	22 39 27	11 29 33	22 26 15	29 28 07	11D49.9	24 32.7	20 22.1	26 43.5	14 12.0	5R47.7	4 56.7	7R48.3	0R53.5	26R27.2
3 Tu	22 43 24	12 29 44	6♑35 14	13♑47 21	11 49.9	26 09.4	21 36.9	27 26.7	14 35.7	5 45.6	5 02.4	7 46.1	0 53.5	26 25.6
4 W	22 47 20	13 29 53	21 04 06	28 24 57	11 50.1	27 47.2	22 51.8	28 09.8	14 59.3	5 43.3	5 08.1	7 43.8	0 53.4	26 24.0
5 Th	22 51 17	14 30 01	5♒49 17	13♒16 17	11 50.3	29 26.1	24 06.6	28 52.8	15 22.9	5 40.9	5 13.8	7 41.5	0 53.4	26 22.4
6 F	22 55 13	15 30 06	20 45 04	28 14 40	11R50.5	1♓06.0	25 21.5	29 35.9	15 46.6	5 38.2	5 19.7	7 39.2	0 53.3	26 20.9
7 Sa	22 59 10	16 30 10	5♓44 01	13♓12 06	11 50.5	2 47.0	26 36.3	0♉18.9	16 10.2	5 35.4	5 25.5	7 36.8	0 53.2	26 19.3
8 Su	23 03 06	17 30 13	20 37 51	28 00 17	11 50.4	4 29.2	27 51.0	1 01.8	16 33.9	5 32.4	5 31.5	7 34.4	0 53.0	26 17.7
9 M	23 07 03	18 30 13	5♈18 32	12♈31 50	11 49.9	6 12.4	29 05.8	1 44.7	16 57.5	5 29.2	5 37.5	7 32.0	0 52.8	26 16.0
10 Tu	23 11 00	19 30 11	19 39 32	26 41 11	11 49.0	7 56.8	0♈20.5	2 27.6	17 21.1	5 25.9	5 43.6	7 29.6	0 52.6	26 14.4
11 W	23 14 56	20 30 07	3♉36 27	10♉25 10	11 48.0	9 42.3	1 35.2	3 10.4	17 44.8	5 22.4	5 49.7	7 27.2	0 52.3	26 12.8
12 Th	23 18 53	21 30 01	17 07 20	23 43 04	11 46.9	11 29.0	2 49.9	3 53.2	18 08.4	5 18.7	5 55.9	7 24.7	0 52.0	26 11.2
13 F	23 22 49	22 29 53	0♊12 36	6♊36 17	11 46.0	13 16.8	4 04.5	4 36.0	18 32.0	5 14.8	6 02.2	7 22.3	0 51.7	26 09.6
14 Sa	23 26 46	23 29 42	12 54 31	19 07 47	11D45.6	15 05.8	5 19.2	5 18.7	18 55.6	5 10.8	6 08.5	7 19.8	0 51.4	26 07.9
15 Su	23 30 42	24 29 30	25 16 38	1♋21 37	11 45.6	16 56.0	6 33.8	6 01.4	19 19.2	5 06.6	6 14.9	7 17.3	0 51.0	26 06.3
16 M	23 34 39	25 29 15	7♋23 19	13 22 20	11 46.3	18 47.3	7 48.4	6 44.0	19 42.8	5 02.2	6 21.3	7 14.7	0 50.6	26 04.7
17 Tu	23 38 35	26 28 58	19 19 15	25 14 40	11 47.4	20 39.9	9 02.9	7 26.6	20 06.4	4 57.7	6 27.8	7 12.2	0 50.1	26 03.0
18 W	23 42 32	27 28 38	1♌09 07	7♌03 09	11 48.9	22 33.6	10 17.4	8 09.2	20 30.0	4 53.0	6 34.4	7 09.7	0 49.6	26 01.4
19 Th	23 46 29	28 28 17	12 57 18	18 52 01	11 50.3	24 28.5	11 31.9	8 51.7	20 53.5	4 48.2	6 40.9	7 07.1	0 49.1	25 59.8
20 F	23 50 25	29 27 53	24 47 45	0♍44 55	11R51.3	26 24.5	12 46.4	9 34.1	21 17.1	4 43.2	6 47.6	7 04.6	0 48.6	25 58.2
21 Sa	23 54 22	0♈27 27	6♍43 53	12 44 57	11 51.7	28 21.7	14 00.8	10 16.6	21 40.6	4 38.1	6 54.3	7 02.0	0 48.0	25 56.5
22 Su	23 58 18	1 26 59	18 48 26	24 54 32	11 51.1	0♈19.8	15 15.2	10 58.9	22 04.2	4 32.8	7 01.0	6 59.4	0 47.4	25 54.9
23 M	0 02 15	2 26 29	1♎03 30	7♎15 28	11 49.5	2 19.0	16 29.6	11 41.3	22 27.7	4 27.4	7 07.8	6 56.8	0 46.7	25 53.3
24 Tu	0 06 11	3 25 56	13 30 34	19 48 54	11 46.9	4 19.1	17 43.9	12 23.6	22 51.2	4 21.9	7 14.6	6 54.2	0 46.1	25 51.7
25 W	0 10 08	4 25 22	26 10 33	2♏35 34	11 43.5	6 20.0	18 58.2	13 05.8	23 14.7	4 16.2	7 21.4	6 51.6	0 45.4	25 50.1
26 Th	0 14 04	5 24 46	9♏03 58	15 35 45	11 39.9	8 21.6	20 12.5	13 48.0	23 38.1	4 10.4	7 28.3	6 49.0	0 44.7	25 48.4
27 F	0 18 01	6 24 09	22 10 58	28 49 36	11 36.3	10 23.7	21 26.8	14 30.2	24 01.6	4 04.4	7 35.3	6 46.4	0 43.9	25 46.8
28 Sa	0 21 58	7 23 29	5♐31 37	12♐17 03	11 33.4	12 26.2	22 41.0	15 12.3	24 25.0	3 58.4	7 42.3	6 43.8	0 43.1	25 45.3
29 Su	0 25 54	8 22 48	19 05 51	25 58 00	11D31.6	14 28.8	23 55.3	15 54.4	24 48.4	3 52.2	7 49.3	6 41.2	0 42.3	25 43.7
30 M	0 29 51	9 22 05	2♑53 28	9♑52 11	11 31.1	16 31.4	25 09.4	16 36.5	25 11.8	3 45.9	7 56.4	6 38.6	0 41.5	25 42.1
31 Tu	0 33 47	10 21 20	16 54 03	23 58 55	11 31.6	18 33.5	26 23.6	17 18.5	25 35.2	3 39.4	8 03.5	6 36.0	0 40.6	25 40.5

April 1970

LONGITUDE

Day	Sid.Time	☉	0 hr ☽	Noon ☽	True ☊	☿	♀	♂	?	♃	♄	♅	♆	♇
1 W	0 37 44	11♈20 34	1♒06 38	8♒16 55	11♓33.0	20♈35.0	27♈37.7	18♉00.5	25♓58.6	3♏32.9	8♉10.6	6♎33.5	0♐39.7	25♍39.0
2 Th	0 41 40	12 19 46	15 29 27	22 43 52	11 34.4	22 35.5	28 51.8	18 42.4	26 21.9	3R26.3	8 17.8	6R30.9	0R38.8	25R37.4
3 F	0 45 37	13 18 56	29 59 40	7♓16 19	11R35.3	24 34.6	0♉05.9	19 24.3	26 45.2	3 19.5	8 25.0	6 28.3	0 37.9	25 35.9
4 Sa	0 49 33	14 18 04	14♓33 10	21 49 33	11 35.0	26 32.0	1 20.0	20 06.2	27 08.5	3 12.7	8 32.3	6 25.7	0 36.9	25 34.3
5 Su	0 53 30	15 17 10	29 04 45	6♈18 00	11 33.1	28 27.3	2 34.0	20 48.0	27 31.8	3 05.8	8 39.6	6 23.1	0 35.9	25 32.8
6 M	0 57 27	16 16 14	13♈28 34	20 35 45	11 29.4	0♉20.2	3 48.0	21 29.8	27 55.0	2 58.8	8 46.9	6 20.6	0 34.8	25 31.3
7 Tu	1 01 23	17 15 16	27 38 53	4♉37 24	11 24.3	2 10.2	5 01.9	22 11.5	28 18.2	2 51.7	8 54.2	6 18.0	0 33.8	25 29.8
8 W	1 05 20	18 14 16	11♉30 50	18 18 49	11 18.3	3 57.0	6 15.9	22 53.2	28 41.4	2 44.5	9 01.6	6 15.5	0 32.7	25 28.3
9 Th	1 09 16	19 13 14	25 01 08	1♊37 40	11 12.2	5 40.2	7 29.8	23 34.9	29 04.6	2 37.3	9 09.0	6 13.0	0 31.6	25 26.8
10 F	1 13 13	20 12 10	8♊08 27	14 33 36	11 06.7	7 19.5	8 43.6	24 16.5	29 27.7	2 30.0	9 16.4	6 10.5	0 30.5	25 25.4
11 Sa	1 17 09	21 11 03	20 53 24	27 08 11	11 02.4	8 54.7	9 57.5	24 58.1	29 50.8	2 22.6	9 23.9	6 08.0	0 29.4	25 24.0
12 Su	1 21 06	22 09 54	3♋18 23	9♋24 29	10 59.7	10 25.4	11 11.3	25 39.6	0♈13.8	2 15.2	9 31.3	6 05.5	0 28.2	25 22.5
13 M	1 25 02	23 08 43	15 27 03	21 26 40	10D58.7	11 51.5	12 25.0	26 21.1	0 36.9	2 07.7	9 38.8	6 03.1	0 27.0	25 21.1
14 Tu	1 28 59	24 07 30	27 23 59	3♌19 37	10 59.1	13 12.7	13 38.8	27 02.6	0 59.9	2 00.2	9 46.3	6 00.6	0 25.8	25 19.7
15 W	1 32 56	25 06 14	9♌14 14	15 08 29	11 00.4	14 28.8	14 52.5	27 44.0	1 22.8	1 52.7	9 53.9	5 58.2	0 24.6	25 18.4
16 Th	1 36 52	26 04 57	21 02 59	26 58 22	11 01.9	15 39.7	16 06.1	28 25.4	1 45.7	1 45.1	10 01.4	5 55.8	0 23.3	25 17.0
17 F	1 40 49	27 03 37	2♍55 13	8♍54 06	11R02.7	16 45.2	17 19.7	29 06.7	2 08.6	1 37.5	10 09.0	5 53.4	0 22.0	25 15.7
18 Sa	1 44 45	28 02 14	14 55 31	20 59 55	11 02.2	17 45.2	18 33.3	29 48.0	2 31.4	1 29.8	10 16.6	5 51.1	0 20.7	25 14.4
19 Su	1 48 42	29 00 50	27 07 42	3♎19 13	10 59.8	18 39.6	19 46.8	0♊29.3	2 54.2	1 22.2	10 24.2	5 48.7	0 19.4	25 13.0
20 M	1 52 38	29 59 24	9♎34 44	15 54 24	10 55.2	19 28.3	21 00.3	1 10.5	3 17.0	1 14.5	10 31.8	5 46.4	0 18.1	25 11.8
21 Tu	1 56 35	0♉57 55	22 18 21	28 46 35	10 48.5	20 11.3	22 13.8	1 51.6	3 39.7	1 06.8	10 39.4	5 44.2	0 16.7	25 10.5
22 W	2 00 31	1 56 25	5♏19 04	11♏55 40	10 40.4	20 48.5	23 27.3	2 32.8	4 02.4	0 59.2	10 47.0	5 41.9	0 15.4	25 09.3
23 Th	2 04 28	2 54 53	18 36 11	25 20 21	10 31.5	21 19.8	24 40.7	3 13.9	4 25.1	0 51.5	10 54.7	5 39.7	0 14.0	25 08.0
24 F	2 08 24	3 53 19	2♐07 53	8♐58 25	10 22.8	21 45.2	25 54.0	3 54.9	4 47.7	0 43.8	11 02.4	5 37.5	0 12.6	25 06.9
25 Sa	2 12 21	4 51 44	15 51 39	22 47 12	10 15.4	22 04.8	27 07.3	4 35.9	5 10.2	0 36.2	11 10.0	5 35.3	0 11.2	25 05.7
26 Su	2 16 18	5 50 07	29 44 44	6♑43 57	10 09.9	22 18.6	28 20.6	5 16.9	5 32.8	0 28.6	11 17.7	5 33.2	0 09.7	25 04.5
27 M	2 20 14	6 48 29	13♑44 33	20 46 17	10 06.6	22R26.7	29 33.9	5 57.9	5 55.2	0 21.0	11 25.4	5 31.1	0 08.3	25 03.4
28 Tu	2 24 11	7 46 48	27 48 57	4♒52 22	10D05.4	22 29.2	0♊47.1	6 38.8	6 17.7	0 13.4	11 33.1	5 29.0	0 06.8	25 02.3
29 W	2 28 07	8 45 07	11♒56 22	19 00 48	10 05.7	22 26.3	2 00.3	7 19.6	6 40.0	0 05.9	11 40.8	5 27.0	0 05.4	25 01.2
30 Th	2 32 04	9 43 24	26 05 31	3♓10 21	10R06.4	22 18.1	3 13.5	8 00.5	7 02.4	29♎58.4	11 48.5	5 24.9	0 03.9	25 00.2

Astro Data

	Dy Hr Mn
♆ R	3 9:00
☽ 0N	8 10:05
♃☍♄	8 14:26
♀0N	12 12:52
☉0N	21 0:56
♄⚻♅	22 7:57
☽ 0S	22 15:48
☿0N	23 19:37
☽ 0N	4 20:16
♄□♇	18 6:03
☽ 0S	18 23:18
☿ R	28 10:51
♃⚺♆	29 13:58

Planet Ingress

	Dy Hr Mn
☿ ♓	5 20:10
♂ ♉	7 1:28
♀ ♈	10 5:25
☉ ♈	21 0:56
☿ ♈	22 7:59
♀ ♉	3 10:05
☿ ♉	6 7:40
? ♈	11 21:36
♂ ♊	18 18:59
☉ ♉	20 12:15
♀ ♊	27 20:33
♃ ♎R	30 6:43

Last Aspect / ☽ Ingress (March)

Last Aspect Dy Hr Mn		☽ Ingress Dy Hr Mn
2 7:05 ♂ △	♑	2 12:54
4 11:34 ♂ □	♒	4 14:34
6 14:17 ♂ ⚹	♓	6 14:49
8 11:44 ♀ ☌	♈	8 15:16
9 3:42 ♅ ☍	♉	10 17:43
12 16:32 ♇ △	♊	12 23:37
15 1:39 ♇ □	♋	15 9:18
17 14:45 ☉ △	♌	17 21:40
18 19:21 ♀ △	♍	20 10:30
22 13:58 ♇ ☌	♎	22 21:56
24 7:37 ♀ ☍	♏	25 7:10
27 6:31 ♇ ⚹	♐	27 14:07
29 11:35 ♇ □	♑	29 19:00
31 16:27 ♀ □	♒	31 22:08

Last Aspect / ☽ Ingress (April)

Last Aspect Dy Hr Mn		☽ Ingress Dy Hr Mn
2 23:04 ♀ ⚹	♓	3 0:01
4 18:11 ♇ ☍	♈	5 1:32
6 4:09 ☉ ☌	♉	7 4:02
9 0:48 ♇ △	♊	9 9:02
11 8:39 ♇ □	♋	11 17:33
13 22:30 ♂ ⚹	♌	14 5:16
16 15:07 ♂ □	♍	16 18:07
18 20:18 ♇ ☌	♎	19 5:35
19 16:47 ♅ ☌	♏	21 14:15
23 11:38 ♇ ⚹	♐	23 20:15
25 15:59 ♇ □	♑	26 0:26
27 19:18 ♇ △	♒	28 3:43
29 17:46 ☿ □	♓	30 6:37

☽ Phases & Eclipses

Dy Hr Mn	
1 2:33	☾ 10♐06
7 17:42	● 16♓44
7 17:37:49	● T 03'28"
14 21:16	☽ 23♊53
23 1:52	○ 2♎01
30 11:04	☾ 9♑20
6 4:09	● 15♈57
13 15:44	☽ 23♋18
21 16:21	○ 1♏09
28 17:18	☾ 8♒00

Astro Data

1 March 1970
Julian Day # 25627
SVP 5♓40'29"
GC 26♐25.4 ⚳ 18♒50.0
Eris 11♈45.0 ⚵ 1♓03.4
⚷ 4♈48.4 ⚶ 13♌48.8R
☽ Mean ☊ 12♓08.1

1 April 1970
Julian Day # 25658
SVP 5♓40'25"
GC 26♐25.4 ⚳ 28♒39.0
Eris 12♈05.1 ⚵ 15♓33.9
⚷ 6♈35.6 ⚶ 11♌10.3
☽ Mean ☊ 10♓29.6

LONGITUDE — May 1970

Day	Sid.Time	☉	0 hr ☽	Noon ☽	True ☊	☿	♀	♂	⚳	♃	♄	♅	♆	♇
1 F	2 36 00	10♉41 39	10♓15 08	17♓19 39	10♓06.3	22♉05.0	4♊26.6	8♊41.3	7♈24.7	29♎50.9	11♉56.2	5♎23.0	0♐02.4	24♍59.1
2 Sa	2 39 57	11 39 53	24 23 36	1♈26 42	10R 04.5	21R 47.2	5 39.7	9 22.0	7 46.9	29R 43.5	12 03.9	5R 21.0	0R 00.9	24R 58.1
3 Su	2 43 53	12 38 05	8♈28 35	15 28 51	10 00.2	21 25.2	6 52.7	10 02.8	8 09.1	29 36.1	12 11.6	5 19.1	29♏59.3	24 57.1
4 M	2 47 50	13 36 16	22 27 02	29 22 43	9 53.3	20 59.4	8 05.8	10 43.5	8 31.2	29 28.8	12 19.3	5 17.2	29 57.8	24 56.2
5 Tu	2 51 47	14 34 25	6♉15 25	13♉04 43	9 44.0	20 30.3	9 18.7	11 24.1	8 53.3	29 21.6	12 27.0	5 15.4	29 56.2	24 55.2
6 W	2 55 43	15 32 32	19 50 10	26 31 28	9 33.2	19 58.4	10 31.7	12 04.8	9 15.3	29 14.4	12 34.7	5 13.6	29 54.7	24 54.3
7 Th	2 59 40	16 30 38	3♊08 18	9♊40 30	9 21.9	19 24.4	11 44.6	12 45.3	9 37.3	29 07.4	12 42.4	5 11.9	29 53.1	24 53.4
8 F	3 03 36	17 28 42	16 07 57	22 30 40	9 11.3	18 48.8	12 57.5	13 25.9	9 59.2	29 00.4	12 50.1	5 10.2	29 51.6	24 52.6
9 Sa	3 07 33	18 26 45	28 48 44	5♋02 21	9 02.3	18 12.4	14 10.3	14 06.4	10 21.0	28 53.5	12 57.8	5 08.5	29 50.0	24 51.8
10 Su	3 11 29	19 24 45	11♋11 49	17 17 30	8 55.5	17 35.7	15 23.1	14 46.9	10 42.8	28 46.6	13 05.5	5 06.9	29 48.4	24 51.0
11 M	3 15 26	20 22 44	23 19 50	29 19 21	8 51.3	16 59.4	16 35.8	15 27.4	11 04.5	28 39.9	13 13.2	5 05.3	29 46.8	24 50.2
12 Tu	3 19 23	21 20 41	5♌16 36	11♌12 12	8D 49.2	16 24.1	17 48.5	16 07.8	11 26.2	28 33.3	13 20.9	5 03.7	29 45.2	24 49.5
13 W	3 23 19	22 18 36	17 06 48	23 01 03	8 48.8	15 50.4	19 01.2	16 48.1	11 47.8	28 26.8	13 28.5	5 02.2	29 43.6	24 48.7
14 Th	3 27 16	23 16 29	28 55 39	4♍51 16	8R 49.0	15 18.9	20 13.8	17 28.5	12 09.3	28 20.3	13 36.2	5 00.8	29 42.0	24 48.1
15 F	3 31 12	24 14 20	10♍48 36	16 48 18	8 48.8	14 50.1	21 26.4	18 08.8	12 30.8	28 14.0	13 43.8	4 59.3	29 40.4	24 47.4
16 Sa	3 35 09	25 12 10	22 51 00	28 57 17	8 47.2	14 24.4	22 38.9	18 49.0	12 52.2	28 07.8	13 51.4	4 58.0	29 38.8	24 46.8
17 Su	3 39 05	26 09 58	5♎07 42	11♎22 42	8 43.5	14 02.2	23 51.3	19 29.3	13 13.5	28 01.8	13 59.0	4 56.6	29 37.1	24 46.2
18 M	3 43 02	27 07 44	17 42 41	24 07 56	8 37.2	13 43.7	25 03.8	20 09.5	13 34.7	27 55.8	14 06.6	4 55.4	29 35.5	24 45.6
19 Tu	3 46 58	28 05 29	0♏38 38	7♏14 52	8 28.3	13 29.3	26 16.2	20 49.6	13 55.9	27 50.0	14 14.2	4 54.1	29 33.9	24 45.1
20 W	3 50 55	29 03 12	13 56 33	20 43 29	8 17.5	13 19.2	27 28.5	21 29.7	14 17.0	27 44.3	14 21.7	4 52.9	29 32.3	24 44.6
21 Th	3 54 52	0♊00 54	27 35 24	4♐31 49	8 05.8	13D 13.4	28 40.8	22 09.8	14 38.1	27 38.7	14 29.3	4 51.8	29 30.6	24 44.1
22 F	3 58 48	0 58 35	11♐32 14	18 36 02	7 54.3	13 12.2	29 53.0	22 49.9	14 59.0	27 33.3	14 36.8	4 50.7	29 29.0	24 43.6
23 Sa	4 02 45	1 56 15	25 42 33	2♑51 05	7 44.2	13 15.4	1♋05.2	23 29.9	15 19.9	27 28.0	14 44.3	4 49.7	29 27.4	24 43.2
24 Su	4 06 41	2 53 54	10♑00 57	17 11 29	7 36.4	13 23.2	2 17.4	24 09.9	15 40.8	27 22.8	14 51.7	4 48.7	29 25.8	24 42.8
25 M	4 10 38	3 51 31	24 22 07	1♒32 17	7 31.4	13 35.5	3 29.5	24 49.9	16 01.5	27 17.8	14 59.2	4 47.7	29 24.2	24 42.5
26 Tu	4 14 34	4 49 08	8♒41 33	15 49 35	7 28.9	13 52.3	4 41.5	25 29.8	16 22.2	27 13.0	15 06.6	4 46.8	29 22.5	24 42.2
27 W	4 18 31	5 46 43	22 56 05	0♓00 51	7 28.2	14 13.5	5 53.5	26 09.7	16 42.7	27 08.2	15 14.0	4 46.0	29 20.9	24 41.9
28 Th	4 22 27	6 44 18	7♓03 47	14 04 46	7 28.1	14 38.9	7 05.5	26 49.6	17 03.2	27 03.7	15 21.4	4 45.2	29 19.3	24 41.6
29 F	4 26 24	7 41 51	21 03 46	28 00 44	7 27.4	15 08.7	8 17.4	27 29.4	17 23.7	26 59.3	15 28.8	4 44.4	29 17.7	24 41.4
30 Sa	4 30 21	8 39 24	4♈55 39	11♈48 27	7 24.9	15 42.5	9 29.3	28 09.3	17 44.0	26 55.0	15 36.1	4 43.7	29 16.1	24 41.2
31 Su	4 34 17	9 36 56	18 39 03	25 27 23	7 19.7	16 20.4	10 41.1	28 49.0	18 04.2	26 50.9	15 43.4	4 43.1	29 14.5	24 41.0

LONGITUDE — June 1970

Day	Sid.Time	☉	0 hr ☽	Noon ☽	True ☊	☿	♀	♂	⚳	♃	♄	♅	♆	♇
1 M	4 38 14	10♊34 28	2♉13 18	8♉56 39	7♓11.6	17♉02.2	11♋52.9	29♊28.8	18♈24.4	26♎47.0	15♉50.6	4♎42.5	29♏12.9	24♍40.9
2 Tu	4 42 10	11 31 58	15 37 14	22 14 52	7R 01.1	17 47.8	13 04.6	0♋08.5	18 44.5	26R 43.2	15 57.9	4R 41.9	29R 11.3	24R 40.8
3 W	4 46 07	12 29 28	28 49 22	5♊20 32	6 48.8	18 37.1	14 16.3	0 48.2	19 04.4	26 39.6	16 05.1	4 41.4	29 09.8	24 40.7
4 Th	4 50 03	13 26 56	11♊48 13	18 12 18	6 35.9	19 30.1	15 27.9	1 27.9	19 24.3	26 36.2	16 12.3	4 41.0	29 08.2	24D 40.7
5 F	4 54 00	14 24 24	24 32 42	0♋49 23	6 23.6	20 26.6	16 39.5	2 07.6	19 44.1	26 32.9	16 19.4	4 40.6	29 06.6	24 40.7
6 Sa	4 57 56	15 21 51	7♋02 26	13 11 57	6 12.9	21 26.5	17 51.0	2 47.2	20 03.8	26 29.8	16 26.5	4 40.3	29 05.1	24 40.7
7 Su	5 01 53	16 19 17	19 18 07	25 21 13	6 04.7	22 29.8	19 02.4	3 26.8	20 23.4	26 26.9	16 33.6	4 40.0	29 03.5	24 40.8
8 M	5 05 50	17 16 41	1♌21 34	7♌19 34	5 59.1	23 36.5	20 13.8	4 06.3	20 42.8	26 24.1	16 40.6	4 39.7	29 02.0	24 40.9
9 Tu	5 09 46	18 14 05	13 15 41	19 10 25	5 56.0	24 46.3	21 25.2	4 45.9	21 02.2	26 21.6	16 47.6	4 39.6	29 00.5	24 41.0
10 W	5 13 43	19 11 27	25 04 21	0♍58 05	5D 55.0	25 59.4	22 36.5	5 25.4	21 21.5	26 19.2	16 54.5	4 39.4	28 59.0	24 41.1
11 Th	5 17 39	20 08 49	6♍52 15	12 47 31	5R 55.0	27 15.6	23 47.7	6 04.8	21 40.6	26 16.9	17 01.4	4D 39.4	28 57.5	24 41.3
12 F	5 21 36	21 06 09	18 44 34	24 44 05	5 55.0	28 34.9	24 58.9	6 44.3	21 59.7	26 14.9	17 08.3	4 39.3	28 56.0	24 41.5
13 Sa	5 25 32	22 03 29	0♎46 45	6♎53 14	5 54.1	29 57.3	26 09.9	7 23.7	22 18.6	26 13.0	17 15.1	4 39.4	28 54.5	24 41.8
14 Su	5 29 29	23 00 47	13 04 09	19 20 06	5 51.3	1♊22.8	27 21.0	8 03.1	22 37.5	26 11.3	17 21.9	4 39.5	28 53.1	24 42.1
15 M	5 33 25	23 58 05	25 41 35	2♏09 01	5 46.3	2 51.2	28 31.9	8 42.4	22 56.2	26 09.8	17 28.6	4 39.6	28 51.6	24 42.4
16 Tu	5 37 22	24 55 22	8♏42 44	15 22 55	5 38.9	4 22.6	29 42.8	9 21.8	23 14.8	26 08.5	17 35.3	4 39.8	28 50.2	24 42.7
17 W	5 41 19	25 52 38	22 09 38	29 02 46	5 29.6	5 57.0	0♌53.7	10 01.1	23 33.3	26 07.4	17 42.0	4 40.0	28 48.8	24 43.1
18 Th	5 45 15	26 49 53	6♐02 03	13♐07 02	5 19.4	7 34.4	2 04.4	10 40.4	23 51.7	26 06.4	17 48.6	4 40.3	28 47.4	24 43.5
19 F	5 49 12	27 47 08	20 17 08	27 31 37	5 09.2	9 14.6	3 15.1	11 19.6	24 09.9	26 05.6	17 55.1	4 40.7	28 46.0	24 44.0
20 Sa	5 53 08	28 44 23	4♑49 37	12♑10 12	5 00.3	10 57.8	4 25.7	11 58.8	24 28.1	26 05.0	18 01.6	4 41.1	28 44.7	24 44.5
21 Su	5 57 05	29 41 37	19 32 25	26 55 15	4 53.4	12 43.7	5 36.2	12 38.0	24 46.1	26 04.6	18 08.1	4 41.6	28 43.3	24 45.0
22 M	6 01 01	0♋38 50	4♒17 49	11♒39 14	4 49.2	14 32.5	6 46.7	13 17.2	25 03.9	26D 04.3	18 14.5	4 42.1	28 42.0	24 45.5
23 Tu	6 04 58	1 36 04	18 58 45	26 15 44	4D 47.3	16 24.0	7 57.1	13 56.4	25 21.7	26 04.2	18 20.8	4 42.6	28 40.7	24 46.1
24 W	6 08 55	2 33 17	3♓29 41	10♓40 12	4 47.1	18 18.1	9 07.4	14 35.5	25 39.3	26 04.4	18 27.1	4 43.2	28 39.4	24 46.7
25 Th	6 12 51	3 30 30	17 47 03	24 50 03	4R 47.7	20 14.7	10 17.7	15 14.6	25 56.8	26 04.6	18 33.3	4 43.9	28 38.2	24 47.3
26 F	6 16 48	4 27 44	1♈49 09	8♈44 21	4 47.8	22 13.7	11 27.8	15 53.7	26 14.2	26 05.1	18 39.5	4 44.6	28 36.9	24 48.0
27 Sa	6 20 44	5 24 57	15 35 42	22 23 17	4 46.5	24 14.9	12 37.9	16 32.8	26 31.4	26 05.7	18 45.6	4 45.4	28 35.7	24 48.7
28 Su	6 24 41	6 22 10	29 07 13	5♉47 37	4 43.1	26 18.1	13 48.0	17 11.8	26 48.4	26 06.6	18 51.7	4 46.2	28 34.5	24 49.4
29 M	6 28 37	7 19 24	12♉24 35	18 58 13	4 37.4	28 23.2	14 57.9	17 50.8	27 05.4	26 07.6	18 57.7	4 47.1	28 33.3	24 50.2
30 Tu	6 32 34	8 16 37	25 28 36	1♊55 49	4 29.5	0♋29.8	16 07.8	18 29.9	27 22.2	26 08.8	19 03.7	4 48.0	28 32.1	24 51.0

Astro Data (Dy Hr Mn)

☽0N 2 3:50
☽0S 16 7:06
☿D 22 6:46
☽0N 29 8:57

♇D 5 2:24
⚳0N 11 8:25
♅D 12 9:40
☽0S 12 14:28
♃D 23 9:44
☽0N 25 13:37

Planet Ingress (Dy Hr Mn)

♆ ♏R 3 1:31
☉ ♊ 21 11:37
♀ ♋ 22 14:19

♂ ♋ 2 6:50
☿ ♊ 13 12:46
♀ ♌ 16 17:49
☉ ♋ 21 19:43
☿ ♋ 30 6:22

Last Aspect Dy Hr Mn		☽ Ingress Dy Hr Mn
2 0:59	♇ ☍	♈ 2 9:32
4 12:11	♃ ☍	♉ 4 13:05
6 18:07	♆ ☍	♊ 6 18:17
9 0:16	♃ △	♋ 9 2:17
11 12:55	♆ △	♌ 11 13:22
14 1:35	♆ □	♍ 14 2:10
16 13:21	♆ ⚹	♎ 16 14:02
18 18:58	♃ ☌	♏ 18 22:49
21 3:38	☉ ☍	♐ 21 4:11
23 3:01	♃ ⚹	♑ 23 7:13
25 8:26	♆ ⚹	♒ 25 9:25
27 10:52	♆ □	♓ 27 11:59
29 14:13	♆ △	♈ 29 15:27
31 18:16	♂ ⚹	♉ 31 20:03

Last Aspect Dy Hr Mn		☽ Ingress Dy Hr Mn
3 0:39	♆ ☍	♊ 3 2:10
5 3:51	♃ △	♋ 5 10:25
7 19:23	♆ △	♌ 7 21:17
10 7:58	♆ □	♍ 10 10:02
12 20:37	♆ △	♎ 12 22:28
15 4:37	♀ □	♏ 15 8:02
17 11:36	♆ ☌	♐ 17 13:39
19 12:27	☉ ☍	♑ 19 16:04
21 14:56	♆ ⚹	♒ 21 17:00
23 16:00	♆ □	♓ 23 18:11
25 18:31	♆ △	♈ 25 20:52
27 18:36	♃ ☍	♉ 28 1:35
30 5:41	♆ ☍	♊ 30 8:24

☽ Phases & Eclipses (Dy Hr Mn)

5 14:51 ● 14♉41
13 10:26 ☽ 22♌15
21 3:38 ○ 29♏41
27 22:32 ☾ 6♓12

4 2:21 ● 13♊04
12 4:06 ☽ 20♍47
19 12:27 ○ 27♐48
26 4:01 ☾ 4♈09

Astro Data

1 May 1970
Julian Day # 25688
SVP 5♓40'22"
GC 26♐25.5 ⚴ 6♓41.6
Eris 12♈24.9 ⚵ 29♓45.4
⚷ 8♈16.3 ⚶ 15♌16.7
☽ Mean ☊ 8♓54.3

1 June 1970
Julian Day # 25719
SVP 5♓40'17"
GC 26♐25.6 ⚴ 12♓33.9
Eris 12♈40.7 ⚵ 14♈18.2
⚷ 9♈37.3 ⚶ 24♌19.8
☽ Mean ☊ 7♓15.8

July 1970 LONGITUDE

Day	Sid.Time	☉	0 hr ☽	Noon ☽	True ☊	☿	♀	♂	⚳	♃	♄	♅	♆	♇
1 W	6 36 30	9♋13 51	8♊19 54	14♊40 54	4♓20.3	2♋37.8	17♌17.6	19♋08.8	27♈38.8	26♎10.1	19♉09.6	4♎49.0	28♏31.0	24♍51.8
2 Th	6 40 27	10 11 05	20 58 53	27 13 53	4R 10.5	4 46.9	18 27.3	19 47.8	27 55.3	26 11.7	19 15.4	4 50.0	28R 29.9	24 52.6
3 F	6 44 24	11 08 18	3♋25 58	9♋35 13	4 01.1	6 56.6	19 36.9	20 26.8	28 11.6	26 13.4	19 21.2	4 51.1	28 28.8	24 53.5
4 Sa	6 48 20	12 05 32	15 41 43	21 45 38	3 53.1	9 06.9	20 46.4	21 05.7	28 27.8	26 15.3	19 26.9	4 52.3	28 27.7	24 54.4
5 Su	6 52 17	13 02 45	27 47 07	3♌46 25	3 46.9	11 17.3	21 55.9	21 44.6	28 43.8	26 17.3	19 32.5	4 53.5	28 26.6	24 55.4
6 M	6 56 13	13 59 59	9♌43 46	15 39 28	3 43.0	13 27.7	23 05.2	22 23.5	28 59.7	26 19.6	19 38.1	4 54.7	28 25.6	24 56.3
7 Tu	7 00 10	14 57 12	21 33 55	27 27 29	3D 41.1	15 37.6	24 14.5	23 02.3	29 15.3	26 22.0	19 43.6	4 56.0	28 24.6	24 57.3
8 W	7 04 06	15 54 25	3♍20 38	9♍13 52	3 41.1	17 47.0	25 23.6	23 41.2	29 30.9	26 24.6	19 49.0	4 57.3	28 23.6	24 58.4
9 Th	7 08 03	16 51 38	15 07 42	21 02 43	3 42.1	19 55.5	26 32.7	24 20.0	29 46.2	26 27.3	19 54.4	4 58.7	28 22.7	24 59.4
10 F	7 11 59	17 48 51	26 59 31	2♎58 44	3 43.5	22 03.0	27 41.6	24 58.8	0♉01.4	26 30.2	19 59.6	5 00.1	28 21.7	25 00.5
11 Sa	7 15 56	18 46 04	9♎00 58	15 06 54	3R 44.3	24 09.3	28 50.5	25 37.6	0 16.4	26 33.3	20 04.9	5 01.6	28 20.8	25 01.6
12 Su	7 19 53	19 43 16	21 17 09	27 32 19	3 44.1	26 14.2	29 59.2	26 16.3	0 31.2	26 36.6	20 10.0	5 03.2	28 20.0	25 02.8
13 M	7 23 49	20 40 29	3♏52 59	10♏19 40	3 42.2	28 17.7	1♍07.9	26 55.1	0 45.8	26 40.0	20 15.1	5 04.8	28 19.1	25 03.9
14 Tu	7 27 46	21 37 42	16 52 47	23 32 41	3 38.7	0♌19.7	2 16.4	27 33.8	1 00.3	26 43.6	20 20.1	5 06.4	28 18.3	25 05.1
15 W	7 31 42	22 34 55	0♐19 34	7♐13 29	3 33.7	2 20.0	3 24.8	28 12.5	1 14.5	26 47.4	20 25.0	5 08.1	28 17.5	25 06.4
16 Th	7 35 39	23 32 08	14 14 21	21 21 52	3 28.0	4 18.6	4 33.1	28 51.2	1 28.6	26 51.3	20 29.9	5 09.8	28 16.8	25 07.6
17 F	7 39 35	24 29 22	28 35 35	5♑54 49	3 22.1	6 15.5	5 41.2	29 29.9	1 42.5	26 55.4	20 34.7	5 11.6	28 16.0	25 08.9
18 Sa	7 43 32	25 26 35	13♑18 48	20 46 31	3 16.9	8 10.7	6 49.3	0♌08.5	1 56.2	26 59.7	20 39.4	5 13.4	28 15.3	25 10.2
19 Su	7 47 28	26 23 49	28 16 56	5♒48 53	3 13.1	10 04.0	7 57.2	0 47.1	2 09.7	27 04.1	20 44.0	5 15.3	28 14.6	25 11.5
20 M	7 51 25	27 21 04	13♒21 14	20 52 51	3D 11.0	11 55.6	9 05.0	1 25.8	2 22.9	27 08.6	20 48.5	5 17.2	28 14.0	25 12.9
21 Tu	7 55 22	28 18 19	28 22 40	5♓49 44	3 10.5	13 45.3	10 12.6	2 04.4	2 36.0	27 13.3	20 53.0	5 19.1	28 13.4	25 14.3
22 W	7 59 18	29 15 35	13♓13 12	20 32 26	3 11.3	15 33.3	11 20.2	2 42.9	2 48.9	27 18.2	20 57.4	5 21.1	28 12.8	25 15.7
23 Th	8 03 15	0♌12 51	27 46 52	4♈56 10	3 12.7	17 19.5	12 27.6	3 21.5	3 01.6	27 23.2	21 01.7	5 23.2	28 12.2	25 17.1
24 F	8 07 11	1 10 09	12♈00 05	18 58 31	3R 13.9	19 03.9	13 34.8	4 00.1	3 14.0	27 28.4	21 05.9	5 25.3	28 11.7	25 18.6
25 Sa	8 11 08	2 07 27	25 51 29	2♉39 04	3 14.4	20 46.6	14 41.9	4 38.6	3 26.2	27 33.7	21 10.0	5 27.4	28 11.2	25 20.1
26 Su	8 15 04	3 04 46	9♉21 26	15 58 48	3 13.7	22 27.4	15 48.9	5 17.1	3 38.2	27 39.2	21 14.1	5 29.6	28 10.7	25 21.6
27 M	8 19 01	4 02 07	22 31 26	28 59 37	3 11.7	24 06.5	16 55.8	5 55.6	3 50.0	27 44.8	21 18.0	5 31.8	28 10.2	25 23.1
28 Tu	8 22 57	4 59 28	5♊23 37	11♊43 44	3 08.5	25 43.9	18 02.5	6 34.2	4 01.5	27 50.6	21 21.9	5 34.1	28 09.8	25 24.7
29 W	8 26 54	5 56 51	18 00 17	24 13 31	3 04.5	27 19.4	19 09.0	7 12.7	4 12.8	27 56.5	21 25.7	5 36.4	28 09.4	25 26.2
30 Th	8 30 51	6 54 14	0♋23 42	6♋31 07	3 00.1	28 53.3	20 15.4	7 51.1	4 23.9	28 02.6	21 29.4	5 38.8	28 09.1	25 27.8
31 F	8 34 47	7 51 38	12 36 00	18 38 35	2 56.0	0♍25.3	21 21.7	8 29.6	4 34.7	28 08.8	21 33.0	5 41.2	28 08.8	25 29.5

August 1970 LONGITUDE

Day	Sid.Time	☉	0 hr ☽	Noon ☽	True ☊	☿	♀	♂	⚳	♃	♄	♅	♆	♇
1 Sa	8 38 44	8♌49 04	24♋39 07	0♌37 49	2♓52.5	1♍55.6	22♍27.7	9♌08.1	4♉45.3	28♎15.1	21♉36.5	5♎43.6	28♏08.5	25♍31.1
2 Su	8 42 40	9 46 30	6♌34 57	12 30 44	2R 50.0	3 24.1	23 33.7	9 46.5	4 55.6	28 21.6	21 39.9	5 46.1	28R 08.2	25 32.8
3 M	8 46 37	10 43 57	18 25 25	24 19 18	2D 48.6	4 50.8	24 39.4	10 24.9	5 05.7	28 28.2	21 43.3	5 48.6	28 08.0	25 34.5
4 Tu	8 50 33	11 41 24	0♍12 41	6♍05 51	2 48.4	6 15.6	25 45.0	11 03.3	5 15.5	28 35.0	21 46.5	5 51.1	28 07.8	25 36.2
5 W	8 54 30	12 38 53	11 59 10	17 53 00	2 49.1	7 38.6	26 50.4	11 41.8	5 25.1	28 41.9	21 49.7	5 53.7	28 07.6	25 37.9
6 Th	8 58 26	13 36 22	23 47 46	29 43 53	2 50.4	8 59.7	27 55.6	12 20.1	5 34.3	28 48.9	21 52.7	5 56.3	28 07.5	25 39.7
7 F	9 02 23	14 33 52	5♎41 50	11♎42 04	2 51.9	10 18.9	29 00.6	12 58.5	5 43.3	28 56.1	21 55.7	5 59.0	28 07.4	25 41.5
8 Sa	9 06 20	15 31 23	17 45 07	23 51 31	2 53.2	11 36.1	0♎05.4	13 36.9	5 52.1	29 03.4	21 58.5	6 01.7	28 07.3	25 43.2
9 Su	9 10 16	16 28 55	0♏01 47	6♏16 28	2R 54.1	12 51.3	1 10.0	14 15.2	6 00.5	29 10.8	22 01.3	6 04.5	28D 07.3	25 45.1
10 M	9 14 13	17 26 28	12 36 04	19 01 06	2 54.4	14 04.4	2 14.5	14 53.6	6 08.7	29 18.3	22 04.0	6 07.2	28 07.3	25 46.9
11 Tu	9 18 09	18 24 02	25 32 01	2♐09 13	2 53.9	15 15.3	3 18.6	15 31.9	6 16.6	29 26.0	22 06.5	6 10.1	28 07.3	25 48.7
12 W	9 22 06	19 21 36	8♐53 00	15 43 34	2 52.9	16 24.0	4 22.6	16 10.2	6 24.2	29 33.8	22 09.0	6 12.9	28 07.4	25 50.6
13 Th	9 26 02	20 19 12	22 41 01	29 45 17	2 51.6	17 30.4	5 26.4	16 48.5	6 31.5	29 41.7	22 11.4	6 15.8	28 07.5	25 52.5
14 F	9 29 59	21 16 48	6♑56 07	14♑13 09	2 50.1	18 34.3	6 29.9	17 26.8	6 38.5	29 49.8	22 13.6	6 18.7	28 07.6	25 54.4
15 Sa	9 33 56	22 14 26	21 35 46	29 03 13	2 48.9	19 35.7	7 33.1	18 05.1	6 45.2	29 58.0	22 15.8	6 21.7	28 07.8	25 56.3
16 Su	9 37 52	23 12 05	6♒34 37	14♒08 53	2 48.1	20 34.5	8 36.2	18 43.4	6 51.6	0♏06.2	22 17.9	6 24.6	28 08.0	25 58.3
17 M	9 41 49	24 09 44	21 44 52	29 21 23	2D 47.8	21 30.4	9 38.9	19 21.7	6 57.8	0 14.6	22 19.8	6 27.7	28 08.2	26 00.2
18 Tu	9 45 45	25 07 25	6♓57 13	14♓31 10	2 47.9	22 23.5	10 41.4	19 59.9	7 03.6	0 23.1	22 21.7	6 30.7	28 08.4	26 02.2
19 W	9 49 42	26 05 08	22 02 09	29 29 10	2 48.3	23 13.4	11 43.6	20 38.2	7 09.0	0 31.8	22 23.5	6 33.8	28 08.7	26 04.2
20 Th	9 53 38	27 02 52	6♈51 23	14♈08 07	2 48.8	24 00.2	12 45.6	21 16.4	7 14.2	0 40.5	22 25.1	6 36.9	28 09.0	26 06.2
21 F	9 57 35	28 00 37	21 18 51	28 23 14	2 49.3	24 43.4	13 47.2	21 54.6	7 19.0	0 49.3	22 26.7	6 40.0	28 09.4	26 08.2
22 Sa	10 01 31	28 58 25	5♉21 06	12♉12 25	2 49.6	25 23.0	14 48.6	22 32.9	7 23.6	0 58.3	22 28.1	6 43.2	28 09.8	26 10.2
23 Su	10 05 28	29 56 14	18 57 15	25 35 50	2R 49.7	25 58.8	15 49.7	23 11.1	7 27.7	1 07.4	22 29.5	6 46.4	28 10.2	26 12.3
24 M	10 09 24	0♍54 05	2♊08 26	8♊35 26	2 49.7	26 30.5	16 50.5	23 49.3	7 31.6	1 16.5	22 30.7	6 49.6	28 10.6	26 14.3
25 Tu	10 13 21	1 51 57	14 57 13	21 14 15	2D 49.6	26 57.8	17 50.9	24 27.5	7 35.1	1 25.8	22 31.9	6 52.8	28 11.1	26 16.4
26 W	10 17 18	2 49 52	27 26 58	3♋35 51	2 49.6	27 20.6	18 51.1	25 05.7	7 38.3	1 35.2	22 32.9	6 56.1	28 11.6	26 18.5
27 Th	10 21 14	3 47 48	9♋41 22	15 43 59	2 49.7	27 38.5	19 50.9	25 43.9	7 41.1	1 44.7	22 33.9	6 59.4	28 12.2	26 20.6
28 F	10 25 11	4 45 46	21 44 07	27 42 13	2 49.8	27 51.3	20 50.4	26 22.1	7 43.5	1 54.2	22 34.7	7 02.7	28 12.8	26 22.7
29 Sa	10 29 07	5 43 46	3♌38 40	9♌33 50	2 50.1	27R 58.7	21 49.5	27 00.3	7 45.7	2 03.9	22 35.4	7 06.1	28 13.4	26 24.8
30 Su	10 33 04	6 41 47	15 28 06	21 21 47	2R 50.3	28 00.5	22 48.2	27 38.5	7 47.4	2 13.7	22 36.0	7 09.5	28 14.0	26 26.9
31 M	10 37 00	7 39 50	27 15 13	3♍08 41	2 50.4	27 56.4	23 46.6	28 16.7	7 48.8	2 23.6	22 36.5	7 12.9	28 14.7	26 29.0

Astro Data

Astro Data	Dy Hr Mn
☽0S	9 21:06
♄⚼♅	10 15:10
☽0N	22 20:06
♃⚺♆	31 12:01
☽0S	6 3:06
♀0S	8 5:44
♆D	10 2:20
☽0N	19 5:16
☿0S	20 12:14
☿R	30 7:27

Planet Ingress

Planet Ingress	Dy Hr Mn
⚳ ♉	10 9:50
♀ ♍	12 12:16
☿ ♌	14 8:06
♂ ♌	18 6:43
☉ ♌	23 6:37
☿ ♍	31 5:21
♀ ♎	8 9:59
♃ ♏	15 17:58
☉ ♍	23 13:34

Last Aspect / ☽ Ingress

Last Aspect Dy Hr Mn		☽ Ingress Dy Hr Mn
2 10:00	♃ △	♋ 2 17:21
5 1:20	♆ △	♌ 5 4:26
7 13:56	♆ □	♍ 7 17:11
10 2:46	♆ ⚹	♎ 10 6:02
12 10:13	♃ ☌	♏ 12 16:41
14 20:26	♆ ☌	♐ 14 23:26
16 21:10	♃ ⚹	♑ 17 2:19
18 23:57	♆ ⚹	♒ 19 2:44
20 23:46	♆ □	♓ 21 2:36
23 3:30	☉ △	♈ 23 3:42
25 2:56	♃ ☍	♉ 25 7:18
27 10:28	♆ ☍	♊ 27 13:53
29 19:17	♃ △	♋ 29 23:14

Last Aspect / ☽ Ingress

Last Aspect Dy Hr Mn		☽ Ingress Dy Hr Mn
1 7:11	♃ □	♌ 1 10:44
3 20:32	♃ ⚹	♍ 3 23:34
6 8:45	♆ ⚹	♎ 6 12:32
8 22:13	♃ ☌	♏ 8 23:57
11 4:43	♆ ☌	♐ 11 8:07
13 11:54	♃ ⚹	♑ 13 12:25
15 13:28	♃ □	♒ 15 13:31
17 10:04	♆ □	♓ 17 13:01
19 9:50	♆ △	♈ 19 12:50
21 11:19	☉ △	♉ 21 14:46
23 16:42	♆ ☍	♊ 23 20:03
25 23:26	☿ □	♋ 26 4:58
28 13:02	♆ △	♌ 28 16:38
31 2:01	♆ □	♍ 31 5:36

☽ Phases & Eclipses

Dy Hr Mn		
3 15:18	●	11♋16
11 19:43	☽	19♎04
18 19:58	○	25♑46
25 11:00	☾	2♉05
2 5:58	●	9♌32
10 8:50	☽	17♏19
17 3:15	○	23♒49
17 3:23	•	P 0.408
23 20:34	☾	0♊17
31 22:01	●	8♍04
31 21:54:49	•	A 06'48"

Astro Data

1 July 1970
Julian Day # 25749
SVP 5♓40'11"
GC 26♐25.6 ⚴ 14♓36.7R
Eris 12♈48.0 ⚵ 27♈53.9
⚷ 10♈18.3 ⚶ 5♍55.4
☽ Mean ☊ 5♓40.5

1 August 1970
Julian Day # 25780
SVP 5♓40'05"
GC 26♐25.7 ⚴ 11♓39.0R
Eris 12♈45.5R ⚵ 10♉45.4
⚷ 10♈13.1R ⚶ 19♍42.8
☽ Mean ☊ 4♓02.1

LONGITUDE — September 1970

Day	Sid.Time	☉	0 hr ☽	Noon ☽	True ☊	☿	♀	♂	⚳	♃	♄	♅	♆	♇
1 Tu	10 40 57	8♍37 54	9♍02 29	14♍56 53	2♓50.3	27♍46.3	24♎44.5	28♌54.9	7♉49.8	2♏33.6	22♉36.9	7♎16.3	28♏15.4	26♍31.2
2 W	10 44 53	9 36 00	20 52 11	26 48 38	2R49.8	27R30.0	25 42.1	29 33.0	7 50.5	2 43.6	22 37.1	7 19.7	28 16.1	26 33.4
3 Th	10 48 50	10 34 08	2♎46 32	8♎46 10	2 49.0	27 07.4	26 39.2	0♍11.2	7R50.8	2 53.8	22 37.3	7 23.2	28 16.9	26 35.5
4 F	10 52 47	11 32 17	14 47 50	20 51 50	2 47.8	26 38.5	27 35.9	0 49.4	7 50.7	3 04.0	22R37.4	7 26.7	28 17.7	26 37.7
5 Sa	10 56 43	12 30 28	26 58 30	3♏08 10	2 46.6	26 03.5	28 32.2	1 27.5	7 50.3	3 14.4	22 37.3	7 30.2	28 18.5	26 39.9
6 Su	11 00 40	13 28 41	9♏21 12	15 37 56	2 45.3	25 22.7	29 27.9	2 05.7	7 49.5	3 24.8	22 37.2	7 33.7	28 19.4	26 42.1
7 M	11 04 36	14 26 55	21 58 46	28 24 02	2 44.4	24 36.4	0♏23.2	2 43.8	7 48.3	3 35.3	22 36.9	7 37.3	28 20.3	26 44.3
8 Tu	11 08 33	15 25 10	4♐54 07	11♐29 21	2D43.9	23 45.2	1 18.0	3 21.9	7 46.8	3 45.9	22 36.6	7 40.8	28 21.2	26 46.5
9 W	11 12 29	16 23 27	18 10 00	24 56 21	2 44.0	22 49.9	2 12.2	4 00.1	7 44.8	3 56.6	22 36.1	7 44.4	28 22.1	26 48.7
10 Th	11 16 26	17 21 46	1♑48 33	8♑46 43	2 44.7	21 51.5	3 05.9	4 38.2	7 42.5	4 07.3	22 35.5	7 48.0	28 23.1	26 50.9
11 F	11 20 22	18 20 06	15 50 48	23 00 42	2 45.8	20 51.0	3 59.0	5 16.3	7 39.9	4 18.2	22 34.8	7 51.6	28 24.1	26 53.1
12 Sa	11 24 19	19 18 28	0♒16 06	7♒36 36	2 46.9	19 49.8	4 51.6	5 54.4	7 36.8	4 29.1	22 34.0	7 55.3	28 25.2	26 55.3
13 Su	11 28 16	20 16 51	15 01 36	22 30 21	2R47.7	18 49.3	5 43.5	6 32.5	7 33.4	4 40.1	22 33.1	7 58.9	28 26.3	26 57.6
14 M	11 32 12	21 15 16	0♓01 58	7♓35 27	2 47.9	17 50.8	6 34.7	7 10.6	7 29.6	4 51.1	22 32.1	8 02.6	28 27.4	26 59.8
15 Tu	11 36 09	22 13 42	15 09 40	22 43 30	2 47.1	16 55.8	7 25.3	7 48.7	7 25.4	5 02.3	22 31.0	8 06.2	28 28.5	27 02.0
16 W	11 40 05	23 12 10	0♈15 44	7♈45 16	2 45.3	16 05.8	8 15.2	8 26.8	7 20.9	5 13.5	22 29.8	8 09.9	28 29.6	27 04.2
17 Th	11 44 02	24 10 41	15 11 01	22 32 02	2 42.7	15 21.9	9 04.4	9 04.9	7 16.0	5 24.8	22 28.5	8 13.6	28 30.8	27 06.5
18 F	11 47 58	25 09 13	29 47 32	6♉56 53	2 39.7	14 45.3	9 52.9	9 43.0	7 10.7	5 36.1	22 27.0	8 17.3	28 32.0	27 08.7
19 Sa	11 51 55	26 07 48	13♉59 36	20 55 26	2 36.7	14 16.9	10 40.5	10 21.1	7 05.0	5 47.6	22 25.5	8 21.0	28 33.3	27 11.0
20 Su	11 55 51	27 06 25	27 44 17	4♊26 12	2 34.2	13 57.6	11 27.4	10 59.2	6 59.0	5 59.1	22 23.9	8 24.8	28 34.6	27 13.2
21 M	11 59 48	28 05 04	11♊01 22	17 30 06	2D32.6	13D47.7	12 13.5	11 37.3	6 52.6	6 10.6	22 22.2	8 28.5	28 35.9	27 15.4
22 Tu	12 03 45	29 03 46	23 52 49	0♋10 00	2 32.1	13 47.6	12 58.7	12 15.4	6 45.8	6 22.2	22 20.3	8 32.3	28 37.2	27 17.7
23 W	12 07 41	0♎02 29	6♋22 11	12 29 56	2 32.8	13 57.3	13 43.1	12 53.5	6 38.7	6 33.9	22 18.4	8 36.0	28 38.5	27 19.9
24 Th	12 11 38	1 01 15	18 33 52	24 34 34	2 34.2	14 16.9	14 26.5	13 31.6	6 31.3	6 45.7	22 16.4	8 39.8	28 39.9	27 22.2
25 F	12 15 34	2 00 03	0♌32 39	6♌28 41	2 36.0	14 46.0	15 08.9	14 09.7	6 23.4	6 57.5	22 14.2	8 43.5	28 41.3	27 24.4
26 Sa	12 19 31	2 58 54	12 23 14	18 16 51	2 37.6	15 24.3	15 50.3	14 47.7	6 15.3	7 09.4	22 12.0	8 47.3	28 42.8	27 26.7
27 Su	12 23 27	3 57 46	24 10 02	0♍03 15	2R38.4	16 11.2	16 30.7	15 25.8	6 06.8	7 21.3	22 09.7	8 51.1	28 44.2	27 28.9
28 M	12 27 24	4 56 40	5♍56 56	11 51 27	2 38.0	17 06.2	17 10.1	16 03.9	5 57.9	7 33.3	22 07.2	8 54.9	28 45.7	27 31.1
29 Tu	12 31 20	5 55 37	17 47 12	23 44 27	2 36.0	18 08.7	17 48.3	16 42.0	5 48.8	7 45.4	22 04.7	8 58.6	28 47.2	27 33.3
30 W	12 35 17	6 54 36	29 43 29	5♎44 33	2 32.3	19 18.0	18 25.3	17 20.1	5 39.3	7 57.5	22 02.1	9 02.4	28 48.8	27 35.6

LONGITUDE — October 1970

Day	Sid.Time	☉	0 hr ☽	Noon ☽	True ☊	☿	♀	♂	⚳	♃	♄	♅	♆	♇
1 Th	12 39 14	7♎53 36	11♎47 51	17♎53 34	2♓27.1	20♍33.2	19♏01.1	17♍58.2	5♉29.5	8♏09.6	21♉59.4	9♎06.2	28♏50.3	27♍37.8
2 F	12 43 10	8 52 39	24 01 50	0♏12 48	2R20.8	21 53.9	19 35.6	18 36.3	5R19.4	8 21.8	21R56.6	9 10.0	28 51.9	27 40.0
3 Sa	12 47 07	9 51 44	6♏26 36	12 43 20	2 14.1	23 19.2	20 08.9	19 14.4	5 09.0	8 34.1	21 53.7	9 13.8	28 53.5	27 42.2
4 Su	12 51 03	10 50 51	19 03 07	25 26 06	2 07.7	24 48.6	20 40.7	19 52.5	4 58.3	8 46.4	21 50.7	9 17.6	28 55.1	27 44.4
5 M	12 55 00	11 49 59	1♐52 23	8♐22 06	2 02.2	26 21.4	21 11.1	20 30.5	4 47.3	8 58.7	21 47.6	9 21.4	28 56.8	27 46.6
6 Tu	12 58 56	12 49 09	14 55 26	21 32 29	1 58.4	27 57.0	21 40.0	21 08.6	4 36.1	9 11.2	21 44.4	9 25.2	28 58.5	27 48.8
7 W	13 02 53	13 48 22	28 13 27	4♑58 28	1D56.4	29 34.9	22 07.3	21 46.7	4 24.6	9 23.6	21 41.2	9 29.0	29 00.2	27 51.0
8 Th	13 06 49	14 47 36	11♑47 41	18 41 12	1 56.1	1♎14.8	22 33.1	22 24.8	4 12.9	9 36.1	21 37.9	9 32.7	29 01.9	27 53.2
9 F	13 10 46	15 46 51	25 39 05	2♒41 22	1 57.0	2 56.1	22 57.1	23 02.8	4 00.9	9 48.6	21 34.5	9 36.5	29 03.6	27 55.3
10 Sa	13 14 43	16 46 08	9♒47 58	16 58 43	1 58.2	4 38.6	23 19.4	23 40.9	3 48.8	10 01.2	21 31.0	9 40.3	29 05.4	27 57.5
11 Su	13 18 39	17 45 27	24 13 23	1♓31 32	1R58.9	6 21.9	23 39.9	24 19.0	3 36.4	10 13.8	21 27.4	9 44.1	29 07.2	27 59.6
12 M	13 22 36	18 44 48	8♓52 41	16 16 10	1 58.1	8 05.8	23 58.5	24 57.1	3 23.8	10 26.5	21 23.8	9 47.8	29 09.0	28 01.8
13 Tu	13 26 32	19 44 11	23 41 13	1♈06 55	1 55.1	9 50.0	24 15.2	25 35.1	3 11.1	10 39.2	21 20.1	9 51.6	29 10.8	28 03.9
14 W	13 30 29	20 43 35	8♈32 20	15 56 26	1 50.0	11 34.3	24 29.9	26 13.2	2 58.2	10 51.9	21 16.3	9 55.3	29 12.7	28 06.0
15 Th	13 34 25	21 43 02	23 18 12	0♉36 39	1 42.9	13 18.7	24 42.5	26 51.3	2 45.1	11 04.6	21 12.4	9 59.0	29 14.5	28 08.1
16 F	13 38 22	22 42 31	7♉50 52	15 00 02	1 34.6	15 03.0	24 53.0	27 29.3	2 31.9	11 17.4	21 08.5	10 02.8	29 16.4	28 10.2
17 Sa	13 42 18	23 42 01	22 03 30	29 00 47	1 26.2	16 47.0	25 01.3	28 07.4	2 18.6	11 30.3	21 04.5	10 06.5	29 18.3	28 12.3
18 Su	13 46 15	24 41 35	5♊51 31	12♊35 33	1 18.5	18 30.7	25 07.4	28 45.5	2 05.1	11 43.1	21 00.5	10 10.2	29 20.2	28 14.3
19 M	13 50 12	25 41 10	19 12 53	25 43 41	1 12.5	20 14.0	25 11.3	29 23.6	1 51.6	11 56.0	20 56.3	10 13.9	29 22.2	28 16.4
20 Tu	13 54 08	26 40 48	2♋08 14	8♋26 56	1 08.5	21 56.9	25R12.8	0♎01.7	1 37.9	12 08.9	20 52.2	10 17.6	29 24.1	28 18.4
21 W	13 58 05	27 40 28	14 40 15	20 48 47	1D06.6	23 39.3	25 12.1	0 39.8	1 24.2	12 21.9	20 47.9	10 21.3	29 26.1	28 20.4
22 Th	14 02 01	28 40 10	26 53 07	2♌53 56	1 06.4	25 21.3	25 08.9	1 17.9	1 10.4	12 34.8	20 43.6	10 24.9	29 28.1	28 22.4
23 F	14 05 58	29 39 54	8♌51 53	14 47 41	1 07.1	27 02.7	25 03.3	1 55.9	0 56.6	12 47.8	20 39.3	10 28.6	29 30.1	28 24.4
24 Sa	14 09 54	0♏39 41	20 41 58	26 35 26	1R07.9	28 43.6	24 55.4	2 34.0	0 42.8	13 00.9	20 34.9	10 32.2	29 32.1	28 26.4
25 Su	14 13 51	1 39 29	2♍28 43	8♍22 25	1 07.7	0♏23.9	24 45.0	3 12.1	0 29.0	13 13.9	20 30.5	10 35.8	29 34.2	28 28.4
26 M	14 17 47	2 39 20	14 17 07	20 13 19	1 05.7	2 03.7	24 32.2	3 50.2	0 15.2	13 27.0	20 26.0	10 39.4	29 36.2	28 30.3
27 Tu	14 21 44	3 39 13	26 11 30	2♎12 06	1 01.2	3 43.0	24 17.1	4 28.3	0 01.4	13 40.1	20 21.4	10 43.0	29 38.3	28 32.2
28 W	14 25 40	4 39 08	8♎15 26	14 21 48	0 54.0	5 21.8	23 59.6	5 06.4	29♈47.6	13 53.2	20 16.8	10 46.5	29 40.3	28 34.2
29 Th	14 29 37	5 39 06	20 31 25	26 44 26	0 44.4	7 00.0	23 39.8	5 44.5	29 33.9	14 06.3	20 12.2	10 50.1	29 42.4	28 36.0
30 F	14 33 34	6 39 05	3♏00 57	9♏20 58	0 33.0	8 37.8	23 17.8	6 22.6	29 20.3	14 19.4	20 07.6	10 53.6	29 44.5	28 37.9
31 Sa	14 37 30	7 39 06	15 44 29	22 11 23	0 20.8	10 15.0	22 53.7	7 00.7	29 06.7	14 32.6	20 02.9	10 57.1	29 46.7	28 39.8

Astro Data

	Dy Hr Mn
☽0S	2 8:59
⚳R	3 19:37
♄R	4 13:57
♄□♅	7 9:50
☿0N	11 2:50
☽0N	15 16:09
☿D	22 0:15
☉0S	23 10:59
☽0S	29 15:13
♃⚺♅	8 2:46
☿0S	10 8:57
☽0N	13 2:35
♀R	20 15:57
♂0S	24 11:44
⚳0S	25 5:23

Planet Ingress

	Dy Hr Mn
♂ ♍	3 4:57
♀ ♏	7 1:54
☉ ♎	23 10:59
☿ ♎	7 18:04
♂ ♎	20 10:57
☉ ♏	23 20:04
☿ ♏	25 6:16
⚳ ♈R	27 14:22
♃∠∠	26 19:13
☽0S	26 22:00

Last Aspect / ☽ Ingress

Last Aspect Dy Hr Mn		☽ Ingress	Dy Hr Mn
2 14:56	♆ ⚹	♎	2 18:25
5 2:19	♀ ☌	♏	5 5:54
7 11:53	♆ ☌	♐	7 14:58
9 15:18	♇ □	♑	9 20:51
11 20:56	♆ ⚹	♒	11 23:34
13 21:28	♆ □	♓	13 23:57
15 21:10	♆ △	♈	15 23:35
16 12:40	♅ ☍	♉	18 0:21
20 1:28	♆ ☍	♊	20 4:02
22 9:42	☉ □	♋	22 11:41
24 20:14	♆ △	♌	24 22:54
27 9:19	♆ □	♍	27 11:53
29 22:09	♆ ⚹	♎	30 0:33

Last Aspect Dy Hr Mn		☽ Ingress	Dy Hr Mn
30 18:35	♅ ☌	♏	2 11:35
4 18:31	♆ ☌	♐	4 20:31
7 1:06	☿ □	♑	7 3:10
9 5:49	♆ ⚹	♒	9 7:26
11 8:03	♆ □	♓	11 9:30
13 8:52	♆ △	♈	13 10:12
14 20:21	☉ ☍	♉	15 11:00
17 12:31	♆ ☍	♊	17 13:43
19 19:12	♂ □	♋	19 19:59
22 5:07	♆ △	♌	22 6:12
24 18:01	♆ □	♍	24 18:57
27 6:53	♆ ⚹	♎	27 7:37
28 4:56	♅ ☌	♏	29 18:15

☽ Phases & Eclipses

Dy Hr Mn	
8 19:38	☽ 15♐44
15 11:09	○ 22♓12
22 9:42	☾ 28♊58
30 14:31	● 7♎01
8 4:43	☽ 14♑30
14 20:21	○ 21♈04
22 2:47	☾ 28♋17
30 6:28	● 6♏25

Astro Data

1 September 1970
Julian Day # 25811
SVP 5♓40'01"
GC 26♐25.8 ⚴ 4♓24.4R
Eris 12♈33.7R ⚵ 21♉02.6
⚷ 9♈22.2R ⚶ 4♎42.3
☽ Mean ☊ 2♓23.6

1 October 1970
Julian Day # 25841
SVP 5♓39'58"
GC 26♐25.8 ⚴ 27♒58.6R
Eris 12♈16.6R ⚵ 26♉11.2
⚷ 8♈05.7R ⚶ 19♎58.8
☽ Mean ☊ 0♓48.2

November 1970 LONGITUDE

Day	Sid.Time	☉	0 hr ☽	Noon ☽	True ☊	☿	♀	♂	⚳	♃	♄	♅	♆	♇
1 Su	14 41 27	8♏39 09	28♏41 36	5♐14 57	0♓08.9	11♏51.8	22♏27.5	7♎38.9	28♈53.3	14♏45.7	19♉58.1	11♎00.6	29♏48.8	28♍41.6
2 M	14 45 23	9 39 14	11♐51 19	18 30 31	29♒58.5	13 28.1	21R59.5	8 17.0	28R40.0	14 58.9	19R53.4	11 04.0	29 50.9	28 43.4
3 Tu	14 49 20	10 39 20	25 12 26	1♑56 55	29R50.5	15 03.9	21 29.7	8 55.1	28 26.9	15 12.1	19 48.6	11 07.5	29 53.1	28 45.2
4 W	14 53 16	11 39 28	8♑43 54	15 33 17	29 45.3	16 39.3	20 58.3	9 33.2	28 13.9	15 25.3	19 43.8	11 10.9	29 55.2	28 47.0
5 Th	14 57 13	12 39 38	22 25 02	29 19 09	29 42.7	18 14.3	20 25.5	10 11.3	28 01.0	15 38.5	19 39.0	11 14.3	29 57.4	28 48.8
6 F	15 01 10	13 39 49	6♒15 36	13♒14 24	29D42.1	19 48.9	19 51.5	10 49.4	27 48.3	15 51.7	19 34.2	11 17.6	29 59.6	28 50.5
7 Sa	15 05 06	14 40 01	20 15 33	27 19 00	29R42.2	21 23.1	19 16.5	11 27.5	27 35.9	16 04.9	19 29.3	11 21.0	0♐01.8	28 52.2
8 Su	15 09 03	15 40 15	4♓24 39	11♓32 23	29 41.8	22 57.0	18 40.8	12 05.6	27 23.6	16 18.2	19 24.5	11 24.3	0 04.0	28 53.9
9 M	15 12 59	16 40 30	18 41 57	25 53 02	29 39.7	24 30.5	18 04.5	12 43.7	27 11.6	16 31.4	19 19.6	11 27.5	0 06.2	28 55.5
10 Tu	15 16 56	17 40 47	3♈05 14	10♈18 01	29 34.8	26 03.6	17 27.9	13 21.8	26 59.8	16 44.6	19 14.7	11 30.8	0 08.4	28 57.2
11 W	15 20 52	18 41 05	17 30 48	24 42 53	29 27.1	27 36.5	16 51.4	13 59.9	26 48.2	16 57.8	19 09.8	11 34.0	0 10.6	28 58.8
12 Th	15 24 49	19 41 25	1♉53 32	9♉01 59	29 16.6	29 09.0	16 15.0	14 38.0	26 36.9	17 11.0	19 04.9	11 37.2	0 12.8	29 00.4
13 F	15 28 45	20 41 47	16 07 29	23 09 19	29 04.5	0♐41.2	15 39.2	15 16.1	26 25.9	17 24.3	19 00.1	11 40.4	0 15.0	29 02.0
14 Sa	15 32 42	21 42 10	0♊06 49	6♊59 27	28 51.8	2 13.1	15 04.1	15 54.2	26 15.1	17 37.5	18 55.2	11 43.5	0 17.3	29 03.5
15 Su	15 36 39	22 42 35	13 46 45	20 28 27	28 40.0	3 44.7	14 30.0	16 32.3	26 04.7	17 50.7	18 50.3	11 46.6	0 19.5	29 05.0
16 M	15 40 35	23 43 02	27 04 21	3♋34 27	28 30.0	5 16.0	13 57.1	17 10.4	25 54.5	18 03.9	18 45.5	11 49.7	0 21.8	29 06.5
17 Tu	15 44 32	24 43 31	9♋58 51	16 17 48	28 22.7	6 47.1	13 25.6	17 48.5	25 44.6	18 17.1	18 40.6	11 52.7	0 24.0	29 08.0
18 W	15 48 28	25 44 01	22 31 37	28 40 46	28 18.0	8 17.8	12 55.8	18 26.6	25 35.1	18 30.3	18 35.8	11 55.8	0 26.3	29 09.4
19 Th	15 52 25	26 44 33	4♌45 45	10♌47 10	28 15.8	9 48.3	12 27.7	19 04.7	25 25.9	18 43.5	18 31.0	11 58.7	0 28.5	29 10.8
20 F	15 56 21	27 45 07	16 45 39	22 41 52	28 15.2	11 18.5	12 01.6	19 42.8	25 17.0	18 56.6	18 26.2	12 01.7	0 30.8	29 12.2
21 Sa	16 00 18	28 45 43	28 36 31	4♍30 19	28 15.2	12 48.3	11 37.6	20 21.0	25 08.4	19 09.8	18 21.4	12 04.6	0 33.0	29 13.6
22 Su	16 04 14	29 46 20	10♍23 57	16 18 09	28 14.5	14 17.8	11 15.7	20 59.1	25 00.2	19 22.9	18 16.7	12 07.4	0 35.3	29 14.9
23 M	16 08 11	0♐46 59	22 13 33	28 10 50	28 12.1	15 47.0	10 56.1	21 37.2	24 52.3	19 36.0	18 11.9	12 10.3	0 37.5	29 16.2
24 Tu	16 12 08	1 47 39	4♎10 35	10♎13 21	28 07.3	17 15.7	10 38.9	22 15.3	24 44.8	19 49.2	18 07.2	12 13.1	0 39.8	29 17.5
25 W	16 16 04	2 48 22	16 19 37	22 29 48	27 59.6	18 44.0	10 24.1	22 53.5	24 37.7	20 02.2	18 02.6	12 15.8	0 42.1	29 18.7
26 Th	16 20 01	3 49 05	28 44 15	5♏03 12	27 49.2	20 11.9	10 11.8	23 31.6	24 30.9	20 15.3	17 58.0	12 18.5	0 44.3	29 20.0
27 F	16 23 57	4 49 51	11♏26 47	17 55 03	27 36.8	21 39.1	10 01.9	24 09.7	24 24.5	20 28.4	17 53.4	12 21.2	0 46.6	29 21.1
28 Sa	16 27 54	5 50 37	24 27 57	1♐05 18	27 23.4	23 05.8	9 54.5	24 47.8	24 18.5	20 41.4	17 48.9	12 23.8	0 48.8	29 22.3
29 Su	16 31 50	6 51 25	7♐46 53	14 32 21	27 10.2	24 31.7	9 49.6	25 26.0	24 12.9	20 54.4	17 44.4	12 26.4	0 51.1	29 23.4
30 M	16 35 47	7 52 15	21 21 20	28 13 24	26 58.6	25 56.8	9D47.1	26 04.1	24 07.6	21 07.4	17 40.0	12 29.0	0 53.3	29 24.5

December 1970 LONGITUDE

Day	Sid.Time	☉	0 hr ☽	Noon ☽	True ☊	☿	♀	♂	⚳	♃	♄	♅	♆	♇
1 Tu	16 39 43	8♐53 05	5♑08 05	12♑04 57	26♒49.6	27♐21.0	9♏47.1	26♎42.2	24♈02.8	21♏20.4	17♉35.6	12♎31.5	0♐55.6	29♍25.6
2 W	16 43 40	9 53 57	19 03 34	26 03 31	26R43.6	28 44.1	9 49.5	27 20.3	23R58.3	21 33.3	17R31.2	12 34.0	0 57.8	29 26.6
3 Th	16 47 37	10 54 49	3♒04 29	10♒06 09	26 40.4	0♑06.0	9 54.3	27 58.4	23 54.3	21 46.2	17 27.0	12 36.4	1 00.1	29 27.6
4 F	16 51 33	11 55 42	17 08 16	24 10 41	26D39.5	1 26.4	10 01.4	28 36.5	23 50.6	21 59.0	17 22.7	12 38.8	1 02.3	29 28.6
5 Sa	16 55 30	12 56 36	1♓13 14	8♓15 49	26R39.7	2 45.1	10 10.7	29 14.6	23 47.4	22 11.9	17 18.6	12 41.2	1 04.5	29 29.6
6 Su	16 59 26	13 57 30	15 18 21	22 20 46	26 39.5	4 01.9	10 22.3	29 52.7	23 44.5	22 24.7	17 14.5	12 43.4	1 06.7	29 30.5
7 M	17 03 23	14 58 25	29 22 57	6♈24 47	26 37.7	5 16.4	10 36.0	0♏30.8	23 42.0	22 37.4	17 10.4	12 45.7	1 08.9	29 31.3
8 Tu	17 07 19	15 59 21	13♈26 07	20 26 43	26 33.5	6 28.3	10 51.9	1 08.9	23 40.0	22 50.1	17 06.5	12 47.9	1 11.1	29 32.2
9 W	17 11 16	17 00 18	27 26 21	4♉24 41	26 26.5	7 37.2	11 09.8	1 47.0	23 38.3	23 02.8	17 02.6	12 50.1	1 13.3	29 33.0
10 Th	17 15 12	18 01 15	11♉21 20	18 15 56	26 16.9	8 42.6	11 29.7	2 25.1	23 37.0	23 15.5	16 58.7	12 52.2	1 15.5	29 33.8
11 F	17 19 09	19 02 13	25 08 04	1♊57 16	26 05.7	9 44.0	11 51.5	3 03.2	23 36.2	23 28.1	16 55.0	12 54.2	1 17.7	29 34.5
12 Sa	17 23 06	20 03 12	8♊43 10	15 25 21	25 53.9	10 40.7	12 15.2	3 41.3	23D35.7	23 40.6	16 51.3	12 56.3	1 19.9	29 35.3
13 Su	17 27 02	21 04 12	22 03 32	28 37 26	25 42.7	11 32.2	12 40.7	4 19.4	23 35.6	23 53.1	16 47.7	12 58.2	1 22.0	29 35.9
14 M	17 30 59	22 05 12	5♋06 52	11♋31 47	25 33.2	12 17.7	13 07.9	4 57.5	23 35.9	24 05.6	16 44.2	13 00.2	1 24.2	29 36.6
15 Tu	17 34 55	23 06 14	17 52 10	24 08 06	25 26.1	12 56.4	13 36.9	5 35.6	23 36.6	24 18.0	16 40.8	13 02.0	1 26.3	29 37.2
16 W	17 38 52	24 07 16	0♌19 49	6♌27 35	25 21.6	13 27.3	14 07.4	6 13.7	23 37.7	24 30.4	16 37.4	13 03.8	1 28.5	29 37.8
17 Th	17 42 48	25 08 19	12 31 46	18 32 47	25D19.6	13 49.7	14 39.5	6 51.7	23 39.2	24 42.7	16 34.1	13 05.6	1 30.6	29 38.3
18 F	17 46 45	26 09 23	24 31 09	0♍27 26	25 19.5	14R02.7	15 13.2	7 29.8	23 41.0	24 55.0	16 30.9	13 07.3	1 32.7	29 38.9
19 Sa	17 50 42	27 10 27	6♍22 12	12 16 08	25 20.3	14 05.3	15 48.2	8 07.9	23 43.3	25 07.2	16 27.8	13 09.0	1 34.8	29 39.3
20 Su	17 54 38	28 11 33	18 09 51	24 04 04	25R21.1	13 57.0	16 24.7	8 46.0	23 45.9	25 19.4	16 24.8	13 10.6	1 36.8	29 39.8
21 M	17 58 35	29 12 39	29 59 27	5♎56 41	25 21.0	13 37.1	17 02.5	9 24.1	23 48.8	25 31.5	16 21.9	13 12.2	1 38.9	29 40.2
22 Tu	18 02 31	0♑13 46	11♎56 27	17 59 24	25 19.0	13 05.5	17 41.6	10 02.1	23 52.2	25 43.6	16 19.1	13 13.7	1 40.9	29 40.6
23 W	18 06 28	1 14 54	24 06 07	0♏17 10	25 14.9	12 22.3	18 21.9	10 40.2	23 55.9	25 55.6	16 16.3	13 15.2	1 43.0	29 40.9
24 Th	18 10 24	2 16 02	6♏33 03	12 54 09	25 08.6	11 28.1	19 03.4	11 18.3	24 00.0	26 07.5	16 13.7	13 16.6	1 45.0	29 41.2
25 F	18 14 21	3 17 11	19 20 47	25 53 10	25 00.5	10 24.1	19 46.0	11 56.3	24 04.5	26 19.4	16 11.2	13 17.9	1 47.0	29 41.5
26 Sa	18 18 17	4 18 21	2♐31 22	9♐15 19	24 51.4	9 12.1	20 29.7	12 34.4	24 09.3	26 31.2	16 08.7	13 19.2	1 49.0	29 41.7
27 Su	18 22 14	5 19 31	16 04 52	22 59 39	24 42.4	7 54.1	21 14.5	13 12.4	24 14.4	26 43.0	16 06.4	13 20.5	1 51.0	29 41.9
28 M	18 26 11	6 20 41	29 59 15	7♑03 07	24 34.4	6 32.7	22 00.3	13 50.5	24 20.0	26 54.7	16 04.1	13 21.7	1 52.9	29 42.1
29 Tu	18 30 07	7 21 52	14♑10 36	21 20 59	24 28.3	5 10.7	22 47.0	14 28.5	24 25.9	27 06.3	16 02.0	13 22.8	1 54.8	29 42.3
30 W	18 34 04	8 23 03	28 33 32	5♒47 30	24 24.5	3 50.8	23 34.6	15 06.5	24 32.1	27 17.8	16 00.0	13 23.9	1 56.8	29 42.4
31 Th	18 38 00	9 24 14	13♒02 10	20 16 51	24D23.0	2 35.4	24 23.1	15 44.6	24 38.6	27 29.3	15 58.0	13 25.0	1 58.7	29 42.4

Astro Data Dy Hr Mn	Planet Ingress Dy Hr Mn
☽0N 9 10:32	☊ ♒R 2 8:14
♃☍♄ 18 19:20	♆ ♐ 6 16:32
☽0S 23 5:09	☿ ♐ 13 1:16
⚳0N 29 16:35	☉ ♐ 22 17:25
♀D 1 0:03	☿ ♑ 3 10:14
☽0N 6 15:43	♂ ♏ 6 16:34
⚳D 13 5:01	☉ ♑ 22 6:36
☿R 19 5:58	
☽0S 20 12:24	

Last Aspect Dy Hr Mn	☽ Ingress Dy Hr Mn	Last Aspect Dy Hr Mn	☽ Ingress Dy Hr Mn
1 2:02 ♆ ☌	♐ 1 2:24	2 17:48 ♇ △	♒ 2 18:45
3 6:19 ♇ □	♑ 3 8:32	4 19:54 ♂ △	♓ 4 21:55
5 13:06 ♆ ⚹	♒ 5 13:11	7 0:14 ♇ ☍	♈ 7 1:03
7 0:39 ♆ □	♓ 7 16:33	8 3:46 ☉ △	♉ 9 4:24
9 17:05 ♇ ☍	♈ 9 18:52	11 7:48 ♇ △	♊ 11 8:33
10 17:20 ♂ ☍	♉ 11 20:50	13 13:48 ♇ □	♋ 13 14:32
13 22:09 ♇ △	♊ 13 23:48	15 22:38 ♇ ⚹	♌ 15 23:21
16 3:43 ♇ □	♋ 16 5:23	18 2:29 ☉ △	♍ 18 11:04
18 12:56 ♇ ⚹	♌ 18 14:36	20 23:21 ♇ ☌	♎ 21 0:01
20 23:13 ☉ □	♍ 21 2:50	22 2:44 ☿ □	♏ 23 11:27
23 14:11 ♇ ☌	♎ 23 15:39	25 18:54 ♇ ⚹	♐ 25 19:28
25 12:48 ♂ ☌	♏ 26 2:25	27 23:31 ♇ □	♑ 28 0:01
28 8:54 ♇ ⚹	♐ 28 10:02	30 1:54 ♇ △	♒ 30 2:24
30 14:04 ♇ □	♑ 30 15:05		

☽ Phases & Eclipses Dy Hr Mn	
6 12:47	☽ 13♒42
13 7:28	○ 20♉30
20 23:13	☾ 28♌13
28 21:14	● 6♐14
5 20:36	☽ 13♓18
12 21:03	○ 20♊26
20 21:09	☾ 28♍35
28 10:43	● 6♑17

Astro Data

1 November 1970
Julian Day # 25872
SVP 5♓39'54"
GC 26♐25.9 ⚵ 26♒12.1
Eris 11♈58.1R ✱ 23♉54.3R
⚷ 6♈47.0R ⚶ 6♏15.8
☽ Mean ☊ 29♒09.7

1 December 1970
Julian Day # 25902
SVP 5♓39'49"
GC 26♐26.0 ⚵ 29♒24.3
Eris 11♈44.8R ✱ 17♉37.9R
⚷ 5♈59.3R ⚶ 22♏14.2
☽ Mean ☊ 27♒34.4

LONGITUDE — January 1971

Day	Sid.Time	☉	0 hr ☽	Noon ☽	True ☊	☿	♀	♂	⚳	♃	♄	♅	♆	♇
1 F	18 41 57	10♑25 24	27♒30 55	4♓43 51	24♒23.3	1♑26.5	25♏12.5	16♏22.6	24♈45.6	27♏40.7	15♉56.2	13♎25.9	2♐00.5	29♍42.5
2 Sa	18 45 53	11 26 34	11♓55 13	19 04 37	24 24.6	0R 26.0	26 02.7	17 00.6	24 52.8	27 52.0	15R 54.5	13 26.8	2 02.4	29R 42.5
3 Su	18 49 50	12 27 44	26 11 48	3♈16 33	24R 25.8	29♐34.8	26 53.6	17 38.6	25 00.4	28 03.2	15 52.9	13 27.7	2 04.2	29 42.4
4 M	18 53 46	13 28 54	10♈18 42	17 18 10	24 26.0	28 53.6	27 45.4	18 16.5	25 08.3	28 14.4	15 51.4	13 28.5	2 06.0	29 42.4
5 Tu	18 57 43	14 30 03	24 14 51	1♉08 44	24 24.7	28 22.6	28 37.8	18 54.5	25 16.5	28 25.5	15 50.0	13 29.3	2 07.8	29 42.3
6 W	19 01 40	15 31 12	7♉59 46	14 47 55	24 21.5	28 01.8	29 30.9	19 32.5	25 25.0	28 36.5	15 48.7	13 30.0	2 09.6	29 42.1
7 Th	19 05 36	16 32 21	21 33 07	28 15 20	24 16.6	27D 50.8	0♐24.8	20 10.4	25 33.8	28 47.4	15 47.5	13 30.6	2 11.4	29 41.9
8 F	19 09 33	17 33 30	4♊54 31	11♊30 36	24 10.6	27 49.1	1 19.2	20 48.4	25 43.0	28 58.2	15 46.4	13 31.2	2 13.1	29 41.7
9 Sa	19 13 29	18 34 38	18 03 30	24 33 09	24 04.1	27 56.0	2 14.3	21 26.3	25 52.4	29 09.0	15 45.5	13 31.7	2 14.8	29 41.5
10 Su	19 17 26	19 35 45	0♋59 30	7♋22 31	23 57.9	28 10.9	3 10.0	22 04.2	26 02.2	29 19.6	15 44.7	13 32.2	2 16.5	29 41.2
11 M	19 21 22	20 36 53	13 42 12	19 58 32	23 52.7	28 33.1	4 06.3	22 42.1	26 12.2	29 30.2	15 43.9	13 32.6	2 18.2	29 40.9
12 Tu	19 25 19	21 38 00	26 11 35	2♌21 27	23 49.1	29 01.9	5 03.2	23 20.0	26 22.6	29 40.7	15 43.3	13 32.9	2 19.8	29 40.6
13 W	19 29 15	22 39 06	8♌28 16	14 32 16	23D 47.1	29 36.7	6 00.5	23 58.0	26 33.2	29 51.1	15 42.8	13 33.2	2 21.4	29 40.2
14 Th	19 33 12	23 40 13	20 33 39	26 32 44	23 46.7	0♑16.9	6 58.5	24 35.8	26 44.1	0♐01.4	15 42.4	13 33.5	2 23.0	29 39.8
15 F	19 37 09	24 41 19	2♍29 51	8♍25 25	23 47.5	1 02.0	7 56.9	25 13.7	26 55.2	0 11.6	15 42.1	13 33.7	2 24.5	29 39.4
16 Sa	19 41 05	25 42 24	14 19 53	20 13 42	23 49.2	1 51.4	8 55.8	25 51.6	27 06.7	0 21.6	15 41.9	13 33.8	2 26.1	29 38.9
17 Su	19 45 02	26 43 30	26 07 25	2♎01 35	23 51.1	2 44.8	9 55.2	26 29.5	27 18.4	0 31.6	15D 41.9	13R 33.9	2 27.6	29 38.4
18 M	19 48 58	27 44 35	7♎56 48	13 53 39	23 52.7	3 41.6	10 55.0	27 07.3	27 30.3	0 41.5	15 41.9	13 33.9	2 29.1	29 37.9
19 Tu	19 52 55	28 45 40	19 52 47	25 54 48	23R 53.5	4 41.7	11 55.2	27 45.2	27 42.6	0 51.3	15 42.1	13 33.9	2 30.5	29 37.3
20 W	19 56 51	29 46 44	2♏00 20	8♏10 00	23 53.2	5 44.6	12 55.9	28 23.0	27 55.1	1 01.0	15 42.4	13 33.8	2 32.0	29 36.7
21 Th	20 00 48	0♒47 49	14 24 22	20 43 57	23 51.8	6 50.1	13 57.0	29 00.8	28 07.8	1 10.6	15 42.8	13 33.6	2 33.4	29 36.1
22 F	20 04 44	1 48 52	27 09 15	3♐40 38	23 49.5	7 57.9	14 58.4	29 38.6	28 20.8	1 20.1	15 43.3	13 33.4	2 34.8	29 35.4
23 Sa	20 08 41	2 49 56	10♐18 23	17 02 43	23 46.6	9 07.9	16 00.3	0♐16.4	28 34.1	1 29.5	15 43.9	13 33.1	2 36.1	29 34.7
24 Su	20 12 38	3 50 59	23 53 37	0♑51 02	23 43.5	10 19.8	17 02.5	0 54.2	28 47.5	1 38.7	15 44.6	13 32.8	2 37.4	29 34.0
25 M	20 16 34	4 52 01	7♑54 40	15 04 07	23 40.8	11 33.5	18 05.0	1 32.0	29 01.3	1 47.9	15 45.5	13 32.5	2 38.7	29 33.2
26 Tu	20 20 31	5 53 03	22 18 48	29 37 59	23 38.8	12 48.8	19 07.8	2 09.7	29 15.2	1 56.9	15 46.4	13 32.0	2 40.0	29 32.5
27 W	20 24 27	6 54 04	7♒00 50	14♒26 25	23D 37.7	14 05.6	20 11.0	2 47.5	29 29.4	2 05.8	15 47.5	13 31.5	2 41.2	29 31.7
28 Th	20 28 24	7 55 03	21 53 44	29 21 45	23 37.6	15 23.8	21 14.5	3 25.2	29 43.8	2 14.6	15 48.7	13 31.0	2 42.4	29 30.8
29 F	20 32 20	8 56 02	6♓49 27	14♓15 53	23 38.2	16 43.3	22 18.2	4 02.9	29 58.5	2 23.2	15 50.0	13 30.4	2 43.6	29 29.9
30 Sa	20 36 17	9 57 00	21 40 10	29 01 31	23 39.3	18 04.0	23 22.3	4 40.5	0♉13.4	2 31.8	15 51.4	13 29.7	2 44.7	29 29.1
31 Su	20 40 14	10 57 56	6♈19 17	13♈32 55	23 40.4	19 25.9	24 26.6	5 18.2	0 28.4	2 40.2	15 52.9	13 29.0	2 45.9	29 28.1

LONGITUDE — February 1971

Day	Sid.Time	☉	0 hr ☽	Noon ☽	True ☊	☿	♀	♂	⚳	♃	♄	♅	♆	♇
1 M	20 44 10	11♒58 51	20♈42 03	27♈46 22	23♒41.2	20♑48.8	25♐31.2	5♐55.8	0♉43.7	2♐48.5	15♉54.5	13♎28.3	2♐46.9	29♍27.2
2 Tu	20 48 07	12 59 44	4♉45 44	11♉40 05	23R 41.5	22 12.8	26 36.0	6 33.4	0 59.2	2 56.6	15 56.3	13R 27.5	2 48.0	29R 26.2
3 W	20 52 03	14 00 37	18 29 27	25 13 56	23 41.3	23 37.8	27 41.1	7 11.0	1 14.9	3 04.7	15 58.1	13 26.6	2 49.0	29 25.2
4 Th	20 56 00	15 01 28	1♊53 40	8♊28 53	23 40.6	25 03.8	28 46.4	7 48.5	1 30.8	3 12.6	16 00.1	13 25.7	2 50.0	29 24.2
5 F	20 59 56	16 02 17	14 59 47	21 26 37	23 39.7	26 30.6	29 51.9	8 26.1	1 46.9	3 20.3	16 02.2	13 24.7	2 51.0	29 23.1
6 Sa	21 03 53	17 03 05	27 49 37	4♋09 02	23 38.8	27 58.4	0♑57.7	9 03.6	2 03.2	3 28.0	16 04.3	13 23.7	2 51.9	29 22.0
7 Su	21 07 49	18 03 52	10♋25 08	16 38 09	23 38.0	29 27.1	2 03.7	9 41.1	2 19.7	3 35.5	16 06.6	13 22.6	2 52.8	29 20.9
8 M	21 11 46	19 04 37	22 48 18	28 55 50	23 37.4	0♒56.6	3 09.9	10 18.6	2 36.4	3 42.8	16 09.0	13 21.5	2 53.6	29 19.8
9 Tu	21 15 43	20 05 21	5♌00 56	11♌03 52	23 37.0	2 27.0	4 16.3	10 56.1	2 53.3	3 50.1	16 11.5	13 20.4	2 54.5	29 18.6
10 W	21 19 39	21 06 04	17 04 48	23 04 00	23D 36.9	3 58.2	5 22.9	11 33.5	3 10.3	3 57.1	16 14.1	13 19.1	2 55.3	29 17.4
11 Th	21 23 36	22 06 45	29 01 40	4♍58 03	23 37.0	5 30.3	6 29.7	12 10.9	3 27.5	4 04.1	16 16.8	13 17.9	2 56.0	29 16.2
12 F	21 27 32	23 07 25	10♍53 26	16 48 04	23R 37.1	7 03.3	7 36.7	12 48.3	3 44.9	4 10.9	16 19.6	13 16.6	2 56.8	29 15.0
13 Sa	21 31 29	24 08 03	22 42 16	28 36 22	23 37.0	8 37.1	8 43.9	13 25.7	4 02.4	4 17.5	16 22.5	13 15.2	2 57.5	29 13.8
14 Su	21 35 25	25 08 40	4♎30 43	10♎25 43	23 36.9	10 11.7	9 51.3	14 03.1	4 20.1	4 24.0	16 25.5	13 13.8	2 58.1	29 12.5
15 M	21 39 22	26 09 16	16 21 47	22 19 21	23 36.6	11 47.3	10 58.8	14 40.4	4 38.0	4 30.4	16 28.6	13 12.3	2 58.8	29 11.2
16 Tu	21 43 18	27 09 51	28 18 55	4♏20 57	23 36.3	13 23.6	12 06.5	15 17.7	4 56.1	4 36.6	16 31.8	13 10.8	2 59.4	29 09.9
17 W	21 47 15	28 10 25	10♏25 59	16 34 32	23 36.0	15 00.9	13 14.3	15 55.0	5 14.3	4 42.6	16 35.1	13 09.3	2 59.9	29 08.6
18 Th	21 51 11	29 10 57	22 47 09	29 04 21	23D 35.9	16 39.1	14 22.3	16 32.2	5 32.7	4 48.5	16 38.5	13 07.7	3 00.5	29 07.2
19 F	21 55 08	0♓11 28	5♐26 39	11♐54 31	23 36.0	18 18.1	15 30.5	17 09.5	5 51.2	4 54.3	16 42.0	13 06.1	3 01.0	29 05.9
20 Sa	21 59 05	1 11 58	18 28 24	25 08 38	23 36.5	19 58.1	16 38.8	17 46.7	6 09.9	4 59.8	16 45.6	13 04.4	3 01.4	29 04.5
21 Su	22 03 01	2 12 27	1♑55 30	8♑49 10	23 37.2	21 39.0	17 47.3	18 23.8	6 28.7	5 05.3	16 49.3	13 02.7	3 01.9	29 03.1
22 M	22 06 58	3 12 54	15 49 39	22 56 49	23 38.1	23 20.8	18 55.8	19 01.0	6 47.7	5 10.5	16 53.1	13 01.0	3 02.3	29 01.7
23 Tu	22 10 54	4 13 20	0♒10 24	7♒29 55	23 38.8	25 03.6	20 04.5	19 38.1	7 06.8	5 15.6	16 57.0	12 59.2	3 02.6	29 00.2
24 W	22 14 51	5 13 44	14 53 58	22 23 58	23R 39.1	26 47.4	21 13.4	20 15.1	7 26.0	5 20.6	17 00.9	12 57.3	3 03.0	28 58.8
25 Th	22 18 47	6 14 07	29 56 43	7♓31 49	23 38.8	28 32.2	22 22.3	20 52.2	7 45.4	5 25.3	17 05.0	12 55.4	3 03.3	28 57.3
26 F	22 22 44	7 14 28	15♓08 06	22 44 18	23 37.8	0♓17.9	23 31.4	21 29.2	8 05.0	5 29.9	17 09.2	12 53.5	3 03.5	28 55.8
27 Sa	22 26 40	8 14 47	0♈19 12	7♈51 36	23 36.2	2 04.7	24 40.5	22 06.1	8 24.7	5 34.4	17 13.4	12 51.6	3 03.7	28 54.3
28 Su	22 30 37	9 15 04	15 20 25	22 44 42	23 34.3	3 52.4	25 49.8	22 43.0	8 44.5	5 38.6	17 17.7	12 49.6	3 03.9	28 52.8

Astro Data

	Dy Hr Mn
♇ R	1 22:00
☽ 0N	2 20:24
♃∠♅	5 20:49
☿ D	8 4:36
♃⚹♇	12 11:47
☽ 0S	16 19:29
♄ D	17 13:01
♅ R	18 6:54
☽ 0N	30 3:32
♃☌♆	1 6:49
☽ 0S	13 2:17
☽ 0N	26 13:45

Planet Ingress

		Dy Hr Mn
☿	♐R	2 23:36
♀	♐	7 1:00
☿	♑	14 2:16
♃	♐	14 8:49
☉	♒	20 17:13
♂	♐	23 1:34
⚳	♉	29 14:27
♀	♑	5 14:57
☿	♒	7 20:51
☉	♓	19 7:27
☿	♓	26 7:57

Last Aspect / ☽ Ingress (January)

Last Aspect Dy Hr Mn			☽ Ingress	Dy Hr Mn
1 0:07	♃	□	♓	1 4:08
3 6:03	☿	□	♈	3 6:26
5 7:20	☿	△	♉	5 10:00
7 14:36	♇	△	♊	7 15:08
9 21:34	♇	□	♋	9 22:09
12 6:46	♇	⚹	♌	12 7:24
14 7:52	♂	□	♍	14 18:57
17 7:09	♇	☌	♎	17 7:53
19 18:08	☉	□	♏	19 20:04
22 4:31	♇	⚹	♐	22 5:16
24 9:48	♇	□	♑	24 10:33
26 11:51	♇	△	♒	26 12:36
27 21:57	♀	⚹	♓	28 13:01
30 12:45	♇	☍	♈	30 13:36

Last Aspect / ☽ Ingress (February)

Last Aspect Dy Hr Mn			☽ Ingress	Dy Hr Mn
1 7:51	♀	△	♉	1 15:49
3 19:31	♇	△	♊	3 20:34
6 2:56	♇	□	♋	6 4:07
8 12:47	♇	⚹	♌	8 14:06
10 7:41	☉	☍	♍	11 1:58
13 13:16	♇	☌	♎	13 14:50
15 20:23	☉	△	♏	16 3:22
18 12:14	☉	□	♐	18 13:45
20 18:58	♇	□	♑	20 20:37
22 22:05	♇	△	♒	22 23:43
24 19:54	☿	☌	♓	25 0:05
26 21:47	♇	☍	♈	26 23:30
28 17:28	♀	□	♉	28 23:54

☽ Phases & Eclipses

Dy Hr Mn	
4 4:55	☽ 13♈11
11 13:20	○ 20♋40
19 18:08	☾ 29♎01
26 22:55	● 6♒21
2 14:31	☽ 13♉06
10 7:41	○ 20♌55
10 7:45	T 1.308
18 12:14	☾ 29♏12
25 9:49	● 6♓09
25 9:37:26	P 0.787

Astro Data

1 January 1971
Julian Day # 25933
SVP 5♓39'43"
GC 26♐26.1 ⚴ 6♓18.7
Eris 11♈40.0 ⚵ 16♉40.8
⚷ 5♈58.0 ⚶ 8♐38.2
☽ Mean ☊ 25♒56.0

1 February 1971
Julian Day # 25964
SVP 5♓39'38"
GC 26♐26.1 ⚴ 15♓30.5
Eris 11♈46.1 ⚵ 23♉43.8
⚷ 6♈47.4 ⚶ 24♐31.2
☽ Mean ☊ 24♒17.5

March 1971 — LONGITUDE

Day	Sid.Time	☉	0 hr ☽	Noon ☽	True ☊	☿	♀	♂	⚳	♃	♄	♅	♆	♇
1 M	22 34 34	10♓15 19	0♉03 40	7♉16 42	23♒32.2	5♓41.2	26♑59.2	23♐19.9	9♉04.4	5♐42.7	17♉22.2	12♎47.6	3♐04.1	28♍51.3
2 Tu	22 38 30	11 15 32	14 23 23	21 23 29	23R 30.6	7 31.0	28 08.6	23 56.7	9 24.5	5 46.6	17 26.7	12R 45.5	3 04.2	28R 49.7
3 W	22 42 27	12 15 43	28 16 55	5♊03 44	23D 29.7	9 21.8	29 18.2	24 33.5	9 44.7	5 50.4	17 31.3	12 43.4	3 04.3	28 48.2
4 Th	22 46 23	13 15 52	11♊44 09	18 18 28	23 29.6	11 13.6	0♒27.9	25 10.3	10 05.0	5 53.9	17 36.0	12 41.3	3 04.4	28 46.6
5 F	22 50 20	14 15 59	24 47 01	1♋10 15	23 30.4	13 06.4	1 37.6	25 47.0	10 25.4	5 57.3	17 40.7	12 39.2	3R 04.4	28 45.1
6 Sa	22 54 16	15 16 04	7♋28 39	13 42 40	23 31.8	15 00.1	2 47.5	26 23.6	10 46.0	6 00.6	17 45.6	12 37.0	3 04.4	28 43.5
7 Su	22 58 13	16 16 07	19 52 48	25 59 32	23 33.5	16 54.8	3 57.4	27 00.3	11 06.6	6 03.6	17 50.5	12 34.8	3 04.3	28 41.9
8 M	23 02 10	17 16 07	2♌03 21	8♌04 42	23 35.0	18 50.3	5 07.4	27 36.9	11 27.4	6 06.5	17 55.5	12 32.5	3 04.3	28 40.3
9 Tu	23 06 06	18 16 06	14 03 58	20 01 36	23R 35.8	20 46.5	6 17.5	28 13.4	11 48.3	6 09.1	18 00.6	12 30.3	3 04.2	28 38.7
10 W	23 10 03	19 16 02	25 57 56	1♍53 18	23 35.6	22 43.5	7 27.7	28 49.9	12 09.3	6 11.6	18 05.7	12 28.0	3 04.0	28 37.1
11 Th	23 13 59	20 15 57	7♍48 02	13 42 24	23 34.0	24 41.1	8 37.9	29 26.3	12 30.3	6 14.0	18 11.0	12 25.6	3 03.8	28 35.5
12 F	23 17 56	21 15 49	19 36 41	25 31 08	23 30.9	26 39.1	9 48.3	0♑02.8	12 51.5	6 16.1	18 16.3	12 23.3	3 03.6	28 33.9
13 Sa	23 21 52	22 15 40	1♎25 59	7♎21 29	23 26.7	28 37.3	10 58.7	0 39.1	13 12.8	6 18.0	18 21.7	12 20.9	3 03.4	28 32.3
14 Su	23 25 49	23 15 28	13 17 51	19 15 20	23 21.4	0♈35.7	12 09.1	1 15.4	13 34.2	6 19.8	18 27.1	12 18.5	3 03.1	28 30.6
15 M	23 29 45	24 15 15	25 14 12	1♏14 42	23 15.8	2 33.9	13 19.7	1 51.7	13 55.7	6 21.4	18 32.7	12 16.1	3 02.8	28 29.0
16 Tu	23 33 42	25 15 00	7♏17 08	13 21 48	23 10.4	4 31.8	14 30.3	2 27.9	14 17.3	6 22.8	18 38.3	12 13.7	3 02.5	28 27.4
17 W	23 37 38	26 14 43	19 29 03	25 39 13	23 05.9	6 28.9	15 41.0	3 04.1	14 39.0	6 24.0	18 43.9	12 11.3	3 02.1	28 25.7
18 Th	23 41 35	27 14 25	1♐52 43	8♐09 56	23 02.6	8 25.0	16 51.8	3 40.2	15 00.8	6 25.1	18 49.7	12 08.8	3 01.7	28 24.1
19 F	23 45 32	28 14 05	14 31 16	20 57 10	23D 00.9	10 19.7	18 02.6	4 16.2	15 22.7	6 25.9	18 55.5	12 06.3	3 01.2	28 22.5
20 Sa	23 49 28	29 13 43	27 28 02	4♑04 16	23 00.8	12 12.7	19 13.5	4 52.2	15 44.7	6 26.6	19 01.3	12 03.8	3 00.8	28 20.8
21 Su	23 53 25	0♈13 19	10♑46 13	17 34 11	23 01.7	14 03.4	20 24.5	5 28.2	16 06.8	6 27.0	19 07.3	12 01.3	3 00.3	28 19.2
22 M	23 57 21	1 12 54	24 28 24	1♒29 00	23 03.2	15 51.5	21 35.5	6 04.1	16 28.9	6R 27.3	19 13.3	11 58.8	2 59.8	28 17.6
23 Tu	0 01 18	2 12 27	8♒35 58	15 49 08	23R 04.3	17 36.6	22 46.6	6 39.9	16 51.1	6 27.4	19 19.4	11 56.3	2 59.2	28 15.9
24 W	0 05 14	3 11 58	23 08 12	0♓32 39	23 04.3	19 18.1	23 57.7	7 15.6	17 13.5	6 27.3	19 25.5	11 53.7	2 58.6	28 14.3
25 Th	0 09 11	4 11 27	8♓01 46	15 34 40	23 02.5	20 55.6	25 08.8	7 51.3	17 35.9	6 27.0	19 31.7	11 51.2	2 58.0	28 12.6
26 F	0 13 07	5 10 54	23 10 17	0♈47 26	22 58.7	22 28.7	26 20.1	8 26.9	17 58.4	6 26.5	19 37.9	11 48.6	2 57.3	28 11.0
27 Sa	0 17 04	6 10 19	8♈24 49	16 01 05	22 53.1	23 57.1	27 31.3	9 02.4	18 20.9	6 25.9	19 44.2	11 46.0	2 56.6	28 09.4
28 Su	0 21 01	7 09 42	23 34 55	1♉05 07	22 46.4	25 20.3	28 42.6	9 37.9	18 43.6	6 25.0	19 50.6	11 43.4	2 55.9	28 07.8
29 M	0 24 57	8 09 03	8♉30 32	15 50 14	22 39.4	26 37.9	29 54.0	10 13.3	19 06.3	6 24.0	19 57.0	11 40.8	2 55.2	28 06.2
30 Tu	0 28 54	9 08 22	23 03 29	0♊09 45	22 33.1	27 49.8	1♓05.4	10 48.6	19 29.1	6 22.8	20 03.5	11 38.2	2 54.4	28 04.5
31 W	0 32 50	10 07 39	7♊08 44	14 00 18	22 28.3	28 55.5	2 16.8	11 23.8	19 52.0	6 21.3	20 10.0	11 35.7	2 53.6	28 03.0

April 1971 — LONGITUDE

Day	Sid.Time	☉	0 hr ☽	Noon ☽	True ☊	☿	♀	♂	⚳	♃	♄	♅	♆	♇
1 Th	0 36 47	11♈06 53	20♊44 33	27♊21 40	22♒25.4	29♈54.9	3♓28.2	11♑59.0	20♉15.0	6♐19.7	20♉16.6	11♎33.1	2♐52.8	28♍01.4
2 F	0 40 43	12 06 05	3♋52 03	10♋16 08	22D 24.3	0♉47.8	4 39.7	12 34.0	20 38.0	6R 18.0	20 23.2	11R 30.5	2R 51.9	27R 59.8
3 Sa	0 44 40	13 05 15	16 34 27	22 47 37	22 24.7	1 33.9	5 51.3	13 09.0	21 01.1	6 16.0	20 29.9	11 27.9	2 51.1	27 58.2
4 Su	0 48 36	14 04 22	28 56 14	5♌00 57	22 25.9	2 13.2	7 02.9	13 43.9	21 24.2	6 13.8	20 36.6	11 25.3	2 50.2	27 56.6
5 M	0 52 33	15 03 27	11♌02 22	17 01 07	22R 26.8	2 45.6	8 14.5	14 18.7	21 47.4	6 11.5	20 43.4	11 22.7	2 49.2	27 55.1
6 Tu	0 56 30	16 02 29	22 57 48	28 52 58	22 26.7	3 11.0	9 26.1	14 53.4	22 10.7	6 09.0	20 50.2	11 20.1	2 48.3	27 53.5
7 W	1 00 26	17 01 30	4♍47 09	10♍40 49	22 24.8	3 29.5	10 37.8	15 28.1	22 34.1	6 06.3	20 57.1	11 17.5	2 47.3	27 52.0
8 Th	1 04 23	18 00 28	16 34 25	22 28 21	22 20.6	3 41.0	11 49.5	16 02.6	22 57.5	6 03.4	21 04.0	11 15.0	2 46.3	27 50.5
9 F	1 08 19	18 59 24	28 22 57	4♎18 31	22 13.8	3R 45.8	13 01.2	16 37.1	23 20.9	6 00.4	21 11.0	11 12.4	2 45.2	27 49.0
10 Sa	1 12 16	19 58 18	10♎15 19	16 13 36	22 04.9	3 43.9	14 13.0	17 11.4	23 44.4	5 57.2	21 18.0	11 09.8	2 44.1	27 47.5
11 Su	1 16 12	20 57 09	22 13 31	28 15 16	21 54.3	3 35.7	15 24.8	17 45.7	24 08.0	5 53.8	21 25.0	11 07.3	2 43.1	27 46.0
12 M	1 20 09	21 55 59	4♏18 59	10♏24 47	21 42.9	3 21.5	16 36.6	18 19.8	24 31.7	5 50.2	21 32.1	11 04.7	2 42.0	27 44.5
13 Tu	1 24 05	22 54 47	16 32 50	22 43 13	21 31.8	3 01.6	17 48.5	18 53.9	24 55.4	5 46.5	21 39.2	11 02.2	2 40.8	27 43.1
14 W	1 28 02	23 53 34	28 56 07	5♐11 40	21 22.0	2 36.5	19 00.4	19 27.9	25 19.1	5 42.6	21 46.3	10 59.7	2 39.7	27 41.6
15 Th	1 31 59	24 52 18	11♐30 03	17 51 28	21 14.3	2 06.9	20 12.3	20 01.7	25 42.9	5 38.5	21 53.5	10 57.2	2 38.5	27 40.2
16 F	1 35 55	25 51 01	24 16 10	0♑44 22	21 09.0	1 33.2	21 24.3	20 35.5	26 06.8	5 34.3	22 00.8	10 54.7	2 37.3	27 38.8
17 Sa	1 39 52	26 49 42	7♑16 22	13 52 26	21 06.3	0 56.3	22 36.3	21 09.1	26 30.7	5 29.9	22 08.0	10 52.3	2 36.1	27 37.4
18 Su	1 43 48	27 48 22	20 32 53	27 17 58	21D 05.5	0 16.8	23 48.3	21 42.6	26 54.7	5 25.4	22 15.3	10 49.8	2 34.8	27 36.0
19 M	1 47 45	28 46 59	4♒07 57	11♒03 02	21R 05.8	29♈35.5	25 00.4	22 16.0	27 18.7	5 20.7	22 22.6	10 47.4	2 33.6	27 34.7
20 Tu	1 51 41	29 45 35	18 03 21	25 08 54	21 06.0	28 53.3	26 12.4	22 49.3	27 42.7	5 15.8	22 30.0	10 45.0	2 32.3	27 33.3
21 W	1 55 38	0♉44 10	2♓19 38	9♓35 17	21 04.8	28 10.8	27 24.5	23 22.4	28 06.9	5 10.8	22 37.4	10 42.6	2 31.0	27 32.0
22 Th	1 59 34	1 42 42	16 55 28	24 19 36	21 01.3	27 29.0	28 36.6	23 55.4	28 31.0	5 05.6	22 44.8	10 40.2	2 29.7	27 30.7
23 F	2 03 31	2 41 13	1♈46 57	9♈16 35	20 55.2	26 48.4	29 48.8	24 28.3	28 55.2	5 00.3	22 52.2	10 37.8	2 28.3	27 29.4
24 Sa	2 07 28	3 39 43	16 47 28	24 18 25	20 46.5	26 09.9	1♈00.9	25 01.0	29 19.5	4 54.9	22 59.7	10 35.5	2 27.0	27 28.2
25 Su	2 11 24	4 38 10	1♉48 14	9♉15 42	20 36.1	25 34.0	2 13.1	25 33.6	29 43.8	4 49.3	23 07.2	10 33.2	2 25.6	27 26.9
26 M	2 15 21	5 36 36	16 39 40	23 59 03	20 25.1	25 01.2	3 25.3	26 06.0	0♊08.1	4 43.6	23 14.7	10 30.9	2 24.2	27 25.7
27 Tu	2 19 17	6 34 59	1♊12 57	8♊20 39	20 14.8	24 32.1	4 37.5	26 38.2	0 32.5	4 37.8	23 22.2	10 28.7	2 22.8	27 24.5
28 W	2 23 14	7 33 21	15 21 38	22 15 32	20 06.3	24 06.9	5 49.8	27 10.3	0 56.9	4 31.8	23 29.8	10 26.4	2 21.4	27 23.4
29 Th	2 27 10	8 31 41	29 02 16	5♋41 52	20 00.2	23 46.0	7 02.0	27 42.3	1 21.4	4 25.7	23 37.4	10 24.2	2 19.9	27 22.2
30 F	2 31 07	9 29 59	12♋14 34	18 40 43	19 56.6	23 29.7	8 14.3	28 14.1	1 45.9	4 19.5	23 45.0	10 22.1	2 18.5	27 21.1

Astro Data (Dy Hr Mn)	Planet Ingress (Dy Hr Mn)	Last Aspect (Dy Hr Mn)	☽ Ingress (Dy Hr Mn)	Last Aspect (Dy Hr Mn)	☽ Ingress (Dy Hr Mn)	☽ Phases & Eclipses (Dy Hr Mn)
♆R 5 18:08	♀ ♒ 4 2:24	3 0:56 ♇ △	♊ 3 3:01	1 13:13 ♇ □	♋ 1 16:51	4 2:01 ☽ 12♊51
☽0S 12 8:41	♂ ♑ 12 10:11	5 7:27 ♇ □	♋ 5 9:47	3 22:05 ♇ ⚹	♌ 4 2:05	12 2:34 ○ 20♍52
☿0N 14 23:45	☿ ♈ 14 4:46	7 17:20 ♇ ⚹	♌ 7 19:55	5 19:33 ♄ □	♍ 6 14:16	20 2:30 ☾ 28♐50
☉0N 21 6:38	☉ ♈ 21 6:38	10 5:28 ♂ △	♍ 10 8:10	8 22:53 ♇ ☌	♎ 9 3:17	26 19:23 ● 5♈29
♃R 23 11:33	♀ ♓ 29 14:02	12 18:10 ♇ ☌	♎ 12 21:06	10 20:10 ☉ ☍	♏ 11 15:28	
☽0N 26 1:05		13 22:03 ♅ ☌	♏ 15 9:31	13 21:38 ♇ ⚹	♐ 14 2:03	2 15:46 ☽ 12♋15
	☿ ♉ 1 14:11	17 17:21 ♇ ⚹	♐ 17 20:23	16 6:17 ♇ □	♑ 16 10:38	10 20:10 ○ 20♎18
☽0S 8 14:45	☿ ♈R 18 21:52	20 2:30 ☉ □	♑ 20 4:37	18 12:58 ☉ □	♒ 18 16:46	18 12:58 ☾ 27♑51
☿R 9 17:11	☉ ♉ 20 17:54	22 6:34 ♇ △	♒ 22 9:29	20 17:58 ☿ ⚹	♓ 20 20:08	25 4:02 ● 4♉19
☽0N 22 10:58	♀ ♈ 23 15:44	24 0:25 ♀ ☌	♓ 24 11:07	22 19:30 ♀ ☌	♈ 22 21:08	
♀0N 26 16:54	⚳ ♊ 26 4:00	26 7:54 ♇ ☍	♈ 26 10:45	24 14:51 ☿ ☌	♉ 24 21:06	
		28 7:52 ♀ ⚹	♉ 28 10:15	26 17:41 ♇ △	♊ 26 21:58	
		30 8:28 ♇ △	♊ 30 11:43	28 21:03 ♇ □	♋ 29 1:43	

Astro Data

1 March 1971
Julian Day # 25992
SVP 5♓39'34"
GC 26♐26.2 ⚴ 25♓00.0
Eris 11♈59.5 ⚵ 4♊24.8
⚷ 8♈05.7 ⚶ 7♑57.7
☽ Mean ☊ 22♒48.5

1 April 1971
Julian Day # 26023
SVP 5♓39'30"
GC 26♐26.3 ⚴ 6♈15.4
Eris 12♈19.6 ⚵ 18♊34.8
⚷ 9♈51.7 ⚶ 21♑05.9
☽ Mean ☊ 21♒10.0

LONGITUDE — May 1971

Day	Sid.Time	☉	0 hr ☽	Noon ☽	True ☊	☿	♀	♂	⚳	♃	♄	♅	♆	♇
1 Sa	2 35 03	10♉28 14	25♋00 47	1♌15 19	19♒55.2	23♈18.0	9♈26.6	28♑45.7	2♊10.5	4♐13.2	23♉52.6	10♎19.9	2♐17.0	27♍20.0
2 Su	2 39 00	11 26 28	7♌24 56	13 30 17	19R 54.9	23D 11.1	10 38.9	29 17.1	2 35.0	4R 06.7	24 00.2	10R 17.8	2R 15.5	27R 18.9
3 M	2 42 57	12 24 39	19 32 03	25 30 56	19 54.9	23 09.0	11 51.2	29 48.4	2 59.7	4 00.2	24 07.9	10 15.8	2 14.0	27 17.9
4 Tu	2 46 53	13 22 49	1♍27 35	7♍22 41	19 53.9	23 11.8	13 03.5	0♒19.5	3 24.3	3 53.6	24 15.5	10 13.7	2 12.5	27 16.8
5 W	2 50 50	14 20 56	13 16 51	19 10 43	19 51.1	23 19.2	14 15.8	0 50.4	3 49.0	3 46.8	24 23.2	10 11.7	2 11.0	27 15.8
6 Th	2 54 46	15 19 02	25 04 48	0♎59 39	19 45.7	23 31.4	15 28.2	1 21.1	4 13.7	3 40.0	24 30.9	10 09.7	2 09.5	27 14.9
7 F	2 58 43	16 17 06	6♎55 42	12 53 22	19 37.6	23 48.2	16 40.5	1 51.6	4 38.4	3 33.1	24 38.6	10 07.8	2 07.9	27 13.9
8 Sa	3 02 39	17 15 08	18 53 00	24 54 52	19 27.0	24 09.4	17 52.9	2 22.0	5 03.2	3 26.1	24 46.3	10 05.9	2 06.4	27 13.0
9 Su	3 06 36	18 13 08	0♏59 12	7♏06 12	19 14.4	24 35.0	19 05.3	2 52.1	5 28.0	3 19.0	24 54.0	10 04.0	2 04.8	27 12.1
10 M	3 10 32	19 11 07	13 15 58	19 28 35	19 00.9	25 04.8	20 17.7	3 22.1	5 52.9	3 11.9	25 01.8	10 02.2	2 03.2	27 11.2
11 Tu	3 14 29	20 09 04	25 44 05	2♐02 29	18 47.7	25 38.6	21 30.1	3 51.8	6 17.7	3 04.7	25 09.5	10 00.4	2 01.7	27 10.4
12 W	3 18 26	21 06 59	8♐23 45	14 47 53	18 35.9	26 16.5	22 42.6	4 21.3	6 42.6	2 57.4	25 17.3	9 58.6	2 00.1	27 09.5
13 Th	3 22 22	22 04 53	21 14 50	27 44 37	18 26.4	26 58.1	23 55.0	4 50.6	7 07.6	2 50.1	25 25.0	9 56.9	1 58.5	27 08.8
14 F	3 26 19	23 02 46	4♑17 13	10♑52 39	18 19.7	27 43.4	25 07.5	5 19.7	7 32.5	2 42.7	25 32.8	9 55.3	1 56.9	27 08.0
15 Sa	3 30 15	24 00 38	17 30 59	24 12 18	18 15.9	28 32.2	26 20.0	5 48.5	7 57.5	2 35.3	25 40.5	9 53.6	1 55.3	27 07.3
16 Su	3 34 12	24 58 28	0♒56 40	7♒44 14	18D 14.4	29 24.4	27 32.5	6 17.1	8 22.5	2 27.8	25 48.3	9 52.0	1 53.7	27 06.6
17 M	3 38 08	25 56 17	14 35 06	21 29 23	18R 14.2	0♉19.9	28 45.0	6 45.4	8 47.5	2 20.3	25 56.1	9 50.5	1 52.1	27 05.9
18 Tu	3 42 05	26 54 05	28 27 09	5♓28 28	18 14.1	1 18.7	29 57.6	7 13.5	9 12.6	2 12.7	26 03.8	9 49.0	1 50.5	27 05.2
19 W	3 46 01	27 51 52	12♓33 17	19 41 28	18 12.8	2 20.5	1♉10.1	7 41.4	9 37.7	2 05.1	26 11.6	9 47.5	1 48.9	27 04.6
20 Th	3 49 58	28 49 38	26 52 50	4♈07 00	18 09.3	3 25.3	2 22.7	8 08.9	10 02.8	1 57.5	26 19.3	9 46.1	1 47.2	27 04.0
21 F	3 53 55	29 47 22	11♈23 32	18 41 49	18 03.2	4 33.0	3 35.3	8 36.2	10 27.9	1 49.9	26 27.1	9 44.7	1 45.6	27 03.5
22 Sa	3 57 51	0♊45 06	26 01 09	3♉20 41	17 54.6	5 43.6	4 47.9	9 03.1	10 53.1	1 42.2	26 34.8	9 43.4	1 44.0	27 02.9
23 Su	4 01 48	1 42 48	10♉39 33	17 56 48	17 44.2	6 56.9	6 00.5	9 29.8	11 18.3	1 34.6	26 42.6	9 42.1	1 42.4	27 02.4
24 M	4 05 44	2 40 29	25 11 32	2♊22 49	17 33.1	8 13.0	7 13.2	9 56.2	11 43.5	1 26.9	26 50.3	9 40.8	1 40.7	27 02.0
25 Tu	4 09 41	3 38 09	9♊29 52	16 32 00	17 22.5	9 31.7	8 25.8	10 22.2	12 08.7	1 19.3	26 58.1	9 39.7	1 39.1	27 01.6
26 W	4 13 37	4 35 48	23 28 37	0♋19 20	17 13.6	10 53.0	9 38.5	10 47.9	12 33.9	1 11.7	27 05.8	9 38.5	1 37.5	27 01.2
27 Th	4 17 34	5 33 26	7♋03 54	13 42 13	17 07.1	12 16.9	10 51.1	11 13.3	12 59.2	1 04.0	27 13.5	9 37.4	1 35.9	27 00.8
28 F	4 21 30	6 31 02	20 14 32	26 40 31	17 03.1	13 43.3	12 03.8	11 38.4	13 24.5	0 56.4	27 21.2	9 36.4	1 34.3	27 00.4
29 Sa	4 25 27	7 28 36	3♌01 01	9♌16 15	17D 01.4	15 12.3	13 16.5	12 03.1	13 49.8	0 48.9	27 28.9	9 35.4	1 32.6	27 00.1
30 Su	4 29 24	8 26 09	15 26 45	21 33 04	17 01.2	16 43.8	14 29.2	12 27.5	14 15.1	0 41.3	27 36.6	9 34.4	1 31.0	26 59.9
31 M	4 33 20	9 23 41	27 35 49	3♍35 38	17R 01.6	18 17.8	15 41.9	12 51.5	14 40.4	0 33.8	27 44.3	9 33.5	1 29.4	26 59.6

LONGITUDE — June 1971

Day	Sid.Time	☉	0 hr ☽	Noon ☽	True ☊	☿	♀	♂	⚳	♃	♄	♅	♆	♇
1 Tu	4 37 17	10♊21 12	9♍33 13	15♍29 12	17♒01.6	19♉54.2	16♉54.6	13♒15.1	15♊05.7	0♐26.4	27♉51.9	9♎32.6	1♐27.8	26♍59.4
2 W	4 41 13	11 18 41	21 24 17	27 19 06	17R 00.2	21 33.2	18 07.3	13 38.4	15 31.1	0R 19.0	27 59.6	9R 31.8	1R 26.2	26R 59.2
3 Th	4 45 10	12 16 08	3♎14 17	9♎10 26	16 56.8	23 14.6	19 20.0	14 01.3	15 56.4	0 11.6	28 07.2	9 31.1	1 24.6	26 59.1
4 F	4 49 06	13 13 35	15 08 07	21 07 50	16 51.1	24 58.4	20 32.8	14 23.7	16 21.8	0 04.3	28 14.8	9 30.4	1 23.0	26 58.9
5 Sa	4 53 03	14 11 00	27 10 01	3♏15 06	16 43.2	26 44.7	21 45.6	14 45.8	16 47.2	29♏57.1	28 22.4	9 29.7	1 21.5	26 58.9
6 Su	4 56 59	15 08 25	9♏23 23	15 35 09	16 33.5	28 33.4	22 58.3	15 07.5	17 12.6	29 49.9	28 29.9	9 29.1	1 19.9	26 58.8
7 M	5 00 56	16 05 48	21 50 34	28 09 45	16 23.0	0♊24.5	24 11.1	15 28.8	17 38.0	29 42.8	28 37.5	9 28.6	1 18.3	26D 58.8
8 Tu	5 04 53	17 03 11	4♐32 45	10♐59 32	16 12.7	2 18.0	25 23.9	15 49.6	18 03.4	29 35.8	28 45.0	9 28.1	1 16.8	26 58.8
9 W	5 08 49	18 00 33	17 30 03	24 04 08	16 03.5	4 13.8	26 36.7	16 10.0	18 28.8	29 28.8	28 52.5	9 27.6	1 15.2	26 58.8
10 Th	5 12 46	18 57 53	0♑41 38	7♑22 21	15 56.2	6 11.8	27 49.6	16 30.0	18 54.2	29 22.0	29 00.0	9 27.2	1 13.7	26 58.9
11 F	5 16 42	19 55 14	14 06 03	20 52 33	15 51.2	8 12.0	29 02.4	16 49.5	19 19.7	29 15.2	29 07.4	9 26.9	1 12.2	26 59.0
12 Sa	5 20 39	20 52 33	27 41 36	4♒33 02	15D 48.8	10 14.2	0♊15.3	17 08.5	19 45.1	29 08.5	29 14.8	9 26.6	1 10.7	26 59.2
13 Su	5 24 35	21 49 52	11♒26 39	18 22 18	15 48.2	12 18.3	1 28.2	17 27.0	20 10.6	29 01.9	29 22.2	9 26.4	1 09.2	26 59.3
14 M	5 28 32	22 47 11	25 19 52	2♓19 13	15 48.9	14 24.2	2 41.1	17 45.0	20 36.1	28 55.5	29 29.6	9 26.2	1 07.7	26 59.5
15 Tu	5 32 28	23 44 29	9♓20 15	16 22 50	15R 49.8	16 31.6	3 54.0	18 02.5	21 01.5	28 49.1	29 36.9	9 26.0	1 06.2	26 59.8
16 W	5 36 25	24 41 47	23 26 51	0♈32 09	15 49.8	18 40.4	5 07.0	18 19.4	21 27.0	28 42.8	29 44.2	9 25.9	1 04.8	27 00.0
17 Th	5 40 22	25 39 04	7♈38 32	14 45 45	15 48.3	20 50.3	6 19.9	18 35.9	21 52.5	28 36.7	29 51.5	9D 25.9	1 03.3	27 00.3
18 F	5 44 18	26 36 21	21 53 29	29 01 24	15 44.8	23 01.1	7 32.9	18 51.7	22 18.0	28 30.6	29 58.8	9 25.9	1 01.9	27 00.7
19 Sa	5 48 15	27 33 38	6♉09 02	13♉15 57	15 39.3	25 12.4	8 45.9	19 07.0	22 43.5	28 24.7	0♊06.0	9 26.0	1 00.5	27 01.0
20 Su	5 52 11	28 30 55	20 21 35	27 25 23	15 32.5	27 24.1	9 58.9	19 21.7	23 09.0	28 18.9	0 13.1	9 26.1	0 59.1	27 01.4
21 M	5 56 08	29 28 12	4♊26 49	11♊25 18	15 25.1	29 35.8	11 11.9	19 35.8	23 34.5	28 13.3	0 20.3	9 26.3	0 57.7	27 01.9
22 Tu	6 00 04	0♋25 28	18 20 19	25 11 26	15 18.0	1♋47.3	12 25.0	19 49.3	24 00.0	28 07.8	0 27.4	9 26.5	0 56.3	27 02.3
23 W	6 04 01	1 22 44	1♋58 13	8♋40 23	15 12.1	3 58.3	13 38.1	20 02.2	24 25.6	28 02.4	0 34.5	9 26.8	0 54.9	27 02.8
24 Th	6 07 58	2 19 59	15 17 43	21 50 06	15 07.9	6 08.5	14 51.1	20 14.4	24 51.1	27 57.1	0 41.5	9 27.2	0 53.6	27 03.4
25 F	6 11 54	3 17 14	28 17 31	4♌40 04	15D 05.6	8 17.8	16 04.2	20 26.0	25 16.6	27 52.0	0 48.5	9 27.6	0 52.3	27 03.9
26 Sa	6 15 51	4 14 29	10♌57 57	17 11 25	15 05.1	10 25.8	17 17.3	20 37.0	25 42.1	27 47.1	0 55.4	9 28.0	0 51.0	27 04.5
27 Su	6 19 47	5 11 43	23 20 50	29 26 37	15 05.9	12 32.5	18 30.5	20 47.3	26 07.6	27 42.3	1 02.3	9 28.5	0 49.7	27 05.1
28 M	6 23 44	6 08 56	5♍29 16	11♍29 17	15 07.4	14 37.7	19 43.6	20 56.9	26 33.1	27 37.6	1 09.2	9 29.1	0 48.5	27 05.8
29 Tu	6 27 40	7 06 09	17 27 14	23 23 45	15 08.9	16 41.3	20 56.8	21 05.8	26 58.6	27 33.1	1 16.0	9 29.7	0 47.2	27 06.5
30 W	6 31 37	8 03 21	29 19 24	5♎14 50	15R 09.7	18 43.1	22 09.9	21 14.1	27 24.1	27 28.8	1 22.8	9 30.3	0 46.0	27 07.2

Astro Data (Dy Hr Mn)

☿ D 3 10:25
☽0S 5 20:51
♄⚼♅ 10 13:02
☽0N 19 18:01
♃☌♆ 22 4:57
♄△♇ 25 22:15

☽0S 2 3:23
♇ D 7 15:16
♃☍♄ 12 1:14
☽0N 15 22:58
♅ D 17 14:51
♄☍♆ 25 23:04
☽0S 29 10:31

Planet Ingress (Dy Hr Mn)

♂ ♒ 3 20:57
☿ ♉ 17 3:32
♀ ♉ 18 12:48
☉ ♊ 21 17:15

♃ ♏R 5 2:12
☿ ♊ 7 6:45
♀ ♊ 12 6:58
♄ ♊ 18 16:09
☿ ♋ 21 16:25
☉ ♋ 22 1:20

Last Aspect Dy Hr Mn		☽ Ingress Dy Hr Mn
1 6:58	♂ ☍	♌ 1 9:34
3 9:11	♄ □	♍ 3 21:03
6 4:25	♇ ☌	♎ 6 9:59
8 10:27	☿ ☍	♏ 8 22:03
11 2:45	♇ ⚹	♐ 11 8:08
13 10:54	♇ □	♑ 13 16:09
15 20:15	☿ □	♒ 15 22:19
18 1:42	♀ ⚹	♓ 18 2:39
20 2:37	☉ ⚹	♈ 20 5:11
20 21:19	♅ ☍	♉ 22 6:31
24 3:04	♇ △	♊ 24 8:01
26 6:11	♇ □	♋ 26 11:26
28 13:17	♄ ⚹	♌ 28 18:16
31 0:09	♄ □	♍ 31 4:48

Last Aspect Dy Hr Mn		☽ Ingress Dy Hr Mn
2 13:23	♄ △	♎ 2 17:26
3 22:05	♂ △	♏ 5 5:36
7 14:54	♃ ☌	♐ 7 15:28
9 17:17	♇ □	♑ 9 22:45
12 3:46	♀ △	♒ 12 4:03
14 7:07	♄ □	♓ 14 8:01
16 10:38	♄ ⚹	♈ 16 11:06
18 7:38	☉ ⚹	♉ 18 13:39
20 13:31	♃ ☍	♊ 20 16:24
22 15:16	♇ □	♋ 22 20:30
24 23:17	♃ △	♌ 25 3:12
27 8:35	♃ □	♍ 27 13:06
29 20:22	♃ ⚹	♎ 30 1:22

☽ Phases & Eclipses (Dy Hr Mn)

2 7:34 ☽ 11♌16
10 11:24 ○ 19♏10
17 20:15 ☾ 26♒16
24 12:32 ● 2♊42

1 0:42 ☽ 9♍54
9 0:04 ○ 17♐32
16 1:24 ☾ 24♓16
22 21:57 ● 0♋49
30 18:11 ☽ 8♎18

Astro Data

1 May 1971
Julian Day # 26053
SVP 5♓39'26"
GC 26♐26.3 ⚴ 17♈31.1
Eris 12♈39.3 ⚵ 3♋15.1
⚷ 11♈33.7 ⚶ 0♒54.4
☽ Mean ☊ 19♒34.7

1 June 1971
Julian Day # 26084
SVP 5♓39'21"
GC 26♐26.4 ⚴ 29♈13.2
Eris 12♈55.2 ⚵ 18♋37.9
⚷ 12♈58.5 ⚶ 6♒04.0
☽ Mean ☊ 17♒56.2

July 1971

LONGITUDE

Day	Sid.Time	☉	0 hr ☽	Noon ☽	True ☊	☿	♀	♂	⚳	♃	♄	♅	♆	♇
1 Th	6 35 33	9♋00 33	11♎10 41	17♎07 33	15♒09.4	20♋43.2	23♊23.1	21♒21.6	27♊49.6	27♏24.6	1♊29.5	9♎31.1	0♐44.8	27♍07.9
2 F	6 39 30	9 57 45	23 06 03	29 06 45	15R 07.6	22 41.3	24 36.3	21 28.5	28 15.1	27R 20.6	1 36.2	9 31.8	0R 43.6	27 08.7
3 Sa	6 43 27	10 54 57	5♏10 12	11♏16 55	15 04.4	24 37.5	25 49.6	21 34.7	28 40.6	27 16.7	1 42.8	9 32.6	0 42.5	27 09.5
4 Su	6 47 23	11 52 08	17 27 19	23 41 49	15 00.1	26 31.7	27 02.8	21 40.1	29 06.1	27 13.0	1 49.4	9 33.5	0 41.3	27 10.4
5 M	6 51 20	12 49 19	0♐00 44	6♐24 17	14 55.1	28 24.0	28 16.1	21 44.8	29 31.5	27 09.5	1 56.0	9 34.4	0 40.2	27 11.2
6 Tu	6 55 16	13 46 30	12 52 38	19 25 50	14 50.1	0♌14.2	29 29.4	21 48.8	29 57.0	27 06.2	2 02.4	9 35.4	0 39.2	27 12.1
7 W	6 59 13	14 43 40	26 03 53	2♑46 39	14 45.6	2 02.4	0♋42.7	21 52.0	0♋22.5	27 03.0	2 08.9	9 36.4	0 38.1	27 13.1
8 Th	7 03 09	15 40 51	9♑33 55	16 25 25	14 42.2	3 48.6	1 56.0	21 54.5	0 47.9	27 00.0	2 15.2	9 37.5	0 37.1	27 14.0
9 F	7 07 06	16 38 02	23 20 47	0♒19 37	14 40.1	5 32.8	3 09.3	21 56.2	1 13.3	26 57.1	2 21.6	9 38.6	0 36.1	27 15.0
10 Sa	7 11 02	17 35 13	7♒21 27	14 25 49	14D 39.5	7 14.9	4 22.7	21R 57.2	1 38.8	26 54.4	2 27.8	9 39.8	0 35.1	27 16.0
11 Su	7 14 59	18 32 24	21 32 12	28 40 06	14 40.0	8 55.1	5 36.1	21 57.4	2 04.2	26 51.9	2 34.1	9 41.0	0 34.1	27 17.1
12 M	7 18 56	19 29 36	5♓49 04	12♓58 37	14 41.2	10 33.2	6 49.5	21 56.9	2 29.6	26 49.6	2 40.2	9 42.3	0 33.2	27 18.2
13 Tu	7 22 52	20 26 48	20 08 20	27 17 49	14 42.6	12 09.3	8 02.9	21 55.5	2 55.0	26 47.5	2 46.3	9 43.6	0 32.2	27 19.3
14 W	7 26 49	21 24 01	4♈26 43	11♈34 41	14R 43.6	13 43.3	9 16.3	21 53.4	3 20.4	26 45.5	2 52.3	9 45.0	0 31.4	27 20.4
15 Th	7 30 45	22 21 14	18 41 26	25 46 41	14 43.8	15 15.4	10 29.8	21 50.5	3 45.8	26 43.7	2 58.3	9 46.4	0 30.5	27 21.6
16 F	7 34 42	23 18 28	2♉50 11	9♉51 42	14 43.1	16 45.3	11 43.3	21 46.8	4 11.2	26 42.1	3 04.2	9 47.9	0 29.7	27 22.8
17 Sa	7 38 38	24 15 43	16 51 00	23 47 53	14 41.4	18 13.2	12 56.8	21 42.4	4 36.5	26 40.7	3 10.1	9 49.4	0 28.9	27 24.0
18 Su	7 42 35	25 12 58	0♊42 07	7♊33 31	14 39.1	19 39.1	14 10.4	21 37.2	5 01.9	26 39.4	3 15.9	9 51.0	0 28.1	27 25.2
19 M	7 46 31	26 10 14	14 21 53	21 07 02	14 36.5	21 02.8	15 24.0	21 31.3	5 27.2	26 38.4	3 21.6	9 52.6	0 27.3	27 26.5
20 Tu	7 50 28	27 07 31	27 48 48	4♋27 04	14 34.1	22 24.4	16 37.6	21 24.6	5 52.5	26 37.5	3 27.3	9 54.3	0 26.6	27 27.8
21 W	7 54 25	28 04 49	11♋01 41	17 32 35	14 32.1	23 43.8	17 51.2	21 17.1	6 17.8	26 36.8	3 32.9	9 56.0	0 25.9	27 29.1
22 Th	7 58 21	29 02 06	23 59 43	0♌23 05	14 30.9	25 00.9	19 04.8	21 09.0	6 43.1	26 36.3	3 38.4	9 57.8	0 25.2	27 30.5
23 F	8 02 18	29 59 25	6♌42 43	12 58 44	14D 30.4	26 15.8	20 18.5	21 00.2	7 08.4	26 36.0	3 43.9	9 59.6	0 24.6	27 31.9
24 Sa	8 06 14	0♌56 44	19 11 15	25 20 27	14 30.6	27 28.3	21 32.2	20 50.7	7 33.6	26D 35.8	3 49.3	10 01.4	0 24.0	27 33.3
25 Su	8 10 11	1 54 03	1♍26 36	7♍29 59	14 31.4	28 38.5	22 45.9	20 40.6	7 58.8	26 35.9	3 54.6	10 03.3	0 23.4	27 34.7
26 M	8 14 07	2 51 23	13 30 56	19 29 50	14 32.5	29 46.1	23 59.6	20 29.8	8 24.0	26 36.1	3 59.8	10 05.3	0 22.9	27 36.2
27 Tu	8 18 04	3 48 43	25 27 07	1♎23 15	14 33.6	0♍51.1	25 13.3	20 18.5	8 49.2	26 36.5	4 05.0	10 07.3	0 22.3	27 37.6
28 W	8 22 00	4 46 04	7♎18 44	13 14 04	14 34.5	1 53.5	26 27.1	20 06.6	9 14.4	26 37.1	4 10.1	10 09.3	0 21.9	27 39.1
29 Th	8 25 57	5 43 25	19 09 49	25 06 33	14R 35.0	2 53.1	27 40.9	19 54.1	9 39.5	26 37.8	4 15.1	10 11.4	0 21.4	27 40.7
30 F	8 29 54	6 40 47	1♏04 50	7♏05 16	14 35.2	3 49.8	28 54.7	19 41.2	10 04.6	26 38.8	4 20.1	10 13.5	0 21.0	27 42.2
31 Sa	8 33 50	7 38 09	13 08 24	19 14 49	14 35.0	4 43.5	0♌08.5	19 27.8	10 29.7	26 39.9	4 24.9	10 15.7	0 20.6	27 43.8

August 1971

LONGITUDE

Day	Sid.Time	☉	0 hr ☽	Noon ☽	True ☊	☿	♀	♂	⚳	♃	♄	♅	♆	♇
1 Su	8 37 47	8♌35 32	25♏25 02	1♐39 34	14♒34.6	5♍34.1	1♌22.3	19♒14.0	10♋54.8	26♏41.2	4♊29.7	10♎17.9	0♐20.2	27♍45.4
2 M	8 41 43	9 32 55	7♐58 53	14 23 22	14R 34.1	6 21.3	2 36.2	18R 59.8	11 19.8	26 42.7	4 34.4	10 20.2	0R 19.9	27 47.0
3 Tu	8 45 40	10 30 20	20 53 21	27 29 04	14 33.5	7 05.1	3 50.0	18 45.2	11 44.8	26 44.4	4 39.1	10 22.5	0 19.6	27 48.7
4 W	8 49 36	11 27 45	4♑10 39	10♑58 08	14 33.1	7 45.2	5 03.9	18 30.4	12 09.8	26 46.3	4 43.6	10 24.8	0 19.3	27 50.4
5 Th	8 53 33	12 25 11	17 51 26	24 50 20	14 32.9	8 21.6	6 17.9	18 15.3	12 34.7	26 48.3	4 48.1	10 27.2	0 19.1	27 52.1
6 F	8 57 30	13 22 37	1♒54 28	9♒03 23	14D 32.8	8 53.9	7 31.8	17 59.9	12 59.6	26 50.5	4 52.5	10 29.6	0 18.8	27 53.8
7 Sa	9 01 26	14 20 05	16 16 30	23 33 07	14R 32.8	9 22.1	8 45.7	17 44.3	13 24.5	26 52.9	4 56.8	10 32.1	0 18.7	27 55.5
8 Su	9 05 23	15 17 33	0♓52 29	8♓13 44	14 32.8	9 45.8	9 59.7	17 28.6	13 49.4	26 55.5	5 01.0	10 34.6	0 18.5	27 57.3
9 M	9 09 19	16 15 03	15 36 03	22 58 34	14 32.7	10 05.0	11 13.7	17 12.8	14 14.2	26 58.2	5 05.2	10 37.2	0 18.4	27 59.0
10 Tu	9 13 16	17 12 34	0♈20 26	7♈40 52	14 32.5	10 19.4	12 27.7	16 56.9	14 39.0	27 01.1	5 09.2	10 39.7	0 18.3	28 00.8
11 W	9 17 12	18 10 06	14 59 10	22 14 42	14 32.2	10 28.8	13 41.8	16 41.0	15 03.8	27 04.2	5 13.2	10 42.4	0 18.3	28 02.6
12 Th	9 21 09	19 07 40	29 26 58	6♉35 31	14D 31.9	10R 33.1	14 55.9	16 25.1	15 28.5	27 07.4	5 17.1	10 45.0	0D 18.2	28 04.5
13 F	9 25 05	20 05 16	13♉40 03	20 40 22	14 31.8	10 32.0	16 09.9	16 09.3	15 53.2	27 10.9	5 20.9	10 47.7	0 18.2	28 06.3
14 Sa	9 29 02	21 02 52	27 36 19	4♊27 53	14 32.0	10 25.5	17 24.1	15 53.5	16 17.9	27 14.4	5 24.6	10 50.4	0 18.3	28 08.2
15 Su	9 32 58	22 00 31	11♊15 03	17 57 55	14 32.5	10 13.4	18 38.2	15 38.0	16 42.5	27 18.2	5 28.2	10 53.2	0 18.4	28 10.1
16 M	9 36 55	22 58 11	24 36 35	1♋11 11	14 33.2	9 55.7	19 52.4	15 22.6	17 07.1	27 22.1	5 31.7	10 56.0	0 18.5	28 12.0
17 Tu	9 40 52	23 55 52	7♋41 55	14 08 55	14 34.0	9 32.6	21 06.5	15 07.5	17 31.6	27 26.2	5 35.1	10 58.9	0 18.6	28 13.9
18 W	9 44 48	24 53 35	20 32 23	26 52 30	14 34.8	9 03.9	22 20.7	14 52.7	17 56.2	27 30.5	5 38.5	11 01.7	0 18.8	28 15.9
19 Th	9 48 45	25 51 20	3♌09 26	9♌23 23	14R 35.2	8 30.1	23 35.0	14 38.3	18 20.6	27 34.9	5 41.7	11 04.6	0 19.0	28 17.9
20 F	9 52 41	26 49 06	15 34 32	21 43 02	14 35.2	7 51.4	24 49.2	14 24.2	18 45.0	27 39.5	5 44.9	11 07.6	0 19.2	28 19.8
21 Sa	9 56 38	27 46 53	27 49 06	3♍52 55	14 34.5	7 08.2	26 03.5	14 10.6	19 09.4	27 44.3	5 47.9	11 10.6	0 19.5	28 21.8
22 Su	10 00 34	28 44 41	9♍54 42	15 54 40	14 33.1	6 21.1	27 17.7	13 57.4	19 33.8	27 49.2	5 50.9	11 13.6	0 19.8	28 23.8
23 M	10 04 31	29 42 31	21 53 03	27 50 08	14 31.0	5 30.9	28 32.0	13 44.8	19 58.1	27 54.2	5 53.7	11 16.6	0 20.2	28 25.9
24 Tu	10 08 27	0♍40 22	3♎46 12	9♎41 35	14 28.6	4 38.4	29 46.3	13 32.7	20 22.3	27 59.5	5 56.5	11 19.7	0 20.5	28 27.9
25 W	10 12 24	1 38 14	15 36 37	21 31 42	14 26.0	3 44.5	1♍00.6	13 21.2	20 46.5	28 04.8	5 59.1	11 22.8	0 20.9	28 29.9
26 Th	10 16 21	2 36 08	27 27 15	3♏23 43	14 23.7	2 50.2	2 15.0	13 10.3	21 10.6	28 10.4	6 01.7	11 25.9	0 21.4	28 32.0
27 F	10 20 17	3 34 03	9♏21 35	15 21 20	14 21.9	1 56.7	3 29.3	13 00.0	21 34.7	28 16.1	6 04.1	11 29.1	0 21.8	28 34.1
28 Sa	10 24 14	4 32 00	21 23 30	27 28 39	14D 20.9	1 05.2	4 43.7	12 50.4	21 58.7	28 21.9	6 06.5	11 32.2	0 22.3	28 36.2
29 Su	10 28 10	5 29 58	3♐37 18	9♐50 02	14 20.8	0 16.6	5 58.1	12 41.5	22 22.7	28 27.9	6 08.7	11 35.5	0 22.9	28 38.3
30 M	10 32 07	6 27 57	16 07 22	22 29 49	14 21.5	29♌32.2	7 12.5	12 33.4	22 46.6	28 34.1	6 10.9	11 38.7	0 23.4	28 40.4
31 Tu	10 36 03	7 25 57	28 57 52	5♑31 57	14 22.8	28 53.0	8 26.9	12 25.9	23 10.5	28 40.4	6 12.9	11 42.0	0 24.0	28 42.5

Astro Data
Dy Hr Mn
♃✱♇ 5 2:31
♂ R 11 6:30
☽ 0N 13 4:02
♃ D 24 19:09
☽ 0S 26 18:00

☽ 0N 9 11:10
♆ D 12 15:14
☿ R 12 19:14
☽ 0S 23 1:14

Planet Ingress
Dy Hr Mn
☿ ♌ 6 8:53
⚳ ♋ 6 14:50
♀ ♋ 6 22:02
☉ ♌ 23 12:15
☿ ♍ 26 17:03
♀ ♌ 31 9:15

☉ ♍ 23 19:15
♀ ♍ 24 16:25
☿ ♌R 29 20:41

Last Aspect / ☽ Ingress
Dy Hr Mn / Dy Hr Mn
2 2:00 ♀ △ ♏ 2 13:46
4 18:40 ♃ ☌ ♐ 4 23:59
7 2:04 ♇ □ ♑ 7 7:03
9 6:43 ♇ △ ♒ 9 11:26
11 8:59 ♃ □ ♓ 11 14:14
13 12:02 ♇ ☍ ♈ 13 16:32
15 5:47 ☉ □ ♉ 15 19:10
17 18:16 ♇ △ ♊ 17 22:47
19 23:21 ♇ □ ♋ 20 3:56
22 9:15 ☉ ☌ ♌ 22 11:16
24 16:38 ☿ ☌ ♍ 24 21:09
27 4:23 ♇ ☌ ♎ 27 9:12
29 17:46 ♀ □ ♏ 29 21:50

Last Aspect / ☽ Ingress
Dy Hr Mn / Dy Hr Mn
1 4:30 ♇ ⚹ ♐ 1 8:49
3 12:35 ♇ □ ♑ 3 16:32
5 17:10 ♇ △ ♒ 5 20:47
7 17:29 ♃ □ ♓ 7 22:34
9 20:10 ♇ ☍ ♈ 9 23:27
11 4:46 ☉ △ ♉ 12 0:55
14 0:54 ♇ △ ♊ 14 4:10
16 6:31 ♇ □ ♋ 16 9:50
18 14:39 ♇ ⚹ ♌ 18 17:57
20 23:46 ♃ □ ♍ 21 4:19
23 13:12 ♇ ☌ ♎ 23 16:22
24 19:41 ♂ △ ♏ 26 5:09
28 14:13 ♇ ⚹ ♐ 28 16:56
31 0:25 ☿ △ ♑ 31 1:54

☽ Phases & Eclipses
Dy Hr Mn
8 10:37 ○ 15♑38
15 5:47 ☾ 22♈06
22 9:15 ● 28♋56
22 9:31:08 • P 0.069
30 11:07 ☽ 6♏39

6 19:42 ○ 13♒41
6 19:43 • T 1.728
13 10:55 ☾ 20♉03
20 22:53 ● 27♌15
20 22:38:50 • P 0.508
29 2:56 ☽ 5♐08

Astro Data
1 July 1971
Julian Day # 26114
SVP 5♓39'16"
GC 26♐26.5 ⚴ 10♉16.8
Eris 13♈02.6 ⚵ 3♌20.1
⚷ 13♈44.8 ⚶ 4♒14.0R
☽ Mean ☊ 16♒20.9

1 August 1971
Julian Day # 26145
SVP 5♓39'11"
GC 26♐26.5 ⚴ 20♉54.6
Eris 13♈00.3R ⚵ 18♌07.0
⚷ 13♈45.8R ⚶ 27♑12.7R
☽ Mean ☊ 14♒42.5

LONGITUDE — September 1971

Day	Sid.Time	☉	0 hr ☽	Noon ☽	True ☊	☿	♀	♂	⚳	♃	♄	♅	♆	♇
1 W	10 40 00	8♍23 59	12♑12 23	18♑59 26	14♒24.3	28♌19.8	9♍41.3	12♒19.2	23♋34.3	28♏46.8	6♊14.9	11♎45.3	0♐24.6	28♍44.7
2 Th	10 43 56	9 22 02	25 53 14	2♒53 45	14R 25.5	27R 53.6	10 55.7	12R 13.2	23 58.1	28 53.4	6 16.7	11 48.6	0 25.3	28 46.8
3 F	10 47 53	10 20 07	10♒00 50	17 14 09	14 25.8	27 34.8	12 10.2	12 08.1	24 21.8	29 00.1	6 18.4	11 52.0	0 26.0	28 49.0
4 Sa	10 51 50	11 18 13	24 33 11	1♓57 13	14 24.9	27D 24.2	13 24.6	12 03.6	24 45.4	29 07.0	6 20.1	11 55.3	0 26.7	28 51.1
5 Su	10 55 46	12 16 21	9♓25 25	16 56 44	14 22.7	27 22.1	14 39.1	12 00.0	25 09.0	29 14.0	6 21.6	11 58.7	0 27.5	28 53.3
6 M	10 59 43	13 14 30	24 30 04	2♈04 12	14 19.4	27 28.6	15 53.6	11 57.2	25 32.5	29 21.1	6 23.0	12 02.1	0 28.3	28 55.5
7 Tu	11 03 39	14 12 41	9♈37 55	17 10 01	14 15.3	27 43.9	17 08.1	11 55.1	25 55.9	29 28.4	6 24.3	12 05.6	0 29.1	28 57.7
8 W	11 07 36	15 10 55	24 39 23	2♉05 01	14 11.1	28 08.1	18 22.6	11 53.9	26 19.3	29 35.8	6 25.5	12 09.0	0 29.9	28 59.9
9 Th	11 11 32	16 09 10	9♉26 04	16 41 50	14 07.6	28 40.9	19 37.1	11D 53.4	26 42.6	29 43.3	6 26.6	12 12.5	0 30.8	29 02.1
10 F	11 15 29	17 07 28	23 51 50	0♊55 45	14 05.1	29 22.1	20 51.6	11 53.8	27 05.9	29 51.0	6 27.6	12 16.0	0 31.7	29 04.3
11 Sa	11 19 25	18 05 47	7♊53 25	14 44 52	14D 04.0	0♍11.5	22 06.2	11 54.9	27 29.1	29 58.8	6 28.5	12 19.5	0 32.6	29 06.5
12 Su	11 23 22	19 04 09	21 30 13	28 09 41	14 04.3	1 08.5	23 20.8	11 56.8	27 52.2	0♐06.8	6 29.3	12 23.1	0 33.6	29 08.8
13 M	11 27 19	20 02 33	4♋43 36	11♋12 20	14 05.5	2 12.8	24 35.4	11 59.6	28 15.2	0 14.8	6 30.0	12 26.6	0 34.6	29 11.0
14 Tu	11 31 15	21 00 59	17 36 18	23 55 56	14 07.1	3 23.9	25 49.9	12 03.1	28 38.2	0 23.0	6 30.5	12 30.2	0 35.6	29 13.2
15 W	11 35 12	21 59 27	0♌11 39	6♌23 53	14R 08.4	4 41.0	27 04.6	12 07.4	29 01.0	0 31.4	6 31.0	12 33.8	0 36.7	29 15.5
16 Th	11 39 08	22 57 57	12 33 03	18 39 31	14 08.5	6 03.8	28 19.2	12 12.5	29 23.8	0 39.8	6 31.3	12 37.4	0 37.8	29 17.7
17 F	11 43 05	23 56 29	24 43 39	0♍45 48	14 07.1	7 31.5	29 33.8	12 18.5	29 46.6	0 48.4	6 31.6	12 41.0	0 38.9	29 20.0
18 Sa	11 47 01	24 55 03	6♍46 14	12 45 15	14 03.6	9 03.7	0♎48.4	12 25.1	0♌09.2	0 57.0	6R 31.7	12 44.7	0 40.0	29 22.2
19 Su	11 50 58	25 53 39	18 43 05	24 39 58	13 58.2	10 39.6	2 03.1	12 32.6	0 31.7	1 05.8	6 31.7	12 48.3	0 41.2	29 24.5
20 M	11 54 54	26 52 17	0♎36 07	6♎31 45	13 51.0	12 18.8	3 17.7	12 40.9	0 54.2	1 14.8	6 31.6	12 52.0	0 42.4	29 26.8
21 Tu	11 58 51	27 50 57	12 27 05	18 22 19	13 42.7	14 00.6	4 32.4	12 49.9	1 16.6	1 23.8	6 31.4	12 55.7	0 43.7	29 29.0
22 W	12 02 48	28 49 39	24 17 41	0♏13 26	13 34.0	15 44.7	5 47.1	12 59.6	1 38.8	1 32.9	6 31.1	12 59.4	0 44.9	29 31.3
23 Th	12 06 44	29 48 23	6♏09 50	12 07 12	13 25.7	17 30.6	7 01.8	13 10.1	2 01.0	1 42.2	6 30.6	13 03.1	0 46.2	29 33.5
24 F	12 10 41	0♎47 08	18 05 51	24 06 09	13 18.7	19 17.7	8 16.4	13 21.3	2 23.1	1 51.6	6 30.1	13 06.8	0 47.5	29 35.8
25 Sa	12 14 37	1 45 55	0♐08 31	6♐13 23	13 13.4	21 05.9	9 31.1	13 33.3	2 45.1	2 01.1	6 29.5	13 10.5	0 48.9	29 38.1
26 Su	12 18 34	2 44 45	12 21 12	18 32 31	13 10.3	22 54.8	10 45.8	13 46.0	3 07.0	2 10.7	6 28.7	13 14.3	0 50.2	29 40.3
27 M	12 22 30	3 43 35	24 47 48	1♑07 36	13D 09.1	24 44.1	12 00.5	13 59.3	3 28.8	2 20.4	6 27.9	13 18.0	0 51.6	29 42.6
28 Tu	12 26 27	4 42 28	7♑32 28	14 02 53	13 09.4	26 33.6	13 15.2	14 13.3	3 50.5	2 30.2	6 26.9	13 21.8	0 53.1	29 44.8
29 W	12 30 23	5 41 22	20 39 20	27 22 14	13 10.4	28 23.0	14 29.9	14 28.0	4 12.1	2 40.1	6 25.8	13 25.5	0 54.5	29 47.1
30 Th	12 34 20	6 40 18	4♒11 56	11♒08 40	13R 11.1	0♎12.2	15 44.6	14 43.4	4 33.5	2 50.1	6 24.6	13 29.3	0 56.0	29 49.3

LONGITUDE — October 1971

Day	Sid.Time	☉	0 hr ☽	Noon ☽	True ☊	☿	♀	♂	⚳	♃	♄	♅	♆	♇
1 F	12 38 17	7♎39 16	18♒12 28	25♒23 18	13♒10.5	2♎01.2	16♎59.4	14♒59.4	4♌54.9	3♐00.2	6♊23.3	13♎33.1	0♐57.5	29♍51.6
2 Sa	12 42 13	8 38 15	2♓40 52	10♓04 39	13R 07.9	3 49.6	18 14.1	15 16.0	5 16.2	3 10.4	6R 21.9	13 36.8	0 59.0	29 53.8
3 Su	12 46 10	9 37 17	17 33 58	25 07 52	13 02.9	5 37.6	19 28.8	15 33.2	5 37.3	3 20.7	6 20.4	13 40.6	1 00.5	29 56.1
4 M	12 50 06	10 36 20	2♈45 13	10♈24 42	12 55.7	7 25.0	20 43.5	15 51.0	5 58.3	3 31.1	6 18.8	13 44.4	1 02.1	29 58.3
5 Tu	12 54 03	11 35 25	18 04 57	25 44 29	12 47.0	9 11.7	21 58.2	16 09.4	6 19.2	3 41.6	6 17.1	13 48.2	1 03.7	0♎00.5
6 W	12 57 59	12 34 33	3♉21 52	10♉55 46	12 38.0	10 57.8	23 12.9	16 28.4	6 40.0	3 52.1	6 15.3	13 52.0	1 05.3	0 02.8
7 Th	13 01 56	13 33 43	18 24 59	25 48 31	12 29.7	12 43.1	24 27.7	16 47.9	7 00.7	4 02.8	6 13.4	13 55.7	1 07.0	0 05.0
8 F	13 05 52	14 32 55	3♊05 35	10♊15 39	12 23.2	14 27.7	25 42.4	17 07.9	7 21.3	4 13.6	6 11.4	13 59.5	1 08.6	0 07.2
9 Sa	13 09 49	15 32 09	17 18 22	24 13 40	12 19.0	16 11.6	26 57.1	17 28.5	7 41.7	4 24.4	6 09.3	14 03.3	1 10.3	0 09.4
10 Su	13 13 46	16 31 26	1♋01 36	7♋42 26	12D 17.0	17 54.7	28 11.9	17 49.6	8 02.0	4 35.4	6 07.1	14 07.1	1 12.1	0 11.6
11 M	13 17 42	17 30 45	14 16 33	20 44 23	12 16.6	19 37.1	29 26.6	18 11.2	8 22.1	4 46.4	6 04.7	14 10.9	1 13.8	0 13.8
12 Tu	13 21 39	18 30 06	27 06 30	3♌23 28	12R 17.1	21 18.8	0♏41.4	18 33.3	8 42.1	4 57.5	6 02.3	14 14.7	1 15.5	0 16.0
13 W	13 25 35	19 29 30	9♌35 52	15 44 20	12 17.3	22 59.7	1 56.2	18 55.9	9 02.0	5 08.7	5 59.8	14 18.5	1 17.3	0 18.1
14 Th	13 29 32	20 28 56	21 49 26	27 51 44	12 16.1	24 39.9	3 10.9	19 19.0	9 21.8	5 20.0	5 57.2	14 22.2	1 19.1	0 20.3
15 F	13 33 28	21 28 24	3♍51 45	9♍50 00	12 12.6	26 19.4	4 25.7	19 42.5	9 41.4	5 31.3	5 54.5	14 26.0	1 20.9	0 22.4
16 Sa	13 37 25	22 27 55	15 46 54	21 42 53	12 06.3	27 58.2	5 40.5	20 06.5	10 00.8	5 42.7	5 51.7	14 29.8	1 22.8	0 24.6
17 Su	13 41 21	23 27 27	27 38 17	3♎33 24	11 57.2	29 36.3	6 55.2	20 31.0	10 20.1	5 54.2	5 48.8	14 33.5	1 24.6	0 26.7
18 M	13 45 18	24 27 02	9♎28 31	15 23 53	11 45.6	1♏13.8	8 10.0	20 55.9	10 39.2	6 05.8	5 45.8	14 37.3	1 26.5	0 28.8
19 Tu	13 49 14	25 26 38	21 19 40	27 16 04	11 32.2	2 50.6	9 24.8	21 21.2	10 58.2	6 17.5	5 42.7	14 41.0	1 28.4	0 30.9
20 W	13 53 11	26 26 17	3♏13 15	9♏11 21	11 18.1	4 26.8	10 39.6	21 47.0	11 17.0	6 29.2	5 39.6	14 44.8	1 30.3	0 33.0
21 Th	13 57 08	27 25 58	15 10 33	21 11 00	11 04.5	6 02.4	11 54.3	22 13.1	11 35.7	6 41.0	5 36.3	14 48.5	1 32.2	0 35.1
22 F	14 01 04	28 25 41	27 12 53	3♐16 25	10 52.5	7 37.4	13 09.1	22 39.7	11 54.1	6 52.9	5 33.0	14 52.2	1 34.2	0 37.1
23 Sa	14 05 01	29 25 25	9♐21 50	15 29 25	10 43.0	9 11.8	14 23.9	23 06.6	12 12.4	7 04.8	5 29.6	14 55.9	1 36.2	0 39.2
24 Su	14 08 57	0♏25 12	21 39 28	27 52 21	10 36.4	10 45.7	15 38.7	23 34.0	12 30.6	7 16.8	5 26.1	14 59.6	1 38.2	0 41.2
25 M	14 12 54	1 25 00	4♑08 28	10♑28 13	10 32.7	12 19.0	16 53.5	24 01.7	12 48.5	7 28.9	5 22.5	15 03.3	1 40.2	0 43.3
26 Tu	14 16 50	2 24 50	16 52 04	23 20 29	10D 31.2	13 51.7	18 08.2	24 29.7	13 06.3	7 41.0	5 18.9	15 07.0	1 42.2	0 45.3
27 W	14 20 47	3 24 41	29 53 55	6♒32 50	10R 31.0	15 24.0	19 23.0	24 58.1	13 23.9	7 53.2	5 15.1	15 10.6	1 44.2	0 47.3
28 Th	14 24 43	4 24 34	13♒17 37	20 08 38	10 30.9	16 55.7	20 37.8	25 26.9	13 41.3	8 05.5	5 11.3	15 14.3	1 46.2	0 49.2
29 F	14 28 40	5 24 29	27 06 06	4♓10 09	10 29.5	18 26.9	21 52.5	25 56.0	13 58.5	8 17.8	5 07.4	15 17.9	1 48.3	0 51.2
30 Sa	14 32 37	6 24 25	11♓20 44	18 37 39	10 25.8	19 57.6	23 07.3	26 25.4	14 15.5	8 30.2	5 03.5	15 21.5	1 50.4	0 53.1
31 Su	14 36 33	7 24 23	26 00 25	3♈28 26	10 19.3	21 27.8	24 22.1	26 55.1	14 32.3	8 42.6	4 59.5	15 25.1	1 52.5	0 55.0

Astro Data

	Dy Hr Mn
♃✶♇	1 0:08
☿D	5 6:01
☽0N	5 20:52
♂D	9 13:51
♃☌♆	16 5:28
♄R	19 2:17
☽0S	19 7:45
♀0S	20 5:56
☉0S	23 16:44
☿0S	2 10:59
☽0N	3 7:51
☽0S	16 13:28
♃☍♄	17 2:59
☽0N	30 17:53

Planet Ingress

	Dy Hr Mn
☿ ♍	11 6:45
♃ ♐	11 15:33
♀ ♎	17 20:25
⚳ ♌	18 2:15
☉ ♎	23 16:45
☿ ♎	30 9:19
♇ ♎	5 6:14
♀ ♏	11 22:43
☿ ♏	17 17:49
☉ ♏	24 1:53

Last Aspect / ☽ Ingress (September)

Last Aspect Dy Hr Mn		☽ Ingress	Dy Hr Mn
2 5:07	♃ ✶	♒	2 7:04
4 7:23	♃ □	♓	4 8:51
6 7:39	♃ △	♈	6 8:43
8 5:24	☿ △	♉	8 8:37
10 10:08	♃ ☍	♊	10 10:25
12 13:48	♇ □	♋	12 15:21
14 22:09	♇ ✶	♌	14 23:38
16 0:05	♅ ✶	♍	17 10:29
19 21:37	♇ ☌	♎	19 22:47
21 0:55	♅ ☌	♏	22 11:33
24 22:57	♇ ✶	♐	24 23:43
27 9:19	♇ □	♑	27 9:53
29 16:17	♇ △	♒	29 16:39

Last Aspect / ☽ Ingress (October)

Last Aspect Dy Hr Mn		☽ Ingress	Dy Hr Mn
30 20:35	♀ △	♓	1 19:37
3 19:35	♇ ☍	♈	3 19:40
5 5:34	♀ ☍	♉	5 18:42
6 21:04	♂ □	♊	7 18:53
9 17:16	♀ △	♋	9 22:10
11 9:35	☿ □	♌	12 5:30
14 4:37	☿ ✶	♍	14 16:16
15 4:08	♄ □	♎	17 4:47
19 7:59	☉ ☌	♏	19 17:31
21 14:09	♂ □	♐	22 5:31
24 3:23	♂ ✶	♑	24 16:05
26 1:20	♀ ✶	♒	27 0:11
28 21:30	♂ ☌	♓	29 4:57
30 20:00	♀ △	♈	31 6:26

☽ Phases & Eclipses

Dy Hr Mn	
5 4:02	○ 11♓57
11 18:23	☾ 18♊21
19 14:42	● 26♍00
27 17:17	☽ 3♑57
4 12:19	○ 10♈37
11 5:29	☾ 17♋15
19 7:59	● 25♎17
27 5:54	☽ 3♒09

Astro Data

1 September 1971
Julian Day # 26176
SVP 5♓39'06"
GC 26♐26.6 ⚴ 29♉41.0
Eris 12♈48.7R ⚵ 2♍18.6
⚷ 12♈59.9R ⚶ 23♑03.5R
☽ Mean ☊ 13♒04.0

1 October 1971
Julian Day # 26206
SVP 5♓39'03"
GC 26♐26.7 ⚴ 4♊23.4
Eris 12♈31.6R ⚵ 15♍17.3
⚷ 11♈45.4R ⚶ 25♑46.6
☽ Mean ☊ 11♒28.6

November 1971 — LONGITUDE

Day	Sid.Time	☉	0 hr ☽	Noon ☽	True ☊	☿	♀	♂	⚳	♃	♄	♅	♆	♇
1 M	14 40 30	8♏24 23	11♈00 46	18♈36 23	10♒10.2	22♏57.5	25♏36.8	27♒25.1	14♌48.9	8♐55.1	4♊55.4	15♎28.7	1♐54.6	0♎56.9
2 Tu	14 44 26	9 24 24	26 13 59	3♉52 13	9R 59.2	24 26.7	26 51.6	27 55.4	15 05.3	9 07.6	4R 51.3	15 32.2	1 56.7	0 58.8
3 W	14 48 23	10 24 27	11♉29 38	19 04 49	9 47.6	25 55.3	28 06.3	28 26.0	15 21.5	9 20.2	4 47.1	15 35.8	1 58.8	1 00.7
4 Th	14 52 19	11 24 33	26 36 25	4♊03 12	9 36.6	27 23.5	29 21.1	28 56.8	15 37.5	9 32.8	4 42.8	15 39.3	2 00.9	1 02.5
5 F	14 56 16	12 24 40	11♊24 11	18 38 33	9 27.6	28 51.1	0♐35.8	29 27.9	15 53.3	9 45.5	4 38.5	15 42.8	2 03.1	1 04.3
6 Sa	15 00 12	13 24 50	25 45 44	2♋45 25	9 21.2	0♐18.2	1 50.5	29 59.3	16 08.9	9 58.2	4 34.1	15 46.3	2 05.2	1 06.1
7 Su	15 04 09	14 25 01	9♋37 29	16 22 01	9 17.6	1 44.6	3 05.3	0♓31.0	16 24.2	10 11.0	4 29.7	15 49.7	2 07.4	1 07.9
8 M	15 08 06	15 25 14	22 59 18	29 29 42	9D 16.1	3 10.5	4 20.0	1 02.8	16 39.3	10 23.9	4 25.2	15 53.1	2 09.6	1 09.7
9 Tu	15 12 02	16 25 30	5♌53 44	12♌11 58	9R 15.9	4 35.7	5 34.8	1 35.0	16 54.1	10 36.7	4 20.7	15 56.6	2 11.8	1 11.4
10 W	15 15 59	17 25 47	18 25 03	24 33 37	9 15.8	6 00.1	6 49.5	2 07.3	17 08.8	10 49.7	4 16.1	15 59.9	2 13.9	1 13.1
11 Th	15 19 55	18 26 06	0♍38 21	6♍39 55	9 14.6	7 23.8	8 04.2	2 39.9	17 23.1	11 02.6	4 11.5	16 03.3	2 16.1	1 14.8
12 F	15 23 52	19 26 28	12 38 58	18 36 06	9 11.3	8 46.7	9 19.0	3 12.7	17 37.2	11 15.6	4 06.9	16 06.6	2 18.4	1 16.5
13 Sa	15 27 48	20 26 51	24 31 54	0♎26 54	9 05.2	10 08.6	10 33.7	3 45.8	17 51.1	11 28.7	4 02.2	16 09.9	2 20.6	1 18.1
14 Su	15 31 45	21 27 16	6♎21 36	12 16 26	8 56.2	11 29.6	11 48.5	4 19.0	18 04.7	11 41.7	3 57.4	16 13.2	2 22.8	1 19.8
15 M	15 35 41	22 27 43	18 11 47	24 07 58	8 44.7	12 49.3	13 03.2	4 52.5	18 18.1	11 54.8	3 52.7	16 16.5	2 25.0	1 21.4
16 Tu	15 39 38	23 28 12	0♏05 17	6♏03 58	8 31.3	14 07.9	14 17.9	5 26.2	18 31.1	12 08.0	3 47.9	16 19.7	2 27.3	1 22.9
17 W	15 43 35	24 28 42	12 04 11	18 06 05	8 17.1	15 24.9	15 32.7	6 00.1	18 43.9	12 21.2	3 43.1	16 22.9	2 29.5	1 24.5
18 Th	15 47 31	25 29 14	24 09 49	0♐15 27	8 03.4	16 40.4	16 47.4	6 34.2	18 56.4	12 34.4	3 38.2	16 26.1	2 31.7	1 26.0
19 F	15 51 28	26 29 48	6♐23 05	12 32 48	7 51.3	17 54.1	18 02.1	7 08.4	19 08.7	12 47.7	3 33.4	16 29.2	2 34.0	1 27.5
20 Sa	15 55 24	27 30 23	18 44 41	24 58 50	7 41.6	19 05.7	19 16.8	7 42.9	19 20.6	13 00.9	3 28.5	16 32.3	2 36.2	1 29.0
21 Su	15 59 21	28 30 59	1♑15 23	7♑34 28	7 34.9	20 15.0	20 31.5	8 17.6	19 32.3	13 14.3	3 23.6	16 35.4	2 38.5	1 30.4
22 M	16 03 17	29 31 37	13 56 17	20 21 04	7 31.1	21 21.6	21 46.3	8 52.4	19 43.6	13 27.6	3 18.7	16 38.4	2 40.7	1 31.8
23 Tu	16 07 14	0♐32 16	26 49 02	3♒20 29	7D 29.7	22 25.2	23 01.0	9 27.4	19 54.7	13 41.0	3 13.8	16 41.4	2 43.0	1 33.2
24 W	16 11 11	1 32 56	9♒55 43	16 35 01	7 29.9	23 25.4	24 15.6	10 02.5	20 05.4	13 54.3	3 08.9	16 44.4	2 45.3	1 34.6
25 Th	16 15 07	2 33 37	23 18 43	0♓07 03	7R 30.3	24 21.7	25 30.3	10 37.9	20 15.8	14 07.7	3 03.9	16 47.3	2 47.5	1 35.9
26 F	16 19 04	3 34 19	7♓00 15	13 58 28	7 29.9	25 13.5	26 45.0	11 13.3	20 26.0	14 21.2	2 59.0	16 50.2	2 49.8	1 37.2
27 Sa	16 23 00	4 35 02	21 01 45	28 10 02	7 27.6	26 00.3	27 59.7	11 49.0	20 35.7	14 34.6	2 54.1	16 53.1	2 52.0	1 38.5
28 Su	16 26 57	5 35 47	5♈23 05	12♈40 33	7 22.8	26 41.4	29 14.3	12 24.7	20 45.2	14 48.1	2 49.2	16 55.9	2 54.3	1 39.7
29 M	16 30 53	6 36 32	20 01 52	27 26 18	7 15.7	27 16.1	0♑29.0	13 00.6	20 54.3	15 01.6	2 44.3	16 58.7	2 56.6	1 40.9
30 Tu	16 34 50	7 37 18	4♉52 59	12♉20 54	7 06.8	27 43.6	1 43.6	13 36.7	21 03.1	15 15.1	2 39.4	17 01.5	2 58.8	1 42.1

December 1971 — LONGITUDE

Day	Sid.Time	☉	0 hr ☽	Noon ☽	True ☊	☿	♀	♂	⚳	♃	♄	♅	♆	♇
1 W	16 38 46	8♐38 05	19♉48 56	27♉15 57	6♒57.2	28♐03.1	2♑58.2	14♓12.8	21♌11.6	15♐28.6	2♊34.5	17♎04.2	3♐01.1	1♎43.3
2 Th	16 42 43	9 38 54	4♊40 46	12♊02 17	6R 48.1	28R 13.8	4 12.8	14 49.1	21 19.7	15 42.1	2R 29.6	17 06.9	3 03.3	1 44.4
3 F	16 46 40	10 39 44	19 19 31	26 31 35	6 40.6	28 14.8	5 27.4	15 25.5	21 27.5	15 55.6	2 24.7	17 09.5	3 05.6	1 45.5
4 Sa	16 50 36	11 40 35	3♋37 49	10♋37 41	6 35.2	28 05.5	6 42.0	16 02.1	21 34.9	16 09.2	2 19.9	17 12.1	3 07.8	1 46.6
5 Su	16 54 33	12 41 27	17 30 54	24 17 17	6D 32.3	27 45.3	7 56.6	16 38.7	21 41.9	16 22.8	2 15.1	17 14.6	3 10.0	1 47.6
6 M	16 58 29	13 42 21	0♌56 55	7♌29 57	6 31.6	27 13.8	9 11.2	17 15.5	21 48.6	16 36.3	2 10.3	17 17.2	3 12.3	1 48.6
7 Tu	17 02 26	14 43 15	13 56 43	20 17 38	6 32.3	26 31.0	10 25.7	17 52.3	21 54.9	16 49.9	2 05.6	17 19.6	3 14.5	1 49.6
8 W	17 06 22	15 44 11	26 33 13	2♍44 02	6 33.5	25 37.5	11 40.3	18 29.3	22 00.8	17 03.5	2 00.9	17 22.1	3 16.7	1 50.5
9 Th	17 10 19	16 45 08	8♍50 41	14 53 50	6R 34.3	24 34.1	12 54.8	19 06.3	22 06.4	17 17.1	1 56.2	17 24.4	3 18.9	1 51.4
10 F	17 14 15	17 46 07	20 54 07	26 52 11	6 33.7	23 22.4	14 09.3	19 43.5	22 11.6	17 30.6	1 51.5	17 26.8	3 21.1	1 52.3
11 Sa	17 18 12	18 47 06	2♎48 41	8♎44 15	6 31.3	22 04.3	15 23.8	20 20.8	22 16.3	17 44.2	1 46.9	17 29.1	3 23.3	1 53.1
12 Su	17 22 09	19 48 07	14 39 27	20 34 52	6 26.8	20 42.4	16 38.3	20 58.2	22 20.7	17 57.8	1 42.3	17 31.3	3 25.5	1 53.9
13 M	17 26 05	20 49 08	26 31 00	2♏28 20	6 20.4	19 19.3	17 52.8	21 35.6	22 24.7	18 11.4	1 37.8	17 33.5	3 27.7	1 54.7
14 Tu	17 30 02	21 50 11	8♏27 16	14 28 10	6 12.5	17 58.0	19 07.3	22 13.2	22 28.2	18 25.0	1 33.3	17 35.7	3 29.9	1 55.5
15 W	17 33 58	22 51 15	20 31 21	26 37 04	6 03.9	16 41.0	20 21.8	22 50.8	22 31.4	18 38.6	1 28.9	17 37.8	3 32.1	1 56.2
16 Th	17 37 55	23 52 19	2♐45 30	8♐56 49	5 55.5	15 30.8	21 36.2	23 28.6	22 34.1	18 52.2	1 24.5	17 39.8	3 34.2	1 56.8
17 F	17 41 51	24 53 25	15 11 05	21 28 23	5 48.1	14 29.1	22 50.7	24 06.4	22 36.5	19 05.8	1 20.2	17 41.9	3 36.4	1 57.5
18 Sa	17 45 48	25 54 31	27 48 44	4♑12 06	5 42.3	13 37.4	24 05.1	24 44.3	22 38.4	19 19.3	1 16.0	17 43.8	3 38.5	1 58.1
19 Su	17 49 44	26 55 37	10♑38 27	17 07 47	5 38.6	12 56.3	25 19.5	25 22.3	22 39.8	19 32.9	1 11.8	17 45.8	3 40.6	1 58.7
20 M	17 53 41	27 56 44	23 40 02	0♒15 10	5D 37.0	12 26.2	26 33.9	26 00.4	22 40.9	19 46.4	1 07.7	17 47.6	3 42.7	1 59.2
21 Tu	17 57 38	28 57 51	6♒53 09	13 33 59	5 37.1	12 07.0	27 48.3	26 38.5	22R 41.5	20 00.0	1 03.6	17 49.4	3 44.8	1 59.7
22 W	18 01 34	29 58 59	20 17 40	27 04 12	5 38.4	11D 58.4	29 02.6	27 16.7	22 41.7	20 13.5	0 59.6	17 51.2	3 46.9	2 00.2
23 Th	18 05 31	1♑00 07	3♓53 37	10♓45 55	5 40.0	11 59.6	0♒16.9	27 55.0	22 41.5	20 27.0	0 55.7	17 52.9	3 49.0	2 00.6
24 F	18 09 27	2 01 15	17 41 08	24 39 14	5R 41.2	12 10.1	1 31.2	28 33.4	22 40.8	20 40.5	0 51.8	17 54.6	3 51.0	2 01.0
25 Sa	18 13 24	3 02 23	1♈40 10	8♈43 49	5 41.2	12 29.1	2 45.5	29 11.8	22 39.7	20 54.0	0 48.0	17 56.2	3 53.1	2 01.4
26 Su	18 17 20	4 03 31	15 50 01	22 58 31	5 39.8	12 55.7	3 59.7	29 50.3	22 38.1	21 07.4	0 44.3	17 57.8	3 55.1	2 01.7
27 M	18 21 17	5 04 39	0♉09 00	7♉21 01	5 37.0	13 29.2	5 13.9	0♈28.8	22 36.2	21 20.8	0 40.7	17 59.3	3 57.1	2 02.0
28 Tu	18 25 13	6 05 47	14 34 06	21 47 37	5 33.1	14 08.9	6 28.1	1 07.4	22 33.8	21 34.2	0 37.2	18 00.7	3 59.1	2 02.3
29 W	18 29 10	7 06 55	29 00 58	6♊13 25	5 28.7	14 54.2	7 42.2	1 46.0	22 30.9	21 47.6	0 33.7	18 02.1	4 01.1	2 02.5
30 Th	18 33 07	8 08 03	13♊24 16	20 32 47	5 24.4	15 44.3	8 56.3	2 24.7	22 27.6	22 01.0	0 30.3	18 03.5	4 03.0	2 02.7
31 F	18 37 03	9 09 11	27 38 17	4♋40 09	5 21.0	16 38.8	10 10.4	3 03.4	22 23.9	22 14.3	0 27.1	18 04.8	4 05.0	2 02.9

Astro Data (Dy Hr Mn)

☽0S 12 19:00
☽0N 27 1:16
♄☍♆ 27 18:50

☿R 3 2:31
♄Q♅ 5 13:32
☽0S 10 1:21
♃✱♅ 10 3:44
♄△♇ 10 8:37
⚳R 22 10:41
☿D 22 20:48
☽0N 24 6:20
♂0N 27 16:45

Planet Ingress (Dy Hr Mn)

♀ ♐ 5 0:30
☿ ♐ 6 6:59
♂ ♓ 6 12:31
☉ ♐ 22 23:14
♀ ♑ 29 2:41

☉ ♑ 22 12:24
♀ ♒ 23 6:32
♂ ♈ 26 18:04

Last Aspect Dy Hr Mn			☽ Ingress	Dy Hr Mn
2 2:20	♂	✱	♉	2 5:55
4 3:43	♀	☍	♊	4 5:27
6 7:02	♂	△	♋	6 7:15
7 11:02	♅	□	♌	8 12:56
9 20:51	☉	□	♍	10 22:44
12 13:51	☉	✱	♎	13 11:05
14 20:02	♅	☌	♏	15 23:49
18 1:46	☉	☌	♐	18 11:30
19 23:49	♀	☌	♑	20 21:36
22 5:02	♅	□	♒	23 5:52
25 3:04	♀	✱	♓	25 11:48
27 11:41	♀	□	♈	27 15:04
29 11:43	☿	△	♉	29 16:08

Last Aspect Dy Hr Mn			☽ Ingress	Dy Hr Mn
30 14:07	♂	✱	♊	1 16:25
3 14:53	☿	☍	♋	3 17:51
4 23:29	♅	□	♌	5 22:17
7 23:10	☿	△	♍	8 6:40
10 5:37	☿	□	♎	10 18:19
12 12:14	☿	✱	♏	13 7:01
15 4:11	♂	△	♐	15 18:37
17 19:03	☉	☌	♑	18 4:07
20 4:36	♀	☌	♒	20 11:32
21 23:40	♃	✱	♓	22 17:10
24 19:00	♂	☌	♈	24 21:09
26 8:51	♃	△	♉	26 23:45
27 8:08	♀	□	♊	29 1:38
30 14:31	♃	☍	♋	31 4:01

☽ Phases & Eclipses (Dy Hr Mn)

2 21:19 ○ 9♉48
9 20:51 ☾ 16♌48
18 1:46 ● 25♏03
25 16:37 ☽ 2♓45

2 7:48 ○ 9♊28
9 16:02 ☾ 16♍55
17 19:03 ● 25♐11
25 1:35 ☽ 2♈36
31 20:20 ○ 9♋30

Astro Data

1 November 1971
Julian Day # 26237
SVP 5♓39'00"
GC 26♐26.8 ⚴ 1♊56.9R
Eris 12♈13.1R ⚵ 27♍35.3
⚷ 10♈24.8R ⚶ 4♒00.8
☽ Mean ☊ 9♒50.1

1 December 1971
Julian Day # 26267
SVP 5♓38'55"
GC 26♐26.8 ⚴ 22♉36.8R
Eris 11♈59.7R ⚵ 7♎52.3
⚷ 9♈32.3R ⚶ 15♒08.3
☽ Mean ☊ 8♒14.8

LONGITUDE — January 1972

Day	Sid.Time	☉	0 hr ☽	Noon ☽	True ☊	☿	♀	♂	⚳	♃	♄	♅	♆	♇
1 Sa	18 41 00	10♑10 20	11♋37 49	18♋30 49	5♒18.7	17♐37.2	11♒24.5	3♈42.2	22♌19.8	22♐27.6	0♊23.9	18♎06.0	4♐06.9	2♎03.0
2 Su	18 44 56	11 11 28	25 18 48	2♌01 31	5D 17.7	18 39.0	12 38.5	4 21.0	22R 15.2	22 40.9	0R 20.7	18 07.2	4 08.8	2 03.1
3 M	18 48 53	12 12 37	8♌38 52	15 10 49	5 18.0	19 43.8	13 52.5	4 59.9	22 10.2	22 54.2	0 17.7	18 08.4	4 10.7	2 03.2
4 Tu	18 52 49	13 13 46	21 37 30	27 59 05	5 19.2	20 51.3	15 06.4	5 38.8	22 04.8	23 07.4	0 14.8	18 09.4	4 12.6	2R 03.2
5 W	18 56 46	14 14 54	4♍15 52	10♍28 14	5 20.8	22 01.2	16 20.3	6 17.7	21 58.9	23 20.6	0 12.0	18 10.5	4 14.4	2 03.2
6 Th	19 00 43	15 16 03	16 36 38	22 41 31	5 22.5	23 13.3	17 34.2	6 56.7	21 52.7	23 33.7	0 09.2	18 11.4	4 16.2	2 03.1
7 F	19 04 39	16 17 13	28 43 28	4♎43 01	5 23.7	24 27.3	18 48.0	7 35.7	21 46.0	23 46.8	0 06.6	18 12.4	4 18.0	2 03.0
8 Sa	19 08 36	17 18 22	10♎40 46	16 37 20	5R 24.1	25 43.0	20 01.8	8 14.8	21 38.9	23 59.9	0 04.0	18 13.2	4 19.8	2 02.9
9 Su	19 12 32	18 19 31	22 33 19	28 29 20	5 23.8	27 00.2	21 15.6	8 53.9	21 31.3	24 12.9	0 01.6	18 14.0	4 21.6	2 02.8
10 M	19 16 29	19 20 41	4♏25 58	10♏23 48	5 22.6	28 18.9	22 29.3	9 33.0	21 23.4	24 25.9	29♉59.2	18 14.8	4 23.3	2 02.6
11 Tu	19 20 25	20 21 50	16 23 23	22 25 13	5 20.8	29 38.8	23 43.0	10 12.2	21 15.1	24 38.9	29 56.9	18 15.5	4 25.0	2 02.4
12 W	19 24 22	21 22 59	28 29 46	4♐37 29	5 18.7	0♑59.9	24 56.6	10 51.4	21 06.4	24 51.8	29 54.8	18 16.1	4 26.7	2 02.1
13 Th	19 28 18	22 24 09	10♐48 42	17 03 45	5 16.6	2 22.1	26 10.2	11 30.6	20 57.3	25 04.7	29 52.8	18 16.7	4 28.4	2 01.8
14 F	19 32 15	23 25 18	23 22 51	29 46 10	5 14.9	3 45.3	27 23.8	12 09.9	20 47.9	25 17.5	29 50.8	18 17.2	4 30.1	2 01.5
15 Sa	19 36 12	24 26 27	6♑13 49	12♑45 48	5 13.6	5 09.4	28 37.3	12 49.1	20 38.1	25 30.3	29 49.0	18 17.7	4 31.7	2 01.2
16 Su	19 40 08	25 27 35	19 22 04	26 02 30	5D 12.9	6 34.3	29 50.7	13 28.5	20 27.9	25 43.1	29 47.3	18 18.1	4 33.3	2 00.8
17 M	19 44 05	26 28 43	2♒46 54	9♒35 02	5 12.8	8 00.1	1♓04.2	14 07.8	20 17.4	25 55.7	29 45.7	18 18.5	4 34.9	2 00.4
18 Tu	19 48 01	27 29 50	16 26 36	23 21 17	5 13.2	9 26.6	2 17.5	14 47.2	20 06.5	26 08.4	29 44.2	18 18.7	4 36.4	1 59.9
19 W	19 51 58	28 30 57	0♓18 43	7♓18 31	5 13.7	10 53.9	3 30.8	15 26.6	19 55.4	26 20.9	29 42.8	18 19.0	4 37.9	1 59.4
20 Th	19 55 54	29 32 03	14 20 19	21 23 43	5 14.4	12 21.9	4 44.1	16 06.0	19 43.9	26 33.5	29 41.5	18 19.2	4 39.4	1 58.9
21 F	19 59 51	0♒33 07	28 28 22	5♈33 54	5 14.9	13 50.5	5 57.3	16 45.5	19 32.2	26 45.9	29 40.3	18 19.3	4 40.9	1 58.3
22 Sa	20 03 47	1 34 11	12♈39 58	19 46 15	5R 15.1	15 19.8	7 10.4	17 24.9	19 20.2	26 58.3	29 39.2	18R 19.4	4 42.3	1 57.8
23 Su	20 07 44	2 35 14	26 52 26	3♉58 16	5 15.2	16 49.8	8 23.4	18 04.4	19 07.9	27 10.7	29 38.3	18 19.4	4 43.7	1 57.1
24 M	20 11 41	3 36 16	11♉03 26	18 07 40	5 15.1	18 20.5	9 36.4	18 43.9	18 55.4	27 23.0	29 37.4	18 19.3	4 45.1	1 56.5
25 Tu	20 15 37	4 37 17	25 10 44	2♊12 21	5D 15.1	19 51.7	10 49.4	19 23.4	18 42.6	27 35.2	29 36.7	18 19.2	4 46.5	1 55.8
26 W	20 19 34	5 38 17	9♊12 16	16 10 13	5 15.1	21 23.7	12 02.2	20 02.9	18 29.7	27 47.3	29 36.1	18 19.1	4 47.8	1 55.1
27 Th	20 23 30	6 39 16	23 05 56	29 59 10	5 15.2	22 56.2	13 15.0	20 42.5	18 16.6	27 59.4	29 35.6	18 18.9	4 49.1	1 54.4
28 F	20 27 27	7 40 13	6♋49 39	13♋37 09	5 15.3	24 29.5	14 27.7	21 22.0	18 03.2	28 11.5	29 35.2	18 18.6	4 50.4	1 53.6
29 Sa	20 31 23	8 41 10	20 21 26	27 02 18	5R 15.5	26 03.3	15 40.4	22 01.6	17 49.7	28 23.4	29 34.9	18 18.3	4 51.6	1 52.8
30 Su	20 35 20	9 42 05	3♌39 34	10♌13 07	5 15.5	27 37.9	16 52.9	22 41.1	17 36.1	28 35.3	29D 34.8	18 17.9	4 52.9	1 52.0
31 M	20 39 16	10 43 00	16 42 49	23 08 40	5 15.3	29 13.1	18 05.4	23 20.7	17 22.3	28 47.1	29 34.7	18 17.5	4 54.1	1 51.1

LONGITUDE — February 1972

Day	Sid.Time	☉	0 hr ☽	Noon ☽	True ☊	☿	♀	♂	⚳	♃	♄	♅	♆	♇
1 Tu	20 43 13	11♒43 53	29♌30 39	5♍48 51	5♒14.7	0♒48.9	19♓17.8	24♈00.3	17♌08.5	28♐58.9	29♉34.8	18♎17.0	4♐55.2	1♎50.3
2 W	20 47 10	12 44 46	12♍03 22	18 14 24	5R 13.8	2 25.5	20 30.1	24 39.8	16R 54.5	29 10.5	29 35.0	18R 16.5	4 56.3	1R 49.3
3 Th	20 51 06	13 45 38	24 22 11	0♎27 02	5 12.6	4 02.8	21 42.3	25 19.4	16 40.5	29 22.1	29 35.3	18 15.9	4 57.4	1 48.4
4 F	20 55 03	14 46 28	6♎29 16	12 29 19	5 11.3	5 40.8	22 54.5	25 59.0	16 26.4	29 33.6	29 35.7	18 15.2	4 58.5	1 47.4
5 Sa	20 58 59	15 47 18	18 27 37	24 24 40	5 10.2	7 19.6	24 06.6	26 38.6	16 12.2	29 45.1	29 36.2	18 14.5	4 59.5	1 46.4
6 Su	21 02 56	16 48 07	0♏20 57	6♏17 03	5D 09.4	8 59.0	25 18.5	27 18.2	15 58.1	29 56.4	29 36.8	18 13.8	5 00.5	1 45.4
7 M	21 06 52	17 48 55	12 13 32	18 10 59	5 09.1	10 39.3	26 30.4	27 57.8	15 43.9	0♑07.7	29 37.6	18 12.9	5 01.5	1 44.4
8 Tu	21 10 49	18 49 42	24 10 00	0♐11 11	5 09.4	12 20.4	27 42.2	28 37.4	15 29.8	0 18.9	29 38.4	18 12.1	5 02.4	1 43.3
9 W	21 14 45	19 50 28	6♐15 06	12 22 20	5 10.3	14 02.2	28 53.9	29 17.0	15 15.7	0 30.0	29 39.4	18 11.2	5 03.4	1 42.2
10 Th	21 18 42	20 51 13	18 33 25	24 48 51	5 11.6	15 44.9	0♈05.6	29 56.6	15 01.6	0 41.0	29 40.5	18 10.2	5 04.2	1 41.1
11 F	21 22 39	21 51 57	1♑09 05	7♑34 29	5 13.0	17 28.3	1 17.1	0♉36.2	14 47.7	0 51.9	29 41.7	18 09.2	5 05.1	1 39.9
12 Sa	21 26 35	22 52 40	14 05 21	20 41 53	5 14.2	19 12.6	2 28.5	1 15.8	14 33.8	1 02.8	29 43.0	18 08.1	5 05.9	1 38.8
13 Su	21 30 32	23 53 22	27 24 10	4♒12 12	5R 14.7	20 57.8	3 39.8	1 55.4	14 20.1	1 13.5	29 44.4	18 07.0	5 06.7	1 37.6
14 M	21 34 28	24 54 02	11♒05 49	18 04 44	5 14.3	22 43.7	4 51.0	2 35.1	14 06.4	1 24.2	29 45.9	18 05.9	5 07.4	1 36.4
15 Tu	21 38 25	25 54 41	25 08 33	2♓16 43	5 12.7	24 30.6	6 02.1	3 14.7	13 53.0	1 34.7	29 47.6	18 04.6	5 08.1	1 35.1
16 W	21 42 21	26 55 18	9♓28 35	16 43 27	5 10.3	26 18.2	7 13.1	3 54.3	13 39.7	1 45.2	29 49.3	18 03.4	5 08.8	1 33.9
17 Th	21 46 18	27 55 54	24 00 29	1♈18 51	5 07.1	28 06.7	8 24.0	4 33.9	13 26.6	1 55.5	29 51.2	18 02.1	5 09.5	1 32.6
18 F	21 50 14	28 56 28	8♈37 43	15 56 16	5 03.7	29 56.0	9 34.8	5 13.6	13 13.7	2 05.8	29 53.2	18 00.7	5 10.1	1 31.3
19 Sa	21 54 11	29 57 00	23 13 44	0♉29 25	5 00.8	1♓46.0	10 45.4	5 53.2	13 01.0	2 16.0	29 55.2	17 59.3	5 10.6	1 29.9
20 Su	21 58 08	0♓57 30	7♉42 44	14 53 12	4 58.7	3 36.8	11 55.9	6 32.8	12 48.5	2 26.0	29 57.4	17 57.8	5 11.2	1 28.6
21 M	22 02 04	1 57 59	22 00 26	29 04 08	4D 57.8	5 28.3	13 06.3	7 12.4	12 36.4	2 35.9	29 59.7	17 56.3	5 11.7	1 27.2
22 Tu	22 06 01	2 58 26	6♊04 10	13♊00 24	4 58.1	7 20.4	14 16.6	7 52.0	12 24.4	2 45.8	0♊02.1	17 54.8	5 12.2	1 25.8
23 W	22 09 57	3 58 50	19 52 51	26 41 31	4 59.4	9 13.1	15 26.7	8 31.6	12 12.8	2 55.5	0 04.6	17 53.2	5 12.6	1 24.4
24 Th	22 13 54	4 59 13	3♋26 31	10♋07 57	5 01.0	11 06.2	16 36.7	9 11.2	12 01.5	3 05.1	0 07.2	17 51.6	5 13.1	1 23.0
25 F	22 17 50	5 59 34	16 45 55	23 20 34	5R 02.4	12 59.6	17 46.5	9 50.8	11 50.5	3 14.6	0 10.0	17 49.9	5 13.4	1 21.6
26 Sa	22 21 47	6 59 53	29 52 01	6♌20 23	5 02.9	14 53.2	18 56.2	10 30.4	11 39.8	3 24.0	0 12.8	17 48.2	5 13.8	1 20.2
27 Su	22 25 43	8 00 10	12♌45 46	19 08 16	5 02.0	16 46.8	20 05.8	11 09.9	11 29.4	3 33.3	0 15.7	17 46.5	5 14.1	1 18.7
28 M	22 29 40	9 00 25	25 27 58	1♍44 55	4 59.3	18 40.1	21 15.1	11 49.5	11 19.3	3 42.4	0 18.7	17 44.7	5 14.4	1 17.2
29 Tu	22 33 37	10 00 39	7♍59 14	14 10 58	4 54.9	20 33.0	22 24.4	12 29.0	11 09.7	3 51.5	0 21.8	17 42.8	5 14.6	1 15.7

Astro Data Dy Hr Mn	Planet Ingress Dy Hr Mn	Last Aspect Dy Hr Mn	☽ Ingress Dy Hr Mn	Last Aspect Dy Hr Mn	☽ Ingress Dy Hr Mn	☽ Phases & Eclipses Dy Hr Mn	Astro Data
♇ R 4 14:44	♄ ♉R 10 3:43	1 11:17 ♅ □	♌ 2 8:22	1 0:08 ♄ □	♍ 1 0:56	8 13:31 ☾ 17♎22	1 January 1972
☽ 0S 6 9:07	☿ ♑ 11 18:18	4 2:39 ♃ △	♍ 4 15:50	3 10:18 ♄ △	♎ 3 11:06	16 10:52 ● 25♑25	Julian Day # 26298
☽ 0N 20 11:38	♀ ♓ 16 15:01	6 13:45 ♃ □	♎ 7 2:33	5 22:58 ♃ ⚹	♏ 5 23:18	16 11:02:37 ● A 01'53"	SVP 5♓38'48"
♅ R 23 5:26	☉ ♒ 20 22:59	9 8:38 ☿ ⚹	♏ 9 15:03	8 10:55 ♄ ☍	♐ 8 11:38	23 9:29 ☽ 2♉29	GC 26♐26.9 ⚴ 16♉43.6R
♄ D 31 10:22	☿ ♒ 31 23:46	12 2:49 ♄ ☍	♐ 12 2:57	10 3:45 ☉ ⚹	♑ 10 21:50	30 10:58 ○ 9♌39	Eris 11♈54.8 ⚵ 15♎51.8
		14 7:05 ♀ ⚹	♑ 14 12:26	13 4:08 ♄ △	♒ 13 4:36	30 10:53 • T 1.050	⚷ 9♈24.7 ⚶ 28♒27.2
☽ 0S 2 17:46	♃ ♑ 6 19:37	16 18:40 ♄ △	♒ 16 19:04	15 7:49 ♄ □	♓ 15 8:11		☽ Mean ☊ 6♒36.4
♃⚻♄ 4 16:28	♀ ♈ 10 10:08	18 22:59 ♄ □	♓ 18 23:28	17 9:36 ♄ ⚹	♈ 17 9:51	7 11:11 ☾ 17♏47	
♀0N 11 12:10	♂ ♉ 10 14:04	21 2:03 ♄ ⚹	♈ 21 2:35	19 11:02 ☉ ⚹	♉ 19 11:11	15 0:29 ● 25♒26	1 February 1972
♃□♇ 15 12:47	☿ ♓ 18 12:53	23 0:21 ♃ △	♉ 23 5:17	21 13:35 ♄ ☌	♊ 21 13:35	21 17:20 ☽ 2♊11	Julian Day # 26329
☽ 0N 16 19:27	☉ ♓ 19 13:11	25 7:34 ♄ ☌	♊ 25 8:14	22 20:32 ♅ △	♋ 23 17:52	29 3:12 ○ 9♍39	SVP 5♓38'43"
	♄ ♊ 21 14:52	27 8:28 ♃ ☍	♋ 27 12:01	25 1:58 ♅ □	♌ 26 0:15		GC 26♐27.0 ⚴ 21♉17.4
		29 16:36 ♄ ⚹	♌ 29 17:21	27 14:00 ♀ △	♍ 28 8:39		Eris 12♈00.7 ⚵ 19♎40.3
							⚷ 10♈08.5 ⚶ 12♓43.3
							☽ Mean ☊ 4♒57.9

March 1972

LONGITUDE

Day	Sid.Time	☉	0 hr ☽	Noon ☽	True ☊	☿	♀	♂	⚳	♃	♄	♅	♆	♇
1 W	22 37 33	11♓00 50	20♍20 13	26♍27 06	4♒49.0	22♓25.1	23♈33.4	13♉08.5	11♌00.3	4♑00.4	0♊25.1	17♎41.0	5♐14.8	1♎14.2
2 Th	22 41 30	12 01 00	2♎31 44	8♎34 18	4R42.0	24 16.0	24 42.3	13 48.0	10R51.4	4 09.2	0 28.4	17R39.1	5 15.0	1R12.7
3 F	22 45 26	13 01 08	14 35 00	20 34 03	4 34.8	26 05.5	25 51.1	14 27.5	10 42.8	4 17.9	0 31.8	17 37.1	5 15.1	1 11.1
4 Sa	22 49 23	14 01 15	26 31 46	2♏28 27	4 27.9	27 53.2	26 59.6	15 07.0	10 34.6	4 26.4	0 35.3	17 35.1	5 15.2	1 09.6
5 Su	22 53 19	15 01 20	8♏24 30	14 20 19	4 22.2	29 38.4	28 08.0	15 46.5	10 26.8	4 34.8	0 38.9	17 33.1	5 15.3	1 08.0
6 M	22 57 16	16 01 23	20 16 23	26 13 11	4 18.2	1♈20.9	29 16.2	16 26.0	10 19.4	4 43.1	0 42.6	17 31.1	5R15.3	1 06.5
7 Tu	23 01 12	17 01 25	2♐11 16	8♐11 13	4D16.0	3 00.1	0♉24.3	17 05.4	10 12.4	4 51.3	0 46.4	17 29.0	5 15.3	1 04.9
8 W	23 05 09	18 01 25	14 13 36	20 19 04	4 15.5	4 35.4	1 32.1	17 44.9	10 05.8	4 59.3	0 50.3	17 26.9	5 15.3	1 03.3
9 Th	23 09 06	19 01 24	26 28 13	2♑41 40	4 16.3	6 06.3	2 39.8	18 24.3	9 59.6	5 07.2	0 54.3	17 24.7	5 15.3	1 01.7
10 F	23 13 02	20 01 20	9♑00 00	15 23 48	4 17.7	7 32.3	3 47.3	19 03.8	9 53.8	5 15.0	0 58.4	17 22.6	5 15.2	1 00.1
11 Sa	23 16 59	21 01 16	21 53 32	28 29 39	4R18.8	8 52.9	4 54.6	19 43.2	9 48.5	5 22.6	1 02.5	17 20.4	5 15.0	0 58.5
12 Su	23 20 55	22 01 09	5♒12 28	12♒02 11	4 18.6	10 07.5	6 01.7	20 22.6	9 43.6	5 30.1	1 06.8	17 18.1	5 14.9	0 56.9
13 M	23 24 52	23 01 01	18 58 50	26 02 19	4 16.6	11 15.7	7 08.5	21 02.0	9 39.1	5 37.5	1 11.1	17 15.9	5 14.7	0 55.3
14 Tu	23 28 48	24 00 51	3♓12 18	10♓28 18	4 12.4	12 17.1	8 15.2	21 41.4	9 35.1	5 44.7	1 15.6	17 13.6	5 14.5	0 53.6
15 W	23 32 45	25 00 38	17 49 37	25 15 20	4 06.0	13 11.2	9 21.7	22 20.8	9 31.5	5 51.7	1 20.1	17 11.3	5 14.2	0 52.0
16 Th	23 36 41	26 00 24	2♈44 24	10♈15 41	3 58.2	13 57.8	10 27.9	23 00.1	9 28.3	5 58.6	1 24.7	17 08.9	5 13.9	0 50.4
17 F	23 40 38	27 00 08	17 47 56	25 19 53	3 49.8	14 36.5	11 33.9	23 39.5	9 25.6	6 05.4	1 29.4	17 06.6	5 13.6	0 48.7
18 Sa	23 44 35	27 59 50	2♉50 19	10♉18 08	3 42.0	15 07.2	12 39.6	24 18.8	9 23.3	6 12.0	1 34.2	17 04.2	5 13.2	0 47.1
19 Su	23 48 31	28 59 29	17 42 21	25 02 08	3 35.8	15 29.8	13 45.1	24 58.2	9 21.5	6 18.5	1 39.0	17 01.8	5 12.8	0 45.4
20 M	23 52 28	29 59 07	2♊16 53	9♊26 08	3 31.7	15 44.2	14 50.4	25 37.5	9 20.1	6 24.8	1 44.0	16 59.4	5 12.4	0 43.8
21 Tu	23 56 24	0♈58 42	16 29 38	23 27 19	3D29.9	15R50.4	15 55.4	26 16.8	9 19.1	6 30.9	1 49.0	16 56.9	5 12.0	0 42.1
22 W	0 00 21	1 58 15	0♋19 12	7♋05 29	3 29.7	15 48.6	17 00.1	26 56.1	9D18.6	6 36.9	1 54.1	16 54.5	5 11.5	0 40.5
23 Th	0 04 17	2 57 45	13 46 25	20 22 20	3 30.4	15 39.2	18 04.6	27 35.3	9 18.5	6 42.8	1 59.3	16 52.0	5 11.0	0 38.8
24 F	0 08 14	3 57 13	26 53 35	3♌20 34	3R30.9	15 22.3	19 08.8	28 14.6	9 18.8	6 48.5	2 04.5	16 49.5	5 10.4	0 37.2
25 Sa	0 12 10	4 56 39	9♌43 41	16 03 18	3 30.1	14 58.6	20 12.6	28 53.8	9 19.6	6 54.0	2 09.8	16 47.0	5 09.8	0 35.6
26 Su	0 16 07	5 56 02	22 19 46	28 33 25	3 27.2	14 28.5	21 16.2	29 33.1	9 20.8	6 59.4	2 15.2	16 44.5	5 09.2	0 33.9
27 M	0 20 04	6 55 23	4♍44 34	10♍53 28	3 21.6	13 53.0	22 19.5	0♊12.2	9 22.4	7 04.6	2 20.7	16 41.9	5 08.6	0 32.3
28 Tu	0 24 00	7 54 42	17 00 20	23 05 23	3 13.2	13 12.6	23 22.4	0 51.4	9 24.4	7 09.6	2 26.2	16 39.4	5 07.9	0 30.6
29 W	0 27 57	8 53 59	29 08 47	5♎10 42	3 02.5	12 28.4	24 25.0	1 30.6	9 26.9	7 14.5	2 31.9	16 36.9	5 07.2	0 29.0
30 Th	0 31 53	9 53 13	11♎11 15	17 10 37	2 50.2	11 41.4	25 27.3	2 09.7	9 29.7	7 19.2	2 37.5	16 34.3	5 06.5	0 27.4
31 F	0 35 50	10 52 26	23 08 54	29 06 18	2 37.2	10 52.4	26 29.2	2 48.9	9 33.0	7 23.7	2 43.3	16 31.7	5 05.7	0 25.8

April 1972

LONGITUDE

Day	Sid.Time	☉	0 hr ☽	Noon ☽	True ☊	☿	♀	♂	⚳	♃	♄	♅	♆	♇
1 Sa	0 39 46	11♈51 37	5♏02 58	10♏59 08	2♒24.7	10♈02.6	27♉30.7	3♊28.0	9♌36.7	7♑28.1	2♊49.1	16♎29.2	5♐04.9	0♎24.2
2 Su	0 43 43	12 50 46	16 55 02	22 50 57	2R13.7	9R12.9	28 31.9	4 07.1	9 40.8	7 32.3	2 55.0	16R26.6	5R04.1	0R22.5
3 M	0 47 39	13 49 53	28 47 13	4♐44 12	2 05.0	8 24.3	29 32.8	4 46.1	9 45.2	7 36.3	3 00.9	16 24.0	5 03.3	0 21.0
4 Tu	0 51 36	14 48 58	10♐42 21	16 42 06	1 59.0	7 37.7	0♊33.2	5 25.2	9 50.1	7 40.2	3 07.0	16 21.4	5 02.4	0 19.4
5 W	0 55 32	15 48 02	22 43 58	28 48 31	1 55.7	6 53.9	1 33.2	6 04.3	9 55.4	7 43.9	3 13.0	16 18.8	5 01.5	0 17.8
6 Th	0 59 29	16 47 03	4♑56 19	11♑07 59	1D54.4	6 13.5	2 32.9	6 43.3	10 01.0	7 47.4	3 19.2	16 16.2	5 00.6	0 16.2
7 F	1 03 26	17 46 03	17 24 07	23 45 21	1R54.4	5 37.1	3 32.1	7 22.3	10 07.0	7 50.7	3 25.4	16 13.7	4 59.7	0 14.7
8 Sa	1 07 22	18 45 02	0♒12 16	6♒45 24	1 54.4	5 05.2	4 30.8	8 01.3	10 13.4	7 53.9	3 31.6	16 11.1	4 58.7	0 13.1
9 Su	1 11 19	19 43 58	13 25 15	20 12 13	1 53.3	4 38.2	5 29.1	8 40.3	10 20.2	7 56.9	3 37.9	16 08.5	4 57.7	0 11.6
10 M	1 15 15	20 42 53	27 06 31	4♓08 18	1 50.2	4 16.2	6 27.0	9 19.3	10 27.3	7 59.7	3 44.3	16 05.9	4 56.7	0 10.0
11 Tu	1 19 12	21 41 45	11♓17 26	18 33 38	1 44.4	3 59.5	7 24.4	9 58.2	10 34.8	8 02.3	3 50.7	16 03.3	4 55.6	0 08.5
12 W	1 23 08	22 40 36	25 56 22	3♈24 50	1 36.0	3 48.1	8 21.3	10 37.2	10 42.7	8 04.7	3 57.2	16 00.8	4 54.5	0 07.0
13 Th	1 27 05	23 39 25	10♈58 03	18 34 48	1 25.6	3D42.1	9 17.7	11 16.1	10 50.9	8 07.0	4 03.8	15 58.2	4 53.4	0 05.5
14 F	1 31 01	24 38 13	26 13 44	3♉53 23	1 14.5	3 41.3	10 13.5	11 55.0	10 59.5	8 09.0	4 10.4	15 55.6	4 52.3	0 04.1
15 Sa	1 34 58	25 36 58	11♉32 18	19 09 01	1 03.8	3 45.7	11 08.8	12 33.9	11 08.4	8 10.9	4 17.0	15 53.1	4 51.2	0 02.6
16 Su	1 38 55	26 35 41	26 42 15	4♊10 52	0 55.0	3 55.2	12 03.6	13 12.8	11 17.7	8 12.6	4 23.7	15 50.6	4 50.0	0 01.2
17 M	1 42 51	27 34 22	11♊33 54	18 50 39	0 48.6	4 09.6	12 57.7	13 51.7	11 27.3	8 14.1	4 30.4	15 48.0	4 48.8	29♍59.8
18 Tu	1 46 48	28 33 01	26 00 41	3♋03 42	0 44.9	4 28.8	13 51.3	14 30.5	11 37.2	8 15.4	4 37.2	15 45.5	4 47.6	29 58.3
19 W	1 50 44	29 31 38	9♋59 42	16 48 47	0 43.4	4 52.6	14 44.2	15 09.4	11 47.4	8 16.5	4 44.1	15 43.0	4 46.4	29 57.0
20 Th	1 54 41	0♉30 12	23 31 13	0♌07 23	0 43.2	5 20.7	15 36.5	15 48.2	11 58.0	8 17.5	4 51.0	15 40.6	4 45.1	29 55.6
21 F	1 58 37	1 28 44	6♌37 43	13 02 45	0 43.0	5 53.1	16 28.0	16 27.0	12 08.9	8 18.2	4 57.9	15 38.1	4 43.8	29 54.2
22 Sa	2 02 34	2 27 14	19 22 59	25 38 57	0 41.6	6 29.4	17 18.9	17 05.8	12 20.1	8 18.8	5 04.9	15 35.6	4 42.5	29 52.9
23 Su	2 06 30	3 25 41	1♍51 12	8♍00 13	0 38.1	7 09.7	18 09.0	17 44.6	12 31.6	8 19.2	5 11.9	15 33.2	4 41.2	29 51.6
24 M	2 10 27	4 24 07	14 06 29	20 10 25	0 31.9	7 53.6	18 58.4	18 23.3	12 43.4	8R19.4	5 18.9	15 30.8	4 39.9	29 50.3
25 Tu	2 14 24	5 22 30	26 12 25	2♎12 52	0 22.7	8 41.0	19 46.9	19 02.0	12 55.5	8 19.4	5 26.0	15 28.4	4 38.6	29 49.0
26 W	2 18 20	6 20 52	8♎12 02	14 10 12	0 11.1	9 31.8	20 34.7	19 40.7	13 07.8	8 19.2	5 33.1	15 26.0	4 37.2	29 47.8
27 Th	2 22 17	7 19 12	20 07 37	26 04 29	29♑57.7	10 25.8	21 21.5	20 19.4	13 20.5	8 18.8	5 40.3	15 23.7	4 35.8	29 46.5
28 F	2 26 13	8 17 29	2♏00 59	7♏57 18	29 43.7	11 22.9	22 07.6	20 58.1	13 33.4	8 18.3	5 47.5	15 21.4	4 34.4	29 45.3
29 Sa	2 30 10	9 15 45	13 53 34	19 50 00	29 30.0	12 23.0	22 52.6	21 36.8	13 46.7	8 17.5	5 54.7	15 19.1	4 33.0	29 44.1
30 Su	2 34 06	10 14 00	25 46 44	1♐44 00	29 18.0	13 26.0	23 36.8	22 15.4	14 00.1	8 16.6	6 02.0	15 16.8	4 31.6	29 42.9

Astro Data	Dy Hr Mn
☽0S	1 1:53
☿0N	5 11:44
♆R	7 5:19
♃⚺♆	10 12:31
♄△♇	10 19:16
☽0N	15 5:38
☉0N	20 12:21
☿R	21 18:39
♄⚻♅	22 13:09
⚳D	23 5:05
☽0S	28 8:27
☽0N	11 16:14
☿D	14 3:28
♄☍♆	19 18:47
☽0S	24 13:41

Planet Ingress		Dy Hr Mn
☿	♈	5 16:59
♀	♉	7 3:25
☉	♈	20 12:21
♂	♊	27 4:30
♀	♊	3 22:48
♇	♍R	17 7:50
☉	♉	19 23:37
☊	♑R	27 8:04
♃	R	25 0:18

Last Aspect Dy Hr Mn			☽ Ingress	Dy Hr Mn
1 2:39	☿	☍	♎	1 19:00
3 23:46	♀	☍	♏	4 7:00
5 15:05	♂	☍	♐	6 19:36
8 7:05	☉	□	♑	9 6:49
10 21:17	☉	✶	♒	11 14:43
13 3:06	♂	□	♓	13 18:39
15 11:35	☉	☌	♈	15 19:37
16 22:56	♅	☍	♉	17 19:27
19 19:01	☉	✶	♊	19 20:12
21 0:49	♅	△	♋	21 23:26
24 2:00	♂	✶	♌	24 5:46
26 14:02	♂	□	♍	26 14:48
28 12:37	♀	△	♎	29 1:42
30 10:47	♅	☌	♏	31 13:48

Last Aspect Dy Hr Mn			☽ Ingress	Dy Hr Mn
3 0:34	♀	☍	♐	3 2:27
4 11:19	♅	✶	♑	5 14:20
6 23:44	☉	□	♒	7 23:37
9 11:06	☉	✶	♓	10 4:58
10 21:08	♂	□	♈	12 6:32
13 20:31	☉	☌	♉	14 5:54
14 18:42	♃	△	♊	16 5:16
18 6:44	♇	□	♋	18 6:46
20 11:38	♇	✶	♌	20 11:46
21 18:56	♀	✶	♍	22 20:24
25 7:13	♇	☌	♎	25 7:34
27 1:49	♀	△	♏	27 19:56
30 7:57	♇	✶	♐	30 8:31

☽ Phases & Eclipses Dy Hr Mn		
8 7:05	☾	17♐49
15 11:35	●	25♓00
22 2:12	☽	1♋34
29 20:05	○	9♎14
6 23:44	☾	17♑16
13 20:31	●	24♈00
20 12:45	☽	0♌32
28 12:44	○	8♏19

Astro Data

1 March 1972
Julian Day # 26358
SVP 5♓38'39"
GC 26♐27.0 ⚴ 2♊14.6
Eris 12♈14.6 ⚵ 18♎03.3R
⚷ 11♈26.5 ⚶ 26♓25.3
☽ Mean ☊ 3♒25.7

1 April 1972
Julian Day # 26389
SVP 5♓38'36"
GC 26♐27.1 ⚴ 17♊35.2
Eris 12♈34.6 ⚵ 11♎35.8R
⚷ 13♈11.6 ⚶ 11♈03.2
☽ Mean ☊ 1♒47.2

LONGITUDE — May 1972

Day	Sid.Time	☉	0 hr ☽	Noon ☽	True ☊	☿	♀	♂	⚳	♃	♄	♅	♆	♇
1 M	2 38 03	11♉12 12	7♐42 00	13♐41 00	29♑08.3	14♈31.7	24♊19.9	22♊54.0	14♌13.9	8♑15.5	6♊09.3	15♎14.6	4♐30.1	29♍41.8
2 Tu	2 41 59	12 10 23	19 41 17	25 43 11	29R01.4	15 40.0	25 02.1	23 32.7	14 27.9	8R14.2	6 16.7	15R12.3	4R28.7	29R40.7
3 W	2 45 56	13 08 33	1♑47 06	7♑53 25	28 57.3	16 50.9	25 43.1	24 11.3	14 42.2	8 12.7	6 24.0	15 10.1	4 27.2	29 39.6
4 Th	2 49 53	14 06 41	14 02 36	20 15 10	28D55.6	18 04.3	26 23.1	24 49.8	14 56.7	8 11.0	6 31.4	15 08.0	4 25.7	29 38.5
5 F	2 53 49	15 04 48	26 31 36	2♒52 26	28 55.3	19 20.1	27 02.0	25 28.4	15 11.4	8 09.1	6 38.9	15 05.8	4 24.2	29 37.5
6 Sa	2 57 46	16 02 53	9♒18 15	15 49 31	28R55.6	20 38.3	27 39.6	26 07.0	15 26.5	8 07.1	6 46.3	15 03.7	4 22.7	29 36.4
7 Su	3 01 42	17 00 56	22 26 46	29 10 24	28 55.0	21 58.8	28 16.1	26 45.5	15 41.7	8 04.8	6 53.8	15 01.7	4 21.2	29 35.4
8 M	3 05 39	17 58 59	6♓00 46	12♓58 04	28 52.8	23 21.5	28 51.2	27 24.0	15 57.2	8 02.4	7 01.3	14 59.6	4 19.6	29 34.5
9 Tu	3 09 35	18 57 00	20 02 25	27 13 39	28 48.2	24 46.5	29 25.1	28 02.5	16 12.9	7 59.8	7 08.9	14 57.6	4 18.1	29 33.5
10 W	3 13 32	19 54 59	4♈31 30	11♈55 24	28 41.2	26 13.7	29 57.6	28 41.0	16 28.8	7 57.1	7 16.4	14 55.6	4 16.5	29 32.6
11 Th	3 17 28	20 52 58	19 24 35	26 58 05	28 32.4	27 43.0	0♋28.6	29 19.5	16 45.0	7 54.1	7 24.0	14 53.7	4 15.0	29 31.7
12 F	3 21 25	21 50 55	4♉34 42	12♉13 09	28 22.6	29 14.4	0 58.2	29 58.0	17 01.4	7 51.0	7 31.6	14 51.8	4 13.4	29 30.8
13 Sa	3 25 22	22 48 50	19 51 59	27 29 47	28 13.2	0♉48.0	1 26.3	0♋36.5	17 18.0	7 47.6	7 39.2	14 49.9	4 11.8	29 30.0
14 Su	3 29 18	23 46 44	5♊05 10	12♊36 50	28 05.3	2 23.7	1 52.8	1 14.9	17 34.9	7 44.2	7 46.9	14 48.1	4 10.2	29 29.2
15 M	3 33 15	24 44 37	20 03 41	27 24 47	27 59.6	4 01.5	2 17.6	1 53.4	17 51.9	7 40.5	7 54.5	14 46.3	4 08.6	29 28.4
16 Tu	3 37 11	25 42 28	4♋39 26	11♋47 10	27 56.4	5 41.4	2 40.7	2 31.8	18 09.2	7 36.7	8 02.2	14 44.5	4 07.0	29 27.7
17 W	3 41 08	26 40 17	18 47 44	25 41 03	27D55.3	7 23.5	3 02.1	3 10.2	18 26.6	7 32.7	8 09.9	14 42.8	4 05.4	29 26.9
18 Th	3 45 04	27 38 04	2♌27 15	9♌06 36	27 55.7	9 07.6	3 21.6	3 48.6	18 44.3	7 28.5	8 17.6	14 41.1	4 03.8	29 26.3
19 F	3 49 01	28 35 50	15 39 28	22 06 19	27R56.4	10 53.8	3 39.2	4 27.0	19 02.1	7 24.2	8 25.3	14 39.5	4 02.2	29 25.6
20 Sa	3 52 57	29 33 34	28 27 39	4♍44 03	27 56.4	12 42.1	3 54.8	5 05.4	19 20.1	7 19.7	8 33.1	14 37.9	4 00.6	29 24.9
21 Su	3 56 54	0♊31 16	10♍56 05	17 04 20	27 54.9	14 32.5	4 08.4	5 43.7	19 38.4	7 15.1	8 40.8	14 36.4	3 59.0	29 24.3
22 M	4 00 51	1 28 57	23 09 22	29 11 44	27 51.2	16 24.9	4 20.0	6 22.1	19 56.8	7 10.3	8 48.6	14 34.8	3 57.4	29 23.8
23 Tu	4 04 47	2 26 36	5♎11 56	11♎10 28	27 45.4	18 19.5	4 29.4	7 00.4	20 15.3	7 05.4	8 56.3	14 33.4	3 55.7	29 23.2
24 W	4 08 44	3 24 14	17 07 47	23 04 16	27 37.5	20 16.1	4 36.6	7 38.7	20 34.1	7 00.3	9 04.1	14 32.0	3 54.1	29 22.7
25 Th	4 12 40	4 21 51	29 00 18	4♏56 12	27 28.2	22 14.6	4 41.5	8 17.0	20 53.0	6 55.0	9 11.9	14 30.6	3 52.5	29 22.2
26 F	4 16 37	5 19 26	10♏52 15	16 48 43	27 18.3	24 15.2	4R44.2	8 55.3	21 12.1	6 49.6	9 19.6	14 29.2	3 50.9	29 21.8
27 Sa	4 20 33	6 17 00	22 45 49	28 43 46	27 08.7	26 17.6	4 44.5	9 33.6	21 31.4	6 44.1	9 27.4	14 28.0	3 49.2	29 21.3
28 Su	4 24 30	7 14 32	4♐42 45	10♐42 56	27 00.2	28 21.8	4 42.4	10 11.8	21 50.8	6 38.5	9 35.2	14 26.7	3 47.6	29 20.9
29 M	4 28 26	8 12 04	16 44 31	22 47 40	26 53.6	0♊27.6	4 38.0	10 50.1	22 10.4	6 32.7	9 43.0	14 25.5	3 46.0	29 20.6
30 Tu	4 32 23	9 09 35	28 52 36	4♑59 31	26 49.1	2 35.0	4 31.1	11 28.3	22 30.2	6 26.8	9 50.8	14 24.4	3 44.4	29 20.3
31 W	4 36 20	10 07 04	11♑08 39	17 20 16	26D46.8	4 43.7	4 21.8	12 06.5	22 50.1	6 20.8	9 58.6	14 23.3	3 42.8	29 20.0

LONGITUDE — June 1972

Day	Sid.Time	☉	0 hr ☽	Noon ☽	True ☊	☿	♀	♂	⚳	♃	♄	♅	♆	♇
1 Th	4 40 16	11♊04 33	23♑34 38	29♑52 06	26♑46.4	6♊53.5	4♋10.1	12♋44.7	23♌10.1	6♑14.6	10♊06.4	14♎22.2	3♐41.2	29♍19.7
2 F	4 44 13	12 02 01	6♒12 59	12♒37 38	26 47.2	9 04.3	3R56.0	13 22.9	23 30.3	6R08.3	10 14.2	14R21.2	3R39.6	29R19.5
3 Sa	4 48 09	12 59 28	19 06 24	25 39 41	26 48.6	11 15.8	3 39.5	14 01.1	23 50.7	6 01.9	10 22.0	14 20.2	3 38.0	29 19.3
4 Su	4 52 06	13 56 55	2♓17 48	9♓01 04	26R49.5	13 27.8	3 20.7	14 39.3	24 11.2	5 55.4	10 29.8	14 19.3	3 36.4	29 19.1
5 M	4 56 02	14 54 20	15 49 44	22 43 59	26 49.4	15 39.9	2 59.7	15 17.5	24 31.8	5 48.8	10 37.6	14 18.5	3 34.8	29 18.9
6 Tu	4 59 59	15 51 45	29 43 55	6♈49 28	26 47.6	17 51.9	2 36.4	15 55.7	24 52.6	5 42.1	10 45.4	14 17.6	3 33.2	29 18.8
7 W	5 03 55	16 49 10	14♈00 27	21 16 32	26 44.2	20 03.6	2 11.1	16 33.8	25 13.5	5 35.3	10 53.1	14 16.9	3 31.6	29 18.8
8 Th	5 07 52	17 46 34	28 37 12	6♉01 46	26 39.5	22 14.6	1 43.8	17 12.0	25 34.6	5 28.4	11 00.9	14 16.2	3 30.1	29D18.7
9 F	5 11 49	18 43 57	13♉29 23	20 59 04	26 34.1	24 24.7	1 14.6	17 50.1	25 55.8	5 21.4	11 08.7	14 15.5	3 28.5	29 18.7
10 Sa	5 15 45	19 41 20	28 29 44	6♊00 14	26 28.8	26 33.7	0 43.7	18 28.3	26 17.1	5 14.3	11 16.4	14 14.9	3 27.0	29 18.7
11 Su	5 19 42	20 38 43	13♊29 24	20 56 06	26 24.3	28 41.4	0 11.3	19 06.4	26 38.5	5 07.2	11 24.2	14 14.3	3 25.4	29 18.8
12 M	5 23 38	21 36 04	28 19 18	5♋38 04	26 21.2	0♋47.5	29♊37.5	19 44.5	27 00.1	5 00.0	11 31.9	14 13.8	3 23.9	29 18.9
13 Tu	5 27 35	22 33 25	12♋51 37	19 59 20	26D19.8	2 51.9	29 02.5	20 22.7	27 21.8	4 52.7	11 39.6	14 13.4	3 22.4	29 19.0
14 W	5 31 31	23 30 45	27 00 48	3♌55 45	26 19.9	4 54.5	28 26.6	21 00.8	27 43.7	4 45.3	11 47.3	14 13.0	3 20.9	29 19.2
15 Th	5 35 28	24 28 04	10♌44 05	17 25 52	26 21.0	6 55.1	27 49.9	21 38.9	28 05.6	4 37.9	11 55.0	14 12.6	3 19.4	29 19.4
16 F	5 39 25	25 25 22	24 01 16	0♍30 37	26 22.5	8 53.7	27 12.6	22 17.0	28 27.7	4 30.5	12 02.7	14 12.3	3 17.9	29 19.6
17 Sa	5 43 21	26 22 39	6♍54 17	13 12 44	26 23.9	10 50.1	26 35.1	22 55.0	28 49.8	4 23.0	12 10.4	14 12.1	3 16.4	29 19.8
18 Su	5 47 18	27 19 56	19 26 28	25 36 02	26R24.6	12 44.4	25 57.5	23 33.1	29 12.1	4 15.4	12 18.0	14 11.9	3 15.0	29 20.1
19 M	5 51 14	28 17 11	1♎42 01	7♎44 57	26 24.2	14 36.5	25 20.1	24 11.2	29 34.5	4 07.8	12 25.6	14 11.7	3 13.5	29 20.4
20 Tu	5 55 11	29 14 26	13 45 27	19 44 02	26 22.5	16 26.3	24 43.1	24 49.2	29 57.0	4 00.2	12 33.2	14 11.6	3 12.1	29 20.8
21 W	5 59 07	0♋11 41	25 41 16	1♏37 39	26 19.8	18 13.8	24 06.8	25 27.3	0♍19.6	3 52.6	12 40.8	14D11.6	3 10.7	29 21.2
22 Th	6 03 04	1 08 54	7♏33 41	13 29 49	26 16.3	19 59.0	23 31.4	26 05.3	0 42.4	3 45.0	12 48.3	14 11.6	3 09.3	29 21.6
23 F	6 07 00	2 06 07	19 26 27	25 23 58	26 12.3	21 42.0	22 57.1	26 43.4	1 05.2	3 37.3	12 55.9	14 11.7	3 07.9	29 22.0
24 Sa	6 10 57	3 03 20	1♐22 44	7♐23 03	26 08.5	23 22.6	22 24.1	27 21.4	1 28.1	3 29.6	13 03.4	14 11.8	3 06.6	29 22.5
25 Su	6 14 54	4 00 32	13 25 10	19 29 20	26 05.1	25 00.9	21 52.6	27 59.4	1 51.1	3 21.9	13 10.9	14 12.0	3 05.2	29 23.0
26 M	6 18 50	4 57 44	25 35 46	1♑44 39	26 02.7	26 36.9	21 22.8	28 37.4	2 14.2	3 14.3	13 18.3	14 12.2	3 03.9	29 23.6
27 Tu	6 22 47	5 54 56	7♑56 07	14 10 21	26D01.2	28 10.5	20 54.8	29 15.4	2 37.4	3 06.6	13 25.7	14 12.5	3 02.6	29 24.2
28 W	6 26 43	6 52 07	20 27 26	26 47 31	26 00.8	29 41.8	20 28.8	29 53.4	3 00.7	2 58.9	13 33.1	14 12.8	3 01.3	29 24.8
29 Th	6 30 40	7 49 19	3♒10 41	9♒37 05	26 01.3	1♌10.7	20 04.9	0♌31.4	3 24.1	2 51.3	13 40.5	14 13.2	3 00.0	29 25.4
30 F	6 34 36	8 46 30	16 06 47	22 39 55	26 02.3	2 37.2	19 43.2	1 09.4	3 47.6	2 43.7	13 47.9	14 13.6	2 58.8	29 26.1

Astro Data	Planet Ingress	Last Aspect	☽ Ingress	Last Aspect	☽ Ingress	☽ Phases & Eclipses	Astro Data
Dy Hr Mn	Dy Hr Mn	Dy Hr Mn	Dy Hr Mn	Dy Hr Mn	Dy Hr Mn	Dy Hr Mn	
☽0N 9 1:14	♀ ♋ 10 13:51	2 19:50 ♇ □	♑ 2 20:29	1 10:58 ♇ △	♒ 1 12:15	6 12:26 ☾ 16♒04	1 May 1972
♃⚻♄ 14 6:12	♂ ♋ 12 13:14	5 5:53 ♇ △	♒ 5 6:35	2 15:12 ♅ △	♓ 3 19:52	13 4:08 ● 22♉30	Julian Day # 26419
☽0S 21 18:56	☿ ♉ 12 23:45	7 10:19 ♀ △	♓ 7 13:28	5 23:17 ♇ ☍	♈ 6 0:27	20 1:16 ☽ 29♌08	SVP 5♓38'33"
♀R 27 3:14	☉ ♊ 20 23:00	9 15:51 ♇ ☍	♈ 9 16:35	7 9:39 ☿ ⚹	♉ 8 2:15	28 4:28 ○ 6♐56	GC 26♐27.2 ⚳ 3♋55.9
	☿ ♊ 29 6:46	11 15:53 ♂ ⚹	♉ 11 16:47	10 1:18 ♇ △	♊ 10 2:24		Eris 12♈54.3 ⚵ 5♎34.3R
☽0N 5 7:52		13 15:10 ♇ △	♊ 13 15:57	12 2:43 ☿ ☌	♋ 12 2:45	4 21:22 ☾ 14♓19	⚷ 14♈54.6 ⚶ 24♈55.0
♇D 9 5:43	♀ ♊R 11 20:08	15 15:24 ♇ □	♋ 15 16:16	14 3:59 ♇ ⚹	♌ 14 5:10	11 11:30 ● 20♊38	☽ Mean ☊ 0♒11.9
☽0S 18 1:30	☿ ♋ 12 2:56	17 18:39 ♇ ⚹	♌ 17 19:38	16 6:09 ♀ ⚹	♍ 16 11:03	18 15:41 ☽ 27♍29	
♅D 21 17:28	⚳ ♍ 20 15:09	20 1:16 ☉ □	♍ 20 2:56	18 19:20 ♇ ☌	♎ 18 20:39	26 18:46 ○ 5♑14	1 June 1972
♃⚺♆ 28 3:05	☉ ♋ 21 7:06	22 12:24 ♇ ☌	♎ 22 13:36	20 22:50 ♂ □	♏ 21 8:43		Julian Day # 26450
	♂ ♌ 28 16:09	23 18:48 ♅ ☌	♏ 25 2:01	23 19:58 ♇ ⚹	♐ 23 21:14		SVP 5♓38'27"
	☿ ♌ 28 16:52	27 13:15 ♇ ⚹	♐ 27 14:33	26 7:25 ♇ □	♑ 26 8:36		GC 26♐27.2 ⚳ 21♋09.2
		30 0:55 ♇ □	♑ 30 2:13	28 16:56 ♇ △	♒ 28 18:02		Eris 13♈10.1 ⚵ 4♎03.6
							⚷ 16♈22.2 ⚶ 8♉39.2
							☽ Mean ☊ 28♑33.4

July 1972 — LONGITUDE

Day	Sid.Time	☉	0 hr ☽	Noon☽	True☊	☿	♀	♂	⚳	♃	♄	♅	♆	♇
1 Sa	6 38 33	9♋43 41	29♒16 34	5♓56 50	26♑03.6	4♌01.3	19♊23.7	1♌47.4	4♍11.1	2♑36.1	13♊55.2	14♎14.1	2♐57.6	29♍26.8
2 Su	6 42 29	10 40 53	12♓40 49	19 28 34	26 04.7	5 22.9	19R 06.5	2 25.4	4 34.8	2R 28.6	14 02.4	14 14.7	2R 56.4	29 27.5
3 M	6 46 26	11 38 04	26 20 07	3♈15 28	26R 05.4	6 42.1	18 51.7	3 03.4	4 58.5	2 21.0	14 09.7	14 15.3	2 55.2	29 28.3
4 Tu	6 50 23	12 35 16	10♈14 34	17 17 19	26 05.4	7 58.7	18 39.3	3 41.4	5 22.3	2 13.6	14 16.9	14 15.9	2 54.0	29 29.1
5 W	6 54 19	13 32 29	24 23 30	1♉32 52	26 04.9	9 12.7	18 29.3	4 19.4	5 46.2	2 06.1	14 24.1	14 16.6	2 52.9	29 29.9
6 Th	6 58 16	14 29 41	8♉45 04	15 59 39	26 04.0	10 24.1	18 21.8	4 57.3	6 10.2	1 58.8	14 31.2	14 17.3	2 51.7	29 30.7
7 F	7 02 12	15 26 54	23 16 05	0♊33 44	26 02.8	11 32.8	18 16.6	5 35.3	6 34.3	1 51.5	14 38.3	14 18.2	2 50.6	29 31.6
8 Sa	7 06 09	16 24 08	7♊51 57	15 09 58	26 01.6	12 38.7	18D 13.8	6 13.3	6 58.4	1 44.2	14 45.4	14 19.0	2 49.6	29 32.6
9 Su	7 10 05	17 21 21	22 27 02	29 42 24	26 00.7	13 41.7	18 13.3	6 51.3	7 22.6	1 37.0	14 52.4	14 19.9	2 48.5	29 33.5
10 M	7 14 02	18 18 35	6♋55 17	14♋04 59	26D 00.2	14 41.8	18 15.1	7 29.3	7 46.9	1 29.9	14 59.4	14 20.9	2 47.5	29 34.5
11 Tu	7 17 58	19 15 50	21 10 52	28 12 23	26 00.1	15 38.8	18 19.2	8 07.3	8 11.3	1 22.9	15 06.3	14 21.9	2 46.5	29 35.5
12 W	7 21 55	20 13 04	5♌09 05	12♌00 35	26 00.3	16 32.6	18 25.5	8 45.3	8 35.8	1 16.0	15 13.2	14 23.0	2 45.5	29 36.5
13 Th	7 25 52	21 10 18	18 46 42	25 27 18	26 00.7	17 23.2	18 33.9	9 23.2	9 00.3	1 09.1	15 20.1	14 24.1	2 44.6	29 37.6
14 F	7 29 48	22 07 33	2♍02 22	8♍32 02	26 01.1	18 10.3	18 44.5	10 01.2	9 24.9	1 02.4	15 26.9	14 25.2	2 43.6	29 38.7
15 Sa	7 33 45	23 04 47	14 56 28	21 15 58	26 01.4	18 53.8	18 57.0	10 39.2	9 49.5	0 55.7	15 33.6	14 26.5	2 42.7	29 39.8
16 Su	7 37 41	24 02 02	27 30 53	3♎41 39	26 01.7	19 33.7	19 11.6	11 17.2	10 14.2	0 49.2	15 40.4	14 27.7	2 41.9	29 41.0
17 M	7 41 38	24 59 17	9♎48 44	15 52 38	26 01.8	20 09.7	19 28.1	11 55.1	10 39.0	0 42.7	15 47.0	14 29.0	2 41.0	29 42.2
18 Tu	7 45 34	25 56 32	21 53 54	27 53 05	26 01.8	20 41.6	19 46.5	12 33.1	11 03.9	0 36.4	15 53.6	14 30.4	2 40.2	29 43.4
19 W	7 49 31	26 53 47	3♏50 45	9♏47 29	26 01.8	21 09.5	20 06.7	13 11.1	11 28.8	0 30.2	16 00.2	14 31.8	2 39.4	29 44.6
20 Th	7 53 27	27 51 03	15 43 51	21 40 24	26 01.9	21 33.0	20 28.6	13 49.1	11 53.8	0 24.1	16 06.7	14 33.3	2 38.6	29 45.9
21 F	7 57 24	28 48 19	27 37 40	3♐36 10	26 02.1	21 52.0	20 52.3	14 27.0	12 18.8	0 18.2	16 13.2	14 34.8	2 37.9	29 47.2
22 Sa	8 01 21	29 45 35	9♐36 22	15 38 44	26 02.5	22 06.4	21 17.6	15 05.0	12 43.9	0 12.3	16 19.6	14 36.4	2 37.2	29 48.5
23 Su	8 05 17	0♌42 51	21 43 41	27 51 32	26 02.9	22 16.1	21 44.5	15 43.0	13 09.1	0 06.6	16 25.9	14 38.0	2 36.5	29 49.9
24 M	8 09 14	1 40 09	4♑02 39	10♑17 16	26 03.3	22R 20.8	22 12.9	16 20.9	13 34.3	0 01.1	16 32.2	14 39.6	2 35.9	29 51.2
25 Tu	8 13 10	2 37 26	16 35 35	22 57 46	26R 03.5	22 20.6	22 42.8	16 58.9	13 59.5	29♐55.6	16 38.5	14 41.3	2 35.2	29 52.6
26 W	8 17 07	3 34 44	29 23 53	5♒54 00	26 03.5	22 15.4	23 14.1	17 36.9	14 24.8	29 50.4	16 44.6	14 43.1	2 34.7	29 54.1
27 Th	8 21 03	4 32 03	12♒28 05	19 06 02	26 03.0	22 05.1	23 46.8	18 14.9	14 50.2	29 45.2	16 50.8	14 44.9	2 34.1	29 55.5
28 F	8 25 00	5 29 23	25 47 46	2♓33 05	26 02.1	21 49.7	24 20.8	18 52.9	15 15.6	29 40.2	16 56.8	14 46.7	2 33.6	29 57.0
29 Sa	8 28 57	6 26 43	9♓21 47	16 13 38	26 00.9	21 29.5	24 56.2	19 30.8	15 41.1	29 35.4	17 02.8	14 48.6	2 33.0	29 58.5
30 Su	8 32 53	7 24 05	23 08 23	0♈05 43	25 59.6	21 04.4	25 32.7	20 08.8	16 06.6	29 30.7	17 08.8	14 50.6	2 32.6	0♎00.0
31 M	8 36 50	8 21 27	7♈05 22	14 07 02	25 58.4	20 34.8	26 10.4	20 46.8	16 32.2	29 26.1	17 14.7	14 52.6	2 32.1	0 01.6

August 1972 — LONGITUDE

Day	Sid.Time	☉	0 hr ☽	Noon☽	True☊	☿	♀	♂	⚳	♃	♄	♅	♆	♇
1 Tu	8 40 46	9♌18 51	21♈10 24	28♈15 10	25♑57.6	20♌01.0	26♊49.3	21♌24.8	16♍57.8	29♐21.8	17♊20.5	14♎54.6	2♐31.7	0♎03.1
2 W	8 44 43	10 16 16	5♉21 03	12♉27 43	25D 57.4	19R 23.3	27 29.3	22 02.8	17 23.5	29R 17.5	17 26.2	14 56.7	2R 31.3	0 04.7
3 Th	8 48 39	11 13 42	19 34 53	26 42 14	25 57.8	18 42.3	28 10.4	22 40.8	17 49.2	29 13.5	17 31.9	14 58.8	2 31.0	0 06.4
4 F	8 52 36	12 11 09	3♊49 28	10♊56 16	25 58.7	17 58.7	28 52.4	23 18.8	18 15.0	29 09.6	17 37.5	15 00.9	2 30.6	0 08.0
5 Sa	8 56 32	13 08 38	18 02 16	25 07 10	25 59.9	17 13.0	29 35.5	23 56.9	18 40.8	29 05.9	17 43.1	15 03.1	2 30.4	0 09.7
6 Su	9 00 29	14 06 08	2♋10 36	9♋12 11	26 01.0	16 26.1	0♋19.5	24 34.9	19 06.6	29 02.3	17 48.6	15 05.4	2 30.1	0 11.4
7 M	9 04 26	15 03 39	16 11 34	23 08 24	26R 01.6	15 38.8	1 04.4	25 13.0	19 32.5	28 58.9	17 54.0	15 07.7	2 29.9	0 13.1
8 Tu	9 08 22	16 01 12	0♌02 18	6♌52 56	26 01.3	14 51.9	1 50.1	25 51.0	19 58.5	28 55.7	17 59.3	15 10.0	2 29.7	0 14.8
9 W	9 12 19	16 58 45	13 40 01	20 23 17	26 00.0	14 06.3	2 36.7	26 29.1	20 24.5	28 52.7	18 04.6	15 12.4	2 29.5	0 16.6
10 Th	9 16 15	17 56 19	27 02 29	3♍37 29	25 57.6	13 23.0	3 24.1	27 07.1	20 50.5	28 49.9	18 09.8	15 14.8	2 29.4	0 18.4
11 F	9 20 12	18 53 55	10♍08 10	16 34 31	25 54.4	12 42.9	4 12.3	27 45.2	21 16.6	28 47.2	18 14.9	15 17.3	2 29.3	0 20.2
12 Sa	9 24 08	19 51 31	22 56 35	29 14 28	25 50.7	12 06.6	5 01.2	28 23.2	21 42.7	28 44.7	18 20.0	15 19.8	2 29.2	0 22.0
13 Su	9 28 05	20 49 09	5♎28 22	11♎38 33	25 47.0	11 35.1	5 50.8	29 01.3	22 08.8	28 42.4	18 24.9	15 22.3	2D 29.2	0 23.8
14 M	9 32 01	21 46 47	17 45 20	23 49 06	25 43.7	11 08.9	6 41.1	29 39.4	22 35.0	28 40.3	18 29.8	15 24.9	2 29.2	0 25.7
15 Tu	9 35 58	22 44 27	29 50 17	5♏49 23	25 41.4	10 48.7	7 32.2	0♍17.5	23 01.2	28 38.3	18 34.6	15 27.5	2 29.2	0 27.6
16 W	9 39 54	23 42 07	11♏46 55	17 43 27	25D 40.1	10 35.0	8 23.8	0 55.6	23 27.5	28 36.6	18 39.3	15 30.1	2 29.3	0 29.5
17 Th	9 43 51	24 39 49	23 39 32	29 35 48	25 40.1	10D 28.3	9 16.1	1 33.7	23 53.8	28 35.0	18 44.0	15 32.8	2 29.4	0 31.4
18 F	9 47 48	25 37 32	5♐32 51	11♐31 16	25 41.0	10 28.7	10 09.0	2 11.8	24 20.1	28 33.6	18 48.6	15 35.5	2 29.5	0 33.3
19 Sa	9 51 44	26 35 15	17 31 41	23 34 39	25 42.6	10 36.5	11 02.5	2 49.9	24 46.5	28 32.5	18 53.1	15 38.3	2 29.6	0 35.3
20 Su	9 55 41	27 33 00	29 40 45	5♑50 30	25 44.3	10 52.0	11 56.5	3 28.0	25 12.8	28 31.5	18 57.5	15 41.1	2 29.8	0 37.2
21 M	9 59 37	28 30 47	12♑04 21	18 22 43	25R 45.4	11 15.1	12 51.1	4 06.2	25 39.2	28 30.6	19 01.8	15 43.9	2 30.1	0 39.2
22 Tu	10 03 34	29 28 34	24 45 58	1♒14 19	25 45.5	11 45.9	13 46.3	4 44.3	26 05.7	28 30.0	19 06.0	15 46.8	2 30.3	0 41.2
23 W	10 07 30	0♍26 23	7♒47 57	14 26 56	25 44.1	12 24.2	14 42.0	5 22.5	26 32.2	28 29.6	19 10.2	15 49.7	2 30.6	0 43.2
24 Th	10 11 27	1 24 13	21 11 12	28 00 34	25 41.1	13 09.9	15 38.1	6 00.6	26 58.7	28D 29.3	19 14.2	15 52.6	2 30.9	0 45.2
25 F	10 15 24	2 22 04	4♓54 46	11♓53 25	25 36.6	14 02.9	16 34.8	6 38.8	27 25.2	28 29.3	19 18.2	15 55.6	2 31.3	0 47.3
26 Sa	10 19 20	3 19 57	18 55 59	26 01 55	25 31.0	15 02.8	17 32.0	7 17.0	27 51.7	28 29.4	19 22.1	15 58.6	2 31.7	0 49.3
27 Su	10 23 17	4 17 52	3♈10 33	10♈21 14	25 25.2	16 09.5	18 29.6	7 55.1	28 18.3	28 29.7	19 25.9	16 01.6	2 32.1	0 51.4
28 M	10 27 13	5 15 48	17 33 14	24 45 52	25 19.8	17 22.5	19 27.6	8 33.3	28 44.9	28 30.2	19 29.6	16 04.7	2 32.5	0 53.5
29 Tu	10 31 10	6 13 46	1♉58 30	9♉10 32	25 15.6	18 41.4	20 26.2	9 11.6	29 11.5	28 30.9	19 33.2	16 07.8	2 33.0	0 55.6
30 W	10 35 06	7 11 46	16 21 27	23 30 47	25 13.0	20 05.9	21 25.1	9 49.8	29 38.2	28 31.8	19 36.7	16 10.9	2 33.5	0 57.7
31 Th	10 39 03	8 09 48	0♊38 11	7♊43 24	25D 12.2	21 35.4	22 24.4	10 28.0	0♎04.9	28 32.8	19 40.1	16 14.1	2 34.1	0 59.8

Astro Data Dy Hr Mn	Planet Ingress Dy Hr Mn	Last Aspect Dy Hr Mn	☽ Ingress Dy Hr Mn	Last Aspect Dy Hr Mn	☽ Ingress Dy Hr Mn	☽ Phases & Eclipses Dy Hr Mn	Astro Data
☽0N 2 13:05	☉ ♌ 22 18:03	30 6:45 ♀ △	♓ 1 1:18	1 13:52 ♃ △	♉ 1 14:57	4 3:25 ☾ 12♈15	1 July 1972
♄△♅ 4 8:22	♃ ♐R 24 16:42	3 5:27 ♇ ☍	♈ 3 6:22	3 4:54 ♂ □	♊ 3 17:33	10 19:39 ● 18♋37	Julian Day # 26480
♀D 9 4:55	♇ ♎ 30 11:39	4 14:17 ♀ ⚹	♉ 5 9:25	5 20:01 ♀ ☌	♋ 5 20:18	10 19:45:53 ● T 02'36"	SVP 5♓38'22"
☽0S 15 9:43		7 10:18 ♇ △	♊ 7 11:05	6 22:08 ♅ □	♌ 7 23:56	18 7:46 ☽ 25♎46	GC 26♐27.3 ⚵ 7♌33.5
☿R 24 23:03	♀ ♋ 6 1:26	9 11:45 ♇ □	♋ 9 12:29	10 3:17 ♃ △	♍ 10 5:23	26 7:24 ○ 3♒24	Eris 13♈17.3 ✱ 7♎17.9
♃□♇ 25 22:42	♂ ♍ 15 0:59	11 14:23 ♇ ⚹	♌ 11 15:05	12 11:03 ♃ □	♎ 12 13:27	26 7:16 • P 0.543	⚷ 17♈12.6 ⚶ 21♉03.0
☽0N 29 18:42	☉ ♍ 23 1:03	12 23:29 ♀ ⚹	♍ 13 20:16	15 0:17 ♂ ⚹	♏ 15 0:19		☽ Mean ☊ 26♑58.1
	⚳ ♎ 31 7:38	16 4:11 ♇ ☌	♎ 16 4:49	17 1:09 ☉ □	♐ 17 12:49	2 8:02 ☾ 10♉07	
☽0S 11 18:42		18 7:46 ☉ □	♏ 18 16:15	19 21:45 ♃ ☌	♑ 20 0:38	9 5:26 ● 16♌43	1 August 1972
♆D 14 3:08		21 4:20 ♇ ⚹	♐ 21 4:46	21 6:58 ♅ □	♒ 22 9:43	17 1:09 ☽ 24♏14	Julian Day # 26511
☿D 17 22:39		23 15:51 ♇ □	♑ 23 16:10	24 12:50 ♃ ⚹	♓ 24 15:28	24 18:22 ○ 1♓40	SVP 5♓38'17"
♃D 25 8:01		26 0:55 ♇ △	♒ 26 1:07	26 16:08 ♃ □	♈ 26 18:40	31 12:48 ☾ 8♊12	GC 26♐27.4 ⚵ 23♌58.9
☽0N 26 2:10		28 6:56 ♃ ⚹	♓ 28 7:29	28 18:14 ♃ △	♉ 28 20:43		Eris 13♈14.9R ✱ 13♎58.4
		30 11:00 ♃ □	♈ 30 11:50	30 8:13 ♀ ⚹	♊ 30 22:56		⚷ 17♈18.2R ⚶ 2♊24.8
							☽ Mean ☊ 25♑19.6

LONGITUDE — September 1972

Day	Sid.Time	☉	0 hr ☽	Noon ☽	True ☊	☿	♀	♂	⚳	♃	♄	♅	♆	♇
1 F	10 42 59	9♍07 53	14♊46 12	21♊46 27	25♑12.8	23♌09.5	23♋24.2	11♍06.3	0♎31.6	28♐34.1	19♊43.4	16♎17.2	2♐34.7	1♎02.0
2 Sa	10 46 56	10 05 59	28 44 05	5♋39 02	25 14.0	24 47.7	24 24.3	11 44.5	0 58.3	28 35.5	19 46.7	16 20.5	2 35.3	1 04.1
3 Su	10 50 53	11 04 07	12♋31 16	19 20 48	25R 15.0	26 29.5	25 24.8	12 22.8	1 25.0	28 37.2	19 49.8	16 23.7	2 35.9	1 06.3
4 M	10 54 49	12 02 17	26 07 35	2♌51 37	25 14.8	28 14.4	26 25.7	13 01.1	1 51.8	28 39.0	19 52.9	16 27.0	2 36.6	1 08.5
5 Tu	10 58 46	13 00 29	9♌32 51	16 11 15	25 12.9	0♍01.8	27 26.9	13 39.4	2 18.6	28 41.0	19 55.8	16 30.2	2 37.3	1 10.6
6 W	11 02 42	13 58 42	22 46 45	29 19 16	25 08.6	1 51.4	28 28.5	14 17.7	2 45.4	28 43.2	19 58.7	16 33.6	2 38.0	1 12.8
7 Th	11 06 39	14 56 58	5♍48 44	12♍15 05	25 02.1	3 42.7	29 30.4	14 56.1	3 12.2	28 45.5	20 01.4	16 36.9	2 38.8	1 15.0
8 F	11 10 35	15 55 15	18 38 14	24 58 09	24 53.8	5 35.2	0♌32.6	15 34.4	3 39.1	28 48.1	20 04.0	16 40.3	2 39.6	1 17.2
9 Sa	11 14 32	16 53 34	1♎14 51	7♎28 21	24 44.3	7 28.7	1 35.1	16 12.8	4 05.9	28 50.8	20 06.6	16 43.7	2 40.4	1 19.4
10 Su	11 18 28	17 51 54	13 38 43	19 46 07	24 34.5	9 22.8	2 37.9	16 51.2	4 32.8	28 53.7	20 09.0	16 47.1	2 41.3	1 21.7
11 M	11 22 25	18 50 17	25 50 43	1♏52 46	24 25.4	11 17.2	3 41.1	17 29.5	4 59.7	28 56.8	20 11.4	16 50.5	2 42.2	1 23.9
12 Tu	11 26 21	19 48 41	7♏52 35	13 50 31	24 17.9	13 11.6	4 44.5	18 07.9	5 26.6	29 00.1	20 13.6	16 54.0	2 43.1	1 26.1
13 W	11 30 18	20 47 06	19 47 01	25 42 32	24 12.4	15 05.9	5 48.2	18 46.4	5 53.6	29 03.6	20 15.7	16 57.4	2 44.1	1 28.4
14 Th	11 34 15	21 45 34	1♐37 36	7♐32 47	24 09.1	16 59.9	6 52.1	19 24.8	6 20.5	29 07.2	20 17.8	17 00.9	2 45.1	1 30.6
15 F	11 38 11	22 44 03	13 28 41	19 25 55	24D 07.9	18 53.4	7 56.4	20 03.2	6 47.4	29 11.0	20 19.7	17 04.5	2 46.1	1 32.9
16 Sa	11 42 08	23 42 33	25 25 09	1♑27 02	24 08.1	20 46.3	9 00.9	20 41.7	7 14.4	29 15.0	20 21.5	17 08.0	2 47.1	1 35.1
17 Su	11 46 04	24 41 06	7♑32 14	13 41 23	24R 08.9	22 38.6	10 05.6	21 20.1	7 41.4	29 19.2	20 23.2	17 11.6	2 48.2	1 37.4
18 M	11 50 01	25 39 40	19 55 06	26 13 59	24 09.2	24 30.0	11 10.6	21 58.6	8 08.3	29 23.5	20 24.8	17 15.1	2 49.3	1 39.7
19 Tu	11 53 57	26 38 15	2♒38 32	9♒09 11	24 08.1	26 20.6	12 15.9	22 37.1	8 35.3	29 28.0	20 26.3	17 18.7	2 50.4	1 41.9
20 W	11 57 54	27 36 53	15 46 15	22 29 57	24 04.9	28 10.3	13 21.4	23 15.6	9 02.3	29 32.7	20 27.7	17 22.3	2 51.6	1 44.2
21 Th	12 01 50	28 35 32	29 20 19	6♓17 16	23 59.2	29 59.1	14 27.1	23 54.2	9 29.3	29 37.5	20 29.0	17 25.9	2 52.8	1 46.5
22 F	12 05 47	29 34 12	13♓20 30	20 29 33	23 51.2	1♎47.0	15 33.1	24 32.7	9 56.3	29 42.5	20 30.2	17 29.6	2 54.0	1 48.8
23 Sa	12 09 44	0♎32 55	27 43 46	5♈02 21	23 41.5	3 33.9	16 39.3	25 11.2	10 23.3	29 47.7	20 31.2	17 33.2	2 55.3	1 51.0
24 Su	12 13 40	1 31 40	12♈24 21	19 48 43	23 31.2	5 19.9	17 45.7	25 49.8	10 50.4	29 53.0	20 32.2	17 36.9	2 56.5	1 53.3
25 M	12 17 37	2 30 27	27 14 23	4♉40 14	23 21.5	7 05.0	18 52.3	26 28.4	11 17.4	29 58.5	20 33.0	17 40.6	2 57.8	1 55.6
26 Tu	12 21 33	3 29 16	12♉05 12	19 28 20	23 13.5	8 49.1	19 59.2	27 07.0	11 44.4	0♑04.2	20 33.8	17 44.3	2 59.2	1 57.9
27 W	12 25 30	4 28 07	26 48 47	4♊05 52	23 07.9	10 32.2	21 06.3	27 45.6	12 11.5	0 10.0	20 34.4	17 48.0	3 00.5	2 00.1
28 Th	12 29 26	5 27 01	11♊19 01	18 27 52	23 04.8	12 14.5	22 13.5	28 24.3	12 38.5	0 16.0	20 34.9	17 51.7	3 01.9	2 02.4
29 F	12 33 23	6 25 57	25 32 11	2♋31 53	23D 03.7	13 55.8	23 21.0	29 03.0	13 05.5	0 22.1	20 35.3	17 55.4	3 03.3	2 04.7
30 Sa	12 37 19	7 24 55	9♋26 59	16 17 35	23R 03.8	15 36.3	24 28.7	29 41.6	13 32.6	0 28.4	20 35.6	17 59.1	3 04.8	2 07.0

LONGITUDE — October 1972

Day	Sid.Time	☉	0 hr ☽	Noon ☽	True ☊	☿	♀	♂	⚳	♃	♄	♅	♆	♇
1 Su	12 41 16	8♎23 56	23♋03 51	29♋46 02	23♑03.8	17♎15.9	25♌36.6	0♎20.3	13♎59.7	0♑34.8	20♊35.8	18♎02.9	3♐06.2	2♎09.3
2 M	12 45 13	9 22 59	6♌24 21	12♌59 03	23R 02.4	18 54.6	26 44.6	0 59.1	14 26.7	0 41.4	20R 35.9	18 06.6	3 07.7	2 11.5
3 Tu	12 49 09	10 22 04	19 30 23	25 58 33	22 58.6	20 32.5	27 52.9	1 37.8	14 53.8	0 48.2	20 35.9	18 10.4	3 09.2	2 13.8
4 W	12 53 06	11 21 11	2♍23 46	8♍46 10	22 51.9	22 09.6	29 01.3	2 16.6	15 20.8	0 55.1	20 35.7	18 14.1	3 10.8	2 16.1
5 Th	12 57 02	12 20 21	15 05 54	21 23 04	22 42.3	23 45.9	0♍09.9	2 55.4	15 47.9	1 02.1	20 35.5	18 17.9	3 12.3	2 18.3
6 F	13 00 59	13 19 33	27 37 44	3♎49 59	22 30.1	25 21.3	1 18.6	3 34.2	16 14.9	1 09.3	20 35.1	18 21.7	3 13.9	2 20.6
7 Sa	13 04 55	14 18 46	9♎59 52	16 07 27	22 16.4	26 56.0	2 27.5	4 13.0	16 42.0	1 16.7	20 34.6	18 25.4	3 15.5	2 22.8
8 Su	13 08 52	15 18 02	22 12 48	28 16 00	22 02.1	28 30.0	3 36.6	4 51.8	17 09.0	1 24.2	20 34.0	18 29.2	3 17.2	2 25.0
9 M	13 12 48	16 17 20	4♏17 11	10♏16 30	21 48.7	0♏03.2	4 45.8	5 30.7	17 36.1	1 31.8	20 33.3	18 33.0	3 18.8	2 27.3
10 Tu	13 16 45	17 16 40	16 14 09	22 10 24	21 37.0	1 35.6	5 55.2	6 09.6	18 03.1	1 39.6	20 32.5	18 36.8	3 20.5	2 29.5
11 W	13 20 41	18 16 02	28 05 33	3♐59 57	21 27.9	3 07.4	7 04.8	6 48.5	18 30.1	1 47.5	20 31.6	18 40.6	3 22.2	2 31.7
12 Th	13 24 38	19 15 26	9♐54 02	15 48 13	21 21.7	4 38.4	8 14.4	7 27.4	18 57.2	1 55.5	20 30.5	18 44.4	3 23.9	2 33.9
13 F	13 28 35	20 14 51	21 43 04	27 39 07	21 18.2	6 08.7	9 24.3	8 06.3	19 24.2	2 03.7	20 29.4	18 48.2	3 25.7	2 36.1
14 Sa	13 32 31	21 14 18	3♑36 59	9♑37 18	21D 16.8	7 38.2	10 34.2	8 45.3	19 51.2	2 12.0	20 28.2	18 51.9	3 27.4	2 38.3
15 Su	13 36 28	22 13 47	15 40 44	21 47 57	21R 16.7	9 07.1	11 44.3	9 24.2	20 18.2	2 20.5	20 26.8	18 55.7	3 29.2	2 40.5
16 M	13 40 24	23 13 18	27 59 39	4♒16 29	21 16.5	10 35.2	12 54.6	10 03.2	20 45.2	2 29.0	20 25.3	18 59.5	3 31.0	2 42.7
17 Tu	13 44 21	24 12 51	10♒39 05	17 08 02	21 15.1	12 02.6	14 05.0	10 42.2	21 12.1	2 37.7	20 23.8	19 03.3	3 32.9	2 44.9
18 W	13 48 17	25 12 25	23 43 50	0♓26 52	21 11.6	13 29.2	15 15.5	11 21.2	21 39.1	2 46.6	20 22.1	19 07.1	3 34.7	2 47.0
19 Th	13 52 14	26 12 01	7♓17 23	14 15 27	21 05.5	14 55.0	16 26.1	12 00.3	22 06.1	2 55.5	20 20.3	19 10.8	3 36.6	2 49.1
20 F	13 56 10	27 11 39	21 20 58	28 33 36	20 56.8	16 20.1	17 36.8	12 39.3	22 33.0	3 04.6	20 18.4	19 14.6	3 38.5	2 51.3
21 Sa	14 00 07	28 11 18	5♈52 48	13♈17 45	20 46.2	17 44.4	18 47.7	13 18.4	22 59.9	3 13.8	20 16.4	19 18.3	3 40.4	2 53.4
22 Su	14 04 04	29 11 00	20 47 29	28 20 48	20 34.8	19 07.8	19 58.7	13 57.5	23 26.8	3 23.1	20 14.3	19 22.1	3 42.3	2 55.5
23 M	14 08 00	0♏10 44	5♉56 25	13♉32 57	20 23.8	20 30.3	21 09.9	14 36.7	23 53.7	3 32.6	20 12.2	19 25.8	3 44.3	2 57.6
24 Tu	14 11 57	1 10 29	21 09 01	28 43 18	20 14.6	21 51.8	22 21.1	15 15.8	24 20.6	3 42.1	20 09.9	19 29.6	3 46.2	2 59.6
25 W	14 15 53	2 10 17	6♊14 35	13♊41 51	20 08.0	23 12.4	23 32.5	15 55.0	24 47.5	3 51.8	20 07.5	19 33.3	3 48.2	3 01.7
26 Th	14 19 50	3 10 07	21 04 15	28 21 08	20 04.2	24 31.9	24 44.0	16 34.2	25 14.3	4 01.6	20 05.0	19 37.0	3 50.2	3 03.7
27 F	14 23 46	4 10 00	5♋32 06	12♋36 54	20D 02.7	25 50.2	25 55.6	17 13.4	25 41.1	4 11.5	20 02.4	19 40.7	3 52.2	3 05.8
28 Sa	14 27 43	5 09 54	19 35 30	26 27 59	20R 02.6	27 07.3	27 07.3	17 52.7	26 07.9	4 21.5	19 59.7	19 44.4	3 54.2	3 07.8
29 Su	14 31 40	6 09 51	3♌14 33	9♌55 30	20 02.7	28 23.0	28 19.1	18 31.9	26 34.7	4 31.6	19 56.9	19 48.1	3 56.3	3 09.8
30 M	14 35 36	7 09 50	16 31 13	23 02 04	20 01.7	29 37.3	29 31.0	19 11.2	27 01.5	4 41.8	19 54.1	19 51.7	3 58.3	3 11.8
31 Tu	14 39 33	8 09 51	29 28 29	5♍50 52	19 58.5	0♐49.9	0♎43.0	19 50.5	27 28.3	4 52.1	19 51.1	19 55.4	4 00.4	3 13.7

Astro Data

	Dy Hr Mn
☽0S	8 3:03
☽0N	22 11:34
☉0S	22 22:33
☿0S	23 2:48
♄ R	2 16:25
♅∠♆	2 23:40
♂0S	4 6:34
☽0S	5 9:43
⚳0S	6 6:46
♃□♇	18 13:32
☽0N	19 21:45
♃⊻♆	25 0:50
♄△♅	30 20:26

Planet Ingress

		Dy Hr Mn
☿	♍	5 11:36
♀	♌	7 23:27
☿	♎	21 12:11
☉	♎	22 22:33
♃	♑	25 18:20
♂	♎	30 23:23
♀	♍	5 8:33
☿	♏	9 11:11
☉	♏	23 7:41
☿	♐	30 19:27
♀	♎	30 21:40

Last Aspect / ☽ Ingress

Last Aspect Dy Hr Mn			☽ Ingress	Dy Hr Mn
1 23:44	♃	☍	♋	2 2:11
3 23:36	♀	☌	♌	4 6:54
6 10:53	♃	△	♍	6 13:15
8 19:20	♃	□	♎	8 21:36
11 6:08	♃	✱	♏	11 8:15
13 1:08	☉	✱	♐	13 20:42
16 7:37	♃	☌	♑	16 9:07
18 10:50	☉	△	♒	18 19:04
21 0:26	♃	✱	♓	21 1:09
23 3:21	♃	□	♈	23 3:44
25 4:22	♃	△	♉	25 4:27
27 1:04	♂	△	♊	27 5:14
29 5:43	♂	□	♋	29 7:39

Last Aspect / ☽ Ingress

Last Aspect Dy Hr Mn			☽ Ingress	Dy Hr Mn
30 15:00	♅	□	♌	1 12:25
3 15:54	♀	☌	♍	3 19:31
5 10:29	♄	□	♎	6 4:35
8 12:32	☿	☌	♏	8 15:27
8 23:47	♀	✱	♐	11 3:52
12 21:32	♄	☍	♑	13 16:44
15 12:55	☉	□	♒	16 3:51
18 1:54	☉	△	♓	18 11:12
19 22:17	♄	□	♈	20 14:22
22 13:25	☉	☍	♉	22 14:37
24 1:03	♀	△	♊	24 14:02
26 5:29	♀	□	♋	26 14:44
28 13:16	☿	△	♌	28 18:14
30 6:14	♄	✱	♍	31 0:59

☽ Phases & Eclipses

Dy Hr Mn	
7 17:28	● 15♍10
15 19:13	☽ 23♐02
23 4:07	○ 0♈14
29 19:16	☾ 6♋44
7 8:08	● 14♎09
15 12:55	☽ 22♑16
22 13:25	○ 29♈15
29 4:41	☾ 5♌52

Astro Data

1 September 1972
Julian Day # 26542
SVP 5♓38'13"
GC 26♐27.5 ⚴ 9♍46.9
Eris 13♈03.1R ⚵ 22♎42.7
⚷ 16♈36.2R ⚶ 11♊22.5
☽ Mean ☊ 23♑41.2

1 October 1972
Julian Day # 26572
SVP 5♓38'09"
GC 26♐27.5 ⚴ 24♍25.5
Eris 12♈46.0R ⚵ 2♏17.9
⚷ 15♈23.3R ⚶ 16♊13.9
☽ Mean ☊ 22♑05.8

November 1972 LONGITUDE

Day	Sid.Time	☉	0 hr ☽	Noon ☽	True ☊	☿	♀	♂	⚳	♃	♄	♅	♆	♇
1 W	14 43 29	9♏09 54	12♍09 38	18♍25 08	19♑52.6	2♐00.7	1♎55.2	20♎29.9	27♎55.0	5♑02.6	19♊48.0	19♎59.0	4♐02.5	3♎15.7
2 Th	14 47 26	10 09 59	24 37 43	0♎47 42	19R 43.9	3 09.5	3 07.4	21 09.2	28 21.7	5 13.1	19R 44.9	20 02.7	4 04.6	3 17.6
3 F	14 51 22	11 10 06	6♎55 20	13 00 53	19 32.8	4 16.1	4 19.7	21 48.6	28 48.4	5 23.8	19 41.6	20 06.3	4 06.7	3 19.5
4 Sa	14 55 19	12 10 15	19 04 32	25 06 28	19 20.1	5 20.2	5 32.1	22 28.0	29 15.1	5 34.5	19 38.3	20 09.9	4 08.8	3 21.4
5 Su	14 59 15	13 10 26	1♏06 52	7♏05 52	19 06.9	6 21.6	6 44.6	23 07.5	29 41.7	5 45.3	19 34.9	20 13.4	4 10.9	3 23.3
6 M	15 03 12	14 10 39	13 03 38	19 00 18	18 54.4	7 19.8	7 57.1	23 46.9	0♏08.3	5 56.3	19 31.4	20 17.0	4 13.0	3 25.1
7 Tu	15 07 08	15 10 54	24 56 03	0♐51 04	18 43.5	8 14.6	9 09.8	24 26.4	0 34.9	6 07.3	19 27.8	20 20.5	4 15.2	3 27.0
8 W	15 11 05	16 11 11	6♐45 35	12 39 51	18 35.1	9 05.6	10 22.5	25 05.9	1 01.5	6 18.4	19 24.2	20 24.0	4 17.4	3 28.8
9 Th	15 15 02	17 11 29	18 34 09	24 28 50	18 29.3	9 52.1	11 35.4	25 45.4	1 28.0	6 29.7	19 20.5	20 27.5	4 19.5	3 30.6
10 F	15 18 58	18 11 49	0♑24 17	6♑20 55	18 26.3	10 33.8	12 48.2	26 25.0	1 54.5	6 41.0	19 16.7	20 31.0	4 21.7	3 32.3
11 Sa	15 22 55	19 12 10	12 19 13	18 19 43	18D 25.4	11 10.0	14 01.2	27 04.5	2 20.9	6 52.4	19 12.8	20 34.5	4 23.9	3 34.1
12 Su	15 26 51	20 12 33	24 22 56	0♒29 30	18 26.0	11 40.0	15 14.2	27 44.1	2 47.4	7 03.9	19 08.8	20 37.9	4 26.1	3 35.8
13 M	15 30 48	21 12 57	6♒40 00	12 55 03	18R 26.9	12 03.3	16 27.3	28 23.7	3 13.8	7 15.4	19 04.8	20 41.3	4 28.3	3 37.5
14 Tu	15 34 44	22 13 22	19 15 17	25 41 17	18 27.1	12 19.1	17 40.5	29 03.4	3 40.1	7 27.1	19 00.7	20 44.7	4 30.5	3 39.2
15 W	15 38 41	23 13 49	2♓13 36	8♓52 43	18 25.8	12R 26.7	18 53.8	29 43.0	4 06.5	7 38.8	18 56.6	20 48.0	4 32.8	3 40.8
16 Th	15 42 37	24 14 17	15 39 01	22 32 45	18 22.4	12 25.3	20 07.1	0♏22.7	4 32.7	7 50.6	18 52.3	20 51.4	4 35.0	3 42.4
17 F	15 46 34	25 14 46	29 34 02	6♈42 44	18 16.8	12 14.3	21 20.4	1 02.4	4 59.0	8 02.5	18 48.1	20 54.7	4 37.2	3 44.0
18 Sa	15 50 31	26 15 17	13♈58 35	21 21 02	18 09.6	11 53.1	22 33.9	1 42.1	5 25.2	8 14.5	18 43.7	20 57.9	4 39.4	3 45.6
19 Su	15 54 27	27 15 49	28 49 19	6♉22 27	18 01.5	11 21.5	23 47.3	2 21.8	5 51.4	8 26.6	18 39.3	21 01.2	4 41.7	3 47.1
20 M	15 58 24	28 16 22	13♉59 17	21 38 28	17 53.6	10 39.3	25 00.9	3 01.6	6 17.5	8 38.7	18 34.9	21 04.4	4 43.9	3 48.7
21 Tu	16 02 20	29 16 57	29 18 36	6♊58 15	17 47.0	9 46.9	26 14.5	3 41.4	6 43.6	8 50.9	18 30.4	21 07.6	4 46.2	3 50.2
22 W	16 06 17	0♐17 34	14♊36 00	22 10 36	17 42.4	8 45.0	27 28.2	4 21.2	7 09.6	9 03.1	18 25.9	21 10.8	4 48.4	3 51.6
23 Th	16 10 13	1 18 12	29 40 52	7♋05 52	17D 40.0	7 34.9	28 41.9	5 01.1	7 35.7	9 15.5	18 21.3	21 13.9	4 50.7	3 53.1
24 F	16 14 10	2 18 52	14♋24 53	21 37 21	17 39.6	6 18.3	29 55.7	5 40.9	8 01.6	9 27.9	18 16.7	21 17.0	4 53.0	3 54.5
25 Sa	16 18 07	3 19 33	28 43 00	5♌41 41	17 40.5	4 57.6	1♏09.6	6 20.8	8 27.5	9 40.4	18 12.0	21 20.1	4 55.2	3 55.9
26 Su	16 22 03	4 20 16	12♌33 27	19 18 29	17 41.9	3 35.3	2 23.5	7 00.7	8 53.4	9 52.9	18 07.3	21 23.1	4 57.5	3 57.3
27 M	16 26 00	5 21 00	25 57 06	2♍29 40	17R 42.8	2 14.2	3 37.4	7 40.7	9 19.3	10 05.5	18 02.6	21 26.1	4 59.7	3 58.6
28 Tu	16 29 56	6 21 46	8♍56 38	15 18 28	17 42.4	0 57.0	4 51.5	8 20.7	9 45.0	10 18.2	17 57.8	21 29.1	5 02.0	3 59.9
29 W	16 33 53	7 22 33	21 35 42	27 48 49	17 40.2	29♏46.3	6 05.5	9 00.7	10 10.8	10 30.9	17 53.0	21 32.0	5 04.3	4 01.2
30 Th	16 37 49	8 23 22	3♎58 19	10♎04 41	17 36.1	28 43.9	7 19.6	9 40.7	10 36.5	10 43.7	17 48.1	21 34.9	5 06.5	4 02.4

December 1972 LONGITUDE

Day	Sid.Time	☉	0 hr ☽	Noon ☽	True ☊	☿	♀	♂	⚳	♃	♄	♅	♆	♇
1 F	16 41 46	9♐24 13	16♎08 22	22♎09 48	17♑30.4	27♏51.5	8♏33.8	10♏20.7	11♏02.1	10♑56.5	17♊43.3	21♎37.8	5♐08.8	4♎03.6
2 Sa	16 45 42	10 25 04	28 09 21	4♏07 25	17R 23.6	27R 10.1	9 48.0	11 00.8	11 27.7	11 09.4	17R 38.4	21 40.6	5 11.0	4 04.8
3 Su	16 49 39	11 25 57	10♏04 17	16 00 16	17 16.4	26 40.2	11 02.2	11 40.9	11 53.2	11 22.4	17 33.5	21 43.4	5 13.3	4 06.0
4 M	16 53 36	12 26 52	21 55 39	27 50 39	17 09.5	26 21.7	12 16.5	12 21.0	12 18.7	11 35.4	17 28.6	21 46.1	5 15.5	4 07.1
5 Tu	16 57 32	13 27 47	3♐45 31	9♐40 28	17 03.7	26D 14.4	13 30.8	13 01.2	12 44.1	11 48.5	17 23.6	21 48.8	5 17.8	4 08.2
6 W	17 01 29	14 28 44	15 35 43	21 31 29	16 59.3	26 17.6	14 45.1	13 41.4	13 09.5	12 01.6	17 18.7	21 51.5	5 20.0	4 09.2
7 Th	17 05 25	15 29 41	27 27 59	3♑25 29	16 56.6	26 30.7	15 59.5	14 21.6	13 34.8	12 14.8	17 13.7	21 54.1	5 22.3	4 10.3
8 F	17 09 22	16 30 40	9♑24 13	15 24 29	16D 55.6	26 52.8	17 13.9	15 01.8	14 00.0	12 28.0	17 08.8	21 56.7	5 24.5	4 11.3
9 Sa	17 13 18	17 31 39	21 26 34	27 30 51	16 56.1	27 23.1	18 28.4	15 42.1	14 25.2	12 41.3	17 03.8	21 59.3	5 26.7	4 12.2
10 Su	17 17 15	18 32 39	3♒37 40	9♒47 26	16 57.6	28 00.7	19 42.8	16 22.3	14 50.3	12 54.6	16 58.9	22 01.8	5 28.9	4 13.2
11 M	17 21 11	19 33 39	16 00 34	22 17 29	16 59.3	28 44.8	20 57.4	17 02.6	15 15.4	13 07.9	16 53.9	22 04.2	5 31.1	4 14.1
12 Tu	17 25 08	20 34 40	28 38 40	5♓04 33	17 00.9	29 34.7	22 11.9	17 42.9	15 40.4	13 21.3	16 49.0	22 06.7	5 33.4	4 14.9
13 W	17 29 05	21 35 42	11♓35 33	18 12 06	17R 01.7	0♐29.6	23 26.4	18 23.3	16 05.3	13 34.8	16 44.0	22 09.0	5 35.5	4 15.8
14 Th	17 33 01	22 36 44	24 54 31	1♈43 06	17 01.4	1 28.9	24 41.0	19 03.6	16 30.1	13 48.2	16 39.1	22 11.4	5 37.7	4 16.6
15 F	17 36 58	23 37 46	8♈38 01	15 39 20	17 00.0	2 32.1	25 55.6	19 44.0	16 54.9	14 01.7	16 34.2	22 13.7	5 39.9	4 17.3
16 Sa	17 40 54	24 38 49	22 46 57	0♉00 38	16 57.7	3 38.8	27 10.3	20 24.4	17 19.6	14 15.3	16 29.3	22 15.9	5 42.1	4 18.1
17 Su	17 44 51	25 39 53	7♉19 57	14 44 17	16 54.8	4 48.4	28 24.9	21 04.8	17 44.2	14 28.9	16 24.5	22 18.1	5 44.2	4 18.8
18 M	17 48 47	26 40 56	22 12 52	29 44 43	16 51.9	6 00.6	29 39.6	21 45.3	18 08.8	14 42.5	16 19.6	22 20.2	5 46.4	4 19.5
19 Tu	17 52 44	27 42 01	7♊18 47	14♊53 52	16 49.5	7 15.1	0♐54.3	22 25.8	18 33.3	14 56.1	16 14.8	22 22.4	5 48.5	4 20.1
20 W	17 56 40	28 43 05	22 28 45	0♋02 11	16 48.0	8 31.5	2 09.0	23 06.3	18 57.7	15 09.8	16 10.0	22 24.4	5 50.7	4 20.7
21 Th	18 00 37	29 44 11	7♋32 59	15 00 06	16D 47.4	9 49.7	3 23.8	23 46.8	19 22.0	15 23.5	16 05.3	22 26.4	5 52.8	4 21.3
22 F	18 04 34	0♑45 17	22 22 32	29 39 31	16 47.7	11 09.5	4 38.5	24 27.4	19 46.3	15 37.3	16 00.6	22 28.4	5 54.9	4 21.8
23 Sa	18 08 30	1 46 23	6♌50 26	13♌54 49	16 48.6	12 30.6	5 53.3	25 08.0	20 10.5	15 51.1	15 55.9	22 30.3	5 57.0	4 22.3
24 Su	18 12 27	2 47 30	20 52 26	27 43 12	16 49.9	13 52.9	7 08.1	25 48.6	20 34.6	16 04.8	15 51.3	22 32.2	5 59.0	4 22.8
25 M	18 16 23	3 48 37	4♍27 09	11♍04 29	16 51.0	15 16.2	8 23.0	26 29.2	20 58.6	16 18.7	15 46.7	22 34.0	6 01.1	4 23.2
26 Tu	18 20 20	4 49 45	17 35 30	24 00 36	16R 51.8	16 40.5	9 37.8	27 09.9	21 22.5	16 32.5	15 42.1	22 35.7	6 03.1	4 23.6
27 W	18 24 16	5 50 54	0♎20 13	6♎34 53	16 52.0	18 05.7	10 52.7	27 50.6	21 46.4	16 46.4	15 37.6	22 37.4	6 05.2	4 23.9
28 Th	18 28 13	6 52 03	12 45 08	18 51 30	16 51.7	19 31.6	12 07.6	28 31.3	22 10.1	17 00.3	15 33.2	22 39.1	6 07.2	4 24.3
29 F	18 32 09	7 53 13	24 54 35	0♏54 55	16 51.0	20 58.2	13 22.5	29 12.1	22 33.8	17 14.2	15 28.8	22 40.7	6 09.2	4 24.6
30 Sa	18 36 06	8 54 23	6♏53 03	12 49 31	16 50.0	22 25.4	14 37.4	29 52.9	22 57.4	17 28.1	15 24.4	22 42.3	6 11.2	4 24.8
31 Su	18 40 03	9 55 33	18 44 50	24 39 26	16 48.9	23 53.3	15 52.4	0♐33.7	23 20.9	17 42.0	15 20.2	22 43.8	6 13.1	4 25.0

Astro Data

	Dy Hr Mn
☽0S	1 14:47
♀0S	2 22:55
☿R	15 20:27
☽0N	16 6:51
☽0S	28 19:49
☿D	5 16:23
☽0N	13 13:47
♃⊼♄	23 18:20
☽0S	26 2:50

Planet Ingress

		Dy Hr Mn
⚳	♏	6 4:30
♂	♏	15 22:17
☉	♐	22 5:03
♀	♏	24 13:23
☿	♏R	29 7:08
☿	♐	12 23:20
♀	♐	18 18:34
☉	♑	21 18:13
♂	♐	30 16:12

Last Aspect / ☽ Ingress

Last Aspect Dy Hr Mn		☽ Ingress Dy Hr Mn
1 14:39 ♄ □	♎	2 10:27
4 6:26 ♂ ☌	♏	4 21:46
6 1:21 ☉ ☌	♐	7 10:16
9 14:44 ♂ ⚹	♑	9 23:11
12 6:18 ♂ □	♒	12 11:02
14 18:32 ♂ △	♓	14 19:56
16 15:08 ☉ △	♈	17 0:44
18 14:08 ♀ ☍	♉	19 1:53
20 23:07 ☉ ☍	♊	21 1:05
22 21:12 ♀ △	♋	23 0:31
24 11:26 ♅ □	♌	25 2:12
26 15:45 ♅ ⚹	♍	27 7:24
29 15:29 ☿ ⚹	♎	29 16:15

Last Aspect / ☽ Ingress

Last Aspect Dy Hr Mn		☽ Ingress Dy Hr Mn
1 10:56 ♅ ☌	♏	2 3:42
4 9:03 ☿ ☌	♐	4 16:22
6 12:41 ♅ ⚹	♑	7 5:06
9 11:44 ☿ ⚹	♒	9 16:53
12 1:01 ☿ □	♓	12 2:33
13 22:21 ♀ △	♈	14 8:59
16 2:26 ☉ △	♉	16 11:59
18 11:51 ♀ ☍	♊	18 12:24
20 9:45 ☉ ☍	♋	20 11:57
22 3:00 ♂ △	♌	22 12:34
24 8:27 ♂ □	♍	24 16:03
26 18:18 ♂ ⚹	♎	26 23:21
28 19:32 ♅ ☌	♏	29 10:10
30 21:36 ♃ ⚹	♐	31 22:51

☽ Phases & Eclipses

Dy Hr Mn	
6 1:21	● 13♏44
14 5:01	☽ 21♒56
20 23:07	○ 28♉44
27 17:45	☾ 5♍36
5 20:24	● 13♐49
13 18:36	☽ 21♓52
20 9:45	○ 28♊37
27 10:27	☾ 5♎47

Astro Data

1 November 1972
Julian Day # 26603
SVP 5♓38'06"
GC 26♐27.6 ⚴ 8♎46.3
Eris 12♈27.6R ⚵ 12♏46.7
⚷ 14♈01.5R ⚶ 15♊12.9R
☽ Mean ☊ 20♑27.3

1 December 1972
Julian Day # 26633
SVP 5♓38'02"
GC 26♐27.7 ⚴ 21♎36.8
Eris 12♈14.3R ⚵ 22♏59.5
⚷ 13♈05.4R ⚶ 8♊31.7R
☽ Mean ☊ 18♑52.0

LONGITUDE — January 1973

Day	Sid.Time	☉	0 hr ☽	Noon ☽	True ☊	☿	♀	♂	⚳	♃	♄	♅	♆	♇
1 M	18 43 59	10♑56 44	0♐33 48	6♐28 18	16♑48.0	25♐21.7	17♐07.3	1♐14.5	23♏44.3	17♑56.0	15♊15.9	22♎45.2	6♐15.1	4♎25.2
2 Tu	18 47 56	11 57 55	12 23 21	18 19 16	16R47.3	26 50.6	18 22.3	1 55.3	24 07.6	18 10.0	15R11.8	22 46.6	6 17.0	4 25.4
3 W	18 51 52	12 59 06	24 16 22	0♑14 55	16 46.8	28 20.0	19 37.3	2 36.2	24 30.8	18 23.9	15 07.7	22 48.0	6 18.9	4 25.5
4 Th	18 55 49	14 00 17	6♑15 11	12 17 24	16D46.7	29 49.9	20 52.2	3 17.1	24 53.9	18 37.9	15 03.7	22 49.3	6 20.8	4 25.6
5 F	18 59 45	15 01 28	18 21 44	24 28 25	16 46.7	1♑20.3	22 07.2	3 58.0	25 16.9	18 51.9	14 59.7	22 50.5	6 22.7	4R25.6
6 Sa	19 03 42	16 02 39	0♒37 37	6♒49 29	16R46.8	2 51.1	23 22.2	4 39.0	25 39.7	19 06.0	14 55.8	22 51.7	6 24.6	4 25.6
7 Su	19 07 39	17 03 50	13 04 12	19 21 56	16 46.8	4 22.3	24 37.3	5 20.0	26 02.5	19 20.0	14 52.0	22 52.8	6 26.4	4 25.6
8 M	19 11 35	18 05 00	25 42 50	2♓07 06	16 46.7	5 54.0	25 52.3	6 01.0	26 25.2	19 34.0	14 48.3	22 53.9	6 28.2	4 25.5
9 Tu	19 15 32	19 06 10	8♓34 52	15 06 20	16 46.5	7 26.1	27 07.3	6 42.0	26 47.8	19 48.0	14 44.7	22 54.9	6 30.0	4 25.4
10 W	19 19 28	20 07 19	21 41 38	28 20 58	16 46.2	8 58.6	28 22.3	7 23.0	27 10.2	20 02.0	14 41.1	22 55.9	6 31.8	4 25.3
11 Th	19 23 25	21 08 28	5♈04 27	11♈52 12	16D46.0	10 31.6	29 37.4	8 04.1	27 32.6	20 16.1	14 37.6	22 56.8	6 33.5	4 25.1
12 F	19 27 21	22 09 36	18 44 18	25 40 47	16 45.9	12 05.0	0♑52.4	8 45.1	27 54.8	20 30.1	14 34.2	22 57.7	6 35.2	4 24.9
13 Sa	19 31 18	23 10 44	2♉41 35	9♉46 37	16 46.1	13 38.9	2 07.4	9 26.2	28 16.9	20 44.1	14 30.9	22 58.5	6 36.9	4 24.7
14 Su	19 35 14	24 11 51	16 55 40	24 08 26	16 46.7	15 13.3	3 22.5	10 07.4	28 38.9	20 58.1	14 27.7	22 59.2	6 38.6	4 24.4
15 M	19 39 11	25 12 57	1♊24 31	8♊43 24	16 47.4	16 48.2	4 37.5	10 48.5	29 00.7	21 12.2	14 24.5	22 59.9	6 40.3	4 24.1
16 Tu	19 43 08	26 14 03	16 04 27	23 26 57	16 48.2	18 23.5	5 52.6	11 29.7	29 22.5	21 26.2	14 21.5	23 00.5	6 41.9	4 23.8
17 W	19 47 04	27 15 08	0♋50 08	8♋13 07	16R48.7	19 59.4	7 07.6	12 10.9	29 44.1	21 40.2	14 18.5	23 01.1	6 43.5	4 23.5
18 Th	19 51 01	28 16 12	15 35 01	22 54 57	16 48.7	21 35.7	8 22.7	12 52.1	0♐05.6	21 54.2	14 15.7	23 01.6	6 45.1	4 23.1
19 F	19 54 57	29 17 15	0♌12 03	7♌25 30	16 48.1	23 12.6	9 37.7	13 33.4	0 27.0	22 08.2	14 12.9	23 02.1	6 46.7	4 22.6
20 Sa	19 58 54	0♒18 18	14 34 35	21 38 40	16 46.8	24 50.1	10 52.8	14 14.7	0 48.2	22 22.2	14 10.3	23 02.5	6 48.2	4 22.2
21 Su	20 02 50	1 19 20	28 37 16	5♍30 02	16 44.9	26 28.1	12 07.8	14 56.0	1 09.3	22 36.1	14 07.7	23 02.8	6 49.7	4 21.7
22 M	20 06 47	2 20 22	12♍16 44	18 57 16	16 42.7	28 06.8	13 22.9	15 37.3	1 30.3	22 50.1	14 05.2	23 03.1	6 51.2	4 21.1
23 Tu	20 10 43	3 21 23	25 31 42	2♎00 12	16 40.5	29 46.0	14 38.0	16 18.7	1 51.1	23 04.0	14 02.8	23 03.4	6 52.6	4 20.6
24 W	20 14 40	4 22 24	8♎23 01	14 40 31	16 38.7	1♒25.8	15 53.1	17 00.0	2 11.8	23 17.9	14 00.6	23 03.5	6 54.1	4 20.0
25 Th	20 18 37	5 23 24	20 53 10	27 01 27	16D37.6	3 06.3	17 08.1	17 41.4	2 32.3	23 31.8	13 58.4	23 03.7	6 55.5	4 19.3
26 F	20 22 33	6 24 24	3♏05 55	9♏07 10	16 37.4	4 47.4	18 23.2	18 22.9	2 52.7	23 45.7	13 56.4	23R03.7	6 56.8	4 18.7
27 Sa	20 26 30	7 25 23	15 05 47	21 02 24	16 38.0	6 29.1	19 38.3	19 04.3	3 13.0	23 59.6	13 54.4	23 03.8	6 58.2	4 18.0
28 Su	20 30 26	8 26 21	26 57 39	2♐52 07	16 39.4	8 11.5	20 53.4	19 45.8	3 33.1	24 13.4	13 52.5	23 03.7	6 59.5	4 17.3
29 M	20 34 23	9 27 19	8♐46 24	14 41 06	16 41.2	9 54.6	22 08.5	20 27.3	3 53.1	24 27.3	13 50.8	23 03.6	7 00.8	4 16.5
30 Tu	20 38 19	10 28 16	20 36 45	26 33 51	16 42.9	11 38.3	23 23.6	21 08.9	4 12.9	24 41.1	13 49.2	23 03.5	7 02.0	4 15.7
31 W	20 42 16	11 29 12	2♑32 52	8♑34 15	16R44.1	13 22.6	24 38.7	21 50.4	4 32.5	24 54.8	13 47.6	23 03.2	7 03.3	4 14.9

LONGITUDE — February 1973

Day	Sid.Time	☉	0 hr ☽	Noon ☽	True ☊	☿	♀	♂	⚳	♃	♄	♅	♆	♇
1 Th	20 46 12	12♒30 08	14♑38 21	20♑45 29	16♑44.3	15♒07.6	25♑53.8	22♐32.0	4♐52.0	25♑08.6	13♊46.2	23♎03.0	7♐04.5	4♎14.1
2 F	20 50 09	13 31 02	26 55 56	3♒09 53	16R43.2	16 53.2	27 08.8	23 13.6	5 11.3	25 22.3	13R44.9	23R02.7	7 05.6	4R13.2
3 Sa	20 54 06	14 31 55	9♒27 30	15 48 51	16 40.6	18 39.4	28 23.9	23 55.2	5 30.5	25 36.0	13 43.7	23 02.3	7 06.8	4 12.3
4 Su	20 58 02	15 32 47	22 13 58	28 42 49	16 36.7	20 26.2	29 39.0	24 36.9	5 49.5	25 49.7	13 42.6	23 01.8	7 07.9	4 11.4
5 M	21 01 59	16 33 38	5♓15 20	11♓51 24	16 31.9	22 13.5	0♒54.1	25 18.5	6 08.3	26 03.3	13 41.7	23 01.4	7 09.0	4 10.4
6 Tu	21 05 55	17 34 28	18 30 53	25 13 36	16 26.7	24 01.2	2 09.1	26 00.2	6 26.9	26 16.9	13 40.8	23 00.8	7 10.0	4 09.5
7 W	21 09 52	18 35 16	1♈59 22	8♈47 59	16 21.8	25 49.3	3 24.2	26 41.9	6 45.4	26 30.4	13 40.1	23 00.2	7 11.0	4 08.4
8 Th	21 13 48	19 36 02	15 39 15	22 33 00	16 17.8	27 37.6	4 39.3	27 23.6	7 03.6	26 44.0	13 39.4	22 59.6	7 12.0	4 07.4
9 F	21 17 45	20 36 47	29 29 01	6♉27 10	16 15.3	29 26.1	5 54.3	28 05.4	7 21.7	26 57.4	13 38.9	22 58.8	7 13.0	4 06.3
10 Sa	21 21 41	21 37 31	13♉27 16	20 29 10	16D14.5	1♓14.6	7 09.4	28 47.1	7 39.7	27 10.9	13 38.5	22 58.1	7 13.9	4 05.3
11 Su	21 25 38	22 38 12	27 32 41	4♊37 41	16 15.0	3 02.9	8 24.4	29 28.9	7 57.4	27 24.3	13 38.2	22 57.3	7 14.8	4 04.1
12 M	21 29 35	23 38 53	11♊43 57	18 51 17	16 16.3	4 50.9	9 39.4	0♑10.7	8 14.9	27 37.6	13 38.0	22 56.4	7 15.6	4 03.0
13 Tu	21 33 31	24 39 31	25 59 24	3♋08 01	16R17.7	6 38.2	10 54.4	0 52.6	8 32.2	27 50.9	13D38.0	22 55.5	7 16.5	4 01.8
14 W	21 37 28	25 40 08	10♋16 45	17 25 13	16 18.3	8 24.7	12 09.4	1 34.4	8 49.4	28 04.2	13 38.0	22 54.5	7 17.3	4 00.7
15 Th	21 41 24	26 40 43	24 32 57	1♌39 26	16 17.3	10 09.9	13 24.5	2 16.3	9 06.3	28 17.4	13 38.2	22 53.5	7 18.0	3 59.5
16 F	21 45 21	27 41 16	8♌44 09	15 46 32	16 14.3	11 53.5	14 39.4	2 58.2	9 23.1	28 30.6	13 38.5	22 52.5	7 18.7	3 58.2
17 Sa	21 49 17	28 41 48	22 46 02	29 42 08	16 09.1	13 35.0	15 54.4	3 40.1	9 39.6	28 43.7	13 38.9	22 51.4	7 19.4	3 57.0
18 Su	21 53 14	29 42 19	6♍34 21	13♍22 15	16 02.3	15 14.1	17 09.4	4 22.0	9 55.9	28 56.8	13 39.4	22 50.2	7 20.1	3 55.7
19 M	21 57 10	0♓42 47	20 05 29	26 43 48	15 54.3	16 50.1	18 24.4	5 04.0	10 12.1	29 09.8	13 40.0	22 49.0	7 20.7	3 54.4
20 Tu	22 01 07	1 43 15	3♎17 04	9♎45 13	15 46.2	18 22.6	19 39.4	5 46.0	10 28.0	29 22.8	13 40.7	22 47.7	7 21.3	3 53.1
21 W	22 05 04	2 43 40	16 08 20	22 26 34	15 38.8	19 50.9	20 54.3	6 28.0	10 43.6	29 35.7	13 41.6	22 46.4	7 21.9	3 51.7
22 Th	22 09 00	3 44 05	28 40 10	4♏49 30	15 32.9	21 14.4	22 09.3	7 10.0	10 59.1	29 48.5	13 42.5	22 45.0	7 22.4	3 50.4
23 F	22 12 57	4 44 28	10♏55 00	16 57 08	15 28.9	22 32.5	23 24.2	7 52.0	11 14.4	0♒01.3	13 43.6	22 43.6	7 22.9	3 49.0
24 Sa	22 16 53	5 44 50	22 56 28	28 53 37	15D26.9	23 44.5	24 39.2	8 34.1	11 29.4	0 14.1	13 44.7	22 42.2	7 23.4	3 47.6
25 Su	22 20 50	6 45 10	4♐49 11	10♐43 50	15 26.7	24 49.8	25 54.1	9 16.2	11 44.1	0 26.8	13 46.0	22 40.7	7 23.8	3 46.2
26 M	22 24 46	7 45 29	16 38 14	22 33 03	15 27.6	25 47.7	27 09.1	9 58.3	11 58.7	0 39.4	13 47.4	22 39.2	7 24.2	3 44.8
27 Tu	22 28 43	8 45 46	28 28 57	4♑26 36	15R28.8	26 37.8	28 24.0	10 40.5	12 13.0	0 52.0	13 49.0	22 37.6	7 24.5	3 43.3
28 W	22 32 39	9 46 02	10♑26 36	16 29 33	15 29.3	27 19.5	29 38.9	11 22.6	12 27.1	1 04.4	13 50.6	22 36.0	7 24.9	3 41.9

Astro Data

	Dy Hr Mn
♇ R	6 6:56
☽ 0N	9 19:17
♃∠♆	17 18:27
☽ 0S	22 12:20
♃□♅	23 10:53
♅ R	27 5:30
☽ 0N	6 1:18
♄ D	13 12:49
♃♇♄	17 2:49
☽ 0S	18 22:36
☿0N	26 19:10

Planet Ingress

	Dy Hr Mn
☿ ♑	4 14:41
♀ ♑	11 19:15
⚳ ♐	18 5:45
☉ ♒	20 4:48
☿ ♒	23 15:23
♀ ♒	4 18:43
☿ ♓	9 19:30
♂ ♑	12 5:51
☉ ♓	18 19:01
♃ ♒	23 9:28
♀ ♓	28 18:45

Last Aspect / ☽ Ingress

Last Aspect Dy Hr Mn		☽ Ingress Dy Hr Mn
3 7:37	☿ ☌	♑ 3 11:30
5 8:48	♅ □	♒ 5 22:47
7 23:01	♀ ✶	♓ 8 8:03
10 12:03	♀ □	♈ 10 14:57
12 7:19	♅ ☍	♉ 12 19:24
14 12:06	☉ △	♊ 14 21:41
16 11:17	♅ △	♋ 16 22:39
18 21:28	☉ ☍	♌ 18 23:40
20 14:24	♅ ✶	♍ 21 2:23
23 7:13	☿ △	♎ 23 8:16
25 5:01	♃ □	♏ 25 17:52
27 18:06	♃ ✶	♐ 28 6:10
30 4:56	♅ ✶	♑ 30 18:54

Last Aspect / ☽ Ingress

Last Aspect Dy Hr Mn		☽ Ingress Dy Hr Mn
1 23:07	♀ ☌	♒ 2 5:55
4 4:00	♂ ✶	♓ 4 14:22
6 13:55	♃ ✶	♈ 6 20:29
8 22:06	☿ ✶	♉ 9 0:53
10 23:34	♃ △	♊ 11 4:10
12 20:41	☉ △	♋ 13 6:44
15 6:13	♃ ☍	♌ 15 9:12
17 10:07	☉ ☍	♍ 17 12:31
19 16:31	♃ △	♎ 19 17:58
22 2:02	♃ □	♏ 22 2:35
24 2:27	♀ □	♐ 24 14:14
26 22:24	♀ ✶	♑ 27 3:04

☽ Phases & Eclipses

Dy Hr Mn	
4 15:42	● 14♑10
4 15:45:37	● A 07'49"
12 5:27	☽ 21♈53
18 21:28	○ 28♋40
18 21:17	● A 0.866
26 6:05	☾ 6♏09
3 9:23	● 14♒25
10 14:05	☽ 21♉43
17 10:07	○ 28♌37
25 3:10	☾ 6♐23

Astro Data

1 January 1973
Julian Day # 26664
SVP 5♓37'56"
GC 26♐27.7 ⚵ 3♏12.8
Eris 12♈09.6 ✱ 3♐04.9
⚷ 12♈53.2 ⚶ 1♊58.6R
☽ Mean ☊ 17♑13.5

1 February 1973
Julian Day # 26695
SVP 5♓37'50"
GC 26♐27.8 ⚵ 11♏59.0
Eris 12♈15.6 ✱ 12♐00.6
⚷ 13♈32.9 ⚶ 1♊41.7
☽ Mean ☊ 15♑35.1

March 1973

LONGITUDE

Day	Sid.Time	☉	0 hr ☽	Noon ☽	True ☊	☿	♀	♂	⚳	♃	♄	♅	♆	♇
1 Th	22 36 36	10♓46 17	22♑35 59	28♑46 22	15♑28.3	27♓52.4	0♓53.8	12♑04.8	12♐40.9	1♒16.9	13♊52.3	22♎34.3	7♐25.2	3♎40.4
2 F	22 40 33	11 46 29	5♒01 09	11♒20 37	15R 25.1	28 16.2	2 08.7	12 47.0	12 54.4	1 29.2	13 54.1	22R 32.6	7 25.4	3R 38.9
3 Sa	22 44 29	12 46 40	17 45 01	24 14 30	15 19.4	28 30.6	3 23.6	13 29.2	13 07.7	1 41.5	13 56.1	22 30.8	7 25.6	3 37.4
4 Su	22 48 26	13 46 50	0♓49 04	7♓28 38	15 11.3	28R 35.7	4 38.5	14 11.4	13 20.8	1 53.7	13 58.2	22 29.1	7 25.8	3 35.9
5 M	22 52 22	14 46 57	14 13 01	21 01 54	15 01.6	28 31.4	5 53.4	14 53.7	13 33.6	2 05.9	14 00.3	22 27.2	7 26.0	3 34.3
6 Tu	22 56 19	15 47 03	27 54 53	4♈51 30	14 51.1	28 18.1	7 08.3	15 35.9	13 46.1	2 18.0	14 02.6	22 25.4	7 26.1	3 32.8
7 W	23 00 15	16 47 06	11♈51 11	18 53 23	14 41.0	27 56.1	8 23.1	16 18.2	13 58.3	2 29.9	14 05.0	22 23.5	7 26.2	3 31.2
8 Th	23 04 12	17 47 08	25 57 30	3♉02 58	14 32.4	27 26.0	9 37.9	17 00.5	14 10.3	2 41.9	14 07.5	22 21.5	7 26.2	3 29.6
9 F	23 08 08	18 47 07	10♉09 15	17 15 50	14 26.1	26 48.7	10 52.8	17 42.8	14 22.0	2 53.7	14 10.0	22 19.5	7R 26.3	3 28.1
10 Sa	23 12 05	19 47 04	24 22 18	1♊28 19	14 22.5	26 05.0	12 07.6	18 25.1	14 33.4	3 05.5	14 12.7	22 17.5	7 26.3	3 26.5
11 Su	23 16 02	20 47 00	8♊33 35	15 37 54	14D 21.1	25 16.0	13 22.4	19 07.4	14 44.5	3 17.1	14 15.5	22 15.5	7 26.2	3 24.9
12 M	23 19 58	21 46 53	22 41 06	29 43 05	14 21.1	24 22.9	14 37.2	19 49.8	14 55.3	3 28.7	14 18.4	22 13.4	7 26.1	3 23.3
13 Tu	23 23 55	22 46 43	6♋43 46	13♋43 05	14R 21.5	23 27.0	15 51.9	20 32.1	15 05.9	3 40.2	14 21.4	22 11.3	7 26.0	3 21.7
14 W	23 27 51	23 46 32	20 40 58	27 37 20	14 20.8	22 29.6	17 06.7	21 14.5	15 16.1	3 51.6	14 24.6	22 09.2	7 25.9	3 20.0
15 Th	23 31 48	24 46 18	4♌32 05	11♌25 05	14 18.1	21 32.0	18 21.4	21 56.9	15 26.0	4 03.0	14 27.8	22 07.0	7 25.7	3 18.4
16 F	23 35 44	25 46 01	18 16 09	25 05 04	14 12.6	20 35.4	19 36.1	22 39.3	15 35.7	4 14.2	14 31.1	22 04.8	7 25.5	3 16.8
17 Sa	23 39 41	26 45 43	1♍51 36	8♍35 30	14 04.2	19 40.9	20 50.8	23 21.7	15 45.0	4 25.4	14 34.4	22 02.6	7 25.2	3 15.1
18 Su	23 43 37	27 45 23	15 16 28	21 54 15	13 53.4	18 49.5	22 05.5	24 04.1	15 54.1	4 36.4	14 37.9	22 00.3	7 25.0	3 13.5
19 M	23 47 34	28 45 00	28 28 36	4♎59 17	13 40.9	18 02.2	23 20.2	24 46.5	16 02.8	4 47.4	14 41.5	21 58.0	7 24.6	3 11.9
20 Tu	23 51 30	29 44 35	11♎26 10	17 49 07	13 28.0	17 19.6	24 34.8	25 29.0	16 11.2	4 58.3	14 45.2	21 55.7	7 24.3	3 10.2
21 W	23 55 27	0♈44 09	24 08 06	0♏23 10	13 15.8	16 42.2	25 49.5	26 11.5	16 19.2	5 09.0	14 49.0	21 53.4	7 23.9	3 08.6
22 Th	23 59 24	1 43 41	6♏34 26	12 42 07	13 05.3	16 10.4	27 04.1	26 54.0	16 27.0	5 19.7	14 52.9	21 51.0	7 23.5	3 06.9
23 F	0 03 20	2 43 11	18 46 28	24 47 51	12 57.3	15 44.5	28 18.7	27 36.5	16 34.4	5 30.3	14 56.8	21 48.7	7 23.1	3 05.2
24 Sa	0 07 17	3 42 39	0♐46 43	6♐43 31	12 52.1	15 24.6	29 33.4	28 19.0	16 41.5	5 40.8	15 00.9	21 46.3	7 22.6	3 03.6
25 Su	0 11 13	4 42 05	12 38 50	18 33 14	12 49.3	15 10.7	0♈48.0	29 01.5	16 48.3	5 51.1	15 05.0	21 43.9	7 22.1	3 01.9
26 M	0 15 10	5 41 30	24 27 22	0♑21 52	12D 48.4	15D 02.9	2 02.5	29 44.1	16 54.7	6 01.4	15 09.2	21 41.4	7 21.6	3 00.3
27 Tu	0 19 06	6 40 53	6♑17 28	12 14 49	12R 48.4	15 00.9	3 17.1	0♒26.6	17 00.7	6 11.6	15 13.6	21 39.0	7 21.0	2 58.6
28 W	0 23 03	7 40 14	18 14 39	24 17 37	12 48.1	15 04.6	4 31.7	1 09.2	17 06.5	6 21.6	15 18.0	21 36.5	7 20.4	2 57.0
29 Th	0 26 59	8 39 33	0♒24 25	6♒35 37	12 46.4	15 13.8	5 46.2	1 51.8	17 11.8	6 31.6	15 22.5	21 34.0	7 19.8	2 55.3
30 F	0 30 56	9 38 50	12 51 50	19 13 31	12 42.5	15 28.2	7 00.8	2 34.4	17 16.8	6 41.4	15 27.1	21 31.5	7 19.1	2 53.7
31 Sa	0 34 53	10 38 06	25 41 04	2♓14 46	12 36.0	15 47.8	8 15.3	3 17.0	17 21.5	6 51.1	15 31.7	21 29.0	7 18.5	2 52.0

April 1973

LONGITUDE

Day	Sid.Time	☉	0 hr ☽	Noon ☽	True ☊	☿	♀	♂	⚳	♃	♄	♅	♆	♇
1 Su	0 38 49	11♈37 19	8♓54 47	15♓41 07	12♑26.8	16♓12.1	9♈29.8	3♒59.5	17♐25.8	7♒00.7	15♊36.5	21♎26.5	7♐17.7	2♎50.4
2 M	0 42 46	12 36 31	22 33 35	29 31 54	12R 15.6	16 40.9	10 44.3	4 42.1	17 29.7	7 10.2	15 41.3	21R 24.0	7R 17.0	2R 48.8
3 Tu	0 46 42	13 35 41	6♈35 35	13♈44 00	12 03.4	17 14.1	11 58.8	5 24.8	17 33.2	7 19.6	15 46.2	21 21.4	7 16.2	2 47.2
4 W	0 50 39	14 34 48	20 56 23	28 11 54	11 51.5	17 51.4	13 13.2	6 07.4	17 36.4	7 28.8	15 51.2	21 18.9	7 15.4	2 45.5
5 Th	0 54 35	15 33 54	5♉29 38	12♉48 38	11 41.3	18 32.6	14 27.7	6 50.0	17 39.2	7 38.0	15 56.3	21 16.3	7 14.6	2 43.9
6 F	0 58 32	16 32 57	20 07 59	27 26 50	11 33.6	19 17.4	15 42.1	7 32.6	17 41.6	7 47.0	16 01.4	21 13.7	7 13.7	2 42.3
7 Sa	1 02 28	17 31 59	4♊44 25	12♊00 03	11 28.8	20 05.7	16 56.5	8 15.2	17 43.6	7 55.9	16 06.6	21 11.2	7 12.9	2 40.7
8 Su	1 06 25	18 30 58	19 13 13	26 23 30	11 26.5	20 57.3	18 10.9	8 57.8	17 45.3	8 04.6	16 12.0	21 08.6	7 11.9	2 39.2
9 M	1 10 22	19 29 54	3♋30 37	10♋34 23	11 26.0	21 52.1	19 25.3	9 40.4	17 46.6	8 13.2	16 17.3	21 06.0	7 11.0	2 37.6
10 Tu	1 14 18	20 28 49	17 34 45	24 31 41	11 26.0	22 49.7	20 39.6	10 23.0	17 47.5	8 21.7	16 22.8	21 03.4	7 10.1	2 36.0
11 W	1 18 15	21 27 41	1♌25 15	8♌15 31	11 25.2	23 50.3	21 53.9	11 05.6	17R 48.0	8 30.1	16 28.3	21 00.9	7 09.1	2 34.5
12 Th	1 22 11	22 26 30	15 02 37	21 46 38	11 22.5	24 53.5	23 08.3	11 48.2	17 48.1	8 38.3	16 33.9	20 58.3	7 08.0	2 32.9
13 F	1 26 08	23 25 18	28 27 40	5♍05 47	11 17.0	25 59.3	24 22.6	12 30.8	17 47.8	8 46.4	16 39.6	20 55.7	7 07.0	2 31.4
14 Sa	1 30 04	24 24 03	11♍41 02	18 13 27	11 08.8	27 07.6	25 36.8	13 13.5	17 47.2	8 54.4	16 45.3	20 53.1	7 05.9	2 29.9
15 Su	1 34 01	25 22 45	24 43 01	1♎09 43	10 58.1	28 18.2	26 51.1	13 56.1	17 46.2	9 02.2	16 51.1	20 50.6	7 04.9	2 28.4
16 M	1 37 57	26 21 26	7♎33 32	13 54 25	10 45.7	29 31.2	28 05.3	14 38.7	17 44.7	9 09.9	16 56.9	20 48.0	7 03.7	2 26.9
17 Tu	1 41 54	27 20 05	20 12 21	26 27 18	10 32.9	0♈46.3	29 19.5	15 21.3	17 42.9	9 17.4	17 02.9	20 45.4	7 02.6	2 25.4
18 W	1 45 51	28 18 42	2♏39 18	8♏48 24	10 20.7	2 03.6	0♉33.7	16 03.9	17 40.7	9 24.8	17 08.8	20 42.9	7 01.5	2 24.0
19 Th	1 49 47	29 17 17	14 54 42	20 58 19	10 10.2	3 23.0	1 47.9	16 46.5	17 38.2	9 32.1	17 14.9	20 40.3	7 00.3	2 22.5
20 F	1 53 44	0♉15 50	26 59 28	2♐58 25	10 02.0	4 44.5	3 02.1	17 29.1	17 35.2	9 39.2	17 21.0	20 37.8	6 59.1	2 21.1
21 Sa	1 57 40	1 14 22	8♐55 27	14 50 58	9 56.5	6 07.9	4 16.3	18 11.7	17 31.8	9 46.2	17 27.2	20 35.3	6 57.9	2 19.7
22 Su	2 01 37	2 12 52	20 45 22	26 39 09	9 53.6	7 33.2	5 30.4	18 54.3	17 28.1	9 53.0	17 33.4	20 32.7	6 56.6	2 18.3
23 M	2 05 33	3 11 20	2♑32 50	8♑26 59	9D 52.7	9 00.5	6 44.5	19 36.9	17 23.9	9 59.7	17 39.7	20 30.2	6 55.4	2 16.9
24 Tu	2 09 30	4 09 46	14 22 13	20 19 10	9 53.0	10 29.7	7 58.7	20 19.4	17 19.4	10 06.2	17 46.1	20 27.8	6 54.1	2 15.6
25 W	2 13 26	5 08 11	26 18 30	2♒20 54	9R 53.5	12 00.7	9 12.8	21 02.0	17 14.5	10 12.5	17 52.5	20 25.3	6 52.8	2 14.3
26 Th	2 17 23	6 06 34	8♒27 02	14 37 33	9 53.2	13 33.5	10 26.8	21 44.6	17 09.3	10 18.8	17 58.9	20 22.8	6 51.4	2 12.9
27 F	2 21 20	7 04 56	20 53 06	27 14 16	9 51.2	15 08.2	11 40.9	22 27.1	17 03.6	10 24.8	18 05.5	20 20.4	6 50.1	2 11.6
28 Sa	2 25 16	8 03 16	3♓41 34	10♓15 26	9 47.0	16 44.7	12 55.0	23 09.7	16 57.6	10 30.7	18 12.0	20 18.0	6 48.7	2 10.4
29 Su	2 29 13	9 01 35	16 56 10	23 43 56	9 40.7	18 23.0	14 09.0	23 52.2	16 51.2	10 36.4	18 18.6	20 15.5	6 47.4	2 09.1
30 M	2 33 09	9 59 52	0♈38 45	7♈40 27	9 32.5	20 03.2	15 23.0	24 34.7	16 44.4	10 42.0	18 25.3	20 13.2	6 46.0	2 07.9

Astro Data

	Dy Hr Mn
☿ R	4 12:58
☽ 0N	5 9:06
♅∠♆	6 2:57
♆ R	9 14:32
♃△♇	12 2:05
☿0S	14 21:03
☽ 0S	18 7:25
☉0N	20 18:13
☿ D	27 8:18
♀0N	27 11:02
☽ 0N	1 18:18
♃⚹♆	3 4:00
⚳ R	12 7:48
☽ 0S	14 13:44
☿0N	21 14:34

Planet Ingress

	Dy Hr Mn
☉ ♈	20 18:12
♀ ♈	24 20:34
♂ ♒	26 20:59
☿ ♈	16 21:17
♀ ♉	18 1:05
☉ ♉	20 5:30
☽ 0N29	3:33

Last Aspect / ☽ Ingress

Last Aspect Dy Hr Mn		☽ Ingress	Dy Hr Mn
1 10:11	☿ ⚹	♒	1 14:22
3 8:50	♅ △	♓	3 22:31
6 0:53	☿ ☌	♈	6 3:37
7 17:56	♅ ☍	♉	8 6:51
10 3:21	☿ ⚹	♊	10 9:31
12 3:26	☿ □	♋	12 12:29
14 4:50	☉ △	♌	14 16:07
16 6:43	♅ ⚹	♍	16 20:42
18 23:33	☉ ☍	♎	19 2:48
21 3:27	♂ □	♏	21 11:15
23 19:52	♀ △	♐	23 22:26
25 18:26	♅ ⚹	♑	26 11:16
28 6:42	♅ □	♒	28 23:12
30 16:17	♅ △	♓	31 7:55

Last Aspect / ☽ Ingress

Last Aspect Dy Hr Mn		☽ Ingress	Dy Hr Mn
1 12:56	☿ ☌	♈	2 12:48
4 0:39	♅ ☍	♉	4 14:58
5 21:53	☿ ⚹	♊	6 16:12
8 3:14	♅ △	♋	8 18:04
10 8:50	☿ △	♌	10 21:31
12 14:41	♀ △	♍	13 2:47
15 6:07	☿ ☍	♎	15 9:50
17 18:10	♀ ☍	♏	17 18:51
19 3:10	♂ □	♐	20 6:02
21 23:37	♅ ⚹	♑	22 18:49
24 12:17	♅ □	♒	25 7:21
27 2:26	♂ ☌	♓	27 17:10
29 2:22	♄ □	♈	29 22:53

☽ Phases & Eclipses

Dy Hr Mn	
5 0:07	● 14♓17
11 21:26	☽ 21♊11
18 23:33	○ 28♍14
26 23:46	☾ 6♑11
3 11:45	● 13♈35
10 4:28	☽ 20♋10
17 13:51	○ 27♎25
25 17:59	☾ 5♒23

Astro Data

1 March 1973
Julian Day # 26723
SVP 5♓37'47"
GC 26♐27.9 ⚴ 15♏50.6
Eris 12♈29.0 ⚵ 18♐16.6
⚷ 14♈45.3 ⚶ 6♊38.5
☽ Mean ☊ 14♑06.1

1 April 1973
Julian Day # 26754
SVP 5♓37'44"
GC 26♐27.9 ⚴ 13♏23.8R
Eris 12♈49.0 ⚵ 21♐59.8
⚷ 16♈29.1 ⚶ 15♊48.3
☽ Mean ☊ 12♑27.6

LONGITUDE May 1973

Day	Sid.Time	☉	0 hr ☽	Noon ☽	True ☊	☿	♀	♂	⚴	♃	♄	♅	♆	♇
1 Tu	2 37 06	10♉58 07	14♈48 41	22♈02 53	9♑23.4	21♈45.1	16♉37.1	25♒17.1	16♐37.3	10♒47.4	18♊32.0	20♎10.8	6♐44.6	2♎06.7
2 W	2 41 02	11 56 21	29 22 20	6♉46 06	9R14.4	23 28.9	17 51.1	25 59.6	16R29.8	10 52.7	18 38.8	20R08.4	6R43.1	2R05.5
3 Th	2 44 59	12 54 33	14♉13 10	21 42 24	9 06.6	25 14.5	19 05.0	26 42.0	16 22.0	10 57.7	18 45.6	20 06.1	6 41.7	2 04.3
4 F	2 48 55	13 52 43	29 12 40	6♊42 46	9 00.8	27 01.9	20 19.0	27 24.5	16 13.9	11 02.7	18 52.5	20 03.8	6 40.3	2 03.2
5 Sa	2 52 52	14 50 52	14♊11 39	21 38 17	8 57.4	28 51.2	21 33.0	28 06.8	16 05.4	11 07.4	18 59.4	20 01.6	6 38.8	2 02.1
6 Su	2 56 49	15 48 58	29 01 50	6♋21 35	8D56.2	0♉42.3	22 46.9	28 49.2	15 56.5	11 12.0	19 06.4	19 59.3	6 37.3	2 01.0
7 M	3 00 45	16 47 03	13♋36 58	20 47 36	8 56.6	2 35.2	24 00.8	29 31.5	15 47.4	11 16.4	19 13.4	19 57.1	6 35.8	1 59.9
8 Tu	3 04 42	17 45 06	27 53 14	4♌53 46	8 57.5	4 30.0	25 14.7	0♓13.8	15 38.0	11 20.6	19 20.4	19 54.9	6 34.3	1 58.9
9 W	3 08 38	18 43 07	11♌49 12	18 39 37	8R58.1	6 26.5	26 28.6	0 56.1	15 28.2	11 24.6	19 27.5	19 52.7	6 32.8	1 57.8
10 Th	3 12 35	19 41 06	25 25 10	2♍06 04	8 57.3	8 24.9	27 42.5	1 38.3	15 18.2	11 28.5	19 34.6	19 50.6	6 31.3	1 56.8
11 F	3 16 31	20 39 03	8♍42 33	15 14 53	8 54.6	10 25.0	28 56.3	2 20.6	15 07.9	11 32.2	19 41.8	19 48.5	6 29.7	1 55.9
12 Sa	3 20 28	21 36 58	21 43 18	28 08 04	8 49.9	12 26.8	0♊10.1	3 02.7	14 57.3	11 35.7	19 49.0	19 46.4	6 28.2	1 54.9
13 Su	3 24 24	22 34 51	4♎29 24	10♎47 32	8 43.4	14 30.3	1 23.9	3 44.9	14 46.5	11 39.1	19 56.2	19 44.4	6 26.6	1 54.0
14 M	3 28 21	23 32 43	17 02 40	23 15 00	8 35.7	16 35.3	2 37.7	4 27.0	14 35.4	11 42.2	20 03.4	19 42.4	6 25.0	1 53.1
15 Tu	3 32 18	24 30 33	29 24 41	5♏31 55	8 27.6	18 41.8	3 51.5	5 09.1	14 24.1	11 45.2	20 10.7	19 40.4	6 23.5	1 52.3
16 W	3 36 14	25 28 22	11♏36 50	17 39 36	8 19.8	20 49.5	5 05.3	5 51.1	14 12.5	11 48.0	20 18.1	19 38.5	6 21.9	1 51.4
17 Th	3 40 11	26 26 09	23 40 24	29 39 25	8 13.2	22 58.5	6 19.0	6 33.2	14 00.8	11 50.6	20 25.4	19 36.6	6 20.3	1 50.6
18 F	3 44 07	27 23 55	5♐36 51	11♐32 56	8 08.3	25 08.5	7 32.7	7 15.1	13 48.8	11 53.1	20 32.8	19 34.7	6 18.7	1 49.9
19 Sa	3 48 04	28 21 39	17 27 55	23 22 07	8 05.2	27 19.2	8 46.4	7 57.1	13 36.6	11 55.3	20 40.2	19 32.9	6 17.1	1 49.1
20 Su	3 52 00	29 19 22	29 15 51	5♑09 28	8D04.0	29 30.4	10 00.1	8 39.0	13 24.3	11 57.4	20 47.7	19 31.1	6 15.5	1 48.4
21 M	3 55 57	0♊17 04	11♑03 24	16 58 05	8 04.4	1♊42.0	11 13.8	9 20.9	13 11.8	11 59.3	20 55.2	19 29.3	6 13.9	1 47.7
22 Tu	3 59 53	1 14 45	22 53 59	28 51 39	8 05.7	3 53.6	12 27.5	10 02.7	12 59.1	12 01.0	21 02.7	19 27.6	6 12.3	1 47.1
23 W	4 03 50	2 12 25	4♒51 35	10♒54 23	8 07.4	6 04.9	13 41.2	10 44.5	12 46.3	12 02.5	21 10.2	19 25.9	6 10.7	1 46.4
24 Th	4 07 47	3 10 04	17 00 38	23 10 55	8R08.7	8 15.7	14 54.8	11 26.2	12 33.4	12 03.8	21 17.7	19 24.3	6 09.1	1 45.8
25 F	4 11 43	4 07 41	29 25 49	5♓45 54	8 09.1	10 25.8	16 08.4	12 07.9	12 20.4	12 05.0	21 25.3	19 22.7	6 07.4	1 45.3
26 Sa	4 15 40	5 05 18	12♓11 43	18 43 43	8 08.3	12 34.7	17 22.0	12 49.5	12 07.3	12 05.9	21 32.9	19 21.1	6 05.8	1 44.7
27 Su	4 19 36	6 02 54	25 22 19	2♈07 48	8 06.1	14 42.3	18 35.7	13 31.0	11 54.0	12 06.7	21 40.5	19 19.6	6 04.2	1 44.2
28 M	4 23 33	7 00 29	9♈00 20	15 59 56	8 02.7	16 48.4	19 49.2	14 12.5	11 40.8	12 07.2	21 48.2	19 18.1	6 02.6	1 43.7
29 Tu	4 27 29	7 58 03	23 06 28	0♉19 35	7 58.6	18 52.8	21 02.8	14 54.0	11 27.4	12 07.6	21 55.8	19 16.7	6 00.9	1 43.3
30 W	4 31 26	8 55 36	7♉38 46	15 03 18	7 54.4	20 55.2	22 16.4	15 35.4	11 14.1	12R07.8	22 03.5	19 15.3	5 59.3	1 42.9
31 Th	4 35 22	9 53 09	22 32 17	0♊04 41	7 50.8	22 55.5	23 30.0	16 16.7	11 00.7	12 07.7	22 11.2	19 14.0	5 57.7	1 42.5

LONGITUDE June 1973

Day	Sid.Time	☉	0 hr ☽	Noon ☽	True ☊	☿	♀	♂	⚴	♃	♄	♅	♆	♇
1 F	4 39 19	10♊50 40	7♊39 21	15♊15 03	7♑48.3	24♊53.5	24♊43.5	16♓57.9	10♐47.3	12♒07.5	22♊18.9	19♎12.7	5♐56.1	1♎42.2
2 Sa	4 43 16	11 48 11	22 50 34	0♋24 42	7D47.0	26 49.3	25 57.0	17 39.1	10R33.9	12R07.1	22 26.7	19R11.5	5R54.5	1R41.8
3 Su	4 47 12	12 45 40	7♋56 18	15 24 23	7 47.0	28 42.6	27 10.6	18 20.2	10 20.6	12 06.5	22 34.4	19 10.3	5 52.8	1 41.6
4 M	4 51 09	13 43 08	22 48 05	0♌06 43	7 47.9	0♋33.5	28 24.1	19 01.2	10 07.3	12 05.8	22 42.1	19 09.1	5 51.2	1 41.3
5 Tu	4 55 05	14 40 35	7♌19 44	14 26 47	7 49.3	2 21.7	29 37.6	19 42.1	9 54.0	12 04.8	22 49.9	19 08.0	5 49.6	1 41.1
6 W	4 59 02	15 38 01	21 27 40	28 22 19	7 50.6	4 07.4	0♋51.0	20 23.0	9 40.8	12 03.6	22 57.7	19 06.9	5 48.0	1 40.9
7 Th	5 02 58	16 35 25	5♍10 50	11♍53 21	7R51.3	5 50.5	2 04.5	21 03.7	9 27.7	12 02.3	23 05.5	19 05.9	5 46.4	1 40.7
8 F	5 06 55	17 32 48	18 30 07	25 01 28	7 51.2	7 30.9	3 17.9	21 44.4	9 14.8	12 00.7	23 13.2	19 05.0	5 44.9	1 40.6
9 Sa	5 10 51	18 30 10	1♎27 44	7♎49 19	7 50.2	9 08.6	4 31.3	22 25.0	9 01.9	11 59.0	23 21.0	19 04.0	5 43.3	1 40.5
10 Su	5 14 48	19 27 31	14 06 37	20 20 01	7 48.4	10 43.6	5 44.7	23 05.5	8 49.2	11 57.1	23 28.8	19 03.2	5 41.7	1 40.4
11 M	5 18 45	20 24 52	26 29 56	2♏36 46	7 46.0	12 15.9	6 58.1	23 45.9	8 36.6	11 55.0	23 36.6	19 02.4	5 40.2	1D40.4
12 Tu	5 22 41	21 22 11	8♏40 52	14 42 37	7 43.5	13 45.4	8 11.5	24 26.3	8 24.1	11 52.7	23 44.5	19 01.6	5 38.6	1 40.4
13 W	5 26 38	22 19 29	20 42 20	26 40 22	7 41.2	15 12.2	9 24.8	25 06.5	8 11.9	11 50.2	23 52.3	19 00.9	5 37.1	1 40.5
14 Th	5 30 34	23 16 47	2♐37 01	8♐32 34	7 39.2	16 36.2	10 38.2	25 46.7	7 59.8	11 47.6	24 00.1	19 00.2	5 35.5	1 40.5
15 F	5 34 31	24 14 04	14 27 19	20 21 33	7 37.9	17 57.3	11 51.5	26 26.7	7 47.9	11 44.7	24 07.9	18 59.6	5 34.0	1 40.6
16 Sa	5 38 27	25 11 20	26 15 31	2♑09 31	7D37.3	19 15.5	13 04.8	27 06.7	7 36.2	11 41.7	24 15.7	18 59.0	5 32.5	1 40.8
17 Su	5 42 24	26 08 36	8♑03 50	13 58 46	7 37.3	20 30.9	14 18.0	27 46.5	7 24.7	11 38.5	24 23.5	18 58.5	5 31.0	1 40.9
18 M	5 46 20	27 05 52	19 54 36	25 51 41	7 37.9	21 43.2	15 31.3	28 26.2	7 13.5	11 35.1	24 31.3	18 58.0	5 29.5	1 41.1
19 Tu	5 50 17	28 03 07	1♒50 20	7♒50 57	7 38.7	22 52.6	16 44.6	29 05.9	7 02.5	11 31.6	24 39.1	18 57.6	5 28.0	1 41.4
20 W	5 54 14	29 00 21	13 53 53	19 59 33	7 39.6	23 58.8	17 57.8	29 45.4	6 51.7	11 27.9	24 46.9	18 57.3	5 26.6	1 41.6
21 Th	5 58 10	29 57 35	26 08 23	2♓20 47	7 40.3	25 01.9	19 11.0	0♈24.8	6 41.2	11 24.0	24 54.7	18 57.0	5 25.1	1 41.9
22 F	6 02 07	0♋54 50	8♓37 12	14 58 05	7 40.9	26 01.7	20 24.2	1 04.1	6 31.0	11 19.9	25 02.5	18 56.7	5 23.7	1 42.3
23 Sa	6 06 03	1 52 04	21 23 51	27 54 53	7R41.1	26 58.3	21 37.4	1 43.2	6 21.0	11 15.7	25 10.3	18 56.5	5 22.3	1 42.6
24 Su	6 10 00	2 49 17	4♈31 34	11♈14 11	7 41.1	27 51.3	22 50.6	2 22.2	6 11.4	11 11.3	25 18.1	18 56.3	5 20.9	1 43.0
25 M	6 13 56	3 46 31	18 02 58	24 58 03	7 40.9	28 40.9	24 03.8	3 01.1	6 02.0	11 06.7	25 25.9	18 56.2	5 19.5	1 43.5
26 Tu	6 17 53	4 43 45	1♉59 26	9♉07 00	7 40.6	29 26.8	25 16.9	3 39.9	5 52.9	11 02.0	25 33.6	18D56.2	5 18.1	1 43.9
27 W	6 21 49	5 40 59	16 20 29	23 39 28	7 40.3	0♌09.0	26 30.1	4 18.5	5 44.1	10 57.1	25 41.4	18 56.2	5 16.8	1 44.4
28 Th	6 25 46	6 38 13	1♊03 20	8♊31 21	7 40.2	0 47.3	27 43.2	4 57.0	5 35.7	10 52.1	25 49.1	18 56.2	5 15.4	1 45.0
29 F	6 29 43	7 35 28	16 02 36	23 36 05	7 40.2	1 21.6	28 56.3	5 35.3	5 27.5	10 46.9	25 56.8	18 56.4	5 14.1	1 45.5
30 Sa	6 33 39	8 32 42	1♋10 42	8♋45 15	7 40.2	1 51.8	0♌09.4	6 13.4	5 19.7	10 41.5	26 04.6	18 56.5	5 12.8	1 46.1

Astro Data

	Dy Hr Mn
☽0S	11 18:32
♄△♅	12 5:28
☽0N	26 11:41
♃ R	30 22:10
☽0S	7 23:54
♇ D	11 20:11
☽0N	22 18:21
♅ D	26 22:01
♃□♄	28 17:30

Planet Ingress

		Dy Hr Mn
☿	♉	6 2:55
♂	♓	8 4:09
♀	♊	12 8:42
☿	♊	20 17:24
☉	♊	21 4:54
☿	♋	4 4:42
♀	♋	5 19:20
♂	♈	20 20:54
☉	♋	21 13:01
☿	♌	27 6:42
♀	♌	30 8:55

Last Aspect / ☽ Ingress (May)

Last Aspect Dy Hr Mn			☽ Ingress	Dy Hr Mn
1 17:35	♂	⚹	♉	2 1:01
3 20:23	♂	□	♊	4 1:16
6 1:23	☿	⚹	♋	6 1:35
7 17:57	♀	⚹	♌	8 3:36
10 3:18	♀	□	♍	10 8:13
11 22:49	☉	△	♎	12 15:31
14 5:45	♄	△	♏	15 1:09
17 4:58	☉	☍	♐	17 12:41
19 6:27	♄	☍	♑	20 1:30
21 17:06	♅	□	♒	22 14:17
24 8:19	♄	△	♓	25 1:05
26 17:10	♄	□	♈	27 8:14
28 21:54	♄	⚹	♉	29 11:28
30 12:54	♂	⚹	♊	31 11:53

Last Aspect / ☽ Ingress (June)

Last Aspect Dy Hr Mn			☽ Ingress	Dy Hr Mn
2 5:29	☿	☌	♋	2 11:21
3 18:05	♅	□	♌	4 11:49
6 2:30	♄	⚹	♍	6 14:51
8 8:38	♄	□	♎	8 21:16
10 18:11	♄	△	♏	11 6:52
13 8:40	♂	△	♐	13 18:43
16 1:07	♂	□	♑	16 7:37
18 17:29	♂	⚹	♒	18 20:19
21 7:01	☉	△	♓	21 7:29
23 10:09	☿	△	♈	23 15:48
25 18:45	☿	□	♉	25 20:37
27 17:02	♀	⚹	♊	27 22:18
29 15:45	♄	☌	♋	29 22:08

☽ Phases & Eclipses

Dy Hr Mn		
2 20:55	●	12♉18
9 12:07	☽	18♌43
17 4:58	○	26♏09
25 8:40	☾	4♓00
1 4:34	●	10♊33
7 21:11	☽	16♍57
15 20:35	○	24♐35
15 20:50	☍	A 0.468
23 19:45	☾	2♈11
30 11:39	●	8♋32
30 11:37:57	☌	T 07'04"

Astro Data

1 May 1973
Julian Day # 26784
SVP 5♓37'40"
GC 26♐28.0 ⚳ 5♏04.9R
Eris 13♈08.7 ⚵ 21♐03.8R
⚷ 18♈13.5 ⚶ 26♊50.1
☽ Mean ☊ 10♑52.2

1 June 1973
Julian Day # 26815
SVP 5♓37'36"
GC 26♐28.1 ⚳ 27♎56.3R
Eris 13♈24.5 ⚵ 15♐28.7R
⚷ 19♈44.9 ⚶ 9♋31.0
☽ Mean ☊ 9♑13.8

July 1973 — LONGITUDE

Day	Sid.Time	☉	0 hr ☽	Noon ☽	True ☊	☿	♀	♂	⚳	♃	♄	♅	♆	♇
1 Su	6 37 36	9♋29 55	16♋18 37	23♋49 37	7♑40.1	2♌17.8	1♌22.5	6♈51.4	5♐12.2	10♒36.0	26♊12.2	18♎56.7	5♐11.5	1♎46.7
2 M	6 41 32	10 27 09	1♌17 15	8♌40 32	7R40.0	2 39.5	2 35.5	7 29.2	5R05.1	10R30.4	26 19.9	18 57.0	5R10.3	1 47.4
3 Tu	6 45 29	11 24 22	15 58 41	23 11 03	7 39.6	2 56.7	3 48.6	8 06.9	4 58.3	10 24.6	26 27.6	18 57.3	5 09.1	1 48.1
4 W	6 49 25	12 21 35	0♍17 11	7♍16 45	7 39.2	3 09.3	5 01.6	8 44.4	4 51.9	10 18.7	26 35.2	18 57.7	5 07.8	1 48.8
5 Th	6 53 22	13 18 48	14 09 36	20 55 47	7 38.7	3 17.3	6 14.6	9 21.7	4 45.8	10 12.7	26 42.8	18 58.1	5 06.6	1 49.6
6 F	6 57 19	14 16 01	27 35 23	4♎08 42	7D38.3	3R20.7	7 27.6	9 58.8	4 40.1	10 06.5	26 50.4	18 58.6	5 05.5	1 50.3
7 Sa	7 01 15	15 13 13	10♎36 01	16 57 47	7 38.2	3 19.3	8 40.5	10 35.7	4 34.8	10 00.3	26 58.0	18 59.2	5 04.3	1 51.2
8 Su	7 05 12	16 10 25	23 14 27	29 26 32	7 38.5	3 13.2	9 53.4	11 12.5	4 29.8	9 53.9	27 05.5	18 59.7	5 03.2	1 52.0
9 M	7 09 08	17 07 37	5♏34 32	11♏39 00	7 39.1	3 02.5	11 06.3	11 49.0	4 25.1	9 47.3	27 13.1	19 00.4	5 02.1	1 52.9
10 Tu	7 13 05	18 04 49	17 40 28	23 39 27	7 40.0	2 47.2	12 19.2	12 25.4	4 20.9	9 40.7	27 20.6	19 01.1	5 01.0	1 53.8
11 W	7 17 01	19 02 01	29 36 28	5♐32 00	7 41.1	2 27.6	13 32.1	13 01.6	4 17.0	9 34.0	27 28.0	19 01.8	4 59.9	1 54.7
12 Th	7 20 58	19 59 13	11♐26 31	17 20 27	7 42.1	2 03.8	14 44.9	13 37.6	4 13.4	9 27.2	27 35.5	19 02.6	4 58.9	1 55.7
13 F	7 24 54	20 56 25	23 14 12	29 08 10	7R42.8	1 36.1	15 57.7	14 13.3	4 10.3	9 20.2	27 42.9	19 03.5	4 57.9	1 56.7
14 Sa	7 28 51	21 53 37	5♑02 41	10♑58 06	7 42.9	1 04.9	17 10.5	14 48.9	4 07.5	9 13.2	27 50.3	19 04.4	4 56.9	1 57.7
15 Su	7 32 48	22 50 50	16 54 41	22 52 43	7 42.3	0 30.6	18 23.3	15 24.2	4 05.1	9 06.1	27 57.7	19 05.3	4 55.9	1 58.8
16 M	7 36 44	23 48 03	28 52 29	4♒54 12	7 41.0	29♋53.8	19 36.0	15 59.3	4 03.0	8 58.9	28 05.0	19 06.3	4 55.0	1 59.9
17 Tu	7 40 41	24 45 16	10♒58 06	17 04 25	7 39.0	29 14.9	20 48.7	16 34.2	4 01.3	8 51.7	28 12.3	19 07.4	4 54.1	2 01.0
18 W	7 44 37	25 42 30	23 13 22	29 25 08	7 36.4	28 34.7	22 01.4	17 08.8	4 00.0	8 44.3	28 19.5	19 08.5	4 53.2	2 02.1
19 Th	7 48 34	26 39 45	5♓39 58	11♓58 03	7 33.7	27 53.8	23 14.1	17 43.3	3 59.0	8 36.9	28 26.8	19 09.6	4 52.3	2 03.3
20 F	7 52 30	27 37 00	18 19 38	24 44 55	7 31.1	27 12.8	24 26.7	18 17.4	3 58.4	8 29.5	28 34.0	19 10.8	4 51.5	2 04.5
21 Sa	7 56 27	28 34 15	1♈14 07	7♈47 28	7 29.1	26 32.6	25 39.3	18 51.3	3D58.2	8 21.9	28 41.1	19 12.1	4 50.7	2 05.7
22 Su	8 00 23	29 31 32	14 25 10	21 07 24	7D27.9	25 53.8	26 51.9	19 25.0	3 58.3	8 14.4	28 48.2	19 13.4	4 49.9	2 07.0
23 M	8 04 20	0♌28 49	27 54 20	4♉46 04	7 27.8	25 17.2	28 04.5	19 58.3	3 58.8	8 06.7	28 55.3	19 14.7	4 49.1	2 08.3
24 Tu	8 08 17	1 26 08	11♉42 40	18 44 08	7 28.5	24 43.5	29 17.0	20 31.4	3 59.6	7 59.1	29 02.4	19 16.1	4 48.4	2 09.6
25 W	8 12 13	2 23 27	25 50 22	3♊01 11	7 29.8	24 13.2	0♍29.6	21 04.3	4 00.8	7 51.4	29 09.4	19 17.6	4 47.7	2 10.9
26 Th	8 16 10	3 20 48	10♊16 17	17 35 13	7 31.1	23 46.9	1 42.1	21 36.8	4 02.3	7 43.6	29 16.3	19 19.1	4 47.0	2 12.3
27 F	8 20 06	4 18 09	24 57 27	2♋22 18	7R32.0	23 25.3	2 54.5	22 09.0	4 04.3	7 35.9	29 23.2	19 20.6	4 46.4	2 13.7
28 Sa	8 24 03	5 15 32	9♋48 58	17 16 35	7 31.8	23 08.7	4 07.0	22 40.9	4 06.5	7 28.1	29 30.1	19 22.2	4 45.8	2 15.1
29 Su	8 27 59	6 12 55	24 44 11	2♌10 44	7 30.2	22 57.5	5 19.4	23 12.5	4 09.1	7 20.3	29 36.9	19 23.9	4 45.2	2 16.6
30 M	8 31 56	7 10 18	9♌35 15	16 56 44	7 27.3	22D52.1	6 31.8	23 43.7	4 12.1	7 12.5	29 43.7	19 25.6	4 44.7	2 18.0
31 Tu	8 35 52	8 07 43	24 14 17	1♍27 05	7 23.2	22 52.7	7 44.2	24 14.6	4 15.4	7 04.7	29 50.5	19 27.3	4 44.2	2 19.5

August 1973 — LONGITUDE

Day	Sid.Time	☉	0 hr ☽	Noon ☽	True ☊	☿	♀	♂	⚳	♃	♄	♅	♆	♇
1 W	8 39 49	9♌05 08	8♍34 28	15♍35 52	7♑18.6	22♋59.4	8♍56.5	24♈45.2	4♐19.0	6♒56.9	29♊57.1	19♎29.1	4♐43.7	2♎21.1
2 Th	8 43 46	10 02 34	22 30 57	29 19 29	7R14.0	23 12.6	10 08.8	25 15.4	4 23.0	6R49.1	0♋03.8	19 31.0	4R43.2	2 22.6
3 F	8 47 42	11 00 01	6♎01 25	12♎36 50	7 10.1	23 32.1	11 21.1	25 45.3	4 27.3	6 41.4	0 10.3	19 32.8	4 42.8	2 24.2
4 Sa	8 51 39	11 57 28	19 05 58	25 29 07	7 07.4	23 58.2	12 33.3	26 14.8	4 31.9	6 33.6	0 16.9	19 34.8	4 42.4	2 25.8
5 Su	8 55 35	12 54 56	1♏46 45	7♏59 19	7D06.1	24 30.7	13 45.5	26 43.9	4 36.9	6 25.9	0 23.4	19 36.8	4 42.0	2 27.4
6 M	8 59 32	13 52 25	14 07 24	20 11 35	7 06.2	25 09.7	14 57.7	27 12.7	4 42.2	6 18.2	0 29.8	19 38.8	4 41.7	2 29.0
7 Tu	9 03 28	14 49 54	26 12 29	2♐10 43	7 07.3	25 55.2	16 09.8	27 41.0	4 47.8	6 10.6	0 36.1	19 40.8	4 41.4	2 30.7
8 W	9 07 25	15 47 25	8♐06 56	14 01 44	7 08.9	26 47.0	17 21.9	28 09.0	4 53.7	6 03.0	0 42.5	19 43.0	4 41.1	2 32.4
9 Th	9 11 21	16 44 56	19 55 44	25 49 29	7R10.3	27 45.0	18 34.0	28 36.6	4 59.9	5 55.5	0 48.7	19 45.1	4 40.8	2 34.1
10 F	9 15 18	17 42 28	1♑43 33	7♑38 26	7 10.9	28 49.0	19 46.0	29 03.8	5 06.5	5 48.0	0 54.9	19 47.3	4 40.6	2 35.8
11 Sa	9 19 15	18 40 01	13 34 36	19 32 29	7 10.1	29 58.9	20 58.0	29 30.5	5 13.3	5 40.6	1 01.1	19 49.5	4 40.5	2 37.6
12 Su	9 23 11	19 37 35	25 32 26	1♒34 47	7 07.4	1♌14.6	22 09.9	29 56.8	5 20.5	5 33.2	1 07.1	19 51.8	4 40.3	2 39.4
13 M	9 27 08	20 35 10	7♒39 49	13 47 45	7 02.7	2 35.6	23 21.8	0♉22.7	5 27.9	5 25.9	1 13.2	19 54.1	4 40.2	2 41.2
14 Tu	9 31 04	21 32 47	19 58 45	26 12 56	6 56.4	4 01.8	24 33.7	0 48.1	5 35.7	5 18.7	1 19.1	19 56.5	4 40.1	2 43.0
15 W	9 35 01	22 30 24	2♓30 24	8♓51 10	6 48.8	5 32.9	25 45.5	1 13.1	5 43.7	5 11.6	1 25.0	19 58.9	4 40.1	2 44.8
16 Th	9 38 57	23 28 03	15 15 16	21 42 40	6 40.7	7 08.5	26 57.2	1 37.5	5 52.0	5 04.5	1 30.8	20 01.4	4D40.0	2 46.7
17 F	9 42 54	24 25 43	28 13 20	4♈47 14	6 33.0	8 48.2	28 09.0	2 01.5	6 00.6	4 57.6	1 36.6	20 03.8	4 40.0	2 48.6
18 Sa	9 46 50	25 23 25	11♈24 18	18 04 30	6 26.5	10 31.7	29 20.7	2 25.0	6 09.4	4 50.7	1 42.3	20 06.4	4 40.1	2 50.5
19 Su	9 50 47	26 21 08	24 47 48	1♉34 08	6 21.9	12 18.5	0♎32.3	2 48.0	6 18.6	4 43.9	1 47.9	20 08.9	4 40.2	2 52.4
20 M	9 54 44	27 18 53	8♉23 32	15 15 57	6D19.3	14 08.3	1 43.9	3 10.5	6 28.0	4 37.3	1 53.5	20 11.5	4 40.3	2 54.3
21 Tu	9 58 40	28 16 40	22 11 22	29 09 46	6 18.7	16 00.5	2 55.5	3 32.4	6 37.6	4 30.7	1 59.0	20 14.2	4 40.4	2 56.3
22 W	10 02 37	29 14 29	6♊11 07	13♊15 20	6 19.2	17 54.9	4 07.1	3 53.8	6 47.6	4 24.3	2 04.4	20 16.9	4 40.6	2 58.2
23 Th	10 06 33	0♍12 19	20 22 16	27 31 46	6R20.1	19 50.9	5 18.6	4 14.6	6 57.8	4 18.0	2 09.7	20 19.6	4 40.8	3 00.2
24 F	10 10 30	1 10 11	4♋43 32	11♋57 14	6 20.2	21 48.2	6 30.0	4 34.9	7 08.2	4 11.8	2 15.0	20 22.3	4 41.0	3 02.2
25 Sa	10 14 26	2 08 05	19 12 26	26 28 33	6 18.6	23 46.4	7 41.4	4 54.5	7 18.9	4 05.7	2 20.2	20 25.1	4 41.3	3 04.2
26 Su	10 18 23	3 06 00	3♌45 00	11♌01 03	6 14.7	25 45.2	8 52.8	5 13.5	7 29.9	3 59.8	2 25.3	20 27.9	4 41.6	3 06.3
27 M	10 22 19	4 03 57	18 15 57	25 28 55	6 08.3	27 44.2	10 04.1	5 31.9	7 41.1	3 54.0	2 30.4	20 30.8	4 42.0	3 08.3
28 Tu	10 26 16	5 01 56	2♍39 08	9♍45 52	5 59.8	29 43.3	11 15.4	5 49.7	7 52.5	3 48.3	2 35.4	20 33.7	4 42.3	3 10.4
29 W	10 30 13	5 59 56	16 48 24	23 46 08	5 50.2	1♍42.2	12 26.6	6 06.8	8 04.2	3 42.8	2 40.3	20 36.6	4 42.7	3 12.5
30 Th	10 34 09	6 57 57	0♎38 35	7♎25 23	5 40.3	3 40.7	13 37.8	6 23.2	8 16.1	3 37.5	2 45.1	20 39.6	4 43.2	3 14.6
31 F	10 38 06	7 56 00	14 06 18	20 41 16	5 31.3	5 38.5	14 49.0	6 39.0	8 28.3	3 32.2	2 49.8	20 42.6	4 43.6	3 16.7

Astro Data

	Dy Hr Mn
♂0N	1 2:19
☽0S	5 7:26
☿ R	6 17:00
☽0N	20 0:12
⚳ D	21 16:04
☿ D	30 21:48
☽0S	1 17:03
♅∠♆	7 17:14
☽0N	16 6:19
♆ D	16 16:05
♃⚹♆	20 1:20
♀0S	20 11:28
☽0S	29 3:17

Planet Ingress

		Dy Hr Mn
☿	♋R	16 8:03
☉	♌	22 23:56
♀	♍	25 2:13
♄	♋	1 22:20
☿	♌	11 12:21
♂	♉	12 14:56
♀	♎	19 1:10
☉	♍	23 6:53
☿	♍	28 15:22

Last Aspect / ☽ Ingress

Dy Hr Mn	Aspect	☽ Ingress	Dy Hr Mn
1 4:12	♅ □	♌	1 21:55
3 17:34	♄ ⚹	♍	3 23:31
5 22:31	♄ □	♎	6 4:23
8 7:23	♄ △	♏	8 13:05
9 23:51	☉ △	♐	11 0:48
13 9:05	♄ ☍	♑	13 13:45
15 11:56	☉ ☍	♒	16 2:15
18 9:52	♄ △	♓	18 13:07
20 19:09	♄ □	♈	20 21:43
23 1:42	♄ ⚹	♉	23 3:41
24 21:46	☿ ⚹	♊	25 6:58
27 7:08	♄ ☌	♋	27 8:10
28 21:18	☿ ☌	♌	29 8:29
31 9:17	♄ ⚹	♍	31 9:34

Last Aspect / ☽ Ingress

Dy Hr Mn	Aspect	☽ Ingress	Dy Hr Mn
2 1:01	☿ ⚹	♎	2 13:12
4 13:30	♂ ☍	♏	4 20:35
6 22:33	☿ △	♐	7 7:37
9 17:54	♂ △	♑	9 20:30
12 8:39	♂ □	♒	12 8:52
14 2:16	☉ ☍	♓	14 19:14
16 22:39	♀ ☍	♈	17 3:16
19 2:03	☉ △	♉	19 9:14
21 10:22	☉ □	♊	21 13:26
22 23:53	♅ △	♋	23 16:08
25 1:58	♅ □	♌	25 17:49
27 16:22	☿ ☌	♍	27 19:33
28 5:12	♂ △	♎	29 22:52

☽ Phases & Eclipses

Dy Hr Mn	
7 8:26	☽ 15♎05
15 11:56	○ 22♑51
15 11:39	☍ A 0.104
23 3:58	☾ 0♉10
29 18:59	● 6♌30
5 22:27	☽ 13♏20
14 2:16	○ 21♒09
21 10:22	☾ 28♉13
28 3:25	● 4♍41

Astro Data

1 July 1973
Julian Day # 26845
SVP 5♓37'30"
GC 26♐28.1 ⚴ 27♎41.7
Eris 13♈31.9 ⚵ 9♐12.0R
⚷ 20♈40.7 ⚶ 22♋31.0
☽ Mean ☊ 7♑38.5

1 August 1973
Julian Day # 26876
SVP 5♓37'25"
GC 26♐28.2 ⚴ 3♏19.2
Eris 13♈29.6R ⚵ 6♐32.5
⚷ 20♈52.7R ⚶ 6♌22.7
☽ Mean ☊ 6♑00.0

LONGITUDE — September 1973

Day	Sid.Time	☉	0 hr ☽	Noon ☽	True ☊	☿	♀	♂	⚳	♃	♄	♅	♆	♇
1 Sa	10 42 02	8♍54 05	27♎10 20	3♏33 41	5♑24.1	7♍35.7	16♎00.0	6♉54.1	8♐40.7	3♒27.2	2♋54.5	20♎45.6	4♐44.1	3♎18.8
2 Su	10 45 59	9 52 11	9♏51 37	16 04 31	5R19.2	9 32.0	17 11.1	7 08.5	8 53.3	3R22.3	2 59.0	20 48.6	4 44.7	3 20.9
3 M	10 49 55	10 50 18	22 12 54	28 17 17	5 16.5	11 27.4	18 22.1	7 22.2	9 06.1	3 17.5	3 03.5	20 51.7	4 45.2	3 23.1
4 Tu	10 53 52	11 48 27	4♐18 17	10♐16 32	5D15.6	13 21.8	19 33.0	7 35.2	9 19.2	3 13.0	3 07.9	20 54.9	4 45.8	3 25.2
5 W	10 57 48	12 46 37	16 12 43	22 07 30	5 15.9	15 15.2	20 43.9	7 47.5	9 32.5	3 08.6	3 12.2	20 58.0	4 46.5	3 27.4
6 Th	11 01 45	13 44 49	28 01 35	3♑55 37	5R16.3	17 07.4	21 54.7	7 59.0	9 45.9	3 04.3	3 16.5	21 01.2	4 47.1	3 29.6
7 F	11 05 42	14 43 02	9♑50 17	15 46 11	5 15.8	18 58.6	23 05.4	8 09.8	9 59.6	3 00.2	3 20.6	21 04.4	4 47.8	3 31.8
8 Sa	11 09 38	15 41 17	21 43 56	27 44 03	5 13.5	20 48.6	24 16.1	8 19.8	10 13.5	2 56.3	3 24.7	21 07.6	4 48.5	3 34.0
9 Su	11 13 35	16 39 33	3♒47 04	9♒53 22	5 08.8	22 37.4	25 26.7	8 29.0	10 27.6	2 52.6	3 28.6	21 10.9	4 49.3	3 36.2
10 M	11 17 31	17 37 51	16 03 21	22 17 17	5 01.4	24 25.2	26 37.3	8 37.4	10 41.9	2 49.1	3 32.5	21 14.2	4 50.1	3 38.4
11 Tu	11 21 28	18 36 11	28 35 22	4♓57 43	4 51.7	26 11.8	27 47.8	8 45.1	10 56.4	2 45.7	3 36.3	21 17.5	4 50.9	3 40.6
12 W	11 25 24	19 34 32	11♓24 21	17 55 14	4 40.2	27 57.2	28 58.2	8 51.9	11 11.0	2 42.5	3 40.0	21 20.8	4 51.7	3 42.9
13 Th	11 29 21	20 32 55	24 30 12	1♈09 04	4 28.0	29 41.6	0♏08.6	8 57.9	11 25.9	2 39.5	3 43.6	21 24.2	4 52.6	3 45.1
14 F	11 33 17	21 31 20	7♈51 33	14 37 20	4 16.2	1♎24.8	1 18.8	9 03.1	11 40.9	2 36.7	3 47.1	21 27.5	4 53.5	3 47.3
15 Sa	11 37 14	22 29 48	21 26 05	28 17 27	4 06.1	3 07.0	2 29.1	9 07.5	11 56.2	2 34.1	3 50.5	21 30.9	4 54.5	3 49.6
16 Su	11 41 10	23 28 17	5♉11 05	12♉06 39	3 58.3	4 48.0	3 39.2	9 11.0	12 11.6	2 31.6	3 53.8	21 34.4	4 55.4	3 51.9
17 M	11 45 07	24 26 48	19 03 51	26 02 27	3 53.4	6 28.1	4 49.3	9 13.6	12 27.1	2 29.4	3 57.0	21 37.8	4 56.4	3 54.1
18 Tu	11 49 04	25 25 22	3♊02 13	10♊02 59	3 51.1	8 07.1	5 59.3	9 15.3	12 42.9	2 27.3	4 00.1	21 41.3	4 57.5	3 56.4
19 W	11 53 00	26 23 58	17 04 37	24 07 01	3 50.5	9 45.0	7 09.3	9R16.2	12 58.8	2 25.5	4 03.2	21 44.8	4 58.5	3 58.7
20 Th	11 56 57	27 22 36	1♋10 05	8♋13 44	3 50.5	11 22.0	8 19.2	9 16.2	13 14.9	2 23.8	4 06.1	21 48.3	4 59.6	4 01.0
21 F	12 00 53	28 21 16	15 17 50	22 22 16	3 49.7	12 58.0	9 29.0	9 15.2	13 31.2	2 22.3	4 08.9	21 51.8	5 00.7	4 03.2
22 Sa	12 04 50	29 19 59	29 26 50	6♌31 17	3 47.0	14 33.0	10 38.7	9 13.4	13 47.6	2 21.0	4 11.7	21 55.4	5 01.9	4 05.5
23 Su	12 08 46	0♎18 43	13♌35 20	20 38 36	3 41.6	16 07.1	11 48.4	9 10.7	14 04.2	2 19.9	4 14.3	21 58.9	5 03.1	4 07.8
24 M	12 12 43	1 17 30	27 40 39	4♍41 02	3 33.2	17 40.2	12 58.0	9 07.1	14 21.0	2 19.0	4 16.8	22 02.5	5 04.3	4 10.1
25 Tu	12 16 39	2 16 19	11♍39 14	18 34 43	3 22.3	19 12.3	14 07.5	9 02.5	14 37.9	2 18.3	4 19.2	22 06.1	5 05.5	4 12.4
26 W	12 20 36	3 15 10	25 27 00	2♎15 35	3 09.8	20 43.5	15 16.9	8 57.1	14 54.9	2 17.8	4 21.5	22 09.7	5 06.8	4 14.7
27 Th	12 24 33	4 14 03	9♎00 04	15 40 05	2 57.0	22 13.8	16 26.3	8 50.8	15 12.2	2 17.5	4 23.7	22 13.4	5 08.1	4 17.0
28 F	12 28 29	5 12 58	22 15 22	28 45 47	2 45.1	23 43.2	17 35.6	8 43.6	15 29.5	2D17.4	4 25.8	22 17.0	5 09.4	4 19.3
29 Sa	12 32 26	6 11 55	5♏11 15	11♏31 51	2 35.1	25 11.6	18 44.7	8 35.5	15 47.0	2 17.5	4 27.8	22 20.7	5 10.7	4 21.6
30 Su	12 36 22	7 10 54	17 47 44	23 59 09	2 27.6	26 39.0	19 53.8	8 26.6	16 04.7	2 17.7	4 29.7	22 24.4	5 12.1	4 23.9

LONGITUDE — October 1973

Day	Sid.Time	☉	0 hr ☽	Noon ☽	True ☊	☿	♀	♂	⚳	♃	♄	♅	♆	♇
1 M	12 40 19	8♎09 54	0♐06 29	6♐10 08	2♑23.0	28♎05.5	21♏02.8	8♉16.9	16♐22.5	2♒18.2	4♋31.5	22♎28.0	5♐13.5	4♎26.2
2 Tu	12 44 15	9 08 57	12 10 37	18 08 30	2R20.7	29 31.0	22 11.7	8R06.3	16 40.4	2 18.9	4 33.2	22 31.7	5 14.9	4 28.5
3 W	12 48 12	10 08 01	24 04 24	29 58 58	2 20.1	0♏55.5	23 20.5	7 55.0	16 58.5	2 19.8	4 34.8	22 35.5	5 16.4	4 30.8
4 Th	12 52 08	11 07 07	5♑52 52	11♑46 49	2 20.1	2 19.0	24 29.2	7 42.8	17 16.7	2 20.9	4 36.2	22 39.2	5 17.9	4 33.1
5 F	12 56 05	12 06 15	17 41 28	23 37 34	2 19.7	3 41.5	25 37.8	7 29.9	17 35.1	2 22.1	4 37.6	22 42.9	5 19.4	4 35.4
6 Sa	13 00 02	13 05 24	29 35 45	5♒36 42	2 17.7	5 02.8	26 46.3	7 16.3	17 53.6	2 23.6	4 38.8	22 46.6	5 20.9	4 37.6
7 Su	13 03 58	14 04 36	11♒41 00	17 49 14	2 13.5	6 23.1	27 54.6	7 02.0	18 12.2	2 25.3	4 40.0	22 50.4	5 22.5	4 39.9
8 M	13 07 55	15 03 49	24 01 53	0♓19 22	2 06.7	7 42.1	29 02.9	6 47.1	18 30.9	2 27.1	4 41.0	22 54.1	5 24.0	4 42.2
9 Tu	13 11 51	16 03 04	6♓42 00	13 10 00	1 57.4	8 59.9	0♐11.0	6 31.5	18 49.7	2 29.2	4 41.9	22 57.9	5 25.6	4 44.4
10 W	13 15 48	17 02 20	19 43 28	26 22 24	1 46.3	10 16.4	1 19.0	6 15.3	19 08.7	2 31.4	4 42.7	23 01.6	5 27.3	4 46.7
11 Th	13 19 44	18 01 39	3♈06 37	9♈55 53	1 34.3	11 31.4	2 26.8	5 58.5	19 27.8	2 33.9	4 43.4	23 05.4	5 28.9	4 49.0
12 F	13 23 41	19 01 00	16 49 47	23 47 50	1 22.7	12 45.0	3 34.6	5 41.2	19 47.0	2 36.5	4 44.0	23 09.2	5 30.6	4 51.2
13 Sa	13 27 37	20 00 23	0♉49 29	7♉54 04	1 12.7	13 57.0	4 42.2	5 23.4	20 06.3	2 39.3	4 44.4	23 13.0	5 32.3	4 53.4
14 Su	13 31 34	20 59 48	15 00 58	22 09 29	1 05.1	15 07.2	5 49.6	5 05.1	20 25.7	2 42.3	4 44.8	23 16.7	5 34.0	4 55.7
15 M	13 35 31	21 59 15	29 19 00	6♊28 56	1 00.3	16 15.6	6 57.0	4 46.5	20 45.3	2 45.5	4 45.0	23 20.5	5 35.7	4 57.9
16 Tu	13 39 27	22 58 45	13♊38 44	20 47 58	0D58.1	17 21.9	8 04.2	4 27.4	21 04.9	2 48.9	4R45.2	23 24.3	5 37.5	5 00.1
17 W	13 43 24	23 58 16	27 56 15	5♋03 18	0 57.8	18 26.0	9 11.2	4 08.1	21 24.7	2 52.5	4 45.2	23 28.1	5 39.3	5 02.3
18 Th	13 47 20	24 57 51	12♋08 54	19 12 53	0R58.3	19 27.7	10 18.1	3 48.4	21 44.6	2 56.2	4 45.1	23 31.9	5 41.1	5 04.5
19 F	13 51 17	25 57 27	26 15 09	3♌15 36	0 58.2	20 26.7	11 24.8	3 28.6	22 04.5	3 00.1	4 44.9	23 35.6	5 42.9	5 06.7
20 Sa	13 55 13	26 57 06	10♌14 11	17 10 49	0 56.4	21 22.8	12 31.4	3 08.5	22 24.6	3 04.2	4 44.6	23 39.4	5 44.7	5 08.9
21 Su	13 59 10	27 56 47	24 05 27	0♍57 58	0 52.3	22 15.7	13 37.8	2 48.3	22 44.8	3 08.5	4 44.2	23 43.2	5 46.6	5 11.1
22 M	14 03 06	28 56 30	7♍48 16	14 36 11	0 45.5	23 04.9	14 44.1	2 28.1	23 05.0	3 13.0	4 43.7	23 47.0	5 48.5	5 13.2
23 Tu	14 07 03	29 56 15	21 21 33	28 04 11	0 36.6	23 50.3	15 50.1	2 07.8	23 25.4	3 17.7	4 43.0	23 50.7	5 50.4	5 15.3
24 W	14 10 59	0♏56 03	4♎43 52	11♎20 24	0 26.1	24 31.2	16 56.0	1 47.5	23 45.9	3 22.5	4 42.2	23 54.5	5 52.3	5 17.5
25 Th	14 14 56	1 55 52	17 53 35	24 23 15	0 15.3	25 07.3	18 01.8	1 27.4	24 06.5	3 27.5	4 41.4	23 58.3	5 54.2	5 19.6
26 F	14 18 53	2 55 44	0♏49 16	7♏11 32	0 05.2	25 38.1	19 07.3	1 07.4	24 27.1	3 32.7	4 40.4	24 02.0	5 56.2	5 21.7
27 Sa	14 22 49	3 55 38	13 30 02	19 44 46	29♐56.7	26 02.9	20 12.6	0 47.5	24 47.9	3 38.1	4 39.3	24 05.8	5 58.1	5 23.8
28 Su	14 26 46	4 55 33	25 55 51	2♐03 27	29 50.5	26 21.3	21 17.8	0 28.0	25 08.7	3 43.6	4 38.1	24 09.5	6 00.1	5 25.8
29 M	14 30 42	5 55 31	8♐07 48	14 09 12	29 46.8	26R32.5	22 22.7	0 08.7	25 29.6	3 49.3	4 36.8	24 13.2	6 02.1	5 27.9
30 Tu	14 34 39	6 55 30	20 08 02	26 04 42	29D45.3	26 36.1	23 27.4	29♈49.7	25 50.7	3 55.2	4 35.4	24 17.0	6 04.2	5 29.9
31 W	14 38 35	7 55 30	1♑59 43	7♑53 37	29 45.5	26 31.3	24 31.8	29 31.2	26 11.8	4 01.2	4 33.8	24 20.7	6 06.2	5 32.0

Astro Data

	Dy Hr Mn
♃△♇	2 16:39
♃⊼♄	5 1:47
☽0N	12 13:32
♄□♇	14 17:26
☿0S	14 18:13
♂R	19 23:20
☉0S	23 4:21
☽0S	25 12:16
♃D	28 13:26
♄□♇	7 12:48
☽0N	9 21:58
♄R	17 5:50
☽0S	22 18:51
☿R	30 10:29

Planet Ingress

	Dy Hr Mn
♀ ♏	13 9:05
☿ ♎	13 16:16
☉ ♎	23 4:21
☿ ♏	2 20:12
♀ ♐	9 8:08
☉ ♏	23 13:30
☊ ♐R	27 2:02
♂ ♈R	29 22:56

Last Aspect / ☽ Ingress

Last Aspect Dy Hr Mn		☽ Ingress Dy Hr Mn
31 12:02	♅ ☌	♏ 1 5:17
1 23:01	☉ ⚹	♐ 3 15:24
5 9:38	♅ ⚹	♑ 6 4:01
8 4:20	♀ □	♒ 8 16:30
10 21:07	♀ △	♓ 11 2:40
13 8:59	☿ ☍	♈ 13 9:56
15 0:06	♅ ☍	♉ 15 14:59
17 9:03	☉ △	♊ 17 18:48
19 16:11	☉ □	♋ 19 22:01
21 22:54	☉ ⚹	♌ 22 0:56
23 14:17	♅ ⚹	♍ 24 3:58
25 3:34	♀ ⚹	♎ 26 8:00
28 1:30	☿ ☌	♏ 28 14:18
30 3:15	♀ ☌	♐ 30 23:47

Last Aspect / ☽ Ingress

Last Aspect Dy Hr Mn		☽ Ingress Dy Hr Mn
2 20:55	♅ ⚹	♑ 3 12:02
5 16:28	♀ ⚹	♒ 6 0:49
8 9:20	♀ □	♓ 8 11:23
9 3:26	☿ △	♈ 10 18:29
12 10:53	♅ ☍	♉ 12 22:36
13 23:07	☿ ☍	♊ 15 1:09
16 16:24	♅ △	♋ 17 3:28
18 22:33	☉ □	♌ 19 6:25
21 6:19	☉ ⚹	♍ 21 10:19
23 3:59	☿ ⚹	♎ 23 15:28
25 11:13	♅ ☌	♏ 25 22:28
28 0:34	☿ ☌	♐ 28 7:57
30 19:24	♂ △	♑ 30 19:57

☽ Phases & Eclipses

Dy Hr Mn	
4 15:22	☽ 11♐57
12 15:16	○ 19♓42
19 16:11	☾ 26♊34
26 13:54	● 3♎20
4 10:32	☽ 11♑04
12 3:09	○ 18♈39
18 22:33	☾ 25♋24
26 3:17	● 2♏34

Astro Data

1 September 1973
Julian Day # 26907
SVP 5♓37'21"
GC 26♐28.3 ⚴ 12♏35.2
Eris 13♈18.0R ✱ 9♐00.4
⚷ 20♈16.1R ⚶ 20♌25.6
☽ Mean ☊ 4♑21.5

1 October 1973
Julian Day # 26937
SVP 5♓37'18"
GC 26♐28.4 ⚴ 23♏30.9
Eris 13♈01.0R ✱ 15♐11.4
⚷ 19♈05.8R ⚶ 3♍57.1
☽ Mean ☊ 2♑46.1

November 1973

LONGITUDE

Day	Sid.Time	☉	0 hr ☽	Noon ☽	True ☊	☿	♀	♂	⚳	♃	♄	♅	♆	♇
1 Th	14 42 32	8♏55 33	13♑46 57	19♑40 22	29♐46.7	26♏17.7	25♐36.1	29♈13.1	26♐32.9	4♒07.5	4♋32.2	24♎24.4	6♐08.2	5♎34.0
2 F	14 46 28	9 55 37	25 34 29	1♒29 58	29R 47.9	25R 54.7	26 40.1	28R 55.4	26 54.2	4 13.8	4R 30.4	24 28.1	6 10.3	5 36.0
3 Sa	14 50 25	10 55 42	7♒27 30	13 27 45	29 48.2	25 22.2	27 43.8	28 38.3	27 15.6	4 20.4	4 28.6	24 31.7	6 12.4	5 37.9
4 Su	14 54 22	11 55 50	19 31 22	25 39 00	29 47.0	24 40.0	28 47.2	28 21.7	27 37.0	4 27.1	4 26.6	24 35.4	6 14.5	5 39.9
5 M	14 58 18	12 55 58	1♓51 16	8♓08 41	29 43.9	23 48.5	29 50.4	28 05.7	27 58.5	4 33.9	4 24.6	24 39.0	6 16.6	5 41.8
6 Tu	15 02 15	13 56 08	14 31 44	21 00 48	29 38.9	22 48.2	0♑53.3	27 50.3	28 20.0	4 40.9	4 22.4	24 42.7	6 18.7	5 43.7
7 W	15 06 11	14 56 20	27 36 10	4♈17 59	29 32.4	21 40.3	1 55.9	27 35.6	28 41.7	4 48.1	4 20.2	24 46.3	6 20.8	5 45.6
8 Th	15 10 08	15 56 33	11♈06 15	18 00 50	29 25.1	20 26.4	2 58.2	27 21.5	29 03.4	4 55.4	4 17.8	24 49.9	6 22.9	5 47.5
9 F	15 14 04	16 56 48	25 01 27	2♉07 37	29 17.8	19 08.3	4 00.1	27 08.1	29 25.2	5 02.9	4 15.3	24 53.5	6 25.1	5 49.4
10 Sa	15 18 01	17 57 05	9♉18 44	16 34 05	29 11.6	17 48.5	5 01.7	26 55.4	29 47.0	5 10.5	4 12.8	24 57.0	6 27.3	5 51.2
11 Su	15 21 57	18 57 23	23 52 49	1♊14 02	29 07.1	16 29.4	6 03.0	26 43.5	0♑08.9	5 18.3	4 10.1	25 00.6	6 29.4	5 53.0
12 M	15 25 54	19 57 44	8♊36 48	16 00 10	29D 04.5	15 13.7	7 03.9	26 32.3	0 30.9	5 26.2	4 07.4	25 04.1	6 31.6	5 54.8
13 Tu	15 29 51	20 58 06	23 23 14	0♋45 10	29 03.8	14 03.9	8 04.5	26 21.8	0 53.0	5 34.3	4 04.5	25 07.6	6 33.8	5 56.6
14 W	15 33 47	21 58 30	8♋05 13	15 22 44	29 04.6	13 02.0	9 04.6	26 12.1	1 15.1	5 42.5	4 01.6	25 11.1	6 36.0	5 58.3
15 Th	15 37 44	22 58 55	22 37 14	29 48 16	29 06.1	12 09.7	10 04.4	26 03.2	1 37.2	5 50.8	3 58.5	25 14.6	6 38.2	6 00.1
16 F	15 41 40	23 59 23	6♌55 34	13♌58 56	29R 07.4	11 28.2	11 03.8	25 55.1	1 59.5	5 59.3	3 55.4	25 18.0	6 40.4	6 01.8
17 Sa	15 45 37	24 59 53	20 58 14	27 53 27	29 07.7	10 58.3	12 02.7	25 47.8	2 21.8	6 07.9	3 52.2	25 21.5	6 42.6	6 03.4
18 Su	15 49 33	26 00 24	4♍44 37	11♍31 46	29 06.6	10 40.0	13 01.2	25 41.2	2 44.1	6 16.7	3 48.9	25 24.9	6 44.8	6 05.1
19 M	15 53 30	27 00 57	18 15 00	24 54 25	29 04.0	10D 33.4	13 59.3	25 35.5	3 06.5	6 25.6	3 45.5	25 28.2	6 47.1	6 06.7
20 Tu	15 57 26	28 01 32	1♎30 09	8♎02 18	29 00.0	10 37.8	14 56.9	25 30.6	3 29.0	6 34.6	3 42.0	25 31.6	6 49.3	6 08.3
21 W	16 01 23	29 02 08	14 30 58	20 56 17	28 55.1	10 52.6	15 54.0	25 26.5	3 51.5	6 43.8	3 38.5	25 34.9	6 51.6	6 09.9
22 Th	16 05 20	0♐02 47	27 18 20	3♏37 13	28 49.9	11 17.0	16 50.6	25 23.3	4 14.1	6 53.1	3 34.8	25 38.2	6 53.8	6 11.5
23 F	16 09 16	1 03 27	9♏53 03	16 05 55	28 45.0	11 50.1	17 46.7	25 20.8	4 36.8	7 02.5	3 31.1	25 41.5	6 56.0	6 13.0
24 Sa	16 13 13	2 04 08	22 15 56	28 23 13	28 41.1	12 31.0	18 42.2	25 19.2	4 59.5	7 12.0	3 27.3	25 44.7	6 58.3	6 14.5
25 Su	16 17 09	3 04 51	4♐27 56	10♐30 15	28 38.3	13 18.8	19 37.1	25D 18.4	5 22.2	7 21.7	3 23.5	25 48.0	7 00.6	6 16.0
26 M	16 21 06	4 05 35	16 30 22	22 28 30	28D 37.0	14 12.8	20 31.5	25 18.4	5 45.0	7 31.5	3 19.5	25 51.1	7 02.8	6 17.4
27 Tu	16 25 02	5 06 20	28 24 56	4♑19 58	28 37.0	15 12.1	21 25.2	25 19.2	6 07.8	7 41.4	3 15.5	25 54.3	7 05.1	6 18.8
28 W	16 28 59	6 07 07	10♑13 57	16 07 17	28 38.0	16 16.0	22 18.3	25 20.8	6 30.7	7 51.5	3 11.4	25 57.4	7 07.3	6 20.2
29 Th	16 32 56	7 07 54	22 00 22	27 53 41	28 39.6	17 24.0	23 10.7	25 23.2	6 53.6	8 01.6	3 07.3	26 00.5	7 09.6	6 21.6
30 F	16 36 52	8 08 43	3♒47 44	9♒43 02	28 41.4	18 35.5	24 02.4	25 26.3	7 16.6	8 11.9	3 03.1	26 03.6	7 11.9	6 22.9

December 1973

LONGITUDE

Day	Sid.Time	☉	0 hr ☽	Noon ☽	True ☊	☿	♀	♂	⚳	♃	♄	♅	♆	♇
1 Sa	16 40 49	9♐09 32	15♒40 10	21♒39 41	28♐42.8	19♏49.9	24♑53.4	25♈30.2	7♑39.6	8♒22.3	2♋58.8	26♎06.6	7♐14.1	6♎24.2
2 Su	16 44 45	10 10 23	27 42 13	3♓48 20	28R 43.7	21 06.9	25 43.6	25 34.9	8 02.7	8 32.8	2R 54.5	26 09.6	7 16.4	6 25.5
3 M	16 48 42	11 11 14	9♓58 39	16 13 45	28 43.7	22 26.2	26 33.0	25 40.4	8 25.8	8 43.4	2 50.1	26 12.6	7 18.6	6 26.7
4 Tu	16 52 38	12 12 06	22 34 11	29 00 27	28 43.0	23 47.3	27 21.6	25 46.5	8 48.9	8 54.1	2 45.6	26 15.5	7 20.9	6 27.9
5 W	16 56 35	13 12 59	5♈32 59	12♈12 07	28 41.5	25 10.0	28 09.3	25 53.4	9 12.1	9 04.9	2 41.1	26 18.4	7 23.1	6 29.1
6 Th	17 00 31	14 13 53	18 58 06	25 51 02	28 39.7	26 34.1	28 56.1	26 01.0	9 35.3	9 15.8	2 36.6	26 21.2	7 25.4	6 30.3
7 F	17 04 28	15 14 47	2♉50 54	9♉57 28	28 37.8	27 59.4	29 41.9	26 09.3	9 58.5	9 26.8	2 32.0	26 24.0	7 27.6	6 31.4
8 Sa	17 08 25	16 15 43	17 10 22	24 29 02	28 36.2	29 25.6	0♒26.7	26 18.3	10 21.8	9 38.0	2 27.4	26 26.8	7 29.9	6 32.5
9 Su	17 12 21	17 16 39	1♊52 45	9♊20 39	28 35.1	0♐52.8	1 10.6	26 27.9	10 45.1	9 49.2	2 22.7	26 29.6	7 32.1	6 33.5
10 M	17 16 18	18 17 36	16 51 41	24 24 47	28D 34.6	2 20.7	1 53.3	26 38.2	11 08.5	10 00.5	2 18.0	26 32.3	7 34.4	6 34.6
11 Tu	17 20 14	19 18 34	1♋58 46	9♋32 29	28 34.7	3 49.2	2 35.0	26 49.1	11 31.9	10 12.0	2 13.2	26 34.9	7 36.6	6 35.6
12 W	17 24 11	20 19 33	17 04 47	24 34 36	28 35.3	5 18.3	3 15.4	27 00.6	11 55.3	10 23.5	2 08.5	26 37.6	7 38.8	6 36.5
13 Th	17 28 07	21 20 33	2♌01 01	9♌23 13	28 35.9	6 47.9	3 54.7	27 12.8	12 18.7	10 35.1	2 03.6	26 40.1	7 41.0	6 37.5
14 F	17 32 04	22 21 34	16 40 30	23 52 25	28 36.6	8 17.9	4 32.7	27 25.5	12 42.2	10 46.8	1 58.8	26 42.7	7 43.2	6 38.4
15 Sa	17 36 00	23 22 36	0♍58 35	7♍58 50	28 37.0	9 48.2	5 09.5	27 38.8	13 05.7	10 58.6	1 53.9	26 45.2	7 45.4	6 39.2
16 Su	17 39 57	24 23 39	14 53 06	21 41 25	28R 37.2	11 18.9	5 44.8	27 52.7	13 29.2	11 10.4	1 49.0	26 47.6	7 47.6	6 40.1
17 M	17 43 54	25 24 42	28 23 58	5♎00 58	28 37.1	12 49.9	6 18.8	28 07.1	13 52.7	11 22.4	1 44.1	26 50.0	7 49.8	6 40.9
18 Tu	17 47 50	26 25 47	11♎32 43	17 59 33	28 37.0	14 21.2	6 51.3	28 22.1	14 16.3	11 34.5	1 39.2	26 52.4	7 52.0	6 41.6
19 W	17 51 47	27 26 53	24 21 49	0♏39 55	28 36.8	15 52.8	7 22.3	28 37.6	14 39.9	11 46.6	1 34.3	26 54.7	7 54.2	6 42.4
20 Th	17 55 43	28 27 59	6♏54 12	13 05 04	28D 36.7	17 24.6	7 51.8	28 53.7	15 03.5	11 58.8	1 29.3	26 57.0	7 56.3	6 43.0
21 F	17 59 40	29 29 06	19 12 51	25 17 55	28 36.8	18 56.6	8 19.6	29 10.2	15 27.2	12 11.1	1 24.4	26 59.3	7 58.4	6 43.7
22 Sa	18 03 36	0♑30 14	1♐20 35	7♐21 10	28 36.9	20 28.8	8 45.7	29 27.3	15 50.8	12 23.5	1 19.4	27 01.5	8 00.6	6 44.3
23 Su	18 07 33	1 31 23	13 19 58	19 17 16	28R 37.1	22 01.3	9 10.0	29 44.9	16 14.5	12 35.9	1 14.4	27 03.6	8 02.7	6 44.9
24 M	18 11 29	2 32 32	25 13 18	1♑08 22	28 37.1	23 34.0	9 32.5	0♉02.9	16 38.2	12 48.5	1 09.5	27 05.7	8 04.8	6 45.5
25 Tu	18 15 26	3 33 41	7♑02 43	12 56 35	28 37.0	25 07.0	9 53.1	0 21.5	17 02.0	13 01.1	1 04.5	27 07.7	8 06.9	6 46.0
26 W	18 19 23	4 34 51	18 50 15	24 43 59	28 36.5	26 40.2	10 11.8	0 40.4	17 25.7	13 13.8	0 59.5	27 09.8	8 09.0	6 46.5
27 Th	18 23 19	5 36 00	0♒38 04	6♒32 48	28 35.6	28 13.6	10 28.4	0 59.9	17 49.5	13 26.5	0 54.6	27 11.7	8 11.1	6 47.0
28 F	18 27 16	6 37 10	12 28 32	18 25 36	28 34.5	29 47.3	10 42.9	1 19.8	18 13.2	13 39.3	0 49.6	27 13.6	8 13.1	6 47.4
29 Sa	18 31 12	7 38 20	24 24 23	0♓25 17	28 33.2	1♑21.3	10 55.2	1 40.1	18 37.0	13 52.2	0 44.7	27 15.5	8 15.2	6 47.8
30 Su	18 35 09	8 39 30	6♓28 43	12 35 10	28 32.0	2 55.5	11 05.3	2 00.8	19 00.8	14 05.2	0 39.8	27 17.3	8 17.2	6 48.1
31 M	18 39 05	9 40 40	18 45 04	24 58 55	28 31.1	4 30.1	11 13.2	2 21.9	19 24.6	14 18.2	0 34.9	27 19.0	8 19.2	6 48.4

Astro Data

	Dy Hr Mn
♃⚻♄	4 10:50
☽0N	6 6:53
♃△♇	16 20:35
☽0S	18 23:42
☿D	19 14:14
♃⚹♆	22 14:30
♂D	26 0:06
☽0N	3 15:12
☽0S	16 5:14
☽0N	30 22:20

Planet Ingress

		Dy Hr Mn
♀	♑	5 15:39
⚳	♑	11 2:14
☉	♐	22 10:54
♀	♒	7 21:37
☿	♐	8 21:29
☉	♑	22 0:08
♂	♉	24 8:09
☿	♑	28 15:14

Last Aspect / ☽ Ingress (November)

Last Aspect Dy Hr Mn		☽ Ingress	Dy Hr Mn
2 6:55	♂□	♒	2 8:58
4 18:39	♀⚹	♓	4 20:26
6 15:02	☿△	♈	7 4:19
9 3:43	♂☌	♉	9 8:25
10 14:27	☉☍	♊	11 9:59
13 4:56	♂⚹	♋	13 10:46
15 5:47	♂□	♌	15 12:20
17 8:23	♂△	♍	17 15:41
19 16:08	☉⚹	♎	19 21:15
21 20:47	♅☌	♏	22 5:06
23 15:31	♀⚹	♐	24 15:11
26 18:51	♅⚹	♑	27 3:13
29 8:09	♅□	♒	29 16:17

Last Aspect / ☽ Ingress (December)

Last Aspect Dy Hr Mn		☽ Ingress	Dy Hr Mn
1 20:53	♅△	♓	2 4:32
4 8:45	♀⚹	♈	4 13:50
6 17:37	♀□	♉	6 19:08
8 20:54	☿☍	♊	8 20:58
10 15:34	♂⚹	♋	10 20:52
12 15:58	♂□	♌	12 20:44
14 18:04	♂△	♍	14 22:20
16 17:13	☉□	♎	17 2:53
19 8:01	♂☍	♏	19 10:44
20 9:49	♃□	♐	21 21:20
24 3:46	♅⚹	♑	24 9:41
26 16:57	♅□	♒	26 22:43
29 5:41	♅△	♓	29 11:10
30 3:36	☉⚹	♈	31 21:34

☽ Phases & Eclipses

Dy Hr Mn	
3 6:29	☽ 10♒42
10 14:27	○ 18♉03
17 6:34	☾ 24♌46
24 19:55	● 2♐24
3 1:29	☽ 10♓45
10 1:35	○ 17♊51
10 1:44	• P 0.101
16 17:13	☾ 24♍37
24 15:07	● 2♑40
24 15:02:00	• A 12'02"

Astro Data

1 November 1973
Julian Day # 26968
SVP 5♓37'15"
GC 26♐28.4 ⚴ 5♐54.4
Eris 12♈42.6R ⚵ 24♐11.8
⚷ 17♈42.6R ⚶ 17♍29.5
☽ Mean ☊ 1♑07.6

1 December 1973
Julian Day # 26998
SVP 5♓37'10"
GC 26♐28.5 ⚴ 18♐21.5
Eris 12♈29.2R ⚵ 4♑32.3
⚷ 16♈42.0R ⚶ 29♍35.7
☽ Mean ☊ 29♐32.3

LONGITUDE — January 1974

Day	Sid.Time	☉	0 hr ☽	Noon ☽	True ☊	☿	♀	♂	⚳	♃	♄	♅	♆	♇
1 Tu	18 43 02	10♑41 49	1♈17 12	7♈40 23	28♐30.6	6♑04.9	11♒18.6	2♉43.4	19♑48.4	14♒31.2	0♋30.1	27♎20.7	8♐21.2	6♎48.7
2 W	18 46 58	11 42 58	14 08 56	20 43 17	28D30.8	7 40.1	11R21.7	3 05.3	20 12.3	14 44.4	0R25.3	27 22.4	8 23.1	6 49.0
3 Th	18 50 55	12 44 07	27 23 47	4♉10 45	28 31.5	9 15.6	11 22.3	3 27.6	20 36.1	14 57.6	0 20.5	27 24.0	8 25.1	6 49.2
4 F	18 54 52	13 45 16	11♉04 23	18 04 45	28 32.7	10 51.4	11 20.5	3 50.3	20 59.9	15 10.8	0 15.7	27 25.5	8 27.0	6 49.3
5 Sa	18 58 48	14 46 25	25 11 49	2♊25 22	28 33.9	12 27.7	11 16.1	4 13.3	21 23.8	15 24.1	0 11.0	27 27.0	8 29.0	6 49.5
6 Su	19 02 45	15 47 33	9♊45 00	17 10 09	28R34.8	14 04.3	11 09.2	4 36.6	21 47.6	15 37.5	0 06.3	27 28.5	8 30.9	6 49.6
7 M	19 06 41	16 48 41	24 40 04	2♋13 47	28 35.1	15 41.3	10 59.8	5 00.3	22 11.5	15 50.9	0 01.6	27 29.9	8 32.7	6 49.7
8 Tu	19 10 38	17 49 49	9♋50 15	17 28 14	28 34.3	17 18.7	10 47.8	5 24.3	22 35.3	16 04.4	29♊57.0	27 31.2	8 34.6	6R49.7
9 W	19 14 34	18 50 57	25 06 29	2♌43 40	28 32.5	18 56.5	10 33.3	5 48.6	22 59.2	16 17.9	29 52.5	27 32.5	8 36.4	6 49.7
10 Th	19 18 31	19 52 04	10♌18 31	17 49 50	28 29.9	20 34.8	10 16.4	6 13.2	23 23.0	16 31.5	29 47.9	27 33.7	8 38.3	6 49.7
11 F	19 22 28	20 53 11	25 16 34	2♍37 49	28 26.7	22 13.5	9 57.0	6 38.1	23 46.9	16 45.1	29 43.5	27 34.9	8 40.1	6 49.6
12 Sa	19 26 24	21 54 18	9♍52 50	17 01 08	28 23.6	23 52.7	9 35.4	7 03.3	24 10.8	16 58.7	29 39.1	27 36.0	8 41.8	6 49.5
13 Su	19 30 21	22 55 25	24 02 23	0♎56 27	28 21.1	25 32.3	9 11.5	7 28.8	24 34.6	17 12.4	29 34.7	27 37.1	8 43.6	6 49.4
14 M	19 34 17	23 56 32	7♎43 22	14 23 20	28D19.5	27 12.4	8 45.5	7 54.6	24 58.5	17 26.2	29 30.4	27 38.1	8 45.3	6 49.2
15 Tu	19 38 14	24 57 39	20 56 39	27 23 43	28 19.2	28 53.0	8 17.5	8 20.6	25 22.4	17 40.0	29 26.2	27 39.1	8 47.0	6 49.0
16 W	19 42 10	25 58 45	3♏45 02	10♏01 06	28 20.0	0♒34.0	7 47.7	8 46.9	25 46.2	17 53.8	29 22.0	27 40.0	8 48.7	6 48.7
17 Th	19 46 07	26 59 52	16 12 31	22 19 49	28 21.5	2 15.4	7 16.2	9 13.5	26 10.1	18 07.7	29 17.9	27 40.8	8 50.4	6 48.4
18 F	19 50 03	28 00 58	28 23 35	4♐24 24	28 23.4	3 57.3	6 43.3	9 40.3	26 33.9	18 21.6	29 13.8	27 41.6	8 52.1	6 48.1
19 Sa	19 54 00	29 02 04	10♐22 47	16 19 16	28 25.0	5 39.5	6 09.1	10 07.3	26 57.8	18 35.5	29 09.9	27 42.4	8 53.7	6 47.8
20 Su	19 57 57	0♒03 09	22 14 19	28 08 23	28R25.6	7 22.1	5 33.9	10 34.7	27 21.6	18 49.5	29 06.0	27 43.0	8 55.3	6 47.4
21 M	20 01 53	1 04 14	4♑01 53	9♑55 11	28 24.9	9 05.0	4 57.9	11 02.2	27 45.4	19 03.5	29 02.1	27 43.7	8 56.8	6 47.0
22 Tu	20 05 50	2 05 18	15 48 38	21 42 30	28 22.4	10 48.1	4 21.3	11 30.0	28 09.3	19 17.6	28 58.4	27 44.2	8 58.4	6 46.6
23 W	20 09 46	3 06 22	27 37 06	3♒32 38	28 18.2	12 31.4	3 44.4	11 58.0	28 33.1	19 31.7	28 54.7	27 44.8	8 59.9	6 46.1
24 Th	20 13 43	4 07 25	9♒29 22	15 27 28	28 12.3	14 14.8	3 07.5	12 26.2	28 56.9	19 45.8	28 51.1	27 45.2	9 01.4	6 45.6
25 F	20 17 39	5 08 27	21 27 09	27 28 36	28 05.4	15 58.1	2 30.8	12 54.7	29 20.7	19 59.9	28 47.6	27 45.6	9 02.9	6 45.0
26 Sa	20 21 36	6 09 28	3♓32 01	9♓37 37	27 58.0	17 41.2	1 54.5	13 23.3	29 44.4	20 14.1	28 44.2	27 45.9	9 04.3	6 44.4
27 Su	20 25 32	7 10 28	15 45 34	21 56 09	27 50.9	19 23.9	1 18.9	13 52.2	0♒08.2	20 28.2	28 40.8	27 46.2	9 05.7	6 43.8
28 M	20 29 29	8 11 26	28 09 36	4♈26 12	27 44.9	21 06.1	0 44.2	14 21.2	0 31.9	20 42.4	28 37.6	27 46.5	9 07.1	6 43.2
29 Tu	20 33 26	9 12 24	10♈46 14	17 10 02	27 40.7	22 47.5	0 10.7	14 50.5	0 55.6	20 56.7	28 34.4	27 46.6	9 08.4	6 42.5
30 W	20 37 22	10 13 21	23 37 55	0♉10 14	27D38.3	24 27.8	29♑38.5	15 19.9	1 19.3	21 10.9	28 31.3	27 46.8	9 09.8	6 41.8
31 Th	20 41 19	11 14 16	6♉47 20	13 29 30	27 37.8	26 06.6	29 07.9	15 49.5	1 43.0	21 25.2	28 28.4	27R46.8	9 11.1	6 41.1

LONGITUDE — February 1974

Day	Sid.Time	☉	0 hr ☽	Noon ☽	True ☊	☿	♀	♂	⚳	♃	♄	♅	♆	♇
1 F	20 45 15	12♒15 10	20♉17 02	27♉10 10	27♐38.6	27♒43.7	28♑39.1	16♉19.3	2♒06.7	21♒39.5	28♊25.5	27♎46.8	9♐12.3	6♎40.3
2 Sa	20 49 12	13 16 03	4♊09 02	11♊13 42	27 39.9	29 18.6	28R12.1	16 49.3	2 30.3	21 53.8	28R22.7	27R46.8	9 13.6	6R39.5
3 Su	20 53 08	14 16 54	18 24 05	25 39 58	27R40.7	0♓50.7	27 47.2	17 19.4	2 54.0	22 08.1	28 20.0	27 46.7	9 14.8	6 38.7
4 M	20 57 05	15 17 44	3♋00 57	10♋26 29	27 40.1	2 19.6	27 24.5	17 49.7	3 17.6	22 22.4	28 17.4	27 46.5	9 16.0	6 37.8
5 Tu	21 01 01	16 18 33	17 55 49	25 28 02	27 37.3	3 44.7	27 04.0	18 20.1	3 41.1	22 36.8	28 14.9	27 46.3	9 17.1	6 37.0
6 W	21 04 58	17 19 20	3♌02 04	10♌36 43	27 32.2	5 05.2	26 45.9	18 50.7	4 04.7	22 51.1	28 12.5	27 46.0	9 18.2	6 36.1
7 Th	21 08 55	18 20 06	18 10 45	25 42 51	27 25.1	6 20.6	26 30.2	19 21.5	4 28.2	23 05.5	28 10.3	27 45.7	9 19.3	6 35.1
8 F	21 12 51	19 20 51	3♍11 48	10♍36 28	27 16.7	7 30.0	26 17.0	19 52.3	4 51.7	23 19.9	28 08.1	27 45.3	9 20.4	6 34.1
9 Sa	21 16 48	20 21 34	17 55 49	25 09 02	27 08.1	8 32.7	26 06.3	20 23.3	5 15.2	23 34.2	28 06.0	27 44.9	9 21.4	6 33.1
10 Su	21 20 44	21 22 17	2♎15 30	9♎14 48	27 00.4	9 28.0	25 58.0	20 54.5	5 38.7	23 48.6	28 04.0	27 44.4	9 22.4	6 32.1
11 M	21 24 41	22 22 58	16 06 42	22 51 13	26 54.4	10 15.2	25 52.3	21 25.8	6 02.1	24 03.0	28 02.1	27 43.8	9 23.4	6 31.1
12 Tu	21 28 37	23 23 38	29 28 28	5♏58 48	26 50.5	10 53.5	25D49.1	21 57.2	6 25.5	24 17.4	28 00.3	27 43.3	9 24.3	6 30.0
13 W	21 32 34	24 24 17	12♏22 37	18 40 27	26D48.8	11 22.3	25 48.3	22 28.7	6 48.8	24 31.8	27 58.7	27 42.6	9 25.2	6 28.9
14 Th	21 36 30	25 24 55	24 52 53	1♐00 34	26 48.8	11 41.2	25 50.0	23 00.4	7 12.2	24 46.2	27 57.1	27 41.9	9 26.1	6 27.8
15 F	21 40 27	26 25 32	7♐04 09	13 04 21	26 49.6	11R49.8	25 54.0	23 32.2	7 35.5	25 00.6	27 55.7	27 41.1	9 26.9	6 26.6
16 Sa	21 44 24	27 26 08	19 01 50	24 57 14	26R50.2	11 47.9	26 00.4	24 04.1	7 58.7	25 15.0	27 54.3	27 40.3	9 27.7	6 25.4
17 Su	21 48 20	28 26 43	0♑51 14	6♑44 24	26 49.7	11 35.7	26 09.1	24 36.2	8 22.0	25 29.4	27 53.1	27 39.5	9 28.5	6 24.3
18 M	21 52 17	29 27 16	12 37 19	18 30 29	26 47.1	11 13.3	26 20.0	25 08.3	8 45.2	25 43.8	27 52.0	27 38.6	9 29.3	6 23.0
19 Tu	21 56 13	0♓27 48	24 24 24	0♒19 28	26 41.9	10 41.3	26 33.1	25 40.6	9 08.3	25 58.1	27 51.0	27 37.6	9 30.0	6 21.8
20 W	22 00 10	1 28 18	6♒16 02	12 14 26	26 33.9	10 00.6	26 48.2	26 13.0	9 31.5	26 12.5	27 50.1	27 36.6	9 30.6	6 20.5
21 Th	22 04 06	2 28 47	18 14 55	24 17 41	26 23.5	9 12.2	27 05.4	26 45.5	9 54.6	26 26.9	27 49.3	27 35.5	9 31.3	6 19.2
22 F	22 08 03	3 29 14	0♓22 53	6♓30 38	26 11.3	8 17.3	27 24.6	27 18.1	10 17.6	26 41.3	27 48.6	27 34.4	9 31.9	6 17.9
23 Sa	22 11 59	4 29 39	12 41 01	18 54 05	25 58.3	7 17.5	27 45.6	27 50.7	10 40.6	26 55.6	27 48.1	27 33.2	9 32.5	6 16.6
24 Su	22 15 56	5 30 03	25 09 52	1♈28 24	25 45.7	6 14.3	28 08.5	28 23.5	11 03.6	27 09.9	27 47.6	27 32.0	9 33.0	6 15.2
25 M	22 19 52	6 30 25	7♈49 41	14 13 47	25 34.6	5 09.4	28 33.1	28 56.4	11 26.5	27 24.3	27 47.3	27 30.8	9 33.5	6 13.9
26 Tu	22 23 49	7 30 45	20 40 43	27 10 36	25 25.9	4 04.4	28 59.4	29 29.4	11 49.4	27 38.6	27 47.1	27 29.4	9 34.0	6 12.5
27 W	22 27 46	8 31 03	3♉43 30	10♉19 33	25 20.2	3 00.9	29 27.4	0♊02.5	12 12.2	27 52.8	27D47.0	27 28.1	9 34.4	6 11.1
28 Th	22 31 42	9 31 20	16 58 55	23 41 46	25 17.1	2 00.1	29 56.9	0 35.7	12 35.0	28 07.1	27 47.0	27 26.7	9 34.8	6 09.6

Astro Data

	Dy Hr Mn
♀R	3 6:06
♃⚼♄	4 18:29
♇R	9 0:52
☽0S	12 13:37
☽0N	27 4:38
♅R	1 2:57
♃⚼♇	1 13:20
☽0S	9 0:31
♀D	13 7:28
☿R	15 19:47
☽0N	23 11:01
♃△♅	25 22:00
♃△♄	27 2:13
♄D	27 21:14

Planet Ingress

	Dy Hr Mn
♄ ♊R	7 20:26
☿ ♒	16 3:56
☉ ♒	20 10:46
⚳ ♒	27 3:44
♀ ♑R	29 19:51
☿ ♓	2 22:42
☉ ♓	19 0:59
♂ ♊	27 10:11
♀ ♒	28 14:25

Last Aspect / ☽ Ingress (January)

Last Aspect Dy Hr Mn		☽ Ingress Dy Hr Mn
2 23:59	♅ ☍	♉ 3 4:38
4 6:59	♃ □	♊ 5 8:00
7 4:29	♅ △	♋ 7 8:28
9 3:49	♅ □	♌ 9 7:42
11 7:16	♄ ⚹	♍ 11 7:41
13 9:38	♄ □	♎ 13 10:21
15 15:49	♄ △	♏ 15 16:54
17 22:05	☉ ⚹	♐ 18 3:12
20 13:57	♄ ☍	♑ 20 15:47
23 0:15	♅ □	♒ 23 4:50
25 14:36	♄ △	♓ 25 17:00
28 0:57	♄ □	♈ 28 3:32
30 11:04	♀ □	♉ 30 11:41

Last Aspect / ☽ Ingress (February)

Last Aspect Dy Hr Mn		☽ Ingress Dy Hr Mn
1 14:29	♀ △	♊ 1 16:53
3 16:21	♄ ☌	♋ 3 19:06
5 15:39	♅ □	♌ 5 19:11
7 15:55	♄ ⚹	♍ 7 18:52
9 16:57	♄ □	♎ 9 20:10
11 21:21	♄ △	♏ 12 0:58
14 1:49	♀ ⚹	♐ 14 10:01
16 17:59	♄ ☍	♑ 16 22:16
19 6:33	♅ □	♒ 19 11:21
21 18:57	♄ △	♓ 21 23:15
24 5:53	♂ ⚹	♈ 24 9:12
26 15:27	♀ □	♉ 26 17:11
28 19:59	♃ □	♊ 28 23:10

☽ Phases & Eclipses

Dy Hr Mn	
1 18:06	☽ 10♈57
8 12:36	○ 17♋51
15 7:04	☾ 24♎45
23 11:02	● 3♒04
31 7:39	☽ 11♉03
6 23:24	○ 17♌48
14 0:04	☾ 24♏55
22 5:34	● 3♓13

Astro Data

1 January 1974
Julian Day # 27029
SVP 5♓37'05"
GC 26♐28.6 ⚴ 1♑11.3
Eris 12♈24.3 ⚵ 16♑14.2
⚷ 16♈23.5 ⚶ 10♒01.3
☽ Mean ☊ 27♐53.9

1 February 1974
Julian Day # 27060
SVP 5♓37'00"
GC 26♐28.6 ⚴ 13♑28.1
Eris 12♈30.1 ⚵ 28♑26.7
⚷ 16♈57.4 ⚶ 16♒29.8
☽ Mean ☊ 26♐15.4

March 1974

LONGITUDE

Day	Sid.Time	☉	0 hr ☽	Noon ☽	True ☊	☿	♀	♂	⚳	♃	♄	♅	♆	♇
1 F	22 35 39	10♓31 34	0♊28 16	7♊18 37	25♐16.2	1♓03.4	0♒28.0	1♊08.9	12♒57.7	28♒21.4	27♊47.1	27♎25.2	9♐35.2	6♎08.2
2 Sa	22 39 35	11 31 46	14 12 57	21 11 23	25R 16.3	0R 11.7	1 00.5	1 42.3	13 20.4	28 35.6	27 47.4	27R 23.7	9 35.5	6R 06.7
3 Su	22 43 32	12 31 56	28 14 00	5♋20 43	25 16.1	29♒25.7	1 34.4	2 15.7	13 43.0	28 49.8	27 47.7	27 22.2	9 35.9	6 05.3
4 M	22 47 28	13 32 04	12♋31 27	19 45 53	25 14.2	28 46.0	2 09.7	2 49.2	14 05.6	29 04.0	27 48.2	27 20.6	9 36.1	6 03.8
5 Tu	22 51 25	14 32 10	27 03 39	4♌24 11	25 09.9	28 13.0	2 46.3	3 22.8	14 28.1	29 18.2	27 48.8	27 19.0	9 36.4	6 02.3
6 W	22 55 22	15 32 14	11♌46 48	19 10 38	25 02.7	27 46.8	3 24.1	3 56.4	14 50.6	29 32.3	27 49.5	27 17.4	9 36.6	6 00.8
7 Th	22 59 18	16 32 16	26 34 45	3♍58 08	24 52.9	27 27.5	4 03.2	4 30.2	15 13.0	29 46.4	27 50.3	27 15.7	9 36.7	5 59.2
8 F	23 03 15	17 32 15	11♍19 44	18 38 30	24 41.3	27 14.9	4 43.4	5 03.9	15 35.4	0♓00.5	27 51.2	27 13.9	9 36.9	5 57.7
9 Sa	23 07 11	18 32 13	25 53 26	3♎03 39	24 29.2	27D 09.0	5 24.7	5 37.8	15 57.7	0 14.5	27 52.2	27 12.1	9 37.0	5 56.1
10 Su	23 11 08	19 32 09	10♎08 25	17 07 08	24 18.0	27 09.4	6 07.1	6 11.7	16 19.9	0 28.5	27 53.4	27 10.3	9 37.0	5 54.6
11 M	23 15 04	20 32 03	23 59 24	0♏44 59	24 08.6	27 16.0	6 50.5	6 45.7	16 42.1	0 42.5	27 54.6	27 08.4	9R 37.1	5 53.0
12 Tu	23 19 01	21 31 56	7♏23 51	13 56 06	24 01.9	27 28.4	7 34.9	7 19.7	17 04.3	0 56.5	27 56.0	27 06.5	9 37.1	5 51.4
13 W	23 22 57	22 31 47	20 21 59	26 41 53	23 57.8	27 46.2	8 20.3	7 53.8	17 26.3	1 10.4	27 57.4	27 04.6	9 37.0	5 49.8
14 Th	23 26 54	23 31 36	2♐56 17	9♐05 45	23 56.0	28 09.3	9 06.6	8 28.0	17 48.3	1 24.3	27 59.0	27 02.6	9 37.0	5 48.2
15 F	23 30 50	24 31 23	15 10 54	21 12 25	23 55.6	28 37.2	9 53.7	9 02.2	18 10.3	1 38.2	28 00.7	27 00.6	9 36.9	5 46.6
16 Sa	23 34 47	25 31 09	27 10 58	3♑07 17	23 55.5	29 09.7	10 41.7	9 36.5	18 32.2	1 52.0	28 02.5	26 58.6	9 36.8	5 44.9
17 Su	23 38 44	26 30 53	9♑02 02	14 55 55	23 54.6	29 46.5	11 30.5	10 10.9	18 54.0	2 05.7	28 04.4	26 56.5	9 36.6	5 43.3
18 M	23 42 40	27 30 36	20 49 36	26 43 43	23 51.8	0♓27.4	12 20.1	10 45.3	19 15.8	2 19.5	28 06.4	26 54.4	9 36.4	5 41.7
19 Tu	23 46 37	28 30 16	2♒38 52	8♒35 35	23 46.5	1 11.9	13 10.4	11 19.8	19 37.5	2 33.2	28 08.5	26 52.3	9 36.2	5 40.0
20 W	23 50 33	29 29 55	14 34 22	20 35 38	23 38.4	2 00.1	14 01.4	11 54.3	19 59.1	2 46.8	28 10.7	26 50.1	9 35.9	5 38.4
21 Th	23 54 30	0♈29 32	26 39 45	2♓47 01	23 27.6	2 51.5	14 53.1	12 28.9	20 20.6	3 00.4	28 13.1	26 47.9	9 35.6	5 36.7
22 F	23 58 26	1 29 07	8♓57 38	15 11 46	23 14.9	3 46.1	15 45.5	13 03.5	20 42.1	3 14.0	28 15.5	26 45.7	9 35.3	5 35.1
23 Sa	0 02 23	2 28 39	21 29 30	27 50 49	23 01.3	4 43.6	16 38.5	13 38.2	21 03.5	3 27.5	28 18.0	26 43.5	9 34.9	5 33.4
24 Su	0 06 19	3 28 10	4♈15 41	10♈43 59	22 48.1	5 43.9	17 32.1	14 12.9	21 24.8	3 41.0	28 20.7	26 41.2	9 34.5	5 31.8
25 M	0 10 16	4 27 39	17 15 36	23 50 20	22 36.4	6 46.8	18 26.2	14 47.7	21 46.1	3 54.4	28 23.4	26 38.9	9 34.1	5 30.1
26 Tu	0 14 13	5 27 06	0♉28 02	7♉08 30	22 27.2	7 52.2	19 21.0	15 22.5	22 07.3	4 07.7	28 26.3	26 36.6	9 33.6	5 28.4
27 W	0 18 09	6 26 31	13 51 33	20 37 03	22 20.9	8 59.9	20 16.2	15 57.4	22 28.3	4 21.0	28 29.2	26 34.2	9 33.1	5 26.8
28 Th	0 22 06	7 25 53	27 24 53	4♊14 57	22 17.5	10 09.9	21 12.0	16 32.3	22 49.4	4 34.3	28 32.3	26 31.8	9 32.6	5 25.1
29 F	0 26 02	8 25 13	11♊07 12	18 01 34	22D 16.4	11 22.1	22 08.3	17 07.3	23 10.3	4 47.5	28 35.4	26 29.5	9 32.1	5 23.4
30 Sa	0 29 59	9 24 31	24 58 05	1♋56 43	22R 16.5	12 36.3	23 05.0	17 42.3	23 31.1	5 00.6	28 38.7	26 27.1	9 31.5	5 21.8
31 Su	0 33 55	10 23 47	8♋57 27	16 00 14	22 16.5	13 52.5	24 02.2	18 17.4	23 51.9	5 13.7	28 42.0	26 24.6	9 30.9	5 20.1

April 1974

LONGITUDE

Day	Sid.Time	☉	0 hr ☽	Noon ☽	True ☊	☿	♀	♂	⚳	♃	♄	♅	♆	♇
1 M	0 37 52	11♈23 00	23♋04 59	0♌11 34	22♐15.2	15♓10.6	24♒59.9	18♊52.5	24♒12.6	5♓26.7	28♊45.5	26♎22.2	9♐30.2	5♎18.5
2 Tu	0 41 48	12 22 11	7♌19 45	14 29 13	22R 11.7	16 30.5	25 58.0	19 27.6	24 33.1	5 39.7	28 49.0	26R 19.7	9R 29.6	5R 16.8
3 W	0 45 45	13 21 19	21 39 35	28 50 23	22 05.6	17 52.3	26 56.4	20 02.8	24 53.6	5 52.6	28 52.6	26 17.2	9 28.9	5 15.2
4 Th	0 49 42	14 20 25	6♍01 00	13♍10 50	21 57.0	19 15.8	27 55.4	20 38.0	25 14.0	6 05.4	28 56.4	26 14.8	9 28.1	5 13.5
5 F	0 53 38	15 19 29	20 19 11	27 25 21	21 46.8	20 41.0	28 54.6	21 13.2	25 34.3	6 18.2	29 00.2	26 12.3	9 27.4	5 11.9
6 Sa	0 57 35	16 18 30	4♎28 37	11♎28 21	21 36.1	22 07.9	29 54.3	21 48.5	25 54.5	6 30.9	29 04.1	26 09.7	9 26.6	5 10.3
7 Su	1 01 31	17 17 30	18 23 57	25 14 54	21 26.0	23 36.4	0♓54.4	22 23.8	26 14.7	6 43.5	29 08.1	26 07.2	9 25.8	5 08.7
8 M	1 05 28	18 16 28	2♏00 49	8♏41 24	21 17.5	25 06.6	1 54.7	22 59.1	26 34.7	6 56.1	29 12.2	26 04.7	9 24.9	5 07.0
9 Tu	1 09 24	19 15 23	15 16 32	21 46 11	21 11.4	26 38.4	2 55.5	23 34.5	26 54.6	7 08.6	29 16.4	26 02.1	9 24.1	5 05.4
10 W	1 13 21	20 14 17	28 10 27	4♐29 33	21 07.7	28 11.7	3 56.6	24 09.9	27 14.4	7 21.0	29 20.6	25 59.6	9 23.2	5 03.8
11 Th	1 17 17	21 13 10	10♐43 47	16 53 35	21D 06.3	29 46.7	4 58.0	24 45.3	27 34.2	7 33.3	29 25.0	25 57.0	9 22.2	5 02.3
12 F	1 21 14	22 12 00	22 59 24	29 01 48	21 06.4	1♈23.2	5 59.7	25 20.7	27 53.8	7 45.6	29 29.4	25 54.5	9 21.3	5 00.7
13 Sa	1 25 11	23 10 49	5♑01 22	10♑58 43	21 07.3	3 01.4	7 01.7	25 56.2	28 13.3	7 57.8	29 33.9	25 51.9	9 20.3	4 59.1
14 Su	1 29 07	24 09 36	16 54 31	22 49 26	21R 07.9	4 41.1	8 03.9	26 31.8	28 32.7	8 09.9	29 38.6	25 49.3	9 19.3	4 57.6
15 M	1 33 04	25 08 21	28 44 08	4♒39 16	21 07.4	6 22.3	9 06.5	27 07.3	28 52.0	8 22.0	29 43.2	25 46.8	9 18.3	4 56.0
16 Tu	1 37 00	26 07 04	10♒35 30	16 33 26	21 05.0	8 05.2	10 09.3	27 42.9	29 11.2	8 33.9	29 48.0	25 44.2	9 17.2	4 54.5
17 W	1 40 57	27 05 46	22 33 41	28 36 45	21 00.5	9 49.7	11 12.4	28 18.5	29 30.3	8 45.8	29 52.9	25 41.6	9 16.2	4 53.0
18 Th	1 44 53	28 04 26	4♓43 09	10♓53 18	20 54.0	11 35.7	12 15.8	28 54.1	29 49.3	8 57.6	29 57.8	25 39.0	9 15.1	4 51.5
19 F	1 48 50	29 03 04	17 07 32	23 26 08	20 45.8	13 23.4	13 19.4	29 29.8	0♓08.1	9 09.3	0♋02.8	25 36.5	9 13.9	4 50.0
20 Sa	1 52 46	0♉01 40	29 49 16	6♈17 03	20 36.9	15 12.7	14 23.2	0♋05.5	0 26.9	9 20.9	0 07.9	25 33.9	9 12.8	4 48.5
21 Su	1 56 43	1 00 15	12♈49 28	19 26 24	20 28.0	17 03.6	15 27.2	0 41.2	0 45.5	9 32.5	0 13.1	25 31.3	9 11.6	4 47.0
22 M	2 00 39	1 58 48	26 07 43	2♉53 07	20 20.2	18 56.1	16 31.5	1 17.0	1 04.0	9 43.9	0 18.3	25 28.8	9 10.4	4 45.6
23 Tu	2 04 36	2 57 19	9♉42 18	16 34 54	20 14.2	20 50.3	17 35.9	1 52.8	1 22.4	9 55.3	0 23.6	25 26.2	9 09.2	4 44.2
24 W	2 08 33	3 55 48	23 30 30	0♊28 41	20 10.4	22 46.1	18 40.6	2 28.6	1 40.6	10 06.5	0 29.0	25 23.7	9 08.0	4 42.8
25 Th	2 12 29	4 54 15	7♊29 01	14 31 05	20D 08.8	24 43.5	19 45.4	3 04.4	1 58.7	10 17.7	0 34.5	25 21.2	9 06.7	4 41.4
26 F	2 16 26	5 52 40	21 34 31	28 38 57	20 08.9	26 42.5	20 50.5	3 40.3	2 16.7	10 28.8	0 40.0	25 18.6	9 05.5	4 40.0
27 Sa	2 20 22	6 51 03	5♋44 03	12♋49 34	20 10.0	28 43.0	21 55.7	4 16.2	2 34.5	10 39.8	0 45.7	25 16.1	9 04.2	4 38.7
28 Su	2 24 19	7 49 24	19 55 13	27 00 48	20R 11.2	0♉45.1	23 01.1	4 52.1	2 52.3	10 50.6	0 51.3	25 13.6	9 02.9	4 37.3
29 M	2 28 15	8 47 42	4♌06 06	11♌10 55	20 11.6	2 48.6	24 06.6	5 28.0	3 09.8	11 01.4	0 57.1	25 11.1	9 01.5	4 36.0
30 Tu	2 32 12	9 45 59	18 15 03	25 18 16	20 10.5	4 53.4	25 12.4	6 04.0	3 27.3	11 12.1	1 02.9	25 08.7	9 00.2	4 34.7

Astro Data	Dy Hr Mn
☽0S	8 11:37
☿D	9 22:17
♆R	12 1:20
☉0N	21 0:06
☽0N	22 18:06
♃⊼♇	31 22:28
☽0S	4 20:34
☿0N	15 1:01
☽0N	19 1:54
♃□♆	19 20:40
♃⚼♅	25 18:03

Planet Ingress		Dy Hr Mn
☿	♒R	2 17:49
♃	♓	8 11:11
☿	♓	17 20:11
☉	♈	21 0:07
♀	♓	6 14:17
☿	♈	11 15:20
♄	♋	18 22:34
⚳	♓	19 1:37
♂	♋	20 8:18
☉	♉	20 11:19
☿	♉	28 3:10

Last Aspect Dy Hr Mn			☽ Ingress	Dy Hr Mn
3 2:31	☿	△	♋	3 3:00
5 0:26	♅	□	♌	5 4:49
7 5:04	♃	☍	♍	7 5:33
9 3:17	♄	□	♎	9 6:52
11 6:56	♄	△	♏	11 10:40
13 14:07	☿	□	♐	13 18:20
16 3:36	☿	⚹	♑	16 5:41
18 13:44	☉	⚹	♒	18 18:38
21 3:02	♄	△	♓	21 6:33
23 12:51	♄	□	♈	23 16:02
25 20:17	♄	⚹	♉	25 23:09
27 11:20	♀	□	♊	28 4:33
30 6:18	♄	☌	♋	30 8:40

Last Aspect Dy Hr Mn			☽ Ingress	Dy Hr Mn
1 5:34	♅	□	♌	1 11:41
3 12:04	♄	⚹	♍	3 13:56
5 14:42	♄	□	♎	5 16:22
7 18:55	♄	△	♏	7 20:25
9 22:22	☿	△	♐	10 3:27
12 12:55	♄	☍	♑	12 13:56
14 18:04	♅	□	♒	15 2:34
17 14:31	♄	△	♓	17 14:44
19 23:57	♂	□	♈	20 0:20
21 22:53	♅	☍	♉	22 6:53
23 13:55	♀	⚹	♊	24 11:11
26 8:10	☿	⚹	♋	26 14:17
28 8:59	♅	□	♌	28 17:03
30 11:44	♅	⚹	♍	30 20:00

☽ Phases & Eclipses Dy Hr Mn	
1 18:03	☽ 10♊47
8 10:03	○ 17♍27
15 19:15	☾ 24♐49
23 21:24	● 2♈52
31 1:44	☽ 9♋58
6 21:00	○ 16♎41
14 14:57	☾ 24♑17
22 10:16	● 1♉55
29 7:39	☽ 8♌37

Astro Data

1 March 1974
Julian Day # 27088
SVP 5♓36'56"
GC 26♐28.7 ⚴ 23♑35.3
Eris 12♈43.4 ⚵ 9♒31.7
⚷ 18♈06.3 ⚶ 16♎48.5R
☽ Mean ☊ 24♐46.4

1 April 1974
Julian Day # 27119
SVP 5♓36'53"
GC 26♐28.8 ⚴ 2♒59.0
Eris 13♈03.3 ⚵ 21♒26.4
⚷ 19♈48.8 ⚶ 10♎38.4R
☽ Mean ☊ 23♐07.9

LONGITUDE — May 1974

Day	Sid.Time	☉	0 hr ☽	Noon ☽	True ☊	☿	♀	♂	⚳	♃	♄	♅	♆	♇
1 W	2 36 08	10♉44 13	2♍20 23	9♍21 06	20♐07.7	6♉59.5	26♓18.3	6♋39.9	3♓44.6	11♓22.6	1♋08.8	25♎06.2	8♐58.8	4♎33.4
2 Th	2 40 05	11 42 25	16 20 11	23 17 19	20R 03.3	9 06.8	27 24.3	7 15.9	4 01.7	11 33.1	1 14.7	25R 03.8	8R 57.4	4R 32.2
3 F	2 44 02	12 40 36	0♎12 11	7♎04 29	19 57.8	11 15.1	28 30.5	7 51.9	4 18.7	11 43.4	1 20.7	25 01.4	8 56.0	4 31.0
4 Sa	2 47 58	13 38 44	13 53 52	20 40 04	19 51.9	13 24.1	29 36.9	8 27.9	4 35.6	11 53.7	1 26.8	24 59.0	8 54.6	4 29.8
5 Su	2 51 55	14 36 51	27 22 46	4♏01 44	19 46.3	15 33.8	0♈43.4	9 04.0	4 52.3	12 03.8	1 32.9	24 56.6	8 53.2	4 28.6
6 M	2 55 51	15 34 56	10♏36 47	17 07 46	19 41.7	17 43.9	1 50.0	9 40.0	5 08.8	12 13.8	1 39.1	24 54.2	8 51.7	4 27.4
7 Tu	2 59 48	16 32 59	23 34 36	29 57 17	19 38.5	19 54.1	2 56.8	10 16.1	5 25.3	12 23.8	1 45.3	24 51.9	8 50.3	4 26.3
8 W	3 03 44	17 31 01	6♐15 52	12♐30 30	19D 36.9	22 04.1	4 03.7	10 52.2	5 41.5	12 33.6	1 51.6	24 49.6	8 48.8	4 25.2
9 Th	3 07 41	18 29 01	18 41 22	24 48 46	19 36.8	24 13.8	5 10.8	11 28.3	5 57.6	12 43.3	1 58.0	24 47.3	8 47.3	4 24.1
10 F	3 11 37	19 27 00	0♑53 01	6♑54 30	19 37.8	26 22.7	6 18.0	12 04.5	6 13.6	12 52.8	2 04.4	24 45.0	8 45.8	4 23.0
11 Sa	3 15 34	20 24 58	12 53 41	18 51 02	19 39.5	28 30.6	7 25.3	12 40.6	6 29.3	13 02.3	2 10.8	24 42.8	8 44.3	4 22.0
12 Su	3 19 31	21 22 54	24 47 04	0♒42 23	19 41.2	0♊37.3	8 32.8	13 16.8	6 44.9	13 11.6	2 17.4	24 40.6	8 42.8	4 21.0
13 M	3 23 27	22 20 48	6♒37 32	12 33 08	19R 42.5	2 42.4	9 40.4	13 53.0	7 00.4	13 20.8	2 23.9	24 38.4	8 41.3	4 20.0
14 Tu	3 27 24	23 18 42	18 29 47	24 28 06	19 42.9	4 45.6	10 48.0	14 29.2	7 15.6	13 29.9	2 30.6	24 36.2	8 39.7	4 19.0
15 W	3 31 20	24 16 34	0♓28 41	6♓32 08	19 42.3	6 46.9	11 55.8	15 05.4	7 30.7	13 38.9	2 37.2	24 34.1	8 38.2	4 18.1
16 Th	3 35 17	25 14 25	12 39 00	18 49 49	19 40.5	8 45.9	13 03.8	15 41.7	7 45.7	13 47.7	2 43.9	24 32.0	8 36.6	4 17.2
17 F	3 39 13	26 12 15	25 05 04	1♈25 08	19 37.9	10 42.4	14 11.8	16 18.0	8 00.4	13 56.4	2 50.7	24 29.9	8 35.0	4 16.3
18 Sa	3 43 10	27 10 03	7♈50 22	14 21 01	19 34.7	12 36.4	15 19.9	16 54.2	8 14.9	14 05.0	2 57.5	24 27.9	8 33.4	4 15.4
19 Su	3 47 06	28 07 51	20 57 15	27 39 07	19 31.5	14 27.6	16 28.1	17 30.6	8 29.3	14 13.4	3 04.4	24 25.9	8 31.9	4 14.6
20 M	3 51 03	29 05 37	4♉26 31	11♉19 17	19 28.6	16 16.0	17 36.4	18 06.9	8 43.5	14 21.7	3 11.3	24 23.9	8 30.3	4 13.8
21 Tu	3 55 00	0♊03 22	18 17 08	25 19 38	19 26.6	18 01.5	18 44.9	18 43.2	8 57.5	14 29.9	3 18.3	24 21.9	8 28.7	4 13.0
22 W	3 58 56	1 01 06	2♊26 17	9♊36 29	19D 25.4	19 44.0	19 53.4	19 19.6	9 11.3	14 37.9	3 25.3	24 20.0	8 27.1	4 12.3
23 Th	4 02 53	1 58 48	16 49 35	24 04 52	19 25.3	21 23.4	21 01.9	19 56.0	9 24.9	14 45.8	3 32.3	24 18.2	8 25.5	4 11.6
24 F	4 06 49	2 56 29	1♋21 36	8♋39 05	19 25.9	22 59.7	22 10.6	20 32.4	9 38.2	14 53.5	3 39.4	24 16.3	8 23.8	4 10.9
25 Sa	4 10 46	3 54 09	15 56 35	23 13 28	19 26.9	24 32.9	23 19.4	21 08.8	9 51.4	15 01.1	3 46.5	24 14.6	8 22.2	4 10.3
26 Su	4 14 42	4 51 47	0♌29 07	7♌43 00	19 28.0	26 02.8	24 28.2	21 45.3	10 04.4	15 08.6	3 53.7	24 12.8	8 20.6	4 09.6
27 M	4 18 39	5 49 23	14 54 38	22 03 38	19 28.8	27 29.5	25 37.1	22 21.7	10 17.2	15 15.9	4 00.8	24 11.1	8 19.0	4 09.0
28 Tu	4 22 35	6 46 58	29 09 41	6♍12 33	19R 29.2	28 52.9	26 46.1	22 58.2	10 29.7	15 23.1	4 08.1	24 09.4	8 17.4	4 08.5
29 W	4 26 32	7 44 32	13♍12 01	20 07 58	19 28.9	0♋13.0	27 55.2	23 34.7	10 42.0	15 30.1	4 15.3	24 07.8	8 15.7	4 08.0
30 Th	4 30 29	8 42 04	27 00 19	3♎49 00	19 28.1	1 29.7	29 04.3	24 11.2	10 54.2	15 37.0	4 22.6	24 06.2	8 14.1	4 07.5
31 F	4 34 25	9 39 34	10♎34 01	17 15 21	19 27.1	2 42.9	0♉13.5	24 47.7	11 06.0	15 43.7	4 30.0	24 04.6	8 12.5	4 07.0

LONGITUDE — June 1974

Day	Sid.Time	☉	0 hr ☽	Noon ☽	True ☊	☿	♀	♂	⚳	♃	♄	♅	♆	♇
1 Sa	4 38 22	10♊37 04	23♎53 02	0♏27 07	19♐25.9	3♋52.7	1♉22.8	25♋24.2	11♓17.7	15♓50.2	4♋37.3	24♎03.1	8♐10.9	4♎06.6
2 Su	4 42 18	11 34 32	6♏57 38	13 24 39	19R 24.9	4 59.0	2 32.2	26 00.7	11 29.2	15 56.6	4 44.7	24R 01.6	8R 09.2	4R 06.1
3 M	4 46 15	12 31 59	19 48 15	26 08 31	19 24.1	6 01.7	3 41.6	26 37.3	11 40.4	16 02.9	4 52.1	24 00.2	8 07.6	4 05.8
4 Tu	4 50 11	13 29 25	2♐25 33	8♐39 28	19D 23.7	7 00.7	4 51.1	27 13.9	11 51.3	16 09.0	4 59.6	23 58.8	8 06.0	4 05.4
5 W	4 54 08	14 26 51	14 50 25	20 58 33	19 23.6	7 56.0	6 00.7	27 50.5	12 02.1	16 14.9	5 07.0	23 57.5	8 04.4	4 05.1
6 Th	4 58 04	15 24 15	27 04 04	3♑07 12	19 23.7	8 47.5	7 10.3	28 27.1	12 12.6	16 20.7	5 14.5	23 56.2	8 02.8	4 04.9
7 F	5 02 01	16 21 38	9♑08 11	15 07 17	19 24.0	9 35.1	8 20.0	29 03.7	12 22.8	16 26.3	5 22.1	23 54.9	8 01.2	4 04.6
8 Sa	5 05 58	17 19 01	21 04 51	27 01 13	19 24.3	10 18.7	9 29.8	29 40.3	12 32.8	16 31.7	5 29.6	23 53.7	7 59.6	4 04.4
9 Su	5 09 54	18 16 23	2♒56 45	8♒51 54	19 24.5	10 58.2	10 39.7	0♌16.9	12 42.6	16 37.0	5 37.2	23 52.6	7 58.0	4 04.2
10 M	5 13 51	19 13 44	14 47 05	20 42 48	19R 24.5	11 33.6	11 49.6	0 53.6	12 52.1	16 42.1	5 44.8	23 51.5	7 56.4	4 04.1
11 Tu	5 17 47	20 11 05	26 39 32	2♓37 49	19 24.5	12 04.7	12 59.6	1 30.3	13 01.3	16 47.1	5 52.4	23 50.4	7 54.8	4 04.0
12 W	5 21 44	21 08 26	8♓38 12	14 41 14	19D 24.5	12 31.5	14 09.6	2 07.0	13 10.3	16 51.9	6 00.0	23 49.4	7 53.3	4 03.9
13 Th	5 25 40	22 05 45	20 47 27	26 57 26	19 24.5	12 53.9	15 19.7	2 43.7	13 19.0	16 56.5	6 07.7	23 48.4	7 51.7	4 03.8
14 F	5 29 37	23 03 05	3♈11 41	9♈30 44	19 24.6	13 11.8	16 29.9	3 20.4	13 27.5	17 00.9	6 15.3	23 47.5	7 50.1	4D 03.8
15 Sa	5 33 33	24 00 24	15 55 02	22 25 00	19 24.9	13 25.2	17 40.1	3 57.2	13 35.6	17 05.1	6 23.0	23 46.6	7 48.6	4 03.8
16 Su	5 37 30	24 57 43	29 00 57	5♉43 08	19 25.4	13 34.0	18 50.4	4 33.9	13 43.5	17 09.2	6 30.7	23 45.8	7 47.0	4 03.9
17 M	5 41 27	25 55 01	12♉31 42	19 26 39	19 26.0	13R 38.3	20 00.7	5 10.7	13 51.1	17 13.1	6 38.4	23 45.0	7 45.5	4 04.0
18 Tu	5 45 23	26 52 19	26 27 51	3♊35 03	19 26.4	13 38.1	21 11.1	5 47.5	13 58.5	17 16.8	6 46.2	23 44.3	7 44.0	4 04.1
19 W	5 49 20	27 49 37	10♊47 48	18 05 31	19R 26.7	13 33.3	22 21.6	6 24.4	14 05.5	17 20.4	6 53.9	23 43.6	7 42.5	4 04.2
20 Th	5 53 16	28 46 54	25 27 30	2♋52 52	19 26.5	13 24.2	23 32.1	7 01.2	14 12.2	17 23.7	7 01.7	23 43.0	7 41.0	4 04.4
21 F	5 57 13	29 44 11	10♋20 42	17 49 57	19 25.8	13 10.9	24 42.7	7 38.1	14 18.7	17 26.9	7 09.4	23 42.4	7 39.5	4 04.6
22 Sa	6 01 09	0♋41 27	25 19 33	2♌48 29	19 24.7	12 53.5	25 53.3	8 14.9	14 24.8	17 29.9	7 17.2	23 41.9	7 38.0	4 04.9
23 Su	6 05 06	1 38 43	10♌15 42	17 40 18	19 23.4	12 32.3	27 04.0	8 51.8	14 30.6	17 32.7	7 25.0	23 41.4	7 36.6	4 05.2
24 M	6 09 03	2 35 58	25 01 27	2♍18 28	19 22.0	12 07.6	28 14.7	9 28.8	14 36.2	17 35.3	7 32.8	23 41.0	7 35.2	4 05.5
25 Tu	6 12 59	3 33 12	9♍30 47	16 37 59	19 20.9	11 39.8	29 25.4	10 05.7	14 41.4	17 37.7	7 40.6	23 40.6	7 33.7	4 05.8
26 W	6 16 56	4 30 26	23 39 50	0♎36 11	19D 20.4	11 09.4	0♊36.2	10 42.6	14 46.3	17 40.0	7 48.4	23 40.3	7 32.3	4 06.2
27 Th	6 20 52	5 27 39	7♎27 01	14 12 25	19 20.5	10 36.7	1 47.1	11 19.6	14 50.9	17 42.0	7 56.2	23 40.1	7 30.9	4 06.6
28 F	6 24 49	6 24 52	20 52 34	27 27 40	19 21.3	10 02.3	2 58.0	11 56.6	14 55.2	17 43.9	8 04.0	23 39.8	7 29.5	4 07.0
29 Sa	6 28 45	7 22 04	3♏58 02	10♏23 57	19 22.6	9 26.8	4 08.9	12 33.5	14 59.1	17 45.5	8 11.8	23 39.7	7 28.2	4 07.5
30 Su	6 32 42	8 19 16	16 45 46	23 03 47	19 24.0	8 50.7	5 19.9	13 10.5	15 02.8	17 47.0	8 19.6	23 39.6	7 26.8	4 08.0

Astro Data

	Dy Hr Mn
☽0S	2 2:48
♀0N	7 21:16
☽0N	16 10:00
♄□♇	28 13:16
☽0S	29 7:48
☽0N	12 17:53
♇ D	14 13:17
☿ R	17 22:38
♄⊼♆	24 18:07
☽0S	25 13:51

Planet Ingress

		Dy Hr Mn
♀	♈	4 20:21
☿	♊	12 4:55
☉	♊	21 10:36
☿	♋	29 8:03
♀	♉	31 7:19
♂	♌	9 0:54
☉	♋	21 18:38
♀	♊	25 23:44

Last Aspect / ☽ Ingress (May)

Last Aspect Dy Hr Mn		☽ Ingress	Dy Hr Mn
2 19:45	♀ ☍	♎	2 23:39
4 19:41	♅ ☌	♏	5 4:43
6 13:20	☿ ☍	♐	7 12:05
9 11:57	♅ ⚹	♑	9 22:15
11 23:49	♅ □	♒	12 10:34
14 12:16	♅ △	♓	14 23:03
17 1:19	☉ ⚹	♈	17 9:20
19 6:16	♅ ☍	♉	19 16:10
21 0:14	♂ ⚹	♊	21 19:54
23 12:22	♅ △	♋	23 21:46
25 13:41	♅ □	♌	25 23:12
27 22:11	☿ ⚹	♍	28 1:25
29 18:17	♂ ⚹	♎	30 5:16

Last Aspect / ☽ Ingress (June)

Last Aspect Dy Hr Mn		☽ Ingress	Dy Hr Mn
1 2:19	♂ □	♏	1 11:10
3 12:58	♂ △	♐	3 19:21
5 17:51	♅ ⚹	♑	6 5:48
8 17:40	♂ ☍	♒	8 18:02
10 18:21	♅ △	♓	11 6:43
13 1:45	☉ □	♈	13 17:52
15 15:08	☉ ⚹	♉	16 1:46
17 13:04	♀ ☌	♊	18 5:59
20 4:56	☉ ☌	♋	20 7:21
21 23:57	♀ ⚹	♌	22 7:30
24 4:42	♀ □	♍	24 8:11
25 13:42	♃ ☍	♎	26 10:57
28 5:04	♅ ☌	♏	28 16:40

☽ Phases & Eclipses

Dy Hr Mn		
6 8:55	○	15♏27
14 9:29	☾	23♒13
21 20:34	●	0♊24
28 13:03	☽	6♍49
4 22:10	○	13♐54
4 22:16	☍	P 0.827
13 1:45	☾	21♓41
20 4:56	●	28♊30
20 4:47:20	●	T 05'09"
26 19:20	☽	4♎48

Astro Data

1 May 1974
Julian Day # 27149
SVP 5♓36'50"
GC 26♐28.8 ⚴ 9♒12.7
Eris 13♈23.1 ⚵ 2♓05.2
⚷ 21♈34.4 ⚶ 4♎23.5R
☽ Mean ☊ 21♐32.6

1 June 1974
Julian Day # 27180
SVP 5♓36'45"
GC 26♐28.9 ⚴ 11♒06.5R
Eris 13♈39.0 ⚵ 11♓21.7
⚷ 23♈09.7 ⚶ 4♎37.4
☽ Mean ☊ 19♐54.1

July 1974 LONGITUDE

Day	Sid.Time	☉	0 hr ☽	Noon ☽	True ☊	☿	♀	♂	⚳	♃	♄	♅	♆	♇
1 M	6 36 38	9♋16 27	29♏18 22	5♐29 50	19♐25.1	8♋14.8	6♊31.0	13♌47.6	15♓06.1	17♓48.3	8♋27.4	23♎39.5	7♐25.5	4♎08.6
2 Tu	6 40 35	10 13 38	11♐38 30	17 44 38	19R 25.7	7R 39.5	7 42.1	14 24.6	15 09.0	17 49.4	8 35.2	23D 39.5	7R 24.2	4 09.2
3 W	6 44 32	11 10 49	23 48 33	29 50 31	19 25.3	7 05.6	8 53.2	15 01.7	15 11.7	17 50.3	8 43.1	23 39.6	7 22.9	4 09.8
4 Th	6 48 28	12 08 00	5♑50 46	11♑49 34	19 23.8	6 33.6	10 04.4	15 38.7	15 14.0	17 51.0	8 50.9	23 39.7	7 21.7	4 10.4
5 F	6 52 25	13 05 11	17 47 09	23 43 45	19 21.2	6 04.0	11 15.6	16 15.8	15 16.0	17 51.6	8 58.7	23 39.8	7 20.4	4 11.1
6 Sa	6 56 21	14 02 22	29 39 38	5♒35 03	19 17.7	5 37.5	12 26.9	16 52.9	15 17.6	17 51.9	9 06.5	23 40.0	7 19.2	4 11.8
7 Su	7 00 18	14 59 33	11♒30 15	17 25 33	19 13.5	5 14.4	13 38.3	17 30.0	15 18.9	17R 52.0	9 14.2	23 40.3	7 18.0	4 12.5
8 M	7 04 14	15 56 45	23 21 14	29 17 38	19 09.1	4 55.3	14 49.7	18 07.2	15 19.9	17 52.0	9 22.0	23 40.6	7 16.8	4 13.3
9 Tu	7 08 11	16 53 56	5♓15 08	11♓14 06	19 05.1	4 40.4	16 01.1	18 44.3	15 20.5	17 51.7	9 29.8	23 41.0	7 15.6	4 14.1
10 W	7 12 07	17 51 08	17 14 58	23 18 10	19 01.8	4 30.1	17 12.6	19 21.5	15R 20.7	17 51.2	9 37.6	23 41.4	7 14.5	4 14.9
11 Th	7 16 04	18 48 20	29 24 10	5♈33 27	18 59.7	4D 24.6	18 24.2	19 58.7	15 20.6	17 50.6	9 45.3	23 41.9	7 13.4	4 15.8
12 F	7 20 01	19 45 33	11♈46 33	18 03 56	18D 58.9	4 24.2	19 35.8	20 35.9	15 20.2	17 49.7	9 53.1	23 42.4	7 12.3	4 16.7
13 Sa	7 23 57	20 42 47	24 26 08	0♉53 37	18 59.3	4 29.0	20 47.4	21 13.2	15 19.4	17 48.7	10 00.8	23 43.0	7 11.2	4 17.6
14 Su	7 27 54	21 40 01	7♉26 50	14 06 12	19 00.5	4 39.1	21 59.1	21 50.4	15 18.2	17 47.5	10 08.5	23 43.6	7 10.1	4 18.5
15 M	7 31 50	22 37 15	20 52 00	27 44 29	19 02.0	4 54.7	23 10.9	22 27.7	15 16.7	17 46.0	10 16.2	23 44.3	7 09.1	4 19.5
16 Tu	7 35 47	23 34 30	4♊43 45	11♊49 45	19R 03.0	5 15.7	24 22.7	23 05.0	15 14.8	17 44.4	10 23.9	23 45.0	7 08.1	4 20.5
17 W	7 39 43	24 31 46	19 02 17	26 20 57	19 03.0	5 42.2	25 34.5	23 42.3	15 12.6	17 42.6	10 31.6	23 45.8	7 07.1	4 21.6
18 Th	7 43 40	25 29 03	3♋45 10	11♋14 10	19 01.4	6 14.2	26 46.4	24 19.7	15 10.0	17 40.6	10 39.2	23 46.6	7 06.2	4 22.7
19 F	7 47 36	26 26 20	18 46 58	26 22 28	18 58.2	6 51.6	27 58.3	24 57.1	15 07.0	17 38.4	10 46.9	23 47.5	7 05.2	4 23.8
20 Sa	7 51 33	27 23 37	3♌59 26	11♌36 33	18 53.5	7 34.5	29 10.3	25 34.5	15 03.7	17 36.0	10 54.5	23 48.5	7 04.3	4 24.9
21 Su	7 55 30	28 20 54	19 12 30	26 46 02	18 47.9	8 22.8	0♋22.3	26 11.9	15 00.0	17 33.4	11 02.1	23 49.5	7 03.5	4 26.1
22 M	7 59 26	29 18 12	4♍15 56	11♍41 12	18 42.2	9 16.4	1 34.4	26 49.3	14 56.0	17 30.6	11 09.7	23 50.5	7 02.6	4 27.3
23 Tu	8 03 23	0♌15 31	19 00 58	26 14 35	18 37.3	10 15.2	2 46.5	27 26.8	14 51.6	17 27.7	11 17.2	23 51.6	7 01.8	4 28.5
24 W	8 07 19	1 12 49	3♎21 35	10♎21 44	18 33.8	11 19.2	3 58.6	28 04.2	14 46.8	17 24.5	11 24.7	23 52.7	7 01.0	4 29.7
25 Th	8 11 16	2 10 08	17 14 57	24 01 20	18D 32.0	12 28.3	5 10.8	28 41.7	14 41.7	17 21.2	11 32.2	23 53.9	7 00.2	4 31.0
26 F	8 15 12	3 07 28	0♏41 07	7♏14 38	18 31.8	13 42.4	6 23.1	29 19.2	14 36.3	17 17.7	11 39.7	23 55.2	6 59.5	4 32.3
27 Sa	8 19 09	4 04 47	13 42 18	20 04 37	18 32.7	15 01.4	7 35.3	29 56.8	14 30.5	17 14.0	11 47.1	23 56.5	6 58.8	4 33.6
28 Su	8 23 05	5 02 08	26 22 04	2♐35 12	18 34.0	16 25.2	8 47.7	0♍34.3	14 24.3	17 10.1	11 54.6	23 57.8	6 58.1	4 35.0
29 M	8 27 02	5 59 29	8♐44 33	14 50 37	18R 34.9	17 53.5	10 00.0	1 11.9	14 17.9	17 06.1	12 02.0	23 59.2	6 57.5	4 36.4
30 Tu	8 30 59	6 56 50	20 53 56	26 54 56	18 34.6	19 26.2	11 12.4	1 49.5	14 11.1	17 01.9	12 09.3	24 00.7	6 56.8	4 37.8
31 W	8 34 55	7 54 12	2♑54 05	8♑51 47	18 32.4	21 03.1	12 24.9	2 27.1	14 03.9	16 57.5	12 16.6	24 02.2	6 56.2	4 39.3

August 1974 LONGITUDE

Day	Sid.Time	☉	0 hr ☽	Noon ☽	True ☊	☿	♀	♂	⚳	♃	♄	♅	♆	♇
1 Th	8 38 52	8♌51 35	14♑48 24	20♑44 15	18♐28.0	22♋44.0	13♋37.4	3♍04.7	13♓56.4	16♓52.9	12♋23.9	24♎03.7	6♐55.7	4♎40.7
2 F	8 42 48	9 48 58	26 39 39	2♒34 52	18R 21.5	24 28.5	14 49.9	3 42.4	13R 48.7	16R 48.2	12 31.2	24 05.3	6R 55.1	4 42.2
3 Sa	8 46 45	10 46 22	8♒30 08	14 25 40	18 13.0	26 16.5	16 02.5	4 20.1	13 40.5	16 43.3	12 38.4	24 06.9	6 54.6	4 43.7
4 Su	8 50 41	11 43 48	20 21 41	26 18 23	18 03.2	28 07.6	17 15.2	4 57.8	13 32.1	16 38.3	12 45.6	24 08.6	6 54.2	4 45.3
5 M	8 54 38	12 41 14	2♓15 58	8♓14 38	17 53.0	0♌01.5	18 27.8	5 35.5	13 23.4	16 33.1	12 52.8	24 10.4	6 53.7	4 46.8
6 Tu	8 58 34	13 38 41	14 14 37	20 16 09	17 43.3	1 57.7	19 40.6	6 13.2	13 14.3	16 27.7	12 59.9	24 12.1	6 53.3	4 48.4
7 W	9 02 31	14 36 10	26 19 31	2♈24 59	17 34.9	3 56.0	20 53.4	6 51.0	13 05.0	16 22.2	13 06.9	24 14.0	6 52.9	4 50.0
8 Th	9 06 28	15 33 39	8♈32 53	14 43 35	17 28.6	5 56.0	22 06.2	7 28.8	12 55.4	16 16.6	13 14.0	24 15.8	6 52.6	4 51.7
9 F	9 10 24	16 31 10	20 57 28	27 14 56	17 24.5	7 57.2	23 19.0	8 06.6	12 45.5	16 10.8	13 21.0	24 17.7	6 52.2	4 53.3
10 Sa	9 14 21	17 28 42	3♉36 26	10♉02 25	17D 22.7	9 59.5	24 32.0	8 44.5	12 35.3	16 04.8	13 27.9	24 19.7	6 51.9	4 55.0
11 Su	9 18 17	18 26 16	16 33 20	23 09 37	17 22.5	12 02.3	25 44.9	9 22.3	12 24.9	15 58.7	13 34.8	24 21.7	6 51.7	4 56.7
12 M	9 22 14	19 23 52	29 51 39	6♊39 47	17R 23.1	14 05.5	26 57.9	10 00.2	12 14.2	15 52.5	13 41.7	24 23.8	6 51.5	4 58.5
13 Tu	9 26 10	20 21 28	13♊34 18	20 35 20	17 23.3	16 08.6	28 11.0	10 38.2	12 03.3	15 46.2	13 48.5	24 25.9	6 51.3	5 00.2
14 W	9 30 07	21 19 07	27 42 53	4♋56 50	17 22.1	18 11.6	29 24.1	11 16.1	11 52.1	15 39.7	13 55.3	24 28.0	6 51.1	5 02.0
15 Th	9 34 03	22 16 47	12♋16 48	19 42 16	17 18.8	20 14.1	0♌37.3	11 54.1	11 40.7	15 33.1	14 02.1	24 30.2	6 51.0	5 03.8
16 F	9 38 00	23 14 28	27 12 28	4♌46 25	17 12.9	22 16.0	1 50.5	12 32.1	11 29.0	15 26.4	14 08.7	24 32.4	6 50.9	5 05.6
17 Sa	9 41 57	24 12 10	12♌23 00	20 00 54	17 04.7	24 17.1	3 03.7	13 10.1	11 17.2	15 19.6	14 15.4	24 34.7	6 50.8	5 07.5
18 Su	9 45 53	25 09 54	27 38 45	5♍15 09	16 55.1	26 17.3	4 17.0	13 48.2	11 05.2	15 12.6	14 22.0	24 37.0	6D 50.8	5 09.3
19 M	9 49 50	26 07 39	12♍48 45	20 18 15	16 45.1	28 16.4	5 30.3	14 26.3	10 53.0	15 05.6	14 28.5	24 39.4	6 50.8	5 11.2
20 Tu	9 53 46	27 05 25	27 42 36	5♎00 51	16 36.1	0♍14.4	6 43.6	15 04.4	10 40.6	14 58.5	14 35.0	24 41.8	6 50.8	5 13.1
21 W	9 57 43	28 03 12	12♎12 21	19 16 37	16 28.9	2 11.2	7 57.0	15 42.5	10 28.1	14 51.2	14 41.4	24 44.2	6 50.8	5 15.0
22 Th	10 01 39	29 01 01	26 13 27	3♏02 48	16 24.1	4 06.8	9 10.5	16 20.7	10 15.4	14 43.9	14 47.7	24 46.7	6 50.9	5 16.9
23 F	10 05 36	29 58 51	9♏44 49	16 19 56	16 21.6	6 01.1	10 24.0	16 58.9	10 02.6	14 36.5	14 54.0	24 49.2	6 51.1	5 18.9
24 Sa	10 09 32	0♍56 42	22 48 15	29 10 36	16D 20.9	7 54.0	11 37.5	17 37.1	9 49.7	14 29.1	15 00.3	24 51.8	6 51.2	5 20.9
25 Su	10 13 29	1 54 34	5♐27 27	11♐39 26	16R 21.1	9 45.7	12 51.0	18 15.3	9 36.7	14 21.5	15 06.5	24 54.4	6 51.4	5 22.9
26 M	10 17 26	2 52 28	17 47 11	23 51 20	16 20.9	11 36.0	14 04.6	18 53.6	9 23.6	14 13.9	15 12.6	24 57.0	6 51.6	5 24.9
27 Tu	10 21 22	3 50 22	29 52 32	5♑51 23	16 19.4	13 25.1	15 18.2	19 31.9	9 10.4	14 06.3	15 18.7	24 59.7	6 51.9	5 26.9
28 W	10 25 19	4 48 18	11♑48 27	17 44 17	16 15.8	15 12.8	16 31.9	20 10.2	8 57.2	13 58.5	15 24.7	25 02.4	6 52.2	5 28.9
29 Th	10 29 15	5 46 16	23 39 21	29 34 08	16 09.4	16 59.1	17 45.6	20 48.6	8 43.9	13 50.8	15 30.6	25 05.1	6 52.5	5 31.0
30 F	10 33 12	6 44 14	5♒28 59	11♒24 18	16 00.2	18 44.2	18 59.3	21 26.9	8 30.6	13 43.0	15 36.5	25 07.9	6 52.9	5 33.1
31 Sa	10 37 08	7 42 15	17 20 20	23 17 22	15 48.6	20 28.0	20 13.1	22 05.3	8 17.2	13 35.1	15 42.3	25 10.7	6 53.3	5 35.1

Astro Data	Dy Hr Mn
♅ D	2 0:16
♃ R	7 16:13
☽ 0N	10 1:11
⚳ R	10 17:22
☿ D	12 1:55
☽ 0S	22 22:16
☽ 0N	6 7:49
♆ D	19 3:37
☽ 0S	19 8:44
♃△♄	22 5:19

Planet Ingress	Dy Hr Mn
♀ ♋	21 4:34
☉ ♌	23 5:30
♂ ♍	27 14:04
☿ ♌	5 11:42
♀ ♌	14 23:47
☿ ♍	20 9:04
☉ ♍	23 12:29

Last Aspect Dy Hr Mn	☽ Ingress Dy Hr Mn
30 1:55 ♃ △	♐ 1 1:20
2 23:42 ♅ ✶	♑ 3 12:19
5 11:52 ♅ □	♒ 6 0:41
8 0:39 ♅ △	♓ 8 13:25
10 1:13 ♃ ☌	♈ 11 1:10
12 22:39 ♅ ☍	♉ 13 10:21
15 2:25 ☉ ✶	♊ 15 15:54
17 10:37 ♀ ☌	♋ 17 17:56
19 12:06 ☉ ☌	♌ 19 17:43
21 11:03 ♂ ☌	♍ 21 17:10
22 21:29 ♃ ☍	♎ 23 18:19
25 20:49 ♂ ✶	♏ 25 22:45
27 6:39 ♃ △	♐ 28 7:00
30 6:11 ♅ ✶	♑ 30 18:11

Last Aspect Dy Hr Mn	☽ Ingress Dy Hr Mn
1 18:45 ♅ □	♒ 2 6:46
4 7:38 ♅ △	♓ 4 19:26
6 10:41 ♀ △	♈ 7 7:15
9 6:22 ♅ ☍	♉ 9 17:13
11 17:07 ♀ ✶	♊ 12 0:15
13 18:31 ♅ △	♋ 14 3:49
15 19:42 ♅ □	♌ 16 4:26
17 19:44 ☿ ☌	♍ 18 3:42
19 3:42 ♃ ☍	♎ 20 3:45
22 4:21 ☉ ✶	♏ 22 6:37
23 13:16 ♂ ✶	♐ 24 13:34
26 14:11 ♅ ✶	♑ 27 0:15
29 2:52 ♅ □	♒ 29 12:53

☽ Phases & Eclipses Dy Hr Mn	
4 12:40	○ 12♑10
12 15:28	☾ 19♈54
19 12:06	● 26♋27
26 3:51	☽ 2♏48
3 3:57	○ 10♒27
11 2:46	☾ 18♉04
17 19:02	● 24♌29
24 15:38	☽ 1♐05

Astro Data

1 July 1974
Julian Day # 27210
SVP 5♓36'40"
GC 26♐29.0 ⚵ 7♒17.2R
Eris 13♈46.5 ✱ 17♓21.6
⚷ 24♈11.0 ⚶ 11♎13.4
☽ Mean ☊ 18♐18.8

1 August 1974
Julian Day # 27241
SVP 5♓36'35"
GC 26♐29.1 ⚵ 29♑21.7R
Eris 13♈44.4R ✱ 18♓25.8R
⚷ 24♈29.6R ⚶ 22♎15.2
☽ Mean ☊ 16♐40.3

LONGITUDE — September 1974

Day	Sid.Time	☉	0 hr ☽	Noon ☽	True ☊	☿	♀	♂	⚳	♃	♄	♅	♆	♇
1 Su	10 41 05	8♍40 16	29♒15 37	5♓15 15	15♐35.4	22♍10.6	21♌26.9	22♍43.8	8♓03.9	13♓27.3	15♋48.1	25♎13.6	6♐53.7	5♎37.2
2 M	10 45 01	9 38 20	11♓16 26	17 19 17	15R 21.5	23 51.9	22 40.8	23 22.2	7R 50.6	13R 19.4	15 53.8	25 16.5	6 54.1	5 39.3
3 Tu	10 48 58	10 36 25	23 23 56	29 30 30	15 08.2	25 31.9	23 54.7	24 00.7	7 37.2	13 11.4	15 59.4	25 19.4	6 54.6	5 41.5
4 W	10 52 55	11 34 32	5♈39 05	11♈49 51	14 56.6	27 10.7	25 08.6	24 39.2	7 24.0	13 03.5	16 04.9	25 22.3	6 55.1	5 43.6
5 Th	10 56 51	12 32 40	18 02 56	24 18 32	14 47.4	28 48.3	26 22.6	25 17.8	7 10.7	12 55.6	16 10.4	25 25.3	6 55.7	5 45.8
6 F	11 00 48	13 30 51	0♉36 51	6♉58 07	14 41.1	0♎24.8	27 36.6	25 56.3	6 57.6	12 47.6	16 15.8	25 28.3	6 56.3	5 47.9
7 Sa	11 04 44	14 29 03	13 22 38	19 50 42	14 37.5	2 00.0	28 50.7	26 34.9	6 44.5	12 39.7	16 21.2	25 31.4	6 56.9	5 50.1
8 Su	11 08 41	15 27 18	26 22 39	2♊58 48	14D 36.2	3 34.1	0♍04.8	27 13.6	6 31.5	12 31.7	16 26.4	25 34.5	6 57.5	5 52.3
9 M	11 12 37	16 25 35	9♊39 31	16 25 06	14R 36.0	5 07.0	1 18.9	27 52.3	6 18.6	12 23.8	16 31.6	25 37.6	6 58.2	5 54.5
10 Tu	11 16 34	17 23 54	23 15 49	0♋11 55	14 35.7	6 38.8	2 33.1	28 31.0	6 05.8	12 15.9	16 36.7	25 40.7	6 58.9	5 56.7
11 W	11 20 30	18 22 15	7♋13 28	14 20 30	14 34.2	8 09.3	3 47.3	29 09.7	5 53.2	12 08.0	16 41.8	25 43.9	6 59.6	5 58.9
12 Th	11 24 27	19 20 38	21 32 52	28 50 15	14 30.3	9 38.8	5 01.5	29 48.5	5 40.7	12 00.2	16 46.7	25 47.1	7 00.4	6 01.1
13 F	11 28 24	20 19 03	6♌12 09	13♌37 54	14 23.8	11 07.0	6 15.8	0♎27.3	5 28.4	11 52.4	16 51.6	25 50.3	7 01.2	6 03.4
14 Sa	11 32 20	21 17 30	21 06 38	28 37 19	14 14.7	12 34.1	7 30.1	1 06.1	5 16.2	11 44.7	16 56.4	25 53.6	7 02.1	6 05.6
15 Su	11 36 17	22 15 59	6♍08 48	13♍39 51	14 03.9	14 00.0	8 44.4	1 45.0	5 04.2	11 36.9	17 01.1	25 56.8	7 02.9	6 07.9
16 M	11 40 13	23 14 30	21 09 12	28 35 39	13 52.6	15 24.7	9 58.8	2 23.9	4 52.4	11 29.3	17 05.7	26 00.1	7 03.8	6 10.1
17 Tu	11 44 10	24 13 03	5♎58 02	13♎15 24	13 42.1	16 48.2	11 13.2	3 02.8	4 40.9	11 21.7	17 10.3	26 03.5	7 04.7	6 12.4
18 W	11 48 06	25 11 38	20 26 53	27 31 54	13 33.6	18 10.4	12 27.6	3 41.8	4 29.5	11 14.2	17 14.8	26 06.8	7 05.7	6 14.7
19 Th	11 52 03	26 10 14	4♏30 00	11♏21 01	13 27.6	19 31.4	13 42.1	4 20.8	4 18.4	11 06.8	17 19.1	26 10.2	7 06.7	6 17.0
20 F	11 55 59	27 08 53	18 04 54	24 41 48	13 24.2	20 51.0	14 56.6	4 59.8	4 07.5	10 59.4	17 23.4	26 13.6	7 07.7	6 19.2
21 Sa	11 59 56	28 07 32	1♐12 03	7♐36 02	13D 22.9	22 09.2	16 11.1	5 38.8	3 56.9	10 52.1	17 27.6	26 17.0	7 08.8	6 21.5
22 Su	12 03 52	29 06 14	13 54 17	20 07 22	13R 22.9	23 25.9	17 25.6	6 17.9	3 46.6	10 45.0	17 31.8	26 20.5	7 09.8	6 23.8
23 M	12 07 49	0♎04 57	26 15 55	2♑20 36	13 23.0	24 41.2	18 40.2	6 57.0	3 36.5	10 37.9	17 35.8	26 23.9	7 10.9	6 26.1
24 Tu	12 11 46	1 03 43	8♑22 05	14 21 02	13 22.2	25 54.9	19 54.8	7 36.2	3 26.7	10 30.9	17 39.7	26 27.4	7 12.1	6 28.4
25 W	12 15 42	2 02 29	20 18 05	26 13 54	13 19.5	27 06.9	21 09.4	8 15.4	3 17.2	10 24.0	17 43.6	26 30.9	7 13.2	6 30.7
26 Th	12 19 39	3 01 18	2♒09 03	8♒04 06	13 14.4	28 17.2	22 24.0	8 54.6	3 07.9	10 17.3	17 47.3	26 34.5	7 14.4	6 33.1
27 F	12 23 35	4 00 08	13 59 33	19 55 53	13 06.6	29 25.6	23 38.7	9 33.8	2 59.0	10 10.6	17 51.0	26 38.0	7 15.7	6 35.4
28 Sa	12 27 32	4 59 00	25 53 29	1♓52 42	12 56.6	0♏32.0	24 53.4	10 13.1	2 50.4	10 04.1	17 54.5	26 41.6	7 16.9	6 37.7
29 Su	12 31 28	5 57 54	7♓53 51	13 57 10	12 44.9	1 36.3	26 08.1	10 52.4	2 42.1	9 57.7	17 58.0	26 45.1	7 18.2	6 40.0
30 M	12 35 25	6 56 49	20 02 50	26 10 59	12 32.6	2 38.3	27 22.8	11 31.8	2 34.2	9 51.4	18 01.4	26 48.7	7 19.5	6 42.3

LONGITUDE — October 1974

Day	Sid.Time	☉	0 hr ☽	Noon ☽	True ☊	☿	♀	♂	⚳	♃	♄	♅	♆	♇
1 Tu	12 39 21	7♎55 47	2♈21 43	8♈35 06	12♐20.8	3♏37.8	28♍37.6	12♎11.2	2♓26.6	9♓45.3	18♋04.7	26♎52.3	7♐20.8	6♎44.6
2 W	12 43 18	8 54 47	14 51 10	21 09 56	12R 10.5	4 34.6	29 52.4	12 50.6	2R 19.3	9R 39.3	18 07.8	26 56.0	7 22.2	6 46.9
3 Th	12 47 15	9 53 48	27 31 23	3♉55 33	12 02.4	5 28.5	1♎07.2	13 30.0	2 12.3	9 33.5	18 10.9	26 59.6	7 23.6	6 49.2
4 F	12 51 11	10 52 52	10♉22 25	16 52 02	11 57.1	6 19.3	2 22.0	14 09.5	2 05.7	9 27.8	18 13.9	27 03.3	7 25.0	6 51.5
5 Sa	12 55 08	11 51 59	23 24 27	29 59 45	11D 54.3	7 06.6	3 36.9	14 49.0	1 59.4	9 22.2	18 16.8	27 06.9	7 26.4	6 53.9
6 Su	12 59 04	12 51 07	6♊38 01	13♊19 22	11 53.7	7 50.2	4 51.7	15 28.6	1 53.5	9 16.8	18 19.6	27 10.6	7 27.9	6 56.2
7 M	13 03 01	13 50 18	20 03 57	26 51 54	11 54.3	8 29.7	6 06.6	16 08.2	1 47.9	9 11.6	18 22.3	27 14.3	7 29.4	6 58.5
8 Tu	13 06 57	14 49 31	3♋43 20	10♋38 22	11R 54.9	9 04.7	7 21.6	16 47.8	1 42.7	9 06.5	18 24.9	27 18.0	7 30.9	7 00.8
9 W	13 10 54	15 48 47	17 37 03	24 39 24	11 54.7	9 34.8	8 36.5	17 27.5	1 37.9	9 01.6	18 27.3	27 21.7	7 32.4	7 03.1
10 Th	13 14 50	16 48 05	1♌45 18	8♌54 34	11 52.6	9 59.7	9 51.5	18 07.2	1 33.4	8 56.8	18 29.7	27 25.4	7 34.0	7 05.4
11 F	13 18 47	17 47 25	16 06 55	23 21 55	11 48.3	10 18.7	11 06.5	18 46.9	1 29.3	8 52.2	18 32.0	27 29.2	7 35.6	7 07.6
12 Sa	13 22 44	18 46 47	0♍39 00	7♍57 31	11 41.9	10 31.4	12 21.5	19 26.7	1 25.5	8 47.8	18 34.2	27 32.9	7 37.2	7 09.9
13 Su	13 26 40	19 46 12	15 16 41	22 35 39	11 34.1	10R 37.4	13 36.5	20 06.6	1 22.1	8 43.6	18 36.2	27 36.6	7 38.9	7 12.2
14 M	13 30 37	20 45 39	29 53 31	7♎09 21	11 25.7	10 36.1	14 51.5	20 46.4	1 19.1	8 39.5	18 38.2	27 40.4	7 40.5	7 14.5
15 Tu	13 34 33	21 45 08	14♎22 16	21 31 27	11 17.9	10 27.0	16 06.6	21 26.3	1 16.5	8 35.7	18 40.0	27 44.2	7 42.2	7 16.7
16 W	13 38 30	22 44 39	28 36 10	5♏35 49	11 11.5	10 09.7	17 21.7	22 06.2	1 14.2	8 32.0	18 41.7	27 47.9	7 43.9	7 19.0
17 Th	13 42 26	23 44 12	12♏29 55	19 18 09	11 07.1	9 44.0	18 36.8	22 46.2	1 12.3	8 28.5	18 43.4	27 51.7	7 45.6	7 21.2
18 F	13 46 23	24 43 47	26 00 22	2♐36 31	11D 05.0	9 09.7	19 51.9	23 26.2	1 10.8	8 25.2	18 44.9	27 55.5	7 47.4	7 23.5
19 Sa	13 50 19	25 43 23	9♐06 45	15 31 16	11 04.7	8 26.8	21 07.0	24 06.3	1 09.6	8 22.1	18 46.3	27 59.2	7 49.2	7 25.7
20 Su	13 54 16	26 43 02	21 50 25	28 04 38	11 05.7	7 35.5	22 22.1	24 46.3	1 08.9	8 19.1	18 47.6	28 03.0	7 51.0	7 27.9
21 M	13 58 13	27 42 42	4♑14 26	10♑20 21	11 07.2	6 36.7	23 37.3	25 26.5	1D 08.5	8 16.4	18 48.8	28 06.8	7 52.8	7 30.1
22 Tu	14 02 09	28 42 24	16 22 58	22 22 56	11R 08.4	5 31.1	24 52.4	26 06.6	1 08.4	8 13.9	18 49.8	28 10.6	7 54.6	7 32.3
23 W	14 06 06	29 42 08	28 20 53	4♒17 27	11 08.5	4 20.3	26 07.6	26 46.8	1 08.8	8 11.6	18 50.8	28 14.3	7 56.5	7 34.5
24 Th	14 10 02	0♏41 53	10♒13 16	16 08 57	11 07.0	3 05.9	27 22.7	27 27.0	1 09.5	8 09.4	18 51.7	28 18.1	7 58.3	7 36.7
25 F	14 13 59	1 41 40	22 05 06	28 02 17	11 03.8	1 49.9	28 37.9	28 07.3	1 10.6	8 07.5	18 52.4	28 21.9	8 00.2	7 38.9
26 Sa	14 17 55	2 41 29	4♓01 01	10♓01 48	10 58.9	0 34.7	29 53.1	28 47.6	1 12.0	8 05.8	18 53.0	28 25.7	8 02.1	7 41.0
27 Su	14 21 52	3 41 20	16 05 02	22 11 06	10 52.9	29♎22.5	1♏08.3	29 27.9	1 13.8	8 04.2	18 53.5	28 29.4	8 04.1	7 43.1
28 M	14 25 48	4 41 12	28 20 19	4♈32 56	10 46.3	28 15.5	2 23.5	0♏08.3	1 15.9	8 02.9	18 53.9	28 33.2	8 06.0	7 45.3
29 Tu	14 29 45	5 41 06	10♈49 08	17 09 02	10 39.9	27 15.9	3 38.7	0 48.7	1 18.4	8 01.8	18 54.2	28 36.9	8 08.0	7 47.4
30 W	14 33 41	6 41 02	23 32 41	0♉00 05	10 34.3	26 25.2	4 53.9	1 29.1	1 21.3	8 00.9	18 54.4	28 40.7	8 10.0	7 49.5
31 Th	14 37 38	7 41 00	6♉31 11	13 05 51	10 30.1	25 44.8	6 09.2	2 09.6	1 24.5	8 00.1	18R 54.5	28 44.4	8 12.0	7 51.6

Astro Data Dy Hr Mn	Planet Ingress Dy Hr Mn	Last Aspect Dy Hr Mn	☽ Ingress Dy Hr Mn	Last Aspect Dy Hr Mn	☽ Ingress Dy Hr Mn	☽ Phases & Eclipses Dy Hr Mn	Astro Data
☽0N 2 14:06	☿ ♎ 6 5:48	31 15:49 ♅ △	♓ 1 1:29	2 22:56 ♅ ☍	♉ 3 4:39	1 19:25 ○ 8♓58	1 September 1974
☿0S 6 14:44	♀ ♍ 8 10:28	3 2:58 ☿ ☍	♈ 3 12:58	4 14:31 ♄ ✶	♊ 5 12:00	9 12:01 ☾ 16♊26	Julian Day # 27272
♂0S 15 13:04	♂ ♎ 12 19:08	5 16:22 ♀ △	♉ 5 22:50	7 12:40 ♅ △	♋ 7 17:30	16 2:45 ● 22♍52	SVP 5♓36'31"
☽0S 15 19:32	☉ ♎ 23 9:58	8 6:12 ♀ □	♊ 8 6:36	9 16:36 ♅ □	♌ 9 21:03	23 7:08 ☽ 29♐53	GC 26♐29.1 ⚴ 23♑23.9R
♃□♅ 19 4:22	☿ ♏ 28 0:20	10 8:58 ♂ □	♋ 10 11:40	11 18:49 ♅ ✶	♍ 11 22:56		Eris 13♈32.9R ⚵ 13♓10.5R
☉0S 23 9:59		12 13:40 ♂ ✶	♌ 12 13:54	13 5:26 ♄ ✶	♎ 14 0:11	1 10:38 ○ 7♈52	⚷ 23♈58.8R ⚶ 5♏49.3
☽0N 29 20:38	♀ ♎ 2 14:27	14 7:38 ♅ ✶	♍ 14 14:12	15 22:34 ♅ ☌	♏ 16 2:23	8 19:46 ☾ 15♋09	☽ Mean ☊ 15♐01.8
	☉ ♏ 23 19:11	16 2:45 ☉ ☌	♎ 16 14:17	17 10:58 ♄ △	♐ 18 7:14	15 12:25 ● 21♎46	
♀0S 5 6:12	♀ ♏ 26 14:12	18 9:34 ♅ ☌	♏ 18 16:14	20 11:57 ♅ ✶	♑ 20 15:44	23 1:53 ☽ 29♑17	1 October 1974
☽0S 13 4:47	☿ ♎R 26 23:21	20 16:52 ☉ ✶	♐ 20 21:46	23 1:53 ☉ □	♒ 23 3:20	31 1:19 ○ 7♉14	Julian Day # 27302
☿R 13 19:48	♂ ♏ 28 7:05	23 7:08 ☉ □	♑ 23 7:22	25 13:20 ♀ △	♓ 25 15:57		SVP 5♓36'29"
⚳D 22 1:56		25 13:59 ☿ □	♒ 25 19:38	27 5:32 ♄ △	♈ 28 3:13		GC 26♐29.2 ⚴ 22♑55.7
☽0N 27 3:52		28 1:33 ♅ △	♓ 28 8:14	30 9:32 ♅ ☍	♉ 30 12:00		Eris 13♈16.0R ⚵ 6♓28.9R
♃□♆ 27 13:10		30 14:36 ♀ ☍	♈ 30 19:25				⚷ 22♈51.3R ⚶ 20♏24.7
♄R 31 14:56							☽ Mean ☊ 13♐26.5

November 1974 — LONGITUDE

Day	Sid.Time	☉	0 hr ☽	Noon ☽	True ☊	☿	♀	♂	⚳	♃	♄	♅	♆	♇
1 F	14 41 35	8♏41 00	19♉43 57	26♉25 19	10♐27.7	25♎15.6	7♏24.4	2♏50.2	1♓28.0	7♓59.6	18♋54.4	28♎48.2	8♐14.0	7♎53.6
2 Sa	14 45 31	9 41 01	3♊09 46	9♊57 04	10D 26.9	24R 57.9	8 39.7	3 30.7	1 31.9	7R 59.3	18R 54.3	28 51.9	8 16.0	7 55.7
3 Su	14 49 28	10 41 05	16 47 02	23 39 27	10 27.4	24D 51.8	9 54.9	4 11.3	1 36.1	7D 59.2	18 54.0	28 55.6	8 18.0	7 57.7
4 M	14 53 24	11 41 11	0♋34 08	7♋30 54	10 28.8	24 57.0	11 10.2	4 52.0	1 40.7	7 59.3	18 53.7	28 59.4	8 20.1	7 59.7
5 Tu	14 57 21	12 41 19	14 29 35	21 29 59	10 30.4	25 12.9	12 25.5	5 32.7	1 45.6	7 59.6	18 53.2	29 03.1	8 22.2	8 01.7
6 W	15 01 17	13 41 29	28 31 57	5♌35 18	10R 31.5	25 38.8	13 40.8	6 13.4	1 50.8	8 00.1	18 52.6	29 06.8	8 24.3	8 03.7
7 Th	15 05 14	14 41 41	12♌39 51	19 45 22	10 31.6	26 13.9	14 56.1	6 54.2	1 56.3	8 00.8	18 51.8	29 10.4	8 26.4	8 05.7
8 F	15 09 10	15 41 55	26 51 37	3♍58 18	10 30.5	26 57.3	16 11.4	7 35.0	2 02.2	8 01.8	18 51.0	29 14.1	8 28.5	8 07.6
9 Sa	15 13 07	16 42 11	11♍05 06	18 11 40	10 28.4	27 48.2	17 26.7	8 15.8	2 08.4	8 02.9	18 50.1	29 17.8	8 30.6	8 09.5
10 Su	15 17 04	17 42 29	25 17 34	2♎22 21	10 25.4	28 45.6	18 42.0	8 56.7	2 14.9	8 04.2	18 49.0	29 21.4	8 32.7	8 11.4
11 M	15 21 00	18 42 49	9♎25 35	16 26 47	10 22.1	29 48.7	19 57.3	9 37.7	2 21.7	8 05.7	18 47.9	29 25.0	8 34.9	8 13.3
12 Tu	15 24 57	19 43 11	23 25 27	0♏21 08	10 19.1	0♏56.9	21 12.7	10 18.6	2 28.8	8 07.4	18 46.6	29 28.6	8 37.0	8 15.2
13 W	15 28 53	20 43 35	7♏13 25	14 01 55	10 16.7	2 09.3	22 28.0	10 59.7	2 36.3	8 09.4	18 45.2	29 32.2	8 39.2	8 17.0
14 Th	15 32 50	21 44 01	20 46 19	27 26 21	10D 15.2	3 25.4	23 43.4	11 40.7	2 44.0	8 11.5	18 43.7	29 35.8	8 41.4	8 18.9
15 F	15 36 46	22 44 28	4♐01 53	10♐32 48	10 14.7	4 44.6	24 58.7	12 21.8	2 52.1	8 13.9	18 42.1	29 39.4	8 43.5	8 20.7
16 Sa	15 40 43	23 44 57	16 59 06	23 20 53	10 15.2	6 06.5	26 14.1	13 03.0	3 00.4	8 16.4	18 40.4	29 42.9	8 45.7	8 22.4
17 Su	15 44 39	24 45 27	29 38 17	5♑51 35	10 16.2	7 30.6	27 29.5	13 44.1	3 09.1	8 19.1	18 38.6	29 46.5	8 47.9	8 24.2
18 M	15 48 36	25 45 58	12♑01 04	18 07 07	10 17.6	8 56.5	28 44.8	14 25.4	3 18.0	8 22.1	18 36.7	29 50.0	8 50.2	8 25.9
19 Tu	15 52 33	26 46 31	24 10 09	0♒10 40	10 19.0	10 24.0	0♐00.2	15 06.6	3 27.2	8 25.2	18 34.6	29 53.5	8 52.4	8 27.6
20 W	15 56 29	27 47 05	6♒09 10	12 06 13	10 20.0	11 52.8	1 15.6	15 47.9	3 36.7	8 28.5	18 32.5	29 56.9	8 54.6	8 29.3
21 Th	16 00 26	28 47 40	18 02 23	23 58 16	10R 20.5	13 22.7	2 30.9	16 29.2	3 46.5	8 32.1	18 30.3	0♏00.4	8 56.8	8 31.0
22 F	16 04 22	29 48 17	29 54 27	5♓51 33	10 20.5	14 53.4	3 46.3	17 10.6	3 56.6	8 35.8	18 27.9	0 03.8	8 59.1	8 32.6
23 Sa	16 08 19	0♐48 54	11♓50 08	17 50 49	10 19.9	16 24.8	5 01.6	17 52.0	4 06.9	8 39.7	18 25.5	0 07.2	9 01.3	8 34.2
24 Su	16 12 15	1 49 33	23 54 08	0♈00 36	10 19.1	17 56.7	6 17.0	18 33.5	4 17.5	8 43.8	18 23.0	0 10.5	9 03.5	8 35.8
25 M	16 16 12	2 50 13	6♈10 43	12 24 53	10 18.1	19 29.1	7 32.4	19 15.0	4 28.3	8 48.1	18 20.3	0 13.9	9 05.8	8 37.3
26 Tu	16 20 08	3 50 54	18 43 28	25 06 47	10 17.1	21 01.9	8 47.7	19 56.5	4 39.4	8 52.5	18 17.6	0 17.2	9 08.0	8 38.9
27 W	16 24 05	4 51 36	1♉35 02	8♉08 20	10 16.4	22 34.9	10 03.1	20 38.1	4 50.8	8 57.2	18 14.8	0 20.5	9 10.3	8 40.4
28 Th	16 28 02	5 52 19	14 46 44	21 30 10	10 15.9	24 08.1	11 18.5	21 19.7	5 02.4	9 02.0	18 11.9	0 23.7	9 12.6	8 41.8
29 F	16 31 58	6 53 04	28 18 28	5♊11 22	10D 15.7	25 41.5	12 33.8	22 01.3	5 14.2	9 07.0	18 08.8	0 27.0	9 14.8	8 43.3
30 Sa	16 35 55	7 53 50	12♊08 32	19 09 32	10 15.7	27 15.0	13 49.2	22 43.0	5 26.3	9 12.2	18 05.7	0 30.2	9 17.1	8 44.7

December 1974 — LONGITUDE

Day	Sid.Time	☉	0 hr ☽	Noon ☽	True ☊	☿	♀	♂	⚳	♃	♄	♅	♆	♇
1 Su	16 39 51	8♐54 37	26♊13 53	3♋21 00	10♐15.8	28♏48.6	15♐04.6	23♏24.7	5♓38.6	9♓17.6	18♋02.6	0♏33.4	9♐19.3	8♎46.1
2 M	16 43 48	9 55 26	10♋30 19	17 41 12	10R 15.9	0♐22.3	16 19.9	24 06.5	5 51.2	9 23.2	17R 59.3	0 36.5	9 21.6	8 47.5
3 Tu	16 47 44	10 56 16	24 53 05	2♌05 20	10 15.9	1 56.0	17 35.3	24 48.3	6 04.0	9 28.9	17 55.9	0 39.6	9 23.9	8 48.8
4 W	16 51 41	11 57 07	9♌17 25	16 28 47	10 15.8	3 29.7	18 50.7	25 30.2	6 17.0	9 34.8	17 52.5	0 42.7	9 26.1	8 50.1
5 Th	16 55 38	12 57 59	23 39 01	0♍47 41	10D 15.7	5 03.5	20 06.1	26 12.1	6 30.3	9 40.9	17 48.9	0 45.8	9 28.4	8 51.4
6 F	16 59 34	13 58 53	7♍54 25	14 58 58	10 15.6	6 37.2	21 21.4	26 54.1	6 43.7	9 47.2	17 45.3	0 48.8	9 30.6	8 52.6
7 Sa	17 03 31	14 59 48	22 01 05	29 00 34	10 15.7	8 11.0	22 36.8	27 36.0	6 57.4	9 53.6	17 41.6	0 51.8	9 32.9	8 53.8
8 Su	17 07 27	16 00 45	5♎57 17	12♎51 07	10 16.1	9 44.8	23 52.2	28 18.1	7 11.3	10 00.2	17 37.8	0 54.7	9 35.1	8 55.0
9 M	17 11 24	17 01 42	19 41 58	26 29 47	10 16.7	11 18.7	25 07.6	29 00.2	7 25.4	10 06.9	17 34.0	0 57.6	9 37.4	8 56.2
10 Tu	17 15 20	18 02 41	3♏14 29	9♏56 03	10 17.5	12 52.5	26 23.0	29 42.3	7 39.8	10 13.8	17 30.1	1 00.5	9 39.6	8 57.3
11 W	17 19 17	19 03 41	16 34 24	23 09 32	10 18.1	14 26.5	27 38.4	0♐24.4	7 54.3	10 20.9	17 26.1	1 03.4	9 41.9	8 58.4
12 Th	17 23 13	20 04 42	29 41 24	6♐09 59	10R 18.5	16 00.4	28 53.7	1 06.6	8 09.0	10 28.2	17 22.0	1 06.2	9 44.1	8 59.4
13 F	17 27 10	21 05 44	12♐35 17	18 57 19	10 18.4	17 34.5	0♑09.1	1 48.9	8 24.0	10 35.6	17 17.9	1 08.9	9 46.4	9 00.5
14 Sa	17 31 07	22 06 47	25 16 05	1♑31 41	10 17.7	19 08.6	1 24.5	2 31.2	8 39.1	10 43.1	17 13.7	1 11.7	9 48.6	9 01.4
15 Su	17 35 03	23 07 50	7♑44 11	13 53 44	10 16.3	20 42.8	2 39.9	3 13.5	8 54.4	10 50.9	17 09.4	1 14.4	9 50.8	9 02.4
16 M	17 39 00	24 08 54	20 00 28	26 04 38	10 14.3	22 17.1	3 55.3	3 55.9	9 10.0	10 58.7	17 05.1	1 17.0	9 53.0	9 03.3
17 Tu	17 42 56	25 09 59	2♒06 28	8♒06 16	10 11.9	23 51.6	5 10.6	4 38.3	9 25.7	11 06.7	17 00.7	1 19.6	9 55.2	9 04.2
18 W	17 46 53	26 11 04	14 04 22	20 01 11	10 09.5	25 26.1	6 26.0	5 20.7	9 41.5	11 14.9	16 56.3	1 22.2	9 57.4	9 05.1
19 Th	17 50 49	27 12 09	25 57 09	1♓52 42	10 07.3	27 00.9	7 41.4	6 03.2	9 57.6	11 23.2	16 51.8	1 24.7	9 59.6	9 05.9
20 F	17 54 46	28 13 15	7♓48 22	13 44 41	10 05.7	28 35.7	8 56.7	6 45.7	10 13.9	11 31.7	16 47.3	1 27.2	10 01.8	9 06.7
21 Sa	17 58 42	29 14 21	19 42 13	25 41 33	10D 05.0	0♑10.8	10 12.1	7 28.3	10 30.3	11 40.3	16 42.7	1 29.7	10 03.9	9 07.5
22 Su	18 02 39	0♑15 27	1♈43 16	7♈47 58	10 05.2	1 46.1	11 27.4	8 10.9	10 46.9	11 49.1	16 38.1	1 32.1	10 06.1	9 08.2
23 M	18 06 36	1 16 33	13 56 15	20 08 41	10 06.1	3 21.5	12 42.8	8 53.5	11 03.6	11 58.0	16 33.4	1 34.4	10 08.2	9 08.9
24 Tu	18 10 32	2 17 40	26 25 49	2♉48 10	10 07.7	4 57.2	13 58.1	9 36.2	11 20.5	12 07.0	16 28.7	1 36.8	10 10.4	9 09.5
25 W	18 14 29	3 18 46	9♉16 08	15 50 07	10 09.3	6 33.1	15 13.4	10 18.9	11 37.6	12 16.2	16 24.0	1 39.0	10 12.5	9 10.2
26 Th	18 18 25	4 19 53	22 30 22	29 17 01	10R 10.5	8 09.3	16 28.7	11 01.7	11 54.9	12 25.4	16 19.2	1 41.3	10 14.6	9 10.7
27 F	18 22 22	5 21 00	6♊10 07	13♊09 31	10 10.9	9 45.7	17 44.1	11 44.5	12 12.3	12 34.9	16 14.4	1 43.4	10 16.7	9 11.3
28 Sa	18 26 18	6 22 07	20 14 55	27 25 53	10 09.9	11 22.3	18 59.4	12 27.3	12 29.8	12 44.4	16 09.6	1 45.6	10 18.8	9 11.8
29 Su	18 30 15	7 23 15	4♋41 48	12♋01 54	10 07.6	12 59.2	20 14.7	13 10.2	12 47.5	12 54.1	16 04.7	1 47.7	10 20.9	9 12.3
30 M	18 34 11	8 24 22	19 25 17	26 50 59	10 04.0	14 36.4	21 29.9	13 53.1	13 05.4	13 03.9	15 59.8	1 49.7	10 22.9	9 12.8
31 Tu	18 38 08	9 25 30	4♌17 55	11♌45 03	9 59.7	16 13.8	22 45.2	14 36.1	13 23.3	13 13.9	15 54.9	1 51.7	10 25.0	9 13.2

Astro Data

	Dy Hr Mn
♃ D	3 12:13
☿ D	3 12:51
♃⚻♇	4 6:43
☽0S	9 11:31
♃⚻♇	20 22:21
☽0N	23 11:54
♃□♆	2 0:34
☽0S	6 16:46
☽0N	20 20:18

Planet Ingress

	Dy Hr Mn
☿ ♏	11 16:05
♀ ♐	19 11:56
♅ ♏	21 9:32
☉ ♐	22 16:38
☿ ♐	2 6:17
♂ ♐	10 22:05
♀ ♑	13 9:06
☿ ♑	21 9:16
☉ ♑	22 5:56

Last Aspect / ☽ Ingress

Last Aspect Dy Hr Mn		☽ Ingress Dy Hr Mn
31 22:31	♄ ⚹	♊ 1 18:23
3 21:12	♅ △	♋ 3 23:01
6 0:56	♅ □	♌ 6 2:30
8 3:58	♅ ⚹	♍ 8 5:18
9 13:05	♄ ⚹	♎ 10 7:58
12 10:28	♅ ☌	♏ 12 11:23
14 4:36	♀ ☌	♐ 14 16:39
17 0:12	♅ ⚹	♑ 17 0:42
19 11:37	♀ ⚹	♒ 19 11:39
21 22:39	☉ □	♓ 22 0:11
23 13:09	♄ △	♈ 24 11:59
25 23:14	♄ □	♉ 26 21:05
28 17:16	☿ ☍	♊ 29 2:58

Last Aspect / ☽ Ingress

Last Aspect Dy Hr Mn		☽ Ingress Dy Hr Mn
30 1:59	♀ ☍	♋ 1 6:22
2 23:15	♂ △	♌ 3 8:31
5 3:53	♂ □	♍ 5 10:40
7 9:27	♂ ⚹	♎ 7 13:42
9 9:20	♀ ⚹	♏ 9 18:13
11 1:37	♄ △	♐ 12 0:34
13 16:25	☉ ☌	♑ 14 9:04
15 18:21	♄ ☍	♒ 16 19:48
19 1:38	☉ ⚹	♓ 19 8:12
21 19:43	☉ □	♈ 21 20:35
23 5:07	♀ □	♉ 24 6:45
25 13:01	♄ ⚹	♊ 26 13:15
27 11:00	♃ □	♋ 28 16:15
30 2:34	♀ ☍	♌ 30 17:05

☽ Phases & Eclipses

Dy Hr Mn	
7 2:47	☾ 14♌19
14 0:53	● 21♏16
21 22:39	☽ 29♒15
29 15:10	○ 7♊01
29 15:13	☍ T 1.289
6 10:10	☾ 13♍54
13 16:25	● 21♐17
13 16:12:29	☌ P 0.827
21 19:43	☽ 29♓34
29 3:51	○ 7♋02

Astro Data

1 November 1974
Julian Day # 27333
SVP 5♓36'25"
GC 26♐29.3 ⚴ 27♑13.4
Eris 12♈57.5R ⚵ 5♓22.7
⚷ 21♈27.2R ⚶ 6♐24.1
☽ Mean ☊ 11♐47.9

1 December 1974
Julian Day # 27363
SVP 5♓36'21"
GC 26♐29.3 ⚴ 4♒22.6
Eris 12♈44.0R ⚵ 11♓20.8
⚷ 20♈22.1R ⚶ 22♐22.0
☽ Mean ☊ 10♐12.6

LONGITUDE

January 1975

Day	Sid.Time	☉	0 hr ☽	Noon ☽	True ☊	☿	♀	♂	⚳	♃	♄	♅	♆	♇
1 W	18 42 05	10♑26 38	19♌11 18	26♌35 42	9♐55.3	17♑51.5	24♑00.5	15♐19.1	13♓41.5	13♓23.9	15♋50.0	1♏53.6	10♐27.0	9♎13.6
2 Th	18 46 01	11 27 47	3♍57 22	11♍15 32	9R51.5	19 29.3	25 15.8	16 02.1	13 59.8	13 34.1	15R45.1	1 55.5	10 29.0	9 13.9
3 F	18 49 58	12 28 55	18 29 36	25 39 06	9 48.8	21 07.4	26 31.0	16 45.2	14 18.2	13 44.4	15 40.1	1 57.4	10 31.0	9 14.2
4 Sa	18 53 54	13 30 04	2♎43 44	9♎43 20	9D47.6	22 45.6	27 46.3	17 28.3	14 36.7	13 54.8	15 35.2	1 59.2	10 33.0	9 14.5
5 Su	18 57 51	14 31 13	16 37 51	23 27 22	9 47.9	24 24.0	29 01.5	18 11.5	14 55.4	14 05.3	15 30.2	2 00.9	10 35.0	9 14.7
6 M	19 01 47	15 32 23	0♏12 00	6♏51 59	9 49.2	26 02.4	0♒16.8	18 54.7	15 14.2	14 16.0	15 25.2	2 02.6	10 36.9	9 14.9
7 Tu	19 05 44	16 33 33	13 27 34	19 59 03	9 50.8	27 40.8	1 32.0	19 38.0	15 33.2	14 26.7	15 20.3	2 04.3	10 38.8	9 15.1
8 W	19 09 40	17 34 43	26 26 43	2♐50 50	9R52.1	29 19.2	2 47.2	20 21.3	15 52.2	14 37.6	15 15.3	2 05.8	10 40.7	9 15.2
9 Th	19 13 37	18 35 53	9♐11 43	15 29 36	9 52.1	0♒57.4	4 02.4	21 04.6	16 11.4	14 48.6	15 10.4	2 07.4	10 42.6	9 15.3
10 F	19 17 34	19 37 02	21 44 44	27 57 19	9 50.4	2 35.3	5 17.6	21 48.0	16 30.8	14 59.7	15 05.4	2 08.9	10 44.5	9 15.4
11 Sa	19 21 30	20 38 12	4♑07 33	10♑15 36	9 46.5	4 12.8	6 32.8	22 31.4	16 50.2	15 10.9	15 00.5	2 10.3	10 46.4	9R15.4
12 Su	19 25 27	21 39 22	16 21 38	22 25 46	9 40.6	5 49.7	7 48.0	23 14.8	17 09.8	15 22.2	14 55.6	2 11.7	10 48.2	9 15.4
13 M	19 29 23	22 40 31	28 28 09	4♒28 57	9 32.9	7 25.8	9 03.2	23 58.3	17 29.5	15 33.6	14 50.7	2 13.0	10 50.0	9 15.3
14 Tu	19 33 20	23 41 39	10♒28 18	16 26 23	9 24.0	9 00.8	10 18.4	24 41.8	17 49.3	15 45.1	14 45.8	2 14.3	10 51.8	9 15.3
15 W	19 37 16	24 42 47	22 23 24	28 19 35	9 14.8	10 34.5	11 33.5	25 25.4	18 09.2	15 56.6	14 40.9	2 15.5	10 53.6	9 15.1
16 Th	19 41 13	25 43 55	4♓15 13	10♓10 36	9 06.2	12 06.6	12 48.6	26 09.0	18 29.2	16 08.3	14 36.1	2 16.7	10 55.3	9 15.0
17 F	19 45 09	26 45 01	16 06 05	22 02 04	8 58.9	13 36.6	14 03.8	26 52.6	18 49.3	16 20.1	14 31.3	2 17.8	10 57.0	9 14.8
18 Sa	19 49 06	27 46 07	27 59 00	3♈57 22	8 53.6	15 04.2	15 18.9	27 36.3	19 09.5	16 32.0	14 26.5	2 18.9	10 58.7	9 14.6
19 Su	19 53 03	28 47 13	9♈57 40	16 00 30	8 50.5	16 28.8	16 33.9	28 20.0	19 29.9	16 43.9	14 21.8	2 19.9	11 00.4	9 14.3
20 M	19 56 59	29 48 17	22 06 25	28 16 03	8D49.4	17 49.9	17 49.0	29 03.8	19 50.3	16 56.0	14 17.1	2 20.8	11 02.1	9 14.0
21 Tu	20 00 56	0♒49 21	4♉30 00	10♉48 52	8 49.9	19 06.9	19 04.0	29 47.5	20 10.8	17 08.1	14 12.4	2 21.7	11 03.7	9 13.7
22 W	20 04 52	1 50 23	17 13 16	23 43 43	8 50.9	20 19.0	20 19.1	0♑31.4	20 31.5	17 20.3	14 07.8	2 22.6	11 05.3	9 13.4
23 Th	20 08 49	2 51 25	0♊20 44	7♊04 42	8R51.7	21 25.5	21 34.1	1 15.2	20 52.2	17 32.6	14 03.3	2 23.3	11 06.9	9 13.0
24 F	20 12 45	3 52 26	13 55 53	20 54 27	8 51.0	22 25.6	22 49.1	1 59.1	21 13.0	17 45.0	13 58.7	2 24.1	11 08.4	9 12.5
25 Sa	20 16 42	4 53 25	28 00 19	5♋13 16	8 48.2	23 18.5	24 04.0	2 43.0	21 33.9	17 57.5	13 54.3	2 24.8	11 09.9	9 12.1
26 Su	20 20 39	5 54 24	12♋32 50	19 58 20	8 43.0	24 03.4	25 19.0	3 27.0	21 54.9	18 10.0	13 49.9	2 25.4	11 11.4	9 11.6
27 M	20 24 35	6 55 22	27 28 52	5♌03 19	8 35.4	24 39.3	26 33.9	4 11.0	22 16.0	18 22.7	13 45.5	2 25.9	11 12.9	9 11.1
28 Tu	20 28 32	7 56 19	12♌40 25	20 18 47	8 26.3	25 05.6	27 48.8	4 55.0	22 37.2	18 35.3	13 41.2	2 26.4	11 14.4	9 10.5
29 W	20 32 28	8 57 15	27 57 00	5♍33 38	8 16.7	25R21.4	29 03.6	5 39.1	22 58.4	18 48.1	13 37.0	2 26.9	11 15.8	9 09.9
30 Th	20 36 25	9 58 10	13♍07 23	20 37 03	8 08.0	25 26.5	0♓18.5	6 23.2	23 19.8	19 00.9	13 32.8	2 27.3	11 17.2	9 09.3
31 F	20 40 21	10 59 04	28 01 40	5♎20 25	8 01.0	25 20.3	1 33.3	7 07.3	23 41.2	19 13.8	13 28.7	2 27.6	11 18.5	9 08.7

LONGITUDE

February 1975

Day	Sid.Time	☉	0 hr ☽	Noon ☽	True ☊	☿	♀	♂	⚳	♃	♄	♅	♆	♇
1 Sa	20 44 18	11♒59 58	12♎32 47	19♎38 25	7♐56.5	25♒02.8	2♓48.1	7♑51.5	24♓02.7	19♓26.8	13♋24.6	2♏27.9	11♐19.9	9♎08.0
2 Su	20 48 14	13 00 51	26 37 12	3♏29 10	7D54.3	24R34.3	4 02.9	8 35.8	24 24.2	19 39.8	13R20.6	2 28.1	11 21.2	9R07.3
3 M	20 52 11	14 01 43	10♏14 32	16 53 38	7 53.9	23 55.3	5 17.6	9 20.0	24 45.9	19 52.9	13 16.7	2 28.3	11 22.5	9 06.5
4 Tu	20 56 07	15 02 34	23 26 51	29 54 40	7R54.4	23 06.8	6 32.4	10 04.3	25 07.6	20 06.1	13 12.9	2 28.4	11 23.7	9 05.7
5 W	21 00 04	16 03 25	6♐17 34	12♐36 06	7 54.5	22 10.1	7 47.1	10 48.7	25 29.4	20 19.3	13 09.1	2R28.5	11 25.0	9 04.9
6 Th	21 04 01	17 04 14	18 50 44	25 02 00	7 53.0	21 06.8	9 01.7	11 33.0	25 51.3	20 32.6	13 05.4	2 28.5	11 26.2	9 04.1
7 F	21 07 57	18 05 03	1♑10 20	7♑16 10	7 49.2	19 58.7	10 16.4	12 17.4	26 13.2	20 46.0	13 01.8	2 28.4	11 27.3	9 03.2
8 Sa	21 11 54	19 05 51	13 19 53	19 21 50	7 42.4	18 47.8	11 31.0	13 01.9	26 35.3	20 59.4	12 58.3	2 28.3	11 28.5	9 02.3
9 Su	21 15 50	20 06 37	25 22 18	1♒21 34	7 32.6	17 36.0	12 45.6	13 46.3	26 57.3	21 12.9	12 54.8	2 28.2	11 29.6	9 01.4
10 M	21 19 47	21 07 22	7♒19 51	13 17 20	7 20.3	16 25.4	14 00.2	14 30.8	27 19.5	21 26.4	12 51.5	2 27.9	11 30.6	9 00.5
11 Tu	21 23 43	22 08 06	19 14 13	25 10 37	7 06.3	15 17.7	15 14.8	15 15.4	27 41.7	21 40.0	12 48.2	2 27.7	11 31.7	8 59.5
12 W	21 27 40	23 08 49	1♓06 43	7♓02 40	6 51.7	14 14.4	16 29.3	15 59.9	28 04.0	21 53.6	12 45.0	2 27.3	11 32.7	8 58.5
13 Th	21 31 36	24 09 30	12 58 38	18 54 47	6 37.6	13 16.7	17 43.8	16 44.5	28 26.3	22 07.3	12 41.9	2 26.9	11 33.7	8 57.4
14 F	21 35 33	25 10 09	24 51 22	0♈48 37	6 25.4	12 25.7	18 58.2	17 29.2	28 48.7	22 21.0	12 38.9	2 26.5	11 34.6	8 56.4
15 Sa	21 39 30	26 10 47	6♈46 49	12 46 19	6 15.7	11 41.9	20 12.6	18 13.8	29 11.2	22 34.8	12 36.0	2 26.0	11 35.5	8 55.3
16 Su	21 43 26	27 11 24	18 47 30	24 50 46	6 08.9	11 05.7	21 27.0	18 58.5	29 33.7	22 48.6	12 33.2	2 25.5	11 36.4	8 54.2
17 M	21 47 23	28 11 58	0♉56 36	7♉05 32	6 05.1	10 37.3	22 41.3	19 43.2	29 56.3	23 02.4	12 30.5	2 24.8	11 37.3	8 53.0
18 Tu	21 51 19	29 12 31	13 18 05	19 34 49	6D03.6	10 16.7	23 55.6	20 27.9	0♈18.9	23 16.3	12 27.9	2 24.2	11 38.1	8 51.9
19 W	21 55 16	0♓13 02	25 56 21	2♊23 14	6R03.4	10 03.7	25 09.9	21 12.7	0 41.6	23 30.3	12 25.4	2 23.5	11 38.9	8 50.7
20 Th	21 59 12	1 13 32	8♊56 01	15 35 15	6 03.2	9D58.0	26 24.1	21 57.5	1 04.3	23 44.3	12 22.9	2 22.7	11 39.6	8 49.5
21 F	22 03 09	2 13 59	22 21 19	29 14 34	6 01.9	9 59.2	27 38.3	22 42.3	1 27.1	23 58.3	12 20.6	2 21.9	11 40.3	8 48.2
22 Sa	22 07 05	3 14 25	6♋15 12	13♋23 13	5 58.3	10 07.1	28 52.4	23 27.2	1 49.9	24 12.3	12 18.4	2 21.1	11 41.0	8 47.0
23 Su	22 11 02	4 14 48	20 38 26	28 00 26	5 52.0	10 21.2	0♈06.5	24 12.1	2 12.8	24 26.4	12 16.3	2 20.1	11 41.7	8 45.7
24 M	22 14 59	5 15 10	5♌28 34	13♌01 54	5 43.1	10 41.2	1 20.6	24 57.0	2 35.7	24 40.6	12 14.3	2 19.2	11 42.3	8 44.4
25 Tu	22 18 55	6 15 30	20 39 20	28 19 31	5 32.2	11 06.5	2 34.6	25 41.9	2 58.7	24 54.7	12 12.4	2 18.2	11 42.9	8 43.1
26 W	22 22 52	7 15 48	6♍01 00	13♍42 16	5 20.6	11 36.9	3 48.6	26 26.9	3 21.7	25 08.9	12 10.6	2 17.1	11 43.4	8 41.7
27 Th	22 26 48	8 16 05	21 21 46	28 58 06	5 09.7	12 11.9	5 02.5	27 11.9	3 44.8	25 23.1	12 08.9	2 16.0	11 44.0	8 40.4
28 F	22 30 45	9 16 19	6♎29 56	13♎56 11	5 00.7	12 51.3	6 16.3	27 56.9	4 07.8	25 37.3	12 07.3	2 14.8	11 44.5	8 39.0

Astro Data

	Dy Hr Mn
☽0S	2 23:10
♃△♄	10 20:34
♇R	11 17:39
☽0N	17 4:18
♃⚼♅	22 16:38
☽0S	30 8:26
☿R	30 10:47
♅R	6 1:48
☽0N	13 11:23
☿D	20 19:28
♀0N	25 7:04
☽0S	26 19:47

Planet Ingress

		Dy Hr Mn
♀	♒	6 6:39
☿	♒	8 21:58
☉	♒	20 16:36
♂	♑	21 18:49
♀	♓	30 6:05
⚳	♈	17 15:56
☉	♓	19 6:50
♀	♈	23 9:53

Last Aspect / ☽ Ingress (January)

Last Aspect Dy Hr Mn			☽ Ingress	Dy Hr Mn
31 16:50	♂	△	♍	1 17:32
3 13:36	♀	△	♎	3 19:21
5 22:55	♀	□	♏	5 23:39
8 4:24	☿	⚹	♐	8 6:39
9 23:22	♂	☌	♑	10 15:58
12 10:20	☉	☌	♒	13 3:03
15 5:45	♂	⚹	♓	15 15:23
17 22:24	♂	□	♈	18 4:03
20 15:14	☉	□	♉	20 15:21
22 5:07	☿	□	♊	22 23:23
24 15:34	♀	△	♋	25 3:20
26 9:03	♃	△	♌	27 4:00
29 0:50	♀	☍	♍	29 3:14
30 9:23	♃	☍	♎	31 3:13

Last Aspect / ☽ Ingress (February)

Last Aspect Dy Hr Mn			☽ Ingress	Dy Hr Mn
1 21:00	☿	△	♏	2 5:53
4 0:09	☿	□	♐	4 12:10
6 5:00	☿	⚹	♑	6 21:42
8 15:18	♃	⚹	♒	9 9:16
11 5:17	☉	☌	♓	11 21:45
13 18:36	♃	☌	♈	14 10:22
16 17:03	☉	⚹	♉	16 22:09
18 21:06	♀	⚹	♊	19 7:35
21 8:57	♀	□	♋	21 13:18
23 6:07	♃	△	♌	23 15:13
24 9:54	♆	△	♍	25 14:37
27 9:03	♂	△	♎	27 13:38

☽ Phases & Eclipses

Dy Hr Mn		
4 19:04	☾	13♎48
12 10:20	●	21♑35
20 15:14	☽	29♈57
27 15:09	○	7♌03
3 6:23	☾	13♏47
11 5:17	●	21♒51
19 7:38	☽	0♊02
26 1:15	○	6♍49

Astro Data

1 January 1975
Julian Day # 27394
SVP 5♓36'15"
GC 26♐29.4 ⚴ 13♒33.0
Eris 12♈39.0 ⚵ 22♓41.5
⚷ 19♈57.2 ⚶ 9♑01.7
☽ Mean ☊ 8♐34.2

1 February 1975
Julian Day # 27425
SVP 5♓36'10"
GC 26♐29.5 ⚴ 23♒37.6
Eris 12♈44.7 ⚵ 7♈19.1
⚷ 20♈25.1 ⚶ 25♑31.8
☽ Mean ☊ 6♐55.7

March 1975

LONGITUDE

Day	Sid.Time	☉	0 hr ☽	Noon ☽	True ☊	☿	♀	♂	⚳	♃	♄	♅	♆	♇
1 Sa	22 34 41	10♓16 33	21♎16 01	28♎28 47	4♐54.3	13♒34.7	7♈30.1	28♑42.0	4♈31.0	25♓51.6	12♋05.8	2♏13.6	11♐44.9	8♎37.6
2 Su	22 38 38	11 16 45	5♏34 08	12♏31 55	4R 50.7	14 21.8	8 43.9	29 27.1	4 54.2	26 05.9	12R 04.5	2R 12.3	11 45.3	8R 36.2
3 M	22 42 34	12 16 55	19 22 12	26 05 12	4D 49.3	15 12.4	9 57.7	0♒12.2	5 17.4	26 20.2	12 03.2	2 11.0	11 45.7	8 34.7
4 Tu	22 46 31	13 17 04	2♐41 19	9♐10 58	4R 49.2	16 06.2	11 11.3	0 57.3	5 40.6	26 34.6	12 02.0	2 09.7	11 46.1	8 33.3
5 W	22 50 28	14 17 11	15 34 44	21 53 10	4 49.1	17 03.0	12 25.0	1 42.5	6 03.9	26 48.9	12 01.0	2 08.3	11 46.4	8 31.8
6 Th	22 54 24	15 17 17	28 06 55	4♑16 33	4 47.7	18 02.6	13 38.6	2 27.7	6 27.2	27 03.3	12 00.1	2 06.8	11 46.7	8 30.3
7 F	22 58 21	16 17 21	10♑22 42	16 25 56	4 44.2	19 04.8	14 52.1	3 12.9	6 50.6	27 17.7	11 59.2	2 05.4	11 46.9	8 28.8
8 Sa	23 02 17	17 17 24	22 26 48	28 25 47	4 37.9	20 09.5	16 05.6	3 58.1	7 14.0	27 32.2	11 58.5	2 03.8	11 47.2	8 27.3
9 Su	23 06 14	18 17 25	4♒23 21	10♒19 54	4 28.7	21 16.5	17 19.1	4 43.4	7 37.4	27 46.6	11 57.9	2 02.3	11 47.3	8 25.8
10 M	23 10 10	19 17 24	16 15 49	22 11 25	4 17.0	22 25.6	18 32.5	5 28.7	8 00.9	28 01.1	11 57.4	2 00.6	11 47.5	8 24.2
11 Tu	23 14 07	20 17 21	28 06 58	4♓02 42	4 03.6	23 36.8	19 45.8	6 14.0	8 24.4	28 15.5	11 57.1	1 59.0	11 47.6	8 22.7
12 W	23 18 03	21 17 16	9♓58 49	15 55 31	3 49.6	24 50.0	20 59.1	6 59.3	8 47.9	28 30.0	11 56.8	1 57.3	11 47.7	8 21.1
13 Th	23 22 00	22 17 10	21 52 57	27 51 15	3 36.0	26 05.0	22 12.3	7 44.7	9 11.5	28 44.5	11D 56.6	1 55.5	11R 47.7	8 19.5
14 F	23 25 57	23 17 01	3♈50 35	9♈51 07	3 24.2	27 21.9	23 25.5	8 30.0	9 35.0	28 59.0	11 56.6	1 53.7	11 47.8	8 17.9
15 Sa	23 29 53	24 16 50	15 53 01	21 56 29	3 14.7	28 40.4	24 38.7	9 15.4	9 58.6	29 13.5	11 56.7	1 51.9	11 47.7	8 16.3
16 Su	23 33 50	25 16 38	28 01 44	4♉09 03	3 08.2	0♓00.6	25 51.7	10 00.8	10 22.3	29 28.0	11 56.9	1 50.1	11 47.7	8 14.7
17 M	23 37 46	26 16 23	10♉18 43	16 31 06	3 04.5	1 22.3	27 04.7	10 46.2	10 45.9	29 42.6	11 57.2	1 48.2	11 47.6	8 13.1
18 Tu	23 41 43	27 16 06	22 46 33	29 05 29	3D 03.2	2 45.7	28 17.7	11 31.7	11 09.6	29 57.1	11 57.6	1 46.2	11 47.5	8 11.5
19 W	23 45 39	28 15 47	5♊28 20	11♊55 34	3 03.3	4 10.5	29 30.6	12 17.1	11 33.3	0♈11.6	11 58.1	1 44.3	11 47.3	8 09.9
20 Th	23 49 36	29 15 26	18 27 37	25 04 55	3R 03.8	5 36.8	0♉43.4	13 02.6	11 57.0	0 26.2	11 58.7	1 42.3	11 47.1	8 08.2
21 F	23 53 32	0♈15 02	1♋47 53	8♋36 50	3 03.6	7 04.5	1 56.1	13 48.1	12 20.8	0 40.7	11 59.5	1 40.2	11 46.9	8 06.6
22 Sa	23 57 29	1 14 36	15 32 00	22 33 32	3 01.6	8 33.7	3 08.8	14 33.6	12 44.5	0 55.2	12 00.3	1 38.2	11 46.7	8 04.9
23 Su	0 01 26	2 14 08	29 41 24	6♌55 25	2 57.4	10 04.2	4 21.4	15 19.1	13 08.3	1 09.8	12 01.3	1 36.1	11 46.4	8 03.3
24 M	0 05 22	3 13 37	14♌15 10	21 40 04	2 50.9	11 36.1	5 34.0	16 04.6	13 32.1	1 24.3	12 02.4	1 33.9	11 46.1	8 01.6
25 Tu	0 09 19	4 13 04	29 09 19	6♍41 54	2 42.8	13 09.4	6 46.5	16 50.2	13 55.9	1 38.8	12 03.6	1 31.8	11 45.7	8 00.0
26 W	0 13 15	5 12 29	14♍16 41	21 52 23	2 33.8	14 44.1	7 58.9	17 35.7	14 19.7	1 53.3	12 04.9	1 29.6	11 45.4	7 58.3
27 Th	0 17 12	6 11 51	29 27 39	7♎01 09	2 25.3	16 20.1	9 11.2	18 21.3	14 43.5	2 07.9	12 06.3	1 27.4	11 44.9	7 56.6
28 F	0 21 08	7 11 12	14♎31 36	21 57 51	2 18.2	17 57.5	10 23.4	19 06.9	15 07.4	2 22.4	12 07.8	1 25.1	11 44.5	7 55.0
29 Sa	0 25 05	8 10 31	29 18 54	6♏33 57	2 13.3	19 36.3	11 35.6	19 52.5	15 31.2	2 36.9	12 09.4	1 22.9	11 44.0	7 53.3
30 Su	0 29 01	9 09 48	13♏42 23	20 43 50	2D 10.7	21 16.4	12 47.7	20 38.1	15 55.1	2 51.3	12 11.2	1 20.6	11 43.5	7 51.6
31 M	0 32 58	10 09 03	27 38 07	4♐25 14	2 10.1	22 57.9	13 59.8	21 23.7	16 19.0	3 05.8	12 13.0	1 18.3	11 43.0	7 49.9

April 1975

LONGITUDE

Day	Sid.Time	☉	0 hr ☽	Noon ☽	True ☊	☿	♀	♂	⚳	♃	♄	♅	♆	♇
1 Tu	0 36 54	11♈08 16	11♐05 22	17♐38 48	2♐10.9	24♓40.8	15♉11.7	22♒09.3	16♈42.9	3♈20.3	12♋14.9	1♏15.9	11♐42.4	7♎48.3
2 W	0 40 51	12 07 28	24 05 57	0♑27 19	2 12.0	26 25.1	16 23.6	22 55.0	17 06.8	3 34.7	12 17.0	1R 13.6	11R 41.8	7R 46.6
3 Th	0 44 48	13 06 38	6♑43 26	12 54 54	2R 12.6	28 10.8	17 35.4	23 40.6	17 30.7	3 49.2	12 19.1	1 11.2	11 41.2	7 45.0
4 F	0 48 44	14 05 46	19 02 20	25 06 21	2 11.9	29 57.9	18 47.2	24 26.3	17 54.6	4 03.6	12 21.4	1 08.8	11 40.6	7 43.3
5 Sa	0 52 41	15 04 52	1♒07 33	7♒06 32	2 09.3	1♈46.5	19 58.8	25 12.0	18 18.6	4 18.0	12 23.8	1 06.4	11 39.9	7 41.6
6 Su	0 56 37	16 03 56	13 03 51	19 00 02	2 04.6	3 36.5	21 10.4	25 57.7	18 42.5	4 32.4	12 26.2	1 04.0	11 39.1	7 40.0
7 M	1 00 34	17 02 59	24 55 35	0♓50 58	1 58.2	5 27.9	22 21.9	26 43.4	19 06.4	4 46.8	12 28.8	1 01.5	11 38.4	7 38.3
8 Tu	1 04 30	18 01 59	6♓46 35	12 42 48	1 50.4	7 20.8	23 33.3	27 29.1	19 30.4	5 01.1	12 31.5	0 59.0	11 37.6	7 36.7
9 W	1 08 27	19 00 58	18 39 56	24 38 17	1 42.1	9 15.1	24 44.7	28 14.8	19 54.4	5 15.4	12 34.3	0 56.5	11 36.8	7 35.1
10 Th	1 12 23	19 59 55	0♈38 04	6♈39 32	1 34.1	11 10.9	25 55.9	29 00.5	20 18.3	5 29.7	12 37.1	0 54.0	11 36.0	7 33.4
11 F	1 16 20	20 58 50	12 42 50	18 48 08	1 27.1	13 08.1	27 07.1	29 46.2	20 42.3	5 44.0	12 40.1	0 51.5	11 35.1	7 31.8
12 Sa	1 20 17	21 57 43	24 55 34	1♉05 16	1 21.7	15 06.7	28 18.2	0♓31.9	21 06.2	5 58.3	12 43.2	0 49.0	11 34.2	7 30.2
13 Su	1 24 13	22 56 34	7♉17 22	13 31 59	1 18.2	17 06.7	29 29.2	1 17.6	21 30.2	6 12.5	12 46.4	0 46.5	11 33.3	7 28.6
14 M	1 28 10	23 55 22	19 49 16	26 09 22	1D 16.7	19 08.0	0♊40.1	2 03.3	21 54.2	6 26.7	12 49.6	0 44.0	11 32.4	7 27.0
15 Tu	1 32 06	24 54 09	2♊32 27	8♊58 42	1 16.8	21 10.6	1 50.9	2 49.0	22 18.1	6 40.8	12 53.0	0 41.4	11 31.4	7 25.4
16 W	1 36 03	25 52 54	15 28 19	22 01 30	1 18.0	23 14.4	3 01.6	3 34.7	22 42.1	6 55.0	12 56.5	0 38.9	11 30.4	7 23.9
17 Th	1 39 59	26 51 36	28 38 29	5♋19 28	1 19.6	25 19.3	4 12.2	4 20.4	23 06.1	7 09.1	13 00.0	0 36.3	11 29.4	7 22.3
18 F	1 43 56	27 50 17	12♋04 38	18 54 10	1R 20.8	27 25.1	5 22.8	5 06.1	23 30.0	7 23.2	13 03.7	0 33.7	11 28.4	7 20.8
19 Sa	1 47 52	28 48 55	25 48 09	2♌46 40	1 21.0	29 31.7	6 33.2	5 51.8	23 54.0	7 37.2	13 07.4	0 31.2	11 27.3	7 19.2
20 Su	1 51 49	29 47 30	9♌49 39	16 56 57	1 19.9	1♉39.0	7 43.5	6 37.5	24 17.9	7 51.2	13 11.3	0 28.6	11 26.2	7 17.7
21 M	1 55 46	0♉46 04	24 08 21	1♍23 25	1 17.5	3 46.7	8 53.7	7 23.1	24 41.8	8 05.1	13 15.2	0 26.1	11 25.1	7 16.2
22 Tu	1 59 42	1 44 35	8♍41 40	16 02 26	1 13.9	5 54.6	10 03.8	8 08.8	25 05.8	8 19.1	13 19.2	0 23.5	11 24.0	7 14.7
23 W	2 03 39	2 43 04	23 24 58	0♎48 24	1 09.9	8 02.4	11 13.8	8 54.5	25 29.7	8 32.9	13 23.3	0 20.9	11 22.8	7 13.3
24 Th	2 07 35	3 41 31	8♎11 50	15 34 17	1 06.0	10 09.9	12 23.6	9 40.1	25 53.6	8 46.8	13 27.5	0 18.4	11 21.6	7 11.8
25 F	2 11 32	4 39 56	22 54 48	0♏12 28	1 02.8	12 16.8	13 33.4	10 25.8	26 17.5	9 00.6	13 31.8	0 15.8	11 20.4	7 10.4
26 Sa	2 15 28	5 38 19	7♏26 27	14 35 59	1 00.8	14 22.7	14 43.0	11 11.4	26 41.4	9 14.3	13 36.1	0 13.2	11 19.2	7 08.9
27 Su	2 19 25	6 36 40	21 40 28	28 39 25	1D 00.0	16 27.3	15 52.5	11 57.0	27 05.3	9 28.0	13 40.6	0 10.7	11 18.0	7 07.5
28 M	2 23 21	7 35 00	5♐32 31	12♐19 34	1 00.3	18 30.4	17 01.9	12 42.7	27 29.1	9 41.7	13 45.1	0 08.2	11 16.7	7 06.1
29 Tu	2 27 18	8 33 18	19 00 31	25 35 28	1 01.5	20 31.7	18 11.2	13 28.3	27 53.0	9 55.3	13 49.7	0 05.6	11 15.4	7 04.8
30 W	2 31 15	9 31 35	2♑04 35	8♑28 11	1 03.0	22 30.7	19 20.3	14 13.9	28 16.8	10 08.9	13 54.4	0 03.1	11 14.1	7 03.4

Astro Data Dy Hr Mn	Planet Ingress Dy Hr Mn	Last Aspect Dy Hr Mn	☽ Ingress Dy Hr Mn	Last Aspect Dy Hr Mn	☽ Ingress Dy Hr Mn	☽ Phases & Eclipses Dy Hr Mn	Astro Data
☽0N 12 17:40	♂ ♒ 3 5:32	1 12:24 ♂ □	♏ 1 14:33	2 3:09 ☿ □	♑ 2 11:08	4 20:20 ☾ 13♐38	1 March 1975
♄ D 14 8:32	☿ ♓ 16 11:50	3 12:28 ♃ △	♐ 3 19:05	3 22:09 ♀ △	♒ 4 21:45	12 23:47 ● 21♓47	Julian Day # 27453
♆ R 14 10:02	♃ ♈ 18 16:47	5 21:40 ♃ □	♑ 6 3:39	7 3:04 ♂ ☌	♓ 7 10:17	20 20:05 ☽ 29♊35	SVP 5♓36'07"
☉0N 21 5:57	♀ ♉ 19 21:42	8 10:10 ♃ ⚹	♒ 8 15:09	9 12:14 ♀ ⚹	♈ 9 22:44	27 10:36 ○ 6♎08	GC 26♐29.5 ⚴ 2♓57.0
♃⚻♅ 25 1:53	☉ ♈ 21 5:57	10 12:32 ☿ ☌	♓ 11 3:49	11 16:39 ☉ ☌	♉ 12 9:53		Eris 12♈57.8 ⚵ 22♈15.4
☽0S 26 6:54		13 13:49 ♃ ☌	♈ 13 16:18	13 10:32 ♄ ⚹	♊ 14 19:14	3 12:25 ☾ 13♑08	⚷ 21♈30.4 ⚶ 10♒00.9
♃0N 28 22:42	☿ ♈ 4 12:28	16 2:53 ☿ ⚹	♉ 16 3:52	16 19:34 ☉ ⚹	♋ 17 2:27	11 16:39 ● 21♈10	☽ Mean ☊ 5♐26.7
⚳0N 31 19:12	♂ ♓ 11 19:15	18 13:39 ♃ ⚹	♊ 18 13:43	19 5:26 ☿ □	♌ 19 7:14	19 4:41 ☽ 28♋31	
	♀ ♊ 13 22:26	20 20:05 ☉ □	♋ 20 20:48	20 2:44 ♆ △	♍ 21 9:42	25 19:55 ○ 4♏59	1 April 1975
☿0N 7 1:51	☿ ♉ 19 17:20	21 17:53 ♄ ☌	♌ 23 0:31	22 7:32 ♄ ⚹	♎ 23 10:41		Julian Day # 27484
☽0N 8 23:47	☉ ♉ 20 17:07	24 2:28 ♂ ☍	♍ 25 1:21	24 8:32 ♄ □	♏ 25 11:39		SVP 5♓36'04"
♃☍♇ 18 8:20		25 23:25 ☿ ☍	♎ 27 0:51	26 11:34 ☿ ☍	♐ 27 14:20		GC 26♐29.6 ⚴ 13♓00.6
☽0S 22 15:52		28 7:08 ♂ △	♏ 29 1:08	28 21:14 ♀ ☍	♑ 29 20:08		Eris 13♈17.6 ⚵ 9♉54.3
		30 13:04 ☿ △	♐ 31 4:10				⚷ 23♈11.4 ⚶ 25♒14.1
							☽ Mean ☊ 3♐48.2

LONGITUDE — May 1975

Day	Sid.Time	☉	0 hr ☽	Noon ☽	True ☊	☿	♀	♂	⚳	♃	♄	♅	♆	♇
1 Th	2 35 11	10♉29 50	14♑46 40	21♑00 26	1♐04.4	24♉27.4	20♊29.4	14♓59.5	28♈40.7	10♈22.4	13♋59.2	0♏00.6	11♐12.8	7♎02.1
2 F	2 39 08	11 28 03	27 10 01	3♒15 57	1R 05.4	26 21.3	21 38.3	15 45.1	29 04.5	10 35.9	14 04.0	29♎58.1	11R 11.5	7R 00.8
3 Sa	2 43 04	12 26 15	9♒18 47	15 19 07	1 05.6	28 12.4	22 47.0	16 30.6	29 28.3	10 49.3	14 09.0	29R 55.6	11 10.1	6 59.5
4 Su	2 47 01	13 24 25	21 17 31	27 14 35	1 04.9	0♊00.4	23 55.7	17 16.2	29 52.1	11 02.7	14 14.0	29 53.1	11 08.7	6 58.2
5 M	2 50 57	14 22 34	3♓10 52	9♓06 55	1 03.6	1 45.1	25 04.2	18 01.7	0♉15.9	11 16.0	14 19.1	29 50.7	11 07.3	6 57.0
6 Tu	2 54 54	15 20 42	15 03 16	21 00 26	1 01.6	3 26.4	26 12.6	18 47.3	0 39.6	11 29.3	14 24.2	29 48.2	11 05.9	6 55.7
7 W	2 58 50	16 18 48	26 58 51	2♈58 57	0 59.4	5 04.3	27 20.8	19 32.8	1 03.4	11 42.5	14 29.5	29 45.8	11 04.5	6 54.5
8 Th	3 02 47	17 16 52	9♈01 06	15 05 40	0 57.3	6 38.4	28 28.9	20 18.3	1 27.1	11 55.6	14 34.8	29 43.4	11 03.1	6 53.3
9 F	3 06 43	18 14 55	21 12 56	27 23 08	0 55.5	8 08.9	29 36.9	21 03.7	1 50.8	12 08.7	14 40.2	29 41.0	11 01.6	6 52.2
10 Sa	3 10 40	19 12 57	3♉36 29	9♉53 07	0 54.2	9 35.5	0♋44.7	21 49.2	2 14.5	12 21.7	14 45.6	29 38.6	11 00.1	6 51.0
11 Su	3 14 37	20 10 57	16 13 10	22 36 42	0D 53.6	10 58.3	1 52.3	22 34.6	2 38.2	12 34.7	14 51.2	29 36.2	10 58.7	6 49.9
12 M	3 18 33	21 08 55	29 03 44	5♊34 17	0 53.5	12 17.2	2 59.8	23 20.0	3 01.8	12 47.6	14 56.8	29 33.9	10 57.2	6 48.8
13 Tu	3 22 30	22 06 52	12♊08 20	18 45 49	0 53.9	13 32.0	4 07.2	24 05.3	3 25.5	13 00.5	15 02.4	29 31.6	10 55.7	6 47.8
14 W	3 26 26	23 04 48	25 26 40	2♋10 47	0 54.5	14 42.8	5 14.4	24 50.7	3 49.1	13 13.2	15 08.2	29 29.3	10 54.2	6 46.8
15 Th	3 30 23	24 02 41	8♋58 05	15 48 27	0 55.2	15 49.5	6 21.4	25 36.0	4 12.6	13 25.9	15 14.0	29 27.0	10 52.6	6 45.7
16 F	3 34 19	25 00 33	22 41 44	29 37 49	0 55.8	16 51.9	7 28.2	26 21.2	4 36.2	13 38.6	15 19.8	29 24.8	10 51.1	6 44.8
17 Sa	3 38 16	25 58 23	6♌36 31	13♌37 40	0R 56.1	17 50.2	8 34.9	27 06.5	4 59.7	13 51.1	15 25.7	29 22.6	10 49.5	6 43.8
18 Su	3 42 13	26 56 12	20 41 03	27 46 25	0 56.2	18 44.1	9 41.4	27 51.7	5 23.2	14 03.6	15 31.7	29 20.4	10 48.0	6 42.9
19 M	3 46 09	27 53 58	4♍53 32	12♍02 03	0 56.1	19 33.6	10 47.7	28 36.8	5 46.7	14 16.0	15 37.8	29 18.3	10 46.4	6 42.0
20 Tu	3 50 06	28 51 43	19 11 38	26 21 54	0 55.9	20 18.7	11 53.7	29 22.0	6 10.1	14 28.3	15 43.9	29 16.1	10 44.8	6 41.1
21 W	3 54 02	29 49 26	3♎32 23	10♎42 38	0 55.8	20 59.3	12 59.6	0♈07.1	6 33.5	14 40.6	15 50.1	29 14.0	10 43.3	6 40.2
22 Th	3 57 59	0♊47 08	17 52 09	25 00 24	0D 55.7	21 35.3	14 05.3	0 52.2	6 56.9	14 52.8	15 56.3	29 12.0	10 41.7	6 39.4
23 F	4 01 55	1 44 48	2♏06 53	9♏11 04	0 55.8	22 06.6	15 10.8	1 37.2	7 20.2	15 04.9	16 02.6	29 09.9	10 40.1	6 38.6
24 Sa	4 05 52	2 42 27	16 12 27	23 10 33	0R 55.8	22 33.3	16 16.1	2 22.2	7 43.5	15 16.9	16 08.9	29 07.9	10 38.5	6 37.9
25 Su	4 09 48	3 40 04	0♐04 57	6♐55 18	0 55.8	22 55.3	17 21.2	3 07.2	8 06.8	15 28.9	16 15.3	29 06.0	10 36.9	6 37.1
26 M	4 13 45	4 37 40	13 41 17	20 22 43	0 55.7	23 12.5	18 26.0	3 52.1	8 30.0	15 40.7	16 21.8	29 04.0	10 35.3	6 36.4
27 Tu	4 17 42	5 35 16	26 59 25	3♑31 21	0 55.3	23 25.0	19 30.6	4 37.0	8 53.3	15 52.5	16 28.3	29 02.1	10 33.6	6 35.8
28 W	4 21 38	6 32 50	9♑58 34	16 21 09	0 54.7	23 32.7	20 35.0	5 21.9	9 16.4	16 04.2	16 34.8	29 00.3	10 32.0	6 35.1
29 Th	4 25 35	7 30 23	22 39 18	28 53 18	0 53.9	23R 35.8	21 39.1	6 06.7	9 39.6	16 15.8	16 41.4	28 58.4	10 30.4	6 34.5
30 F	4 29 31	8 27 55	5♒03 27	11♒10 10	0 53.1	23 34.3	22 43.0	6 51.5	10 02.7	16 27.3	16 48.1	28 56.6	10 28.8	6 33.9
31 Sa	4 33 28	9 25 26	17 13 53	23 15 04	0 52.4	23 28.3	23 46.6	7 36.2	10 25.8	16 38.8	16 54.8	28 54.9	10 27.2	6 33.4

LONGITUDE — June 1975

Day	Sid.Time	☉	0 hr ☽	Noon ☽	True ☊	☿	♀	♂	⚳	♃	♄	♅	♆	♇
1 Su	4 37 24	10♊22 57	29♒14 14	5♓11 58	0♐52.0	23♊18.0	24♋50.0	8♈20.9	10♉48.8	16♈50.1	17♋01.5	28♎53.2	10♐25.5	6♎32.9
2 M	4 41 21	11 20 26	11♓08 47	17 05 18	0D 52.0	23R 03.7	25 53.1	9 05.6	11 11.8	17 01.4	17 08.3	28R 51.5	10R 23.9	6R 32.4
3 Tu	4 45 17	12 17 55	23 02 04	28 59 41	0 52.5	22 45.5	26 56.0	9 50.2	11 34.8	17 12.5	17 15.1	28 49.9	10 22.3	6 31.9
4 W	4 49 14	13 15 23	4♈58 42	10♈59 40	0 53.4	22 23.7	27 58.5	10 34.7	11 57.7	17 23.6	17 22.0	28 48.3	10 20.7	6 31.5
5 Th	4 53 11	14 12 51	17 03 07	23 09 33	0 54.6	21 58.9	29 00.8	11 19.2	12 20.5	17 34.5	17 28.9	28 46.7	10 19.1	6 31.1
6 F	4 57 07	15 10 17	29 19 23	5♉33 02	0 55.7	21 31.3	0♌02.8	12 03.7	12 43.4	17 45.4	17 35.9	28 45.2	10 17.4	6 30.7
7 Sa	5 01 04	16 07 43	11♉50 50	18 13 04	0R 56.6	21 01.5	1 04.5	12 48.1	13 06.2	17 56.1	17 42.9	28 43.7	10 15.8	6 30.4
8 Su	5 05 00	17 05 09	24 39 55	1♊11 30	0 57.0	20 29.9	2 05.9	13 32.4	13 28.9	18 06.8	17 50.0	28 42.3	10 14.2	6 30.1
9 M	5 08 57	18 02 33	7♊47 51	14 28 56	0 56.6	19 57.0	3 07.0	14 16.7	13 51.6	18 17.4	17 57.1	28 40.9	10 12.6	6 29.8
10 Tu	5 12 53	18 59 57	21 14 34	28 04 33	0 55.3	19 23.6	4 07.8	15 01.0	14 14.3	18 27.8	18 04.2	28 39.5	10 11.0	6 29.6
11 W	5 16 50	19 57 20	4♋58 34	11♋56 14	0 53.2	18 50.0	5 08.2	15 45.1	14 36.9	18 38.1	18 11.4	28 38.3	10 09.4	6 29.4
12 Th	5 20 46	20 54 42	18 57 06	26 00 41	0 50.6	18 16.9	6 08.2	16 29.3	14 59.4	18 48.4	18 18.6	28 37.0	10 07.8	6 29.2
13 F	5 24 43	21 52 03	3♌06 28	10♌13 54	0 47.9	17 44.9	7 07.9	17 13.3	15 21.9	18 58.5	18 25.8	28 35.8	10 06.2	6 29.1
14 Sa	5 28 40	22 49 24	17 22 28	24 31 40	0 45.5	17 14.4	8 07.3	17 57.3	15 44.4	19 08.5	18 33.1	28 34.6	10 04.6	6 29.0
15 Su	5 32 36	23 46 43	1♍40 59	8♍49 59	0 43.9	16 46.1	9 06.2	18 41.2	16 06.7	19 18.4	18 40.4	28 33.5	10 03.1	6 28.9
16 M	5 36 33	24 44 01	15 58 17	23 05 31	0D 43.3	16 20.3	10 04.7	19 25.1	16 29.1	19 28.2	18 47.7	28 32.5	10 01.5	6D 28.9
17 Tu	5 40 29	25 41 18	0♎11 23	7♎15 37	0 43.6	15 57.6	11 02.8	20 08.8	16 51.4	19 37.8	18 55.1	28 31.4	10 00.0	6 28.9
18 W	5 44 26	26 38 35	14 18 00	21 18 21	0 44.8	15 38.3	12 00.5	20 52.6	17 13.6	19 47.3	19 02.5	28 30.5	9 58.4	6 28.9
19 Th	5 48 22	27 35 51	28 16 30	5♏12 17	0 46.2	15 22.7	12 57.7	21 36.2	17 35.7	19 56.8	19 09.9	28 29.5	9 56.9	6 29.0
20 F	5 52 19	28 33 06	12♏05 33	18 56 12	0R 47.4	15 11.1	13 54.5	22 19.8	17 57.9	20 06.1	19 17.3	28 28.7	9 55.4	6 29.1
21 Sa	5 56 15	29 30 20	25 44 04	2♐29 02	0 47.8	15 03.8	14 50.8	23 03.3	18 19.9	20 15.2	19 24.8	28 27.8	9 53.8	6 29.2
22 Su	6 00 12	0♋27 34	9♐10 57	15 49 43	0 47.0	15D 00.9	15 46.6	23 46.8	18 41.9	20 24.3	19 32.3	28 27.1	9 52.3	6 29.3
23 M	6 04 09	1 24 47	22 25 11	28 57 16	0 44.7	15 02.5	16 41.9	24 30.1	19 03.8	20 33.2	19 39.8	28 26.3	9 50.9	6 29.5
24 Tu	6 08 05	2 22 00	5♑25 52	11♑50 58	0 40.9	15 08.9	17 36.7	25 13.4	19 25.7	20 42.0	19 47.4	28 25.7	9 49.4	6 29.8
25 W	6 12 02	3 19 13	18 12 32	24 30 35	0 36.0	15 20.0	18 30.9	25 56.7	19 47.5	20 50.7	19 54.9	28 25.0	9 47.9	6 30.0
26 Th	6 15 58	4 16 25	0♒45 13	6♒56 33	0 30.4	15 35.8	19 24.6	26 39.8	20 09.2	20 59.2	20 02.5	28 24.5	9 46.5	6 30.3
27 F	6 19 55	5 13 37	13 04 46	19 10 07	0 24.7	15 56.4	20 17.6	27 22.9	20 30.9	21 07.6	20 10.1	28 23.9	9 45.1	6 30.6
28 Sa	6 23 51	6 10 49	25 12 54	1♓13 27	0 19.6	16 21.8	21 10.1	28 05.9	20 52.5	21 15.9	20 17.7	28 23.4	9 43.6	6 31.0
29 Su	6 27 48	7 08 01	7♓12 11	13 09 32	0 15.5	16 51.9	22 02.0	28 48.8	21 14.1	21 24.0	20 25.4	28 23.0	9 42.2	6 31.4
30 M	6 31 44	8 05 13	19 06 01	25 02 09	0 13.0	17 26.7	22 53.2	29 31.7	21 35.5	21 32.0	20 33.0	28 22.6	9 40.8	6 31.8

Astro Data

	Dy Hr Mn
♃△♆	4 21:51
☽0N	6 6:34
☽0S	19 22:26
♂0N	26 9:01
☿R	29 16:01
☽0N	2 14:24
♃□♄	4 3:02
☽0S	16 4:03
♇D	17 4:03
☿D	22 15:19
☽0N	29 22:53

Planet Ingress

	Dy Hr Mn
♅ ♎R	1 17:46
☿ ♊	4 11:55
⚳ ♉	4 19:58
♀ ♋	9 20:11
♂ ♈	21 8:14
☉ ♊	21 16:24
♀ ♌	6 10:54
☉ ♋	22 0:26

Last Aspect / ☽ Ingress

Last Aspect Dy Hr Mn		☽ Ingress Dy Hr Mn
2 5:31	♅ □	♒ 2 5:34
4 17:19	♅ △	♓ 4 17:34
6 23:33	♀ □	♈ 7 6:03
9 16:44	♀ ✶	♉ 9 17:03
11 11:56	♂ ✶	♊ 12 1:44
14 7:14	♅ △	♋ 14 8:08
16 11:38	♅ □	♌ 16 12:38
18 14:38	♅ ✶	♍ 18 15:45
20 17:18	♂ ☍	♎ 20 18:05
22 19:03	♅ ☌	♏ 22 20:25
23 23:48	♄ △	♐ 24 23:51
27 3:46	♅ ✶	♑ 27 5:31
29 12:10	♅ □	♒ 29 14:09

Last Aspect / ☽ Ingress

Last Aspect Dy Hr Mn		☽ Ingress Dy Hr Mn
31 23:19	♅ △	♓ 1 1:32
3 7:27	♀ △	♈ 3 14:01
6 0:26	♀ □	♉ 6 1:19
7 11:03	♄ ✶	♊ 8 9:49
10 13:01	♅ △	♋ 10 15:21
12 16:24	♅ □	♌ 12 18:45
14 18:47	♅ ✶	♍ 14 21:11
16 14:58	☉ □	♎ 16 23:41
19 0:23	♅ ☌	♏ 19 2:59
20 12:38	♄ △	♐ 21 7:34
23 11:03	♅ ✶	♑ 23 13:56
25 19:29	♅ □	♒ 25 22:33
28 6:20	♅ △	♓ 28 9:33
30 2:50	♄ △	♈ 30 22:02

☽ Phases & Eclipses

Dy Hr Mn	
3 5:44	☾ 12♒11
11 7:05	● 19♉59
11 7:16:44	P 0.864
18 10:29	☽ 26♌53
25 5:51	○ 3♐25
25 5:48	T 1.426
1 23:22	☾ 10♓50
9 18:49	● 18♊19
16 14:58	☽ 24♍51
23 16:54	○ 1♑36

Astro Data

1 May 1975
Julian Day # 27514
SVP 5♓36'01"
GC 26♐29.7 ⚳ 21♓58.8
Eris 13♈37.4 ✱ 27♉30.6
⚷ 24♈58.3 ⚵ 8♓42.1
☽ Mean ☊ 2♐12.9

1 June 1975
Julian Day # 27545
SVP 5♓35'57"
GC 26♐29.8 ⚳ 29♓47.0
Eris 13♈53.4 ✱ 15♊45.7
⚷ 26♈37.4 ⚵ 20♓35.4
☽ Mean ☊ 0♐34.4

July 1975 — LONGITUDE

Day	Sid.Time	☉	0 hr ☽	Noon ☽	True ☊	☿	♀	♂	⚳	♃	♄	♅	♆	♇
1 Tu	6 35 41	9♋02 26	0♈58 29	6♈55 37	0♐12.0	18♊06.2	23♌43.8	0♉14.5	21♉56.9	21♈39.9	20♋40.7	28♎22.3	9♐39.5	6♎32.3
2 W	6 39 38	9 59 38	12 54 10	18 54 44	0D 12.3	18 50.3	24 33.7	0 57.1	22 18.3	21 47.6	20 48.4	28R 22.0	9R 38.1	6 32.8
3 Th	6 43 34	10 56 50	24 57 56	1♉04 23	0 13.6	19 38.9	25 22.9	1 39.7	22 39.5	21 55.2	20 56.1	28 21.8	9 36.8	6 33.3
4 F	6 47 31	11 54 03	7♉14 40	13 29 20	0 15.1	20 32.0	26 11.3	2 22.2	23 00.7	22 02.6	21 03.8	28 21.7	9 35.5	6 33.8
5 Sa	6 51 27	12 51 16	19 48 53	26 13 45	0R 16.0	21 29.5	26 59.0	3 04.7	23 21.8	22 09.9	21 11.6	28 21.5	9 34.2	6 34.4
6 Su	6 55 24	13 48 29	2♊44 18	9♊20 47	0 15.7	22 31.4	27 45.9	3 47.0	23 42.8	22 17.0	21 19.3	28D 21.5	9 32.9	6 35.1
7 M	6 59 20	14 45 43	16 03 22	22 52 02	0 13.6	23 37.7	28 32.0	4 29.2	24 03.8	22 24.0	21 27.1	28 21.5	9 31.6	6 35.7
8 Tu	7 03 17	15 42 57	29 46 40	6♋46 59	0 09.6	24 48.1	29 17.3	5 11.4	24 24.7	22 30.8	21 34.8	28 21.5	9 30.4	6 36.4
9 W	7 07 13	16 40 11	13♋52 32	21 02 46	0 03.8	26 02.8	0♍01.6	5 53.4	24 45.4	22 37.5	21 42.6	28 21.6	9 29.2	6 37.1
10 Th	7 11 10	17 37 24	28 16 57	5♌34 16	29♏56.8	27 21.6	0 45.1	6 35.3	25 06.1	22 44.0	21 50.4	28 21.8	9 28.0	6 37.9
11 F	7 15 07	18 34 38	12♌53 49	20 14 40	29 49.5	28 44.5	1 27.6	7 17.1	25 26.7	22 50.4	21 58.1	28 22.0	9 26.8	6 38.7
12 Sa	7 19 03	19 31 52	27 35 53	4♍56 32	29 42.8	0♋11.3	2 09.1	7 58.9	25 47.3	22 56.6	22 05.9	28 22.2	9 25.6	6 39.5
13 Su	7 23 00	20 29 06	12♍15 47	19 32 55	29 37.6	1 42.1	2 49.5	8 40.5	26 07.7	23 02.6	22 13.7	28 22.5	9 24.5	6 40.3
14 M	7 26 56	21 26 20	26 47 17	3♎58 25	29 34.3	3 16.7	3 28.9	9 22.0	26 28.0	23 08.5	22 21.5	28 22.9	9 23.4	6 41.2
15 Tu	7 30 53	22 23 34	11♎05 57	18 09 37	29D 33.0	4 55.1	4 07.2	10 03.4	26 48.2	23 14.2	22 29.3	28 23.3	9 22.3	6 42.1
16 W	7 34 49	23 20 48	25 09 18	2♏04 59	29 33.1	6 37.0	4 44.3	10 44.7	27 08.4	23 19.7	22 37.0	28 23.8	9 21.2	6 43.0
17 Th	7 38 46	24 18 02	8♏56 42	15 44 32	29 34.0	8 22.4	5 20.2	11 25.8	27 28.4	23 25.1	22 44.8	28 24.3	9 20.2	6 44.0
18 F	7 42 42	25 15 16	22 28 38	29 09 10	29R 34.6	10 11.0	5 54.8	12 06.9	27 48.4	23 30.3	22 52.6	28 24.8	9 19.2	6 45.0
19 Sa	7 46 39	26 12 30	5♐46 17	12♐20 09	29 33.8	12 02.7	6 28.1	12 47.9	28 08.2	23 35.3	23 00.4	28 25.5	9 18.2	6 46.0
20 Su	7 50 36	27 09 45	18 50 55	25 18 42	29 31.0	13 57.2	7 00.1	13 28.7	28 28.0	23 40.2	23 08.2	28 26.1	9 17.2	6 47.1
21 M	7 54 32	28 07 00	1♑43 37	8♑05 45	29 25.7	15 54.3	7 30.7	14 09.4	28 47.6	23 44.9	23 15.9	28 26.9	9 16.3	6 48.2
22 Tu	7 58 29	29 04 15	14 25 11	20 41 57	29 18.0	17 53.7	7 59.7	14 50.0	29 07.2	23 49.4	23 23.7	28 27.6	9 15.4	6 49.3
23 W	8 02 25	0♌01 31	26 56 07	3♒07 44	29 08.2	19 55.1	8 27.3	15 30.5	29 26.6	23 53.8	23 31.5	28 28.5	9 14.5	6 50.5
24 Th	8 06 22	0 58 48	9♒16 53	15 23 38	28 57.2	21 58.2	8 53.3	16 10.9	29 45.9	23 57.9	23 39.2	28 29.4	9 13.6	6 51.7
25 F	8 10 18	1 56 05	21 28 07	27 30 28	28 45.9	24 02.6	9 17.7	16 51.1	0♊05.1	24 01.9	23 46.9	28 30.3	9 12.8	6 52.9
26 Sa	8 14 15	2 53 22	3♓30 53	9♓29 36	28 35.3	26 08.1	9 40.3	17 31.3	0 24.2	24 05.7	23 54.7	28 31.3	9 12.0	6 54.1
27 Su	8 18 11	3 50 41	15 26 54	21 23 07	28 26.4	28 14.2	10 01.3	18 11.3	0 43.2	24 09.4	24 02.4	28 32.3	9 11.2	6 55.4
28 M	8 22 08	4 48 01	27 18 39	3♈13 54	28 19.6	0♌20.7	10 20.4	18 51.1	1 02.1	24 12.8	24 10.1	28 33.4	9 10.5	6 56.7
29 Tu	8 26 05	5 45 21	9♈09 24	15 05 39	28 15.3	2 27.3	10 37.7	19 30.9	1 20.8	24 16.1	24 17.8	28 34.5	9 09.7	6 58.0
30 W	8 30 01	6 42 43	21 03 13	27 02 42	28D 13.2	4 33.7	10 53.1	20 10.5	1 39.5	24 19.2	24 25.5	28 35.7	9 09.0	6 59.3
31 Th	8 33 58	7 40 05	3♉04 45	9♉10 00	28 12.7	6 39.8	11 06.5	20 49.9	1 58.0	24 22.0	24 33.1	28 36.9	9 08.4	7 00.7

August 1975 — LONGITUDE

Day	Sid.Time	☉	0 hr ☽	Noon ☽	True ☊	☿	♀	♂	⚳	♃	♄	♅	♆	♇
1 F	8 37 54	8♌37 29	15♉19 06	21♉32 42	28♏13.0	8♌45.1	11♍17.9	21♉29.3	2♊16.4	24♈24.7	24♋40.8	28♎38.2	9♐07.7	7♎02.1
2 Sa	8 41 51	9 34 54	27 51 25	4♊15 50	28R 13.0	10 49.7	11 27.2	22 08.4	2 34.6	24 27.3	24 48.4	28 39.6	9R 07.1	7 03.5
3 Su	8 45 47	10 32 20	10♊46 27	17 23 44	28 11.7	12 53.3	11 34.4	22 47.5	2 52.8	24 29.6	24 56.0	28 40.9	9 06.5	7 05.0
4 M	8 49 44	11 29 47	24 07 57	0♋59 19	28 08.1	14 55.8	11 39.4	23 26.4	3 10.7	24 31.7	25 03.6	28 42.4	9 06.0	7 06.5
5 Tu	8 53 40	12 27 15	7♋57 48	15 03 15	28 02.0	16 57.1	11R 42.2	24 05.1	3 28.6	24 33.6	25 11.2	28 43.9	9 05.5	7 08.0
6 W	8 57 37	13 24 45	22 15 16	29 33 15	27 53.6	18 57.0	11 42.7	24 43.7	3 46.3	24 35.4	25 18.7	28 45.4	9 05.0	7 09.5
7 Th	9 01 34	14 22 15	6♌56 26	14♌23 48	27 43.4	20 55.6	11 40.9	25 22.1	4 03.9	24 36.9	25 26.3	28 47.0	9 04.5	7 11.1
8 F	9 05 30	15 19 47	21 54 13	29 26 28	27 32.7	22 52.8	11 36.8	26 00.4	4 21.3	24 38.3	25 33.8	28 48.6	9 04.1	7 12.7
9 Sa	9 09 27	16 17 19	6♍59 16	14♍31 20	27 22.7	24 48.5	11 30.3	26 38.5	4 38.6	24 39.4	25 41.2	28 50.3	9 03.7	7 14.3
10 Su	9 13 23	17 14 52	22 01 29	29 28 38	27 14.5	26 42.7	11 21.4	27 16.4	4 55.7	24 40.4	25 48.7	28 52.0	9 03.3	7 15.9
11 M	9 17 20	18 12 27	6♎51 52	14♎10 26	27 08.8	28 35.5	11 10.1	27 54.2	5 12.7	24 41.1	25 56.1	28 53.8	9 03.0	7 17.6
12 Tu	9 21 16	19 10 02	21 23 49	28 31 40	27 05.7	0♍26.7	10 56.4	28 31.8	5 29.5	24 41.7	26 03.5	28 55.6	9 02.7	7 19.2
13 W	9 25 13	20 07 38	5♏33 47	12♏30 11	27D 04.6	2 16.5	10 40.4	29 09.2	5 46.2	24 42.1	26 10.9	28 57.5	9 02.4	7 21.0
14 Th	9 29 09	21 05 15	19 20 58	26 06 20	27R 04.5	4 04.7	10 22.1	29 46.4	6 02.7	24R 42.2	26 18.2	28 59.4	9 02.1	7 22.7
15 F	9 33 06	22 02 53	2♐46 35	9♐22 02	27 04.2	5 51.5	10 01.5	0♊23.5	6 19.0	24 42.2	26 25.5	29 01.4	9 01.9	7 24.4
16 Sa	9 37 03	23 00 32	15 53 04	22 20 03	27 02.5	7 36.8	9 38.6	1 00.4	6 35.2	24 41.9	26 32.8	29 03.4	9 01.8	7 26.2
17 Su	9 40 59	23 58 12	28 43 20	5♑03 16	26 58.5	9 20.6	9 13.7	1 37.1	6 51.2	24 41.5	26 40.0	29 05.4	9 01.6	7 28.0
18 M	9 44 56	24 55 53	11♑20 11	17 34 20	26 51.6	11 02.9	8 46.8	2 13.6	7 07.0	24 40.9	26 47.2	29 07.5	9 01.5	7 29.8
19 Tu	9 48 52	25 53 35	23 46 00	29 55 23	26 42.0	12 43.8	8 17.9	2 49.9	7 22.7	24 40.0	26 54.4	29 09.6	9 01.4	7 31.7
20 W	9 52 49	26 51 18	6♒00 40	12♒08 02	26 29.9	14 23.3	7 47.4	3 26.1	7 38.2	24 39.0	27 01.5	29 11.8	9 01.4	7 33.5
21 Th	9 56 45	27 49 03	18 11 37	24 13 33	26 16.4	16 01.4	7 15.2	4 02.0	7 53.5	24 37.8	27 08.6	29 14.0	9D 01.3	7 35.4
22 F	10 00 42	28 46 49	0♓13 58	6♓13 00	26 02.5	17 38.1	6 41.7	4 37.8	8 08.6	24 36.4	27 15.6	29 16.3	9 01.4	7 37.3
23 Sa	10 04 38	29 44 36	12 10 49	18 07 35	25 49.3	19 13.3	6 07.0	5 13.3	8 23.5	24 34.7	27 22.6	29 18.6	9 01.4	7 39.2
24 Su	10 08 35	0♍42 25	24 03 30	29 58 48	25 38.0	20 47.2	5 31.3	5 48.6	8 38.2	24 32.9	27 29.6	29 20.9	9 01.5	7 41.1
25 M	10 12 32	1 40 15	5♈53 48	11♈48 48	25 29.1	22 19.7	4 54.9	6 23.8	8 52.8	24 30.9	27 36.5	29 23.3	9 01.6	7 43.1
26 Tu	10 16 28	2 38 08	17 44 10	23 40 21	25 23.0	23 50.8	4 17.9	6 58.7	9 07.1	24 28.7	27 43.4	29 25.8	9 01.7	7 45.1
27 W	10 20 25	3 36 02	29 37 48	5♉37 03	25 19.6	25 20.5	3 40.7	7 33.4	9 21.3	24 26.3	27 50.3	29 28.2	9 01.9	7 47.0
28 Th	10 24 21	4 33 57	11♉38 38	17 43 10	25D 18.4	26 48.8	3 03.4	8 07.9	9 35.3	24 23.7	27 57.1	29 30.7	9 02.1	7 49.1
29 F	10 28 18	5 31 55	23 51 14	0♊03 30	25R 18.2	28 15.7	2 26.4	8 42.2	9 49.0	24 20.9	28 03.8	29 33.3	9 02.4	7 51.1
30 Sa	10 32 14	6 29 54	6♊20 35	12 43 07	25 18.2	29 41.2	1 49.8	9 16.2	10 02.5	24 17.9	28 10.5	29 35.9	9 02.6	7 53.1
31 Su	10 36 11	7 27 56	19 11 40	25 46 47	25 17.1	1♎05.2	1 13.8	9 50.0	10 15.9	24 14.7	28 17.2	29 38.5	9 02.9	7 55.2

Astro Data	Dy Hr Mn
♅D	7 3:58
☽0S	13 10:41
☽0N	27 7:09
♃⚼♆	27 22:23
♄⚼♆	28 13:02
♃□♄	29 2:51
♀R	6 5:21
☽0S	9 19:25
♃R	14 19:32
♆D	21 14:53
☽0N	23 14:27
☿0S	29 23:02

Planet Ingress		Dy Hr Mn
♂	♉	1 3:53
♀	♍	9 11:06
☊	♏R	10 1:19
☿	♋	12 8:56
☉	♌	23 11:22
⚳	♊	25 5:35
☿	♌	28 8:05
☿	♍	12 6:12
♂	♊	14 20:47
☉	♍	23 18:24
☿	♎	30 17:20

Last Aspect Dy Hr Mn			☽ Ingress	Dy Hr Mn
3 6:42	♅	☍	♉	3 9:54
5 13:29	♀	□	♊	5 18:58
7 22:25	♀	⚹	♋	8 0:23
10 0:08	♅	□	♌	10 2:50
12 3:22	☿	⚹	♍	12 3:55
13 16:28	♄	⚹	♎	14 5:21
16 5:36	♅	☌	♏	16 8:23
18 4:26	☉	△	♐	18 13:32
20 17:50	♅	⚹	♑	20 20:46
23 5:28	☉	☍	♒	23 5:56
25 13:59	♅	△	♓	25 16:58
28 4:53	☿	△	♈	28 5:27
30 15:06	♅	☍	♉	30 17:53

Last Aspect Dy Hr Mn			☽ Ingress	Dy Hr Mn
1 18:02	♄	⚹	♊	2 4:02
4 8:01	♅	△	♋	4 10:17
6 10:42	♅	□	♌	6 12:44
8 11:00	♅	⚹	♍	8 12:53
10 8:17	♂	△	♎	10 12:51
12 12:41	♅	☌	♏	12 14:30
14 18:54	♂	☍	♐	14 18:59
17 0:40	♅	⚹	♑	17 2:25
19 10:30	♅	□	♒	19 12:09
21 22:02	♅	△	♓	21 23:32
24 6:55	♄	△	♈	24 12:02
26 23:38	♅	☍	♉	27 0:45
29 8:07	♄	⚹	♊	29 11:53
31 18:58	♅	△	♋	31 19:35

☽ Phases & Eclipses Dy Hr Mn		
1 16:37	☾	9♈13
9 4:10	●	16♋21
15 19:47	☽	22♎42
23 5:28	○	29♑46
31 8:48	☾	7♉32
7 11:57	●	14♌22
14 2:24	☽	20♏42
21 19:48	○	28♒08
29 23:20	☾	5♊59

Astro Data

1 July 1975
Julian Day # 27575
SVP 5♓35'52"
GC 26♐29.8 ⚴ 4♈57.2
Eris 14♈01.0 ⚵ 3♋06.3
⚷ 27♈44.5 ⚶ 28♓58.7
☽ Mean ☊ 28♏59.1

1 August 1975
Julian Day # 27606
SVP 5♓35'47"
GC 26♐29.9 ⚴ 6♈20.7R
Eris 13♈59.1R ⚵ 20♋21.9
⚷ 28♈09.9 ⚶ 2♈29.2
☽ Mean ☊ 27♏20.6

LONGITUDE — September 1975

Day	Sid.Time	☉	0 hr ☽	Noon ☽	True ☊	☿	♀	♂	⚳	♃	♄	♅	♆	♇
1 M	10 40 07	8♍25 59	2♋28 54	9♋18 20	25♏14.0	2♎27.8	0♍38.8	10♊23.6	10♊28.9	24♈11.4	28♋23.8	29♎41.2	9♐03.3	7♎57.3
2 Tu	10 44 04	9 24 04	16 15 17	23 19 44	25R 08.4	3 48.8	0R 04.9	10 56.9	10 41.8	24R 07.8	28 30.3	29 43.9	9 03.6	7 59.3
3 W	10 48 01	10 22 12	0♌31 29	7♌50 07	25 00.4	5 08.3	29♌32.4	11 30.0	10 54.5	24 04.1	28 36.8	29 46.6	9 04.1	8 01.4
4 Th	10 51 57	11 20 20	15 14 57	22 45 06	24 50.7	6 26.3	29 01.3	12 02.8	11 06.9	24 00.1	28 43.3	29 49.4	9 04.5	8 03.6
5 F	10 55 54	12 18 31	0♍19 28	7♍56 46	24 40.2	7 42.5	28 31.9	12 35.3	11 19.1	23 56.0	28 49.7	29 52.2	9 05.0	8 05.7
6 Sa	10 59 50	13 16 43	15 35 37	23 14 34	24 30.4	8 57.1	28 04.3	13 07.6	11 31.0	23 51.7	28 56.0	29 55.0	9 05.5	8 07.8
7 Su	11 03 47	14 14 58	0♎52 13	8♎27 12	24 22.2	10 09.9	27 38.6	13 39.6	11 42.7	23 47.3	29 02.3	29 57.9	9 06.0	8 10.0
8 M	11 07 43	15 13 13	15 58 20	23 24 37	24 16.5	11 20.9	27 15.0	14 11.3	11 54.1	23 42.6	29 08.5	0♏00.8	9 06.6	8 12.2
9 Tu	11 11 40	16 11 31	0♏45 13	7♏59 35	24 13.4	12 30.0	26 53.6	14 42.8	12 05.3	23 37.8	29 14.6	0 03.8	9 07.2	8 14.4
10 W	11 15 36	17 09 49	15 07 21	22 08 22	24D 12.5	13 36.9	26 34.4	15 13.9	12 16.2	23 32.8	29 20.7	0 06.7	9 07.8	8 16.5
11 Th	11 19 33	18 08 10	29 02 37	5♐50 18	24R 12.7	14 41.8	26 17.5	15 44.8	12 26.9	23 27.7	29 26.8	0 09.8	9 08.4	8 18.8
12 F	11 23 30	19 06 32	12♐31 40	19 07 07	24 13.1	15 44.4	26 02.9	16 15.3	12 37.3	23 22.4	29 32.8	0 12.8	9 09.1	8 21.0
13 Sa	11 27 26	20 04 55	25 37 04	2♑01 58	24 12.4	16 44.5	25 50.7	16 45.6	12 47.4	23 16.9	29 38.7	0 15.9	9 09.9	8 23.2
14 Su	11 31 23	21 03 21	8♑22 19	14 38 37	24 09.7	17 42.0	25 41.0	17 15.6	12 57.3	23 11.3	29 44.5	0 19.0	9 10.6	8 25.4
15 M	11 35 19	22 01 47	20 51 18	27 00 51	24 04.7	18 36.8	25 33.6	17 45.2	13 06.9	23 05.5	29 50.3	0 22.1	9 11.4	8 27.7
16 Tu	11 39 16	23 00 16	3♒07 40	9♒12 09	23 57.2	19 28.6	25 28.6	18 14.5	13 16.2	22 59.6	29 56.0	0 25.3	9 12.2	8 29.9
17 W	11 43 12	23 58 46	15 14 37	21 15 25	23 47.6	20 17.3	25D 26.1	18 43.5	13 25.2	22 53.5	0♌01.7	0 28.5	9 13.1	8 32.2
18 Th	11 47 09	24 57 17	27 14 49	3♓13 04	23 36.7	21 02.5	25 25.9	19 12.2	13 34.0	22 47.3	0 07.2	0 31.7	9 14.0	8 34.5
19 F	11 51 05	25 55 51	9♓10 24	15 07 00	23 25.4	21 44.1	25 28.1	19 40.5	13 42.4	22 40.9	0 12.7	0 34.9	9 14.9	8 36.7
20 Sa	11 55 02	26 54 26	21 03 04	26 58 48	23 14.8	22 21.6	25 32.6	20 08.5	13 50.6	22 34.5	0 18.2	0 38.2	9 15.8	8 39.0
21 Su	11 58 58	27 53 04	2♈54 23	8♈50 01	23 05.7	22 54.9	25 39.3	20 36.2	13 58.4	22 27.9	0 23.5	0 41.5	9 16.8	8 41.3
22 M	12 02 55	28 51 43	14 45 56	20 42 20	22 58.6	23 23.6	25 48.3	21 03.4	14 06.0	22 21.1	0 28.8	0 44.8	9 17.8	8 43.6
23 Tu	12 06 52	29 50 25	26 39 32	2♉37 48	22 54.1	23 47.3	25 59.5	21 30.4	14 13.2	22 14.3	0 34.0	0 48.1	9 18.8	8 45.9
24 W	12 10 48	0♎49 08	8♉37 30	14 39 00	22D 51.8	24 05.6	26 12.7	21 56.9	14 20.1	22 07.3	0 39.2	0 51.5	9 19.9	8 48.2
25 Th	12 14 45	1 47 54	20 42 42	26 49 05	22 51.5	24 18.2	26 28.1	22 23.1	14 26.7	22 00.2	0 44.2	0 54.9	9 21.0	8 50.5
26 F	12 18 41	2 46 42	2♊58 36	9♊11 47	22 52.4	24R 24.7	26 45.4	22 48.8	14 33.0	21 53.1	0 49.2	0 58.3	9 22.1	8 52.9
27 Sa	12 22 38	3 45 32	15 29 10	21 51 15	22R 53.6	24 24.6	27 04.7	23 14.2	14 39.0	21 45.8	0 54.1	1 01.8	9 23.3	8 55.2
28 Su	12 26 34	4 44 25	28 18 35	4♋51 38	22 54.2	24 17.6	27 25.8	23 39.2	14 44.6	21 38.4	0 59.0	1 05.2	9 24.4	8 57.5
29 M	12 30 31	5 43 20	11♋30 52	18 16 38	22 53.4	24 03.4	27 48.8	24 03.7	14 49.9	21 30.9	1 03.7	1 08.7	9 25.7	8 59.8
30 Tu	12 34 27	6 42 17	25 09 11	2♌08 41	22 50.8	23 41.7	28 13.5	24 27.8	14 54.8	21 23.4	1 08.4	1 12.2	9 26.9	9 02.2

LONGITUDE — October 1975

Day	Sid.Time	☉	0 hr ☽	Noon ☽	True ☊	☿	♀	♂	⚳	♃	♄	♅	♆	♇
1 W	12 38 24	7♎41 17	9♌15 05	16♌28 11	22♏46.3	23♎12.4	28♌40.0	24♊51.5	14♊59.4	21♈15.8	1♌13.0	1♏15.7	9♐28.2	9♎04.5
2 Th	12 42 21	8 40 19	23 47 33	1♍12 34	22R 40.4	22R 35.5	29 08.0	25 14.7	15 03.7	21R 08.1	1 17.5	1 19.3	9 29.5	9 06.8
3 F	12 46 17	9 39 22	8♍42 25	16 16 03	22 33.9	21 51.1	29 37.7	25 37.5	15 07.6	21 00.3	1 21.9	1 22.8	9 30.8	9 09.1
4 Sa	12 50 14	10 38 29	23 52 18	1♎29 52	22 27.5	20 59.7	0♍08.8	25 59.8	15 11.1	20 52.4	1 26.2	1 26.4	9 32.1	9 11.5
5 Su	12 54 10	11 37 37	9♎07 24	16 43 33	22 22.3	20 01.9	0 41.4	26 21.6	15 14.2	20 44.6	1 30.5	1 30.0	9 33.5	9 13.8
6 M	12 58 07	12 36 47	24 17 03	1♏46 42	22 18.9	18 58.7	1 15.4	26 42.9	15 17.0	20 36.6	1 34.6	1 33.6	9 34.9	9 16.1
7 Tu	13 02 03	13 35 59	9♏11 31	16 30 40	22D 17.3	17 51.3	1 50.8	27 03.7	15 19.5	20 28.6	1 38.7	1 37.2	9 36.3	9 18.5
8 W	13 06 00	14 35 13	23 43 32	0♐49 43	22 17.5	16 41.3	2 27.5	27 24.0	15 21.5	20 20.6	1 42.7	1 40.9	9 37.8	9 20.8
9 Th	13 09 56	15 34 29	7♐48 59	14 41 17	22 18.7	15 30.4	3 05.4	27 43.8	15 23.2	20 12.6	1 46.5	1 44.5	9 39.3	9 23.1
10 F	13 13 53	16 33 47	21 26 45	28 05 36	22 20.2	14 20.6	3 44.5	28 03.0	15 24.5	20 04.5	1 50.3	1 48.2	9 40.8	9 25.4
11 Sa	13 17 50	17 33 07	4♑38 11	11♑04 55	22R 21.3	13 13.8	4 24.8	28 21.7	15 25.4	19 56.4	1 54.0	1 51.8	9 42.3	9 27.7
12 Su	13 21 46	18 32 28	17 26 18	23 42 50	22 21.4	12 11.9	5 06.2	28 39.9	15R 26.0	19 48.3	1 57.6	1 55.5	9 43.9	9 30.1
13 M	13 25 43	19 31 51	29 55 03	6♒03 30	22 20.0	11 16.8	5 48.8	28 57.5	15 26.1	19 40.2	2 01.1	1 59.2	9 45.5	9 32.4
14 Tu	13 29 39	20 31 16	12♒08 42	18 11 11	22 17.1	10 30.0	6 32.3	29 14.5	15 25.9	19 32.1	2 04.5	2 02.9	9 47.1	9 34.7
15 W	13 33 36	21 30 42	24 11 26	0♓09 55	22 13.0	9 52.8	7 16.9	29 31.0	15 25.2	19 24.0	2 07.8	2 06.7	9 48.7	9 37.0
16 Th	13 37 32	22 30 11	6♓07 06	12 03 21	22 08.0	9 25.9	8 02.4	29 46.8	15 24.2	19 15.9	2 11.1	2 10.4	9 50.3	9 39.2
17 F	13 41 29	23 29 41	17 59 02	23 54 31	22 02.7	9D 10.0	8 48.9	0♋02.0	15 22.8	19 07.9	2 14.2	2 14.1	9 52.0	9 41.5
18 Sa	13 45 25	24 29 13	29 50 06	5♈46 03	21 57.7	9 05.2	9 36.3	0 16.7	15 21.0	18 59.8	2 17.2	2 17.8	9 53.7	9 43.8
19 Su	13 49 22	25 28 47	11♈42 38	17 40 04	21 53.5	9 11.5	10 24.5	0 30.7	15 18.8	18 51.8	2 20.1	2 21.6	9 55.4	9 46.1
20 M	13 53 18	26 28 23	23 38 36	29 38 26	21 50.5	9 28.5	11 13.7	0 44.0	15 16.2	18 43.9	2 22.9	2 25.3	9 57.2	9 48.3
21 Tu	13 57 15	27 28 01	5♉39 46	11♉42 49	21D 48.8	9 55.7	12 03.6	0 56.7	15 13.3	18 36.0	2 25.6	2 29.1	9 58.9	9 50.6
22 W	14 01 12	28 27 41	17 47 49	23 54 59	21 48.4	10 32.3	12 54.3	1 08.8	15 09.9	18 28.1	2 28.2	2 32.9	10 00.7	9 52.8
23 Th	14 05 08	29 27 24	0♊04 34	6♊16 50	21 49.1	11 17.5	13 45.8	1 20.1	15 06.1	18 20.3	2 30.7	2 36.6	10 02.5	9 55.0
24 F	14 09 05	0♏27 08	12 32 03	18 50 31	21 50.4	12 10.7	14 38.0	1 30.8	15 01.9	18 12.5	2 33.2	2 40.4	10 04.4	9 57.3
25 Sa	14 13 01	1 26 55	25 12 33	1♋38 27	21 52.0	13 10.8	15 31.0	1 40.7	14 57.4	18 04.9	2 35.5	2 44.2	10 06.2	9 59.5
26 Su	14 16 58	2 26 44	8♋08 33	14 43 08	21 53.3	14 17.1	16 24.6	1 49.9	14 52.4	17 57.2	2 37.7	2 47.9	10 08.1	10 01.7
27 M	14 20 54	3 26 35	21 22 31	28 06 55	21R 54.1	15 28.8	17 18.9	1 58.4	14 47.0	17 49.7	2 39.7	2 51.7	10 10.0	10 03.9
28 Tu	14 24 51	4 26 28	4♌56 32	11♌51 29	21 54.0	16 45.2	18 13.8	2 06.2	14 41.3	17 42.3	2 41.7	2 55.5	10 11.9	10 06.0
29 W	14 28 47	5 26 24	18 51 48	25 57 23	21 53.1	18 05.6	19 09.4	2 13.1	14 35.2	17 34.9	2 43.6	2 59.2	10 13.8	10 08.2
30 Th	14 32 44	6 26 21	3♍08 02	10♍23 23	21 51.6	19 29.3	20 05.5	2 19.3	14 28.6	17 27.6	2 45.4	3 03.0	10 15.7	10 10.4
31 F	14 36 41	7 26 21	17 42 56	25 06 04	21 49.8	20 55.9	21 02.2	2 24.7	14 21.7	17 20.5	2 47.0	3 06.8	10 17.7	10 12.5

Astro Data	Dy Hr Mn
♃⚼♆	3 12:03
☽0S	6 5:56
♀D	18 1:46
☽0N	19 20:40
☉0S	23 15:56
☿R	26 23:46
☽0S	3 16:47
♄□♅	4 18:04
⚳R	13 9:26
☽0N	17 2:29
♄□♅	17 14:05
☿D	18 10:15
☽0S	31 2:15

Planet Ingress		Dy Hr Mn
♀	♌R	2 15:34
♅	♏	8 5:16
♄	♌	17 4:57
☉	♎	23 15:55
♀	♍	4 5:19
♂	♋	17 8:44
☉	♏	24 1:06

Last Aspect Dy Hr Mn		☽ Ingress Dy Hr Mn
2 22:43	♅ □	♌ 2 23:08
4 23:15	♅ ⚹	♍ 4 23:29
6 21:01	♄ ⚹	♎ 6 22:38
8 21:25	♄ □	♏ 8 22:46
11 0:37	♄ △	♐ 11 1:41
13 0:36	♀ △	♑ 13 8:11
15 17:35	♄ ☍	♒ 15 17:51
17 20:21	♀ ☍	♓ 18 5:32
20 11:50	☉ ☍	♈ 20 18:07
22 22:26	♀ △	♉ 23 6:43
25 11:18	♀ □	♊ 25 18:13
27 21:59	♀ ⚹	♋ 28 3:07
29 21:52	☿ □	♌ 30 8:20

Last Aspect Dy Hr Mn		☽ Ingress Dy Hr Mn
2 8:33	♀ ☌	♍ 2 10:03
4 3:08	♂ □	♎ 4 9:39
6 3:41	♂ △	♏ 6 9:09
6 11:41	♄ □	♐ 8 10:35
10 11:55	♂ ☍	♑ 10 15:29
12 4:35	♃ □	♒ 13 0:10
15 10:40	♂ △	♓ 15 11:40
16 7:30	♆ □	♈ 18 0:20
20 5:06	☉ ☍	♉ 20 12:43
21 12:44	♀ △	♊ 22 23:51
24 10:49	♃ ⚹	♋ 25 8:57
26 17:48	♃ □	♌ 27 15:20
28 21:56	♃ △	♍ 29 18:47
31 4:57	♀ ☌	♎ 31 19:55

☽ Phases & Eclipses Dy Hr Mn	
5 19:19	● 12♍36
12 11:59	☽ 19♐06
20 11:50	○ 26♓54
28 11:46	☾ 4♋44
5 3:23	● 11♎16
12 1:15	☽ 18♑06
20 5:06	○ 26♈11
27 22:07	☾ 3♌52

Astro Data

1 September 1975
Julian Day # 27637
SVP 5♓35'43"
GC 26♐30.0 ⚴ 2♈17.2R
Eris 13♈47.7R ⚵ 6♌37.6
⚷ 27♈45.1R ⚶ 28♓59.5R
☽ Mean ☊ 25♏42.1

1 October 1975
Julian Day # 27667
SVP 5♓35'41"
GC 26♐30.0 ⚴ 24♓33.0R
Eris 13♈30.9R ⚵ 21♌02.4
⚷ 26♈41.0R ⚶ 21♓41.7R
☽ Mean ☊ 24♏06.7

November 1975 LONGITUDE

Day	Sid.Time	☉	0 hr ☽	Noon ☽	True ☊	☿	♀	♂	⚳	♃	♄	♅	♆	♇
1 Sa	14 40 37	8♏26 23	2♎31 58	9♎59 45	21♏48.0	22♎24.8	21♍59.5	2♋29.3	14♊14.4	17♈13.4	2♌48.6	3♏10.5	10♐19.6	10♎14.6
2 Su	14 44 34	9 26 27	17 28 26	24 56 58	21R46.7	23 55.7	22 57.3	2 33.1	14R06.7	17R06.5	2 50.0	3 14.3	10 21.6	10 16.7
3 M	14 48 30	10 26 33	2♏24 17	9♏49 22	21D45.8	25 28.2	23 55.6	2 36.1	13 58.7	16 59.7	2 51.3	3 18.0	10 23.6	10 18.8
4 Tu	14 52 27	11 26 41	17 11 13	24 28 58	21 45.7	27 01.9	24 54.4	2 38.2	13 50.3	16 53.0	2 52.6	3 21.8	10 25.7	10 20.9
5 W	14 56 23	12 26 51	1♐41 51	8♐49 14	21 46.0	28 36.6	25 53.7	2 39.5	13 41.5	16 46.4	2 53.7	3 25.5	10 27.7	10 23.0
6 Th	15 00 20	13 27 03	15 50 41	22 45 51	21 46.7	0♏12.1	26 53.4	2R39.9	13 32.4	16 40.0	2 54.7	3 29.3	10 29.8	10 25.0
7 F	15 04 16	14 27 16	29 34 38	6♑16 59	21 47.4	1 48.2	27 53.6	2 39.5	13 23.0	16 33.7	2 55.5	3 33.0	10 31.8	10 27.0
8 Sa	15 08 13	15 27 30	12♑53 02	19 23 02	21 48.1	3 24.7	28 54.2	2 38.2	13 13.2	16 27.5	2 56.3	3 36.7	10 33.9	10 29.0
9 Su	15 12 10	16 27 46	25 47 17	2♒06 13	21 48.6	5 01.5	29 55.2	2 36.0	13 03.1	16 21.5	2 57.0	3 40.4	10 36.0	10 31.0
10 M	15 16 06	17 28 04	8♒20 18	14 30 03	21R48.8	6 38.4	0♎56.7	2 33.0	12 52.7	16 15.7	2 57.5	3 44.1	10 38.1	10 33.0
11 Tu	15 20 03	18 28 23	20 36 01	26 38 47	21 48.7	8 15.4	1 58.5	2 29.1	12 41.9	16 10.0	2 57.9	3 47.8	10 40.2	10 34.9
12 W	15 23 59	19 28 43	2♓38 54	8♓36 57	21 48.6	9 52.4	3 00.7	2 24.3	12 30.9	16 04.4	2 58.3	3 51.5	10 42.4	10 36.9
13 Th	15 27 56	20 29 05	14 33 31	20 29 08	21 48.4	11 29.4	4 03.3	2 18.7	12 19.6	15 59.0	2 58.5	3 55.1	10 44.5	10 38.8
14 F	15 31 52	21 29 28	26 24 19	2♈19 35	21D48.3	13 06.3	5 06.2	2 12.2	12 08.0	15 53.8	2R58.5	3 58.8	10 46.7	10 40.7
15 Sa	15 35 49	22 29 52	8♈15 24	14 12 12	21 48.3	14 43.1	6 09.5	2 04.8	11 56.2	15 48.8	2 58.5	4 02.4	10 48.8	10 42.5
16 Su	15 39 45	23 30 18	20 10 21	26 10 14	21 48.4	16 19.7	7 13.2	1 56.5	11 44.1	15 43.9	2 58.4	4 06.0	10 51.0	10 44.4
17 M	15 43 42	24 30 46	2♉12 10	8♉16 25	21 48.6	17 56.1	8 17.1	1 47.4	11 31.8	15 39.2	2 58.1	4 09.6	10 53.2	10 46.2
18 Tu	15 47 39	25 31 15	14 23 14	20 32 48	21R48.7	19 32.3	9 21.4	1 37.4	11 19.2	15 34.7	2 57.8	4 13.2	10 55.4	10 48.0
19 W	15 51 35	26 31 46	26 45 17	3♊00 50	21 48.6	21 08.4	10 26.0	1 26.6	11 06.5	15 30.4	2 57.3	4 16.8	10 57.6	10 49.8
20 Th	15 55 32	27 32 18	9♊19 33	15 41 29	21 48.2	22 44.2	11 31.0	1 14.9	10 53.5	15 26.2	2 56.7	4 20.4	10 59.8	10 51.6
21 F	15 59 28	28 32 52	22 06 44	28 35 17	21 47.5	24 19.8	12 36.2	1 02.4	10 40.4	15 22.3	2 56.1	4 23.9	11 02.0	10 53.3
22 Sa	16 03 25	29 33 27	5♋07 13	11♋42 29	21 46.6	25 55.3	13 41.7	0 49.1	10 27.1	15 18.5	2 55.2	4 27.4	11 04.2	10 55.0
23 Su	16 07 21	0♐34 04	18 21 08	25 03 08	21 45.5	27 30.6	14 47.4	0 35.0	10 13.6	15 14.9	2 54.3	4 30.9	11 06.4	10 56.7
24 M	16 11 18	1 34 43	1♌48 28	8♌37 08	21 44.5	29 05.6	15 53.5	0 20.1	10 00.0	15 11.5	2 53.3	4 34.4	11 08.7	10 58.4
25 Tu	16 15 14	2 35 23	15 29 04	22 24 12	21D43.9	0♐40.6	16 59.8	0 04.4	9 46.3	15 08.3	2 52.2	4 37.8	11 10.9	11 00.0
26 W	16 19 11	3 36 05	29 22 29	6♍23 46	21 43.7	2 15.3	18 06.4	29♊47.9	9 32.4	15 05.3	2 50.9	4 41.3	11 13.1	11 01.6
27 Th	16 23 08	4 36 49	13♍27 55	20 34 42	21 44.1	3 50.0	19 13.2	29 30.8	9 18.5	15 02.5	2 49.6	4 44.7	11 15.4	11 03.2
28 F	16 27 04	5 37 34	27 43 52	4♎55 05	21 45.0	5 24.5	20 20.2	29 12.9	9 04.5	14 59.9	2 48.1	4 48.1	11 17.6	11 04.8
29 Sa	16 31 01	6 38 21	12♎07 57	19 22 01	21 46.2	6 58.9	21 27.5	28 54.3	8 50.4	14 57.5	2 46.5	4 51.4	11 19.9	11 06.3
30 Su	16 34 57	7 39 09	26 36 45	3♏51 33	21 47.3	8 33.2	22 35.0	28 35.2	8 36.3	14 55.3	2 44.8	4 54.7	11 22.2	11 07.8

December 1975 LONGITUDE

Day	Sid.Time	☉	0 hr ☽	Noon ☽	True ☊	☿	♀	♂	⚳	♃	♄	♅	♆	♇
1 M	16 38 54	8♐39 59	11♏05 49	18♏18 52	21♏47.8	10♐07.4	23♎42.7	28♊15.4	8♊22.1	14♈53.3	2♌43.0	4♏58.1	11♐24.4	11♎09.3
2 Tu	16 42 50	9 40 50	25 30 00	2♐38 35	21R47.6	11 41.5	24 50.6	27R55.0	8R08.0	14R51.6	2R41.1	5 01.3	11 26.7	11 10.7
3 W	16 46 47	10 41 42	9♐43 57	16 45 30	21 46.3	13 15.6	25 58.7	27 34.2	7 53.8	14 50.0	2 39.1	5 04.6	11 28.9	11 12.1
4 Th	16 50 43	11 42 35	23 42 44	0♑35 12	21 44.1	14 49.7	27 07.1	27 12.8	7 39.7	14 48.6	2 37.0	5 07.8	11 31.2	11 13.5
5 F	16 54 40	12 43 30	7♑22 33	14 04 35	21 41.0	16 23.7	28 15.6	26 51.0	7 25.7	14 47.4	2 34.8	5 11.0	11 33.5	11 14.9
6 Sa	16 58 37	13 44 25	20 41 09	27 12 16	21 37.5	17 57.8	29 24.2	26 28.9	7 11.7	14 46.5	2 32.5	5 14.2	11 35.7	11 16.2
7 Su	17 02 33	14 45 21	3♒38 02	9♒58 40	21 34.1	19 31.8	0♏33.1	26 06.4	6 57.8	14 45.8	2 30.1	5 17.3	11 38.0	11 17.5
8 M	17 06 30	15 46 18	16 14 26	22 25 44	21 31.3	21 05.8	1 42.1	25 43.6	6 44.0	14 45.2	2 27.6	5 20.4	11 40.3	11 18.8
9 Tu	17 10 26	16 47 15	28 33 02	4♓36 48	21 29.4	22 39.9	2 51.3	25 20.5	6 30.3	14 44.9	2 25.0	5 23.5	11 42.5	11 20.0
10 W	17 14 23	17 48 13	10♓37 36	16 36 02	21D28.7	24 14.0	4 00.6	24 57.3	6 16.7	14D44.8	2 22.2	5 26.6	11 44.8	11 21.3
11 Th	17 18 19	18 49 12	22 32 42	28 28 13	21 29.1	25 48.1	5 10.1	24 33.9	6 03.3	14 44.9	2 19.4	5 29.6	11 47.0	11 22.4
12 F	17 22 16	19 50 11	4♈23 13	10♈18 20	21 30.5	27 22.3	6 19.8	24 10.5	5 50.1	14 45.2	2 16.5	5 32.5	11 49.3	11 23.6
13 Sa	17 26 12	20 51 11	16 14 11	22 11 20	21 32.3	28 56.5	7 29.6	23 47.0	5 37.0	14 45.7	2 13.5	5 35.5	11 51.5	11 24.7
14 Su	17 30 09	21 52 11	28 10 23	4♉11 50	21 34.1	0♑30.8	8 39.5	23 23.5	5 24.2	14 46.5	2 10.5	5 38.4	11 53.7	11 25.8
15 M	17 34 06	22 53 13	10♉16 11	16 23 52	21R35.2	2 05.1	9 49.6	23 00.1	5 11.5	14 47.4	2 07.3	5 41.3	11 56.0	11 26.8
16 Tu	17 38 02	23 54 14	22 35 14	28 50 36	21 35.1	3 39.4	10 59.8	22 36.8	4 59.1	14 48.5	2 04.0	5 44.1	11 58.2	11 27.9
17 W	17 41 59	24 55 16	5♊10 12	11♊34 11	21 33.4	5 13.8	12 10.2	22 13.7	4 46.9	14 49.9	2 00.7	5 46.9	12 00.4	11 28.9
18 Th	17 45 55	25 56 19	18 02 37	24 35 29	21 29.9	6 48.1	13 20.6	21 50.7	4 34.9	14 51.4	1 57.2	5 49.6	12 02.6	11 29.8
19 F	17 49 52	26 57 23	1♋12 40	7♋54 01	21 24.9	8 22.4	14 31.3	21 28.1	4 23.3	14 53.2	1 53.7	5 52.4	12 04.9	11 30.7
20 Sa	17 53 48	27 58 27	14 39 17	21 28 08	21 18.9	9 56.7	15 42.0	21 05.7	4 11.9	14 55.2	1 50.1	5 55.1	12 07.1	11 31.6
21 Su	17 57 45	28 59 31	28 20 13	5♌15 09	21 12.5	11 30.8	16 52.8	20 43.6	4 00.7	14 57.3	1 46.5	5 57.7	12 09.2	11 32.5
22 M	18 01 42	0♑00 37	12♌12 31	19 11 54	21 06.6	13 04.7	18 03.8	20 22.0	3 49.9	14 59.7	1 42.7	6 00.3	12 11.4	11 33.3
23 Tu	18 05 38	1 01 43	26 12 53	3♍15 06	21 02.0	14 38.4	19 14.9	20 00.7	3 39.4	15 02.3	1 38.9	6 02.9	12 13.6	11 34.1
24 W	18 09 35	2 02 49	10♍18 13	17 21 54	20 59.1	16 11.7	20 26.1	19 39.9	3 29.2	15 05.0	1 35.0	6 05.4	12 15.8	11 34.9
25 Th	18 13 31	3 03 57	24 25 55	1♎30 01	20D58.1	17 44.7	21 37.4	19 19.6	3 19.3	15 08.0	1 31.0	6 07.9	12 17.9	11 35.6
26 F	18 17 28	4 05 05	8♎34 00	15 37 43	20 58.6	19 17.0	22 48.8	18 59.9	3 09.7	15 11.2	1 27.0	6 10.3	12 20.1	11 36.3
27 Sa	18 21 24	5 06 13	22 41 01	29 43 43	20 59.8	20 48.7	24 00.3	18 40.7	3 00.5	15 14.5	1 22.9	6 12.7	12 22.2	11 36.9
28 Su	18 25 21	6 07 23	6♏45 40	13♏46 42	21R01.0	22 19.5	25 12.0	18 22.1	2 51.7	15 18.1	1 18.7	6 15.0	12 24.3	11 37.5
29 M	18 29 17	7 08 32	20 46 34	27 45 04	21 01.0	23 49.2	26 23.7	18 04.2	2 43.2	15 21.8	1 14.4	6 17.3	12 26.4	11 38.1
30 Tu	18 33 14	8 09 43	4♐41 54	11♐36 45	20 59.0	25 17.6	27 35.4	17 46.9	2 35.1	15 25.8	1 10.1	6 19.6	12 28.5	11 38.7
31 W	18 37 11	9 10 53	18 29 18	25 19 12	20 54.7	26 44.4	28 47.3	17 30.3	2 27.4	15 29.9	1 05.8	6 21.8	12 30.6	11 39.2

Astro Data	Dy Hr Mn
♂ R	6 12:01
♀0S	12 2:56
☽0N	13 9:06
♄ R	14 19:25
☽0S	27 9:29
♃ D	10 12:39
☽0N	10 17:15
☽0S	24 15:30

Planet Ingress		Dy Hr Mn
☿	♏	6 8:58
♀	♎	9 13:52
☉	♐	22 22:31
☿	♐	25 1:44
♂	♊R	25 18:30
♀	♏	7 0:29
☿	♑	14 4:10
☉	♑	22 11:46

Last Aspect Dy Hr Mn			☽ Ingress	Dy Hr Mn
2 10:10	☿	☌	♏	2 20:07
4 12:45	♀	⚹	♐	4 21:10
6 19:49	♀	□	♑	7 0:45
9 7:28	♀	△	♒	9 7:59
10 18:21	☉	□	♓	11 18:42
13 12:00	☉	△	♈	14 7:17
15 15:13	♃	☌	♉	16 19:38
18 22:28	☉	☍	♊	19 6:14
20 11:32	♃	⚹	♋	21 14:36
23 16:58	☿	△	♌	23 20:48
26 0:57	♂	⚹	♍	26 1:04
28 2:41	♂	□	♎	28 3:48
30 3:27	♂	△	♏	30 5:37

Last Aspect Dy Hr Mn			☽ Ingress	Dy Hr Mn
30 13:45	♅	☌	♐	2 7:33
4 6:15	♂	☍	♑	4 10:58
6 16:29	♀	□	♒	6 17:12
8 18:15	♂	△	♓	9 2:52
11 5:46	☿	□	♈	11 15:06
14 3:34	☿	△	♉	14 3:39
14 21:46	♀	☍	♊	16 14:12
18 14:39	☉	☍	♋	18 21:49
20 0:53	♀	△	♌	21 2:54
22 13:57	♂	⚹	♍	23 6:28
24 17:42	♀	⚹	♎	25 9:27
26 18:58	☿	□	♏	27 12:28
29 9:27	♀	☌	♐	29 15:53
30 22:33	♂	☍	♑	31 20:16

☽ Phases & Eclipses Dy Hr Mn		
3 13:05	●	10♏29
3 13:15:06	●	P 0.959
10 18:21	☽	17♒44
18 22:28	○	25♉58
18 22:23	●	T 1.064
26 6:52	☾	3♍23
3 0:50	●	10♐13
10 14:39	☽	17♓55
18 14:39	○	26♊03
25 14:52	☾	3♎11

Astro Data

1 November 1975
Julian Day # 27698
SVP 5♓35'38"
GC 26♐30.1 ⚴ 18♓25.5R
Eris 13♈12.4R ⚵ 3♍58.3
⚷ 25♈16.1R ⚶ 17♓53.6R
☽ Mean ☊ 22♏28.2

1 December 1975
Julian Day # 27728
SVP 5♓35'34"
GC 26♐30.2 ⚴ 18♓10.8
Eris 12♈58.8R ⚵ 13♍36.8
⚷ 24♈06.7R ⚶ 20♓47.0
☽ Mean ☊ 20♏52.9

LONGITUDE

January 1976

Day	Sid.Time	☉	0 hr ☽	Noon ☽	True☊	☿	♀	♂	⚳	♃	♄	♅	♆	♇
1 Th	18 41 07	10♑12 04	2♑06 06	8♑49 39	20♏48.0	28♑09.3	29♏59.3	17♊14.4	2♊20.0	15♈34.3	1♌01.4	6♏24.0	12♐32.6	11♎39.7
2 F	18 45 04	11 13 15	15 29 34	22 05 33	20R 39.4	29 31.9	1♐11.3	16R 59.3	2R 13.1	15 38.8	0R 56.9	6 26.1	12 34.7	11 40.1
3 Sa	18 49 00	12 14 26	28 37 25	5♒05 02	20 29.6	0♒51.6	2 23.4	16 44.9	2 06.5	15 43.5	0 52.4	6 28.2	12 36.7	11 40.5
4 Su	18 52 57	13 15 36	11♒28 19	17 47 18	20 19.6	2 08.2	3 35.6	16 31.3	2 00.4	15 48.4	0 47.9	6 30.2	12 38.8	11 40.9
5 M	18 56 53	14 16 47	24 02 06	0♓12 54	20 10.6	3 20.9	4 47.8	16 18.5	1 54.6	15 53.5	0 43.2	6 32.2	12 40.8	11 41.2
6 Tu	19 00 50	15 17 57	6♓20 00	12 23 44	20 03.2	4 29.1	6 00.1	16 06.5	1 49.3	15 58.7	0 38.6	6 34.1	12 42.7	11 41.5
7 W	19 04 46	16 19 07	18 24 33	24 22 55	19 58.1	5 32.1	7 12.5	15 55.3	1 44.3	16 04.2	0 33.9	6 36.0	12 44.7	11 41.8
8 Th	19 08 43	17 20 16	0♈19 24	6♈14 35	19 55.3	6 29.2	8 24.9	15 44.9	1 39.8	16 09.8	0 29.2	6 37.8	12 46.7	11 42.0
9 F	19 12 40	18 21 25	12 09 06	18 03 36	19D 54.5	7 19.4	9 37.4	15 35.3	1 35.7	16 15.6	0 24.4	6 39.6	12 48.6	11 42.2
10 Sa	19 16 36	19 22 34	23 58 46	29 55 16	19 55.0	8 02.0	10 50.0	15 26.5	1 32.0	16 21.6	0 19.6	6 41.4	12 50.5	11 42.4
11 Su	19 20 33	20 23 42	5♉53 49	11♉55 04	19R 55.8	8 35.9	12 02.6	15 18.6	1 28.7	16 27.7	0 14.8	6 43.0	12 52.4	11 42.5
12 M	19 24 29	21 24 49	17 59 39	24 08 10	19 56.0	9 00.4	13 15.3	15 11.5	1 25.9	16 34.0	0 10.0	6 44.7	12 54.3	11 42.6
13 Tu	19 28 26	22 25 56	0♊21 12	6♊39 13	19 54.5	9R 14.6	14 28.0	15 05.3	1 23.4	16 40.5	0 05.1	6 46.3	12 56.2	11R 42.6
14 W	19 32 22	23 27 03	13 02 37	19 31 43	19 50.6	9 17.7	15 40.8	14 59.8	1 21.4	16 47.2	0 00.3	6 47.8	12 58.0	11 42.6
15 Th	19 36 19	24 28 09	26 06 41	2♋47 34	19 44.2	9 09.4	16 53.6	14 55.2	1 19.8	16 54.0	29♋55.4	6 49.3	12 59.8	11 42.6
16 F	19 40 15	25 29 14	9♋34 17	16 26 37	19 35.2	8 49.2	18 06.5	14 51.3	1 18.6	17 00.9	29 50.5	6 50.7	13 01.6	11 42.6
17 Sa	19 44 12	26 30 19	23 24 11	0♌26 28	19 24.5	8 17.4	19 19.4	14 48.3	1 17.8	17 08.1	29 45.5	6 52.1	13 03.4	11 42.5
18 Su	19 48 09	27 31 23	7♌32 49	14 42 31	19 13.2	7 34.5	20 32.4	14 46.1	1D 17.5	17 15.4	29 40.6	6 53.4	13 05.1	11 42.3
19 M	19 52 05	28 32 27	21 54 46	29 08 43	19 02.5	6 41.3	21 45.4	14 44.6	1 17.5	17 22.8	29 35.7	6 54.6	13 06.9	11 42.2
20 Tu	19 56 02	29 33 30	6♍23 33	13♍38 28	18 53.5	5 39.2	22 58.5	14D 43.9	1 18.0	17 30.4	29 30.7	6 55.9	13 08.6	11 42.0
21 W	19 59 58	0♒34 33	20 52 45	28 05 45	18 47.1	4 30.1	24 11.6	14 44.0	1 18.8	17 38.2	29 25.8	6 57.0	13 10.3	11 41.8
22 Th	20 03 55	1 35 35	5♎16 57	12♎25 57	18 43.4	3 16.1	25 24.8	14 44.8	1 20.1	17 46.1	29 20.8	6 58.1	13 11.9	11 41.5
23 F	20 07 51	2 36 37	19 32 27	26 36 14	18D 42.1	1 59.5	26 38.0	14 46.4	1 21.8	17 54.2	29 15.9	6 59.2	13 13.6	11 41.2
24 Sa	20 11 48	3 37 39	3♏37 13	10♏35 22	18R 42.0	0 42.5	27 51.3	14 48.8	1 23.8	18 02.4	29 11.0	7 00.2	13 15.2	11 40.9
25 Su	20 15 44	4 38 40	17 30 43	24 23 18	18 42.0	29♑27.6	29 04.6	14 51.8	1 26.3	18 10.7	29 06.1	7 01.1	13 16.8	11 40.5
26 M	20 19 41	5 39 41	1♐13 13	8♐00 31	18 40.7	28 16.7	0♑17.9	14 55.6	1 29.1	18 19.2	29 01.2	7 02.0	13 18.3	11 40.1
27 Tu	20 23 38	6 40 41	14 45 16	21 27 31	18 37.1	27 11.5	1 31.3	15 00.1	1 32.4	18 27.9	28 56.3	7 02.8	13 19.9	11 39.7
28 W	20 27 34	7 41 41	28 07 14	4♑44 24	18 30.4	26 13.3	2 44.7	15 05.2	1 36.0	18 36.6	28 51.4	7 03.6	13 21.4	11 39.2
29 Th	20 31 31	8 42 40	11♑18 58	17 50 50	18 20.6	25 23.0	3 58.1	15 11.1	1 40.1	18 45.6	28 46.6	7 04.3	13 22.9	11 38.7
30 F	20 35 27	9 43 38	24 19 54	0♒46 02	18 08.2	24 41.2	5 11.6	15 17.6	1 44.5	18 54.6	28 41.8	7 05.0	13 24.3	11 38.2
31 Sa	20 39 24	10 44 35	7♒09 09	13 29 10	17 54.2	24 08.2	6 25.0	15 24.8	1 49.3	19 03.8	28 37.0	7 05.6	13 25.8	11 37.6

LONGITUDE

February 1976

Day	Sid.Time	☉	0 hr ☽	Noon ☽	True☊	☿	♀	♂	⚳	♃	♄	♅	♆	♇
1 Su	20 43 20	11♒45 31	19♒45 59	25♒59 37	17♏39.9	23♑43.9	7♑38.6	15♊32.7	1♊54.4	19♈13.1	28♋32.2	7♏06.2	13♐27.2	11♎37.0
2 M	20 47 17	12 46 25	2♓10 04	8♓17 27	17R 26.4	23R 28.2	8 52.1	15 41.2	2 00.0	19 22.6	28R 27.5	7 06.7	13 28.5	11R 36.4
3 Tu	20 51 13	13 47 19	14 21 54	20 23 38	17 14.9	23D 20.8	10 05.6	15 50.3	2 05.9	19 32.2	28 22.8	7 07.1	13 29.9	11 35.7
4 W	20 55 10	14 48 11	26 22 56	2♈20 10	17 06.1	23 21.1	11 19.2	16 00.1	2 12.1	19 41.9	28 18.2	7 07.5	13 31.2	11 35.0
5 Th	20 59 07	15 49 02	8♈15 43	14 10 06	17 00.2	23 28.7	12 32.8	16 10.4	2 18.8	19 51.7	28 13.6	7 07.8	13 32.5	11 34.3
6 F	21 03 03	16 49 52	20 03 50	25 57 29	16 57.1	23 43.1	13 46.4	16 21.3	2 25.7	20 01.7	28 09.0	7 08.1	13 33.8	11 33.5
7 Sa	21 07 00	17 50 40	1♉51 42	7♉47 07	16 56.0	24 03.9	15 00.1	16 32.8	2 33.1	20 11.7	28 04.5	7 08.3	13 35.0	11 32.7
8 Su	21 10 56	18 51 27	13 44 26	19 44 21	16 55.9	24 30.4	16 13.7	16 44.9	2 40.7	20 21.9	28 00.1	7 08.5	13 36.2	11 31.9
9 M	21 14 53	19 52 12	25 47 35	1♊54 49	16 55.6	25 02.3	17 27.4	16 57.5	2 48.7	20 32.2	27 55.6	7 08.6	13 37.4	11 31.1
10 Tu	21 18 49	20 52 56	8♊06 43	14 23 57	16 53.9	25 39.0	18 41.1	17 10.7	2 57.1	20 42.7	27 51.3	7R 08.6	13 38.5	11 30.2
11 W	21 22 46	21 53 38	20 47 03	27 16 31	16 50.1	26 20.3	19 54.8	17 24.3	3 05.8	20 53.2	27 47.0	7 08.6	13 39.6	11 29.3
12 Th	21 26 42	22 54 18	3♋52 44	10♋35 55	16 43.5	27 05.6	21 08.6	17 38.5	3 14.8	21 03.8	27 42.8	7 08.6	13 40.7	11 28.3
13 F	21 30 39	23 54 57	17 26 12	24 23 27	16 34.3	27 54.7	22 22.3	17 53.2	3 24.1	21 14.6	27 38.6	7 08.4	13 41.8	11 27.4
14 Sa	21 34 36	24 55 35	1♌27 25	8♌37 36	16 23.2	28 47.3	23 36.1	18 08.4	3 33.7	21 25.4	27 34.5	7 08.3	13 42.8	11 26.4
15 Su	21 38 32	25 56 11	15 53 19	23 13 45	16 11.2	29 43.1	24 49.8	18 24.0	3 43.7	21 36.4	27 30.4	7 08.0	13 43.8	11 25.4
16 M	21 42 29	26 56 45	0♍37 52	8♍04 35	15 59.7	0♒41.8	26 03.6	18 40.1	3 53.9	21 47.5	27 26.5	7 07.8	13 44.8	11 24.3
17 Tu	21 46 25	27 57 18	15 32 44	23 01 08	15 50.0	1 43.1	27 17.5	18 56.6	4 04.5	21 58.6	27 22.6	7 07.4	13 45.7	11 23.2
18 W	21 50 22	28 57 49	0♎28 40	7♎54 20	15 42.9	2 47.0	28 31.3	19 13.6	4 15.3	22 09.9	27 18.7	7 07.0	13 46.6	11 22.2
19 Th	21 54 18	29 58 19	15 17 12	22 36 34	15 38.6	3 53.3	29 45.1	19 31.0	4 26.5	22 21.2	27 15.0	7 06.6	13 47.4	11 21.0
20 F	21 58 15	0♓58 48	29 51 51	7♏02 38	15D 36.9	5 01.6	0♒59.0	19 48.9	4 37.9	22 32.7	27 11.3	7 06.1	13 48.3	11 19.9
21 Sa	22 02 11	1 59 16	14♏08 41	21 09 54	15R 36.8	6 12.0	2 12.9	20 07.1	4 49.6	22 44.3	27 07.7	7 05.5	13 49.1	11 18.7
22 Su	22 06 08	2 59 42	28 06 18	4♐57 58	15 36.9	7 24.4	3 26.7	20 25.7	5 01.6	22 55.9	27 04.1	7 04.9	13 49.8	11 17.5
23 M	22 10 05	4 00 08	11♐45 06	18 27 55	15 36.1	8 38.5	4 40.7	20 44.8	5 13.9	23 07.6	27 00.7	7 04.3	13 50.6	11 16.3
24 Tu	22 14 01	5 00 31	25 06 40	1♑41 36	15 33.2	9 54.3	5 54.6	21 04.2	5 26.5	23 19.5	26 57.3	7 03.6	13 51.3	11 15.0
25 W	22 17 58	6 00 54	8♑12 57	14 40 59	15 27.6	11 11.6	7 08.5	21 24.0	5 39.3	23 31.4	26 54.1	7 02.8	13 52.0	11 13.8
26 Th	22 21 54	7 01 15	21 05 52	27 27 48	15 19.2	12 30.6	8 22.4	21 44.1	5 52.3	23 43.4	26 50.9	7 02.0	13 52.6	11 12.5
27 F	22 25 51	8 01 34	3♒46 55	10♒03 22	15 08.4	13 51.0	9 36.4	22 04.6	6 05.7	23 55.4	26 47.8	7 01.1	13 53.2	11 11.2
28 Sa	22 29 47	9 01 52	16 17 14	22 28 36	14 56.1	15 12.7	10 50.3	22 25.5	6 19.3	24 07.6	26 44.8	7 00.2	13 53.8	11 09.8
29 Su	22 33 44	10 02 08	28 37 33	4♓44 11	14 43.4	16 35.9	12 04.3	22 46.7	6 33.1	24 19.8	26 41.8	6 59.3	13 54.3	11 08.5

Astro Data Dy Hr Mn	Planet Ingress Dy Hr Mn	Last Aspect Dy Hr Mn	☽ Ingress Dy Hr Mn	Last Aspect Dy Hr Mn	☽ Ingress Dy Hr Mn	☽ Phases & Eclipses Dy Hr Mn	Astro Data
☽0N 7 2:34	♀ ♐ 1 12:14	2 0:13 ♃ □	♒ 3 2:33	31 22:47 ♃ ⚹	♓ 1 19:47	1 14:40 ● 10♑19	1 January 1976
☿R 14 6:41	☿ ♒ 2 20:22	4 9:38 ♂ △	♓ 5 11:35	4 3:55 ♄ △	♈ 4 7:17	9 12:40 ☽ 18♈23	Julian Day # 27759
♇R 14 11:41	♄ ♋R 14 13:16	6 19:17 ♂ □	♈ 7 23:21	6 16:26 ♄ □	♉ 6 20:13	17 4:47 ○ 26♋12	SVP 5♓35'28"
⚳D 18 21:22	☉ ♒ 20 22:25	9 12:40 ☉ □	♉ 10 12:10	9 4:15 ♄ ⚹	♊ 9 8:16	23 23:04 ☾ 3♏05	GC 26♐30.2 ⚴ 23♓22.2
♂D 20 21:27	☿ ♑R 25 1:30	12 6:13 ☉ △	♊ 12 23:19	11 1:13 ☉ △	♋ 11 16:59	31 6:20 ● 10♒30	Eris 12♈53.6 ⚵ 18♍56.0
☽0S 20 22:29	♀ ♑ 26 6:09	14 6:54 ♃ ⚹	♋ 15 7:00	13 18:23 ☿ ☍	♌ 13 21:32		⚷ 23♈35.3R ⚶ 28♓48.1
		17 10:51 ♄ ☌	♌ 17 11:15	15 16:43 ☉ ☍	♍ 15 22:59		☽ Mean ☊ 19♏14.4
♄□♆ 2 7:56	☿ ♒ 15 19:03	18 22:37 ♀ △	♍ 19 13:25	17 19:29 ♀ △	♎ 17 23:14	8 10:05 ☽ 18♉47	
☽0N 3 11:40	☉ ♓ 19 12:40	21 14:13 ♄ ⚹	♎ 21 15:10	19 19:38 ♄ □	♏ 20 0:14	15 16:43 ○ 26♌08	1 February 1976
☿D 3 22:57	♀ ♒ 19 16:50	23 16:31 ♄ □	♏ 23 17:48	21 22:16 ♄ △	♐ 22 3:18	22 8:16 ☾ 2♐50	Julian Day # 27790
♅R 10 22:11		25 20:13 ♄ △	♐ 25 21:51	23 20:32 ♃ △	♑ 24 8:54	29 23:25 ● 10♓31	SVP 5♓35'23"
☽0S 17 7:46		27 6:34 ♃ △	♑ 28 3:24	26 10:50 ♄ ☍	♒ 26 16:48		GC 26♐30.3 ⚴ 2♈22.6
		30 8:09 ♄ ☍	♒ 30 10:34	28 15:16 ♃ ⚹	♓ 29 2:42		Eris 12♈59.1 ⚵ 17♍35.1R
							⚷ 23♈57.1 ⚶ 9♈48.2
							☽ Mean ☊ 17♏35.9

March 1976 — LONGITUDE

Day	Sid.Time	☉	0 hr ☽	Noon ☽	True ☊	☿	♀	♂	⚳	♃	♄	♅	♆	♇
1 M	22 37 40	11♓02 22	10♓48 33	16♓50 48	14♏31.4	18♒00.3	13♒18.3	23♊08.3	6♊47.2	24♈32.2	26♋39.0	6♏58.2	13♐54.8	11♎07.1
2 Tu	22 41 37	12 02 34	22 51 02	28 49 27	14R 21.1	19 26.0	14 32.2	23 30.1	7 01.6	24 44.6	26R 36.3	6R 57.2	13 55.3	11R 05.7
3 W	22 45 34	13 02 45	4♈46 14	10♈41 38	14 13.2	20 53.0	15 46.2	23 52.3	7 16.2	24 57.0	26 33.6	6 56.1	13 55.7	11 04.3
4 Th	22 49 30	14 02 53	16 35 58	22 29 34	14 08.0	22 21.2	17 00.2	24 14.9	7 31.0	25 09.6	26 31.1	6 54.9	13 56.1	11 02.9
5 F	22 53 27	15 03 00	28 22 51	4♉16 16	14D 05.5	23 50.6	18 14.1	24 37.7	7 46.0	25 22.2	26 28.7	6 53.7	13 56.5	11 01.4
6 Sa	22 57 23	16 03 05	10♉10 18	16 05 30	14 04.9	25 21.2	19 28.1	25 00.8	8 01.3	25 34.9	26 26.3	6 52.4	13 56.8	11 00.0
7 Su	23 01 20	17 03 07	22 02 28	28 01 47	14 05.6	26 52.9	20 42.1	25 24.2	8 16.8	25 47.6	26 24.1	6 51.1	13 57.1	10 58.5
8 M	23 05 16	18 03 07	4♊04 07	10♊10 07	14R 06.5	28 25.8	21 56.1	25 47.9	8 32.5	26 00.5	26 22.0	6 49.8	13 57.4	10 57.0
9 Tu	23 09 13	19 03 06	16 20 26	22 35 45	14 06.7	29 59.9	23 10.1	26 11.8	8 48.5	26 13.4	26 19.9	6 48.4	13 57.6	10 55.5
10 W	23 13 09	20 03 02	28 56 39	5♋23 44	14 05.4	1♓35.1	24 24.0	26 36.1	9 04.6	26 26.3	26 18.0	6 46.9	13 57.8	10 54.0
11 Th	23 17 06	21 02 56	11♋57 28	18 38 18	14 02.1	3 11.5	25 38.0	27 00.5	9 21.0	26 39.3	26 16.2	6 45.4	13 58.0	10 52.4
12 F	23 21 03	22 02 47	25 26 28	2♌22 06	13 56.6	4 49.0	26 52.0	27 25.3	9 37.5	26 52.4	26 14.4	6 43.9	13 58.1	10 50.9
13 Sa	23 24 59	23 02 37	9♌25 08	16 35 19	13 49.6	6 27.8	28 06.0	27 50.3	9 54.3	27 05.5	26 12.8	6 42.3	13 58.2	10 49.3
14 Su	23 28 56	24 02 24	23 52 11	1♍15 02	13 41.7	8 07.7	29 20.0	28 15.5	10 11.3	27 18.7	26 11.3	6 40.7	13 58.3	10 47.7
15 M	23 32 52	25 02 09	8♍42 59	16 14 58	13 34.0	9 48.8	0♓33.9	28 40.9	10 28.4	27 32.0	26 09.9	6 39.0	13R 58.3	10 46.2
16 Tu	23 36 49	26 01 52	23 49 47	1♎26 08	13 27.4	11 31.0	1 47.9	29 06.6	10 45.7	27 45.3	26 08.6	6 37.4	13 58.3	10 44.6
17 W	23 40 45	27 01 33	9♎02 42	16 38 11	13 22.8	13 14.6	3 01.9	29 32.5	11 03.3	27 58.6	26 07.4	6 35.6	13 58.3	10 42.9
18 Th	23 44 42	28 01 12	24 11 22	1♏41 11	13D 20.3	14 59.3	4 15.9	29 58.6	11 21.0	28 12.0	26 06.4	6 33.8	13 58.2	10 41.3
19 F	23 48 38	29 00 50	9♏06 44	16 27 14	13 19.8	16 45.3	5 29.9	0♋25.0	11 38.9	28 25.5	26 05.4	6 32.0	13 58.1	10 39.7
20 Sa	23 52 35	0♈00 26	23 42 11	0♐51 12	13 20.6	18 32.5	6 43.9	0 51.5	11 56.9	28 39.0	26 04.5	6 30.2	13 57.9	10 38.1
21 Su	23 56 31	1 00 00	7♐54 05	14 50 50	13 22.0	20 21.0	7 57.9	1 18.3	12 15.2	28 52.5	26 03.8	6 28.3	13 57.8	10 36.4
22 M	0 00 28	1 59 32	21 41 29	28 26 16	13R 22.9	22 10.8	9 11.9	1 45.2	12 33.6	29 06.1	26 03.1	6 26.4	13 57.6	10 34.8
23 Tu	0 04 25	2 59 03	5♑05 26	11♑39 19	13 22.6	24 01.8	10 25.9	2 12.3	12 52.2	29 19.7	26 02.6	6 24.4	13 57.3	10 33.1
24 W	0 08 21	3 58 32	18 08 16	24 32 40	13 20.6	25 54.1	11 39.9	2 39.7	13 10.9	29 33.4	26 02.2	6 22.4	13 57.1	10 31.5
25 Th	0 12 18	4 57 59	0♒52 54	7♒09 21	13 16.8	27 47.8	12 53.9	3 07.2	13 29.8	29 47.1	26 01.9	6 20.4	13 56.8	10 29.8
26 F	0 16 14	5 57 24	13 22 22	19 32 19	13 11.4	29 42.7	14 07.9	3 34.9	13 48.9	0♉00.9	26 01.7	6 18.3	13 56.4	10 28.2
27 Sa	0 20 11	6 56 47	25 39 31	1♓44 16	13 05.1	1♈38.8	15 21.9	4 02.8	14 08.1	0 14.7	26D 01.6	6 16.2	13 56.1	10 26.5
28 Su	0 24 07	7 56 09	7♓46 51	13 47 31	12 58.4	3 36.2	16 35.9	4 30.9	14 27.5	0 28.6	26 01.6	6 14.1	13 55.7	10 24.8
29 M	0 28 04	8 55 28	19 46 30	25 44 03	12 52.1	5 34.8	17 49.9	4 59.1	14 47.1	0 42.4	26 01.7	6 12.0	13 55.3	10 23.1
30 Tu	0 32 00	9 54 46	1♈40 23	7♈35 43	12 46.7	7 34.5	19 03.8	5 27.5	15 06.8	0 56.3	26 02.0	6 09.8	13 54.8	10 21.5
31 W	0 35 57	10 54 01	13 30 17	19 24 19	12 42.8	9 35.4	20 17.8	5 56.1	15 26.6	1 10.3	26 02.3	6 07.6	13 54.3	10 19.8

April 1976 — LONGITUDE

Day	Sid.Time	☉	0 hr ☽	Noon ☽	True ☊	☿	♀	♂	⚳	♃	♄	♅	♆	♇
1 Th	0 39 54	11♈53 15	25♈18 05	1♉11 51	12♏40.6	11♈37.2	21♓31.8	6♋24.8	15♊46.6	1♉24.3	26♋02.8	6♏05.3	13♐53.8	10♎18.1
2 F	0 43 50	12 52 26	7♉05 55	13 00 37	12D 39.9	13 39.9	22 45.8	6 53.7	16 06.7	1 38.3	26 03.3	6R 03.1	13R 53.2	10R 16.4
3 Sa	0 47 47	13 51 35	18 56 18	24 53 23	12 40.5	15 43.4	23 59.7	7 22.8	16 27.0	1 52.3	26 04.0	6 00.8	13 52.6	10 14.8
4 Su	0 51 43	14 50 42	0♊52 17	6♊53 27	12 42.0	17 47.5	25 13.7	7 52.0	16 47.4	2 06.4	26 04.8	5 58.5	13 52.0	10 13.1
5 M	0 55 40	15 49 47	12 57 23	19 04 35	12 43.8	19 52.1	26 27.6	8 21.4	17 07.9	2 20.5	26 05.7	5 56.1	13 51.4	10 11.4
6 Tu	0 59 36	16 48 50	25 15 35	1♋30 54	12 45.3	21 56.8	27 41.6	8 50.9	17 28.6	2 34.6	26 06.8	5 53.8	13 50.7	10 09.8
7 W	1 03 33	17 47 50	7♋51 04	14 16 37	12R 46.0	24 01.6	28 55.5	9 20.5	17 49.4	2 48.8	26 07.9	5 51.4	13 50.0	10 08.1
8 Th	1 07 29	18 46 48	20 47 59	27 25 35	12 45.8	26 06.0	0♈09.4	9 50.3	18 10.3	3 02.9	26 09.1	5 49.0	13 49.3	10 06.5
9 F	1 11 26	19 45 43	4♌09 47	11♌00 48	12 44.5	28 09.9	1 23.4	10 20.2	18 31.4	3 17.1	26 10.5	5 46.6	13 48.5	10 04.8
10 Sa	1 15 23	20 44 36	17 58 45	25 03 35	12 42.4	0♉12.8	2 37.3	10 50.3	18 52.6	3 31.3	26 11.9	5 44.2	13 47.7	10 03.2
11 Su	1 19 19	21 43 27	2♍15 05	9♍32 51	12 39.7	2 14.5	3 51.2	11 20.4	19 13.9	3 45.5	26 13.5	5 41.7	13 46.9	10 01.5
12 M	1 23 16	22 42 16	16 56 18	24 24 41	12 37.0	4 14.6	5 05.1	11 50.7	19 35.3	3 59.8	26 15.1	5 39.3	13 46.1	9 59.9
13 Tu	1 27 12	23 41 03	1♎57 01	9♎32 14	12 34.7	6 12.8	6 19.0	12 21.2	19 56.8	4 14.0	26 16.9	5 36.8	13 45.2	9 58.3
14 W	1 31 09	24 39 47	17 09 08	24 46 28	12 33.2	8 08.7	7 32.9	12 51.7	20 18.4	4 28.3	26 18.8	5 34.3	13 44.3	9 56.7
15 Th	1 35 05	25 38 30	2♏22 58	9♏57 24	12D 32.6	10 02.0	8 46.7	13 22.3	20 40.2	4 42.6	26 20.7	5 31.8	13 43.4	9 55.1
16 F	1 39 02	26 37 10	17 28 39	24 55 41	12 32.8	11 52.3	10 00.6	13 53.1	21 02.0	4 56.9	26 22.8	5 29.3	13 42.4	9 53.5
17 Sa	1 42 58	27 35 49	2♐17 40	9♐33 55	12 33.7	13 39.4	11 14.5	14 24.0	21 24.0	5 11.2	26 25.0	5 26.8	13 41.4	9 51.9
18 Su	1 46 55	28 34 26	16 43 55	23 47 22	12 34.8	15 22.9	12 28.4	14 55.0	21 46.1	5 25.5	26 27.3	5 24.3	13 40.4	9 50.3
19 M	1 50 51	29 33 02	0♑44 06	7♑34 06	12 35.8	17 02.8	13 42.2	15 26.1	22 08.3	5 39.8	26 29.7	5 21.8	13 39.4	9 48.8
20 Tu	1 54 48	0♉31 36	14 17 31	20 54 33	12R 36.5	18 38.6	14 56.1	15 57.3	22 30.5	5 54.2	26 32.2	5 19.2	13 38.4	9 47.2
21 W	1 58 45	1 30 08	27 25 33	3♒50 55	12 36.7	20 10.3	16 10.0	16 28.6	22 52.9	6 08.5	26 34.8	5 16.7	13 37.3	9 45.7
22 Th	2 02 41	2 28 39	10♒11 04	16 26 29	12 36.3	21 37.6	17 23.8	17 00.0	23 15.4	6 22.9	26 37.5	5 14.1	13 36.2	9 44.2
23 F	2 06 38	3 27 08	22 37 39	28 45 05	12 35.5	23 00.4	18 37.7	17 31.5	23 38.0	6 37.2	26 40.3	5 11.6	13 35.1	9 42.7
24 Sa	2 10 34	4 25 35	4♓49 15	10♓50 39	12 34.5	24 18.6	19 51.5	18 03.1	24 00.7	6 51.6	26 43.1	5 09.0	13 33.9	9 41.2
25 Su	2 14 31	5 24 01	16 49 45	22 46 59	12 33.5	25 32.1	21 05.4	18 34.9	24 23.4	7 06.0	26 46.1	5 06.4	13 32.7	9 39.7
26 M	2 18 27	6 22 24	28 42 46	4♈37 30	12 32.6	26 40.7	22 19.2	19 06.7	24 46.3	7 20.3	26 49.2	5 03.9	13 31.6	9 38.2
27 Tu	2 22 24	7 20 47	10♈31 34	16 25 17	12 31.9	27 44.5	23 33.0	19 38.6	25 09.3	7 34.7	26 52.4	5 01.3	13 30.3	9 36.8
28 W	2 26 20	8 19 07	22 19 00	28 13 00	12 31.5	28 43.2	24 46.9	20 10.6	25 32.3	7 49.0	26 55.7	4 58.8	13 29.1	9 35.4
29 Th	2 30 17	9 17 26	4♉07 36	10♉03 03	12D 31.3	29 36.8	26 00.7	20 42.7	25 55.4	8 03.4	26 59.0	4 56.2	13 27.8	9 34.0
30 F	2 34 14	10 15 43	15 59 38	21 57 37	12 31.4	0♊25.2	27 14.5	21 14.9	26 18.7	8 17.8	27 02.5	4 53.7	13 26.6	9 32.6

Astro Data

	Dy Hr Mn
☽0N	1 19:18
♃□♄	9 22:34
☽0S	15 18:41
♆R	15 20:40
☉0N	20 11:50
♃⚻♆	21 21:12
♄D	27 19:58
☿0N	28 12:23
☽0N	29 1:20
♀0N	11 5:08
☽0S	12 5:27
♃☍♅	18 10:16
☽0N	25 6:57

Planet Ingress

	Dy Hr Mn
☿ ♓	9 12:02
♀ ♓	15 0:59
♂ ♋	18 13:15
☉ ♈	20 11:50
♃ ♉	26 10:25
☿ ♈	26 15:36
♀ ♈	8 8:56
☿ ♉	10 9:29
☉ ♉	19 23:03
☿ ♊	29 23:11

Last Aspect / ☽ Ingress (March)

Last Aspect Dy Hr Mn		☽ Ingress Dy Hr Mn
2 7:33 ♄ △	♈	2 14:22
4 20:11 ♄ □	♉	5 3:18
7 9:22 ☿ □	♊	7 15:56
9 19:03 ♂ ☌	♋	10 1:59
12 2:21 ♃ □	♌	12 7:55
14 8:37 ♀ ☍	♍	14 9:59
16 8:14 ♂ □	♎	16 9:44
18 9:10 ♂ △	♏	18 9:17
20 10:28 ☉ △	♐	20 10:34
22 13:13 ♃ △	♑	22 14:48
24 21:39 ♃ □	♒	24 22:19
26 1:06 ♆ ⚹	♓	27 8:34
29 12:36 ♄ △	♈	29 20:37

Last Aspect / ☽ Ingress (April)

Last Aspect Dy Hr Mn		☽ Ingress Dy Hr Mn
1 1:31 ♄ □	♉	1 9:34
3 14:22 ♄ ⚹	♊	3 22:15
6 3:53 ♀ □	♋	6 9:06
8 9:42 ♄ ☌	♌	8 16:36
10 4:10 ☉ △	♍	10 20:16
12 14:57 ♄ ⚹	♎	12 20:54
14 14:26 ♄ □	♏	14 20:14
16 14:22 ♄ △	♐	16 20:15
18 20:52 ☉ △	♑	18 22:43
20 22:23 ♄ ☍	♒	21 4:47
22 23:20 ☿ □	♓	23 14:28
25 20:06 ♄ △	♈	26 2:37
28 9:22 ♄ □	♉	28 15:37

☽ Phases & Eclipses

Dy Hr Mn	
9 4:38	☽ 18♊45
16 2:53	○ 25♍39
22 18:54	☾ 2♑17
30 17:08	● 10♈07
7 19:02	☽ 18♋05
14 11:49	○ 24♎39
21 7:14	☾ 1♒19
29 10:19	● 9♉13
29 10:23:30	● A 06'41"

Astro Data

1 March 1976
Julian Day # 27819
SVP 5♓35'20"
GC 26♐30.4 ⚴ 13♈05.3
Eris 13♈12.7 ⚵ 11♍05.5R
⚷ 25♈01.4 ⚶ 21♈33.6
☽ Mean ☊ 16♏03.8

1 April 1976
Julian Day # 27850
SVP 5♓35'17"
GC 26♐30.5 ⚴ 26♈14.2
Eris 13♈32.6 ⚵ 4♍50.2R
⚷ 26♈41.5 ⚶ 4♉54.1
☽ Mean ☊ 14♏25.3

LONGITUDE — May 1976

Day	Sid.Time	☉	0 hr ☽	Noon ☽	True ☊	☿	♀	♂	⚳	♃	♄	♅	♆	♇
1 Sa	2 38 10	11♉13 58	27♉57 15	3♊58 49	12♏31.5	1♊08.5	28♈28.3	21♋47.2	26♊42.0	8♉32.1	27♋06.1	4♏51.1	13♐25.3	9♎31.2
2 Su	2 42 07	12 12 12	10♊02 34	16 08 49	12R31.6	1 46.5	29 42.1	22 19.6	27 05.4	8 46.5	27 09.7	4R48.6	13R24.0	9R29.8
3 M	2 46 03	13 10 23	22 17 51	28 29 57	12 31.5	2 19.2	0♉55.9	22 52.0	27 28.9	9 00.8	27 13.5	4 46.1	13 22.6	9 28.5
4 Tu	2 50 00	14 08 33	4♋45 28	11♋04 41	12 31.4	2 46.5	2 09.7	23 24.6	27 52.4	9 15.1	27 17.3	4 43.6	13 21.3	9 27.2
5 W	2 53 56	15 06 41	17 27 57	23 55 34	12 31.2	3 08.5	3 23.5	23 57.2	28 16.1	9 29.5	27 21.3	4 41.1	13 19.9	9 25.9
6 Th	2 57 53	16 04 47	0♌27 52	7♌05 07	12D31.1	3 25.2	4 37.3	24 29.9	28 39.8	9 43.8	27 25.3	4 38.6	13 18.5	9 24.6
7 F	3 01 49	17 02 50	13 47 34	20 35 25	12 31.0	3 36.6	5 51.0	25 02.7	29 03.6	9 58.1	27 29.4	4 36.1	13 17.1	9 23.4
8 Sa	3 05 46	18 00 52	27 28 47	4♍27 44	12 31.2	3R42.8	7 04.8	25 35.6	29 27.4	10 12.3	27 33.6	4 33.6	13 15.7	9 22.2
9 Su	3 09 43	18 58 52	11♍32 11	18 41 59	12 31.6	3 43.9	8 18.5	26 08.6	29 51.3	10 26.6	27 37.8	4 31.2	13 14.3	9 21.0
10 M	3 13 39	19 56 50	25 56 49	3♎16 14	12 32.2	3 40.0	9 32.3	26 41.6	0♋15.3	10 40.8	27 42.2	4 28.7	13 12.8	9 19.8
11 Tu	3 17 36	20 54 46	10♎39 40	18 06 24	12 32.9	3 31.3	10 46.0	27 14.7	0 39.4	10 55.1	27 46.6	4 26.3	13 11.4	9 18.6
12 W	3 21 32	21 52 41	25 35 35	3♏06 16	12R33.3	3 18.1	11 59.7	27 47.8	1 03.6	11 09.3	27 51.1	4 23.9	13 09.9	9 17.5
13 Th	3 25 29	22 50 34	10♏37 25	18 07 59	12 33.4	3 00.7	13 13.5	28 21.0	1 27.8	11 23.5	27 55.7	4 21.5	13 08.4	9 16.4
14 F	3 29 25	23 48 25	25 36 53	3♐03 04	12 32.9	2 39.4	14 27.2	28 54.3	1 52.0	11 37.7	28 00.4	4 19.1	13 06.9	9 15.3
15 Sa	3 33 22	24 46 15	10♐25 34	17 43 33	12 31.8	2 14.6	15 40.9	29 27.7	2 16.4	11 51.8	28 05.2	4 16.8	13 05.4	9 14.3
16 Su	3 37 18	25 44 04	24 56 14	2♑03 04	12 30.3	1 46.8	16 54.6	0♌01.2	2 40.8	12 06.0	28 10.0	4 14.5	13 03.9	9 13.2
17 M	3 41 15	26 41 51	9♑03 36	15 57 35	12 28.6	1 16.4	18 08.3	0 34.7	3 05.3	12 20.1	28 15.0	4 12.2	13 02.4	9 12.2
18 Tu	3 45 12	27 39 37	22 44 54	29 25 35	12 26.9	0 44.2	19 22.1	1 08.2	3 29.8	12 34.2	28 20.0	4 09.9	13 00.8	9 11.2
19 W	3 49 08	28 37 22	5♒59 49	12♒27 50	12 25.6	0 10.5	20 35.8	1 41.9	3 54.4	12 48.2	28 25.0	4 07.6	12 59.3	9 10.3
20 Th	3 53 05	29 35 06	18 50 03	25 06 53	12D25.0	29♉36.0	21 49.5	2 15.6	4 19.0	13 02.2	28 30.2	4 05.4	12 57.7	9 09.4
21 F	3 57 01	0♊32 49	1♓18 52	7♓26 31	12 25.0	29 01.4	23 03.2	2 49.3	4 43.7	13 16.3	28 35.4	4 03.2	12 56.1	9 08.5
22 Sa	4 00 58	1 30 31	13 30 25	19 31 10	12 25.9	28 27.2	24 16.9	3 23.2	5 08.5	13 30.2	28 40.7	4 01.0	12 54.5	9 07.6
23 Su	4 04 54	2 28 11	25 29 20	1♈25 31	12 27.2	27 54.0	25 30.6	3 57.0	5 33.3	13 44.2	28 46.0	3 58.9	12 53.0	9 06.8
24 M	4 08 51	3 25 51	7♈20 17	13 14 10	12 28.8	27 22.4	26 44.3	4 31.0	5 58.2	13 58.1	28 51.5	3 56.7	12 51.4	9 05.9
25 Tu	4 12 47	4 23 30	19 07 42	25 01 23	12 30.3	26 52.8	27 58.0	5 05.0	6 23.2	14 12.0	28 57.0	3 54.6	12 49.8	9 05.2
26 W	4 16 44	5 21 07	0♉55 40	6♉50 59	12R31.2	26 25.8	29 11.7	5 39.1	6 48.2	14 25.8	29 02.5	3 52.6	12 48.2	9 04.4
27 Th	4 20 41	6 18 44	12 47 42	18 46 10	12 31.1	26 01.8	0♊25.4	6 13.3	7 13.2	14 39.7	29 08.2	3 50.5	12 46.6	9 03.7
28 F	4 24 37	7 16 19	24 46 41	0♊49 33	12 29.9	25 41.2	1 39.1	6 47.5	7 38.3	14 53.4	29 13.9	3 48.5	12 44.9	9 03.0
29 Sa	4 28 34	8 13 54	6♊54 58	13 03 08	12 27.5	25 24.2	2 52.8	7 21.8	8 03.5	15 07.2	29 19.6	3 46.6	12 43.3	9 02.3
30 Su	4 32 30	9 11 27	19 14 14	25 28 23	12 24.0	25 11.2	4 06.5	7 56.1	8 28.7	15 20.9	29 25.5	3 44.6	12 41.7	9 01.7
31 M	4 36 27	10 08 59	1♋45 43	8♋06 19	12 19.7	25 02.3	5 20.2	8 30.5	8 54.0	15 34.6	29 31.4	3 42.7	12 40.1	9 01.1

LONGITUDE — June 1976

Day	Sid.Time	☉	0 hr ☽	Noon ☽	True ☊	☿	♀	♂	⚳	♃	♄	♅	♆	♇
1 Tu	4 40 23	11♊06 30	14♋30 16	20♋57 38	12♏15.2	24♉57.7	6♊33.9	9♌04.9	9♋19.3	15♉48.2	29♋37.3	3♏40.9	12♐38.5	9♎00.5
2 W	4 44 20	12 04 00	27 28 28	4♌02 50	12R11.0	24D57.4	7 47.6	9 39.5	9 44.6	16 01.8	29 43.4	3R39.1	12R36.8	8R59.9
3 Th	4 48 16	13 01 28	10♌40 47	17 22 22	12 07.6	25 01.6	9 01.3	10 14.0	10 10.0	16 15.3	29 49.4	3 37.3	12 35.2	8 59.4
4 F	4 52 13	13 58 56	24 07 36	0♍56 33	12 05.6	25 10.3	10 15.0	10 48.6	10 35.5	16 28.8	29 55.6	3 35.5	12 33.6	8 59.0
5 Sa	4 56 10	14 56 22	7♍49 13	14 45 36	12D04.9	25 23.5	11 28.7	11 23.3	11 01.0	16 42.2	0♌01.8	3 33.8	12 32.0	8 58.5
6 Su	5 00 06	15 53 46	21 45 38	28 49 15	12 05.4	25 41.2	12 42.4	11 58.0	11 26.5	16 55.6	0 08.0	3 32.1	12 30.4	8 58.1
7 M	5 04 03	16 51 10	5♎56 17	13♎06 33	12 06.7	26 03.2	13 56.1	12 32.8	11 52.1	17 09.0	0 14.3	3 30.5	12 28.7	8 57.7
8 Tu	5 07 59	17 48 32	20 19 44	27 35 27	12R08.0	26 29.7	15 09.8	13 07.6	12 17.7	17 22.2	0 20.7	3 28.9	12 27.1	8 57.3
9 W	5 11 56	18 45 54	4♏53 13	12♏12 29	12 08.6	27 00.4	16 23.4	13 42.5	12 43.3	17 35.5	0 27.1	3 27.3	12 25.5	8 57.0
10 Th	5 15 52	19 43 14	19 32 35	26 52 46	12 07.8	27 35.4	17 37.1	14 17.4	13 09.0	17 48.7	0 33.6	3 25.8	12 23.9	8 56.7
11 F	5 19 49	20 40 34	4♐12 15	11♐30 13	12 05.3	28 14.5	18 50.8	14 52.4	13 34.8	18 01.8	0 40.1	3 24.4	12 22.3	8 56.5
12 Sa	5 23 45	21 37 53	18 45 50	25 58 17	12 01.0	28 57.7	20 04.5	15 27.4	14 00.5	18 14.9	0 46.7	3 22.9	12 20.7	8 56.2
13 Su	5 27 42	22 35 11	3♑06 49	10♑10 45	11 55.3	29 44.8	21 18.2	16 02.5	14 26.4	18 27.9	0 53.3	3 21.5	12 19.1	8 56.1
14 M	5 31 39	23 32 29	17 09 33	24 02 45	11 48.8	0♊35.9	22 31.9	16 37.6	14 52.2	18 40.9	0 59.9	3 20.2	12 17.5	8 55.9
15 Tu	5 35 35	24 29 46	0♒50 03	7♒31 18	11 42.3	1 30.8	23 45.6	17 12.8	15 18.1	18 53.8	1 06.6	3 18.9	12 15.9	8 55.8
16 W	5 39 32	25 27 02	14 06 28	20 35 39	11 36.6	2 29.5	24 59.2	17 48.0	15 44.0	19 06.7	1 13.4	3 17.7	12 14.4	8 55.7
17 Th	5 43 28	26 24 19	26 59 04	3♓17 04	11 32.3	3 31.8	26 12.9	18 23.3	16 10.0	19 19.5	1 20.2	3 16.4	12 12.8	8 55.6
18 F	5 47 25	27 21 35	9♓30 04	15 38 33	11 29.8	4 37.8	27 26.7	18 58.6	16 36.0	19 32.2	1 27.0	3 15.3	12 11.2	8D55.6
19 Sa	5 51 21	28 18 50	21 43 04	27 44 13	11D29.0	5 47.3	28 40.4	19 34.0	17 02.0	19 44.9	1 33.9	3 14.2	12 09.7	8 55.6
20 Su	5 55 18	29 16 06	3♈42 38	9♈38 58	11 29.5	7 00.4	29 54.1	20 09.4	17 28.0	19 57.5	1 40.8	3 13.1	12 08.1	8 55.6
21 M	5 59 14	0♋13 21	15 33 51	21 27 57	11 30.7	8 17.0	1♋07.8	20 44.9	17 54.1	20 10.0	1 47.8	3 12.1	12 06.6	8 55.7
22 Tu	6 03 11	1 10 36	27 21 54	3♉16 19	11R31.8	9 37.0	2 21.5	21 20.4	18 20.3	20 22.5	1 54.8	3 11.1	12 05.1	8 55.8
23 W	6 07 08	2 07 51	9♉11 47	15 08 52	11 32.1	11 00.4	3 35.2	21 56.0	18 46.4	20 34.9	2 01.9	3 10.2	12 03.6	8 55.9
24 Th	6 11 04	3 05 06	21 08 03	27 09 50	11 30.7	12 27.2	4 49.0	22 31.6	19 12.6	20 47.2	2 09.0	3 09.3	12 02.1	8 56.1
25 F	6 15 01	4 02 21	3♊14 35	9♊22 39	11 27.2	13 57.3	6 02.7	23 07.2	19 38.8	20 59.5	2 16.1	3 08.5	12 00.6	8 56.3
26 Sa	6 18 57	4 59 35	15 34 18	21 49 45	11 21.5	15 30.6	7 16.5	23 43.0	20 05.1	21 11.7	2 23.2	3 07.7	11 59.1	8 56.6
27 Su	6 22 54	5 56 50	28 09 08	4♋32 31	11 13.9	17 07.3	8 30.2	24 18.7	20 31.4	21 23.8	2 30.4	3 06.9	11 57.7	8 56.8
28 M	6 26 50	6 54 04	10♋59 52	17 31 07	11 04.8	18 47.1	9 44.0	24 54.5	20 57.7	21 35.8	2 37.7	3 06.3	11 56.2	8 57.1
29 Tu	6 30 47	7 51 18	24 06 09	0♌44 46	10 55.2	20 30.1	10 57.7	25 30.4	21 24.0	21 47.8	2 44.9	3 05.6	11 54.8	8 57.5
30 W	6 34 44	8 48 31	7♌26 46	14 11 53	10 46.1	22 16.1	12 11.5	26 06.3	21 50.4	21 59.7	2 52.2	3 05.1	11 53.4	8 57.8

Astro Data (Dy Hr Mn)

	Dy	Hr Mn
♃⊼♇	5	6:33
☿ R	9	5:03
☽ 0S	9	14:36
♄□♆	15	12:48
♃⊼♆	20	5:00
☽ 0N	22	13:37
☿ D	2	1:19
☽ 0S	5	21:51
♇ D	18	21:43
☽ 0N	18	21:59

Planet Ingress (Dy Hr Mn)

		Dy	Hr Mn
♀	♉	2	17:49
⚳	♋	9	20:40
♂	♌	16	11:10
☿	♉R	19	19:21
☉	♊	20	22:21
♀	♊	27	3:43
♄	♌	5	5:09
☿	♊	13	19:20
♀	♋	20	13:56
☉	♋	21	6:24

Last Aspect / ☽ Ingress (May)

Last Aspect Dy Hr Mn		☽ Ingress	Dy Hr Mn
30 22:14	♄ ⚹	♊	1 4:05
2 6:37	♆ ☍	♋	3 14:53
5 18:21	♄ ☌	♌	5 23:09
7 5:17	☉ □	♍	8 4:21
10 2:51	♄ ⚹	♎	10 6:39
12 3:34	♄ □	♏	12 7:03
14 5:02	♂ △	♐	14 7:04
15 4:23	♆ ☌	♑	16 8:31
18 10:01	♄ ☍	♒	18 13:02
20 21:22	☉ □	♓	20 21:27
23 6:35	♄ △	♈	23 9:07
25 20:03	♄ □	♉	25 22:07
28 8:49	♄ ⚹	♊	28 10:22
29 11:21	♆ ☍	♋	30 20:39

Last Aspect / ☽ Ingress (June)

Last Aspect Dy Hr Mn		☽ Ingress	Dy Hr Mn
2 4:03	♄ ☌	♌	2 4:37
4 1:43	☿ □	♍	4 10:21
6 6:34	☿ △	♎	6 14:00
7 18:40	☉ △	♏	8 15:58
10 13:13	☿ ☍	♐	10 17:07
12 4:15	☉ ☍	♑	12 18:45
14 2:29	♃ △	♒	14 22:31
16 21:51	☉ △	♓	17 5:43
19 14:05	♀ □	♈	19 16:32
21 10:28	♂ △	♉	22 5:21
24 2:18	♂ □	♊	24 17:37
26 15:46	♂ ⚹	♋	27 3:29
28 19:34	♃ ⚹	♌	29 10:39

☽ Phases & Eclipses (Dy Hr Mn)

Dy Hr Mn	
7 5:17	☽ 16♌47
13 20:04	○ 23♏10
13 19:54	☍ P 0.122
20 21:22	☾ 29♒58
29 1:47	● 7♊49
5 12:20	☽ 14♍57
12 4:15	○ 21♐19
19 13:15	☾ 28♓22
27 14:50	● 6♋04

Astro Data

1 May 1976
Julian Day # 27880
SVP 5♓35'14"
GC 26♐30.5 ⚴ 10♉14.0
Eris 13♈52.2 ⚵ 4♍11.6
⚷ 28♈29.7 ⚶ 18♉06.3
☽ Mean ☊ 12♏49.9

1 June 1976
Julian Day # 27911
SVP 5♓35'10"
GC 26♐30.6 ⚴ 25♉46.9
Eris 14♈08.1 ⚵ 8♍40.8
⚷ 0♉12.1 ⚶ 1♊42.8
☽ Mean ☊ 11♏11.4

July 1976 — LONGITUDE

Day	Sid.Time	☉	0 hr ☽	Noon ☽	True ☊	☿	♀	♂	⚳	♃	♄	♅	♆	♇
1 Th	6 38 40	9♋45 45	20♌59 54	27♌50 32	10♏38.5	24♊05.1	13♋25.3	26♌42.3	22♋16.8	22♉11.5	2♌59.5	3♏04.5	11♐52.0	8♎58.3
2 F	6 42 37	10 42 58	4♍43 33	11♍38 44	10R 33.0	25 56.9	14 39.0	27 18.3	22 43.2	22 23.2	3 06.9	3R 04.0	11R 50.6	8 58.7
3 Sa	6 46 33	11 40 10	18 35 53	25 34 48	10 29.8	27 51.5	15 52.8	27 54.3	23 09.6	22 34.8	3 14.3	3 03.6	11 49.3	8 59.2
4 Su	6 50 30	12 37 22	2♎35 22	9♎37 25	10D 28.7	29 48.7	17 06.5	28 30.4	23 36.1	22 46.3	3 21.7	3 03.2	11 47.9	8 59.7
5 M	6 54 26	13 34 34	16 40 51	23 45 31	10 28.9	1♋48.2	18 20.3	29 06.5	24 02.6	22 57.8	3 29.1	3 02.9	11 46.6	9 00.2
6 Tu	6 58 23	14 31 46	0♏51 18	7♏57 59	10R 29.4	3 49.9	19 34.1	29 42.7	24 29.1	23 09.2	3 36.6	3 02.6	11 45.3	9 00.8
7 W	7 02 19	15 28 57	15 05 24	22 13 15	10 28.9	5 53.5	20 47.9	0♍18.9	24 55.6	23 20.4	3 44.0	3 02.4	11 44.0	9 01.4
8 Th	7 06 16	16 26 09	29 21 12	6♐28 53	10 26.5	7 58.8	22 01.6	0 55.2	25 22.1	23 31.6	3 51.5	3 02.2	11 42.7	9 02.0
9 F	7 10 13	17 23 20	13♐35 50	20 41 33	10 21.7	10 05.5	23 15.4	1 31.5	25 48.7	23 42.7	3 59.1	3 02.1	11 41.5	9 02.7
10 Sa	7 14 09	18 20 32	27 45 29	4♑47 04	10 14.2	12 13.2	24 29.2	2 07.9	26 15.3	23 53.7	4 06.6	3D 02.1	11 40.3	9 03.4
11 Su	7 18 06	19 17 43	11♑45 44	18 40 56	10 04.5	14 21.8	25 43.0	2 44.3	26 41.9	24 04.7	4 14.2	3 02.0	11 39.1	9 04.1
12 M	7 22 02	20 14 55	25 32 10	2♒19 01	9 53.6	16 30.9	26 56.8	3 20.7	27 08.5	24 15.5	4 21.7	3 02.1	11 37.9	9 04.9
13 Tu	7 25 59	21 12 07	9♒01 06	15 38 12	9 42.5	18 40.1	28 10.5	3 57.2	27 35.1	24 26.2	4 29.3	3 02.2	11 36.7	9 05.7
14 W	7 29 55	22 09 19	22 10 09	28 36 57	9 32.3	20 49.3	29 24.3	4 33.7	28 01.8	24 36.8	4 37.0	3 02.3	11 35.6	9 06.5
15 Th	7 33 52	23 06 32	4♓58 40	11♓15 30	9 23.9	22 58.1	0♌38.1	5 10.3	28 28.4	24 47.3	4 44.6	3 02.5	11 34.4	9 07.4
16 F	7 37 48	24 03 45	17 27 44	23 35 46	9 17.9	25 06.3	1 51.9	5 46.9	28 55.1	24 57.7	4 52.2	3 02.8	11 33.3	9 08.3
17 Sa	7 41 45	25 00 59	29 40 01	5♈41 03	9 14.3	27 13.8	3 05.8	6 23.5	29 21.8	25 08.0	4 59.9	3 03.0	11 32.3	9 09.2
18 Su	7 45 42	25 58 14	11♈39 26	17 35 46	9D 12.8	29 20.3	4 19.6	7 00.2	29 48.6	25 18.2	5 07.6	3 03.4	11 31.2	9 10.1
19 M	7 49 38	26 55 29	23 30 44	29 25 00	9R 12.6	1♌25.6	5 33.4	7 37.0	0♌15.3	25 28.3	5 15.2	3 03.8	11 30.2	9 11.1
20 Tu	7 53 35	27 52 45	5♉19 14	11♉14 09	9 12.6	3 29.6	6 47.2	8 13.8	0 42.0	25 38.3	5 22.9	3 04.3	11 29.2	9 12.1
21 W	7 57 31	28 50 02	17 10 23	23 08 38	9 12.0	5 32.3	8 01.0	8 50.6	1 08.8	25 48.2	5 30.6	3 04.8	11 28.2	9 13.2
22 Th	8 01 28	29 47 20	29 09 29	5♊13 31	9 09.6	7 33.5	9 14.9	9 27.5	1 35.6	25 58.0	5 38.3	3 05.3	11 27.2	9 14.2
23 F	8 05 24	0♌44 38	11♊21 17	17 33 13	9 04.9	9 33.2	10 28.7	10 04.4	2 02.4	26 07.6	5 46.1	3 05.9	11 26.3	9 15.4
24 Sa	8 09 21	1 41 57	23 49 43	0♋11 03	8 57.6	11 31.2	11 42.6	10 41.4	2 29.2	26 17.1	5 53.8	3 06.6	11 25.4	9 16.5
25 Su	8 13 17	2 39 18	6♋37 25	13 08 54	8 47.9	13 27.7	12 56.4	11 18.4	2 56.0	26 26.6	6 01.5	3 07.3	11 24.5	9 17.7
26 M	8 17 14	3 36 39	19 45 29	26 27 00	8 36.4	15 22.5	14 10.3	11 55.5	3 22.9	26 35.9	6 09.3	3 08.1	11 23.7	9 18.9
27 Tu	8 21 11	4 34 00	3♌13 12	10♌03 45	8 24.2	17 15.6	15 24.2	12 32.6	3 49.7	26 45.0	6 17.0	3 08.9	11 22.9	9 20.1
28 W	8 25 07	5 31 22	16 58 12	23 56 01	8 12.6	19 07.0	16 38.0	13 09.8	4 16.6	26 54.1	6 24.8	3 09.8	11 22.1	9 21.3
29 Th	8 29 04	6 28 45	0♍56 42	7♍59 38	8 02.6	20 56.7	17 51.9	13 47.0	4 43.4	27 03.0	6 32.5	3 10.7	11 21.3	9 22.6
30 F	8 33 00	7 26 09	15 04 16	22 10 03	7 55.2	22 44.8	19 05.8	14 24.2	5 10.3	27 11.8	6 40.2	3 11.7	11 20.6	9 23.9
31 Sa	8 36 57	8 23 33	29 16 30	6♎23 10	7 50.6	24 31.2	20 19.6	15 01.5	5 37.2	27 20.4	6 48.0	3 12.7	11 19.9	9 25.3

August 1976 — LONGITUDE

Day	Sid.Time	☉	0 hr ☽	Noon ☽	True ☊	☿	♀	♂	⚳	♃	♄	♅	♆	♇
1 Su	8 40 53	9♌20 57	13♎29 42	20♎35 47	7♏48.5	26♌15.9	21♌33.5	15♍38.9	6♌04.0	27♉29.0	6♌55.7	3♏13.8	11♐19.2	9♎26.6
2 M	8 44 50	10 18 23	27 41 11	4♏45 43	7R 48.0	27 59.0	22 47.3	16 16.2	6 30.9	27 37.4	7 03.4	3 14.9	11R 18.5	9 28.0
3 Tu	8 48 46	11 15 48	11♏49 16	18 51 43	7 48.0	29 40.4	24 01.2	16 53.7	6 57.8	27 45.6	7 11.2	3 16.1	11 17.9	9 29.4
4 W	8 52 43	12 13 15	25 52 59	2♐52 58	7 47.0	1♍20.2	25 15.1	17 31.1	7 24.7	27 53.8	7 18.9	3 17.3	11 17.3	9 30.9
5 Th	8 56 40	13 10 42	9♐51 34	16 48 40	7 44.1	2 58.3	26 28.9	18 08.6	7 51.6	28 01.8	7 26.6	3 18.6	11 16.7	9 32.4
6 F	9 00 36	14 08 10	23 44 05	0♑37 37	7 38.5	4 34.8	27 42.8	18 46.2	8 18.5	28 09.6	7 34.3	3 20.0	11 16.2	9 33.9
7 Sa	9 04 33	15 05 39	7♑29 03	14 18 06	7 30.2	6 09.7	28 56.6	19 23.8	8 45.4	28 17.4	7 42.0	3 21.3	11 15.7	9 35.4
8 Su	9 08 29	16 03 09	21 04 30	27 47 56	7 19.5	7 43.0	0♍10.5	20 01.4	9 12.3	28 24.9	7 49.7	3 22.8	11 15.2	9 36.9
9 M	9 12 26	17 00 40	4♒28 07	11♒04 48	7 07.5	9 14.6	1 24.3	20 39.1	9 39.2	28 32.4	7 57.4	3 24.2	11 14.8	9 38.5
10 Tu	9 16 22	17 58 11	17 37 44	24 06 44	6 55.1	10 44.6	2 38.2	21 16.8	10 06.1	28 39.6	8 05.1	3 25.8	11 14.4	9 40.1
11 W	9 20 19	18 55 44	0♓31 41	6♓52 33	6 43.7	12 12.9	3 52.0	21 54.6	10 33.0	28 46.8	8 12.7	3 27.3	11 14.0	9 41.7
12 Th	9 24 15	19 53 18	13 09 20	19 22 09	6 34.1	13 39.6	5 05.9	22 32.4	10 59.9	28 53.8	8 20.4	3 29.0	11 13.6	9 43.4
13 F	9 28 12	20 50 53	25 31 11	1♈36 43	6 27.0	15 04.6	6 19.7	23 10.2	11 26.8	29 00.6	8 28.0	3 30.6	11 13.3	9 45.1
14 Sa	9 32 08	21 48 30	7♈39 05	13 38 41	6 22.5	16 27.9	7 33.5	23 48.1	11 53.7	29 07.3	8 35.6	3 32.3	11 13.0	9 46.8
15 Su	9 36 05	22 46 08	19 36 01	25 31 35	6D 20.3	17 49.4	8 47.4	24 26.1	12 20.7	29 13.8	8 43.2	3 34.1	11 12.7	9 48.5
16 M	9 40 02	23 43 48	1♉26 00	7♉19 51	6 19.9	19 09.2	10 01.2	25 04.1	12 47.6	29 20.2	8 50.8	3 35.9	11 12.5	9 50.2
17 Tu	9 43 58	24 41 30	13 13 47	19 08 30	6R 20.1	20 27.2	11 15.1	25 42.1	13 14.5	29 26.4	8 58.4	3 37.8	11 12.3	9 52.0
18 W	9 47 55	25 39 12	25 04 39	1♊02 56	6 20.1	21 43.3	12 28.9	26 20.2	13 41.4	29 32.5	9 05.9	3 39.7	11 12.2	9 53.8
19 Th	9 51 51	26 36 57	7♊04 01	13 08 35	6 18.8	22 57.5	13 42.7	26 58.3	14 08.3	29 38.4	9 13.4	3 41.6	11 12.0	9 55.6
20 F	9 55 48	27 34 43	19 17 13	25 30 31	6 15.5	24 09.8	14 56.6	27 36.5	14 35.2	29 44.1	9 20.9	3 43.6	11 11.9	9 57.4
21 Sa	9 59 44	28 32 31	1♋48 58	8♋13 01	6 09.9	25 19.9	16 10.4	28 14.8	15 02.1	29 49.7	9 28.4	3 45.7	11 11.9	9 59.3
22 Su	10 03 41	29 30 21	14 42 57	21 18 59	6 01.9	26 27.9	17 24.2	28 53.0	15 29.0	29 55.1	9 35.9	3 47.7	11D 11.8	10 01.2
23 M	10 07 37	0♍28 12	28 01 12	4♌49 32	5 52.4	27 33.7	18 38.1	29 31.4	15 55.8	0♊00.3	9 43.3	3 49.9	11 11.8	10 03.1
24 Tu	10 11 34	1 26 04	11♌43 43	18 43 26	5 42.0	28 37.2	19 51.9	0♎09.7	16 22.7	0 05.4	9 50.7	3 52.0	11 11.8	10 05.0
25 W	10 15 31	2 23 59	25 48 07	2♍57 09	5 32.1	29 38.1	21 05.7	0 48.2	16 49.6	0 10.3	9 58.1	3 54.3	11 11.9	10 06.9
26 Th	10 19 27	3 21 54	10♍09 47	17 25 11	5 23.6	0♎36.5	22 19.6	1 26.6	17 16.4	0 15.0	10 05.4	3 56.5	11 12.0	10 08.9
27 F	10 23 24	4 19 51	24 42 31	2♎00 54	5 17.4	1 32.2	23 33.4	2 05.1	17 43.3	0 19.5	10 12.8	3 58.8	11 12.1	10 10.8
28 Sa	10 27 20	5 17 50	9♎19 31	16 37 35	5 13.7	2 24.9	24 47.2	2 43.7	18 10.1	0 23.9	10 20.0	4 01.1	11 12.3	10 12.8
29 Su	10 31 17	6 15 50	23 54 25	1♏09 27	5D 12.3	3 14.6	26 01.0	3 22.3	18 36.9	0 28.1	10 27.3	4 03.5	11 12.5	10 14.8
30 M	10 35 13	7 13 51	8♏22 12	15 32 17	5 12.6	4 01.0	27 14.8	4 01.0	19 03.7	0 32.1	10 34.5	4 06.0	11 12.7	10 16.8
31 Tu	10 39 10	8 11 54	22 39 27	29 43 30	5R 13.3	4 43.9	28 28.6	4 39.7	19 30.5	0 35.9	10 41.7	4 08.4	11 13.0	10 18.9

Astro Data

	Dy Hr Mn
♄□♅	2 3:14
☽0S	3 4:09
♅ D	11 6:05
♃⚻♇	11 10:44
☽0N	16 7:27
☽0S	30 10:58
☽0N	12 16:40
☿0S	22 10:27
♆ D	23 2:04
♂0S	26 12:23
☽0S	26 19:22
♄✶♇	27 3:20

Planet Ingress

		Dy Hr Mn
☿	♋	4 14:18
♂	♍	6 23:27
♀	♌	14 23:36
☿	♌	18 19:35
⚳	♌	18 22:16
☉	♌	22 17:18
☿	♍	3 16:41
♀	♍	8 8:36
☉	♍	23 0:18
♃	♊	23 10:24
♂	♎	24 5:55
☿	♎	25 20:52

Last Aspect / ☽ Ingress (July)

Last Aspect Dy Hr Mn			☽ Ingress	Dy Hr Mn
1 9:55	♂	☌	♍	1 15:46
3 16:32	☿	□	♎	3 19:34
5 21:27	♂	✶	♏	5 22:33
7 13:55	♃	☍	♐	8 1:05
8 20:48	♆	☌	♑	10 3:49
12 1:32	♀	☍	♒	12 7:53
14 4:26	♃	□	♓	14 14:36
16 15:36	☿	△	♈	17 0:40
19 6:29	☉	□	♉	19 13:11
22 0:20	☉	✶	♊	22 1:40
23 0:11	♆	☍	♋	24 11:39
26 12:16	♃	✶	♌	26 18:19
28 17:09	♃	□	♍	28 22:23
30 20:35	♃	△	♎	31 1:13

Last Aspect / ☽ Ingress (August)

Last Aspect Dy Hr Mn			☽ Ingress	Dy Hr Mn
1 22:55	☿	✶	♏	2 3:55
4 3:22	♃	☍	♐	4 7:03
6 6:25	♀	△	♑	6 10:54
8 13:07	♃	△	♒	8 15:57
10 20:34	♃	□	♓	10 23:00
13 6:49	♃	✶	♈	13 8:49
15 5:55	☉	△	♉	15 21:05
18 8:57	♃	☌	♊	18 9:54
20 16:17	☉	✶	♋	20 20:34
23 3:28	♃	✶	♌	23 3:31
23 23:05	♆	△	♍	25 7:04
26 20:50	♀	☌	♎	27 8:42
28 3:05	♆	✶	♏	29 10:05
31 9:40	♀	✶	♐	31 12:28

☽ Phases & Eclipses

Dy Hr Mn		
4 17:28	☽	12♎50
11 13:09	○	19♑20
19 6:29	☾	26♈42
27 1:39	●	4♌09
2 22:06	☽	10♏43
9 23:43	○	17♒29
18 0:13	☾	25♉11
25 11:01	●	2♍22

Astro Data

1 July 1976
Julian Day # 27941
SVP 5♓35'05"
GC 26♐30.7 ⚴ 11♊42.8
Eris 14♈15.6 ⚵ 16♍09.4
⚷ 1♉23.8 ⚶ 14♊35.5
☽ Mean ☊ 9♏36.1

1 August 1976
Julian Day # 27972
SVP 5♓35'00"
GC 26♐30.7 ⚴ 28♊51.4
Eris 14♈13.5R ⚵ 25♍42.8
⚷ 1♉54.7 ⚶ 27♊17.7
☽ Mean ☊ 7♏57.6

LONGITUDE — September 1976

Day	Sid.Time	☉	0 hr ☽	Noon ☽	True ☊	☿	♀	♂	⚳	♃	♄	♅	♆	♇
1 W	10 43 06	9♍09 58	6♐44 20	13♐41 55	5♏13.4	5♎23.1	29♍42.4	5♎18.4	19♌57.3	0♊39.5	10♌48.8	4♏10.9	11♐13.3	10♎21.0
2 Th	10 47 03	10 08 03	20 36 13	27 27 17	5R 12.0	5 58.3	0♎56.1	5 57.2	20 24.1	0 43.0	10 56.0	4 13.5	11 13.6	10 23.0
3 F	10 51 00	11 06 10	4♑15 07	10♑59 46	5 08.5	6 29.3	2 09.9	6 36.0	20 50.8	0 46.3	11 03.0	4 16.1	11 13.9	10 25.1
4 Sa	10 54 56	12 04 18	17 41 15	24 19 35	5 02.8	6 55.8	3 23.6	7 14.9	21 17.6	0 49.4	11 10.1	4 18.7	11 14.3	10 27.2
5 Su	10 58 53	13 02 28	0♒54 48	7♒26 51	4 55.1	7 17.5	4 37.4	7 53.8	21 44.3	0 52.2	11 17.1	4 21.3	11 14.8	10 29.4
6 M	11 02 49	14 00 39	13 55 44	20 21 27	4 46.3	7 34.2	5 51.1	8 32.8	22 11.0	0 55.0	11 24.0	4 24.0	11 15.2	10 31.5
7 Tu	11 06 46	14 58 52	26 43 57	3♓03 16	4 37.3	7 45.4	7 04.8	9 11.8	22 37.6	0 57.5	11 30.9	4 26.8	11 15.7	10 33.6
8 W	11 10 42	15 57 06	9♓19 23	15 32 21	4 28.9	7R 50.9	8 18.5	9 50.9	23 04.3	0 59.8	11 37.8	4 29.5	11 16.2	10 35.8
9 Th	11 14 39	16 55 22	21 42 16	27 49 13	4 22.0	7 50.4	9 32.2	10 30.0	23 30.9	1 01.9	11 44.6	4 32.3	11 16.8	10 38.0
10 F	11 18 35	17 53 40	3♈53 23	9♈54 58	4 17.0	7 43.6	10 45.9	11 09.2	23 57.6	1 03.9	11 51.4	4 35.1	11 17.3	10 40.2
11 Sa	11 22 32	18 52 00	15 54 13	21 51 27	4 14.1	7 30.3	11 59.6	11 48.4	24 24.2	1 05.6	11 58.1	4 38.0	11 18.0	10 42.4
12 Su	11 26 29	19 50 22	27 47 03	3♉41 23	4D 13.2	7 10.4	13 13.2	12 27.6	24 50.7	1 07.2	12 04.8	4 40.9	11 18.6	10 44.6
13 M	11 30 25	20 48 46	9♉34 56	15 28 12	4 13.8	6 43.7	14 26.9	13 06.9	25 17.3	1 08.5	12 11.5	4 43.9	11 19.3	10 46.8
14 Tu	11 34 22	21 47 13	21 21 44	27 16 05	4 15.2	6 10.3	15 40.5	13 46.3	25 43.8	1 09.7	12 18.1	4 46.8	11 20.0	10 49.0
15 W	11 38 18	22 45 41	3♊11 52	9♊09 42	4 16.7	5 30.4	16 54.2	14 25.7	26 10.3	1 10.6	12 24.6	4 49.8	11 20.7	10 51.3
16 Th	11 42 15	23 44 12	15 10 15	21 14 08	4R 17.6	4 44.3	18 07.8	15 05.1	26 36.8	1 11.4	12 31.1	4 52.9	11 21.5	10 53.5
17 F	11 46 11	24 42 44	27 22 00	3♋34 27	4 17.2	3 52.5	19 21.4	15 44.6	27 03.3	1 12.0	12 37.5	4 55.9	11 22.3	10 55.8
18 Sa	11 50 08	25 41 19	9♋52 05	16 15 24	4 15.2	2 55.8	20 35.0	16 24.2	27 29.7	1 12.3	12 43.9	4 59.0	11 23.1	10 58.1
19 Su	11 54 04	26 39 56	22 44 52	29 20 50	4 11.7	1 55.2	21 48.7	17 03.8	27 56.1	1R 12.5	12 50.3	5 02.2	11 24.0	11 00.3
20 M	11 58 01	27 38 35	6♌03 33	12♌53 06	4 06.9	0 51.9	23 02.3	17 43.5	28 22.5	1 12.4	12 56.5	5 05.3	11 24.9	11 02.6
21 Tu	12 01 58	28 37 17	19 49 27	26 52 24	4 01.4	29♍47.1	24 15.8	18 23.2	28 48.9	1 12.2	13 02.8	5 08.5	11 25.8	11 04.9
22 W	12 05 54	29 36 00	4♍01 32	11♍16 19	3 56.0	28 42.5	25 29.4	19 02.9	29 15.2	1 11.7	13 08.9	5 11.7	11 26.8	11 07.2
23 Th	12 09 51	0♎34 46	18 36 00	25 59 45	3 51.5	27 39.7	26 43.0	19 42.7	29 41.5	1 11.1	13 15.0	5 14.9	11 27.8	11 09.5
24 F	12 13 47	1 33 33	3♎26 33	10♎55 22	3 48.3	26 40.2	27 56.6	20 22.6	0♍07.7	1 10.2	13 21.0	5 18.2	11 28.8	11 11.8
25 Sa	12 17 44	2 32 23	18 25 06	25 54 42	3D 46.7	25 45.6	29 10.1	21 02.5	0 33.9	1 09.2	13 27.0	5 21.5	11 29.9	11 14.2
26 Su	12 21 40	3 31 14	3♏23 07	10♏49 25	3 46.7	24 57.5	0♏23.6	21 42.5	1 00.1	1 07.9	13 32.9	5 24.8	11 30.9	11 16.5
27 M	12 25 37	4 30 07	18 12 46	25 32 28	3 47.7	24 17.1	1 37.2	22 22.5	1 26.2	1 06.4	13 38.8	5 28.2	11 32.1	11 18.8
28 Tu	12 29 33	5 29 02	2♐47 58	9♐58 50	3 49.2	23 45.4	2 50.7	23 02.5	1 52.3	1 04.8	13 44.5	5 31.5	11 33.2	11 21.1
29 W	12 33 30	6 27 59	17 04 48	24 05 41	3R 50.4	23 23.2	4 04.2	23 42.7	2 18.4	1 02.9	13 50.3	5 34.9	11 34.4	11 23.5
30 Th	12 37 26	7 26 58	1♑01 26	7♑52 06	3 50.9	23D 11.1	5 17.7	24 22.8	2 44.4	1 00.8	13 55.9	5 38.3	11 35.6	11 25.8

LONGITUDE — October 1976

Day	Sid.Time	☉	0 hr ☽	Noon ☽	True ☊	☿	♀	♂	⚳	♃	♄	♅	♆	♇
1 F	12 41 23	8♎25 58	14♑37 46	21♑18 37	3♏50.3	23♍09.4	6♏31.1	25♎03.0	3♍10.4	0♊58.6	14♌01.5	5♏41.8	11♐36.8	11♎28.2
2 Sa	12 45 20	9 25 00	27 54 51	4♒26 40	3R 48.5	23 18.1	7 44.6	25 43.3	3 36.3	0R 56.1	14 07.0	5 45.2	11 38.1	11 30.5
3 Su	12 49 16	10 24 03	10♒54 21	17 18 07	3 45.7	23 36.9	8 58.0	26 23.6	4 02.2	0 53.5	14 12.4	5 48.7	11 39.3	11 32.9
4 M	12 53 13	11 23 09	23 38 14	29 54 57	3 42.3	24 05.7	10 11.4	27 03.9	4 28.1	0 50.6	14 17.8	5 52.2	11 40.6	11 35.2
5 Tu	12 57 09	12 22 16	6♓08 29	12♓19 04	3 38.8	24 43.8	11 24.8	27 44.3	4 53.9	0 47.6	14 23.1	5 55.7	11 42.0	11 37.5
6 W	13 01 06	13 21 25	18 26 57	24 32 19	3 35.5	25 30.6	12 38.2	28 24.8	5 19.6	0 44.3	14 28.3	5 59.2	11 43.3	11 39.9
7 Th	13 05 02	14 20 36	0♈35 23	6♈36 22	3 32.9	26 25.5	13 51.5	29 05.3	5 45.3	0 40.9	14 33.4	6 02.8	11 44.7	11 42.2
8 F	13 08 59	15 19 49	12 35 30	18 33 00	3 31.3	27 27.7	15 04.9	29 45.8	6 11.0	0 37.3	14 38.5	6 06.3	11 46.1	11 44.6
9 Sa	13 12 55	16 19 05	24 29 07	0♉24 06	3D 30.6	28 36.5	16 18.2	0♏26.4	6 36.6	0 33.5	14 43.5	6 09.9	11 47.6	11 46.9
10 Su	13 16 52	17 18 22	6♉18 14	12 11 50	3 30.8	29 51.0	17 31.5	1 07.1	7 02.1	0 29.5	14 48.4	6 13.5	11 49.1	11 49.2
11 M	13 20 49	18 17 42	18 05 14	23 58 48	3 31.6	1♎10.7	18 44.8	1 47.8	7 27.6	0 25.3	14 53.2	6 17.1	11 50.6	11 51.6
12 Tu	13 24 45	19 17 03	29 52 56	5♊48 03	3 32.9	2 34.7	19 58.0	2 28.5	7 53.1	0 21.0	14 57.9	6 20.8	11 52.1	11 53.9
13 W	13 28 42	20 16 27	11♊44 36	17 43 06	3 34.2	4 02.5	21 11.3	3 09.3	8 18.5	0 16.4	15 02.6	6 24.4	11 53.6	11 56.2
14 Th	13 32 38	21 15 54	23 44 01	29 47 54	3 35.3	5 33.4	22 24.5	3 50.2	8 43.8	0 11.7	15 07.2	6 28.1	11 55.2	11 58.6
15 F	13 36 35	22 15 22	5♋55 17	12♋06 44	3R 36.0	7 06.9	23 37.8	4 31.1	9 09.1	0 06.9	15 11.7	6 31.7	11 56.8	12 00.9
16 Sa	13 40 31	23 14 53	18 22 46	24 43 55	3 36.2	8 42.5	24 51.0	5 12.1	9 34.3	0 01.8	15 16.1	6 35.4	11 58.4	12 03.2
17 Su	13 44 28	24 14 26	1♌10 41	7♌43 29	3 36.0	10 19.9	26 04.2	5 53.1	9 59.5	29♉56.6	15 20.4	6 39.1	12 00.1	12 05.5
18 M	13 48 24	25 14 02	14 22 42	21 08 37	3 35.3	11 58.6	27 17.3	6 34.2	10 24.6	29 51.2	15 24.7	6 42.8	12 01.7	12 07.8
19 Tu	13 52 21	26 13 39	28 01 23	5♍01 02	3 34.5	13 38.3	28 30.5	7 15.3	10 49.6	29 45.6	15 28.8	6 46.5	12 03.4	12 10.1
20 W	13 56 18	27 13 19	12♍07 28	19 20 21	3 33.6	15 18.8	29 43.6	7 56.5	11 14.6	29 39.9	15 32.9	6 50.2	12 05.1	12 12.4
21 Th	14 00 14	28 13 02	26 39 15	4♎03 30	3 33.0	16 59.9	0♐56.8	8 37.7	11 39.5	29 34.1	15 36.9	6 54.0	12 06.9	12 14.7
22 F	14 04 11	29 12 46	11♎32 17	19 04 38	3D 32.7	18 41.2	2 09.9	9 19.0	12 04.3	29 28.0	15 40.7	6 57.7	12 08.6	12 17.0
23 Sa	14 08 07	0♏12 32	26 39 27	4♏15 33	3 32.6	20 22.8	3 23.0	10 00.3	12 29.1	29 21.9	15 44.5	7 01.4	12 10.4	12 19.2
24 Su	14 12 04	1 12 21	11♏51 43	19 26 44	3 32.6	22 04.3	4 36.0	10 41.7	12 53.8	29 15.6	15 48.2	7 05.2	12 12.2	12 21.5
25 M	14 16 00	2 12 11	26 59 27	4♐28 47	3 32.8	23 45.8	5 49.1	11 23.2	13 18.4	29 09.1	15 51.8	7 08.9	12 14.0	12 23.7
26 Tu	14 19 57	3 12 03	11♐53 49	19 13 45	3R 32.9	25 27.2	7 02.1	12 04.7	13 42.9	29 02.5	15 55.3	7 12.7	12 15.8	12 26.0
27 W	14 23 53	4 11 57	26 27 59	3♑36 03	3 32.8	27 08.3	8 15.1	12 46.2	14 07.4	28 55.8	15 58.7	7 16.4	12 17.7	12 28.2
28 Th	14 27 50	5 11 52	10♑37 43	17 32 50	3 32.8	28 49.1	9 28.1	13 27.8	14 31.7	28 49.0	16 02.1	7 20.2	12 19.6	12 30.4
29 F	14 31 47	6 11 49	24 21 27	1♒03 43	3D 32.7	0♏29.6	10 41.0	14 09.5	14 56.0	28 42.0	16 05.3	7 24.0	12 21.5	12 32.6
30 Sa	14 35 43	7 11 48	7♒39 53	14 10 16	3 32.7	2 09.7	11 54.0	14 51.2	15 20.2	28 35.0	16 08.4	7 27.7	12 23.4	12 34.8
31 Su	14 39 40	8 11 48	20 35 15	26 55 17	3 32.9	3 49.5	13 06.9	15 32.9	15 44.4	28 27.8	16 11.4	7 31.5	12 25.3	12 37.0

Astro Data

Aspect	Dy Hr Mn
♀0S	3 18:35
♄△♆	5 3:32
☿ R	8 22:04
☽0N	9 0:30
♃ R	19 18:39
☉0S	22 21:48
☽0S	23 5:24
☿0N	25 11:40
☿ D	1 3:58
☽0N	6 6:46
♆⚹♇	10 6:49
☿0S	13 20:32
☽0S	20 16:04

Planet Ingress

	Dy Hr Mn
♀ ♎	1 17:44
☿ ♍R	21 7:15
☉ ♎	22 21:48
⚳ ♍	24 4:57
♀ ♏	26 4:17
♂ ♏	8 20:23
☿ ♎	10 14:47
♃ ♉R	16 20:24
♀ ♐	20 17:22
☉ ♏	23 6:58
☿ ♏	29 4:55

Last Aspect / ☽ Ingress (September)

Last Aspect Dy Hr Mn		☽ Ingress	Dy Hr Mn
1 7:43	♆ ☌	♑	2 16:29
3 12:12	☉ △	♒	4 22:20
5 19:09	♄ ☍	♓	7 6:11
8 12:52	☉ ☍	♈	9 16:18
10 15:55	♄ △	♉	12 4:30
13 23:52	☉ △	♊	14 17:32
16 17:20	☉ □	♋	17 5:07
19 6:46	☉ ⚹	♌	19 13:11
21 7:09	♀ ⚹	♍	21 17:16
23 14:31	☿ ☌	♎	23 18:28
25 17:41	♀ ☌	♏	25 18:34
27 10:01	☿ ⚹	♐	27 19:21
29 11:18	♂ ⚹	♑	29 22:13

Last Aspect / ☽ Ingress (October)

Last Aspect Dy Hr Mn		☽ Ingress	Dy Hr Mn
1 19:09	♂ □	♒	2 3:49
4 6:14	♂ △	♓	4 12:10
6 14:04	☿ ☍	♈	6 22:50
8 4:55	☉ ☍	♉	9 11:11
11 0:07	♀ ☍	♊	12 0:14
13 17:34	☉ △	♋	14 12:24
16 21:49	♃ ⚹	♌	16 21:49
19 3:04	♃ □	♍	19 3:25
21 4:47	♃ △	♎	21 5:26
23 5:10	☉ ☌	♏	23 5:17
25 3:31	♃ ☍	♐	25 4:49
26 23:41	☿ ⚹	♑	27 5:55
29 7:47	♃ △	♒	29 10:05
31 14:55	♃ □	♓	31 17:53

☽ Phases & Eclipses

Dy Hr Mn		
1 3:35	☽	8♐50
8 12:52	○	15♓59
16 17:20	☾	23♊57
23 19:55	●	0♎54
30 11:12	☽	7♑25
8 4:55	○	15♈02
16 8:59	☾	23♋07
23 5:10	●	29♎55
23 5:12:58	●	T 04'47"
29 22:05	☽	6♒37

Astro Data

1 September 1976
Julian Day # 28003
SVP 5♓34'57"
GC 26♐30.8 ⚴ 16♋14.4
Eris 14♈02.0R ⚵ 6♎16.4
⚷ 1♉34.8R ⚶ 8♋55.4
☽ Mean ☊ 6♏19.1

1 October 1976
Julian Day # 28033
SVP 5♓34'54"
GC 26♐30.9 ⚴ 2♌31.1
Eris 13♈45.1R ⚵ 16♎55.3
⚷ 0♉33.3R ⚶ 18♋23.6
☽ Mean ☊ 4♏43.8

November 1976 LONGITUDE

Day	Sid.Time	☉	0 hr ☽	Noon ☽	True ☊	☿	♀	♂	⚳	♃	♄	♅	♆	♇
1 M	14 43 36	9♏11 50	3♓10 48	9♓22 16	3♏33.4	5♏28.8	14♐19.7	16♏14.7	16♍08.4	28♉20.5	16♌14.3	7♏35.3	12♐27.3	12♎39.1
2 Tu	14 47 33	10 11 54	15 30 10	21 34 56	3 34.1	7 07.7	15 32.5	16 56.6	16 32.3	28R 13.1	16 17.1	7 39.0	12 29.3	12 41.3
3 W	14 51 29	11 11 59	27 37 02	3♈36 52	3 34.8	8 46.2	16 45.3	17 38.5	16 56.2	28 05.6	16 19.8	7 42.8	12 31.2	12 43.4
4 Th	14 55 26	12 12 05	9♈34 50	15 31 18	3 35.6	10 24.3	17 58.1	18 20.4	17 20.0	27 58.1	16 22.4	7 46.5	12 33.2	12 45.5
5 F	14 59 22	13 12 14	21 26 39	27 21 11	3R 36.0	12 01.9	19 10.9	19 02.4	17 43.6	27 50.4	16 24.9	7 50.3	12 35.3	12 47.6
6 Sa	15 03 19	14 12 24	3♉15 13	9♉09 03	3 36.0	13 39.2	20 23.6	19 44.5	18 07.2	27 42.7	16 27.3	7 54.0	12 37.3	12 49.7
7 Su	15 07 15	15 12 36	15 02 56	20 57 09	3 35.4	15 16.1	21 36.2	20 26.6	18 30.7	27 34.9	16 29.6	7 57.8	12 39.3	12 51.8
8 M	15 11 12	16 12 50	26 51 58	2♊47 38	3 34.2	16 52.5	22 48.9	21 08.7	18 54.1	27 27.1	16 31.8	8 01.5	12 41.4	12 53.8
9 Tu	15 15 09	17 13 06	8♊44 25	14 42 35	3 32.4	18 28.7	24 01.5	21 50.9	19 17.3	27 19.1	16 33.9	8 05.2	12 43.5	12 55.8
10 W	15 19 05	18 13 23	20 42 26	26 44 14	3 30.2	20 04.4	25 14.0	22 33.2	19 40.5	27 11.2	16 35.9	8 09.0	12 45.6	12 57.9
11 Th	15 23 02	19 13 43	2♋48 19	8♋55 02	3 27.8	21 39.9	26 26.6	23 15.5	20 03.6	27 03.2	16 37.8	8 12.7	12 47.7	12 59.9
12 F	15 26 58	20 14 04	15 04 43	21 17 44	3 25.6	23 15.0	27 39.1	23 57.9	20 26.6	26 55.1	16 39.5	8 16.4	12 49.8	13 01.8
13 Sa	15 30 55	21 14 27	27 34 30	3♌55 22	3 24.0	24 49.8	28 51.5	24 40.3	20 49.4	26 47.0	16 41.2	8 20.1	12 51.9	13 03.8
14 Su	15 34 51	22 14 52	10♌20 45	16 51 02	3D 23.1	26 24.3	0♑03.9	25 22.8	21 12.2	26 38.9	16 42.7	8 23.8	12 54.0	13 05.7
15 M	15 38 48	23 15 19	23 26 36	0♍07 44	3 23.1	27 58.5	1 16.3	26 05.3	21 34.8	26 30.7	16 44.2	8 27.5	12 56.2	13 07.6
16 Tu	15 42 44	24 15 48	6♍54 45	13 47 49	3 24.0	29 32.5	2 28.6	26 47.9	21 57.3	26 22.5	16 45.5	8 31.1	12 58.3	13 09.5
17 W	15 46 41	25 16 19	20 47 04	27 52 28	3 25.4	1♐06.3	3 40.9	27 30.5	22 19.7	26 14.3	16 46.7	8 34.8	13 00.5	13 11.4
18 Th	15 50 38	26 16 52	5♎03 53	12♎21 01	3 26.8	2 39.8	4 53.2	28 13.2	22 41.9	26 06.2	16 47.8	8 38.4	13 02.7	13 13.3
19 F	15 54 34	27 17 26	19 43 24	27 10 24	3R 27.7	4 13.1	6 05.4	28 56.0	23 04.1	25 58.0	16 48.8	8 42.0	13 04.9	13 15.1
20 Sa	15 58 31	28 18 02	4♏41 11	12♏14 49	3 27.6	5 46.2	7 17.6	29 38.8	23 26.1	25 49.8	16 49.7	8 45.7	13 07.1	13 16.9
21 Su	16 02 27	29 18 40	19 50 10	27 26 03	3 26.1	7 19.1	8 29.7	0♐21.6	23 48.0	25 41.6	16 50.4	8 49.3	13 09.3	13 18.7
22 M	16 06 24	0♐19 19	5♐01 15	12♐34 29	3 23.4	8 51.8	9 41.8	1 04.5	24 09.7	25 33.5	16 51.1	8 52.8	13 11.5	13 20.5
23 Tu	16 10 20	1 19 59	20 04 35	27 30 26	3 19.5	10 24.4	10 53.9	1 47.5	24 31.3	25 25.4	16 51.6	8 56.4	13 13.7	13 22.2
24 W	16 14 17	2 20 41	4♑51 06	12♑05 47	3 15.2	11 56.8	12 05.9	2 30.5	24 52.8	25 17.3	16 52.1	9 00.0	13 15.9	13 23.9
25 Th	16 18 13	3 21 24	19 13 54	26 15 02	3 10.9	13 29.0	13 17.8	3 13.5	25 14.1	25 09.3	16 52.4	9 03.5	13 18.2	13 25.6
26 F	16 22 10	4 22 08	3♒08 59	9♒55 45	3 07.5	15 01.1	14 29.7	3 56.7	25 35.3	25 01.3	16 52.6	9 07.0	13 20.4	13 27.3
27 Sa	16 26 07	5 22 53	16 35 26	23 08 19	3 05.3	16 33.0	15 41.5	4 39.8	25 56.3	24 53.3	16R 52.7	9 10.5	13 22.7	13 28.9
28 Su	16 30 03	6 23 39	29 34 48	5♓55 20	3D 04.5	18 04.7	16 53.2	5 23.0	26 17.2	24 45.5	16 52.7	9 13.9	13 24.9	13 30.5
29 M	16 34 00	7 24 26	12♓10 28	18 20 47	3 05.1	19 36.2	18 04.9	6 06.3	26 37.9	24 37.7	16 52.5	9 17.4	13 27.2	13 32.1
30 Tu	16 37 56	8 25 14	24 26 54	0♈29 25	3 06.6	21 07.6	19 16.5	6 49.6	26 58.4	24 29.9	16 52.3	9 20.8	13 29.4	13 33.7

December 1976 LONGITUDE

Day	Sid.Time	☉	0 hr ☽	Noon ☽	True ☊	☿	♀	♂	⚳	♃	♄	♅	♆	♇
1 W	16 41 53	9♐26 03	6♈28 59	12♈26 10	3♏08.4	22♐38.7	20♑28.0	7♐32.9	27♍18.8	24♉22.3	16♌51.9	9♏24.2	13♐31.7	13♎35.2
2 Th	16 45 49	10 26 52	18 21 35	24 15 45	3R 09.9	24 09.5	21 39.5	8 16.3	27 39.1	24R 14.7	16R 51.4	9 27.6	13 33.9	13 36.7
3 F	16 49 46	11 27 43	0♉09 13	6♉02 27	3 10.2	25 40.1	22 50.9	8 59.8	27 59.2	24 07.2	16 50.9	9 30.9	13 36.2	13 38.2
4 Sa	16 53 42	12 28 35	11 55 53	17 49 54	3 08.9	27 10.3	24 02.2	9 43.3	28 19.1	23 59.9	16 50.2	9 34.2	13 38.4	13 39.7
5 Su	16 57 39	13 29 27	23 44 53	29 41 08	3 05.7	28 40.2	25 13.4	10 26.8	28 38.8	23 52.6	16 49.3	9 37.5	13 40.7	13 41.1
6 M	17 01 36	14 30 21	5♊38 53	11♊38 25	3 00.4	0♑09.6	26 24.5	11 10.4	28 58.4	23 45.4	16 48.4	9 40.8	13 43.0	13 42.5
7 Tu	17 05 32	15 31 16	17 39 54	23 43 30	2 53.3	1 38.5	27 35.6	11 54.1	29 17.7	23 38.3	16 47.4	9 44.0	13 45.2	13 43.8
8 W	17 09 29	16 32 11	29 49 23	5♋57 39	2 45.0	3 06.8	28 46.5	12 37.8	29 36.9	23 31.4	16 46.3	9 47.3	13 47.5	13 45.2
9 Th	17 13 25	17 33 08	12♋08 27	18 21 52	2 36.4	4 34.4	29 57.4	13 21.5	29 56.0	23 24.6	16 45.0	9 50.4	13 49.8	13 46.5
10 F	17 17 22	18 34 06	24 38 03	0♌57 07	2 28.2	6 01.1	1♒08.2	14 05.3	0♎14.8	23 17.9	16 43.7	9 53.6	13 52.0	13 47.8
11 Sa	17 21 18	19 35 05	7♌19 12	13 44 28	2 21.3	7 26.8	2 18.9	14 49.1	0 33.4	23 11.3	16 42.2	9 56.7	13 54.3	13 49.0
12 Su	17 25 15	20 36 04	20 13 06	26 45 17	2 16.4	8 51.4	3 29.4	15 33.0	0 51.9	23 04.8	16 40.6	9 59.8	13 56.5	13 50.2
13 M	17 29 12	21 37 05	3♍21 15	10♍01 13	2D 13.7	10 14.5	4 39.9	16 17.0	1 10.1	22 58.5	16 38.9	10 02.9	13 58.8	13 51.4
14 Tu	17 33 08	22 38 07	16 45 22	23 33 57	2 12.9	11 36.0	5 50.3	17 01.0	1 28.2	22 52.4	16 37.2	10 05.9	14 01.0	13 52.5
15 W	17 37 05	23 39 10	0♎27 06	7♎24 57	2 13.6	12 55.5	7 00.6	17 45.0	1 46.0	22 46.4	16 35.3	10 08.9	14 03.3	13 53.7
16 Th	17 41 01	24 40 14	14 27 34	21 34 53	2R 14.6	14 12.8	8 10.7	18 29.1	2 03.6	22 40.5	16 33.3	10 11.9	14 05.5	13 54.7
17 F	17 44 58	25 41 19	28 46 47	6♏02 57	2 14.9	15 27.4	9 20.8	19 13.3	2 21.0	22 34.8	16 31.2	10 14.8	14 07.7	13 55.8
18 Sa	17 48 54	26 42 24	13♏22 59	20 46 17	2 13.4	16 38.9	10 30.7	19 57.5	2 38.2	22 29.3	16 29.0	10 17.7	14 10.0	13 56.8
19 Su	17 52 51	27 43 31	28 12 07	5♐39 37	2 09.6	17 46.8	11 40.6	20 41.7	2 55.2	22 23.9	16 26.7	10 20.6	14 12.2	13 57.8
20 M	17 56 47	28 44 38	13♐07 46	20 35 30	2 03.1	18 50.5	12 50.3	21 26.0	3 11.9	22 18.7	16 24.2	10 23.4	14 14.4	13 58.8
21 Tu	18 00 44	29 45 46	28 01 42	5♑25 14	1 54.5	19 49.4	13 59.8	22 10.4	3 28.4	22 13.7	16 21.7	10 26.2	14 16.6	13 59.7
22 W	18 04 41	0♑46 55	12♑45 02	20 00 09	1 44.6	20 42.7	15 09.3	22 54.8	3 44.7	22 08.8	16 19.1	10 28.9	14 18.8	14 00.6
23 Th	18 08 37	1 48 03	27 09 46	4♒13 12	1 34.6	21 29.7	16 18.6	23 39.2	4 00.7	22 04.1	16 16.4	10 31.6	14 21.0	14 01.4
24 F	18 12 34	2 49 12	11♒10 01	17 59 55	1 25.7	22 09.5	17 27.7	24 23.7	4 16.5	21 59.6	16 13.6	10 34.3	14 23.2	14 02.3
25 Sa	18 16 30	3 50 21	24 42 48	1♓18 46	1 18.7	22 41.2	18 36.7	25 08.2	4 32.0	21 55.3	16 10.7	10 36.9	14 25.3	14 03.0
26 Su	18 20 27	4 51 30	7♓48 02	14 10 57	1 14.1	23 03.9	19 45.6	25 52.8	4 47.3	21 51.2	16 07.8	10 39.5	14 27.5	14 03.8
27 M	18 24 23	5 52 39	20 28 01	26 39 47	1D 11.9	23R 16.6	20 54.3	26 37.4	5 02.3	21 47.3	16 04.7	10 42.1	14 29.6	14 04.5
28 Tu	18 28 20	6 53 48	2♈46 51	8♈49 53	1 11.4	23 18.7	22 02.8	27 22.1	5 17.0	21 43.5	16 01.5	10 44.6	14 31.8	14 05.2
29 W	18 32 16	7 54 56	14 49 35	20 46 38	1R 11.9	23 09.5	23 11.1	28 06.8	5 31.5	21 40.0	15 58.3	10 47.0	14 33.9	14 05.8
30 Th	18 36 13	8 56 05	26 41 45	2♉35 36	1 12.2	22 48.4	24 19.3	28 51.5	5 45.7	21 36.6	15 54.9	10 49.5	14 36.0	14 06.4
31 F	18 40 10	9 57 14	8♉28 51	14 22 08	1 11.3	22 15.5	25 27.3	29 36.3	5 59.6	21 33.5	15 51.5	10 51.8	14 38.1	14 07.0

Astro Data

	Dy Hr Mn
☽0N	2 12:26
♃⚻♇	5 18:58
☽0S	17 1:53
♄ R	27 18:46
☽0N	29 19:15
♆⚹♇	5 22:20
☽0S	14 9:52
☽0N	27 4:11
☿ R	28 4:32

Planet Ingress

	Dy Hr Mn
♀ ♑	14 10:42
☿ ♐	16 19:02
♂ ♐	20 23:53
☉ ♐	22 4:22
☿ ♑	6 9:25
♀ ♒	9 12:53
⚳ ♎	9 17:07
☉ ♑	21 17:35

Last Aspect / ☽ Ingress (November)

Last Aspect Dy Hr Mn		☽ Ingress Dy Hr Mn
3 1:04	♃ ⚹	♈ 3 4:46
4 17:31	♀ △	♉ 5 17:23
8 1:18	♃ ☌	♊ 8 6:21
10 8:41	♀ ☍	♋ 10 18:28
12 22:38	♃ ⚹	♌ 13 4:36
15 7:39	☿ □	♍ 15 11:46
17 11:21	♂ ⚹	♎ 17 15:34
18 19:16	♄ ⚹	♏ 19 16:32
21 15:11	☉ ☌	♐ 21 16:03
22 18:50	♄ △	♑ 23 16:03
25 10:08	♃ △	♒ 25 18:30
27 15:13	♃ □	♓ 28 0:47
30 0:13	♃ ⚹	♈ 30 11:01

Last Aspect / ☽ Ingress (December)

Last Aspect Dy Hr Mn		☽ Ingress Dy Hr Mn
2 11:45	☿ △	♉ 2 23:41
5 1:59	♀ △	♊ 5 12:38
6 22:17	♄ ⚹	♋ 8 0:21
9 21:35	♃ ⚹	♌ 10 10:12
12 5:19	♃ □	♍ 12 17:55
14 10:48	♃ △	♎ 14 23:13
16 17:33	☉ ⚹	♏ 17 2:01
18 14:46	♃ ☍	♐ 19 2:54
21 2:08	☉ ☌	♑ 21 3:12
22 15:34	♃ △	♒ 23 4:48
25 0:06	♂ ⚹	♓ 25 9:36
27 11:55	♂ □	♈ 27 18:32
30 3:53	♂ △	♉ 30 6:43

☽ Phases & Eclipses

Dy Hr Mn	
6 23:15	○ 14♉41
6 23:01	☊ A 0.838
14 22:39	☾ 22♌42
21 15:11	● 29♏27
28 12:59	☽ 6♓26
6 18:15	○ 14♊46
14 10:14	☾ 22♍34
21 2:08	● 29♐21
28 7:48	☽ 6♈43

Astro Data

1 November 1976
Julian Day # 28064
SVP 5♓34'51"
GC 26♐30.9 ⚴ 17♌26.4
Eris 13♈26.7R ⚵ 27♎55.7
⚷ 29♈08.0R ⚶ 24♋56.5
☽ Mean ☊ 3♏05.3

1 December 1976
Julian Day # 28094
SVP 5♓34'47"
GC 26♐31.0 ⚴ 27♌56.8
Eris 13♈13.2R ⚵ 8♏08.7
⚷ 27♈55.1R ⚶ 26♋05.8R
☽ Mean ☊ 1♏30.0

LONGITUDE

January 1977

Day	Sid.Time	☉	0 hr ☽	Noon ☽	True ☊	☿	♀	♂	⚳	♃	♄	♅	♆	♇
1 Sa	18 44 06	10♑58 22	20♉16 00	26♉11 02	1♏08.2	21♑31.1	26♒35.0	0♑21.1	6♎13.3	21♉30.5	15♌48.0	10♏54.2	14♐40.2	14♎07.6
2 Su	18 48 03	11 59 31	2♊07 41	8♊06 25	1R 02.4	20R 35.9	27 42.6	1 06.0	6 26.6	21R 27.7	15R 44.4	10 56.5	14 42.3	14 08.1
3 M	18 51 59	13 00 39	14 07 33	20 11 26	0 53.8	19 31.3	28 50.0	1 50.9	6 39.7	21 25.2	15 40.8	10 58.7	14 44.3	14 08.5
4 Tu	18 55 56	14 01 47	26 18 16	2♋28 14	0 42.6	18 19.1	29 57.2	2 35.9	6 52.5	21 22.8	15 37.0	11 00.9	14 46.4	14 09.0
5 W	18 59 52	15 02 56	8♋41 26	14 57 55	0 29.7	17 01.5	1♓04.1	3 20.9	7 05.0	21 20.7	15 33.2	11 03.1	14 48.4	14 09.4
6 Th	19 03 49	16 04 04	21 17 41	27 40 41	0 16.1	15 41.1	2 10.8	4 05.9	7 17.2	21 18.7	15 29.3	11 05.2	14 50.4	14 09.7
7 F	19 07 45	17 05 11	4♌06 48	10♌35 58	0 03.1	14 20.5	3 17.3	4 51.0	7 29.1	21 17.0	15 25.4	11 07.2	14 52.4	14 10.1
8 Sa	19 11 42	18 06 19	17 08 03	23 42 55	29♎51.8	13 02.3	4 23.5	5 36.1	7 40.6	21 15.4	15 21.4	11 09.3	14 54.4	14 10.4
9 Su	19 15 39	19 07 27	0♍20 28	7♍00 38	29 43.1	11 48.7	5 29.5	6 21.3	7 51.9	21 14.1	15 17.3	11 11.2	14 56.3	14 10.6
10 M	19 19 35	20 08 35	13 43 21	20 28 36	29 37.4	10 41.7	6 35.3	7 06.5	8 02.8	21 13.0	15 13.1	11 13.1	14 58.3	14 10.8
11 Tu	19 23 32	21 09 42	27 16 22	4♎06 43	29 34.6	9 42.7	7 40.7	7 51.8	8 13.4	21 12.0	15 08.9	11 15.0	15 00.2	14 11.0
12 W	19 27 28	22 10 50	10♎59 40	17 55 18	29 33.7	8 52.7	8 46.0	8 37.1	8 23.7	21 11.3	15 04.6	11 16.8	15 02.1	14 11.2
13 Th	19 31 25	23 11 57	24 53 40	1♏54 48	29 33.7	8 12.3	9 50.9	9 22.4	8 33.6	21 10.8	15 00.3	11 18.6	15 04.0	14 11.3
14 F	19 35 21	24 13 05	8♏58 39	16 05 08	29 33.1	7 41.6	10 55.6	10 07.8	8 43.2	21D 10.5	14 55.9	11 20.3	15 05.8	14 11.4
15 Sa	19 39 18	25 14 12	23 14 07	0♐25 17	29 30.6	7 20.6	11 59.9	10 53.2	8 52.4	21 10.4	14 51.5	11 22.0	15 07.7	14R 11.4
16 Su	19 43 14	26 15 20	7♐38 17	14 52 36	29 25.4	7D 08.9	13 04.0	11 38.7	9 01.3	21 10.5	14 47.0	11 23.6	15 09.5	14 11.4
17 M	19 47 11	27 16 27	22 07 39	29 22 42	29 17.1	7 06.0	14 07.7	12 24.2	9 09.8	21 10.8	14 42.5	11 25.2	15 11.3	14 11.4
18 Tu	19 51 08	28 17 33	6♑36 59	13♑49 41	29 06.2	7 11.5	15 11.2	13 09.7	9 18.0	21 11.4	14 37.9	11 26.7	15 13.1	14 11.4
19 W	19 55 04	29 18 40	20 59 55	28 06 54	28 53.6	7 24.5	16 14.2	13 55.3	9 25.8	21 12.1	14 33.3	11 28.2	15 14.9	14 11.3
20 Th	19 59 01	0♒19 45	5♒09 51	12♒08 06	28 40.6	7 44.7	17 17.0	14 40.9	9 33.2	21 13.0	14 28.6	11 29.6	15 16.6	14 11.1
21 F	20 02 57	1 20 50	19 01 06	25 48 26	28 28.7	8 11.2	18 19.4	15 26.6	9 40.2	21 14.2	14 23.9	11 31.0	15 18.3	14 11.0
22 Sa	20 06 54	2 21 53	2♓29 51	9♓05 14	28 18.8	8 43.6	19 21.4	16 12.3	9 46.8	21 15.5	14 19.2	11 32.3	15 20.0	14 10.7
23 Su	20 10 50	3 22 56	15 34 37	21 58 10	28 11.8	9 21.3	20 23.0	16 58.0	9 53.1	21 17.1	14 14.5	11 33.5	15 21.7	14 10.5
24 M	20 14 47	4 23 58	28 16 11	4♈29 05	28 07.5	10 03.9	21 24.2	17 43.7	9 59.0	21 18.9	14 09.7	11 34.7	15 23.3	14 10.2
25 Tu	20 18 43	5 24 59	10♈37 21	16 41 33	28D 05.6	10 50.7	22 25.0	18 29.5	10 04.4	21 20.8	14 04.9	11 35.9	15 25.0	14 09.9
26 W	20 22 40	6 25 59	22 42 19	28 40 18	28R 05.3	11 41.5	23 25.4	19 15.4	10 09.5	21 23.0	14 00.0	11 37.0	15 26.6	14 09.6
27 Th	20 26 37	7 26 57	4♉36 11	10♉30 42	28 05.3	12 35.9	24 25.3	20 01.2	10 14.2	21 25.4	13 55.2	11 38.0	15 28.1	14 09.2
28 F	20 30 33	8 27 55	16 24 31	22 18 23	28 04.5	13 33.5	25 24.8	20 47.1	10 18.4	21 27.9	13 50.3	11 39.0	15 29.7	14 08.8
29 Sa	20 34 30	9 28 51	28 12 56	4♊08 51	28 02.0	14 34.0	26 23.7	21 33.0	10 22.3	21 30.7	13 45.4	11 39.9	15 31.2	14 08.3
30 Su	20 38 26	10 29 46	10♊06 43	16 07 08	27 56.9	15 37.2	27 22.2	22 19.0	10 25.8	21 33.6	13 40.5	11 40.8	15 32.7	14 07.9
31 M	20 42 23	11 30 40	22 10 34	28 17 29	27 49.2	16 42.9	28 20.1	23 04.9	10 28.8	21 36.8	13 35.7	11 41.6	15 34.2	14 07.4

LONGITUDE

February 1977

Day	Sid.Time	☉	0 hr ☽	Noon ☽	True ☊	☿	♀	♂	⚳	♃	♄	♅	♆	♇
1 Tu	20 46 19	12♒31 33	4♋28 14	10♋43 06	27♎38.9	17♑50.8	29♓17.5	23♑50.9	10♎31.4	21♉40.1	13♌30.7	11♏42.4	15♐35.6	14♎06.8
2 W	20 50 16	13 32 24	17 02 16	23 25 51	27R 26.7	19 00.7	0♈14.4	24 37.0	10 33.6	21 43.7	13R 25.8	11 43.1	15 37.0	14R 06.2
3 Th	20 54 12	14 33 15	29 53 51	6♌26 11	27 13.8	20 12.5	1 10.6	25 23.1	10 35.4	21 47.4	13 20.9	11 43.7	15 38.4	14 05.6
4 F	20 58 09	15 34 04	13♌02 40	19 43 05	27 01.4	21 26.1	2 06.3	26 09.2	10 36.7	21 51.3	13 16.0	11 44.3	15 39.8	14 05.0
5 Sa	21 02 06	16 34 52	26 27 06	3♍14 24	26 50.6	22 41.4	3 01.3	26 55.3	10 37.6	21 55.4	13 11.1	11 44.9	15 41.1	14 04.3
6 Su	21 06 02	17 35 38	10♍04 35	16 57 16	26 42.3	23 58.1	3 55.7	27 41.4	10R 38.1	21 59.7	13 06.3	11 45.4	15 42.4	14 03.6
7 M	21 09 59	18 36 24	23 52 06	0♎48 43	26 36.9	25 16.3	4 49.5	28 27.6	10 38.1	22 04.2	13 01.4	11 45.8	15 43.7	14 02.9
8 Tu	21 13 55	19 37 09	7♎46 49	14 46 06	26D 34.3	26 35.9	5 42.5	29 13.9	10 37.8	22 08.8	12 56.5	11 46.2	15 44.9	14 02.1
9 W	21 17 52	20 37 52	21 46 22	28 47 26	26 33.8	27 56.7	6 34.8	0♒00.1	10 36.9	22 13.6	12 51.7	11 46.5	15 46.2	14 01.3
10 Th	21 21 48	21 38 35	5♏49 09	12♏51 26	26R 34.2	29 18.8	7 26.4	0 46.4	10 35.7	22 18.6	12 46.8	11 46.8	15 47.3	14 00.5
11 F	21 25 45	22 39 16	19 54 09	26 57 13	26 34.4	0♒42.1	8 17.2	1 32.7	10 34.0	22 23.8	12 42.0	11 47.0	15 48.5	13 59.6
12 Sa	21 29 41	23 39 57	4♐00 31	11♐03 55	26 33.0	2 06.4	9 07.3	2 19.0	10 31.8	22 29.2	12 37.3	11 47.1	15 49.6	13 58.7
13 Su	21 33 38	24 40 37	18 07 15	25 10 16	26 29.4	3 31.9	9 56.5	3 05.4	10 29.3	22 34.7	12 32.5	11 47.2	15 50.7	13 57.8
14 M	21 37 35	25 41 15	2♑12 41	9♑14 09	26 23.2	4 58.4	10 44.8	3 51.8	10 26.2	22 40.4	12 27.8	11R 47.3	15 51.8	13 56.9
15 Tu	21 41 31	26 41 52	16 14 18	23 12 40	26 14.7	6 25.9	11 32.3	4 38.2	10 22.8	22 46.3	12 23.1	11 47.3	15 52.8	13 55.9
16 W	21 45 28	27 42 28	0♒08 48	7♒02 15	26 04.8	7 54.5	12 18.9	5 24.6	10 18.9	22 52.3	12 18.4	11 47.2	15 53.9	13 54.9
17 Th	21 49 24	28 43 02	13 52 32	20 39 13	25 54.4	9 24.0	13 04.5	6 11.1	10 14.5	22 58.5	12 13.8	11 47.1	15 54.8	13 53.9
18 F	21 53 21	29 43 35	27 21 57	4♓00 25	25 44.7	10 54.5	13 49.1	6 57.6	10 09.8	23 04.9	12 09.3	11 46.9	15 55.8	13 52.8
19 Sa	21 57 17	0♓44 06	10♓34 21	17 03 40	25 36.8	12 26.0	14 32.6	7 44.1	10 04.6	23 11.5	12 04.7	11 46.7	15 56.7	13 51.7
20 Su	22 01 14	1 44 36	23 28 17	29 48 15	25 31.1	13 58.5	15 15.1	8 30.6	9 59.0	23 18.1	12 00.2	11 46.4	15 57.6	13 50.6
21 M	22 05 10	2 45 04	6♈03 45	12♈15 01	25 27.8	15 31.9	15 56.5	9 17.1	9 52.9	23 25.0	11 55.8	11 46.0	15 58.4	13 49.5
22 Tu	22 09 07	3 45 30	18 22 21	24 26 10	25D 26.8	17 06.2	16 36.7	10 03.7	9 46.5	23 32.0	11 51.4	11 45.6	15 59.2	13 48.3
23 W	22 13 04	4 45 54	0♉26 57	6♉25 13	25 27.3	18 41.5	17 15.6	10 50.3	9 39.6	23 39.2	11 47.1	11 45.2	16 00.0	13 47.1
24 Th	22 17 00	5 46 17	12 21 32	18 16 31	25 28.6	20 17.8	17 53.3	11 36.9	9 32.4	23 46.5	11 42.8	11 44.7	16 00.7	13 45.9
25 F	22 20 57	6 46 37	24 10 48	0♊05 03	25R 29.7	21 55.1	18 29.7	12 23.5	9 24.7	23 54.0	11 38.6	11 44.1	16 01.5	13 44.7
26 Sa	22 24 53	7 46 55	5♊59 56	11 56 06	25 29.9	23 33.4	19 04.7	13 10.1	9 16.7	24 01.6	11 34.5	11 43.5	16 02.1	13 43.5
27 Su	22 28 50	8 47 12	17 54 15	23 54 59	25 28.4	25 12.6	19 38.3	13 56.7	9 08.3	24 09.4	11 30.4	11 42.9	16 02.8	13 42.2
28 M	22 32 46	9 47 27	29 58 54	6♋06 35	25 25.0	26 52.9	20 10.4	14 43.4	8 59.5	24 17.3	11 26.4	11 42.2	16 03.4	13 40.9

Astro Data

	Dy Hr Mn
☽0S	10 16:32
♄△♆	12 21:54
♃D	15 10:56
♇R	16 7:05
☿D	17 8:00
☽0N	23 14:35
♄✱♇	24 9:01
♀0N	31 0:16
☽0S	6 23:33
⚳R	7 2:43
♅R	14 19:50
☽0N	20 0:33
♄□♅	24 0:04

Planet Ingress

		Dy Hr Mn
♂	♑	1 0:42
♀	♓	4 13:01
☊	♎R	7 18:05
☉	♒	20 4:14
♀	♈	2 5:54
♂	♒	9 11:57
☿	♒	10 23:55
☉	♓	18 18:30

Last Aspect / ☽ Ingress

Last Aspect Dy Hr Mn		☽ Ingress Dy Hr Mn
1 12:54	♀ □	♊ 1 19:43
4 6:37	♀ △	♋ 4 7:12
6 0:04	♃ ✱	♌ 6 16:20
8 7:32	♃ □	♍ 8 23:23
10 13:18	♃ △	♎ 11 4:48
12 19:55	☉ □	♏ 13 8:44
15 2:41	☉ ✱	♐ 15 11:18
16 12:28	♆ ☌	♑ 17 13:02
19 14:11	☉ ☌	♒ 19 15:12
21 3:53	♃ □	♓ 21 19:30
23 10:42	♃ ✱	♈ 24 3:19
25 15:49	♂ □	♉ 26 14:41
28 18:53	♀ ✱	♊ 29 3:37
31 12:06	♀ □	♋ 31 15:20

Last Aspect / ☽ Ingress

Last Aspect Dy Hr Mn		☽ Ingress Dy Hr Mn
2 14:21	♂ ☍	♌ 3 0:11
4 15:50	♃ □	♍ 5 6:17
7 7:42	♂ △	♎ 7 10:36
9 10:24	☿ △	♏ 9 14:04
11 4:12	♃ ☍	♐ 11 17:11
13 11:06	☉ ✱	♑ 13 20:14
15 11:14	♃ △	♒ 15 23:45
18 3:37	☉ ☌	♓ 18 4:45
19 23:34	♃ ✱	♈ 20 12:22
21 19:39	♀ ☌	♉ 22 23:06
24 23:18	♃ ☌	♊ 25 11:50
27 14:59	☿ △	♋ 28 0:02

☽ Phases & Eclipses

Dy Hr Mn		
5 12:10	○	15♋03
12 19:55	☾	22♎31
19 14:11	●	29♑24
27 5:11	☽	7♉10
4 3:56	○	15♌14
11 4:07	☾	22♏19
18 3:37	●	29♒22
26 2:50	☽	7♊24

Astro Data

1 January 1977
Julian Day # 28125
SVP 5♓34'42"
GC 26♐31.1 ⚵ 1♍19.6R
Eris 13♈08.2 ⚶ 17♏38.9
⚷ 27♈18.7R ⚴ 20♋42.0R
☽ Mean ☊ 29♎51.5

1 February 1977
Julian Day # 28156
SVP 5♓34'37"
GC 26♐31.2 ⚵ 24♌40.6R
Eris 13♈13.9 ⚶ 25♏12.3
⚷ 27♈35.9 ⚴ 13♋08.1R
☽ Mean ☊ 28♎13.0

March 1977 — LONGITUDE

Day	Sid.Time	☉	0 hr ☽	Noon ☽	True ☊	☿	♀	♂	⚳	♃	♄	♅	♆	♇
1 Tu	22 36 43	10♓47 39	12♋18 32	18♋35 10	25♎19.8	28♒34.2	20♈41.0	15♒30.1	8♎50.3	24♉25.3	11♌22.4	11♏41.4	16♐04.0	13♎39.6
2 W	22 40 39	11 47 49	24 56 52	1♌23 52	25R 13.1	0♓16.5	21 09.9	16 16.7	8R 40.8	24 33.5	11R 18.5	11R 40.6	16 04.5	13R 38.2
3 Th	22 44 36	12 47 58	7♌56 20	14 34 19	25 05.7	1 59.9	21 37.2	17 03.4	8 31.0	24 41.8	11 14.7	11 39.7	16 05.1	13 36.9
4 F	22 48 33	13 48 04	21 17 44	28 06 23	24 58.4	3 44.3	22 02.8	17 50.1	8 20.8	24 50.3	11 11.0	11 38.8	16 05.5	13 35.5
5 Sa	22 52 29	14 48 09	4♍59 57	11♍58 03	24 52.1	5 29.8	22 26.5	18 36.9	8 10.4	24 58.9	11 07.3	11 37.8	16 06.0	13 34.1
6 Su	22 56 26	15 48 12	19 00 09	26 05 41	24 47.5	7 16.4	22 48.5	19 23.6	7 59.6	25 07.6	11 03.7	11 36.8	16 06.4	13 32.7
7 M	23 00 22	16 48 12	3♎14 00	10♎24 28	24D 44.8	9 04.1	23 08.5	20 10.3	7 48.5	25 16.5	11 00.2	11 35.7	16 06.8	13 31.2
8 Tu	23 04 19	17 48 11	17 36 25	24 49 12	24 43.9	10 53.0	23 26.5	20 57.1	7 37.1	25 25.5	10 56.8	11 34.6	16 07.1	13 29.8
9 W	23 08 15	18 48 09	2♏02 13	9♏14 56	24 44.6	12 42.9	23 42.6	21 43.9	7 25.4	25 34.6	10 53.4	11 33.5	16 07.4	13 28.3
10 Th	23 12 12	19 48 05	16 26 49	23 37 30	24 46.0	14 33.9	23 56.5	22 30.6	7 13.5	25 43.8	10 50.2	11 32.2	16 07.7	13 26.8
11 F	23 16 08	20 47 59	0♐46 35	7♐53 47	24R 47.3	16 26.1	24 08.3	23 17.4	7 01.4	25 53.2	10 47.0	11 31.0	16 08.0	13 25.3
12 Sa	23 20 05	21 47 52	14 58 53	22 01 41	24 47.9	18 19.4	24 17.9	24 04.2	6 49.0	26 02.7	10 43.9	11 29.7	16 08.2	13 23.8
13 Su	23 24 01	22 47 43	29 02 02	5♑59 47	24 47.2	20 13.7	24 25.2	24 51.0	6 36.4	26 12.3	10 40.9	11 28.3	16 08.4	13 22.3
14 M	23 27 58	23 47 32	12♑54 52	19 47 08	24 45.0	22 09.2	24 30.3	25 37.9	6 23.6	26 22.0	10 38.0	11 26.9	16 08.5	13 20.7
15 Tu	23 31 55	24 47 19	26 36 32	3♒22 57	24 41.5	24 05.6	24R 33.0	26 24.7	6 10.6	26 31.8	10 35.1	11 25.5	16 08.6	13 19.2
16 W	23 35 51	25 47 05	10♒06 18	16 46 29	24 37.1	26 03.0	24 33.3	27 11.5	5 57.4	26 41.8	10 32.4	11 24.0	16 08.7	13 17.6
17 Th	23 39 48	26 46 49	23 23 24	29 56 59	24 32.4	28 01.3	24 31.2	27 58.4	5 44.1	26 51.8	10 29.8	11 22.5	16R 08.8	13 16.0
18 F	23 43 44	27 46 31	6♓27 10	12♓53 52	24 28.1	0♈00.3	24 26.6	28 45.2	5 30.7	27 02.0	10 27.2	11 20.9	16 08.8	13 14.4
19 Sa	23 47 41	28 46 12	19 17 06	25 36 50	24 24.6	2 00.1	24 19.5	29 32.0	5 17.1	27 12.3	10 24.8	11 19.3	16 08.8	13 12.8
20 Su	23 51 37	29 45 50	1♈53 07	8♈06 04	24 22.2	4 00.4	24 10.0	0♓18.9	5 03.5	27 22.7	10 22.4	11 17.6	16 08.7	13 11.2
21 M	23 55 34	0♈45 26	14 15 46	20 22 25	24D 21.2	6 01.1	23 57.9	1 05.7	4 49.8	27 33.2	10 20.2	11 15.9	16 08.6	13 09.6
22 Tu	23 59 30	1 45 00	26 26 15	2♉27 31	24 21.4	8 02.0	23 43.4	1 52.6	4 36.0	27 43.8	10 18.0	11 14.2	16 08.5	13 07.9
23 W	0 03 27	2 44 32	8♉26 34	14 23 46	24 22.5	10 02.9	23 26.5	2 39.4	4 22.2	27 54.4	10 16.0	11 12.4	16 08.3	13 06.3
24 Th	0 07 24	3 44 02	20 19 31	26 14 18	24 24.1	12 03.4	23 07.1	3 26.3	4 08.3	28 05.2	10 14.0	11 10.6	16 08.1	13 04.6
25 F	0 11 20	4 43 29	2♊08 35	8♊02 55	24 25.7	14 03.4	22 45.4	4 13.1	3 54.5	28 16.1	10 12.2	11 08.8	16 07.9	13 03.0
26 Sa	0 15 17	5 42 54	13 57 51	19 53 59	24 27.1	16 02.5	22 21.5	4 59.9	3 40.7	28 27.1	10 10.5	11 06.9	16 07.7	13 01.3
27 Su	0 19 13	6 42 17	25 51 52	1♋52 09	24R 27.8	18 00.3	21 55.4	5 46.7	3 26.9	28 38.2	10 08.8	11 05.0	16 07.4	12 59.7
28 M	0 23 10	7 41 38	7♋55 25	14 02 15	24 27.7	19 56.5	21 27.2	6 33.6	3 13.2	28 49.4	10 07.3	11 03.0	16 07.1	12 58.0
29 Tu	0 27 06	8 40 56	20 13 14	26 28 54	24 26.9	21 50.7	20 57.2	7 20.4	2 59.6	29 00.6	10 05.9	11 01.0	16 06.7	12 56.3
30 W	0 31 03	9 40 12	2♌49 44	9♌16 10	24 25.5	23 42.5	20 25.4	8 07.2	2 46.0	29 12.0	10 04.6	10 59.0	16 06.3	12 54.7
31 Th	0 34 59	10 39 26	15 48 31	22 27 04	24 23.8	25 31.4	19 52.1	8 54.0	2 32.6	29 23.4	10 03.3	10 57.0	16 05.9	12 53.0

April 1977 — LONGITUDE

Day	Sid.Time	☉	0 hr ☽	Noon ☽	True ☊	☿	♀	♂	⚳	♃	♄	♅	♆	♇
1 F	0 38 56	11♈38 38	29♌11 56	6♍03 07	24♎22.0	27♈17.1	19♈17.4	9♓40.8	2♎19.2	29♉34.9	10♌02.2	10♏54.9	16♐05.5	12♎51.3
2 Sa	0 42 53	12 37 47	13♍00 30	20 03 48	24R 20.5	28 59.2	18R 41.6	10 27.5	2R 06.0	29 46.5	10R 01.2	10R 52.7	16R 05.0	12R 49.6
3 Su	0 46 49	13 36 54	27 12 37	4♎26 23	24 19.4	0♉37.3	18 04.9	11 14.3	1 53.0	29 58.2	10 00.3	10 50.6	16 04.5	12 47.9
4 M	0 50 46	14 35 59	11♎44 24	19 05 53	24D 19.0	2 11.0	17 27.5	12 01.1	1 40.2	0♊09.9	9 59.6	10 48.4	16 03.9	12 46.3
5 Tu	0 54 42	15 35 02	26 29 56	3♏55 38	24 19.0	3 40.2	16 49.7	12 47.8	1 27.5	0 21.8	9 58.9	10 46.2	16 03.4	12 44.6
6 W	0 58 39	16 34 03	11♏22 00	18 48 06	24 19.5	5 04.3	16 11.8	13 34.6	1 15.0	0 33.7	9 58.3	10 44.0	16 02.8	12 42.9
7 Th	1 02 35	17 33 02	26 13 02	3♐35 55	24 20.1	6 23.3	15 33.9	14 21.3	1 02.8	0 45.7	9 57.9	10 41.8	16 02.2	12 41.2
8 F	1 06 32	18 31 59	10♐56 03	18 12 47	24 20.6	7 36.9	14 56.5	15 08.1	0 50.8	0 57.7	9 57.5	10 39.5	16 01.5	12 39.6
9 Sa	1 10 28	19 30 55	25 25 35	2♑34 03	24 21.0	8 44.8	14 19.6	15 54.8	0 39.0	1 09.9	9 57.3	10 37.2	16 00.8	12 37.9
10 Su	1 14 25	20 29 49	9♑37 54	16 36 59	24R 21.2	9 47.0	13 43.6	16 41.5	0 27.5	1 22.1	9D 57.1	10 34.9	16 00.1	12 36.2
11 M	1 18 21	21 28 42	23 31 11	0♒20 32	24 21.2	10 43.2	13 08.7	17 28.2	0 16.2	1 34.3	9 57.1	10 32.5	15 59.3	12 34.6
12 Tu	1 22 18	22 27 32	7♒05 07	13 45 02	24 21.1	11 33.3	12 35.0	18 14.9	0 05.3	1 46.7	9 57.2	10 30.2	15 58.6	12 32.9
13 W	1 26 15	23 26 21	20 20 29	26 51 39	24D 20.9	12 17.3	12 02.9	19 01.6	29♍54.6	1 59.1	9 57.4	10 27.8	15 57.8	12 31.3
14 Th	1 30 11	24 25 08	3♓18 46	9♓42 04	24 20.9	12 55.0	11 32.4	19 48.2	29 44.3	2 11.6	9 57.7	10 25.4	15 56.9	12 29.6
15 F	1 34 08	25 23 53	16 01 47	22 18 10	24 21.0	13 26.5	11 03.8	20 34.8	29 34.2	2 24.1	9 58.1	10 23.0	15 56.1	12 28.0
16 Sa	1 38 04	26 22 37	28 31 25	4♈41 47	24 21.1	13 51.6	10 37.1	21 21.5	29 24.5	2 36.7	9 58.6	10 20.5	15 55.2	12 26.4
17 Su	1 42 01	27 21 19	10♈49 29	16 54 45	24R 21.2	14 10.5	10 12.5	22 08.1	29 15.1	2 49.3	9 59.2	10 18.1	15 54.3	12 24.8
18 M	1 45 57	28 19 58	22 57 48	28 58 50	24 21.2	14 23.2	9 50.1	22 54.6	29 06.1	3 02.0	10 00.0	10 15.6	15 53.3	12 23.2
19 Tu	1 49 54	29 18 36	4♉58 07	10♉55 52	24 21.0	14R 29.7	9 29.9	23 41.2	28 57.4	3 14.8	10 00.8	10 13.1	15 52.4	12 21.6
20 W	1 53 50	0♉17 12	16 52 21	22 47 50	24 20.5	14 30.2	9 12.1	24 27.7	28 49.1	3 27.6	10 01.8	10 10.6	15 51.4	12 20.0
21 Th	1 57 47	1 15 46	28 42 38	4♊37 02	24 19.7	14 25.0	8 56.7	25 14.2	28 41.2	3 40.5	10 02.8	10 08.1	15 50.4	12 18.4
22 F	2 01 44	2 14 18	10♊31 24	16 26 07	24 18.6	14 14.2	8 43.6	26 00.7	28 33.7	3 53.5	10 04.0	10 05.6	15 49.3	12 16.9
23 Sa	2 05 40	3 12 48	22 21 34	28 18 12	24 17.5	13 58.2	8 33.0	26 47.2	28 26.5	4 06.4	10 05.3	10 03.1	15 48.3	12 15.3
24 Su	2 09 37	4 11 15	4♋16 27	10♋16 50	24 16.4	13 37.4	8 24.8	27 33.6	28 19.7	4 19.5	10 06.6	10 00.6	15 47.2	12 13.8
25 M	2 13 33	5 09 41	16 19 50	22 25 58	24 15.6	13 12.2	8 19.1	28 20.0	28 13.4	4 32.6	10 08.1	9 58.0	15 46.1	12 12.3
26 Tu	2 17 30	6 08 05	28 35 46	4♌49 46	24D 15.3	12 43.1	8D 15.7	29 06.4	28 07.4	4 45.7	10 09.7	9 55.5	15 44.9	12 10.8
27 W	2 21 26	7 06 26	11♌08 29	17 32 25	24 15.5	12 10.8	8 14.8	29 52.7	28 01.8	4 58.9	10 11.4	9 53.0	15 43.8	12 09.3
28 Th	2 25 23	8 04 45	24 02 01	0♍37 41	24 16.3	11 35.7	8 16.1	0♈39.1	27 56.7	5 12.1	10 13.2	9 50.4	15 42.6	12 07.8
29 F	2 29 19	9 03 02	7♍19 44	14 08 25	24 17.4	10 58.7	8 19.8	1 25.3	27 51.9	5 25.3	10 15.1	9 47.9	15 41.4	12 06.3
30 Sa	2 33 16	10 01 18	21 03 51	28 06 00	24 18.5	10 20.4	8 25.8	2 11.6	27 47.6	5 38.6	10 17.1	9 45.3	15 40.1	12 04.9

Astro Data

	Dy Hr Mn
☽0S	6 8:10
♀R	16 3:01
♆R	18 7:35
☽0N	19 8:37
☿0N	19 16:57
☉0N	20 17:42
♃⚻♇	24 10:51
☽0S	2 18:15
♄D	11 5:41
☽0N	15 14:48
☿R	20 2:08
♄□♅	22 22:25
♀D	27 9:49
☽0S	30 4:40

Planet Ingress

	Dy Hr Mn
☿ ♓	2 8:09
☿ ♈	18 11:56
♂ ♓	20 2:19
☉ ♈	20 17:42
☿ ♉	3 2:46
♃ ♊	3 15:42
⚳ ♍R	12 23:48
☉ ♉	20 4:57
♂ ♈	27 15:46

Last Aspect / ☽ Ingress (March)

Last Aspect Dy Hr Mn		☽ Ingress	Dy Hr Mn
1 23:08	♃ ⚹	♌	2 9:25
4 6:12	♃ □	♍	4 15:19
6 10:21	♃ △	♎	6 18:34
8 9:40	♀ ☍	♏	8 20:37
10 15:34	♃ ☍	♐	10 22:42
12 15:55	♀ △	♑	13 1:40
14 23:43	♃ △	♒	15 6:00
17 8:09	♂ ☌	♓	17 12:06
19 18:33	☉ ☌	♈	19 20:23
21 18:58	♀ ☌	♉	22 7:05
24 15:49	♃ ☌	♊	24 19:39
26 16:47	♀ ⚹	♋	27 8:16
29 16:52	♃ ⚹	♌	29 18:40

Last Aspect / ☽ Ingress (April)

Last Aspect Dy Hr Mn		☽ Ingress	Dy Hr Mn
1 0:31	♃ □	♍	1 1:25
3 4:30	♃ △	♎	3 4:39
4 9:26	♀ ☍	♏	5 5:40
6 3:06	♂ △	♐	7 6:08
8 12:34	☉ △	♑	9 7:40
10 19:15	☉ □	♒	11 11:24
13 5:10	☉ ⚹	♓	13 17:49
15 8:29	♂ ☌	♈	16 2:52
18 10:35	☉ ☌	♉	18 14:02
20 15:37	♂ ⚹	♊	21 2:37
23 8:44	♂ □	♋	23 15:25
26 0:15	♂ △	♌	26 2:43
27 8:38	♆ △	♍	28 10:52
29 14:42	♆ □	♎	30 15:13

☽ Phases & Eclipses

Dy Hr Mn	
5 17:13	○ 15♍01
12 11:35	☾ 21♐47
19 18:33	● 29♓02
27 22:27	☽ 7♋08
4 4:09	○ 14♎17
4 4:18	P 0.193
10 19:15	☾ 20♑48
18 10:35	● 28♈17
18 10:30:42	A 07'04"
26 14:42	☽ 6♌15

Astro Data

1 March 1977
Julian Day # 28184
SVP 5♓34'34"
GC 26♐31.2 ⚴ 16♌01.8R
Eris 13♈27.0 ⚵ 29♏18.6
⚷ 28♈34.6 ⚶ 10♋46.5
☽ Mean ☊ 26♎44.0

1 April 1977
Julian Day # 28215
SVP 5♓34'32"
GC 26♐31.3 ⚴ 13♌30.9
Eris 13♈46.8 ⚵ 29♏28.3R
⚷ 0♉13.0 ⚶ 14♋35.4
☽ Mean ☊ 25♎05.5

LONGITUDE

May 1977

Day	Sid.Time	☉	0 hr ☽	Noon ☽	True ☊	☿	♀	♂	⚳	♃	♄	♅	♆	♇
1 Su	2 37 13	10♉59 31	5♎14 42	12♎29 37	24♎19.4	9♉41.5	8♈34.0	2♈57.8	27♍43.7	5♊51.9	10♌19.3	9♏42.8	15♐38.9	12♎03.5
2 M	2 41 09	11 57 42	19 50 13	27 15 49	24R19.6	9R02.7	8 44.3	3 44.0	27R40.1	6 05.3	10 21.5	9R40.2	15R37.6	12R02.1
3 Tu	2 45 06	12 55 51	4♏45 33	12♏18 25	24 19.0	8 24.7	8 56.8	4 30.2	27 37.0	6 18.7	10 23.8	9 37.7	15 36.4	12 00.7
4 W	2 49 02	13 53 59	19 53 18	27 28 58	24 17.4	7 48.1	9 11.3	5 16.4	27 34.4	6 32.2	10 26.2	9 35.2	15 35.1	11 59.3
5 Th	2 52 59	14 52 06	5♐04 14	12♐37 50	24 15.1	7 13.6	9 27.8	6 02.5	27 32.1	6 45.7	10 28.7	9 32.6	15 33.7	11 58.0
6 F	2 56 55	15 50 10	20 08 40	27 35 41	24 12.3	6 41.6	9 46.2	6 48.5	27 30.2	6 59.2	10 31.3	9 30.1	15 32.4	11 56.6
7 Sa	3 00 52	16 48 14	4♑58 00	12♑14 53	24 09.6	6 12.8	10 06.5	7 34.6	27 28.8	7 12.7	10 34.0	9 27.6	15 31.0	11 55.3
8 Su	3 04 48	17 46 16	19 25 48	26 30 23	24 07.5	5 47.5	10 28.6	8 20.6	27 27.7	7 26.3	10 36.8	9 25.1	15 29.7	11 54.0
9 M	3 08 45	18 44 16	3♒28 27	10♒19 58	24D06.2	5 26.0	10 52.5	9 06.6	27 27.1	7 39.9	10 39.7	9 22.6	15 28.3	11 52.8
10 Tu	3 12 42	19 42 15	17 05 03	23 43 55	24 06.0	5 08.6	11 18.0	9 52.5	27D26.8	7 53.5	10 42.7	9 20.1	15 26.9	11 51.5
11 W	3 16 38	20 40 13	0♓16 53	6♓44 19	24 06.8	4 55.5	11 45.1	10 38.5	27 27.0	8 07.2	10 45.8	9 17.6	15 25.4	11 50.3
12 Th	3 20 35	21 38 10	13 06 40	19 24 23	24 08.3	4 47.0	12 13.8	11 24.3	27 27.6	8 20.9	10 49.0	9 15.1	15 24.0	11 49.1
13 F	3 24 31	22 36 05	25 37 56	1♈47 48	24 10.0	4D42.9	12 44.0	12 10.2	27 28.6	8 34.6	10 52.3	9 12.6	15 22.5	11 47.9
14 Sa	3 28 28	23 33 59	7♈54 26	13 58 16	24R11.3	4 43.5	13 15.6	12 56.0	27 30.0	8 48.3	10 55.7	9 10.2	15 21.1	11 46.8
15 Su	3 32 24	24 31 52	19 59 44	25 59 14	24 11.7	4 48.8	13 48.6	13 41.7	27 31.7	9 02.1	10 59.2	9 07.8	15 19.6	11 45.6
16 M	3 36 21	25 29 43	1♉57 08	7♉53 45	24 10.8	4 58.6	14 22.9	14 27.5	27 33.9	9 15.9	11 02.7	9 05.3	15 18.1	11 44.5
17 Tu	3 40 17	26 27 34	13 49 24	19 44 24	24 08.3	5 12.9	14 58.5	15 13.1	27 36.5	9 29.7	11 06.4	9 02.9	15 16.6	11 43.4
18 W	3 44 14	27 25 22	25 38 59	1♊33 25	24 04.2	5 31.7	15 35.3	15 58.8	27 39.5	9 43.5	11 10.1	9 00.6	15 15.1	11 42.4
19 Th	3 48 11	28 23 10	7♊27 57	13 22 49	23 58.8	5 54.9	16 13.3	16 44.4	27 42.8	9 57.4	11 13.9	8 58.2	15 13.6	11 41.4
20 F	3 52 07	29 20 56	19 18 16	25 14 32	23 52.5	6 22.3	16 52.4	17 29.9	27 46.6	10 11.2	11 17.9	8 55.9	15 12.0	11 40.4
21 Sa	3 56 04	0♊18 40	1♋11 53	7♋10 36	23 46.0	6 53.9	17 32.5	18 15.4	27 50.7	10 25.1	11 21.9	8 53.5	15 10.5	11 39.4
22 Su	4 00 00	1 16 23	13 10 58	19 13 19	23 39.9	7 29.5	18 13.8	19 00.9	27 55.2	10 39.0	11 26.0	8 51.2	15 08.9	11 38.4
23 M	4 03 57	2 14 05	25 18 00	1♌25 23	23 34.8	8 09.0	18 56.0	19 46.3	28 00.1	10 52.9	11 30.2	8 49.0	15 07.3	11 37.5
24 Tu	4 07 53	3 11 45	7♌35 53	13 49 54	23 31.3	8 52.3	19 39.1	20 31.7	28 05.3	11 06.8	11 34.4	8 46.7	15 05.8	11 36.6
25 W	4 11 50	4 09 23	20 07 55	26 30 20	23D29.5	9 39.2	20 23.2	21 17.0	28 10.9	11 20.7	11 38.8	8 44.5	15 04.2	11 35.8
26 Th	4 15 46	5 07 00	2♍57 38	9♍30 15	23 29.3	10 29.8	21 08.2	22 02.2	28 16.9	11 34.6	11 43.2	8 42.3	15 02.6	11 34.9
27 F	4 19 43	6 04 35	16 08 34	22 52 58	23 30.2	11 23.7	21 54.0	22 47.4	28 23.2	11 48.6	11 47.7	8 40.1	15 01.0	11 34.1
28 Sa	4 23 40	7 02 09	29 43 43	6♎41 00	23 31.5	12 21.1	22 40.6	23 32.6	28 29.8	12 02.5	11 52.3	8 38.0	14 59.4	11 33.3
29 Su	4 27 36	7 59 42	13♎44 53	20 55 18	23R32.3	13 21.7	23 28.1	24 17.7	28 36.9	12 16.5	11 57.0	8 35.9	14 57.8	11 32.6
30 M	4 31 33	8 57 13	28 12 00	5♏34 31	23 31.8	14 25.6	24 16.3	25 02.8	28 44.2	12 30.4	12 01.7	8 33.8	14 56.2	11 31.9
31 Tu	4 35 29	9 54 43	13♏02 14	20 34 19	23 29.4	15 32.5	25 05.2	25 47.8	28 51.9	12 44.4	12 06.5	8 31.7	14 54.6	11 31.2

LONGITUDE

June 1977

Day	Sid.Time	☉	0 hr ☽	Noon ☽	True ☊	☿	♀	♂	⚳	♃	♄	♅	♆	♇
1 W	4 39 26	10♊52 12	28♏09 44	5♐47 19	23♎24.9	16♉42.6	25♈54.8	26♈32.7	28♍59.9	12♊58.3	12♌11.4	8♏29.7	14♐53.0	11♎30.5
2 Th	4 43 22	11 49 40	13♐25 46	21 03 43	23R18.8	17 55.6	26 45.2	27 17.6	29 08.2	13 12.3	12 16.4	8R27.7	14R51.3	11R29.9
3 F	4 47 19	12 47 07	28 39 48	6♑12 45	23 11.6	19 11.6	27 36.2	28 02.5	29 16.9	13 26.2	12 21.4	8 25.7	14 49.7	11 29.3
4 Sa	4 51 15	13 44 33	13♑41 21	21 04 36	23 04.3	20 30.4	28 27.8	28 47.3	29 25.8	13 40.2	12 26.6	8 23.8	14 48.1	11 28.7
5 Su	4 55 12	14 41 59	28 21 39	5♒31 54	22 57.9	21 52.2	29 20.0	29 32.1	29 35.1	13 54.1	12 31.8	8 21.9	14 46.5	11 28.2
6 M	4 59 09	15 39 23	12♒34 57	19 30 37	22 53.1	23 16.8	0♉12.9	0♉16.8	29 44.7	14 08.1	12 37.0	8 20.1	14 44.9	11 27.7
7 Tu	5 03 05	16 36 47	26 18 54	2♓59 59	22 50.3	24 44.2	1 06.3	1 01.4	29 54.6	14 22.0	12 42.4	8 18.2	14 43.2	11 27.2
8 W	5 07 02	17 34 11	9♓34 11	16 01 55	22D49.3	26 14.3	2 00.3	1 46.0	0♎04.8	14 36.0	12 47.8	8 16.5	14 41.6	11 26.8
9 Th	5 10 58	18 31 33	22 23 41	28 40 03	22 49.7	27 47.3	2 54.8	2 30.6	0 15.2	14 49.9	12 53.2	8 14.7	14 40.0	11 26.3
10 F	5 14 55	19 28 56	4♈51 38	10♈59 02	22R50.6	29 23.0	3 49.8	3 15.0	0 26.0	15 03.8	12 58.8	8 13.0	14 38.4	11 26.0
11 Sa	5 18 51	20 26 18	17 02 51	23 03 43	22 51.1	1♊01.4	4 45.3	3 59.5	0 37.0	15 17.8	13 04.4	8 11.3	14 36.8	11 25.6
12 Su	5 22 48	21 23 39	29 02 11	4♉58 49	22 50.3	2 42.5	5 41.2	4 43.8	0 48.4	15 31.7	13 10.0	8 09.7	14 35.1	11 25.3
13 M	5 26 44	22 21 00	10♉54 08	16 48 34	22 47.4	4 26.4	6 37.6	5 28.2	1 00.0	15 45.6	13 15.8	8 08.1	14 33.5	11 25.0
14 Tu	5 30 41	23 18 20	22 42 35	28 36 32	22 42.1	6 12.8	7 34.5	6 12.4	1 11.9	15 59.5	13 21.6	8 06.5	14 31.9	11 24.8
15 W	5 34 38	24 15 40	4♊30 47	10♊25 38	22 34.3	8 01.9	8 31.8	6 56.6	1 24.0	16 13.4	13 27.4	8 05.0	14 30.3	11 24.5
16 Th	5 38 34	25 12 59	16 21 19	22 18 05	22 24.3	9 53.6	9 29.5	7 40.7	1 36.4	16 27.2	13 33.3	8 03.5	14 28.7	11 24.4
17 F	5 42 31	26 10 18	28 16 07	4♋15 37	22 13.0	11 47.8	10 27.6	8 24.8	1 49.1	16 41.1	13 39.3	8 02.1	14 27.2	11 24.2
18 Sa	5 46 27	27 07 36	10♋16 44	16 19 37	22 01.1	13 44.4	11 26.0	9 08.8	2 02.0	16 54.9	13 45.4	8 00.7	14 25.6	11 24.1
19 Su	5 50 24	28 04 54	22 24 27	28 31 22	21 49.8	15 43.3	12 24.8	9 52.7	2 15.2	17 08.7	13 51.5	7 59.4	14 24.0	11 24.0
20 M	5 54 20	29 02 11	4♌40 35	10♌52 16	21 40.0	17 44.4	13 24.0	10 36.6	2 28.7	17 22.5	13 57.6	7 58.1	14 22.4	11 24.0
21 Tu	5 58 17	29 59 27	17 06 41	23 24 04	21 32.5	19 47.6	14 23.6	11 20.4	2 42.3	17 36.3	14 03.8	7 56.8	14 20.9	11D23.9
22 W	6 02 13	0♋56 43	29 44 43	6♍08 56	21 27.6	21 52.5	15 23.4	12 04.1	2 56.2	17 50.0	14 10.1	7 55.6	14 19.3	11 24.0
23 Th	6 06 10	1 53 58	12♍37 04	19 09 26	21 25.2	23 59.2	16 23.6	12 47.8	3 10.4	18 03.8	14 16.4	7 54.5	14 17.8	11 24.0
24 F	6 10 07	2 51 12	25 46 25	2♎28 21	21D24.5	26 07.2	17 24.1	13 31.4	3 24.8	18 17.5	14 22.8	7 53.4	14 16.3	11 24.1
25 Sa	6 14 03	3 48 26	9♎15 32	16 08 14	21R24.7	28 16.4	18 24.9	14 14.9	3 39.4	18 31.1	14 29.2	7 52.3	14 14.8	11 24.2
26 Su	6 18 00	4 45 39	23 06 37	0♏10 46	21 24.6	0♋26.5	19 26.0	14 58.3	3 54.2	18 44.8	14 35.7	7 51.3	14 13.3	11 24.3
27 M	6 21 56	5 42 51	7♏20 38	14 36 01	21 22.9	2 37.2	20 27.3	15 41.7	4 09.3	18 58.4	14 42.2	7 50.3	14 11.8	11 24.5
28 Tu	6 25 53	6 40 03	21 56 31	29 21 36	21 19.0	4 48.2	21 29.0	16 25.1	4 24.5	19 12.0	14 48.8	7 49.4	14 10.3	11 24.7
29 W	6 29 49	7 37 15	6♐50 28	14♐22 12	21 12.4	6 59.3	22 30.9	17 08.3	4 40.0	19 25.6	14 55.4	7 48.5	14 08.9	11 25.0
30 Th	6 33 46	8 34 27	21 55 41	29 29 43	21 03.5	9 10.1	23 33.1	17 51.5	4 55.7	19 39.1	15 02.1	7 47.7	14 07.4	11 25.3

Astro Data (Dy Hr Mn)

Aspect	Dy Hr Mn
♂0N	1 6:24
⚳D	10 13:40
☽0N	12 20:36
☿D	13 20:52
♃⊼♅	15 20:22
♄✶♇	24 22:11
♃△♇	26 12:28
♃✶♄	27 9:46
☽0S	27 14:10
♃☍♆	8 20:41
☽0N	9 3:41
♇D	21 13:21
♄△♆	23 16:13
☽0S	23 22:07

Planet Ingress (Dy Hr Mn)

		Dy Hr Mn
☉	♊	21 4:14
♂	♉	6 3:00
♀	♉	6 6:10
⚳	♎	8 0:52
☿	♊	10 21:07
☉	♋	21 12:14
☿	♋	26 7:07

Last Aspect / ☽ Ingress (Dy Hr Mn)

Last Aspect		☽ Ingress	
1 17:10	♆ ✶	♏	2 16:24
3 13:03	☉ ☍	♐	4 15:59
5 16:40	♅ ✶	♑	6 15:54
7 20:09	☉ △	♒	8 18:00
10 4:08	☉ □	♓	10 23:29
12 16:39	☉ ✶	♈	13 8:29
14 14:44	♆ △	♉	15 20:04
18 2:51	☉ ☌	♊	18 8:50
19 19:16	♂ ✶	♋	20 21:35
22 11:34	♂ □	♌	23 9:13
25 1:33	♂ △	♍	25 18:31
26 22:00	♆ □	♎	28 0:28
29 17:53	♂ ☍	♏	30 2:57

Last Aspect		☽ Ingress	
31 3:21	♅ ☍	♐	1 2:54
2 22:21	♂ △	♑	3 2:07
5 1:24	♂ □	♒	5 2:44
6 19:24	♅ □	♓	7 6:35
9 10:04	♅ ✶	♈	9 14:34
11 6:18	☉ ✶	♉	12 1:56
13 4:44	♄ □	♊	14 14:50
16 18:23	☉ ☌	♋	17 3:28
18 2:14	♇ □	♌	19 14:53
21 3:47	♅ ✶	♍	22 0:29
23 22:27	♅ □	♎	24 7:35
25 16:11	♃ △	♏	26 11:42
27 22:18	♀ ☍	♐	28 13:02
29 20:09	♃ ☍	♑	30 12:48

☽ Phases & Eclipses (Dy Hr Mn)

Dy Hr Mn	
3 13:03	○ 12♏58
10 4:08	☾ 19♒23
18 2:51	● 27♉03
26 3:20	☽ 4♍46
1 20:31	○ 11♐13
8 15:07	☾ 17♓42
16 18:23	● 25♊28
24 12:44	☽ 2♎53

Astro Data

1 May 1977
Julian Day # 28245
SVP 5♓34'29"
GC 26♐31.4 ⚴ 18♌18.0
Eris 14♈06.4 ⚵ 24♏51.6R
⚷ 2♉02.4 ⚶ 22♋47.9
☽ Mean ☊ 23♎30.2

1 June 1977
Julian Day # 28276
SVP 5♓34'25"
GC 26♐31.4 ⚴ 27♌29.9
Eris 14♈22.4 ⚵ 18♏09.2R
⚷ 3♉48.9 ⚶ 4♌04.8
☽ Mean ☊ 21♎51.7

July 1977 LONGITUDE

Day	Sid.Time	☉	0 hr ☽	Noon ☽	True ☊	☿	♀	♂	⚳	♃	♄	♅	♆	♇
1 F	6 37 42	9♋31 38	7♑03 00	14♑34 15	20♎53.1	11♋20.4	24♉35.6	18♉34.6	5♎11.5	19♊52.6	15♌08.8	7♏46.9	14♐06.0	11♎25.6
2 Sa	6 41 39	10 28 49	22 02 13	29 25 46	20R42.5	13 30.0	25 38.3	19 17.6	5 27.6	20 06.1	15 15.5	7R46.2	14R04.6	11 26.0
3 Su	6 45 36	11 26 00	6♒43 54	13♒55 50	20 32.8	15 38.7	26 41.3	20 00.6	5 43.9	20 19.5	15 22.3	7 45.5	14 03.2	11 26.3
4 M	6 49 32	12 23 12	21 00 58	27 58 57	20 25.0	17 46.2	27 44.5	20 43.5	6 00.4	20 32.9	15 29.2	7 44.8	14 01.8	11 26.8
5 Tu	6 53 29	13 20 23	4♓49 36	11♓32 56	20 19.7	19 52.5	28 47.9	21 26.3	6 17.0	20 46.3	15 36.1	7 44.3	14 00.4	11 27.2
6 W	6 57 25	14 17 35	18 09 11	24 38 39	20 16.8	21 57.2	29 51.6	22 09.1	6 33.8	20 59.6	15 43.0	7 43.7	13 59.1	11 27.7
7 Th	7 01 22	15 14 47	1♈01 48	7♈19 11	20D15.7	24 00.5	0♊55.5	22 51.8	6 50.9	21 12.9	15 49.9	7 43.2	13 57.7	11 28.2
8 F	7 05 18	16 11 59	13 31 23	19 39 03	20R15.6	26 02.1	1 59.6	23 34.4	7 08.0	21 26.1	15 56.9	7 42.8	13 56.4	11 28.7
9 Sa	7 09 15	17 09 12	25 42 52	1♉43 30	20 15.3	28 01.9	3 04.0	24 16.9	7 25.4	21 39.4	16 04.0	7 42.4	13 55.1	11 29.3
10 Su	7 13 11	18 06 25	7♉41 37	13 37 50	20 13.9	0♌00.0	4 08.5	24 59.4	7 43.0	21 52.5	16 11.0	7 42.1	13 53.8	11 29.9
11 M	7 17 08	19 03 39	19 32 49	25 27 06	20 10.3	1 56.3	5 13.3	25 41.8	8 00.7	22 05.7	16 18.1	7 41.8	13 52.6	11 30.6
12 Tu	7 21 05	20 00 53	1♊21 16	7♊15 46	20 04.1	3 50.7	6 18.2	26 24.1	8 18.6	22 18.7	16 25.3	7 41.6	13 51.3	11 31.3
13 W	7 25 01	20 58 08	13 11 04	19 07 33	19 55.1	5 43.3	7 23.3	27 06.3	8 36.7	22 31.8	16 32.5	7 41.4	13 50.1	11 32.0
14 Th	7 28 58	21 55 23	25 05 32	1♋05 20	19 43.8	7 34.0	8 28.6	27 48.5	8 54.9	22 44.8	16 39.7	7 41.3	13 48.9	11 32.7
15 F	7 32 54	22 52 38	7♋07 08	13 11 09	19 30.8	9 22.8	9 34.1	28 30.5	9 13.3	22 57.7	16 46.9	7D41.2	13 47.7	11 33.5
16 Sa	7 36 51	23 49 54	19 17 31	25 26 18	19 17.3	11 09.7	10 39.8	29 12.5	9 31.8	23 10.6	16 54.2	7 41.2	13 46.6	11 34.3
17 Su	7 40 47	24 47 10	1♌37 37	7♌51 30	19 04.4	12 54.7	11 45.6	29 54.4	9 50.5	23 23.4	17 01.5	7 41.2	13 45.4	11 35.2
18 M	7 44 44	25 44 27	14 07 59	20 27 07	18 53.1	14 37.9	12 51.6	0♊36.2	10 09.4	23 36.2	17 08.8	7 41.3	13 44.3	11 36.0
19 Tu	7 48 40	26 41 44	26 48 57	3♍13 33	18 44.3	16 19.2	13 57.7	1 17.9	10 28.4	23 49.0	17 16.2	7 41.4	13 43.2	11 36.9
20 W	7 52 37	27 39 01	9♍41 00	16 11 24	18 38.4	17 58.6	15 04.0	1 59.6	10 47.5	24 01.6	17 23.5	7 41.6	13 42.2	11 37.9
21 Th	7 56 34	28 36 18	22 44 53	29 21 39	18 35.2	19 36.2	16 10.5	2 41.1	11 06.8	24 14.3	17 30.9	7 41.9	13 41.1	11 38.8
22 F	8 00 30	29 33 36	6♎01 50	12♎45 40	18D34.1	21 11.8	17 17.1	3 22.6	11 26.2	24 26.8	17 38.4	7 42.2	13 40.1	11 39.8
23 Sa	8 04 27	0♌30 54	19 33 20	26 24 59	18R34.1	22 45.6	18 23.9	4 04.0	11 45.8	24 39.3	17 45.8	7 42.5	13 39.1	11 40.9
24 Su	8 08 23	1 28 12	3♏20 47	10♏20 49	18 33.9	24 17.6	19 30.8	4 45.2	12 05.5	24 51.7	17 53.3	7 42.9	13 38.1	11 41.9
25 M	8 12 20	2 25 30	17 25 04	24 33 28	18 32.4	25 47.6	20 37.8	5 26.4	12 25.3	25 04.1	18 00.8	7 43.4	13 37.2	11 43.0
26 Tu	8 16 16	3 22 49	1♐45 46	9♐01 38	18 28.7	27 15.7	21 45.0	6 07.5	12 45.3	25 16.4	18 08.3	7 43.9	13 36.3	11 44.1
27 W	8 20 13	4 20 09	16 20 33	23 41 53	18 22.5	28 41.9	22 52.3	6 48.6	13 05.4	25 28.7	18 15.8	7 44.4	13 35.4	11 45.3
28 Th	8 24 09	5 17 29	1♑04 51	8♑28 32	18 13.9	0♍06.1	23 59.8	7 29.5	13 25.6	25 40.9	18 23.3	7 45.0	13 34.5	11 46.5
29 F	8 28 06	6 14 49	15 51 58	23 14 06	18 03.9	1 28.3	25 07.4	8 10.3	13 46.0	25 53.0	18 30.9	7 45.7	13 33.7	11 47.7
30 Sa	8 32 03	7 12 11	0♒33 54	7♒50 24	17 53.5	2 48.5	26 15.2	8 51.1	14 06.4	26 05.0	18 38.5	7 46.4	13 32.9	11 48.9
31 Su	8 35 59	8 09 33	15 02 40	22 09 56	17 43.9	4 06.7	27 23.1	9 31.7	14 27.0	26 17.0	18 46.1	7 47.2	13 32.1	11 50.2

August 1977 LONGITUDE

Day	Sid.Time	☉	0 hr ☽	Noon ☽	True ☊	☿	♀	♂	⚳	♃	♄	♅	♆	♇
1 M	8 39 56	9♌06 56	29♒11 33	6♓07 05	17♎36.1	5♍22.7	28♊31.1	10♊12.3	14♎47.7	26♊28.9	18♌53.7	7♏48.0	13♐31.4	11♎51.5
2 Tu	8 43 52	10 04 19	12♓56 13	19 38 50	17R30.7	6 36.6	29 39.2	10 52.8	15 08.5	26 40.8	19 01.3	7 48.9	13R30.6	11 52.8
3 W	8 47 49	11 01 44	26 14 59	2♈44 50	17 27.7	7 48.3	0♋47.5	11 33.2	15 29.4	26 52.5	19 08.9	7 49.8	13 30.0	11 54.1
4 Th	8 51 45	11 59 10	9♈08 42	15 27 00	17D26.8	8 57.6	1 55.9	12 13.4	15 50.4	27 04.2	19 16.5	7 50.8	13 29.3	11 55.5
5 F	8 55 42	12 56 38	21 40 14	27 48 57	17 27.0	10 04.6	3 04.4	12 53.6	16 11.6	27 15.8	19 24.2	7 51.8	13 28.6	11 56.9
6 Sa	8 59 38	13 54 06	3♉53 46	9♉55 20	17R27.6	11 09.1	4 13.1	13 33.7	16 32.8	27 27.3	19 31.8	7 52.8	13 28.0	11 58.4
7 Su	9 03 35	14 51 36	15 54 18	21 51 21	17 27.4	12 11.0	5 21.9	14 13.7	16 54.2	27 38.8	19 39.5	7 54.0	13 27.4	11 59.8
8 M	9 07 32	15 49 07	27 47 07	3♊42 15	17 25.6	13 10.3	6 30.8	14 53.6	17 15.6	27 50.2	19 47.1	7 55.1	13 26.9	12 01.3
9 Tu	9 11 28	16 46 40	9♊37 22	15 33 02	17 21.8	14 06.7	7 39.8	15 33.4	17 37.2	28 01.5	19 54.8	7 56.4	13 26.4	12 02.8
10 W	9 15 25	17 44 14	21 29 48	27 28 09	17 15.6	15 00.2	8 48.9	16 13.1	17 58.9	28 12.7	20 02.5	7 57.6	13 25.9	12 04.4
11 Th	9 19 21	18 41 49	3♋28 32	9♋31 20	17 07.4	15 50.6	9 58.1	16 52.7	18 20.6	28 23.8	20 10.2	7 59.0	13 25.4	12 05.9
12 F	9 23 18	19 39 26	15 36 52	21 45 23	16 57.7	16 37.8	11 07.5	17 32.2	18 42.5	28 34.8	20 17.9	8 00.3	13 25.0	12 07.5
13 Sa	9 27 14	20 37 03	27 57 05	4♌12 07	16 47.4	17 21.5	12 16.9	18 11.6	19 04.4	28 45.8	20 25.5	8 01.8	13 24.6	12 09.2
14 Su	9 31 11	21 34 42	10♌30 32	16 52 21	16 37.5	18 01.6	13 26.5	18 50.9	19 26.5	28 56.6	20 33.2	8 03.2	13 24.2	12 10.8
15 M	9 35 07	22 32 23	23 17 34	29 46 06	16 29.0	18 37.9	14 36.2	19 30.1	19 48.6	29 07.4	20 40.9	8 04.7	13 23.9	12 12.5
16 Tu	9 39 04	23 30 04	6♍17 50	12♍52 42	16 22.5	19 10.2	15 45.9	20 09.1	20 10.9	29 18.0	20 48.6	8 06.3	13 23.6	12 14.2
17 W	9 43 01	24 27 47	19 30 32	26 11 14	16 18.4	19 38.2	16 55.8	20 48.1	20 33.2	29 28.6	20 56.3	8 07.9	13 23.3	12 15.9
18 Th	9 46 57	25 25 31	2♎54 41	9♎40 48	16D16.6	20 01.8	18 05.8	21 26.9	20 55.6	29 39.1	21 03.9	8 09.6	13 23.1	12 17.6
19 F	9 50 54	26 23 16	16 29 28	23 20 39	16 16.6	20 20.7	19 15.8	22 05.6	21 18.1	29 49.4	21 11.6	8 11.3	13 22.8	12 19.4
20 Sa	9 54 50	27 21 02	0♏14 17	7♏10 20	16 17.6	20 34.6	20 26.0	22 44.2	21 40.7	29 59.7	21 19.3	8 13.1	13 22.7	12 21.1
21 Su	9 58 47	28 18 49	14 08 45	21 09 27	16R18.5	20 43.3	21 36.3	23 22.7	22 03.3	0♋09.9	21 26.9	8 14.9	13 22.5	12 23.0
22 M	10 02 43	29 16 37	28 12 22	5♐17 22	16 18.6	20R46.6	22 46.6	24 01.0	22 26.1	0 19.9	21 34.5	8 16.7	13 22.4	12 24.8
23 Tu	10 06 40	0♍14 27	12♐24 14	19 32 45	16 17.0	20 44.3	23 57.1	24 39.3	22 48.9	0 29.9	21 42.2	8 18.6	13 22.3	12 26.6
24 W	10 10 36	1 12 18	26 42 33	3♑53 14	16 13.5	20 36.2	25 07.6	25 17.4	23 11.8	0 39.7	21 49.8	8 20.6	13 22.3	12 28.5
25 Th	10 14 33	2 10 09	11♑04 20	18 15 17	16 08.3	20 22.3	26 18.2	25 55.4	23 34.8	0 49.5	21 57.4	8 22.6	13D22.3	12 30.4
26 F	10 18 30	3 08 03	25 25 28	2♒34 15	16 02.0	20 02.3	27 28.9	26 33.3	23 57.8	0 59.1	22 05.0	8 24.6	13 22.3	12 32.3
27 Sa	10 22 26	4 05 57	9♒40 58	16 44 58	15 55.3	19 36.4	28 39.8	27 11.1	24 20.9	1 08.6	22 12.6	8 26.7	13 22.3	12 34.2
28 Su	10 26 23	5 03 53	23 45 38	0♓42 25	15 49.2	19 04.6	29 50.7	27 48.7	24 44.1	1 18.0	22 20.1	8 28.8	13 22.4	12 36.2
29 M	10 30 19	6 01 50	7♓34 49	14 22 28	15 44.3	18 27.3	1♌01.7	28 26.2	25 07.4	1 27.3	22 27.7	8 31.0	13 22.5	12 38.2
30 Tu	10 34 16	6 59 49	21 05 04	27 42 29	15 41.0	17 44.6	2 12.8	29 03.6	25 30.7	1 36.5	22 35.2	8 33.2	13 22.7	12 40.1
31 W	10 38 12	7 57 50	4♈14 39	10♈41 37	15D39.6	16 57.2	3 23.9	29 40.9	25 54.1	1 45.5	22 42.7	8 35.4	13 22.8	12 42.2

Astro Data Dy Hr Mn	Planet Ingress Dy Hr Mn	Last Aspect Dy Hr Mn	☽ Ingress Dy Hr Mn	Last Aspect Dy Hr Mn	☽ Ingress Dy Hr Mn	☽ Phases & Eclipses Dy Hr Mn	Astro Data
☽0N 6 12:42	♀ ♊ 6 15:09	2 5:22 ♀ △	♒ 2 12:56	31 21:41 ♀ △	♓ 1 1:23	1 3:24 ○ 9♑11	1 July 1977
♃□♅ 14 5:36	☿ ♌ 10 12:00	4 11:33 ♀ □	♓ 4 15:31	3 0:59 ♃ □	♈ 3 6:54	8 4:39 ☾ 15♈54	Julian Day # 28306
♅D 16 8:41	♂ ♊ 17 15:13	6 7:06 ♂ ⚹	♈ 6 22:03	5 10:54 ♃ ⚹	♉ 5 16:18	16 8:36 ● 23♋42	SVP 5♓34'20"
☽0S 21 4:50	☉ ♌ 22 23:04	9 3:09 ☿ □	♉ 9 8:33	7 7:31 ♄ □	♊ 8 4:29	23 19:38 ☽ 0♏49	GC 26♐31.5 ⚴ 8♍33.1
	☿ ♍ 28 10:15	11 12:32 ♂ ☌	♊ 11 21:15	10 13:31 ♃ ☌	♋ 10 17:04	30 10:52 ○ 7♒09	Eris 14♈30.0 ⚵ 14♏30.9R
☽0N 2 22:52		13 18:59 ♃ ☌	♋ 14 9:50	12 1:19 ☿ ⚹	♌ 13 3:57		⚷ 5♉06.6 ⚶ 16♌39.2
⚳0S 4 10:51	♀ ♋ 2 19:19	16 19:45 ♂ ⚹	♌ 16 20:51	15 10:48 ♃ ⚹	♍ 15 12:26	6 20:40 ☾ 14♉15	☽ Mean ☊ 20♎16.4
☽0S 17 11:25	♃ ♋ 20 12:43	18 18:03 ♃ ⚹	♍ 19 5:58	17 17:57 ♃ □	♎ 17 18:49	14 21:31 ● 21♌58	
☿0S 22 3:56	☉ ♍ 23 6:00	21 10:32 ☉ ⚹	♎ 21 13:09	19 23:25 ♃ △	♏ 19 23:35	22 1:04 ☽ 28♏50	1 August 1977
☿R 22 14:19	♀ ♌ 28 15:09	23 8:53 ♃ △	♏ 23 18:13	22 1:04 ☉ □	♐ 22 3:03	28 20:10 ○ 5♓24	Julian Day # 28337
♆D 25 12:07		25 14:18 ☿ □	♐ 25 21:04	23 20:58 ♂ ☍	♑ 24 5:30		SVP 5♓34'15"
☿0N 27 14:27		27 20:59 ☿ △	♑ 27 22:15	26 2:41 ♀ ☍	♒ 26 7:41		GC 26♐31.6 ⚴ 21♍10.3
☽0N 30 8:49		28 17:22 ♇ □	♒ 29 23:04	28 6:45 ♂ △	♓ 28 10:46		Eris 14♈28.0R ⚵ 15♏39.3
				30 14:36 ♂ □	♈ 30 16:11		⚷ 5♉45.0 ⚶ 0♍44.3
							☽ Mean ☊ 18♎37.9

LONGITUDE September 1977

Day	Sid.Time	☉	0 hr ☽	Noon ☽	True ☊	☿	♀	♂	⚳	♃	♄	♅	♆	♇
1 Th	10 42 09	8♍55 52	17♈03 33	23♈20 42	15♎39.7	16♍05.8	4♌35.2	0♋18.0	26♎17.5	1♋54.4	22♌50.2	8♏37.7	13♐23.0	12♎44.2
2 F	10 46 05	9 53 57	29 33 25	5♉42 06	15 41.0	15R 11.1	5 46.6	0 55.1	26 41.0	2 03.3	22 57.7	8 40.0	13 23.3	12 46.2
3 Sa	10 50 02	10 52 03	11♉47 14	17 49 20	15 42.6	14 14.1	6 58.0	1 31.9	27 04.6	2 11.9	23 05.1	8 42.4	13 23.6	12 48.3
4 Su	10 53 58	11 50 11	23 48 58	29 46 42	15 44.1	13 15.9	8 09.6	2 08.7	27 28.3	2 20.5	23 12.6	8 44.8	13 23.9	12 50.3
5 M	10 57 55	12 48 22	5♊43 11	11♊39 01	15R 44.8	12 17.8	9 21.2	2 45.3	27 52.0	2 28.9	23 20.0	8 47.3	13 24.2	12 52.4
6 Tu	11 01 52	13 46 34	17 34 49	23 31 11	15 44.3	11 21.1	10 32.9	3 21.8	28 15.8	2 37.2	23 27.4	8 49.8	13 24.6	12 54.5
7 W	11 05 48	14 44 48	29 28 45	5♋28 03	15 42.4	10 27.0	11 44.7	3 58.2	28 39.6	2 45.4	23 34.7	8 52.3	13 25.0	12 56.7
8 Th	11 09 45	15 43 04	11♋29 40	17 34 03	15 39.3	9 36.8	12 56.6	4 34.4	29 03.5	2 53.4	23 42.1	8 54.9	13 25.4	12 58.8
9 F	11 13 41	16 41 22	23 41 41	29 52 57	15 35.2	8 51.7	14 08.5	5 10.4	29 27.4	3 01.4	23 49.4	8 57.5	13 25.9	13 01.0
10 Sa	11 17 38	17 39 43	6♌08 11	12♌27 37	15 30.7	8 12.9	15 20.6	5 46.3	29 51.4	3 09.1	23 56.6	9 00.1	13 26.4	13 03.1
11 Su	11 21 34	18 38 05	18 51 28	25 19 49	15 26.2	7 41.4	16 32.7	6 22.1	0♏15.5	3 16.7	24 03.9	9 02.8	13 26.9	13 05.3
12 M	11 25 31	19 36 29	1♍52 42	8♍30 02	15 22.4	7 17.8	17 44.9	6 57.7	0 39.6	3 24.2	24 11.1	9 05.6	13 27.5	13 07.5
13 Tu	11 29 27	20 34 55	15 11 42	21 57 29	15 19.7	7 02.9	18 57.1	7 33.1	1 03.8	3 31.6	24 18.3	9 08.3	13 28.1	13 09.7
14 W	11 33 24	21 33 22	28 47 07	5♎40 16	15D 18.2	6D 57.0	20 09.5	8 08.4	1 28.0	3 38.8	24 25.4	9 11.1	13 28.7	13 11.9
15 Th	11 37 21	22 31 52	12♎36 35	19 35 41	15 18.0	7 00.5	21 21.9	8 43.6	1 52.3	3 45.8	24 32.5	9 13.9	13 29.4	13 14.1
16 F	11 41 17	23 30 23	26 37 08	3♏40 33	15 18.7	7 13.5	22 34.3	9 18.5	2 16.6	3 52.7	24 39.6	9 16.8	13 30.1	13 16.4
17 Sa	11 45 14	24 28 56	10♏45 30	17 51 37	15 20.0	7 35.8	23 46.9	9 53.4	2 41.0	3 59.5	24 46.6	9 19.7	13 30.8	13 18.6
18 Su	11 49 10	25 27 31	24 58 31	2♐05 50	15 21.3	8 07.3	24 59.5	10 28.0	3 05.4	4 06.0	24 53.6	9 22.6	13 31.6	13 20.9
19 M	11 53 07	26 26 08	9♐13 15	16 20 26	15R 22.3	8 47.6	26 12.2	11 02.5	3 29.9	4 12.5	25 00.6	9 25.6	13 32.4	13 23.2
20 Tu	11 57 03	27 24 46	23 27 08	0♑33 01	15 22.5	9 36.3	27 24.9	11 36.8	3 54.4	4 18.8	25 07.5	9 28.6	13 33.2	13 25.4
21 W	12 01 00	28 23 25	7♑37 51	14 41 20	15 21.9	10 32.9	28 37.7	12 10.9	4 18.9	4 24.9	25 14.4	9 31.6	13 34.1	13 27.7
22 Th	12 04 56	29 22 07	21 43 14	28 43 16	15 20.6	11 36.9	29 50.6	12 44.9	4 43.5	4 30.9	25 21.2	9 34.7	13 34.9	13 30.0
23 F	12 08 53	0♎20 50	5♒41 10	12♒36 40	15 18.8	12 47.6	1♍03.6	13 18.7	5 08.2	4 36.7	25 28.0	9 37.8	13 35.9	13 32.3
24 Sa	12 12 50	1 19 34	19 29 32	26 19 28	15 16.8	14 04.3	2 16.6	13 52.3	5 32.8	4 42.3	25 34.7	9 40.9	13 36.8	13 34.6
25 Su	12 16 46	2 18 21	3♓06 16	9♓49 42	15 15.1	15 26.5	3 29.6	14 25.7	5 57.6	4 47.8	25 41.4	9 44.1	13 37.8	13 37.0
26 M	12 20 43	3 17 09	16 29 35	23 05 46	15 13.8	16 53.4	4 42.8	14 58.9	6 22.3	4 53.1	25 48.1	9 47.2	13 38.8	13 39.3
27 Tu	12 24 39	4 15 59	29 38 07	6♈06 35	15D 13.1	18 24.4	5 56.0	15 32.0	6 47.1	4 58.3	25 54.7	9 50.4	13 39.8	13 41.6
28 W	12 28 36	5 14 52	12♈31 08	18 51 49	15 13.0	19 59.0	7 09.2	16 04.9	7 11.9	5 03.3	26 01.2	9 53.7	13 40.9	13 43.9
29 Th	12 32 32	6 13 46	25 08 43	1♉21 59	15 13.3	21 36.5	8 22.6	16 37.5	7 36.8	5 08.1	26 07.7	9 56.9	13 42.0	13 46.3
30 F	12 36 29	7 12 42	7♉31 50	13 38 31	15 14.0	23 16.5	9 36.0	17 10.0	8 01.7	5 12.7	26 14.2	10 00.2	13 43.1	13 48.6

LONGITUDE October 1977

Day	Sid.Time	☉	0 hr ☽	Noon ☽	True ☊	☿	♀	♂	⚳	♃	♄	♅	♆	♇
1 Sa	12 40 25	8♎11 41	19♉42 20	25♉43 40	15♎14.8	24♍58.4	10♍49.4	17♋42.3	8♏26.6	5♋17.2	26♌20.6	10♏03.5	13♐44.3	13♎51.0
2 Su	12 44 22	9 10 42	1♊42 55	7♊40 32	15 15.5	26 41.9	12 02.9	18 14.4	8 51.6	5 21.5	26 26.9	10 06.8	13 45.5	13 53.3
3 M	12 48 19	10 09 45	13 37 00	19 32 50	15 16.0	28 26.5	13 16.5	18 46.3	9 16.6	5 25.6	26 33.2	10 10.2	13 46.7	13 55.7
4 Tu	12 52 15	11 08 51	25 28 35	1♋24 48	15R 16.3	0♎12.0	14 30.1	19 18.0	9 41.6	5 29.5	26 39.5	10 13.6	13 47.9	13 58.0
5 W	12 56 12	12 07 59	7♋22 06	13 21 01	15 16.4	1 58.1	15 43.8	19 49.5	10 06.7	5 33.3	26 45.6	10 17.0	13 49.2	14 00.4
6 Th	13 00 08	13 07 09	19 22 10	25 26 07	15 16.3	3 44.5	16 57.6	20 20.7	10 31.8	5 36.9	26 51.7	10 20.4	13 50.5	14 02.8
7 F	13 04 05	14 06 21	1♌33 25	7♌44 36	15 16.2	5 31.1	18 11.4	20 51.7	10 56.9	5 40.3	26 57.8	10 23.9	13 51.8	14 05.1
8 Sa	13 08 01	15 05 36	14 00 09	20 20 29	15D 16.2	7 17.6	19 25.2	21 22.5	11 22.1	5 43.5	27 03.8	10 27.3	13 53.2	14 07.5
9 Su	13 11 58	16 04 53	26 46 00	3♍16 57	15 16.2	9 03.9	20 39.1	21 53.1	11 47.2	5 46.5	27 09.7	10 30.8	13 54.5	14 09.8
10 M	13 15 54	17 04 12	9♍53 34	16 35 55	15 16.3	10 50.0	21 53.1	22 23.4	12 12.4	5 49.3	27 15.6	10 34.3	13 55.9	14 12.2
11 Tu	13 19 51	18 03 33	23 24 00	0♎17 40	15 16.5	12 35.7	23 07.1	22 53.5	12 37.7	5 52.0	27 21.4	10 37.8	13 57.4	14 14.5
12 W	13 23 47	19 02 57	7♎16 40	14 20 36	15R 16.6	14 20.9	24 21.2	23 23.3	13 03.0	5 54.4	27 27.2	10 41.4	13 58.8	14 16.9
13 Th	13 27 44	20 02 22	21 28 58	28 41 10	15 16.5	16 05.6	25 35.3	23 52.9	13 28.2	5 56.7	27 32.8	10 45.0	14 00.3	14 19.3
14 F	13 31 41	21 01 50	5♏56 30	13♏14 11	15 16.1	17 49.8	26 49.4	24 22.3	13 53.6	5 58.7	27 38.4	10 48.5	14 01.8	14 21.6
15 Sa	13 35 37	22 01 19	20 33 26	27 53 25	15 15.4	19 33.4	28 03.6	24 51.3	14 18.9	6 00.6	27 44.0	10 52.1	14 03.4	14 24.0
16 Su	13 39 34	23 00 51	5♐13 18	12♐32 20	15 14.6	21 16.3	29 17.9	25 20.1	14 44.3	6 02.3	27 49.5	10 55.7	14 04.9	14 26.3
17 M	13 43 30	24 00 24	19 49 48	27 05 04	15 13.7	22 58.7	0♎32.1	25 48.7	15 09.6	6 03.7	27 54.9	10 59.4	14 06.5	14 28.6
18 Tu	13 47 27	24 59 59	4♑17 36	11♑26 57	15 13.1	24 40.4	1 46.5	26 16.9	15 35.0	6 05.0	28 00.2	11 03.0	14 08.1	14 31.0
19 W	13 51 23	25 59 36	18 32 46	25 34 49	15D 12.8	26 21.5	3 00.8	26 44.9	16 00.5	6 06.1	28 05.4	11 06.7	14 09.8	14 33.3
20 Th	13 55 20	26 59 14	2♒32 56	9♒27 02	15 13.1	28 02.0	4 15.2	27 12.6	16 25.9	6 07.0	28 10.6	11 10.3	14 11.4	14 35.6
21 F	13 59 16	27 58 54	16 17 07	23 03 12	15 13.8	29 41.8	5 29.6	27 40.0	16 51.3	6 07.7	28 15.7	11 14.0	14 13.1	14 37.9
22 Sa	14 03 13	28 58 35	29 45 22	6♓23 44	15 15.0	1♏21.0	6 44.1	28 07.1	17 16.8	6 08.1	28 20.7	11 17.7	14 14.8	14 40.2
23 Su	14 07 10	29 58 19	12♓58 24	19 29 32	15 16.2	2 59.7	7 58.6	28 34.0	17 42.3	6R 08.4	28 25.7	11 21.4	14 16.5	14 42.5
24 M	14 11 06	0♏58 04	25 57 14	2♈21 39	15 17.1	4 37.7	9 13.1	29 00.5	18 07.8	6 08.5	28 30.5	11 25.1	14 18.3	14 44.8
25 Tu	14 15 03	1 57 51	8♈42 56	15 01 11	15R 17.5	6 15.2	10 27.7	29 26.7	18 33.3	6 08.4	28 35.3	11 28.8	14 20.1	14 47.1
26 W	14 18 59	2 57 40	21 16 34	27 29 11	15 17.1	7 52.1	11 42.3	29 52.6	18 58.8	6 08.1	28 40.0	11 32.5	14 21.8	14 49.4
27 Th	14 22 56	3 57 30	3♉39 11	9♉46 43	15 15.7	9 28.5	12 57.0	0♌18.2	19 24.3	6 07.6	28 44.6	11 36.2	14 23.7	14 51.7
28 F	14 26 52	4 57 23	15 51 55	21 55 00	15 13.3	11 04.3	14 11.7	0 43.4	19 49.9	6 06.9	28 49.2	11 39.9	14 25.5	14 53.9
29 Sa	14 30 49	5 57 18	27 56 08	3♊55 34	15 10.1	12 39.7	15 26.4	1 08.3	20 15.4	6 05.9	28 53.6	11 43.7	14 27.3	14 56.2
30 Su	14 34 45	6 57 15	9♊53 32	15 50 21	15 06.4	14 14.6	16 41.1	1 32.9	20 41.0	6 04.8	28 58.0	11 47.4	14 29.2	14 58.4
31 M	14 38 42	7 57 14	21 46 20	27 41 51	15 02.7	15 49.0	17 55.9	1 57.1	21 06.6	6 03.5	29 02.3	11 51.2	14 31.1	15 00.6

Astro Data (Dy Hr Mn)

☽0S 13 19:06
☿D 14 15:05
⊙0S 23 3:30
♆✶♇ 26 2:58
☽0N 26 17:16

☿0S 6 17:54
☽0S 11 4:27
♀0S 19 22:39
☽0N 24 0:01
♃R 24 10:13

Planet Ingress (Dy Hr Mn)

♂ ♋ 1 0:20
⚳ ♏ 10 20:32
♀ ♍ 22 15:05
⊙ ♎ 23 3:29

☿ ♎ 4 9:16
♀ ♎ 17 1:37
☿ ♏ 21 16:23
⊙ ♏ 23 12:41
♂ ♌ 26 18:56

Last Aspect / ☽ Ingress (September)

Last Aspect Dy Hr Mn		☽ Ingress Dy Hr Mn
1 11:01 ♄ △	♉	2 0:52
3 22:39 ♄ □	♊	4 12:27
6 11:52 ♄ ✶	♋	7 1:03
8 8:02 ⊙ ✶	♌	9 12:14
11 9:38 ♄ ☌	♍	11 20:34
13 9:23 ⊙ ☌	♎	14 2:07
15 20:32 ♄ ✶	♏	16 5:45
17 23:59 ⊙ ✶	♐	18 8:28
20 6:18 ⊙ □	♑	20 11:04
22 13:12 ⊙ △	♒	22 14:12
24 10:41 ♄ ☍	♓	24 18:30
25 23:19 ☿ ☍	♈	27 0:40
29 1:48 ♄ △	♉	29 9:21

Last Aspect / ☽ Ingress (October)

Last Aspect Dy Hr Mn		☽ Ingress Dy Hr Mn
1 13:14 ♄ □	♊	1 20:33
4 9:07 ☿ □	♋	4 9:09
6 1:29 ♂ ☌	♌	6 20:58
9 0:39 ♄ ☌	♍	9 5:59
10 22:37 ♂ ✶	♎	11 11:29
13 10:06 ♄ ✶	♏	13 14:11
15 12:18 ♀ ✶	♐	15 15:27
17 13:23 ♄ △	♑	17 16:51
19 14:04 ♂ ☍	♒	19 19:36
21 21:31 ⊙ △	♓	22 0:26
24 5:29 ♂ △	♈	24 7:34
26 16:48 ♂ □	♉	26 16:53
29 1:51 ♄ □	♊	29 4:08
31 14:44 ♄ ✶	♋	31 16:40

☽ Phases & Eclipses (Dy Hr Mn)

5 14:33 ☾ 12♊55
13 9:23 ● 20♍29
20 6:18 ☽ 27♐11
27 8:17 ○ 4♈07
27 8:29 • A 0.901

5 9:21 ☾ 12♋01
12 20:31 ● 19♎24
12 20:26:39 • T 02'37"
19 12:46 ☽ 26♑01
26 23:35 ○ 3♉27

Astro Data

1 September 1977
Julian Day # 28368
SVP 5♓34'12"
GC 26♐31.6 ⚴ 4♎29.1
Eris 14♈16.7R ⚵ 20♏53.9
⚷ 5♉32.1R ⚶ 15♍34.3
☽ Mean ☊ 16♎59.4

1 October 1977
Julian Day # 28398
SVP 5♓34'10"
GC 26♐31.7 ⚴ 17♎43.5
Eris 13♈59.9R ⚵ 28♏35.5
⚷ 4♉34.8R ⚶ 0♎23.5
☽ Mean ☊ 15♎24.0

November 1977 LONGITUDE

Day	Sid.Time	☉	0 hr ☽	Noon ☽	True ☊	☿	♀	♂	⚳	♃	♄	♅	♆	♇
1 Tu	14 42 39	8♏57 15	3♋37 19	9♋33 09	14♎59.3	17♏22.9	19♎10.8	2♌21.0	21♏32.2	6♋02.0	29♌06.5	11♏54.9	14♐33.0	15♎02.8
2 W	14 46 35	9 57 18	15 29 50	21 27 53	14R 56.8	18 56.5	20 25.6	2 44.5	21 57.8	6R 00.3	29 10.6	11 58.7	14 34.9	15 05.0
3 Th	14 50 32	10 57 23	27 27 50	3♌30 14	14D 55.4	20 29.6	21 40.5	3 07.6	22 23.4	5 58.4	29 14.6	12 02.4	14 36.9	15 07.2
4 F	14 54 28	11 57 31	9♌35 40	15 44 43	14 55.2	22 02.3	22 55.4	3 30.3	22 49.0	5 56.2	29 18.6	12 06.2	14 38.8	15 09.4
5 Sa	14 58 25	12 57 40	21 57 57	28 15 56	14 56.1	23 34.5	24 10.3	3 52.7	23 14.6	5 53.9	29 22.4	12 09.9	14 40.8	15 11.5
6 Su	15 02 21	13 57 51	4♍39 12	11♍08 14	14 57.6	25 06.4	25 25.3	4 14.6	23 40.2	5 51.4	29 26.2	12 13.7	14 42.8	15 13.7
7 M	15 06 18	14 58 05	17 43 28	24 25 13	14 59.2	26 38.0	26 40.3	4 36.2	24 05.8	5 48.7	29 29.8	12 17.4	14 44.8	15 15.8
8 Tu	15 10 14	15 58 20	1♎13 43	8♎09 03	15R 00.4	28 09.1	27 55.3	4 57.3	24 31.5	5 45.8	29 33.4	12 21.2	14 46.8	15 17.9
9 W	15 14 11	16 58 38	15 11 09	22 19 48	15 00.3	29 39.9	29 10.4	5 18.0	24 57.1	5 42.7	29 36.8	12 24.9	14 48.9	15 20.0
10 Th	15 18 08	17 58 57	29 34 35	6♏54 52	14 58.7	1♐10.3	0♏25.5	5 38.2	25 22.7	5 39.4	29 40.2	12 28.7	14 50.9	15 22.1
11 F	15 22 04	18 59 18	14♏19 53	21 48 40	14 55.4	2 40.3	1 40.6	5 58.0	25 48.4	5 35.9	29 43.5	12 32.4	14 53.0	15 24.1
12 Sa	15 26 01	19 59 41	29 20 07	6♐53 04	14 50.8	4 09.9	2 55.7	6 17.3	26 14.0	5 32.3	29 46.7	12 36.2	14 55.1	15 26.2
13 Su	15 29 57	21 00 06	14♐26 17	21 58 31	14 45.3	5 39.1	4 10.8	6 36.2	26 39.7	5 28.4	29 49.7	12 39.9	14 57.2	15 28.2
14 M	15 33 54	22 00 32	29 28 37	6♑55 30	14 39.8	7 07.9	5 26.0	6 54.6	27 05.3	5 24.3	29 52.7	12 43.6	14 59.3	15 30.2
15 Tu	15 37 50	23 00 59	14♑18 16	21 36 08	14 35.2	8 36.3	6 41.2	7 12.5	27 30.9	5 20.1	29 55.6	12 47.4	15 01.4	15 32.2
16 W	15 41 47	24 01 28	28 48 35	5♒55 12	14 32.0	10 04.2	7 56.3	7 29.9	27 56.6	5 15.7	29 58.4	12 51.1	15 03.6	15 34.2
17 Th	15 45 43	25 01 58	12♒55 47	19 50 17	14D 30.5	11 31.6	9 11.5	7 46.8	28 22.2	5 11.1	0♍01.0	12 54.8	15 05.7	15 36.1
18 F	15 49 40	26 02 29	26 38 49	3♓21 34	14 30.6	12 58.5	10 26.8	8 03.2	28 47.8	5 06.4	0 03.6	12 58.5	15 07.9	15 38.0
19 Sa	15 53 37	27 03 01	9♓58 50	16 30 57	14 31.8	14 24.8	11 42.0	8 19.1	29 13.4	5 01.4	0 06.0	13 02.1	15 10.0	15 39.9
20 Su	15 57 33	28 03 35	22 58 20	29 21 23	14 33.3	15 50.4	12 57.2	8 34.4	29 39.0	4 56.3	0 08.4	13 05.8	15 12.2	15 41.8
21 M	16 01 30	29 04 09	5♈40 32	11♈56 10	14R 34.2	17 15.3	14 12.5	8 49.2	0♐04.6	4 51.1	0 10.7	13 09.4	15 14.4	15 43.7
22 Tu	16 05 26	0♐04 45	18 08 41	24 18 26	14 33.7	18 39.3	15 27.8	9 03.5	0 30.2	4 45.6	0 12.8	13 13.1	15 16.6	15 45.5
23 W	16 09 23	1 05 23	0♉25 47	6♉31 00	14 31.1	20 02.5	16 43.0	9 17.1	0 55.8	4 40.0	0 14.8	13 16.7	15 18.8	15 47.3
24 Th	16 13 19	2 06 01	12 34 22	18 36 08	14 26.2	21 24.6	17 58.3	9 30.2	1 21.3	4 34.3	0 16.8	13 20.3	15 21.0	15 49.1
25 F	16 17 16	3 06 41	24 36 31	0♊35 41	14 19.1	22 45.5	19 13.6	9 42.8	1 46.9	4 28.4	0 18.6	13 23.9	15 23.2	15 50.9
26 Sa	16 21 12	4 07 23	6♊33 50	12 31 09	14 10.0	24 05.1	20 29.0	9 54.7	2 12.4	4 22.4	0 20.3	13 27.5	15 25.4	15 52.6
27 Su	16 25 09	5 08 05	18 27 47	24 23 56	13 59.7	25 23.1	21 44.3	10 06.0	2 37.9	4 16.2	0 21.9	13 31.1	15 27.7	15 54.4
28 M	16 29 06	6 08 49	0♋19 48	6♋15 36	13 49.2	26 39.4	22 59.7	10 16.7	3 03.4	4 09.9	0 23.4	13 34.6	15 29.9	15 56.0
29 Tu	16 33 02	7 09 35	12 11 35	18 08 01	13 39.3	27 53.7	24 15.0	10 26.7	3 29.0	4 03.4	0 24.8	13 38.2	15 32.2	15 57.7
30 W	16 36 59	8 10 22	24 05 15	0♌03 38	13 31.0	29 05.7	25 30.4	10 36.1	3 54.4	3 56.8	0 26.1	13 41.7	15 34.4	15 59.4

December 1977 LONGITUDE

Day	Sid.Time	☉	0 hr ☽	Noon ☽	True ☊	☿	♀	♂	⚳	♃	♄	♅	♆	♇
1 Th	16 40 55	9♐11 10	6♌03 34	12♌05 30	13♎24.8	0♑15.0	26♏45.8	10♌44.9	4♐19.9	3♋50.1	0♍27.3	13♏45.2	15♐36.7	16♎01.0
2 F	16 44 52	10 12 00	18 09 56	24 17 22	13R 21.0	1 21.3	28 01.2	10 52.9	4 45.4	3R 43.2	0 28.4	13 48.7	15 38.9	16 02.6
3 Sa	16 48 48	11 12 51	0♍28 21	6♍43 28	13D 19.5	2 24.0	29 16.6	11 00.3	5 10.8	3 36.3	0 29.3	13 52.1	15 41.2	16 04.1
4 Su	16 52 45	12 13 43	13 03 18	19 28 25	13 19.6	3 22.8	0♐32.0	11 07.0	5 36.2	3 29.2	0 30.2	13 55.5	15 43.4	16 05.7
5 M	16 56 41	13 14 37	25 59 21	2♎36 38	13R 20.4	4 16.9	1 47.4	11 12.9	6 01.6	3 22.0	0 30.9	13 58.9	15 45.7	16 07.2
6 Tu	17 00 38	14 15 32	9♎20 41	16 11 50	13 20.7	5 05.9	3 02.9	11 18.1	6 27.0	3 14.7	0 31.5	14 02.3	15 47.9	16 08.7
7 W	17 04 35	15 16 28	23 10 17	0♏16 05	13 19.4	5 48.9	4 18.3	11 22.6	6 52.4	3 07.3	0 32.0	14 05.7	15 50.2	16 10.1
8 Th	17 08 31	16 17 26	7♏29 04	14 48 53	13 15.8	6 25.1	5 33.8	11 26.4	7 17.7	2 59.8	0 32.4	14 09.0	15 52.5	16 11.5
9 F	17 12 28	17 18 25	22 14 55	29 46 20	13 09.5	6 53.9	6 49.3	11 29.4	7 43.0	2 52.3	0 32.7	14 12.3	15 54.7	16 12.9
10 Sa	17 16 24	18 19 25	7♐22 03	15♐00 51	13 00.9	7 14.2	8 04.7	11 31.6	8 08.3	2 44.6	0 32.9	14 15.6	15 57.0	16 14.3
11 Su	17 20 21	19 20 25	22 41 17	0♑21 55	12 50.7	7R 25.2	9 20.2	11 33.0	8 33.6	2 36.9	0R 32.9	14 18.9	15 59.3	16 15.6
12 M	17 24 17	20 21 27	8♑01 13	15 37 45	12 40.3	7 26.1	10 35.7	11R 33.6	8 58.9	2 29.1	0 32.9	14 22.1	16 01.5	16 16.9
13 Tu	17 28 14	21 22 29	23 10 13	0♒37 29	12 30.9	7 16.2	11 51.2	11 33.5	9 24.1	2 21.2	0 32.7	14 25.3	16 03.8	16 18.2
14 W	17 32 10	22 23 32	7♒58 40	15 13 04	12 23.5	6 55.0	13 06.7	11 32.5	9 49.3	2 13.3	0 32.4	14 28.5	16 06.1	16 19.5
15 Th	17 36 07	23 24 35	22 20 17	29 20 07	12 18.7	6 22.2	14 22.2	11 30.7	10 14.4	2 05.3	0 32.0	14 31.6	16 08.3	16 20.7
16 F	17 40 04	24 25 39	6♓12 35	12♓57 50	12D 16.4	5 37.8	15 37.7	11 28.1	10 39.6	1 57.3	0 31.5	14 34.8	16 10.6	16 21.9
17 Sa	17 44 00	25 26 42	19 36 14	26 08 11	12 15.9	4 42.7	16 53.1	11 24.7	11 04.7	1 49.3	0 30.9	14 37.8	16 12.8	16 23.0
18 Su	17 47 57	26 27 47	2♈34 14	8♈54 54	12R 16.1	3 37.7	18 08.6	11 20.5	11 29.7	1 41.2	0 30.2	14 40.9	16 15.0	16 24.1
19 M	17 51 53	27 28 51	15 10 48	21 22 32	12 15.8	2 24.8	19 24.1	11 15.5	11 54.7	1 33.1	0 29.3	14 43.9	16 17.3	16 25.2
20 Tu	17 55 50	28 29 56	27 30 40	3♉35 45	12 13.9	1 05.9	20 39.6	11 09.6	12 19.7	1 24.9	0 28.4	14 46.9	16 19.5	16 26.2
21 W	17 59 46	29 31 01	9♉38 19	15 38 52	12 09.5	29♐43.8	21 55.1	11 02.9	12 44.7	1 16.8	0 27.3	14 49.8	16 21.7	16 27.3
22 Th	18 03 43	0♑32 07	21 37 48	27 35 33	12 02.0	28 21.2	23 10.6	10 55.3	13 09.6	1 08.6	0 26.1	14 52.7	16 23.9	16 28.3
23 F	18 07 39	1 33 12	3♊32 27	9♊28 47	11 51.5	27 00.8	24 26.1	10 47.0	13 34.5	1 00.5	0 24.9	14 55.6	16 26.1	16 29.2
24 Sa	18 11 36	2 34 18	15 24 50	21 20 47	11 38.5	25 45.1	25 41.6	10 37.8	13 59.4	0 52.4	0 23.5	14 58.5	16 28.3	16 30.1
25 Su	18 15 33	3 35 25	27 16 52	3♋13 13	11 23.9	24 36.5	26 57.1	10 27.8	14 24.2	0 44.2	0 22.0	15 01.3	16 30.5	16 31.0
26 M	18 19 29	4 36 32	9♋10 00	15 07 21	11 08.8	23 36.4	28 12.6	10 17.0	14 49.0	0 36.1	0 20.4	15 04.0	16 32.7	16 31.9
27 Tu	18 23 26	5 37 39	21 05 25	27 04 23	10 54.4	22 46.1	29 28.1	10 05.3	15 13.7	0 28.0	0 18.7	15 06.8	16 34.9	16 32.7
28 W	18 27 22	6 38 46	3♌04 23	9♌05 40	10 41.9	22 06.2	0♑43.6	9 52.9	15 38.4	0 19.9	0 16.9	15 09.5	16 37.0	16 33.5
29 Th	18 31 19	7 39 54	15 08 26	21 13 00	10 32.2	21 36.9	1 59.1	9 39.6	16 03.0	0 11.9	0 15.0	15 12.1	16 39.2	16 34.2
30 F	18 35 15	8 41 02	27 19 40	3♍28 49	10 25.5	21 18.1	3 14.6	9 25.6	16 27.6	0 03.9	0 13.0	15 14.7	16 41.3	16 34.9
31 Sa	18 39 12	9 42 11	9♍40 51	15 56 12	10 21.7	21D 09.3	4 30.1	9 10.8	16 52.2	29♊56.0	0 10.9	15 17.3	16 43.5	16 35.6

Astro Data	Dy Hr Mn
☽ 0S	7 14:56
☽ 0N	20 6:08
☽ 0S	5 1:07
♄ R	11 12:11
☿ R	12 2:09
♂ R	12 19:12
☽ 0N	17 13:25
♆✱♇	25 20:43
♃✱♄	28 23:53
♃⚼♅	29 11:30
☿ D	31 22:03

Planet Ingress		Dy Hr Mn
☿	♐	9 17:20
♀	♏	10 3:52
♄	♍	17 2:43
⚳	♐	21 7:41
☉	♐	22 10:07
☿	♑	1 6:43
♀	♐	4 1:49
☿	♐R	21 7:18
☉	♑	21 23:23
♀	♑	27 22:09
♃	♊R	30 23:50

Last Aspect Dy Hr Mn			☽ Ingress	Dy Hr Mn
2 9:40	♀	□	♌	3 5:03
5 14:06	♄	☌	♍	5 15:17
7 16:25	☿	⚹	♎	7 21:51
10 0:24	♀	☌	♏	10 0:42
12 0:40	♄	□	♐	12 1:03
14 0:36	♄	△	♑	14 0:50
15 14:31	☉	⚹	♒	16 2:00
17 21:52	☉	□	♓	18 5:58
20 9:20	☉	△	♈	20 13:13
21 23:35	☿	△	♉	22 23:09
24 10:36	♀	☍	♊	25 10:48
27 14:14	☿	☍	♋	27 23:20
30 1:47	♀	△	♌	30 11:53

Last Aspect Dy Hr Mn			☽ Ingress	Dy Hr Mn
2 20:04	♀	□	♍	2 23:05
4 4:59	♆	□	♎	5 7:18
6 11:54	♇	☌	♏	7 11:33
8 10:55	♅	☌	♐	9 12:22
10 17:33	☉	☌	♑	11 11:26
12 13:02	♇	□	♒	13 10:59
15 1:02	☉	⚹	♓	15 13:09
17 10:37	☉	□	♈	17 19:11
20 1:02	☉	△	♉	20 4:54
21 10:21	♅	☍	♊	22 16:51
24 21:50	♀	☍	♋	25 5:30
26 14:50	♇	□	♌	27 17:52
29 12:46	☿	△	♍	30 5:13

☽ Phases & Eclipses Dy Hr Mn		
4 3:58	☾	11♌37
11 7:09	●	18♏47
17 21:52	☽	25♒27
25 17:31	○	3♊21
3 21:16	☾	11♍36
10 17:33	●	18♐34
17 10:37	☽	25♓23
25 12:49	○	3♋37

Astro Data

1 November 1977
Julian Day # 28429
SVP 5♓34'07"
GC 26♐31.8 ⚴ 1♏30.3
Eris 13♈41.4R ⚵ 8♐14.6
⚷ 3♉09.5R ⚶ 15♎56.5
☽ Mean ☊ 13♎45.5

1 December 1977
Julian Day # 28459
SVP 5♓34'02"
GC 26♐31.8 ⚴ 14♏38.4
Eris 13♈27.9R ⚵ 18♐33.1
⚷ 1♉52.4R ⚶ 0♏55.8
☽ Mean ☊ 12♎10.2

LONGITUDE — January 1978

Day	Sid.Time	☉	0 hr ☽	Noon ☽	True ☊	☿	♀	♂	⚳	♃	♄	♅	♆	♇
1 Su	18 43 08	10♑43 19	22♍15 22	28♍38 51	10♎20.3	21♐10.1	5♑45.6	8♌55.3	17♐16.7	29♊48.1	0♍08.6	15♏19.9	16♐45.6	16♎36.2
2 M	18 47 05	11 44 29	5♎07 09	11♎40 47	10R 20.1	21 19.6	7 01.1	8R 39.0	17 41.2	29R 40.3	0R 06.3	15 22.3	16 47.7	16 36.9
3 Tu	18 51 02	12 45 38	18 20 13	25 05 52	10 19.8	21 37.2	8 16.6	8 21.9	18 05.6	29 32.5	0 03.9	15 24.8	16 49.8	16 37.4
4 W	18 54 58	13 46 48	1♏58 05	8♏57 06	10 18.2	22 02.2	9 32.1	8 04.2	18 30.0	29 24.8	0 01.4	15 27.2	16 51.8	16 38.0
5 Th	18 58 55	14 47 58	16 02 58	23 15 36	10 14.3	22 33.9	10 47.6	7 45.8	18 54.3	29 17.2	29♌58.8	15 29.6	16 53.9	16 38.5
6 F	19 02 51	15 49 08	0♐34 42	7♐59 43	10 07.5	23 11.6	12 03.1	7 26.8	19 18.6	29 09.6	29 56.1	15 31.9	16 56.0	16 38.9
7 Sa	19 06 48	16 50 19	15 29 54	23 04 15	9 58.0	23 54.6	13 18.6	7 07.2	19 42.9	29 02.2	29 53.3	15 34.2	16 58.0	16 39.4
8 Su	19 10 44	17 51 29	0♑41 34	8♑20 31	9 46.8	24 42.4	14 34.1	6 46.9	20 07.0	28 54.8	29 50.4	15 36.4	17 00.0	16 39.8
9 M	19 14 41	18 52 40	15 59 37	23 37 26	9 35.0	25 34.5	15 49.6	6 26.1	20 31.2	28 47.6	29 47.4	15 38.6	17 02.0	16 40.1
10 Tu	19 18 38	19 53 50	1♒12 29	8♒43 28	9 24.1	26 30.5	17 05.1	6 04.8	20 55.2	28 40.4	29 44.3	15 40.7	17 04.0	16 40.5
11 W	19 22 34	20 54 59	16 09 14	23 28 50	9 15.3	27 29.8	18 20.6	5 43.1	21 19.2	28 33.4	29 41.1	15 42.8	17 06.0	16 40.7
12 Th	19 26 31	21 56 08	0♓41 33	7♓46 57	9 09.2	28 32.2	19 36.0	5 20.9	21 43.2	28 26.5	29 37.9	15 44.9	17 07.9	16 41.0
13 F	19 30 27	22 57 17	14 44 46	21 34 59	9 05.9	29 37.4	20 51.5	4 58.3	22 07.1	28 19.7	29 34.5	15 46.9	17 09.9	16 41.2
14 Sa	19 34 24	23 58 24	28 17 48	4♈53 30	9D 04.8	0♑45.0	22 07.0	4 35.4	22 30.9	28 13.0	29 31.1	15 48.8	17 11.8	16 41.4
15 Su	19 38 20	24 59 31	11♈22 32	17 45 26	9R 04.9	1 54.9	23 22.4	4 12.1	22 54.7	28 06.5	29 27.6	15 50.7	17 13.7	16 41.5
16 M	19 42 17	26 00 38	24 02 48	0♉15 16	9 04.9	3 06.7	24 37.9	3 48.7	23 18.4	28 00.1	29 24.0	15 52.6	17 15.5	16 41.6
17 Tu	19 46 13	27 01 43	6♉23 29	12 28 05	9 03.7	4 20.4	25 53.3	3 25.0	23 42.0	27 53.8	29 20.4	15 54.4	17 17.4	16 41.7
18 W	19 50 10	28 02 48	18 29 44	24 29 02	9 00.4	5 35.7	27 08.8	3 01.1	24 05.6	27 47.7	29 16.7	15 56.2	17 19.2	16R 41.7
19 Th	19 54 06	29 03 52	0♊26 33	6♊22 50	8 54.4	6 52.5	28 24.2	2 37.2	24 29.1	27 41.7	29 12.9	15 57.9	17 21.0	16 41.7
20 F	19 58 03	0♒04 55	12 18 23	18 13 38	8 45.6	8 10.8	29 39.6	2 13.2	24 52.5	27 35.9	29 09.0	15 59.5	17 22.8	16 41.7
21 Sa	20 02 00	1 05 57	24 08 59	0♋04 45	8 34.5	9 30.3	0♒55.0	1 49.1	25 15.8	27 30.2	29 05.0	16 01.1	17 24.6	16 41.6
22 Su	20 05 56	2 06 59	6♋01 16	11 58 45	8 21.9	10 51.0	2 10.4	1 25.1	25 39.1	27 24.7	29 01.0	16 02.7	17 26.4	16 41.5
23 M	20 09 53	3 08 00	17 57 25	23 57 27	8 08.7	12 12.8	3 25.8	1 01.2	26 02.4	27 19.3	28 57.0	16 04.2	17 28.1	16 41.4
24 Tu	20 13 49	4 09 00	29 58 59	6♌02 08	7 56.2	13 35.7	4 41.2	0 37.4	26 25.5	27 14.2	28 52.8	16 05.6	17 29.8	16 41.2
25 W	20 17 46	5 09 59	12♌07 01	18 13 45	7 45.3	14 59.5	5 56.6	0 13.7	26 48.6	27 09.1	28 48.6	16 07.0	17 31.5	16 41.0
26 Th	20 21 42	6 10 57	24 22 25	0♍33 10	7 36.8	16 24.3	7 12.0	29♋50.2	27 11.6	27 04.3	28 44.4	16 08.4	17 33.1	16 40.8
27 F	20 25 39	7 11 54	6♍46 09	13 01 32	7 31.1	17 50.0	8 27.3	29 27.0	27 34.5	26 59.6	28 40.1	16 09.7	17 34.8	16 40.5
28 Sa	20 29 35	8 12 51	19 19 31	25 40 21	7D 28.2	19 16.6	9 42.7	29 04.1	27 57.3	26 55.1	28 35.7	16 10.9	17 36.4	16 40.2
29 Su	20 33 32	9 13 47	2♎04 17	8♎31 39	7 27.5	20 44.0	10 58.0	28 41.6	28 20.1	26 50.8	28 31.3	16 12.1	17 37.9	16 39.8
30 M	20 37 29	10 14 43	15 02 44	21 37 53	7 28.1	22 12.2	12 13.4	28 19.4	28 42.8	26 46.6	28 26.9	16 13.2	17 39.5	16 39.4
31 Tu	20 41 25	11 15 37	28 17 25	5♏01 39	7R 28.9	23 41.2	13 28.7	27 57.6	29 05.4	26 42.7	28 22.4	16 14.3	17 41.0	16 39.0

LONGITUDE — February 1978

Day	Sid.Time	☉	0 hr ☽	Noon ☽	True ☊	☿	♀	♂	⚳	♃	♄	♅	♆	♇
1 W	20 45 22	12♒16 31	11♏50 50	18♏45 12	7♎28.9	25♑11.0	14♒44.0	27♋36.2	29♐27.9	26♊38.9	28♌17.8	16♏15.3	17♐42.5	16♎38.6
2 Th	20 49 18	13 17 24	25 44 51	2♐49 47	7R 27.1	26 41.5	15 59.3	27R 15.4	29 50.3	26R 35.3	28R 13.2	16 16.3	17 44.0	16R 38.1
3 F	20 53 15	14 18 17	9♐59 53	17 14 50	7 23.1	28 12.9	17 14.6	26 55.1	0♑12.7	26 31.9	28 08.6	16 17.2	17 45.5	16 37.6
4 Sa	20 57 11	15 19 09	24 34 13	1♑57 21	7 17.0	29 45.0	18 29.9	26 35.3	0 34.9	26 28.7	28 04.0	16 18.1	17 46.9	16 37.0
5 Su	21 01 08	16 19 59	9♑23 28	16 51 35	7 09.3	1♒17.8	19 45.2	26 16.1	0 57.1	26 25.7	27 59.3	16 18.9	17 48.3	16 36.4
6 M	21 05 05	17 20 49	24 20 39	1♒49 31	7 01.1	2 51.4	21 00.5	25 57.6	1 19.2	26 22.9	27 54.6	16 19.7	17 49.7	16 35.8
7 Tu	21 09 01	18 21 38	9♒17 00	16 41 57	6 53.4	4 25.8	22 15.8	25 39.6	1 41.2	26 20.3	27 49.8	16 20.4	17 51.0	16 35.2
8 W	21 12 58	19 22 25	24 03 17	1♓20 04	6 47.1	6 01.0	23 31.1	25 22.4	2 03.0	26 17.8	27 45.0	16 21.0	17 52.4	16 34.5
9 Th	21 16 54	20 23 11	8♓31 28	15 36 52	6 43.0	7 37.0	24 46.3	25 05.9	2 24.8	26 15.6	27 40.2	16 21.6	17 53.6	16 33.8
10 F	21 20 51	21 23 55	22 35 49	29 28 04	6D 41.0	9 13.7	26 01.5	24 50.0	2 46.5	26 13.6	27 35.4	16 22.1	17 54.9	16 33.0
11 Sa	21 24 47	22 24 38	6♈13 33	12♈52 21	6 40.9	10 51.3	27 16.7	24 34.9	3 08.1	26 11.8	27 30.6	16 22.6	17 56.1	16 32.2
12 Su	21 28 44	23 25 20	19 24 39	25 50 50	6 42.0	12 29.6	28 31.9	24 20.6	3 29.6	26 10.1	27 25.8	16 23.0	17 57.3	16 31.4
13 M	21 32 40	24 25 59	2♉11 20	8♉26 39	6 43.6	14 08.8	29 47.1	24 07.0	3 50.9	26 08.7	27 20.9	16 23.4	17 58.5	16 30.6
14 Tu	21 36 37	25 26 37	14 37 20	20 44 01	6R 44.6	15 48.9	1♓02.3	23 54.2	4 12.2	26 07.5	27 16.1	16 23.7	17 59.6	16 29.7
15 W	21 40 33	26 27 14	26 47 19	2♊47 51	6 44.5	17 29.8	2 17.4	23 42.2	4 33.4	26 06.5	27 11.2	16 24.0	18 00.7	16 28.8
16 Th	21 44 30	27 27 48	8♊46 16	14 43 09	6 42.7	19 11.5	3 32.6	23 31.0	4 54.4	26 05.7	27 06.3	16 24.2	18 01.8	16 27.9
17 F	21 48 27	28 28 21	20 39 06	26 34 41	6 39.2	20 54.2	4 47.7	23 20.5	5 15.4	26 05.0	27 01.5	16 24.3	18 02.9	16 27.0
18 Sa	21 52 23	29 28 52	2♋30 25	8♋26 47	6 34.1	22 37.7	6 02.8	23 10.9	5 36.2	26 04.6	26 56.6	16 24.4	18 03.9	16 26.0
19 Su	21 56 20	0♓29 22	14 24 14	20 23 08	6 27.9	24 22.2	7 17.9	23 02.0	5 56.9	26D 04.4	26 51.8	16R 24.4	18 04.9	16 25.0
20 M	22 00 16	1 29 49	26 23 50	2♌26 39	6 21.2	26 07.6	8 32.9	22 54.0	6 17.5	26 04.4	26 46.9	16 24.4	18 05.8	16 23.9
21 Tu	22 04 13	2 30 15	8♌31 48	14 39 29	6 14.8	27 54.0	9 48.0	22 46.7	6 38.0	26 04.6	26 42.1	16 24.3	18 06.8	16 22.9
22 W	22 08 09	3 30 39	20 49 53	27 03 05	6 09.3	29 41.2	11 03.0	22 40.3	6 58.3	26 05.0	26 37.3	16 24.2	18 07.6	16 21.8
23 Th	22 12 06	4 31 02	3♍19 10	9♍38 12	6 05.2	1♓29.5	12 18.0	22 34.6	7 18.6	26 05.6	26 32.5	16 24.0	18 08.5	16 20.7
24 F	22 16 02	5 31 23	16 00 14	22 25 15	6 02.8	3 18.6	13 33.0	22 29.7	7 38.7	26 06.3	26 27.7	16 23.8	18 09.3	16 19.5
25 Sa	22 19 59	6 31 42	28 53 16	5♎24 20	6D 01.9	5 08.7	14 47.9	22 25.6	7 58.7	26 07.3	26 23.0	16 23.5	18 10.1	16 18.3
26 Su	22 23 56	7 31 59	11♎58 25	18 35 33	6 02.5	6 59.7	16 02.9	22 22.3	8 18.5	26 08.5	26 18.2	16 23.1	18 10.9	16 17.1
27 M	22 27 52	8 32 15	25 15 47	1♏59 07	6 03.9	8 51.6	17 17.8	22 19.7	8 38.3	26 09.9	26 13.5	16 22.7	18 11.6	16 15.9
28 Tu	22 31 49	9 32 30	8♏45 35	15 35 14	6 05.5	10 44.4	18 32.7	22 17.9	8 57.9	26 11.4	26 08.9	16 22.3	18 12.3	16 14.7

Astro Data Dy Hr Mn	Planet Ingress Dy Hr Mn	Last Aspect Dy Hr Mn	☽ Ingress Dy Hr Mn	Last Aspect Dy Hr Mn	☽ Ingress Dy Hr Mn	☽ Phases & Eclipses Dy Hr Mn	Astro Data
☽0S 1 9:39	♄ ♌R 5 0:44	1 14:08 ♃ □	♎ 1 14:31	2 4:15 ♄ □	♐ 2 7:13	2 12:07 ☾ 11♎45	1 January 1978
☽0N 13 22:55	☿ ♑ 13 20:07	3 19:43 ♃ △	♏ 3 20:35	4 5:43 ♄ △	♑ 4 8:50	9 4:00 ● 18♑32	Julian Day # 28490
♇R 19 0:47	☉ ♒ 20 10:04	5 22:59 ♄ □	♐ 5 23:03	6 2:47 ♂ ☍	♒ 6 9:04	16 3:03 ☽ 25♈38	SVP 5♓33'57"
☽0S 28 16:31	♀ ♒ 20 18:29	7 22:42 ♄ △	♑ 7 22:55	8 6:07 ♄ ☍	♓ 8 9:47	24 7:56 ○ 3♌59	GC 26♐31.9 ⚴ 27♏33.9
	♂ ♋R 26 1:59	9 4:00 ☉ ☌	♒ 9 22:05	10 6:20 ♃ □	♈ 10 12:56	31 23:51 ☾ 11♏46	Eris 13♈22.7 ⚵ 29♐38.7
☽0N 10 9:52		11 22:16 ♄ ☍	♓ 11 22:50	12 17:37 ♀ ⚹	♉ 12 19:50		⚷ 1♉09.2R ⚶ 15♏55.6
♅R 19 15:25	⚳ ♑ 2 22:23	13 23:57 ♃ □	♈ 14 3:05	15 0:52 ♄ □	♊ 15 6:24	7 14:54 ● 18♒29	☽ Mean ☊ 10♎31.7
♅⊻♇ 20 0:26	☿ ♒ 4 15:54	16 10:21 ♄ △	♉ 16 11:30	17 16:12 ☉ △	♋ 17 18:56	14 22:11 ☽ 25♉52	
♃D 20 1:24	♀ ♓ 13 16:07	18 21:36 ♄ □	♊ 18 23:06	19 17:14 ♂ ☌	♌ 20 7:10	23 1:26 ○ 4♍04	1 February 1978
☽0S 24 23:05	☉ ♓ 19 0:21	21 10:00 ♄ ⚹	♋ 21 11:50	22 11:11 ♄ ☌	♍ 22 17:39		Julian Day # 28521
♃⚹♄ 28 2:10	☿ ♓ 22 16:11	22 21:28 ♇ □	♌ 24 0:02	24 18:51 ♃ □	♎ 25 2:03		SVP 5♓33'53"
		26 8:30 ♄ ☌	♍ 26 10:56	27 1:47 ♄ ⚹	♏ 27 8:28		GC 26♐32.0 ⚴ 9♐09.0
		28 18:12 ♂ ⚹	♎ 28 20:08				Eris 13♈28.2 ⚵ 10♑39.7
		31 0:13 ♄ ⚹	♏ 31 3:04				⚷ 1♉19.7 ⚶ 29♏45.2
							☽ Mean ☊ 8♎53.2

March 1978 LONGITUDE

Day	Sid.Time	☉	0 hr ☽	Noon☽	True☊	☿	♀	♂	⚳	♃	♄	♅	♆	♇
1 W	22 35 45	10♓32 43	22♏28 04	29♏24 05	6♎06.7	12♓38.0	19♓47.6	22♋16.9	9♑17.3	26♊13.2	26♌04.2	16♏21.8	18♐13.0	16♎13.4
2 Th	22 39 42	11 32 55	6♐23 13	13♐25 24	6R 07.1	14 32.3	21 02.5	22D 16.6	9 36.7	26 15.2	25R 59.6	16R 21.2	18 13.6	16R 12.2
3 F	22 43 38	12 33 06	20 30 28	27 38 11	6 06.4	16 27.3	22 17.3	22 17.0	9 55.9	26 17.3	25 55.1	16 20.6	18 14.2	16 10.8
4 Sa	22 47 35	13 33 14	4♑48 16	12♑00 19	6 04.6	18 22.8	23 32.2	22 18.2	10 15.0	26 19.7	25 50.5	16 20.0	18 14.8	16 09.5
5 Su	22 51 31	14 33 22	19 13 51	26 28 19	6 02.0	20 18.8	24 47.0	22 20.0	10 33.9	26 22.2	25 46.1	16 19.2	18 15.3	16 08.2
6 M	22 55 28	15 33 27	3♒43 06	10♒57 30	5 59.1	22 15.1	26 01.8	22 22.6	10 52.6	26 24.9	25 41.6	16 18.5	18 15.8	16 06.8
7 Tu	22 59 25	16 33 31	18 10 49	25 22 20	5 56.3	24 11.5	27 16.6	22 25.9	11 11.3	26 27.8	25 37.2	16 17.7	18 16.3	16 05.4
8 W	23 03 21	17 33 33	2♓31 18	9♓37 06	5 54.2	26 07.9	28 31.3	22 29.9	11 29.7	26 30.9	25 32.9	16 16.8	18 16.7	16 04.0
9 Th	23 07 18	18 33 34	16 39 04	23 36 43	5D 52.9	28 03.8	29 46.1	22 34.6	11 48.1	26 34.2	25 28.6	16 15.9	18 17.1	16 02.6
10 F	23 11 14	19 33 32	0♈29 36	7♈17 24	5 52.5	29 59.2	1♈00.8	22 39.9	12 06.2	26 37.7	25 24.4	16 14.9	18 17.5	16 01.1
11 Sa	23 15 11	20 33 28	13 59 55	20 37 02	5 53.0	1♈53.6	2 15.5	22 45.9	12 24.2	26 41.3	25 20.2	16 13.9	18 17.8	15 59.7
12 Su	23 19 07	21 33 23	27 08 47	3♉35 18	5 54.0	3 46.7	3 30.1	22 52.5	12 42.1	26 45.2	25 16.1	16 12.8	18 18.1	15 58.2
13 M	23 23 04	22 33 15	9♉56 46	16 13 31	5 55.3	5 38.1	4 44.8	22 59.8	12 59.7	26 49.2	25 12.1	16 11.7	18 18.4	15 56.7
14 Tu	23 27 00	23 33 05	22 25 55	28 34 24	5 56.4	7 27.4	5 59.4	23 07.7	13 17.3	26 53.4	25 08.1	16 10.5	18 18.6	15 55.2
15 W	23 30 57	24 32 53	4♊39 28	10♊41 38	5 57.3	9 14.1	7 13.9	23 16.3	13 34.6	26 57.8	25 04.2	16 09.3	18 18.8	15 53.7
16 Th	23 34 53	25 32 38	16 41 27	22 39 31	5R 57.7	10 57.7	8 28.5	23 25.4	13 51.8	27 02.3	25 00.3	16 08.0	18 18.9	15 52.1
17 F	23 38 50	26 32 22	28 36 24	4♋32 43	5 57.6	12 37.9	9 43.0	23 35.1	14 08.8	27 07.0	24 56.5	16 06.7	18 19.1	15 50.6
18 Sa	23 42 47	27 32 03	10♋29 02	16 25 56	5 57.0	14 14.1	10 57.5	23 45.4	14 25.6	27 11.9	24 52.8	16 05.4	18 19.2	15 49.0
19 Su	23 46 43	28 31 42	22 23 58	28 23 39	5 56.2	15 45.7	12 12.0	23 56.2	14 42.3	27 17.0	24 49.2	16 04.0	18 19.2	15 47.4
20 M	23 50 40	29 31 18	4♌25 30	10♌29 57	5 55.4	17 12.5	13 26.4	24 07.6	14 58.8	27 22.2	24 45.6	16 02.5	18R 19.2	15 45.8
21 Tu	23 54 36	0♈30 53	16 37 24	22 48 14	5 54.6	18 33.8	14 40.9	24 19.5	15 15.0	27 27.6	24 42.2	16 01.1	18 19.2	15 44.2
22 W	23 58 33	1 30 25	29 02 45	5♍21 10	5 54.0	19 49.4	15 55.2	24 32.0	15 31.1	27 33.1	24 38.8	15 59.5	18 19.2	15 42.6
23 Th	0 02 29	2 29 55	11♍43 40	18 10 21	5 53.6	20 58.9	17 09.6	24 44.9	15 47.1	27 38.8	24 35.5	15 58.0	18 19.1	15 41.0
24 F	0 06 26	3 29 22	24 41 17	1♎16 25	5D 53.5	22 01.8	18 23.9	24 58.4	16 02.8	27 44.7	24 32.2	15 56.4	18 19.0	15 39.4
25 Sa	0 10 22	4 28 48	7♎55 39	14 38 52	5 53.5	22 58.0	19 38.2	25 12.3	16 18.3	27 50.7	24 29.1	15 54.7	18 18.9	15 37.7
26 Su	0 14 19	5 28 12	21 25 50	28 16 17	5R 53.5	23 47.1	20 52.5	25 26.7	16 33.7	27 56.9	24 26.0	15 53.0	18 18.7	15 36.1
27 M	0 18 16	6 27 34	5♏09 57	12♏06 30	5 53.5	24 29.1	22 06.7	25 41.6	16 48.8	28 03.3	24 23.0	15 51.3	18 18.5	15 34.4
28 Tu	0 22 12	7 26 54	19 05 34	26 06 48	5 53.4	25 03.6	23 20.9	25 57.0	17 03.8	28 09.8	24 20.1	15 49.5	18 18.3	15 32.8
29 W	0 26 09	8 26 13	3♐09 50	10♐14 19	5 53.2	25 30.8	24 35.1	26 12.8	17 18.5	28 16.4	24 17.3	15 47.7	18 18.0	15 31.1
30 Th	0 30 05	9 25 29	17 19 52	24 26 08	5 53.0	25 50.4	25 49.2	26 29.0	17 33.0	28 23.2	24 14.6	15 45.9	18 17.7	15 29.5
31 F	0 34 02	10 24 44	1♑32 48	8♑39 33	5D 52.8	26 02.7	27 03.4	26 45.7	17 47.4	28 30.1	24 12.0	15 44.0	18 17.4	15 27.8

April 1978 LONGITUDE

Day	Sid.Time	☉	0 hr ☽	Noon☽	True☊	☿	♀	♂	⚳	♃	♄	♅	♆	♇
1 Sa	0 37 58	11♈23 58	15♑46 03	22♑52 01	5♎52.9	26♈07.5	28♈17.5	27♋02.8	18♑01.5	28♊37.2	24♌09.5	15♏42.1	18♐17.0	15♎26.1
2 Su	0 41 55	12 23 09	29 57 10	7♒01 12	5 53.3	26R 05.3	29 31.5	27 20.2	18 15.4	28 44.4	24R 07.0	15R 40.1	18R 16.6	15R 24.4
3 M	0 45 51	13 22 19	14♒03 50	21 04 48	5 53.9	25 56.1	0♉45.6	27 38.1	18 29.0	28 51.8	24 04.7	15 38.1	18 16.2	15 22.8
4 Tu	0 49 48	14 21 27	28 03 48	5♓00 34	5 54.7	25 40.4	1 59.6	27 56.4	18 42.5	28 59.3	24 02.5	15 36.1	18 15.7	15 21.1
5 W	0 53 45	15 20 33	11♓54 49	18 46 17	5 55.3	25 18.6	3 13.6	28 15.1	18 55.7	29 07.0	24 00.3	15 34.1	18 15.2	15 19.4
6 Th	0 57 41	16 19 37	25 34 42	2♈19 50	5R 55.7	24 51.3	4 27.5	28 34.2	19 08.7	29 14.7	23 58.3	15 32.0	18 14.7	15 17.7
7 F	1 01 38	17 18 39	9♈01 29	15 39 26	5 55.5	24 19.0	5 41.4	28 53.6	19 21.4	29 22.7	23 56.3	15 29.9	18 14.1	15 16.0
8 Sa	1 05 34	18 17 39	22 13 34	28 43 48	5 54.8	23 42.4	6 55.3	29 13.4	19 33.9	29 30.7	23 54.5	15 27.8	18 13.5	15 14.3
9 Su	1 09 31	19 16 37	5♉10 04	11♉32 23	5 53.3	23 02.4	8 09.2	29 33.6	19 46.2	29 38.9	23 52.7	15 25.6	18 12.9	15 12.7
10 M	1 13 27	20 15 33	17 50 51	24 05 34	5 51.4	22 19.8	9 23.0	29 54.1	19 58.2	29 47.2	23 51.1	15 23.4	18 12.3	15 11.0
11 Tu	1 17 24	21 14 27	0♊16 44	6♊24 38	5 49.1	21 35.3	10 36.8	0♌15.0	20 10.0	29 55.7	23 49.6	15 21.2	18 11.6	15 09.3
12 W	1 21 20	22 13 18	12 29 33	18 31 52	5 46.8	20 50.0	11 50.6	0 36.1	20 21.5	0♋04.2	23 48.1	15 18.9	18 10.9	15 07.6
13 Th	1 25 17	23 12 08	24 31 59	0♋30 23	5 44.9	20 04.6	13 04.3	0 57.6	20 32.7	0 12.9	23 46.8	15 16.7	18 10.2	15 06.0
14 F	1 29 13	24 10 55	6♋27 32	12 23 59	5 43.6	19 20.0	14 18.0	1 19.5	20 43.7	0 21.7	23 45.6	15 14.4	18 09.4	15 04.3
15 Sa	1 33 10	25 09 40	18 20 18	24 17 02	5D 43.1	18 37.0	15 31.6	1 41.6	20 54.5	0 30.7	23 44.5	15 12.1	18 08.6	15 02.7
16 Su	1 37 07	26 08 23	0♌14 48	6♌14 12	5 43.5	17 56.4	16 45.3	2 04.1	21 05.0	0 39.7	23 43.5	15 09.7	18 07.8	15 01.0
17 M	1 41 03	27 07 04	12 15 47	18 20 10	5 44.6	17 18.7	17 58.8	2 26.8	21 15.2	0 48.9	23 42.5	15 07.4	18 07.0	14 59.4
18 Tu	1 45 00	28 05 42	24 27 53	0♍39 29	5 46.1	16 44.5	19 12.4	2 49.8	21 25.1	0 58.1	23 41.7	15 05.0	18 06.1	14 57.7
19 W	1 48 56	29 04 18	6♍55 25	13 16 07	5 47.7	16 14.3	20 25.9	3 13.1	21 34.8	1 07.5	23 41.0	15 02.6	18 05.2	14 56.1
20 Th	1 52 53	0♉02 52	19 41 57	26 13 10	5R 48.8	15 48.4	21 39.3	3 36.7	21 44.1	1 17.0	23 40.5	15 00.2	18 04.3	14 54.5
21 F	1 56 49	1 01 24	2♎49 57	9♎32 23	5 49.0	15 27.1	22 52.8	4 00.5	21 53.2	1 26.6	23 40.0	14 57.8	18 03.3	14 52.9
22 Sa	2 00 46	1 59 54	16 20 23	23 13 48	5 48.0	15 10.7	24 06.2	4 24.6	22 02.1	1 36.3	23 39.6	14 55.3	18 02.3	14 51.3
23 Su	2 04 42	2 58 22	0♏12 19	7♏15 32	5 45.8	14 59.3	25 19.5	4 49.0	22 10.6	1 46.1	23 39.3	14 52.9	18 01.3	14 49.7
24 M	2 08 39	3 56 48	14 22 54	21 33 46	5 42.4	14D 52.8	26 32.8	5 13.6	22 18.8	1 56.1	23 39.2	14 50.4	18 00.3	14 48.1
25 Tu	2 12 36	4 55 12	28 47 26	6♐03 07	5 38.3	14 51.4	27 46.1	5 38.4	22 26.8	2 06.1	23D 39.1	14 47.9	17 59.2	14 46.6
26 W	2 16 32	5 53 35	13♐20 00	20 37 18	5 34.1	14 55.0	28 59.3	6 03.5	22 34.4	2 16.2	23 39.2	14 45.4	17 58.2	14 45.0
27 Th	2 20 29	6 51 56	27 54 15	5♑10 08	5 30.4	15 03.4	0♊12.5	6 28.8	22 41.8	2 26.4	23 39.3	14 42.9	17 57.1	14 43.5
28 F	2 24 25	7 50 16	12♑24 19	19 36 16	5 27.8	15 16.7	1 25.7	6 54.4	22 48.8	2 36.7	23 39.6	14 40.4	17 55.9	14 42.0
29 Sa	2 28 22	8 48 34	26 45 32	3♒51 47	5D 26.6	15 34.6	2 38.8	7 20.2	22 55.5	2 47.1	23 40.0	14 37.9	17 54.8	14 40.5
30 Su	2 32 18	9 46 51	10♒54 47	17 54 21	5 26.7	15 57.1	3 51.9	7 46.2	23 01.9	2 57.6	23 40.4	14 35.4	17 53.6	14 39.0

Astro Data	Dy Hr Mn
♂ D	2 9:56
☽ 0N	9 20:22
☿ 0N	10 22:48
♀ 0N	11 23:44
♆ R	20 18:47
☉ 0N	20 23:34
☽ 0S	24 6:47
☿ R	1 16:18
☽ 0N	6 5:00
♃⚼♅	13 20:07
☽ 0S	20 16:03
☿ D	25 6:47
♄ D	25 12:16
♅⚺♇	26 22:16

Planet Ingress		Dy Hr Mn
♀	♈	9 16:29
☿	♈	10 12:10
☉	♈	20 23:34
♀	♉	2 21:14
♂	♌	10 18:50
♃	♋	12 0:12
☉	♉	20 10:50
♀	♊	27 7:53

Last Aspect Dy Hr Mn			☽ Ingress	Dy Hr Mn
1 6:17	♄	□	♐	1 13:02
3 9:44	♃	☍	♑	3 15:58
5 8:56	♀	⚹	♒	5 17:51
7 13:50	♃	△	♓	7 19:45
9 21:01	☿	☌	♈	9 23:08
11 23:13	♃	⚹	♉	12 5:18
14 5:18	♄	□	♊	14 14:48
16 20:53	♃	☌	♋	17 2:49
19 12:17	☉	△	♌	19 15:12
21 21:02	♃	⚹	♍	22 1:49
24 5:32	♃	□	♎	24 9:41
26 11:26	♃	△	♏	26 15:01
28 11:43	♂	△	♐	28 18:37
30 18:43	♃	☍	♑	30 21:23

Last Aspect Dy Hr Mn			☽ Ingress	Dy Hr Mn
1 22:04	♀	□	♒	2 0:05
4 1:30	♃	△	♓	4 3:20
6 6:27	♃	□	♈	6 7:51
8 13:28	♃	⚹	♉	8 14:21
10 11:32	♄	□	♊	10 23:27
12 22:31	♄	⚹	♋	13 10:59
15 13:56	☉	□	♌	15 23:30
18 6:38	☉	△	♍	18 10:44
20 2:45	♀	△	♎	20 18:53
22 12:45	♄	⚹	♏	22 23:39
24 21:03	♀	☍	♐	25 2:00
26 17:00	♄	△	♑	27 3:27
28 4:39	☿	□	♒	29 5:28

☽ Phases & Eclipses Dy Hr Mn	
2 8:34	☾ 11♐24
9 2:36	● 18♓10
16 18:21	☽ 25♊48
24 16:20	○ 3♎40
24 16:22	T 1.451
31 15:11	☾ 10♑33
7 15:15	● 17♈27
7 15:02:58	P 0.788
15 13:56	☽ 25♋14
23 4:11	○ 2♏39
29 21:02	☾ 9♒11

Astro Data

1 March 1978
Julian Day # 28549
SVP 5♓33'50"
GC 26♐32.1 ⚴ 17♐33.7
Eris 13♈41.2 ⚵ 20♑03.8
⚷ 2♉14.0 ⚶ 10♐20.6
☽ Mean ☊ 7♎24.2

1 April 1978
Julian Day # 28580
SVP 5♓33'47"
GC 26♐32.1 ⚴ 23♐00.0
Eris 14♈00.8 ⚵ 29♑11.3
⚷ 3♉50.5 ⚶ 18♐20.9
☽ Mean ☊ 5♎45.7

LONGITUDE

May 1978

Day	Sid.Time	☉	0 hr ☽	Noon☽	True☊	☿	♀	♂	⚳	♃	♄	♅	♆	♇
1 M	2 36 15	10♉45 06	24♒50 26	1♓43 00	5♎27.8	16♈23.9	5♊05.0	8♌12.4	23♑08.0	3♋08.2	23♌41.0	14♏32.9	17♐52.4	14♎37.5
2 Tu	2 40 11	11 43 19	8♓32 05	15 17 44	5 29.3	16 54.9	6 18.0	8 38.9	23 13.8	3 18.9	23 41.7	14R30.3	17R51.2	14R36.0
3 W	2 44 08	12 41 32	22 00 02	28 39 05	5R30.4	17 30.0	7 31.0	9 05.5	23 19.3	3 29.7	23 42.5	14 27.8	17 50.0	14 34.6
4 Th	2 48 05	13 39 42	5♈14 56	11♈47 41	5 30.4	18 09.0	8 44.0	9 32.4	23 24.4	3 40.5	23 43.4	14 25.3	17 48.7	14 33.2
5 F	2 52 01	14 37 51	18 17 24	24 44 08	5 28.8	18 51.7	9 56.9	9 59.4	23 29.2	3 51.5	23 44.4	14 22.7	17 47.5	14 31.8
6 Sa	2 55 58	15 35 59	1♉07 55	7♉28 49	5 25.2	19 38.0	11 09.7	10 26.7	23 33.6	4 02.5	23 45.5	14 20.2	17 46.2	14 30.4
7 Su	2 59 54	16 34 05	13 46 51	20 02 05	5 19.7	20 27.7	12 22.6	10 54.2	23 37.7	4 13.6	23 46.8	14 17.6	17 44.8	14 29.0
8 M	3 03 51	17 32 09	26 14 34	2♊24 23	5 12.6	21 20.8	13 35.4	11 21.8	23 41.5	4 24.8	23 48.1	14 15.1	17 43.5	14 27.7
9 Tu	3 07 47	18 30 12	8♊31 39	14 36 30	5 04.7	22 17.1	14 48.1	11 49.7	23 44.9	4 36.1	23 49.5	14 12.6	17 42.2	14 26.3
10 W	3 11 44	19 28 13	20 39 07	26 39 45	4 56.6	23 16.4	16 00.9	12 17.7	23 48.0	4 47.4	23 51.0	14 10.1	17 40.8	14 25.0
11 Th	3 15 40	20 26 12	2♋38 39	8♋36 08	4 49.3	24 18.7	17 13.5	12 46.0	23 50.7	4 58.8	23 52.7	14 07.5	17 39.4	14 23.7
12 F	3 19 37	21 24 09	14 32 36	20 28 26	4 43.2	25 23.9	18 26.2	13 14.4	23 53.1	5 10.3	23 54.4	14 05.0	17 38.0	14 22.5
13 Sa	3 23 34	22 22 05	26 24 08	2♌20 10	4 39.1	26 31.9	19 38.7	13 42.9	23 55.1	5 21.9	23 56.3	14 02.5	17 36.6	14 21.2
14 Su	3 27 30	23 19 59	8♌17 06	14 15 30	4D36.9	27 42.6	20 51.3	14 11.7	23 56.8	5 33.5	23 58.2	14 00.0	17 35.2	14 20.0
15 M	3 31 27	24 17 51	20 15 59	26 19 09	4 36.4	28 55.9	22 03.8	14 40.6	23 58.1	5 45.2	24 00.3	13 57.5	17 33.7	14 18.8
16 Tu	3 35 23	25 15 41	2♍25 38	8♍36 03	4 37.1	0♉11.8	23 16.2	15 09.7	23 59.1	5 57.0	24 02.4	13 55.1	17 32.3	14 17.6
17 W	3 39 20	26 13 30	14 51 02	21 11 08	4 38.2	1 30.2	24 28.6	15 38.9	23 59.7	6 08.9	24 04.7	13 52.6	17 30.8	14 16.5
18 Th	3 43 16	27 11 17	27 36 53	4♎08 44	4R38.8	2 51.0	25 41.0	16 08.3	23R59.9	6 20.8	24 07.0	13 50.1	17 29.3	14 15.4
19 F	3 47 13	28 09 02	10♎47 04	17 32 07	4 38.1	4 14.3	26 53.3	16 37.8	23 59.8	6 32.7	24 09.4	13 47.7	17 27.8	14 14.3
20 Sa	3 51 09	29 06 46	24 24 00	1♏22 41	4 35.3	5 40.0	28 05.5	17 07.5	23 59.3	6 44.8	24 12.0	13 45.3	17 26.3	14 13.2
21 Su	3 55 06	0♊04 28	8♏27 55	15 39 18	4 30.3	7 08.0	29 17.7	17 37.4	23 58.5	6 56.8	24 14.6	13 42.9	17 24.8	14 12.1
22 M	3 59 03	1 02 09	22 56 14	0♐17 56	4 23.3	8 38.5	0♋29.9	18 07.3	23 57.3	7 09.0	24 17.4	13 40.5	17 23.2	14 11.1
23 Tu	4 02 59	1 59 49	7♐43 27	15 11 42	4 14.9	10 11.2	1 42.0	18 37.5	23 55.7	7 21.2	24 20.2	13 38.1	17 21.7	14 10.1
24 W	4 06 56	2 57 27	22 41 31	0♑11 44	4 06.2	11 46.3	2 54.0	19 07.7	23 53.8	7 33.5	24 23.1	13 35.8	17 20.2	14 09.1
25 Th	4 10 52	3 55 05	7♑41 08	15 08 39	3 58.3	13 23.7	4 06.1	19 38.1	23 51.5	7 45.8	24 26.1	13 33.4	17 18.6	14 08.2
26 F	4 14 49	4 52 41	22 33 15	29 54 07	3 52.1	15 03.4	5 18.0	20 08.7	23 48.8	7 58.1	24 29.3	13 31.1	17 17.0	14 07.3
27 Sa	4 18 45	5 50 17	7♒10 34	14♒22 06	3 48.1	16 45.4	6 29.9	20 39.4	23 45.7	8 10.6	24 32.5	13 28.9	17 15.5	14 06.4
28 Su	4 22 42	6 47 51	21 28 23	28 29 16	3D46.2	18 29.7	7 41.8	21 10.2	23 42.3	8 23.0	24 35.8	13 26.6	17 13.9	14 05.5
29 M	4 26 38	7 45 25	5♓24 45	12♓14 54	3 46.0	20 16.3	8 53.6	21 41.1	23 38.6	8 35.6	24 39.1	13 24.3	17 12.3	14 04.7
30 Tu	4 30 35	8 42 58	18 59 55	25 40 04	3R46.5	22 05.1	10 05.3	22 12.2	23 34.4	8 48.1	24 42.6	13 22.1	17 10.7	14 03.9
31 W	4 34 32	9 40 29	2♈15 39	8♈47 01	3 46.6	23 56.3	11 17.1	22 43.4	23 29.9	9 00.8	24 46.2	13 19.9	17 09.1	14 03.1

LONGITUDE

June 1978

Day	Sid.Time	☉	0 hr ☽	Noon☽	True☊	☿	♀	♂	⚳	♃	♄	♅	♆	♇
1 Th	4 38 28	10♊38 01	15♈14 28	21♈38 22	3♎45.2	25♉49.7	12♋28.7	23♌14.7	23♑25.1	9♋13.4	24♌49.8	13♏17.8	17♐07.5	14♎02.4
2 F	4 42 25	11 35 31	27 59 00	4♉16 39	3R41.5	27 45.3	13 40.3	23 46.1	23R19.9	9 26.1	24 53.6	13R15.6	17R05.9	14R01.7
3 Sa	4 46 21	12 33 01	10♉31 36	16 44 02	3 35.0	29 43.0	14 51.9	24 17.7	23 14.3	9 38.9	24 57.4	13 13.5	17 04.2	14 01.0
4 Su	4 50 18	13 30 29	22 54 11	29 02 12	3 25.9	1♊42.8	16 03.4	24 49.4	23 08.3	9 51.7	25 01.3	13 11.4	17 02.6	14 00.3
5 M	4 54 14	14 27 57	5♊08 13	11♊12 24	3 14.6	3 44.6	17 14.8	25 21.3	23 02.1	10 04.5	25 05.3	13 09.4	17 01.0	13 59.7
6 Tu	4 58 11	15 25 24	17 14 52	23 15 44	3 01.9	5 48.4	18 26.2	25 53.2	22 55.4	10 17.4	25 09.4	13 07.4	16 59.4	13 59.1
7 W	5 02 07	16 22 51	29 15 09	5♋13 17	2 48.9	7 53.8	19 37.6	26 25.3	22 48.5	10 30.3	25 13.6	13 05.4	16 57.8	13 58.5
8 Th	5 06 04	17 20 16	11♋10 19	17 06 29	2 36.7	10 00.9	20 48.8	26 57.4	22 41.2	10 43.3	25 17.9	13 03.4	16 56.1	13 58.0
9 F	5 10 01	18 17 40	23 02 01	28 57 14	2 26.3	12 09.4	22 00.1	27 29.7	22 33.5	10 56.3	25 22.2	13 01.5	16 54.5	13 57.5
10 Sa	5 13 57	19 15 03	4♌52 29	10♌48 10	2 18.3	14 19.1	23 11.2	28 02.1	22 25.6	11 09.3	25 26.6	12 59.6	16 52.9	13 57.0
11 Su	5 17 54	20 12 25	16 44 43	22 42 37	2 12.9	16 29.7	24 22.3	28 34.6	22 17.3	11 22.4	25 31.1	12 57.7	16 51.3	13 56.6
12 M	5 21 50	21 09 47	28 42 25	4♍44 41	2 10.1	18 41.1	25 33.3	29 07.3	22 08.7	11 35.5	25 35.7	12 55.9	16 49.6	13 56.2
13 Tu	5 25 47	22 07 07	10♍50 01	16 59 03	2D09.1	20 52.9	26 44.3	29 40.0	21 59.8	11 48.6	25 40.4	12 54.1	16 48.0	13 55.8
14 W	5 29 43	23 04 26	23 12 23	29 30 41	2R09.1	23 04.9	27 55.2	0♍12.8	21 50.6	12 01.7	25 45.1	12 52.4	16 46.4	13 55.5
15 Th	5 33 40	24 01 44	5♎54 34	12♎24 34	2 08.9	25 16.9	29 06.0	0 45.8	21 41.2	12 14.9	25 49.9	12 50.7	16 44.8	13 55.2
16 F	5 37 36	24 59 02	19 01 12	25 44 53	2 07.4	27 28.4	0♌16.8	1 18.8	21 31.4	12 28.1	25 54.8	12 49.0	16 43.2	13 54.9
17 Sa	5 41 33	25 56 19	2♏35 55	9♏34 25	2 03.7	29 39.3	1 27.4	1 51.9	21 21.4	12 41.3	25 59.7	12 47.4	16 41.6	13 54.7
18 Su	5 45 30	26 53 34	16 40 20	23 53 25	1 57.4	1♋49.3	2 38.0	2 25.2	21 11.1	12 54.6	26 04.8	12 45.8	16 40.0	13 54.4
19 M	5 49 26	27 50 50	1♐13 11	8♐38 55	1 48.8	3 58.3	3 48.6	2 58.5	21 00.6	13 07.9	26 09.9	12 44.3	16 38.4	13 54.3
20 Tu	5 53 23	28 48 04	16 09 41	23 44 21	1 38.6	6 05.9	4 59.0	3 31.9	20 49.8	13 21.2	26 15.0	12 42.8	16 36.8	13 54.1
21 W	5 57 19	29 45 19	1♑21 36	9♑00 02	1 27.8	8 12.1	6 09.4	4 05.4	20 38.8	13 34.5	26 20.3	12 41.3	16 35.3	13 54.0
22 Th	6 01 16	0♋42 33	16 38 15	24 14 49	1 17.8	10 16.6	7 19.7	4 39.0	20 27.5	13 47.8	26 25.6	12 39.9	16 33.7	13 53.9
23 F	6 05 12	1 39 46	1♒48 27	9♒17 59	1 09.6	12 19.4	8 29.9	5 12.7	20 16.0	14 01.2	26 31.0	12 38.5	16 32.2	13D53.9
24 Sa	6 09 09	2 36 59	16 42 29	24 01 11	1 04.0	14 20.4	9 40.1	5 46.5	20 04.4	14 14.5	26 36.4	12 37.2	16 30.6	13 53.9
25 Su	6 13 05	3 34 13	1♓13 36	8♓19 24	1 01.0	16 19.4	10 50.1	6 20.4	19 52.5	14 27.9	26 41.9	12 35.9	16 29.1	13 53.9
26 M	6 17 02	4 31 26	15 18 30	22 10 57	0 59.9	18 16.5	12 00.1	6 54.4	19 40.5	14 41.3	26 47.5	12 34.6	16 27.5	13 54.0
27 Tu	6 20 59	5 28 39	28 56 58	5♈36 50	0 59.8	20 11.5	13 10.0	7 28.5	19 28.2	14 54.8	26 53.1	12 33.4	16 26.0	13 54.1
28 W	6 24 55	6 25 52	12♈10 59	18 39 50	0 59.4	22 04.4	14 19.8	8 02.6	19 15.8	15 08.2	26 58.8	12 32.2	16 24.5	13 54.2
29 Th	6 28 52	7 23 05	25 03 51	1♉23 33	0 57.8	23 55.3	15 29.6	8 36.9	19 03.3	15 21.6	27 04.6	12 31.1	16 23.0	13 54.3
30 F	6 32 48	8 20 19	7♉39 22	13 51 47	0 53.8	25 44.0	16 39.2	9 11.2	18 50.6	15 35.1	27 10.4	12 30.1	16 21.5	13 54.5

Astro Data

	Dy Hr Mn
☽ 0N	3 11:48
☽ 0S	18 2:10
⚳ R	18 15:56
☽ 0N	30 18:06
♃∠♄	5 14:14
☽ 0S	14 11:53
♃△♅	17 21:49
♃□♇	22 22:59
♇ D	24 7:43
☽ 0N	27 1:26

Planet Ingress

	Dy Hr Mn
☿ ♉	16 8:20
☉ ♊	21 10:08
♀ ♋	22 2:03
☿ ♊	3 15:26
♂ ♍	14 2:38
♀ ♌	16 6:19
☿ ♋	17 15:49
☉ ♋	21 18:10

Last Aspect / ☽ Ingress

Last Aspect Dy Hr Mn		☽ Ingress Dy Hr Mn
30 21:59 ♄ ☍	♓	1 9:00
2 16:34 ♆ □	♈	3 14:27
5 10:08 ♄ △	♉	5 21:52
7 19:14 ♄ □	♊	8 7:18
10 6:22 ♄ ⚹	♋	10 18:41
12 23:01 ☿ □	♌	13 7:17
15 17:44 ☿ △	♍	15 19:15
17 22:11 ☉ △	♎	18 4:24
20 5:50 ♀ △	♏	20 9:39
22 2:11 ♄ □	♐	22 11:31
24 2:41 ♄ △	♑	24 11:41
25 10:23 ♇ □	♒	26 12:10
28 5:18 ♄ ☍	♓	28 14:36
30 4:31 ☿ ⚹	♈	30 19:52

Last Aspect / ☽ Ingress

Last Aspect Dy Hr Mn		☽ Ingress Dy Hr Mn
1 18:03 ♄ △	♉	2 3:50
4 4:06 ♄ □	♊	4 13:53
6 17:30 ♂ ⚹	♋	7 1:30
8 20:20 ♀ ☌	♌	9 14:07
12 0:18 ♂ ☌	♍	12 2:35
14 8:41 ♀ ⚹	♎	14 12:55
16 15:37 ☿ △	♏	16 19:28
18 15:37 ♄ □	♐	18 22:01
20 20:30 ☉ ☍	♑	20 21:52
21 19:42 ♇ □	♒	22 21:07
24 16:19 ♄ ☍	♓	24 21:57
26 4:02 ☿ △	♈	27 1:53
29 3:44 ♄ △	♉	29 9:21

☽ Phases & Eclipses

Dy Hr Mn	
7 4:47	● 16♉17
15 7:39	☽ 24♌07
22 13:17	○ 1♐05
29 3:30	☾ 7♓25
5 19:01	● 14♊45
13 22:44	☽ 22♍33
20 20:30	○ 29♐08
27 11:44	☾ 5♈28

Astro Data

1 May 1978
Julian Day # 28610
SVP 5♓33'44"
GC 26♐32.2 ⚴ 22♐17.0R
Eris 14♈20.5 ⚵ 5♒45.8
⚷ 5♉41.1 ⚶ 20♐05.5R
☽ Mean ☊ 4♎10.4

1 June 1978
Julian Day # 28641
SVP 5♓33'40"
GC 26♐32.3 ⚴ 14♐58.3R
Eris 14♈36.5 ⚵ 8♒43.3
⚷ 7♉31.8 ⚶ 14♐51.1R
☽ Mean ☊ 2♎31.9

July 1978 LONGITUDE

Day	Sid.Time	☉	0 hr ☽	Noon ☽	True ☊	☿	♀	♂	⚳	♃	♄	♅	♆	♇
1 Sa	6 36 45	9♋17 32	20♉01 14	26♉08 05	0♎47.1	27♋30.6	17♌48.8	9♍45.7	18♑37.9	15♋48.6	27♌16.3	12♏29.0	16♐20.1	13♎54.8
2 Su	6 40 41	10 14 46	2♊12 43	8♊15 27	0R 37.6	29 15.1	18 58.3	10 20.2	18R 25.0	16 02.1	27 22.3	12R 28.1	16R 18.6	13 55.0
3 M	6 44 38	11 12 00	14 16 32	20 16 15	0 25.9	0♌57.5	20 07.7	10 54.8	18 12.0	16 15.6	27 28.3	12 27.1	16 17.2	13 55.3
4 Tu	6 48 34	12 09 14	26 14 49	2♋12 24	0 12.8	2 37.7	21 17.0	11 29.5	17 58.9	16 29.1	27 34.3	12 26.2	16 15.7	13 55.6
5 W	6 52 31	13 06 27	8♋09 13	14 05 25	29♍59.3	4 15.8	22 26.2	12 04.3	17 45.8	16 42.6	27 40.4	12 25.4	16 14.3	13 56.0
6 Th	6 56 28	14 03 41	20 01 12	25 56 43	29 46.5	5 51.7	23 35.3	12 39.2	17 32.6	16 56.1	27 46.6	12 24.6	16 12.9	13 56.4
7 F	7 00 24	15 00 55	1♌52 11	7♌47 50	29 35.5	7 25.5	24 44.3	13 14.1	17 19.4	17 09.6	27 52.8	12 23.9	16 11.6	13 56.8
8 Sa	7 04 21	15 58 09	13 43 54	19 40 41	29 27.0	8 57.1	25 53.3	13 49.2	17 06.2	17 23.1	27 59.1	12 23.2	16 10.2	13 57.3
9 Su	7 08 17	16 55 22	25 38 31	1♍37 46	29 21.3	10 26.5	27 02.1	14 24.3	16 52.9	17 36.6	28 05.5	12 22.6	16 08.9	13 57.8
10 M	7 12 14	17 52 36	7♍38 51	13 42 13	29 18.1	11 53.8	28 10.8	14 59.5	16 39.7	17 50.1	28 11.8	12 22.0	16 07.5	13 58.3
11 Tu	7 16 10	18 49 49	19 48 22	25 57 50	29D 17.1	13 18.8	29 19.4	15 34.8	16 26.5	18 03.6	28 18.3	12 21.5	16 06.2	13 58.8
12 W	7 20 07	19 47 03	2♎11 10	8♎28 56	29R 17.2	14 41.5	0♍27.9	16 10.1	16 13.3	18 17.1	28 24.7	12 21.0	16 04.9	13 59.4
13 Th	7 24 03	20 44 16	14 51 42	21 20 02	29 17.5	16 02.0	1 36.2	16 45.6	16 00.2	18 30.6	28 31.3	12 20.5	16 03.7	14 00.1
14 F	7 28 00	21 41 30	27 54 28	4♏35 25	29 16.8	17 20.1	2 44.5	17 21.1	15 47.1	18 44.1	28 37.8	12 20.2	16 02.4	14 00.7
15 Sa	7 31 57	22 38 44	11♏23 17	18 18 19	29 14.3	18 35.8	3 52.6	17 56.7	15 34.2	18 57.6	28 44.5	12 19.8	16 01.2	14 01.4
16 Su	7 35 53	23 35 57	25 20 36	2♐30 04	29 09.6	19 49.1	5 00.6	18 32.4	15 21.3	19 11.1	28 51.1	12 19.6	16 00.0	14 02.1
17 M	7 39 50	24 33 11	9♐46 26	17 09 10	29 02.7	20 59.9	6 08.5	19 08.2	15 08.5	19 24.5	28 57.8	12 19.3	15 58.8	14 02.9
18 Tu	7 43 46	25 30 25	24 37 34	2♑10 38	28 54.2	22 08.1	7 16.2	19 44.0	14 55.9	19 38.0	29 04.6	12 19.2	15 57.6	14 03.7
19 W	7 47 43	26 27 39	9♑47 14	17 26 03	28 45.1	23 13.6	8 23.8	20 19.9	14 43.3	19 51.5	29 11.4	12 19.0	15 56.5	14 04.5
20 Th	7 51 39	27 24 54	25 05 41	2♒44 42	28 36.6	24 16.4	9 31.3	20 55.9	14 31.0	20 04.9	29 18.2	12D 19.0	15 55.4	14 05.4
21 F	7 55 36	28 22 09	10♒21 41	17 55 20	28 29.7	25 16.3	10 38.6	21 31.9	14 18.7	20 18.3	29 25.1	12 18.9	15 54.3	14 06.3
22 Sa	7 59 33	29 19 25	25 24 31	2♓48 15	28 25.1	26 13.3	11 45.8	22 08.0	14 06.7	20 31.7	29 32.0	12 19.0	15 53.2	14 07.2
23 Su	8 03 29	0♌16 42	10♓05 48	17 16 40	28D 22.7	27 07.2	12 52.9	22 44.2	13 54.8	20 45.1	29 38.9	12 19.0	15 52.1	14 08.1
24 M	8 07 26	1 13 59	24 20 30	1♈17 14	28 22.2	27 57.9	13 59.8	23 20.5	13 43.1	20 58.5	29 45.9	12 19.2	15 51.1	14 09.1
25 Tu	8 11 22	2 11 17	8♈06 55	14 49 46	28 22.9	28 45.3	15 06.5	23 56.9	13 31.6	21 11.9	29 52.9	12 19.4	15 50.1	14 10.1
26 W	8 15 19	3 08 36	21 26 06	27 56 20	28R 23.7	29 29.2	16 13.1	24 33.3	13 20.4	21 25.2	29 60.0	12 19.6	15 49.1	14 11.1
27 Th	8 19 15	4 05 57	4♉20 58	10♉40 31	28 23.5	0♍09.4	17 19.6	25 09.8	13 09.3	21 38.6	0♍07.1	12 19.9	15 48.2	14 12.2
28 F	8 23 12	5 03 18	16 55 30	23 06 29	28 21.8	0 45.9	18 25.9	25 46.3	12 58.5	21 51.9	0 14.2	12 20.2	15 47.2	14 13.3
29 Sa	8 27 08	6 00 40	29 13 59	5♊18 31	28 18.0	1 18.4	19 32.0	26 23.0	12 47.9	22 05.2	0 21.3	12 20.6	15 46.3	14 14.4
30 Su	8 31 05	6 58 03	11♊20 36	17 20 40	28 12.0	1 46.8	20 38.0	26 59.7	12 37.6	22 18.4	0 28.5	12 21.1	15 45.5	14 15.6
31 M	8 35 01	7 55 27	23 19 08	29 16 24	28 04.3	2 10.8	21 43.8	27 36.5	12 27.5	22 31.7	0 35.7	12 21.6	15 44.6	14 16.8

August 1978 LONGITUDE

Day	Sid.Time	☉	0 hr ☽	Noon ☽	True ☊	☿	♀	♂	⚳	♃	♄	♅	♆	♇
1 Tu	8 38 58	8♌52 53	5♋12 48	11♋08 40	27♍55.4	2♍30.3	22♍49.4	28♍13.4	12♑17.7	22♋44.9	0♍43.0	12♏22.1	15♐43.8	14♎18.0
2 W	8 42 55	9 50 19	17 04 15	22 59 50	27R 46.2	2 45.2	23 54.9	28 50.3	12R 08.2	22 58.1	0 50.3	12 22.7	15R 43.0	14 19.3
3 Th	8 46 51	10 47 46	28 55 39	4♌51 54	27 37.5	2 55.1	25 00.2	29 27.4	11 59.0	23 11.2	0 57.5	12 23.4	15 42.2	14 20.6
4 F	8 50 48	11 45 14	10♌48 47	16 46 31	27 30.0	3R 00.1	26 05.3	0♎04.5	11 50.1	23 24.4	1 04.9	12 24.1	15 41.5	14 21.9
5 Sa	8 54 44	12 42 43	22 45 19	28 45 22	27 24.5	2 59.9	27 10.2	0 41.6	11 41.5	23 37.5	1 12.2	12 24.9	15 40.8	14 23.2
6 Su	8 58 41	13 40 13	4♍46 56	10♍50 15	27 21.0	2 54.4	28 14.9	1 18.9	11 33.1	23 50.6	1 19.6	12 25.7	15 40.1	14 24.6
7 M	9 02 37	14 37 43	16 55 37	23 03 18	27D 19.5	2 43.7	29 19.4	1 56.2	11 25.1	24 03.6	1 27.0	12 26.5	15 39.4	14 26.0
8 Tu	9 06 34	15 35 15	29 13 41	5♎27 06	27 19.7	2 27.5	0♎23.7	2 33.6	11 17.5	24 16.6	1 34.4	12 27.4	15 38.8	14 27.4
9 W	9 10 30	16 32 47	11♎43 57	18 04 38	27 20.9	2 06.1	1 27.8	3 11.0	11 10.1	24 29.6	1 41.8	12 28.4	15 38.2	14 28.8
10 Th	9 14 27	17 30 21	24 29 34	0♏59 09	27 22.4	1 39.5	2 31.6	3 48.5	11 03.1	24 42.5	1 49.2	12 29.4	15 37.6	14 30.3
11 F	9 18 24	18 27 55	7♏33 48	14 13 52	27R 23.3	1 08.0	3 35.3	4 26.1	10 56.5	24 55.4	1 56.7	12 30.5	15 37.1	14 31.8
12 Sa	9 22 20	19 25 30	20 59 39	27 51 24	27 23.0	0 31.8	4 38.7	5 03.8	10 50.1	25 08.2	2 04.2	12 31.6	15 36.6	14 33.3
13 Su	9 26 17	20 23 06	4♐49 13	11♐53 08	27 21.3	29♌51.4	5 41.8	5 41.5	10 44.2	25 21.0	2 11.7	12 32.8	15 36.1	14 34.9
14 M	9 30 13	21 20 43	19 03 00	26 18 29	27 18.1	29 07.3	6 44.7	6 19.3	10 38.5	25 33.8	2 19.2	12 34.0	15 35.7	14 36.5
15 Tu	9 34 10	22 18 21	3♑39 07	11♑04 13	27 13.8	28 20.1	7 47.3	6 57.2	10 33.2	25 46.5	2 26.7	12 35.3	15 35.3	14 38.1
16 W	9 38 06	23 15 59	18 32 58	26 04 20	27 08.9	27 30.7	8 49.7	7 35.1	10 28.3	25 59.2	2 34.3	12 36.6	15 34.9	14 39.7
17 Th	9 42 03	24 13 39	3♒37 15	11♒10 31	27 04.4	26 39.8	9 51.8	8 13.1	10 23.7	26 11.9	2 41.8	12 38.0	15 34.5	14 41.4
18 F	9 45 59	25 11 21	18 42 54	26 13 24	27 00.7	25 48.4	10 53.6	8 51.2	10 19.5	26 24.5	2 49.4	12 39.4	15 34.2	14 43.1
19 Sa	9 49 56	26 09 03	3♓40 23	11♓03 21	26 58.4	24 57.6	11 55.1	9 29.3	10 15.7	26 37.0	2 56.9	12 40.8	15 33.9	14 44.8
20 Su	9 53 53	27 06 47	18 21 16	25 33 29	26D 57.6	24 08.2	12 56.3	10 07.5	10 12.1	26 49.5	3 04.5	12 42.4	15 33.7	14 46.5
21 M	9 57 49	28 04 32	2♈39 27	9♈38 51	26 58.0	23 21.5	13 57.2	10 45.7	10 09.0	27 01.9	3 12.1	12 43.9	15 33.4	14 48.2
22 Tu	10 01 46	29 02 19	16 31 33	23 17 32	26 59.3	22 38.3	14 57.8	11 24.1	10 06.2	27 14.3	3 19.7	12 45.5	15 33.3	14 50.0
23 W	10 05 42	0♍00 08	29 56 58	6♉30 04	27 00.9	21 59.6	15 58.0	12 02.5	10 03.8	27 26.7	3 27.3	12 47.2	15 33.1	14 51.8
24 Th	10 09 39	0 57 58	12♉57 13	19 18 51	27 02.1	21 26.3	16 58.0	12 40.9	10 01.7	27 39.0	3 34.9	12 48.9	15 33.0	14 53.6
25 F	10 13 35	1 55 50	25 35 26	1♊47 31	27R 02.7	20 59.2	17 57.6	13 19.5	10 00.0	27 51.2	3 42.5	12 50.6	15 32.9	14 55.5
26 Sa	10 17 32	2 53 44	7♊55 38	14 00 22	27 02.1	20 38.8	18 56.8	13 58.1	9 58.6	28 03.4	3 50.1	12 52.4	15 32.8	14 57.3
27 Su	10 21 28	3 51 40	20 02 14	26 01 49	27 00.5	20 25.9	19 55.7	14 36.8	9 57.6	28 15.5	3 57.7	12 54.3	15D 32.8	14 59.2
28 M	10 25 25	4 49 38	1♋59 39	7♋56 14	26 58.0	20D 20.6	20 54.2	15 15.5	9 57.0	28 27.5	4 05.3	12 56.2	15 32.8	15 01.1
29 Tu	10 29 22	5 47 37	13 52 02	19 47 32	26 54.9	20 23.5	21 52.3	15 54.3	9D 56.7	28 39.5	4 12.9	12 58.1	15 32.8	15 03.1
30 W	10 33 18	6 45 38	25 43 07	1♌39 12	26 51.6	20 34.5	22 50.0	16 33.2	9 56.8	28 51.5	4 20.5	13 00.1	15 32.9	15 05.0
31 Th	10 37 15	7 43 41	7♌36 06	13 34 10	26 48.4	20 53.9	23 47.3	17 12.2	9 57.2	29 03.3	4 28.1	13 02.1	15 32.9	15 07.0

Astro Data

	Dy Hr Mn
♃⚻♆	3 14:36
☽0S	11 20:09
♄∠♇	18 8:22
♅D	21 10:04
☽0N	24 10:30
☿R	4 23:08
♂0S	6 4:49
♀0S	7 20:35
☽0S	8 2:51
☽0N	20 20:52
♆D	28 0:54
☿D	28 15:42
⚳D	29 18:54

Planet Ingress

		Dy Hr Mn
☿	♌	2 22:28
☊	♍R	5 10:41
♀	♍	12 2:14
☉	♌	23 5:00
♄	♍	26 12:02
☿	♍	27 6:10
♂	♎	4 9:07
♀	♎	8 3:08
☿	♌R	13 7:05
☉	♍	23 11:57

Last Aspect / ☽ Ingress

Last Aspect Dy Hr Mn			☽ Ingress	Dy Hr Mn
1 15:10	☿	⚹	♊	1 19:37
4 2:35	♄	⚹	♋	4 7:33
5 17:24	♃	☌	♌	6 20:13
9 4:51	♄	☌	♍	9 8:44
10 20:55	☉	⚹	♎	11 19:48
14 1:13	♄	⚹	♏	14 3:47
16 5:51	♄	□	♐	16 7:50
18 7:03	♄	△	♑	18 8:33
20 3:05	☉	☍	♒	20 7:41
22 6:38	♄	☍	♓	22 7:26
23 21:40	♂	☍	♈	24 9:46
26 15:03	☿	△	♉	26 15:50
28 17:29	♂	△	♊	29 1:31
31 8:28	♂	□	♋	31 13:28

Last Aspect / ☽ Ingress

Last Aspect Dy Hr Mn			☽ Ingress	Dy Hr Mn
3 0:28	♂	⚹	♌	3 2:10
4 9:49	♆	△	♍	5 14:29
8 1:20	♀	☌	♎	8 1:30
10 0:12	♃	□	♏	10 10:11
12 7:11	♃	△	♐	12 15:43
14 16:23	☿	△	♑	14 18:03
16 11:52	♃	☍	♒	16 18:15
18 11:22	☿	☍	♓	18 18:04
20 14:10	♃	△	♈	20 19:29
22 23:10	☉	△	♉	23 0:06
25 4:14	♃	⚹	♊	25 8:31
27 0:57	☿	⚹	♋	27 19:59
30 6:15	♃	☌	♌	30 8:40

☽ Phases & Eclipses

Dy Hr Mn		
5 9:50	●	13♋01
13 10:49	☽	20♎41
20 3:05	○	27♑04
26 22:31	☾	3♉34
4 1:01	●	11♌19
11 20:06	☽	18♏47
18 10:14	○	25♒07
25 12:18	☾	1♊57

Astro Data

1 July 1978
Julian Day # 28671
SVP 5♓33'36"
GC 26♐32.3 ⚳ 7♐08.5R
Eris 14♈44.3 ⚵ 6♒23.2R
⚷ 8♉55.8 ⚶ 8♐39.1R
☽ Mean ☊ 0♎56.6

1 August 1978
Julian Day # 28702
SVP 5♓33'31"
GC 26♐32.4 ⚳ 4♐51.4
Eris 14♈42.5R ⚵ 29♑35.1R
⚷ 9♉42.1 ⚶ 8♐28.1
☽ Mean ☊ 29♍18.1

LONGITUDE — September 1978

Day	Sid.Time	☉	0 hr ☽	Noon ☽	True ☊	☿	♀	♂	⚳	♃	♄	♅	♆	♇
1 F	10 41 11	8♍41 45	19♌33 39	25♌34 50	26♍45.8	21♌21.6	24♎44.1	17♎51.2	9♑58.0	29♋15.1	4♍35.7	13♏04.2	15♐33.1	15♎09.0
2 Sa	10 45 08	9 39 51	1♍37 55	7♍43 08	26R44.0	21 57.5	25 40.6	18 30.3	9 59.1	29 26.9	4 43.3	13 06.3	15 33.2	15 11.0
3 Su	10 49 04	10 37 59	13 50 39	20 00 39	26D43.2	22 41.4	26 36.5	19 09.4	10 00.6	29 38.6	4 50.9	13 08.5	15 33.4	15 13.0
4 M	10 53 01	11 36 09	26 13 17	2♎28 44	26 43.1	23 33.0	27 32.0	19 48.7	10 02.4	29 50.1	4 58.5	13 10.7	15 33.7	15 15.0
5 Tu	10 56 57	12 34 20	8♎47 09	15 08 41	26 43.7	24 31.9	28 27.0	20 28.0	10 04.6	0♌01.7	5 06.1	13 12.9	15 33.9	15 17.1
6 W	11 00 54	13 32 32	21 33 30	28 01 45	26 44.8	25 37.9	29 21.5	21 07.3	10 07.2	0 13.1	5 13.6	13 15.2	15 34.2	15 19.1
7 Th	11 04 51	14 30 46	4♏33 37	11♏09 14	26 45.9	26 50.4	0♏15.4	21 46.8	10 10.0	0 24.5	5 21.2	13 17.5	15 34.5	15 21.2
8 F	11 08 47	15 29 02	17 48 46	24 32 20	26 46.8	28 09.0	1 08.8	22 26.3	10 13.3	0 35.8	5 28.7	13 19.9	15 34.9	15 23.3
9 Sa	11 12 44	16 27 20	1♐20 03	8♐11 58	26R47.3	29 33.1	2 01.6	23 05.8	10 16.8	0 47.0	5 36.2	13 22.3	15 35.3	15 25.5
10 Su	11 16 40	17 25 38	15 08 07	22 08 27	26 47.4	1♍02.2	2 53.8	23 45.4	10 20.7	0 58.2	5 43.8	13 24.8	15 35.7	15 27.6
11 M	11 20 37	18 23 59	29 12 49	6♑21 02	26 47.0	2 35.7	3 45.4	24 25.1	10 24.9	1 09.2	5 51.3	13 27.3	15 36.2	15 29.8
12 Tu	11 24 33	19 22 20	13♑32 46	20 47 38	26 46.4	4 13.0	4 36.3	25 04.9	10 29.5	1 20.2	5 58.7	13 29.8	15 36.7	15 31.9
13 W	11 28 30	20 20 44	28 05 06	5♒24 33	26 45.7	5 53.7	5 26.5	25 44.7	10 34.3	1 31.1	6 06.2	13 32.4	15 37.2	15 34.1
14 Th	11 32 26	21 19 09	12♒45 18	20 06 35	26 45.0	7 37.3	6 16.1	26 24.6	10 39.5	1 41.9	6 13.7	13 35.0	15 37.7	15 36.3
15 F	11 36 23	22 17 35	27 27 33	4♓47 23	26 44.6	9 23.1	7 04.9	27 04.6	10 45.0	1 52.6	6 21.1	13 37.6	15 38.3	15 38.5
16 Sa	11 40 19	23 16 04	12♓05 14	19 20 19	26D44.4	11 10.8	7 52.9	27 44.6	10 50.8	2 03.2	6 28.5	13 40.3	15 38.9	15 40.7
17 Su	11 44 16	24 14 34	26 31 51	3♈39 10	26 44.4	12 59.9	8 40.2	28 24.6	10 56.9	2 13.8	6 35.9	13 43.0	15 39.6	15 43.0
18 M	11 48 13	25 13 06	10♈41 44	17 39 05	26 44.4	14 50.2	9 26.6	29 04.8	11 03.4	2 24.2	6 43.2	13 45.8	15 40.3	15 45.2
19 Tu	11 52 09	26 11 40	24 30 53	1♉16 57	26R44.5	16 41.1	10 12.2	29 45.0	11 10.1	2 34.6	6 50.6	13 48.5	15 41.0	15 47.5
20 W	11 56 06	27 10 16	7♉57 11	14 31 39	26 44.5	18 32.5	10 57.0	0♏25.3	11 17.1	2 44.8	6 57.9	13 51.4	15 41.7	15 49.7
21 Th	12 00 02	28 08 55	21 00 28	27 23 54	26 44.4	20 24.1	11 40.8	1 05.6	11 24.4	2 55.0	7 05.2	13 54.2	15 42.5	15 52.0
22 F	12 03 59	29 07 35	3♊42 18	9♊56 01	26 44.3	22 15.7	12 23.6	1 46.0	11 32.0	3 05.1	7 12.4	13 57.1	15 43.3	15 54.3
23 Sa	12 07 55	0♎06 18	16 05 34	22 11 25	26D44.1	24 07.1	13 05.5	2 26.5	11 39.9	3 15.1	7 19.7	14 00.0	15 44.2	15 56.6
24 Su	12 11 52	1 05 03	28 14 08	4♋14 17	26 44.1	25 58.1	13 46.4	3 07.0	11 48.1	3 24.9	7 26.9	14 03.0	15 45.0	15 58.9
25 M	12 15 48	2 03 51	10♋12 25	16 09 09	26 44.3	27 48.7	14 26.1	3 47.7	11 56.6	3 34.7	7 34.0	14 06.0	15 45.9	16 01.2
26 Tu	12 19 45	3 02 40	22 05 02	28 00 40	26 44.7	29 38.7	15 04.8	4 28.3	12 05.3	3 44.3	7 41.2	14 09.0	15 46.9	16 03.5
27 W	12 23 42	4 01 32	3♌56 35	9♌53 19	26 45.4	1♎28.0	15 42.4	5 09.1	12 14.3	3 53.9	7 48.3	14 12.1	15 47.8	16 05.8
28 Th	12 27 38	5 00 26	15 51 21	21 51 11	26 46.3	3 16.7	16 18.7	5 49.9	12 23.6	4 03.3	7 55.4	14 15.2	15 48.8	16 08.2
29 F	12 31 35	5 59 22	27 53 12	3♍57 48	26 47.1	5 04.6	16 53.8	6 30.8	12 33.1	4 12.7	8 02.4	14 18.3	15 49.8	16 10.5
30 Sa	12 35 31	6 58 21	10♍05 19	16 16 02	26R47.7	6 51.7	17 27.7	7 11.7	12 43.0	4 21.9	8 09.4	14 21.4	15 50.9	16 12.8

LONGITUDE — October 1978

Day	Sid.Time	☉	0 hr ☽	Noon ☽	True ☊	☿	♀	♂	⚳	♃	♄	♅	♆	♇
1 Su	12 39 28	7♎57 21	22♍30 10	28♍47 55	26♍47.9	8♎38.0	18♏00.1	7♏52.7	12♑53.0	4♌31.0	8♍16.4	14♏24.6	15♐52.0	16♎15.2
2 M	12 43 24	8 56 24	5♎09 23	11♎34 39	26R47.5	10 23.4	18 31.2	8 33.8	13 03.4	4 40.0	8 23.3	14 27.8	15 53.1	16 17.5
3 Tu	12 47 21	9 55 28	18 03 43	24 36 34	26 46.4	12 08.0	19 00.8	9 15.0	13 14.0	4 48.9	8 30.2	14 31.0	15 54.2	16 19.9
4 W	12 51 17	10 54 35	1♏13 06	7♏53 13	26 44.8	13 51.8	19 28.9	9 56.2	13 24.8	4 57.6	8 37.1	14 34.3	15 55.4	16 22.3
5 Th	12 55 14	11 53 43	14 36 45	21 23 32	26 42.7	15 34.8	19 55.5	10 37.5	13 35.9	5 06.2	8 43.9	14 37.5	15 56.6	16 24.6
6 F	12 59 11	12 52 53	28 13 21	5♐06 01	26 40.6	17 16.9	20 20.3	11 18.8	13 47.3	5 14.7	8 50.7	14 40.8	15 57.8	16 27.0
7 Sa	13 03 07	13 52 05	12♐01 17	18 58 56	26 38.8	18 58.3	20 43.5	12 00.2	13 58.8	5 23.1	8 57.4	14 44.2	15 59.1	16 29.4
8 Su	13 07 04	14 51 19	25 58 44	3♑00 27	26D37.6	20 38.8	21 05.0	12 41.7	14 10.7	5 31.4	9 04.1	14 47.5	16 00.4	16 31.7
9 M	13 11 00	15 50 35	10♑03 50	17 08 40	26 37.3	22 18.5	21 24.6	13 23.2	14 22.7	5 39.5	9 10.7	14 50.9	16 01.7	16 34.1
10 Tu	13 14 57	16 49 52	24 14 41	1♒21 38	26 37.8	23 57.5	21 42.3	14 04.8	14 35.0	5 47.5	9 17.3	14 54.3	16 03.1	16 36.5
11 W	13 18 53	17 49 11	8♒29 13	15 37 09	26 39.0	25 35.7	21 58.0	14 46.5	14 47.5	5 55.3	9 23.8	14 57.7	16 04.4	16 38.9
12 Th	13 22 50	18 48 32	22 45 06	29 52 42	26 40.4	27 13.2	22 11.7	15 28.2	15 00.2	6 03.0	9 30.3	15 01.2	16 05.8	16 41.2
13 F	13 26 46	19 47 55	6♓59 33	14♓05 16	26R41.5	28 49.9	22 23.3	16 10.0	15 13.2	6 10.6	9 36.7	15 04.6	16 07.2	16 43.6
14 Sa	13 30 43	20 47 19	21 09 23	28 11 29	26 41.9	0♏26.0	22 32.8	16 51.9	15 26.3	6 18.1	9 43.1	15 08.1	16 08.7	16 46.0
15 Su	13 34 39	21 46 45	5♈11 04	12♈07 44	26 41.2	2 01.4	22 40.1	17 33.8	15 39.7	6 25.4	9 49.4	15 11.6	16 10.2	16 48.3
16 M	13 38 36	22 46 13	19 01 03	25 50 38	26 39.1	3 36.1	22 45.1	18 15.7	15 53.3	6 32.6	9 55.7	15 15.1	16 11.7	16 50.7
17 Tu	13 42 33	23 45 44	2♉36 08	9♉17 18	26 35.7	5 10.1	22R47.8	18 57.8	16 07.1	6 39.6	10 01.9	15 18.7	16 13.2	16 53.1
18 W	13 46 29	24 45 16	15 53 55	22 25 52	26 31.3	6 43.5	22 48.2	19 39.9	16 21.0	6 46.5	10 08.1	15 22.2	16 14.7	16 55.4
19 Th	13 50 26	25 44 51	28 53 08	5♊15 46	26 26.5	8 16.3	22 46.2	20 22.0	16 35.2	6 53.2	10 14.2	15 25.8	16 16.3	16 57.8
20 F	13 54 22	26 44 27	11♊33 53	17 47 44	26 21.7	9 48.5	22 41.8	21 04.3	16 49.6	6 59.8	10 20.2	15 29.4	16 17.9	17 00.1
21 Sa	13 58 19	27 44 06	23 57 37	0♋03 53	26 17.7	11 20.1	22 35.1	21 46.6	17 04.2	7 06.2	10 26.2	15 33.0	16 19.5	17 02.5
22 Su	14 02 15	28 43 48	6♋06 59	12 07 24	26 14.8	12 51.1	22 25.9	22 28.9	17 18.9	7 12.5	10 32.1	15 36.6	16 21.2	17 04.8
23 M	14 06 12	29 43 31	18 05 40	24 02 22	26D13.3	14 21.5	22 14.3	23 11.4	17 33.9	7 18.6	10 38.0	15 40.2	16 22.9	17 07.2
24 Tu	14 10 08	0♏43 17	29 58 05	5♌53 28	26 13.3	15 51.3	22 00.3	23 53.8	17 49.0	7 24.6	10 43.8	15 43.9	16 24.6	17 09.5
25 W	14 14 05	1 43 05	11♌49 07	17 45 42	26 14.4	17 20.5	21 43.9	24 36.4	18 04.3	7 30.4	10 49.6	15 47.5	16 26.3	17 11.8
26 Th	14 18 02	2 42 55	23 43 48	29 44 04	26 16.1	18 49.1	21 25.3	25 19.0	18 19.8	7 36.1	10 55.2	15 51.2	16 28.0	17 14.1
27 F	14 21 58	3 42 47	5♍47 04	11♍53 21	26 17.7	20 17.1	21 04.3	26 01.7	18 35.5	7 41.6	11 00.8	15 54.9	16 29.8	17 16.4
28 Sa	14 25 55	4 42 42	18 03 26	24 17 44	26R18.5	21 44.5	20 41.3	26 44.4	18 51.3	7 46.9	11 06.4	15 58.5	16 31.6	17 18.7
29 Su	14 29 51	5 42 38	0♎36 38	7♎00 26	26 18.0	23 11.2	20 16.1	27 27.3	19 07.4	7 52.1	11 11.8	16 02.2	16 33.4	17 21.0
30 M	14 33 48	6 42 37	13 29 19	20 03 24	26 15.6	24 37.3	19 49.0	28 10.1	19 23.6	7 57.1	11 17.2	16 05.9	16 35.2	17 23.3
31 Tu	14 37 44	7 42 37	26 42 39	3♏26 58	26 11.2	26 02.7	19 20.1	28 53.1	19 39.9	8 01.9	11 22.5	16 09.7	16 37.0	17 25.5

Astro Data (Dy Hr Mn)

☽0S 4 8:57
♃□♆ 8 10:01
♆⚹♇ 15 9:09
☽0N 17 7:19
☉0S 23 9:25
☿0S 28 13:45

☽0S 1 15:55
☽0N 14 16:37
♀R 18 3:58
☽0S 29 0:41

Planet Ingress (Dy Hr Mn)

♃ ♌ 5 8:31
♀ ♏ 7 5:07
☿ ♍ 9 19:23
♂ ♏ 19 20:57
☉ ♎ 23 9:25
☿ ♎ 26 16:40

☿ ♏ 14 5:30
☉ ♏ 23 18:37

Last Aspect (Dy Hr Mn) — **☽ Ingress** (Dy Hr Mn)

1 10:11 ♀ ⚹ ♍ 1 20:46
4 6:52 ♃ ⚹ ♎ 4 7:15
6 14:38 ♀ ☌ ♏ 6 15:38
8 19:06 ☿ □ ♐ 8 21:39
10 14:53 ♂ ⚹ ♑ 11 1:20
12 19:24 ♂ □ ♒ 13 3:09
14 22:46 ♂ △ ♓ 15 4:09
16 19:01 ☉ ☍ ♈ 17 5:50
19 9:08 ♂ ☍ ♉ 19 9:43
21 13:32 ☉ △ ♊ 21 16:56
23 16:30 ☿ □ ♋ 24 3:31
26 15:55 ☿ ⚹ ♌ 26 16:02
28 0:31 ♇ ⚹ ♍ 29 4:11

Last Aspect (Dy Hr Mn) — **☽ Ingress** (Dy Hr Mn)

30 14:25 ♀ ⚹ ♎ 1 14:17
2 20:46 ♇ ☌ ♏ 3 21:48
5 9:19 ♀ ☌ ♐ 6 3:07
7 11:59 ☿ ⚹ ♑ 8 6:52
9 21:53 ☿ □ ♒ 10 9:42
12 6:57 ☿ △ ♓ 12 12:12
14 2:16 ♀ △ ♈ 14 15:06
16 6:10 ☉ ☍ ♉ 16 19:22
18 12:41 ♀ ☍ ♊ 19 2:05
21 7:00 ☉ △ ♋ 21 11:52
23 10:10 ♂ △ ♌ 24 0:04
26 2:37 ♂ □ ♍ 26 12:32
28 16:57 ♂ ⚹ ♎ 28 22:51
30 7:08 ♇ ☌ ♏ 31 5:53

☽ Phases & Eclipses (Dy Hr Mn)

2 16:09 ● 9♍50
10 3:20 ☽ 17♐05
16 19:01 ○ 23♓33
16 19:04 T 1.327
24 5:07 ☾ 0♋48

2 6:41 ● 8♎43
2 6:27:54 P 0.691
9 9:38 ☽ 15♑45
16 6:10 ○ 22♈32
24 0:34 ☾ 0♌15
31 20:06 ● 8♏03

Astro Data

1 September 1978
Julian Day # 28733
SVP 5♓33'27"
GC 26♐32.5 ⚴ 8♐44.4
Eris 14♈31.3R ⚵ 24♑02.1R
⚷ 9♉36.7R ⚶ 14♐59.9
☽ Mean ☊ 27♍39.6

1 October 1978
Julian Day # 28763
SVP 5♓33'25"
GC 26♐32.5 ⚴ 16♐17.3
Eris 14♈14.5R ⚵ 24♑15.7
⚷ 8♉44.2R ⚶ 25♐26.0
☽ Mean ☊ 26♍04.2

November 1978 LONGITUDE

Day	Sid.Time	☉	0 hr ☽	Noon ☽	True ☊	☿	♀	♂	⚳	♃	♄	♅	♆	♇
1 W	14 41 41	8♏42 40	10♏16 05	17♏09 41	26♍05.1	27♏27.4	18♏49.6	29♏36.1	19♑56.4	8♌06.6	11♍27.8	16♏13.4	16♐38.9	17♎27.8
2 Th	14 45 37	9 42 44	24 07 18	1♐08 26	25R57.9	28 51.4	18R17.5	0♐19.1	20 13.1	8 11.1	11 33.0	16 17.1	16 40.8	17 30.0
3 F	14 49 34	10 42 50	8♐12 30	15 18 51	25 50.5	0♐14.5	17 44.2	1 02.3	20 30.0	8 15.4	11 38.1	16 20.8	16 42.7	17 32.3
4 Sa	14 53 31	11 42 58	22 26 51	29 35 53	25 43.8	1 36.7	17 09.8	1 45.5	20 47.0	8 19.5	11 43.1	16 24.6	16 44.6	17 34.5
5 Su	14 57 27	12 43 08	6♑45 20	13♑54 41	25 38.7	2 58.0	16 34.4	2 28.7	21 04.1	8 23.5	11 48.1	16 28.3	16 46.5	17 36.7
6 M	15 01 24	13 43 19	21 03 26	28 11 10	25 35.5	4 18.3	15 58.5	3 12.0	21 21.4	8 27.2	11 52.9	16 32.1	16 48.5	17 38.9
7 Tu	15 05 20	14 43 31	5♒17 36	12♒22 26	25D34.4	5 37.4	15 22.1	3 55.4	21 38.9	8 30.8	11 57.7	16 35.8	16 50.5	17 41.1
8 W	15 09 17	15 43 45	19 25 31	26 26 42	25 34.8	6 55.3	14 45.5	4 38.8	21 56.5	8 34.3	12 02.4	16 39.5	16 52.5	17 43.2
9 Th	15 13 13	16 44 00	3♓25 54	10♓23 04	25 35.8	8 11.8	14 09.1	5 22.3	22 14.2	8 37.5	12 07.0	16 43.3	16 54.5	17 45.4
10 F	15 17 10	17 44 17	17 18 08	24 11 04	25R36.5	9 26.7	13 33.0	6 05.8	22 32.1	8 40.5	12 11.6	16 47.0	16 56.5	17 47.5
11 Sa	15 21 06	18 44 35	1♈01 48	7♈50 16	25 35.8	10 40.0	12 57.5	6 49.4	22 50.1	8 43.4	12 16.1	16 50.8	16 58.5	17 49.6
12 Su	15 25 03	19 44 55	14 36 21	21 19 56	25 32.9	11 51.3	12 22.8	7 33.1	23 08.3	8 46.1	12 20.4	16 54.5	17 00.6	17 51.7
13 M	15 29 00	20 45 16	28 00 53	4♉39 01	25 27.4	13 00.4	11 49.2	8 16.8	23 26.5	8 48.6	12 24.7	16 58.3	17 02.6	17 53.8
14 Tu	15 32 56	21 45 39	11♉14 11	17 46 12	25 19.5	14 07.2	11 16.9	9 00.6	23 44.9	8 50.9	12 28.9	17 02.0	17 04.7	17 55.9
15 W	15 36 53	22 46 03	24 14 55	0♊40 13	25 09.5	15 11.2	10 46.0	9 44.4	24 03.5	8 53.0	12 33.0	17 05.7	17 06.8	17 57.9
16 Th	15 40 49	23 46 29	7♊02 01	13 20 15	24 58.4	16 12.1	10 16.9	10 28.3	24 22.1	8 54.9	12 37.1	17 09.5	17 08.9	18 00.0
17 F	15 44 46	24 46 57	19 34 58	25 46 13	24 47.2	17 09.6	9 49.6	11 12.2	24 40.9	8 56.7	12 41.0	17 13.2	17 11.0	18 02.0
18 Sa	15 48 42	25 47 27	1♋54 10	7♋59 01	24 37.0	18 03.1	9 24.3	11 56.2	24 59.8	8 58.2	12 44.9	17 16.9	17 13.2	18 04.0
19 Su	15 52 39	26 47 58	14 01 04	20 00 40	24 28.7	18 52.1	9 01.2	12 40.3	25 18.9	8 59.6	12 48.6	17 20.6	17 15.3	18 05.9
20 M	15 56 35	27 48 31	25 58 13	1♌54 13	24 22.7	19 36.2	8 40.3	13 24.4	25 38.0	9 00.7	12 52.3	17 24.3	17 17.5	18 07.9
21 Tu	16 00 32	28 49 06	7♌49 11	13 43 42	24 19.1	20 14.5	8 21.7	14 08.6	25 57.3	9 01.7	12 55.9	17 28.0	17 19.6	18 09.8
22 W	16 04 29	29 49 42	19 38 23	25 33 53	24D17.8	20 46.6	8 05.5	14 52.9	26 16.7	9 02.5	12 59.3	17 31.7	17 21.8	18 11.7
23 Th	16 08 25	0♐50 20	1♍30 52	7♍30 00	24 17.8	21 11.5	7 51.7	15 37.2	26 36.1	9 03.0	13 02.7	17 35.4	17 24.0	18 13.6
24 F	16 12 22	1 51 00	13 32 01	19 37 33	24R18.3	21 28.6	7 40.4	16 21.5	26 55.7	9 03.4	13 06.0	17 39.1	17 26.2	18 15.5
25 Sa	16 16 18	2 51 41	25 47 16	2♎01 48	24 18.1	21R37.0	7 31.6	17 05.9	27 15.4	9R03.6	13 09.2	17 42.7	17 28.4	18 17.3
26 Su	16 20 15	3 52 24	8♎21 41	14 47 24	24 16.2	21 36.1	7 25.3	17 50.4	27 35.3	9 03.5	13 12.3	17 46.4	17 30.6	18 19.1
27 M	16 24 11	4 53 09	21 19 20	27 57 46	24 11.9	21 25.0	7 21.5	18 34.9	27 55.2	9 03.3	13 15.3	17 50.0	17 32.8	18 20.9
28 Tu	16 28 08	5 53 55	4♏42 47	11♏34 23	24 04.8	21 03.3	7D20.2	19 19.5	28 15.2	9 02.9	13 18.2	17 53.6	17 35.0	18 22.7
29 W	16 32 04	6 54 42	18 32 20	25 36 15	23 55.2	20 30.7	7 21.3	20 04.2	28 35.3	9 02.3	13 21.0	17 57.2	17 37.2	18 24.5
30 Th	16 36 01	7 55 31	2♐45 35	9♐59 37	23 43.9	19 47.0	7 24.7	20 48.9	28 55.6	9 01.4	13 23.7	18 00.8	17 39.5	18 26.2

December 1978 LONGITUDE

Day	Sid.Time	☉	0 hr ☽	Noon ☽	True ☊	☿	♀	♂	⚳	♃	♄	♅	♆	♇
1 F	16 39 58	8♐56 21	17♐17 27	24♐38 07	23♍32.1	18♐52.9	7♏30.6	21♐33.6	29♑15.9	9♌00.4	13♍26.3	18♏04.4	17♐41.7	18♎27.9
2 Sa	16 43 54	9 57 13	2♑00 36	9♑23 50	23R21.2	17R49.1	7 38.7	22 18.5	29 36.3	8R59.2	13 28.8	18 07.9	17 44.0	18 29.6
3 Su	16 47 51	10 58 05	16 46 47	24 08 30	23 12.3	16 37.2	7 49.1	23 03.3	29 56.9	8 57.8	13 31.1	18 11.5	17 46.2	18 31.2
4 M	16 51 47	11 58 58	1♒28 09	8♒45 01	23 06.1	15 19.0	8 01.7	23 48.2	0♒17.5	8 56.1	13 33.4	18 15.0	17 48.5	18 32.8
5 Tu	16 55 44	12 59 52	15 58 32	23 08 18	23 02.7	13 57.2	8 16.4	24 33.2	0 38.2	8 54.3	13 35.6	18 18.5	17 50.7	18 34.4
6 W	16 59 40	14 00 46	0♓14 03	7♓15 41	23D01.5	12 34.2	8 33.2	25 18.2	0 59.0	8 52.3	13 37.6	18 22.0	17 53.0	18 36.0
7 Th	17 03 37	15 01 41	14 13 08	21 06 30	23R01.5	11 13.1	8 52.0	26 03.3	1 19.8	8 50.1	13 39.6	18 25.5	17 55.3	18 37.5
8 F	17 07 33	16 02 37	27 55 56	4♈41 35	23 01.2	9 56.5	9 12.8	26 48.4	1 40.8	8 47.7	13 41.5	18 28.9	17 57.5	18 39.0
9 Sa	17 11 30	17 03 34	11♈23 39	18 02 22	22 59.3	8 46.7	9 35.4	27 33.6	2 01.8	8 45.1	13 43.2	18 32.3	17 59.8	18 40.5
10 Su	17 15 27	18 04 31	24 37 55	1♉10 27	22 54.9	7 45.7	9 59.9	28 18.8	2 22.9	8 42.3	13 44.8	18 35.7	18 02.1	18 42.0
11 M	17 19 23	19 05 29	7♉40 09	14 07 06	22 47.4	6 54.7	10 26.1	29 04.0	2 44.1	8 39.3	13 46.4	18 39.1	18 04.3	18 43.4
12 Tu	17 23 20	20 06 28	20 31 23	26 53 03	22 36.9	6 14.7	10 54.1	29 49.3	3 05.4	8 36.2	13 47.8	18 42.4	18 06.6	18 44.8
13 W	17 27 16	21 07 27	3♊12 09	9♊28 40	22 23.9	5 46.0	11 23.7	0♑34.7	3 26.8	8 32.8	13 49.1	18 45.7	18 08.8	18 46.2
14 Th	17 31 13	22 08 27	15 42 37	21 54 00	22 09.5	5 28.3	11 54.9	1 20.1	3 48.2	8 29.3	13 50.3	18 49.0	18 11.1	18 47.5
15 F	17 35 09	23 09 28	28 02 52	4♋09 15	21 54.8	5D21.5	12 27.6	2 05.6	4 09.7	8 25.5	13 51.4	18 52.3	18 13.4	18 48.8
16 Sa	17 39 06	24 10 30	10♋13 14	16 14 57	21 41.2	5 24.8	13 01.8	2 51.1	4 31.3	8 21.6	13 52.4	18 55.6	18 15.6	18 50.1
17 Su	17 43 02	25 11 32	22 14 34	28 12 20	21 29.6	5 37.5	13 37.5	3 36.6	4 52.9	8 17.6	13 53.3	18 58.8	18 17.9	18 51.3
18 M	17 46 59	26 12 36	4♌08 30	10♌03 27	21 20.7	5 58.8	14 14.5	4 22.2	5 14.6	8 13.3	13 54.0	19 02.0	18 20.1	18 52.5
19 Tu	17 50 56	27 13 40	15 57 33	21 51 17	21 14.9	6 27.9	14 52.8	5 07.9	5 36.4	8 08.9	13 54.7	19 05.1	18 22.4	18 53.7
20 W	17 54 52	28 14 44	27 45 09	3♍39 42	21 11.8	7 04.0	15 32.4	5 53.5	5 58.2	8 04.2	13 55.2	19 08.2	18 24.6	18 54.9
21 Th	17 58 49	29 15 50	9♍35 34	15 33 23	21D10.7	7 46.4	16 13.2	6 39.3	6 20.1	7 59.5	13 55.7	19 11.3	18 26.9	18 56.0
22 F	18 02 45	0♑16 56	21 33 49	27 37 33	21R10.7	8 34.2	16 55.2	7 25.1	6 42.1	7 54.5	13 56.0	19 14.4	18 29.1	18 57.1
23 Sa	18 06 42	1 18 03	3♎45 17	9♎57 43	21 10.5	9 27.0	17 38.3	8 10.9	7 04.1	7 49.4	13 56.2	19 17.4	18 31.3	18 58.1
24 Su	18 10 38	2 19 11	16 15 31	22 39 17	21 08.9	10 24.1	18 22.5	8 56.8	7 26.2	7 44.1	13R56.3	19 20.4	18 33.5	18 59.1
25 M	18 14 35	3 20 19	29 09 35	5♏46 51	21 05.2	11 24.9	19 07.7	9 42.7	7 48.4	7 38.7	13 56.3	19 23.4	18 35.7	19 00.1
26 Tu	18 18 31	4 21 28	12♏31 27	19 23 31	20 58.7	12 29.2	19 53.9	10 28.7	8 10.6	7 33.1	13 56.2	19 26.3	18 37.9	19 01.1
27 W	18 22 28	5 22 38	26 23 04	3♐29 53	20 49.7	13 36.4	20 41.1	11 14.7	8 32.9	7 27.3	13 55.9	19 29.2	18 40.1	19 02.0
28 Th	18 26 25	6 23 48	10♐43 33	18 03 25	20 38.9	14 46.2	21 29.2	12 00.7	8 55.2	7 21.4	13 55.6	19 32.1	18 42.3	19 02.9
29 F	18 30 21	7 24 58	25 28 37	2♑58 05	20 27.3	15 58.3	22 18.1	12 46.8	9 17.6	7 15.4	13 55.1	19 34.9	18 44.5	19 03.7
30 Sa	18 34 18	8 26 09	10♑30 37	18 04 55	20 16.5	17 12.5	23 07.9	13 33.0	9 40.1	7 09.2	13 54.6	19 37.7	18 46.7	19 04.5
31 Su	18 38 14	9 27 20	25 39 39	3♒13 29	20 07.5	18 28.5	23 58.5	14 19.2	10 02.6	7 02.9	13 53.9	19 40.5	18 48.8	19 05.3

Astro Data	Planet Ingress	Last Aspect	☽ Ingress	Last Aspect	☽ Ingress	☽ Phases & Eclipses	Astro Data
Dy Hr Mn	Dy Hr Mn	Dy Hr Mn	Dy Hr Mn	Dy Hr Mn	Dy Hr Mn	Dy Hr Mn	
☽0N 11 0:12	♂ ♐ 2 1:20	2 7:40 ☿ ☌	♐ 2 10:03	1 6:43 ♂ ☌	♑ 1 20:44	7 16:18 ☽ 14♒54	1 November 1978
♅∠♆ 16 3:53	☿ ♐ 3 7:48	3 15:45 ♇ ⚹	♑ 4 12:40	3 2:49 ♇ □	♒ 3 21:35	14 20:00 ○ 22♉06	Julian Day # 28794
☽0S 25 10:55	☉ ♐ 22 16:05	5 18:14 ♇ □	♒ 6 15:04	5 14:31 ♂ ⚹	♓ 5 23:36	22 21:24 ☾ 0♍13	SVP 5♓33'23"
♃ R 25 20:30		7 21:03 ♇ △	♓ 8 18:06	7 21:12 ♂ □	♈ 8 3:40	30 8:19 ● 7♐46	GC 26♐32.6 ⚴ 26♐18.3
☿ R 25 21:43	⚳ ♒ 3 15:40	9 23:53 ☉ △	♈ 10 22:11	10 6:25 ♂ △	♉ 10 9:50		Eris 13♈56.1R ✱ 0♒09.1
♀ D 28 13:10	♂ ♑ 12 17:39	12 5:47 ♇ ☍	♉ 13 3:35	11 20:31 ♅ ☍	♊ 12 17:54	7 0:34 ☽ 14♓33	⚷ 7♉19.4R ⚶ 8♑40.7
	☉ ♑ 22 5:21	14 20:00 ☉ ☍	♊ 15 10:45	14 12:31 ☉ ☍	♋ 15 3:50	14 12:31 ○ 22♊10	☽ Mean ☊ 24♍25.7
☽0N 8 6:48		16 20:58 ♇ △	♋ 17 20:16	16 17:23 ♅ △	♌ 17 15:37	22 17:42 ☾ 0♎31	
♅∠♇ 13 17:12		20 2:57 ☉ △	♌ 20 8:09	19 23:58 ☉ △	♍ 20 4:34	29 19:36 ● 7♑44	1 December 1978
☿ D 15 15:57		22 1:53 ♀ △	♍ 22 20:57	21 19:18 ♅ ⚹	♎ 22 16:40		Julian Day # 28824
☽0S 22 21:03		24 15:41 ☿ □	♎ 25 8:07	24 5:08 ♇ ☌	♏ 25 1:32		SVP 5♓33'18"
♄ R 24 21:12		27 0:22 ☿ ⚹	♏ 27 15:39	26 12:56 ♀ ☌	♐ 27 6:07		GC 26♐32.7 ⚴ 7♑07.7
		28 22:57 ♅ ☌	♐ 29 19:23	28 13:37 ♇ ⚹	♑ 29 7:15		Eris 13♈42.4R ✱ 9♒42.9
				30 20:28 ♀ ⚹	♒ 31 6:53		⚷ 5♉58.4R ⚶ 22♑51.3
							☽ Mean ☊ 22♍50.4

LONGITUDE — January 1979

Day	Sid.Time	☉	0 hr ☽	Noon ☽	True ☊	☿	♀	♂	⚳	♃	♄	♅	♆	♇
1 M	18 42 11	10♑28 30	10♒45 13	18♒13 46	20♍01.2	19♐46.0	24♏49.8	15♑05.4	10♒25.1	6♌56.5	13♍53.1	19♏43.2	18♐51.0	19♎06.1
2 Tu	18 46 07	11 29 41	25 38 11	2♓57 45	19R57.8	21 05.0	25 41.9	15 51.6	10 47.7	6R49.9	13R52.2	19 45.9	18 53.1	19 06.8
3 W	18 50 04	12 30 51	10♓11 58	17 20 28	19D56.7	22 25.3	26 34.7	16 37.9	11 10.3	6 43.2	13 51.2	19 48.5	18 55.2	19 07.4
4 Th	18 54 00	13 32 01	24 23 08	1♈19 56	19R56.9	23 46.8	27 28.2	17 24.3	11 33.0	6 36.4	13 50.1	19 51.1	18 57.3	19 08.1
5 F	18 57 57	14 33 11	8♈11 00	14 56 33	19 57.3	25 09.3	28 22.3	18 10.6	11 55.8	6 29.5	13 48.8	19 53.7	18 59.4	19 08.7
6 Sa	19 01 54	15 34 20	21 36 53	28 12 21	19 56.5	26 32.8	29 17.1	18 57.0	12 18.5	6 22.4	13 47.5	19 56.2	19 01.5	19 09.3
7 Su	19 05 50	16 35 29	4♉43 17	11♉10 05	19 53.6	27 57.1	0♐12.4	19 43.5	12 41.3	6 15.3	13 46.1	19 58.7	19 03.6	19 09.8
8 M	19 09 47	17 36 37	17 33 06	23 52 40	19 48.1	29 22.3	1 08.4	20 29.9	13 04.2	6 08.1	13 44.5	20 01.1	19 05.6	19 10.3
9 Tu	19 13 43	18 37 45	0♊09 07	6♊22 44	19 40.0	0♑48.3	2 05.0	21 16.4	13 27.1	6 00.7	13 42.9	20 03.5	19 07.7	19 10.7
10 W	19 17 40	19 38 53	12 33 45	18 42 26	19 29.7	2 14.9	3 02.1	22 02.9	13 50.0	5 53.3	13 41.1	20 05.8	19 09.7	19 11.2
11 Th	19 21 36	20 40 00	24 48 56	0♋53 27	19 18.1	3 42.2	3 59.7	22 49.5	14 13.0	5 45.8	13 39.3	20 08.2	19 11.7	19 11.6
12 F	19 25 33	21 41 07	6♋56 08	12 57 07	19 06.3	5 10.2	4 57.8	23 36.1	14 36.0	5 38.3	13 37.3	20 10.4	19 13.7	19 11.9
13 Sa	19 29 30	22 42 14	18 56 34	24 54 37	18 55.3	6 38.8	5 56.5	24 22.7	14 59.0	5 30.6	13 35.3	20 12.6	19 15.7	19 12.2
14 Su	19 33 26	23 43 20	0♌51 26	6♌47 11	18 46.0	8 07.9	6 55.6	25 09.4	15 22.1	5 22.9	13 33.1	20 14.8	19 17.6	19 12.5
15 M	19 37 23	24 44 26	12 42 07	18 36 28	18 39.0	9 37.7	7 55.2	25 56.1	15 45.2	5 15.2	13 30.8	20 16.9	19 19.6	19 12.8
16 Tu	19 41 19	25 45 31	24 30 30	0♍24 34	18 34.5	11 08.0	8 55.2	26 42.8	16 08.3	5 07.3	13 28.5	20 19.0	19 21.5	19 13.0
17 W	19 45 16	26 46 36	6♍19 02	12 14 19	18D32.5	12 38.9	9 55.6	27 29.6	16 31.5	4 59.5	13 26.0	20 21.0	19 23.4	19 13.2
18 Th	19 49 12	27 47 41	18 10 52	24 09 12	18 32.4	14 10.3	10 56.5	28 16.3	16 54.7	4 51.6	13 23.5	20 23.0	19 25.3	19 13.3
19 F	19 53 09	28 48 45	0♎09 52	6♎13 26	18 33.5	15 42.4	11 57.8	29 03.2	17 17.9	4 43.6	13 20.8	20 25.0	19 27.2	19 13.4
20 Sa	19 57 05	29 49 50	12 20 30	18 31 41	18R34.8	17 14.9	12 59.4	29 50.0	17 41.2	4 35.6	13 18.1	20 26.8	19 29.0	19 13.5
21 Su	20 01 02	0♒50 53	24 47 37	1♏08 53	18 35.4	18 48.1	14 01.4	0♒36.9	18 04.5	4 27.6	13 15.3	20 28.7	19 30.8	19R13.5
22 M	20 04 58	1 51 57	7♏36 05	14 09 43	18 34.5	20 21.8	15 03.8	1 23.8	18 27.8	4 19.6	13 12.4	20 30.5	19 32.6	19 13.5
23 Tu	20 08 55	2 52 59	20 50 14	27 37 58	18 31.8	21 56.1	16 06.5	2 10.7	18 51.1	4 11.6	13 09.3	20 32.2	19 34.4	19 13.4
24 W	20 12 52	3 54 02	4♐33 07	11♐35 42	18 27.1	23 31.0	17 09.6	2 57.6	19 14.5	4 03.5	13 06.2	20 33.9	19 36.2	19 13.4
25 Th	20 16 48	4 55 04	18 45 33	26 02 19	18 21.0	25 06.5	18 12.9	3 44.6	19 37.9	3 55.5	13 03.1	20 35.6	19 37.9	19 13.3
26 F	20 20 45	5 56 06	3♑25 23	10♑53 58	18 14.2	26 42.6	19 16.6	4 31.6	20 01.3	3 47.5	12 59.8	20 37.1	19 39.6	19 13.1
27 Sa	20 24 41	6 57 06	18 27 01	26 03 23	18 07.6	28 19.3	20 20.5	5 18.7	20 24.7	3 39.4	12 56.5	20 38.7	19 41.3	19 12.9
28 Su	20 28 38	7 58 06	3♒41 44	11♒20 42	18 02.2	29 56.7	21 24.8	6 05.7	20 48.2	3 31.4	12 53.0	20 40.2	19 43.0	19 12.7
29 M	20 32 34	8 59 05	18 58 55	26 35 03	17 58.5	1♒34.7	22 29.3	6 52.8	21 11.6	3 23.4	12 49.5	20 41.6	19 44.6	19 12.5
30 Tu	20 36 31	10 00 03	4♓07 53	11♓36 22	17D56.9	3 13.4	23 34.0	7 39.9	21 35.1	3 15.5	12 45.9	20 43.0	19 46.2	19 12.2
31 W	20 40 28	11 01 00	18 59 37	26 16 59	17 56.9	4 52.7	24 39.1	8 27.0	21 58.6	3 07.6	12 42.3	20 44.3	19 47.8	19 11.9

LONGITUDE — February 1979

Day	Sid.Time	☉	0 hr ☽	Noon ☽	True ☊	☿	♀	♂	⚳	♃	♄	♅	♆	♇
1 Th	20 44 24	12♒01 55	3♈27 59	10♈32 21	17♍58.2	6♒32.8	25♐44.3	9♒14.1	22♒22.1	2♌59.7	12♍38.5	20♏45.6	19♐49.4	19♎11.5
2 F	20 48 21	13 02 49	17 29 58	24 20 55	17 59.7	8 13.6	26 49.8	10 01.3	22 45.7	2R51.8	12R34.7	20 46.8	19 50.9	19R11.1
3 Sa	20 52 17	14 03 42	1♉05 22	7♉43 36	18R00.8	9 55.1	27 55.5	10 48.4	23 09.2	2 44.1	12 30.9	20 48.0	19 52.5	19 10.7
4 Su	20 56 14	15 04 33	14 15 59	20 42 57	18 00.8	11 37.3	29 01.4	11 35.6	23 32.8	2 36.4	12 26.9	20 49.1	19 54.0	19 10.2
5 M	21 00 10	16 05 23	27 04 55	3♊22 23	17 59.4	13 20.2	0♑07.6	12 22.8	23 56.3	2 28.7	12 22.9	20 50.2	19 55.4	19 09.7
6 Tu	21 04 07	17 06 11	9♊35 48	15 45 39	17 56.5	15 04.0	1 13.9	13 10.0	24 19.9	2 21.1	12 18.9	20 51.2	19 56.9	19 09.2
7 W	21 08 03	18 06 58	21 52 22	27 56 23	17 52.2	16 48.4	2 20.5	13 57.2	24 43.5	2 13.7	12 14.7	20 52.2	19 58.3	19 08.6
8 Th	21 12 00	19 07 44	3♋58 07	9♋57 54	17 47.2	18 33.7	3 27.2	14 44.4	25 07.1	2 06.2	12 10.6	20 53.1	19 59.7	19 08.0
9 F	21 15 57	20 08 28	15 56 07	21 53 03	17 42.0	20 19.7	4 34.1	15 31.6	25 30.7	1 58.9	12 06.3	20 53.9	20 01.0	19 07.4
10 Sa	21 19 53	21 09 11	27 49 02	3♌44 18	17 37.2	22 06.4	5 41.3	16 18.9	25 54.3	1 51.7	12 02.0	20 54.7	20 02.3	19 06.8
11 Su	21 23 50	22 09 52	9♌39 07	15 33 44	17 33.1	23 53.9	6 48.5	17 06.2	26 17.9	1 44.5	11 57.7	20 55.4	20 03.6	19 06.1
12 M	21 27 46	23 10 32	21 28 23	27 23 18	17 30.3	25 42.1	7 56.0	17 53.4	26 41.5	1 37.5	11 53.3	20 56.1	20 04.9	19 05.3
13 Tu	21 31 43	24 11 11	3♍18 44	9♍14 55	17D28.8	27 31.0	9 03.7	18 40.7	27 05.1	1 30.6	11 48.9	20 56.8	20 06.2	19 04.6
14 W	21 35 39	25 11 48	15 12 09	21 10 40	17 28.6	29 20.5	10 11.5	19 28.0	27 28.7	1 23.8	11 44.4	20 57.3	20 07.4	19 03.8
15 Th	21 39 36	26 12 24	27 10 49	3♎12 55	17 29.4	1♓10.6	11 19.4	20 15.3	27 52.3	1 17.1	11 39.9	20 57.9	20 08.5	19 03.0
16 F	21 43 32	27 12 58	9♎17 20	15 24 27	17 30.8	3 01.1	12 27.5	21 02.6	28 15.9	1 10.5	11 35.4	20 58.3	20 09.7	19 02.2
17 Sa	21 47 29	28 13 31	21 34 39	27 48 23	17 32.4	4 52.1	13 35.8	21 49.9	28 39.5	1 04.0	11 30.8	20 58.7	20 10.8	19 01.3
18 Su	21 51 25	29 14 03	4♏06 05	10♏28 11	17 33.8	6 43.4	14 44.2	22 37.2	29 03.2	0 57.7	11 26.1	20 59.1	20 11.9	19 00.4
19 M	21 55 22	0♓14 34	16 55 07	23 27 18	17R34.6	8 34.9	15 52.8	23 24.6	29 26.8	0 51.5	11 21.5	20 59.4	20 13.0	18 59.4
20 Tu	21 59 19	1 15 04	0♐05 06	6♐48 50	17 34.7	10 26.3	17 01.4	24 11.9	29 50.4	0 45.4	11 16.8	20 59.6	20 14.0	18 58.5
21 W	22 03 15	2 15 32	13 38 45	20 34 58	17 34.0	12 17.5	18 10.3	24 59.3	0♓14.0	0 39.5	11 12.1	20 59.8	20 15.0	18 57.5
22 Th	22 07 12	3 15 59	27 37 30	4♑46 14	17 32.6	14 08.3	19 19.2	25 46.6	0 37.6	0 33.7	11 07.4	21 00.0	20 16.0	18 56.5
23 F	22 11 08	4 16 25	12♑00 53	19 20 58	17 31.0	15 58.3	20 28.3	26 34.0	1 01.2	0 28.1	11 02.6	21R00.1	20 16.9	18 55.4
24 Sa	22 15 05	5 16 49	26 45 52	4♒14 47	17 29.4	17 47.4	21 37.4	27 21.3	1 24.8	0 22.6	10 57.9	21 00.1	20 17.8	18 54.4
25 Su	22 19 01	6 17 12	11♒46 45	19 20 42	17 28.1	19 35.0	22 46.7	28 08.7	1 48.4	0 17.3	10 53.1	21 00.1	20 18.7	18 53.3
26 M	22 22 58	7 17 33	26 55 28	4♓29 52	17D27.3	21 20.8	23 56.1	28 56.0	2 12.0	0 12.1	10 48.3	21 00.0	20 19.5	18 52.1
27 Tu	22 26 54	8 17 52	12♓02 41	19 32 46	17 27.1	23 04.3	25 05.6	29 43.4	2 35.6	0 07.1	10 43.5	20 59.8	20 20.4	18 51.0
28 W	22 30 51	9 18 09	26 59 06	4♈20 44	17 27.4	24 45.2	26 15.2	0♓30.7	2 59.1	0 02.3	10 38.7	20 59.6	20 21.1	18 49.8

Astro Data

	Dy Hr Mn
☽0N	4 14:09
♆✶♇	11 9:43
☽0S	19 5:34
♃◻♆	21 4:14
♇R	21 20:47
☽0N	31 23:29
☽0S	15 12:13
♅R	24 11:58
☽0N	28 10:23

Planet Ingress

		Dy Hr Mn
♀	♐	7 6:38
☿	♑	8 22:33
☉	♒	20 16:00
♂	♒	20 17:07
☿	♒	28 12:49
♀	♑	5 9:16
☿	♓	14 20:38
☉	♓	19 6:13
⚳	♓	20 21:47
♂	♓	27 20:25
♃	♋R	28 23:35

Last Aspect / ☽ Ingress (January)

Dy Hr Mn				Dy Hr Mn
1 23:21	♀	◻	♓	2 7:08
4 4:51	♀	△	♈	4 9:41
6 8:36	☿	△	♉	6 15:17
8 5:09	♂	△	♊	8 23:42
10 12:56	♇	△	♋	11 10:14
13 10:51	♂	☍	♌	13 22:16
15 15:25	♅	◻	♍	16 11:10
18 20:48	♂	△	♎	18 23:40
20 13:51	♆	✶	♏	21 9:51
23 0:38	☿	✶	♐	23 16:08
25 1:26	♆	☌	♑	25 18:27
27 15:59	☿	☌	♒	27 18:12
29 5:02	♀	✶	♓	29 17:25
31 9:05	♀	◻	♈	31 18:11

Last Aspect / ☽ Ingress (February)

Dy Hr Mn				Dy Hr Mn
2 16:47	♀	△	♉	2 22:03
4 12:12	♅	☍	♊	5 5:33
6 20:14	♆	☍	♋	7 16:06
9 10:00	♅	△	♌	10 4:25
12 7:58	☿	☍	♍	12 17:18
14 11:33	♅	✶	♎	15 5:37
17 12:52	☉	△	♏	17 16:12
19 11:55	♂	◻	♐	19 23:51
21 19:58	♂	✶	♑	22 4:00
23 14:41	♅	✶	♒	24 5:12
26 2:42	♂	☌	♓	26 4:52
27 21:42	♀	✶	♈	28 4:54

☽ Phases & Eclipses

Dy Hr Mn		
5 11:15	☽	14♈31
13 7:09	○	22♋30
21 11:23	☾	0♏49
28 6:20	●	7♒44
4 0:36	☽	14♉36
12 2:39	○	22♌47
20 1:17	☾	0♐48
26 16:45	●	7♓29
26 16:54:16	●	T 02'49"

Astro Data

1 January 1979
Julian Day # 28855
SVP 5♓33'13"
GC 26♐32.8 ⚴ 18♑46.0
Eris 13♈37.1 ⚵ 22♒13.8
⚷ 5♉08.2R ⚶ 8♒14.4
☽ Mean ☊ 21♍11.9

1 February 1979
Julian Day # 28886
SVP 5♓33'08"
GC 26♐32.8 ⚴ 0♒17.8
Eris 13♈42.4 ⚵ 6♓32.0
⚷ 5♉11.5 ⚶ 23♒54.3
☽ Mean ☊ 19♍33.4

March 1979 — LONGITUDE

Day	Sid.Time	☉	0 hr ☽	Noon ☽	True ☊	☿	♀	♂	⚳	♃	♄	♅	♆	♇
1 Th	22 34 48	10♓18 25	11♈36 55	18♈47 04	17♍28.0	26♓22.7	27♑24.9	1♓18.1	3♓22.7	29♋57.6	10♍33.9	20♏59.4	20♐21.9	18♎48.6
2 F	22 38 44	11 18 38	25 50 44	2♉47 41	17 28.6	27 56.5	28 34.7	2 05.4	3 46.2	29R 53.1	10R 29.1	20R 59.1	20 22.6	18R 47.4
3 Sa	22 42 41	12 18 50	9♉37 51	16 21 17	17 29.2	29 25.9	29 44.5	2 52.8	4 09.7	29 48.8	10 24.3	20 58.7	20 23.3	18 46.1
4 Su	22 46 37	13 19 00	22 58 09	29 28 47	17 29.5	0♈50.3	0♒54.5	3 40.1	4 33.2	29 44.6	10 19.5	20 58.3	20 23.9	18 44.9
5 M	22 50 34	14 19 07	5♊53 32	12♊12 53	17R 29.6	2 09.1	2 04.5	4 27.4	4 56.7	29 40.7	10 14.7	20 57.9	20 24.5	18 43.6
6 Tu	22 54 30	15 19 12	18 27 18	24 37 19	17 29.6	3 21.9	3 14.6	5 14.8	5 20.2	29 36.9	10 09.9	20 57.3	20 25.1	18 42.3
7 W	22 58 27	16 19 16	0♋43 30	6♋46 23	17 29.5	4 28.0	4 24.8	6 02.1	5 43.6	29 33.3	10 05.1	20 56.8	20 25.6	18 40.9
8 Th	23 02 23	17 19 17	12 46 32	18 44 28	17D 29.5	5 26.9	5 35.1	6 49.4	6 07.1	29 29.8	10 00.4	20 56.2	20 26.2	18 39.6
9 F	23 06 20	18 19 16	24 40 44	0♌35 48	17 29.5	6 18.3	6 45.5	7 36.7	6 30.5	29 26.6	9 55.6	20 55.5	20 26.6	18 38.2
10 Sa	23 10 17	19 19 12	6♌30 09	12 24 14	17 29.7	7 01.6	7 55.9	8 23.9	6 53.9	29 23.5	9 50.9	20 54.8	20 27.1	18 36.8
11 Su	23 14 13	20 19 07	18 18 26	24 13 08	17 29.9	7 36.6	9 06.4	9 11.2	7 17.3	29 20.7	9 46.2	20 54.0	20 27.5	18 35.4
12 M	23 18 10	21 19 00	0♍08 42	6♍05 25	17R 30.2	8 03.1	10 16.9	9 58.5	7 40.6	29 18.0	9 41.5	20 53.2	20 27.9	18 34.0
13 Tu	23 22 06	22 18 50	12 03 36	18 03 30	17 30.2	8 20.9	11 27.6	10 45.7	8 03.9	29 15.5	9 36.9	20 52.3	20 28.2	18 32.5
14 W	23 26 03	23 18 39	24 05 21	0♎09 23	17 30.1	8R 30.0	12 38.3	11 32.9	8 27.2	29 13.2	9 32.3	20 51.4	20 28.5	18 31.0
15 Th	23 29 59	24 18 26	6♎15 47	12 24 46	17 29.6	8 30.5	13 49.1	12 20.2	8 50.5	29 11.0	9 27.7	20 50.4	20 28.8	18 29.6
16 F	23 33 56	25 18 11	18 36 30	24 51 10	17 28.7	8 22.5	14 59.9	13 07.4	9 13.8	29 09.1	9 23.2	20 49.4	20 29.0	18 28.0
17 Sa	23 37 52	26 17 54	1♏08 56	7♏30 00	17 27.6	8 06.4	16 10.8	13 54.5	9 37.0	29 07.4	9 18.7	20 48.3	20 29.3	18 26.5
18 Su	23 41 49	27 17 35	13 54 31	20 22 40	17 26.3	7 42.8	17 21.8	14 41.7	10 00.2	29 05.8	9 14.2	20 47.2	20 29.4	18 25.0
19 M	23 45 45	28 17 14	26 54 38	3♐30 34	17 25.2	7 12.2	18 32.8	15 28.9	10 23.4	29 04.5	9 09.8	20 46.0	20 29.6	18 23.5
20 Tu	23 49 42	29 16 52	10♐10 37	16 54 57	17D 24.4	6 35.4	19 43.9	16 16.0	10 46.6	29 03.3	9 05.4	20 44.8	20 29.7	18 21.9
21 W	23 53 39	0♈16 28	23 43 38	0♑36 45	17 24.1	5 53.2	20 55.0	17 03.2	11 09.7	29 02.3	9 01.1	20 43.6	20 29.8	18 20.3
22 Th	23 57 35	1 16 03	7♑34 20	14 36 18	17 24.4	5 06.7	22 06.2	17 50.3	11 32.8	29 01.5	8 56.8	20 42.3	20R 29.8	18 18.8
23 F	0 01 32	2 15 35	21 42 32	28 52 49	17 25.3	4 16.9	23 17.5	18 37.4	11 55.8	29 01.0	8 52.6	20 40.9	20 29.8	18 17.2
24 Sa	0 05 28	3 15 06	6♒06 50	13♒24 09	17 26.4	3 24.9	24 28.8	19 24.5	12 18.9	29 00.6	8 48.5	20 39.5	20 29.8	18 15.6
25 Su	0 09 25	4 14 35	20 44 15	28 06 27	17 27.5	2 31.9	25 40.1	20 11.6	12 41.9	29D 00.4	8 44.4	20 38.1	20 29.7	18 13.9
26 M	0 13 21	5 14 03	5♓30 03	12♓54 13	17R 28.1	1 38.9	26 51.5	20 58.6	13 04.8	29 00.4	8 40.3	20 36.6	20 29.6	18 12.3
27 Tu	0 17 18	6 13 28	20 18 04	27 40 42	17 28.0	0 47.0	28 02.9	21 45.6	13 27.8	29 00.5	8 36.3	20 35.1	20 29.5	18 10.7
28 W	0 21 14	7 12 51	5♈01 12	12♈18 41	17 26.7	29♓57.3	29 14.4	22 32.6	13 50.7	29 00.9	8 32.4	20 33.5	20 29.4	18 09.0
29 Th	0 25 11	8 12 12	19 32 20	26 41 25	17 24.5	29 10.5	0♓25.9	23 19.6	14 13.5	29 01.5	8 28.5	20 31.9	20 29.2	18 07.4
30 F	0 29 08	9 11 31	3♉45 20	10♉43 35	17 21.6	28 27.3	1 37.5	24 06.5	14 36.3	29 02.3	8 24.7	20 30.2	20 28.9	18 05.7
31 Sa	0 33 04	10 10 48	17 35 49	24 21 52	17 18.2	27 48.5	2 49.1	24 53.5	14 59.1	29 03.2	8 21.0	20 28.5	20 28.7	18 04.1

April 1979 — LONGITUDE

Day	Sid.Time	☉	0 hr ☽	Noon ☽	True ☊	☿	♀	♂	⚳	♃	♄	♅	♆	♇
1 Su	0 37 01	11♈10 03	1♊01 38	7♊35 14	17♍15.0	27♓14.5	4♓00.7	25♓40.4	15♓21.8	29♋04.4	8♍17.3	20♏26.8	20♐28.4	18♎02.4
2 M	0 40 57	12 09 15	14 02 49	20 24 44	17R 12.4	26R 45.6	5 12.4	26 27.2	15 44.5	29 05.7	8R 13.8	20R 25.1	20R 28.1	18R 00.7
3 Tu	0 44 54	13 08 26	26 41 20	2♋53 06	17D 10.8	26 22.2	6 24.1	27 14.1	16 07.2	29 07.2	8 10.3	20 23.2	20 27.7	17 59.0
4 W	0 48 50	14 07 33	9♋00 34	15 04 18	17 10.3	26 04.2	7 35.8	28 00.9	16 29.8	29 08.9	8 06.8	20 21.4	20 27.3	17 57.4
5 Th	0 52 47	15 06 39	21 04 52	27 02 55	17 11.0	25 51.9	8 47.5	28 47.7	16 52.3	29 10.8	8 03.5	20 19.5	20 26.9	17 55.7
6 F	0 56 43	16 05 42	2♌59 04	8♌53 56	17 12.4	25D 45.2	9 59.3	29 34.4	17 14.9	29 12.9	8 00.2	20 17.6	20 26.5	17 54.0
7 Sa	1 00 40	17 04 43	14 48 07	20 42 13	17 14.2	25 44.0	11 11.1	0♈21.1	17 37.3	29 15.2	7 57.0	20 15.7	20 26.0	17 52.3
8 Su	1 04 37	18 03 41	26 36 48	2♍32 23	17 15.8	25 48.1	12 23.0	1 07.8	17 59.7	29 17.6	7 53.9	20 13.7	20 25.5	17 50.6
9 M	1 08 33	19 02 38	8♍29 28	14 28 30	17R 16.7	25 57.5	13 34.8	1 54.5	18 22.1	29 20.2	7 50.9	20 11.7	20 25.0	17 48.9
10 Tu	1 12 30	20 01 32	20 29 54	26 34 00	17 16.3	26 12.0	14 46.7	2 41.1	18 44.4	29 23.1	7 48.0	20 09.6	20 24.4	17 47.3
11 W	1 16 26	21 00 24	2♎41 08	8♎51 31	17 14.3	26 31.4	15 58.7	3 27.7	19 06.7	29 26.0	7 45.1	20 07.6	20 23.8	17 45.6
12 Th	1 20 23	21 59 14	15 05 21	21 22 46	17 10.7	26 55.4	17 10.6	4 14.3	19 28.9	29 29.2	7 42.4	20 05.5	20 23.1	17 43.9
13 F	1 24 19	22 58 02	27 43 50	4♏08 35	17 05.7	27 23.9	18 22.6	5 00.8	19 51.0	29 32.5	7 39.7	20 03.3	20 22.5	17 42.2
14 Sa	1 28 16	23 56 48	10♏36 59	17 08 59	16 59.7	27 56.6	19 34.6	5 47.3	20 13.2	29 36.0	7 37.1	20 01.2	20 21.8	17 40.5
15 Su	1 32 12	24 55 32	23 44 29	0♐23 20	16 53.3	28 33.4	20 46.7	6 33.7	20 35.2	29 39.7	7 34.6	19 59.0	20 21.1	17 38.9
16 M	1 36 09	25 54 15	7♐05 25	13 50 33	16 47.5	29 14.1	21 58.7	7 20.2	20 57.2	29 43.6	7 32.2	19 56.8	20 20.3	17 37.2
17 Tu	1 40 05	26 52 55	20 38 36	27 29 25	16 42.8	29 58.5	23 10.8	8 06.6	21 19.2	29 47.6	7 29.9	19 54.6	20 19.6	17 35.5
18 W	1 44 02	27 51 35	4♑22 50	11♑18 42	16 39.8	0♈46.3	24 23.0	8 52.9	21 41.0	29 51.8	7 27.7	19 52.3	20 18.8	17 33.9
19 Th	1 47 59	28 50 12	18 16 55	25 17 20	16D 38.6	1 37.5	25 35.1	9 39.3	22 02.9	29 56.1	7 25.6	19 50.0	20 17.9	17 32.2
20 F	1 51 55	29 48 48	2♒19 49	9♒24 13	16 38.8	2 31.9	26 47.3	10 25.6	22 24.7	0♌00.7	7 23.6	19 47.7	20 17.1	17 30.6
21 Sa	1 55 52	0♉47 22	16 30 23	23 38 06	16 40.0	3 29.3	27 59.5	11 11.8	22 46.4	0 05.4	7 21.7	19 45.4	20 16.2	17 29.0
22 Su	1 59 48	1 45 54	0♓47 08	7♓57 11	16R 41.1	4 29.6	29 11.7	11 58.0	23 08.0	0 10.2	7 19.8	19 43.0	20 15.3	17 27.3
23 M	2 03 45	2 44 25	15 07 53	22 18 50	16 41.2	5 32.8	0♈24.0	12 44.2	23 29.6	0 15.2	7 18.1	19 40.7	20 14.3	17 25.7
24 Tu	2 07 41	3 42 54	29 29 32	6♈39 27	16 39.6	6 38.5	1 36.2	13 30.4	23 51.1	0 20.4	7 16.5	19 38.3	20 13.4	17 24.1
25 W	2 11 38	4 41 22	13♈48 00	20 54 35	16 35.7	7 46.9	2 48.5	14 16.5	24 12.6	0 25.7	7 15.0	19 35.9	20 12.4	17 22.5
26 Th	2 15 34	5 39 47	27 58 34	4♉59 21	16 29.7	8 57.7	4 00.8	15 02.5	24 33.9	0 31.2	7 13.6	19 33.5	20 11.4	17 20.9
27 F	2 19 31	6 38 11	11♉56 22	18 49 07	16 22.0	10 10.9	5 13.1	15 48.5	24 55.3	0 36.8	7 12.2	19 31.0	20 10.3	17 19.3
28 Sa	2 23 28	7 36 33	25 37 10	2♊20 11	16 13.2	11 26.5	6 25.5	16 34.5	25 16.5	0 42.6	7 11.0	19 28.6	20 09.3	17 17.8
29 Su	2 27 24	8 34 53	8♊57 59	15 30 25	16 04.5	12 44.3	7 37.8	17 20.5	25 37.7	0 48.6	7 09.9	19 26.1	20 08.2	17 16.2
30 M	2 31 21	9 33 11	21 57 31	28 19 25	15 56.8	14 04.3	8 50.2	18 06.4	25 58.8	0 54.7	7 08.9	19 23.7	20 07.0	17 14.7

Astro Data

	Dy Hr Mn
☿0N	2 20:25
☽0S	14 18:16
☿R	15 1:14
☉0N	21 5:21
♆R	23 7:34
♃D	26 0:55
☽0N	27 21:14
♅⊻♆	31 9:35
☿0S	2 0:56
☿D	7 5:21
♂0N	9 21:12
☽0S	11 1:17
☿0N	24 1:50
☽0N	24 6:36
♀0N	26 5:03

Planet Ingress

	Dy Hr Mn
♀ ♒	3 17:18
☿ ♈	3 21:32
☉ ♈	21 5:22
☿ ♓R	28 10:39
♀ ♓	29 3:18
♂ ♈	7 1:08
☿ ♈	17 12:48
♃ ♌	20 8:30
☉ ♉	20 16:35
♀ ♈	23 4:02

Last Aspect / ☽ Ingress (March)

Last Aspect Dy Hr Mn		☽ Ingress Dy Hr Mn
2 6:59	♃ □	♉ 2 7:09
4 12:29	♃ ⚹	♊ 4 12:58
6 3:48	♆ ☍	♋ 6 22:34
9 9:40	♃ ☌	♌ 9 10:47
11 5:16	♅ □	♍ 11 23:42
14 10:09	♃ ⚹	♎ 14 11:42
16 20:11	♃ □	♏ 16 21:49
19 3:58	♃ △	♐ 19 5:38
20 18:19	♆ ☌	♑ 21 10:56
23 12:13	♃ ☍	♒ 23 13:52
25 7:41	♀ ☌	♓ 25 15:04
27 14:10	♃ △	♈ 27 15:47
29 15:57	♃ □	♉ 29 17:36
31 20:26	♃ ⚹	♊ 31 22:08

Last Aspect / ☽ Ingress (April)

Last Aspect Dy Hr Mn		☽ Ingress Dy Hr Mn
3 0:19	♂ □	♋ 3 6:24
5 16:19	♃ ☌	♌ 5 17:58
7 11:27	♆ △	♍ 8 6:52
10 17:34	♃ ⚹	♎ 10 18:45
13 3:22	♃ □	♏ 13 4:16
15 10:41	♃ △	♐ 15 11:18
17 10:51	☉ △	♑ 17 16:23
19 19:58	♃ ☍	♒ 19 20:02
21 6:21	♆ ⚹	♓ 21 22:41
23 8:32	♆ □	♈ 24 0:51
25 10:49	♆ △	♉ 26 3:27
27 13:13	♅ ☍	♊ 28 7:49
29 20:35	♆ ☍	♋ 30 15:11

☽ Phases & Eclipses

Dy Hr Mn	
5 16:23	☽ 14♊30
13 21:14	○ 22♍42
13 21:08	☍ P 0.854
21 11:22	☾ 0♑15
28 3:00	● 6♈51
4 9:57	☽ 14♋03
12 13:15	○ 22♎02
19 18:30	☾ 29♑06
26 13:15	● 5♉43

Astro Data

1 March 1979
Julian Day # 28914
SVP 5♓33'05"
GC 26♐32.9 ⚴ 10♒10.1
Eris 13♈55.2 ⚵ 20♓31.0
⚷ 6♉01.2 ⚶ 7♓59.0
☽ Mean ☊ 18♍04.4

1 April 1979
Julian Day # 28945
SVP 5♓33'03"
GC 26♐33.0 ⚴ 19♒56.3
Eris 14♈14.8 ⚵ 6♈49.6
⚷ 7♉35.5 ⚶ 23♓12.3
☽ Mean ☊ 16♍25.9

LONGITUDE

May 1979

Day	Sid.Time	☉	0 hr ☽	Noon ☽	True ☊	☿	♀	♂	⚳	♃	♄	♅	♆	♇
1 Tu	2 35 17	10♉31 28	4♋36 20	10♋48 36	15♍50.7	15♈26.4	10♈02.5	18♈52.2	26♓19.8	1♌00.9	7♍08.0	19♏21.2	20♐05.9	17♎13.2
2 W	2 39 14	11 29 42	16 56 37	23 00 52	15R 46.7	16 50.7	11 14.9	19 38.0	26 40.7	1 07.3	7R 07.2	19R 18.7	20R 04.8	17R 11.7
3 Th	2 43 10	12 27 54	29 01 54	5♌00 19	15D 44.7	18 17.0	12 27.3	20 23.8	27 01.6	1 13.8	7 06.5	19 16.2	20 03.6	17 10.2
4 F	2 47 07	13 26 04	10♌56 44	16 51 48	15 44.5	19 45.4	13 39.7	21 09.5	27 22.4	1 20.5	7 05.9	19 13.7	20 02.4	17 08.7
5 Sa	2 51 03	14 24 12	22 46 12	28 40 35	15 45.2	21 15.7	14 52.1	21 55.1	27 43.1	1 27.3	7 05.4	19 11.2	20 01.2	17 07.2
6 Su	2 55 00	15 22 18	4♍35 37	10♍31 57	15R 46.0	22 48.1	16 04.6	22 40.7	28 03.7	1 34.3	7 05.1	19 08.7	19 59.9	17 05.8
7 M	2 58 57	16 20 22	16 30 13	22 31 01	15 45.8	24 22.5	17 17.0	23 26.3	28 24.2	1 41.4	7 04.8	19 06.1	19 58.6	17 04.4
8 Tu	3 02 53	17 18 25	28 34 52	4♎42 16	15 44.0	25 58.8	18 29.5	24 11.8	28 44.7	1 48.6	7 04.6	19 03.6	19 57.4	17 03.0
9 W	3 06 50	18 16 25	10♎53 39	17 09 21	15 39.9	27 37.1	19 41.9	24 57.3	29 05.1	1 55.9	7D 04.6	19 01.1	19 56.1	17 01.6
10 Th	3 10 46	19 14 24	23 29 39	29 54 43	15 33.3	29 17.4	20 54.4	25 42.7	29 25.3	2 03.4	7 04.6	18 58.6	19 54.7	17 00.2
11 F	3 14 43	20 12 21	6♏24 36	12♏59 19	15 24.6	0♉59.7	22 06.9	26 28.1	29 45.5	2 11.0	7 04.7	18 56.0	19 53.4	16 58.9
12 Sa	3 18 39	21 10 16	19 38 42	26 22 32	15 14.3	2 43.9	23 19.4	27 13.4	0♈05.6	2 18.8	7 05.0	18 53.5	19 52.0	16 57.6
13 Su	3 22 36	22 08 11	3♐10 30	10♐02 14	15 03.5	4 30.1	24 32.0	27 58.7	0 25.7	2 26.6	7 05.3	18 51.0	19 50.7	16 56.2
14 M	3 26 32	23 06 03	16 57 16	23 55 06	14 53.3	6 18.3	25 44.5	28 43.9	0 45.6	2 34.6	7 05.8	18 48.5	19 49.3	16 55.0
15 Tu	3 30 29	24 03 55	0♑55 16	7♑57 15	14 44.8	8 08.5	26 57.1	29 29.1	1 05.4	2 42.7	7 06.4	18 46.0	19 47.9	16 53.7
16 W	3 34 26	25 01 45	15 00 34	22 04 47	14 38.7	10 00.7	28 09.7	0♉14.3	1 25.2	2 51.0	7 07.0	18 43.5	19 46.5	16 52.5
17 Th	3 38 22	25 59 33	29 09 31	6♒14 27	14 35.1	11 54.8	29 22.2	0 59.3	1 44.8	2 59.3	7 07.8	18 41.0	19 45.0	16 51.2
18 F	3 42 19	26 57 21	13♒19 19	20 23 52	14D 33.7	13 50.9	0♉34.9	1 44.4	2 04.3	3 07.8	7 08.7	18 38.5	19 43.6	16 50.0
19 Sa	3 46 15	27 55 08	27 27 59	4♓31 29	14R 33.6	15 48.9	1 47.5	2 29.4	2 23.8	3 16.4	7 09.7	18 36.0	19 42.1	16 48.9
20 Su	3 50 12	28 52 53	11♓34 17	18 36 17	14 33.7	17 48.8	3 00.1	3 14.3	2 43.1	3 25.1	7 10.7	18 33.5	19 40.6	16 47.7
21 M	3 54 08	29 50 37	25 37 21	2♈37 21	14 32.7	19 50.5	4 12.8	3 59.2	3 02.4	3 33.9	7 11.9	18 31.0	19 39.1	16 46.6
22 Tu	3 58 05	0♊48 21	9♈36 07	16 33 26	14 29.5	21 54.0	5 25.4	4 44.1	3 21.5	3 42.8	7 13.2	18 28.6	19 37.6	16 45.5
23 W	4 02 01	1 46 03	23 29 05	0♉22 45	14 23.6	23 59.1	6 38.1	5 28.8	3 40.5	3 51.8	7 14.6	18 26.1	19 36.1	16 44.4
24 Th	4 05 58	2 43 44	7♉14 08	14 02 53	14 14.9	26 05.8	7 50.8	6 13.6	3 59.4	4 01.0	7 16.1	18 23.7	19 34.6	16 43.4
25 F	4 09 55	3 41 24	20 48 41	27 31 10	14 03.9	28 13.8	9 03.5	6 58.3	4 18.2	4 10.2	7 17.7	18 21.3	19 33.0	16 42.4
26 Sa	4 13 51	4 39 03	4♊10 02	10♊45 01	13 51.5	0♊23.1	10 16.2	7 42.9	4 36.9	4 19.6	7 19.4	18 18.9	19 31.5	16 41.4
27 Su	4 17 48	5 36 40	17 15 55	23 42 35	13 39.0	2 33.4	11 28.9	8 27.5	4 55.5	4 29.0	7 21.2	18 16.5	19 29.9	16 40.4
28 M	4 21 44	6 34 17	0♋04 58	6♋23 04	13 27.5	4 44.5	12 41.7	9 12.0	5 13.9	4 38.6	7 23.1	18 14.1	19 28.4	16 39.5
29 Tu	4 25 41	7 31 52	12 37 02	18 47 02	13 17.9	6 56.2	13 54.4	9 56.5	5 32.3	4 48.2	7 25.1	18 11.8	19 26.8	16 38.5
30 W	4 29 37	8 29 26	24 53 22	0♌56 23	13 10.9	9 08.1	15 07.2	10 40.9	5 50.5	4 58.0	7 27.2	18 09.5	19 25.2	16 37.7
31 Th	4 33 34	9 26 58	6♌56 32	12 54 17	13 06.5	11 20.2	16 20.0	11 25.2	6 08.5	5 07.9	7 29.4	18 07.2	19 23.6	16 36.8

LONGITUDE

June 1979

Day	Sid.Time	☉	0 hr ☽	Noon ☽	True ☊	☿	♀	♂	⚳	♃	♄	♅	♆	♇
1 F	4 37 30	10♊24 29	18♌50 14	24♌44 56	13♍04.4	13♊31.9	17♉32.7	12♉09.5	6♈26.5	5♌17.8	7♍31.7	18♏04.9	19♐22.0	16♎36.0
2 Sa	4 41 27	11 21 59	0♍39 03	6♍33 14	13R 03.8	15 43.2	18 45.5	12 53.7	6 44.3	5 27.8	7 34.1	18R 02.6	19R 20.4	16R 35.2
3 Su	4 45 24	12 19 27	12 28 11	18 24 34	13 03.8	17 53.7	19 58.3	13 37.9	7 02.0	5 38.0	7 36.6	18 00.4	19 18.8	16 34.4
4 M	4 49 20	13 16 54	24 23 05	0♎24 24	13 03.2	20 03.1	21 11.1	14 22.0	7 19.6	5 48.2	7 39.2	17 58.2	19 17.2	16 33.7
5 Tu	4 53 17	14 14 20	6♎29 10	12 37 59	13 01.0	22 11.3	22 23.9	15 06.1	7 37.0	5 58.5	7 41.8	17 56.0	19 15.6	16 32.9
6 W	4 57 13	15 11 45	18 51 25	25 09 57	12 56.6	24 18.0	23 36.8	15 50.1	7 54.3	6 08.9	7 44.6	17 53.9	19 14.0	16 32.3
7 Th	5 01 10	16 09 09	1♏33 58	8♏03 46	12 49.7	26 23.0	24 49.6	16 34.0	8 11.4	6 19.3	7 47.5	17 51.7	19 12.4	16 31.6
8 F	5 05 06	17 06 32	14 39 30	21 21 14	12 40.3	28 26.2	26 02.4	17 17.9	8 28.5	6 29.9	7 50.5	17 49.6	19 10.8	16 31.0
9 Sa	5 09 03	18 03 53	28 08 52	5♐02 07	12 29.3	0♋27.5	27 15.3	18 01.8	8 45.3	6 40.5	7 53.5	17 47.6	19 09.1	16 30.4
10 Su	5 12 59	19 01 14	12♐00 37	19 03 51	12 17.7	2 26.6	28 28.2	18 45.5	9 02.1	6 51.3	7 56.7	17 45.5	19 07.5	16 29.9
11 M	5 16 56	19 58 34	26 11 09	3♑21 47	12 06.6	4 23.5	29 41.1	19 29.2	9 18.6	7 02.1	7 59.9	17 43.5	19 05.9	16 29.3
12 Tu	5 20 53	20 55 54	10♑34 57	17 49 52	11 57.3	6 18.2	0♊54.0	20 12.9	9 35.1	7 12.9	8 03.2	17 41.5	19 04.3	16 28.8
13 W	5 24 49	21 53 13	25 05 40	2♒21 37	11 50.5	8 10.6	2 06.9	20 56.5	9 51.4	7 23.9	8 06.6	17 39.6	19 02.7	16 28.4
14 Th	5 28 46	22 50 31	9♒36 59	16 51 10	11 46.4	10 00.6	3 19.9	21 40.0	10 07.5	7 34.9	8 10.1	17 37.7	19 01.0	16 27.9
15 F	5 32 42	23 47 49	24 03 39	1♓14 02	11D 44.6	11 48.3	4 32.9	22 23.5	10 23.5	7 46.0	8 13.7	17 35.8	18 59.4	16 27.5
16 Sa	5 36 39	24 45 07	8♓21 59	15 27 20	11R 44.4	13 33.5	5 45.8	23 07.0	10 39.3	7 57.2	8 17.4	17 33.9	18 57.8	16 27.2
17 Su	5 40 35	25 42 24	22 29 55	29 29 40	11 44.5	15 16.3	6 58.8	23 50.3	10 54.9	8 08.4	8 21.2	17 32.1	18 56.2	16 26.8
18 M	5 44 32	26 39 41	6♈26 35	13♈20 40	11 43.6	16 56.6	8 11.9	24 33.6	11 10.4	8 19.7	8 25.0	17 30.3	18 54.6	16 26.5
19 Tu	5 48 28	27 36 58	20 11 56	27 00 25	11 40.7	18 34.5	9 24.9	25 16.9	11 25.7	8 31.1	8 28.9	17 28.6	18 53.0	16 26.3
20 W	5 52 25	28 34 15	3♉46 06	10♉28 59	11 35.2	20 09.9	10 37.9	26 00.1	11 40.9	8 42.6	8 33.0	17 26.9	18 51.4	16 26.0
21 Th	5 56 22	29 31 31	17 09 02	23 46 13	11 27.1	21 42.8	11 51.0	26 43.2	11 55.9	8 54.1	8 37.1	17 25.2	18 49.8	16 25.8
22 F	6 00 18	0♋28 47	0♊20 26	6♊51 37	11 16.8	23 13.2	13 04.1	27 26.3	12 10.7	9 05.7	8 41.2	17 23.6	18 48.2	16 25.7
23 Sa	6 04 15	1 26 03	13 19 40	19 44 31	11 05.2	24 41.1	14 17.2	28 09.3	12 25.3	9 17.3	8 45.5	17 22.0	18 46.6	16 25.5
24 Su	6 08 11	2 23 19	26 06 05	2♋24 21	10 53.4	26 06.5	15 30.3	28 52.3	12 39.7	9 29.0	8 49.9	17 20.5	18 45.1	16 25.4
25 M	6 12 08	3 20 34	8♋39 18	14 50 59	10 42.5	27 29.2	16 43.5	29 35.2	12 54.0	9 40.8	8 54.3	17 19.0	18 43.5	16 25.4
26 Tu	6 16 04	4 17 49	20 59 29	27 04 58	10 33.4	28 49.3	17 56.6	0♊18.0	13 08.0	9 52.6	8 58.8	17 17.5	18 42.0	16D 25.3
27 W	6 20 01	5 15 03	3♌07 37	9♌07 43	10 26.7	0♌06.8	19 09.8	1 00.7	13 21.9	10 04.5	9 03.4	17 16.1	18 40.4	16 25.3
28 Th	6 23 58	6 12 17	15 05 36	21 01 38	10 22.5	1 21.6	20 23.0	1 43.4	13 35.5	10 16.4	9 08.0	17 14.7	18 38.9	16 25.3
29 F	6 27 54	7 09 31	26 56 17	2♍50 03	10D 20.5	2 33.5	21 36.2	2 26.1	13 49.0	10 28.4	9 12.7	17 13.4	18 37.4	16 25.4
30 Sa	6 31 51	8 06 44	8♍43 27	14 37 05	10 20.3	3 42.7	22 49.4	3 08.6	14 02.3	10 40.4	9 17.6	17 12.1	18 35.8	16 25.5

Astro Data	Dy Hr Mn
☽0S	8 9:53
♄ D	9 14:53
☽0N	21 14:09
♃⚼♆	27 13:59
☽0S	4 19:33
☽0N	17 20:42
♃⚺♄	19 4:59
♇ D	27 1:26

Planet Ingress		Dy Hr Mn
☿	♉	10 22:03
⚳	♈	12 5:16
♂	♉	16 4:25
♀	♉	18 0:29
☉	♊	21 15:54
☿	♊	26 7:44
☿	♋	9 6:32
♀	♊	11 18:13
☉	♋	21 23:56
♂	♊	26 1:55
☿	♌	27 9:51

Last Aspect Dy Hr Mn		☽ Ingress	Dy Hr Mn
2 4:51	♂ □	♌	3 1:56
4 21:19	♂ △	♍	5 14:41
7 6:57	♆ □	♎	8 2:48
10 10:40	☿ ☍	♏	10 12:10
12 2:01	☉ ☍	♐	12 18:25
14 20:43	♂ △	♑	14 22:25
16 23:16	♀ □	♒	17 1:26
18 23:57	☉ □	♓	19 4:18
21 6:53	☉ ⚹	♈	21 7:30
22 17:18	♆ △	♉	23 11:20
25 13:31	☿ ☌	♊	25 16:28
27 4:10	♆ ☍	♋	27 23:51
29 10:51	♅ △	♌	30 10:08

Last Aspect Dy Hr Mn		☽ Ingress	Dy Hr Mn
1 1:06	♆ △	♍	1 22:41
3 15:30	♀ △	♎	4 11:12
6 10:02	☿ △	♏	6 21:05
8 21:06	♀ ☍	♐	9 3:15
10 12:06	♆ ☌	♑	11 6:23
12 16:09	♂ △	♒	13 8:06
14 22:41	☉ △	♓	15 9:56
17 5:01	☉ □	♈	17 12:52
19 13:10	☉ ⚹	♉	19 17:18
21 17:41	♂ ☌	♊	21 23:23
23 10:12	♆ ☍	♋	24 7:24
26 15:52	☿ ☌	♌	26 17:47
28 10:33	♀ ⚹	♍	29 6:14

☽ Phases & Eclipses Dy Hr Mn	
4 4:25	☽ 13♌08
12 2:01	○ 20♏46
18 23:57	☾ 27♒26
26 0:00	● 4♊10
2 22:37	☽ 11♍47
10 11:55	○ 19♐01
17 5:01	☾ 25♓26
24 11:58	● 2♋23

Astro Data

1 May 1979
Julian Day # 28975
SVP 5♓33'00"
GC 26♐33.0 ⚴ 27♒30.5
Eris 14♈34.5 ⚵ 23♈11.6
⚷ 9♉27.2 ⚶ 7♈17.5
☽ Mean ☊ 14♍50.6

1 June 1979
Julian Day # 29006
SVP 5♓32'56"
GC 26♐33.1 ⚴ 2♓15.7
Eris 14♈50.6 ⚵ 10♉28.4
⚷ 11♉22.1 ⚶ 20♈50.1
☽ Mean ☊ 13♍12.1

July 1979 — LONGITUDE

Day	Sid.Time	☉	0 hr ☽	Noon ☽	True ☊	☿	♀	♂	⚳	♃	♄	♅	♆	♇
1 Su	6 35 47	9♋03 57	20♍31 33	26♍27 31	10♍21.0	4♌48.9	24♊02.6	3♊51.1	14♈15.3	10♌52.5	9♍22.4	17♏10.8	18♐34.3	16♎25.6
2 M	6 39 44	10 01 09	2♎25 38	8♎26 34	10R 21.5	5 52.2	25 15.9	4 33.6	14 28.2	11 04.6	9 27.4	17R 09.6	18R 32.9	16 25.8
3 Tu	6 43 40	10 58 21	14 31 00	20 39 35	10 21.0	6 52.3	26 29.2	5 16.0	14 40.8	11 16.8	9 32.4	17 08.5	18 31.4	16 26.0
4 W	6 47 37	11 55 33	26 52 55	3♏11 36	10 18.8	7 49.4	27 42.4	5 58.3	14 53.3	11 29.1	9 37.5	17 07.4	18 29.9	16 26.2
5 Th	6 51 33	12 52 44	9♏36 09	16 06 57	10 14.5	8 43.1	28 55.7	6 40.5	15 05.5	11 41.3	9 42.7	17 06.3	18 28.5	16 26.5
6 F	6 55 30	13 49 55	22 44 21	29 28 31	10 08.2	9 33.4	0♋09.1	7 22.7	15 17.5	11 53.7	9 47.9	17 05.3	18 27.0	16 26.8
7 Sa	6 59 26	14 47 06	6♐19 30	13♐17 09	10 00.5	10 20.3	1 22.4	8 04.8	15 29.2	12 06.0	9 53.2	17 04.3	18 25.6	16 27.1
8 Su	7 03 23	15 44 18	20 21 11	27 31 06	9 52.1	11 03.5	2 35.7	8 46.8	15 40.8	12 18.5	9 58.6	17 03.4	18 24.2	16 27.5
9 M	7 07 20	16 41 29	4♑46 16	12♑05 53	9 44.0	11 42.9	3 49.1	9 28.8	15 52.1	12 30.9	10 04.0	17 02.5	18 22.8	16 27.9
10 Tu	7 11 16	17 38 40	19 29 00	26 54 38	9 37.2	12 18.5	5 02.5	10 10.8	16 03.2	12 43.4	10 09.5	17 01.7	18 21.5	16 28.4
11 W	7 15 13	18 35 51	4♒21 43	11♒49 11	9 32.4	12 50.0	6 15.9	10 52.6	16 14.1	12 55.9	10 15.0	17 00.9	18 20.1	16 28.8
12 Th	7 19 09	19 33 03	19 16 00	26 41 16	9D 29.8	13 17.3	7 29.4	11 34.4	16 24.7	13 08.5	10 20.7	17 00.2	18 18.8	16 29.3
13 F	7 23 06	20 30 15	4♓04 07	11♓23 51	9 29.2	13 40.4	8 42.8	12 16.1	16 35.0	13 21.1	10 26.3	16 59.5	18 17.5	16 29.9
14 Sa	7 27 02	21 27 28	18 39 55	25 51 53	9 29.9	13 58.9	9 56.3	12 57.8	16 45.2	13 33.7	10 32.1	16 58.9	18 16.2	16 30.4
15 Su	7 30 59	22 24 41	2♈59 27	10♈02 26	9R 31.0	14 13.0	11 09.8	13 39.4	16 55.0	13 46.4	10 37.9	16 58.3	18 14.9	16 31.0
16 M	7 34 56	23 21 55	17 00 48	23 54 31	9 31.5	14 22.3	12 23.3	14 21.0	17 04.6	13 59.1	10 43.7	16 57.7	18 13.6	16 31.7
17 Tu	7 38 52	24 19 09	0♉43 41	7♉28 27	9 30.7	14R 26.9	13 36.9	15 02.4	17 14.0	14 11.9	10 49.7	16 57.3	18 12.4	16 32.3
18 W	7 42 49	25 16 24	14 08 56	20 45 20	9 28.1	14 26.6	14 50.5	15 43.8	17 23.1	14 24.6	10 55.6	16 56.8	18 11.2	16 33.0
19 Th	7 46 45	26 13 40	27 17 50	3♊46 36	9 23.6	14 21.5	16 04.0	16 25.2	17 31.9	14 37.4	11 01.7	16 56.4	18 10.0	16 33.8
20 F	7 50 42	27 10 57	10♊11 51	16 33 43	9 17.5	14 11.5	17 17.7	17 06.5	17 40.5	14 50.3	11 07.8	16 56.1	18 08.8	16 34.5
21 Sa	7 54 38	28 08 14	22 52 23	29 07 58	9 10.5	13 56.7	18 31.3	17 47.7	17 48.8	15 03.1	11 13.9	16 55.8	18 07.6	16 35.3
22 Su	7 58 35	29 05 32	5♋20 39	11♋30 33	9 03.3	13 37.2	19 45.0	18 28.8	17 56.8	15 16.0	11 20.1	16 55.6	18 06.5	16 36.2
23 M	8 02 31	0♌02 51	17 37 48	23 42 34	8 56.7	13 13.1	20 58.7	19 09.9	18 04.5	15 28.9	11 26.3	16 55.4	18 05.4	16 37.0
24 Tu	8 06 28	1 00 10	29 45 02	5♌45 21	8 51.2	12 44.8	22 12.4	19 50.9	18 11.9	15 41.9	11 32.6	16 55.3	18 04.3	16 37.9
25 W	8 10 25	1 57 30	11♌43 45	17 40 28	8 47.4	12 12.6	23 26.1	20 31.9	18 19.0	15 54.8	11 39.0	16D 55.2	18 03.3	16 38.8
26 Th	8 14 21	2 54 50	23 35 46	29 29 58	8D 45.4	11 36.8	24 39.9	21 12.7	18 25.9	16 07.8	11 45.4	16 55.2	18 02.2	16 39.8
27 F	8 18 18	3 52 11	5♍23 24	11♍16 28	8 44.9	10 57.9	25 53.6	21 53.5	18 32.4	16 20.8	11 51.8	16 55.2	18 01.2	16 40.8
28 Sa	8 22 14	4 49 32	17 09 35	23 03 12	8 45.8	10 16.7	27 07.4	22 34.3	18 38.7	16 33.8	11 58.3	16 55.3	18 00.2	16 41.8
29 Su	8 26 11	5 46 54	28 57 49	4♎53 58	8 47.3	9 33.5	28 21.2	23 14.9	18 44.6	16 46.8	12 04.9	16 55.4	17 59.2	16 42.9
30 M	8 30 07	6 44 16	10♎52 13	16 53 08	8 49.0	8 49.3	29 35.0	23 55.5	18 50.2	16 59.9	12 11.4	16 55.6	17 58.3	16 44.0
31 Tu	8 34 04	7 41 39	22 57 19	29 05 22	8R 50.2	8 04.8	0♌48.9	24 36.0	18 55.5	17 12.9	12 18.1	16 55.9	17 57.4	16 45.1

August 1979 — LONGITUDE

Day	Sid.Time	☉	0 hr ☽	Noon ☽	True ☊	☿	♀	♂	⚳	♃	♄	♅	♆	♇
1 W	8 38 00	8♌39 03	5♏17 53	11♏35 26	8♍50.5	7♌20.7	2♌02.7	25♊16.5	19♈00.5	17♌26.0	12♍24.7	16♏56.1	17♐56.5	16♎46.2
2 Th	8 41 57	9 36 27	17 58 34	24 27 45	8R 49.6	6R 37.9	3 16.6	25 56.8	19 05.2	17 39.1	12 31.4	16 56.5	17R 55.6	16 47.4
3 F	8 45 53	10 33 52	1♐03 26	7♐45 53	8 47.4	5 57.2	4 30.5	26 37.1	19 09.6	17 52.2	12 38.2	16 56.9	17 54.8	16 48.6
4 Sa	8 49 50	11 31 17	14 35 21	21 31 51	8 44.4	5 19.4	5 44.4	27 17.3	19 13.6	18 05.3	12 45.0	16 57.3	17 54.0	16 49.8
5 Su	8 53 47	12 28 44	28 35 17	5♑45 23	8 40.8	4 45.3	6 58.4	27 57.5	19 17.3	18 18.4	12 51.8	16 57.8	17 53.2	16 51.1
6 M	8 57 43	13 26 11	13♑01 42	20 23 33	8 37.3	4 15.4	8 12.3	28 37.6	19 20.7	18 31.6	12 58.7	16 58.4	17 52.5	16 52.4
7 Tu	9 01 40	14 23 38	27 50 09	5♒20 30	8 34.4	3 50.5	9 26.3	29 17.6	19 23.8	18 44.7	13 05.6	16 59.0	17 51.7	16 53.7
8 W	9 05 36	15 21 07	12♒53 33	20 28 07	8 32.5	3 31.1	10 40.3	29 57.5	19 26.5	18 57.9	13 12.5	16 59.6	17 51.0	16 55.1
9 Th	9 09 33	16 18 37	28 03 00	5♓37 02	8D 31.7	3 17.7	11 54.3	0♋37.4	19 28.9	19 11.0	13 19.5	17 00.3	17 50.4	16 56.4
10 F	9 13 29	17 16 08	13♓09 06	20 38 10	8 32.0	3D 10.6	13 08.3	1 17.2	19 30.9	19 24.2	13 26.5	17 01.1	17 49.7	16 57.8
11 Sa	9 17 26	18 13 40	28 03 21	5♈23 54	8 33.0	3 10.2	14 22.4	1 57.0	19 32.6	19 37.3	13 33.5	17 01.9	17 49.1	16 59.3
12 Su	9 21 22	19 11 14	12♈39 15	19 48 58	8 34.3	3 16.6	15 36.5	2 36.6	19 33.9	19 50.5	13 40.6	17 02.8	17 48.5	17 00.7
13 M	9 25 19	20 08 49	26 52 48	3♉50 35	8 35.4	3 30.1	16 50.6	3 16.2	19 34.9	20 03.6	13 47.7	17 03.7	17 48.0	17 02.2
14 Tu	9 29 16	21 06 26	10♉42 21	17 28 12	8R 36.0	3 50.8	18 04.7	3 55.7	19 35.5	20 16.8	13 54.8	17 04.6	17 47.5	17 03.7
15 W	9 33 12	22 04 04	24 08 19	0♊42 58	8 35.8	4 18.6	19 18.8	4 35.2	19R 35.8	20 29.9	14 02.0	17 05.6	17 47.0	17 05.3
16 Th	9 37 09	23 01 44	7♊12 27	13 37 08	8 34.9	4 53.5	20 33.0	5 14.5	19 35.7	20 43.1	14 09.2	17 06.7	17 46.5	17 06.8
17 F	9 41 05	23 59 25	19 57 21	26 13 30	8 33.4	5 35.5	21 47.2	5 53.8	19 35.2	20 56.2	14 16.4	17 07.8	17 46.1	17 08.4
18 Sa	9 45 02	24 57 08	2♋25 57	8♋35 04	8 31.6	6 24.5	23 01.4	6 33.1	19 34.4	21 09.4	14 23.6	17 09.0	17 45.7	17 10.1
19 Su	9 48 58	25 54 52	14 41 13	20 44 44	8 29.7	7 20.3	24 15.6	7 12.2	19 33.2	21 22.5	14 30.9	17 10.2	17 45.3	17 11.7
20 M	9 52 55	26 52 38	26 45 58	2♌45 12	8 28.0	8 22.6	25 29.9	7 51.3	19 31.7	21 35.7	14 38.2	17 11.5	17 45.0	17 13.4
21 Tu	9 56 51	27 50 25	8♌42 45	14 38 55	8 26.7	9 31.3	26 44.1	8 30.3	19 29.8	21 48.8	14 45.5	17 12.8	17 44.7	17 15.1
22 W	10 00 48	28 48 14	20 33 57	26 28 10	8 25.9	10 46.0	27 58.4	9 09.2	19 27.5	22 01.9	14 52.8	17 14.1	17 44.4	17 16.8
23 Th	10 04 45	29 46 04	2♍21 49	8♍15 12	8D 25.7	12 06.5	29 12.7	9 48.0	19 24.8	22 15.0	15 00.1	17 15.6	17 44.2	17 18.5
24 F	10 08 41	0♍43 56	14 08 36	20 02 18	8 25.9	13 32.2	0♍27.0	10 26.8	19 21.8	22 28.1	15 07.5	17 17.0	17 44.0	17 20.3
25 Sa	10 12 38	1 41 49	25 56 37	1♎51 55	8 26.3	15 03.0	1 41.4	11 05.5	19 18.4	22 41.2	15 14.9	17 18.5	17 43.8	17 22.1
26 Su	10 16 34	2 39 43	7♎48 31	13 46 49	8 27.0	16 38.3	2 55.7	11 44.1	19 14.6	22 54.3	15 22.3	17 20.1	17 43.6	17 23.9
27 M	10 20 31	3 37 38	19 47 13	25 50 07	8 27.5	18 17.6	4 10.1	12 22.6	19 10.5	23 07.3	15 29.7	17 21.7	17 43.5	17 25.7
28 Tu	10 24 27	4 35 35	1♏55 58	8♏05 14	8 28.0	20 00.6	5 24.4	13 01.0	19 06.0	23 20.3	15 37.1	17 23.3	17 43.4	17 27.6
29 W	10 28 24	5 33 34	14 18 22	20 35 51	8 28.2	21 46.8	6 38.8	13 39.3	19 01.1	23 33.3	15 44.6	17 25.0	17D 43.4	17 29.5
30 Th	10 32 20	6 31 33	26 58 07	3♐25 38	8R 28.3	23 35.6	7 53.2	14 17.6	18 55.9	23 46.3	15 52.0	17 26.8	17 43.4	17 31.4
31 F	10 36 17	7 29 34	9♐58 47	16 37 56	8D 28.3	25 26.6	9 07.6	14 55.8	18 50.3	23 59.3	15 59.5	17 28.6	17 43.4	17 33.3

Astro Data (Dy Hr Mn)

☽0S 2 4:59
☽0N 15 3:42
☿R 17 22:43
♅D 26 10:59
♃✶♇ 29 4:04
☽0S 29 13:05
♃□♅ 30 4:03

♃△♆ 3 16:27
☿D 11 1:31
☽0N 11 12:14
⚳R 15 17:59
♅⚺♇ 16 5:19
☽0S 25 19:33
♆D 30 11:14

Planet Ingress (Dy Hr Mn)

♀ ♋ 6 9:02
☉ ♌ 23 10:49
♀ ♌ 30 20:07

♂ ♋ 8 13:28
☉ ♍ 23 17:47
♀ ♍ 24 3:16

Last Aspect / ☽ Ingress (Dy Hr Mn)

Last Aspect		☽ Ingress	
1 6:34	♀ □	♎	1 19:08
4 0:27	♀ △	♏	4 5:57
5 13:48	♅ ☌	♐	6 12:56
7 20:44	♆ ☌	♑	8 16:07
9 20:02	♅ ✶	♒	10 16:59
11 22:29	♆ ✶	♓	12 17:23
14 4:07	☉ △	♈	14 18:57
16 10:59	☉ □	♉	16 22:43
18 20:56	☉ ✶	♊	19 5:00
20 15:00	♆ ☍	♋	21 13:40
23 5:59	♀ ☌	♌	24 0:30
25 18:08	♂ ✶	♍	26 13:01
28 21:14	♀ ✶	♎	29 2:06
31 2:43	☉ △	♏	31 13:46

Last Aspect		☽ Ingress	
1 23:11	♃ □	♐	2 22:05
4 22:17	♂ ☍	♑	5 2:23
6 6:26	♅ ✶	♒	7 3:28
8 9:35	♃ ☍	♓	9 3:05
10 7:30	♆ □	♈	11 3:10
12 12:03	♃ △	♉	13 5:21
14 19:02	☉ □	♊	15 10:41
17 7:21	☉ ✶	♋	17 19:17
19 4:56	♇ □	♌	20 6:28
22 17:10	☉ ☌	♍	22 19:11
24 7:19	♆ □	♎	25 8:13
27 6:32	♃ ✶	♏	27 20:12
29 17:41	♃ □	♐	30 5:39

☽ Phases & Eclipses (Dy Hr Mn)

2 15:24 ☽ 10♎09
9 19:59 ○ 17♑01
16 10:59 ☾ 23♈19
24 1:41 ● 0♌36

1 5:57 ☽ 8♏25
8 3:21 ○ 15♒00
14 19:02 ☾ 21♉23
22 17:10 ● 29♌01
22 17:21:48 ● A 06'03"
30 18:09 ☽ 6♐46

Astro Data

1 July 1979
Julian Day # 29036
SVP 5♓32'51"
GC 26♐33.2 ⚴ 2♓29.2R
Eris 14♈58.5 ⚵ 27♉17.8
⚷ 12♉52.8 ⚶ 2♉28.2
☽ Mean ☊ 11♍36.8

1 August 1979
Julian Day # 29067
SVP 5♓32'47"
GC 26♐33.2 ⚴ 27♒25.3R
Eris 14♈56.8R ⚵ 14♊23.8
⚷ 13♉47.3 ⚶ 12♉06.4
☽ Mean ☊ 9♍58.3

LONGITUDE — September 1979

Day	Sid.Time	☉	0 hr ☽	Noon ☽	True ☊	☿	♀	♂	⚳	♃	♄	♅	♆	♇
1 Sa	10 40 14	8♍27 37	23♐23 22	0♑15 16	8♍28.3	27♌19.5	10♍22.1	15♋33.9	18♈44.4	24♌12.3	16♍07.0	17♏30.4	17♐43.4	17♎35.2
2 Su	10 44 10	9 25 40	7♑13 43	14 18 40	8 28.4	29 13.8	11 36.5	16 11.9	18R 38.1	24 25.2	16 14.5	17 32.3	17 43.5	17 37.2
3 M	10 48 07	10 23 45	21 29 56	28 47 09	8 28.5	1♍09.1	12 51.0	16 49.8	18 31.4	24 38.1	16 22.0	17 34.3	17 43.6	17 39.2
4 Tu	10 52 03	11 21 52	6♒09 46	13♒37 07	8 28.7	3 05.1	14 05.4	17 27.7	18 24.4	24 50.9	16 29.5	17 36.2	17 43.8	17 41.2
5 W	10 56 00	12 20 00	21 08 19	28 42 24	8R 28.9	5 01.4	15 19.9	18 05.4	18 17.1	25 03.8	16 37.0	17 38.3	17 44.0	17 43.2
6 Th	10 59 56	13 18 10	6♓18 13	13♓54 36	8 28.9	6 57.9	16 34.4	18 43.1	18 09.5	25 16.6	16 44.5	17 40.3	17 44.2	17 45.2
7 F	11 03 53	14 16 21	21 30 21	29 04 16	8 28.7	8 54.2	17 48.8	19 20.7	18 01.5	25 29.4	16 52.0	17 42.4	17 44.4	17 47.3
8 Sa	11 07 49	15 14 34	6♈35 12	14♈02 07	8 28.1	10 50.3	19 03.3	19 58.2	17 53.1	25 42.2	16 59.6	17 44.6	17 44.7	17 49.3
9 Su	11 11 46	16 12 49	21 24 09	28 40 32	8 27.3	12 45.8	20 17.9	20 35.6	17 44.5	25 54.9	17 07.1	17 46.8	17 45.0	17 51.4
10 M	11 15 43	17 11 06	5♉50 42	12♉54 17	8 26.4	14 40.8	21 32.4	21 13.0	17 35.5	26 07.6	17 14.6	17 49.0	17 45.4	17 53.5
11 Tu	11 19 39	18 09 25	19 51 03	26 40 58	8 25.5	16 35.0	22 46.9	21 50.2	17 26.2	26 20.2	17 22.1	17 51.3	17 45.7	17 55.6
12 W	11 23 36	19 07 47	3♊24 07	10♊00 42	8D 24.9	18 28.4	24 01.5	22 27.4	17 16.6	26 32.9	17 29.7	17 53.6	17 46.1	17 57.8
13 Th	11 27 32	20 06 10	16 31 02	22 55 32	8 24.8	20 20.9	25 16.1	23 04.4	17 06.8	26 45.5	17 37.2	17 56.0	17 46.6	17 59.9
14 F	11 31 29	21 04 36	29 14 39	5♋28 52	8 25.2	22 12.5	26 30.6	23 41.4	16 56.6	26 58.0	17 44.7	17 58.4	17 47.1	18 02.1
15 Sa	11 35 25	22 03 04	11♋38 43	17 44 45	8 26.1	24 03.1	27 45.2	24 18.3	16 46.1	27 10.5	17 52.2	18 00.8	17 47.6	18 04.3
16 Su	11 39 22	23 01 34	23 47 29	29 47 28	8 27.4	25 52.7	28 59.8	24 55.1	16 35.4	27 23.0	17 59.8	18 03.3	17 48.1	18 06.5
17 M	11 43 18	24 00 06	5♌45 11	11♌41 10	8 28.7	27 41.3	0♎14.4	25 31.8	16 24.4	27 35.4	18 07.3	18 05.9	17 48.7	18 08.7
18 Tu	11 47 15	24 58 40	17 35 50	23 29 39	8 29.9	29 28.9	1 29.1	26 08.4	16 13.1	27 47.8	18 14.8	18 08.4	17 49.3	18 10.9
19 W	11 51 12	25 57 16	29 23 01	5♍16 18	8R 30.5	1♎15.4	2 43.7	26 45.0	16 01.6	28 00.2	18 22.3	18 11.0	17 49.9	18 13.1
20 Th	11 55 08	26 55 54	11♍09 52	17 04 00	8 30.3	3 00.9	3 58.4	27 21.4	15 49.9	28 12.5	18 29.7	18 13.7	17 50.6	18 15.4
21 F	11 59 05	27 54 33	22 59 02	28 55 13	8 29.1	4 45.4	5 13.0	27 57.7	15 38.0	28 24.7	18 37.2	18 16.3	17 51.3	18 17.6
22 Sa	12 03 01	28 53 15	4♎52 49	10♎52 04	8 26.9	6 28.9	6 27.7	28 33.9	15 25.8	28 36.9	18 44.7	18 19.0	17 52.0	18 19.9
23 Su	12 06 58	29 51 59	16 53 11	22 56 25	8 23.8	8 11.4	7 42.3	29 10.0	15 13.5	28 49.1	18 52.1	18 21.8	17 52.8	18 22.2
24 M	12 10 54	0♎50 45	29 01 58	5♏10 05	8 20.2	9 52.9	8 57.0	29 46.0	15 00.9	29 01.1	18 59.6	18 24.6	17 53.6	18 24.5
25 Tu	12 14 51	1 49 33	11♏21 00	17 34 57	8 16.5	11 33.4	10 11.7	0♌21.9	14 48.2	29 13.2	19 07.0	18 27.4	17 54.4	18 26.8
26 W	12 18 47	2 48 22	23 52 11	0♐12 58	8 13.2	13 13.0	11 26.4	0 57.7	14 35.4	29 25.2	19 14.4	18 30.3	17 55.2	18 29.1
27 Th	12 22 44	3 47 13	6♐37 35	13 06 18	8 10.6	14 51.7	12 41.0	1 33.4	14 22.4	29 37.1	19 21.8	18 33.2	17 56.1	18 31.4
28 F	12 26 40	4 46 06	19 39 23	26 17 06	8D 09.2	16 29.4	13 55.7	2 09.0	14 09.3	29 49.0	19 29.1	18 36.1	17 57.1	18 33.7
29 Sa	12 30 37	5 45 01	2♑59 42	9♑47 23	8 09.0	18 06.3	15 10.4	2 44.4	13 56.0	0♍00.8	19 36.5	18 39.0	17 58.0	18 36.0
30 Su	12 34 34	6 43 57	16 40 19	23 38 34	8 09.8	19 42.2	16 25.1	3 19.8	13 42.7	0 12.5	19 43.8	18 42.0	17 59.0	18 38.4

LONGITUDE — October 1979

Day	Sid.Time	☉	0 hr ☽	Noon ☽	True ☊	☿	♀	♂	⚳	♃	♄	♅	♆	♇
1 M	12 38 30	7♎42 55	0♒42 08	7♒50 56	8♍11.2	21♎17.3	17♎39.8	3♌55.1	13♈29.3	0♍24.2	19♍51.1	18♏45.0	18♐00.0	18♎40.7
2 Tu	12 42 27	8 41 55	15 04 45	22 23 12	8 12.6	22 51.6	18 54.5	4 30.2	13R 15.8	0 35.9	19 58.4	18 48.1	18 01.1	18 43.1
3 W	12 46 23	9 40 57	29 45 47	7♓11 51	8R 13.3	24 25.0	20 09.2	5 05.2	13 02.2	0 47.4	20 05.6	18 51.2	18 02.1	18 45.4
4 Th	12 50 20	10 40 00	14♓40 37	22 11 09	8 12.6	25 57.5	21 23.9	5 40.1	12 48.6	0 58.9	20 12.9	18 54.3	18 03.2	18 47.8
5 F	12 54 16	11 39 05	29 42 25	7♈13 19	8 10.4	27 29.3	22 38.6	6 14.9	12 35.0	1 10.3	20 20.1	18 57.4	18 04.4	18 50.2
6 Sa	12 58 13	12 38 12	14♈42 44	22 09 33	8 06.5	29 00.2	23 53.3	6 49.6	12 21.4	1 21.7	20 27.2	19 00.6	18 05.5	18 52.5
7 Su	13 02 09	13 37 22	29 32 42	6♉51 15	8 01.4	0♏30.3	25 08.0	7 24.2	12 07.8	1 33.0	20 34.4	19 03.8	18 06.7	18 54.9
8 M	13 06 06	14 36 33	14♉04 23	21 11 25	7 55.8	1 59.6	26 22.7	7 58.7	11 54.2	1 44.2	20 41.5	19 07.0	18 07.9	18 57.3
9 Tu	13 10 03	15 35 47	28 11 53	5♊05 30	7 50.3	3 28.1	27 37.4	8 33.0	11 40.6	1 55.3	20 48.6	19 10.2	18 09.2	18 59.7
10 W	13 13 59	16 35 03	11♊52 08	18 31 50	7 45.8	4 55.7	28 52.1	9 07.2	11 27.0	2 06.4	20 55.6	19 13.5	18 10.4	19 02.0
11 Th	13 17 56	17 34 22	25 04 46	1♋31 17	7 42.8	6 22.6	0♏06.9	9 41.3	11 13.6	2 17.4	21 02.7	19 16.8	18 11.7	19 04.4
12 F	13 21 52	18 33 43	7♋51 48	14 06 48	7D 41.4	7 48.6	1 21.6	10 15.3	11 00.2	2 28.3	21 09.7	19 20.1	18 13.1	19 06.8
13 Sa	13 25 49	19 33 06	20 16 51	26 22 36	7 41.5	9 13.7	2 36.3	10 49.1	10 46.9	2 39.1	21 16.6	19 23.5	18 14.4	19 09.2
14 Su	13 29 45	20 32 31	2♌24 39	8♌23 39	7 42.7	10 38.0	3 51.0	11 22.9	10 33.7	2 49.9	21 23.5	19 26.8	18 15.8	19 11.6
15 M	13 33 42	21 31 59	14 20 16	20 15 08	7 44.3	12 01.3	5 05.8	11 56.4	10 20.6	3 00.5	21 30.4	19 30.2	18 17.2	19 14.0
16 Tu	13 37 38	22 31 29	26 08 51	2♍02 01	7R 45.4	13 23.7	6 20.5	12 29.9	10 07.6	3 11.1	21 37.3	19 33.6	18 18.7	19 16.4
17 W	13 41 35	23 31 01	7♍55 11	13 48 52	7 45.4	14 45.1	7 35.3	13 03.2	9 54.8	3 21.6	21 44.1	19 37.1	18 20.1	19 18.7
18 Th	13 45 32	24 30 35	19 43 32	25 39 36	7 43.5	16 05.4	8 50.0	13 36.4	9 42.2	3 32.0	21 50.8	19 40.5	18 21.6	19 21.1
19 F	13 49 28	25 30 12	1♎37 27	7♎37 23	7 39.4	17 24.7	10 04.7	14 09.4	9 29.7	3 42.3	21 57.5	19 44.0	18 23.1	19 23.5
20 Sa	13 53 25	26 29 50	13 39 42	19 44 35	7 33.1	18 42.7	11 19.5	14 42.3	9 17.4	3 52.5	22 04.2	19 47.5	18 24.7	19 25.9
21 Su	13 57 21	27 29 31	25 52 13	2♏02 44	7 24.9	19 59.5	12 34.2	15 15.0	9 05.4	4 02.6	22 10.9	19 51.0	18 26.2	19 28.2
22 M	14 01 18	28 29 13	8♏16 13	14 32 43	7 15.5	21 14.9	13 49.0	15 47.6	8 53.5	4 12.7	22 17.4	19 54.5	18 27.8	19 30.6
23 Tu	14 05 14	29 28 58	20 52 16	27 14 52	7 05.7	22 28.9	15 03.7	16 20.1	8 41.9	4 22.6	22 24.0	19 58.1	18 29.5	19 33.0
24 W	14 09 11	0♏28 44	3♐40 32	10♐09 15	6 56.6	23 41.3	16 18.5	16 52.3	8 30.5	4 32.4	22 30.5	20 01.7	18 31.1	19 35.3
25 Th	14 13 07	1 28 32	16 41 02	23 15 54	6 49.0	24 51.9	17 33.2	17 24.5	8 19.4	4 42.2	22 36.9	20 05.2	18 32.8	19 37.7
26 F	14 17 04	2 28 23	29 53 53	6♑35 02	6 43.7	26 00.5	18 48.0	17 56.4	8 08.5	4 51.8	22 43.3	20 08.8	18 34.4	19 40.0
27 Sa	14 21 00	3 28 14	13♑19 25	20 07 07	6 40.7	27 07.1	20 02.7	18 28.2	7 57.9	5 01.3	22 49.6	20 12.5	18 36.2	19 42.4
28 Su	14 24 57	4 28 07	26 58 12	3♒52 46	6D 39.8	28 11.4	21 17.5	18 59.9	7 47.6	5 10.7	22 55.9	20 16.1	18 37.9	19 44.7
29 M	14 28 54	5 28 02	10♒50 51	17 52 27	6 40.3	29 13.0	22 32.2	19 31.4	7 37.6	5 20.0	23 02.2	20 19.7	18 39.6	19 47.0
30 Tu	14 32 50	6 27 59	24 57 34	2♓06 02	6R 41.0	0♐11.8	23 46.9	20 02.7	7 27.9	5 29.2	23 08.3	20 23.4	18 41.4	19 49.3
31 W	14 36 47	7 27 57	9♓17 41	16 32 11	6 40.6	1 07.3	25 01.7	20 33.8	7 18.5	5 38.3	23 14.5	20 27.0	18 43.2	19 51.6

Astro Data	Planet Ingress	Last Aspect	☽ Ingress	Last Aspect	☽ Ingress	☽ Phases & Eclipses	Astro Data
Dy Hr Mn	Dy Hr Mn	Dy Hr Mn	Dy Hr Mn	Dy Hr Mn	Dy Hr Mn	Dy Hr Mn	1 September 1979
♆⚹♇ 5 22:25	☿ ♍ 2 21:39	1 6:05 ☿ △	♑ 1 11:34	2 12:52 ☿ △	♓ 3 0:23	6 10:59 ○ 13♓16	Julian Day # 29098
☽0N 7 22:24	♀ ♎ 17 7:21	2 17:33 ♇ □	♒ 3 13:59	4 8:50 ♄ ☍	♈ 5 0:28	6 10:54 ☍ T 1.094	SVP 5♓32'43"
♅⊻♆ 8 13:23	☿ ♎ 18 18:59	5 6:09 ♃ ☍	♓ 5 14:03	7 0:23 ☿ ☍	♉ 7 0:45	13 6:15 ☾ 19♊52	GC 26♐33.3 ⚵ 19♒42.5R
♄□♆ 14 19:58	☉ ♎ 23 15:16	6 19:55 ♂ △	♈ 7 13:29	8 11:09 ♄ △	♊ 9 3:07	21 9:47 ● 27♍49	Eris 14♈45.8R ⚵ 0♋34.8
♄⚹♅ 17 5:12	♂ ♌ 24 21:21	9 7:22 ♃ △	♉ 9 14:12	11 9:05 ♀ △	♋ 11 9:09	29 4:20 ☽ 5♑26	⚷ 13♉50.2R ⚶ 17♉47.1
♄⊻♇ 17 18:24	♃ ♍ 29 10:23	11 11:23 ♃ □	♊ 11 17:54	13 1:51 ♄ ⚹	♌ 13 19:12		☽ Mean ☊ 8♍19.8
♀0S 19 16:41		13 19:23 ♃ ⚹	♋ 14 1:27	15 14:51 ☉ ⚹	♍ 16 7:51	5 19:35 ○ 11♈58	
☿0S 20 4:39	☿ ♏ 7 3:55	16 10:13 ♀ ⚹	♌ 16 12:25	18 4:13 ♄ ☌	♎ 18 20:44	12 21:24 ☾ 18♋57	1 October 1979
☽0S 22 1:20	♀ ♏ 11 9:48	18 20:55 ♃ ☌	♍ 19 1:15	21 2:23 ☉ ☌	♏ 21 8:02	21 2:23 ● 27♎06	Julian Day # 29128
☉0S 23 15:17	☉ ♏ 24 0:28	21 9:58 ♂ ⚹	♎ 21 14:11	23 2:48 ♄ ⚹	♐ 23 17:09	28 13:06 ☽ 4♒31	SVP 5♓32'41"
♅⊻♇ 24 6:11	☿ ♐ 30 7:06	24 0:54 ♂ □	♏ 24 1:54	25 10:49 ♄ □	♑ 26 0:11		GC 26♐33.4 ⚵ 15♒00.0R
		26 10:29 ♃ □	♐ 26 11:36	28 1:18 ☿ ⚹	♒ 28 5:16		Eris 14♈29.1R ⚵ 14♋22.8
☽0N 5 9:20		28 18:26 ♃ △	♑ 28 18:40	29 20:40 ♀ □	♓ 30 8:29		⚷ 13♉03.3R ⚶ 17♉29.8R
☽0S 19 7:54		30 5:13 ♄ △	♒ 30 22:49				☽ Mean ☊ 6♍44.4
♃∠♇ 24 21:21							

November 1979 LONGITUDE

Day	Sid.Time	☉	0 hr ☽	Noon ☽	True ☊	☿	♀	♂	⚳	♃	♄	♅	♆	♇
1 Th	14 40 43	8♏27 56	23♓49 06	1♈07 53	6♍38.4	1♐59.4	26♏16.4	21♌04.8	7♈09.4	5♍47.3	23♍20.5	20♏30.7	18♐45.0	19♎53.9
2 F	14 44 40	9 27 58	8♈27 52	15 48 17	6R 33.5	2 47.4	27 31.1	21 35.6	7R 00.6	5 56.1	23 26.5	20 34.4	18 46.9	19 56.2
3 Sa	14 48 36	10 28 01	23 08 16	0♉26 55	6 25.9	3 31.1	28 45.8	22 06.2	6 52.2	6 04.9	23 32.5	20 38.0	18 48.7	19 58.5
4 Su	14 52 33	11 28 05	7♉43 17	14 56 28	6 16.2	4 09.8	0♐00.5	22 36.6	6 44.1	6 13.5	23 38.3	20 41.7	18 50.6	20 00.7
5 M	14 56 29	12 28 12	22 05 37	29 09 59	6 05.3	4 43.0	1 15.2	23 06.9	6 36.4	6 22.0	23 44.2	20 45.4	18 52.5	20 03.0
6 Tu	15 00 26	13 28 21	6♊08 56	13♊02 00	5 54.5	5 10.2	2 29.9	23 37.0	6 29.0	6 30.4	23 49.9	20 49.1	18 54.4	20 05.2
7 W	15 04 23	14 28 32	19 48 50	26 29 18	5 44.8	5 30.6	3 44.6	24 06.8	6 21.9	6 38.6	23 55.6	20 52.9	18 56.3	20 07.5
8 Th	15 08 19	15 28 44	3♋03 23	9♋31 14	5 37.2	5 43.6	4 59.3	24 36.5	6 15.2	6 46.8	24 01.3	20 56.6	18 58.3	20 09.7
9 F	15 12 16	16 28 59	15 53 06	22 09 24	5 32.1	5R 48.6	6 14.0	25 06.0	6 08.9	6 54.8	24 06.8	21 00.3	19 00.3	20 11.9
10 Sa	15 16 12	17 29 16	28 20 36	4♌27 16	5 29.4	5 44.8	7 28.7	25 35.3	6 02.9	7 02.7	24 12.3	21 04.0	19 02.2	20 14.1
11 Su	15 20 09	18 29 34	10♌30 01	16 29 30	5D 28.6	5 31.7	8 43.4	26 04.4	5 57.3	7 10.4	24 17.8	21 07.8	19 04.2	20 16.2
12 M	15 24 05	19 29 55	22 26 26	28 21 29	5R 28.7	5 08.8	9 58.1	26 33.3	5 52.1	7 18.0	24 23.1	21 11.5	19 06.3	20 18.4
13 Tu	15 28 02	20 30 17	4♍15 23	10♍08 48	5 28.7	4 35.7	11 12.8	27 02.0	5 47.2	7 25.5	24 28.4	21 15.2	19 08.3	20 20.5
14 W	15 31 58	21 30 41	16 02 26	21 56 54	5 27.5	3 52.5	12 27.5	27 30.4	5 42.8	7 32.8	24 33.6	21 19.0	19 10.3	20 22.7
15 Th	15 35 55	22 31 08	27 52 49	3♎50 44	5 24.2	2 59.5	13 42.2	27 58.6	5 38.7	7 40.0	24 38.8	21 22.7	19 12.4	20 24.8
16 F	15 39 52	23 31 36	9♎51 10	15 54 33	5 18.1	1 57.4	14 56.9	28 26.6	5 35.0	7 47.1	24 43.8	21 26.4	19 14.5	20 26.9
17 Sa	15 43 48	24 32 05	22 01 15	28 11 33	5 09.2	0 47.4	16 11.6	28 54.4	5 31.7	7 54.0	24 48.8	21 30.2	19 16.6	20 28.9
18 Su	15 47 45	25 32 37	4♏25 42	10♏43 48	4 57.7	29♏31.3	17 26.2	29 21.9	5 28.7	8 00.8	24 53.7	21 33.9	19 18.7	20 31.0
19 M	15 51 41	26 33 10	17 05 54	23 32 00	4 44.6	28 11.4	18 40.9	29 49.2	5 26.2	8 07.4	24 58.6	21 37.6	19 20.8	20 33.0
20 Tu	15 55 38	27 33 45	0♐01 58	6♐35 38	4 30.9	26 50.0	19 55.6	0♍16.2	5 24.0	8 13.9	25 03.3	21 41.4	19 22.9	20 35.0
21 W	15 59 34	28 34 21	13 12 48	19 53 12	4 17.9	25 29.9	21 10.3	0 43.0	5 22.3	8 20.2	25 08.0	21 45.1	19 25.0	20 37.0
22 Th	16 03 31	29 34 59	26 36 33	3♑22 33	4 06.9	24 13.7	22 24.9	1 09.5	5 20.9	8 26.4	25 12.6	21 48.8	19 27.2	20 39.0
23 F	16 07 27	0♐35 38	10♑10 57	17 01 29	3 58.7	23 04.0	23 39.6	1 35.7	5 19.9	8 32.4	25 17.1	21 52.5	19 29.4	20 41.0
24 Sa	16 11 24	1 36 18	23 53 56	0♒48 07	3 53.6	22 02.7	24 54.3	2 01.7	5 19.3	8 38.3	25 21.6	21 56.2	19 31.5	20 42.9
25 Su	16 15 21	2 36 59	7♒43 53	14 41 08	3 51.2	21 11.4	26 08.9	2 27.4	5D 19.1	8 44.0	25 25.9	21 59.9	19 33.7	20 44.8
26 M	16 19 17	3 37 41	21 39 49	28 39 52	3 50.6	20 31.1	27 23.5	2 52.8	5 19.3	8 49.5	25 30.2	22 03.6	19 35.9	20 46.7
27 Tu	16 23 14	4 38 24	5♓41 16	12♓43 56	3 50.5	20 02.4	28 38.2	3 17.9	5 19.8	8 54.9	25 34.4	22 07.3	19 38.1	20 48.6
28 W	16 27 10	5 39 09	19 47 50	26 52 49	3 49.6	19 45.3	29 52.8	3 42.8	5 20.8	9 00.1	25 38.4	22 11.0	19 40.3	20 50.5
29 Th	16 31 07	6 39 54	3♈58 43	11♈05 17	3 46.5	19D 39.5	1♑07.4	4 07.3	5 22.1	9 05.2	25 42.4	22 14.6	19 42.5	20 52.3
30 F	16 35 03	7 40 40	18 12 12	25 19 03	3 40.7	19 44.5	2 22.0	4 31.6	5 23.7	9 10.1	25 46.4	22 18.2	19 44.7	20 54.1

December 1979 LONGITUDE

Day	Sid.Time	☉	0 hr ☽	Noon ☽	True ☊	☿	♀	♂	⚳	♃	♄	♅	♆	♇
1 Sa	16 39 00	8♐41 27	2♉25 21	9♉30 34	3♍31.8	19♏59.5	3♑36.5	4♍55.5	5♈25.8	9♍14.8	25♍50.2	22♏21.9	19♐47.0	20♎55.8
2 Su	16 42 56	9 42 15	16 34 05	23 35 18	3R 20.5	20 23.6	4 51.1	5 19.2	5 28.2	9 19.4	25 53.9	22 25.5	19 49.2	20 57.6
3 M	16 46 53	10 43 04	0♊33 35	7♊28 21	3 07.8	20 56.0	6 05.6	5 42.5	5 31.0	9 23.8	25 57.5	22 29.1	19 51.4	20 59.3
4 Tu	16 50 50	11 43 55	14 19 04	21 05 15	2 55.0	21 35.9	7 20.2	6 05.5	5 34.2	9 28.0	26 01.1	22 32.7	19 53.7	21 01.0
5 W	16 54 46	12 44 47	27 46 35	4♋22 46	2 43.2	22 22.3	8 34.7	6 28.2	5 37.7	9 32.0	26 04.5	22 36.3	19 55.9	21 02.7
6 Th	16 58 43	13 45 39	10♋53 43	17 19 23	2 33.6	23 14.6	9 49.2	6 50.5	5 41.5	9 35.9	26 07.9	22 39.8	19 58.2	21 04.4
7 F	17 02 39	14 46 33	23 39 54	29 55 29	2 26.8	24 11.9	11 03.7	7 12.5	5 45.8	9 39.6	26 11.2	22 43.4	20 00.4	21 06.0
8 Sa	17 06 36	15 47 29	6♌06 27	12♌13 13	2 22.7	25 13.8	12 18.2	7 34.2	5 50.3	9 43.1	26 14.3	22 46.9	20 02.7	21 07.6
9 Su	17 10 32	16 48 25	18 16 16	24 16 10	2D 21.0	26 19.5	13 32.7	7 55.4	5 55.2	9 46.5	26 17.4	22 50.4	20 05.0	21 09.1
10 M	17 14 29	17 49 22	0♍13 32	6♍09 00	2 20.8	27 28.5	14 47.2	8 16.3	6 00.5	9 49.6	26 20.4	22 53.9	20 07.2	21 10.7
11 Tu	17 18 25	18 50 21	12 03 15	17 56 59	2R 21.0	28 40.5	16 01.6	8 36.8	6 06.1	9 52.6	26 23.3	22 57.4	20 09.5	21 12.2
12 W	17 22 22	19 51 21	23 50 54	29 45 43	2 20.6	29 55.0	17 16.1	8 57.0	6 12.0	9 55.4	26 26.0	23 00.8	20 11.8	21 13.7
13 Th	17 26 19	20 52 21	5♎42 06	11♎40 42	2 18.4	1♐11.8	18 30.5	9 16.7	6 18.3	9 58.0	26 28.7	23 04.2	20 14.0	21 15.1
14 F	17 30 15	21 53 23	17 42 11	23 47 05	2 13.9	2 30.4	19 44.9	9 36.0	6 24.9	10 00.4	26 31.3	23 07.6	20 16.3	21 16.6
15 Sa	17 34 12	22 54 26	29 55 56	6♏09 11	2 06.7	3 50.7	20 59.3	9 54.9	6 31.8	10 02.7	26 33.7	23 11.0	20 18.6	21 18.0
16 Su	17 38 08	23 55 30	12♏27 11	18 50 11	1 57.1	5 12.5	22 13.7	10 13.4	6 39.0	10 04.7	26 36.1	23 14.4	20 20.8	21 19.3
17 M	17 42 05	24 56 35	25 18 21	1♐51 43	1 45.9	6 35.4	23 28.1	10 31.5	6 46.6	10 06.6	26 38.4	23 17.7	20 23.1	21 20.7
18 Tu	17 46 01	25 57 40	8♐30 13	15 13 39	1 33.9	7 59.5	24 42.4	10 49.1	6 54.5	10 08.3	26 40.5	23 21.0	20 25.3	21 22.0
19 W	17 49 58	26 58 46	22 01 44	28 54 03	1 22.6	9 24.6	25 56.8	11 06.2	7 02.7	10 09.7	26 42.6	23 24.3	20 27.6	21 23.3
20 Th	17 53 55	27 59 53	5♑50 08	12♑49 27	1 12.9	10 50.5	27 11.1	11 22.9	7 11.2	10 11.0	26 44.5	23 27.6	20 29.9	21 24.5
21 F	17 57 51	29 01 00	19 51 24	26 55 26	1 05.8	12 17.1	28 25.4	11 39.1	7 20.0	10 12.1	26 46.4	23 30.8	20 32.1	21 25.7
22 Sa	18 01 48	0♑02 08	4♒00 58	11♒07 27	1 01.5	13 44.4	29 39.7	11 54.9	7 29.1	10 13.0	26 48.1	23 34.0	20 34.4	21 26.9
23 Su	18 05 44	1 03 16	18 14 25	25 21 25	0D 59.8	15 12.3	0♒53.9	12 10.1	7 38.5	10 13.7	26 49.7	23 37.2	20 36.6	21 28.0
24 M	18 09 41	2 04 24	2♓28 07	9♓34 14	0 59.9	16 40.7	2 08.1	12 24.8	7 48.2	10 14.2	26 51.3	23 40.3	20 38.8	21 29.2
25 Tu	18 13 37	3 05 32	16 39 30	23 43 47	1R 00.7	18 09.6	3 22.3	12 39.0	7 58.1	10 14.6	26 52.7	23 43.4	20 41.1	21 30.2
26 W	18 17 34	4 06 40	0♈46 56	7♈48 51	1 00.9	19 38.9	4 36.5	12 52.7	8 08.4	10R 14.7	26 54.0	23 46.5	20 43.3	21 31.3
27 Th	18 21 30	5 07 48	14 49 25	21 48 34	0 59.5	21 08.7	5 50.6	13 05.9	8 18.9	10 14.6	26 55.2	23 49.5	20 45.5	21 32.3
28 F	18 25 27	6 08 56	28 46 10	5♉42 05	0 55.9	22 38.9	7 04.7	13 18.5	8 29.8	10 14.3	26 56.3	23 52.6	20 47.7	21 33.3
29 Sa	18 29 24	7 10 04	12♉36 10	19 28 12	0 49.9	24 09.4	8 18.8	13 30.6	8 40.8	10 13.9	26 57.2	23 55.5	20 49.9	21 34.2
30 Su	18 33 20	8 11 12	26 17 59	3♊05 16	0 41.9	25 40.3	9 32.8	13 42.1	8 52.2	10 13.2	26 58.1	23 58.5	20 52.1	21 35.1
31 M	18 37 17	9 12 20	9♊49 46	16 31 16	0 32.7	27 11.6	10 46.9	13 53.0	9 03.8	10 12.4	26 58.9	24 01.4	20 54.3	21 36.0

Astro Data Dy Hr Mn	Planet Ingress Dy Hr Mn	Last Aspect Dy Hr Mn	☽ Ingress Dy Hr Mn	Last Aspect Dy Hr Mn	☽ Ingress Dy Hr Mn	☽ Phases & Eclipses Dy Hr Mn	Astro Data
☽0N 1 19:31	♀ ♐ 4 11:50	1 3:17 ♀ △	♈ 1 10:09	2 15:59 ♄ △	♊ 2 23:02	4 5:47 ○ 11♉13	1 November 1979
☿R 9 13:55	☿ ♏R 18 3:08	2 21:49 ♂ △	♉ 3 11:16	4 20:52 ♄ □	♋ 5 4:01	11 16:24 ☾ 18♌41	Julian Day # 29159
☽0S 15 16:12	♂ ♍ 19 21:36	5 2:43 ♄ △	♊ 5 13:25	7 4:47 ♄ ⚹	♌ 7 12:09	19 18:04 ● 26♏48	SVP 5♓32'38"
⚳D 25 13:20	☉ ♐ 22 21:54	7 7:33 ♂ ⚹	♋ 7 18:24	9 16:34 ☿ □	♍ 9 23:33	26 21:09 ☽ 4♓01	GC 26♐33.5 ⚴ 15♒26.5
☽0N 29 3:51	♀ ♑ 28 14:20	9 15:49 ♄ ⚹	♌ 10 3:14	12 12:21 ☿ ⚹	♎ 12 12:29		Eris 14♈10.6R ⚵ 24♋58.3
☿D 29 12:41		12 8:11 ♂ ☌	♍ 12 15:20	14 7:56 ☉ ⚹	♏ 15 0:08	3 18:08 ○ 10♊59	⚷ 11♉39.7R ⚶ 11♉01.0R
	☿ ♐ 12 13:34	14 17:20 ♄ ☌	♎ 15 4:16	17 2:26 ♄ ⚹	♐ 17 8:36	11 13:59 ☾ 18♍55	☽ Mean ☊ 5♍05.9
☽0S 13 1:51	☉ ♑ 22 11:10	17 13:26 ♂ ⚹	♏ 17 15:29	19 8:23 ☉ ☌	♑ 19 13:55	19 8:23 ● 26♐50	
☽0N 26 10:32	♀ ♒ 22 18:35	19 19:48 ☿ ☌	♐ 19 23:56	21 14:47 ♀ ☌	♒ 21 17:13	26 5:11 ☽ 3♈49	1 December 1979
♃R 26 14:59		21 21:26 ♄ □	♑ 22 6:01	23 9:04 ♅ □	♓ 23 19:50		Julian Day # 29189
		24 2:30 ♄ △	♒ 24 10:37	25 17:22 ♄ ☍	♈ 25 22:40		SVP 5♓32'34"
		26 9:37 ♀ ⚹	♓ 26 14:17	27 11:32 ♇ ☍	♉ 28 2:08		GC 26♐33.5 ⚴ 20♒08.0
		28 9:53 ♄ ☍	♈ 28 17:17	30 1:10 ♄ △	♊ 30 6:32		Eris 13♈56.9R ⚵ 29♋04.3
		30 4:32 ♇ ☍	♉ 30 19:54				⚷ 10♉14.8R ⚶ 4♉23.0R
							☽ Mean ☊ 3♍30.6

LONGITUDE — January 1980

Day	Sid.Time	☉	0 hr ☽	Noon ☽	True ☊	☿	♀	♂	⚳	♃	♄	♅	♆	♇
1 Tu	18 41 13	10♑13 28	23♊09 28	29♊44 10	0♍23.2	28♐43.2	12♒00.8	14♍03.4	9♈15.6	10♍11.3	26♍59.5	24♏04.3	20♐56.5	21♎36.9
2 W	18 45 10	11 14 36	6♋15 11	12♋42 20	0R 14.6	0♑15.2	13 14.8	14 13.2	9 27.8	10R 10.1	27 00.1	24 07.1	20 58.6	21 37.7
3 Th	18 49 06	12 15 44	19 05 34	25 24 50	0 07.6	1 47.5	14 28.7	14 22.3	9 40.1	10 08.7	27 00.5	24 10.0	21 00.8	21 38.5
4 F	18 53 03	13 16 52	1♌40 13	7♌51 48	0 02.8	3 20.2	15 42.5	14 30.9	9 52.7	10 07.1	27 00.8	24 12.7	21 02.9	21 39.2
5 Sa	18 56 59	14 18 01	13 59 48	20 04 28	0D 00.2	4 53.2	16 56.3	14 38.8	10 05.6	10 05.2	27 01.0	24 15.5	21 05.0	21 39.9
6 Su	19 00 56	15 19 09	26 06 09	2♍05 15	29♌59.6	6 26.7	18 10.1	14 46.0	10 18.6	10 03.2	27R 01.2	24 18.2	21 07.1	21 40.6
7 M	19 04 53	16 20 18	8♍02 12	13 57 32	0♍00.5	8 00.4	19 23.9	14 52.7	10 32.0	10 01.0	27 01.1	24 20.8	21 09.2	21 41.2
8 Tu	19 08 49	17 21 26	19 51 48	25 45 34	0 02.1	9 34.6	20 37.6	14 58.6	10 45.5	9 58.7	27 01.0	24 23.4	21 11.3	21 41.8
9 W	19 12 46	18 22 35	1♎39 28	7♎34 10	0 03.6	11 09.2	21 51.2	15 03.9	10 59.3	9 56.1	27 00.8	24 26.0	21 13.4	21 42.4
10 Th	19 16 42	19 23 43	13 30 17	19 28 31	0R 04.2	12 44.2	23 04.8	15 08.4	11 13.3	9 53.3	27 00.5	24 28.6	21 15.5	21 42.9
11 F	19 20 39	20 24 52	25 29 29	1♏33 52	0 03.4	14 19.6	24 18.4	15 12.3	11 27.5	9 50.4	27 00.0	24 31.1	21 17.5	21 43.4
12 Sa	19 24 35	21 26 01	7♏42 15	13 55 12	0 00.9	15 55.5	25 32.0	15 15.5	11 41.9	9 47.2	26 59.5	24 33.5	21 19.5	21 43.9
13 Su	19 28 32	22 27 09	20 13 14	26 36 47	29♌56.8	17 31.8	26 45.4	15 17.9	11 56.6	9 43.9	26 58.8	24 35.9	21 21.6	21 44.3
14 M	19 32 28	23 28 18	3♐06 11	9♐41 40	29 51.4	19 08.6	27 58.9	15 19.6	12 11.4	9 40.4	26 58.0	24 38.3	21 23.6	21 44.7
15 Tu	19 36 25	24 29 26	16 23 21	23 11 13	29 45.4	20 45.9	29 12.3	15R 20.6	12 26.5	9 36.7	26 57.2	24 40.6	21 25.5	21 45.0
16 W	19 40 22	25 30 34	0♑05 06	7♑04 40	29 39.5	22 23.7	0♓25.6	15 20.8	12 41.8	9 32.9	26 56.2	24 42.9	21 27.5	21 45.3
17 Th	19 44 18	26 31 42	14 09 30	21 18 59	29 34.5	24 02.0	1 38.9	15 20.2	12 57.2	9 28.8	26 55.1	24 45.2	21 29.5	21 45.6
18 F	19 48 15	27 32 49	28 32 26	5♒49 05	29 31.0	25 40.9	2 52.2	15 18.9	13 12.9	9 24.6	26 53.9	24 47.4	21 31.4	21 45.9
19 Sa	19 52 11	28 33 56	13♒08 04	20 28 31	29D 29.2	27 20.2	4 05.4	15 16.8	13 28.8	9 20.2	26 52.6	24 49.5	21 33.3	21 46.1
20 Su	19 56 08	29 35 02	27 49 34	5♓10 24	29 29.1	29 00.2	5 18.5	15 13.9	13 44.8	9 15.7	26 51.2	24 51.6	21 35.2	21 46.2
21 M	20 00 04	0♒36 07	12♓30 14	19 48 23	29 30.1	0♒40.6	6 31.6	15 10.2	14 01.1	9 10.9	26 49.6	24 53.7	21 37.1	21 46.4
22 Tu	20 04 01	1 37 11	27 04 16	4♈17 24	29 31.6	2 21.7	7 44.6	15 05.7	14 17.5	9 06.0	26 48.0	24 55.7	21 38.9	21 46.5
23 W	20 07 57	2 38 14	11♈27 22	18 33 54	29 32.9	4 03.3	8 57.5	15 00.4	14 34.1	9 01.0	26 46.3	24 57.7	21 40.8	21 46.5
24 Th	20 11 54	3 39 16	25 36 46	2♉35 53	29R 33.6	5 45.5	10 10.4	14 54.4	14 50.9	8 55.8	26 44.4	24 59.6	21 42.6	21R 46.5
25 F	20 15 51	4 40 17	9♉31 09	16 22 33	29 33.1	7 28.2	11 23.2	14 47.5	15 07.8	8 50.4	26 42.5	25 01.5	21 44.4	21 46.5
26 Sa	20 19 47	5 41 17	23 10 09	29 53 58	29 31.4	9 11.5	12 35.9	14 39.9	15 25.0	8 44.9	26 40.5	25 03.3	21 46.1	21 46.5
27 Su	20 23 44	6 42 16	6♊34 05	13♊10 34	29 28.6	10 55.4	13 48.5	14 31.4	15 42.3	8 39.3	26 38.4	25 05.1	21 47.9	21 46.4
28 M	20 27 40	7 43 13	19 43 32	26 13 03	29 25.3	12 39.7	15 01.1	14 22.2	15 59.7	8 33.5	26 36.1	25 06.8	21 49.6	21 46.3
29 Tu	20 31 37	8 44 10	2♋39 11	9♋02 03	29 21.8	14 24.6	16 13.6	14 12.2	16 17.3	8 27.6	26 33.8	25 08.5	21 51.3	21 46.1
30 W	20 35 33	9 45 06	15 21 44	21 38 19	29 18.7	16 09.8	17 26.0	14 01.4	16 35.1	8 21.5	26 31.4	25 10.1	21 53.0	21 45.9
31 Th	20 39 30	10 46 00	27 51 54	4♌02 36	29 16.3	17 55.5	18 38.4	13 49.8	16 53.0	8 15.3	26 28.9	25 11.7	21 54.6	21 45.7

LONGITUDE — February 1980

Day	Sid.Time	☉	0 hr ☽	Noon ☽	True ☊	☿	♀	♂	⚳	♃	♄	♅	♆	♇
1 F	20 43 26	11♒46 54	10♌10 34	16♌15 55	29♌14.8	19♒41.4	19♓50.6	13♍37.4	17♈11.1	8♍09.0	26♍26.3	25♏13.2	21♐56.3	21♎45.5
2 Sa	20 47 23	12 47 46	22 18 52	28 19 36	29D 14.3	21 27.6	21 02.8	13R 24.3	17 29.3	8R 02.5	26R 23.6	25 14.6	21 57.9	21R 45.2
3 Su	20 51 20	13 48 37	4♍18 23	10♍15 29	29 14.6	23 13.9	22 14.8	13 10.5	17 47.7	7 56.0	26 20.8	25 16.1	21 59.4	21 44.8
4 M	20 55 16	14 49 28	16 11 12	22 05 55	29 15.6	25 00.1	23 26.8	12 55.9	18 06.2	7 49.3	26 17.9	25 17.4	22 01.0	21 44.5
5 Tu	20 59 13	15 50 17	28 00 01	3♎53 54	29 16.9	26 46.2	24 38.7	12 40.5	18 24.9	7 42.5	26 15.0	25 18.7	22 02.5	21 44.1
6 W	21 03 09	16 51 05	9♎48 04	15 42 59	29 18.2	28 31.9	25 50.5	12 24.5	18 43.7	7 35.6	26 11.9	25 20.0	22 04.0	21 43.6
7 Th	21 07 06	17 51 53	21 39 11	27 37 14	29 19.3	0♓17.0	27 02.2	12 07.7	19 02.6	7 28.6	26 08.8	25 21.2	22 05.5	21 43.2
8 F	21 11 02	18 52 39	3♏37 41	9♏41 07	29R 19.9	2 01.2	28 13.8	11 50.3	19 21.7	7 21.5	26 05.6	25 22.4	22 06.9	21 42.7
9 Sa	21 14 59	19 53 25	15 48 08	21 59 17	29 20.1	3 44.2	29 25.3	11 32.2	19 40.9	7 14.3	26 02.3	25 23.5	22 08.4	21 42.1
10 Su	21 18 55	20 54 09	28 15 10	4♐36 16	29 19.8	5 25.6	0♈36.7	11 13.5	20 00.2	7 07.1	25 58.9	25 24.5	22 09.8	21 41.6
11 M	21 22 52	21 54 53	11♐03 05	17 36 01	29 19.2	7 05.1	1 48.0	10 54.2	20 19.7	6 59.7	25 55.5	25 25.5	22 11.1	21 41.0
12 Tu	21 26 49	22 55 35	24 15 24	1♑01 27	29 18.4	8 42.2	2 59.2	10 34.3	20 39.3	6 52.3	25 51.9	25 26.5	22 12.5	21 40.4
13 W	21 30 45	23 56 17	7♑54 15	14 53 46	29 17.7	10 16.3	4 10.3	10 13.9	20 59.0	6 44.8	25 48.3	25 27.4	22 13.8	21 39.7
14 Th	21 34 42	24 56 57	21 59 47	29 11 56	29 17.2	11 47.0	5 21.3	9 53.0	21 18.9	6 37.2	25 44.7	25 28.2	22 15.1	21 39.0
15 F	21 38 38	25 57 36	6♒29 40	13♒52 16	29 16.9	13 13.5	6 32.2	9 31.6	21 38.8	6 29.6	25 40.9	25 29.0	22 16.3	21 38.3
16 Sa	21 42 35	26 58 13	21 18 55	28 48 37	29D 16.8	14 35.3	7 43.0	9 09.7	21 58.9	6 21.9	25 37.1	25 29.7	22 17.6	21 37.5
17 Su	21 46 31	27 58 49	6♓20 18	13♓52 50	29 16.8	15 51.6	8 53.6	8 47.5	22 19.1	6 14.2	25 33.2	25 30.4	22 18.8	21 36.7
18 M	21 50 28	28 59 23	21 25 07	28 56 00	29R 16.9	17 01.9	10 04.2	8 24.9	22 39.4	6 06.4	25 29.3	25 31.0	22 19.9	21 35.9
19 Tu	21 54 24	29 59 56	6♈24 30	13♈49 39	29 16.8	18 05.2	11 14.6	8 02.0	22 59.8	5 58.6	25 25.3	25 31.6	22 21.1	21 35.0
20 W	21 58 21	1♓00 27	21 10 40	28 26 55	29 16.7	19 01.1	12 24.8	7 38.8	23 20.4	5 50.8	25 21.2	25 32.1	22 22.2	21 34.2
21 Th	22 02 18	2 00 55	5♉37 53	12♉43 14	29 16.5	19 48.9	13 35.0	7 15.4	23 41.0	5 43.0	25 17.1	25 32.5	22 23.2	21 33.2
22 F	22 06 14	3 01 23	19 42 47	26 36 27	29D 16.4	20 28.0	14 45.0	6 51.8	24 01.7	5 35.1	25 12.9	25 32.9	22 24.3	21 32.3
23 Sa	22 10 11	4 01 48	3♊24 19	10♊06 30	29 16.4	20 57.9	15 54.8	6 28.1	24 22.6	5 27.2	25 08.7	25 33.3	22 25.3	21 31.3
24 Su	22 14 07	5 02 11	16 43 16	23 14 52	29 16.6	21 18.2	17 04.5	6 04.3	24 43.5	5 19.3	25 04.4	25 33.6	22 26.3	21 30.3
25 M	22 18 04	6 02 32	29 41 40	6♋03 59	29 17.2	21R 28.7	18 14.1	5 40.5	25 04.6	5 11.4	25 00.1	25 33.8	22 27.2	21 29.3
26 Tu	22 22 00	7 02 52	12♋22 13	18 36 43	29 17.9	21 29.4	19 23.5	5 16.6	25 25.7	5 03.5	24 55.7	25 34.0	22 28.2	21 28.3
27 W	22 25 57	8 03 09	24 47 52	0♌56 00	29 18.8	21 20.2	20 32.7	4 52.9	25 46.9	4 55.7	24 51.3	25 34.1	22 29.0	21 27.2
28 Th	22 29 53	9 03 25	7♌01 29	13 04 38	29 19.6	21 01.6	21 41.8	4 29.2	26 08.2	4 47.8	24 46.9	25R 34.2	22 29.9	21 26.1
29 F	22 33 50	10 03 38	19 05 44	25 05 06	29R 20.0	20 33.9	22 50.7	4 05.6	26 29.6	4 40.0	24 42.4	25 34.2	22 30.7	21 25.0

Astro Data

	Dy Hr Mn
♄ R	6 22:42
☽ 0S	9 11:25
♂ R	16 6:18
☽ 0N	22 17:20
♇ R	24 15:49
♆✶♇	26 16:49
⚳ 0N	30 3:17
☽ 0S	5 19:33
♀ 0N	11 0:49
♃∠♇	14 5:52
♄✶♅	18 2:55
☽ 0N	19 1:58
☿ R	26 1:30
♅ R	29 6:39

Planet Ingress

	Dy Hr Mn
☿ ♑	2 8:02
☊ ♌R	5 14:53
☊ ♍	7 2:39
☊ ♌R	12 18:20
♀ ♓	16 3:37
☉ ♒	20 21:49
☿ ♒	21 2:18
☿ ♓	7 8:07
♀ ♈	9 23:39
☉ ♓	19 12:02

Last Aspect / ☽ Ingress (January)

Last Aspect Dy Hr Mn		☽ Ingress Dy Hr Mn
1 9:54	☿ ☍	♋ 1 12:29
3 15:03	♄ ✶	♌ 3 20:47
5 20:21	♅ □	♍ 6 7:48
8 14:34	♄ ☌	♎ 8 20:38
10 20:01	♀ △	♏ 11 8:55
13 12:41	♄ ✶	♐ 13 18:17
15 23:29	♀ ✶	♑ 15 23:51
17 21:19	☉ ☌	♒ 18 2:25
19 19:07	♅ □	♓ 20 3:33
21 23:34	♄ ☍	♈ 22 4:52
23 17:27	♇ ☍	♉ 24 7:31
26 6:15	♄ △	♊ 26 12:11
28 12:43	♄ □	♋ 28 19:02
30 21:23	♄ ✶	♌ 31 4:08

Last Aspect / ☽ Ingress (February)

Last Aspect Dy Hr Mn		☽ Ingress Dy Hr Mn
2 5:50	♅ □	♍ 2 15:21
4 20:30	♄ ☌	♎ 5 4:04
7 0:52	♆ ✶	♏ 7 16:46
9 19:45	♄ ✶	♐ 10 3:19
12 2:55	♄ □	♑ 12 10:12
14 6:17	♄ △	♒ 14 13:20
16 8:51	☉ ☌	♓ 16 13:54
18 6:32	♅ △	♈ 18 13:42
20 1:57	♆ △	♉ 20 14:35
22 10:09	♅ ☍	♊ 22 17:58
24 15:22	♄ □	♋ 25 0:34
27 1:30	♅ △	♌ 27 10:10
29 12:58	♅ □	♍ 29 21:53

☽ Phases & Eclipses

Dy Hr Mn		
2 9:02	○	11♋07
10 11:50	☾	19♎23
17 21:19	●	26♑55
24 13:58	☽	3♉44
1 2:21	○	11♌22
9 7:35	☾	19♏42
16 8:51	●	26♒50
16 8:53:11	●	T 04'08"
23 0:14	☽	3♊32

Astro Data

1 January 1980
Julian Day # 29220
SVP 5♓32'28"
GC 26♐33.6 ⚴ 27♒50.6
Eris 13♈51.4R ⚵ 25♋01.9R
⚷ 9♉17.4R ⚶ 3♉29.1
☽ Mean ☊ 1♍52.1

1 February 1980
Julian Day # 29251
SVP 5♓32'23"
GC 26♐33.7 ⚴ 7♓16.2
Eris 13♈56.5 ⚵ 17♋53.5R
⚷ 9♉13.1 ⚶ 8♉45.8
☽ Mean ☊ 0♍13.6

March 1980 — LONGITUDE

Day	Sid.Time	☉	0 hr ☽	Noon☽	True☊	☿	♀	♂	⚳	♃	♄	♅	♆	♇
1 Sa	22 37 46	11♓03 50	1♍03 00	6♍59 41	29♌19.9	19♓58.0	23♈59.5	3♍42.2	26♈51.1	4♍32.2	24♍37.9	25♏34.1	22♐31.5	21♎23.8
2 Su	22 41 43	12 04 00	12 55 25	18 50 27	29R 19.2	19R 14.8	25 08.0	3R 19.1	27 12.7	4R 24.4	24R 33.3	25R 34.1	22 32.3	21R 22.6
3 M	22 45 40	13 04 08	24 45 02	0♎39 26	29 17.7	18 25.2	26 16.4	2 56.2	27 34.4	4 16.7	24 28.7	25 33.9	22 33.0	21 21.4
4 Tu	22 49 36	14 04 14	6♎33 55	12 28 47	29 15.6	17 30.7	27 24.7	2 33.6	27 56.1	4 09.0	24 24.1	25 33.7	22 33.7	21 20.2
5 W	22 53 33	15 04 19	18 24 18	24 20 49	29 13.1	16 32.7	28 32.7	2 11.3	28 18.0	4 01.3	24 19.5	25 33.4	22 34.3	21 18.9
6 Th	22 57 29	16 04 22	0♏18 41	6♏18 16	29 10.5	15 32.4	29 40.5	1 49.4	28 39.9	3 53.7	24 14.8	25 33.1	22 35.0	21 17.7
7 F	23 01 26	17 04 23	12 19 59	18 24 14	29 08.2	14 31.4	0♉48.2	1 28.0	29 01.9	3 46.2	24 10.1	25 32.8	22 35.6	21 16.4
8 Sa	23 05 22	18 04 23	24 31 29	0♐42 12	29 06.4	13 31.1	1 55.6	1 07.0	29 23.9	3 38.7	24 05.4	25 32.4	22 36.1	21 15.0
9 Su	23 09 19	19 04 21	6♐56 52	13 15 57	29D 05.4	12 32.8	3 02.9	0 46.4	29 46.1	3 31.3	24 00.7	25 31.9	22 36.7	21 13.7
10 M	23 13 15	20 04 18	19 39 56	26 09 17	29 05.4	11 37.6	4 10.0	0 26.4	0♉08.3	3 24.0	23 56.0	25 31.4	22 37.2	21 12.3
11 Tu	23 17 12	21 04 13	2♑44 24	9♑25 40	29 06.3	10 46.4	5 16.8	0 07.0	0 30.6	3 16.8	23 51.2	25 30.8	22 37.6	21 11.0
12 W	23 21 09	22 04 06	16 13 23	23 07 43	29 07.7	10 00.2	6 23.4	29♌48.1	0 53.0	3 09.6	23 46.5	25 30.2	22 38.0	21 09.6
13 Th	23 25 05	23 03 57	0♒08 45	7♒16 26	29 09.1	9 19.4	7 29.8	29 29.8	1 15.4	3 02.5	23 41.7	25 29.5	22 38.4	21 08.1
14 F	23 29 02	24 03 47	14 30 32	21 50 38	29R 10.1	8 44.6	8 36.0	29 12.2	1 37.9	2 55.6	23 37.0	25 28.8	22 38.8	21 06.7
15 Sa	23 32 58	25 03 35	29 16 07	6♓46 14	29 10.1	8 15.9	9 42.0	28 55.2	2 00.5	2 48.7	23 32.2	25 28.0	22 39.1	21 05.2
16 Su	23 36 55	26 03 21	14♓20 01	21 56 21	29 08.7	7 53.6	10 47.7	28 38.9	2 23.1	2 41.9	23 27.5	25 27.2	22 39.4	21 03.8
17 M	23 40 51	27 03 05	29 34 00	7♈11 41	29 06.0	7 37.7	11 53.2	28 23.3	2 45.9	2 35.3	23 22.7	25 26.3	22 39.7	21 02.3
18 Tu	23 44 48	28 02 47	14♈48 04	22 21 55	29 02.2	7 28.0	12 58.4	28 08.4	3 08.6	2 28.7	23 18.0	25 25.4	22 39.9	21 00.8
19 W	23 48 44	29 02 27	29 52 02	7♉17 22	28 57.9	7D 24.5	14 03.4	27 54.3	3 31.5	2 22.3	23 13.3	25 24.4	22 40.1	20 59.2
20 Th	23 52 41	0♈02 05	14♉37 04	21 50 28	28 53.7	7 26.9	15 08.1	27 40.9	3 54.4	2 16.0	23 08.6	25 23.4	22 40.3	20 57.7
21 F	23 56 38	1 01 40	28 57 05	5♊56 39	28 50.2	7 35.1	16 12.6	27 28.3	4 17.3	2 09.8	23 03.9	25 22.3	22 40.4	20 56.2
22 Sa	0 00 34	2 01 14	12♊49 06	19 34 29	28 48.1	7 48.8	17 16.7	27 16.4	4 40.3	2 03.8	22 59.2	25 21.2	22 40.5	20 54.6
23 Su	0 04 31	3 00 45	26 13 03	2♋45 08	28D 47.4	8 07.6	18 20.6	27 05.3	5 03.4	1 57.9	22 54.6	25 20.0	22 40.5	20 53.0
24 M	0 08 27	4 00 13	9♋11 10	15 31 38	28 47.9	8 31.4	19 24.1	26 55.1	5 26.5	1 52.1	22 49.9	25 18.8	22R 40.6	20 51.4
25 Tu	0 12 24	4 59 39	21 47 04	27 58 03	28 49.4	8 59.9	20 27.3	26 45.5	5 49.7	1 46.5	22 45.4	25 17.5	22 40.5	20 49.8
26 W	0 16 20	5 59 03	4♌05 07	10♌08 52	28 51.1	9 32.8	21 30.2	26 36.8	6 12.9	1 41.0	22 40.8	25 16.2	22 40.5	20 48.2
27 Th	0 20 17	6 58 25	16 09 48	22 08 29	28R 52.3	10 09.9	22 32.8	26 28.9	6 36.2	1 35.7	22 36.3	25 14.9	22 40.4	20 46.6
28 F	0 24 13	7 57 44	28 05 23	4♍00 58	28 52.4	10 50.8	23 35.1	26 21.8	6 59.5	1 30.5	22 31.8	25 13.5	22 40.3	20 45.0
29 Sa	0 28 10	8 57 01	9♍55 38	15 49 48	28 50.8	11 35.5	24 36.9	26 15.4	7 22.9	1 25.5	22 27.3	25 12.0	22 40.2	20 43.3
30 Su	0 32 06	9 56 16	21 43 47	27 37 54	28 47.2	12 23.7	25 38.5	26 09.8	7 46.3	1 20.6	22 22.9	25 10.6	22 40.0	20 41.7
31 M	0 36 03	10 55 29	3♎32 27	9♎27 40	28 41.7	13 15.2	26 39.6	26 05.0	8 09.8	1 15.9	22 18.5	25 09.0	22 39.8	20 40.0

April 1980 — LONGITUDE

Day	Sid.Time	☉	0 hr ☽	Noon☽	True☊	☿	♀	♂	⚳	♃	♄	♅	♆	♇
1 Tu	0 40 00	11♈54 40	15♎23 48	21♎21 01	28♌34.5	14♓09.8	27♉40.4	26♌01.0	8♉33.3	1♍11.3	22♍14.1	25♏07.5	22♐39.5	20♎38.4
2 W	0 43 56	12 53 49	27 19 34	3♏19 37	28R 26.2	15 07.4	28 40.7	25R 57.7	8 56.9	1R 06.9	22R 09.9	25R 05.9	22R 39.3	20R 36.7
3 Th	0 47 53	13 52 56	9♏21 22	15 25 02	28 17.5	16 07.8	29 40.7	25 55.2	9 20.5	1 02.7	22 05.6	25 04.2	22 39.0	20 35.0
4 F	0 51 49	14 52 01	21 30 49	27 38 57	28 09.4	17 10.8	0♊40.2	25 53.5	9 44.1	0 58.6	22 01.4	25 02.5	22 38.6	20 33.4
5 Sa	0 55 46	15 51 04	3♐49 43	10♐03 22	28 02.7	18 16.4	1 39.3	25D 52.5	10 07.8	0 54.7	21 57.3	25 00.8	22 38.3	20 31.7
6 Su	0 59 42	16 50 05	16 20 14	22 40 38	27 57.8	19 24.5	2 38.0	25 52.2	10 31.5	0 51.0	21 53.2	24 59.0	22 37.9	20 30.0
7 M	1 03 39	17 49 05	29 04 55	5♑33 27	27 55.0	20 34.8	3 36.2	25 52.7	10 55.3	0 47.4	21 49.2	24 57.2	22 37.4	20 28.3
8 Tu	1 07 35	18 48 03	12♑06 37	18 44 44	27D 54.2	21 47.4	4 34.0	25 53.9	11 19.1	0 44.1	21 45.2	24 55.4	22 37.0	20 26.6
9 W	1 11 32	19 46 59	25 28 10	2♒17 12	27 54.7	23 02.2	5 31.2	25 55.8	11 43.0	0 40.9	21 41.3	24 53.5	22 36.5	20 25.0
10 Th	1 15 29	20 45 54	9♒12 03	16 12 51	27R 55.7	24 19.0	6 28.0	25 58.4	12 06.9	0 37.8	21 37.4	24 51.6	22 36.0	20 23.3
11 F	1 19 25	21 44 46	23 19 37	0♓32 13	27 56.1	25 37.8	7 24.2	26 01.8	12 30.8	0 35.0	21 33.6	24 49.7	22 35.4	20 21.6
12 Sa	1 23 22	22 43 37	7♓50 23	15 13 38	27 54.9	26 58.6	8 19.9	26 05.8	12 54.8	0 32.3	21 29.9	24 47.7	22 34.8	20 19.9
13 Su	1 27 18	23 42 26	22 41 18	0♈12 33	27 51.4	28 21.3	9 15.1	26 10.4	13 18.7	0 29.9	21 26.3	24 45.7	22 34.2	20 18.2
14 M	1 31 15	24 41 13	7♈46 22	15 21 35	27 45.5	29 45.8	10 09.7	26 15.8	13 42.8	0 27.5	21 22.7	24 43.7	22 33.6	20 16.5
15 Tu	1 35 11	25 39 59	22 56 56	0♉31 07	27 37.6	1♈12.2	11 03.7	26 21.8	14 06.8	0 25.4	21 19.2	24 41.6	22 32.9	20 14.8
16 W	1 39 08	26 38 42	8♉02 50	15 30 51	27 28.6	2 40.4	11 57.1	26 28.5	14 30.9	0 23.5	21 15.7	24 39.5	22 32.2	20 13.1
17 Th	1 43 04	27 37 23	22 54 03	0♊11 32	27 19.5	4 10.3	12 49.8	26 35.8	14 55.1	0 21.8	21 12.4	24 37.4	22 31.4	20 11.5
18 F	1 47 01	28 36 03	7♊22 31	14 26 31	27 11.4	5 41.9	13 41.9	26 43.7	15 19.2	0 20.2	21 09.1	24 35.2	22 30.7	20 09.8
19 Sa	1 50 58	29 34 40	21 23 12	28 12 28	27 05.3	7 15.3	14 33.3	26 52.3	15 43.4	0 18.8	21 05.9	24 33.1	22 29.9	20 08.1
20 Su	1 54 54	0♉33 15	4♋54 24	11♋29 14	27 01.4	8 50.4	15 24.0	27 01.4	16 07.6	0 17.7	21 02.8	24 30.9	22 29.1	20 06.5
21 M	1 58 51	1 31 47	17 57 21	24 19 13	26D 59.6	10 27.2	16 14.0	27 11.2	16 31.8	0 16.7	20 59.7	24 28.6	22 28.2	20 04.8
22 Tu	2 02 47	2 30 18	0♌35 24	6♌46 32	26 59.5	12 05.7	17 03.2	27 21.5	16 56.1	0 15.8	20 56.8	24 26.4	22 27.4	20 03.2
23 W	2 06 44	3 28 46	12 53 15	18 56 12	27R 00.0	13 45.9	17 51.6	27 32.4	17 20.4	0 15.2	20 53.9	24 24.1	22 26.5	20 01.5
24 Th	2 10 40	4 27 12	24 56 05	0♍53 31	27 00.1	15 27.8	18 39.1	27 43.9	17 44.7	0 14.8	20 51.1	24 21.8	22 25.5	19 59.9
25 F	2 14 37	5 25 36	6♍49 09	12 43 35	26 58.9	17 11.4	19 25.8	27 55.9	18 09.0	0D 14.5	20 48.4	24 19.5	22 24.6	19 58.3
26 Sa	2 18 33	6 23 58	18 37 21	24 31 00	26 55.4	18 56.7	20 11.6	28 08.4	18 33.4	0 14.5	20 45.8	24 17.1	22 23.6	19 56.7
27 Su	2 22 30	7 22 18	0♎24 59	6♎19 42	26 49.4	20 43.8	20 56.4	28 21.5	18 57.7	0 14.6	20 43.3	24 14.8	22 22.6	19 55.1
28 M	2 26 27	8 20 36	12 15 33	18 12 50	26 40.7	22 32.6	21 40.3	28 35.0	19 22.1	0 14.9	20 40.8	24 12.4	22 21.6	19 53.5
29 Tu	2 30 23	9 18 52	24 11 49	0♏12 43	26 29.7	24 23.1	22 23.2	28 49.1	19 46.5	0 15.4	20 38.5	24 10.0	22 20.5	19 51.9
30 W	2 34 20	10 17 06	6♏15 43	12 20 57	26 17.1	26 15.4	23 05.1	29 03.7	20 11.0	0 16.0	20 36.3	24 07.6	22 19.4	19 50.4

Astro Data	Dy Hr Mn
☽0S	4 2:04
☽0N	17 12:33
☿D	19 13:59
☉0N	20 11:10
♆R	24 17:42
♄□♆	26 13:32
☽0S	31 8:01
♂D	6 8:27
☽0N	13 23:40
☿0N	18 17:26
♃D	26 8:47
☽0S	27 14:41

Planet Ingress	Dy Hr Mn
♀ ♉	6 18:54
⚳ ♉	10 3:03
♂ ♌R	11 20:46
☉ ♈	20 11:10
♀ ♊	3 19:46
☿ ♈	14 15:58
☉ ♉	19 22:23

Last Aspect Dy Hr Mn		☽ Ingress Dy Hr Mn
3 1:39	♅ ⚹	♎ 3 10:40
5 21:20	♀ ☍	♏ 5 23:22
8 1:59	♅ ☌	♐ 8 10:38
10 7:56	♄ □	♑ 10 19:02
12 16:05	♅ ⚹	♒ 12 23:45
14 23:40	♂ ☍	♓ 15 1:10
16 18:56	☉ ☌	♈ 17 0:41
18 21:05	♂ △	♉ 19 0:13
20 21:42	♂ □	♊ 21 1:47
23 1:44	♂ ⚹	♋ 23 6:55
25 6:48	♅ △	♌ 25 15:58
27 20:40	♂ ☌	♍ 28 3:52
30 7:34	♀ △	♎ 30 16:49

Last Aspect Dy Hr Mn		☽ Ingress Dy Hr Mn
1 21:20	♂ ⚹	♏ 2 5:21
4 8:35	♂ □	♐ 4 16:35
6 18:00	♂ △	♑ 7 1:43
8 23:00	♅ ⚹	♒ 9 8:00
11 4:29	♂ ☍	♓ 11 11:07
13 8:45	☿ ☌	♈ 13 11:40
15 5:22	♂ △	♉ 15 11:11
17 6:01	♂ □	♊ 17 11:41
19 14:38	☉ ⚹	♋ 19 15:11
21 12:18	♅ △	♌ 21 22:52
24 5:31	♂ ☌	♍ 24 10:12
26 11:32	♅ ⚹	♎ 26 23:09
29 9:10	♂ ⚹	♏ 29 11:35

☽ Phases & Eclipses Dy Hr Mn	
1 21:00	○ 11♍26
1 20:45	☊ A 0.654
9 23:49	☾ 19♐34
16 18:56	● 26♓21
23 12:31	☽ 3♋02
31 15:14	○ 11♎03
8 12:06	☾ 18♑48
15 3:46	● 25♈20
22 2:59	☽ 2♌08
30 7:35	○ 10♏06

Astro Data

1 March 1980
Julian Day # 29280
SVP 5♓32'20"
GC 26♐33.7 ⚴ 16♓54.8
Eris 14♈09.8 ⚵ 16♋24.8
⚷ 10♉00.0 ⚶ 17♉17.7
☽ Mean ☊ 28♌41.5

1 April 1980
Julian Day # 29311
SVP 5♓32'18"
GC 26♐33.8 ⚴ 27♓33.5
Eris 14♈29.5 ⚵ 21♋24.6
⚷ 11♉32.9 ⚶ 28♉35.9
☽ Mean ☊ 27♌03.0

LONGITUDE — May 1980

Day	Sid.Time	☉	0 hr ☽	Noon ☽	True ☊	☿	♀	♂	⚳	♃	♄	♅	♆	♇
1 Th	2 38 16	11♉15 19	18♏28 32	24♏38 33	26♌04.1	28♈09.5	23♊45.9	29♌18.7	20♉35.4	0♍16.9	20♍34.1	24♏05.2	22♐18.3	19♎48.8
2 F	2 42 13	12 13 30	0♐51 03	7♐06 08	25R51.7	0♉05.2	24 25.5	29 34.2	20 59.9	0 17.9	20R32.0	24R02.8	22R17.2	19R47.3
3 Sa	2 46 09	13 11 39	13 23 51	19 44 16	25 41.0	2 02.7	25 04.0	29 50.2	21 24.4	0 19.1	20 30.1	24 00.3	22 16.1	19 45.8
4 Su	2 50 06	14 09 47	26 07 31	2♑33 41	25 32.8	4 01.9	25 41.3	0♍06.6	21 48.9	0 20.5	20 28.2	23 57.9	22 14.9	19 44.3
5 M	2 54 02	15 07 53	9♑02 57	15 35 28	25 27.3	6 02.7	26 17.4	0 23.4	22 13.4	0 22.1	20 26.4	23 55.4	22 13.7	19 42.8
6 Tu	2 57 59	16 05 58	22 11 26	28 51 04	25 24.6	8 05.2	26 52.2	0 40.7	22 37.9	0 23.9	20 24.8	23 52.9	22 12.5	19 41.3
7 W	3 01 56	17 04 02	5♒34 36	12♒22 15	25 23.7	10 09.2	27 25.6	0 58.4	23 02.5	0 25.8	20 23.2	23 50.4	22 11.3	19 39.8
8 Th	3 05 52	18 02 04	19 14 12	26 10 37	25 23.7	12 14.6	27 57.6	1 16.6	23 27.0	0 27.9	20 21.7	23 47.9	22 10.0	19 38.4
9 F	3 09 49	19 00 04	3♓11 36	10♓17 08	25 23.2	14 21.4	28 28.2	1 35.1	23 51.6	0 30.2	20 20.3	23 45.4	22 08.7	19 37.0
10 Sa	3 13 45	19 58 04	17 27 07	24 41 20	25 21.1	16 29.5	28 57.3	1 54.0	24 16.2	0 32.7	20 19.0	23 42.9	22 07.5	19 35.6
11 Su	3 17 42	20 56 02	1♈59 22	9♈20 42	25 16.5	18 38.5	29 24.9	2 13.4	24 40.8	0 35.3	20 17.8	23 40.4	22 06.1	19 34.2
12 M	3 21 38	21 53 59	16 44 37	24 10 16	25 09.2	20 48.4	29 50.8	2 33.1	25 05.4	0 38.1	20 16.8	23 37.9	22 04.8	19 32.8
13 Tu	3 25 35	22 51 54	1♉36 40	9♉02 47	24 59.4	22 59.0	0♋15.1	2 53.2	25 30.1	0 41.1	20 15.8	23 35.4	22 03.5	19 31.5
14 W	3 29 31	23 49 48	16 27 30	23 49 41	24 48.2	25 10.0	0 37.7	3 13.6	25 54.7	0 44.2	20 14.9	23 32.9	22 02.1	19 30.1
15 Th	3 33 28	24 47 41	1♊08 19	8♊22 25	24 36.7	27 21.1	0 58.5	3 34.5	26 19.3	0 47.6	20 14.1	23 30.3	22 00.7	19 28.8
16 F	3 37 25	25 45 32	15 31 11	22 33 58	24 26.3	29 32.2	1 17.4	3 55.7	26 44.0	0 51.1	20 13.5	23 27.8	21 59.3	19 27.6
17 Sa	3 41 21	26 43 21	29 30 17	6♋19 53	24 17.9	1♊42.8	1 34.4	4 17.2	27 08.7	0 54.7	20 12.9	23 25.3	21 57.9	19 26.3
18 Su	3 45 18	27 41 09	13♋02 38	19 38 39	24 12.1	3 52.8	1 49.5	4 39.1	27 33.3	0 58.6	20 12.4	23 22.8	21 56.5	19 25.1
19 M	3 49 14	28 38 55	26 08 07	2♌31 25	24 08.8	6 01.8	2 02.5	5 01.4	27 58.0	1 02.5	20 12.1	23 20.3	21 55.0	19 23.8
20 Tu	3 53 11	29 36 40	8♌49 00	15 01 24	24D07.5	8 09.5	2 13.4	5 23.9	28 22.7	1 06.7	20 11.8	23 17.8	21 53.6	19 22.7
21 W	3 57 07	0♊34 23	21 09 14	27 13 08	24R07.4	10 15.8	2 22.2	5 46.8	28 47.3	1 11.0	20D11.7	23 15.3	21 52.1	19 21.5
22 Th	4 01 04	1 32 04	3♍13 47	9♍11 53	24 07.2	12 20.4	2 28.8	6 10.0	29 12.0	1 15.5	20 11.6	23 12.8	21 50.6	19 20.3
23 F	4 05 00	2 29 44	15 08 05	21 03 03	24 06.1	14 23.1	2 33.0	6 33.5	29 36.7	1 20.1	20 11.7	23 10.3	21 49.1	19 19.2
24 Sa	4 08 57	3 27 22	26 57 28	2♎51 54	24 02.9	16 23.6	2R35.0	6 57.3	0♊01.4	1 24.9	20 11.8	23 07.9	21 47.6	19 18.1
25 Su	4 12 54	4 24 59	8♎46 57	14 43 09	23 57.3	18 21.9	2 34.6	7 21.3	0 26.1	1 29.9	20 12.1	23 05.4	21 46.1	19 17.0
26 M	4 16 50	5 22 34	20 40 57	26 40 47	23 49.1	20 17.7	2 31.9	7 45.7	0 50.8	1 35.0	20 12.4	23 03.0	21 44.6	19 16.0
27 Tu	4 20 47	6 20 08	2♏43 01	8♏47 55	23 38.5	22 11.1	2 26.7	8 10.4	1 15.4	1 40.2	20 12.9	23 00.6	21 43.0	19 15.0
28 W	4 24 43	7 17 41	14 55 45	21 06 40	23 26.5	24 01.8	2 19.1	8 35.3	1 40.1	1 45.6	20 13.5	22 58.1	21 41.5	19 14.0
29 Th	4 28 40	8 15 13	27 20 46	3♐38 07	23 13.8	25 49.9	2 09.0	9 00.5	2 04.8	1 51.2	20 14.1	22 55.7	21 39.9	19 13.0
30 F	4 32 36	9 12 43	9♐58 43	16 22 32	23 01.8	27 35.2	1 56.6	9 26.0	2 29.5	1 56.9	20 14.9	22 53.4	21 38.3	19 12.1
31 Sa	4 36 33	10 10 13	22 49 29	29 19 30	22 51.4	29 17.7	1 41.7	9 51.7	2 54.2	2 02.7	20 15.8	22 51.0	21 36.8	19 11.2

LONGITUDE — June 1980

Day	Sid.Time	☉	0 hr ☽	Noon ☽	True ☊	☿	♀	♂	⚳	♃	♄	♅	♆	♇
1 Su	4 40 29	11♊07 41	5♑52 28	12♑28 17	22♌43.5	0♋57.4	1♋24.4	10♍17.7	3♊18.9	2♍08.7	20♍16.8	22♏48.6	21♐35.2	19♎10.3
2 M	4 44 26	12 05 09	19 06 53	25 48 11	22R38.3	2 34.3	1R04.9	10 43.9	3 43.5	2 14.8	20 17.8	22R46.3	21R33.6	19R09.5
3 Tu	4 48 23	13 02 36	2♒32 08	9♒18 44	22D35.7	4 08.2	0 43.1	11 10.4	4 08.2	2 21.1	20 19.0	22 44.0	21 32.0	19 08.6
4 W	4 52 19	14 00 02	16 07 58	22 59 51	22 35.0	5 39.3	0 19.1	11 37.1	4 32.9	2 27.5	20 20.3	22 41.7	21 30.4	19 07.8
5 Th	4 56 16	14 57 27	29 54 25	6♓51 41	22R35.4	7 07.4	29♊53.0	12 04.0	4 57.5	2 34.0	20 21.7	22 39.4	21 28.8	19 07.1
6 F	5 00 12	15 54 52	13♓51 39	20 54 17	22 35.4	8 32.5	29 25.0	12 31.2	5 22.2	2 40.7	20 23.2	22 37.2	21 27.2	19 06.3
7 Sa	5 04 09	16 52 16	27 59 30	5♈07 07	22 34.1	9 54.6	28 55.2	12 58.6	5 46.9	2 47.5	20 24.7	22 35.0	21 25.6	19 05.6
8 Su	5 08 05	17 49 40	12♈16 54	19 28 31	22 30.7	11 13.7	28 23.7	13 26.3	6 11.5	2 54.5	20 26.4	22 32.8	21 24.0	19 04.9
9 M	5 12 02	18 47 03	26 41 31	3♉55 22	22 24.9	12 29.7	27 50.8	13 54.1	6 36.1	3 01.6	20 28.2	22 30.6	21 22.3	19 04.3
10 Tu	5 15 58	19 44 26	11♉09 26	18 23 00	22 17.0	13 42.6	27 16.5	14 22.2	7 00.8	3 08.8	20 30.1	22 28.4	21 20.7	19 03.7
11 W	5 19 55	20 41 48	25 35 19	2♊45 37	22 07.7	14 52.2	26 41.2	14 50.5	7 25.4	3 16.1	20 32.1	22 26.3	21 19.1	19 03.1
12 Th	5 23 52	21 39 09	9♊53 08	16 57 08	21 58.1	15 58.7	26 04.9	15 19.1	7 50.0	3 23.6	20 34.1	22 24.2	21 17.5	19 02.5
13 F	5 27 48	22 36 30	23 56 57	0♋52 04	21 49.3	17 01.8	25 28.0	15 47.8	8 14.6	3 31.2	20 36.3	22 22.1	21 15.9	19 02.0
14 Sa	5 31 45	23 33 50	7♋42 00	14 26 29	21 42.3	18 01.5	24 50.7	16 16.7	8 39.2	3 38.9	20 38.6	22 20.1	21 14.2	19 01.5
15 Su	5 35 41	24 31 10	21 05 18	27 38 26	21 37.4	18 57.7	24 13.2	16 45.9	9 03.8	3 46.7	20 40.9	22 18.1	21 12.6	19 01.1
16 M	5 39 38	25 28 28	4♌05 59	10♌28 07	21D34.9	19 50.4	23 35.7	17 15.3	9 28.4	3 54.7	20 43.4	22 16.1	21 11.0	19 00.6
17 Tu	5 43 34	26 25 46	16 45 09	22 57 30	21 34.3	20 39.4	22 58.4	17 44.8	9 52.9	4 02.8	20 46.0	22 14.2	21 09.4	19 00.3
18 W	5 47 31	27 23 03	29 05 39	5♍10 06	21 34.9	21 24.6	22 21.7	18 14.5	10 17.5	4 11.0	20 48.6	22 12.3	21 07.8	18 59.9
19 Th	5 51 27	28 20 19	11♍11 27	17 10 19	21 35.9	22 06.0	21 45.7	18 44.5	10 42.0	4 19.3	20 51.4	22 10.4	21 06.2	18 59.6
20 F	5 55 24	29 17 35	23 07 20	29 03 10	21R36.5	22 43.3	21 10.7	19 14.6	11 06.5	4 27.7	20 54.2	22 08.6	21 04.6	18 59.3
21 Sa	5 59 21	0♋14 50	4♎58 27	10♎53 50	21 35.8	23 16.6	20 36.8	19 44.9	11 31.0	4 36.3	20 57.1	22 06.8	21 03.0	18 59.0
22 Su	6 03 17	1 12 04	16 49 57	22 47 22	21 33.3	23 45.7	20 04.3	20 15.4	11 55.5	4 44.9	21 00.1	22 05.0	21 01.4	18 58.8
23 M	6 07 14	2 09 17	28 46 41	4♏48 24	21 28.8	24 10.5	19 33.4	20 46.0	12 19.9	4 53.6	21 03.2	22 03.3	20 59.8	18 58.6
24 Tu	6 11 10	3 06 30	10♏52 58	17 00 50	21 22.6	24 30.9	19 04.2	21 16.8	12 44.3	5 02.5	21 06.4	22 01.6	20 58.2	18 58.4
25 W	6 15 07	4 03 42	23 12 19	29 27 43	21 15.2	24 46.8	18 36.8	21 47.8	13 08.7	5 11.5	21 09.7	21 59.9	20 56.6	18 58.3
26 Th	6 19 03	5 00 55	5♐47 11	12♐10 53	21 07.2	24 58.2	18 11.5	22 19.0	13 33.1	5 20.5	21 13.1	21 58.3	20 55.1	18 58.2
27 F	6 23 00	5 58 06	18 38 49	25 10 59	20 59.5	25R05.0	17 48.2	22 50.3	13 57.5	5 29.7	21 16.6	21 56.7	20 53.5	18 58.1
28 Sa	6 26 56	6 55 18	1♑47 15	8♑27 28	20 52.9	25 07.1	17 27.1	23 21.8	14 21.9	5 39.0	21 20.1	21 55.2	20 52.0	18D58.1
29 Su	6 30 53	7 52 29	15 11 23	21 58 45	20 48.1	25 04.7	17 08.4	23 53.5	14 46.2	5 48.4	21 23.8	21 53.7	20 50.4	18 58.1
30 M	6 34 50	8 49 40	28 49 15	5♒42 34	20 45.2	24 57.6	16 51.9	24 25.3	15 10.5	5 57.8	21 27.5	21 52.2	20 48.9	18 58.1

Astro Data	Dy Hr Mn
☽0N	11 9:38
♄ D	22 11:50
♀ R	24 20:10
☽0S	24 22:41
☽0N	7 17:36
♃∠♇	17 4:51
☽0S	21 7:37
♄□♆	22 18:21
☿ R	28 11:12
♇ D	28 20:09

Planet Ingress		Dy Hr Mn
☿	♉	2 10:56
♂	♍	4 2:27
♀	♋	12 20:53
☿	♊	16 17:06
☉	♊	20 21:42
⚳	♊	24 10:39
☿	♋	31 22:05
♀	♊R	5 5:44
☉	♋	21 5:47

Last Aspect Dy Hr Mn			☽ Ingress	Dy Hr Mn
1 21:13	♂	□	♐	1 22:22
3 22:32	♀	☍	♑	4 7:14
6 3:05	♅	⚹	♒	6 14:03
8 15:11	♀	△	♓	8 18:33
10 19:15	♀	□	♈	10 20:44
12 8:38	♆	△	♉	12 21:24
14 14:34	☿	☌	♊	14 22:07
16 11:01	♆	☍	♋	17 0:52
19 4:06	☉	⚹	♌	19 7:14
21 4:10	♅	□	♍	21 17:32
23 16:18	♅	⚹	♎	24 6:11
26 2:09	♆	⚹	♏	26 18:37
28 15:34	♅	☌	♐	29 5:05
31 11:56	☿	☍	♑	31 13:14

Last Aspect Dy Hr Mn			☽ Ingress	Dy Hr Mn
2 6:35	♅	⚹	♒	2 19:29
4 11:28	♅	□	♓	5 0:10
7 1:55	♀	□	♈	7 3:23
9 2:17	♀	⚹	♉	9 5:29
10 18:47	♅	☍	♊	11 7:22
13 3:01	♀	☌	♋	13 10:29
15 2:14	♅	△	♌	15 16:22
17 19:21	☉	⚹	♍	18 1:47
20 12:32	☉	□	♎	20 13:55
22 14:02	☿	□	♏	23 2:26
25 2:51	☿	△	♐	25 13:02
27 7:32	♂	□	♑	27 20:46
29 17:25	☿	☍	♒	30 2:04

☽ Phases & Eclipses Dy Hr Mn	
7 20:51	☾ 17♒25
14 12:00	● 23♉50
21 19:16	☽ 0♍52
29 21:28	○ 8♐38
6 2:53	☾ 15♓33
12 20:38	● 22♊00
20 12:32	☽ 29♍19
28 9:02	○ 6♑48

Astro Data

1 May 1980
Julian Day # 29341
SVP 5♓32'15"
GC 26♐33.9 ⚴ 7♈45.9
Eris 14♈49.1 ⚵ 0♌12.1
⚷ 13♉26.1 ⚶ 10♊43.2
☽ Mean ☊ 25♌27.6

1 June 1980
Julian Day # 29372
SVP 5♓32'11"
GC 26♐33.9 ⚴ 17♈45.7
Eris 15♈05.0 ⚵ 11♌21.3
⚷ 15♉25.0 ⚶ 23♊53.0
☽ Mean ☊ 23♌49.1

July 1980 — LONGITUDE

Day	Sid.Time	☉	0 hr ☽	Noon ☽	True ☊	☿	♀	♂	⚳	♃	♄	♅	♆	♇
1 Tu	6 38 46	9♋46 51	12♒38 24	19♒36 24	20♌44.3	24♋46.2	16♊37.8	24♍57.2	15♊34.8	6♍07.4	21♍31.3	21♏50.8	20♐47.4	18♎58.2
2 W	6 42 43	10 44 03	26 36 17	3♓37 46	20D 44.8	24R 30.3	16R 26.2	25 29.4	15 59.1	6 17.0	21 35.2	21R 49.4	20R 45.9	18 58.3
3 Th	6 46 39	11 41 14	10♓40 34	17 44 27	20 46.1	24 10.4	16 16.9	26 01.6	16 23.3	6 26.8	21 39.1	21 48.1	20 44.4	18 58.4
4 F	6 50 36	12 38 25	24 49 10	1♈54 31	20R 47.3	23 46.6	16 10.0	26 34.0	16 47.5	6 36.6	21 43.2	21 46.8	20 42.9	18 58.6
5 Sa	6 54 32	13 35 37	9♈00 16	16 06 12	20 47.6	23 19.2	16 05.6	27 06.6	17 11.7	6 46.6	21 47.3	21 45.6	20 41.4	18 58.8
6 Su	6 58 29	14 32 50	23 12 05	0♉17 39	20 46.6	22 48.6	16D 03.5	27 39.3	17 35.9	6 56.6	21 51.5	21 44.4	20 40.0	18 59.1
7 M	7 02 25	15 30 02	7♉22 36	14 26 37	20 44.1	22 15.4	16 03.8	28 12.2	18 00.0	7 06.7	21 55.8	21 43.2	20 38.6	18 59.3
8 Tu	7 06 22	16 27 15	21 29 23	28 30 30	20 40.2	21 39.9	16 06.3	28 45.2	18 24.1	7 16.9	22 00.2	21 42.1	20 37.1	18 59.6
9 W	7 10 19	17 24 29	5♊29 36	12♊26 16	20 35.4	21 02.7	16 11.2	29 18.4	18 48.2	7 27.2	22 04.6	21 41.0	20 35.7	19 00.0
10 Th	7 14 15	18 21 43	19 20 09	26 10 50	20 30.4	20 24.5	16 18.2	29 51.7	19 12.2	7 37.6	22 09.1	21 40.0	20 34.3	19 00.4
11 F	7 18 12	19 18 57	2♋58 00	9♋41 20	20 25.9	19 45.9	16 27.4	0♎25.1	19 36.3	7 48.0	22 13.8	21 39.1	20 32.9	19 00.8
12 Sa	7 22 08	20 16 11	16 20 36	22 55 38	20 22.3	19 07.6	16 38.6	0 58.7	20 00.3	7 58.5	22 18.4	21 38.1	20 31.6	19 01.2
13 Su	7 26 05	21 13 26	29 26 17	5♌52 33	20 20.0	18 30.1	16 51.9	1 32.5	20 24.2	8 09.2	22 23.2	21 37.3	20 30.2	19 01.7
14 M	7 30 01	22 10 41	12♌14 28	18 32 09	20D 19.2	17 54.3	17 07.2	2 06.3	20 48.1	8 19.9	22 28.0	21 36.4	20 28.9	19 02.2
15 Tu	7 33 58	23 07 56	24 45 48	0♍55 41	20 19.6	17 20.6	17 24.4	2 40.3	21 12.0	8 30.6	22 32.9	21 35.7	20 27.6	19 02.8
16 W	7 37 54	24 05 11	7♍02 07	13 05 31	20 20.9	16 49.8	17 43.4	3 14.5	21 35.8	8 41.5	22 37.9	21 34.9	20 26.3	19 03.3
17 Th	7 41 51	25 02 27	19 06 17	25 04 56	20 22.5	16 22.4	18 04.2	3 48.7	21 59.6	8 52.4	22 42.9	21 34.2	20 25.1	19 03.9
18 F	7 45 48	25 59 42	1♎01 59	6♎58 00	20 24.1	15 58.9	18 26.7	4 23.1	22 23.4	9 03.4	22 48.0	21 33.6	20 23.8	19 04.6
19 Sa	7 49 44	26 56 58	12 53 32	18 49 11	20R 25.1	15 39.8	18 50.9	4 57.6	22 47.1	9 14.4	22 53.2	21 33.0	20 22.6	19 05.3
20 Su	7 53 41	27 54 14	24 45 35	0♏43 18	20 25.4	15 25.4	19 16.8	5 32.3	23 10.8	9 25.5	22 58.4	21 32.5	20 21.4	19 06.0
21 M	7 57 37	28 51 30	6♏42 56	12 45 04	20 24.6	15 16.2	19 44.2	6 07.1	23 34.5	9 36.7	23 03.7	21 32.0	20 20.2	19 06.7
22 Tu	8 01 34	29 48 47	18 50 15	24 58 59	20 23.0	15D 12.3	20 13.1	6 42.0	23 58.1	9 48.0	23 09.1	21 31.6	20 19.0	19 07.5
23 W	8 05 30	0♌46 04	1♐11 46	7♐29 00	20 20.7	15 14.1	20 43.4	7 17.0	24 21.6	9 59.3	23 14.5	21 31.2	20 17.9	19 08.3
24 Th	8 09 27	1 43 21	13 51 00	20 18 05	20 18.1	15 21.6	21 15.2	7 52.1	24 45.1	10 10.7	23 20.0	21 30.9	20 16.7	19 09.1
25 F	8 13 23	2 40 39	26 50 23	3♑28 01	20 15.6	15 35.1	21 48.3	8 27.4	25 08.6	10 22.1	23 25.6	21 30.6	20 15.6	19 10.0
26 Sa	8 17 20	3 37 58	10♑10 56	16 59 03	20 13.5	15 54.5	22 22.7	9 02.7	25 32.0	10 33.6	23 31.2	21 30.4	20 14.6	19 10.9
27 Su	8 21 17	4 35 17	23 52 08	0♒49 50	20 12.0	16 20.0	22 58.4	9 38.2	25 55.4	10 45.2	23 36.9	21 30.2	20 13.5	19 11.9
28 M	8 25 13	5 32 36	7♒51 46	14 57 25	20D 11.4	16 51.5	23 35.3	10 13.8	26 18.7	10 56.8	23 42.6	21 30.1	20 12.5	19 12.8
29 Tu	8 29 10	6 29 57	22 06 13	29 17 34	20 11.4	17 29.1	24 13.4	10 49.5	26 42.0	11 08.5	23 48.4	21D 30.0	20 11.5	19 13.8
30 W	8 33 06	7 27 18	6♓30 49	13♓45 18	20 12.1	18 12.6	24 52.6	11 25.4	27 05.2	11 20.2	23 54.3	21 30.0	20 10.5	19 14.9
31 Th	8 37 03	8 24 41	21 00 24	28 15 29	20 13.0	19 02.1	25 32.9	12 01.3	27 28.4	11 32.0	24 00.2	21 30.0	20 09.6	19 15.9

August 1980 — LONGITUDE

Day	Sid.Time	☉	0 hr ☽	Noon ☽	True ☊	☿	♀	♂	⚳	♃	♄	♅	♆	♇
1 F	8 40 59	9♌22 04	5♈29 58	12♈43 18	20♌13.8	19♋57.5	26♊14.2	12♎37.3	27♊51.6	11♍43.9	24♍06.1	21♏30.1	20♐08.6	19♎17.0
2 Sa	8 44 56	10 19 29	19 55 02	27 04 45	20 14.5	20 58.7	26 56.6	13 13.5	28 14.6	11 55.8	24 12.2	21 30.2	20R 07.7	19 18.1
3 Su	8 48 52	11 16 55	4♉12 05	11♉16 45	20R 14.7	22 05.4	27 39.9	13 49.8	28 37.7	12 07.7	24 18.2	21 30.4	20 06.9	19 19.3
4 M	8 52 49	12 14 22	18 18 30	25 17 09	20 14.5	23 17.7	28 24.1	14 26.2	29 00.6	12 19.7	24 24.4	21 30.6	20 06.0	19 20.5
5 Tu	8 56 46	13 11 50	2♊12 33	9♊04 36	20 14.0	24 35.3	29 09.3	15 02.7	29 23.6	12 31.8	24 30.5	21 30.9	20 05.2	19 21.7
6 W	9 00 42	14 09 20	15 53 14	22 38 22	20 13.3	25 58.1	29 55.3	15 39.3	29 46.4	12 43.9	24 36.8	21 31.2	20 04.4	19 22.9
7 Th	9 04 39	15 06 51	29 19 59	5♋58 03	20 12.7	27 25.7	0♋42.2	16 16.0	0♋09.2	12 56.0	24 43.1	21 31.6	20 03.6	19 24.2
8 F	9 08 35	16 04 23	12♋32 36	19 03 36	20 12.1	28 58.0	1 29.8	16 52.9	0 32.0	13 08.2	24 49.4	21 32.1	20 02.9	19 25.5
9 Sa	9 12 32	17 01 57	25 31 07	1♌55 11	20 11.8	0♌34.7	2 18.2	17 29.8	0 54.6	13 20.4	24 55.8	21 32.6	20 02.2	19 26.8
10 Su	9 16 28	17 59 31	8♌15 51	14 33 13	20D 11.7	2 15.4	3 07.4	18 06.8	1 17.2	13 32.7	25 02.2	21 33.1	20 01.5	19 28.2
11 M	9 20 25	18 57 07	20 47 23	26 58 29	20 11.7	3 59.9	3 57.3	18 44.0	1 39.8	13 45.0	25 08.7	21 33.7	20 00.8	19 29.6
12 Tu	9 24 21	19 54 44	3♍06 42	9♍12 12	20R 11.7	5 47.7	4 47.8	19 21.3	2 02.3	13 57.4	25 15.2	21 34.4	20 00.2	19 31.0
13 W	9 28 18	20 52 22	15 15 15	21 16 05	20 11.7	7 38.5	5 39.0	19 58.6	2 24.7	14 09.8	25 21.7	21 35.1	19 59.6	19 32.4
14 Th	9 32 15	21 50 01	27 15 03	3♎12 27	20 11.6	9 31.8	6 30.9	20 36.1	2 47.0	14 22.2	25 28.3	21 35.8	19 59.1	19 33.9
15 F	9 36 11	22 47 41	9♎08 42	15 04 12	20 11.3	11 27.3	7 23.4	21 13.7	3 09.3	14 34.7	25 35.0	21 36.6	19 58.5	19 35.4
16 Sa	9 40 08	23 45 22	20 59 23	26 54 46	20 10.9	13 24.7	8 16.4	21 51.4	3 31.5	14 47.2	25 41.6	21 37.5	19 58.0	19 36.9
17 Su	9 44 04	24 43 04	2♏50 49	8♏48 06	20 10.6	15 23.4	9 10.1	22 29.1	3 53.6	14 59.7	25 48.4	21 38.4	19 57.5	19 38.5
18 M	9 48 01	25 40 48	14 47 08	20 48 30	20D 10.4	17 23.1	10 04.3	23 07.0	4 15.6	15 12.3	25 55.1	21 39.4	19 57.1	19 40.1
19 Tu	9 51 57	26 38 32	26 52 45	3♐00 28	20 10.4	19 23.6	10 59.1	23 45.0	4 37.6	15 24.9	26 01.9	21 40.4	19 56.7	19 41.7
20 W	9 55 54	27 36 18	9♐12 11	15 28 25	20 10.7	21 24.4	11 54.4	24 23.1	4 59.5	15 37.5	26 08.8	21 41.4	19 56.3	19 43.3
21 Th	9 59 50	28 34 04	21 49 40	28 16 21	20 11.4	23 25.3	12 50.2	25 01.3	5 21.3	15 50.2	26 15.6	21 42.6	19 56.0	19 45.0
22 F	10 03 47	29 31 52	4♑48 51	11♑27 26	20 12.2	25 26.0	13 46.4	25 39.5	5 43.0	16 02.9	26 22.5	21 43.7	19 55.6	19 46.7
23 Sa	10 07 44	0♍29 41	18 12 18	25 03 30	20 13.0	27 26.4	14 43.2	26 17.9	6 04.6	16 15.6	26 29.5	21 44.9	19 55.4	19 48.4
24 Su	10 11 40	1 27 32	2♒00 57	9♒04 29	20R 13.6	29 26.2	15 40.5	26 56.3	6 26.2	16 28.3	26 36.4	21 46.2	19 55.1	19 50.1
25 M	10 15 37	2 25 23	16 13 41	23 28 05	20 13.8	1♍25.3	16 38.2	27 34.9	6 47.6	16 41.1	26 43.4	21 47.5	19 54.9	19 51.8
26 Tu	10 19 33	3 23 17	0♓47 01	8♓09 40	20 13.3	3 23.6	17 36.3	28 13.5	7 09.0	16 53.8	26 50.4	21 48.9	19 54.7	19 53.6
27 W	10 23 30	4 21 11	15 35 10	23 02 31	20 12.2	5 20.9	18 34.9	28 52.3	7 30.3	17 06.6	26 57.5	21 50.3	19 54.5	19 55.4
28 Th	10 27 26	5 19 08	0♈30 42	7♈58 40	20 10.5	7 17.2	19 33.9	29 31.1	7 51.5	17 19.5	27 04.6	21 51.7	19 54.4	19 57.2
29 F	10 31 23	6 17 06	15 25 26	22 50 03	20 08.6	9 12.4	20 33.3	0♏10.0	8 12.6	17 32.3	27 11.7	21 53.2	19 54.3	19 59.1
30 Sa	10 35 19	7 15 06	0♉11 40	7♉29 34	20 06.7	11 06.4	21 33.1	0 49.0	8 33.6	17 45.2	27 18.8	21 54.8	19 54.2	20 00.9
31 Su	10 39 16	8 13 07	14 43 10	21 52 01	20 05.4	12 59.3	22 33.3	1 28.1	8 54.5	17 58.0	27 26.0	21 56.4	19D 54.2	20 02.8

Astro Data (Dy Hr Mn)	Planet Ingress (Dy Hr Mn)	Last Aspect (Dy Hr Mn)	☽ Ingress (Dy Hr Mn)	Last Aspect (Dy Hr Mn)	☽ Ingress (Dy Hr Mn)	☽ Phases & Eclipses (Dy Hr Mn)	Astro Data
☽0N 4 23:58	♂ ♎ 10 17:59	1 15:50 ♅ □	♓ 2 5:48	2 11:46 ♀ ⚹	♉ 2 16:55	5 7:27 ☾ 13♈25	1 July 1980
♄⚹♅ 5 4:16	☉ ♌ 22 16:42	4 2:36 ♂ ☍	♈ 4 8:46	4 10:28 ♄ △	♊ 4 20:10	12 6:46 ● 20♋04	Julian Day # 29402
♀ D 6 21:15		5 23:47 ☿ □	♉ 6 11:30	6 15:33 ♄ □	♋ 7 1:12	20 5:51 ☽ 27♎40	SVP 5♓32'06"
♂0S 12 5:07	♀ ♋ 6 14:25	8 12:26 ♂ △	♊ 8 14:33	8 22:47 ♄ ⚹	♌ 9 8:23	27 18:54 ○ 4♒52	GC 26♐34.0 ⚴ 26♈19.0
☽0S 18 16:28	⚳ ♋ 7 2:18	10 4:53 ♄ □	♋ 10 18:44	11 1:29 ♅ □	♍ 11 17:54	27 19:08 • A 0.253	Eris 15♈12.8 ⚵ 23♌05.6
☿ D 22 16:37	☿ ♌ 9 3:31	12 10:52 ♄ ⚹	♌ 13 1:03	13 20:17 ♄ ☌	♎ 14 5:32		⚷ 17♉01.7 ⚶ 6♋53.7
♅ D 30 11:39	☉ ♍ 22 23:41	14 17:54 ♅ □	♍ 15 10:11	16 5:02 ☉ ⚹	♏ 16 18:15	3 12:00 ☾ 11♉17	☽ Mean ☊ 22♌13.8
	☿ ♍ 24 18:47	17 11:55 ☉ ⚹	♎ 17 21:55	18 22:28 ☉ □	♐ 19 6:08	10 19:09 ● 18♌17	
☽0N 1 6:15	♂ ♏ 29 5:50	20 5:51 ☉ □	♏ 20 10:33	21 12:35 ☉ △	♑ 21 15:11	10 19:11:30 • A 03'23"	1 August 1980
☽0S 15 0:16		22 8:25 ♄ ⚹	♐ 22 21:42	23 14:30 ♄ △	♒ 23 20:32	18 22:28 ☽ 26♏06	Julian Day # 29433
♆⚹♇ 27 1:00		24 17:37 ♄ □	♑ 25 5:45	25 19:04 ♂ △	♓ 25 22:43	26 3:42 ○ 3♓03	SVP 5♓32'01"
☽0N 28 14:02		26 23:28 ♄ △	♒ 27 10:34	27 18:21 ♄ ☍	♈ 27 23:11	26 3:30 • A 0.709	GC 26♐34.1 ⚴ 2♉58.8
♆ D 31 23:39		29 3:09 ♀ △	♓ 29 13:11	29 8:02 ♀ □	♉ 29 23:41		Eris 15♈10.9R ⚵ 5♍36.5
		31 7:18 ♀ □	♈ 31 14:53				⚷ 18♉03.7 ⚶ 20♋21.4
							☽ Mean ☊ 20♌35.3

LONGITUDE — September 1980

Day	Sid.Time	☉	0 hr ☽	Noon ☽	True ☊	☿	♀	♂	⚳	♃	♄	♅	♆	♇
1 M	10 43 13	9♍11 11	28♉55 49	5♊54 23	20♌04.7	14♍50.9	23♋33.8	2♏07.3	9♋15.4	18♍10.9	27♍33.2	21♏58.0	19♐54.2	20♎04.7
2 Tu	10 47 09	10 09 17	12♊47 40	19 35 43	20D 04.9	16 41.4	24 34.7	2 46.6	9 36.1	18 23.8	27 40.4	21 59.7	19 54.2	20 06.7
3 W	10 51 06	11 07 25	26 18 40	2♋56 42	20 05.9	18 30.7	25 36.0	3 26.0	9 56.7	18 36.8	27 47.6	22 01.5	19 54.3	20 08.6
4 Th	10 55 02	12 05 35	9♋30 06	15 59 07	20 07.3	20 18.7	26 37.6	4 05.5	10 17.2	18 49.7	27 54.9	22 03.3	19 54.4	20 10.6
5 F	10 58 59	13 03 47	22 24 02	28 45 11	20 08.9	22 05.5	27 39.6	4 45.1	10 37.6	19 02.7	28 02.2	22 05.1	19 54.5	20 12.6
6 Sa	11 02 55	14 02 00	5♌02 52	11♌17 21	20R 09.9	23 51.2	28 41.9	5 24.8	10 57.9	19 15.6	28 09.4	22 07.0	19 54.7	20 14.6
7 Su	11 06 52	15 00 16	17 28 56	23 37 52	20 10.2	25 35.6	29 44.4	6 04.5	11 18.1	19 28.6	28 16.8	22 08.9	19 54.9	20 16.6
8 M	11 10 48	15 58 33	29 44 24	5♍48 47	20 09.2	27 18.9	0♌47.3	6 44.4	11 38.1	19 41.6	28 24.1	22 10.9	19 55.1	20 18.7
9 Tu	11 14 45	16 56 52	11♍51 13	17 51 56	20 06.9	29 01.0	1 50.5	7 24.3	11 58.1	19 54.5	28 31.4	22 12.9	19 55.4	20 20.7
10 W	11 18 41	17 55 13	23 51 08	29 49 03	20 03.2	0♎41.9	2 54.0	8 04.4	12 17.9	20 07.5	28 38.8	22 15.0	19 55.7	20 22.8
11 Th	11 22 38	18 53 36	5♎45 53	11♎41 53	19 58.5	2 21.8	3 57.7	8 44.5	12 37.6	20 20.5	28 46.2	22 17.1	19 56.0	20 24.9
12 F	11 26 35	19 52 00	17 37 17	23 32 24	19 53.2	4 00.5	5 01.7	9 24.7	12 57.1	20 33.5	28 53.5	22 19.2	19 56.4	20 27.0
13 Sa	11 30 31	20 50 27	29 27 30	5♏22 57	19 47.8	5 38.1	6 06.0	10 05.0	13 16.6	20 46.5	29 00.9	22 21.4	19 56.7	20 29.2
14 Su	11 34 28	21 48 55	11♏19 06	17 16 21	19 43.0	7 14.7	7 10.5	10 45.4	13 35.9	20 59.5	29 08.3	22 23.7	19 57.2	20 31.3
15 M	11 38 24	22 47 24	23 15 08	29 15 55	19 39.3	8 50.1	8 15.3	11 25.9	13 55.0	21 12.5	29 15.8	22 26.0	19 57.6	20 33.5
16 Tu	11 42 21	23 45 55	5♐19 12	11♐25 31	19 37.0	10 24.6	9 20.3	12 06.5	14 14.1	21 25.5	29 23.2	22 28.3	19 58.1	20 35.7
17 W	11 46 17	24 44 28	17 35 22	23 49 20	19D 36.2	11 57.9	10 25.6	12 47.1	14 33.0	21 38.5	29 30.6	22 30.6	19 58.7	20 37.9
18 Th	11 50 14	25 43 03	0♑07 57	6♑31 45	19 36.7	13 30.3	11 31.1	13 27.8	14 51.7	21 51.5	29 38.0	22 33.0	19 59.2	20 40.1
19 F	11 54 10	26 41 39	13 01 15	19 36 53	19 38.0	15 01.5	12 36.9	14 08.7	15 10.4	22 04.4	29 45.5	22 35.5	19 59.8	20 42.3
20 Sa	11 58 07	27 40 17	26 19 02	3♒08 00	19 39.5	16 31.8	13 42.8	14 49.6	15 28.8	22 17.4	29 52.9	22 38.0	20 00.4	20 44.5
21 Su	12 02 04	28 38 57	10♒03 58	17 06 56	19R 40.3	18 01.0	14 49.0	15 30.5	15 47.2	22 30.4	0♎00.4	22 40.5	20 01.1	20 46.8
22 M	12 06 00	29 37 38	24 16 47	1♓33 11	19 39.8	19 29.2	15 55.4	16 11.6	16 05.3	22 43.3	0 07.8	22 43.1	20 01.8	20 49.0
23 Tu	12 09 57	0♎36 21	8♓55 35	16 23 15	19 37.5	20 56.3	17 02.1	16 52.7	16 23.3	22 56.3	0 15.3	22 45.7	20 02.5	20 51.3
24 W	12 13 53	1 35 06	23 55 16	1♈30 31	19 33.3	22 22.4	18 08.9	17 34.0	16 41.2	23 09.2	0 22.7	22 48.3	20 03.2	20 53.6
25 Th	12 17 50	2 33 53	9♈07 46	16 45 40	19 27.5	23 47.4	19 16.0	18 15.3	16 58.9	23 22.1	0 30.1	22 51.0	20 04.0	20 55.9
26 F	12 21 46	3 32 41	24 22 52	1♉58 02	19 20.9	25 11.2	20 23.2	18 56.6	17 16.4	23 35.0	0 37.6	22 53.7	20 04.8	20 58.2
27 Sa	12 25 43	4 31 33	9♉29 56	16 57 29	19 14.4	26 34.0	21 30.7	19 38.1	17 33.8	23 47.9	0 45.0	22 56.4	20 05.7	21 00.5
28 Su	12 29 39	5 30 26	24 19 44	1♊35 58	19 09.0	27 55.6	22 38.3	20 19.7	17 51.0	24 00.8	0 52.5	22 59.2	20 06.5	21 02.8
29 M	12 33 36	6 29 22	8♊45 43	15 48 39	19 05.1	29 16.1	23 46.2	21 01.3	18 08.1	24 13.6	0 59.9	23 02.0	20 07.5	21 05.1
30 Tu	12 37 33	7 28 20	22 44 41	29 33 52	19D 03.2	0♏35.2	24 54.2	21 43.0	18 24.9	24 26.5	1 07.3	23 04.9	20 08.4	21 07.5

LONGITUDE — October 1980

Day	Sid.Time	☉	0 hr ☽	Noon ☽	True ☊	☿	♀	♂	⚳	♃	♄	♅	♆	♇
1 W	12 41 29	8♎27 20	6♋16 25	12♋52 39	19♌03.0	1♏53.1	26♌02.4	22♏24.8	18♋41.6	24♍39.3	1♎14.7	23♏07.7	20♐09.4	21♎09.8
2 Th	12 45 26	9 26 23	19 22 59	25 47 53	19 03.9	3 09.7	27 10.8	23 06.7	18 58.1	24 52.1	1 22.1	23 10.7	20 10.4	21 12.1
3 F	12 49 22	10 25 28	2♌07 51	8♌23 25	19R 05.0	4 24.8	28 19.4	23 48.6	19 14.4	25 04.9	1 29.5	23 13.6	20 11.4	21 14.5
4 Sa	12 53 19	11 24 35	14 35 05	20 43 22	19 05.4	5 38.4	29 28.1	24 30.7	19 30.5	25 17.6	1 36.9	23 16.6	20 12.4	21 16.9
5 Su	12 57 15	12 23 45	26 48 46	2♍51 42	19 04.3	6 50.4	0♍37.0	25 12.8	19 46.5	25 30.3	1 44.3	23 19.6	20 13.5	21 19.2
6 M	13 01 12	13 22 56	8♍52 38	14 51 55	19 01.0	8 00.6	1 46.1	25 55.0	20 02.2	25 43.0	1 51.7	23 22.6	20 14.7	21 21.6
7 Tu	13 05 08	14 22 10	20 49 53	26 46 52	18 55.1	9 09.1	2 55.3	26 37.3	20 17.7	25 55.7	1 59.0	23 25.7	20 15.8	21 24.0
8 W	13 09 05	15 21 26	2♎43 06	8♎38 52	18 46.8	10 15.5	4 04.7	27 19.7	20 33.0	26 08.3	2 06.3	23 28.8	20 17.0	21 26.4
9 Th	13 13 01	16 20 44	14 34 20	20 29 44	18 36.5	11 19.7	5 14.2	28 02.1	20 48.1	26 20.9	2 13.6	23 32.0	20 18.2	21 28.8
10 F	13 16 58	17 20 04	26 25 15	2♏21 03	18 24.9	12 21.7	6 23.9	28 44.6	21 03.0	26 33.5	2 20.9	23 35.1	20 19.4	21 31.1
11 Sa	13 20 55	18 19 26	8♏17 20	14 14 19	18 13.1	13 21.0	7 33.7	29 27.2	21 17.7	26 46.0	2 28.2	23 38.3	20 20.7	21 33.5
12 Su	13 24 51	19 18 50	20 12 12	26 11 14	18 02.2	14 17.6	8 43.7	0♐09.9	21 32.1	26 58.5	2 35.5	23 41.5	20 22.0	21 35.9
13 M	13 28 48	20 18 16	2♐11 43	8♐13 56	17 53.0	15 11.1	9 53.8	0 52.6	21 46.3	27 11.0	2 42.7	23 44.8	20 23.3	21 38.3
14 Tu	13 32 44	21 17 44	14 18 17	20 25 07	17 46.1	16 01.3	11 04.0	1 35.5	22 00.3	27 23.4	2 49.9	23 48.0	20 24.6	21 40.7
15 W	13 36 41	22 17 13	26 34 53	2♑48 03	17 41.8	16 47.8	12 14.4	2 18.4	22 14.1	27 35.8	2 57.1	23 51.3	20 26.0	21 43.1
16 Th	13 40 37	23 16 45	9♑05 06	15 26 33	17D 40.0	17 30.2	13 24.9	3 01.3	22 27.6	27 48.2	3 04.3	23 54.6	20 27.4	21 45.5
17 F	13 44 34	24 16 18	21 52 54	28 24 41	17 39.7	18 08.2	14 35.5	3 44.4	22 40.8	28 00.5	3 11.4	23 58.0	20 28.9	21 47.9
18 Sa	13 48 30	25 15 53	5♒02 23	11♒46 24	17R 40.2	18 41.2	15 46.2	4 27.5	22 53.9	28 12.7	3 18.5	24 01.4	20 30.3	21 50.3
19 Su	13 52 27	26 15 29	18 37 06	25 34 43	17 40.0	19 08.9	16 57.1	5 10.7	23 06.6	28 25.0	3 25.6	24 04.7	20 31.8	21 52.7
20 M	13 56 24	27 15 07	2♓39 21	9♓50 57	17 38.2	19 30.6	18 08.1	5 54.0	23 19.1	28 37.1	3 32.6	24 08.1	20 33.3	21 55.1
21 Tu	14 00 20	28 14 47	17 09 14	24 33 43	17 34.0	19 45.9	19 19.2	6 37.3	23 31.4	28 49.3	3 39.6	24 11.6	20 34.8	21 57.5
22 W	14 04 17	29 14 29	2♈03 42	9♈38 12	17 27.1	19R 54.1	20 30.4	7 20.7	23 43.4	29 01.3	3 46.6	24 15.0	20 36.4	21 59.9
23 Th	14 08 13	0♏14 12	17 16 05	24 56 02	17 17.8	19 54.7	21 41.7	8 04.2	23 55.1	29 13.3	3 53.6	24 18.5	20 38.0	22 02.2
24 F	14 12 10	1 13 58	2♉36 35	10♉16 17	17 07.2	19 47.2	22 53.1	8 47.7	24 06.6	29 25.3	4 00.5	24 22.0	20 39.6	22 04.6
25 Sa	14 16 06	2 13 46	17 53 37	25 27 15	16 56.4	19 31.1	24 04.7	9 31.3	24 17.7	29 37.2	4 07.4	24 25.5	20 41.2	22 07.0
26 Su	14 20 03	3 13 35	2♊55 57	10♊18 42	16 46.9	19 06.0	25 16.4	10 15.0	24 28.6	29 49.1	4 14.2	24 29.0	20 42.9	22 09.4
27 M	14 23 59	4 13 27	17 34 44	24 43 28	16 39.5	18 31.7	26 28.1	10 58.7	24 39.3	0♎00.9	4 21.1	24 32.5	20 44.5	22 11.7
28 Tu	14 27 56	5 13 21	1♋44 38	8♋38 08	16 34.6	17 48.2	27 40.0	11 42.6	24 49.6	0 12.6	4 27.8	24 36.1	20 46.2	22 14.1
29 W	14 31 53	6 13 18	15 24 06	22 02 48	16 32.3	16 55.9	28 52.0	12 26.5	24 59.6	0 24.3	4 34.6	24 39.7	20 48.0	22 16.4
30 Th	14 35 49	7 13 16	28 34 38	5♌00 07	16 31.6	15 55.4	0♎04.1	13 10.4	25 09.3	0 36.0	4 41.3	24 43.3	20 49.7	22 18.8
31 F	14 39 46	8 13 17	11♌19 50	17 34 24	16 31.6	14 47.7	1 16.3	13 54.5	25 18.7	0 47.5	4 47.9	24 46.9	20 51.5	22 21.1

Astro Data	Dy Hr Mn
♃□♆	9 13:34
☿0S	10 21:36
☽0S	11 6:51
♃⚺♇	11 21:43
♃⚹♅	22 11:22
☉0S	22 21:09
☽0N	24 23:58
☽0S	8 12:51
☽0N	22 11:16
☿R	23 1:58

Planet Ingress		Dy Hr Mn
♀	♌	7 17:57
☿	♎	10 2:00
♄	♎	21 10:48
☉	♎	22 21:09
☿	♏	30 1:16
♀	♍	4 23:07
♂	♐	12 6:27
☉	♏	23 6:18
♃	♎	27 10:10
♀	♎	30 10:38

Last Aspect Dy Hr Mn			☽ Ingress	Dy Hr Mn
31 21:32	♄	△	♊	1 1:50
3 2:35	♄	□	♋	3 6:39
5 10:38	♄	⚹	♌	5 14:22
7 9:06	♅	□	♍	8 0:31
10 9:37	♄	☌	♎	10 12:22
12 5:43	♇	☌	♏	13 1:06
15 12:00	♄	⚹	♐	15 13:28
17 22:56	♄	□	♑	17 23:45
20 6:15	♄	△	♒	20 6:31
21 21:21	♅	□	♓	22 9:27
23 22:35	♃	☍	♈	24 9:37
26 0:11	☿	☍	♉	26 8:53
27 23:18	♃	△	♊	28 9:21
30 3:02	♀	⚹	♋	30 12:46

Last Aspect Dy Hr Mn			☽ Ingress	Dy Hr Mn
2 10:13	♃	⚹	♌	2 19:57
4 19:55	♂	□	♍	5 6:19
7 11:39	♂	⚹	♎	7 18:30
9 14:00	♇	☌	♏	10 7:15
12 13:36	♃	⚹	♐	12 19:37
15 1:48	♃	□	♑	15 6:37
17 11:15	♃	△	♒	17 14:54
19 13:15	☉	△	♓	19 19:31
21 18:55	♃	☍	♈	21 20:43
23 7:27	♇	☍	♉	23 19:55
25 18:45	♃	△	♊	25 19:17
27 15:14	♀	□	♋	27 21:00
30 1:49	♀	⚹	♌	30 2:38

☽ Phases & Eclipses Dy Hr Mn		
1 18:08	☾	9♊26
9 10:00	●	16♍52
17 13:54	☽	24♐49
24 12:08	○	1♈35
1 3:18	☾	8♋06
9 2:50	●	15♎58
17 3:47	☽	23♑56
23 20:52	○	0♉36
30 16:33	☾	7♌25

Astro Data

1 September 1980
Julian Day # 29464
SVP 5♓31'58"
GC 26♐34.2 ⚴ 5♉37.0R
Eris 14♈59.8R ⚵ 18♍08.9
⚷ 18♉13.8R ⚶ 3♌34.0
☽ Mean ☊ 18♌56.8

1 October 1980
Julian Day # 29494
SVP 5♓31'55"
GC 26♐34.2 ⚴ 2♉05.6R
Eris 14♈43.0R ⚵ 0♎01.5
⚷ 17♉31.8R ⚶ 15♌44.4
☽ Mean ☊ 17♌21.5

November 1980 — LONGITUDE

Day	Sid.Time	☉	0 hr ☽	Noon ☽	True ☊	☿	♀	♂	⚳	♃	♄	♅	♆	♇
1 Sa	14 43 42	9♏13 19	23♌44 27	29♌50 38	16♌31.1	13♏34.5	2♎28.6	14♐38.5	25♋27.8	0♎59.0	4♎54.5	24♏50.5	20♐53.3	22♎23.4
2 Su	14 47 39	10 13 24	5♍53 35	11♍53 54	16R 28.9	12R 17.7	3 41.0	15 22.7	25 36.6	1 10.5	5 01.1	24 54.1	20 55.1	22 25.7
3 M	14 51 35	11 13 31	17 52 09	23 48 53	16 24.2	10 59.3	4 53.4	16 07.0	25 45.0	1 21.9	5 07.6	24 57.7	20 56.9	22 28.0
4 Tu	14 55 32	12 13 40	29 44 35	5♎39 40	16 16.5	9 42.0	6 06.0	16 51.3	25 53.2	1 33.2	5 14.1	25 01.4	20 58.7	22 30.3
5 W	14 59 28	13 13 51	11♎34 32	17 29 31	16 05.8	8 28.1	7 18.6	17 35.6	26 01.0	1 44.4	5 20.5	25 05.1	21 00.6	22 32.6
6 Th	15 03 25	14 14 03	23 24 53	29 20 55	15 52.6	7 20.1	8 31.3	18 20.1	26 08.4	1 55.6	5 26.9	25 08.7	21 02.5	22 34.9
7 F	15 07 22	15 14 18	5♏17 48	11♏15 42	15 38.0	6 19.9	9 44.1	19 04.6	26 15.5	2 06.6	5 33.2	25 12.4	21 04.4	22 37.1
8 Sa	15 11 18	16 14 34	17 14 46	23 15 09	15 23.0	5 29.3	10 57.0	19 49.1	26 22.3	2 17.6	5 39.5	25 16.1	21 06.3	22 39.4
9 Su	15 15 15	17 14 53	29 16 57	5♐20 18	15 08.9	4 49.4	12 10.0	20 33.8	26 28.7	2 28.6	5 45.7	25 19.8	21 08.3	22 41.6
10 M	15 19 11	18 15 12	11♐25 20	17 32 13	14 56.7	4 21.0	13 23.0	21 18.5	26 34.7	2 39.4	5 51.9	25 23.5	21 10.2	22 43.8
11 Tu	15 23 08	19 15 34	23 41 07	29 52 15	14 47.4	4D 04.2	14 36.1	22 03.2	26 40.4	2 50.2	5 58.0	25 27.2	21 12.2	22 46.1
12 W	15 27 04	20 15 57	6♑05 53	12♑22 17	14 41.2	3 59.1	15 49.3	22 48.1	26 45.7	3 00.9	6 04.0	25 30.9	21 14.2	22 48.2
13 Th	15 31 01	21 16 21	18 41 48	25 04 47	14 37.9	4 05.0	17 02.5	23 32.9	26 50.7	3 11.5	6 10.0	25 34.6	21 16.2	22 50.4
14 F	15 34 57	22 16 47	1♒31 38	8♒02 44	14D 36.7	4 21.5	18 15.8	24 17.9	26 55.2	3 22.0	6 16.0	25 38.4	21 18.3	22 52.6
15 Sa	15 38 54	23 17 14	14 38 32	21 19 23	14R 36.7	4 47.6	19 29.2	25 02.9	26 59.4	3 32.5	6 21.9	25 42.1	21 20.3	22 54.7
16 Su	15 42 51	24 17 43	28 05 41	4♓57 43	14 36.4	5 22.6	20 42.6	25 48.0	27 03.3	3 42.8	6 27.7	25 45.8	21 22.4	22 56.9
17 M	15 46 47	25 18 12	11♓55 42	18 59 44	14 34.6	6 05.5	21 56.1	26 33.1	27 06.7	3 53.1	6 33.4	25 49.5	21 24.4	22 59.0
18 Tu	15 50 44	26 18 43	26 09 44	3♈25 30	14 30.5	6 55.4	23 09.6	27 18.2	27 09.7	4 03.2	6 39.1	25 53.2	21 26.5	23 01.1
19 W	15 54 40	27 19 15	10♈46 36	18 12 25	14 23.6	7 51.5	24 23.2	28 03.5	27 12.4	4 13.3	6 44.7	25 57.0	21 28.6	23 03.2
20 Th	15 58 37	28 19 48	25 42 06	3♉14 39	14 14.3	8 53.1	25 36.9	28 48.7	27 14.6	4 23.3	6 50.3	26 00.7	21 30.7	23 05.2
21 F	16 02 33	29 20 23	10♉48 51	18 23 27	14 03.4	9 59.3	26 50.6	29 34.1	27 16.5	4 33.1	6 55.8	26 04.4	21 32.8	23 07.3
22 Sa	16 06 30	0♐20 59	25 57 05	3♊28 25	13 52.2	11 09.6	28 04.4	0♑19.5	27 17.9	4 42.9	7 01.2	26 08.1	21 35.0	23 09.3
23 Su	16 10 26	1 21 37	10♊56 12	18 19 17	13 42.1	12 23.4	29 18.2	1 04.9	27 19.0	4 52.6	7 06.6	26 11.9	21 37.1	23 11.3
24 M	16 14 23	2 22 16	25 36 44	2♋47 46	13 34.0	13 40.2	0♏32.1	1 50.4	27 19.6	5 02.2	7 11.9	26 15.6	21 39.3	23 13.3
25 Tu	16 18 20	3 22 57	9♋51 53	16 48 45	13 28.6	14 59.6	1 46.0	2 36.0	27R 19.8	5 11.7	7 17.1	26 19.3	21 41.5	23 15.2
26 W	16 22 16	4 23 39	23 38 15	0♌20 29	13 25.9	16 21.1	3 00.0	3 21.6	27 19.6	5 21.0	7 22.3	26 23.0	21 43.6	23 17.2
27 Th	16 26 13	5 24 23	6♌55 41	13 24 13	13D 25.1	17 44.4	4 14.0	4 07.2	27 19.0	5 30.3	7 27.4	26 26.7	21 45.8	23 19.1
28 F	16 30 09	6 25 08	19 46 35	26 03 20	13R 25.5	19 09.3	5 28.1	4 53.0	27 18.0	5 39.4	7 32.4	26 30.4	21 48.0	23 21.0
29 Sa	16 34 06	7 25 55	2♍15 05	8♍22 29	13 25.8	20 35.5	6 42.3	5 38.7	27 16.5	5 48.5	7 37.3	26 34.1	21 50.2	23 22.9
30 Su	16 38 02	8 26 43	14 26 12	20 26 55	13 25.0	22 02.9	7 56.4	6 24.5	27 14.7	5 57.4	7 42.1	26 37.7	21 52.4	23 24.7

December 1980 — LONGITUDE

Day	Sid.Time	☉	0 hr ☽	Noon ☽	True ☊	☿	♀	♂	⚳	♃	♄	♅	♆	♇
1 M	16 41 59	9♐27 32	26♍25 16	2♎21 54	13♌22.2	23♏31.1	9♏10.7	7♑10.4	27♋12.4	6♎06.2	7♎46.9	26♏41.4	21♐54.6	23♎26.6
2 Tu	16 45 55	10 28 23	8♎17 25	14 12 22	13R 16.8	25 00.1	10 24.9	7 56.3	27R 09.6	6 14.9	7 51.6	26 45.0	21 56.9	23 28.4
3 W	16 49 52	11 29 16	20 07 17	26 02 37	13 08.9	26 29.8	11 39.2	8 42.3	27 06.5	6 23.5	7 56.2	26 48.7	21 59.1	23 30.1
4 Th	16 53 49	12 30 10	1♏58 47	7♏56 10	12 58.8	28 00.0	12 53.6	9 28.3	27 02.9	6 32.0	8 00.8	26 52.3	22 01.3	23 31.9
5 F	16 57 45	13 31 05	13 55 05	19 55 45	12 47.3	29 30.6	14 08.0	10 14.4	26 58.9	6 40.3	8 05.2	26 55.9	22 03.6	23 33.6
6 Sa	17 01 42	14 32 01	25 58 24	2♐03 12	12 35.3	1♐01.7	15 22.4	11 00.5	26 54.4	6 48.5	8 09.6	26 59.5	22 05.8	23 35.3
7 Su	17 05 38	15 32 58	8♐10 15	14 19 40	12 24.1	2 33.1	16 36.8	11 46.7	26 49.6	6 56.6	8 13.9	27 03.1	22 08.1	23 37.0
8 M	17 09 35	16 33 56	20 31 30	26 45 47	12 14.5	4 04.7	17 51.3	12 32.9	26 44.3	7 04.6	8 18.1	27 06.7	22 10.4	23 38.7
9 Tu	17 13 31	17 34 55	3♑02 34	9♑21 55	12 07.2	5 36.6	19 05.8	13 19.2	26 38.6	7 12.4	8 22.2	27 10.3	22 12.6	23 40.3
10 W	17 17 28	18 35 55	15 43 52	22 08 29	12 02.7	7 08.7	20 20.4	14 05.5	26 32.5	7 20.1	8 26.2	27 13.8	22 14.9	23 41.9
11 Th	17 21 24	19 36 56	28 35 52	5♒06 09	12D 00.6	8 40.9	21 35.0	14 51.9	26 26.0	7 27.6	8 30.2	27 17.4	22 17.1	23 43.5
12 F	17 25 21	20 37 57	11♒39 28	18 16 00	12 00.5	10 13.3	22 49.6	15 38.2	26 19.1	7 35.1	8 34.0	27 20.9	22 19.4	23 45.0
13 Sa	17 29 18	21 38 59	24 55 55	1♓39 24	12 01.5	11 45.9	24 04.2	16 24.7	26 11.7	7 42.4	8 37.8	27 24.4	22 21.7	23 46.5
14 Su	17 33 14	22 40 01	8♓26 40	15 17 51	12R 02.6	13 18.6	25 18.8	17 11.1	26 04.0	7 49.5	8 41.4	27 27.8	22 23.9	23 48.0
15 M	17 37 11	23 41 03	22 13 05	29 12 26	12 02.6	14 51.4	26 33.5	17 57.7	25 55.9	7 56.5	8 45.0	27 31.3	22 26.2	23 49.5
16 Tu	17 41 07	24 42 06	6♈15 53	13♈23 18	12 01.0	16 24.4	27 48.2	18 44.2	25 47.4	8 03.4	8 48.5	27 34.7	22 28.5	23 50.9
17 W	17 45 04	25 43 09	20 34 27	27 48 58	11 57.3	17 57.5	29 02.9	19 30.8	25 38.6	8 10.1	8 51.9	27 38.1	22 30.7	23 52.3
18 Th	17 49 00	26 44 13	5♉06 20	12♉25 56	11 51.8	19 30.8	0♐17.6	20 17.4	25 29.4	8 16.7	8 55.2	27 41.5	22 33.0	23 53.6
19 F	17 52 57	27 45 17	19 47 00	27 08 41	11 44.9	21 04.2	1 32.3	21 04.0	25 19.8	8 23.1	8 58.4	27 44.9	22 35.3	23 55.0
20 Sa	17 56 53	28 46 21	4♊30 01	11♊50 04	11 37.8	22 37.8	2 47.1	21 50.7	25 09.9	8 29.4	9 01.5	27 48.2	22 37.5	23 56.3
21 Su	18 00 50	29 47 26	19 07 50	26 22 26	11 31.2	24 11.5	4 01.9	22 37.5	24 59.6	8 35.5	9 04.5	27 51.5	22 39.8	23 57.6
22 M	18 04 47	0♑48 32	3♋33 00	10♋38 49	11 26.1	25 45.5	5 16.7	23 24.2	24 49.0	8 41.5	9 07.4	27 54.8	22 42.0	23 58.8
23 Tu	18 08 43	1 49 38	17 39 18	24 34 00	11 22.8	27 19.6	6 31.6	24 11.0	24 38.1	8 47.3	9 10.3	27 58.1	22 44.3	24 00.0
24 W	18 12 40	2 50 44	1♌22 38	8♌05 05	11D 21.5	28 53.9	7 46.4	24 57.8	24 26.9	8 53.0	9 13.0	28 01.3	22 46.5	24 01.2
25 Th	18 16 36	3 51 51	14 41 21	21 11 35	11 21.9	0♑28.5	9 01.3	25 44.7	24 15.4	8 58.5	9 15.6	28 04.5	22 48.8	24 02.3
26 F	18 20 33	4 52 58	27 36 04	3♍55 10	11 23.3	2 03.3	10 16.2	26 31.6	24 03.6	9 03.9	9 18.1	28 07.7	22 51.0	24 03.5
27 Sa	18 24 29	5 54 06	10♍09 18	16 19 01	11 25.0	3 38.4	11 31.1	27 18.5	23 51.5	9 09.1	9 20.5	28 10.9	22 53.2	24 04.5
28 Su	18 28 26	6 55 14	22 24 52	28 27 27	11R 26.4	5 13.7	12 46.0	28 05.4	23 39.2	9 14.1	9 22.8	28 14.0	22 55.4	24 05.6
29 M	18 32 23	7 56 23	4♎27 24	10♎25 19	11 26.8	6 49.3	14 00.9	28 52.4	23 26.6	9 19.0	9 25.1	28 17.1	22 57.7	24 06.6
30 Tu	18 36 19	8 57 32	16 21 52	22 17 38	11 25.7	8 25.3	15 15.9	29 39.4	23 13.8	9 23.7	9 27.2	28 20.1	22 59.9	24 07.6
31 W	18 40 16	9 58 42	28 13 15	4♏09 17	11 23.2	10 01.5	16 30.9	0♒26.5	23 00.7	9 28.2	9 29.2	28 23.2	23 02.1	24 08.5

Astro Data

	Dy Hr Mn
♄0S	1 12:52
♀0S	2 11:46
☽0S	4 19:22
♃0S	10 4:08
☿ D	12 10:56
☽0N	18 22:03
⚳ R	25 13:02
☽0S	2 3:06
☽0N	16 6:33
☽0S	29 11:54
♃☌♄	31 21:23

Planet Ingress

		Dy Hr Mn
♂	♑	22 1:42
☉	♐	22 3:41
♀	♏	24 1:35
☿	♐	5 19:45
♀	♐	18 6:21
☉	♑	21 16:56
☿	♑	25 4:46
♂	♒	30 22:30

Last Aspect / ☽ Ingress (November)

Last Aspect Dy Hr Mn			☽ Ingress	Dy Hr Mn
1 2:06	♅	□	♍	1 12:19
3 14:20	♅	⚹	♎	4 0:31
5 22:16	♇	☌	♏	6 13:19
8 16:02	♅	☌	♐	9 1:25
10 22:10	♇	⚹	♑	11 12:15
13 12:56	♅	⚹	♒	13 21:10
15 19:49	♅	□	♓	16 3:21
18 1:20	♂	□	♈	18 6:22
20 4:35	♂	△	♉	20 6:51
22 0:15	♅	☍	♊	22 6:27
23 20:01	♇	△	♋	24 7:18
26 4:51	♅	△	♌	26 11:23
28 12:52	♅	□	♍	28 19:37

Last Aspect / ☽ Ingress (December)

Last Aspect Dy Hr Mn			☽ Ingress	Dy Hr Mn
1 0:29	♅	⚹	♎	1 7:13
3 6:50	♇	☌	♏	3 20:00
6 1:58	♅	☌	♐	6 7:57
8 6:00	♇	⚹	♑	8 18:12
10 21:31	♅	⚹	♒	11 2:36
13 4:24	♅	□	♓	13 9:03
15 9:06	♅	△	♈	15 13:21
17 8:16	☉	△	♉	17 15:36
19 12:59	♅	☍	♊	19 16:39
21 7:59	♇	△	♋	21 18:03
23 18:00	♅	△	♌	23 21:34
26 0:57	♅	□	♍	26 4:32
28 11:33	♅	⚹	♎	28 15:05
30 15:43	♇	☌	♏	31 3:36

☽ Phases & Eclipses

Dy Hr Mn		
7 20:43	●	15♏36
15 15:47	☽	23♒27
22 6:39	○	0♊07
29 9:59	☾	7♍21
7 14:35	●	15♐40
15 1:47	☽	23♓15
21 18:08	○	0♋03
29 6:32	☾	7♎42

Astro Data

1 November 1980
Julian Day # 29525
SVP 5♓31'52"
GC 26♐34.3 ⚴ 23♈02.6R
Eris 14♈24.6R ⚵ 11♎41.8
⚷ 16♉09.4R ⚶ 27♌02.9
☽ Mean ☊ 15♌43.0

1 December 1980
Julian Day # 29555
SVP 5♓31'48"
GC 26♐34.4 ⚴ 16♈40.3R
Eris 14♈11.0R ⚵ 21♎56.8
⚷ 14♉41.3R ⚶ 5♍40.1
☽ Mean ☊ 14♌07.7

LONGITUDE

January 1981

Day	Sid.Time	☉	0 hr ☽	Noon ☽	True ☊	☿	♀	♂	⚳	♃	♄	♅	♆	♇
1 Th	18 44 12	10♑59 51	10♏06 16	16♏04 43	11♌19.3	11♑38.1	17♐45.9	1♒13.5	22♋47.5	9♎32.6	9♎31.1	28♏26.2	23♐04.2	24♎09.4
2 F	18 48 09	12 01 02	22 05 05	28 07 47	11R 14.4	13 15.0	19 00.9	2 00.6	22R 34.1	9 36.8	9 32.9	28 29.1	23 06.4	24 10.3
3 Sa	18 52 05	13 02 12	4♐13 10	10♐21 32	11 09.3	14 52.3	20 15.9	2 47.7	22 20.5	9 40.8	9 34.6	28 32.1	23 08.6	24 11.2
4 Su	18 56 02	14 03 23	16 33 07	22 48 06	11 04.3	16 30.0	21 30.9	3 34.9	22 06.8	9 44.6	9 36.2	28 35.0	23 10.7	24 12.0
5 M	18 59 58	15 04 34	29 06 37	5♑28 42	11 00.1	18 08.0	22 45.9	4 22.1	21 52.9	9 48.3	9 37.6	28 37.8	23 12.9	24 12.7
6 Tu	19 03 55	16 05 44	11♑54 24	18 23 38	10 57.2	19 46.3	24 01.0	5 09.3	21 38.9	9 51.8	9 39.0	28 40.7	23 15.0	24 13.5
7 W	19 07 52	17 06 55	24 56 22	1♒32 28	10D 55.6	21 25.1	25 16.0	5 56.5	21 24.9	9 55.1	9 40.3	28 43.5	23 17.1	24 14.2
8 Th	19 11 48	18 08 05	8♒11 49	14 54 16	10 55.3	23 04.2	26 31.1	6 43.7	21 10.7	9 58.3	9 41.4	28 46.2	23 19.3	24 14.9
9 F	19 15 45	19 09 15	21 39 39	28 27 48	10 56.1	24 43.7	27 46.1	7 31.0	20 56.5	10 01.2	9 42.5	28 48.9	23 21.4	24 15.5
10 Sa	19 19 41	20 10 24	5♓18 35	12♓11 49	10 57.5	26 23.5	29 01.2	8 18.3	20 42.3	10 04.0	9 43.4	28 51.6	23 23.4	24 16.1
11 Su	19 23 38	21 11 33	19 07 21	26 05 02	10 59.0	28 03.6	0♑16.2	9 05.6	20 28.0	10 06.6	9 44.3	28 54.3	23 25.5	24 16.6
12 M	19 27 34	22 12 41	3♈04 44	10♈06 16	11R 00.1	29 44.1	1 31.3	9 52.9	20 13.7	10 09.0	9 45.0	28 56.9	23 27.6	24 17.2
13 Tu	19 31 31	23 13 49	17 09 28	24 14 07	11 00.4	1♒24.8	2 46.4	10 40.2	19 59.5	10 11.2	9 45.6	28 59.4	23 29.6	24 17.7
14 W	19 35 27	24 14 56	1♉20 00	8♉26 50	10 59.9	3 05.8	4 01.4	11 27.5	19 45.3	10 13.3	9 46.1	29 01.9	23 31.6	24 18.1
15 Th	19 39 24	25 16 02	15 34 20	22 42 07	10 58.6	4 46.9	5 16.5	12 14.9	19 31.1	10 15.1	9 46.5	29 04.4	23 33.6	24 18.5
16 F	19 43 21	26 17 07	29 49 48	6♊56 56	10 56.9	6 28.0	6 31.6	13 02.3	19 17.1	10 16.8	9 46.8	29 06.9	23 35.6	24 18.9
17 Sa	19 47 17	27 18 12	14♊03 04	21 07 41	10 55.0	8 09.2	7 46.7	13 49.6	19 03.1	10 18.3	9 47.0	29 09.2	23 37.6	24 19.3
18 Su	19 51 14	28 19 16	28 10 18	5♋10 25	10 53.3	9 50.3	9 01.7	14 37.0	18 49.2	10 19.6	9R 47.0	29 11.6	23 39.5	24 19.6
19 M	19 55 10	29 20 19	12♋07 33	19 01 15	10 52.0	11 31.1	10 16.8	15 24.4	18 35.5	10 20.7	9 47.0	29 13.9	23 41.5	24 19.8
20 Tu	19 59 07	0♒21 22	25 51 09	2♌36 55	10D 51.3	13 11.5	11 31.9	16 11.8	18 21.9	10 21.6	9 46.9	29 16.2	23 43.4	24 20.1
21 W	20 03 03	1 22 24	9♌18 17	15 55 05	10 51.3	14 51.3	12 47.0	16 59.2	18 08.4	10 22.3	9 46.6	29 18.4	23 45.3	24 20.3
22 Th	20 07 00	2 23 25	22 27 14	28 54 42	10 51.7	16 30.3	14 02.1	17 46.7	17 55.2	10 22.8	9 46.3	29 20.6	23 47.2	24 20.4
23 F	20 10 56	3 24 26	5♍17 35	11♍36 03	10 52.4	18 08.2	15 17.2	18 34.1	17 42.1	10 23.2	9 45.8	29 22.7	23 49.0	24 20.6
24 Sa	20 14 53	4 25 26	17 50 19	24 00 42	10 53.1	19 44.7	16 32.3	19 21.5	17 29.3	10R 23.3	9 45.2	29 24.8	23 50.9	24 20.7
25 Su	20 18 50	5 26 25	0♎07 34	6♎11 21	10 53.8	21 19.5	17 47.4	20 09.0	17 16.6	10 23.3	9 44.6	29 26.8	23 52.7	24 20.7
26 M	20 22 46	6 27 24	12 12 31	18 11 36	10 54.3	22 52.1	19 02.5	20 56.4	17 04.2	10 23.1	9 43.8	29 28.8	23 54.5	24R 20.7
27 Tu	20 26 43	7 28 22	24 09 07	0♏05 39	10R 54.5	24 22.0	20 17.6	21 43.9	16 52.1	10 22.7	9 42.9	29 30.8	23 56.3	24 20.7
28 W	20 30 39	8 29 20	6♏01 47	11 58 07	10 54.5	25 48.7	21 32.7	22 31.3	16 40.2	10 22.0	9 41.9	29 32.7	23 58.0	24 20.7
29 Th	20 34 36	9 30 16	17 55 15	23 53 45	10 54.5	27 11.7	22 47.8	23 18.8	16 28.6	10 21.2	9 40.8	29 34.5	23 59.8	24 20.6
30 F	20 38 32	10 31 13	29 54 13	5♐57 11	10D 54.4	28 30.3	24 02.9	24 06.3	16 17.3	10 20.2	9 39.6	29 36.3	24 01.5	24 20.5
31 Sa	20 42 29	11 32 08	12♐03 11	18 12 40	10 54.4	29 43.7	25 18.0	24 53.8	16 06.3	10 19.1	9 38.3	29 38.1	24 03.2	24 20.3

LONGITUDE

February 1981

Day	Sid.Time	☉	0 hr ☽	Noon ☽	True ☊	☿	♀	♂	⚳	♃	♄	♅	♆	♇
1 Su	20 46 25	12♒33 03	24♐26 06	0♑43 49	10♌54.6	0♓51.3	26♑33.1	25♒41.2	15♋55.6	10♎17.7	9♎36.8	29♏39.8	24♐04.8	24♎20.1
2 M	20 50 22	13 33 57	7♑06 07	13 33 15	10 54.8	1 52.2	27 48.2	26 28.7	15R 45.3	10R 16.1	9R 35.3	29 41.5	24 06.5	24R 19.9
3 Tu	20 54 19	14 34 50	20 05 19	26 42 23	10 55.0	2 45.6	29 03.3	27 16.2	15 35.3	10 14.4	9 33.7	29 43.1	24 08.1	24 19.6
4 W	20 58 15	15 35 42	3♒24 25	10♒11 14	10R 55.2	3 30.8	0♒18.4	28 03.7	15 25.6	10 12.4	9 32.0	29 44.6	24 09.7	24 19.3
5 Th	21 02 12	16 36 32	17 02 37	23 58 14	10 55.0	4 07.0	1 33.5	28 51.2	15 16.4	10 10.3	9 30.2	29 46.1	24 11.2	24 19.0
6 F	21 06 08	17 37 22	0♓57 40	8♓00 27	10 54.6	4 33.5	2 48.6	29 38.6	15 07.5	10 08.0	9 28.2	29 47.6	24 12.8	24 18.6
7 Sa	21 10 05	18 38 10	15 06 02	22 13 52	10 53.8	4 49.8	4 03.7	0♓26.1	14 58.9	10 05.4	9 26.2	29 49.0	24 14.3	24 18.2
8 Su	21 14 01	19 38 57	29 23 21	6♈33 54	10 52.7	4R 55.4	5 18.7	1 13.6	14 50.8	10 02.7	9 24.1	29 50.3	24 15.8	24 17.8
9 M	21 17 58	20 39 42	13♈44 55	20 55 53	10 51.6	4 50.2	6 33.8	2 01.0	14 43.1	9 59.9	9 21.9	29 51.6	24 17.2	24 17.3
10 Tu	21 21 54	21 40 25	28 06 16	5♉15 39	10 50.8	4 34.2	7 48.9	2 48.4	14 35.7	9 56.8	9 19.6	29 52.9	24 18.7	24 16.8
11 W	21 25 51	22 41 07	12♉23 38	19 29 51	10D 50.4	4 07.7	9 03.9	3 35.9	14 28.8	9 53.6	9 17.1	29 54.1	24 20.1	24 16.2
12 Th	21 29 48	23 41 47	26 34 04	3♊36 02	10 50.5	3 31.3	10 19.0	4 23.3	14 22.3	9 50.2	9 14.7	29 55.2	24 21.5	24 15.7
13 F	21 33 44	24 42 26	10♊35 34	17 32 33	10 51.3	2 45.9	11 34.0	5 10.7	14 16.2	9 46.6	9 12.1	29 56.3	24 22.8	24 15.1
14 Sa	21 37 41	25 43 03	24 26 49	1♋18 19	10 52.4	1 52.8	12 49.0	5 58.1	14 10.6	9 42.8	9 09.4	29 57.3	24 24.1	24 14.4
15 Su	21 41 37	26 43 38	8♋06 58	14 52 41	10 53.7	0 53.3	14 04.0	6 45.5	14 05.3	9 38.9	9 06.6	29 58.3	24 25.4	24 13.8
16 M	21 45 34	27 44 12	21 35 23	28 15 03	10R 54.7	29♒49.2	15 19.1	7 32.9	14 00.5	9 34.8	9 03.8	29 59.2	24 26.7	24 13.1
17 Tu	21 49 30	28 44 44	4♌51 36	11♌24 58	10 55.1	28 42.1	16 34.1	8 20.2	13 56.1	9 30.5	9 00.8	0♐00.1	24 27.9	24 12.3
18 W	21 53 27	29 45 14	17 55 07	24 22 01	10 54.6	27 33.9	17 49.1	9 07.6	13 52.2	9 26.1	8 57.8	0 00.9	24 29.2	24 11.6
19 Th	21 57 23	0♓45 42	0♍45 40	7♍06 02	10 53.0	26 26.4	19 04.0	9 54.9	13 48.7	9 21.5	8 54.7	0 01.7	24 30.3	24 10.8
20 F	22 01 20	1 46 09	13 23 12	19 37 12	10 50.3	25 21.2	20 19.0	10 42.2	13 45.6	9 16.7	8 51.5	0 02.4	24 31.5	24 09.9
21 Sa	22 05 17	2 46 35	25 48 09	1♎56 13	10 46.9	24 19.7	21 34.0	11 29.5	13 42.9	9 11.8	8 48.3	0 03.1	24 32.6	24 09.1
22 Su	22 09 13	3 46 59	8♎01 36	14 04 31	10 43.0	23 23.0	22 49.0	12 16.8	13 40.7	9 06.8	8 44.9	0 03.7	24 33.7	24 08.2
23 M	22 13 10	4 47 21	20 05 18	26 04 17	10 39.1	22 32.2	24 03.9	13 04.0	13 38.9	9 01.5	8 41.5	0 04.2	24 34.7	24 07.3
24 Tu	22 17 06	5 47 42	2♏01 50	7♏58 25	10 35.7	21 47.9	25 18.9	13 51.3	13 37.5	8 56.2	8 38.0	0 04.7	24 35.8	24 06.3
25 W	22 21 03	6 48 02	13 54 30	19 50 35	10 33.2	21 10.5	26 33.8	14 38.5	13 36.6	8 50.7	8 34.5	0 05.1	24 36.8	24 05.4
26 Th	22 24 59	7 48 20	25 47 14	1♐45 00	10D 31.9	20 40.3	27 48.8	15 25.7	13D 36.1	8 45.0	8 30.8	0 05.5	24 37.7	24 04.4
27 F	22 28 56	8 48 37	7♐44 30	13 46 19	10 31.8	20 17.4	29 03.7	16 12.9	13 36.0	8 39.2	8 27.1	0 05.9	24 38.7	24 03.3
28 Sa	22 32 52	9 48 53	19 51 04	25 59 21	10 32.8	20 01.7	0♓18.7	17 00.1	13 36.4	8 33.3	8 23.4	0 06.1	24 39.6	24 02.3

Astro Data Dy Hr Mn	Planet Ingress Dy Hr Mn	Last Aspect Dy Hr Mn	☽ Ingress Dy Hr Mn	Last Aspect Dy Hr Mn	☽ Ingress Dy Hr Mn	☽ Phases & Eclipses Dy Hr Mn	Astro Data
☽0N 12 12:46	♀ ♑ 11 6:48	2 12:42 ♅ ☌	♐ 2 15:42	1 1:45 ♂ ⚹	♑ 1 10:37	6 7:24 ● 15♑54	1 January 1981
♄R 18 16:58	☿ ♒ 12 15:48	4 14:40 ♇ ⚹	♑ 5 1:41	3 17:25 ♅ ⚹	♒ 3 17:55	13 10:10 ☽ 23♈09	Julian Day # 29586
♃R 24 19:23	☉ ♒ 20 3:36	7 6:52 ♅ ⚹	♒ 7 9:12	5 21:59 ♅ □	♓ 5 22:21	20 7:39 ○ 0♌10	SVP 5♓31'43"
☽0S 25 20:50	☿ ♓ 31 17:35	9 12:37 ♅ □	♓ 9 14:42	8 0:44 ♅ △	♈ 8 1:01	20 7:50 • A 1.014	GC 26♐34.4 ⚴ 18♈09.3
♇R 26 12:51		11 16:52 ♅ △	♈ 11 18:43	9 17:37 ♆ △	♉ 10 3:11	28 4:19 ☾ 8♏10	Eris 14♈05.6 ⚵ 0♏42.5
	♀ ♒ 4 6:07	13 12:06 ♇ ☍	♉ 13 21:45	12 5:42 ♅ ☍	♊ 12 5:51		⚷ 13♉37.8R ⚶ 10♍13.7
☿R 8 12:31	♂ ♓ 6 22:48	15 22:45 ♅ ☍	♊ 16 0:17	14 1:26 ☉ △	♋ 14 9:43		☽ Mean ☊ 12♌29.2
☽0N 8 18:44	☿ ♒R 16 8:02	17 17:26 ♇ △	♋ 18 3:08	16 15:09 ♅ △	♌ 16 15:10	4 22:14 ● 16♒02	
♆⚹♇ 9 12:39	♅ ♐ 17 9:02	20 6:02 ♅ △	♌ 20 7:21	18 17:30 ☿ ☍	♍ 18 22:34	4 22:08:31 • A 00'33"	1 February 1981
☽0S 22 4:56	☉ ♓ 18 17:52	22 12:49 ♅ □	♍ 22 14:02	20 21:32 ♆ □	♎ 21 8:12	11 17:49 ☽ 22♉56	Julian Day # 29617
⚳D 27 3:44	♀ ♓ 28 6:01	24 22:38 ♅ ⚹	♎ 24 23:45	23 9:00 ♅ ⚹	♏ 23 19:54	18 22:58 ○ 0♍13	SVP 5♓31'38"
		27 0:23 ♇ ☌	♏ 27 11:49	26 3:09 ♀ □	♐ 26 8:29	27 1:14 ☾ 8♐22	GC 26♐34.5 ⚴ 26♈38.3
		29 23:23 ♅ ☌	♐ 30 0:12	28 9:24 ♆ ☌	♑ 28 19:46		Eris 14♈10.9 ⚵ 6♏26.1
							⚷ 13♉27.1 ⚶ 8♍02.5R
							☽ Mean ☊ 10♌50.7

March 1981 — LONGITUDE

Day	Sid.Time	☉	0 hr ☽	Noon ☽	True ☊	☿	♀	♂	⚳	♃	♄	♅	♆	♇
1 Su	22 36 49	10♓49 06	2♑11 45	8♑28 48	10♌34.4	19♒53.0	1♓33.6	17♓47.2	13♋37.2	8♎27.3	8♎19.5	0♐06.4	24♐40.4	24♎01.2
2 M	22 40 45	11 49 19	14 51 00	21 18 48	10 36.1	19D 51.0	2 48.5	18 34.4	13 38.4	8R 21.1	8R 15.6	0 06.5	24 41.3	24R 00.1
3 Tu	22 44 42	12 49 30	27 52 34	4♒32 32	10R 37.2	19 55.5	4 03.4	19 21.5	13 40.0	8 14.8	8 11.7	0 06.6	24 42.1	23 58.9
4 W	22 48 39	13 49 39	11♒18 50	18 11 30	10 37.1	20 06.1	5 18.3	20 08.6	13 42.1	8 08.4	8 07.7	0R 06.7	24 42.9	23 57.8
5 Th	22 52 35	14 49 46	25 10 21	2♓15 05	10 35.4	20 22.5	6 33.2	20 55.6	13 44.6	8 01.9	8 03.6	0 06.7	24 43.6	23 56.6
6 F	22 56 32	15 49 52	9♓25 14	16 40 09	10 32.0	20 44.4	7 48.1	21 42.7	13 47.5	7 55.2	7 59.5	0 06.7	24 44.3	23 55.4
7 Sa	23 00 28	16 49 55	23 59 05	1♈21 08	10 27.1	21 11.3	9 02.9	22 29.7	13 50.8	7 48.5	7 55.3	0 06.6	24 45.0	23 54.1
8 Su	23 04 25	17 49 57	8♈45 17	16 10 32	10 21.4	21 42.9	10 17.8	23 16.7	13 54.5	7 41.6	7 51.1	0 06.4	24 45.6	23 52.9
9 M	23 08 21	18 49 57	23 35 49	1♉00 07	10 15.6	22 19.0	11 32.6	24 03.6	13 58.6	7 34.7	7 46.8	0 06.2	24 46.2	23 51.6
10 Tu	23 12 18	19 49 54	8♉22 32	15 42 12	10 10.6	22 59.1	12 47.4	24 50.6	14 03.1	7 27.6	7 42.5	0 05.9	24 46.8	23 50.3
11 W	23 16 14	20 49 50	22 58 27	0♊10 44	10 07.1	23 43.2	14 02.2	25 37.5	14 08.0	7 20.5	7 38.1	0 05.6	24 47.4	23 49.0
12 Th	23 20 11	21 49 43	7♊18 38	14 21 55	10D 05.3	24 30.8	15 17.0	26 24.3	14 13.3	7 13.3	7 33.7	0 05.2	24 47.9	23 47.6
13 F	23 24 08	22 49 34	21 20 25	28 14 10	10 05.2	25 21.8	16 31.8	27 11.2	14 19.0	7 06.1	7 29.3	0 04.8	24 48.3	23 46.3
14 Sa	23 28 04	23 49 23	5♋03 13	11♋47 45	10 06.2	26 16.0	17 46.6	27 58.0	14 25.1	6 58.7	7 24.8	0 04.3	24 48.8	23 44.9
15 Su	23 32 01	24 49 09	18 27 57	25 04 05	10 07.6	27 13.1	19 01.3	28 44.7	14 31.5	6 51.4	7 20.3	0 03.8	24 49.2	23 43.5
16 M	23 35 57	25 48 53	1♌36 23	8♌05 07	10R 08.4	28 13.0	20 16.0	29 31.5	14 38.4	6 43.9	7 15.8	0 03.2	24 49.6	23 42.0
17 Tu	23 39 54	26 48 35	14 30 33	20 52 55	10 07.8	29 15.5	21 30.8	0♈18.2	14 45.5	6 36.4	7 11.2	0 02.6	24 49.9	23 40.6
18 W	23 43 50	27 48 15	27 12 24	3♍29 14	10 05.2	0♓20.4	22 45.4	1 04.8	14 53.1	6 28.8	7 06.6	0 01.9	24 50.2	23 39.1
19 Th	23 47 47	28 47 53	9♍43 33	15 55 30	10 00.2	1 27.7	24 00.1	1 51.5	15 01.0	6 21.2	7 02.0	0 01.2	24 50.5	23 37.7
20 F	23 51 43	29 47 28	22 05 14	28 12 50	9 53.0	2 37.3	25 14.8	2 38.1	15 09.2	6 13.6	6 57.4	0 00.4	24 50.7	23 36.2
21 Sa	23 55 40	0♈47 02	4♎18 27	10♎22 12	9 43.9	3 48.9	26 29.5	3 24.6	15 17.8	6 05.9	6 52.8	29♏59.6	24 50.9	23 34.7
22 Su	23 59 37	1 46 33	16 24 11	22 24 35	9 33.8	5 02.6	27 44.1	4 11.1	15 26.8	5 58.2	6 48.1	29 58.7	24 51.1	23 33.1
23 M	0 03 33	2 46 03	28 23 33	4♏21 19	9 23.5	6 18.2	28 58.7	4 57.6	15 36.1	5 50.5	6 43.5	29 57.7	24 51.2	23 31.6
24 Tu	0 07 30	3 45 31	10♏18 08	16 14 15	9 14.0	7 35.6	0♈13.3	5 44.1	15 45.7	5 42.8	6 38.8	29 56.8	24 51.4	23 30.0
25 W	0 11 26	4 44 57	22 10 03	28 05 53	9 06.1	8 54.9	1 27.9	6 30.5	15 55.6	5 35.0	6 34.1	29 55.7	24 51.4	23 28.5
26 Th	0 15 23	5 44 21	4♐02 12	9♐59 27	9 00.3	10 15.9	2 42.5	7 16.9	16 05.9	5 27.3	6 29.4	29 54.7	24R 51.5	23 26.9
27 F	0 19 19	6 43 43	15 58 09	21 58 53	8 56.9	11 38.6	3 57.1	8 03.2	16 16.4	5 19.5	6 24.7	29 53.5	24 51.5	23 25.3
28 Sa	0 23 16	7 43 04	28 02 11	4♑08 43	8D 55.6	13 02.9	5 11.7	8 49.6	16 27.3	5 11.8	6 20.0	29 52.4	24 51.5	23 23.7
29 Su	0 27 12	8 42 23	10♑19 03	16 33 51	8 55.8	14 28.9	6 26.2	9 35.8	16 38.5	5 04.0	6 15.3	29 51.1	24 51.4	23 22.1
30 M	0 31 09	9 41 40	22 53 43	29 19 14	8R 56.5	15 56.4	7 40.7	10 22.1	16 50.0	4 56.3	6 10.7	29 49.9	24 51.3	23 20.5
31 Tu	0 35 06	10 40 55	5♒50 56	12♒29 16	8 56.7	17 25.4	8 55.3	11 08.3	17 01.8	4 48.6	6 06.0	29 48.6	24 51.2	23 18.8

April 1981 — LONGITUDE

Day	Sid.Time	☉	0 hr ☽	Noon ☽	True ☊	☿	♀	♂	⚳	♃	♄	♅	♆	♇
1 W	0 39 02	11♈40 09	19♒14 36	26♒07 09	8♌55.4	18♓56.0	10♈09.8	11♈54.4	17♋13.9	4♎40.9	6♎01.3	29♏47.2	24♐51.0	23♎17.2
2 Th	0 42 59	12 39 20	3♓06 59	10♓13 58	8R 51.9	20 28.1	11 24.3	12 40.5	17 26.3	4R 33.3	5R 56.7	29R 45.8	24R 50.8	23R 15.5
3 F	0 46 55	13 38 30	17 27 48	24 47 55	8 45.8	22 01.7	12 38.7	13 26.6	17 39.0	4 25.7	5 52.0	29 44.4	24 50.6	23 13.9
4 Sa	0 50 52	14 37 38	2♈13 34	9♈43 46	8 37.4	23 36.8	13 53.2	14 12.7	17 52.0	4 18.1	5 47.4	29 42.9	24 50.3	23 12.2
5 Su	0 54 48	15 36 43	17 17 22	24 53 05	8 27.6	25 13.4	15 07.7	14 58.7	18 05.2	4 10.6	5 42.8	29 41.4	24 50.1	23 10.6
6 M	0 58 45	16 35 47	2♉29 32	10♉05 21	8 17.5	26 51.4	16 22.1	15 44.6	18 18.7	4 03.2	5 38.2	29 39.8	24 49.7	23 08.9
7 Tu	1 02 41	17 34 49	17 39 13	25 09 53	8 08.3	28 30.9	17 36.5	16 30.5	18 32.5	3 55.8	5 33.7	29 38.2	24 49.4	23 07.2
8 W	1 06 38	18 33 48	2♊36 19	9♊57 38	8 01.1	0♈12.0	18 50.9	17 16.4	18 46.6	3 48.4	5 29.2	29 36.6	24 49.0	23 05.5
9 Th	1 10 34	19 32 45	17 13 12	24 22 35	7 56.5	1 54.5	20 05.3	18 02.2	19 00.9	3 41.2	5 24.7	29 34.9	24 48.6	23 03.8
10 F	1 14 31	20 31 40	1♋25 32	8♋22 00	7D 54.2	3 38.5	21 19.6	18 48.0	19 15.5	3 34.0	5 20.2	29 33.2	24 48.1	23 02.1
11 Sa	1 18 28	21 30 33	15 12 06	21 56 05	7 53.7	5 24.0	22 34.0	19 33.7	19 30.3	3 26.9	5 15.8	29 31.4	24 47.7	23 00.5
12 Su	1 22 24	22 29 23	28 34 15	5♌07 01	7R 53.9	7 11.0	23 48.3	20 19.4	19 45.4	3 19.9	5 11.4	29 29.6	24 47.1	22 58.8
13 M	1 26 21	23 28 11	11♌34 49	17 58 08	7 53.6	8 59.5	25 02.6	21 05.0	20 00.7	3 13.0	5 07.1	29 27.8	24 46.6	22 57.1
14 Tu	1 30 17	24 26 57	24 17 24	0♍33 06	7 51.6	10 49.6	26 16.9	21 50.6	20 16.2	3 06.1	5 02.8	29 25.9	24 46.0	22 55.4
15 W	1 34 14	25 25 40	6♍45 39	12 55 26	7 47.2	12 41.2	27 31.1	22 36.1	20 32.0	2 59.4	4 58.6	29 24.0	24 45.4	22 53.7
16 Th	1 38 10	26 24 21	19 02 50	25 08 10	7 39.9	14 34.4	28 45.4	23 21.6	20 48.0	2 52.8	4 54.4	29 22.1	24 44.8	22 52.0
17 F	1 42 07	27 23 00	1♎11 42	7♎13 41	7 29.8	16 29.1	29 59.6	24 07.1	21 04.2	2 46.3	4 50.2	29 20.1	24 44.1	22 50.3
18 Sa	1 46 03	28 21 37	13 14 20	19 13 51	7 17.4	18 25.4	1♉13.8	24 52.5	21 20.7	2 39.8	4 46.1	29 18.1	24 43.5	22 48.6
19 Su	1 50 00	29 20 12	25 12 23	1♏10 06	7 03.5	20 23.2	2 28.0	25 37.8	21 37.4	2 33.5	4 42.0	29 16.1	24 42.7	22 46.9
20 M	1 53 57	0♉18 46	7♏07 09	13 03 41	6 49.4	22 22.5	3 42.1	26 23.1	21 54.2	2 27.4	4 38.0	29 14.0	24 42.0	22 45.3
21 Tu	1 57 53	1 17 17	18 59 54	24 55 58	6 36.1	24 23.3	4 56.3	27 08.3	22 11.3	2 21.3	4 34.1	29 11.9	24 41.2	22 43.6
22 W	2 01 50	2 15 47	0♐52 07	6♐48 37	6 24.7	26 25.5	6 10.4	27 53.5	22 28.6	2 15.4	4 30.2	29 09.8	24 40.4	22 41.9
23 Th	2 05 46	3 14 15	12 45 46	18 43 55	6 15.9	28 29.0	7 24.6	28 38.7	22 46.1	2 09.6	4 26.4	29 07.7	24 39.6	22 40.3
24 F	2 09 43	4 12 41	24 43 26	0♑44 46	6 09.9	0♉33.8	8 38.7	29 23.8	23 03.8	2 03.9	4 22.6	29 05.5	24 38.7	22 38.6
25 Sa	2 13 39	5 11 05	6♑48 24	12 54 50	6 06.7	2 39.8	9 52.8	0♉08.9	23 21.7	1 58.4	4 18.9	29 03.3	24 37.8	22 37.0
26 Su	2 17 36	6 09 28	19 04 39	25 18 24	6 05.4	4 46.8	11 06.8	0 53.9	23 39.8	1 53.0	4 15.3	29 01.1	24 36.9	22 35.3
27 M	2 21 32	7 07 50	1♒36 41	8♒00 06	6 05.3	6 54.7	12 20.9	1 38.8	23 58.0	1 47.7	4 11.8	28 58.8	24 36.0	22 33.7
28 Tu	2 25 29	8 06 10	14 29 13	21 04 34	6 05.0	9 03.3	13 34.9	2 23.8	24 16.5	1 42.6	4 08.3	28 56.6	24 35.0	22 32.1
29 W	2 29 26	9 04 28	27 46 36	4♓35 43	6 03.5	11 12.4	14 49.0	3 08.6	24 35.1	1 37.6	4 04.8	28 54.3	24 34.0	22 30.5
30 Th	2 33 22	10 02 45	11♓32 08	18 35 55	5 59.7	13 21.7	16 03.0	3 53.4	24 53.9	1 32.8	4 01.5	28 52.0	24 33.0	22 28.9

Astro Data

	Dy Hr Mn
☿ D	2 7:05
♃☌♄	4 19:07
♅ R	5 1:46
☽ 0N	8 2:42
♂0N	19 9:29
☉0N	20 17:02
☽ 0S	21 11:54
♀0N	26 21:59
♆ R	27 6:08
♄0N	30 23:41
☽ 0N	4 12:57
♃0N	9 17:29
☿0N	11 9:40
☽ 0S	17 18:14

Planet Ingress

	Dy Hr Mn
♂ ♈	17 2:40
☿ ♓	18 4:33
☉ ♈	20 17:03
♅ ♏R	20 23:15
♀ ♈	24 7:43
☿ ♈	8 9:11
♀ ♉	17 12:08
☉ ♉	20 4:19
☿ ♉	24 5:31
♂ ♉	25 7:17

Last Aspect / ☽ Ingress (March)

Last Aspect Dy Hr Mn		☽ Ingress Dy Hr Mn
2 16:56	♇ □	♒ 3 3:51
4 23:14	♆ ⚹	♓ 5 8:12
7 1:14	♆ □	♈ 7 9:48
9 1:54	♆ △	♉ 9 10:22
11 3:58	♂ ⚹	♊ 11 11:42
13 10:03	♂ □	♋ 13 15:06
15 19:10	♂ △	♌ 15 21:02
17 19:29	♆ △	♍ 18 5:20
20 15:22	☉ ☍	♎ 20 15:31
22 16:54	♆ ⚹	♏ 23 3:14
25 15:42	♅ ☌	♐ 25 15:51
27 17:43	♆ ☌	♑ 28 3:52
30 12:57	♅ ⚹	♒ 30 13:15

Last Aspect / ☽ Ingress (April)

Last Aspect Dy Hr Mn		☽ Ingress Dy Hr Mn
1 18:18	♅ □	♓ 1 18:41
3 19:59	♅ △	♈ 3 20:25
5 11:55	♆ △	♉ 5 20:04
7 19:11	♅ ☍	♊ 7 19:47
9 12:44	♆ ☍	♋ 9 21:34
12 1:42	♅ △	♌ 12 2:36
14 9:51	♅ □	♍ 14 10:56
16 20:21	♅ ⚹	♎ 16 21:38
19 7:59	☉ ☍	♏ 19 9:39
21 20:36	♅ ☌	♐ 21 22:15
24 9:08	♂ △	♑ 24 10:31
26 19:04	♅ ⚹	♒ 26 20:57
29 2:02	♅ □	♓ 29 3:56

☽ Phases & Eclipses

Dy Hr Mn	
6 10:31	● 15♓46
13 1:51	☽ 22♊24
20 15:22	○ 29♍56
28 19:34	☾ 8♑02
4 20:19	● 14♈58
11 11:11	☽ 21♋29
19 7:59	○ 29♎10
27 10:14	☾ 7♒04

Astro Data

1 March 1981
Julian Day # 29645
SVP 5♓31'35"
GC 26♐34.6 ⚴ 8♉14.4
Eris 14♈23.8 ⚵ 7♏41.7R
⚷ 14♉07.7 ⚶ 1♍14.8R
☽ Mean ☊ 9♌21.7

1 April 1981
Julian Day # 29676
SVP 5♓31'32"
GC 26♐34.6 ⚴ 23♉50.9
Eris 14♈43.4 ⚵ 3♏55.0R
⚷ 15♉37.7 ⚶ 25♌42.7R
☽ Mean ☊ 7♌43.2

LONGITUDE May 1981

Day	Sid.Time	☉	0 hr ☽	Noon ☽	True ☊	☿	♀	♂	⚳	♃	♄	♅	♆	♇
1 F	2 37 19	11♉01 00	25♓46 59	3♈04 59	5♌53.3	15♉31.0	17♉17.0	4♉38.2	25♋12.9	1♎28.1	3♎58.2	28♏49.6	24♐32.0	22♎27.3
2 Sa	2 41 15	11 59 14	10♈29 22	17 59 19	5R44.5	17 40.0	18 31.0	5 22.9	25 32.1	1R23.6	3R55.0	28R47.3	24R30.9	22R25.7
3 Su	2 45 12	12 57 26	25 33 48	3♉11 36	5 34.0	19 48.4	19 45.0	6 07.6	25 51.5	1 19.3	3 51.9	28 44.9	24 29.8	22 24.2
4 M	2 49 08	13 55 36	10♉51 19	18 31 31	5 23.0	21 55.9	20 58.9	6 52.2	26 11.0	1 15.1	3 48.9	28 42.5	24 28.7	22 22.6
5 Tu	2 53 05	14 53 45	26 10 41	3♊47 24	5 13.0	24 02.3	22 12.9	7 36.8	26 30.6	1 11.1	3 45.9	28 40.1	24 27.6	22 21.1
6 W	2 57 01	15 51 52	11♊20 21	18 48 25	5 04.9	26 07.2	23 26.8	8 21.3	26 50.5	1 07.2	3 43.0	28 37.7	24 26.4	22 19.6
7 Th	3 00 58	16 49 57	26 10 41	3♋26 27	4 59.4	28 10.4	24 40.7	9 05.8	27 10.5	1 03.5	3 40.2	28 35.3	24 25.2	22 18.1
8 F	3 04 55	17 48 01	10♋35 15	17 36 53	4 56.5	0♊11.5	25 54.6	9 50.2	27 30.7	1 00.0	3 37.5	28 32.8	24 24.0	22 16.6
9 Sa	3 08 51	18 46 02	24 31 18	1♌18 40	4D55.5	2 10.4	27 08.5	10 34.5	27 51.0	0 56.7	3 34.9	28 30.4	24 22.8	22 15.1
10 Su	3 12 48	19 44 02	7♌59 14	14 33 25	4R55.6	4 06.8	28 22.3	11 18.8	28 11.4	0 53.5	3 32.4	28 27.9	24 21.6	22 13.6
11 M	3 16 44	20 41 59	21 01 41	27 24 33	4 55.5	6 00.5	29 36.2	12 03.0	28 32.0	0 50.5	3 29.9	28 25.5	24 20.3	22 12.2
12 Tu	3 20 41	21 39 55	3♍42 34	9♍56 18	4 54.1	7 51.4	0♊50.0	12 47.2	28 52.8	0 47.7	3 27.6	28 23.0	24 19.0	22 10.8
13 W	3 24 37	22 37 49	16 06 18	22 13 06	4 50.6	9 39.3	2 03.8	13 31.4	29 13.7	0 45.0	3 25.3	28 20.5	24 17.7	22 09.4
14 Th	3 28 34	23 35 41	28 17 12	4♎19 05	4 44.4	11 24.1	3 17.6	14 15.4	29 34.7	0 42.6	3 23.2	28 18.0	24 16.4	22 08.0
15 F	3 32 30	24 33 32	10♎19 11	16 17 52	4 35.7	13 05.8	4 31.3	14 59.5	29 55.9	0 40.3	3 21.1	28 15.5	24 15.1	22 06.6
16 Sa	3 36 27	25 31 21	22 15 31	28 12 24	4 24.9	14 44.2	5 45.1	15 43.4	0♌17.2	0 38.1	3 19.1	28 13.0	24 13.7	22 05.3
17 Su	3 40 24	26 29 08	4♏08 49	10♏04 59	4 12.7	16 19.2	6 58.8	16 27.4	0 38.6	0 36.2	3 17.2	28 10.5	24 12.4	22 04.0
18 M	3 44 20	27 26 54	16 01 09	21 57 28	4 00.2	17 50.8	8 12.5	17 11.2	1 00.2	0 34.4	3 15.4	28 08.0	24 11.0	22 02.6
19 Tu	3 48 17	28 24 38	27 54 08	3♐51 20	3 48.5	19 19.0	9 26.2	17 55.0	1 21.9	0 32.9	3 13.7	28 05.5	24 09.6	22 01.4
20 W	3 52 13	29 22 21	9♐49 15	15 48 03	3 38.4	20 43.7	10 39.9	18 38.8	1 43.7	0 31.5	3 12.1	28 03.0	24 08.1	22 00.1
21 Th	3 56 10	0♊20 03	21 47 58	27 49 13	3 30.7	22 04.8	11 53.5	19 22.5	2 05.6	0 30.2	3 10.6	28 00.5	24 06.7	21 58.9
22 F	4 00 06	1 17 44	3♑52 04	9♑56 50	3 25.6	23 22.3	13 07.2	20 06.1	2 27.7	0 29.2	3 09.2	27 58.0	24 05.3	21 57.7
23 Sa	4 04 03	2 15 24	16 03 50	22 13 26	3D23.0	24 36.2	14 20.8	20 49.7	2 49.8	0 28.3	3 07.8	27 55.5	24 03.8	21 56.5
24 Su	4 07 59	3 13 02	28 26 04	4♒42 08	3 22.4	25 46.4	15 34.4	21 33.3	3 12.1	0 27.7	3 06.6	27 53.0	24 02.3	21 55.3
25 M	4 11 56	4 10 40	11♒02 07	17 26 28	3 23.0	26 52.8	16 48.1	22 16.8	3 34.5	0 27.2	3 05.5	27 50.5	24 00.8	21 54.2
26 Tu	4 15 53	5 08 16	23 55 40	0♓30 10	3R23.6	27 55.4	18 01.6	23 00.2	3 57.0	0 26.8	3 04.5	27 48.0	23 59.3	21 53.0
27 W	4 19 49	6 05 52	7♓10 24	13 56 42	3 23.4	28 54.2	19 15.2	23 43.6	4 19.7	0D26.7	3 03.5	27 45.6	23 57.8	21 51.9
28 Th	4 23 46	7 03 26	20 49 20	27 48 28	3 21.6	29 48.9	20 28.8	24 26.9	4 42.4	0 26.7	3 02.7	27 43.1	23 56.3	21 50.9
29 F	4 27 42	8 01 00	4♈54 06	12♈06 04	3 17.7	0♋39.7	21 42.4	25 10.2	5 05.2	0 27.0	3 02.0	27 40.6	23 54.8	21 49.8
30 Sa	4 31 39	8 58 33	19 24 02	26 47 26	3 11.8	1 26.4	22 55.9	25 53.5	5 28.2	0 27.4	3 01.4	27 38.2	23 53.2	21 48.8
31 Su	4 35 35	9 56 05	4♉15 31	11♉47 19	3 04.4	2 08.9	24 09.4	26 36.6	5 51.2	0 28.0	3 00.9	27 35.7	23 51.7	21 47.8

LONGITUDE June 1981

Day	Sid.Time	☉	0 hr ☽	Noon ☽	True ☊	☿	♀	♂	⚳	♃	♄	♅	♆	♇
1 M	4 39 32	10♊53 37	19♉21 43	26♉57 29	2♌56.6	2♋47.2	25♊22.9	27♉19.8	6♌14.4	0♎28.7	3♎00.4	27♏33.3	23♐50.1	21♎46.9
2 Tu	4 43 28	11 51 07	4♊33 18	12♊07 49	2R49.3	3 21.1	26 36.4	28 02.8	6 37.7	0 29.7	3R00.1	27R30.9	23R48.5	21R45.9
3 W	4 47 25	12 48 37	19 39 46	27 07 58	2 43.5	3 50.7	27 49.9	28 45.9	7 01.0	0 30.8	2 59.9	27 28.5	23 46.9	21 45.0
4 Th	4 51 22	13 46 05	4♋31 23	11♋49 11	2 39.7	4 15.7	29 03.4	29 28.8	7 24.5	0 32.1	2D59.8	27 26.2	23 45.4	21 44.1
5 F	4 55 18	14 43 32	19 00 42	26 05 30	2D37.9	4 36.3	0♋16.9	0♊11.7	7 48.0	0 33.6	2 59.8	27 23.8	23 43.8	21 43.3
6 Sa	4 59 15	15 40 58	3♌03 20	9♌54 10	2 38.0	4 52.2	1 30.3	0 54.6	8 11.7	0 35.3	2 59.9	27 21.5	23 42.2	21 42.5
7 Su	5 03 11	16 38 23	16 38 06	23 15 21	2 39.0	5 03.6	2 43.7	1 37.4	8 35.4	0 37.1	3 00.1	27 19.1	23 40.6	21 41.7
8 M	5 07 08	17 35 47	29 46 18	6♍11 22	2R40.2	5R10.4	3 57.2	2 20.1	8 59.3	0 39.1	3 00.4	27 16.8	23 39.0	21 40.9
9 Tu	5 11 04	18 33 10	12♍31 04	18 45 57	2 40.8	5 12.6	5 10.5	3 02.8	9 23.2	0 41.3	3 00.8	27 14.5	23 37.4	21 40.2
10 W	5 15 01	19 30 32	24 56 34	1♎03 30	2 40.0	5 10.3	6 23.9	3 45.4	9 47.2	0 43.6	3 01.3	27 12.3	23 35.7	21 39.5
11 Th	5 18 57	20 27 52	7♎07 19	13 08 35	2 37.5	5 03.5	7 37.3	4 28.0	10 11.2	0 46.2	3 01.9	27 10.0	23 34.1	21 38.8
12 F	5 22 54	21 25 12	19 07 50	25 05 34	2 33.2	4 52.5	8 50.6	5 10.5	10 35.4	0 48.9	3 02.6	27 07.8	23 32.5	21 38.2
13 Sa	5 26 51	22 22 30	1♏02 15	6♏58 20	2 27.5	4 37.4	10 03.9	5 52.9	10 59.7	0 51.7	3 03.4	27 05.6	23 30.9	21 37.5
14 Su	5 30 47	23 19 48	12 54 13	18 50 15	2 20.8	4 18.5	11 17.2	6 35.3	11 24.0	0 54.8	3 04.3	27 03.5	23 29.3	21 37.0
15 M	5 34 44	24 17 05	24 46 47	0♐44 04	2 13.8	3 56.0	12 30.5	7 17.7	11 48.4	0 58.0	3 05.3	27 01.3	23 27.6	21 36.4
16 Tu	5 38 40	25 14 22	6♐42 24	12 41 59	2 07.2	3 30.4	13 43.8	8 00.0	12 12.9	1 01.4	3 06.4	26 59.2	23 26.0	21 35.9
17 W	5 42 37	26 11 38	18 43 02	24 45 45	2 01.7	3 01.9	14 57.0	8 42.2	12 37.4	1 04.9	3 07.6	26 57.1	23 24.4	21 35.4
18 Th	5 46 33	27 08 53	0♑50 19	6♑56 54	1 57.7	2 31.2	16 10.2	9 24.4	13 02.0	1 08.6	3 08.9	26 55.1	23 22.8	21 35.0
19 F	5 50 30	28 06 08	13 05 40	19 16 48	1 55.3	1 58.6	17 23.4	10 06.5	13 26.7	1 12.5	3 10.3	26 53.1	23 21.2	21 34.5
20 Sa	5 54 26	29 03 22	25 30 31	1♒46 59	1D54.6	1 24.8	18 36.6	10 48.6	13 51.5	1 16.5	3 11.8	26 51.1	23 19.6	21 34.1
21 Su	5 58 23	0♋00 37	8♒06 27	14 29 07	1 55.1	0 50.2	19 49.8	11 30.6	14 16.4	1 20.7	3 13.4	26 49.1	23 18.0	21 33.8
22 M	6 02 20	0 57 50	20 55 16	27 25 07	1 56.5	0 15.6	21 03.0	12 12.6	14 41.3	1 25.0	3 15.1	26 47.2	23 16.4	21 33.5
23 Tu	6 06 16	1 55 04	3♓58 57	10♓37 00	1 58.1	29♊41.4	22 16.1	12 54.5	15 06.2	1 29.5	3 16.8	26 45.3	23 14.8	21 33.2
24 W	6 10 13	2 52 18	17 19 30	24 06 39	1R59.2	29 08.3	23 29.2	13 36.4	15 31.3	1 34.1	3 18.7	26 43.4	23 13.2	21 32.9
25 Th	6 14 09	3 49 31	0♈58 35	7♈55 21	1 59.4	28 36.8	24 42.4	14 18.2	15 56.4	1 38.9	3 20.7	26 41.6	23 11.6	21 32.7
26 F	6 18 06	4 46 45	14 56 59	22 03 19	1 58.4	28 07.5	25 55.4	15 00.0	16 21.6	1 43.9	3 22.8	26 39.8	23 10.0	21 32.5
27 Sa	6 22 02	5 43 58	29 14 09	6♉29 05	1 56.3	27 40.9	27 08.5	15 41.7	16 46.8	1 49.0	3 25.0	26 38.0	23 08.4	21 32.3
28 Su	6 25 59	6 41 12	13♉47 38	21 09 08	1 53.4	27 17.5	28 21.6	16 23.4	17 12.1	1 54.3	3 27.2	26 36.3	23 06.8	21 32.2
29 M	6 29 55	7 38 26	28 32 51	5♊57 54	1 50.2	26 57.6	29 34.7	17 05.0	17 37.5	1 59.7	3 29.6	26 34.6	23 05.3	21 32.1
30 Tu	6 33 52	8 35 39	13♊23 22	20 48 13	1 47.1	26 41.6	0♌47.7	17 46.5	18 02.9	2 05.2	3 32.1	26 32.9	23 03.7	21 32.1

Astro Data Dy Hr Mn	Planet Ingress Dy Hr Mn	Last Aspect Dy Hr Mn	☽ Ingress Dy Hr Mn	Last Aspect Dy Hr Mn	☽ Ingress Dy Hr Mn	☽ Phases & Eclipses Dy Hr Mn	Astro Data
☽0N 2 0:05	☿ ♊ 8 9:42	1 5:03 ♅ △	♈ 1 6:57	1 12:56 ♅ ☍	♊ 1 16:48	4 4:19 ● 13♉37	1 May 1981
☽0S 15 0:45	♀ ♊ 11 19:45	2 22:20 ♆ △	♉ 3 6:59	3 13:14 ♀ ☌	♋ 3 16:38	10 22:22 ☽ 20♌09	Julian Day # 29706
♃D 27 18:26	⚳ ♌ 15 16:39	5 3:56 ♅ ☍	♊ 5 6:01	5 14:14 ♅ △	♌ 5 18:43	19 0:04 ○ 27♏56	SVP 5♓31'29"
☽0N 29 10:08	☉ ♊ 21 3:39	6 21:09 ♆ ☍	♋ 7 6:18	7 19:26 ♅ □	♍ 8 0:25	26 21:00 ☾ 5♓30	GC 26♐34.7 ⚴ 10♊40.2
	☿ ♋ 28 17:04	9 7:02 ♅ △	♌ 9 9:40	10 4:27 ♅ ⚹	♎ 10 9:55		Eris 15♈03.0 ⚵ 27♎15.7R
♄D 5 2:13		11 16:37 ♀ □	♍ 11 16:55	12 8:53 ♆ ⚹	♏ 12 21:54	2 11:32 ● 11♊50	⚷ 17♉31.8 ⚶ 27♎08.6
☿R 9 11:36	♂ ♊ 5 5:26	14 0:04 ♅ ⚹	♎ 14 3:24	15 4:33 ♅ ☌	♐ 15 10:31	9 11:33 ☽ 18♍32	☽ Mean ☊ 6♌07.9
☽0S 11 8:04	♀ ♋ 5 6:29	16 3:59 ♆ ⚹	♏ 16 15:37	17 15:04 ☉ ☍	♑ 17 22:21	17 15:04 ○ 26♐19	
☽0N 25 17:56	☉ ♋ 21 11:45	19 0:25 ♅ ☌	♐ 19 4:14	20 2:36 ♅ ⚹	♒ 20 8:36	25 4:25 ☾ 3♈31	1 June 1981
	☿ ♊R 22 22:51	21 4:38 ♆ ☌	♑ 21 16:20	22 10:50 ♅ □	♓ 22 16:44		Julian Day # 29737
	♀ ♌ 29 20:20	23 22:59 ♅ ⚹	♒ 24 3:01	24 20:28 ♅ □	♈ 24 22:18		SVP 5♓31'25"
		26 7:06 ♅ □	♓ 26 11:05	26 21:50 ☿ ⚹	♉ 27 1:16		GC 26♐34.8 ⚴ 28♊57.9
		28 15:38 ☿ □	♈ 28 15:44	29 0:45 ♀ ⚹	♊ 29 2:21		Eris 15♈19.0 ⚵ 22♎31.4R
		30 7:18 ♆ △	♉ 30 17:10				⚷ 19♉35.3 ⚶ 4♍33.6
							☽ Mean ☊ 4♌29.4

July 1981 — LONGITUDE

Day	Sid.Time	☉	0 hr ☽	Noon ☽	True ☊	☿	♀	♂	⚳	♃	♄	♅	♆	♇
1 W	6 37 49	9♋32 53	28♊11 30	5♋32 15	1♌44.8	26♊29.9	2♌00.7	18♊28.0	18♌28.4	2♎10.9	3♎34.6	26♏31.3	23♐02.2	21♎32.0
2 Th	6 41 45	10 30 07	12♋49 34	20 02 39	1D43.4	26R22.6	3 13.7	19 09.5	18 54.0	2 16.8	3 37.3	26R29.8	23R00.7	21D32.0
3 F	6 45 42	11 27 21	27 10 51	4♌13 36	1 43.1	26D20.0	4 26.7	19 50.9	19 19.6	2 22.8	3 40.0	26 28.2	22 59.1	21 32.1
4 Sa	6 49 38	12 24 34	11♌10 32	18 01 25	1 43.6	26 22.3	5 39.7	20 32.2	19 45.3	2 28.9	3 42.8	26 26.7	22 57.6	21 32.2
5 Su	6 53 35	13 21 47	24 46 09	1♍24 46	1 44.8	26 29.5	6 52.6	21 13.5	20 11.0	2 35.2	3 45.8	26 25.3	22 56.1	21 32.3
6 M	6 57 31	14 19 00	7♍57 25	14 24 22	1 46.1	26 41.7	8 05.5	21 54.7	20 36.8	2 41.6	3 48.8	26 23.9	22 54.6	21 32.4
7 Tu	7 01 28	15 16 13	20 45 59	27 02 39	1 47.3	26 59.1	9 18.4	22 35.9	21 02.6	2 48.2	3 51.9	26 22.5	22 53.2	21 32.6
8 W	7 05 24	16 13 25	3♎14 52	9♎23 08	1R48.0	27 21.5	10 31.3	23 17.0	21 28.5	2 54.8	3 55.1	26 21.2	22 51.7	21 32.8
9 Th	7 09 21	17 10 38	15 28 01	21 30 03	1 48.1	27 49.1	11 44.1	23 58.1	21 54.4	3 01.7	3 58.3	26 19.9	22 50.3	21 33.1
10 F	7 13 18	18 07 50	27 29 49	3♏27 53	1 47.5	28 21.8	12 57.0	24 39.1	22 20.4	3 08.6	4 01.7	26 18.6	22 48.8	21 33.3
11 Sa	7 17 14	19 05 02	9♏24 48	15 21 06	1 46.4	28 59.6	14 09.8	25 20.0	22 46.4	3 15.7	4 05.2	26 17.5	22 47.4	21 33.6
12 Su	7 21 11	20 02 15	21 17 18	27 13 54	1 44.9	29 42.4	15 22.5	26 00.9	23 12.5	3 22.9	4 08.7	26 16.3	22 46.0	21 34.0
13 M	7 25 07	20 59 27	3♐11 21	9♐10 04	1 43.4	0♋30.2	16 35.3	26 41.8	23 38.6	3 30.2	4 12.3	26 15.2	22 44.6	21 34.4
14 Tu	7 29 04	21 56 40	15 10 27	21 12 50	1 42.0	1 23.0	17 48.0	27 22.6	24 04.8	3 37.7	4 16.0	26 14.1	22 43.3	21 34.8
15 W	7 33 00	22 53 52	27 17 32	3♑24 49	1 40.9	2 20.7	19 00.7	28 03.3	24 31.0	3 45.3	4 19.8	26 13.1	22 41.9	21 35.3
16 Th	7 36 57	23 51 05	9♑34 54	15 47 59	1 40.2	3 23.2	20 13.4	28 44.0	24 57.2	3 53.0	4 23.7	26 12.2	22 40.6	21 35.7
17 F	7 40 54	24 48 19	22 04 13	28 23 42	1D39.9	4 30.5	21 26.0	29 24.7	25 23.5	4 00.8	4 27.6	26 11.3	22 39.3	21 36.3
18 Sa	7 44 50	25 45 32	4♒46 33	11♒12 47	1 40.0	5 42.5	22 38.6	0♋05.2	25 49.9	4 08.7	4 31.7	26 10.4	22 38.0	21 36.8
19 Su	7 48 47	26 42 47	17 42 29	24 15 37	1 40.3	6 59.1	23 51.2	0 45.8	26 16.3	4 16.8	4 35.8	26 09.6	22 36.7	21 37.4
20 M	7 52 43	27 40 02	0♓52 11	7♓32 10	1 40.7	8 20.2	25 03.8	1 26.3	26 42.7	4 25.0	4 40.0	26 08.8	22 35.4	21 38.0
21 Tu	7 56 40	28 37 17	14 15 31	21 02 12	1 41.0	9 45.7	26 16.3	2 06.7	27 09.1	4 33.3	4 44.2	26 08.1	22 34.2	21 38.7
22 W	8 00 36	29 34 33	27 52 07	4♈45 11	1 41.2	11 15.5	27 28.8	2 47.1	27 35.6	4 41.7	4 48.6	26 07.4	22 33.0	21 39.3
23 Th	8 04 33	0♌31 50	11♈41 17	18 40 18	1 41.3	12 49.5	28 41.3	3 27.4	28 02.2	4 50.2	4 53.0	26 06.7	22 31.8	21 40.1
24 F	8 08 29	1 29 08	25 42 02	2♉46 18	1 41.4	14 27.5	29 53.8	4 07.7	28 28.7	4 58.8	4 57.5	26 06.2	22 30.6	21 40.8
25 Sa	8 12 26	2 26 27	9♉52 51	17 01 23	1 41.4	16 09.3	1♍06.2	4 47.9	28 55.4	5 07.6	5 02.1	26 05.6	22 29.4	21 41.6
26 Su	8 16 22	3 23 47	24 11 34	1♊22 59	1 41.5	17 54.7	2 18.6	5 28.1	29 22.0	5 16.4	5 06.7	26 05.1	22 28.3	21 42.4
27 M	8 20 19	4 21 08	8♊35 12	15 47 44	1 41.7	19 43.4	3 31.0	6 08.2	29 48.7	5 25.4	5 11.4	26 04.7	22 27.2	21 43.2
28 Tu	8 24 16	5 18 30	23 00 32	0♋11 32	1 42.0	21 35.2	4 43.3	6 48.3	0♍15.4	5 34.4	5 16.2	26 04.3	22 26.1	21 44.1
29 W	8 28 12	6 15 53	7♋21 40	14 29 51	1 42.3	23 29.8	5 55.7	7 28.3	0 42.2	5 43.6	5 21.1	26 04.0	22 25.0	21 45.0
30 Th	8 32 09	7 13 17	21 35 30	28 38 05	1R42.5	25 26.8	7 08.0	8 08.3	1 09.0	5 52.8	5 26.0	26 03.7	22 24.0	21 46.0
31 F	8 36 05	8 10 42	5♌37 05	12♌32 05	1 42.4	27 26.0	8 20.2	8 48.2	1 35.8	6 02.2	5 31.0	26 03.5	22 23.0	21 47.0

August 1981 — LONGITUDE

Day	Sid.Time	☉	0 hr ☽	Noon ☽	True ☊	☿	♀	♂	⚳	♃	♄	♅	♆	♇
1 Sa	8 40 02	9♌08 07	19♌22 41	26♌08 37	1♌41.9	29♋27.0	9♍32.5	9♋28.1	2♍02.7	6♎11.7	5♎36.1	26♏03.3	22♐22.0	21♎48.0
2 Su	8 43 58	10 05 33	2♍49 40	9♍25 45	1R41.1	1♌29.3	10 44.7	10 07.9	2 29.6	6 21.2	5 41.2	26R03.2	22R21.0	21 49.0
3 M	8 47 55	11 03 00	15 56 49	22 22 58	1 40.0	3 32.8	11 56.9	10 47.7	2 56.5	6 30.9	5 46.4	26D03.1	22 20.1	21 50.1
4 Tu	8 51 52	12 00 28	28 44 22	5♎01 15	1 38.7	5 37.0	13 09.0	11 27.4	3 23.5	6 40.6	5 51.7	26 03.1	22 19.2	21 51.2
5 W	8 55 48	12 57 56	11♎13 56	17 22 47	1 37.4	7 41.6	14 21.1	12 07.0	3 50.4	6 50.5	5 57.0	26 03.1	22 18.3	21 52.3
6 Th	8 59 45	13 55 26	23 28 16	29 30 50	1 36.5	9 46.3	15 33.2	12 46.6	4 17.4	7 00.4	6 02.4	26 03.2	22 17.4	21 53.5
7 F	9 03 41	14 52 55	5♏31 02	11♏29 24	1D36.0	11 50.9	16 45.2	13 26.2	4 44.5	7 10.4	6 07.9	26 03.3	22 16.6	21 54.7
8 Sa	9 07 38	15 50 26	17 26 30	23 22 55	1 36.2	13 55.2	17 57.2	14 05.7	5 11.5	7 20.6	6 13.4	26 03.5	22 15.8	21 55.9
9 Su	9 11 34	16 47 58	29 19 14	5♐16 03	1 36.9	15 58.8	19 09.1	14 45.1	5 38.6	7 30.8	6 19.0	26 03.8	22 15.0	21 57.1
10 M	9 15 31	17 45 30	11♐13 55	17 13 24	1 38.1	18 01.7	20 21.1	15 24.5	6 05.7	7 41.0	6 24.6	26 04.1	22 14.3	21 58.4
11 Tu	9 19 27	18 43 04	23 15 02	29 19 17	1 39.5	20 03.7	21 32.9	16 03.8	6 32.8	7 51.4	6 30.3	26 04.4	22 13.5	21 59.7
12 W	9 23 24	19 40 38	5♑26 38	11♑37 28	1 40.8	22 04.6	22 44.8	16 43.1	7 00.0	8 01.9	6 36.1	26 04.8	22 12.8	22 01.1
13 Th	9 27 20	20 38 14	17 52 10	24 10 59	1R41.6	24 04.4	23 56.5	17 22.3	7 27.2	8 12.4	6 41.9	26 05.2	22 12.2	22 02.5
14 F	9 31 17	21 35 50	0♒34 10	7♒01 51	1 41.7	26 03.0	25 08.3	18 01.5	7 54.4	8 23.0	6 47.8	26 05.7	22 11.5	22 03.9
15 Sa	9 35 14	22 33 28	13 34 06	20 10 54	1 40.8	28 00.3	26 20.0	18 40.6	8 21.6	8 33.7	6 53.7	26 06.3	22 10.9	22 05.3
16 Su	9 39 10	23 31 07	26 52 08	3♓37 40	1 38.8	29 56.2	27 31.6	19 19.7	8 48.8	8 44.4	6 59.7	26 06.9	22 10.3	22 06.7
17 M	9 43 07	24 28 47	10♓27 12	17 20 27	1 36.1	1♍50.8	28 43.2	19 58.7	9 16.1	8 55.3	7 05.7	26 07.5	22 09.8	22 08.2
18 Tu	9 47 03	25 26 28	24 17 01	1♈16 29	1 32.8	3 44.0	29 54.8	20 37.7	9 43.3	9 06.2	7 11.8	26 08.2	22 09.3	22 09.7
19 W	9 51 00	26 24 11	8♈18 25	15 22 20	1 29.4	5 35.8	1♎06.3	21 16.6	10 10.6	9 17.2	7 17.9	26 09.0	22 08.8	22 11.3
20 Th	9 54 56	27 21 56	22 27 45	29 34 15	1 26.6	7 26.3	2 17.8	21 55.5	10 37.9	9 28.2	7 24.1	26 09.8	22 08.3	22 12.8
21 F	9 58 53	28 19 42	6♉41 22	13♉48 43	1 24.7	9 15.3	3 29.3	22 34.3	11 05.3	9 39.3	7 30.4	26 10.6	22 07.9	22 14.4
22 Sa	10 02 49	29 17 30	20 55 56	28 02 41	1D24.0	11 02.9	4 40.6	23 13.1	11 32.6	9 50.5	7 36.6	26 11.6	22 07.5	22 16.0
23 Su	10 06 46	0♍15 20	5♊08 41	12♊13 41	1 24.4	12 49.2	5 52.0	23 51.8	12 00.0	10 01.8	7 43.0	26 12.5	22 07.1	22 17.7
24 M	10 10 43	1 13 12	19 17 26	26 19 45	1 25.7	14 34.1	7 03.3	24 30.5	12 27.4	10 13.1	7 49.3	26 13.5	22 06.8	22 19.3
25 Tu	10 14 39	2 11 06	3♋20 26	10♋19 16	1 27.1	16 17.6	8 14.6	25 09.1	12 54.8	10 24.5	7 55.8	26 14.6	22 06.5	22 21.0
26 W	10 18 36	3 09 01	17 16 06	24 10 41	1R28.2	17 59.9	9 25.8	25 47.7	13 22.2	10 36.0	8 02.2	26 15.7	22 06.2	22 22.7
27 Th	10 22 32	4 06 58	1♌02 52	7♌52 24	1 28.2	19 40.8	10 37.0	26 26.2	13 49.6	10 47.5	8 08.7	26 16.9	22 06.0	22 24.5
28 F	10 26 29	5 04 56	14 39 05	21 22 42	1 26.8	21 20.3	11 48.1	27 04.6	14 17.1	10 59.1	8 15.3	26 18.1	22 05.8	22 26.2
29 Sa	10 30 25	6 02 57	28 03 03	4♍39 57	1 23.6	22 58.6	12 59.2	27 43.1	14 44.5	11 10.8	8 21.9	26 19.3	22 05.6	22 28.0
30 Su	10 34 22	7 00 58	11♍13 14	17 42 47	1 18.8	24 35.6	14 10.2	28 21.4	15 12.0	11 22.5	8 28.5	26 20.6	22 05.5	22 29.8
31 M	10 38 18	7 59 02	24 08 31	0♎30 25	1 12.7	26 11.3	15 21.2	28 59.7	15 39.5	11 34.2	8 35.2	26 22.0	22 05.3	22 31.7

Astro Data	Dy Hr Mn	Planet Ingress	Dy Hr Mn	Last Aspect Dy Hr Mn		☽ Ingress Dy Hr Mn	Last Aspect Dy Hr Mn		☽ Ingress Dy Hr Mn	☽ Phases & Eclipses Dy Hr Mn	
♇ D	1 16:12	☿ ♋	12 21:08	30 21:25	☿ ☌	♋ 1 2:57	1 11:51	♅ □	♍ 1 18:54	1 19:03	● 9♋50
☿ D	3 12:58	♂ ♋	18 8:54	2 22:49	♅ △	♌ 3 4:47	3 18:55	♅ ⚹	♎ 4 2:24	9 2:39	☽ 16♎48
♃0S	8 15:38	☉ ♌	22 22:40	5 3:00	☿ ⚹	♍ 5 9:26	5 21:41	♆ ⚹	♏ 6 12:58	17 4:39	○ 24♑31
☽0S	8 16:10	♀ ♍	24 14:04	7 11:53	☿ □	♎ 7 17:42	8 17:25	♅ ☌	♐ 9 1:22	17 4:47	◑ P 0.548
☽0N	22 23:46	⚳ ♍	27 22:09	10 1:14	☿ △	♏ 10 5:02	10 21:59	♆ ☌	♑ 11 13:20	24 9:40	☾ 1♉24
♃☌♄	24 4:15			12 10:04	♅ ☌	♐ 12 17:35	13 15:36	♅ ⚹	♒ 13 22:56	31 3:52	● 7♌51
♄0S	29 6:48	☿ ♌	1 18:30	15 0:53	♂ ☍	♑ 15 5:19	16 4:23	☿ ☍	♓ 16 5:34	31 3:45:44	● T 02'03"
		☿ ♍	16 12:47	17 7:50	♅ ⚹	♒ 17 15:02	18 9:27	♀ ☍	♈ 18 9:49		
♅ D	4 10:49	♀ ♎	18 13:44	19 15:27	♅ □	♓ 19 22:26	20 8:01	☉ △	♉ 20 12:43	7 19:26	☽ 15♏11
☽0S	5 0:34	☉ ♍	23 5:38	22 2:19	☉ △	♈ 22 3:43	22 14:16	☉ □	♊ 22 15:18	15 16:37	○ 22♒45
♆⚹♇	18 6:43			24 6:40	♀ △	♉ 24 7:18	24 5:09	♇ △	♋ 24 18:17	22 14:16	☾ 29♉23
☽0N	19 5:18			26 3:10	♅ ☍	♊ 26 9:42	26 15:38	♅ △	♌ 26 22:10	29 14:43	● 6♍10
♀0S	19 23:26			27 23:04	♆ ☍	♋ 28 11:41	28 20:51	♅ □	♍ 29 3:32		
♃∠♅	30 7:47			30 7:36	♅ △	♌ 30 14:20	31 8:59	♂ ⚹	♎ 31 11:02		

Astro Data

1 July 1981
Julian Day # 29767
SVP 5♓31'19"
GC 26♐34.9 ⚴ 16♋52.4
Eris 15♈26.9 ⚵ 22♎40.8
⚷ 21♉19.3 ⚶ 15♍20.7
☽ Mean ☊ 2♌54.1

1 August 1981
Julian Day # 29798
SVP 5♓31'14"
GC 26♐34.9 ⚴ 5♌01.5
Eris 15♈25.2R ⚵ 27♎07.2
⚷ 22♉31.0 ⚶ 28♍44.8
☽ Mean ☊ 1♌15.6

LONGITUDE — September 1981

Day	Sid.Time	☉	0 hr ☽	Noon ☽	True ☊	☿	♀	♂	⚳	♃	♄	♅	♆	♇
1 Tu	10 42 15	8♍57 06	6♎48 31	13♎02 54	1♌06.2	27♍45.8	16♎32.1	29♋37.9	16♍06.9	11♎46.0	8♎41.9	26♏23.4	22♐05.3	22♎33.5
2 W	10 46 12	9 55 13	19 13 45	25 21 17	0R 59.7	29 19.0	17 43.0	0♌16.1	16 34.4	11 57.9	8 48.6	26 24.9	22D 05.2	22 35.4
3 Th	10 50 08	10 53 21	1♏25 47	7♏27 38	0 54.1	0♎50.9	18 53.8	0 54.3	17 01.9	12 09.8	8 55.4	26 26.4	22 05.2	22 37.3
4 F	10 54 05	11 51 30	13 27 13	19 25 00	0 49.9	2 21.6	20 04.5	1 32.3	17 29.5	12 21.8	9 02.2	26 27.9	22 05.2	22 39.2
5 Sa	10 58 01	12 49 41	25 21 30	1♐17 16	0 47.3	3 51.0	21 15.2	2 10.3	17 57.0	12 33.8	9 09.1	26 29.5	22 05.3	22 41.2
6 Su	11 01 58	13 47 53	7♐12 54	13 08 59	0D 46.5	5 19.1	22 25.9	2 48.3	18 24.5	12 45.9	9 16.0	26 31.2	22 05.3	22 43.1
7 M	11 05 54	14 46 07	19 06 09	25 05 02	0 47.0	6 46.0	23 36.4	3 26.2	18 52.0	12 58.1	9 22.9	26 32.9	22 05.5	22 45.1
8 Tu	11 09 51	15 44 22	1♑06 16	7♑10 30	0 48.4	8 11.6	24 46.9	4 04.1	19 19.6	13 10.2	9 29.8	26 34.6	22 05.6	22 47.1
9 W	11 13 47	16 42 39	13 18 18	19 30 15	0R 49.7	9 35.8	25 57.4	4 41.8	19 47.1	13 22.4	9 36.8	26 36.4	22 05.8	22 49.1
10 Th	11 17 44	17 40 58	25 46 52	2♒08 37	0 50.2	10 58.7	27 07.8	5 19.6	20 14.7	13 34.7	9 43.8	26 38.3	22 06.0	22 51.2
11 F	11 21 41	18 39 18	8♒35 51	15 08 51	0 49.2	12 20.3	28 18.1	5 57.3	20 42.2	13 47.0	9 50.8	26 40.1	22 06.3	22 53.2
12 Sa	11 25 37	19 37 40	21 47 47	28 32 43	0 46.1	13 40.4	29 28.3	6 34.9	21 09.7	13 59.3	9 57.9	26 42.1	22 06.5	22 55.3
13 Su	11 29 34	20 36 03	5♓23 30	12♓19 56	0 41.0	14 59.1	0♏38.5	7 12.4	21 37.3	14 11.7	10 04.9	26 44.0	22 06.9	22 57.4
14 M	11 33 30	21 34 28	19 21 36	26 27 58	0 34.0	16 16.3	1 48.5	7 50.0	22 04.8	14 24.1	10 12.0	26 46.0	22 07.2	22 59.5
15 Tu	11 37 27	22 32 55	3♈38 24	10♈52 06	0 25.9	17 31.9	2 58.6	8 27.4	22 32.4	14 36.6	10 19.2	26 48.1	22 07.6	23 01.6
16 W	11 41 23	23 31 24	18 08 16	25 25 59	0 17.6	18 45.9	4 08.5	9 04.8	22 59.9	14 49.1	10 26.3	26 50.2	22 08.0	23 03.8
17 Th	11 45 20	24 29 55	2♉44 23	10♉02 37	0 10.3	19 58.2	5 18.4	9 42.2	23 27.5	15 01.6	10 33.5	26 52.4	22 08.4	23 05.9
18 F	11 49 16	25 28 29	17 19 53	24 35 29	0 04.7	21 08.8	6 28.2	10 19.5	23 55.0	15 14.2	10 40.7	26 54.5	22 08.9	23 08.1
19 Sa	11 53 13	26 27 04	1♊48 50	8♊59 27	0 01.2	22 17.4	7 37.9	10 56.7	24 22.6	15 26.8	10 47.9	26 56.8	22 09.4	23 10.3
20 Su	11 57 09	27 25 42	16 06 59	23 11 12	29♋59.9	23 24.1	8 47.5	11 33.9	24 50.1	15 39.4	10 55.1	26 59.1	22 10.0	23 12.5
21 M	12 01 06	28 24 22	0♋11 57	7♋09 13	0♌00.0	24 28.6	9 57.1	12 11.0	25 17.7	15 52.1	11 02.4	27 01.4	22 10.5	23 14.7
22 Tu	12 05 03	29 23 05	14 02 59	20 53 21	0 00.8	25 30.9	11 06.6	12 48.1	25 45.2	16 04.8	11 09.6	27 03.7	22 11.1	23 17.0
23 W	12 08 59	0♎21 49	27 40 23	4♌24 13	0 00.9	26 30.7	12 16.0	13 25.1	26 12.8	16 17.5	11 16.9	27 06.1	22 11.8	23 19.2
24 Th	12 12 56	1 20 36	11♌04 58	17 42 43	29♋59.5	27 28.0	13 25.3	14 02.0	26 40.3	16 30.3	11 24.2	27 08.6	22 12.5	23 21.5
25 F	12 16 52	2 19 25	24 17 35	0♍49 35	29 55.6	28 22.4	14 34.6	14 38.9	27 07.9	16 43.0	11 31.5	27 11.1	22 13.2	23 23.7
26 Sa	12 20 49	3 18 16	7♍18 47	13 45 11	29 49.1	29 13.8	15 43.7	15 15.7	27 35.4	16 55.8	11 38.8	27 13.6	22 13.9	23 26.0
27 Su	12 24 45	4 17 09	20 08 48	26 29 36	29 39.9	0♏01.9	16 52.8	15 52.5	28 02.9	17 08.7	11 46.1	27 16.1	22 14.7	23 28.3
28 M	12 28 42	5 16 04	2♎47 36	9♎02 46	29 28.6	0 46.4	18 01.8	16 29.2	28 30.4	17 21.5	11 53.5	27 18.7	22 15.5	23 30.6
29 Tu	12 32 38	6 15 01	15 15 07	21 24 43	29 16.3	1 27.1	19 10.7	17 05.8	28 57.9	17 34.4	12 00.8	27 21.4	22 16.3	23 32.9
30 W	12 36 35	7 14 01	27 31 38	3♏35 59	29 03.9	2 03.5	20 19.5	17 42.4	29 25.4	17 47.3	12 08.2	27 24.0	22 17.2	23 35.2

LONGITUDE — October 1981

Day	Sid.Time	☉	0 hr ☽	Noon ☽	True ☊	☿	♀	♂	⚳	♃	♄	♅	♆	♇
1 Th	12 40 32	8♎13 02	9♏37 57	15♏37 45	28♋52.6	2♏35.4	21♏28.1	18♌18.9	29♍52.9	18♎00.2	12♎15.5	27♏26.7	22♐18.0	23♎37.6
2 F	12 44 28	9 12 05	21 35 42	27 32 06	28R 43.3	3 02.4	22 36.7	18 55.4	0♎20.3	18 13.1	12 22.9	27 29.5	22 19.0	23 39.9
3 Sa	12 48 25	10 11 09	3♐27 23	9♐22 00	28 36.6	3 23.9	23 45.2	19 31.7	0 47.8	18 26.0	12 30.3	27 32.3	22 19.9	23 42.2
4 Su	12 52 21	11 10 16	15 16 26	21 11 16	28 32.4	3 39.6	24 53.6	20 08.0	1 15.2	18 39.0	12 37.6	27 35.1	22 20.9	23 44.6
5 M	12 56 18	12 09 25	27 07 04	3♑04 30	28D 30.6	3R 49.1	26 01.9	20 44.3	1 42.7	18 52.0	12 45.0	27 37.9	22 21.9	23 47.0
6 Tu	13 00 14	13 08 35	9♑04 11	15 06 49	28 30.2	3 51.8	27 10.0	21 20.4	2 10.1	19 04.9	12 52.4	27 40.8	22 23.0	23 49.3
7 W	13 04 11	14 07 47	21 13 05	27 23 39	28R 30.4	3 47.3	28 18.0	21 56.6	2 37.5	19 17.9	12 59.7	27 43.7	22 24.1	23 51.7
8 Th	13 08 07	15 07 01	3♒39 09	10♒00 13	28 30.0	3 35.2	29 25.9	22 32.6	3 04.9	19 30.9	13 07.1	27 46.7	22 25.2	23 54.1
9 F	13 12 04	16 06 16	16 27 23	23 01 08	28 27.9	3 15.2	0♐33.7	23 08.6	3 32.2	19 43.9	13 14.5	27 49.6	22 26.3	23 56.5
10 Sa	13 16 01	17 05 34	29 41 46	6♓29 33	28 23.3	2 47.1	1 41.3	23 44.5	3 59.6	19 57.0	13 21.8	27 52.6	22 27.5	23 58.9
11 Su	13 19 57	18 04 53	13♓24 29	20 26 28	28 16.1	2 10.7	2 48.8	24 20.3	4 26.9	20 10.0	13 29.2	27 55.7	22 28.7	24 01.2
12 M	13 23 54	19 04 14	27 35 10	4♈50 00	28 06.5	1 26.3	3 56.1	24 56.0	4 54.2	20 23.0	13 36.5	27 58.7	22 29.9	24 03.6
13 Tu	13 27 50	20 03 37	12♈10 15	19 34 59	27 55.4	0 34.1	5 03.3	25 31.7	5 21.5	20 36.0	13 43.9	28 01.8	22 31.1	24 06.0
14 W	13 31 47	21 03 02	27 03 06	4♉33 25	27 43.9	29♎34.9	6 10.4	26 07.3	5 48.7	20 49.0	13 51.2	28 05.0	22 32.4	24 08.4
15 Th	13 35 43	22 02 29	12♉04 41	19 35 40	27 33.4	28 29.6	7 17.3	26 42.9	6 16.0	21 02.1	13 58.6	28 08.1	22 33.7	24 10.8
16 F	13 39 40	23 01 58	27 05 09	4♊32 05	27 25.0	27 19.7	8 24.0	27 18.4	6 43.2	21 15.1	14 05.9	28 11.3	22 35.1	24 13.2
17 Sa	13 43 36	24 01 30	11♊55 33	19 14 47	27 19.4	26 06.8	9 30.6	27 53.8	7 10.4	21 28.1	14 13.2	28 14.5	22 36.4	24 15.7
18 Su	13 47 33	25 01 04	26 29 14	3♋38 31	27 16.4	24 52.8	10 37.0	28 29.1	7 37.6	21 41.1	14 20.5	28 17.8	22 37.8	24 18.1
19 M	13 51 30	26 00 40	10♋42 27	17 40 58	27 15.4	23 39.9	11 43.3	29 04.4	8 04.7	21 54.2	14 27.8	28 21.0	22 39.2	24 20.5
20 Tu	13 55 26	27 00 19	24 34 08	1♌22 09	27 15.4	22 30.2	12 49.4	29 39.6	8 31.8	22 07.2	14 35.0	28 24.3	22 40.7	24 22.9
21 W	13 59 23	28 00 00	8♌05 16	14 43 45	27 14.9	21 25.9	13 55.3	0♍14.7	8 58.9	22 20.2	14 42.3	28 27.6	22 42.1	24 25.3
22 Th	14 03 19	28 59 43	21 17 58	27 48 14	27 12.7	20 28.9	15 01.0	0 49.7	9 26.0	22 33.2	14 49.5	28 31.0	22 43.6	24 27.7
23 F	14 07 16	29 59 28	4♍14 51	10♍38 10	27 07.9	19 40.8	16 06.6	1 24.7	9 53.1	22 46.2	14 56.7	28 34.3	22 45.2	24 30.1
24 Sa	14 11 12	0♏59 15	16 58 25	23 15 51	27 00.1	19 02.7	17 11.9	1 59.6	10 20.1	22 59.2	15 03.9	28 37.7	22 46.7	24 32.5
25 Su	14 15 09	1 59 05	29 30 42	5♎43 06	26 49.3	18 35.6	18 17.1	2 34.4	10 47.1	23 12.2	15 11.1	28 41.1	22 48.3	24 34.9
26 M	14 19 05	2 58 57	11♎53 14	18 01 12	26 36.3	18D 19.8	19 22.0	3 09.1	11 14.0	23 25.1	15 18.3	28 44.5	22 49.9	24 37.3
27 Tu	14 23 02	3 58 50	24 07 07	0♏11 05	26 21.9	18 15.5	20 26.8	3 43.7	11 40.9	23 38.1	15 25.4	28 48.0	22 51.5	24 39.6
28 W	14 26 58	4 58 46	6♏13 12	12 13 34	26 07.5	18 22.3	21 31.3	4 18.3	12 07.8	23 51.0	15 32.5	28 51.4	22 53.1	24 42.0
29 Th	14 30 55	5 58 44	18 12 20	24 09 40	25 54.1	18 39.9	22 35.5	4 52.7	12 34.7	24 03.9	15 39.6	28 54.9	22 54.8	24 44.4
30 F	14 34 52	6 58 43	0♐05 44	6♐00 48	25 42.9	19 07.5	23 39.6	5 27.1	13 01.5	24 16.8	15 46.7	28 58.4	22 56.5	24 46.8
31 Sa	14 38 48	7 58 44	11 55 08	17 49 04	25 34.4	19 44.3	24 43.4	6 01.3	13 28.3	24 29.7	15 53.7	29 01.9	22 58.2	24 49.1

Astro Data

	Dy Hr Mn
☽0S	1 8:39
☿0S	2 22:03
♆ D	3 11:07
☽0N	15 12:33
☉0S	23 3:05
☽0S	28 16:01
♄∠♅	3 22:29
☿ R	6 9:15
☽0N	12 22:20
♃⚹♆	23 9:49
☽0S	25 22:40
☿ D	27 9:09

Planet Ingress

	Dy Hr Mn
♂ ♌	2 1:52
☿ ♎	2 22:40
♀ ♏	12 22:51
☊ ♋R	20 7:19
☊ ♌	21 10:24
☉ ♎	23 3:05
☊ ♋R	24 6:27
☿ ♏	27 11:02
⚳ ♎	1 18:13
♀ ♐	9 0:04
☿ ♎R	14 2:09
♂ ♍	21 1:56
☉ ♏	23 12:13

Last Aspect / ☽ Ingress (September)

Last Aspect Dy Hr Mn		☽ Ingress Dy Hr Mn
2 6:33	♇ ☌	♏ 2 21:10
5 2:16	♅ ☌	♐ 5 9:24
7 8:43	♀ ⚹	♑ 7 21:48
10 1:36	♅ ⚹	♒ 10 7:59
12 13:47	♀ △	♓ 12 14:34
14 12:30	♅ △	♈ 14 17:55
16 8:06	♇ ☍	♉ 16 19:30
18 15:51	♅ ☍	♊ 18 20:59
20 19:47	☉ □	♋ 20 23:39
22 22:57	♅ △	♌ 23 4:08
25 7:09	☿ ⚹	♍ 25 10:29
27 13:29	♅ ⚹	♎ 27 18:40
29 16:12	♇ ☌	♏ 30 4:53

Last Aspect / ☽ Ingress (October)

Last Aspect Dy Hr Mn		☽ Ingress Dy Hr Mn
2 11:55	♅ ☌	♐ 2 16:59
4 17:12	♇ ⚹	♑ 5 5:49
7 13:55	♀ ⚹	♒ 7 17:01
9 20:42	♅ □	♓ 10 0:32
12 0:37	♅ △	♈ 12 4:01
14 4:33	☿ ☍	♉ 14 4:43
16 1:44	♅ ☍	♊ 16 4:41
18 2:58	♂ ⚹	♋ 18 5:52
20 6:44	♅ △	♌ 20 9:34
22 14:24	☉ ⚹	♍ 22 16:05
24 22:21	♅ ⚹	♎ 25 0:56
27 1:02	♇ ☌	♏ 27 11:38
29 21:39	♅ ☌	♐ 29 23:48

☽ Phases & Eclipses

Dy Hr Mn	
6 13:26	☽ 13♐51
14 3:09	○ 21♓13
20 19:47	☾ 27♊45
28 4:07	● 4♎57
6 7:45	☽ 12♑58
13 12:49	○ 20♈06
20 3:40	☾ 26♋40
27 20:13	● 4♏19

Astro Data

1 September 1981
Julian Day # 29829
SVP 5♓31'11"
GC 26♐35.0 ⚵ 22♌23.7
Eris 15♈14.2R ⚶ 4♏28.0
⚷ 22♉51.1R ⚴ 13♎36.3
☽ Mean ☊ 29♋37.1

1 October 1981
Julian Day # 29859
SVP 5♓31'09"
GC 26♐35.1 ⚵ 8♍09.6
Eris 14♈57.5R ⚶ 13♏17.0
⚷ 22♉16.6R ⚴ 28♎53.6
☽ Mean ☊ 28♋01.7

November 1981 LONGITUDE

Day	Sid.Time	☉	0 hr ☽	Noon ☽	True ☊	☿	♀	♂	⚳	♃	♄	♅	♆	♇
1 Su	14 42 45	8♏58 47	23♐43 00	29♐37 22	25♋28.9	20♎29.5	25♐46.9	6♍35.5	13♎55.0	24♎42.5	16♎00.7	29♏05.5	23♐00.0	24♎51.5
2 M	14 46 41	9 58 52	5♑32 38	11♑29 22	25R 26.1	21 22.2	26 50.2	7 09.6	14 21.7	24 55.4	16 07.7	29 09.0	23 01.7	24 53.8
3 Tu	14 50 38	10 58 58	17 28 07	23 29 31	25D 25.3	22 21.5	27 53.2	7 43.6	14 48.4	25 08.2	16 14.6	29 12.6	23 03.5	24 56.2
4 W	14 54 34	11 59 06	29 34 11	5♒42 49	25R 25.5	23 26.7	28 55.9	8 17.5	15 15.0	25 21.0	16 21.5	29 16.2	23 05.3	24 58.5
5 Th	14 58 31	12 59 15	11♒56 04	18 14 35	25 25.4	24 37.0	29 58.3	8 51.3	15 41.6	25 33.7	16 28.4	29 19.8	23 07.1	25 00.8
6 F	15 02 28	13 59 26	24 39 00	1♓09 53	25 24.2	25 51.6	1♑00.4	9 25.0	16 08.1	25 46.4	16 35.2	29 23.4	23 09.0	25 03.1
7 Sa	15 06 24	14 59 39	7♓47 45	14 32 59	25 20.8	27 10.0	2 02.1	9 58.6	16 34.6	25 59.1	16 42.0	29 27.0	23 10.8	25 05.4
8 Su	15 10 21	15 59 52	21 25 49	28 26 20	25 14.9	28 31.5	3 03.6	10 32.1	17 01.1	26 11.8	16 48.8	29 30.6	23 12.7	25 07.7
9 M	15 14 17	17 00 08	5♈34 25	12♈49 43	25 06.6	29 55.6	4 04.6	11 05.5	17 27.5	26 24.4	16 55.5	29 34.3	23 14.6	25 10.0
10 Tu	15 18 14	18 00 24	20 11 40	27 39 27	24 56.8	1♏22.0	5 05.3	11 38.9	17 53.8	26 37.0	17 02.2	29 37.9	23 16.5	25 12.3
11 W	15 22 10	19 00 43	5♉12 02	12♉48 11	24 46.4	2 50.2	6 05.7	12 12.1	18 20.1	26 49.6	17 08.9	29 41.6	23 18.5	25 14.5
12 Th	15 26 07	20 01 03	20 26 34	28 05 45	24 36.9	4 19.9	7 05.6	12 45.2	18 46.4	27 02.1	17 15.5	29 45.2	23 20.4	25 16.8
13 F	15 30 03	21 01 25	5♊44 19	13♊20 51	24 29.3	5 50.9	8 05.1	13 18.2	19 12.6	27 14.6	17 22.1	29 48.9	23 22.4	25 19.0
14 Sa	15 34 00	22 01 49	20 54 08	28 23 04	24 24.1	7 22.9	9 04.2	13 51.1	19 38.7	27 27.1	17 28.6	29 52.6	23 24.4	25 21.2
15 Su	15 37 57	23 02 14	5♋46 47	13♋04 36	24D 21.6	8 55.7	10 02.9	14 23.9	20 04.8	27 39.5	17 35.1	29 56.3	23 26.4	25 23.4
16 M	15 41 53	24 02 42	20 16 04	27 20 57	24 21.1	10 29.1	11 01.1	14 56.6	20 30.9	27 51.8	17 41.5	29 60.0	23 28.4	25 25.6
17 Tu	15 45 50	25 03 11	4♌19 11	11♌10 52	24 21.8	12 03.0	11 58.9	15 29.1	20 56.9	28 04.2	17 47.9	0♐03.7	23 30.4	25 27.8
18 W	15 49 46	26 03 42	17 56 12	24 35 31	24R 22.3	13 37.2	12 56.2	16 01.6	21 22.8	28 16.5	17 54.2	0 07.4	23 32.5	25 29.9
19 Th	15 53 43	27 04 15	1♍09 13	7♍37 42	24 21.8	15 11.7	13 53.0	16 33.9	21 48.7	28 28.7	18 00.5	0 11.1	23 34.6	25 32.1
20 F	15 57 39	28 04 50	14 01 27	20 20 54	24 19.2	16 46.4	14 49.2	17 06.1	22 14.5	28 40.9	18 06.8	0 14.8	23 36.6	25 34.2
21 Sa	16 01 36	29 05 26	26 36 31	2♎48 45	24 14.2	18 21.3	15 45.0	17 38.2	22 40.3	28 53.0	18 13.0	0 18.5	23 38.7	25 36.3
22 Su	16 05 32	0♐06 04	8♎57 58	15 04 35	24 06.8	19 56.2	16 40.2	18 10.2	23 06.0	29 05.1	18 19.1	0 22.3	23 40.8	25 38.4
23 M	16 09 29	1 06 44	21 08 54	27 11 15	23 57.5	21 31.1	17 34.7	18 42.1	23 31.6	29 17.2	18 25.2	0 25.9	23 43.0	25 40.4
24 Tu	16 13 25	2 07 25	3♏11 54	9♏11 06	23 47.1	23 06.0	18 28.7	19 13.8	23 57.2	29 29.1	18 31.2	0 29.7	23 45.1	25 42.5
25 W	16 17 22	3 08 07	15 09 03	21 05 58	23 36.6	24 40.8	19 22.1	19 45.4	24 22.7	29 41.1	18 37.2	0 33.4	23 47.2	25 44.5
26 Th	16 21 19	4 08 52	27 02 02	2♐57 27	23 26.8	26 15.6	20 14.8	20 16.8	24 48.1	29 52.9	18 43.1	0 37.1	23 49.4	25 46.5
27 F	16 25 15	5 09 37	8♐52 23	14 47 04	23 18.7	27 50.4	21 06.8	20 48.2	25 13.5	0♏04.8	18 49.0	0 40.8	23 51.6	25 48.5
28 Sa	16 29 12	6 10 24	20 41 41	26 36 29	23 12.8	29 25.1	21 58.2	21 19.3	25 38.8	0 16.5	18 54.8	0 44.5	23 53.7	25 50.5
29 Su	16 33 08	7 11 12	2♑31 45	8♑27 47	23 09.2	0♐59.7	22 48.7	21 50.4	26 04.0	0 28.2	19 00.5	0 48.2	23 55.9	25 52.4
30 M	16 37 05	8 12 01	14 24 55	20 23 33	23D 07.9	2 34.2	23 38.5	22 21.3	26 29.2	0 39.8	19 06.2	0 51.9	23 58.1	25 54.3

December 1981 LONGITUDE

Day	Sid.Time	☉	0 hr ☽	Noon ☽	True ☊	☿	♀	♂	⚳	♃	♄	♅	♆	♇
1 Tu	16 41 01	9♐12 51	26♑24 06	2♒27 01	23♋08.3	4♐08.6	24♑27.5	22♍52.0	26♎54.2	0♏51.4	19♎11.8	0♐55.6	24♐00.3	25♎56.2
2 W	16 44 58	10 13 42	8♒32 49	14 42 00	23 09.7	5 43.0	25 15.7	23 22.6	27 19.2	1 02.9	19 17.3	0 59.3	24 02.5	25 58.1
3 Th	16 48 55	11 14 34	20 55 07	27 12 44	23 11.2	7 17.3	26 03.0	23 53.0	27 44.1	1 14.3	19 22.8	1 03.0	24 04.8	26 00.0
4 F	16 52 51	12 15 26	3♓35 24	10♓03 39	23R 12.0	8 51.6	26 49.3	24 23.3	28 09.0	1 25.7	19 28.2	1 06.6	24 07.0	26 01.8
5 Sa	16 56 48	13 16 19	16 37 58	23 18 47	23 11.5	10 25.8	27 34.7	24 53.4	28 33.7	1 37.0	19 33.6	1 10.3	24 09.2	26 03.6
6 Su	17 00 44	14 17 13	0♈06 27	7♈01 10	23 09.3	12 00.0	28 19.1	25 23.4	28 58.4	1 48.2	19 38.8	1 13.9	24 11.4	26 05.4
7 M	17 04 41	15 18 08	14 03 02	21 11 57	23 05.5	13 34.2	29 02.4	25 53.2	29 23.0	1 59.3	19 44.0	1 17.6	24 13.7	26 07.1
8 Tu	17 08 37	16 19 04	28 27 37	5♉49 33	23 00.4	15 08.4	29 44.7	26 22.9	29 47.5	2 10.4	19 49.2	1 21.2	24 15.9	26 08.9
9 W	17 12 34	17 20 00	13♉17 01	20 49 06	22 54.8	16 42.7	0♒25.8	26 52.3	0♏11.9	2 21.3	19 54.2	1 24.8	24 18.2	26 10.6
10 Th	17 16 30	18 20 57	28 24 42	6♊02 36	22 49.6	18 16.9	1 05.7	27 21.7	0 36.2	2 32.3	19 59.2	1 28.4	24 20.4	26 12.3
11 F	17 20 27	19 21 55	13♊41 26	21 19 52	22 45.5	19 51.2	1 44.4	27 50.8	1 00.4	2 43.1	20 04.1	1 32.0	24 22.7	26 13.9
12 Sa	17 24 24	20 22 54	28 56 31	6♋30 09	22 42.9	21 25.6	2 21.8	28 19.8	1 24.6	2 53.8	20 09.0	1 35.6	24 25.0	26 15.5
13 Su	17 28 20	21 23 54	13♋59 39	21 24 01	22D 42.0	23 00.1	2 57.9	28 48.6	1 48.6	3 04.5	20 13.7	1 39.2	24 27.2	26 17.1
14 M	17 32 17	22 24 54	28 42 31	5♌54 35	22 42.5	24 34.6	3 32.6	29 17.2	2 12.6	3 15.1	20 18.4	1 42.7	24 29.5	26 18.7
15 Tu	17 36 13	23 25 56	12♌59 50	19 58 07	22 43.9	26 09.3	4 05.9	29 45.6	2 36.4	3 25.5	20 23.0	1 46.2	24 31.8	26 20.3
16 W	17 40 10	24 26 58	26 49 24	3♍33 50	22 45.5	27 44.1	4 37.7	0♎13.8	3 00.2	3 35.9	20 27.6	1 49.7	24 34.0	26 21.8
17 Th	17 44 06	25 28 01	10♍11 41	16 43 19	22R 46.7	29 19.0	5 07.9	0 41.8	3 23.8	3 46.3	20 32.0	1 53.2	24 36.3	26 23.3
18 F	17 48 03	26 29 06	23 09 08	29 29 38	22 47.0	0♑54.1	5 36.6	1 09.7	3 47.4	3 56.5	20 36.4	1 56.7	24 38.6	26 24.7
19 Sa	17 51 59	27 30 11	5♎45 20	11♎56 45	22 46.1	2 29.4	6 03.5	1 37.3	4 10.8	4 06.6	20 40.7	2 00.2	24 40.8	26 26.1
20 Su	17 55 56	28 31 17	18 04 26	24 08 53	22 44.0	4 04.8	6 28.8	2 04.7	4 34.2	4 16.6	20 44.9	2 03.6	24 43.1	26 27.5
21 M	17 59 53	29 32 23	0♏10 37	6♏10 08	22 40.8	5 40.3	6 52.2	2 31.9	4 57.4	4 26.5	20 49.0	2 07.0	24 45.4	26 28.9
22 Tu	18 03 49	0♑33 31	12 07 52	18 04 16	22 37.1	7 16.1	7 13.8	2 58.9	5 20.5	4 36.4	20 53.0	2 10.4	24 47.6	26 30.2
23 W	18 07 46	1 34 39	23 59 42	29 54 33	22 33.2	8 52.0	7 33.5	3 25.7	5 43.5	4 46.1	20 56.9	2 13.8	24 49.9	26 31.5
24 Th	18 11 42	2 35 47	5♐49 09	11♐43 47	22 29.7	10 28.1	7 51.2	3 52.2	6 06.4	4 55.7	21 00.8	2 17.1	24 52.1	26 32.8
25 F	18 15 39	3 36 56	17 38 45	23 34 18	22 26.9	12 04.3	8 06.8	4 18.5	6 29.2	5 05.2	21 04.6	2 20.5	24 54.4	26 34.1
26 Sa	18 19 35	4 38 06	29 30 41	5♑28 07	22 25.0	13 40.6	8 20.3	4 44.6	6 51.8	5 14.7	21 08.3	2 23.8	24 56.6	26 35.3
27 Su	18 23 32	5 39 16	11♑26 49	17 27 02	22D 24.1	15 17.1	8 31.6	5 10.4	7 14.3	5 24.0	21 11.8	2 27.0	24 58.9	26 36.5
28 M	18 27 28	6 40 26	23 28 58	29 32 53	22 24.2	16 53.6	8 40.7	5 36.0	7 36.7	5 33.1	21 15.3	2 30.3	25 01.1	26 37.6
29 Tu	18 31 25	7 41 36	5♒39 00	11♒47 36	22 25.0	18 30.2	8 47.5	6 01.3	7 59.0	5 42.2	21 18.7	2 33.5	25 03.4	26 38.7
30 W	18 35 22	8 42 46	17 58 58	24 13 23	22 26.2	20 06.8	8 51.9	6 26.4	8 21.1	5 51.2	21 22.0	2 36.7	25 05.6	26 39.8
31 Th	18 39 18	9 43 56	0♓31 11	6♓52 41	22 27.4	21 43.3	8R 54.0	6 51.1	8 43.1	6 00.0	21 25.3	2 39.8	25 07.8	26 40.8

Astro Data Dy Hr Mn	Planet Ingress Dy Hr Mn	Last Aspect Dy Hr Mn	☽ Ingress Dy Hr Mn	Last Aspect Dy Hr Mn	☽ Ingress Dy Hr Mn	☽ Phases & Eclipses Dy Hr Mn	Astro Data
♃☌♇ 2 8:27	♀ ♑ 5 12:39	1 3:26 ♀ ☌	♑ 1 12:46	30 23:02 ♇ □	♒ 1 7:09	5 1:09 ☽ 12♒32	1 November 1981
☽0N 9 9:40	☿ ♏ 9 13:14	3 23:21 ♅ ⚹	♒ 4 0:51	3 9:42 ♇ △	♓ 3 17:16	11 22:26 ○ 19♉27	Julian Day # 29890
⚳0S 11 12:53	♅ ♐ 16 12:05	6 8:44 ♅ □	♓ 6 9:52	5 20:00 ♀ ⚹	♈ 5 23:49	18 14:54 ☾ 26♌11	SVP 5♓31'05"
☽0S 22 5:07	☉ ♐ 22 9:36	8 13:49 ♅ △	♈ 8 14:39	8 1:36 ♀ □	♉ 8 2:31	26 14:38 ● 4♐16	GC 26♐35.1 ⚴ 23♍03.2
	♃ ♏ 27 2:19	10 10:19 ♃ ☍	♉ 10 15:44	9 21:53 ♂ △	♊ 10 2:30		Eris 14♈39.1R ⚵ 23♏24.5
♃⚺♅ 2 0:55	☿ ♐ 28 20:52	12 14:37 ♅ ☍	♊ 12 14:59	11 22:36 ♂ □	♋ 12 1:40	4 16:22 ☽ 12♓27	⚷ 20♉56.9R ⚶ 15♏17.1
☽0N 6 20:15		14 10:29 ♃ △	♋ 14 14:37	14 0:35 ♂ ⚹	♌ 14 2:08	11 8:41 ○ 19♊14	☽ Mean ☊ 26♋23.2
☽0S 19 12:06	♀ ♒ 8 20:52	16 12:54 ♃ □	♌ 16 16:32	16 0:15 ☿ △	♍ 16 5:38	18 5:47 ☾ 26♍13	
♂0S 27 17:06	⚳ ♏ 9 0:19	18 18:49 ♃ ⚹	♍ 18 21:53	18 5:47 ☉ □	♎ 18 12:58	26 10:10 ● 4♑33	1 December 1981
♀R 31 19:45	♂ ♎ 16 0:14	21 4:09 ☉ ⚹	♎ 21 6:33	20 21:30 ☉ ⚹	♏ 20 23:39		Julian Day # 29920
	☿ ♑ 17 22:21	23 16:15 ♃ ☌	♏ 23 17:36	21 13:27 ♀ □	♐ 23 12:11		SVP 5♓31'01"
	☉ ♑ 21 22:51	25 20:21 ☿ ☌	♐ 26 6:00	25 18:04 ♇ ⚹	♑ 26 0:59		GC 26♐35.2 ⚴ 5♎37.5
		28 10:26 ♇ ⚹	♑ 28 18:53	28 6:13 ♇ □	♒ 28 12:53		Eris 14♈25.4R ⚵ 3♐38.5
				30 16:40 ♇ △	♓ 30 23:01		⚷ 19♉25.7R ⚶ 1♐26.1
							☽ Mean ☊ 24♋47.9

LONGITUDE

January 1982

Day	Sid.Time	☉	0 hr ☽	Noon ☽	True ☊	☿	♀	♂	⚳	♃	♄	♅	♆	♇
1 F	18 43 15	10♑45 06	13♓18 13	19♓48 06	22♋28.5	23♑19.6	8♒53.5	7♎15.7	9♏05.0	6♏08.8	21♎28.4	2♐43.0	25♐10.0	26♎41.8
2 Sa	18 47 11	11 46 15	26 22 41	3♈02 13	22R 29.1	24 55.7	8R 50.6	7 39.9	9 26.7	6 17.4	21 31.4	2 46.1	25 12.2	26 42.8
3 Su	18 51 08	12 47 24	9♈46 58	16 37 08	22 29.2	26 31.4	8 45.1	8 03.9	9 48.3	6 25.9	21 34.3	2 49.2	25 14.4	26 43.8
4 M	18 55 04	13 48 33	23 32 48	0♉34 01	22 28.8	28 06.6	8 37.2	8 27.5	10 09.8	6 34.2	21 37.1	2 52.2	25 16.6	26 44.7
5 Tu	18 59 01	14 49 42	7♉40 39	14 52 30	22 28.2	29 41.1	8 26.6	8 50.9	10 31.1	6 42.5	21 39.9	2 55.2	25 18.7	26 45.5
6 W	19 02 57	15 50 50	22 09 10	29 30 08	22 27.4	1♒14.8	8 13.6	9 14.0	10 52.2	6 50.6	21 42.5	2 58.2	25 20.9	26 46.4
7 Th	19 06 54	16 51 58	6♊54 45	14♊22 12	22 26.7	2 47.4	7 58.1	9 36.8	11 13.2	6 58.6	21 45.0	3 01.1	25 23.1	26 47.2
8 F	19 10 51	17 53 06	21 51 33	29 21 49	22 26.2	4 18.7	7 40.1	9 59.3	11 34.1	7 06.4	21 47.5	3 04.0	25 25.2	26 48.0
9 Sa	19 14 47	18 54 14	6♋51 54	14♋20 44	22D 26.0	5 48.3	7 19.7	10 21.5	11 54.8	7 14.2	21 49.8	3 06.9	25 27.3	26 48.7
10 Su	19 18 44	19 55 21	21 47 16	29 10 28	22 25.9	7 15.9	6 57.0	10 43.3	12 15.4	7 21.8	21 52.1	3 09.8	25 29.4	26 49.4
11 M	19 22 40	20 56 28	6♌29 27	13♌43 25	22 26.0	8 41.0	6 32.2	11 04.8	12 35.7	7 29.2	21 54.2	3 12.6	25 31.5	26 50.1
12 Tu	19 26 37	21 57 34	20 51 47	27 54 01	22R 26.1	10 03.2	6 05.2	11 26.0	12 56.0	7 36.6	21 56.2	3 15.3	25 33.6	26 50.7
13 W	19 30 33	22 58 41	4♍49 51	11♍39 05	22 26.1	11 22.0	5 36.4	11 46.9	13 16.0	7 43.7	21 58.2	3 18.1	25 35.7	26 51.3
14 Th	19 34 30	23 59 47	18 21 45	24 57 56	22 26.0	12 36.7	5 05.7	12 07.3	13 35.9	7 50.8	22 00.0	3 20.8	25 37.8	26 51.9
15 F	19 38 27	25 00 53	1♎27 54	7♎51 59	22 25.8	13 46.6	4 33.6	12 27.5	13 55.7	7 57.7	22 01.7	3 23.4	25 39.8	26 52.4
16 Sa	19 42 23	26 01 59	14 10 37	20 24 16	22D 25.7	14 51.1	4 00.0	12 47.2	14 15.2	8 04.5	22 03.3	3 26.1	25 41.8	26 52.9
17 Su	19 46 20	27 03 04	26 33 28	2♏38 47	22 25.7	15 49.2	3 25.3	13 06.6	14 34.6	8 11.1	22 04.8	3 28.6	25 43.8	26 53.3
18 M	19 50 16	28 04 10	8♏40 49	14 40 08	22 25.9	16 40.2	2 49.6	13 25.6	14 53.8	8 17.5	22 06.2	3 31.2	25 45.8	26 53.7
19 Tu	19 54 13	29 05 15	20 37 19	26 32 59	22 26.5	17 23.1	2 13.3	13 44.2	15 12.8	8 23.9	22 07.5	3 33.7	25 47.8	26 54.1
20 W	19 58 09	0♒06 19	2♐27 39	8♐21 52	22 27.3	17 57.2	1 36.6	14 02.4	15 31.7	8 30.0	22 08.7	3 36.1	25 49.8	26 54.4
21 Th	20 02 06	1 07 24	14 16 08	20 10 57	22 28.2	18 21.5	0 59.6	14 20.1	15 50.3	8 36.1	22 09.8	3 38.6	25 51.7	26 54.8
22 F	20 06 02	2 08 28	26 06 43	2♑03 52	22 29.1	18R 35.4	0 22.8	14 37.5	16 08.8	8 41.9	22 10.8	3 40.9	25 53.7	26 55.0
23 Sa	20 09 59	3 09 31	8♑02 44	14 03 39	22R 29.7	18 38.3	29♑46.3	14 54.4	16 27.0	8 47.6	22 11.7	3 43.3	25 55.6	26 55.3
24 Su	20 13 56	4 10 34	20 06 54	26 12 43	22 29.8	18 29.7	29 10.3	15 10.9	16 45.1	8 53.2	22 12.5	3 45.6	25 57.5	26 55.5
25 M	20 17 52	5 11 35	2♒21 17	8♒32 47	22 29.3	18 09.6	28 35.2	15 26.9	17 02.9	8 58.6	22 13.1	3 47.8	25 59.3	26 55.6
26 Tu	20 21 49	6 12 36	14 47 21	21 05 04	22 28.0	17 38.1	28 01.1	15 42.4	17 20.6	9 03.8	22 13.7	3 50.0	26 01.2	26 55.7
27 W	20 25 45	7 13 36	27 26 01	3♓50 17	22 26.2	16 56.0	27 28.3	15 57.5	17 38.0	9 08.9	22 14.1	3 52.2	26 03.0	26 55.8
28 Th	20 29 42	8 14 35	10♓17 52	16 43 49	22 23.8	16 04.2	26 57.0	16 12.1	17 55.2	9 13.8	22 14.5	3 54.3	26 04.8	26R 55.9
29 F	20 33 38	9 15 33	23 23 09	0♈00 52	22 21.4	15 04.1	26 27.3	16 26.1	18 12.2	9 18.5	22 14.7	3 56.3	26 06.6	26 55.9
30 Sa	20 37 35	10 16 30	6♈42 00	13 26 32	22 19.3	13 57.3	25 59.4	16 39.7	18 29.0	9 23.1	22R 14.8	3 58.4	26 08.4	26 55.9
31 Su	20 41 31	11 17 25	20 14 27	27 05 46	22 17.8	12 46.0	25 33.5	16 52.8	18 45.6	9 27.5	22 14.8	4 00.3	26 10.1	26 55.8

LONGITUDE

February 1982

Day	Sid.Time	☉	0 hr ☽	Noon ☽	True ☊	☿	♀	♂	⚳	♃	♄	♅	♆	♇
1 M	20 45 28	12♒18 19	4♉00 25	10♉58 22	22♋17.2	11♒32.3	25♑09.7	17♎05.4	19♏01.9	9♏31.7	22♎14.8	4♐02.3	26♐11.8	26♎55.7
2 Tu	20 49 24	13 19 12	17 59 31	25 03 43	22D 17.6	10R 18.2	24R 48.0	17 17.4	19 18.0	9 35.8	22R 14.6	4 04.1	26 13.5	26R 55.6
3 W	20 53 21	14 20 03	2♊10 48	9♊20 31	22 18.7	9 05.8	24 28.7	17 28.9	19 33.9	9 39.7	22 14.3	4 06.0	26 15.2	26 55.4
4 Th	20 57 18	15 20 53	16 32 32	23 46 29	22 20.2	7 57.1	24 11.8	17 39.8	19 49.5	9 43.4	22 13.9	4 07.8	26 16.9	26 55.2
5 F	21 01 14	16 21 42	1♋01 52	8♋18 10	22R 21.5	6 53.5	23 57.2	17 50.2	20 04.9	9 46.9	22 13.3	4 09.5	26 18.5	26 55.0
6 Sa	21 05 11	17 22 29	15 34 45	22 50 57	22 22.0	5 56.3	23 45.2	18 00.0	20 20.0	9 50.3	22 12.7	4 11.2	26 20.1	26 54.7
7 Su	21 09 07	18 23 15	0♌06 04	7♌19 21	22 21.3	5 06.4	23 35.6	18 09.2	20 34.9	9 53.5	22 12.0	4 12.8	26 21.7	26 54.4
8 M	21 13 04	19 24 00	14 30 05	21 37 33	22 19.1	4 24.4	23 28.5	18 17.8	20 49.6	9 56.5	22 11.2	4 14.4	26 23.2	26 54.1
9 Tu	21 17 00	20 24 43	28 41 07	5♍40 12	22 15.7	3 50.5	23 23.9	18 25.8	21 04.0	9 59.3	22 10.3	4 15.9	26 24.7	26 53.7
10 W	21 20 57	21 25 25	12♍34 20	19 23 09	22 11.1	3 24.8	23D 21.8	18 33.3	21 18.1	10 02.0	22 09.2	4 17.4	26 26.2	26 53.3
11 Th	21 24 54	22 26 05	26 06 23	2♎43 55	22 06.1	3 07.3	23 22.1	18 40.0	21 32.0	10 04.5	22 08.1	4 18.8	26 27.7	26 52.8
12 F	21 28 50	23 26 45	9♎15 44	15 41 59	22 01.3	2D 57.5	23 24.9	18 46.2	21 45.6	10 06.8	22 06.8	4 20.2	26 29.2	26 52.4
13 Sa	21 32 47	24 27 23	22 02 51	28 18 40	21 57.3	2 55.3	23 30.0	18 51.6	21 58.9	10 08.9	22 05.5	4 21.6	26 30.6	26 51.9
14 Su	21 36 43	25 28 01	4♏29 51	10♏36 51	21 54.6	3 00.2	23 37.5	18 56.5	22 11.9	10 10.8	22 04.1	4 22.8	26 32.0	26 51.3
15 M	21 40 40	26 28 37	16 40 13	22 40 31	21D 53.3	3 11.7	23 47.2	19 00.6	22 24.7	10 12.5	22 02.5	4 24.1	26 33.3	26 50.7
16 Tu	21 44 36	27 29 12	28 38 22	4♐34 24	21 53.5	3 29.5	23 59.1	19 04.1	22 37.2	10 14.1	22 00.9	4 25.2	26 34.7	26 50.1
17 W	21 48 33	28 29 46	10♐29 17	16 23 37	21 54.8	3 53.0	24 13.2	19 06.8	22 49.4	10 15.5	21 59.1	4 26.4	26 36.0	26 49.5
18 Th	21 52 29	29 30 18	22 18 05	28 13 17	21 56.6	4 21.8	24 29.3	19 08.9	23 01.3	10 16.6	21 57.3	4 27.4	26 37.3	26 48.8
19 F	21 56 26	0♓30 49	4♑09 49	10♑08 16	21R 58.2	4 55.6	24 47.5	19 10.2	23 12.9	10 17.6	21 55.3	4 28.4	26 38.5	26 48.1
20 Sa	22 00 22	1 31 19	16 09 08	22 12 54	21 58.8	5 33.9	25 07.6	19R 10.8	23 24.2	10 18.4	21 53.3	4 29.4	26 39.7	26 47.4
21 Su	22 04 19	2 31 48	28 20 00	4♒30 46	21 57.9	6 16.4	25 29.6	19 10.6	23 35.2	10 19.1	21 51.2	4 30.3	26 40.9	26 46.6
22 M	22 08 16	3 32 15	10♒45 30	17 04 25	21 55.1	7 02.8	25 53.3	19 09.7	23 45.9	10 19.5	21 49.0	4 31.2	26 42.1	26 45.8
23 Tu	22 12 12	4 32 40	23 27 38	29 55 12	21 50.2	7 52.7	26 18.8	19 08.1	23 56.3	10R 19.7	21 46.6	4 32.0	26 43.2	26 45.0
24 W	22 16 09	5 33 04	6♓27 05	13♓03 11	21 43.6	8 46.0	26 46.0	19 05.7	24 06.3	10 19.8	21 44.2	4 32.7	26 44.3	26 44.1
25 Th	22 20 05	6 33 26	19 43 17	26 27 09	21 35.8	9 42.2	27 14.8	19 02.5	24 16.0	10 19.6	21 41.7	4 33.4	26 45.4	26 43.2
26 F	22 24 02	7 33 46	3♈14 29	10♈04 56	21 27.8	10 41.4	27 45.2	18 58.5	24 25.4	10 19.3	21 39.1	4 34.1	26 46.4	26 42.3
27 Sa	22 27 58	8 34 04	16 58 08	23 53 44	21 20.5	11 43.2	28 17.0	18 53.8	24 34.5	10 18.8	21 36.4	4 34.6	26 47.4	26 41.3
28 Su	22 31 55	9 34 20	0♉51 21	7♉50 38	21 14.6	12 47.4	28 50.3	18 48.3	24 43.2	10 18.1	21 33.7	4 35.2	26 48.4	26 40.3

Astro Data

	Dy Hr Mn
☽0N	3 4:08
☽0S	15 20:07
☿R	23 6:01
♇R	29 8:18
☽0N	30 9:33
♄R	31 3:46
♀D	10 20:38
☽0S	12 5:00
☿D	13 7:17
♂R	20 19:13
♃R	24 5:41
♆⚹♇	24 9:04
☽0N	26 14:58

Planet Ingress

	Dy Hr Mn
☿ ♒	5 16:49
☉ ♒	20 9:31
♀ ♑R	23 2:56
☉ ♓	18 23:47

Last Aspect / ☽ Ingress

Last Aspect Dy Hr Mn		☽ Ingress Dy Hr Mn
1 21:50 ♆ □	♈	2 6:33
4 7:17 ☿ □	♉	4 11:02
5 11:55 ☉ △	♊	6 12:49
8 7:54 ♇ △	♋	8 13:01
10 8:10 ♇ □	♌	10 13:21
12 10:11 ♇ ⚹	♍	12 15:37
14 13:13 ♆ □	♎	14 21:17
17 0:39 ♇ ☌	♏	17 6:46
19 17:38 ☉ ⚹	♐	19 19:00
22 1:37 ♇ ⚹	♑	22 7:51
24 17:32 ♀ ☌	♒	24 19:25
26 23:03 ♇ △	♓	27 4:49
29 5:48 ♀ ⚹	♈	29 11:58
31 11:43 ♇ ☍	♉	31 17:03

Last Aspect / ☽ Ingress

Last Aspect Dy Hr Mn		☽ Ingress Dy Hr Mn
2 11:34 ♀ △	♊	2 20:20
4 17:12 ♇ △	♋	4 22:18
6 18:43 ♇ □	♌	6 23:50
8 20:57 ♇ ⚹	♍	9 2:15
11 0:37 ♆ □	♎	11 7:02
13 9:13 ♇ ☌	♏	13 15:16
15 20:21 ☉ □	♐	16 2:45
18 14:50 ☉ ⚹	♑	18 15:36
20 20:58 ♇ □	♒	21 3:15
23 6:08 ♇ △	♓	23 12:09
25 13:28 ♀ ⚹	♈	25 18:17
27 19:53 ♀ □	♉	27 22:32

☽ Phases & Eclipses

Dy Hr Mn	
3 4:45	☽ 12♈29
9 19:53	○ 19♋14
9 19:56	T 1.331
16 23:58	☾ 26♎32
25 4:56	● 4♒54
25 4:41:59	P 0.566
1 14:28	☽ 12♉25
8 7:57	○ 19♌14
15 20:21	☾ 26♏50
23 21:13	● 4♓56

Astro Data

1 January 1982
Julian Day # 29951
SVP 5♓30'55"
GC 26♐35.3 ⚳ 15♎45.5
Eris 14♈19.9R ⚵ 14♐08.5
⚷ 18♉14.3R ⚶ 18♐06.3
☽ Mean ☊ 23♋09.4

1 February 1982
Julian Day # 29982
SVP 5♓30'51"
GC 26♐35.3 ⚳ 21♎12.8
Eris 14♈25.0 ⚵ 23♐58.0
⚷ 17♉54.8 ⚶ 4♑23.5
☽ Mean ☊ 21♋31.0

March 1982 — LONGITUDE

Day	Sid.Time	☉	0 hr ☽	Noon ☽	True ☊	☿	♀	♂	⚳	♃	♄	♅	♆	♇
1 M	22 35 51	10♓34 35	14♉51 16	21♉52 58	21♋10.9	13♒53.9	29♑24.9	18♎42.0	24♏51.6	10♏17.2	21♎30.8	4♐35.7	26♐49.4	26♎39.3
2 Tu	22 39 48	11 34 47	28 55 30	5♊58 40	21D 09.3	15 02.6	0♒00.9	18R 35.0	24 59.6	10R 16.1	21R 27.9	4 36.1	26 50.3	26R 38.3
3 W	22 43 45	12 34 57	13♊02 16	20 06 08	21 09.3	16 13.4	0 38.1	18 27.2	25 07.3	10 14.8	21 24.9	4 36.4	26 51.2	26 37.2
4 Th	22 47 41	13 35 06	27 10 09	4♋14 09	21 10.3	17 26.0	1 16.6	18 18.6	25 14.6	10 13.3	21 21.8	4 36.8	26 52.0	26 36.1
5 F	22 51 38	14 35 12	11♋17 59	18 21 27	21R 11.0	18 40.5	1 56.2	18 09.2	25 21.6	10 11.7	21 18.6	4 37.0	26 52.8	26 35.0
6 Sa	22 55 34	15 35 16	25 24 19	2♌26 21	21 10.5	19 56.8	2 37.0	17 59.1	25 28.2	10 09.8	21 15.4	4 37.2	26 53.6	26 33.9
7 Su	22 59 31	16 35 17	9♌27 13	16 26 34	21 07.9	21 14.7	3 18.8	17 48.2	25 34.5	10 07.8	21 12.0	4 37.4	26 54.4	26 32.7
8 M	23 03 27	17 35 17	23 24 01	0♍19 10	21 02.7	22 34.2	4 01.7	17 36.6	25 40.4	10 05.6	21 08.6	4 37.5	26 55.1	26 31.5
9 Tu	23 07 24	18 35 15	7♍11 35	14 00 50	20 55.0	23 55.2	4 45.6	17 24.2	25 45.9	10 03.2	21 05.2	4R 37.5	26 55.8	26 30.3
10 W	23 11 20	19 35 10	20 46 33	27 28 21	20 45.3	25 17.7	5 30.5	17 11.0	25 51.1	10 00.7	21 01.6	4 37.5	26 56.5	26 29.1
11 Th	23 15 17	20 35 04	4♎05 58	10♎39 09	20 34.6	26 41.7	6 16.3	16 57.2	25 55.9	9 57.9	20 58.0	4 37.5	26 57.1	26 27.8
12 F	23 19 14	21 34 56	17 07 47	23 31 49	20 23.8	28 07.0	7 03.0	16 42.6	26 00.3	9 55.0	20 54.3	4 37.3	26 57.7	26 26.5
13 Sa	23 23 10	22 34 47	29 51 17	6♏06 21	20 14.2	29 33.8	7 50.6	16 27.4	26 04.3	9 51.9	20 50.6	4 37.2	26 58.2	26 25.2
14 Su	23 27 07	23 34 35	12♏17 14	18 24 15	20 06.4	1♓01.9	8 39.0	16 11.4	26 07.9	9 48.6	20 46.8	4 37.0	26 58.8	26 23.9
15 M	23 31 03	24 34 22	24 27 48	0♐28 23	20 01.0	2 31.3	9 28.2	15 54.8	26 11.2	9 45.2	20 42.9	4 36.7	26 59.2	26 22.5
16 Tu	23 35 00	25 34 07	6♐26 29	12 22 43	19 58.0	4 02.0	10 18.1	15 37.5	26 14.0	9 41.6	20 39.0	4 36.4	26 59.7	26 21.2
17 W	23 38 56	26 33 51	18 17 41	24 12 03	19D 57.0	5 34.1	11 08.8	15 19.6	26 16.5	9 37.8	20 35.0	4 36.0	27 00.1	26 19.8
18 Th	23 42 53	27 33 33	0♑06 30	6♑01 41	19 57.2	7 07.4	12 00.2	15 01.1	26 18.5	9 33.8	20 31.0	4 35.5	27 00.5	26 18.4
19 F	23 46 49	28 33 13	11 58 20	17 57 06	19R 57.6	8 42.0	12 52.3	14 42.0	26 20.2	9 29.7	20 26.9	4 35.1	27 00.9	26 16.9
20 Sa	23 50 46	29 32 51	23 58 38	0♒03 35	19 57.2	10 17.9	13 45.0	14 22.4	26 21.4	9 25.4	20 22.8	4 34.5	27 01.2	26 15.5
21 Su	23 54 43	0♈32 27	6♒12 31	12 25 56	19 54.9	11 55.0	14 38.4	14 02.2	26 22.3	9 21.0	20 18.6	4 33.9	27 01.5	26 14.0
22 M	23 58 39	1 32 02	18 44 17	25 07 56	19 50.2	13 33.4	15 32.3	13 41.6	26R 22.7	9 16.4	20 14.4	4 33.3	27 01.8	26 12.6
23 Tu	0 02 36	2 31 35	1♓37 06	8♓11 56	19 42.8	15 13.2	16 26.8	13 20.5	26 22.7	9 11.6	20 10.1	4 32.6	27 02.0	26 11.1
24 W	0 06 32	3 31 06	14 52 26	21 38 28	19 32.9	16 54.2	17 21.9	12 59.0	26 22.3	9 06.7	20 05.8	4 31.9	27 02.2	26 09.5
25 Th	0 10 29	4 30 34	28 29 44	5♈25 52	19 21.5	18 36.5	18 17.5	12 37.2	26 21.5	9 01.6	20 01.4	4 31.1	27 02.3	26 08.0
26 F	0 14 25	5 30 01	12♈26 21	19 30 32	19 09.5	20 20.1	19 13.5	12 15.0	26 20.3	8 56.4	19 57.0	4 30.2	27 02.5	26 06.5
27 Sa	0 18 22	6 29 26	26 37 44	3♉47 13	18 58.4	22 05.1	20 10.1	11 52.5	26 18.7	8 51.0	19 52.6	4 29.3	27 02.5	26 04.9
28 Su	0 22 18	7 28 49	10♉58 15	18 10 04	18 49.2	23 51.4	21 07.2	11 29.8	26 16.6	8 45.5	19 48.2	4 28.4	27 02.6	26 03.3
29 M	0 26 15	8 28 09	25 22 01	2♊33 29	18 42.7	25 39.0	22 04.7	11 06.8	26 14.2	8 39.9	19 43.7	4 27.4	27R 02.6	26 01.7
30 Tu	0 30 11	9 27 27	9♊43 56	16 52 57	18 39.0	27 28.0	23 02.6	10 43.8	26 11.3	8 34.1	19 39.2	4 26.4	27 02.6	26 00.2
31 W	0 34 08	10 26 43	24 00 12	1♋05 28	18D 37.5	29 18.3	24 01.0	10 20.6	26 08.0	8 28.2	19 34.6	4 25.3	27 02.6	25 58.5

April 1982 — LONGITUDE

Day	Sid.Time	☉	0 hr ☽	Noon ☽	True ☊	☿	♀	♂	⚳	♃	♄	♅	♆	♇
1 Th	0 38 05	11♈25 56	8♋08 35	15♋09 27	18♋37.4	1♈10.0	24♒59.7	9♎57.4	26♏04.4	8♏22.2	19♎30.1	4♐24.2	27♐02.5	25♎56.9
2 F	0 42 01	12 25 08	22 08 03	29 04 23	18R 37.2	3 03.1	25 58.9	9R 34.1	26R 00.3	8R 16.0	19R 25.5	4R 23.0	27R 02.4	25R 55.3
3 Sa	0 45 58	13 24 16	5♌58 27	12♌50 16	18 35.6	4 57.6	26 58.4	9 10.9	25 55.8	8 09.8	19 20.9	4 21.8	27 02.2	25 53.7
4 Su	0 49 54	14 23 23	19 39 48	26 27 02	18 31.8	6 53.4	27 58.3	8 47.7	25 51.0	8 03.4	19 16.3	4 20.5	27 02.1	25 52.0
5 M	0 53 51	15 22 27	3♍11 55	9♍54 21	18 25.0	8 50.6	28 58.5	8 24.7	25 45.7	7 56.9	19 11.7	4 19.2	27 01.9	25 50.4
6 Tu	0 57 47	16 21 29	16 34 12	23 11 19	18 15.3	10 49.1	29 59.1	8 01.8	25 40.0	7 50.3	19 07.1	4 17.8	27 01.6	25 48.7
7 W	1 01 44	17 20 28	29 45 33	6♎16 45	18 03.3	12 48.9	1♓00.1	7 39.1	25 34.0	7 43.6	19 02.5	4 16.4	27 01.3	25 47.1
8 Th	1 05 40	18 19 26	12♎44 44	19 09 23	17 50.0	14 49.9	2 01.3	7 16.7	25 27.6	7 36.8	18 57.8	4 15.0	27 01.0	25 45.4
9 F	1 09 37	19 18 21	25 30 36	1♏48 20	17 36.6	16 52.2	3 02.9	6 54.5	25 20.8	7 30.0	18 53.2	4 13.5	27 00.7	25 43.7
10 Sa	1 13 34	20 17 15	8♏02 35	14 13 24	17 24.3	18 55.5	4 04.8	6 32.7	25 13.6	7 23.0	18 48.6	4 12.0	27 00.3	25 42.0
11 Su	1 17 30	21 16 07	20 20 56	26 25 24	17 14.0	20 59.7	5 06.9	6 11.2	25 06.1	7 16.0	18 44.0	4 10.4	26 59.9	25 40.3
12 M	1 21 27	22 14 57	2♐27 02	8♐26 13	17 06.3	23 04.9	6 09.4	5 50.1	24 58.2	7 08.9	18 39.3	4 08.8	26 59.5	25 38.6
13 Tu	1 25 23	23 13 45	14 23 19	20 18 50	17 01.4	25 10.7	7 12.1	5 29.4	24 49.9	7 01.7	18 34.7	4 07.2	26 59.0	25 37.0
14 W	1 29 20	24 12 32	26 13 16	2♑07 12	16 59.0	27 17.0	8 15.1	5 09.3	24 41.3	6 54.4	18 30.1	4 05.5	26 58.5	25 35.3
15 Th	1 33 16	25 11 17	8♑01 15	13 56 03	16D 58.3	29 23.6	9 18.4	4 49.6	24 32.4	6 47.1	18 25.5	4 03.8	26 58.0	25 33.6
16 F	1 37 13	26 10 00	19 52 17	25 50 37	16R 58.4	1♉30.3	10 21.9	4 30.4	24 23.1	6 39.7	18 20.9	4 02.0	26 57.5	25 31.9
17 Sa	1 41 09	27 08 41	1♒51 47	7♒56 26	16 58.0	3 36.7	11 25.6	4 11.8	24 13.5	6 32.3	18 16.4	4 00.2	26 56.9	25 30.2
18 Su	1 45 06	28 07 21	14 05 16	20 18 53	16 56.2	5 42.6	12 29.6	3 53.8	24 03.6	6 24.8	18 11.9	3 58.4	26 56.3	25 28.5
19 M	1 49 03	29 05 59	26 37 51	3♓02 42	16 52.2	7 47.7	13 33.8	3 36.5	23 53.4	6 17.3	18 07.3	3 56.5	26 55.6	25 26.8
20 Tu	1 52 59	0♉04 35	9♓33 48	16 11 28	16 45.6	9 51.7	14 38.2	3 19.7	23 42.9	6 09.7	18 02.8	3 54.6	26 54.9	25 25.1
21 W	1 56 56	1 03 09	22 55 49	29 46 52	16 36.7	11 54.2	15 42.8	3 03.7	23 32.1	6 02.1	17 58.4	3 52.7	26 54.2	25 23.4
22 Th	2 00 52	2 01 42	6♈44 25	13♈48 06	16 26.1	13 54.9	16 47.6	2 48.3	23 21.0	5 54.5	17 53.9	3 50.7	26 53.5	25 21.7
23 F	2 04 49	3 00 13	20 57 24	28 11 37	16 14.9	15 53.4	17 52.6	2 33.6	23 09.7	5 46.8	17 49.5	3 48.7	26 52.7	25 20.1
24 Sa	2 08 45	3 58 42	5♉29 53	12♉51 15	16 04.4	17 49.6	18 57.8	2 19.7	22 58.1	5 39.2	17 45.2	3 46.7	26 51.9	25 18.4
25 Su	2 12 42	4 57 09	20 14 42	27 39 12	15 55.6	19 43.1	20 03.2	2 06.5	22 46.3	5 31.5	17 40.8	3 44.7	26 51.1	25 16.7
26 M	2 16 38	5 55 35	5♊03 41	12♊27 13	15 49.4	21 33.6	21 08.8	1 54.1	22 34.3	5 23.8	17 36.6	3 42.6	26 50.3	25 15.1
27 Tu	2 20 35	6 53 58	19 48 55	27 08 03	15 45.9	23 20.9	22 14.5	1 42.5	22 22.1	5 16.2	17 32.3	3 40.5	26 49.4	25 13.4
28 W	2 24 32	7 52 19	4♋24 02	11♋36 23	15D 44.7	25 04.8	23 20.4	1 31.6	22 09.7	5 08.5	17 28.1	3 38.3	26 48.5	25 11.8
29 Th	2 28 28	8 50 38	18 44 48	25 49 05	15 44.8	26 45.1	24 26.4	1 21.6	21 57.1	5 00.8	17 23.9	3 36.1	26 47.6	25 10.1
30 F	2 32 25	9 48 55	2♌49 10	9♌45 02	15R 45.1	28 21.7	25 32.6	1 12.3	21 44.3	4 53.2	17 19.8	3 34.0	26 46.6	25 08.5

Astro Data	Dy Hr Mn
♅ R	9 19:41
☽ 0S	11 13:52
☉ 0N	20 22:56
⚳ R	23 1:04
☽ 0N	25 22:32
♆ R	29 16:38
☿ 0N	3 3:12
♄∠♅	3 5:59
☽ 0S	7 21:48
♂ 0N	11 20:12
☽ 0N	22 8:23

Planet Ingress		Dy Hr Mn
♀	♒	2 11:25
☿	♓	13 19:11
☉	♈	20 22:56
☿	♈	31 20:59
♀	♓	6 12:20
☿	♉	15 18:54
☉	♉	20 10:07

Last Aspect Dy Hr Mn			☽ Ingress	Dy Hr Mn
2 1:24	♀	△	♊	2 1:50
3 23:28	♆	☍	♋	4 4:48
6 1:59	♇	□	♌	6 7:50
8 6:05	♆	△	♍	8 11:27
10 11:03	♆	□	♎	10 16:34
12 21:49	☿	△	♏	13 0:17
14 23:09	☉	△	♐	15 11:03
17 17:42	♆	☌	♑	17 23:47
20 10:54	☉	⚹	♒	20 11:53
22 15:32	♆	⚹	♓	22 21:01
24 21:28	♆	□	♈	25 2:37
27 0:42	♆	△	♉	27 5:39
28 22:50	☿	⚹	♊	29 7:44
31 8:31	☿	□	♋	31 10:09

Last Aspect Dy Hr Mn			☽ Ingress	Dy Hr Mn
2 6:33	♇	□	♌	2 13:36
4 14:55	♀	☍	♍	4 18:18
6 19:00	♆	□	♎	7 0:26
9 2:51	♆	⚹	♏	9 8:33
9 22:51	♃	☌	♐	11 19:07
14 1:33	♆	☌	♑	14 7:41
16 12:42	☉	□	♒	16 20:18
19 4:02	☉	⚹	♓	19 6:20
21 6:59	♆	□	♈	21 12:23
23 9:50	♆	△	♉	23 14:59
24 22:43	♀	⚹	♊	25 15:48
27 11:29	♆	☍	♋	27 16:43
29 13:48	☿	⚹	♌	29 19:09

☽ Phases & Eclipses Dy Hr Mn	
2 22:15	☽ 12♊00
9 20:45	○ 18♍57
17 17:15	☾ 26♐47
25 10:17	● 4♈26
1 5:08	☽ 11♋09
8 10:18	○ 18♎15
16 12:42	☾ 26♑12
23 20:29	● 3♉21
30 12:07	☽ 9♌49

Astro Data

1 March 1982
Julian Day # 30010
SVP 5♓30'47"
GC 26♐35.4 ⚴ 20♎02.5R
Eris 14♈37.7 ⚵ 1♑36.8
⚷ 18♉29.0 ⚶ 18♑23.8
☽ Mean ☊ 20♋02.0

1 April 1982
Julian Day # 30041
SVP 5♓30'44"
GC 26♐35.5 ⚴ 11♎58.3R
Eris 14♈57.2 ⚵ 7♑43.4
⚷ 19♉55.7 ⚶ 2♒33.3
☽ Mean ☊ 18♋23.5

LONGITUDE May 1982

Day	Sid.Time	☉	0 hr ☽	Noon ☽	True ☊	☿	♀	♂	⚳	♃	♄	♅	♆	♇
1 Sa	2 36 21	10♉47 10	16♌36 47	23♌24 31	15♋44.4	29♉54.4	26♓38.9	1♎03.8	21♏31.4	4♏45.6	17♎15.8	3♐31.7	26♐45.7	25♎06.9
2 Su	2 40 18	11 45 23	0♍08 25	6♍48 37	15R 41.8	1♊23.1	27 45.4	0R 56.2	21R 18.4	4R 38.0	17R 11.8	3R 29.5	26R 44.7	25R 05.3
3 M	2 44 14	12 43 34	13 25 18	19 58 36	15 36.7	2 47.7	28 52.0	0 49.3	21 05.3	4 30.5	17 07.8	3 27.2	26 43.6	25 03.7
4 Tu	2 48 11	13 41 43	26 28 41	2♎55 40	15 29.2	4 08.0	29 58.8	0 43.2	20 52.0	4 23.0	17 03.9	3 25.0	26 42.6	25 02.1
5 W	2 52 07	14 39 50	9♎19 37	15 40 39	15 19.7	5 24.1	1♈05.7	0 38.0	20 38.7	4 15.5	17 00.1	3 22.6	26 41.5	25 00.5
6 Th	2 56 04	15 37 55	21 58 49	28 14 10	15 09.1	6 35.9	2 12.7	0 33.5	20 25.3	4 08.1	16 56.3	3 20.3	26 40.4	24 59.0
7 F	3 00 01	16 35 58	4♏26 47	10♏36 44	14 58.3	7 43.2	3 19.9	0 29.8	20 11.9	4 00.8	16 52.6	3 18.0	26 39.3	24 57.4
8 Sa	3 03 57	17 34 00	16 44 05	22 48 58	14 48.4	8 46.1	4 27.1	0 26.9	19 58.4	3 53.5	16 48.9	3 15.6	26 38.1	24 55.9
9 Su	3 07 54	18 32 00	28 51 29	4♐51 51	14 40.1	9 44.3	5 34.6	0 24.7	19 44.9	3 46.2	16 45.3	3 13.3	26 37.0	24 54.4
10 M	3 11 50	19 29 59	10♐50 16	16 47 00	14 34.1	10 38.0	6 42.1	0 23.4	19 31.4	3 39.1	16 41.8	3 10.9	26 35.8	24 52.8
11 Tu	3 15 47	20 27 56	22 42 21	28 36 40	14 30.5	11 27.0	7 49.8	0D 22.8	19 17.9	3 32.0	16 38.4	3 08.5	26 34.6	24 51.4
12 W	3 19 43	21 25 52	4♑30 23	10♑23 56	14D 29.0	12 11.2	8 57.5	0 23.0	19 04.4	3 25.0	16 35.0	3 06.0	26 33.3	24 49.9
13 Th	3 23 40	22 23 46	16 17 48	22 12 34	14 29.2	12 50.7	10 05.4	0 23.9	18 51.0	3 18.0	16 31.7	3 03.6	26 32.1	24 48.4
14 F	3 27 36	23 21 40	28 08 45	4♒07 00	14 30.2	13 25.3	11 13.4	0 25.6	18 37.6	3 11.2	16 28.4	3 01.2	26 30.8	24 47.0
15 Sa	3 31 33	24 19 32	10♒07 56	16 12 11	14R 31.3	13 55.0	12 21.5	0 28.0	18 24.3	3 04.4	16 25.3	2 58.7	26 29.5	24 45.6
16 Su	3 35 30	25 17 22	22 20 24	28 33 13	14 31.6	14 19.8	13 29.7	0 31.1	18 11.1	2 57.7	16 22.2	2 56.3	26 28.2	24 44.2
17 M	3 39 26	26 15 12	4♓51 14	11♓15 01	14 30.3	14 39.6	14 38.0	0 34.9	17 58.0	2 51.2	16 19.1	2 53.8	26 26.9	24 42.8
18 Tu	3 43 23	27 13 00	17 45 05	24 21 48	14 27.3	14 54.6	15 46.4	0 39.5	17 45.0	2 44.7	16 16.2	2 51.3	26 25.6	24 41.4
19 W	3 47 19	28 10 47	1♈05 30	7♈56 19	14 22.5	15 04.6	16 54.9	0 44.7	17 32.2	2 38.4	16 13.3	2 48.8	26 24.2	24 40.1
20 Th	3 51 16	29 08 33	14 54 16	21 59 09	14 16.3	15R 09.8	18 03.5	0 50.7	17 19.4	2 32.1	16 10.6	2 46.3	26 22.8	24 38.7
21 F	3 55 12	0♊06 18	29 10 37	6♉28 05	14 09.5	15 10.2	19 12.2	0 57.3	17 06.9	2 26.0	16 07.9	2 43.9	26 21.4	24 37.4
22 Sa	3 59 09	1 04 02	13♉50 48	21 17 51	14 03.0	15 06.0	20 21.0	1 04.6	16 54.5	2 20.0	16 05.3	2 41.4	26 20.0	24 36.2
23 Su	4 03 05	2 01 44	28 48 10	6♊20 35	13 57.6	14 57.3	21 29.8	1 12.6	16 42.4	2 14.1	16 02.7	2 38.9	26 18.6	24 34.9
24 M	4 07 02	2 59 25	13♊53 55	21 26 57	13 54.0	14 44.3	22 38.8	1 21.3	16 30.4	2 08.4	16 00.3	2 36.4	26 17.1	24 33.7
25 Tu	4 10 59	3 57 05	28 58 33	6♋27 40	13D 52.3	14 27.4	23 47.8	1 30.5	16 18.6	2 02.7	15 58.0	2 33.9	26 15.7	24 32.4
26 W	4 14 55	4 54 44	13♋53 22	21 14 54	13 52.3	14 06.7	24 56.9	1 40.5	16 07.1	1 57.3	15 55.7	2 31.4	26 14.2	24 31.3
27 Th	4 18 52	5 52 21	28 31 38	5♌43 10	13 53.4	13 42.8	26 06.0	1 51.0	15 55.8	1 51.9	15 53.5	2 28.9	26 12.7	24 30.1
28 F	4 22 48	6 49 57	12♌49 12	19 49 36	13 54.7	13 15.9	27 15.2	2 02.2	15 44.8	1 46.7	15 51.5	2 26.4	26 11.2	24 29.0
29 Sa	4 26 45	7 47 31	26 44 20	3♍33 31	13R 55.6	12 46.6	28 24.5	2 13.9	15 34.1	1 41.6	15 49.5	2 23.9	26 09.7	24 27.8
30 Su	4 30 41	8 45 03	10♍17 17	16 55 54	13 55.4	12 15.4	29 33.9	2 26.3	15 23.6	1 36.7	15 47.6	2 21.4	26 08.2	24 26.7
31 M	4 34 38	9 42 34	23 29 36	29 58 44	13 53.7	11 42.8	0♉43.3	2 39.2	15 13.4	1 32.0	15 45.8	2 19.0	26 06.7	24 25.7

LONGITUDE June 1982

Day	Sid.Time	☉	0 hr ☽	Noon ☽	True ☊	☿	♀	♂	⚳	♃	♄	♅	♆	♇
1 Tu	4 38 34	10♊40 04	6♎23 34	12♎44 27	13♋50.5	11♊09.3	1♉52.8	2♎52.6	15♏03.5	1♏27.3	15♎44.1	2♐16.5	26♐05.1	24♎24.6
2 W	4 42 31	11 37 33	19 01 42	25 15 36	13R 46.1	10R 35.7	3 02.4	3 06.7	14R 54.0	1R 22.9	15R 42.5	2R 14.0	26R 03.6	24R 23.6
3 Th	4 46 28	12 35 00	1♏26 27	7♏34 31	13 41.0	10 02.4	4 12.0	3 21.2	14 44.7	1 18.6	15 40.9	2 11.6	26 02.0	24 22.6
4 F	4 50 24	13 32 27	13 40 04	19 43 22	13 35.8	9 30.0	5 21.7	3 36.3	14 35.7	1 14.4	15 39.5	2 09.2	26 00.5	24 21.7
5 Sa	4 54 21	14 29 52	25 44 37	1♐44 05	13 31.0	8 59.0	6 31.5	3 51.9	14 27.1	1 10.5	15 38.2	2 06.7	25 58.9	24 20.7
6 Su	4 58 17	15 27 16	7♐41 58	13 38 32	13 27.1	8 30.1	7 41.3	4 08.1	14 18.8	1 06.6	15 37.0	2 04.3	25 57.3	24 19.8
7 M	5 02 14	16 24 40	19 34 00	25 28 37	13 24.5	8 03.6	8 51.2	4 24.7	14 10.8	1 03.0	15 35.8	2 01.9	25 55.7	24 19.0
8 Tu	5 06 10	17 22 02	1♑22 41	7♑16 28	13D 23.3	7 40.1	10 01.2	4 41.8	14 03.2	0 59.5	15 34.8	1 59.6	25 54.1	24 18.1
9 W	5 10 07	18 19 24	13 10 17	19 04 30	13 23.2	7 19.8	11 11.2	4 59.4	13 56.0	0 56.2	15 33.9	1 57.2	25 52.5	24 17.3
10 Th	5 14 03	19 16 45	24 59 29	0♒55 38	13 24.2	7 03.2	12 21.3	5 17.4	13 49.1	0 53.0	15 33.0	1 54.9	25 50.9	24 16.5
11 F	5 18 00	20 14 06	6♒53 23	12 53 13	13 25.7	6 50.4	13 31.4	5 35.9	13 42.5	0 50.0	15 32.3	1 52.5	25 49.3	24 15.7
12 Sa	5 21 57	21 11 26	18 55 35	25 01 01	13 27.3	6 41.8	14 41.6	5 54.9	13 36.3	0 47.2	15 31.6	1 50.2	25 47.7	24 15.0
13 Su	5 25 53	22 08 46	1♓10 03	7♓23 11	13 28.5	6D 37.5	15 51.9	6 14.3	13 30.5	0 44.5	15 31.1	1 47.9	25 46.1	24 14.3
14 M	5 29 50	23 06 05	13 40 58	20 03 54	13R 29.2	6 37.7	17 02.2	6 34.1	13 25.0	0 42.1	15 30.6	1 45.6	25 44.5	24 13.6
15 Tu	5 33 46	24 03 23	26 32 27	3♈07 03	13 29.0	6 42.3	18 12.6	6 54.4	13 19.9	0 39.8	15 30.3	1 43.4	25 42.9	24 13.0
16 W	5 37 43	25 00 42	9♈48 03	16 35 42	13 27.9	6 51.5	19 23.0	7 15.1	13 15.2	0 37.7	15 30.0	1 41.2	25 41.2	24 12.4
17 Th	5 41 39	25 58 00	23 30 09	0♉31 24	13 26.2	7 05.4	20 33.5	7 36.2	13 10.9	0 35.7	15D 29.9	1 38.9	25 39.6	24 11.8
18 F	5 45 36	26 55 17	7♉39 19	14 53 33	13 24.2	7 23.8	21 44.1	7 57.7	13 06.9	0 33.9	15 29.8	1 36.8	25 38.0	24 11.3
19 Sa	5 49 32	27 52 35	22 13 36	29 38 48	13 22.3	7 46.8	22 54.7	8 19.6	13 03.3	0 32.4	15 29.9	1 34.6	25 36.4	24 10.7
20 Su	5 53 29	28 49 52	7♊08 18	14♊41 06	13 20.7	8 14.4	24 05.3	8 41.9	13 00.1	0 30.9	15 30.1	1 32.5	25 34.8	24 10.3
21 M	5 57 26	29 47 09	22 16 04	29 52 03	13D 19.7	8 46.4	25 16.1	9 04.6	12 57.3	0 29.7	15 30.3	1 30.4	25 33.2	24 09.8
22 Tu	6 01 22	0♋44 26	7♋27 48	15♋02 09	13 19.5	9 22.9	26 26.8	9 27.7	12 54.9	0 28.7	15 30.7	1 28.3	25 31.5	24 09.4
23 W	6 05 19	1 41 42	22 33 56	0♌02 09	13 19.8	10 03.7	27 37.6	9 51.1	12 52.9	0 27.8	15 31.1	1 26.3	25 29.9	24 09.0
24 Th	6 09 15	2 38 57	7♌25 53	14 44 24	13 20.6	10 48.9	28 48.5	10 14.9	12 51.2	0 27.1	15 31.7	1 24.2	25 28.3	24 08.7
25 F	6 13 12	3 36 12	21 57 08	29 03 40	13 21.4	11 38.2	29 59.4	10 39.1	12 49.9	0 26.6	15 32.4	1 22.2	25 26.7	24 08.3
26 Sa	6 17 08	4 33 26	6♍03 47	12♍57 23	13 22.1	12 31.8	1♊10.3	11 03.6	12 49.0	0 26.3	15 33.1	1 20.3	25 25.1	24 08.1
27 Su	6 21 05	5 30 40	19 44 31	26 25 21	13R 22.5	13 29.4	2 21.3	11 28.5	12D 48.5	0D 26.2	15 34.0	1 18.4	25 23.5	24 07.8
28 M	6 25 01	6 27 53	3♎00 08	9♎29 13	13 22.6	14 31.1	3 32.3	11 53.7	12 48.4	0 26.2	15 34.9	1 16.5	25 21.9	24 07.6
29 Tu	6 28 58	7 25 05	15 52 58	22 11 49	13 22.4	15 36.8	4 43.4	12 19.2	12 48.6	0 26.5	15 36.0	1 14.6	25 20.4	24 07.4
30 W	6 32 55	8 22 17	28 26 13	4♏36 39	13 22.0	16 46.5	5 54.5	12 45.0	12 49.3	0 26.9	15 37.1	1 12.8	25 18.8	24 07.2

Astro Data Dy Hr Mn	Planet Ingress Dy Hr Mn	Last Aspect Dy Hr Mn	☽ Ingress Dy Hr Mn	Last Aspect Dy Hr Mn	☽ Ingress Dy Hr Mn	☽ Phases & Eclipses Dy Hr Mn
☽0S 5 4:37	☿ ♊ 1 13:29	1 17:57 ♆ △	♍ 1 23:45	2 13:33 ♆ ⚹	♏ 2 21:12	8 0:45 ○ 17♏07
♀0N 7 13:34	♀ ♈ 4 12:27	4 5:59 ♀ ☍	♎ 4 6:32	3 4:42 ♀ ☍	♐ 5 8:31	16 5:11 ☾ 25♒01
♂ D 11 18:36	☉ ♊ 21 9:23	6 9:00 ♆ ⚹	♏ 6 15:24	7 12:55 ♆ ☌	♑ 7 21:12	23 4:40 ● 1♊44
♃⚺♅ 16 20:35	♀ ♉ 30 21:02	8 0:45 ☉ ☍	♐ 9 2:17	9 22:34 ♇ □	♒ 10 10:08	29 20:07 ☽ 8♍07
☽0N 19 18:59		11 7:52 ♆ ☌	♑ 11 14:50	12 13:31 ♆ ⚹	♓ 12 21:44	
☿ R 21 2:05	☉ ♋ 21 17:23	13 17:15 ♇ □	♒ 14 3:44	14 22:30 ♆ □	♈ 15 6:20	6 15:59 ○ 15♐37
♂0S 26 22:43	♀ ♊ 25 12:13	16 8:00 ♆ ⚹	♓ 16 14:46	17 3:43 ♆ △	♉ 17 11:07	14 18:06 ☾ 23♓21
		18 17:30 ☉ ⚹	♈ 18 22:04	19 0:10 ♀ ☌	♊ 19 12:34	21 11:52 ● 29♊47
☽0S 1 10:49		20 19:20 ♆ △	♉ 21 1:22	21 11:52 ☉ ☌	♋ 21 12:13	21 12:03:42 ● P 0.617
☿ D 13 23:22		21 5:25 ♃ ☍	♊ 23 1:54	23 7:47 ♀ ⚹	♌ 23 11:57	28 5:56 ☽ 6♎13
☽0N 16 4:23		24 19:42 ♆ ☍	♋ 25 1:38	25 5:53 ♆ △	♍ 25 13:36	
♄ D 18 11:05		26 18:36 ♀ □	♌ 27 2:27	27 10:09 ♆ □	♎ 27 18:30	
♃ D 27 18:16		29 2:05 ♀ △	♍ 29 5:43	29 18:01 ♆ ⚹	♏ 30 3:02	
⚳ D 28 8:30		31 4:50 ♆ □	♎ 31 12:02			
☽0S 28 17:19						

Astro Data

1 May 1982
Julian Day # 30071
SVP 5♓30'41"
GC 26♐35.5 ⚴ 4♎08.1R
Eris 15♈16.9 ⚵ 9♑56.1R
⚷ 21♉50.5 ⚶ 14♒04.3
☽ Mean ☊ 16♋48.1

1 June 1982
Julian Day # 30102
SVP 5♓30'37"
GC 26♐35.6 ⚴ 2♎45.2
Eris 15♈33.0 ⚵ 7♑09.0R
⚷ 23♉58.6 ⚶ 22♒14.7
☽ Mean ☊ 15♋09.7

July 1982

LONGITUDE

Day	Sid.Time	☉	0 hr ☽	Noon ☽	True ☊	☿	♀	♂	⚳	♃	♄	♅	♆	♇
1 Th	6 36 51	9♋19 29	10♏43 34	16♏47 26	13♋21.5	18♊00.0	7♊05.7	13♎11.2	12♏50.2	0♏27.4	15♎38.4	1♐11.0	25♐17.2	24♎07.1
2 F	6 40 48	10 16 40	22 48 42	28 47 47	13R 21.0	19 17.4	8 16.9	13 37.7	12 51.6	0 28.2	15 39.7	1R 09.2	25R 15.7	24R 07.0
3 Sa	6 44 44	11 13 52	4♐45 07	10♐41 03	13 20.7	20 38.6	9 28.2	14 04.4	12 53.3	0 29.2	15 41.2	1 07.5	25 14.1	24 07.0
4 Su	6 48 41	12 11 03	16 36 00	22 30 16	13 20.6	22 03.6	10 39.5	14 31.5	12 55.4	0 30.3	15 42.7	1 05.8	25 12.6	24D 07.0
5 M	6 52 37	13 08 14	28 24 13	4♑18 08	13 20.5	23 32.2	11 50.8	14 58.9	12 57.9	0 31.6	15 44.4	1 04.2	25 11.1	24 07.0
6 Tu	6 56 34	14 05 25	10♑12 20	16 07 05	13 20.5	25 04.5	13 02.2	15 26.5	13 00.7	0 33.0	15 46.1	1 02.6	25 09.6	24 07.0
7 W	7 00 31	15 02 36	22 02 41	27 59 25	13 20.5	26 40.3	14 13.7	15 54.4	13 03.8	0 34.7	15 48.0	1 01.0	25 08.1	24 07.1
8 Th	7 04 27	15 59 47	3♒57 32	9♒57 21	13 20.3	28 19.7	15 25.2	16 22.6	13 07.3	0 36.5	15 49.9	0 59.5	25 06.6	24 07.2
9 F	7 08 24	16 56 58	15 59 08	22 03 12	13 20.0	0♋02.5	16 36.7	16 51.1	13 11.2	0 38.5	15 51.9	0 58.0	25 05.1	24 07.4
10 Sa	7 12 20	17 54 10	28 09 52	4♓19 26	13 19.5	1 48.5	17 48.3	17 19.8	13 15.4	0 40.7	15 54.0	0 56.6	25 03.6	24 07.5
11 Su	7 16 17	18 51 22	10♓32 15	16 48 40	13 18.9	3 37.7	19 00.0	17 48.8	13 19.9	0 43.0	15 56.2	0 55.2	25 02.2	24 07.8
12 M	7 20 13	19 48 34	23 09 01	29 33 39	13 18.3	5 29.8	20 11.7	18 18.0	13 24.8	0 45.5	15 58.5	0 53.8	25 00.7	24 08.0
13 Tu	7 24 10	20 45 47	6♈02 54	12♈37 05	13D 17.9	7 24.7	21 23.4	18 47.6	13 30.0	0 48.2	16 00.9	0 52.5	24 59.3	24 08.3
14 W	7 28 06	21 43 00	19 16 29	26 01 22	13 17.9	9 22.3	22 35.2	19 17.3	13 35.5	0 51.1	16 03.4	0 51.2	24 57.9	24 08.6
15 Th	7 32 03	22 40 14	2♉51 52	9♉48 06	13 18.2	11 22.1	23 47.0	19 47.3	13 41.3	0 54.1	16 06.0	0 50.0	24 56.5	24 09.0
16 F	7 36 00	23 37 29	16 50 04	23 57 39	13 18.9	13 24.0	24 58.9	20 17.6	13 47.5	0 57.3	16 08.7	0 48.8	24 55.1	24 09.4
17 Sa	7 39 56	24 34 45	1♊10 37	8♊28 34	13 19.7	15 27.7	26 10.9	20 48.1	13 54.0	1 00.7	16 11.5	0 47.6	24 53.8	24 09.8
18 Su	7 43 53	25 32 01	15 51 00	23 17 12	13 20.5	17 32.8	27 22.8	21 18.8	14 00.8	1 04.2	16 14.3	0 46.6	24 52.4	24 10.2
19 M	7 47 49	26 29 18	0♋46 22	8♋17 36	13R 21.0	19 39.1	28 34.9	21 49.8	14 08.0	1 07.9	16 17.3	0 45.5	24 51.1	24 10.7
20 Tu	7 51 46	27 26 35	15 49 50	23 21 59	13 20.9	21 46.2	29 46.9	22 21.0	14 15.4	1 11.8	16 20.3	0 44.5	24 49.8	24 11.2
21 W	7 55 42	28 23 53	0♌52 57	8♌21 39	13 20.1	23 53.8	0♋59.1	22 52.4	14 23.1	1 15.8	16 23.4	0 43.5	24 48.5	24 11.8
22 Th	7 59 39	29 21 11	15 47 01	23 08 08	13 18.5	26 01.7	2 11.2	23 24.1	14 31.2	1 20.0	16 26.6	0 42.6	24 47.2	24 12.4
23 F	8 03 35	0♌18 29	0♍24 11	7♍34 30	13 16.4	28 09.5	3 23.4	23 56.0	14 39.5	1 24.3	16 29.9	0 41.8	24 46.0	24 13.0
24 Sa	8 07 32	1 15 48	14 38 35	21 36 07	13 14.2	0♌16.9	4 35.6	24 28.1	14 48.2	1 28.8	16 33.3	0 40.9	24 44.8	24 13.7
25 Su	8 11 29	2 13 08	28 26 54	5♎10 57	13 12.1	2 23.9	5 47.9	25 00.4	14 57.1	1 33.5	16 36.8	0 40.2	24 43.5	24 14.4
26 M	8 15 25	3 10 27	11♎48 23	18 19 27	13 10.6	4 30.0	7 00.2	25 32.9	15 06.3	1 38.3	16 40.3	0 39.4	24 42.4	24 15.1
27 Tu	8 19 22	4 07 47	24 44 30	1♏03 57	13D 09.9	6 35.2	8 12.6	26 05.7	15 15.8	1 43.3	16 44.0	0 38.8	24 41.2	24 15.8
28 W	8 23 18	5 05 08	7♏18 18	13 28 06	13 10.2	8 39.4	9 25.0	26 38.6	15 25.6	1 48.4	16 47.7	0 38.1	24 40.0	24 16.6
29 Th	8 27 15	6 02 29	19 33 54	25 36 17	13 11.2	10 42.3	10 37.5	27 11.8	15 35.6	1 53.7	16 51.5	0 37.6	24 38.9	24 17.5
30 F	8 31 11	6 59 51	1♐35 50	7♐33 08	13 12.7	12 43.9	11 49.9	27 45.1	15 45.9	1 59.1	16 55.4	0 37.0	24 37.8	24 18.3
31 Sa	8 35 08	7 57 13	13 28 45	19 23 12	13 14.4	14 44.1	13 02.5	28 18.6	15 56.5	2 04.7	16 59.4	0 36.6	24 36.8	24 19.2

August 1982

LONGITUDE

Day	Sid.Time	☉	0 hr ☽	Noon ☽	True ☊	☿	♀	♂	⚳	♃	♄	♅	♆	♇
1 Su	8 39 04	8♌54 36	25♐17 02	1♑10 43	13♋15.7	16♌42.8	14♋15.0	28♎52.4	16♏07.3	2♏10.4	17♎03.4	0♐36.1	24♐35.7	24♎20.1
2 M	8 43 01	9 51 59	7♑04 43	12 59 25	13R 16.3	18 40.0	15 27.7	29 26.3	16 18.4	2 16.3	17 07.5	0R 35.8	24R 34.7	24 21.1
3 Tu	8 46 58	10 49 24	18 55 13	24 52 28	13 15.7	20 35.7	16 40.3	0♏00.3	16 29.7	2 22.3	17 11.7	0 35.4	24 33.7	24 22.1
4 W	8 50 54	11 46 49	0♒51 28	6♒52 29	13 13.8	22 29.8	17 53.0	0 34.6	16 41.3	2 28.5	17 16.0	0 35.2	24 32.7	24 23.1
5 Th	8 54 51	12 44 15	12 55 44	19 01 27	13 10.5	24 22.4	19 05.8	1 09.1	16 53.1	2 34.8	17 20.4	0 34.9	24 31.8	24 24.1
6 F	8 58 47	13 41 42	25 09 48	1♓20 56	13 06.0	26 13.4	20 18.6	1 43.7	17 05.2	2 41.2	17 24.8	0 34.8	24 30.8	24 25.2
7 Sa	9 02 44	14 39 10	7♓35 00	13 52 07	13 00.9	28 02.8	21 31.4	2 18.5	17 17.5	2 47.8	17 29.3	0 34.6	24 29.9	24 26.3
8 Su	9 06 40	15 36 40	20 12 23	26 35 55	12 55.7	29 50.6	22 44.3	2 53.5	17 30.0	2 54.5	17 33.8	0D 34.6	24 29.0	24 27.4
9 M	9 10 37	16 34 10	3♈02 50	9♈33 13	12 50.9	1♍36.9	23 57.2	3 28.6	17 42.8	3 01.4	17 38.5	0 34.6	24 28.2	24 28.6
10 Tu	9 14 33	17 31 42	16 07 11	22 44 51	12 47.3	3 21.6	25 10.2	4 03.9	17 55.8	3 08.4	17 43.2	0 34.6	24 27.4	24 29.8
11 W	9 18 30	18 29 15	29 26 20	6♉11 42	12D 45.1	5 04.8	26 23.2	4 39.4	18 09.0	3 15.5	17 48.0	0 34.7	24 26.6	24 31.0
12 Th	9 22 27	19 26 50	13♉01 04	19 54 30	12 44.4	6 46.5	27 36.3	5 15.0	18 22.4	3 22.7	17 52.9	0 34.8	24 25.8	24 32.3
13 F	9 26 23	20 24 26	26 52 00	3♊53 34	12 45.0	8 26.6	28 49.4	5 50.9	18 36.0	3 30.1	17 57.8	0 35.0	24 25.1	24 33.6
14 Sa	9 30 20	21 22 04	10♊59 07	18 08 29	12 46.3	10 05.2	0♌02.6	6 26.8	18 49.9	3 37.6	18 02.8	0 35.2	24 24.4	24 34.9
15 Su	9 34 16	22 19 43	25 21 25	2♋37 33	12R 47.5	11 42.4	1 15.8	7 03.0	19 03.9	3 45.3	18 07.9	0 35.5	24 23.7	24 36.3
16 M	9 38 13	23 17 24	9♋56 26	17 17 28	12 47.7	13 18.1	2 29.0	7 39.3	19 18.2	3 53.0	18 13.0	0 35.9	24 23.0	24 37.6
17 Tu	9 42 09	24 15 07	24 39 59	2♌03 10	12 46.4	14 52.2	3 42.3	8 15.8	19 32.7	4 00.9	18 18.2	0 36.3	24 22.4	24 39.1
18 W	9 46 06	25 12 50	9♌26 11	16 48 06	12 43.1	16 24.9	4 55.7	8 52.4	19 47.4	4 08.9	18 23.5	0 36.7	24 21.8	24 40.5
19 Th	9 50 02	26 10 35	24 07 59	1♍24 55	12 37.8	17 56.1	6 09.0	9 29.2	20 02.3	4 17.1	18 28.8	0 37.2	24 21.3	24 41.9
20 F	9 53 59	27 08 22	8♍38 03	15 46 36	12 31.2	19 25.8	7 22.5	10 06.1	20 17.3	4 25.3	18 34.2	0 37.7	24 20.7	24 43.4
21 Sa	9 57 56	28 06 09	22 49 54	29 47 27	12 23.9	20 54.0	8 35.9	10 43.2	20 32.6	4 33.7	18 39.6	0 38.3	24 20.2	24 45.0
22 Su	10 01 52	29 03 58	6♎38 53	13♎23 58	12 16.9	22 20.7	9 49.4	11 20.4	20 48.0	4 42.2	18 45.1	0 39.0	24 19.7	24 46.5
23 M	10 05 49	0♍01 48	20 02 39	26 35 01	12 11.0	23 45.9	11 02.9	11 57.8	21 03.7	4 50.8	18 50.7	0 39.7	24 19.3	24 48.1
24 Tu	10 09 45	0 59 39	3♏01 18	9♏21 47	12 06.7	25 09.4	12 16.5	12 35.4	21 19.5	4 59.5	18 56.3	0 40.5	24 18.9	24 49.7
25 W	10 13 42	1 57 32	15 36 57	21 47 16	12D 04.6	26 31.4	13 30.1	13 13.1	21 35.5	5 08.3	19 02.0	0 41.3	24 18.5	24 51.3
26 Th	10 17 38	2 55 25	27 53 18	3♐55 41	12 03.8	27 51.8	14 43.7	13 50.9	21 51.6	5 17.3	19 07.8	0 42.1	24 18.2	24 52.9
27 F	10 21 35	3 53 20	9♐55 03	15 52 03	12 04.4	29 10.5	15 57.4	14 28.8	22 08.0	5 26.3	19 13.6	0 43.0	24 17.8	24 54.6
28 Sa	10 25 31	4 51 17	21 47 21	27 41 36	12 05.6	0♎27.5	17 11.1	15 06.9	22 24.5	5 35.5	19 19.4	0 44.0	24 17.6	24 56.3
29 Su	10 29 28	5 49 15	3♑35 26	9♑29 29	12R 06.3	1 42.7	18 24.9	15 45.2	22 41.2	5 44.7	19 25.4	0 45.0	24 17.3	24 58.0
30 M	10 33 25	6 47 14	15 24 18	21 20 28	12 05.9	2 56.1	19 38.7	16 23.5	22 58.0	5 54.1	19 31.3	0 46.1	24 17.1	24 59.8
31 Tu	10 37 21	7 45 14	27 18 27	3♒18 43	12 03.5	4 07.6	20 52.5	17 02.1	23 15.0	6 03.6	19 37.3	0 47.2	24 16.9	25 01.6

Astro Data
Dy Hr Mn
♇ D 4 13:11
♄∠♅ 11 5:01
☽0N 13 11:28
♃⊻♅ 14 12:44
☽0S 26 0:51

♆✶♇ 9 7:02
♅ D 9 10:21
☽0N 9 16:41
☽0S 22 9:28
☿0S 26 14:41

Planet Ingress
Dy Hr Mn
☿ ♋ 9 11:26
♀ ♋ 20 16:21
☉ ♌ 23 4:15
☿ ♌ 24 8:48

♂ ♏ 3 11:45
☿ ♍ 8 14:06
♀ ♌ 14 11:09
☉ ♍ 23 11:15
☿ ♎ 28 3:22

Last Aspect Dy Hr Mn		☽ Ingress Dy Hr Mn
30 19:59	☉ △	♐ 2 14:25
4 17:29	♆ ☌	♑ 5 3:15
7 4:11	♇ □	♒ 7 16:03
9 17:57	♆ ✶	♓ 10 3:35
12 3:31	♆ □	♈ 12 12:49
14 10:08	♆ △	♉ 14 19:00
16 11:24	☉ ✶	♊ 16 22:03
18 19:09	♀ ☌	♋ 18 22:46
20 18:57	☉ ☌	♌ 20 22:35
22 14:43	♆ △	♍ 22 23:20
24 17:29	♆ □	♎ 25 2:45
27 2:08	♂ ☌	♏ 27 9:58
28 3:14	♀ △	♐ 29 20:48

Last Aspect Dy Hr Mn		☽ Ingress Dy Hr Mn
1 7:04	♂ ✶	♑ 1 9:36
3 10:59	♇ □	♒ 3 22:17
6 0:19	☿ ☍	♓ 6 9:23
8 8:03	♆ □	♈ 8 18:21
10 16:48	♀ □	♉ 11 1:00
13 2:32	♀ ✶	♊ 13 5:22
14 22:44	♇ △	♋ 15 7:40
16 23:57	♇ □	♌ 17 8:40
19 2:45	☉ ☌	♍ 19 9:40
21 2:35	♆ □	♎ 21 12:22
23 8:42	♇ ☌	♏ 23 18:21
25 22:28	☿ ✶	♐ 26 4:11
28 6:23	♇ ✶	♑ 28 16:42
30 19:23	♇ □	♒ 31 5:23

☽ Phases & Eclipses
Dy Hr Mn
6 7:32 ○ 13♑55
6 7:31 ● T 1.718
14 3:47 ☾ 21♈23
20 18:57 ● 27♋43
20 18:43:50 ● P 0.464
27 18:22 ☽ 4♏23

4 22:34 ○ 12♒12
12 11:08 ☾ 19♉25
19 2:45 ● 25♌48
26 9:49 ☽ 2♐50

Astro Data
1 July 1982
Julian Day # 30132
SVP 5♓30'32"
GC 26♐35.7 ⚴ 7♎31.7
Eris 15♈41.0 ⚵ 0♏43.0R
⚷ 25♉50.4 ⚶ 24♒27.5R
☽ Mean ☊ 13♋34.3

1 August 1982
Julian Day # 30163
SVP 5♓30'26"
GC 26♐35.8 ⚴ 16♎23.5
Eris 15♈39.5R ⚵ 25♐12.1R
⚷ 27♉12.5 ⚶ 19♒42.0R
☽ Mean ☊ 11♋55.9

LONGITUDE — September 1982

Day	Sid.Time	☉	0 hr ☽	Noon ☽	True ☊	☿	♀	♂	⚳	♃	♄	♅	♆	♇
1 W	10 41 18	8♍43 16	9♒21 39	15♒27 35	11♋58.9	5♎17.1	22♌06.3	17♏40.7	23♏32.2	6♏13.1	19♎43.4	0♐48.3	24♐16.7	25♎03.4
2 Th	10 45 14	9 41 19	21 36 46	27 49 26	11R51.9	6 24.5	23 20.2	18 19.4	23 49.5	6 22.8	19 49.5	0 49.6	24R16.6	25 05.2
3 F	10 49 11	10 39 24	4♓05 41	10♓25 35	11 42.9	7 29.8	24 34.2	18 58.3	24 06.9	6 32.5	19 55.7	0 50.8	24 16.5	25 07.0
4 Sa	10 53 07	11 37 31	16 49 10	23 16 22	11 32.7	8 32.7	25 48.1	19 37.3	24 24.5	6 42.4	20 01.9	0 52.1	24 16.4	25 08.9
5 Su	10 57 04	12 35 39	29 47 06	6♈21 13	11 22.1	9 33.2	27 02.2	20 16.5	24 42.3	6 52.4	20 08.2	0 53.5	24D16.4	25 10.8
6 M	11 01 00	13 33 50	12♈58 33	19 38 58	11 12.4	10 31.2	28 16.2	20 55.7	25 00.2	7 02.4	20 14.5	0 54.9	24 16.4	25 12.7
7 Tu	11 04 57	14 32 02	26 22 14	3♉08 13	11 04.4	11 26.4	29 30.3	21 35.1	25 18.2	7 12.5	20 20.8	0 56.3	24 16.4	25 14.6
8 W	11 08 53	15 30 16	9♉56 44	16 47 39	10 58.8	12 18.7	0♍44.4	22 14.6	25 36.4	7 22.8	20 27.2	0 57.8	24 16.5	25 16.6
9 Th	11 12 50	16 28 32	23 40 51	0♊36 16	10 55.6	13 07.9	1 58.6	22 54.3	25 54.7	7 33.1	20 33.6	0 59.4	24 16.6	25 18.5
10 F	11 16 47	17 26 51	7♊33 48	14 33 24	10D54.6	13 53.8	3 12.7	23 34.0	26 13.2	7 43.5	20 40.1	1 01.0	24 16.7	25 20.5
11 Sa	11 20 43	18 25 11	21 35 00	28 38 32	10R54.8	14 36.1	4 27.0	24 13.9	26 31.8	7 54.0	20 46.6	1 02.7	24 16.9	25 22.5
12 Su	11 24 40	19 23 34	5♋43 54	12♋50 56	10 55.0	15 14.6	5 41.3	24 53.9	26 50.5	8 04.6	20 53.2	1 04.4	24 17.1	25 24.6
13 M	11 28 36	20 21 59	19 59 26	27 09 07	10 54.1	15 49.0	6 55.6	25 34.0	27 09.3	8 15.2	20 59.8	1 06.1	24 17.3	25 26.6
14 Tu	11 32 33	21 20 26	4♌19 39	11♌30 33	10 51.0	16 19.0	8 09.9	26 14.3	27 28.3	8 26.0	21 06.4	1 07.9	24 17.6	25 28.7
15 W	11 36 29	22 18 55	18 41 20	25 51 23	10 45.1	16 44.3	9 24.3	26 54.7	27 47.4	8 36.8	21 13.1	1 09.7	24 17.9	25 30.8
16 Th	11 40 26	23 17 26	3♍00 04	10♍06 41	10 36.6	17 04.5	10 38.7	27 35.1	28 06.7	8 47.7	21 19.8	1 11.6	24 18.2	25 32.9
17 F	11 44 22	24 15 59	17 10 34	24 11 04	10 25.9	17 19.3	11 53.1	28 15.7	28 26.0	8 58.7	21 26.6	1 13.5	24 18.6	25 35.0
18 Sa	11 48 19	25 14 33	1♎07 32	7♎59 28	10 14.1	17R28.4	13 07.5	28 56.4	28 45.5	9 09.8	21 33.4	1 15.5	24 19.0	25 37.1
19 Su	11 52 16	26 13 10	14 46 25	21 28 04	10 02.4	17 31.3	14 22.0	29 37.3	29 05.1	9 21.0	21 40.2	1 17.5	24 19.4	25 39.3
20 M	11 56 12	27 11 48	28 04 13	4♏34 49	9 52.0	17 27.7	15 36.5	0♐18.2	29 24.8	9 32.2	21 47.0	1 19.6	24 19.9	25 41.4
21 Tu	12 00 09	28 10 29	10♏59 55	17 19 42	9 43.7	17 17.4	16 51.1	0 59.3	29 44.6	9 43.5	21 53.9	1 21.7	24 20.4	25 43.6
22 W	12 04 05	29 09 11	23 34 28	29 44 36	9 38.1	17 00.1	18 05.6	1 40.4	0♐04.6	9 54.8	22 00.8	1 23.8	24 20.9	25 45.8
23 Th	12 08 02	0♎07 54	5♐50 35	11♐52 56	9 34.9	16 35.5	19 20.2	2 21.7	0 24.6	10 06.3	22 07.7	1 26.0	24 21.5	25 48.0
24 F	12 11 58	1 06 40	17 52 17	23 49 16	9D33.7	16 03.7	20 34.9	3 03.1	0 44.8	10 17.8	22 14.7	1 28.3	24 22.1	25 50.3
25 Sa	12 15 55	2 05 27	29 44 32	5♑38 48	9R33.6	15 24.7	21 49.5	3 44.5	1 05.0	10 29.3	22 21.7	1 30.5	24 22.7	25 52.5
26 Su	12 19 51	3 04 16	11♑32 44	17 27 04	9 33.5	14 38.9	23 04.2	4 26.1	1 25.4	10 41.0	22 28.7	1 32.9	24 23.4	25 54.8
27 M	12 23 48	4 03 07	23 22 26	29 19 31	9 32.2	13 46.5	24 18.8	5 07.8	1 45.8	10 52.7	22 35.7	1 35.2	24 24.0	25 57.0
28 Tu	12 27 45	5 01 59	5♒18 56	11♒21 14	9 29.0	12 48.5	25 33.6	5 49.6	2 06.4	11 04.4	22 42.8	1 37.6	24 24.8	25 59.3
29 W	12 31 41	6 00 53	17 26 58	23 36 34	9 23.2	11 45.8	26 48.3	6 31.5	2 27.0	11 16.3	22 49.9	1 40.0	24 25.5	26 01.6
30 Th	12 35 38	6 59 49	29 50 25	6♓08 47	9 14.7	10 39.7	28 03.0	7 13.5	2 47.8	11 28.1	22 57.0	1 42.5	24 26.3	26 03.9

LONGITUDE — October 1982

Day	Sid.Time	☉	0 hr ☽	Noon ☽	True ☊	☿	♀	♂	⚳	♃	♄	♅	♆	♇
1 F	12 39 34	7♎58 47	12♓31 52	18♓59 46	9♋03.7	9♎31.6	29♍17.8	7♐55.5	3♐08.6	11♏40.1	23♎04.1	1♐45.0	24♐27.1	26♎06.2
2 Sa	12 43 31	8 57 47	25 32 27	2♈09 49	8R51.3	8R23.2	0♎32.6	8 37.7	3 29.6	11 52.1	23 11.2	1 47.6	24 28.0	26 08.5
3 Su	12 47 27	9 56 49	8♈51 38	15 37 37	8 38.5	7 16.3	1 47.4	9 20.0	3 50.6	12 04.1	23 18.4	1 50.2	24 28.8	26 10.8
4 M	12 51 24	10 55 53	22 27 22	29 20 26	8 26.5	6 12.8	3 02.3	10 02.3	4 11.7	12 16.2	23 25.6	1 52.8	24 29.8	26 13.2
5 Tu	12 55 20	11 54 59	6♉16 23	13♉14 41	8 16.5	5 14.4	4 17.1	10 44.8	4 32.9	12 28.4	23 32.8	1 55.5	24 30.7	26 15.5
6 W	12 59 17	12 54 07	20 14 52	27 16 28	8 09.2	4 22.8	5 32.0	11 27.3	4 54.2	12 40.6	23 40.0	1 58.2	24 31.7	26 17.9
7 Th	13 03 13	13 53 17	4♊19 05	11♊22 21	8 04.9	3 39.3	6 46.9	12 10.0	5 15.6	12 52.9	23 47.2	2 00.9	24 32.7	26 20.3
8 F	13 07 10	14 52 30	18 25 58	25 29 41	8D03.0	3 05.2	8 01.8	12 52.7	5 37.0	13 05.2	23 54.4	2 03.7	24 33.7	26 22.6
9 Sa	13 11 07	15 51 46	2♋33 18	9♋36 42	8R02.7	2 41.3	9 16.8	13 35.5	5 58.6	13 17.6	24 01.7	2 06.5	24 34.8	26 25.0
10 Su	13 15 03	16 51 03	16 39 46	23 42 24	8 02.7	2D28.0	10 31.8	14 18.5	6 20.2	13 30.0	24 08.9	2 09.3	24 35.9	26 27.4
11 M	13 19 00	17 50 23	0♌44 31	7♌46 01	8 01.5	2 25.6	11 46.8	15 01.5	6 41.9	13 42.5	24 16.2	2 12.2	24 37.0	26 29.8
12 Tu	13 22 56	18 49 46	14 46 45	21 46 34	7 58.2	2 33.9	13 01.8	15 44.6	7 03.7	13 55.0	24 23.5	2 15.1	24 38.1	26 32.2
13 W	13 26 53	19 49 10	28 45 15	5♍42 32	7 52.1	2 52.8	14 16.8	16 27.8	7 25.5	14 07.5	24 30.8	2 18.1	24 39.3	26 34.6
14 Th	13 30 49	20 48 37	12♍38 06	19 31 37	7 43.2	3 21.7	15 31.8	17 11.0	7 47.4	14 20.1	24 38.1	2 21.1	24 40.5	26 37.0
15 F	13 34 46	21 48 06	26 22 43	3♎10 59	7 32.0	3 59.9	16 46.9	17 54.4	8 09.5	14 32.7	24 45.3	2 24.1	24 41.8	26 39.4
16 Sa	13 38 42	22 47 37	9♎56 05	16 37 37	7 19.6	4 46.9	18 02.0	18 37.9	8 31.5	14 45.4	24 52.6	2 27.1	24 43.0	26 41.8
17 Su	13 42 39	23 47 10	23 15 18	29 48 51	7 07.2	5 41.7	19 17.1	19 21.4	8 53.7	14 58.1	24 59.9	2 30.2	24 44.3	26 44.2
18 M	13 46 36	24 46 45	6♏18 07	12♏42 58	6 56.1	6 43.6	20 32.2	20 05.0	9 15.9	15 10.9	25 07.2	2 33.3	24 45.7	26 46.6
19 Tu	13 50 32	25 46 22	19 03 23	25 19 28	6 47.0	7 51.7	21 47.3	20 48.8	9 38.2	15 23.7	25 14.5	2 36.4	24 47.0	26 49.0
20 W	13 54 29	26 46 01	1♐31 23	7♐39 22	6 40.6	9 05.3	23 02.5	21 32.6	10 00.6	15 36.5	25 21.8	2 39.5	24 48.4	26 51.4
21 Th	13 58 25	27 45 42	13 43 46	19 45 00	6 36.9	10 23.7	24 17.6	22 16.4	10 23.0	15 49.3	25 29.1	2 42.7	24 49.8	26 53.8
22 F	14 02 22	28 45 25	25 43 32	1♑39 55	6D35.5	11 46.1	25 32.8	23 00.4	10 45.5	16 02.2	25 36.4	2 45.9	24 51.2	26 56.3
23 Sa	14 06 18	29 45 09	7♑34 44	13 28 37	6 35.5	13 12.0	26 47.9	23 44.4	11 08.0	16 15.2	25 43.7	2 49.2	24 52.7	26 58.7
24 Su	14 10 15	0♏44 55	19 22 13	25 16 12	6R36.1	14 40.8	28 03.1	24 28.6	11 30.6	16 28.1	25 51.0	2 52.4	24 54.2	27 01.1
25 M	14 14 11	1 44 43	1♒11 18	7♒08 10	6 36.0	16 12.0	29 18.3	25 12.7	11 53.3	16 41.1	25 58.3	2 55.7	24 55.7	27 03.5
26 Tu	14 18 08	2 44 33	13 07 29	19 09 57	6 34.5	17 45.1	0♏33.5	25 57.0	12 16.0	16 54.1	26 05.6	2 59.0	24 57.2	27 05.9
27 W	14 22 05	3 44 24	25 16 09	1♓26 41	6 30.8	19 19.8	1 48.7	26 41.3	12 38.8	17 07.1	26 12.8	3 02.3	24 58.8	27 08.3
28 Th	14 26 01	4 44 17	7♓42 03	14 02 42	6 24.8	20 55.7	3 03.9	27 25.7	13 01.7	17 20.1	26 20.1	3 05.7	25 00.4	27 10.7
29 F	14 29 58	5 44 11	20 28 58	27 01 04	6 16.6	22 32.7	4 19.1	28 10.2	13 24.6	17 33.2	26 27.3	3 09.1	25 02.0	27 13.1
30 Sa	14 33 54	6 44 07	3♈39 08	10♈23 07	6 06.9	24 10.3	5 34.3	28 54.8	13 47.5	17 46.3	26 34.6	3 12.5	25 03.6	27 15.5
31 Su	14 37 51	7 44 05	17 12 52	24 08 03	5 56.8	25 48.5	6 49.6	29 39.4	14 10.5	17 59.4	26 41.8	3 15.9	25 05.3	27 17.9

Astro Data

	Dy Hr Mn
☽0N	5 21:52
♆D	5 23:36
☽0S	18 18:32
♃∠♆	19 8:35
☿R	19 11:03
☉0S	23 8:47
☽0N	3 4:56
♀0S	4 17:08
☿D	11 5:20
♄⚹♆	14 21:50
☽0S	16 3:05
☽0N	30 14:26

Planet Ingress

	Dy Hr Mn
♀ ♍	7 21:38
♂ ♐	20 1:20
⚳ ♐	22 6:32
☉ ♎	23 8:46
♀ ♎	2 1:32
☉ ♏	23 17:58
♀ ♏	26 1:19
♂ ♑	31 23:05

Last Aspect / ☽ Ingress

Last Aspect Dy Hr Mn		☽ Ingress Dy Hr Mn
2 6:43	♇ △	♓ 2 16:11
4 13:51	♆ □	♈ 5 0:24
7 4:55	♀ △	♉ 7 6:27
8 21:59	♂ ☍	♊ 9 10:57
11 6:26	♇ △	♋ 11 14:18
13 9:13	♂ △	♌ 13 16:46
15 13:51	♂ □	♍ 15 18:57
17 19:24	♂ ⚹	♎ 17 22:03
19 19:37	♇ ☌	♏ 20 3:32
22 10:45	☉ ⚹	♐ 22 12:30
24 16:06	♇ ⚹	♑ 25 0:31
27 5:11	♇ □	♒ 27 13:21
29 16:41	♇ △	♓ 30 0:18

Last Aspect / ☽ Ingress

Last Aspect Dy Hr Mn		☽ Ingress Dy Hr Mn
1 22:01	♆ □	♈ 2 8:06
4 6:33	♇ ☍	♉ 4 13:09
5 10:39	♃ ☍	♊ 6 16:39
8 13:30	♇ △	♋ 8 19:39
10 16:42	♇ □	♌ 10 22:44
12 20:12	♇ ⚹	♍ 13 2:09
14 21:01	♆ □	♎ 15 6:23
17 6:20	♇ ☌	♏ 17 12:21
18 16:44	♃ ☌	♐ 19 21:02
22 5:35	☉ ⚹	♑ 22 8:38
24 18:19	♀ □	♒ 24 21:36
27 3:37	♇ △	♓ 27 9:12
29 14:13	♂ □	♈ 29 17:25
31 22:00	♂ △	♉ 31 22:04

☽ Phases & Eclipses

Dy Hr Mn	
3 12:28	○ 10♓41
10 17:19	☾ 17♊40
17 12:09	● 24♍16
25 4:07	☽ 1♑46
3 1:09	○ 9♈30
9 23:26	☾ 16♋20
17 0:04	● 23♎18
25 0:08	☽ 1♒15

Astro Data

1 September 1982
Julian Day # 30194
SVP 5♓30'23"
GC 26♐35.8 ⚴ 27♎34.2
Eris 15♈28.6R ⚵ 24♐47.4
⚷ 27♉43.7 ⚶ 12♒43.1R
☽ Mean ☊ 10♋17.4

1 October 1982
Julian Day # 30224
SVP 5♓30'20"
GC 26♐35.9 ⚴ 9♏39.4
Eris 15♈12.0R ⚵ 29♐15.0
⚷ 27♉18.0R ⚶ 11♒11.5
☽ Mean ☊ 8♋42.0

November 1982 LONGITUDE

Day	Sid.Time	☉	0 hr ☽	Noon ☽	True ☊	☿	♀	♂	⚳	♃	♄	♅	♆	♇
1 M	14 41 47	8♏44 05	1♉08 14	8♉12 52	5♋47.3	27♎27.0	8♏04.8	0♑24.1	14♐33.6	18♏12.5	26♎49.0	3♐19.3	25♐07.0	27♎20.2
2 Tu	14 45 44	9 44 07	15 21 16	22 32 42	5R39.4	29 05.7	9 20.0	1 08.8	14 56.7	18 25.7	26 56.2	3 22.8	25 08.7	27 22.6
3 W	14 49 40	10 44 11	29 46 24	7♊01 34	5 33.8	0♏44.6	10 35.3	1 53.6	15 19.8	18 38.8	27 03.4	3 26.2	25 10.4	27 25.0
4 Th	14 53 37	11 44 17	14♊17 25	21 33 14	5D30.7	2 23.5	11 50.6	2 38.5	15 43.0	18 52.0	27 10.5	3 29.7	25 12.2	27 27.4
5 F	14 57 34	12 44 24	28 48 23	6♋02 16	5 29.9	4 02.2	13 05.8	3 23.5	16 06.3	19 05.2	27 17.7	3 33.2	25 13.9	27 29.7
6 Sa	15 01 30	13 44 34	13♋14 25	20 24 28	5 30.5	5 40.9	14 21.1	4 08.5	16 29.5	19 18.4	27 24.8	3 36.8	25 15.7	27 32.1
7 Su	15 05 27	14 44 46	27 32 07	4♌37 09	5R31.6	7 19.4	15 36.4	4 53.5	16 52.9	19 31.6	27 31.9	3 40.3	25 17.5	27 34.4
8 M	15 09 23	15 45 00	11♌39 27	18 38 55	5 31.9	8 57.6	16 51.7	5 38.7	17 16.3	19 44.8	27 39.0	3 43.9	25 19.4	27 36.7
9 Tu	15 13 20	16 45 16	25 35 31	2♍29 12	5 30.7	10 35.6	18 07.0	6 23.9	17 39.7	19 58.1	27 46.0	3 47.4	25 21.2	27 39.0
10 W	15 17 16	17 45 35	9♍19 58	16 07 49	5 27.4	12 13.4	19 22.4	7 09.2	18 03.2	20 11.3	27 53.0	3 51.0	25 23.1	27 41.3
11 Th	15 21 13	18 45 55	22 52 43	29 34 39	5 21.9	13 50.9	20 37.7	7 54.5	18 26.7	20 24.6	28 00.0	3 54.6	25 25.0	27 43.6
12 F	15 25 09	19 46 16	6♎13 34	12♎49 24	5 14.8	15 28.0	21 53.0	8 39.9	18 50.2	20 37.8	28 07.0	3 58.2	25 26.9	27 45.9
13 Sa	15 29 06	20 46 40	19 22 07	25 51 39	5 06.6	17 04.9	23 08.3	9 25.3	19 13.8	20 51.1	28 14.0	4 01.9	25 28.8	27 48.2
14 Su	15 33 03	21 47 06	2♏17 55	8♏40 53	4 58.5	18 41.5	24 23.7	10 10.9	19 37.4	21 04.3	28 20.9	4 05.5	25 30.8	27 50.5
15 M	15 36 59	22 47 33	15 00 31	21 16 49	4 51.1	20 17.9	25 39.0	10 56.4	20 01.1	21 17.6	28 27.8	4 09.1	25 32.8	27 52.7
16 Tu	15 40 56	23 48 02	27 29 51	3♐39 40	4 45.2	21 53.9	26 54.4	11 42.1	20 24.8	21 30.9	28 34.6	4 12.8	25 34.7	27 54.9
17 W	15 44 52	24 48 33	9♐46 25	15 50 17	4 41.3	23 29.7	28 09.8	12 27.8	20 48.6	21 44.1	28 41.5	4 16.5	25 36.7	27 57.2
18 Th	15 48 49	25 49 05	21 51 29	27 50 19	4D39.4	25 05.2	29 25.1	13 13.5	21 12.3	21 57.4	28 48.3	4 20.1	25 38.8	27 59.4
19 F	15 52 45	26 49 38	3♑47 08	9♑42 19	4 39.3	26 40.4	0♐40.5	13 59.3	21 36.1	22 10.6	28 55.0	4 23.8	25 40.8	28 01.6
20 Sa	15 56 42	27 50 13	15 36 19	21 29 37	4 40.4	28 15.5	1 55.8	14 45.2	22 00.0	22 23.9	29 01.7	4 27.5	25 42.8	28 03.7
21 Su	16 00 38	28 50 49	27 22 46	3♒16 19	4 42.2	29 50.3	3 11.2	15 31.1	22 23.8	22 37.1	29 08.4	4 31.2	25 44.9	28 05.9
22 M	16 04 35	29 51 26	9♒10 52	15 07 03	4 43.9	1♐24.9	4 26.6	16 17.0	22 47.7	22 50.3	29 15.1	4 34.9	25 47.0	28 08.0
23 Tu	16 08 32	0♐52 05	21 05 30	27 06 52	4R44.9	2 59.3	5 41.9	17 03.0	23 11.7	23 03.6	29 21.7	4 38.6	25 49.1	28 10.2
24 W	16 12 28	1 52 44	3♓11 47	9♓20 53	4 44.6	4 33.6	6 57.3	17 49.0	23 35.6	23 16.8	29 28.2	4 42.3	25 51.2	28 12.3
25 Th	16 16 25	2 53 25	15 34 46	21 53 59	4 43.0	6 07.7	8 12.7	18 35.1	23 59.6	23 30.0	29 34.8	4 46.0	25 53.3	28 14.3
26 F	16 20 21	3 54 06	28 19 01	4♈50 17	4 39.9	7 41.6	9 28.0	19 21.2	24 23.6	23 43.1	29 41.2	4 49.7	25 55.4	28 16.4
27 Sa	16 24 18	4 54 49	11♈28 04	18 12 34	4 35.8	9 15.5	10 43.4	20 07.4	24 47.6	23 56.3	29 47.7	4 53.3	25 57.6	28 18.5
28 Su	16 28 14	5 55 33	25 03 49	2♉01 43	4 31.3	10 49.2	11 58.7	20 53.6	25 11.6	24 09.4	29 54.1	4 57.1	25 59.7	28 20.5
29 M	16 32 11	6 56 18	9♉05 58	16 16 10	4 27.0	12 22.8	13 14.1	21 39.9	25 35.7	24 22.6	0♏00.4	5 00.8	26 01.9	28 22.5
30 Tu	16 36 07	7 57 04	23 31 41	0♊51 46	4 23.4	13 56.3	14 29.5	22 26.2	25 59.8	24 35.7	0 06.7	5 04.5	26 04.0	28 24.5

December 1982 LONGITUDE

Day	Sid.Time	☉	0 hr ☽	Noon ☽	True ☊	☿	♀	♂	⚳	♃	♄	♅	♆	♇
1 W	16 40 04	8♐57 52	8♊15 32	15♊42 01	4♋21.1	15♐29.8	15♐44.8	23♑12.5	26♐23.9	24♏48.7	0♏12.9	5♐08.2	26♐06.2	28♎26.5
2 Th	16 44 01	9 58 40	23 10 10	0♋38 57	4D20.1	17 03.2	17 00.2	23 58.9	26 48.0	25 01.8	0 19.1	5 11.9	26 08.4	28 28.4
3 F	16 47 57	10 59 30	8♋07 19	15 34 19	4 20.4	18 36.6	18 15.5	24 45.3	27 12.2	25 14.9	0 25.3	5 15.6	26 10.6	28 30.3
4 Sa	16 51 54	12 00 21	22 59 03	0♌20 43	4 21.5	20 09.9	19 30.9	25 31.7	27 36.3	25 27.9	0 31.4	5 19.2	26 12.8	28 32.2
5 Su	16 55 50	13 01 14	7♌38 43	14 52 30	4 22.9	21 43.1	20 46.3	26 18.2	28 00.5	25 40.9	0 37.4	5 22.9	26 15.0	28 34.1
6 M	16 59 47	14 02 08	22 01 42	29 06 03	4 24.2	23 16.4	22 01.6	27 04.7	28 24.7	25 53.8	0 43.4	5 26.6	26 17.3	28 36.0
7 Tu	17 03 43	15 03 03	6♍05 26	12♍59 47	4R24.8	24 49.5	23 17.0	27 51.3	28 48.9	26 06.8	0 49.3	5 30.3	26 19.5	28 37.8
8 W	17 07 40	16 03 59	19 49 10	26 33 41	4 24.4	26 22.7	24 32.4	28 37.8	29 13.1	26 19.7	0 55.2	5 33.9	26 21.7	28 39.6
9 Th	17 11 36	17 04 56	3♎13 29	9♎48 48	4 23.2	27 55.7	25 47.7	29 24.5	29 37.4	26 32.5	1 01.0	5 37.6	26 24.0	28 41.4
10 F	17 15 33	18 05 55	16 19 49	22 46 48	4 21.3	29 28.8	27 03.1	0♒11.1	0♑01.6	26 45.4	1 06.8	5 41.2	26 26.2	28 43.2
11 Sa	17 19 30	19 06 55	29 09 59	5♏29 35	4 19.1	1♑01.7	28 18.5	0 57.8	0 25.9	26 58.2	1 12.5	5 44.9	26 28.5	28 44.9
12 Su	17 23 26	20 07 56	11♏45 52	17 59 03	4 16.7	2 34.4	29 33.8	1 44.5	0 50.2	27 11.0	1 18.1	5 48.5	26 30.7	28 46.6
13 M	17 27 23	21 08 58	24 09 20	0♐16 57	4 14.7	4 07.1	0♑49.2	2 31.3	1 14.5	27 23.7	1 23.7	5 52.1	26 33.0	28 48.3
14 Tu	17 31 19	22 10 01	6♐22 06	12 24 59	4 13.2	5 39.5	2 04.6	3 18.1	1 38.8	27 36.4	1 29.2	5 55.7	26 35.2	28 49.9
15 W	17 35 16	23 11 04	18 25 49	24 24 48	4D12.4	7 11.6	3 20.0	4 04.9	2 03.1	27 49.0	1 34.7	5 59.3	26 37.5	28 51.6
16 Th	17 39 12	24 12 09	0♑22 10	6♑18 10	4 12.2	8 43.4	4 35.3	4 51.7	2 27.4	28 01.6	1 40.0	6 02.9	26 39.8	28 53.2
17 F	17 43 09	25 13 14	12 13 03	18 07 06	4 12.6	10 14.8	5 50.7	5 38.6	2 51.7	28 14.2	1 45.3	6 06.4	26 42.1	28 54.7
18 Sa	17 47 06	26 14 19	24 00 38	29 53 59	4 13.2	11 45.7	7 06.0	6 25.5	3 16.0	28 26.7	1 50.6	6 10.0	26 44.3	28 56.3
19 Su	17 51 02	27 15 25	5♒47 31	11♒41 39	4 14.1	13 15.9	8 21.4	7 12.4	3 40.3	28 39.2	1 55.8	6 13.5	26 46.6	28 57.8
20 M	17 54 59	28 16 32	17 36 49	23 33 28	4 14.8	14 45.4	9 36.8	7 59.3	4 04.7	28 51.6	2 00.9	6 17.0	26 48.9	28 59.3
21 Tu	17 58 55	29 17 38	29 32 07	5♓33 15	4 15.4	16 13.9	10 52.1	8 46.2	4 29.0	29 04.0	2 05.9	6 20.5	26 51.1	29 00.7
22 W	18 02 52	0♑18 45	11♓37 25	17 45 11	4 15.8	17 41.3	12 07.4	9 33.2	4 53.3	29 16.3	2 10.8	6 24.0	26 53.4	29 02.2
23 Th	18 06 48	1 19 52	23 57 05	0♈13 40	4R15.9	19 07.2	13 22.8	10 20.2	5 17.7	29 28.6	2 15.7	6 27.4	26 55.7	29 03.6
24 F	18 10 45	2 20 59	6♈35 27	13 02 57	4 15.8	20 31.6	14 38.1	11 07.2	5 42.0	29 40.8	2 20.5	6 30.9	26 57.9	29 04.9
25 Sa	18 14 41	3 22 06	19 36 34	26 16 41	4D15.7	21 53.9	15 53.4	11 54.2	6 06.3	29 53.0	2 25.3	6 34.3	27 00.2	29 06.3
26 Su	18 18 38	4 23 14	3♉03 34	9♉57 23	4 15.7	23 13.9	17 08.7	12 41.2	6 30.6	0♐05.1	2 29.9	6 37.7	27 02.4	29 07.6
27 M	18 22 35	5 24 21	16 58 08	24 05 40	4 15.8	24 31.2	18 24.0	13 28.3	6 54.9	0 17.1	2 34.5	6 41.1	27 04.7	29 08.8
28 Tu	18 26 31	6 25 29	1♊19 43	8♊39 45	4 15.9	25 45.2	19 39.3	14 15.3	7 19.2	0 29.1	2 39.0	6 44.4	27 06.9	29 10.1
29 W	18 30 28	7 26 36	16 05 06	23 34 57	4R16.1	26 55.4	20 54.6	15 02.4	7 43.5	0 41.0	2 43.4	6 47.7	27 09.2	29 11.3
30 Th	18 34 24	8 27 44	1♋08 16	8♋43 57	4 16.1	28 01.2	22 09.8	15 49.5	8 07.8	0 52.9	2 47.8	6 51.0	27 11.4	29 12.5
31 F	18 38 21	9 28 52	16 20 47	23 57 31	4 15.9	29 01.9	23 25.1	16 36.5	8 32.1	1 04.7	2 52.0	6 54.3	27 13.7	29 13.6

Astro Data

	Dy Hr Mn
♄☌♇	8 0:44
☽0S	12 10:17
☽0N	27 1:05
♃⊻♆	8 16:39
☽0S	9 16:19
♃⊻♇	21 4:50
☽0N	24 10:30

Planet Ingress

	Dy Hr Mn
☿ ♏	3 1:10
♀ ♐	18 23:07
☿ ♐	21 14:28
☉ ♐	22 15:23
♄ ♏	29 10:29
♂ ♒	10 6:17
⚳ ♑	10 10:23
☿ ♑	10 20:04
♀ ♑	12 20:20
☉ ♑	22 4:38
♃ ♐	26 1:57

Last Aspect / ☽ Ingress (November)

Last Aspect Dy Hr Mn		☽ Ingress Dy Hr Mn
2 5:02	♃ ☍	♊ 3 0:23
4 21:47	♇ △	♋ 5 1:59
7 0:02	♇ □	♌ 7 4:10
9 3:42	♄ ⚹	♍ 9 7:40
11 4:31	♆ □	♎ 11 12:46
13 16:27	♄ ☌	♏ 13 19:42
15 21:22	♀ ☌	♐ 16 4:52
18 13:58	♄ ⚹	♑ 18 16:21
21 3:56	☿ ⚹	♒ 21 5:20
23 16:29	♄ △	♓ 23 17:43
25 19:30	♆ □	♈ 26 3:07
28 8:19	♄ ☍	♉ 28 8:31
30 1:36	♃ ☍	♊ 30 10:36

Last Aspect / ☽ Ingress (December)

Last Aspect Dy Hr Mn		☽ Ingress Dy Hr Mn
2 8:30	♇ △	♋ 2 10:58
4 9:02	♇ □	♌ 4 11:26
6 11:09	♇ ⚹	♍ 6 13:32
8 15:57	♂ △	♎ 8 18:11
10 23:11	♇ ☌	♏ 11 1:34
13 6:14	♃ ☌	♐ 13 11:27
15 20:58	♇ ⚹	♑ 15 23:15
18 10:02	♇ □	♒ 18 12:12
20 22:56	♇ △	♓ 21 0:56
23 10:33	♃ △	♈ 23 11:34
25 17:02	♇ ☍	♉ 25 18:37
27 12:47	☿ △	♊ 27 21:49
29 20:55	♇ △	♋ 29 22:12
31 20:33	☿ ☍	♌ 31 21:33

☽ Phases & Eclipses

Dy Hr Mn	
1 12:57	○ 8♉46
8 6:38	☾ 15♌32
15 15:10	● 22♏56
23 20:06	☽ 1♓13
1 0:21	○ 8♊28
7 15:53	☾ 15♍13
15 9:18	● 23♐04
15 9:31:18	● P 0.735
23 14:17	☽ 1♈26
30 11:33	○ 8♋27
30 11:29	● T 1.182

Astro Data

1 November 1982
Julian Day # 30255
SVP 5♓30'17"
GC 26♐36.0 ⚴ 22♏51.0
Eris 14♈53.6R ⚵ 7♑27.3
⚷ 26♉02.4R ⚶ 16♒15.4
☽ Mean ☊ 7♋03.5

1 December 1982
Julian Day # 30285
SVP 5♓30'12"
GC 26♐36.0 ⚴ 5♐50.7
Eris 14♈39.8R ⚵ 17♑41.9
⚷ 24♉28.5R ⚶ 25♒29.0
☽ Mean ☊ 5♋28.2

LONGITUDE — January 1983

Day	Sid.Time	☉	0 hr ☽	Noon ☽	True ☊	☿	♀	♂	⚳	♃	♄	♅	♆	♇
1 Sa	18 42 17	10♑30 00	1♌32 55	9♌05 48	4♋15.4	29♑56.7	24♑40.4	17♒23.6	8♑56.4	1♐16.4	2♏56.2	6♐57.6	27♐15.9	29♎14.7
2 Su	18 46 14	11 31 08	16 35 06	23 59 53	4R 14.7	0♒44.8	25 55.6	18 10.7	9 20.7	1 28.0	3 00.3	7 00.8	27 18.1	29 15.8
3 M	18 50 10	12 32 17	1♍19 20	8♍32 54	4 13.7	1 25.4	27 10.8	18 57.8	9 44.9	1 39.6	3 04.3	7 04.0	27 20.3	29 16.8
4 Tu	18 54 07	13 33 26	15 40 07	22 40 45	4 12.9	1 57.4	28 26.1	19 44.9	10 09.2	1 51.1	3 08.2	7 07.2	27 22.5	29 17.8
5 W	18 58 04	14 34 34	29 34 44	6♎22 07	4D 12.3	2 20.0	29 41.3	20 32.0	10 33.4	2 02.6	3 12.0	7 10.3	27 24.7	29 18.8
6 Th	19 02 00	15 35 44	13♎03 05	19 37 55	4 12.2	2R 32.4	0♒56.5	21 19.2	10 57.6	2 14.0	3 15.8	7 13.4	27 26.9	29 19.8
7 F	19 05 57	16 36 53	26 06 58	2♏30 40	4 12.7	2 33.8	2 11.7	22 06.3	11 21.9	2 25.3	3 19.4	7 16.5	27 29.1	29 20.7
8 Sa	19 09 53	17 38 03	8♏49 28	15 03 49	4 13.7	2 23.6	3 26.9	22 53.4	11 46.1	2 36.5	3 23.0	7 19.6	27 31.3	29 21.5
9 Su	19 13 50	18 39 12	21 14 14	27 21 11	4 15.0	2 01.6	4 42.1	23 40.6	12 10.2	2 47.6	3 26.5	7 22.6	27 33.4	29 22.4
10 M	19 17 46	19 40 22	3♐25 06	9♐26 28	4 16.4	1 27.9	5 57.3	24 27.7	12 34.4	2 58.7	3 29.9	7 25.6	27 35.6	29 23.2
11 Tu	19 21 43	20 41 31	15 25 42	21 23 10	4 17.5	0 42.9	7 12.5	25 14.9	12 58.6	3 09.7	3 33.2	7 28.5	27 37.7	29 24.0
12 W	19 25 39	21 42 41	27 19 16	3♑14 19	4R 18.0	29♑47.5	8 27.6	26 02.0	13 22.7	3 20.6	3 36.4	7 31.5	27 39.8	29 24.7
13 Th	19 29 36	22 43 50	9♑08 38	15 02 32	4 17.6	28 43.2	9 42.8	26 49.1	13 46.8	3 31.4	3 39.5	7 34.4	27 41.9	29 25.4
14 F	19 33 33	23 44 59	20 56 15	26 50 04	4 16.2	27 31.8	10 57.9	27 36.3	14 10.9	3 42.1	3 42.5	7 37.2	27 44.0	29 26.0
15 Sa	19 37 29	24 46 07	2♒44 14	8♒39 00	4 13.6	26 15.6	12 13.0	28 23.4	14 35.0	3 52.7	3 45.4	7 40.0	27 46.1	29 26.7
16 Su	19 41 26	25 47 15	14 34 35	20 31 16	4 10.2	24 57.1	13 28.2	29 10.6	14 59.0	4 03.3	3 48.3	7 42.8	27 48.2	29 27.3
17 M	19 45 22	26 48 22	26 29 17	2♓28 56	4 06.3	23 38.6	14 43.2	29 57.7	15 23.1	4 13.7	3 51.0	7 45.6	27 50.2	29 27.8
18 Tu	19 49 19	27 49 28	8♓30 30	14 34 18	4 02.2	22 22.6	15 58.3	0♓44.8	15 47.1	4 24.0	3 53.6	7 48.3	27 52.3	29 28.3
19 W	19 53 15	28 50 34	20 40 42	26 50 02	3 58.6	21 11.1	17 13.4	1 31.9	16 11.0	4 34.3	3 56.1	7 51.0	27 54.3	29 28.8
20 Th	19 57 12	29 51 39	3♈02 42	9♈19 06	3 55.8	20 05.9	18 28.4	2 19.1	16 35.0	4 44.4	3 58.6	7 53.6	27 56.3	29 29.3
21 F	20 01 08	0♒52 43	15 39 40	22 04 48	3D 54.2	19 08.2	19 43.4	3 06.1	16 58.9	4 54.5	4 00.9	7 56.2	27 58.3	29 29.7
22 Sa	20 05 05	1 53 46	28 34 55	5♉10 26	3 53.9	18 19.1	20 58.4	3 53.2	17 22.8	5 04.4	4 03.1	7 58.7	28 00.2	29 30.0
23 Su	20 09 02	2 54 48	11♉51 40	18 38 57	3 54.8	17 39.0	22 13.4	4 40.3	17 46.7	5 14.3	4 05.2	8 01.3	28 02.2	29 30.4
24 M	20 12 58	3 55 49	25 32 31	2♊32 27	3 56.2	17 08.0	23 28.4	5 27.4	18 10.5	5 24.0	4 07.3	8 03.7	28 04.1	29 30.7
25 Tu	20 16 55	4 56 49	9♊38 48	16 51 23	3 57.8	16 46.2	24 43.3	6 14.4	18 34.3	5 33.7	4 09.2	8 06.2	28 06.0	29 30.9
26 W	20 20 51	5 57 48	24 09 55	1♋33 54	3R 58.6	16 33.3	25 58.2	7 01.4	18 58.0	5 43.2	4 11.0	8 08.6	28 07.9	29 31.2
27 Th	20 24 48	6 58 46	9♋02 39	16 35 18	3 58.0	16D 28.7	27 13.1	7 48.5	19 21.8	5 52.6	4 12.8	8 10.9	28 09.8	29 31.4
28 F	20 28 44	7 59 43	24 10 51	1♌48 05	3 55.8	16 32.1	28 28.0	8 35.5	19 45.5	6 01.9	4 14.4	8 13.2	28 11.7	29 31.5
29 Sa	20 32 41	9 00 39	9♌25 46	17 02 34	3 51.9	16 43.0	29 42.8	9 22.4	20 09.1	6 11.1	4 15.9	8 15.5	28 13.5	29 31.6
30 Su	20 36 38	10 01 34	24 37 10	2♍08 21	3 46.7	17 00.6	0♓57.6	10 09.4	20 32.8	6 20.2	4 17.3	8 17.7	28 15.3	29 31.7
31 M	20 40 34	11 02 28	9♍34 57	16 56 00	3 40.8	17 24.6	2 12.4	10 56.3	20 56.3	6 29.2	4 18.6	8 19.9	28 17.1	29R 31.8

LONGITUDE — February 1983

Day	Sid.Time	☉	0 hr ☽	Noon ☽	True ☊	☿	♀	♂	⚳	♃	♄	♅	♆	♇
1 Tu	20 44 31	12♒03 21	24♍10 45	1♎18 36	3♋35.2	17♑54.3	3♓27.1	11♓43.3	21♑19.9	6♐38.0	4♏19.9	8♐22.0	28♐18.9	29♎31.8
2 W	20 48 27	13 04 13	8♎19 11	15 12 21	3R 30.6	18 29.3	4 41.9	12 30.2	21 43.4	6 46.8	4 21.0	8 24.1	28 20.7	29R 31.7
3 Th	20 52 24	14 05 05	21 58 08	28 36 42	3 27.5	19 09.1	5 56.6	13 17.1	22 06.9	6 55.4	4 22.0	8 26.2	28 22.4	29 31.7
4 F	20 56 20	15 05 56	5♏08 23	11♏33 37	3D 26.2	19 53.3	7 11.3	14 03.9	22 30.3	7 03.9	4 22.9	8 28.2	28 24.1	29 31.6
5 Sa	21 00 17	16 06 46	17 52 56	24 06 53	3 26.5	20 41.5	8 25.9	14 50.8	22 53.7	7 12.2	4 23.6	8 30.1	28 25.8	29 31.5
6 Su	21 04 13	17 07 35	0♐16 05	6♐21 12	3 27.7	21 33.3	9 40.6	15 37.6	23 17.0	7 20.5	4 24.3	8 32.0	28 27.4	29 31.3
7 M	21 08 10	18 08 23	12 22 50	18 21 37	3 29.3	22 28.4	10 55.2	16 24.4	23 40.3	7 28.6	4 24.9	8 33.9	28 29.1	29 31.1
8 Tu	21 12 06	19 09 10	24 18 10	0♑13 03	3R 30.3	23 26.6	12 09.8	17 11.2	24 03.6	7 36.6	4 25.4	8 35.7	28 30.7	29 30.8
9 W	21 16 03	20 09 56	6♑06 49	11 59 59	3 29.9	24 27.6	13 24.3	17 58.0	24 26.8	7 44.4	4 25.8	8 37.5	28 32.3	29 30.6
10 Th	21 20 00	21 10 41	17 52 59	23 46 14	3 27.5	25 31.2	14 38.8	18 44.7	24 50.0	7 52.1	4 26.0	8 39.2	28 33.8	29 30.3
11 F	21 23 56	22 11 25	29 40 08	5♒34 59	3 22.8	26 37.1	15 53.3	19 31.5	25 13.1	7 59.7	4R 26.2	8 40.8	28 35.4	29 29.9
12 Sa	21 27 53	23 12 07	11♒31 04	17 28 38	3 15.7	27 45.2	17 07.8	20 18.2	25 36.2	8 07.1	4 26.2	8 42.5	28 36.9	29 29.5
13 Su	21 31 49	24 12 48	23 27 53	29 29 00	3 06.7	28 55.3	18 22.2	21 04.8	25 59.2	8 14.4	4 26.2	8 44.0	28 38.4	29 29.1
14 M	21 35 46	25 13 28	5♓32 08	11♓37 25	2 56.5	0♒07.3	19 36.6	21 51.5	26 22.2	8 21.6	4 26.0	8 45.5	28 39.8	29 28.7
15 Tu	21 39 42	26 14 06	17 44 58	23 54 55	2 45.9	1 21.0	20 51.0	22 38.1	26 45.1	8 28.6	4 25.7	8 47.0	28 41.3	29 28.2
16 W	21 43 39	27 14 43	0♈07 23	6♈22 31	2 36.1	2 36.5	22 05.3	23 24.7	27 07.9	8 35.5	4 25.4	8 48.4	28 42.7	29 27.7
17 Th	21 47 35	28 15 17	12 40 28	19 01 25	2 27.9	3 53.5	23 19.6	24 11.2	27 30.7	8 42.2	4 24.9	8 49.8	28 44.0	29 27.1
18 F	21 51 32	29 15 50	25 25 34	1♉53 09	2 22.0	5 11.9	24 33.9	24 57.8	27 53.4	8 48.7	4 24.3	8 51.1	28 45.4	29 26.5
19 Sa	21 55 29	0♓16 22	8♉24 25	14 59 38	2 18.5	6 31.8	25 48.1	25 44.3	28 16.1	8 55.2	4 23.6	8 52.3	28 46.7	29 25.9
20 Su	21 59 25	1 16 51	21 39 03	28 22 58	2D 17.3	7 53.1	27 02.2	26 30.7	28 38.7	9 01.4	4 22.8	8 53.5	28 48.0	29 25.3
21 M	22 03 22	2 17 19	5♊11 37	12♊05 12	2 17.6	9 15.6	28 16.4	27 17.2	29 01.3	9 07.6	4 21.9	8 54.7	28 49.3	29 24.6
22 Tu	22 07 18	3 17 45	19 03 52	26 07 41	2R 18.3	10 39.4	29 30.5	28 03.5	29 23.8	9 13.5	4 20.9	8 55.8	28 50.5	29 23.9
23 W	22 11 15	4 18 09	3♋16 36	10♋30 26	2 18.1	12 04.3	0♈44.5	28 49.9	29 46.2	9 19.3	4 19.9	8 56.8	28 51.7	29 23.1
24 Th	22 15 11	5 18 31	17 48 51	25 11 22	2 16.1	13 30.5	1 58.5	29 36.2	0♒08.6	9 25.0	4 18.7	8 57.8	28 52.9	29 22.4
25 F	22 19 08	6 18 51	2♌37 19	10♌05 51	2 11.6	14 57.8	3 12.4	0♈22.5	0 30.9	9 30.5	4 17.4	8 58.8	28 54.0	29 21.5
26 Sa	22 23 04	7 19 09	17 36 00	25 06 40	2 04.3	16 26.2	4 26.3	1 08.8	0 53.1	9 35.8	4 16.0	8 59.7	28 55.2	29 20.7
27 Su	22 27 01	8 19 25	2♍36 39	10♍04 46	1 54.9	17 55.8	5 40.2	1 55.0	1 15.2	9 41.0	4 14.5	9 00.5	28 56.2	29 19.8
28 M	22 30 58	9 19 40	17 29 50	24 50 45	1 44.2	19 26.4	6 54.0	2 41.1	1 37.3	9 46.0	4 12.9	9 01.3	28 57.3	29 18.9

Astro Data

	Dy Hr Mn
☽0S	5 22:30
☿R	7 2:57
♃⚺♄	14 13:20
☽0N	20 17:15
☿D	27 13:26
♇R	1 5:53
☽0S	2 6:18
♄R	12 11:17
☽0N	16 22:10
♃☌♅	18 22:41
♀0N	24 18:24
♂0N	26 19:50

Planet Ingress

		Dy Hr Mn
☿	♒	1 13:32
♀	♒	5 17:58
☿	♑R	12 6:55
♂	♓	17 13:10
☉	♒	20 15:17
♀	♓	29 17:31
☿	♒	14 9:36
☉	♓	19 5:31
♀	♈	22 21:35
⚳	♒	24 2:49
♂	♈	25 0:19

Last Aspect / ☽ Ingress (January)

Last Aspect Dy Hr Mn			☽ Ingress	Dy Hr Mn
2 20:37	♇	⚹	♍	2 21:49
4 23:00	♀	△	♎	5 0:44
7 6:02	♇	☌	♏	7 7:16
9 4:17	♂	□	♐	9 17:14
12 4:14	♇	⚹	♑	12 5:26
14 17:17	♇	□	♒	14 18:26
17 6:37	♂	☌	♓	17 7:02
19 16:15	☉	⚹	♈	19 18:08
22 1:41	♇	☍	♉	22 2:36
23 18:52	♀	□	♊	24 7:40
26 8:42	♇	△	♋	26 9:28
28 8:25	♇	□	♌	28 9:10
30 7:49	♇	⚹	♍	30 8:35

Last Aspect / ☽ Ingress (February)

Last Aspect Dy Hr Mn			☽ Ingress	Dy Hr Mn
1 6:56	♆	□	♎	1 9:47
3 13:40	♇	☌	♏	3 14:32
5 4:55	☿	⚹	♐	5 23:28
8 10:34	♇	⚹	♑	8 11:33
10 23:40	♇	□	♒	11 0:40
13 12:00	♇	△	♓	13 13:02
15 21:15	♆	□	♈	15 23:46
18 7:29	♇	☍	♉	18 8:30
20 9:22	♀	⚹	♊	20 14:52
22 18:14	♀	□	♋	22 18:31
24 19:32	♂	△	♌	24 19:47
26 18:46	♇	⚹	♍	26 19:49
28 18:47	♆	□	♎	28 20:30

☽ Phases & Eclipses

Dy Hr Mn		
6 4:00	☾	15♎15
14 5:08	●	23♑27
22 5:33	☽	1♉37
28 22:26	○	8♌26
4 19:17	☾	15♏24
13 0:32	●	23♒44
20 17:32	☽	1♊31
27 8:58	○	8♍12

Astro Data

1 January 1983
Julian Day # 30316
SVP 5♓30'06"
GC 26♐36.1 ⚴ 19♐02.8
Eris 14♈34.1R ⚵ 29♑49.2
⚷ 23♉09.1R ⚶ 7♓34.6
☽ Mean ☊ 3♋49.7

1 February 1983
Julian Day # 30347
SVP 5♓30'01"
GC 26♐36.2 ⚴ 1♑28.7
Eris 14♈39.1 ⚵ 12♒55.5
⚷ 22♉39.9 ⚶ 21♓04.1
☽ Mean ☊ 2♋11.3

March 1983 LONGITUDE

Day	Sid.Time	☉	0 hr ☽	Noon ☽	True ☊	☿	♀	♂	⚳	♃	♄	♅	♆	♇
1 Tu	22 34 54	10♓19 53	2♎06 32	9♎16 24	1♋33.6	20♒58.1	8♈07.7	3♈27.3	1♒59.4	9♐50.9	4♏11.2	9♐02.0	28♐58.3	29♎18.0
2 W	22 38 51	11 20 04	16 19 44	23 16 06	1R 24.2	22 31.0	9 21.4	4 13.4	2 21.3	9 55.6	4R 09.4	9 02.7	28 59.3	29R 17.1
3 Th	22 42 47	12 20 14	0♏05 17	6♏47 17	1 17.0	24 04.8	10 35.1	4 59.4	2 43.2	10 00.1	4 07.5	9 03.3	29 00.3	29 16.1
4 F	22 46 44	13 20 22	13 22 15	19 50 27	1 12.2	25 39.8	11 48.7	5 45.5	3 05.0	10 04.5	4 05.6	9 03.9	29 01.2	29 15.1
5 Sa	22 50 40	14 20 28	26 12 19	2♐28 22	1 09.8	27 15.9	13 02.2	6 31.5	3 26.7	10 08.6	4 03.5	9 04.4	29 02.1	29 14.0
6 Su	22 54 37	15 20 34	8♐39 13	14 45 29	1D 09.2	28 53.0	14 15.7	7 17.4	3 48.4	10 12.7	4 01.3	9 04.9	29 03.0	29 13.0
7 M	22 58 33	16 20 37	20 47 51	26 47 02	1R 09.4	0♓31.3	15 29.2	8 03.3	4 10.0	10 16.5	3 59.1	9 05.3	29 03.8	29 11.9
8 Tu	23 02 30	17 20 39	2♑43 44	8♑38 37	1 09.2	2 10.6	16 42.6	8 49.2	4 31.5	10 20.2	3 56.7	9 05.6	29 04.6	29 10.7
9 W	23 06 27	18 20 39	14 32 22	20 25 36	1 07.6	3 51.1	17 56.0	9 35.1	4 52.9	10 23.7	3 54.3	9 05.9	29 05.4	29 09.6
10 Th	23 10 23	19 20 38	26 18 56	2♒12 54	1 03.8	5 32.6	19 09.3	10 20.9	5 14.2	10 27.0	3 51.8	9 06.2	29 06.1	29 08.4
11 F	23 14 20	20 20 35	8♒08 02	14 04 45	0 57.1	7 15.4	20 22.5	11 06.6	5 35.5	10 30.1	3 49.2	9 06.4	29 06.8	29 07.2
12 Sa	23 18 16	21 20 30	20 03 27	26 04 27	0 47.6	8 59.2	21 35.7	11 52.4	5 56.6	10 33.1	3 46.5	9 06.5	29 07.5	29 06.0
13 Su	23 22 13	22 20 23	2♓08 01	8♓14 22	0 35.6	10 44.2	22 48.9	12 38.0	6 17.7	10 35.8	3 43.7	9 06.6	29 08.1	29 04.8
14 M	23 26 09	23 20 14	14 23 37	20 35 53	0 22.0	12 30.4	24 02.0	13 23.7	6 38.7	10 38.4	3 40.8	9R 06.6	29 08.7	29 03.5
15 Tu	23 30 06	24 20 04	26 51 10	3♈09 31	0 08.0	14 17.8	25 15.0	14 09.3	6 59.6	10 40.9	3 37.9	9 06.6	29 09.3	29 02.2
16 W	23 34 02	25 19 51	9♈30 51	15 55 08	29♊54.7	16 06.4	26 28.0	14 54.8	7 20.4	10 43.1	3 34.8	9 06.5	29 09.9	29 00.9
17 Th	23 37 59	26 19 36	22 22 19	28 52 19	29 43.4	17 56.2	27 40.9	15 40.3	7 41.1	10 45.1	3 31.7	9 06.4	29 10.4	28 59.6
18 F	23 41 56	27 19 19	5♉25 07	12♉00 39	29 34.8	19 47.1	28 53.7	16 25.8	8 01.7	10 47.0	3 28.6	9 06.2	29 10.8	28 58.2
19 Sa	23 45 52	28 19 00	18 38 56	25 20 00	29 29.3	21 39.3	0♉06.5	17 11.2	8 22.2	10 48.7	3 25.3	9 06.0	29 11.3	28 56.8
20 Su	23 49 49	29 18 39	2♊03 54	8♊50 43	29 26.6	23 32.7	1 19.2	17 56.6	8 42.7	10 50.2	3 22.0	9 05.7	29 11.7	28 55.4
21 M	23 53 45	0♈18 16	15 40 32	22 33 28	29 25.8	25 27.3	2 31.9	18 41.9	9 03.0	10 51.5	3 18.6	9 05.3	29 12.0	28 54.0
22 Tu	23 57 42	1 17 50	29 29 36	6♋29 01	29 25.7	27 23.1	3 44.5	19 27.2	9 23.2	10 52.6	3 15.1	9 04.9	29 12.4	28 52.6
23 W	0 01 38	2 17 22	13♋31 42	20 37 36	29 25.0	29 20.0	4 57.0	20 12.5	9 43.3	10 53.5	3 11.6	9 04.5	29 12.7	28 51.1
24 Th	0 05 35	3 16 51	27 46 35	4♌58 24	29 22.5	1♈18.0	6 09.4	20 57.7	10 03.3	10 54.3	3 08.0	9 04.0	29 13.0	28 49.7
25 F	0 09 31	4 16 19	12♌12 41	19 28 56	29 17.4	3 17.1	7 21.8	21 42.8	10 23.2	10 54.8	3 04.3	9 03.5	29 13.2	28 48.2
26 Sa	0 13 28	5 15 43	26 46 32	4♍04 45	29 09.5	5 17.2	8 34.1	22 27.9	10 43.0	10 55.2	3 00.6	9 02.9	29 13.4	28 46.7
27 Su	0 17 25	6 15 06	11♍22 46	18 39 42	28 59.2	7 18.1	9 46.3	23 12.9	11 02.7	10R 55.4	2 56.8	9 02.2	29 13.6	28 45.2
28 M	0 21 21	7 14 27	25 54 37	3♎06 39	28 47.4	9 19.9	10 58.4	23 57.9	11 22.2	10 55.4	2 52.9	9 01.5	29 13.7	28 43.6
29 Tu	0 25 18	8 13 45	10♎14 57	17 18 44	28 35.6	11 22.2	12 10.5	24 42.9	11 41.7	10 55.2	2 49.0	9 00.8	29 13.8	28 42.1
30 W	0 29 14	9 13 01	24 17 22	1♏10 22	28 24.9	13 25.1	13 22.4	25 27.8	12 01.0	10 54.8	2 45.1	9 00.0	29 13.9	28 40.5
31 Th	0 33 11	10 12 16	7♏57 23	14 38 13	28 16.2	15 28.2	14 34.3	26 12.6	12 20.3	10 54.3	2 41.1	8 59.1	29R 13.9	28 39.0

April 1983 LONGITUDE

Day	Sid.Time	☉	0 hr ☽	Noon ☽	True ☊	☿	♀	♂	⚳	♃	♄	♅	♆	♇
1 F	0 37 07	11♈11 29	21♏12 50	27♏41 22	28♊10.3	17♈31.4	15♉46.2	26♈57.4	12♒39.4	10♐53.5	2♏37.0	8♐58.2	29♐13.9	28♎37.4
2 Sa	0 41 04	12 10 39	4♐04 03	10♐21 15	28R 06.9	19 34.4	16 57.9	27 42.2	12 58.4	10R 52.6	2R 32.9	8R 57.3	29R 13.9	28R 35.8
3 Su	0 45 00	13 09 49	16 33 26	22 41 06	28D 05.7	21 36.9	18 09.6	28 26.9	13 17.2	10 51.5	2 28.8	8 56.3	29 13.9	28 34.2
4 M	0 48 57	14 08 56	28 44 53	4♑45 24	28R 05.7	23 38.6	19 21.2	29 11.6	13 36.0	10 50.2	2 24.6	8 55.2	29 13.8	28 32.6
5 Tu	0 52 53	15 08 02	10♑43 19	16 39 20	28 05.8	25 39.2	20 32.7	29 56.2	13 54.6	10 48.7	2 20.3	8 54.2	29 13.6	28 30.9
6 W	0 56 50	16 07 05	22 34 09	28 28 25	28 05.1	27 38.3	21 44.1	0♉40.8	14 13.1	10 47.0	2 16.1	8 53.0	29 13.5	28 29.3
7 Th	1 00 47	17 06 07	4♒22 50	10♒18 00	28 02.5	29 35.6	22 55.4	1 25.3	14 31.5	10 45.1	2 11.7	8 51.9	29 13.3	28 27.6
8 F	1 04 43	18 05 08	16 14 34	22 13 04	27 57.6	1♉30.6	24 06.7	2 09.8	14 49.7	10 43.1	2 07.4	8 50.6	29 13.1	28 26.0
9 Sa	1 08 40	19 04 06	28 14 01	4♓17 51	27 50.1	3 23.0	25 17.9	2 54.2	15 07.8	10 40.9	2 03.0	8 49.4	29 12.8	28 24.3
10 Su	1 12 36	20 03 02	10♓24 58	16 35 40	27 40.4	5 12.5	26 29.0	3 38.6	15 25.7	10 38.4	1 58.6	8 48.0	29 12.5	28 22.7
11 M	1 16 33	21 01 57	22 50 11	29 08 41	27 29.1	6 58.7	27 40.0	4 22.9	15 43.5	10 35.8	1 54.2	8 46.7	29 12.2	28 21.0
12 Tu	1 20 29	22 00 50	5♈31 12	11♈57 45	27 17.4	8 41.3	28 50.9	5 07.2	16 01.2	10 33.1	1 49.7	8 45.3	29 11.8	28 19.3
13 W	1 24 26	22 59 40	18 28 16	25 02 34	27 06.2	10 20.0	0♊01.7	5 51.4	16 18.7	10 30.1	1 45.2	8 43.8	29 11.5	28 17.6
14 Th	1 28 22	23 58 29	1♉40 29	8♉21 46	26 56.7	11 54.5	1 12.4	6 35.6	16 36.1	10 27.0	1 40.7	8 42.3	29 11.0	28 15.9
15 F	1 32 19	24 57 16	15 06 09	21 53 22	26 49.6	13 24.6	2 23.0	7 19.7	16 53.3	10 23.7	1 36.2	8 40.8	29 10.6	28 14.2
16 Sa	1 36 16	25 56 01	28 43 06	5♊35 08	26 45.2	14 50.1	3 33.6	8 03.8	17 10.4	10 20.2	1 31.6	8 39.3	29 10.1	28 12.5
17 Su	1 40 12	26 54 43	12♊29 12	19 25 06	26D 43.4	16 10.8	4 44.0	8 47.9	17 27.3	10 16.6	1 27.1	8 37.6	29 09.6	28 10.9
18 M	1 44 09	27 53 24	26 22 39	3♋21 43	26 43.3	17 26.4	5 54.3	9 31.9	17 44.1	10 12.7	1 22.5	8 36.0	29 09.1	28 09.2
19 Tu	1 48 05	28 52 02	10♋22 09	17 23 51	26R 44.0	18 37.0	7 04.5	10 15.8	18 00.7	10 08.8	1 17.9	8 34.3	29 08.5	28 07.5
20 W	1 52 02	29 50 38	24 26 43	1♌30 37	26 44.4	19 42.3	8 14.6	10 59.7	18 17.2	10 04.6	1 13.4	8 32.6	29 07.9	28 05.8
21 Th	1 55 58	0♉49 12	8♌35 25	15 40 56	26 43.4	20 42.2	9 24.6	11 43.5	18 33.4	10 00.3	1 08.8	8 30.8	29 07.3	28 04.1
22 F	1 59 55	1 47 43	22 46 57	29 53 10	26 40.3	21 36.6	10 34.5	12 27.3	18 49.6	9 55.8	1 04.2	8 29.0	29 06.6	28 02.4
23 Sa	2 03 51	2 46 13	6♍59 15	14♍04 48	26 35.1	22 25.5	11 44.3	13 11.0	19 05.5	9 51.2	0 59.6	8 27.2	29 05.9	28 00.7
24 Su	2 07 48	3 44 40	21 09 20	28 12 23	26 27.9	23 08.8	12 53.9	13 54.7	19 21.3	9 46.4	0 55.0	8 25.3	29 05.2	27 59.0
25 M	2 11 45	4 43 05	5♎13 25	12♎11 53	26 19.6	23 46.5	14 03.4	14 38.3	19 36.9	9 41.5	0 50.5	8 23.5	29 04.4	27 57.3
26 Tu	2 15 41	5 41 28	19 07 17	25 59 07	26 11.1	24 18.4	15 12.8	15 21.9	19 52.3	9 36.5	0 45.9	8 21.5	29 03.7	27 55.6
27 W	2 19 38	6 39 49	2♏46 59	9♏30 29	26 03.4	24 44.6	16 22.1	16 05.4	20 07.6	9 31.2	0 41.4	8 19.6	29 02.9	27 54.0
28 Th	2 23 34	7 38 08	16 09 23	22 43 28	25 57.3	25 05.1	17 31.3	16 48.8	20 22.7	9 25.9	0 36.8	8 17.6	29 02.0	27 52.3
29 F	2 27 31	8 36 26	29 12 42	5♐37 04	25 53.2	25 20.0	18 40.3	17 32.2	20 37.6	9 20.4	0 32.3	8 15.5	29 01.2	27 50.6
30 Sa	2 31 27	9 34 42	11♐56 43	18 11 51	25D 51.2	25 29.2	19 49.2	18 15.6	20 52.3	9 14.8	0 27.8	8 13.5	29 00.3	27 49.0

Astro Data	Dy Hr Mn
☽ 0S	1 15:53
♆ ⚹ ♇	11 17:16
♅ R	14 13:03
☽ 0N	16 3:33
☉ 0N	21 4:39
☿ 0N	25 10:26
♃ R	27 23:56
☽ 0S	29 1:54
♆ R	1 4:28
☽ 0N	12 10:56
☽ 0S	25 10:44

Planet Ingress	Dy Hr Mn
☿ ♓	7 4:24
☊ ♊R	16 2:05
♀ ♉	19 9:51
☉ ♈	21 4:39
☿ ♈	23 20:09
♂ ♉	5 14:03
☿ ♉	7 17:04
♀ ♊	13 11:26
☉ ♉	20 15:50

Last Aspect Dy Hr Mn		☽ Ingress Dy Hr Mn
2 22:34	♇ ☌	♏ 2 23:51
5 0:34	☿ □	♐ 5 7:15
7 16:51	♇ ⚹	♑ 7 18:29
10 5:46	♇ □	♒ 10 7:30
12 18:03	♆ ⚹	♓ 12 19:47
15 4:23	♆ □	♈ 15 6:00
17 12:33	♆ △	♉ 17 14:04
19 17:45	☉ ⚹	♊ 19 20:20
21 23:30	♆ ☍	♋ 22 0:52
24 1:47	♇ □	♌ 24 3:43
26 4:01	♆ △	♍ 26 5:18
28 5:31	♆ □	♎ 28 6:48
30 8:36	♆ ⚹	♏ 30 9:57

Last Aspect Dy Hr Mn		☽ Ingress Dy Hr Mn
31 11:52	♀ ☍	♐ 1 16:20
4 0:58	♆ ☌	♑ 4 2:30
6 12:02	♇ □	♒ 6 15:06
9 1:57	♆ ⚹	♓ 9 3:30
11 12:07	♆ □	♈ 11 13:37
13 19:31	♆ △	♉ 13 20:59
14 19:08	☿ ☌	♊ 16 2:15
18 4:46	♆ ☍	♋ 18 6:14
20 8:58	☉ □	♌ 20 9:26
22 10:41	♆ △	♍ 22 12:12
24 13:30	♆ □	♎ 24 15:04
26 17:25	♆ ⚹	♏ 26 19:04
28 16:27	☿ ☍	♐ 29 1:28

☽ Phases & Eclipses Dy Hr Mn	
6 13:16	☾ 15♐24
14 17:43	● 23♓35
22 2:25	☽ 0♋54
28 19:27	○ 7♎33
5 8:38	☾ 15♑00
13 7:58	● 22♈50
20 8:58	☽ 29♋43
27 6:31	○ 6♏26

Astro Data

1 March 1983
Julian Day # 30375
SVP 5♓29'58"
GC 26♐36.2 ⚴ 11♑27.3
Eris 14♈51.7 ⚵ 25♒14.8
⚷ 23♉07.0 ⚶ 3♈49.6
☽ Mean ☊ 0♋42.3

1 April 1983
Julian Day # 30406
SVP 5♓29'55"
GC 26♐36.3 ⚴ 20♑10.3
Eris 15♈11.1 ⚵ 9♓06.6
⚷ 24♉29.5 ⚶ 18♈08.3
☽ Mean ☊ 29♊03.8

LONGITUDE — May 1983

Day	Sid.Time	☉	0 hr ☽	Noon ☽	True ☊	☿	♀	♂	⚷	♃	♄	♅	♆	♇
1 Su	2 35 24	10♉32 57	24♐22 46	0♑29 52	25♊51.0	25♉32.9	20♊57.9	18♉58.9	21♒06.8	9♐09.0	0♏23.4	8♐11.4	28♐59.4	27♎47.4
2 M	2 39 20	11 31 10	6♑33 34	12 34 23	25 52.0	25R31.3	22 06.6	19 42.2	21 21.1	9R03.1	0R18.9	8R09.3	28R58.5	27R45.7
3 Tu	2 43 17	12 29 21	18 32 52	24 29 36	25 53.5	25 24.5	23 15.0	20 25.4	21 35.3	8 57.1	0 14.5	8 07.2	28 57.5	27 44.1
4 W	2 47 14	13 27 31	0♒25 11	6♒20 16	25R54.7	25 12.8	24 23.4	21 08.6	21 49.2	8 51.0	0 10.1	8 05.0	28 56.5	27 42.5
5 Th	2 51 10	14 25 39	12 15 29	18 11 28	25 54.9	24 56.5	25 31.6	21 51.7	22 03.0	8 44.7	0 05.7	8 02.8	28 55.5	27 40.9
6 F	2 55 07	15 23 46	24 08 52	0♓08 16	25 53.6	24 35.9	26 39.7	22 34.8	22 16.5	8 38.4	0 01.3	8 00.6	28 54.5	27 39.3
7 Sa	2 59 03	16 21 52	6♓10 17	12 15 28	25 50.6	24 11.5	27 47.6	23 17.8	22 29.8	8 31.9	29♎57.0	7 58.4	28 53.4	27 37.7
8 Su	3 03 00	17 19 56	18 24 17	24 37 11	25 46.2	23 43.7	28 55.4	24 00.8	22 43.0	8 25.3	29 52.8	7 56.1	28 52.3	27 36.1
9 M	3 06 56	18 17 59	0♈54 33	7♈16 39	25 40.6	23 13.1	0♋03.0	24 43.7	22 55.9	8 18.6	29 48.5	7 53.8	28 51.2	27 34.5
10 Tu	3 10 53	19 16 00	13 43 43	20 15 50	25 34.5	22 40.2	1 10.4	25 26.5	23 08.5	8 11.9	29 44.3	7 51.5	28 50.1	27 33.0
11 W	3 14 49	20 14 00	26 53 00	3♉35 09	25 28.6	22 05.7	2 17.8	26 09.4	23 21.0	8 05.0	29 40.2	7 49.2	28 48.9	27 31.4
12 Th	3 18 46	21 11 58	10♉22 04	17 13 29	25 23.7	21 30.0	3 24.9	26 52.1	23 33.3	7 58.0	29 36.1	7 46.9	28 47.7	27 29.9
13 F	3 22 43	22 09 55	24 09 00	1♊08 13	25 20.2	20 54.0	4 31.9	27 34.9	23 45.3	7 51.0	29 32.0	7 44.5	28 46.5	27 28.4
14 Sa	3 26 39	23 07 51	8♊10 36	15 15 39	25D18.3	20 18.2	5 38.7	28 17.6	23 57.1	7 43.9	29 28.0	7 42.2	28 45.3	27 26.9
15 Su	3 30 36	24 05 45	22 22 50	29 31 34	25 18.0	19 43.2	6 45.3	29 00.2	24 08.6	7 36.7	29 24.1	7 39.8	28 44.1	27 25.5
16 M	3 34 32	25 03 37	6♋41 20	13♋51 39	25 18.9	19 09.6	7 51.8	29 42.8	24 19.9	7 29.5	29 20.2	7 37.4	28 42.8	27 24.0
17 Tu	3 38 29	26 01 27	21 02 02	28 12 04	25 20.3	18 38.0	8 58.1	0♊25.3	24 31.0	7 22.1	29 16.3	7 35.0	28 41.5	27 22.6
18 W	3 42 25	26 59 16	5♌21 23	12♌29 38	25 21.6	18 08.9	10 04.1	1 07.8	24 41.9	7 14.8	29 12.5	7 32.6	28 40.2	27 21.1
19 Th	3 46 22	27 57 03	19 36 32	26 41 50	25R22.2	17 42.7	11 10.0	1 50.2	24 52.4	7 07.4	29 08.8	7 30.1	28 38.9	27 19.7
20 F	3 50 18	28 54 48	3♍45 18	10♍46 43	25 21.7	17 19.9	12 15.7	2 32.6	25 02.8	6 59.9	29 05.1	7 27.7	28 37.6	27 18.4
21 Sa	3 54 15	29 52 32	17 45 53	24 42 37	25 20.1	17 00.7	13 21.1	3 14.9	25 12.9	6 52.4	29 01.5	7 25.2	28 36.2	27 17.0
22 Su	3 58 12	0♊50 14	1♎36 45	8♎28 07	25 17.4	16 45.4	14 26.4	3 57.1	25 22.7	6 44.9	28 58.0	7 22.8	28 34.8	27 15.7
23 M	4 02 08	1 47 54	15 16 31	22 01 49	25 14.2	16 34.3	15 31.4	4 39.4	25 32.3	6 37.3	28 54.5	7 20.3	28 33.5	27 14.3
24 Tu	4 06 05	2 45 33	28 43 51	5♏32 30	25 10.8	16 27.5	16 36.2	5 21.5	25 41.6	6 29.7	28 51.1	7 17.8	28 32.1	27 13.0
25 W	4 10 01	3 43 10	11♏57 37	18 29 08	25 07.8	16D25.1	17 40.8	6 03.6	25 50.6	6 22.1	28 47.7	7 15.4	28 30.6	27 11.7
26 Th	4 13 58	4 40 47	24 57 00	1♐21 11	25 05.5	16 27.2	18 45.1	6 45.7	25 59.4	6 14.5	28 44.5	7 12.9	28 29.2	27 10.5
27 F	4 17 54	5 38 22	7♐41 42	13 58 37	25D04.2	16 33.8	19 49.2	7 27.7	26 07.9	6 06.8	28 41.3	7 10.4	28 27.8	27 09.3
28 Sa	4 21 51	6 35 56	20 12 03	26 22 10	25 03.8	16 45.0	20 53.0	8 09.7	26 16.1	5 59.2	28 38.1	7 07.9	28 26.3	27 08.0
29 Su	4 25 47	7 33 28	2♑29 11	8♑33 22	25 04.3	17 00.6	21 56.6	8 51.6	26 24.1	5 51.6	28 35.1	7 05.4	28 24.8	27 06.9
30 M	4 29 44	8 31 00	14 35 01	20 34 30	25 05.4	17 20.6	22 59.9	9 33.5	26 31.8	5 43.9	28 32.1	7 02.9	28 23.3	27 05.7
31 Tu	4 33 41	9 28 31	26 32 13	2♒28 36	25 06.7	17 44.9	24 02.9	10 15.3	26 39.2	5 36.3	28 29.2	7 00.5	28 21.8	27 04.6

LONGITUDE — June 1983

Day	Sid.Time	☉	0 hr ☽	Noon ☽	True ☊	☿	♀	♂	⚷	♃	♄	♅	♆	♇
1 W	4 37 37	10♊26 01	8♒24 09	14♒19 22	25♊08.0	18♉13.6	25♋05.7	10♊57.1	26♒46.3	5♐28.7	28♎26.4	6♐58.0	28♐20.3	27♎03.4
2 Th	4 41 34	11 23 31	20 14 47	26 10 58	25 09.0	18 46.4	26 08.2	11 38.9	26 53.1	5R21.2	28R23.7	6R55.5	28R18.8	27R02.3
3 F	4 45 30	12 20 59	2♓08 29	8♓07 55	25R09.5	19 23.3	27 10.4	12 20.6	26 59.6	5 13.6	28 21.0	6 53.0	28 17.3	27 01.3
4 Sa	4 49 27	13 18 27	14 09 51	20 14 52	25 09.5	20 04.1	28 12.3	13 02.2	27 05.8	5 06.1	28 18.4	6 50.6	28 15.7	27 00.2
5 Su	4 53 23	14 15 54	26 23 31	2♈36 20	25 08.9	20 48.9	29 13.8	13 43.8	27 11.7	4 58.6	28 15.9	6 48.1	28 14.2	26 59.2
6 M	4 57 20	15 13 20	8♈53 48	15 16 20	25 08.0	21 37.5	0♌15.1	14 25.4	27 17.3	4 51.1	28 13.5	6 45.6	28 12.6	26 58.2
7 Tu	5 01 16	16 10 46	21 44 19	28 18 02	25 06.9	22 29.7	1 16.1	15 06.9	27 22.6	4 43.8	28 11.2	6 43.2	28 11.0	26 57.3
8 W	5 05 13	17 08 11	4♉57 39	11♉43 15	25 05.8	23 25.6	2 16.7	15 48.3	27 27.5	4 36.4	28 09.0	6 40.7	28 09.5	26 56.3
9 Th	5 09 10	18 05 35	18 34 48	25 32 08	25 05.0	24 25.0	3 17.0	16 29.8	27 32.2	4 29.1	28 06.8	6 38.3	28 07.9	26 55.4
10 F	5 13 06	19 02 59	2♊34 55	9♊42 44	25 04.5	25 27.8	4 16.9	17 11.1	27 36.5	4 21.9	28 04.8	6 35.9	28 06.3	26 54.6
11 Sa	5 17 03	20 00 22	16 55 03	24 11 10	25D04.4	26 34.1	5 16.5	17 52.5	27 40.5	4 14.8	28 02.8	6 33.5	28 04.7	26 53.7
12 Su	5 20 59	20 57 44	1♋30 21	8♋51 45	25 04.5	27 43.7	6 15.7	18 33.8	27 44.2	4 07.7	28 00.9	6 31.1	28 03.1	26 52.9
13 M	5 24 56	21 55 06	16 14 32	23 37 48	25 04.7	28 56.5	7 14.5	19 15.0	27 47.5	4 00.7	27 59.1	6 28.8	28 01.5	26 52.1
14 Tu	5 28 52	22 52 26	1♌00 42	8♌22 24	25 05.0	0♊12.6	8 12.9	19 56.2	27 50.6	3 53.8	27 57.5	6 26.4	27 59.9	26 51.4
15 W	5 32 49	23 49 46	15 42 10	22 59 20	25 05.1	1 31.9	9 10.9	20 37.3	27 53.2	3 47.0	27 55.9	6 24.1	27 58.3	26 50.6
16 Th	5 36 46	24 47 05	0♍13 19	7♍23 41	25R05.2	2 54.3	10 08.5	21 18.4	27 55.6	3 40.2	27 54.4	6 21.7	27 56.7	26 49.9
17 F	5 40 42	25 44 23	14 30 02	21 32 09	25D05.2	4 19.8	11 05.6	21 59.5	27 57.6	3 33.6	27 52.9	6 19.4	27 55.0	26 49.3
18 Sa	5 44 39	26 41 39	28 29 51	5♎23 05	25 05.2	5 48.4	12 02.2	22 40.5	27 59.2	3 27.1	27 51.6	6 17.1	27 53.4	26 48.6
19 Su	5 48 35	27 38 55	12♎11 48	18 56 06	25 05.3	7 20.1	12 58.4	23 21.5	28 00.5	3 20.6	27 50.4	6 14.9	27 51.8	26 48.0
20 M	5 52 32	28 36 11	25 36 04	2♏11 50	25 05.6	8 54.8	13 54.1	24 02.4	28 01.5	3 14.3	27 49.3	6 12.6	27 50.2	26 47.4
21 Tu	5 56 28	29 33 25	8♏43 34	15 11 27	25 06.0	10 32.6	14 49.2	24 43.2	28 02.1	3 08.1	27 48.3	6 10.4	27 48.6	26 46.9
22 W	6 00 25	0♋30 39	21 35 40	27 56 25	25 06.5	12 13.3	15 43.8	25 24.1	28R02.4	3 02.0	27 47.3	6 08.2	27 46.9	26 46.4
23 Th	6 04 21	1 27 53	4♐13 53	10♐28 17	25 06.9	13 57.0	16 37.9	26 04.8	28 02.3	2 56.1	27 46.5	6 06.1	27 45.3	26 45.9
24 F	6 08 18	2 25 06	16 39 49	22 48 39	25R07.1	15 43.5	17 31.4	26 45.6	28 01.9	2 50.2	27 45.8	6 03.9	27 43.7	26 45.5
25 Sa	6 12 15	3 22 18	28 55 01	4♑59 07	25 07.0	17 32.9	18 24.3	27 26.3	28 01.1	2 44.5	27 45.1	6 01.8	27 42.1	26 45.1
26 Su	6 16 11	4 19 31	11♑01 09	17 01 22	25 06.4	19 24.9	19 16.6	28 06.9	28 00.0	2 38.9	27 44.6	5 59.7	27 40.5	26 44.7
27 M	6 20 08	5 16 43	23 00 00	28 57 19	25 05.4	21 19.7	20 08.2	28 47.5	27 58.5	2 33.5	27 44.1	5 57.6	27 38.9	26 44.3
28 Tu	6 24 04	6 13 55	4♒53 36	10♒49 11	25 04.0	23 16.9	20 59.2	29 28.1	27 56.6	2 28.2	27 43.8	5 55.6	27 37.3	26 44.0
29 W	6 28 01	7 11 06	16 44 23	22 39 34	25 02.3	25 16.5	21 49.5	0♋08.6	27 54.4	2 23.0	27 43.6	5 53.6	27 35.7	26 43.7
30 Th	6 31 57	8 08 18	28 35 09	4♓31 33	25 00.6	27 18.3	22 39.2	0 49.1	27 51.9	2 18.0	27 43.4	5 51.6	27 34.1	26 43.5

Astro Data
Dy Hr Mn
☿R 1 16:37
☽0N 9 20:02
♃☌♅ 14 20:36
☽0S 22 17:40
☿D 25 12:49

☽0N 6 5:26
♄⚹♆ 7 17:33
☽0S 18 23:18
♄⚹♆ 21 22:59
⚷R 22 18:48

Planet Ingress
Dy Hr Mn
♄ ♎R 6 19:29
♀ ♋ 9 10:56
♂ ♊ 16 21:43
☉ ♊ 21 15:06

♀ ♌ 6 6:04
☿ ♊ 14 8:06
☉ ♋ 21 23:09
♂ ♋ 29 6:54

Last Aspect / ☽ Ingress
Dy Hr Mn / Dy Hr Mn
1 9:02 ♆ ☌ ♑ 1 11:01
3 18:33 ♇ □ ♒ 3 23:09
6 9:33 ♆ ⚹ ♓ 6 11:43
8 21:02 ♀ □ ♈ 8 22:16
11 5:02 ♄ ☍ ♉ 11 5:36
13 5:35 ♂ ☌ ♊ 13 10:03
15 11:47 ♄ △ ♋ 15 12:48
17 13:47 ♄ □ ♌ 17 15:01
19 16:08 ♄ ⚹ ♍ 19 17:37
21 18:45 ♆ □ ♎ 21 21:11
24 0:16 ♄ ☌ ♏ 24 2:17
25 10:23 ♀ △ ♐ 26 9:27
28 16:25 ♄ ⚹ ♑ 28 19:07
31 3:58 ♄ □ ♒ 31 7:00

Last Aspect / ☽ Ingress
Dy Hr Mn / Dy Hr Mn
2 16:27 ♄ △ ♓ 2 19:42
5 4:55 ♀ △ ♈ 5 6:59
7 11:48 ♄ ☍ ♉ 7 15:05
9 9:56 ☿ ☌ ♊ 9 19:37
11 18:23 ♆ ☍ ♋ 11 21:32
13 21:26 ☿ ⚹ ♌ 13 22:21
15 20:14 ♆ △ ♍ 15 23:38
17 22:58 ♆ □ ♎ 18 2:36
20 4:56 ☉ △ ♏ 20 7:59
21 11:15 ♀ □ ♐ 22 15:55
24 21:43 ♄ ⚹ ♑ 25 2:08
27 9:32 ♄ □ ♒ 27 14:07
29 22:15 ♄ △ ♓ 30 2:52

☽ Phases & Eclipses
Dy Hr Mn
5 3:43 ☾ 14♒06
12 19:25 ● 21♉30
19 14:17 ☽ 28♌03
26 18:48 ○ 4♐57

3 21:07 ☾ 12♓43
11 4:37 ● 19♊43
11 4:42:41 • T 05'11"
17 19:46 ☽ 26♍03
25 8:32 ○ 3♑14
25 8:22 • P 0.335

Astro Data
1 May 1983
Julian Day # 30436
SVP 5♓29'51"
GC 26♐36.4 ⚳ 24♑52.5
Eris 15♈30.8 ⚵ 22♓27.7
⚷ 26♉24.6 ⚶ 1♉51.3
☽ Mean ☊ 27♊28.4

1 June 1983
Julian Day # 30467
SVP 5♓29'47"
GC 26♐36.5 ⚳ 24♑00.7R
Eris 15♈47.0 ⚵ 5♈49.7
⚷ 28♉37.4 ⚶ 15♉36.7
☽ Mean ☊ 25♊50.0

July 1983 LONGITUDE

Day	Sid.Time	☉	0 hr ☽	Noon ☽	True ☊	☿	♀	♂	⚳	♃	♄	♅	♆	♇
1 F	6 35 54	9♋05 30	10♓29 13	16♓28 39	24♊59.1	29♊22.0	23♌28.1	1♋29.5	27♒49.0	2♐13.1	27♎43.4	5♐49.7	27♐32.5	26♎43.2
2 Sa	6 39 50	10 02 42	22 30 20	28 34 47	24R 58.1	1♋27.5	24 16.3	2 09.9	27R 45.7	2R 08.3	27D 43.4	5R 47.7	27R 31.0	26R 43.1
3 Su	6 43 47	10 59 54	4♈42 33	10♈54 10	24D 57.7	3 34.5	25 03.6	2 50.3	27 42.0	2 03.7	27 43.5	5 45.9	27 29.4	26 42.9
4 M	6 47 44	11 57 06	17 10 08	23 30 59	24 58.0	5 42.7	25 50.2	3 30.6	27 38.1	1 59.3	27 43.8	5 44.0	27 27.8	26 42.8
5 Tu	6 51 40	12 54 19	29 57 11	6♉29 10	24 59.0	7 51.8	26 36.0	4 10.9	27 33.7	1 55.0	27 44.1	5 42.2	27 26.3	26 42.7
6 W	6 55 37	13 51 31	13♉07 17	19 51 50	25 00.3	10 01.5	27 20.9	4 51.2	27 29.0	1 50.9	27 44.6	5 40.4	27 24.7	26D 42.6
7 Th	6 59 33	14 48 45	26 42 58	3♊40 44	25 01.5	12 11.6	28 04.9	5 31.4	27 23.9	1 47.0	27 45.1	5 38.7	27 23.2	26 42.6
8 F	7 03 30	15 45 58	10♊45 03	17 55 38	25R 02.3	14 21.8	28 48.0	6 11.5	27 18.5	1 43.2	27 45.8	5 37.0	27 21.7	26 42.6
9 Sa	7 07 26	16 43 12	25 12 04	2♋33 45	25 02.3	16 31.7	29 30.1	6 51.7	27 12.8	1 39.6	27 46.5	5 35.3	27 20.2	26 42.7
10 Su	7 11 23	17 40 26	9♋59 53	17 29 35	25 01.2	18 41.2	0♍11.2	7 31.7	27 06.7	1 36.1	27 47.4	5 33.6	27 18.7	26 42.8
11 M	7 15 19	18 37 40	25 01 46	2♌35 18	24 59.1	20 49.9	0 51.3	8 11.8	27 00.2	1 32.8	27 48.3	5 32.1	27 17.2	26 42.9
12 Tu	7 19 16	19 34 54	10♌08 59	17 41 38	24 56.1	22 57.8	1 30.2	8 51.8	26 53.5	1 29.7	27 49.3	5 30.5	27 15.7	26 43.1
13 W	7 23 13	20 32 09	25 12 07	2♍39 23	24 52.8	25 04.5	2 08.1	9 31.8	26 46.4	1 26.8	27 50.5	5 29.0	27 14.3	26 43.3
14 Th	7 27 09	21 29 23	10♍02 30	17 20 43	24 49.6	27 10.0	2 44.8	10 11.7	26 38.9	1 24.0	27 51.7	5 27.5	27 12.8	26 43.5
15 F	7 31 06	22 26 37	24 33 26	1♎40 14	24 47.2	29 14.1	3 20.2	10 51.6	26 31.1	1 21.4	27 53.0	5 26.1	27 11.4	26 43.7
16 Sa	7 35 02	23 23 51	8♎40 53	15 35 17	24D 45.9	1♌16.8	3 54.4	11 31.4	26 23.1	1 19.0	27 54.5	5 24.7	27 10.0	26 44.0
17 Su	7 38 59	24 21 06	22 23 30	29 05 42	24 45.7	3 17.8	4 27.3	12 11.2	26 14.7	1 16.8	27 56.0	5 23.3	27 08.6	26 44.3
18 M	7 42 55	25 18 20	5♏42 07	12♏13 08	24 46.6	5 17.2	4 58.8	12 51.0	26 06.0	1 14.7	27 57.6	5 22.0	27 07.2	26 44.7
19 Tu	7 46 52	26 15 35	18 39 05	25 00 26	24 48.2	7 15.0	5 28.8	13 30.7	25 57.0	1 12.9	27 59.3	5 20.7	27 05.8	26 45.1
20 W	7 50 48	27 12 50	1♐17 34	7♐30 57	24 49.7	9 11.0	5 57.4	14 10.4	25 47.7	1 11.2	28 01.1	5 19.5	27 04.5	26 45.5
21 Th	7 54 45	28 10 05	13 41 00	19 48 08	24R 50.7	11 05.2	6 24.4	14 50.0	25 38.1	1 09.7	28 03.0	5 18.3	27 03.1	26 46.0
22 F	7 58 42	29 07 21	25 52 43	1♑55 09	24 50.6	12 57.8	6 49.8	15 29.6	25 28.3	1 08.4	28 05.1	5 17.2	27 01.8	26 46.5
23 Sa	8 02 38	0♌04 37	7♑55 44	13 54 47	24 48.9	14 48.5	7 13.6	16 09.2	25 18.2	1 07.2	28 07.1	5 16.1	27 00.5	26 47.0
24 Su	8 06 35	1 01 53	19 52 36	25 49 27	24 45.5	16 37.5	7 35.7	16 48.7	25 07.8	1 06.2	28 09.3	5 15.1	26 59.2	26 47.6
25 M	8 10 31	1 59 10	1♒45 35	7♒41 13	24 40.5	18 24.7	7 56.0	17 28.2	24 57.2	1 05.5	28 11.6	5 14.1	26 58.0	26 48.2
26 Tu	8 14 28	2 56 28	13 36 36	19 31 58	24 34.2	20 10.2	8 14.4	18 07.7	24 46.3	1 04.9	28 14.0	5 13.1	26 56.7	26 48.8
27 W	8 18 24	3 53 46	25 27 31	1♓23 33	24 27.1	21 53.9	8 31.0	18 47.1	24 35.2	1 04.4	28 16.5	5 12.2	26 55.5	26 49.5
28 Th	8 22 21	4 51 05	7♓20 17	13 18 02	24 19.9	23 35.8	8 45.7	19 26.5	24 23.9	1D 04.2	28 19.0	5 11.3	26 54.3	26 50.2
29 F	8 26 17	5 48 25	19 17 05	25 17 47	24 13.4	25 16.1	8 58.3	20 05.9	24 12.4	1 04.2	28 21.7	5 10.5	26 53.1	26 50.9
30 Sa	8 30 14	6 45 46	1♈20 30	7♈25 37	24 08.2	26 54.6	9 08.9	20 45.2	24 00.6	1 04.3	28 24.4	5 09.7	26 52.0	26 51.6
31 Su	8 34 11	7 43 08	13 33 36	19 44 52	24 04.6	28 31.3	9 17.3	21 24.5	23 48.7	1 04.6	28 27.2	5 09.0	26 50.9	26 52.4

August 1983 LONGITUDE

Day	Sid.Time	☉	0 hr ☽	Noon ☽	True ☊	☿	♀	♂	⚳	♃	♄	♅	♆	♇
1 M	8 38 07	8♌40 31	25♈59 54	2♉19 11	24♊03.0	0♍06.4	9♍23.7	22♋03.7	23♒36.6	1♐05.1	28♎30.1	5♐08.4	26♐49.7	26♎53.3
2 Tu	8 42 04	9 37 56	8♉43 12	15 12 28	24D 02.9	1 39.7	9 27.8	22 42.9	23R 24.3	1 05.8	28 33.1	5R 07.7	26R 48.7	26 54.1
3 W	8 46 00	10 35 21	21 47 23	28 28 24	24 03.8	3 11.3	9R 29.7	23 22.1	23 11.9	1 06.6	28 36.2	5 07.2	26 47.6	26 55.0
4 Th	8 49 57	11 32 48	5♊15 49	12♊09 54	24R 05.0	4 41.2	9 29.2	24 01.3	22 59.3	1 07.7	28 39.4	5 06.6	26 46.6	26 55.9
5 F	8 53 53	12 30 16	19 10 47	26 18 25	24 05.4	6 09.3	9 26.5	24 40.4	22 46.6	1 08.9	28 42.6	5 06.2	26 45.5	26 56.9
6 Sa	8 57 50	13 27 45	3♋32 38	10♋53 01	24 04.3	7 35.6	9 21.5	25 19.5	22 33.7	1 10.3	28 46.0	5 05.7	26 44.6	26 57.9
7 Su	9 01 46	14 25 16	18 19 00	25 49 46	24 01.1	9 00.2	9 14.0	25 58.5	22 20.8	1 11.9	28 49.4	5 05.4	26 43.6	26 58.9
8 M	9 05 43	15 22 47	3♌24 19	11♌01 29	23 55.8	10 22.9	9 04.2	26 37.5	22 07.8	1 13.7	28 53.0	5 05.1	26 42.6	27 00.0
9 Tu	9 09 40	16 20 20	18 39 59	26 18 25	23 48.7	11 43.8	8 52.1	27 16.5	21 54.7	1 15.6	28 56.6	5 04.8	26 41.7	27 01.0
10 W	9 13 36	17 17 53	3♍55 24	11♍29 37	23 40.8	13 02.8	8 37.5	27 55.5	21 41.5	1 17.7	29 00.2	5 04.6	26 40.8	27 02.2
11 Th	9 17 33	18 15 28	18 59 49	26 24 56	23 33.0	14 19.8	8 20.7	28 34.4	21 28.2	1 20.0	29 04.0	5 04.4	26 40.0	27 03.3
12 F	9 21 29	19 13 03	3♎44 05	10♎56 38	23 26.4	15 34.9	8 01.5	29 13.2	21 15.0	1 22.5	29 07.8	5 04.3	26 39.1	27 04.5
13 Sa	9 25 26	20 10 39	18 02 08	25 00 22	23 21.7	16 47.9	7 40.1	29 52.1	21 01.7	1 25.2	29 11.8	5D 04.2	26 38.3	27 05.7
14 Su	9 29 22	21 08 16	1♏51 18	8♏35 06	23 19.0	17 58.7	7 16.6	0♌30.9	20 48.4	1 28.0	29 15.8	5 04.2	26 37.6	27 06.9
15 M	9 33 19	22 05 55	15 12 02	21 42 32	23D 18.3	19 07.4	6 50.9	1 09.6	20 35.1	1 31.0	29 19.9	5 04.2	26 36.8	27 08.2
16 Tu	9 37 15	23 03 34	28 07 03	4♐26 09	23 18.7	20 13.7	6 23.3	1 48.4	20 21.9	1 34.2	29 24.0	5 04.3	26 36.1	27 09.5
17 W	9 41 12	24 01 14	10♐40 25	16 50 26	23R 19.4	21 17.7	5 53.9	2 27.1	20 08.7	1 37.6	29 28.3	5 04.5	26 35.4	27 10.8
18 Th	9 45 09	24 58 55	22 56 47	29 00 03	23 19.4	22 19.1	5 22.7	3 05.7	19 55.5	1 41.1	29 32.6	5 04.7	26 34.7	27 12.2
19 F	9 49 05	25 56 38	5♑00 47	10♑59 31	23 17.8	23 18.0	4 50.1	3 44.4	19 42.4	1 44.8	29 37.0	5 04.9	26 34.1	27 13.6
20 Sa	9 53 02	26 54 21	16 56 43	22 52 49	23 13.9	24 14.0	4 16.1	4 23.0	19 29.4	1 48.7	29 41.4	5 05.2	26 33.5	27 15.0
21 Su	9 56 58	27 52 06	28 48 14	4♒43 19	23 07.3	25 07.2	3 41.1	5 01.5	19 16.5	1 52.7	29 46.0	5 05.5	26 32.9	27 16.4
22 M	10 00 55	28 49 52	10♒38 22	16 33 41	22 58.3	25 57.3	3 05.0	5 40.0	19 03.7	1 56.9	29 50.6	5 05.9	26 32.4	27 17.9
23 Tu	10 04 51	29 47 39	22 29 28	28 25 57	22 47.2	26 44.1	2 28.4	6 18.5	18 51.0	2 01.3	29 55.3	5 06.4	26 31.8	27 19.4
24 W	10 08 48	0♍45 28	4♓23 20	10♓21 45	22 34.9	27 27.5	1 51.2	6 57.0	18 38.4	2 05.8	0♏00.0	5 06.9	26 31.4	27 20.9
25 Th	10 12 44	1 43 18	16 21 25	22 22 27	22 22.4	28 07.3	1 13.9	7 35.4	18 26.0	2 10.5	0 04.8	5 07.4	26 30.9	27 22.4
26 F	10 16 41	2 41 10	28 25 03	4♈29 25	22 10.8	28 43.1	0 36.6	8 13.8	18 13.7	2 15.3	0 09.7	5 08.0	26 30.5	27 24.0
27 Sa	10 20 38	3 39 04	10♈35 44	16 44 14	22 00.9	29 14.9	29♌59.6	8 52.2	18 01.6	2 20.4	0 14.7	5 08.7	26 30.1	27 25.6
28 Su	10 24 34	4 36 59	22 55 13	29 08 59	21 53.6	29 42.3	29 23.1	9 30.6	17 49.6	2 25.5	0 19.7	5 09.4	26 29.7	27 27.3
29 M	10 28 31	5 34 56	5♉25 51	11♉46 12	21 49.0	0♎05.1	28 47.4	10 08.9	17 37.9	2 30.8	0 24.8	5 10.2	26 29.4	27 28.9
30 Tu	10 32 27	6 32 55	18 10 24	24 38 54	21D 46.8	0 23.1	28 12.7	10 47.1	17 26.4	2 36.3	0 29.9	5 11.0	26 29.1	27 30.6
31 W	10 36 24	7 30 56	1♊12 06	7♊50 24	21 46.3	0 35.8	27 39.1	11 25.4	17 15.0	2 41.9	0 35.2	5 11.8	26 28.8	27 32.3

Astro Data	Planet Ingress	Last Aspect	☽ Ingress	Last Aspect	☽ Ingress	☽ Phases & Eclipses	Astro Data
Dy Hr Mn	Dy Hr Mn	Dy Hr Mn	Dy Hr Mn	Dy Hr Mn	Dy Hr Mn	Dy Hr Mn	
♄ D 1 12:31	☿ ♋ 1 19:18	2 9:55 ♆ □	♈ 2 14:47	1 7:13 ☿ △	♉ 1 7:37	3 12:12 ☾ 11♈00	1 July 1983
☽ 0N 3 13:37	♀ ♍ 10 5:25	4 19:53 ♄ ☍	♉ 5 0:05	3 2:23 ♂ ⚹	♊ 3 14:43	10 12:18 ● 17♋41	Julian Day # 30497
♇ D 7 11:25	☿ ♌ 15 20:57	7 1:50 ♀ □	♊ 7 5:41	5 16:01 ♄ △	♋ 5 18:09	17 2:50 ☽ 23♎59	SVP 5♓29'41"
☽ 0S 16 5:09	☉ ♌ 23 10:04	9 6:47 ♀ ⚹	♋ 9 7:50	7 16:46 ♄ □	♌ 7 18:37	24 23:27 ○ 1♒29	GC 26♐36.5 ⚴ 17♑24.5R
♃ D 29 7:04		11 4:24 ♄ □	♌ 11 7:54	9 16:10 ♄ ⚹	♍ 9 17:49		Eris 15♈55.1 ⚵ 17♈49.1
♆⚹♇ 30 16:25	☿ ♍ 1 10:22	13 4:14 ♄ ⚹	♍ 13 7:43	11 15:41 ♂ ⚹	♎ 11 17:51	2 0:52 ☾ 9♉11	⚷ 0♊37.4 ⚶ 28♉14.1
☽ 0N 30 19:53	♂ ♌ 13 16:54	15 7:10 ☿ ⚹	♎ 15 9:10	13 19:21 ♄ ☌	♏ 13 20:44	8 19:18 ● 15♌40	☽ Mean ☊ 24♊14.7
	☉ ♍ 23 17:07	17 9:54 ♄ ☌	♏ 17 13:38	15 12:47 ☉ □	♐ 16 3:33	15 12:47 ☽ 22♏08	
♀ R 3 19:44	♄ ♏ 24 11:54	19 14:35 ☉ △	♐ 19 21:31	18 13:05 ♄ ⚹	♑ 18 13:59	23 14:59 ○ 29♒55	1 August 1983
☽ 0S 12 12:36	♀ ♌R 27 11:43	22 4:21 ♄ ⚹	♑ 22 8:11	21 1:53 ♄ □	♒ 21 2:25	31 11:22 ☾ 7♊29	Julian Day # 30528
♅ D 14 7:10	☿ ♎ 29 6:07	24 16:44 ♄ □	♒ 24 20:26	23 15:01 ♄ △	♓ 23 15:10		SVP 5♓29'37"
☿ 0S 21 3:01		27 5:40 ♄ △	♓ 27 9:11	26 0:01 ☿ ☍	♈ 26 3:08		GC 26♐36.6 ⚴ 9♑30.5R
☽ 0N 27 0:55		29 15:09 ♆ □	♈ 29 21:21	28 12:26 ♀ △	♉ 28 13:38		Eris 15♈53.8R ⚵ 28♈13.2
				30 18:16 ♀ □	♊ 30 21:49		⚷ 2♊10.8 ⚶ 10♊08.6
							☽ Mean ☊ 22♊36.2

LONGITUDE — September 1983

Day	Sid.Time	☉	0 hr ☽	Noon ☽	True ☊	☿	♀	♂	⚳	♃	♄	♅	♆	♇
1 Th	10 40 20	8♍28 58	14♊34 11	21♊23 46	21♊46.4	0♎43.1	27♌07.0	12♌03.6	17♒03.9	2♐47.7	0♏40.5	5♐12.7	26♐28.5	27♎34.0
2 F	10 44 17	9 27 03	28 19 24	5♋21 14	21R45.9	0R44.7	26R36.5	12 41.8	16R53.0	2 53.7	0 45.8	5 13.7	26R28.3	27 35.8
3 Sa	10 48 13	10 25 10	12♋29 16	19 43 21	21 43.7	0 40.4	26 07.7	13 20.0	16 42.4	2 59.8	0 51.2	5 14.7	26 28.2	27 37.6
4 Su	10 52 10	11 23 19	27 03 07	4♌28 03	21 38.9	0 30.0	25 40.7	13 58.1	16 32.0	3 06.0	0 56.7	5 15.8	26 28.0	27 39.4
5 M	10 56 07	12 21 29	11♌57 23	19 30 08	21 31.5	0 13.2	25 15.8	14 36.2	16 21.9	3 12.4	1 02.2	5 16.9	26 27.9	27 41.2
6 Tu	11 00 03	13 19 41	27 05 13	4♍41 20	21 21.7	29♍50.1	24 53.0	15 14.3	16 12.1	3 18.9	1 07.8	5 18.1	26 27.8	27 43.1
7 W	11 04 00	14 17 55	12♍17 08	19 51 15	21 10.7	29 20.6	24 32.4	15 52.3	16 02.5	3 25.6	1 13.5	5 19.3	26D27.8	27 44.9
8 Th	11 07 56	15 16 11	27 22 22	4♎49 14	20 59.7	28 44.8	24 14.0	16 30.3	15 53.3	3 32.4	1 19.2	5 20.5	26 27.8	27 46.8
9 F	11 11 53	16 14 28	12♎10 49	19 26 14	20 50.0	28 03.1	23 58.0	17 08.3	15 44.3	3 39.4	1 24.9	5 21.8	26 27.8	27 48.7
10 Sa	11 15 49	17 12 47	26 34 50	3♏36 13	20 42.5	27 15.8	23 44.3	17 46.3	15 35.6	3 46.5	1 30.7	5 23.2	26 27.8	27 50.7
11 Su	11 19 46	18 11 08	10♏30 10	17 16 41	20 37.6	26 23.5	23 33.0	18 24.2	15 27.3	3 53.7	1 36.6	5 24.6	26 27.9	27 52.6
12 M	11 23 42	19 09 30	23 55 58	0♐28 19	20 35.1	25 27.1	23 24.1	19 02.0	15 19.3	4 01.1	1 42.5	5 26.1	26 28.0	27 54.6
13 Tu	11 27 39	20 07 54	6♐54 12	13 14 09	20 34.4	24 27.6	23 17.7	19 39.9	15 11.5	4 08.6	1 48.5	5 27.6	26 28.2	27 56.6
14 W	11 31 36	21 06 20	19 28 45	25 38 39	20 34.3	23 26.1	23 13.6	20 17.7	15 04.2	4 16.3	1 54.5	5 29.1	26 28.4	27 58.6
15 Th	11 35 32	22 04 47	1♑44 31	7♑47 00	20 33.8	22 24.0	23D11.9	20 55.5	14 57.1	4 24.1	2 00.6	5 30.7	26 28.6	28 00.7
16 F	11 39 29	23 03 16	13 46 46	19 44 27	20 31.7	21 22.6	23 12.5	21 33.2	14 50.5	4 32.0	2 06.7	5 32.4	26 28.9	28 02.7
17 Sa	11 43 25	24 01 46	25 40 39	1♒35 54	20 27.2	20 23.5	23 15.5	22 10.9	14 44.1	4 40.0	2 12.9	5 34.1	26 29.1	28 04.8
18 Su	11 47 22	25 00 18	7♒30 46	13 25 40	20 20.0	19 28.1	23 20.7	22 48.6	14 38.1	4 48.2	2 19.1	5 35.8	26 29.5	28 06.9
19 M	11 51 18	25 58 52	19 21 03	25 17 17	20 10.0	18 38.0	23 28.2	23 26.2	14 32.4	4 56.5	2 25.4	5 37.6	26 29.8	28 09.0
20 Tu	11 55 15	26 57 27	1♓14 40	7♓13 27	19 57.8	17 54.2	23 37.9	24 03.9	14 27.1	5 04.9	2 31.7	5 39.5	26 30.2	28 11.1
21 W	11 59 11	27 56 04	13 13 53	19 16 07	19 44.2	17 18.1	23 49.7	24 41.4	14 22.2	5 13.4	2 38.0	5 41.3	26 30.6	28 13.3
22 Th	12 03 08	28 54 44	25 20 17	1♈26 31	19 30.4	16 50.5	24 03.7	25 19.0	14 17.6	5 22.1	2 44.4	5 43.3	26 31.0	28 15.4
23 F	12 07 04	29 53 25	7♈34 52	13 45 26	19 17.5	16 32.2	24 19.6	25 56.5	14 13.4	5 30.9	2 50.8	5 45.2	26 31.5	28 17.6
24 Sa	12 11 01	0♎52 08	19 58 17	26 13 30	19 06.6	16D23.5	24 37.6	26 34.0	14 09.5	5 39.8	2 57.3	5 47.3	26 32.0	28 19.8
25 Su	12 14 58	1 50 53	2♉31 09	8♉51 23	18 58.3	16 24.9	24 57.4	27 11.5	14 06.0	5 48.8	3 03.8	5 49.3	26 32.6	28 22.0
26 M	12 18 54	2 49 41	15 14 20	21 40 09	18 52.9	16 36.2	25 19.1	27 48.9	14 02.8	5 57.9	3 10.4	5 51.4	26 33.2	28 24.2
27 Tu	12 22 51	3 48 31	28 09 04	4♊41 18	18 50.3	16 57.4	25 42.6	28 26.3	14 00.0	6 07.1	3 17.0	5 53.6	26 33.8	28 26.5
28 W	12 26 47	4 47 23	11♊17 06	17 56 44	18D49.6	17 28.3	26 07.9	29 03.7	13 57.6	6 16.5	3 23.6	5 55.8	26 34.4	28 28.7
29 Th	12 30 44	5 46 17	24 40 28	1♋28 33	18R49.8	18 08.2	26 34.8	29 41.0	13 55.5	6 25.9	3 30.3	5 58.0	26 35.1	28 31.0
30 F	12 34 40	6 45 14	8♋21 12	15 18 33	18 49.6	18 56.7	27 03.4	0♍18.3	13 53.8	6 35.5	3 37.0	6 00.3	26 35.8	28 33.2

LONGITUDE — October 1983

Day	Sid.Time	☉	0 hr ☽	Noon ☽	True ☊	☿	♀	♂	⚳	♃	♄	♅	♆	♇
1 Sa	12 38 37	7♎44 13	22♋20 41	29♋27 33	18♊47.9	19♍53.3	27♌33.5	0♍55.6	13♒52.5	6♐45.2	3♏43.7	6♐02.6	26♐36.5	28♎35.5
2 Su	12 42 33	8 43 15	6♌38 59	13♌54 40	18R43.8	20 57.1	28 05.1	1 32.9	13R51.5	6 55.0	3 50.5	6 04.9	26 37.3	28 37.8
3 M	12 46 30	9 42 18	21 14 07	28 36 40	18 37.2	22 07.5	28 38.2	2 10.1	13 50.9	7 04.9	3 57.3	6 07.3	26 38.1	28 40.1
4 Tu	12 50 27	10 41 24	6♍01 33	13♍27 48	18 28.4	23 23.7	29 12.6	2 47.3	13D50.7	7 14.9	4 04.1	6 09.8	26 38.9	28 42.5
5 W	12 54 23	11 40 32	20 54 22	28 20 10	18 18.3	24 45.1	29 48.4	3 24.5	13 50.8	7 25.0	4 11.0	6 12.2	26 39.8	28 44.8
6 Th	12 58 20	12 39 42	5♎44 03	13♎04 56	18 08.0	26 11.0	0♍25.5	4 01.6	13 51.3	7 35.2	4 17.8	6 14.8	26 40.7	28 47.1
7 F	13 02 16	13 38 54	20 21 48	27 33 48	17 58.8	27 40.6	1 03.8	4 38.7	13 52.1	7 45.4	4 24.7	6 17.3	26 41.6	28 49.5
8 Sa	13 06 13	14 38 09	4♏40 10	11♏40 22	17 51.7	29 13.6	1 43.3	5 15.7	13 53.3	7 55.8	4 31.7	6 19.9	26 42.6	28 51.8
9 Su	13 10 09	15 37 25	18 34 04	25 21 02	17 47.0	0♎49.2	2 24.0	5 52.7	13 54.9	8 06.3	4 38.7	6 22.5	26 43.6	28 54.2
10 M	13 14 06	16 36 43	2♐01 19	8♐35 01	17D44.8	2 27.0	3 05.8	6 29.7	13 56.8	8 16.9	4 45.6	6 25.2	26 44.6	28 56.6
11 Tu	13 18 02	17 36 03	15 02 27	21 24 00	17 44.4	4 06.5	3 48.6	7 06.7	13 59.0	8 27.6	4 52.7	6 27.9	26 45.7	28 58.9
12 W	13 21 59	18 35 25	27 40 09	3♑51 29	17 45.1	5 47.4	4 32.5	7 43.6	14 01.7	8 38.4	4 59.7	6 30.7	26 46.7	29 01.3
13 Th	13 25 56	19 34 48	9♑58 34	16 02 05	17R45.8	7 29.4	5 17.3	8 20.4	14 04.6	8 49.2	5 06.7	6 33.4	26 47.9	29 03.7
14 F	13 29 52	20 34 13	22 02 40	28 00 59	17 45.5	9 12.1	6 03.2	8 57.3	14 07.9	9 00.2	5 13.8	6 36.2	26 49.0	29 06.1
15 Sa	13 33 49	21 33 40	3♒57 41	9♒53 25	17 43.5	10 55.3	6 49.9	9 34.1	14 11.6	9 11.2	5 20.9	6 39.1	26 50.2	29 08.5
16 Su	13 37 45	22 33 09	15 48 45	21 44 18	17 39.3	12 38.8	7 37.5	10 10.8	14 15.6	9 22.3	5 28.0	6 42.0	26 51.4	29 10.9
17 M	13 41 42	23 32 40	27 40 34	3♓38 03	17 32.9	14 22.4	8 26.0	10 47.6	14 19.9	9 33.5	5 35.1	6 44.9	26 52.6	29 13.3
18 Tu	13 45 38	24 32 12	9♓37 11	15 38 21	17 24.6	16 06.1	9 15.3	11 24.3	14 24.5	9 44.8	5 42.3	6 47.8	26 53.9	29 15.7
19 W	13 49 35	25 31 46	21 41 51	27 47 58	17 15.0	17 49.5	10 05.5	12 00.9	14 29.5	9 56.1	5 49.4	6 50.8	26 55.1	29 18.1
20 Th	13 53 31	26 31 22	3♈56 53	10♈08 46	17 05.2	19 32.8	10 56.4	12 37.5	14 34.8	10 07.5	5 56.6	6 53.8	26 56.4	29 20.6
21 F	13 57 28	27 31 00	16 23 43	22 41 45	16 56.0	21 15.7	11 48.0	13 14.1	14 40.4	10 19.1	6 03.8	6 56.8	26 57.8	29 23.0
22 Sa	14 01 25	28 30 40	29 02 54	5♉27 08	16 48.3	22 58.3	12 40.4	13 50.7	14 46.3	10 30.6	6 11.0	6 59.9	26 59.2	29 25.4
23 Su	14 05 21	29 30 22	11♉54 24	18 24 38	16 42.7	24 40.4	13 33.5	14 27.2	14 52.6	10 42.3	6 18.2	7 03.0	27 00.5	29 27.8
24 M	14 09 18	0♏30 07	24 57 46	1♊33 45	16 39.5	26 22.2	14 27.2	15 03.7	14 59.1	10 54.0	6 25.4	7 06.1	27 02.0	29 30.2
25 Tu	14 13 14	1 29 53	8♊12 32	14 54 03	16D38.3	28 03.4	15 21.6	15 40.1	15 06.0	11 05.8	6 32.6	7 09.2	27 03.4	29 32.6
26 W	14 17 11	2 29 42	21 38 18	28 25 17	16 38.8	29 44.1	16 16.7	16 16.5	15 13.1	11 17.7	6 39.8	7 12.4	27 04.9	29 35.1
27 Th	14 21 07	3 29 32	5♋15 00	12♋07 27	16 40.1	1♏24.4	17 12.4	16 52.9	15 20.6	11 29.7	6 47.0	7 15.6	27 06.4	29 37.5
28 F	14 25 04	4 29 26	19 02 40	26 00 36	16R41.3	3 04.1	18 08.6	17 29.2	15 28.4	11 41.7	6 54.3	7 18.8	27 07.9	29 39.9
29 Sa	14 29 00	5 29 21	3♌01 15	10♌04 29	16 41.5	4 43.4	19 05.4	18 05.5	15 36.4	11 53.8	7 01.5	7 22.1	27 09.5	29 42.3
30 Su	14 32 57	6 29 18	17 10 12	24 18 08	16 40.1	6 22.1	20 02.8	18 41.8	15 44.7	12 05.9	7 08.7	7 25.4	27 11.1	29 44.7
31 M	14 36 54	7 29 18	1♍28 01	8♍39 26	16 36.9	8 00.4	21 00.7	19 18.0	15 53.4	12 18.1	7 16.0	7 28.7	27 12.7	29 47.1

Astro Data

	Dy Hr Mn
☿ R	2 6:41
♆ D	8 11:00
☽ 0S	8 21:59
☿ 0N	15 13:23
♀ D	15 17:22
☽ 0N	23 6:19
☉ 0S	23 14:41
☿ D	24 20:51
♃ ☌ ♅	25 13:54
⚳ D	4 16:16
☽ 0S	6 8:19
☿ 0S	11 17:35
☽ 0N	20 13:22

Planet Ingress

	Dy Hr Mn
☿ ♍R	6 2:30
☉ ♎	23 14:42
♂ ♍	30 0:12
♀ ♍	5 19:35
☿ ♎	8 23:44
☉ ♏	23 23:54
☿ ♏	26 15:47

Last Aspect / ☽ Ingress (September)

Last Aspect Dy Hr Mn		☽ Ingress Dy Hr Mn
1 22:43 ♇ △	♋	2 2:53
4 0:58 ♇ □	♌	4 4:47
6 0:58 ♇ ✱	♍	6 4:36
8 2:36 ☿ ☌	♎	8 4:13
10 2:07 ♇ ☌	♏	10 5:49
12 3:24 ☿ ✱	♐	12 11:08
14 16:35 ♇ ✱	♑	14 20:34
17 4:51 ♇ □	♒	17 8:46
19 17:47 ♇ △	♓	19 21:30
22 6:36 ☉ ☍	♈	22 9:10
24 16:02 ♇ ☍	♉	24 19:12
26 23:57 ♂ □	♊	27 3:24
29 8:42 ♂ ✱	♋	29 9:24

Last Aspect / ☽ Ingress (October)

Last Aspect Dy Hr Mn		☽ Ingress Dy Hr Mn
1 10:32 ♇ □	♌	1 12:54
3 12:06 ♇ ✱	♍	3 14:15
5 9:18 ♆ □	♎	5 14:42
7 14:08 ♇ ☌	♏	7 16:06
8 0:30 ♂ ✱	♐	9 20:21
12 2:35 ♇ ✱	♑	12 4:30
14 14:12 ♇ □	♒	14 16:00
17 3:05 ♇ △	♓	17 4:41
19 10:16 ♆ □	♈	19 16:18
22 0:40 ♇ ☍	♉	22 1:47
23 4:21 ♂ △	♊	24 9:10
26 14:38 ☿ △	♋	26 14:47
28 18:17 ♇ □	♌	28 18:50
30 21:09 ♇ ✱	♍	30 21:33

☽ Phases & Eclipses

Dy Hr Mn	
7 2:35	● 13♍55
14 2:24	☽ 20♐43
22 6:36	○ 28♓42
29 20:05	☾ 6♋06
6 11:16	● 12♎38
13 19:42	☽ 19♑54
21 21:53	○ 27♈56
29 3:37	☾ 5♌08

Astro Data

1 September 1983
Julian Day # 30559
SVP 5♓29'33"
GC 26♐36.7 ⚴ 6♑32.9
Eris 15♈43.1R ⚵ 4♉40.6
⚷ 2♊54.5 ⚶ 20♊09.7
☽ Mean ☊ 20♊57.7

1 October 1983
Julian Day # 30589
SVP 5♓29'29"
GC 26♐36.7 ⚴ 9♑10.0
Eris 15♈26.6R ⚵ 4♉33.7R
⚷ 2♊39.2R ⚶ 26♊49.4
☽ Mean ☊ 19♊22.3

November 1983 — LONGITUDE

Day	Sid.Time	☉	0 hr ☽	Noon ☽	True ☊	☿	♀	♂	⚳	♃	♄	♅	♆	♇
1 Tu	14 40 50	8♏29 20	15♍51 54	23♍04 52	16♊32.2	9♏38.2	21♍59.1	19♍54.2	16♒02.3	12♐30.4	7♏23.2	7♐32.0	27♐14.3	29♎49.5
2 W	14 44 47	9 29 24	0♎17 42	7♎29 42	16R 26.5	11 15.5	22 58.1	20 30.3	16 11.5	12 42.7	7 30.5	7 35.3	27 15.9	29 51.9
3 Th	14 48 43	10 29 29	14 40 09	21 48 20	16 20.6	12 52.3	23 57.5	21 06.4	16 20.9	12 55.1	7 37.7	7 38.7	27 17.6	29 54.3
4 F	14 52 40	11 29 37	28 53 34	5♏55 11	16 15.3	14 28.7	24 57.3	21 42.5	16 30.6	13 07.5	7 44.9	7 42.1	27 19.3	29 56.7
5 Sa	14 56 36	12 29 47	12♏52 38	19 45 25	16 11.3	16 04.7	25 57.6	22 18.5	16 40.7	13 20.0	7 52.2	7 45.5	27 21.0	29 59.1
6 Su	15 00 33	13 29 59	26 33 11	3♐15 41	16D 08.9	17 40.3	26 58.3	22 54.4	16 50.9	13 32.6	7 59.4	7 49.0	27 22.8	0♏01.5
7 M	15 04 29	14 30 12	9♐52 47	16 24 28	16 08.2	19 15.4	27 59.5	23 30.4	17 01.5	13 45.2	8 06.6	7 52.4	27 24.5	0 03.8
8 Tu	15 08 26	15 30 27	22 50 50	29 12 06	16 08.8	20 50.2	29 01.0	24 06.2	17 12.3	13 57.9	8 13.8	7 55.9	27 26.3	0 06.2
9 W	15 12 23	16 30 44	5♑28 33	11♑40 35	16 10.4	22 24.6	0♎02.9	24 42.1	17 23.3	14 10.6	8 21.0	7 59.4	27 28.1	0 08.6
10 Th	15 16 19	17 31 02	17 48 37	23 53 11	16 12.2	23 58.7	1 05.2	25 17.8	17 34.6	14 23.4	8 28.2	8 02.9	27 30.0	0 10.9
11 F	15 20 16	18 31 22	29 54 48	5♒54 05	16 13.7	25 32.5	2 07.9	25 53.6	17 46.1	14 36.2	8 35.4	8 06.4	27 31.8	0 13.2
12 Sa	15 24 12	19 31 43	11♒51 37	17 48 01	16R 14.4	27 05.9	3 10.9	26 29.3	17 57.9	14 49.1	8 42.5	8 09.9	27 33.7	0 15.6
13 Su	15 28 09	20 32 05	23 43 54	29 39 53	16 14.0	28 39.0	4 14.3	27 04.9	18 10.0	15 02.0	8 49.7	8 13.5	27 35.6	0 17.9
14 M	15 32 05	21 32 29	5♓36 35	11♓34 34	16 12.4	0♐11.8	5 18.0	27 40.5	18 22.2	15 14.9	8 56.8	8 17.0	27 37.5	0 20.2
15 Tu	15 36 02	22 32 54	17 34 22	23 36 31	16 09.8	1 44.4	6 22.0	28 16.0	18 34.7	15 27.9	9 03.9	8 20.6	27 39.4	0 22.4
16 W	15 39 58	23 33 20	29 41 30	5♈49 42	16 06.4	3 16.7	7 26.3	28 51.5	18 47.4	15 40.9	9 11.0	8 24.2	27 41.3	0 24.7
17 Th	15 43 55	24 33 48	12♈01 29	18 17 10	16 02.8	4 48.7	8 31.0	29 26.9	19 00.4	15 54.0	9 18.1	8 27.8	27 43.3	0 27.0
18 F	15 47 52	25 34 18	24 36 57	1♉00 59	15 59.4	6 20.4	9 35.9	0♎02.3	19 13.5	16 07.1	9 25.2	8 31.4	27 45.3	0 29.2
19 Sa	15 51 48	26 34 48	7♉29 22	14 02 04	15 56.7	7 51.9	10 41.2	0 37.6	19 26.9	16 20.2	9 32.2	8 35.0	27 47.3	0 31.5
20 Su	15 55 45	27 35 21	20 39 03	27 20 08	15 54.8	9 23.1	11 46.7	1 12.9	19 40.5	16 33.4	9 39.2	8 38.7	27 49.3	0 33.7
21 M	15 59 41	28 35 54	4♊05 09	10♊53 49	15D 54.0	10 54.1	12 52.5	1 48.2	19 54.3	16 46.6	9 46.2	8 42.3	27 51.3	0 35.9
22 Tu	16 03 38	29 36 30	17 45 50	24 40 52	15 54.1	12 24.8	13 58.6	2 23.4	20 08.3	16 59.9	9 53.2	8 46.0	27 53.3	0 38.1
23 W	16 07 34	0♐37 07	1♋38 34	8♋38 34	15 54.9	13 55.3	15 04.9	2 58.5	20 22.5	17 13.1	10 00.1	8 49.6	27 55.4	0 40.3
24 Th	16 11 31	1 37 46	15 40 28	22 43 55	15 56.0	15 25.4	16 11.5	3 33.6	20 37.0	17 26.4	10 07.1	8 53.3	27 57.5	0 42.4
25 F	16 15 27	2 38 26	29 48 33	6♌54 02	15 57.2	16 55.2	17 18.4	4 08.6	20 51.6	17 39.8	10 14.0	8 57.0	27 59.6	0 44.6
26 Sa	16 19 24	3 39 08	14♌00 02	21 06 16	15R 58.0	18 24.7	18 25.4	4 43.6	21 06.4	17 53.1	10 20.8	9 00.7	28 01.7	0 46.7
27 Su	16 23 21	4 39 51	28 12 26	5♍18 14	15 58.2	19 53.9	19 32.8	5 18.5	21 21.4	18 06.5	10 27.7	9 04.3	28 03.8	0 48.8
28 M	16 27 17	5 40 36	12♍23 26	19 27 44	15 57.9	21 22.6	20 40.3	5 53.4	21 36.6	18 20.0	10 34.5	9 08.0	28 05.9	0 50.9
29 Tu	16 31 14	6 41 23	26 30 53	3♎32 37	15 57.2	22 50.8	21 48.0	6 28.2	21 51.9	18 33.4	10 41.2	9 11.7	28 08.0	0 53.0
30 W	16 35 10	7 42 11	10♎32 39	17 30 44	15 56.2	24 18.5	22 56.0	7 02.9	22 07.5	18 46.9	10 48.0	9 15.4	28 10.2	0 55.0

December 1983 — LONGITUDE

Day	Sid.Time	☉	0 hr ☽	Noon ☽	True ☊	☿	♀	♂	⚳	♃	♄	♅	♆	♇
1 Th	16 39 07	8♐43 01	24♎26 33	1♏19 51	15♊55.2	25♐45.6	24♎04.2	7♎37.6	22♒23.3	19♐00.3	10♏54.7	9♐19.1	28♐12.3	0♏57.1
2 F	16 43 03	9 43 52	8♏10 21	14 57 48	15R 54.4	27 12.0	25 12.5	8 12.2	22 39.2	19 13.8	11 01.3	9 22.8	28 14.5	0 59.1
3 Sa	16 47 00	10 44 44	21 41 57	28 22 35	15 53.9	28 37.6	26 21.1	8 46.8	22 55.3	19 27.4	11 08.0	9 26.5	28 16.7	1 01.1
4 Su	16 50 56	11 45 38	4♐59 33	11♐32 41	15D 53.7	0♑02.2	27 29.8	9 21.3	23 11.5	19 40.9	11 14.6	9 30.2	28 18.9	1 03.0
5 M	16 54 53	12 46 32	18 01 54	24 27 10	15 53.7	1 25.7	28 38.7	9 55.7	23 28.0	19 54.5	11 21.1	9 33.8	28 21.1	1 05.0
6 Tu	16 58 50	13 47 28	0♑48 31	7♑06 01	15 53.9	2 48.0	29 47.8	10 30.1	23 44.6	20 08.0	11 27.6	9 37.5	28 23.3	1 06.9
7 W	17 02 46	14 48 25	13 19 48	19 30 06	15 54.0	4 08.8	0♏57.0	11 04.3	24 01.4	20 21.6	11 34.1	9 41.2	28 25.5	1 08.8
8 Th	17 06 43	15 49 22	25 37 08	1♒41 16	15R 54.1	5 27.9	2 06.4	11 38.6	24 18.3	20 35.2	11 40.5	9 44.9	28 27.7	1 10.7
9 F	17 10 39	16 50 21	7♒42 49	13 42 15	15 54.0	6 45.0	3 16.0	12 12.7	24 35.4	20 48.8	11 46.9	9 48.6	28 29.9	1 12.6
10 Sa	17 14 36	17 51 20	19 39 59	25 36 32	15 53.9	7 59.7	4 25.7	12 46.8	24 52.7	21 02.4	11 53.3	9 52.2	28 32.2	1 14.4
11 Su	17 18 32	18 52 19	1♓32 27	7♓28 15	15 53.7	9 11.8	5 35.5	13 20.8	25 10.1	21 16.1	11 59.6	9 55.9	28 34.4	1 16.2
12 M	17 22 29	19 53 19	13 24 33	19 21 54	15D 53.6	10 20.7	6 45.5	13 54.7	25 27.6	21 29.7	12 05.8	9 59.6	28 36.7	1 18.0
13 Tu	17 26 25	20 54 20	25 20 56	1♈22 14	15 53.7	11 26.1	7 55.6	14 28.5	25 45.3	21 43.3	12 12.0	10 03.2	28 38.9	1 19.7
14 W	17 30 22	21 55 21	7♈26 22	13 33 53	15 54.1	12 27.2	9 05.9	15 02.3	26 03.2	21 56.9	12 18.1	10 06.8	28 41.2	1 21.5
15 Th	17 34 19	22 56 23	19 45 21	26 01 13	15 54.7	13 23.6	10 16.3	15 36.0	26 21.2	22 10.6	12 24.2	10 10.5	28 43.4	1 23.2
16 F	17 38 15	23 57 25	2♉21 55	8♉47 50	15 55.6	14 14.4	11 26.8	16 09.6	26 39.3	22 24.2	12 30.3	10 14.1	28 45.7	1 24.9
17 Sa	17 42 12	24 58 27	15 19 13	21 56 15	15 56.4	14 59.0	12 37.4	16 43.1	26 57.5	22 37.8	12 36.3	10 17.7	28 48.0	1 26.5
18 Su	17 46 08	25 59 31	28 39 02	5♊27 31	15R 57.0	15 36.5	13 48.2	17 16.6	27 15.9	22 51.5	12 42.2	10 21.3	28 50.2	1 28.1
19 M	17 50 05	27 00 34	12♊21 33	19 20 49	15 57.1	16 06.1	14 59.1	17 50.0	27 34.5	23 05.1	12 48.1	10 24.9	28 52.5	1 29.7
20 Tu	17 54 01	28 01 39	26 24 56	3♋33 21	15 56.6	16 26.8	16 10.1	18 23.3	27 53.1	23 18.7	12 53.9	10 28.4	28 54.8	1 31.3
21 W	17 57 58	29 02 44	10♋45 27	18 00 30	15 55.5	16R 37.7	17 21.2	18 56.5	28 11.9	23 32.3	12 59.7	10 32.0	28 57.0	1 32.9
22 Th	18 01 55	0♑03 49	25 17 43	2♌36 17	15 53.8	16 38.1	18 32.4	19 29.6	28 30.8	23 45.9	13 05.4	10 35.5	28 59.3	1 34.4
23 F	18 05 51	1 04 55	9♌55 22	17 14 11	15 51.9	16 27.2	19 43.8	20 02.6	28 49.8	23 59.5	13 11.0	10 39.1	29 01.6	1 35.9
24 Sa	18 09 48	2 06 02	24 31 57	1♍47 59	15 50.0	16 04.7	20 55.2	20 35.6	29 09.0	24 13.1	13 16.6	10 42.6	29 03.9	1 37.3
25 Su	18 13 44	3 07 09	9♍01 43	16 12 37	15 48.5	15 30.4	22 06.7	21 08.5	29 28.3	24 26.7	13 22.1	10 46.1	29 06.1	1 38.7
26 M	18 17 41	4 08 17	23 20 18	0♎24 29	15D 47.8	14 44.6	23 18.4	21 41.2	29 47.6	24 40.3	13 27.6	10 49.5	29 08.4	1 40.1
27 Tu	18 21 37	5 09 26	7♎24 57	14 21 37	15 48.0	13 48.0	24 30.1	22 13.9	0♓07.2	24 53.8	13 33.0	10 53.0	29 10.6	1 41.5
28 W	18 25 34	6 10 35	21 14 25	28 03 23	15 49.0	12 42.1	25 41.9	22 46.5	0 26.8	25 07.3	13 38.3	10 56.4	29 12.9	1 42.8
29 Th	18 29 30	7 11 45	4♏48 34	11♏30 05	15 50.5	11 28.6	26 53.8	23 19.0	0 46.5	25 20.9	13 43.6	10 59.9	29 15.2	1 44.1
30 F	18 33 27	8 12 55	18 08 03	24 42 34	15 52.0	10 09.8	28 05.8	23 51.4	1 06.3	25 34.4	13 48.8	11 03.3	29 17.4	1 45.4
31 Sa	18 37 24	9 14 06	1♐13 46	7♐41 46	15R 53.1	8 48.3	29 17.9	24 23.6	1 26.3	25 47.9	13 53.9	11 06.6	29 19.7	1 46.6

Astro Data Dy Hr Mn	Planet Ingress Dy Hr Mn	Last Aspect Dy Hr Mn	☽ Ingress Dy Hr Mn	Last Aspect Dy Hr Mn	☽ Ingress Dy Hr Mn	☽ Phases & Eclipses Dy Hr Mn
☽0S 2 17:46	♇ ♏ 5 21:07	1 18:56 ♆ □	♎ 1 23:31	1 6:32 ♆ ⚹	♏ 1 9:41	4 22:21 ● 11♏56
♄⊻♅ 3 18:24	♀ ♎ 9 10:52	4 1:46 ♇ ☌	♏ 4 1:53	2 4:58 ♄ ☌	♐ 3 14:56	12 15:49 ☽ 19♒41
♀0S 12 1:36	☿ ♐ 14 8:56	5 23:50 ♀ ⚹	♐ 6 6:09	5 20:41 ♀ ⚹	♑ 5 22:28	20 12:29 ○ 27♉37
♃∠♇ 14 23:49	♂ ♎ 18 10:26	8 11:37 ♀ □	♑ 8 13:31	6 20:28 ♄ ⚹	♒ 8 8:39	27 10:50 ☾ 4♍37
☽0N 16 22:07	☉ ♐ 22 21:18	10 14:57 ♂ △	♒ 11 0:10	10 17:56 ♆ ⚹	♓ 10 20:53	
♂0S 24 10:19		13 9:38 ♀ □	♓ 13 12:41	13 6:34 ♆ □	♈ 13 9:17	4 12:26 ● 11♐47
☽0S 30 0:59	☿ ♑ 4 11:22	15 21:40 ♂ ☍	♈ 16 0:36	15 17:09 ♆ △	♉ 15 19:33	4 12:30:22 ● A 04'01"
	♀ ♏ 6 16:15	18 5:53 ♆ △	♉ 18 10:06	16 22:39 ♆ ☍	♊ 18 2:23	12 13:09 ☽ 19♓56
☽0N 14 7:14	☉ ♑ 22 10:30	20 12:29 ☉ ☍	♊ 20 16:45	20 4:11 ♆ ☍	♋ 20 6:02	20 2:00 ○ 27♊36
☿R 22 0:51	⚳ ♓ 27 3:13	22 17:33 ♆ ☍	♋ 22 21:10	21 13:36 ♂ □	♌ 22 7:44	20 1:49 ○ A 0.889
☽0S 27 6:18		23 23:56 ♀ □	♌ 25 0:19	24 7:28 ♆ △	♍ 24 9:01	26 18:52 ☾ 4♎26
		26 23:44 ♆ △	♍ 27 3:02	26 9:50 ♆ □	♎ 26 11:18	
		29 2:44 ♆ □	♎ 29 5:57	28 14:03 ♆ ⚹	♏ 28 15:27	
				30 18:51 ♀ ☌	♐ 30 21:44	

Astro Data

1 November 1983
Julian Day # 30620
SVP 5♓29'26"
GC 26♐36.8 ⚴ 15♑45.9
Eris 15♈08.1R ⚵ 28♈17.6R
⚷ 1♊29.2R ⚶ 28♊33.6R
☽ Mean ☊ 17♊43.8

1 December 1983
Julian Day # 30650
SVP 5♓29'21"
GC 26♐36.9 ⚴ 24♑22.4
Eris 14♈54.2R ⚵ 24♈27.0R
⚷ 29♉53.7R ⚶ 23♊53.4R
☽ Mean ☊ 16♊08.5

LONGITUDE — January 1984

Day	Sid.Time	☉	0 hr ☽	Noon ☽	True ☊	☿	♀	♂	⚳	♃	♄	♅	♆	♇
1 Su	18 41 20	10♑15 17	14♐06 42	20♐28 38	15♊53.3	7♑26.9	0♐30.1	24♎55.8	1♓46.3	26♐01.3	13♏59.0	11♐10.0	29♐21.9	1♏47.8
2 M	18 45 17	11 16 28	26 47 42	3♑03 58	15R 52.1	6R 08.0	1 42.3	25 27.9	2 06.5	26 14.8	14 03.9	11 13.3	29 24.1	1 49.0
3 Tu	18 49 13	12 17 39	9♑17 32	15 28 29	15 49.5	4 54.2	2 54.6	25 59.8	2 26.8	26 28.2	14 08.9	11 16.6	29 26.4	1 50.2
4 W	18 53 10	13 18 50	21 36 57	27 43 03	15 45.6	3 47.4	4 07.0	26 31.7	2 47.1	26 41.6	14 13.7	11 19.9	29 28.6	1 51.3
5 Th	18 57 06	14 20 01	3♒46 56	9♒48 46	15 40.6	2 49.1	5 19.4	27 03.4	3 07.6	26 54.9	14 18.5	11 23.2	29 30.8	1 52.3
6 F	19 01 03	15 21 12	15 48 45	21 47 10	15 35.0	2 00.1	6 31.9	27 35.0	3 28.1	27 08.3	14 23.2	11 26.4	29 33.0	1 53.4
7 Sa	19 04 59	16 22 23	27 44 18	3♓40 27	15 29.5	1 21.2	7 44.5	28 06.5	3 48.8	27 21.6	14 27.8	11 29.6	29 35.2	1 54.4
8 Su	19 08 56	17 23 33	9♓36 01	15 31 25	15 24.6	0 52.4	8 57.1	28 37.8	4 09.5	27 34.8	14 32.3	11 32.8	29 37.4	1 55.4
9 M	19 12 53	18 24 43	21 27 07	27 23 36	15 20.9	0 33.5	10 09.7	29 09.1	4 30.4	27 48.1	14 36.8	11 35.9	29 39.6	1 56.3
10 Tu	19 16 49	19 25 52	3♈21 24	9♈21 05	15D 18.8	0D 24.2	11 22.5	29 40.2	4 51.3	28 01.3	14 41.1	11 39.1	29 41.8	1 57.2
11 W	19 20 46	20 27 01	15 23 15	21 28 30	15 18.2	0 24.0	12 35.2	0♏11.2	5 12.3	28 14.5	14 45.4	11 42.1	29 43.9	1 58.1
12 Th	19 24 42	21 28 09	27 37 26	3♉50 40	15 18.9	0 32.1	13 48.1	0 42.0	5 33.4	28 27.6	14 49.6	11 45.2	29 46.1	1 58.9
13 F	19 28 39	22 29 17	10♉08 46	16 32 18	15 20.5	0 48.1	15 00.9	1 12.7	5 54.5	28 40.7	14 53.8	11 48.2	29 48.2	1 59.7
14 Sa	19 32 35	23 30 24	23 01 47	29 37 36	15 22.0	1 11.1	16 13.9	1 43.3	6 15.8	28 53.7	14 57.8	11 51.2	29 50.3	2 00.5
15 Su	19 36 32	24 31 30	6♊20 07	13♊09 32	15R 22.9	1 40.5	17 26.9	2 13.8	6 37.1	29 06.7	15 01.8	11 54.2	29 52.5	2 01.2
16 M	19 40 28	25 32 36	20 05 54	27 09 09	15 22.3	2 15.8	18 39.9	2 44.1	6 58.5	29 19.7	15 05.7	11 57.1	29 54.6	2 01.9
17 Tu	19 44 25	26 33 41	4♋18 58	11♋34 53	15 19.8	2 56.4	19 52.9	3 14.3	7 20.0	29 32.6	15 09.5	12 00.0	29 56.6	2 02.5
18 W	19 48 22	27 34 46	18 56 14	26 22 10	15 15.3	3 41.7	21 06.1	3 44.3	7 41.5	29 45.5	15 13.2	12 02.9	29 58.7	2 03.2
19 Th	19 52 18	28 35 50	3♌51 39	11♌23 32	15 09.2	4 31.2	22 19.2	4 14.2	8 03.2	29 58.4	15 16.8	12 05.7	0♑00.8	2 03.7
20 F	19 56 15	29 36 54	18 56 35	26 29 32	15 02.2	5 24.7	23 32.4	4 43.9	8 24.8	0♑11.2	15 20.3	12 08.5	0 02.8	2 04.3
21 Sa	20 00 11	0♒37 56	4♍01 10	11♍30 18	14 55.2	6 21.5	24 45.7	5 13.5	8 46.6	0 23.9	15 23.8	12 11.3	0 04.8	2 04.8
22 Su	20 04 08	1 38 59	18 55 56	26 17 12	14 49.2	7 21.5	25 59.0	5 43.0	9 08.4	0 36.6	15 27.1	12 14.0	0 06.9	2 05.3
23 M	20 08 04	2 40 01	3♎33 23	10♎44 01	14 45.0	8 24.3	27 12.3	6 12.2	9 30.3	0 49.2	15 30.4	12 16.7	0 08.9	2 05.7
24 Tu	20 12 01	3 41 02	17 48 48	24 47 35	14D 42.8	9 29.7	28 25.6	6 41.3	9 52.3	1 01.8	15 33.6	12 19.4	0 10.8	2 06.1
25 W	20 15 57	4 42 03	1♏40 24	8♏27 23	14 42.5	10 37.4	29 39.1	7 10.3	10 14.3	1 14.3	15 36.7	12 22.0	0 12.8	2 06.5
26 Th	20 19 54	5 43 04	15 08 49	21 44 59	14 43.3	11 47.3	0♑52.5	7 39.1	10 36.4	1 26.8	15 39.6	12 24.5	0 14.7	2 06.8
27 F	20 23 51	6 44 04	28 16 16	4♐43 05	14R 44.4	12 59.0	2 06.0	8 07.7	10 58.6	1 39.2	15 42.5	12 27.1	0 16.7	2 07.1
28 Sa	20 27 47	7 45 04	11♐05 50	17 24 55	14 44.8	14 12.6	3 19.5	8 36.1	11 20.8	1 51.5	15 45.3	12 29.6	0 18.6	2 07.4
29 Su	20 31 44	8 46 02	23 40 44	29 53 37	14 43.5	15 27.7	4 33.0	9 04.3	11 43.1	2 03.8	15 48.0	12 32.0	0 20.5	2 07.6
30 M	20 35 40	9 47 00	6♑03 55	12♑11 56	14 39.8	16 44.4	5 46.6	9 32.3	12 05.4	2 16.1	15 50.6	12 34.5	0 22.3	2 07.8
31 Tu	20 39 37	10 47 58	18 17 54	24 22 04	14 33.4	18 02.5	7 00.2	10 00.2	12 27.8	2 28.2	15 53.2	12 36.8	0 24.2	2 08.0

LONGITUDE — February 1984

Day	Sid.Time	☉	0 hr ☽	Noon ☽	True ☊	☿	♀	♂	⚳	♃	♄	♅	♆	♇
1 W	20 43 33	11♒48 54	0♒24 37	6♒25 44	14♊24.4	19♑22.0	8♑13.8	10♏27.8	12♓50.3	2♑40.3	15♏55.6	12♐39.2	0♑26.0	2♏08.1
2 Th	20 47 30	12 49 49	12 25 34	18 24 16	14R 13.4	20 42.6	9 27.4	10 55.3	13 12.8	2 52.4	15 57.9	12 41.4	0 27.8	2 08.1
3 F	20 51 26	13 50 43	24 22 00	0♓18 54	14 01.2	22 04.5	10 41.1	11 22.5	13 35.3	3 04.3	16 00.1	12 43.7	0 29.6	2R 08.2
4 Sa	20 55 23	14 51 36	6♓15 10	12 10 58	13 48.9	23 27.4	11 54.8	11 49.5	13 57.9	3 16.2	16 02.2	12 45.9	0 31.4	2 08.2
5 Su	20 59 20	15 52 27	18 06 34	24 02 12	13 37.5	24 51.4	13 08.5	12 16.4	14 20.6	3 28.0	16 04.2	12 48.0	0 33.1	2 08.2
6 M	21 03 16	16 53 18	29 58 11	5♈54 52	13 28.0	26 16.5	14 22.2	12 42.9	14 43.3	3 39.8	16 06.1	12 50.1	0 34.8	2 08.1
7 Tu	21 07 13	17 54 06	11♈52 40	17 52 00	13 21.0	27 42.5	15 35.9	13 09.3	15 06.0	3 51.4	16 07.9	12 52.2	0 36.5	2 08.0
8 W	21 11 09	18 54 54	23 53 22	29 57 18	13 16.7	29 09.4	16 49.7	13 35.4	15 28.8	4 03.0	16 09.6	12 54.2	0 38.2	2 07.8
9 Th	21 15 06	19 55 39	6♉04 22	12♉15 08	13D 14.8	0♒37.3	18 03.5	14 01.3	15 51.6	4 14.5	16 11.3	12 56.2	0 39.8	2 07.7
10 F	21 19 02	20 56 24	18 30 14	24 50 17	13 14.5	2 06.1	19 17.2	14 27.0	16 14.5	4 25.9	16 12.8	12 58.1	0 41.4	2 07.5
11 Sa	21 22 59	21 57 07	1♊15 51	7♊47 32	13R 14.9	3 35.8	20 31.0	14 52.4	16 37.4	4 37.3	16 14.2	13 00.0	0 43.0	2 07.2
12 Su	21 26 55	22 57 48	14 25 50	21 11 10	13 14.8	5 06.4	21 44.9	15 17.6	17 00.4	4 48.5	16 15.5	13 01.8	0 44.6	2 06.9
13 M	21 30 52	23 58 27	28 03 50	5♋04 01	13 13.0	6 37.9	22 58.7	15 42.6	17 23.4	4 59.7	16 16.7	13 03.6	0 46.2	2 06.6
14 Tu	21 34 49	24 59 05	12♋11 42	19 26 38	13 08.7	8 10.2	24 12.5	16 07.2	17 46.4	5 10.8	16 17.8	13 05.4	0 47.7	2 06.3
15 W	21 38 45	25 59 41	26 48 23	4♌16 14	13 01.7	9 43.5	25 26.4	16 31.6	18 09.5	5 21.8	16 18.8	13 07.0	0 49.2	2 05.9
16 Th	21 42 42	27 00 16	11♌49 15	19 26 17	12 52.3	11 17.6	26 40.3	16 55.8	18 32.6	5 32.7	16 19.7	13 08.7	0 50.7	2 05.5
17 F	21 46 38	28 00 49	27 06 00	4♍46 56	12 41.4	12 52.5	27 54.1	17 19.7	18 55.7	5 43.5	16 20.4	13 10.3	0 52.1	2 05.0
18 Sa	21 50 35	29 01 20	12♍27 34	20 06 25	12 30.4	14 28.4	29 08.0	17 43.3	19 18.9	5 54.2	16 21.1	13 11.8	0 53.5	2 04.5
19 Su	21 54 31	0♓01 50	27 42 05	5♎13 18	12 20.5	16 05.2	0♒21.9	18 06.6	19 42.1	6 04.9	16 21.7	13 13.3	0 54.9	2 04.0
20 M	21 58 28	1 02 19	12♎39 03	19 58 30	12 12.9	17 42.9	1 35.9	18 29.6	20 05.3	6 15.4	16 22.2	13 14.7	0 56.3	2 03.4
21 Tu	22 02 24	2 02 46	27 11 06	4♏16 30	12 07.9	19 21.5	2 49.8	18 52.3	20 28.6	6 25.9	16 22.6	13 16.1	0 57.6	2 02.9
22 W	22 06 21	3 03 12	11♏14 35	18 05 27	12 05.5	21 01.0	4 03.8	19 14.7	20 51.9	6 36.2	16 22.8	13 17.5	0 58.9	2 02.2
23 Th	22 10 18	4 03 37	24 49 19	1♐26 33	12 04.8	22 41.5	5 17.7	19 36.8	21 15.2	6 46.4	16 23.0	13 18.8	1 00.2	2 01.6
24 F	22 14 14	5 04 01	7♐57 37	14 23 01	12 04.8	24 22.9	6 31.7	19 58.6	21 38.5	6 56.6	16R 23.1	13 20.0	1 01.4	2 00.9
25 Sa	22 18 11	6 04 23	20 43 20	26 59 06	12 04.2	26 05.4	7 45.7	20 20.0	22 01.9	7 06.6	16 23.0	13 21.2	1 02.7	2 00.2
26 Su	22 22 07	7 04 43	3♑10 55	9♑19 19	12 01.9	27 48.8	8 59.7	20 41.1	22 25.3	7 16.5	16 22.9	13 22.3	1 03.8	1 59.4
27 M	22 26 04	8 05 02	15 24 49	21 27 54	11 56.8	29 33.2	10 13.7	21 01.9	22 48.8	7 26.4	16 22.6	13 23.4	1 05.0	1 58.7
28 Tu	22 30 00	9 05 20	27 29 00	3♒28 32	11 48.8	1♓18.6	11 27.7	21 22.3	23 12.2	7 36.1	16 22.3	13 24.4	1 06.1	1 57.8
29 W	22 33 57	10 05 36	9♒26 50	15 24 12	11 37.7	3 05.1	12 41.7	21 42.3	23 35.7	7 45.7	16 21.8	13 25.4	1 07.2	1 57.0

Astro Data

	Dy Hr Mn
☽0N	10 15:06
♄∠♆	10 19:00
☿D	11 0:37
♃☌♆	19 17:23
♃∠♄	21 11:44
☽0S	23 12:01
♃✶♇	29 19:31
♇R	4 2:05
☽0N	6 21:10
☽0S	19 20:12
♄R	24 14:36

Planet Ingress

	Dy Hr Mn
♀ ♐	1 2:00
♂ ♏	11 3:20
☿ ♑	19 2:55
♃ ♑	19 15:04
☉ ♒	20 21:05
♀ ♑	25 18:51
☿ ♒	9 1:50
♀ ♒	19 4:53
☉ ♓	19 11:16
☿ ♓	27 18:07

Last Aspect / ☽ Ingress

Last Aspect Dy Hr Mn		☽ Ingress Dy Hr Mn
2 4:57 ♆ ☌	♑	2 6:07
4 9:33 ♂ □	♒	4 16:30
7 3:43 ♆ ✶	♓	7 4:34
9 16:35 ♆ □	♈	9 17:15
12 4:08 ♆ △	♉	12 4:36
13 23:56 ☉ △	♊	14 12:40
16 16:39 ♆ ☍	♋	16 16:47
18 14:05 ☉ ☍	♌	18 17:50
20 6:54 ♀ △	♍	20 17:35
22 11:27 ♀ □	♎	22 18:07
24 18:56 ♀ ✶	♏	24 21:04
26 0:53 ♄ ☌	♐	27 3:12
28 2:37 ♅ ☌	♑	29 12:12
30 22:00 ☿ ☌	♒	31 23:11

Last Aspect / ☽ Ingress

Last Aspect Dy Hr Mn		☽ Ingress Dy Hr Mn
2 7:05 ♄ □	♓	3 11:22
5 13:53 ☿ ✶	♈	6 0:04
8 10:13 ☿ □	♉	8 12:05
10 4:00 ☉ □	♊	10 21:39
12 15:22 ☉ △	♋	13 3:20
14 20:30 ♀ ☍	♌	15 5:09
17 0:41 ☉ ☍	♍	17 4:32
19 3:33 ☿ △	♎	19 3:39
20 7:49 ☿ △	♏	21 4:44
22 17:56 ☿ □	♐	23 9:22
25 10:00 ☿ ✶	♑	25 17:49
27 11:07 ♂ ✶	♒	28 5:02

☽ Phases & Eclipses

Dy Hr Mn	
3 5:16	● 12♑00
11 9:48	☽ 20♈21
18 14:05	○ 27♋40
25 4:48	☾ 4♏24
1 23:46	● 12♒19
10 4:00	☽ 20♉36
17 0:41	○ 27♌32
23 17:12	☾ 4♐17

Astro Data

1 January 1984
Julian Day # 30681
SVP 5♓29'16"
GC 26♐36.9 ⚴ 4♒29.1
Eris 14♈48.4R ⚵ 28♈42.9
⚷ 28♉26.1R ⚶ 16♊10.0R
☽ Mean ☊ 14♊30.1

1 February 1984
Julian Day # 30712
SVP 5♓29'10"
GC 26♐37.0 ⚴ 15♒04.9
Eris 14♈53.3 ⚵ 9♉31.7
⚷ 27♉46.3R ⚶ 13♊00.1
☽ Mean ☊ 12♊51.6

March 1984

LONGITUDE

Day	Sid.Time	☉	0 hr ☽	Noon ☽	True ☊	☿	♀	♂	⚳	♃	♄	♅	♆	♇
1 Th	22 37 53	11♓05 50	21♒20 54	27♒17 10	11♊24.3	4♓52.6	13♒55.8	22♏02.0	23♓59.2	7♑55.2	16♏21.2	13♐26.3	1♑08.3	1♏56.1
2 F	22 41 50	12 06 03	3♓13 11	9♓09 07	11R 09.5	6 41.1	15 09.8	22 21.2	24 22.7	8 04.5	16R 20.6	13 27.2	1 09.3	1R 55.2
3 Sa	22 45 47	13 06 13	15 05 09	21 01 25	10 54.4	8 30.7	16 23.8	22 40.1	24 46.2	8 13.8	16 19.8	13 28.0	1 10.3	1 54.3
4 Su	22 49 43	14 06 22	26 58 05	2♈55 19	10 40.3	10 21.3	17 37.9	22 58.6	25 09.8	8 22.9	16 18.9	13 28.8	1 11.3	1 53.3
5 M	22 53 40	15 06 29	8♈53 18	14 52 15	10 28.2	12 13.0	18 51.9	23 16.6	25 33.4	8 31.9	16 18.0	13 29.5	1 12.3	1 52.3
6 Tu	22 57 36	16 06 34	20 52 25	26 54 07	10 19.0	14 05.6	20 05.9	23 34.3	25 56.9	8 40.8	16 16.9	13 30.1	1 13.2	1 51.3
7 W	23 01 33	17 06 37	2♉57 39	9♉03 26	10 12.9	15 59.3	21 20.0	23 51.5	26 20.5	8 49.6	16 15.7	13 30.7	1 14.1	1 50.3
8 Th	23 05 29	18 06 37	15 11 51	21 23 23	10 09.6	17 53.9	22 34.0	24 08.3	26 44.2	8 58.2	16 14.5	13 31.3	1 14.9	1 49.2
9 F	23 09 26	19 06 36	27 38 32	3♊57 48	10D 08.4	19 49.4	23 48.0	24 24.6	27 07.8	9 06.8	16 13.1	13 31.8	1 15.7	1 48.1
10 Sa	23 13 22	20 06 33	10♊21 45	16 50 54	10R 08.4	21 45.8	25 02.1	24 40.5	27 31.4	9 15.1	16 11.6	13 32.2	1 16.5	1 47.0
11 Su	23 17 19	21 06 27	23 25 46	0♋06 50	10 08.2	23 43.0	26 16.1	24 56.0	27 55.1	9 23.4	16 10.1	13 32.6	1 17.3	1 45.8
12 M	23 21 16	22 06 19	6♋54 28	13 49 00	10 06.6	25 40.8	27 30.2	25 10.9	28 18.7	9 31.5	16 08.4	13 33.0	1 18.0	1 44.7
13 Tu	23 25 12	23 06 09	20 50 34	27 59 10	10 02.8	27 39.2	28 44.2	25 25.4	28 42.4	9 39.5	16 06.7	13 33.2	1 18.7	1 43.5
14 W	23 29 09	24 05 57	5♌14 36	12♌36 27	9 56.4	29 38.0	29 58.2	25 39.4	29 06.1	9 47.4	16 04.8	13 33.5	1 19.3	1 42.2
15 Th	23 33 05	25 05 42	20 04 04	27 36 33	9 47.6	1♈37.0	1♓12.2	25 52.9	29 29.8	9 55.1	16 02.9	13 33.6	1 19.9	1 41.0
16 F	23 37 02	26 05 25	5♍12 49	12♍51 33	9 37.2	3 36.0	2 26.3	26 05.9	29 53.5	10 02.7	16 00.9	13 33.8	1 20.5	1 39.7
17 Sa	23 40 58	27 05 06	20 31 23	28 10 49	9 26.5	5 34.8	3 40.3	26 18.4	0♈17.2	10 10.2	15 58.7	13R 33.8	1 21.1	1 38.4
18 Su	23 44 55	28 04 45	5♎48 24	13♎22 44	9 16.8	7 33.1	4 54.3	26 30.3	0 40.8	10 17.5	15 56.5	13 33.8	1 21.6	1 37.1
19 M	23 48 51	29 04 22	20 52 35	28 16 53	9 09.1	9 30.5	6 08.4	26 41.7	1 04.6	10 24.6	15 54.2	13 33.8	1 22.1	1 35.8
20 Tu	23 52 48	0♈03 57	5♏34 49	12♏45 46	9 04.0	11 26.9	7 22.4	26 52.6	1 28.3	10 31.6	15 51.8	13 33.7	1 22.5	1 34.4
21 W	23 56 45	1 03 31	19 49 24	26 45 32	9D 01.5	13 21.7	8 36.4	27 02.9	1 52.0	10 38.5	15 49.4	13 33.6	1 23.0	1 33.0
22 Th	0 00 41	2 03 03	3♐34 15	10♐15 45	9 00.9	15 14.5	9 50.5	27 12.6	2 15.7	10 45.3	15 46.8	13 33.4	1 23.4	1 31.6
23 F	0 04 38	3 02 33	16 50 24	23 18 38	9R 01.3	17 05.1	11 04.5	27 21.7	2 39.4	10 51.8	15 44.2	13 33.1	1 23.7	1 30.2
24 Sa	0 08 34	4 02 01	29 41 00	5♑58 05	9 01.6	18 52.8	12 18.5	27 30.2	3 03.1	10 58.3	15 41.4	13 32.8	1 24.0	1 28.8
25 Su	0 12 31	5 01 28	12♑10 28	18 18 48	9 00.6	20 37.4	13 32.6	27 38.1	3 26.8	11 04.6	15 38.6	13 32.5	1 24.3	1 27.3
26 M	0 16 27	6 00 53	24 23 40	0♒25 41	8 57.6	22 18.3	14 46.6	27 45.3	3 50.5	11 10.7	15 35.7	13 32.1	1 24.6	1 25.9
27 Tu	0 20 24	7 00 16	6♒25 24	12 23 21	8 52.1	23 55.2	16 00.6	27 51.9	4 14.3	11 16.7	15 32.8	13 31.6	1 24.8	1 24.4
28 W	0 24 20	7 59 37	18 20 02	24 15 54	8 44.2	25 27.6	17 14.7	27 57.9	4 38.0	11 22.5	15 29.7	13 31.1	1 25.0	1 22.9
29 Th	0 28 17	8 58 56	0♓11 19	6♓06 41	8 34.2	26 55.1	18 28.7	28 03.2	5 01.7	11 28.1	15 26.6	13 30.6	1 25.2	1 21.4
30 F	0 32 14	9 58 13	12 02 17	17 58 24	8 22.9	28 17.5	19 42.7	28 07.8	5 25.4	11 33.6	15 23.4	13 29.9	1 25.3	1 19.8
31 Sa	0 36 10	10 57 29	23 55 16	29 53 06	8 11.4	29 34.4	20 56.7	28 11.8	5 49.1	11 39.0	15 20.1	13 29.3	1 25.4	1 18.3

April 1984

LONGITUDE

Day	Sid.Time	☉	0 hr ☽	Noon ☽	True ☊	☿	♀	♂	⚳	♃	♄	♅	♆	♇
1 Su	0 40 07	11♈56 42	5♈52 03	11♈52 18	8♊00.6	0♉45.5	22♓10.7	28♏15.0	6♈12.8	11♑44.1	15♏16.8	13♐28.6	1♑25.4	1♏16.7
2 M	0 44 03	12 55 53	17 54 00	23 57 18	7R 51.5	1 50.6	23 24.7	28 17.5	6 36.5	11 49.1	15R 13.4	13R 27.8	1R 25.4	1R 15.1
3 Tu	0 48 00	13 55 02	0♉02 21	6♉09 20	7 44.7	2 49.4	24 38.7	28 19.3	7 00.1	11 54.0	15 09.9	13 27.0	1 25.4	1 13.5
4 W	0 51 56	14 54 09	12 18 25	18 29 51	7 40.3	3 41.8	25 52.7	28 20.5	7 23.8	11 58.6	15 06.3	13 26.1	1 25.4	1 11.9
5 Th	0 55 53	15 53 14	24 43 50	1♊00 41	7D 38.4	4 27.7	27 06.7	28R 20.8	7 47.4	12 03.1	15 02.7	13 25.2	1 25.3	1 10.3
6 F	0 59 49	16 52 17	7♊20 40	13 44 08	7 38.3	5 06.9	28 20.7	28 20.5	8 11.1	12 07.5	14 59.1	13 24.3	1 25.2	1 08.7
7 Sa	1 03 46	17 51 18	20 11 26	26 42 54	7 39.3	5 39.3	29 34.7	28 19.4	8 34.7	12 11.6	14 55.3	13 23.3	1 25.0	1 07.1
8 Su	1 07 42	18 50 16	3♋18 54	9♋59 46	7R 40.4	6 04.9	0♈48.6	28 17.5	8 58.3	12 15.6	14 51.5	13 22.2	1 24.9	1 05.4
9 M	1 11 39	19 49 12	16 45 48	23 37 14	7 40.6	6 23.8	2 02.6	28 15.0	9 21.9	12 19.4	14 47.7	13 21.1	1 24.7	1 03.8
10 Tu	1 15 36	20 48 05	0♌34 14	7♌36 50	7 39.3	6 35.9	3 16.5	28 11.6	9 45.5	12 23.0	14 43.8	13 20.0	1 24.4	1 02.1
11 W	1 19 32	21 46 57	14 44 56	21 58 19	7 36.1	6R 41.4	4 30.5	28 07.5	10 09.1	12 26.5	14 39.9	13 18.8	1 24.1	1 00.5
12 Th	1 23 29	22 45 45	29 16 34	6♍39 06	7 31.1	6 40.5	5 44.4	28 02.7	10 32.6	12 29.8	14 35.9	13 17.6	1 23.8	0 58.8
13 F	1 27 25	23 44 32	14♍05 10	21 33 51	7 24.9	6 33.3	6 58.3	27 57.1	10 56.2	12 32.9	14 31.8	13 16.3	1 23.5	0 57.1
14 Sa	1 31 22	24 43 16	29 04 07	6♎34 49	7 18.4	6 20.2	8 12.2	27 50.7	11 19.7	12 35.8	14 27.7	13 15.0	1 23.1	0 55.4
15 Su	1 35 18	25 41 59	14♎04 47	21 32 51	7 12.3	6 01.6	9 26.1	27 43.6	11 43.2	12 38.6	14 23.6	13 13.6	1 22.7	0 53.8
16 M	1 39 15	26 40 39	28 57 53	6♏18 52	7 07.6	5 37.9	10 40.0	27 35.7	12 06.7	12 41.1	14 19.4	13 12.2	1 22.3	0 52.1
17 Tu	1 43 11	27 39 18	13♏34 55	20 45 20	7 04.7	5 09.5	11 53.9	27 27.1	12 30.1	12 43.5	14 15.2	13 10.8	1 21.8	0 50.4
18 W	1 47 08	28 37 54	27 49 34	4♐47 17	7D 03.6	4 37.3	13 07.8	27 17.7	12 53.6	12 45.7	14 10.9	13 09.3	1 21.3	0 48.7
19 Th	1 51 05	29 36 29	11♐38 17	18 22 35	7 04.1	4 01.7	14 21.7	27 07.5	13 17.0	12 47.8	14 06.7	13 07.8	1 20.8	0 47.0
20 F	1 55 01	0♉35 03	25 00 17	1♑31 41	7 05.4	3 23.5	15 35.6	26 56.6	13 40.4	12 49.6	14 02.3	13 06.2	1 20.3	0 45.3
21 Sa	1 58 58	1 33 34	7♑57 07	14 17 03	7 07.0	2 43.4	16 49.5	26 45.0	14 03.8	12 51.3	13 58.0	13 04.6	1 19.7	0 43.6
22 Su	2 02 54	2 32 04	20 31 59	26 42 29	7R 08.1	2 02.2	18 03.4	26 32.6	14 27.1	12 52.7	13 53.6	13 02.9	1 19.1	0 41.9
23 M	2 06 51	3 30 33	2♒49 07	8♒52 28	7 08.1	1 20.7	19 17.2	26 19.5	14 50.4	12 54.0	13 49.2	13 01.3	1 18.4	0 40.2
24 Tu	2 10 47	4 29 00	14 53 10	20 51 47	7 06.7	0 39.6	20 31.1	26 05.7	15 13.7	12 55.1	13 44.8	12 59.5	1 17.7	0 38.5
25 W	2 14 44	5 27 25	26 48 53	2♓45 02	7 03.9	29♈59.7	21 45.0	25 51.2	15 37.0	12 56.0	13 40.3	12 57.8	1 17.0	0 36.8
26 Th	2 18 40	6 25 48	8♓40 44	14 36 29	6 59.9	29 21.6	22 58.8	25 36.1	16 00.3	12 56.7	13 35.9	12 56.0	1 16.3	0 35.2
27 F	2 22 37	7 24 10	20 32 43	26 29 52	6 55.1	28 45.9	24 12.7	25 20.3	16 23.5	12 57.2	13 31.4	12 54.1	1 15.6	0 33.5
28 Sa	2 26 34	8 22 30	2♈28 15	8♈28 14	6 50.0	28 13.3	25 26.5	25 03.8	16 46.7	12 57.6	13 26.9	12 52.3	1 14.8	0 31.8
29 Su	2 30 30	9 20 48	14 30 06	20 34 04	6 45.2	27 44.0	26 40.4	24 46.8	17 09.9	12R 57.7	13 22.3	12 50.4	1 13.9	0 30.1
30 M	2 34 27	10 19 05	26 40 21	2♉49 08	6 41.3	27 18.7	27 54.2	24 29.2	17 33.0	12 57.7	13 17.8	12 48.5	1 13.1	0 28.4

Astro Data	Planet Ingress	Last Aspect	☽ Ingress	Last Aspect	☽ Ingress	☽ Phases & Eclipses	Astro Data
Dy Hr Mn	Dy Hr Mn	Dy Hr Mn	Dy Hr Mn	Dy Hr Mn	Dy Hr Mn	Dy Hr Mn	1 March 1984
☽0N 5 2:26	♀ ♓ 14 12:35	1 1:05 ♂ □	♓ 1 17:29	1 15:12 ♅ △	♉ 2 23:55	2 18:31 ● 12♓22	Julian Day # 30741
♄∠♆ 8 7:11	☿ ♈ 14 16:27	3 15:25 ♂ △	♈ 4 6:07	5 6:55 ♂ ☍	♊ 5 10:04	10 18:27 ☽ 20♊23	SVP 5♓29'06"
☿0N 15 14:28	⚳ ♈ 16 18:37	5 20:54 ♀ ⚹	♉ 6 18:09	7 17:46 ♀ □	♋ 7 17:59	17 10:10 ○ 27♍01	GC 26♐37.1 ⚴ 24♒54.2
♅ R 18 6:13	☉ ♈ 20 10:24	8 17:25 ♂ ☍	♊ 9 4:30	9 19:59 ♂ △	♌ 9 23:01	24 7:58 ☾ 3♑52	Eris 15♈06.3 ⚵ 22♉54.0
☽0S 18 6:42	☿ ♉ 31 20:25	11 4:25 ♀ △	♋ 11 11:48	11 22:04 ♂ □	♍ 12 1:11		⚷ 28♉06.8 ⚶ 16♊05.9
☉0N 20 10:24		13 11:21 ☿ △	♌ 13 15:21	13 22:09 ♂ ⚹	♎ 14 1:29	1 12:10 ● 11♈57	☽ Mean ☊ 11♊19.4
♆⚹♇ 27 5:55	♀ ♈ 7 20:13	15 9:13 ♂ □	♍ 15 15:47	15 19:11 ☉ ☍	♏ 16 1:41	9 4:51 ☽ 19♋32	
☽0N 1 8:15	☉ ♉ 19 21:38	17 10:10 ☉ ☍	♎ 17 14:51	17 23:14 ♂ ☌	♐ 18 3:44	15 19:11 ○ 26♎00	1 April 1984
♆ R 2 14:04	☿ ♈R 25 11:49	18 12:18 ♅ ⚹	♏ 19 14:49	19 4:06 ♀ △	♑ 20 9:10	23 0:26 ☾ 3♒02	Julian Day # 30772
♂ R 5 12:22		21 12:31 ♂ ☌	♐ 21 17:41	22 11:41 ♂ ⚹	♒ 22 18:27		SVP 5♓29'03"
♀0N 10 16:14		22 22:34 ☿ △	♑ 24 0:36	24 22:20 ♂ □	♓ 25 6:26		GC 26♐37.2 ⚴ 4♓47.0
☿ R 11 20:25		26 6:37 ♂ ⚹	♒ 26 11:09	27 9:43 ♂ △	♈ 27 19:03		Eris 15♈25.8 ⚵ 8♊49.0
☽0S 14 17:33		28 19:33 ♂ □	♓ 28 23:37	30 1:36 ☿ ☌	♉ 30 6:30		⚷ 29♉25.8 ⚶ 24♊01.4
♃⚺♅ 26 4:47		31 8:35 ♂ △	♈ 31 12:14				☽ Mean ☊ 9♊40.9
☽0N 28 15:16	♃ R29 18:37						

LONGITUDE May 1984

Day	Sid.Time	☉	0 hr ☽	Noon ☽	True ☊	☿	♀	♂	⚳	♃	♄	♅	♆	♇
1 Tu	2 38 23	11♉17 20	9♉00 33	15♉14 44	6♊38.5	26♈57.5	29♈08.0	24♏11.0	17♈56.1	12♑57.5	13♏13.3	12♐46.5	1♑12.2	0♏26.8
2 W	2 42 20	12 15 34	21 31 46	27 51 46	6D37.0	26R40.7	0♉21.9	23R52.4	18 19.2	12R57.0	13R08.8	12R44.5	1R11.3	0R25.1
3 Th	2 46 16	13 13 45	4♊14 48	10♊40 57	6 36.8	26 28.5	1 35.7	23 33.3	18 42.2	12 56.4	13 04.2	12 42.5	1 10.4	0 23.5
4 F	2 50 13	14 11 55	17 10 18	23 42 55	6 37.5	26 20.9	2 49.5	23 13.7	19 05.2	12 55.6	12 59.7	12 40.4	1 09.5	0 21.8
5 Sa	2 54 09	15 10 03	0♋18 53	6♋58 18	6 38.9	26D18.1	4 03.3	22 53.7	19 28.1	12 54.6	12 55.2	12 38.3	1 08.5	0 20.2
6 Su	2 58 06	16 08 09	13 41 13	20 27 43	6 40.3	26 20.1	5 17.1	22 33.4	19 51.1	12 53.5	12 50.6	12 36.2	1 07.5	0 18.6
7 M	3 02 03	17 06 13	27 17 50	4♌11 36	6R41.4	26 26.8	6 30.9	22 12.7	20 14.0	12 52.1	12 46.1	12 34.1	1 06.5	0 17.0
8 Tu	3 05 59	18 04 15	11♌08 59	18 09 54	6 41.8	26 38.1	7 44.7	21 51.8	20 36.8	12 50.6	12 41.6	12 31.9	1 05.4	0 15.4
9 W	3 09 56	19 02 15	25 14 14	2♍21 45	6 41.4	26 54.0	8 58.4	21 30.7	20 59.6	12 48.8	12 37.1	12 29.8	1 04.3	0 13.8
10 Th	3 13 52	20 00 14	9♍32 09	16 45 04	6 40.2	27 14.4	10 12.2	21 09.3	21 22.4	12 46.9	12 32.6	12 27.6	1 03.2	0 12.2
11 F	3 17 49	20 58 10	24 00 00	1♎16 24	6 38.5	27 39.1	11 25.9	20 47.8	21 45.1	12 44.8	12 28.2	12 25.3	1 02.1	0 10.7
12 Sa	3 21 45	21 56 04	8♎33 38	15 50 58	6 36.6	28 08.1	12 39.7	20 26.2	22 07.8	12 42.5	12 23.7	12 23.1	1 01.0	0 09.1
13 Su	3 25 42	22 53 57	23 07 41	0♏23 01	6 34.9	28 41.1	13 53.4	20 04.5	22 30.4	12 40.1	12 19.3	12 20.8	0 59.8	0 07.6
14 M	3 29 38	23 51 48	7♏36 12	14 46 32	6 33.7	29 18.2	15 07.2	19 42.9	22 53.0	12 37.4	12 14.9	12 18.5	0 58.6	0 06.1
15 Tu	3 33 35	24 49 38	21 53 19	28 56 00	6D33.0	29 59.0	16 20.9	19 21.2	23 15.5	12 34.6	12 10.5	12 16.2	0 57.4	0 04.6
16 W	3 37 32	25 47 27	5♐54 03	12♐47 05	6 33.0	0♉43.6	17 34.6	18 59.6	23 38.1	12 31.6	12 06.2	12 13.9	0 56.2	0 03.1
17 Th	3 41 28	26 45 14	19 34 51	26 17 10	6 33.5	1 31.7	18 48.4	18 38.1	24 00.5	12 28.4	12 01.9	12 11.5	0 54.9	0 01.6
18 F	3 45 25	27 42 59	2♑53 59	9♑25 22	6 34.2	2 23.3	20 02.1	18 16.8	24 22.9	12 25.1	11 57.6	12 09.2	0 53.7	0 00.2
19 Sa	3 49 21	28 40 44	15 51 28	22 12 33	6 35.0	3 18.3	21 15.8	17 55.7	24 45.3	12 21.6	11 53.3	12 06.8	0 52.4	29♎58.7
20 Su	3 53 18	29 38 27	28 28 56	4♒41 01	6 35.7	4 16.4	22 29.5	17 34.8	25 07.6	12 17.9	11 49.1	12 04.4	0 51.1	29 57.3
21 M	3 57 14	0♊36 10	10♒49 15	16 54 08	6 36.2	5 17.8	23 43.2	17 14.2	25 29.9	12 14.0	11 45.0	12 02.0	0 49.7	29 55.9
22 Tu	4 01 11	1 33 51	22 56 11	28 55 58	6R36.4	6 22.2	24 57.0	16 53.9	25 52.1	12 10.0	11 40.8	11 59.6	0 48.4	29 54.5
23 W	4 05 07	2 31 31	4♓54 04	10♓51 01	6 36.3	7 29.5	26 10.7	16 34.0	26 14.2	12 05.8	11 36.7	11 57.2	0 47.0	29 53.2
24 Th	4 09 04	3 29 10	16 47 25	22 43 51	6 36.1	8 39.8	27 24.4	16 14.5	26 36.4	12 01.5	11 32.7	11 54.7	0 45.7	29 51.8
25 F	4 13 01	4 26 48	28 40 50	4♈38 54	6 35.9	9 52.8	28 38.1	15 55.5	26 58.4	11 56.9	11 28.7	11 52.3	0 44.3	29 50.5
26 Sa	4 16 57	5 24 25	10♈38 34	16 40 18	6 35.7	11 08.7	29 51.8	15 36.9	27 20.4	11 52.3	11 24.7	11 49.8	0 42.9	29 49.2
27 Su	4 20 54	6 22 01	22 44 31	28 51 36	6D35.6	12 27.3	1♊05.5	15 18.8	27 42.3	11 47.4	11 20.8	11 47.4	0 41.4	29 47.9
28 M	4 24 50	7 19 36	5♉01 54	11♉15 41	6 35.6	13 48.5	2 19.3	15 01.4	28 04.2	11 42.4	11 17.0	11 44.9	0 40.0	29 46.6
29 Tu	4 28 47	8 17 10	17 33 12	23 54 35	6R35.7	15 12.4	3 33.0	14 44.5	28 26.1	11 37.3	11 13.2	11 42.4	0 38.5	29 45.4
30 W	4 32 43	9 14 43	0♊19 58	6♊49 24	6 35.8	16 39.0	4 46.7	14 28.2	28 47.8	11 32.0	11 09.4	11 40.0	0 37.1	29 44.2
31 Th	4 36 40	10 12 16	13 22 52	20 00 19	6 35.7	18 08.1	6 00.4	14 12.5	29 09.5	11 26.6	11 05.8	11 37.5	0 35.6	29 43.0

LONGITUDE June 1984

Day	Sid.Time	☉	0 hr ☽	Noon ☽	True ☊	☿	♀	♂	⚳	♃	♄	♅	♆	♇
1 F	4 40 36	11♊09 47	26♊41 36	3♋26 35	6♊35.4	19♉39.8	7♊14.1	13♏57.6	29♈31.2	11♑21.1	11♏02.2	11♐35.0	0♑34.1	29♎41.8
2 Sa	4 44 33	12 07 17	10♋15 03	17 06 44	6R34.9	21 14.0	8 27.8	13R43.4	29 52.7	11R15.4	10R58.6	11R32.5	0R32.6	29R40.7
3 Su	4 48 30	13 04 45	24 01 24	0♌58 44	6 34.2	22 50.8	9 41.5	13 29.9	0♉14.2	11 09.5	10 55.1	11 30.1	0 31.1	29 39.6
4 M	4 52 26	14 02 13	7♌58 26	15 00 11	6 33.4	24 30.1	10 55.2	13 17.1	0 35.7	11 03.6	10 51.7	11 27.6	0 29.5	29 38.5
5 Tu	4 56 23	14 59 39	22 03 39	29 08 32	6 32.9	26 11.9	12 08.9	13 05.1	0 57.0	10 57.5	10 48.3	11 25.1	0 28.0	29 37.4
6 W	5 00 19	15 57 04	6♍14 30	13♍21 13	6D32.6	27 56.3	13 22.6	12 53.9	1 18.3	10 51.3	10 45.0	11 22.6	0 26.5	29 36.4
7 Th	5 04 16	16 54 28	20 28 24	27 35 43	6 32.7	29 43.1	14 36.3	12 43.4	1 39.6	10 45.0	10 41.8	11 20.2	0 24.9	29 35.4
8 F	5 08 12	17 51 51	4♎42 51	11♎49 29	6 33.3	1♊32.4	15 50.0	12 33.8	2 00.7	10 38.5	10 38.7	11 17.7	0 23.3	29 34.4
9 Sa	5 12 09	18 49 12	18 55 17	25 59 55	6 34.2	3 24.1	17 03.7	12 25.0	2 21.8	10 32.0	10 35.6	11 15.3	0 21.8	29 33.4
10 Su	5 16 05	19 46 33	3♏03 03	10♏04 20	6 35.2	5 18.3	18 17.4	12 17.0	2 42.8	10 25.4	10 32.6	11 12.8	0 20.2	29 32.5
11 M	5 20 02	20 43 53	17 03 25	24 00 00	6R35.9	7 14.7	19 31.1	12 09.8	3 03.7	10 18.6	10 29.7	11 10.4	0 18.6	29 31.6
12 Tu	5 23 59	21 41 11	0♐53 43	7♐44 17	6 36.2	9 13.4	20 44.8	12 03.5	3 24.5	10 11.8	10 26.8	11 08.0	0 17.0	29 30.7
13 W	5 27 55	22 38 30	14 31 23	21 14 48	6 35.8	11 14.2	21 58.5	11 57.9	3 45.3	10 04.9	10 24.1	11 05.5	0 15.4	29 29.9
14 Th	5 31 52	23 35 47	27 54 19	4♑29 47	6 34.5	13 17.1	23 12.2	11 53.2	4 06.0	9 57.9	10 21.4	11 03.1	0 13.8	29 29.1
15 F	5 35 48	24 33 04	11♑01 05	17 28 12	6 32.4	15 21.8	24 25.8	11 49.3	4 26.6	9 50.8	10 18.8	11 00.8	0 12.2	29 28.3
16 Sa	5 39 45	25 30 20	23 51 08	0♒10 00	6 29.8	17 28.2	25 39.6	11 46.3	4 47.2	9 43.6	10 16.2	10 58.4	0 10.6	29 27.6
17 Su	5 43 41	26 27 36	6♒24 58	12 36 15	6 26.8	19 36.1	26 53.3	11 44.0	5 07.6	9 36.4	10 13.8	10 56.0	0 09.0	29 26.8
18 M	5 47 38	27 24 52	18 44 08	24 48 58	6 24.0	21 45.2	28 07.0	11 42.6	5 28.0	9 29.1	10 11.4	10 53.7	0 07.4	29 26.1
19 Tu	5 51 35	28 22 07	0♓51 10	6♓51 10	6 21.8	23 55.4	29 20.7	11D42.0	5 48.2	9 21.8	10 09.2	10 51.3	0 05.7	29 25.5
20 W	5 55 31	29 19 22	12 49 28	18 46 35	6D20.3	26 06.3	0♋34.4	11 42.2	6 08.4	9 14.3	10 07.0	10 49.0	0 04.1	29 24.8
21 Th	5 59 28	0♋16 36	24 43 06	0♈39 33	6 19.8	28 17.7	1 48.1	11 43.2	6 28.5	9 06.9	10 04.9	10 46.7	0 02.5	29 24.2
22 F	6 03 24	1 13 51	6♈36 33	12 34 41	6 20.3	0♋29.3	3 01.8	11 45.0	6 48.5	8 59.3	10 02.8	10 44.5	0 00.9	29 23.6
23 Sa	6 07 21	2 11 05	18 34 33	24 36 44	6 21.6	2 40.8	4 15.5	11 47.5	7 08.4	8 51.8	10 00.9	10 42.2	29♐59.3	29 23.1
24 Su	6 11 17	3 08 20	0♉41 48	6♉50 17	6 23.2	4 51.9	5 29.3	11 50.9	7 28.2	8 44.2	9 59.1	10 40.0	29 57.6	29 22.6
25 M	6 15 14	4 05 34	13 02 40	19 19 23	6 24.7	7 02.5	6 43.0	11 55.1	7 48.0	8 36.6	9 57.3	10 37.8	29 56.0	29 22.1
26 Tu	6 19 10	5 02 48	25 40 50	2♊07 20	6R25.6	9 12.1	7 56.8	12 00.0	8 07.6	8 28.9	9 55.7	10 35.6	29 54.4	29 21.7
27 W	6 23 07	6 00 02	8♊39 03	15 16 09	6 25.4	11 20.8	9 10.5	12 05.8	8 27.1	8 21.2	9 54.1	10 33.4	29 52.8	29 21.2
28 Th	6 27 04	6 57 17	21 58 37	28 46 22	6 23.8	13 28.1	10 24.3	12 12.2	8 46.5	8 13.6	9 52.6	10 31.3	29 51.2	29 20.9
29 F	6 31 00	7 54 31	5♋39 09	12♋36 40	6 20.7	15 34.1	11 38.0	12 19.5	9 05.8	8 05.9	9 51.3	10 29.2	29 49.6	29 20.5
30 Sa	6 34 57	8 51 44	19 38 27	26 43 58	6 16.5	17 38.5	12 51.8	12 27.4	9 25.0	7 58.2	9 50.0	10 27.1	29 48.0	29 20.2

Astro Data	Dy Hr Mn
⚳0N	1 22:17
☿ D	5 14:06
♃⚹♄	5 15:38
☽0S	12 2:40
♄⚺♅	12 19:12
☽0N	25 23:09
♃⚺♅	27 12:33
☽0S	8 9:16
♃⚹♄	8 11:04
♂ D	19 18:17
☽0N	22 7:04

Planet Ingress		Dy Hr Mn
♀	♉	2 4:53
☿	♉	15 12:33
♇	♎R	18 14:35
☉	♊	20 20:58
♀	♊	26 14:40
⚳	♉	2 20:06
☿	♊	7 15:45
♀	♋	20 0:48
☉	♋	21 5:02
☿	♋	22 6:39
♆	♐R	23 1:10

Last Aspect Dy Hr Mn			☽ Ingress	Dy Hr Mn
2 4:38	♂	☍	♊	2 16:02
4 16:46	☿	⚹	♋	4 23:26
6 22:23	☿	□	♌	7 4:43
9 2:37	☿	△	♍	9 8:02
10 19:07	♂	⚹	♎	11 9:54
13 9:04	☿	☍	♏	13 11:22
15 4:29	☉	☍	♐	15 13:50
16 11:02	♅	☌	♑	17 18:43
20 2:51	♇	□	♒	20 2:55
22 13:57	♇	△	♓	22 14:09
24 22:31	♀	⚹	♈	25 2:39
27 13:50	♇	☍	♉	27 14:13
28 19:02	♂	☍	♊	29 23:23

Last Aspect Dy Hr Mn			☽ Ingress	Dy Hr Mn
1 5:22	♇	△	♋	1 5:54
3 9:44	♇	□	♌	3 10:19
5 12:49	♇	⚹	♍	5 13:27
6 16:42	☉	□	♎	7 16:03
9 18:03	♇	☌	♏	9 18:48
10 15:45	♂	☌	♐	11 22:26
14 2:52	♇	⚹	♑	14 3:48
16 10:39	♇	□	♒	16 11:41
18 21:10	♇	△	♓	18 22:18
21 6:09	☿	□	♈	21 10:40
23 22:35	♆	△	♉	23 22:38
24 21:45	♂	☍	♊	26 8:04
28 13:53	♆	☍	♋	28 14:09
30 16:23	♇	□	♌	30 17:30

☽ Phases & Eclipses Dy Hr Mn		
1 3:45	●	10♉57
8 11:50	☽	18♌04
15 4:29	○	24♏32
15 4:40	☊	A 0.807
22 17:45	☾	1♓48
30 16:48	●	9♊26
30 16:44:47	☊	A 00'11"
6 16:42	☽	16♍08
13 14:42	○	22♐45
13 14:26	☊	A 0.064
21 11:10	☾	0♈15
29 3:18	●	7♋34

Astro Data

1 May 1984
Julian Day # 30802
SVP 5♓29'00"
GC 26♐37.2 ⚴ 13♓09.5
Eris 15♈45.4 ⚵ 24♊46.8
⚷ 1♊21.7 ⚶ 4♋24.8
☽ Mean ☊ 8♊05.6

1 June 1984
Julian Day # 30833
SVP 5♓28'55"
GC 26♐37.3 ⚴ 19♓45.8
Eris 16♈01.5 ⚵ 11♋14.0
⚷ 3♊39.4 ⚶ 16♋47.1
☽ Mean ☊ 6♊27.1

July 1984 — LONGITUDE

Day	Sid.Time	☉	0 hr ☽	Noon ☽	True ☊	☿	♀	♂	⚳	♃	♄	♅	♆	♇
1 Su	6 38 53	9♋48 58	3♌52 36	11♌03 39	6♊11.7	19♋41.3	14♋05.5	12♏36.1	9♉44.1	7♑50.5	9♏48.8	10♐25.0	29♐46.4	29♎19.9
2 M	6 42 50	10 46 11	18 16 25	25 30 12	6R 06.8	21 42.3	15 19.3	12 45.5	10 03.1	7R 42.8	9R 47.7	10R 23.0	29R 44.8	29R 19.7
3 Tu	6 46 46	11 43 24	2♍44 16	9♍57 58	6 02.7	23 41.5	16 33.1	12 55.7	10 22.0	7 35.1	9 46.7	10 21.0	29 43.3	29 19.5
4 W	6 50 43	12 40 37	17 10 42	24 21 58	5 59.9	25 38.8	17 46.8	13 06.5	10 40.7	7 27.5	9 45.8	10 19.0	29 41.7	29 19.3
5 Th	6 54 39	13 37 49	1♎31 18	8♎38 22	5D 58.7	27 34.1	19 00.6	13 18.0	10 59.3	7 19.9	9 45.0	10 17.1	29 40.1	29 19.1
6 F	6 58 36	14 35 01	15 42 53	22 44 40	5 58.8	29 27.6	20 14.4	13 30.2	11 17.8	7 12.3	9 44.3	10 15.2	29 38.6	29 19.0
7 Sa	7 02 33	15 32 12	29 43 35	6♏39 34	5 59.9	1♌19.0	21 28.1	13 43.1	11 36.2	7 04.7	9 43.7	10 13.3	29 37.0	29 18.9
8 Su	7 06 29	16 29 24	13♏32 34	20 22 35	6 01.2	3 08.5	22 41.9	13 56.6	11 54.5	6 57.2	9 43.2	10 11.5	29 35.5	29D 18.9
9 M	7 10 26	17 26 36	27 09 38	3♐53 41	6R 02.0	4 56.0	23 55.7	14 10.7	12 12.6	6 49.7	9 42.7	10 09.7	29 34.0	29 18.9
10 Tu	7 14 22	18 23 47	10♐34 47	17 12 55	6 01.5	6 41.5	25 09.5	14 25.5	12 30.7	6 42.3	9 42.4	10 07.9	29 32.4	29 18.9
11 W	7 18 19	19 20 59	23 48 03	0♑20 12	5 59.1	8 25.1	26 23.2	14 40.8	12 48.6	6 35.0	9 42.2	10 06.2	29 30.9	29 19.0
12 Th	7 22 15	20 18 10	6♑49 19	13 15 22	5 54.7	10 06.6	27 37.0	14 56.8	13 06.3	6 27.7	9D 42.1	10 04.5	29 29.4	29 19.0
13 F	7 26 12	21 15 22	19 38 21	25 58 15	5 48.3	11 46.2	28 50.8	15 13.4	13 23.9	6 20.5	9 42.1	10 02.8	29 28.0	29 19.2
14 Sa	7 30 08	22 12 34	2♒15 05	8♒28 52	5 40.5	13 23.8	0♌04.6	15 30.5	13 41.4	6 13.3	9 42.1	10 01.2	29 26.5	29 19.3
15 Su	7 34 05	23 09 47	14 39 43	20 47 44	5 32.0	14 59.4	1 18.4	15 48.2	13 58.8	6 06.2	9 42.3	9 59.6	29 25.1	29 19.5
16 M	7 38 02	24 07 00	26 53 05	2♓55 59	5 23.7	16 33.0	2 32.2	16 06.4	14 16.0	5 59.2	9 42.6	9 58.0	29 23.6	29 19.7
17 Tu	7 41 58	25 04 14	8♓56 43	14 55 35	5 16.2	18 04.6	3 46.0	16 25.2	14 33.1	5 52.3	9 42.9	9 56.5	29 22.2	29 20.0
18 W	7 45 55	26 01 28	20 52 59	26 49 20	5 10.3	19 34.2	4 59.8	16 44.5	14 50.0	5 45.5	9 43.4	9 55.1	29 20.8	29 20.3
19 Th	7 49 51	26 58 42	2♈45 06	8♈40 49	5 06.4	21 01.7	6 13.6	17 04.3	15 06.8	5 38.8	9 43.9	9 53.6	29 19.4	29 20.6
20 F	7 53 48	27 55 58	14 37 02	20 34 21	5D 04.5	22 27.3	7 27.4	17 24.7	15 23.4	5 32.1	9 44.6	9 52.2	29 18.0	29 21.0
21 Sa	7 57 44	28 53 14	26 33 21	2♉34 42	5 04.2	23 50.7	8 41.2	17 45.5	15 39.9	5 25.6	9 45.3	9 50.9	29 16.6	29 21.4
22 Su	8 01 41	29 50 31	8♉39 01	14 46 56	5 05.0	25 12.0	9 55.0	18 06.9	15 56.2	5 19.2	9 46.2	9 49.6	29 15.3	29 21.8
23 M	8 05 37	0♌47 49	20 59 05	27 16 03	5R 05.9	26 31.2	11 08.8	18 28.7	16 12.4	5 12.9	9 47.2	9 48.3	29 14.0	29 22.3
24 Tu	8 09 34	1 45 08	3♊38 22	10♊06 31	5 06.0	27 48.2	12 22.7	18 51.0	16 28.4	5 06.7	9 48.2	9 47.1	29 12.7	29 22.8
25 W	8 13 31	2 42 28	16 40 52	23 21 43	5 04.5	29 03.0	13 36.5	19 13.8	16 44.2	5 00.6	9 49.3	9 45.9	29 11.4	29 23.3
26 Th	8 17 27	3 39 49	0♋09 10	7♋03 15	5 00.8	0♍15.4	14 50.3	19 37.1	16 59.9	4 54.7	9 50.6	9 44.8	29 10.1	29 23.9
27 F	8 21 24	4 37 10	14 03 46	21 10 23	4 54.8	1 25.5	16 04.2	20 00.8	17 15.4	4 48.9	9 51.9	9 43.7	29 08.9	29 24.5
28 Sa	8 25 20	5 34 33	28 22 32	5♌39 33	4 46.8	2 33.1	17 18.0	20 25.0	17 30.7	4 43.2	9 53.4	9 42.7	29 07.6	29 25.1
29 Su	8 29 17	6 31 56	13♌00 31	20 24 30	4 37.6	3 38.2	18 31.9	20 49.6	17 45.9	4 37.7	9 54.9	9 41.7	29 06.4	29 25.8
30 M	8 33 13	7 29 19	27 50 23	5♍17 05	4 28.4	4 40.7	19 45.7	21 14.6	18 00.8	4 32.3	9 56.5	9 40.7	29 05.2	29 26.5
31 Tu	8 37 10	8 26 44	12♍43 29	20 08 34	4 20.2	5 40.4	20 59.6	21 40.1	18 15.6	4 27.0	9 58.2	9 39.8	29 04.1	29 27.2

August 1984 — LONGITUDE

Day	Sid.Time	☉	0 hr ☽	Noon ☽	True ☊	☿	♀	♂	⚳	♃	♄	♅	♆	♇
1 W	8 41 07	9♌24 09	27♍31 21	4♎51 04	4♊14.0	6♍37.2	22♌13.4	22♏06.0	18♉30.2	4♑21.9	10♏00.1	9♐39.0	29♐02.9	29♎28.0
2 Th	8 45 03	10 21 34	12♎07 02	19 18 45	4R 10.1	7 31.1	23 27.2	22 32.2	18 44.6	4R 16.9	10 02.0	9R 38.2	29R 01.8	29 28.8
3 F	8 49 00	11 19 00	26 25 54	3♏28 16	4D 08.4	8 21.8	24 41.1	22 58.9	18 58.8	4 12.1	10 04.0	9 37.4	29 00.7	29 29.6
4 Sa	8 52 56	12 16 27	10♏25 50	17 18 37	4 08.3	9 09.3	25 54.9	23 26.0	19 12.8	4 07.5	10 06.1	9 36.7	28 59.6	29 30.5
5 Su	8 56 53	13 13 55	24 06 45	0♐50 28	4R 08.6	9 53.3	27 08.8	23 53.4	19 26.6	4 03.0	10 08.3	9 36.0	28 58.6	29 31.4
6 M	9 00 49	14 11 23	7♐29 59	14 05 34	4 08.3	10 33.7	28 22.6	24 21.3	19 40.2	3 58.7	10 10.6	9 35.4	28 57.5	29 32.3
7 Tu	9 04 46	15 08 52	20 37 29	27 05 59	4 06.2	11 10.3	29 36.4	24 49.5	19 53.6	3 54.5	10 12.9	9 34.9	28 56.5	29 33.2
8 W	9 08 42	16 06 22	3♑31 19	9♑53 41	4 01.7	11 42.9	0♍50.2	25 18.0	20 06.8	3 50.5	10 15.4	9 34.4	28 55.6	29 34.2
9 Th	9 12 39	17 03 53	16 13 17	22 30 15	3 54.4	12 11.3	2 04.1	25 46.9	20 19.8	3 46.7	10 18.0	9 33.9	28 54.6	29 35.3
10 F	9 16 36	18 01 25	28 44 45	4♒56 52	3 44.4	12 35.4	3 17.9	26 16.1	20 32.6	3 43.0	10 20.6	9 33.5	28 53.7	29 36.3
11 Sa	9 20 32	18 58 57	11♒06 42	17 14 20	3 32.4	12 54.8	4 31.7	26 45.7	20 45.2	3 39.5	10 23.3	9 33.1	28 52.8	29 37.4
12 Su	9 24 29	19 56 31	23 19 53	29 23 26	3 19.4	13 09.4	5 45.5	27 15.6	20 57.5	3 36.2	10 26.2	9 32.8	28 51.9	29 38.5
13 M	9 28 25	20 54 06	5♓25 07	11♓25 04	3 06.3	13 19.0	6 59.3	27 45.8	21 09.6	3 33.1	10 29.1	9 32.5	28 51.1	29 39.7
14 Tu	9 32 22	21 51 43	17 23 28	23 20 34	2 54.4	13R 23.3	8 13.1	28 16.3	21 21.5	3 30.1	10 32.1	9 32.3	28 50.2	29 40.9
15 W	9 36 18	22 49 21	29 16 36	5♈11 54	2 44.4	13 22.3	9 26.9	28 47.1	21 33.1	3 27.3	10 35.2	9 32.2	28 49.4	29 42.1
16 Th	9 40 15	23 47 00	11♈06 51	17 01 50	2 37.1	13 15.8	10 40.7	29 18.2	21 44.6	3 24.7	10 38.3	9 32.0	28 48.7	29 43.3
17 F	9 44 11	24 44 41	22 57 20	28 53 53	2 32.4	13 03.6	11 54.5	29 49.7	21 55.7	3 22.3	10 41.6	9D 32.0	28 47.9	29 44.6
18 Sa	9 48 08	25 42 23	4♉52 00	10♉52 19	2 30.1	12 45.8	13 08.3	0♐21.4	22 06.6	3 20.0	10 44.9	9 32.0	28 47.2	29 45.9
19 Su	9 52 04	26 40 07	16 55 26	23 02 00	2 29.5	12 22.3	14 22.1	0 53.4	22 17.3	3 17.9	10 48.4	9 32.0	28 46.5	29 47.2
20 M	9 56 01	27 37 52	29 12 41	5♊28 08	2 29.4	11 53.3	15 35.9	1 25.7	22 27.8	3 16.1	10 51.9	9 32.1	28 45.9	29 48.6
21 Tu	9 59 58	28 35 40	11♊48 58	18 15 48	2 28.9	11 18.9	16 49.7	1 58.3	22 37.9	3 14.4	10 55.5	9 32.2	28 45.3	29 50.0
22 W	10 03 54	29 33 29	24 49 08	1♋29 25	2 26.8	10 39.5	18 03.5	2 31.2	22 47.8	3 12.9	10 59.1	9 32.4	28 44.7	29 51.4
23 Th	10 07 51	0♍31 20	8♋16 57	15 11 55	2 22.3	9 55.6	19 17.3	3 04.3	22 57.5	3 11.5	11 02.9	9 32.7	28 44.1	29 52.8
24 F	10 11 47	1 29 12	22 14 17	29 23 51	2 15.2	9 07.7	20 31.1	3 37.7	23 06.8	3 10.4	11 06.7	9 33.0	28 43.6	29 54.3
25 Sa	10 15 44	2 27 06	6♌40 10	14♌02 34	2 05.7	8 16.6	21 44.9	4 11.4	23 15.9	3 09.5	11 10.7	9 33.3	28 43.1	29 55.8
26 Su	10 19 40	3 25 02	21 30 11	29 01 55	1 54.9	7 23.1	22 58.6	4 45.3	23 24.7	3 08.7	11 14.7	9 33.7	28 42.6	29 57.3
27 M	10 23 37	4 22 59	6♍36 32	14♍12 42	1 43.8	6 28.2	24 12.4	5 19.5	23 33.3	3 08.1	11 18.7	9 34.2	28 42.2	29 58.9
28 Tu	10 27 33	5 20 58	21 49 03	29 24 11	1 33.7	5 32.9	25 26.2	5 53.9	23 41.5	3 07.8	11 22.9	9 34.7	28 41.7	0♏00.5
29 W	10 31 30	6 18 58	6♎56 52	14♎25 57	1 25.9	4 38.4	26 39.9	6 28.6	23 49.4	3D 07.6	11 27.1	9 35.2	28 41.4	0 02.1
30 Th	10 35 27	7 16 59	21 50 30	29 09 46	1 20.7	3 46.0	27 53.7	7 03.6	23 57.1	3 07.6	11 31.4	9 35.9	28 41.0	0 03.7
31 F	10 39 23	8 15 02	6♏23 13	13♏30 31	1 18.1	2 56.7	29 07.4	7 38.8	24 04.4	3 07.8	11 35.8	9 36.5	28 40.7	0 05.4

Astro Data	Dy Hr Mn
☽ 0S	5 14:17
♇ D	9 8:22
♄ D	13 6:16
♆ ⚹ ♇	18 18:49
☽ 0N	19 14:13
♄ ⚺ ♅	24 0:26
☽ 0S	1 19:49
☿ R	14 19:34
☽ 0N	15 20:25
♅ D	18 5:40
☽ 0S	29 3:37
♃ D	29 23:02

Planet Ingress		Dy Hr Mn
☿	♌	6 18:56
♀	♌	14 10:30
☉	♌	22 15:58
☿	♍	26 6:49
♀	♍	7 19:40
♂	♐	17 19:50
☉	♍	22 23:00
♇	♏	28 4:44

Last Aspect Dy Hr Mn			☽ Ingress	Dy Hr Mn
2 19:02	♆	△	♍	2 19:28
4 20:55	♆	□	♎	4 21:27
6 23:50	♆	⚹	♏	7 0:28
8 16:30	♀	△	♐	9 5:03
11 10:29	♆	☌	♑	11 11:23
13 18:23	♇	□	♒	13 19:41
16 4:59	♆	⚹	♓	16 6:10
18 17:06	♆	□	♈	18 18:26
21 5:35	♇	☍	♉	21 6:52
23 10:25	☿	□	♊	23 17:10
25 23:03	☿	⚹	♋	25 23:44
28 1:43	♇	□	♌	28 2:41
30 2:34	♇	⚹	♍	30 3:29

Last Aspect Dy Hr Mn			☽ Ingress	Dy Hr Mn
1 2:30	♆	□	♎	1 4:03
3 5:12	♇	☌	♏	3 6:04
5 4:44	♀	□	♐	5 10:30
7 17:10	♀	△	♑	7 17:24
10 1:39	♇	□	♒	10 2:25
12 12:30	♇	△	♓	12 13:13
14 23:06	♆	□	♈	15 1:28
17 13:42	♇	☍	♉	17 14:13
19 19:41	☉	□	♊	20 1:31
22 9:04	♇	△	♋	22 9:20
24 12:51	♇	□	♌	24 13:00
26 13:28	♇	⚹	♍	26 13:32
28 10:53	♆	□	♎	28 12:57
30 11:13	♆	⚹	♏	30 13:23

☽ Phases & Eclipses Dy Hr Mn		
5 21:04	☽	13♎59
13 2:20	○	20♑52
21 4:01	☾	28♈34
28 11:51	●	5♌34
4 2:33	☽	11♏54
11 15:43	○	19♒08
19 19:41	☾	26♉59
26 19:25	●	3♍43

Astro Data

1 July 1984
Julian Day # 30863
SVP 5♓28'49"
GC 26♐37.4 ⚴ 23♓00.4
Eris 16♈09.5 ⚵ 26♋47.4
⚷ 5♊47.5 ⚶ 29♋42.8
☽ Mean ☊ 4♊51.8

1 August 1984
Julian Day # 30894
SVP 5♓28'44"
GC 26♐37.4 ⚴ 21♓37.1R
Eris 16♈08.0R ⚵ 12♌17.0
⚷ 7♊31.9 ⚶ 13♌40.7
☽ Mean ☊ 3♊13.3

LONGITUDE — September 1984

Day	Sid.Time	☉	0 hr ☽	Noon ☽	True ☊	☿	♀	♂	⚳	♃	♄	♅	♆	♇
1 Sa	10 43 20	9♍13 06	20♏31 33	27♏26 19	1♊17.3	2♍11.6	0♎21.2	8♐14.2	24♉11.5	3♑08.2	11♏40.3	9♐37.2	28♐40.4	0♏07.1
2 Su	10 47 16	10 11 12	4♐14 59	10♐57 49	1R 17.3	1R 32.0	1 34.9	8 49.8	24 18.2	3 08.8	11 44.8	9 38.0	28R 40.2	0 08.8
3 M	10 51 13	11 09 19	17 35 10	24 07 26	1 16.9	0 58.6	2 48.6	9 25.7	24 24.7	3 09.5	11 49.4	9 38.8	28 39.9	0 10.5
4 Tu	10 55 09	12 07 27	0♑35 00	6♑58 20	1 14.7	0 32.4	4 02.3	10 01.7	24 30.8	3 10.5	11 54.1	9 39.7	28 39.7	0 12.3
5 W	10 59 06	13 05 37	13 17 50	19 33 55	1 10.2	0 13.9	5 16.0	10 38.0	24 36.6	3 11.7	11 58.8	9 40.6	28 39.6	0 14.1
6 Th	11 03 02	14 03 49	25 46 57	1♒57 17	1 02.8	0D 03.7	6 29.7	11 14.5	24 42.0	3 13.0	12 03.6	9 41.6	28 39.5	0 15.9
7 F	11 06 59	15 02 02	8♒05 13	14 11 02	0 52.8	0 02.3	7 43.3	11 51.2	24 47.2	3 14.5	12 08.5	9 42.6	28 39.4	0 17.7
8 Sa	11 10 56	16 00 16	20 14 58	26 17 13	0 40.8	0 09.7	8 57.0	12 28.1	24 52.0	3 16.2	12 13.5	9 43.6	28 39.3	0 19.6
9 Su	11 14 52	16 58 32	2♓17 58	8♓17 24	0 27.6	0 26.1	10 10.6	13 05.2	24 56.5	3 18.1	12 18.5	9 44.8	28D 39.3	0 21.5
10 M	11 18 49	17 56 50	14 15 41	20 12 58	0 14.4	0 51.4	11 24.3	13 42.5	25 00.7	3 20.2	12 23.5	9 45.9	28 39.3	0 23.4
11 Tu	11 22 45	18 55 10	26 09 24	2♈05 11	0 02.3	1 25.5	12 37.9	14 20.0	25 04.5	3 22.5	12 28.7	9 47.1	28 39.3	0 25.3
12 W	11 26 42	19 53 32	8♈00 30	13 55 37	29♉52.2	2 08.1	13 51.5	14 57.7	25 07.9	3 24.9	12 33.9	9 48.4	28 39.4	0 27.2
13 Th	11 30 38	20 51 55	19 50 46	25 46 17	29 44.6	2 58.8	15 05.1	15 35.5	25 11.1	3 27.6	12 39.2	9 49.7	28 39.5	0 29.2
14 F	11 34 35	21 50 21	1♉42 30	7♉39 49	29 39.8	3 57.2	16 18.7	16 13.6	25 13.8	3 30.4	12 44.5	9 51.1	28 39.6	0 31.2
15 Sa	11 38 31	22 48 49	13 38 40	19 39 33	29D 37.5	5 02.7	17 32.2	16 51.8	25 16.2	3 33.4	12 49.9	9 52.5	28 39.8	0 33.2
16 Su	11 42 28	23 47 19	25 42 59	1♊49 31	29 37.1	6 14.9	18 45.8	17 30.2	25 18.3	3 36.5	12 55.3	9 54.0	28 40.0	0 35.2
17 M	11 46 25	24 45 51	7♊59 44	14 14 14	29R 37.5	7 33.1	19 59.4	18 08.8	25 20.0	3 39.9	13 00.9	9 55.5	28 40.2	0 37.2
18 Tu	11 50 21	25 44 25	20 33 37	26 58 30	29 37.9	8 56.8	21 12.9	18 47.5	25 21.3	3 43.4	13 06.4	9 57.0	28 40.5	0 39.3
19 W	11 54 18	26 43 02	3♋29 24	10♋06 50	29 37.0	10 25.3	22 26.5	19 26.4	25 22.3	3 47.1	13 12.1	9 58.6	28 40.8	0 41.4
20 Th	11 58 14	27 41 40	16 51 13	23 42 50	29 34.2	11 57.9	23 40.0	20 05.5	25 22.8	3 51.0	13 17.7	10 00.3	28 41.1	0 43.5
21 F	12 02 11	28 40 21	0♌41 51	7♌48 13	29 29.2	13 34.2	24 53.5	20 44.7	25R 23.0	3 55.1	13 23.5	10 02.0	28 41.5	0 45.6
22 Sa	12 06 07	29 39 05	15 01 44	22 21 56	29 22.0	15 13.6	26 07.0	21 24.2	25 22.9	3 59.3	13 29.3	10 03.7	28 41.9	0 47.7
23 Su	12 10 04	0♎37 50	29 48 09	7♍19 28	29 13.5	16 55.4	27 20.5	22 03.7	25 22.3	4 03.7	13 35.1	10 05.5	28 42.3	0 49.9
24 M	12 14 00	1 36 37	14♍54 46	22 32 47	29 04.5	18 39.4	28 34.0	22 43.5	25 21.4	4 08.3	13 41.0	10 07.4	28 42.8	0 52.1
25 Tu	12 17 57	2 35 27	0♎12 09	7♎51 25	28 56.4	20 24.9	29 47.5	23 23.3	25 20.1	4 13.1	13 47.0	10 09.2	28 43.3	0 54.2
26 W	12 21 54	3 34 18	15 29 10	23 04 05	28 50.1	22 11.7	1♏01.0	24 03.4	25 18.3	4 18.0	13 53.0	10 11.2	28 43.8	0 56.4
27 Th	12 25 50	4 33 11	0♏34 58	8♏00 49	28 46.1	23 59.4	2 14.4	24 43.6	25 16.3	4 23.1	13 59.1	10 13.1	28 44.4	0 58.7
28 F	12 29 47	5 32 06	15 20 51	22 34 27	28D 44.3	25 47.7	3 27.9	25 23.9	25 13.8	4 28.4	14 05.2	10 15.2	28 45.0	1 00.9
29 Sa	12 33 43	6 31 03	29 41 18	6♐41 12	28 44.4	27 36.3	4 41.3	26 04.4	25 10.9	4 33.8	14 11.3	10 17.2	28 45.6	1 03.1
30 Su	12 37 40	7 30 02	13♐34 10	20 20 22	28 45.4	29 25.0	5 54.7	26 45.1	25 07.7	4 39.4	14 17.5	10 19.3	28 46.3	1 05.4

LONGITUDE — October 1984

Day	Sid.Time	☉	0 hr ☽	Noon ☽	True ☊	☿	♀	♂	⚳	♃	♄	♅	♆	♇
1 M	12 41 36	8♎29 03	27♐00 06	3♑33 43	28♉46.3	1♎13.7	7♏08.1	27♐25.9	25♉04.0	4♑45.1	14♏23.8	10♐21.5	28♐47.0	1♏07.6
2 Tu	12 45 33	9 28 05	10♑01 39	16 24 25	28R 46.1	3 02.1	8 21.5	28 06.8	25R 00.0	4 51.0	14 30.0	10 23.7	28 47.7	1 09.9
3 W	12 49 29	10 27 09	22 42 29	28 56 24	28 44.2	4 50.2	9 34.8	28 47.8	24 55.6	4 57.1	14 36.4	10 25.9	28 48.4	1 12.2
4 Th	12 53 26	11 26 15	5♒06 40	11♒13 45	28 40.3	6 37.9	10 48.2	29 29.0	24 50.8	5 03.3	14 42.7	10 28.2	28 49.2	1 14.5
5 F	12 57 23	12 25 22	17 18 08	23 20 15	28 34.3	8 25.0	12 01.5	0♑10.3	24 45.7	5 09.7	14 49.2	10 30.5	28 50.1	1 16.8
6 Sa	13 01 19	13 24 31	29 20 29	5♓19 14	28 26.8	10 11.6	13 14.8	0 51.7	24 40.1	5 16.3	14 55.6	10 32.9	28 50.9	1 19.2
7 Su	13 05 16	14 23 43	11♓16 48	17 13 30	28 18.4	11 57.5	14 28.1	1 33.2	24 34.2	5 23.0	15 02.1	10 35.3	28 51.8	1 21.5
8 M	13 09 12	15 22 56	23 09 36	29 05 20	28 09.9	13 42.7	15 41.3	2 14.9	24 27.9	5 29.8	15 08.6	10 37.7	28 52.7	1 23.8
9 Tu	13 13 09	16 22 11	5♈00 57	10♈56 39	28 02.2	15 27.3	16 54.6	2 56.7	24 21.3	5 36.8	15 15.2	10 40.2	28 53.6	1 26.2
10 W	13 17 05	17 21 28	16 52 39	22 49 09	27 55.8	17 11.2	18 07.8	3 38.6	24 14.3	5 43.9	15 21.8	10 42.7	28 54.6	1 28.5
11 Th	13 21 02	18 20 47	28 46 22	4♉44 33	27 51.3	18 54.3	19 21.0	4 20.6	24 06.9	5 51.2	15 28.4	10 45.3	28 55.6	1 30.9
12 F	13 24 58	19 20 08	10♉43 54	16 44 44	27D 48.8	20 36.8	20 34.2	5 02.7	23 59.1	5 58.6	15 35.1	10 47.8	28 56.7	1 33.3
13 Sa	13 28 55	20 19 32	22 47 18	28 51 58	27 48.2	22 18.5	21 47.3	5 44.9	23 51.1	6 06.2	15 41.8	10 50.5	28 57.7	1 35.7
14 Su	13 32 51	21 18 58	4♊59 05	11♊09 01	27 48.9	23 59.5	23 00.5	6 27.2	23 42.6	6 13.9	15 48.5	10 53.1	28 58.8	1 38.1
15 M	13 36 48	22 18 26	17 22 11	23 39 01	27 50.4	25 39.8	24 13.6	7 09.6	23 33.8	6 21.8	15 55.3	10 55.8	29 00.0	1 40.5
16 Tu	13 40 45	23 17 56	29 59 59	6♋25 30	27 52.0	27 19.4	25 26.7	7 52.2	23 24.7	6 29.8	16 02.1	10 58.6	29 01.1	1 42.9
17 W	13 44 41	24 17 29	12♋56 01	19 31 56	27R 53.0	28 58.4	26 39.8	8 34.8	23 15.3	6 37.9	16 08.9	11 01.4	29 02.3	1 45.3
18 Th	13 48 38	25 17 04	26 13 37	3♌01 23	27 52.9	0♏36.7	27 52.9	9 17.6	23 05.5	6 46.1	16 15.8	11 04.2	29 03.5	1 47.7
19 F	13 52 34	26 16 41	9♌55 23	16 55 44	27 51.3	2 14.4	29 06.0	10 00.4	22 55.4	6 54.5	16 22.7	11 07.0	29 04.8	1 50.1
20 Sa	13 56 31	27 16 21	24 02 22	1♍15 03	27 48.4	3 51.4	0♐19.0	10 43.4	22 45.0	7 03.1	16 29.6	11 09.9	29 06.0	1 52.5
21 Su	14 00 27	28 16 02	8♍33 23	15 56 48	27 44.6	5 27.9	1 32.0	11 26.4	22 34.3	7 11.7	16 36.5	11 12.8	29 07.3	1 54.9
22 M	14 04 24	29 15 46	23 24 30	0♎55 33	27 40.4	7 03.7	2 45.0	12 09.5	22 23.3	7 20.5	16 43.5	11 15.7	29 08.7	1 57.3
23 Tu	14 08 20	0♏15 32	8♎28 53	16 03 19	27 36.5	8 39.0	3 58.0	12 52.8	22 12.0	7 29.4	16 50.4	11 18.7	29 10.0	1 59.8
24 W	14 12 17	1 15 21	23 37 38	1♏10 34	27 33.6	10 13.7	5 11.0	13 36.1	22 00.5	7 38.5	16 57.4	11 21.7	29 11.4	2 02.2
25 Th	14 16 14	2 15 11	8♏40 57	16 07 41	27D 31.9	11 47.9	6 23.9	14 19.5	21 48.7	7 47.6	17 04.4	11 24.7	29 12.8	2 04.6
26 F	14 20 10	3 15 03	23 29 48	0♐46 30	27 31.6	13 21.5	7 36.9	15 03.0	21 36.7	7 56.9	17 11.5	11 27.8	29 14.3	2 07.0
27 Sa	14 24 07	4 14 57	7♐57 12	15 01 25	27 32.3	14 54.7	8 49.8	15 46.6	21 24.4	8 06.3	17 18.5	11 30.9	29 15.7	2 09.5
28 Su	14 28 03	5 14 53	21 58 56	28 49 39	27 33.7	16 27.3	10 02.6	16 30.3	21 12.0	8 15.9	17 25.6	11 34.0	29 17.2	2 11.9
29 M	14 32 00	6 14 50	5♑33 37	12♑11 04	27 35.2	17 59.5	11 15.5	17 14.1	20 59.3	8 25.5	17 32.7	11 37.1	29 18.7	2 14.3
30 Tu	14 35 56	7 14 49	18 42 17	25 07 39	27 36.4	19 31.1	12 28.3	17 57.9	20 46.4	8 35.3	17 39.8	11 40.3	29 20.3	2 16.7
31 W	14 39 53	8 14 50	1♒27 38	7♒42 45	27R 36.9	21 02.3	13 41.1	18 41.9	20 33.4	8 45.2	17 46.9	11 43.5	29 21.9	2 19.2

Astro Data

	Dy Hr Mn
♀0S	3 5:39
☿ D	7 4:00
♆ D	9 22:13
☽0N	12 2:08
⚳ R	21 13:05
☉0S	22 20:33
♄∠♆	24 19:42
☽0S	25 13:51
☿0S	2 23:14
☽0N	9 8:07
☽0S	23 0:58

Planet Ingress

	Dy Hr Mn
♀ ♎	1 5:07
☊ ♉R	11 17:01
☉ ♎	22 20:33
♀ ♏	25 16:05
☿ ♎	30 19:44
♂ ♑	5 6:02
☿ ♏	18 3:01
♀ ♐	20 5:45
☉ ♏	23 5:46

Last Aspect / ☽ Ingress (September)

Last Aspect Dy Hr Mn		☽ Ingress Dy Hr Mn
31 8:45	♄ ☌	♐ 1 16:30
3 20:25	♆ ☌	♑ 3 22:55
4 22:35	☉ △	♒ 6 8:11
8 16:43	♆ ✶	♓ 8 19:24
11 5:03	♆ □	♈ 11 7:47
13 17:50	♆ △	♉ 13 20:33
15 18:49	☉ △	♊ 16 8:26
18 15:09	♆ ☍	♋ 18 17:36
20 19:23	☉ ✶	♌ 20 22:49
22 22:14	♆ △	♍ 23 0:19
24 21:40	♆ □	♎ 24 23:41
26 21:02	♆ ✶	♏ 26 23:04
28 18:12	☿ ✶	♐ 29 0:32

Last Aspect / ☽ Ingress (October)

Last Aspect Dy Hr Mn		☽ Ingress Dy Hr Mn
1 3:14	♆ ☌	♑ 1 5:28
2 8:22	♄ ✶	♒ 3 14:03
5 23:00	♆ ✶	♓ 6 1:19
8 11:34	♆ □	♈ 8 13:51
11 0:18	♆ △	♉ 11 2:28
12 20:27	♀ ☍	♊ 13 14:14
15 22:08	♆ ☍	♋ 16 0:00
18 2:03	♀ △	♌ 18 6:41
20 8:26	♆ △	♍ 20 9:56
22 9:09	♆ □	♎ 22 10:32
24 8:50	♆ ✶	♏ 24 10:08
25 13:33	♄ ☌	♐ 26 10:43
28 12:49	♆ ☌	♑ 28 14:05
30 0:07	☿ ✶	♒ 30 21:13

☽ Phases & Eclipses

Dy Hr Mn	
2 10:30	☽ 10♐08
10 7:01	○ 17♓45
18 9:31	☾ 25♊38
25 3:11	● 2♎14
1 21:52	☽ 8♑53
9 23:58	○ 16♈52
17 21:14	☾ 24♋40
24 12:08	● 1♏16
31 13:07	☽ 8♒18

Astro Data

1 September 1984
Julian Day # 30925
SVP 5♓28'40"
GC 26♐37.5 ⚴ 15♓13.2R
Eris 15♈57.1R ⚵ 27♌01.2
⚷ 8♊27.7 ⚶ 28♌00.1
☽ Mean ☊ 1♊34.8

1 October 1984
Julian Day # 30955
SVP 5♓28'37"
GC 26♐37.6 ⚴ 7♓57.1R
Eris 15♈40.6R ⚵ 10♍21.4
⚷ 8♊22.8R ⚶ 11♍58.4
☽ Mean ☊ 29♉59.5

November 1984 LONGITUDE

Day	Sid.Time	☉	0 hr ☽	Noon ☽	True ☊	☿	♀	♂	⚷	♃	♄	♅	♆	♇
1 Th	14 43 49	9♏14 52	13♒53 31	20♒00 30	27♉36.4	22♏33.0	14♐53.8	19♑25.9	20♉20.2	8♑55.2	17♏54.1	11♐46.7	29♐23.4	2♏21.6
2 F	14 47 46	10 14 56	26 04 15	2♓05 19	27R 35.2	24 03.3	16 06.6	20 09.9	20R 06.8	9 05.3	18 01.2	11 50.0	29 25.1	2 24.0
3 Sa	14 51 43	11 15 02	8♓04 14	14 01 32	27 33.2	25 33.1	17 19.3	20 54.1	19 53.4	9 15.5	18 08.3	11 53.3	29 26.7	2 26.4
4 Su	14 55 39	12 15 09	19 57 41	25 53 09	27 30.9	27 02.3	18 31.9	21 38.3	19 39.8	9 25.8	18 15.5	11 56.6	29 28.4	2 28.8
5 M	14 59 36	13 15 17	1♈48 22	7♈43 44	27 28.5	28 31.1	19 44.5	22 22.5	19 26.1	9 36.2	18 22.6	11 59.9	29 30.1	2 31.2
6 Tu	15 03 32	14 15 27	13 39 36	19 36 17	27 26.4	29 59.5	20 57.1	23 06.9	19 12.3	9 46.7	18 29.8	12 03.2	29 31.8	2 33.6
7 W	15 07 29	15 15 39	25 34 07	1♉33 20	27 24.7	1♐27.2	22 09.7	23 51.3	18 58.5	9 57.3	18 37.0	12 06.6	29 33.5	2 36.0
8 Th	15 11 25	16 15 53	7♉34 12	13 36 55	27 23.7	2 54.5	23 22.2	24 35.7	18 44.6	10 08.1	18 44.2	12 10.0	29 35.2	2 38.3
9 F	15 15 22	17 16 09	19 41 41	25 48 43	27D 23.4	4 21.2	24 34.6	25 20.2	18 30.6	10 18.9	18 51.3	12 13.4	29 37.0	2 40.7
10 Sa	15 19 18	18 16 26	1♊58 11	8♊10 14	27 23.6	5 47.3	25 47.1	26 04.8	18 16.7	10 29.8	18 58.5	12 16.8	29 38.8	2 43.1
11 Su	15 23 15	19 16 45	14 25 04	20 42 50	27 24.1	7 12.8	26 59.5	26 49.4	18 02.7	10 40.8	19 05.7	12 20.3	29 40.6	2 45.4
12 M	15 27 12	20 17 06	27 03 43	3♋27 54	27 24.8	8 37.5	28 11.8	27 34.1	17 48.7	10 51.9	19 12.9	12 23.7	29 42.5	2 47.8
13 Tu	15 31 08	21 17 29	9♋55 35	16 26 55	27 25.6	10 01.6	29 24.1	28 18.9	17 34.8	11 03.1	19 20.1	12 27.2	29 44.3	2 50.1
14 W	15 35 05	22 17 54	23 02 06	29 41 17	27 26.1	11 24.8	0♑36.4	29 03.7	17 20.9	11 14.4	19 27.3	12 30.7	29 46.2	2 52.4
15 Th	15 39 01	23 18 21	6♌24 39	13♌12 18	27R 26.4	12 47.0	1 48.7	29 48.5	17 07.1	11 25.8	19 34.4	12 34.2	29 48.1	2 54.8
16 F	15 42 58	24 18 49	20 04 19	27 00 43	27 26.4	14 08.3	3 00.8	0♒33.4	16 53.3	11 37.3	19 41.6	12 37.7	29 50.0	2 57.1
17 Sa	15 46 54	25 19 19	4♍01 29	11♍06 29	27 26.4	15 28.4	4 13.0	1 18.4	16 39.6	11 48.9	19 48.8	12 41.3	29 52.0	2 59.3
18 Su	15 50 51	26 19 52	18 15 30	25 28 14	27 26.2	16 47.3	5 25.1	2 03.4	16 26.1	12 00.5	19 56.0	12 44.8	29 53.9	3 01.6
19 M	15 54 47	27 20 26	2♎44 14	10♎02 59	27D 26.2	18 04.7	6 37.2	2 48.4	16 12.6	12 12.2	20 03.1	12 48.4	29 55.9	3 03.9
20 Tu	15 58 44	28 21 01	17 23 50	24 46 03	27 26.2	19 20.5	7 49.2	3 33.5	15 59.3	12 24.0	20 10.3	12 52.0	29 57.9	3 06.1
21 W	16 02 41	29 21 39	2♏08 51	9♏31 20	27 26.3	20 34.5	9 01.1	4 18.7	15 46.1	12 35.9	20 17.4	12 55.6	29 59.9	3 08.4
22 Th	16 06 37	0♐22 18	16 52 38	24 11 53	27R 26.4	21 46.3	10 13.0	5 03.9	15 33.1	12 47.9	20 24.5	12 59.2	0♑01.9	3 10.6
23 F	16 10 34	1 22 59	1♐28 12	8♐40 50	27 26.4	22 55.8	11 24.9	5 49.1	15 20.3	13 00.0	20 31.6	13 02.8	0 03.9	3 12.8
24 Sa	16 14 30	2 23 41	15 49 03	22 52 17	27 26.1	24 02.6	12 36.7	6 34.4	15 07.7	13 12.1	20 38.7	13 06.4	0 06.0	3 15.0
25 Su	16 18 27	3 24 24	29 50 03	6♑42 03	27 25.5	25 06.3	13 48.5	7 19.7	14 55.3	13 24.3	20 45.8	13 10.1	0 08.1	3 17.2
26 M	16 22 23	4 25 08	13♑28 04	20 08 02	27 24.6	26 06.4	15 00.2	8 05.1	14 43.2	13 36.6	20 52.9	13 13.7	0 10.2	3 19.4
27 Tu	16 26 20	5 25 54	26 42 01	3♒10 12	27 23.7	27 02.5	16 11.8	8 50.5	14 31.2	13 48.9	20 59.9	13 17.4	0 12.3	3 21.5
28 W	16 30 17	6 26 41	9♒32 51	15 50 20	27 22.8	27 54.0	17 23.3	9 35.9	14 19.6	14 01.3	21 07.0	13 21.0	0 14.4	3 23.6
29 Th	16 34 13	7 27 28	22 03 06	28 11 37	27D 22.1	28 40.3	18 34.8	10 21.4	14 08.2	14 13.8	21 14.0	13 24.7	0 16.5	3 25.7
30 F	16 38 10	8 28 17	4♓16 27	10♓18 10	27 22.0	29 20.7	19 46.2	11 06.9	13 57.0	14 26.4	21 21.0	13 28.4	0 18.6	3 27.8

December 1984 LONGITUDE

Day	Sid.Time	☉	0 hr ☽	Noon ☽	True ☊	☿	♀	♂	⚷	♃	♄	♅	♆	♇
1 Sa	16 42 06	9♐29 06	16♓17 20	22♓14 34	27♉22.4	29♐54.5	20♑57.6	11♒52.4	13♉46.2	14♑39.0	21♏27.9	13♐32.0	0♑20.8	3♏29.9
2 Su	16 46 03	10 29 56	28 10 29	4♈05 39	27 23.3	0♑20.8	22 08.8	12 37.9	13R 35.7	14 51.7	21 34.9	13 35.7	0 22.9	3 32.0
3 M	16 49 59	11 30 47	10♈00 40	15 56 05	27 24.5	0 38.8	23 20.0	13 23.5	13 25.4	15 04.4	21 41.8	13 39.4	0 25.1	3 34.0
4 Tu	16 53 56	12 31 39	21 52 25	27 50 10	27 26.0	0R 47.8	24 31.1	14 09.1	13 15.5	15 17.2	21 48.7	13 43.0	0 27.2	3 36.0
5 W	16 57 52	13 32 32	3♉49 47	9♉51 42	27 27.2	0 46.8	25 42.1	14 54.7	13 05.9	15 30.1	21 55.5	13 46.7	0 29.4	3 38.0
6 Th	17 01 49	14 33 26	15 56 16	22 03 47	27R 28.0	0 35.2	26 53.0	15 40.4	12 56.7	15 43.0	22 02.4	13 50.4	0 31.6	3 40.0
7 F	17 05 46	15 34 21	28 14 32	4♊28 43	27 27.9	0 12.5	28 03.8	16 26.0	12 47.8	15 56.0	22 09.2	13 54.1	0 33.8	3 41.9
8 Sa	17 09 42	16 35 17	10♊46 29	17 07 55	27 26.8	29♐38.4	29 14.6	17 11.7	12 39.2	16 09.0	22 16.0	13 57.7	0 36.0	3 43.8
9 Su	17 13 39	17 36 13	23 33 04	0♋01 56	27 24.8	28 53.0	0♒25.2	17 57.4	12 31.0	16 22.1	22 22.7	14 01.4	0 38.3	3 45.7
10 M	17 17 35	18 37 11	6♋34 27	13 10 31	27 21.8	27 57.0	1 35.7	18 43.1	12 23.2	16 35.2	22 29.4	14 05.1	0 40.5	3 47.6
11 Tu	17 21 32	19 38 10	19 50 00	26 32 46	27 18.4	26 51.4	2 46.1	19 28.8	12 15.7	16 48.4	22 36.1	14 08.8	0 42.7	3 49.5
12 W	17 25 28	20 39 10	3♌18 37	10♌07 23	27 15.0	25 37.8	3 56.5	20 14.6	12 08.6	17 01.6	22 42.8	14 12.4	0 45.0	3 51.3
13 Th	17 29 25	21 40 10	16 58 51	23 52 51	27 12.0	24 18.5	5 06.7	21 00.3	12 01.9	17 14.9	22 49.4	14 16.1	0 47.2	3 53.1
14 F	17 33 21	22 41 12	0♍49 10	7♍47 38	27 10.0	22 56.0	6 16.8	21 46.1	11 55.5	17 28.2	22 56.0	14 19.7	0 49.5	3 54.9
15 Sa	17 37 18	23 42 15	14 48 04	21 50 17	27D 09.2	21 33.1	7 26.7	22 31.9	11 49.6	17 41.6	23 02.5	14 23.4	0 51.7	3 56.7
16 Su	17 41 15	24 43 18	28 54 06	5♎59 18	27 09.6	20 12.6	8 36.6	23 17.7	11 44.0	17 55.0	23 09.0	14 27.0	0 54.0	3 58.4
17 M	17 45 11	25 44 23	13♎05 42	20 13 01	27 10.8	18 57.2	9 46.4	24 03.5	11 38.8	18 08.4	23 15.5	14 30.7	0 56.2	4 00.1
18 Tu	17 49 08	26 45 29	27 21 00	4♏29 20	27 12.4	17 48.9	10 56.0	24 49.3	11 34.0	18 21.9	23 21.9	14 34.3	0 58.5	4 01.8
19 W	17 53 04	27 46 35	11♏37 39	18 45 33	27R 13.6	16 49.6	12 05.5	25 35.1	11 29.7	18 35.5	23 28.2	14 37.9	1 00.8	4 03.4
20 Th	17 57 01	28 47 42	25 52 34	2♐58 14	27 13.7	16 00.3	13 14.8	26 21.0	11 25.7	18 49.0	23 34.6	14 41.5	1 03.0	4 05.1
21 F	18 00 57	29 48 50	10♐02 03	17 03 28	27 12.3	15 21.7	14 24.1	27 06.8	11 22.1	19 02.7	23 40.9	14 45.1	1 05.3	4 06.7
22 Sa	18 04 54	0♑49 59	24 01 59	0♑57 06	27 09.0	14 54.0	15 33.2	27 52.7	11 19.0	19 16.3	23 47.1	14 48.7	1 07.6	4 08.2
23 Su	18 08 50	1 51 08	7♑48 23	14 35 25	27 04.1	14 37.1	16 42.1	28 38.5	11 16.2	19 30.0	23 53.3	14 52.2	1 09.9	4 09.8
24 M	18 12 47	2 52 17	21 17 54	27 55 35	26 58.0	14D 30.5	17 50.9	29 24.4	11 13.9	19 43.7	23 59.4	14 55.8	1 12.1	4 11.3
25 Tu	18 16 44	3 53 27	4♒28 20	10♒56 06	26 51.3	14 33.5	18 59.5	0♓10.3	11 12.0	19 57.5	24 05.5	14 59.3	1 14.4	4 12.8
26 W	18 20 40	4 54 37	17 18 58	23 37 04	26 45.0	14 45.5	20 08.0	0 56.1	11 10.4	20 11.2	24 11.6	15 02.9	1 16.7	4 14.2
27 Th	18 24 37	5 55 46	29 50 40	6♓00 05	26 39.6	15 05.7	21 16.3	1 42.0	11 09.3	20 25.0	24 17.6	15 06.4	1 18.9	4 15.6
28 F	18 28 33	6 56 56	12♓05 45	18 08 08	26 35.8	15 33.4	22 24.4	2 27.9	11 08.6	20 38.9	24 23.5	15 09.9	1 21.2	4 17.0
29 Sa	18 32 30	7 58 06	24 07 46	0♈05 13	26D 33.7	16 07.7	23 32.3	3 13.7	11D 08.3	20 52.7	24 29.4	15 13.3	1 23.5	4 18.4
30 Su	18 36 26	8 59 15	6♈01 07	11 56 06	26 33.3	16 48.1	24 40.0	3 59.6	11 08.4	21 06.6	24 35.2	15 16.8	1 25.7	4 19.7
31 M	18 40 23	10 00 24	17 50 49	23 45 55	26 34.3	17 33.8	25 47.6	4 45.4	11 08.9	21 20.5	24 41.0	15 20.2	1 28.0	4 21.0

Astro Data

	Dy Hr Mn
☽0N	5 14:51
☽0S	19 10:33
♃⚺♅	23 20:03
☽0N	2 22:15
☿R	4 21:47
☽0S	16 17:10
☿D	24 16:12
⚷D	29 18:08
☽0N	30 5:49

Planet Ingress

		Dy Hr Mn
☿	♐	6 12:09
♀	♑	13 23:54
♂	♒	15 18:09
♆	♑	21 13:21
☉	♐	22 3:11
☿	♑	1 16:29
☿	♐R	7 21:46
♀	♒	9 3:26
☉	♑	21 16:23
♂	♓	25 6:38

Last Aspect / ☽ Ingress

Last Aspect Dy Hr Mn		☽ Ingress Dy Hr Mn
2 6:39	♆ ⚹	♓ 2 7:50
4 19:17	♆ □	♈ 4 20:20
7 8:00	♆ △	♉ 7 8:53
9 11:01	♂ △	♊ 9 20:10
12 4:57	♆ ☍	♋ 12 5:31
14 10:48	♂ ☍	♌ 14 12:34
16 16:51	♆ △	♍ 16 17:08
18 19:20	♆ □	♎ 18 19:29
20 20:28	♆ ⚹	♏ 20 20:31
22 5:44	♄ ☌	♐ 22 21:34
24 14:11	☿ ☌	♑ 25 0:17
26 13:22	♄ ⚹	♒ 27 6:06
29 13:00	☿ ⚹	♓ 29 15:33

Last Aspect / ☽ Ingress

Last Aspect Dy Hr Mn		☽ Ingress Dy Hr Mn
1 10:25	♄ △	♈ 2 3:42
4 4:36	♀ □	♉ 4 16:20
6 22:21	♀ △	♊ 7 3:24
9 10:01	☿ ☍	♋ 9 11:56
11 4:54	♄ △	♌ 11 18:08
13 12:40	☿ △	♍ 13 22:35
15 15:25	☉ □	♎ 16 1:52
17 22:00	☉ ⚹	♏ 18 4:27
20 0:10	♂ □	♐ 20 6:58
22 6:21	♂ ⚹	♑ 22 10:21
24 4:48	♄ ⚹	♒ 24 15:47
26 13:07	♄ □	♓ 27 0:18
29 0:38	♄ △	♈ 29 11:49

☽ Phases & Eclipses

Dy Hr Mn		
8 17:43	○	16♉30
8 17:55	☍	A 0.899
16 6:59	☾	24♌06
22 22:57	●	0♐50
22 22:53:22	☌	T 01'60"
30 8:01	☽	8♓18
8 10:53	○	16♊32
15 15:25	☾	23♍51
22 11:47	●	0♑49
30 5:27	☽	8♈43

Astro Data

1 November 1984
Julian Day # 30986
SVP 5♓28'33"
GC 26♐37.6 ⚳ 4♓35.7R
Eris 15♈22.2R ⚴ 22♍49.3
⚷ 7♊18.9R ⚶ 26♍13.4
☽ Mean ☊ 28♉21.0

1 December 1984
Julian Day # 31016
SVP 5♓28'28"
GC 26♐37.7 ⚳ 6♓40.6
Eris 15♈08.4R ⚴ 3♎00.3
⚷ 5♊42.4R ⚶ 9♎23.2
☽ Mean ☊ 26♉45.7

LONGITUDE

January 1985

Day	Sid.Time	☉	0 hr ☽	Noon ☽	True ☊	☿	♀	♂	⚳	♃	♄	♅	♆	♇
1 Tu	18 44 19	11♑01 34	29♈42 04	5♉39 54	26♉35.9	18♐24.2	26♒54.9	5♓31.3	11♉09.8	21♑34.4	24♏46.7	15♐23.6	1♑30.2	4♏22.3
2 W	18 48 16	12 02 43	11♉40 02	17 43 04	26R 37.2	19 18.9	28 02.0	6 17.1	11 11.1	21 48.3	24 52.3	15 27.0	1 32.5	4 23.5
3 Th	18 52 13	13 03 52	23 49 32	29 59 56	26 37.5	20 17.3	29 08.9	7 03.0	11 12.8	22 02.3	24 57.9	15 30.4	1 34.7	4 24.7
4 F	18 56 09	14 05 01	6♊14 40	12♊34 04	26 36.1	21 19.1	0♓15.6	7 48.8	11 14.9	22 16.3	25 03.4	15 33.8	1 36.9	4 25.9
5 Sa	19 00 06	15 06 09	18 58 25	25 27 51	26 32.5	22 23.9	1 22.0	8 34.6	11 17.3	22 30.2	25 08.9	15 37.1	1 39.2	4 27.0
6 Su	19 04 02	16 07 18	2♋02 26	8♋42 05	26 26.6	23 31.2	2 28.2	9 20.4	11 20.2	22 44.2	25 14.3	15 40.4	1 41.4	4 28.1
7 M	19 07 59	17 08 26	15 26 37	22 15 47	26 18.8	24 41.0	3 34.1	10 06.1	11 23.4	22 58.3	25 19.6	15 43.7	1 43.6	4 29.2
8 Tu	19 11 55	18 09 34	29 09 09	6♌06 17	26 09.8	25 52.9	4 39.8	10 51.9	11 27.0	23 12.3	25 24.9	15 46.9	1 45.8	4 30.2
9 W	19 15 52	19 10 42	13♌06 38	20 09 36	26 00.7	27 06.7	5 45.2	11 37.7	11 31.0	23 26.3	25 30.1	15 50.2	1 48.0	4 31.2
10 Th	19 19 49	20 11 50	27 14 35	4♍20 59	25 52.5	28 22.2	6 50.4	12 23.4	11 35.3	23 40.4	25 35.3	15 53.4	1 50.2	4 32.2
11 F	19 23 45	21 12 57	11♍28 12	18 35 44	25 46.1	29 39.2	7 55.2	13 09.1	11 40.1	23 54.4	25 40.3	15 56.6	1 52.4	4 33.1
12 Sa	19 27 42	22 14 05	25 43 05	2♎49 51	25 42.0	0♑57.6	8 59.8	13 54.8	11 45.1	24 08.5	25 45.3	15 59.7	1 54.5	4 34.0
13 Su	19 31 38	23 15 12	9♎55 44	17 00 29	25D 40.3	2 17.4	10 04.0	14 40.5	11 50.6	24 22.5	25 50.3	16 02.8	1 56.7	4 34.9
14 M	19 35 35	24 16 20	24 03 54	1♏05 52	25 40.2	3 38.3	11 08.0	15 26.2	11 56.3	24 36.6	25 55.1	16 05.9	1 58.8	4 35.7
15 Tu	19 39 31	25 17 27	8♏06 17	15 05 07	25R 41.0	5 00.3	12 11.6	16 11.8	12 02.5	24 50.6	25 59.9	16 09.0	2 01.0	4 36.5
16 W	19 43 28	26 18 35	22 02 18	28 57 47	25 41.2	6 23.3	13 14.9	16 57.4	12 09.0	25 04.7	26 04.6	16 12.1	2 03.1	4 37.3
17 Th	19 47 24	27 19 42	5♐51 29	12♐43 19	25 39.9	7 47.2	14 17.9	17 43.1	12 15.8	25 18.8	26 09.3	16 15.1	2 05.2	4 38.0
18 F	19 51 21	28 20 49	19 33 09	26 20 49	25 36.1	9 12.1	15 20.6	18 28.7	12 23.0	25 32.9	26 13.8	16 18.0	2 07.3	4 38.7
19 Sa	19 55 18	29 21 55	3♑06 07	9♑48 51	25 29.4	10 37.7	16 22.8	19 14.3	12 30.5	25 46.9	26 18.3	16 21.0	2 09.4	4 39.4
20 Su	19 59 14	0♒23 01	16 28 47	23 05 39	25 19.9	12 04.2	17 24.7	19 59.8	12 38.4	26 01.0	26 22.7	16 23.9	2 11.4	4 40.0
21 M	20 03 11	1 24 06	29 39 14	6♒09 20	25 08.4	13 31.4	18 26.2	20 45.4	12 46.5	26 15.1	26 27.1	16 26.8	2 13.5	4 40.6
22 Tu	20 07 07	2 25 10	12♒35 47	18 58 28	24 55.8	14 59.4	19 27.3	21 30.9	12 55.0	26 29.1	26 31.3	16 29.6	2 15.5	4 41.1
23 W	20 11 04	3 26 14	25 17 20	1♓32 25	24 43.2	16 28.1	20 28.0	22 16.4	13 03.9	26 43.1	26 35.5	16 32.4	2 17.5	4 41.6
24 Th	20 15 00	4 27 17	7♓43 48	13 51 39	24 31.9	17 57.5	21 28.3	23 01.9	13 13.0	26 57.2	26 39.6	16 35.2	2 19.5	4 42.1
25 F	20 18 57	5 28 18	19 56 13	25 57 50	24 22.8	19 27.5	22 28.1	23 47.4	13 22.5	27 11.2	26 43.6	16 37.9	2 21.5	4 42.5
26 Sa	20 22 53	6 29 19	1♈56 54	7♈53 52	24 16.3	20 58.3	23 27.4	24 32.8	13 32.2	27 25.2	26 47.5	16 40.6	2 23.5	4 42.9
27 Su	20 26 50	7 30 18	13 49 16	19 43 39	24 12.6	22 29.7	24 26.3	25 18.2	13 42.3	27 39.2	26 51.3	16 43.3	2 25.4	4 43.3
28 M	20 30 47	8 31 17	25 37 40	1♉31 58	24D 11.0	24 01.8	25 24.6	26 03.6	13 52.6	27 53.1	26 55.1	16 45.9	2 27.4	4 43.6
29 Tu	20 34 43	9 32 14	7♉27 12	13 24 06	24R 10.8	25 34.6	26 22.5	26 48.9	14 03.3	28 07.1	26 58.7	16 48.5	2 29.3	4 43.9
30 W	20 38 40	10 33 10	19 23 20	25 25 37	24 11.0	27 08.0	27 19.7	27 34.2	14 14.2	28 21.0	27 02.3	16 51.1	2 31.2	4 44.1
31 Th	20 42 36	11 34 05	1♊31 37	7♊41 59	24 10.3	28 42.1	28 16.5	28 19.5	14 25.4	28 34.9	27 05.8	16 53.6	2 33.1	4 44.4

LONGITUDE

February 1985

Day	Sid.Time	☉	0 hr ☽	Noon ☽	True ☊	☿	♀	♂	⚳	♃	♄	♅	♆	♇
1 F	20 46 33	12♒34 58	13♊57 19	20♊18 08	24♉07.7	0♒17.0	29♓12.6	29♓04.8	14♉36.9	28♑48.8	27♏09.2	16♐56.0	2♑34.9	4♏44.5
2 Sa	20 50 29	13 35 50	26 44 52	3♋17 51	24R 02.6	1 52.5	0♈08.1	29 50.0	14 48.7	29 02.7	27 12.5	16 58.5	2 36.8	4 44.7
3 Su	20 54 26	14 36 41	9♋57 18	16 43 15	23 54.7	3 28.7	1 03.0	0♈35.2	15 00.8	29 16.6	27 15.7	17 00.9	2 38.6	4 44.8
4 M	20 58 22	15 37 31	23 35 36	0♌34 04	23 44.3	5 05.7	1 57.2	1 20.3	15 13.1	29 30.4	27 18.9	17 03.2	2 40.4	4 44.9
5 Tu	21 02 19	16 38 19	7♌38 13	14 47 26	23 32.3	6 43.4	2 50.8	2 05.4	15 25.6	29 44.2	27 21.9	17 05.5	2 42.1	4R 44.9
6 W	21 06 16	17 39 06	22 00 56	29 17 52	23 20.0	8 21.8	3 43.7	2 50.5	15 38.5	29 57.9	27 24.8	17 07.8	2 43.9	4 44.9
7 Th	21 10 12	18 39 52	6♍37 16	13♍58 08	23 08.7	10 01.0	4 35.8	3 35.6	15 51.5	0♒11.7	27 27.7	17 10.0	2 45.6	4 44.9
8 F	21 14 09	19 40 37	21 19 28	28 40 19	22 59.5	11 41.0	5 27.2	4 20.6	16 04.9	0 25.4	27 30.4	17 12.1	2 47.3	4 44.8
9 Sa	21 18 05	20 41 21	5♎59 50	13♎17 16	22 53.2	13 21.8	6 17.7	5 05.6	16 18.4	0 39.1	27 33.1	17 14.3	2 49.0	4 44.7
10 Su	21 22 02	21 42 03	20 32 01	27 43 36	22 49.8	15 03.4	7 07.5	5 50.5	16 32.3	0 52.7	27 35.7	17 16.4	2 50.7	4 44.6
11 M	21 25 58	22 42 45	4♏51 42	11♏56 06	22 48.5	16 45.8	7 56.5	6 35.4	16 46.3	1 06.3	27 38.1	17 18.4	2 52.3	4 44.4
12 Tu	21 29 55	23 43 25	18 56 43	25 53 34	22 48.4	18 29.1	8 44.6	7 20.3	17 00.6	1 19.9	27 40.5	17 20.4	2 53.9	4 44.2
13 W	21 33 51	24 44 05	2♐46 44	9♐36 18	22 48.0	20 13.3	9 31.7	8 05.2	17 15.1	1 33.4	27 42.8	17 22.3	2 55.5	4 43.9
14 Th	21 37 48	25 44 43	16 22 27	23 05 20	22 46.0	21 58.2	10 18.0	8 50.0	17 29.9	1 47.0	27 45.0	17 24.2	2 57.0	4 43.6
15 F	21 41 45	26 45 21	29 45 07	6♑21 54	22 41.5	23 44.1	11 03.2	9 34.8	17 44.8	2 00.4	27 47.1	17 26.1	2 58.6	4 43.3
16 Sa	21 45 41	27 45 57	12♑55 50	19 26 58	22 33.9	25 30.8	11 47.5	10 19.5	18 00.0	2 13.8	27 49.1	17 27.9	3 00.1	4 43.0
17 Su	21 49 38	28 46 31	25 55 21	2♒21 01	22 23.3	27 18.4	12 30.7	11 04.2	18 15.4	2 27.2	27 51.0	17 29.7	3 01.6	4 42.6
18 M	21 53 34	29 47 05	8♒43 57	15 04 09	22 10.4	29 06.9	13 12.9	11 48.9	18 31.0	2 40.6	27 52.7	17 31.4	3 03.0	4 42.1
19 Tu	21 57 31	0♓47 36	21 21 34	27 36 13	21 56.3	0♓56.2	13 53.8	12 33.5	18 46.9	2 53.9	27 54.4	17 33.1	3 04.5	4 41.7
20 W	22 01 27	1 48 06	3♓48 04	9♓57 10	21 42.1	2 46.3	14 33.7	13 18.1	19 02.9	3 07.1	27 56.0	17 34.7	3 05.9	4 41.2
21 Th	22 05 24	2 48 35	16 03 34	22 07 23	21 29.2	4 37.2	15 12.2	14 02.7	19 19.1	3 20.3	27 57.5	17 36.2	3 07.2	4 40.7
22 F	22 09 20	3 49 01	28 08 47	4♈07 57	21 18.5	6 28.9	15 49.5	14 47.2	19 35.6	3 33.4	27 58.9	17 37.7	3 08.6	4 40.1
23 Sa	22 13 17	4 49 26	10♈05 11	16 00 48	21 10.5	8 21.2	16 25.5	15 31.7	19 52.2	3 46.5	28 00.2	17 39.2	3 09.9	4 39.5
24 Su	22 17 14	5 49 49	21 55 11	27 48 48	21 05.5	10 14.2	17 00.1	16 16.2	20 09.0	3 59.6	28 01.3	17 40.6	3 11.2	4 38.9
25 M	22 21 10	6 50 11	3♉42 08	9♉35 45	21D 03.1	12 07.8	17 33.2	17 00.6	20 26.1	4 12.5	28 02.4	17 42.0	3 12.4	4 38.2
26 Tu	22 25 07	7 50 30	15 30 14	21 26 14	21 02.6	14 01.7	18 04.9	17 44.9	20 43.3	4 25.5	28 03.4	17 43.3	3 13.7	4 37.5
27 W	22 29 03	8 50 47	27 24 23	3♊25 24	21R 02.8	15 55.9	18 35.0	18 29.3	21 00.6	4 38.3	28 04.3	17 44.6	3 14.9	4 36.8
28 Th	22 33 00	9 51 03	9♊29 58	15 38 46	21 02.8	17 50.3	19 03.4	19 13.5	21 18.2	4 51.2	28 05.0	17 45.8	3 16.0	4 36.0

Astro Data

	Dy Hr Mn
☽0S	12 21:52
♃⚹♄	22 17:26
☽0N	26 13:02
♀0N	30 19:34
♂0N	4 1:55
♇ R	5 23:58
☽0S	9 3:37
♃∠♅	17 17:03
♃⚺♆	20 9:30
☽0N	22 19:46
♃□♇	27 9:16

Planet Ingress

		Dy Hr Mn
♀	♓	4 6:23
☿	♑	11 18:25
☉	♒	20 2:58
☿	♒	1 7:43
♀	♈	2 8:29
♂	♈	2 17:19
♃	♒	6 15:35
☉	♓	18 17:07
☿	♓	18 23:41

Last Aspect / ☽ Ingress

Last Aspect Dy Hr Mn			☽ Ingress	Dy Hr Mn
31 16:32	♀	⚹	♉	1 0:36
3 10:12	♀	□	♊	3 12:00
5 5:50	☿	☍	♋	5 20:18
7 17:23	♄	△	♌	8 1:28
10 0:55	☿	△	♍	10 4:40
11 24:00	♄	⚹	♎	12 7:13
14 0:44	♃	□	♏	14 10:07
16 7:02	☉	⚹	♐	16 13:48
17 21:17	♂	□	♑	18 18:29
20 18:02	♄	⚹	♒	21 0:38
23 2:26	♄	□	♓	23 9:02
25 14:30	♃	⚹	♈	25 20:05
28 4:27	♃	□	♉	28 8:53
30 17:53	♃	△	♊	30 21:01

Last Aspect / ☽ Ingress

Last Aspect Dy Hr Mn			☽ Ingress	Dy Hr Mn
2 5:48	♀	□	♋	2 5:59
4 10:09	♃	☍	♌	4 11:02
6 8:54	♄	□	♍	6 13:09
8 10:05	♄	⚹	♎	8 14:10
10 1:11	☉	△	♏	10 15:49
12 15:06	♄	☌	♐	12 19:09
14 17:10	☉	⚹	♑	15 0:27
17 3:34	♄	⚹	♒	17 7:36
19 12:35	♄	□	♓	19 16:38
21 23:39	♄	△	♈	22 3:43
23 15:20	♅	△	♉	24 16:27
27 1:19	♄	☍	♊	27 5:11

☽ Phases & Eclipses

Dy Hr Mn		
7 2:16	○	16♋44
13 23:27	☾	23♎44
21 2:28	●	1♒00
29 3:29	☽	9♉11
5 15:19	○	16♌47
12 7:57	☾	23♏33
19 18:43	●	1♓05
27 23:41	☽	9♊20

Astro Data

1 January 1985
Julian Day # 31047
SVP 5♓28'23"
GC 26♐37.8 ⚵ 13♓02.2
Eris 15♈02.8R ⚴ 10♎29.4
⚷ 4♊07.6R ⚶ 21♎33.6
☽Mean ☊ 25♉07.2

1 February 1985
Julian Day # 31078
SVP 5♓28'17"
GC 26♐37.9 ⚵ 22♓10.4
Eris 15♈07.8 ⚴ 13♎14.1R
⚷ 3♊17.9R ⚶ 0♏54.4
☽Mean ☊ 23♉28.8

March 1985

LONGITUDE

Day	Sid.Time	☉	0 hr ☽	Noon ☽	True ☊	☿	♀	♂	⚳	♃	♄	♅	♆	♇
1 F	22 36 56	10♓51 16	21♊52 29	28♊11 44	21♉01.3	19♓44.6	19♈30.2	19♈57.8	21♉35.9	5♒03.9	28♏05.7	17♐46.9	3♑17.2	4♏35.3
2 Sa	22 40 53	11 51 27	4♋37 07	11♋09 06	20R 57.8	21 38.5	19 55.2	20 42.0	21 53.8	5 16.6	28 06.3	17 48.0	3 18.3	4R 34.4
3 Su	22 44 49	12 51 36	17 48 05	24 34 19	20 51.8	23 31.9	20 18.5	21 26.1	22 11.9	5 29.2	28 06.7	17 49.1	3 19.4	4 33.6
4 M	22 48 46	13 51 43	1♌27 53	8♌28 42	20 43.4	25 24.4	20 39.8	22 10.2	22 30.1	5 41.8	28 07.1	17 50.1	3 20.4	4 32.7
5 Tu	22 52 43	14 51 49	15 36 29	22 50 43	20 33.6	27 15.7	20 59.2	22 54.3	22 48.5	5 54.3	28 07.4	17 51.1	3 21.5	4 31.8
6 W	22 56 39	15 51 52	0♍10 42	7♍35 32	20 23.2	29 05.4	21 16.7	23 38.3	23 07.1	6 06.7	28 07.5	17 52.0	3 22.4	4 30.9
7 Th	23 00 36	16 51 53	15 04 09	22 35 24	20 13.6	0♈53.0	21 32.0	24 22.3	23 25.8	6 19.1	28R 07.6	17 52.8	3 23.4	4 29.9
8 F	23 04 32	17 51 52	0♎08 00	7♎40 43	20 05.7	2 38.2	21 45.2	25 06.2	23 44.7	6 31.4	28 07.5	17 53.6	3 24.3	4 28.9
9 Sa	23 08 29	18 51 49	15 12 21	22 41 47	20 00.4	4 20.3	21 56.3	25 50.1	24 03.7	6 43.6	28 07.4	17 54.3	3 25.2	4 27.9
10 Su	23 12 25	19 51 45	0♏08 01	7♏30 16	19D 57.7	5 59.0	22 05.1	26 33.9	24 22.9	6 55.7	28 07.1	17 55.0	3 26.1	4 26.9
11 M	23 16 22	20 51 39	14 47 54	22 00 28	19 57.1	7 33.7	22 11.6	27 17.7	24 42.2	7 07.8	28 06.8	17 55.7	3 26.9	4 25.8
12 Tu	23 20 18	21 51 31	29 07 39	6♐09 22	19 57.7	9 03.9	22 15.9	28 01.5	25 01.6	7 19.8	28 06.3	17 56.2	3 27.7	4 24.7
13 W	23 24 15	22 51 22	13♐05 35	19 56 26	19R 58.4	10 29.1	22R 17.7	28 45.2	25 21.2	7 31.8	28 05.8	17 56.8	3 28.5	4 23.6
14 Th	23 28 12	23 51 12	26 42 05	3♑22 49	19 58.0	11 48.7	22 17.1	29 28.9	25 41.0	7 43.6	28 05.1	17 57.3	3 29.2	4 22.4
15 F	23 32 08	24 50 59	9♑58 54	16 30 39	19 55.6	13 02.3	22 14.1	0♉12.5	26 00.8	7 55.4	28 04.4	17 57.7	3 29.9	4 21.2
16 Sa	23 36 05	25 50 45	22 58 22	29 22 22	19 51.0	14 09.5	22 08.6	0 56.1	26 20.8	8 07.1	28 03.5	17 58.1	3 30.6	4 20.0
17 Su	23 40 01	26 50 29	5♒42 55	12♒00 18	19 44.1	15 09.9	22 00.6	1 39.7	26 41.0	8 18.7	28 02.5	17 58.4	3 31.2	4 18.8
18 M	23 43 58	27 50 11	18 14 45	24 26 29	19 35.3	16 03.0	21 50.2	2 23.2	27 01.3	8 30.2	28 01.5	17 58.6	3 31.8	4 17.6
19 Tu	23 47 54	28 49 51	0♓35 41	6♓42 33	19 25.5	16 48.7	21 37.3	3 06.6	27 21.7	8 41.6	28 00.3	17 58.8	3 32.4	4 16.3
20 W	23 51 51	29 49 30	12 47 13	18 49 52	19 15.7	17 26.7	21 21.9	3 50.0	27 42.2	8 53.0	27 59.1	17 59.0	3 33.0	4 15.0
21 Th	23 55 47	0♈49 06	24 50 38	0♈49 42	19 06.7	17 56.8	21 04.1	4 33.4	28 02.8	9 04.2	27 57.7	17 59.1	3 33.5	4 13.7
22 F	23 59 44	1 48 40	6♈47 13	12 43 24	18 59.3	18 18.9	20 43.9	5 16.8	28 23.6	9 15.4	27 56.3	17R 59.2	3 33.9	4 12.3
23 Sa	0 03 41	2 48 13	18 38 28	24 32 40	18 54.0	18 33.0	20 21.4	6 00.0	28 44.5	9 26.4	27 54.7	17 59.1	3 34.4	4 11.0
24 Su	0 07 37	3 47 43	0♉26 18	6♉19 43	18 51.0	18R 39.2	19 56.7	6 43.3	29 05.5	9 37.4	27 53.1	17 59.1	3 34.8	4 09.6
25 M	0 11 34	4 47 11	12 13 15	18 07 20	18D 50.0	18 37.6	19 29.9	7 26.5	29 26.6	9 48.3	27 51.4	17 59.0	3 35.1	4 08.2
26 Tu	0 15 30	5 46 36	24 02 27	29 59 03	18 50.6	18 28.5	19 01.2	8 09.6	29 47.9	9 59.1	27 49.5	17 58.8	3 35.5	4 06.7
27 W	0 19 27	6 46 00	5♊57 42	11♊58 57	18 52.0	18 12.2	18 30.6	8 52.7	0♊09.2	10 09.8	27 47.6	17 58.6	3 35.8	4 05.3
28 Th	0 23 23	7 45 21	18 03 24	24 11 40	18 53.5	17 49.2	17 58.3	9 35.8	0 30.7	10 20.3	27 45.6	17 58.3	3 36.0	4 03.9
29 F	0 27 20	8 44 40	0♋24 19	6♋42 00	18R 54.3	17 20.2	17 24.6	10 18.8	0 52.2	10 30.8	27 43.5	17 58.0	3 36.3	4 02.4
30 Sa	0 31 16	9 43 57	13 05 16	19 34 39	18 53.8	16 45.7	16 49.5	11 01.8	1 13.9	10 41.2	27 41.3	17 57.7	3 36.5	4 00.9
31 Su	0 35 13	10 43 11	26 10 37	2♌53 32	18 51.7	16 06.5	16 13.4	11 44.7	1 35.7	10 51.5	27 39.1	17 57.2	3 36.7	3 59.4

April 1985

LONGITUDE

Day	Sid.Time	☉	0 hr ☽	Noon ☽	True ☊	☿	♀	♂	⚳	♃	♄	♅	♆	♇
1 M	0 39 10	11♈42 23	9♌43 39	16♌41 05	18♉48.1	15♈23.5	15♈36.5	12♉27.6	1♊57.5	11♒01.6	27♏36.7	17♐56.8	3♑36.8	3♏57.9
2 Tu	0 43 06	12 41 33	23 45 46	0♍57 26	18R 43.3	14R 37.7	14R 59.0	13 10.4	2 19.5	11 11.7	27R 34.3	17R 56.3	3 36.9	3R 56.3
3 W	0 47 03	13 40 40	8♍15 39	15 39 44	18 38.0	13 50.0	14 21.1	13 53.2	2 41.6	11 21.6	27 31.7	17 55.7	3 37.0	3 54.8
4 Th	0 50 59	14 39 45	23 08 50	0♎41 54	18 33.0	13 01.4	13 43.2	14 35.9	3 03.7	11 31.4	27 29.1	17 55.1	3R 37.0	3 53.2
5 F	0 54 56	15 38 48	8♎17 47	15 55 12	18 29.0	12 12.8	13 05.4	15 18.6	3 25.9	11 41.2	27 26.4	17 54.4	3 37.0	3 51.6
6 Sa	0 58 52	16 37 49	23 32 51	1♏09 26	18 26.5	11 25.1	12 28.1	16 01.2	3 48.3	11 50.8	27 23.7	17 53.7	3 37.0	3 50.0
7 Su	1 02 49	17 36 48	8♏43 43	16 14 37	18D 25.5	10 39.4	11 51.5	16 43.8	4 10.7	12 00.3	27 20.8	17 52.9	3 36.9	3 48.4
8 M	1 06 45	18 35 45	23 41 09	1♐02 33	18 25.9	9 56.2	11 15.8	17 26.4	4 33.2	12 09.6	27 17.9	17 52.1	3 36.8	3 46.8
9 Tu	1 10 42	19 34 41	8♐18 12	15 27 41	18 27.2	9 16.3	10 41.2	18 08.9	4 55.8	12 18.9	27 14.9	17 51.2	3 36.7	3 45.2
10 W	1 14 38	20 33 35	22 30 47	29 27 23	18 28.7	8 40.3	10 08.0	18 51.3	5 18.5	12 28.0	27 11.8	17 50.3	3 36.5	3 43.6
11 Th	1 18 35	21 32 27	6♑17 33	13♑01 28	18R 29.8	8 08.6	9 36.4	19 33.8	5 41.3	12 37.0	27 08.6	17 49.3	3 36.3	3 41.9
12 F	1 22 32	22 31 17	19 39 23	26 11 37	18 30.1	7 41.7	9 06.6	20 16.1	6 04.1	12 45.9	27 05.4	17 48.3	3 36.1	3 40.3
13 Sa	1 26 28	23 30 06	2♒38 33	9♒00 37	18 29.1	7 19.7	8 38.6	20 58.5	6 27.0	12 54.7	27 02.1	17 47.3	3 35.9	3 38.6
14 Su	1 30 25	24 28 52	15 18 14	21 31 50	18 27.1	7 02.8	8 12.6	21 40.7	6 50.0	13 03.3	26 58.7	17 46.2	3 35.6	3 37.0
15 M	1 34 21	25 27 38	27 41 50	3♓48 40	18 24.1	6 51.2	7 48.8	22 23.0	7 13.1	13 11.8	26 55.3	17 45.0	3 35.3	3 35.3
16 Tu	1 38 18	26 26 21	9♓52 44	15 54 24	18 20.6	6D 44.8	7 27.2	23 05.2	7 36.3	13 20.2	26 51.8	17 43.8	3 34.9	3 33.6
17 W	1 42 14	27 25 02	21 54 02	27 51 58	18 17.0	6 43.6	7 07.9	23 47.4	7 59.5	13 28.4	26 48.2	17 42.6	3 34.5	3 32.0
18 Th	1 46 11	28 23 42	3♈48 31	9♈43 58	18 13.7	6 47.6	6 51.0	24 29.5	8 22.9	13 36.5	26 44.6	17 41.3	3 34.1	3 30.3
19 F	1 50 07	29 22 19	15 38 36	21 32 42	18 11.2	6 56.6	6 36.5	25 11.5	8 46.3	13 44.5	26 40.9	17 40.0	3 33.6	3 28.6
20 Sa	1 54 04	0♉20 55	27 26 32	3♉20 21	18 09.6	7 10.5	6 24.4	25 53.6	9 09.7	13 52.3	26 37.2	17 38.6	3 33.2	3 26.9
21 Su	1 58 01	1 19 29	9♉14 25	15 09 00	18D 08.9	7 29.2	6 14.8	26 35.6	9 33.3	14 00.0	26 33.4	17 37.2	3 32.7	3 25.2
22 M	2 01 57	2 18 01	21 04 25	27 00 57	18 09.1	7 52.4	6 07.6	27 17.5	9 56.9	14 07.6	26 29.5	17 35.7	3 32.1	3 23.5
23 Tu	2 05 54	3 16 31	2♊58 56	8♊58 42	18 09.9	8 20.0	6 02.8	27 59.4	10 20.5	14 15.0	26 25.6	17 34.2	3 31.5	3 21.8
24 W	2 09 50	4 14 59	15 00 37	21 05 05	18 11.1	8 51.8	6D 00.4	28 41.3	10 44.3	14 22.2	26 21.7	17 32.7	3 30.9	3 20.1
25 Th	2 13 47	5 13 25	27 12 30	3♋23 19	18 12.3	9 27.7	6 00.4	29 23.1	11 08.1	14 29.3	26 17.7	17 31.1	3 30.3	3 18.4
26 F	2 17 43	6 11 49	9♋37 57	15 56 51	18 13.3	10 07.4	6 02.7	0♊04.8	11 31.9	14 36.3	26 13.6	17 29.5	3 29.7	3 16.7
27 Sa	2 21 40	7 10 11	22 20 27	28 49 11	18R 13.9	10 50.8	6 07.3	0 46.6	11 55.9	14 43.1	26 09.5	17 27.9	3 29.0	3 15.0
28 Su	2 25 36	8 08 31	5♌23 27	12♌03 34	18 14.0	11 37.8	6 14.1	1 28.2	12 19.8	14 49.8	26 05.4	17 26.2	3 28.2	3 13.3
29 M	2 29 33	9 06 49	18 49 48	25 42 22	18 13.7	12 28.1	6 23.2	2 09.9	12 43.9	14 56.3	26 01.2	17 24.5	3 27.5	3 11.6
30 Tu	2 33 30	10 05 04	2♍41 18	9♍46 35	18 13.0	13 21.8	6 34.3	2 51.5	13 08.0	15 02.7	25 57.0	17 22.7	3 26.7	3 10.0

Astro Data

	Dy Hr Mn
☿0N	7 0:10
♄ R	7 12:38
☽0S	8 12:21
♀ R	13 18:18
☉0N	20 16:14
☽0N	22 2:06
♅ R	22 22:02
☿ R	24 19:01
☽0S	4 23:19
♆ R	5 1:27
♆⚹♇	15 12:59
☿ D	17 5:22
☽0N	18 8:15
♀ D	25 0:09

Planet Ingress

	Dy Hr Mn
☿ ♈	7 0:07
♂ ♉	15 5:06
☉ ♈	20 16:14
⚳ ♊	27 1:38
☉ ♉	20 3:26
♂ ♊	26 9:13

Last Aspect / ☽ Ingress

Last Aspect Dy Hr Mn		☽ Ingress Dy Hr Mn
28 19:21	♂ ⚹	♋ 1 15:23
3 18:11	♄ △	♌ 3 21:28
5 20:39	♄ □	♍ 5 23:43
7 20:48	♄ ⚹	♎ 7 23:47
9 17:19	♂ ☍	♏ 9 23:47
11 22:17	♄ ☌	♐ 12 1:29
14 4:34	♂ △	♑ 14 5:55
16 9:32	♄ ⚹	♒ 16 13:11
18 18:58	♄ □	♓ 18 22:50
21 6:15	♄ △	♈ 21 10:20
23 3:45	♀ ☌	♉ 23 23:06
26 7:40	♄ ☍	♊ 26 12:02
28 0:21	♀ ⚹	♋ 28 23:13
31 2:41	♄ △	♌ 31 6:51

Last Aspect Dy Hr Mn		☽ Ingress Dy Hr Mn
2 6:23	♄ □	♍ 2 10:25
4 6:55	♄ ⚹	♎ 4 10:54
5 15:07	♅ ⚹	♏ 6 10:10
8 5:54	♄ ☌	♐ 8 10:17
9 19:30	☉ △	♑ 10 12:57
12 13:39	♄ ⚹	♒ 12 19:04
14 22:33	♄ □	♓ 15 4:30
17 9:52	♄ △	♈ 17 16:18
19 4:08	♅ △	♉ 20 5:12
22 12:35	♂ ☌	♊ 22 18:01
24 5:02	♅ ☍	♋ 25 5:26
27 7:07	♄ △	♌ 27 14:10
29 12:32	♄ □	♍ 29 19:24

☽ Phases & Eclipses

Dy Hr Mn	
7 2:13	○ 16♍27
13 17:34	☾ 23♐05
21 11:59	● 0♈49
29 16:11	☽ 8♋55
5 11:32	○ 15♎38
12 4:41	☾ 22♑13
20 5:22	● 0♉05
28 4:25	☽ 7♌50

Astro Data

1 March 1985
Julian Day # 31106
SVP 5♓28'13"
GC 26♐37.9 ⚳ 1♈56.4
Eris 15♈20.4 ⚵ 10♎29.0R
⚷ 3♊29.2 ⚶ 5♏03.4
☽ Mean ☊ 21♉59.8

1 April 1985
Julian Day # 31137
SVP 5♓28'10"
GC 26♐38.0 ⚳ 13♈50.1
Eris 15♈39.8 ⚵ 3♎26.9R
⚷ 4♊42.0 ⚶ 2♏44.6R
☽ Mean ☊ 20♉21.3

LONGITUDE May 1985

Day	Sid.Time	☉	0 hr ☽	Noon ☽	True ☊	☿	♀	♂	⚳	♃	♄	♅	♆	♇
1 W	2 37 26	11♉03 17	16♍57 58	24♍15 08	18♉12.2	14♈18.5	6♈47.6	3♊33.0	13♊32.1	15♒08.9	25♏52.8	17♐20.9	3♑25.9	3♏08.3
2 Th	2 41 23	12 01 29	1♎37 30	9♎04 24	18R 11.4	15 18.2	7 02.8	4 14.5	13 56.3	15 14.9	25R 48.5	17R 19.1	3R 25.1	3R 06.6
3 F	2 45 19	12 59 38	16 34 58	24 08 12	18 10.9	16 20.8	7 20.0	4 56.0	14 20.6	15 20.8	25 44.2	17 17.2	3 24.2	3 04.9
4 Sa	2 49 16	13 57 46	1♏43 01	9♏18 15	18D 10.7	17 26.2	7 39.2	5 37.4	14 44.9	15 26.5	25 39.9	17 15.3	3 23.3	3 03.3
5 Su	2 53 12	14 55 52	16 52 42	24 25 13	18 10.6	18 34.3	8 00.1	6 18.7	15 09.3	15 32.1	25 35.5	17 13.4	3 22.4	3 01.6
6 M	2 57 09	15 53 56	1♐54 41	9♐20 07	18 10.8	19 45.0	8 22.9	7 00.1	15 33.7	15 37.5	25 31.1	17 11.4	3 21.5	3 00.0
7 Tu	3 01 05	16 51 59	16 40 38	23 55 32	18 10.9	20 58.2	8 47.3	7 41.4	15 58.2	15 42.8	25 26.7	17 09.4	3 20.5	2 58.3
8 W	3 05 02	17 50 01	1♑04 17	8♑06 31	18R 11.0	22 13.9	9 13.5	8 22.6	16 22.7	15 47.8	25 22.3	17 07.4	3 19.6	2 56.7
9 Th	3 08 59	18 48 01	15 02 01	21 50 44	18 11.0	23 32.0	9 41.2	9 03.8	16 47.3	15 52.8	25 17.9	17 05.4	3 18.5	2 55.1
10 F	3 12 55	19 46 00	28 32 46	5♒08 20	18 10.9	24 52.4	10 10.4	9 45.0	17 11.9	15 57.5	25 13.4	17 03.3	3 17.5	2 53.5
11 Sa	3 16 52	20 43 57	11♒37 45	18 01 22	18D 10.8	26 15.2	10 41.2	10 26.1	17 36.6	16 02.1	25 09.0	17 01.2	3 16.5	2 51.9
12 Su	3 20 48	21 41 53	24 19 41	0♓33 10	18 10.9	27 40.2	11 13.3	11 07.2	18 01.3	16 06.5	25 04.5	16 59.1	3 15.4	2 50.3
13 M	3 24 45	22 39 48	6♓42 21	12 47 46	18 11.1	29 07.5	11 46.8	11 48.2	18 26.1	16 10.7	25 00.0	16 56.9	3 14.3	2 48.7
14 Tu	3 28 41	23 37 41	18 49 58	24 49 29	18 11.6	0♉36.9	12 21.7	12 29.3	18 50.9	16 14.8	24 55.5	16 54.7	3 13.1	2 47.2
15 W	3 32 38	24 35 34	0♈46 51	6♈42 32	18 12.2	2 08.6	12 57.8	13 10.2	19 15.7	16 18.7	24 51.0	16 52.5	3 12.0	2 45.6
16 Th	3 36 34	25 33 25	12 37 04	18 30 52	18 12.9	3 42.4	13 35.1	13 51.2	19 40.6	16 22.4	24 46.5	16 50.3	3 10.8	2 44.1
17 F	3 40 31	26 31 14	24 24 23	0♉17 59	18 13.6	5 18.4	14 13.5	14 32.1	20 05.6	16 25.9	24 42.0	16 48.0	3 09.6	2 42.6
18 Sa	3 44 28	27 29 03	6♉12 05	12 06 58	18R 14.0	6 56.5	14 53.1	15 12.9	20 30.5	16 29.2	24 37.5	16 45.8	3 08.4	2 41.1
19 Su	3 48 24	28 26 50	18 03 00	24 00 26	18 14.0	8 36.8	15 33.7	15 53.7	20 55.6	16 32.4	24 33.0	16 43.5	3 07.1	2 39.6
20 M	3 52 21	29 24 36	29 59 33	6♊00 37	18 13.5	10 19.3	16 15.4	16 34.5	21 20.6	16 35.4	24 28.6	16 41.2	3 05.9	2 38.1
21 Tu	3 56 17	0♊22 20	12♊03 50	18 09 26	18 12.4	12 03.9	16 58.0	17 15.3	21 45.7	16 38.2	24 24.1	16 38.9	3 04.6	2 36.6
22 W	4 00 14	1 20 03	24 17 38	0♋28 39	18 10.8	13 50.7	17 41.6	17 56.0	22 10.9	16 40.8	24 19.6	16 36.5	3 03.3	2 35.2
23 Th	4 04 10	2 17 45	6♋42 41	12 59 56	18 08.8	15 39.6	18 26.1	18 36.6	22 36.1	16 43.2	24 15.2	16 34.2	3 02.0	2 33.8
24 F	4 08 07	3 15 25	19 20 38	25 44 58	18 06.8	17 30.6	19 11.4	19 17.3	23 01.3	16 45.5	24 10.8	16 31.8	3 00.6	2 32.4
25 Sa	4 12 03	4 13 04	2♌13 10	8♌45 25	18 05.1	19 23.7	19 57.6	19 57.9	23 26.5	16 47.6	24 06.4	16 29.4	2 59.3	2 31.0
26 Su	4 16 00	5 10 41	15 21 55	22 02 50	18 03.9	21 19.0	20 44.6	20 38.4	23 51.8	16 49.4	24 02.0	16 27.0	2 57.9	2 29.7
27 M	4 19 57	6 08 17	28 48 21	5♍38 33	18D 03.5	23 16.3	21 32.4	21 18.9	24 17.1	16 51.1	23 57.7	16 24.6	2 56.5	2 28.3
28 Tu	4 23 53	7 05 51	12♍33 31	19 33 15	18 03.8	25 15.6	22 20.9	21 59.4	24 42.5	16 52.6	23 53.4	16 22.2	2 55.1	2 27.0
29 W	4 27 50	8 03 24	26 37 40	3♎46 37	18 04.8	27 16.8	23 10.1	22 39.8	25 07.9	16 53.9	23 49.1	16 19.7	2 53.7	2 25.7
30 Th	4 31 46	9 00 55	10♎59 49	18 16 53	18 06.1	29 20.0	24 00.0	23 20.2	25 33.3	16 55.0	23 44.8	16 17.3	2 52.3	2 24.4
31 F	4 35 43	9 58 25	25 37 20	3♏00 33	18 07.2	1♊24.8	24 50.6	24 00.6	25 58.7	16 56.0	23 40.6	16 14.9	2 50.8	2 23.2

LONGITUDE June 1985

Day	Sid.Time	☉	0 hr ☽	Noon ☽	True ☊	☿	♀	♂	⚳	♃	♄	♅	♆	♇
1 Sa	4 39 39	10♊55 54	10♏25 47	17♏52 14	18♉07.7	3♊31.3	25♈41.9	24♊40.9	26♊24.2	16♒56.7	23♏36.4	16♐12.4	2♑49.4	2♏21.9
2 Su	4 43 36	11 53 21	25 18 58	2♐45 04	18R 07.2	5 39.2	26 33.7	25 21.2	26 49.7	16 57.3	23R 32.2	16R 10.0	2R 47.9	2R 20.7
3 M	4 47 32	12 50 48	10♐09 32	17 31 24	18 05.4	7 48.5	27 26.2	26 01.4	27 15.2	16 57.6	23 28.1	16 07.5	2 46.4	2 19.5
4 Tu	4 51 29	13 48 14	24 49 47	2♑03 51	18 02.6	9 58.8	28 19.3	26 41.7	27 40.7	16R 57.8	23 24.0	16 05.0	2 44.9	2 18.4
5 W	4 55 26	14 45 39	9♑12 52	16 16 16	17 58.9	12 09.9	29 12.9	27 21.8	28 06.3	16 57.8	23 20.0	16 02.6	2 43.4	2 17.2
6 Th	4 59 22	15 43 03	23 13 38	0♒04 39	17 55.0	14 21.7	0♉07.1	28 02.0	28 31.9	16 57.6	23 16.0	16 00.1	2 41.9	2 16.1
7 F	5 03 19	16 40 27	6♒49 11	13 27 17	17 51.4	16 33.7	1 01.8	28 42.1	28 57.6	16 57.2	23 12.1	15 57.6	2 40.4	2 15.0
8 Sa	5 07 15	17 37 50	19 59 04	26 24 47	17 48.5	18 45.8	1 57.0	29 22.2	29 23.2	16 56.6	23 08.2	15 55.2	2 38.8	2 14.0
9 Su	5 11 12	18 35 12	2♓44 50	8♓59 38	17D 46.8	20 57.7	2 52.6	0♋02.2	29 48.9	16 55.8	23 04.4	15 52.7	2 37.3	2 12.9
10 M	5 15 08	19 32 33	15 09 43	21 15 38	17 46.3	23 09.1	3 48.8	0 42.2	0♋14.6	16 54.9	23 00.6	15 50.2	2 35.7	2 11.9
11 Tu	5 19 05	20 29 54	27 17 57	3♈17 20	17 47.0	25 19.7	4 45.4	1 22.2	0 40.3	16 53.7	22 56.8	15 47.8	2 34.1	2 10.9
12 W	5 23 02	21 27 15	9♈14 22	15 09 41	17 48.5	27 29.4	5 42.4	2 02.2	1 06.1	16 52.3	22 53.1	15 45.3	2 32.6	2 10.0
13 Th	5 26 58	22 24 35	21 03 53	26 57 35	17 50.2	29 37.8	6 39.9	2 42.1	1 31.9	16 50.8	22 49.5	15 42.9	2 31.0	2 09.0
14 F	5 30 55	23 21 55	2♉51 20	8♉45 40	17R 51.6	1♋44.8	7 37.8	3 22.0	1 57.7	16 49.1	22 46.0	15 40.4	2 29.4	2 08.1
15 Sa	5 34 51	24 19 15	14 41 06	20 38 04	17 51.9	3 50.2	8 36.0	4 01.8	2 23.5	16 47.1	22 42.5	15 38.0	2 27.8	2 07.3
16 Su	5 38 48	25 16 33	26 37 01	2♊38 17	17 50.8	5 53.9	9 34.7	4 41.7	2 49.3	16 45.0	22 39.0	15 35.6	2 26.2	2 06.4
17 M	5 42 44	26 13 52	8♊42 11	14 49 00	17 47.9	7 55.7	10 33.7	5 21.4	3 15.2	16 42.7	22 35.7	15 33.1	2 24.6	2 05.6
18 Tu	5 46 41	27 11 10	20 58 56	27 12 09	17 43.3	9 55.5	11 33.0	6 01.2	3 41.1	16 40.2	22 32.4	15 30.7	2 23.0	2 04.8
19 W	5 50 37	28 08 28	3♋28 46	9♋48 50	17 37.2	11 53.3	12 32.7	6 41.0	4 07.0	16 37.6	22 29.1	15 28.3	2 21.4	2 04.1
20 Th	5 54 34	29 05 45	16 12 23	22 39 25	17 30.3	13 49.0	13 32.7	7 20.7	4 32.9	16 34.7	22 26.0	15 26.0	2 19.8	2 03.4
21 F	5 58 31	0♋03 01	29 09 53	5♌43 44	17 23.2	15 42.5	14 33.1	8 00.3	4 58.9	16 31.7	22 22.9	15 23.6	2 18.1	2 02.7
22 Sa	6 02 27	1 00 17	12♌20 53	19 01 17	17 16.9	17 33.9	15 33.7	8 40.0	5 24.8	16 28.5	22 19.9	15 21.2	2 16.5	2 02.0
23 Su	6 06 24	1 57 32	25 44 49	2♍31 26	17 11.9	19 23.0	16 34.7	9 19.6	5 50.8	16 25.1	22 16.9	15 18.9	2 14.9	2 01.4
24 M	6 10 20	2 54 46	9♍21 03	16 13 37	17 08.8	21 09.9	17 35.9	9 59.2	6 16.8	16 21.5	22 14.1	15 16.6	2 13.3	2 00.8
25 Tu	6 14 17	3 52 00	23 09 03	0♎07 17	17D 07.5	22 54.5	18 37.4	10 38.7	6 42.7	16 17.8	22 11.3	15 14.3	2 11.7	2 00.2
26 W	6 18 13	4 49 13	7♎08 14	14 11 48	17 07.8	24 36.9	19 39.2	11 18.2	7 08.8	16 13.9	22 08.6	15 12.0	2 10.0	1 59.6
27 Th	6 22 10	5 46 26	21 17 52	28 26 14	17 08.8	26 17.0	20 41.2	11 57.7	7 34.8	16 09.8	22 05.9	15 09.7	2 08.4	1 59.1
28 F	6 26 06	6 43 38	5♏36 40	12♏48 51	17R 09.6	27 54.8	21 43.5	12 37.2	8 00.8	16 05.5	22 03.4	15 07.5	2 06.8	1 58.7
29 Sa	6 30 03	7 40 50	20 02 23	27 16 50	17 09.3	29 30.3	22 46.1	13 16.6	8 26.8	16 01.1	22 00.9	15 05.3	2 05.2	1 58.2
30 Su	6 34 00	8 38 02	4♐31 38	11♐46 11	17 07.0	1♌03.6	23 48.9	13 56.0	8 52.9	15 56.5	21 58.5	15 03.1	2 03.6	1 57.8

Astro Data (Dy Hr Mn)

☽0S 2 10:10
☽0N 15 14:30
♃✶♅ 21 15:10
☽0S 29 18:50

♃R 4 22:24
☽0N 11 21:05
☽0S 26 0:48

Planet Ingress (Dy Hr Mn)

☿ ♉ 14 2:10
☉ ♊ 21 2:43
☿ ♊ 30 19:44

♀ ♉ 6 8:53
♂ ♋ 9 10:40
⚳ ♋ 9 22:23
☿ ♋ 13 16:11
☉ ♋ 21 10:44
☿ ♌ 29 19:34

Last Aspect / ☽ Ingress (Dy Hr Mn)

Last Aspect		☽ Ingress
1 14:39	♄ ✶	♎ 1 21:22
3 1:09	♅ ✶	♏ 3 21:17
5 13:52	♄ ☌	♐ 5 20:56
7 6:38	☿ △	♑ 7 22:11
9 18:08	♄ ✶	♒ 10 2:38
12 5:42	☿ ✶	♓ 12 10:56
14 12:12	♄ △	♈ 14 22:25
16 8:36	♅ △	♉ 17 11:23
19 21:41	☉ ☌	♊ 20 0:01
21 10:07	♂ ☌	♋ 22 11:05
24 9:05	♄ △	♌ 24 19:54
26 15:31	♄ □	♍ 27 2:06
28 23:17	☿ △	♎ 29 5:41
30 21:55	♀ ☍	♏ 31 7:07

Last Aspect		☽ Ingress
1 21:12	♄ ☌	♐ 2 7:33
4 5:22	♀ △	♑ 4 8:34
6 0:08	♄ ✶	♒ 6 11:52
8 17:53	♂ △	♓ 8 18:46
10 16:34	☿ □	♈ 11 5:24
13 1:55	☉ ✶	♉ 13 18:11
15 16:09	♄ ☍	♊ 16 6:45
18 11:58	☉ ☌	♋ 18 17:22
20 11:35	♄ △	♌ 21 1:32
22 17:54	♄ □	♍ 23 7:32
24 22:23	♄ ✶	♎ 25 11:48
27 7:55	☿ □	♏ 27 14:37
29 16:08	☿ △	♐ 29 16:30

☽ Phases & Eclipses (Dy Hr Mn)

4 19:53 ○ 14♏17
4 19:56 ☍ T 1.237
11 17:34 ☾ 20♒57
19 21:41 ● 28♉50
19 21:28:42 ● P 0.841
27 12:56 ☽ 6♍11

3 3:50 ○ 12♐31
10 8:19 ☾ 19♓24
18 11:58 ● 27♊11
25 18:53 ☽ 4♎08

Astro Data

1 May 1985
Julian Day # 31167
SVP 5♓28'06"
GC 26♐38.1 ⚴ 26♈04.0
Eris 15♈59.4 ⚵ 28♍11.4R
⚷ 6♊37.1 ⚶ 25♎41.1R
☽ Mean ☊ 18♉46.0

1 June 1985
Julian Day # 31198
SVP 5♓28'02"
GC 26♐38.1 ⚴ 9♉12.8
Eris 16♈15.6 ⚵ 27♍58.1
⚷ 8♊59.5 ⚶ 21♎48.2R
☽ Mean ☊ 17♉07.5

July 1985 — LONGITUDE

Day	Sid.Time	☉	0 hr ☽	Noon ☽	True ☊	☿	♀	♂	⚳	♃	♄	♅	♆	♇
1 M	6 37 56	9♋35 13	18♐59 47	26♐11 44	17♉02.6	2♌34.5	24♉51.9	14♋35.4	9♋19.0	15♒51.8	21♏56.2	15♐00.9	2♑02.0	1♏57.4
2 Tu	6 41 53	10 32 24	3♑21 19	10♑27 49	16R55.9	4 03.1	25 55.2	15 14.7	9 45.0	15R46.9	21R54.0	14R58.7	2R00.4	1R57.1
3 W	6 45 49	11 29 35	17 30 33	24 28 56	16 47.7	5 29.4	26 58.8	15 54.0	10 11.1	15 41.9	21 51.9	14 56.6	1 58.8	1 56.8
4 Th	6 49 46	12 26 46	1♒22 26	8♒10 40	16 38.7	6 53.3	28 02.5	16 33.3	10 37.2	15 36.7	21 49.8	14 54.5	1 57.2	1 56.5
5 F	6 53 42	13 23 57	14 53 21	21 30 19	16 30.0	8 14.7	29 06.5	17 12.6	11 03.3	15 31.3	21 47.9	14 52.4	1 55.6	1 56.3
6 Sa	6 57 39	14 21 08	28 01 34	4♓27 11	16 22.4	9 33.8	0♊10.7	17 51.8	11 29.4	15 25.8	21 46.0	14 50.4	1 54.1	1 56.0
7 Su	7 01 36	15 18 19	10♓47 24	17 02 32	16 16.7	10 50.3	1 15.0	18 31.0	11 55.5	15 20.2	21 44.2	14 48.4	1 52.5	1 55.9
8 M	7 05 32	16 15 31	23 13 01	29 19 18	16 13.1	12 04.3	2 19.6	19 10.2	12 21.7	15 14.4	21 42.5	14 46.4	1 50.9	1 55.7
9 Tu	7 09 29	17 12 43	5♈21 58	11♈21 36	16D11.5	13 15.7	3 24.4	19 49.4	12 47.8	15 08.5	21 40.9	14 44.4	1 49.4	1 55.6
10 W	7 13 25	18 09 56	17 18 51	23 14 23	16 11.4	14 24.4	4 29.4	20 28.5	13 13.9	15 02.5	21 39.4	14 42.5	1 47.8	1 55.5
11 Th	7 17 22	19 07 09	29 08 50	5♉02 55	16R12.0	15 30.4	5 34.6	21 07.6	13 40.1	14 56.3	21 38.0	14 40.6	1 46.3	1D55.5
12 F	7 21 18	20 04 22	10♉57 16	16 52 32	16 12.4	16 33.5	6 40.0	21 46.7	14 06.2	14 50.0	21 36.6	14 38.7	1 44.8	1 55.5
13 Sa	7 25 15	21 01 36	22 49 20	28 48 17	16 11.6	17 33.8	7 45.5	22 25.8	14 32.4	14 43.6	21 35.4	14 36.9	1 43.3	1 55.5
14 Su	7 29 11	21 58 51	4♊49 52	10♊54 36	16 08.8	18 31.0	8 51.2	23 04.8	14 58.6	14 37.0	21 34.3	14 35.1	1 41.8	1 55.5
15 M	7 33 08	22 56 06	17 02 54	23 15 07	16 03.6	19 25.1	9 57.1	23 43.9	15 24.7	14 30.4	21 33.2	14 33.3	1 40.3	1 55.6
16 Tu	7 37 05	23 53 22	29 31 30	5♋52 14	15 56.0	20 15.9	11 03.2	24 22.9	15 50.9	14 23.6	21 32.3	14 31.6	1 38.8	1 55.8
17 W	7 41 01	24 50 38	12♋17 26	18 47 06	15 46.2	21 03.3	12 09.4	25 01.8	16 17.1	14 16.8	21 31.4	14 29.9	1 37.3	1 55.9
18 Th	7 44 58	25 47 54	25 21 08	1♌59 22	15 35.1	21 47.2	13 15.8	25 40.8	16 43.3	14 09.8	21 30.7	14 28.3	1 35.9	1 56.1
19 F	7 48 54	26 45 11	8♌41 35	15 27 27	15 23.7	22 27.4	14 22.3	26 19.7	17 09.4	14 02.8	21 30.0	14 26.7	1 34.5	1 56.3
20 Sa	7 52 51	27 42 28	22 16 38	29 08 45	15 13.3	23 03.9	15 29.0	26 58.6	17 35.6	13 55.7	21 29.4	14 25.1	1 33.0	1 56.6
21 Su	7 56 47	28 39 46	6♍03 24	13♍00 12	15 04.9	23 36.3	16 35.8	27 37.5	18 01.8	13 48.4	21 29.0	14 23.5	1 31.6	1 56.9
22 M	8 00 44	29 37 04	19 58 47	26 58 48	14 58.9	24 04.6	17 42.7	28 16.4	18 28.0	13 41.1	21 28.6	14 22.0	1 30.3	1 57.2
23 Tu	8 04 40	0♌34 22	3♎59 59	11♎02 04	14 55.6	24 28.6	18 49.8	28 55.2	18 54.1	13 33.8	21 28.3	14 20.6	1 28.9	1 57.6
24 W	8 08 37	1 31 40	18 04 51	25 08 09	14D54.4	24 48.1	19 57.0	29 34.0	19 20.3	13 26.3	21 28.1	14 19.1	1 27.5	1 58.0
25 Th	8 12 34	2 28 59	2♏11 51	9♏15 49	14R54.3	25 02.9	21 04.4	0♌12.8	19 46.4	13 18.9	21D28.1	14 17.8	1 26.2	1 58.4
26 F	8 16 30	3 26 18	16 19 55	23 24 03	14 54.2	25 13.1	22 11.9	0 51.6	20 12.6	13 11.3	21 28.1	14 16.4	1 24.9	1 58.9
27 Sa	8 20 27	4 23 38	0♐28 01	7♐31 39	14 52.8	25R18.2	23 19.6	1 30.3	20 38.7	13 03.7	21 28.2	14 15.1	1 23.6	1 59.4
28 Su	8 24 23	5 20 58	14 34 42	21 36 52	14 49.1	25 18.4	24 27.3	2 09.1	21 04.9	12 56.1	21 28.4	14 13.9	1 22.3	1 59.9
29 M	8 28 20	6 18 19	28 37 49	5♑37 08	14 42.6	25 13.5	25 35.2	2 47.8	21 31.0	12 48.4	21 28.7	14 12.7	1 21.0	2 00.5
30 Tu	8 32 16	7 15 40	12♑34 24	19 29 10	14 33.5	25 03.5	26 43.2	3 26.5	21 57.1	12 40.7	21 29.1	14 11.5	1 19.8	2 01.1
31 W	8 36 13	8 13 02	26 20 59	3♒09 24	14 22.2	24 48.3	27 51.4	4 05.1	22 23.2	12 32.9	21 29.6	14 10.4	1 18.6	2 01.7

August 1985 — LONGITUDE

Day	Sid.Time	☉	0 hr ☽	Noon ☽	True ☊	☿	♀	♂	⚳	♃	♄	♅	♆	♇
1 Th	8 40 09	9♌10 25	9♒54 01	16♒34 29	14♉10.0	24♌28.1	28♊59.7	4♌43.8	22♋49.4	12♒25.2	21♏30.2	14♐09.3	1♑17.4	2♏02.4
2 F	8 44 06	10 07 48	23 10 32	29 41 59	13R57.9	24R03.0	0♋08.1	5 22.4	23 15.5	12R17.4	21 30.9	14R08.3	1R16.2	2 03.1
3 Sa	8 48 03	11 05 13	6♓08 43	12♓30 45	13 47.1	23 33.2	1 16.6	6 01.0	23 41.6	12 09.6	21 31.7	14 07.3	1 15.1	2 03.9
4 Su	8 51 59	12 02 38	18 48 11	25 01 12	13 38.4	22 59.1	2 25.3	6 39.6	24 07.6	12 01.8	21 32.6	14 06.4	1 13.9	2 04.6
5 M	8 55 56	13 00 05	1♈10 07	7♈15 17	13 32.3	22 21.0	3 34.0	7 18.2	24 33.7	11 54.0	21 33.6	14 05.5	1 12.8	2 05.4
6 Tu	8 59 52	13 57 33	13 17 09	19 16 14	13 28.8	21 39.4	4 42.9	7 56.7	24 59.8	11 46.2	21 34.7	14 04.6	1 11.7	2 06.3
7 W	9 03 49	14 55 02	25 13 07	1♉08 24	13 27.3	20 55.1	5 51.9	8 35.3	25 25.8	11 38.4	21 35.9	14 03.8	1 10.7	2 07.1
8 Th	9 07 45	15 52 33	7♉02 43	12 56 46	13 27.0	20 08.5	7 01.0	9 13.8	25 51.9	11 30.6	21 37.1	14 03.1	1 09.6	2 08.0
9 F	9 11 42	16 50 05	18 51 14	24 46 47	13 26.9	19 20.7	8 10.3	9 52.3	26 17.9	11 22.9	21 38.5	14 02.4	1 08.6	2 09.0
10 Sa	9 15 38	17 47 38	0♊44 07	6♊43 54	13 25.9	18 32.3	9 19.6	10 30.8	26 43.9	11 15.1	21 40.0	14 01.7	1 07.6	2 09.9
11 Su	9 19 35	18 45 13	12 46 46	18 53 19	13 23.1	17 44.3	10 29.1	11 09.3	27 09.9	11 07.5	21 41.5	14 01.1	1 06.6	2 10.9
12 M	9 23 32	19 42 49	25 04 05	1♋19 34	13 17.8	16 57.7	11 38.6	11 47.7	27 35.9	10 59.8	21 43.2	14 00.6	1 05.7	2 11.9
13 Tu	9 27 28	20 40 26	7♋40 07	14 06 02	13 10.0	16 13.3	12 48.3	12 26.2	28 01.9	10 52.2	21 45.0	14 00.1	1 04.8	2 13.0
14 W	9 31 25	21 38 05	20 37 30	27 14 34	12 59.9	15 32.0	13 58.1	13 04.6	28 27.9	10 44.6	21 46.8	13 59.6	1 03.9	2 14.1
15 Th	9 35 21	22 35 46	3♌57 10	10♌45 07	12 48.4	14 54.8	15 07.9	13 43.0	28 53.8	10 37.1	21 48.8	13 59.2	1 03.0	2 15.2
16 F	9 39 18	23 33 27	17 38 02	24 35 32	12 36.5	14 22.4	16 17.9	14 21.4	29 19.7	10 29.7	21 50.8	13 58.8	1 02.2	2 16.4
17 Sa	9 43 14	24 31 10	1♍37 01	8♍41 52	12 25.5	13 55.5	17 28.0	14 59.8	29 45.7	10 22.3	21 52.9	13 58.5	1 01.4	2 17.6
18 Su	9 47 11	25 28 54	15 49 25	22 58 57	12 16.5	13 34.7	18 38.1	15 38.2	0♌11.5	10 15.0	21 55.1	13 58.3	1 00.6	2 18.8
19 M	9 51 07	26 26 39	0♎09 47	7♎21 15	12 10.2	13 20.6	19 48.4	16 16.5	0 37.4	10 07.7	21 57.5	13 58.1	0 59.8	2 20.0
20 Tu	9 55 04	27 24 25	14 32 44	21 43 43	12 06.6	13D13.6	20 58.7	16 54.8	1 03.2	10 00.6	21 59.9	13 57.9	0 59.1	2 21.3
21 W	9 59 01	28 22 12	28 53 45	6♏02 27	12D05.3	13 14.0	22 09.2	17 33.2	1 29.0	9 53.5	22 02.4	13 57.8	0 58.4	2 22.6
22 Th	10 02 57	29 20 01	13♏09 34	20 14 53	12R05.3	13 22.0	23 19.7	18 11.5	1 54.8	9 46.6	22 04.9	13D57.7	0 57.8	2 23.9
23 F	10 06 54	0♍17 51	27 18 15	4♐19 35	12 05.4	13 37.8	24 30.3	18 49.8	2 20.6	9 39.7	22 07.6	13 57.7	0 57.1	2 25.3
24 Sa	10 10 50	1 15 42	11♐18 49	18 15 53	12 04.3	14 01.4	25 41.0	19 28.0	2 46.3	9 32.9	22 10.4	13 57.8	0 56.5	2 26.7
25 Su	10 14 47	2 13 34	25 10 45	2♑03 22	12 01.2	14 32.8	26 51.8	20 06.3	3 12.0	9 26.3	22 13.3	13 57.9	0 55.9	2 28.1
26 M	10 18 43	3 11 27	8♑53 38	15 41 27	11 55.4	15 11.9	28 02.7	20 44.5	3 37.7	9 19.8	22 16.2	13 58.1	0 55.4	2 29.6
27 Tu	10 22 40	4 09 22	22 26 42	29 09 14	11 47.2	15 58.6	29 13.7	21 22.7	4 03.4	9 13.3	22 19.2	13 58.3	0 54.9	2 31.1
28 W	10 26 36	5 07 18	5♒48 52	12♒25 27	11 37.0	16 52.6	0♌24.8	22 01.0	4 29.0	9 07.0	22 22.3	13 58.5	0 54.4	2 32.6
29 Th	10 30 33	6 05 15	18 58 48	25 28 45	11 25.8	17 53.6	1 35.9	22 39.1	4 54.6	9 00.9	22 25.5	13 58.8	0 53.9	2 34.1
30 F	10 34 30	7 03 14	1♓55 12	8♓18 02	11 14.8	19 01.3	2 47.1	23 17.3	5 20.2	8 54.8	22 28.8	13 59.2	0 53.5	2 35.7
31 Sa	10 38 26	8 01 15	14 37 13	20 52 45	11 04.8	20 15.4	3 58.5	23 55.5	5 45.7	8 48.9	22 32.2	13 59.6	0 53.1	2 37.3

Astro Data

	Dy Hr Mn
♆⚹♇	5 0:45
☽0N	9 4:05
♇ D	12 8:41
♃⚹♅	14 21:33
☽0S	23 5:24
♄ D	25 19:34
☿ R	28 0:51
☽0N	5 11:25
☽0S	19 11:01
☿ D	20 22:49
♅ D	23 0:18

Planet Ingress

	Dy Hr Mn
♀ ♊	6 8:01
☉ ♌	22 21:36
♂ ♌	25 4:04
♀ ♋	2 9:10
⚳ ♌	18 1:18
☉ ♍	23 4:36
♀ ♌	28 3:39

Last Aspect / ☽ Ingress (July)

Last Aspect Dy Hr Mn		☽ Ingress Dy Hr Mn
30 18:53	♃ ⚹	♑ 1 18:22
3 16:42	♀ △	♒ 3 21:36
6 3:16	♀ □	♓ 6 3:40
7 21:05	♄ △	♈ 8 13:20
10 6:04	♂ □	♉ 11 1:44
12 22:28	♂ ⚹	♊ 13 14:23
15 4:02	☿ ⚹	♋ 16 0:54
18 0:00	♂ ☌	♌ 18 8:25
20 0:54	☿ ☌	♍ 20 13:29
22 16:51	☉ ⚹	♎ 22 17:10
24 19:54	♂ □	♏ 24 20:16
26 15:07	☿ □	♐ 26 23:12
28 18:17	☿ △	♑ 29 2:21
30 15:29	♄ ⚹	♒ 31 6:25

Last Aspect / ☽ Ingress (August)

Last Aspect Dy Hr Mn		☽ Ingress Dy Hr Mn
2 1:56	☿ ☍	♓ 2 12:33
4 5:16	♄ △	♈ 4 21:43
6 16:32	☿ △	♉ 7 9:41
9 5:38	♄ ☍	♊ 9 22:31
11 11:43	☉ ⚹	♋ 12 9:28
14 2:05	♄ △	♌ 14 16:57
16 10:05	☉ ☌	♍ 16 21:15
18 10:13	♄ ⚹	♎ 18 23:44
20 22:11	☉ ⚹	♏ 21 1:51
22 17:42	♀ △	♐ 23 4:36
24 14:11	♂ △	♑ 25 8:24
27 12:09	♀ ☍	♒ 27 13:31
29 6:30	♂ ☍	♓ 29 20:25

☽ Phases & Eclipses

Dy Hr Mn	
2 12:08	○ 10♑33
10 0:49	☾ 17♈43
17 23:56	● 25♋19
24 23:39	☽ 1♏59
31 21:41	○ 8♒36
8 18:29	☾ 16♉08
16 10:05	● 23♌29
23 4:36	☽ 0♐00
30 9:27	○ 6♓57

Astro Data

1 July 1985
Julian Day # 31228
SVP 5♓27'56"
GC 26♐38.2 ⚵ 22♉14.9
Eris 16♈23.7 ⚴ 2♎12.7
⚷ 11♊16.8 ⚶ 25♎08.0
☽ Mean ☊ 15♉32.2

1 August 1985
Julian Day # 31259
SVP 5♓27'50"
GC 26♐38.3 ⚵ 5♊47.5
Eris 16♈22.4R ⚴ 9♎34.7
⚷ 13♊14.7 ⚶ 4♏08.0
☽ Mean ☊ 13♉53.7

LONGITUDE — September 1985

Day	Sid.Time	☉	0 hr ☽	Noon ☽	True ☊	☿	♀	♂	⚳	♃	♄	♅	♆	♇
1 Su	10 42 23	8♍59 17	27♓04 43	3♈13 14	10♉56.8	21♌35.3	5♌09.9	24♌33.7	6♌11.2	8♒43.1	22♏35.7	14♐00.0	0♑52.7	2♏38.9
2 M	10 46 19	9 57 21	9♈18 31	15 20 51	10R51.2	23 00.7	6 21.4	25 11.8	6 36.7	8R37.4	22 39.2	14 00.5	0R52.4	2 40.5
3 Tu	10 50 16	10 55 26	21 20 32	27 17 59	10 48.1	24 31.1	7 32.9	25 49.9	7 02.1	8 31.9	22 42.8	14 01.1	0 52.1	2 42.2
4 W	10 54 12	11 53 34	3♉13 39	9♉08 03	10D47.1	26 05.9	8 44.6	26 28.1	7 27.5	8 26.6	22 46.5	14 01.7	0 51.8	2 43.9
5 Th	10 58 09	12 51 44	15 01 43	20 55 15	10 47.5	27 44.6	9 56.4	27 06.2	7 52.9	8 21.4	22 50.3	14 02.4	0 51.6	2 45.6
6 F	11 02 05	13 49 55	26 49 17	2♊44 28	10 48.4	29 26.8	11 08.2	27 44.3	8 18.2	8 16.3	22 54.1	14 03.1	0 51.4	2 47.3
7 Sa	11 06 02	14 48 09	8♊41 26	14 40 54	10R48.9	1♍11.9	12 20.1	28 22.4	8 43.5	8 11.4	22 58.1	14 03.9	0 51.2	2 49.1
8 Su	11 09 59	15 46 24	20 43 31	26 49 55	10 48.2	2 59.4	13 32.1	29 00.5	9 08.8	8 06.7	23 02.1	14 04.7	0 51.1	2 50.9
9 M	11 13 55	16 44 42	3♋00 45	9♋16 34	10 45.6	4 48.9	14 44.2	29 38.5	9 34.0	8 02.1	23 06.2	14 05.6	0 51.0	2 52.7
10 Tu	11 17 52	17 43 02	15 37 53	22 05 09	10 41.0	6 39.9	15 56.4	0♍16.6	9 59.2	7 57.7	23 10.4	14 06.5	0 50.9	2 54.5
11 W	11 21 48	18 41 24	28 38 40	5♌18 38	10 34.5	8 32.1	17 08.6	0 54.7	10 24.3	7 53.5	23 14.6	14 07.5	0D50.8	2 56.4
12 Th	11 25 45	19 39 48	12♌05 09	18 58 06	10 26.7	10 25.1	18 20.9	1 32.7	10 49.4	7 49.5	23 18.9	14 08.5	0 50.8	2 58.3
13 F	11 29 41	20 38 13	25 57 15	3♍02 12	10 18.5	12 18.6	19 33.3	2 10.8	11 14.5	7 45.6	23 23.3	14 09.6	0 50.8	3 00.2
14 Sa	11 33 38	21 36 41	10♍12 23	17 27 05	10 10.8	14 12.3	20 45.7	2 48.8	11 39.5	7 41.9	23 27.8	14 10.7	0 50.9	3 02.1
15 Su	11 37 34	22 35 11	24 45 29	2♎06 39	10 04.6	16 06.0	21 58.2	3 26.8	12 04.4	7 38.3	23 32.4	14 11.8	0 51.0	3 04.1
16 M	11 41 31	23 33 42	9♎29 40	16 53 32	10 00.4	17 59.6	23 10.8	4 04.8	12 29.3	7 35.0	23 37.0	14 13.1	0 51.1	3 06.0
17 Tu	11 45 27	24 32 15	24 17 19	1♏40 08	9D58.5	19 52.7	24 23.5	4 42.8	12 54.2	7 31.8	23 41.7	14 14.3	0 51.2	3 08.0
18 W	11 49 24	25 30 50	9♏01 12	16 19 50	9 58.3	21 45.4	25 36.2	5 20.8	13 19.0	7 28.8	23 46.4	14 15.7	0 51.4	3 10.0
19 Th	11 53 21	26 29 27	23 35 28	0♐47 41	9 59.3	23 37.4	26 49.0	5 58.7	13 43.7	7 26.0	23 51.3	14 17.0	0 51.7	3 12.1
20 F	11 57 17	27 28 05	7♐56 08	15 00 37	10R00.6	25 28.7	28 01.9	6 36.7	14 08.4	7 23.4	23 56.2	14 18.5	0 51.9	3 14.1
21 Sa	12 01 14	28 26 45	22 01 00	28 57 16	10 01.1	27 19.3	29 14.8	7 14.7	14 33.1	7 21.0	24 01.1	14 19.9	0 52.2	3 16.2
22 Su	12 05 10	29 25 27	5♑49 25	12♑37 31	10 00.3	29 09.0	0♍27.7	7 52.6	14 57.7	7 18.8	24 06.2	14 21.4	0 52.5	3 18.3
23 M	12 09 07	0♎24 10	19 21 39	26 01 57	9 57.7	0♎57.9	1 40.8	8 30.5	15 22.2	7 16.8	24 11.3	14 23.0	0 52.9	3 20.4
24 Tu	12 13 03	1 22 55	2♒38 31	9♒11 29	9 53.4	2 45.8	2 53.9	9 08.4	15 46.6	7 15.0	24 16.4	14 24.6	0 53.3	3 22.5
25 W	12 17 00	2 21 42	15 40 57	22 07 03	9 47.7	4 32.9	4 07.1	9 46.3	16 11.0	7 13.3	24 21.7	14 26.3	0 53.7	3 24.6
26 Th	12 20 56	3 20 30	28 29 52	4♓49 31	9 41.4	6 19.0	5 20.3	10 24.2	16 35.4	7 11.9	24 26.9	14 28.0	0 54.1	3 26.8
27 F	12 24 53	4 19 20	11♓06 05	17 19 40	9 35.0	8 04.2	6 33.6	11 02.1	16 59.6	7 10.6	24 32.3	14 29.7	0 54.6	3 29.0
28 Sa	12 28 50	5 18 12	23 30 23	29 38 21	9 29.4	9 48.5	7 46.9	11 40.0	17 23.8	7 09.6	24 37.7	14 31.5	0 55.1	3 31.2
29 Su	12 32 46	6 17 06	5♈43 43	11♈46 38	9 25.0	11 31.9	9 00.3	12 17.8	17 48.0	7 08.7	24 43.1	14 33.4	0 55.7	3 33.4
30 M	12 36 43	7 16 03	17 47 18	23 45 56	9 22.2	13 14.4	10 13.8	12 55.7	18 12.0	7 08.1	24 48.7	14 35.3	0 56.2	3 35.6

LONGITUDE — October 1985

Day	Sid.Time	☉	0 hr ☽	Noon ☽	True ☊	☿	♀	♂	⚳	♃	♄	♅	♆	♇
1 Tu	12 40 39	8♎15 01	29♈42 49	5♉38 14	9♉21.0	14♎56.0	11♍27.3	13♍33.5	18♌36.0	7♒07.6	24♏54.3	14♐37.2	0♑56.8	3♏37.8
2 W	12 44 36	9 14 01	11♉32 31	17 26 04	9D21.2	16 36.7	12 40.9	14 11.4	19 00.0	7D07.3	24 59.9	14 39.2	0 57.5	3 40.0
3 Th	12 48 32	10 13 04	23 19 17	29 12 38	9 22.5	18 16.6	13 54.5	14 49.2	19 23.8	7 07.3	25 05.6	14 41.2	0 58.2	3 42.3
4 F	12 52 29	11 12 09	5♊06 37	11♊01 46	9 24.3	19 55.6	15 08.2	15 27.1	19 47.6	7 07.4	25 11.3	14 43.2	0 58.9	3 44.6
5 Sa	12 56 25	12 11 16	16 58 37	22 57 47	9 26.0	21 33.9	16 22.0	16 04.9	20 11.4	7 07.7	25 17.1	14 45.4	0 59.6	3 46.9
6 Su	13 00 22	13 10 26	28 59 50	5♋05 22	9R27.1	23 11.3	17 35.8	16 42.7	20 35.0	7 08.3	25 23.0	14 47.5	1 00.4	3 49.2
7 M	13 04 19	14 09 38	11♋15 01	17 29 22	9 27.4	24 47.9	18 49.7	17 20.5	20 58.6	7 09.0	25 28.9	14 49.7	1 01.2	3 51.5
8 Tu	13 08 15	15 08 52	23 48 57	0♌14 18	9 26.5	26 23.8	20 03.6	17 58.3	21 22.0	7 09.9	25 34.9	14 51.9	1 02.0	3 53.8
9 W	13 12 12	16 08 08	6♌45 51	13 23 59	9 24.6	27 58.9	21 17.6	18 36.1	21 45.4	7 11.0	25 40.9	14 54.2	1 02.9	3 56.1
10 Th	13 16 08	17 07 27	20 08 56	27 00 49	9 21.9	29 33.3	22 31.6	19 13.9	22 08.8	7 12.3	25 46.9	14 56.5	1 03.8	3 58.5
11 F	13 20 05	18 06 48	3♍59 38	11♍05 11	9 18.9	1♏06.9	23 45.7	19 51.7	22 32.0	7 13.8	25 53.0	14 58.9	1 04.7	4 00.8
12 Sa	13 24 01	19 06 11	18 17 06	25 34 50	9 16.0	2 39.8	24 59.8	20 29.4	22 55.1	7 15.5	25 59.2	15 01.3	1 05.7	4 03.2
13 Su	13 27 58	20 05 36	2♎57 40	10♎24 45	9 13.7	4 12.1	26 14.0	21 07.2	23 18.2	7 17.4	26 05.4	15 03.7	1 06.7	4 05.5
14 M	13 31 54	21 05 04	17 55 04	25 27 31	9D12.4	5 43.6	27 28.2	21 45.0	23 41.1	7 19.5	26 11.6	15 06.2	1 07.7	4 07.9
15 Tu	13 35 51	22 04 33	3♏00 57	10♏34 13	9 12.0	7 14.5	28 42.4	22 22.7	24 04.0	7 21.8	26 17.9	15 08.7	1 08.8	4 10.3
16 W	13 39 48	23 04 05	18 06 11	25 35 48	9 12.4	8 44.6	29 56.7	23 00.4	24 26.7	7 24.3	26 24.3	15 11.3	1 09.9	4 12.7
17 Th	13 43 44	24 03 38	3♐02 09	10♐24 24	9 13.4	10 14.1	1♎11.1	23 38.2	24 49.4	7 27.0	26 30.6	15 13.9	1 11.0	4 15.1
18 F	13 47 41	25 03 13	17 41 56	24 54 12	9 14.6	11 42.9	2 25.4	24 15.9	25 11.9	7 29.9	26 37.1	15 16.5	1 12.1	4 17.5
19 Sa	13 51 37	26 02 50	2♑00 54	9♑01 49	9 15.5	13 11.0	3 39.8	24 53.6	25 34.4	7 33.0	26 43.5	15 19.2	1 13.3	4 19.9
20 Su	13 55 34	27 02 29	15 56 53	22 46 08	9R16.0	14 38.4	4 54.3	25 31.3	25 56.7	7 36.2	26 50.0	15 21.9	1 14.5	4 22.3
21 M	13 59 30	28 02 09	29 29 43	6♒07 50	9 15.9	16 05.1	6 08.8	26 09.0	26 18.9	7 39.7	26 56.5	15 24.6	1 15.7	4 24.7
22 Tu	14 03 27	29 01 51	12♒40 46	19 08 49	9 15.3	17 31.0	7 23.3	26 46.7	26 41.0	7 43.3	27 03.1	15 27.4	1 17.0	4 27.1
23 W	14 07 23	0♏01 35	25 32 19	1♓51 39	9 14.3	18 56.2	8 37.9	27 24.3	27 03.0	7 47.1	27 09.7	15 30.2	1 18.3	4 29.5
24 Th	14 11 20	1 01 20	8♓07 08	14 19 09	9 13.2	20 20.5	9 52.4	28 02.0	27 24.9	7 51.1	27 16.3	15 33.1	1 19.6	4 32.0
25 F	14 15 17	2 01 07	20 28 01	26 34 05	9 12.1	21 44.1	11 07.1	28 39.6	27 46.7	7 55.3	27 23.0	15 35.9	1 21.0	4 34.4
26 Sa	14 19 13	3 00 56	2♈37 40	8♈39 03	9 11.2	23 06.8	12 21.7	29 17.3	28 08.3	7 59.6	27 29.7	15 38.8	1 22.3	4 36.8
27 Su	14 23 10	4 00 47	14 38 33	20 36 25	9 10.6	24 28.5	13 36.4	29 54.9	28 29.9	8 04.2	27 36.4	15 41.8	1 23.7	4 39.2
28 M	14 27 06	5 00 39	26 32 57	2♉28 22	9D10.3	25 49.3	14 51.1	0♎32.5	28 51.3	8 08.9	27 43.2	15 44.7	1 25.2	4 41.7
29 Tu	14 31 03	6 00 34	8♉22 58	14 17 01	9 10.3	27 09.0	16 05.9	1 10.1	29 12.6	8 13.8	27 50.0	15 47.7	1 26.6	4 44.1
30 W	14 34 59	7 00 30	20 10 46	26 04 30	9 10.4	28 27.6	17 20.7	1 47.7	29 33.7	8 18.9	27 56.8	15 50.8	1 28.1	4 46.5
31 Th	14 38 56	8 00 29	1♊58 32	7♊53 11	9 10.6	29 44.9	18 35.5	2 25.3	29 54.7	8 24.1	28 03.6	15 53.8	1 29.6	4 48.9

Astro Data

	Dy Hr Mn
☽ 0N	1 18:43
♆ D	12 9:17
☽ 0S	15 19:15
☉ 0S	23 2:07
☿ 0S	24 15:42
☽ 0N	29 1:37
♃ D	3 8:17
☽ 0S	13 5:50
♀ 0S	19 9:52
☽ 0N	26 7:55

Planet Ingress

		Dy Hr Mn
☿	♍	6 19:39
♂	♍	10 1:31
♀	♍	22 2:53
☿	♎	22 23:13
☉	♎	23 2:07
☿	♏	10 18:50
♀	♎	16 13:04
☉	♏	23 11:22
♂	♎	27 15:16
☿	♐	31 16:44
⚳	♍	31 18:03

Last Aspect / ☽ Ingress (September)

Last Aspect Dy Hr Mn			☽ Ingress	Dy Hr Mn
31 15:13	♄	△	♈	1 5:42
3 8:52	♂	△	♉	3 17:28
6 4:12	☿	□	♊	6 6:27
8 16:28	♂	⚹	♋	8 18:10
10 14:01	♄	△	♌	11 2:27
12 19:32	♄	□	♍	13 6:52
14 21:56	♄	⚹	♎	15 8:34
16 23:07	♀	⚹	♏	17 9:17
19 4:45	♀	□	♐	19 10:40
21 12:33	♀	△	♑	21 13:49
23 8:39	♄	⚹	♒	23 19:11
25 16:14	♄	□	♓	26 2:50
28 2:07	♄	△	♈	28 12:43

Last Aspect / ☽ Ingress (October)

Last Aspect Dy Hr Mn			☽ Ingress	Dy Hr Mn
29 17:33	♅	△	♉	1 0:35
3 3:33	♄	☍	♊	3 13:36
5 8:46	☿	△	♋	6 1:59
8 3:50	☿	□	♌	8 11:33
10 16:57	☿	⚹	♍	10 17:09
12 12:40	♄	⚹	♎	12 19:12
14 4:33	☉	☌	♏	14 19:13
16 13:19	♄	☌	♐	16 19:05
18 12:16	☉	⚹	♑	18 20:35
20 20:13	☉	□	♒	21 0:54
23 8:12	☉	△	♓	23 8:27
25 16:22	♂	☍	♈	25 18:47
27 2:05	♅	△	♉	28 6:59
30 17:27	☿	☍	♊	30 19:59

☽ Phases & Eclipses

Dy Hr Mn	
7 12:16	☾ 14♊49
14 19:20	● 21♍55
21 11:03	☽ 28♐24
29 0:08	○ 5♈48
7 5:04	☾ 13♋53
14 4:33	● 20♎47
20 20:13	☽ 27♑23
28 17:38	○ 5♉15
28 17:42	• T 1.074

Astro Data

1 September 1985
Julian Day # 31290
SVP 5♓27'46"
GC 26♐38.3 ⚴ 18♊53.9
Eris 16♈11.6R ⚵ 18♎44.7
⚷ 14♊26.2 ⚶ 16♏32.0
☽ Mean ☊ 12♉15.2

1 October 1985
Julian Day # 31320
SVP 5♓27'43"
GC 26♐38.4 ⚴ 0♋04.7
Eris 15♈55.2R ⚵ 28♎34.3
⚷ 14♊36.0R ⚶ 0♐26.3
☽ Mean ☊ 10♉39.9

November 1985 — LONGITUDE

Day	Sid.Time	☉	0 hr ☽	Noon ☽	True ☊	☿	♀	♂	⚳	♃	♄	♅	♆	♇
1 F	14 42 52	9♏00 30	13♊48 47	19♊45 42	9♉10.7	1♐00.9	19♎50.4	3♎02.9	0♍15.6	8♒29.6	28♏10.5	15♐56.9	1♑31.1	4♏51.4
2 Sa	14 46 49	10 00 32	25 44 19	1♋45 02	9R 10.6	2 15.4	21 05.2	3 40.5	0 36.4	8 35.2	28 17.4	16 00.0	1 32.7	4 53.8
3 Su	14 50 46	11 00 37	7♋48 19	13 54 36	9 10.5	3 28.3	22 20.1	4 18.1	0 57.0	8 40.9	28 24.3	16 03.2	1 34.3	4 56.2
4 M	14 54 42	12 00 44	20 04 22	26 18 06	9 10.3	4 39.3	23 35.1	4 55.7	1 17.4	8 46.9	28 31.2	16 06.4	1 35.9	4 58.6
5 Tu	14 58 39	13 00 53	2♌36 16	8♌59 20	9D 10.2	5 48.3	24 50.1	5 33.2	1 37.8	8 53.0	28 38.2	16 09.6	1 37.5	5 01.1
6 W	15 02 35	14 01 04	15 27 47	22 02 00	9 10.2	6 55.1	26 05.1	6 10.8	1 57.9	8 59.2	28 45.1	16 12.8	1 39.2	5 03.5
7 Th	15 06 32	15 01 17	28 42 22	5♍29 09	9 10.5	7 59.4	27 20.1	6 48.3	2 17.9	9 05.7	28 52.1	16 16.0	1 40.8	5 05.9
8 F	15 10 28	16 01 32	12♍22 31	19 22 35	9 11.0	9 00.8	28 35.1	7 25.9	2 37.8	9 12.2	28 59.2	16 19.3	1 42.5	5 08.3
9 Sa	15 14 25	17 01 49	26 29 14	3♎42 15	9 11.7	9 59.1	29 50.2	8 03.4	2 57.5	9 19.0	29 06.2	16 22.6	1 44.3	5 10.7
10 Su	15 18 21	18 02 07	11♎01 15	18 25 38	9 12.4	10 53.8	1♏05.3	8 40.9	3 17.0	9 25.9	29 13.2	16 25.9	1 46.0	5 13.0
11 M	15 22 18	19 02 28	25 54 38	3♏27 22	9R 12.8	11 44.6	2 20.4	9 18.4	3 36.4	9 33.0	29 20.3	16 29.2	1 47.8	5 15.4
12 Tu	15 26 15	20 02 51	11♏02 45	18 39 37	9 12.7	12 30.9	3 35.6	9 55.9	3 55.6	9 40.2	29 27.4	16 32.6	1 49.6	5 17.8
13 W	15 30 11	21 03 16	26 16 43	3♐52 49	9 12.0	13 12.1	4 50.7	10 33.4	4 14.6	9 47.6	29 34.5	16 36.0	1 51.4	5 20.2
14 Th	15 34 08	22 03 42	11♐26 40	18 57 07	9 10.7	13 47.8	6 05.9	11 10.9	4 33.5	9 55.1	29 41.6	16 39.4	1 53.2	5 22.5
15 F	15 38 04	23 04 09	26 23 09	3♑43 54	9 09.0	14 17.1	7 21.1	11 48.4	4 52.1	10 02.8	29 48.7	16 42.8	1 55.1	5 24.9
16 Sa	15 42 01	24 04 38	10♑58 39	18 06 55	9 07.2	14 39.4	8 36.3	12 25.8	5 10.6	10 10.7	29 55.8	16 46.3	1 56.9	5 27.2
17 Su	15 45 57	25 05 09	25 08 21	2♒02 49	9 05.5	14 54.0	9 51.6	13 03.3	5 28.9	10 18.7	0♐02.9	16 49.7	1 58.8	5 29.5
18 M	15 49 54	26 05 40	8♒50 21	15 31 04	9D 04.4	15R 00.1	11 06.8	13 40.7	5 47.0	10 26.8	0 10.1	16 53.2	2 00.8	5 31.9
19 Tu	15 53 50	27 06 13	22 05 17	28 33 22	9 04.1	14 57.0	12 22.1	14 18.1	6 04.9	10 35.1	0 17.2	16 56.7	2 02.7	5 34.2
20 W	15 57 47	28 06 47	4♓55 44	11♓12 55	9 04.7	14 44.0	13 37.3	14 55.5	6 22.6	10 43.5	0 24.3	17 00.2	2 04.6	5 36.5
21 Th	16 01 44	29 07 22	17 25 25	23 33 48	9 05.9	14 20.7	14 52.6	15 32.9	6 40.1	10 52.1	0 31.5	17 03.7	2 06.6	5 38.7
22 F	16 05 40	0♐07 58	29 38 36	5♈40 21	9 07.5	13 46.7	16 07.9	16 10.3	6 57.4	11 00.8	0 38.6	17 07.3	2 08.6	5 41.0
23 Sa	16 09 37	1 08 35	11♈39 36	17 36 50	9 09.2	13 02.1	17 23.2	16 47.6	7 14.5	11 09.6	0 45.8	17 10.8	2 10.6	5 43.2
24 Su	16 13 33	2 09 14	23 32 32	29 27 08	9R 10.4	12 07.2	18 38.5	17 25.0	7 31.3	11 18.5	0 52.9	17 14.4	2 12.6	5 45.5
25 M	16 17 30	3 09 54	5♉21 03	11♉14 40	9 10.8	11 03.1	19 53.8	18 02.3	7 48.0	11 27.6	1 00.0	17 17.9	2 14.6	5 47.7
26 Tu	16 21 26	4 10 35	17 08 18	23 02 17	9 09.9	9 51.0	21 09.2	18 39.6	8 04.4	11 36.9	1 07.2	17 21.5	2 16.7	5 49.9
27 W	16 25 23	5 11 18	28 56 54	4♊52 25	9 07.7	8 33.0	22 24.5	19 16.9	8 20.6	11 46.2	1 14.3	17 25.1	2 18.7	5 52.1
28 Th	16 29 19	6 12 02	10♊49 04	16 47 04	9 04.1	7 11.4	23 39.9	19 54.2	8 36.6	11 55.7	1 21.4	17 28.7	2 20.8	5 54.3
29 F	16 33 16	7 12 47	22 46 38	28 47 59	8 59.5	5 48.9	24 55.3	20 31.5	8 52.4	12 05.3	1 28.6	17 32.3	2 22.9	5 56.5
30 Sa	16 37 13	8 13 34	4♋51 20	10♋56 53	8 54.2	4 28.3	26 10.6	21 08.8	9 07.9	12 15.1	1 35.7	17 36.0	2 25.0	5 58.6

December 1985 — LONGITUDE

Day	Sid.Time	☉	0 hr ☽	Noon ☽	True ☊	☿	♀	♂	⚳	♃	♄	♅	♆	♇
1 Su	16 41 09	9♐14 22	17♋04 51	23♋15 30	8♉48.9	3♐12.3	27♏26.0	21♎46.1	9♍23.2	12♒24.9	1♐42.8	17♐39.6	2♑27.1	6♏00.7
2 M	16 45 06	10 15 11	29 29 05	5♌45 51	8R 44.2	2R 03.2	28 41.4	22 23.3	9 38.2	12 34.9	1 49.9	17 43.2	2 29.2	6 02.8
3 Tu	16 49 02	11 16 02	12♌06 07	18 30 10	8 40.6	1 03.0	29 56.9	23 00.6	9 53.0	12 45.0	1 57.0	17 46.9	2 31.4	6 04.9
4 W	16 52 59	12 16 53	24 58 20	1♍30 55	8D 38.4	0 13.1	1♐12.3	23 37.8	10 07.5	12 55.2	2 04.1	17 50.5	2 33.5	6 07.0
5 Th	16 56 55	13 17 47	8♍08 15	14 50 35	8 37.9	29♏34.3	2 27.7	24 15.0	10 21.7	13 05.5	2 11.1	17 54.2	2 35.7	6 09.1
6 F	17 00 52	14 18 41	21 38 12	28 31 18	8 38.6	29 07.0	3 43.2	24 52.2	10 35.7	13 15.9	2 18.2	17 57.8	2 37.9	6 11.1
7 Sa	17 04 48	15 19 37	5♎30 00	12♎34 20	8 40.0	28D 51.0	4 58.6	25 29.4	10 49.4	13 26.5	2 25.2	18 01.5	2 40.0	6 13.1
8 Su	17 08 45	16 20 34	19 44 12	26 59 24	8R 41.4	28 46.0	6 14.1	26 06.6	11 02.9	13 37.2	2 32.2	18 05.2	2 42.2	6 15.1
9 M	17 12 42	17 21 33	4♏19 32	11♏44 02	8 41.8	28 51.3	7 29.6	26 43.7	11 16.0	13 47.9	2 39.2	18 08.8	2 44.4	6 17.1
10 Tu	17 16 38	18 22 33	19 12 14	26 43 13	8 40.5	29 06.2	8 45.1	27 20.8	11 28.9	13 58.8	2 46.2	18 12.4	2 46.6	6 19.0
11 W	17 20 35	19 23 33	4♐15 58	11♐49 22	8 37.3	29 29.8	10 00.5	27 58.0	11 41.5	14 09.8	2 53.2	18 16.1	2 48.9	6 20.9
12 Th	17 24 31	20 24 35	19 22 12	26 53 15	8 32.0	0♐01.3	11 16.0	28 35.1	11 53.8	14 20.9	3 00.1	18 19.8	2 51.1	6 22.8
13 F	17 28 28	21 25 37	4♑21 19	11♑45 17	8 25.3	0 39.9	12 31.5	29 12.2	12 05.7	14 32.1	3 07.1	18 23.5	2 53.3	6 24.7
14 Sa	17 32 24	22 26 41	19 04 11	26 17 11	8 18.0	1 24.8	13 47.0	29 49.2	12 17.4	14 43.4	3 14.0	18 27.2	2 55.6	6 26.6
15 Su	17 36 21	23 27 44	3♒23 40	10♒23 10	8 11.1	2 15.2	15 02.5	0♏26.3	12 28.8	14 54.8	3 20.8	18 30.8	2 57.8	6 28.4
16 M	17 40 18	24 28 48	17 15 28	24 00 31	8 05.5	3 10.5	16 18.0	1 03.3	12 39.8	15 06.3	3 27.7	18 34.5	3 00.1	6 30.2
17 Tu	17 44 14	25 29 53	0♓38 26	7♓09 29	8 01.6	4 10.1	17 33.5	1 40.3	12 50.5	15 17.8	3 34.5	18 38.1	3 02.3	6 32.0
18 W	17 48 11	26 30 57	13 34 05	19 52 42	7D 59.7	5 13.4	18 49.0	2 17.2	13 00.9	15 29.5	3 41.3	18 41.8	3 04.6	6 33.8
19 Th	17 52 07	27 32 02	26 05 54	2♈14 19	7 59.6	6 20.1	20 04.5	2 54.2	13 10.9	15 41.3	3 48.0	18 45.4	3 06.8	6 35.5
20 F	17 56 04	28 33 08	8♈18 35	14 19 23	8 00.6	7 29.6	21 20.0	3 31.1	13 20.7	15 53.1	3 54.8	18 49.0	3 09.1	6 37.2
21 Sa	18 00 00	29 34 13	20 17 22	26 13 12	8 01.8	8 41.6	22 35.5	4 08.0	13 30.0	16 05.1	4 01.5	18 52.6	3 11.4	6 38.9
22 Su	18 03 57	0♑35 19	2♉07 31	8♉00 56	8R 02.5	9 55.9	23 51.0	4 44.9	13 39.1	16 17.1	4 08.1	18 56.3	3 13.6	6 40.5
23 M	18 07 53	1 36 25	13 54 01	19 47 18	8 01.6	11 12.1	25 06.5	5 21.8	13 47.8	16 29.2	4 14.8	18 59.9	3 15.9	6 42.1
24 Tu	18 11 50	2 37 31	25 41 14	1♊36 18	7 58.5	12 30.0	26 22.0	5 58.6	13 56.1	16 41.4	4 21.4	19 03.5	3 18.2	6 43.7
25 W	18 15 47	3 38 38	7♊32 50	13 31 12	7 52.9	13 49.5	27 37.5	6 35.4	14 04.1	16 53.7	4 27.9	19 07.0	3 20.4	6 45.3
26 Th	18 19 43	4 39 45	19 31 39	25 34 25	7 44.8	15 10.3	28 53.0	7 12.2	14 11.7	17 06.0	4 34.4	19 10.6	3 22.7	6 46.8
27 F	18 23 40	5 40 52	1♋39 40	7♋47 32	7 34.6	16 32.2	0♑08.5	7 49.0	14 18.9	17 18.4	4 40.9	19 14.2	3 25.0	6 48.3
28 Sa	18 27 36	6 42 00	13 58 06	20 11 26	7 23.2	17 55.3	1 24.0	8 25.8	14 25.8	17 30.9	4 47.4	19 17.7	3 27.3	6 49.8
29 Su	18 31 33	7 43 07	26 27 35	2♌46 32	7 11.6	19 19.3	2 39.5	9 02.5	14 32.3	17 43.5	4 53.8	19 21.2	3 29.5	6 51.3
30 M	18 35 29	8 44 16	9♌08 20	15 32 58	7 00.9	20 44.1	3 55.0	9 39.2	14 38.4	17 56.2	5 00.1	19 24.8	3 31.8	6 52.7
31 Tu	18 39 26	9 45 24	22 00 30	28 30 57	6 52.0	22 09.7	5 10.5	10 15.9	14 44.1	18 08.9	5 06.5	19 28.3	3 34.1	6 54.1

Astro Data (Dy Hr Mn)
- ♂0S 1 1:13
- ☽0S 9 16:47
- ☿R 18 16:10
- ☽0N 22 13:48
- ☽0S 7 1:35
- ☿D 8 11:23
- ♄⚺♆ 10 14:06
- ☽0N 19 19:58

Planet Ingress (Dy Hr Mn)
- ♀ ♏ 9 15:08
- ♄ ♐ 17 2:10
- ☉ ♐ 22 8:51
- ♀ ♐ 3 13:00
- ☿ ♏R 4 19:23
- ☿ ♐ 12 11:05
- ♂ ♏ 14 18:59
- ☉ ♑ 21 22:08
- ♀ ♑ 27 9:17

Last Aspect / ☽ Ingress (November)

Last Aspect Dy Hr Mn		☽ Ingress Dy Hr Mn
1 12:10	♀ △	♋ 2 8:31
4 16:17	♄ △	♌ 4 19:04
7 0:11	♄ □	♍ 7 2:18
9 4:18	♄ ⚹	♎ 9 5:52
10 8:46	♅ ⚹	♏ 11 6:31
13 5:09	♄ ☌	♐ 13 5:52
14 8:18	♅ ☌	♑ 15 5:53
16 22:58	☉ ⚹	♒ 17 8:25
19 9:04	☉ □	♓ 19 14:42
21 23:58	☉ △	♈ 22 0:42
23 11:07	♅ △	♉ 24 13:07
26 7:43	♀ ☍	♊ 27 2:08
28 18:36	♂ △	♋ 29 14:23

Last Aspect / ☽ Ingress (December)

Last Aspect Dy Hr Mn		☽ Ingress Dy Hr Mn
1 20:58	♀ △	♌ 2 0:59
3 20:48	♂ ⚹	♍ 4 9:14
6 13:00	☿ ⚹	♎ 6 14:33
8 10:29	♂ ☌	♏ 8 16:56
10 15:53	☿ ☌	♐ 10 17:13
12 14:50	♂ ⚹	♑ 12 16:59
14 18:13	♂ □	♒ 14 18:15
16 12:55	☉ ⚹	♓ 16 22:50
19 1:58	☉ □	♈ 19 7:37
21 19:27	☉ △	♉ 21 19:41
23 5:09	♃ □	♊ 24 8:45
26 19:17	♀ ☍	♋ 26 20:44
27 12:03	♂ △	♌ 29 6:44
30 22:50	☿ △	♍ 31 14:43

☽ Phases & Eclipses (Dy Hr Mn)
- 5 20:07 ☾ 13♌21
- 12 14:20 ● 20♏09
- 12 14:10:31 ☌ T 01'59"
- 19 9:04 ☽ 26♒59
- 27 12:42 ○ 5♊13
- 5 9:01 ☾ 13♍10
- 12 0:54 ● 19♐56
- 19 1:58 ☽ 27♓06
- 27 7:30 ○ 5♋29

Astro Data

1 November 1985
Julian Day # 31351
SVP 5♓27'39"
GC 26♐38.5 ⚵ 7♋34.5
Eris 15♈36.8R ⚴ 9♏09.7
⚷ 13♊42.2R ⚶ 15♐58.4
☽ Mean ☊ 9♉01.4

1 December 1985
Julian Day # 31381
SVP 5♓27'34"
GC 26♐38.6 ⚵ 6♋45.7R
Eris 15♈22.9R ⚴ 19♏21.8
⚷ 12♊06.9R ⚶ 1♑38.6
☽ Mean ☊ 7♉26.1

LONGITUDE — January 1986

Day	Sid.Time	☉	0 hr ☽	Noon ☽	True ☊	☿	♀	♂	⚳	♃	♄	♅	♆	♇
1 W	18 43 22	10♑46 32	5♍04 23	11♍40 55	6♉45.7	23♐36.1	6♑26.0	10♏52.6	14♍49.4	18♒21.7	5♐12.7	19♐31.8	3♑36.3	6♏55.4
2 Th	18 47 19	11 47 41	18 20 39	25 03 44	6R 42.1	25 03.1	7 41.5	11 29.2	14 54.3	18 34.5	5 19.0	19 35.2	3 38.6	6 56.7
3 F	18 51 16	12 48 50	1♎50 17	8♎40 29	6D 40.7	26 30.7	8 57.0	12 05.8	14 58.8	18 47.5	5 25.1	19 38.7	3 40.8	6 58.0
4 Sa	18 55 12	13 50 00	15 34 27	22 32 18	6 40.9	27 58.9	10 12.5	12 42.4	15 03.0	19 00.4	5 31.3	19 42.1	3 43.1	6 59.3
5 Su	18 59 09	14 51 10	29 34 04	6♏39 44	6R 41.2	29 27.7	11 28.0	13 19.0	15 06.6	19 13.5	5 37.4	19 45.5	3 45.3	7 00.5
6 M	19 03 05	15 52 20	13♏49 12	21 02 15	6 40.4	0♑57.0	12 43.5	13 55.5	15 09.9	19 26.6	5 43.4	19 48.9	3 47.5	7 01.7
7 Tu	19 07 02	16 53 30	28 18 29	5♐37 27	6 37.5	2 26.8	13 59.0	14 32.0	15 12.8	19 39.8	5 49.4	19 52.3	3 49.8	7 02.9
8 W	19 10 58	17 54 41	12♐58 30	20 20 52	6 31.7	3 57.1	15 14.5	15 08.5	15 15.2	19 53.1	5 55.3	19 55.7	3 52.0	7 04.0
9 Th	19 14 55	18 55 51	27 43 40	5♑05 56	6 23.1	5 27.8	16 30.0	15 44.9	15 17.2	20 06.4	6 01.2	19 59.0	3 54.2	7 05.1
10 F	19 18 52	19 57 01	12♑26 39	19 44 48	6 12.2	6 59.1	17 45.5	16 21.4	15 18.8	20 19.7	6 07.0	20 02.3	3 56.4	7 06.2
11 Sa	19 22 48	20 58 11	26 59 24	4♒09 34	6 00.1	8 30.8	19 01.0	16 57.7	15 19.9	20 33.1	6 12.8	20 05.6	3 58.6	7 07.2
12 Su	19 26 45	21 59 21	11♒14 32	18 13 40	5 48.3	10 02.9	20 16.5	17 34.1	15 20.6	20 46.6	6 18.5	20 08.9	4 00.8	7 08.2
13 M	19 30 41	23 00 30	25 06 31	1♓52 49	5 37.9	11 35.6	21 32.0	18 10.4	15R 20.9	21 00.1	6 24.2	20 12.1	4 03.0	7 09.2
14 Tu	19 34 38	24 01 38	8♓32 27	15 05 30	5 29.8	13 08.7	22 47.5	18 46.6	15 20.7	21 13.7	6 29.8	20 15.3	4 05.2	7 10.1
15 W	19 38 34	25 02 46	21 32 11	27 52 49	5 24.4	14 42.3	24 02.9	19 22.9	15 20.1	21 27.3	6 35.3	20 18.5	4 07.3	7 11.0
16 Th	19 42 31	26 03 53	4♈07 52	10♈17 53	5 21.7	16 16.4	25 18.4	19 59.0	15 19.0	21 40.9	6 40.8	20 21.6	4 09.5	7 11.9
17 F	19 46 27	27 04 59	16 23 28	22 25 17	5D 20.8	17 51.0	26 33.8	20 35.2	15 17.5	21 54.6	6 46.2	20 24.8	4 11.6	7 12.7
18 Sa	19 50 24	28 06 05	28 24 00	4♉20 21	5R 20.7	19 26.1	27 49.3	21 11.3	15 15.6	22 08.4	6 51.5	20 27.9	4 13.7	7 13.5
19 Su	19 54 21	29 07 09	10♉15 02	16 08 46	5 20.4	21 01.7	29 04.7	21 47.4	15 13.2	22 22.2	6 56.8	20 30.9	4 15.9	7 14.2
20 M	19 58 17	0♒08 13	22 02 12	27 56 01	5 18.7	22 37.9	0♒20.1	22 23.4	15 10.4	22 36.0	7 02.0	20 34.0	4 18.0	7 15.0
21 Tu	20 02 14	1 09 16	3♊50 49	9♊47 12	5 14.6	24 14.6	1 35.6	22 59.4	15 07.2	22 49.9	7 07.2	20 37.0	4 20.0	7 15.6
22 W	20 06 10	2 10 18	15 45 39	21 46 39	5 07.7	25 51.9	2 51.0	23 35.4	15 03.5	23 03.8	7 12.3	20 40.0	4 22.1	7 16.3
23 Th	20 10 07	3 11 19	27 50 35	3♋57 46	4 58.0	27 29.8	4 06.4	24 11.3	14 59.3	23 17.7	7 17.3	20 42.9	4 24.2	7 16.9
24 F	20 14 03	4 12 20	10♋08 28	16 22 49	4 45.8	29 08.2	5 21.8	24 47.2	14 54.8	23 31.7	7 22.2	20 45.8	4 26.2	7 17.5
25 Sa	20 18 00	5 13 19	22 40 56	29 02 49	4 32.1	0♒47.3	6 37.1	25 23.0	14 49.8	23 45.7	7 27.1	20 48.7	4 28.2	7 18.0
26 Su	20 21 56	6 14 18	5♌28 25	11♌57 37	4 18.0	2 27.1	7 52.5	25 58.8	14 44.4	23 59.8	7 31.9	20 51.6	4 30.2	7 18.5
27 M	20 25 53	7 15 16	18 30 15	25 06 07	4 04.9	4 07.4	9 07.9	26 34.6	14 38.5	24 13.9	7 36.6	20 54.4	4 32.2	7 19.0
28 Tu	20 29 50	8 16 13	1♍44 59	8♍26 38	3 53.9	5 48.4	10 23.2	27 10.3	14 32.3	24 28.0	7 41.3	20 57.2	4 34.2	7 19.4
29 W	20 33 46	9 17 09	15 10 49	21 57 21	3 45.8	7 30.1	11 38.6	27 46.0	14 25.6	24 42.1	7 45.9	20 59.9	4 36.2	7 19.8
30 Th	20 37 43	10 18 04	28 46 02	5♎36 45	3 40.8	9 12.5	12 53.9	28 21.6	14 18.5	24 56.2	7 50.4	21 02.6	4 38.1	7 20.2
31 F	20 41 39	11 18 58	12♎29 22	19 23 50	3 38.5	10 55.5	14 09.2	28 57.2	14 11.0	25 10.4	7 54.8	21 05.3	4 40.0	7 20.5

LONGITUDE — February 1986

Day	Sid.Time	☉	0 hr ☽	Noon ☽	True ☊	☿	♀	♂	⚳	♃	♄	♅	♆	♇
1 Sa	20 45 36	12♒19 52	26♎20 06	3♏18 10	3♉38.0	12♒39.3	15♒24.5	29♏32.7	14♍03.1	25♒24.6	7♐59.1	21♐07.9	4♑41.9	7♏20.8
2 Su	20 49 32	13 20 46	10♏17 59	17 19 34	3R 38.0	14 23.7	16 39.9	0♐08.2	13R 54.8	25 38.9	8 03.4	21 10.5	4 43.8	7 21.0
3 M	20 53 29	14 21 38	24 22 52	1♐27 45	3 37.1	16 08.8	17 55.2	0 43.6	13 46.1	25 53.1	8 07.6	21 13.1	4 45.7	7 21.2
4 Tu	20 57 25	15 22 30	8♐34 06	15 41 40	3 34.2	17 54.5	19 10.5	1 19.0	13 37.1	26 07.4	8 11.7	21 15.6	4 47.5	7 21.4
5 W	21 01 22	16 23 21	22 50 08	29 59 05	3 28.5	19 40.9	20 25.8	1 54.4	13 27.6	26 21.7	8 15.8	21 18.1	4 49.4	7 21.6
6 Th	21 05 19	17 24 11	7♑08 02	14♑16 25	3 20.0	21 27.9	21 41.0	2 29.6	13 17.8	26 36.0	8 19.7	21 20.6	4 51.2	7 21.7
7 F	21 09 15	18 25 00	21 23 35	28 28 52	3 09.1	23 15.5	22 56.3	3 04.9	13 07.7	26 50.4	8 23.6	21 23.0	4 53.0	7 21.7
8 Sa	21 13 12	19 25 47	5♒31 36	12♒31 06	2 57.0	25 03.6	24 11.6	3 40.0	12 57.2	27 04.7	8 27.4	21 25.3	4 54.7	7R 21.8
9 Su	21 17 08	20 26 34	19 26 45	26 18 02	2 44.9	26 52.2	25 26.8	4 15.1	12 46.4	27 19.1	8 31.1	21 27.6	4 56.5	7 21.8
10 M	21 21 05	21 27 19	3♓04 28	9♓45 46	2 34.1	28 41.1	26 42.0	4 50.2	12 35.3	27 33.5	8 34.7	21 29.9	4 58.2	7 21.7
11 Tu	21 25 01	22 28 02	16 21 41	22 52 09	2 25.4	0♓30.2	27 57.3	5 25.2	12 23.9	27 47.8	8 38.2	21 32.1	4 59.9	7 21.6
12 W	21 28 58	23 28 44	29 17 14	5♈37 05	2 19.6	2 19.5	29 12.5	6 00.1	12 12.2	28 02.2	8 41.7	21 34.3	5 01.5	7 21.5
13 Th	21 32 54	24 29 25	11♈51 58	18 02 16	2 16.3	4 08.8	0♓27.6	6 34.9	12 00.2	28 16.6	8 45.0	21 36.5	5 03.2	7 21.4
14 F	21 36 51	25 30 04	24 08 26	0♉11 00	2D 15.3	5 57.8	1 42.8	7 09.7	11 48.0	28 31.0	8 48.3	21 38.6	5 04.8	7 21.2
15 Sa	21 40 48	26 30 41	6♉10 34	12 07 45	2 15.6	7 46.4	2 57.9	7 44.4	11 35.5	28 45.5	8 51.4	21 40.6	5 06.4	7 21.0
16 Su	21 44 44	27 31 16	18 03 12	23 57 37	2R 16.1	9 34.3	4 13.1	8 19.0	11 22.8	28 59.9	8 54.5	21 42.6	5 07.9	7 20.7
17 M	21 48 41	28 31 50	29 51 41	5♊46 06	2 15.9	11 21.2	5 28.2	8 53.6	11 09.9	29 14.3	8 57.5	21 44.6	5 09.5	7 20.4
18 Tu	21 52 37	29 32 22	11♊41 31	17 38 38	2 13.9	13 06.8	6 43.3	9 28.1	10 56.8	29 28.7	9 00.4	21 46.5	5 11.0	7 20.1
19 W	21 56 34	0♓32 52	23 38 02	29 40 19	2 09.8	14 50.6	7 58.4	10 02.6	10 43.6	29 43.1	9 03.2	21 48.4	5 12.5	7 19.7
20 Th	22 00 30	1 33 21	5♋46 01	11♋55 35	2 03.2	16 32.2	9 13.4	10 36.9	10 30.2	29 57.5	9 05.9	21 50.2	5 14.0	7 19.3
21 F	22 04 27	2 33 48	18 09 26	24 27 50	1 54.5	18 11.2	10 28.5	11 11.2	10 16.7	0♓12.0	9 08.5	21 52.0	5 15.4	7 18.9
22 Sa	22 08 23	3 34 12	0♌51 01	7♌19 06	1 44.4	19 47.0	11 43.5	11 45.4	10 03.0	0 26.4	9 11.1	21 53.7	5 16.8	7 18.4
23 Su	22 12 20	4 34 35	13 52 05	20 29 52	1 33.9	21 19.0	12 58.5	12 19.6	9 49.2	0 40.8	9 13.5	21 55.4	5 18.2	7 17.9
24 M	22 16 17	5 34 57	27 12 16	3♍59 00	1 24.1	22 46.7	14 13.4	12 53.7	9 35.4	0 55.2	9 15.8	21 57.1	5 19.6	7 17.4
25 Tu	22 20 13	6 35 16	10♍49 41	17 43 55	1 15.9	24 09.4	15 28.4	13 27.7	9 21.5	1 09.6	9 18.1	21 58.7	5 20.9	7 16.8
26 W	22 24 10	7 35 34	24 41 12	1♎41 04	1 10.0	25 26.5	16 43.3	14 01.6	9 07.5	1 23.9	9 20.2	22 00.2	5 22.2	7 16.2
27 Th	22 28 06	8 35 50	8♎42 59	15 46 30	1 06.6	26 37.4	17 58.3	14 35.4	8 53.5	1 38.3	9 22.2	22 01.7	5 23.5	7 15.6
28 F	22 32 03	9 36 05	22 51 10	29 56 32	1D 05.5	27 41.4	19 13.1	15 09.2	8 39.5	1 52.7	9 24.2	22 03.1	5 24.7	7 15.0

Astro Data

	Dy Hr Mn
♃∠♆	2 21:06
☽0S	3 7:19
♃⚹♅	8 18:17
⚳R	13 14:20
☽0N	16 3:11
♄⚻♇	23 9:58
☽0S	30 11:48
♇R	8 20:17
☽0N	12 11:26
☽0S	26 17:58
☿0N	27 17:46

Planet Ingress

		Dy Hr Mn
☿	♑	5 20:42
♀	♒	20 5:36
☉	♒	20 8:46
☿	♒	25 0:33
♂	♐	2 6:27
☿	♓	11 5:21
♀	♓	13 3:11
☉	♓	18 22:58
♃	♓	20 16:05

Last Aspect / ☽ Ingress

Last Aspect Dy Hr Mn		☽ Ingress	Dy Hr Mn
2 11:59	☿ □	♎	2 20:45
4 22:24	☿ ⚹	♏	5 0:44
6 9:19	♃ □	♐	7 2:47
8 11:19	♅ ☌	♑	9 3:42
10 12:22	☉ ☌	♒	11 5:01
12 16:30	♃ ☌	♓	13 8:39
15 6:09	☉ ⚹	♈	15 16:03
17 22:13	☉ □	♉	18 3:14
20 0:56	♃ □	♊	20 16:12
22 14:36	♃ △	♋	23 4:15
25 4:46	♂ △	♌	25 13:47
27 14:48	♂ □	♍	27 20:51
29 22:42	♂ ⚹	♎	30 2:10

Last Aspect / ☽ Ingress

Last Aspect Dy Hr Mn		☽ Ingress	Dy Hr Mn
31 22:10	♃ △	♏	1 6:19
3 2:23	♃ □	♐	3 9:32
5 5:49	♃ ⚹	♑	5 12:02
6 0:23	♇ ⚹	♒	7 14:35
9 13:50	♃ ☌	♓	9 18:32
11 9:31	♅ □	♈	12 1:21
14 8:37	♃ ⚹	♉	14 11:38
16 22:27	♃ □	♊	17 0:17
19 12:06	♃ △	♋	19 12:39
20 22:15	☿ △	♌	21 22:25
23 14:34	♅ △	♍	24 4:58
26 0:14	☿ ☍	♎	26 9:07
27 22:37	♅ ⚹	♏	28 12:06

☽ Phases & Eclipses

Dy Hr Mn	
3 19:47	☾ 13♎09
10 12:22	● 19♑58
17 22:13	☽ 27♈31
26 0:31	○ 5♌45
2 4:41	☾ 13♏02
9 0:55	● 19♒59
16 19:55	☽ 27♉51
24 15:02	○ 5♍43

Astro Data

1 January 1986
Julian Day # 31412
SVP 5♓27'28"
GC 26♐38.6 ⚴ 27♊30.2R
Eris 15♈17.2R ⚵ 29♏18.4
⚷ 10♊24.2R ⚶ 18♑06.5
☽ Mean ☊ 5♉47.6

1 February 1986
Julian Day # 31443
SVP 5♓27'23"
GC 26♐38.7 ⚴ 22♊42.8
Eris 15♈22.0 ⚵ 7♐55.1
⚷ 9♊21.5R ⚶ 4♒30.6
☽ Mean ☊ 4♉09.1

March 1986

LONGITUDE

Day	Sid.Time	☉	0 hr ☽	Noon ☽	True ☊	☿	♀	♂	⚳	♃	♄	♅	♆	♇
1 Sa	22 35 59	10♓36 18	7♏02 17	14♏08 05	1♉06.1	28♓38.1	20♓28.0	15♐42.8	8♍25.6	2♓07.0	9♐26.0	22♐04.5	5♑25.9	7♏14.3
2 Su	22 39 56	11 36 30	21 13 41	28 18 51	1 07.1	29 26.8	21 42.9	16 16.4	8R 11.6	2 21.4	9 27.8	22 05.8	5 27.1	7R 13.5
3 M	22 43 52	12 36 41	5♐23 26	12♐27 15	1R 07.7	0♈07.1	22 57.7	16 49.9	7 57.7	2 35.7	9 29.5	22 07.1	5 28.3	7 12.8
4 Tu	22 47 49	13 36 50	19 30 09	26 32 00	1 06.9	0 38.7	24 12.6	17 23.3	7 43.8	2 50.0	9 31.0	22 08.4	5 29.4	7 12.0
5 W	22 51 46	14 36 57	3♑32 37	10♑31 50	1 04.2	1 01.3	25 27.4	17 56.6	7 30.0	3 04.3	9 32.5	22 09.6	5 30.5	7 11.2
6 Th	22 55 42	15 37 03	17 29 26	24 25 11	0 59.4	1R 14.7	26 42.2	18 29.8	7 16.4	3 18.5	9 33.8	22 10.7	5 31.6	7 10.3
7 F	22 59 39	16 37 07	1♒18 50	8♒10 05	0 52.9	1 18.8	27 56.9	19 02.9	7 02.8	3 32.8	9 35.1	22 11.8	5 32.6	7 09.4
8 Sa	23 03 35	17 37 10	14 58 39	21 44 15	0 45.4	1 13.9	29 11.7	19 36.0	6 49.4	3 47.0	9 36.2	22 12.8	5 33.6	7 08.5
9 Su	23 07 32	18 37 10	28 26 35	5♓05 25	0 37.9	1 00.2	0♈26.4	20 08.8	6 36.1	4 01.2	9 37.3	22 13.8	5 34.6	7 07.6
10 M	23 11 28	19 37 09	11♓40 30	18 11 41	0 31.1	0 38.0	1 41.1	20 41.6	6 23.1	4 15.4	9 38.2	22 14.7	5 35.5	7 06.6
11 Tu	23 15 25	20 37 06	24 38 50	1♈01 54	0 25.9	0 08.0	2 55.7	21 14.3	6 10.2	4 29.6	9 39.1	22 15.6	5 36.4	7 05.6
12 W	23 19 21	21 37 01	7♈20 54	13 35 56	0 22.5	29♓31.0	4 10.4	21 46.9	5 57.5	4 43.7	9 39.8	22 16.4	5 37.3	7 04.6
13 Th	23 23 18	22 36 54	19 47 10	25 54 49	0D 21.0	28 47.9	5 25.0	22 19.3	5 45.0	4 57.8	9 40.5	22 17.2	5 38.1	7 03.6
14 F	23 27 14	23 36 44	1♉59 12	8♉00 42	0 21.2	27 59.7	6 39.6	22 51.6	5 32.8	5 11.9	9 41.0	22 17.9	5 39.0	7 02.5
15 Sa	23 31 11	24 36 33	13 59 43	19 56 45	0 22.5	27 07.6	7 54.2	23 23.8	5 20.8	5 25.9	9 41.5	22 18.6	5 39.7	7 01.4
16 Su	23 35 08	25 36 20	25 52 18	1♊46 57	0 24.3	26 12.8	9 08.7	23 55.9	5 09.1	5 39.9	9 41.8	22 19.2	5 40.5	7 00.2
17 M	23 39 04	26 36 04	7♊41 16	13 35 54	0 25.9	25 16.6	10 23.2	24 27.9	4 57.7	5 53.9	9 42.1	22 19.8	5 41.2	6 59.1
18 Tu	23 43 01	27 35 46	19 31 27	25 28 34	0R 26.7	24 20.1	11 37.7	24 59.7	4 46.6	6 07.8	9R 42.2	22 20.3	5 41.9	6 57.9
19 W	23 46 57	28 35 26	1♋27 54	7♋30 03	0 26.3	23 24.7	12 52.2	25 31.4	4 35.8	6 21.7	9 42.2	22 20.7	5 42.5	6 56.7
20 Th	23 50 54	29 35 03	13 35 37	19 45 10	0 24.5	22 31.3	14 06.6	26 02.9	4 25.4	6 35.6	9 42.2	22 21.1	5 43.2	6 55.5
21 F	23 54 50	0♈34 39	25 59 14	2♌18 16	0 21.4	21 41.0	15 21.0	26 34.4	4 15.2	6 49.4	9 42.0	22 21.5	5 43.7	6 54.2
22 Sa	23 58 47	1 34 12	8♌42 39	15 12 39	0 17.4	20 54.6	16 35.4	27 05.7	4 05.4	7 03.2	9 41.7	22 21.8	5 44.3	6 52.9
23 Su	0 02 43	2 33 42	21 48 29	28 30 13	0 13.0	20 12.7	17 49.7	27 36.8	3 56.0	7 16.9	9 41.4	22 22.0	5 44.8	6 51.6
24 M	0 06 40	3 33 11	5♍17 47	12♍11 02	0 08.7	19 35.9	19 04.0	28 07.8	3 46.9	7 30.6	9 40.9	22 22.2	5 45.3	6 50.3
25 Tu	0 10 37	4 32 37	19 09 39	26 13 12	0 05.3	19 04.6	20 18.3	28 38.7	3 38.2	7 44.3	9 40.4	22 22.3	5 45.8	6 49.0
26 W	0 14 33	5 32 01	3♎21 09	10♎32 51	0 02.9	18 39.1	21 32.5	29 09.4	3 29.8	7 57.9	9 39.7	22 22.4	5 46.2	6 47.6
27 Th	0 18 30	6 31 23	17 47 35	25 04 36	0D 01.9	18 19.4	22 46.7	29 40.0	3 21.9	8 11.5	9 38.9	22R 22.4	5 46.6	6 46.2
28 F	0 22 26	7 30 43	2♏23 07	9♏42 19	0 02.1	18 05.7	24 00.9	0♑10.4	3 14.3	8 25.0	9 38.1	22 22.4	5 46.9	6 44.8
29 Sa	0 26 23	8 30 02	17 01 28	24 19 51	0 03.1	17D 57.8	25 15.0	0 40.7	3 07.1	8 38.5	9 37.1	22 22.3	5 47.2	6 43.4
30 Su	0 30 19	9 29 19	1♐36 49	8♐51 49	0 04.4	17 55.8	26 29.2	1 10.8	3 00.4	8 51.9	9 36.1	22 22.2	5 47.5	6 42.0
31 M	0 34 16	10 28 34	16 04 22	23 14 03	0 05.6	17 59.3	27 43.3	1 40.7	2 54.0	9 05.3	9 34.9	22 22.1	5 47.8	6 40.5

April 1986

LONGITUDE

Day	Sid.Time	☉	0 hr ☽	Noon ☽	True ☊	☿	♀	♂	⚳	♃	♄	♅	♆	♇
1 Tu	0 38 12	11♈27 47	0♑20 34	7♑23 41	0♉06.3	18♓08.3	28♈57.3	2♑10.5	2♍48.0	9♓18.6	9♐33.7	22♐21.8	5♑48.0	6♏39.0
2 W	0 42 09	12 26 58	14 23 15	21 19 08	0R 06.1	18 22.6	0♉11.4	2 40.0	2R 42.5	9 31.8	9R 32.3	22R 21.5	5 48.2	6R 37.5
3 Th	0 46 06	13 26 08	28 11 17	4♒59 40	0 05.2	18 41.8	1 25.4	3 09.4	2 37.4	9 45.1	9 30.9	22 21.2	5 48.3	6 36.0
4 F	0 50 02	14 25 16	11♒44 20	18 25 16	0 03.5	19 05.9	2 39.3	3 38.6	2 32.6	9 58.2	9 29.4	22 20.8	5 48.5	6 34.5
5 Sa	0 53 59	15 24 22	25 02 33	1♓36 14	0 01.5	19 34.5	3 53.3	4 07.6	2 28.4	10 11.3	9 27.7	22 20.4	5 48.6	6 33.0
6 Su	0 57 55	16 23 26	8♓06 22	14 33 03	29♈59.5	20 07.4	5 07.2	4 36.4	2 24.5	10 24.3	9 26.0	22 19.9	5 48.6	6 31.4
7 M	1 01 52	17 22 29	20 56 20	27 16 20	29 57.7	20 44.4	6 21.1	5 05.0	2 21.1	10 37.3	9 24.2	22 19.4	5R 48.6	6 29.9
8 Tu	1 05 48	18 21 29	3♈33 07	9♈46 50	29 56.4	21 25.2	7 34.9	5 33.4	2 18.1	10 50.2	9 22.3	22 18.8	5 48.6	6 28.3
9 W	1 09 45	19 20 27	15 57 35	22 05 32	29D 55.8	22 09.8	8 48.8	6 01.6	2 15.5	11 03.1	9 20.3	22 18.2	5 48.6	6 26.7
10 Th	1 13 41	20 19 24	28 10 51	4♉13 44	29 55.7	22 57.8	10 02.6	6 29.6	2 13.4	11 15.9	9 18.2	22 17.5	5 48.5	6 25.1
11 F	1 17 38	21 18 18	10♉14 26	16 13 12	29 56.1	23 49.2	11 16.3	6 57.3	2 11.7	11 28.6	9 16.1	22 16.7	5 48.4	6 23.5
12 Sa	1 21 35	22 17 10	22 10 21	28 06 12	29 56.7	24 43.7	12 30.0	7 24.8	2 10.4	11 41.2	9 13.8	22 15.9	5 48.2	6 21.8
13 Su	1 25 31	23 16 00	4♊01 08	9♊55 34	29 57.5	25 41.2	13 43.7	7 52.1	2 09.6	11 53.8	9 11.5	22 15.1	5 48.0	6 20.2
14 M	1 29 28	24 14 48	15 49 56	21 44 41	29 58.2	26 41.5	14 57.4	8 19.1	2D 09.2	12 06.3	9 09.0	22 14.2	5 47.8	6 18.6
15 Tu	1 33 24	25 13 34	27 40 22	3♋37 28	29 58.7	27 44.6	16 11.0	8 45.9	2 09.2	12 18.7	9 06.5	22 13.3	5 47.6	6 16.9
16 W	1 37 21	26 12 18	9♋36 33	15 38 10	29R 59.0	28 50.2	17 24.6	9 12.4	2 09.7	12 31.1	9 03.9	22 12.3	5 47.3	6 15.3
17 Th	1 41 17	27 10 59	21 42 54	27 51 19	29 59.1	29 58.4	18 38.1	9 38.7	2 10.5	12 43.4	9 01.2	22 11.3	5 47.0	6 13.6
18 F	1 45 14	28 09 38	4♌03 57	10♌21 21	29 59.0	1♈09.0	19 51.6	10 04.7	2 11.8	12 55.6	8 58.5	22 10.2	5 46.7	6 11.9
19 Sa	1 49 10	29 08 15	16 44 00	23 12 21	29D 58.9	2 21.9	21 05.1	10 30.4	2 13.5	13 07.7	8 55.7	22 09.1	5 46.3	6 10.3
20 Su	1 53 07	0♉06 50	29 46 45	6♍27 30	29 58.9	3 37.0	22 18.5	10 55.9	2 15.7	13 19.8	8 52.8	22 08.0	5 45.9	6 08.6
21 M	1 57 04	1 05 22	13♍14 45	20 08 35	29 59.0	4 54.4	23 31.9	11 21.1	2 18.2	13 31.7	8 49.8	22 06.8	5 45.5	6 06.9
22 Tu	2 01 00	2 03 52	27 08 53	4♎15 26	29 59.1	6 13.8	24 45.2	11 46.0	2 21.1	13 43.6	8 46.7	22 05.5	5 45.0	6 05.2
23 W	2 04 57	3 02 20	11♎27 50	18 45 32	29R 59.3	7 35.3	25 58.5	12 10.6	2 24.5	13 55.4	8 43.6	22 04.2	5 44.5	6 03.5
24 Th	2 08 53	4 00 47	26 07 49	3♏33 50	29 59.3	8 58.8	27 11.8	12 35.0	2 28.2	14 07.1	8 40.4	22 02.9	5 44.0	6 01.8
25 F	2 12 50	4 59 11	11♏02 38	18 33 12	29 59.1	10 24.3	28 25.0	12 59.0	2 32.3	14 18.8	8 37.1	22 01.5	5 43.4	6 00.1
26 Sa	2 16 46	5 57 34	26 04 25	3♐35 13	29 58.7	11 51.7	29 38.2	13 22.7	2 36.8	14 30.3	8 33.8	22 00.1	5 42.8	5 58.4
27 Su	2 20 43	6 55 55	11♐04 31	18 31 22	29 58.0	13 21.0	0♊51.3	13 46.1	2 41.7	14 41.8	8 30.4	21 58.6	5 42.2	5 56.7
28 M	2 24 39	7 54 15	25 54 52	3♑14 16	29 57.2	14 52.3	2 04.4	14 09.2	2 47.0	14 53.1	8 26.9	21 57.1	5 41.6	5 55.0
29 Tu	2 28 36	8 52 33	10♑28 56	17 38 26	29 56.4	16 25.4	3 17.5	14 31.9	2 52.7	15 04.4	8 23.4	21 55.6	5 40.9	5 53.3
30 W	2 32 33	9 50 49	24 42 27	1♒40 48	29D 55.9	18 00.4	4 30.5	14 54.3	2 58.7	15 15.6	8 19.8	21 54.0	5 40.2	5 51.7

Astro Data Dy Hr Mn	Planet Ingress Dy Hr Mn	Last Aspect Dy Hr Mn	☽ Ingress Dy Hr Mn	Last Aspect Dy Hr Mn	☽ Ingress Dy Hr Mn	☽ Phases & Eclipses Dy Hr Mn
♅∠♇ 6 7:23	☿ ♈ 3 7:22	2 14:01 ☿ △	♐ 2 14:51	2 6:47 ☿ ⚹	♒ 3 3:11	3 12:17 ☾ 12♐37
☿ R 7 10:56	♀ ♈ 9 3:32	4 7:39 ♀ □	♑ 4 17:56	4 19:06 ♅ ⚹	♓ 5 9:03	10 14:52 ● 19♓44
♀0N 11 10:33	☿ ♓R 11 17:36	6 16:22 ♀ ⚹	♒ 6 21:42	7 2:37 ♅ □	♈ 7 17:12	18 16:39 ☽ 27♊47
☽0N 11 19:45	☉ ♈ 20 22:03	8 12:51 ♅ ⚹	♓ 9 2:48	9 12:25 ♅ △	♉ 10 3:36	26 3:02 ○ 5♎10
♃⚹♆ 16 13:02	♂ ♑ 28 3:47	10 19:32 ♅ □	♈ 11 10:03	12 4:35 ☿ ⚹	♊ 12 15:51	
♄ R 19 9:27		13 4:53 ♅ △	♉ 13 20:04	14 22:59 ☿ □	♋ 15 4:42	1 19:30 ☾ 11♑46
☿0S 19 20:42	♀ ♉ 2 8:19	16 1:31 ☿ ⚹	♊ 16 8:23	17 10:35 ☉ □	♌ 17 16:10	9 6:08 ● 19♈06
☉0N 20 22:02	☊ ♈R 6 5:31	18 16:39 ☉ □	♋ 18 21:04	19 23:42 ☉ △	♍ 20 0:24	9 6:20:27 ● P 0.824
♃△♇ 21 19:38	☿ ♈ 17 12:33	20 17:00 ☿ △	♌ 21 7:38	21 18:23 ♀ △	♎ 22 4:50	17 10:35 ☽ 27♋08
☽0S 26 2:57	☉ ♉ 20 9:12	23 10:21 ♂ △	♍ 23 14:39	23 17:24 ♅ ⚹	♏ 24 6:15	24 12:46 ○ 4♏03
♅ R 27 14:17	♀ ♊ 26 19:10	25 16:15 ♂ □	♎ 25 18:22	26 5:08 ♀ ☍	♐ 26 6:16	24 12:43 ● T 1.202
☿ D 30 8:42		27 19:49 ♂ ⚹	♏ 27 20:05	27 17:35 ♅ ☌	♑ 28 6:41	
♃□♄ 2 12:49	⚳ D14 22:35	29 1:37 ☿ △	♐ 29 21:20	29 9:42 ☿ □	♒ 30 9:06	
♆ R 7 12:52	☽0S22 13:29	31 20:17 ♀ △	♑ 31 23:25			
☽0N 8 3:01	☿0N22 13:40					

Astro Data

1 March 1986
Julian Day # 31471
SVP 5♓27'19"
GC 26♐38.8 ⚴ 27♊15.5
Eris 15♈34.5 ⚵ 13♐41.6
⚷ 9♊21.7 ⚶ 19♒00.0
☽ Mean ☊ 2♉40.2

1 April 1986
Julian Day # 31502
SVP 5♓27'15"
GC 26♐38.8 ⚴ 8♋11.9
Eris 15♈53.8 ⚵ 16♐35.1
⚷ 10♊26.6 ⚶ 4♓22.2
☽ Mean ☊ 1♉01.7

LONGITUDE — May 1986

Day	Sid.Time	☉	0 hr ☽	Noon ☽	True ☊	☿	♀	♂	⚳	♃	♄	♅	♆	♇
1 Th	2 36 29	10♉49 04	8♒33 25	15♒20 23	29♈55.9	19♈37.3	5♊43.5	15♑16.3	3♍05.1	15♓26.7	8♐16.2	21♐52.4	5♑39.5	5♏50.0
2 F	2 40 26	11 47 17	22 01 51	28 38 03	29 56.3	21 16.0	6 56.5	15 38.0	3 11.8	15 37.7	8R 12.4	21R 50.8	5R 38.7	5R 48.3
3 Sa	2 44 22	12 45 29	5♓09 15	11♓35 45	29 57.2	22 56.6	8 09.4	15 59.2	3 19.0	15 48.6	8 08.7	21 49.1	5 37.9	5 46.6
4 Su	2 48 19	13 43 40	17 57 56	24 16 07	29 58.3	24 39.0	9 22.3	16 20.1	3 26.4	15 59.4	8 04.9	21 47.3	5 37.1	5 44.9
5 M	2 52 15	14 41 49	0♈30 41	6♈41 57	29 59.5	26 23.3	10 35.1	16 40.6	3 34.3	16 10.1	8 01.0	21 45.6	5 36.3	5 43.2
6 Tu	2 56 12	15 39 56	12 50 17	18 55 59	0♉00.4	28 09.4	11 47.9	17 00.7	3 42.4	16 20.7	7 57.1	21 43.8	5 35.4	5 41.6
7 W	3 00 08	16 38 02	24 59 22	1♉00 43	0R 00.7	29 57.5	13 00.7	17 20.3	3 50.9	16 31.1	7 53.1	21 41.9	5 34.5	5 39.9
8 Th	3 04 05	17 36 06	7♉00 20	12 58 27	0 00.2	1♉47.4	14 13.4	17 39.5	3 59.8	16 41.5	7 49.1	21 40.1	5 33.6	5 38.3
9 F	3 08 02	18 34 09	18 55 20	24 51 14	29♈58.8	3 39.1	15 26.1	17 58.3	4 09.0	16 51.8	7 45.0	21 38.2	5 32.6	5 36.6
10 Sa	3 11 58	19 32 10	0♊46 25	6♊41 07	29 56.4	5 32.8	16 38.7	18 16.6	4 18.5	17 01.9	7 40.9	21 36.2	5 31.6	5 35.0
11 Su	3 15 55	20 30 09	12 35 38	18 30 13	29 53.3	7 28.2	17 51.3	18 34.5	4 28.3	17 12.0	7 36.8	21 34.3	5 30.6	5 33.3
12 M	3 19 51	21 28 07	24 25 11	0♋20 52	29 49.8	9 25.6	19 03.9	18 51.9	4 38.5	17 21.9	7 32.6	21 32.3	5 29.6	5 31.7
13 Tu	3 23 48	22 26 03	6♋17 36	12 15 45	29 46.3	11 24.7	20 16.4	19 08.8	4 49.0	17 31.7	7 28.4	21 30.3	5 28.6	5 30.1
14 W	3 27 44	23 23 58	18 15 43	24 17 57	29 43.3	13 25.6	21 28.8	19 25.3	4 59.7	17 41.4	7 24.2	21 28.2	5 27.5	5 28.5
15 Th	3 31 41	24 21 50	0♌22 53	6♌30 59	29 41.0	15 28.2	22 41.3	19 41.2	5 10.8	17 51.0	7 19.9	21 26.1	5 26.4	5 26.9
16 F	3 35 37	25 19 41	12 42 45	18 58 40	29D 39.8	17 32.5	23 53.6	19 56.6	5 22.2	18 00.5	7 15.6	21 24.0	5 25.3	5 25.4
17 Sa	3 39 34	26 17 30	25 19 14	1♍44 56	29 39.8	19 38.2	25 05.9	20 11.6	5 33.9	18 09.8	7 11.3	21 21.9	5 24.1	5 23.8
18 Su	3 43 31	27 15 18	8♍16 13	14 53 29	29 40.7	21 45.4	26 18.2	20 25.9	5 45.8	18 19.0	7 06.9	21 19.7	5 23.0	5 22.3
19 M	3 47 27	28 13 03	21 37 06	28 27 19	29 42.1	23 53.8	27 30.4	20 39.8	5 58.1	18 28.1	7 02.6	21 17.6	5 21.8	5 20.7
20 Tu	3 51 24	29 10 47	5♎24 16	12♎27 58	29 43.5	26 03.4	28 42.6	20 53.1	6 10.6	18 37.1	6 58.2	21 15.4	5 20.6	5 19.2
21 W	3 55 20	0♊08 30	19 38 18	26 54 57	29R 44.3	28 13.8	29 54.7	21 05.9	6 23.4	18 45.9	6 53.8	21 13.1	5 19.3	5 17.7
22 Th	3 59 17	1 06 11	4♏17 24	11♏44 59	29 43.9	0♊25.0	1♋06.8	21 18.1	6 36.5	18 54.7	6 49.3	21 10.9	5 18.1	5 16.2
23 F	4 03 13	2 03 50	19 16 49	26 51 51	29 41.9	2 36.5	2 18.8	21 29.7	6 49.8	19 03.2	6 44.9	21 08.6	5 16.8	5 14.7
24 Sa	4 07 10	3 01 29	4♐28 56	12♐06 46	29 38.6	4 48.3	3 30.7	21 40.7	7 03.4	19 11.7	6 40.5	21 06.3	5 15.5	5 13.3
25 Su	4 11 06	3 59 06	19 44 03	27 19 29	29 34.1	6 59.9	4 42.6	21 51.1	7 17.2	19 20.0	6 36.0	21 04.0	5 14.2	5 11.9
26 M	4 15 03	4 56 42	4♑51 49	12♑19 57	29 29.1	9 11.2	5 54.5	22 00.9	7 31.3	19 28.2	6 31.6	21 01.7	5 12.9	5 10.5
27 Tu	4 19 00	5 54 17	19 42 55	26 59 57	29 24.4	11 21.8	7 06.3	22 10.1	7 45.6	19 36.3	6 27.1	20 59.4	5 11.6	5 09.1
28 W	4 22 56	6 51 51	4♒10 30	11♒14 11	29 20.7	13 31.5	8 18.0	22 18.6	8 00.2	19 44.2	6 22.7	20 57.1	5 10.2	5 07.7
29 Th	4 26 53	7 49 25	18 10 50	25 00 28	29 18.3	15 40.0	9 29.7	22 26.5	8 15.0	19 52.0	6 18.2	20 54.7	5 08.8	5 06.3
30 F	4 30 49	8 46 57	1♓43 13	8♓19 23	29D 17.5	17 47.2	10 41.4	22 33.7	8 30.0	19 59.6	6 13.7	20 52.3	5 07.4	5 05.0
31 Sa	4 34 46	9 44 28	14 49 21	21 13 34	29 18.1	19 52.7	11 53.0	22 40.2	8 45.3	20 07.1	6 09.3	20 49.9	5 06.0	5 03.7

LONGITUDE — June 1986

Day	Sid.Time	☉	0 hr ☽	Noon ☽	True ☊	☿	♀	♂	⚳	♃	♄	♅	♆	♇
1 Su	4 38 42	10♊41 59	27♓32 32	3♈46 48	29♈19.4	21♊56.4	13♋04.5	22♑46.0	9♍00.8	20♓14.4	6♐04.8	20♐47.5	5♑04.6	5♏02.4
2 M	4 42 39	11 39 29	9♈56 55	16 03 24	29 20.8	23 58.1	14 16.0	22 51.2	9 16.5	20 21.6	6R 00.4	20R 45.1	5R 03.2	5R 01.1
3 Tu	4 46 35	12 36 58	22 06 49	28 07 39	29R 21.6	25 57.7	15 27.4	22 55.6	9 32.5	20 28.6	5 56.0	20 42.7	5 01.7	4 59.8
4 W	4 50 32	13 34 26	4♉06 23	10♉03 29	29 20.9	27 55.0	16 38.8	22 59.3	9 48.6	20 35.5	5 51.5	20 40.2	5 00.2	4 58.6
5 Th	4 54 29	14 31 54	15 59 22	21 54 23	29 18.4	29 50.1	17 50.1	23 02.2	10 05.0	20 42.3	5 47.1	20 37.8	4 58.7	4 57.4
6 F	4 58 25	15 29 21	27 48 53	3♊43 10	29 13.7	1♋42.7	19 01.3	23 04.4	10 21.6	20 48.9	5 42.8	20 35.3	4 57.3	4 56.2
7 Sa	5 02 22	16 26 47	9♊37 32	15 32 13	29 07.1	3 32.8	20 12.5	23 05.9	10 38.4	20 55.3	5 38.4	20 32.9	4 55.7	4 55.0
8 Su	5 06 18	17 24 12	21 27 27	27 23 28	28 58.8	5 20.5	21 23.7	23R 06.6	10 55.4	21 01.6	5 34.1	20 30.4	4 54.2	4 53.9
9 M	5 10 15	18 21 36	3♋20 27	9♋18 37	28 49.6	7 05.6	22 34.8	23 06.6	11 12.6	21 07.7	5 29.8	20 28.0	4 52.7	4 52.8
10 Tu	5 14 11	19 18 59	15 18 11	21 19 23	28 40.3	8 48.1	23 45.8	23 05.9	11 30.0	21 13.7	5 25.5	20 25.5	4 51.2	4 51.7
11 W	5 18 08	20 16 22	27 22 26	3♌27 37	28 31.8	10 28.0	24 56.7	23 04.3	11 47.5	21 19.5	5 21.3	20 23.1	4 49.6	4 50.6
12 Th	5 22 05	21 13 43	9♌35 12	15 45 32	28 24.9	12 05.3	26 07.6	23 02.0	12 05.3	21 25.1	5 17.0	20 20.6	4 48.1	4 49.6
13 F	5 26 01	22 11 04	21 58 57	28 15 48	28 20.0	13 39.9	27 18.4	22 59.0	12 23.3	21 30.5	5 12.9	20 18.1	4 46.5	4 48.6
14 Sa	5 29 58	23 08 23	4♍36 30	11♍01 28	28D 17.4	15 11.9	28 29.1	22 55.2	12 41.4	21 35.8	5 08.7	20 15.7	4 44.9	4 47.6
15 Su	5 33 54	24 05 42	17 31 05	24 05 48	28 16.6	16 41.1	29 39.8	22 50.7	12 59.7	21 41.0	5 04.6	20 13.2	4 43.3	4 46.7
16 M	5 37 51	25 03 00	0♎45 58	7♎31 56	28 17.1	18 07.7	0♌50.4	22 45.5	13 18.2	21 45.9	5 00.5	20 10.8	4 41.8	4 45.7
17 Tu	5 41 47	26 00 16	14 24 00	21 22 20	28R 17.8	19 31.5	2 00.9	22 39.5	13 36.8	21 50.7	4 56.5	20 08.3	4 40.2	4 44.8
18 W	5 45 44	26 57 32	28 27 00	5♏37 58	28 17.8	20 52.6	3 11.4	22 32.8	13 55.6	21 55.3	4 52.5	20 05.9	4 38.6	4 44.0
19 Th	5 49 40	27 54 48	12♏54 57	20 17 32	28 16.0	22 10.8	4 21.7	22 25.3	14 14.6	21 59.8	4 48.6	20 03.4	4 37.0	4 43.1
20 F	5 53 37	28 52 02	27 45 06	5♐16 49	28 11.9	23 26.1	5 32.0	22 17.2	14 33.7	22 04.0	4 44.7	20 01.0	4 35.4	4 42.3
21 Sa	5 57 34	29 49 16	12♐51 39	20 28 26	28 05.5	24 38.6	6 42.2	22 08.4	14 53.0	22 08.1	4 40.9	19 58.6	4 33.8	4 41.5
22 Su	6 01 30	0♋46 30	28 05 53	5♑42 37	27 57.2	25 48.1	7 52.3	21 58.9	15 12.5	22 12.1	4 37.1	19 56.2	4 32.1	4 40.8
23 M	6 05 27	1 43 43	13♑17 17	20 48 35	27 48.0	26 54.5	9 02.4	21 48.7	15 32.1	22 15.8	4 33.4	19 53.8	4 30.5	4 40.1
24 Tu	6 09 23	2 40 56	28 15 20	5♒36 32	27 39.0	27 57.9	10 12.3	21 37.9	15 51.8	22 19.4	4 29.7	19 51.4	4 28.9	4 39.4
25 W	6 13 20	3 38 09	12♒51 22	19 59 15	27 31.2	28 58.0	11 22.2	21 26.4	16 11.7	22 22.8	4 26.1	19 49.1	4 27.3	4 38.7
26 Th	6 17 16	4 35 21	26 59 49	3♓52 53	27 25.4	29 54.8	12 32.0	21 14.3	16 31.7	22 26.0	4 22.6	19 46.7	4 25.7	4 38.1
27 F	6 21 13	5 32 34	10♓38 31	17 16 55	27 22.0	0♌48.3	13 41.7	21 01.6	16 51.9	22 29.0	4 19.1	19 44.4	4 24.1	4 37.5
28 Sa	6 25 09	6 29 46	23 48 26	0♈13 31	27D 20.5	1 38.3	14 51.3	20 48.3	17 12.2	22 31.8	4 15.6	19 42.0	4 22.4	4 36.9
29 Su	6 29 06	7 26 59	6♈32 43	12 46 37	27 20.4	2 24.7	16 00.8	20 34.5	17 32.6	22 34.4	4 12.3	19 39.7	4 20.8	4 36.4
30 M	6 33 03	8 24 11	18 55 52	25 01 07	27R 20.7	3 07.4	17 10.2	20 20.1	17 53.2	22 36.9	4 09.0	19 37.4	4 19.2	4 35.9

Astro Data (Dy Hr Mn)

☽ 0N 5 8:58
♆⚹♇ 16 17:11
☽ 0S 19 23:24
♃⚼♇ 31 2:38

☽ 0N 1 14:17
♃□♅ 5 0:12
♂ R 8 23:25
♆⚹♇ 9 8:02
☽ 0S 16 7:03
♄⚺♇ 21 7:05
♄⚺♆ 24 21:49
☽ 0N 28 20:12

Planet Ingress (Dy Hr Mn)

☊ ♉ 5 22:57
☿ ♉ 7 12:33
☊ ♈R 8 17:11
☉ ♊ 21 8:28
♀ ♋ 21 13:46
☿ ♊ 22 7:26

☿ ♋ 5 14:06
♀ ♌ 15 18:52
☉ ♋ 21 16:30
☿ ♌ 26 14:15

Last Aspect (Dy Hr Mn) — **☽ Ingress** (Dy Hr Mn)

1 23:42 ♅ ⚹ — ♓ 2 14:30
4 7:17 ♅ □ — ♈ 4 23:01
7 9:31 ☿ ☌ — ♉ 7 9:59
8 22:10 ☉ ☌ — ♊ 9 22:26
11 18:12 ♅ ☍ — ♋ 12 11:18
14 10:04 ☉ ⚹ — ♌ 14 23:15
17 1:00 ☉ □ — ♍ 17 8:45
19 11:33 ☉ △ — ♎ 19 14:41
21 2:39 ♅ ⚹ — ♏ 21 17:02
23 3:24 ♂ ⚹ — ♐ 23 16:57
25 2:08 ♅ ☌ — ♑ 25 16:15
27 3:56 ♂ ☌ — ♒ 27 17:00
29 4:48 ♅ ⚹ — ♓ 29 20:54

Last Aspect (Dy Hr Mn) — **☽ Ingress** (Dy Hr Mn)

31 14:45 ♂ ⚹ — ♈ 1 4:43
3 6:49 ☿ ⚹ — ♉ 3 15:45
5 14:18 ♂ △ — ♊ 6 4:26
7 23:01 ♃ □ — ♋ 8 17:16
10 17:22 ♀ ☌ — ♌ 11 5:11
12 23:26 ☉ ⚹ — ♍ 13 15:18
15 12:00 ☉ □ — ♎ 15 22:38
17 20:26 ☉ △ — ♏ 18 2:36
19 15:24 ♂ ⚹ — ♐ 20 3:36
21 14:38 ♃ □ — ♑ 22 3:00
23 22:35 ☿ ☍ — ♒ 24 2:50
25 11:43 ♅ ⚹ — ♓ 26 5:12
27 21:35 ♃ ☌ — ♈ 28 11:35
30 2:56 ♂ □ — ♉ 30 21:54

☽ Phases & Eclipses (Dy Hr Mn)

1 3:22 ☾ 10♒28
8 22:10 ● 18♉01
17 1:00 ☽ 25♌51
23 20:45 ○ 2♐25
30 12:55 ☾ 8♓49

7 14:00 ● 16♊32
15 12:00 ☽ 24♍06
22 3:42 ○ 0♑27
29 0:53 ☾ 7♈00

Astro Data

1 May 1986
Julian Day # 31532
SVP 5♓27'11"
GC 26♐38.9 ⚴ 21♋24.1
Eris 16♈13.4 ⚵ 14♐40.4R
⚷ 12♊19.9 ⚶ 18♓12.4
☽ Mean ☊ 29♈26.4

1 June 1986
Julian Day # 31563
SVP 5♓27'07"
GC 26♐39.0 ⚴ 6♌01.6
Eris 16♈29.7 ⚵ 8♐31.6R
⚷ 14♊46.4 ⚶ 0♈52.6
☽ Mean ☊ 27♈47.9

July 1986 LONGITUDE

Day	Sid.Time	☉	0 hr ☽	Noon☽	True☊	☿	♀	♂	⚳	♃	♄	♅	♆	♇
1 Tu	6 36 59	9♋21 24	1♉03 00	7♉02 10	27♈20.4	3♌46.3	18♌19.5	20♑05.3	18♍13.9	22♓39.2	4♐05.7	19♐35.1	4♑17.6	4♏35.4
2 W	6 40 56	10 18 37	12 59 13	18 54 45	27R 18.4	4 21.2	19 28.8	19R 50.0	18 34.8	22 41.2	4R 02.6	19R 32.9	4R 16.0	4R 34.9
3 Th	6 44 52	11 15 50	24 49 17	0♊43 20	27 14.0	4 52.1	20 38.0	19 34.3	18 55.8	22 43.1	3 59.5	19 30.7	4 14.4	4 34.5
4 F	6 48 49	12 13 04	6♊37 20	12 31 41	27 06.9	5 18.8	21 47.0	19 18.2	19 16.9	22 44.8	3 56.4	19 28.4	4 12.8	4 34.1
5 Sa	6 52 45	13 10 17	18 26 46	24 22 52	26 57.2	5 41.1	22 56.0	19 01.8	19 38.1	22 46.3	3 53.5	19 26.3	4 11.2	4 33.8
6 Su	6 56 42	14 07 31	0♋20 14	6♋19 07	26 45.4	5 59.0	24 04.8	18 45.0	19 59.4	22 47.7	3 50.6	19 24.1	4 09.6	4 33.5
7 M	7 00 38	15 04 44	12 19 41	18 22 04	26 32.3	6 12.4	25 13.6	18 28.0	20 20.9	22 48.8	3 47.8	19 21.9	4 08.0	4 33.2
8 Tu	7 04 35	16 01 58	24 26 26	0♌32 52	26 19.0	6 21.1	26 22.3	18 10.9	20 42.5	22 49.7	3 45.1	19 19.8	4 06.4	4 33.0
9 W	7 08 32	16 59 12	6♌41 30	12 52 26	26 06.8	6R 25.1	27 30.8	17 53.5	21 04.2	22 50.4	3 42.4	19 17.7	4 04.8	4 32.8
10 Th	7 12 28	17 56 25	19 05 48	25 21 44	25 56.4	6 24.4	28 39.2	17 36.1	21 26.0	22 51.0	3 39.8	19 15.7	4 03.3	4 32.6
11 F	7 16 25	18 53 39	1♍40 23	8♍01 58	25 48.7	6 19.0	29 47.5	17 18.6	21 47.9	22 51.3	3 37.4	19 13.6	4 01.7	4 32.4
12 Sa	7 20 21	19 50 53	14 26 41	20 54 48	25 43.8	6 08.8	0♍55.7	17 01.0	22 09.9	22R 51.4	3 35.0	19 11.6	4 00.2	4 32.3
13 Su	7 24 18	20 48 06	27 26 35	4♎02 19	25 41.5	5 54.0	2 03.8	16 43.5	22 32.1	22 51.4	3 32.6	19 09.6	3 58.6	4 32.2
14 M	7 28 14	21 45 20	10♎42 18	17 26 49	25 40.8	5 34.8	3 11.8	16 26.1	22 54.3	22 51.1	3 30.4	19 07.7	3 57.1	4D 32.2
15 Tu	7 32 11	22 42 33	24 16 08	1♏10 27	25 40.8	5 11.3	4 19.6	16 08.9	23 16.6	22 50.7	3 28.2	19 05.8	3 55.6	4 32.2
16 W	7 36 07	23 39 47	8♏09 56	15 14 37	25 40.1	4 43.7	5 27.3	15 51.8	23 39.1	22 50.0	3 26.2	19 03.9	3 54.1	4 32.2
17 Th	7 40 04	24 37 01	22 24 24	29 39 06	25 37.6	4 12.5	6 34.8	15 34.9	24 01.6	22 49.2	3 24.2	19 02.0	3 52.6	4 32.3
18 F	7 44 01	25 34 15	6♐58 18	14♐21 27	25 32.6	3 38.1	7 42.3	15 18.3	24 24.3	22 48.2	3 22.3	19 00.2	3 51.1	4 32.4
19 Sa	7 47 57	26 31 29	21 47 49	29 16 29	25 25.0	3 00.9	8 49.5	15 02.0	24 47.0	22 46.9	3 20.5	18 58.4	3 49.6	4 32.5
20 Su	7 51 54	27 28 44	6♑46 26	14♑16 29	25 15.2	2 21.6	9 56.7	14 46.0	25 09.8	22 45.5	3 18.8	18 56.7	3 48.2	4 32.7
21 M	7 55 50	28 25 59	21 45 28	29 12 10	25 04.3	1 40.7	11 03.7	14 30.4	25 32.7	22 43.9	3 17.2	18 55.0	3 46.7	4 32.9
22 Tu	7 59 47	29 23 14	6♒35 26	13♒54 14	24 53.4	0 58.9	12 10.5	14 15.3	25 55.7	22 42.1	3 15.6	18 53.3	3 45.3	4 33.1
23 W	8 03 43	0♌20 30	21 07 40	28 15 00	24 43.8	0 17.1	13 17.2	14 00.6	26 18.8	22 40.1	3 14.2	18 51.7	3 43.9	4 33.4
24 Th	8 07 40	1 17 47	5♓15 45	12♓09 34	24 36.4	29♋35.8	14 23.7	13 46.3	26 41.9	22 38.0	3 12.8	18 50.0	3 42.5	4 33.7
25 F	8 11 37	2 15 05	18 56 20	25 36 05	24 31.5	28 55.8	15 30.0	13 32.6	27 05.2	22 35.6	3 11.6	18 48.5	3 41.1	4 34.0
26 Sa	8 15 33	3 12 23	2♈09 04	8♈35 35	24 29.0	28 18.0	16 36.2	13 19.5	27 28.5	22 33.0	3 10.4	18 46.9	3 39.8	4 34.4
27 Su	8 19 30	4 09 42	14 56 07	21 11 11	24D 28.3	27 42.9	17 42.3	13 06.9	27 51.9	22 30.3	3 09.3	18 45.4	3 38.4	4 34.8
28 M	8 23 26	5 07 03	27 21 24	3♉27 24	24R 28.3	27 11.3	18 48.1	12 55.0	28 15.4	22 27.3	3 08.3	18 44.0	3 37.1	4 35.2
29 Tu	8 27 23	6 04 24	9♉29 52	15 29 27	24 28.0	26 43.8	19 53.8	12 43.7	28 39.0	22 24.2	3 07.5	18 42.6	3 35.8	4 35.7
30 W	8 31 19	7 01 46	21 26 49	27 22 39	24 26.4	26 20.9	20 59.4	12 33.1	29 02.6	22 20.9	3 06.7	18 41.2	3 34.5	4 36.2
31 Th	8 35 16	7 59 10	3♊17 33	9♊12 07	24 22.6	26 03.2	22 04.7	12 23.1	29 26.4	22 17.4	3 06.0	18 39.9	3 33.2	4 36.7

August 1986 LONGITUDE

Day	Sid.Time	☉	0 hr ☽	Noon☽	True☊	☿	♀	♂	⚳	♃	♄	♅	♆	♇
1 F	8 39 12	8♌56 35	15♊06 54	21♊02 26	24♈16.3	25♋50.9	23♍09.9	12♑13.9	29♍50.2	22♓13.7	3♐05.4	18♐38.6	3♑32.0	4♏37.3
2 Sa	8 43 09	9 54 00	26 59 08	2♋57 26	24R 07.4	25D 44.6	24 14.8	12R 05.4	0♎14.1	22R 09.8	3R 04.9	18R 37.4	3R 30.7	4 37.9
3 Su	8 47 06	10 51 27	8♋57 39	15 00 06	23 56.4	25 44.4	25 19.6	11 57.7	0 38.0	22 05.8	3 04.5	18 36.2	3 29.5	4 38.5
4 M	8 51 02	11 48 55	21 05 00	27 12 31	23 44.1	25 50.6	26 24.2	11 50.8	1 02.0	22 01.6	3 04.1	18 35.0	3 28.3	4 39.2
5 Tu	8 54 59	12 46 24	3♌22 48	9♌35 54	23 31.6	26 03.2	27 28.6	11 44.7	1 26.1	21 57.2	3 03.9	18 33.9	3 27.2	4 39.9
6 W	8 58 55	13 43 53	15 51 52	22 10 43	23 20.1	26 22.5	28 32.8	11 39.4	1 50.3	21 52.6	3D 03.8	18 32.8	3 26.0	4 40.6
7 Th	9 02 52	14 41 24	28 32 27	4♍57 02	23 10.3	26 48.5	29 36.7	11 34.9	2 14.5	21 47.9	3 03.8	18 31.8	3 24.9	4 41.4
8 F	9 06 48	15 38 56	11♍24 27	17 54 41	23 03.2	27 21.1	0♎40.4	11 31.2	2 38.8	21 43.0	3 03.9	18 30.8	3 23.8	4 42.2
9 Sa	9 10 45	16 36 28	24 27 45	1♎03 40	22 58.7	28 00.3	1 43.9	11 28.4	3 03.2	21 38.0	3 04.1	18 29.9	3 22.7	4 43.0
10 Su	9 14 41	17 34 01	7♎42 30	14 24 17	22D 56.8	28 46.1	2 47.2	11 26.4	3 27.6	21 32.7	3 04.3	18 29.0	3 21.7	4 43.9
11 M	9 18 38	18 31 36	21 09 09	27 57 09	22 56.6	29 38.4	3 50.2	11D 25.3	3 52.1	21 27.4	3 04.7	18 28.2	3 20.6	4 44.8
12 Tu	9 22 35	19 29 11	4♏48 26	11♏43 04	22R 57.1	0♌37.0	4 53.0	11 25.0	4 16.6	21 21.8	3 05.2	18 27.4	3 19.6	4 45.8
13 W	9 26 31	20 26 47	18 41 06	25 42 33	22 57.1	1 41.8	5 55.5	11 25.6	4 41.2	21 16.2	3 05.7	18 26.7	3 18.7	4 46.7
14 Th	9 30 28	21 24 24	2♐47 21	9♐55 21	22 55.7	2 52.5	6 57.7	11 27.0	5 05.9	21 10.4	3 06.4	18 26.0	3 17.7	4 47.7
15 F	9 34 24	22 22 02	17 06 19	24 19 53	22 52.2	4 09.0	7 59.7	11 29.3	5 30.6	21 04.4	3 07.2	18 25.3	3 16.8	4 48.8
16 Sa	9 38 21	23 19 41	1♑35 34	8♑52 46	22 46.4	5 30.9	9 01.3	11 32.4	5 55.4	20 58.3	3 08.0	18 24.7	3 15.9	4 49.8
17 Su	9 42 17	24 17 21	16 10 48	23 28 51	22 38.7	6 57.9	10 02.7	11 36.3	6 20.2	20 52.1	3 09.0	18 24.2	3 15.0	4 50.9
18 M	9 46 14	25 15 02	0♒46 05	8♒01 36	22 29.9	8 29.8	11 03.7	11 41.0	6 45.1	20 45.8	3 10.0	18 23.7	3 14.2	4 52.1
19 Tu	9 50 10	26 12 44	15 14 32	22 24 05	22 21.1	10 06.2	12 04.5	11 46.6	7 10.0	20 39.3	3 11.2	18 23.2	3 13.3	4 53.2
20 W	9 54 07	27 10 28	29 29 28	6♓30 03	22 13.3	11 46.6	13 04.9	11 52.9	7 35.0	20 32.7	3 12.4	18 22.8	3 12.5	4 54.4
21 Th	9 58 04	28 08 12	13♓25 19	20 14 55	22 07.3	13 30.7	14 04.9	12 00.1	8 00.0	20 26.0	3 13.8	18 22.5	3 11.8	4 55.6
22 F	10 02 00	29 05 59	26 58 36	3♈36 17	22 03.6	15 17.9	15 04.7	12 08.0	8 25.0	20 19.1	3 15.2	18 22.2	3 11.0	4 56.9
23 Sa	10 05 57	0♍03 47	10♈08 03	16 34 04	22D 01.9	17 08.0	16 04.0	12 16.6	8 50.2	20 12.2	3 16.7	18 21.9	3 10.3	4 58.1
24 Su	10 09 53	1 01 37	22 54 38	29 10 09	22 02.0	19 00.4	17 03.0	12 26.1	9 15.3	20 05.2	3 18.3	18 21.7	3 09.6	4 59.5
25 M	10 13 50	1 59 28	5♉21 04	11♉27 56	22 03.0	20 54.8	18 01.7	12 36.3	9 40.5	19 58.0	3 20.1	18 21.6	3 09.0	5 00.8
26 Tu	10 17 46	2 57 21	17 31 20	23 31 51	22R 04.2	22 50.6	18 59.9	12 47.2	10 05.8	19 50.8	3 21.9	18 21.5	3 08.3	5 02.2
27 W	10 21 43	3 55 16	29 30 09	5♊26 52	22 04.6	24 47.6	19 57.8	12 58.9	10 31.1	19 43.5	3 23.8	18D 21.5	3 07.8	5 03.6
28 Th	10 25 39	4 53 13	11♊22 38	17 18 06	22 03.6	26 45.4	20 55.2	13 11.3	10 56.4	19 36.1	3 25.8	18 21.5	3 07.2	5 05.0
29 F	10 29 36	5 51 12	23 13 52	29 10 32	22 00.8	28 43.7	21 52.3	13 24.4	11 21.8	19 28.6	3 27.9	18 21.5	3 06.7	5 06.4
30 Sa	10 33 33	6 49 12	5♋08 38	11♋08 41	21 56.2	0♍42.1	22 48.8	13 38.2	11 47.3	19 21.0	3 30.1	18 21.6	3 06.2	5 07.9
31 Su	10 37 29	7 47 15	17 11 09	23 16 25	21 49.9	2 40.5	23 45.0	13 52.7	12 12.8	19 13.4	3 32.3	18 21.8	3 05.7	5 09.4

Astro Data	Dy Hr Mn
♅∠♇	1 8:54
☿ R	9 20:28
♃ R	12 17:01
☽0S	13 12:24
♇ D	15 6:31
☽0N	26 3:33
☿ D	3 0:47
♄ D	7 4:50
♀0S	7 11:44
☽0S	9 17:02
♂ D	12 7:45
♄⚺♆	20 13:14
☽0N	22 12:13
♃⚼♇	25 4:13
♅ D	27 21:16

Planet Ingress		Dy Hr Mn
♀	♍	11 16:23
☉	♌	23 3:24
☿	♋R	23 21:51
⚳	♎	1 21:53
♀	♎	7 20:46
☿	♌	11 21:09
☉	♍	23 10:26
☿	♍	30 3:28

Last Aspect Dy Hr Mn		☽ Ingress	Dy Hr Mn
2 19:41	♃ ⚹	♊	3 10:32
5 8:46	♀ ⚹	♋	5 23:19
7 20:48	♃ △	♌	8 10:56
10 18:54	♀ ☌	♍	10 20:50
12 15:35	♃ ☍	♎	13 4:40
14 20:10	☉ □	♏	15 9:58
17 3:05	☉ △	♐	17 12:34
19 1:36	♃ □	♑	19 13:10
21 10:40	☉ ☍	♒	21 13:17
22 20:15	♅ ⚹	♓	23 14:59
25 17:47	☿ △	♈	25 20:02
28 0:10	☿ □	♉	28 5:11
30 9:58	☿ ⚹	♊	30 17:19

Last Aspect Dy Hr Mn		☽ Ingress	Dy Hr Mn
1 16:43	♀ □	♋	2 6:04
4 10:17	♀ ⚹	♌	4 17:26
6 5:07	♅ △	♍	7 2:44
9 6:09	☿ ⚹	♎	9 10:05
11 15:11	☿ □	♏	11 15:36
13 4:29	♃ △	♐	13 19:17
15 8:31	☉ △	♑	15 21:22
17 7:44	♃ ⚹	♒	17 22:44
19 18:54	☉ ☍	♓	20 0:52
21 12:20	♃ ☌	♈	22 5:27
23 15:23	♅ △	♉	24 13:36
26 10:21	☿ □	♊	27 1:00
29 10:55	☿ ⚹	♋	29 13:40

☽ Phases & Eclipses Dy Hr Mn	
7 4:55	● 14♋48
14 20:10	☽ 22♎05
21 10:40	○ 28♑23
28 15:34	☾ 5♉16
5 18:36	● 13♌02
13 2:21	☽ 20♏04
19 18:54	○ 26♒29
27 8:39	☾ 3♊47

Astro Data

1 July 1986
Julian Day # 31593
SVP 5♓27'01"
GC 26♐39.0 ⚵ 20♌25.8
Eris 16♈38.0 ⚶ 2♐41.8R
⚷ 17♊13.3 ⚴ 10♈41.4
☽ Mean ☊ 26♈12.6

1 August 1986
Julian Day # 31624
SVP 5♓26'56"
GC 26♐39.1 ⚵ 5♍16.6
Eris 16♈36.8R ⚶ 0♐59.3
⚷ 19♊25.8 ⚴ 16♈44.7
☽ Mean ☊ 24♈34.1

LONGITUDE — September 1986

Day	Sid.Time	☉	0 hr ☽	Noon ☽	True ☊	☿	♀	♂	⚳	♃	♄	♅	♆	♇
1 M	10 41 26	8♍45 19	29♋24 51	5♌36 43	21♈42.6	4♍38.6	24♎40.6	14♑07.8	12♎38.3	19♓05.7	3♐34.7	18♐22.0	3♑05.2	5♏11.0
2 Tu	10 45 22	9 43 25	11♌52 14	18 11 32	21R35.0	6 36.2	25 35.8	14 23.7	13 03.8	18R58.0	3 37.2	18 22.3	3R04.8	5 12.5
3 W	10 49 19	10 41 32	24 34 42	1♍01 44	21 27.9	8 33.2	26 30.5	14 40.2	13 29.4	18 50.2	3 39.7	18 22.6	3 04.4	5 14.1
4 Th	10 53 15	11 39 42	7♍32 35	14 07 09	21 22.1	10 29.4	27 24.7	14 57.4	13 55.1	18 42.4	3 42.4	18 22.9	3 04.1	5 15.7
5 F	10 57 12	12 37 53	20 45 16	27 26 46	21 18.0	12 24.8	28 18.3	15 15.2	14 20.7	18 34.5	3 45.1	18 23.4	3 03.8	5 17.4
6 Sa	11 01 08	13 36 05	4♎11 25	10♎59 01	21D15.8	14 19.3	29 11.3	15 33.6	14 46.4	18 26.6	3 47.9	18 23.8	3 03.5	5 19.1
7 Su	11 05 05	14 34 20	17 49 20	24 42 08	21 15.4	16 12.8	0♏03.8	15 52.6	15 12.2	18 18.6	3 50.8	18 24.3	3 03.2	5 20.8
8 M	11 09 01	15 32 35	1♏37 12	8♏34 21	21 16.3	18 05.2	0 55.7	16 12.3	15 37.9	18 10.7	3 53.8	18 24.9	3 03.0	5 22.5
9 Tu	11 12 58	16 30 53	15 33 23	22 34 06	21 17.8	19 56.6	1 46.9	16 32.5	16 03.7	18 02.7	3 56.9	18 25.5	3 02.8	5 24.2
10 W	11 16 55	17 29 12	29 36 21	6♐39 56	21R19.0	21 46.8	2 37.5	16 53.3	16 29.6	17 54.8	4 00.1	18 26.2	3 02.7	5 26.0
11 Th	11 20 51	18 27 32	13♐44 40	20 50 21	21 19.4	23 36.0	3 27.4	17 14.7	16 55.4	17 46.8	4 03.3	18 26.9	3 02.5	5 27.8
12 F	11 24 48	19 25 54	27 56 45	5♑03 34	21 18.4	25 24.0	4 16.5	17 36.7	17 21.3	17 38.8	4 06.7	18 27.7	3 02.4	5 29.6
13 Sa	11 28 44	20 24 18	12♑10 30	19 17 13	21 16.1	27 10.9	5 05.0	17 59.1	17 47.3	17 30.9	4 10.1	18 28.6	3 02.4	5 31.5
14 Su	11 32 41	21 22 43	26 23 17	3♒28 17	21 12.6	28 56.7	5 52.6	18 22.1	18 13.2	17 22.9	4 13.6	18 29.4	3D02.4	5 33.3
15 M	11 36 37	22 21 10	10♒31 46	17 33 14	21 08.4	0♎41.5	6 39.5	18 45.6	18 39.2	17 15.0	4 17.2	18 30.4	3 02.4	5 35.2
16 Tu	11 40 34	23 19 38	24 32 14	1♓28 18	21 04.1	2 25.1	7 25.5	19 09.6	19 05.2	17 07.2	4 20.9	18 31.3	3 02.4	5 37.1
17 W	11 44 31	24 18 08	8♓20 59	15 09 55	21 00.4	4 07.6	8 10.6	19 34.1	19 31.2	16 59.3	4 24.6	18 32.4	3 02.5	5 39.1
18 Th	11 48 27	25 16 40	21 54 46	28 35 17	20 57.7	5 49.2	8 54.9	19 59.0	19 57.3	16 51.5	4 28.5	18 33.5	3 02.6	5 41.0
19 F	11 52 24	26 15 14	5♈11 16	11♈42 39	20D56.2	7 29.6	9 38.2	20 24.4	20 23.3	16 43.7	4 32.4	18 34.6	3 02.7	5 43.0
20 Sa	11 56 20	27 13 50	18 09 24	24 31 37	20 55.9	9 09.1	10 20.5	20 50.3	20 49.4	16 36.0	4 36.3	18 35.8	3 02.9	5 45.0
21 Su	12 00 17	28 12 28	0♉49 26	7♉03 06	20 56.7	10 47.5	11 01.8	21 16.6	21 15.5	16 28.4	4 40.4	18 37.0	3 03.1	5 47.0
22 M	12 04 13	29 11 08	13 12 55	19 19 15	20 58.1	12 25.0	11 42.1	21 43.3	21 41.7	16 20.8	4 44.6	18 38.3	3 03.3	5 49.0
23 Tu	12 08 10	0♎09 50	25 22 32	1♊23 15	20 59.7	14 01.5	12 21.3	22 10.4	22 07.8	16 13.2	4 48.8	18 39.6	3 03.6	5 51.1
24 W	12 12 06	1 08 34	7♊21 53	13 19 01	21 01.2	15 37.0	12 59.4	22 38.0	22 34.0	16 05.8	4 53.1	18 41.0	3 03.9	5 53.1
25 Th	12 16 03	2 07 21	19 15 12	25 11 01	21R02.1	17 11.6	13 36.2	23 05.9	23 00.2	15 58.4	4 57.4	18 42.4	3 04.2	5 55.2
26 F	12 19 59	3 06 10	1♋07 06	7♋04 01	21 02.2	18 45.3	14 11.9	23 34.3	23 26.4	15 51.1	5 01.9	18 43.9	3 04.6	5 57.3
27 Sa	12 23 56	4 05 02	13 02 23	19 02 46	21 01.5	20 18.0	14 46.3	24 03.0	23 52.7	15 43.9	5 06.4	18 45.4	3 05.0	5 59.5
28 Su	12 27 53	5 03 55	25 05 44	1♌11 47	21 00.1	21 49.9	15 19.4	24 32.1	24 19.0	15 36.8	5 11.0	18 47.0	3 05.4	6 01.6
29 M	12 31 49	6 02 51	7♌21 26	13 35 05	20 58.2	23 20.8	15 51.1	25 01.6	24 45.2	15 29.8	5 15.7	18 48.6	3 05.9	6 03.8
30 Tu	12 35 46	7 01 49	19 53 08	26 15 51	20 56.2	24 50.9	16 21.4	25 31.4	25 11.5	15 22.9	5 20.4	18 50.2	3 06.4	6 05.9

LONGITUDE — October 1986

Day	Sid.Time	☉	0 hr ☽	Noon ☽	True ☊	☿	♀	♂	⚳	♃	♄	♅	♆	♇
1 W	12 39 42	8♎00 49	2♍43 28	9♍16 08	20♈54.3	26♎20.0	16♏50.2	26♑01.6	25♎37.8	15♓16.1	5♐25.2	18♐51.9	3♑06.9	6♏08.1
2 Th	12 43 39	8 59 51	15 53 52	22 36 37	20R52.8	27 48.2	17 17.5	26 32.1	26 04.2	15R09.5	5 30.1	18 53.7	3 07.5	6 10.3
3 F	12 47 35	9 58 55	29 24 15	6♎16 30	20 51.9	29 15.6	17 43.1	27 03.0	26 30.5	15 02.9	5 35.0	18 55.5	3 08.1	6 12.6
4 Sa	12 51 32	10 58 02	13♎13 02	20 13 27	20D51.6	0♏41.9	18 07.2	27 34.2	26 56.9	14 56.5	5 40.0	18 57.4	3 08.7	6 14.8
5 Su	12 55 28	11 57 10	27 17 15	4♏23 55	20 51.8	2 07.4	18 29.5	28 05.8	27 23.2	14 50.2	5 45.1	18 59.2	3 09.4	6 17.0
6 M	12 59 25	12 56 21	11♏32 52	18 43 32	20 52.3	3 31.9	18 50.0	28 37.6	27 49.6	14 44.1	5 50.2	19 01.2	3 10.1	6 19.3
7 Tu	13 03 22	13 55 33	25 55 18	3♐07 36	20 53.0	4 55.4	19 08.7	29 09.8	28 16.0	14 38.1	5 55.4	19 03.2	3 10.8	6 21.6
8 W	13 07 18	14 54 47	10♐19 53	17 31 39	20 53.5	6 17.8	19 25.4	29 42.3	28 42.4	14 32.2	6 00.7	19 05.2	3 11.6	6 23.9
9 Th	13 11 15	15 54 03	24 42 25	1♑51 47	20 53.9	7 39.2	19 40.2	0♒15.0	29 08.8	14 26.5	6 06.0	19 07.3	3 12.3	6 26.2
10 F	13 15 11	16 53 21	8♑59 24	16 04 55	20R54.0	8 59.6	19 52.9	0 48.1	29 35.2	14 20.9	6 11.4	19 09.4	3 13.2	6 28.5
11 Sa	13 19 08	17 52 40	23 08 07	0♒08 45	20 54.0	10 18.7	20 03.5	1 21.4	0♏01.7	14 15.5	6 16.9	19 11.6	3 14.0	6 30.8
12 Su	13 23 04	18 52 01	7♒06 39	14 01 41	20 53.8	11 36.6	20 12.0	1 55.0	0 28.1	14 10.3	6 22.4	19 13.8	3 14.9	6 33.1
13 M	13 27 01	19 51 24	20 53 42	27 42 37	20 53.7	12 53.2	20 18.2	2 28.8	0 54.5	14 05.2	6 27.9	19 16.0	3 15.8	6 35.5
14 Tu	13 30 57	20 50 48	4♓28 20	11♓10 48	20D53.6	14 08.4	20 22.2	3 02.9	1 20.9	14 00.3	6 33.5	19 18.3	3 16.8	6 37.8
15 W	13 34 54	21 50 15	17 49 56	24 25 42	20 53.6	15 22.2	20R23.8	3 37.3	1 47.4	13 55.5	6 39.2	19 20.6	3 17.8	6 40.2
16 Th	13 38 51	22 49 43	0♈58 05	7♈27 02	20 53.7	16 34.3	20 23.0	4 11.9	2 13.8	13 51.0	6 44.9	19 23.0	3 18.8	6 42.6
17 F	13 42 47	23 49 13	13 52 34	20 14 43	20R53.8	17 44.7	20 19.9	4 46.7	2 40.3	13 46.6	6 50.7	19 25.4	3 19.8	6 44.9
18 Sa	13 46 44	24 48 45	26 33 32	2♉49 04	20 53.7	18 53.3	20 14.4	5 21.7	3 06.7	13 42.3	6 56.6	19 27.8	3 20.9	6 47.3
19 Su	13 50 40	25 48 19	9♉01 28	15 10 51	20 53.4	19 59.8	20 06.4	5 57.0	3 33.2	13 38.3	7 02.4	19 30.3	3 22.0	6 49.7
20 M	13 54 37	26 47 56	21 17 26	27 21 25	20 52.8	21 04.0	19 56.0	6 32.4	3 59.6	13 34.4	7 08.4	19 32.8	3 23.1	6 52.1
21 Tu	13 58 33	27 47 34	3♊23 05	9♊22 45	20 51.9	22 05.9	19 43.2	7 08.1	4 26.1	13 30.7	7 14.4	19 35.4	3 24.3	6 54.5
22 W	14 02 30	28 47 15	15 20 46	21 17 32	20 50.8	23 05.0	19 28.0	7 44.0	4 52.5	13 27.3	7 20.4	19 38.0	3 25.5	6 56.9
23 Th	14 06 26	29 46 58	27 13 29	3♋09 04	20 49.7	24 01.2	19 10.5	8 20.1	5 19.0	13 24.0	7 26.5	19 40.6	3 26.7	6 59.3
24 F	14 10 23	0♏46 43	9♋04 48	15 01 13	20 48.9	24 54.0	18 50.7	8 56.3	5 45.4	13 20.8	7 32.6	19 43.3	3 27.9	7 01.7
25 Sa	14 14 20	1 46 30	20 58 52	26 58 18	20D48.4	25 43.3	18 28.7	9 32.8	6 11.9	13 17.9	7 38.8	19 46.0	3 29.2	7 04.2
26 Su	14 18 16	2 46 20	3♌00 07	9♌04 54	20 48.4	26 28.4	18 04.5	10 09.4	6 38.3	13 15.2	7 45.0	19 48.7	3 30.5	7 06.6
27 M	14 22 13	3 46 12	15 13 13	21 25 37	20 49.0	27 09.2	17 38.4	10 46.2	7 04.7	13 12.7	7 51.3	19 51.5	3 31.9	7 09.0
28 Tu	14 26 09	4 46 06	27 42 39	4♍04 46	20 50.1	27 44.9	17 10.3	11 23.3	7 31.2	13 10.3	7 57.6	19 54.3	3 33.2	7 11.4
29 W	14 30 06	5 46 02	10♍32 25	17 05 56	20 51.3	28 15.2	16 40.6	12 00.4	7 57.6	13 08.2	8 04.0	19 57.1	3 34.6	7 13.9
30 Th	14 34 02	6 46 00	23 45 35	0♎31 30	20 52.5	28 39.4	16 09.2	12 37.8	8 24.0	13 06.3	8 10.3	20 00.0	3 36.0	7 16.3
31 F	14 37 59	7 46 00	7♎23 44	14 22 07	20R53.2	28 57.0	15 36.5	13 15.3	8 50.5	13 04.5	8 16.8	20 02.9	3 37.5	7 18.7

Astro Data

	Dy Hr Mn
☽0S	5 23:00
♃□♅	6 19:52
⚳0S	7 21:21
♆ D	14 19:38
☿0S	16 6:46
☽0N	18 21:07
☉0S	23 7:59
☽0S	3 7:22
♀ R	15 16:33
♄⊻♇	15 19:04
☽0N	16 4:55
☽0S	30 17:25

Planet Ingress

		Dy Hr Mn
♀	♏	7 10:15
☿	♎	15 2:28
☉	♎	23 7:59
☿	♏	4 0:19
♂	♒	9 1:01
⚳	♏	11 10:30
☉	♏	23 17:14

Last Aspect / ☽ Ingress (September)

Last Aspect Dy Hr Mn			☽ Ingress	Dy Hr Mn
31 13:01	♀	□	♌	1 1:08
3 2:58	♀	⚹	♍	3 10:06
4 20:14	♃	☍	♎	5 16:33
7 1:01	♅	⚹	♏	7 21:12
9 6:50	☿	⚹	♐	10 0:40
11 17:21	☿	□	♑	12 3:28
14 3:15	☿	△	♒	14 6:07
15 13:38	♅	⚹	♓	16 9:27
18 5:34	☉	☍	♈	18 14:33
20 4:47	♂	□	♉	20 22:25
22 16:56	♂	△	♊	23 9:13
24 22:52	♅	☍	♋	25 21:44
27 22:21	♂	☍	♌	28 9:39
30 9:00	☿	⚹	♍	30 18:57

Last Aspect / ☽ Ingress (October)

Last Aspect Dy Hr Mn			☽ Ingress	Dy Hr Mn
2 19:13	♂	△	♎	3 1:03
5 0:57	♂	□	♏	5 4:35
7 5:09	♂	⚹	♐	7 6:48
8 14:37	♅	☌	♑	9 8:52
10 18:33	♀	⚹	♒	11 11:45
12 22:52	♀	□	♓	13 16:03
15 4:39	♀	△	♈	15 22:13
17 19:22	☉	☍	♉	18 6:35
19 22:22	☿	☍	♊	20 17:15
23 4:33	☉	△	♋	23 5:37
25 9:19	☿	△	♌	25 18:02
27 23:30	☿	□	♍	28 4:20
30 8:37	☿	⚹	♎	30 11:05

☽ Phases & Eclipses

Dy Hr Mn		
4 7:10	●	11♍28
11 7:41	☽	18♐17
18 5:34	○	25♓01
26 3:17	☾	2♋45
3 18:55	●	10♎16
3 19:05:19	●	AT00'00"
10 13:28	☽	16♑57
17 19:22	○	24♈07
17 19:18	●	T 1.246
25 22:26	☾	2♌12

Astro Data

1 September 1986
Julian Day # 31655
SVP 5♓26'51"
GC 26♐39.2 ⚴ 19♍57.7
Eris 16♈26.2R ⚵ 4♐12.1
⚷ 20♊55.3 ⚶ 16♈30.1R
☽ Mean ☊ 22♈55.6

1 October 1986
Julian Day # 31685
SVP 5♓26'48"
GC 26♐39.3 ⚴ 3♎56.1
Eris 16♈09.9R ⚵ 10♐47.6
⚷ 21♊22.5R ⚶ 10♈12.2R
☽ Mean ☊ 21♈20.3

November 1986 LONGITUDE

Day	Sid.Time	☉	0 hr ☽	Noon ☽	True ☊	☿	♀	♂	⚳	♃	♄	♅	♆	♇
1 Sa	14 41 55	8♏46 03	21♎26 25	28♎36 13	20♈53.2	29♏07.2	15♏02.6	13♒53.0	9♏16.9	13♓03.0	8♐23.2	20♐05.9	3♑38.9	7♏21.2
2 Su	14 45 52	9 46 07	5♏50 55	13♏09 49	20R 52.2	29R 09.5	14R 27.8	14 30.8	9 43.3	13R 01.7	8 29.8	20 08.8	3 40.4	7 23.6
3 M	14 49 49	10 46 13	20 32 04	27 56 45	20 50.2	29 03.3	13 52.1	15 08.8	10 09.7	13 00.6	8 36.3	20 11.8	3 41.9	7 26.0
4 Tu	14 53 45	11 46 21	5♐22 50	12♐49 20	20 47.5	28 48.1	13 16.0	15 47.0	10 36.1	12 59.7	8 42.9	20 14.9	3 43.5	7 28.5
5 W	14 57 42	12 46 31	20 15 12	27 39 30	20 44.5	28 23.3	12 39.6	16 25.3	11 02.4	12 59.0	8 49.5	20 17.9	3 45.1	7 30.9
6 Th	15 01 38	13 46 42	5♑01 21	12♑19 58	20 41.8	27 48.7	12 03.1	17 03.7	11 28.8	12 58.5	8 56.2	20 21.0	3 46.7	7 33.3
7 F	15 05 35	14 46 55	19 34 44	26 45 10	20 39.7	27 04.4	11 26.8	17 42.3	11 55.2	12D 58.2	9 02.8	20 24.1	3 48.3	7 35.7
8 Sa	15 09 31	15 47 09	3♒50 55	10♒51 46	20D 38.7	26 10.7	10 51.0	18 21.0	12 21.5	12 58.1	9 09.5	20 27.3	3 49.9	7 38.1
9 Su	15 13 28	16 47 25	17 47 36	24 38 28	20 38.8	25 08.4	10 15.9	18 59.8	12 47.8	12 58.2	9 16.3	20 30.5	3 51.6	7 40.6
10 M	15 17 24	17 47 42	1♓24 27	8♓05 44	20 39.9	23 58.6	9 41.7	19 38.8	13 14.1	12 58.6	9 23.1	20 33.6	3 53.3	7 43.0
11 Tu	15 21 21	18 48 00	14 42 31	21 15 04	20 41.5	22 43.1	9 08.7	20 17.9	13 40.4	12 59.1	9 29.8	20 36.9	3 55.0	7 45.4
12 W	15 25 18	19 48 20	27 43 40	4♈08 34	20 43.1	21 24.0	8 37.1	20 57.1	14 06.6	12 59.8	9 36.7	20 40.1	3 56.8	7 47.8
13 Th	15 29 14	20 48 41	10♈30 03	16 48 23	20R 44.1	20 03.6	8 07.0	21 36.4	14 32.9	13 00.8	9 43.5	20 43.4	3 58.5	7 50.1
14 F	15 33 11	21 49 04	23 03 48	29 16 32	20 43.8	18 44.7	7 38.6	22 15.8	14 59.1	13 01.9	9 50.4	20 46.7	4 00.3	7 52.5
15 Sa	15 37 07	22 49 28	5♉26 48	11♉34 46	20 41.9	17 29.8	7 12.2	22 55.3	15 25.3	13 03.3	9 57.3	20 50.0	4 02.1	7 54.9
16 Su	15 41 04	23 49 54	17 40 38	23 44 34	20 38.3	16 21.3	6 47.8	23 34.9	15 51.5	13 04.8	10 04.2	20 53.3	4 03.9	7 57.3
17 M	15 45 00	24 50 22	29 46 44	5♊47 18	20 33.1	15 21.3	6 25.6	24 14.6	16 17.7	13 06.6	10 11.1	20 56.7	4 05.8	7 59.6
18 Tu	15 48 57	25 50 51	11♊46 26	17 44 21	20 26.7	14 31.3	6 05.6	24 54.4	16 43.8	13 08.6	10 18.1	21 00.1	4 07.6	8 02.0
19 W	15 52 53	26 51 22	23 41 16	29 37 25	20 19.7	13 52.4	5 48.0	25 34.3	17 09.9	13 10.7	10 25.0	21 03.4	4 09.5	8 04.3
20 Th	15 56 50	27 51 55	5♋33 05	11♋28 35	20 12.7	13 25.0	5 32.8	26 14.3	17 36.0	13 13.1	10 32.0	21 06.9	4 11.4	8 06.6
21 F	16 00 47	28 52 29	17 24 15	23 20 29	20 06.6	13D 09.4	5 20.1	26 54.3	18 02.1	13 15.7	10 39.0	21 10.3	4 13.3	8 08.9
22 Sa	16 04 43	29 53 05	29 17 43	5♌16 24	20 01.8	13 05.2	5 09.8	27 34.5	18 28.2	13 18.4	10 46.1	21 13.8	4 15.3	8 11.2
23 Su	16 08 40	0♐53 42	11♌17 03	17 20 12	19 58.8	13 11.9	5 02.1	28 14.7	18 54.2	13 21.4	10 53.1	21 17.2	4 17.2	8 13.5
24 M	16 12 36	1 54 22	23 26 25	29 36 16	19D 57.7	13 28.7	4 56.9	28 55.0	19 20.2	13 24.5	11 00.1	21 20.7	4 19.2	8 15.8
25 Tu	16 16 33	2 55 02	5♍50 22	12♍09 16	19 58.0	13 54.9	4D 54.1	29 35.4	19 46.2	13 27.9	11 07.2	21 24.2	4 21.2	8 18.1
26 W	16 20 29	3 55 45	18 33 33	25 03 45	19 59.3	14 29.4	4 53.8	0♓15.9	20 12.1	13 31.4	11 14.3	21 27.7	4 23.2	8 20.3
27 Th	16 24 26	4 56 29	1♎40 20	8♎23 40	20R 00.7	15 11.5	4 56.0	0 56.4	20 38.0	13 35.1	11 21.4	21 31.2	4 25.2	8 22.6
28 F	16 28 22	5 57 15	15 14 04	22 11 38	20 01.1	16 00.3	5 00.5	1 37.0	21 03.9	13 39.1	11 28.4	21 34.8	4 27.3	8 24.8
29 Sa	16 32 19	6 58 02	29 16 23	6♏28 04	19 59.9	16 55.0	5 07.4	2 17.7	21 29.8	13 43.2	11 35.5	21 38.3	4 29.3	8 27.0
30 Su	16 36 16	7 58 50	13♏46 19	21 10 27	19 56.5	17 54.7	5 16.6	2 58.5	21 55.6	13 47.5	11 42.6	21 41.9	4 31.4	8 29.2

December 1986 LONGITUDE

Day	Sid.Time	☉	0 hr ☽	Noon ☽	True ☊	☿	♀	♂	⚳	♃	♄	♅	♆	♇
1 M	16 40 12	8♐59 40	28♏39 40	6♐12 53	19♈50.9	18♏59.0	5♏28.0	3♓39.3	22♏21.4	13♓52.0	11♐49.8	21♐45.5	4♑33.5	8♏31.4
2 Tu	16 44 09	10 00 32	13♐48 55	21 26 26	19R 43.5	20 07.1	5 41.6	4 20.2	22 47.1	13 56.7	11 56.9	21 49.1	4 35.6	8 33.5
3 W	16 48 05	11 01 24	29 04 03	6♑40 22	19 35.3	21 18.6	5 57.2	5 01.1	23 12.9	14 01.6	12 04.0	21 52.7	4 37.7	8 35.7
4 Th	16 52 02	12 02 18	14♑14 05	21 44 00	19 27.3	22 33.0	6 15.0	5 42.2	23 38.5	14 06.6	12 11.1	21 56.3	4 39.8	8 37.8
5 F	16 55 58	13 03 12	29 09 07	6♒28 35	19 20.7	23 49.8	6 34.7	6 23.2	24 04.2	14 11.8	12 18.2	21 59.9	4 42.0	8 39.9
6 Sa	16 59 55	14 04 07	13♒41 49	20 48 26	19 16.0	25 08.8	6 56.3	7 04.4	24 29.8	14 17.3	12 25.4	22 03.5	4 44.1	8 42.0
7 Su	17 03 52	15 05 02	27 48 16	4♓41 18	19D 13.5	26 29.6	7 19.8	7 45.6	24 55.4	14 22.9	12 32.5	22 07.2	4 46.3	8 44.1
8 M	17 07 48	16 05 58	11♓27 41	18 07 44	19 13.0	27 52.0	7 45.1	8 26.8	25 20.9	14 28.6	12 39.6	22 10.8	4 48.4	8 46.1
9 Tu	17 11 45	17 06 55	24 41 49	1♈10 23	19 13.6	29 15.7	8 12.1	9 08.1	25 46.3	14 34.6	12 46.7	22 14.4	4 50.6	8 48.2
10 W	17 15 41	18 07 53	7♈33 55	13 52 56	19R 14.4	0♐40.6	8 40.8	9 49.4	26 11.8	14 40.7	12 53.8	22 18.1	4 52.8	8 50.2
11 Th	17 19 38	19 08 51	20 07 56	26 19 26	19 14.3	2 06.5	9 11.1	10 30.7	26 37.2	14 47.0	13 00.9	22 21.7	4 55.0	8 52.2
12 F	17 23 34	20 09 50	2♉27 54	8♉33 46	19 12.3	3 33.2	9 42.9	11 12.1	27 02.5	14 53.4	13 08.0	22 25.4	4 57.2	8 54.1
13 Sa	17 27 31	21 10 49	14 37 27	20 39 18	19 07.6	5 00.7	10 16.3	11 53.6	27 27.8	15 00.1	13 15.0	22 29.0	4 59.4	8 56.1
14 Su	17 31 27	22 11 50	26 39 39	2♊38 48	19 00.2	6 28.8	10 51.1	12 35.0	27 53.1	15 06.9	13 22.1	22 32.7	5 01.7	8 58.0
15 M	17 35 24	23 12 51	8♊36 57	14 34 21	18 50.0	7 57.5	11 27.3	13 16.5	28 18.3	15 13.8	13 29.2	22 36.3	5 03.9	8 59.9
16 Tu	17 39 21	24 13 52	20 31 12	26 27 38	18 37.9	9 26.7	12 04.9	13 58.1	28 43.4	15 20.9	13 36.2	22 40.0	5 06.1	9 01.8
17 W	17 43 17	25 14 55	2♋23 50	8♋19 58	18 24.5	10 56.4	12 43.8	14 39.6	29 08.5	15 28.2	13 43.2	22 43.6	5 08.4	9 03.6
18 Th	17 47 14	26 15 58	14 16 11	20 12 41	18 11.1	12 26.4	13 23.9	15 21.2	29 33.6	15 35.7	13 50.2	22 47.3	5 10.6	9 05.4
19 F	17 51 10	27 17 01	26 09 40	2♌07 21	17 58.8	13 56.8	14 05.2	16 02.8	29 58.6	15 43.2	13 57.2	22 50.9	5 12.9	9 07.3
20 Sa	17 55 07	28 18 06	8♌06 01	14 05 59	17 48.6	15 27.5	14 47.6	16 44.5	0♐23.5	15 51.0	14 04.2	22 54.5	5 15.1	9 09.0
21 Su	17 59 03	29 19 11	20 07 37	26 11 17	17 41.0	16 58.5	15 31.2	17 26.1	0 48.4	15 58.9	14 11.2	22 58.2	5 17.4	9 10.8
22 M	18 03 00	0♑20 17	2♍17 26	8♍26 34	17 36.3	18 29.8	16 15.8	18 07.8	1 13.3	16 06.9	14 18.1	23 01.8	5 19.6	9 12.5
23 Tu	18 06 56	1 21 23	14 39 11	20 55 51	17D 34.2	20 01.4	17 01.4	18 49.5	1 38.0	16 15.1	14 25.1	23 05.4	5 21.9	9 14.2
24 W	18 10 53	2 22 30	27 17 06	3♎43 31	17 33.7	21 33.3	17 48.0	19 31.3	2 02.8	16 23.5	14 32.0	23 09.1	5 24.2	9 15.9
25 Th	18 14 50	3 23 38	10♎15 39	16 53 59	17R 33.9	23 05.4	18 35.6	20 13.0	2 27.4	16 32.0	14 38.8	23 12.7	5 26.4	9 17.5
26 F	18 18 46	4 24 47	23 38 59	0♏30 59	17 33.4	24 37.8	19 24.0	20 54.8	2 52.1	16 40.6	14 45.7	23 16.3	5 28.7	9 19.1
27 Sa	18 22 43	5 25 56	7♏30 13	14 36 44	17 31.0	26 10.5	20 13.4	21 36.6	3 16.6	16 49.4	14 52.5	23 19.9	5 31.0	9 20.7
28 Su	18 26 39	6 27 06	21 50 25	29 10 53	17 25.9	27 43.4	21 03.5	22 18.4	3 41.1	16 58.3	14 59.3	23 23.5	5 33.3	9 22.3
29 M	18 30 36	7 28 16	6♐37 35	14♐09 39	17 18.0	29 16.6	21 54.5	23 00.3	4 05.5	17 07.3	15 06.1	23 27.0	5 35.5	9 23.8
30 Tu	18 34 32	8 29 27	21 46 02	29 25 28	17 07.8	0♑50.1	22 46.2	23 42.1	4 29.9	17 16.5	15 12.9	23 30.6	5 37.8	9 25.3
31 W	18 38 29	9 30 38	7♑06 30	14♑47 38	16 56.1	2 23.8	23 38.7	24 24.0	4 54.2	17 25.9	15 19.6	23 34.2	5 40.1	9 26.8

Astro Data

	Dy Hr Mn
☿ R	2 6:47
♃ D	8 9:27
☽ 0N	12 10:55
☿ D	22 9:02
♀ D	26 2:46
☽ 0S	27 3:07
☽ 0N	9 15:53
☽ 0S	24 10:33

Planet Ingress

	Dy Hr Mn
☉ ♐	22 14:44
♂ ♓	26 2:35
☿ ♐	10 0:34
⚳ ♐	19 13:22
☉ ♑	22 4:02
☿ ♑	29 23:09

Last Aspect / ☽ Ingress

Last Aspect Dy Hr Mn		☽ Ingress Dy Hr Mn
31 21:41	♅ ⚹	♏ 1 14:19
3 13:46	☿ ☌	♐ 3 15:19
5 0:02	♅ ☌	♑ 5 15:48
7 12:31	☿ ⚹	♒ 7 17:28
9 12:49	☿ □	♓ 9 21:30
11 14:28	☿ △	♈ 12 4:14
13 21:42	♂ ⚹	♉ 14 13:24
16 12:12	☉ ☍	♊ 17 0:26
19 3:19	♂ △	♋ 19 12:46
22 0:11	☉ △	♌ 22 1:25
24 10:36	♂ ☍	♍ 24 12:46
26 5:21	♅ □	♎ 26 20:59
28 10:57	♅ ⚹	♏ 29 1:13

Last Aspect / ☽ Ingress

Last Aspect Dy Hr Mn		☽ Ingress Dy Hr Mn
30 6:20	☿ ☌	♐ 1 2:08
2 12:36	♅ ☌	♑ 3 1:28
4 13:26	☿ ⚹	♒ 5 1:23
6 20:12	☿ □	♓ 7 3:48
9 8:00	☿ △	♈ 9 9:49
11 4:16	♅ △	♉ 11 19:10
13 0:39	♃ ⚹	♊ 14 6:41
16 7:04	☉ ☍	♋ 16 19:09
18 2:35	♃ △	♌ 19 7:44
21 18:44	☉ △	♍ 21 19:30
23 16:07	♅ □	♎ 24 5:05
26 0:25	☿ ⚹	♏ 26 11:06
28 0:12	♂ △	♐ 28 13:20
30 2:42	♅ ☌	♑ 30 12:54

☽ Phases & Eclipses

Dy Hr Mn		
2 6:02	●	9♏31
8 21:11	☽	16♒10
16 12:12	○	23♉50
24 16:50	☾	2♍07
1 16:43	●	9♐12
8 8:02	☽	15♓56
16 7:04	○	24♊01
24 9:17	☾	2♎16
31 3:10	●	9♑08

Astro Data

1 November 1986
Julian Day # 31716
SVP 5♓26'44"
GC 26♐39.3 ⚴ 17♎59.3
Eris 15♈51.5R ⚵ 19♐57.9
⚷ 20♊42.1R ⚶ 3♈38.4R
☽ Mean ☊ 19♈41.8

1 December 1986
Julian Day # 31746
SVP 5♓26'39"
GC 26♐39.4 ⚴ 0♏57.4
Eris 15♈37.5R ⚵ 0♑17.2
⚷ 19♊10.8R ⚶ 3♈14.5
☽ Mean ☊ 18♈06.5

LONGITUDE — January 1987

Day	Sid.Time	☉	0 hr ☽	Noon ☽	True ☊	☿	♀	♂	⚳	♃	♄	♅	♆	♇
1 Th	18 42 26	10♑31 49	22♑27 21	0♒04 10	16♈44.5	3♑57.9	24♏31.8	25♓05.9	5♐18.4	17♓35.3	15♐26.3	23♐37.7	5♑42.4	9♏28.3
2 F	18 46 22	11 33 00	7♒36 44	15 03 55	16R34.3	5 32.3	25 25.6	25 47.8	5 42.5	17 44.9	15 32.9	23 41.2	5 44.6	9 29.7
3 Sa	18 50 19	12 34 10	22 24 47	29 38 39	16 26.6	7 07.0	26 20.1	26 29.7	6 06.6	17 54.6	15 39.6	23 44.8	5 46.9	9 31.1
4 Su	18 54 15	13 35 21	6♓45 05	13♓43 55	16 21.6	8 42.1	27 15.2	27 11.6	6 30.6	18 04.5	15 46.2	23 48.3	5 49.1	9 32.4
5 M	18 58 12	14 36 31	20 35 08	27 18 56	16 19.2	10 17.5	28 10.9	27 53.6	6 54.6	18 14.5	15 52.7	23 51.7	5 51.4	9 33.7
6 Tu	19 02 08	15 37 40	3♈55 42	10♈25 51	16 18.6	11 53.3	29 07.1	28 35.5	7 18.4	18 24.5	15 59.2	23 55.2	5 53.6	9 35.0
7 W	19 06 05	16 38 50	16 49 58	23 08 36	16 18.5	13 29.4	0♐04.0	29 17.5	7 42.2	18 34.8	16 05.7	23 58.6	5 55.9	9 36.3
8 Th	19 10 01	17 39 59	29 22 24	5♉32 01	16 17.8	15 06.0	1 01.3	29 59.4	8 05.9	18 45.1	16 12.1	24 02.1	5 58.1	9 37.5
9 F	19 13 58	18 41 07	11♉38 02	17 41 04	16 15.2	16 43.0	1 59.2	0♈41.4	8 29.5	18 55.5	16 18.5	24 05.5	6 00.4	9 38.7
10 Sa	19 17 55	19 42 15	23 41 42	29 40 27	16 09.9	18 20.4	2 57.6	1 23.3	8 53.0	19 06.1	16 24.9	24 08.9	6 02.6	9 39.8
11 Su	19 21 51	20 43 23	5♊37 49	11♊34 13	16 01.6	19 58.2	3 56.5	2 05.3	9 16.5	19 16.8	16 31.2	24 12.3	6 04.8	9 41.0
12 M	19 25 48	21 44 30	17 30 02	23 25 38	15 50.3	21 36.5	4 55.8	2 47.2	9 39.9	19 27.6	16 37.5	24 15.6	6 07.0	9 42.1
13 Tu	19 29 44	22 45 37	29 21 16	5♋17 12	15 36.8	23 15.3	5 55.6	3 29.1	10 03.1	19 38.4	16 43.7	24 18.9	6 09.2	9 43.1
14 W	19 33 41	23 46 43	11♋13 39	17 10 47	15 22.1	24 54.6	6 55.8	4 11.1	10 26.3	19 49.5	16 49.9	24 22.2	6 11.4	9 44.1
15 Th	19 37 37	24 47 49	23 08 45	29 07 42	15 07.1	26 34.3	7 56.4	4 53.0	10 49.4	20 00.6	16 56.0	24 25.5	6 13.6	9 45.1
16 F	19 41 34	25 48 55	5♌07 45	11♌09 02	14 53.4	28 14.5	8 57.5	5 34.9	11 12.5	20 11.8	17 02.1	24 28.8	6 15.8	9 46.1
17 Sa	19 45 30	26 50 00	17 11 41	23 15 54	14 41.7	29 55.2	9 58.9	6 16.9	11 35.4	20 23.1	17 08.1	24 32.0	6 17.9	9 47.0
18 Su	19 49 27	27 51 04	29 21 51	5♍29 45	14 32.9	1♒36.4	11 00.8	6 58.8	11 58.2	20 34.5	17 14.1	24 35.2	6 20.1	9 47.9
19 M	19 53 24	28 52 08	11♍39 53	17 52 33	14 27.3	3 18.1	12 03.0	7 40.7	12 21.0	20 46.0	17 20.0	24 38.4	6 22.2	9 48.8
20 Tu	19 57 20	29 53 12	24 08 05	0♎26 52	14 24.4	5 00.2	13 05.5	8 22.6	12 43.6	20 57.6	17 25.9	24 41.6	6 24.4	9 49.6
21 W	20 01 17	0♒54 15	6♎49 20	13 15 53	14D23.6	6 42.8	14 08.4	9 04.5	13 06.2	21 09.3	17 31.7	24 44.7	6 26.5	9 50.4
22 Th	20 05 13	1 55 18	19 46 58	26 23 03	14R23.8	8 25.7	15 11.6	9 46.4	13 28.7	21 21.1	17 37.5	24 47.8	6 28.6	9 51.1
23 F	20 09 10	2 56 21	3♏04 32	9♏51 46	14 23.7	10 09.1	16 15.1	10 28.2	13 51.0	21 33.0	17 43.2	24 50.9	6 30.7	9 51.8
24 Sa	20 13 06	3 57 23	16 45 04	23 44 35	14 22.2	11 52.7	17 19.0	11 10.1	14 13.3	21 44.9	17 48.9	24 53.9	6 32.8	9 52.5
25 Su	20 17 03	4 58 25	0♐50 23	8♐02 21	14 18.3	13 36.6	18 23.1	11 52.0	14 35.4	21 57.0	17 54.5	24 57.0	6 34.8	9 53.2
26 M	20 20 59	5 59 26	15 20 10	22 43 19	14 11.8	15 20.7	19 27.5	12 33.8	14 57.5	22 09.1	18 00.0	24 59.9	6 36.9	9 53.8
27 Tu	20 24 56	7 00 27	0♑11 05	7♑42 33	14 03.0	17 04.8	20 32.2	13 15.7	15 19.4	22 21.4	18 05.5	25 02.9	6 38.9	9 54.3
28 W	20 28 53	8 01 27	15 16 34	22 51 55	13 52.7	18 48.9	21 37.1	13 57.5	15 41.2	22 33.7	18 11.0	25 05.8	6 40.9	9 54.9
29 Th	20 32 49	9 02 27	0♒27 14	8♒01 10	13 42.4	20 32.7	22 42.3	14 39.3	16 03.0	22 46.1	18 16.3	25 08.7	6 42.9	9 55.4
30 F	20 36 46	10 03 25	15 32 23	22 59 39	13 33.1	22 16.1	23 47.8	15 21.2	16 24.6	22 58.6	18 21.6	25 11.6	6 44.9	9 55.8
31 Sa	20 40 42	11 04 22	0♓21 53	7♓38 13	13 25.9	23 58.9	24 53.4	16 03.0	16 46.0	23 11.2	18 26.8	25 14.4	6 46.9	9 56.3

LONGITUDE — February 1987

Day	Sid.Time	☉	0 hr ☽	Noon ☽	True ☊	☿	♀	♂	⚳	♃	♄	♅	♆	♇
1 Su	20 44 39	12♒05 18	14♓47 58	21♓50 41	13♈21.4	25♒40.9	25♐59.3	16♈44.8	17♐07.4	23♓23.8	18♐32.0	25♐17.2	6♑48.8	9♏56.6
2 M	20 48 35	13 06 12	28 46 08	5♈34 16	13D19.3	27 21.6	27 05.4	17 26.5	17 28.6	23 36.5	18 37.1	25 20.0	6 50.8	9 57.0
3 Tu	20 52 32	14 07 06	12♈15 15	18 49 21	13 19.1	29 00.9	28 11.7	18 08.3	17 49.8	23 49.3	18 42.1	25 22.7	6 52.7	9 57.3
4 W	20 56 28	15 07 58	25 16 58	1♉38 38	13 19.9	0♓38.2	29 18.2	18 50.1	18 10.8	24 02.1	18 47.1	25 25.3	6 54.6	9 57.6
5 Th	21 00 25	16 08 48	7♉54 53	14 06 21	13R20.6	2 13.1	0♑24.9	19 31.8	18 31.6	24 15.1	18 52.0	25 28.0	6 56.4	9 57.8
6 F	21 04 22	17 09 37	20 13 40	26 17 29	13 20.1	3 45.2	1 31.8	20 13.5	18 52.4	24 28.0	18 56.8	25 30.6	6 58.3	9 58.0
7 Sa	21 08 18	18 10 25	2♊18 25	8♊17 07	13 17.6	5 13.9	2 38.8	20 55.2	19 13.0	24 41.1	19 01.5	25 33.2	7 00.1	9 58.2
8 Su	21 12 15	19 11 11	14 14 11	20 10 09	13 12.9	6 38.5	3 46.1	21 36.9	19 33.4	24 54.2	19 06.2	25 35.7	7 01.9	9 58.3
9 M	21 16 11	20 11 56	26 05 34	2♋00 54	13 06.0	7 58.4	4 53.5	22 18.5	19 53.8	25 07.4	19 10.8	25 38.2	7 03.7	9 58.4
10 Tu	21 20 08	21 12 39	7♋56 34	13 52 59	12 57.1	9 12.9	6 01.1	23 00.2	20 14.0	25 20.6	19 15.3	25 40.7	7 05.5	9 58.5
11 W	21 24 04	22 13 21	19 50 27	25 49 17	12 47.2	10 21.3	7 08.9	23 41.8	20 34.1	25 33.9	19 19.8	25 43.1	7 07.2	9R58.5
12 Th	21 28 01	23 14 02	1♌49 41	7♌51 54	12 37.1	11 22.8	8 16.8	24 23.4	20 54.0	25 47.3	19 24.2	25 45.4	7 09.0	9 58.5
13 F	21 31 57	24 14 40	13 56 03	20 02 17	12 27.7	12 16.6	9 24.9	25 05.0	21 13.8	26 00.7	19 28.5	25 47.8	7 10.7	9 58.5
14 Sa	21 35 54	25 15 18	26 10 43	2♍21 25	12 19.9	13 02.2	10 33.1	25 46.5	21 33.4	26 14.2	19 32.7	25 50.1	7 12.3	9 58.4
15 Su	21 39 51	26 15 54	8♍34 31	14 50 03	12 14.3	13 38.8	11 41.4	26 28.0	21 52.9	26 27.7	19 36.8	25 52.3	7 14.0	9 58.3
16 M	21 43 47	27 16 28	21 08 08	27 28 53	12 10.9	14 05.9	12 50.0	27 09.5	22 12.3	26 41.3	19 40.9	25 54.5	7 15.6	9 58.1
17 Tu	21 47 44	28 17 02	3♎52 25	10♎18 52	12D09.8	14 23.0	13 58.6	27 51.0	22 31.5	26 54.9	19 44.9	25 56.7	7 17.2	9 57.9
18 W	21 51 40	29 17 34	16 48 25	23 21 16	12 10.2	14R30.0	15 07.4	28 32.4	22 50.5	27 08.6	19 48.8	25 58.8	7 18.8	9 57.7
19 Th	21 55 37	0♓18 04	29 57 35	6♏37 36	12 11.6	14 26.6	16 16.3	29 13.9	23 09.4	27 22.3	19 52.6	26 00.8	7 20.4	9 57.4
20 F	21 59 33	1 18 34	13♏21 31	20 09 30	12R12.9	14 13.0	17 25.4	29 55.3	23 28.1	27 36.1	19 56.3	26 02.9	7 21.9	9 57.1
21 Sa	22 03 30	2 19 02	27 01 43	3♐58 16	12 13.4	13 49.5	18 34.5	0♉36.7	23 46.7	27 49.9	20 00.0	26 04.9	7 23.4	9 56.8
22 Su	22 07 26	3 19 29	10♐59 08	18 04 17	12 12.4	13 16.8	19 43.8	1 18.0	24 05.1	28 03.7	20 03.5	26 06.8	7 24.9	9 56.4
23 M	22 11 23	4 19 55	25 13 31	2♑26 31	12 09.7	12 35.6	20 53.2	1 59.4	24 23.4	28 17.7	20 07.0	26 08.7	7 26.3	9 56.0
24 Tu	22 15 20	5 20 19	9♑42 51	17 01 57	12 05.5	11 47.0	22 02.7	2 40.7	24 41.4	28 31.6	20 10.4	26 10.6	7 27.8	9 55.6
25 W	22 19 16	6 20 42	24 23 06	1♒45 29	12 00.2	10 52.3	23 12.3	3 22.0	24 59.3	28 45.6	20 13.7	26 12.4	7 29.2	9 55.1
26 Th	22 23 13	7 21 03	9♒08 12	16 30 18	11 54.7	9 53.0	24 22.0	4 03.3	25 17.1	28 59.6	20 16.9	26 14.1	7 30.5	9 54.6
27 F	22 27 09	8 21 23	23 50 47	1♓08 44	11 49.7	8 50.6	25 31.8	4 44.6	25 34.6	29 13.7	20 20.1	26 15.8	7 31.9	9 54.1
28 Sa	22 31 06	9 21 41	8♓23 15	15 33 30	11 46.0	7 46.7	26 41.7	5 25.8	25 52.0	29 27.8	20 23.1	26 17.5	7 33.2	9 53.5

Astro Data	Planet Ingress	Last Aspect	☽ Ingress	Last Aspect	☽ Ingress	☽ Phases & Eclipses	Astro Data
Dy Hr Mn	Dy Hr Mn	Dy Hr Mn	Dy Hr Mn	Dy Hr Mn	Dy Hr Mn	Dy Hr Mn	1 January 1987
☽0N 5 21:49	♀ ♐ 7 10:20	1 3:47 ♂ ⚹	♒ 1 11:53	1 19:47 ♀ □	♈ 2 2:09	6 22:34 ☽ 16♈05	Julian Day # 31777
♂0N 9 11:07	♂ ♈ 8 12:20	3 6:07 ♀ □	♓ 3 12:36	4 7:08 ♀ △	♉ 4 8:53	15 2:30 ○ 24♋24	SVP 5♓26'33"
☽0S 20 15:44	☿ ♒ 17 13:08	5 13:41 ♀ △	♈ 5 16:51	6 8:19 ♃ ⚹	♊ 6 19:23	22 22:45 ☾ 2♏23	GC 26♐39.5 ⚴ 13♏12.6
♅∠♇ 23 21:30	☉ ♒ 20 14:40	7 13:36 ♅ △	♉ 8 1:13	8 23:02 ♅ ☍	♋ 9 7:55	29 13:45 ● 9♒07	Eris 15♈31.6R ⚵ 11♑49.0
		9 14:30 ♃ ⚹	♊ 10 12:39	11 11:29 ♃ △	♌ 11 20:21		⚷ 17♊21.0R ⚶ 8♈55.0
☽0N 2 6:08	☿ ♓ 4 2:31	12 13:42 ♅ ☍	♋ 13 1:18	13 23:17 ♅ △	♍ 14 7:26	5 16:21 ☽ 16♉20	☽ Mean ☊ 16♈28.0
♃□♇ 8 19:34	♀ ♑ 5 3:03	15 6:03 ♀ ☍	♌ 15 13:45	16 10:29 ♃ ☍	♎ 16 16:44	13 20:58 ○ 24♌37	
♇R 11 16:56	☉ ♓ 19 4:50	17 14:31 ♅ △	♍ 18 1:15	18 23:41 ☉ △	♏ 19 0:04	21 8:56 ☾ 2♐11	1 February 1987
♃□♅ 12 7:56	♂ ♉ 20 14:44	20 10:51 ☉ △	♎ 20 11:09	21 1:13 ♃ △	♐ 21 5:09	28 0:51 ● 8♓54	Julian Day # 31808
☽0S 16 20:39		22 9:07 ♅ ⚹	♏ 22 18:30	23 5:00 ♃ □	♑ 23 7:57		SVP 5♓26'27"
☿R 18 16:08		24 8:33 ♃ △	♐ 24 22:35	25 7:03 ♃ ⚹	♒ 25 9:08		GC 26♐39.5 ⚴ 23♏24.7
		26 15:41 ♅ ☌	♑ 26 23:42	27 3:57 ♅ ⚹	♓ 27 10:07		Eris 15♈36.3 ⚵ 23♑42.6
		28 11:31 ♃ ⚹	♒ 28 23:17				⚷ 16♊04.2R ⚶ 18♈29.9
		30 15:35 ♅ ⚹	♓ 30 23:24				☽ Mean ☊ 14♈49.5

March 1987 — LONGITUDE

Day	Sid.Time	☉	0 hr ☽	Noon ☽	True ☊	☿	♀	♂	⚳	♃	♄	♅	♆	♇
1 Su	22 35 02	10♓21 57	22♓38 51	29♓38 44	11♈43.8	6♓42.9	27♑51.7	6♉07.0	26♐09.1	29♓41.9	20♐26.0	26♐19.1	7♑34.5	9♏52.9
2 M	22 38 59	11 22 11	6♈32 47	13♈20 45	11D43.2	5R40.6	29 01.8	6 48.2	26 26.1	29 56.1	20 28.9	26 20.6	7 35.7	9R52.3
3 Tu	22 42 55	12 22 23	20 02 34	26 38 16	11 44.0	4 41.1	0♒11.9	7 29.4	26 42.9	0♈10.2	20 31.6	26 22.1	7 36.9	9 51.6
4 W	22 46 52	13 22 34	3♉08 01	9♉32 08	11 45.5	3 45.7	1 22.2	8 10.5	26 59.5	0 24.5	20 34.3	26 23.6	7 38.1	9 50.9
5 Th	22 50 49	14 22 42	15 50 59	22 05 01	11 47.3	2 55.1	2 32.5	8 51.6	27 15.9	0 38.7	20 36.9	26 25.0	7 39.3	9 50.2
6 F	22 54 45	15 22 48	28 14 44	4♊20 42	11R48.6	2 10.3	3 42.9	9 32.7	27 32.1	0 53.0	20 39.4	26 26.4	7 40.4	9 49.4
7 Sa	22 58 42	16 22 52	10♊23 30	16 23 44	11 49.1	1 31.6	4 53.3	10 13.8	27 48.2	1 07.3	20 41.8	26 27.7	7 41.6	9 48.6
8 Su	23 02 38	17 22 54	22 22 00	28 18 55	11 48.6	0 59.4	6 03.8	10 54.8	28 04.0	1 21.6	20 44.1	26 28.9	7 42.6	9 47.8
9 M	23 06 35	18 22 54	4♋15 03	10♋11 00	11 46.9	0 34.0	7 14.4	11 35.8	28 19.6	1 35.9	20 46.2	26 30.2	7 43.7	9 47.0
10 Tu	23 10 31	19 22 52	16 07 18	22 04 28	11 44.2	0 15.2	8 25.1	12 16.8	28 34.9	1 50.3	20 48.4	26 31.3	7 44.7	9 46.1
11 W	23 14 28	20 22 47	28 02 58	4♌03 16	11 40.9	0 03.1	9 35.8	12 57.7	28 50.1	2 04.7	20 50.4	26 32.4	7 45.7	9 45.2
12 Th	23 18 24	21 22 41	10♌05 44	16 10 43	11 37.5	29♒57.5	10 46.6	13 38.6	29 05.1	2 19.1	20 52.3	26 33.5	7 46.6	9 44.2
13 F	23 22 21	22 22 32	22 18 30	28 29 20	11 34.3	29D58.1	11 57.5	14 19.5	29 19.8	2 33.5	20 54.1	26 34.5	7 47.6	9 43.3
14 Sa	23 26 18	23 22 21	4♍43 24	11♍00 50	11 31.7	0♓04.8	13 08.4	15 00.4	29 34.3	2 47.9	20 55.8	26 35.4	7 48.5	9 42.3
15 Su	23 30 14	24 22 08	17 21 45	23 46 09	11 30.0	0 17.2	14 19.4	15 41.2	29 48.6	3 02.4	20 57.4	26 36.3	7 49.3	9 41.2
16 M	23 34 11	25 21 53	0♎14 05	6♎45 29	11D29.3	0 35.1	15 30.4	16 22.0	0♑02.7	3 16.8	20 58.9	26 37.2	7 50.1	9 40.2
17 Tu	23 38 07	26 21 37	13 20 18	19 58 28	11 29.4	0 58.1	16 41.5	17 02.8	0 16.5	3 31.3	21 00.3	26 38.0	7 50.9	9 39.1
18 W	23 42 04	27 21 18	26 39 51	3♏24 22	11 30.1	1 25.9	17 52.7	17 43.5	0 30.1	3 45.8	21 01.7	26 38.7	7 51.7	9 38.0
19 Th	23 46 00	28 20 58	10♏11 52	17 02 14	11 31.2	1 58.3	19 03.9	18 24.2	0 43.5	4 00.3	21 02.9	26 39.4	7 52.4	9 36.8
20 F	23 49 57	29 20 36	23 55 19	0♐50 58	11 32.2	2 35.0	20 15.1	19 04.9	0 56.6	4 14.8	21 04.0	26 40.1	7 53.1	9 35.7
21 Sa	23 53 53	0♈20 12	7♐49 03	14 49 22	11 33.0	3 15.6	21 26.5	19 45.6	1 09.5	4 29.3	21 05.0	26 40.7	7 53.8	9 34.5
22 Su	23 57 50	1 19 46	21 51 45	28 56 00	11R33.4	4 00.1	22 37.8	20 26.2	1 22.1	4 43.8	21 06.0	26 41.2	7 54.4	9 33.3
23 M	0 01 47	2 19 19	6♑01 52	13♑09 04	11 33.2	4 48.0	23 49.3	21 06.8	1 34.5	4 58.4	21 06.8	26 41.7	7 55.0	9 32.1
24 Tu	0 05 43	3 18 50	20 17 17	27 26 11	11 32.7	5 39.3	25 00.7	21 47.4	1 46.6	5 12.9	21 07.5	26 42.1	7 55.6	9 30.8
25 W	0 09 40	4 18 20	4♒35 22	11♒44 22	11 31.9	6 33.8	26 12.3	22 27.9	1 58.5	5 27.4	21 08.2	26 42.5	7 56.1	9 29.5
26 Th	0 13 36	5 17 47	18 52 45	26 00 01	11 31.1	7 31.2	27 23.8	23 08.5	2 10.0	5 42.0	21 08.7	26 42.8	7 56.6	9 28.2
27 F	0 17 33	6 17 13	3♓05 38	10♓09 07	11 30.5	8 31.3	28 35.4	23 49.0	2 21.4	5 56.5	21 09.1	26 43.1	7 57.1	9 26.9
28 Sa	0 21 29	7 16 36	17 09 57	24 07 39	11 30.1	9 34.2	29 47.1	24 29.4	2 32.4	6 11.0	21 09.4	26 43.3	7 57.5	9 25.6
29 Su	0 25 26	8 15 58	1♈01 48	7♈52 02	11D29.9	10 39.5	0♓58.7	25 09.9	2 43.2	6 25.5	21 09.6	26 43.5	7 57.9	9 24.2
30 M	0 29 22	9 15 18	14 38 01	21 19 31	11 30.0	11 47.2	2 10.5	25 50.3	2 53.7	6 40.1	21R09.8	26 43.6	7 58.3	9 22.8
31 Tu	0 33 19	10 14 35	27 56 24	4♉28 33	11 30.1	12 57.2	3 22.2	26 30.7	3 03.9	6 54.6	21 09.8	26R43.7	7 58.6	9 21.4

April 1987 — LONGITUDE

Day	Sid.Time	☉	0 hr ☽	Noon ☽	True ☊	☿	♀	♂	⚳	♃	♄	♅	♆	♇
1 W	0 37 15	11♈13 50	10♉56 01	17♉18 53	11♈30.1	14♓09.3	4♓34.0	27♉11.1	3♑13.8	7♈09.1	21♐09.7	26♐43.7	7♑59.0	9♏20.0
2 Th	0 41 12	12 13 04	23 37 19	29 51 34	11R30.1	15 23.6	5 45.8	27 51.4	3 23.4	7 23.6	21R09.5	26R43.6	7 59.2	9R18.5
3 F	0 45 09	13 12 15	6♊01 57	12♊08 52	11 30.0	16 39.8	6 57.6	28 31.7	3 32.7	7 38.1	21 09.2	26 43.5	7 59.5	9 17.1
4 Sa	0 49 05	14 11 24	18 12 44	24 14 01	11 29.7	17 58.0	8 09.5	29 12.0	3 41.8	7 52.6	21 08.9	26 43.4	7 59.7	9 15.6
5 Su	0 53 02	15 10 30	0♋13 15	6♋10 58	11D29.6	19 18.1	9 21.4	29 52.3	3 50.5	8 07.0	21 08.4	26 43.2	7 59.8	9 14.1
6 M	0 56 58	16 09 34	12 07 44	18 04 07	11 29.5	20 40.0	10 33.3	0♊32.5	3 58.9	8 21.5	21 07.8	26 42.9	8 00.0	9 12.6
7 Tu	1 00 55	17 08 36	24 00 44	29 58 08	11 29.7	22 03.6	11 45.3	1 12.7	4 07.0	8 36.0	21 07.1	26 42.6	8 00.1	9 11.1
8 W	1 04 51	18 07 36	5♌56 55	11♌57 38	11 30.1	23 29.0	12 57.3	1 52.8	4 14.8	8 50.4	21 06.4	26 42.3	8 00.1	9 09.5
9 Th	1 08 48	19 06 33	18 00 48	24 06 57	11 30.8	24 56.2	14 09.3	2 33.0	4 22.3	9 04.8	21 05.5	26 41.9	8R00.2	9 08.0
10 F	1 12 44	20 05 28	0♍16 32	6♍29 57	11 31.6	26 24.9	15 21.3	3 13.1	4 29.5	9 19.2	21 04.5	26 41.4	8 00.2	9 06.4
11 Sa	1 16 41	21 04 20	12 47 33	19 09 39	11 32.4	27 55.4	16 33.3	3 53.2	4 36.4	9 33.6	21 03.5	26 40.9	8 00.1	9 04.8
12 Su	1 20 38	22 03 11	25 36 26	2♎08 03	11R33.0	29 27.5	17 45.4	4 33.2	4 42.9	9 47.9	21 02.3	26 40.4	8 00.1	9 03.3
13 M	1 24 34	23 01 59	8♎44 31	15 25 50	11 33.1	1♈01.2	18 57.5	5 13.2	4 49.1	10 02.2	21 01.1	26 39.8	8 00.0	9 01.7
14 Tu	1 28 31	24 00 46	22 11 50	29 02 18	11 32.6	2 36.5	20 09.6	5 53.2	4 55.0	10 16.5	20 59.7	26 39.1	7 59.8	9 00.0
15 W	1 32 27	24 59 30	5♏56 55	12♏55 19	11 31.5	4 13.4	21 21.8	6 33.1	5 00.5	10 30.8	20 58.3	26 38.4	7 59.7	8 58.4
16 Th	1 36 24	25 58 13	19 57 01	27 01 32	11 29.8	5 52.0	22 34.0	7 13.1	5 05.7	10 45.1	20 56.7	26 37.7	7 59.5	8 56.8
17 F	1 40 20	26 56 54	4♐08 18	11♐16 47	11 27.9	7 32.1	23 46.2	7 53.0	5 10.6	10 59.3	20 55.1	26 36.9	7 59.3	8 55.1
18 Sa	1 44 17	27 55 33	18 26 24	25 36 36	11 26.0	9 13.9	24 58.4	8 32.9	5 15.1	11 13.6	20 53.4	26 36.0	7 59.0	8 53.5
19 Su	1 48 13	28 54 11	2♑46 52	9♑56 43	11 24.5	10 57.3	26 10.7	9 12.7	5 19.2	11 27.7	20 51.6	26 35.1	7 58.7	8 51.8
20 M	1 52 10	29 52 47	17 05 44	24 13 31	11D23.7	12 42.3	27 23.0	9 52.5	5 23.1	11 41.9	20 49.7	26 34.2	7 58.4	8 50.2
21 Tu	1 56 07	0♉51 21	1♒19 45	8♒24 09	11 23.8	14 29.0	28 35.3	10 32.3	5 26.5	11 56.0	20 47.7	26 33.2	7 58.0	8 48.5
22 W	2 00 03	1 49 53	15 26 29	22 26 35	11 24.6	16 17.3	29 47.6	11 12.1	5 29.6	12 10.1	20 45.7	26 32.2	7 57.6	8 46.8
23 Th	2 04 00	2 48 24	29 24 17	6♓19 26	11 25.9	18 07.3	0♈59.9	11 51.8	5 32.4	12 24.2	20 43.5	26 31.1	7 57.2	8 45.2
24 F	2 07 56	3 46 54	13♓11 56	20 01 41	11 27.3	19 58.9	2 12.3	12 31.6	5 34.7	12 38.2	20 41.2	26 30.0	7 56.8	8 43.5
25 Sa	2 11 53	4 45 21	26 48 34	3♈32 29	11R28.3	21 52.1	3 24.7	13 11.3	5 36.7	12 52.2	20 38.9	26 28.8	7 56.3	8 41.8
26 Su	2 15 49	5 43 47	10♈13 22	16 51 05	11 28.4	23 47.1	4 37.1	13 50.9	5 38.4	13 06.2	20 36.5	26 27.6	7 55.8	8 40.1
27 M	2 19 46	6 42 11	23 25 35	29 56 47	11 27.3	25 43.6	5 49.5	14 30.6	5 39.6	13 20.1	20 34.0	26 26.3	7 55.2	8 38.4
28 Tu	2 23 42	7 40 33	6♉24 37	12♉49 03	11 24.8	27 41.8	7 01.9	15 10.2	5 40.5	13 34.0	20 31.4	26 25.0	7 54.7	8 36.7
29 W	2 27 39	8 38 54	19 10 06	25 27 46	11 21.1	29 41.6	8 14.3	15 49.8	5R41.1	13 47.8	20 28.7	26 23.7	7 54.1	8 35.0
30 Th	2 31 36	9 37 13	1♊42 09	7♊53 21	11 16.6	1♉43.0	9 26.8	16 29.4	5 41.2	14 01.6	20 26.0	26 22.3	7 53.4	8 33.3

Astro Data	Dy Hr Mn
☽ 0N	1 16:08
☿ D	12 21:23
♃ 0N	13 6:31
☽ 0S	16 3:16
☉ 0N	21 3:52
☽ 0N	29 1:43
♄ R	31 4:43
♅ R	1 4:35
♃□♆	4 23:53
♃⚻♇	9 16:49
♆ R	10 0:12
☽ 0S	12 11:47
☿ 0N	16 10:02
☽ 0N	25 9:14
♀ 0N	25 16:56

Planet Ingress		Dy Hr Mn
♃	♈	2 18:41
♀	♒	3 7:55
☿	♒R	11 21:55
☿	♓	13 21:09
⚳	♑	16 7:23
☉	♈	21 3:52
♀	♓	28 16:20
♂	♊	5 16:37
☿	♈	12 20:23
☉	♉	20 14:58
♀	♈	22 16:07
☿	♉	29 15:39
⚳ R		30 9:22

Last Aspect Dy Hr Mn		☽ Ingress	Dy Hr Mn
1 12:06	♃ ☌	♈	1 12:37
3 11:30	♅ △	♉	3 18:11
4 19:55	☉ ⚹	♊	6 3:26
8 8:18	♅ ☍	♋	8 15:24
10 6:05	☉ △	♌	11 3:54
13 14:52	☿ ☍	♍	13 14:55
15 17:17	♅ □	♎	15 23:34
17 23:57	♅ ⚹	♏	18 5:57
20 9:12	☉ △	♐	20 10:32
22 8:11	♅ ☌	♑	22 13:48
24 2:03	♂ △	♒	24 16:18
26 14:35	♀ ☌	♓	26 18:46
28 16:30	♅ □	♈	28 22:12
30 21:47	♅ △	♉	31 3:46

Last Aspect Dy Hr Mn		☽ Ingress	Dy Hr Mn
2 7:55	♂ ☌	♊	2 12:16
4 16:59	♅ ☍	♋	4 23:33
6 17:56	☿ △	♌	7 12:04
9 17:03	♅ △	♍	9 23:28
12 6:26	☿ ☍	♎	12 8:06
14 7:50	♅ ⚹	♏	14 13:41
16 3:45	♀ △	♐	16 17:02
18 16:10	☉ △	♑	18 19:21
20 17:49	♀ ⚹	♒	20 21:45
22 19:02	♅ ⚹	♓	23 1:02
24 23:26	♅ □	♈	25 5:41
27 5:33	♅ △	♉	27 12:06
28 4:08	♇ ☍	♊	29 20:43

☽ Phases & Eclipses Dy Hr Mn	
7 11:58	☽ 16♊23
15 13:13	○ 24♍25
22 16:22	☾ 1♑31
29 12:46	● 8♈18
29 12:48:52	◐ AT00'08"
6 7:48	☽ 15♋59
14 2:31	○ 23♎38
14 2:19	◐ A 0.777
20 22:15	☾ 0♒18
28 1:34	● 7♉15

Astro Data

1 March 1987
Julian Day # 31836
SVP 5♓26'23"
GC 26♐39.6 ⚴ 29♏35.6
Eris 15♈48.6 ⚵ 4♒22.0
⚷ 15♊51.2 ⚶ 29♈02.5
☽ Mean ☊ 13♈20.6

1 April 1987
Julian Day # 31867
SVP 5♓26'20"
GC 26♐39.7 ⚴ 0♐56.2R
Eris 16♈07.9 ⚵ 15♒35.3
⚷ 16♊45.9 ⚶ 11♉49.5
☽ Mean ☊ 11♈42.1

LONGITUDE — May 1987

Day	Sid.Time	☉	0 hr ☽	Noon ☽	True ☊	☿	♀	♂	⚳	♃	♄	♅	♆	♇
1 F	2 35 32	10♉35 30	14♊01 32	20♊06 56	11♈11.6	3♉45.9	10♈39.3	17♊08.9	5♑41.0	14♈15.4	20♐23.2	26♐20.9	7♑52.8	8♏31.6
2 Sa	2 39 29	11 33 45	26 09 49	2♋10 30	11R 06.8	5 50.2	11 51.7	17 48.5	5R 40.4	14 29.1	20R 20.3	26R 19.4	7R 52.1	8R 29.9
3 Su	2 43 25	12 31 57	8♋09 21	14 06 49	11 02.7	7 55.9	13 04.2	18 28.0	5 39.4	14 42.7	20 17.3	26 17.9	7 51.4	8 28.2
4 M	2 47 22	13 30 08	20 03 20	25 59 25	10 59.8	10 02.7	14 16.7	19 07.4	5 38.0	14 56.3	20 14.3	26 16.4	7 50.6	8 26.5
5 Tu	2 51 18	14 28 17	1♌55 36	7♌52 28	10D 58.3	12 10.7	15 29.2	19 46.9	5 36.3	15 09.9	20 11.2	26 14.8	7 49.8	8 24.9
6 W	2 55 15	15 26 24	13 50 35	19 50 35	10 58.1	14 19.6	16 41.7	20 26.3	5 34.2	15 23.4	20 08.0	26 13.2	7 49.0	8 23.2
7 Th	2 59 11	16 24 29	25 53 02	1♍58 35	10 59.1	16 29.3	17 54.3	21 05.7	5 31.7	15 36.9	20 04.7	26 11.5	7 48.2	8 21.5
8 F	3 03 08	17 22 32	8♍07 49	14 21 17	11 00.7	18 39.4	19 06.8	21 45.1	5 28.8	15 50.3	20 01.4	26 09.8	7 47.4	8 19.8
9 Sa	3 07 05	18 20 34	20 39 31	27 02 59	11 02.1	20 49.8	20 19.4	22 24.4	5 25.6	16 03.7	19 58.0	26 08.1	7 46.5	8 18.2
10 Su	3 11 01	19 18 33	3♎32 05	10♎07 08	11R 02.8	23 00.3	21 31.9	23 03.7	5 22.0	16 17.0	19 54.6	26 06.3	7 45.6	8 16.5
11 M	3 14 58	20 16 30	16 48 20	23 35 46	11 02.2	25 10.4	22 44.5	23 43.0	5 18.0	16 30.2	19 51.1	26 04.5	7 44.6	8 14.8
12 Tu	3 18 54	21 14 26	0♏29 21	7♏28 53	10 59.7	27 20.1	23 57.1	24 22.3	5 13.6	16 43.4	19 47.5	26 02.6	7 43.7	8 13.2
13 W	3 22 51	22 12 20	14 34 00	21 44 11	10 55.5	29 28.9	25 09.7	25 01.5	5 08.9	16 56.6	19 43.9	26 00.8	7 42.7	8 11.6
14 Th	3 26 47	23 10 13	28 58 44	6♐16 53	10 49.8	1♊36.6	26 22.3	25 40.7	5 03.8	17 09.6	19 40.2	25 58.9	7 41.7	8 09.9
15 F	3 30 44	24 08 05	13♐37 44	21 00 18	10 43.3	3 42.8	27 34.9	26 19.9	4 58.4	17 22.6	19 36.4	25 56.9	7 40.6	8 08.3
16 Sa	3 34 40	25 05 55	28 23 37	5♑46 41	10 37.0	5 47.5	28 47.6	26 59.1	4 52.6	17 35.6	19 32.7	25 55.0	7 39.6	8 06.7
17 Su	3 38 37	26 03 44	13♑08 34	20 28 27	10 31.5	7 50.2	0♉00.2	27 38.2	4 46.4	17 48.5	19 28.8	25 53.0	7 38.5	8 05.1
18 M	3 42 34	27 01 31	27 45 36	4♒59 25	10 27.7	9 50.9	1 12.9	28 17.4	4 39.9	18 01.3	19 24.9	25 51.0	7 37.4	8 03.6
19 Tu	3 46 30	27 59 18	12♒09 26	19 15 21	10D 25.7	11 49.2	2 25.6	28 56.5	4 33.0	18 14.1	19 21.0	25 48.9	7 36.2	8 02.0
20 W	3 50 27	28 57 03	26 16 57	3♓14 10	10 25.4	13 45.1	3 38.3	29 35.6	4 25.8	18 26.8	19 17.0	25 46.8	7 35.1	8 00.4
21 Th	3 54 23	29 54 47	10♓07 01	16 55 35	10 26.3	15 38.4	4 51.0	0♋14.6	4 18.3	18 39.4	19 13.0	25 44.7	7 33.9	7 58.9
22 F	3 58 20	0♊52 30	23 40 01	0♈20 30	10R 27.3	17 29.0	6 03.7	0 53.7	4 10.4	18 52.0	19 08.9	25 42.6	7 32.7	7 57.3
23 Sa	4 02 16	1 50 12	6♈57 15	13 30 27	10 27.6	19 16.8	7 16.5	1 32.7	4 02.1	19 04.5	19 04.8	25 40.5	7 31.5	7 55.8
24 Su	4 06 13	2 47 53	20 00 19	26 27 03	10 26.4	21 01.7	8 29.2	2 11.7	3 53.6	19 16.9	19 00.6	25 38.3	7 30.2	7 54.3
25 M	4 10 09	3 45 33	2♉50 48	9♉11 43	10 22.9	22 43.6	9 42.0	2 50.7	3 44.7	19 29.2	18 56.4	25 36.1	7 29.0	7 52.8
26 Tu	4 14 06	4 43 12	15 29 56	21 45 34	10 16.9	24 22.5	10 54.7	3 29.6	3 35.6	19 41.5	18 52.2	25 33.8	7 27.7	7 51.4
27 W	4 18 03	5 40 50	27 58 42	4♊09 25	10 08.8	25 58.4	12 07.5	4 08.6	3 26.1	19 53.7	18 48.0	25 31.6	7 26.4	7 49.9
28 Th	4 21 59	6 38 26	10♊17 49	16 24 00	9 58.9	27 31.1	13 20.3	4 47.5	3 16.3	20 05.8	18 43.7	25 29.3	7 25.1	7 48.5
29 F	4 25 56	7 36 02	22 28 04	28 30 11	9 48.1	29 00.8	14 33.1	5 26.4	3 06.3	20 17.9	18 39.4	25 27.1	7 23.8	7 47.1
30 Sa	4 29 52	8 33 36	4♋30 30	10♋29 14	9 37.5	0♋27.2	15 46.0	6 05.3	2 56.0	20 29.8	18 35.1	25 24.8	7 22.4	7 45.7
31 Su	4 33 49	9 31 09	16 26 38	22 22 59	9 27.9	1 50.5	16 58.8	6 44.2	2 45.4	20 41.7	18 30.7	25 22.4	7 21.0	7 44.3

LONGITUDE — June 1987

Day	Sid.Time	☉	0 hr ☽	Noon ☽	True ☊	☿	♀	♂	⚳	♃	♄	♅	♆	♇
1 M	4 37 45	10♊28 40	28♋18 39	4♌14 00	9♈20.2	3♋10.5	18♉11.6	7♋23.0	2♑34.5	20♈53.5	18♐26.4	25♐20.1	7♑19.7	7♏42.9
2 Tu	4 41 42	11 26 11	10♌09 29	16 05 35	9R 14.7	4 27.2	19 24.5	8 01.9	2R 23.5	21 05.2	18R 22.0	25R 17.8	7R 18.2	7R 41.6
3 W	4 45 39	12 23 40	22 02 50	28 01 48	9 11.6	5 40.6	20 37.3	8 40.7	2 12.2	21 16.8	18 17.6	25 15.4	7 16.8	7 40.3
4 Th	4 49 35	13 21 08	4♍03 05	10♍07 17	9D 10.5	6 50.6	21 50.2	9 19.5	2 00.6	21 28.3	18 13.2	25 13.0	7 15.4	7 39.0
5 F	4 53 32	14 18 34	16 15 04	22 27 02	9 10.6	7 57.1	23 03.0	9 58.2	1 48.9	21 39.7	18 08.7	25 10.6	7 13.9	7 37.7
6 Sa	4 57 28	15 15 59	28 43 51	5♎06 06	9R 11.1	9 00.2	24 15.9	10 37.0	1 37.0	21 51.0	18 04.3	25 08.2	7 12.5	7 36.5
7 Su	5 01 25	16 13 23	11♎34 19	18 09 01	9 10.9	9 59.6	25 28.8	11 15.7	1 24.9	22 02.3	17 59.9	25 05.8	7 11.0	7 35.2
8 M	5 05 21	17 10 46	24 50 33	1♏39 11	9 08.9	10 55.4	26 41.7	11 54.4	1 12.6	22 13.4	17 55.4	25 03.4	7 09.5	7 34.0
9 Tu	5 09 18	18 08 08	8♏35 03	15 38 03	9 04.7	11 47.4	27 54.6	12 33.1	1 00.2	22 24.5	17 51.0	25 01.0	7 08.0	7 32.8
10 W	5 13 14	19 05 29	22 47 57	0♐04 16	8 58.0	12 35.7	29 07.6	13 11.8	0 47.6	22 35.4	17 46.5	24 58.5	7 06.5	7 31.7
11 Th	5 17 11	20 02 50	7♐26 18	14 53 12	8 49.2	13 19.9	0♊20.5	13 50.5	0 34.9	22 46.3	17 42.1	24 56.1	7 05.0	7 30.5
12 F	5 21 08	21 00 09	22 23 51	29 57 05	8 39.2	14 00.2	1 33.5	14 29.1	0 22.0	22 57.1	17 37.7	24 53.7	7 03.5	7 29.4
13 Sa	5 25 04	21 57 28	7♑31 34	15♑06 00	8 29.2	14 36.4	2 46.4	15 07.7	0 09.1	23 07.7	17 33.2	24 51.2	7 01.9	7 28.4
14 Su	5 29 01	22 54 46	22 39 05	0♒09 37	8 20.3	15 08.4	3 59.4	15 46.3	29♐56.1	23 18.3	17 28.8	24 48.8	7 00.4	7 27.3
15 M	5 32 57	23 52 04	7♒36 32	14 58 57	8 13.6	15 36.1	5 12.4	16 24.9	29 43.0	23 28.7	17 24.4	24 46.3	6 58.8	7 26.3
16 Tu	5 36 54	24 49 21	22 16 11	29 27 44	8 09.3	15 59.4	6 25.5	17 03.5	29 29.8	23 39.1	17 20.0	24 43.9	6 57.2	7 25.3
17 W	5 40 50	25 46 38	6♓33 20	13♓32 51	8D 07.3	16 18.2	7 38.5	17 42.1	29 16.6	23 49.3	17 15.7	24 41.4	6 55.7	7 24.3
18 Th	5 44 47	26 43 54	20 26 21	27 13 58	8R 06.9	16 32.6	8 51.6	18 20.6	29 03.3	23 59.4	17 11.3	24 39.0	6 54.1	7 23.3
19 F	5 48 43	27 41 11	3♈55 59	10♈32 45	8 07.0	16 42.4	10 04.6	18 59.1	28 50.0	24 09.4	17 07.0	24 36.5	6 52.5	7 22.4
20 Sa	5 52 40	28 38 27	17 04 37	23 32 01	8 06.3	16R 47.7	11 17.7	19 37.7	28 36.7	24 19.3	17 02.6	24 34.0	6 50.9	7 21.5
21 Su	5 56 37	29 35 43	29 55 21	6♉15 01	8 03.8	16 48.4	12 30.8	20 16.2	28 23.4	24 29.1	16 58.3	24 31.6	6 49.3	7 20.6
22 M	6 00 33	0♋32 58	12♉31 23	18 44 49	7 58.7	16 44.6	13 44.0	20 54.7	28 10.2	24 38.8	16 54.1	24 29.2	6 47.7	7 19.8
23 Tu	6 04 30	1 30 14	24 55 37	1♊04 04	7 50.8	16 36.4	14 57.1	21 33.2	27 57.0	24 48.4	16 49.8	24 26.7	6 46.1	7 19.0
24 W	6 08 26	2 27 29	7♊10 26	13 14 55	7 40.1	16 23.8	16 10.3	22 11.6	27 43.8	24 57.8	16 45.6	24 24.3	6 44.5	7 18.2
25 Th	6 12 23	3 24 44	19 17 42	25 18 57	7 27.4	16 07.2	17 23.4	22 50.1	27 30.7	25 07.1	16 41.5	24 21.9	6 42.9	7 17.5
26 F	6 16 19	4 21 59	1♋18 49	7♋17 29	7 13.6	15 46.6	18 36.6	23 28.5	27 17.6	25 16.3	16 37.3	24 19.5	6 41.2	7 16.7
27 Sa	6 20 16	5 19 14	13 15 03	19 11 44	6 59.9	15 22.5	19 49.9	24 07.0	27 04.7	25 25.4	16 33.2	24 17.1	6 39.6	7 16.0
28 Su	6 24 13	6 16 28	25 07 41	1♌03 08	6 47.3	14 55.1	21 03.1	24 45.4	26 51.9	25 34.3	16 29.2	24 14.7	6 38.0	7 15.4
29 M	6 28 09	7 13 42	6♌58 18	12 53 31	6 36.7	14 24.8	22 16.3	25 23.8	26 39.2	25 43.1	16 25.2	24 12.3	6 36.4	7 14.8
30 Tu	6 32 06	8 10 55	18 49 04	24 45 21	6 28.9	13 52.2	23 29.6	26 02.2	26 26.6	25 51.8	16 21.2	24 10.0	6 34.8	7 14.2

Astro Data

	Dy Hr Mn
☽0S	9 21:00
☽0N	22 14:37
♃△♄	23 12:26
☽0S	6 5:21
☽0N	18 19:24
☿R	21 3:43
♃△♅	21 16:52

Planet Ingress

	Dy Hr Mn
☿ ♊	13 17:50
♀ ♉	17 11:56
♂ ♋	21 3:01
☉ ♊	21 14:10
☿ ♋	30 4:21
♀ ♊	11 5:15
⚳ ♐R	14 4:48
☉ ♋	21 22:11

Last Aspect / ☽ Ingress

Last Aspect Dy Hr Mn		☽ Ingress Dy Hr Mn
2 0:21	♅ ☍	♋ 2 7:39
3 13:14	♃ □	♌ 4 20:06
7 0:38	♅ △	♍ 7 8:07
9 10:18	♅ □	♎ 9 17:29
11 16:19	♅ ⚹	♏ 11 23:09
13 12:50	☉ ☍	♐ 14 1:41
15 23:38	♀ △	♑ 16 2:37
17 21:51	☉ △	♒ 18 3:42
20 5:23	♂ △	♓ 20 6:24
22 3:41	♅ □	♈ 22 11:23
24 10:29	♅ △	♉ 24 18:39
25 13:03	♀ ☌	♊ 27 3:55
29 13:09	☿ ☌	♋ 29 14:59

Last Aspect Dy Hr Mn		☽ Ingress Dy Hr Mn
31 8:32	♃ □	♌ 1 3:25
3 6:28	♅ △	♍ 3 15:56
5 17:13	♅ □	♎ 6 2:24
8 0:25	♅ ⚹	♏ 8 9:06
10 10:18	♀ ☍	♐ 10 11:53
12 4:00	♅ ☌	♑ 12 12:05
14 0:55	♃ □	♒ 14 11:45
16 4:07	♅ ⚹	♓ 16 12:54
18 11:03	☉ □	♈ 18 16:56
20 22:22	☉ ⚹	♉ 21 0:09
22 16:25	♂ ⚹	♊ 23 9:54
25 11:36	♃ ⚹	♋ 25 21:22
28 0:45	♃ □	♌ 28 9:52
30 14:16	♃ △	♍ 30 22:34

☽ Phases & Eclipses

Dy Hr Mn	
6 2:26	☽ 15♌03
13 12:50	○ 22♏14
20 4:02	☾ 28♒38
27 15:13	● 5♊49
4 18:53	☽ 13♍38
11 20:49	○ 20♐24
18 11:03	☾ 26♓42
26 5:37	● 4♋07

Astro Data

1 May 1987
Julian Day # 31897
SVP 5♓26'16"
GC 26♐39.7 ⚴ 25♏17.0R
Eris 16♈27.5 ⚵ 25♒15.3
⚷ 18♊35.9 ⚶ 24♉43.5
☽ Mean ☊ 10♈06.7

1 June 1987
Julian Day # 31928
SVP 5♓26'11"
GC 26♐39.8 ⚴ 16♏23.4R
Eris 16♈43.9 ⚵ 2♓59.7
⚷ 21♊06.0 ⚶ 8♊12.9
☽ Mean ☊ 8♈28.3

July 1987

LONGITUDE

Day	Sid.Time	☉	0 hr ☽	Noon ☽	True ☊	☿	♀	♂	⚳	♃	♄	♅	♆	♇
1 W	6 36 02	9♋08 08	0♍42 47	6♍41 50	6♈23.9	13♋17.7	24♊42.8	26♋40.6	26♐14.2	26♈00.3	16♐17.3	24♐07.6	6♑33.1	7♏13.6
2 Th	6 39 59	10 05 21	12 43 00	18 46 51	6R 21.4	12R 41.8	25 56.1	27 19.0	26R 01.9	26 08.7	16R 13.4	24R 05.3	6R 31.5	7R 13.1
3 F	6 43 55	11 02 33	24 53 57	1♎04 55	6 20.6	12 05.3	27 09.4	27 57.4	25 49.9	26 17.0	16 09.5	24 02.9	6 29.9	7 12.5
4 Sa	6 47 52	11 59 45	7♎20 22	13 40 55	6 20.6	11 28.7	28 22.8	28 35.7	25 38.0	26 25.1	16 05.8	24 00.6	6 28.3	7 12.1
5 Su	6 51 48	12 56 56	20 07 10	26 39 39	6 20.1	10 52.6	29 36.1	29 14.0	25 26.3	26 33.1	16 02.0	23 58.4	6 26.7	7 11.6
6 M	6 55 45	13 54 08	3♏18 53	10♏05 14	6 18.2	10 17.7	0♋49.4	29 52.4	25 14.8	26 41.0	15 58.4	23 56.1	6 25.1	7 11.2
7 Tu	6 59 42	14 51 19	16 58 59	24 00 14	6 14.0	9 44.5	2 02.8	0♌30.7	25 03.6	26 48.7	15 54.8	23 53.9	6 23.5	7 10.9
8 W	7 03 38	15 48 30	1♐08 54	8♐24 41	6 07.3	9 13.8	3 16.2	1 09.0	24 52.6	26 56.3	15 51.2	23 51.6	6 21.9	7 10.5
9 Th	7 07 35	16 45 41	15 47 05	23 15 18	5 58.5	8 45.9	4 29.6	1 47.3	24 41.8	27 03.7	15 47.7	23 49.4	6 20.3	7 10.2
10 F	7 11 31	17 42 52	0♑48 22	8♑25 05	5 48.3	8 21.4	5 43.0	2 25.6	24 31.3	27 11.0	15 44.3	23 47.3	6 18.7	7 09.9
11 Sa	7 15 28	18 40 03	16 04 08	23 44 02	5 38.0	8 00.8	6 56.5	3 03.9	24 21.0	27 18.2	15 40.9	23 45.1	6 17.1	7 09.7
12 Su	7 19 24	19 37 15	1♒23 22	9♒00 41	5 28.8	7 44.5	8 09.9	3 42.1	24 11.0	27 25.1	15 37.6	23 43.0	6 15.6	7 09.5
13 M	7 23 21	20 34 26	16 34 42	24 04 15	5 21.7	7 32.8	9 23.4	4 20.4	24 01.3	27 32.0	15 34.4	23 40.9	6 14.0	7 09.3
14 Tu	7 27 17	21 31 38	1♓28 24	8♓46 25	5 17.0	7D 26.0	10 36.9	4 58.6	23 51.9	27 38.7	15 31.2	23 38.8	6 12.4	7 09.2
15 W	7 31 14	22 28 51	15 57 49	23 02 19	5D 14.8	7 24.3	11 50.4	5 36.9	23 42.7	27 45.2	15 28.1	23 36.7	6 10.9	7 09.1
16 Th	7 35 11	23 26 04	29 59 50	6♈50 28	5 14.4	7 27.8	13 04.0	6 15.1	23 33.9	27 51.6	15 25.1	23 34.7	6 09.4	7 09.0
17 F	7 39 07	24 23 18	13♈34 27	20 12 07	5R 14.6	7 36.9	14 17.5	6 53.3	23 25.3	27 57.8	15 22.1	23 32.7	6 07.8	7D 08.9
18 Sa	7 43 04	25 20 32	26 43 53	3♉10 13	5 14.5	7 51.4	15 31.1	7 31.6	23 17.1	28 03.8	15 19.2	23 30.7	6 06.3	7 08.9
19 Su	7 47 00	26 17 47	9♉31 37	15 48 38	5 12.8	8 11.6	16 44.7	8 09.8	23 09.2	28 09.7	15 16.4	23 28.8	6 04.8	7 09.0
20 M	7 50 57	27 15 03	22 01 44	28 11 26	5 08.9	8 37.4	17 58.4	8 48.0	23 01.6	28 15.5	15 13.7	23 26.9	6 03.3	7 09.0
21 Tu	7 54 53	28 12 20	4♊18 12	10♊22 27	5 02.4	9 08.7	19 12.0	9 26.2	22 54.3	28 21.0	15 11.0	23 25.0	6 01.9	7 09.1
22 W	7 58 50	29 09 37	16 24 36	22 25 00	4 53.5	9 45.8	20 25.7	10 04.4	22 47.4	28 26.4	15 08.5	23 23.2	6 00.4	7 09.2
23 Th	8 02 46	0♌06 55	28 23 59	4♋21 50	4 42.8	10 28.4	21 39.4	10 42.7	22 40.8	28 31.7	15 06.0	23 21.4	5 59.0	7 09.4
24 F	8 06 43	1 04 14	10♋18 47	16 15 06	4 31.0	11 16.5	22 53.2	11 20.9	22 34.6	28 36.7	15 03.6	23 19.6	5 57.5	7 09.6
25 Sa	8 10 40	2 01 34	22 10 58	28 06 36	4 19.2	12 10.1	24 06.9	11 59.1	22 28.7	28 41.6	15 01.2	23 17.9	5 56.1	7 09.8
26 Su	8 14 36	2 58 54	4♌02 10	9♌57 52	4 08.4	13 09.1	25 20.7	12 37.2	22 23.1	28 46.3	14 59.0	23 16.2	5 54.7	7 10.1
27 M	8 18 33	3 56 14	15 53 55	21 50 31	3 59.5	14 13.4	26 34.5	13 15.4	22 18.0	28 50.8	14 56.8	23 14.5	5 53.3	7 10.4
28 Tu	8 22 29	4 53 36	27 47 55	3♍46 24	3 53.0	15 22.9	27 48.3	13 53.6	22 13.1	28 55.2	14 54.7	23 12.8	5 51.9	7 10.7
29 W	8 26 26	5 50 57	9♍46 15	15 47 48	3 49.0	16 37.5	29 02.1	14 31.8	22 08.7	28 59.4	14 52.7	23 11.2	5 50.6	7 11.1
30 Th	8 30 22	6 48 20	21 51 27	27 57 37	3D 47.2	17 57.0	0♌15.9	15 10.0	22 04.6	29 03.4	14 50.8	23 09.7	5 49.2	7 11.5
31 F	8 34 19	7 45 43	4♎06 44	10♎19 17	3 47.2	19 21.4	1 29.8	15 48.1	22 00.8	29 07.2	14 49.0	23 08.2	5 47.9	7 11.9

August 1987

LONGITUDE

Day	Sid.Time	☉	0 hr ☽	Noon ☽	True ☊	☿	♀	♂	⚳	♃	♄	♅	♆	♇
1 Sa	8 38 15	8♌43 06	16♎35 46	22♎56 42	3♈48.1	20♋50.4	2♌43.7	16♌26.3	21♐57.4	29♈10.8	14♐47.3	23♐06.7	5♑46.6	7♏12.4
2 Su	8 42 12	9 40 31	29 22 36	5♏53 58	3R 48.8	22 23.9	3 57.6	17 04.5	21R 54.4	29 14.3	14R 45.6	23R 05.3	5R 45.3	7 12.9
3 M	8 46 09	10 37 56	12♏31 15	19 14 50	3 48.5	24 01.5	5 11.5	17 42.6	21 51.8	29 17.5	14 44.1	23 03.9	5 44.1	7 13.5
4 Tu	8 50 05	11 35 21	26 05 03	3♐02 04	3 46.5	25 43.1	6 25.4	18 20.8	21 49.5	29 20.6	14 42.6	23 02.5	5 42.8	7 14.0
5 W	8 54 02	12 32 47	10♐05 56	17 16 33	3 42.6	27 28.4	7 39.4	18 58.9	21 47.6	29 23.5	14 41.3	23 01.2	5 41.6	7 14.7
6 Th	8 57 58	13 30 14	24 33 34	1♑56 27	3 36.8	29 17.0	8 53.3	19 37.1	21 46.0	29 26.2	14 40.0	22 59.9	5 40.4	7 15.3
7 F	9 01 55	14 27 42	9♑24 30	16 56 44	3 30.0	1♌08.6	10 07.3	20 15.2	21 44.8	29 28.7	14 38.8	22 58.7	5 39.2	7 16.0
8 Sa	9 05 51	15 25 11	24 32 03	2♒09 12	3 22.8	3 02.8	11 21.3	20 53.4	21 44.0	29 31.0	14 37.7	22 57.5	5 38.1	7 16.7
9 Su	9 09 48	16 22 40	9♒46 50	17 23 37	3 16.4	4 59.3	12 35.4	21 31.5	21D 43.5	29 33.2	14 36.7	22 56.4	5 36.9	7 17.4
10 M	9 13 44	17 20 11	24 58 12	2♓29 23	3 11.5	6 57.7	13 49.4	22 09.7	21 43.4	29 35.1	14 35.8	22 55.3	5 35.8	7 18.2
11 Tu	9 17 41	18 17 42	9♓56 03	17 17 19	3 08.6	8 57.7	15 03.5	22 47.8	21 43.7	29 36.9	14 35.0	22 54.2	5 34.7	7 19.0
12 W	9 21 38	19 15 15	24 32 29	1♈41 02	3D 07.6	10 58.8	16 17.5	23 26.0	21 44.3	29 38.4	14 34.3	22 53.2	5 33.7	7 19.8
13 Th	9 25 34	20 12 50	8♈42 41	15 37 19	3 08.1	13 00.7	17 31.6	24 04.1	21 45.2	29 39.8	14 33.7	22 52.2	5 32.6	7 20.7
14 F	9 29 31	21 10 25	22 25 00	29 05 54	3 09.3	15 03.1	18 45.8	24 42.2	21 46.5	29 41.0	14 33.2	22 51.3	5 31.6	7 21.6
15 Sa	9 33 27	22 08 03	5♉40 22	12♉08 47	3R 10.6	17 05.7	19 59.9	25 20.4	21 48.1	29 41.9	14 32.7	22 50.4	5 30.6	7 22.6
16 Su	9 37 24	23 05 42	18 31 37	24 49 24	3 11.0	19 08.2	21 14.1	25 58.5	21 50.1	29 42.7	14 32.4	22 49.6	5 29.6	7 23.5
17 M	9 41 20	24 03 22	1♊02 39	7♊11 55	3 10.0	21 10.5	22 28.3	26 36.7	21 52.4	29 43.3	14 32.2	22 48.8	5 28.7	7 24.5
18 Tu	9 45 17	25 01 04	13 17 47	19 20 45	3 07.4	23 12.2	23 42.5	27 14.8	21 55.1	29 43.7	14D 32.1	22 48.1	5 27.8	7 25.6
19 W	9 49 13	25 58 48	25 21 21	1♋20 04	3 03.2	25 13.2	24 56.7	27 53.0	21 58.1	29R 43.8	14 32.0	22 47.4	5 26.9	7 26.6
20 Th	9 53 10	26 56 33	7♋17 22	13 13 40	2 57.7	27 13.4	26 11.0	28 31.2	22 01.5	29 43.8	14 32.1	22 46.8	5 26.0	7 27.7
21 F	9 57 07	27 54 20	19 09 22	25 04 49	2 51.5	29 12.6	27 25.2	29 09.3	22 05.2	29 43.6	14 32.2	22 46.2	5 25.2	7 28.9
22 Sa	10 01 03	28 52 08	1♌00 21	6♌56 14	2 45.2	1♍10.8	28 39.5	29 47.5	22 09.2	29 43.2	14 32.5	22 45.7	5 24.4	7 30.0
23 Su	10 05 00	29 49 58	12 52 46	18 50 09	2 39.5	3 07.9	29 53.8	0♍25.7	22 13.5	29 42.5	14 32.9	22 45.2	5 23.6	7 31.2
24 M	10 08 56	0♍47 49	24 48 39	0♍48 27	2 34.9	5 03.7	1♍08.1	1 03.9	22 18.2	29 41.7	14 33.3	22 44.8	5 22.8	7 32.4
25 Tu	10 12 53	1 45 42	6♍49 46	12 52 49	2 31.7	6 58.3	2 22.4	1 42.0	22 23.2	29 40.7	14 33.8	22 44.4	5 22.1	7 33.7
26 W	10 16 49	2 43 36	18 57 47	25 04 54	2D 30.1	8 51.7	3 36.8	2 20.2	22 28.5	29 39.4	14 34.5	22 44.0	5 21.4	7 35.0
27 Th	10 20 46	3 41 31	1♎14 24	7♎26 31	2 30.0	10 43.8	4 51.1	2 58.4	22 34.2	29 38.0	14 35.2	22 43.7	5 20.8	7 36.3
28 F	10 24 42	4 39 28	13 41 32	19 59 44	2 30.9	12 34.5	6 05.5	3 36.6	22 40.1	29 36.4	14 36.1	22 43.5	5 20.1	7 37.6
29 Sa	10 28 39	5 37 26	26 21 24	2♏46 52	2 32.4	14 24.0	7 19.9	4 14.8	22 46.4	29 34.5	14 37.0	22 43.3	5 19.5	7 39.0
30 Su	10 32 36	6 35 26	9♏16 25	15 50 22	2 34.0	16 12.2	8 34.3	4 53.0	22 52.9	29 32.5	14 38.1	22 43.2	5 18.9	7 40.4
31 M	10 36 32	7 33 27	22 29 01	29 12 36	2R 35.0	17 59.1	9 48.7	5 31.2	22 59.8	29 30.3	14 39.2	22 43.1	5 18.4	7 41.8

Astro Data

	Dy Hr Mn
☽ 0S	3 11:59
☿ D	15 7:51
☽ 0N	16 1:33
♇ D	18 6:11
☽ 0S	30 17:15
⚳ D	10 7:56
♃⚼♄	10 18:20
☽ 0N	12 10:04
♄ D	19 8:53
♃ R	19 21:07
☽ 0S	26 22:26
♃⚼♄	28 14:44

Planet Ingress

	Dy Hr Mn
♀ ♋	5 19:50
♂ ♌	6 16:46
☉ ♌	23 9:06
♀ ♌	30 6:49
☿ ♌	6 21:20
☿ ♍	21 21:36
♂ ♍	22 19:51
♀ ♍	23 14:00
☉ ♍	23 16:10

Last Aspect / ☽ Ingress

Last Aspect Dy Hr Mn		☽ Ingress Dy Hr Mn
3 5:37 ♂ ⚹	♎	3 9:55
5 17:52 ♀ △	♏	5 18:03
6 19:10 ☉ △	♐	7 22:05
9 18:07 ♃ △	♑	9 22:43
11 17:38 ♃ □	♒	11 21:49
13 17:38 ♃ ⚹	♓	13 21:36
15 12:59 ♅ □	♈	16 0:00
18 2:24 ♃ ☌	♉	18 6:04
20 10:00 ☉ ⚹	♊	20 15:33
23 0:10 ♃ ⚹	♋	23 3:13
25 13:11 ♃ □	♌	25 15:50
28 2:12 ♃ △	♍	28 4:26
30 2:35 ♅ □	♎	30 15:59

Last Aspect / ☽ Ingress

Last Aspect Dy Hr Mn		☽ Ingress Dy Hr Mn
1 23:41 ♃ ☍	♏	2 1:09
3 21:34 ☿ △	♐	4 6:47
6 7:56 ♃ △	♑	6 8:52
8 7:50 ♃ □	♒	8 8:37
10 7:21 ♃ ⚹	♓	10 8:01
11 21:16 ♅ □	♈	12 9:09
14 13:04 ♃ ☌	♉	14 13:38
16 14:20 ♂ □	♊	16 21:59
19 8:46 ♃ ⚹	♋	19 9:19
21 21:24 ♃ □	♌	21 21:58
24 9:47 ♃ △	♍	24 10:23
26 7:24 ♅ □	♎	26 21:35
29 6:03 ♃ ☍	♏	29 6:49
30 12:46 ☿ ⚹	♐	31 13:24

☽ Phases & Eclipses

Dy Hr Mn	
4 8:34	☽ 11♎52
11 3:33	○ 18♑20
17 20:17	☾ 24♈43
25 20:38	● 2♌22
2 19:24	☽ 9♏58
9 10:17	○ 16♒19
16 8:25	☾ 22♉57
24 11:59	● 0♍48

Astro Data

1 July 1987
Julian Day # 31958
SVP 5♓26'05"
GC 26♐39.9 ⚴ 12♏27.4R
Eris 16♈52.3 ⚵ 6♓45.6
⚷ 23♊42.5 ⚶ 21♊09.0
☽ Mean ☊ 6♈53.0

1 August 1987
Julian Day # 31989
SVP 5♓26'00"
GC 26♐40.0 ⚴ 15♏09.6
Eris 16♈51.3R ⚵ 4♓52.9R
⚷ 26♊10.8 ⚶ 4♋07.2
☽ Mean ☊ 5♈14.5

LONGITUDE — September 1987

Day	Sid.Time	☉	0 hr ☽	Noon ☽	True ☊	☿	♀	♂	⚳	♃	♄	♅	♆	♇
1 Tu	10 40 29	8♍31 29	6♐01 20	12♐55 20	2♈35.1	19♍44.7	11♍03.1	6♍09.4	23♐07.0	29♈27.9	14♐40.4	22♐43.1	5♑17.9	7♏43.3
2 W	10 44 25	9 29 33	19 54 40	26 59 15	2R 34.3	21 29.1	12 17.6	6 47.6	23 14.4	29R 25.3	14 41.7	22D 43.1	5R 17.4	7 44.8
3 Th	10 48 22	10 27 38	4♑08 55	11♑23 19	2 32.4	23 12.2	13 32.0	7 25.8	23 22.2	29 22.5	14 43.2	22 43.2	5 16.9	7 46.3
4 F	10 52 18	11 25 45	18 42 00	26 04 21	2 29.9	24 54.1	14 46.5	8 04.0	23 30.2	29 19.5	14 44.7	22 43.3	5 16.5	7 47.8
5 Sa	10 56 15	12 23 53	3♒29 35	10♒56 50	2 27.3	26 34.7	16 00.9	8 42.2	23 38.5	29 16.3	14 46.3	22 43.5	5 16.1	7 49.4
6 Su	11 00 11	13 22 02	18 25 08	25 53 27	2 24.9	28 14.2	17 15.4	9 20.4	23 47.1	29 12.9	14 48.0	22 43.7	5 15.7	7 51.0
7 M	11 04 08	14 20 13	3♓20 43	10♓45 54	2 23.1	29 52.4	18 29.9	9 58.7	23 56.0	29 09.4	14 49.8	22 44.0	5 15.4	7 52.6
8 Tu	11 08 05	15 18 26	18 08 00	25 26 09	2D 22.3	1♎29.5	19 44.4	10 36.9	24 05.2	29 05.6	14 51.7	22 44.3	5 15.1	7 54.3
9 W	11 12 01	16 16 40	2♈39 34	9♈47 37	2 22.3	3 05.4	20 58.9	11 15.1	24 14.6	29 01.7	14 53.7	22 44.6	5 14.8	7 55.9
10 Th	11 15 58	17 14 57	16 49 50	23 45 52	2 23.0	4 40.2	22 13.4	11 53.4	24 24.2	28 57.6	14 55.8	22 45.1	5 14.6	7 57.6
11 F	11 19 54	18 13 15	0♉35 34	7♉18 54	2 24.1	6 13.9	23 27.9	12 31.6	24 34.2	28 53.3	14 57.9	22 45.6	5 14.4	7 59.3
12 Sa	11 23 51	19 11 36	13 55 59	20 27 00	2 25.2	7 46.4	24 42.5	13 09.9	24 44.3	28 48.8	15 00.2	22 46.1	5 14.2	8 01.1
13 Su	11 27 47	20 09 59	26 52 18	3♊12 15	2 26.2	9 17.7	25 57.0	13 48.2	24 54.8	28 44.2	15 02.6	22 46.7	5 14.0	8 02.9
14 M	11 31 44	21 08 24	9♊27 19	15 38 01	2R 26.7	10 48.0	27 11.6	14 26.4	25 05.5	28 39.4	15 05.0	22 47.3	5 13.9	8 04.7
15 Tu	11 35 40	22 06 51	21 44 52	27 48 26	2 26.7	12 17.1	28 26.2	15 04.7	25 16.4	28 34.4	15 07.6	22 48.0	5 13.9	8 06.5
16 W	11 39 37	23 05 20	3♋49 17	9♋48 00	2 26.2	13 45.1	29 40.7	15 43.0	25 27.6	28 29.3	15 10.2	22 48.7	5D 13.8	8 08.3
17 Th	11 43 34	24 03 51	15 45 07	21 41 11	2 25.4	15 12.0	0♎55.3	16 21.3	25 39.0	28 23.9	15 12.9	22 49.5	5 13.8	8 10.2
18 F	11 47 30	25 02 24	27 36 45	3♌32 17	2 24.4	16 37.7	2 09.9	16 59.7	25 50.7	28 18.5	15 15.7	22 50.3	5 13.8	8 12.1
19 Sa	11 51 27	26 01 00	9♌28 15	15 25 06	2 23.5	18 02.2	3 24.6	17 38.0	26 02.6	28 12.8	15 18.6	22 51.2	5 13.9	8 14.0
20 Su	11 55 23	26 59 38	21 23 14	27 22 59	2 22.7	19 25.5	4 39.2	18 16.3	26 14.7	28 07.0	15 21.6	22 52.2	5 14.0	8 15.9
21 M	11 59 20	27 58 17	3♍24 42	9♍28 40	2 22.1	20 47.6	5 53.8	18 54.7	26 27.1	28 01.1	15 24.7	22 53.2	5 14.1	8 17.9
22 Tu	12 03 16	28 56 59	15 35 06	21 44 15	2D 21.9	22 08.5	7 08.5	19 33.0	26 39.6	27 55.0	15 27.8	22 54.2	5 14.2	8 19.9
23 W	12 07 13	29 55 42	27 56 16	4♎11 19	2 21.8	23 28.0	8 23.1	20 11.4	26 52.4	27 48.8	15 31.1	22 55.3	5 14.4	8 21.9
24 Th	12 11 09	0♎54 28	10♎29 30	16 50 55	2 21.8	24 46.2	9 37.8	20 49.8	27 05.5	27 42.4	15 34.4	22 56.4	5 14.6	8 23.9
25 F	12 15 06	1 53 15	23 15 38	29 43 43	2R 21.9	26 03.0	10 52.4	21 28.2	27 18.7	27 35.9	15 37.8	22 57.6	5 14.9	8 25.9
26 Sa	12 19 03	2 52 05	6♏15 12	12♏50 07	2 21.9	27 18.3	12 07.1	22 06.6	27 32.1	27 29.3	15 41.3	22 58.8	5 15.2	8 28.0
27 Su	12 22 59	3 50 56	19 28 29	26 10 17	2 21.8	28 32.1	13 21.8	22 45.0	27 45.8	27 22.5	15 44.9	23 00.1	5 15.5	8 30.0
28 M	12 26 56	4 49 49	2♐55 33	9♐44 13	2 21.6	29 44.2	14 36.4	23 23.4	27 59.7	27 15.7	15 48.6	23 01.5	5 15.8	8 32.1
29 Tu	12 30 52	5 48 44	16 36 17	23 31 39	2D 21.4	0♏54.5	15 51.1	24 01.8	28 13.7	27 08.7	15 52.3	23 02.9	5 16.2	8 34.3
30 W	12 34 49	6 47 41	0♑30 15	7♑31 56	2 21.3	2 03.1	17 05.8	24 40.2	28 28.0	27 01.6	15 56.2	23 04.3	5 16.7	8 36.4

LONGITUDE — October 1987

Day	Sid.Time	☉	0 hr ☽	Noon ☽	True ☊	☿	♀	♂	⚳	♃	♄	♅	♆	♇
1 Th	12 38 45	7♎46 39	14♑36 31	21♑43 46	2♈21.5	3♏09.6	18♎20.5	25♍18.7	28♐42.4	26♈54.4	16♐00.1	23♐05.8	5♑17.1	8♏38.5
2 F	12 42 42	8 45 39	28 53 24	6♒05 04	2 21.9	4 14.0	19 35.1	25 57.1	28 57.1	26R 47.1	16 04.1	23 07.3	5 17.6	8 40.7
3 Sa	12 46 38	9 44 41	13♒18 19	20 32 40	2 22.5	5 16.1	20 49.8	26 35.6	29 11.9	26 39.7	16 08.1	23 08.9	5 18.1	8 42.9
4 Su	12 50 35	10 43 44	27 47 36	5♓02 30	2 23.1	6 15.7	22 04.5	27 14.1	29 26.9	26 32.2	16 12.3	23 10.5	5 18.7	8 45.1
5 M	12 54 32	11 42 49	12♓16 43	19 29 38	2R 23.7	7 12.7	23 19.2	27 52.5	29 42.1	26 24.7	16 16.5	23 12.2	5 19.2	8 47.3
6 Tu	12 58 28	12 41 56	26 40 32	3♈48 49	2 23.9	8 06.7	24 33.8	28 31.0	29 57.5	26 17.0	16 20.8	23 13.9	5 19.9	8 49.5
7 W	13 02 25	13 41 05	10♈53 50	17 55 03	2 23.5	8 57.5	25 48.5	29 09.5	0♑13.1	26 09.3	16 25.1	23 15.7	5 20.5	8 51.7
8 Th	13 06 21	14 40 17	24 51 57	1♉44 09	2 22.6	9 44.8	27 03.2	29 48.0	0 28.8	26 01.5	16 29.6	23 17.5	5 21.2	8 54.0
9 F	13 10 18	15 39 30	8♉31 19	15 13 15	2 21.0	10 28.4	28 17.9	0♎26.6	0 44.7	25 53.7	16 34.1	23 19.3	5 21.9	8 56.2
10 Sa	13 14 14	16 38 46	21 49 52	28 21 09	2 19.1	11 07.7	29 32.6	1 05.1	1 00.7	25 45.8	16 38.7	23 21.2	5 22.6	8 58.5
11 Su	13 18 11	17 38 04	4♊47 13	11♊08 15	2 17.0	11 42.6	0♏47.3	1 43.7	1 17.0	25 37.8	16 43.3	23 23.2	5 23.4	9 00.8
12 M	13 22 07	18 37 24	17 24 33	23 36 28	2 15.1	12 12.5	2 02.0	2 22.2	1 33.4	25 29.9	16 48.1	23 25.2	5 24.2	9 03.1
13 Tu	13 26 04	19 36 46	29 44 26	5♋48 55	2 13.7	12 36.9	3 16.7	3 00.8	1 49.9	25 21.8	16 52.9	23 27.2	5 25.1	9 05.4
14 W	13 30 01	20 36 11	11♋50 28	17 49 38	2D 13.1	12 55.4	4 31.4	3 39.4	2 06.6	25 13.8	16 57.7	23 29.3	5 25.9	9 07.8
15 Th	13 33 57	21 35 38	23 47 00	29 43 10	2 13.3	13 07.5	5 46.1	4 18.0	2 23.5	25 05.7	17 02.7	23 31.4	5 26.9	9 10.1
16 F	13 37 54	22 35 08	5♌38 44	11♌34 19	2 14.2	13R 12.6	7 00.8	4 56.7	2 40.5	24 57.6	17 07.7	23 33.6	5 27.8	9 12.4
17 Sa	13 41 50	23 34 39	17 30 31	23 27 54	2 15.8	13 10.3	8 15.5	5 35.3	2 57.7	24 49.5	17 12.7	23 35.8	5 28.8	9 14.8
18 Su	13 45 47	24 34 13	29 27 01	5♍28 23	2 17.5	13 00.1	9 30.2	6 14.0	3 15.0	24 41.4	17 17.9	23 38.0	5 29.7	9 17.1
19 M	13 49 43	25 33 49	11♍32 30	17 39 47	2 18.9	12 41.5	10 44.9	6 52.6	3 32.5	24 33.2	17 23.1	23 40.3	5 30.8	9 19.5
20 Tu	13 53 40	26 33 27	23 50 36	0♎05 18	2R 19.6	12 14.2	11 59.6	7 31.3	3 50.1	24 25.1	17 28.3	23 42.6	5 31.8	9 21.9
21 W	13 57 36	27 33 07	6♎24 06	12 47 11	2 19.2	11 38.2	13 14.4	8 10.0	4 07.8	24 17.0	17 33.7	23 45.0	5 32.9	9 24.3
22 Th	14 01 33	28 32 50	19 14 40	25 46 32	2 17.5	10 53.5	14 29.1	8 48.7	4 25.7	24 08.9	17 39.0	23 47.4	5 34.0	9 26.7
23 F	14 05 29	29 32 34	2♏22 45	9♏03 10	2 14.4	10 00.4	15 43.8	9 27.4	4 43.8	24 00.9	17 44.5	23 49.9	5 35.2	9 29.1
24 Sa	14 09 26	0♏32 21	15 47 36	22 35 45	2 10.4	8 59.7	16 58.5	10 06.2	5 02.0	23 52.8	17 50.0	23 52.4	5 36.4	9 31.5
25 Su	14 13 23	1 32 09	29 27 18	6♐21 54	2 05.8	7 52.5	18 13.2	10 44.9	5 20.3	23 44.8	17 55.6	23 54.9	5 37.6	9 33.9
26 M	14 17 19	2 31 59	13♐19 08	20 18 38	2 01.3	6 40.2	19 28.0	11 23.7	5 38.7	23 36.9	18 01.2	23 57.5	5 38.8	9 36.3
27 Tu	14 21 16	3 31 51	27 19 57	4♑22 44	1 57.5	5 24.7	20 42.7	12 02.5	5 57.3	23 29.0	18 06.9	24 00.1	5 40.1	9 38.7
28 W	14 25 12	4 31 45	11♑26 35	18 31 10	1 55.0	4 08.1	21 57.4	12 41.3	6 16.0	23 21.2	18 12.6	24 02.7	5 41.4	9 41.1
29 Th	14 29 09	5 31 40	25 36 12	2♒41 22	1D 53.9	2 52.7	23 12.1	13 20.1	6 34.8	23 13.4	18 18.4	24 05.4	5 42.7	9 43.6
30 F	14 33 05	6 31 37	9♒46 28	16 51 15	1 54.3	1 40.8	24 26.8	13 58.9	6 53.7	23 05.7	18 24.2	24 08.1	5 44.1	9 46.0
31 Sa	14 37 02	7 31 35	23 55 32	0♓59 06	1 55.6	0 34.9	25 41.5	14 37.7	7 12.8	22 58.1	18 30.1	24 10.8	5 45.4	9 48.4

Astro Data

	Dy Hr Mn
♅∠♇	1 8:32
♅D	1 14:23
☿0S	8 2:06
☽0N	8 20:16
♆D	17 8:23
♀0S	19 3:20
☽0S	23 4:46
☉0S	23 13:45
☽0N	6 6:17
♂0S	12 8:49
☿R	16 16:46
☽0S	20 12:36
♃△♅	24 13:04

Planet Ingress

		Dy Hr Mn
☿	♎	7 13:52
♀	♎	16 18:12
☉	♎	23 13:45
☿	♏	28 17:21
⚳	♑	6 15:52
♂	♎	8 19:27
♀	♏	10 20:49
☉	♏	23 23:01

Last Aspect / ☽ Ingress

Last Aspect Dy Hr Mn		☽ Ingress Dy Hr Mn
2 16:05 ♃ △	♑	2 17:04
4 17:15 ♃ □	♒	4 18:22
6 17:20 ♃ ⚹	♓	6 18:37
8 7:33 ♅ □	♈	8 19:34
10 21:04 ♃ ☌	♉	10 22:57
12 20:47 ♀ △	♊	13 5:54
15 13:31 ♃ ⚹	♋	15 16:22
18 1:29 ♃ □	♌	18 4:50
20 13:27 ♃ △	♍	20 17:13
23 3:08 ☉ ☌	♎	23 3:58
25 8:06 ♃ ☍	♏	25 12:30
27 5:34 ♂ ⚹	♐	27 18:49
29 18:11 ♃ △	♑	29 23:08

Last Aspect / ☽ Ingress

Last Aspect Dy Hr Mn		☽ Ingress Dy Hr Mn
1 20:37 ♃ □	♒	2 1:51
3 22:02 ♃ ⚹	♓	4 3:39
6 2:40 ♂ ☍	♈	6 5:35
8 3:00 ♀ ☍	♉	8 8:57
9 3:00 ♀ ☍	♊	10 15:03
12 15:39 ♃ ⚹	♋	13 0:31
15 2:45 ♃ □	♌	15 12:34
17 14:42 ♃ △	♍	18 1:06
19 23:42 ♅ □	♎	20 11:50
22 17:28 ☉ ☌	♏	22 19:41
24 1:05 ♀ ☌	♐	25 0:57
26 18:15 ♅ ☌	♑	27 4:33
28 20:07 ♃ □	♒	29 7:27
31 2:08 ♀ □	♓	31 10:19

☽ Phases & Eclipses

Dy Hr Mn	
1 3:48	☽ 8♐12
7 18:13	○ 14♓35
14 23:44	☾ 21♊37
23 3:08	● 29♍34
23 3:11:26	● A 03'49"
30 10:39	☽ 6♑44
7 4:12	○ 13♈22
7 4:02	● A 0.987
14 18:06	☾ 20♋51
22 17:28	● 28♎46
29 17:10	☽ 5♒45

Astro Data

1 September 1987
Julian Day # 32020
SVP 5♓25'56"
GC 26♐40.0 ⚴ 22♏35.4
Eris 16♈40.8R ⚵ 27♒56.2R
⚷ 28♊00.2 ⚶ 16♋18.6
☽ Mean ☊ 3♈36.0

1 October 1987
Julian Day # 32050
SVP 5♓25'52"
GC 26♐40.1 ⚴ 2♐22.7
Eris 16♈24.6R ⚵ 22♒43.7R
⚷ 28♊48.2 ⚶ 26♋45.9
☽ Mean ☊ 2♈00.7

November 1987 — LONGITUDE

Day	Sid.Time	☉	0 hr ☽	Noon ☽	True ☊	☿	♀	♂	⚳	♃	♄	♅	♆	♇
1 Su	14 40 58	8♏31 35	8♓01 45	15♓03 18	1♈57.0	29♎36.7	26♏56.2	15♎16.5	7♑31.9	22♈50.6	18♐36.1	24♐13.6	5♑46.8	9♏50.9
2 M	14 44 55	9 31 37	22 03 31	29 02 09	1R 57.9	28R 47.9	28 10.9	15 55.4	7 51.2	22R 43.1	18 42.1	24 16.4	5 48.3	9 53.3
3 Tu	14 48 52	10 31 40	5♈58 56	12♈53 35	1 57.4	28 09.8	29 25.6	16 34.2	8 10.6	22 35.8	18 48.1	24 19.3	5 49.7	9 55.7
4 W	14 52 48	11 31 45	19 45 49	26 35 17	1 55.1	27 43.0	0♐40.2	17 13.1	8 30.1	22 28.5	18 54.2	24 22.1	5 51.2	9 58.1
5 Th	14 56 45	12 31 51	3♉21 42	10♉04 46	1 50.7	27D 27.8	1 54.9	17 52.0	8 49.7	22 21.3	19 00.3	24 25.0	5 52.7	10 00.6
6 F	15 00 41	13 32 00	16 44 13	23 19 48	1 44.4	27 24.2	3 09.6	18 30.9	9 09.4	22 14.3	19 06.5	24 28.0	5 54.3	10 03.0
7 Sa	15 04 38	14 32 10	29 51 23	6♊18 48	1 36.9	27 31.7	4 24.3	19 09.9	9 29.2	22 07.4	19 12.7	24 31.0	5 55.8	10 05.4
8 Su	15 08 34	15 32 23	12♊42 02	19 01 06	1 28.8	27 49.8	5 38.9	19 48.8	9 49.2	22 00.5	19 19.0	24 34.0	5 57.4	10 07.9
9 M	15 12 31	16 32 37	25 16 08	1♋27 17	1 21.0	28 17.6	6 53.6	20 27.8	10 09.2	21 53.8	19 25.3	24 37.0	5 59.0	10 10.3
10 Tu	15 16 28	17 32 53	7♋34 49	13 39 06	1 14.4	28 54.4	8 08.2	21 06.7	10 29.3	21 47.3	19 31.6	24 40.1	6 00.7	10 12.7
11 W	15 20 24	18 33 11	19 40 30	25 39 30	1 09.5	29 39.3	9 22.9	21 45.7	10 49.5	21 40.8	19 38.0	24 43.1	6 02.3	10 15.1
12 Th	15 24 21	19 33 31	1♌36 37	7♌32 25	1 06.6	0♏31.3	10 37.6	22 24.7	11 09.9	21 34.5	19 44.5	24 46.3	6 04.0	10 17.5
13 F	15 28 17	20 33 53	13 27 30	19 22 29	1D 05.6	1 29.6	11 52.2	23 03.8	11 30.3	21 28.4	19 50.9	24 49.4	6 05.7	10 19.9
14 Sa	15 32 14	21 34 17	25 18 01	1♍14 47	1 06.0	2 33.3	13 06.9	23 42.8	11 50.8	21 22.4	19 57.4	24 52.6	6 07.4	10 22.3
15 Su	15 36 10	22 34 43	7♍13 26	13 14 38	1 07.2	3 41.9	14 21.5	24 21.9	12 11.4	21 16.5	20 04.0	24 55.8	6 09.2	10 24.7
16 M	15 40 07	23 35 10	19 19 00	25 27 09	1R 08.2	4 54.6	15 36.1	25 01.0	12 32.1	21 10.8	20 10.6	24 59.0	6 10.9	10 27.1
17 Tu	15 44 03	24 35 40	1♎39 38	7♎56 56	1 08.1	6 10.7	16 50.8	25 40.1	12 52.9	21 05.3	20 17.2	25 02.2	6 12.7	10 29.5
18 W	15 48 00	25 36 11	14 19 29	20 47 37	1 06.1	7 29.9	18 05.4	26 19.2	13 13.7	20 59.9	20 23.8	25 05.5	6 14.6	10 31.9
19 Th	15 51 56	26 36 44	27 21 31	4♏01 18	1 01.8	8 51.6	19 20.1	26 58.3	13 34.7	20 54.6	20 30.5	25 08.8	6 16.4	10 34.2
20 F	15 55 53	27 37 19	10♏46 54	17 38 10	0 54.9	10 15.4	20 34.7	27 37.4	13 55.7	20 49.6	20 37.2	25 12.1	6 18.2	10 36.6
21 Sa	15 59 50	28 37 55	24 34 45	1♐36 11	0 46.2	11 41.1	21 49.3	28 16.6	14 16.9	20 44.7	20 43.9	25 15.4	6 20.1	10 38.9
22 Su	16 03 46	29 38 33	8♐41 52	15 51 07	0 36.2	13 08.2	23 03.9	28 55.8	14 38.1	20 40.0	20 50.7	25 18.8	6 22.0	10 41.3
23 M	16 07 43	0♐39 12	23 03 09	0♑17 08	0 26.4	14 36.5	24 18.6	29 35.0	14 59.4	20 35.5	20 57.5	25 22.2	6 23.9	10 43.6
24 Tu	16 11 39	1 39 52	7♑32 13	14 47 37	0 17.6	16 05.9	25 33.2	0♏14.2	15 20.7	20 31.2	21 04.3	25 25.6	6 25.9	10 45.9
25 W	16 15 36	2 40 34	22 02 33	29 16 22	0 11.0	17 36.1	26 47.8	0 53.4	15 42.2	20 27.0	21 11.2	25 29.0	6 27.8	10 48.2
26 Th	16 19 32	3 41 17	6♒28 29	13♒38 26	0 06.9	19 07.0	28 02.4	1 32.6	16 03.7	20 23.1	21 18.0	25 32.4	6 29.8	10 50.5
27 F	16 23 29	4 42 00	20 45 52	27 50 33	0D 05.2	20 38.5	29 17.0	2 11.9	16 25.3	20 19.3	21 24.9	25 35.8	6 31.8	10 52.8
28 Sa	16 27 26	5 42 45	4♓52 20	11♓51 10	0 05.1	22 10.4	0♑31.5	2 51.1	16 46.9	20 15.7	21 31.8	25 39.3	6 33.8	10 55.1
29 Su	16 31 22	6 43 30	18 47 04	25 40 02	0R 05.6	23 42.7	1 46.1	3 30.4	17 08.7	20 12.4	21 38.8	25 42.8	6 35.8	10 57.3
30 M	16 35 19	7 44 17	2♈30 11	9♈17 34	0 05.3	25 15.2	3 00.6	4 09.7	17 30.5	20 09.2	21 45.7	25 46.3	6 37.8	10 59.5

December 1987 — LONGITUDE

Day	Sid.Time	☉	0 hr ☽	Noon ☽	True ☊	☿	♀	♂	⚳	♃	♄	♅	♆	♇
1 Tu	16 39 15	8♐45 04	16♈02 15	22♈44 19	0♈03.2	26♏48.0	4♑15.2	4♏49.0	17♑52.3	20♈06.2	21♐52.7	25♐49.8	6♑39.9	11♏01.8
2 W	16 43 12	9 45 53	29 23 47	6♉00 39	29♓58.3	28 20.9	5 29.7	5 28.3	18 14.2	20R 03.4	21 59.7	25 53.3	6 42.0	11 04.0
3 Th	16 47 08	10 46 42	12♉34 52	19 06 25	29R 50.5	29 54.0	6 44.2	6 07.6	18 36.2	20 00.8	22 06.7	25 56.8	6 44.0	11 06.2
4 F	16 51 05	11 47 33	25 35 11	2♊01 07	29 39.9	1♐27.2	7 58.7	6 47.0	18 58.3	19 58.4	22 13.7	26 00.4	6 46.1	11 08.3
5 Sa	16 55 01	12 48 24	8♊24 07	14 44 06	29 27.3	3 00.5	9 13.2	7 26.3	19 20.4	19 56.3	22 20.7	26 04.0	6 48.2	11 10.5
6 Su	16 58 58	13 49 17	21 01 01	27 14 52	29 13.6	4 33.8	10 27.6	8 05.7	19 42.5	19 54.3	22 27.7	26 07.5	6 50.4	11 12.6
7 M	17 02 55	14 50 11	3♋25 38	9♋33 26	29 00.2	6 07.2	11 42.1	8 45.1	20 04.8	19 52.5	22 34.8	26 11.1	6 52.5	11 14.8
8 Tu	17 06 51	15 51 06	15 38 22	21 40 40	28 48.2	7 40.7	12 56.5	9 24.5	20 27.0	19 51.0	22 41.8	26 14.7	6 54.6	11 16.9
9 W	17 10 48	16 52 02	27 40 33	3♌38 23	28 38.4	9 14.2	14 10.9	10 04.0	20 49.4	19 49.6	22 48.9	26 18.3	6 56.8	11 18.9
10 Th	17 14 44	17 52 59	9♌34 31	15 29 26	28 31.4	10 47.8	15 25.4	10 43.4	21 11.8	19 48.5	22 56.0	26 21.9	6 59.0	11 21.0
11 F	17 18 41	18 53 57	21 23 37	27 17 37	28 27.2	12 21.4	16 39.7	11 22.9	21 34.2	19 47.5	23 03.1	26 25.5	7 01.1	11 23.1
12 Sa	17 22 37	19 54 56	3♍12 04	9♍07 35	28D 25.4	13 55.1	17 54.1	12 02.4	21 56.7	19 46.8	23 10.2	26 29.1	7 03.3	11 25.1
13 Su	17 26 34	20 55 56	15 04 51	21 04 33	28R 25.0	15 28.8	19 08.5	12 41.9	22 19.3	19 46.3	23 17.3	26 32.7	7 05.5	11 27.1
14 M	17 30 30	21 56 58	27 07 24	3♎14 05	28 25.0	17 02.6	20 22.8	13 21.4	22 41.9	19 45.9	23 24.4	26 36.4	7 07.7	11 29.1
15 Tu	17 34 27	22 58 00	9♎25 17	15 41 39	28 24.1	18 36.6	21 37.2	14 01.0	23 04.5	19D 45.8	23 31.5	26 40.0	7 09.9	11 31.0
16 W	17 38 24	23 59 03	22 03 46	28 32 10	28 21.3	20 10.6	22 51.5	14 40.5	23 27.2	19 45.9	23 38.6	26 43.6	7 12.1	11 33.0
17 Th	17 42 20	25 00 08	5♏07 14	11♏49 17	28 15.9	21 44.7	24 05.8	15 20.1	23 49.9	19 46.2	23 45.7	26 47.3	7 14.4	11 34.9
18 F	17 46 17	26 01 13	18 38 27	25 34 40	28 07.7	23 19.0	25 20.1	15 59.7	24 12.7	19 46.8	23 52.8	26 50.9	7 16.6	11 36.8
19 Sa	17 50 13	27 02 19	2♐37 43	9♐47 11	27 57.0	24 53.4	26 34.4	16 39.3	24 35.6	19 47.5	23 59.9	26 54.5	7 18.8	11 38.7
20 Su	17 54 10	28 03 26	17 02 24	24 22 34	27 44.9	26 27.9	27 48.6	17 18.9	24 58.5	19 48.4	24 07.0	26 58.2	7 21.1	11 40.5
21 M	17 58 06	29 04 34	1♑46 41	9♑13 39	27 32.6	28 02.7	29 02.9	17 58.5	25 21.4	19 49.6	24 14.1	27 01.8	7 23.3	11 42.3
22 Tu	18 02 03	0♑05 42	16 42 16	24 11 20	27 21.5	29 37.6	0♒17.1	18 38.2	25 44.4	19 51.0	24 21.1	27 05.5	7 25.6	11 44.1
23 W	18 06 00	1 06 50	1♒39 40	9♒06 13	27 12.9	1♑12.7	1 31.3	19 17.9	26 07.4	19 52.5	24 28.2	27 09.1	7 27.9	11 45.9
24 Th	18 09 56	2 07 58	16 30 00	23 50 14	27 07.1	2 48.0	2 45.4	19 57.5	26 30.4	19 54.3	24 35.3	27 12.7	7 30.1	11 47.7
25 F	18 13 53	3 09 07	1♓06 18	8♓17 46	27 04.2	4 23.6	3 59.5	20 37.2	26 53.5	19 56.3	24 42.3	27 16.4	7 32.4	11 49.4
26 Sa	18 17 49	4 10 15	15 24 20	22 25 55	27 03.3	5 59.4	5 13.6	21 16.9	27 16.6	19 58.5	24 49.4	27 20.0	7 34.7	11 51.1
27 Su	18 21 46	5 11 23	29 22 30	6♈14 12	27 03.3	7 35.4	6 27.7	21 56.6	27 39.7	20 00.9	24 56.4	27 23.6	7 36.9	11 52.7
28 M	18 25 42	6 12 32	13♈01 14	19 43 49	27 02.7	9 11.7	7 41.7	22 36.4	28 02.9	20 03.4	25 03.4	27 27.2	7 39.2	11 54.4
29 Tu	18 29 39	7 13 40	26 22 14	2♉56 47	27 00.4	10 48.3	8 55.7	23 16.1	28 26.1	20 06.2	25 10.4	27 30.8	7 41.5	11 56.0
30 W	18 33 35	8 14 49	9♉27 45	15 55 22	26 55.5	12 25.2	10 09.7	23 55.8	28 49.3	20 09.2	25 17.4	27 34.4	7 43.7	11 57.6
31 Th	18 37 32	9 15 57	22 19 54	28 41 33	26 47.5	14 02.3	11 23.6	24 35.6	29 12.6	20 12.4	25 24.4	27 38.0	7 46.0	11 59.1

Astro Data

	Dy Hr Mn
☽0N	2 14:15
☿D	6 7:38
♇0S	12 23:20
☽0S	16 21:11
♃△♄	21 13:39
☽0N	29 19:38
♅∠♇	9 22:20
☽0S	14 5:08
♃D	15 12:22
☽0N	27 0:13

Planet Ingress

		Dy Hr Mn
☿	♎R	1 1:57
♀	♐	3 23:04
☿	♏	11 21:57
☉	♐	22 20:29
♂	♏	24 3:19
♀	♑	28 1:51
☊	♓R	2 5:13
☿	♐	3 13:33
♀	♒	22 6:29
☉	♑	22 9:46
☿	♑	22 17:40

Last Aspect / ☽ Ingress (November)

Last Aspect Dy Hr Mn			☽ Ingress	Dy Hr Mn
2 10:23	♀	△	♈	2 13:40
4 13:57	☿	☍	♉	4 18:02
5 16:46	☉	☍	♊	7 0:16
9 5:35	☿	△	♋	9 9:10
11 20:39	☿	□	♌	11 20:45
13 23:05	♅	△	♍	14 9:29
16 11:05	♅	□	♎	16 20:48
18 22:38	♂	☌	♏	19 4:47
21 6:33	☉	☌	♐	21 9:16
23 10:47	♂	⚹	♑	23 11:32
24 21:26	♃	□	♒	25 13:13
27 14:41	♀	⚹	♓	27 15:40
29 12:05	♅	□	♈	29 19:36

Last Aspect / ☽ Ingress (December)

Last Aspect Dy Hr Mn			☽ Ingress	Dy Hr Mn
1 17:35	♅	△	♉	2 1:06
2 21:15	♇	☍	♊	4 8:13
6 9:49	♅	☍	♋	6 17:20
8 8:22	♃	□	♌	9 4:40
11 10:14	♅	△	♍	11 17:30
13 22:55	♅	□	♎	14 5:40
16 8:39	♅	⚹	♏	16 14:41
18 11:32	♀	⚹	♐	18 19:33
20 18:25	☉	☌	♑	20 21:08
22 5:02	♃	□	♒	22 21:20
24 17:35	♅	⚹	♓	24 22:10
26 20:30	♅	□	♈	27 1:05
29 2:02	♅	△	♉	29 6:37
31 3:50	♂	☍	♊	31 14:29

☽ Phases & Eclipses

Dy Hr Mn		
5 16:46	○	12♉44
13 14:38	☾	20♌41
21 6:33	●	28♏24
28 0:37	☽	5♓14
5 8:01	○	12♊38
13 11:41	☾	20♍55
20 18:25	●	28♐20
27 10:01	☽	5♈06

Astro Data

1 November 1987
Julian Day # 32081
SVP 5♓25'48"
GC 26♐40.2 ⚴ 13♐57.6
Eris 16♈06.2R ⚵ 24♒09.5
⚷ 28♊25.6R ⚶ 5♌04.6
☽ Mean ☊ 0♈22.2

1 December 1987
Julian Day # 32111
SVP 5♓25'43"
GC 26♐40.2 ⚴ 25♐51.0
Eris 15♈52.1R ⚵ 1♓40.7
⚷ 27♊02.0R ⚶ 8♌54.6
☽ Mean ☊ 28♓46.9

LONGITUDE — January 1988

Day	Sid.Time	☉	0 hr ☽	Noon ☽	True ☊	☿	♀	♂	⚳	♃	♄	♅	♆	♇
1 F	18 41 29	10♑17 05	5♊00 29	11♊16 51	26♓36.7	15♑39.7	12♒37.5	25♏15.4	29♑35.9	20♈15.8	25♐31.4	27♐41.6	7♑48.3	12♏00.7
2 Sa	18 45 25	11 18 14	17 30 45	23 42 17	26R 23.8	17 17.4	13 51.4	25 55.2	29 59.2	20 19.4	25 38.3	27 45.1	7 50.6	12 02.2
3 Su	18 49 22	12 19 22	29 51 33	5♋58 35	26 09.9	18 55.4	15 05.2	26 35.0	0♒22.6	20 23.1	25 45.2	27 48.7	7 52.8	12 03.6
4 M	18 53 18	13 20 30	12♋03 30	18 06 21	25 56.0	20 33.6	16 19.0	27 14.9	0 45.9	20 27.1	25 52.1	27 52.2	7 55.1	12 05.1
5 Tu	18 57 15	14 21 38	24 07 16	0♌06 22	25 43.5	22 12.1	17 32.7	27 54.7	1 09.3	20 31.3	25 59.0	27 55.8	7 57.4	12 06.5
6 W	19 01 11	15 22 47	6♌03 52	11 59 58	25 33.2	23 50.8	18 46.4	28 34.6	1 32.8	20 35.6	26 05.8	27 59.3	7 59.6	12 07.9
7 Th	19 05 08	16 23 55	17 54 55	23 49 05	25 25.7	25 29.7	20 00.0	29 14.4	1 56.2	20 40.1	26 12.7	28 02.8	8 01.9	12 09.2
8 F	19 09 04	17 25 03	29 42 47	5♍36 29	25 21.1	27 08.7	21 13.7	29 54.3	2 19.7	20 44.9	26 19.5	28 06.3	8 04.1	12 10.5
9 Sa	19 13 01	18 26 11	11♍30 39	17 25 48	25D 19.0	28 47.9	22 27.2	0♐34.3	2 43.1	20 49.8	26 26.2	28 09.8	8 06.4	12 11.8
10 Su	19 16 58	19 27 19	23 22 30	29 21 22	25 18.8	0♒27.0	23 40.7	1 14.2	3 06.6	20 54.8	26 33.0	28 13.2	8 08.6	12 13.0
11 M	19 20 54	20 28 28	5♎23 02	11♎28 10	25R 19.4	2 06.0	24 54.2	1 54.1	3 30.2	21 00.1	26 39.7	28 16.7	8 10.9	12 14.3
12 Tu	19 24 51	21 29 36	17 37 27	23 51 32	25 19.6	3 44.9	26 07.6	2 34.1	3 53.7	21 05.5	26 46.4	28 20.1	8 13.1	12 15.4
13 W	19 28 47	22 30 44	0♏11 04	6♏36 41	25 18.5	5 23.5	27 21.0	3 14.1	4 17.3	21 11.2	26 53.0	28 23.5	8 15.3	12 16.6
14 Th	19 32 44	23 31 52	13 08 54	19 48 11	25 15.4	7 01.6	28 34.3	3 54.1	4 40.8	21 17.0	26 59.7	28 26.9	8 17.5	12 17.7
15 F	19 36 40	24 33 00	26 34 51	3♐29 06	25 09.8	8 39.1	29 47.6	4 34.1	5 04.4	21 22.9	27 06.3	28 30.3	8 19.7	12 18.8
16 Sa	19 40 37	25 34 08	10♐30 55	17 40 07	25 02.1	10 15.8	1♓00.8	5 14.1	5 28.0	21 29.1	27 12.8	28 33.6	8 21.9	12 19.9
17 Su	19 44 33	26 35 16	24 56 16	2♑18 42	24 53.0	11 51.3	2 14.0	5 54.1	5 51.7	21 35.4	27 19.3	28 36.9	8 24.1	12 20.9
18 M	19 48 30	27 36 23	9♑46 35	17 18 49	24 43.4	13 25.5	3 27.1	6 34.2	6 15.3	21 41.9	27 25.8	28 40.2	8 26.3	12 21.9
19 Tu	19 52 27	28 37 30	24 54 10	2♒31 19	24 34.8	14 57.9	4 40.2	7 14.2	6 38.9	21 48.5	27 32.3	28 43.5	8 28.5	12 22.8
20 W	19 56 23	29 38 36	10♒08 53	17 45 29	24 28.0	16 28.2	5 53.2	7 54.3	7 02.6	21 55.4	27 38.7	28 46.8	8 30.6	12 23.8
21 Th	20 00 20	0♒39 42	25 19 51	2♓50 49	24 23.6	17 55.8	7 06.1	8 34.4	7 26.3	22 02.3	27 45.0	28 50.0	8 32.8	12 24.6
22 F	20 04 16	1 40 46	10♓17 25	17 38 52	24D 21.7	19 20.4	8 19.0	9 14.5	7 49.9	22 09.5	27 51.3	28 53.2	8 34.9	12 25.5
23 Sa	20 08 13	2 41 50	24 54 34	2♈04 10	24 21.7	20 41.2	9 31.8	9 54.6	8 13.6	22 16.8	27 57.6	28 56.4	8 37.0	12 26.3
24 Su	20 12 09	3 42 52	9♈07 26	16 04 22	24 22.7	21 57.7	10 44.6	10 34.7	8 37.3	22 24.2	28 03.8	28 59.6	8 39.2	12 27.1
25 M	20 16 06	4 43 53	22 55 04	29 39 45	24R 23.6	23 09.2	11 57.2	11 14.8	9 00.9	22 31.9	28 10.0	29 02.7	8 41.3	12 27.8
26 Tu	20 20 02	5 44 54	6♉18 43	12♉52 20	24 23.5	24 14.8	13 09.8	11 54.9	9 24.6	22 39.6	28 16.2	29 05.8	8 43.3	12 28.5
27 W	20 23 59	6 45 53	19 20 59	25 45 06	24 21.5	25 13.8	14 22.3	12 35.1	9 48.3	22 47.6	28 22.3	29 08.9	8 45.4	12 29.2
28 Th	20 27 56	7 46 51	2♊05 04	8♊21 20	24 17.4	26 05.3	15 34.7	13 15.2	10 12.0	22 55.6	28 28.3	29 11.9	8 47.5	12 29.8
29 F	20 31 52	8 47 49	14 34 15	20 44 12	24 11.2	26 48.5	16 47.1	13 55.4	10 35.7	23 03.8	28 34.3	29 15.0	8 49.5	12 30.4
30 Sa	20 35 49	9 48 44	26 51 31	2♋56 31	24 03.5	27 22.6	17 59.4	14 35.6	10 59.4	23 12.2	28 40.2	29 18.0	8 51.5	12 31.0
31 Su	20 39 45	10 49 39	8♋59 27	15 00 35	23 54.9	27 46.9	19 11.5	15 15.8	11 23.0	23 20.7	28 46.1	29 20.9	8 53.5	12 31.5

LONGITUDE — February 1988

Day	Sid.Time	☉	0 hr ☽	Noon ☽	True ☊	☿	♀	♂	⚳	♃	♄	♅	♆	♇
1 M	20 43 42	11♒50 33	21♋00 10	26♋58 22	23♓46.4	28♒00.7	20♓23.6	15♐56.0	11♒46.7	23♈29.4	28♐52.0	29♐23.8	8♑55.5	12♏32.0
2 Tu	20 47 38	12 51 26	2♌55 26	8♌51 31	23R 38.7	28R 03.6	21 35.6	16 36.2	12 10.4	23 38.1	28 57.7	29 26.7	8 57.5	12 32.5
3 W	20 51 35	13 52 17	14 46 51	20 41 39	23 32.5	27 55.4	22 47.5	17 16.4	12 34.1	23 47.0	29 03.5	29 29.6	8 59.5	12 32.9
4 Th	20 55 32	14 53 07	26 36 06	2♍30 29	23 28.2	27 36.0	23 59.3	17 56.7	12 57.7	23 56.1	29 09.1	29 32.4	9 01.4	12 33.3
5 F	20 59 28	15 53 57	8♍25 02	14 20 06	23D 25.9	27 05.8	25 11.0	18 36.9	13 21.4	24 05.3	29 14.8	29 35.2	9 03.3	12 33.6
6 Sa	21 03 25	16 54 45	20 15 58	26 13 03	23 25.5	26 25.4	26 22.6	19 17.2	13 45.0	24 14.6	29 20.3	29 38.0	9 05.2	12 33.9
7 Su	21 07 21	17 55 32	2♎11 44	8♎12 28	23 26.4	25 35.9	27 34.1	19 57.5	14 08.7	24 24.0	29 25.8	29 40.7	9 07.1	12 34.2
8 M	21 11 18	18 56 18	14 15 44	20 22 02	23 28.1	24 38.5	28 45.5	20 37.8	14 32.3	24 33.6	29 31.2	29 43.4	9 08.9	12 34.4
9 Tu	21 15 14	19 57 03	26 31 55	2♏45 54	23 29.8	23 35.0	29 56.9	21 18.1	14 55.9	24 43.3	29 36.6	29 46.0	9 10.8	12 34.6
10 W	21 19 11	20 57 47	9♏04 32	15 28 22	23R 30.9	22 27.1	1♈08.1	21 58.4	15 19.6	24 53.1	29 41.9	29 48.7	9 12.6	12 34.8
11 Th	21 23 07	21 58 30	21 57 54	28 33 36	23 30.9	21 16.8	2 19.1	22 38.7	15 43.2	25 03.1	29 47.2	29 51.2	9 14.4	12 34.9
12 F	21 27 04	22 59 13	5♐15 51	12♐04 57	23 29.4	20 06.0	3 30.1	23 19.1	16 06.8	25 13.1	29 52.4	29 53.8	9 16.2	12 35.0
13 Sa	21 31 01	23 59 54	19 01 03	26 04 10	23 26.7	18 56.5	4 41.0	23 59.4	16 30.4	25 23.3	29 57.5	29 56.3	9 17.9	12 35.1
14 Su	21 34 57	25 00 34	3♑14 10	10♑30 42	23 22.9	17 50.2	5 51.8	24 39.8	16 53.9	25 33.6	0♑02.6	29 58.8	9 19.7	12R 35.1
15 M	21 38 54	26 01 13	17 53 13	25 20 57	23 18.8	16 48.4	7 02.4	25 20.2	17 17.5	25 44.0	0 07.5	0♑01.2	9 21.4	12 35.1
16 Tu	21 42 50	27 01 50	2♒53 00	10♒28 15	23 15.0	15 52.2	8 12.9	26 00.6	17 41.0	25 54.5	0 12.5	0 03.6	9 23.1	12 35.0
17 W	21 46 47	28 02 27	18 05 29	25 43 23	23 12.1	15 02.6	9 23.3	26 40.9	18 04.5	26 05.2	0 17.3	0 05.9	9 24.8	12 34.9
18 Th	21 50 43	29 03 01	3♓20 40	10♓56 02	23D 10.4	14 20.2	10 33.6	27 21.3	18 28.1	26 15.9	0 22.1	0 08.2	9 26.4	12 34.8
19 F	21 54 40	0♓03 34	18 28 18	25 56 23	23 10.0	13 45.3	11 43.8	28 01.7	18 51.5	26 26.8	0 26.8	0 10.5	9 28.0	12 34.7
20 Sa	21 58 36	1 04 05	3♈19 24	10♈36 38	23 10.7	13 18.0	12 53.8	28 42.1	19 15.0	26 37.7	0 31.4	0 12.7	9 29.6	12 34.5
21 Su	22 02 33	2 04 35	17 47 33	24 51 49	23 12.1	12 58.3	14 03.6	29 22.5	19 38.4	26 48.8	0 36.0	0 14.9	9 31.2	12 34.2
22 M	22 06 29	3 05 02	1♉49 15	8♉39 53	23 13.5	12 46.1	15 13.3	0♑03.0	20 01.9	26 59.9	0 40.5	0 17.0	9 32.7	12 34.0
23 Tu	22 10 26	4 05 28	15 23 49	22 01 19	23 14.6	12D 41.0	16 22.9	0 43.4	20 25.3	27 11.2	0 44.9	0 19.1	9 34.2	12 33.7
24 W	22 14 23	5 05 52	28 32 44	4♊58 27	23R 15.0	12 42.8	17 32.3	1 23.8	20 48.6	27 22.5	0 49.2	0 21.1	9 35.7	12 33.3
25 Th	22 18 19	6 06 14	11♊18 57	17 34 42	23 14.6	12 51.1	18 41.6	2 04.2	21 12.0	27 34.0	0 53.4	0 23.1	9 37.2	12 32.9
26 F	22 22 16	7 06 34	23 46 12	29 54 00	23 13.4	13 05.5	19 50.7	2 44.7	21 35.3	27 45.5	0 57.6	0 25.1	9 38.6	12 32.5
27 Sa	22 26 12	8 06 52	5♋58 34	12♋00 23	23 11.5	13 25.7	20 59.7	3 25.1	21 58.6	27 57.1	1 01.7	0 27.0	9 40.0	12 32.1
28 Su	22 30 09	9 07 08	17 59 57	23 57 42	23 09.4	13 51.2	22 08.4	4 05.5	22 21.8	28 08.9	1 05.7	0 28.8	9 41.4	12 31.6
29 M	22 34 05	10 07 22	29 54 02	5♌49 21	23 07.2	14 21.6	23 17.0	4 46.0	22 45.1	28 20.7	1 09.7	0 30.7	9 42.7	12 31.1

Astro Data

	Dy Hr Mn
☽ 0S	10 11:41
♄∠♇	17 18:49
☽ 0N	23 6:54
☿ R	2 6:16
☽ 0S	6 17:19
♀0N	10 13:21
♄☌♅	13 0:58
♇ R	14 14:50
☽ 0N	19 16:39
☿ D	23 17:30
♇0N	26 23:24

Planet Ingress

		Dy Hr Mn
⚳	♒	2 12:48
♂	♐	8 15:24
☿	♒	10 5:28
♀	♓	15 16:04
☉	♒	20 20:24
♀	♈	9 13:04
♄	♑	13 23:51
♅	♑	15 0:11
☉	♓	19 10:35
♂	♑	22 10:15

Last Aspect / ☽ Ingress

Last Aspect Dy Hr Mn			☽ Ingress	Dy Hr Mn
2 19:55	♅	☍	♋	3 0:17
5 7:20	♂	△	♌	5 11:47
7 23:42	♂	□	♍	8 0:35
10 9:43	♅	□	♎	10 13:17
12 20:33	♅	⚹	♏	12 23:39
15 4:59	♀	□	♐	15 5:58
17 5:59	♅	☌	♑	17 8:15
19 5:26	☉	☌	♒	19 8:02
21 5:33	♅	⚹	♓	21 7:27
23 6:43	♅	□	♈	23 8:31
25 10:53	♅	△	♉	25 12:36
27 10:56	☿	□	♊	27 20:02
30 4:47	♅	☍	♋	30 6:11

Last Aspect / ☽ Ingress

Last Aspect Dy Hr Mn			☽ Ingress	Dy Hr Mn
1 4:54	♃	□	♌	1 18:06
4 5:57	♅	△	♍	4 6:54
6 18:53	♅	□	♎	6 19:36
9 6:14	♅	⚹	♏	9 6:42
10 23:50	☿	□	♐	11 14:36
13 18:34	♄	☌	♑	13 18:36
15 12:37	♃	□	♒	15 19:25
17 15:54	☉	☌	♓	17 18:44
19 15:33	♂	□	♈	19 18:35
21 20:09	♂	△	♉	21 20:50
22 19:13	☿	□	♊	24 2:42
26 7:44	♃	⚹	♋	26 12:12
28 20:36	♃	□	♌	29 0:12

☽ Phases & Eclipses

Dy Hr Mn		
4 1:40	○	12♋54
12 7:04	☾	21♎17
19 5:26	●	28♑21
25 21:54	☽	5♉09
2 20:52	○	13♌14
10 23:01	☾	21♏26
17 15:54	●	28♒12
24 12:15	☽	5♊07

Astro Data

1 January 1988
Julian Day # 32142
SVP 5♓25'37"
GC 26♐40.3 ⚴ 8♑16.1
Eris 15♈46.1R ⚵ 13♓44.1
⚷ 25♊07.2R ⚶ 6♌23.1R
☽ Mean ☊ 27♓08.4

1 February 1988
Julian Day # 32173
SVP 5♓25'31"
GC 26♐40.4 ⚴ 20♑18.1
Eris 15♈50.6 ⚵ 28♓34.7
⚷ 23♊35.3R ⚶ 28♋44.5R
☽ Mean ☊ 25♓29.9

March 1988 — LONGITUDE

Day	Sid.Time	☉	0 hr ☽	Noon ☽	True ☊	☿	♀	♂	⚳	♃	♄	♅	♆	♇
1 Tu	22 38 02	11♓07 34	11♌44 01	17♌38 22	23♓05.3	14♒56.7	24♈25.4	5♑26.5	23♒08.3	28♈32.6	1♑13.5	0♑32.4	9♑44.1	12♏30.6
2 W	22 41 59	12 07 45	23 32 43	29 27 20	23R 03.9	15 36.0	25 33.6	6 06.9	23 31.4	28 44.5	1 17.3	0 34.2	9 45.4	12R 30.0
3 Th	22 45 55	13 07 53	5♍22 31	11♍18 31	23D 03.1	16 19.4	26 41.7	6 47.4	23 54.6	28 56.6	1 21.0	0 35.8	9 46.6	12 29.4
4 F	22 49 52	14 07 59	17 15 35	23 13 58	23 02.9	17 06.4	27 49.5	7 27.9	24 17.7	29 08.7	1 24.6	0 37.5	9 47.9	12 28.8
5 Sa	22 53 48	15 08 04	29 13 54	5♎15 39	23 03.1	17 56.9	28 57.2	8 08.4	24 40.7	29 20.9	1 28.1	0 39.0	9 49.1	12 28.1
6 Su	22 57 45	16 08 07	11♎19 27	17 25 36	23 03.6	18 50.6	0♉04.6	8 48.9	25 03.8	29 33.2	1 31.5	0 40.6	9 50.3	12 27.4
7 M	23 01 41	17 08 08	23 34 21	29 46 00	23 04.2	19 47.3	1 11.9	9 29.4	25 26.8	29 45.6	1 34.9	0 42.0	9 51.4	12 26.7
8 Tu	23 05 38	18 08 08	6♏00 52	12♏19 16	23 04.8	20 46.8	2 18.9	10 09.9	25 49.7	29 58.1	1 38.1	0 43.5	9 52.5	12 25.9
9 W	23 09 34	19 08 06	18 41 31	25 07 56	23 05.3	21 48.9	3 25.8	10 50.4	26 12.7	0♉10.6	1 41.3	0 44.9	9 53.6	12 25.1
10 Th	23 13 31	20 08 02	1♐38 52	8♐14 35	23 05.5	22 53.5	4 32.4	11 30.9	26 35.6	0 23.2	1 44.4	0 46.2	9 54.7	12 24.3
11 F	23 17 27	21 07 57	14 55 22	21 41 26	23R 05.6	24 00.5	5 38.8	12 11.4	26 58.4	0 35.8	1 47.4	0 47.5	9 55.7	12 23.4
12 Sa	23 21 24	22 07 50	28 32 57	5♑29 59	23D 05.6	25 09.6	6 44.9	12 51.9	27 21.2	0 48.6	1 50.3	0 48.7	9 56.7	12 22.5
13 Su	23 25 21	23 07 42	12♑32 32	19 40 26	23 05.5	26 20.8	7 50.9	13 32.5	27 44.0	1 01.4	1 53.1	0 49.9	9 57.7	12 21.6
14 M	23 29 17	24 07 32	26 53 28	4♒11 12	23 05.6	27 34.0	8 56.5	14 13.0	28 06.7	1 14.2	1 55.9	0 51.0	9 58.6	12 20.7
15 Tu	23 33 14	25 07 20	11♒33 06	18 58 28	23 05.7	28 49.1	10 02.0	14 53.5	28 29.4	1 27.1	1 58.5	0 52.1	9 59.5	12 19.7
16 W	23 37 10	26 07 06	26 26 31	3♓56 18	23 05.9	0♓06.0	11 07.2	15 34.0	28 52.1	1 40.1	2 01.0	0 53.1	10 00.4	12 18.7
17 Th	23 41 07	27 06 50	11♓26 48	18 56 59	23R 06.1	1 24.6	12 12.1	16 14.6	29 14.7	1 53.2	2 03.5	0 54.1	10 01.3	12 17.7
18 F	23 45 03	28 06 33	26 25 44	3♈52 02	23 06.0	2 44.9	13 16.8	16 55.1	29 37.2	2 06.3	2 05.8	0 55.0	10 02.1	12 16.6
19 Sa	23 49 00	29 06 13	11♈14 54	18 33 25	23 05.7	4 06.8	14 21.2	17 35.6	29 59.7	2 19.5	2 08.1	0 55.9	10 02.8	12 15.5
20 Su	23 52 56	0♈05 51	25 46 51	2♉54 35	23 05.0	5 30.3	15 25.3	18 16.1	0♓22.2	2 32.7	2 10.2	0 56.7	10 03.6	12 14.4
21 M	23 56 53	1 05 27	9♉56 09	16 51 15	23 04.0	6 55.3	16 29.1	18 56.6	0 44.6	2 46.0	2 12.3	0 57.5	10 04.3	12 13.3
22 Tu	0 00 50	2 05 01	23 39 45	0♊21 39	23 03.0	8 21.8	17 32.7	19 37.1	1 06.9	2 59.3	2 14.3	0 58.2	10 05.0	12 12.1
23 W	0 04 46	3 04 33	6♊57 06	13 26 21	23 02.1	9 49.8	18 35.9	20 17.6	1 29.2	3 12.7	2 16.2	0 58.9	10 05.6	12 10.9
24 Th	0 08 43	4 04 02	19 49 44	26 07 43	23D 01.5	11 19.2	19 38.8	20 58.0	1 51.5	3 26.1	2 17.9	0 59.5	10 06.2	12 09.7
25 F	0 12 39	5 03 29	2♋20 46	8♋29 25	23 01.4	12 50.1	20 41.3	21 38.5	2 13.6	3 39.6	2 19.6	1 00.1	10 06.8	12 08.5
26 Sa	0 16 36	6 02 54	14 34 14	20 35 48	23 01.9	14 22.3	21 43.5	22 19.0	2 35.8	3 53.1	2 21.2	1 00.6	10 07.4	12 07.2
27 Su	0 20 32	7 02 17	26 34 43	2♌31 34	23 02.8	15 56.0	22 45.4	22 59.4	2 57.8	4 06.7	2 22.7	1 01.1	10 07.9	12 06.0
28 M	0 24 29	8 01 37	8♌26 54	14 21 18	23 04.2	17 31.1	23 46.9	23 39.9	3 19.8	4 20.3	2 24.1	1 01.5	10 08.4	12 04.6
29 Tu	0 28 25	9 00 55	20 15 16	26 09 19	23 05.6	19 07.5	24 48.0	24 20.3	3 41.8	4 33.9	2 25.4	1 01.8	10 08.8	12 03.3
30 W	0 32 22	10 00 10	2♍03 54	7♍59 28	23 06.8	20 45.3	25 48.7	25 00.8	4 03.7	4 47.6	2 26.6	1 02.1	10 09.2	12 02.0
31 Th	0 36 19	10 59 24	13 56 24	19 55 03	23R 07.4	22 24.6	26 49.0	25 41.2	4 25.5	5 01.4	2 27.7	1 02.4	10 09.6	12 00.6

April 1988 — LONGITUDE

Day	Sid.Time	☉	0 hr ☽	Noon ☽	True ☊	☿	♀	♂	⚳	♃	♄	♅	♆	♇
1 F	0 40 15	11♈58 35	25♍55 45	1♎58 46	23♓07.1	24♓05.2	27♉48.9	26♑21.6	4♓47.3	5♉15.1	2♑28.7	1♑02.6	10♑10.0	11♏59.2
2 Sa	0 44 12	12 57 44	8♎04 20	14 12 39	23R 05.9	25 47.3	28 48.4	27 02.0	5 09.0	5 28.9	2 29.6	1 02.7	10 10.3	11R 57.8
3 Su	0 48 08	13 56 51	20 23 54	26 38 12	23 03.7	27 30.7	29 47.5	27 42.4	5 30.6	5 42.8	2 30.4	1 02.8	10 10.6	11 56.4
4 M	0 52 05	14 55 56	2♏55 41	9♏16 26	23 00.7	29 15.6	0♊46.0	28 22.8	5 52.2	5 56.6	2 31.1	1R 02.8	10 10.8	11 55.0
5 Tu	0 56 01	15 54 59	15 40 30	22 07 57	22 57.1	1♈01.9	1 44.2	29 03.2	6 13.7	6 10.6	2 31.7	1 02.8	10 11.0	11 53.5
6 W	0 59 58	16 54 01	28 38 49	5♐13 08	22 53.6	2 49.7	2 41.8	29 43.6	6 35.1	6 24.5	2 32.2	1 02.8	10 11.2	11 52.0
7 Th	1 03 54	17 53 01	11♐50 57	18 32 16	22 50.5	4 38.9	3 39.0	0♒24.0	6 56.5	6 38.5	2 32.6	1 02.7	10 11.4	11 50.5
8 F	1 07 51	18 51 59	25 17 07	2♑05 30	22 48.3	6 29.6	4 35.6	1 04.3	7 17.8	6 52.5	2 32.9	1 02.5	10 11.5	11 49.0
9 Sa	1 11 48	19 50 55	8♑57 24	15 52 49	22D 47.4	8 21.8	5 31.7	1 44.7	7 39.0	7 06.5	2 33.1	1 02.3	10 11.6	11 47.5
10 Su	1 15 44	20 49 49	22 51 42	29 53 56	22 47.6	10 15.5	6 27.3	2 25.0	8 00.2	7 20.6	2R 33.2	1 02.0	10 11.6	11 46.0
11 M	1 19 41	21 48 42	6♒59 24	14♒07 54	22 48.7	12 10.6	7 22.3	3 05.3	8 21.3	7 34.7	2 33.2	1 01.7	10R 11.7	11 44.4
12 Tu	1 23 37	22 47 33	21 19 10	28 32 52	22 50.1	14 07.2	8 16.8	3 45.6	8 42.3	7 48.8	2 33.1	1 01.3	10 11.6	11 42.9
13 W	1 27 34	23 46 22	5♓48 34	13♓05 45	22R 51.3	16 05.3	9 10.6	4 25.9	9 03.2	8 02.9	2 32.9	1 00.9	10 11.6	11 41.3
14 Th	1 31 30	24 45 10	20 23 49	27 42 08	22 51.5	18 04.7	10 03.8	5 06.2	9 24.0	8 17.0	2 32.6	1 00.4	10 11.5	11 39.7
15 F	1 35 27	25 43 55	4♈59 56	12♈16 29	22 50.2	20 05.6	10 56.4	5 46.4	9 44.8	8 31.2	2 32.2	0 59.9	10 11.4	11 38.1
16 Sa	1 39 23	26 42 39	19 30 58	26 42 39	22 47.3	22 07.8	11 48.4	6 26.6	10 05.5	8 45.4	2 31.8	0 59.3	10 11.2	11 36.5
17 Su	1 43 20	27 41 21	3♉50 47	10♉54 42	22 42.8	24 11.2	12 39.6	7 06.7	10 26.1	8 59.6	2 31.2	0 58.7	10 11.1	11 34.8
18 M	1 47 17	28 40 01	17 53 49	24 47 40	22 37.2	26 15.8	13 30.1	7 46.9	10 46.6	9 13.9	2 30.5	0 58.1	10 10.9	11 33.2
19 Tu	1 51 13	29 38 38	1♊35 56	8♊18 22	22 31.2	28 21.5	14 19.9	8 27.0	11 07.0	9 28.1	2 29.7	0 57.3	10 10.6	11 31.6
20 W	1 55 10	0♉37 14	14 54 54	21 25 35	22 25.6	0♉28.0	15 08.9	9 07.1	11 27.3	9 42.4	2 28.8	0 56.6	10 10.3	11 29.9
21 Th	1 59 06	1 35 48	27 50 35	4♋10 10	22 21.0	2 35.4	15 57.1	9 47.1	11 47.6	9 56.6	2 27.9	0 55.8	10 10.0	11 28.3
22 F	2 03 03	2 34 19	10♋24 42	16 34 39	22 17.9	4 43.2	16 44.5	10 27.2	12 07.7	10 10.9	2 26.8	0 54.9	10 09.7	11 26.6
23 Sa	2 06 59	3 32 49	22 40 30	28 42 51	22D 16.4	6 51.4	17 31.0	11 07.1	12 27.8	10 25.2	2 25.6	0 54.0	10 09.3	11 24.9
24 Su	2 10 56	4 31 16	4♌42 17	10♌39 26	22 16.5	8 59.7	18 16.6	11 47.1	12 47.8	10 39.5	2 24.4	0 53.0	10 08.9	11 23.3
25 M	2 14 52	5 29 40	16 34 56	22 29 28	22 17.6	11 07.9	19 01.2	12 27.0	13 07.6	10 53.8	2 23.0	0 52.0	10 08.5	11 21.6
26 Tu	2 18 49	6 28 03	28 23 38	4♍18 05	22 19.2	13 15.6	19 44.9	13 06.9	13 27.4	11 08.1	2 21.6	0 51.0	10 08.0	11 19.9
27 W	2 22 46	7 26 24	10♍13 26	16 10 15	22R 20.3	15 22.5	20 27.5	13 46.8	13 47.0	11 22.4	2 20.0	0 49.9	10 07.5	11 18.2
28 Th	2 26 42	8 24 43	22 09 03	28 10 22	22 20.3	17 28.3	21 09.2	14 26.6	14 06.6	11 36.8	2 18.4	0 48.7	10 07.0	11 16.5
29 F	2 30 39	9 22 59	4♎14 36	10♎22 09	22 18.6	19 32.8	21 49.7	15 06.3	14 26.1	11 51.1	2 16.7	0 47.6	10 06.4	11 14.8
30 Sa	2 34 35	10 21 14	16 33 20	22 48 24	22 14.7	21 35.6	22 29.1	15 46.1	14 45.4	12 05.4	2 14.9	0 46.3	10 05.8	11 13.1

Astro Data

	Dy Hr Mn
☽0S	4 23:06
♃△♅	12 12:19
☽0N	18 3:48
♃△♄	18 10:57
☉0N	20 9:38
☽0S	1 5:42
♅R	4 19:25
☿0N	7 14:28
♄R	11 2:08
♆R	11 13:17
☽0N	14 13:44
♃△♆	22 9:59
♃☍♇	27 5:39
☽0S	28 13:01

Planet Ingress

	Dy Hr Mn
♀ ♉	6 10:21
♃ ♉	8 15:44
☿ ♓	16 10:09
⚳ ♓	19 12:18
☉ ♈	20 9:39
♀ ♊	3 17:07
☿ ♈	4 22:04
♂ ♒	6 21:44
☉ ♉	19 20:45
☿ ♉	20 6:42

Last Aspect / ☽ Ingress

Last Aspect Dy Hr Mn		☽ Ingress Dy Hr Mn
2 10:32 ♃ △	♍	2 13:06
3 16:01 ☉ ☍	♎	5 1:32
7 11:59 ♃ ☍	♏	7 12:27
9 5:17 ☿ □	♐	9 20:59
11 16:26 ☿ ✶	♑	12 2:31
13 18:11 ☉ ✶	♒	14 5:08
16 5:17 ☿ ☌	♓	16 5:42
18 2:02 ☉ ☌	♈	18 5:45
19 10:20 ♂ □	♉	20 7:05
21 15:51 ♂ △	♊	22 11:21
23 4:27 ☿ □	♋	24 19:27
26 15:39 ♂ ☍	♌	27 6:54
29 8:59 ♀ □	♍	29 19:49

Last Aspect / ☽ Ingress

Last Aspect Dy Hr Mn		☽ Ingress Dy Hr Mn
1 3:01 ♀ △	♎	1 8:05
3 14:10 ♂ □	♏	3 18:26
6 1:26 ♂ ✶	♐	6 2:29
7 10:44 ☉ △	♑	8 8:19
9 19:21 ☉ □	♒	10 12:10
12 1:45 ☉ ✶	♓	12 14:24
13 9:41 ♇ △	♈	14 15:47
16 12:00 ☉ ☌	♉	16 17:31
17 13:09 ♇ ☍	♊	18 21:10
19 23:40 ♀ ☌	♋	21 4:04
22 2:01 ♇ △	♌	23 14:34
25 4:29 ♀ ✶	♍	26 3:16
27 21:09 ♀ □	♎	28 15:37

☽ Phases & Eclipses

Dy Hr Mn	
3 16:01	○ 13♍18
3 16:13	☍ A 1.091
11 10:56	☾ 21♐05
18 2:02	● 27♓42
18 1:58:00	● T 03'47"
25 4:42	☽ 4♋45
2 9:21	○ 12♎51
9 19:21	☾ 20♑09
16 12:00	● 26♈43
23 22:32	☽ 3♌58

Astro Data

1 March 1988
Julian Day # 32202
SVP 5♓25'27"
GC 26♐40.4 ⚴ 0♒42.7
Eris 16♈03.4 ⚵ 14♈05.3
⚷ 23♊06.9 ⚶ 23♋45.2R
☽ Mean ☊ 23♓57.8

1 April 1988
Julian Day # 32233
SVP 5♓25'24"
GC 26♐40.5 ⚴ 10♒16.4
Eris 16♈22.7 ⚵ 1♉45.5
⚷ 23♊50.8 ⚶ 25♋09.1
☽ Mean ☊ 22♓19.3

LONGITUDE

May 1988

Day	Sid.Time	☉	0 hr ☽	Noon ☽	True ☊	☿	♀	♂	⚳	♃	♄	♅	♆	♇
1 Su	2 38 32	11♉19 27	29♎07 30	5♏30 45	22♓08.8	23♉36.4	23♊07.3	16♒25.8	15♓04.7	12♉19.7	2♑13.0	0♑45.1	10♑05.2	11♏11.4
2 M	2 42 28	12 17 38	11♏58 10	18 29 41	22R 01.2	25 35.0	23 44.2	17 05.4	15 23.8	12 34.1	2R 11.0	0R 43.8	10R 04.6	11R 09.7
3 Tu	2 46 25	13 15 48	25 05 12	1♐44 31	21 52.6	27 31.0	24 20.0	17 45.1	15 42.9	12 48.4	2 08.9	0 42.4	10 03.9	11 08.1
4 W	2 50 21	14 13 56	8♐27 24	15 13 35	21 43.9	29 24.4	24 54.3	18 24.6	16 01.8	13 02.7	2 06.8	0 41.0	10 03.2	11 06.4
5 Th	2 54 18	15 12 02	22 02 46	28 54 39	21 36.0	1♊14.8	25 27.4	19 04.2	16 20.6	13 17.0	2 04.5	0 39.6	10 02.5	11 04.7
6 F	2 58 15	16 10 07	5♑48 55	12♑45 16	21 29.9	3 02.2	25 59.0	19 43.7	16 39.3	13 31.3	2 02.2	0 38.1	10 01.7	11 03.0
7 Sa	3 02 11	17 08 11	19 43 26	26 43 11	21 25.9	4 46.3	26 29.2	20 23.1	16 57.9	13 45.6	1 59.8	0 36.6	10 00.9	11 01.3
8 Su	3 06 08	18 06 13	3♒44 17	10♒46 33	21D 24.1	6 27.0	26 57.8	21 02.5	17 16.4	13 59.9	1 57.3	0 35.0	10 00.1	10 59.6
9 M	3 10 04	19 04 14	17 49 50	24 53 58	21 24.0	8 04.3	27 24.9	21 41.8	17 34.8	14 14.2	1 54.7	0 33.5	9 59.3	10 58.0
10 Tu	3 14 01	20 02 13	1♓58 48	9♓04 12	21R 24.6	9 38.0	27 50.3	22 21.1	17 53.0	14 28.5	1 52.1	0 31.8	9 58.4	10 56.3
11 W	3 17 57	21 00 11	16 09 57	23 15 52	21 25.0	11 08.0	28 14.1	23 00.3	18 11.1	14 42.8	1 49.4	0 30.2	9 57.5	10 54.6
12 Th	3 21 54	21 58 08	0♈21 42	7♈27 07	21 24.0	12 34.3	28 36.1	23 39.5	18 29.1	14 57.1	1 46.5	0 28.4	9 56.6	10 53.0
13 F	3 25 50	22 56 03	14 31 46	21 35 16	21 20.7	13 56.8	28 56.3	24 18.6	18 46.9	15 11.3	1 43.7	0 26.7	9 55.6	10 51.3
14 Sa	3 29 47	23 53 58	28 37 07	5♉36 52	21 14.8	15 15.5	29 14.6	24 57.6	19 04.6	15 25.5	1 40.7	0 24.9	9 54.6	10 49.7
15 Su	3 33 44	24 51 51	12♉34 01	19 28 04	21 06.4	16 30.3	29 31.1	25 36.5	19 22.2	15 39.8	1 37.7	0 23.1	9 53.6	10 48.0
16 M	3 37 40	25 49 42	26 18 32	3♊05 00	20 56.3	17 41.2	29 45.5	26 15.4	19 39.7	15 54.0	1 34.6	0 21.3	9 52.6	10 46.4
17 Tu	3 41 37	26 47 32	9♊47 08	16 24 37	20 45.2	18 48.0	29 57.9	26 54.2	19 57.0	16 08.2	1 31.4	0 19.4	9 51.6	10 44.8
18 W	3 45 33	27 45 21	22 57 18	29 25 05	20 34.5	19 50.7	0♋08.2	27 32.9	20 14.2	16 22.3	1 28.1	0 17.5	9 50.5	10 43.2
19 Th	3 49 30	28 43 08	5♋47 59	12♋06 07	20 25.1	20 49.4	0 16.4	28 11.5	20 31.2	16 36.5	1 24.8	0 15.6	9 49.4	10 41.6
20 F	3 53 26	29 40 53	18 19 43	24 29 06	20 17.8	21 43.8	0 22.3	28 50.1	20 48.1	16 50.6	1 21.5	0 13.6	9 48.3	10 40.0
21 Sa	3 57 23	0♊38 37	0♌34 39	6♌36 51	20 12.8	22 33.9	0 25.9	29 28.5	21 04.8	17 04.7	1 18.0	0 11.6	9 47.1	10 38.5
22 Su	4 01 19	1 36 19	12 36 14	18 33 22	20 10.2	23 19.7	0R 27.2	0♓06.9	21 21.4	17 18.8	1 14.5	0 09.6	9 46.0	10 36.9
23 M	4 05 16	2 34 00	24 28 53	0♍23 26	20D 09.4	24 01.0	0 26.2	0 45.2	21 37.8	17 32.9	1 11.0	0 07.5	9 44.8	10 35.4
24 Tu	4 09 13	3 31 39	6♍17 42	12 12 21	20R 09.6	24 37.9	0 22.7	1 23.3	21 54.1	17 46.9	1 07.3	0 05.4	9 43.6	10 33.8
25 W	4 13 09	4 29 16	18 08 05	24 05 33	20 09.6	25 10.3	0 16.9	2 01.4	22 10.2	18 00.9	1 03.7	0 03.3	9 42.3	10 32.3
26 Th	4 17 06	5 26 52	0♎05 25	6♎08 18	20 08.6	25 38.0	0 08.6	2 39.4	22 26.2	18 14.9	0 59.9	0 01.2	9 41.1	10 30.8
27 F	4 21 02	6 24 27	12 14 45	18 25 18	20 05.6	26 01.1	29♊57.8	3 17.3	22 42.0	18 28.8	0 56.2	29♐59.0	9 39.8	10 29.3
28 Sa	4 24 59	7 22 00	24 40 24	1♏00 23	20 00.2	26 19.5	29 44.7	3 55.1	22 57.6	18 42.7	0 52.3	29 56.9	9 38.5	10 27.9
29 Su	4 28 55	8 19 32	7♏25 32	13 56 00	19 52.2	26 33.2	29 29.1	4 32.8	23 13.1	18 56.6	0 48.4	29 54.7	9 37.2	10 26.4
30 M	4 32 52	9 17 03	20 31 49	27 12 55	19 42.0	26 42.2	29 11.1	5 10.4	23 28.4	19 10.4	0 44.5	29 52.4	9 35.9	10 25.0
31 Tu	4 36 48	10 14 33	3♐59 06	10♐50 03	19 30.5	26R 46.6	28 50.9	5 47.9	23 43.6	19 24.3	0 40.6	29 50.2	9 34.5	10 23.6

LONGITUDE

June 1988

Day	Sid.Time	☉	0 hr ☽	Noon ☽	True ☊	☿	♀	♂	⚳	♃	♄	♅	♆	♇
1 W	4 40 45	11♊12 02	17♐45 19	24♐44 25	19♓18.7	26♊46.3	28♊28.3	6♓25.3	23♓58.5	19♉38.0	0♑36.5	29♐47.9	9♑33.2	10♏22.2
2 Th	4 44 42	12 09 29	1♑46 44	8♑51 40	19R 08.1	26R 41.6	28R 03.7	7 02.6	24 13.3	19 51.8	0R 32.5	29R 45.7	9R 31.8	10R 20.8
3 F	4 48 38	13 06 56	15 58 33	23 06 46	18 59.4	26 32.5	27 36.9	7 39.7	24 28.0	20 05.5	0 28.4	29 43.4	9 30.4	10 19.5
4 Sa	4 52 35	14 04 23	0♒15 41	7♒24 47	18 53.4	26 19.3	27 08.3	8 16.8	24 42.4	20 19.2	0 24.3	29 41.1	9 29.0	10 18.1
5 Su	4 56 31	15 01 48	14 33 34	21 41 40	18 50.1	26 02.2	26 37.9	8 53.7	24 56.6	20 32.8	0 20.1	29 38.7	9 27.6	10 16.8
6 M	5 00 28	15 59 13	28 48 43	5♓54 31	18 48.9	25 41.4	26 05.9	9 30.4	25 10.7	20 46.4	0 15.9	29 36.4	9 26.1	10 15.5
7 Tu	5 04 24	16 56 37	12♓58 53	20 01 41	18 48.8	25 17.4	25 32.4	10 07.1	25 24.6	20 59.9	0 11.7	29 34.0	9 24.7	10 14.3
8 W	5 08 21	17 54 00	27 02 49	4♈02 15	18 48.4	24 50.5	24 57.7	10 43.6	25 38.3	21 13.4	0 07.4	29 31.6	9 23.2	10 13.0
9 Th	5 12 17	18 51 23	10♈59 55	17 55 44	18 46.7	24 21.3	24 22.0	11 19.9	25 51.7	21 26.9	0 03.1	29 29.3	9 21.7	10 11.8
10 F	5 16 14	19 48 46	24 49 39	1♉41 31	18 42.5	23 50.0	23 45.5	11 56.1	26 05.0	21 40.3	29♐58.8	29 26.9	9 20.2	10 10.6
11 Sa	5 20 11	20 46 08	8♉31 12	15 18 32	18 35.5	23 17.4	23 08.4	12 32.1	26 18.1	21 53.7	29 54.5	29 24.5	9 18.7	10 09.4
12 Su	5 24 07	21 43 29	22 03 18	28 45 18	18 25.8	22 43.9	22 30.9	13 08.0	26 31.0	22 07.0	29 50.1	29 22.0	9 17.2	10 08.2
13 M	5 28 04	22 40 50	5♊24 16	12♊00 00	18 14.0	22 10.1	21 53.4	13 43.7	26 43.6	22 20.3	29 45.7	29 19.6	9 15.7	10 07.1
14 Tu	5 32 00	23 38 10	18 32 17	25 00 56	18 01.3	21 36.7	21 15.9	14 19.2	26 56.1	22 33.5	29 41.4	29 17.2	9 14.2	10 06.0
15 W	5 35 57	24 35 30	1♋25 50	7♋46 54	17 48.8	21 04.1	20 38.9	14 54.6	27 08.3	22 46.7	29 37.0	29 14.8	9 12.6	10 04.9
16 Th	5 39 53	25 32 49	14 04 07	20 17 33	17 37.6	20 32.9	20 02.4	15 29.8	27 20.3	22 59.8	29 32.5	29 12.3	9 11.0	10 03.9
17 F	5 43 50	26 30 08	26 27 19	2♌33 39	17 28.5	20 03.7	19 26.7	16 04.7	27 32.1	23 12.9	29 28.1	29 09.9	9 09.5	10 02.8
18 Sa	5 47 47	27 27 25	8♌36 50	14 37 13	17 22.1	19 36.9	18 52.1	16 39.5	27 43.6	23 25.9	29 23.7	29 07.4	9 07.9	10 01.8
19 Su	5 51 43	28 24 42	20 35 12	26 31 18	17 18.3	19 13.0	18 18.7	17 14.1	27 55.0	23 38.8	29 19.3	29 05.0	9 06.3	10 00.8
20 M	5 55 40	29 21 58	2♍26 02	8♍19 59	17D 16.7	18 52.4	17 46.8	17 48.5	28 06.0	23 51.7	29 14.8	29 02.5	9 04.7	9 59.9
21 Tu	5 59 36	0♋19 13	14 13 47	20 08 04	17R 16.5	18 35.5	17 16.4	18 22.7	28 16.9	24 04.5	29 10.4	29 00.1	9 03.1	9 59.0
22 W	6 03 33	1 16 28	26 03 30	2♎00 48	17 16.6	18 22.6	16 47.8	18 56.6	28 27.5	24 17.3	29 05.9	28 57.6	9 01.5	9 58.1
23 Th	6 07 29	2 13 42	8♎00 38	14 03 40	17 16.0	18 13.8	16 21.1	19 30.4	28 37.9	24 30.0	29 01.5	28 55.2	8 59.9	9 57.2
24 F	6 11 26	3 10 55	20 10 34	26 21 57	17 13.9	18D 09.5	15 56.4	20 03.9	28 48.0	24 42.6	28 57.1	28 52.7	8 58.3	9 56.4
25 Sa	6 15 22	4 08 08	2♏38 21	9♏00 17	17 09.5	18 09.8	15 33.9	20 37.3	28 57.9	24 55.2	28 52.7	28 50.3	8 56.7	9 55.6
26 Su	6 19 19	5 05 21	15 28 09	22 02 13	17 02.8	18 14.7	15 13.5	21 10.3	29 07.5	25 07.7	28 48.3	28 47.9	8 55.1	9 54.8
27 M	6 23 16	6 02 33	28 42 38	5♐29 27	16 53.9	18 24.5	14 55.4	21 43.2	29 16.9	25 20.2	28 43.9	28 45.5	8 53.5	9 54.0
28 Tu	6 27 12	6 59 44	12♐22 31	19 21 32	16 43.7	18 39.0	14 39.7	22 15.8	29 26.0	25 32.5	28 39.5	28 43.0	8 51.9	9 53.3
29 W	6 31 09	7 56 56	26 26 01	3♑35 24	16 33.3	18 58.5	14 26.3	22 48.2	29 34.8	25 44.8	28 35.2	28 40.6	8 50.3	9 52.6
30 Th	6 35 05	8 54 07	10♑48 55	18 05 45	16 23.7	19 22.7	14 15.4	23 20.3	29 43.4	25 57.1	28 30.9	28 38.2	8 48.6	9 52.0

Astro Data

	Dy Hr Mn
☽ 0N	11 20:55
♃□♅	14 11:05
♃□♄	18 19:59
♀ R	22 13:26
☽ 0S	25 20:30
☿ R	31 22:44
☽ 0N	8 1:50
♃□♆	21 9:41
☽ 0S	22 3:37
☿ D	24 22:41
♄☌♅	26 17:06

Planet Ingress

		Dy Hr Mn
☿	♊	4 19:40
♀	♋	17 16:26
☉	♊	20 19:57
♂	♓	22 7:42
♅	♐R	27 1:17
♀	♊R	27 7:36
♄	♐R	10 5:22
☉	♋	21 3:57

Last Aspect / ☽ Ingress

Last Aspect Dy Hr Mn			☽ Ingress	Dy Hr Mn
30 11:21	♀	△	♏	1 1:39
3 3:07	☿	☍	♐	3 8:52
5 5:43	♀	☍	♑	5 13:54
6 18:19	☉	△	♒	7 17:37
9 16:24	♀	△	♓	9 20:39
11 20:38	♀	□	♈	11 23:23
14 0:50	♀	⚹	♉	14 2:22
15 23:18	♂	□	♊	16 6:31
18 8:20	♂	△	♋	18 13:05
19 20:50	♃	⚹	♌	20 22:51
22 22:17	☿	⚹	♍	23 11:12
25 14:15	☿	□	♎	25 23:49
28 10:01	♅	⚹	♏	28 10:06
29 21:17	♃	☍	♐	30 16:57

Last Aspect / ☽ Ingress

Last Aspect Dy Hr Mn			☽ Ingress	Dy Hr Mn
1 20:37	♅	☌	♑	1 20:58
3 6:50	♃	△	♒	3 23:34
6 1:22	♅	⚹	♓	6 2:00
8 4:16	♅	□	♈	8 5:04
10 9:01	♄	△	♉	10 9:02
11 23:55	♃	☌	♊	12 14:14
14 20:41	♄	☍	♋	14 21:19
16 17:21	♃	⚹	♌	17 6:57
19 17:39	♄	△	♍	19 19:03
22 6:10	♄	□	♎	22 7:57
24 16:56	♄	⚹	♏	24 18:58
26 17:40	♃	☍	♐	27 2:18
29 3:48	♅	☌	♑	29 6:00

☽ Phases & Eclipses

Dy Hr Mn	
1 23:41	○ 11♏48
9 1:23	☾ 18♒39
15 22:11	● 25♉16
23 16:49	☽ 2♍46
31 10:53	○ 10♐12
7 6:22	☾ 16♓43
14 9:14	● 23♊32
22 10:23	☽ 1♎13
29 19:46	○ 8♑15

Astro Data

1 May 1988
Julian Day # 32263
SVP 5♓25'20"
GC 26♐40.6 ⚴ 17♒04.4
Eris 16♈42.2 ⚵ 19♉27.1
⚷ 25♊36.8 ⚶ 1♌58.6
☽ Mean ☊ 20♓44.0

1 June 1988
Julian Day # 32294
SVP 5♓25'15"
GC 26♐40.6 ⚴ 20♒10.7
Eris 16♈58.5 ⚵ 7♊55.0
⚷ 28♊10.1 ⚶ 12♌32.6
☽ Mean ☊ 19♓05.5

July 1988 — LONGITUDE

Day	Sid.Time	☉	0 hr ☽	Noon ☽	True ☊	☿	♀	♂	⚳	♃	♄	♅	♆	♇
1 F	6 39 02	9♋51 18	25♑24 59	2♒45 40	16♓16.0	19♊51.8	14♊06.8	23♓52.1	29♓51.7	26♉09.2	28♐26.6	28♐35.9	8♑47.0	9♏51.4
2 Sa	6 42 58	10 48 29	10♒06 54	17 27 48	16R 10.7	20 25.7	14R 00.7	24 23.7	29 59.8	26 21.3	28R 22.3	28R 33.5	8R 45.4	9R 50.8
3 Su	6 46 55	11 45 40	24 47 33	2♓05 28	16D 08.0	21 04.4	13 56.9	24 55.0	0♈07.5	26 33.3	28 18.0	28 31.1	8 43.8	9 50.2
4 M	6 50 51	12 42 51	9♓20 58	16 33 36	16 07.3	21 47.8	13D 55.5	25 26.1	0 15.0	26 45.2	28 13.8	28 28.8	8 42.2	9 49.7
5 Tu	6 54 48	13 40 03	23 43 01	0♈48 58	16R 07.7	22 35.8	13 56.5	25 56.8	0 22.2	26 57.1	28 09.6	28 26.4	8 40.5	9 49.2
6 W	6 58 45	14 37 14	7♈51 20	14 50 02	16 08.1	23 28.4	13 59.8	26 27.2	0 29.1	27 08.9	28 05.4	28 24.1	8 38.9	9 48.7
7 Th	7 02 41	15 34 27	21 45 06	28 36 33	16 07.3	24 25.6	14 05.3	26 57.3	0 35.7	27 20.6	28 01.3	28 21.8	8 37.3	9 48.2
8 F	7 06 38	16 31 39	5♉24 29	12♉08 56	16 04.6	25 27.3	14 13.0	27 27.1	0 42.0	27 32.2	27 57.2	28 19.5	8 35.7	9 47.8
9 Sa	7 10 34	17 28 53	18 50 02	25 27 49	15 59.6	26 33.5	14 22.8	27 56.5	0 48.0	27 43.7	27 53.1	28 17.2	8 34.1	9 47.5
10 Su	7 14 31	18 26 06	2♊02 23	8♊33 45	15 52.3	27 44.0	14 34.7	28 25.6	0 53.7	27 55.1	27 49.1	28 15.0	8 32.5	9 47.1
11 M	7 18 27	19 23 20	15 01 58	21 27 03	15 43.4	28 58.8	14 48.7	28 54.4	0 59.1	28 06.5	27 45.2	28 12.7	8 30.9	9 46.8
12 Tu	7 22 24	20 20 34	27 49 01	4♋07 54	15 33.6	0♋17.8	15 04.6	29 22.7	1 04.2	28 17.8	27 41.2	28 10.5	8 29.4	9 46.5
13 W	7 26 20	21 17 49	10♋23 44	16 36 32	15 23.8	1 41.1	15 22.4	29 50.8	1 09.0	28 28.9	27 37.4	28 08.3	8 27.8	9 46.3
14 Th	7 30 17	22 15 04	22 46 24	28 53 26	15 15.2	3 08.4	15 42.0	0♈18.4	1 13.4	28 40.0	27 33.5	28 06.2	8 26.2	9 46.1
15 F	7 34 14	23 12 19	4♌57 45	10♌59 33	15 08.3	4 39.7	16 03.4	0 45.6	1 17.6	28 51.0	27 29.7	28 04.0	8 24.7	9 45.9
16 Sa	7 38 10	24 09 34	16 59 03	22 56 32	15 03.5	6 14.9	16 26.6	1 12.4	1 21.4	29 01.9	27 26.0	28 01.9	8 23.1	9 45.8
17 Su	7 42 07	25 06 50	28 52 20	4♍46 48	15D 01.0	7 53.9	16 51.3	1 38.8	1 24.8	29 12.7	27 22.3	27 59.8	8 21.6	9 45.7
18 M	7 46 03	26 04 06	10♍40 23	16 33 33	15 00.4	9 36.5	17 17.7	2 04.8	1 28.0	29 23.4	27 18.7	27 57.7	8 20.0	9 45.6
19 Tu	7 50 00	27 01 22	22 26 48	28 20 41	15 01.2	11 22.5	17 45.6	2 30.4	1 30.8	29 34.0	27 15.2	27 55.7	8 18.5	9D 45.6
20 W	7 53 56	27 58 38	4♎15 48	10♎12 46	15 02.5	13 11.8	18 15.0	2 55.5	1 33.2	29 44.5	27 11.7	27 53.7	8 17.0	9 45.6
21 Th	7 57 53	28 55 55	16 12 13	22 14 46	15R 03.5	15 04.2	18 45.8	3 20.2	1 35.3	29 54.8	27 08.2	27 51.7	8 15.5	9 45.6
22 F	8 01 49	29 53 12	28 21 06	4♏31 49	15 03.6	16 59.3	19 18.0	3 44.4	1 37.1	0♊05.1	27 04.9	27 49.7	8 14.0	9 45.7
23 Sa	8 05 46	0♌50 29	10♏47 32	17 08 49	15 02.2	18 56.8	19 51.6	4 08.2	1 38.6	0 15.3	27 01.5	27 47.8	8 12.5	9 45.7
24 Su	8 09 43	1 47 46	23 36 10	0♐09 58	14 59.1	20 56.6	20 26.4	4 31.5	1 39.7	0 25.4	26 58.3	27 45.9	8 11.1	9 45.9
25 M	8 13 39	2 45 04	6♐50 33	13 38 05	14 54.4	22 58.3	21 02.4	4 54.3	1 40.4	0 35.3	26 55.1	27 44.0	8 09.6	9 46.0
26 Tu	8 17 36	3 42 23	20 32 36	27 33 57	14 48.7	25 01.5	21 39.7	5 16.6	1R 40.8	0 45.2	26 52.0	27 42.2	8 08.2	9 46.3
27 W	8 21 32	4 39 42	4♑41 48	11♑55 41	14 42.5	27 05.9	22 18.1	5 38.3	1 40.9	0 54.9	26 49.0	27 40.4	8 06.8	9 46.5
28 Th	8 25 29	5 37 02	19 14 54	26 38 38	14 36.9	29 11.2	22 57.6	5 59.6	1 40.6	1 04.5	26 46.0	27 38.7	8 05.4	9 46.8
29 F	8 29 25	6 34 22	4♒05 53	11♒35 37	14 32.4	1♌17.1	23 38.2	6 20.3	1 39.9	1 14.0	26 43.2	27 36.9	8 04.0	9 47.1
30 Sa	8 33 22	7 31 43	19 06 41	26 37 58	14 29.6	3 23.2	24 19.8	6 40.5	1 38.9	1 23.4	26 40.3	27 35.2	8 02.7	9 47.4
31 Su	8 37 19	8 29 05	4♓08 23	11♓36 54	14D 28.5	5 29.3	25 02.4	7 00.1	1 37.6	1 32.7	26 37.6	27 33.6	8 01.3	9 47.8

August 1988 — LONGITUDE

Day	Sid.Time	☉	0 hr ☽	Noon ☽	True ☊	☿	♀	♂	⚳	♃	♄	♅	♆	♇
1 M	8 41 15	9♌26 28	19♓02 36	26♓24 44	14♓28.9	7♌35.1	25♊45.9	7♈19.2	1♈35.8	1♊41.8	26♐34.9	27♐32.0	8♑00.0	9♏48.2
2 Tu	8 45 12	10 23 51	3♈42 40	10♈55 54	14 30.1	9 40.4	26 30.4	7 37.6	1R 33.7	1 50.9	26R 32.4	27R 30.4	7R 58.7	9 48.6
3 W	8 49 08	11 21 17	18 04 07	25 07 05	14 31.5	11 45.0	27 15.8	7 55.5	1 31.3	1 59.8	26 29.9	27 28.8	7 57.4	9 49.1
4 Th	8 53 05	12 18 43	2♉04 45	8♉57 07	14R 32.3	13 48.7	28 02.1	8 12.7	1 28.5	2 08.5	26 27.4	27 27.3	7 56.1	9 49.6
5 F	8 57 01	13 16 11	15 44 16	22 26 24	14 32.0	15 51.4	28 49.1	8 29.3	1 25.3	2 17.2	26 25.1	27 25.9	7 54.9	9 50.1
6 Sa	9 00 58	14 13 40	29 03 42	5♊36 24	14 30.4	17 53.0	29 37.0	8 45.2	1 21.7	2 25.7	26 22.8	27 24.4	7 53.6	9 50.7
7 Su	9 04 54	15 11 10	12♊04 48	18 29 07	14 27.4	19 53.3	0♋25.6	9 00.5	1 17.8	2 34.1	26 20.7	27 23.1	7 52.4	9 51.3
8 M	9 08 51	16 08 42	24 49 39	1♋06 40	14 23.5	21 52.4	1 15.0	9 15.1	1 13.6	2 42.4	26 18.6	27 21.7	7 51.2	9 52.0
9 Tu	9 12 48	17 06 15	7♋20 25	13 31 09	14 19.0	23 50.0	2 05.1	9 28.9	1 09.0	2 50.5	26 16.6	27 20.4	7 50.1	9 52.6
10 W	9 16 44	18 03 49	19 39 05	25 44 28	14 14.5	25 46.2	2 55.8	9 42.1	1 04.0	2 58.5	26 14.7	27 19.1	7 48.9	9 53.3
11 Th	9 20 41	19 01 25	1♌47 32	7♌48 28	14 10.6	27 41.0	3 47.3	9 54.6	0 58.6	3 06.3	26 12.8	27 17.9	7 47.8	9 54.1
12 F	9 24 37	19 59 01	13 47 31	19 44 55	14 07.7	29 34.3	4 39.3	10 06.3	0 52.9	3 14.0	26 11.1	27 16.8	7 46.7	9 54.9
13 Sa	9 28 34	20 56 39	25 40 54	1♍35 43	14 05.9	1♍26.2	5 32.0	10 17.2	0 46.9	3 21.5	26 09.4	27 15.6	7 45.6	9 55.7
14 Su	9 32 30	21 54 18	7♍29 40	13 23 02	14D 05.3	3 16.6	6 25.2	10 27.4	0 40.5	3 29.0	26 07.9	27 14.5	7 44.5	9 56.5
15 M	9 36 27	22 51 58	19 16 09	25 09 23	14 05.7	5 05.5	7 19.0	10 36.9	0 33.7	3 36.2	26 06.4	27 13.5	7 43.5	9 57.4
16 Tu	9 40 23	23 49 39	1♎03 06	6♎57 44	14 06.8	6 52.9	8 13.4	10 45.5	0 26.6	3 43.3	26 05.0	27 12.5	7 42.5	9 58.3
17 W	9 44 20	24 47 21	12 53 44	18 51 35	14 08.3	8 38.9	9 08.3	10 53.4	0 19.2	3 50.3	26 03.8	27 11.5	7 41.5	9 59.2
18 Th	9 48 17	25 45 04	24 51 46	0♏54 49	14 09.8	10 23.5	10 03.7	11 00.5	0 11.5	3 57.1	26 02.6	27 10.6	7 40.6	10 00.2
19 F	9 52 13	26 42 49	7♏01 16	13 11 42	14 10.9	12 06.6	10 59.7	11 06.8	0 03.4	4 03.8	26 01.5	27 09.8	7 39.6	10 01.2
20 Sa	9 56 10	27 40 34	19 26 37	25 46 33	14R 11.4	13 48.3	11 56.1	11 12.3	29♓55.0	4 10.3	26 00.5	27 09.0	7 38.7	10 02.3
21 Su	10 00 06	28 38 21	2♐12 02	8♐43 30	14 11.1	15 28.6	12 52.9	11 16.9	29 46.3	4 16.6	25 59.6	27 08.2	7 37.8	10 03.3
22 M	10 04 03	29 36 09	15 21 19	22 05 48	14 10.2	17 07.5	13 50.3	11 20.8	29 37.3	4 22.8	25 58.8	27 07.5	7 37.0	10 04.4
23 Tu	10 07 59	0♍33 58	28 57 09	5♑55 25	14 08.9	18 45.0	14 48.1	11 23.8	29 28.0	4 28.8	25 58.0	27 06.8	7 36.2	10 05.6
24 W	10 11 56	1 31 48	13♑00 30	20 12 09	14 07.3	20 21.2	15 46.3	11 26.0	29 18.4	4 34.7	25 57.4	27 06.2	7 35.4	10 06.7
25 Th	10 15 52	2 29 40	27 29 55	4♒53 12	14 05.9	21 56.0	16 44.9	11 27.3	29 08.5	4 40.4	25 56.9	27 05.6	7 34.6	10 07.9
26 F	10 19 49	3 27 33	12♒21 13	19 53 00	14 04.8	23 29.4	17 44.0	11R 27.8	28 58.3	4 45.9	25 56.5	27 05.1	7 33.9	10 09.1
27 Sa	10 23 46	4 25 27	27 27 30	5♓03 32	14D 04.3	25 01.5	18 43.4	11 27.5	28 47.9	4 51.3	25 56.2	27 04.7	7 33.2	10 10.4
28 Su	10 27 42	5 23 23	12♓39 55	20 15 25	14 04.2	26 32.2	19 43.3	11 26.3	28 37.2	4 56.5	25 55.9	27 04.2	7 32.5	10 11.7
29 M	10 31 39	6 21 20	27 48 53	5♈19 14	14 04.6	28 01.5	20 43.5	11 24.3	28 26.2	5 01.5	25D 55.8	27 03.9	7 31.8	10 13.0
30 Tu	10 35 35	7 19 19	12♈45 30	20 06 53	14 05.1	29 29.5	21 44.1	11 21.4	28 15.0	5 06.4	25 55.7	27 03.5	7 31.2	10 14.3
31 W	10 39 32	8 17 21	27 22 44	4♉32 33	14 05.7	0♎56.1	22 45.0	11 17.7	28 03.6	5 11.1	25 55.8	27 03.3	7 30.6	10 15.7

Astro Data

	Dy Hr Mn
♀ D	4 14:09
☽ 0N	5 6:38
♃⚻♄	10 2:38
♃⚻♅	11 23:04
☽ 0S	19 10:09
♇ D	20 4:21
⚳ R	27 3:40
☽ 0N	1 13:30
☽ 0S	15 16:14
♂ R	26 14:40
☽ 0N	28 23:03
☿0S	30 7:50
♄ D	30 10:06

Planet Ingress

		Dy Hr Mn
⚳	♈	2 12:44
☿	♋	12 6:42
♂	♈	13 20:00
♃	♊	21 24:00
☉	♌	22 14:51
☿	♌	28 21:19
♀	♋	6 23:24
☿	♍	12 17:29
⚳	♓R	19 21:48
☉	♍	22 21:54
☿	♎	30 20:25

Last Aspect / ☽ Ingress (July)

Last Aspect Dy Hr Mn			☽ Ingress	Dy Hr Mn
1 1:03	♃	△	♒	1 7:30
3 6:08	♅	⚹	♓	3 8:33
5 7:59	♅	□	♈	5 10:37
7 11:34	♅	△	♉	7 14:27
9 16:41	♂	⚹	♊	9 20:16
12 3:50	☿	☌	♋	12 4:08
14 11:33	♃	⚹	♌	14 14:11
17 0:31	♃	□	♍	17 2:17
19 14:31	♃	△	♎	19 15:22
22 2:14	☉	□	♏	22 3:13
23 15:59	☿	△	♐	24 11:42
26 12:14	♅	☌	♑	26 16:07
28 16:46	☿	☍	♒	28 17:25
30 13:31	♅	⚹	♓	30 17:23

Last Aspect / ☽ Ingress (August)

Last Aspect Dy Hr Mn			☽ Ingress	Dy Hr Mn
1 13:50	♅	□	♈	1 17:53
3 16:03	♅	△	♉	3 20:24
4 22:07	☿	□	♊	6 1:43
8 4:50	♅	☍	♋	8 9:52
9 4:55	♇	△	♌	10 20:26
13 3:13	♅	△	♍	13 8:46
15 16:12	♅	□	♎	15 21:52
18 4:37	♅	⚹	♏	18 10:12
20 15:51	☉	□	♐	20 19:55
22 20:49	♅	☌	♑	23 1:49
24 12:17	☿	△	♒	25 4:05
26 23:24	♅	⚹	♓	27 4:01
28 23:04	☿	☍	♈	29 3:29
30 23:28	♅	△	♉	31 4:22

☽ Phases & Eclipses

Dy Hr Mn		
6 11:36	☾	14♈36
13 21:53	●	21♋41
22 2:14	☽	29♎30
29 3:25	○	6♒14
4 18:22	☾	12♉34
12 12:31	●	20♌00
20 15:51	☽	27♏50
27 10:56	○	4♓23
27 11:05	☍	P 0.291

Astro Data

1 July 1988
Julian Day # 32324
SVP 5♓25'09"
GC 26♐40.7 ⚴ 17♒58.0R
Eris 17♈06.7 ⚵ 25♊35.1
⚷ 0♋56.4 ⚶ 24♌50.1
☽ Mean ☊ 17♓30.2

1 August 1988
Julian Day # 32355
SVP 5♓25'04"
GC 26♐40.8 ⚴ 10♒51.5R
Eris 17♈05.5R ⚵ 13♋15.1
⚷ 3♋40.6 ⚶ 8♍53.6
☽ Mean ☊ 15♓51.7

LONGITUDE — September 1988

Day	Sid.Time	☉	0 hr ☽	Noon ☽	True ☊	☿	♀	♂	⚳	♃	♄	♅	♆	♇
1 Th	10 43 28	9♍15 24	11♉36 04	18♉33 05	14♓06.1	2♎21.3	23♋46.3	11♈13.2	27♓51.9	5♊15.6	25♐56.0	27♐03.0	7♑30.0	10♏17.1
2 F	10 47 25	10 13 29	25 23 37	2♊07 46	14R 06.3	3 45.1	24 48.0	11R 07.8	27R 40.1	5 20.0	25 56.2	27R 02.9	7R 29.5	10 18.5
3 Sa	10 51 21	11 11 36	8♊45 45	15 17 53	14 06.4	5 07.4	25 50.0	11 01.5	27 28.0	5 24.1	25 56.6	27 02.7	7 29.0	10 20.0
4 Su	10 55 18	12 09 45	21 44 30	28 06 00	14 06.3	6 28.3	26 52.3	10 54.5	27 15.8	5 28.1	25 57.0	27D 02.7	7 28.5	10 21.5
5 M	10 59 15	13 07 56	4♋22 51	10♋35 30	14D 06.2	7 47.6	27 54.9	10 46.6	27 03.3	5 31.9	25 57.6	27 02.6	7 28.1	10 23.0
6 Tu	11 03 11	14 06 08	16 44 23	22 49 58	14 06.1	9 05.4	28 57.8	10 37.9	26 50.7	5 35.5	25 58.2	27 02.7	7 27.7	10 24.5
7 W	11 07 08	15 04 23	28 52 41	4♌52 59	14 06.2	10 21.6	0♌01.0	10 28.4	26 38.0	5 39.0	25 58.9	27 02.8	7 27.3	10 26.1
8 Th	11 11 04	16 02 40	10♌51 14	16 47 51	14 06.3	11 36.2	1 04.5	10 18.2	26 25.1	5 42.2	25 59.8	27 02.9	7 26.9	10 27.7
9 F	11 15 01	17 00 59	22 43 10	28 37 34	14 06.5	12 48.9	2 08.3	10 07.3	26 12.1	5 45.3	26 00.7	27 03.1	7 26.6	10 29.3
10 Sa	11 18 57	17 59 19	4♍31 20	10♍24 47	14R 06.7	13 59.9	3 12.3	9 55.6	25 58.9	5 48.1	26 01.8	27 03.3	7 26.3	10 31.0
11 Su	11 22 54	18 57 41	16 18 14	22 11 56	14 06.6	15 08.9	4 16.6	9 43.3	25 45.7	5 50.8	26 02.9	27 03.6	7 26.1	10 32.7
12 M	11 26 50	19 56 06	28 06 11	4♎01 15	14 06.3	16 16.0	5 21.2	9 30.3	25 32.4	5 53.3	26 04.1	27 03.9	7 25.8	10 34.4
13 Tu	11 30 47	20 54 31	9♎57 26	15 54 59	14 05.6	17 20.9	6 26.0	9 16.7	25 19.0	5 55.6	26 05.4	27 04.3	7 25.6	10 36.1
14 W	11 34 43	21 52 59	21 54 14	27 55 29	14 04.7	18 23.5	7 31.0	9 02.5	25 05.6	5 57.7	26 06.9	27 04.7	7 25.5	10 37.8
15 Th	11 38 40	22 51 29	3♏59 03	10♏05 17	14 03.5	19 23.7	8 36.3	8 47.8	24 52.1	5 59.6	26 08.4	27 05.2	7 25.4	10 39.6
16 F	11 42 37	23 50 00	16 14 32	22 27 11	14 02.3	20 21.3	9 41.9	8 32.6	24 38.6	6 01.3	26 10.0	27 05.8	7 25.3	10 41.4
17 Sa	11 46 33	24 48 33	28 43 37	5♐04 12	14 01.3	21 16.2	10 47.6	8 16.9	24 25.1	6 02.8	26 11.7	27 06.4	7 25.2	10 43.2
18 Su	11 50 30	25 47 07	11♐29 20	17 59 23	14D 00.7	22 08.2	11 53.6	8 00.8	24 11.6	6 04.1	26 13.5	27 07.0	7D 25.2	10 45.1
19 M	11 54 26	26 45 43	24 34 42	1♑15 36	14 00.6	22 56.9	12 59.8	7 44.4	23 58.2	6 05.2	26 15.4	27 07.7	7 25.2	10 47.0
20 Tu	11 58 23	27 44 21	8♑02 19	14 55 03	14 01.1	23 42.2	14 06.2	7 27.6	23 44.7	6 06.1	26 17.4	27 08.5	7 25.2	10 48.8
21 W	12 02 19	28 43 01	21 53 52	28 58 46	14 02.1	24 23.8	15 12.8	7 10.6	23 31.4	6 06.8	26 19.5	27 09.3	7 25.3	10 50.8
22 Th	12 06 16	29 41 42	6♒09 35	13♒26 00	14 03.2	25 01.4	16 19.6	6 53.3	23 18.0	6 07.4	26 21.7	27 10.1	7 25.4	10 52.7
23 F	12 10 12	0♎40 25	20 47 34	28 13 40	14 04.2	25 34.6	17 26.7	6 35.8	23 04.8	6 07.7	26 24.0	27 11.0	7 25.5	10 54.7
24 Sa	12 14 09	1 39 10	5♓43 30	13♓16 10	14R 04.6	26 03.2	18 33.9	6 18.2	22 51.7	6R 07.8	26 26.3	27 12.0	7 25.7	10 56.6
25 Su	12 18 06	2 37 56	20 50 35	28 25 38	14 04.2	26 26.7	19 41.3	6 00.5	22 38.6	6 07.7	26 28.8	27 13.0	7 25.9	10 58.6
26 M	12 22 02	3 36 44	6♈00 07	13♈32 51	14 02.8	26 44.8	20 48.9	5 42.8	22 25.7	6 07.4	26 31.3	27 14.0	7 26.2	11 00.6
27 Tu	12 25 59	4 35 35	21 02 42	28 28 34	14 00.5	26 57.0	21 56.7	5 25.1	22 12.9	6 06.9	26 34.0	27 15.1	7 26.4	11 02.7
28 W	12 29 55	5 34 27	5♉49 32	13♉04 48	13 57.6	27R 03.0	23 04.7	5 07.4	22 00.3	6 06.3	26 36.7	27 16.3	7 26.7	11 04.7
29 Th	12 33 52	6 33 22	20 13 47	27 16 03	13 54.6	27 02.3	24 12.9	4 49.8	21 47.8	6 05.4	26 39.5	27 17.5	7 27.1	11 06.8
30 F	12 37 48	7 32 20	4♊11 21	10♊59 36	13 52.0	26 54.5	25 21.3	4 32.3	21 35.5	6 04.3	26 42.4	27 18.7	7 27.4	11 08.9

LONGITUDE — October 1988

Day	Sid.Time	☉	0 hr ☽	Noon ☽	True ☊	☿	♀	♂	⚳	♃	♄	♅	♆	♇
1 Sa	12 41 45	8♎31 19	17♊40 54	24♊15 28	13♓50.1	26♎39.4	26♌29.8	4♈15.1	21♓23.4	6♊03.0	26♐45.4	27♐20.0	7♑27.8	11♏11.0
2 Su	12 45 41	9 30 21	0♋43 37	7♋05 48	13D 49.3	26R 16.7	27 38.5	3R 58.0	21R 11.5	6R 01.5	26 48.5	27 21.4	7 28.3	11 13.2
3 M	12 49 38	10 29 25	13 22 30	19 34 16	13 49.6	25 46.2	28 47.4	3 41.3	20 59.8	5 59.8	26 51.7	27 22.8	7 28.7	11 15.3
4 Tu	12 53 35	11 28 32	25 41 40	1♌45 19	13 50.9	25 07.9	29 56.4	3 24.8	20 48.3	5 57.9	26 54.9	27 24.2	7 29.2	11 17.5
5 W	12 57 31	12 27 41	7♌45 49	13 43 44	13 52.6	24 22.0	1♍05.6	3 08.7	20 37.0	5 55.8	26 58.3	27 25.7	7 29.8	11 19.6
6 Th	13 01 28	13 26 51	19 39 40	25 34 10	13 54.3	23 29.1	2 15.0	2 53.1	20 26.0	5 53.5	27 01.7	27 27.3	7 30.3	11 21.8
7 F	13 05 24	14 26 05	1♍27 44	7♍20 53	13R 55.5	22 29.8	3 24.5	2 37.9	20 15.2	5 51.0	27 05.2	27 28.8	7 30.9	11 24.1
8 Sa	13 09 21	15 25 20	13 14 04	19 07 41	13 55.6	21 25.1	4 34.1	2 23.1	20 04.7	5 48.4	27 08.8	27 30.5	7 31.6	11 26.3
9 Su	13 13 17	16 24 37	25 02 07	0♎57 42	13 54.1	20 16.4	5 43.9	2 08.9	19 54.5	5 45.5	27 12.5	27 32.2	7 32.2	11 28.5
10 M	13 17 14	17 23 57	6♎54 44	12 53 28	13 51.0	19 05.3	6 53.9	1 55.3	19 44.5	5 42.4	27 16.3	27 33.9	7 32.9	11 30.8
11 Tu	13 21 10	18 23 19	18 54 10	24 57 00	13 46.3	17 53.6	8 03.9	1 42.3	19 34.8	5 39.1	27 20.1	27 35.7	7 33.7	11 33.0
12 W	13 25 07	19 22 42	1♏02 08	7♏09 46	13 40.3	16 43.4	9 14.2	1 29.9	19 25.5	5 35.6	27 24.0	27 37.5	7 34.4	11 35.3
13 Th	13 29 04	20 22 08	13 20 01	19 33 01	13 33.7	15 36.7	10 24.5	1 18.1	19 16.5	5 32.0	27 28.0	27 39.3	7 35.2	11 37.6
14 F	13 33 00	21 21 36	25 48 55	2♐07 50	13 27.0	14 35.4	11 35.0	1 07.1	19 07.7	5 28.1	27 32.1	27 41.3	7 36.0	11 39.9
15 Sa	13 36 57	22 21 06	8♐29 56	14 55 21	13 21.2	13 41.3	12 45.6	0 56.8	18 59.3	5 24.1	27 36.3	27 43.2	7 36.9	11 42.2
16 Su	13 40 53	23 20 37	21 24 15	27 56 50	13 16.7	12 55.9	13 56.3	0 47.1	18 51.3	5 19.9	27 40.5	27 45.2	7 37.8	11 44.5
17 M	13 44 50	24 20 10	4♑33 16	11♑13 44	13 14.1	12 20.3	15 07.1	0 38.3	18 43.6	5 15.5	27 44.8	27 47.3	7 38.7	11 46.9
18 Tu	13 48 46	25 19 45	17 58 25	24 47 29	13D 13.2	11 55.5	16 18.1	0 30.2	18 36.2	5 10.9	27 49.2	27 49.4	7 39.7	11 49.2
19 W	13 52 43	26 19 22	1♒41 02	8♒39 12	13 13.8	11D 41.8	17 29.2	0 22.9	18 29.1	5 06.2	27 53.7	27 51.5	7 40.7	11 51.6
20 Th	13 56 39	27 19 00	15 41 57	22 49 15	13 15.0	11 39.3	18 40.4	0 16.3	18 22.5	5 01.2	27 58.2	27 53.7	7 41.7	11 53.9
21 F	14 00 36	28 18 40	0♓00 55	7♓16 41	13R 16.1	11 47.8	19 51.7	0 10.6	18 16.1	4 56.1	28 02.8	27 55.9	7 42.7	11 56.3
22 Sa	14 04 33	29 18 22	14 36 05	21 58 36	13 15.9	12 06.9	21 03.1	0 05.6	18 10.2	4 50.9	28 07.5	27 58.1	7 43.8	11 58.7
23 Su	14 08 29	0♏18 05	29 23 32	6♈50 02	13 13.8	12 36.1	22 14.6	0 01.5	18 04.6	4 45.4	28 12.3	28 00.4	7 44.9	12 01.1
24 M	14 12 26	1 17 50	14♈17 11	21 43 58	13 09.5	13 14.5	23 26.2	29♓58.1	17 59.3	4 39.9	28 17.1	28 02.8	7 46.0	12 03.5
25 Tu	14 16 22	2 17 37	29 09 20	6♉32 12	13 03.0	14 01.3	24 37.9	29 55.6	17 54.5	4 34.1	28 22.0	28 05.1	7 47.2	12 05.9
26 W	14 20 19	3 17 27	13♉51 35	21 06 31	12 55.1	14 55.8	25 49.8	29 53.8	17 50.0	4 28.2	28 26.9	28 07.6	7 48.4	12 08.3
27 Th	14 24 15	4 17 18	28 16 13	5♊20 01	12 46.6	15 57.0	27 01.7	29D 52.9	17 45.9	4 22.2	28 31.9	28 10.0	7 49.6	12 10.7
28 F	14 28 12	5 17 11	12♊17 26	19 08 10	12 38.6	17 04.1	28 13.8	29 52.7	17 42.1	4 16.0	28 37.0	28 12.5	7 50.9	12 13.1
29 Sa	14 32 08	6 17 07	25 52 04	2♋29 09	12 32.0	18 16.4	29 25.9	29 53.3	17 38.7	4 09.7	28 42.2	28 15.0	7 52.2	12 15.5
30 Su	14 36 05	7 17 05	8♋59 38	15 23 49	12 27.3	19 33.2	0♎38.2	29 54.7	17 35.7	4 03.2	28 47.4	28 17.6	7 53.5	12 17.9
31 M	14 40 02	8 17 05	21 42 07	27 55 03	12D 24.7	20 53.8	1 50.5	29 56.9	17 33.1	3 56.6	28 52.7	28 20.2	7 54.8	12 20.4

Astro Data

	Dy Hr Mn
♇0S	5 6:53
♅D	5 9:41
☽0S	11 22:13
♆D	18 18:19
☉0S	22 19:28
♃R	24 13:58
☽0N	25 10:06
☿R	28 21:37
☽0S	9 4:26
♄☌♅	18 13:26
☿D	20 5:20
☽0N	22 20:22
♂D	28 5:07

Planet Ingress

	Dy Hr Mn
♀ ♌	7 11:37
☉ ♎	22 19:29
♀ ♍	4 13:15
☉ ♏	23 4:44
♂ ♓R	23 22:01
♀ ♎	29 23:20

Last Aspect / ☽ Ingress

Last Aspect Dy Hr Mn		☽ Ingress Dy Hr Mn
1 21:53	♀ ⚹	♊ 2 8:11
4 10:00	♅ ☍	♋ 4 15:37
7 1:20	♀ ☌	♌ 7 2:14
9 8:48	♅ △	♍ 9 14:48
11 21:53	♅ □	♎ 12 3:51
14 10:19	♅ ⚹	♏ 14 16:07
16 14:52	☉ ⚹	♐ 17 2:25
19 4:36	♅ ☌	♑ 19 9:45
21 11:31	☉ △	♒ 21 13:43
23 10:19	♅ ⚹	♓ 23 14:51
25 10:05	♅ □	♈ 25 14:29
27 10:01	♅ △	♉ 27 14:29
29 6:19	♀ □	♊ 29 16:43

Last Aspect / ☽ Ingress

Last Aspect Dy Hr Mn		☽ Ingress Dy Hr Mn
1 17:42	♅ ☍	♋ 1 22:39
3 23:34	☿ □	♌ 4 8:31
6 15:51	♅ △	♍ 6 21:01
9 5:03	♅ □	♎ 9 10:03
11 17:14	♅ ⚹	♏ 11 21:58
12 20:39	♇ ☌	♐ 14 7:58
16 11:39	♅ ☌	♑ 16 15:44
18 13:01	☉ □	♒ 18 21:05
20 20:39	♄ ⚹	♓ 20 23:58
22 22:00	♄ □	♈ 23 0:59
24 22:39	♄ △	♉ 25 1:22
27 2:44	♂ ⚹	♊ 27 2:55
29 7:16	♂ □	♋ 29 7:28
31 15:58	♂ △	♌ 31 16:03

☽ Phases & Eclipses

Dy Hr Mn	
3 3:50	☾ 10♊52
11 4:49	● 18♍40
11 4:43:33	● A 06'57"
19 3:18	☽ 26♐24
25 19:07	○ 2♈55
2 16:59	☾ 9♋43
10 21:49	● 17♎48
18 13:01	☽ 25♑22
25 4:36	○ 1♉59

Astro Data

1 September 1988
Julian Day # 32386
SVP 5♓25'00"
GC 26♐40.9 ⚴ 3♒49.3R
Eris 16♈55.0R ⚵ 29♋54.4
⚷ 5♋50.9 ⚶ 23♍52.7
☽ Mean ☊ 14♓13.2

1 October 1988
Julian Day # 32416
SVP 5♓24'56"
GC 26♐40.9 ⚴ 1♒38.4
Eris 16♈38.6R ⚵ 14♌34.8
⚷ 7♋01.2 ⚶ 8♎58.6
☽ Mean ☊ 12♓37.9

November 1988 LONGITUDE

Day	Sid.Time	☉	0 hr ☽	Noon ☽	True ☊	☿	♀	♂	⚳	♃	♄	♅	♆	♇
1 Tu	14 43 58	9♏17 07	4♌03 13	10♌07 13	12♓24.1	22♎17.5	3♎02.9	29♓59.9	17♓30.8	3♊49.9	28♐58.0	28♐22.9	7♑56.2	12♏22.8
2 W	14 47 55	10 17 11	16 07 44	22 05 26	12 24.6	23 44.0	4 15.5	0♈03.6	17R 29.0	3R 43.0	29 03.4	28 25.5	7 57.6	12 25.2
3 Th	14 51 51	11 17 17	28 01 01	3♍55 09	12R 25.6	25 12.7	5 28.1	0 08.1	17 27.5	3 36.0	29 08.9	28 28.3	7 59.0	12 27.6
4 F	14 55 48	12 17 25	9♍48 30	15 41 41	12 25.8	26 43.2	6 40.8	0 13.3	17 26.3	3 28.9	29 14.4	28 31.0	8 00.4	12 30.1
5 Sa	14 59 44	13 17 36	21 35 19	27 29 56	12 24.4	28 15.3	7 53.5	0 19.3	17 25.6	3 21.7	29 20.0	28 33.8	8 01.9	12 32.5
6 Su	15 03 41	14 17 48	3♎26 02	9♎24 06	12 20.8	29 48.5	9 06.4	0 26.0	17D 25.2	3 14.4	29 25.6	28 36.6	8 03.4	12 34.9
7 M	15 07 37	15 18 02	15 24 31	21 27 36	12 14.5	1♏22.7	10 19.3	0 33.4	17 25.2	3 07.0	29 31.3	28 39.4	8 04.9	12 37.4
8 Tu	15 11 34	16 18 18	27 33 38	3♏42 49	12 05.5	2 57.6	11 32.3	0 41.6	17 25.6	2 59.5	29 37.1	28 42.3	8 06.5	12 39.8
9 W	15 15 31	17 18 36	9♏55 17	16 11 07	11 54.5	4 33.0	12 45.4	0 50.5	17 26.4	2 51.9	29 42.9	28 45.2	8 08.1	12 42.2
10 Th	15 19 27	18 18 56	22 30 21	28 52 56	11 42.3	6 08.9	13 58.6	1 00.1	17 27.5	2 44.2	29 48.8	28 48.2	8 09.7	12 44.6
11 F	15 23 24	19 19 18	5♐18 48	11♐47 51	11 30.1	7 45.1	15 11.8	1 10.3	17 29.0	2 36.5	29 54.7	28 51.2	8 11.3	12 47.1
12 Sa	15 27 20	20 19 41	18 19 59	24 55 04	11 18.9	9 21.4	16 25.1	1 21.3	17 30.9	2 28.7	0♑00.6	28 54.2	8 12.9	12 49.5
13 Su	15 31 17	21 20 05	1♑32 58	8♑13 35	11 09.9	10 57.9	17 38.5	1 32.9	17 33.1	2 20.8	0 06.7	28 57.2	8 14.6	12 51.9
14 M	15 35 13	22 20 31	14 56 50	21 42 39	11 03.6	12 34.3	18 51.9	1 45.2	17 35.7	2 12.8	0 12.7	29 00.3	8 16.3	12 54.3
15 Tu	15 39 10	23 20 59	28 31 01	5♒21 54	11 00.1	14 10.7	20 05.4	1 58.1	17 38.7	2 04.8	0 18.8	29 03.4	8 18.0	12 56.7
16 W	15 43 06	24 21 27	12♒15 21	19 11 22	10D 58.8	15 47.1	21 18.9	2 11.6	17 42.0	1 56.8	0 25.0	29 06.5	8 19.8	12 59.1
17 Th	15 47 03	25 21 57	26 09 58	3♓11 11	10R 58.8	17 23.3	22 32.5	2 25.8	17 45.7	1 48.7	0 31.2	29 09.6	8 21.6	13 01.5
18 F	15 51 00	26 22 28	10♓14 58	17 21 13	10 58.8	18 59.4	23 46.1	2 40.5	17 49.7	1 40.6	0 37.4	29 12.8	8 23.3	13 03.9
19 Sa	15 54 56	27 23 01	24 29 47	1♈40 25	10 57.5	20 35.4	24 59.8	2 55.9	17 54.0	1 32.5	0 43.7	29 16.0	8 25.1	13 06.3
20 Su	15 58 53	28 23 34	8♈52 47	16 06 24	10 53.7	22 11.1	26 13.6	3 11.7	17 58.7	1 24.3	0 50.0	29 19.2	8 27.0	13 08.6
21 M	16 02 49	29 24 09	23 20 43	0♉35 05	10 47.0	23 46.8	27 27.4	3 28.2	18 03.8	1 16.1	0 56.4	29 22.4	8 28.8	13 11.0
22 Tu	16 06 46	0♐24 45	7♉48 47	15 01 00	10 37.4	25 22.2	28 41.3	3 45.2	18 09.2	1 08.0	1 02.8	29 25.7	8 30.7	13 13.4
23 W	16 10 42	1 25 22	22 10 56	29 17 47	10 25.8	26 57.5	29 55.2	4 02.7	18 14.9	0 59.8	1 09.3	29 29.0	8 32.6	13 15.7
24 Th	16 14 39	2 26 01	6♊20 49	13♊19 22	10 13.2	28 32.6	1♏09.2	4 20.7	18 20.9	0 51.6	1 15.8	29 32.3	8 34.5	13 18.0
25 F	16 18 35	3 26 42	20 12 50	27 00 49	10 00.9	0♐07.6	2 23.2	4 39.2	18 27.3	0 43.4	1 22.3	29 35.6	8 36.4	13 20.4
26 Sa	16 22 32	4 27 24	3♋43 00	10♋19 15	9 50.2	1 42.5	3 37.2	4 58.2	18 34.0	0 35.3	1 28.8	29 39.0	8 38.4	13 22.7
27 Su	16 26 29	5 28 07	16 49 33	23 14 03	9 41.9	3 17.2	4 51.4	5 17.7	18 41.0	0 27.2	1 35.4	29 42.4	8 40.3	13 25.0
28 M	16 30 25	6 28 52	29 32 59	5♌46 44	9 36.3	4 51.7	6 05.5	5 37.7	18 48.3	0 19.1	1 42.1	29 45.8	8 42.3	13 27.3
29 Tu	16 34 22	7 29 38	11♌55 46	18 00 37	9 33.4	6 26.2	7 19.7	5 58.1	18 55.9	0 11.0	1 48.7	29 49.2	8 44.3	13 29.5
30 W	16 38 18	8 30 26	24 01 54	0♍00 15	9 32.3	8 00.6	8 34.0	6 18.9	19 03.8	0 03.0	1 55.4	29 52.6	8 46.3	13 31.8

December 1988 LONGITUDE

Day	Sid.Time	☉	0 hr ☽	Noon ☽	True ☊	☿	♀	♂	⚳	♃	♄	♅	♆	♇
1 Th	16 42 15	9♐31 15	5♍56 22	11♍50 55	9♓32.2	9♐34.9	9♏48.3	6♈40.2	19♓12.0	29♉55.0	2♑02.1	29♐56.0	8♑48.3	13♏34.0
2 F	16 46 11	10 32 06	17 44 40	23 38 16	9R 31.9	11 09.1	11 02.6	7 01.9	19 20.5	29R 47.1	2 08.9	29 59.5	8 50.4	13 36.3
3 Sa	16 50 08	11 32 57	29 32 27	5♎27 52	9 30.2	12 43.3	12 17.0	7 24.0	19 29.4	29 39.2	2 15.7	0♑03.0	8 52.4	13 38.5
4 Su	16 54 04	12 33 51	11♎25 09	17 24 53	9 26.2	14 17.5	13 31.4	7 46.5	19 38.5	29 31.4	2 22.5	0 06.4	8 54.5	13 40.7
5 M	16 58 01	13 34 45	23 27 30	29 33 48	9 19.4	15 51.7	14 45.9	8 09.5	19 47.9	29 23.7	2 29.3	0 09.9	8 56.6	13 42.9
6 Tu	17 01 58	14 35 41	5♏43 51	11♏58 03	9 09.8	17 25.8	16 00.4	8 32.8	19 57.6	29 16.0	2 36.1	0 13.5	8 58.7	13 45.0
7 W	17 05 54	15 36 38	18 16 39	24 39 45	8 57.8	19 00.0	17 14.9	8 56.5	20 07.5	29 08.5	2 43.0	0 17.0	9 00.8	13 47.2
8 Th	17 09 51	16 37 36	1♐07 24	7♐39 30	8 44.5	20 34.2	18 29.4	9 20.6	20 17.8	29 01.0	2 49.9	0 20.5	9 02.9	13 49.3
9 F	17 13 47	17 38 36	14 15 56	20 56 25	8 30.9	22 08.4	19 44.0	9 45.0	20 28.3	28 53.6	2 56.8	0 24.1	9 05.1	13 51.5
10 Sa	17 17 44	18 39 36	27 40 40	4♑28 17	8 18.5	23 42.7	20 58.6	10 09.8	20 39.1	28 46.3	3 03.8	0 27.7	9 07.2	13 53.6
11 Su	17 21 40	19 40 37	11♑18 54	18 12 04	8 08.3	25 17.0	22 13.3	10 34.9	20 50.1	28 39.2	3 10.8	0 31.2	9 09.4	13 55.6
12 M	17 25 37	20 41 38	25 07 24	2♒04 30	8 01.1	26 51.4	23 27.9	11 00.4	21 01.5	28 32.1	3 17.7	0 34.8	9 11.6	13 57.7
13 Tu	17 29 34	21 42 40	9♒03 00	16 02 36	7 56.9	28 25.9	24 42.6	11 26.2	21 13.0	28 25.2	3 24.7	0 38.4	9 13.8	13 59.8
14 W	17 33 30	22 43 43	23 03 03	0♓04 10	7D 55.3	0♑00.4	25 57.3	11 52.3	21 24.9	28 18.4	3 31.7	0 42.0	9 16.0	14 01.8
15 Th	17 37 27	23 44 46	7♓05 46	14 07 45	7R 55.2	1 35.1	27 12.0	12 18.7	21 36.9	28 11.7	3 38.8	0 45.6	9 18.2	14 03.8
16 F	17 41 23	24 45 49	21 10 03	28 12 33	7 55.3	3 09.8	28 26.8	12 45.5	21 49.3	28 05.1	3 45.8	0 49.2	9 20.4	14 05.8
17 Sa	17 45 20	25 46 53	5♈15 12	12♈17 52	7 54.2	4 44.5	29 41.5	13 12.5	22 01.8	27 58.7	3 52.8	0 52.8	9 22.6	14 07.7
18 Su	17 49 16	26 47 57	19 20 26	26 22 43	7 51.0	6 19.3	0♐56.3	13 39.8	22 14.6	27 52.5	3 59.9	0 56.4	9 24.8	14 09.6
19 M	17 53 13	27 49 01	3♉24 27	10♉25 20	7 45.0	7 54.2	2 11.1	14 07.3	22 27.7	27 46.3	4 07.0	1 00.0	9 27.0	14 11.6
20 Tu	17 57 09	28 50 06	17 25 02	24 23 08	7 36.4	9 29.1	3 25.9	14 35.2	22 40.9	27 40.4	4 14.0	1 03.7	9 29.3	14 13.4
21 W	18 01 06	29 51 11	1♊19 12	8♊12 45	7 25.6	11 03.9	4 40.8	15 03.3	22 54.4	27 34.6	4 21.1	1 07.3	9 31.5	14 15.3
22 Th	18 05 03	0♑52 16	15 03 20	21 50 30	7 13.9	12 38.7	5 55.6	15 31.6	23 08.1	27 28.9	4 28.2	1 10.9	9 33.8	14 17.2
23 F	18 08 59	1 53 22	28 33 52	5♋13 06	7 02.4	14 13.4	7 10.5	16 00.2	23 22.0	27 23.4	4 35.3	1 14.5	9 36.0	14 19.0
24 Sa	18 12 56	2 54 28	11♋47 54	18 18 07	6 52.2	15 47.9	8 25.4	16 29.1	23 36.2	27 18.1	4 42.4	1 18.2	9 38.3	14 20.8
25 Su	18 16 52	3 55 35	24 43 40	1♌04 33	6 44.2	17 22.2	9 40.3	16 58.1	23 50.5	27 12.9	4 49.5	1 21.8	9 40.6	14 22.5
26 M	18 20 49	4 56 42	7♌20 54	13 32 55	6 38.9	18 56.2	10 55.3	17 27.4	24 05.1	27 07.9	4 56.6	1 25.4	9 42.8	14 24.3
27 Tu	18 24 45	5 57 50	19 40 54	25 45 14	6D 36.1	20 29.7	12 10.2	17 56.9	24 19.9	27 03.1	5 03.7	1 29.0	9 45.1	14 26.0
28 W	18 28 42	6 58 58	1♍46 23	7♍44 50	6 35.4	22 02.7	13 25.2	18 26.6	24 34.8	26 58.4	5 10.8	1 32.6	9 47.4	14 27.7
29 Th	18 32 38	8 00 06	13 41 11	19 36 02	6 36.1	23 35.0	14 40.2	18 56.5	24 50.0	26 54.0	5 17.9	1 36.2	9 49.6	14 29.3
30 F	18 36 35	9 01 15	25 30 02	1♎23 51	6R 37.0	25 06.3	15 55.1	19 26.6	25 05.4	26 49.7	5 25.0	1 39.8	9 51.9	14 31.0
31 Sa	18 40 32	10 02 24	7♎18 10	13 13 40	6 37.2	26 36.5	17 10.2	19 57.0	25 20.9	26 45.6	5 32.1	1 43.4	9 54.2	14 32.6

Astro Data

	Dy Hr Mn
♀0S	2 0:18
☽0S	5 11:02
⚳ D	6 23:30
♂0N	17 11:08
☽0N	19 3:53
♃⊼♄	22 20:25
♃⊼♅	1 9:48
☽0S	2 17:59
☽0N	16 8:46
☽0S	30 1:08

Planet Ingress

		Dy Hr Mn
♂	♈	1 12:57
☿	♏	6 14:57
♄	♑	12 9:26
☉	♐	22 2:12
♀	♏	23 13:34
☿	♐	25 10:04
♃	♉R	30 20:53
♅	♑	2 15:35
☿	♑	14 11:53
♀	♐	17 17:56
☉	♑	21 15:28

Last Aspect / ☽ Ingress (November)

Last Aspect Dy Hr Mn			☽ Ingress	Dy Hr Mn
3 2:13	♄	△	♍	3 4:02
5 15:45	♄	□	♎	5 17:04
8 3:58	♄	⚹	♏	8 4:46
9 14:20	☉	☌	♐	10 14:06
12 19:15	♅	☌	♑	12 21:12
14 13:12	☉	⚹	♒	15 2:36
17 5:06	♅	⚹	♓	17 6:34
19 7:58	♅	□	♈	19 9:12
21 9:59	♅	△	♉	21 11:02
23 7:33	☿	☍	♊	23 13:12
25 16:37	♅	☍	♋	25 17:19
26 17:38	♇	△	♌	28 0:52
30 11:44	♅	△	♍	30 11:59

Last Aspect / ☽ Ingress (December)

Last Aspect Dy Hr Mn			☽ Ingress	Dy Hr Mn
3 0:21	♃	△	♎	3 0:56
4 4:49	☿	⚹	♏	5 12:51
7 20:15	♃	☍	♐	7 21:55
9 14:26	☿	☌	♑	10 4:07
12 5:57	♃	△	♒	12 8:25
14 11:53	☿	⚹	♓	14 11:53
16 12:27	♀	△	♈	16 15:03
18 12:46	☉	△	♉	18 18:11
20 17:38	♃	☌	♊	20 21:43
22 0:26	♂	⚹	♋	23 2:35
25 4:44	♃	⚹	♌	25 9:57
27 14:34	♃	□	♍	27 20:27
30 2:45	♃	△	♎	30 9:09

☽ Phases & Eclipses

Dy Hr Mn		
1 10:11	☾	9♌13
9 14:20	●	17♏24
16 21:35	☽	24♒46
23 15:53	○	1♊35
1 6:49	☾	9♍18
9 5:36	●	17♐22
16 5:40	☽	24♓30
23 5:29	○	1♋37
31 4:57	☾	9♎44

Astro Data

1 November 1988
Julian Day # 32447
SVP 5♓24'52"
GC 26♐41.0 ⚴ 4♒31.0
Eris 16♈20.3R ⚵ 27♌29.6
⚷ 6♋59.2R ⚶ 24♎56.7
☽ Mean ☊ 10♓59.4

1 December 1988
Julian Day # 32477
SVP 5♓24'47"
GC 26♐41.1 ⚴ 10♒46.4
Eris 16♈06.4R ⚵ 6♍36.8
⚷ 5♋46.7R ⚶ 10♏29.0
☽ Mean ☊ 9♓24.1

LONGITUDE — January 1989

Day	Sid.Time	☉	0 hr ☽	Noon ☽	True ☊	☿	♀	♂	⚳	♃	♄	♅	♆	♇
1 Su	18 44 28	11♑03 33	19♎11 02	25♎10 57	6♓35.9	28♑05.3	18♐25.2	20♈27.5	25♓36.7	26♉41.7	5♑39.1	1♑47.0	9♑56.4	14♏34.2
2 M	18 48 25	12 04 43	1♏14 02	7♏20 52	6R32.5	29 32.5	19 40.2	20 58.2	25 52.6	26R38.0	5 46.2	1 50.6	9 58.7	14 35.7
3 Tu	18 52 21	13 05 54	13 32 01	19 47 56	6 26.9	0♒57.6	20 55.3	21 29.1	26 08.7	26 34.4	5 53.3	1 54.2	10 01.0	14 37.2
4 W	18 56 18	14 07 04	26 08 59	2♐35 30	6 19.3	2 20.4	22 10.3	22 00.1	26 25.0	26 31.1	6 00.3	1 57.8	10 03.3	14 38.7
5 Th	19 00 14	15 08 15	9♐07 38	15 45 27	6 10.4	3 40.2	23 25.4	22 31.4	26 41.5	26 28.0	6 07.4	2 01.3	10 05.5	14 40.2
6 F	19 04 11	16 09 25	22 28 52	29 17 43	6 01.2	4 56.6	24 40.5	23 02.8	26 58.1	26 25.1	6 14.4	2 04.9	10 07.8	14 41.6
7 Sa	19 08 08	17 10 36	6♑11 38	13♑10 13	5 52.6	6 09.0	25 55.5	23 34.4	27 15.0	26 22.3	6 21.5	2 08.4	10 10.1	14 43.0
8 Su	19 12 04	18 11 47	20 12 55	27 19 05	5 45.7	7 16.7	27 10.6	24 06.2	27 32.0	26 19.8	6 28.5	2 11.9	10 12.3	14 44.4
9 M	19 16 01	19 12 57	4♒28 04	11♒39 09	5 41.0	8 19.1	28 25.7	24 38.1	27 49.1	26 17.5	6 35.5	2 15.5	10 14.6	14 45.7
10 Tu	19 19 57	20 14 07	18 51 37	26 04 47	5D38.7	9 15.1	29 40.8	25 10.2	28 06.5	26 15.3	6 42.5	2 19.0	10 16.8	14 47.0
11 W	19 23 54	21 15 16	3♓18 02	10♓30 48	5 38.4	10 04.2	0♑55.9	25 42.4	28 23.9	26 13.4	6 49.4	2 22.4	10 19.1	14 48.3
12 Th	19 27 50	22 16 25	17 42 33	24 52 55	5 39.4	10 45.2	2 11.0	26 14.8	28 41.6	26 11.7	6 56.4	2 25.9	10 21.3	14 49.6
13 F	19 31 47	23 17 33	2♈01 31	9♈08 07	5 40.7	11 17.4	3 26.1	26 47.4	28 59.4	26 10.2	7 03.3	2 29.4	10 23.5	14 50.8
14 Sa	19 35 43	24 18 40	16 12 31	23 14 33	5R41.4	11 39.9	4 41.2	27 20.0	29 17.3	26 08.9	7 10.2	2 32.8	10 25.8	14 51.9
15 Su	19 39 40	25 19 46	0♉14 07	7♉11 08	5 40.8	11R51.9	5 56.3	27 52.8	29 35.4	26 07.8	7 17.1	2 36.2	10 28.0	14 53.1
16 M	19 43 37	26 20 52	14 05 32	20 57 15	5 38.3	11 52.7	7 11.4	28 25.8	29 53.7	26 06.9	7 23.9	2 39.6	10 30.2	14 54.2
17 Tu	19 47 33	27 21 57	27 46 14	4♊32 24	5 34.0	11 41.9	8 26.6	28 58.8	0♈12.1	26 06.2	7 30.8	2 43.0	10 32.4	14 55.3
18 W	19 51 30	28 23 02	11♊15 40	17 55 57	5 28.3	11 19.4	9 41.7	29 32.0	0 30.6	26 05.8	7 37.6	2 46.4	10 34.6	14 56.3
19 Th	19 55 26	29 24 05	24 33 08	1♋07 09	5 21.9	10 45.4	10 56.8	0♉05.3	0 49.2	26D05.5	7 44.4	2 49.7	10 36.8	14 57.4
20 F	19 59 23	0♒25 08	7♋37 53	14 05 16	5 15.6	10 00.5	12 11.9	0 38.7	1 08.0	26 05.5	7 51.1	2 53.1	10 39.0	14 58.3
21 Sa	20 03 19	1 26 10	20 29 15	26 49 48	5 10.0	9 05.7	13 27.0	1 12.2	1 27.0	26 05.6	7 57.8	2 56.4	10 41.1	14 59.3
22 Su	20 07 16	2 27 12	3♌06 55	9♌20 40	5 05.8	8 02.5	14 42.1	1 45.8	1 46.0	26 06.0	8 04.5	2 59.6	10 43.3	15 00.2
23 M	20 11 12	3 28 12	15 31 08	21 38 28	5 03.2	6 52.8	15 57.2	2 19.6	2 05.2	26 06.5	8 11.2	3 02.9	10 45.4	15 01.1
24 Tu	20 15 09	4 29 12	27 42 53	3♍44 37	5D02.3	5 38.7	17 12.3	2 53.4	2 24.5	26 07.3	8 17.8	3 06.1	10 47.5	15 01.9
25 W	20 19 06	5 30 11	9♍43 59	15 41 21	5 02.8	4 22.5	18 27.5	3 27.3	2 44.0	26 08.3	8 24.4	3 09.3	10 49.6	15 02.7
26 Th	20 23 02	6 31 10	21 37 07	27 31 44	5 04.3	3 06.4	19 42.6	4 01.3	3 03.5	26 09.4	8 31.0	3 12.5	10 51.7	15 03.5
27 F	20 26 59	7 32 08	3♎25 43	9♎19 35	5 06.2	1 52.8	20 57.7	4 35.4	3 23.2	26 10.8	8 37.5	3 15.7	10 53.8	15 04.2
28 Sa	20 30 55	8 33 05	15 13 55	21 09 17	5 07.9	0 43.3	22 12.8	5 09.7	3 43.0	26 12.4	8 44.0	3 18.8	10 55.9	15 04.9
29 Su	20 34 52	9 34 01	27 06 19	3♏05 39	5R09.0	29♑39.8	23 27.9	5 43.9	4 02.9	26 14.2	8 50.5	3 21.9	10 58.0	15 05.6
30 M	20 38 48	10 34 57	9♏07 53	15 13 39	5 09.1	28 43.3	24 43.1	6 18.3	4 22.9	26 16.2	8 56.9	3 25.0	11 00.0	15 06.2
31 Tu	20 42 45	11 35 53	21 23 33	27 38 10	5 08.1	27 54.8	25 58.2	6 52.8	4 43.0	26 18.3	9 03.3	3 28.0	11 02.0	15 06.8

LONGITUDE — February 1989

Day	Sid.Time	☉	0 hr ☽	Noon ☽	True ☊	☿	♀	♂	⚳	♃	♄	♅	♆	♇
1 W	20 46 41	12♒36 47	3♐57 59	10♐23 28	5♓06.0	27♑14.7	27♑13.3	7♉27.4	5♈03.3	26♉20.7	9♑09.6	3♑31.1	11♑04.1	15♏07.4
2 Th	20 50 38	13 37 41	16 55 01	23 32 52	5R03.2	26R43.2	28 28.4	8 02.0	5 23.6	26 23.3	9 15.9	3 34.1	11 06.1	15 07.9
3 F	20 54 35	14 38 34	0♑17 11	7♑08 00	5 00.1	26 20.3	29 43.6	8 36.7	5 44.1	26 26.1	9 22.1	3 37.0	11 08.0	15 08.4
4 Sa	20 58 31	15 39 26	14 05 12	21 08 29	4 57.2	26 05.8	0♒58.7	9 11.5	6 04.7	26 29.0	9 28.4	3 40.0	11 10.0	15 08.8
5 Su	21 02 28	16 40 16	28 17 26	5♒31 28	4 54.9	25D59.3	2 13.8	9 46.4	6 25.3	26 32.2	9 34.5	3 42.9	11 12.0	15 09.2
6 M	21 06 24	17 41 06	12♒49 52	20 11 48	4D53.4	26 00.5	3 28.9	10 21.4	6 46.1	26 35.6	9 40.6	3 45.7	11 13.9	15 09.6
7 Tu	21 10 21	18 41 55	27 36 21	5♓02 32	4 53.0	26 08.9	4 44.0	10 56.4	7 07.0	26 39.1	9 46.7	3 48.6	11 15.8	15 09.9
8 W	21 14 17	19 42 41	12♓29 22	19 55 52	4 53.4	26 23.9	5 59.1	11 31.5	7 27.9	26 42.9	9 52.7	3 51.4	11 17.7	15 10.2
9 Th	21 18 14	20 43 27	27 21 08	4♈44 17	4 54.3	26 45.0	7 14.2	12 06.7	7 49.0	26 46.8	9 58.7	3 54.1	11 19.6	15 10.5
10 F	21 22 10	21 44 11	12♈04 35	19 21 25	4 55.4	27 11.9	8 29.3	12 41.9	8 10.1	26 50.9	10 04.6	3 56.9	11 21.4	15 10.7
11 Sa	21 26 07	22 44 53	26 34 16	3♉42 45	4 56.3	27 44.0	9 44.4	13 17.2	8 31.3	26 55.2	10 10.4	3 59.6	11 23.2	15 10.9
12 Su	21 30 04	23 45 34	10♉46 36	17 45 41	4R56.9	28 20.9	10 59.4	13 52.6	8 52.7	26 59.7	10 16.3	4 02.2	11 25.0	15 11.1
13 M	21 34 00	24 46 13	24 39 54	1♊29 19	4 56.8	29 02.3	12 14.5	14 28.0	9 14.1	27 04.4	10 22.0	4 04.8	11 26.8	15 11.2
14 Tu	21 37 57	25 46 51	8♊13 59	14 54 04	4 56.3	29 47.7	13 29.6	15 03.5	9 35.6	27 09.2	10 27.7	4 07.4	11 28.6	15 11.3
15 W	21 41 53	26 47 26	21 29 44	28 01 11	4 55.5	0♒36.8	14 44.6	15 39.1	9 57.1	27 14.2	10 33.3	4 10.0	11 30.3	15R11.4
16 Th	21 45 50	27 48 01	4♋28 39	10♋52 21	4 54.5	1 29.3	15 59.6	16 14.7	10 18.8	27 19.4	10 38.9	4 12.5	11 32.1	15 11.4
17 F	21 49 46	28 48 33	17 12 30	23 29 21	4 53.6	2 25.1	17 14.7	16 50.3	10 40.5	27 24.8	10 44.4	4 15.0	11 33.8	15 11.3
18 Sa	21 53 43	29 49 03	29 43 06	5♌53 58	4 52.9	3 23.7	18 29.7	17 26.0	11 02.3	27 30.4	10 49.9	4 17.4	11 35.4	15 11.3
19 Su	21 57 39	0♓49 32	12♌02 11	18 07 56	4 52.5	4 25.0	19 44.7	18 01.7	11 24.2	27 36.1	10 55.3	4 19.8	11 37.1	15 11.2
20 M	22 01 36	1 49 59	24 11 25	0♍12 53	4D52.3	5 28.8	20 59.7	18 37.5	11 46.2	27 41.9	11 00.7	4 22.1	11 38.7	15 11.1
21 Tu	22 05 33	2 50 25	6♍12 31	12 10 34	4 52.3	6 34.9	22 14.7	19 13.3	12 08.2	27 48.0	11 05.9	4 24.4	11 40.3	15 10.9
22 W	22 09 29	3 50 49	18 07 15	24 02 52	4 52.4	7 43.3	23 29.6	19 49.2	12 30.3	27 54.2	11 11.1	4 26.7	11 41.9	15 10.7
23 Th	22 13 26	4 51 11	29 57 42	5♎52 02	4R52.5	8 53.6	24 44.6	20 25.1	12 52.5	28 00.6	11 16.3	4 28.9	11 43.4	15 10.5
24 F	22 17 22	5 51 32	11♎46 14	17 40 39	4 52.4	10 05.9	25 59.6	21 01.1	13 14.7	28 07.1	11 21.4	4 31.1	11 45.0	15 10.2
25 Sa	22 21 19	6 51 52	23 35 42	29 31 48	4 52.2	11 19.9	27 14.5	21 37.1	13 37.0	28 13.8	11 26.4	4 33.3	11 46.5	15 09.9
26 Su	22 25 15	7 52 09	5♏29 25	11♏29 02	4 51.9	12 35.7	28 29.5	22 13.1	13 59.4	28 20.6	11 31.3	4 35.4	11 47.9	15 09.5
27 M	22 29 12	8 52 26	17 31 09	23 36 18	4 51.6	13 53.1	29 44.4	22 49.1	14 21.8	28 27.6	11 36.2	4 37.4	11 49.4	15 09.2
28 Tu	22 33 08	9 52 41	29 45 01	5♐57 51	4D51.4	15 12.1	0♓59.4	23 25.3	14 44.3	28 34.8	11 41.0	4 39.4	11 50.8	15 08.8

Astro Data	Planet Ingress	Last Aspect	☽ Ingress	Last Aspect	☽ Ingress	☽ Phases & Eclipses
Dy Hr Mn	Dy Hr Mn	Dy Hr Mn	Dy Hr Mn	Dy Hr Mn	Dy Hr Mn	Dy Hr Mn
☽0N 12 13:39	☿ ♒ 2 19:41	1 18:34 ☿ □	♏ 1 21:34	1 16:27 ☉ ⚹	♑ 2 23:30	7 19:22 ● 17♑29
☿R 16 1:43	♀ ♑ 10 18:08	4 0:44 ♃ ☍	♐ 4 7:12	4 21:01 ♃ △	♒ 5 2:51	14 13:58 ☽ 24♈24
♃D 20 6:12	⚳ ♈ 16 20:17	6 3:03 ♀ ☌	♑ 6 13:14	6 22:24 ♃ □	♓ 7 3:52	21 21:34 ○ 1♌50
☽0S 26 8:20	♂ ♉ 19 8:11	8 10:20 ♃ △	♒ 8 16:31	8 23:01 ♃ ⚹	♈ 9 4:18	30 2:02 ☾ 10♏10
	☉ ♒ 20 2:07	10 12:18 ♃ □	♓ 10 18:31	11 1:32 ☿ □	♉ 11 5:45	
☿D 5 20:08	☿ ♑R 29 4:06	12 14:12 ♃ ⚹	♈ 12 20:36	13 7:26 ☿ △	♊ 13 9:22	6 7:37 ● 17♒30
☽0N 8 21:16		14 19:18 ♂ ☌	♉ 14 23:36	15 9:32 ☉ △	♋ 15 15:40	12 23:15 ☽ 24♉14
♇R 16 9:46	♀ ♒ 3 17:15	16 22:15 ☉ △	♊ 17 3:57	17 19:36 ♃ ⚹	♌ 18 0:33	20 15:32 ○ 1♍59
☽0S 22 15:15	☿ ♒ 14 18:11	18 0:29 ☿ △	♋ 19 9:57	20 6:56 ♃ □	♍ 20 11:34	20 15:35 ☍ T 1.275
	☉ ♓ 18 16:21	21 10:36 ♃ ⚹	♌ 21 18:02	22 19:53 ♃ △	♎ 23 0:05	28 20:08 ☾ 10♐13
	♀ ♓ 27 16:59	23 20:50 ♃ □	♍ 24 4:32	25 6:50 ♀ △	♏ 25 12:57	
		26 9:12 ♃ △	♎ 26 17:01	27 21:35 ♃ ☍	♐ 28 0:29	
		29 5:40 ☿ □	♏ 29 5:49			
		31 12:30 ♀ ⚹	♐ 31 16:30			

Astro Data

1 January 1989
Julian Day # 32508
SVP 5♓24'41"
GC 26♐41.1 ⚴ 19♒23.6
Eris 16♈00.5R ⚵ 10♍34.1
⚷ 3♋49.7R ⚶ 26♏15.6
☽ Mean ☊ 7♓45.6

1 February 1989
Julian Day # 32539
SVP 5♓24'36"
GC 26♐41.2 ⚴ 29♒12.0
Eris 16♈05.1 ⚵ 7♍14.5R
⚷ 2♋03.8R ⚶ 11♐13.9
☽ Mean ☊ 6♓07.2

March 1989 — LONGITUDE

Day	Sid.Time	☉	0 hr ☽	Noon ☽	True ☊	☿	♀	♂	⚳	♃	♄	♅	♆	♇
1 W	22 37 05	10♓52 55	12♐15 18	18♐37 54	4♓51.5	16♒32.5	2♓14.3	24♉01.4	15♈06.9	28♉42.1	11♑45.8	4♑41.4	11♑52.2	15♏08.3
2 Th	22 41 02	11 53 07	25 06 06	1♑40 21	4 51.8	17 54.4	3 29.2	24 37.6	15 29.5	28 49.6	11 50.5	4 43.3	11 53.6	15R 07.8
3 F	22 44 58	12 53 17	8♑20 59	15 08 15	4 52.4	19 17.7	4 44.2	25 13.8	15 52.2	28 57.2	11 55.1	4 45.2	11 54.9	15 07.3
4 Sa	22 48 55	13 53 27	22 02 18	29 03 08	4 53.2	20 42.3	5 59.1	25 50.1	16 14.9	29 04.9	11 59.6	4 47.0	11 56.2	15 06.8
5 Su	22 52 51	14 53 34	6♒10 37	13♒24 26	4 54.0	22 08.2	7 14.0	26 26.4	16 37.7	29 12.8	12 04.1	4 48.8	11 57.5	15 06.2
6 M	22 56 48	15 53 40	20 44 05	28 08 55	4R 54.5	23 35.3	8 28.8	27 02.7	17 00.6	29 20.9	12 08.4	4 50.6	11 58.7	15 05.6
7 Tu	23 00 44	16 53 43	5♓38 04	13♓10 34	4 54.5	25 03.7	9 43.7	27 39.0	17 23.5	29 29.0	12 12.7	4 52.3	12 00.0	15 05.0
8 W	23 04 41	17 53 45	20 45 18	28 21 04	4 53.8	26 33.4	10 58.6	28 15.4	17 46.4	29 37.4	12 16.9	4 53.9	12 01.2	15 04.3
9 Th	23 08 37	18 53 45	5♈56 38	13♈30 48	4 52.4	28 04.3	12 13.4	28 51.8	18 09.5	29 45.8	12 21.1	4 55.5	12 02.3	15 03.6
10 F	23 12 34	19 53 43	21 02 24	28 30 22	4 50.6	29 36.3	13 28.3	29 28.3	18 32.5	29 54.4	12 25.2	4 57.0	12 03.5	15 02.8
11 Sa	23 16 31	20 53 39	5♉53 47	13♉11 53	4 48.6	1♓09.6	14 43.1	0♊04.8	18 55.6	0♊03.1	12 29.1	4 58.5	12 04.6	15 02.1
12 Su	23 20 27	21 53 33	20 24 07	27 30 05	4 46.8	2 44.0	15 57.9	0 41.3	19 18.8	0 12.0	12 33.0	5 00.0	12 05.6	15 01.3
13 M	23 24 24	22 53 25	4♊29 32	11♊22 26	4D 45.6	4 19.6	17 12.7	1 17.8	19 42.0	0 21.0	12 36.9	5 01.4	12 06.7	15 00.4
14 Tu	23 28 20	23 53 14	18 08 51	24 48 59	4 45.3	5 56.5	18 27.5	1 54.4	20 05.2	0 30.1	12 40.6	5 02.7	12 07.7	14 59.6
15 W	23 32 17	24 53 01	1♋23 07	7♋51 38	4 45.8	7 34.5	19 42.2	2 31.0	20 28.5	0 39.3	12 44.3	5 04.1	12 08.7	14 58.7
16 Th	23 36 13	25 52 46	14 14 56	20 33 30	4 47.0	9 13.7	20 57.0	3 07.6	20 51.9	0 48.7	12 47.8	5 05.3	12 09.6	14 57.8
17 F	23 40 10	26 52 29	26 47 46	2♌58 13	4 48.6	10 54.1	22 11.7	3 44.2	21 15.3	0 58.1	12 51.3	5 06.5	12 10.6	14 56.8
18 Sa	23 44 06	27 52 09	9♌05 20	15 09 33	4 50.2	12 35.8	23 26.4	4 20.8	21 38.7	1 07.7	12 54.7	5 07.7	12 11.4	14 55.9
19 Su	23 48 03	28 51 47	21 11 19	27 11 02	4R 51.3	14 18.6	24 41.1	4 57.5	22 02.1	1 17.4	12 58.0	5 08.8	12 12.3	14 54.8
20 M	23 52 00	29 51 23	3♍09 04	9♍05 46	4 51.4	16 02.8	25 55.8	5 34.2	22 25.6	1 27.2	13 01.3	5 09.8	12 13.1	14 53.8
21 Tu	23 55 56	0♈50 57	15 01 29	20 56 30	4 50.3	17 48.1	27 10.4	6 10.8	22 49.1	1 37.1	13 04.4	5 10.8	12 13.9	14 52.8
22 W	23 59 53	1 50 29	26 51 05	2♎45 31	4 47.9	19 34.8	28 25.1	6 47.5	23 12.7	1 47.2	13 07.5	5 11.8	12 14.7	14 51.7
23 Th	0 03 49	2 49 58	8♎40 03	14 34 54	4 44.0	21 22.7	29 39.7	7 24.3	23 36.3	1 57.3	13 10.4	5 12.7	12 15.4	14 50.6
24 F	0 07 46	3 49 26	20 30 20	26 26 35	4 39.2	23 11.9	0♈54.3	8 01.0	23 59.9	2 07.6	13 13.3	5 13.5	12 16.1	14 49.4
25 Sa	0 11 42	4 48 52	2♏23 53	8♏22 31	4 33.8	25 02.4	2 08.9	8 37.7	24 23.6	2 17.9	13 16.1	5 14.3	12 16.7	14 48.3
26 Su	0 15 39	5 48 16	14 22 46	20 24 56	4 28.4	26 54.2	3 23.5	9 14.5	24 47.3	2 28.4	13 18.8	5 15.0	12 17.4	14 47.1
27 M	0 19 35	6 47 38	26 29 21	2♐36 22	4 23.6	28 47.4	4 38.1	9 51.3	25 11.0	2 38.9	13 21.4	5 15.7	12 18.0	14 45.9
28 Tu	0 23 32	7 46 59	8♐46 21	14 59 42	4 19.9	0♈41.8	5 52.6	10 28.1	25 34.8	2 49.6	13 23.9	5 16.4	12 18.5	14 44.6
29 W	0 27 28	8 46 17	21 16 51	27 38 14	4D 17.7	2 37.6	7 07.2	11 04.9	25 58.5	3 00.4	13 26.3	5 17.0	12 19.1	14 43.4
30 Th	0 31 25	9 45 34	4♑04 15	10♑35 22	4 17.1	4 34.6	8 21.7	11 41.7	26 22.4	3 11.2	13 28.7	5 17.5	12 19.6	14 42.1
31 F	0 35 22	10 44 49	17 11 57	23 54 23	4 17.8	6 32.8	9 36.2	12 18.6	26 46.2	3 22.2	13 30.9	5 18.0	12 20.0	14 40.8

April 1989 — LONGITUDE

Day	Sid.Time	☉	0 hr ☽	Noon ☽	True ☊	☿	♀	♂	⚳	♃	♄	♅	♆	♇
1 Sa	0 39 18	11♈44 03	0♒42 57	7♒37 52	4♓19.1	8♈32.3	10♈50.7	12♊55.4	27♈10.1	3♊33.2	13♑33.1	5♑18.4	12♑20.5	14♏39.5
2 Su	0 43 15	12 43 14	14 39 16	21 47 05	4R 20.5	10 32.9	12 05.2	13 32.3	27 34.0	3 44.4	13 35.1	5 18.8	12 20.9	14R 38.1
3 M	0 47 11	13 42 24	29 01 09	6♓21 07	4 21.0	12 34.6	13 19.7	14 09.2	27 57.9	3 55.6	13 37.1	5 19.2	12 21.2	14 36.8
4 Tu	0 51 08	14 41 32	13♓46 26	21 16 22	4 19.9	14 37.3	14 34.2	14 46.1	28 21.9	4 06.9	13 38.9	5 19.4	12 21.6	14 35.4
5 W	0 55 04	15 40 38	28 49 57	6♈26 08	4 16.9	16 40.8	15 48.6	15 23.0	28 45.9	4 18.3	13 40.7	5 19.7	12 21.9	14 34.0
6 Th	0 59 01	16 39 42	14♈03 40	21 41 14	4 12.0	18 45.0	17 03.1	15 59.9	29 09.9	4 29.8	13 42.3	5 19.8	12 22.1	14 32.5
7 F	1 02 57	17 38 44	29 17 31	6♉51 11	4 05.7	20 49.9	18 17.5	16 36.9	29 33.9	4 41.3	13 43.9	5 20.0	12 22.4	14 31.1
8 Sa	1 06 54	18 37 44	14♉21 01	21 45 56	3 58.8	22 55.0	19 31.9	17 13.8	29 57.9	4 53.0	13 45.4	5R 20.0	12 22.6	14 29.6
9 Su	1 10 51	19 36 42	29 05 02	6♊17 35	3 52.4	25 00.3	20 46.3	17 50.8	0♉22.0	5 04.7	13 46.7	5 20.0	12 22.7	14 28.2
10 M	1 14 47	20 35 37	13♊23 07	20 21 21	3 47.1	27 05.5	22 00.6	18 27.8	0 46.1	5 16.5	13 48.0	5 20.0	12 22.9	14 26.7
11 Tu	1 18 44	21 34 30	27 12 12	3♋55 45	3 43.6	29 10.3	23 15.0	19 04.7	1 10.2	5 28.4	13 49.2	5 19.9	12 23.0	14 25.2
12 W	1 22 40	22 33 21	10♋32 17	17 02 09	3D 42.0	1♉14.4	24 29.3	19 41.7	1 34.3	5 40.4	13 50.3	5 19.8	12 23.0	14 23.6
13 Th	1 26 37	23 32 10	23 25 49	29 43 51	3 42.1	3 17.4	25 43.6	20 18.7	1 58.4	5 52.4	13 51.3	5 19.6	12R 23.1	14 22.1
14 F	1 30 33	24 30 57	5♌56 48	12♌05 19	3 43.1	5 19.0	26 57.9	20 55.7	2 22.5	6 04.5	13 52.1	5 19.4	12 23.1	14 20.6
15 Sa	1 34 30	25 29 41	18 10 00	24 11 29	3R 44.2	7 19.0	28 12.1	21 32.8	2 46.7	6 16.7	13 52.9	5 19.1	12 23.0	14 19.0
16 Su	1 38 26	26 28 22	0♍10 22	6♍07 12	3 44.6	9 16.9	29 26.4	22 09.8	3 10.9	6 28.9	13 53.6	5 18.7	12 23.0	14 17.4
17 M	1 42 23	27 27 02	12 02 34	17 56 57	3 43.4	11 12.4	0♉40.6	22 46.8	3 35.0	6 41.2	13 54.2	5 18.3	12 22.9	14 15.8
18 Tu	1 46 20	28 25 40	23 50 48	29 44 34	3 40.0	13 05.2	1 54.8	23 23.8	3 59.2	6 53.6	13 54.7	5 17.9	12 22.7	14 14.2
19 W	1 50 16	29 24 15	5♎38 36	11♎33 15	3 34.1	14 54.9	3 09.0	24 00.8	4 23.4	7 06.0	13 55.1	5 17.4	12 22.6	14 12.6
20 Th	1 54 13	0♉22 49	17 28 48	23 25 30	3 26.0	16 41.4	4 23.2	24 37.9	4 47.6	7 18.5	13 55.4	5 16.9	12 22.4	14 11.0
21 F	1 58 09	1 21 20	29 23 34	5♏23 11	3 16.0	18 24.3	5 37.3	25 14.9	5 11.8	7 31.0	13 55.5	5 16.3	12 22.1	14 09.4
22 Sa	2 02 06	2 19 50	11♏24 32	17 27 46	3 04.9	20 03.5	6 51.4	25 51.9	5 36.1	7 43.7	13R 55.6	5 15.6	12 21.9	14 07.7
23 Su	2 06 02	3 18 18	23 33 00	29 40 25	2 53.8	21 38.7	8 05.6	26 29.0	6 00.3	7 56.3	13 55.6	5 15.0	12 21.6	14 06.1
24 M	2 09 59	4 16 44	5♐50 08	12♐02 20	2 43.6	23 09.8	9 19.7	27 06.0	6 24.5	8 09.0	13 55.5	5 14.2	12 21.3	14 04.4
25 Tu	2 13 55	5 15 09	18 17 11	24 34 54	2 35.2	24 36.6	10 33.7	27 43.1	6 48.8	8 21.8	13 55.3	5 13.4	12 20.9	14 02.8
26 W	2 17 52	6 13 32	0♑55 42	7♑19 52	2 29.2	25 59.0	11 47.8	28 20.2	7 13.1	8 34.7	13 55.1	5 12.6	12 20.5	14 01.1
27 Th	2 21 49	7 11 53	13 47 40	20 19 23	2 25.7	27 16.8	13 01.9	28 57.2	7 37.3	8 47.5	13 54.7	5 11.7	12 20.1	13 59.4
28 F	2 25 45	8 10 13	26 55 22	3♒35 53	2D 24.4	28 30.1	14 15.9	29 34.3	8 01.6	9 00.5	13 54.2	5 10.8	12 19.7	13 57.8
29 Sa	2 29 42	9 08 32	10♒21 15	17 11 43	2 24.5	29 38.5	15 29.9	0♋11.4	8 25.9	9 13.5	13 53.6	5 09.9	12 19.2	13 56.1
30 Su	2 33 38	10 06 48	24 07 30	1♓08 41	2R 24.8	0♊42.2	16 43.9	0 48.5	8 50.2	9 26.5	13 52.9	5 08.8	12 18.7	13 54.4

Astro Data (Dy Hr Mn)

♄☌♆ 3 10:44
⚳0N 3 12:14
☽0N 8 7:46
☉0N 20 15:28
☽0S 21 21:38
♀0N 26 8:38
☿0N 30 2:43

☽0N 4 18:57
♅R 9 8:54
♃⚻♅ 10 18:59
♆R 13 23:36
☽0S 18 3:33
♄R 22 23:37

Planet Ingress (Dy Hr Mn)

☿ ♓ 10 18:07
♃ ♊ 11 3:26
♂ ♊ 11 8:51
☉ ♈ 20 15:28
♀ ♈ 23 18:32
☿ ♈ 28 3:16

⚳ ♉ 8 14:05
☿ ♉ 11 21:36
♀ ♉ 16 22:52
☉ ♉ 20 2:39
♂ ♋ 29 4:37
☿ ♊ 29 19:53

Last Aspect Dy Hr Mn		☽ Ingress Dy Hr Mn	
1 7:37	☿ ⚹	♑	2 8:58
4 12:03	♃ △	♒	4 13:36
6 13:57	♃ □	♓	6 14:59
8 14:02	♃ ⚹	♈	8 14:36
10 13:59	☿ ⚹	♉	10 14:25
12 1:47	☉ ⚹	♊	12 16:16
14 10:11	☉ □	♋	14 21:27
16 23:07	☉ △	♌	17 6:13
18 11:33	♇ □	♍	19 17:39
22 2:09	♀ ☍	♎	22 6:24
23 9:08	♄ □	♏	24 19:10
27 3:09	☿ △	♐	27 6:54
28 2:50	♂ ☍	♑	29 16:25
30 19:28	♇ ⚹	♒	31 22:45

Last Aspect Dy Hr Mn		☽ Ingress Dy Hr Mn	
1 23:59	♇ □	♓	3 1:37
4 1:20	♇ △	♈	5 1:51
6 6:39	☿ ☌	♉	7 1:07
8 0:15	♇ ☍	♊	9 1:31
11 1:57	☿ ⚹	♋	11 4:58
13 3:31	♀ □	♌	13 12:31
15 20:58	♀ △	♍	15 23:39
17 22:22	♂ □	♎	18 12:31
20 14:34	♂ △	♏	21 1:13
22 17:54	☿ ☍	♐	23 12:38
25 18:15	♂ ☍	♑	25 22:15
28 1:57	☿ △	♒	28 5:33
29 8:45	♀ □	♓	30 10:03

☽ Phases & Eclipses (Dy Hr Mn)

7 18:19 ● 17♓10
7 18:07:44 ● P 0.827
14 10:11 ☽ 23♊49
22 9:58 ○ 1♎45
30 10:21 ☾ 9♑42

6 3:33 ● 16♈19
12 23:13 ☽ 23♋01
21 3:13 ○ 1♏00
28 20:46 ☾ 8♒32

Astro Data

1 March 1989
Julian Day # 32567
SVP 5♓24'32"
GC 26♐41.3 ⚳ 8♓28.7
Eris 16♈17.5 ✱ 0♍19.4R
⚷ 1♋19.0R ⚶ 23♐24.8
☽ Mean ☊ 4♓38.2

1 April 1989
Julian Day # 32598
SVP 5♓24'28"
GC 26♐41.3 ⚳ 18♓42.4
Eris 16♈36.7 ✱ 25♌30.3R
⚷ 1♋46.0 ⚶ 4♑16.0
☽ Mean ☊ 2♓59.7

LONGITUDE — May 1989

Day	Sid.Time	☉	0 hr ☽	Noon ☽	True ☊	☿	♀	♂	⚳	♃	♄	♅	♆	♇
1 M	2 37 35	11♉05 04	8♓15 19	15♓27 16	2♓24.2	1♊41.0	17♉57.9	1♋25.6	9♉14.4	9♊39.6	13♑52.1	5♑07.8	12♑18.1	13♏52.7
2 Tu	2 41 31	12 03 17	22 44 15	0♈05 51	2R 21.7	2 34.9	19 11.9	2 02.7	9 38.7	9 52.7	13R 51.2	5R 06.7	12R 17.5	13R 51.0
3 W	2 45 28	13 01 29	7♈31 25	15 00 10	2 16.6	3 23.7	20 25.9	2 39.8	10 03.0	10 05.9	13 50.3	5 05.5	12 16.9	13 49.3
4 Th	2 49 24	13 59 40	22 31 08	0♉03 12	2 08.9	4 07.5	21 39.8	3 16.9	10 27.3	10 19.1	13 49.2	5 04.3	12 16.3	13 47.6
5 F	2 53 21	14 57 49	7♉35 10	15 05 47	1 59.1	4 46.1	22 53.8	3 54.0	10 51.6	10 32.3	13 48.0	5 03.1	12 15.6	13 45.9
6 Sa	2 57 18	15 55 57	22 33 50	29 58 08	1 48.4	5 19.6	24 07.7	4 31.1	11 15.9	10 45.6	13 46.8	5 01.8	12 15.0	13 44.3
7 Su	3 01 14	16 54 03	7♊17 38	14♊31 27	1 37.9	5 47.8	25 21.6	5 08.3	11 40.2	10 59.0	13 45.4	5 00.5	12 14.2	13 42.6
8 M	3 05 11	17 52 07	21 38 53	28 39 27	1 28.9	6 10.9	26 35.5	5 45.4	12 04.4	11 12.3	13 44.0	4 59.1	12 13.5	13 40.9
9 Tu	3 09 07	18 50 09	5♋32 51	12♋19 01	1 22.1	6 28.7	27 49.3	6 22.6	12 28.7	11 25.8	13 42.4	4 57.7	12 12.7	13 39.2
10 W	3 13 04	19 48 10	18 58 01	25 30 08	1 17.8	6 41.4	29 03.2	6 59.7	12 53.0	11 39.2	13 40.8	4 56.3	12 11.9	13 37.5
11 Th	3 17 00	20 46 08	1♌55 43	8♌15 17	1 15.7	6R 48.9	0♊17.0	7 36.9	13 17.3	11 52.7	13 39.1	4 54.8	12 11.1	13 35.9
12 F	3 20 57	21 44 05	14 29 23	20 38 38	1 15.2	6 51.3	1 30.8	8 14.0	13 41.5	12 06.2	13 37.3	4 53.3	12 10.2	13 34.2
13 Sa	3 24 53	22 41 59	26 43 43	2♍45 18	1 15.3	6 48.9	2 44.6	8 51.2	14 05.8	12 19.7	13 35.4	4 51.7	12 09.3	13 32.5
14 Su	3 28 50	23 39 52	8♍44 04	14 40 41	1 14.7	6 41.7	3 58.4	9 28.3	14 30.0	12 33.3	13 33.4	4 50.1	12 08.4	13 30.9
15 M	3 32 47	24 37 44	20 35 48	26 30 02	1 12.6	6 29.9	5 12.1	10 05.5	14 54.2	12 46.9	13 31.3	4 48.4	12 07.5	13 29.2
16 Tu	3 36 43	25 35 33	2♎23 58	8♎18 09	1 08.1	6 13.9	6 25.9	10 42.6	15 18.4	13 00.5	13 29.2	4 46.8	12 06.5	13 27.6
17 W	3 40 40	26 33 21	14 13 04	20 09 08	1 00.9	5 54.0	7 39.6	11 19.8	15 42.7	13 14.1	13 26.9	4 45.1	12 05.5	13 25.9
18 Th	3 44 36	27 31 07	26 06 46	2♏06 16	0 51.0	5 30.5	8 53.3	11 57.0	16 06.9	13 27.8	13 24.6	4 43.3	12 04.5	13 24.3
19 F	3 48 33	28 28 52	8♏07 56	14 11 57	0 39.0	5 03.9	10 07.0	12 34.1	16 31.0	13 41.5	13 22.2	4 41.5	12 03.5	13 22.7
20 Sa	3 52 29	29 26 36	20 18 29	26 27 40	0 25.7	4 34.6	11 20.6	13 11.3	16 55.2	13 55.2	13 19.7	4 39.7	12 02.4	13 21.1
21 Su	3 56 26	0♊24 18	2♐39 35	8♐54 15	0 12.3	4 03.2	12 34.3	13 48.5	17 19.4	14 08.9	13 17.1	4 37.9	12 01.3	13 19.5
22 M	4 00 22	1 21 59	15 11 42	21 31 56	29♒60.0	3 30.3	13 47.9	14 25.6	17 43.6	14 22.7	13 14.5	4 36.0	12 00.2	13 17.9
23 Tu	4 04 19	2 19 39	27 54 57	4♑20 46	29 49.6	2 56.4	15 01.5	15 02.8	18 07.7	14 36.4	13 11.8	4 34.1	11 59.1	13 16.3
24 W	4 08 16	3 17 17	10♑49 24	17 20 52	29 42.0	2 22.1	16 15.1	15 40.0	18 31.8	14 50.2	13 09.0	4 32.1	11 57.9	13 14.7
25 Th	4 12 12	4 14 55	23 55 16	0♒32 39	29 37.2	1 48.0	17 28.7	16 17.2	18 55.9	15 04.0	13 06.1	4 30.2	11 56.8	13 13.2
26 F	4 16 09	5 12 31	7♒13 10	13 56 56	29 35.0	1 14.7	18 42.3	16 54.4	19 20.1	15 17.9	13 03.1	4 28.2	11 55.6	13 11.6
27 Sa	4 20 05	6 10 07	20 44 05	27 34 47	29 34.4	0 42.8	19 55.8	17 31.6	19 44.1	15 31.7	13 00.1	4 26.1	11 54.4	13 10.1
28 Su	4 24 02	7 07 42	4♓29 09	11♓27 17	29 34.4	0 12.8	21 09.4	18 08.8	20 08.2	15 45.5	12 57.0	4 24.1	11 53.1	13 08.6
29 M	4 27 58	8 05 15	18 29 12	25 34 53	29 33.7	29♉45.2	22 22.9	18 46.0	20 32.3	15 59.4	12 53.9	4 22.0	11 51.9	13 07.1
30 Tu	4 31 55	9 02 48	2♈44 11	9♈56 50	29 31.0	29 20.5	23 36.4	19 23.2	20 56.3	16 13.3	12 50.6	4 19.9	11 50.6	13 05.6
31 W	4 35 51	10 00 21	17 12 29	24 30 36	29 25.9	28 58.9	24 49.9	20 00.4	21 20.3	16 27.2	12 47.3	4 17.8	11 49.3	13 04.2

LONGITUDE — June 1989

Day	Sid.Time	☉	0 hr ☽	Noon ☽	True ☊	☿	♀	♂	⚳	♃	♄	♅	♆	♇
1 Th	4 39 48	10♊57 52	1♉50 31	9♉11 30	29♒18.1	28♉41.0	26♊03.4	20♋37.6	21♉44.3	16♊41.1	12♑44.0	4♑15.6	11♑48.0	13♏02.7
2 F	4 43 45	11 55 23	16 32 38	23 52 59	29R 08.3	28R 26.8	27 16.9	21 14.8	22 08.3	16 55.0	12R 40.5	4R 13.4	11R 46.6	13R 01.3
3 Sa	4 47 41	12 52 52	1♊11 35	8♊27 28	28 57.3	28 16.8	28 30.4	21 52.1	22 32.3	17 08.9	12 37.0	4 11.2	11 45.3	12 59.9
4 Su	4 51 38	13 50 21	15 39 42	22 47 30	28 46.5	28D 10.9	29 43.8	22 29.3	22 56.2	17 22.8	12 33.5	4 09.0	11 43.9	12 58.5
5 M	4 55 34	14 47 49	29 50 08	6♋47 05	28 37.0	28 09.4	0♋57.3	23 06.6	23 20.1	17 36.7	12 29.9	4 06.8	11 42.5	12 57.1
6 Tu	4 59 31	15 45 16	13♋37 56	20 22 29	28 29.7	28 12.4	2 10.7	23 43.8	23 44.0	17 50.6	12 26.2	4 04.5	11 41.1	12 55.8
7 W	5 03 27	16 42 42	27 00 40	3♌32 35	28 24.9	28 19.8	3 24.1	24 21.1	24 07.9	18 04.5	12 22.5	4 02.2	11 39.7	12 54.4
8 Th	5 07 24	17 40 07	9♌58 28	16 18 38	28D 22.5	28 31.7	4 37.5	24 58.4	24 31.7	18 18.4	12 18.7	3 59.9	11 38.3	12 53.1
9 F	5 11 21	18 37 30	22 33 34	28 43 46	28 21.9	28 48.2	5 50.8	25 35.6	24 55.5	18 32.4	12 14.9	3 57.6	11 36.8	12 51.8
10 Sa	5 15 17	19 34 52	4♍49 50	10♍52 22	28R 22.2	29 09.1	7 04.2	26 12.9	25 19.3	18 46.3	12 11.0	3 55.3	11 35.4	12 50.6
11 Su	5 19 14	20 32 14	16 52 02	22 49 31	28 22.4	29 34.4	8 17.5	26 50.2	25 43.0	19 00.2	12 07.1	3 52.9	11 33.9	12 49.3
12 M	5 23 10	21 29 34	28 45 29	4♎40 34	28 21.5	0♊04.0	9 30.8	27 27.5	26 06.7	19 14.1	12 03.1	3 50.6	11 32.4	12 48.1
13 Tu	5 27 07	22 26 54	10♎35 27	16 30 43	28 18.7	0 38.0	10 44.1	28 04.7	26 30.4	19 28.0	11 59.1	3 48.2	11 30.9	12 46.9
14 W	5 31 03	23 24 12	22 26 58	28 24 45	28 13.6	1 16.1	11 57.3	28 42.0	26 54.1	19 41.9	11 55.0	3 45.8	11 29.4	12 45.7
15 Th	5 35 00	24 21 30	4♏24 31	10♏26 44	28 06.2	1 58.4	13 10.6	29 19.3	27 17.7	19 55.7	11 51.0	3 43.4	11 27.8	12 44.6
16 F	5 38 56	25 18 47	16 31 45	22 39 53	27 56.9	2 44.8	14 23.8	29 56.6	27 41.3	20 09.6	11 46.8	3 41.0	11 26.3	12 43.4
17 Sa	5 42 53	26 16 03	28 51 22	5♐06 22	27 46.4	3 35.2	15 37.0	0♌33.9	28 04.9	20 23.5	11 42.7	3 38.6	11 24.8	12 42.3
18 Su	5 46 50	27 13 19	11♐25 00	17 47 18	27 35.8	4 29.4	16 50.2	1 11.2	28 28.4	20 37.3	11 38.5	3 36.2	11 23.2	12 41.3
19 M	5 50 46	28 10 34	24 13 13	0♑42 42	27 25.9	5 27.6	18 03.4	1 48.5	28 51.9	20 51.2	11 34.3	3 33.8	11 21.7	12 40.2
20 Tu	5 54 43	29 07 49	7♑15 38	13 51 50	27 17.8	6 29.5	19 16.6	2 25.9	29 15.3	21 05.0	11 30.0	3 31.4	11 20.1	12 39.2
21 W	5 58 39	0♋05 03	20 31 10	27 13 26	27 11.9	7 35.1	20 29.7	3 03.2	29 38.8	21 18.8	11 25.7	3 28.9	11 18.5	12 38.2
22 Th	6 02 36	1 02 17	3♒58 28	10♒46 05	27 08.6	8 44.4	21 42.8	3 40.5	0♊02.2	21 32.6	11 21.4	3 26.5	11 16.9	12 37.2
23 F	6 06 32	1 59 30	17 36 07	24 28 28	27D 07.4	9 57.3	22 55.9	4 17.9	0 25.5	21 46.4	11 17.1	3 24.1	11 15.3	12 36.3
24 Sa	6 10 29	2 56 44	1♓23 00	8♓19 38	27 07.7	11 13.8	24 09.0	4 55.2	0 48.8	22 00.1	11 12.7	3 21.6	11 13.7	12 35.3
25 Su	6 14 25	3 53 57	15 18 16	22 18 50	27R 08.6	12 33.8	25 22.0	5 32.6	1 12.1	22 13.9	11 08.4	3 19.2	11 12.1	12 34.4
26 M	6 18 22	4 51 11	29 21 13	6♈25 19	27 09.0	13 57.4	26 35.1	6 09.9	1 35.3	22 27.6	11 04.0	3 16.7	11 10.5	12 33.6
27 Tu	6 22 19	5 48 24	13♈30 58	20 37 58	27 08.1	15 24.3	27 48.1	6 47.3	1 58.5	22 41.3	10 59.6	3 14.3	11 08.9	12 32.7
28 W	6 26 15	6 45 38	27 46 02	4♉54 52	27 05.2	16 54.7	29 01.1	7 24.7	2 21.7	22 55.0	10 55.2	3 11.9	11 07.3	12 31.9
29 Th	6 30 12	7 42 51	12♉04 01	19 13 04	27 00.3	18 28.5	0♌14.1	8 02.1	2 44.8	23 08.6	10 50.7	3 09.4	11 05.7	12 31.2
30 F	6 34 08	8 40 05	26 21 27	3♊28 36	26 53.8	20 05.6	1 27.1	8 39.5	3 07.9	23 22.3	10 46.3	3 07.0	11 04.1	12 30.4

Astro Data

	Dy Hr Mn
☽0N	2 4:23
♄✱♇	2 5:26
☿R	12 11:52
♃⚻♆	12 18:45
☽0S	15 9:27
♃⚻♇	18 6:30
♃⚻♄	18 7:13
♄✱♇	18 21:50
☽0N	29 11:00
☿D	5 8:06
☽0S	11 15:56
♄☌♆	24 3:11
☽0N	25 15:48

Planet Ingress

		Dy Hr Mn
♀	♊	11 6:28
☉	♊	21 1:54
☊	♒R	22 11:56
☿	♉R	28 22:53
♀	♋	4 17:17
☿	♊	12 8:56
♂	♌	16 14:10
☉	♋	21 9:53
⚳	♊	22 9:47
♀	♌	29 7:21

Last Aspect / ☽ Ingress (May)

Last Aspect Dy Hr Mn		☽ Ingress	Dy Hr Mn
1 16:32	♀ ✱	♈	2 11:51
3 10:08	♄ □	♉	4 11:55
6 1:40	♀ ☌	♊	6 12:03
7 6:01	♃ ☌	♋	8 14:19
10 19:18	♀ ✱	♌	10 20:23
12 14:20	☉ □	♍	13 6:30
15 7:51	☉ △	♎	15 19:07
16 22:29	♄ □	♏	18 7:48
20 18:16	☉ ☍	♐	20 18:52
21 22:12	♃ ☍	♑	23 3:54
24 8:46	♂ ☍	♒	25 11:01
26 21:15	♀ △	♓	27 16:13
29 18:48	☿ ✱	♈	29 19:25
31 12:35	♀ ✱	♉	31 20:59

Last Aspect / ☽ Ingress (June)

Last Aspect Dy Hr Mn		☽ Ingress	Dy Hr Mn
2 19:23	☿ ☌	♊	2 22:02
4 2:44	♃ ☌	♋	5 0:17
7 2:18	☿ ✱	♌	7 5:28
9 12:09	☿ □	♍	9 14:29
12 2:14	☿ △	♎	12 2:31
14 12:37	♂ □	♏	14 15:11
15 18:00	♀ △	♐	17 2:12
19 6:57	☉ ☍	♑	19 10:41
20 22:45	♀ ☍	♒	21 16:57
23 7:13	♃ △	♓	23 21:36
25 17:42	♀ △	♈	26 1:06
28 1:11	♀ □	♉	28 3:45
29 0:46	♇ ☍	♊	30 6:08

☽ Phases & Eclipses

Dy Hr Mn		
5 11:46	●	14♉57
12 14:20	☽	21♌50
20 18:16	○	29♏42
28 4:01	☾	6♓49
3 19:53	●	13♊12
11 6:59	☽	20♍20
19 6:57	○	27♐59
26 9:09	☾	4♈44

Astro Data

1 May 1989
Julian Day # 32628
SVP 5♓24'24"
GC 26♐41.4 ⚴ 28♓05.3
Eris 16♈56.3 ✱ 26♌46.7
⚷ 3♋23.3 ⚶ 10♑19.3
☽ Mean ☊ 1♓24.4

1 June 1989
Julian Day # 32659
SVP 5♓24'20"
GC 26♐41.5 ⚴ 6♈39.7
Eris 17♈12.6 ✱ 2♍45.7
⚷ 5♋56.8 ⚶ 9♑39.6R
☽ Mean ☊ 29♒45.9

July 1989 — LONGITUDE

Day	Sid.Time	☉	0 hr ☽	Noon ☽	True ☊	☿	♀	♂	⚳	♃	♄	♅	♆	♇
1 Sa	6 38 05	9♋37 19	10♊33 55	17♊36 48	26♒46.4	21♊46.0	2♌40.1	9♌16.9	3♊30.9	23♊35.9	10♑41.9	3♑04.6	11♑02.5	12♏29.7
2 Su	6 42 01	10 34 33	24 36 39	1♋32 56	26R39.0	23 29.5	3 53.0	9 54.3	3 53.9	23 49.5	10R37.5	3R02.2	11R00.8	12R29.0
3 M	6 45 58	11 31 47	8♋25 08	15 12 53	26 32.5	25 16.2	5 06.0	10 31.7	4 16.8	24 03.0	10 33.0	2 59.7	10 59.2	12 28.4
4 Tu	6 49 55	12 29 01	21 55 50	28 33 47	26 27.6	27 05.8	6 18.9	11 09.2	4 39.7	24 16.6	10 28.6	2 57.3	10 57.6	12 27.7
5 W	6 53 51	13 26 14	5♌06 39	11♌34 25	26 24.7	28 58.3	7 31.8	11 46.7	5 02.5	24 30.1	10 24.2	2 55.0	10 56.0	12 27.1
6 Th	6 57 48	14 23 28	17 57 12	24 15 13	26D23.6	0♋53.6	8 44.6	12 24.1	5 25.3	24 43.5	10 19.7	2 52.6	10 54.4	12 26.6
7 F	7 01 44	15 20 41	0♍28 45	6♍38 11	26 24.0	2 51.3	9 57.5	13 01.6	5 48.0	24 57.0	10 15.3	2 50.2	10 52.7	12 26.1
8 Sa	7 05 41	16 17 54	12 43 58	18 46 35	26 25.3	4 51.4	11 10.3	13 39.1	6 10.6	25 10.4	10 10.9	2 47.8	10 51.1	12 25.6
9 Su	7 09 37	17 15 07	24 46 35	0♎44 33	26 26.9	6 53.6	12 23.1	14 16.6	6 33.2	25 23.7	10 06.5	2 45.5	10 49.5	12 25.1
10 M	7 13 34	18 12 20	6♎41 04	12 36 48	26R27.9	8 57.6	13 35.8	14 54.1	6 55.8	25 37.0	10 02.2	2 43.2	10 47.9	12 24.6
11 Tu	7 17 30	19 09 33	18 32 20	24 28 19	26 27.9	11 03.2	14 48.6	15 31.6	7 18.3	25 50.3	9 57.8	2 40.9	10 46.3	12 24.2
12 W	7 21 27	20 06 46	0♏25 21	6♏24 01	26 26.5	13 10.1	16 01.3	16 09.1	7 40.7	26 03.6	9 53.5	2 38.6	10 44.7	12 23.9
13 Th	7 25 23	21 03 59	12 24 55	18 28 34	26 23.6	15 17.9	17 14.0	16 46.6	8 03.1	26 16.8	9 49.2	2 36.3	10 43.1	12 23.5
14 F	7 29 20	22 01 12	24 35 26	0♐45 58	26 19.4	17 26.4	18 26.6	17 24.1	8 25.4	26 29.9	9 44.9	2 34.0	10 41.5	12 23.2
15 Sa	7 33 17	22 58 25	7♐00 31	13 19 24	26 14.4	19 35.2	19 39.2	18 01.7	8 47.7	26 43.0	9 40.6	2 31.8	10 39.9	12 23.0
16 Su	7 37 13	23 55 38	19 42 48	26 10 52	26 09.1	21 44.1	20 51.8	18 39.2	9 09.9	26 56.1	9 36.4	2 29.6	10 38.4	12 22.7
17 M	7 41 10	24 52 52	2♑43 39	9♑21 06	26 04.2	23 52.8	22 04.4	19 16.8	9 32.0	27 09.1	9 32.2	2 27.4	10 36.8	12 22.5
18 Tu	7 45 06	25 50 06	16 03 06	22 49 26	26 00.2	26 01.1	23 17.0	19 54.4	9 54.1	27 22.1	9 28.0	2 25.2	10 35.3	12 22.4
19 W	7 49 03	26 47 20	29 39 51	6♒33 59	25 57.6	28 08.7	24 29.5	20 32.0	10 16.1	27 35.1	9 23.9	2 23.0	10 33.7	12 22.2
20 Th	7 52 59	27 44 35	13♒31 26	20 31 49	25D56.4	0♌15.4	25 42.0	21 09.6	10 38.0	27 48.0	9 19.8	2 20.9	10 32.2	12 22.1
21 F	7 56 56	28 41 50	27 34 39	4♓39 29	25 56.5	2 21.1	26 54.4	21 47.2	10 59.9	28 00.8	9 15.7	2 18.8	10 30.7	12 22.0
22 Sa	8 00 53	29 39 06	11♓45 53	18 53 24	25 57.6	4 25.5	28 06.8	22 24.8	11 21.7	28 13.6	9 11.7	2 16.7	10 29.1	12D22.0
23 Su	8 04 49	0♌36 23	26 01 38	3♈10 10	25 59.0	6 28.7	29 19.2	23 02.4	11 43.4	28 26.3	9 07.7	2 14.6	10 27.6	12 22.0
24 M	8 08 46	1 33 40	10♈18 40	17 26 46	26 00.2	8 30.5	0♍31.6	23 40.1	12 05.0	28 39.0	9 03.8	2 12.6	10 26.1	12 22.0
25 Tu	8 12 42	2 30 59	24 34 12	1♉40 39	26R00.7	10 30.7	1 43.9	24 17.8	12 26.6	28 51.6	8 59.9	2 10.6	10 24.7	12 22.1
26 W	8 16 39	3 28 19	8♉45 52	15 49 34	26 00.2	12 29.4	2 56.2	24 55.4	12 48.1	29 04.2	8 56.1	2 08.6	10 23.2	12 22.2
27 Th	8 20 35	4 25 39	22 51 30	29 51 27	25 58.8	14 26.6	4 08.5	25 33.1	13 09.5	29 16.7	8 52.3	2 06.7	10 21.7	12 22.3
28 F	8 24 32	5 23 01	6♊49 08	13♊44 20	25 56.6	16 22.1	5 20.8	26 10.9	13 30.9	29 29.2	8 48.5	2 04.8	10 20.3	12 22.5
29 Sa	8 28 28	6 20 24	20 36 49	27 26 20	25 53.9	18 16.0	6 33.0	26 48.6	13 52.2	29 41.6	8 44.9	2 02.9	10 18.9	12 22.7
30 Su	8 32 25	7 17 47	4♋12 41	10♋55 40	25 51.3	20 08.2	7 45.2	27 26.3	14 13.4	29 53.9	8 41.2	2 01.1	10 17.5	12 22.9
31 M	8 36 22	8 15 12	17 35 06	24 10 51	25 49.0	21 58.8	8 57.4	28 04.1	14 34.5	0♋06.2	8 37.7	1 59.2	10 16.1	12 23.2

August 1989 — LONGITUDE

Day	Sid.Time	☉	0 hr ☽	Noon ☽	True ☊	☿	♀	♂	⚳	♃	♄	♅	♆	♇
1 Tu	8 40 18	9♌12 37	0♌42 49	7♌10 55	25♒47.4	23♌47.8	10♍09.5	28♌41.9	14♊55.5	0♋18.4	8♑34.2	1♑57.5	10♑14.7	12♏23.5
2 W	8 44 15	10 10 04	13 35 10	19 55 34	25D46.7	25 35.1	11 21.6	29 19.7	15 16.4	0 30.6	8R30.7	1R55.7	10R13.4	12 23.8
3 Th	8 48 11	11 07 31	26 12 14	2♍25 17	25 46.7	27 20.7	12 33.7	29 57.5	15 37.2	0 42.6	8 27.3	1 54.0	10 12.0	12 24.2
4 F	8 52 08	12 04 59	8♍34 57	14 41 27	25 47.3	29 04.7	13 45.7	0♍35.3	15 58.0	0 54.6	8 24.0	1 52.3	10 10.7	12 24.6
5 Sa	8 56 04	13 02 27	20 45 07	26 46 17	25 48.4	0♍47.1	14 57.7	1 13.2	16 18.6	1 06.6	8 20.8	1 50.7	10 09.4	12 25.1
6 Su	9 00 01	13 59 57	2♎45 22	8♎42 48	25 49.5	2 27.9	16 09.7	1 51.0	16 39.2	1 18.4	8 17.6	1 49.0	10 08.1	12 25.5
7 M	9 03 57	14 57 27	14 39 03	20 34 38	25 50.6	4 07.1	17 21.6	2 28.9	16 59.6	1 30.2	8 14.5	1 47.5	10 06.8	12 26.0
8 Tu	9 07 54	15 54 58	26 30 06	2♏25 59	25 51.3	5 44.7	18 33.5	3 06.8	17 20.0	1 41.9	8 11.4	1 45.9	10 05.6	12 26.6
9 W	9 11 51	16 52 30	8♏22 53	14 21 22	25R51.6	7 20.7	19 45.3	3 44.7	17 40.2	1 53.6	8 08.4	1 44.5	10 04.4	12 27.2
10 Th	9 15 47	17 50 03	20 22 01	26 25 24	25 51.5	8 55.1	20 57.1	4 22.6	18 00.4	2 05.1	8 05.6	1 43.0	10 03.2	12 27.8
11 F	9 19 44	18 47 36	2♐32 05	8♐42 36	25 51.1	10 27.9	22 08.9	5 00.5	18 20.4	2 16.6	8 02.7	1 41.6	10 02.0	12 28.4
12 Sa	9 23 40	19 45 11	14 57 26	21 17 02	25 50.4	11 59.1	23 20.6	5 38.5	18 40.4	2 28.0	8 00.0	1 40.2	10 00.8	12 29.1
13 Su	9 27 37	20 42 47	27 41 46	4♑11 57	25 49.8	13 28.7	24 32.2	6 16.5	19 00.2	2 39.3	7 57.3	1 38.9	9 59.7	12 29.8
14 M	9 31 33	21 40 23	10♑47 48	17 29 25	25 49.3	14 56.7	25 43.9	6 54.4	19 19.9	2 50.6	7 54.7	1 37.6	9 58.6	12 30.6
15 Tu	9 35 30	22 38 01	24 16 50	1♒09 56	25 48.9	16 23.1	26 55.4	7 32.4	19 39.5	3 01.7	7 52.2	1 36.4	9 57.5	12 31.3
16 W	9 39 26	23 35 40	8♒08 27	15 12 04	25D48.7	17 47.8	28 07.0	8 10.5	19 59.0	3 12.8	7 49.8	1 35.2	9 56.4	12 32.2
17 Th	9 43 23	24 33 19	22 20 18	29 32 32	25 48.7	19 10.8	29 18.4	8 48.5	20 18.4	3 23.8	7 47.5	1 34.0	9 55.4	12 33.0
18 F	9 47 20	25 31 01	6♓48 08	14♓06 19	25R48.7	20 32.1	0♎29.9	9 26.5	20 37.7	3 34.6	7 45.2	1 32.9	9 54.4	12 33.9
19 Sa	9 51 16	26 28 43	21 26 18	28 47 16	25 48.7	21 51.7	1 41.2	10 04.6	20 56.8	3 45.4	7 43.0	1 31.8	9 53.4	12 34.8
20 Su	9 55 13	27 26 27	6♈08 22	13♈28 49	25 48.6	23 09.5	2 52.6	10 42.7	21 15.9	3 56.1	7 40.9	1 30.8	9 52.4	12 35.7
21 M	9 59 09	28 24 13	20 47 52	28 04 53	25 48.4	24 25.5	4 03.9	11 20.8	21 34.8	4 06.8	7 38.9	1 29.8	9 51.4	12 36.7
22 Tu	10 03 06	29 22 01	5♉19 14	12♉30 28	25 48.1	25 39.6	5 15.1	11 58.9	21 53.5	4 17.3	7 37.0	1 28.9	9 50.5	12 37.7
23 W	10 07 02	0♍19 50	19 38 10	26 42 03	25D48.0	26 51.7	6 26.3	12 37.1	22 12.2	4 27.7	7 35.2	1 28.0	9 49.6	12 38.7
24 Th	10 10 59	1 17 41	3♊41 54	10♊37 36	25 48.1	28 01.8	7 37.5	13 15.3	22 30.7	4 38.0	7 33.4	1 27.1	9 48.8	12 39.8
25 F	10 14 55	2 15 34	17 29 07	24 16 26	25 48.4	29 09.8	8 48.6	13 53.5	22 49.1	4 48.2	7 31.8	1 26.4	9 47.9	12 40.9
26 Sa	10 18 52	3 13 29	0♋59 38	7♋38 47	25 49.0	0♎15.6	9 59.6	14 31.7	23 07.3	4 58.4	7 30.2	1 25.6	9 47.1	12 42.0
27 Su	10 22 49	4 11 25	14 14 01	20 45 28	25 49.8	1 19.0	11 10.6	15 09.9	23 25.4	5 08.4	7 28.7	1 24.9	9 46.3	12 43.2
28 M	10 26 45	5 09 23	27 13 17	3♌37 37	25 50.5	2 20.1	12 21.6	15 48.2	23 43.4	5 18.3	7 27.4	1 24.3	9 45.6	12 44.4
29 Tu	10 30 42	6 07 23	9♌58 37	16 16 27	25R51.1	3 18.5	13 32.5	16 26.5	24 01.2	5 28.1	7 26.1	1 23.6	9 44.8	12 45.6
30 W	10 34 38	7 05 24	22 31 16	28 43 14	25 51.2	4 14.2	14 43.3	17 04.8	24 18.9	5 37.8	7 24.9	1 23.1	9 44.1	12 46.9
31 Th	10 38 35	8 03 27	4♍52 31	10♍59 17	25 50.8	5 07.0	15 54.1	17 43.2	24 36.4	5 47.4	7 23.8	1 22.6	9 43.5	12 48.2

Astro Data

	Dy Hr Mn
☽0S	8 23:11
♃⚼♇	18 12:24
☽0N	22 21:01
♇ D	23 3:55
☽0S	5 6:51
♃☍♅	8 19:18
☽0N	19 4:29
♀0S	19 11:05
☿0S	23 12:50

Planet Ingress

		Dy Hr Mn
☿	♋	6 0:55
☿	♌	20 9:04
☉	♌	22 20:45
♀	♍	24 1:31
♃	♋	30 23:50
♂	♍	3 13:35
☿	♍	5 0:54
♀	♎	18 1:58
☉	♍	23 3:46
☿	♎	26 6:14

Last Aspect / ☽ Ingress (July)

Last Aspect Dy Hr Mn			☽ Ingress	Dy Hr Mn
1 22:26	♃	☌	♋	2 9:19
3 7:09	♇	△	♌	4 14:37
6 12:55	♃	⚹	♍	6 23:04
9 1:02	♃	□	♎	9 10:30
11 14:49	♃	△	♏	11 23:09
13 17:32	☉	△	♐	14 10:31
16 13:25	♃	☍	♑	16 19:01
18 18:39	☿	☍	♒	19 0:35
21 0:34	♃	△	♓	21 4:07
23 3:56	♃	□	♈	23 6:41
25 7:10	♃	⚹	♉	25 9:10
27 4:16	♂	□	♊	27 12:15
29 16:03	♃	☌	♋	29 16:32
30 14:37	♇	△	♌	31 22:41

Last Aspect / ☽ Ingress (August)

Last Aspect Dy Hr Mn			☽ Ingress	Dy Hr Mn
3 6:59	♂	☌	♍	3 7:19
4 9:58	♀	☌	♎	5 18:28
6 23:37	☉	⚹	♏	8 7:05
9 23:58	♀	⚹	♐	10 19:02
12 16:16	♀	□	♑	13 4:16
15 3:55	♀	△	♒	15 9:59
17 3:07	☉	☍	♓	17 12:46
18 23:35	☿	☍	♈	19 13:59
21 12:34	☉	△	♉	21 15:10
23 12:18	☿	△	♊	23 17:39
25 21:30	☿	□	♋	25 22:13
27 1:11	♂	⚹	♌	28 5:12
29 6:14	♀	⚹	♍	30 14:29

☽ Phases & Eclipses

Dy Hr Mn		
3 4:59	●	11♋15
11 0:19	☽	18♎42
18 17:42	○	26♑04
25 13:31	☾	2♉35
1 16:06	●	9♌22
9 17:29	☽	17♏06
17 3:07	○	24♒12
17 3:08	☍	T 1.598
23 18:40	☾	0♊36
31 5:45	●	7♍48
31 5:30:50	☌	P 0.634

Astro Data

1 July 1989
Julian Day # 32689
SVP 5♓24'14"
GC 26♐41.6 ⚴ 13♈02.5
Eris 17♈21.0 ⚵ 11♍11.9
⚷ 8♋52.0 ⚶ 3♑14.8R
☽ Mean ☊ 28♒10.6

1 August 1989
Julian Day # 32720
SVP 5♓24'08"
GC 26♐41.6 ⚴ 16♈16.4
Eris 17♈19.9R ⚵ 21♍24.4
⚷ 11♋53.6 ⚶ 28♐20.6R
☽ Mean ☊ 26♒32.1

LONGITUDE — September 1989

Day	Sid.Time	☉	0 hr ☽	Noon ☽	True ☊	☿	♀	♂	⚳	♃	♄	♅	♆	♇
1 F	10 42 31	9♍01 32	17♍03 43	23♍06 02	25♒49.6	5♎56.8	17♎04.9	18♍21.5	24♊53.7	5♋56.8	7♑22.8	1♑22.1	9♑42.8	12♏49.5
2 Sa	10 46 28	9 59 38	29 06 26	5♎05 11	25R47.9	6 43.3	18 15.6	18 59.9	25 10.9	6 06.2	7R21.9	1R21.7	9R42.2	12 50.8
3 Su	10 50 24	10 57 46	11♎02 33	16 58 49	25 45.7	7 26.3	19 26.2	19 38.3	25 27.9	6 15.4	7 21.1	1 21.3	9 41.6	12 52.2
4 M	10 54 21	11 55 55	22 54 20	28 49 28	25 43.2	8 05.6	20 36.7	20 16.7	25 44.8	6 24.5	7 20.3	1 21.0	9 41.1	12 53.6
5 Tu	10 58 18	12 54 06	4♏44 37	10♏40 12	25 40.9	8 40.9	21 47.2	20 55.1	26 01.5	6 33.5	7 19.7	1 20.8	9 40.6	12 55.0
6 W	11 02 14	13 52 18	16 36 42	22 34 35	25 38.9	9 12.0	22 57.7	21 33.6	26 18.0	6 42.4	7 19.2	1 20.6	9 40.1	12 56.5
7 Th	11 06 11	14 50 32	28 34 24	4♐36 40	25D37.7	9 38.5	24 08.1	22 12.1	26 34.3	6 51.1	7 18.8	1 20.4	9 39.6	12 58.0
8 F	11 10 07	15 48 48	10♐41 57	16 50 48	25 37.4	10 00.3	25 18.4	22 50.6	26 50.5	6 59.7	7 18.5	1 20.3	9 39.2	12 59.5
9 Sa	11 14 04	16 47 05	23 03 46	29 21 24	25 37.9	10 16.8	26 28.6	23 29.1	27 06.5	7 08.2	7 18.2	1D20.3	9 38.8	13 01.1
10 Su	11 18 00	17 45 23	5♑44 13	12♑12 41	25 39.0	10 27.9	27 38.8	24 07.7	27 22.3	7 16.6	7D18.1	1 20.3	9 38.4	13 02.6
11 M	11 21 57	18 43 43	18 47 13	25 28 07	25 40.5	10R33.2	28 48.9	24 46.3	27 38.0	7 24.8	7 18.1	1 20.3	9 38.1	13 04.2
12 Tu	11 25 53	19 42 05	2♒15 39	9♒09 54	25 41.9	10 32.4	29 58.9	25 24.9	27 53.4	7 32.9	7 18.1	1 20.4	9 37.8	13 05.9
13 W	11 29 50	20 40 28	16 10 50	23 18 15	25R42.5	10 25.2	1♏08.9	26 03.5	28 08.6	7 40.9	7 18.3	1 20.6	9 37.5	13 07.5
14 Th	11 33 47	21 38 53	0♓31 48	7♓50 55	25 42.1	10 11.4	2 18.7	26 42.2	28 23.7	7 48.8	7 18.6	1 20.7	9 37.3	13 09.2
15 F	11 37 43	22 37 20	15 14 53	22 42 50	25 40.4	9 50.8	3 28.5	27 20.8	28 38.5	7 56.4	7 18.9	1 21.0	9 37.1	13 10.9
16 Sa	11 41 40	23 35 48	0♈13 44	7♈46 27	25 37.5	9 23.3	4 38.2	27 59.5	28 53.2	8 04.0	7 19.4	1 21.3	9 36.9	13 12.6
17 Su	11 45 36	24 34 18	15 19 47	22 52 33	25 33.6	8 49.0	5 47.8	28 38.2	29 07.6	8 11.4	7 19.9	1 21.6	9 36.8	13 14.4
18 M	11 49 33	25 32 51	0♉23 35	7♉51 47	25 29.5	8 08.1	6 57.4	29 17.0	29 21.9	8 18.7	7 20.6	1 22.1	9 36.6	13 16.1
19 Tu	11 53 29	26 31 26	15 16 11	22 36 00	25 25.7	7 20.8	8 06.8	29 55.8	29 35.9	8 25.8	7 21.4	1 22.5	9 36.6	13 17.9
20 W	11 57 26	27 30 03	29 50 35	6♊59 28	25 22.9	6 27.8	9 16.2	0♎34.6	29 49.7	8 32.8	7 22.2	1 23.0	9D36.5	13 19.8
21 Th	12 01 22	28 28 42	14♊02 22	20 59 11	25D21.3	5 29.9	10 25.5	1 13.4	0♋03.3	8 39.7	7 23.2	1 23.6	9 36.5	13 21.6
22 F	12 05 19	29 27 24	27 49 55	4♋34 42	25 21.2	4 28.0	11 34.7	1 52.3	0 16.6	8 46.4	7 24.2	1 24.2	9 36.5	13 23.5
23 Sa	12 09 16	0♎26 07	11♋13 48	17 47 31	25 22.2	3 23.5	12 43.9	2 31.1	0 29.8	8 52.9	7 25.4	1 24.8	9 36.6	13 25.4
24 Su	12 13 12	1 24 53	24 16 13	0♌40 17	25 23.8	2 17.7	13 52.9	3 10.1	0 42.7	8 59.3	7 26.6	1 25.6	9 36.7	13 27.3
25 M	12 17 09	2 23 42	7♌00 10	13 16 15	25R25.2	1 12.3	15 01.9	3 49.0	0 55.3	9 05.5	7 27.9	1 26.3	9 36.8	13 29.2
26 Tu	12 21 05	3 22 32	19 28 56	25 38 37	25 25.8	0 08.9	16 10.7	4 28.0	1 07.7	9 11.6	7 29.4	1 27.1	9 37.0	13 31.2
27 W	12 25 02	4 21 24	1♍45 40	7♍50 24	25 25.0	29♍09.1	17 19.5	5 07.0	1 19.9	9 17.5	7 30.9	1 28.0	9 37.1	13 33.2
28 Th	12 28 58	5 20 19	13 53 09	19 54 09	25 22.3	28 14.7	18 28.1	5 46.0	1 31.8	9 23.2	7 32.5	1 28.9	9 37.4	13 35.2
29 F	12 32 55	6 19 15	25 53 42	1♎52 00	25 17.5	27 27.1	19 36.7	6 25.1	1 43.4	9 28.8	7 34.3	1 29.9	9 37.6	13 37.2
30 Sa	12 36 51	7 18 14	7♎49 18	13 45 46	25 10.9	26 47.4	20 45.2	7 04.1	1 54.8	9 34.2	7 36.1	1 30.9	9 37.9	13 39.2

LONGITUDE — October 1989

Day	Sid.Time	☉	0 hr ☽	Noon ☽	True ☊	☿	♀	♂	⚳	♃	♄	♅	♆	♇
1 Su	12 40 48	8♎17 15	19♎41 39	25♎37 07	25♒03.0	26♍16.9	21♏53.5	7♎43.3	2♋05.9	9♋39.5	7♑38.0	1♑31.9	9♑38.2	13♏41.3
2 M	12 44 44	9 16 17	1♏32 24	7♏27 45	24R54.3	25R56.2	23 01.8	8 22.4	2 16.7	9 44.5	7 40.0	1 33.1	9 38.6	13 43.3
3 Tu	12 48 41	10 15 22	13 23 23	19 19 38	24 45.8	25D45.7	24 09.9	9 01.6	2 27.3	9 49.4	7 42.1	1 34.2	9 39.0	13 45.4
4 W	12 52 38	11 14 29	25 16 47	1♐15 11	24 38.3	25 45.8	25 17.9	9 40.8	2 37.6	9 54.2	7 44.3	1 35.4	9 39.4	13 47.6
5 Th	12 56 34	12 13 37	7♐15 14	13 17 21	24 32.5	25 56.4	26 25.8	10 20.0	2 47.6	9 58.7	7 46.6	1 36.7	9 39.8	13 49.7
6 F	13 00 31	13 12 47	19 22 00	25 29 40	24 28.6	26 17.2	27 33.6	10 59.3	2 57.3	10 03.1	7 49.0	1 38.0	9 40.3	13 51.8
7 Sa	13 04 27	14 11 59	1♑40 52	7♑56 08	24D26.8	26 47.8	28 41.3	11 38.5	3 06.7	10 07.3	7 51.5	1 39.4	9 40.9	13 54.0
8 Su	13 08 24	15 11 13	14 16 02	20 41 05	24 26.8	27 27.7	29 48.8	12 17.8	3 15.9	10 11.4	7 54.1	1 40.8	9 41.4	13 56.2
9 M	13 12 20	16 10 29	27 11 49	3♒48 42	24 27.7	28 16.2	0♐56.2	12 57.2	3 24.7	10 15.2	7 56.8	1 42.3	9 42.0	13 58.4
10 Tu	13 16 17	17 09 46	10♒32 10	17 22 31	24R28.6	29 12.5	2 03.4	13 36.5	3 33.2	10 18.9	7 59.5	1 43.8	9 42.6	14 00.6
11 W	13 20 13	18 09 05	24 19 59	1♓24 37	24 28.6	0♎16.0	3 10.5	14 15.9	3 41.4	10 22.4	8 02.4	1 45.3	9 43.3	14 02.8
12 Th	13 24 10	19 08 25	8♓36 17	15 54 42	24 26.8	1 25.8	4 17.4	14 55.4	3 49.3	10 25.7	8 05.3	1 46.9	9 43.9	14 05.0
13 F	13 28 07	20 07 48	23 19 18	0♈49 21	24 22.6	2 41.2	5 24.2	15 34.8	3 56.9	10 28.8	8 08.3	1 48.6	9 44.7	14 07.3
14 Sa	13 32 03	21 07 12	8♈23 50	16 01 37	24 16.1	4 01.4	6 30.8	16 14.3	4 04.2	10 31.7	8 11.4	1 50.3	9 45.4	14 09.6
15 Su	13 36 00	22 06 39	23 41 21	1♉21 38	24 07.8	5 25.8	7 37.2	16 53.8	4 11.1	10 34.5	8 14.6	1 52.0	9 46.2	14 11.8
16 M	13 39 56	23 06 07	9♉00 58	16 37 58	23 58.8	6 53.7	8 43.5	17 33.3	4 17.7	10 37.0	8 17.9	1 53.8	9 47.0	14 14.1
17 Tu	13 43 53	24 05 38	24 11 18	1♊39 47	23 50.1	8 24.6	9 49.6	18 12.9	4 24.0	10 39.4	8 21.3	1 55.6	9 47.8	14 16.4
18 W	13 47 49	25 05 11	9♊02 28	16 18 37	23 42.9	9 58.0	10 55.5	18 52.5	4 29.9	10 41.6	8 24.7	1 57.5	9 48.7	14 18.7
19 Th	13 51 46	26 04 47	23 27 44	0♋29 31	23 37.9	11 33.3	12 01.2	19 32.2	4 35.5	10 43.6	8 28.3	1 59.4	9 49.6	14 21.1
20 F	13 55 42	27 04 25	7♋23 55	14 11 02	23 35.1	13 10.3	13 06.8	20 11.8	4 40.7	10 45.4	8 31.9	2 01.4	9 50.6	14 23.4
21 Sa	13 59 39	28 04 05	20 51 09	27 24 40	23D34.3	14 48.5	14 12.1	20 51.5	4 45.6	10 47.0	8 35.6	2 03.4	9 51.5	14 25.8
22 Su	14 03 36	29 03 47	3♌52 02	10♌13 49	23 34.6	16 27.7	15 17.3	21 31.3	4 50.1	10 48.4	8 39.4	2 05.5	9 52.5	14 28.1
23 M	14 07 32	0♏03 31	16 30 34	22 42 53	23R35.1	18 07.6	16 22.2	22 11.1	4 54.2	10 49.6	8 43.3	2 07.6	9 53.6	14 30.5
24 Tu	14 11 29	1 03 18	28 51 22	4♍56 35	23 34.4	19 47.9	17 27.0	22 50.9	4 58.0	10 50.6	8 47.2	2 09.7	9 54.6	14 32.8
25 W	14 15 25	2 03 07	10♍59 05	16 59 22	23 31.8	21 28.6	18 31.5	23 30.7	5 01.4	10 51.4	8 51.3	2 11.9	9 55.7	14 35.2
26 Th	14 19 22	3 02 58	22 57 54	28 55 07	23 26.5	23 09.4	19 35.8	24 10.6	5 04.4	10 52.0	8 55.4	2 14.1	9 56.9	14 37.6
27 F	14 23 18	4 02 51	4♎51 23	10♎47 04	23 18.2	24 50.3	20 39.9	24 50.5	5 07.1	10 52.4	8 59.6	2 16.4	9 58.0	14 40.0
28 Sa	14 27 15	5 02 46	16 42 25	22 37 42	23 07.3	26 31.1	21 43.7	25 30.4	5 09.3	10R52.6	9 03.8	2 18.7	9 59.2	14 42.4
29 Su	14 31 11	6 02 43	28 33 09	4♏28 56	22 54.3	28 11.7	22 47.3	26 10.4	5 11.2	10 52.6	9 08.2	2 21.0	10 00.4	14 44.8
30 M	14 35 08	7 02 42	10♏25 14	16 22 13	22 40.2	29 52.1	23 50.6	26 50.4	5 12.7	10 52.4	9 12.6	2 23.4	10 01.6	14 47.2
31 Tu	14 39 05	8 02 43	22 20 02	28 18 50	22 26.2	1♏32.3	24 53.7	27 30.4	5 13.7	10 52.0	9 17.1	2 25.8	10 02.9	14 49.6

Astro Data (Dy Hr Mn)
☽0S 1 14:12
♅D 10 1:14
♃☍♆ 10 16:19
♄D 11 7:10
☿R 11 20:58
☽0N 15 14:24
♆D 21 6:53
♂0S 22 13:31
☉0S 23 1:20
☽0S 28 20:39
☿0N 29 18:25
♃☍♆ 1 5:52
☿D 3 23:50
☽0N 13 1:19
☿0S 14 20:26

Planet Ingress (Dy Hr Mn)
♀ ♏ 12 12:22
♂ ♎ 19 14:38
⚳ ♋ 21 6:11
☉ ♎ 23 1:20
☿ ♍R 26 15:28

♀ ♐ 8 16:00
☿ ♎ 11 6:11
☉ ♏ 23 10:35
☿ ♏ 30 13:53

☽0S26 2:12
♃ R29 0:03

Last Aspect / ☽ Ingress (September)

Last Aspect Dy Hr Mn		☽ Ingress Dy Hr Mn
1 2:03	♂ ☌	♎ 2 1:47
3 17:31	♀ ☌	♏ 4 14:23
6 9:51	♂ ✶	♐ 7 2:51
9 5:58	♀ ✶	♑ 9 13:13
11 18:30	♀ □	♒ 11 20:02
12 18:46	♇ □	♓ 13 23:08
15 19:44	♂ ☍	♈ 15 23:38
16 14:55	♆ □	♉ 17 23:22
19 18:57	☉ △	♊ 20 0:16
22 2:10	☉ □	♋ 22 3:50
23 3:58	♇ △	♌ 24 10:44
25 15:44	♀ □	♍ 26 20:32
29 3:39	☿ ☌	♎ 29 8:15

Last Aspect / ☽ Ingress (October)

Last Aspect Dy Hr Mn		☽ Ingress Dy Hr Mn
30 3:39	♆ □	♏ 1 20:53
4 0:56	☿ ✶	♐ 4 9:29
6 13:36	☿ □	♑ 6 20:45
9 1:16	☿ △	♒ 9 5:07
10 11:36	☉ △	♓ 11 9:37
12 9:00	♇ △	♈ 13 10:41
14 20:32	☉ ☍	♉ 15 9:52
16 8:12	♇ ☍	♊ 17 9:19
19 3:52	☉ △	♋ 19 11:09
21 13:19	☉ □	♌ 21 16:47
23 10:55	♂ ✶	♍ 24 2:15
25 15:23	☿ □	♎ 26 14:11
28 21:11	☿ ☌	♏ 29 2:56
30 8:48	♇ ☌	♐ 31 15:23

☽ Phases & Eclipses (Dy Hr Mn)
8 9:49 ☽ 15♐44
15 11:50 ○ 22♓37
22 2:10 ☾ 29♊03
29 21:47 ● 6♎43

8 0:52 ☽ 14♑44
14 20:32 ○ 21♈28
21 13:19 ☾ 28♋07
29 15:27 ● 6♏11

Astro Data
1 September 1989
Julian Day # 32751
SVP 5♓24'04"
GC 26♐41.7 ⚴ 14♈14.8R
Eris 17♈09.5R ⚵ 2♎23.3
⚷ 14♋28.6 ⚶ 0♑29.9
☽ Mean ☊ 24♒53.6

1 October 1989
Julian Day # 32781
SVP 5♓24'01"
GC 26♐41.8 ⚴ 7♈04.6R
Eris 16♈53.2R ⚵ 13♎17.2
⚷ 16♋07.4 ⚶ 8♑12.9
☽ Mean ☊ 23♒18.3

November 1989 — LONGITUDE

Day	Sid.Time	☉	0 hr ☽	Noon ☽	True ☊	☿	♀	♂	⚳	♃	♄	♅	♆	♇
1 W	14 43 01	9♏02 46	4♐18 49	10♐20 09	22♒13.5	3♏12.1	25♐56.5	28♎10.5	5♋14.4	10♋51.4	9♑21.7	2♑28.3	10♑04.2	14♏52.0
2 Th	14 46 58	10 02 50	16 23 05	22 27 53	22R 03.0	4 51.6	26 59.0	28 50.6	5R 14.7	10R 50.6	9 26.3	2 30.8	10 05.5	14 54.5
3 F	14 50 54	11 02 56	28 34 49	4♑44 15	21 55.3	6 30.7	28 01.1	29 30.7	5 14.6	10 49.6	9 31.1	2 33.3	10 06.9	14 56.9
4 Sa	14 54 51	12 03 04	10♑56 34	17 12 10	21 50.5	8 09.5	29 03.0	0♏10.9	5 14.0	10 48.4	9 35.8	2 35.9	10 08.3	14 59.3
5 Su	14 58 47	13 03 14	23 31 30	29 55 04	21 48.4	9 47.9	0♑04.6	0 51.1	5 13.1	10 47.0	9 40.7	2 38.5	10 09.7	15 01.7
6 M	15 02 44	14 03 25	6♒23 19	12♒56 46	21 47.9	11 25.8	1 05.8	1 31.3	5 11.8	10 45.4	9 45.6	2 41.2	10 11.1	15 04.2
7 Tu	15 06 40	15 03 37	19 35 51	26 20 59	21 47.8	13 03.4	2 06.6	2 11.6	5 10.0	10 43.5	9 50.6	2 43.9	10 12.6	15 06.6
8 W	15 10 37	16 03 51	3♓12 31	10♓10 42	21 47.0	14 40.7	3 07.1	2 51.9	5 07.9	10 41.5	9 55.7	2 46.6	10 14.1	15 09.0
9 Th	15 14 34	17 04 06	17 15 37	24 27 12	21 44.2	16 17.5	4 07.2	3 32.2	5 05.3	10 39.3	10 00.8	2 49.3	10 15.6	15 11.4
10 F	15 18 30	18 04 23	1♈45 13	9♈09 10	21 38.8	17 54.0	5 06.9	4 12.6	5 02.3	10 36.9	10 06.0	2 52.1	10 17.1	15 13.9
11 Sa	15 22 27	19 04 41	16 38 22	24 11 52	21 30.5	19 30.1	6 06.2	4 52.9	4 58.9	10 34.3	10 11.3	2 54.9	10 18.7	15 16.3
12 Su	15 26 23	20 05 01	1♉48 34	9♉27 08	21 20.0	21 05.9	7 05.0	5 33.4	4 55.1	10 31.5	10 16.6	2 57.8	10 20.3	15 18.7
13 M	15 30 20	21 05 22	17 06 10	24 44 12	21 08.4	22 41.4	8 03.5	6 13.8	4 50.9	10 28.6	10 22.0	3 00.7	10 21.9	15 21.1
14 Tu	15 34 16	22 05 45	2♊19 47	9♊51 34	20 57.0	24 16.6	9 01.4	6 54.3	4 46.3	10 25.4	10 27.4	3 03.6	10 23.5	15 23.6
15 W	15 38 13	23 06 10	17 18 22	24 39 11	20 47.2	25 51.5	9 58.9	7 34.8	4 41.3	10 22.0	10 32.9	3 06.6	10 25.2	15 26.0
16 Th	15 42 09	24 06 37	1♋53 14	9♋00 00	20 39.8	27 26.1	10 55.9	8 15.4	4 35.9	10 18.5	10 38.5	3 09.5	10 26.9	15 28.4
17 F	15 46 06	25 07 06	15 59 11	22 50 43	20 35.1	29 00.5	11 52.3	8 56.0	4 30.1	10 14.7	10 44.1	3 12.5	10 28.6	15 30.8
18 Sa	15 50 03	26 07 36	29 34 44	6♌11 29	20 33.0	0♐34.6	12 48.3	9 36.7	4 23.9	10 10.8	10 49.8	3 15.6	10 30.3	15 33.2
19 Su	15 53 59	27 08 08	12♌41 25	19 05 02	20 32.5	2 08.5	13 43.7	10 17.3	4 17.3	10 06.7	10 55.5	3 18.6	10 32.1	15 35.6
20 M	15 57 56	28 08 42	25 22 55	1♍35 43	20 32.5	3 42.2	14 38.5	10 58.0	4 10.3	10 02.4	11 01.3	3 21.7	10 33.9	15 38.0
21 Tu	16 01 52	29 09 17	7♍44 06	13 48 43	20 31.7	5 15.7	15 32.7	11 38.8	4 02.9	9 57.9	11 07.1	3 24.8	10 35.7	15 40.4
22 W	16 05 49	0♐09 55	19 50 14	25 49 17	20 29.2	6 49.1	16 26.3	12 19.6	3 55.1	9 53.3	11 13.0	3 28.0	10 37.5	15 42.7
23 Th	16 09 45	1 10 34	1♎46 28	7♎42 20	20 24.0	8 22.2	17 19.3	13 00.4	3 46.9	9 48.4	11 19.0	3 31.2	10 39.3	15 45.1
24 F	16 13 42	2 11 14	13 37 26	19 32 12	20 16.0	9 55.2	18 11.6	13 41.2	3 38.4	9 43.4	11 25.0	3 34.4	10 41.2	15 47.5
25 Sa	16 17 38	3 11 56	25 27 05	1♏22 26	20 05.1	11 28.1	19 03.2	14 22.1	3 29.4	9 38.3	11 31.0	3 37.6	10 43.1	15 49.8
26 Su	16 21 35	4 12 40	7♏18 34	13 15 45	19 52.1	13 00.8	19 54.1	15 03.1	3 20.2	9 32.9	11 37.1	3 40.8	10 45.0	15 52.1
27 M	16 25 32	5 13 25	19 14 12	25 14 05	19 37.9	14 33.4	20 44.2	15 44.0	3 10.6	9 27.4	11 43.2	3 44.1	10 46.9	15 54.5
28 Tu	16 29 28	6 14 12	1♐15 33	7♐18 44	19 23.8	16 05.8	21 33.6	16 25.0	3 00.6	9 21.8	11 49.4	3 47.4	10 48.8	15 56.8
29 W	16 33 25	7 15 00	13 23 43	19 30 36	19 10.8	17 38.2	22 22.1	17 06.1	2 50.3	9 16.0	11 55.7	3 50.7	10 50.8	15 59.1
30 Th	16 37 21	8 15 49	25 39 28	1♑50 26	19 00.1	19 10.4	23 09.8	17 47.1	2 39.7	9 10.0	12 02.0	3 54.0	10 52.8	16 01.4

December 1989 — LONGITUDE

Day	Sid.Time	☉	0 hr ☽	Noon ☽	True ☊	☿	♀	♂	⚳	♃	♄	♅	♆	♇
1 F	16 41 18	9♐16 39	8♑03 37	14♑19 10	18♒52.3	20♐42.4	23♑56.6	18♏28.2	2♋28.7	9♋03.9	12♑08.3	3♑57.4	10♑54.8	16♏03.7
2 Sa	16 45 14	10 17 30	20 37 15	26 58 07	18R 47.4	22 14.3	24 42.5	19 09.4	2R 17.5	8R 57.7	12 14.7	4 00.7	10 56.8	16 06.0
3 Su	16 49 11	11 18 22	3♒21 58	9♒49 07	18D 45.2	23 46.0	25 27.4	19 50.5	2 06.0	8 51.3	12 21.1	4 04.1	10 58.8	16 08.2
4 M	16 53 08	12 19 15	16 19 52	22 54 32	18 45.0	25 17.5	26 11.3	20 31.7	1 54.2	8 44.8	12 27.5	4 07.5	11 00.8	16 10.5
5 Tu	16 57 04	13 20 08	29 33 27	6♓16 55	18R 45.4	26 48.8	26 54.1	21 13.0	1 42.1	8 38.1	12 34.0	4 11.0	11 02.9	16 12.7
6 W	17 01 01	14 21 03	13♓05 15	19 58 39	18 45.5	28 19.9	27 35.9	21 54.2	1 29.8	8 31.3	12 40.5	4 14.4	11 05.0	16 14.9
7 Th	17 04 57	15 21 57	26 57 18	4♈01 13	18 43.9	29 50.6	28 16.4	22 35.5	1 17.3	8 24.4	12 47.1	4 17.8	11 07.0	16 17.1
8 F	17 08 54	16 22 53	11♈10 20	18 24 24	18 40.1	1♑21.0	28 55.8	23 16.9	1 04.5	8 17.4	12 53.7	4 21.3	11 09.1	16 19.3
9 Sa	17 12 50	17 23 50	25 43 00	3♉05 34	18 33.8	2 50.9	29 33.9	23 58.3	0 51.5	8 10.3	13 00.3	4 24.8	11 11.2	16 21.4
10 Su	17 16 47	18 24 47	10♉31 20	17 59 22	18 25.4	4 20.3	0♒10.8	24 39.7	0 38.3	8 03.1	13 06.9	4 28.3	11 13.4	16 23.6
11 M	17 20 43	19 25 45	25 28 36	2♊57 54	18 15.9	5 49.1	0 46.2	25 21.1	0 25.0	7 55.8	13 13.6	4 31.8	11 15.5	16 25.7
12 Tu	17 24 40	20 26 43	10♊26 03	17 51 53	18 06.5	7 17.2	1 20.3	26 02.6	0 11.5	7 48.3	13 20.4	4 35.3	11 17.7	16 27.8
13 W	17 28 37	21 27 43	25 14 16	2♋32 11	17 58.3	8 44.4	1 52.8	26 44.1	29♊57.9	7 40.8	13 27.1	4 38.9	11 19.8	16 29.9
14 Th	17 32 33	22 28 43	9♋44 48	16 51 24	17 52.1	10 10.6	2 23.9	27 25.7	29 44.1	7 33.3	13 33.9	4 42.4	11 22.0	16 32.0
15 F	17 36 30	23 29 44	23 51 31	0♌44 51	17 48.3	11 35.6	2 53.4	28 07.3	29 30.2	7 25.6	13 40.7	4 46.0	11 24.2	16 34.1
16 Sa	17 40 26	24 30 46	7♌31 16	14 10 51	17D 46.9	12 59.2	3 21.2	28 48.9	29 16.2	7 17.8	13 47.5	4 49.5	11 26.4	16 36.1
17 Su	17 44 23	25 31 49	20 43 48	27 10 27	17 47.2	14 21.0	3 47.3	29 30.6	29 02.1	7 10.0	13 54.4	4 53.1	11 28.6	16 38.1
18 M	17 48 19	26 32 53	3♍31 14	9♍46 42	17 48.3	15 40.8	4 11.7	0♐12.3	28 48.0	7 02.2	14 01.3	4 56.7	11 30.8	16 40.1
19 Tu	17 52 16	27 33 57	15 57 23	22 03 57	17R 49.3	16 58.3	4 34.2	0 54.0	28 33.8	6 54.2	14 08.2	5 00.3	11 33.0	16 42.1
20 W	17 56 12	28 35 03	28 07 01	4♎07 15	17 49.3	18 13.0	4 54.9	1 35.8	28 19.5	6 46.3	14 15.1	5 03.8	11 35.2	16 44.0
21 Th	18 00 09	29 36 09	10♎05 18	16 01 48	17 47.6	19 24.5	5 13.6	2 17.6	28 05.3	6 38.2	14 22.0	5 07.4	11 37.4	16 46.0
22 F	18 04 06	0♑37 16	21 57 21	27 52 33	17 43.7	20 32.2	5 30.3	2 59.5	27 51.1	6 30.2	14 29.0	5 11.0	11 39.7	16 47.9
23 Sa	18 08 02	1 38 23	3♏47 56	9♏44 01	17 37.8	21 35.6	5 44.9	3 41.4	27 36.9	6 22.1	14 36.0	5 14.6	11 41.9	16 49.7
24 Su	18 11 59	2 39 32	15 41 14	21 39 59	17 30.3	22 33.9	5 57.3	4 23.3	27 22.7	6 14.0	14 43.0	5 18.2	11 44.1	16 51.6
25 M	18 15 55	3 40 41	27 40 39	3♐43 29	17 21.8	23 26.5	6 07.6	5 05.2	27 08.6	6 05.8	14 50.0	5 21.9	11 46.4	16 53.4
26 Tu	18 19 52	4 41 50	9♐48 46	15 56 39	17 13.1	24 12.4	6 15.6	5 47.3	26 54.6	5 57.7	14 57.0	5 25.5	11 48.7	16 55.3
27 W	18 23 48	5 43 00	22 07 18	28 20 48	17 05.2	24 50.9	6 21.3	6 29.3	26 40.7	5 49.5	15 04.1	5 29.1	11 50.9	16 57.0
28 Th	18 27 45	6 44 10	4♑37 12	10♑56 32	16 58.8	25 21.0	6R 24.6	7 11.4	26 26.9	5 41.4	15 11.1	5 32.7	11 53.2	16 58.8
29 F	18 31 41	7 45 20	17 18 49	23 44 00	16 54.3	25 41.8	6 25.5	7 53.5	26 13.3	5 33.3	15 18.2	5 36.3	11 55.5	17 00.5
30 Sa	18 35 38	8 46 31	0♒12 07	6♒43 07	16D 51.9	25R 52.4	6 23.9	8 35.6	25 59.7	5 25.1	15 25.3	5 39.9	11 57.7	17 02.3
31 Su	18 39 35	9 47 41	13 16 59	19 53 46	16 51.5	25 52.1	6 19.9	9 17.8	25 46.4	5 17.0	15 32.4	5 43.5	12 00.0	17 03.9

Astro Data

	Dy Hr Mn
⚳ R	2 16:36
☽ 0N	9 10:57
♄☌♆	13 11:39
♃☍♄	14 6:27
♃☍♆	14 20:54
☽ 0S	22 7:36
☽ 0N	6 17:46
☽ 0S	19 14:05
♃☍♅	29 5:46
♀ R	29 8:50
☿ R	30 23:31

Planet Ingress

	Dy Hr Mn
♂ ♏	4 5:29
♀ ♑	5 10:13
☿ ♐	18 3:10
☉ ♐	22 8:05
☿ ♑	7 14:30
♀ ♒	10 4:54
⚳ ♊R	13 8:15
♂ ♐	18 4:57
☉ ♑	21 21:22

Last Aspect / ☽ Ingress

Last Aspect Dy Hr Mn		☽ Ingress Dy Hr Mn
3 1:14	♂ ⚹	♑ 3 2:46
4 7:45	♇ ⚹	♒ 5 12:09
6 15:52	♇ □	♓ 7 18:25
8 22:45	☉ △	♈ 9 21:08
10 14:21	♃ □	♉ 11 21:09
13 8:24	☿ ☍	♊ 13 20:19
13 8:24	☿ ☍	♋ 15 20:51
18 0:26	☿ △	♌ 18 0:45
20 4:44	☉ □	♍ 20 8:54
21 15:43	♀ △	♎ 22 20:25
24 9:03	♀ □	♏ 25 9:13
27 2:20	♀ ⚹	♐ 27 21:30
29 7:48	☿ ☌	♑ 30 8:26

Last Aspect / ☽ Ingress

Last Aspect Dy Hr Mn		☽ Ingress Dy Hr Mn
2 7:28	♀ ☌	♒ 2 17:42
4 16:53	☿ ⚹	♓ 5 0:48
7 4:04	☿ □	♈ 7 5:11
9 6:01	♀ □	♉ 9 6:59
10 23:13	♂ ☍	♊ 11 7:15
12 16:30	☉ ☍	♋ 13 7:49
15 7:10	♂ △	♌ 15 10:41
17 16:39	♂ □	♍ 17 17:19
19 23:55	☉ □	♎ 20 3:45
21 19:35	☿ □	♏ 22 16:18
24 13:57	☿ ⚹	♐ 25 4:37
25 16:48	♀ ⚹	♑ 27 15:10
29 15:43	☿ ☌	♒ 29 23:38

☽ Phases & Eclipses

Dy Hr Mn	
6 14:11	☽ 14♒09
13 5:51	○ 20♉50
20 4:44	☾ 27♌50
28 9:41	● 6♐08
6 1:26	☽ 13♓54
12 16:30	○ 20♊38
19 23:55	☾ 28♍04
28 3:20	● 6♑22

Astro Data

1 November 1989
Julian Day # 32812
SVP 5♓23'57"
GC 26♐41.8 ⚴ 29♓18.6R
Eris 16♈34.8R ⚵ 24♎25.4
⚷ 16♋34.6R ⚶ 19♑43.5
☽ Mean ☊ 21♒39.8

1 December 1989
Julian Day # 32842
SVP 5♓23'52"
GC 26♐41.9 ⚴ 27♓15.3
Eris 16♈20.9R ⚵ 4♏38.3
⚷ 15♋42.1R ⚶ 2♒49.0
☽ Mean ☊ 20♒04.5

LONGITUDE — January 1990

Day	Sid.Time	☉	0 hr ☽	Noon ☽	True ☊	☿	♀	♂	⚳	♃	♄	♅	♆	♇
1 M	18 43 31	10♑48 51	26♒33 26	3♓16 04	16♒52.4	25♑40.4	6♒13.3	10♐00.0	25♊33.2	5♋08.9	15♑39.4	5♑47.1	12♑02.3	17♏05.6
2 Tu	18 47 28	11 50 01	10♓01 40	16 50 18	16 54.0	25R 16.7	6R 04.2	10 42.2	25R 20.3	5R 00.9	15 46.5	5 50.7	12 04.6	17 07.2
3 W	18 51 24	12 51 11	23 42 00	0♈36 49	16R 55.4	24 41.3	5 52.6	11 24.5	25 07.6	4 52.9	15 53.7	5 54.3	12 06.8	17 08.8
4 Th	18 55 21	13 52 20	7♈34 44	14 35 41	16 55.9	23 54.5	5 38.5	12 06.8	24 55.1	4 44.9	16 00.8	5 57.9	12 09.1	17 10.4
5 F	18 59 17	14 53 30	21 39 36	28 46 17	16 55.1	22 57.2	5 21.9	12 49.2	24 42.8	4 37.0	16 07.9	6 01.5	12 11.4	17 11.9
6 Sa	19 03 14	15 54 38	5♉55 28	13♉06 50	16 52.8	21 50.9	5 02.9	13 31.5	24 30.8	4 29.1	16 15.0	6 05.1	12 13.6	17 13.4
7 Su	19 07 10	16 55 47	20 19 54	27 34 09	16 49.3	20 37.7	4 41.6	14 14.0	24 19.1	4 21.3	16 22.1	6 08.6	12 15.9	17 14.9
8 M	19 11 07	17 56 55	4♊48 57	12♊03 37	16 45.0	19 19.6	4 18.0	14 56.4	24 07.7	4 13.6	16 29.2	6 12.2	12 18.2	17 16.4
9 Tu	19 15 04	18 58 03	19 17 26	26 29 37	16 40.6	17 59.4	3 52.2	15 38.9	23 56.5	4 06.0	16 36.3	6 15.7	12 20.5	17 17.8
10 W	19 19 00	19 59 10	3♋39 26	10♋46 10	16 36.8	16 39.6	3 24.4	16 21.4	23 45.7	3 58.4	16 43.4	6 19.3	12 22.7	17 19.2
11 Th	19 22 57	21 00 17	17 49 10	24 47 51	16 34.1	15 22.6	2 54.7	17 04.0	23 35.2	3 50.9	16 50.5	6 22.8	12 25.0	17 20.6
12 F	19 26 53	22 01 24	1♌41 45	8♌30 30	16D 32.6	14 10.7	2 23.3	17 46.6	23 25.0	3 43.5	16 57.6	6 26.3	12 27.2	17 21.9
13 Sa	19 30 50	23 02 30	15 13 53	21 51 47	16 32.5	13 05.6	1 50.5	18 29.2	23 15.2	3 36.2	17 04.7	6 29.8	12 29.5	17 23.2
14 Su	19 34 46	24 03 36	28 24 11	4♍51 12	16 33.4	12 08.6	1 16.3	19 11.8	23 05.7	3 29.1	17 11.8	6 33.3	12 31.7	17 24.5
15 M	19 38 43	25 04 42	11♍13 04	17 30 04	16 34.9	11 20.7	0 41.1	19 54.5	22 56.5	3 22.0	17 18.9	6 36.8	12 33.9	17 25.7
16 Tu	19 42 40	26 05 47	23 42 36	29 51 06	16 36.6	10 42.2	0 05.1	20 37.3	22 47.8	3 15.0	17 25.9	6 40.3	12 36.2	17 26.9
17 W	19 46 36	27 06 52	5♎56 05	11♎58 06	16 38.0	10 13.4	29♑28.5	21 20.1	22 39.4	3 08.1	17 33.0	6 43.7	12 38.4	17 28.1
18 Th	19 50 33	28 07 58	17 57 43	23 55 31	16R 38.7	9 54.1	28 51.6	22 02.9	22 31.4	3 01.4	17 40.0	6 47.1	12 40.6	17 29.2
19 F	19 54 29	29 09 02	29 52 07	5♏48 08	16 38.6	9D 43.8	28 14.7	22 45.7	22 23.7	2 54.8	17 47.1	6 50.5	12 42.8	17 30.3
20 Sa	19 58 26	0♒10 07	11♏44 10	17 40 47	16 37.7	9 42.2	27 37.9	23 28.6	22 16.5	2 48.3	17 54.1	6 53.9	12 45.0	17 31.4
21 Su	20 02 22	1 11 11	23 38 35	29 38 05	16 36.1	9 48.7	27 01.7	24 11.5	22 09.6	2 41.9	18 01.1	6 57.3	12 47.2	17 32.4
22 M	20 06 19	2 12 15	5♐39 47	11♐44 10	16 34.1	10 02.7	26 26.1	24 54.5	22 03.2	2 35.7	18 08.1	7 00.7	12 49.4	17 33.4
23 Tu	20 10 15	3 13 18	17 51 37	24 02 29	16 31.9	10 23.5	25 51.5	25 37.5	21 57.2	2 29.6	18 15.0	7 04.0	12 51.5	17 34.4
24 W	20 14 12	4 14 20	0♑17 05	6♑35 38	16 30.0	10 50.6	25 18.0	26 20.5	21 51.6	2 23.7	18 22.0	7 07.4	12 53.7	17 35.3
25 Th	20 18 09	5 15 22	12 58 18	19 25 09	16 28.5	11 23.5	24 45.9	27 03.5	21 46.4	2 18.0	18 28.9	7 10.7	12 55.9	17 36.2
26 F	20 22 05	6 16 24	25 56 14	2♒31 28	16 27.6	12 01.5	24 15.4	27 46.6	21 41.6	2 12.3	18 35.8	7 13.9	12 58.0	17 37.1
27 Sa	20 26 02	7 17 24	9♒10 47	15 53 58	16D 27.3	12 44.2	23 46.6	28 29.8	21 37.3	2 06.9	18 42.7	7 17.2	13 00.1	17 38.0
28 Su	20 29 58	8 18 23	22 40 48	29 31 02	16 27.5	13 31.3	23 19.8	29 12.9	21 33.4	2 01.6	18 49.6	7 20.4	13 02.2	17 38.7
29 M	20 33 55	9 19 22	6♓24 21	13♓20 26	16 28.0	14 22.1	22 54.9	29 56.1	21 29.9	1 56.5	18 56.4	7 23.6	13 04.3	17 39.5
30 Tu	20 37 51	10 20 19	20 18 56	27 19 30	16 28.7	15 16.5	22 32.2	0♑39.3	21 26.8	1 51.5	19 03.2	7 26.8	13 06.4	17 40.2
31 W	20 41 48	11 21 15	4♈21 47	11♈25 27	16 29.2	16 14.1	22 11.8	1 22.5	21 24.2	1 46.7	19 10.0	7 30.0	13 08.5	17 40.9

LONGITUDE — February 1990

Day	Sid.Time	☉	0 hr ☽	Noon ☽	True ☊	☿	♀	♂	⚳	♃	♄	♅	♆	♇
1 Th	20 45 44	12♒22 09	18♈30 10	25♈35 37	16♒29.6	17♑14.6	21♑53.7	2♑05.8	21♊22.0	1♋42.1	19♑16.7	7♑33.1	13♑10.5	17♏41.6
2 F	20 49 41	13 23 03	2♉41 29	9♉47 30	16R 29.7	18 17.7	21R 38.0	2 49.1	21R 20.3	1R 37.7	19 23.4	7 36.2	13 12.5	17 42.2
3 Sa	20 53 38	14 23 55	16 53 21	23 58 47	16 29.7	19 23.3	21 24.7	3 32.5	21 18.9	1 33.4	19 30.1	7 39.3	13 14.6	17 42.8
4 Su	20 57 34	15 24 45	1♊03 29	8♊07 13	16 29.6	20 31.1	21 13.8	4 15.8	21 18.0	1 29.4	19 36.8	7 42.3	13 16.6	17 43.3
5 M	21 01 31	16 25 35	15 09 41	22 10 35	16D 29.6	21 40.9	21 05.5	4 59.2	21D 17.5	1 25.5	19 43.4	7 45.4	13 18.6	17 43.9
6 Tu	21 05 27	17 26 22	29 09 39	6♋06 35	16 29.8	22 52.7	20 59.6	5 42.7	21 17.5	1 21.8	19 50.0	7 48.4	13 20.5	17 44.3
7 W	21 09 24	18 27 09	13♋01 05	19 52 52	16 29.8	24 06.2	20D 56.2	6 26.1	21 17.9	1 18.3	19 56.6	7 51.3	13 22.5	17 44.8
8 Th	21 13 20	19 27 54	26 41 40	3♌27 13	16R 29.9	25 21.4	20 55.3	7 09.6	21 18.6	1 15.0	20 03.1	7 54.3	13 24.4	17 45.2
9 F	21 17 17	20 28 37	10♌09 18	16 47 43	16 30.0	26 38.1	20 56.8	7 53.2	21 19.8	1 11.9	20 09.6	7 57.2	13 26.3	17 45.5
10 Sa	21 21 13	21 29 19	23 22 19	29 53 00	16 29.9	27 56.2	21 00.6	8 36.7	21 21.5	1 08.9	20 16.0	8 00.0	13 28.2	17 45.9
11 Su	21 25 10	22 30 00	6♍19 42	12♍42 26	16 29.4	29 15.7	21 06.9	9 20.3	21 23.5	1 06.2	20 22.4	8 02.9	13 30.1	17 46.2
12 M	21 29 07	23 30 40	19 01 16	25 16 20	16 28.7	0♒36.6	21 15.4	10 03.9	21 25.9	1 03.6	20 28.8	8 05.7	13 32.0	17 46.4
13 Tu	21 33 03	24 31 18	1♎27 49	7♎35 58	16 27.6	1 58.7	21 26.1	10 47.6	21 28.8	1 01.3	20 35.1	8 08.4	13 33.8	17 46.7
14 W	21 37 00	25 31 55	13 41 06	19 43 35	16 26.3	3 21.9	21 39.1	11 31.3	21 32.0	0 59.1	20 41.4	8 11.2	13 35.6	17 46.8
15 Th	21 40 56	26 32 31	25 43 49	1♏42 16	16 25.2	4 46.4	21 54.1	12 15.0	21 35.6	0 57.2	20 47.6	8 13.9	13 37.4	17 47.0
16 F	21 44 53	27 33 06	7♏39 25	13 35 48	16 24.2	6 11.9	22 11.2	12 58.8	21 39.6	0 55.4	20 53.8	8 16.5	13 39.2	17 47.1
17 Sa	21 48 49	28 33 39	19 31 59	25 28 33	16D 23.8	7 38.5	22 30.3	13 42.6	21 44.1	0 53.8	21 00.0	8 19.2	13 40.9	17 47.2
18 Su	21 52 46	29 34 11	1♐26 03	7♐25 08	16 23.9	9 06.2	22 51.3	14 26.4	21 48.9	0 52.5	21 06.1	8 21.8	13 42.7	17R 47.2
19 M	21 56 42	0♓34 43	13 26 21	19 30 18	16 24.6	10 34.9	23 14.2	15 10.2	21 54.1	0 51.3	21 12.1	8 24.3	13 44.4	17 47.2
20 Tu	22 00 39	1 35 12	25 37 32	1♑48 36	16 25.8	12 04.6	23 38.9	15 54.1	21 59.6	0 50.3	21 18.1	8 26.8	13 46.1	17 47.2
21 W	22 04 36	2 35 41	8♑03 58	14 24 05	16 27.2	13 35.4	24 05.2	16 38.0	22 05.6	0 49.6	21 24.1	8 29.3	13 47.7	17 47.2
22 Th	22 08 32	3 36 08	20 49 17	27 19 53	16 28.5	15 07.1	24 33.3	17 22.0	22 11.9	0 49.0	21 30.0	8 31.8	13 49.4	17 47.1
23 F	22 12 29	4 36 33	3♒56 02	10♒37 50	16R 29.3	16 39.9	25 02.9	18 05.9	22 18.6	0 48.7	21 35.8	8 34.2	13 51.0	17 46.9
24 Sa	22 16 25	5 36 57	17 25 15	24 18 07	16 29.2	18 13.6	25 34.1	18 49.9	22 25.6	0D 48.5	21 41.6	8 36.5	13 52.6	17 46.8
25 Su	22 20 22	6 37 20	1♓16 10	8♓18 58	16 28.1	19 48.3	26 06.7	19 34.0	22 33.0	0 48.5	21 47.4	8 38.8	13 54.1	17 46.6
26 M	22 24 18	7 37 40	15 26 00	22 36 39	16 26.0	21 24.1	26 40.7	20 18.0	22 40.8	0 48.8	21 53.1	8 41.1	13 55.7	17 46.3
27 Tu	22 28 15	8 37 59	29 50 12	7♈05 52	16 23.0	23 00.8	27 16.1	21 02.1	22 48.9	0 49.2	21 58.7	8 43.4	13 57.2	17 46.0
28 W	22 32 11	9 38 16	14♈22 52	21 40 23	16 19.7	24 38.5	27 52.7	21 46.2	22 57.4	0 49.9	22 04.2	8 45.6	13 58.7	17 45.7

Astro Data

	Dy Hr Mn
☽ 0N	2 22:37
☽ 0S	15 22:14
♄✱♇	16 15:56
☿ D	20 4:31
♃⚻♇	22 19:42
☽ 0N	30 4:11
⚳ D	6 2:55
♀ D	8 9:16
☽ 0S	12 7:10
♇ R	19 6:31
♃ D	24 19:14
☽ 0N	26 12:18

Planet Ingress

	Dy Hr Mn
♀ ♑R	16 15:23
☉ ♒	20 8:02
♂ ♑	29 14:10
☿ ♒	12 1:11
☉ ♓	18 22:14

Last Aspect / ☽ Ingress (January)

Last Aspect Dy Hr Mn		☽ Ingress Dy Hr Mn
31 6:52	♇ □	♓ 1 6:10
3 2:11	☿ ✱	♈ 3 10:56
5 2:50	☿ □	♉ 5 14:04
7 1:24	☿ △	♊ 7 16:02
8 17:01	♂ ☍	♋ 9 17:52
11 4:57	☉ ☍	♌ 11 21:02
13 5:31	♂ △	♍ 14 2:57
16 3:59	☉ △	♎ 16 12:17
18 21:28	♀ □	♏ 19 0:16
21 7:02	♀ ✱	♐ 21 12:44
23 15:14	♂ ☌	♑ 23 23:27
25 21:29	♀ ☌	♒ 26 7:25
28 11:27	♂ ✱	♓ 28 12:51
30 4:01	♀ ✱	♈ 30 16:34

Last Aspect / ☽ Ingress (February)

Last Aspect Dy Hr Mn		☽ Ingress Dy Hr Mn
1 5:52	♀ □	♉ 1 19:27
3 7:43	♀ △	♊ 3 22:12
5 1:24	☉ △	♋ 6 1:27
7 20:10	☿ ☍	♌ 8 5:51
9 19:16	☉ ☍	♍ 10 12:13
12 4:11	♀ △	♎ 12 21:09
15 0:40	☉ △	♏ 15 8:34
17 18:48	☉ □	♐ 17 21:07
18 15:50	☿ ✱	♑ 20 8:30
22 6:42	♀ ☌	♒ 22 16:52
24 0:38	♇ □	♓ 24 21:49
26 19:03	♀ ✱	♈ 27 0:16

☽ Phases & Eclipses

Dy Hr Mn	
4 10:40	☽ 13♈49
11 4:57	○ 20♋42
18 21:17	☾ 28♎32
26 19:20	● 6♒35
26 19:30:24	● A 02'03"
2 18:32	☽ 13♉40
9 19:16	○ 20♌47
9 19:11	● T 1.075
17 18:48	☾ 28♏51
25 8:54	● 6♓30

Astro Data

1 January 1990
Julian Day # 32873
SVP 5♓23'46"
GC 26♐42.0 ⚴ 1♈33.6
Eris 16♈14.8R ⚵ 13♏59.5
⚷ 13♋48.8R ⚶ 17♒26.6
☽ Mean ☊ 18♒26.0

1 February 1990
Julian Day # 32904
SVP 5♓23'41"
GC 26♐42.0 ⚴ 10♈35.0
Eris 16♈19.3 ⚵ 21♏11.4
⚷ 11♋48.6R ⚶ 2♓34.8
☽ Mean ☊ 16♒47.6

March 1990 LONGITUDE

Day	Sid.Time	☉	0 hr ☽	Noon ☽	True ☊	☿	♀	♂	⚳	♃	♄	♅	♆	♇
1 Th	22 36 08	10♓38 31	28♈57 39	6♉13 56	16♒16.6	26♒17.3	28♑30.6	22♑30.3	23♊06.2	0♋50.7	22♑09.8	8♑47.7	14♑00.1	17♏45.4
2 F	22 40 05	11 38 43	13♉28 35	20 41 02	16R14.2	27 57.0	29 09.7	23 14.4	23 15.3	0 51.7	22 15.2	8 49.8	14 01.6	17R45.0
3 Sa	22 44 01	12 38 54	27 50 48	4♊57 33	16D12.9	29 37.8	29 50.0	23 58.6	23 24.8	0 53.0	22 20.6	8 51.9	14 03.0	17 44.6
4 Su	22 47 58	13 39 03	12♊01 01	19 01 00	16 12.8	1♓19.7	0♒31.4	24 42.8	23 34.6	0 54.4	22 25.9	8 53.9	14 04.3	17 44.1
5 M	22 51 54	14 39 10	25 57 25	2♋50 14	16 13.7	3 02.6	1 13.8	25 27.0	23 44.7	0 56.0	22 31.2	8 55.9	14 05.7	17 43.6
6 Tu	22 55 51	15 39 14	9♋39 29	16 25 14	16 15.3	4 46.7	1 57.2	26 11.2	23 55.2	0 57.9	22 36.4	8 57.8	14 07.0	17 43.1
7 W	22 59 47	16 39 17	23 07 32	29 46 30	16 16.8	6 31.8	2 41.6	26 55.5	24 05.9	0 59.9	22 41.5	8 59.7	14 08.3	17 42.6
8 Th	23 03 44	17 39 17	6♌22 14	12♌54 49	16R17.7	8 18.0	3 27.0	27 39.8	24 17.0	1 02.1	22 46.6	9 01.6	14 09.6	17 42.0
9 F	23 07 40	18 39 15	19 24 20	25 50 53	16 17.3	10 05.3	4 13.3	28 24.1	24 28.3	1 04.5	22 51.6	9 03.4	14 10.8	17 41.4
10 Sa	23 11 37	19 39 11	2♍14 30	8♍35 17	16 15.3	11 53.7	5 00.4	29 08.4	24 39.9	1 07.1	22 56.5	9 05.1	14 12.0	17 40.7
11 Su	23 15 34	20 39 05	14 53 15	21 08 29	16 11.6	13 43.3	5 48.4	29 52.8	24 51.9	1 09.8	23 01.4	9 06.8	14 13.2	17 40.1
12 M	23 19 30	21 38 58	27 21 02	3♎31 01	16 06.2	15 34.1	6 37.2	0♒37.2	25 04.1	1 12.8	23 06.2	9 08.5	14 14.3	17 39.4
13 Tu	23 23 27	22 38 48	9♎38 30	15 43 39	15 59.7	17 25.9	7 26.8	1 21.6	25 16.6	1 15.9	23 10.9	9 10.1	14 15.4	17 38.6
14 W	23 27 23	23 38 36	21 46 38	27 47 38	15 52.6	19 18.9	8 17.2	2 06.0	25 29.4	1 19.3	23 15.6	9 11.7	14 16.5	17 37.8
15 Th	23 31 20	24 38 23	3♏46 56	9♏44 49	15 45.7	21 13.1	9 08.2	2 50.5	25 42.4	1 22.8	23 20.1	9 13.2	14 17.6	17 37.0
16 F	23 35 16	25 38 08	15 41 38	21 37 45	15 39.7	23 08.3	10 00.0	3 35.0	25 55.7	1 26.4	23 24.6	9 14.6	14 18.6	17 36.2
17 Sa	23 39 13	26 37 51	27 33 38	3♐29 45	15 35.1	25 04.6	10 52.4	4 19.5	26 09.3	1 30.3	23 29.1	9 16.1	14 19.6	17 35.4
18 Su	23 43 09	27 37 33	9♐26 36	15 24 46	15 32.4	27 01.9	11 45.5	5 04.0	26 23.1	1 34.3	23 33.4	9 17.4	14 20.6	17 34.5
19 M	23 47 06	28 37 13	21 24 48	27 27 20	15D31.4	29 00.2	12 39.1	5 48.5	26 37.2	1 38.6	23 37.7	9 18.8	14 21.5	17 33.5
20 Tu	23 51 03	29 36 51	3♑32 58	9♑42 19	15 31.9	0♈59.3	13 33.4	6 33.1	26 51.6	1 43.0	23 41.9	9 20.0	14 22.4	17 32.6
21 W	23 54 59	0♈36 27	15 56 00	22 14 36	15 33.2	2 59.2	14 28.3	7 17.7	27 06.2	1 47.5	23 46.1	9 21.3	14 23.3	17 31.6
22 Th	23 58 56	1 36 02	28 38 40	5♒08 42	15R34.5	4 59.8	15 23.6	8 02.3	27 21.0	1 52.3	23 50.1	9 22.4	14 24.1	17 30.6
23 F	0 02 52	2 35 34	11♒45 05	18 28 07	15 34.9	7 00.9	16 19.5	8 46.9	27 36.1	1 57.2	23 54.1	9 23.6	14 24.9	17 29.6
24 Sa	0 06 49	3 35 05	25 17 59	2♓14 42	15 33.6	9 02.3	17 16.0	9 31.6	27 51.5	2 02.2	23 58.0	9 24.6	14 25.7	17 28.5
25 Su	0 10 45	4 34 34	9♓18 08	16 27 56	15 30.1	11 03.8	18 12.8	10 16.2	28 07.0	2 07.5	24 01.8	9 25.7	14 26.5	17 27.4
26 M	0 14 42	5 34 01	23 43 34	1♈04 20	15 24.6	13 05.2	19 10.2	11 00.9	28 22.8	2 12.9	24 05.5	9 26.6	14 27.2	17 26.3
27 Tu	0 18 38	6 33 26	8♈29 19	15 57 30	15 17.2	15 06.3	20 08.0	11 45.6	28 38.8	2 18.5	24 09.2	9 27.6	14 27.8	17 25.2
28 W	0 22 35	7 32 49	23 27 43	0♉58 45	15 09.1	17 06.6	21 06.2	12 30.3	28 55.0	2 24.2	24 12.7	9 28.4	14 28.5	17 24.0
29 Th	0 26 31	8 32 10	8♉29 24	15 58 30	15 01.1	19 05.9	22 04.9	13 15.0	29 11.5	2 30.1	24 16.2	9 29.2	14 29.1	17 22.8
30 F	0 30 28	9 31 29	23 24 57	0♊47 51	14 54.3	21 03.8	23 03.9	13 59.7	29 28.2	2 36.1	24 19.6	9 30.0	14 29.7	17 21.6
31 Sa	0 34 25	10 30 45	8♊06 25	15 20 03	14 49.5	22 59.9	24 03.3	14 44.5	29 45.1	2 42.4	24 22.9	9 30.7	14 30.2	17 20.4

April 1990 LONGITUDE

Day	Sid.Time	☉	0 hr ☽	Noon ☽	True ☊	☿	♀	♂	⚳	♃	♄	♅	♆	♇
1 Su	0 38 21	11♈30 00	22♊28 22	29♊31 07	14♒46.9	24♈53.9	25♒03.1	15♒29.2	0♋02.1	2♋48.7	24♑26.1	9♑31.4	14♑30.7	17♏19.1
2 M	0 42 18	12 29 11	6♋28 15	13♋19 48	14D46.3	26 45.4	26 03.2	16 14.0	0 19.4	2 55.2	24 29.3	9 32.0	14 31.2	17R17.8
3 Tu	0 46 14	13 28 21	20 05 57	26 46 58	14 46.8	28 33.9	27 03.7	16 58.7	0 36.9	3 01.9	24 32.3	9 32.6	14 31.7	17 16.5
4 W	0 50 11	14 27 28	3♌23 08	9♌54 49	14R47.5	0♉19.1	28 04.5	17 43.5	0 54.6	3 08.7	24 35.3	9 33.1	14 32.1	17 15.2
5 Th	0 54 07	15 26 33	16 22 23	22 46 11	14 47.3	2 00.6	29 05.7	18 28.3	1 12.5	3 15.7	24 38.1	9 33.5	14 32.5	17 13.9
6 F	0 58 04	16 25 35	29 06 35	5♍23 55	14 45.2	3 38.0	0♓07.1	19 13.1	1 30.5	3 22.8	24 40.9	9 33.9	14 32.8	17 12.5
7 Sa	1 02 00	17 24 35	11♍38 28	17 50 30	14 40.6	5 11.1	1 08.9	19 57.9	1 48.8	3 30.0	24 43.6	9 34.3	14 33.1	17 11.1
8 Su	1 05 57	18 23 33	24 00 16	0♎07 58	14 33.3	6 39.5	2 10.9	20 42.7	2 07.2	3 37.4	24 46.2	9 34.6	14 33.4	17 09.7
9 M	1 09 54	19 22 29	6♎13 48	12 17 53	14 23.5	8 03.0	3 13.3	21 27.5	2 25.8	3 44.9	24 48.7	9 34.9	14 33.7	17 08.3
10 Tu	1 13 50	20 21 23	18 20 23	24 21 26	14 11.8	9 21.4	4 15.9	22 12.3	2 44.5	3 52.5	24 51.1	9 35.1	14 33.9	17 06.9
11 W	1 17 47	21 20 15	0♏21 10	6♏19 45	13 59.1	10 34.4	5 18.8	22 57.2	3 03.5	4 00.3	24 53.4	9 35.2	14 34.0	17 05.4
12 Th	1 21 43	22 19 05	12 17 19	18 14 05	13 46.6	11 41.9	6 22.0	23 42.0	3 22.6	4 08.3	24 55.6	9 35.3	14 34.2	17 03.9
13 F	1 25 40	23 17 53	24 10 15	0♐06 06	13 35.2	12 43.7	7 25.4	24 26.9	3 41.9	4 16.3	24 57.8	9R35.3	14 34.3	17 02.4
14 Sa	1 29 36	24 16 39	6♐01 56	11 58 05	13 25.8	13 39.7	8 29.0	25 11.7	4 01.3	4 24.5	24 59.8	9 35.3	14 34.4	17 00.9
15 Su	1 33 33	25 15 24	17 54 58	23 53 00	13 19.0	14 29.7	9 32.9	25 56.6	4 20.9	4 32.8	25 01.8	9 35.3	14 34.4	16 59.4
16 M	1 37 29	26 14 07	29 52 41	5♑54 33	13 14.9	15 13.7	10 37.1	26 41.5	4 40.7	4 41.2	25 03.6	9 35.2	14R34.5	16 57.9
17 Tu	1 41 26	27 12 48	11♑59 09	18 07 06	13D13.1	15 51.7	11 41.4	27 26.4	5 00.6	4 49.8	25 05.4	9 35.0	14 34.4	16 56.3
18 W	1 45 23	28 11 27	24 19 00	0♒35 28	13R12.8	16 23.5	12 46.0	28 11.3	5 20.6	4 58.5	25 07.0	9 34.8	14 34.4	16 54.8
19 Th	1 49 19	29 10 05	6♒57 08	13 24 35	13 12.9	16 49.2	13 50.7	28 56.1	5 40.8	5 07.3	25 08.6	9 34.6	14 34.3	16 53.2
20 F	1 53 16	0♉08 41	19 58 21	26 38 55	13 12.4	17 08.8	14 55.7	29 41.0	6 01.2	5 16.2	25 10.1	9 34.2	14 34.2	16 51.6
21 Sa	1 57 12	1 07 15	3♓26 37	10♓21 42	13 10.0	17 22.3	16 00.9	0♓25.9	6 21.7	5 25.2	25 11.4	9 33.9	14 34.1	16 50.0
22 Su	2 01 09	2 05 48	17 24 14	24 34 05	13 05.2	17R29.8	17 06.2	1 10.8	6 42.3	5 34.4	25 12.7	9 33.5	14 33.9	16 48.4
23 M	2 05 05	3 04 19	1♈50 53	9♈14 04	12 57.8	17 31.5	18 11.8	1 55.7	7 03.1	5 43.6	25 13.9	9 33.0	14 33.7	16 46.8
24 Tu	2 09 02	4 02 48	16 42 50	24 16 07	12 48.1	17 27.4	19 17.5	2 40.5	7 24.1	5 53.0	25 15.0	9 32.5	14 33.4	16 45.2
25 W	2 12 58	5 01 16	1♉52 43	9♉31 15	12 37.1	17 18.0	20 23.3	3 25.4	7 45.1	6 02.5	25 15.9	9 31.9	14 33.1	16 43.5
26 Th	2 16 55	5 59 42	17 10 17	24 48 21	12 26.3	17 03.4	21 29.4	4 10.3	8 06.3	6 12.1	25 16.8	9 31.3	14 32.8	16 41.9
27 F	2 20 52	6 58 06	2♊24 05	9♊56 11	12 16.8	16 44.1	22 35.5	4 55.1	8 27.7	6 21.8	25 17.6	9 30.7	14 32.5	16 40.2
28 Sa	2 24 48	7 56 28	17 23 34	24 45 22	12 09.5	16 20.3	23 41.9	5 39.9	8 49.1	6 31.6	25 18.3	9 30.0	14 32.1	16 38.6
29 Su	2 28 45	8 54 47	2♋00 55	9♋09 49	12 05.0	15 52.7	24 48.3	6 24.8	9 10.7	6 41.5	25 18.9	9 29.2	14 31.7	16 36.9
30 M	2 32 41	9 53 05	16 11 49	23 06 56	12 02.9	15 21.8	25 55.0	7 09.6	9 32.4	6 51.5	25 19.4	9 28.4	14 31.3	16 35.2

Astro Data

	Dy Hr Mn
☽0S	11 15:15
☉0N	20 21:20
☿0N	21 7:49
☽0N	25 22:29
♃□♇	28 11:22
☽0S	7 21:34
♅ R	13 22:21
♆ R	16 12:55
☽0N	22 8:42
☿ R	23 6:54

Planet Ingress

		Dy Hr Mn
☿	♓	3 17:14
♀	♒	3 17:52
♂	♒	11 15:54
☿	♈	20 0:04
☉	♈	20 21:19
⚳	♋	1 9:01
☿	♉	4 7:35
♀	♓	6 9:13
☉	♉	20 8:27
♂	♓	20 22:09

Last Aspect / ☽ Ingress (March)

Last Aspect Dy Hr Mn			☽ Ingress	Dy Hr Mn
28 22:41	♀	□	♉	1 1:43
3 2:55	♀	△	♊	3 3:37
4 2:05	☉	□	♋	5 7:02
7 6:33	♂	☍	♌	7 12:24
8 20:50	♇	□	♍	9 19:47
11 15:39	♄	△	♎	12 5:09
14 2:54	♄	□	♏	14 16:25
16 20:51	☉	△	♐	17 4:56
19 15:39	☿	□	♑	19 17:01
21 14:53	♄	☌	♒	22 2:31
23 10:16	♇	□	♓	24 8:09
26 0:33	♄	⚹	♈	26 10:15
28 1:09	♄	□	♉	28 10:26
30 1:26	♄	△	♊	30 10:42

Last Aspect / ☽ Ingress (April)

Last Aspect Dy Hr Mn			☽ Ingress	Dy Hr Mn
1 3:48	♀	△	♋	1 12:50
3 15:44	☿	□	♌	3 17:50
6 1:02	♀	☍	♍	6 1:42
8 1:27	♄	△	♎	8 11:44
10 12:59	♄	□	♏	10 23:18
13 1:34	♄	⚹	♐	13 11:48
15 16:24	♂	⚹	♑	16 0:15
18 7:03	☉	□	♒	18 10:53
20 17:42	♂	☌	♓	20 17:57
22 13:04	♄	⚹	♈	22 20:58
24 13:33	♄	□	♉	24 21:03
26 12:45	♄	△	♊	26 20:12
28 10:08	♀	□	♋	28 20:39

☽ Phases & Eclipses

Dy Hr Mn		
4 2:05	☽	13♊14
11 10:59	○	20♍37
19 14:30	☾	28♐43
26 19:48	●	5♈53
2 10:24	☽	12♋25
10 3:18	○	20♎00
18 7:03	☾	27♑59
25 4:27	●	4♉43

Astro Data

1 March 1990
Julian Day # 32932
SVP 5♓23'37"
GC 26♐42.1 ⚴ 21♈27.2
Eris 16♈31.5 ⚵ 24♏44.1
⚷ 10♋42.6R ⚶ 16♓19.8
☽ Mean ☊ 15♒18.6

1 April 1990
Julian Day # 32963
SVP 5♓23'33"
GC 26♐42.2 ⚴ 5♉36.1
Eris 16♈50.7 ⚵ 24♏02.5R
⚷ 10♋47.6 ⚶ 1♈19.6
☽ Mean ☊ 13♒40.1

LONGITUDE

May 1990

Day	Sid.Time	☉	0 hr ☽	Noon ☽	True ☊	☿	♀	♂	⚳	♃	♄	♅	♆	♇
1 Tu	2 36 38	10♉51 21	29♋55 18	6♌37 11	12♒02.3	14♉48.1	27♓01.7	7♓54.4	9♋54.3	7♋01.6	25♑19.8	9♑27.6	14♑30.8	16♏33.6
2 W	2 40 34	11 49 34	13♌12 59	19 43 09	12R 02.3	14R 12.3	28 08.6	8 39.2	10 16.2	7 11.8	25 20.0	9R 26.7	14R 30.3	16R 31.9
3 Th	2 44 31	12 47 46	26 08 09	2♍28 30	12 01.4	13 35.1	29 15.6	9 23.9	10 38.3	7 22.1	25 20.2	9 25.7	14 29.8	16 30.2
4 F	2 48 27	13 45 55	8♍44 44	14 57 20	11 58.8	12 57.1	0♈22.8	10 08.7	11 00.4	7 32.5	25R 20.3	9 24.8	14 29.2	16 28.5
5 Sa	2 52 24	14 44 03	21 06 48	27 13 34	11 53.5	12 19.0	1 30.0	10 53.4	11 22.7	7 43.0	25 20.3	9 23.7	14 28.6	16 26.8
6 Su	2 56 21	15 42 08	3♎18 02	9♎20 35	11 45.4	11 41.5	2 37.4	11 38.2	11 45.1	7 53.6	25 20.2	9 22.6	14 28.0	16 25.2
7 M	3 00 17	16 40 12	15 21 32	21 21 11	11 34.5	11 05.3	3 44.9	12 22.9	12 07.6	8 04.2	25 20.0	9 21.5	14 27.4	16 23.5
8 Tu	3 04 14	17 38 14	27 19 46	3♏17 31	11 21.7	10 30.9	4 52.6	13 07.6	12 30.2	8 15.0	25 19.7	9 20.4	14 26.7	16 21.8
9 W	3 08 10	18 36 14	9♏14 38	15 11 16	11 07.8	9 59.0	6 00.3	13 52.3	12 52.9	8 25.8	25 19.3	9 19.1	14 26.0	16 20.1
10 Th	3 12 07	19 34 13	21 07 37	27 03 51	10 54.0	9 29.9	7 08.2	14 37.0	13 15.7	8 36.7	25 18.8	9 17.9	14 25.2	16 18.4
11 F	3 16 03	20 32 11	3♐00 07	8♐56 37	10 41.4	9 04.1	8 16.2	15 21.6	13 38.7	8 47.7	25 18.3	9 16.6	14 24.5	16 16.7
12 Sa	3 20 00	21 30 07	14 53 33	20 51 11	10 30.9	8 42.1	9 24.2	16 06.2	14 01.7	8 58.8	25 17.6	9 15.3	14 23.7	16 15.1
13 Su	3 23 56	22 28 01	26 49 47	2♑49 40	10 23.1	8 24.0	10 32.4	16 50.9	14 24.8	9 10.0	25 16.8	9 13.9	14 22.9	16 13.4
14 M	3 27 53	23 25 54	8♑51 10	14 54 43	10 18.1	8 10.2	11 40.7	17 35.5	14 48.0	9 21.2	25 15.9	9 12.5	14 22.0	16 11.7
15 Tu	3 31 50	24 23 46	21 00 44	27 09 43	10 15.7	8 00.7	12 49.1	18 20.0	15 11.3	9 32.5	25 15.0	9 11.0	14 21.2	16 10.0
16 W	3 35 46	25 21 37	3♒22 10	9♒38 38	10D 15.1	7D 55.8	13 57.6	19 04.6	15 34.7	9 43.9	25 13.9	9 09.5	14 20.3	16 08.4
17 Th	3 39 43	26 19 26	15 59 39	22 25 47	10R 15.2	7 55.4	15 06.2	19 49.1	15 58.2	9 55.4	25 12.7	9 08.0	14 19.4	16 06.7
18 F	3 43 39	27 17 14	28 57 33	5♓35 27	10 15.0	7 59.6	16 14.8	20 33.6	16 21.7	10 06.9	25 11.5	9 06.4	14 18.4	16 05.1
19 Sa	3 47 36	28 15 01	12♓19 53	19 11 12	10 13.4	8 08.4	17 23.6	21 18.1	16 45.4	10 18.5	25 10.1	9 04.8	14 17.4	16 03.4
20 Su	3 51 32	29 12 47	26 09 34	3♈15 03	10 09.6	8 21.7	18 32.5	22 02.5	17 09.1	10 30.2	25 08.7	9 03.2	14 16.4	16 01.8
21 M	3 55 29	0♊10 32	10♈27 29	17 46 31	10 03.4	8 39.5	19 41.4	22 46.9	17 33.0	10 41.9	25 07.2	9 01.5	14 15.4	16 00.2
22 Tu	3 59 25	1 08 16	25 11 32	2♉41 45	9 55.1	9 01.6	20 50.4	23 31.3	17 56.9	10 53.7	25 05.6	8 59.8	14 14.3	15 58.6
23 W	4 03 22	2 05 58	10♉16 07	17 53 25	9 45.6	9 28.1	21 59.5	24 15.6	18 20.9	11 05.6	25 03.8	8 58.0	14 13.3	15 56.9
24 Th	4 07 19	3 03 40	25 32 19	3♊11 21	9 35.9	9 58.7	23 08.7	24 59.9	18 45.0	11 17.5	25 02.0	8 56.2	14 12.2	15 55.4
25 F	4 11 15	4 01 20	10♊49 07	18 24 13	9 27.4	10 33.4	24 17.9	25 44.2	19 09.2	11 29.5	25 00.2	8 54.4	14 11.1	15 53.8
26 Sa	4 15 12	4 58 59	25 55 25	3♋21 36	9 20.8	11 12.0	25 27.2	26 28.4	19 33.4	11 41.6	24 58.2	8 52.5	14 09.9	15 52.2
27 Su	4 19 08	5 56 37	10♋41 56	17 55 43	9 16.8	11 54.5	26 36.6	27 12.6	19 57.8	11 53.7	24 56.1	8 50.7	14 08.7	15 50.6
28 M	4 23 05	6 54 13	25 02 33	2♌02 14	9D 15.0	12 40.7	27 46.1	27 56.7	20 22.2	12 05.9	24 54.0	8 48.7	14 07.6	15 49.1
29 Tu	4 27 01	7 51 48	8♌54 42	15 40 08	9 14.9	13 30.5	28 55.6	28 40.8	20 46.6	12 18.1	24 51.7	8 46.8	14 06.4	15 47.6
30 W	4 30 58	8 49 21	22 18 48	28 51 06	9R 15.6	14 23.9	0♉05.2	29 24.8	21 11.2	12 30.4	24 49.4	8 44.8	14 05.1	15 46.0
31 Th	4 34 54	9 46 53	5♍17 30	11♍38 31	9 15.9	15 20.7	1 14.8	0♈08.8	21 35.8	12 42.8	24 47.0	8 42.8	14 03.9	15 44.5

LONGITUDE

June 1990

Day	Sid.Time	☉	0 hr ☽	Noon ☽	True ☊	☿	♀	♂	⚳	♃	♄	♅	♆	♇
1 F	4 38 51	10♊44 24	17♍54 42	24♍06 38	9♒14.9	16♉20.8	2♉24.5	0♈52.8	22♋00.5	12♋55.2	24♑44.5	8♑40.8	14♑02.6	15♏43.0
2 Sa	4 42 48	11 41 53	0♎14 53	6♎19 59	9R 11.9	17 24.2	3 34.3	1 36.7	22 25.2	13 07.6	24R 42.0	8R 38.7	14R 01.3	15R 41.6
3 Su	4 46 44	12 39 21	12 22 29	18 22 51	9 06.7	18 30.7	4 44.1	2 20.5	22 50.1	13 20.1	24 39.3	8 36.6	14 00.0	15 40.1
4 M	4 50 41	13 36 48	24 21 35	0♏19 05	8 59.3	19 40.4	5 54.0	3 04.3	23 14.9	13 32.6	24 36.6	8 34.5	13 58.7	15 38.7
5 Tu	4 54 37	14 34 14	6♏15 45	12 11 55	8 50.3	20 53.2	7 03.9	3 48.0	23 39.9	13 45.2	24 33.8	8 32.4	13 57.3	15 37.2
6 W	4 58 34	15 31 39	18 07 52	24 03 55	8 40.4	22 09.0	8 13.9	4 31.7	24 04.9	13 57.9	24 30.9	8 30.2	13 56.0	15 35.8
7 Th	5 02 30	16 29 02	0♐00 17	5♐57 12	8 30.5	23 27.7	9 24.0	5 15.4	24 30.0	14 10.5	24 28.0	8 28.0	13 54.6	15 34.5
8 F	5 06 27	17 26 25	11 54 51	17 53 26	8 21.5	24 49.4	10 34.1	5 59.0	24 55.1	14 23.3	24 25.0	8 25.8	13 53.2	15 33.1
9 Sa	5 10 24	18 23 47	23 53 09	29 54 09	8 14.1	26 14.0	11 44.3	6 42.5	25 20.3	14 36.0	24 21.9	8 23.6	13 51.8	15 31.7
10 Su	5 14 20	19 21 09	5♑56 40	12♑00 54	8 08.8	27 41.5	12 54.6	7 26.0	25 45.5	14 48.8	24 18.7	8 21.4	13 50.4	15 30.4
11 M	5 18 17	20 18 29	18 07 05	24 15 28	8 05.7	29 11.9	14 04.9	8 09.4	26 10.9	15 01.7	24 15.5	8 19.1	13 48.9	15 29.1
12 Tu	5 22 13	21 15 49	0♒26 21	6♒40 03	8D 04.7	0♊45.1	15 15.2	8 52.8	26 36.2	15 14.5	24 12.2	8 16.8	13 47.5	15 27.8
13 W	5 26 10	22 13 09	12 56 54	19 17 15	8 05.2	2 21.1	16 25.6	9 36.1	27 01.6	15 27.4	24 08.8	8 14.6	13 46.0	15 26.6
14 Th	5 30 06	23 10 28	25 41 31	2♓10 03	8 06.4	3 59.9	17 36.1	10 19.3	27 27.1	15 40.4	24 05.4	8 12.2	13 44.5	15 25.3
15 F	5 34 03	24 07 46	8♓43 15	15 21 29	8R 07.5	5 41.4	18 46.7	11 02.5	27 52.7	15 53.4	24 01.9	8 09.9	13 43.0	15 24.1
16 Sa	5 37 59	25 05 05	22 05 03	28 54 15	8 07.8	7 25.8	19 57.2	11 45.6	28 18.2	16 06.4	23 58.4	8 07.6	13 41.5	15 22.9
17 Su	5 41 56	26 02 22	5♈49 13	12♈50 02	8 06.5	9 12.8	21 07.9	12 28.6	28 43.9	16 19.4	23 54.8	8 05.2	13 40.0	15 21.7
18 M	5 45 53	26 59 40	19 56 39	27 08 51	8 03.6	11 02.5	22 18.6	13 11.6	29 09.6	16 32.5	23 51.1	8 02.8	13 38.5	15 20.6
19 Tu	5 49 49	27 56 58	4♉26 15	11♉48 18	7 59.2	12 54.8	23 29.3	13 54.5	29 35.3	16 45.6	23 47.4	8 00.5	13 36.9	15 19.4
20 W	5 53 46	28 54 15	19 14 14	26 43 13	7 53.8	14 49.7	24 40.1	14 37.3	0♌01.1	16 58.8	23 43.6	7 58.1	13 35.4	15 18.3
21 Th	5 57 42	29 51 32	4♊14 09	11♊45 56	7 48.3	16 46.9	25 51.0	15 20.0	0 27.0	17 11.9	23 39.8	7 55.7	13 33.8	15 17.3
22 F	6 01 39	0♋48 49	19 17 24	26 47 21	7 43.4	18 46.5	27 01.9	16 02.6	0 52.9	17 25.1	23 35.9	7 53.3	13 32.3	15 16.2
23 Sa	6 05 35	1 46 05	4♋14 38	11♋38 13	7 39.7	20 48.2	28 12.8	16 45.2	1 18.8	17 38.4	23 32.0	7 50.9	13 30.7	15 15.2
24 Su	6 09 32	2 43 21	18 57 09	26 10 42	7D 37.6	22 51.9	29 23.8	17 27.7	1 44.8	17 51.6	23 28.0	7 48.5	13 29.1	15 14.2
25 M	6 13 28	3 40 37	3♌18 16	10♌19 28	7 37.2	24 57.4	0♊34.8	18 10.1	2 10.9	18 04.9	23 24.0	7 46.0	13 27.5	15 13.2
26 Tu	6 17 25	4 37 51	17 14 02	24 01 56	7 38.0	27 04.5	1 45.9	18 52.3	2 37.0	18 18.1	23 20.0	7 43.6	13 25.9	15 12.3
27 W	6 21 22	5 35 06	0♍43 15	7♍18 12	7 39.5	29 12.9	2 57.0	19 34.5	3 03.1	18 31.5	23 15.9	7 41.2	13 24.3	15 11.4
28 Th	6 25 18	6 32 20	13 47 06	20 10 21	7 41.0	1♋22.3	4 08.2	20 16.6	3 29.2	18 44.8	23 11.7	7 38.7	13 22.7	15 10.5
29 F	6 29 15	7 29 33	26 28 25	2♎41 51	7R 41.9	3 32.5	5 19.4	20 58.6	3 55.4	18 58.1	23 07.6	7 36.3	13 21.1	15 09.6
30 Sa	6 33 11	8 26 46	8♎51 09	14 56 56	7 41.8	5 43.1	6 30.6	21 40.6	4 21.7	19 11.5	23 03.4	7 33.9	13 19.5	15 08.8

Astro Data

Astro Data	Dy Hr Mn
♄R	4 22:43
☽0S	5 2:36
♀0N	7 5:08
♃☍♅	13 19:31
☿D	17 2:01
☽0N	19 17:09
☽0S	1 7:52
♃☍♆	6 8:45
♂0N	6 9:20
♃△♇	13 10:30
☽0N	15 23:23
☽0S	28 14:43

Planet Ingress

Planet Ingress	Dy Hr Mn
♀ ♈	4 3:52
☉ ♊	21 7:37
♀ ♉	30 10:13
♂ ♈	31 7:11
☿ ♊	12 0:29
⚳ ♌	20 10:57
☉ ♋	21 15:33
♀ ♊	25 0:14
☿ ♋	27 20:46

Last Aspect / ☽ Ingress (May)

Last Aspect Dy Hr Mn		☽ Ingress	Dy Hr Mn
30 17:21	♀ △	♌	1 0:08
2 6:07	♇ □	♍	3 7:18
5 8:17	♄ △	♎	5 17:28
7 19:59	♄ □	♏	8 5:22
10 8:28	♄ ✶	♐	10 17:56
12 1:48	♂ □	♑	13 6:21
15 8:17	♄ ☌	♒	15 17:30
17 19:45	☉ □	♓	18 1:54
20 4:42	☉ ✶	♈	20 6:31
21 23:52	♄ □	♉	22 7:42
23 23:14	♄ △	♊	24 7:00
26 0:18	♂ □	♋	26 6:34
28 4:34	♂ △	♌	28 8:29
29 12:13	♇ □	♍	30 14:08

Last Aspect / ☽ Ingress (June)

Last Aspect Dy Hr Mn		☽ Ingress	Dy Hr Mn
1 13:13	♄ △	♎	1 23:31
4 0:33	♄ □	♏	4 11:22
6 12:54	♄ ✶	♐	6 23:59
8 11:01	☉ ☍	♑	9 12:12
11 22:58	☿ △	♒	11 23:09
13 17:57	☉ △	♓	14 8:00
16 4:48	☉ □	♈	16 13:55
18 11:44	☉ ✶	♉	18 16:43
20 8:26	♀ ☌	♊	20 17:15
21 21:13	☿ ☌	♋	22 17:09
24 17:53	♀ ✶	♌	24 18:25
26 18:28	☿ ✶	♍	26 22:42
28 17:42	♄ △	♎	29 6:47

☽ Phases & Eclipses

Dy Hr Mn	
1 20:18	☽ 11♌11
9 19:31	○ 18♏54
17 19:45	☾ 26♒38
24 11:47	● 3♊03
31 8:11	☽ 9♍38
8 11:01	○ 17♐24
16 4:48	☾ 24♓48
22 18:55	● 1♋05
29 22:07	☽ 7♎54

Astro Data

1 May 1990
Julian Day # 32993
SVP 5♓23'29"
GC 26♐42.3 ⚴ 20♉53.1
Eris 17♈10.2 ⚵ 18♏46.8R
⚷ 12♋11.4 ⚶ 15♈20.8
☽ Mean ☊ 12♒04.8

1 June 1990
Julian Day # 33024
SVP 5♓23'25"
GC 26♐42.3 ⚴ 7♊56.8
Eris 17♈26.6 ⚵ 12♏14.8R
⚷ 14♋41.6 ⚶ 29♈00.9
☽ Mean ☊ 10♒26.3

July 1990 — LONGITUDE

Day	Sid.Time	☉	0 hr ☽	Noon ☽	True ☊	☿	♀	♂	⚳	♃	♄	♅	♆	♇
1 Su	6 37 08	9♋23 58	20♎59 44	27♎00 07	7♒40.4	7♋54.0	7♊41.9	22♈22.4	4♌48.0	19♋24.8	22♑59.1	7♑31.4	13♑17.9	15♏08.0
2 M	6 41 04	10 21 10	2♏58 39	8♏55 51	7R 37.9	10 04.8	8 53.2	23 04.1	5 14.3	19 38.2	22R 54.9	7R 29.0	13R 16.3	15R 07.2
3 Tu	6 45 01	11 18 22	14 52 12	20 48 12	7 34.4	12 15.2	10 04.6	23 45.7	5 40.7	19 51.6	22 50.6	7 26.6	13 14.6	15 06.5
4 W	6 48 57	12 15 34	26 44 16	2♐40 49	7 30.4	14 25.1	11 16.0	24 27.2	6 07.1	20 05.0	22 46.3	7 24.1	13 13.0	15 05.8
5 Th	6 52 54	13 12 45	8♐38 12	14 36 44	7 26.3	16 34.1	12 27.5	25 08.6	6 33.5	20 18.4	22 41.9	7 21.7	13 11.4	15 05.1
6 F	6 56 51	14 09 56	20 36 45	26 38 29	7 22.6	18 42.0	13 39.0	25 49.9	7 00.0	20 31.9	22 37.6	7 19.3	13 09.8	15 04.4
7 Sa	7 00 47	15 07 08	2♑42 10	8♑48 00	7 19.7	20 48.8	14 50.6	26 31.1	7 26.5	20 45.3	22 33.2	7 16.9	13 08.2	15 03.8
8 Su	7 04 44	16 04 19	14 56 11	21 06 53	7 17.8	22 54.3	16 02.2	27 12.2	7 53.0	20 58.8	22 28.8	7 14.5	13 06.5	15 03.2
9 M	7 08 40	17 01 31	27 20 13	3♒36 22	7D 17.0	24 58.2	17 13.8	27 53.2	8 19.6	21 12.2	22 24.4	7 12.1	13 04.9	15 02.7
10 Tu	7 12 37	17 58 42	9♒55 27	16 17 35	7 17.2	27 00.6	18 25.5	28 34.0	8 46.2	21 25.7	22 20.0	7 09.7	13 03.3	15 02.1
11 W	7 16 33	18 55 54	22 42 56	29 11 37	7 18.1	29 01.3	19 37.2	29 14.8	9 12.8	21 39.1	22 15.6	7 07.4	13 01.7	15 01.6
12 Th	7 20 30	19 53 06	5♓43 46	12♓19 32	7 19.4	1♌00.2	20 49.0	29 55.4	9 39.5	21 52.6	22 11.1	7 05.0	13 00.1	15 01.2
13 F	7 24 26	20 50 19	18 59 01	25 42 21	7 20.6	2 57.4	22 00.9	0♉35.9	10 06.2	22 06.0	22 06.7	7 02.7	12 58.5	15 00.7
14 Sa	7 28 23	21 47 32	2♈29 38	9♈20 54	7R 21.5	4 52.8	23 12.7	1 16.3	10 32.9	22 19.5	22 02.3	7 00.3	12 56.9	15 00.3
15 Su	7 32 20	22 44 46	16 16 11	23 15 25	7 21.8	6 46.4	24 24.7	1 56.5	10 59.7	22 32.9	21 57.8	6 58.0	12 55.3	15 00.0
16 M	7 36 16	23 42 01	0♉18 32	7♉25 18	7 21.4	8 38.1	25 36.7	2 36.6	11 26.5	22 46.4	21 53.4	6 55.7	12 53.7	14 59.6
17 Tu	7 40 13	24 39 16	14 35 29	21 48 40	7 20.5	10 28.0	26 48.7	3 16.6	11 53.3	22 59.9	21 48.9	6 53.4	12 52.1	14 59.3
18 W	7 44 09	25 36 32	29 04 24	6♊22 07	7 19.3	12 16.0	28 00.7	3 56.5	12 20.2	23 13.3	21 44.5	6 51.1	12 50.5	14 59.1
19 Th	7 48 06	26 33 49	13♊41 09	21 00 47	7 18.0	14 02.2	29 12.9	4 36.2	12 47.1	23 26.8	21 40.1	6 48.9	12 49.0	14 58.8
20 F	7 52 02	27 31 06	28 20 14	5♋38 43	7 16.9	15 46.6	0♋25.0	5 15.8	13 14.0	23 40.3	21 35.7	6 46.7	12 47.4	14 58.6
21 Sa	7 55 59	28 28 24	12♋55 23	20 09 29	7 16.2	17 29.1	1 37.2	5 55.2	13 40.9	23 53.7	21 31.3	6 44.5	12 45.8	14 58.5
22 Su	7 59 56	29 25 43	27 20 17	4♌27 06	7D 15.9	19 09.8	2 49.5	6 34.4	14 07.9	24 07.1	21 26.9	6 42.3	12 44.3	14 58.3
23 M	8 03 52	0♌23 02	11♌29 23	18 26 41	7 16.0	20 48.6	4 01.8	7 13.5	14 34.9	24 20.6	21 22.5	6 40.1	12 42.8	14 58.2
24 Tu	8 07 49	1 20 21	25 18 39	2♍05 04	7 16.4	22 25.6	5 14.1	7 52.5	15 01.9	24 34.0	21 18.2	6 38.0	12 41.3	14 58.2
25 W	8 11 45	2 17 41	8♍45 50	15 20 59	7 16.9	24 00.8	6 26.4	8 31.2	15 28.9	24 47.4	21 13.8	6 35.8	12 39.7	14D 58.1
26 Th	8 15 42	3 15 01	21 50 36	28 14 56	7 17.3	25 34.1	7 38.8	9 09.8	15 56.0	25 00.8	21 09.5	6 33.7	12 38.2	14 58.1
27 F	8 19 38	4 12 22	4♎34 17	10♎49 01	7 17.7	27 05.6	8 51.3	9 48.3	16 23.1	25 14.1	21 05.2	6 31.7	12 36.8	14 58.1
28 Sa	8 23 35	5 09 43	16 59 35	23 06 28	7 17.8	28 35.3	10 03.8	10 26.6	16 50.1	25 27.5	21 01.0	6 29.6	12 35.3	14 58.2
29 Su	8 27 31	6 07 04	29 10 11	5♏11 16	7R 17.9	0♍03.0	11 16.3	11 04.7	17 17.3	25 40.8	20 56.8	6 27.6	12 33.8	14 58.3
30 M	8 31 28	7 04 27	11♏10 18	17 07 50	7D 17.9	1 28.9	12 28.9	11 42.6	17 44.4	25 54.2	20 52.6	6 25.6	12 32.4	14 58.5
31 Tu	8 35 25	8 01 49	23 04 28	29 00 44	7 17.9	2 52.8	13 41.5	12 20.3	18 11.6	26 07.5	20 48.4	6 23.7	12 30.9	14 58.6

August 1990 — LONGITUDE

Day	Sid.Time	☉	0 hr ☽	Noon ☽	True ☊	☿	♀	♂	⚳	♃	♄	♅	♆	♇
1 W	8 39 21	8♌59 13	4♐57 12	10♐54 23	7♒18.0	4♍14.8	14♋54.1	12♉57.9	18♌38.7	26♋20.7	20♑44.3	6♑21.7	12♑29.5	14♏58.8
2 Th	8 43 18	9 56 37	16 52 48	22 52 53	7 18.3	5 34.9	16 06.8	13 35.3	19 05.9	26 34.0	20R 40.3	6R 19.8	12R 28.1	14 59.1
3 F	8 47 14	10 54 02	28 55 06	4♑59 49	7 18.6	6 52.9	17 19.6	14 12.5	19 33.1	26 47.3	20 36.2	6 18.0	12 26.8	14 59.3
4 Sa	8 51 11	11 51 27	11♑07 24	17 18 09	7 19.0	8 08.8	18 32.3	14 49.5	20 00.3	27 00.5	20 32.2	6 16.1	12 25.4	14 59.7
5 Su	8 55 07	12 48 53	23 32 17	29 50 02	7R 19.2	9 22.5	19 45.1	15 26.3	20 27.6	27 13.7	20 28.3	6 14.3	12 24.0	15 00.0
6 M	8 59 04	13 46 21	6♒11 31	12♒36 51	7 19.3	10 34.1	20 58.0	16 03.0	20 54.8	27 26.8	20 24.4	6 12.6	12 22.7	15 00.4
7 Tu	9 03 00	14 43 49	19 06 02	25 39 04	7 19.0	11 43.4	22 10.9	16 39.4	21 22.1	27 40.0	20 20.5	6 10.8	12 21.4	15 00.8
8 W	9 06 57	15 41 18	2♓15 54	8♓56 25	7 18.3	12 50.4	23 23.9	17 15.6	21 49.4	27 53.1	20 16.7	6 09.1	12 20.1	15 01.2
9 Th	9 10 54	16 38 48	15 40 27	22 27 51	7 17.2	13 54.9	24 36.8	17 51.6	22 16.7	28 06.1	20 13.0	6 07.5	12 18.8	15 01.7
10 F	9 14 50	17 36 20	29 18 24	6♈11 52	7 16.0	14 56.8	25 49.9	18 27.4	22 44.0	28 19.2	20 09.3	6 05.8	12 17.6	15 02.2
11 Sa	9 18 47	18 33 53	13♈08 01	20 06 35	7 14.8	15 56.1	27 03.0	19 03.0	23 11.3	28 32.2	20 05.7	6 04.3	12 16.3	15 02.7
12 Su	9 22 43	19 31 27	27 07 18	4♉09 54	7 14.0	16 52.6	28 16.1	19 38.4	23 38.6	28 45.2	20 02.1	6 02.7	12 15.1	15 03.3
13 M	9 26 40	20 29 03	11♉14 07	18 19 39	7D 13.6	17 46.2	29 29.3	20 13.5	24 06.0	28 58.2	19 58.6	6 01.2	12 13.9	15 03.9
14 Tu	9 30 36	21 26 40	25 26 14	2♊33 34	7 13.8	18 36.7	0♌42.5	20 48.4	24 33.3	29 11.1	19 55.1	5 59.7	12 12.7	15 04.6
15 W	9 34 33	22 24 19	9♊41 19	16 49 11	7 14.5	19 24.0	1 55.7	21 23.1	25 00.7	29 24.0	19 51.7	5 58.3	12 11.6	15 05.3
16 Th	9 38 29	23 22 00	23 56 50	1♋03 54	7 15.7	20 07.9	3 09.0	21 57.5	25 28.1	29 36.8	19 48.4	5 56.9	12 10.5	15 06.0
17 F	9 42 26	24 19 42	8♋10 00	15 14 45	7 16.8	20 48.2	4 22.4	22 31.7	25 55.5	29 49.6	19 45.1	5 55.5	12 09.4	15 06.7
18 Sa	9 46 23	25 17 26	22 17 45	29 18 35	7R 17.6	21 24.6	5 35.8	23 05.6	26 22.9	0♌02.4	19 41.9	5 54.2	12 08.3	15 07.5
19 Su	9 50 19	26 15 11	6♌16 52	13♌12 11	7 17.6	21 57.1	6 49.2	23 39.3	26 50.3	0 15.1	19 38.8	5 52.9	12 07.2	15 08.3
20 M	9 54 16	27 12 57	20 04 11	26 52 30	7 16.7	22 25.3	8 02.7	24 12.6	27 17.7	0 27.8	19 35.7	5 51.7	12 06.2	15 09.2
21 Tu	9 58 12	28 10 44	3♍36 53	10♍17 04	7 14.8	22 49.0	9 16.2	24 45.7	27 45.1	0 40.4	19 32.7	5 50.5	12 05.2	15 10.0
22 W	10 02 09	29 08 33	16 52 54	23 24 16	7 11.9	23 08.0	10 29.7	25 18.6	28 12.5	0 53.0	19 29.8	5 49.4	12 04.2	15 11.0
23 Th	10 06 05	0♍06 24	29 51 10	6♎13 37	7 08.4	23 22.0	11 43.3	25 51.1	28 39.9	1 05.6	19 27.0	5 48.3	12 03.2	15 11.9
24 F	10 10 02	1 04 15	12♎31 47	18 45 52	7 04.8	23 30.7	12 56.9	26 23.3	29 07.4	1 18.1	19 24.2	5 47.2	12 02.3	15 12.9
25 Sa	10 13 58	2 02 08	24 56 08	1♏02 55	7 01.5	23R 34.0	14 10.6	26 55.3	29 34.8	1 30.5	19 21.5	5 46.2	12 01.4	15 13.9
26 Su	10 17 55	3 00 02	7♏06 39	13 07 45	6 58.9	23 31.7	15 24.3	27 26.9	0♍02.2	1 42.9	19 18.9	5 45.2	12 00.5	15 14.9
27 M	10 21 51	3 57 57	19 06 46	25 04 12	6D 57.4	23 23.5	16 38.0	27 58.3	0 29.7	1 55.2	19 16.4	5 44.3	11 59.7	15 16.0
28 Tu	10 25 48	4 55 54	1♐00 38	6♐56 40	6 57.0	23 09.2	17 51.7	28 29.3	0 57.1	2 07.5	19 14.0	5 43.5	11 58.8	15 17.1
29 W	10 29 45	5 53 52	12 52 53	18 49 54	6 57.7	22 48.9	19 05.5	29 00.0	1 24.6	2 19.8	19 11.6	5 42.6	11 58.1	15 18.2
30 Th	10 33 41	6 51 52	24 48 20	0♑48 46	6 59.2	22 22.6	20 19.4	29 30.4	1 52.0	2 31.9	19 09.4	5 41.9	11 57.3	15 19.4
31 F	10 37 38	7 49 52	6♑51 46	12 57 54	7 00.9	21 50.3	21 33.2	0♊00.4	2 19.4	2 44.1	19 07.2	5 41.1	11 56.5	15 20.6

Astro Data	Dy Hr Mn
☽0N	13 4:29
♃☍♄	13 12:53
☽0S	25 23:17
♇ D	26 1:25
☽0N	9 10:15
☿0S	20 10:18
☽0S	22 8:31
☿ R	25 14:08

Planet Ingress		Dy Hr Mn
☿	♌	11 23:48
♂	♉	12 14:44
♀	♋	20 3:41
☉	♌	23 2:22
☿	♍	29 11:10
♀	♌	13 22:05
♃	♌	18 7:30
☉	♍	23 9:21
⚳	♍	26 10:02
♂	♊	31 11:40

Last Aspect Dy Hr Mn			☽ Ingress	Dy Hr Mn
1 4:01	♄	□	♏	1 18:01
3 16:06	♄	⚹	♐	4 6:35
6 10:18	♂	△	♑	6 18:39
9 0:25	♂	□	♒	9 5:07
11 12:06	♂	⚹	♓	11 13:29
13 5:38	♄	⚹	♈	13 19:36
15 14:09	♀	⚹	♉	15 23:29
17 17:02	☉	⚹	♊	18 1:32
20 2:39	♀	☌	♋	20 2:44
22 2:54	☉	☌	♌	22 4:29
23 16:40	☿	☌	♍	24 8:17
26 5:49	♃	⚹	♎	26 15:18
29 0:21	☿	⚹	♏	29 1:39
31 6:03	♃	△	♐	31 14:00

Last Aspect Dy Hr Mn			☽ Ingress	Dy Hr Mn
1 7:48	☉	△	♑	3 2:09
5 6:57	♃	☍	♒	5 12:19
6 18:41	♂	□	♓	7 19:54
9 22:03	♃	△	♈	10 1:13
12 2:38	♃	□	♉	12 4:55
14 6:14	♃	⚹	♊	14 7:41
15 22:05	☉	⚹	♋	16 10:12
18 0:55	♂	⚹	♌	18 13:11
20 12:39	☉	☌	♍	20 17:33
22 15:41	♂	△	♎	23 0:17
24 13:14	♄	□	♏	25 9:56
27 18:07	♂	☍	♐	27 21:57
29 19:45	☿	□	♑	30 10:23

☽ Phases & Eclipses Dy Hr Mn		
8 1:23	○	15♑39
15 11:04	☾	22♈43
22 2:54	●	29♋04
22 3:02:08	●	T 02'33"
29 14:01	☽	6♏12
6 14:19	○	13♒52
6 14:12	●	P 0.676
13 15:54	☾	20♉38
20 12:39	●	27♌15
28 7:34	☽	4♐45

Astro Data

1 July 1990
Julian Day # 33054
SVP 5♓23'19"
GC 26♐42.4 ⚵ 25♊20.4
Eris 17♈35.1 ✱ 9♏22.9R
⚷ 17♋43.6 ⚶ 11♉03.0
☽ Mean ☊ 8♒51.0

1 August 1990
Julian Day # 33085
SVP 5♓23'14"
GC 26♐42.5 ⚵ 13♋45.6
Eris 17♈34.3R ✱ 11♏16.7
⚷ 21♋02.3 ⚶ 21♉34.2
☽ Mean ☊ 7♒12.5

LONGITUDE

September 1990

Day	Sid.Time	☉	0 hr ☽	Noon ☽	True ☊	☿	♀	♂	⚳	♃	♄	♅	♆	♇
1 Sa	10 41 34	8♍47 55	19♑07 40	25♑21 31	7♒02.3	21♍12.2	22♌47.1	0♊30.1	2♍46.9	2♌56.1	19♑05.1	5♑40.4	11♑55.8	15♏21.8
2 Su	10 45 31	9 45 58	1♒39 50	8♒02 56	7R 02.8	20R 28.8	24 01.1	0 59.5	3 14.3	3 08.1	19R 03.1	5R 39.8	11R 55.1	15 23.1
3 M	10 49 27	10 44 03	14 31 04	21 04 23	7 02.0	19 40.5	25 15.1	1 28.5	3 41.7	3 20.0	19 01.1	5 39.2	11 54.5	15 24.4
4 Tu	10 53 24	11 42 10	27 42 54	4♓26 33	6 59.6	18 48.0	26 29.1	1 57.2	4 09.2	3 31.9	18 59.3	5 38.7	11 53.9	15 25.7
5 W	10 57 20	12 40 18	11♓15 09	18 08 26	6 55.5	17 52.2	27 43.1	2 25.5	4 36.6	3 43.7	18 57.6	5 38.2	11 53.3	15 27.0
6 Th	11 01 17	13 38 28	25 05 59	2♈07 20	6 50.3	16 54.2	28 57.2	2 53.5	5 04.0	3 55.4	18 55.9	5 37.8	11 52.7	15 28.4
7 F	11 05 14	14 36 39	9♈11 55	16 19 06	6 44.5	15 54.9	0♍11.3	3 21.0	5 31.4	4 07.1	18 54.3	5 37.4	11 52.2	15 29.8
8 Sa	11 09 10	15 34 53	23 28 16	0♉38 44	6 38.9	14 55.8	1 25.4	3 48.2	5 58.8	4 18.7	18 52.9	5 37.0	11 51.7	15 31.2
9 Su	11 13 07	16 33 09	7♉49 52	15 01 05	6 34.3	13 58.2	2 39.6	4 15.0	6 26.2	4 30.3	18 51.5	5 36.7	11 51.2	15 32.7
10 M	11 17 03	17 31 26	22 11 48	29 21 33	6 31.1	13 03.4	3 53.8	4 41.3	6 53.6	4 41.7	18 50.2	5 36.5	11 50.7	15 34.2
11 Tu	11 21 00	18 29 46	6♊29 57	13♊36 38	6D 29.7	12 12.7	5 08.1	5 07.3	7 21.0	4 53.1	18 49.0	5 36.3	11 50.3	15 35.7
12 W	11 24 56	19 28 08	20 41 22	27 43 57	6 29.9	11 27.4	6 22.4	5 32.8	7 48.4	5 04.4	18 47.9	5 36.2	11 49.9	15 37.2
13 Th	11 28 53	20 26 33	4♋44 15	11♋42 11	6 31.0	10 48.6	7 36.7	5 57.9	8 15.8	5 15.7	18 46.9	5 36.1	11 49.6	15 38.8
14 F	11 32 49	21 24 59	18 37 40	25 30 40	6R 32.2	10 17.3	8 51.1	6 22.5	8 43.1	5 26.8	18 46.0	5D 36.0	11 49.3	15 40.4
15 Sa	11 36 46	22 23 28	2♌21 09	9♌09 02	6 32.6	9 54.3	10 05.5	6 46.6	9 10.5	5 37.9	18 45.2	5 36.0	11 49.0	15 42.0
16 Su	11 40 43	23 21 58	15 54 18	22 36 50	6 31.3	9 40.2	11 19.9	7 10.3	9 37.9	5 48.9	18 44.5	5 36.1	11 48.7	15 43.7
17 M	11 44 39	24 20 30	29 16 35	5♍53 25	6 28.0	9D 35.4	12 34.3	7 33.5	10 05.2	5 59.8	18 43.9	5 36.2	11 48.5	15 45.4
18 Tu	11 48 36	25 19 05	12♍27 15	18 57 57	6 22.3	9 40.2	13 48.8	7 56.2	10 32.5	6 10.7	18 43.4	5 36.4	11 48.3	15 47.1
19 W	11 52 32	26 17 41	25 25 26	1♎49 37	6 14.6	9 54.5	15 03.3	8 18.4	10 59.8	6 21.4	18 42.9	5 36.6	11 48.2	15 48.8
20 Th	11 56 29	27 16 19	8♎10 27	14 27 55	6 05.4	10 18.3	16 17.9	8 40.1	11 27.1	6 32.1	18 42.6	5 36.9	11 48.0	15 50.5
21 F	12 00 25	28 15 00	20 42 02	26 52 54	5 55.7	10 51.4	17 32.4	9 01.2	11 54.4	6 42.6	18 42.4	5 37.2	11 47.9	15 52.3
22 Sa	12 04 22	29 13 41	3♏00 39	9♏05 30	5 46.4	11 33.3	18 47.0	9 21.9	12 21.7	6 53.1	18D 42.3	5 37.6	11 47.9	15 54.1
23 Su	12 08 18	0♎12 25	15 07 43	21 07 36	5 38.3	12 23.5	20 01.6	9 41.9	12 48.9	7 03.5	18 42.3	5 38.0	11D 47.9	15 55.9
24 M	12 12 15	1 11 11	27 05 33	3♐02 01	5 32.2	13 21.6	21 16.3	10 01.4	13 16.1	7 13.8	18 42.3	5 38.4	11 47.9	15 57.8
25 Tu	12 16 12	2 09 58	8♐57 30	14 52 31	5 28.3	14 26.9	22 30.9	10 20.4	13 43.3	7 24.0	18 42.5	5 39.0	11 47.9	15 59.7
26 W	12 20 08	3 08 47	20 47 39	26 43 32	5D 26.5	15 38.8	23 45.6	10 38.7	14 10.5	7 34.1	18 42.8	5 39.6	11 48.0	16 01.6
27 Th	12 24 05	4 07 38	2♑40 48	8♑40 07	5 26.4	16 56.5	25 00.3	10 56.5	14 37.7	7 44.0	18 43.2	5 40.2	11 48.1	16 03.5
28 F	12 28 01	5 06 31	14 42 07	20 47 29	5 27.1	18 19.5	26 15.0	11 13.7	15 04.8	7 53.9	18 43.6	5 40.9	11 48.2	16 05.4
29 Sa	12 31 58	6 05 25	26 56 51	3♒10 50	5R 27.7	19 47.0	27 29.8	11 30.2	15 31.9	8 03.7	18 44.2	5 41.6	11 48.4	16 07.4
30 Su	12 35 54	7 04 21	9♒30 00	15 54 50	5 27.2	21 18.4	28 44.6	11 46.2	15 59.0	8 13.4	18 44.9	5 42.4	11 48.6	16 09.4

LONGITUDE

October 1990

Day	Sid.Time	☉	0 hr ☽	Noon ☽	True ☊	☿	♀	♂	⚳	♃	♄	♅	♆	♇
1 M	12 39 51	8♎03 19	22♒25 45	29♒03 02	5♒24.8	22♍53.2	29♍59.3	12♊01.5	16♍26.1	8♌23.0	18♑45.7	5♑43.2	11♑48.8	16♏11.4
2 Tu	12 43 47	9 02 18	5♓46 53	12♓37 19	5R 19.9	24 30.7	1♎14.1	12 16.1	16 53.1	8 32.4	18 46.5	5 44.1	11 49.1	16 13.4
3 W	12 47 44	10 01 20	19 34 10	26 37 09	5 12.6	26 10.5	2 29.0	12 30.1	17 20.2	8 41.8	18 47.5	5 45.0	11 49.4	16 15.4
4 Th	12 51 41	11 00 23	3♈45 46	10♈59 21	5 03.3	27 52.2	3 43.8	12 43.4	17 47.1	8 51.0	18 48.6	5 46.0	11 49.8	16 17.5
5 F	12 55 37	11 59 28	18 17 06	25 38 04	4 53.0	29 35.2	4 58.7	12 56.1	18 14.1	9 00.2	18 49.7	5 47.0	11 50.1	16 19.5
6 Sa	12 59 34	12 58 36	3♉01 14	10♉25 31	4 42.8	1♎19.3	6 13.6	13 08.0	18 41.0	9 09.2	18 51.0	5 48.1	11 50.5	16 21.6
7 Su	13 03 30	13 57 46	17 49 53	25 13 20	4 34.0	3 04.2	7 28.5	13 19.2	19 08.0	9 18.1	18 52.4	5 49.2	11 51.0	16 23.7
8 M	13 07 27	14 56 58	2♊34 55	9♊53 52	4 27.5	4 49.7	8 43.4	13 29.7	19 34.8	9 26.9	18 53.8	5 50.4	11 51.4	16 25.9
9 Tu	13 11 23	15 56 12	17 09 32	24 21 25	4 23.5	6 35.3	9 58.4	13 39.5	20 01.7	9 35.6	18 55.4	5 51.6	11 52.0	16 28.0
10 W	13 15 20	16 55 29	1♋29 10	8♋32 37	4D 21.8	8 21.1	11 13.3	13 48.5	20 28.5	9 44.1	18 57.1	5 52.9	11 52.5	16 30.2
11 Th	13 19 16	17 54 48	15 31 39	22 26 20	4R 21.6	10 06.9	12 28.3	13 56.7	20 55.3	9 52.5	18 58.8	5 54.3	11 53.1	16 32.4
12 F	13 23 13	18 54 10	29 16 45	6♌03 06	4 21.8	11 52.4	13 43.3	14 04.1	21 22.1	10 00.8	19 00.7	5 55.6	11 53.7	16 34.6
13 Sa	13 27 10	19 53 33	12♌45 33	19 24 21	4 21.0	13 37.7	14 58.4	14 10.7	21 48.8	10 09.0	19 02.6	5 57.1	11 54.3	16 36.8
14 Su	13 31 06	20 52 59	25 59 42	2♍31 49	4 18.1	15 22.5	16 13.4	14 16.6	22 15.5	10 17.0	19 04.7	5 58.5	11 55.0	16 39.0
15 M	13 35 03	21 52 28	9♍00 54	15 27 06	4 12.5	17 07.0	17 28.5	14 21.5	22 42.1	10 24.9	19 06.8	6 00.0	11 55.7	16 41.2
16 Tu	13 38 59	22 51 58	21 50 32	28 11 18	4 03.8	18 50.9	18 43.6	14 25.7	23 08.8	10 32.7	19 09.0	6 01.6	11 56.4	16 43.5
17 W	13 42 56	23 51 30	4♎29 29	10♎45 08	3 52.4	20 34.3	19 58.6	14 29.0	23 35.3	10 40.3	19 11.3	6 03.2	11 57.2	16 45.7
18 Th	13 46 52	24 51 05	16 58 17	23 08 58	3 39.1	22 17.2	21 13.8	14 31.4	24 01.9	10 47.8	19 13.8	6 04.9	11 58.0	16 48.0
19 F	13 50 49	25 50 42	29 17 15	5♏23 10	3 24.8	23 59.4	22 28.9	14 33.0	24 28.4	10 55.2	19 16.3	6 06.6	11 58.8	16 50.3
20 Sa	13 54 45	26 50 20	11♏26 50	17 28 21	3 10.9	25 41.1	23 44.0	14R 33.7	24 54.8	11 02.4	19 18.9	6 08.4	11 59.7	16 52.6
21 Su	13 58 42	27 50 01	23 27 55	29 25 42	2 58.5	27 22.2	24 59.2	14 33.6	25 21.2	11 09.5	19 21.6	6 10.2	12 00.6	16 54.9
22 M	14 02 38	28 49 43	5♐22 00	11♐17 08	2 48.4	29 02.6	26 14.3	14 32.5	25 47.6	11 16.4	19 24.4	6 12.0	12 01.5	16 57.2
23 Tu	14 06 35	29 49 28	17 11 28	23 05 26	2 41.2	0♏42.5	27 29.5	14 30.6	26 13.9	11 23.2	19 27.3	6 13.9	12 02.4	16 59.6
24 W	14 10 32	0♏49 14	28 59 32	4♑54 16	2 36.8	2 21.8	28 44.7	14 27.8	26 40.2	11 29.8	19 30.3	6 15.8	12 03.4	17 01.9
25 Th	14 14 28	1 49 02	10♑50 15	16 48 05	2 34.9	4 00.5	29 59.8	14 24.1	27 06.4	11 36.3	19 33.3	6 17.8	12 04.5	17 04.3
26 F	14 18 25	2 48 51	22 48 25	28 51 56	2 34.4	5 38.7	1♏15.0	14 19.5	27 32.5	11 42.6	19 36.5	6 19.8	12 05.5	17 06.6
27 Sa	14 22 21	3 48 42	4♒59 20	11♒11 17	2 34.3	7 16.3	2 30.2	14 14.0	27 58.7	11 48.8	19 39.7	6 21.9	12 06.6	17 09.0
28 Su	14 26 18	4 48 35	17 28 26	23 51 27	2 33.5	8 53.4	3 45.4	14 07.6	28 24.7	11 54.8	19 43.0	6 24.0	12 07.7	17 11.4
29 M	14 30 14	5 48 29	0♓20 52	6♓57 11	2 30.8	10 29.9	5 00.6	14 00.3	28 50.7	12 00.7	19 46.5	6 26.2	12 08.8	17 13.8
30 Tu	14 34 11	6 48 25	13 40 45	20 31 48	2 25.5	12 06.0	6 15.9	13 52.2	29 16.7	12 06.4	19 50.0	6 28.4	12 10.0	17 16.2
31 W	14 38 07	7 48 23	27 30 22	4♈36 18	2 17.6	13 41.5	7 31.1	13 43.2	29 42.5	12 11.9	19 53.5	6 30.6	12 11.2	17 18.5

Astro Data Dy Hr Mn	Planet Ingress Dy Hr Mn	Last Aspect Dy Hr Mn	☽ Ingress Dy Hr Mn	Last Aspect Dy Hr Mn	☽ Ingress Dy Hr Mn	☽ Phases & Eclipses Dy Hr Mn
☿0N 3 8:08	♀ ♍ 7 8:21	1 4:25 ☿ △	♒ 1 20:51	30 12:27 ♇ □	♓ 1 13:42	5 1:46 ○ 12♓15
☽0N 5 17:54	☉ ♎ 23 6:56	3 20:20 ♀ ☍	♓ 4 4:06	3 11:09 ☿ ☍	♈ 3 17:42	11 20:53 ☾ 18♊51
♅D 14 18:29		5 13:25 ♄ ⚹	♈ 6 8:23	5 0:53 ♄ □	♉ 5 19:06	19 0:46 ● 25♍50
♃⚻♅ 15 7:55	♀ ♎ 1 12:13	7 16:20 ♄ □	♉ 8 10:55	7 1:40 ♄ △	♊ 7 19:47	27 2:06 ☽ 3♑43
☿D 17 12:06	☿ ♎ 5 17:44	9 18:24 ♄ △	♊ 10 13:05	8 20:57 ☉ △	♋ 9 21:29	
☽0S 18 16:51	☿ ♏ 23 1:46	11 20:53 ☉ □	♋ 12 15:53	11 5:58 ♄ ☍	♌ 12 1:16	4 12:02 ○ 11♈00
♄D 23 5:10	☉ ♏ 23 16:14	14 4:19 ☉ ⚹	♌ 14 19:52	13 12:57 ☉ ⚹	♍ 14 7:21	11 3:31 ☾ 17♋34
☉0S 23 6:55	♀ ♏ 25 12:03	15 23:40 ♇ □	♍ 17 1:19	15 18:53 ♄ △	♎ 16 15:26	18 15:37 ● 25♎00
♆D 23 18:37		19 0:46 ☉ ☌	♎ 19 8:34	18 15:37 ☉ ☌	♏ 19 1:24	26 20:26 ☽ 3♒10
☽0N 3 3:21		20 20:09 ♄ □	♏ 21 18:06	20 15:42 ♄ ⚹	♐ 21 13:09	
♀0S 4 3:38		23 9:32 ♀ ⚹	♐ 24 5:52	23 22:01 ♀ ⚹	♑ 24 2:03	
☿0S 8 4:34		26 5:18 ♀ □	♑ 26 18:36	25 17:32 ♄ ☌	♒ 26 14:14	
☽0S 15 23:15		28 23:50 ♀ △	♒ 29 5:54	27 23:25 ♇ □	♓ 28 23:22	
♂R 20 19:30				30 10:47 ♄ ⚹	♈ 31 4:14	
☽0N 30 13:12	♃⚻⚻31 8:04					

Astro Data

1 September 1990
Julian Day # 33116
SVP 5♓23'10"
GC 26♐42.5 ⚴ 2♌01.2
Eris 17♈24.0R ⚵ 17♏00.7
⚷ 24♋03.4 ⚶ 28♉54.6
☽ Mean ☊ 5♒34.0

1 October 1990
Julian Day # 33146
SVP 5♓23'06"
GC 26♐42.6 ⚴ 18♌49.2
Eris 17♈07.7R ⚵ 24♏57.4
⚷ 26♋14.4 ⚶ 1♊06.9R
☽ Mean ☊ 3♒58.7

November 1990

LONGITUDE

Day	Sid.Time	☉	0 hr ☽	Noon ☽	True ☊	☿	♀	♂	⚳	♃	♄	♅	♆	♇
1 Th	14 42 04	8♏48 22	11♈49 15	19♈08 36	2♒07.4	15♏16.6	8♏46.3	13♊33.3	0♎08.4	12♌17.3	19♑57.2	6♑32.9	12♑12.4	17♏20.9
2 F	14 46 01	9 48 24	26 33 33	4♉03 04	1R56.0	16 51.3	10 01.5	13R22.6	0 34.2	12 22.5	20 01.0	6 35.2	12 13.7	17 23.3
3 Sa	14 49 57	10 48 27	11♉35 58	19 10 58	1 44.6	18 25.5	11 16.8	13 11.1	0 59.9	12 27.6	20 04.8	6 37.6	12 15.0	17 25.8
4 Su	14 53 54	11 48 32	26 46 40	4♊21 45	1 34.5	19 59.3	12 32.0	12 58.7	1 25.5	12 32.4	20 08.7	6 39.9	12 16.3	17 28.2
5 M	14 57 50	12 48 39	11♊54 54	19 24 59	1 26.8	21 32.6	13 47.3	12 45.5	1 51.1	12 37.2	20 12.7	6 42.4	12 17.6	17 30.6
6 Tu	15 01 47	13 48 48	26 51 01	4♋12 11	1 21.9	23 05.6	15 02.6	12 31.5	2 16.7	12 41.7	20 16.8	6 44.9	12 19.0	17 33.0
7 W	15 05 43	14 48 59	11♋27 54	18 37 47	1D19.7	24 38.3	16 17.9	12 16.7	2 42.1	12 46.1	20 21.0	6 47.4	12 20.4	17 35.4
8 Th	15 09 40	15 49 12	25 41 39	2♌39 27	1 19.2	26 10.5	17 33.1	12 01.1	3 07.6	12 50.3	20 25.2	6 49.9	12 21.8	17 37.9
9 F	15 13 37	16 49 27	9♌31 19	16 17 27	1R19.4	27 42.4	18 48.4	11 44.9	3 32.9	12 54.3	20 29.5	6 52.5	12 23.3	17 40.3
10 Sa	15 17 33	17 49 44	22 58 09	29 33 47	1 18.9	29 14.0	20 03.7	11 27.9	3 58.2	12 58.2	20 33.9	6 55.1	12 24.8	17 42.7
11 Su	15 21 30	18 50 04	6♍04 43	12♍31 21	1 16.5	0♐45.2	21 19.0	11 10.2	4 23.4	13 01.8	20 38.4	6 57.8	12 26.3	17 45.1
12 M	15 25 26	19 50 25	18 54 06	25 13 19	1 11.6	2 16.0	22 34.4	10 51.9	4 48.5	13 05.3	20 42.9	7 00.5	12 27.8	17 47.6
13 Tu	15 29 23	20 50 48	1♎29 21	7♎42 32	1 03.8	3 46.5	23 49.7	10 32.9	5 13.5	13 08.6	20 47.5	7 03.2	12 29.4	17 50.0
14 W	15 33 19	21 51 12	13 53 08	20 01 24	0 53.3	5 16.7	25 05.0	10 13.4	5 38.5	13 11.7	20 52.2	7 06.0	12 30.9	17 52.4
15 Th	15 37 16	22 51 39	26 07 33	2♏11 45	0 41.0	6 46.5	26 20.3	9 53.3	6 03.4	13 14.7	20 57.0	7 08.8	12 32.5	17 54.8
16 F	15 41 12	23 52 07	8♏14 12	14 15 01	0 27.8	8 16.0	27 35.7	9 32.8	6 28.2	13 17.4	21 01.8	7 11.6	12 34.2	17 57.2
17 Sa	15 45 09	24 52 37	20 14 22	26 12 22	0 14.8	9 45.0	28 51.0	9 11.8	6 53.0	13 20.0	21 06.7	7 14.4	12 35.8	17 59.7
18 Su	15 49 06	25 53 09	2♐09 11	8♐05 00	0 03.2	11 13.7	0♐06.4	8 50.4	7 17.6	13 22.4	21 11.7	7 17.3	12 37.5	18 02.1
19 M	15 53 02	26 53 42	14 00 00	19 54 24	29♑53.7	12 41.9	1 21.7	8 28.7	7 42.2	13 24.5	21 16.8	7 20.3	12 39.2	18 04.5
20 Tu	15 56 59	27 54 17	25 48 29	1♑42 34	29 47.0	14 09.6	2 37.1	8 06.7	8 06.7	13 26.5	21 21.9	7 23.2	12 40.9	18 06.9
21 W	16 00 55	28 54 53	7♑36 59	13 32 09	29 43.1	15 36.9	3 52.4	7 44.4	8 31.0	13 28.3	21 27.1	7 26.2	12 42.7	18 09.3
22 Th	16 04 52	29 55 30	19 28 30	25 26 33	29D41.5	17 03.5	5 07.8	7 22.0	8 55.3	13 29.9	21 32.3	7 29.2	12 44.5	18 11.7
23 F	16 08 48	0♐56 08	1♒26 49	7♒29 53	29 41.7	18 29.5	6 23.1	6 59.4	9 19.5	13 31.4	21 37.6	7 32.3	12 46.3	18 14.1
24 Sa	16 12 45	1 56 48	13 36 21	19 46 50	29 42.6	19 54.8	7 38.5	6 36.7	9 43.6	13 32.6	21 43.0	7 35.3	12 48.1	18 16.4
25 Su	16 16 41	2 57 28	26 01 58	2♓22 23	29R43.1	21 19.3	8 53.8	6 13.9	10 07.7	13 33.6	21 48.4	7 38.4	12 49.9	18 18.8
26 M	16 20 38	3 58 10	8♓48 41	15 21 24	29 42.4	22 42.9	10 09.2	5 51.2	10 31.6	13 34.4	21 53.9	7 41.5	12 51.8	18 21.2
27 Tu	16 24 35	4 58 53	22 01 00	28 47 53	29 39.7	24 05.4	11 24.5	5 28.6	10 55.4	13 35.0	21 59.5	7 44.7	12 53.6	18 23.5
28 W	16 28 31	5 59 36	5♈42 16	12♈44 13	29 34.9	25 26.8	12 39.9	5 06.0	11 19.1	13 35.5	22 05.1	7 47.9	12 55.5	18 25.9
29 Th	16 32 28	7 00 21	19 53 38	27 10 09	29 28.1	26 46.7	13 55.2	4 43.7	11 42.7	13R35.7	22 10.7	7 51.1	12 57.4	18 28.2
30 F	16 36 24	8 01 07	4♉33 14	12♉02 03	29 20.1	28 05.2	15 10.6	4 21.6	12 06.2	13 35.8	22 16.5	7 54.3	12 59.4	18 30.5

December 1990

LONGITUDE

Day	Sid.Time	☉	0 hr ☽	Noon ☽	True ☊	☿	♀	♂	⚳	♃	♄	♅	♆	♇
1 Sa	16 40 21	9♐01 54	19♉35 37	27♉12 43	29♑12.0	29♐21.8	16♐25.9	3♊59.7	12♎29.6	13♌35.6	22♑22.3	7♑57.5	13♑01.3	18♏32.8
2 Su	16 44 17	10 02 42	4♊52 01	12♊32 06	29R04.7	0♑36.3	17 41.3	3R38.1	12 52.8	13R35.3	22 28.1	8 00.8	13 03.3	18 35.1
3 M	16 48 14	11 03 31	20 11 31	27 48 55	28 59.2	1 48.5	18 56.6	3 16.9	13 16.0	13 34.7	22 34.0	8 04.1	13 05.3	18 37.4
4 Tu	16 52 10	12 04 22	5♋23 01	12♋52 42	28 56.0	2 58.0	20 12.0	2 56.1	13 39.1	13 34.0	22 39.9	8 07.4	13 07.3	18 39.7
5 W	16 56 07	13 05 14	20 17 03	27 35 22	28D54.9	4 04.2	21 27.3	2 35.7	14 02.0	13 33.0	22 45.9	8 10.7	13 09.3	18 42.0
6 Th	17 00 04	14 06 07	4♌47 10	11♌52 09	28 55.4	5 06.9	22 42.7	2 15.8	14 24.8	13 31.9	22 52.0	8 14.1	13 11.3	18 44.2
7 F	17 04 00	15 07 01	18 50 14	25 41 29	28 56.8	6 05.4	23 58.0	1 56.4	14 47.6	13 30.5	22 58.1	8 17.4	13 13.4	18 46.4
8 Sa	17 07 57	16 07 56	2♍26 05	9♍04 22	28R57.9	6 59.1	25 13.3	1 37.5	15 10.1	13 29.0	23 04.2	8 20.8	13 15.4	18 48.7
9 Su	17 11 53	17 08 53	15 36 41	22 03 30	28 58.0	7 47.4	26 28.7	1 19.2	15 32.6	13 27.3	23 10.4	8 24.2	13 17.5	18 50.9
10 M	17 15 50	18 09 51	28 25 18	4♎42 33	28 56.5	8 29.6	27 44.0	1 01.5	15 54.9	13 25.3	23 16.6	8 27.6	13 19.6	18 53.1
11 Tu	17 19 46	19 10 50	10♎55 46	17 05 26	28 53.1	9 04.7	28 59.4	0 44.4	16 17.1	13 23.2	23 22.9	8 31.1	13 21.7	18 55.2
12 W	17 23 43	20 11 50	23 11 59	29 15 54	28 47.9	9 32.1	0♑14.7	0 28.1	16 39.2	13 20.9	23 29.2	8 34.5	13 23.8	18 57.4
13 Th	17 27 39	21 12 52	5♏17 33	11♏17 20	28 41.3	9 50.7	1 30.1	0 12.4	17 01.1	13 18.4	23 35.6	8 38.0	13 26.0	18 59.5
14 F	17 31 36	22 13 54	17 15 35	23 12 37	28 34.1	9R59.8	2 45.4	29♉57.4	17 22.9	13 15.6	23 42.0	8 41.5	13 28.1	19 01.7
15 Sa	17 35 33	23 14 57	29 08 43	5♐04 09	28 27.0	9 58.5	4 00.8	29 43.2	17 44.6	13 12.7	23 48.5	8 45.0	13 30.3	19 03.8
16 Su	17 39 29	24 16 01	10♐59 08	16 53 54	28 20.7	9 46.1	5 16.1	29 29.7	18 06.1	13 09.6	23 55.0	8 48.5	13 32.4	19 05.9
17 M	17 43 26	25 17 06	22 48 41	28 43 41	28 15.7	9 22.3	6 31.5	29 17.1	18 27.4	13 06.4	24 01.5	8 52.0	13 34.6	19 07.9
18 Tu	17 47 22	26 18 11	4♑39 07	10♑35 14	28 12.4	8 46.8	7 46.8	29 05.2	18 48.6	13 02.9	24 08.1	8 55.5	13 36.8	19 10.0
19 W	17 51 19	27 19 17	16 32 17	22 30 32	28D10.9	7 59.8	9 02.2	28 54.1	19 09.7	12 59.2	24 14.7	8 59.0	13 39.0	19 12.0
20 Th	17 55 15	28 20 24	28 30 17	4♒31 51	28 10.9	7 02.3	10 17.5	28 43.8	19 30.6	12 55.4	24 21.3	9 02.6	13 41.2	19 14.0
21 F	17 59 12	29 21 30	10♒35 36	16 41 55	28 12.1	5 55.3	11 32.8	28 34.4	19 51.3	12 51.4	24 28.0	9 06.2	13 43.4	19 16.0
22 Sa	18 03 08	0♑22 37	22 51 12	29 03 56	28 13.8	4 40.8	12 48.2	28 25.8	20 11.9	12 47.2	24 34.7	9 09.7	13 45.6	19 18.0
23 Su	18 07 05	1 23 44	5♓20 31	11♓41 28	28 15.5	3 21.1	14 03.5	28 18.0	20 32.3	12 42.8	24 41.4	9 13.3	13 47.8	19 19.9
24 M	18 11 02	2 24 52	18 07 12	24 38 12	28R16.7	1 58.8	15 18.8	28 11.1	20 52.5	12 38.3	24 48.2	9 16.9	13 50.1	19 21.8
25 Tu	18 14 58	3 25 59	1♈14 51	7♈57 30	28 16.8	0 36.7	16 34.1	28 05.0	21 12.6	12 33.5	24 55.0	9 20.4	13 52.3	19 23.7
26 W	18 18 55	4 27 07	14 46 27	21 41 52	28 15.8	29♐17.4	17 49.4	27 59.7	21 32.5	12 28.6	25 01.8	9 24.0	13 54.6	19 25.6
27 Th	18 22 51	5 28 14	28 43 47	5♉52 07	28 13.7	28 03.5	19 04.6	27 55.2	21 52.2	12 23.6	25 08.7	9 27.6	13 56.8	19 27.5
28 F	18 26 48	6 29 22	13♉06 35	20 26 44	28 11.0	26 56.8	20 19.9	27 51.6	22 11.8	12 18.4	25 15.5	9 31.2	13 59.1	19 29.3
29 Sa	18 30 44	7 30 29	27 51 56	5♊21 22	28 08.0	25 59.1	21 35.2	27 48.8	22 31.1	12 13.0	25 22.4	9 34.8	14 01.3	19 31.1
30 Su	18 34 41	8 31 37	12♊54 04	20 28 54	28 05.4	25 11.1	22 50.4	27 46.8	22 50.3	12 07.5	25 29.3	9 38.4	14 03.6	19 32.9
31 M	18 38 38	9 32 45	28 04 40	5♋40 07	28 03.5	24 33.6	24 05.7	27 45.6	23 09.3	12 01.8	25 36.3	9 42.0	14 05.9	19 34.6

Astro Data	Planet Ingress	Last Aspect	☽ Ingress	Last Aspect	☽ Ingress	☽ Phases & Eclipses	Astro Data
Dy Hr Mn	Dy Hr Mn	Dy Hr Mn	Dy Hr Mn	Dy Hr Mn	Dy Hr Mn	Dy Hr Mn	1 November 1990
☽0S 12 4:05	⚳ ♎ 1 4:12	1 13:19 ♄ □	♉ 2 5:31	1 4:20 ♄ △	♊ 1 16:23	2 21:48 ○ 10♉13	Julian Day # 33177
☽0N 26 21:45	☿ ♐ 11 0:06	3 13:25 ♄ △	♊ 4 5:06	2 20:48 ♀ ☍	♋ 3 15:27	9 13:02 ☾ 16♌52	SVP 5♓23'03"
♃R 30 5:03	♀ ♐ 18 9:58	5 1:30 ♂ ☌	♋ 6 5:07	5 4:00 ♄ ☍	♌ 5 16:00	17 9:05 ● 24♏45	GC 26♐42.7 ⚵ 4♍23.7
	☊ ♑R 18 19:23	7 23:27 ☿ △	♌ 8 7:24	7 8:39 ♀ △	♍ 7 19:39	25 13:11 ☽ 3♓00	Eris 16♈49.3R ⚴ 4♐42.0
☽0S 9 9:15	☉ ♐ 22 13:47	10 11:19 ☿ □	♍ 10 12:48	9 21:14 ♀ □	♎ 10 3:00		⚷ 27♋17.8 ⚶ 26♉47.8R
♃⚻♆ 11 20:13		12 6:24 ♀ ⚹	♎ 12 21:08	12 0:28 ♄ □	♏ 12 13:28	2 7:50 ○ 9♊52	☽ Mean ☊ 2♒20.2
☿R 14 21:10	☿ ♑ 2 0:13	14 13:40 ♄ □	♏ 15 7:39	15 1:22 ♂ ☍	♐ 15 1:44	9 2:04 ☾ 16♍44	
☽0N 24 4:10	♀ ♑ 12 7:18	17 17:58 ♀ ☌	♐ 17 19:39	17 4:22 ☉ ☌	♑ 17 14:35	17 4:22 ● 24♐58	1 December 1990
	♂ ♉R 14 7:46	18 22:46 ♃ △	♑ 20 8:31	20 0:37 ♂ △	♒ 20 2:59	25 3:16 ☽ 3♈04	Julian Day # 33207
	☉ ♑ 22 3:07	22 4:06 ♄ ☌	♒ 22 21:07	22 10:47 ♂ □	♓ 22 13:48	31 18:35 ○ 9♋50	SVP 5♓22'58"
	☿ ♐R 25 22:57	24 12:17 ☿ ⚹	♓ 25 7:32	24 18:25 ♂ ⚹	♈ 24 21:45		GC 26♐42.7 ⚵ 16♍35.2
		27 2:45 ☿ □	♈ 27 14:06	26 23:54 ☿ △	♉ 27 2:09		Eris 16♈35.3R ⚴ 14♐58.3
		29 11:18 ☿ △	♉ 29 16:37	28 23:57 ♂ ☌	♊ 29 3:26		⚷ 26♋54.6R ⚶ 19♉17.5R
				30 19:07 ☿ ☍	♋ 31 3:02		☽ Mean ☊ 0♒44.9

LONGITUDE — January 1991

Day	Sid.Time	☉	0 hr ☽	Noon ☽	True ☊	☿	♀	♂	⚳	♃	♄	♅	♆	♇
1 Tu	18 42 34	10♑33 53	13♋14 02	20♋45 11	28♑02.5	24♐06.5	25♑20.9	27♉45.2	23♎28.1	11♌56.0	25♑43.3	9♑45.6	14♑08.1	19♏36.3
2 W	18 46 31	11 35 01	28 12 31	5♌35 04	28D 02.5	23R 49.7	26 36.1	27D 45.6	23 46.7	11R 50.1	25 50.2	9 49.2	14 10.4	19 38.0
3 Th	18 50 27	12 36 09	12♌52 04	20 02 55	28 03.3	23D 42.7	27 51.4	27 46.7	24 05.1	11 43.9	25 57.2	9 52.8	14 12.7	19 39.7
4 F	18 54 24	13 37 17	27 07 11	4♍04 37	28 04.5	23 45.0	29 06.6	27 48.6	24 23.3	11 37.7	26 04.3	9 56.4	14 15.0	19 41.4
5 Sa	18 58 20	14 38 25	10♍55 10	17 38 54	28 05.7	23 55.8	0♒21.8	27 51.2	24 41.3	11 31.3	26 11.3	10 00.0	14 17.2	19 43.0
6 Su	19 02 17	15 39 34	24 16 01	0♎46 50	28 06.6	24 14.6	1 37.0	27 54.5	24 59.1	11 24.8	26 18.3	10 03.5	14 19.5	19 44.6
7 M	19 06 13	16 40 43	7♎11 44	13 31 12	28R 07.0	24 40.4	2 52.1	27 58.6	25 16.7	11 18.2	26 25.4	10 07.1	14 21.8	19 46.1
8 Tu	19 10 10	17 41 52	19 45 44	25 55 53	28 06.9	25 12.8	4 07.3	28 03.4	25 34.0	11 11.4	26 32.5	10 10.7	14 24.1	19 47.7
9 W	19 14 07	18 43 01	2♏02 11	8♏05 12	28 06.3	25 50.9	5 22.5	28 08.9	25 51.2	11 04.6	26 39.6	10 14.3	14 26.3	19 49.2
10 Th	19 18 03	19 44 10	14 05 29	20 03 36	28 05.4	26 34.3	6 37.6	28 15.2	26 08.1	10 57.6	26 46.7	10 17.8	14 28.6	19 50.6
11 F	19 22 00	20 45 19	26 00 02	1♐55 17	28 04.3	27 22.4	7 52.8	28 22.0	26 24.8	10 50.5	26 53.8	10 21.4	14 30.9	19 52.1
12 Sa	19 25 56	21 46 28	7♐49 49	13 44 04	28 03.3	28 14.7	9 07.9	28 29.6	26 41.2	10 43.3	27 00.9	10 24.9	14 33.1	19 53.5
13 Su	19 29 53	22 47 37	19 38 25	25 33 16	28 02.4	29 10.7	10 23.0	28 37.8	26 57.4	10 36.1	27 08.0	10 28.5	14 35.4	19 54.9
14 M	19 33 49	23 48 46	1♑28 54	7♑25 40	28 01.9	0♑10.0	11 38.2	28 46.7	27 13.4	10 28.7	27 15.1	10 32.0	14 37.6	19 56.3
15 Tu	19 37 46	24 49 54	13 23 49	19 23 36	28D 01.7	1 12.4	12 53.3	28 56.2	27 29.1	10 21.2	27 22.3	10 35.5	14 39.9	19 57.6
16 W	19 41 42	25 51 02	25 25 15	1♒28 58	28 01.6	2 17.5	14 08.3	29 06.3	27 44.6	10 13.7	27 29.4	10 39.1	14 42.1	19 58.9
17 Th	19 45 39	26 52 10	7♒34 57	13 43 24	28 01.7	3 25.0	15 23.4	29 17.1	27 59.8	10 06.1	27 36.6	10 42.6	14 44.4	20 00.1
18 F	19 49 36	27 53 16	19 54 28	26 08 22	28R 01.8	4 34.8	16 38.5	29 28.4	28 14.8	9 58.4	27 43.7	10 46.0	14 46.6	20 01.4
19 Sa	19 53 32	28 54 22	2♓25 16	8♓45 22	28 01.7	5 46.5	17 53.5	29 40.4	28 29.5	9 50.7	27 50.8	10 49.5	14 48.8	20 02.6
20 Su	19 57 29	29 55 27	15 08 49	21 35 51	28 01.5	7 00.0	19 08.5	29 52.9	28 43.9	9 42.9	27 58.0	10 53.0	14 51.1	20 03.7
21 M	20 01 25	0♒56 32	28 06 38	4♈41 23	28 01.3	8 15.2	20 23.5	0♊05.9	28 58.0	9 35.1	28 05.1	10 56.4	14 53.3	20 04.8
22 Tu	20 05 22	1 57 35	11♈20 15	18 03 25	28 01.0	9 31.9	21 38.5	0 19.5	29 11.9	9 27.2	28 12.2	10 59.8	14 55.5	20 05.9
23 W	20 09 18	2 58 38	24 50 59	1♉43 05	28D 00.9	10 50.0	22 53.4	0 33.7	29 25.5	9 19.2	28 19.4	11 03.2	14 57.7	20 07.0
24 Th	20 13 15	3 59 39	8♉39 43	15 40 52	28 01.0	12 09.3	24 08.3	0 48.3	29 38.8	9 11.3	28 26.5	11 06.6	14 59.8	20 08.0
25 F	20 17 11	5 00 40	22 46 25	29 56 08	28 01.4	13 29.9	25 23.3	1 03.5	29 51.9	9 03.3	28 33.6	11 10.0	15 02.0	20 09.0
26 Sa	20 21 08	6 01 39	7♊09 45	14♊26 47	28 02.1	14 51.7	26 38.1	1 19.2	0♏04.6	8 55.3	28 40.7	11 13.4	15 04.2	20 10.0
27 Su	20 25 05	7 02 37	21 46 44	29 08 57	28 02.8	16 14.4	27 53.0	1 35.3	0 17.0	8 47.3	28 47.8	11 16.7	15 06.3	20 10.9
28 M	20 29 01	8 03 35	6♋32 39	13♋57 03	28R 03.5	17 38.2	29 07.8	1 52.0	0 29.2	8 39.3	28 54.9	11 20.0	15 08.5	20 11.8
29 Tu	20 32 58	9 04 31	21 21 13	28 44 16	28 03.7	19 03.0	0♓22.6	2 09.0	0 41.0	8 31.3	29 02.0	11 23.3	15 10.6	20 12.7
30 W	20 36 54	10 05 26	6♌05 15	13♌23 19	28 03.4	20 28.7	1 37.4	2 26.6	0 52.6	8 23.3	29 09.0	11 26.6	15 12.7	20 13.5
31 Th	20 40 51	11 06 20	20 37 36	27 47 23	28 02.3	21 55.3	2 52.2	2 44.5	1 03.8	8 15.3	29 16.1	11 29.8	15 14.8	20 14.3

LONGITUDE — February 1991

Day	Sid.Time	☉	0 hr ☽	Noon ☽	True ☊	☿	♀	♂	⚳	♃	♄	♅	♆	♇
1 F	20 44 47	12♒07 13	4♍52 02	11♍51 05	28♑00.7	23♑22.7	4♓06.9	3♊02.9	1♏14.7	8♌07.3	29♑23.1	11♑33.1	15♑16.9	20♏15.0
2 Sa	20 48 44	13 08 05	18 44 09	25 31 03	27R 58.6	24 51.0	5 21.6	3 21.7	1 25.3	7R 59.3	29 30.1	11 36.3	15 19.0	20 15.8
3 Su	20 52 40	14 08 57	2♎11 42	8♎46 09	27 56.4	26 20.1	6 36.2	3 40.8	1 35.5	7 51.4	29 37.1	11 39.4	15 21.0	20 16.4
4 M	20 56 37	15 09 47	15 14 36	21 37 20	27 54.4	27 50.0	7 50.9	4 00.4	1 45.4	7 43.5	29 44.1	11 42.6	15 23.1	20 17.1
5 Tu	21 00 34	16 10 37	27 54 44	4♏07 14	27 53.1	29 20.7	9 05.5	4 20.4	1 55.0	7 35.6	29 51.1	11 45.7	15 25.1	20 17.7
6 W	21 04 30	17 11 25	10♏15 22	16 19 41	27D 52.5	0♒52.2	10 20.1	4 40.7	2 04.3	7 27.8	29 58.0	11 48.8	15 27.1	20 18.3
7 Th	21 08 27	18 12 13	22 20 47	28 19 16	27 52.9	2 24.5	11 34.7	5 01.4	2 13.1	7 20.0	0♒04.9	11 51.9	15 29.1	20 18.8
8 F	21 12 23	19 13 00	4♐15 45	10♐10 52	27 54.1	3 57.6	12 49.2	5 22.5	2 21.7	7 12.3	0 11.8	11 55.0	15 31.1	20 19.3
9 Sa	21 16 20	20 13 46	16 05 13	21 59 22	27 55.8	5 31.5	14 03.7	5 43.9	2 29.9	7 04.6	0 18.7	11 58.0	15 33.0	20 19.8
10 Su	21 20 16	21 14 31	27 53 55	3♑49 23	27 57.6	7 06.2	15 18.2	6 05.7	2 37.7	6 57.0	0 25.6	12 01.0	15 35.0	20 20.2
11 M	21 24 13	22 15 15	9♑46 16	15 45 02	27 59.0	8 41.7	16 32.6	6 27.8	2 45.2	6 49.5	0 32.4	12 04.0	15 36.9	20 20.6
12 Tu	21 28 09	23 15 57	21 46 05	27 49 47	27R 59.5	10 18.1	17 47.0	6 50.2	2 52.2	6 42.0	0 39.2	12 06.9	15 38.8	20 21.0
13 W	21 32 06	24 16 39	3♒56 26	10♒06 19	27 58.9	11 55.2	19 01.4	7 13.0	2 59.0	6 34.7	0 46.0	12 09.8	15 40.7	20 21.3
14 Th	21 36 03	25 17 19	16 19 36	22 36 27	27 56.9	13 33.2	20 15.8	7 36.1	3 05.3	6 27.4	0 52.7	12 12.7	15 42.6	20 21.6
15 F	21 39 59	26 17 57	28 56 56	5♓21 05	27 53.4	15 12.0	21 30.1	7 59.4	3 11.2	6 20.2	0 59.4	12 15.5	15 44.4	20 21.9
16 Sa	21 43 56	27 18 34	11♓48 54	18 20 19	27 48.9	16 51.8	22 44.4	8 23.1	3 16.8	6 13.2	1 06.1	12 18.3	15 46.2	20 22.1
17 Su	21 47 52	28 19 09	24 55 14	1♈33 33	27 43.8	18 32.3	23 58.6	8 47.1	3 22.0	6 06.2	1 12.7	12 21.1	15 48.0	20 22.3
18 M	21 51 49	29 19 43	8♈15 05	14 59 43	27 38.7	20 13.8	25 12.8	9 11.3	3 26.7	5 59.3	1 19.3	12 23.8	15 49.8	20 22.4
19 Tu	21 55 45	0♓20 15	21 47 15	28 37 34	27 34.4	21 56.2	26 26.9	9 35.8	3 31.1	5 52.6	1 25.9	12 26.5	15 51.6	20 22.5
20 W	21 59 42	1 20 45	5♉30 28	12♉25 49	27 31.3	23 39.5	27 41.1	10 00.6	3 35.1	5 45.9	1 32.4	12 29.2	15 53.3	20 22.6
21 Th	22 03 38	2 21 13	19 23 28	26 23 17	27D 29.9	25 23.7	28 55.1	10 25.7	3 38.6	5 39.4	1 38.9	12 31.8	15 55.1	20R 22.6
22 F	22 07 35	3 21 40	3♊25 07	10♊28 50	27 29.9	27 08.9	0♈09.2	10 51.0	3 41.8	5 33.1	1 45.4	12 34.4	15 56.7	20 22.6
23 Sa	22 11 32	4 22 04	17 34 14	24 41 09	27 31.0	28 55.0	1 23.1	11 16.6	3 44.6	5 26.8	1 51.8	12 37.0	15 58.4	20 22.6
24 Su	22 15 28	5 22 27	1♋49 19	8♋58 30	27 32.5	0♓42.1	2 37.1	11 42.4	3 46.9	5 20.7	1 58.1	12 39.5	16 00.1	20 22.5
25 M	22 19 25	6 22 47	16 08 19	23 18 25	27R 33.5	2 30.2	3 51.0	12 08.4	3 48.9	5 14.8	2 04.5	12 42.0	16 01.7	20 22.4
26 Tu	22 23 21	7 23 06	0♌28 19	7♌37 33	27 33.1	4 19.2	5 04.8	12 34.7	3 50.4	5 09.0	2 10.8	12 44.5	16 03.3	20 22.3
27 W	22 27 18	8 23 23	14 45 33	21 51 44	27 30.9	6 09.2	6 18.6	13 01.2	3 51.5	5 03.3	2 17.0	12 46.9	16 04.9	20 22.1
28 Th	22 31 14	9 23 38	28 55 32	5♍56 21	27 26.6	8 00.1	7 32.3	13 27.9	3 52.2	4 57.7	2 23.2	12 49.2	16 06.4	20 21.9

Astro Data

	Dy Hr Mn
♂ D	1 12:49
☿ D	3 17:52
☽ 0S	5 16:47
⚳ 0S	8 12:39
♃⚻♅	14 4:40
☽ 0N	20 9:33
☽ 0S	2 2:46
☽ 0N	16 15:44
♇ R	22 1:29
♀ 0N	24 5:30

Planet Ingress

	Dy Hr Mn
♀ ♒	5 5:03
☿ ♑	14 8:02
☉ ♒	20 13:47
♂ ♊	21 1:15
⚳ ♏	26 3:17
♀ ♓	29 4:44
☿ ♒	5 22:20
♄ ♒	6 18:51
☉ ♓	19 3:58
♀ ♈	22 9:02
☿ ♓	24 2:35

Last Aspect / ☽ Ingress (January)

Last Aspect Dy Hr Mn		☽ Ingress Dy Hr Mn
1 23:16 ♂ ⚹	♌	2 2:54
4 1:09 ♂ □	♍	4 4:57
6 6:40 ♂ △	♎	6 10:33
8 13:12 ♄ □	♏	8 19:59
11 4:43 ♂ ☍	♐	11 8:06
13 20:00 ☿ ☌	♑	13 21:00
16 7:14 ♂ △	♒	16 9:04
18 18:29 ♂ □	♓	18 19:23
20 23:51 ♄ ⚹	♈	21 3:28
23 6:02 ♄ □	♉	23 9:01
25 9:41 ♄ △	♊	25 12:06
27 9:45 ♀ ☍	♋	27 13:23
29 12:29 ♄ ☍	♌	29 14:03
30 23:21 ♇ □	♍	31 15:44

Last Aspect / ☽ Ingress (February)

Last Aspect Dy Hr Mn		☽ Ingress Dy Hr Mn
2 19:12 ♄ △	♎	2 20:02
5 3:39 ♄ □	♏	5 4:01
6 19:55 ♇ ☌	♐	7 15:23
9 8:05 ☉ ⚹	♑	10 4:16
11 21:10 ♇ ⚹	♒	12 16:16
14 17:32 ☉ ☌	♓	15 1:59
16 20:52 ♀ ☌	♈	17 9:11
18 22:35 ☿ ⚹	♉	19 14:24
21 16:45 ♀ ⚹	♊	21 18:10
23 20:08 ☿ △	♋	23 20:56
25 7:05 ♇ △	♌	25 23:13
27 9:28 ♇ □	♍	28 1:50

☽ Phases & Eclipses

Dy Hr Mn	
7 18:36	☾ 16♎58
15 23:50	● 25♑20
15 23:52:53	● A 07'36"
23 14:21	☽ 3♉05
30 6:10	○ 9♌51
30 5:59	• A 0.881
6 13:52	☾ 17♏16
14 17:32	● 25♒31
21 22:58	☽ 2♊49
28 18:25	○ 9♍40

Astro Data

1 January 1991
Julian Day # 33238
SVP 5♓22'52"
GC 26♐42.8 ⚴ 24♍17.3
Eris 16♈29.1R ⚵ 25♐54.6
⚷ 25♋14.4R ⚶ 15♉33.6R
☽ Mean ☊ 29♑06.4

1 February 1991
Julian Day # 33269
SVP 5♓22'47"
GC 26♐42.9 ⚴ 24♍11.2R
Eris 16♈33.4 ⚵ 6♑38.4
⚷ 23♋04.2R ⚶ 18♉31.1
☽ Mean ☊ 27♑27.9

March 1991 — LONGITUDE

Day	Sid.Time	☉	0 hr ☽	Noon ☽	True ☊	☿	♀	♂	⚳	♃	♄	♅	♆	♇
1 F	22 35 11	10♓23 51	12♍53 39	19♍46 54	27♑20.4	9♓52.0	8♈46.0	13♊54.8	3♏52.5	4♌52.4	2♒29.4	12♑51.6	16♑07.9	20♏21.6
2 Sa	22 39 07	11 24 02	26 35 41	3♎19 38	27R 12.9	11 44.8	9 59.6	14 21.9	3R 52.3	4R 47.2	2 35.5	12 53.8	16 09.4	20R 21.4
3 Su	22 43 04	12 24 12	9♎58 32	16 32 13	27 04.9	13 38.4	11 13.2	14 49.2	3 51.7	4 42.1	2 41.5	12 56.1	16 10.9	20 21.0
4 M	22 47 01	13 24 20	23 00 40	29 23 57	26 57.3	15 32.8	12 26.7	15 16.7	3 50.7	4 37.2	2 47.5	12 58.3	16 12.3	20 20.7
5 Tu	22 50 57	14 24 26	5♏42 16	11♏55 52	26 50.9	17 28.0	13 40.2	15 44.4	3 49.3	4 32.5	2 53.5	13 00.5	16 13.8	20 20.3
6 W	22 54 54	15 24 31	18 05 10	24 10 34	26 46.4	19 23.9	14 53.6	16 12.3	3 47.5	4 27.9	2 59.4	13 02.6	16 15.1	20 19.9
7 Th	22 58 50	16 24 34	0♐12 36	6♐11 50	26D 43.8	21 20.3	16 07.0	16 40.3	3 45.2	4 23.5	3 05.2	13 04.7	16 16.5	20 19.4
8 F	23 02 47	17 24 36	12 08 53	18 04 21	26 43.1	23 17.1	17 20.3	17 08.6	3 42.5	4 19.3	3 11.0	13 06.7	16 17.8	20 19.0
9 Sa	23 06 43	18 24 36	23 58 56	29 53 17	26 43.7	25 14.1	18 33.6	17 37.0	3 39.3	4 15.2	3 16.8	13 08.7	16 19.2	20 18.4
10 Su	23 10 40	19 24 35	5♑48 04	11♑43 57	26 44.9	27 11.2	19 46.8	18 05.6	3 35.8	4 11.3	3 22.5	13 10.6	16 20.4	20 17.9
11 M	23 14 36	20 24 32	17 41 34	23 41 31	26R 45.8	29 08.2	21 00.0	18 34.4	3 31.8	4 07.6	3 28.1	13 12.6	16 21.7	20 17.3
12 Tu	23 18 33	21 24 27	29 44 25	5♒50 44	26 45.3	1♈04.7	22 13.1	19 03.3	3 27.4	4 04.1	3 33.7	13 14.4	16 22.9	20 16.7
13 W	23 22 30	22 24 20	12♒00 58	18 15 30	26 42.9	3 00.4	23 26.1	19 32.4	3 22.6	4 00.8	3 39.2	13 16.2	16 24.1	20 16.0
14 Th	23 26 26	23 24 12	24 34 38	0♓58 35	26 38.1	4 55.1	24 39.1	20 01.6	3 17.3	3 57.6	3 44.7	13 18.0	16 25.3	20 15.4
15 F	23 30 23	24 24 01	7♓27 28	14 01 18	26 30.9	6 48.4	25 52.1	20 31.0	3 11.7	3 54.6	3 50.1	13 19.7	16 26.4	20 14.7
16 Sa	23 34 19	25 23 49	20 40 00	27 23 21	26 21.7	8 39.9	27 04.9	21 00.6	3 05.6	3 51.8	3 55.4	13 21.4	16 27.5	20 13.9
17 Su	23 38 16	26 23 35	4♈11 03	11♈02 45	26 11.4	10 29.0	28 17.7	21 30.3	2 59.2	3 49.3	4 00.7	13 23.0	16 28.6	20 13.1
18 M	23 42 12	27 23 18	17 57 57	24 56 10	26 01.1	12 15.5	29 30.5	22 00.2	2 52.3	3 46.8	4 05.9	13 24.6	16 29.6	20 12.3
19 Tu	23 46 09	28 23 00	1♉56 52	8♉59 29	25 52.0	13 58.8	0♉43.2	22 30.2	2 45.1	3 44.6	4 11.0	13 26.1	16 30.6	20 11.5
20 W	23 50 05	29 22 39	16 03 31	23 08 26	25 44.9	15 38.4	1 55.8	23 00.3	2 37.5	3 42.6	4 16.1	13 27.6	16 31.6	20 10.6
21 Th	23 54 02	0♈22 16	0♊13 50	7♊19 18	25 40.3	17 13.9	3 08.3	23 30.6	2 29.5	3 40.8	4 21.1	13 29.1	16 32.5	20 09.7
22 F	23 57 59	1 21 51	14 24 32	21 29 16	25D 38.1	18 44.9	4 20.8	24 01.0	2 21.1	3 39.1	4 26.0	13 30.4	16 33.4	20 08.8
23 Sa	0 01 55	2 21 24	28 33 18	5♋36 31	25 37.8	20 10.8	5 33.2	24 31.5	2 12.4	3 37.7	4 30.9	13 31.8	16 34.3	20 07.9
24 Su	0 05 52	3 20 54	12♋38 46	19 39 59	25R 38.2	21 31.3	6 45.5	25 02.2	2 03.3	3 36.4	4 35.7	13 33.1	16 35.2	20 06.9
25 M	0 09 48	4 20 22	26 40 05	3♌38 59	25 38.1	22 46.1	7 57.8	25 32.9	1 53.9	3 35.4	4 40.4	13 34.3	16 36.0	20 05.9
26 Tu	0 13 45	5 19 48	10♌36 32	17 32 38	25 36.2	23 54.7	9 09.9	26 03.8	1 44.2	3 34.5	4 45.1	13 35.5	16 36.8	20 04.8
27 W	0 17 41	6 19 11	24 27 05	1♍19 39	25 31.9	24 56.9	10 22.0	26 34.8	1 34.1	3 33.8	4 49.7	13 36.7	16 37.6	20 03.8
28 Th	0 21 38	7 18 32	8♍10 06	14 58 09	25 24.7	25 52.3	11 34.0	27 06.0	1 23.7	3 33.3	4 54.2	13 37.7	16 38.3	20 02.7
29 F	0 25 34	8 17 50	21 43 29	28 25 49	25 14.8	26 40.9	12 46.0	27 37.2	1 13.1	3 33.0	4 58.6	13 38.8	16 39.0	20 01.6
30 Sa	0 29 31	9 17 07	5♎04 49	11♎40 16	25 02.9	27 22.4	13 57.8	28 08.5	1 02.1	3D 32.9	5 03.0	13 39.8	16 39.6	20 00.4
31 Su	0 33 27	10 16 22	18 11 54	24 39 33	24 50.2	27 56.7	15 09.6	28 39.9	0 50.9	3 33.0	5 07.3	13 40.7	16 40.3	19 59.3

April 1991 — LONGITUDE

Day	Sid.Time	☉	0 hr ☽	Noon ☽	True ☊	☿	♀	♂	⚳	♃	♄	♅	♆	♇
1 M	0 37 24	11♈15 34	1♏03 07	7♏22 36	24♑37.9	28♈23.7	16♉21.3	29♊11.4	0♏39.4	3♌33.3	5♒11.5	13♑41.6	16♑40.8	19♏58.1
2 Tu	0 41 21	12 14 45	13 38 01	19 49 31	24R 26.9	28 43.4	17 32.9	29 43.1	0R 27.7	3 33.8	5 15.6	13 42.5	16 41.4	19R 56.9
3 W	0 45 17	13 13 54	25 57 19	2♐01 45	24 18.3	28 55.8	18 44.4	0♋14.8	0 15.7	3 34.4	5 19.7	13 43.2	16 41.9	19 55.6
4 Th	0 49 14	14 13 01	8♐03 09	14 02 00	24 12.2	29R 01.1	19 55.8	0 46.6	0 03.5	3 35.3	5 23.7	13 44.0	16 42.4	19 54.4
5 F	0 53 10	15 12 07	19 58 47	25 54 05	24 08.8	28 59.5	21 07.2	1 18.5	29♎51.0	3 36.3	5 27.6	13 44.7	16 42.9	19 53.1
6 Sa	0 57 07	16 11 10	1♑48 29	7♑42 39	24D 07.4	28 51.1	22 18.4	1 50.6	29 38.4	3 37.5	5 31.4	13 45.3	16 43.3	19 51.8
7 Su	1 01 03	17 10 12	13 37 15	19 32 57	24R 07.2	28 36.3	23 29.6	2 22.7	29 25.6	3 38.9	5 35.1	13 45.9	16 43.7	19 50.5
8 M	1 05 00	18 09 12	25 30 29	1♒30 30	24 07.1	28 15.6	24 40.7	2 54.9	29 12.7	3 40.5	5 38.8	13 46.4	16 44.1	19 49.1
9 Tu	1 08 56	19 08 11	7♒33 42	13 40 44	24 06.0	27 49.4	25 51.7	3 27.1	28 59.6	3 42.3	5 42.4	13 46.9	16 44.4	19 47.8
10 W	1 12 53	20 07 07	19 52 12	26 08 37	24 03.0	27 18.3	27 02.6	3 59.5	28 46.3	3 44.3	5 45.8	13 47.4	16 44.7	19 46.4
11 Th	1 16 50	21 06 02	2♓30 29	8♓58 08	23 57.3	26 43.1	28 13.4	4 32.0	28 33.0	3 46.4	5 49.3	13 47.7	16 45.0	19 45.0
12 F	1 20 46	22 04 54	15 31 50	22 11 42	23 49.0	26 04.4	29 24.2	5 04.5	28 19.5	3 48.7	5 52.6	13 48.1	16 45.2	19 43.6
13 Sa	1 24 43	23 03 45	28 57 43	5♈49 43	23 38.4	25 23.0	0♊34.8	5 37.1	28 06.0	3 51.2	5 55.8	13 48.3	16 45.4	19 42.1
14 Su	1 28 39	24 02 34	12♈47 21	19 50 09	23 26.4	24 39.8	1 45.3	6 09.8	27 52.4	3 53.9	5 58.9	13 48.6	16 45.6	19 40.7
15 M	1 32 36	25 01 22	26 57 28	4♉08 35	23 14.4	23 55.7	2 55.8	6 42.6	27 38.7	3 56.8	6 02.0	13 48.7	16 45.7	19 39.2
16 Tu	1 36 32	26 00 07	11♉22 40	18 38 50	23 03.5	23 11.3	4 06.1	7 15.5	27 25.0	3 59.9	6 05.0	13 48.9	16 45.8	19 37.7
17 W	1 40 29	26 58 50	25 56 12	3♊13 54	22 54.8	22 27.7	5 16.3	7 48.4	27 11.3	4 03.1	6 07.8	13R 48.9	16 45.9	19 36.2
18 Th	1 44 25	27 57 31	10♊31 07	17 47 09	22 49.0	21 45.4	6 26.4	8 21.5	26 57.7	4 06.5	6 10.6	13 49.0	16R 45.9	19 34.7
19 F	1 48 22	28 56 10	25 01 23	2♋13 20	22 45.9	21 05.4	7 36.5	8 54.6	26 44.0	4 10.1	6 13.3	13 48.9	16 45.9	19 33.2
20 Sa	1 52 19	29 54 47	9♋22 37	16 29 00	22D 44.9	20 28.1	8 46.4	9 27.7	26 30.4	4 13.8	6 15.9	13 48.8	16 45.9	19 31.6
21 Su	1 56 15	0♉53 21	23 32 18	0♌32 27	22R 44.9	19 54.2	9 56.1	10 01.0	26 16.9	4 17.7	6 18.5	13 48.7	16 45.8	19 30.1
22 M	2 00 12	1 51 53	7♌29 27	14 23 19	22 44.5	19 24.0	11 05.8	10 34.3	26 03.4	4 21.8	6 20.9	13 48.5	16 45.7	19 28.5
23 Tu	2 04 08	2 50 23	21 14 09	28 02 01	22 42.5	18 58.1	12 15.3	11 07.6	25 50.0	4 26.1	6 23.2	13 48.3	16 45.6	19 26.9
24 W	2 08 05	3 48 51	4♍46 58	11♍29 04	22 38.1	18 36.7	13 24.8	11 41.1	25 36.7	4 30.5	6 25.4	13 48.0	16 45.4	19 25.3
25 Th	2 12 01	4 47 16	18 08 21	24 44 50	22 30.9	18 19.9	14 34.0	12 14.6	25 23.6	4 35.1	6 27.6	13 47.7	16 45.2	19 23.7
26 F	2 15 58	5 45 39	1♎18 30	7♎49 18	22 21.1	18 08.0	15 43.2	12 48.1	25 10.6	4 39.8	6 29.6	13 47.3	16 45.0	19 22.1
27 Sa	2 19 54	6 44 01	14 17 12	20 42 07	22 09.3	18D 01.1	16 52.2	13 21.7	24 57.8	4 44.7	6 31.6	13 46.9	16 44.7	19 20.5
28 Su	2 23 51	7 42 21	27 04 01	3♏22 51	21 56.6	17 59.0	18 01.1	13 55.4	24 45.1	4 49.8	6 33.5	13 46.4	16 44.4	19 18.8
29 M	2 27 48	8 40 39	9♏38 34	15 51 13	21 44.2	18 01.9	19 09.9	14 29.1	24 32.6	4 55.0	6 35.2	13 45.8	16 44.1	19 17.2
30 Tu	2 31 44	9 38 55	22 00 50	28 07 31	21 33.1	18 09.7	20 18.5	15 02.9	24 20.3	5 00.4	6 36.9	13 45.3	16 43.7	19 15.5

Astro Data

	Dy Hr Mn
☽0S	1 13:09
⚳R	1 15:18
⚳0N	8 17:38
☿0N	12 12:51
☽0N	15 23:37
♃☍♄	16 1:26
☉0N	21 3:02
☽0S	28 21:40
♃D	30 13:15
☿R	4 18:10
☽0N	12 8:34
♅R	18 10:33
♆R	19 0:11
☽0S	25 3:37
☿D	28 9:49

Planet Ingress

		Dy Hr Mn
☿	♈	11 22:40
♀	♉	18 21:45
☉	♈	21 3:02
♂	♋	3 0:49
⚳	♎R	4 18:44
♀	♊	13 0:10
☉	♉	20 14:08

Last Aspect / ☽ Ingress (March)

Last Aspect Dy Hr Mn			☽ Ingress	Dy Hr Mn
1 13:01	♇	⚹	♎	2 6:03
3 11:21	♆	□	♏	4 13:08
6 4:25	♇	☌	♐	6 23:35
9 0:41	☿	□	♑	9 12:14
11 6:01	♀	□	♒	12 0:31
13 22:53	♀	⚹	♓	14 10:11
16 8:10	☉	☌	♈	16 16:38
18 20:34	♀	☌	♉	18 20:40
20 23:21	☉	⚹	♊	20 23:37
22 16:27	♂	☌	♋	23 2:27
24 15:30	☿	□	♌	25 5:43
27 3:23	♂	⚹	♍	27 9:41
29 10:29	♂	□	♎	29 14:49
31 19:50	♂	△	♏	31 22:01

Last Aspect / ☽ Ingress (April)

Last Aspect Dy Hr Mn			☽ Ingress	Dy Hr Mn
2 12:14	♇	☌	♐	3 7:59
5 18:13	☿	△	♑	5 20:19
8 5:43	☿	□	♒	8 9:00
10 14:07	☿	⚹	♓	10 19:18
12 7:35	♇	△	♈	13 1:49
14 19:45	☿	☌	♉	15 5:06
16 13:37	♇	☍	♊	17 6:41
19 6:07	☉	⚹	♋	19 8:17
20 18:30	☿	□	♌	21 11:04
22 20:53	♇	□	♍	23 15:29
25 2:18	♇	⚹	♎	25 21:36
27 7:00	☿	☍	♏	28 5:34
29 18:40	♇	☌	♐	30 15:42

☽ Phases & Eclipses

Dy Hr Mn		
8 10:32	☾	17♐21
16 8:10	●	25♓14
23 6:03	☽	2♋07
30 7:17	○	9♎05
7 6:45	☾	16♑57
14 19:38	●	24♈21
21 12:39	☽	0♌55
28 20:59	○	8♏04

Astro Data

1 March 1991
Julian Day # 33297
SVP 5♓22'43"
GC 26♐43.0 ⚴ 16♍51.5R
Eris 16♈45.5 ⚵ 15♑38.4
⚷ 21♋35.2R ⚶ 25♉24.8
☽ Mean ☊ 25♑59.0

1 April 1991
Julian Day # 33328
SVP 5♓22'40"
GC 26♐43.0 ⚴ 8♍09.4R
Eris 17♈04.5 ⚵ 24♑05.1
⚷ 21♋11.9 ⚶ 5♊49.3
☽ Mean ☊ 24♑20.4

LONGITUDE

May 1991

Day	Sid.Time	☉	0 hr ☽	Noon ☽	True ☊	☿	♀	♂	⚳	♃	♄	♅	♆	♇
1 W	2 35 41	10♉37 09	4♐11 25	10♐12 46	21♑24.2	18♈22.2	21♊27.0	15♋36.7	24♎08.3	5♌05.9	6♒38.5	13♑44.6	16♑43.3	19♏13.9
2 Th	2 39 37	11 35 22	16 11 50	22 08 56	21R17.8	18 39.4	22 35.3	16 10.6	23R56.4	5 11.6	6 40.0	13R44.0	16R42.9	19R12.2
3 F	2 43 34	12 33 33	28 04 28	3♑58 53	21 14.1	19 01.1	23 43.5	16 44.6	23 44.8	5 17.4	6 41.4	13 43.3	16 42.5	19 10.6
4 Sa	2 47 30	13 31 43	9♑52 41	15 46 24	21D12.7	19 27.2	24 51.5	17 18.6	23 33.4	5 23.4	6 42.6	13 42.5	16 42.0	19 08.9
5 Su	2 51 27	14 29 51	21 40 38	27 36 00	21 12.7	19 57.5	25 59.4	17 52.7	23 22.3	5 29.5	6 43.8	13 41.7	16 41.5	19 07.2
6 M	2 55 23	15 27 58	3♒33 09	9♒32 45	21R13.2	20 31.8	27 07.2	18 26.8	23 11.5	5 35.8	6 44.9	13 40.8	16 40.9	19 05.6
7 Tu	2 59 20	16 26 03	15 35 29	21 42 01	21 13.2	21 10.1	28 14.8	19 00.9	23 00.9	5 42.2	6 45.9	13 39.9	16 40.4	19 03.9
8 W	3 03 17	17 24 07	27 53 01	4♓09 06	21 11.8	21 52.2	29 22.2	19 35.2	22 50.7	5 48.8	6 46.8	13 38.9	16 39.8	19 02.2
9 Th	3 07 13	18 22 10	10♓30 49	16 58 41	21 08.3	22 37.9	0♋29.5	20 09.4	22 40.7	5 55.5	6 47.6	13 37.9	16 39.1	19 00.5
10 F	3 11 10	19 20 11	23 33 05	0♈14 18	21 02.6	23 27.1	1 36.6	20 43.8	22 31.1	6 02.3	6 48.3	13 36.9	16 38.5	18 58.8
11 Sa	3 15 06	20 18 11	7♈02 29	13 57 36	20 54.9	24 19.6	2 43.5	21 18.1	22 21.8	6 09.3	6 48.9	13 35.8	16 37.8	18 57.1
12 Su	3 19 03	21 16 09	20 59 27	28 07 38	20 45.9	25 15.4	3 50.3	21 52.6	22 12.8	6 16.4	6 49.5	13 34.7	16 37.1	18 55.5
13 M	3 22 59	22 14 06	5♉21 34	12♉40 31	20 36.6	26 14.3	4 56.9	22 27.1	22 04.2	6 23.7	6 49.9	13 33.5	16 36.3	18 53.8
14 Tu	3 26 56	23 12 02	20 03 34	27 29 42	20 28.2	27 16.2	6 03.3	23 01.6	21 55.9	6 31.0	6 50.2	13 32.3	16 35.5	18 52.1
15 W	3 30 52	24 09 56	4♊57 49	12♊26 46	20 21.6	28 21.1	7 09.6	23 36.2	21 48.0	6 38.6	6 50.4	13 31.0	16 34.7	18 50.4
16 Th	3 34 49	25 07 49	19 55 27	27 22 51	20 17.3	29 28.8	8 15.6	24 10.8	21 40.4	6 46.2	6R50.5	13 29.7	16 33.9	18 48.8
17 F	3 38 46	26 05 40	4♋47 59	12♋10 04	20D15.4	0♉39.2	9 21.4	24 45.5	21 33.2	6 54.0	6 50.5	13 28.3	16 33.1	18 47.1
18 Sa	3 42 42	27 03 29	19 28 27	26 42 35	20 15.3	1 52.3	10 27.1	25 20.2	21 26.4	7 01.9	6 50.4	13 27.0	16 32.2	18 45.4
19 Su	3 46 39	28 01 17	3♌52 10	10♌56 56	20 16.1	3 08.0	11 32.5	25 55.0	21 20.0	7 09.9	6 50.3	13 25.5	16 31.3	18 43.8
20 M	3 50 35	28 59 03	17 56 49	24 51 48	20R16.9	4 26.3	12 37.7	26 29.8	21 13.9	7 18.0	6 50.0	13 24.1	16 30.3	18 42.1
21 Tu	3 54 32	29 56 47	1♍42 00	8♍27 33	20 16.6	5 47.1	13 42.7	27 04.7	21 08.2	7 26.3	6 49.6	13 22.5	16 29.4	18 40.5
22 W	3 58 28	0♊54 29	15 08 38	21 45 28	20 14.6	7 10.4	14 47.5	27 39.5	21 03.0	7 34.7	6 49.1	13 21.0	16 28.4	18 38.8
23 Th	4 02 25	1 52 10	28 18 18	4♎47 20	20 10.5	8 36.2	15 52.0	28 14.5	20 58.1	7 43.2	6 48.6	13 19.4	16 27.4	18 37.2
24 F	4 06 21	2 49 50	11♎12 47	17 34 53	20 04.5	10 04.3	16 56.3	28 49.5	20 53.6	7 51.8	6 47.9	13 17.8	16 26.3	18 35.6
25 Sa	4 10 18	3 47 28	23 53 48	0♏09 43	19 57.0	11 34.9	18 00.4	29 24.5	20 49.5	8 00.5	6 47.1	13 16.1	16 25.3	18 34.0
26 Su	4 14 15	4 45 04	6♏22 49	12 33 13	19 48.9	13 07.9	19 04.1	29 59.5	20 45.8	8 09.3	6 46.3	13 14.4	16 24.2	18 32.4
27 M	4 18 11	5 42 39	18 41 05	24 46 34	19 40.9	14 43.2	20 07.7	0♌34.6	20 42.5	8 18.2	6 45.3	13 12.7	16 23.1	18 30.8
28 Tu	4 22 08	6 40 14	0♐49 49	6♐51 01	19 33.8	16 20.9	21 10.9	1 09.8	20 39.5	8 27.3	6 44.3	13 10.9	16 21.9	18 29.2
29 W	4 26 04	7 37 47	12 50 19	18 47 57	19 28.2	18 01.0	22 13.9	1 44.9	20 37.0	8 36.4	6 43.1	13 09.2	16 20.8	18 27.7
30 Th	4 30 01	8 35 19	24 44 10	0♑39 12	19 24.5	19 43.4	23 16.6	2 20.1	20 34.9	8 45.7	6 41.9	13 07.3	16 19.6	18 26.1
31 F	4 33 57	9 32 49	6♑33 24	12 27 05	19D22.7	21 28.2	24 19.0	2 55.4	20 33.2	8 55.1	6 40.6	13 05.5	16 18.4	18 24.6

LONGITUDE

June 1991

Day	Sid.Time	☉	0 hr ☽	Noon ☽	True ☊	☿	♀	♂	⚳	♃	♄	♅	♆	♇
1 Sa	4 37 54	10♊30 19	18♑20 38	24♑14 30	19♑22.5	23♉15.3	25♋21.2	3♌30.7	20♎31.8	9♌04.5	6♒39.2	13♑03.6	16♑17.2	18♏23.0
2 Su	4 41 50	11 27 48	0♒09 07	6♒05 00	19 23.6	25 04.8	26 23.0	4 06.0	20R30.9	9 14.1	6R37.6	13R01.7	16R15.9	18R21.5
3 M	4 45 47	12 25 17	12 02 40	18 02 42	19 25.2	26 56.5	27 24.5	4 41.4	20D30.3	9 23.7	6 36.0	12 59.7	16 14.7	18 20.0
4 Tu	4 49 44	13 22 44	24 05 40	0♓12 09	19 26.7	28 50.5	28 25.6	5 16.8	20 30.1	9 33.5	6 34.4	12 57.7	16 13.4	18 18.5
5 W	4 53 40	14 20 11	6♓22 47	12 38 07	19R27.4	0♊46.8	29 26.5	5 52.2	20 30.4	9 43.3	6 32.6	12 55.7	16 12.1	18 17.1
6 Th	4 57 37	15 17 37	18 58 45	25 25 11	19 26.9	2 45.2	0♌27.0	6 27.7	20 31.0	9 53.3	6 30.7	12 53.7	16 10.8	18 15.6
7 F	5 01 33	16 15 02	1♈57 53	8♈37 15	19 25.1	4 45.7	1 27.2	7 03.2	20 31.9	10 03.3	6 28.7	12 51.6	16 09.5	18 14.2
8 Sa	5 05 30	17 12 27	15 23 31	22 16 52	19 21.9	6 48.2	2 27.0	7 38.7	20 33.3	10 13.5	6 26.7	12 49.5	16 08.1	18 12.7
9 Su	5 09 26	18 09 52	29 17 15	6♉24 30	19 17.9	8 52.6	3 26.4	8 14.3	20 35.1	10 23.7	6 24.5	12 47.4	16 06.7	18 11.3
10 M	5 13 23	19 07 15	13♉38 14	20 57 53	19 13.6	10 58.7	4 25.5	8 50.0	20 37.2	10 34.0	6 22.3	12 45.3	16 05.3	18 10.0
11 Tu	5 17 19	20 04 39	28 22 44	5♊51 50	19 09.6	13 06.3	5 24.2	9 25.6	20 39.7	10 44.4	6 20.0	12 43.1	16 03.9	18 08.6
12 W	5 21 16	21 02 01	13♊24 09	20 58 31	19 06.5	15 15.2	6 22.5	10 01.4	20 42.6	10 54.9	6 17.6	12 40.9	16 02.5	18 07.3
13 Th	5 25 13	21 59 23	28 33 43	6♋08 33	19D04.7	17 25.3	7 20.3	10 37.1	20 45.8	11 05.4	6 15.2	12 38.7	16 01.1	18 05.9
14 F	5 29 09	22 56 44	13♋41 49	21 12 28	19 04.3	19 36.3	8 17.7	11 12.9	20 49.5	11 16.1	6 12.6	12 36.5	15 59.7	18 04.6
15 Sa	5 33 06	23 54 04	28 39 30	6♌02 06	19 05.0	21 47.8	9 14.7	11 48.7	20 53.4	11 26.8	6 10.0	12 34.3	15 58.2	18 03.4
16 Su	5 37 02	24 51 24	13♌19 38	20 31 36	19 06.2	23 59.7	10 11.2	12 24.6	20 57.8	11 37.6	6 07.3	12 32.0	15 56.7	18 02.1
17 M	5 40 59	25 48 42	27 37 40	4♍37 41	19 07.6	26 11.6	11 07.3	13 00.5	21 02.5	11 48.5	6 04.5	12 29.7	15 55.2	18 00.9
18 Tu	5 44 55	26 46 00	11♍31 35	18 19 29	19R08.5	28 23.3	12 02.8	13 36.4	21 07.5	11 59.4	6 01.6	12 27.4	15 53.7	17 59.6
19 W	5 48 52	27 43 16	25 01 31	1♎37 57	19 08.7	0♋34.5	12 57.8	14 12.4	21 12.9	12 10.5	5 58.7	12 25.1	15 52.2	17 58.4
20 Th	5 52 49	28 40 32	8♎09 06	14 35 18	19 07.9	2 45.0	13 52.3	14 48.4	21 18.7	12 21.6	5 55.7	12 22.8	15 50.7	17 57.3
21 F	5 56 45	29 37 47	20 56 55	27 14 20	19 06.2	4 54.5	14 46.2	15 24.4	21 24.7	12 32.7	5 52.6	12 20.4	15 49.2	17 56.1
22 Sa	6 00 42	0♋35 02	3♏27 58	9♏38 09	19 03.9	7 02.8	15 39.5	16 00.4	21 31.2	12 44.0	5 49.4	12 18.1	15 47.6	17 55.0
23 Su	6 04 38	1 32 16	15 45 17	21 49 43	19 01.3	9 09.8	16 32.2	16 36.5	21 37.9	12 55.3	5 46.2	12 15.7	15 46.1	17 53.9
24 M	6 08 35	2 29 29	27 51 48	3♐51 50	18 58.7	11 15.2	17 24.3	17 12.7	21 45.0	13 06.7	5 42.9	12 13.3	15 44.5	17 52.8
25 Tu	6 12 31	3 26 42	9♐50 08	15 47 01	18 56.5	13 19.0	18 15.8	17 48.8	21 52.4	13 18.1	5 39.5	12 11.0	15 42.9	17 51.8
26 W	6 16 28	4 23 55	21 42 45	27 37 36	18 54.9	15 21.0	19 06.6	18 25.0	22 00.1	13 29.6	5 36.1	12 08.6	15 41.4	17 50.8
27 Th	6 20 24	5 21 07	3♑31 52	9♑25 49	18D54.0	17 21.1	19 56.7	19 01.2	22 08.1	13 41.2	5 32.6	12 06.2	15 39.8	17 49.8
28 F	6 24 21	6 18 19	15 19 43	21 13 53	18 53.8	19 19.3	20 46.1	19 37.5	22 16.4	13 52.8	5 29.1	12 03.8	15 38.2	17 48.8
29 Sa	6 28 18	7 15 31	27 08 35	3♒04 10	18 54.2	21 15.6	21 34.8	20 13.8	22 25.0	14 04.5	5 25.5	12 01.4	15 36.6	17 47.9
30 Su	6 32 14	8 12 42	9♒00 58	14 59 20	18 55.0	23 09.8	22 22.7	20 50.1	22 33.9	14 16.2	5 21.8	11 58.9	15 35.0	17 47.0

Astro Data	Dy Hr Mn
☽0N	9 17:20
♃☍♄	17 1:24
♄ R	17 4:04
☽0S	22 8:17
⚳ D	4 10:33
☽0N	6 0:58
⚳0S	16 5:18
☽0S	18 13:53
♃⚻♅	20 14:10

Planet Ingress		Dy Hr Mn
♀	♋	9 1:28
☿	♉	16 22:45
☉	♊	21 13:20
♂	♌	26 12:19
☿	♊	5 2:24
♀	♌	6 1:16
☿	♋	19 5:40
☉	♋	21 21:19

Last Aspect Dy Hr Mn			☽ Ingress	Dy Hr Mn
2 12:59	♀	☍	♑	3 3:54
4 19:48	☿	□	♒	5 16:51
8 1:57	♀	△	♓	8 4:04
9 18:06	♂	△	♈	10 11:35
12 6:51	☿	☌	♉	12 15:07
14 4:36	☉	☌	♊	14 16:02
16 15:40	☿	⚹	♋	16 16:14
18 12:37	☉	⚹	♌	18 17:30
20 19:46	☉	□	♍	20 21:00
22 23:19	♂	⚹	♎	23 3:08
25 10:29	♂	□	♏	25 11:41
27 1:58	♀	△	♐	27 22:21
28 15:15	♃	△	♑	30 10:40

Last Aspect Dy Hr Mn			☽ Ingress	Dy Hr Mn
1 14:28	♀	☍	♒	1 23:42
4 8:51	☿	□	♓	4 11:36
5 22:40	♇	△	♈	6 20:25
8 2:31	☉	⚹	♉	9 1:13
10 7:26	♇	☍	♊	11 2:36
12 12:06	☉	☌	♋	13 2:16
14 7:00	♇	△	♌	15 2:10
16 19:49	☉	⚹	♍	17 4:03
19 4:19	☉	□	♎	19 9:01
21 16:58	☉	△	♏	21 17:18
23 4:14	♇	☌	♐	24 4:16
25 17:24	♀	△	♑	26 16:49
28 7:21	☿	☍	♒	29 5:47

☽ Phases & Eclipses Dy Hr Mn	
7 0:46	☾ 15♒59
14 4:36	● 22♉54
20 19:46	☽ 29♌18
28 11:37	○ 6♐39
5 15:30	☾ 14♓29
12 12:06	● 21♊02
19 4:19	☽ 27♍25
27 2:58	○ 5♑00
27 3:15	☍ A 0.312

Astro Data

1 May 1991
Julian Day # 33358
SVP 5♓22'37"
GC 26♐43.1 ⚴ 6♍33.9
Eris 17♈24.1 ✴ 29♑39.8
⚷ 22♋15.7 ⚵ 17♊28.9
☽ Mean ☊ 22♑45.1

1 June 1991
Julian Day # 33389
SVP 5♓22'31"
GC 26♐43.2 ⚴ 11♍32.3
Eris 17♈40.6 ✴ 1♒10.4R
⚷ 24♋36.8 ⚵ 0♋26.1
☽ Mean ☊ 21♑06.6

July 1991 — LONGITUDE

Day	Sid.Time	☉	0 hr ☽	Noon ☽	True ☊	☿	♀	♂	⚳	♃	♄	♅	♆	♇
1 M	6 36 11	9♋09 54	20♒59 39	27♒02 19	18♑56.0	25♋01.9	23♌09.8	21♌26.4	22♎43.1	14♌28.0	5♒18.1	11♑56.5	15♑33.4	17♏46.1
2 Tu	6 40 07	10 07 06	3♓07 45	9♓16 24	18 56.9	26 52.0	23 56.1	22 02.8	22 52.6	14 39.9	5R 14.4	11R 54.1	15R 31.8	17R 45.2
3 W	6 44 04	11 04 18	15 28 42	21 45 07	18 57.5	28 40.0	24 41.6	22 39.2	23 02.4	14 51.8	5 10.5	11 51.7	15 30.1	17 44.4
4 Th	6 48 00	12 01 30	28 06 06	4♈32 05	18R 57.9	0♌25.9	25 26.1	23 15.7	23 12.5	15 03.8	5 06.7	11 49.2	15 28.5	17 43.6
5 F	6 51 57	12 58 42	11♈03 29	17 40 38	18 58.0	2 09.7	26 09.8	23 52.2	23 22.8	15 15.8	5 02.7	11 46.8	15 26.9	17 42.8
6 Sa	6 55 53	13 55 54	24 23 51	1♉13 22	18 57.7	3 51.5	26 52.5	24 28.7	23 33.4	15 27.9	4 58.8	11 44.4	15 25.3	17 42.1
7 Su	6 59 50	14 53 07	8♉09 17	15 11 35	18 57.4	5 31.1	27 34.2	25 05.3	23 44.3	15 40.0	4 54.8	11 42.0	15 23.7	17 41.4
8 M	7 03 47	15 50 21	22 20 09	29 34 39	18 57.0	7 08.7	28 15.0	25 41.9	23 55.5	15 52.2	4 50.7	11 39.5	15 22.0	17 40.7
9 Tu	7 07 43	16 47 35	6♊54 39	14♊19 30	18 56.8	8 44.1	28 54.6	26 18.5	24 06.9	16 04.4	4 46.6	11 37.1	15 20.4	17 40.1
10 W	7 11 40	17 44 49	21 48 26	29 20 29	18 56.7	10 17.5	29 33.2	26 55.2	24 18.6	16 16.7	4 42.5	11 34.7	15 18.8	17 39.4
11 Th	7 15 36	18 42 03	6♋54 37	14♋29 42	18 56.6	11 48.7	0♍10.6	27 31.9	24 30.5	16 29.0	4 38.3	11 32.3	15 17.2	17 38.9
12 F	7 19 33	19 39 18	22 04 34	29 38 02	18 56.6	13 17.8	0 46.9	28 08.6	24 42.7	16 41.4	4 34.1	11 29.9	15 15.6	17 38.3
13 Sa	7 23 29	20 36 33	7♌08 58	14♌36 20	18 56.6	14 44.7	1 21.9	28 45.4	24 55.1	16 53.8	4 29.8	11 27.5	15 13.9	17 37.8
14 Su	7 27 26	21 33 47	21 59 13	29 16 50	18 56.4	16 09.4	1 55.6	29 22.2	25 07.8	17 06.2	4 25.6	11 25.1	15 12.3	17 37.3
15 M	7 31 22	22 31 02	6♍28 35	13♍34 00	18 56.0	17 32.0	2 28.0	29 59.1	25 20.7	17 18.7	4 21.3	11 22.8	15 10.7	17 36.8
16 Tu	7 35 19	23 28 17	20 32 50	27 24 58	18 55.6	18 52.2	2 59.1	0♍36.0	25 33.9	17 31.2	4 16.9	11 20.4	15 09.1	17 36.4
17 W	7 39 16	24 25 32	4♎10 25	10♎49 22	18 55.3	20 10.2	3 28.6	1 12.9	25 47.3	17 43.8	4 12.6	11 18.0	15 07.5	17 36.0
18 Th	7 43 12	25 22 47	17 22 04	23 48 51	18D 55.1	21 25.9	3 56.7	1 49.8	26 00.9	17 56.4	4 08.2	11 15.7	15 05.9	17 35.6
19 F	7 47 09	26 20 02	0♏10 10	6♏26 29	18 55.2	22 39.1	4 23.2	2 26.8	26 14.7	18 09.0	4 03.8	11 13.4	15 04.3	17 35.3
20 Sa	7 51 05	27 17 18	12 38 16	18 46 04	18 55.7	23 49.8	4 48.1	3 03.8	26 28.8	18 21.6	3 59.4	11 11.1	15 02.8	17 35.0
21 Su	7 55 02	28 14 34	24 50 24	0♐51 48	18 56.5	24 58.1	5 11.3	3 40.8	26 43.1	18 34.3	3 55.0	11 08.8	15 01.2	17 34.7
22 M	7 58 58	29 11 50	6♐50 46	12 47 47	18 57.5	26 03.6	5 32.8	4 17.9	26 57.5	18 47.1	3 50.6	11 06.5	14 59.6	17 34.5
23 Tu	8 02 55	0♌09 06	18 43 21	24 37 54	18 58.4	27 06.5	5 52.5	4 55.0	27 12.2	18 59.8	3 46.1	11 04.3	14 58.1	17 34.3
24 W	8 06 52	1 06 23	0♑31 50	6♑25 35	18 59.2	28 06.6	6 10.3	5 32.1	27 27.1	19 12.6	3 41.7	11 02.0	14 56.5	17 34.1
25 Th	8 10 48	2 03 40	12 19 30	18 13 55	18R 59.5	29 03.7	6 26.2	6 09.3	27 42.2	19 25.4	3 37.2	10 59.8	14 55.0	17 34.0
26 F	8 14 45	3 00 58	24 09 09	0♒05 30	18 59.3	29 57.8	6 40.2	6 46.5	27 57.5	19 38.2	3 32.8	10 57.6	14 53.5	17 33.9
27 Sa	8 18 41	3 58 17	6♒03 13	12 02 35	18 58.2	0♍48.7	6 52.1	7 23.8	28 13.0	19 51.1	3 28.3	10 55.4	14 51.9	17 33.8
28 Su	8 22 38	4 55 36	18 03 51	24 07 13	18 56.5	1 36.4	7 01.9	8 01.0	28 28.7	20 04.0	3 23.8	10 53.3	14 50.4	17D 33.8
29 M	8 26 34	5 52 56	0♓12 57	6♓21 15	18 54.2	2 20.5	7 09.6	8 38.3	28 44.5	20 16.9	3 19.4	10 51.2	14 48.9	17 33.8
30 Tu	8 30 31	6 50 17	12 32 22	18 46 31	18 51.6	3 01.0	7 15.1	9 15.7	29 00.6	20 29.8	3 14.9	10 49.1	14 47.5	17 33.8
31 W	8 34 27	7 47 39	25 03 57	1♈24 55	18 49.0	3 37.8	7R 18.4	9 53.1	29 16.8	20 42.8	3 10.5	10 47.0	14 46.0	17 33.9

August 1991 — LONGITUDE

Day	Sid.Time	☉	0 hr ☽	Noon ☽	True ☊	☿	♀	♂	⚳	♃	♄	♅	♆	♇
1 Th	8 38 24	8♌45 02	7♈49 39	14♈18 23	18♑46.9	4♍10.6	7♍19.4	10♍30.5	29♎33.2	20♌55.7	3♒06.1	10♑44.9	14♑44.5	17♏34.0
2 F	8 42 20	9 42 26	20 51 23	27 28 52	18D 45.5	4 39.2	7R 18.1	11 07.9	29 49.8	21 08.7	3R 01.6	10R 42.9	14R 43.1	17 34.1
3 Sa	8 46 17	10 39 51	4♉11 03	10♉58 06	18 45.0	5 03.6	7 14.5	11 45.4	0♏06.5	21 21.7	2 57.2	10 40.9	14 41.7	17 34.3
4 Su	8 50 14	11 37 18	17 50 08	24 47 14	18 45.5	5 23.4	7 08.5	12 22.9	0 23.5	21 34.8	2 52.8	10 38.9	14 40.3	17 34.5
5 M	8 54 10	12 34 46	1♊49 24	8♊56 30	18 46.6	5 38.5	7 00.2	13 00.5	0 40.6	21 47.8	2 48.5	10 37.0	14 38.9	17 34.8
6 Tu	8 58 07	13 32 15	16 08 21	23 24 37	18 48.0	5 48.7	6 49.5	13 38.1	0 57.8	22 00.9	2 44.1	10 35.0	14 37.5	17 35.0
7 W	9 02 03	14 29 45	0♋44 50	8♋08 25	18R 49.1	5R 53.9	6 36.4	14 15.7	1 15.3	22 13.9	2 39.8	10 33.2	14 36.1	17 35.4
8 Th	9 06 00	15 27 17	15 34 39	23 02 41	18 49.3	5 53.9	6 21.0	14 53.4	1 32.8	22 27.0	2 35.5	10 31.3	14 34.8	17 35.7
9 F	9 09 56	16 24 49	0♌31 35	8♌00 21	18 48.3	5 48.5	6 03.3	15 31.1	1 50.6	22 40.1	2 31.2	10 29.5	14 33.5	17 36.1
10 Sa	9 13 53	17 22 23	15 27 56	22 53 18	18 45.9	5 37.8	5 43.3	16 08.9	2 08.5	22 53.2	2 27.0	10 27.7	14 32.2	17 36.5
11 Su	9 17 50	18 19 58	0♍15 26	7♍33 25	18 42.3	5 21.7	5 21.2	16 46.7	2 26.5	23 06.3	2 22.7	10 26.0	14 30.9	17 36.9
12 M	9 21 46	19 17 34	14 46 28	21 53 53	18 38.0	5 00.2	4 56.9	17 24.5	2 44.7	23 19.5	2 18.6	10 24.2	14 29.6	17 37.4
13 Tu	9 25 43	20 15 10	28 55 11	5♎50 00	18 33.4	4 33.4	4 30.6	18 02.3	3 03.1	23 32.6	2 14.4	10 22.5	14 28.4	17 37.9
14 W	9 29 39	21 12 48	12♎38 09	19 19 37	18 29.3	4 01.5	4 02.3	18 40.2	3 21.6	23 45.7	2 10.3	10 20.9	14 27.1	17 38.5
15 Th	9 33 36	22 10 27	25 54 31	2♏23 06	18 26.3	3 24.9	3 32.3	19 18.2	3 40.2	23 58.8	2 06.2	10 19.3	14 25.9	17 39.0
16 F	9 37 32	23 08 07	8♏45 43	15 02 49	18D 24.6	2 43.9	3 00.7	19 56.1	3 59.0	24 12.0	2 02.2	10 17.7	14 24.8	17 39.7
17 Sa	9 41 29	24 05 47	21 14 55	27 22 34	18 24.4	1 59.1	2 27.6	20 34.1	4 17.9	24 25.1	1 58.3	10 16.2	14 23.6	17 40.3
18 Su	9 45 25	25 03 29	3♐26 23	9♐26 59	18 25.3	1 11.1	1 53.3	21 12.2	4 36.9	24 38.2	1 54.3	10 14.7	14 22.5	17 41.0
19 M	9 49 22	26 01 12	15 24 58	21 21 00	18 26.8	0 20.8	1 17.9	21 50.3	4 56.1	24 51.4	1 50.5	10 13.2	14 21.3	17 41.7
20 Tu	9 53 19	26 58 56	27 15 39	3♑09 33	18 28.4	29♌28.9	0 41.6	22 28.4	5 15.4	25 04.5	1 46.6	10 11.8	14 20.3	17 42.5
21 W	9 57 15	27 56 41	9♑03 14	14 57 13	18R 29.4	28 36.5	0 04.8	23 06.5	5 34.8	25 17.6	1 42.9	10 10.4	14 19.2	17 43.2
22 Th	10 01 12	28 54 28	20 52 02	26 48 06	18 29.0	27 44.6	29♌27.6	23 44.7	5 54.4	25 30.7	1 39.1	10 09.1	14 18.1	17 44.1
23 F	10 05 08	29 52 16	2♒45 49	8♒45 34	18 27.0	26 54.3	28 50.2	24 22.9	6 14.1	25 43.9	1 35.5	10 07.8	14 17.1	17 44.9
24 Sa	10 09 05	0♍50 04	14 47 39	20 52 18	18 23.0	26 06.6	28 12.9	25 01.2	6 33.9	25 57.0	1 31.9	10 06.6	14 16.1	17 45.8
25 Su	10 13 01	1 47 55	26 59 45	3♓10 10	18 17.2	25 22.5	27 36.0	25 39.5	6 53.8	26 10.1	1 28.3	10 05.3	14 15.2	17 46.7
26 M	10 16 58	2 45 47	9♓23 40	15 40 19	18 10.0	24 43.1	26 59.8	26 17.8	7 13.8	26 23.1	1 24.8	10 04.2	14 14.2	17 47.6
27 Tu	10 20 54	3 43 40	22 00 10	28 23 16	18 02.1	24 09.2	26 24.3	26 56.2	7 33.9	26 36.2	1 21.4	10 03.0	14 13.3	17 48.6
28 W	10 24 51	4 41 35	4♈49 36	11♈19 08	17 54.2	23 41.6	25 49.9	27 34.6	7 54.2	26 49.3	1 18.1	10 02.0	14 12.4	17 49.6
29 Th	10 28 47	5 39 32	17 51 54	24 27 50	17 47.3	23 21.1	25 16.7	28 13.0	8 14.5	27 02.3	1 14.8	10 00.9	14 11.5	17 50.6
30 F	10 32 44	6 37 30	1♉06 57	7♉49 15	17 42.0	23 08.1	24 45.0	28 51.5	8 35.0	27 15.4	1 11.6	9 59.9	14 10.7	17 51.7
31 Sa	10 36 41	7 35 31	14 34 44	21 23 25	17 38.7	23D 03.2	24 15.0	29 30.1	8 55.6	27 28.4	1 08.4	9 59.0	14 09.9	17 52.8

Astro Data

	Dy Hr Mn
☽ 0N	3 7:19
♃⚻♆	6 7:28
☽ 0S	15 21:50
♃□♇	16 21:37
♇ D	28 23:47
☽ 0N	30 13:06
♀ R	1 10:35
☿ R	7 23:58
☽ 0S	12 7:48
♃⚼♅	21 0:06
☽ 0N	26 19:17
☿ D	31 14:35

Planet Ingress

		Dy Hr Mn
☿	♌	4 6:05
♀	♍	11 5:06
♂	♍	15 12:36
☉	♌	23 8:11
☿	♍	26 13:00
⚳	♏	3 2:39
☿	♌R	19 21:40
♀	♌R	21 15:06
☉	♍	23 15:13

Last Aspect / ☽ Ingress

Last Aspect Dy Hr Mn			☽ Ingress	Dy Hr Mn
1 3:47	♀	☍	♓	1 17:51
4 3:09	☿	△	♈	4 3:33
6 3:58	♀	△	♉	6 9:52
8 9:42	♀	□	♊	8 12:42
10 12:21	♀	⚹	♋	10 13:03
11 19:06	☉	☌	♌	12 12:35
14 12:09	♂	☌	♍	14 13:12
16 4:34	☉	⚹	♎	16 16:34
18 15:11	☉	□	♏	18 23:41
21 6:19	☉	△	♐	21 10:16
23 17:31	☿	△	♑	23 22:55
25 10:39	♇	⚹	♒	26 11:49
28 3:50	♃	☍	♓	28 23:35
30 9:41	♇	△	♈	31 9:20

Last Aspect / ☽ Ingress

Last Aspect Dy Hr Mn			☽ Ingress	Dy Hr Mn
2 0:20	♃	△	♉	2 16:32
4 6:24	♃	□	♊	4 20:54
6 9:40	♃	⚹	♋	6 22:47
8 3:15	♇	△	♌	8 23:09
10 12:00	♃	☌	♍	10 23:35
12 4:47	♇	⚹	♎	13 1:52
14 20:12	♃	⚹	♏	15 7:34
17 6:05	♃	□	♐	17 17:11
20 5:02	☿	△	♑	20 5:34
22 5:29	♂	△	♒	22 18:27
25 1:42	♀	☍	♓	25 5:51
27 9:08	♂	☍	♈	27 15:01
29 16:44	♃	△	♉	29 22:00

☽ Phases & Eclipses

Dy Hr Mn	
5 2:50	☾ 12♈37
11 19:06	● 18♋59
11 19:06:03	● T 06'53"
18 15:11	☽ 25♎30
26 18:24	○ 3♒16
26 18:08	● A 0.254
3 11:25	☾ 10♉38
10 2:28	● 17♌00
17 5:01	☽ 23♏49
25 9:07	○ 1♓41

Astro Data

1 July 1991
Julian Day # 33419
SVP 5♓22'26"
GC 26♐43.2 ⚴ 20♍12.0
Eris 17♈49.2 ⚵ 27♑24.3R
⚷ 27♋41.9 ⚶ 13♋26.5
☽ Mean ☊ 19♑31.3

1 August 1991
Julian Day # 33450
SVP 5♓22'21"
GC 26♐43.3 ⚴ 1♎22.9
Eris 17♈48.5R ⚵ 20♑19.2R
⚷ 1♌15.4 ⚶ 27♋05.0
☽ Mean ☊ 17♑52.9

LONGITUDE

September 1991

Day	Sid.Time	☉	0 hr ☽	Noon ☽	True ☊	☿	♀	♂	⚳	♃	♄	♅	♆	♇
1 Su	10 40 37	8♍33 33	28♉15 19	5♊10 26	17♑37.5	23♌06.4	23♌46.7	0♎08.6	9♏16.2	27♌41.4	1♒05.3	9♑58.1	14♑09.1	17♏54.0
2 M	10 44 34	9 31 38	12♊08 47	19 10 20	17D37.7	23 18.2	23R20.4	0 47.2	9 37.0	27 54.4	1R02.3	9R57.2	14R08.3	17 55.1
3 Tu	10 48 30	10 29 44	26 15 00	3♋22 39	17R38.6	23 38.4	22 56.2	1 25.9	9 57.9	28 07.4	0 59.4	9 56.4	14 07.6	17 56.3
4 W	10 52 27	11 27 52	10♋33 06	17 46 03	17 39.2	24 07.1	22 34.1	2 04.6	10 18.9	28 20.4	0 56.5	9 55.7	14 06.9	17 57.6
5 Th	10 56 23	12 26 03	25 01 07	2♌17 48	17 38.3	24 44.1	22 14.2	2 43.3	10 40.0	28 33.3	0 53.8	9 55.0	14 06.2	17 58.8
6 F	11 00 20	13 24 15	9♌35 32	16 53 37	17 35.3	25 29.2	21 56.7	3 22.1	11 01.2	28 46.2	0 51.1	9 54.3	14 05.6	18 00.1
7 Sa	11 04 16	14 22 29	24 11 18	1♍27 46	17 29.8	26 22.0	21 41.5	4 00.9	11 22.4	28 59.1	0 48.4	9 53.7	14 05.0	18 01.4
8 Su	11 08 13	15 20 45	8♍42 10	15 53 42	17 22.0	27 22.2	21 28.6	4 39.8	11 43.8	29 12.0	0 45.9	9 53.1	14 04.4	18 02.8
9 M	11 12 10	16 19 02	23 01 33	0♎05 00	17 12.7	28 29.5	21 18.2	5 18.7	12 05.3	29 24.8	0 43.4	9 52.6	14 03.9	18 04.1
10 Tu	11 16 06	17 17 21	7♎03 27	13 56 24	17 02.9	29 43.1	21 10.2	5 57.7	12 26.8	29 37.6	0 41.1	9 52.1	14 03.3	18 05.5
11 W	11 20 03	18 15 42	20 43 30	27 24 34	16 53.6	1♍02.8	21 04.6	6 36.6	12 48.5	29 50.4	0 38.8	9 51.7	14 02.8	18 07.0
12 Th	11 23 59	19 14 05	3♏59 31	10♏28 28	16 45.8	2 27.8	21D01.3	7 15.7	13 10.2	0♍03.2	0 36.6	9 51.3	14 02.4	18 08.4
13 F	11 27 56	20 12 29	16 51 35	23 09 14	16 40.2	3 57.6	21 00.4	7 54.7	13 32.0	0 15.9	0 34.4	9 51.0	14 01.9	18 09.9
14 Sa	11 31 52	21 10 55	29 21 50	5♐29 52	16 36.8	5 31.8	21 01.9	8 33.9	13 53.9	0 28.6	0 32.4	9 50.7	14 01.6	18 11.4
15 Su	11 35 49	22 09 23	11♐33 56	17 34 38	16D35.5	7 09.6	21 05.7	9 13.0	14 15.9	0 41.3	0 30.5	9 50.5	14 01.2	18 13.0
16 M	11 39 45	23 07 52	23 32 39	29 28 37	16 35.5	8 50.6	21 11.7	9 52.2	14 38.0	0 53.9	0 28.6	9 50.3	14 00.9	18 14.6
17 Tu	11 43 42	24 06 23	5♑23 15	11♑17 13	16R36.0	10 34.2	21 19.9	10 31.4	15 00.1	1 06.5	0 26.9	9 50.2	14 00.6	18 16.2
18 W	11 47 39	25 04 55	17 11 11	23 05 49	16 35.9	12 19.9	21 30.3	11 10.7	15 22.3	1 19.0	0 25.2	9D50.2	14 00.3	18 17.8
19 Th	11 51 35	26 03 29	29 01 42	4♒59 27	16 34.3	14 07.4	21 42.8	11 50.0	15 44.6	1 31.5	0 23.7	9 50.1	14 00.1	18 19.4
20 F	11 55 32	27 02 05	10♒59 34	17 02 31	16 30.4	15 56.2	21 57.4	12 29.4	16 06.9	1 44.0	0 22.2	9 50.2	13 59.8	18 21.1
21 Sa	11 59 28	28 00 42	23 08 44	29 18 32	16 23.9	17 45.9	22 14.0	13 08.8	16 29.4	1 56.4	0 20.8	9 50.2	13 59.7	18 22.8
22 Su	12 03 25	28 59 21	5♓32 11	11♓49 52	16 14.8	19 36.3	22 32.5	13 48.2	16 51.9	2 08.8	0 19.5	9 50.4	13 59.5	18 24.5
23 M	12 07 21	29 58 02	18 11 41	24 37 39	16 03.6	21 27.0	22 52.9	14 27.7	17 14.4	2 21.1	0 18.3	9 50.6	13 59.4	18 26.3
24 Tu	12 11 18	0♎56 45	1♈07 41	7♈41 40	15 51.4	23 17.9	23 15.1	15 07.2	17 37.1	2 33.4	0 17.2	9 50.8	13 59.3	18 28.1
25 W	12 15 14	1 55 30	14 19 23	21 00 35	15 39.2	25 08.7	23 39.1	15 46.7	17 59.8	2 45.6	0 16.2	9 51.1	13D59.3	18 29.9
26 Th	12 19 11	2 54 18	27 44 58	4♉32 15	15 28.3	26 59.2	24 04.8	16 26.4	18 22.6	2 57.8	0 15.3	9 51.4	13 59.3	18 31.7
27 F	12 23 08	3 53 07	11♉22 06	18 14 12	15 19.5	28 49.4	24 32.2	17 06.0	18 45.4	3 10.0	0 14.5	9 51.8	13 59.3	18 33.5
28 Sa	12 27 04	4 51 59	25 08 18	2♊04 07	15 13.6	0♎39.1	25 01.2	17 45.7	19 08.3	3 22.1	0 13.8	9 52.3	13 59.4	18 35.4
29 Su	12 31 01	5 50 52	9♊01 28	16 00 09	15 10.3	2 28.2	25 31.8	18 25.4	19 31.3	3 34.1	0 13.2	9 52.7	13 59.5	18 37.3
30 M	12 34 57	6 49 49	23 00 04	0♋01 06	15D09.2	4 16.7	26 03.8	19 05.2	19 54.3	3 46.1	0 12.7	9 53.3	13 59.6	18 39.2

LONGITUDE

October 1991

Day	Sid.Time	☉	0 hr ☽	Noon ☽	True ☊	☿	♀	♂	⚳	♃	♄	♅	♆	♇
1 Tu	12 38 54	7♎48 47	7♋03 09	14♋06 10	15♑09.1	6♎04.5	26♌37.3	19♎45.1	20♏17.4	3♍58.0	0♒12.3	9♑53.9	13♑59.7	18♏41.1
2 W	12 42 50	8 47 48	21 10 03	28 14 40	15R08.8	7 51.5	27 12.1	20 24.9	20 40.5	4 09.9	0R11.9	9 54.5	13 59.9	18 43.1
3 Th	12 46 47	9 46 51	5♌19 53	12♌25 28	15 06.9	9 37.8	27 48.3	21 04.9	21 03.7	4 21.7	0 11.7	9 55.2	14 00.2	18 45.1
4 F	12 50 43	10 45 57	19 31 10	26 36 36	15 02.5	11 23.3	28 25.8	21 44.8	21 27.0	4 33.5	0D11.6	9 56.0	14 00.4	18 47.1
5 Sa	12 54 40	11 45 04	3♍41 23	10♍45 02	14 55.1	13 07.9	29 04.4	22 24.9	21 50.3	4 45.2	0 11.6	9 56.8	14 00.7	18 49.1
6 Su	12 58 37	12 44 14	17 47 01	24 46 47	14 45.0	14 51.8	29 44.3	23 04.9	22 13.7	4 56.8	0 11.7	9 57.6	14 01.0	18 51.1
7 M	13 02 33	13 43 26	1♎43 47	8♎37 27	14 33.0	16 34.9	0♍25.3	23 45.0	22 37.1	5 08.4	0 11.9	9 58.5	14 01.4	18 53.2
8 Tu	13 06 30	14 42 40	15 27 17	22 12 51	14 20.1	18 17.2	1 07.4	24 25.2	23 00.6	5 19.9	0 12.2	9 59.5	14 01.8	18 55.3
9 W	13 10 26	15 41 56	28 53 46	5♏29 48	14 07.6	19 58.7	1 50.6	25 05.4	23 24.2	5 31.3	0 12.5	10 00.5	14 02.2	18 57.4
10 Th	13 14 23	16 41 14	12♏00 46	18 26 40	13 56.9	21 39.4	2 34.7	25 45.6	23 47.7	5 42.7	0 13.0	10 01.5	14 02.7	18 59.5
11 F	13 18 19	17 40 34	24 47 32	1♐03 34	13 48.5	23 19.4	3 19.9	26 25.9	24 11.4	5 54.0	0 13.6	10 02.6	14 03.1	19 01.6
12 Sa	13 22 16	18 39 56	7♐15 03	13 22 22	13 43.0	24 58.6	4 06.0	27 06.3	24 35.1	6 05.2	0 14.3	10 03.8	14 03.7	19 03.7
13 Su	13 26 12	19 39 20	19 25 58	25 26 22	13 40.0	26 37.1	4 53.0	27 46.6	24 58.8	6 16.4	0 15.1	10 05.0	14 04.2	19 05.9
14 M	13 30 09	20 38 45	1♑24 10	7♑19 59	13D38.9	28 14.8	5 40.8	28 27.1	25 22.6	6 27.4	0 16.0	10 06.2	14 04.8	19 08.1
15 Tu	13 34 05	21 38 13	13 14 30	19 08 22	13R38.9	29 51.9	6 29.5	29 07.5	25 46.4	6 38.4	0 17.0	10 07.5	14 05.4	19 10.3
16 W	13 38 02	22 37 42	25 02 19	0♒57 02	13 38.7	1♏28.3	7 19.1	29 48.0	26 10.3	6 49.3	0 18.1	10 08.9	14 06.1	19 12.5
17 Th	13 41 59	23 37 12	6♒53 13	12 51 31	13 37.3	3 04.0	8 09.4	0♏28.6	26 34.2	7 00.2	0 19.3	10 10.3	14 06.8	19 14.7
18 F	13 45 55	24 36 45	18 52 35	24 57 02	13 33.8	4 39.0	9 00.5	1 09.2	26 58.1	7 10.9	0 20.6	10 11.7	14 07.5	19 16.9
19 Sa	13 49 52	25 36 19	1♓05 23	7♓18 07	13 27.7	6 13.5	9 52.3	1 49.8	27 22.1	7 21.6	0 22.0	10 13.2	14 08.3	19 19.2
20 Su	13 53 48	26 35 55	13 35 37	19 58 12	13 19.0	7 47.3	10 44.8	2 30.5	27 46.1	7 32.2	0 23.5	10 14.7	14 09.0	19 21.4
21 M	13 57 45	27 35 33	26 26 02	2♈59 12	13 08.2	9 20.5	11 38.0	3 11.3	28 10.2	7 42.7	0 25.1	10 16.3	14 09.9	19 23.7
22 Tu	14 01 41	28 35 13	9♈37 40	16 21 16	12 56.2	10 53.1	12 31.9	3 52.0	28 34.3	7 53.1	0 26.7	10 17.9	14 10.7	19 26.0
23 W	14 05 38	29 34 54	23 09 43	0♉02 37	12 44.1	12 25.1	13 26.4	4 32.9	28 58.4	8 03.4	0 28.5	10 19.6	14 11.6	19 28.3
24 Th	14 09 34	0♏34 38	6♉59 30	13 59 49	12 33.2	13 56.6	14 21.6	5 13.7	29 22.6	8 13.6	0 30.4	10 21.3	14 12.5	19 30.6
25 F	14 13 31	1 34 24	21 02 57	28 08 17	12 24.6	15 27.5	15 17.3	5 54.7	29 46.8	8 23.8	0 32.4	10 23.1	14 13.4	19 32.9
26 Sa	14 17 28	2 34 12	5♊15 11	12♊23 05	12 18.6	16 57.8	16 13.7	6 35.6	0♐11.0	8 33.8	0 34.5	10 24.9	14 14.4	19 35.3
27 Su	14 21 24	3 34 02	19 31 25	26 39 44	12 15.5	18 27.6	17 10.6	7 16.7	0 35.3	8 43.7	0 36.6	10 26.8	14 15.4	19 37.6
28 M	14 25 21	4 33 54	3♋47 36	10♋54 42	12D14.6	19 56.8	18 08.1	7 57.7	0 59.6	8 53.6	0 38.9	10 28.7	14 16.5	19 40.0
29 Tu	14 29 17	5 33 49	18 00 47	25 05 39	12R14.9	21 25.4	19 06.0	8 38.8	1 23.9	9 03.3	0 41.3	10 30.7	14 17.5	19 42.3
30 W	14 33 14	6 33 45	2♌09 09	9♌11 12	12 15.1	22 53.5	20 04.6	9 20.0	1 48.3	9 13.0	0 43.7	10 32.6	14 18.6	19 44.7
31 Th	14 37 10	7 33 44	16 11 42	23 10 35	12 14.1	24 21.0	21 03.6	10 01.2	2 12.7	9 22.5	0 46.3	10 34.7	14 19.8	19 47.0

Astro Data	Dy Hr Mn
♂0S	3 17:37
♃□♆	7 22:27
☽0S	8 18:08
♀D	13 8:55
♃⚻♄	14 18:16
♅D	19 8:37
☽0N	23 2:32
⊙0S	23 12:49
♆D	26 7:13
☿0S	30 2:19
♄D	5 3:57
☽0S	6 2:53
☽0N	20 10:46

Planet Ingress		Dy Hr Mn
♂	♎	1 6:38
☿	♍	10 17:14
♃	♍	12 6:00
⊙	♎	23 12:48
☿	♎	28 3:26
♀	♍	6 21:15
☿	♏	15 14:01
♂	♏	16 19:05
⊙	♏	23 22:05
⚳	♐	26 1:06

Last Aspect Dy Hr Mn		☽ Ingress	Dy Hr Mn
1 2:52	♂ △	♊	1 3:02
3 3:02	♃ ✶	♋	3 6:19
4 12:19	♇ △	♌	5 8:13
7 7:51	♃ ☌	♍	7 9:35
8 15:37	♇ ✶	♎	9 11:51
11 16:29	♃ ✶	♏	11 16:42
13 7:53	♀ □	♐	14 1:14
15 22:01	⊙ □	♑	16 13:04
18 16:23	⊙ △	♒	19 1:58
20 21:53	♀ ☍	♓	21 13:20
23 5:06	☿ ☍	♈	23 21:56
25 16:52	♀ △	♉	26 3:59
27 23:21	♀ □	♊	28 8:25
30 4:58	♀ ✶	♋	30 11:58

Last Aspect Dy Hr Mn		☽ Ingress	Dy Hr Mn
1 22:04	♂ □	♌	2 14:58
4 15:14	♀ ☌	♍	4 17:45
6 1:48	♇ ✶	♎	6 21:00
8 16:09	♂ ☌	♏	9 2:00
10 13:02	♇ ☌	♐	11 9:58
13 16:59	♂ ✶	♑	13 21:10
16 9:32	♂ □	♒	16 10:04
18 11:17	⊙ △	♓	18 21:53
20 10:51	♇ △	♈	21 6:33
23 11:08	⊙ ☍	♉	23 11:55
24 21:25	♇ ☍	♊	25 15:09
26 18:55	♀ □	♋	27 17:37
29 5:03	☿ △	♌	29 20:20
31 14:15	☿ □	♍	31 23:47

☽ Phases & Eclipses Dy Hr Mn		
1 18:16	☾	8♊49
8 11:01	●	15♍18
15 22:01	☽	22♐34
23 22:40	○	0♈24
1 0:30	☾	7♋21
7 21:39	●	14♎07
15 17:33	☽	21♑52
23 11:08	○	29♈33
30 7:11	☾	6♌22

Astro Data

1 September 1991
Julian Day # 33481
SVP 5♓22'17"
GC 26♐43.4 ⚴ 13♎52.7
Eris 17♈38.3R ⚵ 15♑58.4R
⚷ 4♌42.7 ⚶ 10♌40.9
☽ Mean ☊ 16♑14.4

1 October 1991
Julian Day # 33511
SVP 5♓22'14"
GC 26♐43.4 ⚴ 26♎41.9
Eris 17♈22.2R ⚵ 17♑27.9
⚷ 7♌28.7 ⚶ 23♌29.8
☽ Mean ☊ 14♑39.0

November 1991

LONGITUDE

Day	Sid.Time	☉	0 hr ☽	Noon☽	True☊	☿	♀	♂	⚳	♃	♄	♅	♆	♇
1 F	14 41 07	8♏33 45	0♍07 46	7♍03 09	12♑10.8	25♏47.9	22♍03.0	10♏42.5	2♐37.1	9♍32.0	0♒48.9	10♑36.8	14♑20.9	19♏49.4
2 Sa	14 45 03	9 33 48	13 56 36	20 47 59	12R 05.0	27 14.1	23 03.0	11 23.8	3 01.5	9 41.3	0 51.7	10 38.9	14 22.1	19 51.8
3 Su	14 49 00	10 33 54	27 37 06	4♎23 44	11 56.7	28 39.7	24 03.3	12 05.2	3 26.0	9 50.5	0 54.5	10 41.1	14 23.3	19 54.2
4 M	14 52 57	11 34 01	11♎07 39	17 48 38	11 46.6	0♐04.6	25 04.1	12 46.6	3 50.5	9 59.6	0 57.4	10 43.3	14 24.6	19 56.6
5 Tu	14 56 53	12 34 10	24 26 25	1♏00 46	11 35.7	1 28.8	26 05.4	13 28.0	4 15.1	10 08.6	1 00.4	10 45.5	14 25.8	19 59.0
6 W	15 00 50	13 34 21	7♏31 32	13 58 31	11 25.1	2 52.2	27 07.0	14 09.5	4 39.6	10 17.5	1 03.6	10 47.8	14 27.1	20 01.4
7 Th	15 04 46	14 34 34	20 21 39	26 40 52	11 16.0	4 14.7	28 09.0	14 51.1	5 04.2	10 26.3	1 06.8	10 50.1	14 28.5	20 03.8
8 F	15 08 43	15 34 49	2♐56 13	9♐07 48	11 08.9	5 36.3	29 11.4	15 32.7	5 28.8	10 34.9	1 10.0	10 52.5	14 29.8	20 06.2
9 Sa	15 12 39	16 35 06	15 15 48	21 20 27	11 04.3	6 56.9	0♎14.1	16 14.3	5 53.4	10 43.4	1 13.4	10 54.9	14 31.2	20 08.6
10 Su	15 16 36	17 35 24	27 22 04	3♑21 03	11D 02.1	8 16.3	1 17.2	16 56.0	6 18.1	10 51.8	1 16.9	10 57.4	14 32.6	20 11.1
11 M	15 20 32	18 35 43	9♑17 50	15 12 56	11 01.8	9 34.5	2 20.7	17 37.8	6 42.7	11 00.1	1 20.4	10 59.8	14 34.1	20 13.5
12 Tu	15 24 29	19 36 04	21 06 53	27 00 18	11 02.7	10 51.3	3 24.4	18 19.6	7 07.4	11 08.3	1 24.1	11 02.4	14 35.6	20 15.9
13 W	15 28 26	20 36 27	2♒53 47	8♒48 00	11 04.0	12 06.6	4 28.5	19 01.4	7 32.1	11 16.3	1 27.8	11 04.9	14 37.1	20 18.3
14 Th	15 32 22	21 36 50	14 43 37	20 41 18	11R 04.7	13 20.2	5 32.9	19 43.3	7 56.8	11 24.2	1 31.6	11 07.5	14 38.6	20 20.8
15 F	15 36 19	22 37 15	26 41 44	2♓45 34	11 04.0	14 31.8	6 37.6	20 25.2	8 21.5	11 31.9	1 35.5	11 10.2	14 40.1	20 23.2
16 Sa	15 40 15	23 37 42	8♓53 26	15 05 56	11 01.5	15 41.2	7 42.6	21 07.2	8 46.2	11 39.6	1 39.5	11 12.8	14 41.7	20 25.6
17 Su	15 44 12	24 38 10	21 23 35	27 46 50	10 57.0	16 48.1	8 47.9	21 49.2	9 11.0	11 47.1	1 43.5	11 15.5	14 43.3	20 28.0
18 M	15 48 08	25 38 39	4♈16 04	10♈51 32	10 50.9	17 52.3	9 53.4	22 31.3	9 35.7	11 54.4	1 47.7	11 18.3	14 44.9	20 30.4
19 Tu	15 52 05	26 39 09	17 33 21	24 21 30	10 43.6	18 53.2	10 59.2	23 13.4	10 00.5	12 01.6	1 51.9	11 21.0	14 46.6	20 32.8
20 W	15 56 01	27 39 41	1♉15 50	8♉16 02	10 36.1	19 50.6	12 05.3	23 55.6	10 25.3	12 08.7	1 56.2	11 23.8	14 48.2	20 35.2
21 Th	15 59 58	28 40 14	15 21 37	22 31 59	10 29.3	20 44.0	13 11.7	24 37.8	10 50.1	12 15.6	2 00.5	11 26.7	14 49.9	20 37.6
22 F	16 03 55	29 40 49	29 46 26	7♊04 06	10 24.0	21 32.7	14 18.3	25 20.0	11 14.9	12 22.4	2 05.0	11 29.5	14 51.6	20 40.0
23 Sa	16 07 51	0♐41 26	14♊24 08	21 45 36	10 20.7	22 16.2	15 25.1	26 02.3	11 39.7	12 29.1	2 09.5	11 32.4	14 53.4	20 42.4
24 Su	16 11 48	1 42 04	29 07 37	6♋29 19	10D 19.3	22 53.9	16 32.2	26 44.7	12 04.5	12 35.6	2 14.1	11 35.4	14 55.1	20 44.8
25 M	16 15 44	2 42 43	13♋49 53	21 08 39	10 19.7	23 25.1	17 39.5	27 27.1	12 29.3	12 42.0	2 18.8	11 38.3	14 56.9	20 47.2
26 Tu	16 19 41	3 43 24	28 25 00	5♌38 26	10 21.0	23 48.9	18 47.1	28 09.5	12 54.2	12 48.2	2 23.5	11 41.3	14 58.7	20 49.6
27 W	16 23 37	4 44 07	12♌48 35	19 55 10	10 22.4	24 04.5	19 54.9	28 52.1	13 19.0	12 54.2	2 28.4	11 44.3	15 00.6	20 52.0
28 Th	16 27 34	5 44 51	26 58 01	3♍57 01	10R 23.2	24R 11.3	21 02.8	29 34.6	13 43.8	13 00.1	2 33.2	11 47.4	15 02.4	20 54.3
29 F	16 31 30	6 45 36	10♍52 07	17 43 21	10 22.7	24 08.4	22 11.0	0♐17.2	14 08.7	13 05.9	2 38.2	11 50.5	15 04.3	20 56.7
30 Sa	16 35 27	7 46 24	24 30 46	1♎14 25	10 20.6	23 55.1	23 19.4	0 59.9	14 33.5	13 11.4	2 43.2	11 53.6	15 06.1	20 59.0

December 1991

LONGITUDE

Day	Sid.Time	☉	0 hr ☽	Noon☽	True☊	☿	♀	♂	⚳	♃	♄	♅	♆	♇
1 Su	16 39 24	8♐47 13	7♎54 23	14♎30 47	10♑17.0	23♐31.0	24♎28.0	1♐42.6	14♐58.4	13♍16.9	2♒48.3	11♑56.7	15♑08.0	21♏01.4
2 M	16 43 20	9 48 03	21 03 41	27 33 11	10R 12.3	22R 55.8	25 36.7	2 25.3	15 23.2	13 22.1	2 53.5	11 59.8	15 10.0	21 03.7
3 Tu	16 47 17	10 48 54	3♏59 21	10♏22 16	10 07.1	22 09.6	26 45.7	3 08.1	15 48.1	13 27.2	2 58.7	12 03.0	15 11.9	21 06.0
4 W	16 51 13	11 49 47	16 42 01	22 58 40	10 02.0	21 12.9	27 54.8	3 51.0	16 12.9	13 32.2	3 04.0	12 06.2	15 13.9	21 08.3
5 Th	16 55 10	12 50 41	29 12 18	5♐23 02	9 57.7	20 06.9	29 04.0	4 33.9	16 37.8	13 36.9	3 09.4	12 09.4	15 15.9	21 10.6
6 F	16 59 06	13 51 37	11♐30 59	17 36 16	9 54.5	18 53.1	0♏13.5	5 16.8	17 02.6	13 41.5	3 14.8	12 12.7	15 17.9	21 12.9
7 Sa	17 03 03	14 52 33	23 39 04	29 39 35	9D 52.7	17 33.7	1 23.1	5 59.8	17 27.5	13 45.9	3 20.3	12 15.9	15 19.9	21 15.2
8 Su	17 07 00	15 53 30	5♑38 03	11♑34 45	9 52.2	16 11.3	2 32.8	6 42.8	17 52.3	13 50.2	3 25.9	12 19.2	15 21.9	21 17.4
9 M	17 10 56	16 54 28	17 29 59	23 24 07	9 52.9	14 48.5	3 42.7	7 25.9	18 17.2	13 54.3	3 31.5	12 22.5	15 23.9	21 19.7
10 Tu	17 14 53	17 55 27	29 17 33	5♒10 43	9 54.4	13 28.2	4 52.7	8 09.1	18 42.0	13 58.2	3 37.2	12 25.9	15 26.0	21 21.9
11 W	17 18 49	18 56 26	11♒04 05	16 58 11	9 56.1	12 13.1	6 02.9	8 52.2	19 06.8	14 01.9	3 42.9	12 29.2	15 28.1	21 24.1
12 Th	17 22 46	19 57 27	22 53 33	28 50 44	9 57.8	11 05.3	7 13.2	9 35.5	19 31.6	14 05.5	3 48.7	12 32.6	15 30.2	21 26.3
13 F	17 26 42	20 58 27	4♓50 21	10♓53 00	9R 58.9	10 06.6	8 23.6	10 18.7	19 56.4	14 08.8	3 54.5	12 36.0	15 32.3	21 28.5
14 Sa	17 30 39	21 59 28	16 59 16	23 09 46	9 59.2	9 18.2	9 34.1	11 02.0	20 21.2	14 12.0	4 00.4	12 39.4	15 34.4	21 30.7
15 Su	17 34 35	23 00 30	29 25 05	5♈45 45	9 58.7	8 40.8	10 44.8	11 45.4	20 46.0	14 15.0	4 06.4	12 42.8	15 36.5	21 32.8
16 M	17 38 32	24 01 32	12♈12 17	18 45 04	9 57.4	8 14.5	11 55.6	12 28.8	21 10.7	14 17.8	4 12.4	12 46.2	15 38.6	21 34.9
17 Tu	17 42 29	25 02 35	25 24 28	2♉10 42	9 55.7	7D 59.3	13 06.5	13 12.2	21 35.5	14 20.5	4 18.5	12 49.7	15 40.8	21 37.0
18 W	17 46 25	26 03 37	9♉03 51	16 03 51	9 53.7	7 54.5	14 17.5	13 55.7	22 00.2	14 22.9	4 24.6	12 53.1	15 43.0	21 39.1
19 Th	17 50 22	27 04 41	23 10 30	0♊23 22	9 52.0	7 59.7	15 28.7	14 39.3	22 24.9	14 25.2	4 30.7	12 56.6	15 45.1	21 41.2
20 F	17 54 18	28 05 45	7♊41 55	15 05 23	9 50.6	8 14.0	16 39.9	15 22.8	22 49.7	14 27.3	4 36.9	13 00.1	15 47.3	21 43.3
21 Sa	17 58 15	29 06 49	22 32 54	0♋03 26	9D 49.9	8 36.6	17 51.3	16 06.5	23 14.3	14 29.2	4 43.2	13 03.6	15 49.5	21 45.3
22 Su	18 02 11	0♑07 54	7♋35 55	15 09 11	9 49.9	9 06.8	19 02.7	16 50.1	23 39.0	14 30.9	4 49.5	13 07.1	15 51.7	21 47.3
23 M	18 06 08	1 09 00	22 42 06	0♌13 32	9 50.3	9 43.7	20 14.3	17 33.9	24 03.7	14 32.5	4 55.8	13 10.6	15 53.9	21 49.4
24 Tu	18 10 04	2 10 06	7♌42 29	15 08 01	9 50.9	10 26.7	21 25.9	18 17.6	24 28.3	14 33.8	5 02.2	13 14.1	15 56.1	21 51.3
25 W	18 14 01	3 11 12	22 29 21	29 45 51	9 51.6	11 15.0	22 37.7	19 01.4	24 52.9	14 34.9	5 08.6	13 17.7	15 58.4	21 53.3
26 Th	18 17 58	4 12 19	6♍57 03	14♍02 36	9 52.1	12 08.0	23 49.5	19 45.3	25 17.5	14 35.9	5 15.1	13 21.2	16 00.6	21 55.2
27 F	18 21 54	5 13 27	21 02 20	27 56 12	9R 52.4	13 05.3	25 01.4	20 29.2	25 42.1	14 36.6	5 21.6	13 24.8	16 02.8	21 57.1
28 Sa	18 25 51	6 14 36	4♎44 15	11♎26 39	9 52.4	14 06.2	26 13.4	21 13.2	26 06.6	14 37.2	5 28.1	13 28.3	16 05.1	21 59.0
29 Su	18 29 47	7 15 44	18 03 38	24 35 28	9 52.3	15 10.5	27 25.6	21 57.2	26 31.2	14 37.6	5 34.7	13 31.9	16 07.3	22 00.9
30 M	18 33 44	8 16 54	1♏02 29	7♏25 03	9 52.1	16 17.6	28 37.7	22 41.2	26 55.7	14R 37.7	5 41.3	13 35.5	16 09.6	22 02.7
31 Tu	18 37 40	9 18 04	13 43 29	19 58 11	9D 52.0	17 27.2	29 50.0	23 25.3	27 20.2	14 37.7	5 48.0	13 39.0	16 11.8	22 04.5

Astro Data

	Dy Hr Mn
☽0S	2 9:05
♃△♅	11 10:51
♀0S	11 22:41
☽0N	16 19:15
☿R	28 17:01
☽0S	29 13:46
☽0N	14 3:04
☿D	18 11:12
☽0S	26 19:38
♃R	30 21:33

Planet Ingress

	Dy Hr Mn
☿ ♐	4 10:41
♀ ♎	9 6:37
☉ ♐	22 19:36
♂ ♐	29 2:19
♀ ♏	6 7:21
☉ ♑	22 8:54
♀ ♐	31 15:19

Last Aspect / ☽ Ingress

Last Aspect Dy Hr Mn		☽ Ingress Dy Hr Mn
3 0:39	☿ ⚹	♎ 3 4:13
4 5:52	♆ □	♏ 5 10:09
7 15:04	♀ ⚹	♐ 7 18:21
8 14:52	♃ □	♑ 10 5:16
11 22:13	♇ ⚹	♒ 12 18:06
14 14:02	☉ □	♓ 15 6:33
17 5:37	☉ △	♈ 17 16:08
19 1:36	☿ △	♉ 19 21:49
21 22:56	☉ ☍	♊ 22 0:22
23 12:52	☿ ☍	♋ 24 1:25
25 22:56	♂ △	♌ 26 2:37
28 4:04	♂ □	♍ 28 5:12
29 23:12	☿ □	♎ 30 9:47

Last Aspect / ☽ Ingress

Last Aspect Dy Hr Mn		☽ Ingress Dy Hr Mn
2 8:03	♀ ☌	♏ 2 16:33
4 8:28	♇ ☌	♐ 5 1:32
6 14:18	☿ ☌	♑ 7 12:41
9 7:46	♇ ⚹	♒ 10 1:27
11 21:01	♇ □	♓ 12 14:19
14 9:32	☉ □	♈ 15 1:06
16 22:18	☉ △	♉ 17 8:10
18 21:28	♇ ☍	♊ 19 11:21
21 10:23	☉ ☍	♋ 21 11:55
22 22:34	♇ △	♌ 23 11:38
24 23:11	♀ □	♍ 25 12:23
27 6:26	♀ ⚹	♎ 27 15:37
29 6:51	♂ ⚹	♏ 29 22:03

☽ Phases & Eclipses

Dy Hr Mn	
6 11:11	● 13♏32
14 14:02	☽ 21♒42
21 22:56	○ 29♉08
28 15:21	☾ 5♍53
6 3:56	● 13♐31
14 9:32	☽ 21♓53
21 10:23	○ 29♊03
21 10:33	• P 0.087
28 1:55	☾ 5♎49

Astro Data

1 November 1991
Julian Day # 33542
SVP 5♓22'10"
GC 26♐43.5 ⚴ 10♏18.7
Eris 17♈03.8R ⚵ 24♑06.7
⚷ 9♌14.8 ⚶ 5♍53.6
☽ Mean ☊ 13♑00.5

1 December 1991
Julian Day # 33572
SVP 5♓22'06"
GC 26♐43.6 ⚴ 23♏29.5
Eris 16♈49.6R ⚵ 3♒56.9
⚷ 9♌31.5R ⚶ 16♍15.0
☽ Mean ☊ 11♑25.2

LONGITUDE — January 1992

Day	Sid.Time	☉	0 hr ☽	Noon ☽	True ☊	☿	♀	♂	⚳	♃	♄	♅	♆	♇
1 W	18 41 37	10♑19 14	26♏09 30	2♐17 45	9♑52.0	18♐39.2	1♐02.3	24♐09.5	27♐44.6	14♍37.5	5♒54.7	13♑42.6	16♑14.1	22♏06.3
2 Th	18 45 33	11 20 25	8♐23 18	14 26 27	9 52.1	19 53.1	2 14.7	24 53.6	28 09.1	14R37.1	6 01.4	13 46.2	16 16.4	22 08.1
3 F	18 49 30	12 21 35	20 27 29	26 26 42	9 52.2	21 08.9	3 27.2	25 37.9	28 33.5	14 36.5	6 08.2	13 49.8	16 18.6	22 09.9
4 Sa	18 53 27	13 22 46	2♑24 22	8♑20 45	9R52.3	22 26.2	4 39.8	26 22.1	28 57.8	14 35.7	6 15.0	13 53.4	16 20.9	22 11.6
5 Su	18 57 23	14 23 57	14 16 04	20 10 37	9 52.3	23 45.0	5 52.4	27 06.5	29 22.2	14 34.7	6 21.8	13 57.0	16 23.2	22 13.3
6 M	19 01 20	15 25 08	26 04 37	1♒58 22	9 51.9	25 05.0	7 05.0	27 50.8	29 46.5	14 33.5	6 28.6	14 00.5	16 25.5	22 14.9
7 Tu	19 05 16	16 26 18	7♒52 07	13 46 10	9 51.2	26 26.3	8 17.7	28 35.2	0♑10.8	14 32.1	6 35.5	14 04.1	16 27.8	22 16.6
8 W	19 09 13	17 27 28	19 40 49	25 36 26	9 50.1	27 48.6	9 30.5	29 19.6	0 35.0	14 30.5	6 42.4	14 07.7	16 30.0	22 18.2
9 Th	19 13 09	18 28 38	1♓33 21	7♓31 59	9 48.9	29 11.8	10 43.3	0♑04.1	0 59.2	14 28.8	6 49.3	14 11.3	16 32.3	22 19.8
10 F	19 17 06	19 29 48	13 32 43	19 36 01	9 47.6	0♑36.0	11 56.2	0 48.6	1 23.4	14 26.8	6 56.3	14 14.9	16 34.6	22 21.3
11 Sa	19 21 02	20 30 57	25 42 20	1♈52 09	9 46.6	2 01.0	13 09.1	1 33.2	1 47.5	14 24.6	7 03.2	14 18.4	16 36.8	22 22.8
12 Su	19 24 59	21 32 05	8♈05 58	14 24 15	9D45.9	3 26.8	14 22.1	2 17.8	2 11.6	14 22.3	7 10.2	14 22.0	16 39.1	22 24.3
13 M	19 28 56	22 33 13	20 47 31	27 16 14	9 45.9	4 53.3	15 35.1	3 02.4	2 35.7	14 19.7	7 17.3	14 25.6	16 41.4	22 25.8
14 Tu	19 32 52	23 34 20	3♉50 48	10♉31 36	9 46.4	6 20.5	16 48.2	3 47.1	2 59.7	14 17.0	7 24.3	14 29.1	16 43.6	22 27.2
15 W	19 36 49	24 35 26	17 18 55	24 12 58	9 47.5	7 48.4	18 01.3	4 31.8	3 23.6	14 14.1	7 31.3	14 32.7	16 45.9	22 28.6
16 Th	19 40 45	25 36 32	1♊13 48	8♊21 22	9 48.7	9 16.9	19 14.4	5 16.6	3 47.6	14 11.0	7 38.4	14 36.2	16 48.2	22 30.0
17 F	19 44 42	26 37 38	15 35 25	22 55 33	9 49.8	10 46.1	20 27.6	6 01.4	4 11.5	14 07.8	7 45.5	14 39.7	16 50.4	22 31.3
18 Sa	19 48 38	27 38 42	0♋21 10	7♋51 29	9R50.3	12 15.8	21 40.9	6 46.2	4 35.3	14 04.3	7 52.6	14 43.3	16 52.7	22 32.7
19 Su	19 52 35	28 39 46	15 25 32	23 02 14	9 50.0	13 46.2	22 54.1	7 31.1	4 59.1	14 00.7	7 59.7	14 46.8	16 54.9	22 33.9
20 M	19 56 32	29 40 49	0♌40 20	8♌18 34	9 48.6	15 17.1	24 07.4	8 16.0	5 22.9	13 56.9	8 06.8	14 50.3	16 57.1	22 35.2
21 Tu	20 00 28	0♒41 52	15 55 37	23 30 14	9 46.2	16 48.7	25 20.8	9 00.9	5 46.6	13 52.9	8 13.9	14 53.8	16 59.4	22 36.4
22 W	20 04 25	1 42 53	1♍01 13	8♍27 31	9 43.2	18 20.8	26 34.2	9 45.9	6 10.2	13 48.7	8 21.1	14 57.2	17 01.6	22 37.6
23 Th	20 08 21	2 43 55	15 48 16	23 02 45	9 40.0	19 53.5	27 47.6	10 31.0	6 33.8	13 44.4	8 28.2	15 00.7	17 03.8	22 38.7
24 F	20 12 18	3 44 56	0♎10 30	7♎11 13	9 37.3	21 26.8	29 01.1	11 16.0	6 57.4	13 39.9	8 35.4	15 04.1	17 06.0	22 39.9
25 Sa	20 16 14	4 45 56	14 04 47	20 51 15	9 35.4	23 00.7	0♑14.6	12 01.1	7 20.9	13 35.2	8 42.6	15 07.6	17 08.2	22 41.0
26 Su	20 20 11	5 46 56	27 30 49	4♏03 49	9D34.6	24 35.3	1 28.1	12 46.3	7 44.4	13 30.4	8 49.7	15 11.0	17 10.4	22 42.0
27 M	20 24 07	6 47 56	10♏30 40	16 51 49	9 35.0	26 10.4	2 41.7	13 31.5	8 07.8	13 25.4	8 56.9	15 14.4	17 12.6	22 43.0
28 Tu	20 28 04	7 48 55	23 07 49	29 19 13	9 36.3	27 46.2	3 55.3	14 16.7	8 31.1	13 20.3	9 04.1	15 17.8	17 14.7	22 44.0
29 W	20 32 01	8 49 53	5♐26 35	11♐30 28	9 38.1	29 22.7	5 08.9	15 02.0	8 54.4	13 15.0	9 11.3	15 21.1	17 16.9	22 45.0
30 Th	20 35 57	9 50 51	17 31 27	23 30 01	9 39.9	0♒59.8	6 22.6	15 47.3	9 17.7	13 09.5	9 18.4	15 24.5	17 19.0	22 45.9
31 F	20 39 54	10 51 47	29 26 42	5♑21 58	9R40.9	2 37.5	7 36.3	16 32.6	9 40.8	13 03.9	9 25.6	15 27.8	17 21.2	22 46.8

LONGITUDE — February 1992

Day	Sid.Time	☉	0 hr ☽	Noon ☽	True ☊	☿	♀	♂	⚳	♃	♄	♅	♆	♇
1 Sa	20 43 50	11♒52 43	11♑16 14	17♑09 54	9♑40.7	4♒16.0	8♑50.0	17♑18.0	10♑04.0	12♍58.2	9♒32.8	15♑31.1	17♑23.3	22♏47.6
2 Su	20 47 47	12 53 39	23 03 19	28 56 50	9R38.8	5 55.2	10 03.7	18 03.4	10 27.0	12R52.3	9 40.0	15 34.4	17 25.4	22 48.4
3 M	20 51 43	13 54 33	4♒50 44	10♒45 16	9 35.2	7 35.0	11 17.5	18 48.8	10 50.0	12 46.3	9 47.2	15 37.7	17 27.5	22 49.2
4 Tu	20 55 40	14 55 25	16 40 40	22 37 11	9 29.9	9 15.6	12 31.3	19 34.3	11 13.0	12 40.1	9 54.3	15 41.0	17 29.6	22 50.0
5 W	20 59 36	15 56 17	28 35 01	4♓34 21	9 23.3	10 57.0	13 45.0	20 19.8	11 35.8	12 33.8	10 01.5	15 44.2	17 31.6	22 50.7
6 Th	21 03 33	16 57 07	10♓35 23	16 38 20	9 16.0	12 39.1	14 58.9	21 05.4	11 58.6	12 27.4	10 08.7	15 47.4	17 33.7	22 51.4
7 F	21 07 30	17 57 56	22 43 25	28 50 51	9 08.7	14 21.9	16 12.7	21 50.9	12 21.4	12 20.9	10 15.8	15 50.6	17 35.7	22 52.0
8 Sa	21 11 26	18 58 44	5♈00 54	11♈13 50	9 02.3	16 05.6	17 26.5	22 36.5	12 44.0	12 14.2	10 22.9	15 53.7	17 37.7	22 52.6
9 Su	21 15 23	19 59 30	17 29 57	23 49 34	8 57.4	17 50.0	18 40.4	23 22.2	13 06.6	12 07.5	10 30.1	15 56.8	17 39.7	22 53.2
10 M	21 19 19	21 00 15	0♉13 02	6♉40 41	8 54.4	19 35.2	19 54.2	24 07.8	13 29.1	12 00.6	10 37.2	15 59.9	17 41.7	22 53.7
11 Tu	21 23 16	22 00 58	13 12 53	19 49 59	8D53.3	21 21.2	21 08.1	24 53.5	13 51.6	11 53.7	10 44.3	16 03.0	17 43.7	22 54.2
12 W	21 27 12	23 01 40	26 32 19	3♊20 09	8 53.7	23 08.0	22 22.0	25 39.2	14 14.0	11 46.6	10 51.4	16 06.1	17 45.6	22 54.7
13 Th	21 31 09	24 02 20	10♊13 45	17 13 14	8 54.9	24 55.6	23 35.9	26 25.0	14 36.2	11 39.5	10 58.4	16 09.1	17 47.6	22 55.1
14 F	21 35 05	25 02 58	24 18 39	1♋29 54	8R56.0	26 43.9	24 49.8	27 10.7	14 58.5	11 32.2	11 05.5	16 12.1	17 49.5	22 55.5
15 Sa	21 39 02	26 03 35	8♋46 45	16 08 47	8 56.0	28 32.9	26 03.8	27 56.5	15 20.6	11 24.9	11 12.5	16 15.1	17 51.4	22 55.8
16 Su	21 42 59	27 04 09	23 35 23	1♌05 47	8 54.1	0♓22.6	27 17.7	28 42.4	15 42.7	11 17.6	11 19.5	16 18.0	17 53.3	22 56.1
17 M	21 46 55	28 04 43	8♌39 02	16 13 59	8 49.9	2 13.0	28 31.6	29 28.2	16 04.7	11 10.1	11 26.5	16 20.9	17 55.1	22 56.4
18 Tu	21 50 52	29 05 14	23 49 27	1♍24 07	8 43.5	4 03.9	29 45.6	0♒14.1	16 26.5	11 02.6	11 33.5	16 23.8	17 57.0	22 56.7
19 W	21 54 48	0♓05 44	8♍56 43	16 25 59	8 35.6	5 55.3	0♒59.6	1 00.0	16 48.4	10 55.0	11 40.4	16 26.6	17 58.8	22 56.9
20 Th	21 58 45	1 06 13	23 50 47	1♎10 07	8 27.1	7 47.1	2 13.6	1 45.9	17 10.1	10 47.4	11 47.4	16 29.4	18 00.6	22 57.1
21 F	22 02 41	2 06 40	8♎23 10	15 29 22	8 19.0	9 39.2	3 27.6	2 31.9	17 31.7	10 39.7	11 54.3	16 32.2	18 02.3	22 57.2
22 Sa	22 06 38	3 07 05	22 28 18	29 19 47	8 12.4	11 31.4	4 41.6	3 17.9	17 53.3	10 32.0	12 01.1	16 34.9	18 04.1	22 57.3
23 Su	22 10 34	4 07 30	6♏03 52	12♏40 41	8 07.9	13 23.6	5 55.6	4 03.9	18 14.8	10 24.2	12 08.0	16 37.6	18 05.8	22 57.4
24 M	22 14 31	5 07 53	19 10 36	25 34 02	8D05.5	15 15.4	7 09.6	4 50.0	18 36.2	10 16.4	12 14.8	16 40.3	18 07.5	22R57.4
25 Tu	22 18 28	6 08 15	1♐51 32	8♐03 42	8 05.0	17 06.8	8 23.7	5 36.0	18 57.4	10 08.6	12 21.6	16 42.9	18 09.2	22 57.4
26 W	22 22 24	7 08 35	14 11 11	20 14 39	8 05.6	18 57.3	9 37.7	6 22.1	19 18.6	10 00.7	12 28.4	16 45.6	18 10.9	22 57.3
27 Th	22 26 21	8 08 54	26 14 47	2♑12 14	8R06.4	20 46.7	10 51.8	7 08.3	19 39.7	9 52.9	12 35.1	16 48.1	18 12.5	22 57.3
28 F	22 30 17	9 09 11	8♑07 39	14 01 41	8 06.4	22 34.5	12 05.9	7 54.4	20 00.8	9 45.0	12 41.8	16 50.7	18 14.1	22 57.2
29 Sa	22 34 14	10 09 27	19 54 55	25 47 53	8 04.6	24 20.4	13 20.0	8 40.6	20 21.7	9 37.1	12 48.5	16 53.1	18 15.7	22 57.0

Astro Data

	Dy	Hr Mn
☽0N	10	9:52
♃△♅	12	13:07
☽0S	23	4:36
☽0N	6	16:08
♃⊼♄	16	8:43
☽0S	19	15:49
♇R	24	21:33

Planet Ingress

		Dy	Hr Mn
⚳	♑	7	1:21
♂	♑	9	9:47
☿	♑	10	1:46
☉	♒	20	19:32
♀	♑	25	7:14
☿	♒	29	21:15
☿	♓	16	7:04
♂	♒	18	4:38
♀	♒	18	16:40
☉	♓	19	9:43

Last Aspect / ☽ Ingress

Last Aspect Dy Hr Mn		☽ Ingress	Dy Hr Mn
31 16:05	♇ ☌	♐	1 7:30
3 10:15	♂ ☌	♑	3 19:09
5 16:10	♇ ⚹	♒	6 7:59
8 20:01	♂ ⚹	♓	8 20:52
10 17:26	♇ △	♈	11 8:22
13 2:32	☉ □	♉	13 17:00
15 12:42	☉ △	♊	15 21:55
17 7:37	♀ ☍	♋	17 23:26
19 21:28	☉ ☍	♌	19 22:57
21 15:12	♀ △	♍	21 22:22
23 20:43	♀ □	♎	23 23:42
25 16:23	☿ □	♏	26 4:32
28 8:32	☿ ⚹	♐	28 13:20
29 15:26	♃ □	♑	31 1:07

Last Aspect / ☽ Ingress

Last Aspect Dy Hr Mn		☽ Ingress	Dy Hr Mn
1 23:29	♇ ⚹	♒	2 14:09
4 12:26	♇ □	♓	5 2:51
7 0:16	♇ △	♈	7 14:15
9 11:05	♂ □	♉	9 23:36
11 21:37	♂ △	♊	12 6:08
14 2:55	☿ △	♋	14 9:31
16 7:59	♂ ☍	♌	16 10:15
18 8:04	☉ ☍	♍	18 9:47
19 22:32	♇ ⚹	♎	20 10:04
21 16:22	♆ □	♏	22 13:11
24 7:04	♇ ☌	♐	24 20:26
26 8:59	♇ ☍	♑	27 7:33
29 8:30	☿ ⚹	♒	29 20:34

☽ Phases & Eclipses

Dy Hr Mn		
4 23:10	●	13♑51
4 23:04:39	☀	A 10'58"
13 2:32	☽	22♈09
19 21:28	○	29♋04
26 15:27	☾	5♏56
3 19:00	●	14♒12
11 16:15	☽	22♉12
18 8:04	○	28♌55
25 7:56	☾	5♐58

Astro Data

1 January 1992
Julian Day # 33603
SVP 5♓22'00"
GC 26♐43.7 ⚴ 6♐40.7
Eris 16♈43.2R ⚵ 16♒26.1
⚷ 8♌17.7R ⚶ 23♍44.5
☽ Mean ☊ 9♑46.7

1 February 1992
Julian Day # 33634
SVP 5♓21'54"
GC 26♐43.7 ⚴ 18♐49.6
Eris 16♈47.4 ⚵ 0♓30.2
⚷ 6♌06.9R ⚶ 25♍35.1R
☽ Mean ☊ 8♑08.3

March 1992

LONGITUDE

Day	Sid.Time	☉	0 hr ☽	Noon ☽	True ☊	☿	♀	♂	⚳	♃	♄	♅	♆	♇
1 Su	22 38 10	11♓09 41	1♒41 06	7♒35 01	8♑00.3	26♓03.9	14♒34.0	9♒26.8	20♑42.5	9♍29.2	12♒55.1	16♑55.6	18♑17.2	22♏56.8
2 M	22 42 07	12 09 54	13 30 01	19 26 29	7R 53.3	27 44.5	15 48.1	10 13.0	21 03.2	9R 21.4	13 01.7	16 58.0	18 18.8	22R 56.6
3 Tu	22 46 03	13 10 05	25 24 40	1♓24 51	7 43.8	29 21.6	17 02.2	10 59.2	21 23.8	9 13.5	13 08.3	17 00.4	18 20.3	22 56.4
4 W	22 50 00	14 10 14	7♓27 12	13 31 54	7 32.1	0♈54.8	18 16.3	11 45.4	21 44.3	9 05.7	13 14.8	17 02.7	18 21.8	22 56.1
5 Th	22 53 56	15 10 21	19 39 02	25 48 42	7 19.3	2 23.5	19 30.4	12 31.7	22 04.6	8 57.9	13 21.3	17 05.0	18 23.2	22 55.8
6 F	22 57 53	16 10 26	2♈00 57	8♈15 51	7 06.5	3 47.1	20 44.5	13 18.0	22 24.9	8 50.1	13 27.7	17 07.3	18 24.7	22 55.4
7 Sa	23 01 50	17 10 29	14 33 26	20 53 45	6 54.9	5 05.0	21 58.6	14 04.3	22 45.1	8 42.4	13 34.1	17 09.5	18 26.1	22 55.0
8 Su	23 05 46	18 10 31	27 16 52	3♉42 51	6 45.4	6 16.7	23 12.7	14 50.6	23 05.1	8 34.7	13 40.5	17 11.7	18 27.4	22 54.6
9 M	23 09 43	19 10 30	10♉11 50	16 43 56	6 38.6	7 21.7	24 26.8	15 36.9	23 25.0	8 27.0	13 46.8	17 13.8	18 28.8	22 54.1
10 Tu	23 13 39	20 10 27	23 19 18	29 58 08	6 34.6	8 19.5	25 40.9	16 23.3	23 44.9	8 19.4	13 53.1	17 15.9	18 30.1	22 53.6
11 W	23 17 36	21 10 22	6♊40 37	13♊26 59	6D 33.1	9 09.7	26 55.0	17 09.6	24 04.6	8 11.9	13 59.3	17 17.9	18 31.4	22 53.1
12 Th	23 21 32	22 10 15	20 17 23	27 12 01	6R 32.9	9 52.0	28 09.0	17 56.0	24 24.1	8 04.4	14 05.5	17 19.9	18 32.6	22 52.6
13 F	23 25 29	23 10 05	4♋10 59	11♋14 20	6 33.0	10 26.1	29 23.1	18 42.4	24 43.6	7 57.0	14 11.6	17 21.9	18 33.9	22 52.0
14 Sa	23 29 25	24 09 54	18 22 02	25 33 54	6 31.9	10 51.8	0♓37.2	19 28.7	25 02.9	7 49.7	14 17.7	17 23.8	18 35.1	22 51.3
15 Su	23 33 22	25 09 39	2♌49 40	10♌08 52	6 28.6	11 08.9	1 51.3	20 15.1	25 22.1	7 42.5	14 23.8	17 25.7	18 36.3	22 50.7
16 M	23 37 19	26 09 23	17 30 54	24 55 01	6 22.5	11R 17.6	3 05.4	21 01.6	25 41.2	7 35.3	14 29.7	17 27.5	18 37.4	22 50.0
17 Tu	23 41 15	27 09 05	2♍20 20	9♍45 51	6 13.7	11 17.8	4 19.4	21 48.0	26 00.1	7 28.2	14 35.7	17 29.3	18 38.5	22 49.3
18 W	23 45 12	28 08 44	17 10 31	24 33 14	6 02.8	11 09.7	5 33.5	22 34.4	26 18.9	7 21.2	14 41.5	17 31.0	18 39.6	22 48.5
19 Th	23 49 08	29 08 21	1♎52 55	9♎08 34	5 50.9	10 53.9	6 47.6	23 20.8	26 37.6	7 14.4	14 47.4	17 32.7	18 40.7	22 47.8
20 F	23 53 05	0♈07 56	16 19 19	23 24 24	5 39.4	10 30.6	8 01.6	24 07.3	26 56.1	7 07.6	14 53.1	17 34.4	18 41.7	22 47.0
21 Sa	23 57 01	1 07 30	0♏23 16	7♏15 33	5 29.4	10 00.6	9 15.7	24 53.8	27 14.5	7 00.9	14 58.9	17 36.0	18 42.7	22 46.1
22 Su	0 00 58	2 07 02	14 01 01	20 39 40	5 21.9	9 24.6	10 29.8	25 40.2	27 32.8	6 54.4	15 04.5	17 37.5	18 43.6	22 45.3
23 M	0 04 54	3 06 32	27 11 39	3♐37 14	5 17.0	8 43.3	11 43.9	26 26.7	27 50.9	6 47.9	15 10.1	17 39.0	18 44.6	22 44.4
24 Tu	0 08 51	4 06 00	9♐56 50	16 10 57	5 14.6	7 57.9	12 57.9	27 13.2	28 08.9	6 41.6	15 15.7	17 40.5	18 45.5	22 43.4
25 W	0 12 48	5 05 26	22 20 10	28 25 07	5 13.8	7 09.2	14 12.0	27 59.7	28 26.7	6 35.4	15 21.2	17 41.9	18 46.3	22 42.5
26 Th	0 16 44	6 04 51	4♑26 27	10♑24 54	5 13.8	6 18.4	15 26.1	28 46.2	28 44.4	6 29.3	15 26.6	17 43.2	18 47.2	22 41.5
27 F	0 20 41	7 04 14	16 21 09	22 15 53	5 13.3	5 26.5	16 40.1	29 32.7	29 01.9	6 23.4	15 31.9	17 44.5	18 48.0	22 40.5
28 Sa	0 24 37	8 03 35	28 09 47	4♒03 31	5 11.2	4 34.6	17 54.2	0♓19.2	29 19.3	6 17.6	15 37.2	17 45.8	18 48.8	22 39.5
29 Su	0 28 34	9 02 54	9♒57 41	15 52 52	5 06.8	3 43.8	19 08.3	1 05.8	29 36.5	6 11.9	15 42.5	17 47.0	18 49.5	22 38.4
30 M	0 32 30	10 02 11	21 49 35	27 48 19	4 59.5	2 55.0	20 22.3	1 52.3	29 53.6	6 06.4	15 47.7	17 48.2	18 50.2	22 37.3
31 Tu	0 36 27	11 01 27	3♓49 28	9♓53 23	4 49.6	2 09.0	21 36.4	2 38.8	0♒10.5	6 01.0	15 52.8	17 49.3	18 50.9	22 36.2

April 1992

LONGITUDE

Day	Sid.Time	☉	0 hr ☽	Noon ☽	True ☊	☿	♀	♂	⚳	♃	♄	♅	♆	♇
1 W	0 40 23	12♈00 40	16♓00 19	22♓10 30	4♑37.5	1♈26.6	22♓50.4	3♓25.3	0♒27.2	5♍55.7	15♒57.8	17♑50.3	18♑51.5	22♏35.1
2 Th	0 44 20	12 59 52	28 24 04	4♈41 04	4R 24.1	0R 48.4	24 04.5	4 11.9	0 43.8	5R 50.7	16 02.8	17 51.4	18 52.1	22R 33.9
3 F	0 48 17	13 59 01	11♈01 32	17 25 23	4 10.7	0 14.8	25 18.5	4 58.4	1 00.2	5 45.7	16 07.7	17 52.3	18 52.7	22 32.7
4 Sa	0 52 13	14 58 09	23 52 34	0♉22 57	3 58.3	29♓46.2	26 32.6	5 44.9	1 16.4	5 41.0	16 12.5	17 53.2	18 53.2	22 31.5
5 Su	0 56 10	15 57 14	6♉56 22	13 32 42	3 48.2	29 22.9	27 46.6	6 31.4	1 32.4	5 36.3	16 17.3	17 54.1	18 53.8	22 30.3
6 M	1 00 06	16 56 18	20 11 47	26 53 30	3 40.9	29 05.0	29 00.6	7 17.9	1 48.3	5 31.9	16 22.0	17 54.9	18 54.2	22 29.0
7 Tu	1 04 03	17 55 19	3♊37 44	10♊24 24	3 36.5	28 52.6	0♈14.6	8 04.4	2 04.0	5 27.6	16 26.6	17 55.7	18 54.7	22 27.7
8 W	1 07 59	18 54 18	17 13 28	24 04 53	3D 34.7	28D 45.8	1 28.6	8 50.9	2 19.5	5 23.5	16 31.1	17 56.4	18 55.1	22 26.4
9 Th	1 11 56	19 53 14	0♋58 40	7♋54 50	3R 34.4	28 44.3	2 42.6	9 37.4	2 34.8	5 19.6	16 35.6	17 57.0	18 55.5	22 25.1
10 F	1 15 52	20 52 09	14 53 23	21 54 18	3 34.6	28 48.2	3 56.6	10 23.9	2 49.9	5 15.8	16 40.0	17 57.6	18 55.8	22 23.8
11 Sa	1 19 49	21 51 01	28 57 33	6♌03 02	3 33.9	28 57.3	5 10.6	11 10.3	3 04.9	5 12.2	16 44.3	17 58.2	18 56.1	22 22.4
12 Su	1 23 46	22 49 50	13♌10 35	20 19 57	3 31.3	29 11.4	6 24.5	11 56.8	3 19.6	5 08.8	16 48.6	17 58.7	18 56.4	22 21.0
13 M	1 27 42	23 48 37	27 30 47	4♍42 40	3 26.1	29 30.3	7 38.5	12 43.2	3 34.1	5 05.5	16 52.7	17 59.2	18 56.7	22 19.6
14 Tu	1 31 39	24 47 22	11♍55 02	19 07 17	3 18.4	29 53.9	8 52.4	13 29.7	3 48.5	5 02.4	16 56.8	17 59.6	18 56.9	22 18.2
15 W	1 35 35	25 46 05	26 18 43	3♎28 36	3 08.8	0♈21.9	10 06.4	14 16.1	4 02.6	4 59.5	17 00.8	17 59.9	18 57.1	22 16.8
16 Th	1 39 32	26 44 46	10♎36 12	17 40 46	2 58.2	0 54.2	11 20.3	15 02.5	4 16.6	4 56.8	17 04.8	18 00.2	18 57.2	22 15.3
17 F	1 43 28	27 43 24	24 41 38	1♏38 11	2 47.9	1 30.5	12 34.2	15 48.9	4 30.3	4 54.3	17 08.6	18 00.5	18 57.3	22 13.8
18 Sa	1 47 25	28 42 01	8♏29 54	15 16 24	2 38.8	2 10.8	13 48.1	16 35.3	4 43.8	4 51.9	17 12.4	18 00.7	18 57.4	22 12.4
19 Su	1 51 21	29 40 36	21 57 26	28 32 51	2 31.9	2 54.7	15 02.1	17 21.7	4 57.1	4 49.7	17 16.1	18 00.8	18 57.4	22 10.9
20 M	1 55 18	0♉39 10	5♐02 40	11♐26 59	2 27.4	3 42.1	16 16.0	18 08.1	5 10.2	4 47.8	17 19.7	18 00.9	18R 57.5	22 09.3
21 Tu	1 59 14	1 37 41	17 46 04	24 00 15	2D 25.3	4 32.9	17 29.9	18 54.4	5 23.1	4 45.9	17 23.2	18R 01.0	18 57.4	22 07.8
22 W	2 03 11	2 36 11	0♑09 58	6♑15 42	2 25.0	5 27.0	18 43.8	19 40.8	5 35.7	4 44.3	17 26.6	18 01.0	18 57.4	22 06.3
23 Th	2 07 08	3 34 39	12 18 01	18 17 32	2 25.8	6 24.1	19 57.7	20 27.1	5 48.2	4 42.9	17 30.0	18 00.9	18 57.3	22 04.7
24 F	2 11 04	4 33 06	24 14 52	0♒10 41	2R 26.5	7 24.1	21 11.6	21 13.4	6 00.4	4 41.6	17 33.3	18 00.8	18 57.2	22 03.2
25 Sa	2 15 01	5 31 31	6♒05 40	12 00 27	2 26.4	8 26.9	22 25.4	21 59.7	6 12.3	4 40.5	17 36.4	18 00.6	18 57.0	22 01.6
26 Su	2 18 57	6 29 54	17 55 42	23 52 05	2 24.6	9 32.5	23 39.3	22 46.0	6 24.0	4 39.6	17 39.5	18 00.4	18 56.9	22 00.0
27 M	2 22 54	7 28 16	29 50 10	5♓50 32	2 20.7	10 40.7	24 53.2	23 32.3	6 35.5	4 38.9	17 42.5	18 00.2	18 56.7	21 58.4
28 Tu	2 26 50	8 26 36	11♓53 42	18 00 09	2 14.7	11 51.3	26 07.1	24 18.5	6 46.8	4 38.4	17 45.5	17 59.9	18 56.4	21 56.8
29 W	2 30 47	9 24 54	24 10 15	0♈24 22	2 07.0	13 04.4	27 20.9	25 04.8	6 57.7	4 38.1	17 48.3	17 59.5	18 56.1	21 55.1
30 Th	2 34 43	10 23 11	6♈42 43	13 05 28	1 58.1	14 19.9	28 34.8	25 51.0	7 08.5	4D 37.9	17 51.0	17 59.1	18 55.8	21 53.5

Astro Data	Dy Hr Mn
☿0N	3 6:02
☽0N	4 22:31
☿R	17 0:31
☽0S	18 2:44
☉0N	20 8:49
☽0N	1 5:26
☿0S	6 18:18
☿D	9 6:26
♀0N	10 3:05
☽0S	14 11:12
♆R	20 12:14
♅R	21 23:19
☿0N	22 21:43
☽0N	28 12:53
♃D	30 19:38

Planet Ingress		Dy Hr Mn
☿	♈	3 21:45
♀	♓	13 23:57
☉	♈	20 8:48
♂	♓	28 2:04
⚳	♒	30 21:04
☿	♓R	3 23:52
♀	♈	7 7:16
☿	♈	14 17:35
☉	♉	19 19:57

Last Aspect Dy Hr Mn			☽ Ingress	Dy Hr Mn
2 19:03	♇	□	♓	3 9:11
5 6:24	♇	△	♈	5 20:07
7 14:15	♀	✶	♉	8 5:05
10 3:29	♀	□	♊	10 12:03
12 13:48	♀	△	♋	12 16:50
14 9:30	☉	△	♌	14 19:20
16 8:38	♇	□	♍	16 20:13
18 18:18	☉	☍	♎	18 20:55
20 13:18	♂	△	♏	20 23:20
22 21:46	♂	□	♐	23 5:13
25 11:06	♂	✶	♑	25 15:08
27 12:50	♇	✶	♒	28 3:44
30 1:37	♇	□	♓	30 16:23

Last Aspect Dy Hr Mn			☽ Ingress	Dy Hr Mn
1 13:26	♀	☌	♈	2 3:04
3 14:43	♆	□	♉	4 11:18
6 16:10	♀	✶	♊	6 17:33
8 20:07	☿	□	♋	8 22:18
10 23:51	☿	△	♌	11 1:46
12 16:29	☉	△	♍	13 4:09
14 17:18	♇	✶	♎	15 6:10
17 4:43	☉	☍	♏	17 9:10
19 0:26	♇	☌	♐	19 14:40
21 1:32	♂	□	♑	21 23:40
23 19:36	♇	✶	♒	24 11:38
26 11:31	♀	✶	♓	27 0:20
29 1:05	♂	☌	♈	29 11:13

☽ Phases & Eclipses Dy Hr Mn		
4 13:22	●	14♓14
12 2:36	☽	21♊47
18 18:18	○	28♍24
26 2:30	☾	5♑41
3 5:01	●	13♈42
10 10:06	☽	20♋47
17 4:43	○	27♎26
24 21:40	☾	4♒57

Astro Data

1 March 1992
Julian Day # 33663
SVP 5♓21'51"
GC 26♐43.8 ⚴ 28♐28.0
Eris 16♈59.9 ⚵ 14♓38.8
⚷ 4♌12.7R ⚶ 20♍49.8R
☽ Mean ☊ 6♑36.1

1 April 1992
Julian Day # 33694
SVP 5♓21'48"
GC 26♐43.9 ⚴ 5♑36.7
Eris 17♈19.0 ⚵ 0♈29.7
⚷ 3♌18.0R ⚶ 13♍22.5R
☽ Mean ☊ 4♑57.6

LONGITUDE May 1992

Day	Sid.Time	☉	0 hr ☽	Noon ☽	True ☊	☿	♀	♂	⚳	♃	♄	♅	♆	♇
1 F	2 38 40	11♉21 27	19♈32 41	26♈04 23	1♑49.0	15♈37.7	29♈48.7	26♓37.1	7♒19.0	4♍38.0	17♒53.7	17♑58.7	18♑55.5	21♏51.9
2 Sa	2 42 37	12 19 40	2♉40 27	9♉20 42	1R 40.7	16 57.7	1♉02.5	27 23.3	7 29.2	4 38.2	17 56.2	17R 58.2	18R 55.1	21R 50.2
3 Su	2 46 33	13 17 52	16 04 54	22 52 44	1 33.9	18 19.9	2 16.3	28 09.4	7 39.1	4 38.6	17 58.7	17 57.6	18 54.7	21 48.6
4 M	2 50 30	14 16 02	29 43 53	6♊37 57	1 29.3	19 44.2	3 30.2	28 55.5	7 48.8	4 39.2	18 01.1	17 57.0	18 54.3	21 46.9
5 Tu	2 54 26	15 14 11	13♊34 34	20 33 21	1D 26.8	21 10.6	4 44.0	29 41.6	7 58.3	4 39.9	18 03.3	17 56.4	18 53.8	21 45.3
6 W	2 58 23	16 12 18	27 33 56	4♋35 58	1 26.4	22 39.2	5 57.8	0♈27.6	8 07.4	4 40.9	18 05.5	17 55.7	18 53.3	21 43.6
7 Th	3 02 19	17 10 22	11♋39 10	18 43 13	1 27.2	24 09.8	7 11.6	1 13.6	8 16.3	4 42.0	18 07.6	17 54.9	18 52.8	21 41.9
8 F	3 06 16	18 08 25	25 47 54	2♌52 58	1 28.5	25 42.4	8 25.4	1 59.6	8 24.9	4 43.4	18 09.6	17 54.1	18 52.2	21 40.3
9 Sa	3 10 12	19 06 26	9♌58 13	17 03 27	1R 29.2	27 17.0	9 39.2	2 45.6	8 33.2	4 44.9	18 11.5	17 53.3	18 51.6	21 38.6
10 Su	3 14 09	20 04 25	24 08 29	1♍13 05	1 28.7	28 53.7	10 53.0	3 31.5	8 41.2	4 46.6	18 13.3	17 52.4	18 51.0	21 36.9
11 M	3 18 06	21 02 22	8♍17 01	15 20 03	1 26.5	0♉32.4	12 06.8	4 17.3	8 48.9	4 48.4	18 15.0	17 51.5	18 50.4	21 35.2
12 Tu	3 22 02	22 00 17	22 21 52	29 22 11	1 22.5	2 13.1	13 20.6	5 03.2	8 56.4	4 50.5	18 16.7	17 50.5	18 49.7	21 33.6
13 W	3 25 59	22 58 10	6♎20 38	13♎16 53	1 17.3	3 55.8	14 34.3	5 49.0	9 03.5	4 52.7	18 18.2	17 49.5	18 49.0	21 31.9
14 Th	3 29 55	23 56 02	20 10 35	27 01 21	1 11.4	5 40.6	15 48.1	6 34.8	9 10.4	4 55.1	18 19.6	17 48.4	18 48.2	21 30.2
15 F	3 33 52	24 53 52	3♏48 51	10♏32 47	1 05.6	7 27.3	17 01.8	7 20.5	9 17.0	4 57.6	18 20.9	17 47.3	18 47.5	21 28.5
16 Sa	3 37 48	25 51 40	17 12 53	23 48 55	1 00.5	9 16.1	18 15.6	8 06.2	9 23.2	5 00.3	18 22.2	17 46.2	18 46.7	21 26.9
17 Su	3 41 45	26 49 27	0♐20 46	6♐48 20	0 56.8	11 06.9	19 29.3	8 51.9	9 29.2	5 03.3	18 23.3	17 45.0	18 45.9	21 25.2
18 M	3 45 41	27 47 13	13 11 37	19 30 41	0D 54.7	12 59.7	20 43.1	9 37.5	9 34.8	5 06.3	18 24.3	17 43.7	18 45.0	21 23.5
19 Tu	3 49 38	28 44 58	25 45 41	1♑56 51	0 54.1	14 54.6	21 56.8	10 23.1	9 40.1	5 09.6	18 25.3	17 42.5	18 44.2	21 21.9
20 W	3 53 35	29 42 41	8♑04 28	14 08 52	0 54.8	16 51.3	23 10.5	11 08.7	9 45.1	5 13.0	18 26.1	17 41.1	18 43.3	21 20.2
21 Th	3 57 31	0♊40 23	20 10 28	26 09 45	0 56.3	18 50.1	24 24.2	11 54.2	9 49.8	5 16.6	18 26.9	17 39.8	18 42.4	21 18.6
22 F	4 01 28	1 38 04	2♒07 11	8♒03 20	0 58.0	20 50.7	25 38.0	12 39.7	9 54.2	5 20.3	18 27.5	17 38.4	18 41.4	21 16.9
23 Sa	4 05 24	2 35 44	13 58 46	19 54 03	0 59.4	22 53.1	26 51.7	13 25.2	9 58.2	5 24.2	18 28.1	17 36.9	18 40.4	21 15.3
24 Su	4 09 21	3 33 23	25 49 50	1♓46 41	1R 00.1	24 57.3	28 05.4	14 10.6	10 01.9	5 28.3	18 28.5	17 35.5	18 39.4	21 13.7
25 M	4 13 17	4 31 00	7♓45 14	13 46 05	0 59.8	27 03.1	29 19.2	14 55.9	10 05.2	5 32.5	18 28.9	17 33.9	18 38.4	21 12.0
26 Tu	4 17 14	5 28 37	19 49 48	25 56 57	0 58.3	29 10.4	0♊32.9	15 41.3	10 08.3	5 36.9	18 29.1	17 32.4	18 37.4	21 10.4
27 W	4 21 10	6 26 13	2♈08 02	8♈23 30	0 55.8	1♊19.1	1 46.6	16 26.6	10 11.0	5 41.4	18 29.3	17 30.8	18 36.3	21 08.8
28 Th	4 25 07	7 23 48	14 43 45	21 09 05	0 52.6	3 28.9	3 00.3	17 11.8	10 13.3	5 46.1	18R 29.3	17 29.2	18 35.2	21 07.2
29 F	4 29 04	8 21 22	27 39 45	4♉15 52	0 49.2	5 39.6	4 14.1	17 57.0	10 15.3	5 51.0	18 29.3	17 27.5	18 34.1	21 05.6
30 Sa	4 33 00	9 18 56	10♉57 28	17 44 27	0 46.1	7 51.1	5 27.8	18 42.1	10 16.9	5 56.0	18 29.1	17 25.8	18 32.9	21 04.1
31 Su	4 36 57	10 16 28	24 36 38	1♊33 42	0 43.6	10 03.0	6 41.5	19 27.2	10 18.2	6 01.2	18 28.9	17 24.0	18 31.8	21 02.5

LONGITUDE June 1992

Day	Sid.Time	☉	0 hr ☽	Noon ☽	True ☊	☿	♀	♂	⚳	♃	♄	♅	♆	♇
1 M	4 40 53	11♊13 59	8♊35 16	15♊40 48	0♑42.1	12♊15.0	7♊55.2	20♈12.3	10♒19.2	6♍06.5	18♒28.6	17♑22.3	18♑30.6	21♏00.9
2 Tu	4 44 50	12 11 30	22 49 45	0♋01 29	0D 41.6	14 27.1	9 09.0	20 57.3	10 19.8	6 12.0	18R 28.1	17R 20.5	18R 29.4	20R 59.4
3 W	4 48 46	13 08 59	7♋15 19	14 30 34	0 41.9	16 38.7	10 22.7	21 42.2	10R 20.0	6 17.6	18 27.6	17 18.6	18 28.1	20 57.9
4 Th	4 52 43	14 06 27	21 46 33	29 02 38	0 42.9	18 49.7	11 36.4	22 27.1	10 19.9	6 23.4	18 27.0	17 16.8	18 26.9	20 56.4
5 F	4 56 40	15 03 54	6♌18 09	13♌32 35	0 44.0	20 59.9	12 50.1	23 11.9	10 19.4	6 29.3	18 26.3	17 14.9	18 25.6	20 54.9
6 Sa	5 00 36	16 01 19	20 45 24	27 56 11	0 45.0	23 08.9	14 03.8	23 56.7	10 18.6	6 35.4	18 25.4	17 12.9	18 24.3	20 53.4
7 Su	5 04 33	16 58 44	5♍04 32	12♍10 10	0R 45.5	25 16.5	15 17.5	24 41.4	10 17.4	6 41.6	18 24.5	17 11.0	18 23.0	20 51.9
8 M	5 08 29	17 56 07	19 12 50	26 12 21	0 45.4	27 22.6	16 31.2	25 26.0	10 15.8	6 47.9	18 23.5	17 09.0	18 21.7	20 50.5
9 Tu	5 12 26	18 53 29	3♎08 32	10♎01 19	0 44.8	29 26.9	17 44.9	26 10.6	10 13.9	6 54.4	18 22.4	17 07.0	18 20.3	20 49.1
10 W	5 16 22	19 50 50	16 50 37	23 36 23	0 43.7	1♋29.4	18 58.6	26 55.2	10 11.6	7 01.0	18 21.2	17 04.9	18 19.0	20 47.6
11 Th	5 20 19	20 48 10	0♏18 36	6♏57 14	0 42.5	3 29.9	20 12.3	27 39.7	10 09.0	7 07.7	18 19.9	17 02.9	18 17.6	20 46.2
12 F	5 24 15	21 45 29	13 32 19	20 03 52	0 41.3	5 28.3	21 26.0	28 24.1	10 06.0	7 14.6	18 18.5	17 00.8	18 16.2	20 44.9
13 Sa	5 28 12	22 42 48	26 31 55	2♐56 30	0 40.3	7 24.4	22 39.7	29 08.4	10 02.7	7 21.6	18 17.0	16 58.7	18 14.8	20 43.5
14 Su	5 32 09	23 40 05	9♐17 43	15 35 37	0 39.7	9 18.4	23 53.4	29 52.8	9 59.0	7 28.8	18 15.4	16 56.5	18 13.4	20 42.2
15 M	5 36 05	24 37 22	21 50 20	28 02 00	0D 39.5	11 10.1	25 07.1	0♉37.0	9 54.9	7 36.0	18 13.8	16 54.4	18 11.9	20 40.9
16 Tu	5 40 02	25 34 39	4♑10 45	10♑16 48	0 39.6	12 59.4	26 20.8	1 21.2	9 50.5	7 43.4	18 12.0	16 52.2	18 10.5	20 39.6
17 W	5 43 58	26 31 55	16 20 22	22 21 42	0 39.8	14 46.4	27 34.5	2 05.3	9 45.8	7 51.0	18 10.2	16 50.0	18 09.0	20 38.3
18 Th	5 47 55	27 29 10	28 21 05	4♒18 52	0 40.2	16 31.0	28 48.2	2 49.4	9 40.7	7 58.6	18 08.3	16 47.7	18 07.5	20 37.0
19 F	5 51 51	28 26 25	10♒15 24	16 11 05	0 40.5	18 13.2	0♋01.9	3 33.4	9 35.2	8 06.4	18 06.2	16 45.5	18 06.1	20 35.8
20 Sa	5 55 48	29 23 40	22 06 21	28 01 39	0 40.7	19 53.0	1 15.6	4 17.3	9 29.4	8 14.2	18 04.1	16 43.2	18 04.5	20 34.6
21 Su	5 59 44	0♋20 54	3♓57 28	9♓54 21	0R 40.8	21 30.4	2 29.4	5 01.2	9 23.2	8 22.2	18 01.9	16 41.0	18 03.0	20 33.4
22 M	6 03 41	1 18 08	15 52 49	21 53 24	0D 40.8	23 05.3	3 43.1	5 45.0	9 16.7	8 30.4	17 59.7	16 38.7	18 01.5	20 32.2
23 Tu	6 07 38	2 15 22	27 56 40	4♈03 12	0 40.8	24 37.9	4 56.8	6 28.8	9 09.9	8 38.6	17 57.3	16 36.4	18 00.0	20 31.1
24 W	6 11 34	3 12 37	10♈13 31	16 28 09	0 40.8	26 07.9	6 10.5	7 12.5	9 02.7	8 46.9	17 54.8	16 34.0	17 58.4	20 30.0
25 Th	6 15 31	4 09 51	22 47 37	29 12 21	0 41.1	27 35.5	7 24.3	7 56.1	8 55.2	8 55.4	17 52.3	16 31.7	17 56.9	20 28.9
26 F	6 19 27	5 07 05	5♉42 45	12♉19 07	0 41.4	29 00.6	8 38.0	8 39.6	8 47.4	9 04.0	17 49.7	16 29.3	17 55.3	20 27.8
27 Sa	6 23 24	6 04 19	19 01 42	25 50 35	0 41.9	0♌23.2	9 51.7	9 23.1	8 39.3	9 12.7	17 47.0	16 27.0	17 53.7	20 26.8
28 Su	6 27 20	7 01 33	2♊45 46	9♊47 05	0 42.4	1 43.2	11 05.5	10 06.5	8 30.8	9 21.5	17 44.2	16 24.6	17 52.1	20 25.8
29 M	6 31 17	7 58 47	16 54 16	24 06 50	0R 42.7	3 00.6	12 19.2	10 49.8	8 22.1	9 30.4	17 41.4	16 22.2	17 50.5	20 24.8
30 Tu	6 35 13	8 56 01	1♋24 12	8♋45 38	0 42.7	4 15.3	13 33.0	11 33.1	8 13.0	9 39.4	17 38.5	16 19.8	17 49.0	20 23.8

Astro Data Dy Hr Mn	Planet Ingress Dy Hr Mn
♄⊻♅ 3 3:19	♀ ♉ 1 15:41
♂0N 9 22:29	♂ ♈ 5 21:36
☽0S 11 17:01	☿ ♉ 11 4:10
☽0N 25 20:36	☉ ♊ 20 19:12
♄ R 28 13:36	♀ ♊ 26 1:18
	☿ ♊ 26 21:16
⚳ R 3 15:51	
♄⊻♆ 4 8:16	☿ ♋ 9 18:27
☽0S 7 21:57	♂ ♉ 14 15:56
♄⊻♆ 19 19:35	♀ ♋ 19 11:22
☽0N 22 4:12	☉ ♋ 21 3:14
	☿ ♌ 27 5:11

Last Aspect Dy Hr Mn	☽ Ingress Dy Hr Mn
30 22:52 ♆ □	♉ 1 19:09
3 21:48 ♂ ⚹	♊ 4 0:28
5 13:11 ☿ ⚹	♋ 6 4:09
7 22:21 ☿ □	♌ 8 7:07
10 7:33 ☿ △	♍ 10 9:56
11 22:39 ♇ ⚹	♎ 12 13:05
13 21:37 ♆ □	♏ 14 17:15
16 16:03 ☉ ☍	♐ 16 23:22
18 9:53 ♄ ⚹	♑ 19 8:13
21 8:04 ♀ △	♒ 21 19:43
24 3:42 ♀ □	♓ 24 8:25
26 19:35 ☿ ⚹	♈ 26 19:52
28 7:14 ♆ □	♉ 29 4:16
30 17:49 ♇ ☍	♊ 31 9:19

Last Aspect Dy Hr Mn	☽ Ingress Dy Hr Mn
1 20:01 ♂ ⚹	♋ 2 11:58
4 0:31 ♂ □	♌ 4 13:35
6 4:57 ♂ △	♍ 6 15:28
8 14:22 ☿ □	♎ 8 18:33
10 18:16 ♂ ☍	♏ 10 23:27
12 13:16 ♇ ☌	♐ 13 6:29
15 5:43 ♀ ☍	♑ 15 15:50
17 8:34 ♇ ⚹	♒ 18 3:19
20 15:01 ☉ △	♓ 20 16:00
22 14:44 ☿ △	♈ 23 4:03
25 8:37 ☿ □	♉ 25 13:28
27 2:31 ♇ ☍	♊ 27 19:14
29 1:21 ♄ △	♋ 29 21:42

☽ Phases & Eclipses Dy Hr Mn	
2 17:44	● 12♉34
9 15:44	☽ 19♌15
16 16:03	○ 26♏01
24 15:53	☾ 3♓43
1 3:57	● 10♊55
7 20:47	☽ 17♍20
15 4:50	○ 24♐20
15 4:57	P 0.682
23 8:11	☾ 2♈06
30 12:18	● 8♋57
30 12:10:24	T 05'20"

Astro Data

1 May 1992
Julian Day # 33724
SVP 5♓21'45"
GC 26♐43.9 ⚳ 7♑32.4R
Eris 17♈38.5 ⚵ 16♈19.5
⚷ 3♌55.8 ⚶ 11♍26.7
☽ Mean ☊ 3♑22.3

1 June 1992
Julian Day # 33755
SVP 5♓21'40"
GC 26♐44.0 ⚳ 2♑47.4R
Eris 17♈54.9 ⚵ 2♉59.2
⚷ 6♌01.6 ⚶ 16♍28.0
☽ Mean ☊ 1♑43.8

July 1992 LONGITUDE

Day	Sid.Time	☉	0 hr ☽	Noon ☽	True ☊	☿	♀	♂	⚳	♃	♄	♅	♆	♇
1 W	6 39 10	9♋53 15	16♋10 18	23♋37 14	0♑42.2	5♌27.4	14♋46.8	12♉16.2	8♒03.7	9♍48.5	17♒35.5	16♑17.4	17♑47.4	20♏22.9
2 Th	6 43 07	10 50 28	1♌05 26	8♌33 53	0R 41.3	6 36.6	16 00.5	12 59.3	7R 54.0	9 57.7	17R 32.4	16R 15.0	17R 45.8	20R 22.0
3 F	6 47 03	11 47 42	16 01 33	23 27 29	0 40.1	7 43.0	17 14.3	13 42.3	7 44.1	10 07.0	17 29.3	16 12.6	17 44.1	20 21.1
4 Sa	6 51 00	12 44 55	0♍50 47	8♍10 39	0 38.9	8 46.4	18 28.1	14 25.3	7 33.9	10 16.4	17 26.1	16 10.2	17 42.5	20 20.2
5 Su	6 54 56	13 42 07	15 26 28	22 37 42	0 37.7	9 46.8	19 41.8	15 08.1	7 23.5	10 26.0	17 22.8	16 07.8	17 40.9	20 19.4
6 M	6 58 53	14 39 20	29 43 58	6♎45 02	0D 37.1	10 44.1	20 55.6	15 50.9	7 12.8	10 35.6	17 19.4	16 05.4	17 39.3	20 18.6
7 Tu	7 02 49	15 36 32	13♎40 47	20 31 12	0 37.0	11 38.2	22 09.4	16 33.6	7 01.9	10 45.3	17 16.0	16 02.9	17 37.7	20 17.9
8 W	7 06 46	16 33 44	27 16 22	3♏56 27	0 37.6	12 28.9	23 23.1	17 16.2	6 50.7	10 55.1	17 12.5	16 00.5	17 36.0	20 17.1
9 Th	7 10 42	17 30 56	10♏31 41	17 02 18	0 38.7	13 16.1	24 36.9	17 58.7	6 39.4	11 04.9	17 09.0	15 58.1	17 34.4	20 16.4
10 F	7 14 39	18 28 08	23 28 37	29 50 56	0 40.0	13 59.8	25 50.7	18 41.1	6 27.8	11 14.9	17 05.4	15 55.7	17 32.8	20 15.7
11 Sa	7 18 36	19 25 20	6♐09 32	12♐24 46	0 41.3	14 39.7	27 04.4	19 23.4	6 16.0	11 25.0	17 01.7	15 53.3	17 31.2	20 15.1
12 Su	7 22 32	20 22 32	18 36 55	24 46 16	0R 42.0	15 15.7	28 18.2	20 05.7	6 04.1	11 35.1	16 58.0	15 50.9	17 29.6	20 14.5
13 M	7 26 29	21 19 44	0♑53 05	6♑57 39	0 42.0	15 47.8	29 32.0	20 47.9	5 52.0	11 45.4	16 54.2	15 48.5	17 27.9	20 13.9
14 Tu	7 30 25	22 16 57	13 00 13	19 01 00	0 41.0	16 15.6	0♌45.8	21 30.0	5 39.7	11 55.7	16 50.4	15 46.1	17 26.3	20 13.4
15 W	7 34 22	23 14 09	25 00 16	0♒58 14	0 38.8	16 39.2	1 59.5	22 12.0	5 27.3	12 06.1	16 46.5	15 43.7	17 24.7	20 12.8
16 Th	7 38 18	24 11 22	6♒55 09	12 51 16	0 35.7	16 58.4	3 13.3	22 53.9	5 14.7	12 16.5	16 42.6	15 41.3	17 23.1	20 12.4
17 F	7 42 15	25 08 36	18 46 49	24 42 07	0 31.8	17 12.9	4 27.1	23 35.7	5 02.0	12 27.1	16 38.7	15 38.9	17 21.5	20 11.9
18 Sa	7 46 11	26 05 50	0♓37 25	6♓33 04	0 27.6	17 22.8	5 40.9	24 17.5	4 49.2	12 37.7	16 34.6	15 36.5	17 19.9	20 11.5
19 Su	7 50 08	27 03 04	12 29 25	18 26 50	0 23.6	17R 27.8	6 54.7	24 59.1	4 36.3	12 48.4	16 30.6	15 34.2	17 18.3	20 11.1
20 M	7 54 05	28 00 20	24 25 43	0♈26 31	0 20.1	17 28.0	8 08.5	25 40.7	4 23.3	12 59.2	16 26.5	15 31.8	17 16.7	20 10.7
21 Tu	7 58 01	28 57 36	6♈29 41	12 35 43	0 17.7	17 23.3	9 22.3	26 22.2	4 10.2	13 10.1	16 22.3	15 29.5	17 15.1	20 10.4
22 W	8 01 58	29 54 52	18 45 06	24 58 22	0D 16.6	17 13.6	10 36.1	27 03.5	3 57.1	13 21.0	16 18.1	15 27.1	17 13.5	20 10.1
23 Th	8 05 54	0♌52 10	1♉16 01	7♉38 35	0 16.6	16 59.0	11 49.9	27 44.8	3 43.9	13 32.0	16 13.9	15 24.8	17 12.0	20 09.8
24 F	8 09 51	1 49 29	14 06 31	20 40 18	0 17.7	16 39.7	13 03.7	28 26.0	3 30.7	13 43.1	16 09.7	15 22.5	17 10.4	20 09.6
25 Sa	8 13 47	2 46 48	27 20 17	4♊06 49	0 19.2	16 15.7	14 17.5	29 07.1	3 17.5	13 54.2	16 05.4	15 20.2	17 08.9	20 09.4
26 Su	8 17 44	3 44 09	11♊00 03	18 00 07	0R 20.5	15 47.3	15 31.3	29 48.1	3 04.3	14 05.5	16 01.1	15 18.0	17 07.3	20 09.2
27 M	8 21 40	4 41 30	25 06 54	2♋20 10	0 20.9	15 14.9	16 45.1	0♊29.0	2 51.1	14 16.7	15 56.7	15 15.7	17 05.8	20 09.1
28 Tu	8 25 37	5 38 53	9♋39 30	17 04 16	0 19.9	14 38.8	17 58.9	1 09.8	2 37.9	14 28.1	15 52.4	15 13.5	17 04.3	20 09.0
29 W	8 29 34	6 36 16	24 33 39	2♌06 40	0 17.3	13 59.5	19 12.8	1 50.4	2 24.7	14 39.5	15 48.0	15 11.3	17 02.8	20 08.9
30 Th	8 33 30	7 33 40	9♌42 10	17 18 54	0 13.1	13 17.7	20 26.6	2 31.0	2 11.6	14 51.0	15 43.6	15 09.1	17 01.3	20D 08.9
31 F	8 37 27	8 31 05	24 55 35	2♍30 53	0 07.9	12 33.8	21 40.4	3 11.5	1 58.6	15 02.5	15 39.1	15 07.0	16 59.8	20 08.9

August 1992 LONGITUDE

Day	Sid.Time	☉	0 hr ☽	Noon ☽	True ☊	☿	♀	♂	⚳	♃	♄	♅	♆	♇
1 Sa	8 41 23	9♌28 30	10♍03 35	17♍32 31	0♑02.3	11♌48.8	22♌54.3	3♊51.8	1♒45.6	15♍14.1	15♒34.7	15♑04.8	16♑58.3	20♏08.9
2 Su	8 45 20	10 25 56	24 56 42	2♎15 19	29♐57.1	11R 03.3	24 08.1	4 32.0	1R 32.8	15 25.7	15R 30.2	15R 02.7	16R 56.8	20 09.0
3 M	8 49 16	11 23 23	9♎27 47	16 33 40	29R 53.2	10 18.2	25 21.9	5 12.1	1 20.0	15 37.4	15 25.7	15 00.6	16 55.4	20 09.1
4 Tu	8 53 13	12 20 50	23 32 45	0♏25 01	29D 50.9	9 34.3	26 35.7	5 52.1	1 07.4	15 49.2	15 21.3	14 58.5	16 54.0	20 09.3
5 W	8 57 09	13 18 18	7♏10 34	13 49 40	29 50.2	8 52.4	27 49.5	6 32.0	0 54.9	16 01.0	15 16.8	14 56.5	16 52.5	20 09.4
6 Th	9 01 06	14 15 47	20 22 39	26 49 57	29 50.9	8 13.5	29 03.3	7 11.8	0 42.6	16 12.9	15 12.3	14 54.5	16 51.1	20 09.6
7 F	9 05 03	15 13 17	3♐12 01	9♐29 24	29 52.1	7 38.2	0♍17.1	7 51.5	0 30.4	16 24.8	15 07.8	14 52.5	16 49.8	20 09.9
8 Sa	9 08 59	16 10 47	15 42 34	21 52 04	29R 53.3	7 07.3	1 30.9	8 31.0	0 18.4	16 36.8	15 03.3	14 50.6	16 48.4	20 10.2
9 Su	9 12 56	17 08 19	27 58 23	4♑02 01	29 53.5	6 41.5	2 44.7	9 10.4	0 06.6	16 48.8	14 58.8	14 48.6	16 47.0	20 10.5
10 M	9 16 52	18 05 51	10♑03 23	16 02 56	29 52.0	6 21.2	3 58.5	9 49.7	29♑55.0	17 00.9	14 54.3	14 46.7	16 45.7	20 10.8
11 Tu	9 20 49	19 03 24	22 01 01	27 58 00	29 48.5	6 07.1	5 12.3	10 28.9	29 43.6	17 13.0	14 49.9	14 44.9	16 44.4	20 11.2
12 W	9 24 45	20 00 58	3♒54 11	9♒49 52	29 42.7	5D 59.4	6 26.1	11 08.0	29 32.4	17 25.1	14 45.4	14 43.0	16 43.1	20 11.6
13 Th	9 28 42	20 58 33	15 45 17	21 40 40	29 34.8	5 58.6	7 39.9	11 46.9	29 21.5	17 37.3	14 40.9	14 41.2	16 41.8	20 12.1
14 F	9 32 38	21 56 10	27 36 14	3♓32 11	29 25.5	6 04.8	8 53.7	12 25.7	29 10.7	17 49.6	14 36.5	14 39.5	16 40.6	20 12.5
15 Sa	9 36 35	22 53 48	9♓28 44	15 26 05	29 15.4	6 18.3	10 07.4	13 04.4	29 00.3	18 01.8	14 32.1	14 37.7	16 39.3	20 13.1
16 Su	9 40 32	23 51 27	21 24 27	27 24 03	29 05.5	6 39.0	11 21.2	13 43.0	28 50.0	18 14.2	14 27.7	14 36.0	16 38.1	20 13.6
17 M	9 44 28	24 49 07	3♈25 10	9♈28 05	28 56.6	7 07.1	12 35.0	14 21.4	28 40.1	18 26.5	14 23.3	14 34.4	16 36.9	20 14.2
18 Tu	9 48 25	25 46 49	15 33 05	21 40 34	28 49.6	7 42.5	13 48.7	14 59.8	28 30.4	18 38.9	14 18.9	14 32.7	16 35.7	20 14.8
19 W	9 52 21	26 44 33	27 50 52	4♉04 26	28 44.9	8 25.2	15 02.5	15 37.9	28 21.0	18 51.4	14 14.6	14 31.1	16 34.6	20 15.4
20 Th	9 56 18	27 42 18	10♉21 41	16 43 06	28D 42.4	9 14.9	16 16.2	16 16.0	28 11.8	19 03.8	14 10.3	14 29.6	16 33.5	20 16.1
21 F	10 00 14	28 40 06	23 09 07	29 40 13	28 41.8	10 11.5	17 30.0	16 53.9	28 03.0	19 16.3	14 06.0	14 28.0	16 32.4	20 16.8
22 Sa	10 04 11	29 37 54	6♊16 51	12♊59 25	28 42.2	11 14.7	18 43.7	17 31.7	27 54.5	19 28.9	14 01.7	14 26.6	16 31.3	20 17.6
23 Su	10 08 07	0♍35 45	19 48 15	26 43 38	28R 42.7	12 24.4	19 57.5	18 09.3	27 46.3	19 41.5	13 57.5	14 25.1	16 30.2	20 18.4
24 M	10 12 04	1 33 37	3♋45 39	10♋54 20	28 42.2	13 40.1	21 11.2	18 46.8	27 38.4	19 54.1	13 53.3	14 23.7	16 29.2	20 19.2
25 Tu	10 16 01	2 31 31	18 09 29	25 30 42	28 39.7	15 01.5	22 25.0	19 24.1	27 30.8	20 06.7	13 49.2	14 22.4	16 28.2	20 20.0
26 W	10 19 57	3 29 27	2♌57 24	10♌28 45	28 34.7	16 28.3	23 38.7	20 01.3	27 23.5	20 19.4	13 45.1	14 21.1	16 27.2	20 20.9
27 Th	10 23 54	4 27 24	18 03 46	25 41 13	28 27.3	17 59.9	24 52.4	20 38.4	27 16.6	20 32.1	13 41.0	14 19.8	16 26.2	20 21.8
28 F	10 27 50	5 25 23	3♍19 48	10♍58 06	28 18.1	19 35.9	26 06.1	21 15.2	27 10.0	20 44.8	13 37.0	14 18.5	16 25.3	20 22.8
29 Sa	10 31 47	6 23 24	18 34 42	26 08 14	28 08.1	21 15.9	27 19.9	21 52.0	27 03.8	20 57.5	13 33.0	14 17.3	16 24.4	20 23.7
30 Su	10 35 43	7 21 25	3♎37 28	11♎01 19	27 58.7	22 59.4	28 33.6	22 28.5	26 57.9	21 10.3	13 29.1	14 16.2	16 23.5	20 24.8
31 M	10 39 40	8 19 29	18 18 55	25 29 38	27 50.8	24 45.9	29 47.3	23 04.9	26 52.3	21 23.1	13 25.3	14 15.1	16 22.6	20 25.8

Astro Data	Planet Ingress	Last Aspect	☽ Ingress	Last Aspect	☽ Ingress	☽ Phases & Eclipses	Astro Data
Dy Hr Mn	Dy Hr Mn	Dy Hr Mn	Dy Hr Mn	Dy Hr Mn	Dy Hr Mn	Dy Hr Mn	1 July 1992
☽0S 5 4:17	♀ ♌ 13 21:07	1 6:48 ♇ △	♌ 1 22:15	1 16:13 ♇ ⚹	♎ 2 8:17	7 2:43 ☽ 15♎14	Julian Day # 33785
☽0N 19 11:20	☉ ♌ 22 14:09	3 6:59 ♇ □	♍ 3 22:37	4 4:39 ♀ ⚹	♏ 4 11:16	14 19:06 ○ 22♑34	SVP 5♓21'34"
☿R 20 0:53	♂ ♊ 26 18:59	5 8:09 ♇ ⚹	♎ 6 0:27	6 16:37 ♀ □	♐ 6 17:57	22 22:12 ☾ 0♉19	GC 26♐44.1 ⚴ 24♐24.8R
♇D 30 21:34		7 15:11 ♀ □	♏ 8 4:53	8 1:35 ♃ □	♑ 9 4:00	29 19:35 ● 6♌54	Eris 18♈03.3 ⚵ 19♉09.7
♃△♅ 31 19:49	☊ ♐R 1 22:09	10 3:38 ♀ △	♐ 10 12:17	10 20:18 ♇ ⚹	♒ 11 16:06		⚷ 9♌04.7 ⚶ 25♍59.0
	♀ ♍ 7 6:26	11 20:53 ♄ ⚹	♑ 12 22:16	13 10:27 ☉ ☍	♓ 14 4:51	5 10:59 ☽ 13♏16	☽ Mean ☊ 0♑08.5
☽0S 1 13:06	⚳ ♑R 10 1:39	14 19:06 ☉ ☍	♒ 15 10:03	15 21:37 ♇ △	♈ 16 17:11	13 10:27 ○ 20♒55	
♃⚻♄ 2 18:39	☉ ♍ 22 21:10	17 9:37 ♂ □	♓ 17 22:44	18 20:40 ☉ △	♉ 19 4:10	21 10:01 ☾ 28♉35	1 August 1992
♃△♆ 9 8:51	♀ ♎ 31 16:09	20 6:44 ☉ △	♈ 20 11:07	21 10:01 ☉ □	♊ 21 12:36	28 2:42 ● 5♍03	Julian Day # 33816
☿D 13 2:52		21 21:15 ☿ △	♉ 22 21:36	22 23:37 ♃ □	♋ 23 17:36		SVP 5♓21'29"
♄⚺♅ 13 9:29		25 2:42 ♂ ☌	♊ 25 4:44	25 6:30 ♀ ⚹	♌ 25 19:15		GC 26♐44.1 ⚴ 19♐07.9R
☽0N 15 17:54		26 8:38 ♄ △	♋ 27 8:08	27 3:44 ♂ ⚹	♍ 27 18:46		Eris 18♈02.4R ⚵ 5♊31.3
♃⚹♇ 26 15:08		28 16:57 ♇ △	♌ 29 8:39	29 14:05 ♀ ☌	♎ 29 18:10		⚷ 12♌49.1 ⚶ 8♎42.7
☽0S 28 23:46		30 17:22 ♀ ☌	♍ 31 8:01	31 10:36 ☿ ⚹	♏ 31 19:38		☽ Mean ☊ 28♐30.0

LONGITUDE — September 1992

Day	Sid.Time	☉	0 hr ☽	Noon ☽	True ☊	☿	♀	♂	⚳	♃	♄	♅	♆	♇
1 Tu	10 43 36	9♍17 33	2♏33 03	9♏28 59	27♐45.2	26♌34.9	1♎01.0	23♊41.2	26♑47.1	21♍35.9	13♒21.4	14♑14.0	16♑21.8	20♏26.9
2 W	10 47 33	10 15 40	16 17 27	22 58 39	27R42.0	28 25.9	2 14.6	24 17.2	26R42.3	21 48.7	13R17.7	14R13.0	16R21.0	20 28.0
3 Th	10 51 30	11 13 47	29 32 53	6♐00 38	27D40.9	0♍18.7	3 28.3	24 53.2	26 37.8	22 01.6	13 14.0	14 12.0	16 20.3	20 29.1
4 F	10 55 26	12 11 56	12♐22 25	18 38 49	27R40.9	2 12.7	4 42.0	25 28.9	26 33.7	22 14.5	13 10.3	14 11.1	16 19.5	20 30.3
5 Sa	10 59 23	13 10 07	24 50 27	0♑57 58	27 40.9	4 07.6	5 55.6	26 04.5	26 30.0	22 27.3	13 06.8	14 10.2	16 18.8	20 31.5
6 Su	11 03 19	14 08 19	7♑02 00	13 03 10	27 40.0	6 03.0	7 09.2	26 39.8	26 26.6	22 40.2	13 03.2	14 09.4	16 18.1	20 32.7
7 M	11 07 16	15 06 32	19 02 04	24 59 14	27 37.1	7 58.7	8 22.9	27 15.1	26 23.5	22 53.1	12 59.8	14 08.6	16 17.5	20 34.0
8 Tu	11 11 12	16 04 47	0♒55 11	6♒50 25	27 31.6	9 54.5	9 36.5	27 50.1	26 20.9	23 06.1	12 56.4	14 07.9	16 16.8	20 35.2
9 W	11 15 09	17 03 04	12 45 19	18 40 18	27 23.3	11 50.1	10 50.1	28 25.0	26 18.5	23 19.0	12 53.1	14 07.2	16 16.2	20 36.6
10 Th	11 19 05	18 01 22	24 35 40	0♓31 42	27 12.3	13 45.3	12 03.6	28 59.6	26 16.6	23 31.9	12 49.8	14 06.6	16 15.7	20 37.9
11 F	11 23 02	18 59 42	6♓28 39	12 26 43	26 59.4	15 40.0	13 17.2	29 34.1	26 15.0	23 44.9	12 46.6	14 06.0	16 15.1	20 39.3
12 Sa	11 26 59	19 58 04	18 26 03	24 26 50	26 45.5	17 34.0	14 30.8	0♋08.4	26 13.8	23 57.9	12 43.5	14 05.4	16 14.6	20 40.7
13 Su	11 30 55	20 56 27	0♈29 11	6♈33 13	26 31.8	19 27.3	15 44.3	0 42.6	26 12.9	24 10.8	12 40.5	14 04.9	16 14.2	20 42.1
14 M	11 34 52	21 54 53	12 39 04	18 46 52	26 19.3	21 19.8	16 57.8	1 16.5	26D12.4	24 23.8	12 37.5	14 04.5	16 13.7	20 43.6
15 Tu	11 38 48	22 53 20	24 56 47	1♉09 00	26 09.1	23 11.4	18 11.3	1 50.2	26 12.2	24 36.8	12 34.6	14 04.1	16 13.3	20 45.1
16 W	11 42 45	23 51 50	7♉23 42	13 41 09	26 01.7	25 02.1	19 24.9	2 23.7	26 12.4	24 49.8	12 31.8	14 03.7	16 12.9	20 46.6
17 Th	11 46 41	24 50 22	20 01 37	26 25 25	25 57.3	26 51.8	20 38.3	2 57.1	26 12.9	25 02.7	12 29.1	14 03.4	16 12.6	20 48.1
18 F	11 50 38	25 48 56	2♊52 52	9♊24 22	25 55.2	28 40.5	21 51.8	3 30.2	26 13.8	25 15.7	12 26.4	14 03.2	16 12.3	20 49.7
19 Sa	11 54 34	26 47 32	16 00 15	22 40 52	25 54.8	0♎28.3	23 05.3	4 03.1	26 15.1	25 28.7	12 23.9	14 03.0	16 12.0	20 51.3
20 Su	11 58 31	27 46 11	29 26 35	6♋17 41	25 54.7	2 15.0	24 18.8	4 35.8	26 16.7	25 41.7	12 21.4	14 02.8	16 11.7	20 52.9
21 M	12 02 28	28 44 51	13♋14 21	20 16 44	25 53.7	4 00.8	25 32.2	5 08.3	26 18.7	25 54.7	12 19.0	14 02.7	16 11.5	20 54.6
22 Tu	12 06 24	29 43 34	27 24 47	4♌38 21	25 50.7	5 45.5	26 45.7	5 40.5	26 20.9	26 07.7	12 16.7	14D02.7	16 11.3	20 56.2
23 W	12 10 21	0♎42 19	11♌57 05	19 20 27	25 45.1	7 29.3	27 59.1	6 12.5	26 23.6	26 20.6	12 14.4	14 02.7	16 11.2	20 57.9
24 Th	12 14 17	1 41 07	26 47 42	4♍17 55	25 36.7	9 12.1	29 12.5	6 44.3	26 26.6	26 33.6	12 12.3	14 02.7	16 11.0	20 59.7
25 F	12 18 14	2 39 56	11♍50 02	19 22 49	25 26.3	10 53.9	0♏25.9	7 15.8	26 29.9	26 46.6	12 10.2	14 02.8	16 10.9	21 01.4
26 Sa	12 22 10	3 38 47	26 55 01	4♎25 20	25 15.0	12 34.8	1 39.3	7 47.1	26 33.5	26 59.5	12 08.3	14 03.0	16 10.9	21 03.2
27 Su	12 26 07	4 37 41	11♎52 31	19 15 25	25 04.0	14 14.7	2 52.7	8 18.2	26 37.5	27 12.5	12 06.4	14 03.2	16D10.8	21 05.0
28 M	12 30 03	5 36 36	26 33 04	3♏44 39	24 54.7	15 53.8	4 06.1	8 49.0	26 41.9	27 25.4	12 04.6	14 03.4	16 10.9	21 06.8
29 Tu	12 34 00	6 35 34	10♏49 34	17 47 27	24 47.7	17 31.9	5 19.4	9 19.5	26 46.5	27 38.3	12 02.9	14 03.7	16 10.9	21 08.7
30 W	12 37 56	7 34 33	24 38 06	1♐21 34	24 43.4	19 09.2	6 32.8	9 49.8	26 51.5	27 51.2	12 01.3	14 04.1	16 11.0	21 10.5

LONGITUDE — October 1992

Day	Sid.Time	☉	0 hr ☽	Noon ☽	True ☊	☿	♀	♂	⚳	♃	♄	♅	♆	♇
1 Th	12 41 53	8♎33 34	7♐58 01	14♐27 47	24♐41.5	20♎45.6	7♏46.1	10♋19.8	26♑56.8	28♍04.1	11♒59.9	14♑04.5	16♑11.1	21♏12.4
2 F	12 45 50	9 32 37	20 51 19	27 09 08	24D41.2	22 21.2	8 59.4	10 49.5	27 02.4	28 17.0	11R58.5	14 05.0	16 11.2	21 14.3
3 Sa	12 49 46	10 31 41	3♑21 51	9♑30 05	24R41.4	23 55.9	10 12.7	11 18.9	27 08.3	28 29.9	11 57.2	14 05.5	16 11.4	21 16.3
4 Su	12 53 43	11 30 47	15 34 31	21 35 49	24 41.0	25 29.8	11 25.9	11 48.1	27 14.6	28 42.7	11 56.0	14 06.0	16 11.6	21 18.2
5 M	12 57 39	12 29 55	27 34 38	3♒31 37	24 38.9	27 03.0	12 39.2	12 17.0	27 21.1	28 55.5	11 54.8	14 06.7	16 11.9	21 20.2
6 Tu	13 01 36	13 29 05	9♒27 24	15 22 33	24 34.5	28 35.3	13 52.4	12 45.6	27 28.0	29 08.3	11 53.8	14 07.3	16 12.1	21 22.2
7 W	13 05 32	14 28 17	21 17 36	27 13 03	24 27.4	0♏06.8	15 05.6	13 13.9	27 35.2	29 21.1	11 52.9	14 08.1	16 12.4	21 24.2
8 Th	13 09 29	15 27 30	3♓09 21	9♓06 53	24 17.9	1 37.5	16 18.8	13 41.9	27 42.6	29 33.8	11 52.1	14 08.8	16 12.8	21 26.2
9 F	13 13 25	16 26 45	15 05 58	21 06 54	24 06.5	3 07.5	17 32.0	14 09.6	27 50.4	29 46.5	11 51.4	14 09.6	16 13.2	21 28.3
10 Sa	13 17 22	17 26 02	27 09 53	3♈15 07	23 54.0	4 36.6	18 45.1	14 36.9	27 58.4	29 59.2	11 50.8	14 10.5	16 13.6	21 30.4
11 Su	13 21 19	18 25 21	9♈22 43	15 32 47	23 41.7	6 05.0	19 58.2	15 04.0	28 06.7	0♎11.9	11 50.3	14 11.4	16 14.0	21 32.5
12 M	13 25 15	19 24 43	21 45 22	28 00 31	23 30.6	7 32.6	21 11.3	15 30.8	28 15.3	0 24.5	11 49.8	14 12.4	16 14.5	21 34.6
13 Tu	13 29 12	20 24 06	4♉18 14	10♉38 35	23 21.5	8 59.4	22 24.4	15 57.2	28 24.2	0 37.1	11 49.5	14 13.4	16 15.0	21 36.7
14 W	13 33 08	21 23 31	17 01 33	23 27 12	23 15.1	10 25.4	23 37.5	16 23.2	28 33.3	0 49.7	11 49.3	14 14.5	16 15.5	21 38.8
15 Th	13 37 05	22 22 59	29 55 35	6♊26 47	23 11.3	11 50.6	24 50.5	16 49.0	28 42.7	1 02.3	11D49.2	14 15.6	16 16.1	21 41.0
16 F	13 41 01	23 22 29	13♊00 55	19 38 07	23D10.0	13 14.9	26 03.5	17 14.4	28 52.4	1 14.8	11 49.2	14 16.8	16 16.7	21 43.2
17 Sa	13 44 58	24 22 01	26 18 32	3♋02 20	23 10.3	14 38.3	27 16.5	17 39.4	29 02.4	1 27.2	11 49.3	14 18.0	16 17.4	21 45.3
18 Su	13 48 54	25 21 36	9♋49 42	16 40 46	23R11.0	16 00.7	28 29.5	18 04.0	29 12.6	1 39.7	11 49.5	14 19.3	16 18.0	21 47.6
19 M	13 52 51	26 21 13	23 35 40	0♌34 28	23 11.2	17 22.3	29 42.4	18 28.3	29 23.0	1 52.1	11 49.8	14 20.6	16 18.7	21 49.8
20 Tu	13 56 48	27 20 52	7♌37 09	14 43 40	23 09.8	18 42.7	0♐55.4	18 52.2	29 33.8	2 04.4	11 50.2	14 21.9	16 19.5	21 52.0
21 W	14 00 44	28 20 33	21 53 46	29 07 10	23 06.3	20 02.1	2 08.3	19 15.7	29 44.7	2 16.8	11 50.7	14 23.3	16 20.2	21 54.3
22 Th	14 04 41	29 20 17	6♍23 23	13♍41 50	23 00.6	21 20.4	3 21.2	19 38.8	29 55.9	2 29.0	11 51.3	14 24.8	16 21.0	21 56.5
23 F	14 08 37	0♏20 03	21 01 48	28 22 28	22 53.0	22 37.4	4 34.1	20 01.5	0♒07.4	2 41.3	11 52.0	14 26.3	16 21.9	21 58.8
24 Sa	14 12 34	1 19 51	5♎42 55	13♎02 13	22 44.6	23 53.0	5 46.9	20 23.7	0 19.1	2 53.4	11 52.8	14 27.9	16 22.7	22 01.1
25 Su	14 16 30	2 19 41	20 19 25	27 33 34	22 36.4	25 07.2	6 59.8	20 45.5	0 31.0	3 05.6	11 53.7	14 29.5	16 23.6	22 03.4
26 M	14 20 27	3 19 33	4♏43 51	11♏49 30	22 29.3	26 19.8	8 12.6	21 06.9	0 43.2	3 17.7	11 54.7	14 31.1	16 24.6	22 05.7
27 Tu	14 24 23	4 19 27	18 49 54	25 44 06	22 24.2	27 30.6	9 25.4	21 27.8	0 55.6	3 29.7	11 55.8	14 32.8	16 25.5	22 08.0
28 W	14 28 20	5 19 23	2♐33 17	9♐15 48	22D21.3	28 39.5	10 38.1	21 48.3	1 08.3	3 41.7	11 57.0	14 34.6	16 26.5	22 10.3
29 Th	14 32 17	6 19 20	15 52 10	22 22 29	22 20.4	29 46.3	11 50.9	22 08.3	1 21.1	3 53.6	11 58.3	14 36.4	16 27.6	22 12.6
30 F	14 36 13	7 19 20	28 47 01	5♑06 09	22 21.1	0♐50.7	13 03.6	22 27.8	1 34.2	4 05.5	11 59.8	14 38.2	16 28.6	22 15.0
31 Sa	14 40 10	8 19 21	11♑20 18	17 30 00	22 22.5	1 52.5	14 16.2	22 46.8	1 47.5	4 17.3	12 01.3	14 40.1	16 29.7	22 17.3

Astro Data	Dy Hr Mn	Planet Ingress	Dy Hr Mn	Last Aspect Dy Hr Mn		☽ Ingress	Dy Hr Mn	Last Aspect Dy Hr Mn		☽ Ingress	Dy Hr Mn	☽ Phases & Eclipses Dy Hr Mn	
♀0S	2 16:25	☿ ♍	3 8:03	2 23:37	☿ □	♐	3 0:50	2 14:13	♃ □	♑	2 17:29	3 22:39	☽ 11♐40
☽0N	12 0:07	♂ ♋	12 6:05	5 1:55	♂ ☍	♑	5 10:06	5 2:33	♃ △	♒	5 4:53	12 2:17	○ 19♓34
⚳ D	15 10:53	☿ ♎	19 5:41	7 7:41	♃ △	♒	7 22:08	7 0:11	♇ □	♓	7 17:38	19 19:53	☾ 27♊07
☿0S	20 17:23	☉ ♎	22 18:43	10 8:44	♂ △	♓	10 10:56	10 5:28	♃ ☍	♈	10 5:36	26 10:40	● 3♎36
☉0S	22 18:43	♀ ♏	25 3:31	12 11:01	♃ ☍	♈	12 23:02	11 18:03	☉ ☍	♉	12 15:48		
♅ D	22 23:45			14 8:03	♀ ☍	♉	15 9:47	14 12:21	♀ ☍	♊	15 0:08	3 14:12	☽ 10♑37
☽0S	25 10:29	☿ ♏	7 10:13	17 12:57	☿ △	♊	17 18:40	16 19:17	☉ △	♋	17 6:36	11 18:03	○ 18♈40
♃Q♄	27 2:07	♃ ♎	10 13:26	19 19:53	☉ □	♋	20 0:59	19 10:22	♀ △	♌	19 11:01	19 4:12	☾ 26♋02
♆ D	27 18:36	♀ ♐	19 17:47	22 3:16	☉ ⚹	♌	22 4:19	21 10:37	☉ ⚹	♍	21 13:27	25 20:34	● 2♏41
		⚳ ♒	22 20:34	24 3:09	♀ ⚹	♍	24 5:08	23 1:42	☿ ⚹	♎	23 14:39		
☽0N	9 6:28	☉ ♏	23 3:57	25 23:57	♃ ☌	♎	26 4:55	25 0:26	♂ □	♏	25 16:04		
♄ D	16 2:06	☿ ♐	29 17:02	27 6:59	♆ □	♏	28 5:44	27 15:23	☿ ☌	♐	27 19:29		
♃0S	22 17:55			30 5:37	♃ ⚹	♐	30 9:33	28 16:52	♄ ⚹	♑	30 2:18		
☽0S	22 19:19												

Astro Data

1 September 1992
Julian Day # 33847
SVP 5♓21'26"
GC 26♐44.2 ⚴ 20♐15.4
Eris 17♈52.1R ⚵ 20♊47.7
⚷ 16♌39.6 ⚶ 23♎14.6
☽ Mean ☊ 26♐51.5

1 October 1992
Julian Day # 33877
SVP 5♓21'23"
GC 26♐44.3 ⚴ 25♐57.7
Eris 17♈35.9R ⚵ 3♋17.0
⚷ 19♌59.5 ⚶ 8♏23.6
☽ Mean ☊ 25♐16.2

November 1992 LONGITUDE

Day	Sid.Time	☉	0 hr ☽	Noon ☽	True ☊	☿	♀	♂	⚳	♃	♄	♅	♆	♇
1 Su	14 44 06	9♏19 23	23♑35 50	29♑38 23	22♐23.8	2♐51.4	15♐28.9	23♋05.3	2♒01.0	4♎29.1	12♒02.9	14♑42.0	16♑30.8	22♏19.7
2 M	14 48 03	10 19 28	5♒38 16	11♒36 10	22R 24.3	3 47.0	16 41.5	23 23.3	2 14.7	4 40.8	12 04.6	14 44.0	16 32.0	22 22.1
3 Tu	14 51 59	11 19 33	17 32 42	23 28 29	22 23.3	4 39.0	17 54.1	23 40.8	2 28.7	4 52.4	12 06.4	14 46.0	16 33.1	22 24.4
4 W	14 55 56	12 19 40	29 24 09	5♓20 17	22 20.6	5 26.9	19 06.6	23 57.8	2 42.8	5 04.0	12 08.3	14 48.0	16 34.3	22 26.8
5 Th	14 59 52	13 19 49	11♓17 26	17 16 07	22 16.1	6 10.3	20 19.1	24 14.3	2 57.1	5 15.5	12 10.4	14 50.1	16 35.6	22 29.2
6 F	15 03 49	14 20 00	23 16 48	29 19 53	22 10.3	6 48.7	21 31.5	24 30.1	3 11.7	5 26.9	12 12.5	14 52.3	16 36.8	22 31.6
7 Sa	15 07 46	15 20 12	5♈25 44	11♈34 38	22 03.7	7 21.4	22 44.0	24 45.5	3 26.4	5 38.3	12 14.7	14 54.4	16 38.1	22 34.0
8 Su	15 11 42	16 20 25	17 46 51	24 02 31	21 57.0	7 47.8	23 56.3	25 00.3	3 41.3	5 49.6	12 17.0	14 56.7	16 39.4	22 36.4
9 M	15 15 39	17 20 40	0♉21 46	6♉44 38	21 50.9	8 07.3	25 08.7	25 14.5	3 56.4	6 00.9	12 19.4	14 58.9	16 40.8	22 38.8
10 Tu	15 19 35	18 20 58	13 11 08	19 41 11	21 46.1	8R 19.2	26 21.0	25 28.1	4 11.6	6 12.0	12 21.9	15 01.2	16 42.2	22 41.2
11 W	15 23 32	19 21 16	26 14 43	2♊51 34	21 43.0	8 22.8	27 33.2	25 41.1	4 27.1	6 23.1	12 24.5	15 03.6	16 43.6	22 43.6
12 Th	15 27 28	20 21 37	9♊31 37	16 14 41	21D 41.6	8 17.4	28 45.4	25 53.4	4 42.7	6 34.1	12 27.2	15 06.0	16 45.0	22 46.0
13 F	15 31 25	21 21 59	23 00 36	29 49 11	21 41.7	8 02.4	29 57.6	26 05.2	4 58.6	6 45.1	12 29.9	15 08.4	16 46.5	22 48.4
14 Sa	15 35 21	22 22 23	6♋40 16	13♋33 42	21 42.9	7 37.3	1♑09.7	26 16.3	5 14.5	6 56.0	12 32.8	15 10.8	16 48.0	22 50.9
15 Su	15 39 18	23 22 49	20 29 19	27 27 00	21 44.5	7 02.0	2 21.8	26 26.8	5 30.7	7 06.7	12 35.8	15 13.3	16 49.5	22 53.3
16 M	15 43 15	24 23 17	4♌26 35	11♌27 57	21R 45.8	6 16.4	3 33.8	26 36.6	5 47.0	7 17.5	12 38.9	15 15.9	16 51.0	22 55.7
17 Tu	15 47 11	25 23 47	18 30 54	25 35 17	21 46.3	5 21.0	4 45.8	26 45.7	6 03.5	7 28.1	12 42.0	15 18.4	16 52.6	22 58.1
18 W	15 51 08	26 24 19	2♍40 53	9♍47 27	21 45.7	4 16.7	5 57.7	26 54.1	6 20.2	7 38.6	12 45.2	15 21.1	16 54.1	23 00.5
19 Th	15 55 04	27 24 52	16 54 40	24 02 13	21 43.9	3 04.8	7 09.6	27 01.8	6 37.0	7 49.1	12 48.6	15 23.7	16 55.8	23 02.9
20 F	15 59 01	28 25 27	1♎09 42	8♎16 41	21 41.2	1 47.3	8 21.4	27 08.8	6 53.9	7 59.4	12 52.0	15 26.4	16 57.4	23 05.3
21 Sa	16 02 57	29 26 04	15 22 41	22 27 13	21 37.9	0 26.3	9 33.2	27 15.0	7 11.1	8 09.7	12 55.5	15 29.1	16 59.1	23 07.7
22 Su	16 06 54	0♐26 43	29 29 44	6♏29 46	21 34.7	29♏04.7	10 44.9	27 20.5	7 28.4	8 19.9	12 59.1	15 31.8	17 00.7	23 10.1
23 M	16 10 50	1 27 23	13♏26 47	20 20 21	21 32.0	27 45.0	11 56.6	27 25.3	7 45.8	8 30.0	13 02.8	15 34.6	17 02.4	23 12.5
24 Tu	16 14 47	2 28 04	27 10 04	3♐55 35	21 30.1	26 30.0	13 08.2	27 29.3	8 03.4	8 40.0	13 06.6	15 37.4	17 04.2	23 14.9
25 W	16 18 44	3 28 47	10♐36 39	17 13 04	21D 29.3	25 21.9	14 19.8	27 32.4	8 21.1	8 49.9	13 10.4	15 40.3	17 05.9	23 17.3
26 Th	16 22 40	4 29 32	23 44 46	0♑11 44	21 29.5	24 22.8	15 31.3	27 34.8	8 39.0	8 59.7	13 14.4	15 43.2	17 07.7	23 19.7
27 F	16 26 37	5 30 17	6♑34 05	12 51 57	21 30.3	23 34.0	16 42.7	27 36.5	8 57.0	9 09.4	13 18.4	15 46.1	17 09.5	23 22.1
28 Sa	16 30 33	6 31 04	19 05 37	25 15 24	21 31.7	22 56.4	17 54.0	27R 37.3	9 15.1	9 19.0	13 22.5	15 49.0	17 11.3	23 24.5
29 Su	16 34 30	7 31 52	1♒21 40	7♒24 53	21 33.1	22 30.4	19 05.3	27 37.2	9 33.4	9 28.5	13 26.7	15 52.0	17 13.2	23 26.8
30 M	16 38 26	8 32 40	13 25 31	19 24 08	21 34.2	22D 15.9	20 16.5	27 36.4	9 51.8	9 37.9	13 31.0	15 55.0	17 15.0	23 29.2

December 1992 LONGITUDE

Day	Sid.Time	☉	0 hr ☽	Noon ☽	True ☊	☿	♀	♂	⚳	♃	♄	♅	♆	♇
1 Tu	16 42 23	9♐33 30	25♒21 15	1♓17 29	21♐34.9	22♏12.5	21♑27.6	27♋34.7	10♒10.4	9♎47.1	13♒35.3	15♑58.0	17♑16.9	23♏31.5
2 W	16 46 19	10 34 20	7♓13 24	13 09 37	21R 35.1	22 19.6	22 38.7	27R 32.2	10 29.1	9 56.3	13 39.7	16 01.0	17 18.8	23 33.9
3 Th	16 50 16	11 35 11	19 06 44	25 05 20	21 34.7	22 36.4	23 49.6	27 28.9	10 47.9	10 05.3	13 44.2	16 04.1	17 20.7	23 36.2
4 F	16 54 13	12 36 03	1♈06 01	7♈09 18	21 33.9	23 02.2	25 00.5	27 24.7	11 06.8	10 14.3	13 48.8	16 07.2	17 22.7	23 38.5
5 Sa	16 58 09	13 36 56	13 15 42	19 25 41	21 32.9	23 35.9	26 11.2	27 19.7	11 25.8	10 23.1	13 53.5	16 10.3	17 24.6	23 40.8
6 Su	17 02 06	14 37 50	25 39 41	1♉58 02	21 31.9	24 16.8	27 21.9	27 13.9	11 45.0	10 31.8	13 58.2	16 13.5	17 26.6	23 43.1
7 M	17 06 02	15 38 44	8♉21 01	14 48 51	21 31.0	25 04.0	28 32.5	27 07.2	12 04.3	10 40.4	14 03.0	16 16.7	17 28.6	23 45.4
8 Tu	17 09 59	16 39 40	21 21 38	27 59 23	21 30.4	25 56.9	29 42.9	26 59.6	12 23.7	10 48.9	14 07.9	16 19.9	17 30.6	23 47.7
9 W	17 13 55	17 40 36	4♊42 03	11♊29 28	21D 30.1	26 53.9	0♒53.3	26 51.2	12 43.2	10 57.2	14 12.9	16 23.1	17 32.6	23 49.9
10 Th	17 17 52	18 41 33	18 21 22	25 17 26	21 30.1	27 56.7	2 03.5	26 42.0	13 02.8	11 05.5	14 17.9	16 26.4	17 34.6	23 52.2
11 F	17 21 48	19 42 31	2♋17 14	9♋20 17	21 30.2	29 02.4	3 13.7	26 31.9	13 22.5	11 13.6	14 23.0	16 29.6	17 36.7	23 54.4
12 Sa	17 25 45	20 43 30	16 26 05	23 34 03	21R 30.3	0♐11.5	4 23.7	26 21.0	13 42.4	11 21.5	14 28.1	16 32.9	17 38.8	23 56.6
13 Su	17 29 42	21 44 30	0♌43 36	7♌54 11	21 30.3	1 23.3	5 33.6	26 09.3	14 02.3	11 29.4	14 33.4	16 36.2	17 40.8	23 58.8
14 M	17 33 38	22 45 31	15 05 14	22 16 13	21 30.3	2 37.7	6 43.4	25 56.7	14 22.3	11 37.1	14 38.7	16 39.6	17 42.9	24 01.0
15 Tu	17 37 35	23 46 33	29 26 39	6♍36 06	21 30.1	3 54.2	7 53.1	25 43.4	14 42.5	11 44.7	14 44.0	16 42.9	17 45.0	24 03.2
16 W	17 41 31	24 47 36	13♍44 10	20 50 31	21D 30.0	5 12.5	9 02.6	25 29.2	15 02.7	11 52.2	14 49.4	16 46.3	17 47.2	24 05.4
17 Th	17 45 28	25 48 40	27 54 53	4♎57 01	21 30.1	6 32.5	10 12.0	25 14.3	15 23.1	11 59.5	14 54.9	16 49.6	17 49.3	24 07.5
18 F	17 49 24	26 49 45	11♎56 45	18 53 54	21 30.4	7 53.9	11 21.3	24 58.5	15 43.5	12 06.6	15 00.5	16 53.0	17 51.4	24 09.6
19 Sa	17 53 21	27 50 50	25 48 20	2♏39 58	21 30.9	9 16.5	12 30.4	24 42.1	16 04.0	12 13.7	15 06.1	16 56.5	17 53.6	24 11.7
20 Su	17 57 17	28 51 57	9♏28 41	16 14 24	21 31.6	10 40.3	13 39.4	24 24.9	16 24.7	12 20.6	15 11.8	16 59.9	17 55.8	24 13.8
21 M	18 01 14	29 53 04	22 57 03	29 36 33	21 32.3	12 05.0	14 48.3	24 07.0	16 45.4	12 27.3	15 17.5	17 03.3	17 58.0	24 15.9
22 Tu	18 05 11	0♑54 12	6♐12 51	12♐45 53	21R 32.8	13 30.5	15 57.0	23 48.4	17 06.2	12 33.9	15 23.3	17 06.8	18 00.1	24 17.9
23 W	18 09 07	1 55 21	19 15 37	25 42 00	21 32.9	14 56.8	17 05.5	23 29.2	17 27.1	12 40.4	15 29.2	17 10.3	18 02.4	24 20.0
24 Th	18 13 04	2 56 30	2♑05 03	8♑24 46	21 32.4	16 23.8	18 13.9	23 09.4	17 48.1	12 46.7	15 35.1	17 13.7	18 04.6	24 22.0
25 F	18 17 00	3 57 39	14 41 13	20 54 29	21 31.2	17 51.4	19 22.1	22 49.0	18 09.1	12 52.9	15 41.0	17 17.2	18 06.8	24 24.0
26 Sa	18 20 57	4 58 48	27 04 41	3♒11 59	21 29.4	19 19.5	20 30.1	22 28.0	18 30.3	12 58.9	15 47.1	17 20.7	18 09.0	24 25.9
27 Su	18 24 53	5 59 58	9♒16 37	15 18 49	21 27.2	20 48.2	21 38.0	22 06.6	18 51.5	13 04.7	15 53.1	17 24.3	18 11.2	24 27.9
28 M	18 28 50	7 01 08	21 18 55	27 17 16	21 24.7	22 17.4	22 45.6	21 44.7	19 12.8	13 10.4	15 59.2	17 27.8	18 13.5	24 29.8
29 Tu	18 32 47	8 02 17	3♓14 16	9♓10 20	21 22.5	23 46.9	23 53.1	21 22.4	19 34.2	13 16.0	16 05.4	17 31.3	18 15.7	24 31.7
30 W	18 36 43	9 03 27	15 05 59	21 01 43	21 20.7	25 17.0	25 00.4	20 59.7	19 55.7	13 21.3	16 11.6	17 34.8	18 18.0	24 33.6
31 Th	18 40 40	10 04 36	26 58 05	2♈55 40	21D 19.6	26 47.4	26 07.4	20 36.7	20 17.2	13 26.5	16 17.9	17 38.4	18 20.2	24 35.4

Astro Data

	Dy Hr Mn
☽0N	5 13:27
☿R	11 9:49
☽0S	19 1:33
♃∠♇	21 5:57
♂R	28 23:31
☿D	1 7:30
☽0N	2 21:12
☽0S	16 6:42
☽0N	30 5:24

Planet Ingress

	Dy Hr Mn
♀ ♑	13 12:48
☿ ♏R	21 19:44
☉ ♐	22 1:26
♀ ♒	8 17:49
☿ ♐	12 8:05
☉ ♑	21 14:43

Last Aspect / ☽ Ingress

Last Aspect Dy Hr Mn		☽ Ingress Dy Hr Mn
31 22:39	♂ ☍	♒ 1 12:43
3 9:50	♇ □	♓ 4 1:13
6 2:13	♂ △	♈ 6 13:19
8 13:52	♂ □	♉ 8 23:19
10 22:46	♂ ⚹	♊ 11 6:49
13 12:16	♀ ☍	♋ 13 12:19
15 10:15	♂ ☌	♌ 15 16:23
17 11:39	☉ □	♍ 17 19:28
19 18:07	☉ ⚹	♎ 19 22:03
21 20:13	♂ □	♏ 22 0:52
24 0:31	♂ △	♐ 24 5:01
25 4:36	♄ ⚹	♑ 26 11:38
28 16:38	♂ ☍	♒ 28 21:19

Last Aspect / ☽ Ingress

Last Aspect Dy Hr Mn		☽ Ingress Dy Hr Mn
30 20:15	♇ □	♓ 1 9:23
3 16:46	♂ △	♈ 3 21:49
6 3:04	♂ □	♉ 6 8:16
8 15:24	♀ △	♊ 8 15:37
9 23:41	☉ ☍	♋ 10 20:05
12 16:36	♂ ☌	♌ 12 22:47
14 14:56	♇ □	♍ 15 0:56
16 19:44	♂ ⚹	♎ 17 3:33
19 2:53	☉ ⚹	♏ 19 7:20
21 2:20	♇ ☌	♐ 21 12:42
22 18:26	♀ ⚹	♑ 23 20:04
25 18:48	♇ ⚹	♒ 26 5:43
28 6:22	♇ □	♓ 28 17:28
30 21:51	☿ □	♈ 31 6:07

☽ Phases & Eclipses

Dy Hr Mn	
2 9:11	☽ 10♒12
10 9:20	○ 18♉14
17 11:39	☾ 25♌23
24 9:11	● 2♐21
2 6:17	☽ 10♓20
9 23:41	○ 18♊10
9 23:44	☍ T 1.271
16 19:13	☾ 25♍06
24 0:43	● 2♑28
24 0:30:43	☌ P 0.842

Astro Data

1 November 1992
Julian Day # 33908
SVP 5♓21'19"
GC 26♐44.4 ⚴ 4♑42.0
Eris 17♈17.6R ⚵ 11♋31.4
⚷ 22♌30.2 ⚶ 24♏45.0
☽ Mean ☊ 23♐37.7

1 December 1992
Julian Day # 33938
SVP 5♓21'15"
GC 26♐44.4 ⚴ 14♑40.3
Eris 17♈03.5R ⚵ 12♋02.1R
⚷ 23♌33.7 ⚶ 10♐56.2
☽ Mean ☊ 22♐02.4

LONGITUDE — January 1993

Day	Sid.Time	☉	0 hr ☽	Noon ☽	True ☊	☿	♀	♂	⚳	♃	♄	♅	♆	♇
1 F	18 44 36	11♑05 45	8♈55 02	14♈56 47	21♐19.5	28♐18.2	27♒14.2	20♋13.4	20♒38.8	13♎31.6	16♒24.2	17♑41.9	18♑22.5	24♏37.3
2 Sa	18 48 33	12 06 54	21 01 31	27 09 51	21 20.2	29 49.4	28 20.8	19R 49.9	21 00.5	13 36.5	16 30.6	17 45.5	18 24.7	24 39.1
3 Su	18 52 29	13 08 03	3♉22 20	9♉39 30	21 21.6	1♑20.9	29 27.2	19 26.2	21 22.3	13 41.2	16 37.0	17 49.1	18 27.0	24 40.9
4 M	18 56 26	14 09 12	16 01 52	22 29 50	21 23.3	2 52.9	0♓33.3	19 02.4	21 44.1	13 45.8	16 43.4	17 52.6	18 29.3	24 42.6
5 Tu	19 00 22	15 10 20	29 03 46	5♊43 54	21 24.7	4 25.2	1 39.2	18 38.5	22 05.9	13 50.1	16 49.9	17 56.2	18 31.5	24 44.3
6 W	19 04 19	16 11 28	12♊30 23	19 23 12	21R 25.4	5 58.0	2 44.8	18 14.5	22 27.9	13 54.4	16 56.4	17 59.8	18 33.8	24 46.1
7 Th	19 08 16	17 12 36	26 22 14	3♋27 09	21 25.0	7 31.1	3 50.1	17 50.6	22 49.9	13 58.4	17 03.0	18 03.3	18 36.1	24 47.7
8 F	19 12 12	18 13 44	10♋37 30	17 52 41	21 23.1	9 04.6	4 55.2	17 26.6	23 12.0	14 02.3	17 09.6	18 06.9	18 38.4	24 49.4
9 Sa	19 16 09	19 14 51	25 11 55	2♌34 20	21 20.0	10 38.5	6 00.0	17 02.8	23 34.1	14 06.0	17 16.3	18 10.5	18 40.6	24 51.0
10 Su	19 20 05	20 15 58	9♌58 57	17 24 44	21 15.9	12 12.8	7 04.4	16 39.2	23 56.3	14 09.5	17 23.0	18 14.0	18 42.9	24 52.6
11 M	19 24 02	21 17 05	24 50 40	2♍15 43	21 11.4	13 47.6	8 08.6	16 15.7	24 18.5	14 12.9	17 29.7	18 17.6	18 45.2	24 54.2
12 Tu	19 27 58	22 18 12	9♍38 56	16 59 29	21 07.3	15 22.8	9 12.4	15 52.5	24 40.8	14 16.1	17 36.4	18 21.2	18 47.5	24 55.7
13 W	19 31 55	23 19 19	24 16 38	1♎29 48	21 04.1	16 58.5	10 16.0	15 29.5	25 03.2	14 19.1	17 43.2	18 24.7	18 49.7	24 57.2
14 Th	19 35 51	24 20 26	8♎38 34	15 42 38	21D 02.4	18 34.7	11 19.2	15 06.9	25 25.6	14 21.9	17 50.0	18 28.3	18 52.0	24 58.7
15 F	19 39 48	25 21 32	22 41 50	29 36 10	21 02.1	20 11.4	12 22.0	14 44.6	25 48.0	14 24.5	17 56.9	18 31.8	18 54.3	25 00.2
16 Sa	19 43 45	26 22 39	6♏25 40	13♏10 28	21 03.1	21 48.5	13 24.5	14 22.7	26 10.6	14 26.9	18 03.7	18 35.4	18 56.5	25 01.6
17 Su	19 47 41	27 23 45	19 50 48	26 26 53	21 04.7	23 26.2	14 26.6	14 01.3	26 33.1	14 29.2	18 10.6	18 38.9	18 58.8	25 03.0
18 M	19 51 38	28 24 51	2♐59 00	9♐27 23	21R 06.2	25 04.4	15 28.4	13 40.3	26 55.7	14 31.3	18 17.6	18 42.5	19 01.1	25 04.4
19 Tu	19 55 34	29 25 57	15 52 21	22 14 07	21 06.7	26 43.2	16 29.8	13 19.9	27 18.4	14 33.2	18 24.5	18 46.0	19 03.3	25 05.7
20 W	19 59 31	0♒27 02	28 32 55	4♑48 59	21 05.7	28 22.5	17 30.7	13 00.0	27 41.1	14 34.9	18 31.5	18 49.5	19 05.6	25 07.0
21 Th	20 03 27	1 28 06	11♑02 30	17 13 38	21 02.6	0♒02.4	18 31.3	12 40.8	28 03.9	14 36.4	18 38.5	18 53.0	19 07.8	25 08.3
22 F	20 07 24	2 29 10	23 22 31	29 29 19	20 57.4	1 42.9	19 31.4	12 22.1	28 26.7	14 37.8	18 45.6	18 56.5	19 10.0	25 09.5
23 Sa	20 11 20	3 30 14	5♒34 08	11♒37 08	20 50.3	3 24.0	20 31.0	12 04.1	28 49.6	14 38.9	18 52.6	19 00.0	19 12.3	25 10.7
24 Su	20 15 17	4 31 16	17 38 25	23 38 11	20 41.8	5 05.7	21 30.2	11 46.8	29 12.4	14 39.8	18 59.7	19 03.5	19 14.5	25 11.9
25 M	20 19 14	5 32 18	29 36 35	5♓33 49	20 32.6	6 48.0	22 28.9	11 30.1	29 35.4	14 40.6	19 06.8	19 07.0	19 16.7	25 13.0
26 Tu	20 23 10	6 33 18	11♓30 10	17 25 52	20 23.8	8 30.8	23 27.1	11 14.2	29 58.3	14 41.2	19 13.9	19 10.4	19 18.9	25 14.1
27 W	20 27 07	7 34 18	23 21 16	29 16 44	20 16.0	10 14.3	24 24.8	10 59.1	0♓21.3	14 41.5	19 21.0	19 13.9	19 21.1	25 15.2
28 Th	20 31 03	8 35 16	5♈12 41	11♈09 34	20 10.0	11 58.3	25 21.9	10 44.6	0 44.4	14R 41.7	19 28.2	19 17.3	19 23.3	25 16.3
29 F	20 35 00	9 36 13	17 07 52	23 08 09	20 06.2	13 43.0	26 18.5	10 31.0	1 07.5	14 41.7	19 35.3	19 20.7	19 25.4	25 17.3
30 Sa	20 38 56	10 37 10	29 10 59	5♉16 56	20D 04.5	15 28.1	27 14.5	10 18.1	1 30.6	14 41.5	19 42.5	19 24.1	19 27.6	25 18.2
31 Su	20 42 53	11 38 04	11♉26 39	17 40 45	20 04.5	17 13.7	28 09.8	10 06.0	1 53.7	14 41.1	19 49.7	19 27.5	19 29.7	25 19.2

LONGITUDE — February 1993

Day	Sid.Time	☉	0 hr ☽	Noon ☽	True ☊	☿	♀	♂	⚳	♃	♄	♅	♆	♇
1 M	20 46 49	12♒38 58	23♉59 49	0♊24 28	20♐05.5	18♒59.8	29♓04.5	9♋54.8	2♓16.9	14♎40.6	19♒56.9	19♑30.9	19♑31.9	25♏20.1
2 Tu	20 50 46	13 39 50	6♊55 14	13 32 34	20R 06.5	20 46.3	29 58.6	9R 44.3	2 40.1	14R 39.8	20 04.1	19 34.2	19 34.0	25 21.0
3 W	20 54 43	14 40 41	20 16 54	27 08 26	20 06.4	22 33.0	0♈52.0	9 34.6	3 03.3	14 38.8	20 11.3	19 37.5	19 36.1	25 21.8
4 Th	20 58 39	15 41 31	4♋07 19	11♋13 29	20 04.5	24 20.0	1 44.7	9 25.8	3 26.6	14 37.7	20 18.5	19 40.8	19 38.2	25 22.6
5 F	21 02 36	16 42 19	18 26 38	25 46 18	20 00.1	26 07.0	2 36.6	9 17.7	3 49.9	14 36.4	20 25.7	19 44.1	19 40.3	25 23.4
6 Sa	21 06 32	17 43 06	3♌11 46	10♌42 06	19 53.3	27 54.0	3 27.8	9 10.4	4 13.2	14 34.8	20 32.9	19 47.4	19 42.4	25 24.1
7 Su	21 10 29	18 43 51	18 16 12	25 52 46	19 44.7	29 40.8	4 18.1	9 04.0	4 36.5	14 33.1	20 40.2	19 50.6	19 44.4	25 24.8
8 M	21 14 25	19 44 36	3♍30 27	11♍07 50	19 35.2	1♓27.1	5 07.6	8 58.3	4 59.9	14 31.2	20 47.4	19 53.8	19 46.5	25 25.5
9 Tu	21 18 22	20 45 19	18 43 32	26 16 15	19 26.1	3 12.8	5 56.3	8 53.4	5 23.3	14 29.1	20 54.6	19 57.0	19 48.5	25 26.1
10 W	21 22 18	21 46 01	3♎44 51	11♎08 24	19 18.4	4 57.5	6 44.1	8 49.4	5 46.7	14 26.9	21 01.8	20 00.2	19 50.5	25 26.7
11 Th	21 26 15	22 46 42	18 26 09	25 37 35	19 13.0	6 40.9	7 31.0	8 46.1	6 10.1	14 24.4	21 09.1	20 03.4	19 52.5	25 27.3
12 F	21 30 12	23 47 22	2♏42 24	9♏40 30	19 10.0	8 22.6	8 16.9	8 43.5	6 33.5	14 21.8	21 16.3	20 06.5	19 54.5	25 27.8
13 Sa	21 34 08	24 48 00	16 31 57	23 16 58	19D 09.1	10 02.2	9 01.8	8 41.8	6 57.0	14 18.9	21 23.5	20 09.6	19 56.4	25 28.3
14 Su	21 38 05	25 48 38	29 55 52	6♐29 03	19R 09.4	11 39.2	9 45.7	8D 40.8	7 20.5	14 15.9	21 30.8	20 12.7	19 58.4	25 28.7
15 M	21 42 01	26 49 15	12♐56 59	19 20 08	19 09.7	13 13.1	10 28.6	8 40.5	7 44.0	14 12.8	21 38.0	20 15.7	20 00.3	25 29.2
16 Tu	21 45 58	27 49 50	25 39 02	1♑54 09	19 09.0	14 43.4	11 10.3	8 41.0	8 07.5	14 09.4	21 45.2	20 18.7	20 02.2	25 29.5
17 W	21 49 54	28 50 24	8♑05 58	14 14 54	19 06.1	16 09.3	11 50.9	8 42.3	8 31.1	14 05.8	21 52.4	20 21.7	20 04.1	25 29.9
18 Th	21 53 51	29 50 57	20 21 22	26 25 44	19 00.4	17 30.3	12 30.3	8 44.3	8 54.6	14 02.1	21 59.6	20 24.7	20 05.9	25 30.2
19 F	21 57 47	0♓51 29	2♒28 18	8♒29 22	18 51.7	18 45.7	13 08.4	8 46.9	9 18.2	13 58.2	22 06.8	20 27.6	20 07.8	25 30.5
20 Sa	22 01 44	1 51 59	14 29 10	20 27 55	18 40.3	19 54.8	13 45.2	8 50.3	9 41.8	13 54.2	22 14.0	20 30.5	20 09.6	25 30.7
21 Su	22 05 41	2 52 27	26 25 46	2♓22 56	18 26.9	20 56.9	14 20.7	8 54.4	10 05.4	13 50.0	22 21.1	20 33.4	20 11.4	25 30.9
22 M	22 09 37	3 52 53	8♓19 31	14 15 42	18 12.4	21 51.4	14 54.9	8 59.2	10 29.0	13 45.6	22 28.3	20 36.3	20 13.2	25 31.1
23 Tu	22 13 34	4 53 18	20 11 39	26 07 31	17 58.2	22 37.7	15 27.5	9 04.7	10 52.6	13 41.0	22 35.4	20 39.1	20 15.0	25 31.2
24 W	22 17 30	5 53 42	2♈03 31	7♈59 52	17 45.3	23 15.3	15 58.6	9 10.8	11 16.2	13 36.3	22 42.5	20 41.9	20 16.7	25 31.3
25 Th	22 21 27	6 54 03	13 56 50	19 54 45	17 34.7	23 43.8	16 28.2	9 17.6	11 39.9	13 31.4	22 49.6	20 44.6	20 18.4	25 31.3
26 F	22 25 23	7 54 22	25 53 57	1♉54 50	17 27.0	24 02.7	16 56.1	9 25.0	12 03.5	13 26.4	22 56.7	20 47.3	20 20.1	25R 31.4
27 Sa	22 29 20	8 54 40	7♉57 51	14 03 31	17 22.3	24R 12.0	17 22.4	9 33.1	12 27.2	13 21.2	23 03.8	20 50.0	20 21.8	25 31.4
28 Su	22 33 16	9 54 56	20 12 19	26 24 51	17 20.1	24 11.5	17 46.8	9 41.8	12 50.8	13 15.9	23 10.8	20 52.6	20 23.4	25 31.3

Astro Data

	Dy Hr Mn
☽0S	12 13:29
♄⊻♅	25 13:18
☽0N	26 13:19
♄⊻♆	27 12:16
♃ R	28 23:09
♀0N	30 15:24
♅☌♆	2 8:06
☽0S	8 23:11
♂ D	15 7:43
☽0N	22 20:17
♇ R	26 14:29
☿0N	26 14:52
☿ R	27 22:56

Planet Ingress

		Dy Hr Mn
☿	♑	2 14:47
♀	♓	3 23:54
☉	♒	20 1:23
☿	♒	21 11:25
⚳	♓	26 13:44
♀	♈	2 12:37
☿	♓	7 16:19
☉	♓	18 15:35

Last Aspect / ☽ Ingress (January)

Last Aspect Dy Hr Mn			☽ Ingress	Dy Hr Mn
2 14:31	♀	⚹	♉	2 17:30
4 16:04	♇	☍	♊	5 1:42
6 7:43	♄	△	♋	7 6:10
8 23:24	♇	△	♌	9 7:49
11 0:04	♇	□	♍	11 8:20
13 1:06	♇	⚹	♎	13 9:30
15 4:01	☉	□	♏	15 12:42
17 13:53	☉	⚹	♐	17 18:30
19 4:42	♄	⚹	♑	20 2:46
22 3:29	♇	⚹	♒	22 13:00
24 15:08	♇	□	♓	25 0:47
27 3:50	♇	△	♈	27 13:28
29 4:51	♄	⚹	♉	30 1:37

Last Aspect / ☽ Ingress (February)

Last Aspect Dy Hr Mn			☽ Ingress	Dy Hr Mn
1 9:20	♀	⚹	♊	1 11:15
3 2:48	☿	△	♋	3 16:56
5 11:23	♇	△	♌	5 18:51
7 11:16	♇	□	♍	7 18:29
9 10:40	♇	⚹	♎	9 17:58
11 6:52	☉	△	♏	11 19:23
13 15:56	♇	☌	♐	14 0:08
16 3:29	☉	⚹	♑	16 8:20
18 10:10	♇	⚹	♒	18 19:05
20 22:09	♇	□	♓	21 7:12
23 10:47	♇	△	♈	23 19:50
25 17:54	♄	⚹	♉	26 8:11
28 10:17	♇	☍	♊	28 18:52

☽ Phases & Eclipses

Dy Hr Mn		
1 3:38	☽	10♈44
8 12:37	○	18♋15
15 4:01	☾	25♎01
22 18:27	●	2♒46
30 23:20	☽	11♉06
6 23:55	○	18♌13
13 14:57	☾	24♏55
21 13:05	●	2♓55

Astro Data

1 January 1993
Julian Day # 33969
SVP 5♓21'10"
GC 26♐44.5 ⚴ 25♑41.9
Eris 16♈57.3R ⚵ 5♋31.2R
⚷ 22♌59.2R ⚶ 27♐43.0
☽ Mean ☊ 20♐23.9

1 February 1993
Julian Day # 34000
SVP 5♓21'04"
GC 26♐44.6 ⚴ 6♒50.0
Eris 17♈01.6 ⚵ 1♋05.6R
⚷ 21♌02.3R ⚶ 14♑12.8
☽ Mean ☊ 18♐45.4

March 1993

LONGITUDE

Day	Sid.Time	☉	0 hr ☽	Noon ☽	True ☊	☿	♀	♂	⚳	♃	♄	♅	♆	♇
1 M	22 37 13	10♓55 09	2♊41 41	9♊03 25	17♐19.6	24♓01.5	18♈09.5	9♋51.0	13♓14.5	13♎10.4	23♒17.8	20♑55.2	20♑25.0	25♏31.2
2 Tu	22 41 10	11 55 21	15 30 37	22 03 52	17R 19.6	23R 42.3	18 30.2	10 00.9	13 38.1	13R 04.8	23 24.8	20 57.8	20 26.6	25R 31.1
3 W	22 45 06	12 55 31	28 43 39	5♋30 24	17 18.8	23 14.3	18 49.0	10 11.3	14 01.8	12 59.0	23 31.8	21 00.3	20 28.2	25 30.9
4 Th	22 49 03	13 55 38	12♋24 25	19 25 53	17 16.1	22 38.3	19 05.8	10 22.3	14 25.4	12 53.2	23 38.8	21 02.8	20 29.7	25 30.8
5 F	22 52 59	14 55 43	26 34 45	3♌50 49	17 10.8	21 55.2	19 20.5	10 33.9	14 49.1	12 47.2	23 45.7	21 05.3	20 31.3	25 30.5
6 Sa	22 56 56	15 55 47	11♌13 38	18 42 28	17 02.8	21 06.2	19 33.0	10 46.0	15 12.7	12 41.0	23 52.6	21 07.7	20 32.8	25 30.3
7 Su	23 00 52	16 55 48	26 16 24	3♍54 15	16 52.6	20 12.4	19 43.3	10 58.6	15 36.4	12 34.8	23 59.5	21 10.1	20 34.2	25 30.0
8 M	23 04 49	17 55 47	11♍34 40	19 16 10	16 41.2	19 15.2	19 51.3	11 11.7	16 00.0	12 28.4	24 06.3	21 12.4	20 35.7	25 29.7
9 Tu	23 08 45	18 55 44	26 57 15	4♎36 23	16 30.0	18 16.0	19 57.1	11 25.3	16 23.6	12 21.9	24 13.1	21 14.7	20 37.1	25 29.3
10 W	23 12 42	19 55 39	12♎12 09	19 43 17	16 20.3	17 16.1	20R 00.4	11 39.4	16 47.3	12 15.3	24 19.9	21 17.0	20 38.5	25 28.9
11 Th	23 16 38	20 55 33	27 08 46	4♏27 45	16 13.0	16 17.0	20 01.4	11 54.0	17 10.9	12 08.6	24 26.7	21 19.2	20 39.8	25 28.5
12 F	23 20 35	21 55 25	11♏39 40	18 44 12	16 08.5	15 19.8	19 59.9	12 09.1	17 34.5	12 01.8	24 33.4	21 21.4	20 41.2	25 28.0
13 Sa	23 24 32	22 55 16	25 41 14	2♐30 51	16 06.4	14 25.6	19 55.9	12 24.6	17 58.2	11 54.9	24 40.1	21 23.6	20 42.5	25 27.5
14 Su	23 28 28	23 55 04	9♐13 18	15 48 58	16 06.0	13 35.5	19 49.5	12 40.5	18 21.8	11 48.0	24 46.7	21 25.7	20 43.7	25 27.0
15 M	23 32 25	24 54 52	22 18 19	28 41 53	16 06.0	12 50.2	19 40.6	12 56.9	18 45.4	11 40.9	24 53.3	21 27.7	20 45.0	25 26.4
16 Tu	23 36 21	25 54 37	5♑00 16	11♑14 03	16 05.2	12 10.2	19 29.2	13 13.7	19 09.0	11 33.7	24 59.9	21 29.7	20 46.2	25 25.8
17 W	23 40 18	26 54 21	17 23 50	23 30 12	16 02.5	11 36.0	19 15.3	13 31.0	19 32.6	11 26.5	25 06.4	21 31.7	20 47.4	25 25.2
18 Th	23 44 14	27 54 03	29 33 43	5♒34 53	15 57.2	11 07.9	18 59.0	13 48.6	19 56.2	11 19.2	25 12.9	21 33.6	20 48.6	25 24.6
19 F	23 48 11	28 53 43	11♒34 11	17 32 05	15 49.0	10 46.0	18 40.3	14 06.7	20 19.7	11 11.8	25 19.4	21 35.5	20 49.7	25 23.9
20 Sa	23 52 07	29 53 21	23 28 56	29 25 07	15 38.2	10 30.4	18 19.3	14 25.2	20 43.3	11 04.4	25 25.8	21 37.4	20 50.8	25 23.2
21 Su	23 56 04	0♈52 57	5♓20 53	11♓16 33	15 25.3	10 20.9	17 56.0	14 44.0	21 06.8	10 56.9	25 32.2	21 39.1	20 51.8	25 22.4
22 M	0 00 01	1 52 32	17 12 18	23 08 21	15 11.4	10D 17.5	17 30.5	15 03.2	21 30.4	10 49.4	25 38.5	21 40.9	20 52.9	25 21.6
23 Tu	0 03 57	2 52 04	29 04 52	5♈02 00	14 57.6	10 20.0	17 03.0	15 22.8	21 53.9	10 41.8	25 44.8	21 42.6	20 53.9	25 20.8
24 W	0 07 54	3 51 34	10♈59 56	16 58 48	14 45.2	10 28.1	16 33.6	15 42.8	22 17.4	10 34.2	25 51.0	21 44.2	20 54.9	25 20.0
25 Th	0 11 50	4 51 03	22 58 48	29 00 06	14 34.9	10 41.7	16 02.4	16 03.1	22 40.8	10 26.5	25 57.2	21 45.9	20 55.8	25 19.1
26 F	0 15 47	5 50 29	5♉02 56	11♉07 33	14 27.3	11 00.4	15 29.6	16 23.7	23 04.3	10 18.8	26 03.3	21 47.4	20 56.7	25 18.2
27 Sa	0 19 43	6 49 53	17 14 15	23 23 20	14 22.7	11 24.1	14 55.4	16 44.7	23 27.7	10 11.1	26 09.4	21 48.9	20 57.6	25 17.3
28 Su	0 23 40	7 49 15	29 35 11	5♊50 12	14D 20.7	11 52.4	14 20.0	17 06.1	23 51.2	10 03.4	26 15.5	21 50.4	20 58.5	25 16.3
29 M	0 27 36	8 48 34	12♊08 49	18 31 30	14 20.4	12 25.0	13 43.7	17 27.7	24 14.6	9 55.6	26 21.4	21 51.8	20 59.3	25 15.3
30 Tu	0 31 33	9 47 52	24 58 42	1♋30 53	14R 20.9	13 01.9	13 06.6	17 49.7	24 37.9	9 47.9	26 27.4	21 53.2	21 00.1	25 14.3
31 W	0 35 30	10 47 06	8♋08 31	14 51 59	14 21.0	13 42.6	12 29.0	18 11.9	25 01.3	9 40.2	26 33.3	21 54.5	21 00.8	25 13.3

April 1993

LONGITUDE

Day	Sid.Time	☉	0 hr ☽	Noon ☽	True ☊	☿	♀	♂	⚳	♃	♄	♅	♆	♇
1 Th	0 39 26	11♈46 19	21♋41 37	28♋37 39	14♐19.8	14♓27.1	11♈51.1	18♋34.5	25♓24.6	9♎32.4	26♒39.1	21♑55.8	21♑01.5	25♏12.2
2 F	0 43 23	12 45 29	5♌40 11	12♌49 11	14R 16.4	15 15.1	11R 13.3	18 57.4	25 47.9	9R 24.7	26 44.8	21 57.0	21 02.2	25R 11.2
3 Sa	0 47 19	13 44 37	20 04 24	27 25 24	14 10.7	16 06.3	10 35.7	19 20.5	26 11.2	9 17.0	26 50.6	21 58.2	21 02.9	25 10.0
4 Su	0 51 16	14 43 43	4♍51 34	12♍22 00	14 03.0	17 00.7	9 58.6	19 43.9	26 34.4	9 09.3	26 56.2	21 59.3	21 03.5	25 08.9
5 M	0 55 12	15 42 46	19 55 42	27 31 26	13 54.3	17 58.1	9 22.3	20 07.6	26 57.6	9 01.7	27 01.8	22 00.4	21 04.1	25 07.7
6 Tu	0 59 09	16 41 47	5♎07 55	12♎43 46	13 45.5	18 58.3	8 47.0	20 31.5	27 20.8	8 54.0	27 07.3	22 01.4	21 04.7	25 06.5
7 W	1 03 05	17 40 46	20 17 39	27 48 17	13 37.8	20 01.2	8 12.9	20 55.7	27 44.0	8 46.4	27 12.8	22 02.4	21 05.2	25 05.3
8 Th	1 07 02	18 39 43	5♏14 31	12♏35 23	13 32.1	21 06.7	7 40.2	21 20.1	28 07.1	8 38.9	27 18.2	22 03.4	21 05.7	25 04.1
9 F	1 10 59	19 38 38	19 50 06	26 58 07	13 28.7	22 14.6	7 09.2	21 44.8	28 30.2	8 31.4	27 23.6	22 04.2	21 06.2	25 02.8
10 Sa	1 14 55	20 37 32	3♐59 05	10♐52 50	13D 27.5	23 24.9	6 40.0	22 09.8	28 53.3	8 24.0	27 28.9	22 05.1	21 06.6	25 01.6
11 Su	1 18 52	21 36 24	17 39 27	24 19 05	13 27.9	24 37.4	6 12.7	22 34.9	29 16.3	8 16.6	27 34.1	22 05.9	21 07.0	25 00.3
12 M	1 22 48	22 35 14	0♑52 04	7♑18 50	13 29.0	25 52.2	5 47.5	23 00.3	29 39.4	8 09.2	27 39.3	22 06.6	21 07.3	24 59.0
13 Tu	1 26 45	23 34 02	13 39 52	19 55 45	13R 29.9	27 09.0	5 24.5	23 25.9	0♈02.3	8 02.0	27 44.4	22 07.3	21 07.7	24 57.6
14 W	1 30 41	24 32 49	26 07 03	2♒14 23	13 29.6	28 27.9	5 03.7	23 51.8	0 25.3	7 54.8	27 49.4	22 07.9	21 08.0	24 56.3
15 Th	1 34 38	25 31 34	8♒18 22	14 19 35	13 27.6	29 48.7	4 45.3	24 17.8	0 48.2	7 47.7	27 54.4	22 08.5	21 08.2	24 54.9
16 F	1 38 34	26 30 17	20 18 37	26 16 00	13 23.5	1♈11.5	4 29.3	24 44.1	1 11.0	7 40.6	27 59.3	22 09.0	21 08.5	24 53.5
17 Sa	1 42 31	27 28 58	2♓12 16	8♓07 53	13 17.6	2 36.2	4 15.7	25 10.6	1 33.9	7 33.7	28 04.1	22 09.5	21 08.7	24 52.1
18 Su	1 46 28	28 27 38	14 03 18	19 58 53	13 10.1	4 02.7	4 04.6	25 37.3	1 56.7	7 26.8	28 08.8	22 09.9	21 08.8	24 50.6
19 M	1 50 24	29 26 16	25 55 01	1♈51 59	13 01.9	5 31.1	3 55.9	26 04.2	2 19.4	7 20.1	28 13.5	22 10.3	21 09.0	24 49.2
20 Tu	1 54 21	0♉24 52	7♈50 04	13 49 30	12 53.6	7 01.2	3 49.7	26 31.3	2 42.1	7 13.4	28 18.1	22 10.6	21 09.1	24 47.7
21 W	1 58 17	1 23 26	19 50 30	25 53 14	12 46.1	8 33.2	3 45.9	26 58.5	3 04.8	7 06.9	28 22.7	22 10.9	21 09.1	24 46.2
22 Th	2 02 14	2 21 58	1♉57 51	8♉04 32	12 40.1	10 06.9	3D 44.5	27 26.0	3 27.4	7 00.4	28 27.1	22 11.1	21R 09.1	24 44.7
23 F	2 06 10	3 20 29	14 13 23	20 24 35	12 35.9	11 42.3	3 45.4	27 53.7	3 50.0	6 54.1	28 31.5	22 11.3	21 09.1	24 43.2
24 Sa	2 10 07	4 18 57	26 38 15	2♊54 35	12D 33.7	13 19.5	3 48.7	28 21.5	4 12.6	6 47.9	28 35.8	22 11.4	21 09.1	24 41.7
25 Su	2 14 03	5 17 24	9♊13 43	15 35 53	12 33.3	14 58.4	3 54.2	28 49.6	4 35.0	6 41.8	28 40.1	22R 11.5	21 09.0	24 40.1
26 M	2 18 00	6 15 48	22 01 17	28 30 09	12 34.2	16 39.1	4 02.0	29 17.8	4 57.5	6 35.8	28 44.2	22 11.5	21 08.9	24 38.6
27 Tu	2 21 56	7 14 11	5♋02 44	11♋39 14	12 35.7	18 21.5	4 11.9	29 46.1	5 19.9	6 30.0	28 48.3	22 11.5	21 08.8	24 37.0
28 W	2 25 53	8 12 31	18 19 56	25 05 01	12 37.1	20 05.7	4 24.0	0♌14.7	5 42.2	6 24.3	28 52.3	22 11.4	21 08.7	24 35.4
29 Th	2 29 50	9 10 49	1♌54 40	8♌49 01	12R 37.7	21 51.6	4 38.1	0 43.4	6 04.5	6 18.7	28 56.2	22 11.3	21 08.5	24 33.9
30 F	2 33 46	10 09 06	15 48 05	22 51 50	12 37.0	23 39.3	4 54.1	1 12.3	6 26.8	6 13.3	29 00.0	22 11.1	21 08.2	24 32.3

Astro Data	Dy Hr Mn
☿0S	5 23:28
☽0S	8 10:35
♀R	11 9:28
♄□♇	20 3:09
☉0N	20 14:41
☽0N	22 2:20
☿D	22 13:44
♃⚻♄	23 6:50
♃∠♇	26 14:09
☽0S	4 21:18
☽0N	18 8:11
☿0N	19 22:06
♀D	22 14:14
♆R	22 22:32
♅R	26 10:03

Planet Ingress	Dy Hr Mn
☉ ♈	20 14:41
⚳ ♈	13 9:34
☿ ♈	15 15:18
☉ ♉	20 1:49
♂ ♌	27 23:40

Last Aspect Dy Hr Mn		☽ Ingress Dy Hr Mn
2 14:53	☿ □	♋ 3 2:16
4 22:13	♇ △	♌ 5 5:40
6 22:47	♇ □	♍ 7 5:52
8 21:43	♇ ⚹	♎ 9 4:46
10 19:29	♄ △	♏ 11 4:40
12 23:37	♇ ☌	♐ 13 7:33
15 4:46	♄ ⚹	♑ 15 14:28
17 19:20	☉ ⚹	♒ 18 0:52
20 3:52	♄ ☌	♓ 20 13:11
22 16:29	♇ △	♈ 23 1:51
25 5:53	♄ ⚹	♉ 25 13:59
27 17:25	♄ □	♊ 28 0:48
30 2:39	♄ △	♋ 30 9:14

Last Aspect Dy Hr Mn		☽ Ingress Dy Hr Mn
1 6:06	♇ △	♌ 1 14:21
3 11:03	♄ ☍	♍ 3 16:10
5 8:13	♇ ⚹	♎ 5 15:54
7 11:03	♄ △	♏ 7 15:32
9 12:44	♄ □	♐ 9 17:10
11 17:58	♄ ⚹	♑ 11 22:24
14 3:41	☿ ⚹	♒ 14 7:36
16 15:30	♄ ☌	♓ 16 19:32
18 23:51	♂ △	♈ 19 8:14
21 16:57	♄ ⚹	♉ 21 20:08
24 3:43	♄ □	♊ 24 6:27
26 12:26	♄ △	♋ 26 14:45
28 11:08	♇ △	♌ 28 20:39

☽ Phases & Eclipses Dy Hr Mn	
1 15:47	☽ 11♊05
8 9:46	○ 17♍50
15 4:17	☾ 24♐36
23 7:14	● 2♈40
31 4:10	☽ 10♋28
6 18:43	○ 16♎58
13 19:39	☾ 23♑53
21 23:49	● 1♉52
29 12:40	☽ 9♌12

Astro Data

1 March 1993
Julian Day # 34028
SVP 5♓21'01"
GC 26♐44.6 ⚴ 16♒31.3
Eris 17♈13.7 ⚵ 3♋37.4
⚷ 18♌56.6R ⚶ 28♑32.8
☽ Mean ☊ 17♐16.4

1 April 1993
Julian Day # 34059
SVP 5♓20'58"
GC 26♐44.7 ⚴ 26♒18.8
Eris 17♈32.7 ⚵ 11♋47.9
⚷ 17♌23.9R ⚶ 13♒20.7
☽ Mean ☊ 15♐37.9

LONGITUDE — May 1993

Day	Sid.Time	☉	0 hr ☽	Noon ☽	True ☊	☿	♀	♂	⚳	♃	♄	♅	♆	♇
1 Sa	2 37 43	11♉07 20	0♍00 06	7♍12 37	12♐35.0	25♈28.7	5♈12.1	1♌41.3	6♈48.9	6♎08.0	29♒03.8	22♑10.8	21♑08.0	24♏30.7
2 Su	2 41 39	12 05 32	14 28 58	21 48 34	12R 31.8	27 19.9	5 32.0	2 10.4	7 11.1	6R 02.9	29 07.4	22R 10.6	21R 07.7	24R 29.0
3 M	2 45 36	13 03 42	29 10 46	6♎34 44	12 27.8	29 12.9	5 53.7	2 39.8	7 33.1	5 57.9	29 11.0	22 10.2	21 07.3	24 27.4
4 Tu	2 49 32	14 01 50	13♎59 34	21 24 18	12 23.7	1♉07.7	6 17.1	3 09.2	7 55.2	5 53.0	29 14.5	22 09.8	21 07.0	24 25.8
5 W	2 53 29	14 59 56	28 47 58	6♏09 32	12 20.2	3 04.2	6 42.2	3 38.8	8 17.1	5 48.3	29 17.9	22 09.4	21 06.6	24 24.1
6 Th	2 57 25	15 58 00	13♏28 06	20 42 48	12 17.6	5 02.4	7 08.9	4 08.6	8 39.0	5 43.8	29 21.3	22 08.9	21 06.2	24 22.5
7 F	3 01 22	16 56 03	27 52 54	4♐57 46	12D 16.4	7 02.4	7 37.2	4 38.4	9 00.9	5 39.4	29 24.5	22 08.4	21 05.7	24 20.9
8 Sa	3 05 19	17 54 05	11♐56 57	18 50 09	12 16.3	9 04.0	8 07.1	5 08.5	9 22.7	5 35.2	29 27.7	22 07.9	21 05.2	24 19.2
9 Su	3 09 15	18 52 05	25 37 11	2♑18 02	12 17.3	11 07.3	8 38.4	5 38.6	9 44.4	5 31.1	29 30.8	22 07.2	21 04.7	24 17.5
10 M	3 13 12	19 50 04	8♑52 49	15 21 45	12 18.7	13 12.1	9 11.1	6 08.9	10 06.1	5 27.2	29 33.7	22 06.6	21 04.2	24 15.9
11 Tu	3 17 08	20 48 01	21 45 08	28 03 22	12 20.2	15 18.2	9 45.1	6 39.3	10 27.7	5 23.5	29 36.6	22 05.9	21 03.6	24 14.2
12 W	3 21 05	21 45 57	4♒16 56	10♒26 19	12 21.4	17 25.7	10 20.4	7 09.8	10 49.3	5 19.9	29 39.4	22 05.1	21 03.0	24 12.5
13 Th	3 25 01	22 43 52	16 32 04	22 34 47	12R 21.8	19 34.4	10 57.0	7 40.5	11 10.7	5 16.5	29 42.2	22 04.3	21 02.4	24 10.9
14 F	3 28 58	23 41 45	28 35 00	4♓33 19	12 21.4	21 44.0	11 34.8	8 11.3	11 32.1	5 13.3	29 44.8	22 03.4	21 01.7	24 09.2
15 Sa	3 32 54	24 39 37	10♓30 19	16 26 34	12 20.1	23 54.4	12 13.7	8 42.2	11 53.5	5 10.2	29 47.3	22 02.5	21 01.0	24 07.5
16 Su	3 36 51	25 37 28	22 22 34	28 18 52	12 18.3	26 05.4	12 53.8	9 13.2	12 14.8	5 07.3	29 49.8	22 01.6	21 00.3	24 05.9
17 M	3 40 48	26 35 17	4♈15 56	10♈14 14	12 16.0	28 16.7	13 34.8	9 44.4	12 36.0	5 04.6	29 52.1	22 00.6	20 59.6	24 04.2
18 Tu	3 44 44	27 33 06	16 14 08	22 16 03	12 13.7	0♊28.0	14 16.9	10 15.6	12 57.1	5 02.1	29 54.4	21 59.5	20 58.8	24 02.5
19 W	3 48 41	28 30 53	28 20 16	4♉27 06	12 11.7	2 39.1	15 00.0	10 47.0	13 18.2	4 59.7	29 56.5	21 58.5	20 58.0	24 00.9
20 Th	3 52 37	29 28 39	10♉36 45	16 49 27	12 10.1	4 49.6	15 44.0	11 18.5	13 39.2	4 57.5	29 58.6	21 57.3	20 57.2	23 59.2
21 F	3 56 34	0♊26 24	23 05 19	29 24 29	12D 09.2	6 59.4	16 28.9	11 50.1	14 00.1	4 55.5	0♓00.6	21 56.2	20 56.3	23 57.5
22 Sa	4 00 30	1 24 07	5♊47 03	12♊13 01	12 08.9	9 08.1	17 14.7	12 21.9	14 20.9	4 53.7	0 02.4	21 55.0	20 55.4	23 55.9
23 Su	4 04 27	2 21 49	18 42 26	25 15 18	12 09.2	11 15.5	18 01.2	12 53.7	14 41.7	4 52.1	0 04.2	21 53.7	20 54.5	23 54.2
24 M	4 08 23	3 19 30	1♋51 34	8♋31 12	12 09.8	13 21.3	18 48.6	13 25.6	15 02.3	4 50.6	0 05.9	21 52.4	20 53.6	23 52.6
25 Tu	4 12 20	4 17 09	15 14 10	22 00 22	12 10.5	15 25.4	19 36.7	13 57.7	15 22.9	4 49.3	0 07.5	21 51.1	20 52.6	23 50.9
26 W	4 16 17	5 14 47	28 49 45	5♌42 12	12 11.2	17 27.4	20 25.6	14 29.8	15 43.4	4 48.2	0 09.0	21 49.7	20 51.6	23 49.3
27 Th	4 20 13	6 12 23	12♌37 36	19 35 49	12 11.7	19 27.3	21 15.2	15 02.1	16 03.9	4 47.3	0 10.4	21 48.3	20 50.6	23 47.7
28 F	4 24 10	7 09 58	26 36 42	3♍40 03	12R 11.9	21 24.9	22 05.4	15 34.4	16 24.2	4 46.6	0 11.7	21 46.8	20 49.6	23 46.1
29 Sa	4 28 06	8 07 32	10♍45 38	17 53 11	12 11.8	23 20.1	22 56.3	16 06.9	16 44.4	4 46.0	0 12.9	21 45.3	20 48.5	23 44.5
30 Su	4 32 03	9 05 04	25 02 22	2♎12 50	12 11.6	25 12.8	23 47.8	16 39.4	17 04.6	4 45.7	0 14.0	21 43.8	20 47.4	23 42.9
31 M	4 35 59	10 02 34	9♎24 09	16 35 51	12 11.4	27 02.9	24 40.0	17 12.1	17 24.6	4D 45.5	0 15.0	21 42.2	20 46.3	23 41.3

LONGITUDE — June 1993

Day	Sid.Time	☉	0 hr ☽	Noon ☽	True ☊	☿	♀	♂	⚳	♃	♄	♅	♆	♇
1 Tu	4 39 56	11♊00 03	23♎47 26	0♏58 22	12♐11.2	28♊50.3	25♈32.7	17♌44.8	17♈44.6	4♎45.5	0♓15.9	21♑40.6	20♑45.2	23♏39.7
2 W	4 43 52	11 57 31	8♏08 05	15 16 01	12D 11.2	0♋35.1	26 26.0	18 17.6	18 04.5	4 45.6	0 16.7	21R 39.0	20R 44.0	23R 38.1
3 Th	4 47 49	12 54 58	22 21 36	29 24 19	12R 11.2	2 17.1	27 19.8	18 50.5	18 24.2	4 46.0	0 17.4	21 37.3	20 42.9	23 36.6
4 F	4 51 46	13 52 24	6♐23 39	13♐19 11	12 11.2	3 56.3	28 14.2	19 23.5	18 43.9	4 46.5	0 18.0	21 35.6	20 41.7	23 35.0
5 Sa	4 55 42	14 49 49	20 10 30	26 57 19	12 11.1	5 32.7	29 09.1	19 56.6	19 03.5	4 47.2	0 18.6	21 33.8	20 40.5	23 33.5
6 Su	4 59 39	15 47 14	3♑39 25	10♑16 39	12 10.9	7 06.3	0♉04.5	20 29.7	19 23.0	4 48.1	0 19.0	21 32.1	20 39.2	23 32.0
7 M	5 03 35	16 44 37	16 49 00	23 16 29	12 10.5	8 37.0	1 00.4	21 03.0	19 42.4	4 49.2	0 19.3	21 30.3	20 38.0	23 30.5
8 Tu	5 07 32	17 42 00	29 39 14	5♒57 28	12 09.8	10 04.9	1 56.7	21 36.3	20 01.7	4 50.4	0 19.5	21 28.4	20 36.7	23 29.0
9 W	5 11 28	18 39 22	12♒11 29	18 21 36	12 09.1	11 29.8	2 53.5	22 09.7	20 20.9	4 51.9	0R 19.6	21 26.5	20 35.4	23 27.5
10 Th	5 15 25	19 36 43	24 28 14	0♓31 51	12 08.5	12 51.8	3 50.8	22 43.2	20 39.9	4 53.4	0 19.7	21 24.6	20 34.1	23 26.1
11 F	5 19 22	20 34 04	6♓32 56	12 32 02	12D 08.0	14 10.9	4 48.4	23 16.8	20 58.9	4 55.2	0 19.6	21 22.7	20 32.7	23 24.6
12 Sa	5 23 18	21 31 24	18 29 40	24 26 26	12 07.9	15 26.9	5 46.4	23 50.5	21 17.8	4 57.2	0 19.4	21 20.7	20 31.4	23 23.2
13 Su	5 27 15	22 28 44	0♈22 54	6♈19 38	12 08.3	16 39.8	6 44.9	24 24.3	21 36.5	4 59.3	0 19.1	21 18.7	20 30.0	23 21.8
14 M	5 31 11	23 26 04	12 17 14	18 16 15	12 09.0	17 49.6	7 43.7	24 58.1	21 55.1	5 01.6	0 18.8	21 16.7	20 28.6	23 20.4
15 Tu	5 35 08	24 23 23	24 17 12	0♉20 38	12 10.1	18 56.3	8 42.9	25 32.0	22 13.6	5 04.0	0 18.3	21 14.7	20 27.2	23 19.0
16 W	5 39 04	25 20 42	6♉27 00	12 36 43	12 11.2	19 59.7	9 42.4	26 06.0	22 32.0	5 06.7	0 17.7	21 12.6	20 25.8	23 17.7
17 Th	5 43 01	26 18 00	18 50 12	25 07 45	12 12.2	20 59.7	10 42.2	26 40.1	22 50.3	5 09.5	0 17.1	21 10.5	20 24.4	23 16.3
18 F	5 46 57	27 15 18	1♊29 37	7♊56 00	12R 12.7	21 56.3	11 42.4	27 14.2	23 08.4	5 12.4	0 16.3	21 08.4	20 22.9	23 15.0
19 Sa	5 50 54	28 12 36	14 26 59	21 02 36	12 12.6	22 49.5	12 42.9	27 48.5	23 26.5	5 15.6	0 15.4	21 06.2	20 21.5	23 13.7
20 Su	5 54 51	29 09 53	27 42 49	4♋27 27	12 11.7	23 39.0	13 43.7	28 22.8	23 44.4	5 18.9	0 14.5	21 04.1	20 20.0	23 12.5
21 M	5 58 47	0♋07 10	11♋16 18	18 09 05	12 09.9	24 24.8	14 44.8	28 57.2	24 02.1	5 22.4	0 13.4	21 01.9	20 18.5	23 11.2
22 Tu	6 02 44	1 04 26	25 05 24	2♌04 53	12 07.6	25 06.8	15 46.2	29 31.6	24 19.7	5 26.0	0 12.3	20 59.7	20 17.0	23 10.0
23 W	6 06 40	2 01 42	9♌07 03	16 11 26	12 05.0	25 44.9	16 47.9	0♍06.2	24 37.2	5 29.8	0 11.0	20 57.4	20 15.5	23 08.8
24 Th	6 10 37	2 58 57	23 17 32	0♍24 52	12 02.6	26 19.0	17 49.8	0 40.8	24 54.6	5 33.8	0 09.7	20 55.2	20 14.0	23 07.6
25 F	6 14 33	3 56 11	7♍32 57	14 41 20	12 00.7	26 48.8	18 52.0	1 15.5	25 11.8	5 37.9	0 08.3	20 52.9	20 12.5	23 06.4
26 Sa	6 18 30	4 53 25	21 49 37	28 57 24	11D 59.8	27 14.5	19 54.4	1 50.2	25 28.9	5 42.2	0 06.7	20 50.6	20 10.9	23 05.3
27 Su	6 22 26	5 50 38	6♎04 23	13♎10 15	11 59.8	27 35.7	20 57.1	2 25.1	25 45.8	5 46.6	0 05.1	20 48.3	20 09.4	23 04.2
28 M	6 26 23	6 47 51	20 14 44	27 17 37	12 00.8	27 52.5	22 00.0	3 00.0	26 02.6	5 51.2	0 03.4	20 46.0	20 07.8	23 03.1
29 Tu	6 30 20	7 45 03	4♏18 41	11♏17 44	12 02.1	28 04.8	23 03.2	3 34.9	26 19.2	5 56.0	0 01.6	20 43.7	20 06.2	23 02.0
30 W	6 34 16	8 42 15	18 14 36	25 09 06	12 03.5	28 12.4	24 06.5	4 10.0	26 35.7	6 00.9	29♒59.7	20 41.4	20 04.6	23 01.0

Astro Data

	Dy Hr Mn
☽0S	2 5:39
☽0N	15 14:46
☽0S	29 11:46
♃ D	1 1:09
♄ R	10 5:27
☽0N	11 22:31
⚳0N	15 0:40
☽0S	25 17:19

Planet Ingress

		Dy Hr Mn
☿	♉	3 21:54
☿	♊	18 6:53
☉	♊	21 1:02
♄	♓	21 4:58
☿	♋	2 3:54
♀	♉	6 10:03
☉	♋	21 9:00
♂	♍	23 7:42
♄	♒R	30 8:29

Last Aspect / ☽ Ingress (May)

Last Aspect Dy Hr Mn			☽ Ingress	Dy Hr Mn
2 16:21	♇	⚹	♎	3 1:20
5 0:46	♄	△	♏	5 1:57
7 2:32	♄	□	♐	7 3:34
9 6:57	♄	⚹	♑	9 7:51
11 4:44	♇	⚹	♒	11 15:44
14 2:18	♄	☌	♓	14 2:50
16 6:30	☿	⚹	♈	16 15:24
19 3:08	♄	⚹	♉	19 3:16
21 1:41	♇	☍	♊	21 13:07
22 21:53	♀	⚹	♋	23 20:38
25 15:15	♇	△	♌	26 2:03
27 19:11	♇	□	♍	28 5:46
29 22:32	☿	□	♎	30 8:18

Last Aspect / ☽ Ingress (June)

Last Aspect Dy Hr Mn			☽ Ingress	Dy Hr Mn
1 7:56	☿	△	♏	1 10:22
3 2:08	♇	☌	♐	3 13:01
5 16:12	♀	△	♑	5 17:26
7 12:26	♇	⚹	♒	8 0:39
9 21:59	♇	□	♓	10 10:57
12 9:53	♇	△	♈	12 23:14
15 2:01	♂	△	♉	15 11:19
17 15:03	♂	□	♊	17 21:12
20 1:52	☉	☌	♋	20 4:05
21 23:25	☿	☌	♌	22 8:26
23 23:44	♇	□	♍	24 11:18
26 9:02	☿	⚹	♎	26 13:45
28 13:01	☿	□	♏	28 16:37
30 20:26	♄	□	♐	30 20:28

☽ Phases & Eclipses

Dy Hr Mn		
6 3:34	○	15♏38
13 12:20	☾	22♒45
21 14:06	●	0♊31
21 14:19:11	•	P 0.735
28 18:21	☽	7♍25
4 13:02	○	13♐55
4 13:00	•	T 1.562
12 5:36	☾	21♓16
20 1:52	●	28♊46
26 22:43	☽	5♎19

Astro Data

1 May 1993
Julian Day # 34089
SVP 5♓20'55"
GC 26♐44.8 ⚴ 4♓11.9
Eris 17♈52.2 ⚵ 22♋34.5
⚷ 17♌22.6 ⚶ 25♒58.2
☽ Mean ☊ 14♐02.6

1 June 1993
Julian Day # 34120
SVP 5♓20'51"
GC 26♐44.8 ⚴ 9♓43.0
Eris 18♈08.7 ⚵ 5♌04.8
⚷ 18♌58.8 ⚶ 6♓12.0
☽ Mean ☊ 12♐24.1

July 1993

LONGITUDE

Day	Sid.Time	☉	0 hr ☽	Noon ☽	True ☊	☿	♀	♂	⚳	♃	♄	♅	♆	♇
1 Th	6 38 13	9♋39 26	2♐01 03	8♐50 18	12♐04.2	28♋15.4	25♉10.1	4♍45.1	26♈52.0	6♎06.0	29♒57.7	20♑39.0	20♑03.1	23♏00.0
2 F	6 42 09	10 36 38	15 36 39	22 19 56	12R 03.9	28R 13.7	26 14.0	5 20.2	27 08.2	6 11.2	29R 55.7	20R 36.7	20R 01.5	22R 59.0
3 Sa	6 46 06	11 33 49	29 00 00	5♑36 42	12 02.2	28 07.5	27 18.0	5 55.5	27 24.2	6 16.5	29 53.5	20 34.3	19 59.9	22 58.1
4 Su	6 50 02	12 31 00	12♑09 55	18 39 32	11 59.0	27 56.7	28 22.3	6 30.8	27 40.1	6 22.0	29 51.3	20 31.9	19 58.3	22 57.1
5 M	6 53 59	13 28 11	25 05 29	1♒27 47	11 54.6	27 41.4	29 26.7	7 06.1	27 55.8	6 27.7	29 49.0	20 29.5	19 56.7	22 56.2
6 Tu	6 57 55	14 25 22	7♒46 26	14 01 31	11 49.3	27 22.0	0♊31.4	7 41.6	28 11.3	6 33.5	29 46.6	20 27.2	19 55.1	22 55.4
7 W	7 01 52	15 22 33	20 13 11	26 21 39	11 43.8	26 58.5	1 36.3	8 17.0	28 26.6	6 39.4	29 44.1	20 24.8	19 53.4	22 54.5
8 Th	7 05 49	16 19 45	2♓27 08	8♓29 58	11 38.6	26 31.3	2 41.3	8 52.6	28 41.8	6 45.5	29 41.5	20 22.4	19 51.8	22 53.7
9 F	7 09 45	17 16 57	14 30 32	20 29 15	11 34.3	26 00.8	3 46.5	9 28.2	28 56.9	6 51.7	29 38.8	20 19.9	19 50.2	22 52.9
10 Sa	7 13 42	18 14 09	26 26 34	2♈23 00	11 31.4	25 27.5	4 52.0	10 03.9	29 11.7	6 58.1	29 36.1	20 17.5	19 48.6	22 52.1
11 Su	7 17 38	19 11 21	8♈19 06	14 15 26	11D 30.0	24 51.7	5 57.6	10 39.7	29 26.3	7 04.6	29 33.3	20 15.1	19 47.0	22 51.4
12 M	7 21 35	20 08 34	20 12 36	26 11 13	11 30.1	24 14.1	7 03.3	11 15.5	29 40.8	7 11.2	29 30.4	20 12.7	19 45.3	22 50.7
13 Tu	7 25 31	21 05 48	2♉11 54	8♉15 16	11 31.2	23 35.3	8 09.3	11 51.4	29 55.1	7 17.9	29 27.4	20 10.3	19 43.7	22 50.0
14 W	7 29 28	22 03 02	14 21 55	20 32 24	11 32.7	22 55.9	9 15.4	12 27.3	0♉09.2	7 24.8	29 24.4	20 07.9	19 42.1	22 49.4
15 Th	7 33 24	23 00 17	26 47 18	3♊07 04	11R 33.9	22 16.6	10 21.7	13 03.4	0 23.1	7 31.9	29 21.2	20 05.5	19 40.5	22 48.8
16 F	7 37 21	23 57 33	9♊32 07	16 02 48	11 34.1	21 38.2	11 28.1	13 39.4	0 36.8	7 39.0	29 18.1	20 03.0	19 38.9	22 48.2
17 Sa	7 41 18	24 54 49	22 39 21	29 21 52	11 32.7	21 01.1	12 34.7	14 15.6	0 50.3	7 46.3	29 14.8	20 00.6	19 37.2	22 47.6
18 Su	7 45 14	25 52 05	6♋10 21	13♋04 38	11 29.4	20 26.3	13 41.4	14 51.8	1 03.6	7 53.7	29 11.5	19 58.2	19 35.6	22 47.1
19 M	7 49 11	26 49 22	20 04 25	27 09 16	11 24.2	19 54.2	14 48.3	15 28.1	1 16.7	8 01.3	29 08.1	19 55.8	19 34.0	22 46.6
20 Tu	7 53 07	27 46 40	4♌18 35	11♌31 41	11 17.6	19 25.5	15 55.3	16 04.5	1 29.6	8 08.9	29 04.6	19 53.4	19 32.4	22 46.2
21 W	7 57 04	28 43 58	18 47 44	26 05 54	11 10.4	19 00.7	17 02.5	16 40.9	1 42.3	8 16.7	29 01.1	19 51.1	19 30.8	22 45.8
22 Th	8 01 00	29 41 16	3♍25 14	10♍44 53	11 03.4	18 40.2	18 09.7	17 17.3	1 54.7	8 24.6	28 57.5	19 48.7	19 29.2	22 45.4
23 F	8 04 57	0♌38 34	18 03 58	25 21 43	10 57.7	18 24.6	19 17.2	17 53.9	2 07.0	8 32.7	28 53.8	19 46.3	19 27.6	22 45.0
24 Sa	8 08 53	1 35 53	2♎37 25	9♎50 31	10 53.8	18 14.2	20 24.7	18 30.5	2 19.0	8 40.8	28 50.1	19 44.0	19 26.0	22 44.7
25 Su	8 12 50	2 33 12	17 00 34	24 07 13	10D 51.9	18D 09.3	21 32.4	19 07.1	2 30.7	8 49.1	28 46.3	19 41.6	19 24.5	22 44.4
26 M	8 16 47	3 30 32	1♏10 15	8♏09 34	10 51.6	18 10.0	22 40.2	19 43.8	2 42.3	8 57.4	28 42.5	19 39.3	19 22.9	22 44.1
27 Tu	8 20 43	4 27 52	15 05 07	21 56 57	10 52.4	18 16.7	23 48.1	20 20.6	2 53.6	9 05.9	28 38.6	19 37.0	19 21.3	22 43.9
28 W	8 24 40	5 25 12	28 45 08	5♐29 49	10R 53.2	18 29.4	24 56.2	20 57.4	3 04.7	9 14.5	28 34.7	19 34.7	19 19.8	22 43.7
29 Th	8 28 36	6 22 33	12♐11 05	18 49 07	10 53.1	18 48.3	26 04.3	21 34.3	3 15.5	9 23.2	28 30.7	19 32.4	19 18.3	22 43.6
30 F	8 32 33	7 19 55	25 24 00	1♑55 52	10 51.1	19 13.4	27 12.6	22 11.3	3 26.1	9 32.1	28 26.7	19 30.2	19 16.7	22 43.4
31 Sa	8 36 29	8 17 17	8♑24 48	14 50 52	10 46.7	19 44.6	28 21.0	22 48.3	3 36.4	9 41.0	28 22.6	19 27.9	19 15.2	22 43.3

August 1993

LONGITUDE

Day	Sid.Time	☉	0 hr ☽	Noon ☽	True ☊	☿	♀	♂	⚳	♃	♄	♅	♆	♇
1 Su	8 40 26	9♌14 40	21♑14 08	27♑34 38	10♐39.8	20♋22.1	29♊29.6	23♍25.4	3♉46.5	9♎50.0	28♒18.5	19♑25.7	19♑13.7	22♏43.3
2 M	8 44 22	10 12 04	3♒52 24	10♒07 27	10R 30.8	21 05.7	0♋38.2	24 02.5	3 56.3	9 59.1	28R 14.4	19R 23.5	19R 12.2	22D 43.3
3 Tu	8 48 19	11 09 28	16 19 51	22 29 39	10 20.2	21 55.4	1 47.0	24 39.7	4 05.9	10 08.4	28 10.2	19 21.3	19 10.7	22 43.3
4 W	8 52 16	12 06 54	28 36 56	4♓41 49	10 09.0	22 51.1	2 55.9	25 16.9	4 15.2	10 17.7	28 05.9	19 19.1	19 09.3	22 43.3
5 Th	8 56 12	13 04 20	10♓44 27	16 45 03	9 58.2	23 52.6	4 04.9	25 54.2	4 24.3	10 27.1	28 01.7	19 17.0	19 07.8	22 43.4
6 F	9 00 09	14 01 48	22 43 51	28 41 10	9 48.8	25 00.0	5 14.0	26 31.6	4 33.0	10 36.6	27 57.4	19 14.8	19 06.4	22 43.5
7 Sa	9 04 05	14 59 17	4♈37 21	10♈32 49	9 41.4	26 12.9	6 23.2	27 09.0	4 41.5	10 46.3	27 53.0	19 12.7	19 05.0	22 43.6
8 Su	9 08 02	15 56 47	16 28 00	22 23 26	9 36.4	27 31.2	7 32.6	27 46.5	4 49.8	10 56.0	27 48.7	19 10.6	19 03.5	22 43.8
9 M	9 11 58	16 54 19	28 19 38	4♉17 13	9 33.7	28 54.7	8 42.0	28 24.0	4 57.7	11 05.8	27 44.3	19 08.6	19 02.2	22 44.0
10 Tu	9 15 55	17 51 51	10♉16 47	16 18 58	9D 32.8	0♌23.1	9 51.6	29 01.6	5 05.3	11 15.7	27 39.9	19 06.6	19 00.8	22 44.2
11 W	9 19 51	18 49 26	22 24 27	28 33 51	9R 33.1	1 56.2	11 01.2	29 39.3	5 12.7	11 25.7	27 35.4	19 04.6	18 59.4	22 44.5
12 Th	9 23 48	19 47 01	4♊47 51	11♊07 02	9 33.3	3 33.7	12 11.0	0♎17.0	5 19.8	11 35.8	27 31.0	19 02.6	18 58.1	22 44.8
13 F	9 27 45	20 44 39	17 31 58	24 03 11	9 32.5	5 15.1	13 20.9	0 54.8	5 26.5	11 45.9	27 26.5	19 00.7	18 56.7	22 45.2
14 Sa	9 31 41	21 42 17	0♋41 03	7♋25 51	9 29.7	7 00.2	14 30.8	1 32.7	5 33.0	11 56.2	27 22.0	18 58.7	18 55.4	22 45.6
15 Su	9 35 38	22 39 57	14 17 44	21 16 41	9 24.5	8 48.5	15 40.9	2 10.6	5 39.1	12 06.5	27 17.5	18 56.9	18 54.2	22 46.0
16 M	9 39 34	23 37 39	28 22 27	5♌34 38	9 16.7	10 39.7	16 51.1	2 48.5	5 45.0	12 17.0	27 13.0	18 55.0	18 52.9	22 46.4
17 Tu	9 43 31	24 35 22	12♌52 35	20 15 30	9 07.0	12 33.3	18 01.3	3 26.6	5 50.5	12 27.5	27 08.5	18 53.2	18 51.6	22 46.9
18 W	9 47 27	25 33 06	27 42 22	5♍12 04	8 56.3	14 29.0	19 11.7	4 04.7	5 55.7	12 38.1	27 04.0	18 51.4	18 50.4	22 47.4
19 Th	9 51 24	26 30 51	12♍43 21	20 14 58	8 45.8	16 26.2	20 22.1	4 42.8	6 00.5	12 48.7	26 59.4	18 49.6	18 49.2	22 48.0
20 F	9 55 20	27 28 38	27 45 43	5♎14 25	8 36.9	18 24.8	21 32.6	5 21.0	6 05.0	12 59.5	26 54.9	18 47.9	18 48.0	22 48.6
21 Sa	9 59 17	28 26 26	12♎40 04	20 01 47	8 30.3	20 24.2	22 43.2	5 59.3	6 09.3	13 10.3	26 50.4	18 46.2	18 46.9	22 49.2
22 Su	10 03 14	29 24 15	27 18 55	4♏30 58	8 26.3	22 24.2	23 53.9	6 37.6	6 13.1	13 21.2	26 45.8	18 44.6	18 45.7	22 49.8
23 M	10 07 10	0♍22 05	11♏37 37	18 38 44	8D 24.6	24 24.5	25 04.7	7 16.0	6 16.7	13 32.2	26 41.3	18 43.0	18 44.6	22 50.5
24 Tu	10 11 07	1 19 56	25 34 20	2♐24 31	8R 24.3	26 24.8	26 15.6	7 54.5	6 19.8	13 43.2	26 36.8	18 41.4	18 43.5	22 51.2
25 W	10 15 03	2 17 49	9♐09 31	15 49 36	8 24.2	28 24.8	27 26.6	8 33.0	6 22.7	13 54.4	26 32.3	18 39.9	18 42.4	22 52.0
26 Th	10 19 00	3 15 43	22 25 07	28 56 24	8 23.1	0♍24.4	28 37.6	9 11.5	6 25.2	14 05.5	26 27.8	18 38.4	18 41.4	22 52.8
27 F	10 22 56	4 13 38	5♑23 46	11♑47 36	8 20.0	2 23.3	29 48.7	9 50.1	6 27.4	14 16.8	26 23.4	18 36.9	18 40.4	22 53.6
28 Sa	10 26 53	5 11 34	18 08 11	24 25 49	8 14.1	4 21.5	0♌59.9	10 28.8	6 29.2	14 28.1	26 18.9	18 35.5	18 39.4	22 54.4
29 Su	10 30 49	6 09 32	0♒40 44	6♒53 11	8 05.3	6 18.9	2 11.2	11 07.5	6 30.6	14 39.5	26 14.5	18 34.1	18 38.4	22 55.3
30 M	10 34 46	7 07 31	13 03 20	19 11 21	7 53.9	8 15.2	3 22.6	11 46.3	6 31.7	14 50.9	26 10.1	18 32.8	18 37.5	22 56.2
31 Tu	10 38 43	8 05 31	25 17 22	1♓21 32	7 40.7	10 10.6	4 34.1	12 25.2	6 32.4	15 02.5	26 05.7	18 31.5	18 36.5	22 57.2

Astro Data

	Dy Hr Mn
☿ R	1 15:29
☽ 0N	9 7:00
♃∠♇	17 16:03
☽ 0S	23 0:10
☿ D	25 20:51
♇ D	2 19:29
☽ 0N	5 15:14
♂0S	14 1:14
♃⚼♄	16 5:41
☽ 0S	19 9:11
♅☌♆	20 7:56

Planet Ingress

		Dy Hr Mn
♀	♊	6 0:21
⚳	♉	13 20:17
☉	♌	22 19:51
♀	♋	1 22:38
☿	♌	10 5:51
♂	♎	12 1:10
☉	♍	23 2:50
☿	♍	26 7:06
♀	♌	27 15:48

Last Aspect / ☽ Ingress (July)

Last Aspect Dy Hr Mn			☽ Ingress	Dy Hr Mn
3 1:38	♄	⚹	♑	3 1:48
5 7:50	♀	△	♒	5 9:14
7 18:37	♄	☌	♓	7 19:09
9 22:39	☿	△	♈	10 7:11
12 18:37	♄	⚹	♉	12 19:37
15 4:55	♄	□	♊	15 6:07
17 11:47	♄	△	♋	17 13:08
19 11:24	☉	☌	♌	19 16:47
21 16:46	♄	☍	♍	21 18:24
23 7:42	♇	⚹	♎	23 19:39
25 19:52	♄	△	♏	25 22:00
27 23:45	♄	□	♐	28 2:13
30 5:37	♄	⚹	♑	30 8:27

Last Aspect / ☽ Ingress (August)

Last Aspect Dy Hr Mn			☽ Ingress	Dy Hr Mn
1 3:44	♂	△	♒	1 16:36
3 23:04	♄	☌	♓	4 2:44
6 7:24	♂	☍	♈	6 14:39
8 23:43	☿	□	♉	9 3:22
11 14:13	♂	△	♊	11 14:47
13 18:07	♄	△	♋	13 22:46
15 14:32	♇	△	♌	16 2:43
17 23:02	♄	☍	♍	18 3:41
19 16:04	♇	⚹	♎	20 3:35
22 2:51	☉	⚹	♏	22 4:27
24 1:52	♄	□	♐	24 7:45
26 7:27	♄	⚹	♑	26 13:58
28 9:05	♇	⚹	♒	28 22:42
31 1:39	♄	☌	♓	31 9:18

☽ Phases & Eclipses

Dy Hr Mn		
3 23:45	○	12♑02
11 22:49	☾	19♈37
19 11:24	●	26♋48
26 3:25	☽	3♏10
2 12:10	○	10♒12
10 15:19	☾	18♉00
17 19:28	●	24♌53
24 9:57	☽	1♐15

Astro Data

1 July 1993
Julian Day # 34150
SVP 5♓20'45"
GC 26♐44.9 ⚴ 11♓11.2R
Eris 18♈17.3 ⚵ 17♌43.1
⚷ 21♌48.2 ⚶ 11♓41.9
☽ Mean ☊ 10♐48.8

1 August 1993
Julian Day # 34181
SVP 5♓20'40"
GC 26♐45.0 ⚴ 7♓31.2R
Eris 18♈16.5R ⚵ 0♍53.4
⚷ 25♌34.3 ⚶ 10♓41.3R
☽ Mean ☊ 9♐10.3

LONGITUDE — September 1993

Day	Sid.Time	☉	0 hr ☽	Noon ☽	True ☊	☿	♀	♂	⚳	♃	♄	♅	♆	♇
1 W	10 42 39	9♍03 34	7♓23 57	13♓24 44	7♐26.7	12♍04.8	5♌45.6	13♎04.1	6♉32.8	15♎14.0	26♒01.3	18♑30.2	18♑35.6	22♏58.1
2 Th	10 46 36	10 01 38	19 24 02	25 22 01	7R 13.1	13 57.9	6 57.3	13 43.0	6R 32.8	15 25.7	25R 57.0	18R 29.0	18R 34.8	22 59.1
3 F	10 50 32	10 59 43	1♈18 50	7♈14 42	7 01.0	15 49.9	8 09.0	14 22.0	6 32.5	15 37.3	25 52.7	18 27.8	18 33.9	23 00.2
4 Sa	10 54 29	11 57 50	13 09 54	19 04 43	6 51.2	17 40.6	9 20.8	15 01.1	6 31.7	15 49.1	25 48.4	18 26.7	18 33.1	23 01.3
5 Su	10 58 25	12 56 00	24 59 30	0♉54 39	6 44.1	19 30.2	10 32.6	15 40.2	6 30.6	16 00.9	25 44.2	18 25.6	18 32.3	23 02.4
6 M	11 02 22	13 54 11	6♉50 36	12 47 50	6 39.9	21 18.6	11 44.6	16 19.4	6 29.1	16 12.8	25 40.0	18 24.6	18 31.6	23 03.5
7 Tu	11 06 18	14 52 24	18 46 55	24 48 25	6D 38.0	23 05.8	12 56.6	16 58.7	6 27.3	16 24.7	25 35.8	18 23.6	18 30.9	23 04.7
8 W	11 10 15	15 50 40	0♊52 56	7♊01 06	6R 37.6	24 51.8	14 08.7	17 38.0	6 25.1	16 36.6	25 31.7	18 22.6	18 30.2	23 05.9
9 Th	11 14 12	16 48 57	13 13 33	19 30 58	6 37.6	26 36.7	15 20.9	18 17.4	6 22.5	16 48.7	25 27.7	18 21.7	18 29.5	23 07.1
10 F	11 18 08	17 47 16	25 53 56	2♋23 04	6 37.0	28 20.4	16 33.2	18 56.8	6 19.5	17 00.7	25 23.6	18 20.9	18 28.8	23 08.3
11 Sa	11 22 05	18 45 38	8♋58 51	15 41 45	6 34.6	0♎03.0	17 45.5	19 36.3	6 16.2	17 12.9	25 19.7	18 20.1	18 28.2	23 09.6
12 Su	11 26 01	19 44 02	22 32 02	29 29 52	6 29.8	1 44.4	18 58.0	20 15.9	6 12.4	17 25.0	25 15.7	18 19.3	18 27.7	23 10.9
13 M	11 29 58	20 42 27	6♌35 12	13♌47 49	6 22.4	3 24.7	20 10.4	20 55.5	6 08.3	17 37.2	25 11.9	18 18.6	18 27.1	23 12.3
14 Tu	11 33 54	21 40 55	21 07 13	28 32 41	6 13.1	5 04.0	21 23.0	21 35.2	6 03.8	17 49.5	25 08.1	18 17.9	18 26.6	23 13.7
15 W	11 37 51	22 39 25	6♍03 18	13♍37 56	6 02.5	6 42.2	22 35.6	22 14.9	5 59.0	18 01.8	25 04.3	18 17.3	18 26.1	23 15.1
16 Th	11 41 47	23 37 56	21 15 16	28 53 54	5 52.2	8 19.3	23 48.3	22 54.7	5 53.7	18 14.1	25 00.6	18 16.7	18 25.6	23 16.5
17 F	11 45 44	24 36 30	6♎32 25	14♎09 24	5 43.2	9 55.4	25 01.1	23 34.6	5 48.1	18 26.5	24 57.0	18 16.2	18 25.2	23 18.0
18 Sa	11 49 40	25 35 05	21 43 33	29 13 43	5 36.5	11 30.4	26 13.9	24 14.5	5 42.1	18 39.0	24 53.4	18 15.7	18 24.8	23 19.4
19 Su	11 53 37	26 33 42	6♏38 55	13♏58 24	5 32.4	13 04.4	27 26.8	24 54.5	5 35.8	18 51.4	24 49.9	18 15.3	18 24.4	23 21.0
20 M	11 57 34	27 32 21	21 11 40	28 18 22	5D 30.8	14 37.5	28 39.8	25 34.5	5 29.1	19 03.9	24 46.4	18 14.9	18 24.1	23 22.5
21 Tu	12 01 30	28 31 01	5♐18 23	12♐11 46	5 30.7	16 09.5	29 52.8	26 14.6	5 22.0	19 16.5	24 43.0	18 14.6	18 23.8	23 24.1
22 W	12 05 27	29 29 43	18 58 43	25 39 30	5R 31.1	17 40.5	1♍05.9	26 54.8	5 14.6	19 29.1	24 39.7	18 14.3	18 23.5	23 25.7
23 Th	12 09 23	0♎28 27	2♑14 30	8♑44 09	5 30.9	19 10.4	2 19.0	27 35.0	5 06.9	19 41.7	24 36.5	18 14.1	18 23.3	23 27.3
24 F	12 13 20	1 27 13	15 08 54	21 29 15	5 28.9	20 39.4	3 32.2	28 15.3	4 58.8	19 54.3	24 33.3	18 13.9	18 23.1	23 28.9
25 Sa	12 17 16	2 26 00	27 45 38	3♒58 32	5 24.7	22 07.4	4 45.4	28 55.6	4 50.3	20 07.0	24 30.3	18 13.8	18 22.9	23 30.6
26 Su	12 21 13	3 24 49	10♒08 21	16 15 29	5 17.8	23 34.4	5 58.8	29 36.0	4 41.6	20 19.7	24 27.2	18 13.7	18 22.8	23 32.3
27 M	12 25 09	4 23 39	22 20 19	28 23 10	5 08.7	25 00.3	7 12.1	0♏16.4	4 32.5	20 32.4	24 24.3	18D 13.7	18 22.7	23 34.0
28 Tu	12 29 06	5 22 32	4♓24 19	10♓24 02	4 58.0	26 25.2	8 25.6	0 56.9	4 23.1	20 45.2	24 21.5	18 13.7	18 22.6	23 35.8
29 W	12 33 03	6 21 26	16 22 32	22 20 03	4 46.5	27 49.0	9 39.0	1 37.5	4 13.4	20 57.9	24 18.7	18 13.8	18D 22.6	23 37.6
30 Th	12 36 59	7 20 22	28 16 45	4♈12 51	4 35.4	29 11.7	10 52.6	2 18.1	4 03.4	21 10.7	24 16.0	18 13.9	18 22.6	23 39.4

LONGITUDE — October 1993

Day	Sid.Time	☉	0 hr ☽	Noon ☽	True ☊	☿	♀	♂	⚳	♃	♄	♅	♆	♇
1 F	12 40 56	8♎19 21	10♈08 31	16♈03 57	4♐25.5	0♏33.3	12♍06.2	2♏58.8	3♉53.1	21♎23.6	24♒13.4	18♑14.1	18♑22.6	23♏41.2
2 Sa	12 44 52	9 18 21	21 59 20	27 54 55	4R 17.6	1 53.7	13 19.8	3 39.5	3R 42.5	21 36.4	24R 10.8	18 14.3	18 22.6	23 43.0
3 Su	12 48 49	10 17 24	3♉50 56	9♉47 41	4 12.1	3 13.0	14 33.5	4 20.3	3 31.6	21 49.3	24 08.4	18 14.6	18 22.7	23 44.9
4 M	12 52 45	11 16 28	15 45 29	21 44 42	4 09.1	4 30.9	15 47.3	5 01.2	3 20.5	22 02.2	24 06.1	18 14.9	18 22.9	23 46.8
5 Tu	12 56 42	12 15 35	27 45 42	3♊48 57	4D 08.2	5 47.5	17 01.1	5 42.1	3 09.1	22 15.1	24 03.8	18 15.3	18 23.0	23 48.7
6 W	13 00 38	13 14 44	9♊54 56	16 04 07	4 08.7	7 02.7	18 15.0	6 23.1	2 57.4	22 28.0	24 01.6	18 15.7	18 23.2	23 50.6
7 Th	13 04 35	14 13 56	22 17 04	28 34 18	4 09.9	8 16.4	19 28.9	7 04.1	2 45.6	22 41.0	23 59.5	18 16.2	18 23.4	23 52.6
8 F	13 08 32	15 13 10	4♋56 24	11♋23 51	4R 10.8	9 28.5	20 42.9	7 45.2	2 33.5	22 53.9	23 57.5	18 16.8	18 23.7	23 54.5
9 Sa	13 12 28	16 12 26	17 57 11	24 36 51	4 10.5	10 38.9	21 57.0	8 26.3	2 21.1	23 06.9	23 55.6	18 17.3	18 24.0	23 56.5
10 Su	13 16 25	17 11 45	1♌23 12	8♌16 29	4 08.5	11 47.4	23 11.0	9 07.6	2 08.6	23 19.9	23 53.8	18 18.0	18 24.3	23 58.5
11 M	13 20 21	18 11 05	15 16 49	22 24 09	4 04.6	12 54.0	24 25.2	9 48.8	1 55.9	23 32.9	23 52.1	18 18.7	18 24.7	24 00.6
12 Tu	13 24 18	19 10 28	29 38 14	6♍58 39	3 59.0	13 58.4	25 39.4	10 30.2	1 43.0	23 45.9	23 50.5	18 19.4	18 25.1	24 02.6
13 W	13 28 14	20 09 54	14♍24 41	21 55 30	3 52.4	15 00.4	26 53.6	11 11.6	1 30.0	23 59.0	23 48.9	18 20.2	18 25.5	24 04.7
14 Th	13 32 11	21 09 21	29 30 01	7♎07 01	3 45.7	15 59.9	28 07.9	11 53.1	1 16.8	24 12.0	23 47.5	18 21.0	18 26.0	24 06.8
15 F	13 36 07	22 08 51	14♎45 11	22 23 08	3 40.0	16 56.6	29 22.2	12 34.6	1 03.5	24 25.0	23 46.2	18 21.9	18 26.5	24 08.9
16 Sa	13 40 04	23 08 22	29 59 31	7♏33 04	3 35.8	17 50.2	0♎36.5	13 16.2	0 50.1	24 38.1	23 44.9	18 22.9	18 27.0	24 11.0
17 Su	13 44 01	24 07 56	15♏02 37	22 27 10	3D 33.5	18 40.3	1 50.9	13 57.8	0 36.5	24 51.1	23 43.8	18 23.9	18 27.5	24 13.1
18 M	13 47 57	25 07 32	29 45 57	6♐58 21	3 33.1	19 26.8	3 05.3	14 39.5	0 22.9	25 04.2	23 42.8	18 24.9	18 28.1	24 15.3
19 Tu	13 51 54	26 07 09	14♐04 01	21 02 44	3 34.0	20 09.1	4 19.8	15 21.3	0 09.2	25 17.2	23 41.8	18 26.0	18 28.8	24 17.5
20 W	13 55 50	27 06 48	27 54 29	4♑39 25	3 35.5	20 46.9	5 34.3	16 03.1	29♈55.5	25 30.3	23 41.0	18 27.1	18 29.4	24 19.7
21 Th	13 59 47	28 06 29	11♑17 47	17 49 56	3R 36.8	21 19.6	6 48.9	16 45.0	29 41.7	25 43.3	23 40.3	18 28.3	18 30.1	24 21.9
22 F	14 03 43	29 06 11	24 16 19	0♒37 24	3 37.3	21 46.9	8 03.4	17 26.9	29 27.9	25 56.4	23 39.6	18 29.6	18 30.8	24 24.1
23 Sa	14 07 40	0♏05 56	6♒53 42	13 05 46	3 36.4	22 08.0	9 18.0	18 08.9	29 14.1	26 09.4	23 39.1	18 30.9	18 31.6	24 26.3
24 Su	14 11 36	1 05 42	19 14 06	25 19 15	3 33.9	22 22.6	10 32.7	18 51.0	29 00.3	26 22.4	23 38.7	18 32.2	18 32.4	24 28.5
25 M	14 15 33	2 05 29	1♓21 43	7♓21 59	3 30.1	22R 29.9	11 47.3	19 33.1	28 46.5	26 35.5	23 38.4	18 33.6	18 33.2	24 30.8
26 Tu	14 19 30	3 05 18	13 20 30	19 17 42	3 25.2	22 29.4	13 02.0	20 15.2	28 32.8	26 48.5	23 38.1	18 35.0	18 34.1	24 33.1
27 W	14 23 26	4 05 09	25 13 57	1♈09 37	3 19.8	22 20.6	14 16.8	20 57.5	28 19.1	27 01.5	23D 38.0	18 36.5	18 35.0	24 35.3
28 Th	14 27 23	5 05 02	7♈05 01	13 00 28	3 14.5	22 03.0	15 31.5	21 39.7	28 05.5	27 14.5	23 38.0	18 38.0	18 35.9	24 37.6
29 F	14 31 19	6 04 57	18 56 13	24 52 31	3 09.9	21 36.1	16 46.3	22 22.1	27 52.0	27 27.5	23 38.1	18 39.6	18 36.8	24 39.9
30 Sa	14 35 16	7 04 53	0♉49 37	6♉47 42	3 06.4	21 00.0	18 01.1	23 04.5	27 38.6	27 40.5	23 38.3	18 41.2	18 37.8	24 42.2
31 Su	14 39 12	8 04 52	12 47 01	18 47 46	3 04.2	20 14.5	19 16.0	23 46.9	27 25.3	27 53.4	23 38.6	18 42.9	18 38.8	24 44.6

Astro Data

	Dy Hr Mn
☽0N	1 22:23
⚳R	2 0:23
☿0S	12 9:35
☽0S	15 19:47
♃□♅	16 16:47
♃□♆	17 9:30
☉0S	23 0:23
♅D	27 12:29
☽0N	29 4:22
♆D	30 6:09
♄□♇	9 6:23
⚳0S	11 15:24
♃△♄	12 19:28
☽0S	13 6:22
♃⊻♇	14 0:35

Planet Ingress

		Dy Hr Mn
☿	♎	11 11:18
♀	♍	21 14:22
☉	♎	23 0:22
♂	♏	27 2:15
☿	♏	1 2:09
♀	♎	16 0:13
⚳	♈R	20 4:06
☉	♏	23 9:37
♀0S		18 20:52
♅☌♆		24 20:07
☿ R		25 22:40
☽0N		26 9:57
♄ D		28 3:39

Last Aspect / ☽ Ingress (September)

Last Aspect Dy Hr Mn		☽ Ingress	Dy Hr Mn
2 7:12	♇ △	♈	2 21:21
5 1:34	♄ ⚹	♉	5 10:09
7 13:34	♄ □	♊	7 22:16
10 3:24	☿ □	♋	10 7:37
12 1:07	♇ △	♌	12 12:51
14 6:32	♄ ☍	♍	14 14:20
16 3:10	☉ ☌	♎	16 13:44
18 6:46	♀ ⚹	♏	18 13:14
20 12:40	♀ □	♐	20 14:53
22 19:32	☉ □	♑	22 19:54
25 1:41	♂ □	♒	25 4:19
27 4:23	☿ △	♓	27 15:13
29 14:37	♇ △	♈	30 3:29

Last Aspect / ☽ Ingress (October)

Last Aspect Dy Hr Mn		☽ Ingress	Dy Hr Mn
2 4:28	♄ ⚹	♉	2 16:13
4 16:42	♄ □	♊	5 4:27
7 3:18	♄ △	♋	7 14:42
9 10:48	♇ △	♌	9 21:34
11 14:41	♇ □	♍	12 0:36
13 20:35	♀ ☌	♎	14 0:47
15 15:15	♃ ☌	♏	16 0:01
17 14:54	♇ ☌	♐	18 0:23
19 21:33	☉ ⚹	♑	20 3:42
22 8:52	☉ □	♒	22 10:49
24 14:07	♃ △	♓	24 21:17
26 22:39	♇ △	♈	27 9:39
29 17:18	♃ ☍	♉	29 22:20

☽ Phases & Eclipses

Dy Hr Mn		
1 2:33	○	8♓41
9 6:26	☾	16♊35
16 3:10	●	23♍16
22 19:32	☽	29♐48
30 18:54	○	7♈37
8 19:35	☾	15♋32
15 11:36	●	22♎08
22 8:52	☽	28♑58
30 12:38	○	7♉06

Astro Data

1 September 1993
Julian Day # 34212
SVP 5♓20'37"
GC 26♐45.0 ⚵ 0♓01.6R
Eris 18♈06.3R ✱ 13♍53.6
⚷ 29♌42.1 ⚶ 3♓46.8R
☽ Mean ☊ 7♐31.8

1 October 1993
Julian Day # 34242
SVP 5♓20'34"
GC 26♐45.1 ⚵ 24♒06.2R
Eris 17♈50.2R ✱ 26♍04.1
⚷ 3♍33.3 ⚶ 28♒29.2R
☽ Mean ☊ 5♐56.5

November 1993 — LONGITUDE

Day	Sid.Time	☉	0 hr ☽	Noon ☽	True ☊	☿	♀	♂	⚳	♃	♄	♅	♆	♇
1 M	14 43 09	9♏04 52	24♉50 11	0♊54 28	3♐03.3	19♏20.1	20♎30.9	24♏29.4	27♈12.2	28♎06.4	23♒39.0	18♑44.6	18♑39.8	24♏46.9
2 Tu	14 47 05	10 04 55	7♊00 54	13 09 43	3D 03.7	18R 17.6	21 45.8	25 12.0	26R 59.2	28 19.3	23 39.5	18 46.4	18 40.9	24 49.2
3 W	14 51 02	11 04 59	19 21 12	25 35 40	3 04.8	17 08.1	23 00.7	25 54.6	26 46.3	28 32.2	23 40.1	18 48.2	18 42.0	24 51.6
4 Th	14 54 58	12 05 06	1♋53 25	8♋14 47	3 06.4	15 53.4	24 15.7	26 37.3	26 33.6	28 45.1	23 40.8	18 50.0	18 43.2	24 53.9
5 F	14 58 55	13 05 14	14 40 06	21 09 43	3 07.9	14 35.4	25 30.7	27 20.1	26 21.1	28 58.0	23 41.6	18 51.9	18 44.3	24 56.3
6 Sa	15 02 52	14 05 25	27 43 58	4♌23 08	3R 08.9	13 16.5	26 45.7	28 02.9	26 08.8	29 10.8	23 42.5	18 53.9	18 45.5	24 58.7
7 Su	15 06 48	15 05 37	11♌07 29	17 57 13	3 09.2	11 59.2	28 00.8	28 45.8	25 56.7	29 23.7	23 43.5	18 55.9	18 46.7	25 01.0
8 M	15 10 45	16 05 52	24 52 28	1♍53 14	3 08.6	10 46.0	29 15.9	29 28.7	25 44.9	29 36.5	23 44.7	18 57.9	18 48.0	25 03.4
9 Tu	15 14 41	17 06 09	8♍59 27	16 10 52	3 07.2	9 39.2	0♏31.0	0♐11.7	25 33.3	29 49.2	23 45.9	19 00.0	18 49.3	25 05.8
10 W	15 18 38	18 06 27	23 27 08	0♎47 43	3 05.4	8 40.8	1 46.1	0 54.7	25 21.9	0♏02.0	23 47.2	19 02.1	18 50.6	25 08.2
11 Th	15 22 34	19 06 48	8♎11 56	15 39 00	3 03.6	7 52.4	3 01.2	1 37.8	25 10.8	0 14.7	23 48.6	19 04.2	18 51.9	25 10.6
12 F	15 26 31	20 07 11	23 07 56	0♏37 46	3 02.0	7 14.9	4 16.4	2 21.0	24 59.9	0 27.4	23 50.2	19 06.4	18 53.3	25 13.0
13 Sa	15 30 27	21 07 35	8♏07 23	15 35 42	3 00.9	6 49.1	5 31.6	3 04.2	24 49.4	0 40.1	23 51.8	19 08.7	18 54.7	25 15.4
14 Su	15 34 24	22 08 01	23 01 40	0♐24 16	3D 00.5	6D 34.9	6 46.8	3 47.5	24 39.1	0 52.7	23 53.5	19 10.9	18 56.1	25 17.8
15 M	15 38 21	23 08 29	7♐42 38	14 56 00	3 00.6	6 32.3	8 02.0	4 30.8	24 29.2	1 05.3	23 55.4	19 13.3	18 57.5	25 20.2
16 Tu	15 42 17	24 08 58	22 03 44	29 05 24	3 01.2	6 40.6	9 17.2	5 14.2	24 19.5	1 17.9	23 57.3	19 15.6	18 59.0	25 22.6
17 W	15 46 14	25 09 29	6♑00 41	12♑49 29	3 02.0	6 59.1	10 32.5	5 57.7	24 10.2	1 30.4	23 59.3	19 18.0	19 00.5	25 25.0
18 Th	15 50 10	26 10 01	19 31 46	26 07 42	3 02.8	7 27.1	11 47.8	6 41.2	24 01.3	1 42.9	24 01.5	19 20.5	19 02.0	25 27.4
19 F	15 54 07	27 10 34	2♒37 32	9♒01 36	3 03.3	8 03.6	13 03.0	7 24.8	23 52.6	1 55.3	24 03.7	19 22.9	19 03.6	25 29.8
20 Sa	15 58 03	28 11 08	15 20 20	21 34 13	3R 03.6	8 47.8	14 18.3	8 08.4	23 44.3	2 07.7	24 06.1	19 25.5	19 05.2	25 32.2
21 Su	16 02 00	29 11 44	27 43 46	3♓49 32	3 03.6	9 38.7	15 33.6	8 52.0	23 36.4	2 20.0	24 08.5	19 28.0	19 06.8	25 34.6
22 M	16 05 56	0♐12 20	9♓52 07	15 52 04	3 03.5	10 35.6	16 48.9	9 35.8	23 28.8	2 32.3	24 11.0	19 30.6	19 08.4	25 37.0
23 Tu	16 09 53	1 12 58	21 49 58	27 46 23	3 03.3	11 37.7	18 04.3	10 19.5	23 21.6	2 44.6	24 13.6	19 33.2	19 10.1	25 39.4
24 W	16 13 50	2 13 37	3♈41 51	9♈36 53	3D 03.1	12 44.3	19 19.6	11 03.4	23 14.8	2 56.8	24 16.4	19 35.9	19 11.7	25 41.8
25 Th	16 17 46	3 14 18	15 31 58	21 27 34	3 03.1	13 54.7	20 34.9	11 47.2	23 08.3	3 09.0	24 19.2	19 38.5	19 13.4	25 44.2
26 F	16 21 43	4 14 59	27 24 07	3♉21 59	3 03.2	15 08.5	21 50.3	12 31.2	23 02.2	3 21.1	24 22.1	19 41.3	19 15.1	25 46.6
27 Sa	16 25 39	5 15 42	9♉21 30	15 23 01	3 03.3	16 25.2	23 05.7	13 15.2	22 56.5	3 33.1	24 25.1	19 44.0	19 16.9	25 49.0
28 Su	16 29 36	6 16 25	21 26 46	27 32 59	3R 03.5	17 44.4	24 21.0	13 59.2	22 51.2	3 45.1	24 28.2	19 46.8	19 18.7	25 51.4
29 M	16 33 32	7 17 10	3♊41 53	9♊53 38	3 03.4	19 05.6	25 36.4	14 43.3	22 46.2	3 57.1	24 31.4	19 49.6	19 20.4	25 53.7
30 Tu	16 37 29	8 17 57	16 08 21	22 26 09	3 03.2	20 28.6	26 51.8	15 27.5	22 41.7	4 09.0	24 34.7	19 52.5	19 22.3	25 56.1

December 1993 — LONGITUDE

Day	Sid.Time	☉	0 hr ☽	Noon ☽	True ☊	☿	♀	♂	⚳	♃	♄	♅	♆	♇
1 W	16 41 26	9♐18 44	28♊47 08	5♋11 21	3♐02.6	21♏53.1	28♏07.2	16♐11.7	22♈37.5	4♏20.8	24♒38.0	19♑55.4	19♑24.1	25♏58.5
2 Th	16 45 22	10 19 33	11♋38 53	18 09 44	3R 01.7	23 18.8	29 22.6	16 55.9	22R 33.7	4 32.6	24 41.5	19 58.3	19 25.9	26 00.8
3 F	16 49 19	11 20 24	24 43 58	1♌21 23	3 00.7	24 45.7	0♐38.1	17 40.2	22 30.4	4 44.3	24 45.1	20 01.2	19 27.8	26 03.2
4 Sa	16 53 15	12 21 15	8♌02 39	14 47 09	2 59.6	26 13.5	1 53.5	18 24.6	22 27.4	4 56.0	24 48.7	20 04.2	19 29.7	26 05.5
5 Su	16 57 12	13 22 08	21 35 04	28 26 24	2 58.8	27 42.0	3 08.9	19 09.0	22 24.8	5 07.6	24 52.4	20 07.2	19 31.6	26 07.8
6 M	17 01 08	14 23 02	5♍21 08	12♍19 10	2D 58.5	29 11.2	4 24.4	19 53.5	22 22.6	5 19.1	24 56.2	20 10.2	19 33.5	26 10.2
7 Tu	17 05 05	15 23 57	19 20 25	26 24 43	2 58.7	0♐41.0	5 39.8	20 38.0	22 20.8	5 30.6	25 00.1	20 13.3	19 35.5	26 12.5
8 W	17 09 01	16 24 54	3♎31 53	10♎41 38	2 59.4	2 11.2	6 55.3	21 22.6	22 19.3	5 41.9	25 04.1	20 16.4	19 37.5	26 14.8
9 Th	17 12 58	17 25 52	17 53 38	25 07 28	3 00.5	3 41.8	8 10.8	22 07.2	22 18.3	5 53.3	25 08.2	20 19.5	19 39.4	26 17.1
10 F	17 16 55	18 26 51	2♏22 39	9♏38 37	3 01.7	5 12.8	9 26.3	22 51.9	22 17.7	6 04.5	25 12.4	20 22.6	19 41.4	26 19.3
11 Sa	17 20 51	19 27 52	16 54 45	24 10 24	3R 02.5	6 44.0	10 41.8	23 36.7	22D 17.5	6 15.7	25 16.6	20 25.8	19 43.5	26 21.6
12 Su	17 24 48	20 28 53	1♐24 50	8♐37 21	3 02.6	8 15.6	11 57.3	24 21.4	22 17.6	6 26.8	25 20.9	20 29.0	19 45.5	26 23.8
13 M	17 28 44	21 29 55	15 47 15	22 53 50	3 01.7	9 47.3	13 12.8	25 06.3	22 18.2	6 37.8	25 25.3	20 32.2	19 47.5	26 26.1
14 Tu	17 32 41	22 30 58	29 56 30	6♑54 43	2 59.8	11 19.3	14 28.3	25 51.2	22 19.2	6 48.7	25 29.8	20 35.4	19 49.6	26 28.3
15 W	17 36 37	23 32 02	13♑48 02	20 36 05	2 57.0	12 51.5	15 43.8	26 36.1	22 20.5	6 59.6	25 34.4	20 38.7	19 51.7	26 30.5
16 Th	17 40 34	24 33 06	27 18 40	3♒55 40	2 53.6	14 23.8	16 59.3	27 21.1	22 22.2	7 10.4	25 39.0	20 41.9	19 53.8	26 32.7
17 F	17 44 30	25 34 11	10♒27 05	16 53 03	2 50.2	15 56.3	18 14.8	28 06.1	22 24.3	7 21.1	25 43.7	20 45.2	19 55.9	26 34.9
18 Sa	17 48 27	26 35 16	23 13 46	29 29 34	2 47.1	17 29.0	19 30.3	28 51.2	22 26.8	7 31.7	25 48.5	20 48.5	19 58.0	26 37.1
19 Su	17 52 24	27 36 21	5♓40 50	11♓48 02	2 44.9	19 01.8	20 45.8	29 36.4	22 29.7	7 42.2	25 53.4	20 51.9	20 00.1	26 39.2
20 M	17 56 20	28 37 26	17 51 42	23 52 22	2D 43.8	20 34.8	22 01.3	0♑21.5	22 32.9	7 52.6	25 58.3	20 55.2	20 02.3	26 41.3
21 Tu	18 00 17	29 38 32	29 50 39	5♈47 10	2 43.9	22 08.0	23 16.8	1 06.7	22 36.5	8 02.9	26 03.3	20 58.6	20 04.4	26 43.4
22 W	18 04 13	0♑39 38	11♈42 32	17 37 24	2 45.0	23 41.4	24 32.3	1 52.0	22 40.5	8 13.2	26 08.4	21 02.0	20 06.6	26 45.5
23 Th	18 08 10	1 40 45	23 32 22	29 28 03	2 46.7	25 14.9	25 47.9	2 37.3	22 44.8	8 23.3	26 13.6	21 05.4	20 08.8	26 47.6
24 F	18 12 06	2 41 51	5♉25 03	11♉23 55	2 48.6	26 48.7	27 03.4	3 22.7	22 49.5	8 33.4	26 18.8	21 08.8	20 11.0	26 49.7
25 Sa	18 16 03	3 42 58	17 25 09	23 29 14	2R 50.0	28 22.7	28 18.9	4 08.1	22 54.6	8 43.3	26 24.1	21 12.2	20 13.2	26 51.7
26 Su	18 19 59	4 44 05	29 36 35	5♊47 34	2 50.3	29 56.9	29 34.4	4 53.5	23 00.0	8 53.2	26 29.4	21 15.6	20 15.4	26 53.7
27 M	18 23 56	5 45 12	12♊02 28	18 21 31	2 49.2	1♑31.4	0♑49.9	5 39.0	23 05.8	9 02.9	26 34.9	21 19.1	20 17.6	26 55.7
28 Tu	18 27 53	6 46 19	24 44 49	1♋12 28	2 46.3	3 06.1	2 05.4	6 24.5	23 11.9	9 12.6	26 40.3	21 22.6	20 19.8	26 57.7
29 W	18 31 49	7 47 26	7♋44 27	14 20 38	2 41.8	4 41.1	3 20.9	7 10.1	23 18.3	9 22.1	26 45.9	21 26.0	20 22.0	26 59.7
30 Th	18 35 46	8 48 34	21 00 53	27 44 56	2 36.0	6 16.4	4 36.4	7 55.7	23 25.1	9 31.6	26 51.5	21 29.5	20 24.3	27 01.6
31 F	18 39 42	9 49 42	4♌32 32	11♌23 18	2 29.7	7 52.0	5 51.9	8 41.4	23 32.2	9 40.9	26 57.2	21 33.0	20 26.5	27 03.5

Astro Data (Dy Hr Mn)

☽0S 9 15:15
☿D 15 5:37
☽0N 22 16:28

☽0S 6 21:55
⚳0N 9 1:45
⚳D 11 13:46
☽0N 20 0:44

Planet Ingress (Dy Hr Mn)

♀ ♏ 9 2:07
♂ ♐ 9 5:29
♃ ♏ 10 8:15
☉ ♐ 22 7:07

♀ ♐ 2 23:54
☿ ♐ 7 1:04
♂ ♑ 20 0:34
☉ ♑ 21 20:26
☿ ♑ 26 12:47
♀ ♑ 26 20:09

Last Aspect Dy Hr Mn		☽ Ingress Dy Hr Mn
31 23:51 ♇ ☍	♊	1 10:13
3 17:43 ♃ △	♋	3 20:25
6 2:28 ♃ □	♌	6 4:06
8 8:03 ♃ ✱	♍	8 8:47
10 2:44 ♇ ✱	♎	10 10:42
12 1:06 ♄ △	♏	12 11:00
14 3:39 ♇ ☌	♐	14 11:20
16 3:12 ♄ ✱	♑	16 13:34
18 12:05 ☉ ✱	♒	18 19:08
21 2:03 ☉ □	♓	21 4:27
23 7:42 ♇ △	♈	23 16:30
25 17:48 ♄ ✱	♉	26 5:14
28 8:40 ♇ ☍	♊	28 16:48

Last Aspect Dy Hr Mn		☽ Ingress Dy Hr Mn
30 16:05 ♄ △	♋	1 2:17
3 2:22 ♇ △	♌	3 9:33
5 10:33 ☿ □	♍	5 14:43
7 11:39 ♇ ✱	♎	7 18:03
9 12:01 ♄ △	♏	9 20:04
11 15:38 ♇ ☌	♐	11 21:39
13 16:19 ♄ ✱	♑	14 0:06
15 22:35 ♇ ✱	♒	16 4:51
18 10:41 ♂ ✱	♓	18 12:59
20 22:26 ☉ □	♈	21 0:19
23 5:24 ♄ ✱	♉	23 13:05
25 18:39 ♇ ☍	♊	26 0:46
28 3:32 ♄ △	♋	28 9:46
30 10:43 ♇ △	♌	30 15:59

☽ Phases & Eclipses (Dy Hr Mn)

7 6:36 ☾ 14♌52
13 21:34 ● 21♏32
13 21:44:48 ● P 0.928
21 2:03 ☽ 28♒47
29 6:31 ○ 7♊03
29 6:26 ● T 1.087

6 15:49 ☾ 14♍33
13 9:27 ● 21♐23
20 22:26 ☽ 29♓04
28 23:05 ○ 7♋15

Astro Data

1 November 1993
Julian Day # 34273
SVP 5♓20'31"
GC 26♐45.2 ⚴ 23♒04.1
Eris 17♈31.8R ✱ 7♎54.4
⚷ 6♍50.9 ⚶ 29♒42.8
☽ Mean ☊ 4♐18.0

1 December 1993
Julian Day # 34303
SVP 5♓20'26"
GC 26♐45.3 ⚴ 26♒47.0
Eris 17♈17.7R ✱ 18♎09.9
⚷ 8♍50.3 ⚶ 6♓29.9
☽ Mean ☊ 2♐42.6

LONGITUDE January 1994

Day	Sid.Time	☉	0 hr ☽	Noon ☽	True ☊	☿	♀	♂	⚳	♃	♄	♅	♆	♇
1 Sa	18 43 39	10♑50 50	18♌16 54	25♌12 56	2♐23.5	9♑27.9	7♑07.3	9♑27.1	23♈39.6	9♏50.1	27♒02.9	21♑36.5	20♑28.7	27♏05.4
2 Su	18 47 35	11 51 58	2♍11 03	9♍10 51	2R 18.3	11 04.1	8 22.8	10 12.8	23 47.3	9 59.3	27 08.7	21 40.0	20 31.0	27 07.3
3 M	18 51 32	12 53 07	16 12 01	23 14 14	2 14.7	12 40.7	9 38.3	10 58.6	23 55.4	10 08.3	27 14.6	21 43.6	20 33.3	27 09.1
4 Tu	18 55 28	13 54 15	0♎17 12	7♎20 43	2D 13.0	14 17.7	10 53.8	11 44.4	24 03.8	10 17.1	27 20.5	21 47.1	20 35.5	27 10.9
5 W	18 59 25	14 55 24	14 24 33	21 28 31	2 12.9	15 55.0	12 09.3	12 30.3	24 12.5	10 25.9	27 26.4	21 50.6	20 37.8	27 12.7
6 Th	19 03 22	15 56 34	28 32 27	5♏36 12	2 14.0	17 32.7	13 24.8	13 16.2	24 21.5	10 34.6	27 32.5	21 54.2	20 40.0	27 14.5
7 F	19 07 18	16 57 44	12♏39 36	19 42 28	2R 15.3	19 10.8	14 40.3	14 02.2	24 30.8	10 43.1	27 38.5	21 57.7	20 42.3	27 16.2
8 Sa	19 11 15	17 58 53	26 44 35	3♐45 42	2 15.8	20 49.3	15 55.8	14 48.2	24 40.4	10 51.5	27 44.7	22 01.3	20 44.6	27 18.0
9 Su	19 15 11	19 00 03	10♐45 34	17 43 50	2 14.7	22 28.3	17 11.3	15 34.2	24 50.3	10 59.8	27 50.9	22 04.8	20 46.9	27 19.7
10 M	19 19 08	20 01 13	24 40 10	1♑34 12	2 11.3	24 07.6	18 26.8	16 20.3	25 00.5	11 08.0	27 57.1	22 08.4	20 49.2	27 21.3
11 Tu	19 23 04	21 02 23	8♑25 33	15 13 49	2 05.5	25 47.3	19 42.3	17 06.4	25 10.9	11 16.0	28 03.4	22 11.9	20 51.4	27 23.0
12 W	19 27 01	22 03 32	21 58 39	28 39 42	1 57.5	27 27.4	20 57.8	17 52.6	25 21.7	11 23.9	28 09.7	22 15.5	20 53.7	27 24.6
13 Th	19 30 57	23 04 41	5♒16 42	11♒49 27	1 48.1	29 07.9	22 13.3	18 38.8	25 32.8	11 31.7	28 16.1	22 19.0	20 56.0	27 26.2
14 F	19 34 54	24 05 49	18 17 46	24 41 38	1 38.2	0♒48.7	23 28.7	19 25.0	25 44.1	11 39.3	28 22.5	22 22.6	20 58.3	27 27.7
15 Sa	19 38 51	25 06 57	1♓01 04	7♓16 11	1 28.8	2 29.9	24 44.2	20 11.2	25 55.7	11 46.8	28 29.0	22 26.2	21 00.5	27 29.2
16 Su	19 42 47	26 08 04	13 27 12	19 34 26	1 20.8	4 11.3	25 59.7	20 57.5	26 07.5	11 54.1	28 35.5	22 29.7	21 02.8	27 30.7
17 M	19 46 44	27 09 10	25 38 14	1♈39 03	1 15.0	5 53.0	27 15.1	21 43.8	26 19.6	12 01.4	28 42.1	22 33.3	21 05.1	27 32.2
18 Tu	19 50 40	28 10 16	7♈37 24	13 33 51	1 11.4	7 34.8	28 30.6	22 30.2	26 32.0	12 08.4	28 48.6	22 36.8	21 07.3	27 33.7
19 W	19 54 37	29 11 20	19 28 59	25 23 27	1D 10.0	9 16.8	29 46.0	23 16.6	26 44.7	12 15.4	28 55.3	22 40.4	21 09.6	27 35.1
20 Th	19 58 33	0♒12 24	1♉17 55	7♉13 04	1 10.2	10 58.7	1♒01.4	24 03.0	26 57.6	12 22.2	29 02.0	22 43.9	21 11.9	27 36.4
21 F	20 02 30	1 13 27	13 09 34	19 08 07	1R 11.0	12 40.5	2 16.8	24 49.4	27 10.7	12 28.8	29 08.7	22 47.4	21 14.1	27 37.8
22 Sa	20 06 26	2 14 30	25 09 23	1♊13 58	1 11.5	14 22.0	3 32.2	25 35.9	27 24.1	12 35.3	29 15.4	22 51.0	21 16.4	27 39.1
23 Su	20 10 23	3 15 31	7♊22 29	13 35 29	1 10.7	16 03.1	4 47.6	26 22.4	27 37.7	12 41.7	29 22.2	22 54.5	21 18.6	27 40.4
24 M	20 14 20	4 16 31	19 53 24	26 16 39	1 07.7	17 43.6	6 03.0	27 09.0	27 51.5	12 47.9	29 29.0	22 58.0	21 20.8	27 41.7
25 Tu	20 18 16	5 17 30	2♋45 29	9♋20 05	1 02.1	19 23.1	7 18.4	27 55.5	28 05.6	12 54.0	29 35.9	23 01.5	21 23.1	27 42.9
26 W	20 22 13	6 18 29	16 00 28	22 46 33	0 54.0	21 01.5	8 33.8	28 42.1	28 19.9	12 59.9	29 42.8	23 05.0	21 25.3	27 44.1
27 Th	20 26 09	7 19 26	29 38 05	6♌34 42	0 43.8	22 38.4	9 49.1	29 28.7	28 34.4	13 05.6	29 49.7	23 08.5	21 27.5	27 45.3
28 F	20 30 06	8 20 23	13♌35 52	20 40 58	0 32.5	24 13.4	11 04.5	0♒15.4	28 49.1	13 11.2	29 56.6	23 11.9	21 29.7	27 46.4
29 Sa	20 34 02	9 21 18	27 49 18	5♍00 05	0 21.4	25 46.1	12 19.8	1 02.0	29 04.1	13 16.6	0♓03.6	23 15.4	21 31.9	27 47.5
30 Su	20 37 59	10 22 13	12♍12 31	19 25 51	0 11.7	27 16.0	13 35.1	1 48.7	29 19.2	13 21.9	0 10.6	23 18.8	21 34.1	27 48.5
31 M	20 41 55	11 23 07	26 39 17	3♎52 11	0 04.3	28 42.6	14 50.4	2 35.5	29 34.6	13 27.0	0 17.6	23 22.3	21 36.3	27 49.6

LONGITUDE February 1994

Day	Sid.Time	☉	0 hr ☽	Noon ☽	True ☊	☿	♀	♂	⚳	♃	♄	♅	♆	♇
1 Tu	20 45 52	12♒24 00	11♎03 56	18♎14 03	29♏59.6	0♓05.2	16♒05.7	3♒22.2	29♈50.2	13♏32.0	0♓24.6	23♑25.7	21♑38.4	27♏50.6
2 W	20 49 49	13 24 52	25 22 11	2♏28 02	29D 57.4	1 23.1	17 21.0	4 09.0	0♉05.9	13 36.8	0 31.7	23 29.1	21 40.6	27 51.5
3 Th	20 53 45	14 25 44	9♏31 25	16 32 16	29R 57.1	2 35.7	18 36.3	4 55.8	0 21.9	13 41.4	0 38.8	23 32.5	21 42.7	27 52.5
4 F	20 57 42	15 26 35	23 30 33	0♐26 15	29 57.2	3 42.2	19 51.6	5 42.6	0 38.1	13 45.9	0 45.9	23 35.9	21 44.9	27 53.4
5 Sa	21 01 38	16 27 25	7♐19 27	14 10 10	29 56.6	4 41.8	21 06.9	6 29.5	0 54.4	13 50.1	0 53.0	23 39.2	21 47.0	27 54.2
6 Su	21 05 35	17 28 14	20 58 27	27 44 20	29 53.9	5 33.8	22 22.2	7 16.4	1 11.0	13 54.3	1 00.2	23 42.6	21 49.1	27 55.1
7 M	21 09 31	18 29 02	4♑27 48	11♑08 49	29 48.4	6 17.3	23 37.4	8 03.3	1 27.7	13 58.2	1 07.4	23 45.9	21 51.2	27 55.9
8 Tu	21 13 28	19 29 50	17 47 20	24 23 14	29 39.8	6 51.7	24 52.7	8 50.2	1 44.6	14 02.0	1 14.6	23 49.2	21 53.3	27 56.6
9 W	21 17 25	20 30 36	0♒56 23	7♒26 40	29 28.4	7 16.4	26 07.9	9 37.2	2 01.7	14 05.6	1 21.8	23 52.5	21 55.3	27 57.3
10 Th	21 21 21	21 31 20	13 53 57	20 18 05	29 15.0	7R 30.8	27 23.1	10 24.1	2 19.0	14 09.0	1 29.0	23 55.7	21 57.4	27 58.0
11 F	21 25 18	22 32 04	26 38 59	2♓56 35	29 00.7	7 34.5	28 38.3	11 11.1	2 36.5	14 12.2	1 36.2	23 59.0	21 59.4	27 58.7
12 Sa	21 29 14	23 32 46	9♓10 51	15 21 48	28 46.9	7 27.6	29 53.5	11 58.1	2 54.1	14 15.3	1 43.5	24 02.2	22 01.4	27 59.3
13 Su	21 33 11	24 33 26	21 29 34	27 34 18	28 34.8	7 10.1	1♓08.7	12 45.1	3 11.9	14 18.2	1 50.7	24 05.4	22 03.4	27 59.9
14 M	21 37 07	25 34 05	3♈36 14	9♈35 39	28 25.1	6 42.3	2 23.8	13 32.1	3 29.8	14 20.9	1 58.0	24 08.5	22 05.4	28 00.4
15 Tu	21 41 04	26 34 42	15 32 57	21 28 33	28 18.4	6 04.9	3 39.0	14 19.2	3 47.9	14 23.4	2 05.3	24 11.7	22 07.4	28 00.9
16 W	21 45 00	27 35 18	27 22 58	3♉16 42	28 14.4	5 18.9	4 54.1	15 06.2	4 06.2	14 25.7	2 12.5	24 14.8	22 09.3	28 01.4
17 Th	21 48 57	28 35 52	9♉10 24	15 04 40	28 12.8	4 25.5	6 09.2	15 53.3	4 24.6	14 27.9	2 19.8	24 17.9	22 11.2	28 01.9
18 F	21 52 53	29 36 24	21 00 12	26 57 39	28 12.5	3 26.2	7 24.3	16 40.4	4 43.2	14 29.9	2 27.1	24 21.0	22 13.2	28 02.3
19 Sa	21 56 50	0♓36 54	2♊57 46	9♊01 13	28 12.3	2 22.5	8 39.4	17 27.4	5 01.9	14 31.7	2 34.4	24 24.0	22 15.0	28 02.6
20 Su	22 00 47	1 37 23	15 08 43	21 20 55	28 11.3	1 16.2	9 54.4	18 14.5	5 20.8	14 33.3	2 41.7	24 27.1	22 16.9	28 03.0
21 M	22 04 43	2 37 50	27 38 26	4♋01 50	28 08.2	0 09.1	11 09.4	19 01.7	5 39.8	14 34.7	2 49.0	24 30.0	22 18.8	28 03.3
22 Tu	22 08 40	3 38 14	10♋31 34	17 07 59	28 02.6	29♒02.8	12 24.4	19 48.8	5 59.0	14 35.9	2 56.3	24 33.0	22 20.6	28 03.5
23 W	22 12 36	4 38 37	23 51 18	0♌41 34	27 54.3	27 58.8	13 39.4	20 35.9	6 18.3	14 37.0	3 03.6	24 35.9	22 22.4	28 03.8
24 Th	22 16 33	5 38 59	7♌38 41	14 42 19	27 43.8	26 58.6	14 54.4	21 23.0	6 37.7	14 37.8	3 10.9	24 38.8	22 24.2	28 04.0
25 F	22 20 29	6 39 18	21 52 00	29 07 02	27 32.0	26 03.3	16 09.3	22 10.2	6 57.2	14 38.5	3 18.2	24 41.7	22 26.0	28 04.1
26 Sa	22 24 26	7 39 35	6♍26 34	13♍49 36	27 20.2	25 13.7	17 24.2	22 57.3	7 16.9	14 39.0	3 25.5	24 44.6	22 27.7	28 04.2
27 Su	22 28 22	8 39 51	21 15 04	28 41 50	27 09.7	24 30.5	18 39.1	23 44.5	7 36.7	14 39.3	3 32.7	24 47.4	22 29.4	28 04.3
28 M	22 32 19	9 40 05	6♎08 47	13♎34 50	27 01.6	23 54.2	19 54.0	24 31.6	7 56.7	14R 39.4	3 40.0	24 50.1	22 31.1	28R 04.4

Astro Data	Dy Hr Mn
♄□♇	2 3:11
☽0S	3 3:49
☽0N	16 10:12
☽0S	30 11:06
☿R	11 8:29
☽0N	12 19:16
☽0S	26 20:38
♃R	28 13:50

Planet Ingress		Dy Hr Mn
☿	♒	14 0:25
♀	♒	19 16:28
☉	♒	20 7:07
♂	♒	28 4:05
♄	♓	28 23:43
☊	♏R	1 9:14
☿	♓	1 10:28
⚳	♉	2 2:59
♀	♓	12 14:04
☉	♓	18 21:22
☿	♒R	21 15:15

Last Aspect Dy Hr Mn			☽ Ingress	Dy Hr Mn
1 15:14	♇	□	♍	1 20:15
3 18:41	♇	⚹	♎	3 23:31
5 22:12	♄	△	♏	6 2:29
8 1:38	♄	□	♐	8 5:34
10 5:39	♄	⚹	♑	10 9:16
12 9:44	♇	⚹	♒	12 14:25
14 19:02	♄	☌	♓	14 22:04
17 3:46	♇	△	♈	17 8:42
19 20:27	☉	□	♉	19 21:22
22 8:04	♄	□	♊	22 9:35
24 18:01	♄	△	♋	24 18:55
26 23:00	♂	☍	♌	27 0:38
28 23:56	♇	□	♍	29 3:39
31 1:56	♇	⚹	♎	31 5:34

Last Aspect Dy Hr Mn			☽ Ingress	Dy Hr Mn
1 20:46	♅	□	♏	2 7:49
4 7:34	♇	☌	♐	4 11:14
6 1:30	♀	⚹	♑	6 16:02
8 18:31	♇	⚹	♒	8 22:16
11 2:52	♀	☌	♓	11 6:22
13 12:51	♇	△	♈	13 16:49
15 23:20	☉	⚹	♉	16 5:20
18 17:47	☉	□	♊	18 18:05
20 5:36	♂	△	♋	21 4:27
23 7:24	♇	△	♌	23 10:48
25 10:16	♇	□	♍	25 13:27
27 11:00	♇	⚹	♎	27 14:06

☽ Phases & Eclipses Dy Hr Mn	
5 0:01	☾ 14♎25
11 23:10	● 21♑31
19 20:27	☽ 29♈33
27 13:23	○ 7♌23
3 8:06	☾ 14♏16
10 14:30	● 21♒38
18 17:47	☽ 29♉51
26 1:15	○ 7♍13

Astro Data

1 January 1994
Julian Day # 34334
SVP 5♓20'21"
GC 26♐45.3 ⚵ 3♓58.0
Eris 17♈11.3R ⚶ 26♎44.0
⚷ 9♍13.0R ⚴ 17♓02.3
☽ Mean ☊ 1♐04.2

1 February 1994
Julian Day # 34365
SVP 5♓20'16"
GC 26♐45.4 ⚵ 13♓14.7
Eris 17♈15.5 ⚶ 1♏58.5
⚷ 7♍52.6R ⚴ 29♓33.5
☽ Mean ☊ 29♏25.7

March 1994 LONGITUDE

Day	Sid.Time	☉	0 hr ☽	Noon☽	True☊	☿	♀	♂	⚳	♃	♄	♅	♆	♇
1 Tu	22 36 16	10♓40 18	20♎59 01	28♎20 30	26♏56.3	23♒24.9	21♓08.9	25♒18.8	8♉16.8	14♏39.3	3♓47.3	24♑52.9	22♑32.8	28♏04.4
2 W	22 40 12	11 40 29	5♏38 35	12♏52 44	26D 53.7	23R 02.7	22 23.7	26 06.0	8 36.9	14R 39.0	3 54.5	24 55.6	22 34.5	28R 04.4
3 Th	22 44 09	12 40 39	20 02 36	27 07 56	26 53.1	22 47.6	23 38.5	26 53.1	8 57.3	14 38.6	4 01.8	24 58.3	22 36.1	28 04.3
4 F	22 48 05	13 40 47	4♐08 40	11♐04 48	26R 53.3	22D 39.3	24 53.3	27 40.3	9 17.7	14 37.9	4 09.0	25 00.9	22 37.7	28 04.2
5 Sa	22 52 02	14 40 54	17 56 27	24 43 47	26 53.0	22 37.8	26 08.1	28 27.5	9 38.2	14 37.1	4 16.3	25 03.5	22 39.3	28 04.1
6 Su	22 55 58	15 40 59	1♑26 59	8♑06 18	26 50.9	22 42.5	27 22.9	29 14.7	9 58.9	14 36.1	4 23.5	25 06.1	22 40.9	28 03.9
7 M	22 59 55	16 41 03	14 41 56	21 14 07	26 46.4	22 53.3	28 37.6	0♓01.9	10 19.7	14 34.9	4 30.7	25 08.7	22 42.4	28 03.8
8 Tu	23 03 51	17 41 05	27 43 03	4♒08 55	26 39.0	23 09.9	29 52.3	0 49.1	10 40.6	14 33.5	4 37.9	25 11.2	22 43.9	28 03.5
9 W	23 07 48	18 41 05	10♒31 50	16 51 56	26 29.1	23 31.7	1♈07.0	1 36.3	11 01.5	14 31.9	4 45.0	25 13.6	22 45.4	28 03.3
10 Th	23 11 45	19 41 03	23 09 19	29 24 04	26 17.3	23 58.6	2 21.7	2 23.5	11 22.6	14 30.1	4 52.2	25 16.1	22 46.8	28 03.0
11 F	23 15 41	20 41 00	5♓36 15	11♓45 56	26 04.7	24 30.2	3 36.4	3 10.7	11 43.9	14 28.1	4 59.3	25 18.5	22 48.3	28 02.6
12 Sa	23 19 38	21 40 55	17 53 10	23 58 03	25 52.4	25 06.2	4 51.0	3 57.9	12 05.2	14 26.0	5 06.4	25 20.8	22 49.7	28 02.3
13 Su	23 23 34	22 40 47	0♈00 41	6♈01 14	25 41.6	25 46.4	6 05.6	4 45.1	12 26.6	14 23.7	5 13.5	25 23.1	22 51.0	28 01.9
14 M	23 27 31	23 40 38	11 59 51	17 56 45	25 32.9	26 30.3	7 20.2	5 32.3	12 48.1	14 21.2	5 20.6	25 25.4	22 52.4	28 01.4
15 Tu	23 31 27	24 40 27	23 52 13	29 46 34	25 26.9	27 17.9	8 34.7	6 19.4	13 09.7	14 18.5	5 27.6	25 27.6	22 53.7	28 00.9
16 W	23 35 24	25 40 14	5♉40 09	11♉33 24	25 23.5	28 08.8	9 49.2	7 06.6	13 31.4	14 15.6	5 34.7	25 29.8	22 55.0	28 00.4
17 Th	23 39 20	26 39 58	17 26 47	23 20 49	25D 22.3	29 02.8	11 03.7	7 53.8	13 53.2	14 12.5	5 41.6	25 32.0	22 56.2	27 59.9
18 F	23 43 17	27 39 40	29 16 04	5♊13 06	25 22.7	29 59.9	12 18.2	8 40.9	14 15.1	14 09.3	5 48.6	25 34.1	22 57.5	27 59.3
19 Sa	23 47 13	28 39 20	11♊12 35	17 15 08	25 23.6	0♓59.7	13 32.6	9 28.0	14 37.0	14 05.9	5 55.6	25 36.1	22 58.7	27 58.8
20 Su	23 51 10	29 38 58	23 21 26	29 32 09	25R 24.2	2 02.1	14 47.0	10 15.2	14 59.1	14 02.4	6 02.5	25 38.2	22 59.8	27 58.1
21 M	23 55 07	0♈38 34	5♋47 54	12♋09 20	25 23.4	3 07.0	16 01.4	11 02.3	15 21.2	13 58.6	6 09.4	25 40.1	23 01.0	27 57.5
22 Tu	23 59 03	1 38 07	18 36 59	25 11 20	25 20.7	4 14.3	17 15.7	11 49.4	15 43.5	13 54.7	6 16.2	25 42.1	23 02.1	27 56.8
23 W	0 03 00	2 37 38	1♌52 46	8♌41 32	25 16.0	5 23.8	18 30.0	12 36.5	16 05.8	13 50.6	6 23.0	25 44.0	23 03.2	27 56.1
24 Th	0 06 56	3 37 07	15 37 42	22 41 12	25 09.4	6 35.4	19 44.3	13 23.6	16 28.1	13 46.4	6 29.8	25 45.8	23 04.2	27 55.3
25 F	0 10 53	4 36 33	29 51 43	7♍08 45	25 01.7	7 49.1	20 58.6	14 10.6	16 50.6	13 42.0	6 36.6	25 47.6	23 05.3	27 54.5
26 Sa	0 14 49	5 35 57	14♍31 36	21 59 21	24 53.8	9 04.7	22 12.8	14 57.7	17 13.1	13 37.5	6 43.3	25 49.4	23 06.2	27 53.7
27 Su	0 18 46	6 35 19	29 30 56	7♎05 08	24 46.7	10 22.2	23 26.9	15 44.7	17 35.8	13 32.8	6 49.9	25 51.1	23 07.2	27 52.9
28 M	0 22 42	7 34 39	14♎40 41	22 16 18	24 41.3	11 41.6	24 41.1	16 31.7	17 58.4	13 27.9	6 56.6	25 52.8	23 08.1	27 52.0
29 Tu	0 26 39	8 33 57	29 50 42	7♏22 44	24 38.0	13 02.7	25 55.2	17 18.7	18 21.2	13 22.9	7 03.2	25 54.4	23 09.0	27 51.1
30 W	0 30 36	9 33 14	14♏51 22	22 15 44	24D 36.8	14 25.5	27 09.3	18 05.7	18 44.0	13 17.7	7 09.8	25 56.0	23 09.9	27 50.2
31 Th	0 34 32	10 32 28	29 35 08	6♐49 03	24 37.2	15 50.0	28 23.3	18 52.7	19 06.9	13 12.4	7 16.3	25 57.5	23 10.7	27 49.2

April 1994 LONGITUDE

Day	Sid.Time	☉	0 hr ☽	Noon☽	True☊	☿	♀	♂	⚳	♃	♄	♅	♆	♇
1 F	0 38 29	11♈31 41	13♐57 10	20♐59 19	24♏38.5	17♓16.1	29♈37.4	19♓39.7	19♉29.9	13♏07.0	7♓22.8	25♑59.0	23♑11.5	27♏48.2
2 Sa	0 42 25	12 30 52	27 55 28	4♑45 43	24R 39.6	18 43.9	0♉51.4	20 26.6	19 53.0	13R 01.4	7 29.2	26 00.4	23 12.3	27R 47.2
3 Su	0 46 22	13 30 01	11♑30 15	18 09 20	24 39.8	20 13.2	2 05.3	21 13.5	20 16.1	12 55.7	7 35.6	26 01.8	23 13.0	27 46.2
4 M	0 50 18	14 29 09	24 43 16	1♒12 25	24 38.4	21 44.1	3 19.3	22 00.4	20 39.2	12 49.9	7 42.0	26 03.1	23 13.8	27 45.1
5 Tu	0 54 15	15 28 14	7♒37 07	13 57 45	24 35.2	23 16.5	4 33.2	22 47.3	21 02.5	12 43.9	7 48.3	26 04.4	23 14.4	27 44.0
6 W	0 58 11	16 27 18	20 14 40	26 28 13	24 30.3	24 50.4	5 47.1	23 34.2	21 25.8	12 37.8	7 54.6	26 05.7	23 15.1	27 42.9
7 Th	1 02 08	17 26 20	2♓38 42	8♓46 26	24 24.2	26 25.9	7 00.9	24 21.0	21 49.2	12 31.6	8 00.8	26 06.9	23 15.7	27 41.8
8 F	1 06 05	18 25 20	14 51 41	20 54 44	24 17.5	28 02.9	8 14.7	25 07.9	22 12.6	12 25.2	8 06.9	26 08.0	23 16.3	27 40.6
9 Sa	1 10 01	19 24 19	26 55 49	2♈55 10	24 11.0	29 41.4	9 28.5	25 54.7	22 36.1	12 18.8	8 13.0	26 09.1	23 16.8	27 39.4
10 Su	1 13 58	20 23 15	8♈53 00	14 49 31	24 05.2	1♈21.4	10 42.2	26 41.4	22 59.6	12 12.2	8 19.1	26 10.2	23 17.3	27 38.2
11 M	1 17 54	21 22 09	20 44 59	26 39 35	24 00.8	3 02.9	11 55.9	27 28.2	23 23.2	12 05.6	8 25.1	26 11.2	23 17.8	27 37.0
12 Tu	1 21 51	22 21 02	2♉33 35	8♉27 16	23 58.0	4 46.0	13 09.6	28 14.9	23 46.9	11 58.8	8 31.1	26 12.1	23 18.2	27 35.7
13 W	1 25 47	23 19 52	14 20 53	20 14 46	23D 56.8	6 30.5	14 23.3	29 01.6	24 10.6	11 52.0	8 37.0	26 13.0	23 18.6	27 34.4
14 Th	1 29 44	24 18 40	26 09 15	2♊04 44	23 57.0	8 16.7	15 36.9	29 48.3	24 34.4	11 45.0	8 42.8	26 13.9	23 19.0	27 33.1
15 F	1 33 40	25 17 26	8♊01 38	14 00 22	23 58.3	10 04.4	16 50.4	0♈34.9	24 58.2	11 38.0	8 48.6	26 14.7	23 19.4	27 31.8
16 Sa	1 37 37	26 16 10	20 01 25	26 05 18	24 00.0	11 53.6	18 04.0	1 21.5	25 22.1	11 30.9	8 54.4	26 15.4	23 19.7	27 30.5
17 Su	1 41 34	27 14 52	2♋12 32	8♋23 39	24 01.6	13 44.4	19 17.5	2 08.1	25 46.0	11 23.8	9 00.1	26 16.1	23 20.0	27 29.1
18 M	1 45 30	28 13 32	14 39 12	20 59 43	24R 02.7	15 36.8	20 30.9	2 54.7	26 09.9	11 16.5	9 05.7	26 16.8	23 20.2	27 27.7
19 Tu	1 49 27	29 12 09	27 25 42	3♌57 37	24 02.8	17 30.7	21 44.3	3 41.2	26 34.0	11 09.2	9 11.2	26 17.4	23 20.4	27 26.3
20 W	1 53 23	0♉10 44	10♌35 54	17 20 51	24 01.8	19 26.2	22 57.7	4 27.6	26 58.0	11 01.9	9 16.7	26 17.9	23 20.6	27 24.9
21 Th	1 57 20	1 09 17	24 12 41	1♍11 29	23 59.8	21 23.3	24 11.0	5 14.1	27 22.1	10 54.5	9 22.2	26 18.4	23 20.7	27 23.5
22 F	2 01 16	2 07 48	8♍17 12	15 29 34	23 57.2	23 21.9	25 24.3	6 00.5	27 46.3	10 47.0	9 27.6	26 18.9	23 20.9	27 22.0
23 Sa	2 05 13	3 06 16	22 48 09	0♎12 20	23 54.4	25 22.1	26 37.6	6 46.9	28 10.4	10 39.5	9 32.9	26 19.3	23 20.9	27 20.6
24 Su	2 09 09	4 04 43	7♎41 19	15 14 07	23 51.8	27 23.7	27 50.8	7 33.2	28 34.7	10 32.0	9 38.1	26 19.6	23R 21.0	27 19.1
25 M	2 13 06	5 03 07	22 49 37	0♏26 38	23 50.0	29 26.7	29 03.9	8 19.5	28 58.9	10 24.4	9 43.3	26 19.9	23 21.0	27 17.6
26 Tu	2 17 02	6 01 30	8♏03 53	15 40 08	23D 49.0	1♉31.1	0♊17.1	9 05.8	29 23.3	10 16.8	9 48.4	26 20.1	23 21.0	27 16.1
27 W	2 20 59	6 59 51	23 14 10	0♐44 52	23 49.0	3 36.7	1 30.2	9 52.0	29 47.6	10 09.2	9 53.5	26 20.3	23 20.9	27 14.6
28 Th	2 24 56	7 58 10	8♐11 15	15 32 30	23 49.7	5 43.4	2 43.2	10 38.2	0♊12.0	10 01.5	9 58.4	26 20.5	23 20.8	27 13.0
29 F	2 28 52	8 56 28	22 47 59	29 57 13	23 50.7	7 51.1	3 56.2	11 24.4	0 36.4	9 53.9	10 03.4	26 20.6	23 20.7	27 11.5
30 Sa	2 32 49	9 54 44	6♑59 55	13♑55 57	23 51.9	9 59.6	5 09.2	12 10.6	1 00.9	9 46.2	10 08.2	26R 20.6	23 20.6	27 09.9

Astro Data	Planet Ingress	Last Aspect	☽ Ingress	Last Aspect	☽ Ingress	☽ Phases & Eclipses	Astro Data
Dy Hr Mn	Dy Hr Mn	Dy Hr Mn	Dy Hr Mn	Dy Hr Mn	Dy Hr Mn	Dy Hr Mn	1 March 1994
♇R 1 10:01	♂ ♓ 7 11:01	1 6:46 ♂ △	♏ 1 14:43	1 9:35 ♂ □	♑ 2 3:37	4 16:53 ☾ 13♐53	Julian Day # 34393
☿D 5 5:48	♀ ♈ 8 14:28	3 13:36 ♇ ☌	♐ 3 16:54	4 5:36 ♇ ✱	♒ 4 9:45	12 7:05 ● 21♓29	SVP 5♓20'13"
♀0N 10 21:16	☿ ♓ 18 12:04	5 19:03 ♂ ✱	♑ 5 21:24	6 14:24 ♇ □	♓ 6 18:51	20 12:14 ☽ 29♊40	GC 26♐45.5 ⚴ 22♓40.7
☽0N 12 2:37	⊙ ♈ 20 20:28	8 3:09 ♀ ✱	♒ 8 4:15	9 4:29 ☿ ☌	♈ 9 6:09	27 11:10 ○ 6♎33	Eris 17♈27.4 ⚵ 2♏30.8R
⊙0N 20 20:29		10 9:24 ♇ □	♓ 10 13:09	11 11:02 ♅ □	♉ 11 18:48		⚷ 5♍46.9R ⚶ 11♈44.9
☽0S 26 7:24	♀ ♉ 1 19:20	12 20:04 ♇ △	♈ 12 23:59	14 7:05 ♂ ✱	♊ 14 7:48	3 2:55 ☾ 13♑08	☽ Mean ☊ 27♏56.7
	☿ ♈ 9 16:30	15 6:35 ☿ ✱	♉ 15 12:27	16 12:23 ⊙ ✱	♋ 16 19:41	11 0:17 ● 20♈53	
☽0N 8 8:18	♂ ♈ 14 18:02	18 0:33 ☿ □	♊ 18 1:29	19 2:34 ⊙ □	♌ 19 4:45	19 2:34 ☽ 28♋49	1 April 1994
♄∠♆ 10 4:12	⊙ ♉ 20 7:36	20 12:14 ⊙ □	♋ 20 12:54	21 5:30 ♇ □	♍ 21 9:58	25 19:45 ○ 5♏22	Julian Day # 34424
☿0N 12 20:26	☿ ♉ 25 18:27	22 16:58 ♇ △	♌ 22 20:39	23 7:23 ♇ ✱	♎ 23 11:40		SVP 5♓20'10"
♂0N 17 20:26	♀ ♊ 26 6:24	24 20:46 ♇ □	♍ 25 0:14	25 10:11 ☿ ☍	♏ 25 11:18		GC 26♐45.5 ⚴ 3♈44.2
☽0S 22 17:38	⚳ ♊ 28 0:12	26 21:25 ♇ ✱	♎ 27 0:46	27 6:24 ♇ ☌	♐ 27 10:48		Eris 17♈46.4 ⚵ 27♎55.6R
♆R 25 10:37		28 17:43 ♅ □	♏ 29 0:15	28 3:32 ♂ △	♑ 29 12:05		⚷ 3♍40.0R ⚶ 25♈39.4
♃△♄ 28 17:56		30 21:07 ♇ ☌	♐ 31 0:41				☽ Mean ☊ 26♏18.2
♅R 30 22:18							

LONGITUDE — May 1994

Day	Sid.Time	☉	0 hr ☽	Noon ☽	True☊	☿	♀	♂	⚳	♃	♄	♅	♆	♇
1 Su	2 36 45	10♉52 59	20♑45 19	27♑28 10	23♏52.7	12♉08.7	6♊22.1	12♈56.7	1♊25.4	9♏38.6	10♓13.0	26♑20.6	23♑20.4	27♏08.4
2 M	2 40 42	11 51 12	4♒04 45	10♒35 24	23R53.0	14 18.3	7 35.0	13 42.7	1 49.9	9R30.9	10 17.7	26R20.6	23R20.2	27R06.8
3 Tu	2 44 38	12 49 24	17 00 29	23 20 28	23 52.8	16 27.9	8 47.8	14 28.8	2 14.5	9 23.3	10 22.3	26 20.5	23 20.0	27 05.2
4 W	2 48 35	13 47 34	29 35 47	5♓46 57	23 52.1	18 37.4	10 00.6	15 14.7	2 39.1	9 15.7	10 26.9	26 20.3	23 19.7	27 03.6
5 Th	2 52 31	14 45 42	11♓54 25	17 58 41	23 51.1	20 46.6	11 13.4	16 00.7	3 03.8	9 08.1	10 31.3	26 20.1	23 19.4	27 02.0
6 F	2 56 28	15 43 50	24 00 12	29 59 26	23 50.0	22 55.0	12 26.1	16 46.6	3 28.4	9 00.5	10 35.7	26 19.8	23 19.0	27 00.4
7 Sa	3 00 25	16 41 55	5♈56 48	11♈52 42	23 48.9	25 02.4	13 38.8	17 32.5	3 53.1	8 52.9	10 40.1	26 19.5	23 18.7	26 58.7
8 Su	3 04 21	17 40 00	17 47 32	23 41 39	23 48.1	27 08.5	14 51.5	18 18.3	4 17.9	8 45.4	10 44.3	26 19.2	23 18.2	26 57.1
9 M	3 08 18	18 38 02	29 35 22	5♉29 01	23 47.5	29 13.1	16 04.1	19 04.1	4 42.6	8 37.9	10 48.5	26 18.8	23 17.8	26 55.5
10 Tu	3 12 14	19 36 04	11♉22 53	17 17 17	23D47.2	1♊15.8	17 16.6	19 49.8	5 07.4	8 30.5	10 52.6	26 18.3	23 17.3	26 53.8
11 W	3 16 11	20 34 03	23 12 28	29 08 44	23 47.2	3 16.4	18 29.2	20 35.5	5 32.3	8 23.1	10 56.6	26 17.8	23 16.9	26 52.2
12 Th	3 20 07	21 32 01	5♊06 19	11♊05 31	23 47.4	5 14.7	19 41.6	21 21.2	5 57.1	8 15.8	11 00.5	26 17.3	23 16.3	26 50.5
13 F	3 24 04	22 29 58	17 06 37	23 09 54	23 47.5	7 10.5	20 54.1	22 06.8	6 22.0	8 08.5	11 04.4	26 16.7	23 15.8	26 48.8
14 Sa	3 28 00	23 27 53	29 15 39	5♋24 12	23R47.6	9 03.6	22 06.4	22 52.3	6 46.9	8 01.3	11 08.1	26 16.0	23 15.2	26 47.2
15 Su	3 31 57	24 25 46	11♋35 53	17 51 00	23 47.6	10 53.9	23 18.8	23 37.8	7 11.9	7 54.2	11 11.8	26 15.4	23 14.6	26 45.5
16 M	3 35 54	25 23 38	24 09 56	0♌33 00	23 47.5	12 41.2	24 31.1	24 23.3	7 36.8	7 47.2	11 15.4	26 14.6	23 13.9	26 43.9
17 Tu	3 39 50	26 21 27	7♌00 33	13 32 54	23 47.4	14 25.5	25 43.3	25 08.7	8 01.8	7 40.2	11 18.9	26 13.8	23 13.3	26 42.2
18 W	3 43 47	27 19 15	20 10 21	26 53 09	23D47.3	16 06.6	26 55.5	25 54.0	8 26.8	7 33.3	11 22.4	26 13.0	23 12.5	26 40.5
19 Th	3 47 43	28 17 02	3♍41 30	10♍35 32	23 47.4	17 44.5	28 07.6	26 39.4	8 51.8	7 26.5	11 25.7	26 12.1	23 11.8	26 38.9
20 F	3 51 40	29 14 46	17 35 17	24 40 41	23 47.7	19 19.1	29 19.7	27 24.6	9 16.8	7 19.9	11 28.9	26 11.2	23 11.1	26 37.2
21 Sa	3 55 36	0♊12 29	1♎51 32	9♎07 30	23 48.2	20 50.4	0♋31.7	28 09.8	9 41.9	7 13.3	11 32.1	26 10.2	23 10.3	26 35.5
22 Su	3 59 33	1 10 10	16 28 06	23 52 44	23 48.8	22 18.3	1 43.7	28 55.0	10 07.0	7 06.8	11 35.2	26 09.2	23 09.4	26 33.9
23 M	4 03 29	2 07 50	1♏20 38	8♏50 56	23R49.3	23 42.8	2 55.6	29 40.1	10 32.1	7 00.4	11 38.2	26 08.2	23 08.6	26 32.2
24 Tu	4 07 26	3 05 29	16 22 37	23 54 38	23 49.5	25 03.8	4 07.4	0♉25.1	10 57.2	6 54.1	11 41.1	26 07.1	23 07.7	26 30.6
25 W	4 11 23	4 03 06	1♐25 54	8♐55 20	23 49.2	26 21.3	5 19.2	1 10.1	11 22.3	6 48.0	11 43.9	26 05.9	23 06.8	26 28.9
26 Th	4 15 19	5 00 42	16 21 51	23 44 32	23 48.4	27 35.3	6 31.0	1 55.1	11 47.5	6 42.0	11 46.6	26 04.7	23 05.9	26 27.3
27 F	4 19 16	5 58 17	1♑02 29	8♑15 00	23 47.2	28 45.6	7 42.7	2 40.0	12 12.6	6 36.0	11 49.3	26 03.5	23 05.0	26 25.6
28 Sa	4 23 12	6 55 51	15 21 31	22 21 39	23 45.6	29 52.3	8 54.3	3 24.9	12 37.8	6 30.3	11 51.8	26 02.3	23 04.0	26 24.0
29 Su	4 27 09	7 53 24	29 15 08	6♒01 55	23 44.0	0♋55.2	10 05.9	4 09.7	13 03.0	6 24.6	11 54.3	26 00.9	23 03.0	26 22.4
30 M	4 31 05	8 50 56	12♒42 02	19 15 42	23 42.7	1 54.4	11 17.4	4 54.4	13 28.2	6 19.1	11 56.6	25 59.6	23 02.0	26 20.8
31 Tu	4 35 02	9 48 28	25 43 11	2♓04 54	23D41.8	2 49.6	12 28.9	5 39.1	13 53.4	6 13.7	11 58.9	25 58.2	23 00.9	26 19.1

LONGITUDE — June 1994

Day	Sid.Time	☉	0 hr ☽	Noon ☽	True☊	☿	♀	♂	⚳	♃	♄	♅	♆	♇
1 W	4 38 59	10♊45 58	8♓21 17	14♓32 52	23♏41.7	3♋41.0	13♋40.3	6♉23.8	14♊18.7	6♏08.4	12♓01.1	25♑56.8	22♑59.9	26♏17.5
2 Th	4 42 55	11 43 28	20 40 12	26 43 50	23 42.3	4 28.3	14 51.6	7 08.4	14 43.9	6R03.3	12 03.1	25R55.3	22R58.8	26R15.9
3 F	4 46 52	12 40 57	2♈44 22	8♈42 23	23 43.5	5 11.6	16 02.9	7 52.9	15 09.2	5 58.3	12 05.1	25 53.8	22 57.6	26 14.4
4 Sa	4 50 48	13 38 25	14 38 27	20 33 07	23 45.0	5 50.7	17 14.1	8 37.4	15 34.5	5 53.5	12 07.0	25 52.3	22 56.5	26 12.8
5 Su	4 54 45	14 35 52	26 26 57	2♉20 25	23 46.6	6 25.5	18 25.3	9 21.8	15 59.8	5 48.8	12 08.8	25 50.7	22 55.3	26 11.2
6 M	4 58 41	15 33 19	8♉14 01	14 08 12	23R47.7	6 56.0	19 36.4	10 06.2	16 25.1	5 44.3	12 10.5	25 49.0	22 54.2	26 09.7
7 Tu	5 02 38	16 30 45	20 03 22	25 59 52	23 48.0	7 22.0	20 47.5	10 50.5	16 50.4	5 39.9	12 12.1	25 47.4	22 53.0	26 08.1
8 W	5 06 34	17 28 10	1♊58 04	7♊58 14	23 47.2	7 43.6	21 58.5	11 34.8	17 15.7	5 35.7	12 13.6	25 45.7	22 51.7	26 06.6
9 Th	5 10 31	18 25 35	14 00 40	20 05 33	23 45.2	8 00.7	23 09.4	12 19.0	17 41.1	5 31.7	12 15.0	25 44.0	22 50.5	26 05.1
10 F	5 14 28	19 22 58	26 13 07	2♋23 31	23 42.2	8 13.2	24 20.3	13 03.2	18 06.4	5 27.8	12 16.3	25 42.2	22 49.2	26 03.6
11 Sa	5 18 24	20 20 21	8♋36 55	14 53 26	23 38.2	8 21.2	25 31.1	13 47.2	18 31.7	5 24.1	12 17.5	25 40.4	22 47.9	26 02.1
12 Su	5 22 21	21 17 43	21 13 10	27 36 13	23 33.9	8R24.5	26 41.8	14 31.3	18 57.1	5 20.5	12 18.6	25 38.6	22 46.6	26 00.7
13 M	5 26 17	22 15 04	4♌02 42	10♌32 42	23 29.6	8 23.4	27 52.5	15 15.2	19 22.5	5 17.1	12 19.6	25 36.8	22 45.3	25 59.2
14 Tu	5 30 14	23 12 24	17 06 17	23 43 32	23 26.1	8 17.8	29 03.0	15 59.1	19 47.8	5 13.9	12 20.5	25 34.9	22 44.0	25 57.8
15 W	5 34 10	24 09 43	0♍24 33	7♍09 23	23 23.6	8 07.8	0♌13.6	16 43.0	20 13.2	5 10.9	12 21.3	25 32.9	22 42.6	25 56.3
16 Th	5 38 07	25 07 02	13 58 06	20 50 40	23D22.5	7 53.8	1 24.0	17 26.7	20 38.5	5 08.0	12 22.0	25 31.0	22 41.2	25 54.9
17 F	5 42 03	26 04 19	27 47 18	4♎47 45	23 22.7	7 35.7	2 34.3	18 10.4	21 03.9	5 05.3	12 22.6	25 29.0	22 39.8	25 53.6
18 Sa	5 46 00	27 01 35	11♎52 00	18 59 53	23 23.8	7 14.1	3 44.6	18 54.1	21 29.3	5 02.8	12 23.1	25 27.0	22 38.4	25 52.2
19 Su	5 49 57	27 58 51	26 11 12	3♏25 37	23 25.2	6 49.1	4 54.8	19 37.7	21 54.6	5 00.4	12 23.5	25 25.0	22 37.0	25 50.9
20 M	5 53 53	28 56 06	10♏42 42	18 01 58	23R26.1	6 21.1	6 04.9	20 21.2	22 20.0	4 58.3	12 23.8	25 22.9	22 35.5	25 49.5
21 Tu	5 57 50	29 53 20	25 22 46	2♐44 24	23 25.9	5 50.7	7 14.9	21 04.7	22 45.4	4 56.3	12 24.1	25 20.9	22 34.1	25 48.2
22 W	6 01 46	0♋50 34	10♐06 06	17 27 00	23 24.1	5 18.2	8 24.8	21 48.1	23 10.8	4 54.4	12R24.2	25 18.8	22 32.6	25 46.9
23 Th	6 05 43	1 47 48	24 46 16	2♑03 00	23 20.5	4 44.3	9 34.7	22 31.4	23 36.1	4 52.8	12 24.2	25 16.6	22 31.1	25 45.7
24 F	6 09 39	2 45 01	9♑16 23	16 25 38	23 15.4	4 09.5	10 44.4	23 14.7	24 01.5	4 51.3	12 24.1	25 14.5	22 29.7	25 44.4
25 Sa	6 13 36	3 42 13	23 30 06	0♒29 13	23 09.2	3 34.3	11 54.1	23 57.9	24 26.9	4 50.1	12 23.9	25 12.3	22 28.2	25 43.2
26 Su	6 17 32	4 39 26	7♒22 32	14 09 49	23 02.9	2 59.5	13 03.7	24 41.0	24 52.2	4 49.0	12 23.6	25 10.1	22 26.6	25 42.0
27 M	6 21 29	5 36 38	20 50 53	27 25 46	22 57.0	2 25.6	14 13.2	25 24.1	25 17.6	4 48.0	12 23.3	25 07.9	22 25.1	25 40.8
28 Tu	6 25 26	6 33 50	3♓54 35	10♓17 35	22 52.4	1 53.1	15 22.5	26 07.2	25 43.0	4 47.3	12 22.8	25 05.7	22 23.6	25 39.7
29 W	6 29 22	7 31 02	16 35 09	22 47 42	22 49.5	1 22.7	16 31.8	26 50.1	26 08.3	4 46.7	12 22.2	25 03.5	22 22.0	25 38.6
30 Th	6 33 19	8 28 15	28 55 46	4♈59 54	22D48.2	0 54.8	17 41.0	27 33.0	26 33.7	4 46.3	12 21.5	25 01.2	22 20.5	25 37.5

Astro Data Dy Hr Mn	Planet Ingress Dy Hr Mn	Last Aspect Dy Hr Mn	☽ Ingress Dy Hr Mn	Last Aspect Dy Hr Mn	☽ Ingress Dy Hr Mn	☽ Phases & Eclipses Dy Hr Mn	Astro Data
☽0N 5 13:44	☿ ♊ 9 21:08	1 11:24 ♇ ⚹	♒ 1 16:34	2 11:05 ♇ △	♈ 2 18:31	2 14:32 ☾ 11♒57	1 May 1994
♄∠♅ 16 7:36	♀ ♋ 21 1:26	3 19:09 ♇ □	♓ 4 0:47	4 22:48 ♅ □	♉ 5 7:14	10 17:07 ● 19♉48	Julian Day # 34454
☽0S 20 2:06	☉ ♊ 21 6:48	6 6:01 ♇ △	♈ 6 12:01	7 12:17 ♇ ☍	♊ 7 20:03	10 17:11:25 ● A 06'14"	SVP 5♓20'07"
	♂ ♉ 23 22:37	8 17:20 ♅ □	♉ 9 0:50	9 8:26 ☉ ☌	♋ 10 7:22	18 12:50 ☽ 27♌21	GC 26♐45.6 ⚴ 14♈39.9
☽0N 1 20:29	☿ ♋ 28 14:52	11 7:25 ♇ ☍	♊ 11 13:43	12 10:08 ♀ ☌	♌ 12 16:29	25 3:39 ○ 3♐43	Eris 18♈05.9 ⚵ 21♎12.5R
☿ R 12 17:49		13 9:47 ♂ ⚹	♋ 14 1:27	14 16:01 ♇ □	♍ 14 23:16	25 3:30 ● P 0.243	⚷ 2♍51.0R ⚶ 9♉09.5
☽0S 16 8:52	♀ ♌ 15 7:23	16 4:51 ♇ △	♌ 16 10:58	16 20:46 ♇ ⚹	♎ 17 3:48		☽ Mean ☊ 24♏42.9
♄ R 23 3:57	☉ ♋ 21 14:48	18 12:50 ☉ □	♍ 18 17:31	19 2:21 ☉ △	♏ 19 6:20	1 4:02 ☾ 10♓27	
☽0N 29 5:05		20 20:30 ♀ □	♎ 20 20:54	21 0:43 ♇ ☌	♐ 21 7:32	9 8:26 ● 18♊17	1 June 1994
		22 20:32 ♂ ☍	♏ 22 21:51	22 3:45 ♄ □	♑ 23 8:37	16 19:56 ☽ 25♍26	Julian Day # 34485
		24 16:08 ♇ ☌	♐ 24 21:43	25 3:48 ♇ ⚹	♒ 25 11:10	23 11:33 ○ 1♑47	SVP 5♓20'02"
		26 18:52 ☿ ☍	♑ 26 22:17	27 8:48 ♇ □	♓ 27 16:44	30 19:31 ☾ 8♈46	GC 26♐45.7 ⚴ 25♈50.0
		28 19:00 ♇ ⚹	♒ 29 1:19	29 20:23 ♂ ⚹	♈ 30 2:06		Eris 18♈22.4 ⚵ 17♎13.7R
		31 1:09 ♇ □	♓ 31 8:03				⚷ 3♍42.9 ⚶ 22♉51.6
							☽ Mean ☊ 23♏04.4

July 1994 LONGITUDE

Day	Sid.Time	☉	0 hr ☽	Noon ☽	True ☊	☿	♀	♂	⚳	♃	♄	♅	♆	♇
1 F	6 37 15	9♋25 27	11♈00 42	16♈58 50	22♏48.4	0♋30.0	18♌50.1	28♉15.9	26♊59.0	4♏46.1	12♓20.7	24♑58.9	22♑18.9	25♏36.4
2 Sa	6 41 12	10 22 40	22 54 56	28 49 39	22 49.5	0R 08.7	19 59.1	28 58.6	27 24.4	4D 46.1	12R 19.9	24R 56.6	22R 17.3	25R 35.3
3 Su	6 45 08	11 19 53	4♉43 37	10♉37 29	22 50.8	29♊51.3	21 08.0	29 41.3	27 49.7	4 46.2	12 18.9	24 54.3	22 15.7	25 34.3
4 M	6 49 05	12 17 06	16 31 50	22 27 16	22R 51.4	29 38.1	22 16.8	0♊24.0	28 15.0	4 46.6	12 17.8	24 52.0	22 14.2	25 33.3
5 Tu	6 53 01	13 14 19	28 24 17	4♊23 25	22 50.7	29 29.4	23 25.6	1 06.5	28 40.4	4 47.1	12 16.7	24 49.6	22 12.6	25 32.3
6 W	6 56 58	14 11 32	10♊25 04	16 29 38	22 48.0	29D 25.3	24 34.1	1 49.0	29 05.7	4 47.8	12 15.4	24 47.3	22 11.0	25 31.3
7 Th	7 00 55	15 08 46	22 37 26	28 48 43	22 43.1	29 26.2	25 42.6	2 31.5	29 31.0	4 48.7	12 14.0	24 44.9	22 09.4	25 30.4
8 F	7 04 51	16 06 00	5♋03 41	11♋22 28	22 36.0	29 32.2	26 51.0	3 13.8	29 56.3	4 49.7	12 12.6	24 42.6	22 07.8	25 29.5
9 Sa	7 08 48	17 03 14	17 45 05	24 11 33	22 27.4	29 43.2	27 59.3	3 56.1	0♋21.6	4 51.0	12 11.1	24 40.2	22 06.1	25 28.7
10 Su	7 12 44	18 00 28	0♌41 47	7♌15 41	22 18.0	29 59.5	29 07.4	4 38.4	0 46.9	4 52.4	12 09.4	24 37.8	22 04.5	25 27.8
11 M	7 16 41	18 57 42	13 53 05	20 33 47	22 08.7	0♋20.9	0♍15.4	5 20.5	1 12.2	4 54.0	12 07.7	24 35.4	22 02.9	25 27.0
12 Tu	7 20 37	19 54 56	27 17 35	4♍04 16	22 00.5	0 47.6	1 23.3	6 02.6	1 37.4	4 55.7	12 05.9	24 33.0	22 01.3	25 26.2
13 W	7 24 34	20 52 10	10♍53 37	17 45 26	21 54.3	1 19.6	2 31.1	6 44.6	2 02.6	4 57.7	12 03.9	24 30.6	21 59.7	25 25.5
14 Th	7 28 30	21 49 24	24 39 34	1♎35 49	21 50.4	1 56.8	3 38.8	7 26.5	2 27.9	4 59.8	12 01.9	24 28.2	21 58.0	25 24.7
15 F	7 32 27	22 46 38	8♎34 04	15 34 11	21D 48.7	2 39.1	4 46.3	8 08.4	2 53.1	5 02.1	11 59.8	24 25.8	21 56.4	25 24.0
16 Sa	7 36 24	23 43 52	22 36 04	29 39 35	21 48.6	3 26.6	5 53.6	8 50.2	3 18.3	5 04.6	11 57.6	24 23.4	21 54.8	25 23.4
17 Su	7 40 20	24 41 06	6♏44 38	13♏51 04	21R 49.1	4 19.1	7 00.9	9 31.9	3 43.4	5 07.2	11 55.4	24 21.0	21 53.2	25 22.7
18 M	7 44 17	25 38 21	20 58 41	28 07 14	21 49.1	5 16.7	8 07.9	10 13.5	4 08.6	5 10.0	11 53.0	24 18.6	21 51.5	25 22.1
19 Tu	7 48 13	26 35 35	5♐16 26	12♐25 54	21 47.6	6 19.3	9 14.9	10 55.1	4 33.7	5 13.0	11 50.6	24 16.2	21 49.9	25 21.6
20 W	7 52 10	27 32 50	19 35 11	26 43 48	21 43.6	7 26.7	10 21.6	11 36.6	4 58.9	5 16.2	11 48.0	24 13.8	21 48.3	25 21.0
21 Th	7 56 06	28 30 05	3♑51 11	10♑56 43	21 37.1	8 38.9	11 28.2	12 18.0	5 24.0	5 19.5	11 45.4	24 11.4	21 46.7	25 20.5
22 F	8 00 03	29 27 21	17 59 49	24 59 52	21 28.2	9 55.9	12 34.7	12 59.4	5 49.0	5 23.0	11 42.8	24 09.0	21 45.1	25 20.0
23 Sa	8 03 59	0♌24 37	1♒56 16	8♒48 32	21 17.8	11 17.5	13 41.0	13 40.7	6 14.1	5 26.6	11 40.0	24 06.6	21 43.5	25 19.6
24 Su	8 07 56	1 21 54	15 36 11	22 18 54	21 06.7	12 43.6	14 47.1	14 21.9	6 39.1	5 30.4	11 37.1	24 04.2	21 41.9	25 19.2
25 M	8 11 53	2 19 11	28 56 26	5♓28 39	20 56.2	14 14.0	15 53.1	15 03.0	7 04.2	5 34.4	11 34.2	24 01.8	21 40.3	25 18.8
26 Tu	8 15 49	3 16 29	11♓55 33	18 17 15	20 47.3	15 48.6	16 58.8	15 44.0	7 29.2	5 38.5	11 31.2	23 59.4	21 38.7	25 18.4
27 W	8 19 46	4 13 48	24 33 58	0♈46 01	20 40.6	17 27.3	18 04.4	16 25.0	7 54.1	5 42.8	11 28.1	23 57.1	21 37.1	25 18.1
28 Th	8 23 42	5 11 08	6♈53 48	12 57 49	20 36.4	19 09.7	19 09.8	17 05.9	8 19.1	5 47.3	11 25.0	23 54.7	21 35.6	25 17.8
29 F	8 27 39	6 08 29	18 58 36	24 56 46	20 34.3	20 55.8	20 15.1	17 46.8	8 44.0	5 51.9	11 21.7	23 52.4	21 34.0	25 17.5
30 Sa	8 31 35	7 05 51	0♉52 55	6♉47 45	20D 33.8	22 45.1	21 20.1	18 27.5	9 08.9	5 56.7	11 18.4	23 50.0	21 32.5	25 17.3
31 Su	8 35 32	8 03 14	12 41 56	18 36 09	20R 33.9	24 37.4	22 25.0	19 08.2	9 33.8	6 01.6	11 15.1	23 47.7	21 30.9	25 17.1

August 1994 LONGITUDE

Day	Sid.Time	☉	0 hr ☽	Noon ☽	True ☊	☿	♀	♂	⚳	♃	♄	♅	♆	♇
1 M	8 39 28	9♌00 38	24♉31 05	0♊27 24	20♏33.6	26♋32.5	23♍29.6	19♊48.8	9♋58.6	6♏06.7	11♓11.6	23♑45.4	21♑29.4	25♏17.0
2 Tu	8 43 25	9 58 04	6♊25 45	12 26 44	20R 31.9	28 29.9	24 34.1	20 29.4	10 23.5	6 11.9	11R 08.1	23R 43.1	21R 27.9	25R 16.8
3 W	8 47 22	10 55 30	18 30 54	24 38 46	20 28.0	0♌29.2	25 38.3	21 09.8	10 48.3	6 17.3	11 04.5	23 40.9	21 26.3	25 16.7
4 Th	8 51 18	11 52 58	0♋50 46	7♋07 15	20 21.4	2 30.3	26 42.4	21 50.2	11 13.0	6 22.8	11 00.9	23 38.6	21 24.8	25 16.7
5 F	8 55 15	12 50 26	13 28 28	19 54 36	20 12.3	4 32.6	27 46.2	22 30.5	11 37.8	6 28.5	10 57.2	23 36.4	21 23.4	25D 16.7
6 Sa	8 59 11	13 47 56	26 25 42	3♌01 43	20 01.2	6 35.9	28 49.8	23 10.7	12 02.5	6 34.3	10 53.5	23 34.1	21 21.9	25 16.7
7 Su	9 03 08	14 45 27	9♌42 29	16 27 46	19 49.0	8 39.8	29 53.1	23 50.8	12 27.2	6 40.3	10 49.6	23 31.9	21 20.4	25 16.7
8 M	9 07 04	15 42 58	23 17 12	0♍10 22	19 37.0	10 43.9	0♎56.3	24 30.9	12 51.8	6 46.4	10 45.8	23 29.8	21 19.0	25 16.8
9 Tu	9 11 01	16 40 31	7♍06 46	14 05 54	19 26.3	12 48.1	1 59.1	25 10.8	13 16.4	6 52.7	10 41.8	23 27.6	21 17.5	25 16.9
10 W	9 14 57	17 38 05	21 07 13	28 10 13	19 17.8	14 52.1	3 01.8	25 50.7	13 41.0	6 59.1	10 37.9	23 25.5	21 16.1	25 17.0
11 Th	9 18 54	18 35 39	5♎14 24	12♎19 19	19 12.2	16 55.6	4 04.1	26 30.5	14 05.5	7 05.7	10 33.8	23 23.4	21 14.7	25 17.2
12 F	9 22 51	19 33 15	19 24 36	26 29 55	19 09.3	18 58.5	5 06.2	27 10.2	14 30.0	7 12.4	10 29.8	23 21.3	21 13.3	25 17.4
13 Sa	9 26 47	20 30 51	3♏35 00	10♏39 40	19 08.3	21 00.5	6 08.0	27 49.8	14 54.4	7 19.2	10 25.6	23 19.2	21 12.0	25 17.7
14 Su	9 30 44	21 28 28	17 43 44	24 47 07	19 08.3	23 01.6	7 09.5	28 29.3	15 18.8	7 26.1	10 21.5	23 17.2	21 10.6	25 18.0
15 M	9 34 40	22 26 07	1♐49 40	8♐51 20	19 07.8	25 01.6	8 10.7	29 08.8	15 43.2	7 33.2	10 17.3	23 15.2	21 09.3	25 18.3
16 Tu	9 38 37	23 23 46	15 51 59	22 51 29	19 05.6	27 00.5	9 11.6	29 48.1	16 07.5	7 40.5	10 13.0	23 13.2	21 08.0	25 18.6
17 W	9 42 33	24 21 26	29 49 40	6♑46 21	19 01.0	28 58.1	10 12.2	0♋27.4	16 31.8	7 47.8	10 08.7	23 11.2	21 06.7	25 19.0
18 Th	9 46 30	25 19 08	13♑41 16	20 34 08	18 53.6	0♍54.5	11 12.5	1 06.6	16 56.0	7 55.3	10 04.4	23 09.3	21 05.4	25 19.4
19 F	9 50 26	26 16 50	27 24 40	4♒12 30	18 43.6	2 49.5	12 12.4	1 45.7	17 20.2	8 02.9	10 00.1	23 07.4	21 04.1	25 19.9
20 Sa	9 54 23	27 14 34	10♒57 19	17 38 48	18 31.8	4 43.1	13 11.9	2 24.7	17 44.4	8 10.7	9 55.7	23 05.6	21 02.9	25 20.4
21 Su	9 58 20	28 12 19	24 16 38	0♓50 35	18 19.4	6 35.4	14 11.1	3 03.6	18 08.5	8 18.5	9 51.3	23 03.7	21 01.7	25 20.9
22 M	10 02 16	29 10 05	7♓20 27	13 46 07	18 07.5	8 26.4	15 09.9	3 42.4	18 32.5	8 26.5	9 46.9	23 01.9	21 00.5	25 21.4
23 Tu	10 06 13	0♍07 53	20 07 31	26 24 42	17 57.2	10 15.9	16 08.3	4 21.2	18 56.5	8 34.6	9 42.4	23 00.2	20 59.3	25 22.0
24 W	10 10 09	1 05 42	2♈37 47	8♈46 59	17 49.2	12 04.1	17 06.4	4 59.8	19 20.5	8 42.9	9 37.9	22 58.4	20 58.2	25 22.6
25 Th	10 14 06	2 03 33	14 52 36	20 54 58	17 43.9	13 50.9	18 04.0	5 38.4	19 44.4	8 51.2	9 33.4	22 56.7	20 57.0	25 23.3
26 F	10 18 02	3 01 26	26 54 33	2♉51 49	17 41.0	15 36.4	19 01.2	6 16.9	20 08.2	8 59.7	9 28.9	22 55.0	20 55.9	25 24.0
27 Sa	10 21 59	3 59 20	8♉47 20	14 41 42	17D 40.1	17 20.6	19 57.9	6 55.3	20 32.0	9 08.2	9 24.4	22 53.4	20 54.8	25 24.7
28 Su	10 25 55	4 57 17	20 35 33	26 29 32	17R 40.2	19 03.4	20 54.3	7 33.6	20 55.8	9 16.9	9 19.8	22 51.8	20 53.8	25 25.4
29 M	10 29 52	5 55 15	2♊24 20	8♊20 38	17 40.4	20 44.9	21 50.1	8 11.8	21 19.5	9 25.7	9 15.2	22 50.3	20 52.7	25 26.2
30 Tu	10 33 49	6 53 15	14 19 08	20 20 29	17 39.5	22 25.2	22 45.5	8 49.9	21 43.1	9 34.7	9 10.7	22 48.8	20 51.7	25 27.0
31 W	10 37 45	7 51 17	26 25 20	2♋34 18	17 36.8	24 04.2	23 40.4	9 27.9	22 06.7	9 43.7	9 06.1	22 47.3	20 50.7	25 27.9

Astro Data	Planet Ingress	Last Aspect	☽ Ingress	Last Aspect	☽ Ingress	☽ Phases & Eclipses	Astro Data
Dy Hr Mn	Dy Hr Mn	Dy Hr Mn	Dy Hr Mn	Dy Hr Mn	Dy Hr Mn	Dy Hr Mn	1 July 1994
♃ D 2 3:33	☿ ♊R 2 23:18	2 4:08 ♅ □	♉ 2 14:23	1 2:34 ☿ ⚹	♊ 1 11:05	8 21:37 ● 16♋29	Julian Day # 34515
☿ D 6 19:43	♂ ♊ 3 22:30	4 18:15 ♇ ☍	♊ 5 3:12	3 14:07 ♀ □	♋ 3 22:22	16 1:12 ☽ 23♎18	SVP 5♓19'58"
☽ 0S 13 15:03	⚳ ♋ 8 15:30	7 13:13 ☿ ☌	♋ 7 14:17	6 3:43 ♀ ⚹	♌ 6 6:31	22 20:16 ○ 29♑47	GC 26♐45.7 ⚳ 6♉07.3
☽ 0N 26 14:44	☿ ♋ 10 12:41	9 14:23 ♇ △	♌ 9 22:43	8 3:29 ♇ □	♍ 8 11:42	30 12:40 ☾ 7♉07	Eris 18♈31.1 ⚴ 18♎13.7
	♀ ♍ 11 6:33	11 20:43 ♇ □	♍ 12 4:48	10 7:51 ♂ □	♎ 10 15:07		⚷ 6♍03.8 ⚶ 5♊36.7
♇ D 5 17:08	☉ ♌ 23 1:41	14 1:19 ♇ ⚹	♎ 14 9:15	12 13:12 ♂ △	♏ 12 17:56	7 8:45 ● 14♌38	☽ Mean ☊ 21♏29.1
♀0S 7 2:56		16 3:04 ♅ □	♏ 16 12:35	14 12:53 ♇ ☌	♐ 14 20:53	14 5:57 ☽ 21♏14	
☽ 0S 9 22:01	☿ ♌ 3 6:09	18 7:32 ☉ △	♐ 18 15:09	16 20:19 ☿ △	♑ 17 0:18	21 6:47 ○ 28♒00	1 August 1994
☽ 0N 22 23:57	♀ ♎ 7 14:36	19 11:01 ♄ □	♑ 20 17:30	18 20:20 ♇ ⚹	♒ 19 4:34	29 6:41 ☾ 5♊42	Julian Day # 34546
♃△♄ 28 17:10	♂ ♋ 16 19:15	22 20:16 ☉ ☍	♒ 22 20:38	21 6:47 ☉ ☍	♓ 21 10:27		SVP 5♓19'53"
	☿ ♍ 18 0:44	24 17:25 ♇ □	♓ 25 1:56	23 10:00 ♇ △	♈ 23 18:55		GC 26♐45.8 ⚳ 15♉32.4
	☉ ♍ 23 8:44	27 1:25 ♇ △	♈ 27 10:30	25 16:03 ♅ □	♉ 26 6:13		Eris 18♈30.5R ⚴ 23♎18.0
		29 9:51 ♅ □	♉ 29 22:13	28 9:50 ♇ ☍	♊ 28 19:07		⚷ 9♍37.7 ⚶ 17♊54.3
				30 17:10 ♀ △	♋ 31 7:00		☽ Mean ☊ 19♏50.6

LONGITUDE — September 1994

Day	Sid.Time	☉	0 hr ☽	Noon ☽	True ☊	☿	♀	♂	⚳	♃	♄	♅	♆	♇
1 Th	10 41 42	8♍49 21	8♋47 57	15♋06 44	17♏31.8	25♍41.9	24♎34.7	10♋05.8	22♋30.2	9♏52.8	9♓01.5	22♑45.8	20♑49.8	25♏28.8
2 F	10 45 38	9 47 26	21 31 03	28 01 13	17R 24.4	27 18.4	25 28.6	10 43.6	22 53.7	10 02.1	8R 57.0	22R 44.4	20R 48.9	25 29.7
3 Sa	10 49 35	10 45 34	4♌37 23	11♌19 36	17 15.1	28 53.6	26 21.8	11 21.3	23 17.1	10 11.4	8 52.4	22 43.1	20 47.9	25 30.6
4 Su	10 53 31	11 43 43	18 07 46	25 01 37	17 04.6	0♎27.6	27 14.6	11 58.9	23 40.4	10 20.9	8 47.8	22 41.8	20 47.1	25 31.6
5 M	10 57 28	12 41 54	2♍00 47	9♍04 44	16 54.2	2 00.4	28 06.7	12 36.4	24 03.6	10 30.4	8 43.2	22 40.5	20 46.2	25 32.6
6 Tu	11 01 24	13 40 07	16 12 48	23 24 17	16 44.9	3 31.9	28 58.2	13 13.9	24 26.8	10 40.1	8 38.7	22 39.2	20 45.4	25 33.6
7 W	11 05 21	14 38 21	0♎38 22	7♎54 13	16 37.7	5 02.2	29 49.1	13 51.2	24 49.9	10 49.9	8 34.1	22 38.0	20 44.6	25 34.7
8 Th	11 09 17	15 36 37	15 11 03	22 28 03	16 33.0	6 31.3	0♏39.3	14 28.3	25 13.0	10 59.7	8 29.6	22 36.9	20 43.8	25 35.8
9 F	11 13 14	16 34 55	29 44 31	6♏59 49	16D 30.8	7 59.2	1 28.8	15 05.4	25 36.0	11 09.7	8 25.1	22 35.8	20 43.1	25 36.9
10 Sa	11 17 11	17 33 14	14♏13 25	21 24 53	16 30.6	9 25.8	2 17.6	15 42.4	25 58.9	11 19.7	8 20.6	22 34.7	20 42.4	25 38.1
11 Su	11 21 07	18 31 35	28 33 53	5♐40 11	16R 31.2	10 51.2	3 05.6	16 19.3	26 21.7	11 29.9	8 16.1	22 33.7	20 41.7	25 39.3
12 M	11 25 04	19 29 57	12♐43 36	19 44 03	16 31.7	12 15.2	3 52.9	16 56.0	26 44.4	11 40.1	8 11.7	22 32.7	20 41.0	25 40.5
13 Tu	11 29 00	20 28 21	26 41 29	3♑35 53	16 30.9	13 38.0	4 39.3	17 32.7	27 07.1	11 50.4	8 07.3	22 31.8	20 40.4	25 41.8
14 W	11 32 57	21 26 47	10♑27 16	17 15 37	16 28.1	14 59.4	5 24.9	18 09.2	27 29.6	12 00.9	8 02.9	22 30.9	20 39.8	25 43.1
15 Th	11 36 53	22 25 14	24 00 57	0♒43 16	16 23.0	16 19.5	6 09.6	18 45.6	27 52.1	12 11.4	7 58.5	22 30.1	20 39.2	25 44.4
16 F	11 40 50	23 23 42	7♒22 33	13 58 46	16 15.8	17 38.1	6 53.4	19 21.9	28 14.6	12 21.9	7 54.2	22 29.3	20 38.7	25 45.7
17 Sa	11 44 46	24 22 13	20 31 52	27 01 48	16 07.2	18 55.2	7 36.3	19 58.1	28 36.9	12 32.6	7 49.9	22 28.6	20 38.2	25 47.1
18 Su	11 48 43	25 20 45	3♓28 32	9♓52 00	15 58.0	20 10.8	8 18.1	20 34.2	28 59.1	12 43.4	7 45.6	22 27.9	20 37.7	25 48.5
19 M	11 52 40	26 19 18	16 12 12	22 29 07	15 49.2	21 24.9	8 58.9	21 10.1	29 21.3	12 54.2	7 41.4	22 27.2	20 37.3	25 49.9
20 Tu	11 56 36	27 17 54	28 42 48	4♈53 17	15 41.6	22 37.2	9 38.6	21 46.0	29 43.3	13 05.1	7 37.2	22 26.6	20 36.9	25 51.4
21 W	12 00 33	28 16 32	11♈00 44	17 05 17	15 35.8	23 47.8	10 17.2	22 21.7	0♌05.3	13 16.1	7 33.1	22 26.1	20 36.5	25 52.9
22 Th	12 04 29	29 15 12	23 07 09	29 06 36	15 32.2	24 56.5	10 54.7	22 57.3	0 27.1	13 27.2	7 29.0	22 25.6	20 36.1	25 54.4
23 F	12 08 26	0♎13 54	5♉03 58	10♉59 38	15D 30.6	26 03.2	11 30.9	23 32.8	0 48.9	13 38.3	7 25.0	22 25.1	20 35.8	25 55.9
24 Sa	12 12 22	1 12 38	16 54 01	22 47 36	15 30.8	27 07.8	12 05.9	24 08.2	1 10.6	13 49.5	7 21.0	22 24.7	20 35.5	25 57.5
25 Su	12 16 19	2 11 24	28 40 53	4♊34 26	15 32.0	28 10.1	12 39.6	24 43.4	1 32.2	14 00.8	7 17.0	22 24.4	20 35.3	25 59.1
26 M	12 20 15	3 10 13	10♊28 50	16 24 43	15 33.5	29 10.1	13 12.0	25 18.5	1 53.6	14 12.2	7 13.2	22 24.1	20 35.1	26 00.7
27 Tu	12 24 12	4 09 03	22 22 42	28 23 26	15R 34.7	0♏07.4	13 43.0	25 53.5	2 15.0	14 23.6	7 09.3	22 23.8	20 34.9	26 02.4
28 W	12 28 09	5 07 57	4♋27 34	10♋35 45	15 34.7	1 01.9	14 12.5	26 28.4	2 36.3	14 35.2	7 05.6	22 23.6	20 34.7	26 04.0
29 Th	12 32 05	6 06 52	16 48 34	23 06 36	15 33.2	1 53.3	14 40.5	27 03.1	2 57.4	14 46.7	7 01.9	22 23.5	20 34.6	26 05.7
30 F	12 36 02	7 05 50	29 30 22	6♌00 17	15 30.0	2 41.4	15 06.9	27 37.7	3 18.5	14 58.4	6 58.2	22 23.4	20 34.5	26 07.5

LONGITUDE — October 1994

Day	Sid.Time	☉	0 hr ☽	Noon ☽	True ☊	☿	♀	♂	⚳	♃	♄	♅	♆	♇
1 Sa	12 39 58	8♎04 49	12♌36 42	19♌19 49	15♏25.4	3♏26.0	15♏31.7	28♋12.1	3♌39.4	15♏10.1	6♓54.6	22♑23.3	20♑34.5	26♏09.2
2 Su	12 43 55	9 03 51	26 09 45	3♍06 22	15R 20.0	4 06.6	15 54.9	28 46.4	4 00.2	15 21.9	6R 51.1	22D 23.3	20D 34.4	26 11.0
3 M	12 47 51	10 02 56	10♍09 28	17 18 38	15 14.3	4 43.0	16 16.2	29 20.6	4 20.9	15 33.7	6 47.7	22 23.3	20 34.4	26 12.8
4 Tu	12 51 48	11 02 02	24 33 15	1♎52 37	15 09.2	5 14.7	16 35.8	29 54.6	4 41.4	15 45.6	6 44.3	22 23.4	20 34.5	26 14.6
5 W	12 55 44	12 01 11	9♎15 50	16 41 57	15 05.4	5 41.4	16 53.6	0♌28.5	5 01.9	15 57.6	6 41.0	22 23.6	20 34.6	26 16.4
6 Th	12 59 41	13 00 21	24 09 54	1♏38 39	15D 03.2	6 02.6	17 09.3	1 02.2	5 22.2	16 09.6	6 37.7	22 23.8	20 34.7	26 18.3
7 F	13 03 37	13 59 34	9♏07 07	16 34 21	15 02.6	6 17.9	17 23.1	1 35.8	5 42.3	16 21.7	6 34.6	22 24.0	20 34.8	26 20.2
8 Sa	13 07 34	14 58 48	23 59 25	1♐21 33	15 03.3	6R 26.8	17 34.9	2 09.2	6 02.4	16 33.8	6 31.5	22 24.3	20 35.0	26 22.1
9 Su	13 11 31	15 58 05	8♐40 05	15 54 29	15 04.7	6 28.8	17 44.5	2 42.5	6 22.3	16 46.0	6 28.5	22 24.7	20 35.2	26 24.0
10 M	13 15 27	16 57 23	23 04 23	0♑09 30	15 06.1	6 23.4	17 51.9	3 15.6	6 42.0	16 58.2	6 25.6	22 25.1	20 35.4	26 26.0
11 Tu	13 19 24	17 56 42	7♑09 42	14 04 56	15R 06.9	6 10.3	17 57.1	3 48.5	7 01.6	17 10.5	6 22.7	22 25.6	20 35.7	26 27.9
12 W	13 23 20	18 56 04	20 55 15	27 40 44	15 06.7	5 49.2	18R 00.0	4 21.3	7 21.1	17 22.9	6 20.0	22 26.1	20 36.0	26 29.9
13 Th	13 27 17	19 55 27	4♒21 33	10♒57 54	15 05.3	5 19.7	18 00.6	4 53.9	7 40.4	17 35.3	6 17.3	22 26.6	20 36.4	26 31.9
14 F	13 31 13	20 54 52	17 29 58	23 58 00	15 02.7	4 41.8	17 58.7	5 26.4	7 59.6	17 47.7	6 14.7	22 27.3	20 36.8	26 34.0
15 Sa	13 35 10	21 54 19	0♓22 14	6♓42 52	14 59.4	3 55.7	17 54.5	5 58.6	8 18.6	18 00.2	6 12.2	22 27.9	20 37.2	26 36.0
16 Su	13 39 06	22 53 47	13 00 08	19 14 16	14 55.7	3 01.9	17 47.9	6 30.8	8 37.5	18 12.7	6 09.8	22 28.6	20 37.6	26 38.1
17 M	13 43 03	23 53 18	25 25 27	1♈33 54	14 52.2	2 01.0	17 38.8	7 02.7	8 56.2	18 25.3	6 07.5	22 29.4	20 38.1	26 40.1
18 Tu	13 47 00	24 52 50	7♈39 48	13 43 22	14 49.3	0 54.1	17 27.3	7 34.5	9 14.7	18 37.9	6 05.3	22 30.2	20 38.6	26 42.2
19 W	13 50 56	25 52 24	19 44 47	25 44 18	14 47.3	29♎42.8	17 13.4	8 06.0	9 33.1	18 50.6	6 03.1	22 31.1	20 39.2	26 44.4
20 Th	13 54 53	26 52 01	1♉42 06	7♉38 26	14D 46.2	28 28.8	16 57.0	8 37.4	9 51.3	19 03.3	6 01.1	22 32.0	20 39.7	26 46.5
21 F	13 58 49	27 51 39	13 33 35	19 27 49	14 46.1	27 14.1	16 38.4	9 08.7	10 09.4	19 16.0	5 59.1	22 33.0	20 40.3	26 48.6
22 Sa	14 02 46	28 51 20	25 21 27	1♊14 50	14 46.8	26 01.0	16 17.5	9 39.7	10 27.2	19 28.8	5 57.2	22 34.0	20 41.0	26 50.8
23 Su	14 06 42	29 51 02	7♊08 21	13 02 24	14 48.0	24 51.5	15 54.4	10 10.6	10 44.9	19 41.6	5 55.5	22 35.0	20 41.7	26 53.0
24 M	14 10 39	0♏50 47	18 57 25	24 53 53	14 49.4	23 48.0	15 29.3	10 41.2	11 02.4	19 54.4	5 53.8	22 36.1	20 42.4	26 55.2
25 Tu	14 14 35	1 50 34	0♋52 17	6♋53 08	14 50.6	22 52.2	15 02.2	11 11.7	11 19.7	20 07.3	5 52.2	22 37.3	20 43.1	26 57.4
26 W	14 18 32	2 50 24	12 57 00	19 04 25	14 51.5	22 05.8	14 33.2	11 41.9	11 36.9	20 20.2	5 50.8	22 38.5	20 43.9	26 59.6
27 Th	14 22 29	3 50 15	25 15 57	1♌32 08	14R 51.9	21 29.7	14 02.6	12 12.0	11 53.8	20 33.2	5 49.4	22 39.8	20 44.7	27 01.9
28 F	14 26 25	4 50 09	7♌53 31	14 20 34	14 51.8	21 04.8	13 30.6	12 41.8	12 10.6	20 46.1	5 48.1	22 41.1	20 45.5	27 04.1
29 Sa	14 30 22	5 50 05	20 53 44	27 33 22	14 51.2	20D 51.5	12 57.2	13 11.4	12 27.1	20 59.1	5 46.9	22 42.5	20 46.4	27 06.4
30 Su	14 34 18	6 50 03	4♍19 45	11♍13 01	14 50.3	20 49.5	12 22.7	13 40.8	12 43.4	21 12.2	5 45.8	22 43.9	20 47.3	27 08.6
31 M	14 38 15	7 50 03	18 13 12	25 20 08	14 49.4	20 58.7	11 47.4	14 10.0	12 59.6	21 25.2	5 44.9	22 45.3	20 48.2	27 10.9

Astro Data

	Dy Hr Mn
☿0S	4 8:23
☽0S	6 6:36
☽0N	19 7:35
☉0S	23 6:19
♄∠♅	23 10:54
♅D	2 1:47
♆D	2 17:47
☽0S	3 16:36
☿R	9 6:43
♀R	13 5:41
☽0N	16 13:30
♃⚹♆	28 10:50
♄∠♆	29 18:10
☿D	30 4:04
☽0S	31 2:53

Planet Ingress

		Dy Hr Mn
☿	♎	4 4:55
♀	♏	7 17:12
⚳	♌	21 6:13
☉	♎	23 6:19
☿	♏	27 8:51
♂	♌	4 15:48
☿	♎R	19 6:19
☉	♏	23 15:36

Last Aspect / ☽ Ingress (September)

Last Aspect Dy Hr Mn			☽ Ingress	Dy Hr Mn
2 10:30	☿	⚹	♌	2 15:37
4 16:05	♀	⚹	♍	4 20:33
6 15:35	♇	⚹	♎	6 22:57
8 12:15	♅	□	♏	9 0:26
10 19:05	♇	☌	♐	11 2:25
12 11:34	☉	□	♑	13 5:44
15 3:04	♇	⚹	♒	15 10:42
17 9:41	♇	□	♓	17 17:31
19 20:01	☉	☍	♈	20 2:30
22 2:46	☿	☍	♉	22 13:47
24 18:28	♇	☍	♊	25 2:41
25 17:29	♄	□	♋	27 15:12
29 19:46	♂	☌	♌	30 0:55

Last Aspect / ☽ Ingress (October)

Last Aspect Dy Hr Mn			☽ Ingress	Dy Hr Mn
2 0:01	♇	□	♍	2 6:39
4 8:40	♂	⚹	♎	4 8:56
5 21:09	♅	□	♏	6 9:22
8 3:51	♇	☌	♐	8 9:47
9 12:07	☉	⚹	♑	10 11:44
12 9:53	♇	⚹	♒	12 16:09
14 16:52	♇	□	♓	14 23:18
17 2:24	♇	△	♈	17 8:56
19 19:15	☿	☍	♉	19 20:34
22 3:00	♇	☍	♊	22 9:28
24 9:58	☿	△	♋	24 22:15
27 3:22	♇	△	♌	27 9:05
29 11:12	♇	□	♍	29 16:21
31 15:05	♇	⚹	♎	31 19:46

☽ Phases & Eclipses

Dy Hr Mn		
5 18:33	●	12♍58
12 11:34	☽	19♐29
19 20:01	○	26♓39
28 0:23	☾	4♋39
5 3:55	●	11♎41
11 19:17	☽	18♑15
19 12:18	○	25♈53
27 16:44	☾	4♌02

Astro Data

1 September 1994
Julian Day # 34577
SVP 5♓19'49"
GC 26♐45.9 ⚴ 22♉24.6
Eris 18♈20.5R ⚵ 1♏02.2
⚷ 13♍51.0 ⚶ 28♊42.5
☽ Mean ☊ 18♏12.1

1 October 1994
Julian Day # 34607
SVP 5♓19'47"
GC 26♐46.0 ⚴ 24♉17.1R
Eris 18♈04.4R ⚵ 10♏03.6
⚷ 18♍03.8 ⚶ 6♋44.5
☽ Mean ☊ 16♏36.7

November 1994 LONGITUDE

Day	Sid.Time	☉	0 hr ☽	Noon☽	True☊	☿	♀	♂	⚳	♃	♄	♅	♆	♇
1 Tu	14 42 11	8♏50 05	2♎33 31	9♎52 51	14♏48.7	21♎18.4	11♏11.5	14♌39.0	13♌15.5	21♏38.3	5♓44.0	22♑46.8	20♑49.2	27♏13.2
2 W	14 46 08	9 50 09	17 17 28	24 46 30	14R48.2	21 48.0	10R35.2	15 07.7	13 31.2	21 51.4	5R43.2	22 48.4	20 50.2	27 15.5
3 Th	14 50 04	10 50 16	2♏18 59	9♏53 49	14D48.0	22 26.5	9 58.7	15 36.2	13 46.6	22 04.5	5 42.6	22 50.0	20 51.2	27 17.8
4 F	14 54 01	11 50 24	17 29 47	25 05 41	14 48.0	23 13.2	9 22.4	16 04.4	14 01.9	22 17.7	5 42.0	22 51.6	20 52.3	27 20.2
5 Sa	14 57 58	12 50 34	2♐40 18	10♐12 30	14 48.2	24 07.1	8 46.3	16 32.4	14 16.9	22 30.8	5 41.5	22 53.3	20 53.4	27 22.5
6 Su	15 01 54	13 50 46	17 41 14	25 05 36	14 48.3	25 07.4	8 10.8	17 00.1	14 31.7	22 44.0	5 41.2	22 55.0	20 54.5	27 24.8
7 M	15 05 51	14 50 59	2♑24 49	9♑38 19	14R48.4	26 13.3	7 36.2	17 27.6	14 46.2	22 57.2	5 40.9	22 56.8	20 55.7	27 27.2
8 Tu	15 09 47	15 51 14	16 45 40	23 46 39	14 48.3	27 24.1	7 02.6	17 54.8	15 00.5	23 10.5	5D40.8	22 58.7	20 56.8	27 29.5
9 W	15 13 44	16 51 30	0♒41 09	7♒29 14	14D48.2	28 39.0	6 30.2	18 21.7	15 14.5	23 23.7	5 40.8	23 00.5	20 58.1	27 31.9
10 Th	15 17 40	17 51 47	14 11 02	20 46 49	14 48.2	29 57.4	5 59.3	18 48.4	15 28.3	23 36.9	5 40.8	23 02.5	20 59.3	27 34.3
11 F	15 21 37	18 52 06	27 16 56	3♓41 45	14 48.3	1♏18.9	5 29.9	19 14.8	15 41.8	23 50.2	5 41.0	23 04.4	21 00.6	27 36.6
12 Sa	15 25 33	19 52 27	10♓01 41	16 17 12	14 48.7	2 42.9	5 02.5	19 40.9	15 55.1	24 03.4	5 41.3	23 06.4	21 01.9	27 39.0
13 Su	15 29 30	20 52 49	22 28 45	28 36 47	14 49.3	4 09.0	4 36.9	20 06.7	16 08.1	24 16.7	5 41.7	23 08.5	21 03.2	27 41.4
14 M	15 33 27	21 53 12	4♈41 44	10♈44 03	14 50.1	5 36.8	4 13.4	20 32.3	16 20.8	24 30.0	5 42.1	23 10.6	21 04.5	27 43.8
15 Tu	15 37 23	22 53 37	16 44 06	22 42 19	14 50.8	7 06.1	3 52.2	20 57.5	16 33.3	24 43.3	5 42.7	23 12.7	21 05.9	27 46.2
16 W	15 41 20	23 54 03	28 39 01	4♉34 34	14R51.4	8 36.6	3 33.2	21 22.5	16 45.4	24 56.6	5 43.4	23 14.9	21 07.3	27 48.6
17 Th	15 45 16	24 54 31	10♉29 16	16 23 26	14 51.5	10 08.1	3 16.6	21 47.1	16 57.3	25 09.9	5 44.2	23 17.1	21 08.8	27 51.0
18 F	15 49 13	25 55 00	22 17 19	28 11 13	14 51.2	11 40.3	3 02.4	22 11.4	17 08.9	25 23.1	5 45.1	23 19.3	21 10.2	27 53.4
19 Sa	15 53 09	26 55 31	4♊05 23	10♊00 04	14 50.2	13 13.1	2 50.7	22 35.4	17 20.3	25 36.4	5 46.2	23 21.6	21 11.7	27 55.8
20 Su	15 57 06	27 56 03	15 55 33	21 52 05	14 48.6	14 46.4	2 41.5	22 59.1	17 31.3	25 49.7	5 47.3	23 24.0	21 13.2	27 58.2
21 M	16 01 02	28 56 38	27 49 57	3♋49 26	14 46.5	16 20.1	2 34.8	23 22.5	17 42.0	26 03.0	5 48.5	23 26.3	21 14.8	28 00.5
22 Tu	16 04 59	29 57 13	9♋50 52	15 54 33	14 44.1	17 54.1	2 30.6	23 45.5	17 52.4	26 16.3	5 49.8	23 28.8	21 16.4	28 02.9
23 W	16 08 56	0♐57 51	22 00 52	28 10 09	14 41.8	19 28.2	2D28.8	24 08.1	18 02.5	26 29.6	5 51.2	23 31.2	21 17.9	28 05.3
24 Th	16 12 52	1 58 30	4♌22 49	10♌39 15	14 40.0	21 02.5	2 29.6	24 30.4	18 12.3	26 42.9	5 52.8	23 33.7	21 19.6	28 07.7
25 F	16 16 49	2 59 10	16 59 53	23 25 06	14D38.8	22 36.9	2 32.7	24 52.4	18 21.7	26 56.2	5 54.4	23 36.2	21 21.2	28 10.1
26 Sa	16 20 45	3 59 55	29 55 19	6♍30 54	14 38.5	24 11.3	2 38.2	25 13.9	18 30.8	27 09.4	5 56.1	23 38.8	21 22.9	28 12.5
27 Su	16 24 42	5 00 36	13♍12 11	19 59 28	14 39.1	25 45.7	2 46.1	25 35.1	18 39.6	27 22.7	5 58.0	23 41.4	21 24.6	28 14.9
28 M	16 28 38	6 01 22	26 52 57	3♎52 42	14 40.4	27 20.2	2 56.2	25 55.9	18 48.1	27 35.9	5 59.9	23 44.0	21 26.3	28 17.3
29 Tu	16 32 35	7 02 09	10♎58 44	18 10 53	14 41.8	28 54.6	3 08.5	26 16.2	18 56.1	27 49.2	6 02.0	23 46.7	21 28.0	28 19.7
30 W	16 36 31	8 02 57	25 28 50	2♏52 04	14R43.0	0♐28.9	3 23.1	26 36.2	19 03.9	28 02.4	6 04.1	23 49.4	21 29.8	28 22.0

December 1994 LONGITUDE

Day	Sid.Time	☉	0 hr ☽	Noon☽	True☊	☿	♀	♂	⚳	♃	♄	♅	♆	♇
1 Th	16 40 28	9♐03 47	10♏19 55	17♏51 34	14♏43.3	2♐03.3	3♏39.7	26♌55.7	19♌11.3	28♏15.6	6♓06.4	23♑52.1	21♑31.5	28♏24.4
2 F	16 44 25	10 04 39	25 26 00	3♐02 05	14R42.4	3 37.6	3 58.3	27 14.9	19 18.3	28 28.8	6 08.7	23 54.9	21 33.3	28 26.8
3 Sa	16 48 21	11 05 31	10♐38 36	18 14 17	14 40.1	5 11.8	4 18.9	27 33.5	19 24.9	28 42.0	6 11.1	23 57.7	21 35.2	28 29.1
4 Su	16 52 18	12 06 25	25 47 52	3♑18 10	14 36.6	6 46.1	4 41.4	27 51.7	19 31.2	28 55.2	6 13.7	24 00.5	21 37.0	28 31.5
5 M	16 56 14	13 07 20	10♑44 04	18 04 38	14 32.4	8 20.2	5 05.7	28 09.5	19 37.1	29 08.3	6 16.3	24 03.4	21 38.9	28 33.8
6 Tu	17 00 11	14 08 15	25 19 07	2♒26 55	14 28.0	9 54.4	5 31.7	28 26.8	19 42.7	29 21.4	6 19.1	24 06.3	21 40.8	28 36.2
7 W	17 04 07	15 09 11	9♒27 40	16 21 12	14 24.3	11 28.5	5 59.5	28 43.6	19 47.8	29 34.5	6 21.9	24 09.2	21 42.7	28 38.5
8 Th	17 08 04	16 10 08	23 07 30	29 46 44	14 21.6	13 02.7	6 28.9	29 00.0	19 52.5	29 47.6	6 24.9	24 12.2	21 44.6	28 40.8
9 F	17 12 00	17 11 06	6♓19 11	12♓45 16	14D20.4	14 36.8	6 59.9	29 15.8	19 56.9	0♐00.6	6 27.9	24 15.2	21 46.5	28 43.1
10 Sa	17 15 57	18 12 04	19 05 28	25 20 18	14 20.5	16 11.0	7 32.5	29 31.1	20 00.9	0 13.6	6 31.0	24 18.2	21 48.5	28 45.4
11 Su	17 19 54	19 13 03	1♈30 23	7♈36 20	14 21.8	17 45.2	8 06.5	29 46.0	20 04.4	0 26.6	6 34.2	24 21.2	21 50.5	28 47.7
12 M	17 23 50	20 14 02	13 38 44	19 38 14	14 23.6	19 19.5	8 41.9	0♍00.3	20 07.6	0 39.5	6 37.5	24 24.3	21 52.5	28 50.0
13 Tu	17 27 47	21 15 02	25 35 24	1♉30 49	14 25.2	20 53.8	9 18.7	0 14.0	20 10.3	0 52.4	6 40.9	24 27.4	21 54.5	28 52.3
14 W	17 31 43	22 16 02	7♉25 01	13 18 30	14R26.0	22 28.2	9 56.8	0 27.3	20 12.7	1 05.3	6 44.4	24 30.5	21 56.5	28 54.5
15 Th	17 35 40	23 17 04	19 11 45	25 05 11	14 25.3	24 02.7	10 36.1	0 40.0	20 14.6	1 18.2	6 48.0	24 33.6	21 58.5	28 56.7
16 F	17 39 36	24 18 05	0♊59 10	6♊54 03	14 22.7	25 37.4	11 16.7	0 52.1	20 16.1	1 31.0	6 51.7	24 36.8	22 00.6	28 59.0
17 Sa	17 43 33	25 19 08	12 50 08	18 47 40	14 18.1	27 12.1	11 58.5	1 03.6	20 17.2	1 43.8	6 55.5	24 40.0	22 02.7	29 01.2
18 Su	17 47 29	26 20 11	24 46 53	0♋47 58	14 11.6	28 47.0	12 41.4	1 14.6	20 17.9	1 56.5	6 59.3	24 43.2	22 04.8	29 03.4
19 M	17 51 26	27 21 15	6♋51 05	12 56 24	14 03.6	0♑22.1	13 25.4	1 24.9	20R18.1	2 09.2	7 03.3	24 46.4	22 06.9	29 05.6
20 Tu	17 55 23	28 22 19	19 04 01	25 14 06	13 54.9	1 57.3	14 10.4	1 34.7	20 17.9	2 21.8	7 07.3	24 49.7	22 09.0	29 07.7
21 W	17 59 19	29 23 24	1♌26 45	7♌42 08	13 46.4	3 32.7	14 56.4	1 43.8	20 17.3	2 34.5	7 11.4	24 52.9	22 11.1	29 09.9
22 Th	18 03 16	0♑24 30	14 00 22	20 21 38	13 39.0	5 08.3	15 43.4	1 52.3	20 16.3	2 47.0	7 15.6	24 56.2	22 13.2	29 12.0
23 F	18 07 12	1 25 36	26 46 08	3♍14 02	13 33.3	6 44.1	16 31.3	2 00.1	20 14.8	2 59.5	7 19.9	24 59.5	22 15.4	29 14.1
24 Sa	18 11 09	2 26 43	9♍45 36	16 21 03	13 29.7	8 20.1	17 20.2	2 07.3	20 12.9	3 12.0	7 24.2	25 02.9	22 17.6	29 16.2
25 Su	18 15 05	3 27 50	23 00 37	29 44 33	13D28.3	9 56.3	18 09.8	2 13.8	20 10.5	3 24.4	7 28.7	25 06.2	22 19.7	29 18.3
26 M	18 19 02	4 28 58	6♎33 05	13♎26 22	13 28.5	11 32.7	19 00.3	2 19.6	20 07.7	3 36.8	7 33.2	25 09.6	22 21.9	29 20.4
27 Tu	18 22 58	5 30 07	20 24 34	27 27 43	13 29.6	13 09.3	19 51.6	2 24.7	20 04.5	3 49.1	7 37.8	25 12.9	22 24.1	29 22.4
28 W	18 26 55	6 31 17	4♏35 47	11♏48 35	13R30.3	14 46.0	20 43.7	2 29.1	20 00.8	4 01.4	7 42.4	25 16.3	22 26.3	29 24.4
29 Th	18 30 52	7 32 27	19 05 49	26 27 02	13 29.6	16 23.0	21 36.5	2 32.8	19 56.7	4 13.6	7 47.2	25 19.8	22 28.5	29 26.4
30 F	18 34 48	8 33 37	3♐51 36	11♐18 45	13 26.6	18 00.0	22 30.0	2 35.7	19 52.2	4 25.8	7 52.0	25 23.2	22 30.7	29 28.4
31 Sa	18 38 45	9 34 48	18 47 34	26 16 59	13 21.1	19 37.2	23 24.1	2 37.9	19 47.2	4 37.9	7 57.0	25 26.6	22 33.0	29 30.4

Astro Data	Dy Hr Mn
♃⚹♅	7 11:09
♄ D	9 8:36
☽0N	12 19:01
♀ D	23 16:57
☽0S	27 12:01
♃☌♇	2 7:30
☽0N	10 2:01
⚳ R	19 13:44
♄∠♆	21 8:36
☽0S	24 19:25

Planet Ingress		Dy Hr Mn
☿	♏	10 12:46
☉	♐	22 13:06
☿	♐	30 4:38
♃	♐	9 10:54
♂	♍	12 11:32
☿	♑	19 6:26
☉	♑	22 2:23

Last Aspect Dy Hr Mn			☽ Ingress	Dy Hr Mn
2 8:51	♅	□	♏	2 20:19
4 15:33	♇	☌	♐	4 19:46
6 12:03	☿	⚹	♑	6 20:02
8 18:53	☿	□	♒	8 22:48
11 0:35	♇	□	♓	11 5:04
13 10:11	♇	△	♈	13 14:44
15 13:01	♅	□	♉	16 2:44
18 11:24	♇	☍	♊	18 15:41
20 14:20	♂	⚹	♋	21 4:21
23 11:51	♇	△	♌	23 15:33
25 20:48	♇	□	♍	26 0:09
28 2:24	♇	⚹	♎	28 5:22
30 1:36	♂	⚹	♏	30 7:21

Last Aspect Dy Hr Mn			☽ Ingress	Dy Hr Mn
2 4:44	♇	☌	♐	2 7:13
4 3:07	♂	△	♑	4 6:42
6 6:42	♃	⚹	♒	6 7:51
8 12:02	♃	□	♓	8 12:24
10 18:39	♇	△	♈	10 21:03
12 21:39	♅	□	♉	13 8:56
15 19:53	♇	☍	♊	15 22:00
18 7:23	☿	☍	♋	18 10:25
20 19:33	♇	△	♌	20 21:13
23 4:34	♇	□	♍	23 6:01
25 11:13	♇	⚹	♎	25 12:27
27 8:11	♅	□	♏	27 16:17
29 16:52	♇	☌	♐	29 17:46
30 6:26	♄	□	♑	31 17:57

☽ Phases & Eclipses Dy Hr Mn	
3 13:35	● 10♏54
3 13:39:05	● T 04'24"
10 6:14	☽ 17♒37
18 6:57	○ 25♉42
18 6:44	● A 0.881
26 7:04	☾ 3♍47
2 23:54	● 10♐35
9 21:06	☽ 17♓34
18 2:17	○ 25♊55
25 19:06	☾ 3♎46

Astro Data

1 November 1994
Julian Day # 34638
SVP 5♓19'44"
GC 26♐46.0 ⚴ 18♉31.9R
Eris 17♈46.1R ⚵ 20♏16.3
⚷ 22♍01.0 ⚶ 10♋46.7
☽ Mean ☊ 14♏58.2

1 December 1994
Julian Day # 34668
SVP 5♓19'40"
GC 26♐46.1 ⚴ 9♉02.0R
Eris 17♈31.8R ⚵ 0♐29.0
⚷ 24♍54.2 ⚶ 8♋34.4R
☽ Mean ☊ 13♏22.9

LONGITUDE — January 1995

Day	Sid.Time	☉	0 hr ☽	Noon ☽	True ☊	☿	♀	♂	⚳	♃	♄	♅	♆	♇
1 Su	18 42 41	10♑35 59	3♑45 54	11♑13 08	13♏13.2	21♑14.4	24♏18.9	2♍39.4	19♌41.8	4♐49.9	8♓01.9	25♑30.1	22♑35.2	29♏32.3
2 M	18 46 38	11 37 10	18 37 34	25 58 05	13R 03.7	22 51.6	25 14.3	2R 40.1	19R 36.0	5 01.9	8 07.0	25 33.5	22 37.4	29 34.3
3 Tu	18 50 34	12 38 21	3♒13 45	10♒23 44	12 53.7	24 28.8	26 10.3	2 40.0	19 29.7	5 13.8	8 12.1	25 37.0	22 39.7	29 36.2
4 W	18 54 31	13 39 32	17 27 22	24 24 15	12 44.3	26 05.8	27 06.9	2 39.1	19 23.1	5 25.7	8 17.3	25 40.5	22 41.9	29 38.0
5 Th	18 58 28	14 40 43	1♓14 05	7♓56 49	12 36.6	27 42.5	28 04.0	2 37.5	19 16.0	5 37.4	8 22.6	25 44.0	22 44.2	29 39.9
6 F	19 02 24	15 41 53	14 32 33	21 01 33	12 31.2	29 18.9	29 01.6	2 35.1	19 08.5	5 49.2	8 28.0	25 47.5	22 46.5	29 41.7
7 Sa	19 06 21	16 43 03	27 24 12	3♈40 59	12 28.2	0♒54.7	29 59.7	2 31.8	19 00.6	6 00.8	8 33.4	25 51.0	22 48.7	29 43.5
8 Su	19 10 17	17 44 12	9♈52 28	15 59 18	12D 27.3	2 29.9	0♐58.4	2 27.8	18 52.3	6 12.4	8 38.8	25 54.5	22 51.0	29 45.3
9 M	19 14 14	18 45 21	22 02 09	28 01 41	12 27.5	4 04.2	1 57.5	2 23.0	18 43.7	6 23.9	8 44.4	25 58.0	22 53.3	29 47.1
10 Tu	19 18 10	19 46 29	3♉58 38	9♉53 40	12R 28.0	5 37.3	2 57.0	2 17.4	18 34.6	6 35.3	8 50.0	26 01.6	22 55.5	29 48.8
11 W	19 22 07	20 47 37	15 47 28	21 40 41	12 27.6	7 09.1	3 57.0	2 10.9	18 25.3	6 46.6	8 55.7	26 05.1	22 57.8	29 50.5
12 Th	19 26 03	21 48 45	27 33 55	3♊27 46	12 25.4	8 39.0	4 57.4	2 03.7	18 15.5	6 57.9	9 01.4	26 08.6	23 00.1	29 52.2
13 F	19 30 00	22 49 52	9♊22 44	15 19 18	12 20.5	10 06.9	5 58.3	1 55.7	18 05.4	7 09.1	9 07.2	26 12.2	23 02.4	29 53.8
14 Sa	19 33 57	23 50 58	21 17 52	27 18 47	12 12.8	11 32.1	6 59.5	1 46.8	17 55.0	7 20.2	9 13.0	26 15.7	23 04.6	29 55.5
15 Su	19 37 53	24 52 04	3♋22 20	9♋28 45	12 02.4	12 54.3	8 01.1	1 37.2	17 44.2	7 31.2	9 19.0	26 19.3	23 06.9	29 57.1
16 M	19 41 50	25 53 10	15 38 11	21 50 45	11 50.0	14 12.9	9 03.1	1 26.7	17 33.1	7 42.2	9 24.9	26 22.8	23 09.2	29 58.6
17 Tu	19 45 46	26 54 15	28 06 28	4♌25 20	11 36.4	15 27.2	10 05.5	1 15.5	17 21.8	7 53.0	9 30.9	26 26.3	23 11.5	0♐00.2
18 W	19 49 43	27 55 19	10♌47 20	17 12 22	11 23.0	16 36.5	11 08.2	1 03.5	17 10.1	8 03.8	9 37.0	26 29.9	23 13.7	0 01.7
19 Th	19 53 39	28 56 23	23 40 22	0♍11 13	11 10.9	17 40.1	12 11.2	0 50.7	16 58.1	8 14.5	9 43.2	26 33.4	23 16.0	0 03.2
20 F	19 57 36	29 57 26	6♍44 52	13 21 12	11 01.2	18 37.1	13 14.6	0 37.1	16 45.9	8 25.1	9 49.3	26 37.0	23 18.3	0 04.6
21 Sa	20 01 32	0♒58 29	20 00 12	26 41 51	10 54.4	19 26.7	14 18.3	0 22.8	16 33.5	8 35.6	9 55.6	26 40.5	23 20.5	0 06.1
22 Su	20 05 29	1 59 32	3♎26 08	10♎13 06	10 50.5	20 08.0	15 22.3	0 07.7	16 20.8	8 46.0	10 01.9	26 44.1	23 22.8	0 07.5
23 M	20 09 26	3 00 34	17 02 50	23 55 24	10D 49.1	20 40.2	16 26.5	29♌51.9	16 07.9	8 56.3	10 08.2	26 47.6	23 25.1	0 08.8
24 Tu	20 13 22	4 01 35	0♏50 52	7♏49 19	10R 48.9	21 02.5	17 31.1	29 35.3	15 54.7	9 06.5	10 14.6	26 51.1	23 27.3	0 10.2
25 W	20 17 19	5 02 37	14 50 46	21 55 12	10 48.7	21R 14.2	18 35.9	29 18.1	15 41.4	9 16.7	10 21.0	26 54.6	23 29.6	0 11.5
26 Th	20 21 15	6 03 38	29 02 30	6♐12 31	10 47.0	21 14.8	19 41.0	29 00.2	15 27.9	9 26.7	10 27.5	26 58.2	23 31.8	0 12.7
27 F	20 25 12	7 04 38	13♐24 54	20 39 16	10 42.9	21 03.9	20 46.4	28 41.7	15 14.3	9 36.6	10 34.0	27 01.7	23 34.0	0 14.0
28 Sa	20 29 08	8 05 38	27 55 04	5♑11 38	10 35.8	20 41.7	21 52.0	28 22.5	15 00.5	9 46.4	10 40.6	27 05.2	23 36.3	0 15.2
29 Su	20 33 05	9 06 37	12♑28 14	19 44 01	10 25.8	20 08.4	22 57.8	28 02.7	14 46.6	9 56.1	10 47.2	27 08.7	23 38.5	0 16.4
30 M	20 37 01	10 07 35	26 58 07	4♒09 40	10 13.8	19 24.6	24 03.8	27 42.4	14 32.6	10 05.7	10 53.9	27 12.2	23 40.7	0 17.5
31 Tu	20 40 58	11 08 32	11♒17 48	18 21 44	10 01.0	18 31.6	25 10.1	27 21.5	14 18.6	10 15.2	11 00.6	27 15.6	23 42.9	0 18.7

LONGITUDE — February 1995

Day	Sid.Time	☉	0 hr ☽	Noon ☽	True ☊	☿	♀	♂	⚳	♃	♄	♅	♆	♇
1 W	20 44 55	12♒09 28	25♒20 48	2♓14 26	9♏48.6	17♒30.7	26♐16.5	27♌00.2	14♌04.4	10♐24.6	11♓07.3	27♑19.1	23♑45.1	0♐19.7
2 Th	20 48 51	13 10 22	9♓02 15	15 43 59	9R 38.0	16R 23.7	27 23.2	26R 38.4	13R 50.3	10 33.9	11 14.1	27 22.5	23 47.3	0 20.8
3 F	20 52 48	14 11 16	22 19 34	28 49 03	9 30.0	15 12.6	28 30.0	26 16.2	13 36.1	10 43.0	11 20.9	27 26.0	23 49.4	0 21.8
4 Sa	20 56 44	15 12 08	5♈12 37	11♈30 36	9 24.9	13 59.4	29 37.1	25 53.6	13 21.9	10 52.1	11 27.8	27 29.4	23 51.6	0 22.8
5 Su	21 00 41	16 12 59	17 43 26	23 51 37	9 22.3	12 46.4	0♑44.3	25 30.7	13 07.7	11 01.0	11 34.6	27 32.8	23 53.7	0 23.7
6 M	21 04 37	17 13 48	29 55 44	5♉56 25	9D 21.6	11 35.3	1 51.7	25 07.5	12 53.6	11 09.8	11 41.6	27 36.2	23 55.9	0 24.7
7 Tu	21 08 34	18 14 36	11♉54 21	17 50 13	9R 21.6	10 28.1	2 59.2	24 44.0	12 39.6	11 18.4	11 48.5	27 39.6	23 58.0	0 25.5
8 W	21 12 30	19 15 23	23 44 43	29 38 35	9 21.2	9 26.1	4 06.9	24 20.4	12 25.6	11 27.0	11 55.5	27 43.0	24 00.1	0 26.4
9 Th	21 16 27	20 16 08	5♊32 29	11♊27 06	9 19.3	8 30.5	5 14.8	23 56.6	12 11.7	11 35.4	12 02.5	27 46.3	24 02.2	0 27.2
10 F	21 20 24	21 16 51	17 23 04	23 20 59	9 15.2	7 42.2	6 22.9	23 32.7	11 57.9	11 43.7	12 09.5	27 49.6	24 04.3	0 28.0
11 Sa	21 24 20	22 17 33	29 21 23	5♋24 45	9 08.3	7 01.6	7 31.0	23 08.8	11 44.3	11 51.9	12 16.6	27 53.0	24 06.4	0 28.7
12 Su	21 28 17	23 18 14	11♋31 32	17 42 03	8 58.8	6 29.0	8 39.4	22 44.8	11 30.8	11 59.9	12 23.7	27 56.3	24 08.4	0 29.5
13 M	21 32 13	24 18 53	23 56 34	0♌15 16	8 47.2	6 04.5	9 47.8	22 20.9	11 17.4	12 07.8	12 30.8	27 59.5	24 10.4	0 30.1
14 Tu	21 36 10	25 19 30	6♌38 14	13 05 27	8 34.4	5 48.0	10 56.4	21 57.0	11 04.3	12 15.6	12 37.9	28 02.8	24 12.5	0 30.8
15 W	21 40 06	26 20 06	19 36 51	26 12 15	8 21.6	5D 39.1	12 05.2	21 33.3	10 51.4	12 23.3	12 45.1	28 06.0	24 14.5	0 31.4
16 Th	21 44 03	27 20 40	2♍51 26	9♍34 07	8 10.1	5 37.6	13 14.1	21 09.7	10 38.6	12 30.8	12 52.3	28 09.2	24 16.5	0 32.0
17 F	21 47 59	28 21 13	16 19 59	23 08 40	8 00.8	5 43.0	14 23.1	20 46.4	10 26.1	12 38.1	12 59.5	28 12.4	24 18.4	0 32.5
18 Sa	21 51 56	29 21 44	29 59 51	6♎53 12	7 54.4	5 54.9	15 32.2	20 23.2	10 13.9	12 45.4	13 06.7	28 15.6	24 20.4	0 33.0
19 Su	21 55 52	0♓22 14	13♎48 23	20 45 09	7 50.8	6 13.0	16 41.4	20 00.4	10 01.9	12 52.5	13 13.9	28 18.7	24 22.3	0 33.5
20 M	21 59 49	1 22 43	27 43 17	4♏42 34	7D 49.4	6 36.7	17 50.8	19 37.9	9 50.1	12 59.4	13 21.2	28 21.8	24 24.3	0 33.9
21 Tu	22 03 46	2 23 10	11♏42 52	18 44 05	7 49.8	7 05.7	19 00.3	19 15.8	9 38.7	13 06.2	13 28.4	28 24.9	24 26.2	0 34.3
22 W	22 07 42	3 23 37	25 46 05	2♐48 49	7R 50.2	7 39.6	20 09.9	18 54.0	9 27.6	13 12.9	13 35.7	28 28.0	24 28.0	0 34.6
23 Th	22 11 39	4 24 02	9♐52 09	16 56 00	7 49.6	8 17.9	21 19.6	18 32.8	9 16.7	13 19.4	13 43.0	28 31.1	24 29.9	0 35.0
24 F	22 15 35	5 24 25	24 00 47	1♑04 29	7 46.9	9 00.4	22 29.4	18 11.9	9 06.2	13 25.8	13 50.3	28 34.1	24 31.7	0 35.3
25 Sa	22 19 32	6 24 48	8♑08 40	15 12 23	7 41.7	9 46.8	23 39.3	17 51.7	8 56.1	13 32.0	13 57.7	28 37.1	24 33.6	0 35.5
26 Su	22 23 28	7 25 09	22 15 16	29 16 52	7 34.0	10 36.7	24 49.3	17 31.9	8 46.2	13 38.0	14 05.0	28 40.0	24 35.4	0 35.7
27 M	22 27 25	8 25 28	6♒16 43	13♒14 18	7 24.6	11 29.9	25 59.4	17 12.7	8 36.8	13 43.9	14 12.3	28 43.0	24 37.2	0 35.9
28 Tu	22 31 21	9 25 45	20 09 08	27 00 42	7 14.3	12 26.1	27 09.6	16 54.2	8 27.7	13 49.7	14 19.7	28 45.9	24 38.9	0 36.1

Astro Data

	Dy Hr Mn
♂ R	2 21:27
☽ 0N	6 11:25
♃∠♆	19 16:20
☽ 0S	21 1:55
☿ R	26 1:13
☽ 0N	2 22:07
☿ D	16 5:06
☽ 0S	17 9:07
♄∠♅	20 15:55
♃∠♅	27 4:13

Planet Ingress

	Dy Hr Mn
☿ ♒	6 22:17
♀ ♐	7 12:07
♇ ♐	17 9:16
☉ ♒	20 13:00
♂ ♌R	22 23:48
♀ ♑	4 20:12
☉ ♓	19 3:11

Last Aspect / ☽ Ingress

Last Aspect Dy Hr Mn		☽ Ingress	Dy Hr Mn
2 17:57	♇ ⚹	♒	2 18:39
4 21:11	♇ □	♓	4 21:49
7 4:24	♇ △	♈	7 4:56
9 7:50	♅ □	♉	9 15:58
12 4:40	♇ ☍	♊	12 4:57
13 0:01	☿ △	♋	14 17:20
17 3:36	♇ △	♌	17 3:36
18 10:47	☿ ☍	♍	19 11:39
21 11:58	♅ △	♎	21 17:53
23 22:06	♂ ⚹	♏	23 22:32
26 0:11	♂ □	♐	26 1:37
28 1:00	♂ △	♑	28 3:26
30 0:21	♅ ☌	♒	30 5:03

Last Aspect / ☽ Ingress

Last Aspect Dy Hr Mn		☽ Ingress	Dy Hr Mn
1 3:06	♂ ☍	♓	1 8:05
3 11:21	♀ □	♈	3 14:12
5 19:19	♅ □	♉	6 0:08
8 8:04	♅ △	♊	8 12:44
10 12:23	♂ ⚹	♋	11 1:17
13 7:42	♅ ☍	♌	13 11:31
15 12:15	☉ ☍	♍	15 18:52
17 20:54	♅ △	♎	18 0:00
20 1:04	♅ □	♏	20 3:55
22 4:34	♅ ⚹	♐	22 7:13
23 14:40	♂ △	♑	24 10:11
26 10:57	♅ ☌	♒	26 13:14
27 18:44	♂ ☍	♓	28 17:16

☽ Phases & Eclipses

Dy Hr Mn	
1 10:56	● 10♑33
8 15:46	☽ 17♈54
16 20:26	○ 26♋15
24 4:58	☾ 3♏44
30 22:48	● 10♒35
7 12:54	☽ 18♉17
15 12:15	○ 26♌21
22 13:04	☾ 3♐26

Astro Data

1 January 1995
Julian Day # 34699
SVP 5♓19'34"
GC 26♐46.2 ⚴ 6♉00.5
Eris 17♈25.3R ✱ 10♐51.1
⚷ 26♍21.9 ⚶ 1♋05.4R
☽ Mean ☊ 11♏44.4

1 February 1995
Julian Day # 34730
SVP 5♓19'29"
GC 26♐46.2 ⚴ 12♉32.2
Eris 17♈29.3 ✱ 20♐24.6
⚷ 25♍58.5R ⚶ 25♊30.6R
☽ Mean ☊ 10♏05.9

March 1995 LONGITUDE

Day	Sid.Time	☉	0 hr ☽	Noon ☽	True ☊	☿	♀	♂	?	♃	♄	♅	♆	♇
1 W	22 35 18	10♓26 01	3♓48 34	10♓32 19	7♏04.4	13♒25.2	28♑19.8	16♌36.3	8♌19.0	13♐55.3	14♓27.1	28♑48.8	24♑40.6	0♐36.2
2 Th	22 39 15	11 26 15	17 11 40	23 46 22	6R 55.8	14 26.9	29 30.2	16R 19.0	8R 10.6	14 00.7	14 34.4	28 51.6	24 42.4	0 36.3
3 F	22 43 11	12 26 27	0♈16 17	6♈41 24	6 49.3	15 31.1	0♒40.6	16 02.4	8 02.7	14 05.9	14 41.8	28 54.4	24 44.0	0R 36.3
4 Sa	22 47 08	13 26 38	13 01 45	19 17 32	6 45.3	16 37.6	1 51.0	15 46.5	7 55.1	14 11.0	14 49.1	28 57.2	24 45.7	0 36.3
5 Su	22 51 04	14 26 46	25 29 01	1♉36 30	6D 43.6	17 46.3	3 01.6	15 31.4	7 48.0	14 16.0	14 56.5	28 59.9	24 47.4	0 36.3
6 M	22 55 01	15 26 52	7♉40 27	13 41 20	6 43.7	18 57.0	4 12.2	15 17.0	7 41.3	14 20.7	15 03.9	29 02.7	24 49.0	0 36.2
7 Tu	22 58 57	16 26 57	19 39 41	25 36 06	6 44.8	20 09.7	5 22.9	15 03.3	7 35.0	14 25.3	15 11.3	29 05.3	24 50.6	0 36.1
8 W	23 02 54	17 26 59	1♊31 11	7♊25 37	6R 46.0	21 24.2	6 33.7	14 50.4	7 29.1	14 29.8	15 18.6	29 08.0	24 52.1	0 36.0
9 Th	23 06 50	18 26 59	13 20 01	19 15 05	6 46.6	22 40.5	7 44.5	14 38.3	7 23.7	14 34.0	15 26.0	29 10.6	24 53.7	0 35.8
10 F	23 10 47	19 26 57	25 11 27	1♋09 48	6 45.6	23 58.5	8 55.4	14 26.9	7 18.7	14 38.1	15 33.4	29 13.2	24 55.2	0 35.6
11 Sa	23 14 44	20 26 52	7♋10 44	13 14 51	6 42.8	25 18.1	10 06.3	14 16.3	7 14.1	14 42.1	15 40.7	29 15.7	24 56.7	0 35.4
12 Su	23 18 40	21 26 46	19 22 41	25 34 43	6 38.2	26 39.2	11 17.3	14 06.6	7 09.9	14 45.8	15 48.1	29 18.2	24 58.1	0 35.1
13 M	23 22 37	22 26 37	1♌51 23	8♌13 00	6 31.9	28 01.9	12 28.4	13 57.6	7 06.2	14 49.4	15 55.4	29 20.7	24 59.6	0 34.8
14 Tu	23 26 33	23 26 26	14 39 49	21 11 57	6 24.6	29 26.0	13 39.5	13 49.3	7 02.9	14 52.8	16 02.7	29 23.1	25 01.0	0 34.4
15 W	23 30 30	24 26 13	27 49 27	4♍32 12	6 17.2	0♓51.6	14 50.6	13 41.9	7 00.1	14 56.0	16 10.1	29 25.5	25 02.4	0 34.1
16 Th	23 34 26	25 25 58	11♍20 01	18 12 36	6 10.4	2 18.5	16 01.9	13 35.3	6 57.7	14 59.1	16 17.4	29 27.9	25 03.7	0 33.7
17 F	23 38 23	26 25 41	25 09 32	2♎10 20	6 05.1	3 46.8	17 13.1	13 29.4	6 55.7	15 01.9	16 24.7	29 30.2	25 05.1	0 33.2
18 Sa	23 42 19	27 25 22	9♎14 27	16 21 16	6 01.6	5 16.5	18 24.5	13 24.4	6 54.1	15 04.6	16 32.0	29 32.5	25 06.4	0 32.7
19 Su	23 46 16	28 25 01	23 30 11	0♏40 36	6D 00.1	6 47.5	19 35.9	13 20.1	6 53.0	15 07.1	16 39.2	29 34.7	25 07.6	0 32.2
20 M	23 50 13	29 24 38	7♏51 53	15 03 30	6 00.3	8 19.9	20 47.3	13 16.5	6 52.3	15 09.5	16 46.5	29 36.9	25 08.9	0 31.7
21 Tu	23 54 09	0♈24 14	22 14 57	29 25 45	6 01.5	9 53.5	21 58.8	13 13.7	6D 52.1	15 11.6	16 53.8	29 39.1	25 10.1	0 31.1
22 W	23 58 06	1 23 48	6♐35 32	13♐43 57	6 02.9	11 28.5	23 10.3	13 11.7	6 52.3	15 13.6	17 01.0	29 41.2	25 11.3	0 30.5
23 Th	0 02 02	2 23 20	20 50 44	27 55 39	6R 03.9	13 04.8	24 21.9	13 10.5	6 52.9	15 15.4	17 08.2	29 43.3	25 12.4	0 29.9
24 F	0 05 59	3 22 50	4♑58 30	11♑59 08	6 03.6	14 42.4	25 33.5	13D 09.9	6 53.9	15 17.0	17 15.4	29 45.3	25 13.6	0 29.2
25 Sa	0 09 55	4 22 19	18 57 24	25 53 10	6 02.0	16 21.3	26 45.2	13 10.1	6 55.4	15 18.4	17 22.6	29 47.3	25 14.7	0 28.5
26 Su	0 13 52	5 21 46	2♒46 18	9♒36 41	5 58.9	18 01.5	27 56.9	13 11.1	6 57.2	15 19.6	17 29.7	29 49.2	25 15.7	0 27.8
27 M	0 17 48	6 21 11	16 24 11	23 08 41	5 54.7	19 43.1	29 08.7	13 12.7	6 59.5	15 20.7	17 36.8	29 51.1	25 16.8	0 27.1
28 Tu	0 21 45	7 20 34	29 50 02	6♓28 08	5 50.1	21 25.9	0♓20.4	13 15.1	7 02.2	15 21.5	17 44.0	29 53.0	25 17.8	0 26.3
29 W	0 25 41	8 19 55	13♓02 52	19 34 08	5 45.5	23 10.2	1 32.3	13 18.1	7 05.3	15 22.2	17 51.0	29 54.8	25 18.8	0 25.5
30 Th	0 29 38	9 19 14	26 01 51	2♈26 00	5 41.7	24 55.7	2 44.1	13 21.9	7 08.9	15 22.6	17 58.1	29 56.6	25 19.7	0 24.6
31 F	0 33 35	10 18 32	8♈46 35	15 03 36	5 38.9	26 42.7	3 56.0	13 26.3	7 12.8	15 22.9	18 05.1	29 58.3	25 20.6	0 23.7

April 1995 LONGITUDE

Day	Sid.Time	☉	0 hr ☽	Noon ☽	True ☊	☿	♀	♂	?	♃	♄	♅	♆	♇
1 Sa	0 37 31	11♈17 47	21♈17 10	27♈27 25	5♏37.5	28♓31.0	5♓07.9	13♌31.4	7♌17.2	15♐23.0	18♓12.1	29♑60.0	25♑21.5	0♐22.8
2 Su	0 41 28	12 17 00	3♉34 31	9♉38 43	5D 37.3	0♈20.7	6 19.9	13 37.2	7 21.9	15R 22.9	18 19.1	0♒01.6	25 22.3	0R 21.9
3 M	0 45 24	13 16 11	15 40 17	21 39 35	5 38.1	2 11.8	7 31.8	13 43.6	7 27.0	15 22.6	18 26.0	0 03.2	25 23.2	0 20.9
4 Tu	0 49 21	14 15 20	27 36 59	3♊32 56	5 39.6	4 04.3	8 43.8	13 50.7	7 32.6	15 22.2	18 32.9	0 04.8	25 23.9	0 19.9
5 W	0 53 17	15 14 26	9♊27 53	15 22 21	5 41.2	5 58.2	9 55.9	13 58.4	7 38.5	15 21.5	18 39.8	0 06.3	25 24.7	0 18.9
6 Th	0 57 14	16 13 31	21 16 52	27 12 01	5 42.7	7 53.5	11 07.9	14 06.7	7 44.8	15 20.7	18 46.7	0 07.7	25 25.4	0 17.9
7 F	1 01 10	17 12 33	3♋08 22	9♋06 31	5R 43.7	9 50.2	12 20.0	14 15.6	7 51.4	15 19.6	18 53.5	0 09.1	25 26.1	0 16.8
8 Sa	1 05 07	18 11 33	15 07 05	21 10 39	5 43.9	11 48.3	13 32.1	14 25.1	7 58.5	15 18.4	19 00.2	0 10.5	25 26.8	0 15.7
9 Su	1 09 04	19 10 30	27 17 50	3♌29 09	5 43.2	13 47.7	14 44.2	14 35.1	8 05.9	15 17.0	19 07.0	0 11.8	25 27.4	0 14.6
10 M	1 13 00	20 09 25	9♌45 09	16 06 19	5 42.0	15 48.3	15 56.3	14 45.8	8 13.6	15 15.4	19 13.7	0 13.0	25 28.0	0 13.5
11 Tu	1 16 57	21 08 18	22 33 01	29 05 37	5 40.2	17 50.2	17 08.5	14 57.0	8 21.7	15 13.7	19 20.3	0 14.2	25 28.5	0 12.3
12 W	1 20 53	22 07 09	5♍44 18	12♍29 12	5 38.3	19 53.3	18 20.7	15 08.7	8 30.2	15 11.7	19 27.0	0 15.4	25 29.1	0 11.1
13 Th	1 24 50	23 05 57	19 20 18	26 17 27	5 36.6	21 57.4	19 32.9	15 21.0	8 39.0	15 09.6	19 33.5	0 16.5	25 29.6	0 09.9
14 F	1 28 46	24 04 43	3♎20 22	10♎28 37	5 35.4	24 02.5	20 45.1	15 33.8	8 48.2	15 07.2	19 40.1	0 17.6	25 30.0	0 08.7
15 Sa	1 32 43	25 03 27	17 41 40	24 58 47	5D 34.7	26 08.3	21 57.4	15 47.0	8 57.6	15 04.7	19 46.6	0 18.6	25 30.4	0 07.4
16 Su	1 36 39	26 02 10	2♏19 14	9♏42 08	5 34.6	28 14.8	23 09.7	16 00.8	9 07.4	15 02.1	19 53.0	0 19.6	25 30.8	0 06.2
17 M	1 40 36	27 00 50	17 06 34	24 31 38	5 34.9	0♉21.7	24 22.0	16 15.1	9 17.6	14 59.2	19 59.4	0 20.5	25 31.2	0 04.9
18 Tu	1 44 33	27 59 29	1♐56 23	9♐20 00	5 35.5	2 28.8	25 34.3	16 29.8	9 28.0	14 56.2	20 05.8	0 21.3	25 31.5	0 03.5
19 W	1 48 29	28 58 06	16 41 38	24 00 36	5 36.1	4 35.8	26 46.6	16 45.0	9 38.8	14 53.0	20 12.1	0 22.2	25 31.8	0 02.2
20 Th	1 52 26	29 56 41	1♑16 18	8♑28 14	5 36.6	6 42.5	27 59.0	17 00.7	9 49.9	14 49.6	20 18.4	0 22.9	25 32.1	0 00.9
21 F	1 56 22	0♉55 15	15 36 00	22 39 21	5R 36.9	8 48.6	29 11.4	17 16.8	10 01.2	14 46.1	20 24.6	0 23.7	25 32.3	29♏59.5
22 Sa	2 00 19	1 53 47	29 38 07	6♒32 12	5 36.9	10 53.7	0♈23.8	17 33.3	10 12.9	14 42.4	20 30.7	0 24.3	25 32.5	29 58.1
23 Su	2 04 15	2 52 17	13♒21 37	20 06 25	5 36.8	12 57.6	1 36.2	17 50.3	10 24.9	14 38.5	20 36.9	0 25.0	25 32.7	29 56.7
24 M	2 08 12	3 50 46	26 46 43	3♓22 41	5 36.6	14 59.9	2 48.7	18 07.7	10 37.1	14 34.4	20 42.9	0 25.5	25 32.8	29 55.2
25 Tu	2 12 08	4 49 13	9♓54 28	16 22 18	5D 36.5	17 00.2	4 01.1	18 25.5	10 49.7	14 30.2	20 48.9	0 26.0	25 32.9	29 53.8
26 W	2 16 05	5 47 38	22 46 22	29 06 52	5 36.5	18 58.4	5 13.6	18 43.7	11 02.5	14 25.8	20 54.9	0 26.5	25 33.0	29 52.3
27 Th	2 20 02	6 46 02	5♈24 03	11♈38 06	5 36.5	20 54.0	6 26.1	19 02.4	11 15.6	14 21.3	21 00.8	0 26.9	25R 33.0	29 50.9
28 F	2 23 58	7 44 24	17 49 14	23 57 40	5R 36.6	22 47.0	7 38.6	19 21.4	11 29.0	14 16.6	21 06.7	0 27.3	25 33.0	29 49.4
29 Sa	2 27 55	8 42 45	0♉03 35	6♉07 14	5 36.7	24 36.9	8 51.1	19 40.7	11 42.7	14 11.7	21 12.4	0 27.6	25 33.0	29 47.8
30 Su	2 31 51	9 41 03	12 08 48	18 08 31	5 36.6	26 23.6	10 03.7	20 00.5	11 56.6	14 06.7	21 18.2	0 27.9	25 32.9	29 46.3

Astro Data

	Dy Hr Mn
☽0N	2 8:00
♇R	4 2:34
☽0S	16 17:51
☉0N	21 2:14
?D	21 13:59
♂D	24 17:18
☽0N	29 15:40
♃R	1 12:03
☿0N	4 16:32
♅⚹♇	10 16:39
♃∠♅	11 7:23
☽0S	13 3:41
♀0N	25 4:46
☽0N	25 21:29
♆R	27 22:14

Planet Ingress

	Dy Hr Mn
♀ ♒	2 22:10
☿ ♓	14 21:35
☉ ♈	21 2:14
♀ ♓	28 5:10
♅ ♒	1 12:11
☿ ♈	2 7:29
☿ ♉	17 7:54
☉ ♉	20 13:21
♇ ♏R	21 2:56
♀ ♈	22 4:07

Last Aspect / ☽ Ingress

Last Aspect Dy Hr Mn		☽ Ingress Dy Hr Mn
2 21:25	♅ ⚹	♈ 2 23:30
5 6:51	♅ □	♉ 5 8:50
7 19:06	♅ △	♊ 7 20:55
9 19:46	☿ △	♋ 10 9:40
12 19:10	♅ ☍	♌ 12 20:28
14 0:21	♃ △	♍ 15 3:54
17 7:26	♅ △	♎ 17 8:18
19 10:10	♅ □	♏ 19 10:52
21 12:22	♅ ⚹	♐ 21 12:57
23 5:24	♀ ⚹	♑ 23 15:31
25 18:48	♅ ☌	♒ 25 19:10
27 23:49	♀ ☌	♓ 28 0:18
30 7:19	♅ ⚹	♈ 30 7:26

Last Aspect / ☽ Ingress

Last Aspect Dy Hr Mn		☽ Ingress Dy Hr Mn
1 7:54	♆ □	♉ 1 16:59
3 19:31	♆ △	♊ 4 4:49
5 18:45	♄ □	♋ 6 17:40
8 20:23	♆ ☍	♌ 9 5:16
10 20:11	☉ △	♍ 11 13:39
13 10:38	♆ △	♎ 13 18:20
15 14:13	☿ ☍	♏ 15 20:13
17 13:36	♆ ⚹	♐ 17 20:51
19 20:46	☉ △	♑ 19 21:53
22 0:36	♇ ⚹	♒ 22 0:38
24 5:43	♇ □	♓ 24 5:50
26 13:26	♇ △	♈ 26 13:41
28 15:07	♆ □	♉ 28 23:53

☽ Phases & Eclipses

Dy Hr Mn	
1 11:48	● 10♓26
9 10:14	☽ 18♊23
17 1:26	○ 25♍59
23 20:10	☾ 2♑44
31 2:09	● 9♈54
8 5:35	☽ 17♋56
15 12:08	○ 25♎04
15 12:18	• P 0.111
22 3:18	☾ 1♒33
29 17:36	● 8♉56
29 17:32:20	• A 06'37"

Astro Data

1 March 1995
Julian Day # 34758
SVP 5♓19'26"
GC 26♐46.3 ⚳ 23♉50.8
Eris 17♈41.1 ⚴ 27♐39.5
⚷ 24♍16.5R ⚶ 26♊14.1
☽ Mean ☊ 8♏37.0

1 April 1995
Julian Day # 34789
SVP 5♓19'24"
GC 26♐46.4 ⚳ 9♊37.9
Eris 18♈00.0 ⚴ 3♑05.0
⚷ 21♍52.5R ⚶ 2♋30.5
☽ Mean ☊ 6♏58.4

LONGITUDE — May 1995

Day	Sid.Time	☉	0 hr ☽	Noon ☽	True ☊	☿	♀	♂	⚳	♃	♄	♅	♆	♇
1 M	2 35 48	10♉39 20	24♉06 39	0♊03 26	5♏36.2	28♉06.9	11♈16.2	20♌20.6	12♌10.8	14♐01.6	21♓23.9	0♒28.1	25♑32.8	29♏44.8
2 Tu	2 39 44	11 37 35	5♊59 09	11 54 07	5R35.6	29 46.6	12 28.8	20 41.1	12 25.2	13R56.3	21 29.5	0 28.3	25R32.7	29R43.2
3 W	2 43 41	12 35 48	17 48 40	23 43 08	5 34.7	1♊22.6	13 41.3	21 02.0	12 39.9	13 50.9	21 35.0	0 28.4	25 32.5	29 41.7
4 Th	2 47 37	13 33 59	29 37 56	5♋33 28	5 33.7	2 54.8	14 53.9	21 23.2	12 54.9	13 45.3	21 40.5	0R28.4	25 32.3	29 40.1
5 F	2 51 34	14 32 09	11♋30 10	17 28 32	5 32.6	4 23.1	16 06.5	21 44.7	13 10.1	13 39.6	21 45.9	0 28.5	25 32.1	29 38.5
6 Sa	2 55 31	15 30 16	23 29 03	29 32 14	5 31.8	5 47.4	17 19.1	22 06.5	13 25.5	13 33.8	21 51.3	0 28.4	25 31.8	29 37.0
7 Su	2 59 27	16 28 21	5♌38 36	11♌48 42	5D31.4	7 07.5	18 31.7	22 28.7	13 41.1	13 27.8	21 56.6	0 28.3	25 31.5	29 35.4
8 M	3 03 24	17 26 25	18 03 03	24 22 11	5 31.4	8 23.5	19 44.3	22 51.2	13 57.0	13 21.7	22 01.8	0 28.2	25 31.2	29 33.8
9 Tu	3 07 20	18 24 26	0♍46 35	7♍16 41	5 32.0	9 35.2	20 56.9	23 14.0	14 13.1	13 15.5	22 07.0	0 28.0	25 30.9	29 32.1
10 W	3 11 17	19 22 26	13 52 54	20 35 32	5 33.0	10 42.6	22 09.6	23 37.1	14 29.5	13 09.2	22 12.1	0 27.8	25 30.5	29 30.5
11 Th	3 15 13	20 20 24	27 24 47	4♎20 45	5 34.1	11 45.7	23 22.2	24 00.5	14 46.0	13 02.8	22 17.1	0 27.5	25 30.0	29 28.9
12 F	3 19 10	21 18 19	11♎23 23	18 32 29	5 35.1	12 44.3	24 34.8	24 24.1	15 02.8	12 56.3	22 22.1	0 27.2	25 29.6	29 27.2
13 Sa	3 23 06	22 16 14	25 47 42	3♏08 28	5R35.6	13 38.4	25 47.5	24 48.1	15 19.8	12 49.7	22 27.0	0 26.8	25 29.1	29 25.6
14 Su	3 27 03	23 14 06	10♏34 04	18 03 38	5 35.3	14 27.9	27 00.2	25 12.3	15 36.9	12 43.0	22 31.8	0 26.4	25 28.6	29 24.0
15 M	3 30 59	24 11 58	25 36 09	3♐10 29	5 34.1	15 12.8	28 12.9	25 36.8	15 54.3	12 36.1	22 36.5	0 25.9	25 28.1	29 22.3
16 Tu	3 34 56	25 09 47	10♐45 27	18 19 51	5 32.1	15 53.0	29 25.6	26 01.5	16 11.9	12 29.3	22 41.2	0 25.4	25 27.5	29 20.7
17 W	3 38 53	26 07 36	25 52 28	3♑22 14	5 29.5	16 28.4	0♉38.3	26 26.5	16 29.6	12 22.3	22 45.8	0 24.8	25 26.9	29 19.0
18 Th	3 42 49	27 05 23	10♑48 07	18 09 18	5 26.9	16 59.1	1 51.0	26 51.8	16 47.6	12 15.2	22 50.3	0 24.2	25 26.3	29 17.4
19 F	3 46 46	28 03 09	25 25 04	2♒34 57	5 24.6	17 25.0	3 03.8	27 17.3	17 05.7	12 08.1	22 54.8	0 23.5	25 25.6	29 15.7
20 Sa	3 50 42	29 00 54	9♒38 35	16 35 50	5D23.1	17 46.0	4 16.5	27 43.1	17 24.1	12 00.9	22 59.2	0 22.8	25 24.9	29 14.0
21 Su	3 54 39	29 58 38	23 26 40	0♓11 14	5 22.6	18 02.1	5 29.3	28 09.0	17 42.6	11 53.6	23 03.5	0 22.1	25 24.2	29 12.4
22 M	3 58 35	0♊56 20	6♓49 43	13 22 28	5 23.1	18 13.4	6 42.1	28 35.3	18 01.3	11 46.3	23 07.7	0 21.3	25 23.5	29 10.7
23 Tu	4 02 32	1 54 02	19 49 50	26 12 15	5 24.4	18R19.9	7 54.8	29 01.7	18 20.1	11 38.9	23 11.8	0 20.4	25 22.7	29 09.1
24 W	4 06 28	2 51 43	2♈30 08	8♈43 58	5 26.0	18 21.7	9 07.6	29 28.4	18 39.2	11 31.4	23 15.9	0 19.5	25 21.9	29 07.4
25 Th	4 10 25	3 49 22	14 54 12	21 01 15	5 27.5	18 18.8	10 20.5	29 55.3	18 58.4	11 23.9	23 19.9	0 18.6	25 21.1	29 05.8
26 F	4 14 22	4 47 01	27 05 33	3♉07 31	5R28.2	18 11.5	11 33.3	0♍22.5	19 17.8	11 16.4	23 23.8	0 17.6	25 20.2	29 04.1
27 Sa	4 18 18	5 44 38	9♉07 29	15 05 50	5 27.8	17 59.8	12 46.1	0 49.8	19 37.3	11 08.9	23 27.6	0 16.5	25 19.3	29 02.5
28 Su	4 22 15	6 42 15	21 02 53	26 58 55	5 25.9	17 44.1	13 59.0	1 17.4	19 57.0	11 01.3	23 31.3	0 15.5	25 18.4	29 00.8
29 M	4 26 11	7 39 50	2♊54 13	8♊49 02	5 22.5	17 24.7	15 11.8	1 45.1	20 16.9	10 53.7	23 35.0	0 14.3	25 17.5	28 59.2
30 Tu	4 30 08	8 37 24	14 43 38	20 38 15	5 17.6	17 01.8	16 24.7	2 13.1	20 36.9	10 46.0	23 38.5	0 13.2	25 16.5	28 57.5
31 W	4 34 04	9 34 57	26 33 08	2♋28 31	5 11.7	16 36.0	17 37.6	2 41.3	20 57.1	10 38.4	23 42.0	0 12.0	25 15.5	28 55.9

LONGITUDE — June 1995

Day	Sid.Time	☉	0 hr ☽	Noon ☽	True ☊	☿	♀	♂	⚳	♃	♄	♅	♆	♇
1 Th	4 38 01	10♊32 29	8♋24 40	14♋21 51	5♏05.4	16♊07.5	18♉50.5	3♍09.7	21♌17.4	10♐30.7	23♓45.4	0♒10.7	25♑14.5	28♏54.3
2 F	4 41 58	11 30 00	20 20 21	26 20 30	4R59.3	15R37.0	20 03.4	3 38.3	21 37.9	10R23.1	23 48.7	0R09.5	25R13.5	28R52.7
3 Sa	4 45 54	12 27 29	2♌22 38	8♌27 08	4 54.0	15 04.9	21 16.3	4 07.1	21 58.5	10 15.5	23 51.9	0 08.1	25 12.4	28 51.1
4 Su	4 49 51	13 24 58	14 34 22	20 44 47	4 50.1	14 31.8	22 29.2	4 36.0	22 19.2	10 07.8	23 55.0	0 06.8	25 11.3	28 49.5
5 M	4 53 47	14 22 25	26 58 49	3♍16 55	4D47.8	13 58.3	23 42.1	5 05.2	22 40.1	10 00.2	23 58.1	0 05.3	25 10.2	28 47.9
6 Tu	4 57 44	15 19 50	9♍39 33	16 07 11	4 47.2	13 24.9	24 55.1	5 34.5	23 01.2	9 52.6	24 01.0	0 03.9	25 09.1	28 46.3
7 W	5 01 40	16 17 15	22 40 16	29 19 11	4 47.8	12 52.2	26 08.0	6 04.0	23 22.3	9 45.0	24 03.9	0 02.4	25 08.0	28 44.7
8 Th	5 05 37	17 14 38	6♎04 18	12♎55 53	4 49.1	12 20.7	27 21.0	6 33.7	23 43.6	9 37.5	24 06.6	0 00.9	25 06.8	28 43.2
9 F	5 09 33	18 12 01	19 54 07	26 59 01	4R50.2	11 51.1	28 33.9	7 03.5	24 05.0	9 30.0	24 09.3	29♑59.3	25 05.6	28 41.6
10 Sa	5 13 30	19 09 22	4♏10 29	11♏28 13	4 50.2	11 23.8	29 46.9	7 33.5	24 26.6	9 22.5	24 11.9	29 57.7	25 04.4	28 40.1
11 Su	5 17 27	20 06 42	18 51 45	26 20 24	4 48.5	10 59.2	0♊59.9	8 03.7	24 48.2	9 15.1	24 14.4	29 56.1	25 03.1	28 38.6
12 M	5 21 23	21 04 02	3♐53 16	11♐29 18	4 44.9	10 37.8	2 12.9	8 34.1	25 10.0	9 07.8	24 16.8	29 54.4	25 01.9	28 37.1
13 Tu	5 25 20	22 01 20	19 07 17	26 45 54	4 39.4	10 19.9	3 25.9	9 04.6	25 31.9	9 00.5	24 19.1	29 52.7	25 00.6	28 35.6
14 W	5 29 16	22 58 38	4♑23 48	11♑59 37	4 32.6	10 05.9	4 38.9	9 35.2	25 54.0	8 53.2	24 21.3	29 51.0	24 59.3	28 34.1
15 Th	5 33 13	23 55 56	19 32 03	26 59 58	4 25.4	9 55.9	5 52.0	10 06.0	26 16.1	8 46.0	24 23.4	29 49.2	24 58.0	28 32.7
16 F	5 37 09	24 53 13	4♒22 22	11♒38 28	4 18.8	9D50.2	7 05.0	10 37.0	26 38.3	8 38.9	24 25.4	29 47.4	24 56.7	28 31.2
17 Sa	5 41 06	25 50 30	18 47 43	25 49 45	4 13.5	9 48.9	8 18.1	11 08.1	27 00.7	8 31.9	24 27.3	29 45.6	24 55.3	28 29.8
18 Su	5 45 02	26 47 46	2♓44 25	9♓31 46	4 10.1	9 52.1	9 31.2	11 39.3	27 23.2	8 24.9	24 29.2	29 43.7	24 54.0	28 28.4
19 M	5 48 59	27 45 02	16 12 01	22 45 29	4D08.7	9 59.9	10 44.3	12 10.7	27 45.7	8 18.1	24 30.9	29 41.8	24 52.6	28 27.0
20 Tu	5 52 56	28 42 17	29 12 36	5♈33 53	4 08.7	10 12.4	11 57.4	12 42.3	28 08.4	8 11.3	24 32.5	29 39.9	24 51.2	28 25.6
21 W	5 56 52	29 39 33	11♈49 55	18 01 16	4 09.6	10 29.5	13 10.6	13 14.0	28 31.2	8 04.6	24 34.1	29 38.0	24 49.7	28 24.3
22 Th	6 00 49	0♋36 48	24 08 33	0♉12 23	4R10.4	10 51.3	14 23.8	13 45.8	28 54.1	7 58.0	24 35.5	29 36.0	24 48.3	28 22.9
23 F	6 04 45	1 34 03	6♉13 19	12 11 57	4 10.1	11 17.7	15 36.9	14 17.8	29 17.1	7 51.5	24 36.8	29 34.0	24 46.9	28 21.6
24 Sa	6 08 42	2 31 18	18 08 46	24 04 18	4 08.0	11 48.7	16 50.1	14 49.9	29 40.2	7 45.1	24 38.1	29 31.9	24 45.4	28 20.3
25 Su	6 12 38	3 28 33	29 58 58	5♊53 12	4 03.6	12 24.2	18 03.4	15 22.1	0♍03.3	7 38.8	24 39.2	29 29.9	24 43.9	28 19.0
26 M	6 16 35	4 25 48	11♊47 20	17 41 42	3 56.6	13 04.1	19 16.6	15 54.5	0 26.6	7 32.7	24 40.3	29 27.8	24 42.5	28 17.8
27 Tu	6 20 31	5 23 02	23 36 35	29 32 14	3 47.4	13 48.5	20 29.8	16 27.1	0 50.0	7 26.6	24 41.2	29 25.7	24 41.0	28 16.5
28 W	6 24 28	6 20 17	5♋28 52	11♋26 41	3 36.5	14 37.2	21 43.1	16 59.7	1 13.5	7 20.7	24 42.0	29 23.6	24 39.4	28 15.3
29 Th	6 28 25	7 17 31	17 25 51	23 26 33	3 24.8	15 30.2	22 56.4	17 32.5	1 37.0	7 14.9	24 42.8	29 21.4	24 37.9	28 14.1
30 F	6 32 21	8 14 44	29 28 56	5♌33 11	3 13.3	16 27.4	24 09.7	18 05.5	2 00.7	7 09.3	24 43.4	29 19.2	24 36.4	28 13.0

Astro Data

	Dy Hr Mn
♅R	5 7:48
☽0S	10 13:33
☽0N	23 3:14
☿R	24 9:01
♃∠♆	3 23:04
☽0S	6 22:25
☿D	17 6:58
☽0N	19 10:38
♄✶♆	27 9:32

Planet Ingress

	Dy Hr Mn
☿ ♊	2 15:18
♀ ♉	16 23:22
☉ ♊	21 12:34
♂ ♍	25 16:09
♅ ♑R	9 1:42
♀ ♊	10 16:18
☉ ♋	21 20:34
⚳ ♍	25 8:33

Last Aspect / ☽ Ingress (May)

Last Aspect Dy Hr Mn		☽ Ingress Dy Hr Mn
1 11:22	♇ ☍	♊ 1 11:53
3 7:38	♄ □	♋ 4 0:45
6 12:09	♇ △	♌ 6 12:55
8 21:43	♇ □	♍ 8 22:33
11 3:37	♇ ✶	♎ 11 4:30
12 23:30	♆ □	♏ 13 6:53
15 5:59	♇ ☌	♐ 15 6:58
17 0:35	♂ △	♑ 17 6:36
19 6:26	♇ ✶	♒ 19 7:39
21 11:36	☉ □	♓ 21 11:40
23 17:35	♇ △	♈ 23 19:13
25 20:32	♆ □	♉ 26 5:46
28 16:06	♇ ☍	♊ 28 18:07
30 18:08	♄ □	♋ 31 6:59

Last Aspect / ☽ Ingress (June)

Last Aspect Dy Hr Mn		☽ Ingress Dy Hr Mn
2 17:02	♇ △	♌ 2 19:17
5 3:30	♇ □	♍ 5 5:46
7 10:58	♇ ✶	♎ 7 13:13
9 17:02	♅ □	♏ 9 17:03
11 17:43	♅ ✶	♐ 11 17:50
13 8:09	♄ □	♑ 13 17:05
15 16:34	♅ ☌	♒ 15 16:52
17 16:36	♇ □	♓ 17 19:13
20 0:53	♅ ✶	♈ 20 1:29
22 10:48	♅ □	♉ 22 11:35
24 23:03	♅ △	♊ 25 0:02
27 2:10	♄ □	♋ 27 12:56
29 23:43	♅ ☍	♌ 30 1:02

☽ Phases & Eclipses

Dy Hr Mn		
7 21:44	☽	16♌52
14 20:48	○	23♏35
21 11:36	☾	29♒58
29 9:27	●	7♊34
6 10:26	☽	15♍16
13 4:03	○	21♐42
19 22:01	☾	28♓09
28 0:50	●	5♋54

Astro Data

1 May 1995
Julian Day # 34819
SVP 5♓19'21"
GC 26♐46.4 ⚴ 26♊27.3
Eris 18♈19.5 ⚵ 4♑21.7R
⚷ 20♍15.5R ⚶ 12♋02.3
☽ Mean ☊ 5♏23.1

1 June 1995
Julian Day # 34850
SVP 5♓19'17"
GC 26♐46.5 ⚴ 14♋17.0
Eris 18♈36.1 ⚵ 0♑37.0R
⚷ 20♍10.3 ⚶ 23♋59.2
☽ Mean ☊ 3♏44.6

July 1995 — LONGITUDE

Day	Sid.Time	☉	0 hr ☽	Noon ☽	True ☊	☿	♀	♂	⚳	♃	♄	♅	♆	♇
1 Sa	6 36 18	9♋11 58	11♌39 30	17♌48 04	3♏03.0	17♊28.8	25♊23.0	18♍38.5	2♍24.4	7♐03.8	24♓44.0	29♑17.0	24♑34.8	28♏11.8
2 Su	6 40 14	10 09 11	23 59 07	0♍12 54	2R 54.8	18 34.3	26 36.3	19 11.7	2 48.2	6R 58.4	24 44.4	29R 14.8	24R 33.3	28R 10.7
3 M	6 44 11	11 06 24	6♍29 43	12 49 53	2 49.1	19 43.8	27 49.6	19 45.0	3 12.1	6 53.1	24 44.7	29 12.6	24 31.7	28 09.6
4 Tu	6 48 07	12 03 36	19 13 44	25 41 38	2 45.9	20 57.4	29 03.0	20 18.4	3 36.1	6 48.0	24 45.0	29 10.3	24 30.2	28 08.5
5 W	6 52 04	13 00 48	2♎13 57	8♎51 03	2D 44.8	22 14.9	0♋16.4	20 52.0	4 00.2	6 43.1	24R 45.1	29 08.1	24 28.6	28 07.5
6 Th	6 56 00	13 58 00	15 33 18	22 21 01	2R 44.9	23 36.3	1 29.8	21 25.6	4 24.3	6 38.2	24 45.1	29 05.8	24 27.0	28 06.4
7 F	6 59 57	14 55 12	29 14 27	6♏13 47	2 45.0	25 01.5	2 43.2	21 59.4	4 48.5	6 33.6	24 45.1	29 03.5	24 25.4	28 05.4
8 Sa	7 03 54	15 52 23	13♏19 04	20 30 13	2 44.0	26 30.5	3 56.6	22 33.3	5 12.8	6 29.1	24 44.9	29 01.2	24 23.8	28 04.5
9 Su	7 07 50	16 49 34	27 47 01	5♐09 00	2 41.0	28 03.3	5 10.0	23 07.3	5 37.2	6 24.7	24 44.6	28 58.8	24 22.2	28 03.5
10 M	7 11 47	17 46 46	12♐35 34	20 05 55	2 35.3	29 39.6	6 23.5	23 41.5	6 01.6	6 20.6	24 44.3	28 56.5	24 20.6	28 02.6
11 Tu	7 15 43	18 43 57	27 39 00	5♑13 43	2 27.2	1♋19.6	7 36.9	24 15.7	6 26.1	6 16.5	24 43.8	28 54.2	24 19.0	28 01.7
12 W	7 19 40	19 41 08	12♑48 46	20 22 50	2 17.3	3 02.9	8 50.4	24 50.0	6 50.7	6 12.7	24 43.2	28 51.8	24 17.4	28 00.9
13 Th	7 23 36	20 38 20	27 54 37	5♒22 52	2 06.7	4 49.6	10 03.9	25 24.5	7 15.4	6 09.0	24 42.6	28 49.4	24 15.8	28 00.0
14 F	7 27 33	21 35 32	12♒46 25	20 04 21	1 56.6	6 39.4	11 17.5	25 59.0	7 40.1	6 05.5	24 41.8	28 47.1	24 14.1	27 59.2
15 Sa	7 31 29	22 32 44	27 15 53	4♓20 28	1 48.2	8 32.1	12 31.0	26 33.7	8 04.8	6 02.1	24 40.9	28 44.7	24 12.5	27 58.4
16 Su	7 35 26	23 29 57	11♓17 46	18 07 41	1 42.1	10 27.6	13 44.6	27 08.5	8 29.7	5 58.9	24 40.0	28 42.3	24 10.9	27 57.7
17 M	7 39 23	24 27 10	24 50 16	1♈25 44	1 38.5	12 25.7	14 58.2	27 43.3	8 54.6	5 55.9	24 38.9	28 39.9	24 09.3	27 57.0
18 Tu	7 43 19	25 24 24	7♈54 30	14 16 59	1D 36.9	14 25.9	16 11.8	28 18.3	9 19.5	5 53.0	24 37.8	28 37.5	24 07.7	27 56.3
19 W	7 47 16	26 21 39	20 33 48	26 45 31	1R 36.6	16 28.2	17 25.4	28 53.4	9 44.6	5 50.3	24 36.5	28 35.1	24 06.0	27 55.6
20 Th	7 51 12	27 18 54	2♉52 49	8♉56 20	1 36.6	18 32.0	18 39.1	29 28.6	10 09.7	5 47.8	24 35.2	28 32.7	24 04.4	27 55.0
21 F	7 55 09	28 16 11	14 58 47	20 54 46	1 35.6	20 37.3	19 52.8	0♎03.9	10 34.8	5 45.5	24 33.7	28 30.3	24 02.8	27 54.4
22 Sa	7 59 05	29 13 28	26 50 58	2♊45 57	1 32.7	22 43.5	21 06.5	0 39.3	11 00.0	5 43.4	24 32.2	28 27.9	24 01.2	27 53.8
23 Su	8 03 02	0♌10 45	8♊40 18	14 34 31	1 27.3	24 50.5	22 20.2	1 14.8	11 25.3	5 41.4	24 30.5	28 25.5	23 59.6	27 53.3
24 M	8 06 58	1 08 04	20 29 05	26 24 24	1 19.2	26 57.8	23 33.9	1 50.4	11 50.6	5 39.6	24 28.8	28 23.1	23 58.0	27 52.8
25 Tu	8 10 55	2 05 23	2♋20 52	8♋18 46	1 08.5	29 05.3	24 47.7	2 26.2	12 16.0	5 38.0	24 27.0	28 20.7	23 56.3	27 52.3
26 W	8 14 52	3 02 43	14 18 22	20 19 53	0 55.8	1♌12.5	26 01.5	3 02.0	12 41.4	5 36.6	24 25.1	28 18.3	23 54.7	27 51.8
27 Th	8 18 48	4 00 04	26 23 30	2♌29 20	0 42.3	3 19.4	27 15.3	3 37.9	13 06.9	5 35.4	24 23.1	28 15.9	23 53.1	27 51.4
28 F	8 22 45	4 57 26	8♌37 29	14 48 01	0 28.9	5 25.6	28 29.1	4 13.9	13 32.5	5 34.3	24 21.0	28 13.5	23 51.6	27 51.0
29 Sa	8 26 41	5 54 48	21 01 01	27 16 33	0 16.9	7 31.0	29 43.0	4 50.0	13 58.1	5 33.5	24 18.8	28 11.1	23 50.0	27 50.7
30 Su	8 30 38	6 52 11	3♍34 39	9♍55 24	0 07.1	9 35.4	0♌56.9	5 26.2	14 23.7	5 32.8	24 16.5	28 08.7	23 48.4	27 50.4
31 M	8 34 34	7 49 34	16 18 55	22 45 17	0 00.1	11 38.7	2 10.7	6 02.6	14 49.4	5 32.3	24 14.1	28 06.4	23 46.8	27 50.1

August 1995 — LONGITUDE

Day	Sid.Time	☉	0 hr ☽	Noon ☽	True ☊	☿	♀	♂	⚳	♃	♄	♅	♆	♇
1 Tu	8 38 31	8♌46 58	29♍14 41	5♎47 16	29♎56.0	13♌40.7	3♌24.6	6♎39.0	15♍15.2	5♐32.0	24♓11.7	28♑04.0	23♑45.3	27♏49.8
2 W	8 42 27	9 44 23	12♎23 15	19 02 51	29D 54.3	15 41.3	4 38.6	7 15.5	15 40.9	5D 31.8	24R 09.1	28R 01.7	23R 43.7	27R 49.6
3 Th	8 46 24	10 41 48	25 46 17	2♏33 46	29R 54.0	17 40.6	5 52.5	7 52.1	16 06.8	5 31.9	24 06.5	27 59.3	23 42.2	27 49.4
4 F	8 50 21	11 39 14	9♏25 29	16 21 37	29 54.0	19 38.4	7 06.4	8 28.8	16 32.6	5 32.1	24 03.8	27 57.0	23 40.7	27 49.3
5 Sa	8 54 17	12 36 40	23 22 14	0♐27 19	29 53.1	21 34.7	8 20.4	9 05.5	16 58.6	5 32.6	24 01.0	27 54.7	23 39.1	27 49.1
6 Su	8 58 14	13 34 07	7♐36 47	14 50 22	29 50.2	23 29.5	9 34.4	9 42.4	17 24.5	5 33.2	23 58.1	27 52.4	23 37.6	27 49.1
7 M	9 02 10	14 31 35	22 07 41	29 28 11	29 44.8	25 22.7	10 48.4	10 19.4	17 50.5	5 34.0	23 55.2	27 50.2	23 36.1	27 49.0
8 Tu	9 06 07	15 29 04	6♑51 09	14♑15 45	29 36.9	27 14.4	12 02.4	10 56.4	18 16.6	5 34.9	23 52.1	27 47.9	23 34.7	27D 49.0
9 W	9 10 03	16 26 34	21 41 02	29 05 58	29 27.2	29 04.5	13 16.5	11 33.6	18 42.7	5 36.1	23 49.0	27 45.7	23 33.2	27 49.0
10 Th	9 14 00	17 24 05	6♒29 27	13♒50 25	29 16.7	0♍53.1	14 30.5	12 10.8	19 08.8	5 37.4	23 45.9	27 43.4	23 31.7	27 49.0
11 F	9 17 56	18 21 36	21 07 51	28 20 51	29 06.7	2 40.2	15 44.6	12 48.1	19 34.9	5 39.0	23 42.6	27 41.2	23 30.3	27 49.1
12 Sa	9 21 53	19 19 09	5♓28 37	12♓30 33	28 58.1	4 25.7	16 58.7	13 25.5	20 01.1	5 40.6	23 39.3	27 39.0	23 28.9	27 49.2
13 Su	9 25 50	20 16 43	19 26 11	26 15 16	28 51.9	6 09.7	18 12.8	14 03.0	20 27.3	5 42.5	23 35.9	27 36.9	23 27.5	27 49.4
14 M	9 29 46	21 14 18	2♈57 42	9♈33 34	28 48.1	7 52.2	19 26.9	14 40.5	20 53.6	5 44.6	23 32.4	27 34.7	23 26.1	27 49.6
15 Tu	9 33 43	22 11 55	16 03 05	22 26 34	28D 46.5	9 33.2	20 41.1	15 18.2	21 19.9	5 46.8	23 28.9	27 32.6	23 24.7	27 49.8
16 W	9 37 39	23 09 34	28 44 29	4♉57 21	28 46.5	11 12.7	21 55.2	15 56.0	21 46.2	5 49.2	23 25.3	27 30.5	23 23.3	27 50.0
17 Th	9 41 36	24 07 14	11♉05 44	17 10 16	28R 47.0	12 50.7	23 09.4	16 33.8	22 12.6	5 51.8	23 21.6	27 28.4	23 22.0	27 50.3
18 F	9 45 32	25 04 55	23 11 36	29 10 23	28 47.1	14 27.3	24 23.6	17 11.7	22 39.0	5 54.6	23 17.9	27 26.4	23 20.6	27 50.6
19 Sa	9 49 29	26 02 38	5♊07 19	11♊03 01	28 45.8	16 02.4	25 37.8	17 49.7	23 05.4	5 57.5	23 14.1	27 24.4	23 19.3	27 51.0
20 Su	9 53 25	27 00 23	16 58 07	22 53 14	28 42.5	17 36.1	26 52.1	18 27.8	23 31.9	6 00.6	23 10.2	27 22.4	23 18.1	27 51.3
21 M	9 57 22	27 58 09	28 48 56	4♋45 43	28 36.9	19 08.4	28 06.4	19 06.0	23 58.4	6 03.9	23 06.3	27 20.4	23 16.8	27 51.8
22 Tu	10 01 19	28 55 57	10♋44 04	16 44 24	28 29.1	20 39.1	29 20.6	19 44.3	24 24.9	6 07.4	23 02.4	27 18.5	23 15.5	27 52.2
23 W	10 05 15	29 53 47	22 47 05	28 52 25	28 19.6	22 08.5	0♍34.9	20 22.7	24 51.5	6 11.0	22 58.3	27 16.6	23 14.3	27 52.7
24 Th	10 09 12	0♍51 38	5♌00 39	11♌11 56	28 09.2	23 36.3	1 49.3	21 01.1	25 18.1	6 14.8	22 54.3	27 14.7	23 13.1	27 53.2
25 F	10 13 08	1 49 31	17 26 24	23 44 08	27 58.8	25 02.7	3 03.6	21 39.7	25 44.7	6 18.8	22 50.2	27 12.8	23 11.9	27 53.8
26 Sa	10 17 05	2 47 25	0♍05 08	6♍29 22	27 49.5	26 27.5	4 17.9	22 18.3	26 11.4	6 22.9	22 46.0	27 11.0	23 10.7	27 54.4
27 Su	10 21 01	3 45 20	12 56 47	19 27 19	27 42.1	27 50.9	5 32.3	22 57.0	26 38.0	6 27.2	22 41.8	27 09.2	23 09.6	27 55.0
28 M	10 24 58	4 43 17	26 00 52	2♎37 21	27 37.1	29 12.7	6 46.7	23 35.8	27 04.7	6 31.7	22 37.5	27 07.5	23 08.5	27 55.6
29 Tu	10 28 54	5 41 16	9♎16 39	15 58 44	27D 34.4	0♎32.9	8 01.1	24 14.7	27 31.4	6 36.4	22 33.2	27 05.8	23 07.4	27 56.3
30 W	10 32 51	6 39 16	22 43 31	29 30 57	27 33.8	1 51.4	9 15.4	24 53.7	27 58.2	6 41.2	22 28.9	27 04.1	23 06.3	27 57.0
31 Th	10 36 47	7 37 17	6♏21 02	13♏13 44	27 34.5	3 08.3	10 29.9	25 32.7	28 24.9	6 46.1	22 24.5	27 02.5	23 05.3	27 57.8

Astro Data

	Dy Hr Mn
☽0S	4 5:53
♄ R	6 7:46
☽0N	16 20:03
♂0S	22 23:25
☽0S	31 12:25
♃ D	2 16:44
♅⚹♇	8 0:26
♇ D	8 13:33
☽0N	13 6:32
♄⚹♆	17 8:10
☽0S	27 19:05
☿0S	27 21:30

Planet Ingress

		Dy Hr Mn
♀	♋	5 6:39
☿	♋	10 16:58
♂	♎	21 9:21
☉	♌	23 7:30
☿	♌	25 22:19
♀	♌	29 17:32
☊	♎R	31 12:33
☿	♍	10 0:13
♀	♍	23 0:43
☉	♍	23 14:35
☿	♎	29 2:07

Last Aspect / ☽ Ingress

Last Aspect Dy Hr Mn			☽ Ingress	Dy Hr Mn
2 8:06	♇	□	♍	2 11:35
4 18:49	♀	□	♎	4 19:55
6 23:43	♅	□	♏	7 1:19
9 1:59	♅	⚹	♐	9 3:37
10 19:22	♄	□	♑	11 3:43
13 1:29	♅	☌	♒	13 3:21
15 1:12	♇	□	♓	15 4:37
17 6:58	♅	⚹	♈	17 9:23
19 15:33	♅	□	♉	19 18:20
22 4:11	☉	⚹	♊	22 6:23
24 8:07	♄	□	♋	24 19:16
27 3:43	♅	☍	♌	27 7:07
29 13:05	♇	□	♍	29 17:12

Last Aspect / ☽ Ingress

Last Aspect Dy Hr Mn			☽ Ingress	Dy Hr Mn
31 21:52	♅	△	♎	1 1:23
3 3:57	♅	□	♏	3 7:29
5 7:43	♅	⚹	♐	5 11:14
7 4:21	☿	△	♑	7 12:52
9 9:55	♇	⚹	♒	9 13:28
11 11:07	♇	□	♓	11 14:46
13 14:47	♇	△	♈	13 18:41
15 21:41	♅	□	♉	16 2:25
18 9:19	♇	☍	♊	18 13:40
20 21:05	☉	⚹	♋	21 2:24
23 10:03	♇	△	♌	23 14:13
25 19:53	♇	□	♍	25 23:50
28 5:07	☿	☌	♎	28 7:15
30 7:42	♅	□	♏	30 12:51

☽ Phases & Eclipses

Dy Hr Mn		
5 20:02	☽	13♎20
12 10:49	○	19♑38
19 11:10	☾	26♈20
27 15:13	●	4♌08
4 3:16	☽	11♏18
10 18:16	○	17♒39
18 3:04	☾	24♉43
26 4:31	●	2♍29

Astro Data

1 July 1995
Julian Day # 34880
SVP 5♓19'12"
GC 26♐46.6 ⚵ 1♌18.8
Eris 18♈45.0 ⚶ 24♐00.7R
⚷ 21♍45.6 ⚴ 6♌47.3
☽ Mean ☊ 2♏09.3

1 August 1995
Julian Day # 34911
SVP 5♓19'07"
GC 26♐46.7 ⚵ 18♌19.8
Eris 18♈44.6R ⚶ 19♐16.6R
⚷ 24♍49.5 ⚴ 20♌49.9
☽ Mean ☊ 0♏30.8

LONGITUDE September 1995

Day	Sid.Time	☉	0 hr ☽	Noon ☽	True ☊	☿	♀	♂	⚳	♃	♄	♅	♆	♇
1 F	10 40 44	8♍35 20	20♏09 04	27♏06 58	27♎35.6	4♎23.4	11♍44.3	26♎11.8	28♍51.7	6♐51.3	22♓20.1	27♑00.8	23♑04.2	27♏58.6
2 Sa	10 44 41	9 33 24	4♐07 26	11♐10 22	27R36.0	5 36.8	12 58.7	26 51.0	29 18.5	6 56.5	22R15.7	26R59.3	23R03.2	27 59.4
3 Su	10 48 37	10 31 29	18 15 38	25 23 03	27 35.0	6 48.2	14 13.2	27 30.3	29 45.4	7 02.0	22 11.2	26 57.7	23 02.3	28 00.2
4 M	10 52 34	11 29 36	2♑32 20	9♑43 09	27 32.2	7 57.7	15 27.6	28 09.7	0♎12.2	7 07.6	22 06.8	26 56.2	23 01.3	28 01.1
5 Tu	10 56 30	12 27 44	16 55 01	24 07 27	27 27.4	9 05.2	16 42.1	28 49.1	0 39.1	7 13.3	22 02.2	26 54.8	23 00.4	28 02.0
6 W	11 00 27	13 25 54	1♒19 51	8♒31 32	27 21.3	10 10.4	17 56.5	29 28.7	1 05.9	7 19.2	21 57.7	26 53.4	22 59.5	28 03.0
7 Th	11 04 23	14 24 05	15 41 49	22 50 00	27 14.5	11 13.4	19 11.0	0♏08.3	1 32.8	7 25.3	21 53.2	26 52.0	22 58.7	28 04.0
8 F	11 08 20	15 22 18	29 55 24	6♓57 21	27 08.0	12 14.0	20 25.5	0 47.9	1 59.7	7 31.5	21 48.6	26 50.7	22 57.8	28 05.0
9 Sa	11 12 16	16 20 32	13♓55 17	20 48 42	27 02.5	13 12.0	21 40.0	1 27.7	2 26.7	7 37.8	21 44.0	26 49.4	22 57.0	28 06.0
10 Su	11 16 13	17 18 48	27 37 11	4♈20 30	26 58.6	14 07.3	22 54.5	2 07.5	2 53.6	7 44.3	21 39.4	26 48.1	22 56.2	28 07.1
11 M	11 20 10	18 17 07	10♈58 27	17 31 01	26D56.5	14 59.7	24 09.0	2 47.4	3 20.6	7 51.0	21 34.8	26 46.9	22 55.5	28 08.2
12 Tu	11 24 06	19 15 27	23 58 16	0♉20 22	26 56.1	15 48.9	25 23.5	3 27.4	3 47.5	7 57.8	21 30.2	26 45.7	22 54.7	28 09.3
13 W	11 28 03	20 13 49	6♉37 37	12 50 22	26 57.0	16 34.9	26 38.1	4 07.5	4 14.5	8 04.7	21 25.6	26 44.6	22 54.0	28 10.5
14 Th	11 31 59	21 12 13	18 59 02	25 04 08	26 58.6	17 17.2	27 52.6	4 47.6	4 41.5	8 11.8	21 20.9	26 43.5	22 53.4	28 11.7
15 F	11 35 56	22 10 40	1♊06 11	7♊05 45	27 00.2	17 55.8	29 07.2	5 27.9	5 08.5	8 19.0	21 16.3	26 42.5	22 52.7	28 12.9
16 Sa	11 39 52	23 09 08	13 03 28	18 59 56	27R01.2	18 30.1	0♎21.7	6 08.2	5 35.5	8 26.3	21 11.7	26 41.5	22 52.1	28 14.1
17 Su	11 43 49	24 07 39	24 55 46	0♋51 35	27 01.1	19 00.1	1 36.3	6 48.6	6 02.6	8 33.8	21 07.1	26 40.5	22 51.5	28 15.4
18 M	11 47 45	25 06 12	6♋48 01	12 45 38	26 59.5	19 25.3	2 50.9	7 29.0	6 29.6	8 41.4	21 02.5	26 39.6	22 51.0	28 16.7
19 Tu	11 51 42	26 04 47	18 45 00	24 46 39	26 56.7	19 45.3	4 05.5	8 09.6	6 56.7	8 49.2	20 57.9	26 38.8	22 50.5	28 18.1
20 W	11 55 39	27 03 24	0♌51 05	6♌58 42	26 52.7	19 59.9	5 20.1	8 50.2	7 23.7	8 57.1	20 53.3	26 38.0	22 50.0	28 19.5
21 Th	11 59 35	28 02 03	13 09 53	19 24 58	26 48.0	20R08.6	6 34.7	9 30.9	7 50.8	9 05.1	20 48.7	26 37.2	22 49.5	28 20.9
22 F	12 03 32	29 00 45	25 44 10	2♍07 39	26 43.3	20 11.1	7 49.3	10 11.7	8 17.9	9 13.2	20 44.1	26 36.5	22 49.1	28 22.3
23 Sa	12 07 28	29 59 28	8♍35 30	15 07 45	26 39.1	20 07.0	9 03.9	10 52.6	8 45.0	9 21.5	20 39.6	26 35.8	22 48.7	28 23.7
24 Su	12 11 25	0♎58 14	21 44 19	28 25 03	26 35.8	19 56.0	10 18.6	11 33.5	9 12.1	9 29.9	20 35.0	26 35.2	22 48.3	28 25.2
25 M	12 15 21	1 57 01	5♎09 46	11♎58 13	26 33.8	19 37.8	11 33.2	12 14.5	9 39.2	9 38.4	20 30.5	26 34.6	22 48.0	28 26.7
26 Tu	12 19 18	2 55 51	18 50 04	25 45 00	26D33.2	19 12.3	12 47.9	12 55.6	10 06.3	9 47.1	20 26.1	26 34.1	22 47.7	28 28.3
27 W	12 23 14	3 54 42	2♏42 39	9♏42 39	26 33.6	18 39.5	14 02.5	13 36.8	10 33.4	9 55.8	20 21.6	26 33.6	22 47.4	28 29.8
28 Th	12 27 11	4 53 35	16 44 37	23 48 12	26 34.8	17 59.3	15 17.2	14 18.0	11 00.5	10 04.7	20 17.2	26 33.2	22 47.2	28 31.4
29 F	12 31 08	5 52 30	0♐53 02	7♐58 47	26 36.2	17 12.1	16 31.8	14 59.4	11 27.6	10 13.7	20 12.8	26 32.8	22 47.0	28 33.1
30 Sa	12 35 04	6 51 27	15 05 07	22 11 45	26 37.3	16 18.5	17 46.5	15 40.8	11 54.7	10 22.9	20 08.5	26 32.5	22 46.8	28 34.7

LONGITUDE October 1995

Day	Sid.Time	☉	0 hr ☽	Noon ☽	True ☊	☿	♀	♂	⚳	♃	♄	♅	♆	♇
1 Su	12 39 01	7♎50 26	29♐18 23	6♑24 44	26♎37.8	15♎19.1	19♎01.1	16♏22.2	12♎21.8	10♐32.1	20♓04.2	26♑32.2	22♑46.7	28♏36.4
2 M	12 42 57	8 49 26	13♑30 32	20 35 30	26R37.5	14R15.1	20 15.8	17 03.8	12 49.0	10 41.5	19R59.9	26R32.0	22R46.6	28 38.1
3 Tu	12 46 54	9 48 28	27 39 22	4♒41 51	26 36.3	13 07.7	21 30.5	17 45.4	13 16.1	10 50.9	19 55.7	26 31.8	22 46.5	28 39.8
4 W	12 50 50	10 47 32	11♒42 39	18 41 29	26 34.6	11 58.6	22 45.1	18 27.1	13 43.2	11 00.5	19 51.6	26 31.7	22D46.5	28 41.5
5 Th	12 54 47	11 46 37	25 38 03	2♓32 03	26 32.6	10 49.4	23 59.8	19 08.8	14 10.3	11 10.2	19 47.4	26 31.6	22 46.5	28 43.3
6 F	12 58 43	12 45 45	9♓23 13	16 11 15	26 30.7	9 42.2	25 14.4	19 50.7	14 37.4	11 20.0	19 43.4	26D31.6	22 46.5	28 45.1
7 Sa	13 02 40	13 44 54	22 55 56	29 37 01	26 29.1	8 38.6	26 29.1	20 32.6	15 04.5	11 29.9	19 39.4	26 31.6	22 46.5	28 46.9
8 Su	13 06 36	14 44 05	6♈14 21	12♈47 46	26 28.2	7 40.6	27 43.7	21 14.5	15 31.6	11 39.8	19 35.4	26 31.7	22 46.6	28 48.7
9 M	13 10 33	15 43 18	19 17 13	25 42 39	26D27.8	6 49.7	28 58.4	21 56.6	15 58.6	11 49.9	19 31.5	26 31.8	22 46.8	28 50.6
10 Tu	13 14 30	16 42 33	2♉04 06	8♉21 39	26 28.1	6 07.5	0♏13.1	22 38.7	16 25.7	12 00.1	19 27.6	26 32.0	22 46.9	28 52.5
11 W	13 18 26	17 41 51	14 35 28	20 45 46	26 28.7	5 34.9	1 27.7	23 20.9	16 52.8	12 10.4	19 23.8	26 32.2	22 47.1	28 54.4
12 Th	13 22 23	18 41 11	26 52 48	2♊56 54	26 29.5	5 12.7	2 42.4	24 03.2	17 19.9	12 20.8	19 20.1	26 32.5	22 47.3	28 56.3
13 F	13 26 19	19 40 33	8♊58 37	14 57 52	26 30.3	5D01.3	3 57.1	24 45.5	17 46.9	12 31.3	19 16.4	26 32.8	22 47.6	28 58.2
14 Sa	13 30 16	20 39 57	20 55 35	26 52 09	26 30.9	5 01.0	5 11.7	25 27.9	18 14.0	12 41.9	19 12.8	26 33.2	22 47.9	29 00.2
15 Su	13 34 12	21 39 23	2♋48 03	8♋43 52	26 31.3	5 11.4	6 26.4	26 10.4	18 41.0	12 52.6	19 09.3	26 33.6	22 48.2	29 02.2
16 M	13 38 09	22 38 52	14 40 09	20 37 30	26R31.5	5 32.3	7 41.1	26 52.9	19 08.1	13 03.3	19 05.8	26 34.1	22 48.6	29 04.2
17 Tu	13 42 05	23 38 23	26 36 31	2♌37 45	26 31.5	6 03.2	8 55.7	27 35.5	19 35.1	13 14.2	19 02.4	26 34.6	22 49.0	29 06.2
18 W	13 46 02	24 37 57	8♌41 47	14 49 11	26 31.3	6 43.3	10 10.4	28 18.2	20 02.1	13 25.2	18 59.1	26 35.2	22 49.4	29 08.3
19 Th	13 49 59	25 37 32	21 00 28	27 16 05	26D31.2	7 31.8	11 25.1	29 01.0	20 29.1	13 36.2	18 55.9	26 35.8	22 49.9	29 10.3
20 F	13 53 55	26 37 10	3♍36 29	10♍02 00	26 31.1	8 28.0	12 39.8	29 43.8	20 56.1	13 47.3	18 52.7	26 36.5	22 50.4	29 12.4
21 Sa	13 57 52	27 36 50	16 32 55	23 09 24	26 31.2	9 31.0	13 54.5	0♐26.8	21 23.1	13 58.5	18 49.6	26 37.3	22 50.9	29 14.5
22 Su	14 01 48	28 36 32	29 51 32	6♎39 17	26 31.3	10 40.0	15 09.2	1 09.7	21 50.1	14 09.8	18 46.6	26 38.1	22 51.5	29 16.6
23 M	14 05 45	29 36 17	13♎32 30	20 30 54	26R31.5	11 54.3	16 23.8	1 52.8	22 17.0	14 21.2	18 43.7	26 38.9	22 52.1	29 18.7
24 Tu	14 09 41	0♏36 03	27 34 07	4♏41 37	26 31.4	13 13.2	17 38.5	2 35.9	22 44.0	14 32.6	18 40.8	26 39.8	22 52.7	29 20.9
25 W	14 13 38	1 35 52	11♏52 49	19 07 02	26 31.2	14 35.9	18 53.2	3 19.1	23 10.9	14 44.2	18 38.1	26 40.7	22 53.4	29 23.0
26 Th	14 17 34	2 35 42	26 23 31	3♐41 29	26 30.6	16 01.9	20 07.9	4 02.4	23 37.8	14 55.8	18 35.4	26 41.7	22 54.1	29 25.2
27 F	14 21 31	3 35 34	11♐00 08	18 18 43	26 29.9	17 30.6	21 22.6	4 45.7	24 04.7	15 07.5	18 32.8	26 42.8	22 54.8	29 27.4
28 Sa	14 25 28	4 35 28	25 36 28	2♑52 44	26 29.0	19 01.5	22 37.3	5 29.1	24 31.5	15 19.3	18 30.3	26 43.9	22 55.6	29 29.6
29 Su	14 29 24	5 35 24	10♑06 55	17 18 29	26 28.3	20 34.3	23 52.0	6 12.6	24 58.4	15 31.1	18 27.9	26 45.0	22 56.3	29 31.8
30 M	14 33 21	6 35 21	24 27 02	1♒32 14	26D27.9	22 08.6	25 06.6	6 56.1	25 25.2	15 43.0	18 25.6	26 46.2	22 57.2	29 34.1
31 Tu	14 37 17	7 35 20	8♒33 52	15 31 46	26 28.0	23 44.1	26 21.3	7 39.7	25 52.0	15 55.0	18 23.4	26 47.4	22 58.0	29 36.3

Astro Data

	Dy Hr Mn
☽0N	9 16:29
♃∠♆	12 2:19
♀0S	18 13:58
☿R	22 9:15
☉0S	23 12:12
☽0S	24 2:55
♆D	5 3:56
♅D	6 12:58
☽0N	7 0:41
♃∠♅	7 16:12
⚳0S	10 4:05
☿D	14 0:45
☽0S	21 12:13

Planet Ingress

	Dy Hr Mn
⚳ ♎	4 1:06
♂ ♏	7 7:00
♀ ♎	16 5:01
☉ ♎	23 12:13
♀ ♏	10 7:48
♂ ♐	20 21:02
☉ ♏	23 21:32

Last Aspect / ☽ Ingress

Last Aspect Dy Hr Mn		☽ Ingress Dy Hr Mn
1 13:29 ♇ ☌	♐	1 16:57
3 15:44 ♂ ⚹	♑	3 19:45
5 20:11 ♂ □	♒	5 21:47
7 20:51 ♇ □	♓	8 0:08
10 0:52 ♇ △	♈	10 4:14
12 5:15 ♅ □	♉	12 11:21
14 18:13 ♇ ☍	♊	14 21:48
16 21:09 ☉ □	♋	17 10:16
19 18:59 ♇ △	♌	19 22:19
22 4:57 ♇ □	♍	22 8:01
24 12:00 ♇ ⚹	♎	24 14:50
26 13:25 ♅ □	♏	26 19:20
28 20:01 ♇ ☌	♐	28 22:30

Last Aspect / ☽ Ingress

Last Aspect Dy Hr Mn		☽ Ingress Dy Hr Mn
30 8:33 ♄ □	♑	1 1:10
3 1:42 ♇ ⚹	♒	3 3:59
5 5:21 ♇ □	♓	5 7:35
7 10:29 ♇ △	♈	7 12:41
9 18:49 ♀ ☍	♉	9 20:05
12 4:02 ♇ ☍	♊	12 6:09
13 22:20 ☉ △	♋	14 18:20
17 4:58 ♇ △	♌	17 6:46
19 15:38 ♇ □	♍	19 17:11
21 22:56 ♇ ⚹	♎	22 0:15
23 22:27 ♅ □	♏	24 4:06
26 4:58 ♇ ☌	♐	26 5:56
27 12:23 ♄ □	♑	28 7:15
30 8:39 ♇ ⚹	♒	30 9:23

☽ Phases & Eclipses

Dy Hr Mn	
2 9:03	☽ 9♐26
9 3:37	○ 16♓00
16 21:09	☾ 23♊31
24 16:55	● 1♎10
1 14:36	☽ 7♑57
8 15:52	○ 14♈54
8 16:04	A 0.825
16 16:26	☾ 22♋50
24 4:36	● 0♏18
24 4:32:29	T 02'10"
30 21:17	☽ 6♒59

Astro Data

1 September 1995
Julian Day # 34942
SVP 5♓19'04"
GC 26♐46.7 ⚴ 4♍36.1
Eris 18♈34.6R ⚵ 19♐45.9
⚷ 28♍51.2 ⚶ 5♍24.6
☽ Mean ☊ 28♎52.3

1 October 1995
Julian Day # 34972
SVP 5♓19'01"
GC 26♐46.8 ⚴ 19♍33.0
Eris 18♈18.7R ⚵ 24♐46.0
⚷ 3♎10.5 ⚶ 19♍48.1
☽ Mean ☊ 27♎17.0

November 1995 — LONGITUDE

Day	Sid.Time	☉	0 hr ☽	Noon☽	True☊	☿	♀	♂	⚳	♃	♄	♅	♆	♇
1 W	14 41 14	8♏35 20	22♒25 52	29♒16 07	26♎28.5	25♎20.4	27♏36.0	8♐23.3	26♎18.7	16♐07.0	18♓21.3	26♑48.7	22♑58.9	29♏38.6
2 Th	14 45 10	9 35 22	6♓02 34	12♓45 15	26 29.6	26 57.5	28 50.6	9 07.1	26 45.5	16 19.1	18R 19.2	26 50.0	22 59.8	29 40.8
3 F	14 49 07	10 35 25	19 24 17	25 59 44	26 30.7	28 35.0	0♐05.3	9 50.8	27 12.2	16 31.3	18 17.3	26 51.4	23 00.8	29 43.1
4 Sa	14 53 03	11 35 31	2♈31 44	9♈00 22	26 31.8	0♏12.9	1 19.9	10 34.7	27 38.9	16 43.5	18 15.5	26 52.9	23 01.8	29 45.4
5 Su	14 57 00	12 35 37	15 25 46	21 48 02	26R32.5	1 51.0	2 34.6	11 18.6	28 05.5	16 55.8	18 13.7	26 54.3	23 02.8	29 47.7
6 M	15 00 57	13 35 46	28 07 16	4♉23 35	26 32.3	3 29.2	3 49.2	12 02.6	28 32.2	17 08.2	18 12.1	26 55.9	23 03.8	29 50.0
7 Tu	15 04 53	14 35 56	10♉37 05	16 47 54	26 31.3	5 07.4	5 03.8	12 46.6	28 58.8	17 20.6	18 10.5	26 57.4	23 04.9	29 52.3
8 W	15 08 50	15 36 09	22 56 10	29 02 02	26 29.2	6 45.5	6 18.5	13 30.7	29 25.4	17 33.1	18 09.1	26 59.1	23 06.0	29 54.6
9 Th	15 12 46	16 36 23	5♊05 40	11♊07 15	26 26.3	8 23.5	7 33.1	14 14.9	29 51.9	17 45.6	18 07.8	27 00.7	23 07.2	29 57.0
10 F	15 16 43	17 36 39	17 07 03	23 05 19	26 22.8	10 01.4	8 47.7	14 59.1	0♏18.4	17 58.2	18 06.5	27 02.4	23 08.3	29 59.3
11 Sa	15 20 39	18 36 56	29 02 20	4♋58 27	26 19.0	11 39.1	10 02.3	15 43.4	0 44.9	18 10.8	18 05.4	27 04.2	23 09.5	0♐01.6
12 Su	15 24 36	19 37 16	10♋54 03	16 49 32	26 15.6	13 16.5	11 16.9	16 27.7	1 11.4	18 23.5	18 04.3	27 06.0	23 10.8	0 04.0
13 M	15 28 32	20 37 38	22 45 22	28 42 03	26 12.8	14 53.7	12 31.5	17 12.1	1 37.8	18 36.3	18 03.4	27 07.9	23 12.0	0 06.4
14 Tu	15 32 29	21 38 01	4♌40 05	10♌40 01	26D 11.0	16 30.7	13 46.1	17 56.6	2 04.2	18 49.1	18 02.6	27 09.7	23 13.3	0 08.7
15 W	15 36 26	22 38 27	16 42 26	22 47 54	26 10.4	18 07.4	15 00.8	18 41.1	2 30.6	19 01.9	18 01.9	27 11.7	23 14.6	0 11.1
16 Th	15 40 22	23 38 54	28 57 00	5♍10 21	26 10.9	19 43.8	16 15.4	19 25.7	2 56.9	19 14.8	18 01.2	27 13.7	23 16.0	0 13.5
17 F	15 44 19	24 39 23	11♍28 28	17 51 55	26 12.3	21 20.0	17 29.9	20 10.4	3 23.2	19 27.7	18 00.7	27 15.7	23 17.3	0 15.8
18 Sa	15 48 15	25 39 54	24 21 10	0♎56 37	26 14.0	22 56.0	18 44.5	20 55.1	3 49.4	19 40.7	18 00.3	27 17.7	23 18.7	0 18.2
19 Su	15 52 12	26 40 27	7♎38 36	14 27 19	26R 15.4	24 31.7	19 59.1	21 39.9	4 15.6	19 53.8	18 00.0	27 19.9	23 20.1	0 20.6
20 M	15 56 08	27 41 01	21 22 49	28 25 03	26 15.8	26 07.1	21 13.7	22 24.7	4 41.8	20 06.8	17 59.8	27 22.0	23 21.6	0 23.0
21 Tu	16 00 05	28 41 37	5♏33 45	12♏48 28	26 14.8	27 42.4	22 28.3	23 09.6	5 08.0	20 19.9	17D 59.7	27 24.2	23 23.1	0 25.4
22 W	16 04 01	29 42 15	20 08 34	27 33 15	26 12.1	29 17.4	23 42.9	23 54.6	5 34.0	20 33.1	17 59.7	27 26.4	23 24.6	0 27.8
23 Th	16 07 58	0♐42 55	5♐01 33	12♐32 23	26 07.9	0♐52.3	24 57.5	24 39.6	6 00.1	20 46.3	17 59.9	27 28.7	23 26.1	0 30.2
24 F	16 11 55	1 43 35	20 04 34	27 36 53	26 02.6	2 26.9	26 12.0	25 24.7	6 26.1	20 59.5	18 00.1	27 31.0	23 27.7	0 32.5
25 Sa	16 15 51	2 44 17	5♑08 08	12♑37 09	25 57.0	4 01.4	27 26.6	26 09.8	6 52.0	21 12.8	18 00.4	27 33.4	23 29.3	0 34.9
26 Su	16 19 48	3 45 00	20 02 57	27 24 36	25 52.0	5 35.7	28 41.2	26 55.0	7 17.9	21 26.1	18 00.9	27 35.8	23 30.9	0 37.3
27 M	16 23 44	4 45 45	4♒41 26	11♒52 54	25 48.2	7 10.0	29 55.7	27 40.3	7 43.8	21 39.4	18 01.4	27 38.2	23 32.5	0 39.7
28 Tu	16 27 41	5 46 30	18 58 39	25 58 31	25D 46.1	8 44.0	1♑10.2	28 25.6	8 09.6	21 52.8	18 02.1	27 40.7	23 34.2	0 42.1
29 W	16 31 37	6 47 16	2♓52 27	9♓40 34	25 45.7	10 18.0	2 24.7	29 10.9	8 35.3	22 06.1	18 02.9	27 43.2	23 35.8	0 44.5
30 Th	16 35 34	7 48 03	16 23 04	23 00 15	25 46.6	11 51.9	3 39.2	29 56.3	9 01.0	22 19.6	18 03.8	27 45.7	23 37.5	0 46.9

December 1995 — LONGITUDE

Day	Sid.Time	☉	0 hr ☽	Noon☽	True☊	☿	♀	♂	⚳	♃	♄	♅	♆	♇
1 F	16 39 30	8♐48 51	29♓32 27	6♈00 04	25♎48.0	13♐25.7	4♑53.7	0♑41.7	9♏26.7	22♐33.0	18♓04.7	27♑48.3	23♑39.3	0♐49.2
2 Sa	16 43 27	9 49 40	12♈23 28	18 43 04	25R 49.3	14 59.4	6 08.2	1 27.2	9 52.3	22 46.5	18 05.8	27 50.9	23 41.0	0 51.6
3 Su	16 47 24	10 50 30	24 59 16	1♉12 24	25 49.3	16 33.1	7 22.7	2 12.8	10 17.8	22 59.9	18 07.0	27 53.6	23 42.8	0 54.0
4 M	16 51 20	11 51 20	7♉22 51	13 30 53	25 47.6	18 06.8	8 37.1	2 58.4	10 43.3	23 13.4	18 08.3	27 56.2	23 44.6	0 56.3
5 Tu	16 55 17	12 52 12	19 36 48	25 40 51	25 43.5	19 40.4	9 51.6	3 44.0	11 08.7	23 27.0	18 09.7	27 59.0	23 46.4	0 58.7
6 W	16 59 13	13 53 05	1♊43 15	7♊44 12	25 37.1	21 14.0	11 06.0	4 29.7	11 34.1	23 40.5	18 11.3	28 01.7	23 48.2	1 01.0
7 Th	17 03 10	14 53 59	13 43 53	19 42 27	25 28.6	22 47.6	12 20.4	5 15.5	11 59.4	23 54.1	18 12.9	28 04.5	23 50.1	1 03.3
8 F	17 07 06	15 54 54	25 40 06	1♋36 58	25 18.6	24 21.1	13 34.8	6 01.3	12 24.6	24 07.7	18 14.6	28 07.3	23 52.0	1 05.7
9 Sa	17 11 03	16 55 50	7♋33 16	13 29 11	25 08.1	25 54.7	14 49.1	6 47.1	12 49.8	24 21.3	18 16.4	28 10.2	23 53.9	1 08.0
10 Su	17 14 59	17 56 47	19 24 57	25 20 50	24 57.8	27 28.2	16 03.5	7 33.0	13 14.9	24 34.9	18 18.3	28 13.0	23 55.8	1 10.3
11 M	17 18 56	18 57 45	1♌17 07	7♌14 09	24 48.9	29 01.8	17 17.8	8 18.9	13 40.0	24 48.5	18 20.4	28 15.9	23 57.7	1 12.6
12 Tu	17 22 53	19 58 44	13 12 19	19 12 01	24 41.9	0♑35.3	18 32.2	9 04.9	14 04.9	25 02.2	18 22.5	28 18.9	23 59.7	1 14.9
13 W	17 26 49	20 59 44	25 13 44	1♍17 57	24 37.3	2 08.7	19 46.5	9 50.9	14 29.9	25 15.8	18 24.7	28 21.8	24 01.6	1 17.2
14 Th	17 30 46	22 00 45	7♍25 14	13 36 08	24D 35.0	3 42.1	21 00.7	10 37.0	14 54.7	25 29.5	18 27.1	28 24.8	24 03.6	1 19.5
15 F	17 34 42	23 01 47	19 51 14	26 11 08	24 34.6	5 15.3	22 15.0	11 23.2	15 19.5	25 43.1	18 29.5	28 27.8	24 05.6	1 21.7
16 Sa	17 38 39	24 02 51	2♎36 24	9♎07 36	24 35.3	6 48.5	23 29.3	12 09.3	15 44.2	25 56.8	18 32.1	28 30.9	24 07.6	1 24.0
17 Su	17 42 35	25 03 55	15 45 13	22 29 42	24R 35.9	8 21.4	24 43.5	12 55.5	16 08.9	26 10.5	18 34.7	28 34.0	24 09.7	1 26.2
18 M	17 46 32	26 05 00	29 21 22	6♏20 23	24 35.3	9 54.1	25 57.7	13 41.8	16 33.4	26 24.2	18 37.4	28 37.1	24 11.7	1 28.5
19 Tu	17 50 28	27 06 06	13♏26 46	20 40 21	24 32.6	11 26.5	27 11.9	14 28.1	16 57.9	26 37.9	18 40.3	28 40.2	24 13.8	1 30.7
20 W	17 54 25	28 07 13	28 00 44	5♐27 16	24 27.3	12 58.5	28 26.1	15 14.5	17 22.3	26 51.6	18 43.2	28 43.3	24 15.9	1 32.9
21 Th	17 58 22	29 08 20	12♐59 04	20 35 04	24 19.4	14 29.9	29 40.3	16 00.8	17 46.7	27 05.3	18 46.2	28 46.5	24 18.0	1 35.1
22 F	18 02 18	0♑09 29	28 13 58	5♑54 21	24 09.6	16 00.7	0♒54.4	16 47.3	18 10.9	27 19.0	18 49.4	28 49.7	24 20.1	1 37.2
23 Sa	18 06 15	1 10 37	13♑34 44	21 13 37	23 59.1	17 30.7	2 08.5	17 33.8	18 35.1	27 32.7	18 52.6	28 52.9	24 22.2	1 39.4
24 Su	18 10 11	2 11 46	28 49 35	6♒21 22	23 49.2	18 59.8	3 22.6	18 20.3	18 59.2	27 46.3	18 55.9	28 56.1	24 24.4	1 41.5
25 M	18 14 08	3 12 55	13♒47 52	21 08 14	23 41.0	20 27.6	4 36.7	19 06.8	19 23.2	28 00.0	18 59.3	28 59.4	24 26.5	1 43.6
26 Tu	18 18 04	4 14 04	28 21 49	5♓28 14	23 35.2	21 54.1	5 50.7	19 53.4	19 47.1	28 13.7	19 02.8	29 02.7	24 28.7	1 45.7
27 W	18 22 01	5 15 13	12♓27 19	19 19 07	23 32.1	23 18.8	7 04.7	20 40.0	20 10.9	28 27.4	19 06.4	29 06.0	24 30.8	1 47.8
28 Th	18 25 57	6 16 22	26 03 50	2♈41 47	23D 31.0	24 41.4	8 18.7	21 26.7	20 34.7	28 41.0	19 10.1	29 09.3	24 33.0	1 49.9
29 F	18 29 54	7 17 32	9♈13 26	15 39 18	23R 31.1	26 01.7	9 32.6	22 13.4	20 58.3	28 54.6	19 13.9	29 12.6	24 35.2	1 51.9
30 Sa	18 33 51	8 18 41	21 59 55	28 15 53	23 31.2	27 19.0	10 46.5	23 00.1	21 21.8	29 08.3	19 17.8	29 16.0	24 37.4	1 54.0
31 Su	18 37 47	9 19 49	4♉27 46	10♉36 09	23 29.9	28 32.9	12 00.3	23 46.8	21 45.3	29 21.9	19 21.7	29 19.3	24 39.6	1 56.0

Astro Data	Dy Hr Mn
☽ 0N	3 7:05
♃□♄	11 2:30
☽ 0S	17 22:19
♄ D	21 19:48
☽ 0N	30 13:07
♃⚺♆	7 3:48
☽ 0S	15 7:50
☽ 0N	27 20:48
♃⚺♅	31 6:02

Planet Ingress		Dy Hr Mn
♀	♐	3 10:18
☿	♏	4 8:50
⚳	♏	9 19:18
♇	♐	10 19:11
☉	♐	22 19:01
☿	♐	22 22:46
♀	♑	27 13:23
♂	♑	30 13:57
☿	♑	12 2:57
♀	♒	21 18:23
☉	♑	22 8:17

Last Aspect Dy Hr Mn			☽ Ingress	Dy Hr Mn
1 12:40	♇	□	♓	1 13:17
3 18:51	♇	△	♈	3 19:21
5 21:42	♅	□	♉	6 3:35
8 13:44	♇	☍	♊	8 13:54
10 2:00	♄	□	♋	11 1:56
13 8:50	♅	☍	♌	13 14:37
15 11:40	☉	□	♍	16 2:02
18 5:22	♅	△	♎	18 10:18
20 10:13	♅	□	♏	20 14:40
22 15:43	☉	☌	♐	22 15:56
24 9:33	♀	☌	♑	24 15:48
26 12:18	♅	☌	♒	26 16:15
28 16:29	♂	⚹	♓	28 18:59

Last Aspect Dy Hr Mn			☽ Ingress	Dy Hr Mn
30 20:45	♅	⚹	♈	1 0:51
3 5:34	♅	□	♉	3 9:40
5 16:35	♅	△	♊	5 20:35
7 20:36	♃	☍	♋	8 8:44
10 17:50	♅	☍	♌	10 21:24
12 23:50	♃	△	♍	13 9:26
15 16:18	♅	△	♎	15 19:09
17 22:40	♅	□	♏	18 1:07
20 1:07	♅	⚹	♐	20 3:13
22 2:22	☉	☌	♑	22 2:46
24 0:08	♅	☌	♒	24 1:52
25 23:35	♃	⚹	♓	26 2:45
28 5:32	♅	⚹	♈	28 7:06
30 13:56	♅	□	♉	30 15:21

☽ Phases & Eclipses Dy Hr Mn	
7 7:20	○ 14♉24
15 11:40	☾ 22♌38
22 15:43	● 29♏52
29 6:28	☽ 6♓33
7 1:27	○ 14♊27
15 5:31	☾ 22♍45
22 2:22	● 29♐45
28 19:06	☽ 6♈34

Astro Data

1 November 1995
Julian Day # 35003
SVP 5♓18'58"
GC 26♐46.9 ⚴ 4♎01.5
Eris 18♈00.3R ⚵ 3♑12.0
⚷ 7♎32.9 ⚶ 4♎42.5
☽ Mean ☊ 25♎38.4

1 December 1995
Julian Day # 35033
SVP 5♓18'54"
GC 26♐46.9 ⚴ 16♎47.2
Eris 17♈45.9R ⚵ 13♑26.1
⚷ 11♎08.7 ⚶ 18♎49.0
☽ Mean ☊ 24♎03.1

LONGITUDE — January 1996

Day	Sid.Time	☉	0 hr ☽	Noon ☽	True ☊	☿	♀	♂	⚳	♃	♄	♅	♆	♇
1 M	18 41 44	10♑20 58	16♉41 33	22♉44 29	23♎26.4	29♑42.9	13♒14.2	24♑33.6	22♏08.6	29♐35.5	19♓25.8	29♑22.7	24♑41.8	1♐58.0
2 Tu	18 45 40	11 22 07	28 45 26	4♊44 47	23R 20.0	0♒48.3	14 27.9	25 20.4	22 31.9	29 49.1	19 29.9	29 26.1	24 44.0	1 59.9
3 W	18 49 37	12 23 16	10♊42 55	16 40 10	23 10.6	1 48.3	15 41.7	26 07.3	22 55.1	0♑02.6	19 34.1	29 29.5	24 46.3	2 01.9
4 Th	18 53 33	13 24 24	22 36 49	28 33 06	22 58.3	2 42.2	16 55.4	26 54.1	23 18.1	0 16.2	19 38.4	29 32.9	24 48.5	2 03.8
5 F	18 57 30	14 25 33	4♋29 13	10♋25 22	22 44.1	3 29.1	18 09.0	27 41.0	23 41.1	0 29.7	19 42.8	29 36.4	24 50.8	2 05.7
6 Sa	19 01 26	15 26 41	16 21 42	22 18 22	22 29.0	4 08.2	19 22.6	28 28.0	24 03.9	0 43.2	19 47.3	29 39.8	24 53.0	2 07.6
7 Su	19 05 23	16 27 50	28 15 30	4♌13 16	22 14.3	4 38.5	20 36.2	29 14.9	24 26.6	0 56.6	19 51.8	29 43.3	24 55.3	2 09.5
8 M	19 09 20	17 28 58	10♌11 50	16 11 23	22 01.0	4 59.1	21 49.7	0♒01.9	24 49.3	1 10.1	19 56.4	29 46.7	24 57.5	2 11.3
9 Tu	19 13 16	18 30 06	22 12 09	28 14 24	21 50.2	5R 09.2	23 03.1	0 48.9	25 11.8	1 23.5	20 01.1	29 50.2	24 59.8	2 13.1
10 W	19 17 13	19 31 14	4♍18 25	10♍24 33	21 42.4	5 08.2	24 16.5	1 36.0	25 34.2	1 36.9	20 05.9	29 53.7	25 02.1	2 14.9
11 Th	19 21 09	20 32 22	16 33 12	22 44 47	21 37.7	4 55.5	25 29.9	2 23.0	25 56.5	1 50.3	20 10.8	29 57.2	25 04.3	2 16.7
12 F	19 25 06	21 33 30	28 59 47	5♎18 42	21 35.5	4 30.9	26 43.2	3 10.1	26 18.7	2 03.6	20 15.7	0♒00.7	25 06.6	2 18.4
13 Sa	19 29 02	22 34 38	11♎42 02	18 10 20	21 35.0	3 54.8	27 56.5	3 57.2	26 40.7	2 16.9	20 20.7	0 04.2	25 08.9	2 20.1
14 Su	19 32 59	23 35 46	24 44 06	1♏23 50	21 34.9	3 07.5	29 09.7	4 44.4	27 02.7	2 30.2	20 25.8	0 07.7	25 11.2	2 21.8
15 M	19 36 55	24 36 54	8♏09 56	15 02 44	21 33.9	2 10.3	0♓22.8	5 31.5	27 24.5	2 43.4	20 31.0	0 11.2	25 13.4	2 23.5
16 Tu	19 40 52	25 38 02	22 02 28	29 09 11	21 30.9	1 04.7	1 35.9	6 18.7	27 46.2	2 56.7	20 36.2	0 14.8	25 15.7	2 25.1
17 W	19 44 49	26 39 09	6♐22 45	13♐42 50	21 25.2	29♑52.6	2 49.0	7 05.9	28 07.8	3 09.8	20 41.5	0 18.3	25 18.0	2 26.7
18 Th	19 48 45	27 40 16	21 08 51	28 39 59	21 16.7	28 36.2	4 02.0	7 53.2	28 29.2	3 23.0	20 46.9	0 21.8	25 20.3	2 28.3
19 F	19 52 42	28 41 23	6♑15 14	13♑53 19	21 06.0	27 18.1	5 14.9	8 40.4	28 50.5	3 36.0	20 52.3	0 25.4	25 22.5	2 29.9
20 Sa	19 56 38	29 42 30	21 32 54	29 12 28	20 54.2	26 00.5	6 27.8	9 27.7	29 11.7	3 49.1	20 57.9	0 28.9	25 24.8	2 31.4
21 Su	20 00 35	0♒43 36	6♒50 33	14♒25 42	20 42.9	24 45.8	7 40.6	10 15.0	29 32.7	4 02.1	21 03.4	0 32.4	25 27.1	2 32.9
22 M	20 04 31	1 44 41	21 56 37	29 22 09	20 33.2	23 36.0	8 53.3	11 02.3	29 53.6	4 15.1	21 09.1	0 36.0	25 29.4	2 34.4
23 Tu	20 08 28	2 45 45	6♓41 25	13♓53 43	20 26.2	22 32.7	10 06.0	11 49.7	0♐14.3	4 28.0	21 14.8	0 39.5	25 31.6	2 35.8
24 W	20 12 24	3 46 48	20 58 38	27 55 58	20 21.9	21 37.0	11 18.6	12 37.0	0 34.9	4 40.8	21 20.6	0 43.0	25 33.9	2 37.2
25 Th	20 16 21	4 47 50	4♈45 43	11♈28 05	20D 20.2	20 49.7	12 31.1	13 24.3	0 55.4	4 53.6	21 26.4	0 46.6	25 36.2	2 38.6
26 F	20 20 18	5 48 51	18 03 24	24 32 07	20R 20.0	20 11.4	13 43.6	14 11.7	1 15.7	5 06.4	21 32.3	0 50.1	25 38.4	2 40.0
27 Sa	20 24 14	6 49 51	0♉54 47	7♉11 59	20 20.1	19 42.2	14 55.9	14 59.1	1 35.8	5 19.1	21 38.3	0 53.6	25 40.7	2 41.3
28 Su	20 28 11	7 50 49	13 24 22	19 32 34	20 19.5	19 21.9	16 08.2	15 46.5	1 55.8	5 31.8	21 44.3	0 57.1	25 42.9	2 42.6
29 M	20 32 07	8 51 47	25 37 14	1♊38 59	20 17.0	19D 10.2	17 20.4	16 33.9	2 15.7	5 44.4	21 50.3	1 00.6	25 45.1	2 43.9
30 Tu	20 36 04	9 52 44	7♊38 26	13 36 07	20 12.0	19 06.8	18 32.5	17 21.3	2 35.4	5 56.9	21 56.5	1 04.1	25 47.4	2 45.1
31 W	20 40 00	10 53 39	19 32 34	25 28 16	20 04.1	19 11.2	19 44.5	18 08.7	2 54.9	6 09.4	22 02.6	1 07.6	25 49.6	2 46.3

LONGITUDE — February 1996

Day	Sid.Time	☉	0 hr ☽	Noon ☽	True ☊	☿	♀	♂	⚳	♃	♄	♅	♆	♇
1 Th	20 43 57	11♒54 33	1♋23 38	7♋19 03	19♎53.8	19♑22.8	20♓56.4	18♒56.1	3♐14.2	6♑21.8	22♓08.9	1♒11.1	25♑51.8	2♐47.4
2 F	20 47 53	12 55 26	13 14 50	19 11 15	19R 41.5	19 41.0	22 08.2	19 43.5	3 33.4	6 34.2	22 15.2	1 14.6	25 54.0	2 48.6
3 Sa	20 51 50	13 56 17	25 08 34	1♌06 58	19 28.4	20 05.5	23 20.0	20 30.9	3 52.5	6 46.5	22 21.5	1 18.1	25 56.2	2 49.7
4 Su	20 55 47	14 57 08	7♌06 38	13 07 41	19 15.5	20 35.5	24 31.6	21 18.4	4 11.3	6 58.7	22 27.9	1 21.6	25 58.4	2 50.8
5 M	20 59 43	15 57 57	19 10 15	25 14 28	19 04.0	21 10.8	25 43.1	22 05.8	4 30.0	7 10.9	22 34.3	1 25.0	26 00.5	2 51.8
6 Tu	21 03 40	16 58 45	1♍20 26	7♍28 17	18 54.6	21 50.7	26 54.5	22 53.2	4 48.5	7 23.0	22 40.8	1 28.5	26 02.7	2 52.8
7 W	21 07 36	17 59 32	13 38 10	19 50 16	18 47.9	22 35.0	28 05.8	23 40.7	5 06.8	7 35.0	22 47.4	1 31.9	26 04.9	2 53.8
8 Th	21 11 33	19 00 18	26 04 46	2♎21 54	18 44.1	23 23.2	29 17.0	24 28.1	5 25.0	7 47.0	22 53.9	1 35.3	26 07.0	2 54.7
9 F	21 15 29	20 01 03	8♎41 56	15 05 10	18D 42.6	24 15.0	0♈28.1	25 15.6	5 43.0	7 58.9	23 00.5	1 38.7	26 09.1	2 55.6
10 Sa	21 19 26	21 01 47	21 31 56	28 02 34	18 42.9	25 10.1	1 39.1	26 03.0	6 00.7	8 10.7	23 07.2	1 42.1	26 11.2	2 56.5
11 Su	21 23 22	22 02 30	4♏37 24	11♏16 49	18R 43.7	26 08.3	2 49.9	26 50.5	6 18.3	8 22.5	23 13.9	1 45.5	26 13.4	2 57.3
12 M	21 27 19	23 03 12	18 01 07	24 50 34	18 44.1	27 09.2	4 00.7	27 38.0	6 35.7	8 34.2	23 20.7	1 48.8	26 15.4	2 58.1
13 Tu	21 31 16	24 03 53	1♐45 23	8♐45 41	18 43.1	28 12.6	5 11.3	28 25.4	6 52.9	8 45.8	23 27.5	1 52.2	26 17.5	2 58.9
14 W	21 35 12	25 04 32	15 51 27	23 02 31	18 39.9	29 18.5	6 21.8	29 12.9	7 09.9	8 57.3	23 34.3	1 55.5	26 19.6	2 59.6
15 Th	21 39 09	26 05 11	0♑18 35	7♑39 09	18 34.6	0♒26.5	7 32.2	0♓00.3	7 26.7	9 08.7	23 41.2	1 58.8	26 21.6	3 00.3
16 F	21 43 05	27 05 48	15 03 33	22 30 54	18 27.4	1 36.6	8 42.5	0 47.8	7 43.3	9 20.1	23 48.1	2 02.1	26 23.7	3 01.0
17 Sa	21 47 02	28 06 25	0♒00 15	7♒30 28	18 19.3	2 48.5	9 52.6	1 35.3	7 59.6	9 31.4	23 55.0	2 05.4	26 25.7	3 01.6
18 Su	21 50 58	29 06 59	15 00 21	22 28 44	18 11.4	4 02.3	11 02.6	2 22.7	8 15.8	9 42.5	24 02.0	2 08.6	26 27.7	3 02.2
19 M	21 54 55	0♓07 32	29 54 26	7♓16 21	18 04.5	5 17.7	12 12.5	3 10.1	8 31.7	9 53.6	24 09.0	2 11.9	26 29.7	3 02.8
20 Tu	21 58 51	1 08 04	14♓33 32	21 45 13	17 59.6	6 34.7	13 22.2	3 57.6	8 47.4	10 04.6	24 16.0	2 15.1	26 31.6	3 03.3
21 W	22 02 48	2 08 33	28 50 46	5♈49 45	17D 56.9	7 53.2	14 31.8	4 45.0	9 02.9	10 15.6	24 23.1	2 18.3	26 33.6	3 03.8
22 Th	22 06 45	3 09 01	12♈41 58	19 27 21	17 56.2	9 13.1	15 41.2	5 32.4	9 18.2	10 26.4	24 30.2	2 21.4	26 35.5	3 04.2
23 F	22 10 41	4 09 28	26 06 00	2♉38 09	17 57.0	10 34.4	16 50.5	6 19.8	9 33.2	10 37.1	24 37.3	2 24.6	26 37.4	3 04.7
24 Sa	22 14 38	5 09 52	9♉04 11	15 24 32	17 58.4	11 57.1	17 59.6	7 07.2	9 48.0	10 47.7	24 44.5	2 27.7	26 39.3	3 05.0
25 Su	22 18 34	6 10 14	21 39 44	27 50 21	17R 59.7	13 20.9	19 08.5	7 54.6	10 02.5	10 58.3	24 51.6	2 30.8	26 41.2	3 05.4
26 M	22 22 31	7 10 35	3♊56 59	10♊00 15	18 00.0	14 46.1	20 17.3	8 42.0	10 16.8	11 08.7	24 58.8	2 33.8	26 43.0	3 05.7
27 Tu	22 26 27	8 10 53	16 00 48	21 59 15	17 58.8	16 12.4	21 25.9	9 29.3	10 30.9	11 19.1	25 06.1	2 36.9	26 44.9	3 06.0
28 W	22 30 24	9 11 10	27 56 10	3♋52 10	17 55.8	17 39.9	22 34.3	10 16.7	10 44.7	11 29.3	25 13.3	2 39.9	26 46.7	3 06.2
29 Th	22 34 20	10 11 24	9♋47 46	15 43 30	17 51.2	19 08.5	23 42.6	11 04.0	10 58.2	11 39.4	25 20.6	2 42.9	26 48.5	3 06.4

Astro Data (Dy Hr Mn)

☿R 9 21:53
☽0S 11 15:50
♃×♇ 13 18:38
☽0N 24 6:55
☿D 30 10:17

☽0S 7 22:33
♀0N 10 1:54
☽0N 20 18:13

Planet Ingress (Dy Hr Mn)

☿ ♒ 1 18:06
♃ ♑ 3 7:22
♂ ♒ 8 11:02
♅ ♒ 12 7:13
♀ ♓ 15 4:30
☿ ♑R 17 9:37
☉ ♒ 20 18:52
⚳ ♐ 22 19:24

♀ ♈ 9 2:30
☿ ♒ 15 2:44
♂ ♓ 15 11:50
☉ ♓ 19 9:01

Last Aspect Dy Hr Mn		☽ Ingress	Dy Hr Mn
2 1:18	♅ △	♊	2 2:29
3 17:53	♄ □	♋	4 14:56
7 2:54	♅ ☍	♌	7 3:30
9 0:32	♀ ☍	♍	9 15:29
12 1:53	♅ △	♎	12 1:55
14 7:35	♀ △	♏	14 9:30
16 5:38	☉ ⚹	♐	16 13:25
17 23:20	♄ □	♑	18 14:07
20 12:51	☉ ☌	♒	20 13:15
21 5:01	♂ ☌	♓	22 13:02
24 7:53	♆ ⚹	♈	24 15:37
26 14:04	♆ □	♉	26 22:16
29 0:13	♆ △	♊	29 8:42
31 5:00	♄ □	♋	31 21:11

Last Aspect Dy Hr Mn		☽ Ingress	Dy Hr Mn
3 1:34	♅ ☍	♌	3 9:46
5 5:22	♂ ☍	♍	5 21:22
8 5:31	♀ ☍	♎	8 7:30
10 8:35	♆ □	♏	10 15:35
12 17:09	♂ □	♐	12 20:58
14 22:47	♂ ⚹	♑	14 23:29
16 18:14	♆ ☌	♒	16 24:00
18 23:30	♆ ☌	♓	19 0:09
20 20:05	♆ ⚹	♈	21 1:58
23 0:56	♆ □	♉	23 7:08
25 9:45	♆ △	♊	25 16:14
27 18:20	♄ □	♋	28 4:10

☽ Phases & Eclipses (Dy Hr Mn)

5 20:51 ○ 14♋48
13 20:45 ☾ 22♎57
20 12:51 ● 29♑45
27 11:14 ☽ 6♉48

4 15:58 ○ 15♌07
12 8:37 ☾ 22♏55
18 23:30 ● 29♒36
26 5:52 ☽ 6♊55

Astro Data

1 January 1996
Julian Day # 35064
SVP 5♓18'49"
GC 26♐47.0 ⚴ 28♎01.2
Eris 17♈39.3R ⚵ 25♑22.5
⚷ 13♎37.1 ⚶ 2♏29.4
☽ Mean ☊ 22♎24.6

1 February 1996
Julian Day # 35095
SVP 5♓18'44"
GC 26♐47.1 ⚴ 5♏59.6
Eris 17♈43.1 ⚵ 8♒08.5
⚷ 14♎20.2R ⚶ 14♏16.1
☽ Mean ☊ 20♎46.2

March 1996

LONGITUDE

Day	Sid.Time	☉	0 hr ☽	Noon ☽	True ☊	☿	♀	♂	⚳	♃	♄	♅	♆	♇
1 F	22 38 17	11♓11 37	21♋39 49	27♋37 09	17♎45.3	20♒38.3	24♈50.6	11♓51.3	11♐11.5	11♑49.4	25♓27.9	2♒45.9	26♑50.2	3♐06.6
2 Sa	22 42 14	12 11 47	3♌35 52	9♌36 18	17R 38.7	22 09.2	25 58.5	12 38.6	11 24.6	11 59.4	25 35.2	2 48.8	26 52.0	3 06.7
3 Su	22 46 10	13 11 56	15 38 44	21 43 25	17 32.1	23 41.3	27 06.1	13 25.9	11 37.4	12 09.2	25 42.5	2 51.7	26 53.7	3 06.8
4 M	22 50 07	14 12 02	27 50 31	4♍00 12	17 26.2	25 14.4	28 13.6	14 13.1	11 49.9	12 18.9	25 49.8	2 54.6	26 55.4	3 06.9
5 Tu	22 54 03	15 12 07	10♍12 35	16 27 45	17 21.5	26 48.7	29 20.8	15 00.4	12 02.1	12 28.5	25 57.2	2 57.4	26 57.1	3R 06.9
6 W	22 58 00	16 12 09	22 45 47	29 06 44	17 18.5	28 24.0	0♉27.9	15 47.6	12 14.1	12 37.9	26 04.5	3 00.2	26 58.7	3 06.9
7 Th	23 01 56	17 12 10	5♎30 37	11♎57 29	17D 17.1	0♓00.5	1 34.7	16 34.8	12 25.8	12 47.3	26 11.9	3 03.0	27 00.3	3 06.9
8 F	23 05 53	18 12 10	18 27 22	25 00 19	17 17.2	1 38.0	2 41.3	17 21.9	12 37.2	12 56.5	26 19.3	3 05.7	27 01.9	3 06.8
9 Sa	23 09 49	19 12 07	1♏36 23	8♏15 37	17 18.4	3 16.8	3 47.6	18 09.1	12 48.3	13 05.7	26 26.7	3 08.5	27 03.5	3 06.7
10 Su	23 13 46	20 12 03	14 58 06	21 43 51	17 19.9	4 56.6	4 53.8	18 56.2	12 59.1	13 14.7	26 34.1	3 11.1	27 05.1	3 06.6
11 M	23 17 42	21 11 57	28 32 58	5♐25 27	17 21.4	6 37.6	5 59.7	19 43.4	13 09.7	13 23.6	26 41.5	3 13.8	27 06.6	3 06.4
12 Tu	23 21 39	22 11 50	12♐21 19	19 20 33	17R 22.1	8 19.7	7 05.3	20 30.5	13 19.9	13 32.3	26 49.0	3 16.4	27 08.1	3 06.2
13 W	23 25 36	23 11 41	26 23 02	3♑28 37	17 21.8	10 03.0	8 10.7	21 17.6	13 29.9	13 41.0	26 56.4	3 19.0	27 09.6	3 05.9
14 Th	23 29 32	24 11 30	10♑37 04	17 48 04	17 20.4	11 47.5	9 15.9	22 04.6	13 39.5	13 49.5	27 03.8	3 21.5	27 11.1	3 05.7
15 F	23 33 29	25 11 18	25 01 11	2♒15 56	17 18.0	13 33.2	10 20.8	22 51.7	13 48.8	13 57.9	27 11.3	3 24.1	27 12.5	3 05.3
16 Sa	23 37 25	26 11 04	9♒31 42	16 47 50	17 15.2	15 20.1	11 25.4	23 38.7	13 57.9	14 06.1	27 18.7	3 26.5	27 13.9	3 05.0
17 Su	23 41 22	27 10 48	24 03 36	1♓18 16	17 12.3	17 08.2	12 29.7	24 25.6	14 06.5	14 14.3	27 26.2	3 29.0	27 15.2	3 04.6
18 M	23 45 18	28 10 30	8♓31 03	15 41 14	17 09.9	18 57.5	13 33.8	25 12.6	14 14.9	14 22.2	27 33.6	3 31.4	27 16.6	3 04.2
19 Tu	23 49 15	29 10 10	22 48 07	29 51 04	17 08.2	20 48.1	14 37.6	25 59.5	14 22.9	14 30.1	27 41.1	3 33.7	27 17.9	3 03.8
20 W	23 53 11	0♈09 49	6♈49 34	13♈43 09	17D 07.6	22 39.9	15 41.0	26 46.4	14 30.6	14 37.8	27 48.5	3 36.1	27 19.2	3 03.3
21 Th	23 57 08	1 09 25	20 31 32	27 14 30	17 07.8	24 32.9	16 44.2	27 33.3	14 38.0	14 45.4	27 56.0	3 38.3	27 20.4	3 02.8
22 F	0 01 05	2 08 59	3♉51 59	10♉23 59	17 08.6	26 27.1	17 47.0	28 20.2	14 45.0	14 52.8	28 03.4	3 40.6	27 21.7	3 02.2
23 Sa	0 05 01	3 08 31	16 50 40	23 12 16	17 09.8	28 22.6	18 49.5	29 07.0	14 51.7	15 00.1	28 10.8	3 42.8	27 22.9	3 01.6
24 Su	0 08 58	4 08 00	29 29 06	5♊41 32	17 11.1	0♈19.3	19 51.7	29 53.8	14 58.1	15 07.3	28 18.3	3 45.0	27 24.0	3 01.0
25 M	0 12 54	5 07 27	11♊50 02	17 55 07	17 12.1	2 17.1	20 53.5	0♈40.5	15 04.0	15 14.3	28 25.7	3 47.1	27 25.2	3 00.4
26 Tu	0 16 51	6 06 53	23 57 17	29 57 07	17R 12.6	4 16.0	21 54.9	1 27.2	15 09.7	15 21.1	28 33.1	3 49.2	27 26.3	2 59.7
27 W	0 20 47	7 06 15	5♋55 12	11♋52 07	17 12.6	6 16.0	22 56.0	2 13.9	15 15.0	15 27.8	28 40.5	3 51.2	27 27.4	2 59.0
28 Th	0 24 44	8 05 36	17 48 27	23 44 47	17 12.2	8 16.9	23 56.7	3 00.5	15 19.9	15 34.4	28 47.9	3 53.2	27 28.4	2 58.3
29 F	0 28 40	9 04 54	29 41 41	5♌39 41	17 11.4	10 18.7	24 57.0	3 47.2	15 24.5	15 40.8	28 55.3	3 55.2	27 29.5	2 57.5
30 Sa	0 32 37	10 04 10	11♌39 19	17 41 04	17 10.5	12 21.3	25 56.8	4 33.7	15 28.7	15 47.1	29 02.6	3 57.1	27 30.4	2 56.7
31 Su	0 36 34	11 03 23	23 45 20	29 52 33	17 09.6	14 24.4	26 56.2	5 20.3	15 32.5	15 53.2	29 10.0	3 58.9	27 31.4	2 55.9

April 1996

LONGITUDE

Day	Sid.Time	☉	0 hr ☽	Noon ☽	True ☊	☿	♀	♂	⚳	♃	♄	♅	♆	♇
1 M	0 40 30	12♈02 34	6♍03 03	12♍17 08	17♎08.9	16♈27.9	27♉55.2	6♈06.8	15♐36.0	15♑59.1	29♓17.3	4♒00.8	27♑32.3	2♐55.1
2 Tu	0 44 27	13 01 43	18 35 00	24 56 50	17R 08.4	18 31.7	28 53.7	6 53.2	15 39.1	16 04.9	29 24.6	4 02.5	27 33.2	2R 54.2
3 W	0 48 23	14 00 50	1♎22 44	7♎52 45	17D 08.2	20 35.4	29 51.7	7 39.6	15 41.8	16 10.5	29 31.9	4 04.3	27 34.1	2 53.3
4 Th	0 52 20	14 59 55	14 26 51	21 04 58	17 08.1	22 38.8	0♊49.3	8 26.0	15 44.2	16 16.0	29 39.2	4 06.0	27 34.9	2 52.3
5 F	0 56 16	15 58 58	27 46 57	4♏32 37	17 08.2	24 41.6	1 46.3	9 12.4	15 46.1	16 21.3	29 46.5	4 07.6	27 35.7	2 51.4
6 Sa	1 00 13	16 57 59	11♏21 45	18 14 05	17R 08.3	26 43.4	2 42.9	9 58.7	15 47.7	16 26.5	29 53.7	4 09.2	27 36.5	2 50.4
7 Su	1 04 09	17 56 58	25 09 19	2♐07 08	17 08.2	28 44.1	3 38.9	10 45.0	15 48.9	16 31.4	0♈01.0	4 10.8	27 37.2	2 49.4
8 M	1 08 06	18 55 55	9♐07 12	16 09 12	17 08.1	0♉43.1	4 34.3	11 31.2	15 49.8	16 36.3	0 08.2	4 12.3	27 37.9	2 48.3
9 Tu	1 12 03	19 54 51	23 12 48	0♑17 39	17 07.9	2 40.1	5 29.2	12 17.4	15R 50.2	16 40.9	0 15.3	4 13.8	27 38.6	2 47.3
10 W	1 15 59	20 53 45	7♑23 27	14 29 52	17D 07.8	4 34.8	6 23.5	13 03.6	15 50.3	16 45.4	0 22.5	4 15.2	27 39.3	2 46.2
11 Th	1 19 56	21 52 37	21 36 35	28 43 18	17 07.8	6 26.8	7 17.1	13 49.7	15 49.9	16 49.7	0 29.6	4 16.5	27 39.9	2 45.1
12 F	1 23 52	22 51 27	5♒49 43	12♒55 31	17 08.0	8 15.7	8 10.2	14 35.8	15 49.2	16 53.9	0 36.7	4 17.9	27 40.4	2 43.9
13 Sa	1 27 49	23 50 16	20 00 24	27 04 03	17 08.5	10 01.3	9 02.6	15 21.9	15 48.0	16 57.8	0 43.8	4 19.1	27 41.0	2 42.8
14 Su	1 31 45	24 49 03	4♓06 10	11♓06 26	17 09.2	11 43.3	9 54.3	16 07.9	15 46.5	17 01.6	0 50.8	4 20.4	27 41.5	2 41.6
15 M	1 35 42	25 47 48	18 04 32	25 00 08	17 09.9	13 21.3	10 45.3	16 53.8	15 44.6	17 05.2	0 57.9	4 21.5	27 42.0	2 40.4
16 Tu	1 39 38	26 46 32	1♈52 58	8♈42 42	17R 10.3	14 55.2	11 35.6	17 39.7	15 42.3	17 08.7	1 04.8	4 22.7	27 42.4	2 39.1
17 W	1 43 35	27 45 13	15 29 06	22 11 55	17 10.4	16 24.6	12 25.2	18 25.6	15 39.5	17 11.9	1 11.8	4 23.8	27 42.8	2 37.9
18 Th	1 47 31	28 43 53	28 50 57	5♉26 04	17 09.9	17 49.5	13 14.0	19 11.5	15 36.4	17 15.0	1 18.7	4 24.8	27 43.2	2 36.6
19 F	1 51 28	29 42 30	11♉57 08	18 24 07	17 08.7	19 09.7	14 02.0	19 57.3	15 32.9	17 17.9	1 25.6	4 25.8	27 43.5	2 35.3
20 Sa	1 55 25	0♉41 06	24 47 02	1♊05 58	17 07.0	20 24.9	14 49.1	20 43.0	15 29.1	17 20.6	1 32.4	4 26.7	27 43.9	2 34.0
21 Su	1 59 21	1 39 40	7♊21 04	13 32 32	17 04.9	21 35.2	15 35.4	21 28.7	15 24.8	17 23.2	1 39.3	4 27.6	27 44.1	2 32.6
22 M	2 03 18	2 38 11	19 40 39	25 45 43	17 02.8	22 40.3	16 20.7	22 14.4	15 20.1	17 25.5	1 46.0	4 28.4	27 44.4	2 31.3
23 Tu	2 07 14	3 36 40	1♋48 08	7♋48 20	17 00.8	23 40.2	17 05.1	23 00.0	15 15.1	17 27.7	1 52.8	4 29.2	27 44.6	2 29.9
24 W	2 11 11	4 35 08	13 46 47	19 43 59	16 59.3	24 34.7	17 48.6	23 45.5	15 09.7	17 29.7	1 59.5	4 30.0	27 44.8	2 28.5
25 Th	2 15 07	5 33 33	25 40 30	1♌36 52	16D 58.6	25 23.9	18 31.0	24 31.0	15 03.9	17 31.5	2 06.1	4 30.6	27 44.9	2 27.1
26 F	2 19 04	6 31 56	7♌33 41	13 31 32	16 58.8	26 07.5	19 12.3	25 16.5	14 57.7	17 33.1	2 12.7	4 31.3	27 45.0	2 25.7
27 Sa	2 23 00	7 30 17	19 31 01	25 32 42	16 59.6	26 45.7	19 52.5	26 01.9	14 51.2	17 34.5	2 19.3	4 31.9	27 45.1	2 24.2
28 Su	2 26 57	8 28 36	1♍37 11	7♍45 00	17 01.1	27 18.3	20 31.6	26 47.3	14 44.3	17 35.8	2 25.8	4 32.4	27R 45.2	2 22.8
29 M	2 30 54	9 26 52	13 56 39	20 12 36	17 02.6	27 45.3	21 09.5	27 32.6	14 37.1	17 36.8	2 32.3	4 32.9	27 45.2	2 21.3
30 Tu	2 34 50	10 25 07	26 33 16	2♎58 59	17 03.9	28 06.8	21 46.2	28 17.8	14 29.5	17 37.7	2 38.7	4 33.3	27 45.2	2 19.8

Astro Data

	Dy Hr Mn
♇R	5 20:18
☽0S	6 5:14
♅✶♇	8 21:05
♄✶♆	15 16:44
☽0N	19 4:37
☉0N	20 8:03
☿0N	26 0:59
♂0N	27 2:54
☽0S	2 13:01
⚳R	10 2:56
☽0N	15 12:50
♃∠♇	24 3:35
♄△♇	28 2:49
♆R	29 9:52
☽0S	29 22:06

Planet Ingress

	Dy Hr Mn
♀ ♉	6 2:01
☿ ♓	7 11:53
☉ ♈	20 8:03
☿ ♈	24 8:03
♂ ♈	24 15:12
♀ ♊	3 15:26
♄ ♈	7 8:49
☿ ♉	8 3:16
☉ ♉	19 19:10

Last Aspect / ☽ Ingress

Last Aspect Dy Hr Mn		☽ Ingress	Dy Hr Mn
1 10:25	♆ ☍	♌	1 16:47
3 23:37	♀ △	♍	4 4:13
6 7:58	♆ △	♎	6 13:40
8 15:42	♆ □	♏	8 21:05
10 21:27	♆ ✶	♐	11 2:32
13 0:51	♄ □	♑	13 6:08
15 3:37	♆ ☌	♒	15 8:15
16 2:25	♀ □	♓	17 9:50
19 10:45	☉ ☌	♈	19 12:15
21 12:11	♆ □	♉	21 16:59
24 0:03	♂ ✶	♊	24 0:59
26 9:10	♄ □	♋	26 12:06
28 22:18	♄ △	♌	29 0:37
31 5:45	♀ □	♍	31 12:15

Last Aspect / ☽ Ingress

Last Aspect Dy Hr Mn		☽ Ingress	Dy Hr Mn
2 20:25	♄ ☍	♎	2 21:26
4 23:39	♆ □	♏	5 3:57
7 8:21	♄ △	♐	7 8:21
8 17:05	☉ △	♑	9 11:30
11 10:13	♆ ☌	♒	11 14:09
13 6:06	☉ ✶	♓	13 17:00
15 16:42	♆ ✶	♈	15 20:42
17 22:49	☉ ☌	♉	18 2:05
20 5:35	♆ △	♊	20 9:54
22 4:35	♂ ✶	♋	22 20:25
25 4:11	♆ ☍	♌	25 8:44
27 14:32	☿ □	♍	27 20:49
30 2:41	☿ △	♎	30 6:27

☽ Phases & Eclipses

Dy Hr Mn	
5 9:23	○ 15♍06
12 17:15	☾ 22♐25
19 10:45	● 29♓07
27 1:31	☽ 6♋40
4 0:07	○ 14♎31
4 0:10	☍ T 1.379
10 23:36	☾ 21♑22
17 22:49	● 28♈12
17 22:37:10	● P 0.880
25 20:40	☽ 5♌55

Astro Data

1 March 1996
Julian Day # 35124
SVP 5♓18'41"
GC 26♐47.1 ⚴ 8♏35.5R
Eris 17♈55.4 ⚵ 20♒27.1
⚷ 13♎20.6R ⚶ 22♏06.7
☽ Mean ☊ 19♎14.0

1 April 1996
Julian Day # 35155
SVP 5♓18'39"
GC 26♐47.2 ⚴ 4♏10.1R
Eris 18♈14.3 ⚵ 3♓38.9
⚷ 11♎06.5R ⚶ 24♏44.7R
☽ Mean ☊ 17♎35.5

LONGITUDE — May 1996

Day	Sid.Time	☉	0 hr ☽	Noon ☽	True ☊	☿	♀	♂	⚳	♃	♄	♅	♆	♇
1 W	2 38 47	11♉23 20	9♎29 59	16♎06 26	17♎04.5	28♉22.7	22♊21.5	29♈03.1	14♐21.5	17♑38.4	2♈45.1	4♒33.7	27♑45.1	2♐18.3
2 Th	2 42 43	12 21 31	22 48 24	29 35 48	17R04.0	28 33.1	22 55.6	29 48.2	14R13.3	17 38.9	2 51.5	4 34.1	27R45.0	2R16.8
3 F	2 46 40	13 19 40	6♏28 27	13♏26 04	17 02.2	28R38.1	23 28.2	0♉33.3	14 04.7	17 39.2	2 57.8	4 34.3	27 44.9	2 15.3
4 Sa	2 50 36	14 17 48	20 28 13	27 34 23	16 59.3	28 37.8	23 59.4	1 18.4	13 55.8	17R39.3	3 04.0	4 34.6	27 44.8	2 13.7
5 Su	2 54 33	15 15 54	4♐43 57	11♐56 12	16 55.5	28 32.4	24 29.1	2 03.4	13 46.5	17 39.2	3 10.2	4 34.8	27 44.6	2 12.2
6 M	2 58 29	16 13 58	19 10 26	26 25 51	16 51.3	28 22.1	24 57.3	2 48.4	13 37.0	17 39.0	3 16.3	4 34.9	27 44.4	2 10.6
7 Tu	3 02 26	17 12 01	3♑41 44	10♑57 19	16 47.5	28 07.3	25 23.9	3 33.3	13 27.2	17 38.6	3 22.4	4 35.0	27 44.1	2 09.0
8 W	3 06 23	18 10 03	18 11 58	25 25 05	16 44.6	27 48.1	25 48.8	4 18.2	13 17.1	17 37.9	3 28.5	4R35.0	27 43.9	2 07.5
9 Th	3 10 19	19 08 03	2♒36 08	9♒44 44	16D42.9	27 25.1	26 12.0	5 03.0	13 06.6	17 37.1	3 34.4	4 35.0	27 43.6	2 05.9
10 F	3 14 16	20 06 02	16 50 33	23 53 21	16 42.6	26 58.7	26 33.4	5 47.8	12 56.0	17 36.1	3 40.4	4 35.0	27 43.2	2 04.3
11 Sa	3 18 12	21 03 59	0♓52 59	7♓49 21	16 43.5	26 29.3	26 53.0	6 32.5	12 45.0	17 34.9	3 46.2	4 34.9	27 42.8	2 02.6
12 Su	3 22 09	22 01 56	14 42 26	21 32 13	16 44.9	25 57.5	27 10.8	7 17.2	12 33.8	17 33.5	3 52.1	4 34.7	27 42.4	2 01.0
13 M	3 26 05	22 59 51	28 18 44	5♈02 03	16R46.2	25 23.9	27 26.5	8 01.8	12 22.4	17 31.9	3 57.8	4 34.5	27 42.0	1 59.4
14 Tu	3 30 02	23 57 44	11♈42 12	18 19 15	16 46.7	24 49.0	27 40.3	8 46.4	12 10.7	17 30.2	4 03.5	4 34.2	27 41.5	1 57.8
15 W	3 33 58	24 55 37	24 53 13	1♉24 10	16 45.7	24 13.6	27 52.0	9 30.9	11 58.8	17 28.2	4 09.1	4 33.9	27 41.0	1 56.1
16 Th	3 37 55	25 53 28	7♉52 05	14 17 01	16 42.9	23 38.2	28 01.7	10 15.3	11 46.8	17 26.1	4 14.7	4 33.6	27 40.5	1 54.5
17 F	3 41 52	26 51 18	20 38 59	26 57 59	16 38.1	23 03.5	28 09.1	10 59.8	11 34.5	17 23.8	4 20.2	4 33.2	27 40.0	1 52.9
18 Sa	3 45 48	27 49 06	3♊14 04	9♊27 17	16 31.7	22 30.0	28 14.3	11 44.1	11 22.1	17 21.3	4 25.7	4 32.7	27 39.4	1 51.2
19 Su	3 49 45	28 46 53	15 37 44	21 45 29	16 24.2	21 58.2	28R17.2	12 28.4	11 09.5	17 18.6	4 31.0	4 32.2	27 38.8	1 49.6
20 M	3 53 41	29 44 38	27 50 44	3♋53 39	16 16.4	21 28.8	28 17.8	13 12.7	10 56.7	17 15.7	4 36.3	4 31.7	27 38.1	1 47.9
21 Tu	3 57 38	0♊42 22	9♋54 29	15 53 31	16 08.9	21 02.2	28 16.0	13 56.9	10 43.8	17 12.7	4 41.6	4 31.1	27 37.5	1 46.3
22 W	4 01 34	1 40 05	21 51 05	27 47 36	16 02.6	20 38.7	28 11.9	14 41.0	10 30.8	17 09.5	4 46.8	4 30.4	27 36.8	1 44.6
23 Th	4 05 31	2 37 46	3♌43 28	9♌39 11	15 58.0	20 18.7	28 05.3	15 25.1	10 17.7	17 06.1	4 51.9	4 29.7	27 36.0	1 42.9
24 F	4 09 27	3 35 25	15 35 17	21 32 18	15 55.2	20 02.6	27 56.3	16 09.1	10 04.6	17 02.5	4 56.9	4 29.0	27 35.3	1 41.3
25 Sa	4 13 24	4 33 03	27 30 49	3♍31 28	15D54.3	19 50.5	27 44.8	16 53.1	9 51.3	16 58.8	5 01.9	4 28.2	27 34.5	1 39.6
26 Su	4 17 21	5 30 39	9♍34 52	15 41 38	15 54.8	19 42.6	27 31.0	17 37.0	9 38.0	16 54.9	5 06.8	4 27.4	27 33.7	1 38.0
27 M	4 21 17	6 28 14	21 52 24	28 07 45	15 55.9	19D39.1	27 14.7	18 20.9	9 24.7	16 50.8	5 11.6	4 26.5	27 32.8	1 36.3
28 Tu	4 25 14	7 25 47	4♎28 16	10♎54 26	15R56.8	19 40.1	26 56.0	19 04.7	9 11.3	16 46.6	5 16.4	4 25.6	27 31.9	1 34.7
29 W	4 29 10	8 23 19	17 26 43	24 05 26	15 56.6	19 45.5	26 35.1	19 48.4	8 57.9	16 42.2	5 21.0	4 24.6	27 31.1	1 33.1
30 Th	4 33 07	9 20 50	0♏50 48	7♏42 55	15 54.6	19 55.4	26 11.9	20 32.1	8 44.5	16 37.7	5 25.6	4 23.6	27 30.1	1 31.4
31 F	4 37 03	10 18 20	14 41 41	21 46 52	15 50.4	20 09.8	25 46.5	21 15.8	8 31.2	16 32.9	5 30.2	4 22.6	27 29.2	1 29.8

LONGITUDE — June 1996

Day	Sid.Time	☉	0 hr ☽	Noon ☽	True ☊	☿	♀	♂	⚳	♃	♄	♅	♆	♇
1 Sa	4 41 00	11♊15 48	28♏58 00	6♐14 29	15♎44.1	20♉28.6	25♊19.2	21♉59.3	8♐17.9	16♑28.1	5♈34.6	4♒21.5	27♑28.2	1♐28.2
2 Su	4 44 56	12 13 16	13♐35 30	21 00 08	15R36.2	20 51.8	24R49.9	22 42.9	8R04.6	16R23.1	5 39.0	4R20.3	27R27.2	1R26.6
3 M	4 48 53	13 10 42	28 27 17	5♑55 51	15 27.7	21 19.3	24 18.9	23 26.4	7 51.4	16 17.9	5 43.3	4 19.2	27 26.2	1 24.9
4 Tu	4 52 50	14 08 08	13♑24 38	20 52 33	15 19.5	21 51.0	23 46.4	24 09.8	7 38.3	16 12.6	5 47.5	4 17.9	27 25.2	1 23.3
5 W	4 56 46	15 05 33	28 18 30	5♒41 35	15 12.7	22 26.9	23 12.4	24 53.1	7 25.3	16 07.2	5 51.7	4 16.7	27 24.1	1 21.7
6 Th	5 00 43	16 02 57	13♒00 59	20 16 05	15 08.0	23 06.8	22 37.3	25 36.4	7 12.3	16 01.6	5 55.7	4 15.4	27 23.0	1 20.2
7 F	5 04 39	17 00 21	27 26 26	4♓31 44	15D05.5	23 50.7	22 01.2	26 19.7	6 59.5	15 55.9	5 59.7	4 14.0	27 21.9	1 18.6
8 Sa	5 08 36	17 57 44	11♓31 52	18 26 48	15 04.8	24 38.5	21 24.4	27 02.9	6 46.8	15 50.0	6 03.6	4 12.7	27 20.7	1 17.0
9 Su	5 12 32	18 55 06	25 16 38	2♈01 35	15R05.2	25 30.0	20 47.1	27 46.0	6 34.3	15 44.0	6 07.4	4 11.2	27 19.6	1 15.4
10 M	5 16 29	19 52 28	8♈41 53	15 17 49	15 05.6	26 25.2	20 09.5	28 29.1	6 21.9	15 37.9	6 11.1	4 09.8	27 18.4	1 13.9
11 Tu	5 20 25	20 49 50	21 49 42	28 17 49	15 04.8	27 24.0	19 31.9	29 12.2	6 09.7	15 31.7	6 14.8	4 08.3	27 17.2	1 12.4
12 W	5 24 22	21 47 11	4♉42 30	11♉04 00	15 02.0	28 26.4	18 54.5	29 55.2	5 57.7	15 25.4	6 18.4	4 06.7	27 16.0	1 10.8
13 Th	5 28 19	22 44 31	17 22 34	23 38 27	14 56.6	29 32.3	18 17.6	0♊38.1	5 45.9	15 18.9	6 21.8	4 05.2	27 14.7	1 09.3
14 F	5 32 15	23 41 51	29 51 49	6♊02 50	14 48.5	0♊41.5	17 41.4	1 21.0	5 34.2	15 12.3	6 25.2	4 03.5	27 13.4	1 07.8
15 Sa	5 36 12	24 39 11	12♊11 40	18 18 26	14 38.0	1 54.2	17 06.0	2 03.8	5 22.9	15 05.7	6 28.5	4 01.9	27 12.2	1 06.3
16 Su	5 40 08	25 36 30	24 23 15	0♋26 15	14 25.8	3 10.1	16 31.8	2 46.5	5 11.7	14 58.9	6 31.7	4 00.2	27 10.9	1 04.9
17 M	5 44 05	26 33 48	6♋27 32	12 27 16	14 12.9	4 29.3	15 58.9	3 29.2	5 00.8	14 52.0	6 34.8	3 58.5	27 09.5	1 03.4
18 Tu	5 48 01	27 31 06	18 25 37	24 22 45	14 00.5	5 51.8	15 27.5	4 11.9	4 50.2	14 45.1	6 37.9	3 56.7	27 08.2	1 02.0
19 W	5 51 58	28 28 23	0♌18 56	6♌14 26	13 49.6	7 17.5	14 57.8	4 54.5	4 39.8	14 38.0	6 40.8	3 55.0	27 06.8	1 00.6
20 Th	5 55 54	29 25 39	12 09 34	18 04 43	13 40.8	8 46.3	14 29.8	5 37.0	4 29.7	14 30.9	6 43.6	3 53.1	27 05.5	0 59.2
21 F	5 59 51	0♋22 55	24 00 18	29 56 45	13 34.7	10 18.3	14 03.8	6 19.4	4 19.9	14 23.7	6 46.4	3 51.3	27 04.1	0 57.8
22 Sa	6 03 48	1 20 10	5♍54 37	11♍54 27	13 31.2	11 53.4	13 39.9	7 01.9	4 10.4	14 16.4	6 49.0	3 49.4	27 02.7	0 56.4
23 Su	6 07 44	2 17 24	17 56 49	24 02 20	13D29.8	13 31.5	13 18.1	7 44.2	4 01.1	14 09.1	6 51.6	3 47.5	27 01.2	0 55.1
24 M	6 11 41	3 14 38	0♎11 39	6♎25 24	13R29.6	15 12.8	12 58.5	8 26.5	3 52.2	14 01.7	6 54.1	3 45.6	26 59.8	0 53.7
25 Tu	6 15 37	4 11 51	12 44 13	19 08 43	13 29.6	16 57.0	12 41.2	9 08.7	3 43.7	13 54.3	6 56.5	3 43.6	26 58.3	0 52.4
26 W	6 19 34	5 09 04	25 39 26	2♏16 52	13 28.6	18 44.1	12 26.3	9 50.9	3 35.4	13 46.8	6 58.7	3 41.6	26 56.9	0 51.1
27 Th	6 23 30	6 06 16	9♏01 25	15 53 19	13 25.7	20 34.1	12 13.7	10 33.0	3 27.5	13 39.3	7 00.9	3 39.6	26 55.4	0 49.8
28 F	6 27 27	7 03 28	22 52 40	29 59 24	13 20.3	22 26.8	12 03.5	11 15.0	3 19.9	13 31.7	7 03.0	3 37.6	26 53.9	0 48.6
29 Sa	6 31 23	8 00 39	7♐13 10	14♐33 29	13 12.5	24 22.2	11 55.7	11 57.0	3 12.6	13 24.1	7 05.0	3 35.5	26 52.4	0 47.4
30 Su	6 35 20	8 57 50	21 59 34	29 30 27	13 02.6	26 20.0	11 50.3	12 39.0	3 05.7	13 16.4	7 06.9	3 33.4	26 50.9	0 46.2

Astro Data

	Dy Hr Mn
☿ R	3 22:41
♃ R	4 15:37
♅ R	8 19:36
☽ 0N	12 19:18
♄ ⚹ ♅	19 16:50
♀ R	20 6:08
♄ 0N	25 3:37
☽ 0S	27 7:48
☿ D	27 19:03
♃ ∠ ♇	1 11:27
☽ 0N	9 1:37
☽ 0S	23 17:01

Planet Ingress

	Dy Hr Mn
♂ ♉	2 18:16
☉ ♊	20 18:23
♂ ♊	12 14:42
☿ ♊	13 21:45
☉ ♋	21 2:24

Last Aspect / ☽ Ingress

Last Aspect Dy Hr Mn			☽ Ingress Dy Hr Mn
2 12:23	♂ ☍	♏	2 12:42
4 13:46	☿ ☍	♐	4 16:05
6 9:29	♀ ☍	♑	6 17:54
8 15:53	☿ △	♒	8 19:39
10 17:07	☿ □	♓	10 22:29
12 22:55	♆ ⚹	♈	13 3:00
15 5:23	♀ ⚹	♉	15 9:25
17 13:20	♆ △	♊	17 17:48
20 0:54	♀ ☌	♋	20 4:16
22 11:38	♆ ☍	♌	22 16:28
25 0:40	♀ ⚹	♍	25 4:58
27 10:53	♆ △	♎	27 15:33
29 18:06	♆ □	♏	29 22:30

Last Aspect / ☽ Ingress

Last Aspect Dy Hr Mn			☽ Ingress Dy Hr Mn
31 21:32	♆ ⚹	♐	1 1:43
2 17:58	♀ ☍	♑	3 2:29
4 22:33	♆ ☌	♒	5 2:44
6 21:24	♂ □	♓	7 4:19
9 3:59	♂ ⚹	♈	9 8:23
11 10:07	♆ □	♉	11 15:11
13 18:56	♆ △	♊	14 0:16
16 1:36	☉ ☌	♋	16 11:08
18 17:34	♆ ☍	♌	18 23:22
20 5:00	♀ ⚹	♍	21 12:07
23 17:49	♆ △	♎	23 23:37
26 2:22	♆ □	♏	26 7:53
28 6:49	♆ ⚹	♐	28 12:01
30 6:11	☿ ☍	♑	30 12:47

☽ Phases & Eclipses

Dy Hr Mn	
3 11:48	○ 13♏19
10 5:04	☾ 19♒49
17 11:46	● 26♉51
25 14:13	☽ 4♍38
1 20:47	○ 11♐37
8 11:06	☾ 17♓56
16 1:36	● 25♊12
24 5:23	☽ 2♎59

Astro Data

1 May 1996
Julian Day # 35185
SVP 5♓18'36"
GC 26♐47.3 ⚴ 25♎19.4R
Eris 18♈33.8 ⚵ 16♓06.1
⚷ 8♎57.5R ⚶ 20♏17.1R
☽ Mean ☊ 16♎00.1

1 June 1996
Julian Day # 35216
SVP 5♓18'32"
GC 26♐47.4 ⚴ 19♎47.7R
Eris 18♈50.3 ⚵ 28♓09.3
⚷ 7♎55.3R ⚶ 13♏25.1R
☽ Mean ☊ 14♎21.6

July 1996

LONGITUDE

Day	Sid.Time	☉	0 hr ☽	Noon ☽	True ☊	☿	♀	♂	⚳	♃	♄	♅	♆	♇
1 M	6 39 17	9♋55 01	7♑04 58	14♑41 49	12♎51.9	28♊20.2	11♊47.3	13♊20.9	2♐59.1	13♑08.8	7♈08.7	3♒31.3	26♑49.4	0♐45.0
2 Tu	6 43 13	10 52 12	22 19 36	29 56 54	12R 41.5	0♋22.5	11D 46.6	14 02.7	2R 52.9	13R 01.1	7 10.4	3R 29.2	26R 47.8	0R 43.8
3 W	6 47 10	11 49 23	7♒32 21	15♒04 43	12 32.6	2 26.7	11 48.3	14 44.5	2 47.0	12 53.4	7 12.0	3 27.0	26 46.3	0 42.7
4 Th	6 51 06	12 46 34	22 32 54	29 55 59	12 26.1	4 32.5	11 52.2	15 26.2	2 41.5	12 45.7	7 13.5	3 24.8	26 44.7	0 41.6
5 F	6 55 03	13 43 45	7♓13 18	14♓24 23	12 22.2	6 39.8	11 58.4	16 07.8	2 36.3	12 38.0	7 14.9	3 22.6	26 43.2	0 40.5
6 Sa	6 58 59	14 40 56	21 28 58	28 27 00	12 20.5	8 48.1	12 06.7	16 49.4	2 31.6	12 30.3	7 16.2	3 20.4	26 41.6	0 39.4
7 Su	7 02 56	15 38 08	5♈18 33	12♈03 51	12 20.2	10 57.2	12 17.2	17 31.0	2 27.1	12 22.6	7 17.4	3 18.2	26 40.0	0 38.4
8 M	7 06 52	16 35 20	18 43 12	25 17 01	12 20.1	13 06.9	12 29.8	18 12.5	2 23.0	12 15.0	7 18.5	3 15.9	26 38.4	0 37.3
9 Tu	7 10 49	17 32 33	1♉45 43	8♉09 47	12 19.0	15 16.7	12 44.4	18 53.9	2 19.3	12 07.3	7 19.6	3 13.6	26 36.8	0 36.3
10 W	7 14 46	18 29 46	14 29 39	20 45 46	12 15.9	17 26.5	13 00.9	19 35.3	2 16.0	11 59.7	7 20.5	3 11.4	26 35.2	0 35.4
11 Th	7 18 42	19 26 59	26 58 36	3♊08 31	12 10.1	19 36.0	13 19.3	20 16.6	2 13.0	11 52.1	7 21.3	3 09.1	26 33.6	0 34.4
12 F	7 22 39	20 24 13	9♊15 54	15 21 04	12 01.4	21 44.9	13 39.6	20 57.9	2 10.4	11 44.5	7 22.0	3 06.7	26 32.0	0 33.5
13 Sa	7 26 35	21 21 28	21 24 20	27 25 55	11 50.3	23 53.0	14 01.6	21 39.1	2 08.2	11 37.0	7 22.6	3 04.4	26 30.4	0 32.6
14 Su	7 30 32	22 18 42	3♋26 05	9♋25 01	11 37.5	26 00.1	14 25.3	22 20.2	2 06.4	11 29.5	7 23.1	3 02.1	26 28.8	0 31.8
15 M	7 34 28	23 15 58	15 22 54	21 19 54	11 23.9	28 06.0	14 50.6	23 01.3	2 04.9	11 22.1	7 23.5	2 59.7	26 27.2	0 30.9
16 Tu	7 38 25	24 13 13	27 16 12	3♌11 58	11 10.8	0♌10.7	15 17.5	23 42.4	2 03.8	11 14.7	7 23.8	2 57.4	26 25.5	0 30.1
17 W	7 42 22	25 10 29	9♌07 23	15 02 40	10 59.1	2 13.9	15 46.0	24 23.4	2 03.0	11 07.4	7 23.9	2 55.0	26 23.9	0 29.4
18 Th	7 46 18	26 07 45	20 58 03	26 53 48	10 49.6	4 15.7	16 15.9	25 04.3	2D 02.7	11 00.2	7R 24.0	2 52.6	26 22.3	0 28.6
19 F	7 50 15	27 05 01	2♍50 14	8♍47 42	10 42.9	6 15.8	16 47.2	25 45.1	2 02.7	10 53.1	7 24.0	2 50.2	26 20.7	0 27.9
20 Sa	7 54 11	28 02 18	14 46 36	20 47 22	10 38.9	8 14.3	17 19.9	26 25.9	2 03.0	10 46.0	7 23.9	2 47.8	26 19.0	0 27.2
21 Su	7 58 08	28 59 35	26 50 29	2♎56 28	10D 37.3	10 11.2	17 53.8	27 06.7	2 03.7	10 39.0	7 23.7	2 45.5	26 17.4	0 26.6
22 M	8 02 04	29 56 52	9♎05 52	15 19 15	10 37.1	12 06.3	18 29.1	27 47.3	2 04.8	10 32.1	7 23.4	2 43.1	26 15.8	0 25.9
23 Tu	8 06 01	0♌54 10	21 37 13	28 00 21	10R 37.4	13 59.7	19 05.5	28 27.9	2 06.3	10 25.3	7 22.9	2 40.7	26 14.2	0 25.3
24 W	8 09 57	1 51 28	4♏29 12	11♏04 17	10 37.1	15 51.4	19 43.2	29 08.5	2 08.1	10 18.5	7 22.4	2 38.3	26 12.6	0 24.8
25 Th	8 13 54	2 48 46	17 46 04	24 34 54	10 35.2	17 41.4	20 21.9	29 49.0	2 10.2	10 11.9	7 21.8	2 35.9	26 10.9	0 24.2
26 F	8 17 50	3 46 05	1♐30 59	8♐34 26	10 31.2	19 29.6	21 01.8	0♋29.4	2 12.7	10 05.4	7 21.1	2 33.5	26 09.3	0 23.7
27 Sa	8 21 47	4 43 24	15 45 05	23 02 38	10 24.9	21 16.0	21 42.7	1 09.8	2 15.6	9 59.1	7 20.2	2 31.1	26 07.7	0 23.3
28 Su	8 25 44	5 40 44	0♑26 31	7♑55 55	10 16.7	23 00.8	22 24.6	1 50.1	2 18.8	9 52.8	7 19.3	2 28.7	26 06.1	0 22.8
29 M	8 29 40	6 38 04	15 29 52	23 07 08	10 07.6	24 43.8	23 07.5	2 30.4	2 22.3	9 46.6	7 18.3	2 26.3	26 04.5	0 22.4
30 Tu	8 33 37	7 35 25	0♒46 23	8♒26 12	9 58.7	26 25.2	23 51.3	3 10.6	2 26.2	9 40.6	7 17.2	2 23.9	26 03.0	0 22.1
31 W	8 37 33	8 32 47	16 05 09	23 41 49	9 51.1	28 04.8	24 36.0	3 50.7	2 30.4	9 34.7	7 16.0	2 21.5	26 01.4	0 21.7

August 1996

LONGITUDE

Day	Sid.Time	☉	0 hr ☽	Noon ☽	True ☊	☿	♀	♂	⚳	♃	♄	♅	♆	♇
1 Th	8 41 30	9♌30 09	1♓14 56	8♓43 24	9♎45.5	29♌42.7	25♊21.6	4♋30.8	2♐34.9	9♑28.9	7♈14.6	2♒19.1	25♑59.8	0♐21.4
2 F	8 45 26	10 27 33	16 06 17	23 22 54	9R 42.3	1♍18.9	26 08.1	5 10.9	2 39.8	9R 23.3	7R 13.2	2R 16.7	25R 58.2	0R 21.1
3 Sa	8 49 23	11 24 58	0♈32 46	7♈35 37	9D 41.2	2 53.5	26 55.4	5 50.8	2 45.0	9 17.7	7 11.7	2 14.4	25 56.7	0 20.9
4 Su	8 53 19	12 22 24	14 31 24	21 20 12	9 41.6	4 26.3	27 43.5	6 30.7	2 50.5	9 12.4	7 10.1	2 12.0	25 55.1	0 20.6
5 M	8 57 16	13 19 51	28 02 16	4♉37 55	9R 42.4	5 57.5	28 32.3	7 10.6	2 56.3	9 07.1	7 08.4	2 09.7	25 53.6	0 20.5
6 Tu	9 01 13	14 17 20	11♉07 37	17 31 49	9 42.6	7 26.9	29 21.9	7 50.4	3 02.4	9 02.1	7 06.6	2 07.3	25 52.1	0 20.3
7 W	9 05 09	15 14 49	23 51 03	0♊05 51	9 41.4	8 54.7	0♋12.1	8 30.2	3 08.8	8 57.1	7 04.7	2 05.0	25 50.6	0 20.2
8 Th	9 09 06	16 12 21	6♊16 44	12 24 14	9 38.2	10 20.7	1 03.1	9 09.8	3 15.6	8 52.4	7 02.7	2 02.7	25 49.1	0 20.1
9 F	9 13 02	17 09 53	18 28 51	24 31 03	9 32.8	11 44.9	1 54.7	9 49.5	3 22.6	8 47.7	7 00.6	2 00.4	25 47.6	0 20.1
10 Sa	9 16 59	18 07 27	0♋31 17	6♋29 55	9 25.4	13 07.4	2 46.9	10 29.1	3 30.0	8 43.3	6 58.5	1 58.1	25 46.1	0D 20.0
11 Su	9 20 55	19 05 02	12 27 20	18 23 52	9 16.6	14 28.0	3 39.7	11 08.6	3 37.6	8 39.0	6 56.2	1 55.9	25 44.6	0 20.0
12 M	9 24 52	20 02 39	24 19 48	0♌15 24	9 07.1	15 46.8	4 33.2	11 48.0	3 45.6	8 34.8	6 53.9	1 53.6	25 43.2	0 20.1
13 Tu	9 28 48	21 00 16	6♌10 56	12 06 35	8 58.0	17 03.7	5 27.2	12 27.4	3 53.8	8 30.9	6 51.4	1 51.4	25 41.8	0 20.2
14 W	9 32 45	21 57 55	18 02 36	23 59 09	8 49.9	18 18.6	6 21.7	13 06.7	4 02.3	8 27.1	6 48.9	1 49.2	25 40.3	0 20.3
15 Th	9 36 42	22 55 35	29 56 29	5♍54 46	8 43.5	19 31.5	7 16.8	13 46.0	4 11.1	8 23.4	6 46.3	1 47.0	25 38.9	0 20.4
16 F	9 40 38	23 53 17	11♍54 16	17 55 12	8 39.2	20 42.3	8 12.4	14 25.2	4 20.2	8 20.0	6 43.5	1 44.8	25 37.5	0 20.6
17 Sa	9 44 35	24 50 59	23 57 52	0♎02 33	8D 37.1	21 50.9	9 08.4	15 04.4	4 29.5	8 16.7	6 40.8	1 42.7	25 36.2	0 20.8
18 Su	9 48 31	25 48 43	6♎09 36	12 19 21	8 36.8	22 57.3	10 05.0	15 43.4	4 39.1	8 13.6	6 37.9	1 40.5	25 34.8	0 21.1
19 M	9 52 28	26 46 27	18 32 12	24 48 34	8 37.7	24 01.3	11 02.0	16 22.5	4 49.0	8 10.7	6 34.9	1 38.4	25 33.5	0 21.4
20 Tu	9 56 24	27 44 13	1♏08 52	7♏33 33	8 39.1	25 02.8	11 59.4	17 01.4	4 59.2	8 08.0	6 31.9	1 36.3	25 32.2	0 21.7
21 W	10 00 21	28 42 00	14 03 03	20 37 47	8R 40.3	26 01.7	12 57.3	17 40.3	5 09.6	8 05.4	6 28.8	1 34.3	25 30.9	0 22.0
22 Th	10 04 17	29 39 49	27 18 07	4♐04 21	8 40.5	26 57.8	13 55.6	18 19.1	5 20.3	8 03.0	6 25.6	1 32.2	25 29.6	0 22.4
23 F	10 08 14	0♍37 38	10♐56 44	17 55 22	8 39.2	27 51.1	14 54.4	18 57.9	5 31.2	8 00.9	6 22.3	1 30.2	25 28.3	0 22.9
24 Sa	10 12 11	1 35 29	25 00 16	2♑11 15	8 36.4	28 41.3	15 53.5	19 36.6	5 42.3	7 58.9	6 19.0	1 28.3	25 27.1	0 23.3
25 Su	10 16 07	2 33 21	9♑27 57	16 49 53	8 32.2	29 28.3	16 53.0	20 15.3	5 53.7	7 57.1	6 15.6	1 26.3	25 25.9	0 23.8
26 M	10 20 04	3 31 14	24 16 18	1♒46 19	8 27.3	0♎11.8	17 52.9	20 53.8	6 05.4	7 55.4	6 12.1	1 24.4	25 24.7	0 24.3
27 Tu	10 24 00	4 29 08	9♒18 55	16 52 56	8 22.5	0 51.7	18 53.2	21 32.3	6 17.3	7 54.0	6 08.5	1 22.5	25 23.5	0 24.9
28 W	10 27 57	5 27 04	24 27 09	2♓00 19	8 18.3	1 27.7	19 53.8	22 10.8	6 29.4	7 52.7	6 04.9	1 20.7	25 22.3	0 25.5
29 Th	10 31 53	6 25 01	9♓31 14	16 58 47	8 15.4	1 59.6	20 54.8	22 49.2	6 41.7	7 51.7	6 01.2	1 18.8	25 21.2	0 26.1
30 F	10 35 50	7 23 00	24 21 57	1♈39 54	8D 14.0	2 27.1	21 56.2	23 27.5	6 54.3	7 50.8	5 57.5	1 17.0	25 20.1	0 26.7
31 Sa	10 39 46	8 21 01	8♈51 58	15 57 41	8 14.1	2 49.9	22 57.9	24 05.8	7 07.1	7 50.1	5 53.6	1 15.3	25 19.0	0 27.4

Astro Data	Dy Hr Mn
♀ D	2 6:51
☽ 0N	6 9:19
♄ R	18 20:29
⚳ D	18 23:57
☽ 0S	21 0:54
☽ 0N	2 18:54
♇ D	10 12:35
☽ 0S	17 7:29
☿ 0S	20 22:25
☽ 0N	30 5:40
♄ 0S	30 16:56

Planet Ingress		Dy Hr Mn
☿	♋	2 7:37
☿	♌	16 9:56
☉	♌	22 13:19
♂	♋	25 18:32
☿	♍	1 16:17
♀	♋	7 6:15
☉	♍	22 20:23
☿	♎	26 5:17

Last Aspect Dy Hr Mn			☽ Ingress	Dy Hr Mn
2 7:03	♆	☌	♒	2 12:05
3 11:26	♂	△	♓	4 12:07
6 8:58	♆	⚹	♈	6 14:42
8 14:30	♆	□	♉	8 20:43
10 23:13	♆	△	♊	11 5:52
12 23:48	♂	☌	♋	13 17:08
16 4:35	☿	☌	♌	16 5:31
18 8:05	♂	⚹	♍	18 18:16
21 3:35	☉	⚹	♎	21 6:14
23 12:54	♂	△	♏	23 15:43
25 14:47	♆	⚹	♐	25 21:24
27 9:43	♀	☍	♑	27 23:17
29 16:38	♆	☌	♒	29 22:47
31 19:48	☿	☍	♓	31 22:00

Last Aspect Dy Hr Mn			☽ Ingress	Dy Hr Mn
2 16:51	♀	□	♈	2 23:05
5 0:11	♀	⚹	♉	5 3:33
7 3:50	♆	△	♊	7 11:49
8 20:08	☉	⚹	♋	9 22:57
12 2:50	♆	☍	♌	12 11:29
14 7:34	☉	☌	♍	15 0:07
17 3:15	♆	△	♎	17 11:55
19 16:02	☉	⚹	♏	19 21:50
22 3:36	☉	□	♐	22 4:48
24 5:49	☿	□	♑	24 8:22
26 1:51	♆	☌	♒	26 9:10
26 19:01	♄	⚹	♓	28 8:49
30 1:36	♆	⚹	♈	30 9:15

☽ Phases & Eclipses Dy Hr Mn		
1 3:58	○	9♑36
7 18:55	☾	15♈55
15 16:15	●	23♋26
23 17:49	☽	1♏08
30 10:35	○	7♒32
6 5:25	☾	14♉02
14 7:34	●	21♌47
22 3:36	☽	29♏20
28 17:52	○	5♓41

Astro Data

1 July 1996
Julian Day # 35246
SVP 5♓18'27"
GC 26♐47.4 ⚴ 21♎17.3
Eris 18♈59.0 ⚵ 8♈16.0
⚷ 8♎34.7 ⚶ 12♏18.2
☽ Mean ☊ 12♎46.3

1 August 1996
Julian Day # 35277
SVP 5♓18'22"
GC 26♐47.5 ⚴ 28♎05.1
Eris 18♈58.4R ⚵ 15♈40.4
⚷ 10♎53.0 ⚶ 18♏06.3
☽ Mean ☊ 11♎07.9

LONGITUDE

September 1996

Day	Sid.Time	☉	0 hr ☽	Noon ☽	True ☊	☿	♀	♂	⚳	♃	♄	♅	♆	♇
1 Su	10 43 43	9♍19 03	22♈56 43	29♈48 59	8♎15.1	3♎07.8	23♋59.9	24♋44.0	7♐20.1	7♑49.6	5♈49.8	1♒13.5	25♑18.0	0♐28.1
2 M	10 47 40	10 17 08	6♉34 30	13♉13 25	8 16.7	3 20.5	25 02.2	25 22.1	7 33.3	7R49.3	5R45.8	1R11.8	25R16.9	0 28.9
3 Tu	10 51 36	11 15 14	19 46 02	26 12 43	8 18.1	3R27.7	26 04.8	26 00.2	7 46.7	7D49.2	5 41.8	1 10.2	25 15.9	0 29.7
4 W	10 55 33	12 13 22	2♊33 55	8♊50 08	8R18.9	3 29.1	27 07.8	26 38.2	8 00.4	7 49.3	5 37.8	1 08.6	25 14.9	0 30.5
5 Th	10 59 29	13 11 33	15 01 53	21 09 44	8 18.7	3 24.5	28 11.0	27 16.2	8 14.2	7 49.5	5 33.7	1 07.0	25 14.0	0 31.3
6 F	11 03 26	14 09 45	27 14 14	3♋15 56	8 17.3	3 13.7	29 14.5	27 54.1	8 28.2	7 50.0	5 29.6	1 05.4	25 13.0	0 32.2
7 Sa	11 07 22	15 08 00	9♋15 23	15 13 06	8 15.0	2 56.4	0♌18.3	28 31.9	8 42.5	7 50.6	5 25.4	1 03.9	25 12.1	0 33.1
8 Su	11 11 19	16 06 16	21 09 36	27 05 19	8 11.8	2 32.7	1 22.4	29 09.7	8 56.9	7 51.5	5 21.1	1 02.4	25 11.2	0 34.1
9 M	11 15 15	17 04 34	3♌00 42	8♌56 10	8 08.4	2 02.4	2 26.7	29 47.4	9 11.6	7 52.5	5 16.8	1 01.0	25 10.4	0 35.1
10 Tu	11 19 12	18 02 55	14 52 05	20 48 46	8 05.0	1 25.8	3 31.3	0♌25.0	9 26.4	7 53.7	5 12.5	0 59.6	25 09.5	0 36.1
11 W	11 23 09	19 01 17	26 46 32	2♍45 40	8 02.0	0 43.1	4 36.2	1 02.6	9 41.4	7 55.1	5 08.1	0 58.2	25 08.7	0 37.1
12 Th	11 27 05	19 59 41	8♍46 23	14 48 56	7 59.8	29♍54.8	5 41.3	1 40.1	9 56.7	7 56.7	5 03.7	0 56.9	25 08.0	0 38.2
13 F	11 31 02	20 58 07	20 53 31	27 00 19	7D58.6	29 01.4	6 46.6	2 17.5	10 12.0	7 58.5	4 59.3	0 55.6	25 07.2	0 39.3
14 Sa	11 34 58	21 56 34	3♎09 32	9♎21 19	7 58.3	28 03.9	7 52.1	2 54.9	10 27.6	8 00.5	4 54.8	0 54.4	25 06.5	0 40.4
15 Su	11 38 55	22 55 04	15 35 51	21 53 18	7 58.7	27 03.3	8 57.9	3 32.1	10 43.4	8 02.6	4 50.3	0 53.2	25 05.8	0 41.6
16 M	11 42 51	23 53 35	28 13 52	4♏37 43	7 59.6	26 00.7	10 03.9	4 09.3	10 59.3	8 05.0	4 45.7	0 52.1	25 05.2	0 42.8
17 Tu	11 46 48	24 52 08	11♏05 03	17 36 03	8 00.8	24 57.6	11 10.1	4 46.5	11 15.4	8 07.5	4 41.2	0 51.0	25 04.5	0 44.0
18 W	11 50 44	25 50 43	24 10 54	0♐49 46	8 01.9	23 55.5	12 16.5	5 23.5	11 31.7	8 10.2	4 36.6	0 49.9	25 03.9	0 45.2
19 Th	11 54 41	26 49 20	7♐32 49	14 20 10	8R02.6	22 55.9	13 23.2	6 00.5	11 48.1	8 13.1	4 32.0	0 48.9	25 03.4	0 46.5
20 F	11 58 37	27 47 58	21 11 56	28 08 06	8 02.8	22 00.2	14 30.0	6 37.5	12 04.7	8 16.2	4 27.3	0 47.9	25 02.8	0 47.8
21 Sa	12 02 34	28 46 38	5♑08 40	12♑13 30	8 02.6	21 10.1	15 37.0	7 14.3	12 21.4	8 19.5	4 22.7	0 47.0	25 02.3	0 49.2
22 Su	12 06 31	29 45 19	19 22 22	26 34 57	8 02.0	20 26.7	16 44.2	7 51.1	12 38.4	8 23.0	4 18.1	0 46.1	25 01.9	0 50.6
23 M	12 10 27	0♎44 02	3♒50 50	11♒09 28	8 01.2	19 51.2	17 51.6	8 27.8	12 55.4	8 26.6	4 13.4	0 45.3	25 01.4	0 52.0
24 Tu	12 14 24	1 42 47	18 30 12	25 52 19	8 00.4	19 24.5	18 59.2	9 04.4	13 12.6	8 30.4	4 08.7	0 44.5	25 01.0	0 53.4
25 W	12 18 20	2 41 33	3♓14 58	10♓37 19	7 59.8	19 07.4	20 07.0	9 40.9	13 30.0	8 34.4	4 04.0	0 43.8	25 00.6	0 54.8
26 Th	12 22 17	3 40 22	17 58 29	25 17 36	7D59.5	19D00.1	21 15.0	10 17.4	13 47.5	8 38.5	3 59.4	0 43.1	25 00.3	0 56.3
27 F	12 26 13	4 39 12	2♈33 48	9♈46 21	7 59.4	19 03.0	22 23.1	10 53.8	14 05.2	8 42.9	3 54.7	0 42.4	25 00.0	0 57.8
28 Sa	12 30 10	5 38 04	16 54 32	23 57 48	7 59.5	19 16.1	23 31.5	11 30.1	14 22.9	8 47.4	3 50.0	0 41.8	24 59.7	0 59.4
29 Su	12 34 06	6 36 59	0♉55 41	7♉47 53	7 59.7	19 39.1	24 40.0	12 06.4	14 40.9	8 52.0	3 45.3	0 41.3	24 59.4	1 00.9
30 M	12 38 03	7 35 56	14 34 12	21 14 33	7R59.7	20 11.6	25 48.6	12 42.5	14 58.9	8 56.9	3 40.7	0 40.8	24 59.2	1 02.5

LONGITUDE

October 1996

Day	Sid.Time	☉	0 hr ☽	Noon ☽	True ☊	☿	♀	♂	⚳	♃	♄	♅	♆	♇
1 Tu	12 42 00	8♎34 55	27♉49 02	4♊17 47	7♎59.7	20♍53.3	26♌57.5	13♌18.6	15♐17.1	9♑01.9	3♈36.0	0♒40.3	24♑59.0	1♐04.1
2 W	12 45 56	9 33 56	10♊41 05	16 59 17	7R59.6	21 43.4	28 06.5	13 54.6	15 35.5	9 07.1	3R31.4	0R39.9	24R58.9	1 05.8
3 Th	12 49 53	10 33 00	23 12 48	29 22 06	7D59.5	22 41.3	29 15.6	14 30.6	15 53.9	9 12.4	3 26.7	0 39.6	24 58.8	1 07.4
4 F	12 53 49	11 32 05	5♋27 43	11♋30 12	7 59.4	23 46.4	0♍25.0	15 06.4	16 12.5	9 17.9	3 22.1	0 39.3	24 58.7	1 09.1
5 Sa	12 57 46	12 31 14	17 30 07	23 28 03	7 59.5	24 57.9	1 34.5	15 42.2	16 31.3	9 23.6	3 17.5	0 39.0	24 58.6	1 10.9
6 Su	13 01 42	13 30 24	29 24 35	5♌20 18	7 59.9	26 15.0	2 44.1	16 17.9	16 50.1	9 29.5	3 12.9	0 38.8	24D58.6	1 12.6
7 M	13 05 39	14 29 37	11♌15 46	17 11 31	8 00.5	27 37.0	3 53.9	16 53.5	17 09.1	9 35.5	3 08.4	0 38.7	24 58.6	1 14.4
8 Tu	13 09 35	15 28 52	23 08 04	29 05 55	8 01.2	29 03.3	5 03.8	17 29.1	17 28.2	9 41.6	3 03.8	0 38.6	24 58.7	1 16.1
9 W	13 13 32	16 28 09	5♍05 31	11♍07 16	8 02.1	0♎33.3	6 13.8	18 04.5	17 47.4	9 47.9	2 59.3	0D38.5	24 58.7	1 18.0
10 Th	13 17 29	17 27 28	17 11 33	23 18 40	8 02.8	2 06.3	7 24.0	18 39.9	18 06.7	9 54.4	2 54.9	0 38.5	24 58.8	1 19.8
11 F	13 21 25	18 26 50	29 28 55	5♎42 29	8R03.1	3 41.8	8 34.4	19 15.1	18 26.2	10 01.0	2 50.4	0 38.6	24 59.0	1 21.6
12 Sa	13 25 22	19 26 13	11♎59 34	18 20 17	8 02.9	5 19.3	9 44.8	19 50.3	18 45.7	10 07.8	2 46.0	0 38.7	24 59.2	1 23.5
13 Su	13 29 18	20 25 39	24 44 40	1♏12 46	8 02.1	6 58.5	10 55.4	20 25.4	19 05.4	10 14.8	2 41.7	0 38.8	24 59.4	1 25.4
14 M	13 33 15	21 25 07	7♏44 33	14 19 56	8 00.7	8 39.0	12 06.1	21 00.4	19 25.2	10 21.8	2 37.4	0 39.0	24 59.6	1 27.3
15 Tu	13 37 11	22 24 36	20 58 51	27 41 08	7 58.8	10 20.4	13 16.9	21 35.3	19 45.1	10 29.1	2 33.1	0 39.3	24 59.9	1 29.3
16 W	13 41 08	23 24 08	4♐26 40	11♐15 16	7 56.7	12 02.5	14 27.9	22 10.1	20 05.1	10 36.5	2 28.9	0 39.6	25 00.2	1 31.2
17 Th	13 45 04	24 23 41	18 06 45	25 00 57	7 54.8	13 45.1	15 38.9	22 44.8	20 25.2	10 44.0	2 24.7	0 39.9	25 00.6	1 33.2
18 F	13 49 01	25 23 16	1♑57 38	8♑56 37	7 53.4	15 27.9	16 50.1	23 19.4	20 45.4	10 51.7	2 20.6	0 40.4	25 01.0	1 35.2
19 Sa	13 52 57	26 22 53	15 57 43	23 00 42	7D52.7	17 10.8	18 01.4	23 53.9	21 05.7	10 59.5	2 16.5	0 40.8	25 01.4	1 37.2
20 Su	13 56 54	27 22 32	0♒05 20	7♒11 25	7 52.9	18 53.7	19 12.8	24 28.3	21 26.1	11 07.4	2 12.5	0 41.3	25 01.8	1 39.3
21 M	14 00 51	28 22 12	14 18 39	21 26 46	7 53.9	20 36.4	20 24.3	25 02.6	21 46.6	11 15.5	2 08.6	0 41.9	25 02.3	1 41.3
22 Tu	14 04 47	29 21 54	28 35 27	5♓44 22	7 55.3	22 18.9	21 35.9	25 36.8	22 07.2	11 23.8	2 04.7	0 42.5	25 02.8	1 43.4
23 W	14 08 44	0♏21 37	12♓53 06	20 01 14	7 56.6	24 01.1	22 47.6	26 10.9	22 27.9	11 32.1	2 00.8	0 43.2	25 03.4	1 45.5
24 Th	14 12 40	1 21 23	27 08 20	4♈13 55	7R57.3	25 42.9	23 59.4	26 44.9	22 48.6	11 40.6	1 57.1	0 43.9	25 03.9	1 47.6
25 F	14 16 37	2 21 10	11♈17 29	18 18 34	7 57.0	27 24.4	25 11.3	27 18.8	23 09.5	11 49.3	1 53.3	0 44.7	25 04.6	1 49.7
26 Sa	14 20 33	3 20 59	25 16 39	2♉11 18	7 55.4	29 05.4	26 23.3	27 52.6	23 30.4	11 58.0	1 49.7	0 45.5	25 05.2	1 51.9
27 Su	14 24 30	4 20 50	9♉02 06	15 48 42	7 52.5	0♏46.0	27 35.4	28 26.2	23 51.4	12 06.9	1 46.1	0 46.3	25 05.9	1 54.0
28 M	14 28 26	5 20 43	22 30 49	29 08 13	7 48.5	2 26.1	28 47.6	28 59.8	24 12.6	12 15.9	1 42.6	0 47.2	25 06.6	1 56.2
29 Tu	14 32 23	6 20 38	5♊40 50	12♊08 35	7 43.8	4 05.7	29 59.9	29 33.3	24 33.8	12 25.0	1 39.2	0 48.2	25 07.3	1 58.4
30 W	14 36 20	7 20 36	18 31 34	24 49 56	7 39.0	5 44.9	1♎12.3	0♍06.6	24 55.0	12 34.3	1 35.9	0 49.2	25 08.1	2 00.6
31 Th	14 40 16	8 20 35	1♋03 55	7♋13 49	7 34.7	7 23.6	2 24.8	0 39.9	25 16.4	12 43.7	1 32.6	0 50.3	25 08.9	2 02.8

Astro Data

	Dy Hr Mn
♃D	3 14:37
☿R	4 5:47
☽0S	13 13:40
☿0N	18 20:31
♅✱♇	20 12:44
☉0S	22 18:00
☽0N	26 16:12
☿D	26 17:10
♆D	6 15:55
♅D	10 0:55
☽0S	10 20:48
☿0S	12 0:39
☽0N	24 1:15
♄△♇	26 3:03

Planet Ingress

		Dy Hr Mn
♀	♌	7 5:07
♂	♌	9 20:02
☿	♍R	12 9:32
☉	♎	22 18:00
♀	♍	4 3:22
☿	♎	9 3:13
☉	♏	23 3:19
☿	♏	27 1:01
♀	♎	29 12:02
♂	♍	30 7:13

Last Aspect / ☽ Ingress (September)

Last Aspect Dy Hr Mn			☽ Ingress	Dy Hr Mn
1 4:06	♆	□	♉	1 12:19
3 11:44	♀	✱	♊	3 19:08
4 19:06	☉	□	♋	6 5:29
8 16:26	♂	☌	♌	8 17:54
9 4:38	♄	△	♍	11 6:28
13 15:40	☿	☌	♎	13 17:51
15 18:05	♆	□	♏	16 3:20
18 2:18	☉	✱	♐	18 10:31
20 11:23	☉	□	♑	20 15:12
22 17:38	☉	△	♒	22 17:39
23 23:52	♀	☍	♓	24 18:43
26 11:32	♆	✱	♈	26 19:46
28 13:46	♆	□	♉	28 22:23

Last Aspect / ☽ Ingress (October)

Last Aspect Dy Hr Mn			☽ Ingress	Dy Hr Mn
30 21:07	♀	□	♊	1 4:01
3 11:46	♀	✱	♋	3 13:14
5 15:22	☿	✱	♌	6 1:12
7 11:22	♂	☌	♍	8 13:49
10 15:15	♆	△	♎	11 1:00
13 0:27	♆	□	♏	13 9:46
15 7:12	♆	✱	♐	15 16:07
17 10:50	☉	✱	♑	17 20:37
19 18:09	☉	□	♒	19 23:51
22 0:30	☉	△	♓	22 2:22
23 20:29	♆	✱	♈	24 4:50
26 5:52	☿	☍	♉	26 8:11
28 11:44	♂	□	♊	28 13:34
28 17:08	♇	☍	♋	30 21:56

☽ Phases & Eclipses

Dy Hr Mn		
4 19:06	☾	12♊31
12 23:07	●	20♍27
20 11:23	☽	27♐46
27 2:51	○	4♈17
27 2:54	•	T 1.240
4 12:04	☾	11♋32
12 14:14	●	19♎32
12 14:02:02	•	P 0.758
19 18:09	☽	26♑38
26 14:11	○	3♉26

Astro Data

1 September 1996
Julian Day # 35308
SVP 5♓18'19"
GC 26♐47.6 ⚴ 8♏02.8
Eris 18♈48.4R ⚵ 17♈36.4R
⚷ 14♎26.1 ⚶ 28♏36.2
☽ Mean ☊ 9♎29.3

1 October 1996
Julian Day # 35338
SVP 5♓18'17"
GC 26♐47.6 ⚴ 19♏23.9
Eris 18♈32.3R ⚵ 12♈51.9R
⚷ 18♎34.8 ⚶ 11♐22.9
☽ Mean ☊ 7♎54.0

November 1996 LONGITUDE

Day	Sid.Time	☉	0 hr ☽	Noon ☽	True ☊	☿	♀	♂	⚳	♃	♄	♅	♆	♇
1 F	14 44 13	9♏20 36	13♋20 04	19♋23 05	7♎31.4	9♏01.8	3♎37.4	1♍13.0	25♐37.8	12♑53.2	1♈29.4	0♒51.4	25♑09.8	2♐05.0
2 Sa	14 48 09	10 20 40	25 23 23	1♌21 31	7D 29.5	10 39.6	4 50.0	1 46.0	25 59.3	13 02.8	1R 26.3	0 52.6	25 10.7	2 07.2
3 Su	14 52 06	11 20 46	7♌18 04	13 13 39	7 29.1	12 16.9	6 02.8	2 18.9	26 20.9	13 12.6	1 23.3	0 53.8	25 11.6	2 09.5
4 M	14 56 02	12 20 53	19 08 54	25 04 26	7 29.9	13 53.8	7 15.6	2 51.7	26 42.6	13 22.4	1 20.3	0 55.1	25 12.5	2 11.7
5 Tu	14 59 59	13 21 03	1♍00 54	6♍58 55	7 31.4	15 30.3	8 28.5	3 24.4	27 04.3	13 32.4	1 17.4	0 56.4	25 13.5	2 14.0
6 W	15 03 55	14 21 15	12 59 06	19 02 01	7 33.2	17 06.3	9 41.5	3 56.9	27 26.1	13 42.5	1 14.7	0 57.7	25 14.5	2 16.3
7 Th	15 07 52	15 21 29	25 08 12	1♎18 08	7R 34.4	18 42.0	10 54.6	4 29.3	27 48.0	13 52.6	1 12.0	0 59.1	25 15.5	2 18.6
8 F	15 11 49	16 21 45	7♎32 16	13 50 56	7 34.4	20 17.3	12 07.7	5 01.6	28 10.0	14 02.9	1 09.4	1 00.6	25 16.6	2 20.9
9 Sa	15 15 45	17 22 02	20 14 25	26 42 54	7 32.6	21 52.2	13 20.9	5 33.7	28 32.0	14 13.4	1 06.9	1 02.1	25 17.7	2 23.2
10 Su	15 19 42	18 22 22	3♏16 27	9♏55 04	7 28.9	23 26.8	14 34.2	6 05.7	28 54.1	14 23.9	1 04.4	1 03.6	25 18.8	2 25.5
11 M	15 23 38	19 22 43	16 38 35	23 26 47	7 23.3	25 01.1	15 47.5	6 37.5	29 16.2	14 34.5	1 02.1	1 05.2	25 19.9	2 27.8
12 Tu	15 27 35	20 23 06	0♐19 19	7♐15 45	7 16.4	26 35.1	17 01.0	7 09.3	29 38.5	14 45.2	0 59.9	1 06.9	25 21.1	2 30.1
13 W	15 31 31	21 23 31	14 15 35	21 18 14	7 08.9	28 08.8	18 14.4	7 40.8	0♑00.7	14 56.0	0 57.8	1 08.6	25 22.3	2 32.5
14 Th	15 35 28	22 23 58	28 23 09	5♑29 42	7 01.8	29 42.1	19 28.0	8 12.3	0 23.1	15 07.0	0 55.7	1 10.3	25 23.6	2 34.8
15 F	15 39 24	23 24 25	12♑37 18	19 45 23	6 56.0	1♐15.3	20 41.6	8 43.5	0 45.5	15 18.0	0 53.8	1 12.1	25 24.9	2 37.2
16 Sa	15 43 21	24 24 54	26 53 28	4♒01 07	6 52.0	2 48.1	21 55.2	9 14.7	1 08.0	15 29.1	0 51.9	1 13.9	25 26.2	2 39.5
17 Su	15 47 18	25 25 24	11♒07 57	18 13 40	6D 50.2	4 20.7	23 08.9	9 45.6	1 30.5	15 40.3	0 50.2	1 15.8	25 27.5	2 41.9
18 M	15 51 14	26 25 56	25 18 03	2♓20 55	6 50.1	5 53.1	24 22.6	10 16.5	1 53.0	15 51.6	0 48.6	1 17.7	25 28.9	2 44.3
19 Tu	15 55 11	27 26 28	9♓22 09	16 21 39	6 51.0	7 25.2	25 36.4	10 47.1	2 15.7	16 03.0	0 47.0	1 19.7	25 30.2	2 46.6
20 W	15 59 07	28 27 02	23 19 21	0♈15 11	6R 52.0	8 57.1	26 50.3	11 17.6	2 38.3	16 14.5	0 45.6	1 21.7	25 31.7	2 49.0
21 Th	16 03 04	29 27 37	7♈09 04	14 00 56	6 51.9	10 28.8	28 04.2	11 47.9	3 01.1	16 26.1	0 44.3	1 23.7	25 33.1	2 51.4
22 F	16 07 00	0♐28 14	20 50 38	27 38 04	6 49.9	12 00.2	29 18.2	12 18.1	3 23.8	16 37.7	0 43.0	1 25.8	25 34.6	2 53.7
23 Sa	16 10 57	1 28 51	4♉23 03	11♉05 24	6 45.4	13 31.4	0♏32.2	12 48.1	3 46.7	16 49.5	0 41.9	1 28.0	25 36.1	2 56.1
24 Su	16 14 53	2 29 30	17 44 55	24 21 24	6 38.3	15 02.4	1 46.2	13 18.0	4 09.5	17 01.3	0 40.9	1 30.1	25 37.6	2 58.5
25 M	16 18 50	3 30 10	0♊54 40	7♊24 31	6 28.9	16 33.2	3 00.3	13 47.6	4 32.5	17 13.2	0 40.0	1 32.3	25 39.1	3 00.9
26 Tu	16 22 47	4 30 52	13 50 49	20 13 29	6 18.1	18 03.6	4 14.5	14 17.1	4 55.4	17 25.2	0 39.2	1 34.6	25 40.7	3 03.3
27 W	16 26 43	5 31 35	26 32 26	2♋47 44	6 06.9	19 33.8	5 28.7	14 46.4	5 18.4	17 37.2	0 38.5	1 36.9	25 42.3	3 05.6
28 Th	16 30 40	6 32 20	8♋59 26	15 07 43	5 56.3	21 03.7	6 42.9	15 15.6	5 41.5	17 49.4	0 37.9	1 39.2	25 43.9	3 08.0
29 F	16 34 36	7 33 05	21 12 47	27 14 58	5 47.2	22 33.2	7 57.2	15 44.5	6 04.6	18 01.6	0 37.4	1 41.6	25 45.6	3 10.4
30 Sa	16 38 33	8 33 53	3♌14 37	9♌12 10	5 40.4	24 02.3	9 11.5	16 13.3	6 27.7	18 13.9	0 37.0	1 44.0	25 47.2	3 12.8

December 1996 LONGITUDE

Day	Sid.Time	☉	0 hr ☽	Noon ☽	True ☊	☿	♀	♂	⚳	♃	♄	♅	♆	♇
1 Su	16 42 29	9♐34 41	15♌08 08	21♌03 03	5♎36.1	25♐31.0	10♏25.9	16♍41.8	6♑50.9	18♑26.2	0♈36.8	1♒46.4	25♑48.9	3♐15.1
2 M	16 46 26	10 35 32	26 57 30	2♍52 08	5D 34.1	26 59.1	11 40.3	17 10.2	7 14.1	18 38.6	0R 36.6	1 48.9	25 50.7	3 17.5
3 Tu	16 50 22	11 36 23	8♍47 36	14 44 34	5 33.8	28 26.7	12 54.7	17 38.4	7 37.4	18 51.1	0D 36.5	1 51.4	25 52.4	3 19.8
4 W	16 54 19	12 37 16	20 43 44	26 45 48	5R 34.2	29 53.5	14 09.2	18 06.3	8 00.6	19 03.7	0 36.6	1 54.0	25 54.2	3 22.2
5 Th	16 58 16	13 38 10	2♎51 25	9♎01 15	5 34.4	1♑19.5	15 23.7	18 34.1	8 24.0	19 16.3	0 36.7	1 56.6	25 55.9	3 24.5
6 F	17 02 12	14 39 06	15 15 53	21 35 53	5 33.2	2 44.6	16 38.2	19 01.6	8 47.3	19 29.0	0 37.0	1 59.2	25 57.7	3 26.9
7 Sa	17 06 09	15 40 02	28 01 41	4♏33 40	5 29.7	4 08.6	17 52.8	19 28.9	9 10.7	19 41.8	0 37.4	2 01.9	25 59.6	3 29.2
8 Su	17 10 05	16 41 00	11♏12 03	17 56 57	5 23.5	5 31.3	19 07.4	19 56.0	9 34.2	19 54.6	0 37.9	2 04.6	26 01.4	3 31.6
9 M	17 14 02	17 42 00	24 48 17	1♐45 51	5 14.7	6 52.5	20 22.1	20 22.8	9 57.6	20 07.5	0 38.5	2 07.3	26 03.3	3 33.9
10 Tu	17 17 58	18 43 00	8♐49 13	15 57 49	5 03.8	8 11.9	21 36.8	20 49.4	10 21.1	20 20.5	0 39.2	2 10.1	26 05.2	3 36.2
11 W	17 21 55	19 44 01	23 10 56	0♑27 42	4 51.9	9 29.3	22 51.4	21 15.8	10 44.7	20 33.5	0 40.0	2 12.9	26 07.1	3 38.5
12 Th	17 25 51	20 45 03	7♑47 09	15 08 17	4 40.4	10 44.3	24 06.2	21 41.9	11 08.2	20 46.5	0 40.9	2 15.7	26 09.0	3 40.8
13 F	17 29 48	21 46 05	22 30 05	29 51 35	4 30.6	11 56.5	25 20.9	22 07.8	11 31.8	20 59.6	0 42.0	2 18.6	26 11.0	3 43.1
14 Sa	17 33 45	22 47 08	7♒11 50	14♒30 05	4 23.3	13 05.4	26 35.7	22 33.4	11 55.4	21 12.8	0 43.1	2 21.5	26 12.9	3 45.4
15 Su	17 37 41	23 48 12	21 45 39	28 58 02	4 18.9	14 10.6	27 50.5	22 58.7	12 19.1	21 26.0	0 44.4	2 24.4	26 14.9	3 47.7
16 M	17 41 38	24 49 16	6♓06 50	13♓11 50	4D 17.0	15 11.4	29 05.3	23 23.8	12 42.7	21 39.3	0 45.7	2 27.3	26 16.9	3 49.9
17 Tu	17 45 34	25 50 20	20 12 55	27 10 05	4R 16.6	16 07.3	0♐20.1	23 48.6	13 06.4	21 52.6	0 47.2	2 30.3	26 18.9	3 52.2
18 W	17 49 31	26 51 24	4♈03 23	10♈52 58	4 16.6	16 57.4	1 34.9	24 13.1	13 30.1	22 06.0	0 48.8	2 33.3	26 21.0	3 54.4
19 Th	17 53 27	27 52 29	17 39 00	24 21 39	4 15.4	17 41.0	2 49.8	24 37.3	13 53.8	22 19.4	0 50.4	2 36.3	26 23.0	3 56.6
20 F	17 57 24	28 53 34	1♉01 07	7♉37 32	4 12.1	18 17.3	4 04.6	25 01.3	14 17.6	22 32.8	0 52.2	2 39.4	26 25.1	3 58.9
21 Sa	18 01 20	29 54 40	14 11 04	20 41 50	4 05.7	18 45.3	5 19.5	25 25.0	14 41.3	22 46.3	0 54.1	2 42.5	26 27.1	4 01.1
22 Su	18 05 17	0♑55 45	27 09 53	3♊35 17	3 56.3	19 04.1	6 34.4	25 48.3	15 05.1	22 59.8	0 56.1	2 45.6	26 29.2	4 03.2
23 M	18 09 14	1 56 51	9♊58 03	16 18 12	3 44.1	19R 13.0	7 49.3	26 11.4	15 28.9	23 13.4	0 58.2	2 48.7	26 31.3	4 05.4
24 Tu	18 13 10	2 57 58	22 35 41	28 50 31	3 30.1	19 11.0	9 04.3	26 34.2	15 52.7	23 27.0	1 00.4	2 51.9	26 33.5	4 07.6
25 W	18 17 07	3 59 05	5♋02 41	11♋12 12	3 15.3	18 57.6	10 19.2	26 56.6	16 16.5	23 40.7	1 02.7	2 55.0	26 35.6	4 09.7
26 Th	18 21 03	5 00 12	17 19 08	23 23 33	3 01.2	18 32.4	11 34.2	27 18.7	16 40.4	23 54.4	1 05.1	2 58.2	26 37.7	4 11.8
27 F	18 25 00	6 01 19	29 25 35	5♌25 25	2 48.8	17 55.4	12 49.2	27 40.5	17 04.2	24 08.1	1 07.6	3 01.4	26 39.9	4 13.9
28 Sa	18 28 56	7 02 27	11♌23 19	17 19 33	2 39.0	17 07.1	14 04.2	28 02.0	17 28.1	24 21.8	1 10.2	3 04.7	26 42.0	4 16.0
29 Su	18 32 53	8 03 35	23 14 30	29 08 34	2 32.2	16 08.3	15 19.2	28 23.1	17 52.0	24 35.6	1 12.9	3 07.9	26 44.2	4 18.1
30 M	18 36 49	9 04 44	5♍02 15	10♍56 04	2 28.2	15 00.5	16 34.2	28 43.8	18 15.9	24 49.4	1 15.7	3 11.2	26 46.4	4 20.1
31 Tu	18 40 46	10 05 53	16 50 35	22 46 26	2D 26.5	13 45.7	17 49.3	29 04.2	18 39.8	25 03.2	1 18.6	3 14.5	26 48.6	4 22.2

Astro Data	Planet Ingress	Last Aspect	☽ Ingress	Last Aspect	☽ Ingress	☽ Phases & Eclipses	Astro Data
Dy Hr Mn	Dy Hr Mn	Dy Hr Mn	Dy Hr Mn	Dy Hr Mn	Dy Hr Mn	Dy Hr Mn	1 November 1996
♀0S 1 12:52	⚳ ♑ 13 11:12	1 23:34 ♆ ☍	♌ 2 9:16	1 22:22 ☿ △	♍ 2 6:11	3 7:50 ☾ 11♌10	Julian Day # 35369
☽0S 7 5:35	☿ ♐ 14 16:36	3 9:47 ☿ □	♍ 4 21:57	4 10:17 ♆ △	♎ 4 18:23	11 4:16 ● 19♏03	SVP 5♓18'14"
♄✶♅ 10 16:50	☉ ♐ 22 0:49	7 0:13 ♆ △	♎ 7 9:29	6 20:11 ♆ □	♏ 7 3:39	18 1:09 ☽ 25♒59	GC 26♐47.7 ⚴ 2♐05.1
☽0N 20 8:28	♀ ♏ 23 1:34	9 9:23 ♆ □	♏ 9 18:02	9 2:09 ♆ ✶	♐ 9 8:58	25 4:10 ○ 3♊10	Eris 18♈14.0R ⚵ 6♈27.5R
♃∠♇ 30 9:19		11 15:18 ♆ ✶	♐ 11 23:26	10 20:21 ♂ □	♑ 11 11:14		⚷ 23♎03.7 ⚶ 26♐09.5
	☿ ♑ 4 13:48	13 6:18 ♀ ✶	♑ 14 2:44	13 5:59 ♆ ☌	♒ 13 12:14	3 5:06 ☾ 11♍19	☽ Mean ☊ 6♎15.5
♄ D 3 12:39	♀ ♐ 17 5:34	15 21:32 ♆ ☌	♒ 16 5:14	15 9:56 ♀ □	♓ 15 13:44	10 16:56 ● 18♐56	
☽0S 4 15:34	☉ ♑ 21 14:06	18 1:09 ☉ □	♓ 18 8:00	17 10:31 ♆ ✶	♈ 17 16:55	17 9:31 ☽ 25♓44	1 December 1996
☽0N 17 15:01		20 8:38 ☉ △	♈ 20 11:34	19 18:51 ☉ △	♉ 19 22:09	24 20:41 ○ 3♋20	Julian Day # 35399
☿ R 23 19:47		22 15:15 ♀ ☍	♉ 22 16:12	21 22:42 ♆ △	♊ 22 5:17		SVP 5♓18'09"
		24 14:19 ♆ △	♊ 24 22:20	24 7:29 ♂ □	♋ 24 14:14		GC 26♐47.8 ⚴ 14♐44.3
		26 7:22 ☿ ☍	♋ 27 6:37	26 20:02 ♂ ✶	♌ 27 1:09		Eris 17♈59.7R ⚵ 6♈48.6
		29 9:01 ♆ ☍	♌ 29 17:30	28 4:38 ♀ △	♍ 29 13:45		⚷ 27♎03.6 ⚶ 11♑19.2
							☽ Mean ☊ 4♎40.2

LONGITUDE — January 1997

Day	Sid.Time	☉	0 hr ☽	Noon ☽	True ☊	☿	♀	♂	⚳	♃	♄	♅	♆	♇
1 W	18 44 43	11♑07 02	28♍44 17	4♎44 47	2♎26.3	12♑26.3	19♐04.3	29♍24.2	19♑03.7	25♑17.1	1♈21.6	3♒17.8	26♑50.8	4♐24.2
2 Th	18 48 39	12 08 12	10♎48 39	16 56 35	2R 26.3	11R 04.9	20 19.4	29 43.8	19 27.6	25 31.0	1 24.8	3 21.2	26 53.0	4 26.2
3 F	18 52 36	13 09 22	23 09 16	29 27 21	2 25.3	9 44.1	21 34.5	0♎03.0	19 51.5	25 44.9	1 27.9	3 24.5	26 55.2	4 28.1
4 Sa	18 56 32	14 10 32	5♏51 27	12♏22 06	2 22.4	8 26.6	22 49.5	0 21.9	20 15.4	25 58.9	1 31.2	3 27.9	26 57.5	4 30.1
5 Su	19 00 29	15 11 42	18 59 44	25 44 39	2 16.9	7 14.5	24 04.6	0 40.3	20 39.4	26 12.8	1 34.6	3 31.3	26 59.7	4 32.0
6 M	19 04 25	16 12 53	2♐37 01	9♐36 46	2 08.7	6 09.7	25 19.8	0 58.3	21 03.3	26 26.8	1 38.1	3 34.6	27 01.9	4 34.0
7 Tu	19 08 22	17 14 04	16 43 41	23 57 18	1 58.3	5 13.6	26 34.9	1 15.9	21 27.2	26 40.8	1 41.7	3 38.1	27 04.2	4 35.8
8 W	19 12 19	18 15 15	1♑16 58	8♑41 46	1 46.8	4 26.9	27 50.0	1 33.0	21 51.2	26 54.8	1 45.4	3 41.5	27 06.5	4 37.7
9 Th	19 16 15	19 16 25	16 10 40	23 42 27	1 35.5	3 50.1	29 05.1	1 49.7	22 15.1	27 08.9	1 49.2	3 44.9	27 08.7	4 39.6
10 F	19 20 12	20 17 36	1♒15 50	8♒49 31	1 25.7	3 23.3	0♑20.3	2 06.0	22 39.1	27 22.9	1 53.0	3 48.4	27 11.0	4 41.4
11 Sa	19 24 08	21 18 45	16 22 13	23 52 45	1 18.4	3 06.3	1 35.4	2 21.7	23 03.0	27 37.0	1 57.0	3 51.8	27 13.3	4 43.2
12 Su	19 28 05	22 19 55	1♓20 04	8♓43 19	1 13.9	2D 58.7	2 50.5	2 37.0	23 27.0	27 51.1	2 01.0	3 55.3	27 15.5	4 45.0
13 M	19 32 01	23 21 03	16 01 48	23 15 02	1D 12.0	2 59.8	4 05.7	2 51.8	23 50.9	28 05.2	2 05.1	3 58.8	27 17.8	4 46.7
14 Tu	19 35 58	24 22 11	0♈22 43	7♈24 42	1 11.9	3 09.2	5 20.8	3 06.2	24 14.8	28 19.3	2 09.3	4 02.2	27 20.1	4 48.4
15 W	19 39 54	25 23 19	14 21 01	21 11 47	1R 12.3	3 26.1	6 35.9	3 20.0	24 38.8	28 33.4	2 13.6	4 05.7	27 22.3	4 50.1
16 Th	19 43 51	26 24 25	27 57 13	4♉37 37	1 12.1	3 49.9	7 51.1	3 33.3	25 02.7	28 47.5	2 18.0	4 09.2	27 24.6	4 51.8
17 F	19 47 48	27 25 31	11♉13 17	17 44 35	1 10.0	4 19.9	9 06.2	3 46.0	25 26.6	29 01.6	2 22.5	4 12.7	27 26.9	4 53.4
18 Sa	19 51 44	28 26 36	24 11 52	0♊35 27	1 05.5	4 55.7	10 21.4	3 58.3	25 50.5	29 15.7	2 27.0	4 16.2	27 29.2	4 55.1
19 Su	19 55 41	29 27 40	6♊55 40	13 12 49	0 58.3	5 36.6	11 36.5	4 10.0	26 14.4	29 29.9	2 31.7	4 19.7	27 31.5	4 56.7
20 M	19 59 37	0♒28 43	19 27 09	25 38 53	0 48.8	6 22.1	12 51.6	4 21.2	26 38.3	29 44.0	2 36.4	4 23.3	27 33.7	4 58.2
21 Tu	20 03 34	1 29 46	1♋48 15	7♋55 23	0 37.6	7 11.8	14 06.8	4 31.7	27 02.2	29 58.1	2 41.2	4 26.8	27 36.0	4 59.8
22 W	20 07 30	2 30 48	14 00 29	20 03 40	0 25.8	8 05.3	15 21.9	4 41.8	27 26.0	0♒12.2	2 46.0	4 30.3	27 38.3	5 01.3
23 Th	20 11 27	3 31 49	26 05 05	2♌04 51	0 14.4	9 02.1	16 37.1	4 51.2	27 49.9	0 26.3	2 51.0	4 33.8	27 40.6	5 02.8
24 F	20 15 23	4 32 49	8♌03 08	14 00 06	0 04.5	10 02.1	17 52.2	5 00.0	28 13.7	0 40.5	2 56.0	4 37.3	27 42.8	5 04.2
25 Sa	20 19 20	5 33 48	19 55 56	25 50 51	29♍56.7	11 04.8	19 07.3	5 08.3	28 37.5	0 54.6	3 01.1	4 40.9	27 45.1	5 05.6
26 Su	20 23 17	6 34 47	1♍45 07	7♍39 02	29 51.4	12 10.1	20 22.5	5 15.9	29 01.3	1 08.7	3 06.3	4 44.4	27 47.3	5 07.0
27 M	20 27 13	7 35 45	13 32 56	19 27 14	29D 48.6	13 17.7	21 37.6	5 22.9	29 25.1	1 22.8	3 11.5	4 47.9	27 49.6	5 08.4
28 Tu	20 31 10	8 36 42	25 22 20	1♎18 44	29 47.9	14 27.3	22 52.8	5 29.2	29 48.9	1 36.9	3 16.8	4 51.4	27 51.8	5 09.7
29 W	20 35 06	9 37 38	7♎16 57	13 17 32	29 48.7	15 39.0	24 07.9	5 34.9	0♒12.6	1 50.9	3 22.2	4 54.9	27 54.1	5 11.1
30 Th	20 39 03	10 38 34	19 21 05	25 28 13	29 50.0	16 52.4	25 23.0	5 39.9	0 36.4	2 05.0	3 27.7	4 58.4	27 56.3	5 12.3
31 F	20 42 59	11 39 29	1♏39 32	7♏55 41	29R 50.9	18 07.4	26 38.2	5 44.2	1 00.1	2 19.0	3 33.2	5 01.9	27 58.6	5 13.6

LONGITUDE — February 1997

Day	Sid.Time	☉	0 hr ☽	Noon ☽	True ☊	☿	♀	♂	⚳	♃	♄	♅	♆	♇
1 Sa	20 46 56	12♒40 23	14♏17 16	20♏44 51	29♍50.6	19♑24.0	27♑53.3	5♎47.8	1♒23.8	2♒33.1	3♈38.8	5♒05.4	28♑00.8	5♐14.8
2 Su	20 50 52	13 41 17	27 18 57	4♐00 00	29R 48.6	20 42.0	29 08.5	5 50.8	1 47.4	2 47.1	3 44.5	5 08.9	28 03.0	5 16.0
3 M	20 54 49	14 42 10	10♐48 18	17 44 02	29 44.6	22 01.4	0♒23.6	5 53.0	2 11.1	3 01.1	3 50.2	5 12.4	28 05.2	5 17.1
4 Tu	20 58 46	15 43 02	24 47 11	1♑57 36	29 38.9	23 22.0	1 38.8	5 54.5	2 34.7	3 15.1	3 56.0	5 15.9	28 07.4	5 18.2
5 W	21 02 42	16 43 53	9♑14 50	16 38 17	29 32.2	24 43.8	2 53.9	5R 55.3	2 58.3	3 29.1	4 01.8	5 19.4	28 09.6	5 19.3
6 Th	21 06 39	17 44 43	24 07 07	1♒40 17	29 25.4	26 06.8	4 09.0	5 55.3	3 21.9	3 43.0	4 07.8	5 22.9	28 11.8	5 20.4
7 F	21 10 35	18 45 32	9♒16 36	16 54 45	29 19.5	27 30.8	5 24.2	5 54.5	3 45.5	3 57.0	4 13.7	5 26.3	28 14.0	5 21.4
8 Sa	21 14 32	19 46 19	24 33 21	2♓11 04	29 15.1	28 55.9	6 39.3	5 53.1	4 09.0	4 10.9	4 19.8	5 29.8	28 16.1	5 22.4
9 Su	21 18 28	20 47 05	9♓46 35	17 18 43	29D 12.7	0♒22.0	7 54.4	5 50.8	4 32.5	4 24.7	4 25.9	5 33.2	28 18.3	5 23.4
10 M	21 22 25	21 47 50	24 46 28	2♈08 58	29 12.2	1 49.1	9 09.5	5 47.8	4 56.0	4 38.6	4 32.0	5 36.6	28 20.4	5 24.3
11 Tu	21 26 21	22 48 33	9♈25 36	16 35 54	29 13.1	3 17.1	10 24.6	5 44.0	5 19.4	4 52.4	4 38.2	5 40.0	28 22.5	5 25.2
12 W	21 30 18	23 49 14	23 39 39	0♉36 45	29 14.6	4 46.1	11 39.7	5 39.4	5 42.8	5 06.2	4 44.5	5 43.4	28 24.6	5 26.0
13 Th	21 34 14	24 49 54	7♉27 17	14 11 25	29R 16.0	6 16.0	12 54.8	5 34.0	6 06.2	5 19.9	4 50.8	5 46.8	28 26.7	5 26.8
14 F	21 38 11	25 50 32	20 49 27	27 21 45	29 16.4	7 46.8	14 09.8	5 27.9	6 29.5	5 33.7	4 57.2	5 50.2	28 28.8	5 27.6
15 Sa	21 42 08	26 51 09	3♊48 43	10♊10 47	29 15.5	9 18.5	15 24.9	5 21.0	6 52.8	5 47.4	5 03.6	5 53.5	28 30.9	5 28.4
16 Su	21 46 04	27 51 44	16 28 26	22 42 05	29 13.1	10 51.1	16 40.0	5 13.3	7 16.0	6 01.0	5 10.1	5 56.9	28 32.9	5 29.1
17 M	21 50 01	28 52 17	28 52 13	4♋59 15	29 09.3	12 24.6	17 55.0	5 04.8	7 39.3	6 14.6	5 16.6	6 00.2	28 35.0	5 29.8
18 Tu	21 53 57	29 52 48	11♋03 35	17 05 37	29 04.5	13 59.1	19 10.0	4 55.6	8 02.4	6 28.2	5 23.2	6 03.5	28 37.0	5 30.4
19 W	21 57 54	0♓53 17	23 05 42	29 04 10	28 59.3	15 34.4	20 25.1	4 45.6	8 25.6	6 41.8	5 29.8	6 06.8	28 39.0	5 31.0
20 Th	22 01 50	1 53 45	5♌01 18	10♌57 25	28 54.2	17 10.7	21 40.1	4 34.8	8 48.7	6 55.2	5 36.5	6 10.0	28 41.0	5 31.6
21 F	22 05 47	2 54 11	16 52 46	22 47 35	28 49.9	18 47.9	22 55.1	4 23.2	9 11.7	7 08.7	5 43.2	6 13.3	28 43.0	5 32.2
22 Sa	22 09 43	3 54 35	28 42 08	4♍36 38	28 46.6	20 26.0	24 10.1	4 10.9	9 34.7	7 22.1	5 49.9	6 16.5	28 44.9	5 32.7
23 Su	22 13 40	4 54 58	10♍31 20	16 26 29	28 44.7	22 05.1	25 25.1	3 57.8	9 57.7	7 35.5	5 56.7	6 19.7	28 46.9	5 33.2
24 M	22 17 37	5 55 19	22 22 21	28 19 12	28D 44.0	23 45.1	26 40.1	3 44.0	10 20.6	7 48.8	6 03.5	6 22.9	28 48.8	5 33.6
25 Tu	22 21 33	6 55 38	4♎17 20	10♎17 04	28 44.5	25 26.1	27 55.0	3 29.5	10 43.5	8 02.1	6 10.4	6 26.1	28 50.7	5 34.0
26 W	22 25 30	7 55 56	16 18 46	22 22 48	28 45.7	27 08.2	29 10.0	3 14.3	11 06.4	8 15.3	6 17.3	6 29.2	28 52.5	5 34.4
27 Th	22 29 26	8 56 12	28 29 33	4♏39 29	28 47.3	28 51.2	0♓24.9	2 58.3	11 29.2	8 28.5	6 24.2	6 32.3	28 54.4	5 34.7
28 F	22 33 23	9 56 27	10♏53 00	17 10 34	28 48.8	0♓35.2	1 39.9	2 41.7	11 51.9	8 41.6	6 31.2	6 35.4	28 56.2	5 35.0

Astro Data

	Dy Hr Mn
☽0S	1 1:17
♃☌♆	9 11:39
☿ D	12 20:42
☽0N	13 22:50
☽0S	28 9:28
♅⚹♇	5 11:21
♂ R	6 0:37
♃⚹♄	9 15:33
☽0N	10 8:50
♃⚹♇	14 0:47
♃☌♅	16 2:22
♄0N	16 5:26
♄△♇	19 16:56
☽0S	24 16:04

Planet Ingress

	Dy Hr Mn
♂ ♎	3 8:10
♀ ♑	10 5:32
☉ ♒	20 0:43
♃ ♒	21 15:13
☊ ♍R	25 0:51
⚳ ♒	28 23:15
♀ ♒	3 4:28
☿ ♒	9 5:53
☉ ♓	18 14:51
♀ ♓	27 4:01
☿ ♓	28 3:54

Last Aspect / ☽ Ingress (January)

Last Aspect Dy Hr Mn		☽ Ingress Dy Hr Mn
1 1:02	♂ ☌	♎ 1 2:32
3 7:11	♆ □	♏ 3 13:02
5 14:12	♆ ⚹	♐ 5 19:27
7 16:43	♀ ☌	♑ 7 21:55
9 17:33	♃ ☌	♒ 9 22:00
10 5:25	♇ ⚹	♓ 11 21:51
13 20:16	♃ ⚹	♈ 13 23:22
16 1:19	♃ □	♉ 16 3:40
18 9:27	♃ △	♊ 18 10:53
18 20:12	♇ ☍	♋ 20 20:29
23 3:09	♆ ☍	♌ 23 7:50
23 17:58	♇ △	♍ 25 20:26
28 5:01	♆ △	♎ 28 9:21
30 16:49	♆ □	♏ 30 20:48

Last Aspect / ☽ Ingress (February)

Last Aspect Dy Hr Mn		☽ Ingress Dy Hr Mn
2 2:24	♀ ⚹	♐ 2 4:51
3 6:22	☉ ⚹	♑ 4 8:44
6 6:29	♆ ☌	♒ 6 9:21
7 15:06	☉ ☌	♓ 8 8:34
10 5:46	♆ ⚹	♈ 10 8:29
12 8:10	♆ □	♉ 12 10:56
14 14:04	♆ △	♊ 14 16:53
16 22:56	☉ △	♋ 17 2:13
19 11:09	♆ ☍	♌ 19 13:52
21 12:17	♀ ☍	♍ 22 2:38
24 13:00	♆ △	♎ 24 15:23
27 2:49	♀ △	♏ 27 2:57

☽ Phases & Eclipses

Dy Hr Mn		
2 1:45	☾	11♎42
9 4:26	●	18♑57
15 20:02	☽	25♈44
23 15:11	○	3♌40
31 19:40	☾	11♏59
7 15:06	●	18♒53
14 8:58	☽	25♉43
22 10:27	○	3♍51

Astro Data

1 January 1997
Julian Day # 35430
SVP 5♓18'04"
GC 26♐47.8 ⚳ 27♐42.7
Eris 17♈53.3R ✱ 14♈51.0
⚷ 0♏15.2 ⚵ 27♑24.5
☽ Mean ☊ 3♎01.7

1 February 1997
Julian Day # 35461
SVP 5♓18'00"
GC 26♐47.9 ⚳ 10♑03.7
Eris 17♈57.3 ✱ 27♈54.6
⚷ 1♏55.8 ⚵ 13♒33.2
☽ Mean ☊ 1♎23.2

March 1997

LONGITUDE

Day	Sid.Time	☉	0 hr ☽	Noon ☽	True ☊	☿	♀	♂	⚳	♃	♄	♅	♆	♇
1 Sa	22 37 19	10♓56 41	23♏32 38	29♏59 39	28♍49.9	2♓20.3	2♓54.8	2♎24.4	12♒14.6	8♒54.7	6♈38.2	6♒38.5	28♑58.1	5♐35.3
2 Su	22 41 16	11 56 53	6♐32 02	13♐10 10	28R50.2	4 06.4	4 09.8	2R06.5	12 37.3	9 07.7	6 45.3	6 41.5	28 59.9	5 35.5
3 M	22 45 12	12 57 03	19 54 21	26 44 49	28 49.8	5 53.6	5 24.7	1 48.0	12 59.9	9 20.7	6 52.4	6 44.5	29 01.6	5 35.7
4 Tu	22 49 09	13 57 12	3♑41 41	10♑44 58	28 48.6	7 41.8	6 39.6	1 28.8	13 22.4	9 33.6	6 59.5	6 47.5	29 03.4	5 35.9
5 W	22 53 06	14 57 19	17 54 31	25 10 00	28 47.0	9 31.1	7 54.5	1 09.2	13 44.9	9 46.5	7 06.6	6 50.5	29 05.1	5 36.0
6 Th	22 57 02	15 57 25	2♒30 57	9♒56 41	28 45.3	11 21.5	9 09.4	0 48.9	14 07.3	9 59.3	7 13.8	6 53.4	29 06.8	5 36.1
7 F	23 00 59	16 57 29	17 26 23	24 59 04	28 43.9	13 13.0	10 24.3	0 28.2	14 29.7	10 12.0	7 21.0	6 56.3	29 08.5	5 36.1
8 Sa	23 04 55	17 57 31	2♓33 37	10♓08 52	28 42.9	15 05.5	11 39.2	0 07.0	14 52.0	10 24.7	7 28.2	6 59.2	29 10.2	5R36.2
9 Su	23 08 52	18 57 32	17 43 37	25 16 39	28D42.5	16 59.0	12 54.0	29♍45.4	15 14.3	10 37.3	7 35.5	7 02.0	29 11.8	5 36.1
10 M	23 12 48	19 57 30	2♈46 49	10♈13 06	28 42.6	18 53.6	14 08.9	29 23.4	15 36.5	10 49.8	7 42.8	7 04.9	29 13.5	5 36.1
11 Tu	23 16 45	20 57 26	17 34 36	24 50 33	28 43.1	20 49.1	15 23.7	29 01.0	15 58.6	11 02.3	7 50.1	7 07.6	29 15.0	5 36.0
12 W	23 20 41	21 57 21	2♉00 23	9♉03 42	28 43.8	22 45.5	16 38.5	28 38.4	16 20.7	11 14.7	7 57.4	7 10.4	29 16.6	5 35.9
13 Th	23 24 38	22 57 13	16 00 17	22 50 05	28 44.4	24 42.8	17 53.3	28 15.5	16 42.7	11 27.0	8 04.8	7 13.1	29 18.2	5 35.7
14 F	23 28 35	23 57 03	29 33 09	6♊09 42	28 44.8	26 40.8	19 08.1	27 52.3	17 04.7	11 39.3	8 12.1	7 15.8	29 19.7	5 35.5
15 Sa	23 32 31	24 56 51	12♊40 03	19 04 34	28R45.0	28 39.5	20 22.9	27 29.1	17 26.5	11 51.5	8 19.5	7 18.4	29 21.2	5 35.3
16 Su	23 36 28	25 56 36	25 23 43	1♋37 59	28 45.0	0♈38.7	21 37.6	27 05.6	17 48.3	12 03.6	8 26.9	7 21.1	29 22.6	5 35.1
17 M	23 40 24	26 56 19	7♋47 55	13 54 03	28 44.9	2 38.2	22 52.4	26 42.1	18 10.1	12 15.6	8 34.3	7 23.7	29 24.1	5 34.8
18 Tu	23 44 21	27 56 00	19 56 55	25 57 04	28D44.8	4 37.9	24 07.1	26 18.6	18 31.7	12 27.6	8 41.8	7 26.2	29 25.5	5 34.5
19 W	23 48 17	28 55 39	1♌55 02	7♌51 18	28 44.8	6 37.6	25 21.8	25 55.1	18 53.3	12 39.4	8 49.2	7 28.7	29 26.9	5 34.1
20 Th	23 52 14	29 55 15	13 46 23	19 40 43	28 44.9	8 36.9	26 36.5	25 31.6	19 14.9	12 51.2	8 56.7	7 31.2	29 28.2	5 33.7
21 F	23 56 10	0♈54 50	25 34 45	1♍28 51	28 45.1	10 35.6	27 51.1	25 08.2	19 36.3	13 03.0	9 04.1	7 33.6	29 29.5	5 33.3
22 Sa	0 00 07	1 54 22	7♍23 24	13 18 44	28 45.3	12 33.4	29 05.8	24 45.0	19 57.7	13 14.6	9 11.6	7 36.0	29 30.8	5 32.8
23 Su	0 04 03	2 53 51	19 15 11	25 13 00	28R45.4	14 29.8	0♈20.4	24 21.9	20 19.0	13 26.1	9 19.1	7 38.4	29 32.1	5 32.3
24 M	0 08 00	3 53 19	1♎12 28	7♎13 48	28 45.4	16 24.7	1 35.0	23 59.1	20 40.2	13 37.6	9 26.6	7 40.7	29 33.3	5 31.8
25 Tu	0 11 57	4 52 45	13 17 15	19 23 02	28 45.0	18 17.4	2 49.6	23 36.5	21 01.3	13 49.0	9 34.1	7 43.0	29 34.6	5 31.3
26 W	0 15 53	5 52 09	25 31 20	1♏42 21	28 44.3	20 07.7	4 04.2	23 14.2	21 22.4	14 00.2	9 41.6	7 45.3	29 35.7	5 30.7
27 Th	0 19 50	6 51 31	7♏56 17	14 13 20	28 43.3	21 55.0	5 18.8	22 52.3	21 43.4	14 11.4	9 49.1	7 47.5	29 36.9	5 30.1
28 F	0 23 46	7 50 51	20 33 41	26 57 33	28 42.2	23 39.1	6 33.4	22 30.8	22 04.3	14 22.5	9 56.6	7 49.6	29 38.0	5 29.4
29 Sa	0 27 43	8 50 09	3♐25 07	9♐56 35	28 41.0	25 19.3	7 47.9	22 09.6	22 25.1	14 33.6	10 04.2	7 51.8	29 39.1	5 28.8
30 Su	0 31 39	9 49 26	16 32 09	23 11 58	28 40.1	26 55.5	9 02.5	21 48.9	22 45.8	14 44.5	10 11.7	7 53.9	29 40.2	5 28.1
31 M	0 35 36	10 48 41	29 56 11	6♑44 57	28D39.6	28 27.1	10 17.0	21 28.8	23 06.5	14 55.3	10 19.2	7 55.9	29 41.2	5 27.3

April 1997

LONGITUDE

Day	Sid.Time	☉	0 hr ☽	Noon ☽	True ☊	☿	♀	♂	⚳	♃	♄	♅	♆	♇
1 Tu	0 39 32	11♈47 54	13♑38 20	20♑36 20	28♍39.7	29♈53.9	11♈31.5	21♍09.1	23♒27.0	15♒06.0	10♈26.7	7♒57.9	29♑42.2	5♐26.6
2 W	0 43 29	12 47 05	27 38 54	4♒45 55	28 40.4	1♉15.5	12 46.0	20R49.9	23 47.5	15 16.6	10 34.3	7 59.9	29 43.2	5R25.8
3 Th	0 47 26	13 46 15	11♒57 07	19 12 12	28 41.5	2 31.6	14 00.4	20 31.4	24 07.8	15 27.1	10 41.8	8 01.8	29 44.1	5 24.9
4 F	0 51 22	14 45 23	26 30 40	3♓51 59	28 42.6	3 42.0	15 14.9	20 13.5	24 28.1	15 37.6	10 49.3	8 03.7	29 45.1	5 24.1
5 Sa	0 55 19	15 44 28	11♓15 27	18 40 18	28R43.4	4 46.5	16 29.4	19 56.1	24 48.3	15 47.9	10 56.8	8 05.5	29 45.9	5 23.2
6 Su	0 59 15	16 43 32	26 05 41	3♈30 40	28 43.5	5 44.9	17 43.8	19 39.5	25 08.4	15 58.1	11 04.3	8 07.3	29 46.8	5 22.3
7 M	1 03 12	17 42 34	10♈54 19	18 15 43	28 42.8	6 36.9	18 58.2	19 23.5	25 28.4	16 08.2	11 11.8	8 09.1	29 47.6	5 21.4
8 Tu	1 07 08	18 41 34	25 33 56	2♉48 10	28 41.0	7 22.6	20 12.6	19 08.3	25 48.3	16 18.1	11 19.3	8 10.8	29 48.4	5 20.4
9 W	1 11 05	19 40 32	9♉57 40	17 01 50	28 38.3	8 01.7	21 27.0	18 53.7	26 08.0	16 28.0	11 26.8	8 12.4	29 49.1	5 19.4
10 Th	1 15 01	20 39 28	24 00 12	0♊52 26	28 35.2	8 34.2	22 41.3	18 39.9	26 27.7	16 37.8	11 34.3	8 14.1	29 49.9	5 18.4
11 F	1 18 58	21 38 22	7♊38 22	14 17 57	28 32.0	9 00.2	23 55.7	18 26.9	26 47.3	16 47.4	11 41.7	8 15.6	29 50.6	5 17.3
12 Sa	1 22 55	22 37 13	20 51 18	27 18 37	28 29.3	9 19.5	25 10.0	18 14.6	27 06.7	16 56.9	11 49.2	8 17.1	29 51.2	5 16.3
13 Su	1 26 51	23 36 02	3♋40 13	9♋56 32	28 27.4	9 32.2	26 24.3	18 03.1	27 26.1	17 06.3	11 56.6	8 18.6	29 51.8	5 15.2
14 M	1 30 48	24 34 49	16 08 01	22 15 14	28D26.6	9R38.6	27 38.6	17 52.3	27 45.3	17 15.6	12 04.1	8 20.1	29 52.4	5 14.1
15 Tu	1 34 44	25 33 34	28 18 44	4♌19 07	28 26.9	9 38.6	28 52.8	17 42.4	28 04.4	17 24.8	12 11.5	8 21.4	29 53.0	5 12.9
16 W	1 38 41	26 32 16	10♌17 01	16 13 02	28 28.1	9 32.5	0♉07.1	17 33.2	28 23.4	17 33.8	12 18.8	8 22.8	29 53.5	5 11.7
17 Th	1 42 37	27 30 56	22 07 48	28 01 54	28 29.9	9 20.6	1 21.3	17 24.9	28 42.3	17 42.7	12 26.2	8 24.1	29 54.0	5 10.6
18 F	1 46 34	28 29 34	3♍55 55	9♍50 25	28 31.6	9 03.3	2 35.5	17 17.3	29 01.1	17 51.5	12 33.6	8 25.3	29 54.5	5 09.3
19 Sa	1 50 30	29 28 10	15 45 53	21 42 49	28R32.8	8 40.9	3 49.7	17 10.5	29 19.8	18 00.2	12 40.9	8 26.5	29 54.9	5 08.1
20 Su	1 54 27	0♉26 43	27 41 40	3♎42 48	28 32.8	8 14.0	5 03.8	17 04.5	29 38.3	18 08.7	12 48.2	8 27.6	29 55.3	5 06.9
21 M	1 58 23	1 25 15	9♎46 34	15 53 16	28 31.5	7 43.2	6 18.0	16 59.3	29 56.7	18 17.1	12 55.5	8 28.7	29 55.6	5 05.6
22 Tu	2 02 20	2 23 45	22 03 07	28 16 19	28 28.5	7 08.9	7 32.1	16 54.9	0♓15.0	18 25.4	13 02.7	8 29.8	29 56.0	5 04.3
23 W	2 06 17	3 22 12	4♏33 00	10♏53 13	28 24.0	6 32.0	8 46.2	16 51.3	0 33.1	18 33.5	13 10.0	8 30.8	29 56.3	5 03.0
24 Th	2 10 13	4 20 38	17 17 02	23 44 25	28 18.3	5 53.1	10 00.3	16 48.4	0 51.1	18 41.5	13 17.2	8 31.7	29 56.5	5 01.6
25 F	2 14 10	5 19 02	0♐15 19	6♐49 41	28 12.1	5 13.0	11 14.4	16 46.3	1 09.0	18 49.4	13 24.4	8 32.6	29 56.8	5 00.3
26 Sa	2 18 06	6 17 25	13 27 25	20 08 22	28 06.2	4 32.4	12 28.4	16 44.9	1 26.8	18 57.1	13 31.5	8 33.5	29 57.0	4 58.9
27 Su	2 22 03	7 15 46	26 52 27	3♑39 32	28 01.1	3 52.1	13 42.5	16D44.3	1 44.4	19 04.7	13 38.7	8 34.3	29 57.1	4 57.5
28 M	2 25 59	8 14 05	10♑29 30	17 22 13	27 57.6	3 12.7	14 56.5	16 44.5	2 01.9	19 12.1	13 45.8	8 35.0	29 57.3	4 56.1
29 Tu	2 29 56	9 12 23	24 17 36	1♒15 31	27D55.8	2 35.1	16 10.5	16 45.4	2 19.3	19 19.4	13 52.8	8 35.8	29 57.4	4 54.7
30 W	2 33 52	10 10 39	8♒15 53	15 18 33	27 55.6	1 59.6	17 24.5	16 47.0	2 36.5	19 26.6	13 59.9	8 36.4	29 57.4	4 53.2

Astro Data	Dy Hr Mn
♄⚹♅	1 13:23
♇ R	8 12:54
☽ 0N	9 20:06
☿0N	17 5:09
☉0N	20 13:55
☽ 0S	23 22:16
♀0N	25 19:22
☽ 0N	6 6:52
☿ R	14 24:00
☽ 0S	20 5:23
♂ D	27 19:09

Planet Ingress		Dy Hr Mn
♂	♍R	8 19:49
☿	♈	16 4:13
☉	♈	20 13:55
♀	♈	23 5:26
☿	♉	1 13:45
♀	♉	16 9:43
☉	♉	20 1:03
⚳	♓	21 16:20

Last Aspect Dy Hr Mn		☽ Ingress	Dy Hr Mn
1 10:06	♆ ⚹	♐	1 12:01
2 9:37	☉ □	♑	3 17:38
5 18:26	♆ ☌	♒	5 19:54
6 12:04	♃ ☌	♓	7 19:57
9 18:59	♂ ☍	♈	9 19:33
11 19:23	♆ □	♉	11 20:37
13 23:34	♆ △	♊	14 0:48
16 3:31	♂ □	♋	16 8:51
18 19:00	♆ ☍	♌	18 20:08
19 21:54	♃ ☍	♍	21 8:59
23 20:40	♆ △	♎	23 21:35
26 7:55	♆ □	♏	26 8:42
28 16:59	♆ ⚹	♐	28 17:40
30 19:31	☿ △	♑	31 0:07

Last Aspect Dy Hr Mn		☽ Ingress	Dy Hr Mn
2 3:30	♆ ☌	♒	2 3:59
3 5:44	♃ ☌	♓	4 5:42
6 5:57	♆ ⚹	♈	6 6:19
8 7:01	♆ □	♉	8 7:20
10 10:10	♆ △	♊	10 10:28
12 7:34	♀ ⚹	♋	12 17:03
15 3:07	♆ ☍	♌	15 3:22
17 10:51	☉ △	♍	17 16:00
20 4:27	♆ △	♎	20 4:36
22 15:11	♆ □	♏	22 15:19
24 23:26	♆ ⚹	♐	24 23:32
26 9:51	♃ ⚹	♑	27 5:32
29 9:46	♆ ☌	♒	29 9:50

☽ Phases & Eclipses Dy Hr Mn	
2 9:37	☾ 11♐51
9 1:15	● 18♓31
9 1:23:48	◐ T 02'50"
16 0:06	☽ 25♊27
24 4:45	○ 3♎35
24 4:39	◑ P 0.919
31 19:38	☾ 11♑08
7 11:02	● 17♈40
14 17:00	☽ 24♋47
22 20:33	○ 2♏45
30 2:37	☾ 9♒48

Astro Data

1 March 1997
Julian Day # 35489
SVP 5♓17'57"
GC 26♐48.0 ⚴ 20♑09.4
Eris 18♈09.1 ⚵ 12♉05.2
⚷ 1♏51.7R ⚶ 27♒54.4
☽ Mean ☊ 29♍54.2

1 April 1997
Julian Day # 35520
SVP 5♓17'54"
GC 26♐48.1 ⚴ 29♑22.0
Eris 18♈28.0 ⚵ 29♉03.7
⚷ 0♏13.8R ⚶ 13♓15.5
☽ Mean ☊ 28♍15.7

LONGITUDE — May 1997

Day	Sid.Time	☉	0 hr ☽	Noon ☽	True ☊	☿	♀	♂	⚳	♃	♄	♅	♆	♇
1 Th	2 37 49	11♉08 54	22♒23 24	29♒30 14	27♍56.5	1♉27.0	18♉38.5	16♍49.3	2♓53.6	19♒33.6	14♈06.9	8♒37.0	29♑57.5	4♐51.8
2 F	2 41 46	12 07 07	6♓38 52	13♓49 01	27R 57.7	0R 57.7	19 52.4	16 52.4	3 10.5	19 40.5	14 13.9	8 37.6	29R 57.5	4R 50.3
3 Sa	2 45 42	13 05 19	21 00 21	28 12 29	27 58.3	0 32.1	21 06.4	16 56.1	3 27.2	19 47.2	14 20.8	8 38.1	29 57.4	4 48.8
4 Su	2 49 39	14 03 29	5♈24 57	12♈37 13	27 57.4	0 10.5	22 20.3	17 00.6	3 43.9	19 53.7	14 27.7	8 38.5	29 57.4	4 47.3
5 M	2 53 35	15 01 38	19 48 42	26 58 47	27 54.5	29♈53.2	23 34.2	17 05.7	4 00.3	20 00.1	14 34.6	8 39.0	29 57.3	4 45.8
6 Tu	2 57 32	15 59 45	4♉06 48	11♉12 05	27 49.4	29 40.4	24 48.1	17 11.6	4 16.6	20 06.4	14 41.4	8 39.3	29 57.1	4 44.3
7 W	3 01 28	16 57 51	18 14 02	25 12 01	27 42.3	29 32.2	26 02.0	17 18.1	4 32.8	20 12.4	14 48.2	8 39.6	29 57.0	4 42.7
8 Th	3 05 25	17 55 55	2♊05 34	8♊54 14	27 34.0	29D 28.6	27 15.9	17 25.2	4 48.7	20 18.4	14 54.9	8 39.9	29 56.8	4 41.2
9 F	3 09 21	18 53 57	15 37 41	22 15 44	27 25.5	29 29.8	28 29.7	17 33.0	5 04.5	20 24.1	15 01.6	8 40.1	29 56.5	4 39.6
10 Sa	3 13 18	19 51 58	28 48 18	5♋15 25	27 17.5	29 35.6	29 43.6	17 41.5	5 20.2	20 29.7	15 08.3	8 40.2	29 56.3	4 38.1
11 Su	3 17 15	20 49 57	11♋37 13	17 53 58	27 11.0	29 46.1	0♊57.4	17 50.6	5 35.7	20 35.2	15 14.9	8 40.4	29 56.0	4 36.5
12 M	3 21 11	21 47 54	24 06 02	0♌13 49	27 06.5	0♉01.1	2 11.2	18 00.3	5 51.0	20 40.5	15 21.5	8R 40.4	29 55.7	4 34.9
13 Tu	3 25 08	22 45 49	6♌17 51	12 18 41	27D 04.0	0 20.6	3 25.0	18 10.6	6 06.1	20 45.6	15 28.0	8 40.4	29 55.3	4 33.3
14 W	3 29 04	23 43 42	18 16 55	24 13 11	27 03.4	0 44.5	4 38.7	18 21.5	6 21.0	20 50.5	15 34.5	8 40.4	29 54.9	4 31.7
15 Th	3 33 01	24 41 33	0♍08 10	6♍02 30	27 03.9	1 12.6	5 52.5	18 33.0	6 35.8	20 55.3	15 41.0	8 40.3	29 54.5	4 30.1
16 F	3 36 57	25 39 23	11 56 51	17 51 55	27R 04.8	1 44.8	7 06.2	18 45.0	6 50.4	20 59.9	15 47.4	8 40.1	29 54.1	4 28.5
17 Sa	3 40 54	26 37 11	23 48 17	29 46 36	27 05.1	2 21.1	8 19.9	18 57.6	7 04.7	21 04.3	15 53.7	8 40.0	29 53.6	4 26.8
18 Su	3 44 50	27 34 58	5♎47 26	11♎51 18	27 03.9	3 01.1	9 33.5	19 10.7	7 18.9	21 08.6	16 00.0	8 39.7	29 53.1	4 25.2
19 M	3 48 47	28 32 43	17 58 40	24 09 56	27 00.6	3 45.0	10 47.2	19 24.4	7 33.0	21 12.7	16 06.2	8 39.4	29 52.5	4 23.6
20 Tu	3 52 44	29 30 26	0♏25 27	6♏45 25	26 54.9	4 32.4	12 00.8	19 38.6	7 46.8	21 16.6	16 12.4	8 39.1	29 52.0	4 21.9
21 W	3 56 40	0♊28 08	13 10 02	19 39 20	26 46.9	5 23.3	13 14.5	19 53.3	8 00.4	21 20.3	16 18.5	8 38.7	29 51.4	4 20.3
22 Th	4 00 37	1 25 48	26 13 16	2♐51 44	26 37.1	6 17.7	14 28.1	20 08.5	8 13.8	21 23.9	16 24.6	8 38.3	29 50.7	4 18.6
23 F	4 04 33	2 23 28	9♐34 29	16 21 14	26 26.5	7 15.3	15 41.7	20 24.2	8 27.1	21 27.2	16 30.6	8 37.8	29 50.1	4 17.0
24 Sa	4 08 30	3 21 06	23 11 36	0♑05 10	26 16.0	8 16.1	16 55.2	20 40.4	8 40.1	21 30.5	16 36.6	8 37.3	29 49.4	4 15.4
25 Su	4 12 26	4 18 43	7♑01 30	14 00 08	26 06.9	9 20.1	18 08.8	20 57.1	8 52.9	21 33.5	16 42.5	8 36.7	29 48.7	4 13.7
26 M	4 16 23	5 16 19	21 00 37	28 02 31	26 00.0	10 27.1	19 22.3	21 14.2	9 05.5	21 36.3	16 48.4	8 36.1	29 47.9	4 12.1
27 Tu	4 20 19	6 13 54	5♒05 28	12♒09 06	25 55.6	11 37.0	20 35.9	21 31.8	9 17.9	21 39.0	16 54.2	8 35.4	29 47.2	4 10.4
28 W	4 24 16	7 11 28	19 13 08	26 17 21	25D 53.5	12 49.8	21 49.4	21 49.8	9 30.0	21 41.5	16 59.9	8 34.7	29 46.4	4 08.8
29 Th	4 28 13	8 09 01	3♓21 32	10♓25 33	25 53.1	14 05.5	23 02.9	22 08.2	9 42.0	21 43.7	17 05.6	8 34.0	29 45.5	4 07.1
30 F	4 32 09	9 06 33	17 29 16	24 32 33	25R 53.3	15 23.9	24 16.4	22 27.1	9 53.7	21 45.8	17 11.2	8 33.2	29 44.7	4 05.5
31 Sa	4 36 06	10 04 05	1♈35 17	8♈37 20	25 52.9	16 45.1	25 29.8	22 46.4	10 05.2	21 47.8	17 16.7	8 32.3	29 43.8	4 03.9

LONGITUDE — June 1997

Day	Sid.Time	☉	0 hr ☽	Noon ☽	True ☊	☿	♀	♂	⚳	♃	♄	♅	♆	♇
1 Su	4 40 02	11♊01 36	15♈38 32	22♈38 39	25♍50.6	18♉09.0	26♊43.3	23♍06.1	10♓16.4	21♒49.5	17♈22.2	8♒31.4	29♑42.9	4♐02.2
2 M	4 43 59	11 59 06	29 37 27	6♉34 39	25R 45.7	19 35.6	27 56.7	23 26.2	10 27.5	21 51.0	17 27.7	8R 30.5	29R 42.0	4R 00.6
3 Tu	4 47 55	12 56 35	13♉29 53	20 22 49	25 38.1	21 04.9	29 10.1	23 46.8	10 38.2	21 52.4	17 33.0	8 29.5	29 41.0	3 59.0
4 W	4 51 52	13 54 04	27 13 03	4♊00 13	25 27.9	22 36.8	0♋23.6	24 07.7	10 48.8	21 53.5	17 38.3	8 28.4	29 40.0	3 57.3
5 Th	4 55 48	14 51 31	10♊43 56	17 23 54	25 16.0	24 11.3	1 37.0	24 29.0	10 59.1	21 54.5	17 43.5	8 27.4	29 39.0	3 55.7
6 F	4 59 45	15 48 58	23 59 48	0♋31 26	25 03.6	25 48.4	2 50.3	24 50.7	11 09.1	21 55.3	17 48.7	8 26.3	29 38.0	3 54.1
7 Sa	5 03 42	16 46 24	6♋58 40	13 21 27	24 51.8	27 28.1	4 03.7	25 12.7	11 18.9	21 55.8	17 53.8	8 25.1	29 36.9	3 52.5
8 Su	5 07 38	17 43 48	19 39 50	25 53 57	24 41.7	29 10.4	5 17.1	25 35.2	11 28.4	21 56.2	17 58.8	8 23.9	29 35.8	3 50.9
9 M	5 11 35	18 41 12	2♌04 00	8♌10 19	24 34.0	0♊55.3	6 30.4	25 58.0	11 37.7	21R 56.4	18 03.7	8 22.7	29 34.7	3 49.4
10 Tu	5 15 31	19 38 35	14 13 16	20 13 20	24 28.8	2 42.7	7 43.7	26 21.1	11 46.7	21 56.4	18 08.6	8 21.4	29 33.6	3 47.8
11 W	5 19 28	20 35 56	26 11 01	2♍06 53	24 26.1	4 32.6	8 57.0	26 44.6	11 55.4	21 56.2	18 13.3	8 20.1	29 32.5	3 46.2
12 Th	5 23 24	21 33 17	8♍01 33	13 55 41	24 25.2	6 25.0	10 10.3	27 08.4	12 03.9	21 55.9	18 18.1	8 18.7	29 31.3	3 44.7
13 F	5 27 21	22 30 37	19 49 56	25 45 00	24 25.1	8 19.8	11 23.5	27 32.5	12 12.0	21 55.3	18 22.7	8 17.3	29 30.1	3 43.1
14 Sa	5 31 17	23 27 55	1♎41 34	7♎40 19	24 24.8	10 16.9	12 36.7	27 57.0	12 20.0	21 54.5	18 27.3	8 15.8	29 28.9	3 41.6
15 Su	5 35 14	24 25 13	13 41 55	19 47 00	24 23.2	12 16.2	13 50.0	28 21.7	12 27.6	21 53.6	18 31.7	8 14.4	29 27.6	3 40.1
16 M	5 39 11	25 22 30	25 56 08	2♏09 53	24 19.5	14 17.7	15 03.1	28 46.8	12 34.9	21 52.4	18 36.2	8 12.8	29 26.4	3 38.6
17 Tu	5 43 07	26 19 46	8♏28 40	14 52 53	24 13.4	16 21.2	16 16.3	29 12.2	12 42.0	21 51.1	18 40.5	8 11.3	29 25.1	3 37.1
18 W	5 47 04	27 17 02	21 22 46	27 58 28	24 04.7	18 26.5	17 29.5	29 37.8	12 48.8	21 49.6	18 44.7	8 09.7	29 23.8	3 35.6
19 Th	5 51 00	28 14 17	4♐40 01	11♐27 15	23 54.1	20 33.4	18 42.6	0♎03.8	12 55.2	21 47.8	18 48.9	8 08.1	29 22.5	3 34.2
20 F	5 54 57	29 11 31	18 19 55	25 17 37	23 42.5	22 41.7	19 55.7	0 30.0	13 01.4	21 45.9	18 53.0	8 06.4	29 21.2	3 32.7
21 Sa	5 58 53	0♋08 45	2♑19 49	9♑25 53	23 31.0	24 51.2	21 08.8	0 56.6	13 07.3	21 43.9	18 57.0	8 04.7	29 19.8	3 31.3
22 Su	6 02 50	1 05 58	16 35 07	23 46 44	23 21.0	27 01.5	22 21.9	1 23.4	13 12.9	21 41.6	19 00.9	8 03.0	29 18.5	3 29.9
23 M	6 06 46	2 03 11	0♒59 59	8♒14 05	23 13.2	29 12.5	23 34.9	1 50.4	13 18.2	21 39.1	19 04.8	8 01.2	29 17.1	3 28.5
24 Tu	6 10 43	3 00 24	15 28 20	22 42 04	23 08.1	1♋23.9	24 47.9	2 17.7	13 23.1	21 36.5	19 08.5	7 59.4	29 15.7	3 27.1
25 W	6 14 40	3 57 37	29 54 44	7♓05 52	23 05.6	3 35.3	26 00.9	2 45.3	13 27.8	21 33.7	19 12.2	7 57.6	29 14.3	3 25.8
26 Th	6 18 36	4 54 50	14♓15 06	21 22 10	23D 04.9	5 46.5	27 13.9	3 13.2	13 32.1	21 30.7	19 15.8	7 55.7	29 12.8	3 24.4
27 F	6 22 33	5 52 03	28 26 52	5♈29 06	23R 05.0	7 57.2	28 26.9	3 41.3	13 36.1	21 27.5	19 19.3	7 53.9	29 11.4	3 23.1
28 Sa	6 26 29	6 49 16	12♈28 47	19 25 54	23 04.5	10 07.2	29 39.9	4 09.6	13 39.8	21 24.1	19 22.7	7 51.9	29 09.9	3 21.8
29 Su	6 30 26	7 46 29	26 20 26	3♉12 22	23 02.4	12 16.3	0♌52.8	4 38.2	13 43.1	21 20.6	19 26.0	7 50.0	29 08.4	3 20.5
30 M	6 34 22	8 43 42	10♉01 43	16 48 26	22 57.9	14 24.2	2 05.7	5 07.0	13 46.2	21 16.8	19 29.2	7 48.0	29 07.0	3 19.2

Astro Data

	Dy Hr Mn
♆R	1 23:21
☽0N	3 15:52
☿D	8 18:06
♅R	13 4:05
☽0S	17 13:58
☽0N	30 23:05
♃R	10 0:24
☽0S	13 23:28
♄□♇	16 22:00
♂0S	21 6:05
☽0N	27 5:39

Planet Ingress

	Dy Hr Mn
☿ ♈R	5 1:48
♀ ♊	10 17:20
☿ ♉	12 10:25
☉ ♊	21 0:18
♀ ♋	4 4:18
☿ ♊	8 23:25
♂ ♎	19 8:30
☉ ♋	21 8:20
☿ ♋	23 20:41
♀ ♌	28 18:38

Last Aspect / ☽ Ingress (May)

Last Aspect Dy Hr Mn		☽ Ingress Dy Hr Mn
30 19:04	♃ ☌	♓ 1 12:50
3 14:55	♆ ⚹	♈ 3 14:59
5 17:00	♆ □	♉ 5 17:04
7 20:15	♆ △	♊ 7 20:21
10 1:22	♆ ⚹	♋ 10 2:13
12 11:24	♆ ☍	♌ 12 11:33
14 10:55	☉ □	♍ 14 23:43
17 12:14	♆ △	♎ 17 12:27
19 22:57	♆ □	♏ 19 23:11
22 6:34	♆ ⚹	♐ 22 6:51
23 21:00	♆ ⚹	♑ 24 11:51
26 14:59	♆ ☌	♒ 26 15:20
28 4:10	♃ ☌	♓ 28 18:18
30 20:51	♆ ⚹	♈ 30 21:18

Last Aspect / ☽ Ingress (June)

Last Aspect Dy Hr Mn		☽ Ingress Dy Hr Mn
2 0:09	♆ □	♉ 2 0:39
4 4:20	♆ △	♊ 4 4:55
6 1:15	♂ □	♋ 6 11:02
8 19:24	♆ ⚹	♌ 8 19:58
10 15:27	♃ ☍	♍ 11 7:43
13 19:34	♆ △	♎ 13 20:35
16 6:47	♆ □	♏ 16 7:51
18 15:05	♂ ⚹	♐ 18 15:39
20 19:09	☉ ☍	♑ 20 20:02
22 21:11	♆ ☌	♒ 22 22:20
24 10:11	♃ ☌	♓ 25 0:09
27 1:17	♆ ⚹	♈ 27 2:38
29 4:54	♆ □	♉ 29 6:23

☽ Phases & Eclipses

Dy Hr Mn	
6 20:47	● 16♉21
14 10:55	☽ 23♌41
22 9:13	○ 1♐19
29 7:51	☾ 7♓59
5 7:04	● 14♊40
13 4:51	☽ 22♍14
20 19:09	○ 29♐29
27 12:42	☾ 5♈54

Astro Data

1 May 1997
Julian Day # 35550
SVP 5♓17'51"
GC 26♐48.1 ⚴ 5♒09.6
Eris 18♈47.5 ⚵ 15♊56.1
⚷ 27♎56.9R ⚶ 27♓15.5
☽ Mean ☊ 26♍40.4

1 June 1997
Julian Day # 35581
SVP 5♓17'47"
GC 26♐48.2 ⚴ 6♒14.0R
Eris 19♈04.0 ⚵ 3♋15.9
⚷ 26♎06.9R ⚶ 10♈24.0
☽ Mean ☊ 25♍01.9

July 1997 — LONGITUDE

Day	Sid.Time	☉	0 hr ☽	Noon ☽	True ☊	☿	♀	♂	⚳	♃	♄	♅	♆	♇
1 Tu	6 38 19	9♋40 55	23♉32 28	0♊13 44	22♍50.6	16♋30.9	3♌18.6	5♎36.1	13♓48.8	21♒12.9	19♈32.4	7♒46.0	29♑05.5	3♐18.0
2 W	6 42 15	10 38 09	6♊52 10	13 27 38	22R41.0	18 36.0	4 31.5	6 05.4	13 51.2	21R08.9	19 35.4	7R44.0	29R03.9	3R16.8
3 Th	6 46 12	11 35 22	20 00 01	26 29 13	22 29.7	20 39.6	5 44.4	6 34.9	13 53.2	21 04.6	19 38.4	7 41.9	29 02.4	3 15.6
4 F	6 50 09	12 32 36	2♋55 06	9♋17 35	22 17.8	22 41.5	6 57.2	7 04.7	13 54.9	21 00.2	19 41.2	7 39.9	29 00.9	3 14.4
5 Sa	6 54 05	13 29 49	15 36 39	21 52 16	22 06.5	24 41.7	8 10.0	7 34.7	13 56.2	20 55.6	19 44.0	7 37.8	28 59.4	3 13.2
6 Su	6 58 02	14 27 02	28 04 28	4♌13 22	21 56.7	26 40.0	9 22.8	8 04.9	13 57.2	20 50.9	19 46.7	7 35.6	28 57.8	3 12.1
7 M	7 01 58	15 24 16	10♌19 08	16 21 59	21 49.1	28 36.5	10 35.6	8 35.3	13 57.8	20 46.0	19 49.3	7 33.5	28 56.2	3 11.0
8 Tu	7 05 55	16 21 29	22 22 12	28 20 09	21 44.1	0♌31.0	11 48.3	9 06.0	13R58.0	20 41.0	19 51.7	7 31.3	28 54.7	3 09.9
9 W	7 09 51	17 18 42	4♍16 13	10♍10 52	21D41.5	2 23.6	13 01.1	9 36.8	13 58.0	20 35.8	19 54.1	7 29.1	28 53.1	3 08.8
10 Th	7 13 48	18 15 56	16 04 39	21 58 05	21 40.8	4 14.3	14 13.8	10 07.9	13 57.5	20 30.4	19 56.4	7 26.9	28 51.5	3 07.8
11 F	7 17 45	19 13 09	27 51 48	3♎46 24	21 41.2	6 03.1	15 26.4	10 39.2	13 56.7	20 24.9	19 58.6	7 24.7	28 49.9	3 06.8
12 Sa	7 21 41	20 10 22	9♎42 34	15 40 57	21R41.8	7 49.9	16 39.1	11 10.7	13 55.6	20 19.2	20 00.7	7 22.4	28 48.3	3 05.8
13 Su	7 25 38	21 07 35	21 42 14	27 47 05	21 41.7	9 34.7	17 51.7	11 42.3	13 54.1	20 13.5	20 02.7	7 20.2	28 46.7	3 04.8
14 M	7 29 34	22 04 48	3♏56 09	10♏10 01	21 40.0	11 17.6	19 04.3	12 14.2	13 52.2	20 07.5	20 04.6	7 17.9	28 45.1	3 03.9
15 Tu	7 33 31	23 02 01	16 29 17	22 54 24	21 36.3	12 58.6	20 16.8	12 46.2	13 50.0	20 01.5	20 06.4	7 15.6	28 43.5	3 03.0
16 W	7 37 27	23 59 14	29 25 47	6♐03 42	21 30.5	14 37.6	21 29.4	13 18.5	13 47.5	19 55.3	20 08.1	7 13.3	28 41.9	3 02.1
17 Th	7 41 24	24 56 28	12♐48 18	19 39 36	21 22.9	16 14.7	22 41.9	13 50.9	13 44.5	19 49.0	20 09.7	7 11.0	28 40.3	3 01.3
18 F	7 45 20	25 53 42	26 37 26	3♑41 27	21 14.4	17 49.8	23 54.3	14 23.5	13 41.3	19 42.6	20 11.2	7 08.7	28 38.6	3 00.5
19 Sa	7 49 17	26 50 56	10♑51 09	18 05 52	21 06.0	19 22.9	25 06.8	14 56.3	13 37.6	19 36.1	20 12.6	7 06.3	28 37.0	2 59.7
20 Su	7 53 14	27 48 10	25 24 47	2♒47 00	20 58.5	20 54.1	26 19.2	15 29.2	13 33.7	19 29.4	20 14.0	7 04.0	28 35.4	2 58.9
21 M	7 57 10	28 45 25	10♒11 31	17 37 18	20 52.9	22 23.3	27 31.5	16 02.3	13 29.3	19 22.7	20 15.2	7 01.6	28 33.8	2 58.2
22 Tu	8 01 07	29 42 41	25 03 19	2♓28 38	20 49.4	23 50.6	28 43.9	16 35.6	13 24.6	19 15.8	20 16.3	6 59.3	28 32.1	2 57.5
23 W	8 05 03	0♌39 57	9♓52 20	17 13 38	20D48.1	25 15.8	29 56.2	17 09.1	13 19.6	19 08.9	20 17.3	6 56.9	28 30.5	2 56.8
24 Th	8 09 00	1 37 14	24 31 55	1♈46 38	20 48.4	26 39.0	1♍08.4	17 42.7	13 14.2	19 01.8	20 18.2	6 54.5	28 28.9	2 56.1
25 F	8 12 56	2 34 32	8♈57 24	16 03 58	20 49.5	28 00.1	2 20.7	18 16.5	13 08.4	18 54.7	20 19.0	6 52.1	28 27.3	2 55.5
26 Sa	8 16 53	3 31 51	23 06 10	0♉03 56	20R50.2	29 19.1	3 32.9	18 50.5	13 02.4	18 47.5	20 19.6	6 49.7	28 25.7	2 54.9
27 Su	8 20 49	4 29 11	6♉57 19	13 46 21	20 49.9	0♍35.9	4 45.1	19 24.6	12 55.9	18 40.2	20 20.2	6 47.3	28 24.0	2 54.3
28 M	8 24 46	5 26 32	20 31 10	27 11 54	20 47.8	1 50.5	5 57.2	19 58.9	12 49.1	18 32.8	20 20.7	6 44.9	28 22.4	2 53.8
29 Tu	8 28 43	6 23 55	3♊48 43	10♊21 46	20 43.8	3 02.9	7 09.4	20 33.3	12 42.0	18 25.4	20 21.1	6 42.5	28 20.8	2 53.3
30 W	8 32 39	7 21 18	16 51 12	23 17 10	20 38.1	4 12.9	8 21.4	21 07.9	12 34.6	18 17.9	20 21.4	6 40.1	28 19.2	2 52.8
31 Th	8 36 36	8 18 42	29 39 48	5♋59 15	20 31.2	5 20.5	9 33.5	21 42.7	12 26.8	18 10.3	20 21.6	6 37.7	28 17.6	2 52.4

August 1997 — LONGITUDE

Day	Sid.Time	☉	0 hr ☽	Noon ☽	True ☊	☿	♀	♂	⚳	♃	♄	♅	♆	♇
1 F	8 40 32	9♌16 07	12♋15 37	18♋29 02	20♍23.8	6♍25.6	10♍45.5	22♎17.6	12♓18.7	18♒02.7	20♈21.6	6♒35.4	28♑16.0	2♐52.0
2 Sa	8 44 29	10 13 33	24 39 37	0♌47 29	20R16.8	7 28.1	11 57.5	22 52.7	12R10.3	17R55.0	20R21.6	6R33.0	28R14.4	2R51.6
3 Su	8 48 25	11 11 00	6♌52 47	12 55 41	20 10.8	8 27.9	13 09.5	23 27.9	12 01.6	17 47.3	20 21.5	6 30.6	28 12.9	2 51.3
4 M	8 52 22	12 08 28	18 56 22	24 55 02	20 06.3	9 24.8	14 21.4	24 03.3	11 52.6	17 39.6	20 21.2	6 28.2	28 11.3	2 51.0
5 Tu	8 56 18	13 05 57	0♍51 56	6♍47 21	20 03.6	10 18.8	15 33.3	24 38.9	11 43.3	17 31.8	20 20.9	6 25.8	28 09.7	2 50.7
6 W	9 00 15	14 03 26	12 41 36	18 35 03	20D02.6	11 09.7	16 45.1	25 14.5	11 33.7	17 24.0	20 20.4	6 23.4	28 08.2	2 50.5
7 Th	9 04 12	15 00 57	24 28 06	0♎21 10	20 03.1	11 57.4	17 56.9	25 50.4	11 23.8	17 16.2	20 19.9	6 21.1	28 06.6	2 50.3
8 F	9 08 08	15 58 28	6♎14 46	12 09 23	20 04.5	12 41.6	19 08.7	26 26.3	11 13.6	17 08.4	20 19.2	6 18.7	28 05.1	2 50.1
9 Sa	9 12 05	16 56 00	18 05 35	24 03 55	20 06.2	13 22.2	20 20.4	27 02.4	11 03.2	17 00.5	20 18.5	6 16.3	28 03.6	2 49.9
10 Su	9 16 01	17 53 33	0♏04 59	6♏09 24	20 07.6	13 59.1	21 32.1	27 38.7	10 52.5	16 52.7	20 17.6	6 14.0	28 02.1	2 49.8
11 M	9 19 58	18 51 07	12 17 47	18 30 42	20R08.2	14 32.0	22 43.7	28 15.1	10 41.6	16 44.9	20 16.7	6 11.7	28 00.6	2 49.7
12 Tu	9 23 54	19 48 42	24 48 44	1♐12 26	20 07.6	15 00.6	23 55.3	28 51.6	10 30.4	16 37.1	20 15.6	6 09.4	27 59.1	2D49.7
13 W	9 27 51	20 46 18	7♐42 16	14 18 38	20 05.7	15 24.9	25 06.9	29 28.3	10 19.1	16 29.3	20 14.5	6 07.1	27 57.6	2 49.7
14 Th	9 31 47	21 43 55	21 01 50	27 52 01	20 02.8	15 44.6	26 18.4	0♏05.1	10 07.5	16 21.5	20 13.2	6 04.8	27 56.2	2 49.7
15 F	9 35 44	22 41 32	4♑49 14	11♑53 20	19 59.2	15 59.4	27 29.8	0 42.0	9 55.7	16 13.7	20 11.8	6 02.5	27 54.7	2 49.8
16 Sa	9 39 40	23 39 11	19 04 01	26 20 45	19 55.4	16 09.1	28 41.2	1 19.0	9 43.7	16 06.0	20 10.4	6 00.3	27 53.3	2 49.8
17 Su	9 43 37	24 36 51	3♒42 54	11♒09 36	19 52.1	16R13.6	29 52.5	1 56.2	9 31.5	15 58.4	20 08.8	5 58.0	27 51.9	2 50.0
18 M	9 47 34	25 34 32	18 39 52	26 12 37	19 49.7	16 12.6	1♎03.8	2 33.5	9 19.2	15 50.7	20 07.2	5 55.8	27 50.5	2 50.1
19 Tu	9 51 30	26 32 15	3♓46 41	11♓20 53	19D48.5	16 06.1	2 15.1	3 10.9	9 06.7	15 43.2	20 05.4	5 53.6	27 49.1	2 50.3
20 W	9 55 27	27 29 58	18 54 05	26 25 10	19 48.4	15 53.8	3 26.3	3 48.5	8 54.1	15 35.6	20 03.6	5 51.4	27 47.7	2 50.5
21 Th	9 59 23	28 27 44	3♈53 10	11♈17 14	19 49.2	15 35.7	4 37.4	4 26.2	8 41.3	15 28.2	20 01.6	5 49.3	27 46.4	2 50.8
22 F	10 03 20	29 25 31	18 36 40	25 50 55	19 50.5	15 11.9	5 48.5	5 04.0	8 28.5	15 20.8	19 59.6	5 47.1	27 45.1	2 51.1
23 Sa	10 07 16	0♍23 19	2♉59 36	10♉02 28	19 51.7	14 42.4	6 59.5	5 41.9	8 15.5	15 13.5	19 57.5	5 45.0	27 43.8	2 51.4
24 Su	10 11 13	1 21 10	16 59 25	23 50 29	19R52.5	14 07.5	8 10.5	6 19.9	8 02.4	15 06.2	19 55.2	5 42.9	27 42.5	2 51.7
25 M	10 15 09	2 19 02	0♊35 45	7♊15 27	19 52.6	13 27.4	9 21.4	6 58.1	7 49.2	14 59.0	19 52.9	5 40.9	27 41.2	2 52.1
26 Tu	10 19 06	3 16 56	13 49 49	20 19 09	19 51.9	12 42.7	10 32.3	7 36.4	7 36.0	14 52.0	19 50.5	5 38.8	27 39.9	2 52.5
27 W	10 23 03	4 14 52	26 43 48	3♋04 06	19 50.5	11 53.9	11 43.1	8 14.8	7 22.7	14 45.0	19 48.0	5 36.8	27 38.7	2 53.0
28 Th	10 26 59	5 12 50	9♋20 25	15 33 07	19 48.6	11 01.8	12 53.9	8 53.3	7 09.4	14 38.1	19 45.4	5 34.8	27 37.5	2 53.5
29 F	10 30 56	6 10 49	21 42 32	27 49 01	19 46.6	10 07.3	14 04.6	9 32.0	6 56.0	14 31.3	19 42.8	5 32.9	27 36.3	2 54.0
30 Sa	10 34 52	7 08 50	3♌52 53	9♌54 26	19 44.7	9 11.3	15 15.3	10 10.7	6 42.7	14 24.6	19 40.0	5 30.9	27 35.2	2 54.6
31 Su	10 38 49	8 06 53	15 54 00	21 51 50	19 43.1	8 15.0	16 25.9	10 49.6	6 29.3	14 18.0	19 37.1	5 29.0	27 34.0	2 55.2

Astro Data

	Dy Hr Mn
⚳ R	8 18:26
☽ 0S	11 8:42
♃ ✶ ♄	14 20:57
☽ 0N	24 13:02
♄ R	1 16:56
☽ 0S	7 16:38
♇ D	13 8:31
☿ R	17 19:49
♀ 0S	18 23:01
☽ 0N	20 22:07

Planet Ingress

	Dy Hr Mn
☿ ♌	8 5:28
☉ ♌	22 19:15
♀ ♍	23 13:16
☿ ♍	27 0:42
♂ ♏	14 8:42
♀ ♎	17 14:31
☉ ♍	23 2:19

Last Aspect / ☽ Ingress

Last Aspect Dy Hr Mn		☽ Ingress Dy Hr Mn
1 9:57	♆ △	♊ 1 11:35
3 2:02	♃ △	♋ 3 18:33
6 1:45	♆ ☍	♌ 6 3:45
7 20:44	♃ ☍	♍ 8 15:22
11 2:00	♆ △	♎ 11 4:21
13 13:57	♆ □	♏ 13 16:20
15 22:41	♆ ✶	♐ 16 1:02
17 17:45	♀ △	♑ 18 5:45
20 5:12	♆ ☌	♒ 20 7:29
22 5:24	♀ ☍	♓ 22 7:59
24 6:32	♆ ✶	♈ 24 9:03
26 10:34	☿ △	♉ 26 11:53
28 14:07	♆ △	♊ 28 17:04
30 7:47	♂ △	♋ 31 0:38

Last Aspect / ☽ Ingress

Last Aspect Dy Hr Mn		☽ Ingress Dy Hr Mn
2 7:01	♆ ☍	♌ 2 10:27
4 10:11	♂ ✶	♍ 4 22:15
7 7:26	♆ △	♎ 7 11:17
9 19:58	♆ □	♏ 9 23:50
12 5:59	♆ ✶	♐ 12 9:45
14 9:01	♀ □	♑ 14 15:42
16 16:10	♀ △	♒ 16 17:58
18 10:55	☉ ☍	♓ 18 18:01
20 14:12	♆ ✶	♈ 20 17:45
22 18:25	☉ △	♉ 22 18:57
24 18:50	♆ △	♊ 24 22:56
26 11:07	♄ ✶	♋ 27 6:10
29 11:35	♆ ☍	♌ 29 16:19

☽ Phases & Eclipses

Dy Hr Mn	
4 18:40	● 12♋48
12 21:44	☽ 20♎34
20 3:20	○ 27♑28
26 18:28	☾ 3♉47
3 8:14	● 11♌02
11 12:42	☽ 18♏53
18 10:55	○ 25♒32
25 2:24	☾ 1♊56

Astro Data

1 July 1997
Julian Day # 35611
SVP 5♓17'43"
GC 26♐48.3 ⚴ 1♒28.2R
Eris 19♈12.9 ⚵ 19♋36.0
⚷ 25♎44.0 ⚶ 21♈09.9
☽ Mean ☊ 23♍26.6

1 August 1997
Julian Day # 35642
SVP 5♓17'38"
GC 26♐48.3 ⚴ 23♑20.0R
Eris 19♈12.4R ⚵ 5♌48.2
⚷ 27♎02.0 ⚶ 29♈03.9
☽ Mean ☊ 21♍48.1

LONGITUDE

September 1997

Day	Sid.Time	☉	0 hr ☽	Noon ☽	True ☊	☿	♀	♂	⚳	♃	♄	♅	♆	♇
1 M	10 42 45	9♍04 58	27♌48 14	3♍43 29	19♍42.1	7♍19.6	17♎36.5	11♏28.6	6♓16.0	14♒11.6	19♈34.2	5♒27.1	27♑32.9	2♐55.8
2 Tu	10 46 42	10 03 04	9♍37 49	15 31 32	19D 41.7	6R 26.3	18 47.0	12 07.8	6R 02.7	14R 05.3	19R 31.2	5R 25.3	27R 31.8	2 56.4
3 W	10 50 38	11 01 12	21 24 54	27 18 13	19 41.7	5 36.2	19 57.4	12 47.0	5 49.4	13 59.1	19 28.1	5 23.5	27 30.7	2 57.1
4 Th	10 54 35	11 59 21	3♎11 48	9♎05 57	19 42.2	4 50.7	21 07.8	13 26.3	5 36.3	13 53.0	19 24.9	5 21.7	27 29.7	2 57.8
5 F	10 58 32	12 57 32	15 01 02	20 57 24	19 42.8	4 10.7	22 18.1	14 05.8	5 23.1	13 47.0	19 21.6	5 20.0	27 28.6	2 58.6
6 Sa	11 02 28	13 55 45	26 55 27	2♏55 37	19 43.5	3 37.2	23 28.3	14 45.4	5 10.1	13 41.2	19 18.3	5 18.2	27 27.6	2 59.4
7 Su	11 06 25	14 53 59	8♏58 18	15 03 59	19 44.1	3 11.1	24 38.5	15 25.1	4 57.2	13 35.6	19 14.9	5 16.6	27 26.7	3 00.2
8 M	11 10 21	15 52 15	21 13 08	27 26 13	19 44.4	2 53.0	25 48.6	16 04.8	4 44.5	13 30.1	19 11.4	5 14.9	27 25.7	3 01.0
9 Tu	11 14 18	16 50 32	3♐43 44	10♐06 09	19R 44.6	2D 43.5	26 58.6	16 44.7	4 31.8	13 24.7	19 07.8	5 13.3	27 24.8	3 01.9
10 W	11 18 14	17 48 51	16 33 54	23 07 25	19 44.6	2 42.9	28 08.6	17 24.8	4 19.3	13 19.5	19 04.2	5 11.8	27 23.9	3 02.8
11 Th	11 22 11	18 47 11	29 47 02	6♑33 03	19D 44.6	2 51.3	29 18.5	18 04.9	4 07.0	13 14.4	19 00.5	5 10.2	27 23.0	3 03.8
12 F	11 26 07	19 45 33	13♑25 38	20 24 52	19 44.5	3 08.9	0♏28.3	18 45.1	3 54.8	13 09.5	18 56.8	5 08.7	27 22.2	3 04.8
13 Sa	11 30 04	20 43 56	27 30 40	4♒42 49	19 44.6	3 35.6	1 38.0	19 25.4	3 42.8	13 04.8	18 52.9	5 07.3	27 21.4	3 05.8
14 Su	11 34 01	21 42 21	12♒00 56	19 24 26	19 44.7	4 11.0	2 47.6	20 05.8	3 31.1	13 00.2	18 49.1	5 05.9	27 20.6	3 06.8
15 M	11 37 57	22 40 48	26 52 37	4♓24 33	19 44.9	4 55.0	3 57.2	20 46.3	3 19.5	12 55.8	18 45.1	5 04.5	27 19.8	3 07.9
16 Tu	11 41 54	23 39 16	11♓59 15	19 35 33	19R 45.0	5 47.1	5 06.6	21 26.9	3 08.1	12 51.6	18 41.1	5 03.2	27 19.1	3 09.0
17 W	11 45 50	24 37 46	27 12 15	4♈48 08	19 44.9	6 46.9	6 16.0	22 07.6	2 57.0	12 47.6	18 37.0	5 01.9	27 18.4	3 10.1
18 Th	11 49 47	25 36 19	12♈21 59	19 52 43	19 44.5	7 53.7	7 25.3	22 48.4	2 46.1	12 43.7	18 32.9	5 00.6	27 17.7	3 11.3
19 F	11 53 43	26 34 53	27 19 16	4♉40 48	19 43.8	9 07.0	8 34.5	23 29.4	2 35.5	12 40.0	18 28.7	4 59.4	27 17.1	3 12.5
20 Sa	11 57 40	27 33 29	11♉56 34	19 06 04	19 43.0	10 26.2	9 43.6	24 10.4	2 25.1	12 36.5	18 24.5	4 58.2	27 16.5	3 13.7
21 Su	12 01 36	28 32 08	26 08 55	3♊04 58	19 42.1	11 50.7	10 52.6	24 51.5	2 15.0	12 33.1	18 20.2	4 57.1	27 15.9	3 15.0
22 M	12 05 33	29 30 49	9♊54 09	16 36 36	19 41.4	13 19.8	12 01.5	25 32.7	2 05.1	12 30.0	18 15.9	4 56.0	27 15.3	3 16.2
23 Tu	12 09 29	0♎29 32	23 12 33	29 42 20	19D 41.2	14 53.0	13 10.4	26 14.0	1 55.6	12 27.0	18 11.6	4 55.0	27 14.8	3 17.5
24 W	12 13 26	1 28 18	6♋06 21	12♋25 04	19 41.4	16 29.5	14 19.1	26 55.4	1 46.3	12 24.2	18 07.2	4 54.0	27 14.3	3 18.9
25 Th	12 17 23	2 27 05	18 38 59	24 48 37	19 42.2	18 09.0	15 27.8	27 36.9	1 37.3	12 21.6	18 02.7	4 53.1	27 13.9	3 20.3
26 F	12 21 19	3 25 55	0♌54 29	6♌57 09	19 43.3	19 50.8	16 36.3	28 18.4	1 28.7	12 19.2	17 58.2	4 52.2	27 13.4	3 21.7
27 Sa	12 25 16	4 24 47	12 57 06	18 54 50	19 44.6	21 34.5	17 44.7	29 00.1	1 20.3	12 17.0	17 53.7	4 51.3	27 13.0	3 23.1
28 Su	12 29 12	5 23 42	24 50 51	0♍45 35	19 45.9	23 19.7	18 53.1	29 41.9	1 12.3	12 14.9	17 49.2	4 50.5	27 12.7	3 24.5
29 M	12 33 09	6 22 38	6♍39 27	12 32 51	19R 46.7	25 06.0	20 01.3	0♐23.8	1 04.6	12 13.1	17 44.6	4 49.8	27 12.3	3 26.0
30 Tu	12 37 05	7 21 36	18 26 09	24 19 40	19 46.7	26 53.1	21 09.4	1 05.8	0 57.2	12 11.5	17 40.0	4 49.0	27 12.0	3 27.5

LONGITUDE

October 1997

Day	Sid.Time	☉	0 hr ☽	Noon ☽	True ☊	☿	♀	♂	⚳	♃	♄	♅	♆	♇
1 W	12 41 02	8♎20 37	0♎13 43	6♎08 35	19♍45.9	28♍40.7	22♏17.4	1♐47.8	0♓50.2	12♒10.0	17♈35.3	4♒48.4	27♑11.8	3♐29.1
2 Th	12 44 58	9 19 40	12 04 33	18 01 50	19R 44.1	0♎28.6	23 25.3	2 30.0	0R 43.5	12R 08.8	17R 30.7	4R 47.8	27R 11.5	3 30.6
3 F	12 48 55	10 18 44	24 00 42	0♏01 23	19 41.3	2 16.6	24 33.1	3 12.2	0 37.2	12 07.7	17 26.0	4 47.2	27 11.3	3 32.2
4 Sa	12 52 52	11 17 51	6♏04 06	12 09 05	19 37.9	4 04.5	25 40.7	3 54.6	0 31.2	12 06.9	17 21.3	4 46.7	27 11.2	3 33.8
5 Su	12 56 48	12 16 59	18 16 36	24 26 53	19 34.3	5 52.1	26 48.3	4 37.0	0 25.6	12 06.3	17 16.6	4 46.2	27 11.0	3 35.5
6 M	13 00 45	13 16 10	0♐40 12	6♐56 50	19 30.8	7 39.4	27 55.6	5 19.5	0 20.3	12 05.8	17 11.9	4 45.8	27 10.9	3 37.1
7 Tu	13 04 41	14 15 22	13 17 03	19 41 09	19 27.9	9 26.3	29 02.9	6 02.1	0 15.4	12D 05.6	17 07.2	4 45.4	27 10.9	3 38.8
8 W	13 08 38	15 14 36	26 09 27	2♑42 14	19 26.1	11 12.6	0♐10.0	6 44.8	0 10.9	12 05.5	17 02.4	4 45.1	27D 10.8	3 40.5
9 Th	13 12 34	16 13 52	9♑19 47	16 02 22	19D 25.5	12 58.3	1 17.0	7 27.6	0 06.7	12 05.7	16 57.7	4 44.8	27 10.8	3 42.3
10 F	13 16 31	17 13 09	22 50 12	29 43 27	19 26.0	14 43.5	2 23.8	8 10.5	0 02.9	12 06.1	16 53.0	4 44.6	27 10.8	3 44.0
11 Sa	13 20 27	18 12 29	6♒42 11	13♒46 27	19 27.3	16 28.0	3 30.4	8 53.4	29♒59.5	12 06.6	16 48.2	4 44.4	27 10.9	3 45.8
12 Su	13 24 24	19 11 49	20 56 06	28 10 54	19 28.8	18 11.8	4 36.9	9 36.5	29 56.5	12 07.4	16 43.5	4 44.3	27 11.0	3 47.6
13 M	13 28 21	20 11 12	5♓30 28	12♓54 16	19R 29.8	19 54.9	5 43.2	10 19.6	29 53.8	12 08.3	16 38.8	4D 44.2	27 11.1	3 49.4
14 Tu	13 32 17	21 10 37	20 21 36	27 51 37	19 29.7	21 37.4	6 49.3	11 02.7	29 51.5	12 09.5	16 34.0	4 44.2	27 11.3	3 51.3
15 W	13 36 14	22 10 03	5♈23 23	12♈55 48	19 28.1	23 19.1	7 55.3	11 46.0	29 49.5	12 10.9	16 29.3	4 44.2	27 11.5	3 53.2
16 Th	13 40 10	23 09 31	20 27 44	27 58 02	19 24.8	25 00.2	9 01.0	12 29.3	29 47.9	12 12.4	16 24.6	4 44.3	27 11.7	3 55.1
17 F	13 44 07	24 09 02	5♉25 33	12♉49 13	19 20.1	26 40.6	10 06.6	13 12.8	29 46.7	12 14.1	16 20.0	4 44.4	27 12.0	3 57.0
18 Sa	13 48 03	25 08 35	20 08 05	27 21 20	19 14.6	28 20.3	11 12.0	13 56.2	29 45.9	12 16.1	16 15.3	4 44.6	27 12.3	3 58.9
19 Su	13 52 00	26 08 09	4♊28 20	11♊28 37	19 09.1	29 59.4	12 17.2	14 39.8	29D 45.4	12 18.2	16 10.7	4 44.8	27 12.6	4 00.9
20 M	13 55 56	27 07 46	18 21 55	25 08 09	19 04.2	1♏37.9	13 22.2	15 23.5	29 45.3	12 20.6	16 06.0	4 45.1	27 13.0	4 02.8
21 Tu	13 59 53	28 07 26	1♋47 23	8♋19 50	19 00.7	3 15.7	14 26.9	16 07.2	29 45.6	12 23.1	16 01.5	4 45.5	27 13.4	4 04.8
22 W	14 03 49	29 07 08	14 45 50	21 05 51	18D 58.8	4 53.0	15 31.5	16 51.0	29 46.2	12 25.8	15 56.9	4 45.9	27 13.8	4 06.8
23 Th	14 07 46	0♏06 51	27 20 24	3♌30 03	18 58.5	6 29.6	16 35.8	17 34.9	29 47.2	12 28.7	15 52.4	4 46.3	27 14.3	4 08.9
24 F	14 11 43	1 06 37	9♌35 25	15 37 10	18 59.4	8 05.7	17 39.9	18 18.9	29 48.5	12 31.8	15 47.9	4 46.8	27 14.8	4 10.9
25 Sa	14 15 39	2 06 26	21 35 56	27 32 21	19 01.0	9 41.2	18 43.8	19 02.9	29 50.2	12 35.1	15 43.4	4 47.3	27 15.3	4 13.0
26 Su	14 19 36	3 06 16	3♍27 04	9♍20 41	19R 02.4	11 16.2	19 47.4	19 47.0	29 52.3	12 38.6	15 39.0	4 47.9	27 15.9	4 15.1
27 M	14 23 32	4 06 09	15 13 46	21 06 52	19 02.8	12 50.7	20 50.7	20 31.2	29 54.7	12 42.2	15 34.6	4 48.5	27 16.5	4 17.2
28 Tu	14 27 29	5 06 04	27 00 28	2♎55 03	19 01.6	14 24.6	21 53.8	21 15.5	29 57.4	12 46.1	15 30.3	4 49.2	27 17.1	4 19.3
29 W	14 31 25	6 06 00	8♎50 59	14 48 39	18 58.3	15 58.1	22 56.7	21 59.8	0♓00.5	12 50.1	15 26.0	4 50.0	27 17.8	4 21.4
30 Th	14 35 22	7 05 59	20 48 20	26 50 18	18 52.7	17 31.1	23 59.2	22 44.2	0 04.0	12 54.3	15 21.8	4 50.8	27 18.5	4 23.6
31 F	14 39 18	8 06 00	2♏54 46	9♏01 52	18 45.0	19 03.6	25 01.5	23 28.7	0 07.8	12 58.7	15 17.6	4 51.6	27 19.2	4 25.7

Astro Data

	Dy Hr Mn
☽0S	3 23:08
☿D	10 1:41
☽0N	17 8:47
♄□♇	22 10:42
☉0S	22 23:55
☽0S	1 5:05
☿0S	4 11:03
♃D	8 4:37
♆D	9 1:28
♅D	14 10:48
☽0N	14 19:50
⚳D	20 7:10
☽0S	28 11:52

Planet Ingress

		Dy Hr Mn
♀	♏	12 2:17
☉	♎	22 23:56
♂	♐	28 22:22
☿	♎	2 5:38
♀	♐	8 8:25
⚳	♒R	11 8:28
☿	♏	19 12:08
☉	♏	23 9:15
⚳	♓	29 8:07

Last Aspect / ☽ Ingress (September)

Last Aspect Dy Hr Mn			☽ Ingress	Dy Hr Mn
31 7:30	♄	△	♍	1 4:27
3 12:25	♆	△	♎	3 17:30
6 1:05	♆	□	♏	6 6:10
8 11:59	♆	⚹	♐	8 16:54
10 21:55	♀	⚹	♑	11 0:23
12 23:45	♆	☌	♒	13 4:10
14 13:10	♂	□	♓	15 4:59
17 0:10	♆	⚹	♈	17 4:25
18 23:57	♆	□	♉	19 4:21
21 3:31	☉	△	♊	21 6:38
22 14:59	♄	⚹	♋	23 12:33
25 17:50	♂	△	♌	25 22:12
28 9:42	♂	□	♍	28 10:27
30 18:08	☿	☌	♎	30 23:32

Last Aspect / ☽ Ingress (October)

Last Aspect Dy Hr Mn			☽ Ingress	Dy Hr Mn
3 6:21	♆	□	♏	3 11:57
5 17:17	♆	⚹	♐	5 22:43
7 7:14	♄	△	♑	8 7:04
10 7:35	♆	☌	♒	10 12:29
11 20:00	☉	△	♓	12 14:59
14 10:56	♆	⚹	♈	14 15:25
16 10:46	♆	□	♉	16 15:16
18 11:45	♆	△	♊	18 16:26
20 15:52	☉	△	♋	20 20:45
23 4:48	☉	□	♌	23 5:10
24 17:45	♂	△	♍	25 16:59
28 0:33	♆	△	♎	28 6:05
30 12:56	♆	□	♏	30 18:15

☽ Phases & Eclipses

Dy Hr Mn		
1 23:52	●	9♍34
2 0:03:46	•	P 0.899
10 1:31	☽	17♐23
16 18:50	○	23♓56
16 18:47	•	T 1.191
23 13:35	☾	0♋33
1 16:52	●	8♎33
9 12:22	☽	16♑15
16 3:46	○	22♈49
23 4:48	☾	29♋49
31 10:01	●	8♏01

Astro Data

1 September 1997
Julian Day # 35673
SVP 5♓17'34"
GC 26♐48.4 ⚴ 18♑13.7R
Eris 19♈02.5R ⚵ 21♌07.6
⚷ 29♎49.1 ⚶ 1♉43.2R
☽ Mean ☊ 20♍09.6

1 October 1997
Julian Day # 35703
SVP 5♓17'32"
GC 26♐48.5 ⚴ 18♑46.4
Eris 18♈46.6R ⚵ 4♍53.3
⚷ 3♏29.8 ⚶ 27♈45.7R
☽ Mean ☊ 18♍34.2

November 1997 LONGITUDE

Day	Sid.Time	☉	0 hr ☽	Noon ☽	True ☊	☿	♀	♂	⚳	♃	♄	♅	♆	♇
1 Sa	14 43 15	9♏06 03	15♏11 45	21♏24 30	18♍35.8	20♏35.7	26♐03.4	24♐13.3	0♓11.9	13♒03.3	15♈13.4	4♒52.5	27♑20.0	4♐27.9
2 Su	14 47 12	10 06 07	27 40 09	3♐58 46	18R 26.0	22 07.3	27 05.1	24 57.9	0 16.4	13 08.1	15R 09.4	4 53.4	27 20.8	4 30.1
3 M	14 51 08	11 06 13	10♐20 21	16 44 58	18 16.5	23 38.5	28 06.4	25 42.6	0 21.2	13 13.1	15 05.3	4 54.4	27 21.6	4 32.3
4 Tu	14 55 05	12 06 21	23 12 36	29 43 17	18 08.2	25 09.2	29 07.4	26 27.3	0 26.4	13 18.2	15 01.4	4 55.5	27 22.5	4 34.5
5 W	14 59 01	13 06 31	6♑17 06	12♑54 06	18 02.0	26 39.5	0♑08.0	27 12.2	0 31.9	13 23.5	14 57.5	4 56.6	27 23.4	4 36.7
6 Th	15 02 58	14 06 42	19 34 23	26 18 01	17 58.1	28 09.4	1 08.2	27 57.1	0 37.7	13 29.0	14 53.7	4 57.7	27 24.3	4 39.0
7 F	15 06 54	15 06 55	3♒05 08	9♒55 51	17D 56.6	29 38.8	2 08.1	28 42.0	0 43.8	13 34.6	14 49.9	4 58.9	27 25.2	4 41.2
8 Sa	15 10 51	16 07 09	16 50 14	23 48 23	17 56.7	1♐07.8	3 07.6	29 27.0	0 50.3	13 40.5	14 46.2	5 00.2	27 26.2	4 43.5
9 Su	15 14 47	17 07 25	0♓50 18	7♓55 57	17R 57.4	2 36.3	4 06.6	0♑12.1	0 57.1	13 46.5	14 42.6	5 01.5	27 27.3	4 45.8
10 M	15 18 44	18 07 41	15 05 13	22 17 52	17 57.6	4 04.3	5 05.2	0 57.3	1 04.1	13 52.6	14 39.0	5 02.8	27 28.3	4 48.0
11 Tu	15 22 41	19 08 00	29 33 34	6♈51 51	17 56.1	5 31.8	6 03.4	1 42.5	1 11.5	13 58.9	14 35.6	5 04.2	27 29.4	4 50.3
12 W	15 26 37	20 08 19	14♈12 07	21 33 39	17 52.3	6 58.7	7 01.0	2 27.7	1 19.2	14 05.4	14 32.2	5 05.6	27 30.5	4 52.6
13 Th	15 30 34	21 08 41	28 55 38	6♉17 08	17 45.6	8 25.1	7 58.2	3 13.0	1 27.2	14 12.1	14 28.8	5 07.1	27 31.6	4 54.9
14 F	15 34 30	22 09 04	13♉37 13	20 54 54	17 36.6	9 50.9	8 54.9	3 58.4	1 35.5	14 18.9	14 25.6	5 08.6	27 32.8	4 57.2
15 Sa	15 38 27	23 09 28	28 09 15	5♊19 23	17 26.1	11 16.0	9 51.1	4 43.8	1 44.0	14 25.9	14 22.4	5 10.2	27 34.0	4 59.6
16 Su	15 42 23	24 09 55	12♊24 32	19 24 05	17 15.1	12 40.3	10 46.7	5 29.3	1 52.9	14 33.0	14 19.4	5 11.8	27 35.2	5 01.9
17 M	15 46 20	25 10 23	26 17 33	3♋04 38	17 04.9	14 03.9	11 41.8	6 14.9	2 02.0	14 40.3	14 16.4	5 13.5	27 36.5	5 04.2
18 Tu	15 50 16	26 10 53	9♋45 11	16 19 13	16 56.5	15 26.5	12 36.2	7 00.4	2 11.4	14 47.7	14 13.5	5 15.2	27 37.8	5 06.6
19 W	15 54 13	27 11 24	22 46 56	29 08 36	16 50.5	16 48.1	13 30.1	7 46.1	2 21.1	14 55.3	14 10.7	5 17.0	27 39.1	5 08.9
20 Th	15 58 10	28 11 58	5♌24 40	11♌35 36	16 47.1	18 08.6	14 23.3	8 31.8	2 31.1	15 03.1	14 07.9	5 18.8	27 40.5	5 11.3
21 F	16 02 06	29 12 33	17 42 00	23 44 30	16D 45.7	19 27.8	15 15.9	9 17.6	2 41.3	15 11.0	14 05.3	5 20.6	27 41.8	5 13.6
22 Sa	16 06 03	0♐13 09	29 43 46	5♍40 30	16R 45.7	20 45.6	16 07.8	10 03.4	2 51.8	15 19.0	14 02.7	5 22.5	27 43.2	5 16.0
23 Su	16 09 59	1 13 48	11♍35 24	17 29 11	16 45.9	22 01.7	16 59.0	10 49.3	3 02.5	15 27.2	14 00.3	5 24.5	27 44.7	5 18.3
24 M	16 13 56	2 14 28	23 22 31	29 16 04	16 45.2	23 16.0	17 49.4	11 35.2	3 13.5	15 35.5	13 57.9	5 26.5	27 46.1	5 20.7
25 Tu	16 17 52	3 15 09	5♎10 29	11♎06 21	16 42.6	24 28.1	18 39.1	12 21.2	3 24.8	15 44.0	13 55.7	5 28.5	27 47.6	5 23.1
26 W	16 21 49	4 15 53	17 04 12	23 04 32	16 37.5	25 37.7	19 28.0	13 07.2	3 36.3	15 52.6	13 53.5	5 30.5	27 49.1	5 25.4
27 Th	16 25 45	5 16 37	29 07 45	5♏14 13	16 29.4	26 44.6	20 16.1	13 53.3	3 48.1	16 01.3	13 51.4	5 32.7	27 50.6	5 27.8
28 F	16 29 42	6 17 24	11♏24 13	17 37 55	16 18.6	27 48.3	21 03.3	14 39.4	4 00.1	16 10.2	13 49.5	5 34.8	27 52.2	5 30.2
29 Sa	16 33 39	7 18 11	23 55 28	0♐16 53	16 05.8	28 48.3	21 49.6	15 25.6	4 12.4	16 19.3	13 47.6	5 37.0	27 53.8	5 32.5
30 Su	16 37 35	8 19 00	6♐42 08	13 11 07	15 52.0	29 44.2	22 34.9	16 11.8	4 24.9	16 28.4	13 45.8	5 39.2	27 55.4	5 34.9

December 1997 LONGITUDE

Day	Sid.Time	☉	0 hr ☽	Noon ☽	True ☊	☿	♀	♂	⚳	♃	♄	♅	♆	♇
1 M	16 41 32	9♐19 50	19♐43 41	26♐19 38	15♍38.5	0♑35.3	23♑19.3	16♑58.1	4♓37.6	16♒37.7	13♈44.2	5♒41.5	27♑57.0	5♐37.2
2 Tu	16 45 28	10 20 41	2♑58 42	9♑40 39	15R 26.5	1 21.0	24 02.7	17 44.4	4 50.5	16 47.1	13R 42.6	5 43.8	27 58.7	5 39.6
3 W	16 49 25	11 21 34	16 25 14	23 12 12	15 17.1	2 00.6	24 45.0	18 30.7	5 03.7	16 56.7	13 41.2	5 46.2	28 00.4	5 42.0
4 Th	16 53 21	12 22 27	0♒01 20	6♒52 28	15 10.8	2 33.4	25 26.2	19 17.1	5 17.1	17 06.4	13 39.8	5 48.6	28 02.1	5 44.3
5 F	16 57 18	13 23 21	13 45 28	20 40 13	15 07.4	2 58.4	26 06.2	20 03.6	5 30.8	17 16.2	13 38.6	5 51.0	28 03.8	5 46.7
6 Sa	17 01 14	14 24 15	27 36 39	4♓34 44	15 06.3	3 14.9	26 45.0	20 50.1	5 44.6	17 26.1	13 37.4	5 53.5	28 05.6	5 49.0
7 Su	17 05 11	15 25 11	11♓34 27	18 35 45	15 06.2	3R 22.0	27 22.5	21 36.6	5 58.7	17 36.1	13 36.4	5 56.0	28 07.4	5 51.4
8 M	17 09 08	16 26 07	25 38 37	2♈42 58	15 05.7	3 18.9	27 58.7	22 23.1	6 12.9	17 46.3	13 35.5	5 58.5	28 09.2	5 53.7
9 Tu	17 13 04	17 27 03	9♈48 40	16 55 30	15 03.6	3 04.9	28 33.5	23 09.7	6 27.4	17 56.6	13 34.7	6 01.1	28 11.0	5 56.0
10 W	17 17 01	18 28 01	24 03 14	1♉11 28	14 58.8	2 39.6	29 06.9	23 56.4	6 42.1	18 07.0	13 34.0	6 03.7	28 12.8	5 58.4
11 Th	17 20 57	19 28 59	8♉19 46	15 27 36	14 51.1	2 02.9	29 38.8	24 43.0	6 56.9	18 17.5	13 33.4	6 06.3	28 14.7	6 00.7
12 F	17 24 54	20 29 57	22 34 22	29 39 27	14 40.6	1 14.9	0♒09.1	25 29.7	7 12.0	18 28.1	13 32.9	6 09.0	28 16.6	6 03.0
13 Sa	17 28 50	21 30 57	6♊42 09	13♊41 50	14 28.3	0 16.4	0 37.8	26 16.4	7 27.2	18 38.8	13 32.5	6 11.7	28 18.5	6 05.3
14 Su	17 32 47	22 31 57	20 37 52	27 29 42	14 15.3	29♐08.7	1 04.9	27 03.2	7 42.7	18 49.6	13 32.3	6 14.5	28 20.4	6 07.6
15 M	17 36 43	23 32 58	4♋16 52	10♋58 59	14 03.1	27 53.5	1 30.2	27 50.0	7 58.3	19 00.6	13D 32.1	6 17.3	28 22.3	6 09.9
16 Tu	17 40 40	24 34 00	17 35 49	24 07 15	13 52.7	26 33.1	1 53.7	28 36.8	8 14.1	19 11.6	13 32.1	6 20.1	28 24.3	6 12.2
17 W	17 44 37	25 35 02	0♌33 18	6♌54 03	13 44.8	25 10.3	2 15.3	29 23.6	8 30.1	19 22.8	13 32.1	6 22.9	28 26.3	6 14.4
18 Th	17 48 33	26 36 05	13 09 47	19 20 50	13 39.9	23 47.8	2 35.0	0♒10.5	8 46.3	19 34.0	13 32.3	6 25.8	28 28.3	6 16.7
19 F	17 52 30	27 37 09	25 27 37	1♍30 40	13 37.4	22 28.4	2 52.8	0 57.4	9 02.6	19 45.3	13 32.6	6 28.7	28 30.3	6 18.9
20 Sa	17 56 26	28 38 14	7♍30 33	13 27 53	13D 36.8	21 14.6	3 08.4	1 44.4	9 19.1	19 56.8	13 33.0	6 31.6	28 32.3	6 21.2
21 Su	18 00 23	29 39 20	19 23 20	25 17 35	13R 37.0	20 08.4	3 22.0	2 31.3	9 35.8	20 08.3	13 33.5	6 34.6	28 34.3	6 23.4
22 M	18 04 19	0♑40 26	1♎11 21	7♎05 18	13 36.9	19 11.4	3 33.4	3 18.3	9 52.6	20 20.0	13 34.1	6 37.5	28 36.4	6 25.6
23 Tu	18 08 16	1 41 34	13 00 10	18 56 37	13 35.4	18 24.5	3 42.5	4 05.3	10 09.6	20 31.7	13 34.8	6 40.6	28 38.4	6 27.8
24 W	18 12 12	2 42 41	24 55 18	0♏56 50	13 31.7	17 48.4	3 49.4	4 52.4	10 26.8	20 43.5	13 35.6	6 43.6	28 40.5	6 30.0
25 Th	18 16 09	3 43 50	7♏01 46	13 10 36	13 25.4	17 23.1	3 53.9	5 39.5	10 44.1	20 55.4	13 36.6	6 46.7	28 42.6	6 32.1
26 F	18 20 06	4 44 59	19 23 45	25 41 34	13 16.5	17D 08.3	3R 56.1	6 26.6	11 01.6	21 07.4	13 37.6	6 49.7	28 44.7	6 34.3
27 Sa	18 24 02	5 46 09	2♐04 17	8♐32 03	13 05.6	17 03.6	3 55.8	7 13.7	11 19.2	21 19.5	13 38.8	6 52.9	28 46.9	6 36.4
28 Su	18 27 59	6 47 19	15 04 51	21 42 38	12 53.6	17 08.3	3 53.1	8 00.8	11 37.0	21 31.6	13 40.0	6 56.0	28 49.0	6 38.5
29 M	18 31 55	7 48 29	28 25 12	5♑12 14	12 41.9	17 21.7	3 47.9	8 48.0	11 54.9	21 43.9	13 41.4	6 59.2	28 51.2	6 40.6
30 Tu	18 35 52	8 49 40	12♑03 21	18 58 06	12 31.4	17 43.1	3 40.2	9 35.2	12 13.0	21 56.2	13 42.9	7 02.3	28 53.3	6 42.7
31 W	18 39 48	9 50 50	25 55 58	2♒56 25	12 23.2	18 11.8	3 30.0	10 22.4	12 31.2	22 08.6	13 44.5	7 05.5	28 55.5	6 44.8

Astro Data

	Dy Hr Mn
☽ 0N	11 5:47
♃ ⚹ ♄	15 3:53
☽ 0S	24 20:17
☿ R	7 16:57
☽ 0N	8 13:42
♄ D	16 10:29
☽ 0S	22 5:57
♀ R	26 21:21
☿ D	27 11:41

Planet Ingress

	Dy Hr Mn
♀ ♑	5 8:50
☿ ♐	7 17:42
♂ ♑	9 5:33
☉ ♐	22 6:48
☿ ♑	30 19:11
♀ ♒	12 4:39
☿ ♐R	13 18:06
♂ ♒	18 6:37
☉ ♑	21 20:07

Last Aspect Dy Hr Mn		☽ Ingress Dy Hr Mn
1 23:22	♆ ⚹	♐ 2 4:27
4 10:48	♀ ☌	♑ 4 12:31
6 15:42	☿ ⚹	♒ 6 18:33
8 22:11	♂ ⚹	♓ 8 22:35
10 20:34	♆ ⚹	♈ 11 0:44
12 21:42	♆ □	♉ 13 1:45
14 23:00	♆ △	♊ 15 3:05
16 3:35	♃ △	♋ 17 6:32
19 9:10	♆ ☍	♌ 19 13:38
21 23:58	☉ □	♍ 22 0:33
24 8:57	♆ △	♎ 24 13:29
26 21:26	♆ □	♏ 27 1:43
29 7:30	♆ ⚹	♐ 29 11:28

Last Aspect Dy Hr Mn		☽ Ingress Dy Hr Mn
30 18:07	♃ ⚹	♑ 1 18:38
3 20:29	♆ ☌	♒ 3 23:58
5 6:02	♃ ☌	♓ 6 4:07
8 4:15	♆ ⚹	♈ 8 7:24
10 8:22	♀ □	♉ 10 10:00
12 9:39	♆ △	♊ 12 12:35
14 14:40	☿ ☍	♋ 14 16:25
16 20:54	♂ ☍	♌ 16 22:58
19 3:34	☉ △	♍ 19 9:00
21 18:42	♆ △	♎ 21 21:35
24 7:28	♆ □	♏ 24 10:07
26 17:47	♆ ⚹	♐ 26 20:07
28 11:40	♃ ⚹	♑ 29 2:48
31 5:07	♆ ☌	♒ 31 6:58

☽ Phases & Eclipses

Dy Hr Mn	
7 21:43	☽ 15♒31
14 14:12	○ 22♉15
21 23:58	☾ 29♌43
30 2:14	● 7♐54
7 6:09	☽ 15♓10
14 2:37	○ 22♊08
21 21:43	☾ 0♎04
29 16:56	● 8♑01

Astro Data

1 November 1997
Julian Day # 35734
SVP 5♓17'30"
GC 26♐48.5 ⚴ 23♑50.9
Eris 18♈28.2R ⚵ 17♍36.1
⚷ 7♏47.9 ⚶ 20♈06.4R
☽ Mean ☊ 16♍55.7

1 December 1997
Julian Day # 35764
SVP 5♓17'25"
GC 26♐48.6 ⚴ 1♒29.5
Eris 18♈13.9R ⚵ 27♍45.9
⚷ 11♏55.2 ⚶ 16♈31.8R
☽ Mean ☊ 15♍20.4

LONGITUDE — January 1998

Day	Sid.Time	☉	0 hr ☽	Noon ☽	True ☊	☿	♀	♂	⚳	♃	♄	♅	♆	♇
1 Th	18 43 45	10♑52 01	9♒58 54	17♒02 53	12♍17.9	18♐46.9	3♒17.2	11♒09.6	12♓49.6	22♒21.1	13♈46.2	7♒08.8	28♑57.7	6♐46.9
2 F	18 47 42	11 53 11	24 07 52	1♓13 26	12D 15.2	19 27.8	3R 02.1	11 56.8	13 08.1	22 33.7	13 48.0	7 12.0	28 59.9	6 48.9
3 Sa	18 51 38	12 54 21	8♓19 11	15 24 48	12 14.8	20 13.9	2 44.4	12 44.1	13 26.7	22 46.3	13 49.9	7 15.3	29 02.1	6 50.9
4 Su	18 55 35	13 55 31	22 30 01	29 34 39	12 15.4	21 04.6	2 24.4	13 31.3	13 45.4	22 59.1	13 52.0	7 18.6	29 04.3	6 52.9
5 M	18 59 31	14 56 41	6♈38 31	13♈41 31	12R 16.0	21 59.4	2 02.1	14 18.6	14 04.3	23 11.8	13 54.1	7 21.9	29 06.5	6 54.9
6 Tu	19 03 28	15 57 50	20 43 32	27 44 28	12 15.3	22 57.9	1 37.5	15 05.9	14 23.4	23 24.7	13 56.3	7 25.2	29 08.7	6 56.8
7 W	19 07 24	16 58 59	4♉44 11	11♉42 34	12 12.6	23 59.7	1 10.9	15 53.2	14 42.5	23 37.6	13 58.7	7 28.5	29 11.0	6 58.8
8 Th	19 11 21	18 00 07	18 39 27	25 34 38	12 07.5	25 04.4	0 42.3	16 40.5	15 01.8	23 50.6	14 01.1	7 31.9	29 13.2	7 00.7
9 F	19 15 17	19 01 15	2♊27 53	9♊18 56	12 00.2	26 11.6	0 11.9	17 27.8	15 21.1	24 03.6	14 03.7	7 35.2	29 15.4	7 02.6
10 Sa	19 19 14	20 02 23	16 07 32	22 53 21	11 51.3	27 21.2	29♑39.9	18 15.1	15 40.6	24 16.7	14 06.3	7 38.6	29 17.7	7 04.5
11 Su	19 23 11	21 03 30	29 36 06	6♋15 32	11 41.9	28 32.9	29 06.5	19 02.4	16 00.2	24 29.9	14 09.1	7 42.0	29 20.0	7 06.3
12 M	19 27 07	22 04 37	12♋51 21	19 23 23	11 32.9	29 46.5	28 31.8	19 49.7	16 20.0	24 43.2	14 11.9	7 45.4	29 22.2	7 08.1
13 Tu	19 31 04	23 05 43	25 51 27	2♌15 29	11 25.3	1♑01.8	27 56.2	20 37.0	16 39.8	24 56.4	14 14.9	7 48.8	29 24.5	7 10.0
14 W	19 35 00	24 06 49	8♌35 26	14 51 22	11 19.7	2 18.6	27 19.9	21 24.4	16 59.7	25 09.8	14 17.9	7 52.3	29 26.8	7 11.7
15 Th	19 38 57	25 07 55	21 03 25	27 11 48	11 16.3	3 36.9	26 43.1	22 11.7	17 19.8	25 23.2	14 21.1	7 55.7	29 29.0	7 13.5
16 F	19 42 53	26 09 00	3♍16 46	9♍18 42	11D 15.1	4 56.4	26 06.2	22 59.0	17 40.0	25 36.6	14 24.3	7 59.2	29 31.3	7 15.2
17 Sa	19 46 50	27 10 06	15 17 59	21 15 06	11 15.6	6 17.1	25 29.2	23 46.4	18 00.2	25 50.1	14 27.6	8 02.6	29 33.6	7 16.9
18 Su	19 50 46	28 11 10	27 10 34	3♎04 57	11 17.1	7 38.9	24 52.6	24 33.7	18 20.6	26 03.7	14 31.1	8 06.1	29 35.9	7 18.6
19 M	19 54 43	29 12 15	8♎58 52	14 52 55	11 18.7	9 01.8	24 16.6	25 21.0	18 41.0	26 17.3	14 34.6	8 09.5	29 38.1	7 20.3
20 Tu	19 58 40	0♒13 19	20 47 45	26 44 03	11R 19.7	10 25.6	23 41.4	26 08.4	19 01.6	26 31.0	14 38.2	8 13.0	29 40.4	7 21.9
21 W	20 02 36	1 14 23	2♏42 28	8♏43 39	11 19.4	11 50.3	23 07.3	26 55.7	19 22.2	26 44.7	14 42.0	8 16.5	29 42.7	7 23.5
22 Th	20 06 33	2 15 26	14 48 13	20 56 47	11 17.5	13 15.9	22 34.4	27 43.0	19 43.0	26 58.4	14 45.8	8 20.0	29 45.0	7 25.1
23 F	20 10 29	3 16 29	27 09 54	3♐28 04	11 13.8	14 42.3	22 03.1	28 30.4	20 03.8	27 12.2	14 49.7	8 23.5	29 47.2	7 26.6
24 Sa	20 14 26	4 17 31	9♐51 41	16 21 04	11 08.8	16 09.5	21 33.4	29 17.7	20 24.8	27 26.1	14 53.7	8 27.0	29 49.5	7 28.1
25 Su	20 18 22	5 18 33	22 56 26	29 37 54	11 02.9	17 37.5	21 05.5	0♓05.0	20 45.8	27 39.9	14 57.8	8 30.5	29 51.8	7 29.6
26 M	20 22 19	6 19 35	6♑25 24	13♑18 45	10 56.8	19 06.2	20 39.7	0 52.4	21 06.9	27 53.9	15 01.9	8 34.0	29 54.1	7 31.1
27 Tu	20 26 15	7 20 35	20 17 39	27 21 38	10 51.4	20 35.7	20 15.9	1 39.7	21 28.1	28 07.8	15 06.2	8 37.6	29 56.3	7 32.5
28 W	20 30 12	8 21 35	4♒30 08	11♒42 28	10 47.3	22 05.9	19 54.4	2 27.0	21 49.4	28 21.8	15 10.5	8 41.1	29 58.6	7 34.0
29 Th	20 34 09	9 22 34	18 57 51	26 15 30	10D 44.9	23 36.7	19 35.1	3 14.3	22 10.8	28 35.8	15 15.0	8 44.6	0♒00.9	7 35.3
30 F	20 38 05	10 23 32	3♓34 34	10♓54 14	10 44.1	25 08.3	19 18.2	4 01.6	22 32.2	28 49.9	15 19.5	8 48.1	0 03.1	7 36.7
31 Sa	20 42 02	11 24 28	18 13 42	25 32 16	10 44.7	26 40.6	19 03.7	4 48.9	22 53.7	29 04.0	15 24.1	8 51.6	0 05.4	7 38.0

LONGITUDE — February 1998

Day	Sid.Time	☉	0 hr ☽	Noon ☽	True ☊	☿	♀	♂	⚳	♃	♄	♅	♆	♇
1 Su	20 45 58	12♒25 24	2♈49 14	10♈04 06	10♍46.1	28♑13.6	18♑51.7	5♓36.2	23♓15.3	29♒18.1	15♈28.8	8♒55.1	0♒07.6	7♐39.3
2 M	20 49 55	13 26 17	17 16 21	24 25 39	10 47.6	29 47.3	18R 42.1	6 23.5	23 37.0	29 32.3	15 33.5	8 58.6	0 09.8	7 40.5
3 Tu	20 53 51	14 27 10	1♉31 43	8♉34 20	10R 48.6	1♒21.7	18 35.0	7 10.7	23 58.8	29 46.5	15 38.4	9 02.1	0 12.1	7 41.8
4 W	20 57 48	15 28 01	15 33 23	22 28 47	10 48.5	2 56.8	18 30.4	7 57.9	24 20.6	0♓00.7	15 43.3	9 05.6	0 14.3	7 43.0
5 Th	21 01 44	16 28 51	29 20 31	6♊08 36	10 47.3	4 32.7	18D 28.2	8 45.1	24 42.5	0 14.9	15 48.3	9 09.1	0 16.5	7 44.1
6 F	21 05 41	17 29 39	12♊53 03	19 33 55	10 44.9	6 09.3	18 28.5	9 32.3	25 04.4	0 29.2	15 53.4	9 12.6	0 18.7	7 45.3
7 Sa	21 09 38	18 30 26	26 11 14	2♋45 06	10 41.7	7 46.7	18 31.1	10 19.5	25 26.4	0 43.4	15 58.6	9 16.1	0 20.9	7 46.4
8 Su	21 13 34	19 31 12	9♋15 33	15 42 39	10 38.3	9 24.8	18 36.2	11 06.7	25 48.5	0 57.7	16 03.8	9 19.5	0 23.1	7 47.4
9 M	21 17 31	20 31 56	22 06 27	28 27 02	10 35.0	11 03.7	18 43.5	11 53.8	26 10.7	1 12.1	16 09.1	9 23.0	0 25.3	7 48.5
10 Tu	21 21 27	21 32 39	4♌44 29	10♌58 52	10 32.3	12 43.4	18 53.1	12 41.0	26 32.9	1 26.4	16 14.5	9 26.5	0 27.4	7 49.5
11 W	21 25 24	22 33 20	17 10 18	23 18 54	10 30.5	14 23.9	19 04.9	13 28.1	26 55.2	1 40.7	16 19.9	9 29.9	0 29.6	7 50.5
12 Th	21 29 20	23 34 00	29 24 50	5♍28 17	10D 29.6	16 05.3	19 18.8	14 15.1	27 17.5	1 55.1	16 25.4	9 33.4	0 31.7	7 51.4
13 F	21 33 17	24 34 38	11♍29 26	17 28 34	10 29.7	17 47.5	19 34.8	15 02.2	27 39.9	2 09.5	16 31.0	9 36.8	0 33.8	7 52.3
14 Sa	21 37 13	25 35 15	23 25 56	29 21 54	10 30.5	19 30.5	19 52.9	15 49.2	28 02.3	2 23.9	16 36.7	9 40.2	0 35.9	7 53.2
15 Su	21 41 10	26 35 51	5♎16 48	11♎11 03	10 31.7	21 14.5	20 12.9	16 36.2	28 24.8	2 38.3	16 42.4	9 43.6	0 38.0	7 54.0
16 M	21 45 06	27 36 26	17 05 04	22 59 22	10 33.0	22 59.3	20 34.8	17 23.2	28 47.4	2 52.7	16 48.2	9 47.0	0 40.1	7 54.8
17 Tu	21 49 03	28 36 59	28 54 25	4♏50 46	10 34.2	24 44.9	20 58.5	18 10.2	29 10.0	3 07.1	16 54.0	9 50.4	0 42.2	7 55.6
18 W	21 53 00	29 37 31	10♏48 58	16 49 36	10 35.0	26 31.5	21 24.0	18 57.2	29 32.7	3 21.6	16 59.9	9 53.7	0 44.3	7 56.3
19 Th	21 56 56	0♓38 02	22 53 14	29 00 29	10R 35.4	28 19.0	21 51.2	19 44.1	29 55.4	3 36.0	17 05.9	9 57.1	0 46.3	7 57.0
20 F	22 00 53	1 38 32	5♐11 54	11♐28 03	10 35.2	0♓07.4	22 20.1	20 31.0	0♈18.2	3 50.5	17 11.9	10 00.4	0 48.3	7 57.7
21 Sa	22 04 49	2 39 00	17 49 27	24 16 33	10 34.7	1 56.7	22 50.5	21 17.9	0 41.0	4 04.9	17 18.0	10 03.7	0 50.4	7 58.3
22 Su	22 08 46	3 39 27	0♑49 46	7♑29 24	10 33.9	3 46.8	23 22.4	22 04.7	1 03.9	4 19.4	17 24.2	10 07.0	0 52.4	7 58.9
23 M	22 12 42	4 39 53	14 15 39	21 08 35	10 33.1	5 37.8	23 55.8	22 51.5	1 26.8	4 33.8	17 30.4	10 10.3	0 54.3	7 59.5
24 Tu	22 16 39	5 40 17	28 08 09	5♒14 07	10 32.5	7 29.6	24 30.5	23 38.3	1 49.7	4 48.3	17 36.7	10 13.6	0 56.3	8 00.0
25 W	22 20 35	6 40 40	12♒26 05	19 43 30	10 32.1	9 22.1	25 06.6	24 25.1	2 12.7	5 02.8	17 43.0	10 16.8	0 58.3	8 00.5
26 Th	22 24 32	7 41 01	27 05 40	4♓31 44	10D 31.9	11 15.3	25 44.0	25 11.9	2 35.8	5 17.2	17 49.4	10 20.0	1 00.2	8 01.0
27 F	22 28 29	8 41 20	12♓00 42	19 31 33	10 31.9	13 09.2	26 22.5	25 58.6	2 58.9	5 31.7	17 55.8	10 23.2	1 02.1	8 01.4
28 Sa	22 32 25	9 41 37	27 03 10	4♈34 27	10R 32.0	15 03.6	27 02.3	26 45.3	3 22.0	5 46.1	18 02.3	10 26.4	1 04.0	8 01.8

Astro Data	Dy Hr Mn
☽ 0N	4 20:19
☽ 0S	18 15:28
☽ 0N	1 3:34
♃⚺♆	5 15:10
♀ D	5 21:27
♃∠♄	9 4:06
☽ 0S	14 23:37
☽ 0N	28 12:51

Planet Ingress		Dy Hr Mn
♀	♑R	9 21:03
☿	♑	12 16:20
☉	♒	20 6:46
♂	♓	25 9:26
♆	♒	29 2:52
☿	♒	2 15:15
♃	♓	4 10:52
☉	♓	18 20:55
⚳	♈	19 16:51
☿	♓	20 10:22

Last Aspect Dy Hr Mn			☽ Ingress	Dy Hr Mn
1 21:07	♃	☌	♓	2 9:56
4 11:08	♆	⚹	♈	4 12:43
6 14:25	♆	□	♉	6 15:52
8 18:21	♆	△	♊	8 19:42
10 20:45	☿	☍	♋	11 0:43
13 6:38	♆	☍	♌	13 7:45
15 8:23	♃	☍	♍	15 17:31
18 4:54	♆	△	♎	18 5:44
20 17:56	♆	□	♏	20 18:34
23 4:59	♆	⚹	♐	23 5:25
25 8:26	♃	⚹	♑	25 12:39
27 16:21	♆	☌	♒	27 16:27
29 15:54	♃	☌	♓	29 18:08
31 14:06	☿	⚹	♈	31 19:21

Last Aspect Dy Hr Mn			☽ Ingress	Dy Hr Mn
2 20:46	♃	⚹	♉	2 21:25
4 5:08	♀	△	♊	5 1:09
6 7:58	☉	△	♋	7 6:57
8 17:27	♀	☍	♌	9 14:57
11 10:23	☉	☍	♍	12 1:09
13 16:20	♀	△	♎	14 13:17
16 22:14	☉	△	♏	17 2:13
19 10:25	☿	□	♐	19 13:56
21 6:08	♂	□	♑	21 22:30
23 17:00	♀	☌	♒	24 3:10
25 8:41	♄	⚹	♓	26 4:42
27 23:25	♀	⚹	♈	28 4:42

☽ Phases & Eclipses Dy Hr Mn		
5 14:18	☽	15♈03
12 17:24	○	22♋18
20 19:40	☾	0♏33
28 6:01	●	8♒06
3 22:53	☽	14♉55
11 10:23	○	22♌29
19 15:27	☾	0♐47
26 17:26	●	7♓55
26 17:28:24	●	T 04'09"

Astro Data

1 January 1998
Julian Day # 35795
SVP 5♓17'20"
GC 26♐48.7 ⚴ 10♒58.5
Eris 18♈07.3R ⚵ 4♎49.8
⚷ 15♏33.9 ⚶ 19♈30.4
☽ Mean ☊ 13♍41.9

1 February 1998
Julian Day # 35826
SVP 5♓17'15"
GC 26♐48.8 ⚴ 21♒13.0
Eris 18♈11.2 ⚵ 6♎36.7R
⚷ 18♏00.2 ⚶ 27♈24.8
☽ Mean ☊ 12♍03.4

March 1998 LONGITUDE

Day	Sid.Time	☉	0 hr ☽	Noon ☽	True ☊	☿	♀	♂	⚳	♃	♄	♅	♆	♇
1 Su	22 36 22	10♓41 53	12♈04 19	19♈31 46	10♍32.0	16♓58.4	27♑43.2	27♓31.9	3♈45.2	6♓00.5	18♈08.8	10♒29.6	1♒05.8	8♐02.2
2 M	22 40 18	11 42 07	26 55 55	4♉16 00	10R 32.0	18 53.4	28 25.1	28 18.5	4 08.4	6 15.0	18 15.4	10 32.7	1 07.7	8 02.5
3 Tu	22 44 15	12 42 18	11♉31 24	18 41 37	10 31.8	20 48.5	29 08.1	29 05.1	4 31.6	6 29.4	18 22.1	10 35.8	1 09.5	8 02.8
4 W	22 48 11	13 42 28	25 46 22	2♊45 26	10D 31.6	22 43.4	29 52.1	29 51.7	4 54.9	6 43.8	18 28.7	10 38.9	1 11.3	8 03.0
5 Th	22 52 08	14 42 35	9♊38 47	16 26 28	10 31.6	24 38.0	0♒37.1	0♈38.2	5 18.2	6 58.2	18 35.5	10 42.0	1 13.1	8 03.2
6 F	22 56 04	15 42 40	23 08 38	29 45 29	10 31.7	26 31.9	1 23.0	1 24.7	5 41.5	7 12.6	18 42.2	10 45.0	1 14.9	8 03.4
7 Sa	23 00 01	16 42 44	6♋17 19	12♋44 26	10 32.2	28 24.8	2 09.7	2 11.1	6 04.9	7 27.0	18 49.0	10 48.0	1 16.6	8 03.6
8 Su	23 03 58	17 42 45	19 07 11	25 25 54	10 32.8	0♈16.3	2 57.3	2 57.5	6 28.3	7 41.3	18 55.9	10 51.0	1 18.3	8 03.7
9 M	23 07 54	18 42 44	1♌40 57	7♌52 41	10 33.7	2 06.1	3 45.8	3 43.9	6 51.7	7 55.7	19 02.8	10 54.0	1 20.0	8 03.8
10 Tu	23 11 51	19 42 40	14 01 25	20 07 29	10 34.5	3 53.7	4 35.0	4 30.2	7 15.2	8 10.0	19 09.7	10 56.9	1 21.7	8R 03.8
11 W	23 15 47	20 42 35	26 11 12	2♍12 51	10R 35.0	5 38.6	5 25.0	5 16.5	7 38.7	8 24.3	19 16.7	10 59.8	1 23.4	8 03.8
12 Th	23 19 44	21 42 28	8♍12 42	14 11 02	10 35.1	7 20.5	6 15.7	6 02.7	8 02.2	8 38.6	19 23.7	11 02.7	1 25.0	8 03.8
13 F	23 23 40	22 42 18	20 08 06	26 04 09	10 34.6	8 58.7	7 07.1	6 48.9	8 25.7	8 52.8	19 30.7	11 05.5	1 26.6	8 03.7
14 Sa	23 27 37	23 42 07	1♎59 26	7♎54 11	10 33.4	10 32.7	7 59.2	7 35.1	8 49.3	9 07.0	19 37.8	11 08.3	1 28.2	8 03.6
15 Su	23 31 33	24 41 54	13 48 42	19 43 15	10 31.6	12 02.2	8 52.0	8 21.2	9 12.9	9 21.2	19 44.9	11 11.1	1 29.7	8 03.5
16 M	23 35 30	25 41 39	25 38 06	1♏33 36	10 29.3	13 26.4	9 45.4	9 07.3	9 36.5	9 35.4	19 52.1	11 13.8	1 31.3	8 03.3
17 Tu	23 39 27	26 41 22	7♏30 03	13 27 51	10 26.8	14 45.1	10 39.4	9 53.4	10 00.1	9 49.6	19 59.3	11 16.6	1 32.8	8 03.1
18 W	23 43 23	27 41 04	19 27 22	25 29 00	10 24.3	15 57.7	11 34.0	10 39.4	10 23.8	10 03.7	20 06.5	11 19.3	1 34.2	8 02.9
19 Th	23 47 20	28 40 43	1♐33 14	7♐40 30	10 22.4	17 03.9	12 29.1	11 25.4	10 47.4	10 17.8	20 13.7	11 21.9	1 35.7	8 02.6
20 F	23 51 16	29 40 21	13 51 16	20 06 03	10D 21.2	18 03.3	13 24.8	12 11.3	11 11.1	10 31.9	20 21.0	11 24.5	1 37.1	8 02.3
21 Sa	23 55 13	0♈39 58	26 25 20	2♑49 35	10 20.9	18 55.6	14 21.0	12 57.2	11 34.8	10 45.9	20 28.3	11 27.1	1 38.5	8 02.0
22 Su	23 59 09	1 39 32	9♑19 17	15 54 49	10 21.5	19 40.4	15 17.7	13 43.0	11 58.6	10 59.9	20 35.6	11 29.7	1 39.9	8 01.6
23 M	0 03 06	2 39 05	22 36 34	29 24 49	10 22.7	20 17.7	16 14.9	14 28.9	12 22.3	11 13.9	20 42.9	11 32.2	1 41.2	8 01.2
24 Tu	0 07 02	3 38 36	6♒19 44	13♒21 23	10 24.2	20 47.3	17 12.5	15 14.6	12 46.1	11 27.9	20 50.3	11 34.7	1 42.5	8 00.8
25 W	0 10 59	4 38 05	20 29 41	27 44 21	10R 25.4	21 09.1	18 10.6	16 00.4	13 09.9	11 41.8	20 57.7	11 37.1	1 43.8	8 00.4
26 Th	0 14 55	5 37 32	5♓04 58	12♓30 54	10 25.8	21 23.0	19 09.1	16 46.0	13 33.7	11 55.6	21 05.1	11 39.5	1 45.1	7 59.9
27 F	0 18 52	6 36 58	20 01 20	27 35 18	10 25.0	21R 29.3	20 08.1	17 31.7	13 57.5	12 09.5	21 12.5	11 41.9	1 46.3	7 59.3
28 Sa	0 22 49	7 36 21	5♈11 40	12♈49 12	10 22.8	21 27.9	21 07.4	18 17.3	14 21.3	12 23.2	21 20.0	11 44.2	1 47.5	7 58.8
29 Su	0 26 45	8 35 43	20 26 35	28 02 33	10 19.4	21 19.3	22 07.0	19 02.8	14 45.1	12 37.0	21 27.5	11 46.5	1 48.7	7 58.2
30 M	0 30 42	9 35 02	5♉35 49	13♉05 14	10 15.3	21 03.7	23 07.1	19 48.4	15 09.0	12 50.7	21 34.9	11 48.8	1 49.8	7 57.6
31 Tu	0 34 38	10 34 19	20 29 49	27 48 43	10 11.0	20 41.6	24 07.5	20 33.8	15 32.8	13 04.3	21 42.4	11 51.0	1 50.9	7 56.9

April 1998 LONGITUDE

Day	Sid.Time	☉	0 hr ☽	Noon ☽	True ☊	☿	♀	♂	⚳	♃	♄	♅	♆	♇
1 W	0 38 35	11♈33 34	5♊01 17	12♊07 07	10♍07.4	20♈13.5	25♒08.2	21♈19.2	15♈56.7	13♓17.9	21♈50.0	11♒53.2	1♒52.0	7♐56.2
2 Th	0 42 31	12 32 46	19 05 56	25 57 42	10R 04.8	19R 40.1	26 09.3	22 04.6	16 20.6	13 31.5	21 57.5	11 55.3	1 53.0	7R 55.5
3 F	0 46 28	13 31 56	2♋42 31	9♋20 37	10D 03.7	19 02.1	27 10.6	22 49.9	16 44.5	13 45.0	22 05.0	11 57.4	1 54.1	7 54.8
4 Sa	0 50 24	14 31 04	15 52 20	22 18 07	10 03.8	18 20.5	28 12.3	23 35.2	17 08.3	13 58.5	22 12.6	11 59.5	1 55.0	7 54.0
5 Su	0 54 21	15 30 10	28 38 28	4♌53 52	10 05.1	17 35.9	29 14.3	24 20.4	17 32.2	14 11.9	22 20.2	12 01.5	1 56.0	7 53.2
6 M	0 58 18	16 29 13	11♌04 55	17 12 09	10 06.7	16 49.5	0♓16.5	25 05.6	17 56.1	14 25.2	22 27.7	12 03.5	1 56.9	7 52.4
7 Tu	1 02 14	17 28 13	23 16 06	29 17 20	10R 08.2	16 02.0	1 19.1	25 50.7	18 20.0	14 38.5	22 35.3	12 05.4	1 57.8	7 51.5
8 W	1 06 11	18 27 12	5♍16 18	11♍13 31	10 08.7	15 14.5	2 21.9	26 35.8	18 43.9	14 51.7	22 42.9	12 07.3	1 58.7	7 50.6
9 Th	1 10 07	19 26 08	17 09 25	23 04 23	10 07.8	14 27.9	3 24.9	27 20.8	19 07.8	15 04.9	22 50.5	12 09.1	1 59.5	7 49.7
10 F	1 14 04	20 25 03	28 58 47	4♎52 58	10 04.9	13 42.9	4 28.3	28 05.8	19 31.7	15 18.1	22 58.1	12 10.9	2 00.3	7 48.8
11 Sa	1 18 00	21 23 55	10♎47 14	16 41 51	10 00.1	13 00.5	5 31.8	28 50.7	19 55.6	15 31.1	23 05.7	12 12.7	2 01.1	7 47.8
12 Su	1 21 57	22 22 45	22 37 03	28 33 05	9 53.5	12 21.1	6 35.6	29 35.6	20 19.5	15 44.1	23 13.3	12 14.4	2 01.8	7 46.8
13 M	1 25 53	23 21 33	4♏30 08	10♏28 25	9 45.7	11 45.4	7 39.7	0♉20.4	20 43.3	15 57.1	23 20.9	12 16.1	2 02.5	7 45.8
14 Tu	1 29 50	24 20 19	16 28 09	22 29 31	9 37.2	11 14.0	8 44.0	1 05.2	21 07.2	16 10.0	23 28.5	12 17.7	2 03.2	7 44.7
15 W	1 33 47	25 19 04	28 32 45	4♐38 05	9 29.0	10 47.0	9 48.5	1 49.9	21 31.1	16 22.8	23 36.1	12 19.3	2 03.8	7 43.7
16 Th	1 37 43	26 17 47	10♐45 47	16 56 06	9 21.8	10 24.9	10 53.2	2 34.6	21 55.0	16 35.5	23 43.7	12 20.8	2 04.5	7 42.6
17 F	1 41 40	27 16 28	23 09 22	29 25 54	9 16.4	10 07.9	11 58.1	3 19.2	22 18.9	16 48.2	23 51.3	12 22.3	2 05.0	7 41.5
18 Sa	1 45 36	28 15 07	5♑46 03	12♑10 12	9 13.0	9 55.9	13 03.2	4 03.8	22 42.8	17 00.8	23 58.8	12 23.7	2 05.6	7 40.3
19 Su	1 49 33	29 13 44	18 38 44	25 12 01	9D 11.6	9D 49.2	14 08.5	4 48.3	23 06.7	17 13.4	24 06.4	12 25.1	2 06.1	7 39.1
20 M	1 53 29	0♉12 20	1♒50 26	8♒34 19	9 11.8	9 47.6	15 14.0	5 32.8	23 30.5	17 25.9	24 14.0	12 26.5	2 06.6	7 38.0
21 Tu	1 57 26	1 10 55	15 23 58	22 19 34	9 12.7	9 51.0	16 19.6	6 17.3	23 54.4	17 38.3	24 21.6	12 27.8	2 07.0	7 36.7
22 W	2 01 22	2 09 27	29 21 17	6♓29 04	9R 13.5	9 59.5	17 25.5	7 01.6	24 18.2	17 50.6	24 29.2	12 29.1	2 07.4	7 35.5
23 Th	2 05 19	3 07 58	13♓42 48	21 02 08	9 12.9	10 12.9	18 31.5	7 46.0	24 42.1	18 02.8	24 36.7	12 30.3	2 07.8	7 34.3
24 F	2 09 16	4 06 27	28 26 34	5♈55 23	9 10.4	10 31.0	19 37.7	8 30.3	25 05.9	18 15.0	24 44.3	12 31.4	2 08.1	7 33.0
25 Sa	2 13 12	5 04 55	13♈27 42	21 02 27	9 05.4	10 53.6	20 44.0	9 14.5	25 29.8	18 27.1	24 51.8	12 32.5	2 08.5	7 31.7
26 Su	2 17 09	6 03 21	28 38 27	6♉14 23	8 58.3	11 20.6	21 50.5	9 58.7	25 53.6	18 39.1	24 59.3	12 33.6	2 08.7	7 30.4
27 M	2 21 05	7 01 45	13♉48 55	21 20 46	8 49.7	11 51.9	22 57.1	10 42.8	26 17.4	18 51.1	25 06.8	12 34.6	2 09.0	7 29.0
28 Tu	2 25 02	8 00 07	28 48 43	6♊11 40	8 40.7	12 27.2	24 03.8	11 26.9	26 41.2	19 02.9	25 14.3	12 35.6	2 09.2	7 27.7
29 W	2 28 58	8 58 27	13♊28 42	20 39 08	8 32.3	13 06.4	25 10.7	12 11.0	27 04.9	19 14.7	25 21.8	12 36.5	2 09.4	7 26.3
30 Th	2 32 55	9 56 45	27 42 29	4♋38 27	8 25.6	13 49.3	26 17.8	12 55.0	27 28.7	19 26.4	25 29.2	12 37.4	2 09.5	7 24.9

Astro Data	Dy Hr Mn
♂0N	6 16:12
☿0N	8 13:09
♃□♇	10 1:36
♇ R	11 4:55
☽0S	14 6:15
☉0N	20 19:54
♃⚺♅	25 2:17
☿ R	27 19:43
☽0N	27 23:47
⚳0N	2 22:57
♄Q♇	9 9:49
☽0S	10 12:22
♃∠♆	18 21:27
☿ D	20 7:31
☽0N	24 10:50

Planet Ingress		Dy Hr Mn
♀	♒	4 16:14
♂	♈	4 16:18
☿	♈	8 8:28
☉	♈	20 19:55
♀	♓	6 5:38
♂	♉	13 1:05
☉	♉	20 6:57

Last Aspect Dy Hr Mn		☽ Ingress Dy Hr Mn
2 1:57	♀ □	♉ 2 5:00
4 6:44	♀ △	♊ 4 7:15
6 5:09	☿ □	♋ 6 12:27
7 23:32	♄ □	♌ 8 20:46
10 10:05	♄ △	♍ 11 7:35
13 4:34	☉ ☍	♎ 13 19:58
15 12:03	♄ ☍	♏ 16 8:51
18 16:45	☉ △	♐ 18 20:56
20 12:29	♄ △	♑ 21 6:43
22 20:29	♄ □	♒ 23 13:02
25 0:50	☿ ⚹	♓ 25 15:43
26 11:02	♃ ☌	♈ 27 15:49
29 1:59	♀ ⚹	♉ 29 15:06
31 5:29	♀ □	♊ 31 15:37

Last Aspect Dy Hr Mn		☽ Ingress Dy Hr Mn
2 12:22	♀ △	♋ 2 19:09
4 14:34	♂ □	♌ 5 2:36
7 4:40	♂ △	♍ 7 13:25
8 19:30	♃ ☍	♎ 10 2:04
12 14:15	♂ ☍	♏ 12 14:55
13 23:10	♃ △	♐ 15 2:52
17 7:32	☉ △	♑ 17 13:05
19 19:53	☉ □	♒ 19 20:41
21 15:31	♄ ⚹	♓ 22 1:06
23 7:34	♀ ☌	♈ 24 2:30
25 18:05	♄ ☌	♉ 26 2:09
27 14:47	♀ ⚹	♊ 28 1:55
29 20:20	♀ □	♋ 30 3:57

☽ Phases & Eclipses Dy Hr Mn	
5 8:41	☽ 14♊34
13 4:34	○ 22♍24
13 4:20	• A 0.709
21 7:38	☾ 0♑29
28 3:14	● 7♈15
3 20:18	☽ 13♋52
11 22:23	○ 21♎49
19 19:53	☾ 29♑33
26 11:41	● 6♉03

Astro Data

1 March 1998
Julian Day # 35854
SVP 5♓17'12"
GC 26♐48.8 ⚴ 0♓35.1
Eris 18♈22.8 ⚵ 2♎46.6R
⚷ 18♏46.8 ⚶ 7♉02.5
☽ Mean ☊ 10♍34.4

1 April 1998
Julian Day # 35885
SVP 5♓17'10"
GC 26♐48.9 ⚴ 10♓35.0
Eris 18♈41.6 ⚵ 25♍27.0R
⚷ 17♏57.9R ⚶ 19♉13.0
☽ Mean ☊ 8♍55.9

LONGITUDE — May 1998

Day	Sid.Time	☉	0 hr ☽	Noon ☽	True ☊	☿	♀	♂	⚳	♃	♄	♅	♆	♇
1 F	2 36 51	10♉55 02	11♋27 00	18♋08 14	8♍21.1	14♈35.8	27♓24.9	13♉38.9	27♈52.5	19♓38.0	25♈36.7	12♒38.2	2♒09.6	7♐23.5
2 Sa	2 40 48	11 53 16	24 42 25	1♌09 57	8D 18.8	15 25.7	28 32.2	14 22.8	28 16.2	19 49.5	25 44.1	12 39.0	2 09.7	7R 22.1
3 Su	2 44 45	12 51 28	7♌31 19	13 47 07	8 18.2	16 18.9	29 39.6	15 06.6	28 39.9	20 00.9	25 51.5	12 39.7	2R 09.8	7 20.6
4 M	2 48 41	13 49 38	19 57 56	26 04 26	8 18.6	17 15.3	0♈47.1	15 50.4	29 03.6	20 12.2	25 58.9	12 40.4	2 09.8	7 19.2
5 Tu	2 52 38	14 47 46	2♍07 17	8♍07 07	8R 19.0	18 14.6	1 54.7	16 34.1	29 27.3	20 23.4	26 06.2	12 41.0	2 09.8	7 17.7
6 W	2 56 34	15 45 52	14 04 35	20 00 19	8 18.3	19 16.9	3 02.4	17 17.7	29 50.9	20 34.5	26 13.6	12 41.5	2 09.7	7 16.2
7 Th	3 00 31	16 43 56	25 54 51	1♎48 46	8 15.7	20 22.0	4 10.3	18 01.3	0♉14.5	20 45.6	26 20.9	12 42.1	2 09.6	7 14.7
8 F	3 04 27	17 41 58	7♎42 32	13 36 36	8 10.6	21 29.9	5 18.2	18 44.9	0 38.2	20 56.5	26 28.1	12 42.5	2 09.5	7 13.2
9 Sa	3 08 24	18 39 59	19 31 24	25 27 14	8 02.8	22 40.3	6 26.3	19 28.4	1 01.7	21 07.3	26 35.4	12 43.0	2 09.4	7 11.7
10 Su	3 12 20	19 37 58	1♏24 26	7♏23 14	7 52.6	23 53.4	7 34.5	20 11.8	1 25.3	21 18.1	26 42.6	12 43.3	2 09.2	7 10.2
11 M	3 16 17	20 35 55	13 23 51	19 26 27	7 40.6	25 08.9	8 42.7	20 55.2	1 48.8	21 28.7	26 49.8	12 43.7	2 09.0	7 08.6
12 Tu	3 20 13	21 33 51	25 31 11	1♐38 09	7 27.7	26 26.9	9 51.1	21 38.6	2 12.4	21 39.2	26 57.0	12 43.9	2 08.7	7 07.1
13 W	3 24 10	22 31 45	7♐47 26	13 59 09	7 15.1	27 47.3	10 59.6	22 21.8	2 35.9	21 49.6	27 04.1	12 44.2	2 08.5	7 05.5
14 Th	3 28 07	23 29 38	20 13 22	26 30 11	7 03.8	29 10.1	12 08.1	23 05.1	2 59.3	22 00.0	27 11.2	12 44.4	2 08.2	7 03.9
15 F	3 32 03	24 27 29	2♑49 41	9♑12 02	6 54.7	0♉35.1	13 16.8	23 48.3	3 22.8	22 10.2	27 18.3	12 44.5	2 07.8	7 02.3
16 Sa	3 36 00	25 25 20	15 37 22	22 05 52	6 48.4	2 02.5	14 25.5	24 31.4	3 46.2	22 20.3	27 25.3	12 44.6	2 07.4	7 00.7
17 Su	3 39 56	26 23 09	28 37 45	5♒13 14	6 44.8	3 32.1	15 34.4	25 14.5	4 09.6	22 30.3	27 32.4	12R 44.6	2 07.0	6 59.1
18 M	3 43 53	27 20 56	11♒52 34	18 36 00	6D 43.4	5 03.9	16 43.3	25 57.6	4 33.0	22 40.1	27 39.3	12 44.6	2 06.6	6 57.5
19 Tu	3 47 49	28 18 43	25 23 46	2♓16 05	6R 43.3	6 38.0	17 52.3	26 40.6	4 56.3	22 49.9	27 46.3	12 44.5	2 06.2	6 55.9
20 W	3 51 46	29 16 29	9♓13 06	16 14 54	6 43.1	8 14.3	19 01.4	27 23.5	5 19.6	22 59.5	27 53.1	12 44.4	2 05.7	6 54.3
21 Th	3 55 42	0♊14 13	23 21 29	0♈32 43	6 41.7	9 52.8	20 10.5	28 06.4	5 42.9	23 09.1	28 00.0	12 44.2	2 05.1	6 52.7
22 F	3 59 39	1 11 56	7♈48 19	15 07 52	6 38.1	11 33.5	21 19.8	28 49.2	6 06.1	23 18.5	28 06.8	12 44.0	2 04.6	6 51.0
23 Sa	4 03 36	2 09 39	22 30 46	29 56 16	6 31.8	13 16.4	22 29.1	29 32.0	6 29.4	23 27.7	28 13.6	12 43.7	2 04.0	6 49.4
24 Su	4 07 32	3 07 20	7♉23 26	14♉51 17	6 22.9	15 01.5	23 38.5	0♊14.8	6 52.5	23 36.9	28 20.3	12 43.4	2 03.4	6 47.8
25 M	4 11 29	4 05 00	22 18 40	29 44 26	6 12.2	16 48.8	24 48.0	0 57.5	7 15.7	23 45.9	28 27.0	12 43.1	2 02.7	6 46.1
26 Tu	4 15 25	5 02 39	7♊07 29	14♊26 44	6 00.7	18 38.3	25 57.5	1 40.1	7 38.8	23 54.8	28 33.7	12 42.7	2 02.1	6 44.5
27 W	4 19 22	6 00 17	21 41 14	28 50 10	5 50.0	20 30.0	27 07.1	2 22.7	8 01.9	24 03.6	28 40.3	12 42.2	2 01.4	6 42.9
28 Th	4 23 18	6 57 53	5♋52 55	12♋49 03	5 40.9	22 23.8	28 16.8	3 05.2	8 24.9	24 12.2	28 46.8	12 41.7	2 00.6	6 41.2
29 F	4 27 15	7 55 28	19 38 19	26 20 40	5 34.3	24 19.8	29 26.5	3 47.7	8 47.9	24 20.8	28 53.3	12 41.1	1 59.9	6 39.6
30 Sa	4 31 12	8 53 02	2♌56 12	9♌25 11	5 30.3	26 17.8	0♉36.3	4 30.1	9 10.9	24 29.1	28 59.8	12 40.5	1 59.1	6 37.9
31 Su	4 35 08	9 50 34	15 48 00	22 05 08	5 28.5	28 17.9	1 46.1	5 12.5	9 33.8	24 37.4	29 06.2	12 39.9	1 58.3	6 36.3

LONGITUDE — June 1998

Day	Sid.Time	☉	0 hr ☽	Noon ☽	True ☊	☿	♀	♂	⚳	♃	♄	♅	♆	♇
1 M	4 39 05	10♊48 05	28♌17 08	4♍24 38	5♍28.1	0♊19.8	2♉56.0	5♊54.8	9♉56.7	24♓45.5	29♈12.5	12♒39.2	1♒57.4	6♐34.7
2 Tu	4 43 01	11 45 35	10♍28 16	16 28 44	5R 28.0	2 23.7	4 05.9	6 37.1	10 19.5	24 53.4	29 18.8	12R 38.5	1R 56.6	6R 33.0
3 W	4 46 58	12 43 03	22 26 42	28 22 51	5 27.3	4 29.2	5 15.9	7 19.3	10 42.3	25 01.3	29 25.1	12 37.7	1 55.7	6 31.4
4 Th	4 50 54	13 40 30	4♎17 50	10♎12 17	5 24.8	6 36.3	6 26.0	8 01.5	11 05.0	25 08.9	29 31.3	12 36.8	1 54.8	6 29.8
5 F	4 54 51	14 37 56	16 06 48	22 01 55	5 19.9	8 44.8	7 36.1	8 43.6	11 27.7	25 16.5	29 37.4	12 36.0	1 53.8	6 28.2
6 Sa	4 58 47	15 35 21	27 58 10	3♏56 00	5 12.5	10 54.5	8 46.3	9 25.7	11 50.3	25 23.9	29 43.5	12 35.0	1 52.8	6 26.5
7 Su	5 02 44	16 32 45	9♏55 47	15 57 54	5 02.6	13 05.2	9 56.5	10 07.7	12 12.9	25 31.1	29 49.6	12 34.1	1 51.8	6 24.9
8 M	5 06 40	17 30 07	22 02 35	28 10 04	4 50.8	15 16.6	11 06.8	10 49.7	12 35.5	25 38.2	29 55.5	12 33.1	1 50.8	6 23.3
9 Tu	5 10 37	18 27 29	4♐20 30	10♐34 00	4 38.2	17 28.5	12 17.2	11 31.6	12 58.0	25 45.2	0♉01.4	12 32.0	1 49.8	6 21.7
10 W	5 14 34	19 24 50	16 50 36	23 10 18	4 25.8	19 40.6	13 27.6	12 13.4	13 20.5	25 52.0	0 07.3	12 30.9	1 48.7	6 20.1
11 Th	5 18 30	20 22 11	29 33 05	5♑58 54	4 14.7	21 52.6	14 38.0	12 55.2	13 42.9	25 58.6	0 13.1	12 29.8	1 47.6	6 18.6
12 F	5 22 27	21 19 30	12♑27 41	18 59 21	4 05.8	24 04.3	15 48.5	13 37.0	14 05.2	26 05.1	0 18.8	12 28.6	1 46.5	6 17.0
13 Sa	5 26 23	22 16 49	25 33 52	2♒11 10	3 59.6	26 15.3	16 59.1	14 18.7	14 27.5	26 11.5	0 24.5	12 27.4	1 45.4	6 15.4
14 Su	5 30 20	23 14 08	8♒51 13	15 34 01	3 56.1	28 25.5	18 09.7	15 00.4	14 49.8	26 17.7	0 30.1	12 26.1	1 44.2	6 13.9
15 M	5 34 16	24 11 26	22 19 36	29 08 00	3D 54.8	0♋34.6	19 20.4	15 42.0	15 12.0	26 23.7	0 35.7	12 24.8	1 43.0	6 12.3
16 Tu	5 38 13	25 08 43	5♓59 15	12♓53 26	3R 54.9	2 42.4	20 31.1	16 23.6	15 34.1	26 29.5	0 41.2	12 23.5	1 41.8	6 10.8
17 W	5 42 10	26 06 01	19 50 34	26 50 41	3 55.2	4 48.7	21 41.9	17 05.1	15 56.2	26 35.2	0 46.6	12 22.1	1 40.6	6 09.3
18 Th	5 46 06	27 03 18	3♈53 44	10♈59 37	3 54.4	6 53.4	22 52.7	17 46.6	16 18.2	26 40.8	0 51.9	12 20.7	1 39.3	6 07.8
19 F	5 50 03	28 00 34	18 08 11	25 19 09	3 51.8	8 56.3	24 03.6	18 28.0	16 40.2	26 46.1	0 57.2	12 19.2	1 38.1	6 06.3
20 Sa	5 53 59	28 57 51	2♉32 06	9♉46 35	3 46.8	10 57.3	25 14.5	19 09.4	17 02.1	26 51.4	1 02.4	12 17.7	1 36.8	6 04.8
21 Su	5 57 56	29 55 07	17 02 01	24 17 42	3 39.5	12 56.3	26 25.5	19 50.7	17 24.0	26 56.4	1 07.6	12 16.2	1 35.5	6 03.3
22 M	6 01 52	0♋52 24	1♊32 53	8♊46 45	3 30.5	14 53.3	27 36.5	20 32.0	17 45.8	27 01.2	1 12.6	12 14.6	1 34.2	6 01.9
23 Tu	6 05 49	1 49 40	15 58 28	23 07 16	3 20.9	16 48.2	28 47.5	21 13.3	18 07.5	27 05.9	1 17.6	12 13.0	1 32.8	6 00.4
24 W	6 09 45	2 46 55	0♋12 22	7♋13 08	3 11.7	18 41.0	29 58.6	21 54.5	18 29.1	27 10.5	1 22.6	12 11.4	1 31.5	5 59.0
25 Th	6 13 42	3 44 11	14 08 58	20 59 27	3 04.0	20 31.6	1♊09.8	22 35.6	18 50.7	27 14.8	1 27.4	12 09.7	1 30.1	5 57.6
26 F	6 17 39	4 41 26	27 44 17	4♌23 19	2 58.3	22 20.0	2 21.0	23 16.7	19 12.2	27 19.0	1 32.2	12 08.0	1 28.7	5 56.2
27 Sa	6 21 35	5 38 40	10♌56 33	17 24 03	2 55.0	24 06.2	3 32.2	23 57.8	19 33.7	27 22.9	1 36.9	12 06.2	1 27.3	5 54.9
28 Su	6 25 32	6 35 54	23 46 06	0♍03 00	2D 53.8	25 50.3	4 43.5	24 38.8	19 55.1	27 26.7	1 41.5	12 04.4	1 25.9	5 53.5
29 M	6 29 28	7 33 07	6♍15 11	12 23 09	2 54.1	27 32.1	5 54.8	25 19.8	20 16.4	27 30.4	1 46.1	12 02.6	1 24.4	5 52.2
30 Tu	6 33 25	8 30 20	18 27 26	24 28 40	2 55.1	29 11.6	7 06.2	26 00.7	20 37.6	27 33.8	1 50.5	12 00.8	1 23.0	5 50.8

Astro Data

	Dy Hr Mn
♆R	4 10:39
♀0N	6 20:40
☽0S	7 19:11
♅R	17 15:01
☽0N	21 20:27
☽0S	4 3:19
☽0N	18 4:04
♃∠♅	24 15:34
♄□♆	25 22:24

Planet Ingress

	Dy Hr Mn
♀ ♈	3 19:16
⚳ ♉	6 21:14
☿ ♉	15 2:10
☉ ♊	21 6:05
♂ ♊	24 3:42
♀ ♉	29 23:32
☿ ♊	1 8:07
♄ ♉	9 6:07
☿ ♋	15 5:33
☉ ♋	21 14:03
♀ ♊	24 12:27
☿ ♌	30 23:52

Last Aspect / ☽ Ingress (May)

Last Aspect Dy Hr Mn		☽ Ingress Dy Hr Mn
2 6:37 ♀ △	♌	2 9:49
4 11:49 ♄ △	♍	4 19:47
6 13:10 ♃ ☍	♎	7 8:19
9 14:19 ♃ ☍	♏	9 21:10
11 16:05 ♃ △	♐	12 8:48
14 17:42 ☿ △	♑	14 18:39
16 21:53 ♄ □	♒	17 2:30
19 4:35 ☉ □	♓	19 8:03
21 7:44 ♂ ⚹	♈	21 11:06
23 9:13 ♄ ☌	♉	23 12:06
25 2:15 ♃ ⚹	♊	25 12:25
27 11:43 ♄ ⚹	♋	27 13:58
29 18:09 ♀ □	♌	29 18:38

Last Aspect / ☽ Ingress (June)

Last Aspect Dy Hr Mn		☽ Ingress Dy Hr Mn
1 2:24 ☿ □	♍	1 3:21
3 5:08 ♃ ☍	♎	3 15:17
6 3:28 ♄ ☍	♏	6 4:06
8 7:00 ♃ △	♐	8 15:34
10 17:08 ♃ □	♑	11 0:50
13 1:03 ♃ ⚹	♒	13 8:03
15 2:38 ☉ △	♓	15 13:31
17 11:33 ♃ ☌	♈	17 17:23
19 16:48 ☉ ⚹	♉	19 19:47
21 16:24 ♃ ⚹	♊	21 21:26
23 18:46 ♃ □	♋	23 23:39
25 23:11 ♃ △	♌	26 4:04
28 1:05 ♂ ⚹	♍	28 11:54
30 22:57 ☿ ⚹	♎	30 23:05

☽ Phases & Eclipses

Dy Hr Mn	
3 10:04	☽ 12♌47
11 14:29	○ 20♏42
19 4:35	☾ 28♒01
25 19:32	● 4♊23
2 1:45	☽ 11♍21
10 4:18	○ 19♐06
17 10:38	☾ 26♓03
24 3:50	● 2♋27

Astro Data

1 May 1998
Julian Day # 35915
SVP 5♓17'07"
GC 26♐49.0 ⚴ 19♓21.6
Eris 19♈01.2 ⚵ 21♍12.0R
⚷ 15♏58.6R ⚶ 1♊47.8
☽ Mean ☊ 7♍20.6

1 June 1998
Julian Day # 35946
SVP 5♓17'02"
GC 26♐49.0 ⚴ 26♓46.9
Eris 19♈17.8 ⚵ 22♍17.8
⚷ 13♏45.2R ⚶ 15♊09.2
☽ Mean ☊ 5♍42.1

July 1998 — LONGITUDE

Day	Sid.Time	☉	0 hr ☽	Noon ☽	True ☊	☿	♀	♂	⚳	♃	♄	♅	♆	♇
1 W	6 37 21	9♋27 33	0♎27 27	6♎24 26	2♍55.8	0♌49.0	8♊17.6	26♊41.5	20♉58.7	27♓37.0	1♉54.9	11♒58.9	1♒21.5	5♐49.5
2 Th	6 41 18	10 24 45	12 20 16	18 15 36	2R 55.5	2 24.1	9 29.0	27 22.3	21 19.8	27 40.1	1 59.2	11R 57.0	1R 20.0	5R 48.3
3 F	6 45 14	11 21 57	24 11 04	0♏07 18	2 53.5	3 56.9	10 40.5	28 03.1	21 40.8	27 43.0	2 03.4	11 55.1	1 18.5	5 47.0
4 Sa	6 49 11	12 19 09	6♏04 51	12 04 17	2 49.5	5 27.5	11 52.0	28 43.8	22 01.7	27 45.7	2 07.6	11 53.1	1 17.0	5 45.8
5 Su	6 53 08	13 16 20	18 06 06	24 10 45	2 43.7	6 55.8	13 03.6	29 24.5	22 22.5	27 48.2	2 11.6	11 51.1	1 15.5	5 44.6
6 M	6 57 04	14 13 31	0♐18 37	6♐30 00	2 36.3	8 21.8	14 15.2	0♋05.1	22 43.3	27 50.6	2 15.6	11 49.1	1 14.0	5 43.4
7 Tu	7 01 01	15 10 42	12 45 11	19 04 20	2 28.2	9 45.5	15 26.8	0 45.6	23 04.0	27 52.7	2 19.5	11 47.1	1 12.4	5 42.2
8 W	7 04 57	16 07 53	25 27 33	1♑54 52	2 20.2	11 06.8	16 38.5	1 26.2	23 24.5	27 54.6	2 23.3	11 45.0	1 10.9	5 41.1
9 Th	7 08 54	17 05 05	8♑26 14	15 01 32	2 13.0	12 25.7	17 50.3	2 06.7	23 45.0	27 56.4	2 27.0	11 42.9	1 09.3	5 39.9
10 F	7 12 50	18 02 16	21 40 38	28 23 17	2 07.4	13 42.1	19 02.1	2 47.1	24 05.4	27 58.0	2 30.7	11 40.8	1 07.8	5 38.8
11 Sa	7 16 47	18 59 27	5♒09 16	11♒58 19	2 03.7	14 56.1	20 13.9	3 27.5	24 25.8	27 59.4	2 34.2	11 38.7	1 06.2	5 37.8
12 Su	7 20 43	19 56 39	18 50 08	25 44 26	2D 02.1	16 07.5	21 25.7	4 07.8	24 46.0	28 00.5	2 37.7	11 36.5	1 04.6	5 36.7
13 M	7 24 40	20 53 51	2♓40 57	9♓39 26	2 02.1	17 16.2	22 37.7	4 48.1	25 06.1	28 01.5	2 41.0	11 34.4	1 03.0	5 35.7
14 Tu	7 28 37	21 51 04	16 39 38	23 41 19	2 03.2	18 22.3	23 49.6	5 28.4	25 26.2	28 02.3	2 44.3	11 32.2	1 01.4	5 34.7
15 W	7 32 33	22 48 17	0♈44 16	7♈48 18	2 04.5	19 25.5	25 01.6	6 08.6	25 46.1	28 02.9	2 47.5	11 29.9	0 59.8	5 33.7
16 Th	7 36 30	23 45 31	14 53 12	21 58 46	2R 05.2	20 25.9	26 13.7	6 48.8	26 06.0	28 03.3	2 50.6	11 27.7	0 58.2	5 32.7
17 F	7 40 26	24 42 45	29 04 48	6♉11 01	2 04.7	21 23.3	27 25.8	7 28.9	26 25.7	28R 03.6	2 53.6	11 25.5	0 56.6	5 31.8
18 Sa	7 44 23	25 40 00	13♉17 10	20 22 56	2 02.6	22 17.5	28 37.9	8 09.0	26 45.4	28 03.6	2 56.5	11 23.2	0 55.0	5 30.9
19 Su	7 48 19	26 37 16	27 27 58	4♊31 53	1 59.1	23 08.6	29 50.1	8 49.1	27 04.9	28 03.4	2 59.3	11 20.9	0 53.4	5 30.0
20 M	7 52 16	27 34 33	11♊34 17	18 34 44	1 54.4	23 56.3	1♋02.4	9 29.1	27 24.3	28 03.0	3 02.0	11 18.6	0 51.8	5 29.2
21 Tu	7 56 12	28 31 50	25 32 47	2♋28 02	1 49.3	24 40.5	2 14.6	10 09.1	27 43.7	28 02.4	3 04.7	11 16.3	0 50.1	5 28.4
22 W	8 00 09	29 29 09	9♋20 02	16 08 27	1 44.4	25 21.1	3 27.0	10 49.0	28 02.9	28 01.7	3 07.2	11 14.0	0 48.5	5 27.6
23 Th	8 04 06	0♌26 27	22 52 56	29 33 14	1 40.3	25 57.9	4 39.3	11 28.9	28 22.0	28 00.7	3 09.6	11 11.7	0 46.9	5 26.8
24 F	8 08 02	1 23 46	6♌09 10	12♌40 35	1 37.5	26 30.7	5 51.7	12 08.7	28 41.0	27 59.5	3 12.0	11 09.3	0 45.3	5 26.1
25 Sa	8 11 59	2 21 06	19 07 29	25 29 55	1D 36.2	26 59.4	7 04.2	12 48.5	28 59.9	27 58.1	3 14.2	11 07.0	0 43.6	5 25.4
26 Su	8 15 55	3 18 26	1♍48 00	8♍01 57	1 36.2	27 23.8	8 16.6	13 28.3	29 18.6	27 56.6	3 16.3	11 04.6	0 42.0	5 24.7
27 M	8 19 52	4 15 47	14 12 03	20 18 39	1 37.2	27 43.8	9 29.2	14 08.0	29 37.2	27 54.8	3 18.4	11 02.2	0 40.4	5 24.1
28 Tu	8 23 48	5 13 08	26 22 09	2♎23 00	1 38.8	27 59.0	10 41.7	14 47.6	29 55.7	27 52.9	3 20.3	10 59.8	0 38.8	5 23.5
29 W	8 27 45	6 10 30	8♎21 43	14 18 50	1 40.5	28 09.6	11 54.3	15 27.2	0♊14.1	27 50.7	3 22.2	10 57.5	0 37.1	5 22.9
30 Th	8 31 41	7 07 52	20 14 55	26 10 34	1R 41.7	28R 15.1	13 07.0	16 06.8	0 32.4	27 48.4	3 23.9	10 55.1	0 35.5	5 22.3
31 F	8 35 38	8 05 15	2♏06 21	8♏02 53	1 42.2	28 15.6	14 19.6	16 46.3	0 50.5	27 45.9	3 25.5	10 52.7	0 33.9	5 21.8

August 1998 — LONGITUDE

Day	Sid.Time	☉	0 hr ☽	Noon ☽	True ☊	☿	♀	♂	⚳	♃	♄	♅	♆	♇
1 Sa	8 39 35	9♌02 39	14♏00 47	20♏00 38	1♍41.7	28♌11.0	15♋32.4	17♋25.8	1♊08.5	27♓43.2	3♉27.1	10♒50.3	0♒32.3	5♐21.3
2 Su	8 43 31	10 00 03	26 02 59	2♐08 24	1R 40.2	28R 01.2	16 45.1	18 05.3	1 26.3	27R 40.3	3 28.5	10R 47.9	0R 30.7	5R 20.9
3 M	8 47 28	10 57 27	8♐17 22	14 30 20	1 38.0	27 46.2	17 57.9	18 44.7	1 44.0	27 37.2	3 29.8	10 45.5	0 29.1	5 20.4
4 Tu	8 51 24	11 54 53	20 47 42	27 09 47	1 35.3	27 26.0	19 10.7	19 24.0	2 01.6	27 33.9	3 31.0	10 43.1	0 27.5	5 20.0
5 W	8 55 21	12 52 19	3♑36 51	10♑09 02	1 32.5	27 00.9	20 23.6	20 03.3	2 19.0	27 30.4	3 32.2	10 40.7	0 25.9	5 19.7
6 Th	8 59 17	13 49 46	16 46 25	23 28 57	1 30.1	26 30.9	21 36.5	20 42.6	2 36.3	27 26.8	3 33.2	10 38.3	0 24.4	5 19.3
7 F	9 03 14	14 47 14	0♒16 30	7♒08 51	1 28.3	25 56.4	22 49.5	21 21.8	2 53.5	27 23.0	3 34.1	10 35.9	0 22.8	5 19.0
8 Sa	9 07 10	15 44 43	14 05 40	21 06 32	1D 27.3	25 17.9	24 02.5	22 01.0	3 10.5	27 19.0	3 34.9	10 33.6	0 21.3	5 18.8
9 Su	9 11 07	16 42 13	28 10 59	5♓18 28	1 27.1	24 35.7	25 15.6	22 40.2	3 27.3	27 14.8	3 35.6	10 31.2	0 19.7	5 18.5
10 M	9 15 04	17 39 44	12♓28 24	19 40 11	1 27.6	23 50.6	26 28.6	23 19.3	3 44.0	27 10.5	3 36.2	10 28.8	0 18.2	5 18.3
11 Tu	9 19 00	18 37 16	26 53 11	4♈06 49	1 28.5	23 03.2	27 41.8	23 58.4	4 00.5	27 06.0	3 36.7	10 26.4	0 16.6	5 18.2
12 W	9 22 57	19 34 50	11♈20 30	18 33 42	1 29.4	22 14.4	28 54.9	24 37.4	4 16.9	27 01.3	3 37.1	10 24.1	0 15.1	5 18.0
13 Th	9 26 53	20 32 25	25 45 54	2♉56 40	1 30.2	21 24.9	0♌08.2	25 16.4	4 33.1	26 56.4	3 37.4	10 21.7	0 13.6	5 17.9
14 F	9 30 50	21 30 02	10♉05 36	17 12 23	1R 30.6	20 35.9	1 21.4	25 55.3	4 49.2	26 51.4	3 37.6	10 19.4	0 12.1	5 17.8
15 Sa	9 34 46	22 27 40	24 16 44	1♊18 23	1 30.5	19 48.1	2 34.7	26 34.3	5 05.1	26 46.2	3R 37.7	10 17.1	0 10.6	5D 17.8
16 Su	9 38 43	23 25 20	8♊17 10	15 12 54	1 30.1	19 02.6	3 48.1	27 13.2	5 20.8	26 40.9	3 37.7	10 14.7	0 09.2	5 17.8
17 M	9 42 39	24 23 01	22 05 29	28 54 47	1 29.4	18 20.3	5 01.5	27 52.0	5 36.3	26 35.4	3 37.5	10 12.4	0 07.7	5 17.8
18 Tu	9 46 36	25 20 44	5♋40 45	12♋23 17	1 28.6	17 42.1	6 14.9	28 30.8	5 51.6	26 29.8	3 37.3	10 10.1	0 06.3	5 17.9
19 W	9 50 33	26 18 29	19 02 22	25 37 58	1 27.9	17 08.9	7 28.4	29 09.6	6 06.8	26 24.0	3 37.0	10 07.9	0 04.9	5 17.9
20 Th	9 54 29	27 16 15	2♌10 02	8♌38 36	1 27.5	16 41.3	8 41.9	29 48.3	6 21.8	26 18.0	3 36.5	10 05.6	0 03.5	5 18.1
21 F	9 58 26	28 14 02	15 03 40	21 25 18	1D 27.2	16 20.0	9 55.5	0♌27.0	6 36.6	26 12.0	3 36.0	10 03.4	0 02.1	5 18.2
22 Sa	10 02 22	29 11 51	27 43 33	3♍58 30	1 27.2	16 05.6	11 09.0	1 05.6	6 51.2	26 05.8	3 35.3	10 01.1	0 00.7	5 18.4
23 Su	10 06 19	0♍09 41	10♍10 19	16 19 08	1 27.2	15D 58.4	12 22.7	1 44.2	7 05.6	25 59.4	3 34.6	9 58.9	29♑59.3	5 18.6
24 M	10 10 15	1 07 33	22 25 09	28 28 37	1R 27.3	15 58.9	13 36.3	2 22.8	7 19.8	25 52.9	3 33.7	9 56.7	29 58.0	5 18.9
25 Tu	10 14 12	2 05 25	4♎29 49	10♎29 02	1 27.3	16 07.2	14 50.0	3 01.3	7 33.8	25 46.3	3 32.7	9 54.6	29 56.7	5 19.2
26 W	10 18 08	3 03 20	16 26 39	22 23 04	1 27.1	16 23.5	16 03.8	3 39.8	7 47.6	25 39.6	3 31.7	9 52.4	29 55.4	5 19.5
27 Th	10 22 05	4 01 15	28 18 41	4♏13 59	1 26.9	16 47.7	17 17.5	4 18.2	8 01.1	25 32.8	3 30.5	9 50.3	29 54.1	5 19.9
28 F	10 26 01	4 59 12	10♏09 27	16 05 37	1 26.6	17 19.9	18 31.3	4 56.6	8 14.5	25 25.9	3 29.2	9 48.2	29 52.8	5 20.3
29 Sa	10 29 58	5 57 10	22 03 01	28 02 12	1D 26.4	18 00.0	19 45.2	5 35.0	8 27.6	25 18.8	3 27.8	9 46.1	29 51.6	5 20.7
30 Su	10 33 55	6 55 10	4♐03 45	10♐08 13	1 26.3	18 47.6	20 59.1	6 13.3	8 40.6	25 11.7	3 26.4	9 44.1	29 50.4	5 21.1
31 M	10 37 51	7 53 11	16 16 10	22 28 10	1 26.5	19 42.7	22 13.0	6 51.5	8 53.3	25 04.4	3 24.8	9 42.0	29 49.2	5 21.6

Astro Data

	Dy Hr Mn
☽0S	1 12:23
☽0N	15 10:24
♃R	18 1:49
☽0S	28 21:21
☿R	31 2:27
☽0N	11 17:01
♄R	15 19:09
♇D	16 6:08
☿D	23 22:37
☽0S	25 5:19

Planet Ingress

	Dy Hr Mn
♂ ♋	6 9:00
♀ ♋	19 15:17
☉ ♌	23 0:55
⚳ ♊	28 17:33
♀ ♌	13 9:19
♂ ♌	20 19:16
♆ ♑R	23 0:13
☉ ♍	23 7:59

Last Aspect / ☽ Ingress

Last Aspect Dy Hr Mn		☽ Ingress Dy Hr Mn
3 7:34	♂ △	♏ 3 11:45
5 19:08	♃ △	♐ 5 23:24
8 4:33	♃ □	♑ 8 8:27
10 11:15	♃ ⚹	♒ 10 14:52
12 3:48	♀ △	♓ 12 19:22
14 19:25	♃ ☌	♈ 14 22:45
16 19:51	♀ ⚹	♉ 17 1:33
19 1:00	♃ ⚹	♊ 19 4:18
21 4:19	♃ □	♋ 21 7:43
23 9:13	♃ △	♌ 23 12:48
25 14:56	☿ ☌	♍ 25 20:34
28 3:02	♃ ☍	♎ 28 7:14
30 16:13	☿ ⚹	♏ 30 19:44

Last Aspect / ☽ Ingress

Last Aspect Dy Hr Mn		☽ Ingress Dy Hr Mn
2 4:01	☿ □	♐ 2 7:48
4 12:45	♃ □	♑ 4 17:18
6 18:59	♃ ⚹	♒ 6 23:31
8 18:47	☿ ☍	♓ 9 3:04
11 0:25	♃ ☌	♈ 11 5:10
13 6:52	♀ □	♉ 13 7:04
15 4:18	♃ ⚹	♊ 15 9:46
17 7:56	♃ □	♋ 17 13:55
19 18:48	♂ ☌	♌ 19 20:00
22 2:03	☉ ☌	♍ 22 4:21
24 14:57	♆ △	♎ 24 15:02
27 3:14	♆ □	♏ 27 3:25
29 15:38	♆ ⚹	♐ 29 15:55

☽ Phases & Eclipses

Dy Hr Mn		
1 18:43	☽	9♎44
9 16:01	○	17♑15
16 15:13	☾	23♈53
23 13:44	●	0♌31
31 12:05	☽	8♏05
8 2:10	○	15♒21
8 2:25	◐	A 0.120
14 19:48	☾	21♉49
22 2:03	●	28♌48
22 2:06:07	◐	A 03'14"
30 5:06	☽	6♐39

Astro Data

1 July 1998
Julian Day # 35976
SVP 5♓16'58"
GC 26♐49.1 ⚴ 1♈20.3
Eris 19♈26.8 ⚵ 27♍30.5
⚷ 12♏30.7R ⚶ 28♊08.0
☽ Mean ☊ 4♍06.8

1 August 1998
Julian Day # 36007
SVP 5♓16'53"
GC 26♐49.2 ⚴ 1♈49.0R
Eris 19♈26.5R ⚵ 5♎32.7
⚷ 12♏46.9 ⚶ 11♋20.4
☽ Mean ☊ 2♍28.3

LONGITUDE — September 1998

Day	Sid.Time	☉	0 hr ☽	Noon ☽	True ☊	☿	♀	♂	⚳	♃	♄	♅	♆	♇
1 Tu	10 41 48	8♍51 13	28♐44 43	5♑06 17	1♍27.1	20♌44.9	23♌26.9	7♌29.8	9♊05.7	24♓57.1	3♉23.1	9♒40.0	29♑48.0	5♐22.2
2 W	10 45 44	9 49 17	11♑33 18	18 06 07	1 27.8	21 53.7	24 40.9	8 08.0	9 18.0	24R 49.7	3R 21.3	9R 38.1	29R 46.8	5 22.7
3 Th	10 49 41	10 47 22	24 45 00	1♒30 06	1 28.6	23 08.8	25 54.9	8 46.1	9 30.0	24 42.2	3 19.5	9 36.1	29 45.7	5 23.3
4 F	10 53 37	11 45 28	8♒21 27	15 18 58	1 29.3	24 29.8	27 08.9	9 24.2	9 41.8	24 34.7	3 17.5	9 34.2	29 44.6	5 23.9
5 Sa	10 57 34	12 43 36	22 22 25	29 31 25	1R 29.6	25 56.1	28 23.0	10 02.3	9 53.3	24 27.1	3 15.4	9 32.3	29 43.5	5 24.6
6 Su	11 01 30	13 41 46	6♓45 27	14♓03 50	1 29.4	27 27.3	29 37.1	10 40.3	10 04.6	24 19.4	3 13.3	9 30.5	29 42.4	5 25.3
7 M	11 05 27	14 39 57	21 25 46	28 50 24	1 28.5	29 02.7	0♍51.3	11 18.3	10 15.6	24 11.6	3 11.0	9 28.6	29 41.4	5 26.0
8 Tu	11 09 24	15 38 10	6♈16 43	13♈43 45	1 27.1	0♍41.9	2 05.4	11 56.3	10 26.4	24 03.8	3 08.7	9 26.9	29 40.4	5 26.8
9 W	11 13 20	16 36 26	21 10 28	28 35 56	1 25.3	2 24.4	3 19.6	12 34.2	10 36.9	23 56.0	3 06.2	9 25.1	29 39.4	5 27.6
10 Th	11 17 17	17 34 43	5♉59 14	13♉19 33	1 23.4	4 09.6	4 33.9	13 12.1	10 47.2	23 48.1	3 03.7	9 23.4	29 38.4	5 28.4
11 F	11 21 13	18 33 02	20 36 13	27 48 41	1 21.9	5 57.1	5 48.2	13 49.9	10 57.1	23 40.2	3 01.1	9 21.7	29 37.5	5 29.2
12 Sa	11 25 10	19 31 24	4♊56 33	11♊59 30	1D 21.0	7 46.4	7 02.5	14 27.7	11 06.9	23 32.3	2 58.3	9 20.0	29 36.6	5 30.1
13 Su	11 29 06	20 29 47	18 57 25	25 50 13	1 21.0	9 37.2	8 16.8	15 05.5	11 16.3	23 24.3	2 55.5	9 18.4	29 35.7	5 31.0
14 M	11 33 03	21 28 13	2♋37 59	9♋20 51	1 21.7	11 28.9	9 31.2	15 43.2	11 25.5	23 16.3	2 52.6	9 16.8	29 34.8	5 32.0
15 Tu	11 36 59	22 26 41	15 58 59	22 32 37	1 23.0	13 21.4	10 45.6	16 20.9	11 34.3	23 08.3	2 49.7	9 15.3	29 34.0	5 33.0
16 W	11 40 56	23 25 11	29 02 01	5♌27 28	1 24.5	15 14.2	12 00.1	16 58.5	11 42.9	23 00.3	2 46.6	9 13.8	29 33.2	5 34.0
17 Th	11 44 53	24 23 43	11♌49 14	18 07 36	1 25.8	17 07.2	13 14.5	17 36.1	11 51.2	22 52.3	2 43.5	9 12.3	29 32.4	5 35.0
18 F	11 48 49	25 22 17	24 22 49	0♍35 10	1R 26.4	19 00.2	14 29.1	18 13.7	11 59.2	22 44.3	2 40.2	9 10.9	29 31.7	5 36.1
19 Sa	11 52 46	26 20 53	6♍44 52	12 52 09	1 25.9	20 52.8	15 43.6	18 51.2	12 06.9	22 36.4	2 36.9	9 09.5	29 31.0	5 37.2
20 Su	11 56 42	27 19 31	18 57 14	25 00 19	1 24.0	22 45.1	16 58.1	19 28.7	12 14.2	22 28.4	2 33.5	9 08.1	29 30.3	5 38.3
21 M	12 00 39	28 18 11	1♎01 36	7♎01 18	1 20.9	24 36.9	18 12.7	20 06.2	12 21.3	22 20.5	2 30.1	9 06.8	29 29.6	5 39.5
22 Tu	12 04 35	29 16 53	12 59 36	18 56 46	1 16.5	26 28.0	19 27.3	20 43.5	12 28.0	22 12.6	2 26.5	9 05.5	29 29.0	5 40.7
23 W	12 08 32	0♎15 37	24 52 59	0♏48 33	1 11.4	28 18.5	20 42.0	21 20.9	12 34.4	22 04.7	2 22.9	9 04.3	29 28.4	5 41.9
24 Th	12 12 28	1 14 23	6♏43 44	12 38 52	1 06.1	0♎08.2	21 56.6	21 58.2	12 40.5	21 56.9	2 19.2	9 03.1	29 27.8	5 43.1
25 F	12 16 25	2 13 10	18 34 16	24 30 21	1 01.2	1 57.0	23 11.3	22 35.5	12 46.3	21 49.2	2 15.5	9 02.0	29 27.3	5 44.4
26 Sa	12 20 21	3 11 59	0♐27 31	6♐26 13	0 57.1	3 45.0	24 26.0	23 12.7	12 51.7	21 41.5	2 11.7	9 00.9	29 26.8	5 45.7
27 Su	12 24 18	4 10 51	12 26 56	18 30 11	0 54.3	5 32.2	25 40.7	23 49.9	12 56.8	21 33.8	2 07.8	8 59.8	29 26.3	5 47.1
28 M	12 28 15	5 09 43	24 36 31	0♑46 27	0D 53.1	7 18.4	26 55.5	24 27.0	13 01.5	21 26.3	2 03.8	8 58.8	29 25.9	5 48.4
29 Tu	12 32 11	6 08 38	7♑00 33	13 19 23	0 53.2	9 03.8	28 10.2	25 04.1	13 05.9	21 18.8	1 59.8	8 57.9	29 25.5	5 49.8
30 W	12 36 08	7 07 34	19 43 30	26 13 22	0 54.4	10 48.3	29 25.0	25 41.2	13 10.0	21 11.4	1 55.8	8 56.9	29 25.1	5 51.3

LONGITUDE — October 1998

Day	Sid.Time	☉	0 hr ☽	Noon ☽	True ☊	☿	♀	♂	⚳	♃	♄	♅	♆	♇
1 Th	12 40 04	8♎06 32	2♒49 28	9♒32 09	0♍55.9	12♎31.8	0♎39.8	26♌18.2	13♊13.6	21♓04.1	1♉51.6	8♒56.1	29♑24.7	5♐52.7
2 F	12 44 01	9 05 32	16 21 42	23 18 17	0R 57.1	14 14.5	1 54.7	26 55.1	13 17.0	20R 56.8	1R 47.4	8R 55.2	29R 24.4	5 54.2
3 Sa	12 47 57	10 04 34	0♓21 52	7♓32 18	0 57.1	15 56.4	3 09.5	27 32.1	13 20.0	20 49.7	1 43.2	8 54.5	29 24.1	5 55.7
4 Su	12 51 54	11 03 37	14 49 13	22 12 02	0 55.5	17 37.3	4 24.3	28 08.9	13 22.6	20 42.7	1 38.9	8 53.7	29 23.9	5 57.2
5 M	12 55 50	12 02 42	29 40 00	7♈12 09	0 51.9	19 17.5	5 39.2	28 45.8	13 24.8	20 35.8	1 34.6	8 53.1	29 23.7	5 58.8
6 Tu	12 59 47	13 01 50	14♈47 21	22 24 21	0 46.7	20 56.8	6 54.1	29 22.5	13 26.7	20 28.9	1 30.2	8 52.4	29 23.5	6 00.4
7 W	13 03 44	14 00 59	0♉01 48	7♉38 21	0 40.3	22 35.3	8 09.0	29 59.3	13 28.2	20 22.2	1 25.8	8 51.8	29 23.3	6 02.0
8 Th	13 07 40	15 00 11	15 12 44	22 43 41	0 33.7	24 13.0	9 24.0	0♍36.0	13 29.4	20 15.7	1 21.3	8 51.3	29 23.2	6 03.6
9 F	13 11 37	15 59 24	0♊10 11	7♊31 21	0 27.8	25 50.0	10 38.9	1 12.6	13 30.1	20 09.2	1 16.8	8 50.8	29 23.1	6 05.3
10 Sa	13 15 33	16 58 41	14 46 29	21 55 10	0 23.4	27 26.2	11 53.9	1 49.3	13R 30.5	20 02.9	1 12.3	8 50.3	29 23.1	6 07.0
11 Su	13 19 30	17 57 59	28 57 06	5♋52 13	0D 20.8	29 01.7	13 08.9	2 25.8	13 30.5	19 56.7	1 07.7	8 50.0	29D 23.1	6 08.7
12 M	13 23 26	18 57 20	12♋40 37	19 22 32	0 20.0	0♏36.5	14 23.9	3 02.4	13 30.1	19 50.7	1 03.1	8 49.6	29 23.1	6 10.4
13 Tu	13 27 23	19 56 43	25 58 17	2♌28 17	0 20.6	2 10.5	15 38.9	3 38.8	13 29.3	19 44.8	0 58.4	8 49.3	29 23.1	6 12.2
14 W	13 31 19	20 56 09	8♌53 00	15 12 56	0 21.8	3 43.9	16 54.0	4 15.3	13 28.2	19 39.0	0 53.8	8 49.1	29 23.2	6 13.9
15 Th	13 35 16	21 55 37	21 28 35	27 40 27	0R 22.6	5 16.6	18 09.0	4 51.7	13 26.6	19 33.4	0 49.1	8 48.9	29 23.3	6 15.7
16 F	13 39 13	22 55 07	3♍49 03	9♍54 49	0 22.2	6 48.6	19 24.1	5 28.0	13 24.6	19 27.9	0 44.4	8 48.7	29 23.4	6 17.6
17 Sa	13 43 09	23 54 39	15 58 12	21 59 35	0 19.6	8 20.0	20 39.2	6 04.3	13 22.2	19 22.6	0 39.6	8 48.6	29 23.6	6 19.4
18 Su	13 47 06	24 54 13	27 59 20	3♎57 46	0 14.6	9 50.7	21 54.3	6 40.5	13 19.5	19 17.5	0 34.9	8D 48.6	29 23.8	6 21.3
19 M	13 51 02	25 53 49	9♎55 09	15 51 46	0 07.1	11 20.8	23 09.4	7 16.7	13 16.3	19 12.5	0 30.1	8 48.6	29 24.1	6 23.2
20 Tu	13 54 59	26 53 28	21 47 49	27 43 31	29♌57.3	12 50.2	24 24.6	7 52.9	13 12.7	19 07.8	0 25.3	8 48.6	29 24.4	6 25.1
21 W	13 58 55	27 53 08	3♏39 03	9♏34 35	29 46.1	14 19.0	25 39.7	8 29.0	13 08.8	19 03.1	0 20.5	8 48.8	29 24.7	6 27.0
22 Th	14 02 52	28 52 51	15 30 20	21 26 28	29 34.2	15 47.0	26 54.9	9 05.0	13 04.4	18 58.7	0 15.7	8 48.9	29 25.0	6 29.0
23 F	14 06 48	29 52 35	27 23 12	3♐20 46	29 22.8	17 14.5	28 10.0	9 41.0	12 59.6	18 54.4	0 10.9	8 49.1	29 25.4	6 30.9
24 Sa	14 10 45	0♏52 22	9♐19 27	15 19 31	29 12.9	18 41.2	29 25.2	10 16.9	12 54.5	18 50.3	0 06.1	8 49.4	29 25.8	6 32.9
25 Su	14 14 42	1 52 10	21 21 20	27 25 15	29 05.1	20 07.2	0♏40.4	10 52.8	12 48.9	18 46.4	0 01.3	8 49.7	29 26.3	6 34.9
26 M	14 18 38	2 51 59	3♑31 41	9♑41 06	29 00.0	21 32.5	1 55.6	11 28.6	12 43.0	18 42.7	29♈56.5	8 50.1	29 26.8	6 37.0
27 Tu	14 22 35	3 51 51	15 54 00	22 10 52	28D 57.3	22 57.1	3 10.8	12 04.4	12 36.7	18 39.2	29 51.8	8 50.5	29 27.3	6 39.0
28 W	14 26 31	4 51 44	28 32 14	4♒58 39	28 56.7	24 20.8	4 26.0	12 40.1	12 30.0	18 35.9	29 47.0	8 51.0	29 27.8	6 41.1
29 Th	14 30 28	5 51 39	11♒30 38	18 08 39	28R 57.0	25 43.7	5 41.2	13 15.7	12 22.9	18 32.7	29 42.2	8 51.5	29 28.4	6 43.1
30 F	14 34 24	6 51 35	24 53 10	1♓44 29	28 57.2	27 05.7	6 56.4	13 51.3	12 15.5	18 29.8	29 37.5	8 52.1	29 29.1	6 45.2
31 Sa	14 38 21	7 51 33	8♓42 52	15 48 23	28 56.2	28 26.7	8 11.7	14 26.9	12 07.7	18 27.1	29 32.8	8 52.7	29 29.7	6 47.3

Astro Data

	Dy Hr Mn
♃∠♅	4 13:56
☽0N	8 1:22
☽0S	21 12:05
☉0S	23 5:38
☿0S	26 4:33
♀0S	3 14:29
☽0N	5 11:47
⚳R	10 23:36
♆D	11 14:03
☽0S	18 18:17
♅D	18 21:24

Planet Ingress

		Dy Hr Mn
♀	♍	6 19:24
☿	♍	8 1:58
☉	♎	23 5:37
☿	♎	24 10:13
♀	♎	30 23:13
♂	♍	7 12:28
☿	♏	12 2:44
☊	♌R	20 5:51
☉	♏	23 14:59
♀	♏	24 23:06
♄	♈R	25 18:41

Last Aspect / ☽ Ingress (September)

Last Aspect Dy Hr Mn			☽ Ingress	Dy Hr Mn
31 16:57	♃	□	♑	1 2:23
3 8:56	♆	☌	♒	3 9:21
5 9:55	♀	☍	♓	5 12:48
7 13:22	♆	✶	♈	7 13:52
9 13:43	♆	□	♉	9 14:16
11 15:02	♆	△	♊	11 15:40
13 7:47	♃	□	♋	13 19:20
16 0:59	♆	☍	♌	16 1:48
17 10:57	♂	☌	♍	18 10:52
20 20:57	♆	△	♎	20 21:57
23 9:18	♆	□	♏	23 10:22
25 21:58	♆	✶	♐	25 23:05
28 3:41	♀	□	♑	28 10:30
30 18:26	♀	△	♒	30 18:53

Last Aspect / ☽ Ingress (October)

Last Aspect Dy Hr Mn			☽ Ingress	Dy Hr Mn
2 18:27	♂	☍	♓	2 23:23
4 23:34	♆	✶	♈	5 0:32
6 23:26	♂	△	♉	6 23:57
8 22:44	♆	△	♊	8 23:43
10 22:37	☿	△	♋	11 1:48
13 6:17	♆	☍	♌	13 7:25
14 23:54	☉	✶	♍	15 16:32
18 2:49	♆	△	♎	18 4:02
20 15:24	♆	□	♏	20 16:36
23 4:06	♆	✶	♐	23 5:16
24 18:58	♃	□	♑	25 17:05
28 2:24	♄	□	♒	28 2:44
30 8:20	♄	✶	♓	30 8:58

☽ Phases & Eclipses

Dy Hr Mn	
6 11:21	○ 13♓40
6 11:10	☍ A 0.812
13 1:58	☾ 20♊05
20 17:01	● 27♍32
28 21:11	☽ 5♑32
5 20:12	○ 12♈23
12 11:11	☾ 18♋55
20 10:09	● 26♎49
28 11:46	☽ 4♒51

Astro Data

1 September 1998
Julian Day # 36038
SVP 5♓16'50"
GC 26♐49.2 ⚴ 26♓53.1R
Eris 19♈16.8R ⚵ 15♎08.3
⚷ 14♏39.2 ⚶ 24♋00.9
☽ Mean ☊ 0♍49.8

1 October 1998
Julian Day # 36068
SVP 5♓16'47"
GC 26♐49.3 ⚴ 19♓08.9R
Eris 19♈00.9R ⚵ 25♎13.0
⚷ 17♏40.2 ⚶ 5♌17.9
☽ Mean ☊ 29♌14.4

November 1998 LONGITUDE

Day	Sid.Time	☉	0 hr ☽	Noon ☽	True ☊	☿	♀	♂	?	♃	♄	♅	♆	♇
1 Su	14 42 17	8♏51 33	23♓00 56	0♈20 13	28♌52.8	29♏46.6	9♏26.9	15♍02.4	11♊59.5	18♓24.5	29♈28.1	8♒53.3	29♑30.4	6♐49.5
2 M	14 46 14	9 51 34	7♈45 43	15 16 39	28R46.8	1♐05.5	10 42.1	15 37.8	11R51.0	18R22.2	29R23.4	8 54.1	29 31.1	6 51.6
3 Tu	14 50 10	10 51 37	22 52 02	0♉30 40	28 38.3	2 23.1	11 57.4	16 13.1	11 42.1	18 20.0	29 18.7	8 54.8	29 31.9	6 53.8
4 W	14 54 07	11 51 42	8♉11 11	15 52 08	28 28.0	3 39.3	13 12.6	16 48.5	11 32.9	18 18.1	29 14.1	8 55.7	29 32.6	6 55.9
5 Th	14 58 04	12 51 48	23 31 59	1♊09 18	28 17.0	4 54.1	14 27.9	17 23.7	11 23.4	18 16.3	29 09.5	8 56.5	29 33.4	6 58.1
6 F	15 02 00	13 51 57	8♊42 41	16 10 58	28 06.9	6 07.2	15 43.1	17 58.9	11 13.5	18 14.8	29 04.9	8 57.5	29 34.3	7 00.3
7 Sa	15 05 57	14 52 08	23 33 09	0♋48 30	27 58.6	7 18.5	16 58.4	18 34.0	11 03.3	18 13.4	29 00.4	8 58.4	29 35.2	7 02.5
8 Su	15 09 53	15 52 20	7♋56 31	14 56 55	27 52.9	8 27.7	18 13.7	19 09.1	10 52.8	18 12.3	28 55.9	8 59.5	29 36.1	7 04.7
9 M	15 13 50	16 52 35	21 49 41	28 34 56	27 49.7	9 34.7	19 28.9	19 44.1	10 42.0	18 11.4	28 51.5	9 00.5	29 37.0	7 07.0
10 Tu	15 17 46	17 52 51	5♌12 59	11♌44 17	27D48.5	10 39.1	20 44.2	20 19.1	10 30.9	18 10.6	28 47.1	9 01.7	29 38.0	7 09.2
11 W	15 21 43	18 53 10	18 09 19	24 28 40	27R48.5	11 40.7	21 59.5	20 54.0	10 19.5	18 10.1	28 42.7	9 02.8	29 39.0	7 11.5
12 Th	15 25 40	19 53 31	0♍43 00	6♍52 54	27 48.3	12 39.0	23 14.8	21 28.8	10 07.8	18 09.8	28 38.4	9 04.1	29 40.0	7 13.7
13 F	15 29 36	20 53 53	12 59 02	19 02 01	27 46.8	13 33.6	24 30.1	22 03.6	9 55.9	18D09.7	28 34.1	9 05.3	29 41.1	7 16.0
14 Sa	15 33 33	21 54 17	25 02 27	1♎00 51	27 42.9	14 24.2	25 45.4	22 38.3	9 43.7	18 09.8	28 29.9	9 06.6	29 42.2	7 18.3
15 Su	15 37 29	22 54 44	6♎57 47	12 53 40	27 36.2	15 10.1	27 00.8	23 12.9	9 31.3	18 10.1	28 25.8	9 08.0	29 43.3	7 20.5
16 M	15 41 26	23 55 12	18 48 56	24 43 58	27 26.4	15 50.9	28 16.1	23 47.5	9 18.7	18 10.6	28 21.7	9 09.4	29 44.5	7 22.8
17 Tu	15 45 22	24 55 41	0♏39 03	6♏34 29	27 13.9	16 25.9	29 31.4	24 21.9	9 05.8	18 11.3	28 17.7	9 10.9	29 45.7	7 25.1
18 W	15 49 19	25 56 13	12 30 29	18 27 14	26 59.5	16 54.4	0♐46.8	24 56.4	8 52.8	18 12.2	28 13.7	9 12.4	29 46.9	7 27.5
19 Th	15 53 15	26 56 46	24 24 55	0♐23 40	26 44.3	17 15.6	2 02.1	25 30.7	8 39.5	18 13.3	28 09.8	9 13.9	29 48.2	7 29.8
20 F	15 57 12	27 57 20	6♐23 36	12 24 53	26 29.6	17R28.9	3 17.4	26 05.0	8 26.2	18 14.7	28 05.9	9 15.6	29 49.4	7 32.1
21 Sa	16 01 08	28 57 56	18 27 36	24 31 57	26 16.6	17 33.4	4 32.8	26 39.1	8 12.6	18 16.2	28 02.2	9 17.2	29 50.7	7 34.4
22 Su	16 05 05	29 58 34	0♑38 04	6♑46 11	26 06.1	17 28.4	5 48.1	27 13.2	7 59.0	18 18.0	27 58.5	9 18.9	29 52.1	7 36.8
23 M	16 09 02	0♐59 12	12 56 31	19 09 21	25 58.7	17 13.4	7 03.5	27 47.3	7 45.2	18 19.9	27 54.9	9 20.6	29 53.4	7 39.1
24 Tu	16 12 58	1 59 52	25 25 00	1♒43 50	25 54.4	16 47.8	8 18.8	28 21.2	7 31.3	18 22.1	27 51.3	9 22.4	29 54.8	7 41.5
25 W	16 16 55	3 00 33	8♒06 13	14 32 36	25D52.6	16 11.4	9 34.2	28 55.1	7 17.4	18 24.5	27 47.9	9 24.3	29 56.3	7 43.8
26 Th	16 20 51	4 01 15	21 03 23	27 39 01	25R52.3	15 24.3	10 49.5	29 28.9	7 03.3	18 27.0	27 44.5	9 26.1	29 57.7	7 46.1
27 F	16 24 48	5 01 58	4♓19 54	11♓06 25	25 52.2	14 27.1	12 04.8	0♎02.6	6 49.3	18 29.8	27 41.2	9 28.1	29 59.2	7 48.5
28 Sa	16 28 44	6 02 42	17 58 52	24 57 27	25 51.1	13 20.7	13 20.2	0 36.2	6 35.2	18 32.7	27 37.9	9 30.0	0♒00.7	7 50.8
29 Su	16 32 41	7 03 27	2♈02 16	9♈13 14	25 47.9	12 06.9	14 35.5	1 09.7	6 21.1	18 35.9	27 34.8	9 32.0	0 02.2	7 53.2
30 M	16 36 37	8 04 13	16 30 06	23 52 24	25 42.0	10 47.5	15 50.8	1 43.1	6 06.9	18 39.2	27 31.7	9 34.1	0 03.7	7 55.5

December 1998 LONGITUDE

Day	Sid.Time	☉	0 hr ☽	Noon ☽	True ☊	☿	♀	♂	?	♃	♄	♅	♆	♇
1 Tu	16 40 34	9♐05 00	1♉19 29	8♉50 26	25♌33.5	9♐25.2	17♐06.2	2♎16.5	5♊52.9	18♓42.8	27♈28.8	9♒36.2	0♒05.3	7♐57.9
2 W	16 44 31	10 05 48	16 24 12	23 59 34	25R23.0	8R02.8	18 21.5	2 49.8	5R38.8	18 46.5	27R25.9	9 38.3	0 06.9	8 00.2
3 Th	16 48 27	11 06 37	1♊35 11	9♊09 42	25 11.7	6 42.9	19 36.8	3 23.0	5 24.8	18 50.4	27 23.1	9 40.5	0 08.6	8 02.6
4 F	16 52 24	12 07 27	16 41 43	24 10 00	25 01.0	5 28.3	20 52.2	3 56.0	5 10.9	18 54.6	27 20.4	9 42.7	0 10.2	8 05.0
5 Sa	16 56 20	13 08 19	1♋33 25	8♋51 01	24 52.1	4 21.1	22 07.5	4 29.1	4 57.0	18 58.9	27 17.8	9 45.0	0 11.9	8 07.3
6 Su	17 00 17	14 09 11	16 02 04	23 06 03	24 45.7	3 23.2	23 22.8	5 02.0	4 43.3	19 03.4	27 15.3	9 47.3	0 13.6	8 09.6
7 M	17 04 13	15 10 05	0♌02 42	6♌51 55	24 42.1	2 35.9	24 38.1	5 34.8	4 29.7	19 08.1	27 12.9	9 49.6	0 15.3	8 12.0
8 Tu	17 08 10	16 11 00	13 33 50	20 08 42	24D40.7	1 59.7	25 53.5	6 07.5	4 16.2	19 12.9	27 10.6	9 52.0	0 17.0	8 14.3
9 W	17 12 07	17 11 56	26 36 55	2♍59 00	24 40.8	1 34.9	27 08.8	6 40.1	4 02.8	19 18.0	27 08.4	9 54.4	0 18.8	8 16.7
10 Th	17 16 03	18 12 54	9♍15 29	15 27 02	24R41.3	1D21.3	28 24.1	7 12.6	3 49.6	19 23.2	27 06.2	9 56.8	0 20.6	8 19.0
11 F	17 20 00	19 13 52	21 34 17	27 37 55	24 40.9	1 18.5	29 39.4	7 45.1	3 36.6	19 28.6	27 04.2	9 59.3	0 22.4	8 21.3
12 Sa	17 23 56	20 14 52	3♎38 34	9♎36 55	24 38.8	1 25.7	0♑54.8	8 17.4	3 23.8	19 34.2	27 02.3	10 01.8	0 24.2	8 23.6
13 Su	17 27 53	21 15 53	15 33 33	21 29 05	24 34.3	1 42.3	2 10.1	8 49.6	3 11.2	19 40.0	27 00.5	10 04.4	0 26.1	8 25.9
14 M	17 31 49	22 16 54	27 24 04	3♏18 59	24 27.2	2 07.3	3 25.4	9 21.7	2 58.8	19 45.9	26 58.8	10 07.0	0 28.0	8 28.2
15 Tu	17 35 46	23 17 57	9♏14 18	15 10 24	24 17.7	2 40.0	4 40.8	9 53.6	2 46.7	19 52.0	26 57.2	10 09.6	0 29.9	8 30.5
16 W	17 39 42	24 19 01	21 07 39	27 06 20	24 06.4	3 19.5	5 56.1	10 25.5	2 34.8	19 58.3	26 55.7	10 12.3	0 31.8	8 32.8
17 Th	17 43 39	25 20 05	3♐06 42	9♐08 57	23 54.4	4 05.0	7 11.4	10 57.3	2 23.2	20 04.8	26 54.3	10 15.0	0 33.7	8 35.1
18 F	17 47 36	26 21 10	15 13 13	21 19 38	23 42.7	4 55.9	8 26.7	11 28.9	2 11.8	20 11.4	26 53.0	10 17.7	0 35.6	8 37.4
19 Sa	17 51 32	27 22 16	27 28 18	3♑39 16	23 32.4	5 51.5	9 42.1	12 00.4	2 00.8	20 18.2	26 51.8	10 20.4	0 37.6	8 39.6
20 Su	17 55 29	28 23 23	9♑52 37	16 08 23	23 24.2	6 51.3	10 57.4	12 31.8	1 50.0	20 25.1	26 50.7	10 23.2	0 39.6	8 41.9
21 M	17 59 25	29 24 30	22 28 22	28 47 28	23 18.6	7 54.7	12 12.7	13 03.0	1 39.6	20 32.3	26 49.8	10 26.1	0 41.6	8 44.1
22 Tu	18 03 22	0♑25 37	5♒10 57	11♒37 15	23D15.7	9 01.4	13 28.0	13 34.2	1 29.5	20 39.6	26 48.9	10 28.9	0 43.6	8 46.4
23 W	18 07 18	1 26 45	18 06 29	24 38 50	23 14.9	10 10.8	14 43.3	14 05.2	1 19.7	20 47.0	26 48.2	10 31.8	0 45.7	8 48.6
24 Th	18 11 15	2 27 52	1♓14 30	7♓53 42	23 15.7	11 22.7	15 58.6	14 36.0	1 10.3	20 54.6	26 47.6	10 34.7	0 47.7	8 50.8
25 F	18 15 11	3 29 00	14 36 38	21 23 32	23R16.8	12 36.8	17 13.9	15 06.7	1 01.2	21 02.4	26 47.0	10 37.7	0 49.8	8 53.0
26 Sa	18 19 08	4 30 08	28 14 34	5♈09 52	23 17.4	13 52.7	18 29.1	15 37.3	0 52.5	21 10.3	26 46.6	10 40.6	0 51.9	8 55.1
27 Su	18 23 05	5 31 16	12♈09 30	19 13 27	23 16.4	15 10.4	19 44.4	16 07.8	0 44.1	21 18.3	26 46.3	10 43.6	0 54.0	8 57.3
28 M	18 27 01	6 32 23	26 21 34	3♉33 37	23 13.5	16 29.6	20 59.7	16 38.0	0 36.1	21 26.5	26 46.1	10 46.6	0 56.1	8 59.5
29 Tu	18 30 58	7 33 31	10♉49 12	18 07 47	23 08.6	17 50.0	22 14.9	17 08.2	0 28.5	21 34.9	26D46.1	10 49.7	0 58.2	9 01.6
30 W	18 34 54	8 34 39	25 28 40	2♊51 05	23 02.2	19 11.7	23 30.1	17 38.2	0 21.3	21 43.4	26 46.1	10 52.8	1 00.3	9 03.7
31 Th	18 38 51	9 35 47	10♊14 07	17 36 47	22 55.0	20 34.5	24 45.4	18 08.1	0 14.5	21 52.0	26 46.3	10 55.9	1 02.5	9 05.8

Astro Data	Planet Ingress	Last Aspect	☽ Ingress	Last Aspect	☽ Ingress	☽ Phases & Eclipses
Dy Hr Mn	Dy Hr Mn	Dy Hr Mn	Dy Hr Mn	Dy Hr Mn	Dy Hr Mn	Dy Hr Mn
♄□♆ 1 1:36	☿ ♐ 1 16:02	1 11:00 ♆ △	♈ 1 11:27	2 3:43 ♃ ⚹	♊ 2 21:30	4 5:18 ○ 11♉35
☽0N 1 23:12	♀ ♐ 17 21:06	3 10:28 ♆ □	♉ 3 11:12	4 17:07 ♄ ⚹	♋ 4 21:28	11 0:28 ☾ 18♌24
♃D 13 13:02	☉ ♐ 22 12:34	5 9:29 ♆ △	♊ 5 10:11	6 19:08 ♄ □	♌ 6 23:55	19 4:27 ● 26♏38
☽0S 15 0:59	♂ ♎ 27 10:10	7 9:01 ♄ ⚹	♋ 7 10:39	9 1:01 ♄ △	♍ 9 6:21	27 0:23 ☽ 4♓33
☿R 21 11:46	♆ ♒ 28 1:19	9 13:52 ♆ ☍	♌ 9 14:33	11 16:30 ♀ □	♎ 11 16:43	
☽0N 29 9:39		11 20:05 ♄ △	♍ 11 22:37	13 23:10 ♄ ☍	♏ 14 5:16	3 15:19 ○ 11♊15
	♀ ♑ 11 18:33	14 9:21 ♆ △	♎ 14 9:58	15 21:33 ♃ △	♐ 16 17:47	10 17:54 ☾ 18♍28
♂0S 4 13:44	☉ ♑ 22 1:56	16 22:10 ♆ □	♏ 16 22:41	18 22:50 ♄ △	♑ 19 4:55	18 22:42 ● 26♐48
☿D 11 6:29		19 10:49 ♆ ⚹	♐ 19 11:13	21 8:18 ♄ □	♒ 21 14:17	26 10:46 ☽ 4♈27
☽0S 12 8:56		21 18:52 ♄ △	♑ 21 22:45	23 15:56 ♄ ⚹	♓ 23 21:45	
☽0N 26 17:41		24 8:33 ♆ ☌	♒ 24 8:43	25 11:22 ♃ ☌	♈ 26 3:03	
♄D 29 15:45		26 12:10 ♄ ⚹	♓ 26 16:14	28 0:41 ♄ ☌	♉ 28 6:05	
		28 0:56 ♃ ☌	♈ 28 20:34	29 19:22 ♀ △	♊ 30 7:22	
		30 17:53 ♄ ☌	♉ 30 21:52			

Astro Data

1 November 1998
Julian Day # 36099
SVP 5♓16'45"
GC 26♐49.4 ⚳ 13♓55.3R
Eris 18♈42.5R ⚵ 5♏56.3
⚷ 21♏33.3 ⚶ 15♌04.0
☽ Mean ☊ 27♌35.9

1 December 1998
Julian Day # 36129
SVP 5♓16'41"
GC 26♐49.4 ⚳ 14♓29.7
Eris 18♈28.1R ⚵ 16♏09.3
⚷ 25♏32.9 ⚶ 21♌12.7
☽ Mean ☊ 26♌00.6

LONGITUDE — January 1999

Day	Sid.Time	☉	0 hr ☽	Noon ☽	True ☊	☿	♀	♂	⚳	♃	♄	♅	♆	♇
1 F	18 42 47	10♑36 55	24♊58 05	2♋17 01	22♌48.1	21♐58.2	26♑00.6	18♎37.8	0♊08.1	22♓00.8	26♈46.5	10♒59.0	1♒04.6	9♐07.9
2 Sa	18 46 44	11 38 02	9♋32 40	16 44 09	22R 42.4	23 22.8	27 15.8	19 07.3	0R 02.0	22 09.8	26 46.9	11 02.1	1 06.8	9 10.0
3 Su	18 50 40	12 39 10	23 50 44	0♌51 51	22 38.5	24 48.1	28 31.0	19 36.7	29♉56.4	22 18.8	26 47.4	11 05.3	1 09.0	9 12.0
4 M	18 54 37	13 40 18	7♌47 03	14 36 04	22D 36.5	26 14.3	29 46.2	20 06.0	29 51.2	22 28.0	26 48.0	11 08.5	1 11.2	9 14.1
5 Tu	18 58 34	14 41 26	21 18 47	27 55 14	22 36.3	27 41.1	1♒01.3	20 35.0	29 46.4	22 37.3	26 48.7	11 11.7	1 13.3	9 16.1
6 W	19 02 30	15 42 35	4♍25 36	10♍50 08	22 37.4	29 08.5	2 16.5	21 03.9	29 41.9	22 46.8	26 49.5	11 14.9	1 15.6	9 18.1
7 Th	19 06 27	16 43 43	17 09 15	23 23 24	22 39.2	0♑36.5	3 31.6	21 32.7	29 37.9	22 56.4	26 50.4	11 18.2	1 17.8	9 20.1
8 F	19 10 23	17 44 51	29 33 07	5♎38 57	22 40.7	2 05.2	4 46.8	22 01.2	29 34.3	23 06.1	26 51.5	11 21.4	1 20.0	9 22.0
9 Sa	19 14 20	18 46 00	11♎41 32	17 41 29	22R 41.4	3 34.3	6 01.9	22 29.6	29 31.1	23 16.0	26 52.6	11 24.7	1 22.2	9 24.0
10 Su	19 18 16	19 47 08	23 39 24	29 35 57	22 40.9	5 04.0	7 17.0	22 57.8	29 28.4	23 25.9	26 53.9	11 28.0	1 24.5	9 25.9
11 M	19 22 13	20 48 17	5♏31 44	11♏27 20	22 38.8	6 34.3	8 32.2	23 25.8	29 26.0	23 36.0	26 55.2	11 31.4	1 26.7	9 27.8
12 Tu	19 26 09	21 49 26	17 23 20	23 20 15	22 35.3	8 05.0	9 47.3	23 53.6	29 24.1	23 46.2	26 56.7	11 34.7	1 29.0	9 29.6
13 W	19 30 06	22 50 34	29 18 35	5♐18 46	22 30.7	9 36.2	11 02.4	24 21.2	29 22.5	23 56.6	26 58.3	11 38.0	1 31.2	9 31.5
14 Th	19 34 03	23 51 43	11♐21 13	17 26 16	22 25.6	11 08.0	12 17.4	24 48.7	29 21.4	24 07.0	27 00.0	11 41.4	1 33.5	9 33.3
15 F	19 37 59	24 52 51	23 34 12	29 45 15	22 20.4	12 40.2	13 32.5	25 15.9	29 20.7	24 17.6	27 01.8	11 44.8	1 35.7	9 35.1
16 Sa	19 41 56	25 53 59	5♑59 35	12♑17 19	22 15.9	14 13.0	14 47.6	25 42.9	29D 20.4	24 28.3	27 03.7	11 48.2	1 38.0	9 36.9
17 Su	19 45 52	26 55 06	18 38 31	25 03 12	22 12.5	15 46.3	16 02.6	26 09.6	29 20.6	24 39.1	27 05.7	11 51.6	1 40.3	9 38.7
18 M	19 49 49	27 56 13	1♒31 20	8♒02 52	22 10.4	17 20.0	17 17.6	26 36.2	29 21.1	24 50.0	27 07.8	11 55.0	1 42.6	9 40.4
19 Tu	19 53 45	28 57 19	14 37 43	21 15 46	22D 09.7	18 54.3	18 32.6	27 02.5	29 22.1	25 01.0	27 10.1	11 58.4	1 44.8	9 42.2
20 W	19 57 42	29 58 25	27 56 54	4♓40 58	22 10.1	20 29.2	19 47.6	27 28.6	29 23.4	25 12.1	27 12.4	12 01.9	1 47.1	9 43.8
21 Th	20 01 38	0♒59 30	11♓27 53	18 17 28	22 11.3	22 04.6	21 02.6	27 54.4	29 25.2	25 23.3	27 14.9	12 05.3	1 49.4	9 45.5
22 F	20 05 35	2 00 34	25 09 38	2♈04 15	22 12.8	23 40.5	22 17.5	28 20.1	29 27.4	25 34.6	27 17.4	12 08.8	1 51.7	9 47.1
23 Sa	20 09 32	3 01 36	9♈01 12	16 00 20	22 14.1	25 17.0	23 32.4	28 45.4	29 29.9	25 46.0	27 20.1	12 12.2	1 53.9	9 48.7
24 Su	20 13 28	4 02 38	23 01 30	0♉04 34	22R 14.8	26 54.1	24 47.3	29 10.5	29 32.9	25 57.6	27 22.8	12 15.7	1 56.2	9 50.3
25 M	20 17 25	5 03 39	7♉09 19	14 15 31	22 14.6	28 31.8	26 02.2	29 35.4	29 36.2	26 09.2	27 25.7	12 19.2	1 58.5	9 51.9
26 Tu	20 21 21	6 04 39	21 22 53	28 31 06	22 13.6	0♒10.1	27 17.1	0♏00.0	29 40.0	26 20.9	27 28.6	12 22.7	2 00.8	9 53.4
27 W	20 25 18	7 05 37	5♊39 48	12♊48 33	22 12.0	1 49.1	28 31.9	0 24.4	29 44.1	26 32.7	27 31.7	12 26.2	2 03.0	9 54.9
28 Th	20 29 14	8 06 35	19 56 52	27 04 16	22 10.1	3 28.7	29 46.7	0 48.4	29 48.6	26 44.6	27 34.8	12 29.7	2 05.3	9 56.4
29 F	20 33 11	9 07 31	4♋10 13	11♋14 10	22 08.3	5 08.9	1♓01.4	1 12.2	29 53.5	26 56.6	27 38.1	12 33.2	2 07.6	9 57.8
30 Sa	20 37 07	10 08 27	18 15 37	25 14 02	22 06.8	6 49.9	2 16.2	1 35.8	29 58.8	27 08.6	27 41.5	12 36.7	2 09.9	9 59.3
31 Su	20 41 04	11 09 21	2♌08 58	9♌00 00	22D 05.9	8 31.5	3 30.9	1 59.0	0♊04.4	27 20.8	27 44.9	12 40.2	2 12.1	10 00.6

LONGITUDE — February 1999

Day	Sid.Time	☉	0 hr ☽	Noon ☽	True ☊	☿	♀	♂	⚳	♃	♄	♅	♆	♇
1 M	20 45 01	12♒10 14	15♌46 48	22♌29 06	22♌05.7	10♒13.8	4♓45.6	2♏21.9	0♊10.3	27♓33.0	27♈48.4	12♒43.7	2♒14.4	10♐02.0
2 Tu	20 48 57	13 11 06	29 06 43	5♍39 34	22 05.9	11 56.8	6 00.2	2 44.6	0 16.7	27 45.3	27 52.1	12 47.1	2 16.6	10 03.3
3 W	20 52 54	14 11 58	12♍07 38	18 31 01	22 06.5	13 40.5	7 14.9	3 06.9	0 23.4	27 57.7	27 55.8	12 50.6	2 18.9	10 04.6
4 Th	20 56 50	15 12 48	24 49 53	1♎04 29	22 07.3	15 25.0	8 29.5	3 29.0	0 30.4	28 10.2	27 59.6	12 54.1	2 21.1	10 05.9
5 F	21 00 47	16 13 37	7♎15 07	13 22 12	22 08.0	17 10.1	9 44.0	3 50.7	0 37.8	28 22.8	28 03.6	12 57.6	2 23.3	10 07.1
6 Sa	21 04 43	17 14 26	19 26 09	25 27 27	22 08.6	18 56.0	10 58.6	4 12.0	0 45.5	28 35.4	28 07.6	13 01.1	2 25.6	10 08.4
7 Su	21 08 40	18 15 13	1♏26 37	7♏24 13	22 08.9	20 42.5	12 13.1	4 33.1	0 53.5	28 48.1	28 11.7	13 04.6	2 27.8	10 09.5
8 M	21 12 36	19 16 00	13 20 49	19 17 00	22R 09.0	22 29.7	13 27.6	4 53.8	1 01.9	29 00.9	28 15.8	13 08.1	2 30.0	10 10.7
9 Tu	21 16 33	20 16 45	25 13 22	1♐10 31	22 08.9	24 17.5	14 42.0	5 14.1	1 10.6	29 13.7	28 20.1	13 11.6	2 32.2	10 11.8
10 W	21 20 30	21 17 30	7♐09 02	13 09 28	22D 08.8	26 05.9	15 56.5	5 34.1	1 19.7	29 26.7	28 24.5	13 15.1	2 34.4	10 12.9
11 Th	21 24 26	22 18 13	19 12 23	25 18 06	22 08.8	27 54.8	17 10.9	5 53.7	1 29.1	29 39.6	28 28.9	13 18.5	2 36.5	10 13.9
12 F	21 28 23	23 18 56	1♑27 36	7♑40 47	22 08.9	29 44.2	18 25.2	6 12.9	1 38.7	29 52.7	28 33.5	13 22.0	2 38.7	10 14.9
13 Sa	21 32 19	24 19 37	13 58 11	20 20 04	22 09.1	1♓33.9	19 39.5	6 31.8	1 48.7	0♈05.8	28 38.1	13 25.5	2 40.9	10 15.9
14 Su	21 36 16	25 20 17	26 46 40	3♒18 07	22 09.3	3 23.9	20 53.8	6 50.2	1 59.0	0 19.0	28 42.8	13 28.9	2 43.0	10 16.9
15 M	21 40 12	26 20 56	9♒54 25	16 35 33	22R 09.5	5 14.0	22 08.1	7 08.2	2 09.6	0 32.2	28 47.6	13 32.4	2 45.2	10 17.8
16 Tu	21 44 09	27 21 33	23 21 22	0♓11 38	22 09.5	7 04.0	23 22.3	7 25.9	2 20.5	0 45.6	28 52.4	13 35.8	2 47.3	10 18.7
17 W	21 48 05	28 22 09	7♓06 03	14 04 11	22 09.2	8 53.7	24 36.5	7 43.0	2 31.7	0 58.9	28 57.4	13 39.2	2 49.4	10 19.6
18 Th	21 52 02	29 22 43	21 05 37	28 09 51	22 08.5	10 42.9	25 50.6	7 59.8	2 43.2	1 12.3	29 02.4	13 42.6	2 51.5	10 20.4
19 F	21 55 59	0♓23 15	5♈16 19	12♈24 29	22 07.5	12 31.3	27 04.7	8 16.1	2 55.0	1 25.8	29 07.5	13 46.0	2 53.6	10 21.2
20 Sa	21 59 55	1 23 46	19 33 47	26 43 40	22 06.5	14 18.6	28 18.8	8 31.9	3 07.0	1 39.3	29 12.7	13 49.4	2 55.6	10 21.9
21 Su	22 03 52	2 24 15	3♉53 39	11♉03 14	22 05.5	16 04.5	29 32.8	8 47.3	3 19.4	1 52.9	29 18.0	13 52.8	2 57.7	10 22.6
22 M	22 07 48	3 24 42	18 12 00	25 19 34	22D 04.9	17 48.5	0♈46.8	9 02.2	3 32.0	2 06.6	29 23.3	13 56.1	2 59.7	10 23.3
23 Tu	22 11 45	4 25 07	2♊25 38	9♊29 53	22 04.9	19 30.2	2 00.7	9 16.7	3 44.8	2 20.2	29 28.7	13 59.5	3 01.7	10 24.0
24 W	22 15 41	5 25 30	16 32 07	23 32 08	22 05.4	21 09.0	3 14.6	9 30.6	3 58.0	2 34.0	29 34.2	14 02.8	3 03.7	10 24.6
25 Th	22 19 38	6 25 51	0♋29 46	7♋24 53	22 06.4	22 44.5	4 28.4	9 44.1	4 11.4	2 47.7	29 39.7	14 06.1	3 05.7	10 25.2
26 F	22 23 34	7 26 11	14 17 21	21 07 06	22 07.6	24 16.0	5 42.2	9 57.0	4 25.0	3 01.6	29 45.3	14 09.4	3 07.7	10 25.7
27 Sa	22 27 31	8 26 28	27 53 59	4♌37 56	22 08.8	25 43.0	6 55.9	10 09.5	4 38.9	3 15.4	29 51.0	14 12.7	3 09.7	10 26.2
28 Su	22 31 28	9 26 43	11♌18 51	17 56 39	22R 09.4	27 04.9	8 09.6	10 21.4	4 53.0	3 29.3	29 56.8	14 15.9	3 11.6	10 26.7

Astro Data

	Dy Hr Mn
☽ 0S	8 18:03
⚳ D	16 16:16
☽ 0N	22 23:46
♃∠♅	2 16:53
♃⊻♄	3 6:40
☽ 0S	5 3:20
☽ 0N	19 6:10
♀0N	23 16:56
♃0N	24 11:41
♃⚹♆	27 0:24
☿0N	28 21:15

Planet Ingress

		Dy Hr Mn
⚳	♉R	2 20:31
♀	♒	4 16:25
☿	♑	7 2:04
☉	♒	20 12:37
☿	♒	26 9:32
♂	♏	26 11:59
♀	♓	28 16:17
⚳	♊	30 17:28
☿	♓	12 15:28
♃	♈	13 1:23
☉	♓	19 2:47
♀	♈	21 20:49

Last Aspect / ☽ Ingress (January)

Last Aspect Dy Hr Mn			☽ Ingress	Dy Hr Mn
1 2:57	♄	⚹	♋	1 8:15
3 7:34	♀	☍	♌	3 10:31
5 11:31	☿	△	♍	5 15:49
7 11:07	♃	☍	♎	8 0:53
10 6:32	♄	☍	♏	10 12:49
12 12:53	♃	△	♐	13 1:23
15 6:43	♄	△	♑	15 12:29
17 15:49	♄	□	♒	17 21:11
19 22:44	♂	△	♓	20 3:40
22 0:34	♃	☌	♈	22 8:25
24 10:25	♂	☍	♉	24 11:52
26 9:44	♀	□	♊	26 14:29
28 12:52	♄	⚹	♋	28 16:57
30 16:16	♄	□	♌	30 20:16

Last Aspect / ☽ Ingress (February)

Last Aspect Dy Hr Mn			☽ Ingress	Dy Hr Mn
1 21:40	♄	△	♍	2 1:37
4 6:18	♃	☍	♎	4 9:56
6 17:22	♄	☍	♏	6 21:06
9 8:00	♃	△	♐	9 9:38
11 20:39	♃	□	♑	11 21:10
14 3:31	♄	□	♒	14 5:57
16 9:41	♄	⚹	♓	16 11:40
18 7:42	♀	☌	♈	18 15:06
20 16:11	♄	☌	♉	20 17:29
21 21:36	☿	⚹	♊	22 19:54
24 22:28	♄	⚹	♋	24 23:09
27 3:24	♄	□	♌	27 3:44

☽ Phases & Eclipses

Dy Hr Mn	
2 2:50	○ 11♋15
9 14:22	☾ 18♎52
17 15:46	● 27♑05
24 19:15	☽ 4♉21
31 16:07	○ 11♌20
31 16:17	A 1.003
8 11:58	☾ 19♏16
16 6:39	● 27♒08
16 6:33:34	A 00'39"
23 2:43	☽ 4♊02

Astro Data

1 January 1999
Julian Day # 36160
SVP 5♓16'35"
GC 26♐49.5 ⚵ 20♓05.5
Eris 18♈21.4R ⚶ 25♏59.4
⚷ 29♏21.3 ⚴ 21♌51.2R
☽ Mean ☊ 24♌22.1

1 February 1999
Julian Day # 36191
SVP 5♓16'30"
GC 26♐49.6 ⚵ 29♓07.4
Eris 18♈25.1 ⚶ 4♐19.7
⚷ 2♐15.8 ⚴ 15♌47.5R
☽ Mean ☊ 22♌43.6

March 1999 — LONGITUDE

Day	Sid.Time	☉	0 hr ☽	Noon ☽	True ☊	☿	♀	♂	⚳	♃	♄	♅	♆	♇
1 M	22 35 24	10♓26 57	24♌31 15	1♍02 34	22♌09.2	28♓21.0	9♈23.2	10♏32.7	5♊07.4	3♈43.2	0♉02.6	14♒19.2	3♒13.5	10♐27.2
2 Tu	22 39 21	11 27 09	7♍30 34	13 55 13	22R 08.0	29 30.7	10 36.7	10 43.6	5 22.0	3 57.2	0 08.4	14 22.4	3 15.4	10 27.6
3 W	22 43 17	12 27 18	20 16 30	26 34 28	22 05.8	0♈33.6	11 50.2	10 53.8	5 36.9	4 11.2	0 14.4	14 25.6	3 17.3	10 28.0
4 Th	22 47 14	13 27 27	2♎49 10	9♎00 42	22 02.7	1 28.9	13 03.7	11 03.5	5 51.9	4 25.3	0 20.4	14 28.7	3 19.1	10 28.3
5 F	22 51 10	14 27 33	15 09 16	21 15 02	21 59.0	2 16.4	14 17.1	11 12.6	6 07.2	4 39.4	0 26.5	14 31.9	3 21.0	10 28.6
6 Sa	22 55 07	15 27 38	27 18 16	3♏19 17	21 55.1	2 55.4	15 30.4	11 21.1	6 22.7	4 53.5	0 32.6	14 35.0	3 22.8	10 28.9
7 Su	22 59 03	16 27 41	9♏18 27	15 16 09	21 51.5	3 25.8	16 43.7	11 29.0	6 38.5	5 07.6	0 38.8	14 38.1	3 24.6	10 29.1
8 M	23 03 00	17 27 42	21 12 50	27 09 00	21 48.8	3 47.3	17 56.9	11 36.3	6 54.4	5 21.8	0 45.0	14 41.2	3 26.4	10 29.3
9 Tu	23 06 56	18 27 42	3♐05 10	9♐01 53	21D 47.1	3R 59.8	19 10.1	11 42.9	7 10.6	5 36.0	0 51.3	14 44.3	3 28.1	10 29.5
10 W	23 10 53	19 27 41	14 59 45	20 59 20	21 46.7	4 03.2	20 23.3	11 48.9	7 26.9	5 50.3	0 57.7	14 47.3	3 29.8	10 29.6
11 Th	23 14 50	20 27 37	27 01 15	3♑06 07	21 47.4	3 57.7	21 36.3	11 54.2	7 43.5	6 04.5	1 04.1	14 50.3	3 31.6	10 29.7
12 F	23 18 46	21 27 33	9♑14 31	15 27 01	21 48.8	3 43.7	22 49.3	11 58.9	8 00.3	6 18.8	1 10.5	14 53.3	3 33.2	10 29.8
13 Sa	23 22 43	22 27 26	21 44 10	28 06 27	21 50.6	3 21.5	24 02.3	12 02.9	8 17.2	6 33.2	1 17.1	14 56.3	3 34.9	10R 29.8
14 Su	23 26 39	23 27 18	4♒34 17	11♒08 01	21R 51.9	2 51.7	25 15.2	12 06.2	8 34.4	6 47.5	1 23.6	14 59.2	3 36.5	10 29.8
15 M	23 30 36	24 27 08	17 47 53	24 33 59	21 52.3	2 15.2	26 28.0	12 08.7	8 51.7	7 01.9	1 30.2	15 02.1	3 38.2	10 29.8
16 Tu	23 34 32	25 26 56	1♓26 19	8♓24 43	21 51.2	1 32.7	27 40.8	12 10.6	9 09.3	7 16.2	1 36.9	15 05.0	3 39.7	10 29.7
17 W	23 38 29	26 26 42	15 28 51	22 38 14	21 48.5	0 45.4	28 53.5	12 11.8	9 27.0	7 30.6	1 43.6	15 07.8	3 41.3	10 29.6
18 Th	23 42 25	27 26 26	29 52 15	7♈10 08	21 44.1	29♓54.3	0♉06.1	12R 12.2	9 44.9	7 45.1	1 50.4	15 10.7	3 42.8	10 29.4
19 F	23 46 22	28 26 08	14♈30 59	21 53 52	21 38.7	29 00.6	1 18.7	12 11.9	10 03.0	7 59.5	1 57.2	15 13.4	3 44.4	10 29.3
20 Sa	23 50 19	29 25 48	29 17 45	6♉41 39	21 32.9	28 05.5	2 31.2	12 10.8	10 21.3	8 14.0	2 04.0	15 16.2	3 45.8	10 29.1
21 Su	23 54 15	0♈25 26	14♉04 36	21 25 42	21 27.6	27 10.3	3 43.6	12 09.0	10 39.7	8 28.4	2 10.9	15 18.9	3 47.3	10 28.8
22 M	23 58 12	1 25 01	28 44 10	5♊59 21	21 23.6	26 16.0	4 56.0	12 06.4	10 58.3	8 42.9	2 17.9	15 21.6	3 48.7	10 28.5
23 Tu	0 02 08	2 24 35	13♊10 44	20 17 56	21D 21.2	25 23.8	6 08.3	12 03.1	11 17.1	8 57.4	2 24.8	15 24.3	3 50.2	10 28.2
24 W	0 06 05	3 24 06	27 20 43	4♋18 57	21 20.5	24 34.4	7 20.5	11 59.1	11 36.0	9 11.9	2 31.9	15 26.9	3 51.5	10 27.9
25 Th	0 10 01	4 23 34	11♋12 39	18 01 52	21 21.2	23 48.9	8 32.6	11 54.2	11 55.1	9 26.4	2 38.9	15 29.5	3 52.9	10 27.5
26 F	0 13 58	5 23 01	24 46 45	1♌27 30	21 22.6	23 07.8	9 44.6	11 48.6	12 14.4	9 40.9	2 46.0	15 32.0	3 54.2	10 27.1
27 Sa	0 17 54	6 22 25	8♌04 19	14 37 27	21R 23.7	22 31.6	10 56.6	11 42.3	12 33.8	9 55.4	2 53.1	15 34.6	3 55.5	10 26.7
28 Su	0 21 51	7 21 47	21 07 07	27 33 33	21 23.7	22 00.8	12 08.5	11 35.1	12 53.4	10 09.9	3 00.3	15 37.0	3 56.8	10 26.2
29 M	0 25 48	8 21 06	3♍56 58	10♍17 31	21 21.9	21 35.5	13 20.3	11 27.2	13 13.1	10 24.4	3 07.5	15 39.5	3 58.0	10 25.7
30 Tu	0 29 44	9 20 23	16 35 23	22 50 43	21 17.8	21 16.1	14 32.0	11 18.6	13 32.9	10 39.0	3 14.7	15 41.9	3 59.2	10 25.2
31 W	0 33 41	10 19 38	29 03 37	5♎14 13	21 11.5	21 02.4	15 43.6	11 09.2	13 52.9	10 53.5	3 21.9	15 44.3	4 00.4	10 24.6

April 1999 — LONGITUDE

Day	Sid.Time	☉	0 hr ☽	Noon ☽	True ☊	☿	♀	♂	⚳	♃	♄	♅	♆	♇
1 Th	0 37 37	11♈18 51	11♎22 36	17♎28 54	21♌03.1	20♓54.5	16♉55.2	10♏59.0	14♊13.0	11♈08.0	3♉29.2	15♒46.6	4♒01.6	10♐24.0
2 F	0 41 34	12 18 02	23 33 12	29 35 39	20R 53.5	20D 52.3	18 06.7	10R 48.1	14 33.3	11 22.5	3 36.5	15 48.9	4 02.7	10R 23.4
3 Sa	0 45 30	13 17 11	5♏36 24	11♏35 38	20 43.3	20 55.7	19 18.0	10 36.4	14 53.7	11 37.0	3 43.9	15 51.2	4 03.8	10 22.7
4 Su	0 49 27	14 16 19	17 33 35	23 30 29	20 33.6	21 04.5	20 29.3	10 24.0	15 14.2	11 51.5	3 51.2	15 53.4	4 04.8	10 22.0
5 M	0 53 23	15 15 24	29 26 40	5♐22 28	20 25.3	21 18.4	21 40.5	10 10.9	15 34.9	12 06.1	3 58.6	15 55.6	4 05.9	10 21.3
6 Tu	0 57 20	16 14 28	11♐18 18	17 14 36	20 18.9	21 37.4	22 51.6	9 57.0	15 55.6	12 20.6	4 06.1	15 57.7	4 06.9	10 20.5
7 W	1 01 17	17 13 29	23 11 51	29 10 35	20 14.8	22 01.1	24 02.6	9 42.5	16 16.6	12 35.1	4 13.5	15 59.8	4 07.9	10 19.8
8 Th	1 05 13	18 12 29	5♑11 23	11♑14 49	20D 12.9	22 29.3	25 13.5	9 27.2	16 37.6	12 49.6	4 21.0	16 01.9	4 08.8	10 19.0
9 F	1 09 10	19 11 28	17 21 32	23 32 08	20 12.8	23 01.8	26 24.3	9 11.3	16 58.8	13 04.0	4 28.4	16 03.9	4 09.7	10 18.1
10 Sa	1 13 06	20 10 24	29 47 16	6♒07 31	20 13.4	23 38.5	27 35.1	8 54.8	17 20.1	13 18.5	4 35.9	16 05.9	4 10.6	10 17.3
11 Su	1 17 03	21 09 19	12♒33 29	19 05 40	20R 14.0	24 19.0	28 45.7	8 37.6	17 41.5	13 33.0	4 43.5	16 07.8	4 11.4	10 16.4
12 M	1 20 59	22 08 12	25 44 31	2♓30 21	20 13.3	25 03.3	29 56.2	8 19.8	18 03.0	13 47.4	4 51.0	16 09.7	4 12.3	10 15.5
13 Tu	1 24 56	23 07 03	9♓23 23	16 23 37	20 10.6	25 51.0	1♊06.7	8 01.4	18 24.6	14 01.8	4 58.6	16 11.6	4 13.0	10 14.5
14 W	1 28 52	24 05 52	23 30 55	0♈44 55	20 05.5	26 42.1	2 17.0	7 42.5	18 46.4	14 16.3	5 06.1	16 13.4	4 13.8	10 13.5
15 Th	1 32 49	25 04 40	8♈05 03	15 30 31	19 57.9	27 36.3	3 27.2	7 23.0	19 08.2	14 30.7	5 13.7	16 15.2	4 14.5	10 12.5
16 F	1 36 45	26 03 25	23 00 20	0♉33 19	19 48.6	28 33.6	4 37.4	7 03.1	19 30.2	14 45.0	5 21.3	16 16.9	4 15.2	10 11.5
17 Sa	1 40 42	27 02 09	8♉08 13	15 43 40	19 38.5	29 33.7	5 47.4	6 42.7	19 52.3	14 59.4	5 28.9	16 18.6	4 15.9	10 10.5
18 Su	1 44 39	28 00 51	23 18 20	0♊50 55	19 29.0	0♈36.6	6 57.3	6 22.0	20 14.5	15 13.7	5 36.6	16 20.2	4 16.5	10 09.4
19 M	1 48 35	28 59 30	8♊20 15	15 45 21	19 21.2	1 42.2	8 07.1	6 00.8	20 36.8	15 28.1	5 44.2	16 21.8	4 17.1	10 08.3
20 Tu	1 52 32	29 58 08	23 05 22	0♋19 44	19 15.7	2 50.2	9 16.8	5 39.4	20 59.2	15 42.4	5 51.8	16 23.3	4 17.6	10 07.2
21 W	1 56 28	0♉56 43	7♋28 02	14 30 04	19 12.7	4 00.7	10 26.3	5 17.6	21 21.7	15 56.6	5 59.5	16 24.8	4 18.2	10 06.0
22 Th	2 00 25	1 55 16	21 25 49	28 15 23	19D 11.7	5 13.6	11 35.7	4 55.7	21 44.2	16 10.9	6 07.2	16 26.3	4 18.7	10 04.9
23 F	2 04 21	2 53 47	4♌59 01	11♌37 03	19R 11.8	6 28.7	12 45.0	4 33.5	22 06.9	16 25.1	6 14.8	16 27.7	4 19.1	10 03.7
24 Sa	2 08 18	3 52 15	18 09 52	24 37 53	19 11.8	7 46.0	13 54.2	4 11.2	22 29.7	16 39.3	6 22.5	16 29.1	4 19.5	10 02.5
25 Su	2 12 14	4 50 41	1♍01 34	7♍21 21	19 10.6	9 05.4	15 03.3	3 48.8	22 52.6	16 53.4	6 30.1	16 30.4	4 19.9	10 01.2
26 M	2 16 11	5 49 06	13 37 39	19 50 52	19 07.1	10 27.0	16 12.2	3 26.3	23 15.5	17 07.5	6 37.8	16 31.6	4 20.3	10 00.0
27 Tu	2 20 08	6 47 28	26 01 23	2♎09 31	19 00.9	11 50.6	17 20.9	3 03.8	23 38.6	17 21.6	6 45.5	16 32.9	4 20.6	9 58.7
28 W	2 24 04	7 45 48	8♎15 34	14 19 48	18 51.8	13 16.2	18 29.6	2 41.3	24 01.7	17 35.7	6 53.1	16 34.0	4 20.9	9 57.4
29 Th	2 28 01	8 44 06	20 22 26	26 23 39	18 40.2	14 43.8	19 38.0	2 18.9	24 24.9	17 49.7	7 00.8	16 35.2	4 21.2	9 56.1
30 F	2 31 57	9 42 22	2♏23 38	8♏22 33	18 26.9	16 13.3	20 46.4	1 56.6	24 48.2	18 03.7	7 08.5	16 36.2	4 21.4	9 54.7

Astro Data	Dy Hr Mn
☽ 0S	4 11:44
☿ R	10 9:10
♇ R	13 21:34
♂ R	18 13:41
☽ 0N	18 14:41
☉0N	21 1:47
☿0S	24 19:32
♃△♇	29 14:00
☽ 0S	31 18:53
☿ D	2 9:19
♄□♆	6 15:05
☽ 0N	15 1:13
☿0N	23 9:02
♃⚹♅	23 16:55
☽ 0S	28 1:18

Planet Ingress	Dy Hr Mn
♄ ♉	1 1:26
☿ ♈	2 22:50
☿ ♓R	18 9:23
♀ ♉	18 9:59
☉ ♈	21 1:46
♀ ♊	12 13:17
☿ ♈	17 22:09
☉ ♉	20 12:46

Last Aspect Dy Hr Mn		☽ Ingress Dy Hr Mn	
28 5:18	♅ ☍	♍	1 10:04
2 6:58	☉ ☍	♎	3 18:34
4 22:43	♅ △	♏	6 5:22
7 14:38	☉ △	♐	8 17:46
10 10:40	♀ △	♑	11 5:54
13 3:33	♀ □	♒	13 15:32
15 15:40	♀ ⚹	♓	15 21:30
17 18:48	☉ ☌	♈	18 0:13
19 1:07	♅ ⚹	♉	20 1:09
21 20:52	☿ ⚹	♊	22 2:05
23 20:11	☿ □	♋	24 4:33
25 21:46	☿ △	♌	26 9:22
27 13:45	♅ ☍	♍	28 16:34
30 9:02	☿ ☍	♎	31 1:49

Last Aspect Dy Hr Mn		☽ Ingress Dy Hr Mn	
1 8:38	♅ △	♏	2 12:48
4 7:01	☿ △	♐	5 1:07
6 21:07	☿ □	♑	7 13:39
9 18:06	♀ △	♒	10 0:24
12 7:02	♀ □	♓	12 7:35
14 4:53	☿ ☌	♈	14 10:46
16 4:22	☉ ☌	♉	16 11:07
17 12:55	♅ □	♊	18 10:39
20 11:21	☉ ⚹	♋	20 11:27
21 14:32	♃ □	♌	22 15:06
23 20:57	♃ △	♍	24 22:04
26 4:14	♀ □	♎	27 7:46
28 21:07	♀ △	♏	29 19:12

☽ Phases & Eclipses Dy Hr Mn	
2 6:58	○ 11♍15
10 8:40	☾ 19♐19
17 18:48	● 26♓44
24 10:18	☽ 3♋20
31 22:49	○ 10♎46
9 2:51	☾ 18♑49
16 4:22	● 25♈45
22 19:02	☽ 2♌12
30 14:55	○ 9♏49

Astro Data

1 March 1999
Julian Day # 36219
SVP 5♓16'27"
GC 26♐49.7 ⚴ 9♈13.1
Eris 18♈36.6 ⚵ 9♐40.1
⚷ 3♐41.1 ⚶ 9♌07.1R
☽ Mean ☊ 21♌14.7

1 April 1999
Julian Day # 36250
SVP 5♓16'25"
GC 26♐49.7 ⚴ 21♈52.0
Eris 18♈55.4 ⚵ 11♐49.4R
⚷ 3♐39.7R ⚶ 7♌21.6
☽ Mean ☊ 19♌36.1

LONGITUDE May 1999

Day	Sid.Time	☉	0 hr ☽	Noon ☽	True ☊	☿	♀	♂	⚳	♃	♄	♅	♆	♇
1 Sa	2 35 54	10♉40 37	14♏20 32	20♏17 45	18♌12.9	17♈44.8	21♊54.6	1♏34.5	25♊11.6	18♈17.7	7♉16.1	16♒37.3	4♒21.6	9♐53.4
2 Su	2 39 50	11 38 50	26 14 21	2♐10 32	17R 59.3	19 18.2	23 02.6	1R 12.5	25 35.0	18 31.6	7 23.8	16 38.2	4 21.8	9R 52.0
3 M	2 43 47	12 37 01	8♐06 30	14 02 29	17 47.3	20 53.5	24 10.5	0 50.8	25 58.5	18 45.5	7 31.5	16 39.2	4 21.9	9 50.6
4 Tu	2 47 43	13 35 11	19 58 46	25 55 41	17 37.7	22 30.7	25 18.2	0 29.4	26 22.2	18 59.3	7 39.1	16 40.1	4 22.0	9 49.2
5 W	2 51 40	14 33 19	1♑53 35	7♑52 52	17 30.9	24 09.8	26 25.8	0 08.3	26 45.8	19 13.1	7 46.7	16 40.9	4 22.1	9 47.8
6 Th	2 55 37	15 31 26	13 54 02	19 57 32	17 26.9	25 50.8	27 33.2	29♎47.5	27 09.6	19 26.9	7 54.4	16 41.7	4R 22.1	9 46.4
7 F	2 59 33	16 29 31	26 03 57	2♒13 50	17 25.1	27 33.7	28 40.4	29 27.2	27 33.5	19 40.6	8 02.0	16 42.4	4 22.1	9 44.9
8 Sa	3 03 30	17 27 35	8♒27 46	14 46 22	17 24.7	29 18.6	29 47.5	29 07.3	27 57.4	19 54.3	8 09.6	16 43.1	4 22.1	9 43.4
9 Su	3 07 26	18 25 38	21 10 14	27 39 55	17 24.6	1♉05.3	0♋54.4	28 47.9	28 21.4	20 07.9	8 17.2	16 43.8	4 22.0	9 42.0
10 M	3 11 23	19 23 39	4♓15 59	10♓58 50	17 23.6	2 53.9	2 01.1	28 28.9	28 45.4	20 21.5	8 24.8	16 44.4	4 21.9	9 40.5
11 Tu	3 15 19	20 21 39	17 48 51	24 46 14	17 20.7	4 44.4	3 07.7	28 10.6	29 09.6	20 35.0	8 32.4	16 44.9	4 21.8	9 39.0
12 W	3 19 16	21 19 37	1♈51 01	9♈03 04	17 15.2	6 36.9	4 14.1	27 52.8	29 33.8	20 48.5	8 39.9	16 45.4	4 21.6	9 37.4
13 Th	3 23 12	22 17 34	16 21 59	23 47 10	17 07.2	8 31.2	5 20.2	27 35.6	29 58.0	21 01.9	8 47.5	16 45.8	4 21.4	9 35.9
14 F	3 27 09	23 15 30	1♉17 46	8♉52 42	16 57.2	10 27.4	6 26.2	27 19.0	0♋22.4	21 15.3	8 55.0	16 46.2	4 21.2	9 34.4
15 Sa	3 31 06	24 13 24	16 30 43	24 10 24	16 46.3	12 25.5	7 32.0	27 03.1	0 46.8	21 28.6	9 02.5	16 46.6	4 20.9	9 32.8
16 Su	3 35 02	25 11 17	1♊50 18	9♊28 57	16 35.8	14 25.4	8 37.6	26 47.9	1 11.2	21 41.9	9 10.0	16 46.9	4 20.6	9 31.2
17 M	3 38 59	26 09 09	17 04 57	24 37 00	16 27.0	16 27.1	9 43.0	26 33.4	1 35.8	21 55.1	9 17.5	16 47.1	4 20.3	9 29.7
18 Tu	3 42 55	27 06 59	2♋04 03	9♋25 13	16 20.6	18 30.5	10 48.2	26 19.6	2 00.4	22 08.2	9 24.9	16 47.3	4 20.0	9 28.1
19 W	3 46 52	28 04 47	16 39 52	23 47 35	16 16.8	20 35.5	11 53.2	26 06.6	2 25.0	22 21.3	9 32.4	16 47.5	4 19.6	9 26.5
20 Th	3 50 48	29 02 33	0♌48 12	7♌41 42	16D 15.3	22 42.0	12 57.9	25 54.4	2 49.7	22 34.4	9 39.8	16 47.6	4 19.2	9 24.9
21 F	3 54 45	0♊00 18	14 28 17	21 08 13	16R 15.2	24 49.8	14 02.4	25 42.9	3 14.5	22 47.3	9 47.2	16R 47.6	4 18.7	9 23.3
22 Sa	3 58 41	0 58 01	27 41 55	4♍09 50	16 15.3	26 58.9	15 06.7	25 32.2	3 39.3	23 00.3	9 54.5	16 47.6	4 18.2	9 21.7
23 Su	4 02 38	1 55 43	10♍32 31	16 50 30	16 14.4	29 09.0	16 10.7	25 22.3	4 04.2	23 13.1	10 01.8	16 47.5	4 17.7	9 20.1
24 M	4 06 35	2 53 23	23 04 18	29 14 29	16 11.6	1♊19.9	17 14.4	25 13.3	4 29.1	23 25.9	10 09.1	16 47.4	4 17.2	9 18.5
25 Tu	4 10 31	3 51 01	5♎21 33	11♎25 59	16 06.3	3 31.4	18 17.9	25 05.0	4 54.1	23 38.6	10 16.4	16 47.3	4 16.6	9 16.9
26 W	4 14 28	4 48 38	17 28 13	23 28 41	15 58.4	5 43.2	19 21.1	24 57.5	5 19.1	23 51.2	10 23.6	16 47.1	4 16.0	9 15.2
27 Th	4 18 24	5 46 14	29 27 44	5♏25 41	15 48.1	7 55.0	20 24.0	24 50.9	5 44.2	24 03.8	10 30.8	16 46.8	4 15.4	9 13.6
28 F	4 22 21	6 43 48	11♏22 50	17 19 27	15 36.2	10 06.7	21 26.7	24 45.1	6 09.3	24 16.3	10 38.0	16 46.5	4 14.7	9 12.0
29 Sa	4 26 17	7 41 21	23 15 44	29 11 54	15 23.7	12 17.8	22 29.0	24 40.1	6 34.5	24 28.7	10 45.2	16 46.2	4 14.0	9 10.3
30 Su	4 30 14	8 38 53	5♐08 09	11♐04 38	15 11.6	14 28.2	23 31.1	24 35.9	6 59.7	24 41.1	10 52.3	16 45.8	4 13.3	9 08.7
31 M	4 34 10	9 36 24	17 01 33	22 59 05	15 00.9	16 37.5	24 32.8	24 32.5	7 25.0	24 53.4	10 59.3	16 45.4	4 12.6	9 07.1

LONGITUDE June 1999

Day	Sid.Time	☉	0 hr ☽	Noon ☽	True ☊	☿	♀	♂	⚳	♃	♄	♅	♆	♇
1 Tu	4 38 07	10♊33 54	28♐57 27	4♑56 51	14♌52.3	18♊45.6	25♋34.2	24♎29.9	7♋50.4	25♈05.6	11♉06.4	16♒44.9	4♒11.8	9♐05.4
2 W	4 42 04	11 31 23	10♑57 34	16 59 51	14R 46.3	20 52.2	26 35.3	24R 28.1	8 15.7	25 17.7	11 13.4	16R 44.4	4R 11.0	9R 03.8
3 Th	4 46 00	12 28 51	23 04 04	29 10 33	14 42.9	22 57.0	27 36.1	24D 27.1	8 41.1	25 29.8	11 20.4	16 43.8	4 10.2	9 02.2
4 F	4 49 57	13 26 18	5♒19 42	11♒31 56	14D 41.7	25 00.1	28 36.5	24 26.9	9 06.6	25 41.7	11 27.3	16 43.2	4 09.3	9 00.6
5 Sa	4 53 53	14 23 45	17 47 45	24 07 36	14 41.9	27 01.1	29 36.5	24 27.5	9 32.1	25 53.6	11 34.2	16 42.5	4 08.5	8 58.9
6 Su	4 57 50	15 21 10	0♓31 59	7♓01 23	14R 42.6	28 59.9	0♌36.2	24 28.8	9 57.7	26 05.4	11 41.0	16 41.8	4 07.6	8 57.3
7 M	5 01 46	16 18 35	13 36 15	20 17 02	14 42.8	0♋56.5	1 35.5	24 31.0	10 23.3	26 17.1	11 47.8	16 41.0	4 06.6	8 55.7
8 Tu	5 05 43	17 16 00	27 04 04	3♈57 37	14 41.5	2 50.8	2 34.5	24 33.9	10 48.9	26 28.8	11 54.6	16 40.2	4 05.7	8 54.1
9 W	5 09 39	18 13 24	10♈57 48	18 04 37	14 38.3	4 42.7	3 33.0	24 37.5	11 14.6	26 40.3	12 01.3	16 39.3	4 04.7	8 52.5
10 Th	5 13 36	19 10 47	25 17 51	2♉37 07	14 32.9	6 32.2	4 31.1	24 41.9	11 40.3	26 51.8	12 08.0	16 38.4	4 03.7	8 50.9
11 F	5 17 33	20 08 10	10♉01 49	17 31 08	14 25.9	8 19.2	5 28.8	24 47.1	12 06.1	27 03.2	12 14.6	16 37.5	4 02.6	8 49.3
12 Sa	5 21 29	21 05 32	25 04 03	2♊39 26	14 18.1	10 03.7	6 26.1	24 52.9	12 31.9	27 14.4	12 21.2	16 36.5	4 01.6	8 47.7
13 Su	5 25 26	22 02 54	10♊15 59	17 52 21	14 10.4	11 45.7	7 22.9	24 59.6	12 57.7	27 25.6	12 27.7	16 35.5	4 00.5	8 46.1
14 M	5 29 22	23 00 15	25 27 12	2♋59 15	14 03.9	13 25.1	8 19.3	25 06.9	13 23.6	27 36.7	12 34.2	16 34.4	3 59.4	8 44.5
15 Tu	5 33 19	23 57 36	10♋27 20	17 50 27	13 59.3	15 01.9	9 15.1	25 14.9	13 49.5	27 47.7	12 40.7	16 33.3	3 58.3	8 43.0
16 W	5 37 15	24 54 56	25 07 47	2♌18 43	13D 56.9	16 36.1	10 10.5	25 23.7	14 15.4	27 58.6	12 47.1	16 32.1	3 57.1	8 41.4
17 Th	5 41 12	25 52 14	9♌22 52	16 20 02	13 56.3	18 07.8	11 05.3	25 33.1	14 41.4	28 09.4	12 53.4	16 30.9	3 56.0	8 39.9
18 F	5 45 08	26 49 32	23 10 10	29 53 25	13 57.1	19 36.8	11 59.6	25 43.2	15 07.4	28 20.1	12 59.7	16 29.7	3 54.8	8 38.3
19 Sa	5 49 05	27 46 49	6♍30 03	13♍00 27	13 58.3	21 03.1	12 53.4	25 54.0	15 33.5	28 30.7	13 05.9	16 28.4	3 53.5	8 36.8
20 Su	5 53 02	28 44 06	19 25 04	25 44 23	13R 59.1	22 26.8	13 46.5	26 05.4	15 59.6	28 41.1	13 12.1	16 27.1	3 52.3	8 35.3
21 M	5 56 58	29 41 21	1♎58 59	8♎09 24	13 58.8	23 47.8	14 39.1	26 17.4	16 25.7	28 51.5	13 18.2	16 25.7	3 51.0	8 33.8
22 Tu	6 00 55	0♋38 36	14 16 13	20 19 59	13 56.7	25 06.0	15 31.0	26 30.1	16 51.8	29 01.8	13 24.2	16 24.3	3 49.8	8 32.3
23 W	6 04 51	1 35 50	26 21 15	2♏20 32	13 52.9	26 21.4	16 22.3	26 43.4	17 18.0	29 11.9	13 30.2	16 22.8	3 48.5	8 30.8
24 Th	6 08 48	2 33 03	8♏18 20	14 15 05	13 47.5	27 33.9	17 12.9	26 57.3	17 44.2	29 22.0	13 36.1	16 21.4	3 47.2	8 29.4
25 F	6 12 44	3 30 16	20 11 13	26 07 07	13 40.9	28 43.5	18 02.8	27 11.8	18 10.4	29 31.9	13 42.0	16 19.8	3 45.8	8 27.9
26 Sa	6 16 41	4 27 29	2♐03 07	7♐59 32	13 33.7	29 50.1	18 52.0	27 26.9	18 36.6	29 41.7	13 47.8	16 18.3	3 44.5	8 26.5
27 Su	6 20 37	5 24 41	13 56 39	19 54 42	13 26.8	0♌53.7	19 40.4	27 42.5	19 02.9	29 51.4	13 53.6	16 16.7	3 43.1	8 25.1
28 M	6 24 34	6 21 53	25 53 55	1♑54 30	13 20.7	1 54.1	20 28.1	27 58.7	19 29.2	0♉01.0	13 59.3	16 15.1	3 41.7	8 23.7
29 Tu	6 28 31	7 19 05	7♑56 39	14 00 33	13 16.0	2 51.3	21 14.9	28 15.4	19 55.5	0 10.5	14 04.9	16 13.4	3 40.3	8 22.3
30 W	6 32 27	8 16 16	20 06 23	26 14 21	13 13.0	3 45.2	22 00.9	28 32.7	20 21.9	0 19.8	14 10.5	16 11.7	3 38.9	8 21.0

Astro Data	Dy Hr Mn
♆R	7 0:51
☽0N	12 12:12
♄⊼♇	18 20:24
♅R	21 22:25
☽0S	25 7:56
♃⚼♇	28 4:39
♂D	4 6:10
☽0N	8 21:52
☽0S	21 15:28

Planet Ingress		Dy Hr Mn
♂	♎R	5 21:32
♀	♋	8 16:29
☿	♉	8 21:22
⚳	♋	13 13:57
☉	♊	21 11:52
☿	♊	23 21:22
♀	♌	5 21:25
☿	♋	7 0:18
☉	♋	21 19:49
☿	♌	26 15:39
♃	♉	28 9:29

Last Aspect Dy Hr Mn		☽ Ingress Dy Hr Mn
1 4:35	♅ □	♐ 2 7:36
4 10:37	♀ ☍	♑ 4 20:12
7 6:45	♂ □	♒ 7 7:40
9 14:01	♂ △	♓ 9 16:16
11 3:51	☉ ⚹	♈ 11 20:53
13 17:59	♂ ☍	♉ 13 21:56
15 12:05	☉ ☌	♊ 15 21:07
17 15:04	♂ △	♋ 17 20:39
19 19:51	☉ ⚹	♌ 19 22:37
21 20:14	♂ ⚹	♍ 22 4:15
23 10:37	♀ ⚹	♎ 24 13:29
26 14:56	♂ ☌	♏ 27 1:05
28 21:08	♀ △	♐ 29 13:37

Last Aspect Dy Hr Mn		☽ Ingress Dy Hr Mn
31 15:54	♃ △	♑ 1 2:05
3 8:38	♀ ☍	♒ 3 13:37
5 18:26	☿ △	♓ 5 23:00
7 4:20	☉ □	♈ 8 5:08
10 2:27	♃ ☌	♉ 10 7:44
11 10:34	♅ □	♊ 12 7:48
14 3:19	♃ ⚹	♋ 14 7:14
16 4:39	♃ □	♌ 16 8:07
18 9:10	♃ △	♍ 18 12:12
20 18:13	☉ □	♎ 20 20:10
23 5:36	♃ ☍	♏ 23 7:18
25 17:50	☿ △	♐ 25 19:51
28 8:11	♃ △	♑ 28 8:12
30 16:36	♂ □	♒ 30 19:19

☽ Phases & Eclipses Dy Hr Mn		
8 17:29	☾	17♒41
15 12:05	●	24♉14
22 5:34	☽	0♍43
30 6:40	○	8♐26
7 4:20	☾	16♓00
13 19:03	●	22♊20
20 18:13	☽	28♍59
28 21:37	○	6♑45

Astro Data

1 May 1999
Julian Day # 36280
SVP 5♓16'22"
GC 26♐49.8 ⚴ 5♉12.0
Eris 19♈14.9 ⚵ 9♐06.1R
⚷ 2♐12.4R ⚶ 12♌07.7
☽ Mean ☊ 18♌00.8

1 June 1999
Julian Day # 36311
SVP 5♓16'17"
GC 26♐49.9 ⚴ 19♉53.5
Eris 19♈31.7 ⚵ 2♐37.2R
⚷ 29♏59.6R ⚶ 21♌33.7
☽ Mean ☊ 16♌22.3

July 1999

LONGITUDE

Day	Sid.Time	☉	0 hr ☽	Noon ☽	True ☊	☿	♀	♂	⚳	♃	♄	♅	♆	♇
1 Th	6 36 24	9♋13 27	2♒24 39	8♒37 28	13♌11.7	4♌35.6	22♌46.1	28♎50.5	20♋48.3	0♉29.0	14♉16.0	16♒10.0	3♒37.5	8♐19.6
2 F	6 40 20	10 10 39	14 53 04	21 11 40	13D 11.9	5 22.5	23 30.3	29 08.8	21 14.7	0 38.1	14 21.4	16R 08.2	3R 36.0	8R 18.3
3 Sa	6 44 17	11 07 50	27 33 33	3♓58 58	13 13.0	6 05.7	24 13.6	29 27.6	21 41.1	0 47.1	14 26.7	16 06.4	3 34.6	8 17.0
4 Su	6 48 13	12 05 01	10♓28 13	17 01 35	13 14.6	6 45.1	24 56.0	29 46.9	22 07.6	0 56.0	14 32.0	16 04.6	3 33.1	8 15.7
5 M	6 52 10	13 02 13	23 39 20	0♈21 43	13 15.9	7 20.6	25 37.3	0♏06.7	22 34.0	1 04.7	14 37.3	16 02.7	3 31.6	8 14.4
6 Tu	6 56 07	13 59 25	7♈08 56	14 01 09	13R 16.4	7 52.0	26 17.6	0 26.9	23 00.5	1 13.3	14 42.4	16 00.9	3 30.1	8 13.2
7 W	7 00 03	14 56 37	20 58 26	28 00 45	13 15.8	8 19.3	26 56.9	0 47.6	23 27.1	1 21.7	14 47.5	15 58.9	3 28.6	8 11.9
8 Th	7 04 00	15 53 50	5♉08 00	12♉19 54	13 14.0	8 42.3	27 35.0	1 08.8	23 53.6	1 30.1	14 52.5	15 57.0	3 27.1	8 10.7
9 F	7 07 56	16 51 03	19 36 03	26 55 55	13 11.3	9 00.8	28 12.0	1 30.5	24 20.2	1 38.3	14 57.4	15 55.0	3 25.5	8 09.6
10 Sa	7 11 53	17 48 17	4♊18 49	11♊43 56	13 07.9	9 14.8	28 47.8	1 52.6	24 46.7	1 46.3	15 02.3	15 53.0	3 24.0	8 08.4
11 Su	7 15 49	18 45 31	19 10 22	26 37 08	13 04.6	9 24.2	29 22.3	2 15.1	25 13.4	1 54.2	15 07.1	15 51.0	3 22.4	8 07.3
12 M	7 19 46	19 42 45	4♋03 12	11♋27 33	13 01.9	9R 28.9	29 55.5	2 38.1	25 40.0	2 02.0	15 11.8	15 48.9	3 20.9	8 06.1
13 Tu	7 23 42	20 40 00	18 49 12	26 07 14	13 00.1	9 28.8	0♍27.4	3 01.5	26 06.6	2 09.6	15 16.4	15 46.9	3 19.3	8 05.1
14 W	7 27 39	21 37 14	3♌20 52	10♌29 25	12D 59.4	9 23.9	0 57.9	3 25.3	26 33.3	2 17.1	15 20.9	15 44.8	3 17.7	8 04.0
15 Th	7 31 36	22 34 29	17 32 22	24 29 22	12 59.7	9 14.3	1 27.0	3 49.5	27 00.0	2 24.4	15 25.4	15 42.7	3 16.1	8 02.9
16 F	7 35 32	23 31 44	1♍20 11	8♍04 45	13 00.7	8 59.9	1 54.5	4 14.2	27 26.7	2 31.6	15 29.8	15 40.5	3 14.6	8 01.9
17 Sa	7 39 29	24 28 59	14 43 07	21 15 30	13 02.1	8 41.0	2 20.4	4 39.2	27 53.4	2 38.6	15 34.1	15 38.3	3 13.0	8 00.9
18 Su	7 43 25	25 26 15	27 42 08	4♎03 26	13 03.4	8 17.7	2 44.8	5 04.6	28 20.1	2 45.5	15 38.3	15 36.2	3 11.3	8 00.0
19 M	7 47 22	26 23 30	10♎19 48	16 31 43	13R 04.2	7 50.3	3 07.4	5 30.4	28 46.8	2 52.2	15 42.4	15 33.9	3 09.7	7 59.0
20 Tu	7 51 18	27 20 46	22 39 44	28 44 24	13 04.5	7 19.1	3 28.3	5 56.5	29 13.6	2 58.8	15 46.5	15 31.7	3 08.1	7 58.1
21 W	7 55 15	28 18 01	4♏46 15	10♏45 52	13 04.0	6 44.5	3 47.3	6 23.0	29 40.3	3 05.2	15 50.5	15 29.5	3 06.5	7 57.2
22 Th	7 59 11	29 15 17	16 43 49	22 40 38	13 03.0	6 07.0	4 04.5	6 49.9	0♌07.1	3 11.5	15 54.3	15 27.2	3 04.9	7 56.3
23 F	8 03 08	0♌12 34	28 36 51	4♐32 59	13 01.5	5 27.2	4 19.8	7 17.1	0 33.9	3 17.6	15 58.1	15 24.9	3 03.3	7 55.5
24 Sa	8 07 05	1 09 51	10♐29 29	16 26 48	12 59.8	4 45.6	4 33.0	7 44.7	1 00.6	3 23.5	16 01.8	15 22.7	3 01.6	7 54.7
25 Su	8 11 01	2 07 08	22 25 21	28 25 31	12 58.2	4 03.1	4 44.2	8 12.6	1 27.4	3 29.3	16 05.4	15 20.4	3 00.0	7 53.9
26 M	8 14 58	3 04 26	4♑27 36	10♑31 55	12 56.9	3 20.2	4 53.3	8 40.8	1 54.2	3 34.9	16 09.0	15 18.1	2 58.4	7 53.2
27 Tu	8 18 54	4 01 44	16 38 44	22 48 14	12 55.9	2 37.9	5 00.2	9 09.3	2 21.1	3 40.3	16 12.4	15 15.7	2 56.8	7 52.5
28 W	8 22 51	4 59 03	29 00 38	5♒16 05	12D 55.5	1 56.8	5 05.0	9 38.1	2 47.9	3 45.6	16 15.8	15 13.4	2 55.1	7 51.8
29 Th	8 26 47	5 56 23	11♒34 41	17 56 33	12 55.4	1 17.7	5R 07.4	10 07.3	3 14.7	3 50.7	16 19.0	15 11.0	2 53.5	7 51.1
30 F	8 30 44	6 53 43	24 21 44	0♓50 19	12 55.7	0 41.4	5 07.6	10 36.7	3 41.6	3 55.6	16 22.2	15 08.7	2 51.9	7 50.5
31 Sa	8 34 40	7 51 04	7♓22 17	13 57 42	12 56.1	0 08.5	5 05.4	11 06.5	4 08.4	4 00.4	16 25.2	15 06.3	2 50.3	7 49.9

August 1999

LONGITUDE

Day	Sid.Time	☉	0 hr ☽	Noon ☽	True ☊	☿	♀	♂	⚳	♃	♄	♅	♆	♇
1 Su	8 38 37	8♌48 26	20♓36 32	27♓18 48	12♌56.6	29♋39.7	5♍00.9	11♏36.5	4♌35.3	4♉05.0	16♉28.2	15♒04.0	2♒48.6	7♐49.3
2 M	8 42 34	9 45 50	4♈04 27	10♈53 29	12 56.9	29R 15.7	4R 54.0	12 06.8	5 02.1	4 09.4	16 31.1	15R 01.6	2R 47.0	7R 48.7
3 Tu	8 46 30	10 43 14	17 45 48	24 41 19	12 57.1	28 56.8	4 44.7	12 37.4	5 29.0	4 13.6	16 33.9	14 59.2	2 45.4	7 48.2
4 W	8 50 27	11 40 40	1♉39 57	8♉41 32	12R 57.2	28 43.6	4 33.1	13 08.3	5 55.8	4 17.7	16 36.6	14 56.8	2 43.8	7 47.7
5 Th	8 54 23	12 38 07	15 45 52	22 52 44	12D 57.2	28D 36.4	4 19.1	13 39.5	6 22.7	4 21.6	16 39.2	14 54.4	2 42.2	7 47.3
6 F	8 58 20	13 35 35	0♊01 48	7♊12 43	12 57.2	28 35.4	4 02.8	14 10.9	6 49.6	4 25.3	16 41.7	14 52.0	2 40.6	7 46.8
7 Sa	9 02 16	14 33 05	14 25 06	21 38 27	12 57.3	28 41.1	3 44.2	14 42.6	7 16.5	4 28.8	16 44.1	14 49.6	2 39.0	7 46.5
8 Su	9 06 13	15 30 36	28 52 14	6♋05 54	12 57.5	28 53.3	3 23.4	15 14.6	7 43.4	4 32.1	16 46.4	14 47.2	2 37.4	7 46.1
9 M	9 10 09	16 28 08	13♋18 51	20 30 26	12 57.8	29 12.4	3 00.4	15 46.8	8 10.3	4 35.3	16 48.6	14 44.8	2 35.9	7 45.8
10 Tu	9 14 06	17 25 41	27 40 03	4♌47 05	12R 58.0	29 38.3	2 35.3	16 19.3	8 37.2	4 38.2	16 50.7	14 42.4	2 34.3	7 45.5
11 W	9 18 03	18 23 16	11♌50 57	18 51 07	12 58.0	0♌11.1	2 08.3	16 52.1	9 04.1	4 41.0	16 52.7	14 40.1	2 32.8	7 45.2
12 Th	9 21 59	19 20 51	25 47 09	2♍38 38	12 57.7	0 50.6	1 39.4	17 25.0	9 31.0	4 43.5	16 54.6	14 37.7	2 31.2	7 45.0
13 F	9 25 56	20 18 28	9♍25 17	16 06 55	12 57.1	1 36.9	1 08.8	17 58.3	9 57.9	4 45.9	16 56.4	14 35.3	2 29.7	7 44.8
14 Sa	9 29 52	21 16 05	22 43 25	29 14 48	12 56.1	2 29.7	0 36.6	18 31.8	10 24.8	4 48.1	16 58.0	14 32.9	2 28.1	7 44.6
15 Su	9 33 49	22 13 44	5♎41 07	12♎02 36	12 55.0	3 29.0	0 03.1	19 05.5	10 51.7	4 50.1	16 59.6	14 30.5	2 26.6	7 44.5
16 M	9 37 45	23 11 24	18 19 28	24 32 05	12 53.8	4 34.6	29♌28.4	19 39.4	11 18.5	4 51.9	17 01.1	14 28.2	2 25.1	7 44.4
17 Tu	9 41 42	24 09 05	0♏40 50	6♏46 10	12 52.8	5 46.2	28 52.7	20 13.6	11 45.4	4 53.5	17 02.5	14 25.8	2 23.6	7 44.3
18 W	9 45 38	25 06 46	12 48 36	18 48 38	12D 52.3	7 03.5	28 16.3	20 48.0	12 12.3	4 54.9	17 03.8	14 23.5	2 22.2	7D 44.3
19 Th	9 49 35	26 04 29	24 46 52	0♐43 50	12 52.2	8 26.3	27 39.3	21 22.6	12 39.2	4 56.1	17 04.9	14 21.1	2 20.7	7 44.3
20 F	9 53 31	27 02 13	6♐40 09	12 36 24	12 52.8	9 54.3	27 02.1	21 57.5	13 06.0	4 57.1	17 06.0	14 18.8	2 19.3	7 44.3
21 Sa	9 57 28	27 59 59	18 33 08	24 30 57	12 53.8	11 27.0	26 24.7	22 32.5	13 32.9	4 57.9	17 07.0	14 16.5	2 17.8	7 44.4
22 Su	10 01 25	28 57 45	0♑30 22	6♑31 56	12 55.2	13 04.1	25 47.6	23 07.8	13 59.7	4 58.5	17 07.8	14 14.2	2 16.4	7 44.5
23 M	10 05 21	29 55 33	12 36 06	18 43 19	12 56.5	14 45.2	25 10.9	23 43.2	14 26.6	4 58.9	17 08.6	14 11.9	2 15.0	7 44.6
24 Tu	10 09 18	0♍53 21	24 53 58	1♒08 24	12R 57.5	16 29.8	24 34.9	24 18.9	14 53.4	4R 59.2	17 09.2	14 09.7	2 13.6	7 44.8
25 W	10 13 14	1 51 11	7♒26 53	13 49 36	12 57.9	18 17.4	23 59.7	24 54.7	15 20.2	4 59.2	17 09.7	14 07.4	2 12.3	7 45.0
26 Th	10 17 11	2 49 03	20 16 43	26 48 16	12 57.3	20 07.7	23 25.7	25 30.8	15 47.0	4 59.0	17 10.2	14 05.2	2 10.9	7 45.2
27 F	10 21 07	3 46 56	3♓24 14	10♓04 31	12 55.8	22 00.2	22 53.0	26 07.0	16 13.8	4 58.6	17 10.5	14 03.0	2 09.6	7 45.4
28 Sa	10 25 04	4 44 50	16 48 57	23 37 17	12 53.3	23 54.5	22 21.8	26 43.5	16 40.6	4 58.1	17 10.7	14 00.8	2 08.3	7 45.7
29 Su	10 29 00	5 42 46	0♈29 13	7♈24 25	12 50.2	25 50.1	21 52.3	27 20.1	17 07.4	4 57.3	17R 10.8	13 58.6	2 07.0	7 46.1
30 M	10 32 57	6 40 44	14 22 28	21 22 59	12 46.9	27 46.8	21 24.6	27 56.9	17 34.1	4 56.3	17 10.8	13 56.5	2 05.7	7 46.4
31 Tu	10 36 54	7 38 44	28 25 30	5♉29 38	12 43.9	29 44.1	20 58.9	28 33.8	18 00.9	4 55.1	17 10.7	13 54.3	2 04.4	7 46.8

Astro Data (Dy Hr Mn)

☽0N 6 5:18
☿R 12 23:34
♄□♅ 18 3:54
☽0S 18 23:56
♃□♆ 21 15:52
♀R 30 1:41

☽0N 2 11:03
☿D 6 3:26
☽0S 15 8:46
♇D 19 1:46
♃R 25 2:37
☽0N 29 16:54
♄R 30 1:23

Planet Ingress (Dy Hr Mn)

♂ ♏ 5 3:59
♀ ♍ 12 15:18
⚳ ♌ 22 5:40
☉ ♌ 23 6:44
☿ ♋R 31 18:44

☿ ♌ 11 4:25
♀ ♌R 15 14:12
☉ ♍ 23 13:51
☿ ♍ 31 15:15

Last Aspect Dy Hr Mn		☽ Ingress Dy Hr Mn
3 3:21	♂ △	♓ 3 4:34
4 7:25	♄ ⚹	♈ 5 11:21
7 10:06	♀ △	♉ 7 15:22
9 14:09	♀ □	♊ 9 17:00
11 16:37	♀ ⚹	♋ 11 17:27
13 2:24	☉ ☌	♌ 13 18:26
14 20:55	♅ ☍	♍ 15 21:39
17 18:28	☉ ⚹	♎ 18 4:19
20 9:00	☉ □	♏ 20 14:30
23 2:27	☉ △	♐ 23 2:48
24 9:51	♅ ⚹	♑ 25 15:08
26 23:05	♄ △	♒ 28 1:54
29 8:56	♄ □	♓ 30 10:27

Last Aspect Dy Hr Mn		☽ Ingress Dy Hr Mn
1 16:03	☿ △	♈ 1 16:47
3 19:12	☿ □	♉ 3 21:09
5 21:35	☿ ⚹	♊ 5 23:57
7 0:43	♅ △	♋ 8 1:52
10 3:01	☿ ☌	♌ 10 3:55
11 11:09	☉ ☌	♍ 12 7:21
13 15:30	♂ ⚹	♎ 14 13:24
16 21:12	♀ ⚹	♏ 16 22:40
19 6:06	♀ □	♐ 19 10:31
21 19:36	☉ △	♑ 21 22:59
23 22:12	♂ ⚹	♒ 24 9:49
26 9:31	♂ □	♓ 26 17:50
28 17:41	♂ △	♈ 28 23:09
31 0:39	☿ △	♉ 31 2:41

☽ Phases & Eclipses (Dy Hr Mn)

6 11:57 ☾ 13♈59
13 2:24 ● 20♋17
20 9:00 ☽ 27♎14
28 11:25 ○ 4♒58
28 11:34 ☍ P 0.396

4 17:27 ☾ 11♉54
11 11:09 ● 18♌21
11 11:03:05 ● T 02'23"
19 1:47 ☽ 25♏40
26 23:48 ○ 3♓17

Astro Data

1 July 1999
Julian Day # 36341
SVP 5♓16'12"
GC 26♐49.9 ⚴ 4♊51.5
Eris 19♈40.7 ⚵ 27♏18.0R
⚷ 28♏12.5R ⚶ 3♍20.5
☽ Mean ☊ 14♌47.0

1 August 1999
Julian Day # 36372
SVP 5♓16'08"
GC 26♐50.0 ⚴ 20♊55.1
Eris 19♈40.6R ⚵ 26♏23.9
⚷ 27♏36.0 ⚶ 17♍12.9
☽ Mean ☊ 13♌08.5

LONGITUDE — September 1999

Day	Sid.Time	☉	0 hr ☽	Noon ☽	True ☊	☿	♀	♂	⚳	♃	♄	♅	♆	♇
1 W	10 40 50	8♍36 45	12♉34 56	19♉41 02	12♌41.7	1♍41.7	20♌35.3	29♏11.0	18♌27.6	4♉53.8	17♉10.5	13♒52.2	2♒03.2	7♐47.2
2 Th	10 44 47	9 34 49	26 47 33	3♊54 08	12D 40.6	3 39.5	20R 13.9	29 48.3	18 54.4	4R 52.2	17R 10.2	13R 50.1	2R 02.0	7 47.7
3 F	10 48 43	10 32 55	11♊00 31	18 06 24	12 40.7	5 37.1	19 54.8	0♐25.8	19 21.1	4 50.4	17 09.8	13 48.1	2 00.8	7 48.2
4 Sa	10 52 40	11 31 02	25 11 31	2♋15 40	12 41.7	7 34.4	19 38.0	1 03.5	19 47.8	4 48.4	17 09.3	13 46.0	1 59.6	7 48.7
5 Su	10 56 36	12 29 12	9♋18 37	16 20 08	12 43.2	9 31.1	19 23.6	1 41.4	20 14.5	4 46.3	17 08.7	13 44.0	1 58.5	7 49.3
6 M	11 00 33	13 27 24	23 20 01	0♌18 02	12R 44.5	11 27.2	19 11.6	2 19.4	20 41.1	4 43.9	17 07.9	13 42.0	1 57.4	7 49.9
7 Tu	11 04 29	14 25 37	7♌13 57	14 07 30	12 45.0	13 22.5	19 02.0	2 57.6	21 07.8	4 41.3	17 07.1	13 40.1	1 56.3	7 50.5
8 W	11 08 26	15 23 52	20 58 29	27 46 35	12 44.1	15 17.0	18 54.8	3 36.0	21 34.4	4 38.6	17 06.1	13 38.1	1 55.2	7 51.2
9 Th	11 12 23	16 22 10	4♍31 36	11♍13 17	12 41.5	17 10.5	18 50.0	4 14.5	22 01.0	4 35.6	17 05.1	13 36.2	1 54.1	7 51.9
10 F	11 16 19	17 20 29	17 51 24	24 25 47	12 37.3	19 03.1	18D 47.6	4 53.2	22 27.6	4 32.5	17 03.9	13 34.4	1 53.1	7 52.6
11 Sa	11 20 16	18 18 49	0♎56 18	7♎22 51	12 31.8	20 54.6	18 47.5	5 32.0	22 54.2	4 29.1	17 02.6	13 32.5	1 52.1	7 53.3
12 Su	11 24 12	19 17 12	13 45 26	20 04 03	12 25.4	22 45.1	18 49.8	6 11.0	23 20.7	4 25.6	17 01.3	13 30.7	1 51.1	7 54.1
13 M	11 28 09	20 15 36	26 18 50	2♏29 58	12 18.9	24 34.4	18 54.4	6 50.2	23 47.2	4 21.9	16 59.8	13 28.9	1 50.2	7 55.0
14 Tu	11 32 05	21 14 02	8♏37 40	14 42 15	12 13.1	26 22.7	19 01.2	7 29.5	24 13.7	4 18.0	16 58.2	13 27.2	1 49.2	7 55.8
15 W	11 36 02	22 12 29	20 44 07	26 44 07	12 08.5	28 10.0	19 10.2	8 09.0	24 40.2	4 13.9	16 56.5	13 25.5	1 48.4	7 56.7
16 Th	11 39 58	23 10 58	2♐41 24	8♐37 50	12 05.5	29 56.1	19 21.3	8 48.6	25 06.6	4 09.6	16 54.8	13 23.8	1 47.5	7 57.6
17 F	11 43 55	24 09 29	14 33 32	20 29 06	12D 04.2	1♎41.2	19 34.5	9 28.4	25 33.0	4 05.2	16 52.9	13 22.2	1 46.6	7 58.6
18 Sa	11 47 52	25 08 02	26 25 09	2♑22 20	12 04.4	3 25.2	19 49.8	10 08.3	25 59.4	4 00.5	16 50.9	13 20.6	1 45.8	7 59.6
19 Su	11 51 48	26 06 36	8♑21 15	14 22 34	12 05.6	5 08.1	20 07.0	10 48.3	26 25.7	3 55.8	16 48.8	13 19.0	1 45.0	8 00.6
20 M	11 55 45	27 05 12	20 26 53	26 34 49	12 07.0	6 50.0	20 26.1	11 28.5	26 52.0	3 50.8	16 46.6	13 17.5	1 44.3	8 01.6
21 Tu	11 59 41	28 03 49	2♒46 53	9♒03 37	12R 07.9	8 30.9	20 47.1	12 08.8	27 18.3	3 45.7	16 44.4	13 16.0	1 43.5	8 02.7
22 W	12 03 38	29 02 29	15 25 27	21 52 43	12 07.5	10 10.8	21 09.9	12 49.2	27 44.6	3 40.4	16 42.0	13 14.6	1 42.8	8 03.8
23 Th	12 07 34	0♎01 10	28 25 42	5♓04 30	12 05.2	11 49.7	21 34.4	13 29.8	28 10.8	3 34.9	16 39.6	13 13.2	1 42.2	8 04.9
24 F	12 11 31	0 59 53	11♓49 09	18 39 32	12 00.7	13 27.6	22 00.6	14 10.5	28 37.0	3 29.3	16 37.0	13 11.8	1 41.5	8 06.1
25 Sa	12 15 27	1 58 37	25 35 23	2♈36 18	11 54.3	15 04.6	22 28.5	14 51.3	29 03.1	3 23.6	16 34.4	13 10.5	1 40.9	8 07.3
26 Su	12 19 24	2 57 24	9♈41 45	16 51 04	11 46.4	16 40.6	22 57.9	15 32.3	29 29.2	3 17.6	16 31.6	13 09.2	1 40.3	8 08.5
27 M	12 23 20	3 56 13	24 03 30	1♉18 15	11 38.1	18 15.7	23 28.9	16 13.3	29 55.3	3 11.6	16 28.8	13 08.0	1 39.8	8 09.7
28 Tu	12 27 17	4 55 04	8♉34 28	15 51 19	11 30.3	19 50.0	24 01.3	16 54.5	0♍21.3	3 05.4	16 25.9	13 06.8	1 39.3	8 11.0
29 W	12 31 14	5 53 57	23 07 59	0♊23 43	11 24.0	21 23.3	24 35.1	17 35.8	0 47.3	2 59.0	16 22.9	13 05.6	1 38.8	8 12.3
30 Th	12 35 10	6 52 52	7♊37 53	14 49 56	11 19.7	22 55.7	25 10.3	18 17.3	1 13.3	2 52.6	16 19.8	13 04.5	1 38.3	8 13.7

LONGITUDE — October 1999

Day	Sid.Time	☉	0 hr ☽	Noon ☽	True ☊	☿	♀	♂	⚳	♃	♄	♅	♆	♇
1 F	12 39 07	7♎51 50	21♊59 26	29♊06 04	11♌17.7	24♎27.3	25♌46.9	18♐58.8	1♍39.2	2♉46.0	16♉16.6	13♒03.4	1♒37.9	8♐15.0
2 Sa	12 43 03	8 50 51	6♋09 37	13♋09 58	11D 17.4	25 58.0	26 24.7	19 40.5	2 05.1	2R 39.2	16R 13.4	13R 02.4	1R 37.5	8 16.4
3 Su	12 47 00	9 49 53	20 07 04	27 00 57	11 18.1	27 27.8	27 03.7	20 22.3	2 30.9	2 32.4	16 10.0	13 01.4	1 37.1	8 17.9
4 M	12 50 56	10 48 58	3♌51 38	10♌39 15	11R 18.6	28 56.8	27 43.9	21 04.2	2 56.7	2 25.4	16 06.6	13 00.5	1 36.8	8 19.3
5 Tu	12 54 53	11 48 05	17 23 50	24 05 31	11 17.9	0♏24.8	28 25.2	21 46.2	3 22.4	2 18.3	16 03.1	12 59.6	1 36.5	8 20.8
6 W	12 58 49	12 47 15	0♍44 20	7♍20 20	11 15.0	1 52.0	29 07.6	22 28.3	3 48.1	2 11.1	15 59.5	12 58.7	1 36.2	8 22.3
7 Th	13 02 46	13 46 26	13 53 33	20 23 59	11 09.4	3 18.3	29 51.1	23 10.6	4 13.8	2 03.8	15 55.9	12 57.9	1 36.0	8 23.8
8 F	13 06 43	14 45 40	26 51 37	3♎16 24	11 01.0	4 43.7	0♍35.6	23 52.9	4 39.4	1 56.4	15 52.2	12 57.2	1 35.8	8 25.4
9 Sa	13 10 39	15 44 56	9♎38 18	15 57 18	10 50.4	6 08.2	1 21.0	24 35.4	5 04.9	1 48.9	15 48.4	12 56.5	1 35.6	8 27.0
10 Su	13 14 36	16 44 14	22 13 21	28 26 28	10 38.3	7 31.7	2 07.3	25 18.0	5 30.4	1 41.4	15 44.5	12 55.8	1 35.5	8 28.6
11 M	13 18 32	17 43 34	4♏36 41	10♏44 06	10 25.9	8 54.2	2 54.6	26 00.6	5 55.8	1 33.7	15 40.6	12 55.2	1 35.4	8 30.2
12 Tu	13 22 29	18 42 55	16 48 50	22 51 03	10 14.1	10 15.7	3 42.7	26 43.4	6 21.2	1 26.0	15 36.6	12 54.6	1 35.3	8 31.9
13 W	13 26 25	19 42 19	28 51 02	4♐49 03	10 04.1	11 36.1	4 31.7	27 26.3	6 46.5	1 18.2	15 32.5	12 54.1	1D 35.3	8 33.5
14 Th	13 30 22	20 41 45	10♐45 28	16 40 43	9 56.5	12 55.3	5 21.4	28 09.3	7 11.8	1 10.3	15 28.4	12 53.7	1 35.3	8 35.3
15 F	13 34 18	21 41 12	22 35 16	28 29 38	9 51.5	14 13.4	6 11.9	28 52.3	7 37.0	1 02.4	15 24.2	12 53.3	1 35.3	8 37.0
16 Sa	13 38 15	22 40 42	4♑24 24	10♑20 11	9 49.0	15 30.2	7 03.2	29 35.5	8 02.1	0 54.5	15 20.0	12 52.9	1 35.4	8 38.7
17 Su	13 42 12	23 40 13	16 17 38	22 17 23	9D 48.3	16 45.6	7 55.2	0♑18.8	8 27.2	0 46.5	15 15.7	12 52.6	1 35.5	8 40.5
18 M	13 46 08	24 39 46	28 20 09	4♒26 36	9R 48.4	17 59.5	8 47.9	1 02.1	8 52.2	0 38.4	15 11.4	12 52.3	1 35.6	8 42.3
19 Tu	13 50 05	25 39 20	10♒37 25	16 53 13	9 48.3	19 11.9	9 41.3	1 45.6	9 17.1	0 30.4	15 07.0	12 52.1	1 35.7	8 44.1
20 W	13 54 01	26 38 56	23 14 39	29 42 32	9 46.9	20 22.5	10 35.3	2 29.1	9 42.0	0 22.3	15 02.6	12 51.9	1 35.9	8 46.0
21 Th	13 57 58	27 38 34	6♓16 19	12♓57 20	9 43.2	21 31.2	11 29.9	3 12.7	10 06.8	0 14.2	14 58.1	12 51.8	1 36.2	8 47.8
22 F	14 01 54	28 38 14	19 45 26	26 40 38	9 36.8	22 37.9	12 25.2	3 56.4	10 31.5	0 06.0	14 53.6	12D 51.8	1 36.4	8 49.7
23 Sa	14 05 51	29 37 56	3♈42 44	10♈51 25	9 27.9	23 42.4	13 21.1	4 40.2	10 56.2	29♈57.9	14 49.0	12 51.8	1 36.7	8 51.6
24 Su	14 09 47	0♏37 39	18 06 04	25 25 55	9 17.0	24 44.4	14 17.5	5 24.1	11 20.8	29 49.8	14 44.4	12 51.8	1 37.1	8 53.6
25 M	14 13 44	1 37 25	2♉50 03	10♉17 22	9 05.4	25 43.6	15 14.5	6 08.0	11 45.3	29 41.6	14 39.8	12 51.9	1 37.4	8 55.5
26 Tu	14 17 41	2 37 12	17 46 41	25 16 47	8 54.3	26 39.8	16 12.0	6 52.0	12 09.7	29 33.5	14 35.1	12 52.0	1 37.8	8 57.5
27 W	14 21 37	3 37 02	2♊46 26	10♊14 32	8 44.9	27 32.7	17 10.1	7 36.1	12 34.1	29 25.4	14 30.4	12 52.2	1 38.3	8 59.4
28 Th	14 25 34	4 36 54	17 40 02	25 02 04	8 38.2	28 21.9	18 08.7	8 20.3	12 58.3	29 17.4	14 25.7	12 52.5	1 38.8	9 01.4
29 F	14 29 30	5 36 48	2♋19 57	9♋33 09	8 34.3	29 06.9	19 07.8	9 04.6	13 22.5	29 09.3	14 20.9	12 52.7	1 39.3	9 03.5
30 Sa	14 33 27	6 36 44	16 41 20	23 44 21	8 32.7	29 47.4	20 07.3	9 48.9	13 46.7	29 01.3	14 16.2	12 53.1	1 39.8	9 05.5
31 Su	14 37 23	7 36 42	0♌42 09	7♌34 49	8 32.4	0♐22.8	21 07.3	10 33.3	14 10.7	28 53.4	14 11.4	12 53.5	1 40.4	9 07.6

Astro Data

	Dy Hr Mn
♀ D	11 0:23
☽ 0S	11 17:14
☿ 0S	17 19:26
☉ 0S	23 11:32
☽ 0N	26 0:40
☽ 0S	9 0:49
♃□♆	11 6:47
♆ D	14 1:36
♅ D	23 6:12
☽ 0N	23 10:50

Planet Ingress

	Dy Hr Mn
♂ ♐	2 19:29
☿ ♎	16 12:53
☉ ♎	23 11:31
⚳ ♍	27 16:21
☿ ♏	5 5:12
♀ ♍	7 16:51
♂ ♑	17 1:35
♃ ♈R	23 5:48
☉ ♏	23 20:52
☿ ♐	30 20:08

Last Aspect / ☽ Ingress (September)

Last Aspect Dy Hr Mn		☽ Ingress Dy Hr Mn
2 4:46	♂ ☍	♊ 2 5:25
3 15:00	♀ ⚹	♋ 4 8:09
5 13:23	♄ ⚹	♌ 6 11:29
7 20:30	♀ ☌	♍ 8 15:57
10 0:33	☿ ☌	♎ 10 22:16
12 9:38	♀ ⚹	♏ 13 7:08
15 15:24	☿ ⚹	♐ 15 18:35
17 20:06	☉ □	♑ 18 7:13
20 13:04	☉ △	♒ 20 18:38
22 10:38	♀ ☍	♓ 23 2:51
24 8:27	♄ ⚹	♈ 25 7:34
26 22:33	♀ △	♉ 27 9:51
29 2:00	♀ □	♊ 29 11:21

Last Aspect / ☽ Ingress (October)

Last Aspect Dy Hr Mn		☽ Ingress Dy Hr Mn
1 6:08	♀ ⚹	♋ 1 13:31
3 12:53	☿ □	♌ 3 17:13
5 20:14	♀ ☌	♍ 5 22:40
7 17:27	♂ □	♎ 8 5:52
10 5:33	♂ ⚹	♏ 10 15:01
11 21:42	♄ ☍	♐ 13 2:18
15 12:49	♂ ☌	♑ 15 15:04
17 15:00	☉ □	♒ 18 3:17
20 5:53	☉ △	♓ 20 12:33
22 4:24	☿ △	♈ 22 17:42
24 19:05	♃ ☌	♉ 24 19:25
26 14:21	☿ ☍	♊ 26 19:33
28 18:55	♃ ⚹	♋ 28 20:09
30 21:00	♃ □	♌ 30 22:47

☽ Phases & Eclipses

Dy Hr Mn	
2 22:17	☾ 10♊00
9 22:02	● 16♍47
17 20:06	☽ 24♐29
25 10:51	○ 1♈56
2 4:02	☾ 8♋31
9 11:34	● 15♎44
17 15:00	☽ 23♑48
24 21:02	○ 1♉00
31 12:04	☾ 7♌37

Astro Data

1 September 1999
Julian Day # 36403
SVP 5♓16'04"
GC 26♐50.1 ⚴ 7♋12.3
Eris 19♈31.0R ⚵ 0♐12.2
⚷ 28♏33.6 ⚶ 2♎13.7
☽ Mean ☊ 11♌30.0

1 October 1999
Julian Day # 36433
SVP 5♓16'02"
GC 26♐50.1 ⚴ 22♋25.7
Eris 19♈15.2R ⚵ 7♐06.0
⚷ 0♐49.9 ⚶ 17♎29.5
☽ Mean ☊ 9♌54.7

November 1999 LONGITUDE

Day	Sid.Time	☉	0 hr ☽	Noon ☽	True ☊	☿	♀	♂	⚳	♃	♄	♅	♆	♇
1 M	14 41 20	8♏36 43	14♌22 32	21♌05 34	8♌32.2	0♐52.5	22♍07.8	11♑17.8	14♍34.6	28♈45.5	14♉06.6	12♒53.9	1♒41.0	9♐09.6
2 Tu	14 45 16	9 36 46	27 44 12	4♍18 43	8R30.8	1 16.1	23 08.6	12 02.3	14 58.5	28R37.6	14R01.8	12 54.4	1 41.6	9 11.7
3 W	14 49 13	10 36 51	10♍49 27	17 16 41	8 27.0	1 32.8	24 09.9	12 46.9	15 22.2	28 29.8	13 56.9	12 55.0	1 42.3	9 13.8
4 Th	14 53 10	11 36 58	23 40 42	0♎01 45	8 20.2	1R41.9	25 11.6	13 31.6	15 45.9	28 22.1	13 52.1	12 55.6	1 43.0	9 15.9
5 F	14 57 06	12 37 06	6♎20 02	12 35 44	8 10.4	1 43.0	26 13.7	14 16.4	16 09.5	28 14.4	13 47.2	12 56.2	1 43.7	9 18.1
6 Sa	15 01 03	13 37 17	18 49 00	24 59 57	7 57.9	1 35.2	27 16.2	15 01.2	16 32.9	28 06.8	13 42.4	12 56.9	1 44.5	9 20.2
7 Su	15 04 59	14 37 30	1♏08 40	7♏15 16	7 43.8	1 18.2	28 19.0	15 46.1	16 56.3	27 59.3	13 37.5	12 57.7	1 45.3	9 22.4
8 M	15 08 56	15 37 45	13 19 48	19 22 24	7 29.2	0 51.5	29 22.2	16 31.1	17 19.6	27 51.9	13 32.7	12 58.5	1 46.1	9 24.5
9 Tu	15 12 52	16 38 01	25 23 09	1♐22 11	7 15.3	0 14.8	0♎25.7	17 16.1	17 42.7	27 44.6	13 27.8	12 59.3	1 47.0	9 26.7
10 W	15 16 49	17 38 19	7♐19 40	13 15 48	7 03.2	29♏28.3	1 29.5	18 01.2	18 05.8	27 37.4	13 23.0	13 00.2	1 47.9	9 28.9
11 Th	15 20 45	18 38 39	19 10 51	25 05 07	6 53.6	28 32.4	2 33.7	18 46.3	18 28.7	27 30.4	13 18.2	13 01.2	1 48.8	9 31.1
12 F	15 24 42	19 39 00	0♑58 55	6♑52 42	6 47.1	27 28.0	3 38.1	19 31.5	18 51.6	27 23.4	13 13.4	13 02.2	1 49.8	9 33.4
13 Sa	15 28 39	20 39 23	12 46 53	18 41 59	6 43.4	26 16.5	4 42.9	20 16.8	19 14.3	27 16.5	13 08.6	13 03.3	1 50.7	9 35.6
14 Su	15 32 35	21 39 47	24 38 34	0♒37 13	6D42.0	24 59.6	5 47.9	21 02.1	19 36.9	27 09.8	13 03.8	13 04.4	1 51.8	9 37.8
15 M	15 36 32	22 40 13	6♒38 34	12 43 17	6R42.0	23 39.5	6 53.3	21 47.5	19 59.3	27 03.2	12 59.0	13 05.5	1 52.8	9 40.1
16 Tu	15 40 28	23 40 40	18 52 01	25 05 28	6 42.1	22 18.9	7 58.9	22 32.9	20 21.7	26 56.7	12 54.3	13 06.7	1 53.9	9 42.4
17 W	15 44 25	24 41 08	1♓24 16	7♓49 04	6 41.4	21 00.3	9 04.7	23 18.4	20 43.9	26 50.4	12 49.6	13 08.0	1 55.0	9 44.6
18 Th	15 48 21	25 41 38	14 20 25	20 58 48	6 38.7	19 46.4	10 10.8	24 03.9	21 06.0	26 44.2	12 44.9	13 09.3	1 56.2	9 46.9
19 F	15 52 18	26 42 08	27 44 36	4♈38 02	6 33.6	18 39.5	11 17.2	24 49.5	21 28.0	26 38.2	12 40.3	13 10.6	1 57.4	9 49.2
20 Sa	15 56 14	27 42 40	11♈39 09	18 47 47	6 26.1	17 41.6	12 23.9	25 35.1	21 49.8	26 32.3	12 35.7	13 12.0	1 58.6	9 51.5
21 Su	16 00 11	28 43 14	26 03 34	3♉25 53	6 16.6	16 53.9	13 30.7	26 20.8	22 11.5	26 26.6	12 31.1	13 13.5	1 59.8	9 53.8
22 M	16 04 07	29 43 48	10♉53 54	18 26 32	6 06.2	16 17.6	14 37.8	27 06.5	22 33.1	26 21.0	12 26.6	13 15.0	2 01.1	9 56.1
23 Tu	16 08 04	0♐44 25	26 02 33	3♊40 37	5 56.1	15 52.8	15 45.2	27 52.2	22 54.6	26 15.6	12 22.1	13 16.5	2 02.4	9 58.4
24 W	16 12 01	1 45 02	11♊19 18	18 57 11	5 47.6	15D39.7	16 52.7	28 38.0	23 15.9	26 10.3	12 17.7	13 18.1	2 03.7	10 00.7
25 Th	16 15 57	2 45 41	26 32 55	4♋05 17	5 41.4	15 37.9	18 00.5	29 23.8	23 37.0	26 05.3	12 13.3	13 19.7	2 05.0	10 03.0
26 F	16 19 54	3 46 22	11♋33 15	18 55 58	5 38.0	15 46.8	19 08.5	0♒09.7	23 58.0	26 00.4	12 09.0	13 21.4	2 06.4	10 05.4
27 Sa	16 23 50	4 47 04	26 12 49	3♌23 23	5D36.8	16 05.5	20 16.7	0 55.6	24 18.9	25 55.6	12 04.7	13 23.1	2 07.8	10 07.7
28 Su	16 27 47	5 47 48	10♌27 27	17 24 58	5 37.2	16 33.3	21 25.1	1 41.5	24 39.6	25 51.1	12 00.5	13 24.9	2 09.3	10 10.0
29 M	16 31 43	6 48 33	24 16 04	1♍00 59	5R37.9	17 09.2	22 33.7	2 27.5	25 00.1	25 46.7	11 56.3	13 26.7	2 10.7	10 12.4
30 Tu	16 35 40	7 49 20	7♍40 01	14 13 33	5 37.8	17 52.4	23 42.4	3 13.5	25 20.5	25 42.5	11 52.2	13 28.6	2 12.2	10 14.7

December 1999 LONGITUDE

Day	Sid.Time	☉	0 hr ☽	Noon ☽	True ☊	☿	♀	♂	⚳	♃	♄	♅	♆	♇
1 W	16 39 37	8♐50 09	20♍42 01	27♍05 52	5♌36.0	18♏42.0	24♎51.4	3♒59.5	25♍40.8	25♈38.5	11♉48.1	13♒30.5	2♒13.7	10♐17.0
2 Th	16 43 33	9 50 58	3♎25 32	9♎41 27	5R31.8	19 37.3	26 00.5	4 45.6	26 00.8	25R34.7	11R44.1	13 32.4	2 15.2	10 19.4
3 F	16 47 30	10 51 50	15 54 02	22 03 40	5 25.2	20 37.5	27 09.8	5 31.7	26 20.7	25 31.1	11 40.2	13 34.4	2 16.8	10 21.7
4 Sa	16 51 26	11 52 42	28 10 42	4♏15 28	5 16.5	21 42.0	28 19.3	6 17.9	26 40.4	25 27.7	11 36.4	13 36.4	2 18.4	10 24.0
5 Su	16 55 23	12 53 36	10♏18 14	16 19 17	5 06.3	22 50.2	29 28.9	7 04.0	27 00.0	25 24.4	11 32.6	13 38.5	2 20.0	10 26.4
6 M	16 59 19	13 54 31	22 18 48	28 17 02	4 55.6	24 01.7	0♏38.7	7 50.3	27 19.3	25 21.4	11 28.9	13 40.6	2 21.7	10 28.7
7 Tu	17 03 16	14 55 27	4♐14 09	10♐10 20	4 45.4	25 15.9	1 48.6	8 36.5	27 38.5	25 18.6	11 25.2	13 42.8	2 23.3	10 31.1
8 W	17 07 12	15 56 24	16 05 47	22 00 40	4 36.7	26 32.6	2 58.7	9 22.8	27 57.5	25 15.9	11 21.7	13 45.0	2 25.0	10 33.4
9 Th	17 11 09	16 57 23	27 55 12	3♑49 37	4 29.9	27 51.3	4 08.9	10 09.1	28 16.3	25 13.5	11 18.2	13 47.2	2 26.7	10 35.7
10 F	17 15 06	17 58 22	9♑44 09	15 39 05	4 25.5	29 11.8	5 19.3	10 55.4	28 34.9	25 11.3	11 14.8	13 49.5	2 28.5	10 38.1
11 Sa	17 19 02	18 59 21	21 34 46	27 31 32	4D23.4	0♐33.8	6 29.7	11 41.7	28 53.3	25 09.3	11 11.5	13 51.8	2 30.2	10 40.4
12 Su	17 22 59	20 00 22	3♒29 47	9♒29 57	4 23.3	1 57.2	7 40.3	12 28.1	29 11.5	25 07.5	11 08.3	13 54.2	2 32.0	10 42.7
13 M	17 26 55	21 01 23	15 32 33	21 38 03	4 24.4	3 21.7	8 51.0	13 14.5	29 29.5	25 05.9	11 05.1	13 56.6	2 33.8	10 45.0
14 Tu	17 30 52	22 02 25	27 47 01	4♓00 01	4 26.0	4 47.2	10 01.9	14 00.9	29 47.3	25 04.5	11 02.1	13 59.0	2 35.6	10 47.3
15 W	17 34 48	23 03 27	10♓17 36	16 40 19	4R27.1	6 13.6	11 12.8	14 47.3	0♎04.9	25 03.3	10 59.1	14 01.5	2 37.5	10 49.6
16 Th	17 38 45	24 04 29	23 08 45	29 43 21	4 27.2	7 40.7	12 23.9	15 33.7	0 22.2	25 02.4	10 56.2	14 04.0	2 39.3	10 51.9
17 F	17 42 41	25 05 32	6♈24 35	13♈12 45	4 25.6	9 08.4	13 35.0	16 20.2	0 39.4	25 01.6	10 53.5	14 06.5	2 41.2	10 54.2
18 Sa	17 46 38	26 06 35	20 08 04	27 10 37	4 22.3	10 36.8	14 46.3	17 06.6	0 56.3	25 01.1	10 50.8	14 09.1	2 43.1	10 56.5
19 Su	17 50 35	27 07 39	4♉20 15	11♉36 40	4 17.6	12 05.6	15 57.7	17 53.1	1 12.9	25 00.7	10 48.2	14 11.7	2 45.1	10 58.7
20 M	17 54 31	28 08 43	18 59 19	26 27 29	4 12.0	13 34.9	17 09.2	18 39.6	1 29.4	25D00.6	10 45.7	14 14.4	2 47.0	11 01.0
21 Tu	17 58 28	29 09 47	4♊00 12	11♊36 20	4 06.6	15 04.7	18 20.7	19 26.1	1 45.6	25 00.7	10 43.3	14 17.0	2 49.0	11 03.3
22 W	18 02 24	0♑10 52	19 14 39	26 53 46	4 01.9	16 34.8	19 32.4	20 12.6	2 01.6	25 01.0	10 41.0	14 19.8	2 50.9	11 05.5
23 Th	18 06 21	1 11 57	4♋32 20	12♋08 59	3 58.7	18 05.2	20 44.2	20 59.1	2 17.3	25 01.5	10 38.8	14 22.5	2 52.9	11 07.7
24 F	18 10 17	2 13 03	19 42 31	27 11 46	3D57.2	19 36.0	21 56.0	21 45.6	2 32.8	25 02.2	10 36.7	14 25.3	2 55.0	11 10.0
25 Sa	18 14 14	3 14 10	4♌35 50	11♌53 57	3 57.2	21 07.2	23 08.0	22 32.1	2 48.0	25 03.1	10 34.7	14 28.1	2 57.0	11 12.2
26 Su	18 18 10	4 15 16	19 05 36	26 10 26	3 58.4	22 38.6	24 20.0	23 18.6	3 03.0	25 04.2	10 32.9	14 30.9	2 59.0	11 14.4
27 M	18 22 07	5 16 24	3♍08 18	9♍59 12	4 00.0	24 10.3	25 32.1	24 05.1	3 17.7	25 05.5	10 31.1	14 33.8	3 01.1	11 16.6
28 Tu	18 26 04	6 17 32	16 43 18	23 20 52	4 01.4	25 42.3	26 44.4	24 51.7	3 32.2	25 07.0	10 29.4	14 36.7	3 03.2	11 18.7
29 W	18 30 00	7 18 40	29 52 15	6♎17 54	4R02.1	27 14.6	27 56.6	25 38.2	3 46.3	25 08.8	10 27.8	14 39.6	3 05.2	11 20.9
30 Th	18 33 57	8 19 49	12♎38 18	18 53 57	4 01.6	28 47.2	29 09.0	26 24.7	4 00.2	25 10.7	10 26.4	14 42.6	3 07.3	11 23.0
31 F	18 37 53	9 20 58	25 05 22	1♏13 04	3 59.8	0♑20.1	0♐21.4	27 11.3	4 13.8	25 12.8	10 25.0	14 45.5	3 09.5	11 25.2

Astro Data

	Dy Hr Mn
☿ R	5 2:58
☽ 0S	5 7:33
♀ 0S	11 19:37
♄□♅	14 9:36
☽ 0N	19 22:09
☿ D	25 3:53
☽ 0S	2 14:05
♃⚼♇	5 3:29
☽ 0N	17 8:16
♄⚻♇	17 8:29
♃ D	20 14:48
☽ 0S	29 21:21

Planet Ingress

		Dy Hr Mn
♀	♎	9 2:19
☿	♏R	9 20:13
☉	♐	22 18:25
♂	♒	26 6:56
♀	♏	5 22:41
☿	♐	11 2:09
⚳	♎	15 5:19
☉	♑	22 7:44
♀	♐	31 4:54
☿	♑	31 6:48

Last Aspect / ☽ Ingress (November)

Last Aspect Dy Hr Mn			☽ Ingress	Dy Hr Mn
2 1:43	♃	△	♍	2 4:07
4 2:03	♀	☌	♎	4 11:57
6 18:01	♃	☍	♏	6 21:46
8 5:57	♂	⚹	♐	9 9:15
11 16:53	♃	△	♑	11 22:00
14 5:08	♃	□	♒	14 10:46
16 15:31	♃	⚹	♓	16 21:21
18 21:04	☉	△	♈	19 3:57
21 0:42	♃	☌	♉	21 6:26
23 2:24	♂	△	♊	23 6:13
24 23:20	♃	⚹	♋	25 5:29
26 23:36	♃	□	♌	27 6:19
29 2:43	♃	△	♍	29 10:11

Last Aspect / ☽ Ingress (December)

Last Aspect Dy Hr Mn			☽ Ingress	Dy Hr Mn
30 19:11	☿	⚹	♎	1 17:29
3 23:03	♀	☌	♏	4 3:35
6 2:29	☿	☌	♐	6 15:27
8 18:35	♃	△	♑	9 4:14
11 7:14	♃	□	♒	11 16:59
13 18:46	♃	⚹	♓	14 4:18
16 0:50	☉	□	♈	16 12:30
18 10:03	☉	△	♉	18 16:45
19 22:47	♂	□	♊	20 17:39
22 9:03	♃	⚹	♋	22 16:52
24 8:31	♃	□	♌	24 16:32
26 10:07	♃	△	♍	26 18:34
28 18:51	♀	⚹	♎	29 0:14
31 3:34	♂	△	♏	31 9:36

☽ Phases & Eclipses

Dy Hr Mn		
8 3:53	●	15♏17
16 9:03	☽	23♒33
23 7:04	○	0♊32
29 23:19	☾	7♍17
7 22:32	●	15♐22
16 0:50	☽	23♓36
22 17:31	○	0♋25
29 14:04	☾	7♎24

Astro Data

1 November 1999
Julian Day # 36464
SVP 5♓15'58"
GC 26♐50.2 ⚵ 6♌03.5
Eris 18♈56.9R ⚴ 16♐22.7
⚷ 4♐09.8 ⚶ 3♏44.3
☽ Mean ☊ 8♌16.2

1 December 1999
Julian Day # 36494
SVP 5♓15'54"
GC 26♐50.3 ⚵ 14♌28.9
Eris 18♈42.4R ⚴ 26♐39.0
⚷ 7♐51.4 ⚶ 19♏39.2
☽ Mean ☊ 6♌40.8

LONGITUDE — January 2000

Day	Sid.Time	☉	0 hr ☽	Noon ☽	True ☊	☿	♀	♂	⚳	♃	♄	♅	♆	♇
1 Sa	18 41 50	10♑22 08	7♏17 36	13♏19 26	3♌57.0	1♑53.4	1♐33.9	27♒57.8	4♎27.2	25♈15.2	10♉23.7	14♒48.6	3♒11.6	11♐27.3
2 Su	18 45 46	11 23 18	19 19 02	25 16 51	3R 53.4	3 26.9	2 46.5	28 44.3	4 40.2	25 17.7	10R 22.6	14 51.6	3 13.7	11 29.4
3 M	18 49 43	12 24 29	1♐13 19	7♐08 47	3 49.5	5 00.8	3 59.2	29 30.9	4 52.9	25 20.5	10 21.6	14 54.6	3 15.9	11 31.5
4 Tu	18 53 39	13 25 39	13 03 37	18 58 09	3 45.8	6 35.0	5 11.9	0♓17.4	5 05.4	25 23.4	10 20.6	14 57.7	3 18.0	11 33.5
5 W	18 57 36	14 26 50	24 52 40	0♑47 26	3 42.7	8 09.5	6 24.6	1 04.0	5 17.5	25 26.6	10 19.8	15 00.8	3 20.2	11 35.6
6 Th	19 01 33	15 28 01	6♑42 43	12 38 45	3 40.5	9 44.4	7 37.5	1 50.5	5 29.3	25 29.9	10 19.1	15 04.0	3 22.4	11 37.6
7 F	19 05 29	16 29 11	18 35 46	24 34 00	3D 39.2	11 19.7	8 50.3	2 37.0	5 40.8	25 33.5	10 18.6	15 07.1	3 24.6	11 39.7
8 Sa	19 09 26	17 30 22	0♒33 40	6♒35 01	3 39.0	12 55.4	10 03.3	3 23.6	5 52.0	25 37.2	10 18.1	15 10.3	3 26.8	11 41.7
9 Su	19 13 22	18 31 32	12 38 18	18 43 46	3 39.6	14 31.5	11 16.2	4 10.1	6 02.8	25 41.1	10 17.7	15 13.5	3 29.0	11 43.6
10 M	19 17 19	19 32 42	24 51 43	1♓02 26	3 40.7	16 08.0	12 29.3	4 56.6	6 13.3	25 45.3	10 17.5	15 16.7	3 31.2	11 45.6
11 Tu	19 21 15	20 33 51	7♓16 15	13 33 29	3 42.0	17 44.9	13 42.3	5 43.1	6 23.5	25 49.6	10D 17.3	15 20.0	3 33.5	11 47.5
12 W	19 25 12	21 35 00	19 54 29	26 19 36	3 43.1	19 22.3	14 55.4	6 29.6	6 33.3	25 54.1	10 17.3	15 23.2	3 35.7	11 49.4
13 Th	19 29 08	22 36 08	2♈49 11	9♈23 34	3 43.9	21 00.1	16 08.6	7 16.1	6 42.8	25 58.8	10 17.4	15 26.5	3 37.9	11 51.3
14 F	19 33 05	23 37 15	16 03 03	22 47 53	3R 44.2	22 38.4	17 21.8	8 02.5	6 51.9	26 03.6	10 17.6	15 29.8	3 40.2	11 53.2
15 Sa	19 37 02	24 38 22	29 38 17	6♉34 20	3 44.0	24 17.2	18 35.0	8 49.0	7 00.7	26 08.7	10 17.9	15 33.1	3 42.4	11 55.1
16 Su	19 40 58	25 39 28	13♉36 03	20 43 21	3 43.4	25 56.5	19 48.3	9 35.4	7 09.1	26 13.9	10 18.4	15 36.4	3 44.7	11 56.9
17 M	19 44 55	26 40 34	27 55 57	5♊13 29	3 42.6	27 36.3	21 01.6	10 21.8	7 17.2	26 19.4	10 18.9	15 39.7	3 47.0	11 58.7
18 Tu	19 48 51	27 41 38	12♊35 25	20 01 01	3 41.9	29 16.7	22 15.0	11 08.2	7 24.9	26 24.9	10 19.5	15 43.1	3 49.2	12 00.5
19 W	19 52 48	28 42 42	27 29 28	4♋59 49	3 41.3	0♒57.5	23 28.4	11 54.6	7 32.2	26 30.7	10 20.3	15 46.5	3 51.5	12 02.3
20 Th	19 56 44	29 43 46	12♋31 02	20 02 00	3D 41.0	2 38.8	24 41.8	12 41.0	7 39.1	26 36.7	10 21.2	15 49.8	3 53.8	12 04.0
21 F	20 00 41	0♒44 48	27 31 38	4♌58 51	3 40.9	4 20.7	25 55.3	13 27.3	7 45.7	26 42.8	10 22.2	15 53.2	3 56.1	12 05.7
22 Sa	20 04 38	1 45 50	12♌22 37	19 42 03	3 41.0	6 03.0	27 08.8	14 13.6	7 51.9	26 49.1	10 23.3	15 56.6	3 58.3	12 07.4
23 Su	20 08 34	2 46 51	26 56 22	4♍04 56	3R 41.1	7 45.9	28 22.3	14 59.9	7 57.7	26 55.5	10 24.5	16 00.1	4 00.6	12 09.1
24 M	20 12 31	3 47 52	11♍07 18	18 03 09	3 41.1	9 29.2	29 35.9	15 46.2	8 03.0	27 02.1	10 25.8	16 03.5	4 02.9	12 10.7
25 Tu	20 16 27	4 48 52	24 52 22	1♎34 56	3 41.0	11 12.9	0♑49.5	16 32.4	8 08.0	27 08.9	10 27.3	16 06.9	4 05.2	12 12.4
26 W	20 20 24	5 49 52	8♎11 00	14 40 49	3 40.9	12 57.0	2 03.1	17 18.7	8 12.6	27 15.8	10 28.8	16 10.4	4 07.4	12 13.9
27 Th	20 24 20	6 50 50	21 04 45	27 23 13	3D 40.7	14 41.4	3 16.8	18 04.9	8 16.8	27 22.9	10 30.4	16 13.8	4 09.7	12 15.5
28 F	20 28 17	7 51 49	3♏36 43	9♏45 46	3 40.7	16 26.1	4 30.4	18 51.1	8 20.6	27 30.2	10 32.2	16 17.3	4 12.0	12 17.0
29 Sa	20 32 13	8 52 47	15 50 58	21 52 53	3 40.8	18 10.9	5 44.2	19 37.2	8 23.9	27 37.6	10 34.1	16 20.7	4 14.3	12 18.6
30 Su	20 36 10	9 53 44	27 52 05	3♐49 11	3 41.3	19 55.8	6 57.9	20 23.4	8 26.8	27 45.2	10 36.0	16 24.2	4 16.5	12 20.0
31 M	20 40 06	10 54 40	9♐44 44	15 39 18	3 42.0	21 40.5	8 11.7	21 09.5	8 29.3	27 52.9	10 38.1	16 27.7	4 18.8	12 21.5

LONGITUDE — February 2000

Day	Sid.Time	☉	0 hr ☽	Noon ☽	True ☊	☿	♀	♂	⚳	♃	♄	♅	♆	♇
1 Tu	20 44 03	11♒55 36	21♐33 24	27♐27 31	3♌42.9	23♒25.1	9♑25.5	21♓55.6	8♎31.4	28♈00.8	10♉40.3	16♒31.2	4♒21.1	12♐22.9
2 W	20 48 00	12 56 31	3♑22 08	9♑17 41	3 43.8	25 09.1	10 39.3	22 41.7	8 33.0	28 08.8	10 42.6	16 34.7	4 23.3	12 24.3
3 Th	20 51 56	13 57 25	15 14 31	21 13 02	3 44.5	26 52.5	11 53.2	23 27.7	8 34.2	28 17.0	10 45.0	16 38.1	4 25.6	12 25.7
4 F	20 55 53	14 58 18	27 13 31	3♒16 15	3R 44.8	28 35.0	13 07.0	24 13.7	8 35.0	28 25.3	10 47.5	16 41.6	4 27.9	12 27.0
5 Sa	20 59 49	15 59 09	9♒21 28	15 29 22	3 44.5	0♓16.2	14 20.9	24 59.7	8R 35.3	28 33.8	10 50.2	16 45.1	4 30.1	12 28.3
6 Su	21 03 46	17 00 00	21 40 07	27 53 51	3 43.5	1 55.7	15 34.8	25 45.7	8 35.2	28 42.4	10 52.9	16 48.6	4 32.3	12 29.6
7 M	21 07 42	18 00 49	4♓10 41	10♓30 42	3 41.8	3 33.2	16 48.7	26 31.6	8 34.7	28 51.1	10 55.7	16 52.1	4 34.6	12 30.9
8 Tu	21 11 39	19 01 37	16 53 59	23 20 36	3 39.7	5 08.2	18 02.6	27 17.5	8 33.7	29 00.0	10 58.6	16 55.6	4 36.8	12 32.1
9 W	21 15 35	20 02 24	29 50 35	6♈23 59	3 37.2	6 40.2	19 16.6	28 03.4	8 32.3	29 09.0	11 01.6	16 59.1	4 39.0	12 33.3
10 Th	21 19 32	21 03 09	13♈00 50	19 41 10	3 35.0	8 08.5	20 30.5	28 49.3	8 30.4	29 18.2	11 04.8	17 02.6	4 41.2	12 34.4
11 F	21 23 29	22 03 52	26 25 02	3♉12 26	3 33.2	9 32.6	21 44.5	29 35.1	8 28.1	29 27.5	11 08.0	17 06.0	4 43.4	12 35.6
12 Sa	21 27 25	23 04 34	10♉03 22	16 57 50	3D 32.3	10 51.8	22 58.4	0♈20.8	8 25.4	29 36.9	11 11.3	17 09.5	4 45.6	12 36.7
13 Su	21 31 22	24 05 15	23 55 46	0♊57 07	3 32.4	12 05.4	24 12.4	1 06.6	8 22.2	29 46.4	11 14.7	17 13.0	4 47.8	12 37.7
14 M	21 35 18	25 05 53	8♊01 44	15 09 25	3 33.2	13 12.7	25 26.4	1 52.3	8 18.6	29 56.1	11 18.3	17 16.5	4 50.0	12 38.7
15 Tu	21 39 15	26 06 30	22 19 55	29 32 55	3 34.6	14 12.9	26 40.4	2 38.0	8 14.5	0♉05.9	11 21.9	17 19.9	4 52.2	12 39.8
16 W	21 43 11	27 07 05	6♋47 59	14♋04 36	3 36.0	15 05.3	27 54.4	3 23.6	8 10.0	0 15.8	11 25.6	17 23.4	4 54.3	12 40.7
17 Th	21 47 08	28 07 39	21 22 13	28 40 11	3R 36.9	15 49.3	29 08.4	4 09.2	8 05.1	0 25.8	11 29.4	17 26.8	4 56.4	12 41.7
18 F	21 51 04	29 08 11	5♌57 46	13♌14 14	3 36.7	16 24.3	0♒22.5	4 54.7	7 59.8	0 35.9	11 33.3	17 30.3	4 58.6	12 42.6
19 Sa	21 55 01	0♓08 41	20 28 48	27 40 44	3 35.1	16 49.7	1 36.5	5 40.3	7 54.1	0 46.2	11 37.3	17 33.7	5 00.7	12 43.4
20 Su	21 58 58	1 09 10	4♍49 17	11♍53 47	3 32.1	17 05.3	2 50.5	6 25.7	7 47.9	0 56.6	11 41.3	17 37.1	5 02.8	12 44.3
21 M	22 02 54	2 09 37	18 53 40	25 48 27	3 28.0	17R 10.7	4 04.6	7 11.2	7 41.3	1 07.0	11 45.5	17 40.5	5 04.9	12 45.1
22 Tu	22 06 51	3 10 02	2♎37 45	9♎21 20	3 23.2	17 06.0	5 18.7	7 56.6	7 34.4	1 17.6	11 49.8	17 43.9	5 06.9	12 45.8
23 W	22 10 47	4 10 26	15 59 06	22 31 04	3 18.3	16 51.2	6 32.7	8 41.9	7 27.0	1 28.3	11 54.1	17 47.3	5 09.0	12 46.6
24 Th	22 14 44	5 10 49	28 57 20	5♏18 10	3 14.1	16 26.8	7 46.8	9 27.3	7 19.2	1 39.1	11 58.5	17 50.7	5 11.0	12 47.3
25 F	22 18 40	6 11 10	11♏33 54	17 44 57	3 10.9	15 53.5	9 00.9	10 12.5	7 11.0	1 50.0	12 03.0	17 54.1	5 13.1	12 47.9
26 Sa	22 22 37	7 11 30	23 51 49	29 55 02	3D 09.2	15 12.0	10 15.0	10 57.8	7 02.5	2 01.0	12 07.6	17 57.4	5 15.1	12 48.6
27 Su	22 26 33	8 11 48	5♐55 11	11♐52 54	3 09.0	14 23.4	11 29.1	11 43.0	6 53.6	2 12.1	12 12.3	18 00.8	5 17.1	12 49.2
28 M	22 30 30	9 12 05	17 48 49	23 43 34	3 10.0	13 29.1	12 43.3	12 28.2	6 44.3	2 23.3	12 17.1	18 04.1	5 19.1	12 49.7
29 Tu	22 34 27	10 12 21	29 37 49	5♑32 10	3 11.6	12 30.4	13 57.4	13 13.3	6 34.7	2 34.6	12 21.9	18 07.4	5 21.0	12 50.3

Astro Data

	Dy Hr Mn
♄ D	12 4:59
☽ 0N	13 15:37
♃☌♇	26 3:36
☽ 0S	26 5:57
⚳ R	5 18:11
☽ 0N	9 20:59
♂ 0N	13 14:03
☿ R	21 12:47
☽ 0S	22 15:25

Planet Ingress

	Dy Hr Mn
♂ ♓	4 3:01
☿ ♒	18 22:20
☉ ♒	20 18:23
♀ ♑	24 19:52
☿ ♓	5 8:09
♂ ♈	12 1:04
♃ ♉	14 21:40
♀ ♒	18 4:43
☉ ♓	19 8:33

Last Aspect / ☽ Ingress (January)

Last Aspect Dy Hr Mn		☽ Ingress Dy Hr Mn
2 19:28	♂ □	♐ 2 21:32
5 1:06	♃ △	♑ 5 10:24
7 14:00	♃ □	♒ 7 22:53
10 1:41	♃ ⚹	♓ 10 9:59
12 2:23	☉ ⚹	♈ 12 18:48
14 17:47	♃ ☌	♉ 15 0:38
16 21:50	☿ △	♊ 17 3:25
18 22:21	♃ ⚹	♋ 19 4:01
20 22:36	♃ □	♌ 21 3:58
23 1:30	♀ △	♍ 23 5:07
24 7:48	♂ ☍	♎ 25 9:09
27 11:59	♃ ☍	♏ 27 17:01
29 7:11	♂ △	♐ 30 4:17

Last Aspect / ☽ Ingress (February)

Last Aspect Dy Hr Mn		☽ Ingress Dy Hr Mn
1 13:08	♃ △	♑ 1 17:10
4 2:16	♃ □	♒ 4 5:31
6 13:34	♃ ⚹	♓ 6 16:02
8 19:46	♂ ☌	♈ 9 0:17
11 5:19	♃ ☌	♉ 11 6:21
12 23:22	♀ △	♊ 13 10:23
15 5:51	☉ △	♋ 15 12:45
17 12:51	♀ ☍	♌ 17 14:11
18 19:05	♅ ☍	♍ 19 15:53
20 20:59	☿ ☍	♎ 21 19:21
23 3:16	♅ △	♏ 24 1:58
25 12:18	♅ □	♐ 26 12:10
28 0:28	♅ ⚹	♑ 29 0:45

☽ Phases & Eclipses

Dy Hr Mn		
6 18:14	●	15♑44
14 13:34	☽	23♈41
21 4:40	○	0♌26
21 4:43	•	T 1.325
28 7:57	☾	7♏42
5 13:03	●	16♒02
5 12:49:22	•	P 0.580
12 23:21	☽	23♉33
19 16:27	○	0♍20
27 3:54	☾	7♐51

Astro Data

1 January 2000
Julian Day # 36525
SVP 5♓15'49"
GC 26♐50.4 ⚴ 14♌02.6R
Eris 18♈35.5R ⚵ 7♑59.8
⚷ 11♐37.0 ⚶ 5♐58.3
☽ Mean ☊ 5♌02.4

1 February 2000
Julian Day # 36556
SVP 5♓15'44"
GC 26♐50.4 ⚴ 4♌40.9R
Eris 18♈39.0 ⚵ 19♑34.1
⚷ 14♐45.3 ⚶ 21♐43.8
☽ Mean ☊ 3♌23.9

March 2000

LONGITUDE

Day	Sid.Time	☉	0 hr ☽	Noon ☽	True ☊	☿	♀	♂	⚴	♃	♄	♅	♆	♇
1 W	22 38 23	11♓12 35	11♑27 16	17♑23 41	3♌13.4	11♓28.8	15♒11.5	13♈58.4	6♎24.7	2♉46.0	12♉26.9	18♒10.7	5♒23.0	12♐50.8
2 Th	22 42 20	12 12 48	23 21 58	29 22 38	3R 14.4	10R 25.9	16 25.7	14 43.4	6R 14.4	2 57.5	12 31.9	18 13.9	5 24.9	12 51.2
3 F	22 46 16	13 12 58	5♒26 10	11♒32 57	3 14.1	9 23.2	17 39.8	15 28.5	6 03.7	3 09.1	12 37.0	18 17.2	5 26.8	12 51.7
4 Sa	22 50 13	14 13 07	17 43 19	23 57 33	3 12.0	8 22.1	18 54.0	16 13.4	5 52.8	3 20.8	12 42.1	18 20.4	5 28.7	12 52.1
5 Su	22 54 09	15 13 15	0♓15 51	6♓38 21	3 07.8	7 23.9	20 08.1	16 58.4	5 41.5	3 32.5	12 47.4	18 23.6	5 30.5	12 52.4
6 M	22 58 06	16 13 20	13 05 04	19 35 59	3 01.8	6 29.7	21 22.2	17 43.2	5 30.0	3 44.4	12 52.7	18 26.8	5 32.4	12 52.8
7 Tu	23 02 02	17 13 24	26 11 00	2♈49 55	2 54.4	5 40.3	22 36.4	18 28.1	5 18.2	3 56.3	12 58.1	18 30.0	5 34.2	12 53.0
8 W	23 05 59	18 13 26	9♈32 32	16 18 33	2 46.4	4 56.4	23 50.5	19 12.9	5 06.1	4 08.3	13 03.6	18 33.2	5 36.0	12 53.3
9 Th	23 09 56	19 13 25	23 07 40	29 59 33	2 38.8	4 18.7	25 04.7	19 57.7	4 53.9	4 20.4	13 09.1	18 36.3	5 37.8	12 53.5
10 F	23 13 52	20 13 23	6♉53 51	13♉50 17	2 32.4	3 47.3	26 18.8	20 42.4	4 41.3	4 32.6	13 14.7	18 39.4	5 39.6	12 53.7
11 Sa	23 17 49	21 13 18	20 48 30	27 48 14	2 27.9	3 22.4	27 33.0	21 27.0	4 28.6	4 44.9	13 20.4	18 42.5	5 41.3	12 53.9
12 Su	23 21 45	22 13 12	4♊49 14	11♊51 17	2D 25.5	3 04.2	28 47.1	22 11.7	4 15.7	4 57.2	13 26.1	18 45.5	5 43.0	12 54.0
13 M	23 25 42	23 13 03	18 54 12	25 57 48	2 25.1	2 52.5	0♓01.2	22 56.3	4 02.7	5 09.6	13 31.9	18 48.6	5 44.7	12 54.1
14 Tu	23 29 38	24 12 52	3♋01 57	10♋06 30	2 25.8	2D 47.1	1 15.4	23 40.8	3 49.4	5 22.1	13 37.8	18 51.6	5 46.4	12R 54.1
15 W	23 33 35	25 12 38	17 11 16	24 16 05	2R 26.8	2 48.0	2 29.5	24 25.3	3 36.1	5 34.6	13 43.8	18 54.6	5 48.0	12 54.1
16 Th	23 37 31	26 12 22	1♌20 44	8♌24 57	2 26.9	2 54.7	3 43.6	25 09.7	3 22.6	5 47.3	13 49.8	18 57.5	5 49.7	12 54.1
17 F	23 41 28	27 12 04	15 28 26	22 30 50	2 25.1	3 07.2	4 57.7	25 54.1	3 09.0	5 59.9	13 55.8	19 00.4	5 51.3	12 54.1
18 Sa	23 45 25	28 11 44	29 31 45	6♍30 46	2 20.9	3 25.0	6 11.8	26 38.4	2 55.3	6 12.7	14 01.9	19 03.3	5 52.8	12 54.0
19 Su	23 49 21	29 11 22	13♍27 25	20 21 14	2 14.2	3 47.8	7 25.9	27 22.7	2 41.6	6 25.5	14 08.1	19 06.2	5 54.4	12 53.8
20 M	23 53 18	0♈10 57	27 11 47	3♎58 39	2 05.3	4 15.5	8 40.1	28 07.0	2 27.8	6 38.4	14 14.4	19 09.1	5 55.9	12 53.7
21 Tu	23 57 14	1 10 31	10♎41 27	17 19 53	1 55.0	4 47.7	9 54.2	28 51.2	2 14.0	6 51.3	14 20.7	19 11.9	5 57.4	12 53.5
22 W	0 01 11	2 10 02	23 53 44	0♏22 53	1 44.4	5 24.2	11 08.3	29 35.3	2 00.2	7 04.3	14 27.0	19 14.7	5 58.9	12 53.3
23 Th	0 05 07	3 09 32	6♏47 17	13 07 00	1 34.5	6 04.7	12 22.4	0♉19.4	1 46.4	7 17.4	14 33.4	19 17.4	6 00.3	12 53.0
24 F	0 09 04	4 09 00	19 22 11	25 33 07	1 26.2	6 48.9	13 36.5	1 03.5	1 32.6	7 30.5	14 39.9	19 20.1	6 01.8	12 52.7
25 Sa	0 13 00	5 08 26	1♐40 08	7♐43 38	1 20.1	7 36.7	14 50.6	1 47.5	1 18.8	7 43.6	14 46.4	19 22.8	6 03.1	12 52.4
26 Su	0 16 57	6 07 51	13 44 08	19 42 09	1 16.4	8 27.8	16 04.7	2 31.5	1 05.1	7 56.9	14 53.0	19 25.5	6 04.5	12 52.1
27 M	0 20 53	7 07 13	25 38 19	1♑33 15	1D 14.9	9 22.1	17 18.8	3 15.4	0 51.5	8 10.1	14 59.6	19 28.1	6 05.9	12 51.7
28 Tu	0 24 50	8 06 34	7♑27 35	13 22 02	1 14.8	10 19.3	18 32.9	3 59.3	0 37.9	8 23.5	15 06.3	19 30.7	6 07.2	12 51.3
29 W	0 28 47	9 05 53	19 17 17	25 13 59	1R 15.3	11 19.3	19 47.0	4 43.1	0 24.5	8 36.8	15 13.0	19 33.3	6 08.5	12 50.8
30 Th	0 32 43	10 05 11	1♒12 50	7♒14 28	1 15.3	12 22.0	21 01.1	5 26.9	0 11.2	8 50.3	15 19.8	19 35.8	6 09.7	12 50.3
31 F	0 36 40	11 04 26	13 19 30	19 28 28	1 13.7	13 27.3	22 15.2	6 10.6	29♍58.0	9 03.7	15 26.6	19 38.3	6 10.9	12 49.8

April 2000

LONGITUDE

Day	Sid.Time	☉	0 hr ☽	Noon ☽	True ☊	☿	♀	♂	⚴	♃	♄	♅	♆	♇
1 Sa	0 40 36	12♈03 40	25♒41 54	2♓00 11	1♌09.9	14♓34.9	23♓29.2	6♉54.3	29♍45.1	9♉17.3	15♉33.5	19♒40.7	6♒12.1	12♐49.3
2 Su	0 44 33	13 02 51	8♓23 40	14 52 34	1R 03.4	15 44.8	24 43.3	7 38.0	29R 32.2	9 30.8	15 40.4	19 43.1	6 13.3	12R 48.7
3 M	0 48 29	14 02 01	21 27 00	28 06 55	0 54.4	16 57.0	25 57.4	8 21.6	29 19.6	9 44.4	15 47.3	19 45.5	6 14.4	12 48.1
4 Tu	0 52 26	15 01 09	4♈52 11	11♈42 32	0 43.5	18 11.2	27 11.5	9 05.1	29 07.2	9 58.1	15 54.3	19 47.9	6 15.5	12 47.5
5 W	0 56 22	16 00 15	18 37 34	25 36 46	0 31.6	19 27.5	28 25.5	9 48.6	28 55.0	10 11.8	16 01.3	19 50.2	6 16.6	12 46.8
6 Th	1 00 19	16 59 19	2♉39 33	9♉45 14	0 20.1	20 45.8	29 39.6	10 32.1	28 43.1	10 25.5	16 08.4	19 52.4	6 17.7	12 46.1
7 F	1 04 16	17 58 20	16 53 08	24 02 33	0 10.2	22 06.0	0♈53.6	11 15.5	28 31.4	10 39.3	16 15.5	19 54.7	6 18.7	12 45.4
8 Sa	1 08 12	18 57 20	1♊12 48	8♊23 14	0 02.7	23 28.0	2 07.6	11 58.9	28 20.0	10 53.1	16 22.6	19 56.9	6 19.7	12 44.6
9 Su	1 12 09	19 56 17	15 33 20	22 42 35	29♋58.0	24 51.8	3 21.7	12 42.2	28 08.9	11 06.9	16 29.8	19 59.0	6 20.6	12 43.8
10 M	1 16 05	20 55 12	29 50 37	6♋57 08	29 55.9	26 17.4	4 35.7	13 25.5	27 58.1	11 20.8	16 37.0	20 01.1	6 21.6	12 43.0
11 Tu	1 20 02	21 54 05	14♋01 55	21 04 50	29 55.4	27 44.7	5 49.7	14 08.7	27 47.6	11 34.7	16 44.3	20 03.2	6 22.5	12 42.2
12 W	1 23 58	22 52 55	28 05 48	5♌04 46	29 55.4	29 13.8	7 03.7	14 51.8	27 37.4	11 48.6	16 51.6	20 05.2	6 23.3	12 41.3
13 Th	1 27 55	23 51 43	12♌01 43	18 56 38	29 54.5	0♈44.5	8 17.7	15 35.0	27 27.5	12 02.6	16 58.9	20 07.2	6 24.1	12 40.4
14 F	1 31 51	24 50 29	25 49 29	2♍40 14	29 51.6	2 16.9	9 31.7	16 18.0	27 18.0	12 16.5	17 06.2	20 09.2	6 24.9	12 39.5
15 Sa	1 35 48	25 49 12	9♍28 48	16 15 05	29 46.0	3 50.9	10 45.6	17 01.0	27 08.8	12 30.6	17 13.6	20 11.1	6 25.7	12 38.5
16 Su	1 39 45	26 47 54	22 58 57	29 40 13	29 37.4	5 26.6	11 59.6	17 44.0	27 00.0	12 44.6	17 21.0	20 12.9	6 26.4	12 37.6
17 M	1 43 41	27 46 33	6♎18 44	12♎54 17	29 26.3	7 03.9	13 13.5	18 26.9	26 51.6	12 58.6	17 28.4	20 14.7	6 27.1	12 36.6
18 Tu	1 47 38	28 45 10	19 26 40	25 55 44	29 13.5	8 42.9	14 27.5	19 09.8	26 43.5	13 12.7	17 35.8	20 16.5	6 27.8	12 35.5
19 W	1 51 34	29 43 45	2♏21 19	8♏43 19	29 00.2	10 23.5	15 41.4	19 52.6	26 35.8	13 26.8	17 43.3	20 18.2	6 28.5	12 34.5
20 Th	1 55 31	0♉42 18	15 01 41	21 16 25	28 47.5	12 05.8	16 55.4	20 35.4	26 28.4	13 40.9	17 50.8	20 19.9	6 29.1	12 33.4
21 F	1 59 27	1 40 50	27 27 36	3♐35 24	28 36.6	13 49.7	18 09.3	21 18.1	26 21.5	13 55.1	17 58.3	20 21.6	6 29.6	12 32.3
22 Sa	2 03 24	2 39 20	9♐40 01	15 41 45	28 28.2	15 35.3	19 23.2	22 00.8	26 14.9	14 09.2	18 05.8	20 23.2	6 30.2	12 31.2
23 Su	2 07 20	3 37 48	21 40 57	27 38 04	28 22.5	17 22.5	20 37.1	22 43.4	26 08.8	14 23.4	18 13.4	20 24.7	6 30.7	12 30.0
24 M	2 11 17	4 36 15	3♑33 35	9♑28 02	28 19.4	19 11.5	21 51.0	23 26.0	26 03.0	14 37.6	18 21.0	20 26.3	6 31.2	12 28.9
25 Tu	2 15 14	5 34 40	15 22 00	21 16 07	28D 18.3	21 02.1	23 04.9	24 08.5	25 57.6	14 51.8	18 28.6	20 27.7	6 31.6	12 27.7
26 W	2 19 10	6 33 03	27 11 02	3♒07 27	28R 18.2	22 54.4	24 18.8	24 51.0	25 52.7	15 06.0	18 36.2	20 29.1	6 32.0	12 26.5
27 Th	2 23 07	7 31 25	9♒06 02	15 07 29	28 18.1	24 48.4	25 32.7	25 33.4	25 48.1	15 20.3	18 43.8	20 30.5	6 32.4	12 25.2
28 F	2 27 03	8 29 45	21 12 29	27 21 41	28 16.8	26 44.1	26 46.6	26 15.8	25 44.0	15 34.5	18 51.4	20 31.8	6 32.8	12 24.0
29 Sa	2 31 00	9 28 03	3♓35 42	9♓55 04	28 13.5	28 41.4	28 00.5	26 58.2	25 40.3	15 48.8	18 59.1	20 33.1	6 33.1	12 22.7
30 Su	2 34 56	10 26 20	16 20 17	22 51 43	28 07.8	0♉40.4	29 14.4	27 40.5	25 37.0	16 03.0	19 06.8	20 34.4	6 33.3	12 21.4

Astro Data	Dy Hr Mn
♄⊼♇	6 12:14
☽0N	8 2:47
☿D	14 20:40
♇R	15 11:51
♃□♆	16 17:14
☉0N	20 7:35
☽0S	21 0:36
☽0N	4 10:46
♀0N	9 14:16
♃⊼♇	16 0:47
☿0N	16 18:11
☽0S	17 8:37

Planet Ingress		Dy Hr Mn
♀	♓	13 11:36
☉	♈	20 7:35
♂	♉	23 1:25
⚴	♍R	31 8:25
♀	♈	6 18:37
☊	♋R	9 0:11
☿	♈	13 0:17
☉	♉	19 18:40
☿	♉	30 3:53

Last Aspect Dy Hr Mn		☽ Ingress Dy Hr Mn	
1 4:38	♂□	♒	2 13:14
4 1:12	♀☌	♓	4 23:30
6 5:17	☉☌	♈	7 6:54
9 2:34	♀⚹	♉	9 12:01
11 11:31	♀□	♊	11 15:46
13 6:59	☉□	♋	13 18:51
15 13:43	☉△	♌	15 21:43
17 18:07	♂△	♍	18 0:48
20 4:44	☉☍	♎	20 4:57
22 10:26	♂☍	♏	22 11:17
23 23:53	♅□	♐	24 20:43
26 11:26	♅⚹	♑	27 8:51
28 23:43	♀⚹	♒	29 21:34

Last Aspect Dy Hr Mn		☽ Ingress Dy Hr Mn	
31 12:19	♅☌	♓	1 8:12
3 7:44	♀☌	♈	3 15:22
5 2:04	♅⚹	♉	5 19:29
7 8:24	☿⚹	♊	7 21:58
9 16:01	☿□	♋	10 0:16
12 0:45	☿△	♌	12 3:16
13 21:14	☉△	♍	14 7:19
15 13:45	♄△	♎	16 12:36
18 17:42	☉☍	♏	18 19:35
20 10:36	♂☍	♐	21 4:58
22 21:25	♅⚹	♑	23 16:47
25 18:12	♂△	♒	26 5:42
28 10:44	♀⚹	♓	28 17:06

☽ Phases & Eclipses Dy Hr Mn	
6 5:17	● 15♓57
13 6:59	☽ 23♊01
20 4:44	○ 29♍53
28 0:21	☾ 7♑38
4 18:12	● 15♈16
11 13:30	☽ 21♋58
18 17:42	○ 28♎59
26 19:30	☾ 6♒51

Astro Data

1 March 2000
Julian Day # 36585
SVP 5♓15'41"
GC 26♐50.5 ⚳ 28♋42.3R
Eris 18♈51.0 ⚵ 0♒09.0
⚷ 16♐39.2 ⚶ 5♑26.4
☽ Mean ☊ 1♌51.7

1 April 2000
Julian Day # 36616
SVP 5♓15'38"
GC 26♐50.6 ⚳ 1♌06.6
Eris 19♈09.8 ⚵ 10♒38.6
⚷ 17♐13.2R ⚶ 18♑09.6
☽ Mean ☊ 0♌13.2

LONGITUDE — May 2000

Day	Sid.Time	☉	0 hr ☽	Noon ☽	True ☊	☿	♀	♂	⚳	♃	♄	♅	♆	♇
1 M	2 38 53	11♉24 36	29♓29 36	6♈14 04	27♋59.6	2♉41.0	0♉28.3	28♉22.8	25♍34.1	16♉17.3	19♉14.4	20♒35.5	6♒33.6	12♐20.1
2 Tu	2 42 49	12 22 49	13♈05 04	20 02 23	27R49.4	4 43.2	1 42.1	29 05.0	25R31.6	16 31.6	19 22.1	20 36.7	6 33.8	12R18.7
3 W	2 46 46	13 21 02	27 05 39	4♉14 18	27 38.3	6 46.9	2 56.0	29 47.2	25 29.6	16 45.9	19 29.8	20 37.8	6 34.0	12 17.4
4 Th	2 50 42	14 19 12	11♉27 38	18 44 49	27 27.4	8 52.0	4 09.9	0♊29.3	25 27.9	17 00.1	19 37.5	20 38.8	6 34.1	12 16.0
5 F	2 54 39	15 17 21	26 04 55	3♊26 56	27 17.8	10 58.4	5 23.7	1 11.4	25 26.7	17 14.4	19 45.2	20 39.8	6 34.2	12 14.6
6 Sa	2 58 36	16 15 29	10♊49 52	18 12 44	27 10.7	13 06.0	6 37.6	1 53.4	25 25.9	17 28.7	19 53.0	20 40.8	6 34.3	12 13.2
7 Su	3 02 32	17 13 34	25 34 38	2♋54 46	27 06.2	15 14.6	7 51.4	2 35.4	25D25.5	17 43.0	20 00.7	20 41.7	6 34.4	12 11.8
8 M	3 06 29	18 11 38	10♋12 26	17 27 06	27D04.2	17 24.1	9 05.2	3 17.4	25 25.6	17 57.3	20 08.4	20 42.5	6R34.4	12 10.4
9 Tu	3 10 25	19 09 39	24 38 19	1♌45 50	27 04.0	19 34.3	10 19.0	3 59.3	25 26.0	18 11.6	20 16.1	20 43.3	6 34.4	12 08.9
10 W	3 14 22	20 07 39	8♌49 27	15 49 07	27R04.4	21 44.8	11 32.9	4 41.1	25 26.9	18 25.9	20 23.9	20 44.1	6 34.3	12 07.5
11 Th	3 18 18	21 05 37	22 44 50	29 36 40	27 04.2	23 55.6	12 46.7	5 22.9	25 28.1	18 40.1	20 31.6	20 44.8	6 34.2	12 06.0
12 F	3 22 15	22 03 32	6♍24 43	13♍09 08	27 02.3	26 06.2	14 00.4	6 04.7	25 29.8	18 54.4	20 39.3	20 45.4	6 34.1	12 04.5
13 Sa	3 26 12	23 01 26	19 50 01	26 27 32	26 58.1	28 16.4	15 14.2	6 46.4	25 31.9	19 08.7	20 47.0	20 46.0	6 34.0	12 03.0
14 Su	3 30 08	23 59 19	3♎01 47	9♎32 53	26 51.4	0♊26.0	16 28.0	7 28.0	25 34.3	19 22.9	20 54.8	20 46.6	6 33.8	12 01.5
15 M	3 34 05	24 57 09	16 00 54	22 25 54	26 42.5	2 34.6	17 41.8	8 09.7	25 37.2	19 37.1	21 02.5	20 47.1	6 33.6	11 59.9
16 Tu	3 38 01	25 54 58	28 47 57	5♏07 05	26 32.1	4 42.0	18 55.5	8 51.2	25 40.4	19 51.4	21 10.2	20 47.5	6 33.3	11 58.4
17 W	3 41 58	26 52 46	11♏23 19	17 36 44	26 21.3	6 47.9	20 09.3	9 32.7	25 44.1	20 05.6	21 17.9	20 48.0	6 33.1	11 56.9
18 Th	3 45 54	27 50 32	23 47 21	29 55 17	26 11.0	8 52.0	21 23.0	10 14.2	25 48.1	20 19.8	21 25.6	20 48.3	6 32.8	11 55.3
19 F	3 49 51	28 48 16	6♐00 36	12♐03 29	26 02.1	10 54.2	22 36.8	10 55.7	25 52.4	20 34.0	21 33.3	20 48.6	6 32.4	11 53.7
20 Sa	3 53 47	29 46 00	18 04 06	24 02 41	25 55.3	12 54.3	23 50.5	11 37.1	25 57.2	20 48.2	21 41.0	20 48.9	6 32.1	11 52.2
21 Su	3 57 44	0♊43 42	29 59 30	5♑54 53	25 50.9	14 52.0	25 04.3	12 18.4	26 02.3	21 02.3	21 48.7	20 49.1	6 31.7	11 50.6
22 M	4 01 41	1 41 23	11♑49 13	17 42 55	25D48.7	16 47.2	26 18.0	12 59.7	26 07.8	21 16.5	21 56.3	20 49.3	6 31.2	11 49.0
23 Tu	4 05 37	2 39 03	23 36 27	29 30 21	25 48.4	18 39.8	27 31.8	13 41.0	26 13.7	21 30.6	22 04.0	20 49.4	6 30.8	11 47.4
24 W	4 09 34	3 36 42	5♒25 09	11♒21 28	25 49.3	20 29.7	28 45.5	14 22.2	26 19.8	21 44.7	22 11.6	20R49.5	6 30.3	11 45.8
25 Th	4 13 30	4 34 19	17 19 53	23 21 04	25 50.4	22 16.8	29 59.2	15 03.4	26 26.4	21 58.8	22 19.2	20 49.5	6 29.7	11 44.2
26 F	4 17 27	5 31 56	29 25 40	5♓34 18	25R51.0	24 01.1	1♊13.0	15 44.5	26 33.3	22 12.8	22 26.8	20 49.4	6 29.2	11 42.6
27 Sa	4 21 23	6 29 32	11♓47 37	18 06 13	25 50.2	25 42.5	2 26.7	16 25.6	26 40.5	22 26.9	22 34.4	20 49.4	6 28.6	11 41.0
28 Su	4 25 20	7 27 07	24 30 38	1♈01 22	25 47.7	27 20.9	3 40.4	17 06.7	26 48.1	22 40.9	22 42.0	20 49.2	6 28.0	11 39.3
29 M	4 29 16	8 24 41	7♈38 47	14 23 09	25 43.3	28 56.3	4 54.2	17 47.7	26 56.0	22 54.9	22 49.6	20 49.0	6 27.4	11 37.7
30 Tu	4 33 13	9 22 14	21 14 36	28 13 05	25 37.4	0♋28.7	6 07.9	18 28.7	27 04.2	23 08.9	22 57.1	20 48.8	6 26.7	11 36.1
31 W	4 37 09	10 19 46	5♉18 23	12♉30 07	25 30.6	1 58.1	7 21.6	19 09.6	27 12.8	23 22.8	23 04.6	20 48.5	6 26.0	11 34.5

LONGITUDE — June 2000

Day	Sid.Time	☉	0 hr ☽	Noon ☽	True ☊	☿	♀	♂	⚳	♃	♄	♅	♆	♇
1 Th	4 41 06	11♊17 18	19♉47 39	27♉10 14	25♋23.8	3♋24.3	8♊35.4	19♊50.5	27♍21.7	23♉36.7	23♉12.1	20♒48.2	6♒25.3	11♐32.8
2 F	4 45 03	12 14 49	4♊36 54	12♊06 38	25R17.9	4 47.4	9 49.1	20 31.4	27 30.9	23 50.6	23 19.6	20R47.8	6R24.5	11R31.2
3 Sa	4 48 59	13 12 18	19 38 15	27 10 35	25 13.5	6 07.4	11 02.8	21 12.2	27 40.4	24 04.5	23 27.0	20 47.4	6 23.7	11 29.6
4 Su	4 52 56	14 09 47	4♋42 28	12♋12 49	25D11.1	7 24.1	12 16.6	21 53.0	27 50.3	24 18.3	23 34.5	20 47.0	6 22.9	11 28.0
5 M	4 56 52	15 07 14	19 40 36	27 04 58	25 10.5	8 37.6	13 30.3	22 33.7	28 00.4	24 32.1	23 41.9	20 46.4	6 22.1	11 26.3
6 Tu	5 00 49	16 04 41	4♌25 12	11♌40 44	25 11.2	9 47.8	14 44.0	23 14.4	28 10.9	24 45.8	23 49.2	20 45.9	6 21.2	11 24.7
7 W	5 04 45	17 02 06	18 51 10	25 56 15	25 12.6	10 54.6	15 57.7	23 55.1	28 21.6	24 59.6	23 56.6	20 45.3	6 20.3	11 23.1
8 Th	5 08 42	17 59 30	2♍55 51	9♍49 59	25R13.7	11 57.9	17 11.5	24 35.7	28 32.6	25 13.2	24 03.9	20 44.6	6 19.4	11 21.5
9 F	5 12 39	18 56 52	16 38 44	23 22 16	25 13.8	12 57.8	18 25.2	25 16.3	28 43.9	25 26.9	24 11.2	20 43.9	6 18.4	11 19.9
10 Sa	5 16 35	19 54 14	0♎00 49	6♎34 37	25 12.6	13 54.0	19 38.9	25 56.8	28 55.5	25 40.5	24 18.4	20 43.2	6 17.5	11 18.3
11 Su	5 20 32	20 51 35	13 03 58	19 29 09	25 09.8	14 46.6	20 52.6	26 37.3	29 07.4	25 54.0	24 25.6	20 42.4	6 16.5	11 16.7
12 M	5 24 28	21 48 54	25 50 28	2♏08 13	25 05.7	15 35.4	22 06.3	27 17.8	29 19.5	26 07.5	24 32.8	20 41.5	6 15.4	11 15.1
13 Tu	5 28 25	22 46 13	8♏22 39	14 34 04	25 00.6	16 20.4	23 20.0	27 58.2	29 31.9	26 21.0	24 40.0	20 40.6	6 14.4	11 13.5
14 W	5 32 21	23 43 31	20 42 42	26 48 47	24 55.2	17 01.4	24 33.7	28 38.5	29 44.5	26 34.4	24 47.1	20 39.7	6 13.3	11 11.9
15 Th	5 36 18	24 40 48	2♐52 34	8♐54 15	24 50.1	17 38.4	25 47.4	29 18.9	29 57.4	26 47.8	24 54.2	20 38.7	6 12.2	11 10.3
16 F	5 40 14	25 38 05	14 54 04	20 52 15	24 45.8	18 11.2	27 01.1	29 59.2	0♎10.6	27 01.1	25 01.2	20 37.7	6 11.1	11 08.8
17 Sa	5 44 11	26 35 21	26 49 00	2♑44 36	24 42.7	18 39.7	28 14.8	0♋39.4	0 24.0	27 14.4	25 08.2	20 36.7	6 10.0	11 07.2
18 Su	5 48 08	27 32 36	8♑39 16	14 33 19	24D40.9	19 04.0	29 28.5	1 19.7	0 37.7	27 27.7	25 15.2	20 35.6	6 08.8	11 05.7
19 M	5 52 04	28 29 51	20 27 02	26 20 44	24 40.5	19 23.8	0♋42.2	1 59.8	0 51.5	27 40.9	25 22.1	20 34.4	6 07.6	11 04.2
20 Tu	5 56 01	29 27 06	2♒14 48	8♒09 38	24 41.2	19 39.1	1 56.0	2 40.0	1 05.7	27 54.0	25 29.0	20 33.3	6 06.4	11 02.6
21 W	5 59 57	0♋24 20	14 05 38	20 03 15	24 42.5	19 49.8	3 09.7	3 20.1	1 20.0	28 07.1	25 35.8	20 32.0	6 05.2	11 01.1
22 Th	6 03 54	1 21 34	26 02 59	2♓05 19	24 44.2	19R56.0	4 23.4	4 00.2	1 34.6	28 20.1	25 42.6	20 30.8	6 04.0	10 59.6
23 F	6 07 50	2 18 48	8♓10 48	14 19 57	24 45.6	19 57.7	5 37.1	4 40.2	1 49.4	28 33.1	25 49.4	20 29.5	6 02.7	10 58.1
24 Sa	6 11 47	3 16 02	20 33 19	26 51 26	24R46.5	19 54.7	6 50.8	5 20.3	2 04.4	28 46.0	25 56.1	20 28.1	6 01.4	10 56.6
25 Su	6 15 43	4 13 16	3♈14 48	9♈43 54	24 46.5	19 47.3	8 04.6	6 00.2	2 19.7	28 58.9	26 02.8	20 26.7	6 00.1	10 55.2
26 M	6 19 40	5 10 29	16 19 09	23 00 53	24 45.7	19 35.6	9 18.3	6 40.2	2 35.1	29 11.7	26 09.4	20 25.3	5 58.8	10 53.7
27 Tu	6 23 37	6 07 43	29 49 22	6♉44 41	24 44.1	19 19.6	10 32.0	7 20.1	2 50.8	29 24.4	26 15.9	20 23.8	5 57.4	10 52.3
28 W	6 27 33	7 04 57	13♉46 50	20 55 37	24 42.0	18 59.6	11 45.8	8 00.0	3 06.7	29 37.1	26 22.5	20 22.3	5 56.1	10 50.9
29 Th	6 31 30	8 02 11	28 10 42	5♊31 31	24 39.9	18 35.9	12 59.5	8 39.8	3 22.7	29 49.7	26 28.9	20 20.8	5 54.7	10 49.5
30 F	6 35 26	8 59 24	12♊57 22	20 27 21	24 38.0	18 08.9	14 13.3	9 19.6	3 39.0	0♊02.3	26 35.4	20 19.2	5 53.3	10 48.1

Astro Data

	Dy Hr Mn
☽ 0N	1 20:44
⚳ D	7 21:51
♆ R	8 12:30
♄□♅	13 8:34
☽ 0S	14 15:22
♃□♅	20 13:16
♅ R	25 8:20
♃☌♄	28 16:04
☽ 0N	29 7:06
☽ 0S	10 21:37
☿ R	23 8:32
☽ 0N	25 16:05

Planet Ingress

		Dy Hr Mn
♀	♉	1 2:49
♂	♊	3 19:18
☿	♊	14 7:10
☉	♊	20 17:49
♀	♊	25 12:15
☿	♋	30 4:27
⚳	♎	15 16:42
♂	♋	16 12:30
♀	♋	18 22:15
☉	♋	21 1:48
♃	♊	30 7:35

Last Aspect / ☽ Ingress (May)

Last Aspect Dy Hr Mn			☽ Ingress	Dy Hr Mn
30 21:13	♂	⚹	♈	1 0:55
2 12:59	♅	⚹	♉	3 4:54
4 15:07	♅	□	♊	5 6:23
6 16:01	♅	△	♋	7 7:14
8 16:31	♄	⚹	♌	9 9:01
11 0:11	☿	□	♍	11 12:41
13 15:57	☿	△	♎	13 18:27
15 8:55	♅	△	♏	16 2:16
18 7:34	☉	☍	♐	18 12:09
20 5:30	♅	⚹	♑	21 0:01
23 7:31	♀	△	♒	23 13:00
25 9:56	♄	□	♓	26 1:07
28 4:17	☿	□	♈	28 10:08
29 23:15	♅	⚹	♉	30 15:02

Last Aspect / ☽ Ingress (June)

Last Aspect Dy Hr Mn			☽ Ingress	Dy Hr Mn
1 6:08	♃	☌	♊	1 16:34
3 2:03	♂	☌	♋	3 16:30
5 7:48	♃	⚹	♌	5 16:45
7 10:22	♃	□	♍	7 18:57
9 15:48	♃	△	♎	9 23:59
12 2:15	♂	△	♏	12 7:55
14 11:31	♃	☍	♐	14 18:18
17 1:50	♀	☍	♑	17 6:26
19 14:46	♃	△	♒	19 19:26
22 4:25	♃	□	♓	22 7:52
24 15:40	♃	⚹	♈	24 17:55
26 7:23	♅	⚹	♉	27 0:19
29 2:34	♃	☌	♊	29 2:59

☽ Phases & Eclipses

Dy Hr Mn		
4 4:12	●	14♉00
10 20:01	☽	20♌27
18 7:34	○	27♏40
26 11:55	☾	5♓32
2 12:14	●	12♊15
9 3:29	☽	18♍37
16 22:27	○	26♐03
25 1:00	☾	3♈47

Astro Data

1 May 2000
Julian Day # 36646
SVP 5♓15'35"
GC 26♐50.6 ⚴ 9♌08.1
Eris 19♈29.3 ⚵ 19♒15.0
⚷ 16♐18.3R ⚶ 27♑15.5
☽ Mean ☊ 28♋37.9

1 June 2000
Julian Day # 36677
SVP 5♓15'31"
GC 26♐50.7 ⚴ 20♌20.1
Eris 19♈45.9 ⚵ 25♒20.3
⚷ 14♐20.2R ⚶ 1♒12.4
☽ Mean ☊ 26♋59.4

July 2000

LONGITUDE

Day	Sid.Time	☉	0 hr ☽	Noon ☽	True☊	☿	♀	♂	⚳	♃	♄	♅	♆	♇
1 Sa	6 39 23	9♋56 38	28♊00 28	5♋35 35	24♋36.8	17♋38.8	15♋27.0	9♋59.4	3♎55.5	0♊14.8	26♉41.7	20♒17.6	5♒51.9	10♐46.7
2 Su	6 43 19	10 53 52	13♋11 30	20 46 59	24D 36.2	17R 06.2	16 40.8	10 39.2	4 12.2	0 27.2	26 48.0	20R 16.0	5R 50.5	10R 45.4
3 M	6 47 16	11 51 06	28 20 53	5♌52 05	24 36.4	16 31.5	17 54.6	11 18.9	4 29.0	0 39.6	26 54.3	20 14.3	5 49.0	10 44.0
4 Tu	6 51 12	12 48 19	13♌19 34	20 42 29	24 37.0	15 55.4	19 08.3	11 58.6	4 46.1	0 51.9	27 00.5	20 12.6	5 47.6	10 42.7
5 W	6 55 09	13 45 33	28 00 07	5♍11 56	24 37.9	15 18.4	20 22.1	12 38.2	5 03.3	1 04.1	27 06.6	20 10.8	5 46.1	10 41.4
6 Th	6 59 06	14 42 46	12♍17 35	19 16 50	24 38.8	14 41.1	21 35.8	13 17.9	5 20.7	1 16.2	27 12.7	20 09.0	5 44.6	10 40.2
7 F	7 03 02	15 39 58	26 09 39	2♎56 05	24 39.3	14 04.2	22 49.6	13 57.4	5 38.3	1 28.3	27 18.7	20 07.2	5 43.1	10 38.9
8 Sa	7 06 59	16 37 11	9♎36 18	16 10 36	24R 39.5	13 28.3	24 03.4	14 37.0	5 56.1	1 40.3	27 24.7	20 05.4	5 41.6	10 37.7
9 Su	7 10 55	17 34 23	22 39 17	29 02 45	24 39.4	12 54.0	25 17.1	15 16.5	6 14.0	1 52.2	27 30.6	20 03.5	5 40.1	10 36.4
10 M	7 14 52	18 31 35	5♏21 26	11♏35 45	24 38.9	12 22.1	26 30.9	15 56.0	6 32.1	2 04.0	27 36.4	20 01.6	5 38.6	10 35.2
11 Tu	7 18 48	19 28 47	17 46 11	23 53 10	24 38.3	11 52.9	27 44.7	16 35.4	6 50.4	2 15.8	27 42.2	19 59.7	5 37.0	10 34.1
12 W	7 22 45	20 26 00	29 57 09	5♐58 33	24 37.8	11 27.1	28 58.4	17 14.8	7 08.8	2 27.4	27 47.9	19 57.7	5 35.5	10 32.9
13 Th	7 26 41	21 23 12	11♐57 48	17 55 17	24 37.3	11 05.1	0♌12.2	17 54.2	7 27.4	2 39.0	27 53.6	19 55.7	5 33.9	10 31.8
14 F	7 30 38	22 20 24	23 51 23	29 46 26	24 37.0	10 47.4	1 26.0	18 33.6	7 46.1	2 50.5	27 59.2	19 53.7	5 32.4	10 30.7
15 Sa	7 34 35	23 17 37	5♑40 47	11♑34 45	24 36.9	10 34.3	2 39.7	19 12.9	8 05.0	3 01.9	28 04.7	19 51.7	5 30.8	10 29.6
16 Su	7 38 31	24 14 50	17 28 37	23 22 43	24 36.8	10 26.2	3 53.5	19 52.2	8 24.0	3 13.3	28 10.1	19 49.6	5 29.2	10 28.6
17 M	7 42 28	25 12 04	29 17 18	5♒12 39	24 36.8	10D 23.2	5 07.2	20 31.5	8 43.2	3 24.5	28 15.5	19 47.5	5 27.6	10 27.5
18 Tu	7 46 24	26 09 17	11♒09 05	17 06 51	24 36.8	10 25.6	6 21.0	21 10.7	9 02.5	3 35.7	28 20.8	19 45.4	5 26.0	10 26.5
19 W	7 50 21	27 06 32	23 06 15	29 07 37	24 36.6	10 33.6	7 34.8	21 49.9	9 21.9	3 46.7	28 26.0	19 43.3	5 24.4	10 25.5
20 Th	7 54 17	28 03 46	5♓11 14	11♓17 26	24 36.2	10 47.2	8 48.6	22 29.1	9 41.5	3 57.7	28 31.2	19 41.1	5 22.8	10 24.6
21 F	7 58 14	29 01 02	17 26 35	23 39 01	24 35.7	11 06.5	10 02.3	23 08.3	10 01.2	4 08.6	28 36.3	19 38.9	5 21.2	10 23.6
22 Sa	8 02 10	29 58 18	29 55 07	6♈15 13	24 35.2	11 31.6	11 16.1	23 47.4	10 21.1	4 19.4	28 41.3	19 36.7	5 19.6	10 22.7
23 Su	8 06 07	0♌55 35	12♈39 43	19 08 58	24D 34.8	12 02.5	12 29.9	24 26.5	10 41.1	4 30.0	28 46.3	19 34.5	5 18.0	10 21.8
24 M	8 10 04	1 52 53	25 43 16	2♉22 57	24 34.7	12 39.1	13 43.7	25 05.6	11 01.2	4 40.6	28 51.1	19 32.3	5 16.3	10 21.0
25 Tu	8 14 00	2 50 12	9♉08 14	15 59 19	24 34.9	13 21.5	14 57.4	25 44.6	11 21.5	4 51.1	28 55.9	19 30.0	5 14.7	10 20.2
26 W	8 17 57	3 47 32	22 56 17	29 59 08	24 35.4	14 09.5	16 11.2	26 23.6	11 41.9	5 01.5	29 00.6	19 27.8	5 13.1	10 19.4
27 Th	8 21 53	4 44 53	7♊07 42	14♊21 45	24 36.2	15 03.2	17 25.0	27 02.6	12 02.4	5 11.8	29 05.3	19 25.5	5 11.5	10 18.6
28 F	8 25 50	5 42 15	21 40 51	29 04 27	24 37.0	16 02.4	18 38.8	27 41.6	12 23.0	5 21.9	29 09.8	19 23.2	5 09.8	10 17.8
29 Sa	8 29 46	6 39 38	6♋31 49	14♋02 06	24R 37.6	17 07.1	19 52.6	28 20.6	12 43.7	5 32.0	29 14.3	19 20.9	5 08.2	10 17.1
30 Su	8 33 43	7 37 02	21 34 20	29 07 28	24 37.7	18 17.0	21 06.4	28 59.5	13 04.6	5 42.0	29 18.7	19 18.6	5 06.6	10 16.5
31 M	8 37 40	8 34 26	6♌40 21	14♌11 52	24 37.2	19 32.2	22 20.2	29 38.4	13 25.6	5 51.8	29 23.0	19 16.3	5 04.9	10 15.8

August 2000

LONGITUDE

Day	Sid.Time	☉	0 hr ☽	Noon ☽	True☊	☿	♀	♂	⚳	♃	♄	♅	♆	♇
1 Tu	8 41 36	9♌31 52	21♌40 55	29♌06 27	24♋35.9	20♋52.4	23♌34.0	0♌17.3	13♎46.7	6♊01.5	29♉27.3	19♒13.9	5♒03.3	10♐15.2
2 W	8 45 33	10 29 18	6♍27 32	13♍43 23	24R 34.1	22 17.5	24 47.8	0 56.1	14 07.9	6 11.1	29 31.4	19R 11.6	5R 01.7	10R 14.6
3 Th	8 49 29	11 26 45	20 53 21	27 56 58	24 32.0	23 47.3	26 01.6	1 34.9	14 29.2	6 20.6	29 35.4	19 09.2	5 00.1	10 14.0
4 F	8 53 26	12 24 12	4♎53 56	11♎44 07	24 30.0	25 21.5	27 15.4	2 13.7	14 50.6	6 30.0	29 39.4	19 06.8	4 58.5	10 13.5
5 Sa	8 57 22	13 21 40	18 27 31	25 04 19	24 28.4	26 59.9	28 29.2	2 52.5	15 12.1	6 39.3	29 43.3	19 04.4	4 56.8	10 13.0
6 Su	9 01 19	14 19 09	1♏34 45	7♏59 14	24D 27.5	28 42.2	29 43.0	3 31.2	15 33.8	6 48.4	29 47.1	19 02.1	4 55.2	10 12.5
7 M	9 05 15	15 16 39	14 18 10	20 32 04	24 27.4	0♌28.1	0♍56.7	4 09.9	15 55.5	6 57.4	29 50.8	18 59.7	4 53.6	10 12.0
8 Tu	9 09 12	16 14 10	26 41 28	2♐46 58	24 28.2	2 17.3	2 10.5	4 48.6	16 17.3	7 06.3	29 54.4	18 57.3	4 52.0	10 11.6
9 W	9 13 08	17 11 41	8♐49 06	14 48 29	24 29.6	4 09.3	3 24.3	5 27.3	16 39.2	7 15.1	29 57.9	18 54.9	4 50.5	10 11.2
10 Th	9 17 05	18 09 13	20 45 39	26 41 11	24 31.3	6 03.9	4 38.0	6 05.9	17 01.3	7 23.7	0♊01.4	18 52.5	4 48.9	10 10.9
11 F	9 21 02	19 06 46	2♑35 35	8♑29 23	24 32.8	8 00.7	5 51.8	6 44.5	17 23.4	7 32.2	0 04.7	18 50.1	4 47.3	10 10.6
12 Sa	9 24 58	20 04 21	14 23 01	20 16 56	24R 33.6	9 59.1	7 05.6	7 23.1	17 45.6	7 40.6	0 07.9	18 47.7	4 45.8	10 10.3
13 Su	9 28 55	21 01 56	26 11 33	2♒07 13	24 33.5	11 59.0	8 19.3	8 01.7	18 07.9	7 48.8	0 11.1	18 45.3	4 44.2	10 10.0
14 M	9 32 51	21 59 32	8♒04 15	14 02 57	24 32.0	13 59.9	9 33.0	8 40.2	18 30.2	7 56.9	0 14.2	18 42.9	4 42.7	10 09.8
15 Tu	9 36 48	22 57 10	20 03 36	26 02 24	24 29.2	16 01.4	10 46.8	9 18.7	18 52.7	8 04.9	0 17.1	18 40.6	4 41.1	10 09.6
16 W	9 40 44	23 54 48	2♓11 34	8♓19 17	24 25.2	18 03.4	12 00.5	9 57.2	19 15.2	8 12.7	0 20.0	18 38.2	4 39.6	10 09.5
17 Th	9 44 41	24 52 28	14 29 42	20 42 59	24 20.4	20 05.4	13 14.2	10 35.7	19 37.9	8 20.4	0 22.7	18 35.8	4 38.1	10 09.3
18 F	9 48 37	25 50 10	26 59 15	3♈18 39	24 15.2	22 07.3	14 27.9	11 14.1	20 00.6	8 27.9	0 25.4	18 33.4	4 36.6	10 09.2
19 Sa	9 52 34	26 47 53	9♈41 18	16 07 20	24 10.3	24 08.7	15 41.6	11 52.6	20 23.4	8 35.4	0 28.0	18 31.1	4 35.1	10 09.2
20 Su	9 56 31	27 45 37	22 36 54	29 10 07	24 06.3	26 09.6	16 55.3	12 31.0	20 46.2	8 42.6	0 30.5	18 28.7	4 33.7	10D 09.1
21 M	10 00 27	28 43 23	5♉47 09	12♉28 07	24 03.6	28 09.7	18 09.0	13 09.4	21 09.2	8 49.7	0 32.8	18 26.3	4 32.2	10 09.1
22 Tu	10 04 24	29 41 11	19 13 09	26 02 22	24D 02.5	0♍09.0	19 22.7	13 47.7	21 32.2	8 56.7	0 35.1	18 24.0	4 30.8	10 09.2
23 W	10 08 20	0♍39 01	2♊55 50	9♊53 37	24 02.8	2 07.3	20 36.4	14 26.1	21 55.3	9 03.5	0 37.3	18 21.7	4 29.3	10 09.2
24 Th	10 12 17	1 36 53	16 55 41	24 01 58	24 03.9	4 04.5	21 50.1	15 04.4	22 18.5	9 10.2	0 39.4	18 19.4	4 27.9	10 09.3
25 F	10 16 13	2 34 46	1♋12 16	8♋26 19	24 05.2	6 00.6	23 03.8	15 42.8	22 41.7	9 16.7	0 41.3	18 17.1	4 26.5	10 09.5
26 Sa	10 20 10	3 32 41	15 43 45	23 04 03	24R 05.9	7 55.5	24 17.5	16 21.1	23 05.0	9 23.0	0 43.2	18 14.8	4 25.2	10 09.6
27 Su	10 24 06	4 30 38	0♌26 35	7♌50 38	24 05.2	9 49.2	25 31.2	16 59.3	23 28.4	9 29.2	0 45.0	18 12.5	4 23.8	10 09.8
28 M	10 28 03	5 28 36	15 15 20	22 39 47	24 02.7	11 41.6	26 44.8	17 37.6	23 51.9	9 35.3	0 46.6	18 10.3	4 22.4	10 10.1
29 Tu	10 32 00	6 26 36	0♍03 01	7♍24 04	23 58.2	13 32.8	27 58.5	18 15.8	24 15.4	9 41.1	0 48.2	18 08.0	4 21.1	10 10.4
30 W	10 35 56	7 24 38	14 42 00	21 55 54	23 52.0	15 22.7	29 12.2	18 54.0	24 39.0	9 46.8	0 49.6	18 05.8	4 19.8	10 10.7
31 Th	10 39 53	8 22 41	29 05 01	6♎08 42	23 45.0	17 11.4	0♎25.8	19 32.2	25 02.7	9 52.3	0 51.0	18 03.6	4 18.5	10 11.0

Astro Data	Dy Hr Mn
☽ 0S	8 4:25
☿ D	17 13:20
☽ 0N	22 22:50
♃△♆	27 11:22
☽ 0S	4 12:27
⚳ 0S	6 20:11
☽ 0N	19 4:01
♇ D	20 22:43
☽ 0S	31 21:37

Planet Ingress		Dy Hr Mn
♀	♌	13 8:02
☉	♌	22 12:43
♂	♌	1 1:21
♀	♍	6 17:32
☿	♌	7 5:42
♄	♊	10 2:26
☿	♍	22 10:11
☉	♍	22 19:49
♀	♎	31 3:35

Last Aspect Dy Hr Mn			☽ Ingress	Dy Hr Mn
30 11:47	♅	△	♋	1 3:09
2 21:36	♄	⚹	♌	3 2:38
4 22:26	♄	□	♍	5 3:19
7 1:57	♄	△	♎	7 6:47
9 4:10	♀	□	♏	9 13:48
11 20:29	♀	△	♐	12 0:06
13 16:03	♅	⚹	♑	14 12:28
16 21:48	♄	△	♒	17 1:27
19 10:37	♄	□	♓	19 13:44
21 23:08	☉	△	♈	22 0:09
23 22:11	♂	□	♉	24 7:44
26 10:20	♄	☌	♊	26 12:01
27 20:18	♅	△	♋	28 13:30
30 12:18	♄	⚹	♌	30 13:23

Last Aspect Dy Hr Mn			☽ Ingress	Dy Hr Mn
1 12:34	♄	□	♍	1 13:27
3 14:50	♄	△	♎	3 15:31
5 18:56	♀	⚹	♏	5 21:04
8 6:17	♄	☍	♐	8 6:30
9 20:15	♅	⚹	♑	10 18:44
11 6:02	♀	△	♒	13 7:43
15 5:13	☉	☍	♓	15 19:41
16 19:58	♀	☍	♈	18 5:44
20 9:14	☉	△	♉	20 13:31
22 18:51	☉	□	♊	22 18:55
24 7:57	♀	□	♋	24 22:00
26 14:11	♀	⚹	♌	26 23:17
28 4:44	♅	☍	♍	28 23:55
31 1:21	♀	☌	♎	31 1:33

☽ Phases & Eclipses Dy Hr Mn		
1 19:20	●	10♋14
1 19:32:32	•	P 0.477
8 12:53	☽	16♎39
16 13:55	○	24♑19
16 13:56	•	T 1.768
24 11:02	☾	1♉51
31 2:25	●	8♌12
31 2:13:02	•	P 0.603
7 1:02	☽	14♏50
15 5:13	○	22♒41
22 18:51	☾	29♉58
29 10:19	●	6♍23

Astro Data

1 July 2000
Julian Day # 36707
SVP 5♓15'25"
GC 26♐50.8 ⚵ 2♍33.3
Eris 19♈54.9 ⚴ 26♒48.9R
⚷ 12♐20.6R ⚶ 28♑02.2R
☽ Mean ☊ 25♋24.1

1 August 2000
Julian Day # 36738
SVP 5♓15'20"
GC 26♐50.8 ⚵ 15♍54.8
Eris 19♈54.6R ⚴ 22♒29.1R
⚷ 11♐08.5R ⚶ 20♑54.8R
☽ Mean ☊ 23♋45.6

LONGITUDE — September 2000

Day	Sid.Time	☉	0 hr ☽	Noon ☽	True ☊	☿	♀	♂	⚳	♃	♄	♅	♆	♇
1 F	10 43 49	9♍20 46	13♎06 25	19♎57 50	23♋37.9	18♍58.7	1♎39.4	20♌10.4	25♎26.4	9♊57.7	0♊52.2	18♒01.4	4♒17.3	10♐11.3
2 Sa	10 47 46	10 18 52	26 42 45	3♏21 10	23R31.7	20 44.9	2 53.1	20 48.6	25 50.2	10 02.9	0 53.3	17R59.2	4R16.0	10 11.7
3 Su	10 51 42	11 16 59	9♏53 10	16 19 01	23 26.9	22 29.7	4 06.7	21 26.7	26 14.1	10 07.9	0 54.4	17 57.1	4 14.8	10 12.2
4 M	10 55 39	12 15 08	22 39 04	28 53 46	23 24.0	24 13.4	5 20.3	22 04.8	26 38.0	10 12.8	0 55.3	17 55.0	4 13.6	10 12.7
5 Tu	10 59 35	13 13 19	5♐03 39	11♐09 18	23D23.0	25 55.8	6 33.9	22 42.9	27 01.9	10 17.5	0 56.1	17 52.9	4 12.4	10 13.2
6 W	11 03 32	14 11 31	17 11 19	23 10 23	23 23.3	27 37.1	7 47.5	23 21.0	27 26.0	10 22.0	0 56.8	17 50.8	4 11.2	10 13.7
7 Th	11 07 29	15 09 44	29 07 08	5♑02 14	23 24.5	29 17.1	9 01.0	23 59.0	27 50.1	10 26.3	0 57.4	17 48.8	4 10.1	10 14.3
8 F	11 11 25	16 07 59	10♑56 20	16 50 04	23R25.5	0♎56.0	10 14.6	24 37.0	28 14.2	10 30.5	0 57.9	17 46.7	4 09.0	10 14.9
9 Sa	11 15 22	17 06 16	22 44 02	28 38 48	23 25.5	2 33.7	11 28.1	25 15.0	28 38.4	10 34.4	0 58.2	17 44.7	4 07.9	10 15.5
10 Su	11 19 18	18 04 34	4♒34 54	10♒32 48	23 23.9	4 10.3	12 41.6	25 53.0	29 02.6	10 38.2	0 58.5	17 42.8	4 06.8	10 16.2
11 M	11 23 15	19 02 54	16 32 56	22 35 41	23 20.0	5 45.8	13 55.1	26 31.0	29 26.9	10 41.8	0R58.7	17 40.8	4 05.8	10 16.8
12 Tu	11 27 11	20 01 15	28 41 21	4♓50 11	23 13.7	7 20.1	15 08.6	27 08.9	29 51.2	10 45.2	0 58.7	17 38.9	4 04.8	10 17.6
13 W	11 31 08	20 59 38	11♓02 21	17 18 00	23 05.3	8 53.4	16 22.1	27 46.9	0♏15.6	10 48.5	0 58.7	17 37.0	4 03.8	10 18.3
14 Th	11 35 04	21 58 03	23 37 10	29 59 53	22 55.3	10 25.5	17 35.6	28 24.8	0 40.0	10 51.5	0 58.5	17 35.2	4 02.8	10 19.1
15 F	11 39 01	22 56 30	6♈26 05	12♈55 42	22 44.8	11 56.6	18 49.0	29 02.7	1 04.5	10 54.4	0 58.2	17 33.4	4 01.9	10 19.9
16 Sa	11 42 57	23 54 59	19 28 36	26 04 40	22 34.6	13 26.5	20 02.5	29 40.6	1 29.1	10 57.1	0 57.8	17 31.6	4 01.0	10 20.8
17 Su	11 46 54	24 53 30	2♉43 44	9♉25 40	22 25.9	14 55.4	21 15.9	0♍18.4	1 53.6	10 59.6	0 57.4	17 29.8	4 00.1	10 21.7
18 M	11 50 51	25 52 03	16 10 20	22 57 37	22 19.3	16 23.1	22 29.3	0 56.3	2 18.2	11 01.8	0 56.8	17 28.1	3 59.2	10 22.6
19 Tu	11 54 47	26 50 39	29 47 25	6♊39 40	22 15.3	17 49.7	23 42.7	1 34.1	2 42.9	11 03.9	0 56.1	17 26.4	3 58.4	10 23.6
20 W	11 58 44	27 49 16	13♊34 18	20 31 17	22D13.6	19 15.3	24 56.1	2 11.9	3 07.6	11 05.9	0 55.3	17 24.8	3 57.6	10 24.5
21 Th	12 02 40	28 47 56	27 30 35	4♋32 10	22 13.5	20 39.6	26 09.5	2 49.7	3 32.4	11 07.6	0 54.3	17 23.2	3 56.8	10 25.6
22 F	12 06 37	29 46 38	11♋35 57	18 41 50	22R13.9	22 02.8	27 22.8	3 27.5	3 57.1	11 09.1	0 53.3	17 21.6	3 56.1	10 26.6
23 Sa	12 10 33	0♎45 23	25 49 39	2♌59 12	22 13.5	23 24.8	28 36.2	4 05.3	4 22.0	11 10.4	0 52.2	17 20.1	3 55.4	10 27.7
24 Su	12 14 30	1 44 10	10♌10 09	17 22 06	22 11.3	24 45.6	29 49.5	4 43.0	4 46.8	11 11.5	0 50.9	17 18.6	3 54.7	10 28.8
25 M	12 18 26	2 42 58	24 34 35	1♍47 00	22 06.5	26 05.1	1♏02.9	5 20.8	5 11.8	11 12.4	0 49.6	17 17.1	3 54.0	10 29.9
26 Tu	12 22 23	3 41 49	8♍58 43	16 09 02	21 58.9	27 23.3	2 16.2	5 58.5	5 36.7	11 13.2	0 48.2	17 15.7	3 53.4	10 31.1
27 W	12 26 20	4 40 42	23 17 13	0♎22 33	21 48.8	28 40.1	3 29.5	6 36.2	6 01.7	11 13.7	0 46.6	17 14.3	3 52.8	10 32.3
28 Th	12 30 16	5 39 37	7♎24 20	14 21 55	21 37.3	29 55.5	4 42.8	7 13.9	6 26.7	11 14.0	0 44.9	17 12.9	3 52.2	10 33.5
29 F	12 34 13	6 38 34	21 14 45	28 02 25	21 25.4	1♏09.3	5 56.0	7 51.5	6 51.8	11R14.1	0 43.2	17 11.6	3 51.7	10 34.7
30 Sa	12 38 09	7 37 33	4♏44 36	11♏21 06	21 14.5	2 21.5	7 09.3	8 29.2	7 16.8	11 14.0	0 41.3	17 10.4	3 51.2	10 36.0

LONGITUDE — October 2000

Day	Sid.Time	☉	0 hr ☽	Noon ☽	True ☊	☿	♀	♂	⚳	♃	♄	♅	♆	♇
1 Su	12 42 06	8♎36 34	17♏51 53	24♏17 03	21♋05.5	3♏32.0	8♏22.5	9♍06.8	7♏42.0	11♊13.7	0♊39.3	17♒09.1	3♒50.7	10♐37.3
2 M	12 46 02	9 35 37	0♐36 47	6♐51 25	20R59.0	4 40.6	9 35.8	9 44.4	8 07.1	11R13.2	0R37.3	17R08.0	3R50.2	10 38.7
3 Tu	12 49 59	10 34 41	13 01 23	19 07 09	20 55.1	5 47.3	10 49.0	10 22.0	8 32.3	11 12.5	0 35.1	17 06.8	3 49.8	10 40.1
4 W	12 53 55	11 33 48	25 09 18	1♑08 27	20D53.3	6 51.8	12 02.2	10 59.6	8 57.5	11 11.6	0 32.8	17 05.8	3 49.4	10 41.4
5 Th	12 57 52	12 32 56	7♑05 15	13 00 22	20R53.0	7 54.0	13 15.3	11 37.1	9 22.8	11 10.5	0 30.5	17 04.7	3 49.1	10 42.9
6 F	13 01 49	13 32 06	18 54 32	24 48 25	20 53.0	8 53.8	14 28.5	12 14.7	9 48.0	11 09.2	0 28.0	17 03.7	3 48.8	10 44.3
7 Sa	13 05 45	14 31 17	0♒42 43	6♒38 06	20 52.2	9 50.8	15 41.6	12 52.2	10 13.3	11 07.7	0 25.5	17 02.8	3 48.5	10 45.8
8 Su	13 09 42	15 30 31	12 35 14	18 34 41	20 49.7	10 45.0	16 54.7	13 29.7	10 38.6	11 06.0	0 22.8	17 01.9	3 48.3	10 47.3
9 M	13 13 38	16 29 46	24 37 02	0♓42 47	20 44.7	11 35.8	18 07.8	14 07.2	11 04.0	11 04.1	0 20.1	17 01.0	3 48.0	10 48.8
10 Tu	13 17 35	17 29 03	6♓52 21	13 06 04	20 36.9	12 23.2	19 20.8	14 44.6	11 29.3	11 02.0	0 17.3	17 00.2	3 47.8	10 50.4
11 W	13 21 31	18 28 22	19 24 14	25 46 59	20 26.6	13 06.7	20 33.9	15 22.1	11 54.7	10 59.7	0 14.3	16 59.4	3 47.7	10 52.0
12 Th	13 25 28	19 27 43	2♈14 25	8♈46 29	20 14.3	13 46.0	21 46.9	15 59.5	12 20.1	10 57.2	0 11.3	16 58.7	3 47.6	10 53.6
13 F	13 29 24	20 27 06	15 23 03	22 03 54	20 01.3	14 20.7	22 59.8	16 36.9	12 45.6	10 54.5	0 08.2	16 58.0	3 47.5	10 55.2
14 Sa	13 33 21	21 26 30	28 48 45	5♉37 12	19 48.7	14 50.3	24 12.8	17 14.3	13 11.0	10 51.6	0 05.0	16 57.4	3 47.4	10 56.9
15 Su	13 37 18	22 25 57	12♉28 52	19 23 16	19 37.7	15 14.3	25 25.7	17 51.6	13 36.5	10 48.5	0 01.8	16 56.8	3D47.4	10 58.5
16 M	13 41 14	23 25 27	26 19 59	3♊18 34	19 29.3	15 32.3	26 38.7	18 29.0	14 02.0	10 45.2	29♉58.4	16 56.3	3 47.4	11 00.2
17 Tu	13 45 11	24 24 58	10♊18 36	17 19 42	19 23.9	15 43.7	27 51.6	19 06.3	14 27.5	10 41.8	29 55.0	16 55.8	3 47.5	11 02.0
18 W	13 49 07	25 24 32	24 21 36	1♋23 59	19 21.1	15R47.9	29 04.4	19 43.7	14 53.0	10 38.1	29 51.5	16 55.4	3 47.6	11 03.7
19 Th	13 53 04	26 24 08	8♋26 42	15 29 33	19 20.4	15 44.6	0♐17.3	20 21.0	15 18.6	10 34.3	29 47.9	16 55.0	3 47.7	11 05.5
20 F	13 57 00	27 23 47	22 32 26	29 35 16	19 20.4	15 33.1	1 30.1	20 58.3	15 44.1	10 30.2	29 44.2	16 54.6	3 47.8	11 07.3
21 Sa	14 00 57	28 23 28	6♌37 57	13♌40 24	19 19.8	15 13.0	2 42.9	21 35.6	16 09.7	10 26.0	29 40.5	16 54.4	3 48.0	11 09.1
22 Su	14 04 53	29 23 11	20 42 29	27 44 04	19 17.3	14 44.2	3 55.7	22 12.8	16 35.3	10 21.6	29 36.7	16 54.1	3 48.2	11 10.9
23 M	14 08 50	0♏22 56	4♍44 56	11♍44 50	19 12.2	14 06.4	5 08.5	22 50.1	17 00.9	10 17.0	29 32.8	16 53.9	3 48.5	11 12.8
24 Tu	14 12 47	1 22 43	18 43 28	25 40 29	19 04.3	13 19.8	6 21.2	23 27.3	17 26.6	10 12.3	29 28.8	16 53.8	3 48.7	11 14.7
25 W	14 16 43	2 22 33	2♎35 29	9♎28 03	18 53.7	12 24.8	7 33.9	24 04.5	17 52.2	10 07.4	29 24.8	16 53.7	3 49.1	11 16.6
26 Th	14 20 40	3 22 25	16 17 46	23 04 13	18 41.6	11 22.3	8 46.6	24 41.7	18 17.8	10 02.3	29 20.7	16D53.7	3 49.4	11 18.5
27 F	14 24 36	4 22 18	29 47 01	6♏25 48	18 29.0	10 13.4	9 59.3	25 18.8	18 43.5	9 57.0	29 16.6	16 53.7	3 49.8	11 20.4
28 Sa	14 28 33	5 22 14	13♏00 20	19 30 25	18 17.2	8 59.7	11 11.9	25 56.0	19 09.2	9 51.5	29 12.3	16 53.8	3 50.2	11 22.4
29 Su	14 32 29	6 22 11	25 55 56	2♐16 53	18 07.3	7 43.1	12 24.6	26 33.1	19 34.9	9 45.9	29 08.1	16 53.9	3 50.7	11 24.4
30 M	14 36 26	7 22 11	8♐33 22	14 45 33	18 00.0	6 26.0	13 37.1	27 10.2	20 00.6	9 40.2	29 03.8	16 54.1	3 51.2	11 26.4
31 Tu	14 40 22	8 22 12	20 53 44	26 58 15	17 55.4	5 10.6	14 49.7	27 47.3	20 26.3	9 34.3	28 59.4	16 54.3	3 51.7	11 28.4

Astro Data

	Dy Hr Mn
♀0S	2 3:34
♃☍♇	4 11:14
☿0S	8 13:44
♄R	12 11:34
☽0N	15 9:30
☉0S	22 17:28
☽0S	28 7:05
♃R	29 12:52
☽0N	12 17:00
♃☍♇	13 8:04
♆D	15 14:12
☿R	18 13:41
☽0S	25 15:44
♅D	26 15:24

Planet Ingress

	Dy Hr Mn
☿ ♎	7 22:22
⚳ ♏	12 20:38
♂ ♍	17 0:19
☉ ♎	22 17:28
♀ ♏	24 15:26
☿ ♏	28 13:28
♄ ♉R	16 0:44
♀ ♐	19 6:18
☉ ♏	23 2:47

Last Aspect / ☽ Ingress (September)

Last Aspect Dy Hr Mn		☽ Ingress Dy Hr Mn
1 12:23	♂ ✶	♏ 2 5:55
4 1:34	☿ ✶	♐ 4 14:08
6 22:26	☿ □	♑ 7 1:47
8 10:27	☉ △	♒ 9 14:44
11 20:09	♂ ☍	♓ 12 2:34
13 19:37	☉ ☍	♈ 14 12:00
16 18:50	♂ △	♉ 16 19:05
18 17:31	☉ △	♊ 19 0:22
21 1:28	☉ □	♋ 21 4:16
23 3:58	♀ □	♌ 23 7:00
25 1:33	☿ ✶	♍ 25 9:02
26 3:44	♃ □	♎ 27 11:22
28 16:57	♅ △	♏ 29 15:29

Last Aspect / ☽ Ingress (October)

Last Aspect Dy Hr Mn		☽ Ingress Dy Hr Mn
30 22:42	♅ □	♐ 1 22:50
3 8:03	♅ ✶	♑ 4 9:42
5 12:34	♀ ✶	♒ 6 22:33
8 8:55	♅ ☌	♓ 9 10:36
11 1:09	☿ △	♈ 11 19:51
13 8:53	☉ ☍	♉ 14 2:06
16 6:17	♄ ☌	♊ 16 6:19
18 1:01	☉ △	♋ 18 9:37
20 12:15	♄ ✶	♌ 20 12:42
22 15:12	♄ □	♍ 22 15:52
24 18:34	♄ △	♎ 24 19:30
26 1:03	♅ △	♏ 27 0:23
29 6:04	♄ ☍	♐ 29 7:40
31 13:43	♂ □	♑ 31 18:01

☽ Phases & Eclipses

Dy Hr Mn	
5 16:27	☽ 13♐24
13 19:37	○ 21♓18
21 1:28	☾ 28♊22
27 19:53	● 5♎00
5 10:59	☽ 12♑30
13 8:53	○ 20♈19
20 7:59	☾ 27♋14
27 7:58	● 4♏12

Astro Data

1 September 2000
Julian Day # 36769
SVP 5♓15'17"
GC 26♐50.9 ⚴ 29♍39.7
Eris 19♈44.8R ⚵ 15♒12.8R
⚷ 11♐21.2 ⚶ 18♑08.4
☽ Mean ☊ 22♋07.1

1 October 2000
Julian Day # 36799
SVP 5♓15'14"
GC 26♐51.0 ⚴ 13♎07.5
Eris 19♈29.0R ⚵ 12♒00.0
⚷ 12♐56.1 ⚶ 22♑10.3
☽ Mean ☊ 20♋31.8

November 2000 LONGITUDE

Day	Sid.Time	☉	0 hr ☽	Noon ☽	True ☊	☿	♀	♂	⚳	♃	♄	♅	♆	♇
1 W	14 44 19	9♏22 15	2♑59 32	8♑58 05	17♋53.2	3♏59.4	16♐02.2	28♍24.4	20♏52.0	9♊28.2	28♉55.0	16♒54.6	3♒52.2	11♐30.4
2 Th	14 48 16	10 22 19	14 54 29	20 49 18	17D52.9	2R54.5	17 14.7	29 01.4	21 17.7	9R22.0	28R50.5	16 54.9	3 52.8	11 32.5
3 F	14 52 12	11 22 25	26 43 11	2♒36 49	17R53.4	1 58.0	18 27.1	29 38.4	21 43.4	9 15.7	28 46.0	16 55.3	3 53.5	11 34.5
4 Sa	14 56 09	12 22 33	8♒30 53	14 26 04	17 53.6	1 11.3	19 39.5	0♎15.4	22 09.1	9 09.2	28 41.4	16 55.7	3 54.1	11 36.6
5 Su	15 00 05	13 22 42	20 23 04	26 22 33	17 52.6	0 35.5	20 51.9	0 52.4	22 34.9	9 02.6	28 36.8	16 56.2	3 54.8	11 38.7
6 M	15 04 02	14 22 53	2♓25 10	8♓31 34	17 49.6	0 11.2	22 04.2	1 29.3	23 00.6	8 55.8	28 32.2	16 56.7	3 55.5	11 40.8
7 Tu	15 07 58	15 23 05	14 42 16	20 57 47	17 44.3	29♎58.5	23 16.5	2 06.2	23 26.3	8 49.0	28 27.5	16 57.3	3 56.3	11 42.9
8 W	15 11 55	16 23 18	27 18 31	3♈44 49	17 36.6	29D57.3	24 28.8	2 43.1	23 52.0	8 42.0	28 22.8	16 58.0	3 57.1	11 45.1
9 Th	15 15 51	17 23 34	10♈16 51	16 54 43	17 27.2	0♏07.1	25 41.0	3 20.0	24 17.7	8 34.9	28 18.0	16 58.6	3 57.9	11 47.2
10 F	15 19 48	18 23 50	23 38 21	0♉27 36	17 16.9	0 27.3	26 53.1	3 56.9	24 43.5	8 27.7	28 13.3	16 59.4	3 58.7	11 49.4
11 Sa	15 23 44	19 24 09	7♉22 06	14 21 26	17 06.9	0 57.0	28 05.2	4 33.7	25 09.2	8 20.4	28 08.5	17 00.2	3 59.6	11 51.6
12 Su	15 27 41	20 24 29	21 25 02	28 32 14	16 58.1	1 35.4	29 17.3	5 10.5	25 34.9	8 13.0	28 03.7	17 01.0	4 00.5	11 53.7
13 M	15 31 38	21 24 51	5♊42 20	12♊54 36	16 51.6	2 21.5	0♑29.3	5 47.3	26 00.6	8 05.5	27 58.8	17 01.9	4 01.5	11 55.9
14 Tu	15 35 34	22 25 15	20 08 14	27 22 33	16 47.5	3 14.5	1 41.2	6 24.1	26 26.3	7 57.9	27 54.0	17 02.8	4 02.4	11 58.2
15 W	15 39 31	23 25 40	4♋36 52	11♋50 33	16D45.9	4 13.6	2 53.1	7 00.9	26 52.0	7 50.2	27 49.1	17 03.8	4 03.5	12 00.4
16 Th	15 43 27	24 26 08	19 03 05	26 14 03	16 46.1	5 17.9	4 05.0	7 37.6	27 17.8	7 42.5	27 44.2	17 04.8	4 04.5	12 02.6
17 F	15 47 24	25 26 37	3♌23 06	10♌29 57	16 47.1	6 26.9	5 16.8	8 14.3	27 43.5	7 34.7	27 39.4	17 05.9	4 05.6	12 04.9
18 Sa	15 51 20	26 27 08	17 34 25	24 36 23	16R47.8	7 39.7	6 28.6	8 51.0	28 09.2	7 26.8	27 34.5	17 07.1	4 06.7	12 07.1
19 Su	15 55 17	27 27 41	1♍35 45	8♍32 28	16 47.2	8 55.9	7 40.3	9 27.7	28 34.8	7 18.8	27 29.6	17 08.3	4 07.8	12 09.4
20 M	15 59 14	28 28 16	15 26 30	22 17 49	16 44.7	10 15.0	8 51.9	10 04.3	29 00.5	7 10.8	27 24.7	17 09.5	4 09.0	12 11.6
21 Tu	16 03 10	29 28 52	29 06 23	5♎52 08	16 40.0	11 36.4	10 03.5	10 40.9	29 26.2	7 02.8	27 19.8	17 10.8	4 10.2	12 13.9
22 W	16 07 07	0♐29 30	12♎35 02	19 15 00	16 33.3	13 00.0	11 15.0	11 17.5	29 51.9	6 54.7	27 14.9	17 12.1	4 11.4	12 16.2
23 Th	16 11 03	1 30 10	25 51 56	2♏25 45	16 25.4	14 25.2	12 26.5	11 54.1	0♐17.5	6 46.6	27 10.0	17 13.5	4 12.6	12 18.5
24 F	16 15 00	2 30 52	8♏56 22	15 23 41	16 17.1	15 51.9	13 37.9	12 30.6	0 43.2	6 38.4	27 05.1	17 14.9	4 13.9	12 20.8
25 Sa	16 18 56	3 31 34	21 47 37	28 08 10	16 09.3	17 19.9	14 49.2	13 07.1	1 08.8	6 30.3	27 00.3	17 16.4	4 15.2	12 23.1
26 Su	16 22 53	4 32 19	4♐25 17	10♐39 01	16 02.8	18 48.8	16 00.5	13 43.6	1 34.4	6 22.1	26 55.4	17 17.9	4 16.6	12 25.4
27 M	16 26 49	5 33 04	16 49 27	22 56 43	15 58.2	20 18.5	17 11.7	14 20.1	2 00.0	6 13.9	26 50.6	17 19.5	4 17.9	12 27.7
28 Tu	16 30 46	6 33 51	29 01 00	5♑02 32	15D55.6	21 48.9	18 22.9	14 56.5	2 25.6	6 05.7	26 45.8	17 21.1	4 19.3	12 30.0
29 W	16 34 43	7 34 39	11♑01 38	16 58 38	15 54.9	23 19.9	19 33.9	15 32.9	2 51.2	5 57.5	26 41.1	17 22.7	4 20.8	12 32.3
30 Th	16 38 39	8 35 28	22 53 58	28 48 05	15 55.7	24 51.3	20 44.9	16 09.2	3 16.7	5 49.3	26 36.3	17 24.5	4 22.2	12 34.7

December 2000 LONGITUDE

Day	Sid.Time	☉	0 hr ☽	Noon ☽	True ☊	☿	♀	♂	⚳	♃	♄	♅	♆	♇
1 F	16 42 36	9♐36 18	4♒41 29	10♒34 43	15♋57.3	26♏23.1	21♑55.8	16♎45.6	3♐42.3	5♊41.2	26♉31.6	17♒26.2	4♒23.7	12♐37.0
2 Sa	16 46 32	10 37 09	16 28 21	22 23 01	15 59.2	27 55.2	23 06.6	17 21.8	4 07.8	5R33.0	26R26.9	17 28.0	4 25.2	12 39.3
3 Su	16 50 29	11 38 00	28 19 19	4♓17 55	16R00.4	29 27.5	24 17.3	17 58.1	4 33.3	5 24.9	26 22.3	17 29.9	4 26.7	12 41.6
4 M	16 54 25	12 38 53	10♓19 28	16 24 35	16 00.6	1♐00.0	25 27.9	18 34.3	4 58.7	5 16.9	26 17.7	17 31.7	4 28.3	12 43.9
5 Tu	16 58 22	13 39 46	22 33 55	28 48 02	15 59.4	2 32.7	26 38.4	19 10.5	5 24.2	5 08.8	26 13.1	17 33.7	4 29.9	12 46.3
6 W	17 02 18	14 40 40	5♈07 29	11♈32 46	15 56.8	4 05.6	27 48.8	19 46.7	5 49.6	5 00.9	26 08.6	17 35.6	4 31.5	12 48.6
7 Th	17 06 15	15 41 35	18 04 14	24 42 11	15 52.9	5 38.5	28 59.1	20 22.8	6 15.0	4 53.0	26 04.1	17 37.7	4 33.1	12 50.9
8 F	17 10 12	16 42 30	1♉26 47	8♉18 03	15 48.4	7 11.5	0♒09.3	20 58.9	6 40.4	4 45.1	25 59.7	17 39.7	4 34.7	12 53.2
9 Sa	17 14 08	17 43 27	15 15 51	22 19 54	15 43.9	8 44.6	1 19.4	21 35.0	7 05.7	4 37.3	25 55.3	17 41.8	4 36.4	12 55.6
10 Su	17 18 05	18 44 24	29 29 45	6♊44 45	15 39.9	10 17.9	2 29.4	22 11.0	7 31.1	4 29.6	25 51.0	17 44.0	4 38.1	12 57.9
11 M	17 22 01	19 45 22	14♊04 11	21 27 10	15 37.1	11 51.1	3 39.2	22 47.0	7 56.4	4 22.0	25 46.8	17 46.1	4 39.9	13 00.2
12 Tu	17 25 58	20 46 21	28 52 43	6♋19 52	15D35.6	13 24.5	4 49.0	23 23.0	8 21.6	4 14.4	25 42.6	17 48.4	4 41.6	13 02.5
13 W	17 29 54	21 47 21	13♋47 33	21 14 46	15 35.4	14 58.0	5 58.6	23 58.9	8 46.9	4 07.0	25 38.4	17 50.6	4 43.4	13 04.8
14 Th	17 33 51	22 48 22	28 40 37	6♌04 13	15 36.3	16 31.5	7 08.0	24 34.8	9 12.1	3 59.6	25 34.4	17 52.9	4 45.2	13 07.1
15 F	17 37 47	23 49 23	13♌24 50	20 41 51	15 37.7	18 05.1	8 17.3	25 10.6	9 37.3	3 52.3	25 30.4	17 55.3	4 47.0	13 09.4
16 Sa	17 41 44	24 50 26	27 54 47	5♍03 16	15 39.1	19 38.9	9 26.5	25 46.5	10 02.5	3 45.2	25 26.4	17 57.7	4 48.8	13 11.7
17 Su	17 45 41	25 51 29	12♍07 04	19 06 03	15R39.9	21 12.8	10 35.6	26 22.2	10 27.6	3 38.1	25 22.5	18 00.1	4 50.7	13 14.0
18 M	17 49 37	26 52 34	26 00 10	2♎49 28	15 40.0	22 46.8	11 44.5	26 58.0	10 52.7	3 31.2	25 18.7	18 02.5	4 52.6	13 16.3
19 Tu	17 53 34	27 53 39	9♎34 04	16 14 06	15 39.1	24 21.0	12 53.2	27 33.7	11 17.7	3 24.4	25 15.0	18 05.0	4 54.4	13 18.5
20 W	17 57 30	28 54 45	22 49 45	29 21 14	15 37.4	25 55.3	14 01.9	28 09.4	11 42.8	3 17.7	25 11.4	18 07.5	4 56.4	13 20.8
21 Th	18 01 27	29 55 52	5♏48 45	12♏12 32	15 35.2	27 29.8	15 10.3	28 45.0	12 07.7	3 11.1	25 07.8	18 10.1	4 58.3	13 23.0
22 F	18 05 23	0♑57 00	18 32 48	24 49 45	15 32.8	29 04.5	16 18.6	29 20.6	12 32.7	3 04.7	25 04.3	18 12.7	5 00.2	13 25.3
23 Sa	18 09 20	1 58 08	1♐03 37	7♐14 35	15 30.7	0♑39.4	17 26.7	29 56.1	12 57.6	2 58.4	25 00.9	18 15.3	5 02.2	13 27.5
24 Su	18 13 16	2 59 17	13 22 50	19 28 35	15 29.0	2 14.5	18 34.7	0♏31.6	13 22.5	2 52.3	24 57.6	18 18.0	5 04.2	13 29.8
25 M	18 17 13	4 00 26	25 32 01	1♑33 20	15 27.9	3 49.9	19 42.4	1 07.1	13 47.3	2 46.3	24 54.3	18 20.7	5 06.2	13 32.0
26 Tu	18 21 10	5 01 36	7♑32 44	13 30 27	15D27.5	5 25.5	20 50.0	1 42.5	14 12.1	2 40.5	24 51.2	18 23.4	5 08.2	13 34.2
27 W	18 25 06	6 02 45	19 26 44	25 21 50	15 27.7	7 01.3	21 57.4	2 17.8	14 36.9	2 34.9	24 48.1	18 26.2	5 10.3	13 36.4
28 Th	18 29 03	7 03 55	1♒16 02	7♒09 41	15 28.3	8 37.5	23 04.6	2 53.1	15 01.6	2 29.3	24 45.1	18 29.0	5 12.3	13 38.6
29 F	18 32 59	8 05 05	13 03 05	18 56 39	15 29.1	10 13.9	24 11.5	3 28.4	15 26.2	2 24.0	24 42.2	18 31.8	5 14.4	13 40.7
30 Sa	18 36 56	9 06 15	24 50 47	0♓45 56	15 29.9	11 50.6	25 18.3	4 03.6	15 50.9	2 18.8	24 39.5	18 34.7	5 16.5	13 42.9
31 Su	18 40 52	10 07 25	6♓42 34	12 41 12	15 30.6	13 27.7	26 24.8	4 38.7	16 15.4	2 13.8	24 36.8	18 37.6	5 18.6	13 45.0

Astro Data

	Dy Hr Mn
☿ D	8 2:26
♂0S	8 23:23
☽0N	9 2:42
☽0S	21 22:49
☽0N	6 13:06
♃△♆	9 14:16
☽0S	19 4:50

Planet Ingress

	Dy Hr Mn
♂ ♎	4 2:00
☿ ♎R	7 7:28
♀ ♑	13 2:14
☉ ♐	22 0:19
⚳ ♐	22 19:37
☿ ♐	3 20:26
♀ ♒	8 8:48
☉ ♑	21 13:37
☿ ♑	23 2:03
♂ ♏	23 14:37

Last Aspect / ☽ Ingress (November)

Last Aspect Dy Hr Mn		☽ Ingress Dy Hr Mn
3 5:37	♂ △	♒ 3 6:41
5 16:26	♄ □	♓ 5 19:13
8 2:04	♄ ✶	♈ 8 5:02
10 5:07	♀ △	♉ 10 11:12
12 11:12	♄ ☌	♊ 12 14:27
13 18:51	♅ △	♋ 14 16:21
16 14:30	♄ ✶	♌ 16 18:19
18 17:03	♄ □	♍ 18 21:15
20 23:45	☉ ✶	♎ 21 1:35
22 8:18	♅ △	♏ 23 7:33
25 9:52	♄ ☍	♐ 25 15:33
27 0:57	♅ ✶	♑ 28 1:57
30 7:34	♄ △	♒ 30 14:26

Last Aspect / ☽ Ingress (December)

Last Aspect Dy Hr Mn		☽ Ingress Dy Hr Mn
3 0:51	☿ □	♓ 3 3:23
5 7:26	♀ ✶	♈ 5 14:17
7 20:22	♀ □	♉ 7 21:27
9 18:00	♄ ☌	♊ 10 0:50
11 14:15	♂ △	♋ 12 1:48
13 19:04	♄ ✶	♌ 14 2:09
15 19:57	♄ □	♍ 16 3:30
18 0:41	☉ □	♎ 18 7:01
20 11:07	☉ ✶	♏ 20 13:12
22 12:28	♄ ☍	♐ 22 21:57
24 10:03	♀ ✶	♑ 25 8:54
27 10:52	♄ △	♒ 27 21:25
29 23:47	♀ ☌	♓ 30 10:27

☽ Phases & Eclipses

Dy Hr Mn	
4 7:27	☽ 12♒11
11 21:15	○ 19♉47
18 15:24	☾ 26♌36
25 23:11	● 4♐00
4 3:55	☽ 12♓18
11 9:03	○ 19♊38
18 0:41	☾ 26♍24
25 17:22	● 4♑14
25 17:34:55	● P 0.723

Astro Data

1 November 2000
Julian Day # 36830
SVP 5♓15'11"
GC 26♐51.1 ⚴ 26♎59.3
Eris 19♈10.6R ✱ 15♒25.6
⚷ 15♐41.7 ⚶ 1♓17.5
☽ Mean ☊ 18♋53.2

1 December 2000
Julian Day # 36860
SVP 5♓15'06"
GC 26♐51.1 ⚴ 10♏04.5
Eris 18♈56.3R ✱ 23♒57.5
⚷ 19♐00.8 ⚶ 12♓56.3
☽ Mean ☊ 17♋17.9